Associations Canada

Associations du Canada

Additional Publications

For more detailed information or to place an order, see the back of the book.

CANADIAN PARLIAMENTARY GUIDE 2015
Guide parlementaire canadien
1288 pages, 6 x 9, Hardcover
ISBN 978-1-61925-675-0
ISSN 0315-6168

Published annually since before Confederation, this indispensable guide to government in Canada provides information on federal and provincial governments, with biographical sketches of government members, descriptions of government institutions, and historical text and charts. With significant bilingual sections, the Guide covers elections from Confederation to the present, including the most recent provincial elections.

CANADIAN ALMANAC & DIRECTORY 2015
Répetoire et almanach canadien
2470 pages, 8 1/2 x 11, Hardcover
168th edition, November 2014
ISBN 978-1-61925-191-5
ISSN 0068-8193

A combination of textual material, charts, colour photographs and directory listings, the *Canadian Almanac & Directory* provides the most comprehensive picture of Canada, from physical attributes to economic and business summaries to leisure and recreation.

FINANCIAL SERVICES CANADA 2014-2015
Services financiers au Canada
1743 pages, 8 1/2 x 11, Softcover
17th edition, April 2014
ISBN 978-1-61925-197-7
ISSN 1484-2408

This directory of Canadian financial institutions and organizations includes banks and depository institutions, non-depository institutions, investment management firms, financial planners, insurance companies, accountants, major law firms, government and regulatory agencies, and associations. Fully indexed.

LIBRARIES CANADA 2014-2015
Bibliothèques Canada
928 pages, 8 1/2 x 11, Softcover
28th edition, August 2014
ISBN 978-1-61925-199-1
ISSN 1920-2849

Libraries Canada offers comprehensive information on Canadian libraries, resource centres, business information centres, professional associations, regional library systems, archives, library schools, government libraries, and library technical programs.

HEALTH GUIDE CANADA 2013-2014
Guide canadien de la santé
944 pages, 8 1/2 x 11, Softcover
1st edition, May 2013
ISBN: 978-1-61925-185-4

Health Guide Canada contains thousands of ways to deal with the many aspects of chronic or mental health disorder. It includes associations, government agencies, libraries and resource centres, educational facilities, hospitals and publications.

MAJOR CANADIAN CITIES: COMPARED & RANKED
Comparaison et classement des principales villes canadiennes
816 pages, 8 1/2 x 11, Softcover
1st edition, November 2013
ISBN 978-1-61925-260-8

Major Canadian Cities: Compared & Ranked provides an in-depth comparison and analysis of the 50 most populated cities in Canada. Following the city chapters are ranking tables that compare the demographics, economics, education, religion and infrastructure of the cities listed.

CANADIAN ENVIRONMENTAL RESOURCE GUIDE 2014-2015
Guide des ressources environnementales canadiennes
1590 pages, 8 1/2 x 11, Softcover
19th edition, August 2014
ISBN 978-1-61925-193-9
ISSN 1920-2725

Canada's most complete national listing of environmental associations and organizations, governmental regulators and purchasing groups, product and service companies, special libraries, and more! All indexed and categorized for quick and easy reference. Also included are companies registered by ISO 9001, 9002, 9003 and 14001.

2015

36th Edition

Associations Canada

Associations du Canada

Grey House Publishing Canada
PUBLISHER: Leslie Mackenzie
GENERAL MANAGER: Bryon Moore
EDITORIAL TEAM LEADER: Jill McCullough
ASSOCIATE EDITORS: Stuart Paterson; Elysia Cheung

Grey House Publishing
EDITORIAL DIRECTOR: Laura Mars
MARKETING DIRECTOR: Jessica Moody
PRODUCTION MANAGER & COMPOSITION: Kristen Thatcher

Grey House Publishing Canada
555 Richmond Street West, Suite 301
Toronto, ON M5V 3B1
866-433-4739
FAX 416-644-1904
www.greyhouse.ca
e-mail: info@greyhouse.ca

Grey House Publishing Canada is a wholly owned subsidiary of Grey House Publishing, Inc. USA.

Printed in Canada by Webcom Inc.

ISSN: 1186-9798

ISBN: 978-1-61925-667-5

Cataloguing in Publication Data is available from Libraries and Archives Canada.

Table of Contents

Introduction

This 2015 edition of *Associations Canada* published by Grey House Publishing Canada includes over 20,000 associations, both those that are headquartered in Canada, as well as those headquartered elsewhere with branches in Canada. The Canadian associations are followed by a separate section of Foreign Associations that are of a particular interest to Canadians.

Content

Associations Canada has been a valued reference tool for over three decades, providing the most comprehensive picture of Canada's non-profit sector. This 2015 Grey House Canada edition is no exception. The Canadian organizations and international groups in this edition represent industry, commercial and professional associations, registered charities, and special and common interest organizations. This 36th annual edition includes updates or verification of all major associations as well as almost 37,500 executives.

Each listing presents a detailed association profile, including budget, founding date, scope of activity, licensing body, sources of funding, executive information, full address and complete contact information.

Eight indexes offer a variety of ways to search not only for specific associations, but also for specific categories of associations. In addition to association listings, you'll find several valuable articles following this Introduction, including:

- **Associations**, with historical background, types and organization information.
- **Your Conference is a Strategic Asset—Manage it Accordingly**
- **Canada's Anti-Spam Law (CASL): FAQs Relevant to All Registered Charities and Nonprofits**
- **What the Next Generation of Association Leaders Really Wants from Future Employers**

Arrangement

Accessing the factual information contained in the more than 2,000 pages of *Associations Canada* is facilitated by the following organization:

- **Location of Indexes:** The Subject Index in the front of the book is designed to help users quickly find a listing, or group of listings, by subject. The remaining seven indexes are in alphabetical order in the back of the book: ***Acronyms; Budget; Conferences & Conventions; Executive Name; Geographic; Mailing List;*** and ***Registered Charitable Organizations.***
- **Arrangement of Data:** Each profile has boldfaced category headers to help users quickly identify categories of information: ***Previous Name; Overview; Chief Officers; Finances; Staff; Membership; Activities; Publications;*** and ***Mission.***

Available in print, by subscription, and online via Grey House Publishing Canada at www.greyhouse.ca, *Associations Canada* is widely used as a valuable resource of prospects for sales and marketing executives, tourism and convention officials, researchers, government officials—anyone who wants to locate non-profit interest groups and trade associations. To facilitate its use throughout Canada, a significant number of listings appear in French. Some elements, such as select front matter material is offered in both French and English.

We acknowledge the valuable contribution of those individuals and organizations who have responded to our information gathering process throughout the year; your help and timely responses to our questionnaires, phone calls and faxes is greatly appreciated.

Every effort has been made to ensure the accuracy of the information included in this edition of *Associations Canada*. Do not hesitate to contact us if revisions are necessary.

Cette édition 2015 des *Associations du Canada*, publiée par Grey House Publishing Canada, comprend plus de 20 000 associations, dont celles ayant leur siège social au Canada et celles qui, bien qu'ayant leur siège social à l'étranger, ont des succursales ou des divisions au Canada. On y dresse également le profil d'associations étrangères d'un intérêt particulier pour les Canadiens.

Contenu

Associations du Canada, un ouvrage de référence utile et pratique publié depuis plus de trente ans, fournit un tableau complet et actuel du secteur sans but lucratif au Canada. L'édition 2015 de Grey House Canada ne fait pas exception. Les organismes canadiens et internationaux regroupés dans cette édition comprend des associations industrielles, commerciales et professionnelles, des organismes de bienfaisance enregistrés et des organisations d'intérêt public ou particulier. Cette 36e édition annuelle renferme une mise à jour complète de toutes les associations majeures ainsi que près de 37 500 directeurs.

Chaque entrée présente un profil détaillé d'une association avec son budget, sa date de création, ses champs d'activités, l'autorité constituante, ses sources de financement, des renseignements sur ses dirigeants, son adresse et ses coordonnées de contact.

Huit index permettent de rechercher de différentes façons autant une association particulière qu'une catégorie spécifique d'association.

Outre à l'information factuelle des *Associations du Canada*, vous trouverez la présence de quelques articles à la suite de l'Introduction:

- **Associations**, y compris un aperçu historique, les types et l'information relative à l'organisation.
- **Votre Conférence est un Actif Stratégique – Gérez-le Comme Tel**
- **Loi canadienne anti-pourriel (LCAP) : FAQ pertinente pour tous les organismes de bienfaisance enregistrés et les organismes sans but lucratif**
- **What the Next Generation of Association Leaders Really Wants from Future Employers**

Présentation

Outre les modifications apportées à l'information factuelle des *Associations du Canada*, nous avons procédé à des changements importants qui faciliteront la recherche de renseignements contenus dans plus de 2 000 pages:

- **Emplacement des index** : L'index sujet situé au début de l'édition a été conçu pour aider l'utilisateur à trouver plus rapidement une entrée ou un groupe d'entrées classées par sujet. Les autres sept index sont maintenant situés à la fin de l'édition et présentés par ordre alphabétique dans cette suite : ***Acronyms; Budget; Conferences & Conventions; Executive Name; Geographic; Mailing List;*** et ***Registered Charitable Organizations.***
- **Agencement des données** : Pour aider les utilisateurs à retrouver rapidement les catégories de renseignement, chaque catégorie est maintenant identifiée à l'aide d'un titre en caractère gras : ***Nom précédent, Aperçu, Membre(s) du bureau directeur, Finances, Personnel, Membre, Activités, Publications*** et ***Mission.***

Disponible en format imprimée, par souscription, et en ligne sur le site de Grey House Publishing Canada à www.greyhouse.ca, *Associations du Canada* est une ressource pratique de prospection amplement utilisée par les spécialistes de la vente et du marketing, les planificateurs de congrès et d'événements touristiques, les chercheurs, les représentants gouvernementaux et par tous ceux recherchent des groupes oeuvrant dans le secteur sans but lucratif ou des associations commerciales. Pour une consultation pancanadienne, un nombre important d'entrées apparaissent en français.

Nous tenons à souligner la précieuse contribution des personnes et des organismes qui ont collaboré tout au long de l'année à notre procédé de cueillette d'information; votre aide, vos réponses à notre questionnaire dans les délais impartis, nos appels téléphoniques et nos envois par télécopieur sont grandement appréciés.

Nous avons mis tous les efforts pour nous assurer de l'exactitude de l'information contenue dans cette édition des *Associations du Canada*. N'hésitez pas à communiquer avec nous si des modifications s'avèrent nécessaires.

THE LISTINGS

Associations are listed alphabetically by name. Translated names, or the popular name an association is also known as (AKA), are included in the listings with see references attached (for example, if you look up the popularly known *Canadian Auto Workers Union*, you will be pointed to their full listing under their legal corporate name, the *National Automobile, Aerospace, Transportation & General Workers Union of Canada*). Name changes are reflected in the listings as see references.

Please refer to the sample entry (page x), which illustrates the kind of information *Associations Canada* provides on each organization.

THE INDEXES

The association listings are indexed in 8 ways to speed your research.

Most prominent of these indexes is the **Subject Index**, which includes words that generically cover a field of interest (i.e., Sports) and also words that occur specifically in the title of a given association (i.e., Fencing).

An extensive array of *See* and *See Also* references rounds out this index to cover every approach one might take in searching for specific associations or the field of interest to which they belong:

Acadians
***See also* Francophones in Canada**
Association acadienne des artistes professionnel.le.s du Nouveau-Brunswick inc., 289
Beaton Institute, 380
Conseil coopératif acadien de la Nouvelle-Écosse, 642

Geographic Index - associations listed by provinces, then cities or towns; includes branches, divisions, chapters, etc.

Québec
Alcoholics Anonymous - Québec - Northeast Area of Québec Central Office, 262
Alternatives Action & Communication Network for International Development - Québec City Office, 268
Les AmiEs de la Terre de Québec, 275

Acronym Index - associations listed alphabetically by acronym:

ABPAC - Association des bibliothécaires parlementaires au Canada (Association of Parliamentary Librarians in Canada), 335
ABPBC - Association of Book Publishers of British Columbia, 294
ABPNB - Association des bibliothécaires professionnel(le)s du Nouveau-Brunswick, 293

Executive Name Index - key contacts listed alphabetically by surnames:

Abbott, Dr. Jodi L., *Canadian Diabetes Association - Alberta/NWT Division,* 780/423-1232, Fax: 780/423-3322, Email: abbott@diabetes.ca, p. 482
Abbott, Patricia, *Association of Canadian Choral Conductors,* 514/351-4865, Fax: 514/351-2702, p. 296
Abbott, Robert, *Canadian Boating Federation,* 450/699-0584, p. 460

Registered Charitable Organizations Index - associations that identify themselves as registered charitable organizations, listed by subject:

Alcoholism
Al-Anon Family Groups (Canada), Inc., 242
Alcohol & Drug Recovery Association of Ontario, 262
Alcoholics Anonymous, 262

Budget Index - organizations by annual budget size, ranging from less than $50,000 to greater than $5 million:

Less than $50,000
100 Mile & District Arts Council, 227
15th Field Artillery Regiment Museum & Archives Society, 227
Aboriginal Nurses Association of Canada, 229

LES INSCRIPTIONS

Les inscriptions sont classées par ordre alphabétique sous leurs noms officiels. Les noms traduits et noms populaires sous lesquels certaines associations sont connues contiennent la mention See/Voir. (Par exemple, lorsque vous trouvez l'inscription pour l'association connue *Canadian Auto Workers Union,* vous serez dirigé vers leur nom officiel qui est *National Automobile, Aerospace, Transportation & General Workers Union of Canada*). Les changements de nom portent la mention See/Voir.

Veuillez-vous référer à l'exemple d'une inscription (page xi), qui explique le genre de renseignements que vous pouvez obtenir sur les associations inscrites dans *Associations du Canada*.

LES INDEX

Les inscriptions sont indexées de 8 façons différentes afin d'accélérer vos recherches.

Le plus important est **l'index des matières** qui comprend le mot se rapportant au champ d'intérêt générique (ex: Sports) ainsi que les mots spécifiques qui font partie du nom d'une association donnée (ex: Escrime).

Une importante quantité de références avec *See/Voir* et *See Also/Voir aussi* complète cet index pour couvrir tous les angles de recherches possibles lorsque vous êtes en quête d'une association spécifique ou d'un champ d'intérêt dans lequel celle-ci évolue:

Acadians
***See also* Francophones in Canada**
Association acadienne des artistes professionnel.le.s du Nouveau-Brunswick inc., 289
Beaton Institute, 380
Conseil coopératif acadien de la Nouvelle-Écosse, 642

Index géographique - associations inscrites par provinces, puis par ville ou village; comprend les succursales, divisions, chapitres, etc.

Québec
Alcoholics Anonymous - Québec - Northeast Area of Québec Central Office, 262
Alternatives Action & Communication Network for International Development - Québec City Office, 268
Les AmiEs de la Terre de Québec, 275

Index d'acronymes - associations classées alphabétiquement par acronyme:

ABPAC - Association des bibliothécaires parlementaires au Canada (Association of Parliamentary Librarians in Canada), 335
ABPBC - Association of Book Publishers of British Columbia, 294
ABPNB - Association des bibliothécaires professionnel(le)s du Nouveau-Brunswick, 293

Index des dirigeants - associations classées alphabétiquement par nom de famille:

Abbott, Dr. Jodi L., *Canadian Diabetes Association - Alberta/NWT Division,* 780/423-1232, Fax: 780/423-3322, Email: abbott@diabetes.ca, p. 482
Abbott, Patricia, *Association of Canadian Choral Conductors,* 514/351-4865, Fax: 514/351-2702, p. 296
Abbott, Robert, *Canadian Boating Federation,* 450/699-0584, p. 460

Index des organisations sans buts lucratifs - associations s'identifiant comme ayant le statut d'organisations charitables, sont classées par sujet:

Alcoholism
Al-Anon Family Groups (Canada), Inc., 242
Alcohol & Drug Recovery Association of Ontario, 262
Alcoholics Anonymous, 262

Index du budget annuel - Le budget annuel, affiché par certaines associations, varie entre 50 000$ et 5$ millions:

Moins de 50 000$
100 Mile & District Arts Council, 227
15th Field Artillery Regiment Museum & Archives Society, 227
Aboriginal Nurses Association of Canada, 229

Conferences & Conventions Index - 2015–2021 meetings listed by year, date, and city:

Central Alberta Teachers Convention 2015
Date: February 19-20, 2015
Location: Red Deer College
Red Deer, AB
Sponsor/Contact: Alberta Teachers' Association
Barnett House
11010 - 142 St.
Edmonton, AB T5N 2R1
780-447-9400 *Fax:* 780-455-6481
Toll-Free: 800-232-7208
E-mail: government@teachers.ab.ca
URL: www.teachers.ab.ca
Scope: Local

Mailing List Index - mailing lists, available for rental from the association, listed by subject:

Architecture
Alberta Association of Architects, 243
Architectural Institute of British Columbia, 282
Association des Architectes en pratique privée du Québec, 291

MAILING LISTS

Our association database can be sorted to provide you with mailing labels by broad category or specific subject interest. Lists are provided in printed or electronic form (see details at the back of the book or call us at 1-866-433-4739).

Index des conventions et congrès - les rencontres pour 2014–2020 sont inscrites par année, date, et ville:

Central Alberta Teachers Convention 2015
Date: February 19-20, 2015
Location: Red Deer College
Red Deer, AB
Sponsor/Contact: Alberta Teachers' Association
Barnett House
11010 - 142 St.
Edmonton, AB T5N 2R1
780-447-9400 *Fax:* 780-455-6481
Toll-Free: 800-232-7208
E-mail: government@teachers.ab.ca
URL: www.teachers.ab.ca
Scope: Local

Index des listes d'envoi - listes d'envoi à louer, par l'association, sont classées par sujet:

Architecture
Alberta Association of Architects, 243
Architectural Institute of British Columbia, 282
Association des Architectes en pratique privée du Québec, 291

LISTES D'ENVOI

Notre banque de données sur les associations peut être triée par catégorie générale ou par sujet d'intérêt spécifique afin de vous fournir des étiquettes d'envoi. Les listes sont disponibles en format imprimé ou informatisé (voyez les détails à la fin du livre ou téléphonez au 1-866-433-4739).

SAMPLE ENTRY

Listings include the following information where available:

- Official name of the association presented in its language of choice (English or French); where a translated name has been provided, that name will appear next to the official association name, and will also appear as a cross-reference in the alphabetical listings (e.g., Société canadienne des directeurs d'association, *See* Canadian Society of Association Executives). The acronym follows the association's name and appears in parantheses. See also the Acronym Index.
- Full address
- Communication numbers, including crisis-lines, info-lines, TTY, toll-free telephone numbers, email & website addresses.
- Social media addresses, including LinkedIn, Facebook, and Twitter links.
- Previous Name: If the name of an association has changed, the previous name appears with a note to see the entry under its new name.
- Also Known As: If an association is better known by a more popular name, this name appears as well.
- Previous Name/ Merged From: If the name of an association has changed, its former name appears as well.
- Overview: This description includes the size (small, medium-sized, large), the jurisdiction (international, national, provincial, local), whether it's a charitable or licensing organization, the year it was founded in and the name of the organization it is overseen by.
- A mission statement
- The organizations of which it is a member or with which it is affiliated.

Publishers' Association (PA) / Association des éditeurs (AE)

#1313, 666 King Street East, Toronto, ON, M3Q Z09

Tel: 416-666-6666*; Fax:* 416-666-6667

Toll-Free: 800-666-6666*; TTY:* 416-666-6668

Crisis Hotline: 800-READUS1

Email: info@readus1.com

www.readus1.com

www.linkedin.com/readus

www.facebook.com/readus

twitter.com/readus

www.youtube.com/readus

Previous Name*:* Read Books Association

Also Known As*:* Association of Book Lovers

Merged From: BookMakers Association and Editors Association

Overview*:* A small national charitable licensing organization founded in 2012 overseen by The International Association of Publishers.

Mission: To continue to publish

Member of: North American Publishers Association

Affiliation(s): Association of BookBinders

Chief Officer(s)*:*

Bob Gomez, President, *Tel:* 416-666-6669*; Fax:* 416-666-6670

bgomez@readus1.com

Nancy Gomez, Vice President, *Tel:* 416-666-6671; *Fax:* 416-666-6672

ngomez@readus1.com

Finances*: Annual Operating Budget:* $50,000 - $150,000*; Funding Sources:* Membership dues

Staff*:* 2 staff member(s); 1 volunteer(s)

Membership*:* 190; *Fees:* $55.50*; Member Profile:* Publishers*; Committees*: Marketing; Finance

Activities: This lists the association's activities; *Awareness Events:* National Book Day, February; *Internships*: Yes; *Speaker Service:* Yes; *Rents Mailing List:* Yes; *Library:* Yes, Publishing Library; Open to public, by appointment.

Awards:

Best Publisher Award

Here is a description of the award. *Eligibility:* All members of the association*; Location:* Toronto; *Deadline:* 25-Dec; *Amount:* $500*; Contact:* Bob Gomez, President, Tel: 416-666-6667*;* Fax: 416-666-6668; bgomez@readus1.com

Meetings/Conferences:

International Convention; May 25, 2014, Azteca Inn, Mazatlan, MX

Scope: International

Description: This describes what happens at the convention.

Contact Information: Heather Ramsey, *Tel:* 52-669-44-22-99, hramsey@readus1.com

Publications:

The Annual Publishers' Magazine

Type: Magazine*; Frequency:* a.*; Accepts Advertising; No. of Pages:* 999; *Editor:* Susie Brown; *Author:* Kelly Stewart; *Price:* $150; *ISSN* 9999-9999*; ISBN* 99-999-999-99; *Language*: English*, Contact:* info@readus1.com

Profile: Articles & news

Ontario Division

P.O. Box 666, Hamilton, ON, R1R 1R1

Tel: 613-666-6666*; Fax:* 613-666-6667

Toll-Free: 800-654-3210 *; TTY:* 613-666-6668

info@readus1.on.ca

www.readus1.on.ca

Chief Officer(s):

Julie Chavez, Director, *Tel:* 613-666-6669*; Fax:* 613-666-6670

jchavez@readus1.on.ca

- Chief Officers: Titles may include the following: Executive Director, Director, President, Executive Secretary, Treasurer, Sec.-Treas., General Manager, Coordinator, Chair, Superintendent, Representative, Registrar, Program Head, etc.; eligible for inclusion are both permanent and elected staff. See also the Executive Name Index.
- Finances: This includes the annual operating budget and the funding sources of the association.
- Staff: Includes both paid and volunteer staff.
- Membership: The number of members, often in specific categories (e.g. individual, corporate, senior, lifetime); fees; the membership criteria; and committees on the board of members.
- This includes speakers services and internship programs, awareness events, and whether they have a library or sell mailing lists.
- Awards, Scholarships, Grants: Prizes awarded by the association, along with the amount.
- Publications: Includes details on frequency, author/editor, ISSN or ISBN, language(s) the publication is available in, number of pages, price, advertising, and description of bibliographic contents.
- Meetings: The dates and locations for events to be held in 2015–2021. See also the Conferences and Conventions Index.
- Activities: Highlights what the association does, apart from the information contained in its mission statement.
- Branches: The association may have various branches, listed at the bottom.

EXEMPLE D'INSCRIPTION

Les inscriptions comprennent les renseignements suivants:

- Nom officiel de l'association, présenté dans la langue choisie (anglais ou français); lorsque la traduction d'un nom est fournie par l'organisme, celui-ci sera à la suite du nom officiel de l'organisme et paraîtra aussi en renvoi par classement alphabétique (Société canadienne des directeurs d'associations, *Voir* Canadian Society of Association Executives). L'acronyme suit le nom de l'organisation et est montré entre parenthèses. Voir aussi l'Index des acronymes.
- Adresse complète.
- Numéros de communication comprenant les téléphones secours, infolignes, ATS, numéros sans frais, courrier électronique, adresses des médias sociaux et adresse URL.
- Nom précédent: Si le nom d'une association a changé, son nom précédent paraît en inscription principale avec renvoi au nouveau nom.
- Aussi connu comme: Certaines associations sont mieux connues par leur appellation plus populaire. Ce nom modifié paraît aussi.
- Date de fondation de l'association.
- Envergure des opérations: Est classée comme suit: internationale, nationale, régionale, provinciale ou locale. Les groupes étrangers ne sont pas définis de cette façon.
- Organisme sans but lucratif: Associations s'identifiant comme ayant le statut d'organisations charitables. Voir aussi l'index des organisations à buts non-lucratifs.
- Un énoncé de mission
- Membre de et/ou affiliation à d'autres associations: Associations mères se trouvent sous la rubrique Membre de. Les autres organismes avec lesquels il existe un lien plus distant bien que dynamique se trouvent sous la rubrique Affiliation(s).
- Membres du bureau directeur. Les titres d'emploi peuvent comprendre les suivants: directeur(trice) général(e), président(e), secrétaire ou secrétaire trésorier(ère), gérante(e), coordonnateur(trice), surintendant(e), représentant(e), registraire, chargé(e) de programme, etc. Le nom du personnel permanent ou élu est accepté pour inscription. Voir aussi l'Index par dirigeants.

Association des éditeurs (AE)/Publisher's Association (PA)
#1313, 666 rue King est, Toronto, ON M3Q Z09
Tél: 416-666-6666; *Téléc*: 416-666-6667
Ligne sans frais: 800-666-6666; ATS: 416-666-6668
Téléphone secours: 800-READUS1
Courriel: info@readus1.com
www.readus1.com
twitter.com/readus

Nom précédent: Read Books Association
Également appelé: Association of Book Lovers
Fusion de: BookMakers Association et Assocation d'éditeurs
Aperçu: *Dimension*: petite; *Envergure*: national; *Organisme sans but lucratif*; *fondée en 2012*; *surveillé par* The International Association of Publishers.
Mission: Continuer à éditer les livres
Membre de: North American Publishers Association
Affiliation: Association of BookBinders
Membres du bureau directeur:
Bob Gomez, Président, Tél: 416-666-6669; Téléc: 416-666-6670
bgomez@readus1.com
Nancy Gomez, Vice Président, Tél: 416-666-6671; Téléc: 416-666-6672
ngomez@readus1.com

Finances: *Budget de fonctionnement annuel*: 50000$- 150000$; *Fonds*: Subventions
Personnel: 2 membre(s) du personnel; 1 bénévole(s)
Membre: 190; *Montant de la cotisation*: 55.50$; *Critères d'admissibilité*: Editeurs; *Comités*: Le communications, les finances
Activités: Ceci énumère les activités de l'association. *Evénements de sensibilisation*: National Book Day; *Stagiaires*: Oui; *Service de conférenciers*: Oui; *Listes de destinataire*: Oui; *Bibliothèque*: Oui, Publishing Library; rendez-vous
Prix, Bourses:
Best Publisher Award
Ceci décrit le prix. *Critères d'admissibilité*: Tout les membres de l'association. Location: Toronto; Deadline: Dec 25: Amount: 500$; Contact: Bob Gomez, Président, Tél: 416-666-6667; Téléc: 416-666-6668; bgomez@readus1
Conventions et congrés:
International Convention; May 25, 2014, Azteca Inn, Mazatlan, MZ
Scope: International
Description: Ceci décrit ce qui se passe au congrés convention.
Coordonnées: Heather Ramsey, Tél: 52-669-44-22-99, hramsey@readus1.com
Publications:
The Annual Publisher's Magazine
Type: Magazine; *Fréquence*: annuel; Accepte la publicité; No. de pages: 999; Rédacteur: Susie Brown; Auteur: Kelly Stewart; Prix: 150$; ISSN: 9999-9999; ISBN 99-999-999-99; Langue: anglais, Coordonnées: info@readus1.com
Aperçu: Articles et nouvelles

Ontario Division
P.O. Box 666, Hamilton, ON, R1R 1R1
Tél: 613-666-6666; *Téléc*: 613-666-6667
Ligne sans frais: 800-654-3210; *ATP*: 613-666-6668
Membre(s) du bureau directeur:
Julie Chavez, Directrice,
Tél: 613-666-6666; Téléc: 613-666-6667
jchavez@readus1.on.ca

- Budget annuel d'exploitation/fonctionnement. Voir aussi l'Index du budget annuel.
- Sources de financement: Cite fonds publics et privés et méthode de collecte de fonds.
- Personnel: Salariés et bénévoles.
- Profil des membres et critères d'admission: Qualifications pour membres individuels et corporatifs et les cotisations.
- Nombre de membres, souvent sous différentes catégories spécifiques (corporatifs, individuels, aînés, à vie) et comités et conseils.
- Possibilité d'obtenir les services de conférenciers.
- Programme pour stagiaires.
- Bibliothèque: Ouverte au public ou sur rendez-vous.
- Disponibilité de listes d'envoi. Voir aussi l'Index des listes d'envoi.
- Prix décernés, subventions, bourses, avec le montant de ces dernières, si disponible.
- Conventions et congrès: Les dates et endroits où ces réunions auront lieu en 2015–2021.
- Publications: Comprend les renseignements sur la fréquence de publication, les auteurs/rédacteurs, ISSN ou ISBN, la langue (ou langues) dans laquelle la publication est disponible, le nombre de pages, le prix, la publicité et la description du contenu.
- Activités: Énumère les activités qui ne sont pas décrites dans la mission, les buts et objectifs
- Succursales : L'association peut compter diverses succursales, énumérées au bas.

I. ABBREVIATIONS

Academic and other degrees, membership in & degrees conferred by Societies & Institutions, Honours, Labour Union affiliations, Military Titles, etc.

AACI	Accredited Appraiser Canadian Institute
AASA	Associate of the Alberta Society of Artists
AB	Bachelor of Arts (American) (Artium Baccalaureus)
AC	Advanced Certification, Canadian Association of Medical Radiation Technologists
ACAM	Associate C.A.M.
AccSCRP	Associate of the Canadian Public Relations Society Inc.
ACD	Archaeologiae Christianae Doctor
ACIC	Associate of Canadian Institute of Chemistry
ACInstM	- of Institute of Marketing
AIIC	Associate of the Insurance Institute of Canada
ALS	Commissioned Alberta Land Surveyor
AMEIC	Associate Member of the Engineeering Institute of Canada
AMIEE	- of the Institute of Electrical Engineers
APR	Accredited Member of the Canadian Public Relations Society
ARDIO	Associate of Registered Interior Designers of Ontario
ARIC	- of the Royal Institute of Chemistry (London, England)
AScT	Applied Science Technologist
BA	Bachelor of Arts
BAA	- of Applied Arts
B.Acc.	- of Accounting
B.Adm.Pub.	Baccaulauréat spécialisée en administration publique
BAeE(BAeroE)	Bachelor of Aeronautical Engineering
BAS(BASc)	- of Applied Science
BCE	- of Civil Engineering
B.Des.	- of Design
BE(BEng)	- of Engineering
BEE	- of Electrical Engineering (USA)
BES	- of Envrironmental Sciences/Studies
B.ès.A.	Bachelier ès Arts
B.ès.Sc.	- ès Science
B.ès.Sc.App.	- ès Science Appliquée
BEDS	Bachelor of Environmental Design Studies
BFA	- of Fine Arts
BLA	- of Landscape Architecture
BMV	Bachelier en Médicine Vétérinaire
BSA	Bachelor of Science in Agriculture
B.Sc.	- of Science
BSCE	- of Science in Civil Engineering
BSEE	- of Science in Electrical Engineering
BScF(BSF)	- of Science in Forestry
BScFE	- of Science in Forestry Engineering
BTech	- of Technology
CA	Chartered Accountant
CAE	Certified Association Executive
CAE/caé	Chartered Account Executive
CAM	Certified Administrative Manager
Capt.	Captain
CBE	Commander, Order of the British Empire
CBV	Chartered Business Valuator
CC	Companion, Order of Canada
CCU/CSC	Confederation of Canadian Unions/Confédération des syndicats canadiens
CD	Canadian Forces Decoration
Cdr.	Commander
CE	Civil Engineer
CEA	Certified Environmental Auditor
CEQ	Centrale de l'enseignement du Québec/Quebec Teaching Congress
CerE	Ceramic Engineer
CFA	Chartered Financial Analyst
CFP	Chartered Financial Planner
CGA	Certified General Accountant
CHA	Certified Housing Administrator
ChE	Chartered Executive
CHE	- Health Executive
CIF	Canadian Institute of Forestry
CIM	Canadian Investment Manager
CLC/CTC	Canadian Labour Congress/Congrès du travail du Canada
CIM	Canadian Investment Manager
CIM	Certificate in Management
CIM	Certified Industrial Manager
CIS&P	Canadian Institute of Surveying and Photogrammetry
CLM	Certified Industrial Manager
CLS	Canada Land Surveyor C.M. Member, Order of Canada
CLU	Chartered Life Underwriter
CMA	Certified Management Accountant
CMC	Certified Management Consultant
CMM	-Municipal Manager (Ontario)
CMM	Commander, Order of Military Merit
CMOS	Canadian Meteorological and Oceanographic Society Consultant
CNFIU/FCNSI	Canadian National Federation of Independent Unions/Fédération canadienne nationale des syndicats indépendants
Col.	Colonel
CPA	Certified Public Accountant
CPPO	Certified Public Purchasing Officer
CRA	Canadian Residential Appraiser
CRSP	Canadian Registered Safety Professional
CSC	CanadianSecurities Course
CSD/CDU	Centrale des syndicats démocratiques/Congress of Democratic Unions
CSN	Confédération des syndicats nationaux/Confederation of National Trade Unions
CTC	Certified Travel Counsellor
C.Tech.	-Technician
CWO	Chief Warrant Officer
DDS	Doctor of Dental Surgery
DMD	- of Dental Medicine
DEng	- of Engineering
D.en Méd.Vét.	Docteur en médicine vétérinaire
D.ès.Sc.App.	- ès science appliquée
Dip.Ing.	Diploma in Engineering
DLS	Dominion Land Surveyor
Dr.	Doctor
D.Sc.	Doctor of Science
D.Sc.Nat.	- of Natural Science
D.Th.	- of Theology
DVM(DMV)	- of Veterinary Medicine
D.V.Sc.	- of Veterinary Science

EE	Electrical Engineer
EEE/eee	Expert en évaluation d'entreprises
EM	Mining Engineer
FAGS	Fellow of the American Geographical Society
FAOU	- of the American Ornithologists Union
FAPHA	- of the American Public Health Association
FAPS	- of the American Physical Society
FCA	- of the Institute of Chartered Accountants
FCAM	- of the Institute of C.I.C.A.M. (Canadian Institute of Certified Administrative Mangers)
FCGA	- of the Certified General Accountants' Association
FCIC	- of the Chemical Institute of Canada
FCMA	- of the Certified Management Accountants' Association
FCMRT	- of the Canadian Association of Medical Radiation Technologists
FCSI	- of the Canadian Securities Institute
FE	Forest Engineer
FEIC	Fellow of the Engineering Institute of Canada
FGS	- of the Geological Society (British)
FGSA	- of the Geological Society of America
FICE	- of the Institution of Civil Engineers
FIFE	- of the Institution of Electrical Engineers
FMSA	- of the Mineralogical Society of America
FRAIC	- of the Royal Architectural Institute of Canada
FRAS	- of the Royal Astronomical Society
FRGS	- of the Royal Geographical Society
FRHortS	- of the Royal Horticultural Society
FRIC	- of the Royal Institute of Chemistry
FRMS (FRMetS)	- of the Royal Meteorological Society
IA	Investment Advisor
IC	Investment Counselor
IR	Investment Representative
ISP	Information Systems Professional of Canada
Jr.	Junior
L.ès.Sc.	Licencié ès Sciences
L.Gen	Lieutenant General
LL	License in Civil Law
LLB	Bachelor of Laws (Legum Baccalaureus)
LLD	Doctor of Laws (usually honorary)
LLL	Licence en droit
LLM	Master of Law
LRPS	Licentiate in Royal Photographic Society
LS	Land Surveyor
LSA	Licentiate in Agricultural Science
Lt.Col.	Lieutenant Colonel
MA	Master of Arts
MAeE	Master of Aeronautical Engineering
MAIEE	Member of the American Institute of Electrical Engineers
MAIME	- of the American Institute of Mining Engineers
MAP	Maîtrise en administration publique
MASc(MAS)	Master of Applied Science
MASCE	Member of the American Society of Civil Engineers
MASME	- of the American Society of Mechanical Engineers
MBA	Master of Business Administration
MCE	Member of Civil Engineering
MChE	- of Chemical Engineering (USA)
MCIC	- of the Chemical Institute of Canada
MCIF	- of the Canadian Institute of Forestry
MCIM	- of the Canadian Institute of Mining
MCIMM	- of the Canadian Institute of Mining and Metallurgy
MCInstM	Member of the Canadian Institute of Marketing
MD	Doctor of Medicine
ME	Master of Mechanical Engineering
MEDS	Master of Environmental Design Studies
MEE	- of Electrical Engineering (USA)
MEIC	Member of the Engineering Institute of Canada
M.Eng.	- of Environmental Sciences/Studies
MF	- of Forestry
MICE	- of the Institution of Civil Engineers (British)
MIMM	- of the Institute of Mining and Metallurgy (British)
MLS	Master of Library Science
MMM	Member, Order of Military Merit
MP	Member of Parliament
M.Ph.(M.Phil.)	Master of Philosophy
MP	- of Planning
MPM	- of Pest Management
MRM	- of Resource Management
MSA	- of Science in Agriculture
MSc	- of Science
MScA	- of Applied Science
MSCE	- of Science in Civil Engineering
MScF	- of Science in Forestry
M.Sc.(Med.)	- of Science in Medicine
MURP	- of Urban and Rural Planning
MUP	- of Urban Planning
MVSc	- of Veterinary Science
NDA	National Diploma in Agriculture (Royal Agricultural Society of Engineering)
OC	Officer, Order of Canada
OD	Doctor of Optometry
OLS	Ontario Land Surveyor
OMM	Officer, Order of Military Merit
P.Ag.	Professional Agrologist
PC	Privy Councillor
PE	Professional Engineer
PFP	Personal Financial Planner
P.Mgr.	Professional Manager
PhD	Doctor of Philosophy
Pharm.D.	Doctor of Pharmacology
Prof.	Professor
QAA	Qualified Administrative Assistant
QC	Queen's Counsel
QLS	Québec Land Surveyor
Rev.	Reverend
RFP	Registered Financial Planner
RN	Registered Nurse
R.P.Bio.	Registered Professional Biologist
RSW	- Specification Writer
ScD	Doctorat ès Sciences
ScL	Licence ès Sciences
SFC	Specialist in Financial Counseling
SLS	Saskatchewan Land Surveyor
SM	Master of Science
SPA	Service for Photographic Art

II. GEOGRAPHICAL TERMS

Provinces

Alberta	AB	Alberta
British Columbia	BC	Colombie-Britannique
Manitoba	MB	Manitoba
New Brunswick	NB	Nouveau-Brunswick
Newfoundland & Labrador	NL	Terre-Neuve et Labrador
Northwest Territories	NT	Territoires du Nord-Ouest
Nova Scotia	NS	Nouvelle-Écosse
Nunavut	NU	Nunavut
Ontario	ON	Ontario
Prince Edward Island	PE	Île-du-Prince-Édouard
Québec	QC	Québec
Saskatchewan	SK	Saskatchewan
Yukon	YT	Yukon

The United States

Alabama	AL	Montana	MT
Alaska	AK	Nebraska	NE
Arizona	AZ	Nevada	NV
Arkansas	AR	New Hampshire	NH
California	CA	New Jersey	NJ
Colorado	CO	New Mexico	NM
Connecticut	CT	New York	NY
Delaware	DE	North Carolina	NC
District of Columbia	DC	North Dakota	ND
Florida	FL	Ohio	OH
Georgia	GA	Oklahoma	OK
Hawaii	HI	Oregon	OR
Idaho	ID	Pennsylvania	PA
Illinois	IL	Rhode Island	RI
Indiana	IN	South Carolina	SC
Iowa	IA	South Dakota	SD
Kansas	KS	Tennessee	TN
Kentucky	KY	Texas	TX
Louisiana	LA	Utah	UT
Maine	ME	Vermont	VT
Maryland	MD	Virginia	VA
Massachusetts	MA	Washington	WA
Michigan	MI	West Virginia	WV
Minnesota	MN	Wisconsin	WI
Mississippi	MS	Wyoming	WY
Missouri	MO		

III. STREET ADDRESSES

Avenue	Ave./av
Boulevard	Blvd./boul
Building	Bldg./Édifice
Care of/au soins de	c/o / a/s
Court	Ct.
Crescent	Cres.
Drive/Promenade	Dr./promenade
Floor/Étage	Fl./étage
Highway/Route	Hwy./Rte
Parkway	Pkwy.
Place/Place	Pl. /Place
Post Office Bag	PO Bag
Post Office Box/Caisse postal	PO Box/CP
Postal Sub-Station	Postal Sub-Stn./sous-station
Retail Postal Outlet	RPO
Road/Chemin	Rd./ch
Square/Carré	Sq./carré
Station/Succursale	Stn/Succ
Street/Rue	St./rue

IV. DAYS OF THE WEEK*

Sunday	Sun.	dimanche
Monday	Mon.	lundi
Tuesday	Tues.	mardi
Wednesday	Wed.	mercredi
Thursday	Thu.	jeudi
Friday	Fri.	vendredi
Saturday	Sat.	samedi

*Days of the week expressed in French are presented in full

V. MONTHS OF THE YEAR

January/janvier	Jan./jan.
Februrary/février	Feb./fév.
March/mars	March/mars
April/avril	April/avril
May/mai	May/mai
June/juin	June/juin
July/juillet	July/juillet
August/août	Aug./août
September/septembre	Sept./sept.
October/octobre	Oct./oct.
November/novembre	Nov./nov.
December/décembre	Dec./déc.

VI. TRANSLATIONS

Selected titles, tags & phrases

Acronym	Acronyme
Activities	Activités
Administrator	Administrateur(trice)
Also known as	Également appelé
Amount	Montant
Annual Operating Budget	Budget de fonctionnement annuel
Appointment (Library)	Rendez-vous (Bibliothèque)
Attendees	Participants
Author	Auteur(e)
Awards	Attribution de prix
Awareness Events	Événements de sensibilisation
Chief Officers	Membres du bureau directeur
Commissioner	Commissaire
Committees	Comités
Communications Officer	Agent de communications
Conferences	Conférences
Contact Person	Personne ressource/Responsable
Contents (Publications)	Contenu (Publications)
Conventions	Congrès
Coordinator	Coordonnateur(trice)

Corresponding Secretary	Secrétaire correspondancier
Crisis-Line	Ligne secours
Deadline	Date limite d'inscription
Editor	Rédacteur(trice)
Eligibility	Admissibilité
Email	Courriel
Executive Assistant	Adjoint(e) de direction
Executive Director	Directeur(trice) général(e)
Executive Manager	Directeur
Executive Sec.-Treas.	Sec.-trés. de direction
FAX (Facsmile Transmission)	Télécopieur
Fee Schedule	Liste des cotisations
Financial Secretary	Secrétaire financier(ière)
Founding Date	Date de fondation
Grants	Subventions
Info-Line	Infoligne
Information Officer	Agent d'information
Interns	Stagiaires
ISBN	Numéro ISBN
ISSN	Numéro ISSN
Library	Bibliothèque
Licensing Body	Organisme de réglementation professionnelle
Mailing Address	Adresse postale
Mailing Lists/Labels	Listes de diffusion/étiquettes d'adresses
Manager	Administrateur(trice) ou Gérant(e)
Meetings	Réunions
Member of	Membre de
Membership	Nombre de membres
Membership criteria	Critères d'admissibilité
Membership fee	Montant de la cotisation
Merged from	Fusion de
Number of Pages	Nombre de pages
Online Services	Services en ligne
Open to Public	Bibliothèque publique
Organizational Profile	Description
Physical address	Adresse
Previous Name	Nom précédant
President	Président(e)
President-elect	Président(e) désigné(e)
Recording Secretary	Secrétaire archiviste
Registered Charity	Organisme sans but lucratif
Registrar	Secrétaire
Representative	Représentant(e), Délégué(e)
Schedule	Barème
Scholarships	Bourses
Scope of Activity	Envergure des opérations
Secretary	Secrétaire
Secretary General	Secrétaire général(e)
Secretary-Treasurer (Sec.-Treas.)	Secrétaire-trésorier(ière) (Sec.-trés.)
See	Voir
See also	Voir aussi
Speakers Service	Service de conférenciers
Sponsors	Commanditaires
Staff	Personnel
TTY (Text Telephone)	ATS
Telephone	Téléphone
Toll-free (telephone number)	Ligne sans frais
Treasurer	Trésorier(ière)
URL	Site web
Volunteers	Bénévoles

Canadian Associations at a Glance

There are approximately 20,127 in depth, detailed Canadian association profiles in *Associations Canada 2015*, which include the association's various chapters and branch locations. In addition, this resource lists 877 foreign associations — those not headquartered in Canada, but have a Canadian presence, either physically or otherwise. These foreign listings are in their own section, following the extensive Canadian listings. This by-the-numbers summary illustrates the enormous amount of content to be found in the more than 20,000 listings in this edition.

- **36,314 executives:** This high-powered list makes this edition of *Associations Canada* one of our richest contact-filled databases to date.
- **2,029 Meetings**: Find out who goes where and when, and how many attendees you can expect, for strong, business-building information.
- **5,126 Publications**: With details such as editor names, frequency, and submission information, this data is a valuable, go-to source to research the publications that will best get your message out.
- **5,838 Awards**: This section includes who to contact, deadlines, grants, scholarships, and more, and fills a wide range of research and academic needs, from job hunting to grant money.

Number of Associations in *Associations Canada 2015*, including chapters and branches:

By Province

Ontario	7,078
Québec	3,034
British Columbia	2,386
Alberta	1,925
Manitoba	983
Saskatchewan	921
Nova Scotia	914
New Brunswick	650
Newfoundland and Labrador	422
Prince Edward Island	295
Yukon Territory	159
Northwest Territories	108
Nunavut	37

By Size

Large	1,018
Medium	5,673
Small	13,438

By Type

Professional	2,175
Trade	5,392
Special Interest	12,559

By Budget

Less than $50,000	1,056
$50,000-$100,000	490
$100,000-$250,000	656
$250,000-$500,000	535
$500,000-$1.5 Million	619
$1.5 Million -$3 Million	279
$3 Million -$5 Million	194
Greater than $5 Million	345

Associations du Canada en un coup d'œil

Associations du Canada 2015 compte environ 20 127 profils détaillés d'associations canadiennes, y compris celles qui ont plusieurs succursales et emplacements. De plus, cette ressource énumère 877 associations étrangères, celles dont les sièges sociaux ne se trouvent pas au Canada, mais qui y sont présents, physiquement ou autrement. Ces entrées se retrouvent dans leur propre section, à la suite des entrées exhaustives canadiennes. Ce résumé en chiffres illustre la quantité impressionnante de contenu qui se trouve dans plus de 20 000 entrées qui composent ce numéro.

- **36 314 dirigeants :** cette liste puissante fait de ce numéro d'*Associations Canada* une de nos bases de données contenant le plus de contacts à ce jour.
- **2 029 rencontres :** découvrez qui va où et quand et combien de participants vous pouvez vous attendre à recevoir afin de consolider de l'information d'affaires solide.
- **5 126 publications :** grâce à des détails comme les noms des maisons d'édition, la fréquence de publication et l'information relative à la soumission de textes, ces données constituent une source précieuse de référence pour effectuer des recherches parmi les publications qui transmettront le mieux votre message.
- **5 838 prix :** cette section comprend les contacts, les échéances, les subventions, les bourses, entre autres, et comblent la vaste gamme de besoins en matière de recherche et d'études universitaires, de la recherche d'emploi aux fonds d'aide gratuite.

Nombre d'associations comprises dans *Associations Canada 2015*, y compris les chapitres et succursales

Par Province	
Ontario	7 078
Québec	3 034
British Columbia	2 386
Alberta	1 925
Manitoba	983
Saskatchewan	921
Nova Scotia	914
New Brunswick	650
Newfoundland and Labrador	422
Prince Edward Island	295
Yukon Territory	159
Northwest Territories	108
Nunavut	37

Par taille	
Large	1 018
Medium	5 673
Small	13 438

Par Type	
Professional	2 175
Trade	5 392
Other	12 559

Par Budget	
Less than $50,000	1 056
$50,000-$100,000	490
$100,000-$250,000	656
$250,000-$500,000	535
$500,000-$1.5 Million	619
$1.5 Million -$3 Million	279
$3 Million -$5 Million	194
Greater than $5 Million	345

Associations

Associations are voluntary, nongovernmental, nonprofit organizations composed of personal or institutional members, with or without federal or provincial incorporation. Associations are formed for a particular purpose or to advance a common cause, especially of a public nature. Related terms include foundation, society, institute, federation, alliance, club and union.

The freedom of association is one of the fundamental freedoms guaranteed by the Canadian Charter of Rights and Freedoms. It is estimated that individual Canadians on average are associated with at least 3 associations such as business, trade and professional associations, chambers of commerce and boards of trade, labour organizations and unions, health and welfare groups, religious organizations, athletic associations, political organizations, learned societies, cultural groups, fraternal organizations and service clubs, charities, and community and neighbourhood groups.

Historical Background

The history of associations in Canada dates from when Samuel de Champlain founded the Ordre de Bon Temps in 1604, for the promotion of recreation and relaxation at Port-Royal. A few Canadian associations still in existence can trace their origins back to the 18th century. For example, the Halifax Board of Trade was founded in 1750, which predated the first recorded association of this type in the US by approximately 18 years; the Grand Lodge of Upper Canada of the Ancient Free and Accepted Masons was established in 1792; and the Law Society of Upper Canada was organized in 1797. (Most dates given in this article are formation dates, not incorporation dates.)

Associations formed before Confederation include the Montréal Board of Trade (1822); the Nova Scotia Barristers' Society (1825); the Toronto Board of Trade (1845); the Barristers' Society of New Brunswick (1846); Le Collège des Médecins et Chirurgiens de la Province de Québec (1847); the Royal Canadian Institute (1849); Le Barreau du Québec (1849); the Medical Society of Nova Scotia (1854); the Nova Scotia Board of Insurance Underwriters (1857); the Ontario Fruit Growers' Assn (1859); the Ontario Educational Assn (1861); the Nova Scotian Institute of Natural Science (1862); the Law Society of British Columbia (1863); the Nova Scotia Fruit Growers' Assn (1863); the Entomological Society of Canada (1863), the first national association formed in the sciences; the College of Physicians and Surgeons of Ontario (1866); the Canadian Medical Assn and the Ontario Dental Association (1867).

From 1867 to 1900 many new associations were established at both the national and provincial levels. New markets and the growth of factories and manufacturers spawned the expansion of trade associations to ensure fair competition. Examples of national associations formed during this period and still in existence are the Canadian Manufacturers' Assn (1871); the Royal Society of Canada (1882); the Canadian Institute of Surveying (1882, as the Assn of Dominion Land Surveyors); the Engineering Institute of Canada (1887, as the Canadian Society of Civil Engineers); the Canadian Electrical Assn (1889); the Royal Astronomical Society of Canada (1890, as the Astronomical and Physical Society of Toronto); the Canadian Bankers' Assn (1891); the Canadian Education Assn (1892); and the Canadian Institute of Mining and Metallurgy (1898). From 1900 to the end of WWII there was a steady increase in the number of associations. The period of greatest growth coincided with the economic prosperity of the 1960s. More than one-third of the 1500 nonprofit corporations incorporated under federal legislation from 1900 to 1970 were incorporated in the 5-year period 1966-70. There are also hundreds of associations operating without federal or provincial incorporation. Many professional associations have developed evaluation standards for their members and their respective industries and members can be measured using these standards.

Association headquarters are concentrated heavily in the urban centres of Toronto, Ottawa and Montréal. Vancouver, Edmonton, Calgary and Winnipeg and other large urban areas also have significant concentrations.

Origins and Growth

Several Canadian associations owe their origins to foreign parents, particularly American or British. When Canadian membership in foreign associations increased to a significant number, members withdrew from their parent group to form their own associations with headquarters in Canada. There are still scores of foreign associations with Canadian chapters or divisions, such as the American Society of Mechanical Engineers, New York, and the Royal Commonwealth Society, London. In addition, several international associations such as the International Air Transport Assn have their headquarters in Canada. Many Canadian labour unions are affiliated with international unions headquartered in the US, however, the percentage of international union membership in Canada has significantly shifted away from international unions to national unions, continuing a 25-year trend as new national unions and independent local organizations were organized in Canada. By 1995, international union membership had fallen from two-thirds of all union membership in Canada to 29%, and national union representation rose from 21% to 57%. By 2003 more than 4 million Canadians belonged to a union.

Industry associations provide valuable peer-to-peer support. A 2006 study published by Statistics Canada found innovative firms refer to industry associations almost 10 times more frequently than federal government research institutes and up to 4.4 times more frequently than universities for information, solutions, and business ideas.

The proliferation of associations is partially a result of the growth in population, the expansion and diversification of the economy, and greatly increased government activity, especially in health care and social services, as well as the desire for communication with others who share common interests.

Types

There have been various attempts to classify associations into types according to purpose, function and structure. No classification has been satisfactory because of the diversity in membership, objectives, structure, methods of operation and concerns. One classification makes a distinction between those associations that function primarily for the benefit of the public (charitable organizations) and those that carry on their activities primarily for the benefit of their members (membership organizations). Another distinguishes between corporate-type and federation-type organizations. The latter may bring together associations devoted to the same subject, or to several different subjects. It is also possible to classify associations according to their principal activity.

Incorporation

Incorporation is often advantageous or necessary for nonprofit corporations to carry out certain activities. The principal advantages of incorporation as a nonprofit corporation without share capital are that it provides greater continuity and permanency for the organization, frees members from liability for the debts and obligations of the corporation, and facilitates certain activities such as the holding of real estate. Such corporations must be conducted without pecuniary gain for the members.

Federal nonprofit corporations in Canada include many of the large charitable and membership organizations and virtually all the boards of trade and chambers of commerce incorporated under the Boards of Trade Act. For associations whose activities are within a single locality or province, provincial incorporation as a nonprofit corporation is sufficient. Each province has its own requirements and procedures for incorporation.

Organization and Operation

The board of directors of an incorporated nonprofit corporation manages the corporation's business and affairs. The board is legally responsible for adhering to the corporation constitution and bylaws, for making policy to further the attainment of its stated goals and objectives, and for appointing the chief executive officer. A small group of board members, including the officers, constitutes the executive committee, which sits between board meetings to make decisions on behalf of the board.

The usual officers of an association are the president, vice-president, treasurer and secretary. The officers may be selected by the membership or appointed by the board, and their duties are set out in the bylaws or established by the board. The chief executive officer or executive director (the title may vary) performs duties assigned by the board of directors. This officer executes policies as prescribed by the board, selects employees for the operation of the association office, prepares budgets, approves expenditures and attends all meetings of the board and its executive committee.

The committee structure of associations usually reflects its goals and objectives. Typical committee responsibilities include membership, nominations, education, research, publishing, public and government relations. Officers and directors are expected to render a periodic account of their stewardship, usually in the form of an annual report. The requirements for membership are usually stated in the bylaws of the association and there may be several classes of membership, such as member, associate, student and honorary member. Some associations admit anyone interested in its activities; others, such as professional associations, have specific requirements for membership. In general, charitable organizations rely on government grants for their income and on donations from business and the general public, whereas membership organizations obtain most of their income from fees and dues.

Contribution to Society

Associations registered federally as charitable organizations are legally obligated to provide services beneficial to the community at large. Although membership associations have the advancement of the interests of their members as their primary aim, they too may respond to changing conditions in society by engaging in programs and activities in the public interest. Associations have an important role in building consensus in society by providing the mechanism for their members to reach agreement on social values, on objectives to be pursued and on the means to achieve objectives. Through interaction with government, associations participate in shaping public policy. National associations, many of which are bilingual, can contribute to the strengthening of national unity by improving communications and understanding among the different peoples and regions of Canada.

Associations have evolved as peer support or mentoring agencies that offer members the experience and resources within their areas of interest. Associations are also important as sources for information about hundreds of specialized activities in our society. By helping those in need, supporting and publishing worthwhile research, educating members of the public, contributing to the personal development of citizens and pressing for just and humanitarian causes, associations are making significant contributions to Canadian society and its citizens.

Extensive information about associations in Canada is available in the publication, Associations Canada, which is published annually by Grey House Publishing Canada. Associations Canada was created by the merger of two annual directories: Directory of Associations in Canada and Associations Canada: An Encyclopedic Directory. Today, the publication provides details regarding the activities of a variety of associations in Canada including Canadian and foreign associations, professional associations, nonprofit and voluntary organizations. The directory uses more than 1,500 subject classifications ranging from accounting to zoology to describe the activities of more than 20,000 associations listed.

Author R. BRIAN LAND

Source: The Canadian Encyclopedia, Historica-Dominion Institute. www.thecanadianencyclopedia.com

Associations

Les associations sont des organisations volontaires, non gouvernementales, sans but lucratif, composées de membres individuels ou institutionnels, constituées ou non en sociétés en vertu d'une loi fédérale ou provinciale, formées dans un but particulier ou pour la défense d'une cause commune, plus particulièrement d'intérêt public. D'autres termes y sont apparentés, comme « fondation », « société », « institut », « fédération », « alliance », « club » et « syndicat ».

La liberté d'association est une des libertés fondamentales garanties par la . On estime que, en moyenne, chaque Canadien fait partie d'au moins trois associations telles que des associations de gens d'affaires, de métier ou professionnelles, des chambres et des bureaux de commerce, des organisations ouvrières et des syndicats, des groupes de défense et de promotion de la santé ou du bien commun, des organisations religieuses, des associations sportives, des organisations politiques, des sociétés savantes, des associations culturelles, des sociétés d'aide mutuelle et des organisations philanthropiques, des groupes communautaires et de voisinage.

Historique

L'histoire des associations au Canada remonte à Samuel de , qui a fondé l' en 1604 pour favoriser les loisirs et la détente à Port-Royal. Quelques associations canadiennes nées au XVIIIe siècle sont encore actives : l'Halifax Board of Trade, fondé en 1750, soit environ 18 ans avant la première association de ce genre connue aux États-Unis; la Grand Lodge of Upper Canada of the Ancient Free and Accepted Masons, créée en 1792, et le Barreau du Haut-Canada, formé en 1797 (la plupart des dates mentionnées dans cet article sont celles de la formation des associations et non celles de leur constitution juridique).

Parmi les associations formées avant la Confédération, on compte le Bureau de commerce de Montréal (1822), la Nova Scotia Barristers' Society (1825), le Toronto Board of Trade (1845), le Barreau du Nouveau-Brunswick (1846), le Collège des médecins et chirurgiens de la province de Québec (1847), maintenant l'Ordre des médecins du Québec, le Royal Canadian Institute (1849), le Barreau du Québec (1849), la Medical Society of Nova Scotia (1854), le Nova Scotia Board of Insurance Underwriters (1857), l'Association des fruiticulteurs et des maraîchers de l'Ontario (1859), l'Ontario Educational Association (1861), le Nova Scotian Institute of Natural Science (1862), la Law Society of British Columbia (1863), la Nova Scotia Fruit Growers' Association (1863), la Société entomologique du Canada (1863), la première association nationale dans le domaine des sciences, l'Ordre des médecins et chirurgiens de l'Ontario (1866), l'Association médicale canadienne et l'Ontario Dental Association (1867).

De 1867 à 1900, de nombreuses nouvelles associations voient le jour tant à l'échelle provinciale que fédérale. Parmi les associations nationales formées au cours de cette période et qui existent toujours, nommons l' (1871), la (1882), l'Association canadienne des sciences géomatiques (1882), anciennement l'Association canadienne des sciences géodésiques, l'Institut canadien des ingénieurs (1887), anciennement la Canadian Society of Civil Engineers, l'Association canadienne de l'électricité (1889), la Société royale d'astronomie du Canada (1890), d'abord l'Astronomical and Physical Society of Toronto, l'Association des banquiers canadiens (1891), l'Association canadienne d'éducation (1892) et l'Institut canadien des mines, de la métallurgie et du pétrole (1898). De 1900 jusqu'à la fin de la Deuxième Guerre mondiale, le nombre des associations augmente de façon soutenue. Cette période de forte croissance coïncide avec la prospérité économique des années 1960. Plus du tiers des 1500 sociétés sans but lucratif créées au niveau fédéral de 1900 à 1970 l'ont été dans une période de cinq ans, de 1966 à 1970. Il existe aussi des centaines d'associations qui ne sont constituées en personnalité juridique ni au fédéral ni au provincial. Beaucoup d'associations professionnelles ont élaboré des normes régissant les membres et leurs industries respectives et d'après lesquelles ceux-ci peuvent être évalués.

Les sièges sociaux des associations se concentrent fortement dans les centres urbains de Toronto, d'Ottawa et de Montréal, puis de façon significative à Vancouver, Edmonton, Calgary, Winnipeg et dans d'autres grandes régions urbaines.

Origines et développement

Un certain nombre d'associations canadiennes doivent leur existence à des associations mères de l'étranger, en particulier des États-Unis et de la Grande-Bretagne. Quand les membres canadiens au sein des associations étrangères deviennent suffisamment nombreux, ils se retirent pour former leurs propres associations avec des sièges sociaux au Canada. Toutefois, on trouve encore un bon nombre d'associations étrangères qui comptent des sections ou des filiales au Canada, comme l'American Society of Mechanical Engineers, de New York, et la Royal Commonwealth Society, de Londres. De plus, diverses associations internationales, comme l'Association du Transport aérien international, ont leurs sièges sociaux au Canada. Plusieurs organisations syndicales canadiennes sont affiliées à des organisations internationales dirigées à partir des États-Unis. Cependant, sur l'ensemble des syndiqués canadiens, la proportion de membres affiliés à des syndicats internationaux diminue pendant qu'augmente la participation à des syndicats nationaux, parallèlement à la tendance, remarquée depuis 25 ans, à fonder de nouveaux syndicats nationaux et des organisations locales indépendantes au Canada. En 1995, l'appartenance à des syndicats internationaux, qui constituait les deux tiers des syndiqués du Canada, est tombée à 29 %. Pendant ce temps, la représentation par un syndicat national passe de 21 % à 57 %. En 2003, plus de 4 millions de Canadiens sont membres d'un syndicat.

Les associations d'industrie apportent un soutien par les pairs fort utile. Une étude de 2006, publiée par Statistique Canada, constate que, lorsqu'il s'agit d'avoir des renseignements, des solutions et des idées commerciales, des entreprises novatrices s'en remettent à des associations de l'industrie environ 10 fois plus souvent qu'aux instituts de recherche du gouvernement fédéral et jusqu'à 4,4 fois plus souvent qu'aux universités.

La prolifération des associations s'explique par la croissance démographique, l'expansion et la diversification de l'économie et l'accroissement important de l'activité gouvernementale, spécialement en matière de soins de santé et de services sociaux, de même que le désir d'échanger avec des personnes qui partagent les mêmes intérêts.

Types

On a essayé, suivant divers critères, de classifier les associations en fonction de leur but, de leur fonction et de leur structure. Aucune classification ne s'est révélée satisfaisante en raison de la diversité de la composition, des objectifs, de la structure, du mode de fonctionnement et des intérêts des associations. Une classification distingue entre les associations qui s'intéressent avant tout à l'intérêt public (associations de bienfaisance) et celles dont les activités visent d'abord l'intérêt de leurs membres (associations de membres). Une autre distingue entre les organisations de type sociétaire et celles de type fédératif. Ces dernières peuvent regrouper des associations actives dans un même domaine ou dans plusieurs domaines différents. Il est aussi possible de classifier les associations selon leur activité principale.

Constitution

Il est souvent avantageux ou nécessaire pour des organisations sans but lucratif de se constituer juridiquement en personnes morales pour mener à bien certaines de leurs activités. Les principaux avantages de la constitution juridique pour une organisation sans but lucratif et sans capital social consistent à lui assurer une plus grande continuité et la permanence, à dégager les membres de toute responsabilité en ce qui concerne les dettes et les obligations de l'organisation et à faciliter certaines activités comme la possession de biens immobiliers. De telles sociétés doivent fonctionner sans avantages pécuniaires pour les membres.

Au Canada, parmi les sociétés sans but lucratif à charte fédérale se trouvent plusieurs grandes sociétés de bienfaisance et organisations de membres, et pratiquement tous les bureaux et chambres de commerce constitués en vertu de la *Loi sur les chambres de commerce*. Pour les associations qui poursuivent des activités à l'intérieur d'une seule localité ou province, l'obtention d'un acte constitutif provincial comme société à but non lucratif est suffisante. Chaque province a ses propres exigences et procédures en matière de constitution juridique.

Organisation et fonctionnement

Le conseil d'administration d'une société constituée sans but lucratif gère ses activités et ses affaires internes. Il est légalement responsable du respect de la constitution et des règlements, de l'adoption des politiques en vue d'atteindre les buts et objectifs convenus, et de la nomination du directeur général. Un petit groupe de membres du conseil, y compris les dirigeants, forment le comité exécutif, qui se réunit entre les réunions du conseil pour prendre des décisions au nom du conseil.

Habituellement, les dirigeants d'une association sont le président, le vice-président, le trésorier et le secrétaire. Ils peuvent être choisis par les membres ou nommés par le conseil; leurs tâches sont fixées par les règlements ou établis par le conseil. Le directeur général ou chef de la direction (le titre peut varier) assume les tâches que lui confie le conseil d'administration. Il met en oeuvre les politiques définies par le conseil, choisit les employés chargés du fonctionnement du bureau de l'association, prépare les budgets, approuve les dépenses et assiste à toutes les réunions du conseil et de son comité exécutif.

La structure de comités des associations reflète habituellement leurs buts et objectifs. Les responsabilités typiques des comités incluent l'adhésion des membres, les nominations, la formation, la recherche, les publications, les relations publiques et avec le gouvernement. Les dirigeants et les administrateurs sont tenus de rendre compte périodiquement de leur gestion, habituellement sous la forme d'un rapport annuel. Les conditions d'adhésion sont habituellement fixées par les règlements de l'association, et il peut exister plusieurs formes d'adhésion, comme à titre de membres, d'associés, d'étudiants ou de membres honoraires. Certaines associations acceptent toute personne intéressée à leurs activités. D'autres, comme les associations professionnelles, ont des conditions d'admission spécifiques. En général, les organisations de bienfaisance comptent sur des subventions gouvernementales et sur des dons du milieu des affaires ou du grand public pour leur financement, tandis que les associations de membres tirent leurs revenus de droits et de cotisations.

Contribution sociale

Les associations enregistrées au fédéral en tant qu'organisations de bienfaisance sont légalement obligées de fournir des services qui profitent à l'ensemble de la population. Bien que le principal objectif des associations de membres soit la promotion des intérêts de leurs membres, elles peuvent aussi réagir aux conditions sociales changeantes en s'engageant dans des programmes et des activités d'intérêt public. Les associations jouent un rôle important dans l'élaboration d'un consensus au sein de la société, puisqu'elles fournissent les mécanismes permettant à leurs membres de s'entendre sur des valeurs sociales, sur les objectifs à poursuivre et sur les moyens de les atteindre. Par leur interaction avec le gouvernement, les associations contribuent à façonner la politique gouvernementale. Les associations nationales, dont plusieurs sont bilingues, peuvent contribuer au renforcement de l'unité nationale en améliorant la communication et la compréhension entre les différents peuples et régions du Canada.

Les associations ont évolué en tant que groupes d'entraide ou de mentorat offrant à leurs membres l'expérience et les ressources convenant à leur champ d'intérêt. Elles constituent aussi d'importantes sources d'information sur des centaines d'activités spécialisées dans notre société. En aidant ceux qui sont dans le besoin, en soutenant et en publiant des recherches dignes d'intérêt, en faisant de l'éducation auprès du public, en contribuant à l'épanouissement personnel des citoyens et en se portant à la défense de causes justes et humanitaires, les associations fournissent un apport appréciable à la société canadienne et à ses citoyens.

On peut obtenir des renseignements supplémentaires sur les associations au Canada dans la publication annuelle Associations Canada de Grey House Publishing Canada. Elle résulte de la fusion de deux répertoires, le *Répertoire des associations du Canada et Associations Canada: un répertoire encyclopédique*. De nos jours, le répertoire donne des détails concernant les activités d'associations diverses du Canada, qu'elles soient canadiennes ou étrangères, d'associations professionnelles et d'organismes sans but lucratif et bénévoles. Le répertoire utilise plus 1500 classements par sujet, allant de l'administration à la zoologie, pour décrire les activités de plus de 20 000 associations répertoriées.

Auteur R. BRIAN LAND

Source: L'Encyclopédie Canadienne, Historica-Dominion Institute. www.thecanadianencyclopedia.com.

YOUR CONFERENCE IS A STRATEGIC ASSET – MANAGE IT ACCORDINGLY

By Meredith Low

Why do you hold a conference? Professional development for members? Building your organization's brand and profile? Tradition? The opportunity to engage directly with members? Reliance on its proceeds to fund other activities?

Conferences are under more pressure than ever. Technology is changing the relationship between physical proximity and activities like learning, networking, and collaborating. Delegates find it increasingly difficult to secure funding and time to attend. Industry sponsors are questioning their return on investment, seeking to quantify and justify their marketing decisions. Conferences can be complex to manage, and costs difficult to contain.

At the same time, the surpluses generated by conferences are a revenue stream on which organizations are often increasingly reliant.

In our work with professional associations and other non-profits over the last decade, we've identified several conference elements that organizers should understand well. Your answers to the questions in these four areas will tell you if it's time for a full strategic assessment of your event.

1. Objectives

- Does the conference have a clear set of objectives?
- Do the objectives guide decision-making?
- Are the objectives used to evaluate the conference's success?

If the answer to any or all of these questions is no, start with your objectives and ensure they are developed, validated and *used*. If you don't know what you're trying to do, how can you know if you did it? Objectives should be a guide to planning, management, and evaluation of the conference, and should form the basis of your reporting to the Board.

Depending on the conference's governance structure, finalizing these objectives may involve a fairly lengthy and complex process, or may be accomplished within a week via a couple of discussions and followed by Board approval.

We strongly recommend including a financial objective. If this is not specified, staff will be left to make complex tradeoff decisions on their own, without clear guidance.

2. Value Proposition

- Why do delegates attend? Why *don't* they? What are their alternatives?
- Are delegates getting what they want out of the conference?
- What kinds of delegates might you be able to attract for growth?
- What do industry sponsors and trade show participants want to get out of the conference? Are they getting it?

Are you innovating with the conference – whether through programming, facilitating networking, increasing access, leveraging technology, or trade show design – to increase the value for stakeholders? Most conferences conduct delegate satisfaction surveys, and some have methods of consulting with industry participants. However, often these means of engagement are quite tactical, focusing on delegates' satisfaction with the food at a particular meal, or the logistics of booth setup.

It's rare for an organization to step back and ask its stakeholders the kinds of strategic questions that really get at loyalty and motivation. Conference organizers need to go beyond the simple percentage of satisfaction with the conference and understand what the event means to the delegates, and what value it really brings to industry participants. This often requires more in-depth consultation than a simple survey, such as qualitative interviews or focus groups.

For instance, networking seems universally important to delegates. But what do *your* delegates mean by it? Some examples of what "networking" may mean:

- For a premier scientific researcher: *A chance to discuss collaboration on worldwide studies.*
- For a social worker in a community services organization: *Connecting with local peers who work with the same client groups to better coordinate services.*
- For an accountant: *Meet sources of referrals.*
- For a recent graduate: *Get hired.*
- For an industry product manager: *Social opportunities with key opinion leaders.*

These options have very different implications for conference organizers in terms of program offerings, scheduling, venue, even refreshments. If your event is multidisciplinary, all the more reason to recognize the diversity in delegate preferences.

Similarly, if you only evaluate the program you actually offered, you won't get perspectives informed by what delegates have seen at other events, and what opportunities they see for innovation in your conference. An open question at the end of a conference satisfaction survey won't tell you. Knowledgeable volunteers from the delegate communities typically help develop the program, but it is not reasonable to expect them to speak for all the delegates. It may require a scan of best practices in conferences across industries. Without a deep and systematic understanding of delegate priorities, it's very difficult to make good decisions.

The same goes for industry relationships. The pressure to demonstrate a quantified return on marketing investment is intensifying for industry sponsors and exhibitors. If you don't understand, intimately and concretely, what your event does for your industry partners – what motivates them to participate, what alternatives they have, and how strong their commitment is – that portion of your revenue is at risk.

3. Quantitative assessment

- **Attendance:**
  - What are the trends in attendance? Which delegate segments are increasing? Which aren't?
  - Who attends regularly, versus infrequently?
  - Is attendance aligned with your organization's membership trends?
- **Financials:**
  - What are the trends in revenue and expenses, by category, total and per delegate?
  - Are you capturing the event's true costs? Perhaps you have a conference manager which represents a direct cost, but do you analyze the time others, including management, spend supporting the conference on a part-time basis?
  - How do conference fees compare to competitive events?
  - Do you make or lose money on each incremental delegate?

- If you project out the financial trends for the next few years, what happens?
- **Other:**
  - What quantified media impact do you get from the conference?
  - Is interest from presenters changing (e.g. presentation submissions or scientific abstracts)?
  - Is the number of booths in the exhibit hall increasing?

Without adequate data, you are managing blind.

This analysis can point to previously-hidden issues, such as unintended overinvestment in a conference, when fully loaded costs are included. It can also challenge assumptions; it's counterintuitive to think that an incremental delegate may *cost* you money, but this may be true if you are not charging enough to cover variable per-delegate costs, especially if you have tiered registration fees or revenue-sharing agreements with partners. It can also expose both unrealized opportunities for growth as well as long-term strategic risks, such as low attendance by younger members of the profession.

4. **Resourcing, management and governance**

- Are there skill sets and resources within your organization to effectively manage the conference and deliver on stakeholder expectations?
- Do you have appropriate external partners to complement internal resources?
- Is the conference's performance versus its objectives reported to senior management and the Board?
- Especially if the conference is jointly sponsored by more than one organization, is the governance model working?

How much of a conference's management and logistics should be in-house versus outsourced depends on the specific situation. Regardless, the level of commitment should be aligned with the size and complexity of the conference, taking into consideration whatever resources the rest of the organization might be able to bring to bear (e.g. media relations or fund development capabilities). The key is to first assess what is required, and then secondarily determine how that work should be done – in-house or elsewhere.

If the conference is of strategic significance to the organization, the Board should be receiving annual reports on its performance, and senior management should be actively involved in setting its direction.

Governance models for a multi-organization conference can be challenging to manage, and do require regular review to ensure all partners are seeing benefit from the arrangement.

Treat your conference like the strategic asset that it is

Conferences can be an irreplaceable way for associations to provide value to their members in a tangible way, engage with industry, and generate revenue to be used for mission-critical programs and services. They tend to take on a life of their own, with their own culture, history, and brand associations. It can be easy to let an event continue along, year after year, but a strategic board or CEO will ensure they protect this key asset from risk, and maximize its value.

VOTRE CONFÉRENCE EST UN ACTIF STRATÉGIQUE – GÉREZ-LE COMME TEL

Par Meredith Low

Pourquoi organisez-vous une conférence? Pour le perfectionnement professionnel des membres? Pour bâtir la marque et le profil de l'organisation? Pour la tradition? Pour l'occasion de vous engager directement avec les membres? Pour les recettes afin de financer d'autres activités?

Les conférences subissent plus de pression que jamais. La technologie modifie le rapport entre la proximité physique et les activités telles que la formation, le réseautage et la collaboration. Les délégués trouvent de plus en plus difficile de trouver les fonds et le temps pour y assister. Les commanditaires de l'industrie questionnent le rendement sur leur investissement, cherchant à quantifier et justifier leurs décisions marketing. Les conférences sont parfois complexes à gérer, et les coûts difficiles à contenir.

De plus, les surplus générés par les conférences sont souvent une source de revenus sur lesquels les organisations comptent de plus en plus.

Dans notre travail avec des associations professionnelles et d'autres organismes sans but lucratif au cours de la dernière décennie, nous avons identifié plusieurs éléments de conférences que les organisateurs devraient bien comprendre. Vos réponses aux questions dans ces quatre secteurs vous diront s'il est temps de procéder à une évaluation stratégique complète de votre événement.

1. Objectifs

- La conférence est-elle assortie d'un ensemble clair d'objectifs?
- Les objectifs guident-ils la prise de décisions?
- Les objectifs sont-ils utilisés pour évaluer le succès de la conférence?

Si la réponse à l'une ou à toutes ces questions est négative, commencez avec vos objectifs et assurez-vous de les développer, de les valider et de les *utiliser*. Si vous ne savez pas ce que vous essayez de faire, comment pouvez-vous savoir si vous avez réussi? Les objectifs devraient servir de guide de planification, de gestion et d'évaluation de la conférence, et devraient former la base de votre communication de rapports au conseil d'administration.

Selon la structure de gouvernance de la conférence, la finalisation de ces objectifs peut impliquer un processus assez long et complexe, ou se faire en une semaine par le biais de quelques discussions suivies de l'approbation par le conseil.

Nous recommandons fortement d'inclure un objectif financier. S'il n'est pas précisé, le personnel aura à prendre lui-même des décisions de compromis complexes, sans directives claires.

2. Proposition de valeur

- Pourquoi les délégués participent-ils? Pourquoi ne le font-ils *pas*? Quelles sont leurs alternatives?
- Les délégués retirent-ils ce qu'ils attendent de la conférence?
- Quels types de délégués pourriez-vous attirer pour croître?
- Que veulent retirer de la conférence les commanditaires de l'industrie et participants au salon professionnel? L'obtiennent-ils?

Êtes-vous innovateur dans votre conférence – que ce soit par la programmation, la facilitation du réseautage, l'amélioration de l'accès, la technologie ou le concept du salon – pour augmenter la valeur pour les parties prenantes? La plupart des conférences comportent des sondages de satisfaction des délégués, et certaines des méthodes de consultation des participants de l'industrie. Cependant, ces moyens d'engagement sont souvent tactiques, ciblant la satisfaction des délégués face aux aliments servis à un repas spécifiques, ou la logistique entourant la configuration des kiosques.

Il est rare qu'une organisation prenne du recul et demande aux parties prenantes les types de questions stratégiques touchant véritablement la loyauté et la motivation. Les organisateurs de conférences doivent aller au-delà du simple pourcentage de satisfaction face à l'événement, et comprendre ce qu'il signifie pour les délégués, et quelle valeur il apporte réellement aux participants de l'industrie. Cela nécessite souvent une consultation plus approfondie qu'un simple sondage, notamment des entrevues qualitatives ou des groupes de discussion.

Par exemple, le réseautage semble universellement important pour les délégués. Mais que veulent dire *vos* délégués à ce sujet? Voici quelques exemples de ce que peut signifie le « réseautage » :

- Pour un chercheur scientifique principal : *une occasion de discuter de collaboration à des études mondiales.*
- Pour un travailleur social dans un organisme de services communautaires : *entrer en contact avec des collègues locaux qui travaillent avec les mêmes groupes de clients afin de mieux coordonner les services.*
- Pour un comptable : *rencontrer des sources de références.*
- Pour un récent diplômé : *se faire embaucher.*
- Pour un chef de produit de l'industrie : *des occasions sociales avec des leaders d'opinion clés.*

Ces options présentent des implications très différentes pour les organisateurs de conférences en termes d'offre de programme, de calendrier, de site, et même de rafraîchissements. Dans le cas d'un événement multidisciplinaire, les raisons sont encore plus grandes de reconnaître la diversité des préférences des délégués.

De même, si vous n'évaluez que le programme que vous avez offert, vous n'obtiendrez pas des perspectives éclairées par ce que les délégués ont vu à d'autres événements, et quelles possibilités d'innovation ils voient dans votre conférence. Une question ouverte à la fin d'un sondage de satisfaction face à la conférence ne vous le révélera pas. Les bénévoles érudits issus de la communauté des délégués aident généralement à développer le programme, mais il est déraisonnable de s'attendre à ce qu'ils s'expriment au nom de tous les délégués. Il faudra peut-être une analyse des pratiques exemplaires des conférences à travers les industries. Sans une compréhension approfondie et systématique des priorités des délégués, il est très difficile de prendre de bonnes décisions.

Il en va de même dans les relations avec l'industrie. L'urgence de démontrer un rendement de l'investissement marketing quantifié s'intensifie pour les commanditaires et exposants de l'industrie. Si vous ne comprenez pas intimement et concrètement ce que votre événement fait pour vos partenaires de l'industrie – ce qui les motive à participer, quelles sont leurs alternatives et quelle est la force de leur engagement – cette portion de vos revenus est à risque.

3. Évaluation quantitative

- **Taux de participation :**
  - Quelles sont les tendances en matière de taux de participation? Quels segments de délégués augmentent? Lesquels n'augmentent pas?
  - Qui assiste régulièrement ou non?
  - Le taux de participation correspond-il aux tendances de membership de votre organisation?

- **Finances :**
  - Quelles sont les tendances dans les revenus et dépenses, par catégorie, au total, par délégué?
  - Saisissez-vous les coûts réels de l'événement? Vous avez peut-être un directeur de conférence qui représente un coût direct, mais analysez-vous le temps que les autres, y compris la direction, consacrent à appuyer la conférence à temps partiel?
  - Comment les frais de conférence se comparent-ils à ceux d'événements concurrentiels?
  - Gagnez-vous ou perdez-vous de l'argent sur chaque délégué supplémentaire?
  - Si vous projetez les tendances financières pour les quelques années à venir, que se passe-t-il?
- **Autres :**
  - Quel impact médiatique quantifié obtenez-vous de la conférence?
  - L'intérêt des présentateurs change-t-il (p. ex. soumissions de présentations ou de résumés scientifiques)?
  - Le nombre de kiosques dans le hall d'exposition augmente-t-il?

Sans les données adéquates, vous faites de la gestion de non-voyant.

Cette analyse peut identifier des enjeux auparavant cachés, par exemple un surinvestissement involontaire à une conférence, lorsque les coûts comprenant les frais indirects sont inclus. Elle peut également défier des postulats; il est contre-intuitif de penser qu'un délégué supplémentaire puisse vous *coûter* de l'argent, mais ce peut être le cas si vous ne chargez pas assez pour couvrir les coûts variables par délégué, notamment si vous avez des frais d'inscription étagés et des ententes de partage de revenus avec des partenaires. Elle peut aussi exposer des possibilités non réalisées de croissance ainsi que des risques stratégiques à long terme, par exemple un faible taux de participation chez les membres plus jeunes de la profession.

4. Ressourcement, gestion et gouvernance

- Existe-t-il des ensembles de compétences et des ressources dans votre organisation pour gérer efficacement la conférence et livrer les attentes aux parties prenantes?
- Avez-vous des partenaires externes appropriés pour compléter vos ressources internes?
- Le rendement de la conférence par rapport à ses objectifs a-t-il été rapporté à la haute direction et au conseil d'administration?
- Si, en particulier, la conférence est commanditée conjointement par plus d'une organisation, le modèle de gouvernance fonctionne-t-il?

La proportion de la gestion et de la logistique de la conférence qui devrait se faire à l'interne par rapport à des ressources externes dépend de la situation spécifique. Peu importe la situation, le degré d'engagement devrait correspondre à la taille et à la complexité de la conférence, en tenant compte des ressources que le reste de l'organisation peut contribuer (p. ex. les relations avec les médias ou les capacités de développement de fonds). La clé est d'évaluer d'abord ce qui est requis, et de déterminer ensuite comment ce travail devrait être effectué – à l'interne ou ailleurs.

Si la conférence revêt une importance stratégique pour l'organisation, le conseil d'administration devrait recevoir des rapports annuels sur son rendement, et la haute direction devrait être activement impliquée dans l'établissement de son orientation.

Les modèles de gouvernance pour les conférences impliquant plusieurs organisations peuvent représenter des défis, en plus de nécessiter un examen régulier pour s'assurer que tous les partenaires voient les avantages des dispositions prises.

Votre conférence est un actif stratégique, traitez-la comme tel

Les conférences peuvent être un moyen irremplaçable d'ajouter de manière tangible de la valeur pour les membres, de faire participer l'industrie, et de générer des revenus qui serviront à des programmes et services essentiels à la mission. Elles tendent à avoir leur vie propre, leur propre culture, histoire et marque. Il est facile de laisser un événement se poursuivre année après année, mais un conseil d'administration ou chef de la direction stratégique s'assurera de protéger cet actif clé du risque, et de maximiser sa valeur.

Source: Canadian Society of Association Executives (CSAE), http://www.csae.com/Resources/ArticlesTools/View/ArticleId/1826/YOUR-CONFERENCE-IS-A-STRATEGIC-ASSET-MANAGE-IT-ACCORDINGLY, accessed January 5, 2015.

CANADA'S ANTI-SPAM LAW (CASL): FAQS RELEVANT TO ALL REGISTERED CHARITIES AND NONPROFITS

1. How do we know if we need consent to send a message to somebody?

Consent is only required to send a "commercial electronic message" (CEM). A commercial electronic message is:

> *an electronic message that, having regard to the content of the message, the hyperlinks in the message to content on a website or other database, or the contact information contained in the message, it would be reasonable to conclude has as its purpose, or one of its purposes, to encourage participation in a commercial activity, including an electronic message that*
>
> *(a) offers to purchase, sell, barter or lease a product, goods, a service, land or an interest or right in land;*
>
> *(b) offers to provide a business, investment or gaming opportunity;*
>
> *(c) advertises or promotes anything referred to in paragraph (a) or (b); or*
>
> *(d) promotes a person, including the public image of a person, as being a person who does anything referred to in any of paragraphs (a) to (c), or who intends to do so.*

However, it is important to note that the Regulatory Impact Analysis statement issued alongside the regulations specifies several types of message that are not commercial and to which the regulations do not apply:

- surveys, polling, newsletters, and messages soliciting charitable donations, political contributions, or other political activities that do not encourage participation in a commercial activity are not included in the definition;
- if the message involves a pre-existing commercial relationship or activity and provides additional information, clarification or completes the transaction involving a commercial activity that is already underway, it would not be considered a CEM; and,
- the mere fact that a message involves commercial activity, hyperlinks to a person's website, or business related electronic addressing information does not make it a CEM under the Act if none of its purposes is to encourage the recipient in additional commercial activity.

2. We think our organization sends CEMs. Does this mean we have to stop?

CEMs can still be sent to individuals who have given express or implied consent.

3. What is express consent?

Express consent is when an individual gives you permission to send them any type of message, including CEMs.

Express consent can be obtained in a number of ways, including:

- signing up on your website to receive messages;
- checking a box on a paper form (such as a membership application);
- providing an email address, if it is clear that you intend to send CEMs; and,
- oral or written requests to receive messages.

Express consent, once obtained, only expires if the individual withdraws it. In the same way that express consent can be obtained in many ways, it can also be withdrawn in many ways.

4. We send emails asking people to uncheck a box if they want us to stop sending them messages. If they do not uncheck the box, is this express consent?

The CRTC, which will be enforcing the law, has indicated that a "pre-checked box" is not sufficient for obtaining express consent under the new regulations, and has provided guidance as to how express consent could be sought.

However, the regulations grandfather express consent that you may have obtained under the old rules. *If you have been sending CEMs using pre-checked boxes, you likely have express consent for your existing email lists.*

5. What is implied consent?

Various types of relationship between your organization and an individual provide you with implied consent to send them CEMs. These relationships include instances where an individual or organization has:

- donated to you in the last two years (either cash or in-kind contributions);
- volunteered for you in the last two years;
- been a member of your organization in the last two years;
- entered into a contract with your organization in the last two years;
- purchased a good or service from you in the last two years; or
- made an inquiry about your commercial offerings in the last six months.

Implied consent is transactional. For example, every time someone makes a purchase, the two-year implied consent period begins again.

6. We often have clients referred to us by another organization. Are we still allowed to contact these people?

If your message is not commercial, there would be no restrictions on contact.

In the case of a "third party referral" you are allowed to send one CEM, as long as you specify how you obtained the email address. A message asking for consent is itself a CEM, so if you send such a message and do not receive a response, you may no longer send CEMs to that email address.

7. If we have consent, either express or implied, are there any other requirements?

All CEMs have to contain certain information. This information includes:

- clearly identifying your organization;
- providing up-to-date contact information for your organization; and,
- offering an unsubscribe mechanism.

The unsubscribe option is key to establishing due diligence and responding to any complaints made against you. It does not have to be a technically advanced unsubscribe; asking people to reply to your message with the word "unsubscribe" is sufficient to comply.

8. We have implied consent with somebody. If we send a message asking for express consent, and they do not reply, do we have to stop sending them CEMs?

No. The implied consent will still be valid until it expires. See question 5 above for expiration timelines.

9. What do the regulations mean for our use of social media?

Depending on how you use social media, the regulations are not likely to have much effect.

Posting a message on Twitter, Facebook, LinkedIn, or other social media platforms is considered broadcasting, and not affected by these regulations. Similarly, targeted advertisements you may purchase on social media platforms are not affected.

Direct messages to an individual's personal inbox on the social media platform may be affected, depending on the type of message being sent and the terms and conditions to which they agreed when setting up their social media account.

10. We use a third-party service for our electronic communications. Are we liable if they violate the rules?

Where a third-party service provider is used, your contract with them should include a requirement that they be CASL-compliant, and assurance from them that they are. This demonstrates due diligence on your part.

11. We've heard that the penalties are astronomical if we make any mistakes. How worried should we be?

The *maximum* penalties for CASL are significant. The CRTC has the authority to impose large fines, and, as of July 1, 2017, there will be a possibility of class-action lawsuits with significant damages.

A number of factors need to be kept in mind:

- steps you take to show due diligence (such as tracking how you obtain email addresses, or always including an unsubscribe option) will be taken into consideration when assessing the penalty for non-compliance;
- the CRTC is likely to investigate only in cases where there are a significant number of complaints or there appears to be a major transgression;
- the CRTC is likely to emphasize education and compliance, rather than punishment, in cases where mistakes are made;
- in the case of a violation, a compliance agreement with the CRTC eliminates the possibility of private lawsuits; and,
- frivolous lawsuits may be summarily dismissed, with costs, by a judge.

Organizations that can demonstrate they are acting in good faith, taking reasonable steps to comply, and exercising due diligence are unlikely to face serious consequences if an error occurs.

12. Where can I get more information?

Information for businesses, organizations, and consumers is available at www.fightspam.gc.ca.

If you have specific questions about your own activities, you can make inquiries with the CRTC or with Industry Canada.

CRTC: 1-877-249-CRTC (2782)
Industry Canada: 1-800-328-6189

These Qs and As were issued by Imagine Canada on June 5, 2014 and will be updated periodically as warranted. Check the public policy section of Imagine Canada's website for the most up-to-date information.

LOI CANADIENNE ANTI-POURRIEL (LCAP) : FAQ PERTINENTE POUR TOUS LES ORGANISMES DE BIENFAISANCE ENREGISTRÉS ET LES ORGANISMES SANS BUT LUCRATIF

1. Comment saurons-nous si nous devons obtenir le consentement d'une personne pour lui envoyer un message?

Le consentement n'est requis que pour envoyer un « message électronique commercial » (MEC). Un message électronique commercial est :

> *un message électronique dont il est raisonnable de conclure, vu son contenu, le contenu de tout site Web ou autre banque de données auquel il donne accès par hyperlien ou l'information qu'il donne sur la personne à contacter, qu'il a pour but, entre autres, d'encourager la participation à une activité commerciale et, notamment, tout message électronique qui, selon le cas :*
>
> *(a) comporte une offre d'achat, de vente, de troc ou de louage d'un produit, bien, service, terrain ou droit ou intérêt foncier;*
>
> *(b) offre une possibilité d'affaires, d'investissement ou de jeu;*
>
> *(c) annonce ou fait la promotion d'une chose ou possibilité mentionnée aux alinéas (a) ou (b);*
>
> *(d) fait la promotion d'une personne, y compris l'image de celle-ci auprès du public, comme étant une personne qui accomplit – ou a l'intention d'accomplir – un des actes mentionnés aux alinéas (a) à (c).*

Il est toutefois important de souligner que le Résumé de l'étude d'impact de la réglementation définit plusieurs types de messages qui ne sont pas commerciaux et auxquels cette réglementation ne s'applique pas :

- les enquêtes, les sondages, les bulletins et les messages sollicitant des dons de bienfaisance, les contributions politiques, ou d'autres activités politiques qui n'encouragent pas la participation à une activité commerciale ne seraient pas visés par la définition;
- si le message comporte une relation ou une activité commerciale préexistante et fournit des renseignements supplémentaires, des précisions ou complète une transaction liée à la réalisation d'une activité commerciale qui est déjà en cours, ce message ne serait pas considéré comme un message électronique commercial;
- Le simple fait qu'un message soit lié à une activité commerciale, donne accès par hyperlien au site Web d'une personne ou à de l'information électronique liée à des activités commerciales n'en fait pas pour autant un message électronique commercial en vertu de la Loi si aucun de ses buts ne vise à encourager le destinataire à participer à une activité commerciale.

2. Nous pensons que notre organisme envoie des MEC. Cela veut-il dire que nous devons arrêter de le faire?

On peut continuer à envoyer des MEC aux personnes qui ont donné leur consentement exprès ou tacite.

3. Qu'est-ce que le consentement exprès?

Le *consentement exprès* s'obtient quand une personne vous donne la permission de lui envoyer tout type de messages, dont les MEC.

On peut obtenir le *consentement exprès* de plusieurs façons, dont celles-ci :

- l'inscription à votre site Web pour recevoir des messages;
- une case à cocher dans un formulaire papier (comme une demande d'adhésion);

- la fourniture d'une adresse de courriel, s'il est clair que vous avez l'intention d'envoyer des MEC;
- les demandes orales ou écrites de recevoir des messages.

Le *consentement exprès*, une fois obtenu, n'expire que si la personne le retire. Tout comme il est possible d'obtenir le consentement exprès de nombreuses façons, son retrait peut également être effectué de nombreuses façons.

4. Nous envoyons des courriels demandant aux personnes de décocher une case si elles souhaitent que nous cessions de leur envoyer des messages. Si elles ne décochent pas cette case, est-ce que c'est un consentement exprès?

Le CRTC, qui appliquera la *Loi*, a indiqué qu'une « case cochée d'avance » n'est pas suffisante pour obtenir le consentement exprès en vertu de la nouvelle réglementation et a publié des lignes directrices sur les moyens à employer pour solliciter le consentement exprès.

La réglementation maintient cependant le consentement exprès que vous avez obtenu en vertu des anciennes règles. *Si vous avez envoyé des MEC en utilisant des cases cochées à l'avance, vous disposez vraisemblablement du consentement exprès pour vos listes de distribution électronique existantes.*

5. Qu'est-ce que le consentement tacite?

Divers types de relations entre votre organisme et une personne vous fournissent son consentement tacite de lui envoyer des MEC. Ces relations sont notamment celles dans lesquelles une personne ou un organisme :

- vous a fait un don au cours des deux années passées (des contributions soit en espèces soit en nature);
- a fait du bénévolat pour vous au cours des deux années passées;
- est membre de votre organisme au cours des deux années passées;
- a conclu un contrat avec votre organisme au cours des deux années passées;
- vous a acheté un bien ou un service au cours des deux années passées;
- a demandé des renseignements sur vos offres commerciales au cours des six derniers mois.

Le consentement tacite est transactionnel. Par exemple, chaque fois qu'une personne fait un achat, la période de deux ans du consentement tacite débute à nouveau.

6. Il nous arrive souvent qu'un autre organisme aiguille des clients vers nous. Sommes-nous encore autorisés à communiquer avec ces personnes?

Si votre message n'est pas commercial, aucune restriction ne s'appliquerait à cette communication.

Dans le cas d'une « référence d'un tiers », vous êtes autorisés à lui envoyer un seul MEC, à condition d'indiquer comment vous avez obtenu son adresse de courriel. Un message de sollicitation du consentement est un MEC en lui-même, donc, si vous envoyez un tel message et que vous ne recevez pas de réponse, vous ne pourrez plus envoyer de MEC à cette adresse de courriel.

7. Si nous avons le consentement, soit exprès, soit tacite, des autres exigences s'appliquent-elles?

Tous les MEC doivent obligatoirement contenir les éléments suivants :

- les renseignements permettant d'identifier clairement votre organisme;
- les coordonnées valides de votre organisme;
- un mécanisme de désabonnement.

L'option de désabonnement est indispensable pour démontrer votre diligence raisonnable et pour donner suite aux plaintes éventuellement formulées contre vous. Il est inutile que ce mécanisme de désabonnement soit techniquement avancé; il vous suffit de demander aux personnes de répondre à votre message avec le mot « désabonnement » pour vous conformer à la réglementation.

8. Nous avons le consentement tacite d'une personne. Si nous lui envoyons un message sollicitant son consentement exprès et qu'elle n'y répond pas, devons-nous cesser de lui envoyer des MEC?

Non. Le consentement tacite demeurera valide jusqu'à son expiration. Voir les échéances d'expiration à la question 5 ci-dessus.

9. Comment cette réglementation s'applique-t-elle à notre utilisation des médias sociaux?

La réglementation est susceptible de différer selon votre utilisation des médias sociaux, mais son effet ne sera vraisemblablement pas important.

L'affichage d'un message dans Twitter, Facebook, LinkedIn ou dans d'autres plateformes des médias sociaux est considéré comme de la diffusion sélective et cette réglementation ne s'y applique pas, de même qu'aux encarts ciblés que vous pouvez acheter sur les plateformes des médias sociaux.

Il se peut que cette réglementation s'applique aux messages adressés directement à la corbeille d'arrivée d'une personne, selon le type de message envoyé et les conditions qu'elle a acceptées lors de la création de son compte dans une des plateformes des médias sociaux.

10. Nous utilisons un fournisseur de services tiers pour nos communications électroniques. Serons-nous responsables s'il enfreint ces règles?

Quand vous utilisez les services d'un fournisseur tiers, le contrat qui vous lie à ce fournisseur devrait exiger sa conformité à la LCAP et qu'il vous certifie cette conformité, ce qui démontre votre diligence raisonnable.

11. Nous avons entendu dire que les pénalités sont astronomiques si nous commettons des erreurs. Dans quelle mesure cela devrait-il nous inquiéter?

Les pénalités *maximales* pour les infractions à la LCAP sont sévères. Le CRTC a le pouvoir d'imposer de lourdes amendes et, à partir du 1er juillet 2017, il sera possible d'intenter des recours collectifs en réclamant des dommages-intérêts élevés.

Plusieurs facteurs à garder présents à l'esprit :

- les mesures que vous prenez pour démontrer votre diligence raisonnable (comme la surveillance des moyens que vous utilisez pour obtenir des adresses de courriel ou l'inclusion systématique d'une option de désabonnement) seront prises en compte lors de l'évaluation de la pénalité à imposer pour la non-conformité;
- le CRTC ne mènera vraisemblablement une enquête que dans le cas d'un nombre élevé de plaintes ou d'une grave transgression;
- le CRTC mettra vraisemblablement l'accent sur l'information et la conformité, plutôt que sur les sanctions, en cas d'erreur;
- en cas de violation, une entente de conformité avec le CRTC élimine la possibilité d'actions en justice privées;
- les actions en justice frivoles pourront être classées sans suite, avec dépens, par un juge.

Les organismes qui peuvent démontrer qu'ils agissent de bonne foi, en prenant des mesures raisonnables pour se conformer à la *Loi* et en exerçant une diligence raisonnable ne subiront vraisemblablement pas de graves conséquences si une erreur se produit.

12. Où puis-je obtenir de plus amples renseignements?

De l'information pour les entreprises, les organismes et les consommateurs est consultable à l'adresse www.combattrelepourriel.gc.ca.

Si vous avez des questions précises sur vos propres activités, vous pouvez demander des renseignements au CRTC ou à Industrie Canada.

CRTC : 1-877-249-CRTC (2782)
Industrie Canada : 1-800-328-6189

Cette foire aux questions a été publiée le 5 juin 2014 et sera mise à jour périodiquement selon les besoins. Consultez l'information la plus récente dans la section du site Web d'Imagine Canada consacrée aux politiques publiques.

Source: Imagine Canada (2014), http://www.imaginecanada.ca/resources-and-tools/resources/canada%E2%80%99s-anti-spam-law-casl-faqs-relevant-all-registered-charities-and, accessed January 5, 2015.

WHAT THE NEXT GENERATION OF ASSOCIATION LEADERS REALLY WANTS FROM FUTURE EMPLOYERS

By Jack Shand, CAE

What is the emerging generation (40 or younger) of association leaders looking for in their future career and from future employers? How do they see the sector in five or ten years?

Four individuals with senior association management experience were invited to share their thoughts on: career experience and preparation for leadership roles; how future roles will be attractive to future employees; the issues younger leaders foresee for organizations and how the next generation of CEOs may be equipped to help employers with the changes already in play and accelerating.

The four are –

• Nicole Burgess, Executive Director, Supply Chain Management Association Saskatchewan. A graduate of Simon Fraser University, Nicole has been with her current association for seven years. She is a CAE® candidate.
• Chris Conway, President and CEO of the Building Owners and Managers Association of the Greater Toronto Area. Chris has a law degree and MBA, with prior association management experience in government relations following roles on Parliament Hill and as a consultant.
• Marco D'Angelo, Executive Director of the Ontario Traffic Council. Marco has his MBA, is a certified association executive, and had earlier roles in government relations in association management as well as Parliament Hill experience.
• Susie Grynol, Vice President, Government Relations, Retail Council of Canada. Susie is a certified association executive and the current president of CSAE's Ottawa-Gatineau Chapter. Susie worked at the House of Commons for four years after graduating from the University of Ottawa. Prior to her recent move to the Retail Council of Canada, she was a senior manager with a national professional association for eight years.

While there are many outstanding performers currently in the ranks of younger association managers, these four were selected because I know something of their background and, with my own experience in consulting, executive search, and association CEO leadership roles, I think they are representative of a capable new generation of leaders. I am optimistic among this group are the future CEOs of Canada's pre-eminent associations.

Experience for the Future

It has been suggested that the association specialist will be replaced, or already has been, with managers with experience across many sectors – in business, the professions, government, and not-for-profit.

Nicole Burgess observes that as executives are expected to do more with less and perform at a higher level and at faster speeds than ever before, education and diverse sectoral experience (from healthcare to the arts to business) will best equip them to deal with the demands placed upon them.

Chris Conway recognizes that management mastery is expected by employers. Management experience and training, including executive leadership continuing education programs, will help those individuals aspiring to run one of Canada's leading not-for-profits hone their abilities in the coming decade. Managing people continues to be very important, as association executives not only manage staff but a large virtual group of members, directors, working groups such as committees, and in some cases front-line volunteers. Financial literacy is also important (all the more so as traditional revenue sources are under pressure). Last but not least, diverse experience will prepare the CEO to relate to individuals on the Board of Directors who may often comprise leaders in their own sector (private or public sectors), and to deal externally - and substantively - with government on challenging issues globally, domestically, and sector-specifically.

Marco D'Angelo suggests that the new energy and perspectives a younger employee may offer have to be balanced with behaviours demonstrating an ability to lead. He cautions that one cannot facilitate change, with over-confidence or an "I-know-better" attitude that will alienate Boards of Directors and members, no matter how compelling change may be needed. Marco recommends that the best way to overcome age-related questions about experience and preparation are to provide fresh solutions but also recognize there may be a time-honoured way to get things done. Understanding the association's framework (e.g., consultation, compromise, consensus) to adopt and implement change, and understanding the "old guard", will go a long way to increasing the likelihood that new ideas will take root.

Susie Grynol believes the next generation of CEOs will have a tougher job than the current one. Member expectations are higher than before and there are more organizations (both private and public) offering comparable services. CEOs will need to help their organization retain members. This will require fresh thinking and creative ways of delivering value to stay ahead of what Susie predicts will be "fierce" competition for members' support, time, and money.

Career Planning and Ongoing Development

Susie Grynol adds that the young association executive today needs to complement job training and education with a strong network of peers, experience through volunteering, and mentorship. It takes careful planning. She encourages every young person to have a mentor, or several, who are willing to teach and share their wisdom. A strong peer network will help the young executive navigate through the new experiences, identifying industry standards or better practices the executive can apply to their situation. Volunteering opens doors to developing skills in areas where a paid job may not, as well as helping the individual appreciate that "running an association has more to do with people management than any other skill." Drawing upon her own benefits as a volunteer, Susie notes that "one is exposed to different personalities, dynamics and situations" that will be helpful preparation for the demands of being the staff leader of a not-for-profit organization.

Chris Conway also notes that it is harder to market one's self through a résumé and networks are increasingly important, so making those connections is an essential strategy.

Marco D'Angelo feels that the "qualities unique to a single association can be learned on the job" and, therefore, the priority investment should be developing "managerial mental flexibility" through more general programs such as the CAE® (grounding in association management), an MBA degree (learning general business), and certificate programs in the individual's skill gap areas such as group facilitation or web technology.

Motivating Exceptional Talent

The reality for not-for-profit organizations and their Boards is that talented employees have options. The mediocre organization is not likely to attract or retain an extraordinary executive who wants to be part of a well-functioning team achieving stretch goals. So what do these younger leaders feel will be the attractors – or detractors – in considering jobs in the future?

Chris Conway will be drawn to the cause, area or industry that can show forward thinking and recognize global-context. Associations that think beyond Canada and the United States and recognize the value of partner relationships are more likely to be thought-leaders in his view. The environment, sustainability, education standards are all areas that transcend borders. A detractor will be the employer that does not see value or willingness to recognize these trends.

Susie Grynol recognizes that the organization's value proposition is the central issue as members demand more, and associations have to be nimble by quickly adapting or building programs that link to ever-evolving needs. For Susie Grynol, the biggest deterrent is the employer that cannot handle the need for change and the pace at which change must occur.

And the younger association leaders still feel – as is the case for more seasoned CEOs – that alignment with the organization's values and mission are important to job satisfaction and motivation.

Opportunities To Be Met

In the next decade, the younger leaders foresee opportunities for organizations to achieve their goals in the changing landscape of organizational value and stakeholder expectations.

Nicole Burgess sees that many organizations in the not-for-profit sector have evolved to become more competitive and business-minded. For those that have not, she believes that associations must operate more like a business including integration of business systems and approaches, demonstrating high levels of professionalism with all products and services, and attracting the highest caliber of human resources (staff and volunteers) possible. Technology is now so pervasive that the organization that is not already well along integrating technology into their business processes – possibly only because they haven't the resources to be competitive – will likely disappear in the next five years. In Nicole's view this is the most significant change in play and where younger executives have the potential to offer value by pointing out what advances and applications in technology are present or coming. The younger executive is more in tune with technology, perhaps more adaptive and responsive to change, and can help their associations understand how technology's impact will influence future success and growth.

Younger executives and managers, Chris Conway suggests, intuitively understand how the younger demographic communicates and what they expect. Technology has been core to their life experience – in education, at work, and socially. Chris also emphasizes that younger people are inherently more global in their thinking. This may lead to opportunities, for example in China, as more competitive, relevant not-for-profit organizations expand and become enablers of success in other parts of the world.

Susie Grynol predicts the not-for-profit of tomorrow will look very different from the ones today. She thinks that most organizations are held back by historic structure, including inefficient governance models, programs that are not "exactly" in line with members' needs, disjointed communications strategies, and too many committees. These structures are barriers and threats to quick decision-making. Members increasingly see a disconnect between the resources spent on governance meetings or defining roles among provincial divisions or local branches, over what matters most to them: programs and services with value which they demand. Her call to action: "This sounds negative, but it's not. I think there is a tremendous opportunity on the horizon for associations en masse to shake things up, to be more efficient, and to streamline both operations and programs for the betterment of all involved." The younger leaders today are well positioned to help their organizations because they are not afraid of new things and they embrace change. Their frustration when things don't make sense or are not accessible immediately, simply mirror how increasing numbers of members feel.

Marco D'Angelo predicts that as long-time members increasingly retire, transactional members will take their place and the emphasis will be – as is already seen – more on accountability (versus belonging and loyalty). In effect, organizations will face a "daily referendum". Participation in organizations will be experiential. Marco also recognizes that the younger manager may be effective at harnessing technology. However, he reiterates the point that success for the younger CEO will be incorporating legacy knowledge and processes, and then adding value with new ideas and new platforms to reach members. Creating the means for constant feedback from members and on-going demonstrations of membership value will be the hallmarks of managing tomorrow's associations. "Waiting for the annual general meeting to facilitate change" will no longer be an option, he cautions.

Both Marco and Susie Grynol believe the recipe for success includes blending new ideas and fresh thinking with a respect for the past. Change is occurring and it needs new thinking, but Boards will continue to respond to action that is justifiable and constructive. Older colleagues also need to buy-in and can share context and other information that will help make the case for necessary change.

From this representative group of young leaders, the indicators are clear that the not-for-profit sector is in very capable hands as it transitions from current leadership to the next generation of thought-leaders.

Source: Canadian Society of Association Executives (CSAE), http://www.csae.com/Resources/ArticlesTools/View/ArticleId/2082/What-the-Next-Generation-of-Association-Leaders-Really-Wants-from-Future-Employers, accessed January 5, 2015.

Subject Index

- Canadian & foreign headquarters listed here by subject
- *See* & *See also* references direct you through the index
- Subjects are listed alphabetically
- Entries may appear under more than one subject
- Each entry is accompanied by a page number which points you to the corresponding listing in the alphabetical listings of both Canadian and Foreign Associations

Agriculture & Youth

Agrochemicals

Agroforestry

Agrologists

Agronomists

AIDS

Air & Waste Management

Air Ambulance

Air Cadets

Air Conditioning

Air Force

Air Freight

Air Handling

Air Pilots

Air Pollution

Air Quality Testing

Air Rescue

Air Safety

Air Search

Air Shows

Air Sports

Air Transportation

Aircraft

Aircraft Industry

Airlines

Airplanes, Model

Chambers of Mines

Chaplains, Hospital

Charities

Charter Boats

Construction Trades Councils

Consular Service

Consultants & Consulting

Consumer Protection

Consumers

Containers

Continuing Care

Continuing Education

Continuing Legal Education

Contraception

Contractors

Convalescent Homes

Convention Planning

Cookie Industry

Cooks

Cooperative Education

Cooperative Housing

Cooperative Learning

Cooperative Movement

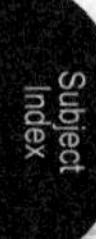
Subject Index

Subject Index

Subject Index

Foundations

Founding

Foundry Industry

Four-Wheel Drive

Fourth World

Fragrances

France

Franchises

Francophones in Canada

Subject Index

Horseshoe Pitching

Horticulture

Hospice Care

Hospital Auxiliaries

Hospital Employees

Hospital Medical Records

Hospitality Industry

Hospitalization Insurance

Hospitals

Hostelling

Hostels for Women

Hot Air Balloons

Hotels & Motels

House Cleaning

House Construction

Houseboats

Household Appliances

Household Employees

Housewares Industry

Housework

Housing

Housing for the Physically Disabled

Housing, Assisted

Housing, Cooperative

Subject Index

Subject Index

Labrador

Lacrosse

Ladies' Golf

Lakes

Lamps & Fixtures

Land Economics

Land Mines

Land Reclamation

Land Surveying

Land Trusts, Community

Land Use

Landfill

Landlords

Landscape Architecture

Language Disorders

Language Teaching

Languages

Native Peoples

Native Women

NATO

Natural Birth Control

Natural Childbirth

Natural Family Planning

Natural Gas

Natural Healing

Natural History

Natural Products Industry

Natural Resource Management

Natural Resources, Conservation of

Subject Index

Subject Index

Religious Orders of Brothers

Religious Orders of Women

Religious Society of Friends

Remote Sensing

Renaissance Studies

Renewable Energy Resources

Renovation

Rent Controls

Rental Housing

Reporters

Reproduction Rights (Literary, Perf

Reproductive Biotechnology

Reproductive Choice

Reproductive Health

Reprographic Equipment Industry

Reprographic Rights

Reprography

Reptiles

Rescue Services

Research

Abbeyfield Houses Society of Canada
PO Box 1, 427 Bloor St. West, Toronto ON M5S 1X7
Tel: 416-920-7483; *Fax:* 416-920-6956
info@abbeyfield.ca
www.abbeyfield.ca
Overview: A small national charitable organization founded in 1984
Mission: To provide accommodation and companionship for lonely older people within their own community.
Affliation(s): Abbeyfield International, U.K.
Activities: *Speaker Service:* Yes
Awards:
• Queen's Jubilee Medals (Award)

Abbotsford Arts Council (AAC)
PO Box 336, 2387 Ware St., Abbotsford BC V2T 6Z6
Tel: 604-852-9358
www.abbotsfordartscouncil.org
www.linkedin.com/company/abbotsford-arts-council
www.facebook.com/AbbotsfordArtsCouncil
twitter.com/AbbyArtsCouncil
Overview: A small local charitable organization founded in 1972
Mission: To promote the vision, creativity & energy of the community through the arts; To develop & enhance all of the arts & culture in the Abbotsford community; To encourage & support arts organizations & individuals including professional & emerging artists & hobbyists by coordinating projects & events; To provide education opportunities that stimulate & promote excellence in the arts
Member of: Assembly of BC Arts Councils
Affiliation(s): BC Touring Council; Festivals BC
Chief Officer(s):
Judy Whyte, Executive Director
Finances: *Annual Operating Budget:* $50,000-$100,000; *Funding Sources:* Government; corporate; private
Staff Member(s): 2; 50 volunteer(s)
Membership: 400; *Fees:* $15 Individual; $25 Group
Activities: Christmas Craft Fair; For the Love of the Arts Studio Tour; Art Walk; unity statue project; Artisans Fair; Art Benches; Arty Awards; *Awareness Events:* Envision Coffee House Concert Series; Snowflake Christmas Market; Art of Marketing
Awards:
• Arty Awards

Abbotsford Chamber of Commerce (ACOC)
207 - 32900 South Fraser Way, Abbotsford BC V2S 5A1
Tel: 604-859-9651; *Fax:* 604-850-6880
acoc@telus.net
www.abbotsfordchamber.com
www.facebook.com/abbotsfordchamber
www.twitter.com/@acoc
Overview: A small local charitable organization founded in 1913
Mission: To represent, serve & connect our members to build & sustain a thriving business community
Member of: British Columbia Chamber of Commerce; Canadian Chamber of Commerce
Chief Officer(s):
Allan Asaph, Executive Director
allan@abbotsfordchamber.com
Finances: *Annual Operating Budget:* $250,000-$500,000; *Funding Sources:* Membership fees; fundraising
Staff Member(s): 4; 150 volunteer(s)
Membership: 700+; *Fees:* $126.89-$452.11; *Member Profile:* Business & non-profit organizations; *Committees:* Agriculture; Membership; Retail & Services; Tourism; Training & Development; Golf; Government Affairs
Activities: Operates business information centre; business luncheons; training & skills seminars & workshops; awards; networking; fundraisers; lobbying; annual gala; Springtime Fashion Show; chamber of commerce week; small business week; *Library:* Resource Centre; Open to public
Awards:
• Business Excellence Awards (Award)

Abbotsford Community Services
2420 Montrose St., Abbotsford BC V2S 3S9
Tel: 604-859-7681; *Fax:* 604-859-6334
info@abbotsfordcommunityservices.com
abbotsfordcommunityservices.com
Overview: A medium-sized local charitable organization founded in 1969
Mission: To provide supportive community social services in partnership with government ministries & the local community
Member of: British Columbia Association for Community Living; Federation of Family & Children Services
Affiliation(s): Social Planning & Research Council of BC; Community Social Services Employers' Association
Chief Officer(s):
Virginia Cooke, President
Finances: *Annual Operating Budget:* Greater than $5 Million; *Funding Sources:* Government; community donors; foundations; sales; membership fees
Staff Member(s): 300; 1000 volunteer(s)
Membership: 75 individual; *Fees:* $2; *Committees:* Board Development; Community Relations; Finance; Health & Safety; Multicultural; Nominations; Fund Development
Activities: Family services; recycling operation; multi-cultural services; senior services; employment services; food bank; services for developmentally disabled; legal services intake; *Awareness Events:* Multi-cultural Week; Substance Abuse Awareness Week; Volunteer Appreciation Day; *Internships:* Yes
Awards:
• Cultural Diversity (Award)

Abbotsford Downtown Business Association
2615A Montrose Ave., Abbotsford BC V2S 3T5
Tel: 604-850-6547; *Fax:* 604-859-6507
info@downtownabbotsford.com
www.downtownabbotsford.com
www.facebook.com/AbbotsfordDowntown
twitter.com/downtownabbybc
Overview: A small local organization
Mission: To attract patrons to Historic Downtown Abbotsford

Abbotsford Female Hockey Association (AFHA)
c/o Paul Unger, Sponsorship Director, 2167 Essex Dr., Abbotsford BC V2S 7R8
www.abbotsfordfemalehockey.com
www.facebook.com/AbbotsfordFemaleHockeyAssociation
twitter.com/AbbyIceGirls
Overview: A small local organization
Mission: The Abbotsford Female Hockey Association seeks to provide an opportunity for females of all ages & all skill levels to play hockey in Abbotsford in an all-female league.
Member of: BC Hockey
Chief Officer(s):
Scott Findlay, President

Abbotsford Food Bank & Christmas Bureau (AFB)
33914 Essendene Ave., Abbotsford BC V2S 2H8
Tel: 604-859-5749; *Fax:* 604-859-2717
Toll-Free: 877-859-5749
afb@telus.net
www.abbotsfordfoodbank.com
www.facebook.com/AbbyFoodbank
Previous Name: Matsqui-Abbotsford Food Bank
Overview: A small local organization founded in 1979
Member of: Canadian Food Bank Association
Chief Officer(s):
Dave Murray, Manager
dave.murray@abbotsfordcommunityservices.com
Finances: *Annual Operating Budget:* $100,000-$250,000; *Funding Sources:* Donations
Activities: Christmas Bureau; Free Dental clinic; mentoring; garden box; comedy tours; kids sports; school breakfast programs; *Speaker Service:* Yes

Abbotsford International Air Show Society (AIAS) / Spectacle aérienne d'Abbotsford
#4, 1276 Tower Rd., Abbotsford BC V2T 6H5
Tel: 604-852-8511; *Fax:* 604-852-6093
info@abbotsfordairshow.com
www.abbotsfordairshow.com
www.facebook.com/360068150851
twitter.com/AbbyAirshow
Overview: A small local organization founded in 1966
Mission: To produce & orchestrate an international flying events show
Member of: Abbotsford Chamber of Commerce; International Council of Airshows
Chief Officer(s):
Ron Price, President & CEO
Staff Member(s): 3; 1000 volunteer(s)
Activities: The Abbotsford International Airshow, August; *Speaker Service:* Yes

Abbotsford Social Activity Association
33889 Essendene Ave., Abbotsford BC V2S 2H6
Tel: 604-853-4014; *Fax:* 604-853-4031
abbysocialactivityassoc@gmail.com
www.abbysocialactivityassoc.com
Overview: A small local charitable organization founded in 1972
Mission: To provide recreational facilities & activities for seniors in the Abbotsford area of British Columbia
Chief Officer(s):
Jim Curran, Acting President, 604-859-6531
Membership: *Fees:* $10 / year
Activities: Dancing; Classes; Crafts; Exercise;

Abbotsford-Mission Nature Club
PO Box 612, Abbotsford BC V2T 6Z8
Tel: 604-853-4283
info@abbymissionnatureclub.org
www.centralvalleynaturalists.org
Previous Name: Central Valley Naturalists
Overview: A small local organization
Affiliation(s): Federation of BC Naturalists
Chief Officer(s):
Hank Roos, President
Membership: 120; *Fees:* $30 individual; $35 family

ABC CANADA Literacy Foundation *See* ABC Life Literacy Canada

ABC Life Literacy Canada
#604, 110 Eglinton Ave. East, Toronto ON M4P 2Y1
Tel: 416-218-0010; *Fax:* 416-218-0457
Toll-Free: 800-303-1004
info@abclifeliteracy.ca
abclifeliteracy.ca
www.linkedin.com/groups?home=&gid=2805444
www.facebook.com/abclifeliteracycanada
twitter.com/Life_Literacy
www.youtube.com/user/abccanadavideo
Previous Name: ABC CANADA Literacy Foundation
Overview: A medium-sized national charitable organization founded in 1990
Mission: A joint initiative of business & labour, supporting the development of an educated & adaptable workforce through the fostering of a lifelong learning culture; ABC CANADA supports the development of a fully literate Canadian population
Chief Officer(s):
Gillian Mason, President, 416-218-0010 Ext. 120
gmason@abclifeliteracy.ca
Anthony Alfred, Director, Communications & Marketing
aalfred@abclifeliteracy.ca
Finances: *Annual Operating Budget:* $1.5 Million-$3 Million; *Funding Sources:* Federal government; private sector
Staff Member(s): 7
Membership: 1-99; *Committees:* Audit; Communications; Executive; Research; Board; Finance
Activities: Public awareness; National LEARN/APPRENDRE campaign; Math Literacy; *Awareness Events:* PGI Golf Tournaments for Literacy; Family Literacy Day; Learn Campaign; *Library:* ABC CANADA Collection at Alpha Plus Centre; Open to public by appointment

Abilities Foundation of Nova Scotia *See* Easter Seals Nova Scotia

Ability New Brunswick / Capacité Nouveau-Brunswick
#102, 440 Wilsey Rd., Fredericton NB E2B 7G5
Tel: 506-462-9555; *Fax:* 506-458-9134
Toll-Free: 866-462-9555
info@abilitynb.ca
www.abilitynb.ca
www.facebook.com/abilitynb
twitter.com/AbilityNB
Previous Name: Canadian Paraplegic Association (New Brunswick) Inc.
Overview: A medium-sized provincial organization overseen by Spinal Cord Injury Canada
Mission: To respond to the needs of people with spinal cord injuries & their families in New Brunswick
Chief Officer(s):
Courtney Keenan, President
Haley Flaro, Executive Director
haley.flaro@abilitynb.ca
Activities: Offering information & support services
Publications:
• Ability Now! [a publication of Ability New Brunswick]
Type: Newsletter

Moncton
#20, 236 St. George St., Moncton NB E1C 1W1
Tel: 506-858-0311; *Fax:* 506-858-8290
Toll-Free: 866-462-9555
info@abilitynb.ca

Ability Online Support Network / En ligne directe
PO Box RPO PO Box 18515, 250 Wincott Dr., Toronto ON M9R 4C8
Tel: 416-650-6207; *Fax:* 866-829-6780
Toll-Free: 866-650-6207
information@abilityonline.org
www.abilityonline.org
www.facebook.com/AbilityOnline
twitter.com/Ability_Online
Also Known As: Ability Online
Overview: A small national charitable organization founded in 1992
Mission: To enhance the lives of children with disabilities or illness by providing an online community for friendship, support & skill development
Chief Officer(s):
Michelle McClure, Executive Director
Michael Teixeira, Chair
miket@abilityonline.org
George Kyriakis, Vice-Chair
Finances: *Annual Operating Budget:* $250,000-$500,000; *Funding Sources:* Corporations; private foundations; special events; private donations
Staff Member(s): 5; 70 volunteer(s)
Membership: 6,300; *Member Profile:* Children, youth, young adults with disabilities or illness, parents & caregivers; *Committees:* Fundraising, Program/Volunteers; Audit; Executive
Activities: Golf tournament; *Awareness Events:* People in Motion, 1st weekend in June; *Internships:* Yes

Ability Society of Alberta (ASA)
#323, 41 Ave. NE, Calgary AB T2E 2N4
Tel: 403-262-9445; *Fax:* 403-262-4539
info@abilitysociety.org
www.abilitysociety.org
www.linkedin.com/in/abilitysociety
www.facebook.com/AbilitySociety
twitter.com/AbilitySociety
plus.google.com/114873957698483644364
Previous Name: Society for Technology & Rehabilitation
Overview: A medium-sized provincial charitable organization founded in 1984
Mission: To build a caring community; to provide innovative, appropriate, & needed technical aids to individuals with any type of disability, seniors, their families, & support systems; to provide access to technology that is used as a tool by a person with a disability to live with dignity
Chief Officer(s):
Adrian Bohach, President/CEO
adrian@abilitysociety.org
Finances: *Annual Operating Budget:* $1.5 Million-$3 Million
Staff Member(s): 43; 100 volunteer(s)
Membership: 100-499; *Fees:* $50
Activities: *Library:* Resource Centre; Open to public by appointment

Aboriginal Agricultural Education Society of British Columbia (AAESBC)
PO Box 1186, Stn. Main, 7410 Dallas Dr., Kamloops BC V2C 6H3
Tel: 778-469-5040; *Fax:* 778-469-5030
info@aaesbc.ca
www.aaesbc.ca
Overview: A small provincial organization founded in 2005
Mission: To provide culturally appropriate & respectful training for First Nations agricultural businesses, so that they may excel in the agricultural industry
Affliation(s): First Nations Agricultural Association; First Nations Agricultural Lending Association
Finances: *Funding Sources:* Government; corporate sponsors

Aboriginal Financial Officers Association *See* AFOA Canada

Aboriginal Firefighters Association of Canada (AFAC) / Association des pompiers autochtones de Canada
12411 Dawson Pl., Maple Ridge BC V4R 2L6
Tel: 250-267- 2579
info@afac-acpi.ca
www.afac-acpi.ca
www.facebook.com/AFAC.ACPI
Overview: A small national organization
Mission: A united body of regional First Nations Fire Protection Associations from across Canada.
Chief Officer(s):
William Moffat, President

Aboriginal Friendship Centre of Calgary
342-14 St. NW, Calgary AB T2N 1Z7
Tel: 403-270-7379
www.afccalgary.org
Overview: A small local organization overseen by Alberta Native Friendship Centres Association
Member of: Alberta Native Friendship Centres Association
Chief Officer(s):
Sandra Sutter, President
Membership: *Fees:* $2 Singles; $10 Families

Aboriginal Friendship Centres of Saskatchewan
1615, 29th St., Saskatoon SK S7L 0N6
Tel: 306-955-0762; *Fax:* 306-955-0972
www.afcs.ca
Overview: A medium-sized provincial organization overseen by National Association of Friendship Centres
Mission: The objectives of the Aboriginal Friendship Centres (AFC) of Sask. are: the promotion of the goals and objectives of its member Friendship Centres; the facilitation of communication and cooperation amongst all Centres w/in SK,.; the providing of information regarding the operation and dvlp. of AFCs to the public; negotiation with all tiers of gov't on matters of concern to the member Centres; assistance in Program Dvlp.; and assistance to all members in terms of funding information, debt recovery plans, financial negotiation, and networking.

Aboriginal Head Start Association of British Columbia (AHSABC)
PO Box 271, Cobble Hill BC V0R 1L0
Tel: 250-858-4543; *Fax:* 250-743-2478
www.ahsabc.com
Overview: A medium-sized provincial organization founded in 1998
Mission: To promote excellence in Aboriginal early childhood learning programs across British Columbia
Chief Officer(s):
Leona Antoine, President, 604-253-5388, Fax: 604-253-5282
coordinator@sf.acc-society.bc.ca
Peggy Abou, Secretary, 250-635-4906, Fax: 250-635-3013
pabou@kermode-fs.ca
Joan Gignac, Executive Director
executivedirector@ahsabc.com
Finances: *Funding Sources:* Federal government
Membership: 12 urban Aboriginal Head Start preschool sites
Activities: Training & workshops; Leadership administration & management program; quality assessment of early childhood programs; conference planning & facilitation;

Aboriginal Healing Foundation
#801, 75 Albert St., Ottawa ON K1P 5E7
Tel: 613-237-4441; *Fax:* 613-237-4442
Toll-Free: 888-725-8886
www.ahf.ca
Overview: A small national organization
Mission: To encourage & support Aboriginal people in building & reinforcing sustainable healing processes that address the legacy of Physical Abuse & Sexual Abuse in the Residential School system, including intergenerational impacts
Chief Officer(s):
Garnet Angeconeb, Secretary

Aboriginal Human Resources Council (AHRC)
708 - 2nd Ave. North, Saskatoon SK S7K 2E1
Tel: 306-956-5360; *Fax:* 306-956-5361
Toll-Free: 866-711-5091
contact.us@aboriginalhr.ca
www.aboriginalhr.ca
www.facebook.com/aboriginalhr
twitter.com/inclusionworks
Overview: A medium-sized national organization founded in 1988
Mission: Working collectively through strategic public & private sector partnerships, we develop innovative employment solutions for Aboriginal people
Chief Officer(s):
Kelly Lendsay, President & CEO
klendsay@aboriginalhr.ca

Aboriginal Legal Services of Toronto (ALST)
#803, 415 Yonge St., Toronto ON M5B 2E7
Tel: 416-408-3967; *Fax:* 416-408-1568
www.aboriginallegal.ca
Overview: A small local organization founded in 1990
Mission: To strengthen the capacity of the Aboriginal community and its citizens to deals with justice issues and provide Aboriginal controlled and culturally based justice alternatives.
Chief Officer(s):
Jonathan Rudin, Program Director
Staff Member(s): 3

Aboriginal Literacy Foundation, Inc.
#403, 181 Higgins Ave., Winnipeg MB R3B 3G1
Tel: 204-989-8860; *Fax:* 204-989-8870
allf@abcentre.org
www.abcentre.org/literacy.html
Overview: A small provincial organization
Mission: To provide programming to Aboriginal adults in Winnipeg
Activities: One-on-one, small & large group instruction; computer-assisted learning

Aboriginal Mentoring & Training Association (AMTA)
274B Halston Connector Rd., Kamloops BC V2H 1J9
Tel: 250-314-9959
Toll-Free: 855-614-9959
info@amta-bc.com
www.amta-bc.com
www.linkedin.com/company/2930667
www.facebook.com/bcamta
twitter.com/BCAMTA
Previous Name: BC Aboriginal Mine Training Association
Overview: A medium-sized provincial charitable organization
Mission: AMTA is a federally registered charity devoted to preparing Aboriginal candidates for sustainable careers within the natural resource sectors.
Chief Officer(s):
Laurie Sterritt, CEO, 604-681-4321 Ext. 112
lsterritt@amta-bc.com
Leonard Jackson, Director of Operations, 250-314-9959
ljackson@amta-bc.com

Aboriginal Multi-Media Society (AMMSA)
13245 - 146th St., Edmonton AB T5L 4S8
Tel: 780-455-2700; *Fax:* 780-455-7639
www.ammsa.com
www.facebook.com/windspeakernews
twitter.com/windspeakernews
Previous Name: Aboriginal Multi-Media Society of Alberta
Overview: A small provincial organization founded in 1983
Mission: Committed to facilitating the exchange of information reflecting Aboriginal culture to a growing & diverse audience; dedicated to providing objective, mature & balanced coverage of news, information & entertainment relevant to Aboriginal issues & peoples while maintaining profound respect for the values, principles & traditions of Aboriginal people
Chief Officer(s):
Bert Crowfoot, CEO
Paul Macedo, Director, Publishing Operations
Staff Member(s): 21

Aboriginal Multi-Media Society of Alberta *See* Aboriginal Multi-Media Society

Aboriginal Nurses Association of Canada (ANAC) / Association des infirmières et infirmiers autochtones du Canada
#600, 16 Concourse Gate, Ottawa ON K2E 7S8
Tel: 613-724-4677; *Fax:* 613-724-4718
Toll-Free: 866-724-3049
info@anac.on.ca
www.anac.on.ca
www.facebook.com/group.php?gid=8896466083
twitter.com/aboriginalnurse
Previous Name: Indian & Inuit Nurses of Canada
Overview: A large national charitable organization founded in 1974
Mission: To work with & on behalf of Aboriginal nurses to promote the development & practice of Aboriginal nursing in order to improve the health of Aboriginal people
Member of: Canadian Nurses Association
Affliation(s): Health Canada; Canadian Nurses Association
Chief Officer(s):
Rhonda Goodtrack, President
Sherri Di Lallo, Vice-President
Lisa Bourque-Bearskin, Secretary-Treasurer
Membership: 100-499; *Fees:* $60 regular; $20 student; $120 organization subscription; *Member Profile:* Regular - registered nurses with Aboriginal ancestry; Associate - health care workers, non-Aboriginal registered nurses & LPNs; Student - any full-time student of nursing

Activities: Recruiting; Supporting members; Consulting; Researching; Educating; *Awareness Events:* Aboriginal Nurses Day, May 13; *Library:* Aboriginal Nurses Association of Canada Library
Meetings/Conferences: • Aboriginal Nurses Association of Canada 2015 Annual General Meeting, 2015
Scope: National
Description: Featuring the election of the Board of Directors
Contact Information: E-mail: info@anac.on.ca
• Aboriginal Nurses Association of Canada 2015 National Conference, 2015
Scope: National
Contact Information: E-mail: info@anac.on.ca
Publications:
• The Aboriginal Nurse
Type: Newsletter; *Frequency:* 3 pa; *Accepts Advertising*; *Editor:* Connie Toulouse; *Price:* Free with membership in the Aboriginal Nurses Association of Canada

Aboriginal Sport & Wellness Council of Ontario (ASWCO)
2425 Matheson Blvd. East, 7th Fl., Mississauga ON L4W 5K4
Tel: 416-479-0928; *Fax:* 866-258-8527
aswco@shaw.ca
www.sijhlhockey.com
www.facebook.com/aswco
twitter.com/aswco
Overview: A medium-sized provincial organization founded in 2011
Mission: To organize sporting events for Aboriginal athletes throughout Ontario
Chief Officer(s):
Rod Jacobs, Senior Manager
rod.jacobs@aswco.ca

Aboriginal Tourism Association of British Columbia
#600 - 100 Park Royal South, West Vancouver BC V7T 1A2
Tel: 604-921-1070; *Fax:* 604-921-1072
Toll-Free: 877-266-2822
info@aboriginalbc.com
www.aboriginalbc.com
www.facebook.com/AboriginalBC
twitter.com/AboriginalBC
www.youtube.com/user/aboriginalbc
Overview: A small provincial organization
Chief Officer(s):
Paula Amos, Executive Director, 604-921-1070 Ext. 223
paula@aboriginalbc.com
Awards:
• Coast Hotels & Resorts Ambassador Award
• Inspirational Leadership Award
• Young Adult Achievement Award
• Power of Education Award
• Cultural Authenticity Award
• Strength in Marketing Award
• Tourism Conservation Award
• Excellence in Customer Service Award
• Industry Partner Award

Aboriginal Tourism Association of Southern Ontario (ATASO)
34 Merton St., Ottawa ON K1Y 1V5
Tel: 613-722-0315; *Fax:* 613-722-2344
Toll-Free: 877-746-5658
info@ataso.ca
www.ataso.ca
Overview: A small provincial organization founded in 1998
Chief Officer(s):
Mae Maracle, President
Kim Porter, Sec.-Treas.

Aboriginal Women of Manitoba *See* Mother of Red Nations Women's Council of Manitoba

Aboriginal Women's Association of Prince Edward Island
172 Eagle Feather Trail, Lennox Island PE C0B 1P0
Tel: 902-831-3059; *Fax:* 902-831-3181
info@awapei.org
www.facebook.com/193334154037222
Overview: A small provincial organization founded in 1975 overseen by Native Women's Association of Canada
Mission: The purpose of the project is to address issues of concern to off-reserve Aboriginal women and to improve the educational, social and economic environments in which they live. The resource centre offers culturally sensitive programs and services to off-reserve Aboriginal families and children from birth to age 6.
Finances: *Annual Operating Budget:* Less than $50,000
Activities: Outreach, Maowmi, drop-in play, traditional parenting, and a community kitchen.

AboutFace
PO Box 72, 1057 Steeles Ave. West, Toronto ON M2R 3X1
Tel: 416-597-2229; *Fax:* 416-597-8494
Toll-Free: 800-665-3223
Other Communication: info-francais@aboutface.ca
info@aboutface.ca
aboutface.ca
www.linkedin.com/pub/anna-pileggi/a/7a2/91a
www.facebook.com/191138150916182
twitter.com/AboutFace0
www.youtube.com/user/AboutFaceEvents?feature=mhum
Overview: A small international charitable organization founded in 1985
Mission: To provide emotional support & information to, & on behalf of, individuals who have a facial difference & their families
Chief Officer(s):
Anna Pileggi, Executive Director
anna@aboutface.ca
Staff Member(s): 3
Membership: 5,000-14,999; *Fees:* $35
Activities: Public education; hospital visits; school programs; volunteer training; *Speaker Service:* Yes

Académie canadienne d'audiologie *See* Canadian Academy of Audiology

L'Académie canadienne d'endodontie *See* Canadian Academy of Endodontics

Académie canadienne d'histoire de la pharmacie *See* Canadian Academy of the History of Pharmacy

Académie canadienne de médecine du sport *See* Canadian Academy of Sport Medicine

Académie canadienne de parodontologie *See* Canadian Academy of Periodontology

Académie canadienne de psychiatrie de l'enfant et de l'adolescent *See* Canadian Academy of Child & Adolescent Psychiatry

L'Académie canadienne de psychiatrie et droit *See* Canadian Academy of Psychiatry & the Law

Académie canadienne des arts et des sciences de l'enregistrement *See* Canadian Academy of Recording Arts & Sciences

Académie canadienne du cinéma et de la télévision *See* Academy of Canadian Cinema & Television

L'Académie canadienne du génie *See* The Canadian Academy of Engineering

Académie de musique du Québec (AMQ)
CP 818, Succ. C, 1231, rue Panet, Montréal QC H2L 4L6
Tél: 514-528-1961; *Téléc:* 514-528-7572
prixdeurope@videotron.ca
Aperçu: *Dimension:* moyenne; *Envergure:* provinciale; fondée en 1870
Mission: Promouvoir le goût et l'avancement de la musique au Québec, aux professeurs oeuvrant dans le secteur privé et soucieux à la fois d'autonomie et d'encadrement, aux élèves qui désirent une reconnaissance officielle de leur travail
Membre de: Conseil québécois de la Musique
Membre(s) du bureau directeur:
Jean Marchand, Président
Finances: *Budget de fonctionnement annuel:* Moins de $50,000; *Fonds:* Ministère de la Culture et des communications du Québec
Membre(s) du personnel: 1; 5 bénévole(s)
Membre: 120; *Montant de la cotisation:* 30$; *Critères d'admissibilite:* Répondre aux besoins de l'AMQ selon les régions et les disciplines; être disponible pour juger des examens, rédiger des épreuves d'examens et/ou des programmes; posséder des talents de communicateur; être parrainé par un membre de l'AMQ
Activités: Gestion d'un concours de musique depuis 1911; sessions d'examens annuels depuis 1870; le concours "Prix d'Europe"
Prix, Bouses:
• Prix John Newmark (Prix)
Amount: 2 000$
• Prix du Centre de Musique canadienne (Prix)
Amount: 500$
• Prix d'Europe (Prix)
Amount: 20 000$

Académie de Réflexologie du Québec
1285, rue de la Visitation, Sainte-Foy QC G1W 3K5
Tél: 418-651-8575
Ligne sans frais: 800-701-8575
www.academiereflexologie.ca
Aperçu: *Dimension:* petite; *Envergure:* provinciale; Organisme sans but lucratif; fondée en 1984
Mission: Faire connaître la remarquable efficacité des thérapies réflexes pour améliorer rapidement de beaucoup la santé; grâce à de meilleures connaissances en biochimie cellulaire et en neurobiologie, l'Académie de Réflexologie du Québec a développé depuis de nombreuses années des nouvelles techniques très performantes (massage articulaire ou massage intégral) qui agissent simultanément pour détecter (prévenir), détendre (relaxer) et qui ont un effet thérapeutique profond pour résoudre d'innombrables problèmes de santé; de ses recherches est née la carrière de Thérapeute Réflexe; toute personne certifiée est assujettie à un code de déontologie et appartient à son regroupement professionnel de même formation; le maître massothérapeute travaille avec les bases majeures du corps humain, dont les réflexes des différents méchanismes du système nerveux autonome
Membre de: Association des maîtres massothérapeutes
Membre(s) du personnel: 3; 4 bénévole(s)
Membre: 1-99; *Montant de la cotisation:* 60-100; *Critères d'admissibilite:* Etre diplomé de l'A.R.Q. en podoreflexologie et maître massotherapeute
Activités: *Evénements de sensibilisation:* Porte Ouverte, mai et sept.; *Stagiaires:* Oui; *Service de conférenciers:* Oui; *Bibliothèque:* Propre à l'École

Académie des lettres du Québec
Stn. Rosemont, CP 417, Montréal QC H1X 3C6
Tél: 514-873-4496; *Téléc:* 514-873-4612
secretariat@academiedeslettresduquebec.ca
www.academiedeslettresduquebec.ca/academie.html
Aperçu: *Dimension:* moyenne; *Envergure:* provinciale; fondée en 1944
Membre(s) du bureau directeur:
Maude Levasseur, Assistant Administratif
Lise Gauvin, Présidente

Académie internationale de droit et de santé mentale *See* International Academy of Law & Mental Health

Académie royale des arts du Canada *See* Royal Canadian Academy of Arts

Academy of Canadian Cinema & Television (ACCT) / Académie canadienne du cinéma et de la télévision
#501, 49 Ontario St., Toronto ON M5A 2V1
Tel: 416-366-2227; *Fax:* 416-366-8454
Toll-Free: 800-644-5194
info@academy.ca
www.academy.ca
www.facebook.com/acctv
Overview: A medium-sized national charitable organization founded in 1979
Mission: To promote & celebrate exceptional creative achievement in the Canadian film & television industries; To heighten public awareness & increase audience appreciation of Canadian film & television productions through its national Award program
Chief Officer(s):
Martin Katz, Chair
Helga Stephenson, Chief Executive Officer, 416-366-2227 Ext. 240
hstephenson@academy.ca
Finances: *Funding Sources:* Government; industry & corporate sponsors; membership dues; award show revenue
Staff Member(s): 24
Membership: 4,000; *Fees:* $25 student; $100 international/friend; $150 voting; *Member Profile:* Professionals working in Canadian film & television industry; *Committees:* Film Governance; Television Governance; Digital Media Governance; News & Sports Governance
Activities: National Apprenticeship Training Program; Academy Speaker Series; Academy Screening Series; *Internships:* Yes; *Speaker Service:* Yes
Awards:
• Canadian Screen Awards (Award)

• Prix Gémeaux (Award)
For excellence & achievement in French-language television production; held annually & presented in 70 categories covering Programs, Performance & Crafts; nominations & voting by peer groups composed of academy members*Eligibility:* Production télévisuelle de langue française du Canada

Montréal Office
#106, 225, rue Roy Est, Montréal QC H2W 1M5
Tél: 514-849-7448; *Téléc:* 514-849-5069
academie@acct.ca
www.acct.ca
www.facebook.com/acct.quebec
twitter.com/acctquebec
Chief Officer(s):
Patrice Lachance, Directrice
plachance@acct.ca

Academy of Canadian Executive Nurses (ACEN)

#1, 136 Lewis St., Ottawa ON K2P 0S7
Tel: 613-235-3033
info@acen.ca
www.acen.ca
Overview: A small national organization founded in 1982
Mission: To advance nursing practice, education, research, & leadership; To work in partnership with other national organizations to influence health policy & set direction of healthcare in Canada to assure quality of care to Canadians
Chief Officer(s):
Nancy Lefebre, President
Finances: *Annual Operating Budget:* $100,000-$250,000; *Funding Sources:* Membership dues
Membership: 54; *Fees:* $400; *Member Profile:* Canadian executive nurses in academic health care organizations associated with university schools / faculties of nursing, who are accountable for strategic, operational practice; Membership is by invitation of the Academy; *Committees:* Leadership/Policy; Finance; The CJNL Editorial Advisory Board
Awards:
• Leadership Award

Acadia Centre for Social & Business Entrepreneurship (ACSBE)

c/o Acadia University, PO Box 142, Wolfville NS B4P 2R6
Tel: 902-585-1180; *Fax:* 902-585-1057
Toll-Free: 866-654-4499
acsbe@acadiau.ca
www.acsbe.com
www.facebook.com/acsbe
Overview: A small local organization
Mission: To foster an entrepreneurial culture through specialized programming
Affliation(s): Acadia University; Centre for Entrepreneurship Education & Development Inc.
Chief Officer(s):
Fred Morley, Chair
Findlay McRae, Executive Director
findlay.macrae@acadiau.ca
Membership: *Member Profile:* Individuals, businesses, non-profits & business development professionals

ACSBE Job Depot
10361 St. Margarets Bay Rd., Hubbards NS B0J 1T0
Tel: 902-858-5627; *Fax:* 902-858-5628
Toll-Free: 877-457-5627

ACSBE Resource Centre
373 Kings St., Bridgewater NS B4V 1B1
Tel: 902-543-1067; *Fax:* 902-543-7042
Toll-Free: 877-232-2723

Acadia Environmental Society

c/o Acadia Students' Union, PO Box 6002, Wolfville NS B4P 2R5
Tel: 902-585-2110
aes@acadiau.ca
Overview: A small local organization founded in 1989
Mission: To provide an information resource on environmental issues; to encourage & help the Acadia community to adopt & maintain environmentally sound & sustainable practices
Finances: *Funding Sources:* Acadia Students' Union

Acadia University Faculty Association (AUFA) / Association des professeurs de l'Université Acadia

Acadia University, #211, Huggins Science Hall, 12 University Ave., Wolfville NS B4P 2R6
Tel: 902-585-1422; *Fax:* 902-585-1153
aufa@acadiau.ca
www.acadiafaculty.ca
Overview: A small local organization
Mission: To promote the interests of faculty at Acadia University; To encourage academic discussion among the members; to provide full support for all activities; To maintain & improve the quality & stature of members
Member of: Canadian Association of University Teachers
Chief Officer(s):
Gillian Poutier, President, 902-585-1289
gillian.poulter@acadiau.ca
Staff Member(s): 1; 9 volunteer(s)
Membership: 272
Awards:
• Lois Vallely-Fischer Award for Democratic Student Citizenship
• CAUT Dedicated Service Award

The Acadian Entomological Society (AES)

Natural Resources Canada, Canadian Forest Service, PO Box 4000, Atlantic Forestry Centre, 1350 Regent St., Fredericton NB E3B 5P7
e-mail: b35ckp@mun.ca
www.acadianes.org/aes.html
Overview: A small local organization founded in 1915
Mission: To bring about a close association of entomologists & those interested in entomology in the four Atlantic provinces & the neighbouring New England States; To cooperate with, & to support the Entomological Society of Canada
Affliation(s): Entomological Society of Canada
Chief Officer(s):
Carolyn Parsons, President, 709-772-5640
b35ckp@mun.ca
Peggy Dixon, Vice-President
dixonpl@agr.gc.ca
Rob Johns, Sec./Treas.
Finances: *Annual Operating Budget:* Less than $50,000; *Funding Sources:* Membership dues; Entomological Society of Canada
5 volunteer(s)
Membership: 50; *Fees:* Regular: $20; Student: $10; *Committees:* Archives; Memberships; Pest Management; Public Education
Meetings/Conferences: • The Acadian Entomological Society 2015 Annual Meeting, 2015
Publications:
• The Journal of the Acadian Entomological Society
Editor: Don Ostaff *ISSN:* 1710-4033

Accelerated Christian Education Canada

PO Box 1360, Portage la Prairie MB R1N 3N9
Tel: 204-428-5332; *Fax:* 204-428-5386
Toll-Free: 800-976-7226
info@acecanada.net
www.acecanada.net
Also Known As: School of Tomorrow Canada
Previous Name: Canadian National Accelerated Christian Education Association
Overview: A small national organization founded in 1974
Mission: To continue to assure Canadians of the freedom to choose alternative Christian education
Affliation(s): Federation of Independent Schools in Canada
Chief Officer(s):
Alfred MacLaren, Manager
amaclaren@acecanada.net
Finances: *Annual Operating Budget:* Less than $50,000; *Funding Sources:* Provincial dues
24 volunteer(s)
Membership: 100-499

A.C.C.E.S. Employment

#100, 489 College St., Toronto ON M6G 1A5
Tel: 416-921-1800; *Fax:* 416-921-3055
www.accestrain.com
www.linkedin.com/company/acces-employment
twitter.com/ACCESEmployment
Also Known As: Accessible Community Counselling & Employment Services
Overview: A small local charitable organization founded in 1986
Mission: To assist job seekers from diverse backgrounds who are facing barriers to employment, to integrate into the Canadian job market; to provide employment services, linking employers to skilled people & building strong networks in collaboration with community partners
Affliation(s): Ontario Coalition of Agencies Serving Immigrants
Chief Officer(s):
Allison Pond, Executive Director
Irene Sihvonen, Sr. Director, Services & Organizational Development
Manjeet Dhiman, Sr. Director, Services & Business Development
Finances: *Annual Operating Budget:* $500,000-$1.5 Million; *Funding Sources:* Provincial government
Staff Member(s): 45; 25 volunteer(s)
Membership: 1-99
Activities: Job Connect Program; information & referral services; job search workshop; resume clinic; computer training; *Library:* Resource Centre

Scarborough
#250, 2100 Ellesmere Rd., Toronto ON M1H 3B7
Tel: 416-431-5326; *Fax:* 416-431-5286
Chief Officer(s):
Manjeet Dhiman, Director of Services, East Region

Access AIDS Network / Access le réseau du SIDA

#203, 111 Elm St., Sudbury ON P3C 1T3
Tel: 705-688-0500; *Fax:* 705-688-0423
Toll-Free: 800-465-2437
access@cyberbeach.net
www.accessaidsnetwork.com
Previous Name: AIDS Committee of Sudbury; Access AIDS Committee
Overview: A small local organization overseen by Canadian AIDS Society
Mission: To serve the needs of HIV positive individuals living in Algoma, Sudbury, & Manitoulin.

Access AIDS Network Sault Ste Marie

167 Gore St., Sault Ste Marie ON P6A 1M3
Tel: 705-256-2437; *Fax:* 705-256-1182
Toll-Free: 800-465-2437
www.accessaidsnetwork.com
Previous Name: Algoma AIDS Network
Overview: A small local charitable organization founded in 1992 overseen by Canadian AIDS Society
Mission: To provide care & support services to people living with HIV/AIDS & those affected to promote awareness of HIV/AIDS through the provision of a resource centre, educational programs & advocacy for positive living
Member of: Ontario AIDS Network
Finances: *Annual Operating Budget:* $50,000-$100,000
Staff Member(s): 2; 12 volunteer(s)
Membership: 50; *Fees:* $5; *Committees:* Fundraising; AIDS Walk; Board of Directors
Activities: Presentations; support groups; *Awareness Events:* Annual Aids Walk - Sept.; AIDS Awareness Week; *Speaker Service:* Yes; *Library* Open to public

Access Copyright

#800, One Yonge St., Toronto ON M5E 1E5
Tel: 416-868-1620; *Fax:* 416-868-1621
Toll-Free: 800-893-5777
info@accesscopyright.ca
www.accesscopyright.ca
Also Known As: Canadian Copyright Licensing Agency
Previous Name: Canadian Reprography Collective
Overview: A medium-sized national licensing organization founded in 1988
Mission: To licence copyright users who wish to reproduce copyright-protected works; to collect a fee for this service & to distribute royalties to the copyright owners whose works have been copied; to provide protection for copyright owners as well as legal access to published works for copyright users
Member of: Book & Periodical Council
Affliation(s): International Federation of Reproduction Rights Organization
Chief Officer(s):
Maureen Cavan, Executive Director
Brian O'Donnell, Director, Business Development
Roanie Levy, Director, Legal & External Affairs
Finances: *Annual Operating Budget:* $3 Million-$5 Million; *Funding Sources:* Licensing revenue
Staff Member(s): 40
Membership: 37 voting members + 8,000 rightsholders; *Member Profile:* Rightsholders - publishers & creators whose work has been published; voting - associations representing Canadian publishers & creators; *Committees:* Executive; Finance; Distribution; Licensing; Nomination; Communications; Membership; Systems
Activities: *Internships:* Yes; *Speaker Service:* Yes; *Library* Open to public

Access Counselling & Family Services

#200, 460 Brant St., Burlington ON L7R 4B6

Tel: 905-637-5256; *Fax:* 905-637-8221
Toll-Free: 866-457-0234
info@accesscounselling.ca
www.accesscounselling.ca
Overview: A small local charitable organization founded in 1968 overseen by Family Service Ontario
Mission: To serve members of the community in times of crisis, assisting people to cope with conflict, grief, loss, violence, abuse.
Member of: United Way Burlington
Chief Officer(s):
Susan Jewett, Executive Director
Finances: *Funding Sources:* Ministry of Community & Social Services; Ministry of the Attorney General; United Way; donations
Activities: Counselling services; Violence Against Women program; Caring Dads program; Employee Assistance program; Family Life Education program; *Internships:* Yes

Access le réseau du SIDA *See* Access AIDS Network

Accessible Housing Society
Deerfoot Junction III, #215, 1212 - 31st Ave. NE, Calgary AB T2E 7S8
Tel: 403-282-1872; *Fax:* 403-284-0304
info@ahscalgary.ca
www.ahscalgary.ca
www.facebook.com/142720319087854
Overview: A small local charitable organization founded in 1974
Mission: To create opportunities for safe, affordable, barrier-free housing for people experiencing mobility problems.
Chief Officer(s):
Jeff Dyer, Executive Director, 403-735-2425
jeff@ahscalgary.ca
Staff Member(s): 4
Activities: Provides housing & coordinated personal care at 3 sites in Calgary; acts as a resource to the community on barrier-free design & modification for accessibility through a residential assessment & design service; library resources; maintains a housing registry; facilitates opportunities for wheelchair accessible housing; *Library:* ACT Library; Open to public
Publications:
• Ramping Up!
Type: Newsletter; *Frequency:* Quarterly; *Editor:* Jason Yule

Accessible Media Inc. (AMI)
#200, 1090 Don Mills Rd., Toronto ON M3C 3R6
Tel: 416-422-4222; *Fax:* 416-422-1633
Toll-Free: 800-567-6755
info@ami.ca
www.ami.ca
www.linkedin.com/company/accessible-media-inc.
www.facebook.com/pages/Accessible-Media-Inc/231158620268882
twitter.com/a11ymedia
www.youtube.com/user/accessiblemedia
Overview: A medium-sized national charitable organization
Mission: Accessible Media Inc. (AMI) is a not-for-profit multimedia organization operating two broadcast services, AMI-audio and AMI-tv, and a multi-functional website (ami.ca) for the purpose of bringing media in an alternate form to those not able to follow traditional ways.
Affiliation(s): Achilles Canada; Canadian Council of the Blind; CNIB; Courage Canada; Sight Night; Foundation Fighting Blindness
Chief Officer(s):
David Errington, President/CEO
John Melville, VP, Human Resources
Awards:
• Accessible Media Inc. Scholarship (Scholarship)
Created to further strengthen AMI's commitment to making media accessible to all Canadians. Eligibility: Canadian citizens or permanent residents of Canada planning to enrol or continuing to be enrolled in full-time studies in a diploma or degree program at a Canadian post-secondary school. *Amount:* $5,000 (2)

ACCIS - The Graduate Workforce Professionals *See* Canadian Association of Career Educators & Employers

Acclaim Health
2370 Speers Rd., Oakville ON L6L 5M2
Tel: 905-827-8800; *Fax:* 905-827-3390
Toll-Free: 800-387-7127
www.acclaimhealth.ca
ca.linkedin.com/company/acclaim-health
www.facebook.com/pages/Acclaim-Health/468827769806318
twitter.com/AcclaimHealth
Overview: A small local charitable organization founded in 1971
Mission: To provide elderly patients with home health care solutions; to help improve their patients' quality of life through volunteer visitors
Chief Officer(s):
Angelia Brewer, CEO
abrewer@acclaimhealth.ca
Staff Member(s): 400; 600 volunteer(s)

Burlington Office
760 Brant St., Burlington ON L7R 4B7
Tel: 905-631-1711

Accreditation Canada / Agrément Canada
1150 Cyrville Rd., Ottawa ON K1J 7S9
Tel: 613-738-3800; *Fax:* 613-738-7755
Toll-Free: 800-814-7769
communications@accreditation.ca
www.accreditation.ca
Previous Name: Canadian Council on Health Services Accreditation; Canadian Council on Health Facilities Accreditation
Overview: A large national licensing charitable organization founded in 1958
Mission: To improve quality in health services through accreditation; To provide health care organizations with a voluntary, external peer review to assess the quality of their services
Chief Officer(s):
Sébastien Audette, Chief Executive Officer & Secretary
Jil Beardmore, Contact
jil.beardmore@accreditation.ca
Finances: *Funding Sources:* Membership fees
Membership: *Fees:* Schedule available (based on budget)
Activities: Qmentum Accreditation Program, which focuses on quality improvement & patient safety
Meetings/Conferences: • Accreditation Canada Quality Conference 2015, March, 2015, Westin Harbour Castle, Toronto, ON
Scope: National
Contact Information: URL: www.accreditation.ca/quality-conference-2015
Publications:
• Accreditation Canada Annual Report
Type: Yearbook; *Frequency:* Annually
• Accreditation Standard
Type: Newsletter; *Frequency:* Semiannually; *Editor:* Sandra Morrison; Leanne Craig; *ISBN:* 978-1-55149-086-1
Profile: Updates & information about accreditation for Accreditation Canada's client organizations
• Canadian Health Accreditation Report
Frequency: Annually; *ISBN:* 978-1-55149-073-1
Profile: Findings from accreditation surveys, highlights of challenges & successes in health care, & leading practices by health organizations across Canada
• In Touch: A Newsletter for Surveyors
Type: Newsletter; *Editor:* Erin Guthrie
Profile: Information for surveyors
• Leadership in the Journey to Quality Heath Care: The History of Accreditation
Type: Book
Profile: Evolution of Accreditation Canada over the past fifty years
• Leading Practices
Frequency: Annually
Profile: Companion report to the annual Canadian Health Accreditation Report which presents a compilation of practices identified by surveyors
• Qmentum Quarterly
Type: Journal; *Frequency:* Quarterly; *Accepts Advertising*; *Editor:* Erin Guthrie
Profile: Educational information for health & social services organizations to improve quality & patient safety
• The Value & Impact of Accreditation in Health Care: A Review of the Literature
Author: Wendy Nicklin; Sarah Dickson
• Within Our Grasp: A Healthy Workplace Action Strategy for Success & Sustainability in Canada's Healthcare System

Accreditation Council for Canadian Physiotherapy Academic Programs *See* Physiotherapy Education Accreditation Canada

Accueil Grossesse *See* Birthright International

Accueil international pour l'enfance *See* Child Haven International

Achilles Canada
123 Snowden Ave., Toronto ON M4N 2A8
Tel: 416-485-6451; *Fax:* 416-485-0823
www.achillescanada.ca
Previous Name: Achilles Track Club Canada
Overview: A medium-sized national charitable organization founded in 1999
Mission: To encourage & assist all persons with disabilities to enjoy running for health in a social environment
Chief Officer(s):
Brian McLean, Contact
bmclean@achillescanada.ca
Membership: *Fees:* $25 donation encouraged
Activities: Provides support, training, & technical expertise to runners at all levels; Achilles welcomes people with all disabilities: visual disability, cerebral palsy, paraplegia, arthritis, epilepsy, multiple sclerosis, amputation, cystic fibrosis, stroke, cancer, traumatic head injury, & many others; runners participate with crutches, in wheelchairs, on prostheses, & without aids; *Awareness Events:* Achilles St. Patrick's Day 5K Run/Walk, March

Achilles Track Club Canada *See* Achilles Canada

Acoustic Neuroma Association of Canada (ANAC) / Association pour les neurinomes acoustiques du Canada
PO Box 193, Buckhorn ON K0L 1J0
Tel: 416-546-6426; *Fax:* 705-657-2365
Toll-Free: 800-561-2622
info@anac.ca
www.anac.ca
Overview: A medium-sized national charitable organization founded in 1984
Mission: To provide support & information for those who have experienced acoustic neuromas or other tumors affecting the cranial nerves; To furnish information on patient rehabilitation to physicians & health care personnel; To promote & support research; To educate the public regarding symptoms suggestive of acoustic neuromas, thus promoting early diagnosis & consequent successful treatment
Chief Officer(s):
Theresa Forson, National Coordinator
Finances: *Funding Sources:* Private; corporate; federal government grant
Staff Member(s): 1
Activities: *Awareness Events:* A-Wear-Ness Day, June 24

Acoustical Association Ontario (AAO)
32 Vancho Cres., Toronto ON M9A 4Z2
Tel: 416-605-6417; *Fax:* 416-246-1993
info@aao-online.ca
www.aao-online.ca
Overview: A small provincial organization founded in 1963
Mission: The Acoustical Association Ontario (AAO) is an association representing unionized employers engaged in Acoustic and Drywall construction in the Industrial, Commercial and Institutional sector of the construction industry in the Province of Ontario.
Chief Officer(s):
Joseph De Caria, Executive Secretary
Membership: 42; *Member Profile:* Unionized contractors engaged in interior finishing construction

Across Boundaries Multifaith Institute
PO Box 437, Stn. A, Toronto ON M5W 1C2
Tel: 416-850-3598; *Fax:* 416-850-3599
info@acrossboundaries.net
www.acrossboundaries.net
Overview: A small national charitable organization
Mission: To strengthen civil society and enhance pluralism in Canada and globallyby promoting dialogue and exchange among faith traditions and between secular and religious perspectives.
Chief Officer(s):
Wanda Romer Taylor, Chair, Secretary
Membership: *Member Profile:* Members come from any religious faith.
Publications:
• Voices Across Boundaries
Frequency: Bimonthly; *Editor:* Bob Chodes
Profile: To promote dialogue and mutual understanding among different religious traditions, and between religious and secular visions of the world

• Vox Feminarum
Frequency: Bi-annual; *Editor:* Ginny Freeman MacOwan
Profile: Canada's only existing multifaith periodical.

ACT for Disarmament Coalition ***See*** **ACT for the Earth**

ACT for the Earth
PO Box 52007, Oakville ON L6J 7N5
Tel: 905-849-5501; *Fax:* 905-849-5501
Toll-Free: 877-457-0409
info@actfortheearth.org
www.actfortheearth.org
Previous Name: ACT for Disarmament Coalition
Overview: A small national organization founded in 1982
Mission: To make Canadians aware of the dangers of the arms race & to mobilize them against Canada's involvement in the arms race; To help build international non-aligned peace movement; To oppose nuclear fuel cycle in Canada; To work on issues related to ecology, the environment, human rights
Affliation(s): International Peace Bureau; Ontario Environment Network; War Resisters International
Chief Officer(s):
Dylan Penner, Executive Officer
Chris Davenport, Webmaster
Finances: *Annual Operating Budget:* Less than $50,000
200 volunteer(s)
Membership: 200; *Fees:* $20
Activities: *Internships:* Yes; *Speaker Service:* Yes; *Library* Open to public
Publications:
• The ACTivist
Frequency: Quarterly; *Editor:* Dylan Penner; *Price:* $4.95

Act To End Violence Against Women
#209, 390 Steeles Ave. West, Thornhill ON L4J 6X2
Tel: 905-695-5372; *Fax:* 905-695-5375
Toll-Free: 866-333-5942
info@acttoendvaw.org
www.acttoendvaw.org
www.facebook.com/acttoendvaw
Previous Name: B'nai Brith Women of Eastern Canada; Jewish Women International of Canada
Overview: A medium-sized national organization
Mission: Works locally, nationally & internationally to strengthen the effectiveness of women in the Jewish community & society; to foster the emotional well-being of children; to perpetuate Jewish values & secure world Jewry. Programs include ending violence towards women, sexual assault awareness, emergency housing for women & children, & advocacy to end child poverty in Canada. Offices in Toronto & Montréal, & chapters in Toronto, Montréal, B.C., Windsor & Winnipeg.
Affliation(s): Jewish Women International
Chief Officer(s):
Penny Krowitz, Executive Director
Finances: *Funding Sources:* Fundraising; membership fees
Staff Member(s): 3
Membership: 3,000; *Fees:* $36+
Activities: Education; advocacy; shelters for abused women; homes for emotionally abused children

Action Autonomie
3958, rue Dandurand, Montréal QC H1X 1P6
Tél: 514-525-5060; *Téléc:* 514-525-5580
lecollectif@actionautonomie.qc.ca
www.actionautonomie.qc.ca
Aperçu: *Dimension:* petite; *Envergure:* locale
Mission: La mission d'Action Autonomie vise la défense des droits des personnes vivant des problèmes de santé mentale par une approche d'éducation
Activités: Information; aide & accompagnement; information & orientation; conscience publique; atelier de formation; support & lobbying

Action Budget Denis Riverin Inc. ***Voir*** Carrefour-Ressources

Action by Christians for the Abolition of Torture ***Voir*** Action des Chrétiens pour l'abolition de la torture

Action Canada for Sexual Health & Rights
251 Bank St., 2nd Fl., Ottawa ON K2P 1X3
Tel: 613-241-4474
Toll-Free: 888-642-2725
access@sexualhealthandrights.ca
www.sexualhealthandrights.ca
www.facebook.com/actioncanadaSHR
twitter.com/acpdcanada
Merged from: Canadians for Choice; Canadian Federation for Sexual Health; Action Canada for Population
Overview: A large national charitable organization founded in 2014
Mission: To advance sexual & reproductive health & rights in Canada & abroad through Public education & awareness; Support for the delivery of programs & services in Canada.
Member of: International Planned Parenthood Federation
Chief Officer(s):
Sandeep Prasad, Executive Director
Frédérique Chabot, Health Information Officer
Finances: *Funding Sources:* Donations; project grants
Staff Member(s): 8
Membership: *Member Profile:* Provincial, territorial or local sexual & reproductive health organizations in Canada with similar objectives & policies; associate - other organizations in sympathy with objectives of the Federation
Activities: Sexuality education & fair access to contraception & abortion services; sexual & reproductive health policy; works toward reaching high risk & hard-to-reach populations of youth & adults; extension of services to visible minority populations; encourages the development of new & safer forms of contraception; monitors the developments of new reproductive technologies; advocacy
Awards:
• Phyllis P. Harris Scholarship (Scholarship)
For students who have worked or volunteered in the general field of human sexuality who intend to work for a degree in the field of family planning or population issues*Deadline:* April 1 *Amount:* $2,500 towards full-time study at a Canadian university
• John & Lois Lamont Scholarship (Scholarship)
Established 2004; awarded to a full-time graduate student in the field of sexual & reproductive health *Amount:* $2,600
• Janssen-Ortho Volunteer of the Year Award (Award)
Sponsored by Ortho Pharmaceutical (Canada) Ltd; established 1979; awarded annually to recognize outstanding volunteer contributions to the family planning movement in Canada*Amount:* Award consists of a certificate, travel expenses to receive the award, & cash prize of $1,000
• Dr. Henry Morgentaler Future Choice Scholarship (Award)
• Helen & Fred Bentley Affiliate Award (Award)
Publications:
• Beyond the Basics: A Sourcebook on Sexual & Reproductive Health Education
Price: $85
Profile: Resource used in schools, public health offices, & community-based health organizations
• Finding Our Way: A Sexual & Reproductive Health Sourcebook for Aboriginal Communities
Price: $55
• Positive Thinking
• Sexual & Reproductive Health Counselling Guidelines
Price: $30
Profile: Resource used throughout Canada in schools, public health offices, & community-based health organizations
• Sexual Health in Canada: Baseline
Profile: Written with an educatioal focus
• Youth Talk Back
Price: $8
• Youth Talk Back Teachers' Guide
Price: $8
Profile: Written with a strong educational focus, the resource is used in Canadian schools

Action Centre-Ville
#210, 105, rue Ontario Est, MontréAl QC H2X 1G9
Tél: 514-878-0847; *Téléc:* 214-878-0452
info@acv-montreal.com
www.acv-montreal.com
Aperçu: *Dimension:* petite; *Envergure:* locale
Mission: Fournit des personnes âgées avec services remisé tels que les repas et les cours d'impôt, ainsi que l'activité physique et de activité récréative
Membre: *Montant de la cotisation:* 10$; *Critères d'admissibilite:* Toute gens qui a 50 ans ou plus
Activités: Activité récréative; activité phsyical; voyages

Action des Chrétiens pour l'abolition de la torture (ACAT) / Action by Christians for the Abolition of Torture
#C-246, 2715, ch de la Côte-Sainte-Catherine, Montréal QC H3T 1B6
Tél: 514-890-6169; *Téléc:* 514-890-6484
info@acatcanada.org
www.acatcanada.org
Également appelé: ACAT Canada
Aperçu: *Dimension:* moyenne; *Envergure:* nationale; Organisme sans but lucratif; fondée en 1984
Mission: Dans un but d'engagement évangélique, encourager les différentes communautés Chrétiennes du Canada à porter ensemble, par la prière, les souffrances des victimes de la torture; dans un but éducatif, sensibiliser particulièrement les Chrétiens au scandale de la torture (par l'information et la formation aux droits de la personne); dans un but de soulager la misère des victimes de la torture, apporter une aide concrète par l'envoi de lettres et pétitions aux responsables de torture et des lettres d'encouragement aux victimes
Affliation(s): Fédération internationale de l'action des Chrétiens pour l'abolition de la torture (FIACAT)
Membre(s) du bureau directeur:
Raoul Lincourt, Président
François Poulin, Coordonnateur
Finances: *Budget de fonctionnement annuel:* $50,000-$100,000; *Fonds:* Organisations philanthropiques et particuliers.
Membre(s) du personnel: 2; 20 bénévole(s)
Membre: 150; *Montant de la cotisation:* 35 $; *Comités:* Commission des interventions; Financement; Relations publiques; Ressourcement
Activités: Campagne annuelle; Bulletins; Appels à l'action; *Stagiaires:* Oui; *Service de conférenciers:* Oui; *Listes de destinataires:* Oui; *Bibliothèque* rendez-vous

Action Dignité de Saint-Léonard
9089A, boul Viau, Saint-Léonard QC H1R 2V6
Tél: 514-251-2874
Aperçu: *Dimension:* petite; *Envergure:* locale
Mission: Groupe de défense des droits des locataires

Action Emploi Papineau Inc. ***Voir*** Carrefour jeunesse-emploi Papineau

Action for Healthy Communities (AHC)
#101, 10554 - 110 St., Edmonton AB T5H 3C5
Tel: 780-944-4687; *Fax:* 780-423-4193
a4hc.ca
www.facebook.com/217084201652707
Previous Name: Edmonton Health Care Citizenship Society
Overview: A small local charitable organization founded in 1995
Mission: Works with individuals, families and groups to build community through the provision of public education and other initiatives to enable individuals to enhance their own lives.
Chief Officer(s):
Idalia Ivon Pereira, Executive Director
Finances: *Funding Sources:* Fundraising projects

Action Intégration Brossard ***Voir*** Action Intégration en Déficience Intellectuelle

Action Intégration en Déficience Intellectuelle (AIDI)
6180, rue Agathe, Brossard QC J4Z 1E1
Tél: 450-676-5058; *Téléc:* 450-676-5686
actionintegration.org
Nom précédent: Action Intégration Brossard
Aperçu: *Dimension:* petite; *Envergure:* locale; Organisme sans but lucratif; fondée en 1978
Mission: Promouvoir les intérêts et défendre les droits des personnes ayant une déficience intellectuelle; favoriser leur intégration sociale; soutenir leur famille
Affliation(s): Association du Québec pour l'intégration sociale
Membre(s) du bureau directeur:
Yves Gougeon, Président
Sylvie Léger, Directrice générale
Finances: *Budget de fonctionnement annuel:* $250,000-$500,000
Membre(s) du personnel: 50; 60 bénévole(s)
Membre: 100-499
Activités: Répits; loisirs; soutien;

Action Life (Ottawa) Inc. / Action pour la vie
#40, 100 Brookfield Rd., Ottawa ON K1V 6J1
Tel: 613-798-4494; *Fax:* 613-798-4496
info@actionlife.org
www.actionlife.org
www.facebook.com/group.php?gid=41938419521
Overview: A small local charitable organization founded in 1976
Mission: To promote respect for human life from conception to natural death through public education
Chief Officer(s):
Louise Harbour, Executive Director
Finances: *Annual Operating Budget:* $100,000-$250,000
Staff Member(s): 2
Membership: 4,000; *Fees:* $25 general; $15 senior/student
Activities: Pro-life education; *Speaker Service:* Yes; *Library* Open to public

Action Nouvelle Vie
740, Saint-Charles Est, Longueuil QC J4H 1C2
Tél: 450-646-5815; *Téléc:* 450-646-3509
info@actionnouvellevie.com
actionnouvellevie.com
Aperçu: *Dimension:* petite; *Envergure:* locale; fondée en 1993
Mission: Pour aider les familles défavorisées, les personnes et les enfants ont accès à la nourriture et à l'éducation
Membre(s) du bureau directeur:
Suzanne Fournier, Directrice générale
Jérémie Olivier, Communications

Action on Smoking & Health (ASH)
PO Box 4500, Stn. S, Edmonton AB T6E 6K2
Tel: 780-426-7867; *Fax:* 780-488-7195
www.ash.ca
Overview: A small national charitable organization founded in 1979
Mission: To act as a tobacco control agency in western Canada
Finances: *Funding Sources:* Donations; Membership fees
Membership: 300; *Fees:* $25 household; $100 corporate
Activities: Reducing tobacco use through advocacy, policy development, & public education;
Publications:
• Action on Smoking & Health Newsletter
Type: Newsletter; *Price:* Free, with membership in Action on Smoking & Health
Profile: News & events from Action on Smoking & Health

Action Patrimoine
82, Grande-Allée ouest, Québec QC G1R 2G6
Tél: 418-647-4347; *Téléc:* 418-647-6483
Ligne sans frais: 800-494-4347
info@actionpatrimoine.ca
www.actionpatrimoine.ca
Aperçu: *Dimension:* petite; *Envergure:* provinciale; fondée en 1975
Mission: Afin de préserver et de promouvoir repères culturels au Québec
Affiliation(s): Continuité; Fonation Québécoise du patriomoine
Membre(s) du bureau directeur:
Louise Mercier, Présidente
Charles Méthé, Vice-président
Guy Drouin, Trésorier
Pierre Landry, Directeur général
direction@actionpatriomoine.ca
Membre: *Critères d'admissibilite:* Ouvert à toute personne intéressée par la sauvegarde et la mise en valeur du patrimoine du Québec
Activités: *Listes de destinataires:* Oui; *Bibliothèque*

Action pour la vie *See* Action Life (Ottawa) Inc.

Action Séro Zéro *Voir* RÉZO

Action to Restore a Clean Humber (ARCH)
147 Stephenson Cres., Richmond Hill ON L4C 5T3
Tel: 416-326-0726
Overview: A small local organization founded in 1991
Mission: To clean up & conserve the Humber watersheds
Chief Officer(s):
Luciano Martin, Executive Director

Action Volunteers for Animals (AVA)
PO Box 64578, Unionville ON L3R 0M9
Tel: 416-439-8770
ava2009@actionvolunteersforanimals.com
www.actionvolunteersforanimals.com
Overview: A medium-sized local charitable organization founded in 1972
Mission: To abolish all cruelty against & suffering of non-human animals
Chief Officer(s):
Josephine Polk
Shana Mortimer-Gibson
Carol Lawson
Finances: *Annual Operating Budget:* $50,000-$100,000
20 volunteer(s)
Membership: 600; *Fees:* $25; *Committees:* Stray Animals; Vet Fund; Anti-Fur; Fundraising
Activities: Meetings, demonstrations, membership parties, lectures, fundraising events; *Library:* AVA Library; Open to public

Active Healthy Kids Canada / Jeunes en forme Canada
#1205, 77 Bloor St. West, Toronto ON M5S 1M2
Tel: 416-913-0238; *Fax:* 416-913-1541
info@activehealthykids.ca
www.activehealthykids.ca
Previous Name: The Foundation for Active Healthy Kids
Overview: A small national charitable organization founded in 1994
Mission: To advocate the importance of quality, accessible & enjoyable physical activity participation experiences for children & youth; To provide expertise & direction to decision makers at all levels, from policy-makers to parents, in order to increase the attention given to, investment in, & effective implementation of physical activity opportunities for all Canadian children & youth
Chief Officer(s):
Jennifer Cowie Bonne, Chief Executive Officer, 416-913-0238 Ext. 111
jencb@activehealthykids.ca
Finances: *Annual Operating Budget:* $250,000-$500,000; *Funding Sources:* Corporate sponsorship
Staff Member(s): 3
Activities: *Awareness Events:* Active Healthy Kids' Day, last Thur. in May; *Speaker Service:* Yes
Meetings/Conferences: • Active Healthy Kids Canada / Jeunes en forme Canada 2015 Global Summit on the Physical Activity of Children, 2015
Scope: International
Description: Brings together those who are working to resolve the growing childhood physical inactivity crisis.
Contact Information: Communications Manager: Katherine Janson, Phone: 416-913-0238, E-mail: kjanson@participACTION.com

Active Living Alliance for Canadians with a Disability (ALACD) / Alliance de vie active pour les canadiens/canadiennes ayant un handicap
#104, 720 Belfast Rd., Ottawa ON K1G 0Z5
Tel: 613-244-0052; *Fax:* 613-244-4857
Toll-Free: 800-771-0663; *TTY:* 888-771-0663
ala@ala.ca
www.ala.ca
Overview: A medium-sized national organization
Mission: To promote inclusion & active living lifestyles of Canadians with disabilities by facilitating communication & collaboration among organizations, agencies & individuals
Affliation(s): Canadian Amputee Sports Association; Canadian Association for Disabled Skiing; Canadian Association for Health, Physical Education, Recreation & Dance; Canadian Blind Sports Association; Canadian Cerebral Palsy Sports Association; Canadian Deaf Sports Association; Canadian Intramural Recreation Association; Canadian National Institute for the Blind; Canadian Paralympic Committee; Canadian Paraplegic Association; Canadian Parks/Recreation Association; Canadian Red Cross Society; Canadian Special Olympics; Learning Disabilities Association of Canada; National Network for Mental Health
Chief Officer(s):
Jane Arkell, Executive Director
jane@ala.ca
Chris Bourne, Manager, Community Development
chris@ala.ca
Finances: *Annual Operating Budget:* $100,000-$250,000; *Funding Sources:* Fitness program
Staff Member(s): 3; 25 volunteer(s)
Membership: 4,000

Active Living Coalition for Older Adults (ALCOA) / Coalition d'une vie active pour les aîné(e)s
PO Box 143, Shelburne ON L0N 1S0
Tel: 519-925-1676
Toll-Free: 800-549-9799
Other Communication: Other URL: www.silvertimes.ca
alcoa3@uniserve.com
www.alcoa.ca
Overview: A medium-sized national organization founded in 1993
Mission: To encourage older Canadians to maintain & enhance their well-being & independence through a lifestyle that embraces daily physical activities
Chief Officer(s):
Patricia Clark, Executive Director
50 volunteer(s)
Membership: 23; *Committees:* Research Update; Reducing Barriers; Older Adult Advisory; Diabetes; Sustainability; Executive; Speakers Bureau

Active Parenting Canada
5409 - 50 Ave., Red Deer AB T4N 4B7
Tel: 403-877-8395; *Fax:* 403-358-7801
Toll-Free: 800-668-5131
apcanada@fsca.ca
www.activeparentingcanada.com
www.facebook.com/ActiveParentingCanada
twitter.com/activeparentcan
Overview: A small national organization founded in 1992
Mission: To provide video-based materials & leader training workshops in the area of parenting, teacher-in-service, self-esteem, loss education & parent involvement in schools
Member of: North American Association of Adlerian Psychologists; College of Alberta Psychologists

Active Support Against Poverty (ASAP)
1188 - 6 Ave., Prince George BC V2L 3M6
Tel: 250-563-6112; *Fax:* 250-563-1612
Toll-Free: 877-563-6112
asap@princegeorge.com
Overview: A small local charitable organization founded in 1987
Mission: To act as a guide for the empowerment, education & self-determination of the financially poor; To act as an agent of change for an inclusive community
Affliation(s): Federated Anti-Poverty Groups of BC
Chief Officer(s):
Audrey Schwartz, Executive Director
Doug Tedford, Chair
Finances: *Annual Operating Budget:* $500,000-$1.5 Million; *Funding Sources:* Regional & provincial government; Law Fdn. of BC
Staff Member(s): 20; 10 volunteer(s)
Activities: *Speaker Service:* Yes

The Actors' Fund of Canada / La Caisse des acteurs du Canada inc.
#301, 1000 Yonge St., Toronto ON M4W 2K2
Tel: 416-975-0304; *Fax:* 416-975-0306
Toll-Free: 877-399-8392
Other Communication: Toll-Free Fax: 1-866-372-0985
contact@actorsfund.ca
www.actorsfund.ca
www.facebook.com/ActorsFund
twitter.com/ActorsFund
www.flickr.com/photos/actorsfundofcanada
Overview: A small national charitable organization founded in 1958
Mission: The Actors' Fund of Canada promotes artistic excellence for performers, creators, technicians & other members of creative & production teams in all entertainment industry sectors. The Fund carries out this mission by providing encouragement & short-term financial aid to help entertainment industry workers maintain their health, housing & ability to work after an illness, injury or sudden unemployment.
Chief Officer(s):
Jane Mallett, Founding President
Maria Topalovich, President
David Hope, CGA, Executive Director
Finances: *Annual Operating Budget:* $500,000-$1.5 Million; *Funding Sources:* Benefits; donations
Staff Member(s): 1
Membership: 1,000; *Fees:* $15

ACTRA Fraternal Benefit Society
1000 Yonge St., Toronto ON M4W 2K2
Tel: 416-967-6600; *Fax:* 416-967-4744
Toll-Free: 800-387-8897
Other Communication: finance@actrafrat.com
benefits@actrafrat.com
www.actrafrat.com
www.facebook.com/17000Stories?ref=hl
twitter.com/AFBSCanada
Overview: A large national organization founded in 1975
Mission: Actra Fraternal Benefit Society is a not-for-profit, member-owned, federally incorporated insurance company operating for over 25 years. Members of the Society are primarily Members of ACTRA and The Writers Guild of Canada.
Chief Officer(s):
Norm Bolen, President & CEO
Membership: 15,000

ACUC International
PO Box 1179, #3, 101 Nelson St. East, Port Dover ON N0A 1N0
Tel: 519-583-9798; *Fax:* 519-583-3247
acuchq@acuc.ca
www.acuc.es
www.facebook.com/acucinternational
Also Known As: American & Canadian Underwater Certification Inc.

Overview: A medium-sized international licensing organization founded in 1968
Mission: To supply quality training for sport scuba divers & instructors; To teach the highest standards in safety, sport, & marine conservation
Affliation(s): World Diving Federation; Undersea Hyperbaric Medical Society
Chief Officer(s):
Juan Rodriguez, President & Chief Executive Officer
jra@acuc.es
Nancy Cronkwright, Vice-President & Officer Manager, 519-750-5767, Fax: 519-750-5769
acuchq@acuc.ca
Patricia Molina, Vice-President & Manager, Clinet Service
comercial@acuc.es
Activities: *Internships:* Yes; *Speaker Service:* Yes

Acupuncture Foundation of Canada Institute (AFCI) / Institut de la fondation d'acupuncture du Canada

#204, 2131 Lawrence Ave. East, Toronto ON M1R 5G4
Tel: 416-752-3988; *Fax:* 416-752-4398
afciweb@afcinstitute.com
www.afcinstitute.com
Overview: A medium-sized national organization founded in 1995
Mission: To define & maintain the highest professional standards for the use of acupuncture; to gain recognition of acupuncture's legitimate place in western medicine as a safe, efficient complement to conventional medical treatment; to design educational training programs for physicians, physiotherapists, RNs, dentists, chiropractors & naturopaths in the methodology & practice of acupuncture
Affliation(s): World Federation of Acupuncture Societies; Pan Pacific Medical Acupuncture Forum
Chief Officer(s):
Mac Mierzejewski, President/Chair
Cathy Donald, Treasurer
Ronda Kellington, Managing Director
Finances: *Annual Operating Budget:* $500,000-$1.5 Million
Staff Member(s): 5
Membership: 1,200; *Fees:* $255; *Member Profile:* Physicians, physiotherapists, dentists, chiropractors, naturopaths & licensed acupuncturists, RNs (baccalaurate)

Adala - Canadian Arab Justice Committee

PO Box 47095, #15, 555 West 12th Ave., Vancouver BC V5Z 4L6
Tel: 604-506-5155; *Fax:* 604-941-5627
info@adala.ca
www.adala.ca
Overview: A small national organization founded in 2002
Mission: To increase the collective understanding on issues of importance to Arab Canadians, such as the Palestine question and the war in Iraq
Membership: *Fees:* $25 basic

Adam Mickiewicz Foundation of Canada

#2102, 61 Richview Rd., Toronto ON M9A 4M8
Tel: 416-243-8984
Overview: A small local organization founded in 1963
Mission: The oldest Polish cultural foundation in Canada; to provide grants & financial support for students of Polish origin studying at Canadian universities; To help various libraries & printing houses; To assist in the development of contacts between universities in Poland & in Canada; To organize lectures in Polish & English
Chief Officer(s):
Krystyna Burska, President, 905-270-6097

Addiction Research Foundation *See* Centre for Addiction & Mental Health

Addiction Services of Thames Valley

#260, 200 Queens Ave., London ON N6A 1J3
Tel: 519-673-3242; *Fax:* 519-673-1022
intake@adstv.on.ca
www.adstv.on.ca
Overview: A small local organization
Mission: Addiction remedial services in the Thames Valley area of Southwestern Ontario
Activities: Service in Middlesex, Elgin & Oxford counties, London, Strathroy, St. Thomas & Woodstock, Ingersoll & Tillsonburg; Substance Abuse; Problem Gambling; Back on Track; Heartspace; Youth Services

Addictions & Mental Health Ontario

#104, 970 Lawrence Ave. West, Toronto ON M6A 2B6
Tel: 416-490-8900; *Fax:* 866-295-6394
info@addictionsandmentalhealthontario.ca
www.addictionsandmentalhealthontario.ca
twitter.com/AMHont
Previous Name: Alcohol and Drug Recovery Association of Ontario
Merged from: Addictions Ontario; Ontario Federation of Community Mental Health & Addiction Programs
Overview: A small provincial charitable organization founded in 1968
Mission: To ensure that the best possible addictions treatment & recovery services are available to people throughout Ontario
Chief Officer(s):
Gail Czukar, Chief Executive Officer
gail.czukar@addictionsandmentalhealthontario.ca
Finances: *Funding Sources:* Membership fees; donations
Staff Member(s): 5
Membership: *Fees:* Schedule available based on budget

Addictions Foundation of Manitoba (AFM) / Fondation manitobaine de lutte contre les dépendances

1031 Portage Ave., Winnipeg MB R3G 0R8
Tel: 204-944-6236; *Fax:* 204-786-7768
Toll-Free: 866-638-2561
wpgreg@afm.mb.ca
afm.mb.ca
Overview: A medium-sized provincial organization founded in 1956
Mission: To be a sensitive, caring, learning organization dedicated to continuously improving our services related to addiction & to collaborate with community members in providing a holistic approach, resulting in an improved quality of life for Manitobans; provides prevention, education & treatment programs related to addictions to individuals & communities; conducts research into the negative effects of addictions
Chief Officer(s):
Heather Mitchell, Chair
Finances: *Annual Operating Budget:* Greater than $5 Million; *Funding Sources:* Dept. of Health, Manitoba Government
Staff Member(s): 226; 20 volunteer(s)
Activities: *Awareness Events:* Manitoba Addiction Awareness Week, Nov.; *Speaker Service:* Yes; *Library:* William Potoroka Memorial Library; Open to public

Northern Region Office
Polaris Place, 90 Princeton Dr., Thompson MB R8N 0L3
Tel: 204-677-7300; *Fax:* 204-677-7328
Toll-Free: 866-291-7774
northreg@afm.mb.ca

Western Region Office
Parkwood Centre, 510 Frederick St., Brandon MB R7A 6Z4
Tel: 204-729-3838; *Fax:* 204-729-3844
Toll-Free: 866-767-3838
parkwood@afm.mb.ca

Winnipeg Region Office
1031 Portage Ave., Winnipeg MB R3G 0R8
Tel: 204-944-6200; *Fax:* 204-786-7768
Toll-Free: 866-638-2561
wpgreg@afm.mb.ca

Adlerian Psychological Association of British Columbia *See* Adlerian Psychology Association of British Columbia

Adlerian Psychology Association of British Columbia (APABC)

#230, 1818 West Broadway, Vancouver BC V6J 1Y9
Tel: 604-742-1818; *Fax:* 604-742-1811
apabc@adler.bc.ca
www.adlercentre.ca
Also Known As: Adler School of Professional Psychology
Previous Name: Adlerian Psychological Association of British Columbia
Overview: A small provincial charitable organization founded in 1973 overseen by North American Society of Adlerian Psychology
Member of: North American Society of Adlerian Psychologists; Canadian Guidance & Counselling Association
Chief Officer(s):
James Skinner, Executive Director, 204-742-1818
Staff Member(s): 2
Membership: *Fees:* $50 individual/family; $35 student/senior; $75 professional; $100 institution
Activities: Graduate programs; lectures; parenting groups; bookstore; *Speaker Service:* Yes; *Library:* Birdie Mosak Library
Publications:
• Canadian Journal of Adlerian Psychology

Administrateurs canadiens des ressources bénévoles *See* Canadian Administrators of Volunteer Resources

Administrative & Professional Staff Association (APSA)

Simon Fraser University, #AQ 5133, 8888 University Dr., Vancouver BC V5A 1S6
Tel: 778-782-4319; *Fax:* 778-782-4245
apsa@sfu.ca
apsa.sfu.ca
Overview: A small local organization founded in 1981
Chief Officer(s):
Neal Baldwin, President
baldwin@sfu.ca
Anne Mason, Director, Association
Staff Member(s): 2
Membership: 587; *Fees:* Monthly fees; *Member Profile:* Administrative & professional staff at Simon Fraser University; *Committees:* Advocacy; Salaries & Benefits; APIN; Nominating; University Affairs; Liaison; Pension
Activities: Participates in deliberations for salaries & benefits; plays a role in forming & revising university policies & procedures that govern the working environment;

Administrative & Supervisory Personnel Association (ASPA)

Kirk Hall, #304, 117 Science Place, Saskatoon SK S7N 5C8
Tel: 306-966-2471; *Fax:* 306-966-2962
aspa@usask.ca
www.aspasask.ca
Overview: A small local organization founded in 1978
Chief Officer(s):
Glen Hauser, President
Finances: *Annual Operating Budget:* $50,000-$100,000
Staff Member(s): 1
Membership: 849; *Fees:* % of monthly salary; *Member Profile:* Administrative, supervisory, professional, instructional personnel of the University

Administrative Sciences Association of Canada (ASAC) / Association des sciences administratives du Canada

c/o Sobey School of Business, Saint Mary's University, Halifax NS B3H 3C3
Tel: 902-496-8139
jean.mills@smu.ca
www.asac.ca
Overview: A medium-sized national organization founded in 1982
Mission: To develop teaching & research in management studies at Canadian universities
Chief Officer(s):
Tanya Mark, Secretary, 519-824-4120 Ext. 53687
markt@uoguelph.ca
Travor Brown, President
Finances: *Annual Operating Budget:* $100,000-$250,000; *Funding Sources:* Membership fees
Membership: 100 student + 700 individual; *Fees:* $45; *Member Profile:* Open to individuals teaching in business school or Ph.D. students
Meetings/Conferences: • Administrative Sciences Association of Canada 2015 Conference, June, 2015, World Trade & Convention Centre, Halifax, NS
Scope: National

Administrators of Volunteer Resources BC (AVRBC)

PO Box 2259, Vancouver BC V6B 3W2
e-mail: info@avrbc.com
www.avrbc.com
www.facebook.com/avrbc
twitter.com/@avrbc
Overview: A small provincial organization founded in 1975
Mission: To promote leadership in the management of volunteer resources & to provide a supportive network for all its members
Member of: Canadian Administrators of Volunteer Resources
Chief Officer(s):
Clare O'Kelly, President
president@avrbc.com
Membership: 130+; *Fees:* Annual - Voting: $75; Non-voting: $65; *Committees:* External Communications; Internal Communications; Membership; Professional Development; Regional Representation; Website

Adoption Council of Canada (ACC) / Conseil d'Adoption du Canada

211 Bronson Ave., Ottawa ON K1R 6H5

Tel: 613-235-0344
Toll-Free: 888-542-3678
info@adoption.ca
www.adoption.ca
www.facebook.com/259196824104313
twitter.com/adoptioncanada
Overview: A medium-sized national charitable organization founded in 1991
Mission: To inform & educate Canadians on all aspects of adoption; to promote the placement of waiting children in permanent homes; to promote openness & honesty in adoption; to work toward legislative reform
Member of: North American Council of Adoptable Children
Affliation(s): Child & Family Canada; Canadian Coalition for Rights of the Child
Chief Officer(s):
Sarah Pedersen, Executive Director
Laura Eggertson, President
Finances: *Annual Operating Budget:* $100,000-$250,000
Staff Member(s): 1; 3 volunteer(s)
Membership: 200+; *Fees:* $60 agency; $35 individual
Activities: Operates Canada's waiting children program to make Canadians aware of Canadian children in need of families; *Awareness Events:* National Adoption Awareness Month, Nov.; *Speaker Service:* Yes; *Library* by appointment

Adoption Council of Ontario (ACO)

#202, 36 Eglinton Ave West, Toronto ON M4R 1A1
Fax: 877-543-0009
Toll-Free: 877-236-7820
info@adoptontario.ca
www.adoption.on.ca
www.facebook.com/adoptioncouncilontario
twitter.com/ontarioadopts
Overview: A medium-sized provincial charitable organization founded in 1987
Mission: To education, support & advocate on behalf of those touched by adoption in Ontario
Member of: Adoption Council of Canada; North American Council on Adoptable Children
Chief Officer(s):
Wendy Hayes, Contact
wendy.hayes@adoptontario.ca
Finances: *Annual Operating Budget:* $100,000-$250,000; *Funding Sources:* Membership dues; donations; programs
Staff Member(s): 4; 20 volunteer(s)
Membership: 15; *Fees:* $50/year; $130/3 years; *Member Profile:* Adoptees; birth parents; adoptive & pre-adoptive parents; professionals; *Committees:* Advocacy; Fundraising; Education; Finance
Activities: Workshops; seminars; helpline; advocacy; *Awareness Events:* Adoption Awareness Month, Nov.; *Internships:* Yes; *Speaker Service:* Yes; *Library:* Adoption Resource Centre; Open to public

Adoption Roots & Rights (ARR)

187 Patricia Ave., Dorchester ON N0L 1G1
Tel: 519-268-3674
fayrath@execulink.com
Overview: A small local organization founded in 1994
Mission: To help people separated by adoption to reconnect with birth family members; To offer search assistance; To help people be informed of their rights
Affliation(s): Parent Finders
Chief Officer(s):
Fay Rath, Co-ordinator
Finances: *Annual Operating Budget:* Less than $50,000
Staff Member(s): 1; 1 volunteer(s)
Membership: 200; *Fees:* $20 individual; *Member Profile:* Adult adoptees; birth relatives; adoptive parents & adult foster persons
Activities: *Library:* Search Resource Material; by appointment

ADR Institute of Canada (ADRIC) / Institut d'arbitrage et de médiation du Canada

#405, 234 Eglinton Ave. East, Toronto ON M4P 1K5
Tel: 416-487-4733; *Fax:* 416-487-4429
Toll-Free: 877-475-4353
admin@adrcanada.ca
www.adrcanada.ca
www.linkedin.com/groups?gid=3303518
www.facebook.com/ADRInstituteOfCanadaADRIC.IAMC
Previous Name: Arbitration & Mediation Institute of Canada Inc.; Canadian Foundation for Dispute Resolution
Overview: A medium-sized national charitable organization founded in 1974
Mission: To promote the use of arbitration & mediation (ADR - alternative dispute resolution) to settle disputes; to provide information & education on ADR to practitioners, parties, the public, & the business, professional & government communities; to assist those wishing to use ADR through the provision of Arbitration & Mediation Rules, administrative services, & information about the process & member arbitrators & mediators
Affliation(s): British Columbia Arbitration & Mediation Institute; ADR Institute of Alberta; ADR Institute of Saskatchewan Inc.; ADR Institute of Ontario, Inc.; Institut de médiation d'arbitrage du Québec; ADR Atlantic Institute
Chief Officer(s):
Mary Anne Harnick, Executive Director
Finances: *Funding Sources:* Membership fees
Staff Member(s): 5
Membership: 1,700 individuals; 60 businesses; *Fees:* Schedule available; *Member Profile:* ADR professionals & corporate users
Activities: ADR Connect; chartered mediators (C.Med.) & chartered arbitrators (C.Arb.) designations;
Awards:
• Lionel J. McGowan Award of Excellence (Award)

ADR Atlantic Institute
PO Box 123, Halifax NS B3J 2M4
Tel: 709-437-2359
admin@adratlantic.ca
www.adratlantic.ca
Chief Officer(s):
Andrew Butt, President
andrewdbutt@nl.rogers.com

ADR Institute of Alberta
Ralph King Athletic Centre, Concordia University, 7128 Ada Blvd., #CE223A, Edmonton AB T5B 4E4
Tel: 780-433-4881; *Fax:* 780-433-9024
Toll-Free: 800-232-7214
temp@adralberta.com
www.adralberta.com
Chief Officer(s):
Erika Deines, Executive Director
edexecutivedirector@adralberta.com

ADR Institute of Ontario, Inc.
#405, 234 Eglinton Ave. East, Toronto ON M4P 1K5
Tel: 416-487-4447; *Fax:* 416-487-4429
admin@adrontario.ca
www.adrontario.ca
www.linkedin.com/groups?gid=2754057
www.facebook.com/ADRInstituteOfOntario
Chief Officer(s):
Mary Anne Harnick, Executive Director

ADR Institute of Saskatchewan Inc.
PO Box 22015, Stn. Wildwood, Saskatoon SK S4H 5P1
Fax: 855-487-4429
Toll-Free: 866-596-7275
info@adrsaskatchewan.ca
www.adrsaskatchewan.ca
Chief Officer(s):
Scott Siemens, President, 306-780-6755
scott.siemens@cra-arc.gc.ca

British Columbia Arbitration & Mediation Institute
#510, 700 West Pender St., Vancouver BC V6C 1G8
Tel: 604-736-6614
Toll-Free: 877-332-2264
info@bcami.com
www.bcami.com
Chief Officer(s):
Glen Bell, President
gwb@belladr.com

Adsum for Women & Children

2421 Brunswick St., Halifax NS B3K 2Z4
Tel: 902-423-5049; *Fax:* 902-423-9336; *Crisis Hot-Line:* 902-423-4443
adsum@adsumforwomen.org
www.adsumforwomen.org
www.facebook.com/pages/Adsum-for-Women-Children/111571128907431
twitter.com/AdsumForWomen
Previous Name: Association for Women's Residential Facilities
Overview: A medium-sized local charitable organization founded in 1983
Mission: To administer Adsum House; To provide emergency shelter for homeless women & children
Chief Officer(s):
Sheri Lecker, Executive Director
sheri.lecker@adsumforwomen.org
Finances: *Annual Operating Budget:* $250,000-$500,000; *Funding Sources:* Government; private & corporate donations; fundraising
Staff Member(s): 12; 50 volunteer(s)
Membership: 30; *Fees:* $5; *Committees:* Public Relations & Fundraising; Personnel; Finance; Property Management
Activities: *Speaker Service:* Yes; *Rents Mailing List:* Yes

Adult Basic Education Association of British Columbia (ABEABC)

5476 - 45th Ave., Delta BC V4K 1L4
Tel: 604-296-6901
www.abeabc.ca
Overview: A small provincial organization
Mission: Fosters and promotes excellence in adult basic education instruction and programming.
Chief Officer(s):
Yvonne Chard, President, 604-594-6100
ychard@deltasd.bc.ca
John Cowan, Treasurer, 604-594-6100
jcowan@deltasd.bc.ca
Membership: *Fees:* $40 non-profit community group/individual; $50 individual outside Canada; $75 Organization (no bursary); *Committees:* Membership; Groundwork; Fundraising & Conference
Meetings/Conferences: • Adult Basic Education Association of British Columbia Conference 2015, 2015, BC
Scope: Provincial
Contact Information: abeabcnews@gmail.com

Adult Children of Alcoholics (ACA)

PO Box 75061, 20 Bloor St. East, Toronto ON M5W 3T3
Tel: 416-631-3614
acatoronto@hotmail.com
acatoronto.org
Overview: A small national organization
Mission: To find freedom & improve members' lives through the 12 step program
Activities: Weekly meetings; annual workshops; *Speaker Service:* Yes

Adult Educators' Provincial Specialist Association (AEPSA)

c/o British Columbia Teachers' Federation, #100, 550 West 6th Ave., Vancouver BC V5Z 4P2
Tel: 604-871-2283; *Fax:* 604-871-2286
adultedpsa.org
twitter.com/AEPSAEditor
Overview: A small provincial organization
Mission: The aims of AEPSA include facilitating communication between adult educators, exchanging ideas & advocating on behalf of them and their students. Most members work in adult education programs, such as Adult Basic Education (ABE), Adult Literacy, Adult Foundations, General Education Development (GED), Grade 10 Completion, English as a Second Language (ESL) or English Language Services for Adults (ELSA), High School Completion (HSC) or Adult Secondary School Completion (ASSC), and Adult Special Education (ASE).
Member of: BC Teachers' Federation
Finances: *Funding Sources:* BCTF union membership dues; membership fees
Membership: *Fees:* $20 BCTF members; $10 students & TAs

Adult Learning Development Association (ALDA)

#608, 409 Granville St., Vancouver BC V6C 1T2
Tel: 604-683-5554; *Fax:* 604-683-2380
aldaexec@telus.net
www.alda-bc.org
Previous Name: Association of Learning Disabled Adults
Overview: A small local charitable organization founded in 1988
Mission: ALDA exclusively represents and works with adults and older youth who have suspected or diagnosed learning disabilities; Provides a compregensive range of services and programs that are adapted and designed to meet the needs of their clients and members and that are accessible to all.
Member of: Affiliation of Multicultural Societies & Service Agencies of BC; SUCCESS; Learning Disabilities Association of Canada; BC Coalition of People with Disabilities; ENET Educational Society
Chief Officer(s):
Dave McNea, CEO/Director of Operations
aldaceo@alda-bc.org
Donna Ginther, Director, Programs & Services
Finances: *Annual Operating Budget:* $250,000-$500,000; *Funding Sources:* Service Canada, City of Vancouver Community Services Grant, Province of British Columbia, memberships and donations

Staff Member(s): 5; 20 volunteer(s)
Membership: 200+; *Member Profile:* Adults & older youth who have learning disabilities/difficulties; professionals
Activities: Information & referrals; assessment; advocacy; employment services; career exploration; transition to work skill; individual counselling & research; videos & DVDs; *Speaker Service:* Yes; *Library:* "I-Improve" Learning Disability Resource Centre; by appointment
Publications:
• ALDA Update Express

Adult Literacy Council of Greater Fort Erie (ALC)
PO Box 86, Fort Erie ON L2A 5M6
Tel: 905-871-6626
info@literacyforterie.ca
www.literacyforterie.ca
Overview: A small local charitable organization founded in 1978
Mission: To promote literacy to adults in the Greater Fort Erie area in order to enhance the lives of individuals & of the community through individual literacy programs & community events
Member of: Laubach Literacy of Canada - Ontario
Affliation(s): United Way
Chief Officer(s):
Jessica Grimes, Chair
Salvati Maria, Program Coordinator
maria@literacyforterie.ca
Finances: *Funding Sources:* Donations; bingo; events; membership fee; United Way; Trillium Fondation; foundations
Staff Member(s): 2
Activities: Provision of literacy services for adults; "Each One, Teach One"; Sponsor-a-Student Learner Group; *Library* by appointment

Advanced Card Technology Association of Canada / Association canadienne de la technologie des cartes à mémoire
85 Mullen Dr., Ajax ON L1T 2B3
Tel: 905-426-6360; *Fax:* 905-619-3275
info@actcda.com
www.actcda.com
Also Known As: ACT Canada
Overview: A small national organization founded in 1989
Mission: To promote the understanding & use of all advanced card technologies across a wide range of applications; to connect users & suppliers; to work with governments, financial institutions & users to advance standards, develop card related policies & prepare the marketplace for a broad based acceptance of advanced cards
Chief Officer(s):
Catherine Johnston, President & CEO
Finances: *Annual Operating Budget:* $100,000-$250,000; *Funding Sources:* Membership dues; seminars; consulting
Staff Member(s): 4; 15 volunteer(s)
Membership: 80+; *Fees:* Based on membership level; *Member Profile:* Users, suppliers & parties interested in smart, optical & other advanced card technologies; *Committees:* Membership; Education; Conference; Communication; Marketing
Activities: Teaching; advocacy; consulting; market research; setting international standards; *Speaker Service:* Yes; *Rents Mailing List:* Yes; *Library* by appointment

Advanced Coronary Treatment (ACT) Foundation of Canada / La fondation des soins avancés en urgence coronarienne du Canada
379 Holland Ave., Ottawa ON K1Y 0Y9
Tel: 613-729-3455; *Fax:* 613-729-5837
Toll-Free: 800-465-9111
Other Communication: www.flickr.com/photos/actfoundation
act@actfoundation.ca
www.actfoundation.ca
www.facebook.com/theactfoundation
twitter.com/actfoundation
www.youtube.com/theactfoundation
Also Known As: ACT Foundation
Overview: A small national charitable organization founded in 1985
Mission: To work with health professionals, governments, & the community in educating the public about the prevention, management, & treatment of illnesses that can lead to prehospital health emergencies
Chief Officer(s):
Sandra Clarke, Executive Director
Finances: *Annual Operating Budget:* $250,000-$500,000
Staff Member(s): 5; 300 volunteer(s)
Membership: 50 individual; *Committees:* Medical Advisory; Media/Communications Advisory; Education Advisory; Community Advisory
Activities: Helping establish high school CPR across Canada;

Advanced Foods & Materials Network / Réseau des aliments et des matériaux d'avant-garde
#215, 150 Research Lane, Guelph ON N1G 4T2
Tel: 519-822-6253; *Fax:* 519-824-8453
www.afmnet.ca
Also Known As: AFMNet
Overview: A medium-sized national organization
Member of: Networks of Centres of Excellence
Chief Officer(s):
Rickey Yada, Scientific Director, 519-824-4120 Ext. 58915, Fax: 519-824-6631
rickey.yada@afmnet.ca

Advancing Canadian Entrepreneurship Inc.; Canada's Future Entrepreneurial Leaders *See* Enactus Canada

Adventist Development & Relief Agency Canada (ADRA)
20 Robert St. W., Newcastle ON L1B 1C6
Tel: 905-446-2372; *Fax:* 905-723-1903
Toll-Free: 888-274-2372
Other Communication: donor-relations@adra.ca
info@adra.ca
www.adra.ca
www.facebook.com/adracanada
twitter.com/adracanada
www.youtube.com/adracanada
Also Known As: ADRA Canada
Overview: A medium-sized international charitable organization founded in 1985
Mission: To provide community development & disaster relief without regard to political or religious association, age, or ethnicity
Member of: Canadian Council of Christian Charities, Canadian Churches in Action, Canadian Council for International Cooperation, Canadian Christian Relief and Development Association
Affliation(s): Canadian Council of Christian Charities
Chief Officer(s):
James Astleford, Executive Director
Finances: *Annual Operating Budget:* $1.5 Million-$3 Million; *Funding Sources:* Resources & donations received from the public & the Canadian government.
Staff Member(s): 14; 1500 volunteer(s)
Membership: 7,000
Activities: Non-sectarian, humanitarian relief agency; community development projects in 50 countries
Publications:
• Global Impact
Type: Newsletter; *Frequency:* Quarterly

Adventive Cross Cultural Initiatives (ACCI)
89 Auriga Dr., Nepean ON K2E 7Z2
Tel: 613-298-1546; *Fax:* 613-225-7455
lauren@adventive.ca
www.adventive.ca
www.facebook.com/AdventiveCCI
Previous Name: New Life League
Overview: A small national charitable organization founded in 1986
Mission: To operate as an international, interdenominational Christian missionary organization; To minister through printing & literature, children's homes, national workers, evangelism, & church planting.
Member of: Canadian Council of Christian Charities
Chief Officer(s):
John Haley, Executive Director
johnhaley@adventive.ca
Lauren Roth, Canadian National Director
lauren@adventive.ca
Finances: *Annual Operating Budget:* Less than $50,000; *Funding Sources:* Donations
Staff Member(s): 4; 1 volunteer(s)
Activities: *Internships:* Yes

The Advertising & Design Club of Canada (ADCC)
#235, 401 Richmond St. West, Toronto ON M5V 3A8
Tel: 416-423-4113; *Fax:* 416-423-3362
info@theadcc.ca
www.theadcc.ca
www.facebook.com/TheADCC
twitter.com/TheADCC
Previous Name: Art Directors' Club of Toronto
Overview: A small national organization founded in 1948
Mission: To recognize, support & promote creative excellence in the Canadian advertising, publishing & design community
Chief Officer(s):
Fidel Pe¤a, President
Dawn Wickstrom, Executive Director
Finances: *Funding Sources:* Memberships; entry fees
Membership: *Fees:* $150 professional; $35 student
Awards:
• The Advertising & Design Club of Canada Awards (Award)
Main categories of awards are: Advertising Print, Advertising Broadcast, Advertising Multiple Media, Graphic Design, Editorial Design & Interactive Design; winners receive gold, silver or merit awards

Advertising Association of Winnipeg Inc. (AAW)
PO Box 2278, 950 Borebank St., Winnipeg MB R3C 4B3
Tel: 204-831-1077; *Fax:* 204-885-6265
www.adwinnipeg.ca
www.linkedin.com/groups/Advertising-Association-Winnipeg-3100170
www.facebook.com/AdWinnipeg
twitter.com/AdWinnipeg
www.youtube.com/AdWinnipeg
Overview: A small local licensing organization founded in 1944
Mission: To encourage professional development amoung its members & those involved in advertisement
Chief Officer(s):
Matt Cohen, President
Membership: 92 individuals; 64 companies; *Fees:* $50 student; $100 single; $285 corporate
Activities: Monthly luncheons with speakers; workshops

The Advertising Club of Toronto
Toronto ON
www.adclub.ca
www.linkedin.com/company/330264
www.facebook.com/AdClubToronto
twitter.com/Adclubtoronto
www.youtube.com/user/AdClubToronto
Overview: A small local organization
Mission: To organize meetings & seminars for ACT members & guests that will present the newest ideas & developments in the advertising industry; create social & business events which will give ACT members opportunities to interact with colleagues in the advertising industry; to establish & maintain an informal structure within the club to promote a sense of accessibility between all members & directors
Chief Officer(s):
Mladen Raickovic, President
Activities: *Rents Mailing List:* Yes

Advertising Standards Canada *Voir* Les normes canadiennes de la publicité

Advertising Standards Canada (ASC) / Les normes canadiennes de la publicité
South Tower, #1801, 175 Bloor St. East, Toronto ON M4W 3R8
Tel: 416-961-6311; *Fax:* 416-961-7904
www.adstandards.com
Previous Name: Advertising Standards Council
Overview: A medium-sized national organization founded in 1957
Mission: To ensure the integrity & viability of advertising through industry self-regulation.
Chief Officer(s):
Linda J. Nagel, President/CEO Ext. 222
Staff Member(s): 16
Membership: 167; *Fees:* Schedule available; *Member Profile:* Advertisers; advertising agencies; media organizations; suppliers
Activities: Standards Division administers the industry's principal self-regulatory code, the Canadian Code of Advertising Standards; handles complaints from consumers regarding advertising & coordinates the Council on Diversity in Advertising; Advertising Clearance Division previews advertisement in six industry categories, helping advertisers adhere to applicable legislation, regulatory codes & industry standards

Québec
#915, 2015, rue Peel, Montréal QC H3A 1T8
Tél: 514-931-8060; *Téléc:* 877-956-8646
www.normespub.com
Chief Officer(s):
Danielle Lefrançois, Directrice, Communications, 514-931-8060 Ext. 260

Advertising Standards Council ***See*** Advertising Standards Canada

Advocacy Centre for the Elderly (ACE)

#701, 2 Carlton St., Toronto ON M5B 1J3
Tel: 416-598-2656; *Fax:* 416-598-7924
www.acelaw.ca
Also Known As: Holly Street Advocacy Centre for the Elderly Inc.
Overview: A small provincial charitable organization founded in 1984
Mission: To provide legal services to low income senior citizens
Chief Officer(s):
Judith Wahl, Executive Director
wahlj@lao.on.ca
Timothy Banks, Chair
Finances: *Funding Sources:* Membership fees; Donations; Legal Aid Ontario
Staff Member(s): 8
Membership: *Fees:* $10 individuals; $25 corporations
Activities: Providing individual & group client advice & representation; Offering public legal education, such as community presentations & workshops; Engaging in law reform activities of importance to the senior population; *Speaker Service:* Yes
Publications:
• ACE [Advocacy Centre for the Elderly] Newsletter
Type: Newsletter; *Frequency:* Semiannually; *Price:* Free with membership in the Advocacy Centre for the Elderly
Profile: Articles on legal issues related to seniors
• Care Homes
• Continuing Power of Attorney for Property
• Elder Abuse: The Hidden Crime
• Every Resident: The Bill of Rights for Residents in Ontario Long-Term Care Facilities
• Home Care Complaints & Appeals
• Long-Term Care Facilities in Ontario: The Advocate's Manual
• Power of Attorney for Personal Care

The Advocates' Society

#2700, 250 Yonge St., Toronto ON M5B 2L7
Tel: 416-597-0243; *Fax:* 416-597-1588
mail@advocates.ca
www.advocates.ca
www.linkedin.com/company/the-advocates%27-society
www.facebook.com/TheAdvocatesSociety
twitter.com/Advocates_Soc
Overview: A large provincial organization founded in 1963
Mission: To teach the skills & ethics of advocacy through information sharing, educational programs, seminars, conferences, & workshops; To speak out on behalf of advocates; To protect the right to representation by an independent bar; To initiate appropriate reforms to the legal system
Chief Officer(s):
Alan H. Mark, President, 416-597-4264
amark@goodmans.ca
Alexandra Chyczij, Executive Director
alex@advocates.ca
Finances: *Annual Operating Budget:* $1.5 Million-$3 Million; *Funding Sources:* Membership fees
Staff Member(s): 16
Membership: 5,000+; *Fees:* Schedule available; *Member Profile:* Lawyers; *Committees:* Advocacy & Practice; Collegiality, Mentoring & Membership; Education; Operations, Governance & Finance; Practice Group; Young Advocates

Advocational International Democratic Party of British Columbia

291 Desent Cove, Vernon BC V1H 1Z1
Tel: 250-503-0728; *Fax:* 250-503-0729
bbirdlf@telus.net
Also Known As: Advocational Party
Overview: A small provincial organization
Chief Officer(s):
Michael Yawney, Party Leader

Advocis

#209, 390 Queens Quay West, Toronto ON M5V 3A2
Tel: 416-444-5251; *Fax:* 416-444-8031
Toll-Free: 800-563-5822
info@advocis.ca
www.advocis.ca
www.linkedin.com/company/advocis
www.facebook.com/advocis
twitter.com/Advocis
www.youtube.com/user/AdvocisTFAAC
Also Known As: The Financial Advisors Association of Canada
Previous Name: Life Underwriters Association of Canada
Merged from: Canadian Association of Insurance & Financial Advisors; Canadian Association of Financial Planners
Overview: A medium-sized national organization founded in 1906
Mission: To represent Advice & Advocacy; to carry on the tradition of effectively representing members' interests with all levels of government, regulators, & industry, always with the intention of putting the interests of consumers first
Member of: Financial Planners Standards Council
Affiliation(s): Advocis Protective Association; The Institute for Advanced Financial Education; GAMA International Canada; Conference for Advanced Life Underwriting
Chief Officer(s):
David Juvet, Chair
chair@advocis.ca
Greg Pollock, President & CEO
president@advocis.ca
Membership: 11,000 in 40 chapters; *Committees:* Governance; Law & Regulatory
Activities: Advocacy; professional development courses towards the CFP & CLU designations; *Library*

AEAQ Inc. ***See*** Association of English Language Publishers of Québec

Aéro Montréal

#8000, 380, rue Saint-Antoine Ouest, Montréal QC H2Y 3X7
Tél: 514-987-9330; *Téléc:* 514-987-1948
info@aeromontreal.ca
www.aeromontreal.ca
www.linkedin.com/company/a-ro-montr-al
www.facebook.com/111264895631870
twitter.com/AeroMontreal
Aperçu: *Dimension:* petite; *Envergure:* provinciale; fondée en 2006
Mission: Pour regrouper les professionnels de l'industrie aérospatiale afin de faire progresser la concurrence au Québec
Membre(s) du bureau directeur:
Suzanne M. Benoît, Présidente-directrice générale
suzanne.benoit@aeromontreal.ca
Maria Della Posta, Présidente, Conseil d'administration
Hélène Séguinotte, Vice-présidente, Conseil d'administration
Denis Giangi, Trésorier
Membre(s) du personnel: 13
Membre: *Montant de la cotisation:* 825$ industriel/institutionnelle; $1,130 renouvellemnt

Aéroclub des cantons de l'est

Aéroport Roland-Désourdy, 101, rue du Ciel, Bromont QC V6B 3X9
Tél: 514-862-1216
www.facebook.com/AeroclubDesCantonsDeLEst
Aperçu: *Dimension:* petite; *Envergure:* locale
Membre de: Soaring Association of Canada
Membre(s) du bureau directeur:
Marc Arsenault, Contact
marcarsenault@sympatico.ca

Aerospace Heritage Foundation of Canada (AHFC)

PO Box 246, Stn. Etobicoke D, Toronto ON M9A 4X2
Tel: 416-410-3350
www.ahfc.org
Overview: A small national charitable organization founded in 1989
Mission: Current emphasis of AHFC is on Avro & Orenda; we are trying to locate former employees of these companies
Chief Officer(s):
Frank Harvey, President
fwbd.harvey@sympatico.ca
Nick Doran, Membership Secretary
dorans@idirect.com
Al Sablatnig, Treasurer
Finances: *Annual Operating Budget:* Less than $50,000
12 volunteer(s)
Membership: 248; *Fees:* $35 new; $25 renewal; $10 student; *Committees:* Shows; Speakers; Executive; Editorial
Activities: Meetings; displays; heritage retrieval; *Speaker Service:* Yes

Aerospace Industries Association of Canada (AIAC) / Association des industries aérospatiales du Canada

#703, 255 Albert St., Ottawa ON K1P 6A9
Tel: 613-232-4297; *Fax:* 613-232-1142
info@aiac.ca
www.aiac.ca
Previous Name: Air Industries Association of Canada
Overview: A large national organization founded in 1962
Mission: To promote & facilitate the continued success & growth of this strategic industry; To establish & maintain a public policy environment that enables sustained aerospace industry growth; To strengthen the international competitiveness of all aerospace firms in Canada; To strengthen Canadian aerospace SME capabilities & position them as "suppliers of choice"; To represent & involve the full range of aerospace companies that operate in Canada
Chief Officer(s):
Jim Quick, President & CEO, 613-232-4297
Barry Kohler, Chair
Staff Member(s): 7
Membership: 400; *Committees:* International Exhibition; Technology Council; Defence Procurement Council; Suppliers Development; Space; Civil Aviation; Public Affairs
Activities: *Library*
Awards:
• James C. Floyd Award (Award)
Acknowledges individuals or a team that has made an outstanding contribution to the Canadian aerospace industry.
Eligibility: Any individual or team from an AIAC member company, Canadian university, college or research institution, or government department may be nominated for this award. Nominees of all ages and experience levels will be considered.
Meetings/Conferences: • 2015 Canadian Aerospace Summit, 2015
Scope: National
Attendance: 1200
Description: Visionaries and practitioners will speak on the new evolution and expectations in aerospace, meet leading industry decision-makers, and gain first-hand intelligence on key business opportunities.
Publications:
• AIAC Guide to Canada's Aerospace Industry
Type: Guide; *Frequency:* Annually
Profile: Resource for aerospace industry statistics, companies, products and services.

Aerospace Industry Association of British Columbia (AIABC)

#102, 211 Columbia St., Vancouver BC V6A 2R5
Tel: 604-638-1477
info@aiabc.com
www.aiabc.com
Overview: A small provincial organization founded in 1994
Mission: To enhance the growth of the provincial aerospace industry by acting as a watchdog, advocate & facilitator for BC companies seeking Canadian & international business opportunities
Member of: Aerospace Industry Association of Canada
Finances: *Funding Sources:* Membership dues

Affairs pour les arts ***See*** Business for the Arts

Affiliation des infirmières et infirmiers d'urgence ***See*** National Emergency Nurses Affiliation

Affiliation of Multicultural Societies & Service Agencies of BC (AMSSA)

#205, 2929 Commercial Dr., Vancouver BC V5N 4C8
Tel: 604-718-2777; *Fax:* 604-298-0747
Toll-Free: 888-355-5560
amssa@amssa.org
www.amssa.org
www.facebook.com/amssabc
twitter.com/safeharbourcdn
Overview: A medium-sized provincial organization founded in 1977
Mission: To provide leadership in advocacy & education in British Columbia for anti-racism, human rights & social justice; to support members in serving immigrants, refugees & culturally diverse communities
Member of: Canadian Immigrant Settlement Sector Alliance
Chief Officer(s):
Tim Welsh, Program Director
Lynn Moran, Executive Director
Finances: *Annual Operating Budget:* $500,000-$1.5 Million; *Funding Sources:* Provincial & federal governments; foundations
Staff Member(s): 10
Membership: 75 organizations; *Fees:* $75 associate; *Member Profile:* Organizations providing immigrant settlement &

multicultural services; *Committees:* Cultures West; Immigrant Integration Coordinating
Activities: Distribute multifaith calendars; diversity health fair; Safe Harbour program; settlement & integration program - support for AMSSA member agencies; *Awareness Events:* Safe Harbour Breakfast; *Library:* AMSSA Resource Database; Open to public

Affirm United / S'affirmer Ensemble
PO Box 57057, Stn. Somerset, Ottawa ON K1R 1A1
e-mail: affirmunited@affirmunited.ca
www.affirmunited.ca
Overview: A medium-sized national organization founded in 1982
Mission: To affirm gay, lesbian, bisexual & transgender people & their friends, within The United Church of Canada; to provide a network of supports among affirming ministries & regional groups; to act as a point of contact for individuals; to speak to the church in a united fashion encouraging it to act prophetically & pastorally both within & beyond the church structure.
Affiliation(s): United Church of Canada
Chief Officer(s):
Read Sherman, Communications Coordinator
Finances: *Annual Operating Budget:* Less than $50,000
20 volunteer(s)
Membership: 500 individual; *Fees:* $40 individual/household; $100 institutional
Activities: *Speaker Service:* Yes

Afghan Association of Ontario
29 Pemican Ct., Toronto ON M9M 2Z3
Tel: 416-744-9289; *Fax:* 416-744-6671
info@aaocanada.ca
www.aaocanada.ca
Overview: A small provincial organization founded in 1982
Mission: To provide services to newly immigrated Afghans in order to help settle in Canada
Member of: Ontario Council of Agencies Serving Immigrants
Chief Officer(s):
Mahmood Baher Formuli, President
fformuli@gmail.com
Membership: *Committees:* Membership; Sponsorship; Cultrual; Youth; Women; Finance; Social; Religous

Afghan Women's Counselling & Integration Community Support Organization
#700, 789 Don Mills Rd., Toronto ON M3C 1T5
Tel: 416-588-3585; *Fax:* 416-588-4552
www.afghanwomen.org
Also Known As: Afghan Women's Organization (AWO)
Overview: A small local charitable organization
Mission: To assist Afghan women in their integration & adaptation to Canadian life; to encourage & motivate Afghan women to participate & contribute to life in Canada; To develop a community support network for Afghan women; To emphasize the acquisition of English language in Afghan women; To organize & implement social programs which will educate children/youth about their current social issues; To encourage & promote the development of skills in Afghan women
Chief Officer(s):
Asma Faizi, President
Adeena Niazi, Executive Director
aniazi@afghanwomen.org
Activities: Language Instruction for Newcomers to Canada (LINC) program; Immigration Settlement and Adaptation Program (ISAP); homework club; job search workshop; family support; Senior Afghan Women's Circle; youth programs; sponsorship; itinerant services;

Mississauga
#302, 3050 Confederation Pkwy., Mississauga ON L5B 3Z6
Tel: 905-279-3679; *Fax:* 905-279-4691

North York
#212, 747 Don Mills Rd., Toronto ON M3C 1T2
Tel: 416-422-2225; *Fax:* 416-429-9111

Scarborough
#211, 2555 Eglinton Ave., Toronto ON M1K 5J1
Tel: 416-266-1777; *Fax:* 416-266-8145

AFOA Canada
#301, 1066 Somerset St. West, Ottawa ON K1Y 4T3
Tel: 613-722-5543; *Fax:* 613-722-3467
Toll-Free: 866-722-2362
info@afoa.ca
www.afoa.ca
www.linkedin.com/company/afoa-canada
www.facebook.com/aboriginalfinancialofficersassociation
twitter.com/afoa_canada
Previous Name: Aboriginal Financial Officers Association
Overview: A medium-sized national organization founded in 1999
Mission: To provide leadership in Aboriginal financial management by developing & promoting quality standards, practices, research, certification, & professional development to members & Aboriginal organizations.
Chief Officer(s):
Terry Goodtrack, President & CEO
tgoodtrack@afoa.ca
Paulette Tremblay, Director, Education & Training
ptremblay@afoa.ca
Finances: *Annual Operating Budget:* $500,000-$1.5 Million
Staff Member(s): 8
Membership: 500-999; *Fees:* Schedule available
Activities: *Awareness Events:* Annual National Conference
Awards:
• AFOA-Xerox Excellence in Leadership Awards (Award)
• AFOA-PotashCorp Aboriginal Youth Financial Management Awards (Award)
• Norman Taylor Memorial Scholarships & Bursaries (Scholarship)
Meetings/Conferences: • AFOA Canada 15th National Conference 2015, February, 2015, RBC Convention Centre Winnipeg, Winnipeg, MB
Scope: National
Publications:
• JAM: The Journal of Aboriginal Management
Type: Journal; *Frequency:* Semiannually; *Accepts Advertising*

AFOA Alberta
PO Box 1010, Siksika AB T0J 3W0
Tel: 403-734-5446; *Fax:* 403-398-0601
administration@afoaab.ca
www.afoaab.com
Chief Officer(s):
Robert Andrews, Executive Director
robert.andrews@afoaab.com

AFOA Atlantic
R15, 150 Cliffe Street, Fredericton NB E3A 0A1
Tel: 902-404-4252
Chief Officer(s):
Debbie Christmas, Chair
deborah_christmas@hotmail.com

AFOA British Columbia
#1010, 100 Park Royal, West Vancouver BC V7T 1A2
Tel: 604-925-6370; *Fax:* 604-925-6390
exec@afoabc.org
www.afoabc.org
www.facebook.com/afoabc
Chief Officer(s):
Michael Mearns, General Manager
mmearns@afoabc.org

AFOA Manitoba
PO Box 137, Scanterbury MB R0E 1W0
Tel: 204-799-4726
info@afoamb.ca
www.afoamb.ca
Chief Officer(s):
Chad Bicklemeier, President
olds_442@hotmail.com

AFOA Northwest Territories
PO Box 1456, Inuvik NT X0E 0T0
Tel: 867-777-2004
okpik@northwestel.net
Chief Officer(s):
Gloria Allen, Officer in Charge
gloria.allen@servicecanada.gc.ca

AFOA Ontario
PO Box 694, Parry Sound ON P2A 2Z1
Tel: 705-746-4497
afoaontario@live.com
Chief Officer(s):
Valerie Pizey, President
vpizey@kmts.ca

AFOA Québec
430 Chef Stanislas-Koska, Wendake QC
Tel: 418-842-8268
Chief Officer(s):
Marc-André Beaudoin, Vice-President

AFOA Saskatchewan
#117, 335 Packham Ave., Saskatoon SK S7N 4S1
Tel: 306-477-1066; *Fax:* 306-665-7577
afoa.sask@sasktel.net
www.afoask.ca
Chief Officer(s):
Eugene McKay, Executive Director

Africa Inland Mission International (Canada) (AIM) / Mission à l'intérieur de l'Afrique (Canada)
1641 Victoria Park Ave., Toronto ON M1R 1P8
Tel: 416-751-6077; *Fax:* 416-751-3467
Toll-Free: 877-407-6077
www.aimint.org/can
www.facebook.com/aimcanada
Also Known As: AIM Canada
Overview: A medium-sized international charitable organization founded in 1895
Mission: Evangelization of people within Eastern & Central Africa & Islands around India Ocean; Planting & establishing churches; Training leadership for those churches; Providing medical, educational, & agricultural services
Member of: Africa Inland Mission International, Bristol, England; Interdenominational Foreign Mission Association
Finances: *Annual Operating Budget:* $1.5 Million-$3 Million; *Funding Sources:* Donations from churches & individuals
Staff Member(s): 8; 3 volunteer(s)
Membership: 135; *Committees:* Finance; Personnel; Projects

African & Caribbean Council on HIV/AIDS in Ontario (ACCHO)
20 Victoria St., 4th Fl., Toronto ON M5C 2N8
Tel: 416-977-9955; *Fax:* 416-977-7664
www.accho.ca
www.facebook.com/ACCHOntario
twitter.com/ACCHOntario
www.youtube.com/ACCHOntario
Overview: A medium-sized provincial organization
Mission: To provide support & resources to members of the African, Caribbean & Black communities in Ontario affected by HIV/AIDS.
Chief Officer(s):
Valérie Pierre-Pierre, Director, 416-977-9955 Ext. 292
v.pierrepierre@accho.ca

African & Caribbean Students' Network of Montréal
c/o Concordia Student Union, #H-711, 1455, boul. de Maisonneuve Ouest, Montréal QC H3G 1M8
Tel: 514-613-0125
acsion@acsionmontreal.org
www.acsionmontreal.org
www.facebook.com/acsionnetwork
twitter.com/ACSioNNetwork
Also Known As: ACSioN Network; Réseau ACSioN
Overview: A small local organization
Mission: To form a more interconnected and self-determined union of Black student organizations, which collaborate to elevate the entire Black community beyond the highest standards of academic, economic, political, and cultural excellence.
Chief Officer(s):
Dwight Best, Chief Executive Coordinator
Membership: *Member Profile:* Black student associations in Montréal Universities and Colleges.

African Canadian Continuing Education Society (ACCES)
PO Box 44986, RPO Ocean Park, Surrey BC V4A 9L1
Tel: 604-688-4880
info@acceskenya.org
www.acceskenya.org
www.facebook.com/138185519562017
twitter.com/acceskenya
Overview: A medium-sized national organization founded in 1993
Mission: To help young Africans obtain the skills & education needed to benefit themselves & their society.
Chief Officer(s):
Donna Van Sant, President
Finances: *Funding Sources:* Private & corporate donations

African Canadian Heritage Association (ACHA)
PO Box 99576, 1095 O'Connor Dr., Toronto ON M4B 3M9
Tel: 416-208-3149
acha@achaonline.org
www.achaonline.org
Overview: A small local organization founded in 1969
Mission: African Heritage and language program for families with children aged 5-16; provides history lessons about African

people in Canada; special events include Black History Challenge, Entrepreneurs' Day, Kwanzaa Open House.
Chief Officer(s):
Cushnie Carole, President
Activities: Parent Committee seminars & workshops

African Community Health Services
#207, 110 Spadina Ave., Toronto ON M5V 2K4
Tel: 416-591-7600; *Fax:* 416-591-7317
Overview: A small local organization
Mission: To offer health & social support services to African immigrants & African Canadians
Chief Officer(s):
Senait Teclam, Contact
Activities: Providing services in Amharic, Ibo, Somali, Trigrinya, & Twi, as well as English and French, & will attempt to arrange translators for other African languages

African Enterprise (Canada) (AE)
4509 West 11th Ave., Vancouver BC V6R 2M5
Tel: 604-228-0930; *Fax:* 604-228-0936
aeinternational.org/canada
Also Known As: AE Canada
Overview: A small national charitable organization founded in 1965
Mission: To service & expand an active partnership among Canadian Christians to raise prayer, financial, material & human resources to enable AE to achieve its mission: to evangelise the cities of Africa through word & deed in partnership with the church
Affliation(s): AE International
Chief Officer(s):
John Radford, Chair
David Richardson, Executive Director
Staff Member(s): 2
Activities: *Internships:* Yes; *Speaker Service:* Yes

African Legacy
Dawson College, 3040, rue Sherbrooke ouest, Montréal QC H3Z 1A4
Tel: 514-931-8731; *Fax:* 514-931-1864
african.legacy@mydsu.ca
Overview: A small local organization
Mission: To serve the social, cultural, & educational needs of the African diaspora both within the Canadian mosaic & in the larger global context

African Medical & Research Foundation Canada (AMREF Canada)
#407, 489 College St., Toronto ON M6G 1A5
Tel: 416-961-6981; *Fax:* 416-961-6984
info@amrefcanada.org
www.amrefcanada.org
www.facebook.com/amrefcanada?ref=profile
twitter.com/amrefcanada
Also Known As: Flying Doctors
Overview: A medium-sized international charitable organization founded in 1973
Mission: Development agency working to enhance community health in East & Southern Africa; headquartered in Nairobi, Kenya; eleven national offices in both Europe & America; acts as support office in raising private & public funds for overseas health programs & also plays active role in maintaining working relations with Canadian International Development Agency (CIDA)
Member of: Canadian Council for International Cooperation
Affliation(s): African Medical & Research Foundations Nairobi; Canadian Centre for Philanthropy; Ontario Council for International Cooperation; Canadian Council for International Cooperation; Canadian Society of International Health
Chief Officer(s):
Anne-Marie Kamanye, Executive Director
akamanye@amrefcanada.org
Finances: *Annual Operating Budget:* $1.5 Million-$3 Million; *Funding Sources:* CIDA; private donations; foundations
Staff Member(s): 3; 90 volunteer(s)
Membership: 1,000-4,999; *Committees:* Finance; Executive; Nominations
Activities: Runs variety of innovative projects which emphasize effective, low-cost health care for rural communities; East African Flying Doctors' Service airlifts medical supplies & services to isolated communities; fundraising & awareness events in Canada to support AMREF projects in Africa; *Awareness Events:* Annual African Marketplace; *Rents Mailing List:* Yes; *Library* Open to public by appointment

African Nova Scotian Music Association (ANSMA)
PO Box 931, Halifax NS B3J 2V9
Tel: 902-404-3036; *Fax:* 902-434-0462
ansma@eastlink.ca
www.ansma.com
www.facebook.com/AfricanNovaScotianMusicAssociationANSMA
www.twitter.com/ANSMA1
Overview: A medium-sized provincial organization founded in 1997
Mission: The African Nova Scotian Music Association (ANSMA) is a not for profit organization dedicated to the development, promotion and enhancement of African Nova Scotia Music locally, nationally and internationally.
Chief Officer(s):
Louis (Lou) Gannon Jr., President
Membership: 131 artist, 10 industry

African Students Association - Universty of Alberta (AFSA)
c/o Student Group Services Office, Students' Union Bldg., Univ. of Alb, #040A, 8900 - 114 St. NW, Edmonton AB
Tel: 780-915-8151
Afsa09@ualberta.ca
www.afsaualberta.org
www.facebook.com/groups/7140648140/
twitter.com/AFSAUAlberta
Overview: A small local organization
Mission: A student group that provides an engaging forum for all students of African descent and all those interested in issues of African concern in Edmonton.
Chief Officer(s):
Isaac Odoom, President
Meetings/Conferences: • University of Alberta African Students' Association 2015 Conference, 2015
Scope: Local

African Students Association of Concordia (ASAC)
K Annex, Concordia University, #K-201, 2150, rue Bishop, Montréal QC H3G 2E9
Tel: 514-848-2424
asac@asac.concordia.ca
asac.concordia.ca
www.facebook.com/asacconcordia
twitter.com/asacconcordia
instagram.com/asacconcordia
Overview: A small local organization
Mission: To represent the students of African descent at Concordia University; To facilitate the social networking of African students; To promote African culture & awareness at Concordia University & in the greater Montreal community
Member of: African & Caribbean Students' Network of Montreal
Chief Officer(s):
Sokhna Fatim Niang, President

African Violet Society of Canada
c/o 349 Hyman Dr., Dollard-des-Ormeaux QC H9B 1L5
e-mail: other@avsc.ca
www.avsc.ca
Overview: A small national organization
Chief Officer(s):
Paul F. Kroll, President
Membership: 400+; *Fees:* $15 annual
Publications:
• Chatter
Type: Magazine; *Frequency:* Quarterly

Africans in Partnership Against AIDS (APAA)
#101, 314 Jarvis St., Toronto ON M5B 2C5
Tel: 416-924-5256; *Fax:* 416-924-6575
info@apaa.ca
www.apaa.ca
www.facebook.com/group.php?gid=23222951493
Overview: A small international charitable organization founded in 1993 overseen by Canadian AIDS Society
Mission: To create a stable organization & community response to the impact of HIV/AIDS through capacity development, partnership, growth, & community development & involvement.
Member of: Ontario AIDS Network, Canadian AIDS Society
Chief Officer(s):
Fanta Ongoiba, Executive Director
Finances: *Annual Operating Budget:* $100,000-$250,000; *Funding Sources:* City of Toronto Department of Public Health, donations
Staff Member(s): 4; 40 volunteer(s)
Membership: 30; *Fees:* $10; *Member Profile:* Community-based organization to respond to the increased need for linguistically & culturally appropriate services & support for Africans living with HIV/AIDS.; *Committees:* Planning; Fundraising/Finance; Community Relations; Organizational Development & Operations; Human Resources
Activities: Emotional support, counselling & advice on testing, treatment, nutrition; advice & help arranging palliative care; *Library* Open to public
Publications:
• Kibaru
Type: Newsletter; *Frequency:* Quarterly

Afro-Canadian Caribbean Association of Hamilton & District Inc. (ACCA)
423 King St. East, Hamilton ON L8N 1C5
Tel: 905-385-0925; *Fax:* 905-385-4914
acca@cogeco.net
accahamilton.ca
Overview: A small local organization founded in 1979
Mission: To provide a vehicle for bringing together the Afro-Canadian Caribbean people residing in Hamilton & District
Chief Officer(s):
Elvis Foster, President
100 volunteer(s)
Membership: 500 individual; *Fees:* $25 individual; $35 family; $12.50 student/senior; *Committees:* Youth; Education; Cultural Arts; Membership; Social; Finance; Walkathon; Spelling Bee

Afro-Caribbean Cultural Association of Saskatchewan Inc.
307 Ave. H North, Saskatoon SK S7K 4J1
Overview: A small provincial organization

AFS Interculture Canada (AFSIC)
1425, boul René-Lévesque ouest, Montréal QC H3G 1T7
Tel: 514-288-3282; *Fax:* 514-843-9119
Toll-Free: 800-361-7248
info-canada@afs.org
www.afscanada.org
www.facebook.com/afsinterculturecanada
Also Known As: Interculture Canada
Previous Name: AFS Programs Canada
Overview: A large international charitable organization founded in 1978
Mission: To promote global education & international development through intercultural exchange programs for both young people & adults; To offer international internships; To work as part of the largest network of international exchange programs in the world
Member of: AFS Intercultural Programs
Affliation(s): United Nations
Chief Officer(s):
M. Miklos Fulop, National Director
miklos.fulop@afs.org
Bernard Roy, Executive Director
Finances: *Annual Operating Budget:* $3 Million-$5 Million; *Funding Sources:* Parents; participants; sponsors; CIDA
Staff Member(s): 15; 500 volunteer(s)
Membership: 30,000 individuals in over 50 countries; *Fees:* $5
Activities: *Internships:* Yes
Awards:
• Thailand Grant (Grant)
• Francine and Robert K Barrett Funds (Grant)
• Dave Turner Scholarship (Scholarship)
• Italy Grant (Grant)
Publications:
• The Adventurer
Type: Newsletter; *Frequency:* Quarterly

AFS Programs Canada See AFS Interculture Canada

Ag Energy Co-operative
#2, 45 Speedvale Ave. East, Guelph ON N1H 1J2
Tel: 519-763-3026; *Fax:* 519-763-5231
Toll-Free: 866-818-8828
www.fireflyenergy.ca
Overview: A small local organization founded in 1988
Mission: To offer energy products & services to its members
Chief Officer(s):
Rose Gage, Chief Executive Officer
Membership: *Fees:* $100; *Member Profile:* Agricultural producers & processors

Aga Khan Foundation Canada
The Delegation of the Ismaili Imamat, 199 Sussex Dr., Ottawa ON K1N 1K6
Tel: 613-237-2532; *Fax:* 613-567-2532
Toll-Free: 800-267-2532

info@akfc.ca
www.akfc.ca
Overview: A medium-sized international charitable organization
Mission: To support cost-effective development projects in Asia & Africa in the fields of primary health care, education & rural development, with special attention paid to the needs of women. Major initiatives include: The Pakistan-Canada Social Institutions Development Program; the Tajikistan Institutional Support Program and the Non-Formal Education Program of the Bangladesh Rural Advancement Committee.
Chief Officer(s):
Khalil Z. Shariff, CEO
Awards:
• Fellowship in International Development Management Program (Scholarship)
Postgraduate studies in the area of International Development*Deadline:* February *Amount:* Dependent on application

Agape Food Bank
c/o Agape Centre, 40 - 5th St., Cornwall ON K6J 2T4
Tel: 613-938-9297
info@agapecentre.ca
www.agapecentre.ca
Overview: A small local charitable organization founded in 1971
Mission: To collect & distribute surplus & donated food for the needy
Member of: Ontario Association of Food Banks
Chief Officer(s):
Johanne Gauthier, Operations Manager
Finances: *Funding Sources:* Donations from events (concerts, marathons, food drives)
Staff Member(s): 2; 20 volunteer(s)
Activities: Food bank; soup kitchen; thrift shop

Agassiz-Harrison Community Services
#7, 7086 Pioneer Ave., Agassiz BC V0M 1A0
Tel: 604-796-2585; *Fax:* 604-796-2517
Overview: A small local organization overseen by Food Banks British Columbia
Mission: A registered, non-profit, multi-service agency that provides over 20 different services and programs to the community, including: Food Bank, Thrift Store, Big Brothers & Big Sisters, Youth Centre, English as a Second Language Settlement Assistance Program.
Member of: Food Banks British Columbia; Food Banks Canada

Age & Opportunity Inc.
#200, 280 Smith St., Winnipeg MB R3C 1K2
Tel: 204-956-6440; *Fax:* 204-946-5667
info@ageopportunity.mb.ca
www.ageopportunity.mb.ca
Overview: A small local organization founded in 1957
Mission: Age & Opportunity Inc. is a not-for-profit, social service agency that offers services and programs to adults aged 55+, living in Manitoba. Services include: legal counselling, housing consultation, therapy dog pairing, crime prevention, settlement & orientation sessions for older immigrants. Programs are numerous, including: language lessons, fitness sessions, arts & crafts, social events.
Chief Officer(s):
Macrae Amanda, CEO

Agence canadienne de l'ISBN *See* Canadian ISBN Agency

Agence canadienne des droits de production musicaux limitée *See* Canadian Musical Reproduction Rights Agency

Agence canadienne des médicaments et des technologies de la santé *See* Canadian Agency for Drugs & Technologies in Health

Agence municipale de financement et de développement des centres d'urgence 9-1-1 du Québec / Municipal finance & development agency for emergency 9-1-1 call centres in Quebec
#300, 2954, boul Laurier, Québec QC G1V 4T2
Tél: 418-653-3911; *Téléc:* 418-653-6198
Ligne sans frais: 888-653-3911
info@agence911.org
www.agence911.org
Aperçu: *Dimension:* moyenne; *Envergure:* provinciale; fondée en 2009
Mission: Pour collecter les recettes fiscales et les répartir entre les centres d'urgence 9-1-1
Membre de: Nena; ACUQ
Affiliation(s): Fédération Québécoise des Municipalités; Union des municipalités du Québec; Ville de Montréal; Ministrère des affaires municipales, des régions et de l'occupation du territoire
Membre(s) du bureau directeur:
Jean-Marc Gibeau, Président
president@agence911.org
Serge Allen, Directeur général
sallen@agence911.org
Membre: 3
Activités: *Service de conférenciers:* Oui

Agence universitaire de la Francophonie (AUF)
CP 49714, Succ. Musée, 3034, boul Edouard-Montpetit, Montréal QC H3T 1J7
Tél: 514-343-6630; *Téléc:* 514-343-5783
recorat@auf.org
www.auf.org
www.facebook.com/profile.php?id=1691871982
twitter.com/planeteauf
www.youtube.com/planeteauf
Nom précédent: Association des universités partiellement ou entièrement de langue française
Aperçu: *Dimension:* moyenne; *Envergure:* internationale; Organisme sans but lucratif; fondée en 1961
Mission: Le but principal est le développement, au sein de l'espace francophone, d'une coopération internationale pour assurer à la fois le dialogue permanent des cultures et la circulation des personnes, des idées, des expériences entre institutions universitaires, dans l'intérêt de l'éducation et du progrès de la science.
Membre(s) du bureau directeur:
Bernard Cerquiglini, Recteur
Finances: *Budget de fonctionnement annuel:* Plus de $5 Million
Membre(s) du personnel: 454
Membre: 710 institutionnel; *Critères d'admissibilite:* Universités; centres de recherche; écoles supérieures
Activités: *Evénements de sensibilisation:* Semaine de la francophonie

Aggregate Producers Association of BC *See* British Columbia Stone, Sand & Gravel Association

Aggregate Producers' Association of Ontario *See* Ontario Stone, Sand & Gravel Association

Agincourt Community Services Association (ACSA)
#100, 4155 Sheppard Ave. East, Toronto ON M1S 1T4
Tel: 416-321-6912; *Fax:* 416-321-6922
info@agincourtcommunityservices.com
www.agincourtcommunityservices.com
www.linkedin.com/company/agincourt-community-services-association
www.facebook.com/AgincourtCommunityServices
twitter.com/AginComServices
Overview: A medium-sized local organization founded in 1970
Mission: To address a variety of issues including systemic poverty, hunger, housing, homelessness, unemployment, accessibility and social isolation in the Scarborough community.
Chief Officer(s):
Lee Soda, Executive Director
Vinitha Gengatharan, Chair
Finances: *Funding Sources:* United Way, Government, Donations
1324 volunteer(s)
Membership: *Fees:* $5

Agincourt Community Services Association (ACSA)
#100, 4155 Sheppard Ave. East, Toronto ON M1S 1T4
Tel: 416-321-6912; *Fax:* 416-321-6922
info@agincourtcommunityservices.com
www.agincourtcommunityservices.com
Previous Name: Information Agincourt; Information Scarborough
Overview: A small local charitable organization founded in 1970 overseen by InformOntario
Mission: A charitable, multi-service neighbourhood agency that exists to identify & provide services, information & programs in response to the diverse needs & interest of the multicultural community; strives to improve the quality of life for individuals & families by mobilizing volunteers, providing links & partnerships between those who wish to help & those who need services
Chief Officer(s):
Vinitha Gengatharan, Chairperson
Finances: *Annual Operating Budget:* $50,000-$100,000
Staff Member(s): 11; 165 volunteer(s)
Membership: 1-99; *Fees:* $5; *Committees:* Management
Activities: Information & referral; emergency food; free income tax clinic; free legal counselling; parent & child program; agency luncheons; job bank; Metro Voice Mail Project; Homeless Drop-In; Housing Connections Access Centre; C.A.P.; shower & laundry facilites; babysitting registry; doctor & dentist listing; volunteer drivers for seniors to medical appointments; food security program; lockers; good food box; cooking clubs; community gardens; *Speaker Service:* Yes

Agrément Canada *See* Accreditation Canada

Agrément de l'enseignement de la physiothérapie au Canada *See* Physiotherapy Education Accreditation Canada

Agricultural Adaptation Council (AAC)
Ontario ArgriCentre, #103, 100 Stone Rd. West, Guelph ON N1G 5L3
Tel: 519-822-7554; *Fax:* 519-822-6248
info@adaptcouncil.org
www.adaptcouncil.org
twitter.com/adaptcouncil
www.youtube.com/user/adaptcouncil
Overview: A small provincial organization founded in 1995
Mission: To provide funding to its members so that they may grow their business
Chief Officer(s):
Terry Thompson, Executive Director
tthompson@adaptcouncil.org
Staff Member(s): 11
Membership: 67; *Fees:* $150; *Member Profile:* Agricultural, agri-food & rural organizations

Agricultural Alliance of New Brunswick (AANB) / Alliance agricole du Nouveau-Brunswick
#303, 259 Brunswick St., Fredericton NB E3B 1G8
Tel: 506-452-8101; *Fax:* 506-452-1085
alliance@fermenbfarm.ca
www.fermenbfarm.ca
Previous Name: New Brunswick Federation of Agriculture
Overview: A medium-sized provincial charitable organization founded in 1876 overseen by Canadian Federation of Agriculture
Mission: To promote & advance the social & economic conditions of those engaged in agricultural pursuits; to formulate & promote agricultural policies to meet changing economic conditions
Member of: Atlantic Farmers Council
Chief Officer(s):
Nicole Arseneau, Office Manager
Mélanie Godin, Coordinator, Environmental Farm Plan
Finances: *Annual Operating Budget:* $100,000-$250,000; *Funding Sources:* Membership fees
Staff Member(s): 3; 12 volunteer(s)
Membership: 1,200 individual; *Fees:* $150-500; *Member Profile:* Farmers maintaining specified level of specific commodity; *Committees:* Training; Sustainable Agriculture; Farm Safety; Farm Finance
Activities: *Speaker Service:* Yes

Agricultural Institute of Canada (AIC) / Institut agricole du Canada
#900, 9 Corvus Crt., Ottawa ON K2E 7Z4
Tel: 613-232-9459; *Fax:* 613-594-5190
Toll-Free: 888-277-7980
office@aic.ca
www.aic.ca
Overview: A large national organization founded in 1920
Mission: To provide the voice for national knowledge & expertise; To promote the creation, production, & delivery of safe foods & sustainable use of related national resources in Canada & beyond
Affliation(s): Canadian Agricultural Economics; Canadian Consulting Agrologists' Association; Canadian Society of Agronomy; Canadian Society of Animal Science; Canadian Society for Horticultural Science; Canadian Society of Soil Science; Canadian Society of Agrometeorology; British Columbia Institute of Agrologists; Alberta Institute of Agrologists; Saskatchewan Institute of Agrologists; Manitoba Institute of Agrologists; Ontario Institute of Agrologists; New Brunswick Institute of Agrologists; Nova Scotia Institute of Agrologists; PEI Institute of Agrologists; Newfoundland/Labrador Institute of Agrologists
Chief Officer(s):
Lynn Lashuk, PAg, President, 250-766-2080
Lianne Dwyer, PhD, Vice-President
ldwyer2416@rogers.com
Frances Rodenburg, Manager, Administration & Communications
frodenburg@aic.ca

Finances: *Annual Operating Budget:* $100,000-$250,000; *Funding Sources:* Membership fees
Staff Member(s): 8
Membership: 9 provincial institutes + 8 agriculture-related scientific societies; *Fees:* $125 individual; $500 corporate; $1,000 association
Activities: News service; international program;
Awards:
• International Recognition Award, Individual (Award)
• International Recognition Award, Organization (Award)
• AIC Fellowship (Award)
• Sustainable Futures Award (Award)
Meetings/Conferences: • Agricultural Institute of Canada 2015 Annual General Meeting, 2015
Scope: National
Publications:
• AIC [Agricultural Institute of Canada] Monthly Report
Type: Newsletter; *Frequency:* Monthly
• GEM (Gender Equality Mainstreaming) Digest [a publication of the Agricultural Institute of Canada]
Type: Newsletter; *Frequency:* Monthly
• Sustainable Futures [a publication of the Agricultural Institute of Canada]
Type: Magazine
Profile: No longer published, but back-issues are archived on AIC's website

Agricultural Institute of Canada Foundation (AICF)
#900, 9 Corvus Crt., Ottawa ON K2E 7Z4
Tel: 613-232-9459; *Fax:* 613-594-5190
Toll-Free: 888-277-7980
aicf@aic.ca
www.aic.ca/about/foundation.cfm
Overview: A large national charitable organization founded in 1987
Mission: To enhance agriculture & the role it plays in providing Canadians with a safe, affordable, nutritious food supply
Affliation(s): Agricultural Institute of Canada
Chief Officer(s):
Corrina Dawe, PAg, President
Frances Rodenburg, General Manager
frodenburg@aic.ca
Finances: *Annual Operating Budget:* Less than $50,000; *Funding Sources:* Personal donations; corporate sponsorship
Staff Member(s): 1
Publications:
• Connections [a publication of the Agricultural Institute of Canada Foundation]
Type: Newsletter

Agricultural Manufacturers of Canada (AMC)
Evraz Place, Stockman's Arena, PO Box 636, Stn. Main, Regina SK S4P 3A3
Tel: 306-522-2710; *Fax:* 306-781-7293
amc@a-m-c.ca
www.a-m-c.ca
Previous Name: Prairie Implement Manufacturers Association; PIMA - Agricultural Manufacturers of Canada
Overview: A medium-sized local licensing charitable organization founded in 1970
Mission: To foster & promote the growth & development of the agricultural equipment manufacturing industry; to identify industry problems & take remedial action; to encourage governments to enact legislation & offer programs that enhance the growth potential of industry; to provide a forum for members to exchange ideas & discuss their industry as it relates to the national & international economy
Chief Officer(s):
James Umlah, Chair, 204-453-6833
Jerry Engel, President
Finances: *Annual Operating Budget:* $250,000-$500,000; *Funding Sources:* Membership fees; special projects
Staff Member(s): 9
Membership: 200 regular + 5 affiliate + 300 associate; *Fees:* Schedule available; *Member Profile:* Regular - manufacturer of farm & ranch equipment; associate - supplier of goods & services; *Committees:* Alberta Provincial; Saskatchewan Provincial; Manitoba Provincial; Ontario Provincial

Agricultural Producers Association of Saskatchewan (APAS)
#100, 2400 College Ave., Regina SK S4P 1C8
Tel: 306-789-7774; *Fax:* 306-789-7779
info@apas.ca
www.apas.ca
Overview: A medium-sized provincial organization overseen by Canadian Federation of Agriculture
Mission: To provide farmers & ranchers with a democratically elected, grassroots, non-partisan producer organization based on rural municipal boundaries
Chief Officer(s):
Nial Kuyek, General Manager
nkuyek@apas.ca
Membership: 114 rural municipalities; *Member Profile:* Producers in rural municipalities of Saskatchewan

Agricultural Research & Extension Council of Alberta (ARECA)
#211, 2 Athabascan Ave., Sherwood Park ON T8A 4E3
Tel: 780-416-6046; *Fax:* 780-416-8915
www.areca.ab.ca
Overview: A medium-sized provincial organization
Mission: To provide agricultural producers with access to field research and new technology, in order to enhance & improve their operations
Chief Officer(s):
Gerald Keufler, Chair
Ty Faechner, Executive Director
faechner@areca.ab.ca
Finances: *Funding Sources:* Government; sponsors
Publications:
• ARECA [Agricultural Research & Extension Council of Alberta] E-Newsletter
Type: Newsletter; *Frequency:* Monthly

Agricultural Technologists Association Inc. *Voir* Association des technologues en agroalimentaire

Agriculture Union
#1000, 233 Gilmour St., Ottawa ON K2P 0P2
Tel: 613-560-4306; *Fax:* 613-235-0517
www.agrunion.com
Overview: A medium-sized national organization overseen by Public Service Alliance of Canada (CLC)
Mission: To advance the workplace interests of its membership; To fight for a society that recognizes the value of the important public services provided by Agriculture Union members
Chief Officer(s):
Bob Kingston, National President
Membership: 8,000+;

Agrienergy Producers' Association of Ontario *See* Biogas Association

Agri-Food Export Group Québec - Canada *Voir* Groupe export agroalimentaire Québec - Canada

AgriVenture International Rural Placements
PO Box 165, Annaheim SK SOK 0G0
Fax: 306-598-4416
Toll-Free: 888-598-4415
canada@agriventure.com
www.agriventure.com
www.facebook.com/people/AgriVenture-Iaea/724272279
twitter.com/AgriVenture
Previous Name: International Agricultural Exchange Association
Overview: A small international organization
Mission: To administer agricultural exchange for young people
Chief Officer(s):
Allison Sarauer, Manager
Membership: 5,000 in 14 countries

Aguasabon Chamber of Commerce
PO Box 695, Terrace Bay ON P0T 2W0
Tel: 807-825-4505; *Fax:* 807-825-9664
Toll-Free: 888-445-9999
jason.nesbitt@investorsgroup.com
www.noacc.ca
Overview: A small local organization
Member of: Northwestern Ontario Associated Chambers of Commerce
Chief Officer(s):
John Lubberdink, Chair
Robert Kirkpatrick, Director
Finances: *Annual Operating Budget:* Less than $50,000; *Funding Sources:* Membership fees
13 volunteer(s)
Membership: 35; *Committees:* Tourism
Activities: Curling Bonspeil; golf tournament; regional trade shows; *Library* Open to public by appointment

Ahmadiyya Muslim Centre
525 Kylemore Ave., Winnipeg MB R3L 1B5
Tel: 204-475-2642; *Fax:* 204-452-2455
www.ahmadiyya.ca
Overview: A small local organization founded in 1979
Membership: 1-99
Activities: *Library*

Ahmadiyya Muslim Jamaat Canada
10610 Jane St., Maple ON L6A 3A2
Tel: 905-303-4000; *Fax:* 905-832-3220
info@ahmadiyya.ca
www.ahmadiyya.ca
Also Known As: Ahmadiyya Muslim Community Canada
Overview: A medium-sized national charitable organization
Mission: To promote interfaith understanding
Affliation(s): The Ahmadiyya Muslim Medical Association of Canada (AMMAC)
Chief Officer(s):
Lal Khan Malik, President
Abdul Aziz Khalifa, Vice-President
Aslam Daud, Secretary
Khalid Naeem, Treasurer
Rana Manzoor Ahmed, Librarian, 905-832-2669 Ext. 2245
Finances: *Annual Operating Budget:* Greater than $5 Million
Staff Member(s): 30; 1,00 volunteer(s)
Activities: Offering religious education; muslim TV (www.mta.tv); *Internships:* Yes; *Speaker Service:* Yes; *Library:* Ahmadiyya Muslim Jamaat Canada Library; Open to public by appointment
Meetings/Conferences: • Ahmadiyya Muslim Jamaat Canada 2015 39th Annual Convention, August, 2015
Scope: National
Description: A Muslim convention, featuring religious addresses & the presentation of awards
Contact Information: jalsa@ahmadiyya.ca, URL: jalsa.ahmadiyya.ca
Publications:
• Ahmadiyya Gazette Canada
Type: Magazine; *Frequency:* Monthly; *Accepts Advertising*; *Editor:* Chaudhary Hadi Ali sahib; *Price:* Free
Profile: Educational material about Islam, summaries of sermons or addresses, announcements & news about the organization

AICA Canada Inc.
#301, 150, rue Berlioz - Ile des Sours, Verdun QC H2E 1K3
Tel: 514-658-2538
www.aica-int.org
www.facebook.com/pages/AICA-International/158887227487940
twitter.com/AICAInt
Also Known As: International Association of Art Critics
Overview: A small national organization founded in 1950
Mission: To broaden communication about the visual arts; To promote the values of art criticism as a discipline; To act on behalf of the physical & moral defense of works of art
Affliation(s): UNESCO
Chief Officer(s):
Ninon Gauthier, President
gauthierninon@yahoo.fr
6 volunteer(s)
Membership: 50; *Fees:* $65
Awards:
• Best Art Review
• Best Art Book in Canada

Aide à l'enfance - Canada *See* Save the Children - Canada

Aide aux aînés (Canada) *See* Help the Aged (Canada)

Aide aux personnes âgées en résidence à Laval inc *Voir* Association pour aînés résidant à Laval

Aide juridique Ontario *See* Legal Aid Ontario

AIDS Action Now / Le groupe d'action sida
Toronto ON
e-mail: aidsactionnowtoronto@gmail.com
www.aidsactionnow.org
www.facebook.com/AidsActionNow
twitter.com/AIDSActionNow
vimeo.com/channels/152729
Overview: A small local organization founded in 1989 overseen by Canadian AIDS Society
Mission: To fight for improved treatment, care & support for people living with AIDS & HIV infection
Finances: *Funding Sources:* Donations
Activities: Advocacy programme, consultation services;

AIDS Brandon Inc.
Willowdale, 22 - 8 Cr., Brandon MB R7A 1A3

Tel: 204-726-4020; *Fax:* 204-728-4344
aidsbrandon@westman.wave.ca
Previous Name: Brandon AIDS Support Inc.
Overview: A small local charitable organization founded in 1989 overseen by Canadian AIDS Society
Mission: To promote & assist in providing a healthy environment within the community for persons with AIDS, their families & friends
Member of: Brandon & District United Way
Chief Officer(s):
Tracey Szucki, Program Coordinator
Finances: *Annual Operating Budget:* Less than $50,000; *Funding Sources:* Donations; grant
Membership: 30

AIDS Calgary Awareness Association (ACAA)

#110, 1603 - 10th Ave. SW, Calgary AB T3C 0J7
Tel: 403-508-2500; *Fax:* 403-263-7358
info@aidscalgary.org
www.aidscalgary.org
www.facebook.com/AIDSCalgary
Also Known As: AIDS Calgary
Overview: A small local charitable organization founded in 1983 overseen by Canadian AIDS Society
Mission: To reduce the harm associated with HIV & AIDS for all individuals & communities in the Calgary region; to provide HIV education & support; to enhance the quality of life & advocate on behalf of people living with HIV; to promote awareness & understanding of HIV issues; to work together with partners in the community to create a caring & compassionate society in the face of HIV & AIDS
Member of: Canadian AIDS Society; Alberta Community Council on HIV/AIDS; Canadian HIV/AIDS Legal Network; Calgary Coalition on HIV & AIDS
Chief Officer(s):
Susan Cress, Executive Director
scress@aidscalgary.org
Finances: *Funding Sources:* Alberta Health; Health Canada; United Way of Calgary; City of Calgary
Staff Member(s): 22
Membership: *Fees:* $5 individual; $20 corporate
Activities: Library resources; annual general meeting; town hall meetings; *Awareness Events:* AIDS Walk; World AIDS Day; *Speaker Service:* Yes; *Library* Open to public

AIDS Coalition of Cape Breton (ACCB)

PO Box 177, 150 Bentinck St., Sydney NS B1P 6H1
Tel: 902-567-1766; *Fax:* 902-567-1766
Toll-Free: 877-597-9255
christineporter@accb.ns.ca
accb.ns.ca
www.facebook.com/CB.4.harmreduction
Overview: A small local organization founded in 1991 overseen by Canadian AIDS Society
Chief Officer(s):
Christine Robinson Porter, Executive Director
christineporter@accb.ns.ca
Frances Macleod, SANE Project Coordinator
francesmacleod@accb.ns.ca
Staff Member(s): 8; 17 volunteer(s)
Membership: *Committees:* Volunteer; Financial; Fundraising; Personnel
Activities: Anonymous testing; drop-in centre; PHA support; public education; safer sex supplies; needle exchange; Queer Youth Matter; Trans Support Group; *Library:* AIDS Coalition of Cape Breton Resource Centre; Open to public

AIDS Coalition of Nova Scotia (ACNS)

#401, 1668 Barrington St., Halifax NS B3J 2A2
Tel: 902-429-7922; *Fax:* 902-422-6200
Toll-Free: 800-566-2437
Other Communication: Alternate Phone: 902-429-7922
acns.ns.ca
Previous Name: Nova Scotia PWA Coalition
Overview: A small provincial charitable organization founded in 1995 overseen by Canadian AIDS Society
Mission: To empower persons living with & affected by HIV/AIDS & those at risk through health promotion & mutual support & to reduce the spread of HIV in Nova Scotia
Member of: Canadian AIDS Society; Canadian HIV/AIDS Legal Network
Finances: *Annual Operating Budget:* $250,000-$500,000
Staff Member(s): 4; 120 volunteer(s)
Membership: 200; *Member Profile:* Full - HIV positive or living with AIDS; associate - supportive of aims & objectives of organization
Activities: Advocacy; anonymous HIV testing clinic; Complimentary & Alternative Therapies (CATS) Program; Haircuts for Health; health fund; hospital tv/telephone services; PHA drop-in; referrals; treatment information; Positive Connections Project; *Awareness Events:* AIDS Awareness Week; World AIDS Day; *Library* Open to public

AIDS Committee of Cambridge, Kitchener/Waterloo & Area (ACCKWA)

#2B, 625 King St. East, Kitchener ON N2G 4V4
Tel: 519-570-3687
Toll-Free: 877-770-3687
volunteer@acckwa.com
www.acckwa.com
www.facebook.com/ACCKWA
twitter.com/AIDSCKW
Overview: A small local charitable organization founded in 1987
Mission: To provide support & education services for people affected by & infected with HIV/AIDS; to mobilize community to respond effectively & with compassion to individuals affected by HIV/AIDS; to advocate on behalf of people infected or affected by HIV
Member of: Canadian Public Health Association
Affliation(s): Ontario AIDS Network; Canadian AIDS Society
Chief Officer(s):
Ruth Cameron, Executive Director
Finances: *Funding Sources:* Ontario Ministry of Health; United Way; fundraising
Activities: Provides counselling either in person or by phone for people living with HIV/AIDS; gives referrals to housing, medical, nutrition, financial & treatment services; offers buddy & practical care services for the partners, families & friends of people living with HIV/AIDS; provides speakers, presentations, & displays; *Awareness Events:* AIDS Awareness Week, Nov.; World AIDS Day, Dec. 1; *Speaker Service:* Yes; *Library* Open to public

AIDS Committee of Durham Region (ACDR)

#202, 22 King St. West, Oshawa ON L1H 1A3
Tel: 905-576-1445; *Fax:* 905-576-4610
Toll-Free: 877-361-8750
info@aidsdurham.com
www.aidsdurham.com
www.facebook.com/AIDSDurham
twitter.com/AIDSDurham
Overview: A small local charitable organization founded in 1992 overseen by Canadian AIDS Society
Mission: To provide HIV/AIDS related services to the infected, affected & general community in the Region of Durham
Member of: Ontario AIDS Network
Affliation(s): Interagency Coalition on AIDS & Development; Canadian AIDS Treatment Information Exchange; Canadian HIV/AIDS Legal Network; Community Networks; Community Advisory Committee; Local Planning & Coordinating Group; Feed The Need in Durham; Affrican & Caribbean Council on HIV/AIDS in Ontario
Chief Officer(s):
Doug Willougby, President
Adrian Betts, Executive Director, 905-576-1445 Ext. 11
director@aidsdurham.com
Finances: *Annual Operating Budget:* $250,000-$500,000; *Funding Sources:* Ministry of Health; Health Canada; private
Staff Member(s): 11; 20 volunteer(s)
Membership: 30; *Fees:* $5-$10; *Committees:* Education; Fundraising; Finance; Personnel; Planning & Evaluation
Activities: Support groups; workshops; individual counselling; prevention education; street program; *Awareness Events:* AIDS Walk; *Speaker Service:* Yes; *Library* Open to public

AIDS Committee of Guelph & Wellington County (ACG)

#115, 89 Dawson Rd., Guelph ON N1H 1B1
Tel: 519-763-2255; *Fax:* 519-763-8125
Toll-Free: 800-282-4505
support@aidsguelph.org
www.aidsguelph.org
www.facebook.com/groups/aidsguelph
twitter.com/AIDSGuelph
Overview: A small local charitable organization founded in 1989
Mission: To provide exemplary services, education & support in the area of HIV & AIDS through innovative health promotion strategies & community partnerships
Member of: Ontario AIDS Network; Canadian AIDS Society
Chief Officer(s):
Tom Hammond, Executive Director
director@aidsguelph.org
Brian Woolsey, Coordinator, Support Services
support@aidsguelph.org
Finances: *Annual Operating Budget:* $500,000-$1.5 Million; *Funding Sources:* Ontario Ministry of Health; Health Canada; United Way
Staff Member(s): 14; 42 volunteer(s)
Membership: 1-99; *Fees:* $24; *Member Profile:* Those infected & affected by HIV & Hepatitis C; *Committees:* Fundraising; Treatment Advisory; Youth Advisory
Activities: Gala Auction; outreach; needle exchange; education; support; *Awareness Events:* Red Ribbon Week, Dec.; AIDS Awareness Campaign, Nov. 24 - Dec. 1; *Speaker Service:* Yes; *Library* Open to public

AIDS Committee of London *See* Regional HIV/AIDS Connection

AIDS Committee of Newfoundland & Labrador (ACNL)

47 Janeway Pl., St. John's NL A1A 1R7
Tel: 709-579-8656; *Fax:* 709-579-0559
Toll-Free: 800-563-1575
info@acnl.net
www.acnl.net
Previous Name: Newfoundland & Labrador AIDS Committee
Overview: A medium-sized provincial charitable organization founded in 1988 overseen by Canadian AIDS Society
Mission: To prevent new HIV infections through education; to provide support to persons living with HIV/AIDS & their families, friends & partners
Member of: Atlantic AIDS Network
Finances: *Annual Operating Budget:* $100,000-$250,000
Staff Member(s): 8; 75 volunteer(s)
Membership: 75; *Member Profile:* Volunteers; *Committees:* Education; Gay & Lesbian Outreach; Support; National AIDS Strategy
Activities: *Awareness Events:* Aids Awareness Week; World Aids Day; AIDS Walk; *Library* Open to public

AIDS Committee of North Bay & Area (ACNBA) / Comité du sida de North Bay et de la région

#201, 269 Main St. West, North Bay ON P1B 2T8
Tel: 705-497-3560; *Fax:* 705-497-7850
Toll-Free: 800-387-3701
acnba@efni.com
www.aidsnorthbay.com
www.facebook.com/groups/78693661361
Overview: A small local organization founded in 1990 overseen by Canadian AIDS Society
Mission: To assist & support all those affected & infected by HIV/AIDS; To limit the spread of the virus through education & awareness strategies
Member of: Ontario AIDS Network
Affliation(s): Chamber of Commerce Downtown Inprovement Area
Chief Officer(s):
Jason Maclennan, President
Stacey L. Mayhill, Ph.D., Executive Director
stacey.mayhall@gmail.com
Finances: *Annual Operating Budget:* $100,000-$250,000; *Funding Sources:* Ontario Ministry of Health; Health Canada
Staff Member(s): 7; 100 volunteer(s)
Membership: 1-99; *Committees:* Executive; Advocacy; Finance; Nominating
Activities: Support groups; one-on-one counselling; safer sex & info phone line; needle exchange; prevention services; bingo nights; *Awareness Events:* AIDS Awareness Week; Krispy Kreme Doughnuts Day, June; Paint the Town Red Gala, Nov.; *Speaker Service:* Yes

AIDS Committee of Ottawa (ACO) / Comité du SIDA d'Ottawa

#700, 251 Bank St., Ottawa ON K2P 1X3
Tel: 613-238-5014; *Fax:* 613-238-3425
officeadministrator@aco-cso.ca
www.aco-cso.ca
www.facebook.com/group.php?gid=17899260494
Overview: A small local charitable organization founded in 1985 overseen by Canadian AIDS Society
Mission: To fight AIDS & HIV infection through advocacy, education & support services
Member of: Ontario AIDS Network
Chief Officer(s):
Kathleen Cummings, Executive Director, 613-238-5014 Ext. 227
ed@aco-cso.ca

Finances: *Annual Operating Budget:* $500,000-$1.5 Million; *Funding Sources:* Provincial, federal & regional government; private; corporate
Staff Member(s): 12; 100 volunteer(s)
Membership: 50; *Fees:* Schedule available; *Committees:* Education; Personnel; Support Services; Finance
Activities: Support Services; Drop In Centre; Education; *Awareness Events:* AIDS Walk Ottawa; *Speaker Service:* Yes; *Library* Open to public

AIDS Committee of Simcoe County (ACSC)
#555, 80 Bradford St., Barrie ON L4N 6S7
Tel: 705-722-6778; *Fax:* 705-722-6560
Toll-Free: 800-372-2272
www.acsc.ca
www.facebook.com/AIDSCommitteeofSimcoeCounty
twitter.com/acsc
Overview: A small local charitable organization overseen by Canadian AIDS Society
Mission: To provide support, education & advocacy to people infected & affected by HIV/AIDS in Simcoe County
Member of: The Canadian AIDS Society; The Ontario AIDS Network; The Greater Barrie Chamber of Commerce
Chief Officer(s):
Gerry L. Croteau, Executive Director
ed@acsc.ca
Finances: *Funding Sources:* Ontario Ministry of Health; Health Canada; community; fundraising
Staff Member(s): 6
Membership: *Fees:* $20
Activities: *Speaker Service:* Yes

AIDS Committee of Sudbury; Access AIDS Committee *See* Access AIDS Network

AIDS Committee of Thunder Bay *See* AIDS Thunder Bay

AIDS Committee of Toronto (ACT)
399 Church St., 4th Fl., Toronto ON M5B 2J6
Tel: 416-340-2437; *Fax:* 416-340-8224; *TTY:* 416-340-8122
Other Communication: volinfo@actoronto.org
ask@actoronto.org
www.actoronto.org
www.facebook.com/ACToronto
twitter.com/ACToronto
www.youtube.com/user/AIDSCommitteeToronto
Overview: A medium-sized local charitable organization founded in 1983 overseen by Canadian AIDS Society
Mission: To provide health promotion, support, education & advocacy for people living with HIV/AIDS & those affected by HIV/AIDS
Member of: Ontario AIDS Network
Chief Officer(s):
Hazelle Palmer, Executive Director, 416-340-2437 Ext. 271
Winston Husbands, Director, Research, 416-340-2437 Ext. 454
Daniel Knox, Director, Development, 416-340-2437 Ext. 268
John Maxwell, Director, Programs & Services, 416-340-2437 Ext. 245
Don Phaneuf, Director, Employment Services, 416-340-2437 Ext. 262
Finances: *Funding Sources:* Private; Corporate; Government
500 volunteer(s)
Membership: 1,000+; *Fees:* $5
Activities: Providing education & outreach to gay & bisexual men & at-risk women & youth; *Awareness Events:* Fashion Cares; *Library* Open to public
Publications:
• Being Well: The PWA/ACT Wellness Newsletter

AIDS Committee of Windsor (ACW)
511 Pelissier St., Windsor ON N9A 4L2
Tel: 519-973-0222; *Fax:* 519-973-7389
Toll-Free: 800-265-4858
www.aidswindsor.org
www.facebook.com/aidswindsor
Overview: A small local charitable organization founded in 1985 overseen by Canadian AIDS Society
Mission: To mobilize our communities through education, advocacy & support to respond effectively & with compassion to the AIDS crisis
Member of: Ontario AIDS Network
Affliation(s): AIDS Support Chatham Kent; Drouillard Road Clinic
Chief Officer(s):
Michael Brennan, Executive Director
mbrennan@aidswindsor.org
Finances: *Funding Sources:* Federal, provincial, private
Staff Member(s): 14
Membership: *Committees:* Executive; Fund Development; Governance; Finance; Nominating & AGM; PHA Advisory; Gay Men's Sexual Health Program Advisory; Women & HIV Program Advisory; African Caribbean B;ack Strategy Program Advisory
Activities: Youth project; needle exchange program; safer sex outreach; support services; speakers' bureau; women's project; phoneline; methadone program; *Awareness Events:* AIDS Walk for Life, Sept.; *Speaker Service:* Yes; *Library:* Resource Library; Open to public

AIDS Support Chatham-Kent
#200, 48 Fifth St., Chatham ON N7M 4V8
Tel: 519-352-2121; *Fax:* 519-351-7067
Toll-Free: 800-265-4858
lbaxter@aidschatham.org
Chief Officer(s):
Lori Baxter, Director, PHA & Harm Reduction Services

Drouillard Rd. Clinic
1052 Drouillard Rd., Windsor ON N8Y 2P8
Tel: 519-977-9772; *Fax:* 519-977-7145
Toll-Free: 800-265-4858
prichtig@aidswindsor.org
Chief Officer(s):
Peter Richtig, Director

AIDS Committee of York Region
194 Eagle St. East, Newmarket ON L3Y 1J6
Tel: 905-953-0248; *Fax:* 905-953-1372
Toll-Free: 800-243-7717
acyr@bellnet.ca
www.acyr.org
www.facebook.com/group.php?gid=2406628135
www.twitter.com/outreachacyr
Overview: A small local organization
Mission: To provide support & education; To promote access to dignified care for people living with HIV/AIDS & those affected by HIV/AIDS
Chief Officer(s):
Radha Bhardwaj, Executive Director, 905-953-0248 Ext. 204
rbhardwaj@acyr.org

The AIDS Foundation of Canada
#302, 1224 Hamilton St., Vancouver BC V6B 2S8
Tel: 604-688-7294; *Fax:* 604-689-4888
contact@aidsfoundationofcanada.ca
www.aidsfoundationofcanada.ca
Overview: A medium-sized national organization founded in 1986
Mission: To address the growing problem of HIV disease in Canada; to fund new & innovative ways of assisting infected/affected people with HIV; to support new ways to heighten awareness of HIV disease among the general population
Finances: *Annual Operating Budget:* Less than $50,000; *Funding Sources:* Casinos; donations
Membership: 1-99
Activities: AIDS/HIV educational services; *Speaker Service:* Yes

AIDS Jasper Society *See* HIV West Yellowhead Society

AIDS Moncton / SIDA Moncton
80 Weldon St., Moncton NB E1C 5V8
Tel: 506-859-9616; *Fax:* 506-855-4726
www.sida-aidsmoncton.com
twitter.com/AIDSMoncton
Overview: A small local charitable organization founded in 1989 overseen by Canadian AIDS Society
Mission: To improve the quality of life for persons infected & affected by HIV / AIDS; To reduce HIV & other sexually transmitted infections
Chief Officer(s):
Deborah Warren, Executive Director
Finances: *Funding Sources:* Fundraising; Donations
Activities: Providing subsidized housing; Delivering a needle distribution service; Offering information & referrals about health promotion & treatment; Presenting prevention education sessions at local schools & other community organizations; Organizing informational displays; Accessing workshops; Training for peer education; Engaging in awareness campaigns; *Library:* AIDS Moncton Resource Library;

AIDS Network of Edmonton Society *See* HIV Network of Edmonton Society

AIDS Network, Outreach & Support Society *See* ANKORS

AIDS New Brunswick / Sida Nouveau Brunswick
G17, 65 Brunswick St., Fredericton NB E3B 1G5
Tel: 506-459-7518; *Fax:* 506-459-5782
Toll-Free: 800-561-4009
info@aidsnb.com
www.aidsnb.com
www.linkedin.com/company/aids-nb
www.facebook.com/aidsnb
twitter.com/aidsnb
www.youtube.com/aidsnb
Overview: A small provincial charitable organization founded in 1987
Mission: To facilitate community-based responses to the issue of HIV/AIDS
Member of: Canadian AIDS Society
Affliation(s): Atlantic AIDS Network
Chief Officer(s):
Tracey Rickards, President
Nick Scott, Executive Director, 506-800-1193 Ext. 104
nick@aidsnb.com
Finances: *Annual Operating Budget:* $100,000-$250,000; *Funding Sources:* Federal government; private donations
Staff Member(s): 3; 100 volunteer(s)
Membership: 300; *Committees:* Advocacy; Policy; Membership; Education & Support
Activities: *Awareness Events:* AIDS Awareness Week; World AIDS Day; Candlelight Memorial; *Speaker Service:* Yes; *Library:* Resource Centre/Centre des ressources; Open to public by appointment

AIDS Niagara
120 Queenston St., St Catharines ON L2R 2Z3
Tel: 905-984-8684; *Fax:* 905-988-1921
Toll-Free: 800-773-9843
info@aidsniagara.com
www.aidsniagara.com
www.facebook.com/AIDSNiagara
twitter.com/aidsniagara
Overview: A small local charitable organization founded in 1987
Mission: To improve quality of life for those infected &/or affected by HIV/AIDS & to reduce the spread of HIV
Member of: United Way
Affliation(s): Ontario AIDS Network; Canadian AIDS Society
Chief Officer(s):
Terry Hunter, Chair
Glen Walker, Executive Director, 905-984-8684 Ext. 112
gwalker@aidsniagara.com
Finances: *Annual Operating Budget:* $500,000-$1.5 Million; *Funding Sources:* Ontario Ministry of Health, Public Health Agency of Canada
Staff Member(s): 29; 90 volunteer(s)
Membership: 60; *Fees:* $50 sustaining; $10 basic
Activities: StreetWorks program; support services; supportive housing; community development & education; women's community development; *Awareness Events:* AIDS Walk for Life: A Scavenger Hunt, Sept. 23; World AIDS Day, Dec. 1; *Speaker Service:* Yes

AIDS PEI
161 St. Peter's Rd., Charlottetown PE C1A 5P7
Tel: 902-566-2437; *Fax:* 902-626-3400
info@aidspei.com
www.aidspei.com
www.facebook.com/pages/AIDS-PEI/156237431556
twitter.com/aidspei
Overview: A small provincial charitable organization founded in 1990 overseen by Canadian AIDS Society
Mission: To provide education & support to Islanders infected or affected by HIV/AIDS; To promote the development of greater understanding & acceptance by the public in relation to persons affected by HIV/AIDS
Member of: Prince Edward Island Literacy Alliance Inc.
Chief Officer(s):
Alana Leard, Executive Director
director@aidspei.com
Finances: *Annual Operating Budget:* $100,000-$250,000; *Funding Sources:* Health Canada; donations; fundraising
Staff Member(s): 3; 100 volunteer(s)
Membership: 100-499; *Member Profile:* People living with HIV/AIDS; community groups; individuals; clergy; *Committe*
Education; Fundraising; Support
Activities: *Awareness Events:* Scotiabank AIDS W
June; *Speaker Service:* Yes

AIDS Programs South Saskatchewa
2911 - 5th Ave., Regina SK S4T 0L4

Tel: 306-924-8420; *Fax:* 306-525-0904
Toll-Free: 877-210-7622
aidsprograms@sasktel.net
www.aidsprogramssouthsask.com
www.facebook.com/96087829094
twitter.com/aidsprograms
Previous Name: AIDS Regina, Inc.
Overview: A small local charitable organization founded in 1985 overseen by Canadian AIDS Society
Mission: To strive to meet the needs of people living with AIDS & HIV positive persons; to strive to educate society about HIV & AIDS; to strive to address issues in society which may arise as a result of HIV & AIDS
Member of: Canadian AIDS Society
Chief Officer(s):
Brian Wiens, Executive Director
executivedirectorapss@sasktel.net
Finances: *Funding Sources:* Government; fundraising
Staff Member(s): 10
Membership: *Fees:* Schedule available
Activities: Community development, advocacy; harm reduction; *Awareness Events:* AIDS Walk for Life, Sept.; *Speaker Service:* Yes; *Library:* AIDS Resource Centre

AIDS Regina, Inc. ***See*** AIDS Programs South Saskatchewan

AIDS Saint John (ASJ)
62 Waterloo St., Saint John NB E2L 3P3
Tel: 506-652-2437; *Fax:* 506-652-2438
info@aidssaintjohn.com
www.aidssaintjohn.com
Overview: A small local charitable organization founded in 1987
Mission: To confront HIV & AIDS through providing education, support, prevention & awareness initiatives; to create supportive social environments to people living with & affected with HIV/AIDS; to share our resources & build partnerships to promote the collaborative development of a community-based response to AIDS locally, provincially & regionally
Chief Officer(s):
Leslie Jeffrey, President
Finances: *Funding Sources:* AIDS Community Action Program (ACAP)
Activities: *Speaker Service:* Yes; *Rents Mailing List:* Yes; *Library* Open to public

AIDS Saskatoon
PO Box 4062, 1143 Ave. F North, Saskatoon SK S7K 4E3
Tel: 306-242-5005; *Fax:* 306-665-9976
Toll-Free: 800-667-6876
info@aidssaskatoon.ca
www.aidssaskatoon.ca
www.facebook.com/aidssaskatoon
Overview: A small local charitable organization founded in 1986 overseen by Canadian AIDS Society
Mission: To provide support to those affected by AIDS & HIV; to educate & inform the community; to have the community embrace the issues addressed by AIDS Saskatoon
Chief Officer(s):
Nanette Breker, President
Nicole White, Executive Coordinator
Finances: *Annual Operating Budget:* $250,000-$500,000
Staff Member(s): 10; 75 volunteer(s)
Membership: 1-99; *Fees:* $10; *Committees:* Support; Education; Advocacy
Activities: Drop-in programming; *Awareness Events:* Red Ribbon Tag Day; AIDS Walk; AIDS Awareness Week; *Speaker Service:* Yes; *Library* Open to public

AIDS Thunder Bay (ATB)
574 Memorial Ave., Thunder Bay ON P7B 3Z2
Tel: 807-345-1516; *Fax:* 807-345-2505
Toll-Free: 800-488-5840; *Crisis Hot-Line:* 807-345-7233
info@aidsthunderbay.org
aidsthunderbay.org
Previous Name: AIDS Committee of Thunder Bay
Overview: A small local charitable organization founded in 1985
Mission: To confront HIV/AIDS infection through prevention, support, education, & advocacy
Member of: Canadian AIDS Society; Ontario AIDS Network
Chief Officer(s):
Dennis Eeles, President
Lawrence Korhonen, Executive Director
lkorhonen@aidsthunderbay.org
Bob Manson, Director, Client Services
bmanson@aidsthunderbay.org
Finances: *Annual Operating Budget:* $500,000-$1.5 Million
Staff Member(s): 9; 150 volunteer(s)
Membership: 100; *Fees:* $10; *Committees:* Education; Support Services
Activities: *Awareness Events:* World Hepatitis Day, July; Opening Doors HIV/AIDS Counselling Conference, Oct.; BINGO; *Speaker Service:* Yes; *Library:* Gabe Kakeeway Memorial HIV/AIDS Library; Open to public

AIDS Vancouver (AV)
1107 Seymour St., Vancouver BC V6B 5S8
Tel: 604-893-2201; *Fax:* 604-893-2205; *Crisis Hot-Line:* 604-696-4666
contact@aidsvancouver.org
www.aidsvancouver.org
www.facebook.com/aidsvancouver
twitter.com/AIDSVancouver
Also Known As: Vancouver AIDS Society
Overview: A small local charitable organization founded in 1983 overseen by Canadian AIDS Society
Mission: To alleviate individual & collective vulnerability to HIV & AIDS, through care, support, education, advocacy, & research
Member of: Canadian Public Health Association
Chief Officer(s):
Brian Chittock, Executive Director, 604-696-4655
brian@aidsvancouver.org
Finances: *Annual Operating Budget:* $1.5 Million-$3 Million; *Funding Sources:* Federal, provincial & municipal grants; private Donations; Fundraising
Staff Member(s): 28; 200 volunteer(s)
Membership: 350; *Fees:* $25; free to people living with HIV/AIDS and active agency volunteers
Activities: *Awareness Events:* AIDS Awareness Week, Nov.; World AIDS Day, Dec. 1; *Library:* Pacific AIDS Resource Centre Library; Open to public

AIDS Vancouver Island (AVI)
Access Health Centre, 713 Johnson St., 3rd Fl., Victoria BC V8W 1M8
Tel: 250-384-2366; *Fax:* 250-380-9411
Toll-Free: 800-665-2437; *Crisis Hot-Line:* 250-384-4554
info@avi.org
www.avi.org
www.facebook.com/aidsvancouverisland?ref=ts
twitter.com/AIDSVanIsle
Overview: A small local charitable organization founded in 1986 overseen by Canadian AIDS Society
Mission: To serve people infected & affected by HIV & Hepatitis C on Vancouver Island & the Gulf Islands, British Columbia; To provide support & combat stigma; To prevent infection
Chief Officer(s):
Katrina Jensen, Executive Director
James Boxshall, Manager, Fund Development & Volunteer Services
Heidi Exner, Manager, Health Promotion & Community Development
George Pine, Manager, Operations
Bryson Hawkins, Director, Finance
Kristen Kvakic, Director, Programs
Heather Hobbs, Coordinator, Street Outreach Services
Finances: *Funding Sources:* Donations; Government funders; Foundations; Businesses; Special event sponsors
Activities: Engaging in research in partnership with university & community-based researchers; Providing prevention information
Publications:
• AVI [AIDS Vancouver Island] Newsletter
Type: Newsletter

Campbell River Office
1371 c. Cedar St., Campbell River BC V9W 2W6
Tel: 250-830-0787; *Fax:* 250-830-0784
Toll-Free: 877-650-8787
Chief Officer(s):
Leanne Cunningham, Contact

Courtenay/Comox Office
355 - 6th St., Courtenay BC V9N 1M2
Tel: 250-338-7400; *Fax:* 250-334-8224
Toll-Free: 877-311-7400
Chief Officer(s):
Sarah Sullivan, Contact

Nanaimo Office
#216, 55 Victoria Rd., Nanaimo BC V9R 5N9
Tel: 250-754-9111; *Fax:* 250-754-9888
health.centre@avi.org
avihealthcentre.org
Chief Officer(s):
Dana Becker, Manager

Port Hardy Office
PO Box 52, Port Hardy BC V0N 2P0
Tel: 250-902-2238; *Fax:* 250-949-9953
Chief Officer(s):
Shane Thomas, Manager

AIDS Yukon Alliance ***See*** Blood Ties Four Directions Centre

AIESEC
#602, 30 Duncan St., Toronto ON M5V 2C3
Tel: 416-368-1001; *Fax:* 416-368-4490
info@aiesec.ca
www.aiesec.ca
www.linkedin.com/groups?home=&gid=22258
www.facebook.com/AIESECCanada
twitter.com/aieseccanada
aiesecstories.wordpress.com
Overview: A large international charitable organization founded in 1958
Mission: To provide an international platform for young people to discover & develop their potential to have a positive impact on society by providing leadership opportunities for students
Chief Officer(s):
Barry Jarvis, Chair
Marie Gwen Castel-Girard, Vice-President, Talent Management, 416-368-1001 Ext. 24
mariegwencg@aiesec.ca
Derek Vollebregt, President, 416-368-1001 Ext. 22
derekv@aiesec.ca
Damien Rambeaud, Vice-President, Exchange, 416-368-1001 Ext. 25
damienr@aiesec.ca
Sarah Guinta, Vice-President, Communications, 416-368-1001 Ext. 23
sarahg@aiesec.ca
Kevin Cornwell, Vice-President, Business Development, 416-368-1001 Ext. 21
kevinc@aiesec.ca
Olivia Lee, Vice-President, Organizational Development, 416-368-1001 Ext. 26
olivial@aiesec.ca
Dominic Tremblay, Vice-President, Corporate Relations, 416-368-1001 Ext. 29
dominict@aiesec.ca
Finances: *Annual Operating Budget:* $500,000-$1.5 Million; *Funding Sources:* Donations; Membership fees
Membership: 60,000; *Member Profile:* Post-secondary students, or indivduals who have graduated from a post-secondary institution in the past two years
Activities: Facilitating leadership opportunities for students through their Global Internship Program (internships are offered in the areas of management, technology, education, & development); Hosting 470 annual conferences, including local, regional, national, & international, which provide members with soft skill & training sessions; *Internships:* Yes
Publications:
• AIESEC Annual Report
Type: Yearbook; *Frequency:* Annually
Profile: Financial statements plus highlights of the organization's activities during the year

Calgary
University of Calgary, Scurfield Hall, #199C, 2500 University Dr. NW, Calgary AB
Tel: 403-220-6454; *Fax:* 403-220-9001
aiesec@ucalgary.ca
www.aiesec.ca/calgary
www.facebook.com/AIESECCalgary
twitter.com/aieseccalgary
www.youtube.com/aieseccalgary;
www.flickr.com/photos/aieseccalgary
Chief Officer(s):
Julie Park, Local Committee President
julie.park@aiesec.net

Carleton
Carleton University, Sprott School of Business, Dunton Tower, #710, 1125 Colonel By Dr., Ottawa ON
Tel: 613-520-2600; *Fax:* 613-520-4427
www.aiesec.ca/carleton
www.linkedin.com/groups?home=&gid=3802950
www.facebook.com/group.php?gid=136553459731961
twitter.com/AIESECCarleton
Chief Officer(s):
Michelle Revzine, Local Committee President
president.aieseccarleton@gmail.com

Chicoutimi
Université du Québec à Chicoutimi, #P0-4105, 555 Boul de L'Universite, Chicoutimi QC G7H 2B1
Tél: 418-545-5011; *Téléc:* 418-545-5012
aiesec@uqac.ca
www.aiesec.ca/chicoutimi
www.facebook.com/group.php?gid=6703004238
twitter.com/AIESECUQAC
Chief Officer(s):
Stéfanie Bérubé, Local Committee President

Concordia
Concordia University, Loyola Campus, #SC 3-07, 7141 rue Sherbrooke ouest, Montreal QC H3G 1M8
Tél: 514-848-7466; *Téléc:* 514-848-7450
concordia@aiesec.ca
www.aiesec.ca/concordia
www.facebook.com/pages/AIESEC-Concordia/309170996359
twitter.com/AIESECConcordia
www.youtube.com/user/aiesecconu
Chief Officer(s):
Jason Patrick Morgan, Local Committee President
jason.morgan@aiesec.net

École des Hautes Études Commerciales
Local RJ.870, 3000 Chemin de la Côte Ste-Catherine, Montreal QC H3T 2A7
Tél: 514-340-6228; *Téléc:* 514-340-6978
aiesec@hec.ca
www.aiesec.ca/hec
www.facebook.com/aiesechecmontreal
Chief Officer(s):
Vincent Landry, Local Committee President
lcp@aiesechec.ca

Edmonton
University of Alberta, School of Business, #2-04H, Edmonton AB T6G 2R6
Tel: 780-492-2453; *Fax:* 780-492-9450
aiesec@ualberta.ca
www.aiesec.ca/edmonton
www.linkedin.com/groups/AIESEC-Edmonton-3643877
www.facebook.com/aiesecedmonton
twitter.com/AIESECEdmonton
www.youtube.com/user/AIESECedmonton
Chief Officer(s):
Sam Turner, Local Committee President
sam3turner@gmail.com

Guelph
University of Guelph, University Centre, #234, Guelph ON N1G 2W1
Tel: 519-834-4120; *Fax:* 519-763-9603
aiesecguelph.ca@gmail.com
www.aiesec.ca/guelph
www.linkedin.com/groups/AIESEC-Guelph-3852109
www.facebook.com/pages/AIESEC-Guelph/186564822203
twitter.com/aiesecguelph
aiesecguelphabroad.wordpress.com
Chief Officer(s):
Kaylee Muise, Local Committee President
lcp.aiesecguelph@gmail.com

Halifax
St. Mary's University, Loyola Bldg., Halifax NS B3H 3C3
Tel: 902-491-8673; *Fax:* 902-491-8673
aiesec.halifax@aiesec.net
www.aiesec.ca/halifax
ca.linkedin.com/pub/aiesec-halifax/38/ab7/692
www.facebook.com/pages/AIESEC-Halifax/25423375792926 8
twitter.com/aiesechalifax
www.youtube.com/user/aiesechalifaxns?feature=mhee
Chief Officer(s):
Ikenna Okoaroafor, Local Committee President
lcp.aiesechalifax@aiesec.net

Kwantlen
12666 72nd Ave., Surrey BC V3W 2M8
Tel: 604-376-3294
kwantlen@aiesec.ca
www.aiesec.ca/kwantlen
www.linkedin.com/groups/AIESEC-KWANTLEN-4089203
www.facebook.com/AIESEC.KPU
twitter.com/AIESEC_KPU/
www.youtube.com/aieseckpu
Chief Officer(s):
Saveena Sehmbey, Local Committee President
saveena.sehmbey@aiesec.net

Laurier
Wilfrid Laurier University, SBE 1250, 75 University Ave. West, Waterloo ON N2L 3C5
e-mail: aieseclaurier@gmail.com
www.aiesec.ca/laurier
www.linkedin.com/company/2266780?trk=tyah
www.facebook.com/AIESECLaurier
twitter.com/aiesec_laurier
www.youtube.com/aieseclaurier
Chief Officer(s):
Michael Fragiskatos, Local Committee President
aieseclaurier.lcp@gmail.com
• Explore AIESEC
Type: Magazine

Laval
Université Laval, Pavillon Palasis-Prince, Local 0413, 2325 rue de la Terrasse, Québec QC G1V 0A6
Tél: 418-656-7810; *Téléc:* 418-656-2352
aiesec.laval@gmail.com
www.aiesec.ca/laval
www.facebook.com/AIESECLaval
Chief Officer(s):
Valérie Côté, Vice-President, Communications
valrie.cote@gmail.com

Manitoba
University of Manitoba, Drake Centre, #127, 181 Freedman Cres., Winnipeg MB R3T 5V4
Tel: 204-275-5539; *Fax:* 204-474-7545
manitoba@aiesec.ca
www.aiesec.ca/manitoba
www.linkedin.com/groups?home=&gid=3255688
www.facebook.com/AIESECmanitoba
twitter.com/AIESECManitoba
www.youtube.com/user/AIESECmanitoba
Chief Officer(s):
Seulmi (Sue) Ahn, Local Committee President Elect
seulmi.ahn@aiesec.net

McGill
McGill University, #407, 3480 McTavish St., Montreal QC H3A 1X9
Tel: 514-398-3001; *Fax:* 514-398-7490
mcgill@aiesec.ca
www.aiesec.ca/mcgill
www.facebook.com/AIESECMcGill
twitter.com/aiesecmcgill
www.youtube.com/user/AIESECMcGill
Chief Officer(s):
David Palkovitz, Local Committee President
president@aiesecmcgill.ca

McMaster
McMaster University, Degroote School of Business, #132, 1280 Main St. West, Hamilton ON L8S 4L8
Tel: 905-525-9140
mcmaster@aiesec.ca
www.aiesec.ca/mcmaster
www.linkedin.com/groups/AIESEC-McMaster-3827920
www.facebook.com/group.php?gid=2347829340
twitter.com/AIESEC_McMaster
www.youtube.com/aiesecmcmaster
Chief Officer(s):
Faheem Kayum, Local Committee President
kayumfaheem@gmail.com

Ottawa
University of Ottawa, Desmarais Bldg., #2105H, 55 Laurier Ave. East, Ottawa ON K1N 6N5
Tel: 613-562-5800; *Fax:* 613-562-5164
aiesecottawa.cr@gmail.com
www.aiesec.ca/ottawa
www.facebook.com/AIESECOttawa
twitter.com/aiesecottawa
Chief Officer(s):
Constance Wong, Local Chapter President
aiesecottawa.lcp@gmail.com

Queen's
Queen's University, #328 JDUC, Kingston ON K7L 3N6
Tel: 613-533-2744; *Fax:* 613-533-2744
vpogx.queens@gmail.com
www.aiesec.ca/queens
www.facebook.com/pages/AIESEC-Queens/1744667226084 30
twitter.com/AIESECQueensU
Chief Officer(s):
Kai Ip Wong, Local Committee President
aiesecqueens.lcp@gmail.com

Ryerson
Ryerson University, TSR 3-173, 575 Bay St., Toronto ON M5G 2C5
Tel: 416-979-5000; *Fax:* 416-979-5266
aiesec@ryerson.ca
www.aiesec.ca/ryerson
www.facebook.com/groups/2202746862
twitter.com/aiesec_ryerson
Chief Officer(s):
Munessa Beehuspoteea, Local Committee President, 647-213-3665
munessa.beehuspoteea@aiesec.net

Saskatoon
University of Saskatchewan, Place Riel Student Centre, #80, 1 Campus Dr., Saskatoon SK S7N 5A3
Tel: 306-966-7767; *Fax:* 306-966-7769
aiesec.saskatoon@gmail.com
www.aiesec.ca/saskatoon
www.facebook.com/AIESEC.Saskatoon
twitter.com/AIESECSaskatoon
www.youtube.com/user/aiesecsk?feature=mhsn
Chief Officer(s):
Carson Widynowski, Local Committee President
aiesec.sk.lcp@gmail.com

Sherbrooke
Université de Sherbrooke, faculté d'administration, #K1-1029, 2500, boul. de l'Université, Sherbrooke QC J1K 2R1
Tél: 819-542-1349; *Téléc:* 819-542-1349
aiesec.sherbrooke@gmail.com
www.aiesec.ca/sherbrooke
www.facebook.com/pages/Aiesec-Sherbrooke/64027988000
twitter.com/AIESEC
www.youtube.com/watch?v=ctkFa1Cf-6I
Chief Officer(s):
Simon Lemieux, Président d'AIESEC Sherbrooke
lcp.aiesec.sherbrooke@gmail.com

Simon Fraser University
Beedie School of Business Administration, Simon Fraser University, #2354, 8888 University Dr., Burnaby BC V5A 1S6
Tel: 778-782-4187; *Fax:* 778-782-5571
aiesec@sfu.ca
www.aiesec.ca/sfu
www.linkedin.com/company/aiesec-simon-fraser-university
www.facebook.com/AIESECsfu
twitter.com/aiesecsfu
www.youtube.com/aiesecsfu; sfubiz.ca/aiesec; flickr.com/aiesecsfu
Chief Officer(s):
Tamara Hombrebueno, Vice-President, Communications
tamara.hombrebueno@aiesec.net

Toronto
University of Toronto, #412, 21 Sussex Ave., Toronto ON M5S 1J6
Tel: 416-978-3335; *Fax:* 416-978-5433
info@aiesectoronto.com
www.aiesec.ca/toronto
www.linkedin.com/pub/aiesec-toronto/2a/a38/100
www.facebook.com/AIESECtoronto
twitter.com/AIESECToronto
www.youtube.com/user/AiesecToronto; aiesectoronto.com/guest
Chief Officer(s):
Medha Agarwal, Local Committee President

Université du Québec à Montréal
CP 8888, Succ. Centre Ville, Montreal QC H3C SP8
Tél: 514-987-3288; *Téléc:* 514-987-6639
info.aiesec.uqam@gmail.com
www.aiesec.ca/uqam
www.linkedin.com/profile/view?id=165621472&goback=.npe_*1_*1_*1_*1_*1_
www.facebook.com/group.php?gid=113395952041930
twitter.com/AIESECESGUQAM
www.youtube.com/aiesecesguqam
Chief Officer(s):
Vladimir Vallès, Président du comité local
lcp.aiesec.uqam@gmail.com

University of British Columbia
PO Box 77, 6138 SUB Boul., Vancouver BC V6T 1Z1
Tel: 604-822-6256; *Fax:* 604-822-8187
info@aiesecubc.ca
www.aiesec.ca/ubc
www.linkedin.com/company/aiesec-ubc
www.facebook.com/AIESECUBC

twitter.com/aiesecubc
aiesecubc.wordpress.com
Chief Officer(s):
Sunga Dominic, Local Committee President
dominic.sunga@aiesecubc.ca

Victoria
University of Victoria, Student Union Bldg., PO Box 3035, Victoria BC V8W 3X3
e-mail: aiesec@uvic.ca
www.aiesec.ca/victoria
www.facebook.com/aiesecvictoria
twitter.com/aiesecvictoria
www.youtube.com/user/AIESECUVic
Chief Officer(s):
Shivangani Murti, Local Committee President
shivimurti@gmail.com

Western
University of Western Ontario, University Community Centre, #340, London ON N6A 3K7
www.aiesec.ca/western
www.facebook.com/aiesecwestern
twitter.com/AIESECWestern
www.youtube.com/delsoltani
Chief Officer(s):
Melissa Nantais, Local Committee President
lcp.aiesecwestern@gmail.com

Windsor
University of Windsor, Odette School of Business, #333, 401 Sunset Ave., Windsor ON N9B 3P4
Tel: 519-253-3000; *Fax:* 519-973-7073
aiesec.windsor@gmail.com
www.aiesec.ca/windsor
www.linkedin.com/groups/AIESEC-Windsor-4390569?home=&gid=4390569&trk=a
www.facebook.com/pages/AIESEC-Windsor/269861425400?ref=ts
twitter.com/AIESEC_Windsor
Chief Officer(s):
Kristie Luk, Local Committee President, 519-990-4308 Ext. 3458
lcp.windsor@gmail.com

York
York University, Schulich School of Business, #W036C, 4700 Keele St., Toronto ON M3J 1P3
e-mail: york@aiesec.ca
www.aiesec.ca/york
www.linkedin.com/groups?mostPopular=&gid=2399333
www.facebook.com/aiesecyork
twitter.com/AIESECyork
aiesecyorkstraveladventures.wordpress.com
Chief Officer(s):
Alex Shum, Vice-President, Communications
aiesecyork.comm@gmail.com

Aikido Yukon Association
c/o Sport Yukon, 4061 - 4th Ave., Whitehorse YT Y1A 1H1
Tel: 867-333-2180; *Fax:* 867-667-4237
info@aikidoyukon.ca
www.aikidoyukon.ca
www.facebook.com/aikidoyukon
twitter.com/aikidoyukon
Overview: A small provincial organization
Mission: To teach the martial art of Aikido in the Yukon.

AiMHi, Prince George Association for Community Living
950 Kerry St., Prince George BC V2M 5A3
Tel: 250-564-6408; *Fax:* 250-564-6801
Other Communication: Room Booking e-mail: bookings@aimhi.ca
aimhi@aimhi.ca
www.aimhi.ca
www.facebook.com/AiMHibc
twitter.com/AiMHiBC
Also Known As: AiMHi
Overview: A medium-sized local charitable organization founded in 1957
Mission: To advocate for adults who have developmental disabilities & children who have special needs; to promote opportunities for community access, education, health care, relationships, freedom from discrimination & equality for all; to encourage choices, respect diversity, & acknowledge each person's rights & contributions to our community
Member of: British Columbia Association for Community Living
Chief Officer(s):
Rory Summers, President
J.W. (Bill) Fildes, Executive Director
Melinda P. Heidsma, Executive Director
Finances: *Annual Operating Budget:* Greater than $5 Million
Staff Member(s): 440
Membership: *Fees:* $10 annually; *Committees:* Executive; Finance; Aging
Activities: Programs & services include: Community Options; Family Support; Home Sharing; Infant Development Program; Infinite Employment Solutions; Kitchen Program; Life Skills; Residential services; Skill Building Library;; *Library:* Skill Building Library; Open to public

Air Cadet League of Canada / Ligue des cadets de l'air du Canada
66 Lisgar St., Ottawa ON K2P 0C1
Tel: 613-991-4349; *Fax:* 613-991-4347
Toll-Free: 877-422-6359
webadmin@aircadetleague.com
www.aircadetleague.com
www.facebook.com/groups/19248248746
Overview: A large national charitable organization founded in 1941
Mission: To promote & encourage a practical interest in aeronautics among young people; To assist those intending to pursue a career in aviation
Chief Officer(s):
Ken Higgins, National President
Sarah Matresky, Executive Director
sarahm@aircadetleague.com
Finances: *Annual Operating Budget:* $250,000-$500,000
Staff Member(s): 4; 7400 volunteer(s)
Membership: 55 corporate + 3,322 associate + 28,000 student + 458 sponsor + 1,935 officers; *Committees:* Executive; National Honours & Awards; National Fund Raising; National Finance; National Flying; Policies & Procedures; Effective Speaking Contest; National Selections
Activities: *Speaker Service:* Yes; *Rents Mailing List:* Yes
Publications:
• Air Cadet League of Canada Newsletter
Type: Newsletter

Air Canada Foundation
e-mail: foundation-fondation@aircanada.ca
www.aircanada.com/en/about/community/foundation
Overview: A medium-sized national charitable organization founded in 2012
Mission: Helps connect sick children to the medical care they need, alleviate child poverty, and make the wishes of ill kids come true.
Chief Officer(s):
Micheline Villeneuve, Manager, 514-422-5973
Activities: Hospital Transportation; Every Bit Counts program; Wings of Courage Program; Volunteer Involvement Program; golf tournament

Air Canada Pilots Association (ACPA) / L'Association des pilotes d'Air Canada
#205, 6299 Airport Rd., Mississauga ON L4V 1N3
Tel: 905-678-9008; *Fax:* 905-678-9016
Toll-Free: 800-634-0944
info@acpa.ca
www.acpa.ca
Overview: A medium-sized national organization founded in 1995
Affiliation(s): Association of Star Alliance Pilots
Chief Officer(s):
Paul Strachan, President
Jon Webster, Secretary-Treasurer, 905-678-9008 Ext. 240
jwebster@acpa.ca
Paul Strachan, Chair, Master Executive Council
50 volunteer(s)
Membership: 3,100;

Air Currency Enhancement Society (ACES)
c/o Bud Bemston, 13 Casavechia Ct., Dartmouth NS B2X 3G7
www.soaraces.ca
www.facebook.com/AirCurrencyEnhancementSociety
twitter.com/soaraces
www.youtube.com/user/soaraces
Overview: A small local organization founded in 1991
Mission: To promote & improve standards in aviation
Member of: Soaring Association of Canada
Chief Officer(s):
Robert Francis, Chairman
robert.francis@soaraces.ca
Patrick Dalton, Communications
patrick.dalton@soaraces.ca
Membership: *Fees:* $50 youth/junior/air cadet; $150 affiliate

Air Force Association of Canada (AFAC) / L'Association des forces aériennes du Canada
PO Box 2460, Stn. D, Ottawa ON K1P 5W6
Tel: 613-232-2303; *Fax:* 613-232-2156
Toll-Free: 866-351-2322
director@airforce.ca
www.airforce.ca
twitter.com/RCAFAssociation
Previous Name: Royal Canadian Air Force Association
Overview: A large national organization founded in 1948
Mission: To promote a viable well-equipped air force & a strong Canadian aerospace industry
Member of: National Council of Veteran Associations
Affliation(s): Air Force Association of United States; Royal Air Forces Association
Chief Officer(s):
Terry Chester, National President
Dean Black, National Executive Director
Finances: *Annual Operating Budget:* $500,000-$1.5 Million; *Funding Sources:* Membership dues; magazine subscriptions
Staff Member(s): 5
Membership: 200 senior/lifetime + 16,000 individual; *Fees:* $35; *Member Profile:* Wartime & peacetime air force veterans; *Committees:* Airpower Advocacy
Activities: Operates 67 wings in Canada; *Awareness Events:* Battle of Britain Sunday, mid-Sept.; *Speaker Service:* Yes; *Library:* AFAC Library
Awards:
• Distinguished Service Award (Award)
• Life Membership Award (Award)
• Meritorious Service Award (Award)
• Award of Distinction (Award)
• Award of Merit (Award)
• The Len Baldock Memorial Award - Memeber of the Year (Award)
• Wing of the Year Award (Award)
• Air Marshall W.A. Curtis Award (Award)
• National President's Award (Award)
• National Vice President's Award (Award)
• Group Efficiency Award (Award)
• 408/437 Wing Award (Award)
• Joe Shkwarek Plaque (Award)
• Christina Handler Memorial Award (Award)
Publications:
• Airforce Magazine
Type: Magazine; *Frequency:* Quarterly; *Editor:* Vic Johnson

Air Industries Association of Canada See Aerospace Industries Association of Canada

Air Line Pilots Association, International - Canada (ALPA)
#1715, 360 Albert St., Ottawa ON K1R 7X7
Tel: 613-569-5668; *Fax:* 613-569-5681
www.alpa.org
www.linkedin.com/companies/air-line-pilots-association
www.facebook.com/pages/We-Are-ALPA/200676905671
twitter.com/WeAreALPA
www.youtube.com/user/WeAreALPA
Previous Name: Canadian Air Line Pilots Association
Overview: A large national organization founded in 1931
Mission: To promote & represent the interests of the airline pilot profession; To safeguard the rights of individual members; To promote & maintain the highest standards of flight safety; To function as a trade union & professional association
Affliation(s): International Federation of Air Line Pilots' Associations; Canadian Labour Congress
Chief Officer(s):
Lee Moak, President
W. Randolph Helling, Sec.-Treas.
Finances: *Funding Sources:* Membership dues
Staff Member(s): 10; 360 volunteer(s)
Membership: 2,200 + 19 locals in Canada; *Member Profile:* Active airline pilots employed by airlines in Canada; *Committees:* Air Safety; Aeromedical; Insurance; Membership
Activities: In Québec call 1-888-337-2033
Publications:
• Air Line Pilot
Type: Magazine

Ottawa Office
#1301, 155 Queen St., Ottawa ON K1P 6L1
Tel: 613-569-5668

Vancouver Regional Office
46484 Lear Dr., Chilliwack BC V2R 5P6
Tel: 604-847-3417
Toll-Free: 866-293-2572

Air Transport Association of Canada (ATAC) / Association du transport aérien du Canada
#700, 255 Albert St., Ottawa ON K1P 6A9
Tel: 613-233-7727; *Fax:* 613-230-8648
atac@atac.ca
www.atac.ca
Overview: A medium-sized national organization founded in 1934
Mission: To advance the issues that affect members from the commercial aviation & flight training industries as well as avaiation industry suppliers
Chief Officer(s):
John McKenna, President & Chief Executive Officer
jmckenna@atac.ca
Fred Gaspar, Vice-President, Policy & Strategic Planning, 613-233-7727 Ext. 314
fgaspar@atac.ca
Bill Boucher, Vice-President, Flight Operations
bboucher@atac.ca
Wayne Gouveia, Vice-President, Commercial General Aviation
wgouveia@atac.ca
Cedric Paillard, Vice-President, Communications & Marketing
cpaillard@atac.ca
Mike Skrobica, Vice-President, Industry Monetary Affairs
mikes@atac.ca
Brian Whitehead, Vice-President, Technical Operations
bwhitehead@atac.ca
Staff Member(s): 7
Membership: 200; *Member Profile:* Operators; Associates; Affiliates; *Committees:* Cabin Operations; Environmental Affairs; Flight Operations; Maintenance, Repair and Overheaul; Safety Advisory; Technical Operations; Accessible Transportation; Air Cargo Carrier; Facilitation; Industry and Monetary Affairs; Legal; Security; Tax; Dangerous Goods; Flight Training and Fixed Wing
Activities: Engaging in lobbying activities; *Speaker Service:* Yes
Awards:
• ATAC Honour Roll Award (Award)
• Paul Mulrooney Memorial Award of Excellence (Award)
• Jim Glass Humanitarian Award (Award)
Meetings/Conferences: • Air Transport Association of Canada 2015 81st Annual General Meeting & Trade Show, November, 2015, Fairmont Queen Elizabeth Hotel, Montréal, QC
Scope: National
Description: A business meeting, the presentation of awards, the chance to view exhibits, & networking opportunities for manufacturers, service providers, flying club & school presidents, operation directors, directors of maintenance, program & procurement managers, chief pilots, & government representatives
Contact Information: E-mail: atac@atac.ca
Publications:
• @ATAC [Air Transport Association of Canada] Newsletter
Type: Newsletter
Profile: Association activities, such as events, awards, & membership information
• Air Transport Association of Canada Annual Report
Type: Magazine; *Frequency:* Annually
• Flightplan
Type: Magazine; *Price:* Free with Air Transport Association of Canada membership

Air Waste Management Association - Québec Section ***Voir*** Association pour la prévention de la contamination de l'air et du sol

Aircraft Operations Group Association (Ind.) ***See*** Canadian Federal Pilots Association

AirCrew Association - Eastern Canada Region
69 Stuart Cr., Toronto ON M2N 1A8
Tel: 416-221-6370
www.torontoaircrewassociation.com
Overview: A small local organization founded in 1987
Mission: To foster comradeship among those who qualified to operate military aircraft & are serving or have served as military aircrew in the armed services of those nations allied to the United Kingdom & the Commonwealth
Chief Officer(s):
John King, President
jking139@rogers.com
Membership: 276; *Fees:* $35

Publications:
• Intercom
Type: Magazine; *Frequency:* Quarterly

AirCrew Association - Western Canada Region (ACA Canada)
PO Box 153, Saanichton BC V8M 2C3
Tel: 250-655-6325
avder@pacificcoast.net
www.aircrew.ca
Also Known As: Vancouver Island Aircrew Association
Overview: A small local organization founded in 1953
Mission: To foster comradeship among those who, having been awarded an official flying badge, have qualified to operate military aircraft & are serving or have served as military aircrew in the armed forces of Canada & its Allies
Chief Officer(s):
Scott Eichel, President, 250-360-0939
Finances: *Funding Sources:* Membership dues
Membership: *Fees:* $40 regular; $25 associate
Activities: Branches in Victoria, Sidney, West Vancouver & Calgary

Airdrie & District Soccer Association
PO Box 80021, Stn. Shoppers Downton, Airdrie AB T4A 0H6
Tel: 403-948-6260; *Fax:* 403-948-6290
admin@airdriesoccer.com
airdriesoccer.com
Overview: A small local organization overseen by Alberta Soccer Association
Member of: Alberta Soccer Association
Chief Officer(s):
Julie Smith, Registrar
Membership: *Fees:* Schedule available

Airdrie Chamber of Commerce
#106, 120 - 2nd Ave. NE, Airdrie AB T4B 2N2
Tel: 403-948-4412; *Fax:* 403-948-3141
info@airdriechamber.ab.ca
www.airdriechamber.ab.ca
Overview: A small local charitable organization founded in 1973
Mission: To promote, represent, & enhance the interests of Airdrie Alberta's business community
Member of: Alberta Chamber of Commerce
Chief Officer(s):
Hunt Lorna, Executive Director
Staff Member(s): 1
Membership: 500; *Fees:* Schedule available

Airdrie Food Bank (AFB)
20 East Lake Way NE, Airdrie AB T4A 2J2
Tel: 403-948-0063; *Fax:* 403-948-9332
info@airdriefoodbank.com
www.airdriefoodbank.com
www.facebook.com/airdriefoodbank
twitter.com/airdriefoodbank
www.youtube.com/playlist?list=FLhMDx5mkeznB3FeSW8LCDOw
Overview: A small local charitable organization founded in 1984 overseen by Alberta Food Bank Network Association
Mission: To collect and distribute food to those in need and educate the community on hunger-related issues
Member of: Food Banks Canada; Alberta Food Bank Network Association; Food Banks Alberta
Chief Officer(s):
Lori McRitchie, Executive Director
Finances: *Funding Sources:* Donations; grants/government funding
Staff Member(s): 6; 150+ volunteer(s)

Airport Management Council of Ontario
#5, 50 Terminal St., North Bay ON P1B 8G2
Tel: 705-474-1080; *Fax:* 705-474-4073
Toll-Free: 877-636-2626
amco@amco.on.ca
www.amco.on.ca
Overview: A small provincial organization founded in 1985
Mission: To monitor the airport industry, lobby, provide networking opportunities & training to airports & businesses that work to enhance airport operations.
Chief Officer(s):
Bryan Avery, Executive Director, 877-636-2626
bryan.avery@amco.on.ca
Membership: 58 airports + 56 businesses; *Fees:* Schedule available
Activities: Workshops, presentations, conventions; *Speaker Service:* Yes; *Library:* Resource Centre

Airspace Action on Smoking & Health
PO Box 18004, 1215c 56th St., Delta BC V4L 2M4
Tel: 778-899-4832
Toll-Free: 888-245-7722
airspace.bc.ca
www.facebook.com/234024210003649
twitter.com/airspace_bc
Previous Name: AIRSPACE Non-Smokers' Rights Society
Overview: A medium-sized provincial organization founded in 1981
Mission: To educate non-smokers on the effects that smoking has on them & of their legal right to smoke-free air; to help establish laws to protect the comfort, safety & health of non-smokers; to help reduce the number of future smokers
Affliation(s): Non-Smokers' Rights Association; Canadian Council on Smoking & Health
Finances: *Funding Sources:* Membership dues
9 volunteer(s)
Membership: 1,700; *Fees:* $20 individual; $25 family; $125 individual lifetime; $130 family; *Committees:* Newsletter Publication; Smoke-Free Restaurant List; Demonstrations; Letter-Writing Campaigns
Activities: *Internships:* Yes; *Speaker Service:* Yes; *Library* Open to public

AIRSPACE Non-Smokers' Rights Society ***See*** Airspace Action on Smoking & Health

Aish HaTorah Learning Centre ***See*** Aish Thornhill Community Shul & Learning Centre

Aish Thornhill Community Shul & Learning Centre
949 Clark Ave. West, Thornhill ON L4J 8G6
Tel: 905-764-1818; *Fax:* 905-764-1606
theshul@aish.com
www.thornhillshul.com
www.facebook.com/groups/2588276462
Previous Name: Aish HaTorah Learning Centre
Overview: A small local charitable organization founded in 1981
Chief Officer(s):
Avram Rothman
arothman@aish.edu
Finances: *Annual Operating Budget:* $1.5 Million-$3 Million
Staff Member(s): 15
Activities: *Speaker Service:* Yes; *Rents Mailing List:* Yes

Aiviq Hunters & Trappers Organization
PO Box 300, Cape Dorset NU X0A 0C0
Tel: 867-897-8214
aiviq_hunters@qiniq.com
Overview: A small local organization
Chief Officer(s):
Quvianatiliaq Tapaungai, Chair

Ajax, Pickering & Whitby Association for Community Living ***See*** Community Living Ajax-Pickering & Whitby

Ajax-Pickering Board of Trade
#3, 144 Old Kingston Rd., Ajax ON L1T 2Z9
Tel: 905-686-0883; *Fax:* 905-686-1057
info@apboardoftrade.com
www.apboardoftrade.com
www.facebook.com/APBOT
twitter.com/APBoardofTrade
Overview: A medium-sized local organization founded in 1955
Member of: Canadian Chamber of Commerce
Chief Officer(s):
Kathy McKay, Executive Director, 905-686-0883 Ext. 223
kmckay@apboardoftrade.com
Kasia Chojecki, Communications, 905-686-0883 Ext. 229
Janet Casey, Administration & Events, 905-686-0883 Ext. 222
Finances: *Annual Operating Budget:* $100,000-$250,000; *Funding Sources:* Membership fees
Staff Member(s): 2; 37 volunteer(s)
Membership: 360; *Fees:* Based on number of employees
Activities: Networking; business excellence; *Speaker Service:* Yes

Ajax-Pickering Chamber Orchestra ***See*** Durham Chamber Orchestra

Ajjiit Nunavut Media Association
PO Box 6011, Iqaluit NU X0A 0H0
e-mail: alethea@unikkaat.com
www.ajjiit.ca
Overview: A small provincial organization
Mission: To advocate for film, television, & new media in Nunavut; To promote Nunavut's film, television, & new media

Canadian Associations

industry; To act as a point of contact for outside organizations & the Government of Nunavut
Chief Officer(s):
Alethea Arnaquq-Baril, President
Finances: *Funding Sources:* Memberships; Sponsorships
Membership: *Fees:* $15 Nunavut elders & youth under 18; $50 individuals, businesses, supporters, & providers of services to the industry; $100 persons outside Nunavut; *Member Profile:* Persons engaged in film, television, & new media occupations in Nunavut; Non-Nunavut based producers who collaborate on northern media projects
Activities: Consulting with the territorial government & Nunavut Film on issues which affect the industry; Hosting workshops; Presenting awards;

Alameda Agricultural Society
PO Box 103, Alameda SK S0C 0A0
Tel: 306-489-4913
Overview: A small local charitable organization
Chief Officer(s):
Melissa Gervais, President
Jamie Neuman, Secretary
Finances: *Funding Sources:* Donations
Activities: Hosting a summer fair, 4-H show, & flower show

Al-Anon Family Groups (Canada), Inc. / Groupe familiaux Al-Anon
PO Box 57012, 163 Bell St. North, Ottawa ON K1R 1A1
Tel: 613-860-3431
wso@al-anon.org
al-anon.alateen.on.ca
www.facebook.com/172402452825446
twitter.com/AlAnon_WSO
Also Known As: AL-ANON/ALATEEN
Overview: A medium-sized national charitable organization founded in 1951
Finances: *Funding Sources:* Literature sales; contributions from members & groups
Membership: *Fees:* Voluntary contributions
Activities: Support groups for families, friends & relatives of alcoholics; Alateen - support groups for youth aged 12 - 20 with alcoholic parents; *Speaker Service:* Yes

Al-Anon Montréal
CP 37322, Succ. Marquette, Montréal QC H2E 3B5
Tél: 514-866-9803
information@al-anon-montreal.org
al-anon-montreal.org
Aperçu: *Dimension:* petite; *Envergure:* locale
Mission: Pour aider les personnes souffrant d'alcoolisme et de leurs familles, et les enfants d'aide qui sont touchés par l'alcoolisme

Albanian Canadian Community Association
85 Ingram Dr., Toronto ON M6M 2L7
Tel: 416-503-4704; *Fax:* 416-503-4704
info@albcan.ca
albcan.ca
www.facebook.com/shoqata.shqiptarokanadeze
Also Known As: Shoqata Bashkesia Shqiptaro Kanadeze; Albcan
Overview: A small national organization founded in 1990
Mission: To develop the culture, art and heritage of Albanians in Ontario
Chief Officer(s):
Ruki Kondaj, President, Board of Directors, 416-876-7665
r.kondaj@albcan.ca
Membership: *Fees:* Students: $20; Adults: $30; Families: $50

Alberni District Historical Society
Alberni Valley Museum, 4255 Wallace St., Port Alberni BC V9Y 7M7
Tel: 250-723-2181
aadhs1@gmail.com
Overview: A small local charitable organization founded in 1965
Mission: To preserve & make available local history, to collect, arrange & maintain community archives with a concentration on "paper treasures."
Member of: BC Historical Federation; Archives Association of BC
Finances: *Funding Sources:* Membership fees; donations
Membership: *Member Profile:* Community residents
Activities: Public education; special speakers; *Library:* Archives; Open to public

Alberni Valley Chamber of Commerce
2533 Port Alberni Hwy., Port Alberni BC V9Y 8P2
Tel: 250-724-6535; *Fax:* 250-724-6560
office@avcoc.com
www.avcoc.com
Overview: A small local organization
Mission: To improve our community through the promotion of business & removal of barriers to business development
Member of: BC Chamber of Commerce
Chief Officer(s):
Neil Malbon, President
neil@alberniheritage.com
Mike Carter, Executive Director
manager@avcoc.com
Finances: *Annual Operating Budget:* $100,000-$250,000
Staff Member(s): 2
Membership: 272; *Fees:* Business: $132.60-$1472.35 (depending on business size); Student/senior: $31.05; Club/organization: $49.45; Individual: $48.30; *Committees:* Membership; Business; Junior Achievement; Fantasy Auction

Alberni Valley Coin Club
4689 - 10th Ave, Port Alberni BC V9Y 4Y1
Overview: A small local organization
Member of: Royal Canadian Numismatic Association

Alberni Valley Outdoor Club
c/o Ursula Knoll, 3941 - 9th Ave., Port Alberni BC V9Y 4V1
Tel: 250-723-6883
uschik@telus.net
www.mountainclubs.org/AVOC.htm
Overview: A small local organization
Member of: Federation of Mountain Clubs of British Columbia
Chief Officer(s):
Harold Carlson, Chairperson, 250-724-4535
Membership: *Fees:* Single: $25; Family: $45; Associate: $5

Alberni Valley Rock & Gem Club
PO Box 1291, Stn. A, Port Alberni BC V9Y 7M2
Tel: 250-723-0281
compudoc@telus.net
Overview: A small local organization founded in 1958
Member of: British Columbia Lapidary Society
Chief Officer(s):
Dave West, Contact
Activities: Meetings are held 1st Sun. of every month in Cherry Creek Community Hall, Moore Rd., Port Alberni.

Alberni Valley Soaring Association
8064 Richards Trail, Duncan BC V9L 6B2
Tel: 250-667-3591
Toll-Free: 866-590-7627
www.avsa.ca
www.facebook.com/AlberniValleySoaringAssociation
ca.groups.yahoo.com/group/albernivalleysoaringasc
Overview: A small local organization
Mission: To offer opportunities to fly to its members & guests
Member of: Soaring Association of Canada
Affliation(s): Vancouver Island Soaring Centre; Vancouver Soaring Association
Chief Officer(s):
Allen Paul, President, 250-455-0722
apaul9@telus.net
Membership: *Fees:* $150 youth; $200 junior; $400 regular

Albert County Chamber of Commerce
PO Box 3051, Hillsborough NB E4H 4W5
Tel: 506-389-6002; *Fax:* 506-387-8331
accofc@gmail.com
www.albertcountychamber.com
Overview: A small local organization
Chief Officer(s):
Brian Keirstead, President, 506-386-3917
Kevin Snair, Secretary, 506-734-2551
Membership: *Fees:* $75
Publications:
• Progress
Type: Magazine

Alberta & Northwest Territories Lung Association
PO Box 4500, Stn. South, #208, 17420 Stony Plain Rd., Edmonton AB T5E 6K2
Tel: 780-488-6819; *Fax:* 780-488-7195
Toll-Free: 888-566-5864
info@ab.lung.ca
www.ab.lung.ca
www.facebook.com/group.php?gid=192015860715
Overview: A medium-sized provincial charitable organization founded in 1939 overseen by Canadian Lung Association
Mission: To educate the public & medical professionals about lung health
Chief Officer(s):
Anne Marie Downey, Chair
Kate Hurlburt, Vice-Chair
Tom Watts, Secretary
Paul Borrett, Treasurer
Finances: *Funding Sources:* Donations; Fundraising; Sponsorships
Membership: *Fees:* $25
Activities: Providing indepth information about asthma, COPD, sleep apnea, tuberculosis, & other lung conditions, as well as smoking & clean air; Organizing & promoting events about lung health to support the association; Funding medical research; *Awareness Events:* Radon Awareness Campaign; Northwest Territories Asthma & Allergies Door-to-Door Campaign, May
Publications:
• Alberta & Northwest Territories Lung Association Annual Report
Type: Yearbook; *Frequency:* Annually
Profile: Highlights of fundraising activities, advocacy activities, & patient support programs

Alberta 5 Pin Bowlers' Association (A5-PBA)
Bowling Headquarters, 432 - 14 St. South, Lethbridge AB T1J 2X7
Tel: 403-320-2695; *Fax:* 403-320-2676
Toll-Free: 800-762-3075
generalenquires@centralalberta5pin.com
www.alberta5pin.com
www.facebook.com/a5pba
Overview: A medium-sized provincial charitable organization founded in 1979 overseen by Canadian 5 Pin Bowlers' Association
Chief Officer(s):
Annette Bruneau, President
Julie Kind, Secretary
Don MacIver, Treasurer
Brian Sudbury, Director, Technical

Alberta Aboriginal Women's Society
PO Box 5168, Stn. Main, Peace River AB T8S 1R8
Tel: 780-624-3416; *Fax:* 780-624-3409
aaws@telusplanet.net
Overview: A medium-sized provincial organization overseen by Native Women's Association of Canada
Chief Officer(s):
Ruth Kidder, President

Alberta Accountants Unification Agency (AAUA)
#300, 1210 - 8th St. SW, Calgary AB T2R 1L3
Tel: 403-269-5341; *Fax:* 403-262-5477
Other Communication: Education: 587-390-1877;
yourpath@albertaaccountants.org
www.albertaaccountants.org
Overview: A large provincial licensing organization overseen by Chartered Professional Accountants Canada
Mission: To oversee the integration of the Certified General Accountants of Alberta (CGA), the Certified Management Accountants of Alberta (CMA) & the Institute of Chartered Accountants of Alberta (ICAA) under the Chartered Professional Accountants (CPA) banner.
Chief Officer(s):
John Carpenter, BA, MBA, FICB, Chief Executive Officer
Janice Harrington, Vice-President, Communications & Government Relations
jharrington@cga-alberta.org

Alberta Aerospace Association *See* Aviation Alberta

Alberta Agricultural Economics Association (AAEA)
Dept. of Resource Economics & Environmental Sociology, U of Alberta, 515 General Services Bldg., Edmonton AB T6G 2H1
Tel: 780-422-3122
info@aaea.ab.ca
aaea.ualberta.ca
Overview: A small provincial charitable organization founded in 1984
Mission: To provide an opportunity for communication among those interested in the agricultural & rural social sciences; To provide a forum for the discussion of issues affecting the rural economy; To encourage research & dissemination of research results & other information relating to Alberta's rural economy; To provide avenues for continuing education & professional upgrading
Chief Officer(s):

Lukas Matejovsky, President, 780-422-2887
lukas.matejovsky@gov.ab.ca
Vitor Dias, Secretary, 780-644-8702
vitor.dias@gov.ab.ca
Finances: *Annual Operating Budget:* Less than $50,000
Membership: 100-499; *Fees:* $30
Activities: Annual 'Visions' Conference in May; regional seminars & luncheon speakers; newsletter; undergraduate & graduate scholarships in agricultural economics at University of Alberta;
Awards:
• AAEA Undergraduate Scholarship (Scholarship)
• AAEA Masters Scholarship (Scholarship)

Alberta Alliance on Mental Illness & Mental Health

Capital Place, #320, 9707 - 110 St., Edmonton AB T5K 2L9
Tel: 780-482-4993; *Fax:* 780-482-6348
www.aamimh.ca
Overview: A small provincial organization
Mission: To act as a voice for the mental health & mental illness community; To ensure mental health & mental illness issues are prominent on health & social policy agendas in Alberta
Chief Officer(s):
Orrin Lyseng, Executive Director
executivedirector@aamimh.ca
Membership: 12; *Member Profile:* Mental health organizations in Alberta

Alberta Alpine Ski Association (AASA)

Bill Warren Training Centre, #100, 1995 Olympic Way, Canmore AB T1W 2T6
Tel: 403-609-4730; *Fax:* 403-678-3644
memberservices@albertaalpine.ca
www.albertaalpine.ca
www.facebook.com/122652134004
Also Known As: Alberta Alpine
Overview: A small provincial organization
Mission: To govern & promote alpine skiing in Alberta.
Chief Officer(s):
Adam Hull, President, 403-609-4731
adam@albertaalpine.ca

Alberta Amateur Baseball Council (AABC)

2425 North Parkside Dr., Lethbridge AB T1J 4W3
Tel: 403-320-2025; *Fax:* 403-320-2053
www.albertabaseball.org
twitter.com/AABC_HPC
Overview: A large provincial organization founded in 1998
Mission: To be the governing body of baseball associations throughout Alberta.
Chief Officer(s):
Ron Van Keulen, President
Kim Brigitzer, Manager, Administration & Communications
k.brigitzer@albertabaseball.org
Aaron Lavorato, Coordinator, High Performance
a.lavorato@albertabaseball.org
Membership: 5 leagues + 31,000 individuals

Alberta Amateur Boxing Association *See* Boxing Alberta

Alberta Amateur Football Association (AAFA)

Percy Page Centre, 11759 Groat Rd., Edmonton AB T5M 3K6
Tel: 780-427-8108; *Fax:* 780-422-2663
admin@footballalberta.ab.ca
www.footballalberta.ab.ca
www.facebook.com/pages/Football-Alberta/503709906338891
twitter.com/FootballAlberta
Also Known As: Football Alberta
Overview: A medium-sized provincial organization founded in 1973
Mission: To provide a consistent representative voice for football of all levels throughout the province of Alberta
Member of: Football Canada
Chief Officer(s):
Jay Hetherington, President
jhetherington@rdpsd.ab.ca
Brian Fryer, Executive Director
bfryer@telus.net
Staff Member(s): 3
Membership: *Fees:* Schedule available

Alberta Amateur Softball Association (AASA)

9860 - 33 Ave., Edmonton AB T6N 1C6
Tel: 780-461-7735; *Fax:* 780-461-7757
info@softballalberta.ca
www.softballalberta.ca
www.facebook.com/238456432957672
Also Known As: Softball Alberta
Overview: A large provincial organization founded in 1971 overseen by Canadian Amateur Softball Association
Mission: To foster & promote the playing of amateur softball; to regulate play in all classifications of the game as may be deemed in its best interests
Member of: Canadian Amateur Softball Association
Affliation(s): Western Canada Softball Association
Chief Officer(s):
Michele Patry, Executive Director
michele@softballalberta.ca
Finances: *Funding Sources:* Alberta Sport, Recreation & Parks; Wildlife Foundation
Staff Member(s): 4
Activities: *Internships:* Yes; *Speaker Service:* Yes; *Library* Open to public
Awards:
• Softball Alberta Scholarships (Scholarship)
Deadline: September 1
• Umpire Recognition Award (Award)
• Minor Player of the Year (Male and Female) (Award)
• Adult Slo-Pitch Player of the Year (Male and Female) (Award)
• Adult Fast-Pitch Player of the Year (Male and Female) (Award)
• Coach of the Year (Minor, Adult Slo-Pitch, Adult Fast-Pitch) (Award)
Publications:
• ASDCC Connecting Coaches
Type: Newsletter

Alberta Amateur Speed Skating Association (AASSA)

2500 University Dr. NW, Calgary AB T2N 1N4
Tel: 403-220-7911; *Fax:* 403-220-9226
aassa@ucalgary.ca
www.albertaspeedskating.ca
Overview: A small provincial organization overseen by Speed Skating Canada
Member of: Speed Skating Canada
Chief Officer(s):
Blair Carbert, President
Wendy Walker, Program Coordinator

Alberta Amateur Wrestling Association (AAWA)

Percy Page Centre, 11759 Groat Rd., Edmonton AB T5M 3K6
Tel: 780-415-0140; *Fax:* 780-427-0524
www.albertaamateurwrestling.ca
www.facebook.com/AlbertaWrestling
twitter.com/AlbertaWrestlin
Overview: A small provincial organization founded in 1974 overseen by Canadian Amateur Wrestling Association
Mission: The AAWA is the governing body for amateur wrestling & grappling in Alberta.
Member of: Canadian Amateur Wrestling Association
Chief Officer(s):
Tammie Bradley, Executive Director
Michael Drought, Technical Director, 780-643-0799
Finances: *Annual Operating Budget:* $100,000-$250,000; *Funding Sources:* Government grants; fundraising
Staff Member(s): 2
Membership: 2,000; *Fees:* $10 individual; *Member Profile:* Male & female ages 13+
Activities: Training camps; officials & coaches clinics; school clinics; major games; coordinate provincial program

Alberta Amputee Sports & Recreation Association (AASRA)

PO Box 708, Stn. M, Calgary AB T2P 2J3
Tel: 403-201-0507; *Fax:* 403-256-7611
Toll-Free: 888-501-0507
info@aasra.ab.ca
www.aasra.ab.ca
www.facebook.com/495810413773520
Overview: A small provincial charitable organization founded in 1977
Mission: To support & provide opportunities for amputees in recreational & sporting activities, in events for both the disabled & able-bodied; To provide moral support to new amputees & family
Chief Officer(s):
Shane Westin, President
Gwen Davies, Executive Director
Finances: *Funding Sources:* Donations; corporate & government support
Membership: *Fees:* $20 Annual; $150 Lifetime; *Member Profile:* People who have lost a limb(s) at a major joint; *Committees:* Volunteer
Activities: Annual Pro/Amp Golf Tournament; cycling clinic, golf clinic; support group meetings; *Speaker Service:* Yes

Alberta Angus Association

PO Box 3725, Olds AB T4H 1P5
Tel: 403-556-9057
Toll-Free: 888-556-9057
office@albertaangus.ca
www.albertaangus.com
Overview: A medium-sized provincial organization founded in 1917
Member of: Canadian Angus Association
Chief Officer(s):
Colton Hamilton, President, 403-224-2353
colt43@hotmail.com
Carol High, Vice-President, 403-553-3524
Finances: *Annual Operating Budget:* $50,000-$100,000
Staff Member(s): 1
Membership: 100-499; *Fees:* $25 + GST
Activities: To perform all administrative & promotional activities for its members;
Awards:
• Purebred Breeder of the Year
• Commercial Breeder of the Year
• Spirit of Angus Award

Alberta Aquaculture Association

c/o Dan Menard, Treasurer, PO Box 26, Site 3, RR#1, Red Deer AB T4N 5E1
Tel: 403-342-5206; *Fax:* 403-342-2646
info@smokytroutfarm.com
www.affa.ab.ca
Previous Name: Alberta Fish Farmers Association
Overview: A small local organization
Mission: To support the pursuit of aquaculture promotion & education
Member of: Canadian Aquaculture Producers' Council
Chief Officer(s):
Dan Menard, Treasurer
rdmenard@telusplanet.net
Victoria Page, Sec.-Treas.
Membership: *Fees:* $10 Assoc.; $100 Full; $250 Corporate; $250 Ed. Inst.

Alberta Assessment Consortium (AAC)

#700, 11010 - 142 St., Edmonton AB T5N 2R1
Tel: 780-761-0530; *Fax:* 780-761-0533
info@aac.ab.ca
www.aac.ab.ca
twitter.com/AACinfo
Overview: A medium-sized provincial organization
Mission: Develops a broad range of classroom assessment materials, directly aligned to Alberta curriculum, that address both formative and summative processes.
Chief Officer(s):
Sherry Bennett, Executive Director
Membership: 100-499; *Fees:* $5,500 regular; $1,100 associate; *Member Profile:* School authorities and other educational organizations having a central role in the education of children.
Activities: Classroom assessment materials

Alberta Assessors' Association (AAA)

10555 - 172 St., Edmonton AB T5S 1P1
Tel: 780-483-4222
membership@assessor.ab.ca
www.assessor.ab.ca
twitter.com/AlbertaAssessor
Overview: A small provincial licensing organization founded in 1962
Mission: To promote assessment as a profession, & to ensure the professional integrity & skill of assessors through, for example, the advancement of educational programming.
Affliation(s): International Association of Assessing Officers
Chief Officer(s):
Laurie Hodge, Executive Administrator/Registrar
registrar@assessor.ab.ca
Finances: *Funding Sources:* Membership fees; seminars
Staff Member(s): 2
Membership: *Fees:* $425 Accredited; $350 Associate/Candidate; $75 Retired; $0 Student; *Committees:* Executive; Registration; Practice Review; Discipline; Legislative Policy; Marketing; Editorial
Meetings/Conferences: • Alberta Assessors' Association Annual Conference and General Meeting 2015, April, 2015, Sheraton Cavalier Hotel Calgary, Calgary, AB
Scope: Provincial

Alberta Association for Community Living (AACL)
11724 Kingsway Ave., Edmonton AB T5G 0X5
Tel: 780-451-3055; *Fax:* 780-453-5779
Toll-Free: 800-252-7556
mail@aacl.org
www.aacl.org
www.facebook.com/123079204428055
twitter.com/aaclorg
Previous Name: Alberta Association for the Mentally Handicapped
Overview: A medium-sized provincial charitable organization founded in 1956 overseen by Canadian Association for Community Living
Mission: To advocate for fully inclusive community lives for children & adults with developmental disabilities
Member of: Canadian Association for Community Living; Inclusion International
Affliation(s): Alberta Community Living Foundation
Chief Officer(s):
Bruce Uditsky, Chief Executive Officer, 780-451-3055 Ext. 417
buditsky@aacl.org
Shawn Ergang, Chief Operating Officer, 780-451-3055 Ext. 405
sergang@aacl.org
Trish Bowman, Executive Director, Community Devlopment, 780-451-3055 Ext. 401
pbowman@aacl.org
Finances: *Funding Sources:* Alberta Community Living Foundation; Provincial government grants; Fundraising; Donations
Staff Member(s): 67
Membership: *Member Profile:* Non-profit community organizations throughout Alberta
Activities: Offering an annual summer institute on inclusive education in partnership with other organizations; Hosting an annual leadership series for families; Developing networks of families, known as Family Voices, throughout the province to advocate regionally; Communicating through social media; *Speaker Service:* Yes; *Library:* Reg Peters Library; Open to public
Publications:
• AACL [Alberta Association for Community Living] Connections Magazine
Type: Magazine; *Editor:* Wes Lafortune
Profile: Alberta Association for Community Living events & stories that connect families across Alberta
• Pocket Guide to Advocacy [a publication of the Alberta Association for Community Living]
Type: Guide; *Number of Pages:* 38
Profile: Advocacy tips for parents who have a child with developmental disabilities

Alberta Association for the Mentally Handicapped *See* Alberta Association for Community Living

Alberta Association of Academic Libraries (AAAL)
c/o Leigh Cunningham, Medicine Hat College Library Services, 299 College Dr. SE, Medicine Hat AB TIA 3Y6
Tel: 403-504-3654
aaal.ca
Overview: A medium-sized provincial organization founded in 1973
Mission: To facilitate planning, cooperation, & communication among Alberta's academic libraries; To promote continuing education.
Chief Officer(s):
Leigh Cunningham, Secretary-Treasurer
lcunningham@mhc.ab.ca
Membership: *Member Profile:* All academic libraries in Alberta
Meetings/Conferences: • Alberta Association of Academic Libraries 2015 Annual General Meeting, 2015, AB
Scope: Provincial

Alberta Association of Agricultural Societies (AAAS)
J.G. O'Donoghue Building, #200, 7000 - 113 St., Edmonton AB T6H 5T6
Tel: 780-427-2174; *Fax:* 780-422-7755
aaas@gov.ab.ca
www.albertaagsocieties.ca
Overview: A medium-sized provincial organization founded in 1947
Mission: To preserve & enhance the viability of agricultural societies in Alberta
Chief Officer(s):
Tim Carson, Chief Executive Officer
tim.carson@xplornet.com
Lisa Hardy, Executive Director
lisa.hardy@gov.ab.ca
Monica Bradley, Treasurer
monica.bradley@shaw.ca
Membership: 294+; *Fees:* $150 service membership; $200 agricultural societies; *Member Profile:* Agricultural societies & communities in Alberta
Activities: Presenting education programs; Lobbying government; Providing information; Facilitating networking
Meetings/Conferences: • Alberta Association of Agricultural Societies 2015 Annual Meeting & Convention, February, 2015, Ramada Conference Center, Edmonton, AB
Scope: Provincial
Description: An event attended by members of the Alberta Association of Agricultural Societies, where agricultural societies can submit resolutions to the annual general meeting & vote
Contact Information: E-mail: aaas@gov.ab.ca
Publications:
• Across the Fence [a publication of the Alberta Association of Agricultural Societies]
Type: Newsletter; *Frequency:* Quarterly; *Accepts Advertising*; *Price:* Free with Alberta Association of Agricultural Societies membership
Profile: Contents include the chief executive officer's message, industry topics, conventions, awards, grant opportunities, & regionalissues
• Alberta Association of Agricultural Societies Membership Directory
Type: Directory; *Price:* Free access on request, with Alberta Association of Agricultural Societies membership

The Alberta Association of Animal Health Technologists (AAAHT)
#950, Weber Centre, 5555 Calgary Trail NW, Edmonton AB T6H 5P9
Tel: 780-489-5007
Toll-Free: 800-404-2862
duane.landals@abvma.ca
www.aaaht.com
Overview: A small provincial organization founded in 1978
Mission: To promote professional & educational advancement of the Animal Health Technologist; to enhance the knowledge & skills of the Animal Health Technologist through continuing education programs; to promote positive legislation & to speak for the Animal Health Technologist in regard to legislative action; to develop & maintain a code of ethics & high professional standards of the Animal Health Technologist; to develop & maintain communication & cooperation amongst Animal Health Technologists, the veterinary medical profession, government & industry; to promote progressive & humane medical care for all animals
Member of: Canadian Association of Animal Health Technologists & Technicians
Chief Officer(s):
Duane Landals, Registrar
Finances: *Annual Operating Budget:* $100,000-$250,000; *Funding Sources:* Membership dues
10 volunteer(s)
Membership: 826; *Fees:* $125; *Member Profile:* 2-year CVMA accredited AHT program & veterinary technician national examination; *Committees:* Membership; Discipline & Ethics; Continuing Education; Advisory Council; Bylaw Revisions; Nominations; Public Relations; Mandatory Continuing Education
Activities: *Awareness Events:* Animal Health Technologist Week
Awards:
• AAAHT Appreciation Award (Award)
Awarded to an active member who has actively served on a AAAHT committee or as a AAAHT director for at least 2 years; promotes & contributes to the AHT profession through conduct at work or in public situations

Alberta Association of Architects (AAA)
Duggan House, 10515 Saskatchewan Dr., Edmonton AB T6E 4S1
Tel: 780-432-0224; *Fax:* 780-439-1431
info@aaa.ab.ca
www.aaa.ab.ca
Overview: A medium-sized provincial licensing organization founded in 1906
Mission: To regulate the practice of architecture & interior design in Alberta for the protection of the public & the administration of the profession; to bring architects together in order to channel the energies of unique, creative individuals spiritually committed to a superior architecture
Member of: Royal Architectural Institute of Canada; Committee of Canadian Architectural Councils
Chief Officer(s):
Dianne Johnstone, Executive Director
execdir@aaa.ab.ca
Finances: *Annual Operating Budget:* $250,000-$500,000
Staff Member(s): 6; 160 volunteer(s)
Membership: 1,100+; *Member Profile:* Degree in architecture + 3 yrs. internship; *Committees:* Communications & Marketing; Complaint Review; Registration; Practice Review; Education
Activities: *Internships:* Yes; *Rents Mailing List:* Yes
Awards:
• Prairie Design Awards (Award)

Alberta Association of Child Care Centres *See* Alberta Association of Services for Children & Families

Alberta Association of Clinic Managers (AACM)
c/o Jennifer Hendricks, Treasurer, 30 Prestwick Row SE, Calgary AB T2Z 3L7
e-mail: info@aacm.ca
aacm.ca
www.facebook.com/AACM.ca
Overview: A small provincial organization founded in 1957
Chief Officer(s):
Renee Puchailo, President
Membership: *Fees:* $150
Meetings/Conferences: • Alberta Association of Clinic Managers Annual Conference 2015, 2015, AB
Scope: Provincial

Alberta Association of Family School Liaison Workers (AAFSLW)
c/o Tonia Koversky, St. Albert Family & Community Support Services, #10, 50 Bellerose Dr., St. Albert AB T8N 3L5
Tel: 780-459-1749; *Fax:* 780-458-1260
www.aafslw.ca
www.linkedin.com/groups/AAFSLW-6609871
www.facebook.com/AAFSLW
Overview: A small provincial organization founded in 1991
Mission: AAFSLW provides an opportunity for networking among professionals through conferences, regional meetings, newsletters, resource sharing, and case conferencing.
Chief Officer(s):
Christine Payne, President, 403-253-9257 Ext. 218
Membership: *Fees:* $40-$50; *Member Profile:* Family School Liaison Workers across the Province of Alberta
Meetings/Conferences: • 24th Annual Alberta Association of Family School Liaison Workers Conference, October, 2015, Calgary, AB
Scope: Provincial

Alberta Association of Fund Raising Executives (AAFRE)
11704 - 44 Ave., Edmonton AB T6J 0Z6
Tel: 780-761-1840; *Fax:* 888-423-5976
info@aafre.org
www.aafre.org
twitter.com/aafreorg
Overview: A small provincial organization founded in 1988
Mission: To foster the use of ethical standards in fund raising programs by providing educational and networking opportunities for fund raisers and to enhance the understanding of the benefits to society accomplished through fund raising.
Chief Officer(s):
Carmen Boyko, President
Membership: *Fees:* $200 Charities, Foundations, Not-for-Profit Organizations, Businesses; $150 Individuals; $50 Associate Members
Publications:
• AAFRE [Alberta Association of Fund Raising Executives] News
Type: Newsletter; *Frequency:* 4 pa

Alberta Association of Insolvency & Restructuring Professionals (AAIRP)
c/o Lethbridge Centre, 400 - 4th Ave. South, Lethbridge AB T1J 4E1
www.aairp.com
Previous Name: Alberta Insolvency Practitioners Association
Overview: A small provincial organization overseen by Canadian Association of Insolvency & Restructuring Professionals
Mission: Non-profit organization that exists to attract, develop and support its members who provide insolvency and restructuring services
Member of: Canadian Association of Insolvency & Restructuring Professionals

Chief Officer(s):
Eric Sirrs, President
eric.sirrs@mnp.ca
Membership: 920; *Member Profile:* Trustees in bankruptcy, receivers, consultants, agents for secured creditors

Alberta Association of Insurance Adjusters (AAIA)
AB
www.aaiacentral.org
Overview: A small provincial organization founded in 1952
Chief Officer(s):
Christopher Trollope, President
chris.trollope@aaladjusters.com
Graham Carstairs, Treasurer
gcarstairs@csadj.ca
Finances: *Annual Operating Budget:* Less than $50,000
10 volunteer(s)
Membership: 200; *Fees:* $35

Alberta Association of Landscape Architects (AALA)
PO Box 21052, Edmonton AB T6R 2V4
Tel: 780-435-9902; *Fax:* 780-413-0076
aala@aala.ab.ca
www.aala.ab.ca
Overview: A medium-sized provincial organization founded in 1970
Mission: To advance the quality of the professional practice of landscape architecture in Alberta
Member of: Canadian Society of Landscape Architects
Chief Officer(s):
Jill Lane, Manager
Mark Nolan, Registrar, 780-428-4000
mnolan7@hotmail.com
Brian Charanduk, Treasurer, 780-917-7219
brian.charanduk@stantec.com
Michelle Lefebre, Secretary
Finances: *Funding Sources:* Membership dues; Sponsorships
Membership: *Fees:* $50; *Committees:* Registration; Discipline & Practice Review; Website; Grievance; Promotions; Continuing Education; Examining Board; Calgary; Edmonton
Activities: Offering a continuing education program; *Internships:* Yes; *Library:* Alberta Association of Landscape Architects Resource Library
Meetings/Conferences: • Alberta Association of Landscape Architects 2015 Annual General Meeting, 2015, AB
Scope: Provincial
Publications:
• Alberta Association of Landscape Architects Newsletter
Type: Newsletter
Profile: Association activities & forthcoming events

Alberta Association of Library Technicians (AALT)
PO Box 700, Edmonton AB T5J 2L4
Toll-Free: 866-350-2258
Other Communication: membership@aalt.org
marketing@aalt.org
www.aalt.org
www.facebook.com/AALTLibraryTec
twitter.com/AALTLibraryTech
Overview: A medium-sized provincial organization founded in 1974
Mission: To foster & enhance the professional image of library technicians in Alberta; To support library technicians throughout the province
Chief Officer(s):
Kirsten Livingstone, President
president@aalt.org
Kristian McInnis, Director, Membership
membership@aalt.org
Joanne Shum, Director, Marketing
marketing@aalt.org
Lynda Shurko, Secretary
Nicole Penton, Treasurer
treasurer@aalt.org
Membership: *Fees:* $20 student membership; $35 affiliate membership; $40 personal & associate membership; $55 institutional membership; *Member Profile:* Library technicians from all types of libraries throughout Alberta; *Committees:* Awards; Conference; Journal; Marketing; Membership; Membership Survey; Mentoring; Nomination; Salary Survey; School Library; Web Site
Activities: Providing information to library technicians; Promoting the profession; Offering educational opportunities
Awards:
• AALT Advocacy (Award)
• AALT Library Technician Award of Excellence (Award)
• AALT Special Service Award (Award)
Meetings/Conferences: • Alberta Association of Library Technicians 2015 41st Annual Conference, May, 2015, Radisson Hotel and Conference Centre, Canmore, Canmore, AB
Scope: Provincial
Description: Keynote speakers, program sessions, & social events of interest to library technicians
Contact Information: Alberta Association of Library Technicians Conference Committee, Toll-Free Phone: 1-866-350-2258, E-mail: conference@aalt.org
• Alberta Association of Library Technicians 2016 42nd Annual Conference, 2016, AB
Scope: Provincial
Description: Keynote speakers, program sessions, & social events of interest to library technicians
Contact Information: Alberta Association of Library Technicians Conference Committee, Toll-Free Phone: 1-866-350-2258, E-mail: conference@aalt.org
Publications:
• The AALT [Alberta Association of Library Technicians] Technician
Type: Journal; *Frequency:* Quarterly; *Accepts Advertising*; *Editor:* Rea Gosine; Joanne Shum *ISSN:* 0703-5276
Profile: Association highlights & business, feature articles, & calendar of events
• AALT [Alberta Association of Library Technicians] Membership Directory
Type: Directory
Profile: Contact information for current association members

Alberta Association of Marriage & Family Therapy (AAMFT)
907 - 25 Ave NW, Calgary AB T2M 2B5
Tel: 403-519-2198
info@aamft.ab.ca
www.aamft.ab.ca
Overview: A small provincial organization founded in 1995
Mission: To provide individual marriage & family therapy; to provide educational seminars for therapists
Affliation(s): American Association for Marriage & Family Therapy; Registry of Marriage & Family Therapists in Canada
Chief Officer(s):
Lori Limacher, Interim President
drlori@shaw.ca
Finances: *Funding Sources:* Membership fees; workshops
Membership: *Member Profile:* Must first become a member of the American Association for Marriage and Family Theraphy (AAMFT) and membership is then drawn from the membership of the national organization.
Activities: *Speaker Service:* Yes; *Rents Mailing List:* Yes

Alberta Association of Medical Radiation Technologists *See* Alberta College of Medical Diagnostic & Therapeutic Technologists

Alberta Association of Midwives (AAM)
#166, 63 - 4307-130 Ave. SE, Calgary AB T2Z 3V8
Tel: 403-214-1882; *Fax:* 888-859-5228
info@alberta-midwives.com
www.alberta-midwives.com
Overview: A small provincial organization founded in 1986
Mission: To promote awareness of the profession of midwifery, supports midwifery-centered research, participates in a provincial education program.
Member of: Canadian Association of Midwives
Affiliation(s): International Confederation of Midwives
Chief Officer(s):
Joan Margaret Laine, President
jmlaine@alberta-midwives.com
Alex Andrews, Executive Director
exec.director@alberta-midwives.com
Finances: *Funding Sources:* Membership dues
Membership: *Fees:* $500 full/restricted; $350 inactive; $100 associate/student
Activities: *Awareness Events:* International Day of Midwife, May 5; *Speaker Service:* Yes

Alberta Association of Municipal Districts & Counties (AAMDC)
2510 Sparrow Dr., Nisku AB T9E 8N5
Tel: 780-955-3639; *Fax:* 780-955-3615
Toll-Free: 855-548-7233
aamdc@aamdc.com
www.aamdc.com
twitter.com/aamdc
www.flickr.com/photos/45829734@N03
Overview: A medium-sized provincial organization founded in 1909
Member of: Federation of Canadian Municipalities
Chief Officer(s):
Bob Barss, President, 780-842-7309
bbarss@aamdc.com
Gerald Rhodes, Executive Director, 780-955-4076
Finances: *Annual Operating Budget:* $500,000-$1.5 Million
Staff Member(s): 13
Membership: 69 regular; 650 associate; *Member Profile:* Rural municipalities, counties & municipal districts in Alberta
Meetings/Conferences: • Alberta Association of Municipal Districts & Counties Spring 2015 Convention & Trade Show, March, 2015, Shaw Conference Centre, Edmonton, AB
• Alberta Association of Municipal Districts & Counties Fall 2015 Convention & Trade Show, November, 2015, Shaw Conference Centre, Edmonton, AB
• Alberta Association of Municipal Districts & Counties Spring 2016 Convention & Trade Show, March, 2016, Shaw Conference Centre, Edmonton, AB
• Alberta Association of Municipal Districts & Counties Fall 2016 Convention & Trade Show, November, 2016, Shaw Conference Centre, Edmonton, AB
• Alberta Association of Municipal Districts & Counties Spring 2017 Convention & Trade Show, March, 2017, Shaw Conference Centre, Edmonton, AB
• Alberta Association of Municipal Districts & Counties Fall 2017 Convention & Trade Show, November, 2017, Shaw Conference Centre, Edmonton, AB
• Alberta Association of Municipal Districts & Counties Spring 2018 Convention & Trade Show, 2018, AB
• Alberta Association of Municipal Districts & Counties Fall 2018 Convention & Trade Show, 2018, AB

Alberta Association of Naturopathic Practitioners *See* College of Naturopathic Doctors of Alberta

Alberta Association of Optometrists (AAD)
#100, 8407 Argyll Rd., Edmonton AB T6C 4B2
Tel: 780-451-6824; *Fax:* 780-452-9918
Toll-Free: 800-272-8843
www.optometrists.ab.ca
Overview: A medium-sized provincial organization overseen by Canadian Association of Optometrists
Mission: To promote excellence in the practice of Optometry, to enhance public recognition of Optometry as the primary vision care provider in Alberta, and to advance the interests of the profession.
Chief Officer(s):
Brian Wik, Executive Director
Finances: *Annual Operating Budget:* $500,000-$1.5 Million
Staff Member(s): 5
Membership: 355
Meetings/Conferences: • Alberta Association of Optometrists - 2015 Annual Convention and Trade Show, October, 2015, Telus Convention Centre, Calgary, AB
Scope: Provincial

Alberta Association of Police Governance (AAPG)
PO Box 36098, Stn. Lakeview Post Office, Calgary AB T3E 7C6
Tel: 587-892-7874
admin@aapg.ca
www.aapg.ca
Overview: A medium-sized provincial organization founded in 2003
Mission: The AAPG is an association of police commissions and RCMP policing committees created pursuant to Alberta's Police Act.
Chief Officer(s):
Terry Noble, Chair
Finances: *Funding Sources:* Membership dues; Conference
Meetings/Conferences: • 2015 Alberta Association of Police Governance Conference and Annual General Meeting, 2015, AB
Scope: Provincial

Alberta Association of Professional Paralegals (AAPP)
PO Box 47211, Stn. Edmonton Centre, Edmonton AB T5J 4N1
alberta-paralegal.com
twitter.com/ABProfParalegal
Overview: A small provincial organization founded in 1981 overseen by Canadian Association of Legal Assistants
Mission: To promote professional unity and mutual assistance among paralegals; to enhance knowledge & expertise for the benefit of members & the practice of law, in general; to support & advance status & interests of all legal assistants.
Chief Officer(s):

Lorretta Klein, President
aapppresident@gmail.com
Finances: *Funding Sources:* Membership dues
Membership: *Fees:* $100 regular; $0 student; *Member Profile:* Full: employed as paralegal & employed for 5 years or successfully graduated from course approved by association, presently employed as paralegal & employed for 3 years; Associate: employed as paralegal & employed in legal field for 3 years or graduated from course approved by association, presently employed as paralegal; Affiliate: graduate from approved paralegal program or approved evening course certificate program, employed by lawyer or law firm but not as paralegal, or person working for lawyer or law firm performing at least 50% paralegal duties
Activities: *Library*

Alberta Association of Prosthetists & Orthotists

c/o Canadian Association for Prosthetics & Orthotics, #605, 294 Portage Ave., Winnipeg MB R3C 0B9
Tel: 780-452-9513
Overview: A small provincial organization overseen by Canadian Association for Prosthetics & Orthotics
Mission: To represent members in Alberta's prosthetic & orthotic field; To promote high standards of patient care & professionalism
Chief Officer(s):
Greg Smith, President
Stephanie Hazelwood, Secretary
Jessie Cornell, Director, Education
Membership: *Member Profile:* Prosthetic & orthotic practitioners, registered technicians, allied health professionals, students, & retired persons across Alberta
Activities: Providing continuing education opportunities

Alberta Association of Prosthetists & Orthotists

c/o Northern Alberta Prosthetic & Orthotic Services Ltd., 11024 - 127 St., Edmonton AB T5M 0T2
Tel: 780-452-9513; *Fax:* 780-452-1902
Overview: A small provincial organization
Member of: Canadian Association of Prosthetists & Orthotists
Chief Officer(s):
Greg Smith, President
Alan Heaver, Northern Representative

Alberta Association of Recreation Facility Personnel (AARFP)

11150 Bonaventure Dr. SE, Calgary AB T2J 6R9
Tel: 403-253-7544; *Fax:* 403-253-9181
Toll-Free: 888-253-7544
office@aarfp.com
www.aarfp.com
www.linkedin.com/company/recreation-facility-personnel
www.facebook.com/aarfp
Also Known As: Recreation Facility Personnel
Overview: A medium-sized provincial organization founded in 1978
Mission: To provide leisure facility advisory services & consultation to Albertans
Member of: Alberta Recreation & Parks Association
Affiliation(s): Canadian Recreation Facilities Council
Chief Officer(s):
Larry Golby, Executive Director, 403-851-7626
larryg@aarfp.com
Kim Snell, President, 780-929-8256
kim.snell@town.beaumont.ab.ca
Amber Miller, Treasurer, 780-980-7165
amiller@leduc.ca
Finances: *Annual Operating Budget:* $250,000-$500,000; *Funding Sources:* Self-generated funds; membership fees; course fees; foundation grant
Staff Member(s): 3; 75 volunteer(s)
Membership: 900; *Fees:* Annual - $76 individual; $203 associate; $289 facility; *Member Profile:* People who work in recreation facilities; *Committees:* Education; Conference; Zones
Activities: Hands-on training courses; technical advice; consultation; advocacy; *Internships:* Yes; *Speaker Service:* Yes
Awards:
• Don Moore Scholarship (Scholarship)
Scholastic achievement; personal qualities & character *Amount:* $750
• William Metcalfe Award (Award)
• Bruce Fowlow Memorial Award (Award)
Eligibility: Staff of a municipal or institutional recreation facility

Alberta Association of Registered Nurses *See* The College & Association of Registered Nurses of Alberta

Alberta Association of Registered Occupational Therapists *See* Alberta College of Occupational Therapists

Alberta Association of Rehabilitation Centres (AARC)

#19, 3220 - 5 Ave. NE, Calgary AB T2A 5N1
Tel: 403-250-9495; *Fax:* 403-291-9864
acds@acds.ca
www.acds.ca
Overview: A medium-sized provincial organization founded in 1972
Mission: To support organizations that provide services & supports to people with disabilities; To act as a voice for the field of community rehabilitation to the political & administrative arms of government; To focus on human resource initiatives for the services sector; To provide in-service training opportunities for people employed in the field; To accredit & certify service in Alberta
Chief Officer(s):
Ann Nicol, CEO, 403-250-9495 Ext. 238
Helen Ficocelli, President
Judy Galbraith, Vice-President
Finances: *Annual Operating Budget:* $500,000-$1.5 Million
Staff Member(s): 10
Membership: 130 institutional; *Member Profile:* Organizations serving persons with disabilities

Alberta Association of School Resources Officers (AASRO)

9620 - 103A Ave., Edmonton AB T5H 0H7
Tel: 780-421-3564; *Fax:* 780-421-3362
admin@aasro.com
www.aasro.com
Overview: A medium-sized provincial organization founded in 1998
Mission: To provide school resource officers in the province of Alberta with additional resources to enhance their ability to work with young people in the school system; To ensure that school resource officers work proactively with students to have a positive impact on the choices that they make
Membership: *Fees:* $20; *Member Profile:* School resource officers in Canada

Alberta Association of Services for Children & Families (AASCF)

Bonnie Doon Mall, #255, 8330 - 82nd Ave., Edmonton AB T6C 4E3
Tel: 780-428-3660; *Fax:* 780-428-3844
aascf@aascf.com
www.aascf.com
Previous Name: Alberta Association of Child Care Centres
Overview: A medium-sized provincial organization founded in 1967
Mission: To provide opportunities for deliverers of services to meet with each other to exchange views & develop quality service in Alberta; to establish a structure which can provide information to membership & the public in support of social policy on behalf of Alberta children & families; to create a mechanism for action in social policy & public attitudes relating to the welfare of children & families; to support ongoing development & implementation of standards of service for human service providers & maintain accountability to these standards through an accreditation process; to advocate on behalf of the membership; to promote professional development of member agencies; to support research into child & family welfare issues relevant to member agencies; to advise government on social policy
Member of: Child Welfare League of Canada; Canadian Council on Social Development
Chief Officer(s):
Rhonda Barraclough, Executive Director, 780-428-3580
rbarraclough@aascf.com
Finances: *Annual Operating Budget:* $250,000-$500,000; *Funding Sources:* Fee for service
Staff Member(s): 3; 100 volunteer(s)
Membership: 143 institutional, associate & corporate; *Fees:* Schedule available; *Member Profile:* Organizational - organizations providing direct service in the areas of child & family welfare; Associate - organizations operating in the area of family or child welfare, but not providing direct service; Individual - those interested in child & family welfare but not employed by a member agency; Honorary Life - may be granted to individuals or organizations in the area of child & family welfare by the recommendation of the Association Executive & unanimous vote by the membership at an Annual Meeting; *Committees:* Accreditation & Certification; Peer Review & Evaluation; Advocacy; Resource; Aboriginal Community Council; Program Councils
Meetings/Conferences: • Alberta Association of Services for Children & Families 2015 Annual Conference, January, 2015, Fantasyland Hotel, Edmonton, AB
Scope: Provincial

Alberta Association of Social Workers; Alberta Association of Registered Social Workers *See* Alberta College of Social Workers

Alberta Association of the Appraisal Institute of Canada (AA-AIC)

#245, 495 - 36 St. NE, Calgary AB T2A 6K3
Tel: 403-207-7892; *Fax:* 403-207-7857
aic.alberta@shawlink.ca
www.appraisal.ab.ca
Overview: A small provincial organization founded in 1979 overseen by Appraisal Institute of Canada
Mission: To maintain professional ethics & standards in real estate valuation; to qualify real estate appraisers
Chief Officer(s):
Dan Ackerman, President
dan.ackerman@gov.ab.ca
Suzanne E. Teal, Executive Director
Finances: *Funding Sources:* Membership dues; fees for services
Staff Member(s): 2
Membership: 700; *Fees:* Schedule available; *Committees:* Admissions; Public Relations; Finance; Executive; Professional Practice Advisory
Activities: Training, certification & membership services;

Alberta Association of the Deaf (AAD)

#204, 11404 - 142 St., Edmonton AB T5M 1V1
Tel: 780-455-1007; *Fax:* 780-455-1007
aadpresident@shaw.ca
www.aadnews.ca
www.facebook.com/deaf.alberta
twitter.com/deafalberta
www.youtube.com/deafalberta
Overview: A small provincial charitable organization
Mission: To promote equal rights for deaf people in Alberta; to improve the quality of life for deaf people in general
Affliation(s): Calgary Association of the Deaf; Edmonton Association for the Deaf; Edmonton Fellowship of the Deaf Blind; Alberta Cultural Society of the Deaf; Alberta Deaf Sports Association; Association of Sign Language Interpreters of Alberta
Chief Officer(s):
Donald McCarthy, President
donmcthy@shaw.ca
Membership: *Fees:* $15 senior; $25 individual

Alberta Association of Travel Health Professionals (AATHP)

North Tower, #440, 10030-107 St., Edmonton AB T5J 3E4
www.aathp.com
Overview: A medium-sized provincial organization founded in 1997
Chief Officer(s):
Catherine Shepherd, President
Membership: *Fees:* $40
Meetings/Conferences: • 2015 Alberta Association of Travel Health Professionals Annual Travel Health Symposium and General Meeting, April, 2015, Matrix Hotel, Edmonton, AB
Scope: Provincial

Alberta Association on Gerontology (AAG)

PO Box 8056, Stn. A, Calgary AB T2H 0H7
Toll-Free: 888-735-0556
info@aagweb.ca
www.aagweb.ca
Overview: A medium-sized provincial charitable organization founded in 1980
Mission: To support persons involved in & concerned with gerontology in their efforts to enhance the lives of the aging population
Member of: Canadian Association on Gerontology
Chief Officer(s):
Jaryll Dunne, President
Tiana Rust, Vice-President
Finances: *Annual Operating Budget:* Less than $50,000; *Funding Sources:* Membership dues
Staff Member(s): 1
Membership: 200; *Fees:* $15 student; $20 senior; $40 individual; $60 organization; *Member Profile:* Professionals

working with seniors/seniors issues; *Committees:* Education; Membership; PR; Publication; Research
Awards:
• AAG Student Bursary (Scholarship)
• Mary Morrison Davis Award of Excellence (Award)

Alberta Associations for Bright Children (AABC)
c/o Action for Bright Children Calgary Society, PO Box 36093, Stn. Lakeview, Calgary AB T3E 7C6
Tel: 403-463-9612
www.edmontonabc.org/aabc
Overview: A medium-sized provincial charitable organization founded in 1981
Mission: To inform & support professionals & parents who are facing the challenge of dealing with bright, gifted, talented children; to advocate at the school board & government levels to ensure that resources & expertise are allocated in a manner that serves the children best
Finances: *Annual Operating Budget:* Less than $50,000; *Funding Sources:* Donations; government grants
Membership: *Fees:* $25
Activities: *Speaker Service:* Yes; *Library:* Bright Site

Alberta Athletic Therapists Association
PO Box 61115, Kensington RPO, Calgary AB T2N 4S6
Tel: 403-220-8957
www.aata.ca
www.facebook.com/452665388145479?ref=ts&fref=ts
twitter.com/AATA_therapy
Overview: A small provincial organization
Member of: Canadian Athletic Therapists Association
Chief Officer(s):
Breda Lau, President
president@aata.ca
Danielle Larsen, Secretary
secretary@aata.ca

Alberta Automotive Recyclers & Dismantlers Association (AARDA)
24650 - 33 St. NE, Edmonton AB T5Y 6J1
Tel: 780-478-5820; *Fax:* 780-628-6463
admin@aarda.com
aarda.com
Overview: A medium-sized provincial organization
Mission: To conserve the valuable resources involved in producing and operating the vehicles driven by Albertans today when they become damaged or inoperable, by recycling the parts.
Member of: Automotive Recyclers of Canada
Chief Officer(s):
Ian Hope, Executive Director
Membership: 50; *Member Profile:* Automotive recyclers (wholesale and retail recycled auto parts dealers); Suppliers of end-of-life vehicles to provincial shredding facilities
Meetings/Conferences: • Alberta Automotive Recyclers and Dismantlers Association Annual General Meeting & Conference 2015, May, 2015, Calgary, AB
Scope: Provincial

Alberta Aviation Museum Association
11410 Kingsway Ave., Edmonton AB T5G 0X4
Tel: 780-451-1175; *Fax:* 780-451-1607
aama@live.ca
www.albertaaviationmuseum.com
Overview: A small provincial organization
Mission: To collect, preserve, restore, research & display the history of aviation in Alberta & the city of Edmonton
Member of: Edmonton Aviation Heritage Society
Activities: Aircraft restoration workshops;

Alberta Badminton Association *See* Badminton Alberta

Alberta Ballet
Nat Christie Centre, 141 - 18 Ave. SW, Calgary AB T2S 0B8
Tel: 403-245-4222
schoolinfo@albertaballet.com
www.albertaballet.com
Overview: A medium-sized provincial charitable organization founded in 1966
Mission: To enrich & bring beauty to people's lives through creating, performing & teaching ballet
Chief Officer(s):
Peter Dala, Music Director
Jean Grand-Maître, Artistic Director
Martin Bragg, Executive Director
Finances: *Annual Operating Budget:* $3 Million-$5 Million; *Funding Sources:* Earned income; Fundraising; Government grants
Staff Member(s): 50; 300 volunteer(s)
Membership: 27; *Fees:* $35
Activities: Presenting live performances in Calgary & Edmonton; Touring nationally & internationally; *Internships:* Yes; *Speaker Service:* Yes

Alberta Band Association (ABA)
#204, 4818 - 50 Ave., Red Deer AB T4N 4A3
Tel: 403-347-2237; *Fax:* 403-237-2241
Toll-Free: 877-687-4239
www.albertabandassociation.com
Overview: A medium-sized provincial organization overseen by Canadian Band Association
Mission: To promote & develop the musical, educational & cultural values of bands & band music in Alberta
Member of: Music Alberta
Chief Officer(s):
Ken Rogers, President
Finances: *Funding Sources:* Alberta Foundation for the Arts
Staff Member(s): 2
Membership: 500-999; *Fees:* $75 regular; $125 institutional; $150 commercial; $25 student
Activities: *Speaker Service:* Yes; *Library:* R. Bruce Marsh Memorial Library

Alberta Barley Commission
#200, 6815 - 8 St. NE, Calgary AB T2E 7H7
Tel: 403-291-9111; *Fax:* 403-291-0190
Toll-Free: 800-265-9111
barleyinfo@albertabarley.com
www.albertabarley.com
www.facebook.com/209980095717832
twitter.com/AlbertaBarley
www.youtube.com/user/GoBarleyTV
Also Known As: Alberta Barley
Overview: A large provincial organization founded in 1991
Mission: To supprt barley farmers & help advance the industry
Member of: Barley Council of Canada; Canadian Agri-food Trade Alliance; Grain Growers of Canada
Affliation(s): Alberta Wheat Commission; Feed Coalition; Gainswest Magazine; Growing Forward 2; Western Canadian Deduction
Chief Officer(s):
Lisa Skierka, General Manager
lskierka@albertabarley.com
Staff Member(s): 12
Membership: 11,000; *Fees:* Schedule available; *Member Profile:* Barley farmers in Alberta; *Committees:* Audit & Finance; Communications; Governance; Market Development Group; Policy; Research; Resolutions

Alberta Baton Twirling Association (ABTA)
Percy Page Centre, 11759 Groat Rd., Edmonton AB T5M 3K6
Tel: 780-415-1440; *Fax:* 780-415-0170
abta@telusplanet.net
www.albertabaton.com
www.facebook.com/106834729351227
Overview: A small provincial organization founded in 1971 overseen by Canadian Baton Twirling Federation
Mission: To be the voice of baton twirling in the province; To promote the values & development of the sport; To unite the province in interest of baton twirling; To provide exposure; To manage the business of baton, inform members, provide opportunity & demonstration/competition
Member of: Canadian Baton Twirling Federation
Affliation(s): Alberta Sport, Recreation, Parks, Wildlife Foundation
Chief Officer(s):
Bonnie Brinker, Chair
Shari Foster, Executive Director
Activities: *Library* Open to public

Alberta Beach & District Chamber of Commerce
PO Box 280, Alberta Beach AB T0E 0A0
Tel: 780-924-3889; *Fax:* 780-924-3425
www.albertabeachchamber.com
www.facebook.com/albertabeach
www.twitter.com/ouralbertabeach
Overview: A small local organization founded in 1965
Chief Officer(s):
Bert Pyper, President
Membership: 71; *Fees:* $45

Alberta Beef Producers (ABP)
#320, 6715 - 8th St. NE, Calgary AB T2E 7H7
Tel: 403-275-4400; *Fax:* 403-274-0007
abpfeedback@albertabeef.org
www.albertabeef.org
twitter.com/albertabeef
Previous Name: Alberta Cattle Commission
Overview: A medium-sized provincial organization founded in 1969
Mission: To strengthen the sustainability & competitiveness of the beef industry; To produce beef in an environmentally sustainable manner; To support responsible animal care & handling
Member of: Canadian Cattlemen's Association (CCA)
Chief Officer(s):
Rich Smith, Executive Director, 403-451-1183
RichS@albertabeef.org
Katelyn Laverdure, Manager, Communications, 403-451-1179
katelynl@albertabeef.org
Barb Sweetland, Manager, Marketing & Education, 403-451-1178
BarbS@albertabeef.org
Fred Hays, Policy Analyst, 403-451-1181
fredh@albertabeef.org
Membership: 15,000-49,999
Activities: Influencing government policy; Improving the beef industry's public image; Engaging in research activities; Providing landowners with information on rangeland health
Awards:
• Environmental Stewardship Award (Award)
Presented annually to the beef producer who best exemplifies environmentally sustainable cattle production
Meetings/Conferences: • Alberta Beef Producers Semi-Annual General Meeting 2015, 2015
Scope: Provincial
Publications:
• Beneficial Management Practices: Environmental Manual for Alberta Cow/Calf Producers
Price: Free to all Alberta cattleproducers
Profile: Developed in partnership with Alberta Beef Producers (ABP) & Alberta Agriculture, Food, & Rural Development
• Recommended Code of Practice for the Care & Handling of Farm Animals: Beef Cattle Edition
Type: Booklet; *Price:* Free

Alberta Beekeepers Association *See* Alberta Beekeepers Commission

Alberta Beekeepers Commission
#102, 11434 - 168 St., Edmonton AB T5M 3T9
Tel: 780-489-6949; *Fax:* 780-487-8640
www.albertabeekeepers.org
Previous Name: Alberta Beekeepers Association
Overview: A small provincial organization founded in 2006
Mission: To work as a refundable commission, under the Marketing of Agriculture Products Act of the Province of Alberta
Chief Officer(s):
Grant Hicks, President, 780-324-3688
grhicks77@gmail.com
Jon Zwiers, Vice-President, 403-701-2804
jon.zwiers@gmail.com
Gertie Adair, General Manager, 780-489-6949, Fax: 780-487-8640
Gertie.Adair@AlbertaBeekeepers.org
Membership: *Fees:* $50 producers + $0.75 per colony, if 100 or more live colonies; $100 affiliate members; $50 keep in touch members; *Member Profile:* Producers in Alberta; Industry related businesses or affiliate members; Beekeepers outside Alberta, or any other individuals, who want to "keep in touch" with Alberta beekeepers; *Committees:* Research; Bee Health; CHC; Crop Spraying - Pollination; Food Safety; Importation; PMRA; AFSC - Crop Insurance; Alberta - BC Liason; Convention; GPRC - Fairview Campus; Labour; Legislative; Marketing Council; Website
Activities: Offering liability insurance to eligible producers & hobby members
Publications:
• Alberta Bee News
Type: Magazine; *Frequency:* Monthly; *Price:* Free with membership in the Alberta Beekeepers Commission

Alberta Bicycle Association (ABA)
11759 Groat Rd., Edmonton AB T5M 3K6
Tel: 780-427-6352; *Fax:* 780-427-6438
Toll-Free: 877-646-2453
info@albertabicycle.ab.ca

www.albertabicycle.ab.ca
www.facebook.com/106959523196
twitter.com/albertabicycle
www.youtube.com/albertabicycle
Overview: A small provincial licensing organization overseen by Cycling Canada Cyclisme
Mission: To promote all aspects of cycling in Alberta
Affliation(s): Canadian Cycling Association; Union Cycliste International
Chief Officer(s):
Heather Lothian, Executive Director
heather@albertabicycle.ab.ca
Staff Member(s): 6
Membership: *Fees:* Schedule available; *Member Profile:* Cyclists; *Committees:* BMX; Racing; Recreation & Transportation
Activities: *Internships:* Yes

Alberta Biotechnology Association
#314, 9707 - 110 St., Edmonton AB T5K 2L9
Tel: 780-425-3804; *Fax:* 780-409-9263
info@bioalberta.com
www.bioalberta.com
www.linkedin.com/company/bioalberta-alberta-biotechnology-association-
www.facebook.com/BioAlberta
twitter.com/Bioalberta
www.bioalberta.com/bioalberta-beat
Also Known As: BioAlberta
Overview: A small provincial organization founded in 1999
Mission: To act as the central voice & organizing hub for life science industries in Alberta
Chief Officer(s):
Ryan Radke, President
Staff Member(s): 6
Membership: 140 organizations
Activities: Representing Alberta's life sciences sector; Providing services & programs to member organizations, such as educational sessions, in order to expand the companies' dollars & reach

Alberta Bison Association
501 - 11 Ave., Nisku AB T9E 7N5
Tel: 780-955-1995; *Fax:* 780-955-1990
info@bisoncentre.com
www.bisoncentre.com
www.facebook.com/199914170156327
Overview: A small provincial organization
Mission: To represent bison producers in Alberta & to conduct research aimed towards increasing productivit & profitability as well as solving issues that surround the industry
Member of: Canadian Bison Association
Chief Officer(s):
Thomas Achermann, Chair
Linda Sautner, Office Manager
Membership: *Fees:* $236.25

Alberta Block Parent Association (ABPA)
220 Doveview Crescent SE, Calgary AB T2B 1Y6
Tel: 403-262-2864
alberta@hotmail.com
www.albertablockparent.ca
Overview: A medium-sized provincial charitable organization overseen by Block Parent Program of Canada Inc.
Mission: To assist with the start-up of new programs; to provide ongoing support & resources for established programs; to ensure that faltering programs are properly closed down
Member of: Block Parent Program of Canada Inc.
Membership: 40 programs; *Fees:* $30-$100 depending on area population

Alberta Blonde d'Aquitaine Association
PO Box 5959, Westlock AB T7P 2P7
Tel: 780-348-5308
aba@clearwave.ca
www.albertablondecattle.com
Overview: A small provincial organization
Mission: To represent breeders of Blonde d'Aquitaine cattle in Alberta
Chief Officer(s):
Reed Rigney, President, 780-348-5308
Ken Mackenzie, Vice-President, 780-542-2268
kenkb@telus.net
Dave Kamelchuk, Treasurer, 780-675-1227
littlecreekagroforestry@gmail.com
Membership: *Member Profile:* Breeders of Blonde d'Aquitaine cattle from Alberta
Activities: Providing information for breeders of Blonde d'Aquitaine cattle; Organizing field days
Publications:
• Blonde Bullet [a publication of the Alberta & Manitoba / Saskatchewan Blonde d'Aquitaine Associations]
Type: Newsletter; *Accepts Advertising*

Alberta Bobsleigh Association (ABA)
Bob Niven Training Centre, #205, 88 Canada Olympic Rd. SW, Calgary AB T3B 5R5
Tel: 403-297-2721; *Fax:* 403-286-7213
slide@albertabobsleigh.com
www.albertabobsleigh.com
www.facebook.com/albertabobsleigh
Overview: A small provincial charitable organization founded in 1983
Mission: To develop a broad interest in bobsleigh in Alberta; to provide opportunities for all Albertans to participate in bobsleigh; to provide opportunities for Albertans to progress to national & international levels
Member of: Bobsleigh Canada
Chief Officer(s):
Grant Miller, President
Sarah Monk, Technical Director
Dennis Marineau, Head Coach
Finances: *Annual Operating Budget:* $100,000-$250,000
Staff Member(s): 1; 70 volunteer(s)
Membership: 560; *Fees:* $50-90 Full; $15 Assoc. Support.; $1 Assoc.
Activities: Summer training programs; *Library*

Alberta Bodybuilding Association (ABBA)
Edmonton Centre, PO Box 47248, Edmonton AB T5J 4N1
Tel: 780-709-5309
www.abba.ab.ca
www.facebook.com/Albertabodybuildingassociation
twitter.com/AlbertaBBAssoc
Overview: A small provincial organization overseen by Canadian Bodybuilding Federation
Mission: To govern the sport of amateur bodybuilding, fitness & figure in Alberta.
Member of: Canadian Bodybuilding Federation; International Federation of Bodybuilding
Chief Officer(s):
Asha Belisle, President
president@abba.ab.ca
Tara Jensen, Secretary-Treasurer
secretary@abba.ab.ca

Alberta Boilers Safety Association (ABSA)
9410 - 20th Ave., Edmonton AB T6N 0A4
Tel: 780-437-9100; *Fax:* 780-437-7787
hr@absa.ca
www.absa.ca
Overview: A small provincial organization
Mission: ABSA is a regulatory authority. Key responsibilities include: reviewing & registering pressure equipment designs, equipment; and certifying/registering pressure welders, power engineers, equipment inspectors. The association also investigates accidents that involve pressure equipment.
Chief Officer(s):
Gordon Campbell, General Manager
Activities: Conducts safety education & training

Alberta Bottle Depot Association (ABDA)
#202, 17850 - 105 Ave., Edmonton AB T5S 2H5
Tel: 780-454-0400; *Fax:* 780-454-0424
www.albertadepot.ca
www.facebook.com/142558085810395
twitter.com/AlbertaDepot
Overview: A small provincial organization
Mission: To educate about industry & to standardize the practices for depot operation
Chief Officer(s):
Jeff Linton, Executive Director
Finances: *Funding Sources:* Membership dues
Staff Member(s): 2; 14 volunteer(s)
Membership: 184
Activities: *Library*

Alberta Bowhunters & Archers Association *See* Alberta Bowhunters Association

Alberta Bowhunters Association (ABA)
202 Copperfield Grove SE, Calgary AB T2Z 4L7
www.bowhunters.ca
Previous Name: Alberta Bowhunters & Archers Association
Overview: A medium-sized provincial organization
Mission: To promote bowhunting in Alberta
Member of: Federation of Canadian Archers
Chief Officer(s):
Brent Watson, President
brent@albertabowhunters.com
Membership: *Fees:* $35 Adult; $25 Youth; $70 Family; $500 Life

Alberta Broomball Association (ABA)
c/o Secretary-Treasurer, 56 Somerset St. SE, Medicine Hat AB T1B 0H4
Tel: 403-529-6999
www.albertabroomball.ca
Overview: A small provincial organization overseen by Ballon sur glace Broomball Canada
Member of: Ballon sur glace Broomball Canada
Chief Officer(s):
Greg Mastervick, President
gregma@telusplanet.net
Wayne Neigel, Secretary-Treasurer
neigel@telus.net

Alberta Building Envelope Council (South) (ABEC)
PO Box 61152, Stn. Kensington, Calgary AB T2N 4S6
Tel: 403-246-4500
webmaster@abecsouth.org
www.abecsouth.org
Overview: A small provincial organization founded in 1983
Mission: To promote the understanding of the building envelope
Member of: National Building Envelope Council
Chief Officer(s):
Mike Dietrich, President
mdietrich@morrisonhershfield.com
Bob Passmore, Secretary, 403-703-7535
bpassmore@bsaa.ca
Anton Vlooswyk, Treasurer, 403-651-1514
anton@beei.ca
Finances: *Funding Sources:* Membership dues
Membership: 163; *Fees:* Individual: $48; Corporate: $65; Student: $10
Activities: The link between architects, building owners, engineers & contractors; *Speaker Service:* Yes

Alberta Building Officials Association
112 Sundown Green SE, Calgary AB T2X 2Y4
www.aboa.ab.ca
Also Known As: ABOA
Overview: A small local organization founded in 1959
Mission: To improve standards of building inspection; to be a discussion forum for shared issues and concerns; to assit in the education of building inspector in the areas of administration, technical, and other branches of the profession; to promote the importance of the building official's role.
Chief Officer(s):
Kerry Crump, President, 403-320-3159
kerry.crump@lethbridge.ca
Syd Reynar, Secretary, 780-980-7126
sreynar@leduc.ca
Membership: *Fees:* $125 regular; $150 associate

Alberta CA Profession's Non-Profit Foundation *See* Chartered Accountants' Education Foundation of Alberta

Alberta Camping Association (ACA)
Percy Page Centre, 11759 Groat Rd., Edmonton AB T5M 3K6
Tel: 780-427-6605; *Fax:* 780-427-6695
info@albertacamping.com
www.albertacamping.com
www.facebook.com/AlbertaCampingAssociation
Overview: A medium-sized provincial charitable organization founded in 1949 overseen by Canadian Camping Association
Mission: To promote & coordinate organized camping in Alberta by providing camp information & leadership direction as well as promoting high standards of camp programs & activities for all populations; to take a leading role in the recognition & promotion of professional standards for organized camps in Alberta
Chief Officer(s):
Jon Olfert, President
Les Waite, Secretary-Treasurer
Finances: *Annual Operating Budget:* $50,000-$100,000; *Funding Sources:* Lotteries; community development; recreation; Parks & Wildlife Foundation
Staff Member(s): 1; 18 volunteer(s)
Membership: 20 corporate + 400 individual + 100 camps; *Fees:* $15 student; $35 general; $150 camps; $100 commercial;

Committees: Conference & Education; Marketing & Fundraising; Standards; Research & Development; Newsletter
Activities: *Speaker Service:* Yes; *Rents Mailing List:* Yes; *Library:* ACA Resource Centre; Open to public
Meetings/Conferences: • Alberta Camping AssociationAnnual Conference 2015, March, 2015, Southern Alberta Bible Camp, Lomond, AB
Scope: Provincial

Alberta Cancer Foundation (ACF)
#710, 10123 - 99 St. NW, Edmonton AB T5J 3H1
Tel: 780-643-4400; *Fax:* 780-643-4398
Toll-Free: 866-412-4222
acfonline@albertacancer.ca
albertacancer.ca
www.facebook.com/albertacancerfoundation
twitter.com/albertacancer
www.youtube.com/user/ABCancerFoundation
Overview: A small provincial charitable organization founded in 1984
Mission: To raise funds to support & enhance the programs & treatment facilities of the Alberta Cancer Board
Member of: Alberta Cancer Board
Chief Officer(s):
Myka Osinchuk, CEO
Finances: *Funding Sources:* Individual & corporate donors
Activities: Fundraising for the Alberta Cancer Board which operates two tertiary care facilities: the Cross Cancer Institute, Edmonton, the Tom Baker Cancer Centre, Calgary & 15 other cancer centres throughout Alberta; cancer research, treatment, prevention & education;

Alberta Canola Producers Commission (ACPC)
#170, 14315 - 118 Ave., Edmonton AB T5L 4S6
Tel: 780-454-0844; *Fax:* 780-465-5473
Toll-Free: 800-551-6652
web@canola.ab.ca
www.canola.ab.ca
www.facebook.com/albertacanola
twitter.com/albertacanola
www.youtube.com/albertacanola
Overview: A medium-sized provincial organization founded in 1989
Mission: To provide leadership in a vibrant canola industry for the benefit of Alberta canola producers; to strive to improve the long-term profitability of Alberta canola producers
Member of: Canola Council of Canada; Food Safety Info Society; Agriculture Education Network
Affliation(s): Canadian Canola Growers Association
Chief Officer(s):
Ward Toma, General Manager, 780-454-0844
ward.toma@canola.ab.ca
Finances: *Annual Operating Budget:* $500,000-$1.5 Million
Staff Member(s): 3
Membership: 26,000; *Fees:* Based on sale of canola seed; *Committees:* Administration & Finance; Market Development; Member Relation & Extension; Research
Activities: *Speaker Service:* Yes

Alberta Caregivers Association (ACGA)
c/o Fulton Place School, 10310 - 56th St. NW, Edmonton AB T6A 2J2
Tel: 780-453-5088; *Fax:* 780-465-5581
Toll-Free: 877-453-5088
office@albertacaregivers.org
www.albertacaregiversassociation.org
www.facebook.com/AlbertaCaregivers
twitter.com/ABcaregivers
www.youtube.com/user/ABcaregivers
Overview: A small provincial charitable organization
Mission: To support family caregivers in Alberta, in order to ensure their well-being
Chief Officer(s):
Laura Fitzgerald, President
Anna Mann, Executive Director
amann@AlbertaCaregivers.org
Colin MacPhail, Communications Coordinator
cmacphail@albertacaregivers.org
Finances: *Funding Sources:* Membership fees; Donations; Fundraising
Membership: *Fees:* $20 individuals; $45 organizations; $150 corporations; *Member Profile:* Family caregivers in Alberta
Activities: Engaging in advocacy activities on behalf of family caregivers in Alberta; Providing educational actitivities, such as community caregiver workshops; Offering the COMPASS program (Caregiver Orientation for Mobilizing Personal Assets & Strengths through Self-care); Facilitating networking opportunities; Organizing information displays
Publications:
• Contact
Type: Newsletter
Profile: Information for family caregivers in Alberta, including articles, caregiver stories, training programs, & forthcoming activities

Alberta Carriage Driving Association (ACDA)
c/o Steve Remus, PO Box 575, Redwater AB T0A 2W0
Tel: 780-942-3452
www.albertadriving-acda.ca
Overview: A small provincial organization founded in 1987
Mission: To promote carriage driving & combined driving; to host events that allow drivers with different levels of experience to interact
Chief Officer(s):
Patty Carley, President
Denise MacDonald, Secretary, 780-853-0305
dennynordin@gmail.com
Membership: *Fees:* $35 individual; $45 family; *Member Profile:* Members are required to join the Alberta Equestrian Federation.

Alberta Catholic School Trustees Association
#205, 9940 - 106 St., Edmonton AB T5K 2N2
Tel: 780-484-6209; *Fax:* 780-484-6248
admin@acsta.ab.ca
www.acsta.ab.ca
twitter.com/acstanews
Overview: A medium-sized provincial organization
Affliation(s): Canadian Catholic School Trustees Association
Chief Officer(s):
Dean Sarnecki, Executive Director

Alberta Cattle Breeders Association
PO Box 1060, Stn. M, Calgary AB T2P 2K8
Tel: 403-261-9316; *Fax:* 403-262-3067
albertacattlebreeders.com
Overview: A medium-sized provincial organization
Chief Officer(s):
Doug Finseth, President
Membership: *Member Profile:* Ranchers; farmers
Activities: Annual bull sale

Alberta Cattle Commission *See* Alberta Beef Producers

Alberta Cattle Feeders' Association (ACFA)
#6, 11010- 46th St. SE, Calgary AB T2C 1G4
Tel: 403-250-2509; *Fax:* 403-209-3255
Toll-Free: 800-363-8598
hmanzara@cattlefeeders.ca
www.cattlefeeders.ca
Overview: A medium-sized provincial organization
Mission: To represent the cattle feeding industry in Alberta, in areas such as market development & access, taxation, water & air quality, & manure management
Chief Officer(s):
Russ Evans, Manager of Policy and Research
revans@cattlefeeders.ca
Bryan Walton, Chief Executive Officer
bwalton@cattlefeeders.ca
Jennifer Brunette, Member Service And Event Manager, Events & Member Services
jbrunette@cattlefeeders.ca
Joe Novecosky, Financial Manager & ALPS Inquiries
jnovecosky@cattlefeeders.ca
Finances: *Funding Sources:* Membership fees; Membership service activities
Membership: *Member Profile:* Cattle producers in Alberta
Activities: Implementing research; Developing new management practices & technology; Liaising with partners to develop new opportunities
Publications:
• Business Directory
Type: Directory
Profile: Listings of companies & organizations which offer specialized services to the cattle feeding industry in Alberta

Alberta Central
#350N, 8500 Macleod Trail South, Calgary AB T2H 2N1
Tel: 403-258-5900; *Fax:* 403-253-7720
email@albertacentral.com
www.albertacentral.com
www.linkedin.com/company/536834
www.facebook.com/346088465461276
twitter.com/ABCreditUnions
www.youtube.com/user/AlbertaCreditUnions
Also Known As: Credit Unions of Alberta
Previous Name: Credit Union Central of Alberta
Overview: A small provincial organization overseen by Credit Union Central of Canada
Mission: To act as the central banking facility, trade association, & service bureau for the credit union system of Alberta; To safeguard the financial stability of the province's credit union system by maintaining liquidity; To provide leadership & support to Alberta's credit unions
Member of: Credit Union Central of Canada
Affliation(s): Alberta Community and Co-operative Association (ACCA); Canadian Co-operative Association; Credit Union Deposit Guarantee Corporation; Credit Union Electronic Transaction Services (CUETS); World Council of Credit Unions; CUPS Payment Services (CUPS); CUSOURCE
Chief Officer(s):
Alison Starke, Chair
Graham Wetter, President & CEO
Staff Member(s): 230
Membership: 45 credit unions; *Member Profile:* Independent credit unions across Alberta
Activities: Offering financial & technological products & services, as well as corporate & strategic planning & legal counsel to credit unions in Alberta; Facilitating credit union system development; Raising the profile of credit unions in Alberta
Publications:
• Credit Union Central of Alberta Annual Report
Type: Yearbook; *Frequency:* Annually

Alberta Cerebral Palsy Sport Association (ACPSA)
Percy Page Centre, 11759 Groat Rd., Edmonton AB T5M 3K6
Tel: 780-422-2904; *Fax:* 780-422-2663
contact@acpsa.ca
www.acpsa.ca
Also Known As: Sportability Alberta
Overview: A small provincial charitable organization founded in 1984 overseen by Canadian Cerebral Palsy Sports Association
Mission: To promote recreational & competitive sporting opportunities for persons with cerebral palsy, brain injury & related conditions
Member of: Canadian Cerebral Palsy Sports Association
Chief Officer(s):
Brennan Hermiston-Nicoll, Provincial Coordinator
Brennan@acpsa.ca
Finances: *Annual Operating Budget:* Less than $50,000
Staff Member(s): 2; 40 volunteer(s)
Membership: 220; *Fees:* $15 individual; $25 family; *Member Profile:* Individuals with cerebral palsy, brain injury & other related conditions
Activities: Track & field; boccia; cycling; swimming; pre-school children's program; *Speaker Service:* Yes

Alberta CGIT Association
2720 Lodge Cres., Calgary AB T3E 5Y7
Tel: 780-532-2947
cgit@telus.net
Also Known As: Canadian Girls in Training - Alberta
Overview: A small provincial organization

Alberta Chamber of Commerce *See* Alberta Chambers of Commerce

Alberta Chamber of Resources
#1940, 10180 - 101 St., Edmonton AB T5J 3S4
Tel: 780-420-1030; *Fax:* 780-425-4623
admin@acr-alberta.com
www.acr-alberta.com
Overview: A medium-sized provincial organization
Chief Officer(s):
Gord Ball, President

Alberta Chambers of Commerce (ACC)
#1808, 10025 - 102A Ave., Edmonton AB T5J 2Z2
Tel: 780-425-4180; *Fax:* 780-429-1061
Toll-Free: 800-272-8854
info@abchamber.ca
www.abchamber.ca
www.facebook.com/alberta.chambers.7
twitter.com/albertachambers
Previous Name: Alberta Chamber of Commerce
Overview: A large provincial organization founded in 1937
Mission: To enhance private enterprise in Alberta
Affliation(s): Canadian Chamber of Commerce
Chief Officer(s):

Tab Pollock, Chair
tpollock@abchamber.ca
Brad Severin, Chair-Elect
bseverin@abchamber.ca
Ken Kobly, President & CEO
kkobly@abchamber.ca
Finances: *Annual Operating Budget:* $100,000-$250,000; *Funding Sources:* Membership dues; programs; events
Staff Member(s): 5
Membership: 126 chambers representing 23,000 businesses; *Fees:* Schedule available; *Committees:* Executive
Activities: *Speaker Service:* Yes
Awards:
• Business Awards of Distinction (Award)
Meetings/Conferences: • Alberta Chambers of Commerce 2015 Provincial Conference & Policy Session, 2015, AB
Scope: Provincial

Alberta Chapter of the Registry of Interpreters for the Deaf, Inc. ***See*** Association of Sign Language Interpreters of Alberta

Alberta Cheerleading Association (ACA)
52 Meadowood Cres., Sherwood Park AB T8A 0L7
Tel: 780-417-0050; *Fax:* 780-417-0093
Toll-Free: 888-756-9220
info@albertacheerleading.ca
www.albertacheerleading.ca
www.facebook.com/115045571883130
Overview: A small provincial organization overseen by Cheer Canada
Mission: To be the provincial regulator of cheerleading in Alberta.
Member of: Cheer Canada
Chief Officer(s):
Katy Kelley, President
president@albertacheerleading.ca
Brianne Moar, Contact, Member Services

Alberta Chess Association (ACA)
PO Box 11839, Stn. Main, Edmonton AB T5J 3K9
Tel: 403-970-8032
www.albertachess.org
Overview: A small provincial organization founded in 1975
Mission: To promote activity in Alberta through chess playing
Member of: Chess Federation of Canada
Chief Officer(s):
Vlad Rekhson, Executive Director
vrekhson@yahoo.ca
Membership: 400; 19 clubs; *Fees:* $28 juniors; $43 adults

Alberta Chicken Producers
2518 Ellwood Dr. SW, Edmonton AB T6X 0A9
Tel: 780-488-2125; *Fax:* 780-488-3570
Toll-Free: 877-822-4425
www.chicken.ab.ca
Overview: A medium-sized provincial organization founded in 1966 overseen by Chicken Farmers of Canada
Mission: To offer an environment for profitable chicken production; To promote a competitive & consumer-focused industry, with safe, high quality chicken products
Chief Officer(s):
Karen Kirkwood, Executive Director
Membership: *Member Profile:* Marketing board representing over 230 chicken producers in Alberta
Activities: Liaising with government; Funding research projects to benefit the industry
Meetings/Conferences: • Alberta Chicken Producers 2015 Annual General Meeting, 2015, AB
Scope: Provincial
Description: An interactive educational event focussing upon biosecurity & emergency preparedness, plus a business meeting, & a keynote speaker
Publications:
• Alberta Chicken Producers Annual Report
Type: Yearbook; *Frequency:* Annually
Profile: Organization reports, upcoming events, market conditions, recipes & industry information
• Alberta Chicken Producers Newsletter
Type: Newsletter; *Frequency:* Bimonthly

Alberta Child Care Association (ACCA)
#54, 9912 - 106 St., Edmonton AB T5K 1C5
Tel: 780-421-7544; *Fax:* 780-428-0080
Toll-Free: 877-421-9937
www.albertachildcare.org
Previous Name: Alberta Child Care Network Association
Overview: A medium-sized provincial organization
Mission: ACCA is non-profit, member-based society with a mission to strengthen and advance the early learning & child care profession in Alberta.
Affiliation(s): Canadian Child Care Federation; Provincial Ministry of Children and Youth Services; FRP Canada
Chief Officer(s):
Rosetta Sanders, Chair
sandersrosetta@hotmail.com
Sheri Magnuson, Administrator
acca.sheri@gmail.com
Membership: *Fees:* $50 student; $125 associate/individual; *Member Profile:* ELCC staff, students, academics, operators and other interested individuals and groups

Alberta Child Care Network Association ***See*** Alberta Child Care Association

Alberta Children's Hospital Foundation
2888 Shaganappi Trail NW, Calgary AB T3B 6A8
Tel: 403-955-8818; *Fax:* 403-955-8840
Toll-Free: 877-715-5437
www.childrenshospital.ab.ca
Overview: A small provincial charitable organization founded in 1957
Mission: To raise money on behalf of the Alberta Children's Hospital in order to improve the services provided to patients & to fund research
Chief Officer(s):
Saifa Koonar, President & CEO

Alberta Choral Federation (ACF)
#103, 10612 - 124 St., Edmonton AB T5N 1S4
Tel: 780-488-7464; *Fax:* 780-488-6403
info@albertachoralfederation.ca
www.albertachoralfederation.ca
Overview: A medium-sized provincial charitable organization founded in 1972
Mission: To promote choral music within the communities of Alberta; to gain support for choral music through public policy
Member of: Music Alberta; Association of Canadian Choral Conductors; Canadian Conference for the Arts
Chief Officer(s):
Laurier Fagnan, President
Kathleen Skinner, Vice President
Finances: *Annual Operating Budget:* $250,000-$500,000; *Funding Sources:* Membership fees; Alberta Foundation for the Arts
Staff Member(s): 2; 125 volunteer(s)
Membership: 450; *Fees:* $25 adult/student; $150 choir/institution/corporate; $95 conductor/educator; *Member Profile:* Interest in choral music; *Committees:* Programs & Services; Finance; Personnel; Advocacy
Activities: Choralfest; Alberta Honour Choirs; Workshops Work; *Library:* Choral Lending Library; Open to public

Alberta Civil Liberties Research Centre (ACLRC)
c/o Murray Fraser Hall, Faculty of Law, University of Calgary, #2350, 2500 University Dr. NW, Calgary AB T2N 1N4
Tel: 403-220-2505; *Fax:* 403-284-0945
aclrc@ucalgary.ca
www.aclrc.com
Previous Name: Calgary Civil Liberties Association
Overview: A small provincial charitable organization founded in 1982
Mission: To promote awareness among Albertans about civil liberties & human rights through research & education
Affliation(s): University of Calgary
Chief Officer(s):
Linda McKay-Panos, Executive Director
lmmckayp@ucalgary.ca
Activities: *Speaker Service:* Yes; *Library* Open to public

Alberta Civil Trial Lawyers' Association (ACTLA)
#550, 10055 - 106 St., Edmonton AB T5J 2Y2
Tel: 780-429-1133; *Fax:* 780-429-1199
Toll-Free: 800-665-7248
admin@actla.com
www.actla.com
Overview: A medium-sized provincial organization founded in 1986
Mission: To advocate for a strong civil justice system that protects the rights of all Albertans
Affliation(s): Association of Trial Lawyers of America
Chief Officer(s):
Lyn Bromilow, Executive Director, 780-429-1133
James D. Cuming, President
Finances: *Funding Sources:* Membership dues; seminar revenue; advertising
Staff Member(s): 2
Membership: 600; *Fees:* Schedule available; *Member Profile:* Members of Law Society of Alberta; students enrolled in law school
Activities: *Library:* Expert Witness Database

Alberta Clydesdale & Shire Association
PO Box 33, Fawcett AB T0G 0Y0
Tel: 780-954-3810
www.albertaclydesdalesandshires.com
Previous Name: Alberta Clydesdale Association
Overview: A small provincial organization
Chief Officer(s):
Fay Campbell, Sec.-Treas.
fcampbell@mcsnet.ca
Membership: 20; *Fees:* $40 individual; $50 family

Alberta Clydesdale Association ***See*** Alberta Clydesdale & Shire Association

Alberta College & Association of Chiropractors (ACAC)
Manulife Place, 11203 - 70 St. NW, Edmonton AB T5B 1T1
Tel: 780-420-0932; *Fax:* 780-425-6583
Other Communication: Blog: www.everydaychiropractic.com
office@albertachiro.com
www.albertachiro.com
www.facebook.com/AlbertaChiropractors
twitter.com/AlbertaChiro
www.youtube.com/user/albertachiro
Previous Name: College of Chiropractors of Alberta; Alberta Chiropractic Association
Overview: A medium-sized provincial licensing organization founded in 1986 overseen by Canadian Chiropractic Association
Mission: To ensure quality chiropractic care that enhances the well-being & protects the rights of the people of Alberta; To promote the art, science, & philosophy of chiropractic & its value in the health care community
Chief Officer(s):
Deb Manz, Chief Executive Officer
dmanz@albertachiro.com
Membership: 850 individual
Activities: *Library*

Alberta College & Association of Respiratory Therapy ***See*** College & Association of Respiratory Therapists of Alberta

Alberta College of Acupuncture & Traditional Chinese Medicine (ACATCM)
#125, 4935 - 40 Ave. NW, Calgary AB T3A 2N1
Tel: 403-286-8788
Toll-Free: 888-789-9984
info@acatcm.com
www.acatcm.com
Overview: A medium-sized provincial organization founded in 1997
Mission: Committed to maintaining and further improving leadership in the field of Acupuncture & Traditional Chinese Medical education, as well as providing the highest quality of education in Acupuncture & TCM; providing enhanced continuing education programs to health care professionals who wish to integrate and upgrade their skills; and enabling all graduates to succeed as primary health care providers using the principles of Traditional Chinese Medicine and to become an integral part of the modern health care system.
Affiliation(s): Beijing University of Chinese Medicine
Chief Officer(s):
Dennis Lee, Co-president
Colton Oswald, Co-president

Alberta College of Combined Laboratory & X-Ray Technologists (ACCLXT)
#830, 4445 Calgary Trail, Edmonton AB T6H 5R7
Tel: 780-438-3323; *Fax:* 855-299-0829
www.acclxt.ca
Overview: A medium-sized provincial organization founded in 1969
Mission: To be responsible for the registration, discipline & competency of all registered Combined Laboratory & X-Ray Technicians / Technologists currently practicing in the province of Alberta; To strive to provide excellence in the combined fields of laboratory, radiography, & electrocardiography medicine
Chief Officer(s):
Sheila Joyce, President
Anna Steblyk, Vice President

Lyndsay Arndt, Executive Director/Registrar
Sandra Toepfer, Competency Co-ordinator
Membership: 550; *Member Profile:* Active Membership is granted upon completion of a 2 year diploma program in Laboratory & X-Ray Sciences or substantial equivalence & successfully challenging the ACCLXT Provincial Registration Examination. Graduates from the NAIT CLXT program or a program deemed as substantially equivalent, who have not yet challenged the ACCLXT Provincial Registration Examination, may apply for a Temporary Membership, which allows them to register with the ACCLXT and work in AB, while waiting to challenge the exam. This membership extends from the date of application until the exam results are received. Honorary Membership may be conferred upon any person who has rendered notable service in the College, for its members or the field of Laboratory, X-Ray or Cardiology testing. Associate Membership may be granted to any individual who has been a registered as a CLXT and who no longer wishes to practice as a CLXT.
Publications:
• Alberta College of Combined Laboratory & X-Ray Technologists By-laws
Number of Pages: 20
Profile: Information about items such as meetings, committees, fees, ethics, & standards of practice
• Alberta College of Combined Laboratory & X-Ray Technologists Annual Report
Type: Yearbook; *Frequency:* Annually
Profile: Information about governance, membership, programs, examinations, & finances
• Competency Profile for Alberta Combined Laboratory & X-Ray Technologists
Number of Pages: 80
Profile: Prepared by the Alberta College of Combined Laboratory & X-Ray Technologists & the Alberta Health & Wellness Health Workforce Policy & Planning Branch
• Wavelengths [a publication of the Alberta College of Combined Laboratory & X-Ray Technologists]
Type: Newsletter
Profile: Information about the college's activities

Alberta College of Medical Diagnostic & Therapeutic Technologists

#800, 4445 Calgary Trail NW, Edmonton AB T6H 5R7
Tel: 780-487-6130; *Fax:* 780-432-9106
Toll-Free: 800-282-2165
info@acmdtt.com
acmdtt.com
Also Known As: ACMDTT
Previous Name: Alberta Association of Medical Radiation Technologists
Overview: A medium-sized provincial organization founded in 1983 overseen by Canadian Association of Medical Radiation Technologists
Mission: To act in accordance with the Province of Alberta Health Professions Act, Medical Diagnostic & Therapeutic Technologists Profession Regulation, & by the ACMDTT Bylaws; To abide by & promote ethical practice as described in the ACMDTT Code of Ethics for diagnostic & therapeutic professionals; To promote standards of practice within the discipline; To advance the profession in Alberta
Chief Officer(s):
Kathy Hilsenteger, Chief Executive Officer & Registrar
Dian G. Smith, Director, Member Services
dgsmith@acmdtt.com
Membership: 1,900; *Member Profile:* Alberta professionals in the disciplines of radiological technology (RTR), radiation therapy (RTT), nuclear medicine technology (RTNM), magnetic resonance imaging (RTMR), & electroneurophysiology (ENP)
Activities: Offering an extensive continuing education course program; Distributing current professional information; Providing networking opportunities; Increasing awareness of the profession
Meetings/Conferences: • Alberta College of Medical Diagnostic & Therapeutic Technologists 2015 Annual Conference, April, 2015, Deerfoot Inn & Casino, Calgary, AB
Scope: Provincial
Description: Educational presentations & breakout sessions
Publications:
• Alberta College of Medical Diagnostic & Therapeutic Technologists Annual Report
Type: Yearbook; *Frequency:* Annually
Profile: A yearly report on the activities of the College, including complaints, hearings, & appeals, & audited financial information
• Alberta College of Medical Diagnostic & Therapeutic Technologists Member Directory
Type: Directory
• The Viewbox
Type: Newsletter; *Frequency:* Quarterly; *Editor:* Dian Smith (dgsmith@acmddtt.com)
Profile: Updates from the College, including branch, education, & awards information

Alberta College of Medical Laboratory Technologists (ACMLT)

#301, 9426 - 51 Ave. NW, Edmonton AB T6E 5A6
Tel: 780-435-5452; *Fax:* 780-437-1442
Toll-Free: 800-265-9351
info@acmlt.org
www.acmlt.org
Overview: A medium-sized provincial licensing charitable organization founded in 1981 overseen by Canadian Society for Medical Laboratory Science
Mission: To ensure excellence in medical laboratory science in Alberta
Chief Officer(s):
Lori Kmet, Executive Director/Registrar
registrar@acmlt.org
Staff Member(s): 5
Membership: *Committees:* Legislation Sub-Committee
Activities: Setting entrance to practice requirements; maintaining a Continuing Competence Program; adjudicating complaints of unprofessional conduct
Awards:
• Award of Merit (Award)
• Member Bursary Awards (Award)
• Award of Distinction (Award)

Alberta College of Occupational Therapists (ACOT)

#300, 10436 - 81 Ave., Edmonton AB T6E 1X6
Tel: 780-436-8381; *Fax:* 780-434-0658
Toll-Free: 800-561-5429
info@acot.ca
www.acot.ca
Previous Name: Alberta Association of Registered Occupational Therapists
Overview: A medium-sized provincial licensing organization founded in 1952 overseen by Canadian Association of Occupational Therapists
Mission: To operate as the regulatory body in Alberta for the profession of occupational therapists; to ensure competent & ethical occupational therapy services for the public of the province; to uphold the Code of Ethics & the Standards of Practice for occupational therapists in Alberta
Chief Officer(s):
Ryan Sommer, President
council@acot.ca
Gina Kroetsch, Vice-President
council@acot.ca
Maggie Fulford, Registrar
registrar@acot.ca
Staff Member(s): 4
Membership: *Fees:* $150; *Member Profile:* Regulated members practising occupational therapy in Alberta
Activities: Investigating complaints about occupational therapists practising in Alberta; Reviewing professional conduct; Disciplining members for unprofessional conduct to protect the public
Awards:
• ACOT Centenary PhD Scholarship, in the Faculty of Rehabilitation Medicine at the University of Alberta (Scholarship)
Amount: $5,000 per annum, for graduate student funding in occupational therapy
• President's Awards (Award)
In recognition of individuals who have shown an exemplary level of service & commitment to the profession of occupational therapy
Publications:
• ACOT News
Type: Newsletter; *Frequency:* 3 pa
Profile: College reports, activities, upcoming events, & articles on the profession
• Alberta College of Occupational Therapists Code of Ethics
Number of Pages: 29
• Alberta College Of Occupational Therapists Standards of Practice
Number of Pages: 15
• Alberta College of Occupational Therapists Annual Report
Type: Yearbook; *Frequency:* Annually
• Alberta OT register
Type: Directory
Profile: Listings of regulated members registered with the Alberta College of Occupational Therapists

Alberta College of Optometrists (ACO)

#102, 8407 Argyll Rd. NW, Edmonton AB T6C 4B2
Tel: 780-466-5999; *Fax:* 780-466-5969
Toll-Free: 800-668-2694
admin@collegeofoptometrists.ab.ca
www.collegeofoptometrists.ab.ca
Overview: A small provincial licensing organization founded in 1993
Mission: To act as the regulatory body for the profession of optometry in Alberta
Chief Officer(s):
Gordon Hensel, Registrar & CEO
registrar@collegeofoptometrists.ab.ca
Staff Member(s): 5
Membership: *Member Profile:* Optometrists; *Committees:* Nominating; Competence; Registration; Legislation; Complaint Review

Alberta College of Paramedics (ACP)

#220, 2755 Broadmoor Blvd., Sherwood Park AB T8H 2W7
Tel: 780-449-3114; *Fax:* 780-417-6911
Toll-Free: 877-351-2267
acp@collegeofparamedics.org
www.collegeofparamedics.org
Overview: A small provincial licensing organization
Mission: To carry out operations in accordance with the Health Disciplines Act; to govern & regulate the practice of paramedicine in Alberta; to maintain & enforce the Code of Ethics, to ensure safe & ethical care for Alberta's citizens; to establish & enforce standards of practice for the profession, to ensure competent care for the protection of the public interest
Chief Officer(s):
Sheldon Thunstrom, President
Tim Essington, Registrar/Executive Director
tim.essington@collegeofparamedics.org
Becky Donelon, Deputy Registrar
becky.donelon@collegeofparamedics.org
Carl Damour, Manager, Education & Equivalency
carl.damour@collegeofparamedics.org
Becky Donelon, Manager, Continuing Education & Standards
becky.donelon@collegeofparamedics.org
Heather Verbaas, Manager, Communications
heather.verbaas@collegeofparamedics.org
Bill Carstairs, Manager, Finance, 780-410-4138
bill.carstairs@collegeofparamedics.org
Membership: *Fees:* Schedule available; *Member Profile:* Individuals in Alberta who are registered emergency medical responders (EMR), emergency medical technicians (EMT), & emergency medical technologist-paramedics (EMT-P); *Committees:* Registration; Registration / Examination Advisory; Professional Conduct; Continuing Competence; Communications; Complaint Review; Practical Exam Appeal Review Working Subcommittee; Educational Institutions Program Approval / Audit Working Subcommittee; Substantial Equivalency Review Working Subcommittee
Activities: Overseeing the resolution of complaints involving alleged professional misconduct by registered practitioners
Publications:
• Alberta College of Paramedics Annual Report
Type: Yearbook; *Frequency:* Annually
• Alberta College of Paramedics Continuing Competency Program Handbook
Type: Handbook
• Emergency Medical Dialogue (EMD)
Frequency: 3 pa
Profile: Alberta College of Paramedics updates from the pre-hospital field, for practitioners
• The Pulse: News from the Alberta College of Paramedics
Type: Newsletter; *Frequency:* Monthly
Profile: Updates & announcements for the Emergency Medical Services profession

Alberta College of Pharmacists (ACP)

#1100, 8215 - 112 St. NW, Edmonton AB T6G 2C8
Tel: 780-990-0321; *Fax:* 780-990-0328
Toll-Free: 877-227-3838
acpinfo@pharmacists.ab.ca
www.pharmacists.ab.ca
Overview: A medium-sized provincial organization overseen by National Association of Pharmacy Regulatory Authorities

Member of: Canadian Council on Continuing Education in Pharmacy
Chief Officer(s):
Greg Eberhart, Registrar
Staff Member(s): 18

Alberta College of Social Workers (ACSW) / Association des travailleurs sociaux de l'Alberta

#550, 10707 - 100 Ave. NW, Edmonton AB T5J 3M1
Tel: 780-421-1167; *Fax:* 780-421-1168
Toll-Free: 800-661-3089
www.acsw.ab.ca
Previous Name: Alberta Association of Social Workers; Alberta Association of Registered Social Workers
Overview: A medium-sized provincial organization founded in 1969
Mission: To promote, regulate & govern the profession of social work in the Province of Alberta; To advocate for skilled & ethical social work practices & for policies, programs & services that promote the profession & protect the best interests of the public
Member of: Canadian Association of Social Workers
Affliation(s): International Federation of Social Workers
Chief Officer(s):
Lynn Labrecque King, Executive Director/Registrar
acswexd@acsw.ab.ca
Staff Member(s): 16
Membership: *Member Profile:* Registered social workers; *Committees:* Registration; Competence; Clinical Social Work; Professional Social Work Education
Activities: *Awareness Events:* Social Work Week
Awards:
• AARSW Award for Excellence in Social Work Practice (Award)
Recognizes Registered Social Workers who have exhibited exemplary skills & commitment to the Code of Ethics & mission of the AARSW while engage in providing direct service to clients
• Honourary Memberships (Award)
Awarded to a person or group that has made a significant contribution to the values & ideals inherent in the profession of social work & who have advanced the goals of the AARSW
• John Hutton Memorial Award for Social Action/Policy (Award)
Recognizes members in good standing who have made an outstanding contribution to the profession of social work & the community through advocacy, social action, policy development/analysis, program development or political action aimed at enhancing social functioning, service delivery systems & the environments in which we work with our clients

Alberta College of Speech-Language Pathologists & Audiologists (ACSLPA)

#209, 3132 Parsons Rd., Edmonton AB T6N 1L6
Tel: 780-944-1609; *Fax:* 780-408-3925
Toll-Free: 800-537-0589
website@acslpa.ab.ca
www.acslpa.ab.ca
Previous Name: Speech Language Hearing Association of Alberta
Overview: A small provincial licensing charitable organization founded in 1965
Mission: To provide leadership & coordination among speech-language pathologists & audiologists & the public in order to promote speech, language, & hearing health for Albertans
Affliation(s): Canadian Association of Speech-Language Pathologists & Audiologists
Chief Officer(s):
Laura Manz, President
Anne Assaly, CEO/Registrar
registrar@acslpa.ab.ca
Membership: *Fees:* $650 general; $175 inactive; $125 out of province renewal; *Member Profile:* Speech-language pathologists & audiologists
Activities: *Rents Mailing List:* Yes

Alberta Colleges Athletic Conference (ACAC)

Percy Page Centre, 11759 Groat Rd., Edmonton AB T5M 3K6
Tel: 780-427-9269; *Fax:* 780-427-9289
www.acac.ab.ca
www.facebook.com/AlbertaCollegesAthleticConference
twitter.com/ACAC_Sport
Previous Name: Western Inter-College Conference (WICC)
Overview: A small provincial charitable organization founded in 1964
Mission: To act as the governing body for intercollegiate athletics in Alberta; To develop student athletes
Member of: Canadian Colleges Athletic Association
Chief Officer(s):
Bill Dean, President, 403-382-6912, Fax: 403-317-3585
bill.dean@lethbridgecollege.ca
Alan Rogan, President Elect & Director, Governance & Finance, 780-853-8405, Fax: 780-853-8711
alan.rogan@lakelandcollege.ca
Robert D. Day, Executive Director
rday@acac.ab.ca
Finances: *Funding Sources:* Membership; Government of Alberta, through the Alberta Sport, Recreation, Parks, & Wildlife Foundation
Membership: *Member Profile:* Colleges & universities in Saskatchewan & Alberta
Activities: Administering intercollegiate athletics
Publications:
• ACAC By-laws
• ACAC Operating Code
• Alberta Colleges Athletic Conference Annual Report
Type: Yearbook; *Frequency:* Annually
• Official's Handbooks
Type: Handbook
Profile: Handbooks include Basketball Off-Court Officials Handbook, Hockey Off-Ice Officials Handbook, & Volleyball Off-Court Officials Handbook
• Outlook: The Newsletter of the ACAC
Type: Newsletter
Profile: Previews & reviews of championships & seasons, sport reports & awards

Alberta Committee of Citizens with Disabilities (ACCD)

#106, 10423 - 178 St. NW, Edmonton AB T5S 1R5
Tel: 780-488-9088; *Fax:* 780-488-3757
Toll-Free: 800-387-2514; *TTY:* 780-488-9090
accd@accd.net
www.accd.net
Overview: A medium-sized provincial charitable organization founded in 1973
Mission: To promote full participation in society for Albertans with disabilities
Member of: Alberta Disability Forum
Affliation(s): Council of Canadians with Disabilities
Chief Officer(s):
Beverley D. Matthiessen, Executive Director
Finances: *Annual Operating Budget:* $500,000-$1.5 Million; *Funding Sources:* Donations; government; fundraising
Staff Member(s): 9; 300 volunteer(s)
Membership: 300; *Fees:* $10 individual; $25 organization; *Member Profile:* Individuals with disabilities & organizations of people with disabilities
Activities: Information sharing & disability awareness; *Speaker Service:* Yes; *Library:* ACCD Resource Centre; by appointment
Awards:
• Education for Life Bursary (Scholarship)

Alberta Community & Co-operative Association (ACCA)

#202, 5013 - 48 St., Stony Plain AB T7Z 1L8
Tel: 780-963-3766; *Fax:* 780-968-6733
info@acca.coop
www.acca.coop
www.facebook.com/181455038572693
twitter.com/CoopAlberta
Previous Name: Rural Education & Development Association
Overview: A small local organization founded in 2005
Mission: To strengthen communities in Alberta, through cooperative & agricultural awareness & development
Member of: Canadian Co-operative Association (CCA)
Affliation(s): Canadian Co-operative Association
Chief Officer(s):
Russell Wolf, Chair
Terry Murray, Vice-Chair
Michele Aasgard, Executive Director
maasgard@acca.coop
Richard Stringham, Director, Co-op Development
coopdev@acca.coop
Cindy Dixon, Manager, Administration
cdixon@acca.coop
Finances: *Funding Sources:* Rural Alberta Development Fund
Membership: *Fees:* Schedule available; *Member Profile:* Organizations & individuals registered or incorporated to carry out business in Alberta on a co-operative basis; Persons & organizations who support ACCA goals & objectives
Activities: Promoting the co-operative model; Launching the Rural Co-operative Outreach & Development Project; Providing training opportunities; Offering networking opportunities amongst co-operatives; Disseminating co-op development resources for agricultural organizations, co-operatives, & credit unions
Publications:
• Alberta Community & Co-operative Association Annual Report
Type: Yearbook; *Frequency:* Annually
• Alberta Farm & Ranch Directory
Type: Directory; *Frequency:* Annually; *Editor:* Lance Johnson
Profile: Listings of farming, ranching, agri-business, & agriculture related services in Alberta
• Leadership Training in Rural Alberta: What's in place, what works, what's needed
• News & Views [a publication of the Alberta Community & Co-operative Association]
Type: Newsletter; *Frequency:* Monthly
Profile: ACCA activities, member profiles, upcoming events, & articles

The Alberta Community Crime Prevention Association (ACCPA)

#219, 1609 - 14 St. SW, Calgary AB T3C 1E4
Tel: 403-313-2566; *Fax:* 403-313-2569
info@accpa.org
www.accpa.org
www.youtube.com/user/ACCPAconnection?gl=CA&hl=en
Overview: A medium-sized provincial organization founded in 1989
Mission: To involve Albertans as active partners in crime prevention
Finances: *Funding Sources:* Government of Alberta
Membership: *Fees:* $40 active; $125 associate
Activities: Organinzing membership meetings; *Awareness Events:* Alberta Crime Prevention Week

Alberta Congress Board (ACB)

PO Box 82092, RPO Yellowbird, Edmonton AB T6J 7E6
Tel: 780-421-9330; *Fax:* 780-426-2987
acb@congressboard.ab.ca
www.congressboard.ab.ca
www.linkedin.com/company/alberta-congress-board
Previous Name: Conference Society of Alberta
Overview: A medium-sized provincial organization founded in 1974
Mission: A non-partisan organization dedicated to improving Alberta's social and economic well-being; to provide a neutral forum for dealing with current issues important to Alberta's business, labour, government, education, health, aboriginal and non-profit sectors.
Chief Officer(s):
Dennis Gane, President
Finances: *Annual Operating Budget:* $100,000-$250,000
Staff Member(s): 2; 20 volunteer(s)
Membership: 400

Alberta Conservation Association (ACA)

#101, 9 Chippewa Rd., Sherwood Park AB T8A 6J7
Tel: 780-410-1999; *Fax:* 780-464-0990
Toll-Free: 877-969-9091
info@ab-conservation.com
www.ab-conservation.com
Overview: A medium-sized provincial charitable organization founded in 1997
Mission: To envision an Alberta where citizens understand & support good stewardship of natural biological resources, & where future generations can value, enjoy & use these natural biological resources
Chief Officer(s):
Todd Zimmerling, President/CEO
Finances: *Funding Sources:* Alberta conservationists: Hunters; Anglers; corporate partners
Staff Member(s): 75
Membership: 1-99
Activities: *Speaker Service:* Yes

Alberta Conservation Tillage Society II (ACTS)

#211, 2 Athabasca Ave., Sherwood Park AB T8A 4E3
Tel: 780-416-6046; *Fax:* 780-416-8915
admin@areca.ab.ca
www.areca.ab.ca/site/acts
Overview: A medium-sized provincial organization founded in 1978
Mission: To protect & enhance soil productivity by promoting environmentally responsible conservation farming systems; to address soil & related water conservation resource concerns including government policy & programming, research, environmental & food safety issues, public awareness, & education
Member of: Soil Conservation Council of Canada

Chief Officer(s):
Ty Faechner, Executive Director
Finances: *Annual Operating Budget:* $500,000-$1.5 Million; *Funding Sources:* Government; industry; membership dues
Staff Member(s): 1; 16 volunteer(s)
Membership: 400 + 4,000 associate; *Fees:* $30; *Member Profile:* Interest in soil conservation
Activities: Alberta Reduced Tillage Initiative; Reduced Tillage Courses; Direct Seeding Demonstration Days; Farm Tours; *Speaker Service:* Yes; *Rents Mailing List:* Yes; *Library* Open to public by appointment
Awards:
• Provincial Conservation Farm Family Award (Award)

Alberta Construction Association (ACA)
18012 - 107 Ave., Edmonton AB T5S 2J5
Tel: 780-455-1122; *Fax:* 780-451-2152
info@albertaconstruction.net
www.albertaconstruction.net
Overview: A medium-sized provincial organization founded in 1958 overseen by Canadian Construction Association
Mission: To represent & promote Alberta's construction industry
Chief Officer(s):
Ken Gibson, Executive Director
Shelley Andrea, Director, Administration
Finances: *Funding Sources:* Membership dues
Staff Member(s): 4; 120 volunteer(s)
Membership: 2,900
Activities: *Speaker Service:* Yes; *Rents Mailing List:* Yes

Alberta Construction Labour Relations Association *See* Construction Labour Relations - An Alberta Association

Alberta Construction Safety Association (ACSA)
225 Parsons Rd. SW, Edmonton AB T6X 0W6
Tel: 780-453-3311; *Fax:* 780-455-1120
Toll-Free: 800-661-2272
edmonton@acsa-safety.org
www.acsa-safety.org
Overview: A medium-sized provincial organization
Chief Officer(s):
Steinley Iris, Chair
Staff Member(s): 4
Membership: *Fees:* Member: Free to construction-based companies in Alberta; Associate Member: $500 i Employees; $750 10 Employees

Alberta Construction Trucking Association (ACTA)
#400, 1040 - 7 Ave. SW, Calgary AB T2P 3G9
Tel: 403-244-4487; *Fax:* 403-244-2340
info@myacta.ca
www.myacta.ca
Previous Name: Alberta Gravel Truckers Association
Overview: A medium-sized provincial organization founded in 1983
Mission: To develop & promote the business of transporting construction & construction-related material
Chief Officer(s):
Jennifer Singer, President
Membership: *Fees:* $210-$525 Regular; $525 Affliate

Alberta Contact Centre Association (ACCA)
Crowchild Square, #200, 6 Crowfoot Circle NW, Calgary AB T3G 2T3
www.abcallcentre.com
www.linkedin.com/groups?homeNewMember=&gid=872257
www.facebook.com/pages/ACCA/234446407363
Overview: A small provincial organization founded in 1997
Mission: The Alberta Call Centre Association is a professional organization that serves as Alberta's central resource for industry information, networking and educational opportunities. Their members represent call centres, suppliers, educational services and other support organizations.
Chief Officer(s):
Shekar Kadaba, President
Sherise Thompson, Director
Membership: *Fees:* $100 individual; $250 corporate; $25 student

Alberta Continuing Care Association (ACCA)
#120, 9405 - 50 St. NW, Edmonton AB T6B 2T4
Tel: 780-435-0699; *Fax:* 780-436-9785
info@ab-cca.ca
www.ab-cca.ca
Overview: A medium-sized provincial organization founded in 1981 overseen by Canadian Alliance for Long Term Care
Mission: To represent owners & operators of long term care & designated assisted living facilities & home care
Member of: Canadian Alliance for Long Term Care
Chief Officer(s):
Bruce West, Executive Director, 780-435-0699
bwest@ab-cca.ca
Denise MacDonald, Director, Communications & Special Projects, 780-435-0699
communication@ab-cca.ca
Kailey O'Neill, Analyst, Planning & Research

Alberta Council for Environmental Education (ACEE)
911 Larch Place, Canmore AB T1W 1S5
abcee.org
www.facebook.com/136684183020723
www.youtube.com/user/AlbertaEE
Overview: A medium-sized provincial organization
Mission: To help deliver on the ideas to advance environmental education.
Chief Officer(s):
Gareth Thomson, Executive Director
Kathy Worobec, Education Director
Finances: *Funding Sources:* Donations
Meetings/Conferences: • Earth Matters Conference 2015, October, 2015, Coast Hotel, Canmore, AB
Scope: Provincial
Contact Information: conference@abcee.org

Alberta Council on Admissions & Transfer (ACAT)
Commerce Place, 10155 - 102 St., 11th Fl., Edmonton AB T5J 4L5
Tel: 780-422-9021; *Fax:* 780-422-3688
acat@gov.ab.ca
www.acat.gov.ab.ca
Overview: A small provincial organization founded in 1974
Mission: To develop policies, guidelines & procedures to facilitate transfer arrangements among post-secondary institutions, including: universities, public colleges, private colleges & technical institutes
Chief Officer(s):
Ron Woodward, Chair

Alberta Council on Aging
#232, 11808 St. Albert Trail, Edmonton AB T5L 4G4
Tel: 780-423-7781; *Fax:* 780-425-9246
Toll-Free: 888-423-9666
info@acaging.ca
www.acaging.ca
Overview: A medium-sized provincial charitable organization
Mission: To define the needs of aging & the aged & to bring the current needs to the attention of government or voluntary agencies & to take action where appropriate; to identify & encourage relevant areas of research & systematic compilation of information affecting aging; to encourage & develop discussion on all problems affecting aging; to inform government at any level on the potential impact of policies & legislation on the aging; to print, publish, distribute & sell publications related to aging; to foster interagency liaison & cooperation
Chief Officer(s):
Gary Pool, President
Paul Lemay, Vice-President
Finances: *Annual Operating Budget:* $250,000-$500,000
Staff Member(s): 3; 300 volunteer(s)
Membership: 3,000 individual + 200 organizations; *Fees:* $22 household; $60 organizations; $200 corporate; *Member Profile:* Groups, individuals & agencies concerned with the process of aging

Alberta Country Vacations Association (ACVA)
PO Box 5245, High River AB T1V 1M4
Tel: 403-217-5740; *Fax:* 403-652-5907
Toll-Free: 866-217-2282
info@albertacountryvacation.com
www.albertacountryvacation.com
twitter.com/acvatweets
Also Known As: Farm/Ranch Vacations
Overview: A small provincial organization founded in 1970
Mission: To promote ranch & farm holidays in Alberta; to act as the voice of country vacation businesses in Alberta; to assist members of the association to be strong & profitable organizations
Membership: *Fees:* $400; *Member Profile:* Rural vacation businesses in Alberta, such as ranches, farms, & backcountry vacation operations
Activities: Providing cooperative marketing; Offering professional development activities; Facilitating the exchange of ideas by arranging networking opportunities; Offering referrals to prospective tourists

Alberta Craft Council (ACC)
10186 - 106 St., Edmonton AB T5J 1H4
Tel: 780-488-6611; *Fax:* 780-488-8855
Toll-Free: 800-362-7238
acc@albertacraft.ab.ca
www.albertacraft.ab.ca
Overview: A medium-sized provincial charitable organization founded in 1979
Mission: To stimulate, develop & support craft in Alberta through communication, education, exhibition, & participation
Member of: Canadian Craft Council
Chief Officer(s):
Tom McFall, Executive Director
James Lavoie, Chair
Finances: *Annual Operating Budget:* $250,000-$500,000
Staff Member(s): 6; 50 volunteer(s)
Membership: 600; *Fees:* $60
Activities: Marketing; networking; exhibitions; education; *Library:* Alberta Craft Resource Centre; by appointment

Alberta Cricket Association *See* Cricket Alberta

Alberta Criminal Justice Association (ACJA)
c/o Carol Lemieux, Victims Services, Alberta Solicitor General, 10365 - 97 St. NW, 10th Fl., Edmonton AB T5J 3W7
Tel: 780-428-7590; *Fax:* 780-425-1699
info@acja.ca
www.acja.ca
Overview: A small provincial organization
Mission: To work towards an improved justice system in Alberta
Affliation(s): Canadian Criminal Justice Association
Chief Officer(s):
Peter Copple, President
PeterCopple@acja.ca
Finances: *Annual Operating Budget:* Less than $50,000
141 volunteer(s)
Membership: 250 individual; *Fees:* $25 student; $60 regular
Activities: Workshops

Alberta Cultural Society of the Deaf (ACSD)
#206, 11404 - 142 St., Edmonton AB T5M 1V1
Tel: 780-453-5053; *Fax:* 780-453-5053; *TTY:* 780-453-5033
info@acsd.ca
www.acsd.ca
www.facebook.com/AlbertaCulturalSocietyOfTheDeaf
Overview: A small provincial charitable organization
Mission: To provide educational programs for deaf & hard of hearing people; to raise awareness of deaf education; to foster & preserve deaf culture
Affliation(s): Canadian Cultural Society of the Deaf
Chief Officer(s):
Sandra Reid, President
sreid04@telus.net
Membership: *Committees:* History of ACSD
Activities: *Library:* ACSD Library; Open to public

Alberta Curling Federation (ACF)
Percy Page Centre, 11759 Groat Rd., 3rd Floor, Edmonton AB T5M 3K6
Tel: 780-643-0809; *Fax:* 780-427-8103
www.albertacurling.ab.ca
Overview: A medium-sized provincial organization overseen by Canadian Curling Association
Mission: To promote curling throughout Alberta
Chief Officer(s):
J.W. (Jim) Pringle, Executive Director
jim@albertacurling.ab.ca
Staff Member(s): 4

Alberta Dance Alliance (ADA)
Percy Page Centre, 11759 Groat Rd., 2nd Fl., Edmonton AB T5M 3K6
Tel: 780-422-8107; *Fax:* 780-422-2663
Toll-Free: 888-422-8107
info@abdancealliance.ab.ca
www.abdancealliance.ab.ca
www.facebook.com/ABDanceAlliance
twitter.com/ABDanceAlliance
Overview: A medium-sized provincial charitable organization founded in 1984
Mission: To foster & promote the appreciation & practice of dance in Alberta, through administrative, technical, & informative services, programs, advocacy, & special events
Member of: Canadian Conference of the Arts; Canadian

Association of Professional Dance Organizations
Affliation(s): Canadian Assembly of Dance; CADA BC, Ontario
Chief Officer(s):
Bobbi Westman, Executive Director
Finances: *Annual Operating Budget:* $50,000-$100,000; *Funding Sources:* Government of Alberta; membership fees; services
Staff Member(s): 2; 165 volunteer(s)
Membership: 1,900; *Fees:* $17 youth; $28 adult; $54-107 organization; *Member Profile:* Professional artists & companies, teachers, academics, other service organizations & general public
Activities: Workshops; conference; dance awards; job listings; equipment rental; FEATS Festival of Dance; *Library:* Resource Centre/Library

Alberta Deaf Sports Association (ADSA)

11404 - 142 St., Edmonton AB T5M 1V1
e-mail: info@albertadeafsports.ca
www.albertadeafsports.ca
www.facebook.com/AlbertaDeafSports
Also Known As: Federation of Silent Sports of Alberta
Overview: A medium-sized provincial charitable organization founded in 1974 overseen by Canadian Deaf Sports Association
Mission: To coordinate sport & recreation activities for the deaf in Alberta; To promote competition at the local, provincial, regional, & national levels; To select Alberta athletes to compete in national championships for the World Games of the Deaf
Member of: Canadian Deaf Sports Association
Chief Officer(s):
Sally Korol, Contact
Brenda Hillcox, President
Membership: *Fees:* $25 regular; $15 senior citizens; free for students; *Member Profile:* Deaf & hard of hearing persons
Publications:
• Alberta Deaf Sports Newsletter
Type: Newsletter
Profile: Highlights of past events & notice of future events

Alberta Debate & Speech Association (ADSA)

PO Box 74144, #148, 555 Strathcona Blvd. SW, Calgary AB T3H 3B6
Tel: 403-921-8531
contact@albertadebate.com
www.albertadebate.com
www.facebook.com/AlbertaDebateandSpeechAssociation
Overview: A small provincial charitable organization founded in 1974
Mission: To promote debate & speech activity, both curricular & extracurricular, among youth of secondary-school age in Alberta; to provide workshops, research packets, skill-based documents, video presentations & personal contact by volunteers & staff
Affliation(s): Canadian Student Debating Federation
Chief Officer(s):
Sylvia Hayward, President
Membership: 46 schools; *Fees:* Institution $150; student $20; *Member Profile:* Junior & senior high schools in Alberta; students
Activities: *Internships:* Yes; *Speaker Service:* Yes

Alberta Dental Association & College (ADAC)

#101, 8230 - 105 St., Edmonton AB T6E 5H9
Tel: 780-432-1012; *Fax:* 780-433-4864
Toll-Free: 800-843-3848
adaadmin@telusplanet.net
www.abda.ab.ca
Overview: A medium-sized provincial licensing organization founded in 1906 overseen by Canadian Dental Association
Finances: *Annual Operating Budget:* $3 Million-$5 Million
Staff Member(s): 10
Membership: 1,150; *Member Profile:* Dentists
Meetings/Conferences: • Jasper Dental Congress 2015, May, 2015, Jasper, AB
Scope: Provincial

Alberta Development Officers Association (ADOA)

PO Box 2232, Stn. Main, Stony Plain AB T7Z 1X7
Tel: 780-913-4214; *Fax:* 780-963-9762
admin@adoa.net
www.adoa.net
Overview: A small provincial organization founded in 1984
Chief Officer(s):
Jerry Brett, President
Betty Ann Fountain, Vice-President
Cheryl Callihoo, Secretary
Diane Burtnick, Treasurer
Membership: 301; *Fees:* $75; *Member Profile:* Development Officers from rural & urban municipalities in Alberta; Municipal & independent planners; Engineers; Surveyors
Activities: Establishing a certified training course through the University of Alberta;
Meetings/Conferences: • Alberta Development Officers Association 2015 Conference, 2015, Slave Lake, AB
Scope: Provincial
Publications:
• The Communicator [a publication of the Alberta Development Officers Association]
Editor: Carol-Lynn Gilchrist
Profile: Association activities, conferences, training, & articles

Alberta Diabetes Foundation

#1-020, HRIF East, University of Alberta, Edmonton AB T6G 2E1
Tel: 780-492-6537; *Fax:* 780-492-6046
Toll-Free: 800-563-2450
info@abdiabetes.com
albertadiabetesfoundation.com
www.linkedin.com/company/alberta-diabetes-foundation
www.facebook.com/AlbertaDiabetesFoundation
twitter.com/adfdiabetes
Overview: A medium-sized provincial charitable organization founded in 1988
Mission: Committed to the search for a cure for diabetes
Affliation(s): Funds pilot projects; studentships; & post-doctoral fellowships.
Chief Officer(s):
Jim Kanerva, Chair
Lynn Hamilton, Vice-Chair
Carla Woodward, Treasurer
Brad Fournier, Executive Director
Finances: *Annual Operating Budget:* $1.5 Million-$3 Million; *Funding Sources:* Personal & corporate donations
Staff Member(s): 8
Membership: *Fees:* $10; *Committees:* Special Events
Activities: *Awareness Events:* Frank J. Flaman Dinner & Auction, March; World Diabetes Day, November
Publications:
• inFocus: Working towards a Cure
Type: Newsletter
Profile: Articles about diabetics, research, & giving options, plus recipes & upcoming events

Alberta Diving

426 Reeves Cres., Edmonton AB T6R 2A4
Tel: 780-988-5571; *Fax:* 780-988-7753
www.albertadiving.ca
Overview: A small provincial organization
Mission: To act as the governing body in Alberta for the Olympic sport of amateur diving; to strive for personal & organizational excellence in all areas of diving
Chief Officer(s):
Curtis Yano, President
Keith Poelzer, Vice-President
Barbara Bush, Executive Director
Jim MacDonald, Secretary
Curtis Yano, Treasurer
Finances: *Funding Sources:* Fundraising; Sponsorships
Activities: Promoting sportsmanship & respect for rules; Encouraging community involvement; Promoting both the physical & mental well being of members

Alberta Dressage Association (ADA)

c/o Rita Behan, PO Box 1032, Black Diamond AB T0L 0H0
e-mail: ada@albertadressage.com
www.albertadressage.com
Also Known As: Canadian Dressage Owners & Riders Association, Western Chapter
Overview: A small provincial organization founded in 1978 overseen by Canadian Dressage Owners & Riders Association
Mission: To promote dressage in Alberta
Member of: Alberta Equestrian Federation
Chief Officer(s):
Lorraine Hill, President
lohill@shockware.com
Rita Behan, Secretary
ritabehan@telus.net
Jennifer Peers, Treasurer
peersj@telus.net
Finances: *Funding Sources:* Fundraising; Membership fee; Sponsorships
Membership: *Member Profile:* Senior & junior dressage riders from throughout Alberta
Activities: Liaising with the Alberta Equestrian Federation; Presenting shows; Coordinating dressage clinics for athletes & coaches; Arranging lectures about dressage; Presenting awards

Calgary Area Chapter

c/o Karen Mercier, 28 Cimarron Estates Way, Okotoks AB T1S 2P3
Tel: 403-982-5700
www.ca-ada.com
www.facebook.com/#!/groups/135205126534392/
Mission: To promote dressage in Calgary
Chief Officer(s):
Sue Hewton-Waters, President, 403-251-1504
suehw@me.com
Karen Mercier, Vice-President, 403-540-5732
kmercier7@gmail.com
Kathy Ogryzlo, Treasurer
ogryzlok@shaw.ca
• CA / ADA [Calgary Area, Alberta Dressage Association] Extensions Newsletter
Type: Newsletter; *Price:* Free with membership in the Alberta Dressage Association CalgaryArea Chapter
Profile: Chapter announcements, such as upcoming events & executive reports

Chinook Country Chapter

c/o Dinah Sailer, 96 Canyoncrest Pt. West, Lethbridge AB T1K 0B4
Tel: 403-381-2664
lohill@shockware.com
Mission: To encourage dressage in Alberta's Chinook Country
Chief Officer(s):
Lorraine Hill, Chair, 403-328-3617
lohill@shockware.com
Barb Edgecombe-Green, Vice-Chair
edgecombegreen@shaw.ca
Audrey Kokesch, Secretary
akokesch@shaw.ca
Lynn Dennis, Treausrer
dlde@telus.net
Doug Orr, Director, Communication
lohill@shockware.com
Hope Olsen, Coordinator, Membership, 403-642-2146
eholsen@telusplanet.net
• Chinook Country Alberta Dressage Association Newsletter
Type: Newsletter; *Price:* Free with Alberta Dressage Association Chinook Country Chapter membership
Profile: Chapter notices, such as upcoming events, meeting summaries, & show reports

Cold Lake Area Chapter

PO Box 1147, Cold Lake AB T9M 1P3
Tel: 780-594-2035
carol.porteous@worldpost.ca
www.albertadressage.com
Mission: To advance the art of dressage
Chief Officer(s):
Carol Porteous, President, 780-594-2035
carol.porteous@worldpost.ca
Nancy Gauthier, Vice-President
hooves_paws@worldpost.ca
Chris Gingell, Secretary, 780-639-2164
caruaidd@worldpost.ca
Shannon Reid Burlinguette, Treasurer
shannonreid@royallepage.com
• Cold Lake Area Alberta Dressage Association Newsletter
Type: Newsletter; *Editor:* Niki Elash
Profile: Chapter information, such as upcoming events, as well as articles about dressage

Edmonton Area Chapter

c/o Caroline Litke, 4536 - 33 Ave., Edmonton AB T6L 4X7
Tel: 780-886-7419
Mission: To advance the sport of dressage in Edmonton & area
Member of: United States Dressage Federation
Chief Officer(s):
Gillian Sutherland, President
gillians@rogers.com
Alex Evans, Vice-President
aeevans@ualberta.ca
Brittany Kroening, Secretary
brittdkroening@gmail.com
Susan Hughes, Treasurer
susanhughes1@hotmail.com
• Bits & Pieces - EAADA
Type: Newsletter; *Accepts Advertising*; *Price:* Free with membership in the Edmonton Area Alberta Dressage

Association
Profile: Chapter information, including upcoming clinics & shows

Parkland Area Chapter
c/o Lix Fletcher, PO Box 614, Alix AB T0C 0B0
Tel: 403-843-4093; *Fax:* 403-843-4261
Mission: To promote the sport of dressage in central Alberta; To increase participation in dressage
Chief Officer(s):
Rebecca Cade, Area Group Chair
pcade@telusplanet.net
Jenni Imeson, Area Group Vice-Chair
jenimeson@hotmail.com
Diane Luxen, Secretary
dluxen@telusplanet.net
Arlene Mackenzie, Treasurer
arlene.mackenzie@gov.ab.ca
Liz Fletcher, Director, Merchandise
flyingfl@yahoo.ca

Alberta Easter Seals Society
#103, 811 Manning Rd. NE, Calgary AB T2E 7L4
Tel: 403-235-5662; *Fax:* 403-248-1716
Toll-Free: 877-732-7837
communications@easterseals.ab.ca
www.easterseals.ab.ca
www.facebook.com/EasterSealsAlberta
twitter.com/eastersealsAB
pinterest.com/clienttell
Previous Name: Alberta Rehabilitation Council for the Disabled
Overview: A medium-sized provincial charitable organization founded in 1951 overseen by Easter Seals Canada
Mission: To represent interests of all people with disabilities in Alberta; to promote change at all policy-making levels through public awareness campaigns, projects, seminars; to provide mobility equipment; to conduct public awareness programs; to provide recreational activities through summer camp - Camp Horizon; to provide a residential home program - Easter Seals McQueen Residence
Chief Officer(s):
Linda Wittig, Coordinator, Marketing & Communications
lindaw@easterseals.ab.ca
Susan Boivin, CEO
susan@easterseals.ab.ca
Membership: *Fees:* $20

Alberta Ecotrust Foundation
#1020, 105 - 12 Ave. SE, Calgary AB TSG 1A1
Tel: 403-209-2245
Toll-Free: 800-465-2147
info@albertaecotrust.com
albertaecotrust.com
twitter.com/AlbertaEcotrust
Overview: A medium-sized provincial charitable organization founded in 1991
Mission: To provide grants to environmental groups that work towards improving Alberta's eco health
Chief Officer(s):
Pat Letizia, Executive Director
pat.letizia@albertaecotrust.com
Staff Member(s): 7
Membership: *Committees:* Grant Review

Alberta Educational Facilities Administrators Association (AEFAA)
7 White Pelican Way, Lake Newell Resort AB T1R 0X5
Tel: 403-376-0461
www.aefaa.ca
twitter.com/AlanKloepper
Overview: A small provincial organization founded in 1971
Chief Officer(s):
Alan Kloepper, Executive Director
alan.kloepper@grasslands.ab.ca
Membership: *Member Profile:* Employees employed by school jurisdictions, colleges, universities, trade schools and the provincial government.
Meetings/Conferences: • Alberta Educational Facilities Administrators Association 2015 Annual Conference, 2015
Scope: Provincial

Alberta Egg Producers' Board (EFA)
#101, 90 Freeport Blvd. NE, Calgary AB T3J 5J9
Tel: 403-250-1197; *Fax:* 403-291-9216
Toll-Free: 877-302-2344
info@eggs.ab.ca
eggs.ab.ca
Also Known As: Egg Farmers of Alberta
Overview: A medium-sized provincial organization founded in 1968
Mission: To be the best producers & marketers of eggs
Affliation(s): Egg Farmers of Canada (EFC); Alberta Agriculture & Rural Development (ARD); Alberta Farm Animal Care (AFAC); Canada Food Inspection Agency (CFIA)
Chief Officer(s):
Ben Waldner, Chair
David Webb, Manager, Marketing & Communications
David.Webb@eggs.ab.ca
Staff Member(s): 10
Membership: 168 egg producers in Alberta; *Committees:* Industry Standards

Alberta Electrical League (AEL)
PO Box 80091, Stn. Towerlane, Airdrie AB T4B 2V8
Tel: 403-514-3085; *Fax:* 403-514-6169
Toll-Free: 800-642-5508
info@elecleague.ab.ca
albertaelectricalleague.com
ca.linkedin.com/pub/tara-ternes/12/735/b06
twitter.com/AELtweets
Overview: A small provincial licensing organization founded in 1994
Mission: To promote the electric industry in Alberta; To develop business opportunities for league members
Chief Officer(s):
Ron Stocks, President
ronald.stocks@rdc.ab.ca
Tara Ternes, Executive Director
Membership: 150+; *Member Profile:* Practitioners & companies from the electrical industry in Alberta, such as engineers, manufacturers, distributors, contractors, inspectors, utilities, & colleges & universities
Activities: Hosting electrical trade shows; Providing educational programs; Offering networking opportunities
Publications:
• Power UP E-News
Type: Newsletter; *Frequency:* Monthly
Profile: Current events in the electrical industry in Alberta
• Power UP Newsletter
Type: Newsletter; *Frequency:* Quarterly
Profile: Information distributed to 5,000 individuals involved in Alberta's electrical industry

Alberta Environmental Network (AEN)
PO Box 4541, Edmonton AB T6E 5G4
Tel: 780-757-4872; *Fax:* 866-868-5563
Other Communication: events@aenweb.ca
admin@aenweb.ca
www.aenweb.ca
twitter.com/ABEnvNet
Overview: A medium-sized provincial organization founded in 1987 overseen by Canadian Environmental Network
Mission: To facilitate communication & cooperation among environmental groups in Alberta in order to contribute to the enhancement & protection of the environment
Chief Officer(s):
Nashina Shariff, Chair
Membership: 70; *Fees:* $30-$200; *Member Profile:* Alberta Environmental NGOs; *Committees:* Clean Air/Energy; Forest; Waste Avoidance/Toxics
Activities: *Rents Mailing List:* Yes

Alberta Equestrian Federation (AEF)
#100, 251 Midpark Blvd. SE, Calgary AB T2X 1S3
Tel: 403-253-4411; *Fax:* 403-252-5260
Toll-Free: 877-463-6233
info@albertaequestrian.com
www.albertaequestrian.com
www.facebook.com/AlbertaEquestrian
twitter.com/ab_equestrian
Overview: A small provincial organization founded in 1978
Member of: Equine Canada
Chief Officer(s):
Les Oakes, President
lesoakes@gmail.com
Sonia Dantu, Executive Director Ext. 4
execdir@albertaequestrian.com
Finances: *Annual Operating Budget:* $100,000-$250,000; *Funding Sources:* Alberta Sport, Recreation, Parks & Wildlife Foundation
Staff Member(s): 6
Membership: 12,000+; *Fees:* $50 individual; $110 family; $75 club; $100 business; *Committees:* Executive; Rec. & Trails; Competitions; Officials; Trail Ride
Activities: Administers equestrian NCCP Level I & II for Western, English & Driving Coaching; coordinating, sanctioning & administering body for equestrian sport & recreation in Alberta; provides assistance & expertise in areas such as competitions, coaching, officials, games & sporting events, recreation & travel insurance, awards, human & equine medication control; *Awareness Events:* Annual Trail Ride

Alberta Falconry Association
22 Chilcotin Way West, Lethbridge AB T1K 7L8
e-mail: info@albertafalconry.com
www.albertafalconry.com
Overview: A small local organization founded in 1965
Mission: In addition to providing guidance for any Alberta resident who is interested in falconry & the care of falcons, the aims of the association are to promote the conservation of raptors and their prey, & to perpetuate the highest standards of the practice.
Chief Officer(s):
Alex Stokes, Contact
Membership: 35; *Fees:* $70; $35 renewal

Alberta Famil Child Care Association (AFCCA)
Gail Blixt, Calgary & Region Family Dayhomes, 3224 - 28 St. SW, Calgary AB T3E 2J6
Tel: 403-217-5394; *Fax:* 403-240-2668
www.afcca.ca
Overview: A medium-sized provincial organization founded in 1989
Mission: To promote a high standard of well being for children & the child care industry
Member of: Canadian Child Care Federation
Chief Officer(s):
Gail Blixt, Contact
gail@calgaryfamilydayhomes.com
Membership: 67; *Fees:* $125; *Member Profile:* Family day home agencies

Alberta Family History Society (AFHS)
712 - 16 Ave. NW, Calgary AB T2M 0J8
Tel: 403-214-1447
www.afhs.ab.ca
Overview: A medium-sized provincial charitable organization founded in 1980
Mission: To encourage accuracy & thoroughness in family histories & genealogical research; to establish relations with related societies to promote common interests
Member of: Canadian Federation of Genealogical & Family History Societies
Affliation(s): Federation of Family History Societies (England)
Chief Officer(s):
Irene Oickle, Membership Chair
membership@afhs.ab.ca
Lorna Loughton, President
president@afhs.ab.ca
Finances: *Annual Operating Budget:* Less than $50,000; *Funding Sources:* Membership dues; grants
10 volunteer(s)
Membership: 300; *Fees:* $35-50; *Member Profile:* Open to anyone tracing his/her family tree or to those who want to learn how to begin; *Committees:* Publications; Projects; Seminar; Publicity; Education; Program; Library
Activities: Seminars, workshops, classes; *Library*

Alberta Family Mediation Society (AFMS)
#1650, 246 Stewart Green SW, Calgary AB T3H 3C8
Tel: 403-233-0143
Toll-Free: 877-233-0143
info@afms.ca
www.afms.ca
Overview: A small provincial organization
Mission: To advocate for the resolution of family conflict through mediation by qualified professionals
Affliation(s): Family Mediation Canada
Chief Officer(s):
Linda Hancock, Chair
Membership: *Fees:* $50 student; $130 general
Awards:
• Dr. John Haynes Memorial Award (Award)
Meetings/Conferences: • Alberta Family Mediation Society 2015 Conference, April, 2015, Providence Renewal Centre, Edmonton, AB
Scope: Provincial

Alberta Farm Fresh Producers Association (AFFPA)
PO Box 56, Kelsey AB T0B 2K0
Tel: 780-373-2503; *Fax:* 780-373-2297
Toll-Free: 800-661-2642
info@albertafarmfresh.com
www.albertafarmfresh.com
www.facebook.com/475524020289
twitter.com/AB_Farm_Fresh
Overview: A small provincial organization
Mission: To develop a sustainable & profitable farm direct marketing industry; To support the production of farm direct market vegetable, berry, & fruit crops, perennials, herbs, flowers, & bedding plants, meat, poulty, & eggs, & other specialty items; To contribute to the health & economic well-being of Albertans
Chief Officer(s):
Ron Erdmann, President, 780-961-3912
erdmannsgardens@mcsnet.ca
Blaine Staples, Vice-President, 403-227-4231
info@thejunglefarm.com
Tim Vrieselaar, Treasurer, 403-393-2059
nblgardens@gmail.com
Membership: 162; *Fees:* $145; *Member Profile:* Agri-preneuers in Alberta
Activities: Promoting the farm direct market industry; Providing educational opportunities, such as courses & workshops; Supporting horticultural research; Collaborating with industry partners & government; Arranging insurance; Branding Alberta products from members; Offering networking opportunities with growers acrossAlberta;
Publications:
• Come To Our Farm Guide
Type: Guide; *Price:* Free
Profile: Contact & product information about Alberta Farm Fresh Producers Association members
• Direct Currents [a publication of the Alberta Farm Fresh Producers Association]
Type: Newsletter; *Frequency:* Quarterly; *Accepts Advertising*; *Price:* Free with Alberta Farm Fresh Producers Association membership
Profile: Association updates

Alberta Farmers' Market Association (AFMA)
PO Box 69071, 13040 - 137 Ave., Edmonton AB T5L 5E3
Fax: 780-669-5779
Toll-Free: 866-754-2362
info@albertamarkets.com
www.albertamarkets.com
Overview: A small provincial organization founded in 1994 overseen by Farmers' Markets Canada
Mission: To provide direction & support to members; To assist Alberta Approved Farmers' Markets in playing a major role in the establishment of vibrant communities; To advocate for farmers' markets in Alberta
Member of: Alberta Farm Fresh Producers Association; Growing Alberta; Dine Alberta; Alberta Association of Agricultural Societies; GO Organic
Affliation(s): Alberta Farmers' Market Program; Alberta Agriculture & Rural Development; RBC Agencies/The Cooperators; Times Two Gifts & Promotions; Whytespace
Chief Officer(s):
Darlene Cavanaugh, Director, 780-644-5377
director@albertamarkets.com
Becky Lipton, Coordinator, Training & Communications, 780-427-6403
becky@albertamarkets.com
Membership: *Member Profile:* Alberta Approved Farmers' Markets in Alberta; Vendors; Managers; Boards; Sponsors; Persons who support the principles by which farmers' markets operate
Activities: Promoting Alberta's farmers' markets; Providing education for members, such as regional workshops & market manager training; Offering networking opportunities; Funding & establishing surveys; Advising government organizations regarding guidelines for markets; Arranging market & vendor group liability insurance; *Awareness Events:* Alberta Farmers' Market Awareness Week
Awards:
• New Product in Make It, Bake It, Grow It, Produce It Award (Award)
• Market Award (Award)
• Community Builder Award (Award)
• Outstanding Volunteer Award (Award)
Publications:
• Market Express
Type: Newsletter; *Frequency:* Quarterly

Profile: Feature articles, recipes, & reports from executive members, committess, & regional directors

Alberta Fashion Market *See* Alberta Men's Wear Agents Association

Alberta Federation of Labour (AFL) / Fédération du travail de l'Alberta
10654 - 101 St., Edmonton AB T5H 2S1
Tel: 780-483-3021; *Fax:* 780-484-5928
Toll-Free: 800-661-3995
afl@afl.org
www.afl.org
www.facebook.com/group.php?gid=14904202843997\0
twitter.com/abfedlabour
Overview: A large provincial organization founded in 1912 overseen by Canadian Labour Congress
Mission: To act as a central labour body, representing Alberta's organized workers & their families; To improve conditions for Alberta's workers, their families & communities
Chief Officer(s):
Gil McGowan, President, 780-483-3021, Fax: 780-218-9888
gmcgowan@afl.org
Nancy Furlong, Secretary-Treasurer, 780-483-3021, Fax: 780-720-8945
nfurlong@afl.org
Tony Clarke, Director, Research
tclark@afl.org
Shannon Phillips, Director, Policy Analysis
sphillips@afl.org
Olav Rokne, Director, Communications
orokne@afl.org
Ishani Weera, Director, Organizing & Outreach
iweera@afl.org
Membership: 145,000; *Member Profile:* Alberta workers & their families from twenty-nine unions & employee organizations of both the public & private sectors; *Committees:* Education; Environment; Health & Safety; Human Rights & International Solidarity; Political Action; Pride & Solidarity; Women's; Workers of Colour & Aboriginal Workers; Young Workers
Activities: Publishing research, reports, submissions to government, policy papers, & speeches; Hosting an AFL Kids Camp for children & youth of AFL affiliates; Speaking out on social issues, such as public health care
Meetings/Conferences: • Alberta Federation of Labour 2015 Convention, 2015, AB
Scope: Provincial
Description: A convention held every two years, attended by delegates from every union affiliated to the federation
Publications:
• Labour Bytes
Type: Newsletter
Profile: Updates on Alberta's labour news, campaigns, & research
• Labour Economic Monitor
Type: Newsletter
Profile: An examination of the Alberta scene
• Union Magazine
Type: Magazine; *Frequency:* 3 pa; *Price:* Free
Profile: A seasonal publication, available in electronic or paper versions, to offer insight & analysis into social, economic, & political issues of interest to union activists, officers, & staff

Alberta Federation of Police Associations (AFPA)
Energy Square, #100, 7024 - 101 Ave., Edmonton AB T6A 0H7
Fax: 403-795-7173
information@albertapolice.ca
www.albertapolice.ca
Overview: A medium-sized provincial organization
Mission: To address local, provincial, & national police association issues
Member of: Canadian Police Association
Chief Officer(s):
Bob Walsh, President
bwalsh@albertapolice.ca

Alberta Federation of Rock Clubs (AFRC)
2073 Blackmud Creek Dr. SW, Edmonton AB T6W 1G8
Tel: 780-430-6694
paulinez8@shaw.ca
www.afrc.ca
Overview: A medium-sized provincial organization founded in 1963
Mission: To assist member clubs by providing information & expertise; to promote the study of the Earth Sciences
Affliation(s): Gem & Mineral Federation of Canada
Chief Officer(s):
Alice Watts, President
Pauline Zeschuk, Secretary
Membership: 10 clubs;

Alberta Federation of Shooting Sports (AFSS)
Percy Page Centre, 11759 Groat Rd., Edmonton AB T5M 3K6
Tel: 780-415-1775; *Fax:* 780-422-2663
afss@abshooters.org
www.abshooters.org
Overview: A small provincial organization
Mission: The AFSS provides funding & support to 11 shooting organizations throughout the province.
Affliation(s): Alberta Handgun Association; Alberta Smallbore Rifle Association; Alberta Provincial Rifle Association; International Practical Shooting Confederation Alberta; Alberta Sporting Clays Association; Alberta Skeet Shooting Association; Alberta International Skeetshooting Association; Alberta International Style Trapshooting Association; Alberta Metallic Silhouette Association; Alberta Black Powder Association; Alberta Frontier Shootists Society
Chief Officer(s):
Bernie Harrison, President
Trudie Snider, Office Manager
Membership: 11 associations; *Member Profile:* Shooting associations in Alberta

Alberta Fencing Association (AFA)
Percy Page Centre, 11759 Groat Rd., Edmonton AB T5M 3K6
Tel: 780-427-9474; *Fax:* 780-447-5959
info@fencing.ab.ca
www.fencing.ab.ca
Overview: A small provincial organization founded in 1976 overseen by Canadian Fencing Federation
Mission: The AFA is a non-profit governing body managed by a volunteer executive promoting the sport of fencing in Alberta.
Member of: Canadian Fencing Federation
Chief Officer(s):
Maja Zaher, Executive Director
Finances: *Annual Operating Budget:* $250,000-$500,000
Staff Member(s): 1; 16 volunteer(s)
Membership: 800+; *Fees:* $20 associate; $55 competitive

Alberta Fire Chiefs Association (AFCA)
AB
Tel: 780-719-7939; *Fax:* 780-892-3333
www.afca.ab.ca
Overview: A small provincial organization
Chief Officer(s):
William Purdy, Executive Director, 780-892-2125
bpurdy@xplornet.com
Membership: *Member Profile:* Assistant Chiefs; Deputy Chiefs; Platoon Chiefs; Battalion Chiefs; District Chiefs; Division Chiefs; Directors of fire departments in Alberta.
Meetings/Conferences: • 2015 Northwest Fire Conference, April, 2015, Sawridge Inn and Conference Centre, Peace River, AB
Scope: Provincial
• Alberta Fire Chiefs Association 2015 Conference and Trade Show, May, 2015, Sheraton Red Deer Hotel, Red Deer, AB
Scope: Provincial

Alberta Fish & Game Association (AFGA)
6924 - 104 St., Edmonton AB T6H 2L7
Tel: 780-437-2342; *Fax:* 780-438-6872
office@afga.org
www.afga.org
Overview: A medium-sized provincial organization overseen by Canadian Wildlife Federation
Mission: To ensure fish & wildlife habitat & resources in Alberta
Chief Officer(s):
Conrad Fennema, President
Martin Sharren, Executive Vice-President
Sandie Buwalda, Coordinator, Programs
Brad Fenson, Coordinator, Habitats
Kerry Grisley, Co-Manager, Operation Grassland Community
Susan Skinner, Co-Manager, Operation Grassland Community
Finances: *Funding Sources:* Membership fees; Donations
Membership: 20,000 members in 100+ clubs; *Fees:* $35 individuals; $55 families; *Committees:* Finance; Environment; Fishing; Hunting; Programs
Activities: Providing educational programs; Liaising with government, industry, & other organizations
Meetings/Conferences: • Alberta Fish & Game Association 2015 Annual General Meeting, February, 2015, AB
Scope: Provincial
Description: Voting on resolutions

Alberta Fish Farmers Association *See* Alberta Aquaculture Association

Alberta Fitness Leadership Certification Association (AFLCA)

Percy Page Bldg., 11759 Groat Rd., 3rd Fl., Edmonton AB T5M 3K6
Tel: 780-492-4435; *Fax:* 780-455-2264
Toll-Free: 866-348-8648
www.provincialfitnessunit.ca
Overview: A medium-sized provincial organization founded in 1984
Member of: National Fitness Leadership Advisory Council; National Fitness Leadership Alliance
Chief Officer(s):
Katherine MacKeigan, Executive Director
katherine.mackeigan@ualberta.ca
Staff Member(s): 6
Membership: 1,000-4,999; *Member Profile:* Fitness leader or trainer
Activities: *Internships:* Yes

Alberta Flatwater Canoe Association *See* Alberta Sprint Racing Canoe Association

Alberta Floor Covering Association (AFCA)

60 Martindale Close NE, Calgary AB T3J 2V1
Tel: 403-280-6006; *Fax:* 403-280-6056
Toll-Free: 800-292-9712
afca@shaw.ca
members.shaw.ca/afca/AFCA/home.htm
Overview: A small provincial organization founded in 1979 overseen by National Floor Covering Association
Mission: To ensure professionalism in Alberta's floor covering industry; to promote high standards within the industry, by upholding the Code of Ethics & the Code of Trade & Practice; To represent members on issues related to the construction industry
Affiliation(s): National Floor Covering Association
Chief Officer(s):
Peggy Alkenbrack, Executive Director
Doug Prostebby, President
Grant Medhurst, Secretary-Treasurer
40 volunteer(s)
Membership: *Fees:* $1,000 manufacturers, distributors & retailers; $500 multi branch dealers; $450 associates & affiliates; $100 installers; $50 apprentice installers; *Member Profile:* Floor covering manufacturers, distributors, retailers, installers, & associates in Alberta
Activities: Liaising between all sectors of the floor covering industry in Alberta; Providing seminars & training; Offering technical support; Conducting an inspection program, approved by the Alberta New Home Warranty & the National Home Warranty Programs Ltd., for association members & consumers; Improving apprenticeship training, by working with the Alberta Provincial Apprenticeship Committee
Publications:
• Alberta Floor Covering Association Inspection Services Policy Manual
Type: Manual
Profile: A guide to the inspection process, disclosure policy, fees, & resolution
• Alberta Floor Covering Association Newsletter
Type: Newsletter; *Frequency:* Quarterly
• Jobsite Preparation Standards Manual
Type: Manual

Alberta Floorball Association

Edmonton AB
Tel: 780-999-5333
info@floorballalberta.com
www.floorballalberta.com
www.facebook.com/FloorballAlberta
www.twitter.com/Floorball_AB
Also Known As: Floorball Alberta
Overview: A small provincial organization founded in 2010 overseen by Floorball Canada
Mission: To be the provincial governing body for the sport of floorball in Ontario.
Member of: Floorball Canada
Chief Officer(s):
Shawn Murray, President
shawn@floorballalberta.com
Membership: 6 regional associations

Alberta Food Bank Network Association (AFBNA)

#30, 50 Bellerose Dr., St Albert AB T8N 3L5
Tel: 780-459-4598; *Fax:* 780-459-6347
Toll-Free: 866-251-2326
Other Communication: 780-459-6893 (Membership)
contact@afbna.ca
www.afbna.ca
www.facebook.com/pages/Alberta-Food-Banks/493996147306687
www.twitter.com/ABFoodBanks
Also Known As: Alberta Food Banks
Overview: A medium-sized provincial charitable organization founded in 1998
Mission: Evaluates and researches programs to benefit Alberta food banks.
Member of: Food Banks Canada
Affiliation(s): Community Kitchen Program of Calgary; WECAN Food Basket Society; Iberta Health Services: Edmonton Collective Kitchens
Chief Officer(s):
Suzan Krecsy, Chair
Finances: *Funding Sources:* Corporate sponsors; private donors
Membership: *Fees:* $50-$1000; *Member Profile:* Small, medium & large food banks across the province; *Committees:* Community Relations; Business; Personnel & nominating; Programs & Services
Activities: Coordination of product from Food Bank Canada; coordination of provincial fundraising; liaising between local food banks & national agency
Awards:
• Alberta Food Banks Grant (Grant)
Eligibility: A member of the Alberta Food Bank Network Association and thus a federally registered charity; demonstrates a need for funding *Amount:* $1000

Alberta Food Processors Association (AFPA)

#100W, 4760 - 72 Ave. SW, Calgary AB T2C 3Z2
Tel: 403-201-3657; *Fax:* 403-201-2513
info@afpa.com
www.afpa.com
Overview: A medium-sized provincial organization
Mission: To help Alberta food & beverage companies compete successfully in marketplace
Chief Officer(s):
Ted Johnson, President & CEO Ext. 27
ted@afpa.com
Membership: 300+ organizations; *Fees:* $1,000 full member; $500 basic/associate member

Alberta Forest Products Association (AFPA)

#900, 10707 - 100 Ave., Edmonton AB T5J 3M1
Tel: 780-452-2841; *Fax:* 780-455-0505
www.albertaforestproducts.ca
Overview: A medium-sized provincial licensing organization founded in 1942
Mission: To represent companies that manufacture forest products throughout Alberta
Chief Officer(s):
Neil Shelly, Executive Director
Brady Whittaker, President & Chief Executive Officer
Norm Dupuis, Director, Grade Bureau, 780-452-2841 Ext. 235
Brock Mulligan, Director, Communications, 780-452-2841 Ext. 229
Keith Murray, Director, Policy & Regulation, 780-452-2841 Ext. 227
Carola von Sass, Director, Health & Safety, 780-452-2841 Ext. 237
Finances: *Funding Sources:* Membership fees; Sponsorships
Membership: *Member Profile:* Manufacturers of pulp & paper, lumber, panelboard, & secondary manufactured wood products in Alberta
Meetings/Conferences: • Alberta Forest Products Association 2015 73rd Annual General Meeting & Conference, 2015
Scope: Provincial
Description: A business meeting, sessions on topics relevant to the industry, networking opportunities, & a recognition dinner
• Alberta Forest Products Association 2016 74th Annual General Meeting & Conference, 2016, AB
Scope: Provincial
Description: A business meeting, sessions on topics relevant to the industry, networking opportunities, & a recognition dinner

Alberta Foster Parent Association (AFPA)

9750 - 35th Ave., Edmonton AB T6E 6J6
Tel: 780-429-9923; *Fax:* 780-426-7151
Toll-Free: 800-667-2372
reception@afpaonline.com
www.afpaonline.com
Overview: A small local charitable organization founded in 1974
Chief Officer(s):
Norm Brownell, President
Sylvia Thompson, Vice-President
Katherine Jones, Executive Director, 780-701-4089
katherinejones@afpaonline.com
Finances: *Funding Sources:* Donations
Membership: *Fees:* $50 household; *Member Profile:* Department foster homes, where children are placed through the department; Agency foster homes, where children are placed through an agency; Associate members (staff members from the Department of Family & Social Services or a partnering agency); Support members (friends of foster care who are not foster parents); Honorary members (appointed lifetime members)
Activities: Offering a support line (1-800-667-2372 or 780-906-3890); Providing supportive materials for adoptive families; Offering financial assistance for legal issues; Providing a conflict resolution program; Facilitating networking opportunities for foster parents & social workers;
Awards:
• Foster Family of the Year Award (Award)
• Bursary Fund (Scholarship)
• Citation Awards (Award)
Meetings/Conferences: • Alberta Foster Parent Association 42nd Annual Conference & Awards Banquet, 2015
Scope: Provincial
Publications:
• The Bridge
Type: Newsletter; *Frequency:* Quarterly
Profile: Association reports & information for foster families

Alberta Foundation for the Arts (AFA)

10708 - 105 Ave., Edmonton AB T5H 0A1
Tel: 780-427-9968; *Fax:* 780-422-1162
Toll-Free: -310-0000
www.affta.ab.ca
www.facebook.com/AlbertaFoundationfortheArts
twitter.com/AFA1991
Overview: A large provincial organization founded in 1991
Mission: To create the best possible climate for the arts in Alberta
Chief Officer(s):
Mark T. Phipps, Chair
Shannon Marchand, Secretary
Jeffrey Anderson, Executive Director, 780-415-0283
jeffrey.anderson@gov.ab.ca
Finances: *Annual Operating Budget:* Greater than $5 Million; *Funding Sources:* Alberta Lotteries
Staff Member(s): 3
Membership: 11; *Member Profile:* Appointment by order in council; *Committees:* Art Collection; Communications; Executive; Grants
Activities: Provides grant funding to artists, art organizations & cultural industries; manages an extensive art collection featuring Alberta artists
Awards:
• Arts Organizations Operational Grants (Grant)
• Arts Organizations Project Grants (Grant)
• Individual Artists Project Grants (Grant)
• Grant MacEwan Creative Writing Scholarship (Scholarship)
Amount: $5,000
• Queen's Golden Jubilee Scholarship for Performing Arts (Scholarship)
Amount: $5,000
• Queen's Golden Jubilee Scholarship for Visual Arts (Scholarship)
Amount: $5,000
• Film & Video Arts Scholarship (Scholarship)
Amount: $5,000

Alberta Freestyle Ski Association (AFSA)

88 Canada Olympic Rd., Calgary AB T3B 5R5
Tel: 403-297-2718; *Fax:* 403-202-2522
info@abfreestyle.com
www.abfreestyle.com
www.facebook.com/AlbertaFreestyleSkiingAssociation
twitter.com/ABFreestyleSki
Overview: A small provincial charitable organization founded in 1990 overseen by Canadian Freestyle Ski Association
Mission: To develop & coordinate the sport of freestyle skiing in Alberta
Member of: Canadian Freestyle Ski Association
Chief Officer(s):

Dan Bowman, Chair
DBowman@shaw.ca
Paulo Kapronczai, Vice-Chair
deekorber@shaw.ca
Dan Jefferies, Treasurer
djefferies@bdo.ca
Maureen Calder, Executive Director
Finances: *Funding Sources:* Sponsorships
Activities: Promoting freestyle skiing at all levels in Alberta; Supporting the high performance Alberta Mogul Team & the Alberta Park & Pipe Team; Offering judges' clinics
Publications:
• Alberta Freestyle Skiing Association Newsletter
Type: Newsletter
Profile: Upcoming events, association updates, & club news

Alberta Friends of Schizophrenics ***See*** Schizophrenia Society of Alberta

Alberta Friends of Schizophrenics ***See*** Schizophrenia Society of Alberta

Alberta Funeral Service Association (AFSA)

3030 - 55 St., Red Deer AB T4P 3S6
Tel: 403-342-2460; *Fax:* 403-342-2495
Toll-Free: 800-803-8809
inquiry@afsa.ca
www.afsa.ca
Overview: A medium-sized provincial licensing organization founded in 1928
Mission: To promote & improve funeral service in Alberta
Affliation(s): Funeral Service Association of Canada
Chief Officer(s):
Deanna Schroeder, Executive Administrator
deanna@afsa.ca
Finances: *Annual Operating Budget:* $50,000-$100,000; *Funding Sources:* Membership fees
Staff Member(s): 1; 8 volunteer(s)
Membership: 95 corporate + 21 associate + 23 senior/lifetime + 225 individual; *Fees:* Schedule available; *Committees:* Consumer Relations; National; Legal; Education; Peacetime Emergency Response
Activities: *Library* by appointment

Alberta Funeral Services Regulatory Board (AFSRB)

11810 Kingsway Ave., Edmonton AB T5G 0X5
Tel: 780-452-6130; *Fax:* 780-452-6085
Toll-Free: 800-563-4652
office@afsrb.ab.ca
www.afsrb.ab.ca
Overview: A small provincial organization founded in 1992
Mission: To establish educational standards for the provision of funeral services in Alberta; To set & maintain ethical standards for the funeral services business in the province; To license pre-need salespeople, funeral directors, funeral businesses, embalmers, & crematories in Alberta; To act in accordance with the Alberta Funeral Services Act
Chief Officer(s):
Marilyn McPherson, Administrator
Marion Wombold, Chair
Peter Portlock, Vice-Chair
Kathy Bruce-Kavanagh, Treasurer
Membership: *Committees:* Education; Complaints
Activities: Monitoring the performance of funeral services in Alberta; Investigating consumer complaints
Publications:
• Alberta Funeral Services Regulatory Board Annual Report
Type: Yearbook; *Frequency:* Annually
• Alberta Funeral Services Regulatory Board Newsletter
Type: Newsletter

Alberta Galloway Association

RR#1, Red Deer AB T4N 5E1
Tel: 403-227-3428; *Fax:* 406-227-3423
www.albertagalloway.ca
Overview: A small provincial organization
Mission: To promote Galloway, White Galloway & Belted Galloway cattle in the use of sustainable agriculture; to encourage improvements in the performance of the Galloway family of cattle
Member of: Canadian Galloway Association
Chief Officer(s):
Bonnie Schweer, Secretary
schweer@xplornet.com
Membership: 27; *Fees:* $60 regular; $30 associate; $10 junior; *Member Profile:* Farmers, ranchers & other Galloway breeders; *Committees:* Advertising & Promotion; 4H - Shows - Sales; Finance
Activities: Promotion of Galloways, White Galloways & Belted Galloways

Alberta Genealogical Society (AGS)

#162, 14315 - 118 Ave., Edmonton AB T5L 4S6
Tel: 780-424-4429; *Fax:* 780-423-8980
agsoffice@abgensoc.ca
abgensoc.ca
www.facebook.com/122764957754850
Overview: A medium-sized provincial organization founded in 1973
Mission: To promote the study of genealogy in Alberta
Member of: The Federation of Family History Societies
Chief Officer(s):
Les Campbell, President
Susan Haga, 1st Vice-President
Maxine Maxwell, 2nd Vice-President
Jock Howard, Vice-President, Finance
Mary Ann Legris, Secretary
Linda Winski, Office Coordinator
Finances: *Funding Sources:* Grants; Fundraising
Membership: *Fees:* $50 individual & family; $45 senior individual & family; *Committees:* Finance; Nominations; Archives; Bylaws, Policies, & Procedures; Communications & Public Relations; Conference; Grants & Fundraising; History; Inventory & Property; Library; Master Surname Database; Membership; Publications; Relatively Speaking; Research; Translations; Treasury; Website; Facilities; Gaming; Policies & Procedures
Activities: Encouraging genealogical research in Alberta; Organizing workshops; Facilitating networking opportunities; Conducting research in response to queries; Recording cemeteries; Indexing; Enabling access to databases, such as Index to Alberta Homestead Records - 1870 to 1930 & Index to Alberta Homestead Records - post 1930, through the AGS website; *Library:* Alberta Genealogical Society Library;
Publications:
• Alberta Index to Registrations of Birth, Marriages, & Deaths 1870 - 1905
Number of Pages: 648; *Price:* $48
Profile: Registrations in the years before Alberta became a province
• Alberta Sources
Profile: Listings of Alberta cemeteries
• Relatively Speaking
Type: Newsletter; *Frequency:* Quarterly; *Editor:* Marilyn Hindmarch; Peter Staveley; *Price:* Free with Alberta Genealogical Society membership
Profile: Genealogical research in Canada, sources, research methods, library news, book reviews, & personal experiences

Brooks - Brooks & District Branch
PO Box 1538, Brooks AB T1R 1C4
Tel: 403-362-8642
info@agsbrooks.com
www.agsbrooks.com
Chief Officer(s):
Robert Franz, President
Eileen French, Vice-President
Karyn Norden, Treasurer
Carol Anderson, Secretary
• B & D Heir Lines
Type: Newsletter; *Frequency:* Semiannually; *Price:* $2.50

Camrose - Camrose Branch
4310 - 50 Ave., Camrose AB T4V 0R3
Tel: 780-608-6243
camrose@abgenealogy.ca
camrose.abgensoc.ca
Chief Officer(s):
Janine Carroll, President
Adele Goa, Secretary
Sharon Olsen, Treasurer
• Roots 'N Shoots
Type: Newsletter; *Frequency:* Semiannually; *Editor:* Norm Prestage & Jack Cunningham
Profile: Branch happenings

Drayton Valley Branch
PO Box 115, Rocky Rapids AB T0E 1Z0
Tel: 780-542-2787
ags.dvbranch@gmail.com
www.abgenealogy.ca
www.facebook.com/DraytonValleyBranchAlbertaGenealogicalSociety
Chief Officer(s):
Connie Stuhl, President
• Past Finder
Type: Newsletter; *Frequency:* Quarterly

Edmonton - Edmonton Branch
#162, 14315 - 118 Ave., Edmonton AB T5L 4S6
Tel: 780-424-4429; *Fax:* 780-423-8980
edmontonbranchags@gmail.com
www.agsedm.edmonton.ab.ca
Chief Officer(s):
Lynne Duigou, President
• Clandigger
Type: Newsletter; *Frequency:* 9 pa

Fort McMurray - Fort McMurray Branch
10011 Franklin Ave., Fort McMurray AB T9H 2K7
Tel: 780-791-5663
ftmacgen@telus.net
www.rootsweb.ancestry.com/~abfmags
Chief Officer(s):
Tammy Grantham, President
tgrant@shaw.ca
Laverne Cormier, Vice-President
blcormier@shaw.ca
Bobbie Driscoll, Secretary
BobbieD@shaw.ca
Cathy Marriott, Treasurer
we4rher@shaw.ca
• Lines of Descent
Type: Newsletter; *Frequency:* Quarterly; *Price:* Free with Fort McMurray Branch membership

Grande Prairie - Grande Prairie & District Branch
PO Box 1257, Grande Prairie AB T8V 2Z1
e-mail: gp@abgenealogy.ca
www.gp.abgensoc.ca
Chief Officer(s):
Jean Gray, President
Carol Thomson, Treasurer
• Heritage Seekers
Type: Newsletter; *Frequency:* Quarterly *ISSN:* 0707-0708
Profile: Information from historical sources in the Peace Country, genealogical articles, & member news

Lethbridge - Lethbridge & District Branch
#128, 909 - 3rd Ave. North, Lethbridge AB T1H 0H5
Tel: 403-328-9564
lethags@theboss.net
lethbridgeags.theboss.net
Mission: To promote genealogy in the Lethbridge area; to maintain standards in genealogy
Chief Officer(s):
Doug McLeod, President
Susan Haga, Vice-President
Alma Berridge, Secretary
Pat Barry, Treasurer
• Yesterday's Footprints
Type: Newsletter; *Frequency:* 3 pa

Medicine Hat - Medicine Hat & District Branch
Hillside Monumental Bldg., 974 - 13th Ave. SW, Medicine Hat AB T1A 7G8
Tel: 403-526-1163
mhgs@telus.net
mhdgs.ca
Mission: To promote the search for family history in the Medicine Hat area
Chief Officer(s):
Doreen Schank, President
Leanne Balfour, Secretary
Kathy Gleisner, Treasurer
• The Saamis Seeker
Type: Newsletter; *Frequency:* 3 pa; *Editor:* Barb Dewald; *Price:* Free with Medicine Hat & District Branch membership

Peace River - Peace River & District Branch
9807 - 97 Ave., Peace River AB T8S 1H6
Tel: 780-624-3269
www.rootsweb.ancestry.com/~abprdgs/index.html
Chief Officer(s):
Joan Wahl, President
Linda Chmielewski, Secretary-Treasurer
• Echoes of the Past
Type: Newsletter

Red Deer - Red Deer & District Branch
PO Box 922, Red Deer AB T4N 5H3
Tel: 403-347-1826
www.rdgensoc.ab.ca
Chief Officer(s):
Diane Lehr, President

Joan Shortt, Secretary
Vic Willouby, Treasurer
• The Tree Climber
Type: Newsletter; *Frequency:* Quarterly; *Editor:* Jim Coutts; *Price:* Free with Red Deer & District Branch membership

Wetaskiwin - Wetaskiwin Branch
RR#1, Site 10, Box 18, Millet AB T0C 1Z0
Tel: 780-387-4978
wetaskiwin@abgenealogy.ca
www.wetaskiwin.abgensoc.ca
Mission: To promote family history searches in the Wetaskiwin area
Chief Officer(s):
Diane Strohschein, President
blueeyes.ds23@gmail.com
Elaine Young, Vice-President
elaineyou@telus.net
Alice Hoyle, Secretary/Treasurer
alihoy@xplornet.com
• Roots & Branches
Type: Newsletter; *Frequency:* 3 pa; *Editor:* Claudia Malloch

Alberta Gerontological Nurses Association (AGNA)
PO Box 67040, Stn. Meadowlark, Edmonton AB T5R 5Y3
e-mail: info@agna.ca
www.agna.ca
twitter.com/AGNAtweets
Overview: A medium-sized provincial organization founded in 1981 overseen by Canadian Gerontological Nursing Association
Mission: To promote a high standard of nursing care & related health services for older adults; To enhance professionalism in the practice of gerontological nursing
Chief Officer(s):
Lynne Moulton, President
president@agna.ca
Membership: *Fees:* $35 associate; $45 student; $67.50 RPN/LPN; $75 RN/NP; *Member Profile:* Nurses interested in gerontology; *Committees:* Advocacy & Political Action
Activities: Offering professional networking opportunities; Providing professional development; Advocating for comprehensive services for older adults; Supporting research related to gerontological nursing; Promoting gerontological nursing to the public
Meetings/Conferences: • Alberta Gerontological Nurses Association Annual Conference & AGM 2015, 2015, AB
Scope: Provincial
Publications:
• AGNA [Alberta Gerontological Nurses Association] Newsletter
Type: Newsletter; *Frequency:* Quarterly; *Editor:* Debbie Lee

Alberta Golf Association (AGA)
#22, 11410 - 27 St. SE, Calgary AB T2Z 3R6
Tel: 403-236-4616; *Fax:* 403-236-2915
Toll-Free: 888-414-4849
info@albertagolf.org
www.albertagolf.org
www.facebook.com/144026188016
twitter.com/AGinthenews
Overview: A medium-sized provincial organization founded in 1912 overseen by Royal Canadian Golf Association
Mission: To fulfill the needs of members
Chief Officer(s):
Brent Ellenton, Executive Director, 403-680-3034
brent@albertagolf.org
Finances: *Funding Sources:* Membership fees; Fundraising; Sponsorships
Staff Member(s): 8
Membership: 57,000 individual + 225 clubs; *Fees:* Schedule available; *Member Profile:* Organized golf clubs in Alberta & member golfers
Activities: *Speaker Service:* Yes; *Library* Open to public by appointment

Alberta Gravel Truckers Association ***See*** Alberta Construction Trucking Association

Alberta Greenhouse Growers Association (AGGA)
#200, 10331 - 178 St., Edmonton AB T5S 1R5
Tel: 780-489-1991; *Fax:* 780-444-2152
www.agga.ca
Overview: A small provincial organization
Mission: To strengthen the greenhouse growing industry in Alberta; To act as the voice of the industry, in areas such as taxation, natural gas rebates, disaster relief, & electricity costs
Chief Officer(s):
Michiel Verheul, President, 780-939-7490
Albert Cramer, Vice-President, 403-526-3059
Carol Maier, Secretary, 780-467-5784
Dietrich Kuhlmann, Treasurer, 780-475-7500
Membership: *Fees:* $27.30 students; $54.60 associates & individuals; $168 growers; $180.60 allied trades people; $105 new member; *Member Profile:* Growers; Allied trades people; Educators; Students; Individuals with an interest in horticulture
Activities: Promoting the greenhouse growing industry in Alberta; Providing workshops & seminars; Conducting research; Liaising with related organizations, such as the Canadian Horticultural Council & the Alberta Professional Horticultural Growers Congress Foundation; Increasing cooperation; Assisting members in marketing
Awards:
• Alberta Greenhouse Growers Association Scholarship (Scholarship)
Eligibility: Awarded to the child of an AGGA grower member *Amount:* $500
• Herb Knodel Award (Award)
Eligibility: Awarded to a grower who has made a major contribution to the industry
• Meritorious Service Award (Award)
Eligibility: Awarded to people who are not growers, but who have contributed to the industry, mainly in terms of research
• Grower of the Year Award (Award)
Publications:
• Alberta Greenhouse Growers Association Newsletter
Type: Newsletter; *Frequency:* Quarterly; *Editor:* Peter Johnston-Berresford
Profile: Association activities, & greenhouse growing industry research, developments, & policy
• Regional Crop Reports

Alberta Gymnastics Federation (AGF)
#207, 5800 - 2 St. SW, Calgary AB T2H 0H2
Tel: 403-259-5500; *Fax:* 403-259-5588
Toll-Free: 800-665-1010
www.abgym.ab.ca
www.facebook.com/AlbertaGymnastics
twitter.com/agf_comm
www.youtube.com/albertagymnastics;
flickr.com/photos/albertagymnastics
Overview: A medium-sized provincial organization founded in 1971
Mission: To operate as the governing body of gymnastics in Alberta; To provide administrative support in the development & delivery of programs & competitions in recreational gymnastics, national coaching certification programs, women's artistic gymnastics, trampoline & tumbling, men's artistic gymnastics, & special events
Chief Officer(s):
Scott Hayes, President & CEO
shayes@abgym.ab.ca
Staff Member(s): 10
Membership: 75 member clubs; *Committees:* Women's Program; Women's Program Judging; Trampoline & Tumbling Technical; Men's Technical; Recreational Development

Alberta Handball Association (AHA)
AB
www.albertahandball.com
www.facebook.com/groups/2390949216
Overview: A small provincial organization
Mission: To promote & develop the sport of handball in Alberta
Activities: Operates three clubs: Calgary, Edmonton & Sherwood Park

Alberta Hereford Association (AHA)
PO Box 570, Hardisty AB T0B 1V0
Tel: 780-888-2813
info@albertaherefords.com
www.albertaherefords.com
Overview: A medium-sized provincial licensing organization founded in 1971
Mission: To promote the benefits of Hereford genetics commercial ranchers & farmers, feedlots, & auction markets; To gather feedback on Hereford cattle
Member of: Canadian Hereford Association
Affliation(s): Calgary District Hereford Club; Central Alberta Hereford Club; East Central Hereford Club; Northern Alberta Hereford Club; Peace River Hereford Club; Southern Alberta Hereford Club
Chief Officer(s):
Nels Nixdorff, President, 403-510-2771
nnixdorff@efirehose.net
Gordon Klein, Vice-President, 403-628-3249
wildcat@jrtwave.com
Leonard Poholka, Executive Director, 780-696-3878
bretonw@telus.net
Membership: 650; *Member Profile:* Alberta seedstock producers who raise purebred Hereford cattle for the commercial industry

Alberta Heritage Foundation for Medical Research ***See*** Alberta Innovates - Health Solutions

Alberta Historical Resources Foundation (AHRF)
Old St. Stephen's College, 8820 - 112 St., Edmonton AB T6G 2P8
Tel: 780-431-2300; *Fax:* 780-427-5598
culture.alberta.ca/ahrf/default.aspx
Overview: A medium-sized provincial organization founded in 1976
Mission: To assist in the preservation of Alberta's historic sites, buildings & objects; to encourage & promote public awareness of the province's past; grants are awarded in the spring & fall at each year to a wide variety of community-based heritage initiatives
Chief Officer(s):
David Link, Director
david.link@gov.ab.ca
Finances: *Annual Operating Budget:* $3 Million-$5 Million; *Funding Sources:* Alberta Lotteries
Staff Member(s): 3
Membership: *Committees:* Geographical Names
Activities: Alberta Main Street Programme; Heritage Preservation Grants; Heritage Awareness Grants
Awards:
• Heritage Awards (Award)
Established in 1981 to stimulate awareness & recognize outstanding contributions to the preservation of Alberta's past
• Roger Soderstrom Scholarship in Historical Preservation (Scholarship)
Encourages professional development & advanced studies in the field of heritage conservation in Alberta; for university students at the graduate level in disciplines relating to heritage preservation & research, focussing on Alberta; includes studies in architectural restoration; area conservation & research preservation planning &/or interpretive development of archaeological, historical or palaeontological sites in the province, as well as related thematic work. *Eligibility:* Canadian citizen or landed immigrant & a resident of Alberta for at least six months prior to applying *Deadline:* February & September *Amount:* up to $3,000 *Contact:* Community Resources Officer

Alberta Home Education Association (AHEA)
AB
www.aheaonline.com
Overview: A small provincial organization
Mission: AHEA serves home schooling parents as needs arise, to support local groups of parents and individuals, and to interact with various levels of government to protect the responsibilities of parents.
Chief Officer(s):
Paul van den Bosch, President
president@aheaonline.com
Meetings/Conferences: • Alberta Home Education Association Convention 2015, April, 2015, AB
Scope: Provincial

Alberta Horse Trials Association (AHTA)
c/o Kristine Haut, RR#1, Blackie AB T0L 0J0
Tel: 403-681-0815
www.albertahorsetrials.com
Overview: A small provincial organization
Mission: To promote & develop 3-day eventing in Alberta & Canada & assist in producing Olympic athletes
Affliation(s): Canadian Equestrian Federation
Chief Officer(s):
Kristine Haut, President
kmhaut@gmail.com
Finances: *Annual Operating Budget:* Less than $50,000; *Funding Sources:* National Government, Provincial Government
13 volunteer(s)
Membership: 170 student; 240 individual; 20 associate; *Fees:* $30 associate; $60 junior; $70 senior; $140 family; *Committees:* Membership; Competitions; Special Events; Communications; Athlete Development; Clinics; Marketing

Alberta Horseshoe Pitchers Association (AHPA)
AB

Tel: 403-946-4109
www.albertahpa.com
Overview: A small provincial organization founded in 1977 overseen by Horseshoe Canada
Mission: To promote the sport of horseshoe pitching in Alberta.
Member of: Horseshoe Canada

Alberta Hospice Palliative Care Association (AHPCA)

#1245, 70 Ave. SE, Calgary AB T2H 2X8
Tel: 403-206-9938; *Fax:* 403-206-9958
director@ahpca.ca
ahpca.ca
www.facebook.com/AlbertaHospicePalliativeCare
twitter.com/AHPCA
www.youtube.com/watch?v=6Z3044hPlrl
Previous Name: Palliative Care Association of Alberta
Overview: A medium-sized provincial charitable organization
Mission: To engage in actions & strategies that result in comprehensive, equitable & quality end of life care for Albertans
Member of: Canadian Palliative Care Association
Chief Officer(s):
Terri Woytkiw, Chair
Leslie Penny, Treasurer
Jennifer Elliott, Executive Director
Theresa Bellows, Road Show Coordinator
Jon Angevine, Web Consultant
Finances: *Annual Operating Budget:* $100,000-$250,000; *Funding Sources:* Donations; 50/50 Draw; Silent Auction
Staff Member(s): 4; 50 volunteer(s)
Membership: 300; *Fees:* $45
Activities: Raising provincial awareness of palliative care within Alberta
Meetings/Conferences: • Alberta Hospice Palliative Care Association 2015 Imagine Conference, 2015, AB
Scope: Provincial
Publications:
• Alberta Hospice Palliative Care Association Newsletter
Type: Newsletter
Profile: Association highlights, including membership information & courses
• Alberta Hospice Palliative Care Association Volunteer Training Manual
Type: Manual
Profile: Information based upon the CHPCA Norms of Practice

Alberta Hotel & Lodging Association

2707 Ellwood Dr. SW, Edmonton AB T6X 0P7
Tel: 780-436-6112; *Fax:* 780-436-5404
Toll-Free: 888-436-6112
www.ahla.ca
www.linkedin.com/company/alberta-hotel-&-lodging-association
www.facebook.com/171333316227097
Overview: A medium-sized provincial organization founded in 1919 overseen by Hotel Association of Canada Inc.
Mission: To enhance the image, the quality & efficiency of the hotel industry in Alberta
Chief Officer(s):
Dave Kaiser, President & CEO
dkaiser@ahla.ca
Meetings/Conferences: • Alberta Hotel and Lodging Association 95th Annual Convention and Trade Show 2015, April, 2015, AB
Scope: Provincial

Alberta Innovates - Health Solutions

#1500, 10104 - 103 Ave., Edmonton AB T5J 4A7
Tel: 780-423-5727; *Fax:* 780-429-3509
Toll-Free: 877-423-5727
health@albertainnovates.ca
www.aihealthsolutions.ca
www.facebook.com/179968058752241?sk=wall
twitter.com/ABInnovates
www.youtube.com/user/AIHSChannel
Previous Name: Alberta Heritage Foundation for Medical Research
Overview: A small provincial organization founded in 1980
Mission: To support basic biomedical, clinical & health research in Alberta; contributes funds to scientific community to carry out research
Chief Officer(s):
Cyril (Cy) B. Frank, CEO
Kathleen Thurber, Director, Communications & Education
Finances: *Annual Operating Budget:* Greater than $5 Million
Staff Member(s): 35
Activities: *Library*

Alberta Insolvency Practitioners Association *See* Alberta Association of Insolvency & Restructuring Professionals

Alberta Institute of Agrologists

#1430, 5555 Calgary Trail NW, Edmonton AB T6H 5P9
Tel: 780-435-0606; *Fax:* 780-464-2155
Toll-Free: 855-435-0606
www.albertaagrologists.ca
Overview: A small provincial licensing organization founded in 1947 overseen by Agricultural Institute of Canada
Mission: To serve as a regulatory body within the province for matters related to agrology
Chief Officer(s):
Don Watson, Chair
David Lloyds, CEO & Registrar
Finances: *Funding Sources:* Membership fees
Membership: 2,500+; *Member Profile:* Professional Agrologists (P.Ag.); Articling Agrologists (A.Ag.)
Activities: In-training programs
Awards:
• Distinguished Agrologist Award (Award)
$1000/year to a University of Saskatchewan agrology student
• Outstanding Young Agrologist Award (Award)
• Professional Recognition Award (Award)
• Honorary Member Award (Award)
Publications:
• AIA [Alberta Institute of Agrologists] Bulletin
Profile: Events of interest to Agrologists
• News Update [a publication of the Alberta Institute of Agrologists]
Type: Newsletter
Profile: Update on Institute issues

Alberta Institute Purchasing Management Association of Canada *See* Supply Chain Management Association - Alberta

Alberta Insurance Council (AIC)

Bell Tower, #600, 10104 - 103rd Ave., Edmonton AB T5J 0H8
Tel: 780-421-4148; *Fax:* 780-425-5745
info@abcouncil.ab.ca
www.abcouncil.ab.ca
Overview: A small provincial organization
Mission: Regulatory body responsible for licensing and discipline of insurance agents, brokers and adjusters in the Province of Alberta
Chief Officer(s):
Ronald Gilbertson, Chair
Joanne Abram, Chief Executive Officer
jabram@abcouncil.ab.ca
Carolyn Janz, Chief Financial Officer
cjanz@abcouncil.ab.ca
Membership: *Committees:* Continuing Education

Calgary Office
#500, 222 - 58th Ave. SW, Calgary AB T2H 2S3
Tel: 403-233-2929; *Fax:* 403-233-2990
Chief Officer(s):
Tom Hampton, Chief Operating Officer
thampton@abcouncil.ab.ca

Alberta Irrigation Projects Association (AIPA)

#909, 400 - 4 Ave. South, Lethbridge AB T1K 7H5
Tel: 403-328-3063; *Fax:* 403-327-1043
info@aipa.org
www.aipa.org
Overview: A medium-sized provincial organization founded in 1946
Mission: To advance understanding of the value of irrigation to Alberta; To promote progressive water management practices
Affliation(s): Canadian Water Resources Association
Chief Officer(s):
Richard Phillips, Chair
Ron McMullin, Executive Director, 403-328-3063, Fax: 403-327-1043
ron.mcmullin@aipa.org
Vicky Kress, Administrator, 403-328-3063, Fax: 403-327-1043
vicky.kress@aipa.org
Membership: *Member Profile:* Incorporated Irrigation Districts in Alberta; Associate members; Honorary members
Activities: Participating in education & outreach activities; Developing policy; Researching; Providing information to federal, provincial, & local government officials, departments & agencies, water management stakeholders, members, the public, & the media; Promoting the benefits of Alberta's irrigations infrastructure; Developing partnerships

Alberta Katahdin Sheep Association

c/o Val Sebree, PO Box 43, Vegreville AB T9C 1R1
Tel: 780-658-2415
www.katahdinsheep.com
Overview: A small provincial organization overseen by Canadian Katahdin Sheep Association Inc.
Mission: To promote the Katahdin sheep breed in Alberta
Chief Officer(s):
Lynette Kreddig, President, 780-786-4754, Fax: 780-786-4754
lynette.kreddig@franklynfarm.ca
Michael King, Vice-President, 403-860-2289
michaelj.king@shaw.ca
Val Sebree, Secretary-Treasurer, 780-658-2415
Membership: *Member Profile:* Owners of Canadian registered Katahdin sheep in Alberta
Activities: Showing Katahdin sheep at various events; Providing information about the breed to members & the public

Alberta Lacrosse Association (ALA)

11759 Groat Rd., Edmonton AB T5M 3K6
Tel: 780-422-0030; *Fax:* 780-451-6414
Toll-Free: 866-696-7694
www.albertalacrosse.com
www.facebook.com/257864104242295
twitter.com/AlbertaLacrosse
Overview: A small provincial organization overseen by Canadian Lacrosse Association
Mission: To oversee the sport of lacrosse in the province of Alberta.
Member of: Canadian Lacrosse Association
Chief Officer(s):
Greg Lintz, President
greg@tarrabain.com
Lisa Grant, Executive Director
lisa@albertalacrosse.com

Alberta Lake Management Society (ALMS)

PO Box 4283, Edmonton AB T6E 4T3
Tel: 780-702-2567; *Fax:* 501-423-6381
info@alms.ca
www.alms.ca
www.facebook.com/176278492417652
twitter.com/AlbertaLake
Also Known As: Lakewatch
Overview: A small provincial charitable organization founded in 1991
Mission: To promote understanding & comprehensive management of lakes & reservoirs & their watersheds
Member of: North American Lake Management Society
Chief Officer(s):
Stephanie Neufeld, President
sneufeld@gmail.com
Sheldon Helbert, Vice-President
7shelbert7@gmail.com
Finances: *Annual Operating Budget:* Less than $50,000; *Funding Sources:* Government; workshops
16 volunteer(s)
Membership: 100+; *Fees:* $50 associations; $25 individual; $15 student; *Member Profile:* Private citizens; municipalities; government organizations
Activities: Water sampling; conservation & lake management; *Speaker Service:* Yes; *Library:* ALMS Library; by appointment
Awards:
• Alberta Lake Management Society Scholarship (Scholarship)
Eligibility: Graduate Student with Alberta research project relevant to managing lakes. *Amount:* $2000

Alberta Land Surveyors' Association (ALSA)

#1000, 10020 - 101A Ave., Edmonton AB T5J 3G2
Tel: 780-429-8805; *Fax:* 888-459-1664
Toll-Free: 800-665-2572
info@alsa.ab.ca
www.alsa.ab.ca
Overview: A medium-sized provincial organization founded in 1910 overseen by Professional Surveyors Canada
Mission: To regulate the practice of land surveying.
Chief Officer(s):
Brian Munday, Executive Director
munday@alsa.ab.ca
David McWilliam, Registrar
alsaregistrar@shaw.ca
Robert Scott, President
Bruce Clark, Secretary-Treasurer
Finances: *Funding Sources:* Membership fees; products
Staff Member(s): 9
Membership: *Fees:* $200 affiliate/articled pupil; $100 associate; *Committees:* Articling Process; Association Finances; Boundary Pane; Discipline; External Relations; Historical and Biographical;

Legislation; Practice Review Board; Professional Development; Registration; RST Implementation; Safety; Standards
Activities: *Library*
Meetings/Conferences: • Alberta Land Surveyors' Association 2015 Annual General Meeting, April, 2015, Fairmont Chateau Lake Louise, Lake Louise, AB
Scope: Provincial

Alberta Law Foundation (ALF)
#300, 407 - 8 Ave. SW, Calgary AB T2P 1E5
Tel: 403-264-4701; *Fax:* 403-294-9238
infoo@albertalawfoundation.org
www.albertalawfoundation.org
Overview: A medium-sized provincial charitable organization founded in 1973
Mission: To conduct research into & recommend reform of law & administration of justice; to establish, maintain & operate law libraries; to contribute to legal education & knowledge of people of Alberta; to provide assistance to Native people's legal & student programs
Affiliation(s): Association of Canadian Law Foundations
Chief Officer(s):
David Aucoin, Executive Director
daucoin@albertalawfoundation.org
Diana M. Porter, Administrative Assistant
dporter@albertalawfoundation.org
Finances: *Annual Operating Budget:* $100,000-$250,000
Staff Member(s): 2; 7 volunteer(s)

Alberta Law Reform Institute (ALRI)
402 Law Centre, University of Alberta, Edmonton AB T6G 2H5
Tel: 780-492-5291; *Fax:* 780-492-1790
reform@alri.ualberta.ca
www.alri.ualberta.ca
Overview: A small provincial organization founded in 1967
Mission: Dedicated to advancing just & effective laws through independent legal research, consultation & analysis
Chief Officer(s):
Peter Lown, Director, 780-492-3374, Fax: 780-492-1790
plown@alri.ualberta.ca
Staff Member(s): 10

Alberta Liberal Party
10247 - 124 St. NW, Edmonton AB T5N 1P8
Tel: 780-414-1124
office@albertaliberal.com
www.albertaliberal.com
www.facebook.com/ablib
www.twitter.com/abliberal
www.youtube.com/albertaliberalcaucus
Overview: A medium-sized provincial organization
Mission: To elect Liberals to the Legislative Assembly of Alberta; to enunciate & promote liberal principles & policies; to initiate & maintain effective electoral constituencies
Chief Officer(s):
Raj Sherman, Leader of the Party
Todd Van Vliet, President
Finances: *Funding Sources:* Donations
Staff Member(s): 5
Membership: Over 50,000; *Fees:* $10

Alberta Library Association *See* Library Association of Alberta

Alberta Library Trustees Association (ALTA)
#6-24, 7 Sir Winston Churchill Sq., Edmonton AB T5J 2V5
Tel: 780-761-2582; *Fax:* 866-419-1451
admin@librarytrustees.ab.ca
www.librarytrustees.ab.ca
twitter.com/librarytrustees
Overview: A small provincial organization founded in 1971
Mission: To act as the collective voice for library trustees in Alberta; To develop effective trustees
Chief Officer(s):
Heather Mayor, Executive Director
Dwight Nagel, President
president@librarytrustees.ab.ca
Kiann McNeill, Vice-President
kiann.mcneill@gmail.com
Kelly Aisenstat, Treasurer
kelly.aisenstat@gov.ab.ca
Finances: *Funding Sources:* Alberta Ministry of Municipal Affairs, Public Library Services
Membership: *Fees:* Schedule available, based upon population served; *Member Profile:* Library trustees, past & present; in the following areas & urban districts of Alberta: Peace, Yellowhead, Parkland, Marigold, Chinook Arch, Shortgrass, Metro Edmonton, Northern Lights, Edmonton, & Calgary; Public library supporters; *Committees:* Advocacy; Communication; Trustee Education; Finance & Administration
Activities: Providing education, including online modules, to members; Promoting effective library service; Engaging in advocacy activities; Presenting awards, such as the Lois Hole Award & the ALTA Award of Excellence
Meetings/Conferences: • Alberta Library Trustees Association 2015 Annual General Meeting, March, 2015, Lethbridge Lodge Hotel & Conference Centre, Lethbridge, AB
Scope: Provincial
Description: Financial statements, a proposed budget, nominations report, & special resolutions
Contact Information: Alberta Library Trustees Association Executive Director: Heather Mayor; President: Dwight Nagel, E-mail: mdnagel@telus.net; president@librarytrustees.ab.ca
• Alberta Library Trustees Association 2016 Annual General Meeting, 2016, AB
Scope: Provincial
Description: Financial statements, a proposed budget, nominations report, & special resolutions
Contact Information: Alberta Library Trustees Association Executive Director: Heather Mayor; President: Dwight Nagel, E-mail: mdnagel@telus.net; president@librarytrustees.ab.ca

Alberta Luge Association (ALA)
#201, BNTC, 88 Canada Olympic Rd. SW, Calgary AB T3B 5R5
Tel: 403-202-6570
admin@albertaluge.com
www.albertaluge.com
Overview: A small provincial organization founded in 1983
Mission: To ensure the continued successful growth of the sport of luge in Alberta through the development of its athletes, coaches & volunteers at the recreational & elite levels
Affiliation(s): Canadian Luge Association
Chief Officer(s):
Jason Hegerfeldt, Executive Director
Finances: *Annual Operating Budget:* $100,000-$250,000
Staff Member(s): 2; 150 volunteer(s)
Membership: 700; *Fees:* $10 single; $15 family

Alberta Magazine Publishers Association (AMPA)
#304, 1240 Kensington Rd. NW, Calgary AB T2N 3P7
Tel: 403-262-0081; *Fax:* 403-670-0492
ampa@albertamagazines.com
www.albertamagazines.com
www.facebook.com/group.php?gid=2332265624
twitter.com/albertamags
pinterest.com/albertamagazine
Overview: A medium-sized provincial organization
Mission: To sustain a healthy magazine industry in Alberta; to act as a voice for the province's magazine publishers
Chief Officer(s):
Suzanne Trudel, Executive Director
director@albertamagazines.com
Joyce Byrne, President
Chris Welner, Vice-President
Allan Lacey, Treasurer
Staff Member(s): 2
Membership: *Fees:* Schedule available; *Member Profile:* Creators, publishers, printers, & distributors of Alberta magazines
Activities: Promoting the magazine industry in Alberta; Engaging in advocacy activities; Providing professional assistance; Disseminating professional development resources; Offering bursaries to members to upgrade skills; Providing a subsidized intern program; Facilitating networking opportunities; Offering a one-on-one training program (Pros on the Road) & seminars; *Internships:* Yes
Meetings/Conferences: • 19th Annual Alberta Magazine Conference 2015, March, 2015, Calgary, AB
Scope: Provincial
Publications:
• Currents
Type: Newsletter; *Frequency:* 3 pa
Profile: Alberta Magazine Publishers Association updates
• MagaScene
Type: Newsletter; *Frequency:* Monthly; *Price:* Free
Profile: Magazine publishing industry news & events, plus profiles of member magazines

Alberta Maine-Anjou Association
PO Box 129, Derwent AB T0B 1C0
Tel: 780-741-2188
albertamaineanjou@hotmail.com
www.albertamaine-anjou.com
Overview: A small provincial organization
Affliation(s): Canadian Maine-Anjou Association
Chief Officer(s):
Kevin Shuckburgh, President, 403-742-6475
kshuck@telus.net
Robert Stenberg, Vice-President, 780-388-2182
rcstenb@gmail.com
Doug Roxburgh, Secretary, 403-748-4030
dunriteag@telus.net
Jean Renton, Treasurer, 780-789-3770
jeanr@jkrconcepts.com
Finances: *Funding Sources:* Sponsorships
Membership: 1-99; *Fees:* $50
Awards:
• Jack Lee Memorial Booster (Award)
• Commercial Cattleman Of The Year (Award)
Publications:
• The Maine Connection
Type: Newsletter; *Frequency:* Semiannually; *Accepts Advertising; Editor:* Ashley Shannon

Alberta Medical Association (AMA)
12230 - 106 Ave. NW, Edmonton AB T5N 3Z1
Tel: 780-482-2626; *Fax:* 780-482-5445
Toll-Free: 800-272-9680
amamail@albertadoctors.org
www.albertadoctors.org
Overview: A medium-sized provincial organization founded in 1905 overseen by Canadian Medical Association
Mission: To advocate on behalf of its physician members; to provide leadership & support for their role in the provision of quality health care
Chief Officer(s):
R. Michael Giuffre, President
Michael A. Gormley, Executive Director
michael.gormley@albertadoctors.org
Cameron N. Plitt, Chief Financial Officer
cameron.plitt@albertadoctors.org
Finances: *Annual Operating Budget:* $3 Million-$5 Million
Membership: 4,400
Activities: *Library*

Alberta Men's Wear Agents Association
PO Box 66037, Stn. Heritage, Edmonton AB T6J 6T4
Tel: 780-455-1881; *Fax:* 780-455-3969
amwa@shaw.ca
www.trendsapparel.com
Previous Name: Alberta Fashion Market
Overview: A medium-sized provincial organization overseen by Canadian Association of Wholesale Sales Representatives
Chief Officer(s):
Ken Melnychuk, President, 780-483-7505
Sue Brochu, Secretary-Treasurer, 780-455-1881
Activities: Sponsoring The Apparel Show, involving wholesale sales representatives showing men's, ladies', children's, work, & western wear
Meetings/Conferences: • TRENDS: The Apparel Show 2015 (sponsored by the Alberta Men's Wear Agents Association), March, 2015, Edmonton Expo Centre, Edmonton, AB
Scope: Provincial
Description: Wholesale sales representatives present men's, ladies', children's, sports, work, & western wear, as well as shoe lines
Contact Information: E-mail: amwa@shaw.ca
• TRENDS: The Apparel Show 2015 (sponsored by the Alberta Men's Wear Agents Association), September, 2015, Edmonton Expo Centre, Edmonton, AB
Scope: Provincial
Description: An event, held twice each year, featuring approximately 250 sales representatives
Contact Information: E-mail: amwa@shaw.ca
• TRENDS: The Apparel Show 2016 (sponsored by the Alberta Men's Wear Agents Association), March, 2016, Edmonton Expo Centre, Edmonton, AB
Scope: Provincial
Description: Items from more than 1,500 manufacturers are shown by 250 sales representatives
Contact Information: E-mail: amwa@shaw.ca
• TRENDS: The Apparel Show 2016 (sponsored by the Alberta Men's Wear Agents Association), September, 2016, Edmonton Expo Centre, Edmonton, AB
Scope: Provincial
Description: A semiannual show involving the participation of wholesale sales representatives showing clothing & shoes
Contact Information: E-mail: amwa@shaw.ca

Alberta Metallic Silhouette Association
2306 - 22nd St. South, Lethbridge AB T1K 2K2
Tel: 403-327-7552
www.absilhouetteassoc.ca
Overview: A small provincial charitable organization founded in 1977
Mission: The association seeks to promote & advance the sport of metallic silhouette shooting. It is the governing body for Rifle Metallic Silhouette Target Shooting in Alberta and as such, it sanctions matches for the following disciplines: small bore rifle, high power rifle, small bore hunting rifle, high power hunting rifle, as well as black powder cartridge rifle.
Affiliation(s): Shooting Federation of Canada; Alberta Federation of Shooting Sports
Chief Officer(s):
Ralph Oler, President
president@silhouette-alberta.org
Kathy Oler, Sec.-Treas.
secretary@silhouette-alberta.org
Finances: *Annual Operating Budget:* Less than $50,000; *Funding Sources:* Provincial government
20 volunteer(s)
Membership: 106 individual; *Fees:* $20 individual; $25 family; $60 club

Alberta Milk
1303 - 91 St. SW, Edmonton AB T6X 1H1
Tel: 780-453-5942; *Fax:* 780-455-2196
Toll-Free: 877-361-1231
cblatz@albertamilk.com
www.albertamilk.com
www.facebook.com/MoreAboutMilk
twitter.com/MoreAboutMilk
www.youtube.com/user/albertamilk
Previous Name: Dairy Nutrition Council of Alberta
Overview: A small provincial organization founded in 2002
Mission: To promote the sustainability of the dairy industry in Alberta
Affiliation(s): Dairy Farmers of Canada
Chief Officer(s):
Bill Feenstra, Chair, 403-335-9290
Gerald Weiss, Executive Director, 403-527-0063
Mike Southwood, General Manager, 780-577-3300
msouthwood@albertamilk.com
Denise Brattinga, Manager, Finance, 780-577-3320
dbrattinga@albertamilk.com
Ray Grapentine, Manager, Industry & Member Services, 780-577-3313
rgrapentine@albertamilk.com
Katherine Loughlin, Manager, Market Development, 780-577-3326
kloughlin@albertamilk.com
Gerd Andres, Manager, Policy & Transportation, 780-577-3308
gandres@albertamilk.com
Membership: *Member Profile:* Milk producers of Alberta; *Committees:* Executive; Animal Health & Environment Advisory; Canadian Milk Supply Management; Corporate Affairs; Dairy Advisory; Dairy Farmers of Canada; Finance; Market Development Advisory; Milk Quality, Component & Measurement Advisory; Research & Extension Advisory; Transportation Advisory; Western Milk Pool Coordinating
Activities: Providing industry-specific information to producers, such as Canadian Quality Milk & production reports; Offering nutritional & educational resources to the public; Supporting research
Publications:
• Alberta Milk Annual Report
Type: Yearbook; *Frequency:* Annually
• Alberta Milk Producer Handbook
Type: Handbook
• Milking Times
Type: Newsletter; *Frequency:* Monthly; *Accepts Advertising*; *Number of Pages:* 12
Profile: Information for Alberta's dairy producers & their industry partners

Alberta Modern Pentathlon Association *See* Pentathlon Alberta

Alberta Motion Picture Industries Association (AMPIA)
#318, 8944 - 182 St. NW, Edmonton AB T5T 2E3
Tel: 780-944-0707; *Fax:* 780-426-3057
Toll-Free: 800-814-7779
info@ampia.org
www.ampia.org
twitter.com/yourampia
Overview: A medium-sized provincial organization founded in 1973
Mission: To develop & sustain the motion picture industry indigenous to Alberta
Chief Officer(s):
Josh Miller, President
Camille Beaudoin, Director
Finances: *Annual Operating Budget:* $100,000-$250,000
Membership: 500-999; *Fees:* Schedule available, $99-$550; *Member Profile:* Those involved in the production of motion pictures & television; *Committees:* Alberta Film & Television Awards; Alberta Industry Study; AMPIA Directory; Broadcast; Corporate Sponsorship; Financial/Fundraising; Government Grants; Government Relations; International Marketing; Labour Relations; Membership Revenue; Professional Development
Activities: *Internships:* Yes; *Library* Open to public
Awards:
• Friend of the Industry Award (Award)
Presented annually to an individual who has made a significant difference in assisting Alberta producers achieving their goals
• Lifetime Achievement Award (Award)
Presented annually to a Canadian who has achieved outstanding international success over many years in film & television industry
• David Billington Awards (Award)
Award to an Albertan who, over many years, has made an outstanding contribution to the film & television industry in Alberta
• Alberta Film & Television Awards (Award)
Annual awards established in 1973; "Rosies" presented to Albertans responsible for creating outstanding film & television works; presentation alternates between Calgary & Edmonton

Alberta Motor Association (AMA)
PO Box 8180, Stn. South, Edmonton AB T6H 5X9
Tel: 780-430-5555
www.ama.ab.ca
Overview: A medium-sized provincial organization overseen by Canadian Automobile Association
Affiliation(s): American Automobile Association
Chief Officer(s):
Tania Willumsen, Chair
Don Smitten, President
Membership: 745,000

Alberta Motor Transport Association (AMTA)
#1, 285005 Wrangler Way, Rocky View AB T1X 0K3
Fax: 403-243-4610
Toll-Free: 800-267-1003
amtamsc@amta.ca
www.amta.ca
Merged from: Alberta Trucking Industry Safety Association; Alberta Trucking Association
Overview: A medium-sized provincial organization overseen by Canadian Trucking Alliance
Mission: To take a leadership role in fostering a healthy, vibrant industry
Member of: Canadian Council of Motor Transport Administrators
Chief Officer(s):
Don Wilson, Executive Director, 403-214-3429
Lorri Christensen, Director, Partners in Compliance, 403-214-3430
Peter Vaudry, Director, Corporate Services, 403-214-3438
Kathleen Brown, Administrator, Registration & Certificates, 403-214-3437
William Raccah, Administrator, Program Development, 403-214-3428
250 volunteer(s)
Membership: 12,000; *Member Profile:* All sectors of the highway transportation industry; *Committees:* Injury Reduction & Training; Compliance & Regulatory Affairs; Member Services
Meetings/Conferences: • Alberta Motor Transport Association 2015 Annual General Meeting & Conference, May, 2015, Chateau Lake Louise Hotel, Banff, AB
Scope: Provincial
Description: An event for transportation leaders to learn about the latest issues facing the industry & to set the direction for the association for the upcoming year
Contact Information: E-mail: amtamsc@amta.ca

Alberta Municipal Clerks Association (AMCA)
c/o City of Spruce Grove, 315 Jespersen Dr., Spruce Grove AB T7X 3E8
Tel: 780-962-7634
communications@albertamunicipalclerks.com
www.albertamunicipalclerks.com
Previous Name: City Clerks & Election Officers Association
Overview: A medium-sized provincial organization founded in 1975
Mission: To provide a forum for exchange of ideas among the municipal clerks of the municipalities of Alberta; to provide a means for presentation of suggested amendments in legislation to senior government; to work in conjunction with any other organization, having as its objective the betterment of administration of local government
Chief Officer(s):
Doug Tymchyshyn, President
dtymchyshyn@parklandcounty.com
Finances: *Annual Operating Budget:* Less than $50,000
35 volunteer(s)
Membership: 35; *Fees:* $125; *Member Profile:* City status

Alberta Museums Association
#404, 10408, 124 St., Edmonton AB T5N 1R5
Tel: 780-424-2626; *Fax:* 780-425-1679
info@museums.ab.ca
www.museums.ab.ca
Also Known As: Museums Alberta
Overview: A medium-sized provincial charitable organization founded in 1971
Mission: To promote understanding, access & excellence within Alberta's museums for the benefit of society
Member of: Canadian Museums Association
Chief Officer(s):
Bill Peters, President
Finances: *Annual Operating Budget:* $1.5 Million-$3 Million; *Funding Sources:* Alberta Lottery Fund; Canadian Heritage; membership fees; donations
Staff Member(s): 8; 30 volunteer(s)
Membership: 450 individual + 230 institutional; *Fees:* Schedule available; *Member Profile:* Associations & institutions interested in preservation & interpretation of Alberta's natural & cultural heritage; historical societies, museums & historic houses; botanical gardens, zoological parks, aquaria & planetaria; art galleries & exhibit centres; *Committees:* Awards; Conference
Activities: Professional development & training; museums advisory service; grants programs; *Internships:* Yes
Awards:
• Individual Awards (Award)
• Institutional Awards (Award)
Meetings/Conferences: • Alberta Museums Association 2015 Annual Conference, 2015
Scope: Provincial
Attendance: 250+

Alberta Music Festival Association
Alberta College, Edmonton AB
Tel: 780-633-3725
info@albertamusicfestival.org
www.albertamusicfestival.org
Overview: A medium-sized provincial organization founded in 1963 overseen by Federation of Canadian Music Festivals
Mission: To coordinate, regulate & assist activities of local Alberta festivals of music & speech arts; to encourage formation of additional local festivals
Chief Officer(s):
Norma Jean Atkinson, President, 780-743-5053
president@albertamusicfestival.org
Wendy Durieux, Provincial Administrator, 403-556-3038
abfest@albertamusicfestival.org
Finances: *Annual Operating Budget:* $50,000-$100,000
Membership: 35 institutional

Alberta Music Industry Association (AMIA)
Western Supplies Bldg., #102, 10722 - 103rd Ave., Edmonton AB T5J 5G7
Tel: 780-428-3372; *Fax:* 780-426-0188
Toll-Free: 800-465-3117
info@amia.ca
www.amia.ca
www.facebook.com/albertamusic
twitter.com/Alberta_Music
Overview: A medium-sized provincial organization
Mission: To help music professionals succeed by providing professional development, education, mentoring & training opportunities; to lobby government agencies in support of the music industry; to conduct fundraising & sponsorship activities
Chief Officer(s):
Glen Erickson, Chair

Chris Wynters, Executive Director
chris@amia.ca
Carly Klassen, Program Manager
carly@amia.ca

Alberta Native Friendship Centres Association (ANFCA)
10336 - 121 St., Edmonton AB T5N 1K8
Tel: 780-423-3138; *Fax:* 780-425-6277
www.anfca.com
Overview: A medium-sized provincial organization overseen by National Association of Friendship Centres
Mission: To assist friendship centres in communication, funding & training
Chief Officer(s):
S. Graystone, Fund Development Officer

Alberta Native Plant Council (ANPC)
PO Box 52099, Stn. Garneau Postal Outlet, Edmonton AB T6G 2T5
www.anpc.ab.ca
Overview: A small provincial organization founded in 1987
Mission: To increase knowledge of native plants in Alberta among individuals, government, & industry; To conserve Alberta's native plant species
Membership: *Fees:* $10 students & seniors; $15 individuals; $25 families; $50 corporate memberships; $500 lifetime memberships; *Member Profile:* Individuals interested in ecology, natural history, conservation, photography, drawing, & hiking; *Committees:* Education & Information; Rare Plants; Reclamation & Horticulture; Conservation Action
Activities: Promoting awareness of native plant issues; Organizing field trips & species counts; Developing collection, salvage, & management guidelines; Providing information about uses for native plants; Awarding grants
Publications:
• Alberta Native Plant Council Guidelines on Plant Recues
• Alberta Native Plant Council Guidelines for Rare Plant Surveys in Alberta
• Alberta Native Plant Council Guidelines for the Purchase & Use of Wildflower Seed Mixes
• Dandelion Recipes: 34 great recipes for salads, jellies, beverages, & appetizers!

• IRIS: The Alberta Native Plant Council Newsletter
Type: Newsletter; *Frequency:* 3-4 pa; *Price:* Free with Alberta Native Plant Council membership
Profile: ANPC activities, articles, & plant happenings
• Plant Collection Guidelines for Horticultural Use of Native Plants
• Plant Collection Guidelines for Researchers, Students, & Consultants
• Plant Collection Guidelines for Wildcrafters

Alberta Natural History Society *See* Red Deer River Naturalists

Alberta Netball Association *See* Netball Alberta

Alberta Neurosurgical Society
c/o Southern Alberta Office, Alberta Medical Association, #350, 708 - 11 Ave. SW, Calgary AB T2R 0E4
Tel: 403-266-3533; *Fax:* 403-269-3538
Toll-Free: 866-830-1274
Overview: A small provincial organization founded in 1947
Affliation(s): Alberta Medical Association
Chief Officer(s):
John H. Wong, President
jwong@ucalgary.ca
18 volunteer(s)
Membership: *Member Profile:* Neurosurgeons in Alberta
Activities: *Speaker Service:* Yes

Alberta Northern Lights Wheelchair Basketball Society
Go Center, University of Alberta, #2-209, 11610 - 65 Ave., Edmonton AB T6G 2E1
e-mail: programs@albertanorthernlights.com
www.albertanorthernlights.com
www.facebook.com/172864392765380
Overview: A medium-sized provincial charitable organization founded in 1976
Mission: To develop health, fitness, & sport for men, women, & children with physical disabilities
Chief Officer(s):
Neil Feser, Manager, Program

Alberta Occupational Health Nurses Association (AOHNA)
c/o College & Association of Registered Nurses of Alberta (CARNA), 11620 - 168 St., Edmonton AB T5M 4A6
Fax: 866-877-0228
Toll-Free: 888-566-3343
info@aohna.ab.ca
www.aohna.ab.ca
Overview: A small provincial organization founded in 1977
Mission: To promote healthy work environments
Member of: College & Association of Registered Nurses of Alberta (CARNA)
Affliation(s): Canadian Occupational Health Nurses Association
Chief Officer(s):
Cathy Sobuliak, President
president@aohna.ab.ca
Gail Ramsden, Secretary
Joanne McCusker, Treasurer
treasurer@aohna.ab.ca
Membership: *Fees:* $75 active memberships; $40 associate memberships; *Member Profile:* Occupational health nurses employed in Alberta
Activities: Protecting the health of workers; Preventing occupational injuries & illnesses; Providing educational & networking opportunities; *Awareness Events:* North American Occupational Safety & Health (NAOSH) Week, May
Awards:
• Ruptash-Mandryk Nurse of the Year Award (Award)
Deadline: March 31
• Chapter- Exemplary Service Award (Award)
Deadline: February 28
• Years of Dedicated Service Award (Award)
Deadline: February 28
• Promising Performer Award (Award)
Deadline: February 28
• ARNET Annual Scholarship (Scholarship)

Alberta Opticians Association; Alberta Guild of Opthalmic Dispensers *See* College of Opticians of Alberta

Alberta Organic Producers Association (AOPA)
RR#1, Morinville AB T8R 1P4
Tel: 780-939-5808; *Fax:* 780-939-6738
aopa@cruzinternet.com
www.albertaorganicproducers.org
Previous Name: Organic Crop Improvement Association - Alberta Chapter #1
Overview: A small local organization founded in 1990
Affliation(s): Organic Crop Improvement Association International (OCIA) Inc.
Chief Officer(s):
Sam Godwin, President
samhillent@hotmail.com
Val Schafers, Vice-President, 780-674-4166
Membership: 100-499; *Fees:* $50; *Member Profile:* Individuals interested in the production, processing, marketing, & consumption of organic products in Alberta
Activities: Offering a certificate to producers who meet the special organic criteria; Providing workshops & seminars
Publications:
• Alberta Organic Producers Association Chapter Binder
Type: Manual
Profile: Information for first time organic producers, with examples of forms & documents
• AOPA [Alberta Organic Producers Association] Newsletter
Type: Newsletter
Profile: Association updates & upcoming events

Alberta Orienteering Association (AOA)
PO Box 1576, Cochrane AB T4C 1B5
Tel: 403-981-4444
www.orienteeringalberta.ca
Overview: A small provincial organization founded in 1974
Mission: To promote, encourage, co-ordinate and administer orienteering as sport and recreation in Alberta which includes providing orienteering opportunities for all levels of ability.
Member of: Canadian Orienteering Federation
Chief Officer(s):
Kim Kasperski, President
Kitty Jones, Treasurer
Pascale Levesque, Executive Director
pascale@orienteeringalberta.ca
Staff Member(s): 1
Membership: *Fees:* $30 individual; $45 group
Activities: Sport orienteering; amateur sport; navigation; map reading; *Library* Open to public

Publications:
• The Reentrant
Type: Newsletter

Alberta Party
PO Box 1045, Stn. Main, Edmonton AB T5J 2M1
Tel: 780-760-0011
Toll-Free: 877-683-3126
info@albertaparty.ca
www.albertaparty.ca
www.facebook.com/albertaparty
twitter.com/AlbertaParty
Overview: A medium-sized provincial organization
Chief Officer(s):
Will Munsey, President
Michael McLaughlin, Chief Financial Officer
Finances: *Funding Sources:* Membership purchases; Donations

Alberta Percheron Club
c/o Julie Roy, RR#1, Markerville AB T0M 1M0
Tel: 403-728-3127
sanlan@platinum.ca
www.albertapercherons.com
Overview: A small provincial organization
Mission: To promote the Alberta Percheron horse in Alberta, throughout Canada, & internationally
Chief Officer(s):
John Ruzicka, President, 780-336-2011
Brian Coleman, Vice-President, 403-637-3700
Julie Roy, Secretary, 403-728-3127
sanlan@platinum.ca
Karen Ruzicka, Treasurer, 780-336-2011
Membership: 1-99; *Fees:* $15 youth & associate members; $25 single members; $35 families; *Member Profile:* Persons in Alberta with an interest in the Percheron horse
Activities: Hosting & participating in various shows, such as the annual Provincial Percheron Show & the annual Percheron Club Draft Horse Foal Show; Offering the Alberta Percheron Club Youth Program
Awards:
• Alberta Percheron Club Yearly Scholarship (Scholarship)
Eligibility: Junior members of the Alberta Percheron Club, from ages 16 to 21 *Amount:* $500
Meetings/Conferences: • Alberta Percheron Club 2015 Annual Meeting, February, 2015, Westerner Park, Red Deer, AB
Scope: Provincial
Contact Information: Julie Roy; sanlan@platinum.ca
Publications:
• Alberta Percheron Club Breed Directory
Type: Directory; *Frequency:* Annually; *Accepts Advertising;* *Editor:* Cam Roy
Profile: Listings of Alberta Percheron Club members their farms, & their horses

Alberta Pharmacists' Association (RxA)
Canadian Western Bank Building, #1725, 10303 Jasper Ave., Edmonton AB T5J 3N6
Tel: 780-990-0326; *Fax:* 780-990-1236
rxa@rxa.ca
www.rxa.ca
Overview: A small provincial organization
Mission: To represent the interests of pharmacists & pharmacies in Alberta to enhance enhance the health of Albertans
Chief Officer(s):
Margaret Wing, Chief Executive Officer
margaret.wing@rxa.ca
Rose Dehod, Manager, Professional Development
rose.dehod@rxa.ca
Jody Johnson, Manager, Member Services
jody.johnson@rxa.ca
Meghan Cooper, Communications Coordinator
meghan.cooper@rxa.ca
Jeff Whissell, Director, Pharmacy Practice
jeff.whissell@rxa.ca
Staff Member(s): 8
Membership: *Fees:* $425 pharmacist; $0 student; *Member Profile:* Pharmacies & pharmacists across Alberta
Activities: Providing continuing education; Offering information to members; Promoting the role of pharmacists; Engaging in advocacy activities
Meetings/Conferences: • Alberta Pharmacists' Association 2015 Spring Professional Development Conference, March, 2015, Fantasyland Hotel, Edmonton, AB
Scope: Provincial

Canadian Associations

Publications:
• The Capsule
Type: Newsletter; *Frequency:* Weekly; *Accepts Advertising*
Profile: Updates sent to approximately 900 pharmacies throughout Alberta
• RxPress
Type: Magazine; *Frequency:* Quarterly; *Accepts Advertising*
Profile: Recent developments in the industry, of interest to pharmacists & stakeholders

Alberta Physiotherapy Association (APA)
Dorchester Building, #300, 10357 - 109 St., Edmonton AB T5J 1N3
Tel: 780-438-0338; *Fax:* 780-436-1908
Toll-Free: 800-291-2782
info@physiotherapyalberta.ca
www.physiotherapyalberta.ca
Overview: A medium-sized provincial organization founded in 1996
Mission: To promote the profession of physiotherapy to decision makers & consumers; To establish standards for education & professional conduct
Member of: Canadian Physiotherapy Association
Chief Officer(s):
Greg Cutforth, Vice President
Membership: *Member Profile:* Students & graduates of accredited physiotherapy programs at Canadian universities; Individuals registered with any physiotherapy regulatory board in Canada
Activities: Engaging in advocacy activities; Liaising with government; Supporting professional education of physiotherapists
Publications:
• Alberta Physiotherapy News
Type: Newsletter; *Frequency:* 3 pa; *Accepts Advertising*; *Price:* Free with Alberta Physiotherapy Association membership; $30 - $50 non-members
Profile: Information for physiotherapists & persons in related health fields

Alberta Pinzgauer Association (APA)
c/o Donna Smith, RR#2, Olds AB T4H 1P3
Tel: 403-556-2290; *Fax:* 403-506-8583
diamondt@airenet.com
www.pinzgauer.ca
Overview: A small provincial organization
Mission: To facilitate the exhibition & sale of Pinzgauer cattle in Alberta
Chief Officer(s):
Donna Smith, Secretary-Treasurer
Membership: *Member Profile:* Breeders of Pinzgauer cattle in Alberta
Activities: Promoting interest in Pinzgauer cattle; Recognizing youth involvement

Alberta Pioneer Auto Club
PO Box 111, Stn. M, Calgary AB T2P 2G9
e-mail: apac.calgary@gmail.com
www.apaccalgary.ca
Overview: A small provincial organization founded in 1959
Mission: To encourage the preservation & restoration of all classic, antique & special interest automobiles
Finances: *Funding Sources:* Membership fees
Membership: 180; *Fees:* $40; *Member Profile:* Owners of cars more than 25 years old
Activities: Meetings held 2nd Tues. of each month

Alberta Pioneer Railway Association (APRA)
24215 - 34 St., Edmonton AB T5Y 6B4
Tel: 780-472-6229; *Fax:* 780-968-0167
www.albertarailwaymuseum.com
Also Known As: Alberta Railway Museum
Overview: A small provincial charitable organization founded in 1968
Mission: To collect, preserve, restore, exhibit & interpret artifacts which represent the history & social impact of the railways in Western Canada, with emphasis on Canadian National Railways & Northern Alberta Railways & their predecessors in northern & central Alberta
Member of: Alberta Museums Association; Museums Canada
Affliation(s): Heritage Canada
Chief Officer(s):
Herb Dixon, President
Finances: *Funding Sources:* Grants; donations
Membership: *Fees:* $34 regular; $45 family; $20 senior/associate; *Member Profile:* Railway enthusiasts; retired railway workers
Activities: Operates Alberta Railway Museum; *Library:* John Rechner Memorial Library; Open to public by appointment

Alberta Plastics Recycling Association (APRA)
PO Box 56092, #115, 1935 - 32nd Ave. NE, Calgary AB T2E 8K5
Tel: 780-690-3667
albertaplastics@gmail.com
www.albertaplasticsrecycling.com
Overview: A medium-sized provincial organization founded in 1991
Mission: To minimize plastic waste to landfill in Alberta
Affliation(s): Canadian Plastics Industry Association (CPIA)
Chief Officer(s):
Grantland M. Cameron, Executive Director
Dave Schwass, President
Otto Parets, Vice-President
Guy West, Secretary-Treasurer
Membership: *Member Profile:* Plastics resin producers; Plastic manufacturers, fabricators, & converters; Packagers & fillers of plastic products; Wholesalers & retailers of plastic products & products in plastics packaging; Plastics recyclers & the recycling community; Industry associations; Interested members of the public
Activities: Collaborating with industry, environmental interest groups, & all levels of government; Providing resources to companies, groups, & individuals
Publications:
• Alberta Plastics Recycling Association News
Type: Newsletter
Profile: Highlights & accomplishments of the Alberta Plastics Recycling Association
• Alberta Post-Consumer Plastics Recycling Strategy, Recycled Plastic Audit
Number of Pages: 36
Profile: An initiative of the Alberta Plastics Recycling Association in partnership with Alberta Environment

Alberta Playwrights' Network (APN)
2633 Hochwald Ave. SW, Calgary AB T3E 7K2
Tel: 403-269-8564; *Fax:* 403-265-6773
Toll-Free: 800-268-8564
dramaturg@albertaplaywrights.com
www.albertaplaywrights.com
www.facebook.com/Albertaplaywrights
twitter.com/APNPlaywrights
Overview: A small provincial charitable organization founded in 1985
Mission: To foster playwriting in Alberta.
Member of: Theatre Alberta
Chief Officer(s):
Trevor Rueger, Executive Director
trevor@albertaplaywrights.com
Finances: *Funding Sources:* Grants; member & program fees
Staff Member(s): 5
Membership: *Fees:* $35 student; $55 individual; $65 organization; *Member Profile:* Playwrights & members of the theatre community resident or formerly resident of Alberta
Activities: Playwright Cabaret Readings; Alberta Playwriting Competition; playwriting retreats; workshops; script reading service; Ales & Tales Fundraiser; *Internships:* Yes; *Library:* Script Library/Reading Room; Open to public

Alberta Podiatry Association (APA)
c/o Dr. Mario Turanovic, 14110 Stony Plain Rd., Edmonton AB T5N 3V8
Tel: 780-452-1444
www.albertapodiatry.com
Overview: A small provincial organization founded in 1932
Mission: To act in accordance with the Podiatry Act, under the Statutes of Alberta; To advance the profession of podiatry in Alberta
Member of: American Podiatric Medical Association, Inc., Region 7
Chief Officer(s):
Jayne Jeneroux, Executive Director, 780-922-7669
Mario Turanovic, President
Brad Sonnemax, Vice-President, 780-482-5565
Tedman Donovan, Secretary-Treasurer, 403-255-1448
Richard Bochinski, Registrar, 780-452-1444
Membership: 1-99; *Member Profile:* Medical doctors in Alberta who specialize in treating ailments of the feet & ankles; Members must act in accordance with the Code of Conduct of the Alberta Podiatry Association
Activities: Disciplining members; Registering candidates who qualify under The Podiatry Act;

Alberta Poison Centre *See* Poison & Drug Information Service

Alberta Potato Marketing Board *See* Potato Growers of Alberta

Alberta Powerlifting Union (APU)
c/o James Bartlett, 4805 Vandyke Rd. NW, Calgary AB T3A 0J6
Tel: 403-471-4754
www.powerliftingab.com
www.youtube.com/user/AlbertaPL
Overview: A small provincial organization founded in 1983 overseen by Canadian Powerlifting Union
Mission: To promote powerlifting in Alberta
Affliation(s): Canadian Powerlifting Union; International Powerlifting Federation
Chief Officer(s):
Shane Martin, Interim President
mr.shane.c.martin@gmail.com
James Bartlett, Chair, Registration
bartlettJ@bennettjones.com
Membership: *Fees:* $60 open; $50 junior; $40 special

Alberta Pro Life Alliance Association *See* Wilberforce Project

Alberta Professional Outfitters Society (APOS)
#103, 6030 - 88 St., Edmonton AB T6E 6G4
Tel: 780-414-0249; *Fax:* 780-465-6801
info@apos.ab.ca
www.apos.ab.ca
Previous Name: Professional Outfitters Association of Alberta
Overview: A small provincial organization founded in 1997
Mission: To provide leadership & direction in the continuing development of Alberta's outfitter-hunting industry; strives for long term sustainability in its approach to wildlife management, business opportunities & global competitiveness
Affliation(s): Safari Club International; Foundation for North American Wild Sheep; Rocky Mountain Elk Foundation
Chief Officer(s):
Glenn Brown, President, 403-443-5718
bluebronna@gmail.com
Ken Bailey, Managing Director, 780-414-0249 Ext. 2
ken@apos.ab.ca
Mabel Brick, Administration Manager, 780-414-0249 Ext. 3
mabel@apos.ab.ca
Finances: *Annual Operating Budget:* $500,000-$1.5 Million
Staff Member(s): 3; 30 volunteer(s)
Membership: 450; *Fees:* OG permit $107
Activities: Provides all administrative services to the industry; government liaison; cooperative marketing; disciplinary function

Alberta Professional Photographers Association
c/o Professional Photographers of Canada, 209 Light St., Woodstock ON N4S 6H6
Tel: 519-537-2555; *Fax:* 888-831-4036
Toll-Free: 888-643-7762
www.ppoc-alberta.ca
Also Known As: PPOC - Alberta
Overview: A small provincial organization overseen by Professional Photographers of Canada
Mission: To maintain a strong national identity for all those involved in the photographic industry and includes provincial factions which abide by a specific code of ethics.
Chief Officer(s):
Cameron Colclough, Director
Membership: 250; *Committees:* Trade Liaison; Education; Convention; Membership; Merits; Newsletter; Website; Social Media; Marketing; Print Salon

Alberta Professional Planners Institute (APPI)
PO Box 596, Edmonton AB T5J 2K8
Tel: 780-435-8716; *Fax:* 780-452-7718
Toll-Free: 888-286-8716
admin@albertaplanners.com
www.albertaplanners.com
Overview: A medium-sized provincial organization founded in 1963 overseen by Canadian Institute of Planners
Mission: To expand the depth & enhance the credibility of the association; To promote professional growth of practicing planners throughout Alberta, the Northwest Territories, & Nunavut; To maximize membership potential; To provide an effective level of service to the membership
Chief Officer(s):
Eleanor Mohammed, RPP, MCIP, President
president@albertaplanners.com
MaryJane Alanko, Executive Director
execdir@albertaplanners.com
Finances: *Funding Sources:* Membership dues; Application fees

40 volunteer(s)
Membership: 400; *Member Profile:* Public & private sector professional planners & academics, practicing in Alberta, the Northwest Territories, or Nunavut, who have met all the membership requirements for education & responsible professional planning experience
Activities: *Rents Mailing List:* Yes
Meetings/Conferences: • Canadian Institute of Planners / Alberta Professional Planners Institute 2015 Conference, September, 2015, Edmonton, AB
Scope: National
Description: An event for planners, architects, academics, engineers, & policy makers. This year's title is "Great Cities, Great Regions: Prairie-Urban Transformations"
Contact Information: Co-Chairs, 2015 Conference Organizing Committee: Peter Ohm RPP, MCIP & Nancy MacDonald RPP, MCIP

Alberta Provincial Council
c/o Edmonton Public School Board, Centre for Education, 1 Kingsway, Edmonton AB T5H 4G9
Tel: 780-429-8000; *Fax:* 780-429-8318
Also Known As: Council No: CE995
Overview: A small provincial organization overseen by International Reading Association
Chief Officer(s):
Su Kerslake, Coordinator, 780-498-8772
su.kerslake@epsb.ca

Alberta Provincial Rifle Association
PO Box 1015, Stn. M, Calgary AB T2P 2K4
e-mail: membership@albertarifle.com
www.albertarifle.com
Overview: A medium-sized provincial organization
Mission: To promote in every lawful way the interests of small arms marksmanship in the province of Alberta; To create public interest for the encouragement of small arms shooting, both as a sport & as a necessary means of national defense
Member of: Dominion of Canada Rifle Association; Shooting Federation of Canada
Chief Officer(s):
Joseph Breslawski, President

Alberta Psychiatric Association (APA)
#400, 1040 - 7 Ave. SW, Calgary AB T2P 3G9
Tel: 403-244-4487; *Fax:* 403-244-2340
info@albertapsych.org
www.albertapsych.org
Overview: A small provincial organization
Affliation(s): Canadian Psychiatric Association
Chief Officer(s):
Thomas Raedler, President
Finances: *Funding Sources:* Membership fees; Donations; Grants
Membership: *Member Profile:* Psychiatrists in Alberta
Meetings/Conferences: • Alberta Psychiatric Association 2015 Scientific Conference and AGM, March, 2015, Rimrock Resort Hotel, Banff, AB
Scope: Provincial

Alberta Public Health Association (APHA)
c/o University of Alberta, 4075 RTF, 8308 - 114th St., Edmonton AB T6G 2E1
Tel: 780-492-6014; *Fax:* 780-492-7154
info@apha.ab.ca
www.apha.ab.ca
Overview: A medium-sized provincial charitable organization founded in 1943 overseen by Canadian Public Health Association
Mission: To promote & protect the health of the public through advocacy, partnerships, & education
Chief Officer(s):
PK (Tish) Doyle-Baker, President
Finances: *Annual Operating Budget:* $100,000-$250,000; *Funding Sources:* Membership dues; conferences; charitable donations; grants
15 volunteer(s)
Membership: 300; *Fees:* $50 regular; student/retired $22; *Member Profile:* Public health practitioners; professionals from NGOs; educators, government & citizens interested in advocating for, promoting & protecting the health of the public; *Committees:* Conference; Program; Communications; Membership
Awards:
• Dr. Jean C. Nelson Foundation Award (Award)
• Dr. John Waters Award (Award)

Alberta Public Housing Administrators' Association (APHAA)
14220 - 109 Ave. NW, Edmonton AB T5N 4B3
Tel: 780-498-1971; *Fax:* 780-464-7039
www.aphaa.org
twitter.com/Aphaalnfo
Overview: A medium-sized provincial organization
Mission: Works with the Province of Alberta in the publicly-funded housing industry to promote excellence in publicly funded housing administration through education, information and networking
Chief Officer(s):
Raymond Swonek, President
Membership: *Member Profile:* Chief Administrative Officers for Management Bodies; *Committees:* Communications; Conference Planning; Education; Membership Selection; Nominations
Meetings/Conferences: • Alberta Public Housing Administrators' Association Spring AGM & Education Sessions 2015, May, 2015, Edmonton Marriott River Cree Resort, Edmonton, AB
Scope: Provincial
• Alberta Public Housing Administrators' Association Fall Conference 2015, October, 2015, The Banff Centre, Banff, AB
Scope: Provincial

Alberta Publishers Association *See* Book Publishers Association of Alberta

Alberta Racquetball Association (ARA)
47 Walden Cres., St Albert AB T8N 3N5
Tel: 780-918-5332
albertaracquetball@shaw.ca
www.albertaracquetball.com
Overview: A small provincial organization founded in 1971 overseen by Racquetball Canada
Mission: To develop the sport of racquetball in Alberta.
Member of: Racquetball Canada
Chief Officer(s):
John Halko, President
johnh@mcleanyoung.com
Barbara May, Executive Director
Membership: *Fees:* $10

Alberta Ready Mixed Concrete Association (ARMCA)
9653 - 45 Ave., Edmonton AB T6E 5Z8
Tel: 780-436-5645; *Fax:* 780-436-6503
info@armca.ca
www.armca.ca
Overview: A medium-sized provincial organization founded in 1963 overseen by Canadian Ready Mixed Concrete Association
Mission: To provide industry representation for the advancement of quality concrete in Alberta; To market & promote the use of concrete; To provide a consolidated industry approach to regulatory bodies; To provide networking opportunities; to provide education & training
Chief Officer(s):
Laura Reschke, Executive Director
laura.reschke@armca.ca
Edward Kalis, Director, Technical Services & Training
ed.kalis@armca.ca
Finances: *Annual Operating Budget:* $100,000-$250,000
Staff Member(s): 3; 40 volunteer(s)
Membership: 100-499; *Committees:* Technical; Marketing & Promotion; Environmental; Residential; Transportation; Pumping; Safety
Activities: *Speaker Service:* Yes; *Library:* ARMCA Technical Information; Open to public by appointment
Awards:
• Scholarship (Scholarship)
Amount: $500

Alberta Real Estate Association (AREA)
#300, 4954 Richard Rd. SW, Calgary AB T3E 6L1
Tel: 403-228-6845; *Fax:* 403-228-4360
Toll-Free: 800-661-0231
info@areahub.ca
www.areahub.ca
Overview: A medium-sized provincial organization founded in 1947
Member of: The Canadian Real Estate Association
Chief Officer(s):
Dan Russel, CEO
Membership: 6,750

Alberta Reappraising AIDS Society (ARAS)
PO Box 61037, Stn. Kensington, Calgary AB T2N 4S6
Tel: 403-220-0129
aras@aras.ab.ca
www.aras.ab.ca
Overview: A small provincial organization founded in 1999
Mission: To provide a science-based alternative information on HIV/AIDS & other infectious diseases; does not provide treatment recommendations
Chief Officer(s):
David Crowe, President, 403-289-6609, Fax: 403-206-7717
david.crowe@aras.ab.ca
Roger Swan, Treasurer
Finances: *Annual Operating Budget:* Less than $50,000
2 volunteer(s)
Membership: 135; *Member Profile:* People interested in questioning the dominant HIV/AIDS paradigm
Activities: Education; information; *Speaker Service:* Yes; *Library* by appointment
Awards:
• Healer (Award)
• Administrator (Award)
Awards to the bravest rethinking administrator, bureaucrat, lawyer, NGO employee or politician in the previous year
• Scribe (Award)
Awarded to journalist, writer or film-maker for rethinking AIDS article in the previous year
• Activist (Award)
Awards to activist, who was most hard working & effective in the previous year
• Researcher (Award)
Awarded to researcher, scientist or academic who effectively challeneds HIV/AIDS dogma in the previous year, through their research or scientific publications

Alberta Recording Industry Association (ARIA)
1205 Energy Square, 10109-106 St NW, Edmonton AB T5J 3L7
Tel: 780-428-3372; *Fax:* 780-426-0188
Toll-Free: 800-465-3117
Overview: A medium-sized provincial organization founded in 1984
Mission: To assist & advance the development of the Canadian recorded music industry; to foster the excellence, diversity & vitality of Alberta artists & the Alberta sound recording industry
Affliation(s): Western Canadian Music Alliance; Factor Caras
Finances: *Annual Operating Budget:* $50,000-$100,000; *Funding Sources:* Government
Staff Member(s): 2; 15 volunteer(s)
Membership: 200; *Fees:* $30 & $45; *Member Profile:* Must be involved in recording industry
Activities: *Library*

Alberta Recreation & Parks Association (ARPA)
11759 Groat Rd., Edmonton AB T5M 3K6
Tel: 780-415-1745; *Fax:* 780-451-7915
Toll-Free: 877-544-1747
arpa@arpaonline.ca
arpaonline.ca
www.facebook.com/arpaonline
twitter.com/arpaonline
Overview: A medium-sized provincial charitable organization overseen by Canadian Parks & Recreation Association
Mission: To promote accessibility to recreation & parks & their benefits to Albertans; To work toward economic sustainability, natural resource protection, & conservation within provincial parks & natural environments
Chief Officer(s):
Rick Curtis, Executive Director, 780-415-1745
rcurtis@arpaonline.ca
Steve Allan, Manager, Finance & Operations
sallan@arpaonline.ca
Shelley Shea, President
shelley.shea@calgary.ca
Carol Petersen, Manager, Recreation & Community Development
cpetersen@arpaonline.ca
Terry Welsh, Secretary
twelsh@brooks.ca
Judi Frank, Treasurer
judfra@medicinehat.ca
Lisa Tink, Manager, Children & Youth Programs
ltink@arpaonline.ca
Mandi Wise, Coordinator, Communications
mwise@arpaonline.ca
Membership: 1,300+; *Member Profile:* Students; Municipal elected officials, staff, volunteers & stakeholders; Business staff,

Canadian Associations

suppliers & clients; Eductional institution staff; Non-profit association & government agency elected officials, staff, volunteers & stakeholders; Individuals interested in or working in areas of recreation, parks, leisure, & tourism
Activities: Providing leadership to Alberta's recreation & parks industry; Facilitating communication & information networking; Maximizing human & financial resources for recreation & parks services; Establishing relations with the provincial government; Advocating recreational safety, fair play & gender equity; Increasing public awareness of recreation & active lifestyles; Monitoring development of formal post-secondary educational opportunities for recreation & parks; Research & preparing position papers on various issues; *Awareness Events:* Recreation & Parks Month, June; Communities in Bloom; Community Choosewell Challenge
Awards:
• Alberta Recreation & Parks Association Merit Award (Award)
• Wild Rose Award (Award)
• A.V. Pettigrew Award (Award)
• Excellence in Youth Development Award (Award)
• Parks Excellence Award (Award)
• Halladay Memorial Scholarship (Scholarship)
• Alberta Advisory Board on Recreation for the Disabled (AABRD) Legacy Award (Award)
• Alberta Advisory Board on Recreation for the Disabled (AABRD) Undergraduate & Graduate Scholarships (Scholarship)
Meetings/Conferences: • Alberta Recreation & Parks Association 2015 Parks Forum, March, 2015, Canmore, AB
Scope: Provincial
Description: A staff development event, with keynote speakers, plenary workshops, & presentations, of interest to practitioners at municipal, provincial, & national parks, allied stakeholders, teachers, & students
Contact Information: E-mail: arpa@arpaonline.ca
• Alberta Recreation & Parks Association 2016 Biennial Youth Development Through Recreation Services Symposium, 2016
Scope: Provincial
Description: A three day educational forum, featuring presenters ranging from frontline staff involved in youth programs to youth policy makers
Contact Information: Coordinator, Children & Youth Programs: Allison Pratley, E-mail: apratley@arpaonline.ca
• 2017 International Play Association Conference, 2017
Scope: International
Description: Organized by IPA Canada, the City of Calgary, ARPA, and other partner organizations.
Publications:
• Alberta Recreation & Parks Association Recreation Buyers Guide
Type: Booklet; *Accepts Advertising*
Profile: Advertisements with contact information
• REConnect [a publication of the Alberta Recreation & Parks Association]
Type: Newsletter; *Frequency:* Monthly
Profile: News about recreation & parks related issues in Alberta

Alberta Registered Music Teachers' Association (ARMTA)
#209, 14218 Stony Plain Rd., Edmonton AB T5N 3R3
Tel: 780-488-7648; *Fax:* 780-488-4132
Toll-Free: 877-687-4239
elizcooper@shaw.ca
www.armtaedmonton.ab.ca
Overview: A medium-sized provincial organization founded in 1982
Mission: To enhance quality of life by promoting the love & knowledge of music through professional music teaching & studies in the community & through providing cultural events of a high standard for the community
Member of: Canadian Federation of Music Teachers Associations
Affliation(s): Alberta Music Education Foundation
Chief Officer(s):
Elizabeth Cooper, President
elizcooper@shaw.ca
Finances: *Annual Operating Budget:* $50,000-$100,000
Staff Member(s): 1; 50 volunteer(s)
Membership: 410; *Fees:* $65 full year, $32.50 half-year; *Member Profile:* Accredited music educators & performers
Activities: *Internships:* Yes; *Speaker Service:* Yes; *Rents Mailing List:* Yes

Alberta Registered Professional Foresters Association *See* College of Alberta Professional Foresters

Alberta Rehabilitation Council for the Disabled *See* Alberta Easter Seals Society

Alberta Reined Cow Horse Association (ARCHA)
PO Box 18, RR#2, Site 13, Olds AB T4H 1P3
Tel: 403-556-2640; *Fax:* 403-556-8766
info@cowhorse.ca
www.cowhorse.ca
Overview: A small provincial organization founded in 1981
Mission: To improve the quality of the western reined stock horse; To perpetuate the early Spanish traditions of highly trained & well reined working cow horse events & contests in expositions & shows; To promote the training of reined cow horses & reining horses among the younger horsemen of the West; To use & encourage the use of standard rules for holding & judging contests of the working cow horse
Affliation(s): NRCHA
Chief Officer(s):
Mel Mabbott, President, 403-558-0135, Fax: 403-558-2390
greenpine@xplornet.com
Terri Loree, Office Manager
Finances: *Annual Operating Budget:* Less than $50,000
Staff Member(s): 1; 12 volunteer(s)
Membership: 400 individual; *Fees:* $25 youth; $50 individual; $90 family

Alberta Research Council Inc. (ARC)
250 Karl Clark Rd., Edmonton AB T6N 1E4
Tel: 780-450-5111; *Fax:* 780-450-5333
referral@albertainnovates.ca
www.albertatechfutures.ca
www.linkedin.com/company/alberta-innovates---technology-futures
www.facebook.com/AlbertaInnovates
twitter.com/TechFuturesAB
www.youtube.com/user/TechFutures
Overview: A medium-sized provincial organization founded in 1921
Mission: To operate as an applied research & development corporation; To develop & commercialize technology to grow innovative enterprises; To specialize in converting early stage ideas into marketable technology products & services
Chief Officer(s):
Stephen Lougheed, President/CEO
Sandra Scott, Executive Vice-President
Finances: *Annual Operating Budget:* Greater than $5 Million; *Funding Sources:* Provincial grants; Fees; Revenue
Activities: *Library:* Information Centre; Open to public

Calgary Office
3608 - 33 St. NW, Calgary AB T2L 2A6
Tel: 403-210-5222; *Fax:* 403-210-5380
www.arc.ab.ca

Devon Branch
1 Oil Patch Dr., Devon AB T9G 1A8
Chief Officer(s):
John McDougall, President/CEO

Vegreville Branch
PO Box 4000, Hwy 16A & 75 St., Vegreville AB T9C 1T4
Tel: 780-632-8211; *Fax:* 780-632-8385
Chief Officer(s):
John McDougall, President/CEO

Alberta Restorative Justice Association (ARJA)
#430, 9810 - 111 St., Edmonton AB T5K 1K1
Tel: 780-451-4013
info@arjassoc.ca
www.arjassoc.ca
www.facebook.com/RJAlberta
twitter.com/RJAlberta
Overview: A small provincial organization
Mission: A collective voice to strengthen Restorative Justice in Alberta communities by establishing and providing information, education, and awareness towards best practices in Restorative Justice.
Chief Officer(s):
Deborah Nowakowski, Chair

Alberta Rhythmic Sportive Gymnastics Federation *See* Rhythmic Gymnastics Alberta

Alberta Roadbuilders & Heavy Construction Association (ARHCA)
#201, 9333 - 45 Ave., Edmonton AB T6E 5Z7
Tel: 780-436-9860; *Fax:* 780-436-4910
Toll-Free: 866-436-9860
administration@arhca.ab.ca
www.arhca.ab.ca
Overview: A medium-sized provincial organization founded in 1954 overseen by Canadian Construction Association
Affliation(s): Western Canada Roadbuilders Association; Alberta Construction Safety Association; Roads & Transportation Association Canada
Chief Officer(s):
Gene Syvenky, Chief Executive Officer
gene@arhca.ab.ca
Kimberley Barrett, Director, Finance & Administration
kimberley@arhca.ab.ca
Heidi Harris-Jensen, Director, External Affairs
heidi@arhca.ab.ca
Dawn Fenske, Coordinator, Communications
dawn@arhca.ab.ca
Finances: *Annual Operating Budget:* $500,000-$1.5 Million
Staff Member(s): 4
Membership: 300 corporate + 200 associate + 26 senior/lifetime; *Fees:* Schedule available; *Member Profile:* Active - firm in roadbuilding; associate - active supplier to the industries; Regular - heavy construction

Alberta Roofing Contractors Association (ARCA)
2380 Pegasus Rd. NE, Calgary AB T2E 8G8
Tel: 403-250-7055; *Fax:* 403-250-1702
Toll-Free: 800-382-8515
info@arcaonline.ca
www.arcaonline.ca
Overview: A medium-sized provincial organization founded in 1961 overseen by Canadian Roofing Contractors' Association
Mission: To provide continuing education for roofing contractors, their personnel & interested others; to represent the roofing contracting industry in its relationships with legislative & regulating bodies; to work closely with affiliate organizations & liaison groups in advancing professionalism of roofing contracting; to provide a forum for interaction of members; to encourage high standards of professional conduct among roofing contractors; to develop a comprehensive body of knowledge about roofing management & technology, & disseminate ideas & knowledge to members & others; to monitor new products & systems; to work for cooperation & greater understanding between contracting, inspection, manufacturing & supply segments of the roofing industry
Affliation(s): National Roofing Contractors Association USA
Finances: *Annual Operating Budget:* $250,000-$500,000
Staff Member(s): 4
Membership: 70; *Fees:* Schedule available; *Member Profile:* Roofing contractors, suppliers & manufacturers
Activities: *Library* by appointment

Alberta Rowing Association (ARA)
11759 Groat Rd., Edmonton AB T5M 3K6
Tel: 780-427-8154
office@albertarowing.ca
www.albertarowing.ca
www.facebook.com/pages/Alberta-Rowing-Association/131265308366
twitter.com/AlbertaRowing
Overview: A medium-sized provincial organization overseen by Rowing Canada Aviron
Mission: To act as the organizing body, which promotes all aspects of rowing in Alberta. The ARA is a not for profit association run by volunteers, relying on membership fees, fundraising, and government support for operating funds.
Member of: Rowing Canada Aviron
Chief Officer(s):
Carol Hermansen, President
Membership: 7 clubs

Alberta Rugby Football Union
Percy Page Centre, 11759 Groat Rd., Edmonton AB T5M 3K6
Tel: 780-415-1773; *Fax:* 780-422-5558
info@rugbyalberta.com
www.rugbyalberta.com
twitter.com/AlbertaRugby
Overview: A medium-sized provincial organization founded in 1961 overseen by Rugby Canada
Mission: To develop & promote an interest in rugby in Alberta
Member of: Rugby Canada
Chief Officer(s):
Sandy Nesbitt, President
Simon Chi, Vice-President
Debby Ashmore, Executive Director, 780-638-4547
Rick Melia, Director, Finance & Administration
Finances: *Funding Sources:* Alberta Sport, Recreation, Parks and Wildlife Foundation
Staff Member(s): 3

Activities: *Library* Open to public

Alberta Rural Municipal Administrators Association
6027 - 4th St. NE, Calgary AB T2K 4Z5
Tel: 403-275-0622; *Fax:* 403-275-8179
www.armaa.ca
Overview: A medium-sized provincial organization founded in 1922
Mission: To represent administrators in Alberta municipal governments
Chief Officer(s):
Valerie Schmaltz, Executive Director
d_vschmaltz@shaw.ca
Sheila Kitz, President
skitz@county.stpaul.ab.ca
Finances: *Funding Sources:* Membership dues; grant
Membership: *Member Profile:* Rural municipal administrator
Meetings/Conferences: • Alberta Rural Municipal Administrators' Association 2015 Conference, September, 2015, Best Western Wayside Inn, Wetaskiwin, AB
Scope: Provincial
Description: 2015 theme: "Making Up Is Hard To Do"
Contact Information: Valerie Schmaltz; d_vschmaltz@shaw.ca

Alberta Safety Council
4831 - 93 Ave., Edmonton AB T6B 3A2
Tel: 780-462-7300; *Fax:* 780-462-7318
Toll-Free: 800-301-6407
info@safetycouncil.ab.ca
www.safetycouncil.ab.ca
www.facebook.com/189043441145255
twitter.com/ABSafetycouncil
Overview: A medium-sized provincial organization founded in 1946
Mission: To create awareness & provide educational & training programs to citizens of Alberta on how to maintain a safe environment at home, in traffic, at work & at play
Affiliation(s): Canada Safety Council; National Safety Council; Safety Services Canada
Chief Officer(s):
Laurie Billings, Executive Director
Membership: 209; *Member Profile:* Companies, organizations, agencies which promote safety
Activities: *Speaker Service:* Yes; *Library* Open to public

Alberta Sailing Association (ASA)
4915 Graham Dr. SW, Calgary AB T3E 4L3
Tel: 403-617-9092
info@albertasailing.com
www.albertasailing.com
Overview: A small provincial organization founded in 1973 overseen by Sail Canada
Mission: Alberta Sailing Association in partnership with its member clubs, sailing schools & Sail Canada addresses the needs of sailors; encourages improved access to water & sailing facilities; sail training & safety programs & opportunities to compete at the club, provincial & international levels
Member of: Sail Canada
Chief Officer(s):
Ron Hewitt, President
president@albertasailing.com
Finances: *Annual Operating Budget:* $50,000-$100,000
Staff Member(s): 1
Membership: 1,500; *Fees:* $14

Alberta Salers Association
5160 Skyline Way NE, Carstairs AB T2E 6V1
Tel: 403-264-5850; *Fax:* 403-264-5895
info@salerscanada.com
www.salerscanada.com
Overview: A small provincial organization founded in 1973
Mission: To promote salers cattle in Alberta
Member of: Salers Association of Canada
Chief Officer(s):
Gar Williams, President, 306-997-4909
gmwilliams@sasktel.net
Ken Sweetland, Vice-President, 204-762-5512
sweetlandsalers@xplornet.ca
Ray Depalme, Treas.
Finances: *Annual Operating Budget:* Less than $50,000
11 volunteer(s)
Membership: 60; *Fees:* $25; *Member Profile:* Purebred cattle breeders
Activities: Raising awareness of salers cattle in Alberta

Alberta School Boards Association (ASBA)
#1200, 9925 - 109 St., Edmonton AB T5K 2J8
Tel: 780-482-7311; *Fax:* 780-482-5659
reception@asba.ab.ca
www.asba.ab.ca
twitter.com/newalberta
Previous Name: Alberta School Trustees' Association
Overview: A medium-sized provincial organization founded in 1907 overseen by Canadian School Boards Association
Mission: To promote the availability of high quality schooling for all; To assist member boards in fulfilling their mission of achieving excellence in education
Chief Officer(s):
Jacquie Hansen, President
Cheryl Smith, Vice-President
csmith@brsd.ab.ca
David Anderson, Executive Director, 780-451-7109
Donna Engel, Director, Finance & Corporate Services, 780-451-7110
dengel@asba.ab.ca
Suzanne Lundrigan, Director, Communications, 780-451-7122
slungrigan@asba.ab.ca
Heather Rogers, Director, Finance & Corporate Services, 780-451-7114
hrogers@asba.ab.ca
Finances: *Annual Operating Budget:* Greater than $5 Million; *Funding Sources:* Membership fees; Government grants; Fee for service
Staff Member(s): 24
Membership: 1-99; *Fees:* Formula; *Member Profile:* All school boards in Alberta are members of the ASBA
Activities: Providing professional development opportunities
Meetings/Conferences: • Alberta School Boards Association 2015 Spring General Meeting, June, 2015, Sheraton Red Deer, Red Deer, AB
Scope: Provincial
Description: An Alberta School Boards Association professional development event
Contact Information: Administrative Assistant, Communications: Noreen Pownall, Phone: 780-451-7102, E-mail: npownall@asba.ab.ca
• Alberta School Boards Association 2015 Fall General Meeting, 2015, AB
Scope: Local
Description: An Alberta School Boards Association professional development event
Contact Information: Administrative Assistant, Communications: Noreen Pownall, Phone: 780-451-7102, E-mail: npownall@asba.ab.ca
Publications:
• Alberta School Boards Association Annual Report
Type: Yearbook; *Frequency:* Annually
Profile: A review of the year's activities

Alberta School Councils' Association (ASCA)
#1200, 9925 - 109 St., Edmonton AB T5K 2J8
Tel: 780-454-9867; *Fax:* 780-455-0167
Toll-Free: 800-661-3470
parents@albertaschoolcouncils.ca
www.albertaschoolcouncils.ca
www.linkedin.com/company/alberta-school-councils%27-association?trk=to
www.facebook.com/180244032050548
twitter.com/ABschoolcouncil
www.youtube.com/channel/UCY9v9ogRloU4GK26D5dmiGw
Overview: A medium-sized provincial organization overseen by Canadian Home & School Federation
Mission: To be the voice of parents/families committed to the best possible education for Alberta children, so that they may reach their potential to participate in society in a meaningful & responsible way
Chief Officer(s):
Michele Mulder, Executive Director
michelem@albertaschoolcouncils.ca
Marilyn Sheptycki, President
president@albertaschoolcouncils.ca
Brad Vonkeman, Vice-President
bradvonk@telus.net
Finances: *Annual Operating Budget:* $50,000-$100,000
Staff Member(s): 6; 20 volunteer(s)
Membership: 500; *Fees:* $25 individual parent; $50 school council; $50 associate; *Member Profile:* School council
Activities: *Speaker Service:* Yes; *Library:* Resource Centre; by appointment
Meetings/Conferences: • Alberta School Councils' Association 2015 Conference and AGM, April, 2015, Delta Edmonton South, Edmonton, AB
Scope: Provincial

Alberta School Trustees' Association *See* Alberta School Boards Association

Alberta Schools' Athletic Association (ASAA)
Percy Page Centre, 11759 Groat Rd., Edmonton AB T5M 3K6
Tel: 780-427-8182; *Fax:* 780-415-1833
info@asaa.ca
www.asaa.ca
twitter.com/ASAA
Overview: A medium-sized provincial organization founded in 1956 overseen by School Sport Canada
Mission: To provide leadership in the promotion of high school sport; to regulate sports competition & promote the belief that education includes development of the whole person
Member of: School Sport Canada
Affliation(s): National Federation of State High School Associations
Chief Officer(s):
John F. Paton, Executive Director
john@asaa.ca
Garret Doll, President
gdoll@gsacrd.ab.ca
Finances: *Funding Sources:* Lotteries; membership dues; fundraising; corporate sponsors
Staff Member(s): 5
Membership: 371 schools + 8,000 student athletes

Alberta Securities Commission (ASC)
#600, 250 - 5th St. SW, Calgary AB T2P 0R4
Tel: 403-297-6454; *Fax:* 403-297-6156
Toll-Free: 877-355-0585
Other Communication: inquiries@asc.ca
www.albertasecurities.com
www.linkedin.com/company/alberta-securities-commission_2
www.facebook.com/113543076837
twitter.com/ASCUpdates
www.youtube.com/user/albertasecurities
Overview: A medium-sized provincial organization overseen by Canadian Securities Administrators
Mission: To regulate securities trading in Alberta, through the administration of the Securities Act (Alberta); To report to the Legislature, through the minister responsible for the administration of the Securities Act; To foster a fair & competitive securities market; To protect investors & market integrity
Member of: Canadian Securities Administrators
Chief Officer(s):
William S. Rice, Q.C., Chair & Chief Executive Officer
Finances: *Funding Sources:* Fees collected from market participants under the legislation
Activities: Regulating in Alberta the Investment Industry Regulatory Organization of Canada (IIROC), the Mutual Fund Dealers Association of Canada (MFDA), the Natural Gas Exchange Inc., the Alberta Watt Exchange Limited & the TSX Venture Exchange (TSXV) (with the British Columbia Securities Commission)
Publications:
• The Alberta Capital Market: A Comparative Overview
Type: Report; *Frequency:* Annually
• Alberta Securities Commission Annual Report
Type: Report; *Frequency:* Annually
• Enforcement Report
Type: Report; *Frequency:* Annually
• Oil & Gas Review Report
Type: Report; *Frequency:* Annually

Alberta Senior Citizens Sport & Recreation Association (ASCSRA)
#400, 7015 Macleod Trail., Calgary AB T2H 2K6
Tel: 403-803-9852; *Fax:* 403-800-5599
info@alberta55plus.ca
www.alberta55plus.ca
Also Known As: Alberta 55 Plus
Overview: A medium-sized provincial organization founded in 1980
Mission: To promote sport & recreation development for seniors (55+) across Alberta; to act as a provincial voice to ensure input by age categories for seniors in Alberta Winter & Summer Games; to promote future Alberta Seniors' Games
Affiliation(s): Alberta Sport, Recreation, Parks & Wildlife Foundation
Chief Officer(s):
Vern Hafso, President, 780-336-2270, Fax: 780-336-3525
tollarav@mscnet.ca

Finances: *Annual Operating Budget:* $100,000-$250,000;
Funding Sources: Government & private sector sponsorhip
Staff Member(s): 2; 100 volunteer(s)
Membership: 4,000; *Fees:* $15/1yr, $25/2yrs individual; $50 association; $25-$50 club
Activities: Workshops & instructional clinics; *Speaker Service:* Yes

Alberta Senior Citizens' Housing Association (ASCHA)

9711 - 47 Ave., Edmonton AB T6E 5M7
Tel: 780-439-6473; *Fax:* 780-433-3717
ascha@ascha.com
www.ascha.com
www.facebook.com/ascha.team
twitter.com/ABSeniorsLiving
Overview: A small provincial organization founded in 1967
Mission: To support the providers of seniors housing & act as a vehicle that provides & promotes leadership, an exchange of ideas, resources, communication & education to the members
Affliation(s): Red Deer College Certificate Programs: Site Manager & Activity Coordinator
Chief Officer(s):
Irene Martin-Lindsay, Executive Director
irene@ascha.com
Staff Member(s): 6
Membership: 139 organizations + 1 individual; *Fees:* Schedule available; *Member Profile:* Operators of seniors' housing (regular & associate members); product & service providers (corporate members) & individual members (mainly students in ASCHA Certificate Program)
Activities: Information & support services; advocacy; standards; educational services; housing registry; *Library*
Meetings/Conferences: • Alberta Senior Citizens' Housing Association 2015 Convention and Tradeshow, April, 2015, Shaw Conference Centre, Edmonton, AB
Scope: Provincial

The Alberta Seventh Step Society

1820 - 27th Ave. SW, Calgary AB T2T 1H1
Tel: 403-228-7778; *Fax:* 403-228-7773
administration@albertaseventhstep.com
www.albertaseventhstep.com
Also Known As: 7th Step Society of Alberta
Overview: A medium-sized provincial organization founded in 1971
Mission: To prevent crime & reduce recidivism through the provision of services & programs to persons in conflict with the law
Affliation(s): The 7th Step Society of Canada
Chief Officer(s):
Bob Alexander, Executive Director
execdirector@albertaseventhstep.com
Finances: *Annual Operating Budget:* $500,000-$1.5 Million
Staff Member(s): 22; 467 volunteer(s)
Membership: 48; *Fees:* $10 individual; $100 corporate; *Committees:* Audit; Finance; Governance & Strategy; Policy & Program

Alberta Sheep Breeders Association (ASBA)

PO Box 82, Clyde AB T0G 0P0
Fax: 780-348-5670
Toll-Free: 866-967-4337
office@albertasheepbreeders.ca
www.albertasheepbreeders.ca
Overview: A small provincial organization overseen by Canadian Sheep Breeders' Association
Mission: To promote the purebred sheep industry within Alberta
Chief Officer(s):
Glen Parker, President
Mike Grimmeyer, Secretary
Finances: *Annual Operating Budget:* Less than $50,000
Staff Member(s): 1; 13 volunteer(s)
Membership: 80; *Fees:* $35; *Member Profile:* Producers of purebred sheep in Alberta
Activities: Sheep sale; Alberta sheep symposium; produces promotional material; developing website
Awards:
• Shepherds Past Memorial Award (Award)
• Good Shepherd Award (Award)
• ASBA Memorial Scholarship (Scholarship)

Alberta Shorthand Reporters Association (ASRA)

38 Rutherford Dr., Red Deer AB T4P 2Z2
Tel: 403-347-8899; *Fax:* 403-340-7986
asra@asraonline.com
www.asraonline.com
Overview: A small provincial organization founded in 1958
Mission: To advance the court reporting profession by promoting court reporters as experts in the field of verbatim shorthand reporting; To provide continuing education to its members; To advocate quality service, high ethical standards & state-of-the-art technology
Affiliation(s): National Court Reporters Association
Chief Officer(s):
Linda Hallworth, President
lindahallworth@asraonline.com
Finances: *Annual Operating Budget:* $50,000-$100,000
8 volunteer(s)
Membership: 275; *Fees:* $125 reporters; $10 associates & students; *Committees:* Practice Review; Communications
Activities: Annual convention; seminars; training programs;

Alberta Shorthorn Association

c/o Albert and Susan Oram, PO Box 939, Castor AB T0C 0X0
Tel: 403-728-2345; *Fax:* 800-387-6909
Toll-Free: 800-387-6909
albertashorthorn@gmail.com
www.albertashorthorn.com
www.facebook.com/pages/Alberta-Shorthorn-Association/201076283271843
Overview: A small provincial organization
Mission: Group of Shorthorn breeders who work together, as a team, to produce and promote the Shorthorn breed of cattle.
Member of: Canadian Shorthorn Association
Chief Officer(s):
Kirk Seaborn, President
Betty Beeby, Executive Director, 403-932-5766
b_beeby5@xplornet.com
Finances: *Annual Operating Budget:* Less than $50,000
Membership: 87

Alberta Sign Association

PO Box 3362, Sherwood Park AB T8H 2T3
Fax: 780-464-3137
info@albertasigns.com
www.albertasigns.com
Overview: A small provincial charitable organization founded in 1992
Mission: To promote the growth & professionalism of the Sign Industry through communication & education
Member of: Sign Association of Canada
Affliation(s): Northwest Sign Council
Chief Officer(s):
Tim Pedrick, President
tpedrick@hisigns.com
Daryl Blanchett, Vice-President

Alberta Simmental Association (ASA)

131 Stonegate Cres., Airdrie AB T4B 2S8
Tel: 403-861-6352; *Fax:* 403-948-2059
info@albertasimmental.com
www.albertasimmental.com
Overview: A small provincial organization founded in 1971
Mission: To promote Simmental as a highly sought after, productive & efficient breed; To recognize the value of both purebred Simmental & Simmental influenced cattle; through continuous public awareness, strive for increased acceptance by the producer & consumer markets resulting in a greater share of the beef production industry
Member of: Canadian Simmental Association
Chief Officer(s):
Ashley Anderson, President
ashleyandblair@gmail.com
Healther Saucier, Office Administrator
Staff Member(s): 1; 9 volunteer(s)
Membership: 16; *Committees:* Show and Sale; 4H/YC3; Feeder Sale; Promotions; Advertising; Website
Activities: Financial prudence, fair & equal representation, support of the provincial 4-H program, encouragement & endorsement of the Alberta Young Canadian Simmentalers
Awards:
• Simmental Double Crown
• Wild Rose Classic

Alberta Ski Jumping & Nordic Combined (ASJNC)

88 Canada Olympic Rd., Calgary AB T3B 5R5
Tel: 403-247-5960
skijumpingalberta.com
www.facebook.com/ASJNC
Also Known As: Ski Jumping Alberta
Overview: A small provincial organization founded in 1991
Mission: To oversee ski jumping & nordic combined programs in Alberta.

Alberta Snowboarding Association (ASA)

Bob Niven Training Centre, Bldg. 140, #202, 88 Canada Olympic Rd. SW, Calgary AB T3B 5R5
Tel: 403-247-5609
admin@albertasnowboarding.com
www.albertasnowboarding.com
www.facebook.com/albertaSnowboardingAssociation
twitter.com/AB_Snowboard
instagram.com/albertasnowboard
Overview: A small provincial organization overseen by Canadian Snowboard Federation
Mission: To be the provincial governing body of competitive snowboarding in Alberta.
Member of: Canadian Snowboard Federation
Chief Officer(s):
Kevin Higgins, President
Aletta de Rooij, Office Manager

Alberta Snowmobile Association (ASA)

11759 Groat Rd., Edmonton AB T5M 3K6
Tel: 780-427-2695; *Fax:* 780-415-1779
www.altasnowmobile.ab.ca
www.facebook.com/103977149653938
twitter.com/Altasnowmobile
Overview: A medium-sized provincial organization founded in 1971
Mission: To promote safe recreational snowmobiling in the province of Alberta
Affliation(s): Canadian Council of Snowmobile Organizations
Chief Officer(s):
Lyle Birnie, President
ljbirnie@telus.net
Denise England, Vice-President
plasticandpowder@hotmail.com
Membership: *Fees:* $60-$70
Meetings/Conferences: • 28th Annual Alberta Snowmobile & Powersports Show 2015, October, 2015, Edmonton, AB
Scope: Provincial

Alberta Soaring Council

PO Box 13, Black Diamond AB T0L 0H0
Tel: 403-813-6658
asc@stade.ca
www.soaring.ab.ca
www.facebook.com/AlbertaSoaringCouncil
Overview: A medium-sized provincial organization founded in 1966 overseen by Soaring Association of Canada
Mission: To promote soaring sports provincially in all aspects; To plan & support local & provincial events & national competitions
Member of: Aero Club of Canada
Chief Officer(s):
Phil Stade, Executive Director
asc@stade.ca
Membership: 5 member associations
Activities: *Library*

Alberta Soccer Association (ASA)

9023 - 111 Ave., Edmonton AB T5B 0C3
Tel: 780-474-2200; *Fax:* 780-474-6300
Toll-Free: 866-250-2200
office@albertasoccer.com
www.albertasoccer.com
twitter.com/AlbertaSoccer
www.youtube.com/SoccerAlberta
Overview: A large provincial organization founded in 1909 overseen by Canadian Soccer Association
Mission: To govern & promote the sport of soccer in Alberta
Member of: Canadian Soccer Association
Chief Officer(s):
Ole Jacobsen, President
jacobsen5@shaw.ca
Richard Adams, Executive Director, 780-378-8108 Ext. 230
execdir@albertasoccer.com
Anthony Traficante, Operations Officer, 780-378-8101 Ext. 221
operations@albertasoccer.com
Carmen Charron, Coordinator, Program, 780-378-8104 Ext. 225
programs@albertasoccer.com
Staff Member(s): 16
Membership: 90,000; *Committees:* Constitution & By-Laws; Technical; Competitions; Referee Development; Appeals & Discipline; Development of Women in Soccer
Awards:
• Golden Shoe (Award)
• Shield of Merit (Award)
• Golden Whistle (Award)

• President's Award (Award)
• Award of Merit (Award)
• Life Membership (Award)
Publications:
• ASA [Alberta Soccer Association] Newsletter
Type: Newsletter

Alberta Social Credit Party
998 Conifer St., Sherwood Park AB T8A 1N5
Tel: 403-226-1786
Toll-Free: 888-762-7331
communicate@socialcredit.com
www.socialcredit.com
Overview: A large provincial organization
Chief Officer(s):
Len Skowronski, Party Leader

Alberta Society for the Prevention of Cruelty to Animals
10806 - 124 St., Edmonton AB T5M 0H3
Tel: 780-447-3600; *Fax:* 780-447-4748
info@albertaspca.org
www.albertaspca.org
www.facebook.com/AlbertaSPCA
Also Known As: Alberta SPCA
Overview: A medium-sized provincial charitable organization founded in 1959
Mission: To promote education of public about welfare of domestic animals & livestock; To deal with wildlife issues; To work on improving legislation; To concentrate on enforcement & education; To have every animal in Alberta humanely treated
Member of: Canadian Federation of Humane Societies
Chief Officer(s):
Terra Johnston, Executive Director
Finances: *Annual Operating Budget:* $500,000-$1.5 Million; *Funding Sources:* Public fundraising
Staff Member(s): 16; 600 volunteer(s)
Membership: 2,000; *Fees:* $20 single; $35 family; $150 corporate; $15 student/senior
Activities: *Library* Open to public by appointment
Meetings/Conferences: • Alberta Animal Welfare Conference 2015, 2015, AB
Scope: Provincial

Alberta Society of Artists (ASA)
PO Box 31085, 112 - 4th St., Edmonton AB T2E 9A3
Tel: 403-265-0012; *Fax:* 403-265-0944
www.artists-society.ab.ca
Overview: A small provincial charitable organization founded in 1931
Mission: To have an active membership of professional visual artists which strive for excellence & shall through exhibition, education & communication, increase public awareness & appreciation of the visual arts
Chief Officer(s):
Joanna Moore, President
Jennifer Akkermans, Artistic Coordinator
jennifer@artists-society.ab.ca
Finances: *Annual Operating Budget:* $50,000-$100,000; *Funding Sources:* Casinos; government; membership
Staff Member(s): 2; 53 volunteer(s)
Membership: 200; *Fees:* $80 full member; $30 supporting member; *Member Profile:* Professional visual Artists
Activities: Exhibitions; Travelling Exhibition Program (TREX); scholarships/awards; education; advocacy

ASA TREX Office
1235 - 26th Ave. SE, 3rd Fl., Calgary AB T2G 1R7
Tel: 403-262-4669; *Fax:* 403-263-4610
asatrex@artists-society.ab.ca
www.artists-society.ab.ca/travelling-exhibitions-trex.aspx
Chief Officer(s):
Caroline Loewen, Manager/Curator

Edmonton Office
PO Box 11334, Stn. Main, Edmonton AB T5J 3K6
Tel: 780-426-0072; *Fax:* 780-420-0944
Chief Officer(s):
Marj Thomson, Assistant Artistic Coordinator
marj@artists-society.ab.ca

Alberta Society of Engineering Technologists *See* Association of Science & Engineering Technology Professionals of Alberta

Alberta Society of Petroleum Geologists *See* Canadian Society of Petroleum Geologists

Alberta Society of Professional Biologists (ASPB)
PO Box 21104, Edmonton AB T6R 2V4
Tel: 780-434-5765; *Fax:* 780-413-0076
pbiol@aspb.ab.ca
www.aspb.ab.ca
Overview: A medium-sized provincial organization founded in 1975
Mission: To promote excellence in the practice of biology; To provide a voice for professional biologists in Alberta
Chief Officer(s):
P. Ross Bradford, Executive Director, 780-469-6196
Executivedirector@aspb.ab.ca
Robin Leech, Executive Director
releech@telusplanet.net
Bette Beswick, Registrar, 403-560-4357
bette_beswick@golder.com
Carol Engstrom, President
carol.engstrom@huskyenergy.ca
Gary Ash, Treasurer
gash@golder.com
Monika Burak, Coordinator, Finance, 780-434-5765
monika@managewise.ca
Shauna Prokopchuk, Coordinator, Membership & Communications, 780-434-5765
shauna@managewise.ca
Joy Sager, Coordinator, Association & Events, 780-434-5765
joy@managewise.ca
Membership: *Fees:* $25 student biologists; $50 biologists in training; $250 professional biologists; *Member Profile:* Persons from all disciplines of biology, such as aquatic biology, botany, ecology, genetics, biotechnology, entomology, physiology, & zoology; Student biologists; *Committees:* Discipline, Practice Review; Communications
Activities: Upholding the code of ethics; Organizing seminars for practitioners; Offering a mentorship program
Meetings/Conferences: • Alberta Society of Professional Biologists 2015 Annual Conference & General Meeting, March, 2015, Coast Canmore Hotel & Conference Centre, Canmore, AB
Scope: Provincial
Description: Theme: "A Generation of Science, Regulation and Conservation"
Contact Information: Association & Event Coordinator: Shauna Prokopchuk, Phone: 780-434-5765, E-mail: shauna@managewise.ca
Publications:
• BIOS [a publication of the Alberta Society of Professional Biologists]
Type: Newsletter; *Frequency:* 3 pa; *Editor:* Linda Zimmerling (lindazim@shaw.ca)
Profile: Articles to inform & educate members of the society & the public

Alberta Society of Radiologists (ASR)
#110, 10350 - 124th St., Edmonton AB T5N 3V9
Tel: 780-443-2615; *Fax:* 780-443-0687
asr@radiologists.ab.ca
www.radiologists.ab.ca
Overview: A small provincial organization founded in 1957
Mission: Voluntary professional association for radiologists & radiology residents in Alberta
Chief Officer(s):
Mary Learning, Executive Director
asrlearning@shawbiz.ca
Christine Molnar, President
chris.molnar@calgaryhealthregion.ca
Staff Member(s): 1; 6 volunteer(s)
Membership: 249; *Committees:* Imaging Advisory Committee
Meetings/Conferences: • 16th Continuing Medical Education Conference, May, 2015, Delta Lodge at Kananaskis, Kananaskis, AB
Scope: Provincial

Alberta Society of Surveying & Mapping Technologies (ASSMT)
PO Box 68168, 28 Crowfoot Terrace NW, Calgary AB T3G 3N8
Tel: 403-214-7504
manager@assmt.ab.ca
www.assmt.ab.ca
Overview: A medium-sized provincial organization founded in 1970
Mission: To promote the knowledge, skill & proficiency of technicians & technologists involved in the field of surveying & mapping in Alberta
Affiliation(s): Alberta Land Surveyors' Association
Chief Officer(s):
Ray Heilman, President
president@assmt.ab.ca
Finances: *Annual Operating Budget:* Less than $50,000
Staff Member(s): 1; 15 volunteer(s)
Membership: 30 student; 250 individual; 10 associate; *Fees:* $75 individual; $40 associate; students free; *Committees:* Legislation; Education; Membership; Publication; Nominating
Activities: Regional meetings; Annual general meeting; certification
Awards:
• SAIT/NAIT (Award)
Amount: $300 Bursary
• OLS College (Award)
Amount: $300 Bursary

Alberta Special Olympics Inc. *See* Special Olympics Alberta

Alberta Special Waste Services Association *See* Environmental Services Association of Alberta

Alberta Speleological Society (ASS)
c/o Andrea Corlett, #1606 924 - 14 Ave. SW, Calgary AB T2R 0N7
e-mail: info@caving.ab.ca
www.caving.ab.ca
Overview: A medium-sized provincial organization founded in 1968
Mission: To promote cave conservation; To facilitate cave explorations, primarily in the Canadian Rockies, with some activities throughout Western Canada & internationally
Member of: Federation of Alberta Naturalists
Chief Officer(s):
Jeremy Burns, President
Finances: *Funding Sources:* Membership fees
Activities: *Library* by appointment
Meetings/Conferences: • Alberta Speleological Society 2015 Annual General Meeting, 2015, AB
Scope: Provincial
Description: A meeting of cavers, featuring the election of executive members, the presentation of awards
Contact Information: E-mail: info@caving.ab.ca
Publications:
• Journal of Subterranean Metaphysics
Type: Newsletter; *Frequency:* Quarterly
Profile: A publication in both paper & digital formats, with articles about exploration, as well as society administrative information & event announcements

Alberta Sport Parachuting Association (ASPA)
c/o Tina Connolly, #4, 9915 - 87th Ave., Edmonton AB T6E 2N8
Tel: 780-996-5266
admin@aspa.ca
www.aspa.ca
Overview: A small provincial organization overseen by Canadian Sport Parachuting Association
Mission: To promote & facilitate the development of the sport of skydiving in Alberta
Member of: Canadian Sport Parachuting Association
Chief Officer(s):
Dale Good, President
Tina Connolly, Program Coordinator
Finances: *Annual Operating Budget:* $50,000-$100,000
Staff Member(s): 2
Membership: 1,400; *Fees:* $10; *Member Profile:* Ages 16-65; 30% female; 70% male
Activities: *Awareness Events:* Provincial Championships, early July; *Speaker Service:* Yes

Alberta Sport, Recreation, Parks & Wildlife Foundation
Standard Life Centre, #903, 10405 Jasper Ave., Edmonton AB T5J 4R7
Tel: 780-415-1167; *Fax:* 780-415-0308
www.asrpwf.ca
Overview: A medium-sized provincial organization founded in 1976
Mission: To facilitate & enhance activities, lifestyles & legacies through the development of active partnerships in sport, recreation, parks & wildlife programs
Chief Officer(s):
Kay Kenny, Chair
Finances: *Annual Operating Budget:* Greater than $5 Million; *Funding Sources:* Private & corporate sector donations; Lottery Board grant, Alberta Gaming
Staff Member(s): 41
Activities: *Library* by appointment

Alberta Sports & Recreation Association for the Blind (ASRAB)
#007, 15 Colonel Baker Pl. NE, Calgary AB T2E 4Z3
Tel: 403-262-5332; *Fax:* 403-265-7221
Toll-Free: 888-882-7722
info@asrab.ab.ca
www.asrab.ab.ca
Overview: A small provincial charitable organization founded in 1975 overseen by Canadian Blind Sports Association Inc.
Mission: To provide recreation & sports opportunities for Albertans who are blind & partially sighted
Member of: CBSA
Chief Officer(s):
Linda MacPhail, Executive Director
execdirector@asrab.ab.ca
Peter Wettlaufer, President
Staff Member(s): 4
Membership: *Fees:* $10 individual; $25 family
Activities: Swimming; Lawn Bowling; Powerlifting; Goalball Athletics; Tandem Cycling; *Awareness Events:* Sight Night, Nov.; *Speaker Service:* Yes

Alberta Sports Hall of Fame & Museum (ASHFM)
#102 - 4200 Hwy 2, Red Deer AB T4N 1E3
Tel: 403-341-8614; *Fax:* 403-341-8619
info@ashfm.ca
www.ashfm.ca
www.facebook.com/148079836636
twitter.com/ashfm1
www.youtube.com/user/ABSportsHallOfFame/videos
Overview: A medium-sized provincial charitable organization founded in 1957
Mission: To honour Albertans who have distinguished themselves in sport & to operate a facility to house artifacts that are significant in Alberta's sports history
Member of: Museums Alberta; Canadian Museums Association; Canadian Association for Sport Heritage; International Sport Heritage Association
Chief Officer(s):
Dennis Allan, Chair
Donna Hateley, Managing Director
Finances: *Annual Operating Budget:* $250,000-$500,000
Staff Member(s): 5; 40 volunteer(s)
Membership: 950
Activities: Induction into Sports Hall of Fame; Museum; fundraising; *Awareness Events:* Induction Banquet; Annual Golf Tournament; *Library:* Alberta Sport History Library; Open to public

Alberta Sprint Racing Canoe Association
11759 Groat Rd., Edmonton AB T5M 3K6
Tel: 780-203-3987
www.asrca.com
Previous Name: Alberta Flatwater Canoe Association
Overview: A small provincial organization overseen by CanoeKayak Canada
Member of: CanoeKayak Canada
Chief Officer(s):
Eric Toffin, President
president@asrca.com

Alberta Square & Round Dance Federation
6501 - 46 Ave., Camrose AB T4V 0E6
Tel: 403-672-5669
www.squaredance.ab.ca
Overview: A medium-sized provincial organization overseen by Canadian Square & Round Dance Society
Chief Officer(s):
Wayne Lowther, Co-President
waylow@telusplanet.net
Helen Lowther, Co-President

Alberta Squash Racquets Association *See* Squash Alberta

Alberta Sulphur Research Ltd. (ASRL)
Center for Applied Catalysts & Industrial Sulfur Chemistry, #6, 3535 Research Rd. NW, Calgary AB T2L 2K8
Tel: 403-220-5346; *Fax:* 403-284-2054
asrinfo@ucalgary.ca
www.chem.ucalgary.ca/asr
Overview: A small international organization founded in 1964
Mission: Provides technological support for producers & users of sulfur; research & technology training through seminars & courses; provides contact between industry & academia for applied catalysis & industrial sulfur chemistry; examination of the chemistry & technology of sulfur & its compunds; emphasis on research relevant to sour gas, sulfur & refining industries
Affliation(s): Chemistry Dept., Univ. of Calgary
Chief Officer(s):
Richard Surprenant, President & Chair
Jon Gorrie, 1st Vice-President & Treasurer
Finances: *Annual Operating Budget:* $500,000-$1.5 Million; *Funding Sources:* Membership research contributions
Staff Member(s): 21
Membership: 62; *Member Profile:* Sulphur producers & users; *Committees:* Technical Advisory; Finance; Executive
Activities: *Library* by appointment
Publications:
• ASRL Alberta Sulphur Research Ltd.] Board Newsletter
Type: Newsletter

Alberta Summer Swimming Association (ASSA)
c/o Swim Alberta, 11759 Groat Rd., Edmonton AB T5M 3K6
Tel: 780-454-7462; *Fax:* 780-415-1788
assaadmin@gmail.com
www.assa.ca
Overview: A medium-sized provincial organization
Mission: To provide a summer swimming program for swimmers of all ages in Alberta.
Chief Officer(s):
Don Smith, President
presidentassa@gmail.com
Membership: 59 clubs + 3,323 individuals

Alberta Table Tennis Association (ATTA)
Percy Page Centre, 11759 Groat Rd., Edmonton AB T5M 3K6
Tel: 780-427-8588; *Fax:* 866-273-6708
atta@abtabletennis.com
www.abtabletennis.com
Overview: A small provincial organization founded in 1970 overseen by Table Tennis Canada
Mission: To foster & promote the play of table tennis in a sportsmanlike manner; to award, sanction &, when necessary, supervise or manage all championship matches & tournaments; to interpret & enforce the laws & rules of table tennis; to provide & keep a permanent & official record of all championships established under its jurisdiction; generally to govern the sport in Alberta
Member of: Table Tennis Canada
Affliation(s): International Table Tennis Federation
Chief Officer(s):
Lijun Xu, President
Lei Jiang, Program Coordinator
Finances: *Annual Operating Budget:* $100,000-$250,000; *Funding Sources:* Fundraising; Alberta Sport, Park & Wildlife Foundation; Alberta Gaming
Staff Member(s): 2; 100 volunteer(s)
Membership: 1,200; *Fees:* Schedule available; *Committees:* Communication; Tournaments; Ratings; Officials; Membership/Marketing; Regional/Junior Developments; Schools
Activities: Coaching & officials development; club assistance; sport outreach; summer camps; high performance athletic training; provincial tournament hosting; preparation & sending of athletes to events; *Rents Mailing List:* Yes

Alberta Taekwondo Association (ATA)
7619 - 104 St., Edmonton AB T6E 4C3
Tel: 780-432-0721
www.taekwondoalberta.com
www.facebook.com/groups/13172614788
twitter.com/TKD_Alberta
Overview: A small provincial organization
Affliation(s): Taekwondo Canada; World Taekwondo Federation
Chief Officer(s):
Ken Froese, Chair
kenf@calgarytkd.com
Kevin Olsen, Secretary General
mu-shimtkd@hotmail.com

Alberta Target Archers Association (ATAA)
AB
Tel: 780-717-2597
membership@ataa-org.ca
www.ataa-org.ca
Overview: A small provincial organization
Mission: To promote all forms of archery in Alberta.
Chief Officer(s):
Rene Schaub, President, 780-689-8488
president@ataa-org.ca
Jan Tollenaar, Coordinator, Membership
Membership: *Fees:* Schedule available

Alberta Teachers of English as a Second Language (ATESL)
c/o University of Alberta, #6, 102 Education North, Edmonton AB T6G 2G5
Tel: 780-455-7649
ask@atesl.ca
www.atesl.ca
www.linkedin.com/pub/atesl-alberta-teachers-of-esl/61/8a6/314
www.facebook.com/170856763052757
twitter.com/ATESLnews
plus.google.com/105900523013702188458
Also Known As: Association of Alberta Teachers of English as a Second Language
Overview: A small provincial organization founded in 1974 overseen by TESL Canada Federation
Mission: To promote the highest standards of teaching & English language program provision for all learners in Alberta whose first language is other than English
Chief Officer(s):
Sheri Rhodes, President
Membership: *Committees:* Accreditation
Activities: Professional development; accreditation; advocacy

Alberta Teachers' Association (ATA)
Barnett House, 11010 - 142 St., Edmonton AB T5N 2R1
Tel: 780-447-9400; *Fax:* 780-455-6481
Toll-Free: 800-232-7208
government@teachers.ab.ca
www.teachers.ab.ca
Overview: A large provincial organization founded in 1918 overseen by Canadian Teachers' Federation
Mission: To advance the cause of education in Alberta; To improve the teaching profession; To increase public interest in & support for education; To cooperate with other bodies having similar objectives
Chief Officer(s):
Carol Henderson, President
carol.henderson@ata.ab.ca
Finances: *Annual Operating Budget:* $3 Million-$5 Million; *Funding Sources:* Membership fees
Staff Member(s): 105
Membership: 43,460; *Member Profile:* Employment of teacher by school board; *Committees:* Curriculum; Professional Conduct; Finance; Pension; Resolutions; Substitute Teachers; Table Officers; Teacher Education & Certification; Teacher Welfare Services
Activities: *Library* Open to public
Meetings/Conferences: • North Central Teachers Convention 2015, February, 2015, Shaw Conference Centre, Edmonton, AB
Scope: Local
• Calgary City Teachers Convention 2015, February, 2015, Telus Convention Centre, Calgary, AB
Scope: Local
• Northeast Teachers Convention 2015, February, 2015, Doubletree by Hilton, Edmonton, AB
Scope: Local
• Central Alberta Teachers Convention 2015, February, 2015, Red Deer College, Red Deer, AB
Scope: Local
• Palliser District Teachers Convention 2015, February, 2015, Telus Convention Centre, Calgary, AB
Scope: Local
• South Western Alberta Teachers Convention 2015, February, 2015, University of Lethbridge, Lethbridge, AB
Scope: Local
• Southeastern Alberta Teachers Convention 2015, February, 2015, AB
Scope: Local
• Central East Alberta Teachers Convention 2015, March, 2015, Shaw Conference Centre, Edmonton, AB
Scope: Local
• Mighty Peace Teachers Convention 2015, March, 2015, Grande Prairie, AB
Scope: Local
Publications:
• ATA Magazine
Type: Magazine

Alberta Team Handball Federation (ATHF)
Percy Page Centre, 11749 Groat Rd., Edmonton AB T5M 3K6
Tel: 780-415-2666; *Fax:* 780-422-2663
Handballalberta@gmail.com
www.teamhandball.ab.ca
www.facebook.com/pages/Alberta-Team-Handball-Federation/111368133359
twitter.com/handballalberta

www.youtube.com/user/HandballAlberta1;
vimeo.com/channels/123390
Overview: A medium-sized provincial organization founded in 1960
Mission: To govern the promotion of team handball throughout Alberta, by encouraging the development of athletes, coaches, referees, & administrators of all ages & abilities
Member of: Canadian Team Handball Federation
Chief Officer(s):
Dan Stetic, CEO
Surroosh Ghofrani, Chief Financial Officer
Finances: *Funding Sources:* Membership & course fees; fundraising; donations; Alberta Sport, Recreation, Parks & Wildlife Foundation
Activities: Organizing provincial championships, regional leagues, coaching courses; programs for 8 years of age to adults, sport outreach clinics, & the City of Champions Tournament

Edmonton Team Handball League
11759 Groat Rd., Edmonton AB T5M 3K6
Tel: 780-415-2666
kbmuir@hotmail.com
Chief Officer(s):
Kelly Muir, Contact

Alberta Tennis Association (ATA)
11759 Groat Rd., Edmonton AB T5M 3K6
Tel: 780-415-1661; *Fax:* 780-415-1693
info@tennisalberta.com
www.tennisalberta.com
www.facebook.com/tennisalberta
twitter.com/tennisalberta
Also Known As: Tennis Alberta
Overview: A medium-sized provincial charitable organization founded in 1973 overseen by Tennis Canada
Mission: To facilitate participation, development, & visibility of tennis throughout Alberta
Member of: International Tennis Federation; Tennis Canada
Chief Officer(s):
Jill Groves, Executive Director
jill.groves@tennisalberta.com
Charlie McLean, Coordinator, High Performance
charlie.mclean@tennisalberta.com
Catlin Westrs, Coordinator, Tournament & Program
Finances: *Funding Sources:* ASRPW Foundation; Tennis Canada; Sponsors; Self-generated revenue
Staff Member(s): 3
Activities: Coaching; Officiating; *Library:* Tennis Resource Centre;

Alberta Texas Longhorn Association (ATLA)
RR#1, Leduc AB T9E 2X1
Tel: 780-387-4874
www.albertatexaslonghorn.com
Overview: A small provincial organization founded in 1982
Mission: To provide new & existing breeders with the opportunity to purchase top quality longhorn cattle for herd improvement; to increase public awareness about longhorn cattle; to provide clinics for judging & evaluating the Texas Longhorn
Affliation(s): Texas Longhorn Breeders Association of America
Chief Officer(s):
Ron Walker, President, 403-548-6684
Membership: 35; *Fees:* $40 Active; $20 Associate

Alberta Therapeutic Recreation Association (ATRA)
8038 Fairmount Dr. SE, Calgary AB T2H 0Y1
Tel: 403-258-2520; *Fax:* 403-255-2234
Toll-Free: 888-258-2520
atra@alberta-tr.org
www.alberta-tr.org
Overview: A small provincial organization founded in 1985
Mission: To offer mentorships, continuing education, bursaries, & awards
Chief Officer(s):
Kari Medd, President
president@alberta-tr.org
Membership: *Fees:* $300; $50 student/supporting; *Member Profile:* Professionals who work in the field of therapeutic recreation in Alberta

Alberta Track & Field Association *See* Athletics Alberta

Alberta Trappers' Association
Industrial Park Lot 14, PO Box 6020, Stn. Main, Hwy. 44 South, Westlock AB T7P 2P7
Tel: 780-349-6626; *Fax:* 780-349-6634
info@albertatrappers.com
www.albertatrappers.com
Overview: A small provincial organization
Mission: To represent registered & resident trappers in Alberta; To promote the harvesting of wild furbearers in a humane & sustainable manner
Chief Officer(s):
Jim Mitchell, Contact, Trapper Education
Membership: 2,000+; *Member Profile:* Licensed trappers in Alberta
Activities: Supporting the protection of threatened & endangered species; Operating a fur depot for tanning & shipping; Providing trapper & public education
Publications:
• Alberta Trapper Magazine
Type: Magazine; *Frequency:* Quarterly; *Accepts Advertising*; *Price:* Free with membership in the Alberta Trappers' Association
Profile: Issues encountered by trappers, plus anecdotes about trapping experiences
• Alberta Trappers' Association Newsletter
Type: Newsletter; *Frequency:* Monthly
Profile: Updates from the association, including upcoming courses

Alberta Triathlon Association (ATA)
Percy Page Centre, 11759 Groat Rd., Edmonton AB T5M 3K6
Tel: 780-427-8616; *Fax:* 780-427-8628
Toll-Free: 866-888-7448
info@triathlon.ab.ca
www.triathlon.ab.ca
www.facebook.com/160835077267482
twitter.com/TriAlberta
Overview: A small provincial organization founded in 1984 overseen by Triathlon Canada
Mission: ATA is the official, non-profit governing body for, & has a mandate to develop, the sports of triathlon, duathlon, aquathlon & other related multi-endurance sports in Alberta.
Member of: Triathlon Canada
Chief Officer(s):
Hugh Brown, President
president@triathlon.ab.ca
Tim Wilson, Executive Director
executive.director@triathlon.ab.ca
Finances: *Annual Operating Budget:* $100,000-$250,000
Staff Member(s): 1; 16 volunteer(s)
Membership: 1,000+; *Fees:* $35 adult; $5 junior
Activities: *Speaker Service:* Yes

Alberta Turkey Producers
4828 - 89 St., Edmonton AB T6E 5K1
Tel: 780-465-5755; *Fax:* 780-465-5528
info@albertaturkey.com
www.albertaturkey.com
Overview: A small provincial organization
Chief Officer(s):
Cara Dary, Executive Director
cara@albertaturkey.com
Finances: *Annual Operating Budget:* $250,000-$500,000
Staff Member(s): 2
Membership: 1-99; *Member Profile:* To provide an environment that will enhance the overall growth of the Alberta turkey industry

Alberta Ukrainian Dance Association
Percy Page Centre, 11759 Groat Rd., Edmonton AB T5M 3K6
Tel: 780-422-9700; *Fax:* 780-422-2663
info@abuda.ca
www.abuda.ca
Overview: A medium-sized provincial organization founded in 1982
Mission: To help serve the needs of the Ukrainian dance community; To promote Ukranian heritage through dance; To provide information about Ukranian dancing; To assist dance groups & instructors in Alberta
Chief Officer(s):
Andrew Wujcik, Executive Director
Membership: 86 dance groups + 4,000 dancers; *Fees:* $15 individual; $25 group
Activities: Ukrainian dance workshops held throughout the year; intensive program offers classes in technique & history seminars; *Library*

Alberta Underwater Council (AUC)
Percy Page Building, 11759 Groat Rd., 2nd Fl., Edmonton AB T5M 3K6
Tel: 780-427-9125; *Fax:* 780-427-8139
Toll-Free: 888-307-8566
info@albertaunderwatercouncil.com
www.albertaunderwatercouncil.com
Overview: A medium-sized local organization founded in 1962
Mission: To represent responsible participation in & awareness of underwater activities
Affliation(s): Canadian Underwater Games Association
Chief Officer(s):
Cathie McCuaig, Executive Director, 780-427-9125, Fax: 780-427-8139
Finances: *Funding Sources:* Alberta Gaming; Alberta Sport Recreation Parks & Wildlife Foundation
Membership: 600 individual; *Fees:* $15
Activities: *Awareness Events:* Divescapes

Alberta Union of Provincial Employees / Syndicat de la fonction publique de l'Alberta
10451 - 170 St., Edmonton AB T5P 4S7
Tel: 780-930-3300; *Fax:* 780-930-3392
Toll-Free: 800-232-7284
www.aupe.org
www.facebook.com/yourAUPE
Overview: A medium-sized provincial organization
Chief Officer(s):
Ron Hodgins, Executive Director
r.hodgins@aupe.org
Jamie Oyarzun, Director, Labour Relations
j.oyarzun@aupe.org
Staff Member(s): 95
Membership: 60,000

Alberta Urban Municipalities Association (AUMA)
#300, 8616 15 Ave., Edmonton AB T6E 6E6
Tel: 780-433-4431; *Fax:* 780-433-4454
Toll-Free: 800-310-2862
main@auma.ca
www.auma.ca
twitter.com/theauma
Overview: A medium-sized provincial organization founded in 1905
Mission: To provide leadership in advocating local government interests to the provincial government & other organizations, & to provide services that address the needs of its membership
Chief Officer(s):
John McGowan, CEO
jmcgowan@auma.ca
Finances: *Funding Sources:* Membership dues
Staff Member(s): 23
Membership: 284 municipalities; *Fees:* $474 + GST affiliate/associate; *Committees:* 15 Committees & Task Forces
Activities: *Rents Mailing List:* Yes
Meetings/Conferences: • Alberta Urban Municipalities Association Convention & AMSC Trade Show 2015, September, 2015, Telus Convention Centre, Calgary, AB
Scope: Provincial
• Alberta Urban Municipalities Association Convention & AMSC Trade Show 2016, October, 2016, Edmonton, AB
Scope: Provincial
• Alberta Urban Municipalities Association Convention & AMSC Trade Show 2017, November, 2017, Calgary, AB
Scope: Provincial

Alberta Veterinary Medical Association (AVMA)
Weber Centre, #950, 5555 Calgary Trail NW, Edmonton AB T6H 5P9
Tel: 780-489-5007
Toll-Free: 800-404-2862
www.avma.ca
www.linkedin.com/company/alberta-veterinary-medical-association
www.facebook.com/ABVMA
twitter.com/abvma
www.youtube.com/abvma
Overview: A medium-sized provincial licensing organization founded in 1905 overseen by Canadian Veterinary Medical Association
Mission: To represent Alberta veterinarians in small animal, large animal & mixed practice as well as those employed in government, industry or other institutions
Chief Officer(s):
Duane Landals, Senior Advisor
duane.landals@avma.ab.ca
Finances: *Funding Sources:* Membership fees
Staff Member(s): 10

Membership: 3,037; *Member Profile:* Veterinarians & animal health technologists; *Committees:* Discipline Hearing Tribunal & Complaint Review; Practice Inspection & Practice Standards; Practice Review Board; Registration; Alternate Livestock & Wildlife; Animal Welfare; Companion Animal; Equine; Food Animal; Vet Med 21

Alberta Walking Horse Association (AWHA)

c/o Shirley Wesslen, RR#1, Blackfalds AB T0M 0J0
Tel: 403-885-5290
albertawalkinghorse@gmail.com
www.walkinghorse.ca
Overview: A small provincial organization
Mission: To promote the Tennessee Walking Horse in Alberta
Chief Officer(s):
Blair Dyberg, President, 780-352-3531
seedsandsteeds@aol.com
Shirley Wesslen, Secretary, 403-885-5290
swesslen@aol.com
Rhonda Lemmon, Chair, Alberta Celebration Show, 403-782-3118
yonafeda@gmail.com
Membership: *Fees:* $30 single members; $50 families; $20 youth; *Member Profile:* Tennessee Walking Horse owners & riders in Alberta
Activities: Participating in horse shows & events; Creating networking opportunities; Presenting awards
Publications:
• Alberta Walking Horse Association Newsletter
Type: Newsletter; *Frequency:* Monthly

Alberta Wall & Ceiling Association (AWCA)

PO Box 21016, Edmonton AB T6R 2V4
Tel: 780-757-9277; *Fax:* 888-280-1172
Toll-Free: 888-240-7045
awca.ed@shaw.ca
www.albertawallandceiling.com
Previous Name: Alberta Wall & Ceiling Bureau
Overview: A small provincial organization overseen by Northwest Wall & Ceiling Bureau
Mission: To act as the provincial voice for the industry, providing & promoting technical information & training to its members, the construction industry & consumers at large.

Alberta Wall & Ceiling Bureau *See* Alberta Wall & Ceiling Association

Alberta Water & Wastewater Operators Association (AWWOA)

11810 Kingsway Ave., Edmonton AB T5G 0X5
Tel: 780-454-7745; *Fax:* 780-454-7748
Toll-Free: 877-454-7745
awwoa@telus.net
www.awwoa.ab.ca
www.facebook.com/group.php?gid=157981630910194
twitter.com/awwoa
Overview: A small provincial organization founded in 1976
Mission: To contribute to the training & upgrading of persons employed in the water & wastewater field in Alberta; To encourage the best possible operation of water & wastewater facilities
Affliation(s): Western Canada Water & Wastewater Association
Chief Officer(s):
John Voyer, Executive Director, Fax: 780-451-6451
awwoa1@telus.net
Cathie Monson, Coordinator, Training Program, Fax: 780-454-7748
awwoa@telus.net
Laura Selcho, Training Course Registrar, Fax: 780-454-7758
awwoa2@telus.net
Activities: Providing manuals to operators
Awards:
• Alberta Water & Wastewater Operators Association Outreach Student Applicant Bursaries (Scholarship)
Available to students entering the Water & Wastewater Technician program at the Northern Alberta Institute of Technology*Eligibility:* Applicant must provide a copy of the Alberta Enviornment approved course completion certificate *Amount:* $300 *Contact:* AWWOA Outreach Student Bursaries, Address: 11810 Kingsway Ave., Edmonton, AB T5G 0X5
• Alberta Water & Wastewater Operators Association Steve Blonsky Honorary Life Membership Award (Award)
For persons retired from the water or sewage field*Deadline:* October *Contact:* Kathy Abramowski, Awards Chair, Phone: 780-427-5204; E-mail: Kathy.Abramowski@gov.ab.ca
• Alberta Water & Wastewater Operators Association NAIT Achievement Award (Award)
Eligibility: The student enrolled in the Northern Alberta Institute of Technology's full time Water & Wastewater Technician Program, who achieves the highest marks *Amount:* $500
• Alberta Water & Wastewater Operators Association Operator of the Year Award (Award)
Eligibility: A member in good standing of the Alberta Water & Wastewater Operators Association who has provided exemplary service to the water or wastewater operations field over an extended period of time*Deadline:* January *Contact:* Kathy Abramowski, Awards Chair, Phone: 780-427-5204; E-mail: Kathy.Abramowski@gov.ab.ca
• Alberta Water & Wastewater Operators Association Ron Bayne Service Award (Award)
To recognize outstanding service to the Alberta Water & Wastewater Operators Association & contribution to the water & wastewater operartions field*Deadline:* January *Contact:* Kathy Abramowski, Awards Chair, Phone: 780-427-5204; E-mail: Kathy.Abramowski@gov.ab.ca
• Alberta Water & Wastewater Operators Association NAIT North Scholarship (Scholarship)
To honour academically outstanding individuals who have made significant contributions in extracurricular or community activities*Eligibility:* Registration in the full-time Water & Wastewater Technician program at the Edmonton Campus of the Northern Alberta Institute of Technology *Amount:* $3,000 *Contact:* Alberta Water & Wastewater Operators Assn, 11810 Kingsway Ave., Edmonton, AB, T5G 0X5
• Alberta Water & Wastewater Operators Association NAIT South Scholarship (Scholarship)
To recognize academic credentials, personal leadership activities, excellence in extracurricular activities, & notable contributions to the community*Eligibility:* Registration in the full-time Water & Wastewater Technician program at the Calgary Campus of the Northern Alberta Institute of Technology *Amount:* $3,000 *Contact:* Alberta Water & Wastewater Operators Assn, 11810 Kingsway Ave., Edmonton, AB, T5G 0X5
Meetings/Conferences: • Alberta Water & Wastewater Operators Association 2015 40th Annual Operators Seminar, 2015, AB
Scope: Provincial
Attendance: 500+
Description: Speakers, including operators, supervisors, technical industry representatives, & other experts in their fields, bring operators up-to-date on numerous topics in the water & wastewater field
Contact Information: Training Program Coordinator: Cathie Monson, Phone: 780-454-7745, Fax: 780-454-7748, E-mail: cmonson@awwoa.ca
Publications:
• Alberta Utility Operator Newsletter
Type: Newsletter; *Frequency:* 3 pa; *Editor:* Gayle Sacuta
Profile: Information about Alberta's water & wastewater operations, outstanding service, new technologies, research, regulatory changes, & trainingopportunities

Alberta Water Council

Petroleum Plaza, South Tower, #1400, 9915 - 108 St., Edmonton AB T5K 2G8
Tel: 780-644-7380
info@awchome.ca
www.albertawatercouncil.ca
Overview: A medium-sized provincial organization
Mission: The Alberta Water Council is a stakeholder partnership that provides leadership, expertise and advocacy, to engage and empower individuals, organizations, business and governments to achieve the outcomes of the Water for Life strategy.
Chief Officer(s):
Gord Edwards, Executive Director, 780-644-7373
g.edwards@awchome.ca
Membership: 24 institutional
Meetings/Conferences: • 2015 Alberta Water Council Symposium, 2015
Scope: Provincial

Alberta Water Polo Association (AWPA)

PO Box 54, 2225 Macleod Trail SE, Calgary AB T2G 5B6
Tel: 403-281-7797; *Fax:* 403-281-7798
office@albertawaterpolo.ca
www.albertawaterpolo.ca
www.facebook.com/group.php?gid=143394719017308
Overview: A medium-sized provincial organization founded in 1974 overseen by Water Polo Canada
Mission: To provide a safe & positive environment for the ongoing development & growth of water polo in Alberta for the recreational to the elite athlete
Member of: Water Polo Canada
Chief Officer(s):
Cori Paul, President
cpaul@gss.org
Dayna Christmas, Executive Director
office@albertawaterpolo.ca
Nicolas Youngblud, Treasurer
Blud_1@hotmail.com

Alberta Water Well Drilling Association (AWWDA)

PO Box 130, Lougheed AB T0B 2V0
Tel: 780-386-2335; *Fax:* 780-386-2344
awwda@telusplanet.net
www.awwda.com
Overview: A medium-sized provincial organization founded in 1958 overseen by Canadian Ground Water Association
Mission: The AWWDA is a non-profit, non-sectarian organization with certain objectives including: assisting, promoting, encouraging, and supporting the interest and welfare of the water well industry in all of its phases; fostering aid and promote scientific education, standard research, and technique in order to improve methods of well construction and development and advance the science of groundwater in the province of Alberta.
Chief Officer(s):
Brad Meyers, Secretary Manager, 403-938-4961, Fax: 403-938-3324
aarondrill@telus.net

Alberta Weekly Newspapers Association (AWNA)

3228 Parsons Rd., Edmonton AB T6H 5R7
Tel: 780-434-8746; *Fax:* 780-438-8356
Toll-Free: 800-282-6903
info@awna.com
www.awna.com
releases@awna.com
Overview: A medium-sized provincial organization overseen by Canadian Community Newspapers Association
Mission: To assist members to publish high quality community newspapers; To serve advertisers by providing information about the markets of community newspapers in Alberta
Chief Officer(s):
Dennis Merrell, Executive Director
dennis@awna.com
Ossie Sheddy, President, 403-823-2580
editor@drumhellermail.com
Murray Elliott, Vice-President, 403-556-7510
melliott@olds.greatwest.ca
Chrissie Hamblin, Controller
chrissie@awna.com
Maurizia Hinse, Coordinator, Professional Development & Communication
maurizia@awna.com
Fred Gorman, Corporate Secretary, 403-314-4311
fgorman@reddeeradvocate.com
Membership: 118 newspapers; *Member Profile:* Community newspapers throughout Alberta & the Northwest Territories; *Committees:* Advertising; AdWest Representatives; Membership; AWSOM Archive / Technology; Community Education / VCOY; Government Relations; Newspaper Symposium; Convention; Better Newspapers Competition; Audit; Nominating; Industry Education; Bing Crosby Golf Tournament
Activities: Providing workshops; Assisting with marketing; Recognizing excellence; Presenting bursaries & scholarships; Offering networking opportunities
Meetings/Conferences: • Alberta Weekly Newspapers Association 2015 Newspaper Symposium, February, 2015, Radisson Hotel Edmonton South, Edmonton, AB
Scope: Provincial
Description: A symposium for persons who work for newspapers, such as managers, editors, photographers, & sales people, featuring a keynote speaker, courses on a variety of topics, & the presentation of awards
Contact Information: Professional Development & Communications Coordinator: Maurizia Hinse, E-mail: maurizia@awna.com
• Alberta Weekly Newspapers Association 2015 95th Annual General Meeting & Convention, 2015
Scope: Provincial
Publications:
• Alberta Weekly Newspapers Association Membership Directory
Type: Directory

Alberta Whitewater Association (AWA)

Percy Page Centre, 11759 Groat Rd., Edmonton AB T5M 3K6
Tel: 403-628-2336
admin@albertawhitewater.ca

www.albertawhitewater.ca
www.facebook.com/alberta.whitewater
Overview: A small provincial organization founded in 1972 overseen by CanoeKayak Canada
Mission: To encourage whitewater paddlesport activities
Member of: CanoeKayak Canada
Affliation(s): International Canoe Federation
Chief Officer(s):
Chuck Lee, Executive Director
Finances: *Annual Operating Budget:* $50,000-$100,000
Staff Member(s): 2
Membership: 500-999; *Fees:* Individual: $15; Club: $120
Activities: Canoe polo; slalom; wild water races; recreational river trips; freestyle events

Alberta Wilderness Association (AWA)

PO Box 6398, Stn. D, 455 - 12 St. NW, Calgary AB T2N 1Y9
Tel: 403-283-2025; *Fax:* 403-270-2743
Toll-Free: 866-313-0713
awa@shaw.ca
albertawilderness.ca
www.facebook.com/AlbertaWilderness
twitter.com/ABWilderness
www.youtube.com/user/AlbertaWilderness
Overview: A large provincial charitable organization founded in 1965
Mission: To promote the protection of Alberta's rivers & wildlands areas; To restore the natural ecosystems of Alberta; To educate Albertans on wilderness conservation & sustainable use of natural lands & waters
Member of: Alberta Environment Network; Environmental Law Centre; Calgary & Area Outdoor Council; Volunteer Centre of Calgary
Affliation(s): Environmental Resource Centre
Chief Officer(s):
Richard Secord, President
Christyann Olson, Executive Director
awa@abwild.ca
Finances: *Annual Operating Budget:* $250,000-$500,000; *Funding Sources:* Provincial grants; Fundraising events; Membership fees; Donations
Staff Member(s): 4; 250 volunteer(s)
Membership: 2,500 individual + 110 organizations; *Fees:* $25 single; $30 family
Activities: Researching wilderness issues; *Awareness Events:* Climb & Run for Wilderness, April; *Speaker Service:* Yes; *Library:* Wilderness Resource Centre; Open to public
Awards:
• Great Gray Owl Award (Award)
For individuals who meet a high standard of volunteerism, dedication & commitment
Publications:
• Bighorn Wildland [a publication of the Alberta Wilderness Association]
Type: Book; *ISBN:* 0-920074-20-0
• Elbow Sheep Wilderness [a publication of the Alberta Wilderness Association]
Type: Book
• Recall of the Wild [a publication of the Alberta Wilderness Association]
Profile: A supplement to the Wild Lands Advocate
• Rivers on Borrowed Time [a publication of the Alberta Wilderness Association]
Type: Book
• Wild Lands Advocate [a publication of the Alberta Wilderness Association]
Type: Journal; *Frequency:* 6 pa.; *Editor:* Ian Urquhart
• Willmore Wilderness Park [a publication of the Alberta Wilderness Association]
Type: Book

Alberta Women Entrepreneurs

Melton Building, #308, 10310 Jasper Ave., Edmonton AB T5J 2W4
Fax: 780-422-0756
Toll-Free: 800-713-3558
info@awebusiness.com
www.awebusiness.com
www.linkedin.com/company/alberta-women-entrepreneurs
www.facebook.com/awebusiness
twitter.com/AWEbusiness
Overview: A medium-sized provincial organization founded in 1995
Mission: AWE is a not-for-profit organization that helps women in Alberta succeed in business through business advice, business skills development, financing & networking.
Member of: Western Canada Business Service Network
Chief Officer(s):
Marie C. Robidoux, Chair
Tracey Scarlett, CEO
Finances: *Funding Sources:* Western Economic Diversification Canada
Staff Member(s): 8
Activities: annual conference

Calgary Office
#370, 105 - 12 Ave. SE, Calgary AB T2G 1A1
Fax: 403-777-4258
Toll-Free: 800-713-3558

Alberta Women's Institutes (AWI)

5407 - 36 Ave., Wetaskiwin AB T9A 3C7
Tel: 780-312-2440; *Fax:* 780-312-2482
evelyne@athabascau.ca
awi.athabascau.ca
Overview: A medium-sized provincial organization founded in 1909 overseen by Federated Women's Institutes of Canada
Affliation(s): Associated Country Women of the World; Federated Women's Institutes of Canada
Chief Officer(s):
Evelyn Ellerman, Contact
evelyne@athabascau.ca
Membership: *Fees:* $30 / year

Albion Neighbourhood Services

#14, 21 Panorama Crt., Toronto ON M9V 4E3
Tel: 416-740-3704; *Fax:* 416-740-7124
ans@albionservices.ca
www.albionservices.ca
Previous Name: Etobicoke North Community Information Centre
Overview: A small local organization founded in 1971 overseen by InformOntario
Mission: To provide accessible programs that educate & enable individuals & families to achieve self-sufficiency & social wellbeing
Chief Officer(s):
Herman Todd, President
Filomena Ferlisi, Executive Director
Activities: Information & referral; language resource bank, interpreting & translating; income tax clinic; immigrant settlement services; advocacy; housing counselling, child & youth recreational activities; child breakfast clubs, after school programs, camps;

Alcohol and Drug Recovery Association of Ontario *See* Addictions & Mental Health Ontario

Alcoholics Anonymous (GTA Intergroup) (AA)

#202, 234 Eglinton Ave. East, Toronto ON M4P 1K5
Tel: 416-487-5591; *Fax:* 416-487-5855
Toll-Free: 877-404-5591; *TTY:* 866-831-4657
office@aatoronto.org
aatoronto.org
Overview: A large national charitable organization founded in 1947
Mission: Fellowship of men & women who share their experience, strength & hope with each other so that they may solve their common problem & help others recover from alcoholism; the primary purpose is to stay sober & help other alcoholics to achieve sobriety
Finances: *Annual Operating Budget:* $100,000-$250,000; *Funding Sources:* Donations; literature sales; conferences
Staff Member(s): 3; 350 volunteer(s)
Membership: 12,000; *Member Profile:* Must have a desire to stop drinking; *Committees:* Access Ability; Archives; Communications; Correctional; Cooperation with the Professional Community; Finance; Information A.A. Day; Ontario Regional Conference; Executive; Public Information; Treatment; Twelfth Step; Winter Season Open House
Activities: Annual Ontario Regional Conference; Christmas Day Open House & Dinner; Archives Breakfast, Nov.; Information AA Day, May; AA Picnic, summer; *Library:* Toronto Intergroup Literature Library; Open to public
Publications:
• Better Times [a publication of Alcoholics Anonymous (GTA Intergroup)]
Type: Newsletter; *Frequency:* Monthly

Abbotsford - Intergroup Committee
#17, 1961 Eagle St., Abbotsford BC V2S 3A7
Crisis Hot-Line: 604-850-0811
abbotsfordintrgrp@hotmail.com
www.theabbotsfordintergroup-aa.org

Barrie - Barrie & Area Intergroup
#622, 80 Bradford St., Barrie ON L4N 6S7
Tel: 705-725-8682
officecoordinator@barrieaa.com
www.barrieaa.com
Chief Officer(s):
Carole M. Keenan, Executive Director

Calgary - Central Service Office
#2, 4015 - 1st St. SE, Calgary AB T2G 4X7
Tel: 403-777-1212; *Fax:* 403-287-6540
info@calgaryaa.org
www.calgaryaa.org

Edmonton - AA Central Office
#8, 11041 - 105 Ave. NW, Edmonton AB T5H 3Y1
Tel: 780-424-5900; *Fax:* 780-426-1929
www.edmontonaa.org

Guelph - Central West District 3
#210, 218 Silvercreek Pkwy. North, Guelph ON N1H 8E8
Tel: 519-836-1522
www.centralwest2district3aa.org

Halifax Central Office
PO Box 31338, Halifax NS B3K 5Z1
Tel: 902-461-1119
help@aahalifax.org
www.aahalifax.org

Hamilton - Central Office
#205, 627 Main St. East, Hamilton ON L8M 1J5
Tel: 905-522-8399; *Fax:* 905-522-1946
www.aahamilton.org

London - London Area Intergroup
201 Consortium Crt., London ON
Tel: 519-438-9006; *Fax:* 905-522-1946; *Crisis Hot-Line:* 519-438-1122
www.aalondon.org

Montréal - Intergroupe de Montréal
3920, rue Rachel est, Montréal QC H1X 1Z3
Tel: 514-374-3688; *Fax:* 514-374-2250
area87@aa-quebec.org
aa87.org

Oshawa - Lakeshore Intergroup
200 Thornton Rd. North, Oshawa ON L1J 6T8
Tel: 905-728-1020
aa.oshawa@live.com
www.aaoshawa.org

Ottawa - Ottawa Area Intergroup
#108, 211 Bronson Ave., Ottawa ON K1R 6H5
Tel: 613-237-6000
info@ottawaaa.org
www.ottawaaa.org

Peterborough - Kawartha District Intergroup
625 Cameron St., Peterborough ON K9J 3Z9
Tel: 705-745-6111
district86aa@hotmail.com
www.peterboroughaa.org

Prince Edward Island - Green Acres Intergroup
5 Summer St., Summerside PE C1N 3H3
Tel: 902-436-7721

Québec - Northeast Area of Québec Central Office
#0-17, 14, rue Soumande, Québec QC G1L 0A4
Tel: 418-523-9993; *Fax:* 418-523-9997
region89@aa-quebec.org
aa-quebec.org/region89

Québec - Northwest Area of Québec Central Office
PO Box 361, Saint-Jérôme QC J7Z 5V2
Tel: 450-560-3902; *Fax:* 450-560-3903
region@aa90.org
www.aa90.org

Regina - Central Office
#312, 845 Broad St., Regina SK S4R 8G9
Tel: 306-545-9300
a.a@sasktel.net
www.aaregina.com

St Catharines - Niagara District Intergroup
Tel: 905-682-2140
Toll-Free: 866-311-9042
info@aaniagara.org
www.aaniagara.org

St. John's - Central Office
#117, 183 Kenmount Rd., St. John's NL A1B 3P9

Tel: 709-579-6091; *TTY:* 709-579-5215
sjintergroup@nl.rogers.com
www.aastjohns.nf.net

Saskatoon - Saskatoon Central Office
#515, 245 - 3rd Ave. South, Saskatoon SK S7K 1M4
Tel: 306-665-6727; *Fax:* 306-665-6753
aasaskatoon@sasktel.net
www.aasaskatoon.org

Trenton - District 30 Quinte West
Toll-Free: 866-951-3711
www.quintewestaa.org

Vancouver - Greater Vancouver Intergroup Society
3457 Kingsway, Vancouver BC V5R 5L5
Tel: 604-434-3933; *Fax:* 604-434-2553
intrgrp@vancouveraa.ca
www.vancouveraa.ca

Victoria - AA Central Office
#8, 2020 Douglas St., Victoria BC V8T 4L1
Tel: 250-383-0415; *Fax:* 250-383-0417; *Crisis Hot-Line:* 250-383-7744
vicintgpco@shaw.ca
www.aavictoria.ca

Whitehorse - Whitehorse Intergroup
c/o BC/Yukon Area 79, PO Box 42114, Vancouver BC V5S 4R5
Tel: 604-435-2181
info@bcyukonaa.org
www.bcyukonaa.org

Winnipeg - Manitoba Central Office
#208, 323 Portage Ave., Winnipeg MB R3B 2C1
Tel: 204-942-0126
Toll-Free: 877-942-0126
aambco@mts.net
www.aamanitoba.org

Alcooliques Anonymes du Québec

Bureau des services de la Région 87, 3920, rue Rachel est, Montréal QC H1X 1Z3
Tél: 514-374-3688; *Téléc:* 514-374-2250
region@aa87.org
aa-quebec.org
Aperçu: *Dimension:* petite; *Envergure:* provinciale; fondée en 1935
Mission: Demeurer abstinent et aider d'autres alcooliques à le devenir
Membre(s) du bureau directeur:
Diane H., Présidente
president@aa87.org
Membre: Over 50,000

Alcooliques Anonymes Groupe La Vallée du Cuivre

CP 21, Chibougamau QC G8P 2K5
Ligne sans frais: 866-376-6279
Aperçu: *Dimension:* petite; *Envergure:* locale

The Alcuin Society

PO Box 3216, Vancouver BC V6B 3X8
e-mail: info@alcuinsociety.com
www.alcuinsociety.com
www.facebook.com/alcuinsociety
twitter.com/alcuin
www.flickr.com/photos/alcuinsociety
Overview: A small provincial charitable organization founded in 1965
Mission: To sponsor educational programs; Yo publish a journal; To offer awards & citations for excellence in book arts
Member of: Fellowship of American Bibliophilic Societies
Chief Officer(s):
Howard Greaves, Chair
Finances: *Annual Operating Budget:* Less than $50,000; *Funding Sources:* Membership dues; donations; BC Gaming Commission
Staff Member(s): 1; 10 volunteer(s)
Membership: 370; *Fees:* Annual - Student: $25; Individual: $50; Institutional: $75; Patron: $125; *Member Profile:* Anyone interested in book arts, fine printing, typography, reading; *Committees:* Publishing; Citation Awards
Activities: Book Fair, March
Awards:
• Alcuin Society Citation Awards for Excellence in Book Design in Canada (Award)

Aldergrove Daylily Society

24642 - 51 Ave., Langley BC V2Z 1H9
Tel: 604-856-5758
www.distinctly.on.ca/chs/aldergrove.html
Overview: A small local organization founded in 1991
Chief Officer(s):
Pam Erikson, President
pamela1@istar.ca
Membership: *Fees:* $10 individual; $15 family

Alexandra Writers' Centre Society (AWCS)

922 - 9th Ave. SE., Calgary AB T2G 0S4
Tel: 403-264-4730
awcs@telusplanet.net
www.alexandrawriters.org
www.facebook.com/alexandra.writers
twitter.com/alexwriters
Overview: A small local charitable organization founded in 1981
Mission: To encourage the voices of new, emerging, & experienced writers & provide a platform for their work
Member of: Alberta Magazine Publishers Association
Chief Officer(s):
Bob Laws, President
awcsboard@alexandrawriters.org
Finances: *Annual Operating Budget:* Less than $50,000
Staff Member(s): 1; 16 volunteer(s)
Membership: 135 individual; *Fees:* $60; *Member Profile:* Writers of all ages & experience; *Committees:* Registration; Publicity; Library; Free Fall Magazine; Events; Volunteer; Writer in Residence
Activities: Writing courses; public readings; Alexandra Café; magazine launches; discussion groups; FreeFall Fiction & Poetry Contest; *Library:* AWCS Library; by appointment
Awards:
• Writer in Residence (Award)
• FreeFall Fiction & Poetry Contest Award (Award)
Publications:
• FreeFall Magazine
Editor: Lynn Fraser

Alexandria & District Chamber of Commerce

PO Box 1058, Alexandria ON K0C 1A0
Tel: 613-525-0588; *Fax:* 613-525-1232
info@alexandriachamber.ca
alexandriachamber.ca
www.facebook.com/AlexOnChamber
twitter.com/AlexOnChamber
Overview: A small local organization
Chief Officer(s):
Michael Madden, President

Alfa Romeo Club of Canada (ARCC)

PO Box 62, Stn. Q, Toronto ON M4T 2L7
Tel: 416-498-6553
www.alfaclub.ca
Overview: A medium-sized national organization founded in 1977
Mission: To share common interest in use, preservation & appreciation of Alfa Romeo automobiles
Chief Officer(s):
Read Collacutt, President, 613-489-3192
Christine Pickering, Secretary
Finances: *Annual Operating Budget:* Less than $50,000; *Funding Sources:* Membership fees
12 volunteer(s)
Membership: 500; *Fees:* $55
Activities: *Library* by appointment

Algoma AIDS Network *See* Access AIDS Network Sault Ste Marie

Algoma Arts Festival Association (AAFA)

680 Albert St. East, Sault Ste Marie ON P6A 2K6
Tel: 705-949-0822
festival@algomafallfestival.com
www.facebook.com/pages/Algoma-Fall-Festival/102504434156
twitter.com/AlgomaFallFest
Also Known As: Algoma Fall Festival
Overview: A small local organization founded in 1972
Mission: To promote the arts; To encourage interest in & the study of the performing & visual arts & their traditions through presentation of performances & exhibitions; To provide opportunity to Sault Ste Marie and district students to learn the performing, literary & visual arts; To provide improved opportunities for Canadian artistic talent
Finances: *Annual Operating Budget:* $100,000-$250,000
Staff Member(s): 2; 200 volunteer(s)
Membership: 300; *Fees:* $25
Activities: *Awareness Events:* Annual Algoma Fall Festival, Sept./Oct.; Festival of Learning

Algoma Cattlemen's Association

Algoma ON
Tel: 705-843-2208
Overview: A small local organization
Affliation(s): Ontario Cattlemen's Association
Chief Officer(s):
Cleave O'Malley, President

Algoma District Law Association (ADLA)

444 Queen St. East, Sault Ste Marie ON P6A 1Z7
Tel: 705-946-5691; *Fax:* 705-946-5630
Toll-Free: 866-840-2540
algomalaw@shaw.ca
Overview: A small local organization founded in 1922
Chief Officer(s):
Amanda Ward-Pereira, Contact
Finances: *Annual Operating Budget:* Less than $50,000
Staff Member(s): 1
Membership: 65 individual
Activities: *Library*

Algoma Kinniwabi Travel Association (AKTA)

334 Bay St., Sault Ste Marie ON P6A 1X1
Tel: 705-254-4293; *Fax:* 705-254-4892
Toll-Free: 800-263-2546
info@algomacountry.com
www.algomacountry.com
www.facebook.com/pages/Ontarios-Algoma-Country/75801493223
twitter.com/AlgomaCountry
www.youtube.com/user/OntarioAlgomaCountry
Also Known As: Algoma Country
Overview: A small local organization founded in 1974
Mission: To promote the Algoma Country region to the travelling public
Member of: Ontario Tourism Marketing Partnership Corp.; Tourism Federation of Ontario
Chief Officer(s):
Lori Johnson, President
Finances: *Funding Sources:* Public & private donations
Membership: *Member Profile:* Tourism industry

Algoma Manitoulin Environmental Awareness (AMEA)

RR#1, Kagawong ON P0P 1J0
Tel: 705-282-2886
Overview: A small local organization
Mission: To encourage participation in environmental matters in the Algoma Manitoulin region of Ontario
Member of: Ontario Clean Air Alliance

Algoma Women's Sexual Assault Services (AWSAS)

PO Box 578, 610 Elgin St., White River ON P0M 3G0
Tel: 807-822-2041; *Fax:* 807-822-2282
Toll-Free: 800-205-7100
Also Known As: Algoma Women's Resource Centre
Overview: A small local organization founded in 1993 overseen by Canadian Association of Sexual Assault Centres
Activities: *Speaker Service:* Yes

Blind River Office
#111, 1 Industrial Park Rd., Blind River ON P0R 1B0
Tel: 705-356-4694; *Fax:* 705-356-4704

Dubreuilville Office
PO Box 416, 851 St. Joseph St., Dubreuilville ON P0S 1B0
Tel: 705-884-2291; *Fax:* 705-884-2437

Algoma-Manitoulin & District Labour Council

20 Alberta Rd., Elliot Lake ON P5A 1Z6
Tel: 705-848-2226; *Fax:* 7 - -
Overview: A small local organization founded in 1983 overseen by Ontario Federation of Labour
Mission: Tp provides free services to non-unionized injured workers and their survivors in workplace insurance matters (formerly called workers' compensation).
Member of: Ontario Federation of Labour

Algonquin Arts Council (AAC)

PO Box 1360, 5 Hastings St. South, Bancroft ON K0L 1C0
Tel: 613-332-5918
info@algonquinarts.ca
www.algonquinarts.ca
Overview: A small local charitable organization founded in 1978
Mission: To promote & foster cultural activities in the the 12 northern townships of Hastings County & surrounding areas
Member of: Community Arts Ontario
Affliation(s): Ontario Association of Art Galleries
Chief Officer(s):

Kim Crawford, President
k.crawford@myc.com
Jeannan Barnaby, Secretary
lagunasunrise86@hotmail.com
Avis Price, Treasurer
avis@wispernet.ca
Finances: *Annual Operating Budget:* Less than $50,000; *Funding Sources:* Village of Bancroft; donations; membership; used book sales; craftshop
25 volunteer(s)
Membership: 120; *Fees:* Individual/Family: $20; Youth/Senior: $15; Non-profit: $30; Patron: $50; Benefactor: $200; Corporate Sponsor: $350; *Member Profile:* Interest in the arts; *Committees:* Bancroft Art Gallery; Performing Arts; School Arts; The Village Playhouse; Theatrics; Rainbow Man Theatre
Activities: Art Gallery of Bancroft; concert series; theatre space; arts resource; amateur theatre; studio tour; Bancroft Theatre Guild Bandshell
Awards:
• Earl W. Smith Award (Award)
For artistic achievement at the senior level

Alianza Hispano-Canadiense Ontario / Hispanic-Canadian Alliance of Ontario
PO Box 14, Pickering ON L1V 2R2
e-mail: info@alianzahispano.org
www.alianzahispano.org
Overview: A small local organization
Mission: To help the Hispanic community living in Durham region
Chief Officer(s):
Karen Kannon, President, Board of Directors
Membership: *Fees:* $15 Indvidual; $25 Families
Activities: Parties; BBQs; Trips

Alix Chamber of Commerce
PO Box 145, Alix AB T0C 0B0
Tel: 403-747-2405; *Fax:* 403-747-2403
www.villageofalix.ca
Overview: A small local organization
Member of: Alberta Chamber of Commerce
Chief Officer(s):
Catherine Hepburn, President
Finances: *Annual Operating Budget:* Less than $50,000
Membership: 20 individual

All Terrain Vehicle Association of Nova Scotia (ATVANS)
PO Box 46020, Stn. Novalea, Halifax NS B3K 5V8
Tel: 902-241-3200
Toll-Free: 877-288-4244
admin@atvans.org
www.atvans.org
www.facebook.com/group.php?gid=104517360362
Overview: A medium-sized provincial organization founded in 1997
Mission: To represent the interest of ATV'ers to Government, Land owners, other recreation user groups and the general public and educate, inform and organize ATV'ers to preserve and expand ATV recreational opportunities to promote safe family activities.
Chief Officer(s):
Vince Sawler, President
president@atvans.org
Barry Barnet, Executive Director
execdirector@atvans.org

All-Canada Committee of the Christian Church (Disciples of Christ) ***See*** Christian Church (Disciples of Christ) in Canada

Allen & Milli Gould Family Foundation
310 Main St. West, Hamilton ON L8P 1J8
Tel: 905-527-1531; *Fax:* 905-527-3624
Toll-Free: 888-527-1531
beng@milli.ca
Overview: A small national organization founded in 1985
Mission: To operate as a foundation whose philanthropic interests are local Jewish charities centred in Hamilton & Toronto, with primary focus on Shalom Village, St Joseph's Hospital, McMaster University, & the National Academy Orchestra
Chief Officer(s):
Ben Gould, Director
Staff Member(s): 1
Awards:
• The Allen and Milli Gould Family Foundation Bursaries (Scholarship)
Eligibility: McMaster students enrolled in the Faculty of Business who demonstrate financial need.

AllerGen NCE Inc.
Michael DeGroote Centre for Learning & Discovery, McMaster University, #3120, 1200 Main St. West, Hamilton ON L8N 2A5
Tel: 905-525-9140; *Fax:* 905-524-0611
info@allergen-nce.ca
www.allergen-nce.ca
Overview: A medium-sized national organization founded in 2004
Mission: To support research, capacity building activities, & networking regarding allergic disease in Canada; To reduce the morbidity, mortality & socio-economic impacts of allergy, asthma, & related immune diseases
Chief Officer(s):
Judah Denburg, CEO & Scientific Director, 905-525-9140 Ext. 26502
Diana Royce, Chief Operating Officer & Managing Director, 905-525-9140 Ext. 26502
Mark Mitchell, Manager, Research & Partnerships, 905-525-9140 Ext. 26092
Marta Rudyk, Manager, Communications & Coordinator, Knowledge Mobilization, 905-525-9140 Ext. 26641
Allison Brown, Coordinator, Research, 905-525-9140 Ext. 26553
Michelle Harkness, Coordinator, Highly Qualified Personnel & Events, 905-525-9140 Ext. 26633
Finances: *Funding Sources:* Government of Canada, through the Networks of Centres of Excellence (NCE) Program
Meetings/Conferences: • AllerGen NCE Inc. 2015 10th Annual Conference, April, 2015, Toronto, ON
Scope: National
Description: Keynote speakers, discussion panels, research presentations, poster viewing, the presentation of awards, networking opportunities, & a social program
Contact Information: Coordinator, Highly Qualified Personnel & Events: Michelle Harkness, Phone: 905-525-9140, ext. 26633, E-mail: michelleharkness@allergen-nce.ca
Publications:
• Agenda [a publication of AllerGen NCE Inc.]
Type: Newsletter
Profile: An overview of research, training, partnerships, & networking
• AirWays [a publication of AllerGen NCE Inc.]
Type: Newsletter
Profile: News about training & professional development opportunities
• AllerGen NCE Inc. Annual Report
Type: Yearbook; *Frequency:* Annually
Profile: Highlights of the year & a financial overview
• AllerGen Network Newsletter
Type: Newsletter; *Frequency:* Quarterly
Profile: Information about the management of the network for board & committee members & investigators
• ReAction [a publication of AllerGen NCE Inc.]
Type: Newsletter
Profile: Partnership, training, & networking opportunities

Allergie Asthme association d'information ***See*** Allergy Asthma Information Association

Allergy & Environmental Health Association ***See*** Environmental Health Association of Ontario

Allergy Asthma Information Association (AAIA) / Allergie Asthme association d'information
#118, 295 The West Mall, Toronto ON M9C 4Z4
Tel: 416-621-4571; *Fax:* 416-621-5034
Toll-Free: 800-611-7011
admin@aaia.ca
www.aaia.ca
www.facebook.com/AllergyAsthmaInformationAssociation
Overview: A large national charitable organization founded in 1964
Mission: To create a safer environment for Canadians with allergies, asthma, & anaphylaxis; To assist persons coping with allergies; To act as a national voice for individuals affected by allergy, asthma, & anaphylaxis
Affliation(s): Canadian Society of Allergy & Immunology
Chief Officer(s):
Sharon Van Gyzen, Chair
Mary Allen, CEO
quebec@aaia.ca
Louis Isabella, Treasurer
Finances: *Funding Sources:* Donations; Corporate partnerships
Membership: *Fees:* $35/one year; $60/two years
Activities: Providing education; Raising money for research; Working with related organizations, government, & the food industry; Engaging in advocacy activities; Offering food allergy summer camps; *Awareness Events:* Walk to Axe Anaphylaxis
Publications:
• Allergy Asthma Information Association Newsletter
Type: Newsletter; *Frequency:* Quarterly
Profile: Information for persons affected by allergy, asthma, & anaphylaxis

AAIA Atlantic
#133, 21 Four Season Pl., Toronto ON M6B 3L8
Tel: 416-621-4571
Toll-Free: 800-611-7011
atlantic@aaia.ca
Chief Officer(s):
Ruth Roberts, Regional Coordinator

AAIA BC/Yukon
4730 Redridge Rd., Kelowna BC V1W 3A6
Tel: 250-764-7507; *Fax:* 250-764-7587
Toll-Free: 877-500-2242
bc@aaia.ca
Chief Officer(s):
Yvonne Rousseau, Regional Coordinator

AAIA Ontario
30 Patton St., Collingwood ON L9Y 0E4
Tel: 705-444-0477; *Fax:* 705-444-5705
Toll-Free: 888-250-2298
ontario@aaia.ca
Chief Officer(s):
Monika Gibson, Regional Coordinator

AAIA Prairies/NWT
16531 - 114 St., Edmonton AB T5X 3V6
Tel: 780-456-6651; *Fax:* 780-456-6651
Toll-Free: 866-456-6651
prairies@aaia.ca
Chief Officer(s):
Lilly Byrtus, Regional Coordinator

AAIA Québec
172 Andover Rd., Beaconsfield QC H9W 2Z8
Tel: 416-621-4571
Toll-Free: 800-611-7011
quebec@aaia.ca
Chief Officer(s):
Mary Allen, Regional Coordinator

Allergy, Asthma & Immunology Society of Ontario
2 Demaris Ave., Toronto ON M3N 1M1
Tel: 416-633-2215
inquiry@allergyasthma.on.ca
www.allergyasthma.on.ca
Previous Name: Ontario Allergy Society
Overview: A small provincial organization founded in 1958
Mission: To strive to provide high quality medical services to the public, through consultation by referral from other physicians, as well as through public service education
Membership: *Member Profile:* Practicing physicians
Activities: *Speaker Service:* Yes

Alliance agricole du Nouveau-Brunswick ***See*** Agricultural Alliance of New Brunswick

Alliance animale du Canada ***See*** Animal Alliance of Canada

Alliance autochtone du Québec inc. / Native Alliance of Québec Inc.
21, rue Brodeur, Gatineau QC J8Y 2P6
Tél: 819-770-7763; *Téléc:* 819-770-6070
info@aaqnaq.com
www.aaqnaq.com
Aperçu: *Dimension:* moyenne; *Envergure:* provinciale surveillé par Congress of Aboriginal Peoples
Membre(s) du bureau directeur:
Robert Bertrand, Président Grand Chef
Membre: 22

Région 1 (Abitibi - Témiscamingue)
QC
Tél: 819-797-8503
jnault@tlb.sympatico.ca
www.aaqnaq.com
Mission: Provides assistance and solidarity to citizens of Quebec who are Metis or off-reserve natives whose Native status is not recognized by the Indian Act of the Government of Canada. It promotes recreational activities for the Metis and off-reserve Indians, to assist them in the development of a social fraternity, a dignified and human understanding to contribute to help our members better understand their

history, their accomplishments and their contribution to the Canadian society.
Membre(s) du bureau directeur:
Johanne Nault, Directrice générale
Région 2 (Outaouais - Pontiac - Gatineau - Labelle)
QC
Tél: 819-438-2158
allianceautochtone080@hotmail.com
www.aaqnaq.com
Mission: Provides assistance and solidarity to citizens of Quebec who are Metis or off-reserve natives whose Native status is not recognized by the Indian Act of the Government of Canada. It promotes recreational activities for the Metis and off-reserve Indians, to assist them in the development of a social fraternity, a dignified and human understanding to contribute to help our people better understand their history, their accomplishments and their contribution to the Canadian society.
Membre(s) du bureau directeur:
Carole Romain, Directrice générale, 819-683-3757
cromain@waskahegen.com
Région 3 (Montréal - Trois-Rivières - Estrie - Gaspésie)
Trois-Rivières QC
Tél: 819-846-3962; *Téléc:* 819-846-1162
bouliane.denis@hotmail.ca
www.aaqnaq.com
Mission: Provides assistance and solidarity to citizens of Quebec who are Metis or off-reserve natives whose Native status is not recognized by the Indian Act of the Government of Canada. It promotes recreational activities for the Metis and off-reserve Indians, to assist them in the development of a social fraternity, a dignified and human understanding to contribute to help our people better understand their history, their accomplishments and their contribution to the Canadian society.
Membre(s) du bureau directeur:
Denis Bouliane, Directeur général
Région 4 (Saguenay - Lac-St-Jean - La Tuque - Québec)
QC
Tél: 418-679-1237; *Téléc:* 418-679-1237
castonguay.roger@videotron.ca
www.aaqnaq.com
Mission: Provides assistance and solidarity to citizens of Quebec who are Metis or off-reserve natives whose Native status is not recognized by the Indian Act of the Government of Canada. It promotes recreational activities for the Metis and off-reserve Indians, to assist them in the development of a social fraternity, a dignified and human understanding to contribute to help our people better understand their history, their accomplishments and their contribution to the Canadian society.
Membre(s) du bureau directeur:
Roger Castonguay, Directeur général
Région 5 (Côte-Nord - Basse-Côte-Nord)
Chute-aux-Outardes QC
Tél: 418-233-2273; *Téléc:* 418-233-2273
gtremblay13@hotmail.com
www.aaqnaq.com
Mission: Provides assistance and solidarity to citizens of Quebec who are Metis or off-reserve natives whose Native status is not recognized by the Indian Act of the Government of Canada. It promotes recreational activities for the Metis and off-reserve Indians, to assist them in the development of a social fraternity, a dignified and human understanding to contribute to help our people better understand their history, their accomplishments and their contribution to the Canadian society.
Membre(s) du bureau directeur:
Ginette Tremblay, Directrice générale

L'Alliance canadienne de l'épilepsie *See* Canadian Epilepsy Alliance

Alliance canadienne de massothérapeutes *See* Massage Therapy Alliance of Canada

Alliance canadienne des associations étudiantes *See* Canadian Alliance of Student Associations

Alliance canadienne des organismes de réglementation de la physiothérapie *See* Canadian Alliance of Physiotherapy Regulators

Alliance canadienne des responsables et enseignants en français (langue maternelle) (ACREF) / Canadian Association for the Teachers of French as a First Language

Place de la Francophonie, Succ. A, #401, 450, rue Reideau, Ottawa ON K1N 5Z4
Tél: 613-744-3192; *Téléc:* 613-744-0154
acref@franco.ca
Aperçu: *Dimension:* moyenne; *Envergure:* nationale; Organisme sans but lucratif; fondée en 1989
Mission: Développer un réseau d'identification nationale des professeurs de français langue maternelle; favoriser le développement et l'épanouissement des associations provinciales vouées à l'enseignement du français langue maternelle; promouvoir la diffusion de l'information en matière de théories pédagogiques, de formation à l'approche communicative, et de pratiques scolaires et d'idéologie visant l'identité des francophones, l'égalité en tant que groupe national et le contrôle des structures éducatives; appuyer les organismes provinciaux lors de leur rencontre annuelle; développer des instruments de diffusion de l'information à l'intention de ses membres; favoriser le développement d'une politique nationale en ce qui a trait à la gestion des institutions d'enseignement et voir à ce qu'elle respecte l'autonomie des francophones
Membre de: Fédération internationale des professeurs de français
Activités: *Stagiaires:* Oui; *Bibliothèque* rendez-vous

Alliance canadienne des services d'évaluation de diplômes *See* Alliance of Credential Evaluation Services of Canada

L'Alliance canadienne des victimes d'accidents et de maladies du travail *See* Canadian Injured Workers Alliance

L'Alliance canadienne du camionnage *See* Canadian Trucking Alliance

Alliance canadienne pour la paix *See* Canadian Peace Alliance

Alliance canadiennes des artistes de danse *See* Canadian Alliance of Dance Artists

Alliance catholique canadienne de la santé *See* Catholic Health Alliance of Canada

Alliance Champlain *Voir* Québec dans le monde

Alliance Chorale Manitoba

340, boul Provencher, Winnipeg MB R2H 0G7
Tél: 204-233-7423; *Téléc:* 204-233-8972
Aperçu: *Dimension:* petite; *Envergure:* provinciale; fondée en 1971
Mission: De promouvoir le chant choral en français et de favoriser ainsi l'épanouissement de la culture francophone du Manitoba.
Affliation(s): Centre culturel franco-manitobain

L'Alliance chrétienne et missionnaire au Canada *See* The Christian & Missionary Alliance in Canada

Alliance de l'industrie canadienne de l'aquiculture *See* Canadian Aquaculture Industry Alliance

Alliance de la Fonction publique du Canada *See* Public Service Alliance of Canada

Alliance de vie active pour les canadiens/canadiennes ayant un handicap *See* Active Living Alliance for Canadians with a Disability

Alliance des artistes canadiens du cinéma, de la télévision et de la radio *See* Alliance of Canadian Cinema, Television & Radio Artists

Alliance des arts médiatiques indépendants *See* Independent Media Arts Alliance

Alliance des cadres de l'État

#306, 1305, ch Ste-Foy, Québec QC G1S 4N5
Tél: 418-681-2028
info@alliancedescadres.com
www.alliancedescadres.com
Aperçu: *Dimension:* moyenne; *Envergure:* provinciale
Mission: Pour protéger et défendre les droits des personnes qui travaillent comme cadres dans les organisations gouvernementales
Membre(s) du bureau directeur:
Carole Roberage, Présidente-directrice générale
Membre: 3,871

L'Alliance des Caisses populaires de l'Ontario limitée (ACPOL)

CP 3500, 1870 Bond St., North Bay ON P1B 4V6
Tél: 705-474-5634; *Téléc:* 705-474-5326
support@acpol.com
www.caissealliance.com
www.linkedin.com/company/l'alliance-des-caisses-populaires-de-l'ontari
www.facebook.com/174831179214242
Aperçu: *Dimension:* moyenne; *Envergure:* provinciale; fondée en 1979 surveillé par Credit Union Central of Canada
Membre de: Credit Union Central of Canada
Membre(s) du bureau directeur:
Pierre Dorval, Directeur général
Membre: 1-99
Activités: *Bibliothèque*

Alliance des chorales du Québec (ACQ)

CP 1000, Succ. M, 4545, av Pierre-de-Coubertin, Montréal QC H1V 3R2
Tél: 514-252-3020; *Téléc:* 514-252-3222
Ligne sans frais: 888-924-6387
information@chorale.qc.ca
www.chorale.qc.ca
Aperçu: *Dimension:* moyenne; *Envergure:* provinciale; Organisme sans but lucratif
Mission: Regrouper des chorales de tous styles et de tous niveaux; donner des moyens de mieux chanter; promouvoir et développer le chant choral au Québec
Membre(s) du bureau directeur:
Catherine Girard, Directrice générale
Finances: *Budget de fonctionnement annuel:* $100,000-$250,000
Membre(s) du personnel: 4
Membre: 235 chorales + 15 organismes régionaux; *Montant de la cotisation:* 250$
Activités: *Stagiaires:* Oui; *Bibliothèque:* Service de ventes de partitions de l'ACQ; rendez-vous

Alliance des communautés culturelles pour l'égalité dans la santé et les services sociaux (ACCÉSSS)

#408, 7000, av Du Parc, Montréal QC H3N 1X1
Tél: 514-287-1106; *Téléc:* 514-287-7443
Ligne sans frais: 866-744-1106
accesss@accesss.net
accesss.net
www.facebook.com/pages/ACCÉSSS/273142908412
Aperçu: *Dimension:* petite; *Envergure:* provinciale; fondée en 1984
Mission: Offre des services facilitant l'intégration et l'adaptation des services sociaux et de santé aux personnes issues de communautés ethnoculturelles; représente les intérêts des communautés ethnoculturelles auprès des instances décisionnelles en matières de santé et services sociaux; mène des recherches sur les besoins d'adaptation et d'adéquation des services sociaux et de santé en vue de leur pleine utilisation par les personnes issues des communautés ethnoculturelles
Membre(s) du bureau directeur:
Carmen Gonzalez, Présidente
Jérôme Di Giovanni, Directeur général
jerome.digiovanni@accesss.net
Finances: *Budget de fonctionnement annuel:* $250,000-$500,000; *Fonds:* Ministère de la Santé et des services sociaux
Membre(s) du personnel: 6; 10 bénévole(s)
Membre: 40; *Montant de la cotisation:* 25$

L'Alliance des conseils sectoriels *See* The Alliance of Sector Councils

Alliance des femmes de la francophonie canadienne (AFFC)

Place de la francophonie, #302, 450, rue Rideau, Ottawa ON K1N 5Z4
Tél: 613-241-3500; *Téléc:* 613-241-6679
Ligne sans frais: 866-535-9422
info@affc.ca
www.affc.ca
www.facebook.com/229810340365531
twitter.com/AFFCfemmes
Nom précédent: Fédération nationale des femmes canadiennes-françaises; Fédération des femmes canadiennes-françaises
Aperçu: *Dimension:* moyenne; *Envergure:* nationale; Organisme sans but lucratif; fondée en 1914
Mission: Favorise l'autonomie des femmes canadiennes-françaises sur tous les plans; assure le respect des

droits des femmes francophones vivant en milieu minoritaire; soutien le développement de l'action collective et politique des femmes au Canada français; souligne la spécificité des femmes francophones auprès des instances gouvernementales, des diverses associations et du grand public
Membre de: Gropues Femmes, Politiques et Démocratie
Affliation(s): Fédération des communautés francophones et acadienne du Canada
Membre(s) du bureau directeur:
Manon Beaulieu, Directrice générale
direction@affc.ca
Lepage Maria, Présidente
lepagemariea@hotmail.com
Membre(s) du personnel: 3; 13 bénévole(s)
Membre: 11 groupes; 7 000 individus; *Montant de la cotisation:* Barème; *Critères d'admissibilité:* Etre un groupe et s'intéresser à la condition féminine, à l'avancement des droits des femmes dans la société; *Comités:* Comité d'études et d'action politique; Comité des statuts et règlements
Activités: Bourses d'études; *Service de conférenciers:* Oui; *Bibliothèque* rendez-vous
Prix, Bouses:
- Bourse d'étude Almanda-Walker-Marchand (Brouse)
- Une femme remarquable (Prix)

Alliance des gais et lesbiennes Laval-Laurentides (AGLLL Inc.)

CP 98030, 95, boul Labelle, Sainte-Thérèse QC J7E 5R4
aglll@hotmail.com
www.algi.qc.ca/asso/aglll/
Aperçu: *Dimension:* petite; *Envergure:* locale
Mission: Groupe de discussion; activités
Membre de: Association des lesbiennes et des gais sur Internet (ALGI)

Alliance des massothérapeutes du Québec (AMQ)

147, boul Laurier, Saint-Basile-le-Grand QC J3N 1A9
Tél: 450-441-1117; *Téléc:* 450-441-1157
Ligne sans frais: 888-687-1786
info@massotherapeutes.qc.ca
www.massotherapeutes.qc.ca
www.facebook.com/147162382012847
twitter.com/AllianceMasso
Aperçu: *Dimension:* petite; *Envergure:* provinciale; Organisme sans but lucratif; fondée en 1999
Mission: Vérifier les qualifications des massothérapeutes et offrir un service de formation afin que nos membres demeurent à l'avant-garde de la profession et des besoins du public
Membre(s) du bureau directeur:
Marie-Josée Poisson, Présidente
Finances: *Budget de fonctionnement annuel:* Moins de $50,000
Membre: 165; *Montant de la cotisation:* 200$/an; *Critères d'admissibilité:* Massothérapeutes; kinésithérapeutes
Activités: Association; formation; *Stagiaires:* Oui

Alliance des moniteurs de ski du Canada *See* Canadian Ski Instructors' Alliance

Alliance des professeures et professeurs de Montréal (APPM)

8225, boul Saint-Laurent, Montréal QC H2P 2M1
Tél: 514-384-5756; *Téléc:* 514-383-4880
presidence@alliancedesprofs.qc.ca
www.alliancedesprofs.qc.ca
Aperçu: *Dimension:* moyenne; *Envergure:* locale; fondée en 1919 surveillé par Centrale des syndicats du Québec
Membre de: Fédération des syndicats de l'enseignements (FSE)
Membre(s) du bureau directeur:
Alain Marois, Président
alain.marois@alliancedesprofs.qc.ca
Finances: *Budget de fonctionnement annuel:* $1.5 Million-$3 Million
Membre(s) du personnel: 20; 500 bénévole(s)
Membre: 8 000
Activités: Services aux membres; défense de leurs droits; *Bibliothèque:* Centre de documentation - APPM; rendez-vous

Alliance des professionels et des professionnelles de la Ville de Québec (ALLPPVQ)

www.allppvq.ca
Aperçu: *Dimension:* petite; *Envergure:* locale; fondée en 2001
Membre(s) du bureau directeur:
Sylvie Dolbec, Présidente
sylvie.dolbec@allppvq.ca
Louise Ouellet, 2e Vice-Présidente
louise-e.ouellet@ville.quebec.qc.ca
Membre: 500; *Critères d'admissibilite:* Professionnels et professionnelles travaillant dans des sphères d'activités requérant un diplôme universitaire; *Comités:* Comité d'évaluation et de classification des emplois; Comité de retraite; Comité des relations professionnelles; Comité santé et sécurité

Alliance des radios communautaires du Canada

#1206, 1, rue Nicholas, Ottawa ON K1N 7B7
Tel: 613-562-0000; *Fax:* 613-562-2182
radiorfa.com
www.facebook.com/arcducanada
twitter.com/arcducanada
www.youtube.com/arcducanada
Also Known As: ARC du Canada
Overview: A medium-sized national organization
Chief Officer(s):
François Coté, Secrétaire général
f.cote@radiorfa.com

Alliance du personnel professionel et administratif de Ville de Laval (APPAVL)

Tél: 450-629-0453; *Téléc:* 450-629-9307
appavl@qc.aira.com
www.appavl.ca
Aperçu: *Dimension:* petite; *Envergure:* locale; fondée en 2005
Membre(s) du bureau directeur:
Philippe Dutin, Président Ext. 5127
Nathalie Sampaio, 1re Vice-Président Ext. 6256
Mireille Fournier, 2e Vice-Président Ext. 8793
Membre: *Critères d'admissibilité:* Personnel professionnel ou administratif travaillant en Laval

Alliance du personnel professionnel et technique de la santé et des services sociaux (APTS)

#1050, 1111 rue Saint-Charles Ouest, Longueuil QC J4K 5G4
Tél: 450-670-2411; *Téléc:* 450-679-0107
Ligne sans frais: 866-521-2411
info@aptsq.com
www.aptsq.com
www.facebook.com/SyndicatAPTS
twitter.com/APTSQ
www.youtube.com/channel/UC1srtPhluOjUv_ohjlMhM0g
Nom précédent: Centrale des professionnelles et professionnels de la santé
Aperçu: *Dimension:* grande; *Envergure:* provinciale; Organisme sans but lucratif; fondée en 2004
Mission: Regrouper les organisations syndicales représentant toutes les catégories des personnes salariées professionnelles ou paramédicales travaillant dans le domaine de la santé; défendre, promouvoir et sauvegarder les intérêts collectifs des membres
Membre(s) du bureau directeur:
Dominique Verreault, Présidente
Dominique Aubertin, Directrice générale
Finances: *Budget de fonctionnement annuel:* $1.5 Million-$3 Million
Membre(s) du personnel: 110
Membre: 27 000; *Critères d'admissibilité:* Personnel professionnel et technique du réseau québécois de la santé.

Alliance évangélique du Canada *See* Evangelical Fellowship of Canada

Alliance for Arts & Culture

#100, 938 Howe St., Vancouver BC V6Z 1N9
Tel: 604-681-3535; *Fax:* 604-681-7848
info@allianceforarts.com
www.allianceforarts.com
www.facebook.com/AllianceforArtsandCulture
twitter.com/AllianceArts
www.youtube.com/user/AllianceArtsCulture
Previous Name: Vancouver Cultural Alliance
Overview: A medium-sized local organization founded in 1986
Mission: To project a strong voice for the local arts community; To promote the activities of the arts through a variety of programs, services, & marketing strategies; To increase public awareness of & accessibility to the arts & culture
Member of: Canadian Conference of the Arts; Tourism Vancouver
Chief Officer(s):
Rob Gloor, Executive Director, 604-681-3535 Ext. 209
Kevin Dale McKeown, Director, Communications & Special Events, 604-681-3535 Ext. 215
Kevin Teichroeb, Director, Interactive Media, 604-681-3535
Melissa Flagg, Administrator, Members Services, 604-681-3535 Ext. 207
Finances: *Funding Sources:* Public & private sector
Membership: 350+; *Fees:* Based on budget of potential member; *Member Profile:* Arts & culture organizations & individuals
Activities: Offering training & employment programs; Providing professional development activities & public education; *Library:* Arts Resource Centre; Open to public

Alliance for Audited Media

Canadian Member Service Office, #850, 151 Bloor St. West, Toronto ON M5S 1S4
Tel: 416-962-5840; *Fax:* 416-962-5844
www.accessabc.com
www.linkedin.com/groups?about=&gid=2975919
www.facebook.com/auditedmedia
twitter.com/auditedmedia
www.youtube.com/auditedmedia
Previous Name: Audit Bureau of Circulations
Overview: A medium-sized national organization founded in 1914
Mission: To be the pre-eminent self-regulatory auditing organization, responsible to advertisers, advertising agencies, & the media they use, for the verification & dissemination of members' circulation data & other information for the benefit of the advertising marketplace in the United States & Canada
Chief Officer(s):
Michael J. Lavery, President & Managing Director
Membership: *Committees:* Newspaper Buyers' Advisory; NAA/AAM Liaison; NAA/AAM Circulation; Magazine Buyers' Advisory; Magazine Directors' Advisory; Business Publication Buyers' Advisory; Business Publication Industry; Digital Advisory
Activities: *Library* by appointment

Alliance for Canadian New Music Projects (ACNMP) / Alliance pour des projets de musique canadienne nouvelle

20 St. Joseph St., Toronto ON M4Y 1J9
Tel: 416-963-5937; *Fax:* 416-961-7198
acnmp@rogers.com
www.acnmp.ca
Also Known As: Contemporary Showcase
Overview: A medium-sized national charitable organization founded in 1978
Mission: To provide young musicians with an opportunity to celebrate & enjoy the music of their own time & country through the organization's syllabus & its festival, Contemporary Showcase
Chief Officer(s):
Paige Reid, General Manager
David Gerry, President
dgerry@nas.net
Finances: *Funding Sources:* Donations; foundations; government
Membership: *Fees:* $25
Activities: Contemporary Showcase Centres across Canada; *Library* by appointment

Contemporary Showcase - Biggar
PO Box 727, Biggar SK S0K 0M0
Tel: 306-948-5231
Chief Officer(s):
Peggy L'Hoir, Contact

Contemporary Showcase - Bradford
150 Artesian Pkwy., Bradford ON L3Z 1E8
Tel: 905-778-0440
Chief Officer(s):
Jeanette Martin, Contact
musicinmotion@sympatico.ca

Contemporary Showcase - Calgary
37 Hollyburn Rd. SW, Calgary AB T2V 3H2
Chief Officer(s):
Roberta Stephen, Coordinator

Contemporary Showcase - Castor
PO Box 295, Castor AB T0C 0X0
Tel: 403-882-4545
Chief Officer(s):
Doreen Renschler, Contact
drrenschler@gmail.com

Contemporary Showcase - Chatham
42 Forsyth Dr., Blenheim ON N0P 1A0
Tel: 519-676-8398
Chief Officer(s):
Roberta Dickson, Contact
RMdickson@southkent.net

Contemporary Showcase - Dunnville
140 Broad St. E, Dunnville ON N1A 1E9
Tel: 905-774-2678

Chief Officer(s):
Colleen Clayton, Coordinator
ccschoolofmusic@bellnet.ca

Contemporary Showcase - Edmonton
410 Walker Rd. NW, Edmonton AB T5T 2X2
Tel: 780-489-4191
Chief Officer(s):
Marlaine Osgoode, Coordinator
jamesosogoode@interbaun.com

Contemporary Showcase - Grand Prairie
c/o Grande Prairie Regional College, 10726-106 Ave., Grande Prairie AB T8V 4C4
Tel: 780-539-2444; *Fax:* 780-539-2446
Chief Officer(s):
Guy Bredeson, Coordinator
fbredeson@gprc.ab.ca

Contemporary Showcase - Grand River Region
#407, 168 Wissler Rd., Waterloo ON N2K 2T4
Tel: 519-746-7051
Chief Officer(s):
Helga Morrison, Coordinator
hgmorrison@rogers.com

Contemporary Showcase - Langley
c/o Langley Community Music School, 4899-207th St., Langley BC V3A 2E4
Tel: 604-534-2848; *Fax:* 604-534-9118
Chief Officer(s):
Joel Stobbe, Coordinator
info@langleymusic.com

Contemporary Showcase - London
#29, 70 Chapman Ct., London ON N6G 4Z4
Tel: 519-472-1402
Chief Officer(s):
Grace Yip, Coordinator
graceyip49@hotmail.com

Contemporary Showcase - Mississauga
3132 Folkway Dr., Mississauga ON L5L 2A2
Tel: 905-820-8529; *Fax:* 905-820-2960
Chief Officer(s):
Jill Kelman, Coordinator
jillkl@eol.ca

Contemporary Showcase - Moncton
34 Llangollen Rd., Moncton NB E1E 3W5
Tel: 506-382-0280
Chief Officer(s):
Doris Sabean, Coordinator
dsabean@nb.aign.com

Contemporary Showcase - Montréal
8591, rue Langelier, Montréal QC H1P 2Z4
Tel: 514-324-6527; *Fax:* 514-324-9051
Chief Officer(s):
Lise Gauthier, Coordinator
lisegautheir@myc.com

Contemporary Showcase - North Bay
140 Pionecreed Rd. North, RR#1, Calandar ON P0H 1H0
Tel: 705-752-3552
Chief Officer(s):
Beth Chartrand, Contact
bemachartrand@hotmail.com

Contemporary Showcase - Oshawa
755 Waverly St. North, Oshawa ON L1J 7E4
Tel: 905-721-0385
Chief Officer(s):
Marianne Turner, Contact
marianne.turner@sympatico.ca

Contemporary Showcase - Ottawa/Carleton
81 Berrigan Dr., Nepean ON K2J 4V6
Tel: 613-447-2618
Chief Officer(s):
Tania Granata, Coordinator
taniag5@sympatico.ca

Contemporary Showcase - Parry Sound
2 Brenda Ave., Parry Sound ON P2A 2Z3
Tel: 705-746-8288
tojudyfreeman@yahoo.ca
www.acnmp.ca
Chief Officer(s):
Judy Freeman, Coordinator
tojudyfreeman@yahoo.ca

Contemporary Showcase - Quispamsis
1 Earles' Crt., Quispamsis NB E2E 1C3
Tel: 506-849-3917
Chief Officer(s):
Rita Raymond-Millett, Coordinator
jrmilray@nb.sympatico.ca

Contemporary Showcase - Red Deer
Red Deer College, 189 Alberts Close, Red Deer AB T4R 3J6
Chief Officer(s):
Rita N. Kennedy, Contact

Contemporary Showcase - Regina
4166 Elphinstone St., Regina SK S4S 3L2
Tel: 306-584-1274
Chief Officer(s):
Corinne Groff, Coordinator
musiclessons@sasktel.net

Contemporary Showcase - Saskatoon
530 Redberry Rd., Saskatoon SK S7K 4S3
Tel: 306-384-1922
Chief Officer(s):
Janet Gieck, Coordinator

Contemporary Showcase - Toronto
145 Pickering St., Toronto ON M4E 3J5
Tel: 416-481-8802
Chief Officer(s):
Janet Fothergill, Coordinator, 416-481-8802
JLFothergill@sympatico.ca
Wendy Potter, Coordinator, 416-694-4205
potter@lycos.com
Heidi Saario, Coordinator, 416-699-0547
heidi@playthepiano.ca

Alliance for Equality of Blind Canadians / Alliance pour l'Égalite des Personnes Aveugles du Canada

RPO Town Centre, PO Box 20262, Kelowna BC V1Y 9H2
Toll-Free: 800-561-4774
info@blindcanadians.ca
www.blindcanadians.ca
Previous Name: National Federation of the Blind: Advocates for Equality
Overview: A medium-sized national organization
Mission: To promote the inclusion of blind, deaf-blind and partially-sighted Canadians in all aspects of social life, from employment to participation in elections
Chief Officer(s):
Donna Jodhan, President
Membership: *Fees:* $5 Annual, $100 Lifetime

Alliance for South Asian AIDS Prevention (ASAAP)

#315, 120 Carlton st., Toronto ON M5A 4K3
Tel: 416-599-2727; *Fax:* 416-599-6011
info@asaap.ca
www.asaap.ca
www.facebook.com/pages/Asaap/262246160480711
twitter.com/ASAAP
www.youtube.com/user/ASAAPTV
Overview: A small local charitable organization founded in 1989 overseen by Canadian AIDS Society
Mission: To prevent the spread of HIV & to promote the health of South Asians infected with & affected by HIV/AIDS.
Member of: Ontario AIDS Network; Council of Agencies Serving South Asians; Interagency Coalition on AIDS & Development
Chief Officer(s):
Rupal Shah, Chair
Vihaya Chikermane, Executive Director
ed@asaap.ca
Finances: *Funding Sources:* Federal & provincial government; City of Toronto: Community Partners of ACT
Staff Member(s): 13
Membership: *Committees:* Board Development & Recruitment; Fund Development; Policies and Bylaw
Activities: HIV/AIDS education & prevention to South Asians; PHA support services; work with other South Asian & AIDS service organizations; information & referral services; materials in South Asian languages; *Library:* ASAAP Resource Centre; Open to public

Alliance Française d'Edmonton

Maison de la France, 10424, 123 rue Nord Ouest, Edmonton AB T5N 1N7
Tél: 780-469-0399; *Téléc:* 780-488-0396
info@afedmonton.ca
www.af.ca/edmonton
www.facebook.com/pages/Alliance-francaise-dEdmonton/14588 0992114853
Aperçu: *Dimension:* petite; *Envergure:* internationale; fondée en 1947
Mission: Promouvoir la langue et la culture française.
Affliation(s): Alliance Française réseau international
Membre(s) du bureau directeur:
Anthony Bertrand, Directeur général
Todd Babiak, Président
Membre(s) du personnel: 7
Membre: *Montant de la cotisation:* 35$ individu; 50$ famille; 100$ organisation; *Critères d'admissibilite:* Francophone et allophone désireux d'entretenir la culture et de la langue française
Activités: culturelles variées et École de langue française

Alliance Française d'Ottawa

352, rue MacLaren, Ottawa ON K2P 0M6
Tél: 613-234-9470; *Téléc:* 613-233-1559
info@af.ca
www.af.ca/ottawa
www.facebook.com/pages/Alliance-Française-Ottawa/28839021 6926
Aperçu: *Dimension:* petite; *Envergure:* internationale; Organisme sans but lucratif; fondée en 1905
Mission: Propagation de la langue et de la culture française; dialogue des cultures; formation.
Affliation(s): Alliance Française réseau international
Membre(s) du bureau directeur:
Julie Desbien, Directrice des cours
french@af.ca
Activités: Cours de français et activités culturelles; *Bibliothèque:* Centre de ressources; Bibliothèque publique rendez-vous

Alliance Française de Calgary (AFC)

#180, 240, 4e av sud-ouest, Calgary AB T2P 4H4
Tél: 403-245-5662
info@afcalgary.ca
www.afcalgary.ca
www.facebook.com/pages/Alliance-Française-de-Calgary/12278 0681081274
twitter.com/AFCalgary
Également appelé: École de langue et centre culturel français
Aperçu: *Dimension:* petite; *Envergure:* internationale; Organisme sans but lucratif; fondée en 1947
Mission: Promotion de la langue et de la culture française.
Affliation(s): Alliance Française réseau international
Membre(s) du bureau directeur:
Lila Kaidomar, Directrice
director@afcalgary.ca
Membre(s) du personnel: 13
Membre: *Montant de la cotisation:* Barème
Activités: Cours de langue; ateliers; centre culturel; événements culturels; centre de ressources

Alliance Française de Winnipeg *Voir* Alliance Française du Manitoba

Alliance Française du Manitoba

934, av Corydon, Winnipeg MB R3M 0Y5
Tél: 204-477-1515
info@afmanitoba.ca
www.afmanitoba.ca
www.facebook.com/AFManitoba
twitter.com/AFManitoba
Nom précédent: Alliance Française de Winnipeg
Aperçu: *Dimension:* petite; *Envergure:* internationale; Organisme sans but lucratif; fondée en 1915
Mission: Promouvoir la langue et la culture française; oeuvrer au rapprochement et à l'amitié des peuples français et canadiens.
Affliation(s): Alliance Française réseau international
Membre(s) du bureau directeur:
Emmanuel Bottiau, Directeur général
direction@afmanitoba.ca
David Woods, Responsable Administratif
dwoods@afmanitoba.ca
Finances: *Fonds:* Gouvernement provincial et national
Membre(s) du personnel: 10
Membre: *Critères d'admissibilite:* Étudiant anglophone, francophone non-étudiant
Activités: Conférences; théâtre; musique; danse; promotion des auteurs français; arts visuels; *Bibliothèque* Bibliothèque publique rendez-vous

Alliance Française Halifax (AFH)

5509, rue Young, Halifax NS B3K 1Z7
Tél: 902-455-4411; *Téléc:* 902-455-4149
info@afhalifax.ca
www.afhalifax.ca
www.facebook.com/pages/Alliance-Francaise-Halifax/10405018 9636630
twitter.com/AFHalifax

Aperçu: *Dimension:* petite; *Envergure:* internationale; Organisme sans but lucratif; fondée en 1903
Mission: Promotion de la langue et de la culture française.
Affiliation(s): Alliance Française réseau international; Fédération des alliances françaises du Canada
Membre(s) du bureau directeur:
Isabelle Pédot, Directrice générale
Membre(s) du personnel: 14
Activités: Enseignement du français; activités culturelles et sociales; *Bibliothèque* rendez-vous

Alliance internationale des employé(e)s de scène, de théâtre et de cinéma (AIESTC) / International Alliance of Theatrical Stage Employees, Moving Picture Technicians, Artists & Allied Crafts of the U.S. (IATSE)

#160, 1945, rue Mullin, Montréal QC H3K 1N9
Tél: 514-937-6855; *Téléc:* 514-272-5163
Ligne sans frais: 866-331-4095
admin@iatselocal262.com
www.iatselocal262.com
www.facebook.com/iatselocal262
Nom précédent: Alliance internationale des opérateurs de machines à vues
Aperçu: *Dimension:* petite; *Envergure:* internationale; fondée en 1912
Mission: Représentation des travailleurs/travailleuses sur les lieux de travail afin de faire respecter leurs droits par l'application de leur convention collective.
Affliation(s): Fédération des travailleurs et travailleuses du Québec
Membre(s) du bureau directeur:
Sylvain Bisaillon, Président
s.bisaillon@iatselocal262.com
Membre: 800+

Alliance internationale des opérateurs de machines à vues
Voir Alliance internationale des employé(e)s de scène, de théâtre et de cinéma

Alliance Médias Jeunesse *See* Youth Media Alliance

Alliance numériQC

métro Place-des-arts, #800, 1450, rue City Councillors, Montréal QC H3A 2E6
Tél: 514-848-7177; *Téléc:* 514-848-7133
Ligne sans frais: 866-848-7177
www.alliancenumerique.com
Également appelé: Réseau de l'industrie numérique du Québec
Aperçu: *Dimension:* moyenne; *Envergure:* provinciale
Mission: Vise à soutenir et à accélérer la croissance et la compétitivité de son industrie dans le respect de tous ses intervenants
Membre(s) du bureau directeur:
Pierre Proulx, Directeur général
pproulx@alliancenumerique.com
Membre: 150;

Alliance of Canadian Cinema, Television & Radio Artists (ACTRA) / Alliance des artistes canadiens du cinéma, de la télévision et de la radio

#300, 625 Church St., Toronto ON M4Y 2G1
Tel: 416-489-1311; *Fax:* 416-489-8076
Toll-Free: 800-387-3516
Other Communication: media@actra.ca
national@actra.ca
www.actra.ca
www.facebook.com/pages/Actra-National/125652344169446
twitter.com/ACTRAnat
www.youtube.com/user/ACTRANational
Previous Name: Association of Canadian Television & Radio Artists
Overview: A large national organization founded in 1943
Mission: To represent performers in recorded media; To negotiate & administer collective agreements which set minimum rates & basic conditions governing work; To advocate public policies designed to create strong Canadian broadcasting & film industries in order to provide work opportunities for members in their own country
Member of: Canadian Conference of the Arts; Fédération internationale d'acteurs
Affliation(s): Canadian Labour Congress
Chief Officer(s):
Daintry Dalton, Regional Executive Director
Stephen Waddell, National Executive Director
Ferne Downey, National President
Theresa Tova, National Treasurer
Finances: *Annual Operating Budget:* $3 Million-$5 Million
Staff Member(s): 110
Membership: 22,000; *Fees:* Schedule available; *Member Profile:* Performers; full - performer with 6 professional engagements in ACTRA's jurisdiction; alternatively, a performer may apply on basis of professional reputation, or may qualify as a member of a guild associated with ACTRA as a member of Canadian Actors' Equity Association or as member of Screen Actors Guild or AFTRA; *Committees:* Communications; Constitution & Bylaws; Disipline; Diversity; Finance; Stunt Performers; Women's
Activities: ACTRA Performers' Rights Society; Face to Face Online, ACTRA's online talent catalog
Awards:
• ACTRA's John Drainie Award (Award)
Presented to a performer who has made a distinguished contribution to Canadian broadcasting.
Publications:
• ACTRA
Type: Magazine; *Frequency:* Quarterly

ACTRA Alberta
#602, 7015 MacLeod Trail SW, Calgary AB T2H 2K6
Tel: 403-228-3123; *Fax:* 403-228-3299
Toll-Free: 866-913-3123
alberta@actra.ca
www.actraalberta.com
Chief Officer(s):
Duval Lang, President
dlang@actraalberta.com

ACTRA BC Branch - Union of B.C. Performers
#400, 1155 West Pender St., Vancouver BC V6E 2P4
Tel: 604-689-0727; *Fax:* 604-689-1145
Toll-Free: 866-689-0727
info@ubcp.com
www.ubcp.com
www.facebook.com/pages/UBCP-Union-of-BC-Performers/156939901031369
twitter.com/UBCP_ACTRA
www.youtube.com/user/UBCPinfo?ob=0&feature=results_main
Chief Officer(s):
Alvin Sanders, President
alvin.sanders@ubcp.com

ACTRA Manitoba
#203, 245 McDermot Ave., Winnipeg MB R3B 0S6
Tel: 204-339-9750; *Fax:* 204-947-5664
manitoba@actra.ca
actramanitoba.ca
Chief Officer(s):
Talia Pura, President

ACTRA Maritimes
#103, 1660 Hollis St., Halifax NS B3J 1V7
Tel: 902-420-1404; *Fax:* 902-422-0589
Toll-Free: 877-272-2872
maritimes@actra.ca
www.actramaritimes.ca
Chief Officer(s):
Jamie Bradley, President
jbradley@actramaritimes.ca

ACTRA Montréal
#530, 1450, rue City Councillors, Montréal QC H3A 2E6
Tel: 514-844-3318; *Fax:* 514-844-2068
montreal@actra.ca
www.actramontreal.ca
Chief Officer(s):
Don Jordan, President
djordan@actra.ca

ACTRA Newfoundland
#202, 245 Duckworth St., St. John's NL A1C 1G8
Tel: 709-722-0430; *Fax:* 709-722-2113
newfoundland@actra.ca
www.actranewfoundland.ca
Chief Officer(s):
Amy House, President

ACTRA Ottawa
The Arts Court, #170, 2 Daly Ave., Ottawa ON K1N 6E2
Tel: 613-565-2168; *Fax:* 613-565-4367
ottawa@actra.ca
www.actraottawa.ca
Chief Officer(s):
Sally Clelford, President

ACTRA Saskatchewan
#212, 1808 Smith St., Regina SK S4P 2N4
Tel: 306-757-0885; *Fax:* 306-359-0044
Toll-Free: 800-615-5041
saskatchewan@actra.ca
www.actrasask.com
Chief Officer(s):
Alan Bratt, President

ACTRA Toronto
625 Church St., 1st Fl., Toronto ON M4Y 2G1
Tel: 416-928-2278; *Fax:* 416-928-2852
Toll-Free: 877-913-2278
info@actratoronto.com
www.actratoronto.com
www.facebook.com/ACTRAToronto
twitter.com/ACTRAToronto
www.youtube.com/user/ACTRAToronto
Chief Officer(s):
Karen Ritson, Director of Finance and Administration, 416-642-6722

Alliance of Cancer Consultants

#206, 2571 Shaughnessy St., Port Coquitlam BC V3C 3G3
Previous Name: International Alliance of Breast Cancer Organizations
Overview: A small local organization
Chief Officer(s):
Tadeusz Slubowski, Director

Alliance of Credential Evaluation Services of Canada (ACESC) / Alliance canadienne des services d'évaluation de diplômes (ACSED)

c/o The Canadian Information Centre for International Credentials, #1106, St. Clair Ave. West, Toronto ON M4V 1N6
Tel: 416-962-9725; *Fax:* 416-962-2800
www.canalliance.org
Overview: A small national organization
Mission: To offer standardized assessment of foreign credentials for education, employment, & professional membership
Chief Officer(s):
Yves E. Beaudin, National Coordinator, Canadian Information Centre for International Credentials, 416-962-8100 Ext. 242
Finances: *Funding Sources:* Human Resources & Skills Development Canada; Citizenship & Immigration Canada; Canadian Heritage
Membership: *Member Profile:* Public or private credential assessment services from across Canada that comply with & maintain standards
Activities: Recommending & implementing policies & standards to develop & maintain quality assurance; Raising awareness of the Alliance

Alliance of Manufacturers & Exporters Canada *See* Canadian Manufacturers & Exporters

The Alliance of Sector Councils (TASC) / L'Alliance des conseils sectoriels

#608, 151 Slater St., Ottawa ON K1P 5H3
Tel: 613-565-3637; *Fax:* 613-231-6853
info@councils.org
www.councils.org
Overview: A medium-sized national organization
Chief Officer(s):
Andrew Cardozo, Executive Director
Staff Member(s): 3

Alliance pour des projets de musique canadienne nouvelle
See Alliance for Canadian New Music Projects

Alliance pour l'Égalite des Personnes Aveugles du Canada
See Alliance for Equality of Blind Canadians

Alliance québécoise des techniciens de l'image et du son (AQTIS)

#300, 533, rue Ontario est, Montréal QC H2L 1N8
Tel: 514-844-2113; *Fax:* 514-844-3540
Toll-Free: 888-647-0681
info@aqtis.qc.ca
www.aqtis.qc.ca
Overview: A medium-sized provincial organization
Chief Officer(s):
Bernard Arseneau, Président
barseneau@aqtis.qc.ca
Jean-Claude Rocheleau, Directeur général
jcrocheleau@aqtis.qc.ca

Alliance Québécoise du Psoriasis / Quebec Psoriasis Alliance

#200, 5700, rue J-B-Michaud, LéVis QC G6V 0B1

Tel: 418-383-9779; Fax: 418-838-3789
Toll-Free: 877-838-9779
info@psoriasisquebec.org
www.psoriasisquebec.org
www.facebook.com/211449008933190
twitter.com/psoriasisquebec
www.youtube.com/PsoriasisQuebec
Overview: A small provincial organization founded in 2008
Mission: Pour représenter les patients atteints de psoriasis et de sensibiliser le public sur le psoriasis
Chief Officer(s):
Paul-François Bourgault, Président
paul-francois.bourgault@psoriasisquebec.org
Yves Poulin, Administrateur
Membership: *Fees:* Gratuit; *Member Profile:* Patients atteints de psoriasis et de leurs familles, les professionnels de soins de santé; tous ceux qui veulent soutenir la cause

Allied Arts Council of Spruce Grove
Melcor Cultural Centre, 35 - 5th Ave., Spruce Grove AB T7X 2C5
Tel: 780-962-0664
alliedac@shaw.ca
www.alliedartscouncil.com
www.facebook.com/193509347393424
Overview: A small local charitable organization founded in 1980
Mission: To encourage, foster & sponsor cultural activites in the region
Affliation(s): Visual Arts Alberta Association
Chief Officer(s):
Bonnie Halliday, President
Finances: *Funding Sources:* Art sales & classes; city grant; Alberta Foundation for the Arts
Membership: *Fees:* $40; *Member Profile:* Artist or arts supporter
Activities: Art classes; *Awareness Events:* Open Art Competition, 3rd week in Aug.; *Speaker Service:* Yes

Allied Beauty Association (ABA)
#26-27, 145 Traders Blvd. East, Mississauga ON L4Z 3L3
Tel: 905-568-0158; *Fax:* 905-568-1581
abashows@abacanada.com
www.abacanada.com
www.facebook.com/ABACanada
twitter.com/abacanada
www.youtube.com/user/TheABACanada
Overview: A small national organization founded in 1934
Mission: To encourage & create a greater understanding & knowledge of the professional beauty industry to the salons, the public, the federal & provincial governments, & to members
Chief Officer(s):
Marc Speir, Executive Director
Finances: *Annual Operating Budget:* $500,000-$1.5 Million; *Funding Sources:* Trade shows; membership dues
Staff Member(s): 4
Membership: 265; *Fees:* $700
Activities: *Speaker Service:* Yes; *Rents Mailing List:* Yes
Meetings/Conferences: • Allied Beauty Association Trade Show - Montréal 2015, March, 2015, Palais des congrès (Convention Centre), Montréal, QC
Scope: National
Description: A trade show for beauty professionals to learn about the new happenings in the industry
• Allied Beauty Association Trade Show - Toronto 2015, April, 2015, Metro Toronto Convention Centre, Toronto, ON
Scope: National
Description: A trade show for beauty professionals only to become aware of future trends in the beauty industry
• Allied Beauty Association Trade Show - Edmonton 2015, May, 2015, Edmonton Expo Centre, Edmonton, AB
Scope: National
Description: A trade show for beauty professionals to learn about new happenings in the beauty industry
• Allied Beauty Association Trade Show - Calgary 2015, Calgary, 2015, Calgary Stampede Park, Calgary, AB
Scope: National
Description: A trade show for beauty professionals to learn about current happenings in the beauty industry
• Allied Beauty Association 2015 Annual General Meeting, 2015, Niagara-on-the-Lake, ON
Scope: National
• Allied Beauty Association 2016 Annual General Meeting, 2016, Montréal, QC
Scope: National

Alliston & District Chamber of Commerce
PO Box 32, 51 Victoria St. East, Alliston ON L9R 1T9
Tel: 705-435-7921; *Fax:* 705-435-0289
Toll-Free: 888-835-3092
info@adcc.ca
www.adcc.ca
Overview: A medium-sized local organization founded in 1981
Member of: Ontario Chamber of Commerce
Chief Officer(s):
Crystal Kellard, Office Coordinator
Finances: *Annual Operating Budget:* $50,000-$100,000
Staff Member(s): 2; 2 volunteer(s)
Membership: 280; *Fees:* $125; *Committees:* Home & Garden Show; Potato Festival; Golf Tournament; Santa Claus Parade; Christmas in the Park

Allstate Foundation of Canada
#100, 27 Allstate Pkwy., Markham ON L3R 5P8
Tel: 905-477-6900; *Fax:* 905-513-4018
foundation@allstate.ca
www.allstate.ca
Overview: A small national charitable organization founded in 1977
Chief Officer(s):
Eric Pickering, Executive Vice-President
Awards:
• Allstate Foundation Grant (Grant)
Eligibility: registered not-for-profit charity; require funding for educational initiatives/crime prevention/road safety/home safety

Almaguin-Nipissing Travel Association
PO Box 351, Stn. Regional Information Centre, North Bay ON P1B 8H5
Tel: 705-474-6634
Toll-Free: 800-387-0516
Also Known As: Ontario's Near North
Overview: A medium-sized local organization founded in 1974
Mission: To market Ontario's Near North as a four-seasons family-oriented outdoor vacation destination on behalf of the organized tourist industry
Member of: Tourism Industry Association of Canada
Activities: *Library:* Photo; Open to public

Almonte & District Arts Council ***See*** Almonte in Concert

Almonte in Concert
PO Box 1199, 14 Bridge St., Almonte ON K0A 1A0
Tel: 613-253-3353
info@almonteinconcert.com
www.almonteinconcert.com
Previous Name: Almonte & District Arts Council
Overview: A small local organization
Chief Officer(s):
, Artistic Director
artisticdirector@almonteinconcert.com
Membership: *Fees:* $10-$500

Almost Home
PO Box 2204, 118 William St., Kingston ON K7L 5J9
Tel: 613-548-8255; *Fax:* 613-547-6948
www.almosthome.on.ca
Overview: A small local charitable organization
Mission: To provide a place where families of children hospitalized in Kingston can stay while their child is in the hospital
Chief Officer(s):
Laurie Morgan, Executive Director
LaurieM@almosthome.on.ca
Finances: *Funding Sources:* Donations

Alouette Field Naturalists (AFN)
12554 Grace St., Maple Ridge BC V2X 5N2
Tel: 604-463-8743
Overview: A small local organization founded in 1973
Mission: To promote the enjoyment of nature through environmental appreciation & conservation; To encourage wise use & conservation of natural resources & environmental protection
Member of: Federation of BC Naturalists
Membership: 30-35; *Fees:* $16-30; *Committees:* Pitt Polder Preservation Society; Blue Mountain-Kanata Creek Conservation Committee
Activities: Rivers Day, Nature Day, with displays; hiking, camping, birding, botanizing, mycologizing; *Awareness Events:* Earth Day, April; Annual Christmas Bird Count, December

Alpaca Livestock Producers & Cooperators Association (ALPACA)
PO Box 78098, RPO Callingwood, Edmonton AB T5T 6A1
e-mail: info@alpaca.ca
www.alpaca.ca
Overview: A small national organization
Mission: To create an environment for small &/or large producers with equal opportunities in today's ever changing market; To create & to maintain a central comprehensive database on Alpacas & Alpaca related industries; To provide members with easy access to the database information resulting in an efficient network of cooperative Alpaca producers, buyers & related businesses; To promote the importance of a strong & united society as it relates to information gathering, information access, national & international affairs concerning purity, integrity & the financial security of the Canadian Alpaca industry
Membership: *Fees:* $74

Alphabétisation mondiale Canada ***See*** World Literacy of Canada

Alphabétisation Nouveau-Brunswick Inc. ***See*** Literacy New Brunswick Inc.

Alpine Canada Alpin
#153, 401 - 9th Ave. SW, Calgary AB T2P 3C5
Tel: 403-777-3200; *Fax:* 403-777-3213
info@alpinecanada.org
alpinecanada.org
www.facebook.com/AlpineCanada
twitter.com/Alpine_Canada
www.youtube.com/user/AlpineCanadaAlpin
Overview: A medium-sized national organization
Mission: The ACA is the governing body for ski racing in Canada. Founded in 1920 & accounting for close to 200,000 supporting members, ACA represents coaches, officials, supporters & athletes, including elite racers of the Canadian Alpine Ski Team & the Canadian Disabled Alpine Ski Team.
Chief Officer(s):
Roger Jackson, Interim President, 403-777-4246
rjackson@alpinecanada.org
Paul Kristofic, Vice-President, Sports
pk@alpinecanada.org
Keith Bradford, Director, Communications
kbradford@alpinecanada.org

Alpine Club of Canada (ACC) / Club alpin du Canada (CAC)
PO Box 8040, Stn. Main, 201 Indian Flats Rd., Canmore AB T1W 2T8
Tel: 403-678-3200; *Fax:* 403-678-3224
info@alpineclubofcanada.ca
www.alpineclubofcanada.ca
www.facebook.com/alpineclubofcanada
twitter.com/alpineclubcan
Overview: A large national charitable organization founded in 1906
Mission: To encourage & promote mountaineering & mountain crafts; To educate Canadians in the appreciation of mountain heritage; To explore alpine & glacial regions primarily in Canada; To preserve the natural beauty of mountains & their fauna & flora; to promote mountain art & literature; To disseminate scientific & educational knowledge concerning mountains & mountaineering through meetings & publications; To conduct summer & ski mountaineering camps
Affiliation(s): International Union of Alpinist Associations
Chief Officer(s):
Lawrence White, Executive Director
lwhite@alpineclubofcanada.ca
Lawrence White, Executive Director
lwhite@AlpineClubofCanada.ca
Toby Harper, Director, Programs
tharper@alpineclubofcanada.ca
Kish Stephenson, Manager, Finance
kstephenson@alpineclubofcanada.ca
Finances: *Funding Sources:* Donations; Grants; Corporate
Staff Member(s): 11
Membership: *Fees:* $38 individual; $58 family; $26 youth
Activities: Providing financial support necessary to advocate protection & preservation of mountain & climbing environments; Enhancing constitutional objective of ACC to work towards preservation of alpine environment & flora & fauna in their natural habitat; *Library* Open to public

Alpine Garden Club of BC
43212 Honeysuckle Dr., Chilliwack BC V2R 4A4

Tel: 604-580-3219
info@agc-bc.ca
www.agc-bc.ca
Overview: A small local organization
Mission: To promote the propagation & display of plants suitable for the alpine garden & alpine house, rare & unusual species of hardy plants, trees, shrubs & ferns, plants suitable for the art of bonsai; to promote an interest in the native plants of British Columbia & their preservation
Member of: North American Rock Garden Society
Chief Officer(s):
Linda Verbeek, President, 604-526-6656
Membership: 500; *Fees:* $30
Activities: Seed exchange; open gardens; field trips; plants sales; *Library*
Publications:
• The Bulletin
Type: Newsletter; *Frequency:* Quarterly

Alpine Ontario Alpin (AOA)
#10, 191 Hurontario St., Collingwood ON L9Y 2M1
Tel: 705-444-5111; *Fax:* 705-444-5116
admin@alpineontario.ca
www.alpineontario.ca
Overview: A medium-sized provincial organization
Mission: To provide skiing opportunities for competitive & recreational athletes
Chief Officer(s):
Scott Barrett, Acting Executive Director
sbarrett@alpineontario.ca
Staff Member(s): 5
Membership: 30,000+ in 44 clubs; *Fees:* Schedule available

Alpine Saskatchewan
1860 Lorne St., Regina SK S4P 2L7
Tel: 306-780-9236; *Fax:* 306-780-9462
office@saskalpine.com
saskalpine.webs.com
Also Known As: Sask Alpine
Overview: A small provincial organization
Mission: To be the provincial governing body for noncompetitive & competitive alpine skiing in Saskatchewan.
Chief Officer(s):
Karen Musgrave, President
president@saskalpine.com
Alana Ottenbreit, Office Manager

ALS Society of Alberta
#250, 4723 -1 St. SW, Calgary AB T2G 4Y8
Tel: 403-228-3857; *Fax:* 403-228-7752
Toll-Free: 888-309-1111
info@alsab.ca
www.alsab.ca
www.facebook.com/ALSALBERTA
twitter.com/ALS_AB
Overview: A small provincial charitable organization overseen by ALS Society Of Canada
Chief Officer(s):
Karen Caughey, Executive Director, 403-228-3857 Ext. 103
karen@alsab.ca
Staff Member(s): 12

Edmonton Chapter
5418 - 97 St. NW, Edmonton AB T6E 5C1
Tel: 780-487-0754; *Fax:* 780-486-3604
Toll-Free: 866-447-0754
societynorth@alsab.ca

ALS Society of British Columbia
1233-133351 Commerce Pkwy., Richmond BC V6V 2X7
Tel: 604-278-2257; *Fax:* 604-278-4257
Toll-Free: 800-708-3228
info@alsbc.ca
www.alsbc.ca
twitter.com/#!ALS_BC
Overview: A medium-sized provincial charitable organization overseen by ALS Society Of Canada
Mission: The ALS Society of BC is dedicated to providing direct support to ALS patients, along with their families and caregivers
Chief Officer(s):
Wendy Toyer, Executive Director, 604-278-2257 Ext. 222
wendy@alsbc.ca
Activities: *Awareness Events:* Annual ALS Memorial Golf Tournament, June; Peoples Drug Mart Walks for ALS, January; Cycle of Hope

North Central Island Chapter
PO Box 166, Bowser BC V0R 1G0
e-mail: ncic@alsbc.ca
Chief Officer(s):
Glenda Reynolds, President, 250-244-3791

Victoria Chapter
PO Box 48038, 3511 Blanshard St., Victoria BC V8Z 7H5
e-mail: victoria@alsbc.ca
Chief Officer(s):
Ellen Mahoney, President, 250-479-4266

ALS Society of Canada (ALS) / La Société canadienne de la SLA (SLA)
#200, 3000 Steeles Ave. East, Markham ON L3R 4T9
Tel: 905-248-2052; *Fax:* 905-248-2019
Toll-Free: 800-267-4257
www.als.ca
www.facebook.com/ALSCanada1
twitter.com/alsassociation
Also Known As: Amyotrophic Lateral Sclerosis Society of Canada
Overview: A large national charitable organization founded in 1977
Mission: To support research towards a cure for ALS; to support ALS partners in their provision of quality care for persons affected by ALS
Member of: Canadian Society of Gift Planners; National Society of Fundraising Executives; International Alliance of ALS/MND Associations; Canadian Centre for Philanthropy; Neuromuscular Research Partnership
Affiliation(s): Health Charities Council of Canada
Chief Officer(s):
Lanny McInnes, Chair
Tammy Moore, Interim Chief Executive Officer, 905-248-2052 Ext. 200
tm@als.ca
Enzo Raponi, Director, National WALK FOR ALS, 905-248-2052 Ext. 205
er@als.ca
David Taylor, PhD, Director, Research, 905-248-2052 Ext. 202
dt@als.ca
Finances: *Annual Operating Budget:* $3 Million-$5 Million; *Funding Sources:* Direct mail campaign; corporate & foundation support; ALS Canada Golf Outing
Staff Member(s): 9; 45 volunteer(s)
Membership: 1,000-4,999; *Member Profile:* 10 provincial societies
Activities: Information & referral; advocacy; public awareness; fundraising for research; supports the work of 11 partner units; *Awareness Events:* Walk for ALS, June-Sept.; ALS Charity Golf Classic, Sept.; Hike for ALS, Sept.; *Internships:* Yes; *Speaker Service:* Yes; *Library:* ALS Canada Library; by appointment
Awards:
• Sidney Valo Exceptional Fundraising Program Award (Award)
• Brett Yerex Exceptional Advocacy Award (Award)
• Tony Proudfoot Exceptional Public Awareness Program Award (Award)
• Marcel Bertrand Exceptional Support Services Program Award (Award)
• Mary Pollock Walk for ALS Volunteer Award (Award)
• William Fraser Leadership Development Award (Award)
• Myra Rosenfeld Volunteer Award (Award)
Publications:
• Manual for People Living with ALS [a publication of the ALS Society of Canada]
Type: Manual; *Editor:* Jane McCarthy
• Research News [a publication of the ALS Society of Canada]
Type: Newsletter

ALS Society of Manitoba / La societe Manitobaine de la SLA
493 Madison St., Winnipeg MB R3J 1J2
Tel: 204-831-1510; *Fax:* 204-837-9023
Toll-Free: 866-718-1642
HOPE@alsmb.ca
www.alsmb.ca
www.facebook.com/pages/ALS-Society-of-Manitoba/133254193405378
twitter.com/ALSmanitoba
Overview: A small provincial charitable organization founded in 1980 overseen by ALS Society Of Canada
Mission: The Society helps those with ALSs and their families by providing information and support.
Chief Officer(s):
Diana Rasmussen, Executive Director
Activities: Support Groups; Caregiver Days; VFAF Program; *Library:* Resource Library

ALS Society of New Brunswick
PO Box 295, Moncton NB E1C 8K9
Tel: 506-532-5786; *Fax:* 506-388-7466
Toll-Free: 866-722-7700
info@alsnb.ca
www.alsnb.ca
Overview: A small provincial charitable organization overseen by ALS Society Of Canada
Mission: The ALS Society of New Brunswick is a non-profit organization that support people living with ALS.
Chief Officer(s):
Karen Grotterod, President

ALS Society of Newfoundland & Labrador
Downtown Health Centre, Upper Level, Suite 3, PO Box 844, Corner Brook NL A2H 6H6
Tel: 709-634-9499; *Fax:* 709-634-9499
Toll-Free: 888-364-9499
alssocietyofnfld@nf.aibn.com
www.envision.ca/webs/alsnl
Overview: A small provincial charitable organization overseen by ALS Society Of Canada
Chief Officer(s):
Cheryl Power, Executive Director
Activities: *Awareness Events:* Walk for ALS, June

ALS Society of Nova Scotia
#113, 900 Windmill Rd., Dartmouth NS B3B 1P7
Tel: 902-454-3636; *Fax:* 902-453-3646
careandhope@alsns.ca
www.alsns.ca
www.facebook.com/pages/ALS-Society-of-Nova-Scotia/100227478015
Overview: A small provincial charitable organization founded in 1987 overseen by ALS Society Of Canada
Mission: The ALS Society raises funds and works to enhance the lives of people affected by ALS through care, information, hope and research.
Chief Officer(s):
Kimberly Carter, President
CareandHope@alsns.ca

ALS Society of Ontario
#402, 3100 Steeles Ave E, Markham ON L3R 8T3
Tel: 905-248-2101; *Fax:* 905-248-5620
Toll-Free: 866-611-8545
www.als.ca
Overview: A medium-sized provincial charitable organization overseen by ALS Society Of Canada
Chief Officer(s):
Robert Webster, President/CEO
robert@alsont.ca

ALS Society of PEI
PO Box 1643, Summerside PE C1N 2V5
Tel: 902-439-1600
als_society_pei@hotmail.com
www.alspei.ca
www.facebook.com/198677326838155
Overview: A small provincial charitable organization founded in 1984 overseen by ALS Society Of Canada
Mission: A fund-raising and awareness building group for ALS
Chief Officer(s):
Maxine Holmes, President, 902-675-4805

ALS Society of Québec / Société de la SLA du Québec
#200, 5415, rue Paré, Montréal QC H4P 1P7
Tél: 514-725-2653; *Téléc:* 514-725-6184
Ligne sans frais: 877-725-7725
info@sla-quebec.ca
www.sla-quebec.ca
www.facebook.com/slaquebec
www.flickr.com/photos/slaquebec/collections/
Aperçu: *Dimension:* petite; *Envergure:* provinciale; Organisme sans but lucratif surveillé par ALS Society Of Canada
Membre(s) du bureau directeur:
Claudia Cook, Executive Director, 514-725-2653 Ext. 101
ccook@sla-quebec.ca
Mélodie Prince, Fund Development Coordinator, 514-725-2653 Ext. 108
mprince@sla-quebec.ca
Activités: *Evénements de sensibilisation:* ALS Awareness Month, June

ALS Society of Saskatchewan
90C Cavendish St., Regina SK S4N 5G7

Tel: 306-949-4100; *Fax:* 306-949-4020
alssask@gmail.com
alssask.ca
www.facebook.com/pages/ALS-Society-of-Saskatchewan/47404 7055603
Overview: A small provincial charitable organization overseen by ALS Society Of Canada
Chief Officer(s):
Lisa Pluhowy, President
Activities: *Library:* Resource Library

Alström Syndrome Canada
PO Box 204, RR#2, Finch ON K0C 1K0
Overview: A small national organization
Mission: To raise awareness within the medical community about the existence of Alström Syndrome & its symptoms; To raise money for research; To support the children & families living with Alström Syndrome
Affliation(s): Alström Syndrome International
Chief Officer(s):
Randy Douglas, Director
randydouglas@sympatico.ca

AlterHéros
CP 56073, Succ. Alexis-Nihon, Montréal QC H3Z 1X5
Tél: 514-360-1320
info@alterheros.com
www.alterheros.com
www.facebook.com/alterheros
twitter.com/alterheros
Aperçu: *Dimension:* petite; *Envergure:* provinciale; fondée en 2003
Mission: Organisme communautaire bénévole à but non lucratif qui favorise l'insertion sociale des personnes d'orientation homosexuelle, bisexuelle et d'identité transsexuelle
Membre(s) du bureau directeur:
Véronique Daneau, Directrice générale
Membre(s) du personnel: 6

Alternatives Action & Communication Network for International Development *Voir* Réseau d'action et de communication pour le développement international

Altona & District Chamber of Commerce
Altona Mall, PO Box 329, Altona MB R0G 0B0
Tel: 204-324-8793; *Fax:* 204-324-1314
chamber@shopaltona.com
www.shopaltona.com
Overview: A small local organization
Member of: Manitoba Chamber of Commerce; Canadian Chamber of Commerce
Chief Officer(s):
Geoff Loewen, President, 204-324-5441
geoffloewen@mts.net
Becky Cianflone, Manager
Finances: *Annual Operating Budget:* $50,000-$100,000
Staff Member(s): 1; 8 volunteer(s)
Membership: 147 institutional; *Fees:* $52.50 - $492.37 (dependent upon business size)
Activities: *Awareness Events:* Canada Day in the Park; Manitoba Sunflower Festival, July

Altruvest Charitable Services
#600, 2 Carlton St., Toronto ON M5B 1J3
Tel: 416-597-2293; *Fax:* 416-597-2294
information@altruvest.org
www.altruvest.org
Overview: A small local charitable organization founded in 1994
Mission: To help improve the charitable sector in Canada by strengthening its employment base, creating volunteer interest & improving charitable leaders through training.
Chief Officer(s):
Robert C. Follows, Chair
Susan Dunne, Executive Director
Activities: BoardMatch and BoardWorx programs; *Speaker Service:* Yes

Aluminium Association of Canada (AAC) / Association de l'aluminium du Canada
#1600, 1010, rue Sherbrooke ouest, Montréal QC H3A 2R7
Tél: 514-288-4842; *Téléc:* 514-288-0944
www.thealuminiumdialog.com
twitter.com/AAC_aluminium
Aperçu: *Dimension:* moyenne; *Envergure:* nationale
Mission: To be a representative for the Canadian aluminium industry & to enhance its presence in industrial sectors, especially road & mass transit infrastructure & the automotive industry.
Membre(s) du bureau directeur:
Jean Simard, President & General Manager

Alva Foundation
c/o Graham Hallward, 199 Albertus Ave., Toronto ON M4R 1J6
e-mail: info@alva.ca
www.alva.ca
Previous Name: Southam Foundation
Overview: A medium-sized local charitable organization founded in 1965
Mission: To fund research into risk factors in early childhood development (pre-natal to 3 years of age); To fund pilot programs on demonstrations of new therapies serving the constituency described above
Chief Officer(s):
Graham F. Hallward, President & Chair, Donations Committee
Finances: *Funding Sources:* Investment portfolio
Membership: *Committees:* Donations

Alzheimer Manitoba
#10, 120 Donald St., Winnipeg MB R3C 4G2
Tel: 204-943-6622; *Fax:* 204-942-5408
Toll-Free: 800-378-6699
alzmb@alzheimer.mb.ca
www.alzheimer.mb.ca/
Also Known As: Alzheimer Society of Manitoba
Overview: A medium-sized provincial charitable organization founded in 1982 overseen by Alzheimer Society of Canada
Mission: To alleviate the individual, family & social consequences of Alzheimer type dementia while supporting the search for a cure
Chief Officer(s):
Sylvia Rothney, Executive Director
srothney@alzheimer.mb.ca
Finances: *Annual Operating Budget:* $500,000-$1.5 Million; *Funding Sources:* Donations; events
Staff Member(s): 20; 800 volunteer(s)
Membership: 250; *Fees:* $15
Activities: Helpline; support groups; education; *Awareness Events:* Alzheimer Awareness Month, Jan.; *Speaker Service:* Yes
Meetings/Conferences: • Alzheimer Manitoba A Night to Remember in Brazil: Gala 2015, February, 2015, RBC Convention Centre, Winnipeg, MB
Scope: Provincial

Alzheimer Society Canada (ASC) / Société Alzheimer Canada
#1600, 20 Eglinton Ave. West, Toronto ON M4R 1K8
Tel: 416-488-8772; *Fax:* 416-322-6656
Toll-Free: 800-616-8816
info@alzheimer.ca
www.alzheimer.ca
www.facebook.com/AlzheimerSociety
twitter.com/AlzSociety
www.youtube.com/thealzheimersociety
Overview: A large national charitable organization founded in 1978
Mission: Identifies, develops & facilitates national priorities that enable members to alleviate personal & social consequences of Alzheimer's disease & related disorders; promotes research & leads the search for a cure
Member of: Alzheimer Disease International
Affliation(s): HealthPartners
Chief Officer(s):
Leslie A. Beck, President
Finances: *Annual Operating Budget:* Greater than $5 Million; *Funding Sources:* Public support, including bequests & in memoria; corporations, foundations & event sponsorships; grants
Staff Member(s): 25; 70 volunteer(s)
Membership: 1-99; *Member Profile:* 10 provincial organizations make up the membership; active in over 150 local communities; *Committees:* Executive; Finance/Audit; Executive Compensation & Performance Review; Governance; Investment; Biomedical Review; Psychology Sociology Review; Support Services & Education; Public Policy; Marketing, Development & Communications
Activities: Provides support, information & education to people with Alzheimer's disease, families, physicians & health-care providers; funds researchers in the search for a cause & a cure; *Awareness Events:* Alzheimer Awareness Month, Jan.
Awards:
• Regular Grants (Grant), Alzheimer Society Research Program
• Young Investigator Grants (Grant), Alzheimer Society Research Program
• Doctoral Awards (Award), Alzheimer Society Research Program
• Post-Doctoral Awards (Award), Alzheimer Society Research Program

Alzheimer Society London & Middlesex (ASLM)
435 Windermere Rd., London ON N5X 2T1
Tel: 519-680-2404; *Fax:* 519-680-2864
Toll-Free: 888-495-5855
info@alzheimerlondon.ca
www.alzheimerlondon.ca
www.facebook.com/group.php?gid=70621362714
www.youtube.com/watch?v=VgsO2LGMVLk
Overview: A small local charitable organization founded in 1979
Mission: To provide support services & education for persons affected by Alzheimer's Disease & related dementias in Ontario's London & Middlesex region
Chief Officer(s):
Betsy Little, Chief Executive Officer
blittle@alzheimerlondon.ca
Rose Brochu, Coordinator, Accounting & Operations
rbrochu@alzheimerlondon.ca
Finances: *Funding Sources:* Donations; Fundraising; Sponsorships
Activities: Advocating on behalf of persons affected by Alzheimer's Disease & related dementias; Promoting research; Providing memory screening for persons experiencing memory concerns; Offering community resource information, sensory stimulation games & activities, plus journals & periodicals; *Awareness Events:* Walk for Memories; *Library:* Weldon Family Welcome & Resource Centre; Open to public
Publications:
• Connections
Type: Newsletter; *Frequency:* Quarterly; *Editor:* Leslie Mitchell
Profile: New developments plus volunteer news, fundraising activities, & upcoming events from the Alzheimer Society of London & Middlesex

Alzheimer Society of Alberta & Northwest Territories
10531 Kingsway Ave., Edmonton AB T5H 4K1
Tel: 780-488-2266; *Fax:* 780-488-3055
Toll-Free: 866-950-5465
info@alzheimer.ab.ca
www.alzheimer.ab.ca
Overview: A medium-sized provincial charitable organization founded in 1988 overseen by Alzheimer Society of Canada
Mission: The Society strives to alleviate the personal & social consequences of Alzheimer disease through the development, support & coordination of local societies & chapters. It also promotes the search for a cure through education & research. It is a registered charity, BN: 129690343RR0001.
Affliation(s): Canadian Association on Gerontology; Alberta Association on Gerontology; Canadian Centre for Philanthropy
Chief Officer(s):
Bill Gaudette, CEO
bgaudette@alzheimer.ab.ca
Christene Gordon, Director, Clinet Services & Programs
cgordon@alzheimer.ab.ca
Finances: *Annual Operating Budget:* $500,000-$1.5 Million; *Funding Sources:* Public donations
Staff Member(s): 20; 140 volunteer(s)
Membership: 1-99; *Committees:* Education/Support Services; Advocacy; Fund Development; Research
Activities: *Awareness Events:* National Alzheimer Awareness Month, Jan.; *Library:* Resource Centre; Open to public

Edmonton & Area Chapter
10531 Kingsway Ave., Edmonton AB T5H 4K1
Tel: 780-488-2266; *Fax:* 780-488-3055
Chief Officer(s):
Arlene Huhn, Manager, Client Services & Programs
ahuhn@alzheimer.ab.ca

Fort McMurray - Wood Buffalo Chapter
#200, 10010 Franklin Ave., Fort McMurray AB T9H 5N9
Tel: 780-743-6175; *Fax:* 780-791-0088
Chief Officer(s):
Jennifer Kennedy, Office Coordinator
jkennedy@alzheimer.ab.ca

Grande Prairie Chapter
#205, 8712 - 116 Ave., Grande Prairie AB T8V 4B4
Tel: 780-882-8870; *Fax:* 780-882-8780
Chief Officer(s):
Cindy McLeod, Coordinator, First Link/Intake
cmcleod@alzheimer.ab.ca

Lethbridge & Area Chapter
#402, 740 - 4th Ave. South, Lethbridge AB T1J 0N9
Tel: 403-329-3766; *Fax:* 403-327-3711
Chief Officer(s):
Brenda Hill, Manager, Client Services & Programs
hill@alzheimer.ab.ca

Medicine Hat & Area - Palliser Chapter
Hammond Bldg., #401D - 3rd St. SE, Medicine Hat AB T1A 0G8
Tel: 403-528-2700; *Fax:* 403-526-4994
Chief Officer(s):
Carol Lees, Regional Manager
clees@alzheimer.ab.ca

Northwest Territories - Yellowknife Chapter
#3, 5710 - 50 Ave., Yellowknife NT X1A 1G1
Tel: 867-873-6110; *Fax:* 403-250-8251
Toll-Free: 866-950-5465
Chief Officer(s):
Martha MacLellan, Volunteer Board Member

Red Deer & Central Alberta Chapter
#105, 4419 - 50 Ave., Red Deer AB T4N 3Z5
Tel: 403-342-0448
Chief Officer(s):
Christine Prysunka, Manager, Client Services & Programs
cprysunka@alzheimer.ab.ca

Alzheimer Society of Barrie & District, Alzheimer Society of Greater Simcoe County *See* Alzheimer Society of Simcoe County

Alzheimer Society of Belleville/Hastings/Quinte
470 Dundas St. East, Belleville ON K8N 1G1
Tel: 613-962-0892; *Fax:* 613-962-1225
Toll-Free: 800-361-8036
info@alzheimersocietyofbhq.com
www.alzheimer.ca/bhq
www.facebook.com/groups/288654961687
twitter.com/AlzBHQ
www.youtube.com/AlzBHQ
Overview: A small local organization founded in 1987
Mission: To alleviate the personal & social consequences of Alzheimer disease & to promote research
Affliation(s): Alzheimer Society of Ontario
Chief Officer(s):
Charmaine Jordan, President
Laura Hare, Executive Director
laura.hare@alzheimersocietyofbhq.com
Finances: *Annual Operating Budget:* $100,000-$250,000; *Funding Sources:* Memorials; donations; memberships; fundraisers; government
Staff Member(s): 6; 80 volunteer(s)
Membership: 100-499
Activities: Support groups; Wandering Person Registry; education; fairs; tag days; in-services; workshops; *Awareness Events:* Awareness Month, Jan.; *Library:* Alzheimer Resource Centre;

North Hastings
1 Manor Lane, Bancroft ON K0K 1C0
Tel: 613-332-4614; *Fax:* 613-332-0432
www.alzheimersocietyofbhq.com
Mission: To alleviate the personal & social consequences of Alzheimer Disease and related disorders and to promote research.
Chief Officer(s):
Sarah Krieger, Contact

Alzheimer Society of Brant
#701, 6 Bell Lane, Brantford ON N3T 0C3
Tel: 519-759-7692; *Fax:* 519-759-8353
www.alzbrant.ca
www.facebook.com/alzhbrant
Overview: A small local organization
Mission: To alleviate the personal & social consequences of Alzheimer Disease and related disorders and to promote research.
Member of: Alzheimer Association of Ontario
Chief Officer(s):
Mary Burnett, CEO

Alzheimer Society of British Columbia
#300, 828 West 8th Ave., Vancouver BC V5Z 1E1
Tel: 604-681-6530; *Fax:* 604-669-6907
Toll-Free: 800-667-3742
info@alzheimerbc.org
www.alzheimerbc.org
www.facebook.com/AlzheimerBC
twitter.com/AlzheimerBC
www.youtube.com/AlzheimerBC
Previous Name: Alzheimer Support Association of BC
Overview: A medium-sized provincial charitable organization founded in 1981 overseen by Alzheimer Society of Canada
Mission: To alleviate the personal & social consequences of Alzheimer disease & related dementias; to promote public awareness & to search for the causes & the cures
Chief Officer(s):
Jean Blake, CEO, 604-742-4901
jblake@alzheimerbc.org
Finances: *Annual Operating Budget:* $1.5 Million-$3 Million; *Funding Sources:* Donations; membership dues; grants; special events
Staff Member(s): 58; 400 volunteer(s)
Membership: 150+; *Fees:* $15 individual; $25 family; $50 corporation; *Committees:* Advocacy; Communication; Conference; Finance; Fund Development; Policy & Procedures; Research; Multicultural; Support; Education
Activities: Support groups, Dementia Helpline, education, information resources, advocacy, research funding, fundraising, marketing & communications; *Awareness Events:* Alzheimer Awareness Month, Jan.; Investors Group Walk for Memories, Jan.; Forget Me Not Golf Tournament, May; Ascent for Alzheimer's, Sept.; Mt. Kilimanjaro Grouse Grind for Alzheimer's, Sept.; Coffee Break, Sept.; *Speaker Service:* Yes; *Library* Open to public

Alzheimer Society of Calgary
#201, 222 - 58 Ave. SW, Calgary AB T2H 2S3
Tel: 403-290-0110
Toll-Free: 877-569-4357
info@alzheimercalgary.com
www.alzheimercalgary.com
www.facebook.com/116306041728999
twitter.com/alzcalgary
Overview: A medium-sized local charitable organization founded in 1981
Mission: To offer educational & support services to individuals & families in the Calgary region experiencing Alzheimer Disease & related disorders (dementia), as well as to professionals in the field; to support research
Affliation(s): Alzheimer Society of Canada; Alzheimer Society of Alberta
Chief Officer(s):
Wendy Benson, Director, Human Resources & Administration
Finances: *Annual Operating Budget:* $500,000-$1.5 Million
Staff Member(s): 15; 150 volunteer(s)
Membership: 450; *Fees:* $10 seniors (over 60) & students (under 18); $15 general; *Committees:* Advocacy; Human Resources; Finance; Strategic Planning
Activities: *Internships:* Yes; *Speaker Service:* Yes; *Library:* Resource Centre; Open to public

Alzheimer Society of Chatham-Kent
36 Memory Lane, Chatham ON N7L 5M8
Tel: 519-352-1043; *Fax:* 519-352-3680
info@alzheimerchathamkent.ca
www.alzheimer.ca/chathamkent
www.facebook.com/321344923495
www.youtube.com/thealzheimersociety
Overview: A small local charitable organization founded in 1983
Mission: To alleviate the personal & social consequences of Alzheimer Disease and related disorders and to promote research.
Member of: Alzheimer Society of Canada
Chief Officer(s):
Mary Ellen Parker, CEO
Staff Member(s): 15

Alzheimer Society of Cornwall & District
106B - 2 St. West, Cornwall ON K6H 6N6
Tel: 613-932-4914; *Fax:* 613-932-6154
Toll-Free: 888-222-1445
alzheimer.info@one-mail.on.ca
www.alzheimer.ca/cornwall
Overview: A small local charitable organization
Mission: To alleviate the personal & social consequences of Alzheimer Disease and related disorders and to promote research.

Alzheimer Society of Dufferin County
#1, 25 Centennial Rd., Orangeville ON L9W 1R1
Tel: 519-941-1221; *Fax:* 519-941-1730
info@alzheimerdufferin.org
www.alzheimerdufferin.org
www.facebook.com/Alzheimerdufferin
Overview: A small local charitable organization founded in 1999
Mission: To alleviate the personal & social consequences of Alzheimer Disease and related disorders and to promote research.
Member of: Alzheimer Society of Ontario
Chief Officer(s):
Diane Cowen, Interim Executive Director
dianecowen@alzheimerdufferin.org
Staff Member(s): 8
Activities: Coffee Break; Physician lunch support groups; Education & awareness

Alzheimer Society of Durham Region (ASDR)
Oshawa Executive Centre, Oshawa Centre, #207, 419 King St. West, Oshawa ON L1J 2K5
Tel: 905-576-2567; *Fax:* 905-576-2033
Toll-Free: 888-301-1106
info@alzheimerdurham.com
www.alzheimerdurham.com
Also Known As: Alzheimer Durham
Overview: A small local charitable organization founded in 1979
Mission: To improve the quality of life of persons with Alzheimer's Disease, or related dementias, & their caregivers in Ontario's Durham Region
Member of: Alzheimer Society of Ontario
Chief Officer(s):
Chris Braney, Chief Executive Officer
cbraney@alzheimerdurham.com
Karen Ouellette, Director, Finance
kouellette@alzheimerdurham.com
Michelle Pepin, Director, Family Support
mpepin@alzheimerdurham.com
Loretta Tanner, Director, Public Education
ltanner@alzheimerdurham.com
Linda Bredin, Coordinator, Administration
lbredin@alzheimerdurham.com
Brenda Davie, Coordinator, Family Support & Education
bdavie@alzheimerdurham.com
Robin Jackson, Coordinator, First Link
rjackson@alzheimerdurham.com
Karen Morley, Coordinator, Caregiver
kmorley@alzheimerdurham.com
Nicolle McNall, Coordinator, First Link Outreach & Events
nmcnall@alzheimerdurham.com
Finances: *Funding Sources:* Donations; Fundraising; Sponsorships; Membership fees
Membership: *Fees:* $10
Activities: Offering support & education programs; Engaging in advocacy activities; Raising public awareness; *Awareness Events:* Walk for Memories
Publications:
• Staying Connected: A Newsletter from Alzheimer Society of Durham Region
Type: Newsletter; *Frequency:* Quarterly; *Price:* Free with membership in the Alzheimer Society of Durham Region
Profile: Notices about forthcoming events, education, & support groups

Alzheimer Society of Grey-Bruce
753 - 2nd Ave. East, Owen Sound ON N4K 2G9
Tel: 519-376-7230; *Fax:* 519-376-2428
Toll-Free: 800-265-9013
info@alzheimergreybruce.com
www.alzheimer.ca/greybruce
www.facebook.com/AlzheimerSocietyofGreyBruce
twitter.com/AlzheimerSGB
Overview: A small local charitable organization founded in 1986
Mission: Exists to alleviate the personal and social consequences of Alzheimer's Disease and related disorders and to promote research.
Member of: Alzheimer Association of Ontario
Chief Officer(s):
Deborah Barker, Executive Director
dbarker@alzheimergreybruce.com
Staff Member(s): 13
Activities: *Library* Open to public

Alzheimer Society of Haldimand Norfolk
645 Norfolk St. North, Simcoe ON N3Y 3R2
Tel: 519-428-7771; *Fax:* 519-428-2968
Toll-Free: 800-565-4614
www.alzhn.ca
www.facebook.com/alzhbrant
Overview: A small local charitable organization founded in 1993
Mission: To help people as they deal with the consequences of Alzheimer's Disease & related disorders

Chief Officer(s):
Mary Burnett, Chief Executive Officer
mary.burnett@alzda.ca
Wendy Tanner, Site Manager & Bookkeeper
wtanner@alzhn.ca
Aileen Bradshaw, Volunteer Coordinator
abradshaw@alzhn.ca
Finances: *Funding Sources:* Donations
Activities: Establishing a Wandering Person Registry; Increasing public awareness; Promoting education; Offering supportive counselling; Providing consultation services to community organization & health care agencies; Engaging in advocacy activities; *Awareness Events:* Walk for Memories; *Library:* Alzheimer Resource Library; Open to public

Alzheimer Society of Hamilton Halton
#700, 1575 Upper Ottawa St., Hamilton ON L8W 3E2
Tel: 905-529-7030; *Fax:* 905-529-3787
Toll-Free: 888-343-1017
www.alzheimerhamiltonhalton.org
www.facebook.com/alzhbrant
Overview: A small local charitable organization founded in 1982
Mission: To provide programs & services to help caregivers handle the challenges associated with caring for people with Alzheimer's Disease & related disorders in the communities of Ancaster, Dundas, Flamborough, Glanbrook, Hamilton, & Stoney Creek within the City of Hamilton, & the the communities of Burlington, Halton Hills, Milton & Oakville within Halton Region
Chief Officer(s):
Mary Burnett, Chief Executive Officer
mary.burnett@alzda.ca
JoAnne Chalifour, Regional Director, Operations
joanne.chalifour@alzda.ca
Trevor Clark, Regional Director, Development
trevor.clark@alzda.ca
Gabriela Luchsinger, Manager, Counselling Program
gluchsinger@alzhh.ca
Katherine Rankin, Manager, Education Programs
katherine.rankin@alzda.ca
Marian Cummins, Coordinator, Public Education — Hamilton
educationhamilton@alzhh.ca
Meaghan Plomp, Coordinator, Volunteers
mplomp@alzhh.ca
Karen Robins, Coordinator, Public Education — Halton
educationhalton@alzhh.ca
Dawn Vince, Coordinator, Fund Development
funddevelopment@alzhh.ca
Finances: *Funding Sources:* Donations; Fundraising
Activities: Establishing the Wandering Person Registries in Hamilton & Halton; Offering education services to professionals who work in dementia related areas & to families affected by Alzheimer's Disease; *Awareness Events:* Walk for Memories; *Library:* Hamilton Resource Centre; Open to public

Alzheimer Society of Huron County
PO Box 639, 317 Huron Rd., Clinton ON N0M 1L0
Tel: 519-482-1482; *Fax:* 519-482-8692
Toll-Free: 800-561-5012
admin@alzheimerhuron.on.ca
www.alzheimerhuron.on.ca
www.facebook.com/AlzheimerSocietyHuron
twitter.com/AlzSociety
www.youtube.com/user/AlzheimerSouthwest
Overview: A small local organization
Mission: To alleviate the personal and social consequences of Alzheimer Disease and related disorders and to promote research.
Chief Officer(s):
Cathy Ritsema, Executive Director
cathy@alzheimerhuron.on.ca
Staff Member(s): 8

Alzheimer Society of Kenora/Rainy River Districts
618 - 9th St. North, Kenora ON P9N 2S9
Tel: 807-468-1516; *Fax:* 807-468-9013
Toll-Free: 800-682-0245
info@alzheimerkrr.com
www.alzheimer.ca/krr
www.facebook.com/Alzheimerkrr
Overview: A small local charitable organization founded in 1991
Mission: To alleviate the personal and social consequences of Alzheimer Disease and related disorders and to promote research.
Chief Officer(s):
Lynn Moffatt, Executive Director
lynn@alzheimerkrr.com
Staff Member(s): 5
Activities: Education sessions & support; fundraising events; lending library;

Alzheimer Society of Kingston, Frontenac, Lennox & Addington
#4, 400 Elliot Ave., Kingston ON K7K 6M9
Tel: 613-544-3078; *Fax:* 613-544-6320
Toll-Free: 800-266-7516
reception@alzking.com
www.alzheimer.ca/kfla
www.facebook.com/AlzheimerKingston
twitter.com/AlzSocKing
www.youtube.com/thealzheimersociety
Overview: A small local charitable organization founded in 1986
Mission: To improve the quality of life of people with Alzheimer disease & other dementias & their caregivers
Member of: Alzheimer Association of Ontario
Chief Officer(s):
Jan White, President
Vicki Poffley, Executive Director
Staff Member(s): 6
Activities: *Awareness Events:* Walk for Memories; *Speaker Service:* Yes; *Library* Open to public

Alzheimer Society of Lanark County
115 Christie Lake Rd., Perth ON K7H 3C6
Tel: 613-264-0307
Toll-Free: 800-511-1911
alz@storm.ca
www.alzheimer.ca/lanark
www.facebook.com/pages/Alzheimer-Society-Lanark-County/715699371806903
twitter.com/1ASLC
Overview: A small local organization
Mission: To alleviate the personal and social consequences of Alzheimer Disease and related disorders and to promote research.
Member of: Alzheimer Association of Ontario
Chief Officer(s):
Don McDiarmid, President
Louise Noble, Executive Director
alzlnoble@storm.ca
Staff Member(s): 12

Alzheimer Society of Leeds-Grenville
c/o Garden Street Site, Brockville General Hospital, 42 Garden St., Brockville ON K6V 2C3
Tel: 613-345-7392; *Fax:* 613-345-3186
Toll-Free: 866-576-8556
office@alzheimerleedsgrenville.ca
www.alzheimerleedsgrenville.ca
www.facebook.com/alzheimerleedsgrenville
Overview: A small local charitable organization founded in 1987
Mission: To help persons diagnosed with Alzheimer's Disease or a related dementia in the Leeds-Grenville region of Ontario
Chief Officer(s):
Denise Wood, Executive Director
administrator@alzheimerleedsgrenville.ca
Sean McFadden, Coordinator, Public Education & Family Support
education@alzheimerleedsgrenville.ca
Erin Cleaver, Assistant, Programs & Services
Finances: *Funding Sources:* Donations; Fundraising
Activities: Providing support groups, such as caregiver support groups, early stage support groups for individuals with dementia, & "Just for You" groups for persons living with Alzheimer's Disease or a related dementia for some time; Offering education for professionals & the public; Advocating on behalf of families of people with Alzheimer's Disease or related dementias; Promoting research to find a cause & cure; Increasing public awareness, through campaigns such as Heads Up for Healthier Brains; *Library:* Resources Centre & Loaning Library; Open to public
Publications:
• Alzheimer Society of Leeds-Grenville Newsletter
Type: Newsletter; *Frequency:* 3 pa; *Price:* Free with membership in the Alzheimer Society of Leeds-Grenville
Profile: Updates about the society's activities, plus educational information, caregiver tips, & research reports
• Alzheimer Update
Type: Newsletter
Profile: Medical information & resources for physicians in the Leeds-Grenville region

Alzheimer Society of Miramichi
PO Box 205, Miramichi NB E1N 3A6
Tel: 506-773-7093; *Fax:* 506-773-7093
Toll-Free: 800-664-8411
alzmir@nb.aibn.com
www.alzheimernb.ca
Overview: A small local organization
Mission: To alleviate the personal and social consequences of Alzheimer Disease and related disorders and to promote research.

Alzheimer Society of Moncton
960 St. George Blvd., Moncton NB E1E 3Y3
Tel: 506-858-8380; *Fax:* 506-855-7697
moncton@alzheimernb.ca
www.alzheimernb.ca
Overview: A small local charitable organization founded in 1986
Mission: To alleviate the personal & social consequences of Alzheimer's Disease & related diseases in the Moncton New Brunswick region
Member of: Société Alzheimer Society New Brunswick / Nouveau-Brunswick
Finances: *Funding Sources:* Donations; Fundraising
Activities: Arranging support groups; Providing information & education; Increasing public awareness

Alzheimer Society of Muskoka
#205, 230 Manitoba St., Bracebridge ON P1L 2E1
Tel: 705-645-5621; *Fax:* 705-645-4397
alzmusk@muskoka.com
Overview: A small local charitable organization founded in 1995
Mission: To assist persons living with Alzheimer's Disease & other dementias in the Muskoka region of Ontario; To provide education programs; To promote research
Member of: Alzheimer Society of Ontario
Finances: *Funding Sources:* Donations; Sponsorships
Activities: Providing referral services; Offering counselling & support groups; Advocating for individuals, families, & caregivers; Visiting; *Library:* Alzheimer Society of Muskoka Lending Library & Resource Centre; Open to public

Alzheimer Society of New Brunswick / Société alzheimer du nouveau brunswick
#100, 320 Maple St., Fredericton NB E3B 5G2
Tel: 506-459-4280; *Fax:* 506-452-0313
Toll-Free: 800-664-8411
info@alzheimernb.ca
www.alzheimernb.ca
www.facebook.com/127071537361985
twitter.com/AlzheimerNB
Overview: A medium-sized provincial organization founded in 1987 overseen by Alzheimer Society of Canada
Mission: To alleviate the personal & social consequences of Alzheimer disease; to promote the search for a cause & cure
Chief Officer(s):
Gloria McIlveen, Executive Director
Finances: *Annual Operating Budget:* $250,000-$500,000
Staff Member(s): 4; 20 volunteer(s)
Membership: 250; *Fees:* $15
Activities: *Speaker Service:* Yes

Alzheimer Society of Newfoundland & Labrador
PO Box 37013, 687 Water St., St. John's NL A1E 1C2
Tel: 709-576-0608; *Fax:* 709-576-0798
Toll-Free: 877-776-0608
alzheimersociety@nf.aibn.com
www.alzheimernl.org
www.facebook.com/ASNL2
twitter.com/asnl2
Overview: A small provincial charitable organization founded in 1988 overseen by Alzheimer Society of Canada
Mission: To support the search for the cause & cure of Alzheimer Disease; To raise public awareness of the personal & social impact of the disease; To promote the provision of support to families & caregivers in Newfoundland
Chief Officer(s):
Christine Caravan, Director
Finances: *Annual Operating Budget:* $50,000-$100,000; *Funding Sources:* Fundraising; donations; sponsorship
Staff Member(s): 2
Membership: 130; *Fees:* $15; $10 seniors; $50 corporate; *Committees:* Education; Finance; Fund Development
Activities: *Awareness Events:* Awareness Month, Jan.; Door to Door, March; Coffee Break, Sept.; *Library* Open to public

Alzheimer Society of Niagara Region
#1, 403 Ontario St., St Catharines ON L2N 1L5
Tel: 905-687-3914; *Fax:* 905-687-9952
Toll-Free: 877-818-3202

niagara@alzheimerniagara.ca
www.alzheimer.ca/niagara
www.facebook.com/106624255247
twitter.com/alzheimerniagar
www.youtube.com/user/alzheimerniagara
Overview: A small local charitable organization founded in 1984
Mission: To ensure quality services for individuals with Alzheimer disease & related dementias; we support & advocate for individuals, families, caregivers & community through counselling, education & the promotion of research to compassionately respond to the very special needs of those experiencing dementia
Chief Officer(s):
Robert Fead, President
Teena Kindt, CEO
Finances: *Annual Operating Budget:* $500,000-$1.5 Million; *Funding Sources:* Ministry of Health; fundraising; donations
Staff Member(s): 27; 196 volunteer(s)
Membership: 150; *Fees:* $10
Activities: Support groups; visiting & driving program; wandering registry; caregiver education series; *Awareness Events:* International Alzheimer Day, Sept. 21; Coffee Break, Sept.; Walk for Memories, Jan.; *Internships:* Yes; *Speaker Service:* Yes; *Library* Open to public

Alzheimer Society of North Bay & District
1180 Cassells St., North Bay ON P1B 4B6
Tel: 705-495-4342; *Fax:* 705-495-0329
www.alzheimer.ca/northbay
www.facebook.com/alzheimersmnbd
Overview: A small local charitable organization founded in 1978
Mission: To alleviate the personal & social consequences of Alzheimer Disease & related disorders & to promote research
Member of: Alzheimer Society of Ontario
Chief Officer(s):
Linda Brown, Family Counsellor & Site Supervisor
lbrown@alzheimernorthbay.com
Staff Member(s): 4
Activities: *Awareness Events:* Walk for Memories; *Library* Open to public

Alzheimer Society of Nova Scotia
#300, 6009 Quinpool Rd., Halifax NS B3K 5J7
Tel: 902-422-7961; *Fax:* 902-422-7971
Toll-Free: 800-611-6345
alzheimer@asns.ca
www.alzheimer.ca/ns
www.facebook.com/profile.php?id=100003124237350
twitter.com/alzheimerns
Overview: A medium-sized provincial charitable organization founded in 1983 overseen by Alzheimer Society of Canada
Mission: To enhance the quality of life of people with Alzheimer disease through providing & promoting public education & family support; to engage in advocacy on behalf of people with Alzheimer disease & their families; to promote research at the provincial & national levels
Chief Officer(s):
Lloyd O. Brown, Executive Director
Justin McDonough, President
Finances: *Annual Operating Budget:* $50,000-$100,000
Staff Member(s): 6; 2000 volunteer(s)
Membership: 2,500; *Fees:* $35 business; $15 individual; *Committees:* Research; Education; Advocacy; Support; Fundraising; Public Relations
Activities: *Awareness Events:* Alzheimer Awareness Month, Jan.; *Speaker Service:* Yes; *Library:* Alzheimer Resource Centre; Open to public

Alzheimer Society of Ottawa *See* Alzheimer Society of Ottawa & Renfrew County

Alzheimer Society of Ottawa & Renfrew County / Société Alzheimer d'Ottawa et Renfrew County
#1742, 1750 Russell Rd., Ottawa ON K1G 5Z6
Tel: 613-523-4004; *Fax:* 613-523-8522
Toll-Free: 888-411-2067
info@asorc.org
alzheimerottawa.ca
www.facebook.com/alzheimerottawa
twitter.com/AlzheimerOttawa
www.youtube.com/user/ASOttawa
Previous Name: Alzheimer Society of Ottawa
Overview: A medium-sized local charitable organization founded in 1980
Mission: To increase the understanding of, & to alleviate the personal & social consequences of Alzheimer disease through patient & family support, information & education & promotion of research
Member of: Alzheimer Society of Ontario; Alzheimer Society of Canada
Affliation(s): Perley & Rideau Veterans' Health Centre; Care for Health & Community Services; Champlain Dementia Network
Chief Officer(s):
Kathy Wright, Executive Director
kwright@asorc.org
Debbie Seto, Manager, Communications
dseto@asorc.org
Harvey Pritchett, Director, Operations & Volunteer Resources
hpritchett@asorc.org
Finances: *Annual Operating Budget:* $1.5 Million-$3 Million; *Funding Sources:* Donations; memberships; bequests; fundraising events; approximately 30% from government
Staff Member(s): 25; 300 volunteer(s)
Activities: Family support & education services; specialized family support groups (wives, daughters, husbands, sons, Early Alzheimer Group); workshops for families & professional caregivers; Safely Home Program; Alzheimer Info Line; Enhancing Care Program; resource centre; speakers' bureau; Alzheimer website; Renfrew County Satellite Office; *Awareness Events:* National Alzheimer Awareness Month, Jan.; *Library:* Resource Centre; Open to public
Publications:
• Société Alzheimer Society Ottawa & Renfrew County Annual Report
Type: Yearbook; *Frequency:* Annually
Profile: A review of the year's events
• Société Alzheimer Society Ottawa & Renfrew County Newsletter
Type: Newsletter
Profile: Information about programs & services provided by the society, plus research & education updates

Alzheimer Society of Oxford (ASO)
575 Peel St., Woodstock ON N4S 1K6
Tel: 519-421-2466; *Fax:* 519-421-3098
info@alzheimer.oxford.on.ca
www.alzheimer.ca/oxford
www.facebook.com/alzoxford
twitter.com/AlzSociety
www.youtube.com/thealzheimersociety
Overview: A small local charitable organization founded in 1989
Mission: To improve the quality of life for people with Alzheimer disease or related dementias & their caregivers
Member of: Alzheimer Society of Ontario
Chief Officer(s):
Andrew Szasz, President
Finances: *Funding Sources:* Donations; provincial government; Nevada ticket sales; bingo; fundraising
Activities: Support Groups; Volunteer Companion; Sensory Stimulation Resource Centre; Children's Information Series; Caring with Respect course; Information Support; advocacy; "Walk for Memories"; Tag Day; "Cuddle Bear" Program; Teen Education Series; Information & support group for individuals in the early stages of the disease; *Library* Open to public

Alzheimer Society of Peel
60 Briarwood Ave., Mississauga ON L5G 3N6
Tel: 905-278-3667; *Fax:* 905-278-3964
www.alzheimerpeel.com
www.facebook.com/pages/Alzheimer-Society-Peel/112857568321
twitter.com/AlzPeel
Overview: A small local charitable organization founded in 1983
Mission: To alleviate the personal and social consequences of Alzheimer Disease and related disorders and to promote research.
Member of: Alzheimer Association of Ontario
Chief Officer(s):
Mary-Lynn Peters, President
Finances: *Annual Operating Budget:* Greater than $5 Million
Membership: *Member Profile:* Caregivers; professionals in community health area
Activities: Counselling; day programs; family support; education

Alzheimer Society of PEI
166 Fitzroy St., Charlottetown PE C1A 1S1
Tel: 902-628-2257; *Fax:* 902-368-2715
Toll-Free: 866-628-2257
society@alzpei.ca
www.alzheimer.ca/pei
www.facebook.com/AlzheimerPEI
twitter.com/AlzheimerPEI
Overview: A small provincial charitable organization founded in 1989 overseen by Alzheimer Society of Canada
Mission: To support & assist Islanders affected by Alzheimer Disease; To raise the level of awareness & educate the public at large about the disease
Chief Officer(s):
Colleen Laybolt, Executive Administrator
Finances: *Annual Operating Budget:* $100,000-$250,000; *Funding Sources:* Fee for services; fundraising
Staff Member(s): 7
Membership: 100-499
Activities: Counselling; mediation; Day Respite support groups; advocacy; Wandering Person Registry - Safely Home; Enhancing care program; music therapy; *Awareness Events:* Alzheimer Awareness Month, Jan.; Coffee Break, Sept.; Memory Wall, June; *Speaker Service:* Yes; *Library* Open to public
Awards:
• Leadership Award (Award)

Alzheimer Society of Perth County
1020 Ontario St., Stratford ON N5A 6Z3
Tel: 519-271-1910
Toll-Free: 888-797-1882
alzperth@wightman.ca
www.alzheimerperthcounty.com
www.facebook.com/group.php?gid=131087190247115
twitter.com/@Alzperth
Overview: A small local charitable organization
Mission: To assist those affected by Alzheimer's Disease & other types of dementia
Chief Officer(s):
Debbie Deichert, Executive Director
debdeichert@wightman.ca
Finances: *Funding Sources:* Donations; Fundraising; Sponsorships
Membership: *Fees:* $10 students & seniors; $15 individuals & families; $25 non-profit organizations; $50 corporate members
Activities: Providing support services; Offering a learning series; Promoting research; *Awareness Events:* Walk for Memories; Alzheimer Awareness Month
Publications:
• The Helping Hand
Type: Newsletter; *Price:* Free with Alzheimer Society of Perth County membership
Profile: Articles to help caregivers & upcoming events

Alzheimer Society of Prince Edward County
90 King St., Picton ON K0K 2T0
Tel: 613-476-2085; *Fax:* 613-476-1537
Overview: A small local charitable organization founded in 1985
Mission: To help people diagnosed with Alzheimer's Disease or a related dementia in Prince Edward County of southeastern Ontario
Member of: South East Local Health Integration Network (LHIN)
Chief Officer(s):
Linda Jackson, Executive Director
Linda.Jackson@alzpec.ca
Finances: *Funding Sources:* Donations; Fundraising
Activities: Offering education programs; Advocating for families of people with Alzheimer's Disease & related dementias; Promoting research;

Alzheimer Society of Sarnia-Lambton
420 East St. North, Sarnia ON N7T 6Y5
Tel: 519-332-4444; *Fax:* 519-332-6673
info@alzheimersarnia.ca
alzheimer.sarnia.com
www.facebook.com/alzheimersarnialambton
twitter.com/AlzheimerSociet
Overview: A small local charitable organization founded in 1986
Mission: To improve the quality of live of people with Alzheimer disease or related dementia, & their caregivers
Member of: Alzheimer Society of Ontario
Affliation(s): Ministry of Health, Long-Term Care; Ontario Trillium Foundation
Chief Officer(s):
Bill Seymour, Chair
Judy Doan, CEO
Staff Member(s): 7
Membership: *Member Profile:* Caregivers, medical personnel, organizations, general public
Activities: Support meetings; library; educational training; fundraising; public & staff education; Caregiver Series, Oct.; information series; Remember Me: Children's Education; cadaver transportation; counselling & referral; wandering registry; mobility monitors; *Awareness Events:* Walk for

Memories, Jan.; *Speaker Service:* Yes; *Library:* Resource Library; Open to public

Alzheimer Society Of Saskatchewan Inc. (ASOS)

#301, 2550 - 12 Ave., Regina SK S4P 3X1
Tel: 306-949-4141; *Fax:* 306-949-3069
Toll-Free: 800-263-3367
office@alzheimer.sk.ca
www.alzheimer.sk.ca
www.facebook.com/217901721605861
twitter.com/AlzheimerSK
Previous Name: Saskatchewan Alzheimer & Related Diseases Association
Overview: A medium-sized provincial charitable organization founded in 1982 overseen by Alzheimer Society of Canada
Mission: To alleviate the personal & social consequences of Alzheimer's disease & related disorders & to promote the search for a cause & a cure
Chief Officer(s):
Joanne Bracken, Executive Director
execdir@alzheimer.sk.ca
Kathleen Defoe, Coordinator, Finance & Administration
finance@alzheimer.sk.ca
Finances: *Annual Operating Budget:* $500,000-$1.5 Million; *Funding Sources:* Donations; fundraising
Staff Member(s): 8
Membership: 400 individual + 200 complimentary; *Fees:* Schedule available; *Member Profile:* Family; professional care providers; interested members of the public; health care organizations; regional health authorities
Activities: *Awareness Events:* Alzheimer Awareness Month, Jan.; Alzheimer Coffee Break, Sept.; Alzheimer Fall Gala, Oct.; *Internships:* Yes; *Speaker Service:* Yes; *Library* Open to public

Alzheimer Society of Sault Ste. Marie & District of Algoma

341 Trunk Rd., Sault Ste Marie ON P6A 3S9
Tel: 705-942-2195; *Fax:* 705-256-6777
Toll-Free: 877-396-7888
info@alzheimeralgoma.org
www.alzheimeralgoma.org
Overview: A small local charitable organization founded in 1987
Mission: To improve the quality of life for people with Alzheimer disease & related disorders & to provide support for their caregivers
Member of: Alzheimer Association of Ontario
Chief Officer(s):
Graham Clark, President
Terry Caporossi, Executive Director
Staff Member(s): 17
Activities: Door-to-door campaign; coffee break; Walk for Memories; *Speaker Service:* Yes; *Library:* Kay L. Punch Resource Centre; Open to public

Alzheimer Society of Simcoe County

#3, 20 Anne St. South, Barrie ON L4M 5R4
Tel: 705-722-1066; *Fax:* 705-722-9392
Toll-Free: 800-265-5391
simcoecounty@alzheimersociety.ca
www.alzheimersociety.ca
www.facebook.com/AlzheimerSocietySimcoeCounty
twitter.com/AlzheimerSimcoe
Previous Name: Alzheimer Society of Barrie & District, Alzheimer Society of Greater Simcoe County
Merged from: Alzheimer Society of Greater Simcoe County & Alzheimer Society of North East Simcoe County
Overview: A small local charitable organization founded in 1985
Mission: To improve the quality of life of persons who are directly affected by Alzheimer's diseases or related dementias
Affliation(s): Alzheimer Society of Ontario; Alzheimer Society of Canada
Chief Officer(s):
Debbie Islam, Executive Director
dislam@alzheimersociety.ca
Debbie Islam, Executive Director
dislam@alzheimersociety.ca
Finances: *Annual Operating Budget:* $250,000-$500,000; *Funding Sources:* Membership dues; donations; fundraising programs/events; provincial government
Staff Member(s): 14; 367 volunteer(s)
Membership: 136; *Fees:* $15 regular; $10 seniors; $50 organizations/corporate; *Member Profile:* Family caregivers; professional caregivers; volunteers; organizations
Activities: Education; support; awareness; advocacy; research funding; *Awareness Events:* Alzheimer Awareness Month, Jan.; *Internships:* Yes; *Speaker Service:* Yes; *Library* Open to public

Alzheimer Society of Thunder Bay (ASTB)

#310, 180 Park Ave., Thunder Bay ON P7B 6J4
Tel: 807-345-9556; *Fax:* 807-345-1518
Toll-Free: 888-887-5140; *TTY:* 888-887-5140
info@alzheimerthunderbay.ca
www.alzheimer.ca/thunderbay
www.facebook.com/ASTBAY
Overview: A small local charitable organization founded in 1986
Mission: To improve the quality of life of persons with Alzheimer disease or related dementia & their caregivers; to promote the rights & well-being of persons with the disease & their caregivers; to support the delivery of programmes for individuals affected by the disease; to provide funds for research
Member of: Alzheimer Society of Ontario
Chief Officer(s):
Laraine Tapak, President
Alison Denton, Executive Director
adenton@alzheimerthunderbay.ca
Finances: *Annual Operating Budget:* $100,000-$250,000; *Funding Sources:* Fundraising; Donations
Staff Member(s): 10; 100 volunteer(s)
Membership: *Committees:* Board Task Forces; Special Events
Activities: Individual & family counselling; education; public awareness; activity lending library; advocacy; support groups; *Awareness Events:* Walk for Memories; Alzheimer Coffee Break Campaign; Alzheimer Rendez-vous; *Speaker Service:* Yes; *Library:* Resource Centre; Open to public

Alzheimer Society of Timmins/Porcupine District

70 Cedar St. South, Timmins ON P4N 2G6
Tel: 705-268-4554; *Fax:* 705-360-4492
mail@alzheimertimmins.org
www.alzheimertimmins.org
Overview: A small local charitable organization founded in 1986
Mission: To alleviate the personal & social consequences of Alzheimer disease; to promote the search for the causes & cure of the disease
Member of: Alzheimer Association of Ontario
Chief Officer(s):
Tracy Koskamp-Bergeron, Executive Director
tracykb@alzheimertimmins.org
Staff Member(s): 7
Membership: *Fees:* $15
Activities: *Speaker Service:* Yes

Alzheimer Society of Toronto

20 Eglinton Ave. West, 16th Fl., Toronto ON M4R 1K8
Tel: 416-322-6560; *Fax:* 416-322-6656
contact@alzheimertoronto.org
www.alzheimertoronto.org
Overview: A medium-sized local charitable organization founded in 1982
Mission: To enhance the lives of persons with Alzheimer Disease & their caregivers by providing family support, raising awareness & advocating for services & research
Member of: Alzheimer Society of Ontario
Chief Officer(s):
Françoise Hébert, Chief Ececutive Officer
fhebert@alzheimertoronto.org
Jane Kinney, Chair
Finances: *Annual Operating Budget:* $500,000-$1.5 Million
Staff Member(s): 14; 250 volunteer(s)
Membership: 1,000; *Fees:* $25; $10 students/seniors
Activities: *Awareness Events:* Annual Walk for Memories; Coffee Break; *Speaker Service:* Yes; *Library:* Alzheimer Resource Centre; Open to public

Alzheimer Society of Windsor/Essex County

2135 Richmond St., Windsor ON N8Y 0A1
Tel: 519-974-2220; *Fax:* 519-974-9727
generalinformation@aswecare.com
www.alzheimerwindsor.com
www.facebook.com/AlzheimerSocietyOfWindsorEssexCounty
twitter.com/ASWE_Care
Overview: A small local charitable organization founded in 1981
Mission: To improve the quality of life of those affected by Alzheimer disease or other dementia
Member of: Alzheimer Association of Ontario
Affliation(s): Windsor & District Chamber of Commerce, Alzheimer Association of Canada.
Chief Officer(s):
Gaston Franklyn, Chair
Sally Bennett Olczak, CEO
Finances: *Annual Operating Budget:* $1.5 Million-$3 Million
Staff Member(s): 44
Membership: *Member Profile:* Windsor businesses, local Alzheimer chapters, public; *Committees:* Executive; Finance/Services; Nominating & Governance; Community Advisory Council
Activities: Day Away; caregiver & client support groups; in-home respite care; public education; volunteer opportunities; one to one caregiver support; *Awareness Events:* Awareness Month, Jan.; National Coffee Break, Sept.; *Library* Open to public

Alzheimer Society of York Region

#6, 800 Davis Dr., Newmarket ON L3Y 2R5
Tel: 905-895-1337; *Fax:* 905-895-1736
Toll-Free: 888-414-5550
info@alzheimer-york.com
www.alzheimer-york.com
en-gb.facebook.com/AlzheimerSocietyYork?ref=mf
twitter.com/AlzheimerYork
Overview: A small local charitable organization founded in 1985
Mission: To support individuals & families, in Ontario's York Region, who cope with Alzheimer's Disease & related disorders; To promote research
Chief Officer(s):
Loren Freid, Executive Director, 905-895-1337 Ext. 23
lfreid@alzheimer-york.com
Janice Clarke, Manager, Finance & Administration, 905-895-1337 Ext. 24
jclarke@alzheimer-york.com
Lynn Conforti, CFRE, Manager, Fund Development, 905-895-1337 Ext. 33
lconforti@alzheimer-york.com
Mary Squires, Manager, Newmarket D.A.Y. Centre
Elaine Ross, Coordinator, Events, 905-895-1337 Ext. 22
eross@alzheimer-york.com
Polly Choi, Social Worker, 905-895-1337 Ext. 31
pchoi@alzheimer-york.com
Linda Hayward, Social Worker, 905-895-1337
lhayward@alzheimer-york.com
Angela Johnston, Contact, Caregiver Support, 905-895-1337 Ext. 27
ajohnston@alzheimer-york.com
Finances: *Funding Sources:* Donations; Central Local Health Integration Network; Ontario Trillium Foundation; United Way of York Region
Activities: Providing dementia specific day program services; Offering education programs & support groups for caregivers; Working in partnership with other agencies in the Region of York to offer services; Providing a Wandering Person Registry; *Awareness Events:* Walk for Memories; Annual Alzheimer Awareness Breakfast; Alzheimer Awareness Month; *Library:* Alzheimer Society of York Region Resource Library; Open to public
Publications:
• Alzheimer Society York Region Newsletter
Type: Newsletter
Profile: Articles about Alzheimer's Disease & dementia, plus information about support groups & workshops for caregivers & forthcoming events in the area

Alzheimer Society Ontario / Société Alzheimer Ontario

20 Eglinton Ave. West, 16th Fl., Toronto ON M4R 1K8
Tel: 416-967-5900; *Fax:* 416-967-3826
Toll-Free: 800-879-4226
staff@alzheimeront.org
www.alzheimer.ca/en/on
www.facebook.com/AlzheimerSocietyofOntario
twitter.com/alzheimeront
Also Known As: Alzheimer Ontario
Overview: A large provincial charitable organization founded in 1983 overseen by Alzheimer Society of Canada
Mission: To improve the quality of life for persons with Alzheimer disease & their families; to inform & educate the public & health care professionals about Alzheimer disease; to coordinate a chapter network & liaison in order to presont a united voice to the Government of Ontario & other provincial groups on matters relating to legal concerns, health care, research, & community needs; to raise funds for research
Chief Officer(s):
Vic Pendergast, President
Lee Ann Stewart, Board Liaison
lstewart@alzheimeront.org
Finances: *Annual Operating Budget:* Greater than $5 Million; *Funding Sources:* Private donations
21 volunteer(s)
Membership: 38 chapters

Activities: Research; education & training; advocacy; member support services; *Awareness Events:* Alzheimer Awareness Month, Jan.; Alzheimer Coffee Break, Sept.; *Speaker Service:* Yes; *Rents Mailing List:* Yes; *Library:* Resource Library; Open to public by appointment

Alzheimer Society Peterborough, Kawartha Lakes, Northumberland, & Haliburton (ASPKLNH)

183 Simcoe St., Peterborough ON K9H 2H6
Tel: 705-748-5131; *Fax:* 705-748-6174
Toll-Free: 800-561-2588
info@alzheimerjourney.ca
www.alzheimer.ca/pklnha
www.facebook.com/1462061730698157
twitter.com/Alzheimerpklnh
www.youtube.com/thealzheimersociety
Overview: A small local charitable organization founded in 1981
Mission: To improve the quality of life of persons affected by Alzheimer's Disease & related dementias in the Peterborough, Kawartha Lakes, Northumberland & Haliburton regions of Ontario
Chief Officer(s):
David Webster, Executive Director
david@alzheimerjourney.ca
Susan Barringer, Coordinator, Client Support
susan@alzheimerjourney.ca
Betty Batten, Coordinator, Volunteer
betty@alzheimerjourney.ca
Sarah Cook, Coordinator, Public Education
sarah@alzheimerjourney.ca
Debra McCarthy, Coordinator, Fund Development
debra@alzhiemerjourney.ca
Finances: *Annual Operating Budget:* $500,000-$1.5 Million; *Funding Sources:* Donations; Fundraising; Ontario Ministry of Health
Staff Member(s): 14; 250 volunteer(s)
Membership: *Fees:* no cost
Activities: Providing information, & support services; Offering a learning series; *Internships:* Yes; *Speaker Service:* Yes; *Library:* Alzheimer Society Lending Library; Open to public
Publications:
• Our Journey Together
Type: Newsletter
Profile: Reports & forthcoming events in the region

Kawartha Lakes & Haliburton Office
#201, 55 Mary St., Lindsay ON K9V 5Z6
Tel: 705-878-0126; *Fax:* 705-878-0127
Toll-Free: 800-765-0515
admin@alzheimerjourney.ca
www.alzheimer.ca/pklnh
Chief Officer(s):
Pat Finkle, Client Support Coordinator
pat@alzheimerjourney.ca

Lindsay Office
#201, 55 Mary St., Lindsay ON K9V 5Z6
Tel: 705-878-0126; *Fax:* 705-878-0127
Toll-Free: 800-765-0515
admin@alzheimerjourney.ca
Chief Officer(s):
Leslie Nemisz, Coordinator, Support Services

Alzheimer Society Waterloo Wellington

1145 Concession Rd., Cambridge ON N3H 4L6
Tel: 519-650-1628; *Fax:* 519-742-1862
asww@alzheimerww.ca
www.alzheimer.ca/ww
www.facebook.com/alzsocww
twitter.com/alzsocww
www.pinterest.com/alzsocietyww
Merged from: Alzheimer Societies of Cambridge, Guelph-Wellington & Kitchener-Waterloo
Overview: A small local charitable organization founded in 2014
Mission: To enhance the lives of persons with Alzheimer disease or related dementias & their care-givers by providing support, information, education, public awareness, advocacy & promotion of research
Member of: Alzheimer Society of Ontario
Affliation(s): Alzheimer Society of Canada
Chief Officer(s):
Nancy Kauffman-Lambert, Chair
Jennifer Gillies, Executive Director
jgillies@alzheimerww.ca
Finances: *Funding Sources:* Memorial & general donations; fundraising; Ministry of Health
Staff Member(s): 13; 200 volunteer(s)
Activities: Walk for Memories; Coffee Break; Caregiver Education Day; *Awareness Events:* Walk for Memories, January; *Speaker Service:* Yes; *Library* Open to public

Guelph Office
#207, 255 Woodlawn Rd. West, Guelph ON N1H 8J1
Tel: 519-836-7672; *Fax:* 519-742-1862

Alzheimer Support Association of BC *See* Alzheimer Society of British Columbia

Alzheimer's Foundation for Caregiving in Canada, Inc. (AFCC) / Fondation d'Alzheimer pour les proches aidants au Canada inc. (FAPAC)

#600, 95 rue Mural, Toronto ON L4B 3G2
Tel: 905-882-3141; *Fax:* 905-882-3132
Toll-Free: 877-321-2594
info@alzfdn.ca
www.alzfdn.ca
Overview: A large national charitable organization
Mission: To provide optimal care & services to individuals confronting dementia & to their caregivers & families - through member organizations dedicated to improving quality of life
Activities: *Awareness Events:* Alzheimer Awareness Month, Jan.

Am Shalom

767 Huronia Rd., Barrie ON L4N 9H2
Tel: 705-792-3949; *Fax:* 705-792-3982
amshalomcongregation@bellnet.ca
www.amshalom.ca
www.facebook.com/pages/Am-Shalom-Congregation/283308275052955
Previous Name: Simcoe County Jewish Association (SCJA)
Overview: A small local charitable organization founded in 1974
Mission: To serve the spiritual & cultural needs of the Jewish population of Barrie & Simcoe County, Ontario; To encourage the observance & study of Jewish religion & culture; To support the Jewish values of social responsibility & knowledge
Chief Officer(s):
Glickman Ilyse
rabbi@amshalom.ca
Membership: *Member Profile:* A Reform Jewish congregation
Activities: Providing weekly services; Offering a children's religious school & adult education programs; Maintaining a Judaica collecion of books that may be borrowed by Am Shalom members; *Library:* Am Shalom's Library

Amalgamated Conservation Society (ACS)

PO Box 8741, Victoria BC V8W 3S3
Tel: 250-382-8502
acsbc.ca
Previous Name: Amalgamated Lower Islands Sportsmen's Association
Overview: A small local organization founded in 1963
Mission: To promote the conservation of fish, game & natural resources; To provide the machinery necessary to put up a united front to combat any program by which the democratic rights of individuals may be threatened; To provide a permanent council through which such joint action may be directed
Chief Officer(s):
Charles Nisbet, President
Wayne Zaccarelli, Sec.-Treas., 250-391-1844
Finances: *Annual Operating Budget:* Less than $50,000; *Funding Sources:* Donations; government grants
3 volunteer(s)
Membership: 8 organizations representing 3,000 individuals; *Fees:* $30; *Member Profile:* Membership restricted to associations with similar objectives; *Committees:* Projects
Activities: Salmonid Enhancement Projects; *Speaker Service:* Yes

Amalgamated Construction Association of British Columbia *See* Vancouver Regional Construction Association

Amalgamated Lower Islands Sportsmen's Association *See* Amalgamated Conservation Society

Amazones des grands espaces

Montréal QC
Tél: 514-525-3663
info@plein-air-amazones.org
www.plein-air-amazones.org
Aperçu: *Dimension:* petite; *Envergure:* locale; fondée en 1993
Mission: Club de plein air pour lesbiennes
Membre: *Montant de la cotisation:* 20$

Ambulance Paramedics of British Columbia

#105, 21900 Westminster Hwy., Richmond BC V6W 1J9
Tel: 604-273-5722; *Fax:* 604-273-5762
Toll-Free: 866-273-5766
info@apbc.ca
www.paramedicsofbc.com
www.facebook.com/APBC873
twitter.com/apbc873
www.youtube.com/user/APBCCUPE873?feature=mhsn
Overview: A small provincial organization
Mission: To provide emergency medical care to the sick & injured in British Columbia
Member of: Paramedic Association of Canada
Membership: 3000+
Activities: Offering the following six levels of services: Emergency Medical Dispatching; Medical Air Evacuations (CCT); Infant Transport (ITT); Advanced Care Paramedics (ACP); Primary Care Paramedics (PCP); & Emergency Medical Responder (EMR)

Ambulance Saint-Jean *See* St. John Ambulance

Amelia Rising Sexual Assault Centre of Nipissing / Amelia Rising: Centre d'agressions sexuelles de Nippissing

#11, 101 Worthington St. East, North Bay ON P1B 1G5
Tel: 705-840-2403; *Fax:* 705-840-5050; *Crisis Hot-Line:* 705-476-3355
info@ameliarising.ca
www.ameliarising.ca
www.facebook.com/AmeliaRising
Overview: A small local charitable organization founded in 1994
Mission: To empower & provide a voice for women & the communities in which they live to eliminate violence against women & children; to create social change with respect to issues of equality & justice; to develop, apply & increase awareness of feminist approaches (with an emphasis on action & healing)
Chief Officer(s):
Brenda Quenneville, Executive Director
executive.director@ameliarising.ca
Finances: *Annual Operating Budget:* $250,000-$500,000
Staff Member(s): 6; 50 volunteer(s)
Membership: 50
Activities: *Awareness Events:* No One Asks for It!, May; Sexual Assault Awareness Month, May; Take Back the Night, Oct; *Library* Open to public by appointment

Amelia Rising: Centre d'agressions sexuelles de Nippissing *See* Amelia Rising Sexual Assault Centre of Nipissing

American Association of Critical Care Nurses - Toronto Chapter; National Society of Critical Care Nurses *See* Canadian Association of Critical Care Nurses

American Connemara Association - Western Canada *See* Canadian Connemara Pony Society

American Council of Co-operative Preschools *See* Parent Cooperative Preschools International

American Galloway Breeders Association (AGBA)

c/o Canadian Livestock Records Corporation, 2417 Holly Lane, Ottawa ON K1V 0M7
Tel: 613-731-7110; *Fax:* 613-731-0704
clrc@clrc.ca
www.americangalloway.com
Overview: A small international organization
Mission: To support the Galloway breed
Affliation(s): Canadian Livestock Records Corporation (guardians of the American Galloway Breeder's Association herdbook)
Chief Officer(s):
Harley Blegen, President
Deb Vance, Vice-President
Joyce Jones, Secretary-Treasurer
Membership: *Fees:* $80 active; $40 junior; $25 associate; *Member Profile:* Galloway breeders
Activities: Offering networking opportunities through shows & events;
Publications:
• AGBA Breeders Directory
Type: Directory; *Price:* Free with American Galloway Breeders Association membership
• The Galloway Dispatch
Type: Newsletter; *Frequency:* Quarterly; *Accepts Advertising*; *Price:* Free with membership in the American Galloway Breeders' Association
Profile: Information about meetings, shows & association happenings

American Immigration Lawyers Association - Canadian Chapter (AILA)
c/o Green & Spiegel LLP, #2800, 390 Bay St., Toronto ON M5H 2Y2
Tel: 416-365-5957; *Fax:* 416-865-9042
Overview: A small international organization
Chief Officer(s):
Evan Green, Chapter Chair

American Saddlebred Horse Association of Alberta (ASHA AB)
10 Lowe Ave., Fort Saskatchewan AB T4N 5E1
Tel: 780-998-4513
rmcwade@xplornet.com
www.saddlebredsofalberta.com
www.facebook.com/groups/14432745893
Overview: A small provincial organization founded in 1960
Mission: To foster good sportsmanship, a healthy lifestyle, a sense of responsibility in all age groups through the involvement in the care, training & breeding of the American Saddlebred Horse for both recreation & participation in all disciplines in the sport of horses
Member of: Alberta Equestrian Federation; ASHA Inc.
Affliation(s): ASHA of Canada
Chief Officer(s):
Suzanne Keglowitsch, President
suekeg@gmail.com
Finances: *Annual Operating Budget:* Less than $50,000
10 volunteer(s)
Membership: 137 individual; *Fees:* $50 family; $30 individual senior; $15 individual junior
Activities: Horse shows; clinics; newsletter; breed promotions

American Saddlebred Horse Association of British Columbia (ASHA of BC)
c/o Carol Court, 7011 Lefeuvre Rd., Abbotsford BC V4X 2C1
Tel: 604-856-4542
courtfarms@telus.net
www.facebook.com/375386385825352
Overview: A small provincial organization overseen by American Saddlebred Horse Association of Canada
Mission: To promote purebred American Saddlebred horses & amateur sport in British Columbia
Chief Officer(s):
Carol Court, Contact
Membership: *Member Profile:* Individuals, partnerships, & companies in British Columbia interested in the American Saddlebred horse breed for show or for pleasure; Members do not need to own an American Saddlebred horse
Activities: Hosting events, clinics, & horse shows to showcase American Saddlebred horses in British Columbia; Organizing monthly general meetings in Abbotsford

American Saddlebred Horse Association of Canada (ASHAC)
c/o Ellen Murray, PO Box Site 170 Box 27 RR#1, Brandon MB R7A 5Y1
Tel: 204-728-2076
info@saddlebredcanada.com
www.saddlebredcanada.com
Overview: A small national organization founded in 1948
Mission: To develop & regulate the breeding of purebred American Saddlebred horses in Canada; To carry out a system of registration under the Canadian Livestock Records Corporation; To establish breeding standards
Affliation(s): Canadian Livestock Records Corporation
Chief Officer(s):
Melodie Schwieger, President, 403-843-0076
fschwieg@albertahighspeed.net
Membership: *Fees:* $50 / year; *Member Profile:* Individuals, partnerships, & companies in Canada; *Committees:* Executive; Versatility; Fundraising; International Affairs; Promotion; Pedigree
Activities: Encouraging the breeding of purebred American Saddlebred horses in Canada; Supervising breeders; Promoting the breed; Keeping records; Compiling statistics about the industry; Publishing documents
Publications:
• American Saddlebred Horse Association of Canada Membership Directory
Type: Directory; *Frequency:* Annually; *Price:* Free with membership in the American Saddlebred Horse Association of Canada
Profile: A reference guide with member contact information

American Saddlebred Horse Association of Ontario
c/o Nancy MacDonald, 2792 Concession 9 Drummond, Balderson ON K0G 1A0
www.ashaontario.com
Overview: A small provincial organization overseen by American Saddlebred Horse Association of Canada
Mission: To promote purebred American Saddlebred horses in Ontario
Chief Officer(s):
Nancy MacDonald, Contact
Membership: *Fees:* $25 youth; $35 adult/associate; $50 family; $150 stable/farm; *Member Profile:* Individuals, partnerships, & companies in Ontario
Activities: Hosting events, clinics, & horse shows to showcase American Saddlebred horses in Ontario

American Society of Insurance Management *See* Risk & Insurance Management Society Inc.

American/Canadian Log Builders' Association *See* International Log Builders' Association

Amethyst Scottish Dancers of Nova Scotia
c/o 61 Richardson Dr., Fall River NS B2T 1E7
www.amethystscottishdancersns.ca
Overview: A small provincial organization
Chief Officer(s):
Marla MacInnis, Artistic Director

Amherst & Area Chamber of Commerce
PO Box 283, 35 Church St., Amherst NS B4H 3Z4
Tel: 902-667-8186; *Fax:* 902-667-2270
info@amherstchamber.ca
www.facebook.com/amherstchamber
twitter.com/amherstchamber
Overview: A small local organization
Chief Officer(s):
David Mosley, President
Patti Colson, Executive Assistant
Membership: *Fees:* $40 students; $5 retirees; $75 individual & non-profit; $150-$325 corporate

Amherst Township Historical Society *See* Cumberland Museum Society

Amherstburg Anderdon & Malden Chamber of Commerce *See* Amherstburg Chamber of Commerce

Amherstburg Chamber of Commerce
PO Box 101, 268 Dalhousie St., Amherstburg ON N9V 2Z3
Tel: 519-736-2001; *Fax:* 519-736-9721
amherstburgchamber@gmail.com
www.amherstburgchamberofcommerce.ca
Previous Name: Amherstburg Anderdon & Malden Chamber of Commerce
Overview: A small local organization
Member of: Ontario Chamber of Commerce
Chief Officer(s):
Scott Deslippe, President
Staff Member(s): 2
Membership: 100-499

Amherstburg Community Services
179 Victoria St., Amherstburg ON N9V 3N5
Tel: 519-736-5471; *Fax:* 519-736-1391
acs@bellnet.ca
www.amherstburg-cs.com
Overview: A small local organization founded in 1973 overseen by InforOntario
Mission: To study the social, health, educational, recreational and other human needs of the Amherstburg area, and services available to satisfy those needs; To promote the orderly development of well-balanced community services.
Chief Officer(s):
Kathy DiBartolomeo, Executive Director
edacs@bellnet.ca
Staff Member(s): 11
Membership: 1-99
Activities: Meals on Wheels; Care A Van Senior Transportation; Security Reassurance Calls; Friendly Visiting; Information and Referral; Coats for Kids; Keep the Heat; NCBS Children's Recreation Program; Jumpstart; Job Bank Computer and Internet Access; Photocopying and Faxing; Free Income Tax Clinic

Amherstburg Historic Sites Association
Kings Navy Yard, 214 Dalhousie St., Amherstburg ON N9V 1W4
Tel: 519-736-2511; *Fax:* 519-736-2511
Other Communication: contact@ParkHouseMuseum.com
info@parkhousemuseum.com
www.parkhousemuseum.com
Overview: A small local charitable organization founded in 1973
Mission: To collect, preserve, & exhibit the heritage of Amherstburg, Ontario
Chief Officer(s):
Valerie Buckie, Curator, 519-736-2511
curator@parkhousemuseum.com
Finances: *Funding Sources:* Donations; Grants
Activities: Operating the Park House Museum
Awards:
• O.H.F. Heritage Community Recognition Award/Cultural Heritage (Award)

Les Ami(e)s de la Terre Canada *See* Friends of the Earth Canada

Amicale des Sommeliers du Québec (ASQ)
5310 boul. de L'Assomption, Montréal QC H1T 2M2
Tél: 514-729-9537; *Téléc:* 514-729-0366
secretaire@amicaledessommeliers.com
www.amicaledessommeliers.com
www.facebook.com/groups/16486893521
Aperçu: *Dimension:* petite; *Envergure:* provinciale; fondée en 1962
Mission: Propager l'amour et la connaissance du vin
Membre(s) du bureau directeur:
Lyne Pelletier, Présidente
Membre: 800; *Montant de la cotisation:* 60$ couple
Activités: Dégustations de vins et des repas gastronomiques; cours sur la connaissance des vins; ateliers sur l'accord des mets et des vins

Amici dell'Enotria Toronto / Friends of the Land of the Wine
31 Shaver Ave. North, Toronto ON M9B 4N5
Tel: 416-234-0079
vico.paloschi@rogers.com
www.amicidellenotria.com
Also Known As: The Italian Wine Club
Overview: A small international organization founded in 1977
Mission: To promote the appreciation of Italian wines; To organize wine tastings & social events
Chief Officer(s):
Vico Paloschi, Chapter Master
Finances: *Annual Operating Budget:* Less than $50,000; *Funding Sources:* Membership dues
6 volunteer(s)
Membership: 150; *Fees:* $45 (plus $20 initiation fee)
Activities: *Speaker Service:* Yes

Ami-e du Quartier
655, rue Filion, Saint-Jérôme QC J7Z 1J6
Tél: 450-431-1424
www.facebook.com/lamie.duquartier
Aperçu: *Dimension:* petite; *Envergure:* locale
Mission: • apporter aide et soutien aux personnes et aux familles moins fortunées
Membre(s) du bureau directeur:
Sophie Desmarais, Responsable
Membre: *Montant de la cotisation:* 3$

Les AmiEs de la Terre de Québec (ATQ)
Centre Frédéric-Back Culture et Environnement, #210, 870, rue Salaberry, Québec QC G1R 2T9
Tél: 418-524-2744
info@atquebec.org
www.atquebec.org
Aperçu: *Dimension:* petite; *Envergure:* locale; Organisme sans but lucratif; fondée en 1978
Mission: Conscientiser la population à la crise écologique mondiale versus le droit de tous à un environnement sain; éduquer les gens à leur propre prise en charge personnelle et collective face à cette crise; améliorer les communications entre écologistes aussi bien qu'entre ceux-ci et la population qu'ils desservent; renforcer la qualité de la vie associative chez-nous aussi bien qu'ailleurs dans la région et au Québec
Membre de: Réseau Québécois des Groupes Écologistes (RQGE); Regroupement d'éducation populaire en action communautaire (Répac)
Membre(s) du bureau directeur:
Yan Grenier, Président
Renaud Blais, Administrator
Finances: *Budget de fonctionnement annuel:* Moins de $50,000
Membre(s) du personnel: 9

Membre: 250; *Montant de la cotisation:* 10$ travailleur; 5$ non-travailleur; *Comités:* Paix; Environnement et mondialisation; Écologie et santé; Eau; Forêt
Activités: RadioTerre; émission hebdomadaire d'écologie politique diffusée sur les ondes de CKIA FM (Québec); une conférence par mois sur des thèmes reliés à l'écologie; *Service de conférenciers:* Oui; *Bibliothèque:* Centre documentation des ATQ;

Les Amis canadiens de la Birmanie *See* Canadian Friends of Burma

Les Amis de Bibliothèque et archives Canada *See* The Friends of Library & Archives Canada

Les Amis de la déficience intellectuelle Rive-Nord
#213, 50, rue Thouin, Repentigny QC J6A 4J4
Tél: 450-585-3632; *Téléc:* 450-585-3633
lesamis@deficienceintellectuel.org
www.lesamisdirn.org
Aperçu: *Dimension:* petite; *Envergure:* locale; Organisme sans but lucratif; fondée en 1979
Mission: L'organisme vise à sensibiliser la communauté et promouvoir la compréhension des besoins de la personne; offrir l'opportunité et les moyens pour bénéficier au maximum des services et ressources disponibles de la région; donner un support technique pour répondre aux besoins individuels de ses membres et promouvoir une plus grande intégration sociale
Membre(s) du bureau directeur:
Paulette Goulet, Présidente
Stéphanie-Claude Leclerc, Coordonnatrice
Finances: *Budget de fonctionnement annuel:* $100,000-$250,000; *Fonds:* Gouvernement national; Autofinancement
Membre(s) du personnel: 4; 65 bénévole(s)
Membre: 210; *Montant de la cotisation:* 10$; *Critères d'admissibilité:* Personnes vivant avec une déficience intellectuelle, leurs parents et leurs proches.
Activités: Promotion et défense des droits de nos membres; Activités de loisirs et et de formations

Les Amis du centre canadien d'architecture / Friends of the Canadian Centre for Architecture
1920, rue Baile, Montréal QC H3H 2S6
Tel: 514-939-7026
info@cca.qc.ca
www.cca.qc.ca
www.facebook.com/cca.conversation
twitter.com/ccawire
www.youtube.com/user/CCAchannel
Overview: A medium-sized local organization
Membership: *Fees:* $25 student; $45 adult/architect; $35 senior; $70 family

Les Amis du Jardin botanique de Montréal / Friends of the Montréal Botanical Garden
#206A, 4101, rue Sherbrooke est, Montréal QC H1X 2B2
Tél: 514-872-1493; *Téléc:* 514-872-3765
amisjardin@ville.montreal.qc.ca
www.amisjardin.qc.ca
www.facebook.com/LesAmisduJardinbotaniquedeMontreal
Nom précédent: Société d'animation du Jardin et de l'Institut botanique
Aperçu: *Dimension:* moyenne; *Envergure:* locale; Organisme sans but lucratif; fondée en 1975
Membre de: Fédération des sociétés d'horticulture et d'écologie du Québec (FSHEQ); Flora Québec
Membre(s) du bureau directeur:
Maud Fillion, Contact
maud-ext.fillion@ville.montreal.qc.ca
Paule Lamontagne, Présidente
Membre(s) du personnel: 6; 70 bénévole(s)
Membre: 28 000; *Montant de la cotisation:* 30$ étudiant/ainé; 45$ individu; 60$ familial; $180 corporatif
Activités: Cours et ateliers donnés par des spécialistes; Conférences; Visites guidées et excursions; Voyages

Les Amis du Musée canadien de la guerre *See* Friends of The Canadian War Museum

Les Amis du Parc Awenda *See* The Friends of Awenda Park

Les Amis du vitrail
Centre Boisvert, 6005, boul. Payer, Saint-Hubert QC J3Y 8A6
Tél: 450-812-3799
lesamisduvitrail@hotmail.com
www.lesamisduvitrail.org
Aperçu: *Dimension:* petite; *Envergure:* locale; fondée en 1980
Mission: De rassembler les gens qui aiment la fabrication de vitraux afin de les encourager et de faire des projets ensemble
Membre(s) du bureau directeur:
Normand Carrière, Président, Conseil d'administraion
Activités: Ateliers; Cours de vitrail; Séminaires

Amis et propriétaires de maisons anciennes du Québec (APMAQ)
2050, rue Amherst, Montréal QC H2L 3L8
Tél: 514-528-8444; *Téléc:* 514-528-8686
apmaq@globetrotter.net
www.maisons-anciennes.qc.ca
Aperçu: *Dimension:* petite; *Envergure:* provinciale; Organisme sans but lucratif; fondée en 1980
Prix, Bouses:
- Prix Robert-Lionel-Séguin (Prix)
- Prix régional (Prix)
- Prix de mérite (Prix)

Amitié Chinoise de Montréal *See* Chinese Neighbourhood Society of Montréal

Amity Goodwill Industries *See* Goodwill, The Amity Group

Amma Foundation of Canada
PO Box 21037, RPO Meadowvale, Mississauga ON L5N 6A2
Tel: 905-785-8175
info@ammacanada.ca
www.ammacanada.ca
Overview: A small national organization
Mission: To help the poor & destitute by seeking out & participating in programs; to follow the example of Amma, who instucts, "compassion to the poor is our duty to God"
Chief Officer(s):
Raman Nair, Contact
toronto@ammacanada.ca
Membership: *Member Profile:* Individuals who are inspired by the love & compassion of Amma & wish to work to help the less fortunate
Activities: Donating money, food, clothing, & education to the less fortunate; Offering assistance to those in need through Amma's Kitchen, Amma's Closet, food banks, garage sales, penny money collection, & empty pop can collectin

Amnesty International - Canadian Section (English Speaking)
312 Laurier Ave. East, Ottawa ON K1N 1H9
Tel: 613-744-7667; *Fax:* 613-746-2411
Toll-Free: 800-266-3789
info@amnesty.ca
www.amnesty.ca
www.facebook.com/amnestycanada
twitter.com/AmnestyNow
Also Known As: Amnesty Canada
Overview: A medium-sized international charitable organization founded in 1973
Mission: AI Canada is part of a worldwide movement which is independent of any government, political grouping, ideology, economic interest or religious creed. It's primary aim is to bring public attention to abuses of human rights standards, particularly cases where people are imprisoned for their beliefs, or "prisoners of conscience." It holds that mass public pressure, expressed through effective forms of action, is critical to preventing & ending human rights violations. It also works to abolish the death penalty, torture, & other cruel treatment of prisoners, to end political killings & "disappearances."
Affiliation(s): Formal relations with United Nations Economic & Social Council (ECOSOC), UNESCO, Council of Europe; Organization of American States, Organization of African Unity & Inter-Parliamentary Union
Chief Officer(s):
David Smith, Chair
dsmith@amnesty.ca
Sharmila Setaram, President
ssetaram@amnesty.ca
Robert Goodfellow, Executive Director
Finances: *Annual Operating Budget:* Greater than $5 Million; *Funding Sources:* Individuals
Staff Member(s): 47
Membership: 58,000; *Fees:* $35; *Member Profile:* All cultures & walks of life; human rights activists & financial supporters
Activities: Film festivals; Meetings; Yoga fundraisers

Toronto Office
1992 Yonge St., 3rd Fl., Toronto ON M4S 1Z7
Tel: 416-363-9933; *Fax:* 416-363-3103
info@aito.ca
www.aito.ca
www.facebook.com/AmnestyToronto
twitter.com/AmnestyToronto
www.youtube.com/user/AmnestyIntlToronto
Mission: To help fight humna rights injustices by raising awareness about them through events
Member of: Amenstry International
Chief Officer(s):
Shanaaz Gokool, Chair
chair@aito.ca

Vancouver Regional Office
#430, 319 West Pender St., Vancouver BC V6B 1T4
Tel: 604-294-5160; *Fax:* 604-294-5130
vancouver.intern@amnesty.ca
www.amnesty.ca
www.facebook.com/128797077188904

Amnesty International, Canadian Section (Francophone) *Voir* Amnistie internationale, Section canadienne (Francophone)

Amnistie internationale, Section canadienne (Francophone) / Amnesty International, Canadian Section (Francophone)
50 rue Ste-Catherine Ouest bureau 500, Montréal QC H2X 3V4
Tél: 514-766-9766; *Téléc:* 514-766-2088
Ligne sans frais: 800-565-9766
info@amnistie.ca
www.amnistie.ca
Aperçu: *Dimension:* moyenne; *Envergure:* internationale; fondée en 1973
Mission: Mouvement d'intervention directe formé de bénévoles qui visent à la libération des prisonniers d'opinion, la tenue de procès équitables pour les prisonniers politiques, l'abolition de la torture et la cessation des "disparitions" et assassinats politiques
Membre(s) du bureau directeur:
Beatrice Vaugrante, Direction
Membre: 20 000
Activités: *Service de conférenciers:* Oui; *Bibliothèque* Bibliothèque publique rendez-vous

Among Equals *See* Inter Pares

Amputee Society of Ottawa & District
#1404, 505 Smyth Rd., Ottawa ON K1H 8M2
Tel: 613-737-7350; *Fax:* 613-737-7056
Overview: A small local organization
Mission: Provides support to new amputees from trained amputee visitors, information on community services available to amputees and ongoing contact with amputees via a visitor program
Chief Officer(s):
Betty Lanigan, President
bblanigan@hotmail.com

Les Amputés de guerre du Canada *See* The War Amputations of Canada

An Cumann/The Irish Association of Nova Scotia
PO Box 27153, Halifax NS B3H 4M8
e-mail: info@ancumann.org
www.ancumann.org
Overview: A small provincial organization founded in 1990
Mission: To foster knowledge & enjoyment of Irish customs, culture & heritage throughout Nova Scotia
Chief Officer(s):
David Moriarity, President
Pat Curran, Secretary
Membership: *Fees:* $15 individual; $20 family
Activities: Irish heritage evenings; workshops; *Speaker Service:* Yes

Analystes des minéraux canadiens *See* Canadian Mineral Analysts

Anaphylaxis Canada
#800, 2005 Sheppard Ave. East, Toronto ON M2J 5B4
Tel: 416-785-5666; *Fax:* 416-785-0458
Toll-Free: 866-785-5666
www.anaphylaxis.ca
www.facebook.com/AnaphylaxisCanada
twitter.com/AnaphylaxisCAN
www.youtube.com/user/anaphylaxiscanada
Overview: A medium-sized national charitable organization
Mission: To inform, support, educate, & advocate for the needs of individuals & families living with anaphylaxis; To conduct & support research related to anaphylaxis
Affiliation(s): Dare Foods; Loblaw Companies Ltd.; Mars Canada; McDonalds Restaurants of Canada; Nestle Canada;

Paladin Labs Inc.; Pepsico Canada; Pfizer Canada; Scotiabank Group; TD Securities
Chief Officer(s):
Phillip Haid, Chair
Jeff Smith, Vice-Chair
Brian Brennan, Treasurer
Laurie Harada, Executive Director
Finances: *Funding Sources:* Membership dues; Donations; Grants; Sales of resources & services
Staff Member(s): 4
Publications:
• Anaphylaxis Canada's Facts & Advice Newsletter
Type: Newsletter
Profile: Information about allergies & anaphylaxis, research, programs, events, & stories from families about managing anaphylaxis
• Kids' Club Newsletter [a publication of Anaphylaxis Canada]
Type: Newsletter; *Editor:* Kemrani Khan
Profile: Information & activities for children living with allergies & anaphylaxis

Ancaster Community Services (ACS)
300 Wilson St. East, Ancaster ON L9G 2B9
Tel: 905-648-6675; *Fax:* 905-648-8949
www.ancastercommunityservices.ca
www.facebook.com/AncasterCommunityServices.ca
Previous Name: Ancaster Information Centre & Community Services Inc.
Overview: A small local charitable organization overseen by InformOntario
Chief Officer(s):
Karen Thomson, Executive Director
Finances: *Annual Operating Budget:* $100,000-$250,000
Staff Member(s): 4; 100 volunteer(s)
Membership: 100-499
Activities: Meals on Wheels; assisted driving; community outreach and counselling; home support; Christmas outreach; senior services; food vouchers; youth empowerment services

Ancaster Information Centre & Community Services Inc. *See* Ancaster Community Services

Anchor Industries Society (AIS)
61 Glendale Ave., Lower Sackville NS B4C 3J4
Tel: 902-865-1797; *Fax:* 902-865-1580
aisociety@accesswave.ca
www.anchorindustriessociety.org
www.facebook.com/AnchorIndustriesSocietyAIS
Overview: A small local organization founded in 1973
Mission: To offer vocational & recreational programs & services to adults with intellectual challenges
Member of: DIRECTIONS Council for Vocational Services Society
Chief Officer(s):
Marilyn Forest, Executive Director
Finances: *Annual Operating Budget:* $500,000-$1.5 Million
Activities: Operates four businesses: The PrintShop, The OffShoot Shop, The Ladle Restaurant & All Wrapped Up; literary classes; employment programs
Publications:
• Anchor Industries Society Newsletter
Type: Newsletter

Les Anciens combattants de l'armée, de la marine et des forces aériennes au Canada *See* Army, Navy & Air Force Veterans in Canada

Ancient, Free & Accepted Masons of Canada - Grand Lodge in the Province of Ontario (AF & AM)
363 King St. West, Hamilton ON L8P 1B4
Tel: 905-528-8644; *Fax:* 905-528-6979
office@grandlodge.on.ca
www.grandlodge.on.ca
Overview: A medium-sized provincial organization
Mission: To promote Freemasonry in Ontario
Publications:
• The Ontario Mason Magazine
Type: Magazine; *Accepts Advertising; Editor:* V.W. Bro. Bruce Miller
Profile: Articles about charitable work, events, & local activities

Ancient, Free & Accepted Masons of Canada - Grand Lodge of Alberta (AF & AM)
330 - 12 Ave. SW, Calgary AB T2R 0H2
Tel: 403-262-1149; *Fax:* 403-290-0671
grandsecretary@freemasons.ab.ca
www.freemasons.ab.ca
www.facebook.com/group.php?gid=39244866333
twitter.com/albertamasons
Overview: A medium-sized provincial organization founded in 1905
Chief Officer(s):
Peter Dunlop, Grand Master
Jerry Kopp, Grand Secretary, 403-262-1149, Fax: 403-290-0671
Staff Member(s): 4
Activities: *Library* by appointment
Awards:
• Masonic Higher Education Bursaries (Grant)
Awarded to worthy students across Alberta & the Northwest Territories*Eligibility:* Students in Alberta & the Northwest Territories who are in financial need & are trying to pursue post-secondary education *Amount:* $2,000
Meetings/Conferences: • Ancient, Free & Accepted Masons of Canada - Grand Lodge of Alberta 2015 Annual Communication, June, 2015, Red Deer Sheraton Hotel, Red Deer, AB
Scope: Provincial
Publications:
• The Alberta Freemason
Type: Magazine; *Frequency:* 10 pa; *Editor:* RW Bro. George Tapley; *Price:* $10 plus mailing costs, non-members
Profile: Updates about programs, activities & events, provided to Freemason of Alberta & the Northwest Territories west of the 4th Meridian who are members of The Grand Lodge of Alberta,A.F. & A.M.

Ancient, Free & Accepted Masons of Canada - Grand Lodge of British Columbia *See* Ancient, Free & Accepted Masons of Canada - Grand Lodge of British Columbia & Yukon

Ancient, Free & Accepted Masons of Canada - Grand Lodge of British Columbia & Yukon
1495 West 8th Ave., Vancouver BC V6H 1C9
Tel: 604-736-8941; *Fax:* 604-736-5097
grand_secretary@freemasonry.bcy.ca
freemasonry.bcy.ca
www.facebook.com/group.php?gid=2399059415
Previous Name: Ancient, Free & Accepted Masons of Canada - Grand Lodge of British Columbia
Overview: A medium-sized provincial organization founded in 1871
Chief Officer(s):
William R. Cave, Grand Master
Staff Member(s): 4
Membership: 13,000
Meetings/Conferences: • Ancient, Free & Accepted Masons of the Grand Lodge of British Columbia & Yukon 2015 Masonic Leadership & Ladies Conference, 2015
Scope: Provincial
Description: Discussions of leadership skills, best practices in lodge leadership, & information about the Grand Lodge
Publications:
• The Freemasons & the Masonic Family of British Columbia & Yukon Information Booklet
Type: Booklet
Profile: Contents include an introductions to Freemasonry, historical highlights of Freemasonry, the organization of the Grand Lodge of BritishColumbia, charity, religion, & Grand Masters of the jurisdiction
• Masonic Bulletin
Type: Newsletter; *Frequency:* Monthly; *Editor:* VW Bro. Trevor W. McKeown
Profile: Distributed though the lodge secretaries to every member of the jurisdiction

Ancient, Free & Accepted Masons of Canada - Grand Lodge of New Brunswick
PO Box 6430, Stn. A, Saint John NB E2L 4R6
e-mail: masonic@nbnet.nb.ca
www.nbmf.org/othrpage/blue0001.htm
Overview: A medium-sized provincial organization founded in 1867
Mission: To improve life by improving the men who live it while never losing sight of the need to preserve the past, serve the present & prepare for the future
Activities: *Library*

Ancient, Free & Accepted Masons of Canada - Grand Lodge of Nova Scotia
167 Coronation Ave., Halifax NS B3N 2N2
Tel: 902-423-6149; *Fax:* 902-423-6254
www.grandlodgens.org
Overview: A medium-sized international charitable organization founded in 1866
Chief Officer(s):
Robert Northup, Grand Secretary
Membership: *Member Profile:* Male, 21 years old & over; belief in God; *Committees:* Public Relations
Activities: *Library* Open to public by appointment
Publications:
• The Nova Scotia Freemason: The Official Bulletin of the Grand Lodge of Nova Scotia
Type: Newsletter
Profile: Articles & information from the lodges & districts

Ancient, Free & Accepted Masons of Canada - Grand Lodge of Prince Edward Island
PO Box 337, Charlottetown PE C1A 7K7
Tel: 902-894-3443
www.freemasonry.pe.ca
Also Known As: Grand Lodge of PEI
Overview: A medium-sized provincial organization founded in 1875
Chief Officer(s):
Edward R. MacLaren, Grand Secretary
Finances: *Annual Operating Budget:* Less than $50,000; *Funding Sources:* Membership fees
Membership: 845
Activities: *Library* by appointment

Ancient, Free & Accepted Masons of Canada - Grand Lodge of Québec *See* Grand Lodge of Québec - Ancient, Free & Accepted Masons

Anemia Institute for Research & Education *See* Institute for Optimizing Health Outcomes

The Anglican Church of Canada (ACC) / L'Église anglicane du Canada
80 Hayden St., Toronto ON M4Y 3G2
Tel: 416-924-9192; *Fax:* 416-968-7983
information@national.anglican.ca
www.anglican.ca
www.facebook.com/canadiananglican
twitter.com/generalsynod
www.youtube.com/generalsynod
Previous Name: Church of England in Canada
Overview: A large national charitable organization founded in 1893
Mission: To proclaim & celebrate the gospel of Jesus Christ in worship & action, as a partner in the world-wide Anglican Communion & the universal church; to value our heritage of faith, reason, liturgy, tradition, bishops & synods, & the rich variety of life in community; to acknowledge that God calls His followers to greater diversity of membership, wider participation in ministry & leadership, better stewardship in God's creation & a strong resolve in challenging attitudes & structures which cause injustice
Member of: Canadian Council of Churches
Chief Officer(s):
Fred Hiltz, Primate, Anglican Church of Canada
primate@national.anglican.ca
Michael Thompson, General Secretary
mthompson@national.anglican.ca
Membership: 500,000+ members; 1,700 churches; *Committees:* Communications & Information Resources; Faith, Worship & Ministry; Financial Management; Partners in MIssions & Ecojustice; Philanthropy
Activities: Operates four incorporated bodies: the Anglican Foundation of Canada, Anglican Journal, Primate's World Relief & Development Fund, & Pension Office Corporation.; *Library* by appointment
Publications:
• Anglican Journal [a publication of the Anglican Church of Canada]
Type: Newspaper; *Frequency:* 10x/yr.; *Editor:* Marites (Tess) N. Sison *ISSN:* 0847-978X
Profile: The national newspaper of the Anglican Church of Canada, with a circulation of 160,000

Diocese of Algoma
PO Box 1168, 619 Wellington St. East, Sault Ste Marie ON P6A 5N7
Tel: 702-256-5061; *Fax:* 702-946-1860
secretary@dioceseofalgoma.com
www.dioceseofalgoma.com
Chief Officer(s):
Stephen Andrews, Bishop
bishop@dioceseofalgoma.com

Diocese of Athabasca
PO Box 6868, Peace River AB T8S 1S6

Tel: 780-624-2767; *Fax:* 780-624-2365
dioath@telusplanet.net
www.dioath.ca
Chief Officer(s):
Fraser W. Lawton, Bishop
bpath@telusplanet.net
Diocese of Brandon
PO Box 21009, Stn. W.E.P.O, Brandon MB R7B 3W8
Tel: 204-727-7550; *Fax:* 204-727-4135
diobran@mts.net
www.dioceseofbrandon.org
Chief Officer(s):
Jim Njegovan, Bishop
bishopbdn@mts.net
Diocese of British Columbia
900 Vancouver St., Victoria BC V8V 3V7
Tel: 250-386-7781; *Fax:* 250-386-4013
synod@bc.anglican.ca
www.bc.anglican.ca
Chief Officer(s):
James A.J. Cowan, Bishop
bishop@bc.anglican.ca
Diocese of Caledonia
#201 - 4716 Lazelle Ave., Terrace BC V8G 1T2
Tel: 250-635-6016; *Fax:* 250-635-6026
caledonia@telus.net
www.caledoniaanglican.ca
Chief Officer(s):
William Anderson, Bishop
bishopbill@telus.net
Diocese of Calgary
#180, 1209 5- 9th Ave. SE, Calgary AB T3C 0M5
Tel: 403-243-3673; *Fax:* 403-243-2182
diocese@calgary.anglican.ca
www.calgary.anglican.ca
Chief Officer(s):
Gregory Kerr-Wilson, Bishop
bishop@calgary.anglican.ca
Diocese of Central Newfoundland
34 Fraser Rd., Gander NL A1V 2E8
Tel: 709-256-2372; *Fax:* 709-256-2396
www.centraldiocese.org
Chief Officer(s):
David Torraville, Bishop
bishopcentral@nfld.net
Diocese of Eastern Newfoundland & Labrador
19 King's Bridge Rd., St. John's NL A1C 3K4
Tel: 709-576-6697; *Fax:* 709-576-7122
ecrisby@anglicanenl.net
www.anglican.nfol.ca
Chief Officer(s):
Cyrus C.J. Pitman, Bishop
cpitman@anglicanenl.net
Diocese of Edmonton
10035 - 103 St., Edmonton AB T5J 0X5
Tel: 780-439-7344; *Fax:* 780-439-6549
churched@edmonton.anglican.ca
edmonton.anglican.org
Chief Officer(s):
Jane Alexander, Bishop
bishop@edmonton.anglican.ca
Diocese of Fredericton
115 Church St., Fredericton NB E3B 4C8
Tel: 506-459-1801; *Fax:* 506-460-0520
diocese@anglican.nb.ca
www.anglican.nb.ca
Chief Officer(s):
Claude E.W. Miller, Bishop
bishop@anglican.nb.ca
Diocese of Huron
190 Queens Ave., London ON N6A 6H7
Tel: 519-434-6893; *Fax:* 519-673-1451
huron@huron.anglican.ca
www.diohuron.org
Chief Officer(s):
Robert F. Bennett, Bishop
bishops@huron.anglican.ca
Diocese of Keewatin
915 Ottawa St., Keewatin ON P0X 1C0
Tel: 807-547-3353; *Fax:* 807-547-3356
dioceseofkeewatin@shaw.ca
www.dioceseofkeewatin.ca
Chief Officer(s):
David Ashdown, Bishop
keewatinbishop@shaw.ca
Diocese of Kootenay
#201 - 380 Leathead, Kelowna BC V1X 1H8
Tel: 778-478-8310; *Fax:* 778-478-8314
admin@kootenay.info
www.kootenay.anglican.ca
Chief Officer(s):
John Privett, Bishop
Diocese of Montréal
1444, av Union, Montréal QC H3A 2B8
Tel: 514-843-6577; *Fax:* 514-843-6344
synod.office@montreal.anglican.ca
www.montreal.anglican.ca
Chief Officer(s):
Barry B. Clarke, Bishop
bishops.office@montreal.anglican.ca
Diocese of Moosonee
331 Fifth Ave., Timmins ON P4N 5L6
Tel: 705-360-1129; *Fax:* 705-360-1120
synod@mooseneeanglican.ca
www.moosoneeanglican.ca
Chief Officer(s):
Thomas Alexander Corston, Bishop
bishop@moosoneeanglican.ca
Diocese of New Westminster
#508, 401 West Georgia St., Vancouver BC V6B 5A1
Tel: 604-684-6306; *Fax:* 604-684-7017
www.vancouver.anglican.ca
Chief Officer(s):
Michael C. Ingham, Bishop
bishop@vancouver.anglican.ca
Diocese of Niagara
Cathedral Place, 252 James St. North, Hamilton ON L8R 2L3
Tel: 905-527-1316; *Fax:* 905-527-1281
www.niagara.anglican.ca
Chief Officer(s):
Michael A. Bird, Bishop
bishop@niagara.anglican.ca
Diocese of Nova Scotia & Prince Edward Island
6017 Quinpool Rd., Halifax NS B3K 5J6
Tel: 902-420-0717; *Fax:* 902-425-0717
office@nspeidiocese.ca
www.nspeidiocese.ca
Chief Officer(s):
Susan Moxley, Bishop
smoxley@nspeidiocese.ca
Diocese of Ontario
90 Johnson St., Kingston ON K7L 1X7
Tel: 613-544-4774; *Fax:* 613-547-3745
www.ontario.anglican.ca
Chief Officer(s):
Michael Oulton, Bishop
moulton@ontario.anglican.ca
Diocese of Ottawa
71 Bronson Ave., Ottawa ON K1R 6G6
Tel: 613-233-7741; *Fax:* 613-232-7088
admin@ottawa.anglican.ca
ottawa.anglican.ca
Chief Officer(s):
John Chapman, Bishop
bishopsoffice@ottawa.anglican.ca
Diocese of Qu'Appelle
1501 College Ave., Regina SK S4P 1B8
Tel: 360-522-1608; *Fax:* 360-352-6808
quappelle@sasktel.net
quappelle.anglican.ca
Chief Officer(s):
Rob Hardwick, Bishop
Diocese of Québec
31, rue des Jardins, Québec QC G1R 4L6
Tel: 418-692-3858; *Fax:* 418-692-3876
synodoffice@quebec.anglican.ca
www.quebec.anglican.org
Chief Officer(s):
Dennis Paul Drainville, Bishop
bishop@quebec.anglican.ca
Diocese of Rupert's Land
935 Nesbitt Bay, Winnipeg MB R3T 1W6
Tel: 204-992-4200; *Fax:* 204-992-4219
general@rupertsland.ca
www.rupertsland.ca
Chief Officer(s):
Don Phillips, Bishop
dphillips@rupertsland.anglican.ca
Diocese of Saskatchewan
1308 - 5th Ave. East, Prince Albert SK S6V 2H7
Tel: 306-763-2455; *Fax:* 306-764-5172
synod@sasktel.net
www.skdiocese.com
Chief Officer(s):
Michael W. Hawkins, Bishop
Diocese of Saskatoon
PO Box 1965, Saskatoon SK S7K 3S5
Tel: 306-244-5651; *Fax:* 306-933-4606
anglicansynod@sasktel.net
www.anglicandiocesesaskatoon.com
Chief Officer(s):
David M. Irving, Bishop
Diocese of the Arctic
PO Box 190, 4910 - 51st St., Yellowknife NT X1A 2N2
Tel: 867-873-5432; *Fax:* 867-873-8478
arctic@arcticnet.org
www.arcticnet.org
Chief Officer(s):
David Parsons, Bishop
Diocese of the Yukon
PO Box 31136, Whitehorse YT Y1A 5P7
Tel: 867-667-7746; *Fax:* 867-667-6125
synodoffice@klondiker.com
anglican.yukon.net
Chief Officer(s):
Larry Robertson, Bishop
Diocese of Toronto
135 Adelaide St. East, Toronto ON M5C 1L8
Tel: 416-363-6021; *Fax:* 416-363-7678
Toll-Free: 800-668-8932
www.toronto.anglican.ca
Chief Officer(s):
Colin R. Johnson, Bishop
cjohnson@toronto.anglican.ca
Diocese of Western Newfoundland
25 Main St., Corner Brook NL A2H 1C2
Tel: 709-639-8712; *Fax:* 709-639-1636
www.westernnewfoundland.anglican.org
Chief Officer(s):
Percy Coffin, Bishop
dsown@nf.aibn.com

Anglican Foundation of Canada

Anglican Church House, 80 Hayden St., Toronto ON M4V 3G2
Tel: 416-924-9199; *Fax:* 416-924-8672
foundation@anglicanfoundation.org
www.anglicanfoundation.org
Overview: A small national charitable organization founded in 1957
Mission: To assist parishes, dioceses & programs of Anglican Church of Canada with low interest loans &/or grants
Affliation(s): World Council of Churches
Chief Officer(s):
Judy Rois, Executive Director
jrois@anglicanfoundation.org
Jonathan Marshall, Executive Assistant
jmarshall@anglicanfoundation.org
Activities: *Speaker Service:* Yes

Anglican Houses *See* LOFT Community Services

Animal Alliance Environment Voters Party of Canada (AAEVPC)

#101, 221 Broadview Ave., Toronto ON M4M 2G3
Tel: 416-462-9541; *Fax:* 416-462-9647
www.environmentvoters.org
www.facebook.com/150318548422896
twitter.com/AAEVPC
Overview: A medium-sized national organization founded in 2005
Mission: To promote a principle of just and equitable human progress that respects, protects, and enhances the environment and the lives of the animals.
Affliation(s): Animal Alliance of Canada
Chief Officer(s):
Liz White, Leader
liz@environmentvoters.org
Stephen Best, Chief Agent
stephen@environmentvoters.org
Finances: *Funding Sources:* Private donations

Canadian Associations

Animal Alliance of Canada (AAC) / Alliance animale du Canada
#101, 221 Broadview Ave., Toronto ON M4M 2G3
Tel: 416-462-9541; *Fax:* 416-462-9647
contact@animalalliance.ca
www.animalalliance.ca
www.facebook.com/132125293547127
Overview: A medium-sized national organization founded in 1990
Mission: To preserve & protect all animals; to promote harmonious relationship between people, animals & the environment; to address issues including pound seizure, cosmetic & product testing, puppy mills, pet overpopulation, exotic pet trade, the fur trade, sport hunting, factory farming, animals as "entertainment"
Chief Officer(s):
Shelly Hawley-Yan, Editor, 519-940-4712
shelly@animalalliance.ca
George Dupras, Director
Jacqui Barnes, Director
Marie Crawford, Director
Barry Kent MacKay, Director
Liz White, Director
Finances: *Funding Sources:* Private donations; garage sales; merchandise; information & displays
Staff Member(s): 5; 130 volunteer(s)
Membership: 20,000
Activities: Promoting cruelty-free, environmentally friendly biodegradable products; currently involved in working to ban pound seizure; information displays; National Wolf Campaign; Endangered Species Campaign; working to end the destruction of over 1,000,000 companion animals (abandoned & unwanted pets) in Canada each year through legislation, spay/neuter programs & public education; working to ban the keeping of exotic animals as pets; *Awareness Events:* "Literary Lions" annual literary benefit; "Animal Magnetism" annual music benefit; *Library:* Animal Alliance Resource Centre

Animal Defence & Anti-Vivisection Society of BC (ADAV)
PO Box 391, Stn. A, Vancouver BC V6C 2N2
vivisectionresearch.ca
Overview: A small provincial organization
Chief Officer(s):
Anne Birthistle, Director
shamrockstudio@shaw.ca
John Pranger, Director, 604-564-1432
prangerjohn@yahoo.ca
Finances: *Funding Sources:* Private
Staff Member(s): 6
Membership: 200; *Fees:* $5 student/senior; $10 individual; $50 lifetime

Animal Defence League of Canada (ADLC)
PO Box 3880, Stn. C, Ottawa ON K1Y 4M5
Tel: 613-233-6117; *Fax:* 613-233-6117
animal-defence.ncf.ca
Overview: A medium-sized national organization founded in 1958
Mission: To promote animal welfare/rights; To disseminate information; To encourage spaying & neutering of cats & dogs; To increase public awareness of oppression of animals & how to prevent or alleviate animal exploitation, cruelty & suffering
Member of: World Society for the Protection of Animals
Finances: *Funding Sources:* Donations; Membership fees
Membership: *Fees:* $50 lifetime; $10 individual; $5 senior/student
Activities: *Speaker Service:* Yes; *Library* Open to public

Animal Health Technologists Association of BC *See* British Columbia Veterinary Technologists Association

Animal Nutrition Association of Canada (ANAC) / Association de nutrition animale du Canada
#1301, 150 Metcalfe St., Ottawa ON K2P 1P1
Tel: 613-241-6421; *Fax:* 613-241-7970
info@anacan.org
www.anacan.org
Previous Name: Canadian Feed Industry Association
Overview: A large national organization founded in 1929
Mission: ANAC advocates on behalf of the livestock & poultry feed industry with government regulators & policy-makers, & works to maintain high standards of feed & food safety.
Member of: International Feed Industry Federation (IFIF)
Affliation(s): Canola Council of Canada; Canada Grains Council; Canadian Egg Marketing Agency; Canadian Chicken Marketing Agency; Canadian Turkey Marketing Agency
Chief Officer(s):
John Brennan, Chair
Graham Cooper, Executive Director
gcooper@anacan.org
Finances: *Funding Sources:* Membership fees
Staff Member(s): 3
Membership: 170 organizations; *Fees:* Variable; *Member Profile:* Manufacturers & suppliers of animal nutrition products to Canada's livestock & poultry industries; *Committees:* FFA; GMP; Certification
Activities: FeedAssure program; Canadian Feed Industry Advisor Certification Program; Canadian Feed Technology Seminar; Canadian Feed Industry Commodity Supplier Course; promotion of environment & animal care issues, & regulations & legislation pertaining to feed products, manufacturing, food safety & salmonella control; monitors regulations pertaining to agricultural trade & international & interprovincial import & export;
Awards:
• ANAC Graduate Scholarship (Scholarship)
Eligibility: Must be enrolled in Animal Science or a related field of study, with an interest in animal nutrition
Meetings/Conferences: • Animal Nutrition Association of Canada Annual General Meeting & Convention 2015, 2015
Scope: National
Publications:
• Directory of Members [a publication of the Animal Nutrition Association of Canada]
Type: Directory

Alberta Division
PO Box 1095, Brooks AB T1R 1B9
Tel: 403-362-2905; *Fax:* 403-501-5456
anac-ab.ca
Chief Officer(s):
Glenn Ravnsborg, Division Manager
glennrav@explornet.com
Rick Walger, Chair
b1grumpelt@wtc.ab.ca

Atlantic Division
53 Elliott Dr., Sussex NB E4E 2K5
Tel: 506-433-5917
anacatla@rogers.com
Chief Officer(s):
Dave Colpitts, Executive Manager & Secretary-Treasurer

British Columbia Division
44370 Simpson Rd., Chilliwack BC V2R 4B7
Tel: 604-866-2378; *Fax:* 604-794-3697
Chief Officer(s):
Robert Dornan, Secretary-Treasurer
rjdornan@telus.net

Manitoba Division
55 River Heights Dr., LaSalle MB R0G 0A2
Tel: 204-736-4833; *Fax:* 204-736-3583
Chief Officer(s):
John Enns, Business Manager
jenns.anac@gmail.com

Ontario Agri Business Association
#104, 160 Research Lane, Guelph ON N1G 5B2
Tel: 519-822-3004; *Fax:* 519-822-8862
info@oaba.on.ca
www.oaba.on.ca
Chief Officer(s):
Dave Buttenham, Chief Executive Officer
dave@oaba.on.ca

Québec Division
#200, 4790, rue Martineau, Saint-Hyacinthe QC J2S 7B4
Tél: 450-799-2440; *Téléc:* 450-799-2445
info@aqinac.com
www.aqinac.com
Chief Officer(s):
Yves Lacroix, Président-directeur général
yvan.lacroix@aqinac.com

Saskatchewan Division
c/o Hood Packaging Corp., 339 Poth Cres., Saskatoon SK S7M 4T7
Tel: 306-978-4720; *Fax:* 306-978-4745
Allen Doherty, Secretary-Treasurer
adoherty@hoodpkg.com

Animal Welfare Foundation of Canada (AWF) / Fondation du bien-être animal du Canada
#343, 300 Earl Grey Dr., Ottawa ON K2T 1C1
e-mail: info@awfc.ca
www.awfc.ca
Overview: A small national charitable organization founded in 1965
Mission: The Animal Welfare Foundation of Canada is a registered charity, supported by donors and administered by a volunteer Board of Directors. The Foundation seeks to improve the quality of life for animals in this country. Since the 1960s the Foundation, an independent watchdog organization, has been at the forefront of issues of humane care of animals in Canada.
Affliation(s): World Society for the Protection of Animals
Chief Officer(s):
Alice Crook, President & Chair
Frances Rodenberg, Secretary
Finances: *Annual Operating Budget:* $100,000-$250,000
14 volunteer(s)
Activities: *Speaker Service:* Yes

ANKORS
West Kootenay Regional Office, 101 Baker St., Nelson BC V1L 4H1
Tel: 250-505-5506; *Fax:* 250-505-5507
information@ankors.bc.ca
www.ankors.bc.ca
www.facebook.com/ankors.west
twitter.com/ankorswest
Also Known As: AIDS Network Kootenay Outreach & Support Society
Previous Name: AIDS Network, Outreach & Support Society
Overview: A small local charitable organization founded in 1992
Mission: To provide support, care, outreach & harm reduction services to individuals living with & affected by HIV, AIDS & HepC
Member of: Pacific AIDS Network; Kootenay Pride; Canadian Aids Society; CATIE; Canadian Treatment Action Council; Positive Living BC; Canadian HIV/AIDS Legal Network; HepC BC; Positive Women's Network; Canadian Aboriginial AIDS Network
Affliation(s): West Kootenay Women's Association; Advocacy Centre; Nelson CARES Society; Nelson Committee on Homelessness
Chief Officer(s):
Cheryl Dowden, Executive Director
cheryl@ankors.bc.ca
Finances: *Funding Sources:* Donations; Health Canada; HRAC; Columbia Basin Trust; Interior Health Authority
Staff Member(s): 9
Membership: *Fees:* Free; *Member Profile:* Those infected or affected by HIV, AIDS or HepC
Activities: Education, prevention, awareness, & advocacy for persons with HCV, HIV/AIDS; *Awareness Events:* Red Ribbon Campaign; AIDS Walk for Life, Sept.; AIDS Memorial, Dec.; *Speaker Service:* Yes; *Library* Open to public by appointment

East Kootenay Regional Office
46 - 17th Ave. South, Cranbrook BC V1C 5A8
Tel: 250-426-3383; *Fax:* 250-426-3221
gary@ankors.bc.ca

Annapolis District Board of Trade (ADBOT)
PO Box 2, Annapolis Royal NS B0S 1A0
Tel: 902-532-5454
info@tradeannapolis.com
www.tradeannapolis.com
Overview: A small local organization founded in 1946
Member of: APCC, NSCC
Chief Officer(s):
Tina Halliday, Administrator
Kevin Burnell, Director
Membership: 70; *Fees:* $125-140

Annapolis Region Community Arts Council (ARCAC)
PO Box 534, 396 St. George St., Annapolis Royal NS B0S 1A0
Tel: 902-532-7069; *Fax:* 902-532-7357
Toll-Free: 800-228-4492
arcac@ns.aliantzinc.ca
rcac-artsplace.weebly.com
Overview: A small local charitable organization founded in 1982
Mission: To foster an understanding & appreciation of the arts in the Annapolis region; to provide creative opportunities for professional artists in all media in the community
Chief Officer(s):
Gene Lane, Executive Director
Finances: *Annual Operating Budget:* $100,000-$250,000; *Funding Sources:* Private; corporate; fundraising
Staff Member(s): 1; 50 volunteer(s)

Membership: 220; *Fees:* $5 student; $20 individual; $35 family; $100 patron; *Committees:* Festival; Fundraising; Programs; Scholarship; Exhibitions
Activities: Workshops in all media; exhibits; advocacy; arts resource for community; annual arts festival; monthly board meetings; *Library:* Art Gallery; Open to public

Annapolis Valley Chamber of Commerce (EKCC)
66 Cornwallis St., Kentville NS B4N 3X1
Tel: 902-678-4634; *Fax:* 902-678-5448
annapolisvalleychamber.ca
www.facebook.com/avcc1
twitter.com/avccommerce
Previous Name: Kentville & Area Board of Trade; Eastern Kings Chamber of Commerce
Overview: A small local organization founded in 1893
Mission: To proactively promote & support the interests of business in Eastern Kings County
Member of: Nova Scotia Chamber of Commerce; Atlantic Provinces Chamber of Commerce
Chief Officer(s):
Scott Roberts, President
Judy Rafuse, Executive Director
Finances: *Annual Operating Budget:* Less than $50,000; *Funding Sources:* Membership fees
Staff Member(s): 1; 16 volunteer(s)
Membership: 225; *Fees:* $10 student; $100 associate member; $125 first member from organization; *Committees:* Advocacy; Membership; Education; Programs & Events; Communications
Awards:
• Business Awards (Award)
• Young Entrepreneur Scholarship (Scholarship)

Annapolis Valley Historical Society (AVHS)
PO Box 925, 21 School St., Middleton NS B0S 1P0
Tel: 902-825-6116; *Fax:* 902-825-0531
macdonald.museum@ns.sympatico.ca
www.macdonaldmuseum.ca
Overview: A small local organization founded in 1978
Mission: To act as the governing body for the Macdonald (Consolidated School) Museum; To collect, preserve, & exhibit the historical artifacts of Nova Scotia's Annapolis Valley; To provide genealogical resources, such as vital statistics for Annapolis, Kings, Digby, & Lunenburg Counties, local newspapers, family files, school records, church registers, obituaries, & cemetery inscriptions
Finances: *Funding Sources:* Donations; Fundraising
Membership: *Fees:* $11.50 individual; $17.25 couple; $20.75 family
Activities: Operating a gallery with the works of local artists; *Library:* Annapolis Valley Historical Society Research Library; Open to public by appointment
Publications:
• Annapolis Valley Historical Society Newsletter
Type: Newsletter; *Frequency:* Quarterly; *Price:* Free with membership in the Annapolis Valley Historical Society
Profile: Information about society activities

Annapolis Valley Real Estate Board
PO Box 117, 2110 Hwy. 1, Auburn NS B0P 1A0
Tel: 902-847-9336; *Fax:* 902-847-9869
avreb@eastlink.ca
Overview: A small local organization overseen by Nova Scotia Association of REALTORS
Member of: The Canadian Real Estate Association
Chief Officer(s):
Cathy Simpson, Executive Officer

ANNISAA Organization of Canada (ANNISAA)
111 - 7 St. Dennis Dr., Toronto ON M3C 1E4
Tel: 647-761-0745
info@annisaa.org
annisaa.org
www.facebook.com/179651935453963
twitter.com/ANNISAAORG
Overview: A medium-sized national organization founded in 2012
Mission: ANNISAA aims to promote the best interest of all Muslim women and their families within the Canadian society, providing a voice for Muslim women. ANNISAA promotes an interest in education, research, sports and recreation, social development, Islamic spiritual advancement and moral values, as well as sponsoring literary, art and other educational and cultural events, festivals, and conventions for the promotion of Islam and Muslims.
Membership: *Member Profile:* Practising Muslim women
Publications:
• ANNISAA Magazine
Type: Magazine; *Frequency:* Quarterly
Profile: Magazine presents various aspects of morality, and of Islamic religion, to be useful both in this life and the Hereafter.

Anthroposophical Society in Canada (ASC) / Société anthroposophique au Canada
#8, 9100 Bathurst St., Thornhill ON L4J 8C7
Tel: 416-892-3656
Toll-Free: 877-892-3656
info@anthroposophy.ca
www.anthroposophy.ca
Overview: A medium-sized national charitable organization founded in 1953
Mission: To further the life of the soul, both in the individual & in human society, on the basis of a true knowledge of the spiritual world, as described by Rudolf Steiner (1861-1925)
Affliation(s): General Anthroposophical Society, Dornach, Switzerland
Chief Officer(s):
Mark McAlister, Administrator
Monique Walsh, Chair
Arie van Ameringen, Secretary
France Beaucage, Treasurer
Philip Thatcher, General Secretary
Finances: *Annual Operating Budget:* $50,000-$100,000
Staff Member(s): 2; 10 volunteer(s)
Membership: 500; *Fees:* $240 (voluntary contribution); *Member Profile:* Adults of all ages & professions
Activities: Offers information about anthroposophy; membership services; outreach; AGM in March/April; *Library:* National Library of the Anthroposophical Society in Canada; Open to public

Anti-Defamation League of B'nai Brith *See* League for Human Rights of B'nai Brith Canada

Antigonish Ceilidh Association
31 Arbor Dr., Antigonish NS B2G 1S8
Tel: 902-735-2014
www.antigonishceilidhs.com
Overview: A small provincial organization
Mission: To promote Celtic culture
Chief Officer(s):
Shelley Anderson, Contact
shelley_anderson76@yahoo.com
Activities: Showcasing Celtic performers

Antigonish Chamber of Commerce
21B James St. Plaza, Antigonish NS B2G 1R6
Tel: 902-863-6308; *Fax:* 902-863-2656
contact@antigonishchamber.com
www.antigonishchamber.com
www.facebook.com/AntigonishChamberofCommerce
twitter.com/AntigonishChmbr
Overview: A small local charitable organization founded in 1904
Mission: To represent businesses in Antigonish
Member of: Nova Scotia Chambers of Commerce; Atlantic Chamber of Commerce; Canadian Chamber of Commerce
Chief Officer(s):
Patrick Curry, President
Finances: *Funding Sources:* Membership dues; Special projects
Membership: *Fees:* $57.50 student/senior; $120.75 1-4 employees; $172.50 5-20 employees; $297.50 20 employees; *Committees:* Member Services & Communications; Events; Finance; Governance & Human Resources
Activities: Networking; Advocacy & policy; Marketing opportunities
Awards:
• Ian Spencer Award
• Outstanding Customer Service Award

Antigonish Culture Alive
PO Box 1175, Antigonish NS B2G 2L6
Tel: 902-783-2948
info@antigonishculturealive.ca
www.antigonishculturealive.ca
Previous Name: Guysborough Antigonish Pictou Arts & Culture Council
Overview: A small local organization
Mission: To promote excellence in art practice; To raise awareness of the arts in our region
Chief Officer(s):
Sarah O'Toole, Coordinator
Membership: *Fees:* $20 individual; $35 associate
Activities: Annual Gathering of the Arts, travelling juried exhibition & workshops, July; special events; concerts & readings

Antigonish Highland Society (AHS)
274 Main St., Antigonish NS B2G 2C4
Tel: 902-863-4275; *Fax:* 902-863-0466
info@antigonishhighlandgames.ca
www.antigonishhighlandgames.ca/highlandsociety
www.facebook.com/210633578958080
Overview: A small local organization
Chief Officer(s):
Irene MacLeod, President
Finances: *Annual Operating Budget:* $100,000-$250,000
Staff Member(s): 1; 50 volunteer(s)
Membership: 50; *Fees:* $10 individual; $15 family
Activities: Antigonish Highland Games

Antigonish Therapeutic Riding Association
42 Lower North Grant Rd., Antigonish NS B2G 2L1
Tel: 902-863-6221
Overview: A small local charitable organization founded in 1987
Mission: To provide a therapeutic and recreational horseback riding program for physically, mentally, and emotionally handicapped people, and to promote public awareness of such a program
Chief Officer(s):
Amanada Workman, President
Activities: Two six-week sessions per year; weekly horseback riding lessons for handicapped children & adults

Antigonish-Eastern Shore Tourist Association (AESTA)
9042 Hwy. 7, General Delivery, Head Jeddore HRM NS B0J 1P0
Tel: 902-889-2362; *Fax:* 902-889-2101
anteast@eastlink.ca
www.novascotiaseacoast.com
www.facebook.com/190599970973071
Overview: A small local organization founded in 1962
Mission: To promote tourism in Antigonish-Eastern Shore Region of Nova Scotia
Finances: *Annual Operating Budget:* $500,000-$1.5 Million; *Funding Sources:* Regional government; private sector
Staff Member(s): 2; 17 volunteer(s)
Membership: 280 individual

The Antiquarian & Numismatic Society of Montréal *Voir* Société d'archéologie et de numismatique de Montréal

Antiquarian Booksellers' Association of Canada (ABAC) / Association de la librairie ancienne du Canada (ALAC)
c/o #301, 368 Dalhousie St., Ottawa ON K1N 7G3
e-mail: info@abac.org
www.abac.org
www.facebook.com/210124119032896
twitter.com/A_B_A_C
Overview: A small national organization founded in 1966
Mission: To maintain high standards in the antiquarian book trade; To promote interest in rare books & manuscripts
Member of: International League of Antiquarian Booksellers
Chief Officer(s):
Roger Auger, President
Alexandre Arjomand, Secretary
Finances: *Annual Operating Budget:* Less than $50,000; *Funding Sources:* Membership dues
Membership: 62; *Fees:* $200-$350; *Member Profile:* Booksellers with minimum of 3 years experience & able to provide four recommendations from members in good standing who can vouch for applicant's expertise & integrity
Activities: Insurance & donation appraisals; stolen book registry; international prize for bibliography (in conjunction with ILAB); *Awareness Events:* Annual Toronto Bookfair, May; *Rents Mailing List:* Yes

Antique Motorcycle Club of Manitoba Inc. (AMCM)
1377 Niakwa Rd. East, Winnipeg MB R2J 3T3
Tel: 204-831-8165
www.amcm.ca
Overview: A small provincial organization
Chief Officer(s):
Ross Metcalfe, President
moose102@escape.ca
Mike Baraschuk, Librarian, 204-757-2368

Anti-Tuberculosis Society *See* British Columbia Lung Association

Anxiety Disorders Association of British Columbia
#103, 237 Columbia St. East, New Westminster BC V3L 3W4
Tel: 604-525-7566; *Fax:* 604-525-7586
info@anxietybc.com
www.anxietybc.com
www.facebook.com/AnxietyBC
twitter.com/#!/AnxietyBC
www.youtube.com/user/AnxietyBC/
Also Known As: AnxietyBC
Overview: A small provincial organization founded in 1999 overseen by Anxiety Disorders Association of Canada
Mission: To increase awareness of anxiety disorders, including panic disorder, phobias, obsessive-compulsive disorder, and post-traumatic stress disorder; To provide information and resources for individuals wanting to manage their own anxiety
Member of: BC Partners for Mental Health and Addictions Information
Affliation(s): Anxiety BC
Chief Officer(s):
Amir Rasheed, President
Judith Law, Executive Director
Finances: *Funding Sources:* Provincial Health Services Authority, the Ministry for Children and Family Development; donations; membership fees
Membership: *Committees:* Scientific; Executive

Anxiety Disorders Association of Canada (ADAC) / Association Canadienne des Troubles Anxieux (ACTA)
PO Box 117, Stn. Cote-St-Luc, MontréAl QC H4V 2Y3
Tel: 514-484-0504
Toll-Free: 888-223-2252
contactus@anxietycanada.ca
www.anxietycanada.ca
www.facebook.com/group.php?gid=96864892735
twitter.com/anxietycanada
Overview: A medium-sized national charitable organization founded in 2002
Mission: Aims to promote the prevention, treatment and management of anxiety disorders and to improve the lives of people who suffer from them.
Chief Officer(s):
Lynn Miller, President
Membership: *Fees:* $25 professional; $10 general; *Committees:* Scientific Advisory; Consumer Advisory

Anxiety Disorders Association of Manitoba (ADAM)
#100, 4 Fort St., Winnipeg MB R3C 1C4
Tel: 204-925-0600; *Fax:* 204-925-0609
Toll-Free: 800-805-8885
adam@adam.mb.ca
www.adam.mb.ca
www.facebook.com/anxietydisordersassociationofmanitoba
Overview: A small provincial charitable organization founded in 1986 overseen by Anxiety Disorders Association of Canada
Mission: A peer-led organization for the support of people with anxiety, and to share knowledge and hope with others.
Chief Officer(s):
Richard Shore, Chair
Activities: Education and Public Awareness; Information and Referral Service; Cognitive Behavioural Groups & Support Groups

Anxiety Disorders Association of Ontario (ADAO)
Heartwood House, 404 McArthur Ave., Ottawa ON K1K 1G5
Tel: 613-729-6761
Toll-Free: 877-308-3843
info@anxietydisordersontario.ca
www.anxietydisordersontario.ca
www.facebook.com/anxietyottawa
twitter.com/AnxietyOttawa
www.youtube.com/user/anxietyottawa
Overview: A small provincial charitable organization founded in 1997 overseen by Anxiety Disorders Association of Canada
Mission: ADAO's mission is to empower, in an holistic way, the lives of those affected by anxiety through advocacy, education, research support and community programming.
Chief Officer(s):
Joan Riggs, BA, B.S.W., M.S, President
Membership: *Committees:* 14-Week Program; Finance; Communications

APCHQ - Montréal Métropolitain
5800, boul Louis H. Lafontaine, Anjou QC H1M 1S7
Tél: 514-354-8722; *Téléc:* 514-355-7777
info@apchqmontreal.ca
www.apchqmontreal.ca
Aperçu: *Dimension:* petite; *Envergure:* provinciale; Organisme sans but lucratif; fondée en 1950
Mission: Représente plus de 3 300 membres oeuvrant dans l'industrie de la construction et de la rénovation résidentielle
Membre(s) du bureau directeur:
Ivan Roger, Président
Marc Savard, Directeur général
Finances: *Budget de fonctionnement annuel:* $1.5 Million-$3 Million
Membre(s) du personnel: 9
Membre: 3,300; *Montant de la cotisation:* 500$; *Critères d'admissibilite:* Entrepreneurs en construction
Activités: *Service de conférenciers:* Oui

Apeetogosan (Metis) Development Inc.
#302, 12308 - 111 Ave., Edmonton AB T5M 2N4
Tel: 780-452-7951
Toll-Free: 800-252-7963
www.apeetogosan.com
www.facebook.com/apeetogosan
twitter.com/Apeetogosan
Overview: A small local organization founded in 1984
Mission: To provide assistance with developing and commercializing community members' business ideas
Member of: Metis Nation of Alberta Association; National Aboriginal Capital Corporation Association
Affliation(s): The Métis Nation of Alberta
Chief Officer(s):
Michael Ivy, General Manager
Staff Member(s): 11
Membership: *Committees:* Audit; HR; Loans
Activities: Louis Riel Week Festivities; Aboriginal Day

APER Santé et services sociaux (APERSSS)
1751, Rue Richardson, Montréal QC H3K 1G6
Tél: 514-933-4118; *Téléc:* 514-933-2397
association@aper.qc.ca
www.aper.qc.ca
Nom précédent: Association des cadres de la santé et des services sociaux du Québec
Aperçu: *Dimension:* moyenne; *Envergure:* provinciale; fondée en 1974
Membre(s) du bureau directeur:
Jean Belhumeur, Président intérimaire
jean_belhumeur@ssss.gouv.qc.ca
Membre(s) du personnel: 4
Membre: 900; *Critères d'admissibilite:* Cadres réseau santé et services sociaux

Aphasie Rive-Sud
790, rue Sainte-Hélne, Longueuil QC J4K 3R6
Tél: 450-616-0688
aphasierivesud.org
Aperçu: *Dimension:* petite; *Envergure:* locale
Mission: Pour amener les gens souffrant d'aphasie ensemble des activités sociales et pour aider à leur réhabilitation
Membre de: Regrouper les associations de personnes aphasiques de Québec
Membre(s) du bureau directeur:
Léandre Joannette, Président, Conseil d'administration
leandre.joannette@aphasierivesud.org
Activités: Sport; Artisanat; Chant et musique

Aplastic Anemia & Myelodysplasia Association of Canada (AAMAC)
#321, 11181 Yonge St., Richmond Hill ON L4S 1L2
Tel: 905-780-0698; *Fax:* 905-780-1648
Toll-Free: 888-840-0039
info@aamac.ca
www.aamac.ca
Previous Name: Aplastic Anemia Association of Canada
Overview: A small national charitable organization founded in 1987
Mission: To disseminate information concerning the disease; To form a nation-wide support network for patients, families & medical professionals; To support Canadian Blood Services & their programs; To raise funds for research
Member of: Health Charities Council of Canada
Affliation(s): Network of Rare Blood Disorders
Chief Officer(s):
Gord Sanford, President
Joyce Burnett, Secretary
Sylvia Scow, Coordinator, British Columbia
Chris Meyer, Coordinator, Ontario
Finances: *Annual Operating Budget:* $50,000-$100,000; *Funding Sources:* Private donors
Staff Member(s): 1; 20 volunteer(s)
Membership: 1,400
Activities: Research; Support; Awareness; *Awareness Events:* Aplastic Anemia & Myelodysplasia Awareness Week, 3rd week of Oct.; *Speaker Service:* Yes

Aplastic Anemia Association of Canada *See* Aplastic Anemia & Myelodysplasia Association of Canada

The Apostolic Church in Canada
220 Adelaide St. North, London ON N6B 3H4
Tel: 519-438-7036; *Fax:* 519-438-5800
cheryl@apostolic.ca
www.apostolic.ca
www.facebook.com/pages/Apostolic-Church-in-Canada/117271988314359
twitter.com/ACCnat
Overview: A small national organization founded in 1934
Mission: A Trinitarian, Pentecostal denomination with a strong commitment to mission.
Chief Officer(s):
D. Karl Thomas, National Leader
Finances: *Annual Operating Budget:* $500,000-$1.5 Million
Staff Member(s): 15
Membership: 500-999
Activities: *Internships:* Yes

Apostolic Church of Pentecost of Canada Inc. (ACOP) / Église apostolique de Pentecôte du Canada inc.
International Office, #119, 2340 Pegasus Way NE, Calgary AB T2E 8M5
Tel: 403-273-5777; *Fax:* 403-273-8102
acop@acop.ca
www.acop.ca
www.facebook.com/ACOPcanada
twitter.com/ACOPcanada
Overview: A small national licensing charitable organization founded in 1921
Mission: To provide fellowship, encouragement & accountability in the proclamation of the Gospel of Jesus Christ by the Power of the Holy Spirit
Affliation(s): Evangelical Fellowship of Canada
Chief Officer(s):
Wes Mills, President & National Director
Finances: *Annual Operating Budget:* $1.5 Million-$3 Million; *Funding Sources:* Donations
Staff Member(s): 30
Membership: 155 affiliated churches + 436 members; *Fees:* Varies
Activities: *Internships:* Yes; *Speaker Service:* Yes; *Library* by appointment

Appalachian Teachers' Association (ATA) / Association des enseignant(e)s des Appalaches (AEA)
#800, 257, rue Queen, Lennoxville QC J1M 1K7
Tel: 819-791-4185; *Fax:* 819-791-4186
ataunion@hotmail.com
www.ataunion.org
Previous Name: Eastern Townships Association of Teachers
Overview: A small local organization founded in 1999
Mission: To protect & advance the professional, economic, & social welfare of members
Affliation(s): Québec Provincial Association of Teachers
Chief Officer(s):
Richard Goldfinch, President
Finances: *Annual Operating Budget:* $50,000-$100,000
Staff Member(s): 1
Membership: 500 individual; *Fees:* $260 individual

Appaloosa Horse Club of Canada (ApHCC)
PO Box 940, Claresholm AB T0L 0T0
Tel: 403-625-3326; *Fax:* 403-625-2274
registry@appaloosa.ca
www.appaloosa.ca
www.facebook.com/255499284509
Overview: A medium-sized national organization founded in 1954
Mission: To collect records & historical data relating to origin of the Appaloosa; to file records & issue certificates of registration; to preserve, improve & standardize the breed
Chief Officer(s):
Sharon Duncan, Executive Secretary
Membership: *Committees:* Executive; Nomination; Personnel; National Show; Rules; Judges & Judging; Shows & Showing; Handbook; Breed Improvement; Racing; Activity & Disciplines; Trail, Sports & Recreation;'Discipline; Promotion & Publicity;

Booth; Membership; Museum Liasion; Recognition & Awards; Youth; Law Review; International Liasion; Inspectors & Inspections
Activities: *Library:* APHCC Museum & Archives; Open to public

Appaloosa Horse Club of Nova Scotia
#320, 331 Lacewood Dr., Halifax NS B3S 1K6
Tel: 902-445-5288
cmca96@hotmail.com
www.aphcns.com
Member of: Appaloosa Horse Club of Canada
Chief Officer(s):
Bill Milligan, President & Treasurer, 905-542-7566
billmilligan@royallepage.ca
Jim Rafferty, Vice-President
rafferjl@ns.aliantzinc.ca

Calgary Regional Appaloosa Club
3438 Cedarville Dr. SW, Calgary AB T2W 5A9
Tel: 403-251-5631
wmtj@telusplanet.com
www.calgaryappaloosa.com
Howard Maerz, President
Pat Hyndman, Vice-President
pat@apxin.com
Sue Gatenby, Treasurer
rodsue@telusplanet.net

Kawartha Regional Appaloosa Club
RR#21, Port Perry ON L9L 1B5
Tel: 905-985-2911
www.appaloosaontario.ca/KRAHC.htm
Chief Officer(s):
Gary Guthrie, President, 705-374-4077
garbetsappy@yahoo.ca
John Walker, Vice-President, 705-324-2404
goldenacreappse@xplornet.ca
Dawn Adams, Treasurer, 905-852-1527
dawnadams@bell.blackberry.net

Manitoba Appaloosa Club
PO Box 125, Boissevain MB R0K 0E0
Tel: 204-534-2552
Dale@gloverequine.com
Chief Officer(s):
Cheryle McClure, President
cmcclure@mymts.net
Jocelyn Kish, Vice-President
horseaddict@yahoo.com
Carol Rea, Sec.-Treas.
sonrea_ranch@yahoo.ca

Mighty Peace Appaloosa Club
PO Box 92, Manning AB T0H 2M0
Tel: 780-836-2793
jimcreekranch@yahoo.com
Chief Officer(s):
Barb Whillans, Contact

New Brunswick Appaloosa Club
12421 Rte. 114, Penobsquis NB E4G 2Z8
Tel: 506-433-5401; *Fax:* 506-433-1130
natalieworth@hotmail.com
www.nbaphc.com
Chief Officer(s):
Chris Bell, Contact

Saskatchewan Appaloosa Club
c/o Eleanor Porth, PO Box 26B, R.R.2, Regina SK S4P 2Z2
Tel: 306-569-2849
www.saskapp.ca
Chief Officer(s):
Karen Bedford, President

Thunder Bay Appaloosa Club
226 Hinton Ave., Thunder Bay ON P7A 7E4
Tel: 807-767-3541
appysmalys@shaw.ca
Chief Officer(s):
Harry Lasn, President
Ian K. Shaw, Vice-President
Eleanor Stewart, Sec.-Treas.

Apparel BC (ABC)
1859 Franklin St., Vancouver BC V5V 1P9
Tel: 604-986-2003; *Fax:* 604-986-2097
Also Known As: BC Apparel Manufacturers Association
Overview: A small provincial licensing organization founded in 1994
Mission: To enhance & strengthen the viability of the BC apparel industry in a competitive & global environment through advocacy, marketing, education, mentorships, liaison & the setting of ethical standards
Member of: Canadian Apparel Federation
Chief Officer(s):
Jacqueline Kirby, Executive Director
jacqueline@apparel-bc.org
Finances: *Annual Operating Budget:* $250,000-$500,000
Staff Member(s): 1
Membership: 100-499; *Member Profile:* BC manufacturers, contractors, designers & suppliers to the industry
Activities: Industry networking events; lobbyist for tariff & trade issues; training seminars; marketing support; *Library*
Awards:
• Annual Recognition Awards (Award)

Apparel Human Resources Council (AHRC) / Conseil des ressources humaines de l'industrie du vêtement
#360, 6750, av de l'Esplanade, Montréal QC H2V 4M1
Tel: 514-388-7779; *Fax:* 888-738-7854
info@apparelconnexion.ca
www.apparelconnexion.com
www.linkedin.com/groups/Apparel-Human-Resources-4801586
www.facebook.com/ApparelConnexionConnexionVetement
twitter.com/Apparel_HR
Overview: A small national organization
Mission: To serve human resources development & adjustment needs of managers & employees in the apparel manufacturing industry
Chief Officer(s):
Patrick Thomas, General Manager, 514-388-7779 Ext. 101
patrick@apparelconnexion.ca
Adrian Bussoli, Co-Chair
Judy Lackner, Co-Chair
Staff Member(s): 3
Membership: *Fees:* $25 partner; $50 members; $75 associate; $300 schools; *Committees:* Executive

Apparel Manufacturers Association of Ontario
#504, 124 O'Connor St., Ottawa ON K1P 5M9
Tel: 613-231-3220; *Fax:* 613-231-2305
Also Known As: Apparel Ontario
Overview: A medium-sized provincial organization
Member of: Canadian Apparel Federation
Chief Officer(s):
Bob Kirke, Executive Director
Membership: 200+; *Fees:* Schedule available

Apparel Manufacturers Institute of Québec *Voir* Institut des manufacturiers du vêtement du Québec

Apparel Quebec (AMIQ) / Vêtement Québec
#1270, 1435, rue Saint-Alexandre, Montréal QC H3A 2G4
Tel: 514-382-3846; *Fax:* 514-940-5336
cs@apparelquebec.com
www.vetementquebec.com
Overview: A medium-sized provincial organization
Mission: To advance the exchange of best practices & technological innovations in such areas as sourcing, design & fashion
Affiliation(s): Canadian Apparel Federation (CAF); Apparel Human Reousrces Council (AHRC); Fashion Bureau of Montreal; Ministry of Economic Development, Innovation & Export Trade; Groupe Sensation Mode; Men's Clothing Manufacturers Association; Quebec Council of Odd Pants Employers; Montreal Clothing Contractors Association Inc., Rainwear & Sportswear Manufacturers Association; The Canadian Trimmings Manufacturers Association
Chief Officer(s):
Oxana Sushilnikova, Project Coordinator
Staff Member(s): 1
Membership: *Member Profile:* Apparel producers, importers, marketers & suppliers
Activities: Labour negotiations & government relations

Apple Growers of New Brunswick / Producteurs de pommes du Nouveau-Brunswick
PO Box 653, Stn. Main, Moncton NB E1C 8M7
www.applesnb.ca
Overview: A small provincial organization
Mission: To represent apple growers in New Brunswick
Activities: Providing information about apple orchards & the purchase of apples in New Brunswick

Applegrove Community Complex
60 Woodfield Rd., Toronto ON M4L 2W6
Tel: 416-461-8143; *Fax:* 416-461-5513
applegrove@applegrovecc.ca
www.applegrovecc.ca
www.facebook.com/pages/Applegrove-Community-Complex/99742456574
Also Known As: Applegrove
Overview: A medium-sized local charitable organization founded in 1979
Mission: To provide social service programs for infants, children, teens, adults and seniors living in the Queen-Greenwood area of Toronto.
Chief Officer(s):
Susan Fletcher, Executive Director
Ann McKechnie, Chair
Finances: *Annual Operating Budget:* $500,000-$1.5 Million; *Funding Sources:* City of Toronto, Government, Donations
Membership: *Committees:* Finance & Fundraising; Personnel

AppleRoute Country Chamber of Commerce *See* Brighton & District Chamber of Commerce

Applied Science Technologists & Technicians of British Columbia (ASTTBC)
10767 - 148 St., Surrey BC V3R 0S4
Tel: 604-585-2788; *Fax:* 604-585-2790
techinfo@asttbc.org
www.asttbc.org
www.youtube.com/user/ASTTBC
Previous Name: Society of Engineering Technologists of BC
Overview: A large provincial organization founded in 1958 overseen by Canadian Council of Technicians & Technologists
Mission: To advance the profession of applied science technology & the professional recognition of applied science technologists, certified technician, & other members in a manner that serves & protects the public interest
Member of: Canadian Council of Technicians & Technologists
Chief Officer(s):
Bill MacPherson, AScT, President
John E. Leech, AScT, CAE, Executive Director
jleech@asttbc.org
Cindy Aitken, Manager, Governance & Events
caitken@asttbc.org
Garry Gaudet, Manager, Media Relations
ggaudet@asttbc.org
Jason Jung, Manager, Member & Program Development
jjung@asttbc.org
Nicky Malli, Manager, Finance
nmalli@asttbc.org
Geoff Sale, AScT, Manager, Internationally Trained Professionals
gsale@asttbc.org
Anne Sharp, BA, Manager, Marketing & Exec. Dir., ASTTBC Foundation
asharp@asttbc.org
Robert Stitt, AScT, Manager, Special Projects
rstitt@asttbc.org
Karen Taylor, DipBM, Manager, Operations
ktaylor@asttbc.org
Finances: *Funding Sources:* Membership dues; Accreditation; Member services; Advertising; Education
250 volunteer(s)
Membership: 8,600; *Fees:* $255; *Committees:* Construction Safety Certification Panel; Fire Protection Certification Board; Public Works Inspection Certification Board
Activities: *Internships:* Yes; *Rents Mailing List:* Yes
Awards:
• Peter Allan AScT Leadership Award (Award)
• Advanced Technology Award (Award)
• Certificate of Appreciation (Award)
• Life Membership (Award)
• Professional Achievement (Award)
• R. Littledale Memorial Award (Award)
• Service Award (Award)
• Special Award (Award)
• Honorary Membership (Award)
• Employer Award For Career Enhancement & Success of Technology Professionals (Award)
• Professional Leadership Award For Women in Technology (Award)
• Top in Technology (Award)
• TechGREEN (Award)
Publications:
• Member Compensation Survey [a publication of Applied Science Technologists & Technicians of British Columbia]
Type: Report
• Member Satisfaction Survey [a publication of Applied Science Technologists & Technicians of British Columbia]
Type: Report

Appraisal Institute of Canada (AIC) / Institut canadien des évaluateurs (ICE)

#403, 200 Catherine St., Ottawa ON K2P 2K9
Tel: 613-234-6533; *Fax:* 613-234-7197
info@aicanada.ca
www.aicanada.ca
www.linkedin.com/groups?gid=2967439
www.facebook.com/AppraisalInstitute.Canada
twitter.com/aic_canada
Overview: A large national organization founded in 1938
Mission: To grant professional designations in real estate appraisal; To strive to maintain high standards in real estate appraisal to protect the public interest
Affiliation(s): Appraisal Institute of Canada - Alberta, British Columbia, Manitoba, New Brunswick, Newfoundland & Labrador, Nova Scotia, Ontario, Prince Edward Island, Québec, Saskatchewan
Chief Officer(s):
Keith Lancastle, Chief Executive Officer
keithl@aicanada.ca
Rosmarie Buxbaum, Director, Finance & Administration
rosmarieb@aicanada.ca
Sheila Roy, Director, Marketing & Communications
sheilar@aicanada.ca
Nathalie Roy-Patenaude, Director, Professional Practice
nathalier@aicanada.ca
Dominique Racine-Dickie, Manager, Professional Affairs
dominiquer@aicanada.ca
Membership: 1,000-4,999; *Member Profile:* Professional real estate appraisers; Valuation consultants; *Committees:* Executive; Professional Practice; Communications; Conference; Audit & Finance; Nominating; Bylaws, Regulations & Procedures; Admissions & Accreditation
Activities: Career awareness & promotion; Professional standards & designation; Research; Education; Career development & continuing education; Communications; Professional & member services
Meetings/Conferences: • Appraisal Institute of Canada / Institut canadien des évaluateurs 2015 Annual Conference, June, 2015, Delta Grand Okanagan Resort and Conference Centre, Kelowna, BC
Scope: National
Contact Information: Conference & Meetings Planner, Kevin Collins, Phone: 613-234-6533, ext. 231, E-Mail: kevinc@aicanada.ca

Apprenp'tits Numismates

CP 81183, Québec QC G2B 3W7
Aperçu: *Dimension:* petite; *Envergure:* locale; Organisme sans but lucratif
Mission: Promouvoir la numismatique auprès de la jeunesse francophone au Canada et partout dans le monde
Membre(s) du bureau directeur:
Claude Bernard, Contact
Membre: *Montant de la cotisation:* 10$

Aquaculture Association of Canada (AAC) / Association Aquacole du Canada

16 Lobster Lane, St. Andrews NB E5B 3T6
Tel: 506-529-4766; *Fax:* 506-529-4609
aac@dfo-mpo.gc.ca
www.aquacultureassociation.ca
Overview: A medium-sized national charitable organization founded in 1984
Mission: To foster an aquaculture industry in Canada; To encourage & support the educational, technological, & scientific advancement of aquaculture
Chief Officer(s):
Susan Waddy, Manager, Association Office, 506-529-4766
Susan.Waddy@dfo-mpo.gc.ca
Tim Jackson, President, 506-636-3728, Fax: 506-636-3479
timothy.jackson@nrc-cnrc.gc.ca
Tim DeJager, Vice-President, 250-751-0634
dejagert@co3.ca
Joy Wade, Vice-President, 250-754-6884
joy2004wade@yahoo.ca
Shelley King, Secretary, 902-421-5646, Fax: 902-421-2733
sking@genomeatlantic.ca
Caroline Graham, Treasurer
cpgraham@rogers.com
Finances: *Funding Sources:* Donations
Membership: 900+; *Member Profile:* Students; Educators; Producers; Suppliers; Scientists; Government representatives; *Committees:* Election; Finance; Rules; Time & Place; Arrangements; Program; Publications; Awards; Student Affairs; Membership; Business Development
Activities: Promoting the study of aquaculture & related sciences; Providing scientific & technical information related to aquaculture; Increasing public awareness & understanding of aquaculture; Liaising with goverment & industry; Providing networking opportunities; Conducting seminars
Meetings/Conferences: • Aquaculture Canada 2015: The Aquaculture Association of Canada's Annual Conference & General Meeting, May, 2015, Nanaimo, BC
Scope: National
Description: Featuring presentations, special sessions, workshops, & posters
Contact Information: Office Administrator: Catriona Wong, Phone: 506-529-4766, Fax: 506-529-4609, E-mail: AAC@dfo-mpo.gc.ca
Publications:
• Aquaculture Canada Abstracts
Profile: Conference program guides, featuring conference sessions
• Aquaculture Canada Proceedings of Contributed Papers
Profile: Proceedings of the contributed papers of the annual meetings of the Aquaculture Association of Canada
• Bulletin of the Aquaculture Association of Canada
Type: Newsletter
Profile: Topics have included sea-urchin aquaculture, application of genome science to sustainable aquaculture, proceedings of the scallop aquaculture session, fish health,aquaculture public awareness & education, water movement & aquatic animal health, aquaculture biotechnology, & progress in cod farming
• The Watermark [a publication of the Aquaculture Association of Canada]
Type: Newsletter; *Frequency:* 3 pa; *Editor:* Gregor Reid; Candace Durston
Profile: Aquaculture Association of Canada updates, such as donations, awards, & meetings

Aquaculture Association of Nova Scotia (AANS)

c/o Starlite Gallery, #215, 7071 Bayers Rd., Halifax NS B3L 2C2
Tel: 902-422-6234; *Fax:* 902-422-6248
Other Communication: aans@eastlink.ca
info@aansonline.ca
www.aansonline.ca
twitter.com/AANSOnline
www.youtube.com/user/aansonline
Overview: A small provincial organization founded in 1977
Member of: Canadian Aquaculture Industry Alliance
Chief Officer(s):
Bruce Hancock, Executive Director
bhancock@seafarmers.ca
Finances: *Funding Sources:* Membership fees
Staff Member(s): 3
Membership: 40; *Fees:* Producers $500-10,000; Suppliers/Processors $375-10,000; Friends $150; Students $25; *Member Profile:* Not-for-profit association of growers, suppliers & industry supporters; *Committees:* Nova Scotia Aquaculture Environmental Coordinating Committee
Awards:
• Cathy Enright Scholarship (Scholarship)
To recognize and help advance students who are demonstrating outstanding research work related to aquaculture. Eligibility: Honours & masters students studying in NS who are conducting research projects related to aquaculture (any field) *Amount:* $1000 *Contact:* Danielle Goodfellow, R&D Coordinator, dgoodfellowaans@eastlink.ca
Meetings/Conferences: • Sea Farmers Conference 2015, January, 2015, Delta Halifax, Halifax, NS
Scope: Provincial
Description: Topic: The Case for Aquaculture

AquaNet - Network in Aquaculture

Ocean Sciences Centre, Memorial University of Newfoundland, St. John's NL A1C 5S7
Tel: 709-737-3245; *Fax:* 709-737-3500
info@aquanet.ca
www.aquanet.ca
Overview: A medium-sized national organization
Mission: To foster a sustainable aquaculture sector in Canada through high quality research & education
Member of: Networks of Centres of Excellence

Aquatic Federation of Canada (AFC) / Fédération aquatique du Canada

c/o Martin Richard, Director, Communications, Swimming Canada, #B140, 2445 St-Laurent Blvd., Ottawa ON K1G 6C3
Tel: 613-260-1348
www.aquaticfederation.ca
Overview: A medium-sized national organization founded in 1968
Mission: To promote olympic aquatic sports in Canada
Affiliation(s): Synchro Canada; Canadian Amateur Diving Association Inc.; Water Polo Canada; Swimming Canada
Chief Officer(s):
Bill Hogan, President

Arab Canadian Association of the Atlantic Provinces (ACAAP)

PO Box 1024, Halifax NS B3J 2X1
Tel: 902-429-9100
Overview: A small local charitable organization founded in 1978
Mission: To promote friendship between Arab & Canadian people
Member of: Multicultural Association of Nova Scotia
Chief Officer(s):
Ismail Zayid, President, 902-429-9100
izayid@hfx.eastlink.ca
Finances: *Funding Sources:* Donations & investments
Membership: *Member Profile:* Persons of Arabic-speaking descent & their spouses
Activities: Social & cultural activities; assist new immigrants to integrate in community; struggle against racism & sterotyping;

Arab Community Centre of Toronto

#209, 555 Burnhamthorpe Rd., Toronto ON M9C 2Y3
Tel: 416-231-7746; *Fax:* 416-231-4770
info@arabnewcomers.org
arabcommunitycentre.com
Overview: A small local organization founded in 1972 overseen by Ontario Council of Agencies Serving Immigrants
Mission: To help integrate Arab immigrants into Canada
Chief Officer(s):
Naglaa Raouf, Executive Director
nraouf@arabnewcomers.org
Staff Member(s): 18
Membership: *Fees:* $6 student; $12 individual; $24 family

Arabian Horse Association of Eastern Canada (AHAEC)

c/o Allan Ehrlick, 8259 Walkers Line, Campbellville ON L0P 1B0
Tel: 905-854-0762; *Fax:* 905-854-1386
aoc@milestoneac.ca
www.ahaec.on.ca
Overview: A small local organization founded in 1955
Mission: To promote multi-discipline Arabian & Half-Arabian horses; To coordinate the activities of horse owners
Member of: Ontario Equestrian Federation
Affiliation(s): Arabian Horse Association
Chief Officer(s):
Allan Ehrlick, President
Jane Whitwell, Vice-President, 905-887-9303
jane.lee.whitwell@sympatico.ca
Doris Woolner, Vice-President
woolhaven.maagic@sympatico.ca
Cyndi Tryon, Secretary
cyndi_tryon@yahoo.ca
Jill Barton, Treasurer, 613-386-3195
jill.barton613@gmail.com
Finances: *Funding Sources:* Membership fees; Fundraising
Membership: *Member Profile:* Arabian & Half-Arabian horse owners, breeders, & enthusiasts in eastern Canada
Activities: Providing networking opportunities for members; Coordinating, sponsoring, & participating in horse shows & competitive trail rides; Offering learning experiences about the Arabian horse breed
Awards:
• Freda Currie Scholarship Awards (Scholarship)
Eligibility: AHAEC members who are a minimum of 18 years of age at a certain date, & who will be attending a post-secondary institution *Amount:* $300 *Contact:* Janet Wojcik, wojcik@simcoe.net
• AHAEC Special Youth Award (Award)
To recognize a young Arabian enthusiasts for hard work in the association & the community *Amount:* $250; $150 *Contact:* Janet Wojcik, wojcik@simcoe.net
Publications:
• Arabian Horse Association of Eastern Canada Newsletter
Type: Newsletter; *Editor:* Jill Barton; *Price:* Free with membership in the Arabian Horse Association of Eastern Canada
Profile: Associaton information

Arbitration & Mediation Institute of Canada Inc.; Canadian Foundation for Dispute Resolution *See* ADR Institute of Canada

Arbitration & Mediation Institute of Nova Scotia *See* ADR Institute of Canada

Les Arbitres Maritimes Associés du Canada *See* The Association of Maritime Arbitrators of Canada

Arborfield Board of Trade
c/o Arborfield Meats, PO Box 236, Arborfield SK S0E 0A0
Tel: 306-769-8627
Overview: A small local organization
Chief Officer(s):
Earl Clarke, President
Bonnie Breadner, Secretary
Finances: *Annual Operating Budget:* Less than $50,000
30 volunteer(s)
Membership: 30; *Fees:* $10

Arborg Chamber of Commerce
PO Box 415, Arborg MB R0C 0A0
Tel: 204-376-2308
www.townofarborg.com
Overview: A small local organization
Chief Officer(s):
Ron Johnston, President, 204-376-5060 Ext. 3
rjohnston@puratone.com

Arbres Canada *See* Tree Canada Foundation

Arbutus Vocational Society; THEO BC *See* Open Door Group

ARC, AIDS Resource Centre, Okanagan & Region *See* Living Positive Resource Centre, Okanagan

ARC: Aînés et retraités de la communauté
Montréal QC
Tél: 514-730-8870
arcssc2@gmail.com
www.algi.qc.ca/asso/retraitesgais
www.facebook.com/arc.montreal
Aperçu: *Dimension:* petite; *Envergure:* locale
Mission: Groupement de personnes gaies aînées ou retraitées; activités sociales, culturelles ou sportives. Contactez Raymond B. au 514-529-7471 ou Nicholas au 514-343-1117
Membre: 175; *Montant de la cotisation:* 25$

L'arc-en-ciel littéraire
CP 180, Succ. C, Montréal QC H2L 4K1
arcenciellitteraire@yahoo.ca
arcenciellitteraire.site.voila.fr
Aperçu: *Dimension:* petite; *Envergure:* provinciale
Mission: Le seul regroupement d'écrivains GLBT au Québec; promouvoit la littérature gaie et des auteurs gais
Membre(s) du bureau directeur:
Réjean Roy, Président fondateur

ARCH Disability Law Centre
#110, 425 Bloor St. East, Toronto ON M4W 3R5
Tel: 416-482-8255; *Fax:* 416-482-2981
Toll-Free: 866-482-2724; *TTY:* 416-482-1254
archlib@lao.on.ca
www.archdisabilitylaw.ca
Previous Name: A Legal Resource Centre for Persons with Disabilities
Overview: A medium-sized provincial charitable organization founded in 1980
Mission: To defend & advance the equality rights of persons with disabilities; assisting individuals with disabilities to understand their rights & how to enforce them; working with groups representing people with disabilities throughout Ontario; representing in precedent setting cases where client cannot be represented appropriately by other legal services; summary advice & referral - lawyers who specialize in areas of law as they relate to disability provide free, confidential, basic legal advice & referral to other sources of assistance
Chief Officer(s):
Ivana Petricone, Executive Director
Finances: *Annual Operating Budget:* $500,000-$1.5 Million; *Funding Sources:* Major source of funding is the Clinic Funding Program of Legal Aid Ontario
Staff Member(s): 15; 20 volunteer(s)
Membership: 60 organizations
Activities: *Speaker Service:* Yes; *Library* Open to public

Archaeological Society of Alberta (ASA)
97 Eton Rd. West, Lethbridge AB T1K 4T9
Tel: 403-381-2655
www.arkyalberta.com
Overview: A medium-sized provincial charitable organization founded in 1975 overseen by Canadian Archaeological Association
Mission: To promote the regulations of the Alberta Historical Act & to disseminate archaeological information by means of publications & seminars
Chief Officer(s):
Janice Andreas, President
Jim McMurchy, Executive Sec.-Treas.
jnemc@telus.net
Christie Grekul, Provincial Coordinator
cgrekul@shaw.ca
Finances: *Annual Operating Budget:* Less than $50,000; *Funding Sources:* Dept. of Culture & Multiculturalism grants; government of Alberta
2 volunteer(s)
Membership: 300+; *Fees:* Schedule available
Activities: Annual seminar; publications; monitors archaeological sites
Publications:
• The Alberta Archaeological Review [a publication of the Archaeological Society of Alberta]
Editor: Dan Meyer

Bodo Archaeological Society
PO Box 1781, Provost AB T0B 2S0
Tel: 780-753-6353; *Fax:* 780-753-6352
bodo@bodoarchaeology.com
www.bodoarchaeology.com
Chief Officer(s):
Kim Larson, President
Beth Mann, Provincial Representative

Calgary Centre
PO Box 65123, Stn. North Hill, Calgary AB T2N 4T6
Tel: 403-239-3970
asacalgary@yahoo.com
Chief Officer(s):
Brian Vivian, President

Lethbridge Centre
c/o Jim McMurchy, 97 Eton Rd. West, Lethbridge AB T1K 4T9
Tel: 403-381-2655
Chief Officer(s):
Jim McMurchy, President
jnemc@telus.net
Shawn Bubel, Provincial Representative

Red Deer Centre
Chief Officer(s):
Jean Kaufman, President
jmkauf7@hotmail.com
Doug Shaw, Provincial Representative

Southeastern Centre
Tel: 403-526-3346
Chief Officer(s):
Karl Mueller, President
Janice Andreas, Vice-President & Prov. Rep.
banjomh1@telusplanet.net

Strathcona Centre
c/o George Chalut, 14716 - 65 St., Edmonton AB T5A 2E1
Tel: 780-431-2329
Chief Officer(s):
George Chalut, President
george.chalut@gov.ab.ca

Archaeological Society of British Columbia (ASBC)
PO Box 520, Stn. Bentall, Vancouver BC V6C 2N3
e-mail: info@asbc.bc.ca
www.asbc.bc.ca
Overview: A small provincial organization founded in 1966 overseen by Canadian Archaeological Association
Mission: To protect the archaeological heritage of British Columbia; to promote public understanding of the scientific approach to archaeology; to encourage government to preserve archaeological & pre-historic sites
Member of: Heritage Council of British Columbia
Affiliation(s): Canadian Archaeological Association
Finances: *Funding Sources:* Membership fees
Membership: *Fees:* $30 individual; $35 family; $23 student/senior
Activities: *Library* by appointment

L'Arche Atlantic Region
1381 Orangedale Rd., Orangedale NS B0E 2K0
Tel: 902-295-0050; *Fax:* 902-895-6349
office@larcheatlantic.ca
www.larcheatlantic.ca
www.facebook.com/pages/LArche-Atlantic-Region-Canada/3827 8664428
Overview: A medium-sized provincial charitable organization founded in 1983 overseen by L'Arche Canada
Mission: Regional office contact information for the Atlantic Canada communities of L'Arche
Member of: L'Arche International
Chief Officer(s):
Jenn Power, Regional Leader
Membership: 5 communities

L'Arche Antigonish
4 West St., Antigonish NS B2G 1R8
Tel: 902-863-5000; *Fax:* 902-863-8224
larche.antigonish@ns.sympatico.ca
www.larcheantigonish.org
Affliation(s): St. Francis Xavier University
Chief Officer(s):
Gus Leuschner, Community Leader

L'Arche Cape Breton
3 L'Arche Lane, Whycocomagh NS B0E 3M0
Tel: 902-756-3162; *Fax:* 902-756-3381
larchecb@larchecapebreton.org
www.larchecapebreton.org
www.facebook.com/pages/LArche-Cape-Breton-Community/1 28981923841453
www.youtube.com/user/larchecapebreton
Chief Officer(s):
Jenn Power, Community Leader

L'Arche Halifax
5512 Sullivan St., Halifax NS B3K 1X7
Tel: 902-407-5512; *Fax:* 902-405-9755
office@larchehalifax.org
www.larchehalifax.org
Chief Officer(s):
Rosaire Blais, Interim Community Leader

L'Arche Homefires
10 Gaspereau Ave., Wolfville NS B4P 2C2
Tel: 902-542-3520; *Fax:* 902-542-7686
office@larchehomefires.org
www.larchehomefires.org
Chief Officer(s):
Ingrid Blais, Community Leader
director@larchehomefires.org

L'Arche Saint-John
623 Lancaster Ave., Saint-John NB E2M 2M3
Tel: 506-672-6504; *Fax:* 506-672-6504
larchesaintjohn@nb.aibn.com
www.larchesaintjohn.org
Chief Officer(s):
Jocelyn Worster, Community Leader

L'Arche Canada
#300, 1280 Bernard Ave. West, Outremont QC H2V 1V9
Tel: 514-844-1661; *Fax:* 514-844-1960
office@larche.ca
www.larche.ca
Overview: A medium-sized national organization founded in 1969
Mission: To provide care & a sense of belonging for people who have developmental disabilities
Member of: L'Arche International
Finances: *Funding Sources:* Donations
Membership: 200 homes & day settings across Canada
Activities: Offering programs & publications to schools, professionals & the general public

L'Arche Foundation
#300, 10271 Yonge St., Richmond Hill ON L4C 3B5
Tel: 905-770-7696; *Fax:* 905-884-4819
foundation@larche.ca
www.larchefoundation.ca
www.facebook.com/larche.canada
Overview: A medium-sized national charitable organization overseen by L'Arche Canada
Mission: To raise money to support the activities of L'Arche Canada
Member of: L'Arche International
Chief Officer(s):
Kathy Adamo, Acting Executive Director
Dean Levitt, Chair
Finances: *Annual Operating Budget:* $1.5 Million-$3 Million; *Funding Sources:* Donations

L'Arche Ontario
186 Floyd Ave., Toronto ON M4J 2J1

Tel: 416-406-2869
larcheontario.org
www.facebook.com/larcheontario
Overview: A medium-sized provincial charitable organization overseen by L'Arche Canada
Mission: Regional office contact information for the Ontario communities of L'Arche
Member of: L'Arche International
Chief Officer(s):
John Guido, Regional Coordinator
johnguido@larche.ca
Membership: 9 communities

L'Arche Arnprior
#103, 16 Edward St., Arnprior ON K7S 3W4
Tel: 613-623-7323
office@larchearnprior.org
www.larche.ca/en/communities/arnprior
Chief Officer(s):
Noreen Lamorie, Community Leader

L'Arche Daybreak
11339 Yonge St., Richmond Hill ON L4S 1L1
Tel: 905-884-3454; *Fax:* 905-884-0584
office@larchedaybreak.com
www.larchedaybreak.com
www.facebook.com/larchedaybreak
Mission: L'Arche Daybreak is a non-denominational, inter-faith community of people with different intellectual capacity, social origin & culture. It is located on a 13-acre property & includes 8 homes, 5 vocational programs & a spiritual centre. Live-in assistants join the core members (people with intellecutal disabilities) in performing tasks of daily living.
Member of: L'Arche International
Chief Officer(s):
Carl MacMillan, Community Leader

L'Arche Hamilton
664 Main St. East, Hamilton ON L8M 1K2
Tel: 905-312-0162; *Fax:* 905-312-0165
office@larcheham.com
www.larche.ca/en/communities/hamilton
Chief Officer(s):
Jeff Gilbreath, Community Leader

L'Arche London
#2, 521 Nottinghill Rd., London ON N6K 4E8
e-mail: office@larchelondon.org
larchelondon.org
Chief Officer(s):
Toinette Parisio, Community Leader

L'Arche North Bay
102 First Ave. East, North Bay ON P1B 1J6
Tel: 705-474-0081; *Fax:* 705-497-3447
office_larchenorthbay@bellnet.ca
www.larchenorthbay.ca
www.facebook.com/pages/Friends-of-LArche-North-Bay/224163822118
Chief Officer(s):
Martina Getz, Community Leader

L'Arche Ottawa
11 Rossland Ave., Ottawa ON K2G 2K2
Tel: 613-228-7136; *Fax:* 613-228-8829
office@larcheottawa.org
www.larche.ca/en/communities/ottawa
Chief Officer(s):
Donna Rietschlin, Community Leader

L'Arche Stratford
PO Box 522, Stn. Main, Stratford ON N5A 6T7
Tel: 519-271-9751; *Fax:* 519-271-1861
info@larche.stratford.on.ca
www.larchestratford.ca
Chief Officer(s):
Marg Van Herk-Paradis, Community Leader
commleader@larche.stratford.on.ca

L'Arche Sudbury
1173 Rideau St., Sudbury ON P3A 3A5
Tel: 705-525-1015; *Fax:* 705-525-4448
larchesudbury@larchesudbury.org
www.larchesudbury.org
Chief Officer(s):
Jennifer McCauley, Community Leader
jennifer.mccauley@larchesudbury.org

L'Arche Toronto
186 Floyd Ave., Toronto ON M4J 2J1
Tel: 416-406-2869; *Fax:* 416-406-2539
office@larchetoronto.org
www.larchetoronto.org
www.facebook.com/larchetoronto
Chief Officer(s):
Amy Demoulin, Community Leader
demoulin@larchetoronto.org

L'Arche Québec

1280, rue Bernard Ouest, Outremont QC H2V 1V9
Tél: 514-849-0110
aaq@larche.ca
archequebec.ca
www.facebook.com/arche.quebec
twitter.com/archequebec
plus.google.com/+ArchequebecCa
Aperçu: *Dimension:* moyenne; *Envergure:* provinciale; Organisme sans but lucratif surveillé par L'Arche Canada
Mission: Régional d'information contacter le bureau pour les collectivités du Québec de L'Arche
Membre de: L'Arche International
Membre(s) du bureau directeur:
Sylvie Morin, Directrice régionale
smorin-aaq@larche.ca
Membre: 8 communities

L'Arche Agapè
19, rue Hanson, Gatineau QC J8Y 3M4
Tél: 819-770-2000; *Téléc:* 819-770-3907
arche.agape@bellnet.ca
www.larche.ca/en/communities/agape

L'Arche Amos
42, rue Principale Sud, Amos QC J9T 3A5
Tél: 819-732-1265; *Téléc:* 819-732-0367
courrier@larcheamos.org
www.larcheamos.org

L'Arche Beloeil
42, rue Bernard-Pilon, Beloeil QC J3G 1V2
Tél: 450-446-1061; *Téléc:* 450-446-2396
archebelo@qc.aira.com
www.larche.ca/en/communities/beloeil

L'Arche Joliette
Local 3-21, 144, rue St-Joseph, Beloeil QC J6E 5C4
Tél: 450-759-0408; *Téléc:* 450-759-0408
larchejoliette@bellnet.ca
www.larche.ca/en/communities/joliette

L'Arche l'Étoile
218, rue St-Sauveur, Québec QC G1N 4S1
Tél: 418-527-8839; *Téléc:* 418-527-8738
larcheletoile@videotron.ca
arche-quebec.ca
www.facebook.com/cdjetoile

L'Arche Le Printemps
1375, rue Principale, Saint-Malachie QC G0R 3N0
archeleprintemps@globetrotter.net
www.larche.ca/en/communities/le_printemps

L'Arche Mauricie
570, rue St-Paul, Trois-Rivières QC G9A 1H8
Tél: 819-373-8781; *Téléc:* 819-373-1910
archemauricie@qc.aira.com
www.larchemauricie.org
www.facebook.com/LARCHEMAURICIE

L'Arche Montréal
6105, rue Jogues, Montréal QC H4E 2W2
Tél: 514-761-7307; *Téléc:* 514-761-0823
larche-montreal@qc.aira.com
www.larche-montreal.org

L'Arche Western Region

307 - 57 Ave. SW, Calgary AB T2H 2T6
Tél: 403-571-0155; *Téléc:* 403-255-1354
Aperçu: *Dimension:* moyenne; *Envergure:* provinciale; Organisme sans but lucratif surveillé par L'Arche Canada
Mission: Regional office contact information for the communities of L'Arche in Western Canada
Membre de: L'Arche International
Membre(s) du bureau directeur:
Pal Favaro, Regional Coordinator
pfavaro@larchecalgary.org
Membre: 7 communities;

L'Arche Calgary
307, 57th Ave. SW, Calgary AB T2H 2T6
Tel: 403-571-0155; *Fax:* 403-255-1354
office@larchecalgary.org
www.larchecalgary.org
Membre(s) du bureau directeur:
Peggy Loescher, Community Leader Ext. 13
ploescher@larchecalgary.org

L'Arche Comox Valley
1001 B Fitzgerald Ave., Courtenay BC V9N 8k8
Tel: 250-871-6288; *Fax:* 250-334-8321
office@larchecomoxvalley.org
www.larchecomoxvalley.org
www.facebook.com/pages/LArche-Comox-Valley/491779427541959

L'Arche Edmonton
10310 - 56 St. NW, Edmonton AB T6A 2J2
Tel: 780-465-0618; *Fax:* 780-465-8091
edmoffice@larcheedmonton.org
www.larcheedmonton.org
Membre(s) du bureau directeur:
Pat Desnoyers, Executive Director & Community Leader Ext. 205
pdesnoyers@larcheedmonton.org

L'Arche Greater Vancouver
7401 Sussex Ave., Burnaby BC V5J 3V6
Tel: 604-435-9544
office@larchevancouver.org
www.larchevancouver.org
www.facebook.com/LArcheV
Member of: British Columbia Association for Community Living
Membre(s) du bureau directeur:
Denise Haskett, Executive Diretor & Community Leader, 604-435-9544 Ext. 27
dhaskett@larchevancouver.org

L'Arche Lethbridge
240, 12C St. North, Lethbridge AB T1H 2M7
Tel: 403-328-3735
larche@telusplanet.net
www.larchelethbridge.org
Membre(s) du bureau directeur:
Doug Wiebe, Community Leader

L'Arche Saskatoon
PO Box 23006, Saskatoon SK S7J 5H3
Tel: 306-262-7243
office@larchesaskatoon.org
www.larchesaskatoon.org
Membre(s) du bureau directeur:
Wyndham Thiessen, Community Leader
wthiessen@larchesaskatoon.org

L'Arche Winnipeg
118 Regent Ave. East, Winnipeg MB R2C 0C1
Tel: 204-237-0300; *Fax:* 204-237-0316
office@larchewinnipeg.org
www.larchewinnipeg.org
Membre(s) du bureau directeur:
Jim Lapp, Community Leader Ext. 6
jimlapp@larchewinnipeg.org

Archelaus Smith Historical Society

PO Box 190, Clarks Harbour NS B0W 1P0
Tel: 902-745-2642
www.archelaus.org
Overview: A small local charitable organization founded in 1970
Mission: To collect & display artifacts pertaining to the history of Cape Sable Island
Member of: Federation of the Nova Scotian Heritage
Chief Officer(s):
Blanche O'Connell, President
blancherossoconnell@hotmail.com
Finances: *Annual Operating Budget:* Less than $50,000
Staff Member(s): 3; 7 volunteer(s)
Membership: 20 individual; *Fees:* $10; *Member Profile:* Interest in local history
Activities: Operates a small museum; *Library* Open to public

Archers & Bowhunters Association of Manitoba (ABAM)

145 Pacific Ave., Winnipeg MB R3B 2Z6
Tel: 204-925-5697; *Fax:* 204-925-5792
www.abam.ca
www.facebook.com/164613433679984
Overview: A small provincial organization
Mission: To oversee the sports of archery & bowhunting in Manitoba.
Member of: Sport Manitoba
Chief Officer(s):
Ryan Van Berkel, Executive Director
execdirector@abam.ca
Activities: Archery development program; olympic program

Archers Association of Nova Scotia (AANS)
c/o Sport Nova Scotia, 5516 Spring Garden Rd., 4th Fl., Halifax NS B3J 1G6
www.aans.ca
Overview: A medium-sized provincial organization founded in 1967 overseen by Archery Canada Tir à l'Arc
Mission: To govern archery in Nova Scotia
Member of: Archery Canada Tir à l'Arc
Chief Officer(s):
William Currie, President, 902-852-4393
wcurrie@dal.ca
Finances: *Annual Operating Budget:* Less than $50,000
Membership: 22 clubs; 450 individuals; *Fees:* $35 individuals; $60 family; includes membership with the Federation of Canadian Archers (FCA)

Archery Association of New Brunswick (AANB)
141 Isington St., Moncton NB E1A 1Y7
Tel: 506-855-6169
archerynb.ca
Overview: A small provincial organization founded in 1969 overseen by Archery Canada Tir à l'Arc
Mission: To promote & encourage archery in New Brunswick
Member of: Archery Canada Tir à l'Arc
Chief Officer(s):
Julie Murphy, President
akt@nbnet.nb.ca
Maurice Levesque, Executive Director
mlevesqu@nbnet.nb.ca
Membership: 19 clubs; *Committees:* Executive

Archery Canada Tir à l'Arc
#108, 2255 St. Laurent Blvd., Ottawa ON K1G 4K3
Tel: 613-260-2113; *Fax:* 613-260-2114
archery@magma.ca
www.archerycanada.ca
www.facebook.com/ArcheryCanada
twitter.com/ArcheryCanada
Previous Name: Federation of Canadian Archers Inc.
Overview: A medium-sized national charitable organization founded in 1927
Mission: To promote & develop the sport of archery in a safe & ethical manner; To act as the official representative for archery to the federal government, & national & international sport organizations
Affiliation(s): World Archery Federation
Chief Officer(s):
Scott Ogilvie, Executive Director
Finances: *Funding Sources:* Government support
Membership: *Member Profile:* Archers
Activities: Promoting archery participation across Canada; Supporting high performance excellence in archery; Presenting awards; Providing a vehicle for communication across Canada; Registering competitions; Maintaining Canadian records; Selecting archers to represent Canada at international events; Coordinating research; Training coaches & officials across Canada; Obtaining support for paralympic programs; *Library*
Publications:
• Archery Canada Annual Report
Type: Yearbook; *Frequency:* Annually
Profile: Featuring the financial statements of the association

Architects Association of Prince Edward Island (AAPEI)
PO Box 1766, Charlottetown PE C1A 7N4
Tel: 902-566-3699; *Fax:* 902-566-1235
info@aapei.com
www.aapei.com
Overview: A small provincial organization
Mission: To increase awareness and understanding of architecture and its professional services.
Chief Officer(s):
Heather Mader, President
Finances: *Funding Sources:* Membership dues
Membership: 71
Activities: *Internships:* Yes

Architects' Association of New Brunswick (AANB) / Association des architectes du Nouveau-Brunswick
PO Box 5093, 36 Maple Ave., Sussex NB E4E 2N5
Tel: 506-433-5811; *Fax:* 506-432-1122
aanb@nb.aibn.com
www.aanb.org
Overview: A small provincial licensing organization founded in 1933
Mission: To govern & regulate persons in New Brunswick who offer architectural services; To advance & maintain the standards of architecture in New Brunswick
Chief Officer(s):
Christian Hébert, President
Fernand Daigie, Treasurer
John Leroux, Registrar
Finances: *Funding Sources:* Membership fees; Sponsorship
Membership: *Fees:* $56.50 students; $118.65 interns; $717.55 registered & reciprocal memberships; *Member Profile:* Students; Persons with a certificate of practice, or a temporary licence; Intern members; Registered members from New Brunswick; Reciprocal membership for persons outside New Brunswick; Retired members, who have left the practice of architecture
Activities: Offering a continuing education program to ensure a safe environment for the public
Publications:
• Intern Architect Program
Type: Manual; *Price:* Free with intern membership in the Architects' Association of New Brunswick

Architectural & Building Technologists Association of Manitoba Inc. (ABTAM)
1447 Waverley St., Winnipeg MB R3T 0P7
Tel: 204-956-4727
abtam.info@gmail.com
www.abtam.ca
Overview: A small provincial organization
Chief Officer(s):
Charlene Kroll, President
ckroll@smithcarter.com
Membership: *Fees:* Technician in training: $60; Certified Technician: $90

The Architectural Conservancy of Ontario (ACO)
#403, 10 Adelaide St. East, Toronto ON M5C 1J3
Tel: 416-367-8075; *Fax:* 416-367-8630
Toll-Free: 877-264-8937
manager@arconserv.ca
www.arconserv.ca
www.facebook.com/119712261437141
twitter.com/arconserve
Overview: A medium-sized provincial charitable organization founded in 1933
Mission: To preserve buildings & structures of architectural merit & places of natural beauty or interest
Affiliation(s): Ontario Heritage Alliance
Chief Officer(s):
Susan Ratcliffe, President
Rollo Myers, Manager
Finances: *Funding Sources:* Donations; government grants; membership dues; fundraising activities
Staff Member(s): 2
Activities: Technical consulting service for property owners, groups & municipalities; neighbourhood & garden tours; conferences & workshops; capital fundraising for repair & restoration work; architectural research; property acquisition

Architectural Glass & Metal Contractors Association (AGMCA)
619 Liverpool Rd., Pickering ON L1W 1R1
Tel: 905-420-7272; *Fax:* 905-420-7288
info@agmca.ca
www.agmca.ca
Overview: A small provincial licensing organization founded in 1979
Chief Officer(s):
Dennis Haatvedt, 416-259-2309, Fax: 416-259-4761
dhaatvedt@rogers.com
Membership: *Member Profile:* Contractors (Ontario) industrial; commercial; institutional

Architectural Heritage Society of Saskatchewan (AHSS)
202 - 1275 Broad St., Regina SK S4R 1Y2
Tel: 306-359-0933; *Fax:* 306-359-3899
sahs@sasktel.net
www.ahsk.ca
Overview: A small provincial organization founded in 1987
Mission: To promote, support & facilitate the preservation, conservation, restoration & reuse of distinct architectural & historical heritage properties (designated or potential) throughout the province, ensuring that our built heritage is maintained for present & future citizens to appreciate the contributions & craftsmanship of past generations; to enhance the current social, economic & environmental quality of life
Member of: Saskatchewan Council of Cultural Organizations; Canadian Heritage Network; National Preservation Trust
Finances: *Annual Operating Budget:* $50,000-$100,000; *Funding Sources:* Private & public sector funding
Staff Member(s): 1
Membership: 230; *Fees:* $20; *Committees:* Membership; Finance; Administration; Policy

Architectural Institute of British Columbia (AIBC)
#100, 440 Cambie St., Vancouver BC V6B 2N5
Tel: 604-683-8588; *Fax:* 604-683-8568
Toll-Free: 800-667-0753
info@aibc.ca
www.aibc.ca
Overview: A medium-sized provincial licensing organization founded in 1914
Mission: To regulate the profession of architecture in accordance with the Architects Act; to promote & increase the knowledge, skill & proficiency of its members in all things relating to the practice of architecture; to advance & maintain high standards of qualification & professional ethics; to promote public appreciation of architecture, allied arts, sciences & the professions
Member of: Committee of Canadian Architectural Councils
Affiliation(s): Royal Architectural Institute of Canada
Chief Officer(s):
Michael Ernest, Interim Executive Director, 604-683-8588 Ext. 304
mernest@aibc.ca
Catherine Bolter, Coordinator, Professional Development
Finances: *Annual Operating Budget:* $1.5 Million-$3 Million; *Funding Sources:* Membership dues; document sales; sponsorship
Staff Member(s): 17; 200 volunteer(s)
Membership: 1,310; *Fees:* $760; *Member Profile:* Architects registered to practice in BC; architectural technologists & interns; *Committees:* Act & Bylaw Review Task Force; Advisory Service; Architects in the Community; Architects in Schools; Architectural Technologist Admissions; Building Envelope Education Program; Building Envelope; Communications Board; Design Panel; Educational Facilities; Energy & Environment; Experience Review; Fees & Services; Health Care Facilities; Intern-Architect; Practice Board; Professional Conduct; Professional Development; Registration Board; Regulatory Coordination
Activities: Free architectural advisory; free architectural summer walking tours; *Internships:* Yes; *Rents Mailing List:* Yes; *Library:* Architecture Centre; Open to public by appointment
Awards:
• Lieutenant Governor of British Columbia Awards (Award)
• AIBC Innovation Awards (Award)
• Barbara Dalrymple Memorial Award for Community Service (Award)

Architectural Millworkers of Ontario *See* Architectural Woodwork Manufacturers Association of Canada - Ontario Chapter

Architectural Woodwork Manufacturers Association of British Columbia (AWMA-BC)
#101, 4238 Lozells Ave., Burnaby BC V5A 0C4
Tel: 604-298-3555; *Fax:* 604-298-3558
bc.awmac.org
Previous Name: Architectural Woodwork Manufacturers Association of Canada - British Columbia
Overview: A medium-sized provincial charitable organization founded in 1926 overseen by Architectural Woodwork Manufacturers Association of Canada
Mission: To advance the highest standards of education, quality workmanship, warranties & business practices in architectural woodwork manufacturing in British Columbia
Member of: Construction Specifications Canada
Chief Officer(s):
Mike Harskamp, President
Finances: *Annual Operating Budget:* $250,000-$500,000; *Funding Sources:* Membership dues; inspections
Staff Member(s): 2; 12 volunteer(s)
Membership: 70; *Fees:* Schedule available, please contact; *Member Profile:* Architectural woodworkers; suppliers; advisory; life members; *Committees:* Apprenticeship; Finance; GIS; Membership Services; Social Affairs
Activities: Lunch & learn for architectural & design firms; seminars; retreats; guarantee & inspection service program
Awards:
• Awards of Excellence in Quality & Service (Award)

Architectural Woodwork Manufacturers Association of Canada (AWMAC)
516 - 4 St. West, High River AB T1V 1B6
Tel: 403-652-7685; *Fax:* 403-652-7384
info@awmac.com
www.awmac.com
Overview: A medium-sized national organization founded in 1970
Mission: To foster & advance the interests of those who are engaged in or who are directly or indirectly connected with or affected by the production & installation of architectural woodwork; to endeavour to achieve a closer relationship & a better understanding among the various branches of the industry
Chief Officer(s):
Rick Koehn, Vice-President
Frank VanDonzel, Secretary/Manager
Myron Jonzon, President
Finances: *Funding Sources:* Association chapters
Membership: 112 individuals + 6 organizations

Architectural Woodwork Manufacturers Association of Canada - Atlantic
135 Driscoll Cres., Moncton NB E1E 4C8
e-mail: info@awmac-atlantic.ca
awmac-atlantic.ca
Also Known As: AWMAC-Atlantic
Overview: A medium-sized provincial organization overseen by Architectural Woodwork Manufacturers Association of Canada
Mission: AWMAC-Atlantic is an association of millwork manufacturers, suppliers, installers, designers and educators in the provinces of Atlantic Canada.
Chief Officer(s):
Drew Parks, President
president@awmac-atlantic.ca
Finances: *Annual Operating Budget:* Less than $50,000

Architectural Woodwork Manufacturers Association of Canada - British Columbia *See* Architectural Woodwork Manufacturers Association of British Columbia

Architectural Woodwork Manufacturers Association of Canada - Manitoba
1447 Waverly St., Winnipeg MB R3T 0P7
e-mail: manitoba@awmac.com
www.awmac.com
Also Known As: AWMAC-Manitoba
Overview: A medium-sized provincial organization overseen by Architectural Woodwork Manufacturers Association of Canada
Mission: To foster and advance the intersts of those who are engaged in or who are directly or indirectly connected with or affected by the production and installation of architectural woodwork; to endeavor to achieve a closer relationship and a better understanding among the various branches of the industry.
Chief Officer(s):
Curtis Popel, President
cpopel@mymts.net
Richard Wroblewski, Vice-President
richardw@rjmillwork.com
Nancy Carpenter, Secretary
Greg Pallone, Treasurer
info@parkavenuemillwork.com
Finances: *Annual Operating Budget:* Less than $50,000
Membership: Contractors - 11; Associates - 17; *Fees:* Contractors $850; Associates $350

Architectural Woodwork Manufacturers Association of Canada - Northern Alberta
c/o Margo Love, 12816 - 89 St. NW, Edmonton AB T5E 3J9
Tel: 780-937-8572
nab.awmac.com
Also Known As: AWMAC-Northern Alberta
Overview: A small local organization overseen by Architectural Woodwork Manufacturers Association of Canada
Chief Officer(s):
Dan Zacharko, President

Architectural Woodwork Manufacturers Association of Canada - Ontario Chapter (AWMAC-ON)
70 Leek Cres., Richmond Hill ON L4B 1H1
Tel: 416-499-4000; *Fax:* 416-499-8752
gis@awmacontario.com
www.awmacontario.com
Also Known As: AWMAC-Ontario
Previous Name: Architectural Millworkers of Ontario
Overview: A small provincial organization founded in 1966 overseen by Architectural Woodwork Manufacturers Association of Canada
Mission: To foster & advance the interests of those engaged in the production & installation of architectural woodwork in Ontario
Chief Officer(s):
Jeff Clemount, President, 905-677-9204, Fax: 905-677-7859
j_clermont@shaw.ca
Micah Gingrich, Secretary-Treasurer
Finances: *Annual Operating Budget:* Less than $50,000
Staff Member(s): 10; 35 volunteer(s)
Membership: 35 corporate; *Member Profile:* Manufacturers & suppliers in the architectural millwork industry; *Committees:* Convention; GIS; Membership

Architectural Woodwork Manufacturers Association of Canada - Québec
3875 Isabelle, Brossard QC J4Y 2R2
Tel: 514-346-2511
quebec@awmac.com
awmac-quebec.blogspot.com
Also Known As: AWMAC-Québec
Overview: A medium-sized provincial organization founded in 2009 overseen by Architectural Woodwork Manufacturers Association of Canada
Chief Officer(s):
Marc Pepin, President
pepin.marc@meublesbusch.com
Finances: *Annual Operating Budget:* Less than $50,000

Architectural Woodwork Manufacturers Association of Canada - Saskatchewan
PO Box 26032, Stn. Lawson Heights, Saskatoon SK S7K 8C1
Tel: 306-652-2704; *Fax:* 306-664-2552
awmac.sask@sasktel.net
www.awmac.com
Also Known As: AWMAC-Saskatchewan
Overview: A medium-sized provincial organization overseen by Architectural Woodwork Manufacturers Association of Canada
Mission: To foster and advance the interests of those who are engaged in or who are directly or indirectly connected with or affected by the production and installation of architectural woodwork; to endeavor to achieve a closer relationship and a better understanding among the various branches of the libirary.
Chief Officer(s):
Kerry DePape, President

Architectural Woodwork Manufacturers Association of Canada - Southern Alberta
#2A, 4803 Centre St. NW, Calgary AB T2E 2Z6
Tel: 403-264-5979; *Fax:* 403-286-9400
southernalberta@awmac.com
sab.awmac.com
Also Known As: AWMAC-Southern Alberta Chapter
Overview: A small local organization overseen by Architectural Woodwork Manufacturers Association of Canada
Mission: To advance the interests of those related to the production & installation of architectural woodwork; to foster a closer relationship among the various branches of the industry.
Chief Officer(s):
Rob Hodgins, President
Blaine Wickerson, Secretary
Larry White, AWNAC Director
Membership: 78; *Fees:* $150 design authority; $1000 associate; $1450 manufacturer
Activities: Awards for excellence in design

Archives Association of British Columbia (AABC)
#249, 34A-2755 Lougheed Hwy., Port Coquitlam BC V3B 5Y9
e-mail: info@aabc.ca
www.aabc.ca
www.facebook.com/576282679111715
Merged from: Association of British Columbia Archivists; British Columbia Archives Council
Overview: A small provincial charitable organization founded in 1990 overseen by Canadian Council of Archives
Mission: To act as the voice of archivists & archival institutions in British Columbia; To undertake projects that strengthen the archival network in the province; To preserve & promote access to British Columbia's documentary heritage
Member of: B.C. Heritage Federation
Chief Officer(s):
Caroline Posynick, President
aabc.president@aabc.ca
Sarah Jensen, Secretary
Sarah.Jensen@gov.bc.ca
Sarah Rpmkey, Treasurer
treasurer@aabc.ca
Finances: *Funding Sources:* Membership dues; National Archival Development Program; Donations
Membership: *Fees:* $30 retired, volunteer, & student; $72 associate institutional & individual; $96 sustaining; $120-$480 institutional (based on operating budget); *Member Profile:* Institutions approved by the AABC executive; Individuals who support the association's objectives; Students who are registered full-time in a community college or university program; *Committees:* Constitution & By-laws; Grants; Membership; Nominations & Elections; Programs; Finance; Communications
Activities: Providing educational opportunities & advisory services; Coordinating grant programs; Offering a job board; Building & maintaining the provincial catalogue; Providing networking opportunities for members; Offering access to a range of free conservation services for members; Developing & maintaining web resources created by the AABC; *Awareness Events:* Archive Week
Meetings/Conferences: • Archives Association of British Columbia Conference 2015, April, 2015, Coquitlam, BC
Scope: Provincial

Archives Association of Ontario (AAO) / L'Association des archives de l'Ontario
#202, 720 Spadina Ave., Toronto ON M5S 2T9
Tel: 647-343-3334
aao@aao-archivists.ca
aao-archivists.ca
www.linkedin.com/company/archives-association-of-ontario
www.facebook.com/ArchivesAssociationOfOntario
twitter.com/AAO_tweet
Merged from: Ontario Association of Archivists; Ontario Council of Archives
Overview: A medium-sized provincial organization founded in 1993
Mission: To encourage, through the establishment of networks, the public knowledge & appreciation of archives & their function; to promote the advancement of general education in the preservation of the cultural heritage & identity of the various regions of the province; to represent the interests of the archival community before the government of Ontario, local government & other provincial institutions of a public or private nature; to provide professional guidance & leadership through communication & cooperation with all persons, groups & associations interested in the preservation & use of records of the human experience in Ontario
Affliation(s): Ontario Heritage Foundation
Chief Officer(s):
Sarah Ferencz, President
Erika Heeson, Secretary
Membership: 300; *Fees:* Schedule available based on budget for institutions; $95 individual; $35 friend of AAO/retired; $30 student; *Member Profile:* Open to any person &/or organization interested in the preservation & use of historical records & the heritage of the province of Ontario & to those who are sympathetic to the aims of the association & who wish to further its work
Activities: Educational workshops (5-year part-time programs); *Awareness Events:* Archives Awareness Day, April 6
Meetings/Conferences: • 2015 Archives Association of Ontario Conference, May, 2015, London, ON
Scope: Provincial
Publications:
• Off The Record [a publication of the Archives Association of Ontario]
Type: Newsletter; *Frequency:* Quarterly
Profile: Activities of the AAO & its chapters; News relating to archives in Ontario; Technical & professional advice; Educational & employment opportunities;Information about grants

Durham Region Area Archives
Chief Officer(s):
Jennifer Weymark, Vice-Chair

Eastern Ontario Chapter (EOC)
ON
e-mail: aaoeast@gmail.com
aao-archivists.ca/eoc
www.facebook.com/pages/AAO-EastEst/209300655827038
aaoeast.blogspot.ca
Chief Officer(s):
John D. Lund, President

Northwestern Ontario Archivists' Association (NOAA)
Chief Officer(s):
Jeremy Mohr, Chair

Southwestern Ontario Chapter (SWOC)
Chief Officer(s):
Theresa M. Regnier, President
Toronto Area Archivists' Group (TAAG)
Chief Officer(s):
Jonathan Lofft, Chair

Archives Council of Prince Edward Island
PO Box 1000, Charlottetown PE C1A 7M4
e-mail: acpei@gov.pe.ca
www.archives.pe.ca
Overview: A small provincial organization founded in 1987 overseen by Canadian Council of Archives
Mission: To facilitate the development of the archival system in PEI; To make recommendations about the system's operation & financing; To develop & facilitate the implementation & management of programs to assist the archival community; To communicate archival needs & concerns to decision-makers, researchers & the general public
Chief Officer(s):
John Boylan, President, 902-368-4227, Fax: 902-368-6327
jeboylan@gov.pe.ca
Membership: 12 institutions

Archives du Centre acadien (ACA)
Université Sainte-Anne, 1695, Rte. 1, Pointe-de-l'Église, Pointe-de-l'Église NS B0W 1M0
Tél: 902-769-2114; *Téléc:* 902-769-0063
ccentre.acadien@usainteanne.ca
centreacadien.usainteanne.ca
Aperçu: *Dimension:* petite; *Envergure:* locale; Organisme sans but lucratif; fondée en 1972 surveillé par Université Sainte-Anne
Mission: Faire connaître et rayonner l'histoire et la culture des Acadiens de la Nouvelle-Écosse, et ce, premièrement au sein des provinces Maritimes et deuxièmement, auprès des autres collectivités et regroupements du Canada, des États-Unis et de l'Europe
Membre de: Council of Nova Scotia Archives
Membre(s) du bureau directeur:
Jean-Pierre Pichette
Finances: *Budget de fonctionnement annuel:* $100,000-$250,000
Membre(s) du personnel: 5
Activités: *Bibliothèque:* Bibliothèque du Centre acadien

Archives Society of Alberta (ASA)
#407, 10408 - 124 St. NW, Edmonton AB T5N 1R5
Tel: 780-424-2697; *Fax:* 780-425-1679
info@archivesalberta.org
www.archivesalberta.org
Merged from: Alberta Archives Council; Alberta Society of Archivists
Overview: A medium-sized provincial organization founded in 1993 overseen by Canadian Council of Archives
Mission: To provide professional leadership among persons engaged in practice of archival science; to promote development of archives & archivists in Alberta; to encourage cooperation of archivists & archives with all those interested in preservation & use of documents of human experience
Member of: Alberta Heritage Council
Chief Officer(s):
Debby Shoctor, President
jahsena@shaw.ca
Rene Georgopalis, Executive Director/Archives Advisor
reneg@archivesalberta.org
Finances: *Annual Operating Budget:* $100,000-$250,000; *Funding Sources:* Membership dues; Alberta Historical Resources Foundation
Staff Member(s): 2
Membership: 88 individual; 46 institutional; 16 honorary; 10 associate institutional; *Fees:* $50 individual; $50+ sustaining individual; $75-$400 institutional; *Committees:* Education; Grants; Communications; Membership; Newsletter
Activities: Education Program; *Awareness Events:* Archives week, September; *Internships:* Yes
Meetings/Conferences: • Archives Society of Alberta 2016 Biennial Conference, 2016, AB
Scope: Provincial

Arctic Bay Housing Association
PO Box 59, Arctic Bay NU X0A 0A0
Tel: 867-439-8833; *Fax:* 867-439-8245
Overview: A small local organization

Arctic Co-operatives Limited
1645 Inkster Blvd., Winnipeg MB R2X 2W7
Tel: 204-697-1625; *Fax:* 204-697-1880
info@ArcticCo-op.com
www.arcticco-op.com
Overview: A small provincial organization founded in 1972
Mission: To provide service to, & foster cooperation among the multi-purpose Cooperative businesses in Canada's North; to provide leadership & expertise; to develop & safeguard the ownership participation of Member Owners
Chief Officer(s):
Andy Morrison, Chief Executive Officer
AMorrison@Arctic.Coop
Rod Wilson, Vice-President, Member Management Services
Membership: 31 Co-ops
Nunavut Regional Office
PO Box 697, 1121 Mivvik St., Iqaluit NU X0A 0H0
Tel: 867-979-2448; *Fax:* 867-979-2535

Arctic Council
Foreign Affairs Canada, 125 Sussex Dr., Ottawa ON K1A 0G2
Tel: 613-995-1874; *Fax:* 613-644-1852
media@international.gc.ca
www.arctic-council.org
Mission: To operate as an intergovernmental forum; To address common concerns & challenges by the member states of Canada, Denmark (including Greenland & the Faroe Islands), Finland, Iceland, Norway, the Russian Federation, Sweden & the United States; To address environmental, social & economic issues; To carry out scientific work in five expert working groups, focusing on such issues as monitoring, assessing & preventing pollution in the Arctic, climate change, biodiversity conservation & sustainable use, emergency preparedness, & prevention; To meet every two years, with the secretariat rotating among the member states
Chief Officer(s):
Magnus Jóhannesson, Director of the Secretariat
magnus@arctic-council.org
Membership: *Member Profile:* Member states include Canada, Denmark (including Greenland & the Faroe Islands), Finland, Iceland, Norway, the Russian Federation, Sweden & the United States; Permananent participants are the Arctic Athabascan Council, the Aleut International Association, the Gwich'in Council International, the Inuit Circumpolar Council, the Russian Association of Indigenous Peoples of the North, and the Saami Council
Activities: Five working groups are as follows: Sustainable Development Working Group; Arctic Monitoring & Assessment Programme; Protection of the Marine Environment; Conservation of Arctic Flora & Fauna; Emergency, Prevention, Preparedness & Response

Arctic Institute of North America (AINA)
University of Calgary, 2500 University Dr. NW, Calgary AB T2N 1N4
Tel: 403-220-7515; *Fax:* 403-282-4609
arctic@ucalgary.ca
www.arctic.ucalgary.ca
www.facebook.com/ArcticInstituteofNorthAmerica
twitter.com/ASTISdatabase
Overview: A medium-sized local organization founded in 1945
Mission: To encourage & support scientific research pertaining to the polar regions
Member of: University of the Arctic; Canadian Heritage Information Network
Affiliation(s): The University of Alaska
Chief Officer(s):
Marybeth Murray, Executive Director, 403-220-7516
Mary Li, Institute Manager, 403-220-8373
mmli@ucalgary.ca
Finances: *Annual Operating Budget:* $500,000-$1.5 Million
Staff Member(s): 10; 5 volunteer(s)
Membership: 1,000+; *Fees:* $65 online; $90 print; $100 print & online
Activities: *Speaker Service:* Yes
Awards:
• Jennifer Robinson Memorial Scholarship (Scholarship)
For Master's or Ph.D. students; must submit a brief statement of research objectives*Deadline:* December 1 *Amount:* $5,000
• Grant-in-Aid (Grant)
Aimed at young investigators, to provide funding to support research.*Deadline:* February 1 *Amount:* $1,000
• Lorraine Allison Scholarship (Scholarship)
Granted on the basis of academic standing, commitment to northern Canadian research & benefit to Northerners; Master's or Ph.D. students from the Yukon & NWT are encouraged to apply*Deadline:* May 1 *Amount:* $2,000
Publications:
• Arctic
Type: Journal; *Editor:* Karen McCullough
Profile: A peer-reviewed journal about northern research (polar & subpolar regions)

Arctic Winter Games International Committee (AWGIC)
#400, 5201 - 50 Ave., Yellowknife NT X1A 3S9
Tel: 867-873-7245; *Fax:* 867-920-6467
www.awg.ca
Overview: A medium-sized local organization founded in 1968
Mission: To provide common ground for developing Northern athletes; to promote cultural & social exchanges among Northern regions of the continent
Chief Officer(s):
Gerry Thick, President
Wendell Shiffler, Vice-President
Lloyd Bentz, Secretary
Ian D. Legaree, Technical Director
Finances: *Annual Operating Budget:* $100,000-$250,000
9 volunteer(s)
Membership: 1-99
Activities: To invite & review bids from communities wanting to host the Games; to select sports for each set of Games & prepare the technical package of rules, categories, events, team composition, medals to be awarded, competition format; to oversee the preparations of a Host Society for the Games; *Library:* Arctic Winter Games Archives; by appointment

ArcticNet Inc.
Pavillon Alexandre-Vachon, Université Laval, #4081, 1045, av de la Médecine, Québec QC G1V 0A6
Tel: 418-656-5830; *Fax:* 418-656-2334
arcticnet@arcticnet.ulaval.ca
www.arcticnet.ulaval.ca
twitter.com/arcticnet
Overview: A medium-sized national organization founded in 2003
Mission: To study the impacts of climate change in the coastal Canadian Arctic; To engage Inuit organizations, northern communities, universities, research institutes, industry, government, & international agencies as partners in the scientific process
Member of: Network of Centres of Excellence of Canada
Chief Officer(s):
Martin Fortier, Executive Director, 418-656-5233
martin.fortier@arcticnet.ulaval.ca
Louis Fortier, Scientific Director, 418-656-5646
louis.fortier@bio.ulaval.ca
Finances: *Funding Sources:* Government of Canada, through the Networks of Centres of Excellence programs
Membership: 1-99; *Member Profile:* Educational institutions; *Committees:* Executive; Communications; Audit & Finance; Environmental Review; Industrial Partnership; Inuit Partnership; Research Management; Inuit Advisory
Activities: Conducting Integrated Regional Impact Studies on marine & terrestrial coastal ecosystems & societies in the Eastern Canadian Arctic, the Canadian High Arctic & in Hudson Bay; Disseminating knowledge; Facilitating networking opportunities
Meetings/Conferences: • Arctic Change 2015 Annual Scientific Meeting, 2015
Scope: National
Publications:
• ArcticNet Inc. Annual Report
Type: Yearbook; *Frequency:* Annually
• ArcticNet Newsletter
Type: Newsletter; *Frequency:*

Argentia Area Chamber of Commerce *See* Placentia Area Chamber of Commerce

ARK II
PO Box 687, Stn. Q, Toronto ON M4T 2N5
Tel: 416-536-2308
info@ark-ii.com
www.ark-ii.com
www.facebook.com/group.php?gid=2355091568
twitter.com/ARKII_TO
Also Known As: Animal Rights Kollective
Overview: A small local charitable organization
Mission: To promote & protect the rights of all animals & foster their individual liberties through direct action, political action, & public awareness campaigns
Membership: *Fees:* Annual: $10; Lifetime: $50

Activities: Anti-fur campaigns, Veganism/Vegetarianism promotion, Anti-animal experimentation campaigns

The Ark/Lunenburg County Association for the Specially Challenged

655 King St., Bridgewater NS B4V 1B5
Tel: 902-543-1189; *Fax:* 902-543-6041
theark@ns.sympatico.ca
Also Known As: The Ark/LCASC
Overview: A small local organization founded in 1963
Mission: To provide disabled adults with programs suited to their needs; to foster happiness through the creation of an environment that focusses on wellness & integration with the larger community
Member of: DIRECTIONS Council for Vocational Services Society
Chief Officer(s):
David Jodrie, Executive Director/Manager
Activities: Services such as antique refurbishment & furniture repair, document shredding, woodcrafts & hand-made braided rugs

Arkona & Area Historical Society

PO Box 83, Arkona ON N0M 1B0
Tel: 519-828-3582
Overview: A small local organization founded in 1976
Mission: To stimulate genealogical & historical research; to record the results of current research & all ongoing events of historical significance in our community; to preserve books, documents & records
Chief Officer(s):
Shirley Perriam, Acting President/Secretary
Finances: *Funding Sources:* Membership fees
Membership: 23; *Fees:* $2

ARMA Canada (ARMA)

c/o Yvonne Perry-White, 195 Summerlea Rd., Brampton ON L6T 4P6
Tel: 905-792-7099
www.armacanada.org
twitter.com/armacanada
Also Known As: Association for Information Management Professionals
Previous Name: Association of Records Managers & Administrators
Overview: A large national organization founded in 1955
Mission: ARMA is a not-for-profit, professional association focussed on managing records & information - both paper & electronic. It works to advance records & information management as a discipline & a profession, & organizes programs of research, education, training & networking.
Chief Officer(s):
Jolynne Guillet, Canadian Regional Manager
jolynne.guillet@gmail.com
Yvonne Perry-White, Sec.-Treas.
yvonne.perry-white@ironmountain.com
Dierdre Bradshaw, Coordinator, Western
dierdre.bradshaw@vancouver.ca
Katherine Chornoboy, Coordinator, Central
katherine@InfoAccessConsulting.com
Ann-Marie McIsaac, Coordinator, Eastern
ammcisaac@gov.pe.ca
Finances: *Annual Operating Budget:* $3 Million-$5 Million
Membership: 10,000; *Fees:* $175 Professional; $95 Associate; *Member Profile:* Records & information managers
Activities: *Speaker Service:* Yes; *Rents Mailing List:* Yes
Awards:
• Leadership Grant (Grant), ARMA Canada Region Grants
Eligibility: Must currently be on a chapter board, or will be holding a board position next year*Deadline:* February 28
Amount: $1,000 or less
• Membership Grant (Grant), ARMA Canada Region Grants
Awarded to the chapter that has the largest increase in membership from the previous year*Eligibility:* Chapter must have held at least two events in the past year, one of which must be related to education*Deadline:* June 28 *Amount:* $1,000
• Education Grant (Grant), ARMA Canada Region Grants
Awarded to an individual who is working towards the CRM designation, but who is not supported by his or her employer*Deadline:* February 28 & June 30 *Amount:* CRM test fee
• Publishing Grant (Grant), ARMA Canada Region Grants
Awarded to an individual who has been published in article or book form, & has mentioned ARMA in that publication*Eligibility:* Must be a member of ARMA*Deadline:* Feb. 28 & Sept. 30
Amount: $250
• Special Projects Grant (Grant), ARMA Canada Region Grants
Eligibility: Must meet one of the region's strategic initiatives*Deadline:* June 30 *Amount:* $5,000 or less
• Coordinator Leadership Grant (Grant), ARMA Canada Region Grants
Awarded to an individual who is supported & chosen by a Regional Coordinator; that person cannot have held a prior leadership position in a chapter*Eligibility:* Must have been an ARMA member for at least 2 years*Deadline:* February 28
Amount: Air & hotel costs
• Speaker Grant (Grant), ARMA Canada Region Grants
Eligibility: The chapter must have a demonstrated need*Deadline:* Sept. 30 & Dec. 31 *Amount:* $500
• Leadership (Academy) Grant (Grant), ARMA Canada Region Grants
Awarded to the chapter that has the most graduates from the Leadership Academy*Deadline:* June 30 *Amount:* $500
• Member Recognition Award (Award), ARMA Canada Awards
To recognize the contributions of ARMA members
• Honourary Membership Recognition (Award), ARMA Canada Awards
To honour ARMA members for their distinguished service to the records & information management profession
Meetings/Conferences: • ARMA 2015 Canada Region Conference & Expo, May, 2015, Westin Calgary, Calgary, AB
Scope: National
Contact Information: Conference Director: Ivan Saunders, E-Mail: isaunders@accesscomm.ca; URL: armacanadaconference.org

Calgary Chapter
PO Box 6624, Stn. D, Calgary AB T2P 2E4
e-mail: president@armacalgary.org
www.armacalgary.org
twitter.com/ARMACalgary
Chief Officer(s):
Miara Vinkle, President
president@armacalgary.org

Edmonton Chapter
PO Box 345, #21, 10405 Jasper Ave., Edmonton AB T5J 3S2
e-mail: communications@armaedmonton.com
www.armaedmonton.com
Chief Officer(s):
Nicholas Fonseca, President, 780-221-5782
president@armaedmonton.com

Halifax Chapter
PO Box 2381, Halifax NS B3J 3E4
e-mail: info@armahalifax.org
www.armahalifax.org
www.facebook.com/145838402163975
Chief Officer(s):
Courtney Bayne, President

Montréal Chapter
PO Box 337, Stn. B, Montréal QC H3B 3J7
www.armamontreal.org
www.linkedin.com/groups?gid=2368275
Chief Officer(s):
Stéphane Bourbonnière, Président
sbourbonniere@kpmg.ca

New Brunswick Chapter
PO Box 382, Stn. A, Fredericton NB E3B 4Z9
e-mail: info@nbarma.org
www.nbarma.org
www.facebook.com/554376717925865
Chief Officer(s):
June Gautreau, President, 506-444-6706

Newfoundland Chapter
PO Box 23061, Stn. Churchill Square, St. John's NL A1B 4J9
e-mail: secretary@armaterranova.org
www.armaterranova.org
twitter.com/armaterranova
Chief Officer(s):
Ryan Kelly, President
vicepresident@armaterranova.org
Virginia Connors, Secretary
secretary@armaterranova.org

Ottawa
PO Box 600, Stn. B, Ottawa ON K1P 5P7
www.armancr.ca
www.facebook.com/ARMANCROttawaChapter
twitter.com/ARMA_NCR
Chief Officer(s):
Trevor Banks, President
president@armancr.ca

Prince Edward Island Chapter
PO Box 22055, Stn. Charlottetown-Parkdale, Charlottetown PE C1A 9J2
e-mail: armapeichapter@gmail.com
www.armapei.org
Chief Officer(s):
Mark Demone, President, 902-438-4839
mxdemone@edu.pe.ca

Saskatchewan Chapter
SK
e-mail: info@armasask.org
www.armasaskatchewan.org
www.linkedin.com/pub/arma-international-saskatchewan-chapter/72/851/17
www.facebook.com/523397911057961
twitter.com/armaskchapter
Chief Officer(s):
Alyssa Daku, President
alyssa.daku@armasask.org

Southwestern Ontario Chapter
785 Petrolia Line, Corunna ON N0N 1G0
e-mail: publicity@armaswo.com
www.armaswo.ca
twitter.com/ARMASWO
Chief Officer(s):
Sue Pruliere, President
president@armaswo.ca

Toronto Chapter
PO Box 6587, Stn. A, Toronto ON M5W 1X4
www.armatoronto.on.ca
Chief Officer(s):
Adele Pantusa, President, 416-345-6310

Vancouver Chapter
#413, 280 Nelson St., Vancouver BC V6B 2E2
Toll-Free: 866-866-3332
info@armavancouver.org
vancouver.arma.org
www.linkedin.com/groups/ARMA-Vancouver-2018278
Chief Officer(s):
Pierrette Hodnett, President

Vancouver Island Chapter
PO Box 8005, Victoria BC V8W 3R7
www.armavi.org
www.linkedin.com/groups/ARMA-Vancouver-Island-5091338
Chief Officer(s):
Ken Oldenburger, President, 250-881-1237
koconsult@shaw.ca

Winnipeg Chapter
PO Box 1908, Stn. Main, Winnipeg MB R3R 3R2
e-mail: info@armawinnipeg.org
www.armawinnipeg.org
linkedin.com/company/arma-winnipeg-chapter-inc
twitter.com/armawinnipeg
Chief Officer(s):
Peggy Neal, President
president@armawinnipeg.org

Armateurs du Saint-Laurent (ASL) / St. Lawrence Shipoperators

#101, 271, rue de l'Estuaire, Québec QC G1K 8S8
Tél: 418-648-4378; *Téléc:* 418-649-6495
info@asl-sls.org
www.armateurs-du-st-laurent.org
Nom précédent: Association des armateurs du Saint-Laurent inc.; Association des opérateurs de navires du Saint-Laurent
Aperçu: *Dimension:* petite; *Envergure:* nationale; Organisme sans but lucratif; fondée en 1936
Mission: Voir à la défense et à la promotion des intérêts des armateurs canadiens actifs sur le fleuve Saint-Laurent, les Grands Lacs et dans l'Arctique canadien
Membre(s) du bureau directeur:
Martin Fournier, Directeur général
martin.fournier@asl-sls.org
Ariane Charette, Agente de communication et coordonnatrice
ariane.charette@asl-sls.org
Finances: *Budget de fonctionnement annuel:* $100,000-$250,000
Membre(s) du personnel: 2
Membre: 14 actifs; 85 associés; *Critères d'admissibilite:* Posséder ou opérer un navire canadien

Armed Forces Communications & Electronics Association (Canada)

Ottawa Chapter, #197, 1 Stratford Rd. East, Nepean ON K2H 1B9

Tel: 613-721-6031; *Fax:* 613-721-0092
www.afceaottawa.org
Also Known As: AFCEA Canada
Overview: A medium-sized national charitable organization founded in 1985
Mission: To provide a forum for information exchange & ethical government-industry dialogue with the Canadian communications, electronics, intelligence & information technology community in support of national security
Chief Officer(s):
Natalie Givans, Chair
Al Grasso, President and CEO
Patrick Miorin, Vice President
Finances: *Annual Operating Budget:* $100,000-$250,000; *Funding Sources:* Membership fees; proceeds of shows & seminars
Staff Member(s): 1; 50 volunteer(s)
Membership: 1,550; *Fees:* $35
Activities: Information exchange, professional development, education fund
Publications:
• Signal Magazine
Profile: Intelligence/technology news magazine

Armed Forces Pensioners'/Annuitants' Association of Canada (AFP/AAC) / Association canadienne des pensionnés et rentiers militaires (ACPRM)

PO Box 370, #3, 247 Barr St., Renfrew ON K7V 4A6
Tel: 613-432-9491; *Fax:* 613-432-6840
www.afpaac.ca
www.facebook.com/AFPAAC
twitter.com/AFPAAC
Overview: A small national organization
Mission: To promote & protect the rights & interests of members
Chief Officer(s):
Anthony E. Huntley, National Chair
Bonnie James, Executive Director
executivedirector@afpaac.ca
Membership: *Fees:* $15; *Member Profile:* Canadian Forces retirees & their survivors

Armenian Canadian Medical Association of Ontario (ACMAO)

2030 Victoria Park Ave., Toronto ON M1R 1V2
Tel: 416-443-9971; *Fax:* 416-443-8865
acmaoexecutive@gmail.com
www.acmao.ca
Overview: A small provincial charitable organization founded in 1988
Mission: The Armenian Canadian Medical Association of Ontario (ACMAO) is a multidisciplinary organization of health care professionals in Ontario
Chief Officer(s):
Avedis Bogosyan, President
Activities: Health education, humanitarian projects and academic endeavors.

Armenian Community Centre *See* Armenian Community Centre of Toronto

Armenian Community Centre of Toronto

45 Hallcrown Pl., Toronto ON M2J 4Y4
Tel: 416-491-2900; *Fax:* 416-491-2211
accmanager@armenian.ca
www.armenian.ca
Previous Name: Armenian Community Centre
Overview: A small local organization

Armenian General Benevolent Union (AGBU)

Toronto Chapter, 930 Progress Ave., Toronto ON M1G 3T5
Tel: 416-431-2428; *Fax:* 416-431-2510
agbutoronto@bellnet.ca
www.agbutoronto.ca
Overview: A small local charitable organization
Chief Officer(s):
Salpi Der Ghazarian, Executive Director
Finances: *Annual Operating Budget:* Less than $50,000
Activities: *Library* Open to public

Armenian Holy Apostolic Church - Canadian Diocese (AHAC)

615, av Stuart, Outremont QC H2V 3H2
Tel: 514-276-9479; *Fax:* 514-276-9960
adiocese@aol.com
www.armenianchurch.ca
www.facebook.com/239802236057531
www.youtube.com/user/CanArmChurch
Overview: A medium-sized national charitable organization founded in 1984
Mission: To preserve & promote Christian & national heritage; humanitarian aid to Armenia
Affliation(s): Canadian Council of Churches
Chief Officer(s):
Bagrat V. Galstanian, Primate
Silva Mangassarian, Executive Secretary
Finances: *Annual Operating Budget:* $250,000-$500,000; *Funding Sources:* Donations; parish dues
Staff Member(s): 6
Membership: Over 50,000; *Member Profile:* Baptized in the Armenian faith; *Committees:* Endowment Fund
Activities: Humanitarian Aid to Armenia; *Library* by appointment

Armenian Relief Society of Canada, Inc. (ARS Canada)

3401 Olivar-Asselin Rd., Montréal QC H4J 1L5
Tel: 514-333-1616
ars-canada@bellnet.ca
www.ars-canada.ca
Overview: A medium-sized international organization founded in 1990
Mission: To serve the humanitarian needs of the Armenian people everywhere, & preserves the cultural heritage & identity of the Armenian nation.
Affliation(s): Armenian Relief Society, Inc.
Chief Officer(s):
Seta Malkhassian, President
Annie Tachejian, Secretary
Finances: *Funding Sources:* Membership fees; donations
Membership: 1,250
Activities: Emergency relief & reconstruction; humanitarian assistance; education; social services; health care services; cultural support; summer camp; orphanage project;

Cambridge Chapter: "Meghri"
15 International Village Dr., Cambridge ON N1R 7M5
Tel: 519-623-4812
Chief Officer(s):
Houry Kassamanian, Chair

Hamilton Chapter: "Arev"
191 Barton St., Stoney Creek ON L8E 2K3
Tel: 905-662-3370
Chief Officer(s):
Nathalie Manoukian, Chair

Laval Chapter: "Shoushi"
397, boul des Prairies, Laval QC H7N 2W6
Tel: 450-688-7270
Chief Officer(s):
Zabel Gulian, Chair

Mississauga Chapter: "Arakasd"
3230 Ridgeleigh Hills, Mississauga ON L5M 6S6
Tel: 905-542-9621
Chief Officer(s):
Lilian Sarian, Chair

Montréal Chapter: "Sosse"
3401, rue Olivar-Asselin, Montréal QC H4J 1L5
Tel: 514-335-2222
Chief Officer(s):
Rita Ohanian, Chair

St. Catharines Chapter: "Araz"
156 Martindale Rd., St Catharines ON L2S 2X9
Tel: 905-682-6178
Chief Officer(s):
Salpi Mazmanian, Chair

Toronto Chapter: "Roubina"
45 Hallcrown Pl., Toronto ON M2J 4Y4
Tel: 416-491-2900
Chief Officer(s):
Iren Telemian, Chair

Vancouver Chapter: "Araz"
13780 Westminster Hwy., Richmond BC V6V 1A2
Tel: 604-276-9627
Chief Officer(s):
Clara Hagopian, Chair

Windsor Chapter: "Roubina"
702 Pierre St., Windsor ON N9A 2K5
Tel: 519-256-1082
Chief Officer(s):
Nalkranian Anie, Chair

Armstrong-Spallumcheen Chamber of Commerce

PO Box 118, 3550 Bridge St., Armstrong BC V0E 1B0
Tel: 250-546-8155; *Fax:* 250-546-8868
armstrong_chamber@telus.net
aschamber.com
pinterest.com/asvisitorcentre
Overview: A small local organization founded in 1951
Mission: To stimulate prosperity by promoting business & tourism in our community; to facilitate & enhance the region's quality of life, through the support of the people & business by working together
Member of: British Columbia Chamber of Commerce
Chief Officer(s):
Patti Noonan, Manager
Sandra Starke, President
Finances: *Annual Operating Budget:* $50,000-$100,000; *Funding Sources:* City/municipality grants; membership dues; government grant; fundraising
Staff Member(s): 1; 100 volunteer(s)
Membership: 140; *Fees:* Schedule available; *Member Profile:* Interest in the community well-being, success & promotion; *Committees:* Finance; Tourism; Government Affairs; Membership; Fundraising; Community Events; IPE Parade; Citizen of the Year; Business Awards; Community Revitalization
Activities: *Library:* Resource Centre; Open to public

Army Cadet League of Canada (ACLC) / Ligue des cadets de l'armée du Canada

66 Lisgar St., Ottawa ON K2P 0C1
Tel: 613-991-4348; *Fax:* 613-990-8701
Toll-Free: 877-276-9223
national@armycadetleague.ca
www.armycadetleague.ca
www.facebook.com/132804156762142
twitter.com/ArmyCadetLeague
Overview: A medium-sized international charitable organization founded in 1971
Mission: To provide accommodation, transportation, & financial support for the army cadets; To promote the corps & assists in recruitment
Affliation(s): Army Cadet Force Association, UK; Deutscher-Bundeswehr-Verband
Chief Officer(s):
Wayne Foster, President
Finances: *Funding Sources:* Government grant; donations
Staff Member(s): 3
Activities: *Library* Open to public

Alberta Branch
c/o 342 Somerset Pk. SW, Calgary AB T2Y 3G6
Fax: 403-454-3120
Toll-Free: 866-230-2769
secretary@armycadetleagueab.ca
www.armycadetleagueab.ca
www.facebook.com/home.php?#/group.php?gid=1928316997 7
Chief Officer(s):
Terry Martin, President, 403-201-2157, Fax: 403-266-1837
trooper5@shaw.ca

British Columbia Branch
4050 West 4th Ave., Vancouver BC V6R 1P6
Tel: 604-733-1980; *Fax:* 604-731-4988
Toll-Free: 877-733-1980
bcleague@telus.net
www.armycadetleague.bc.ca
www.facebook.com/group.php?gid=40484822720
Chief Officer(s):
Roger Prouse, Acting Executive Director

Ligue des cadets de l'armée du Canada (Québec)
CP 1000, Succ. Forces, Courcelette QC G0A 4Z0
Téléc: 418-844-7587
Ligne sans frais: 800-463-1584
info@lcac.qc.ca
www.liguecadetsarmee.qc.ca

Manitoba Branch
c/o 29 Harvest Lane, Winnipeg MB R2Y 0R3
www.armycadetsmb.ca
Chief Officer(s):
Sandy Will, President, 204-832-0501
aswill@mts.net

New Brunswick Branch
c/o 3245 Main St., Salisbury NB E4J 2K8
www.aclc-lcac-nb.net/e_index2.htm
Chief Officer(s):
Doug Sentell, Contact

Nova Scotia Branch
c/o 48 Tamarack Dr., Truro NS
www.armycadetleaguens.ca

Chief Officer(s):
Robert Baxter, President, 902-895-9992
Ontario Branch
#600, 4900 Yonge St., Toronto ON M2N 6B7
Fax: 416-635-2790
Toll-Free: 800-561-4786
www.armycadetleague.on.ca
Chief Officer(s):
Ray Smith, President
Marian MacDonald, Executive Director
Saskatchewan Branch
811 McCarthy Blvd. North, Regina SK S4X 2Y1
Tel: 306-543-8809; *Fax:* 306-949-6534
nonprofits.accesscomm.ca/aclofcsk
Chief Officer(s):
Gil Bellavance, President
Eddie Mathew, Executive Director
ematthew@accesscomm.ca
Yukon Branch
c/o Regional Cadet Support Unit, 45 Fireweed Dr., Whitehorse YT Y1A 5T8
Tel: 867-873-0700; *Fax:* 867-667-6780
cadet-info@forces.gc.ca
Chief Officer(s):
Russ LaChapelle, Contact, 867-393-3383
banzai@klondiker.com

Army, Navy & Air Force Veterans in Canada (ANAVETS) / Les Anciens combattants de l'armée, de la marine et des forces aériennes au Canada

#2, 6 Beechwood Ave., Ottawa ON K1L 8B4
Tel: 613-744-0222; *Fax:* 613-744-0208
anavets@storm.ca
www.anavets.ca
Overview: A medium-sized national organization founded in 1917
Mission: To unite veterans & their supporters to maintain entitlements & benefits; to provide a fraternal milieu for members by acquiring & operating clubs & homes; to strive to promote patriotism in Canada, & nurture cooperation & unity within the British Commonwealth
Chief Officer(s):
George Beaulieu, President
Deanna Fimrite, Secretary-Treasurer
Finances: *Annual Operating Budget:* $100,000-$250,000; *Funding Sources:* Membership dues
Staff Member(s): 2
Membership: 7 provincial commands + 85 units + 74 ladies auxiliaries + 40,000 individuals; *Member Profile:* Service in the Armed Forces; *Committees:* Finance; Publicity; Sports; Constitution; Awards; Resolutions; Membership
Activities: Service to the community & to the nation; *Awareness Events:* Remembrance Day; Veterans' Week
Publications:
• ANAVETS Shoulder to Shoulder
Type: Magazine; *Frequency:* Quarterly; *Accepts Advertising*; *Editor:* Richard Comeau
Alberta Provincial Command
c/o Command Secretary, 9120 - 97 St., Grande Prairie AB T8V 2B5
Tel: 780-532-3144; *Fax:* 780-532-1223
Chief Officer(s):
Carol Nolan, Provincial Secretary
British Columbia Provincial Command
#200, 951 - 8th Ave. East, Vancouver BC V5T 4L2
Tel: 604-874-8105; *Fax:* 604-874-0633
bcanavets@telus.net
Manitoba & Northwestern Ontario Provincial Command
3584 Portage Ave., Winnipeg MB R2Y 0V5
Tel: 204-896-9897; *Fax:* 204-896-8837
anavets@mts.net
Nova Scotia Provincial Command
422 Heelen St., New Waterford NS B1H 3C7
e-mail: anavetsnscommand@gmail.com
Ontario Provincial Command
1655 Weston Rd., Toronto ON M9N 1V2
Tel: 416-259-4145; *Fax:* 416-259-1677
anaf_opc@bellnet.ca
Québec Provincial Command
a/s 18, rue Massawippi, Sherbrooke QC J1M 1L2
Saskatchewan Provincial Command
c/o 510 Fairford St. East, Moose Jaw SK S6H 0E6
Tel: 306-692-4950; *Fax:* 306-692-4412

Chief Officer(s):
Marga Lafond, Provincial Secretary
margalafond@sasktel.net

Arrow Lakes Historical Society

PO Box 819, 92 - 7th Ave., Nakusp BC V0G 1R0
Tel: 250-265-0110
Other Communication: 250-265-3323
alhs1234@telus.net
www.alhs-archives.com
Overview: A small local charitable organization founded in 1984
Mission: To record the history of our area; To keep archives open & staffed; to provide archival information, school tours & educational information
Member of: British Columbia Historical Federation; British Columbia Archives & Records Service; Cultural Community of Nakusp & Area; Heritage Federation of South Eastern BC
Chief Officer(s):
Rosemarie Parent, President
Finances: *Annual Operating Budget:* Less than $50,000; *Funding Sources:* BC Gaming; book sales; research donor
20 volunteer(s)
Membership: 38; *Fees:* $5 annual, $50 lifetime; *Committees:* Archives; Publication
Activities: Centennial series (five) of history books, 9x12 hard-cover; History of Halcyon Hot Springs, "Halcyon, the Captains Paradise"; *Library:* Arrow Lakes Historical Society Archives
Publications:
• Caulkboot Riverdance
Type: Book; *Price:* $25
Profile: The history of logging & mills in the Arrow Lakes region
• Halycon - The Captain's Paradise
Price: $25
Profile: Book on the history of the Halycon Hot Springs

Arrowsmith Natural History Society ***See*** Arrowsmith Naturalists

Arrowsmith Naturalists

PO Box 1542, Parksville BC V9P 2H4
Tel: 250-752-0445
arrowsmithnats@gmail.com
www.arrowsmithnats.org
Previous Name: Arrowsmith Natural History Society
Overview: A small local organization founded in 1970
Mission: To further the understanding & conservation of nature
Member of: Federation of BC Naturalists
Affliation(s): B.C. Nature; Nature Canada
Chief Officer(s):
Sandra Gray, Contact, saninerrshaw.ca, 250-248-5565
Finances: *Annual Operating Budget:* Less than $50,000
Membership: 94; *Fees:* $25 individual; $35 family; $12 junior (up to 18); *Member Profile:* Parksville community members who are interested in nature & who enjoy monthly meetings & field trips; *Committees:* Botany; Birds; Outings
Meetings/Conferences: • Arrowsmith Naturalists Membership Meetings, Fourth Monday of every month, Knox United Church, Parskville, BC

Art Dealers Association of Canada Inc. (ADAC) / Association des marchands d'art du Canada

#393, 401 Richmond St. West, Toronto ON M5V 3A8
Tel: 416-934-1583; *Fax:* 866-280-9432
Toll-Free: 866-435-2322
info@ad-ac.ca
www.ad-ac.ca
www.facebook.com/ArtDealersAssociationofCanada
twitter.com/ADAC_AMAC
Overview: A small international organization founded in 1966
Mission: To promote & encourage public awareness of visual arts in Canada & abroad
Member of: CINOA
Affliation(s): AGAC; CMA
Chief Officer(s):
Elizabeth Edwards, Executive Director
Jeanette Langmann, President
Staff Member(s): 2
Membership: 80 art dealers; *Member Profile:* Commercial gallery must be operating bona fide exhibition space for minimum of 5 years & deal in original fine art
Activities: Provides qualified appraisals to public & cultural institutions for donation purposes; *Internships:* Yes; *Speaker Service:* Yes

Art Directors' Club of Toronto ***See*** The Advertising & Design Club of Canada

Arthritis Health Professions Association (AHPA)

912 Tegal Place, Newmarket ON L3X 1L3
Tel: 416-979-7228; *Fax:* 416-979-8366
chardv@yahoo.com
www.ahpa.ca
Overview: A small national charitable organization founded in 1982
Mission: To improve health care standards for people with rheumatic diseases through the promotion of education & support of research among members
Affliation(s): The Arthritis Society
Chief Officer(s):
Jennifer Burt, President
Finances: *Annual Operating Budget:* Less than $50,000
Staff Member(s): 1; 21 volunteer(s)
Membership: 185; *Fees:* $60; $15 students; *Member Profile:* Health professionals who work in the field of rheumatology; *Committees:* Fundraising; Conference; Research; Newsletter
Awards:
• Best Occupational Therapy Abstract (Award)
• Research Grant (Grant)
Amount: $5,000
• Best Scientific Abstract (Award)
Amount: $100
• Best Educational/Special Interest Abstract (Award)
Amount: $100

Arthritis Research Foundation

R. Fraser Elliott Bldg., 190 Elizabeth St., 5S-801, Toronto ON M5G 2C4
Tel: 416-340-4975; *Fax:* 416-340-3496
info@beatarthritis.ca
www.uhn.ca
Overview: A small local organization
Chief Officer(s):
David Prowten, Executive Director
David.Prowten@beatarthritis.ca
Joy Davidson, Director, Development
Joy.Davidson@beatarthritis.ca
Activities: *Awareness Events:* Day at the Races, September

Arthritis Society / Société de l'arthrite

#1700, 393 University Ave., Toronto ON M5G 1E6
Tel: 416-979-7228; *Fax:* 416-979-8366
Toll-Free: 800-321-1433
info@arthritis.ca
www.arthritis.ca
www.facebook.com/arthritissociety
twitter.com/arthritissoc
Previous Name: Canadian Arthritis & Rheumatism Society
Overview: A large national licensing charitable organization founded in 1948
Mission: To fund & promote arthritis research, programs & patient care. There are division offices in each province & nearly 1,000 community branches throughout Canada
Member of: Canadian Centre for Philanthropy; Coalition of National Voluntary Organizations
Affliation(s): The Bone & Joint Decade
Chief Officer(s):
Ken Ready, Chair
Janet Yale, President & CEO
Derek Rodrigues, CFO
Finances: *Annual Operating Budget:* Greater than $5 Million
Staff Member(s): 250; 1000 volunteer(s)
Membership: *Committees:* Executive; Nominating & Governance; Audit & Finance; Scientific Advisory; Medical Advisory
Activities: Joints in Motion, Arthritis Self-Management Program; *Awareness Events:* Joints in Motion; Walk to Fight Arthritis; *Speaker Service:* Yes
Publications:
• Impact eNewsletter [a publication of the Arthritis Society]
Type: Newsletter
Alberta/NWT Division
#300, 1301 - 8th St. SW, Calgary AB T2R 1B7
Tel: 403-228-2571; *Fax:* 403-229-4232
info@ab.arthritis.ca
www.arthritis.ca/ab
www.facebook.com/TheArthritisSocietyAlberta
Chief Officer(s):
Shirley Philips, Executive Director
British Columbia / Yukon Division
895 West 10 Ave., Vancouver BC V5Z 1L7
Tel: 604-714-5550; *Fax:* 604-714-5555
Toll-Free: 866-414-7766

info@bc.arthritis.ca
www.arthritis.ca/bc
Chief Officer(s):
Nancy Roper, Executive Director
Manitoba / Nunavut Division
#105, 386 Broadway Ave., Winnipeg MB R3C 3R6
Tel: 204-942-4892; *Fax:* 204-942-4894
Toll-Free: 800-321-1433
info@mb.arthritis.ca
www.arthritis.ca/mb
Chief Officer(s):
Carol Hiscock, Executive Director
New Brunswick Division
#107, 146 Main St., Fredericton NB E3A 1C8
Tel: 506-452-7191; *Fax:* 506-459-3925
info@nb.arthritis.ca
www.arthritis.ca/nb
Chief Officer(s):
Susan Tilley-Russell, Executive Director, Maritime Region
stilley-russell@ns.arthritis.ca
Newfoundland & Labrador Division
78 O'Leary Ave., St. John's NL A1B 2C7
Tel: 709-579-8190; *Fax:* 709-579-8191
Toll-Free: 800-321-1433
info@nl.arthritis.ca
www.arthritis.ca/nl
Chief Officer(s):
Susan Tilley-Russell, Executive Director, Maritime Region
Nova Scotia Division
#210, 3770 Kempt Rd., Halifax NS B3K 4X8
Tel: 902-429-7025; *Fax:* 902-423-6479
info@ns.arthritis.ca
www.arthritis.ca/ns
Chief Officer(s):
Susan Tilley-Russell, Executive Director, Maritime Region
stilley-russell@ns.arthritis.ca
Ontario Division
#1700, 393 University Ave., Toronto ON M5G 1E6
Tel: 416-979-7228; *Fax:* 416-979-8366
info@on.arthritis.ca
arthritis.ca/on
www.facebook.com/ArthritisSocietyON
twitter.com/arthritissocON
Chief Officer(s):
Trevor Roberts, Executive Director
Prince Edward Island Division
Leisure World Bldg., 95 Capital Dr., Charlottetown PE C1E 1E8
Tel: 902-628-2288; *Fax:* 902-628-6035
info@pe.arthritis.ca
www.arthritis.ca/pei
Chief Officer(s):
Susan Tilley-Russell, Executive Director, Maritime Region
stilley-russell@ns.arthritis.ca
Québec Division
#3120, 380, rue Saint-Antoine Ouest, Montréal QC H2Y 3X7
Tél: 514-846-8840; *Téléc:* 514-846-8999
info@qc.arthrite.ca
www.arthritis.ca/qc
Chief Officer(s):
Eric Amar, Directeur général
eamar@qc.arthritis.ca
Saskatchewan Division
#110, 2550 - 12th Ave., Regina SK S4P 3X1
Tel: 306-352-3312; *Fax:* 306-565-8731
info@sk.arthritis.ca
www.arthritis.ca/sk
Chief Officer(s):
Coni Evans, Executive Director

Arthur & District Chamber of Commerce
PO Box 519, 146 George St., Arthur ON N0G 1A0
Tel: 519-848-5603; *Fax:* 519-848-4030
achamber@wightman.ca
www.arthurchamber.ca
www.facebook.com/154989094563799
Overview: A small local organization founded in 1993
Mission: To promote & improve trade, commerce & the economic, civic & social welfare of the Village of Arthur & the surrounding area
Member of: Ontario Chamber of Commerce
Chief Officer(s):
Corey Bilton, President
Finances: *Annual Operating Budget:* Less than $50,000; *Funding Sources:* Membership dues; Flowerbag campaign
Staff Member(s): 1; 8 volunteer(s)
Membership: 65; *Fees:* $125
Activities: *Internships:* Yes

Artisan Bakers' Quality Alliance (ABQA)
10 Plastics Ave., Toronto ON M8Z 4B7
Tel: 905-945-6791; *Fax:* 905-945-5767
Overview: A small provincial organization founded in 2002
Chief Officer(s):
Shasha (Shaun) Navazesh, President
shasha@shashabread.com
Membership: *Fees:* $318

Artists in Healthcare Manitoba (AHM)
#2, 1325 Markham Rd., Winnipeg MB R3T 4J6
Tel: 204-999-0057
info@artistsinhealthcare.com
www.artistsinhealthcare.com
Overview: A small provincial charitable organization
Mission: To integrate the creative arts into health care as a way of introducing the healing effects of creative expression to help relieve depression
Membership: 100-499; *Fees:* $20

Artists in Stained Glass (AISG)
c/o Elizabeth Steinebach, PO Box 302, Parry Sound ON P2A 2X4
www.aisg.on.ca
Overview: A small local organization founded in 1975
Mission: To encourage the development of stained glass as a contemporary art form, in Ontario & throughout Canada.
Affiliation(s): Ontario Crafts Council
Chief Officer(s):
Elizabeth Steinebach, Contact
Robert Brown, President
robert@robertbrown.com
Membership: *Fees:* $40; *Member Profile:* glass crafters, architects, hobbyists, galleries, & anyone with an interest
Activities: Gallery shows; workshops; conferences

Artists' Union *Voir* Union des artistes

Arts & Crafts Training & Consultation Center *Voir* Centre de formation et de consultation en métiers d'art

The Arts & Letters Club (ALC)
14 Elm St., Toronto ON M5G 1G7
Tel: 416-597-0223; *Fax:* 416-597-9544
info@artsandlettersclub.ca
www.artsandlettersclub.ca
Also Known As: Arts & Letters Club of Toronto
Overview: A small local organization founded in 1908
Mission: To provide a milieu for the free & vigorous interchange of ideas & opinions
Chief Officer(s):
Fiona McKeown, Club Manager
manager@artsandlettersclub.ca
Scott James, Archivist
archives@artsandlettersclub.ca
Membership: *Fees:* Schedule available; *Committees:* Executive
Activities: New Year's Eve Gala; Robbie Burn's Night; Spring Show; *Library:* Archives; by appointment

Arts Connect TriCities Arts Council
2425 St. Johns St., Port Moody BC V3H 2B2
Tel: 604-931-8255; *Fax:* 604-524-4666
info@artsconnect.ca
www.artsconnect.ca
www.facebook.com/ArtsConnectBC
twitter.com/artsconnectbc
www.youtube.com/user/ArtsConnectBC
Also Known As: ArtsConnect
Previous Name: Coquitlam Area Fine Arts Council; ARC Arts Council
Overview: A small local charitable organization founded in 1969
Mission: To promote & advance the development of the arts & culture in school district #43 Anmore, Belcarra, Coquitlam, Port Coquitlam & Port Moody; To improve arts literacy; To advocate for the arts at municipal & provincial levels; To identify cultural needs & issues & to provide support services, resources & related activities
Member of: Assembly of BC Arts Councils; Alliance for Arts & Culture; Arts in Education Council
Affiliation(s): Canadian Conference of the Arts
Chief Officer(s):
Craig Townsend, President
Roger Loubert, Vice-President
Gabriela Caranfil, Director
Finances: *Annual Operating Budget:* $100,000-$250,000; *Funding Sources:* Provincial & municipal government; private; corporate sponsorship; membership dues
Staff Member(s): 2; 100 volunteer(s)
Membership: 2,000; *Fees:* $5 for 2 years; *Member Profile:* Artists & art groups; general public; municipalities; libraries; educational institutions; arts facilities; *Committees:* Executive; Marketing & Communication; Member Services; Finance; Fundraising; Programs
Activities: *Library* Open to public

Arts Council of Sault Ste Marie & District
#104A, 369 Queen St. East, Sault Ste Marie ON P6A 1Z4
Tel: 705-945-9756; *Fax:* 705-945-8665
arts@ssmarts.org
www.ssmarts.org
Overview: A medium-sized local charitable organization founded in 1978
Mission: To enhance quality of life in the community by promoting & fostering the arts; To encourage education in & appreciation of all aspects of the arts
Member of: Ontario Crafts Council; Ontario Chamber of Commerce; Community Arts Ontario
Affiliation(s): Canadian Conference of the Arts; Ontario Arts Council; Theatre Ontario; Visual Arts Ontario
Chief Officer(s):
Sandra Houston, Executive Director
Chris Rous, President
Finances: *Annual Operating Budget:* Less than $50,000; *Funding Sources:* Ontario Arts Council; Ministry of Culture & Communications; City of Sault Ste Marie; JP Bickell Foundation
Staff Member(s): 2; 50 volunteer(s)
Membership: 50 organizations; 200 individuals; *Fees:* $45 group; $20-$25 individual; *Member Profile:* Artists; *Committees:* Publicity; Membership; Information/Technology; Archives; Strategic Planning
Activities: *Awareness Events:* Art in the Park, Aug.; *Speaker Service:* Yes; *Library* Open to public

Arts Council of Surrey
13530 - 72 Ave., Surrey BC V3W 2P1
Tel: 604-594-2700; *Fax:* 604-585-2777
info@artscouncilofsurrey.ca
www.artscouncilofsurrey.ca
www.facebook.com/ArtsCouncilofSurrey
twitter.com/SurreyArts
Overview: A small local organization founded in 1964
Mission: To promote & foster performing, visual, literary arts in Surrey
Member of: Assembly of BC Arts Councils
Chief Officer(s):
Carol Girardi, President
Maxine Howchin, Vice-President
Finances: *Annual Operating Budget:* $50,000-$100,000; *Funding Sources:* Provincial government; City of Surrey; BC Gaming Commission; membership fees; activity fees; general donations
Staff Member(s): 1; 25 volunteer(s)
Membership: 36 group + 79 individual + 20 honorary + 2 patrons; *Fees:* $50 group; $25 individual; $35 business; *Committees:* Juried Art Exhibition; Grants; Scholarship; Choral Festival
Activities: Arts Forum; Annual Juried Art Exhibition; Air Canada Championship Art Exhibition; Choral Festival; Craft Markets; Literary Fair; Fraser Downs Art Competition; Parade of Lights; Surrey Festival of Dance
Awards:
• Outstanding Service to the Arts Award (Award)
• Scholarships (Scholarship)
Surrey youth aged 12-18 years of age participating in the creative, performing or visual arts
• Business & the Arts Award (Award)

Arts Council of the Central Okanagan
#203, 1905 Evergreen Ct., Kelowna BC V1Y 9L4
Tel: 250-861-4123
info@artsco.ca
www.artsco.ca
www.facebook.com/artsokanagan
Previous Name: Kelowna & District Arts Council
Overview: A small local charitable organization founded in 1966
Mission: To increase & broaden the opportunities for public enjoyment of & participation in cultural activities; To stimulate & encourage the development of cultural projects & activities; To

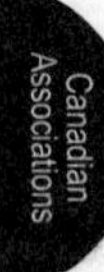

render service to all participating groups; to act as a clearinghouse for information on cultural projects & activities; To foster interest & pride in the cultural heritage of the community; To interpret the work of cultural groups to the community, enlist public interest & promote public understanding
Member of: Assembly of BC Arts Councils
Affliation(s): Kelowna Chamber of Commerce; Okanagan Mainline Region Arts Council; Canadian Conference of the Arts
Chief Officer(s):
Elke Lange, Executive Director
Cheryl Miller, President
Finances: *Funding Sources:* Provincial & municipal governments
Staff Member(s): 2
Membership: 300; *Fees:* $15 youth; $25 individual; $30 family; $50 group; $75 commercial; $100 patron
Activities: Artist registry; Honour in the Arts Program; courses in arts & cultural studies; Artscape Program; grants & fundraising; *Library* Open to public

Arts Council Windsor & Region (ACWR)

1942 Wyandotte St. East, Windsor ON N8Y 1E4
Tel: 519-252-6855; *Fax:* 519-252-6553
info@acwr.net
www.acwr.net
Overview: A medium-sized local organization founded in 1977
Mission: To enrich the quality of life for all by strengthening the arts & the community through leadership, education & promotion
Member of: Community Arts Ontario; Convention & Visitors Bureau of Windsor, Essex County & Pelee Island; Canadian Conference of the Arts; Visual Arts Ontario; Ontario Crafts Council
Chief Officer(s):
Sandra Houston, Executive Director
Finances: *Annual Operating Budget:* $100,000-$250,000; *Funding Sources:* Government; foundation; membership fees; fundraising initiatives
Staff Member(s): 2; 50 volunteer(s)
Membership: 350 individuals/organizations; *Fees:* $125 business; $45 non-profit organizations; $30 individual
Activities: "Articipate" ongoing campaign; "Chair-ity"; "Arts Vote"; "Arthouse"; Awards of Excellence in the Arts; *Library*

Arts Etobicoke

4893A Dundas St. West, Toronto ON M9A 1B2
Tel: 416-622-8731; *Fax:* 416-622-5782
info@artsetobicoke.com
www.artsetobicoke.com
www.facebook.com/123257461082590
twitter.com/artsetobicoke
Overview: A medium-sized local charitable organization founded in 1973
Mission: To engage all people in West Toronto with the arts & artists in their own community
Member of: Community Arts Ontario; Toronto Community Arts Alliance
Affliation(s): Partner & support groups & organizations such as MABELLEarts; Lakeshorte Arts; Expect Theatre; Milkweed Collective; Toronto District School Board; University of Toronto Centre for Community Partnerships; Art Gallery of Ontario; Humber River Shakespeare Company; City of Toronto; Ontario Trillium Foundation; TD Canada Trust; Ontario Arts Council
Chief Officer(s):
Dominique Sanguinetti, Co-Chair
Karl Sprogin, Co-Chair
Louise Garfield, Executive Director
Ruth Cumberbatch, Manager, Fundraising & Communications
Chantelle Grant, Office Manager
Shira Spector, Coordinator, Program & Outreach
Graham Curry, Director, Gallery
Staff Member(s): 6
Membership: 55 groups + 200 individuals; *Fees:* $45 individuals; $65 groups
Activities: Arts Discovery Program; Art Rental/Sales Program; Student Art Show; Annual Juried Art Show; Presidents' Legacy Scholarship Fund; *Library:* Resource Centre; by appointment

Arts Ottawa East-Est (AOE)

Shenkman Arts Centre, #260, 245 Centrum Blvd., Ottawa ON K1E 0A1
Tel: 613-580-2767; *Fax:* 613-580-2767
info@artsoe.ca
www.artsoe.ca
www.facebook.com/313002426106
twitter.com/AOEOttawa
Previous Name: Gloucester Arts Council
Overview: A medium-sized local charitable organization founded in 1987
Mission: To encourage & support the practice & appreciation of the arts in Ottawa
Member of: Community Arts Ontario; Gloucester Chamber of Commerce; Canadian Conference of the Arts
Affliation(s): Volunteer Ottawa
Chief Officer(s):
Christine Tremblay, Executive Director
christine@artsoe.ca
Finances: *Annual Operating Budget:* $100,000-$250,000; *Funding Sources:* Fundraising; corporate; government; earned revenue
Staff Member(s): 4; 450 volunteer(s)
Membership: 6,500; *Fees:* $25 individual; $15 student; $30 family; $75 not-for-profit organizartion; up to $50 individual patrons; *Committees:* Planning; Advocacy; Membership; Volunteer Development & Fundraising; Nominations
Activities: FestivArts; Arts Party; Luncheon for the Arts; Write-on-Workshop; professional development workshops; *Library* Open to public

Arts Richmond Hill

PO Box 139, 10520 Yonge St., Richmond Hill ON L4C 3C7
Tel: 905-508-0789; *Fax:* 888-380-2268
info@artsrichmondhill.org
artsrichmondhill.org
www.facebook.com/pages/ARTS-Richmond-Hill/277643925640177
Also Known As: Art Council of Richmond Hill
Previous Name: Richmond Hill Arts Council
Overview: A small local organization founded in 1986
Mission: To foster & coordinate activities of groups, organizations & individuals engaged in the arts; to encourage education & appreciation for the arts; to provide an information service for the public; to provide forum for exchange of information; to act as liaison between cultural & other art organizations & government organizations
Affliation(s): Community Arts Ontario
Chief Officer(s):
Emmanuel Abara, President
Finances: *Annual Operating Budget:* Less than $50,000; *Funding Sources:* Membership; fundraising; grants
Staff Member(s): 1; 30 volunteer(s)
Membership: 1 institutional + 2 honorary + 30 individual + 30 arts groups; *Fees:* Schedule available; *Member Profile:* Interest/participation in any of the arts; *Committees:* Events; Publicity; Executive; Membership; Nomination
Activities: Music Festival; Heritage Day; Festival of Lights Concert; Workshops; *Rents Mailing List:* Yes

Arts Scarborough *See* Scarborough Arts Council

Arusha Centre Society

The Old "Y" Bldg., #106, 223 - 12 Ave. SW, Calgary AB T2R 0G6
Tel: 403-270-3200; *Fax:* 403-270-8832
arusha@arusha.org
www.arusha.org
www.facebook.com/ArushaCentre
twitter.com/ArushaCentre
Overview: A small local charitable organization founded in 1972
Mission: To provide opportunities for, & remove barriers to, individual & community participation, self-determination & empowerment, especially for those who have been marginalized; To acknowledge, respect & actively value diversity, based on the belief in inherent human dignity; To challenge unjust internal & external assumptions & structures & work toward socially just alternatives; To connect social, economic & ecological issues, both locally & globally; to create a meaningful partnership that fosters social justice internally & externally
Member of: Volunteer Centre of Calgary; Parklands Institute
Chief Officer(s):
Sharon Stevens, Info-activee Coordinator
Finances: *Annual Operating Budget:* $250,000-$500,000; *Funding Sources:* Federal & provincial government; donations; United Way
Staff Member(s): 7; 75 volunteer(s)
Membership: 225; *Fees:* $10; *Member Profile:* Calgary community; *Committees:* Finance; Fundraising; Membership; Programming; Marketing
Activities: *Library:* Resource Centre; Open to public

ARZA-Canada: The Zionist Voice of the Canadian Reform Movement

#301, 3845 Bathurst St., Toronto ON M3H 3N2
Tel: 416-630-0375; *Fax:* 416-630-5089
Toll-Free: 800-560-8242
info@arzacanada.org
www.arzacanada.org
Also Known As: AZRA-Canada
Overview: A medium-sized national organization
Member of: ARZA-World Union-North America
Affliation(s): Canadian Zionist Federation
Chief Officer(s):
Les Rothschild, President
les@arzacanada.org
Cheryl Englander, Vice-President
Dorothy Millman, Vice-President
Miriam Pearlman, Vice-President
Jeff Denaburg, Treasurer
jeff.denaburg@arzacanada.org
Finances: *Funding Sources:* Membership dues; Donations
Membership: 6,000 individual; *Fees:* $36 Household; $18 Adult; $5 Student

ASEAN-Canada Business Council *See* Southeast Asia-Canada Business Council

Ashcroft & Area Food Bank

PO Box 603, 601 Bancroft St., Ashcroft BC V0K 1A0
Tel: 250-453-9656; *Fax:* 250-453-2034
Overview: A small local organization overseen by Food Banks British Columbia
Member of: Food Banks British Columbia
Chief Officer(s):
Denise Fiddick, Contact
scelizfry@telus.net

Ashcroft & District Chamber of Commerce

PO Box 741, Ashcroft BC V0R 1B0
e-mail: ashcroftchamber@hotmail.com
www.ashcroftbc.ca/chamber_of_commerce
Overview: A small local organization
Finances: *Funding Sources:* Membership dues

Ashern & District Chamber of Commerce

PO Box 582, Ashern MB R0C 0E0
Tel: 204-768-3500
secretary@ashern.ca
www.ashern.ca
Overview: A small local organization
Mission: To encourage business growth & economic development; To promote Ashern outside the local area
Member of: Manitoba Chamber of Commerce
Chief Officer(s):
Edith Peterson, President
president@ashern.ca
Finances: *Annual Operating Budget:* Less than $50,000
Staff Member(s): 1
Membership: 74; *Fees:* $75 business; $25 individual; *Member Profile:* Small, independent business; *Committees:* Ashern Trade Fest; Ashern Midnight Madness
Activities: Country Trade Fest; Midnight Madness; Ashern Welcome Wagon; Chamber Golf Tournament

Ashmont & District Agricultural Society

PO Box 23, Ashmont AB T0A 0C0
Tel: 780-726-3897
Overview: A small local organization founded in 1984
Chief Officer(s):
Jenny Bespalko, Contact
jbsbespalko@yahoo.com
Finances: *Funding Sources:* Fundraising; donations
30 volunteer(s)
Membership: 60; *Fees:* $1; *Committees:* Economic Development; Agricultural Services; Aspen Grove Seniors Lodge; Agri-Plex Management; Heritage Day; Minor Sports; Continuing Education; Government Liaison

Asia Pacific Foundation of Canada (APFC) / Fondation Asie Pacifique du Canada

#220, 890 West Pender St., Vancouver BC V6C 1J9
Tel: 604-684-5986; *Fax:* 604-681-1370
info@asiapacific.ca
www.asiapacific.ca
www.facebook.com/asiapacificfoundationofcanada
twitter.com/AsiaPacificFdn
Also Known As: APF Canada
Overview: A medium-sized international organization founded in 1984
Mission: Independent think tank on Canada's relations with Asia; to bring together people & knowledge to provide the most

current & comprehensive research, analysis & information on Canada's transpacific relations; to promote dialogue on economic, security, political & social issues, helping to influence public policy & foster informed decision-making in the Canadian public, private & non-governmental sectors
Chief Officer(s):
Yuen Pau Woo, President & CEO
president@asiapacific.ca
Jill Price, Executive Director
jill.price@asiapacific.ca
Finances: *Annual Operating Budget:* $1.5 Million-$3 Million; *Funding Sources:* Federal & provincial government
Staff Member(s): 30
Activities: Business; media; education; public policy; research; *Internships:* Yes

Asian Community AIDS Services (ACAS)

#410, 260 Spadina Ave., Toronto ON M5T 2E4
Tel: 416-963-4300; *Fax:* 416-963-4371
Toll-Free: 877-630-2227
info@acas.org
www.acas.org
www.facebook.com/AsianCommunityAIDSServices
twitter.com/ACAStoronto
www.youtube.com/user/acasorg; acasconversations.tumblr.com
Overview: A small local charitable organization founded in 1994 overseen by Canadian AIDS Society
Mission: To provide education, prevention & support services on HIV/AIDS to the East & Southeast Asian communities; programs are based on a proactive & holistic approach to HIV/AIDS & are provided in a collaborative, empowering & non-discriminatory manner
Member of: Ontario AIDS Network
Chief Officer(s):
Andre Goh, Chair
Noulmook Sutdhibhasilp, Executive Director, 416-963-4300 Ext. 227
ed@acas.org
Finances: *Annual Operating Budget:* $250,000-$500,000; *Funding Sources:* City of Toronto; Ontario Ministry of Health; Health Canada
Staff Member(s): 6; 70 volunteer(s)
Membership: 1-99; *Member Profile:* People living with HIV/AIDS & program volunteers; *Committees:* Support Program; Education Program; Volunteer Program; Fundraising; Research
Activities: Programs for men, women, & youth; Support Program; Asian Migrant Farmworkers' Research Project; *Awareness Events:* Scotiabank Toronto Waterfront Marathon, Oct.; *Library* Open to public

Asian Heritage Society of Manitoba

MB
Tel: 204-488-8059
www.asianheritagemanitoba.ca
Overview: A small provincial organization
Mission: To bring together members of the Asian Canadian communities in Manitoba; To share the arts, culture, traditions, cuisine, & faiths of Asian Canadians with Manitobans; To reduce racism towards Asian Canadians
Chief Officer(s):
Art Miki, President
Membership: *Member Profile:* Representatives from Chinese, Japanese, Korean, Indian, Vietnamese, Filipino, & Indo-Chinese communities in Manitoba
Activities: Creating partnerships with Asian Canadian groups; Raising public awareness & fostering understanding of Asian cultures; Sharing knowledge of Asian medicinal & meditative traditions; Highlighting the contributions of Asian Canadians in Manitoba; Planning member meeetings; Facilitating networking opportunities; Encouraging participation by Asian Canadian youth; Organizing events, such as the young Asian entrepreneur forum, Asian writers showcase, Asian storytelling, & the Asian Canadian Festival of the Forks; *Awareness Events:* Asian Heritage Month, May

ASK! Community Information Centre (LAMP)

185 Fifth St., Etobicoke ON M8V 2Z5
Tel: 416-252-6471; *Fax:* 416-252-4474; *TTY:* 416-252-1322
www.lampchc.org
www.facebook.com/group.php?gid=111947859235
Previous Name: YMCA ASK! & YMCA ASCC
Overview: A small local organization founded in 1969 overseen by InformOntario
Mission: To offer a range of programs & services to support residents & workers of southern Etobicoke (South/West Toronto); To offer community information, referral, legal advice, immigrant program, & refugee support
Member of: Federation of Community Information Centres of Toronto; Lakeshore Area Multi-Servcies Program
Chief Officer(s):
Russ Ford, Executive Director
Finances: *Annual Operating Budget:* $100,000-$250,000; *Funding Sources:* Municipal, Federal & Regional governments; United Way of Greater Toronto
Staff Member(s): 5; 38 volunteer(s)
Membership: *Committees:* Advisory; Publicity; Promotions
Activities: Medical and dental services; children and youth programs; family programs; community support services

ASM International - Calgary Chapter

PO Box 40411, Stn. Highfield, Calgary AB T2G 5G7
www.asminternational.org/portal/site/calgary
www.facebook.com/AsmInternationalCalgaryChapter
Overview: A small local organization founded in 1999
Chief Officer(s):
Sammy Tang, Vice Chair & Co-Treasurer
smtang@telus.net
Awards:
- M. Brian Ives Lectureship Award
- Best Student Paper
- 5 Star Quality Performance Award

Asociación Venezolana de Estudios Canadienses *See* Venezuelan Association for Canadian Studies

Asparagus Farmers of Ontario (AFO)

PO Box 587, 1283 Blueline Rd., Simcoe ON N3Y 4N5
Tel: 519-426-7529; *Fax:* 519-426-9087
info@asparagus.on.ca
asparagus.on.ca
Previous Name: Ontario Asparagus Growers' Marketing Board
Overview: A large provincial organization
Chief Officer(s):
Marvin Karges, Executive Director
marvin.karges@asparagus.on.ca

ASPECT

975 Alston St., Victoria BC V9A 3S5
Tel: 250-382-9675; *Fax:* 250-382-9677
Toll-Free: 888-287-4957
info@aspect.bc.ca
www.aspect.bc.ca
www.facebook.com/aspect.bc.ca
twitter.com/aspectbc
Also Known As: The Association of Service Providers for Employability & Career Training
Overview: A small provincial organization
Mission: ASPECT is an association of community-based trainers that represents and promotes the interests and activities of members to strengthen their capacity to provide services to people with barriers to employment.
Chief Officer(s):
Norma Strachan, Chief Executive Officer
nstrashan@aspect.bc.ca
Staff Member(s): 5
Membership: 175 agencies; *Fees:* $100 satellite; $200 associate; $300 voting

Aspergers Society of Ontario

#231, 3219 Yonge St., Toronto ON M4N 3S1
Tel: 416-651-4037; *Fax:* 416-651-1935
info@aspergers.ca
www.aspergers.ca
www.facebook.com/AspergerOntario
twitter.com/aspergerontario
Overview: A small provincial charitable organization founded in 2000
Mission: To improve public & professional awareness & understanding of Aspergers Syndrome; To promote & support research & the development of diagnoses, treatment, & education programs for those with Aspergers Syndrome; To provide information & referrals for those interested in Aspergers Syndrome; To initiate programs & services which respond to the needs of those affected by Aspergers Syndrome
Chief Officer(s):
Margot Nelles, Executive Director
Finances: *Funding Sources:* Donations; Membership dues; SickKids Foundation; Centre for Addiction & Mental Health
Staff Member(s): 12
Membership: *Fees:* $30; $50 family; $250 corporate/organizational
Activities: Infoline; Adult social group

ASPHME

#301, 2271, boul Fernand-Lafontaine, Longueuil QC J4G 2R7
Tél: 450-442-7763; *Téléc:* 450-442-2332
info@asphme.org
www.asphme.org
Nom précédent: Association paritaire pour la santé et la sécurité du travail - Habillement
Aperçu: *Dimension:* grande; *Envergure:* provinciale; Organisme sans but lucratif; fondée en 1986
Mission: To prevent work-related injuries in the apparel sector. Full name: Association sectorielle paritaire pour la santé et la sécurité du travail du secteur de la fabrication de produits en métal, de la fabrication de produits électriques et des industries de l'habillement
Membre(s) du bureau directeur:
Normand Durocher, Coprésident
Denis Dufour, Coprésident
Alain Plourde, Directeur général
Finances: *Budget de fonctionnement annuel:* $500,000-$1.5 Million
Membre(s) du personnel: 7
Activités: *Stagiaires:* Oui; *Service de conférenciers:* Oui

Québec
#570, 979, av de Bourgogne, Québec QC G1W 2L4
Tel: 418-652-7682; *Fax:* 418-652-9348

Assaulted Women's Helpline (AWH)

PO Box 369, Stn. B, Toronto ON M5T 2E2
Tel: 416-364-4144; *Fax:* 416-364-0563
Toll-Free: 888-364-1210; *TTY:* 866-863-7868; *Crisis Hot-Line:* 866-863-0511
admin@awhl.org
www.awhl.org
www.facebook.com/AssaultedWomensHelpline
twitter.com/awhl
Overview: A medium-sized local charitable organization founded in 1985
Mission: To provide 24-hour crisis counselling, referral, & an information telephone line, province-wide
Affliation(s): Ontario Association of Interval & Transition Houses; Ontario Network of Sexual Assault/Domestic Treatment Centres; Community Legal Education Ontario; Metropolitan Action Committee on Violence Against Women & Children; Family Law Education for Women; Challenge Sexual Violence; Springtide Resources; Ontario Coalition of Rape Crisis Centres; Women Abuse Council of Toronto;
Chief Officer(s):
Huong Pham, Executive Director
Beth Jordan, Director, Programs & Services
Finances: *Annual Operating Budget:* $1.5 Million-$3 Million; *Funding Sources:* Provincial government
Staff Member(s): 22; 20 volunteer(s)
Membership: 30 institutional; *Fees:* $15 institutional
Activities: *Awareness Events:* Gala, annual (April)
Meetings/Conferences: • Assaulted Women's Helpline Training Programs for the Workplace, 2015
Scope: Local
Description: Customized workshops on topics such as working with abused women, developing non-discriminatory policies, EAP training on woman abuse, cross-cultural perspectives on violence against women, anti-violence initiatives, intervention strategies, & diversity training
Contact Information: Assaulted Women's Helpline, Training, Resource, & Outreach Department, Toll-Free Phone: 1-888-364-1210
• Assaulted Women's Helpline Training Programs for the Non-Profit Sector, 2015
Scope: Local
Description: Specially designed training programs or workshops for organizations & groups on subjects such as impacts of abuse on immigrant & refugee women, cross-cultural perspectives on violence against women, elder abuse, partner abuse, same sex partner abuse, sexual assault, resources for abused women.
Contact Information: Assaulted Women's Helpline, Training, Resource, & Outreach Department, Toll-Free Phone: 1-888-364-1210

Assemblée communautaire fransaskoise (ACF)

#215, 1440, 9 av Nord, Regina SK S4R 8B1
Tél: 306-569-1912; *Téléc:* 306-781-7916
Ligne sans frais: 800-991-1912
acf@sasktel.net
www.fransaskois.sk.ca
www.facebook.com/assembleecommunautairefransaskoise.acf

Nom précédent: Association catholique franco-canadienne de la Saskatchewan; Association culturelle franco-canadienne de la Saskatchewan
Aperçu: *Dimension:* moyenne; *Envergure:* provinciale; Organisme sans but lucratif; fondée en 1912 surveillé par Fédération des communautés francophones et acadienne du Canada
Mission: Travaille au développement, à l'épanouissement et au rayonnement de tous ses membres; est l'entité gouvernante de la communauté fransaskoise
Membre(s) du bureau directeur:
Françoise Sigur-Cloutier, Présidente
francoise.sigur@gmail.com
Marc Masson, Agente aux communications
communication.acf@sasktel.net
Francis Potié, Directeur général
dg.acf@sasktel.net
Membre(s) du personnel: 24
Activités: Réunions publiques; *Bibliothèque:* Archives; rendez-vous

Bureau de Gravelbourg
CP 176, Gravelbourg SK S0H 1X0
Tél: 306-648-3103; *Téléc:* 306-648-3258
acfg1@sasktel.net

Bureau de St-Isidore de Bellevue, Domrémy et St Louis
CP 127, St-Isidor-de-Bellevue SK S0K 3Y0
Tél: 306-423-5303; *Téléc:* 306-423-5606
info@cfbds.ca

Assemblée de la francophonie de l'Ontario
1492B, ch Star Top, Ottawa ON K1B 3W6
Tél: 613-744-6649; *Téléc:* 416-744-8861
Ligne sans frais: 866-596-4692
www.monassemblee.ca
www.facebook.com/monassemblee.ca
twitter.com/MonAssemblee
www.youtube.com/monassemblee
Aperçu: *Dimension:* moyenne; *Envergure:* provinciale surveillé par Fédération des communautés francophones et acadienne du Canada
Mission: Pour représenter la voix politique des francophones en Ontario
Membre(s) du bureau directeur:
Peter Hominuk, Directeur général, 613-744-6649 Ext. 25
dg@monassemblee.ca
Denis B. Vaillancourt, Président
presidence@monassemblee.ca
Membre(s) du personnel: 6
Membre: *Montant de la cotisation:* Barème

L'Assemblée des aînées et aînés francophones du Canada *Voir* Fédération des aînées et aînés francophones du Canada

Assemblée des évêques catholiques de l'Ontario *See* Assembly of Catholic Bishops of Ontario

Assemblée des évêques catholiques du Québec (AEQ) / Assembly of Québec Catholic Bishops
3331, rue Sherbrooke est, Montréal QC H1W 1C5
Tél: 514-274-4323; *Téléc:* 514-274-4383
aeq@eveques.qc.ca
www.eveques.qc.ca
Nom précédent: Assemblée des Évêques du Québec
Aperçu: *Dimension:* moyenne; *Envergure:* provinciale; Organisme sans but lucratif; fondée en 1871 surveillé par Canadian Conference of Catholic Bishops
Mission: Être un lieu d'échange et de concertation où ses membres s'entraident dans la recherche d'actions à entreprendre pour rendre l'Église au Québec toujours plus vivante et engagée dans la société et la culture contemporaines
Affiliation(s): Conférence des évêques catholiques du Canada
Membre(s) du bureau directeur:
Bertrand Ouellet, Secrétaire général
Finances: *Budget de fonctionnement annuel:* $500,000-$1.5 Million
Membre(s) du personnel: 8
Membre: 37; *Critères d'admissibilite:* Évêque diocésain; évêque auxiliaire; *Comités:* Éducation; Laicat; Ministères; Missions; Affaires sociales; Théologie; Communications; Prospective; Législation; Administration; Relations interculturelles; Pastorale des Autochtones

Assemblée des évêques de l'Atlantique *See* Atlantic Episcopal Assembly

Assemblée des Évêques du Québec *Voir* Assemblée des évêques catholiques du Québec

Assemblée des Premières Nations *See* Assembly of First Nations

Assemblée des premières nations du Québec et du Labrador
#201, 250, Place Chef Michel-Laveau, Wendake QC G0A 4V0
Tél: 418-842-5020; *Téléc:* 418-842-2660
apnql@apnql-afnql.com
www.apnql-afnql.com
Aperçu: *Dimension:* moyenne; *Envergure:* provinciale
Membre(s) du bureau directeur:
Ghislain Picard, Chef
Membre: 43

Assemblée internationale des parlementaires de langue française *Voir* Assemblée parlementaire de la Francophonie

Assemblée internationale des parlementaires de langue française (Section canadienne) *Voir* Assemblée parlementaire de la Francophonie (Section canadienne)

Assemblée parlementaire de la Francophonie (APF)
Région Amérique, Assemblée nationale, 1020, rue des Parlementaires, 6e étage, Québec QC G1A 1A3
Tél: 418-643-7391; *Téléc:* 418-643-1865
mvermette@assnat.qc.ca
www.regionamerique-apf.org
Nom précédent: Assemblée internationale des parlementaires de langue française
Aperçu: *Dimension:* moyenne; *Envergure:* internationale; fondée en 1992
Mission: Promouvoir la langue et la culture francaise; promouvoir les droits de l'homme et la démocratie
Membre(s) du bureau directeur:
André Lavoie, Secrétaire administrative régionale
Finances: *Budget de fonctionnement annuel:* Moins de $50,000
Membre: 1-99
Activités: *Service de conférenciers:* Oui

Assemblée parlementaire de la Francophonie (Section canadienne) (APF)
Parliament of Canada, 131 Queen St., 5th Fl., Ottawa ON K1A 0A8
Tél: 613-995-9560; *Téléc:* 613-995-0212
Assem.Franco@parl.gc.ca
Nom précédent: Assemblée internationale des parlementaires de langue française (Section canadienne)
Aperçu: *Dimension:* petite; *Envergure:* provinciale; fondée en 1967
Mission: L'Assemblée parlementaire de la Francophonie est un lieu de débats, de propositions et d'échanges d'informations sur tous les sujets d'intérêt commun à ses membres. Par ses avis et recommandations à la Conférence ministérielle de la Francophonie et au Conseil permanent de la Francophonie, elle participe à la vie institutionnelle de la Francophonie; elle intervient devant les chefs d'État lors des Sommets de la Francophonie. En étroite collaboration avec l'Agence de la Francophonie, elle engage et met en oeuvre des actions dans les domaines de la coopération interparlementaire et du développement de la démocratie. Ses actions visent à renforcer la solidarité entre institutions parlementaires et à promouvoir la démocratie et l'État de droit, plus particulièrement au sein de la communauté francophone
Membre(s) du bureau directeur:
François Michaud, Président

Assemblées de la Pentecôte du Canada *See* Pentecostal Assemblies of Canada

Assembly of BC Arts Councils
PO Box 28533, Stn. Willingdon, Burnaby BC V5C 2H9
Tel: 604-291-0046; *Fax:* 604-648-9454
Toll-Free: 888-315-2288
info@artsbc.org
www.artsbc.org
twitter.com/artsbcdotorg
Also Known As: ArtsBC
Overview: A medium-sized provincial charitable organization founded in 1979
Mission: To promote & advance the role of arts & culture in building community; to work with community based organizations in furthering the impact & contribution of the arts locally, regionally & province-wide
Chief Officer(s):
Stephen Parsons, President
Finances: *Funding Sources:* Public, private & earned revenues
Membership: 300; *Member Profile:* Arts councils & other local arts agencies

Activities: *Library* by appointment

Assembly of Catholic Bishops of Ontario / Assemblée des évêques catholiques de l'Ontario
#800, 10 St. Mary St., Toronto ON M4Y 1P9
Tel: 416-923-1423; *Fax:* 416-923-1509
www.acbo.on.ca
Overview: A small provincial organization overseen by Canadian Conference of Catholic Bishops
Mission: The association of the Catholic bishops of the Province of Ontario in the service of Catholics of Ontario. Involved in providing information and instruction about the principles and moral positions of the Church on all aspects of life
Chief Officer(s):
Luciano (Lou) Piovesan, General Secretary
piovesanl@acbo.on.ca
Thomas Collins, President, 416-934-0606, Fax: 416-934-3452

Assembly of First Nations (AFN) / Assemblée des Premières Nations (APN)
#1600, 55 Metcalfe St., Ottawa ON K1P 6L5
Tel: 613-241-6789; *Fax:* 613-241-5808
Toll-Free: 866-869-6789
www.afn.ca
www.facebook.com/AFN.APN
twitter.com/AFN_Updates
www.youtube.com/user/afnposter
Previous Name: National Indian Brotherhood
Overview: A large national organization
Mission: The AFN Secretariat acts as an advocate for First Nations on many issues, including Aboriginal & Treaty Rights, economic development, education, languages & literacy, health, housing, social development, justice, land claims & the environment
Chief Officer(s):
Perry Bellgarde, National Chief
Finances: *Funding Sources:* Federal grants
Membership: 633 First Nations in Canada

Assembly of Manitoba Chiefs
#200, 275 Portage Ave., Winnipeg MB R3B 2B3
Tel: 204-956-0610; *Fax:* 204-956-2109
Toll-Free: 888-324-5483
info@manitobachiefs.com
www.manitobachiefs.com
Overview: A medium-sized provincial organization
Mission: To promote & preserve Aboriginal and treaty rights while striving to improve the quality of life of the First Nation citizens in Manitoba.
Affliation(s): Assembly of First Nations
Chief Officer(s):
Derek Nepinak, Grand Chief
Membership: 58 member communities

Assembly of Québec Catholic Bishops *Voir* Assemblée des évêques catholiques du Québec

Assiniboia & District Arts Council
PO Box 1596, 122 - 3rd Ave. West, Assiniboia SK S0H 0B0
Tel: 306-642-5294; *Fax:* 306-642-5441
assiniboia.artscouncil@sasktel.net
www.johnnycashtribute.ca
www.facebook.com/assiniboiadistrict.artscouncil
Overview: A small local charitable organization founded in 1981
Mission: To increase & broaden the opportunities for public enjoyment of & participation in cultural activities; To stimulate & encourage the development of cultural projects & activities; To act as a clearinghouse for information on cultural projects & activities
Member of: Organization of Saskatchewan Arts Councils
Chief Officer(s):
Joanne Weiss, Executive Director
Darlene Kowalchuk, President
Finances: *Annual Operating Budget:* Less than $50,000
15 volunteer(s)
Membership: 20; *Fees:* $35; *Member Profile:* All ages & walks of life; *Committees:* Visual Arts; Performing Arts; Art & Craft Sale

Assiniboia & District Chamber of Commerce (SK)
PO Box 1803, 110 - 4th Ave. West, Assiniboia SK S0H 0B0
Tel: 306-642-5553; *Fax:* 306-642-3529
www.assiniboia.net/business/chamber_of_commerce.html
Overview: A small local organization
Chief Officer(s):
Terry L. Sieffert, President
Sonia Dahlman, Treasurer

Bonnie Ruzicka, Executive Assistant
ruzicka@sasktel.net
Activities: *Awareness Events:* Assiniboia & District Chamber of Commerce Light Parade, November; First Responders Day, September; Career Fair, September

Assiniboia Chamber of Commerce (MB) (ACC)
PO Box 42122, Stn. Ferry Road, 1867 Portage Ave., Winnipeg MB R3J 3X7
Tel: 204-774-4154; *Fax:* 204-774-4201
info@assiniboiacc.mb.ca
www.assiniboiacc.mb.ca
twitter.com/assiniboiacc
Overview: A medium-sized local organization founded in 1930
Mission: To promote entrepreneurship & competitive enterprise in West Winnipeg
Member of: Canadian Chamber of Commerce; Manitoba Chamber of Commerce
Chief Officer(s):
Ernie Nairn, Executive Director, 204-774-4154, Fax: 204-774-4201
Marcel Tetrault, Chair, 204-988-5971, Fax: 204-889-4546
macdel.tetrault@rbc.com
Warren Thompson, 1st Vice-Chair, 204-489-5900, Fax: 204-453-9012
warren.thompson2@stantec.com
Michelle Painchaud, 2nd Vice-Chair, 204-489-0673
michelle@ppghr.com
Gerry Glatz, Treasurer, 204-954-2013, Fax: 204-888-0805
E.gglatz@teledisc.com
Raunora Westcott, Secretary, 204-954-9017, Fax: 204-478-4795
E.raunora.westcott@nationalleasing.com
Finances: *Annual Operating Budget:* $100,000-$250,000; *Funding Sources:* Membership fees; Corporate sponsorship
Staff Member(s): 1; 14 volunteer(s)
Membership: 425; *Fees:* $183.75; *Member Profile:* Small to medium size businesses & community groups; *Committees:* Communications/Public Relations; Government Relations; Membership; Programs & Services
Activities: Monthly luncheons; lobbying; programs; *Awareness Events:* Golf Tournament, June; Lobster Fest Dinner, October; *Speaker Service:* Yes; *Rents Mailing List:* Yes

Assiniboine Park Conservancy
55 Pavilion Cres., Winnipeg MB R3P 2N7
Tel: 204-927-6001
Other Communication: comments@assiniboinepark.ca
info@assiniboinepark.ca
www.zoosociety.com
www.facebook.com/assiniboineparkzoo
twitter.com/assiniboinepark
www.youtube.com/user/AssiniboinePark
Previous Name: Zoological Society of Manitoba
Overview: A small provincial charitable organization founded in 1956
Mission: To redevelop & manage the Park's operations & ongoing financial viability.
Chief Officer(s):
Hartley Richardson, Chair
Margaret Redmond, President & CEO
Finances: *Annual Operating Budget:* $1.5 Million-$3 Million
Membership: *Fees:* $10-$95
Activities: School & group programs; workshops & classes; outreach & sleepovers; day campsl guided tours;

Assisted Living Southwestern Ontario (ALSO)
3141 Sandwich St., Windsor ON N9C 1A7
Tel: 519-969-8188; *Fax:* 519-969-0390
info@alsogroup.org
www.appdgroup.org
Previous Name: Association for Persons with Physical Disabilities of Windsor & Essex County
Overview: A small local organization founded in 1985
Mission: Provides personal care, homemaking services and assistance with tasks of daily living to adults with permanent physical disabilities.
Chief Officer(s):
Lyn Calder, Executive Director
Membership: *Committees:* Executive; Finance; Social Recreation; Personnel; Facility Pl; Integration

Associaça Portuguesa de LaSalle / Association Culturelle Recréative Portugaise de Lasalle
2136A, rue Pigeon, LaSalle QC H8N 1A6
Tél: 514-366-6305
Également appelé: LaSalle Portuguese Association
Aperçu: *Dimension:* petite; *Envergure:* locale

Associaça Portuguesa de Ste-Thérèse / Association Portugaise De Sainte-Thérèse
103B, rue Turgeon, Sainte Thérèse QC J7E 3H8
Tél: 450-435-0301
Également appelé: Saint Therese Portuguese Association
Aperçu: *Dimension:* petite; *Envergure:* locale

Associaça Portuguesa Do Canadà (APC) / Portuguese Assocation of Canada
4170 St. Urbain St., Montreal QC H1W 3Y3
Tel: 514-844-2269
apc4170@hotmail.com
www.facebook.com/151731518227684
Overview: A small national organization founded in 1956
Mission: To promote & preserve Portuguese culture; reuinte people of Portuguese origin; to help integrate amd participate in the community

Associaça Portuguesa do West Island / Association Portugaise De L'Ile De L'Ouest
4789, boul des Sources, Pierrefonds QC H8Y 3C6
Tél: 514-684-0857
Également appelé: West Island Portuguese Association
Aperçu: *Dimension:* petite; *Envergure:* locale

Associaça Portuguesa Espirito Santo / Association Portugaise du Saint-Esprit
6024, rue Hochelaga, Montréal QC H1N 1X6
Tél: 514-254-4647
Également appelé: Saint Esprit Portuguese Association
Aperçu: *Dimension:* petite; *Envergure:* locale

Associaçao dos Pais
333 Castelnau St. East, Montreal QC H2R 1P8
Tel: 514-495-3284
Also Known As: Montreal Association of Parents
Overview: A small local organization

Associated Boards of Trade of Ontario *See* Ontario Chamber of Commerce

Associated Business Executives of Canada *See* Associated Senior Executives of Canada Ltd.

Associated Designers of Canada (ADC)
#201, 192 Spadina Ave., Toronto ON M5T 2C2
Tel: 416-410-4209; *Fax:* 416-703-6601
associateddesigners@gmail.com
www.designers.ca
www.linkedin.com/groups?gid=1846687
www.facebook.com/groups/76343880691
Overview: A small national organization founded in 1965
Mission: To promote, pursue & protect the interests & needs of theatrical designers working in Canada
Member of: Theatre Ontario; Toronto Theatre Alliance
Chief Officer(s):
April Viczko, President
William Mackwood, Vice-President
Michael Walsh, Secretary-Treasurer
Finances: *Annual Operating Budget:* $50,000-$100,000; *Funding Sources:* Membership dues; government
Staff Member(s): 2
Membership: 160; *Fees:* $25; *Member Profile:* Portfolio review
Activities: *Library:* Virtual Resource Centre

Associated Environmental Site Assessors of Canada Inc. (AESAC)
PO Box 490, Fenelon Falls ON K0M 1N0
Toll-Free: 877-512-3722
info@aesac.ca
www.aesac.ca
Overview: A small national organization founded in 1992
Mission: To provide services to assist site assessors in meeting the needs of potential clients such as lenders & major property owners; To assist practitioners from many different professional backgrounds in identifying & maintaining appropriate standards for conducting site assessments

Associated Gospel Churches (AGC) / Association des églises évangéliques (AEE)
1500 Kerns Rd., Burlington ON L7P 3A7
Tel: 905-634-8184; *Fax:* 905-634-6283
admin@agcofcanada.com
www.agcofcanada.com
www.facebook.com/home.php?sk=group_192954014073851
www.youtube.com/user/donnaagc
Overview: A medium-sized national charitable organization founded in 1925
Mission: To glorify God by partnering together in obedience to the Great Commandment & the Great Commission; to become a movement of healthy, reproducing churches
Affliation(s): World Relief; World Team; UFM International; Evangelical Fellowship of Canada
Chief Officer(s):
Bill Fietje, President
bill@agcofcanada.com
Susan Page, Church Relations Coordinator
sue@agcofcanada.com
Finances: *Annual Operating Budget:* $250,000-$500,000
Staff Member(s): 5
Membership: 21,400 members; 140+ churches; *Fees:* 4% of revenue minus missions support; *Committees:* Doctrine & Credentials; Finance & Administration; Communication; Church Growth; Church Renting

Canada West Office
92 MacEwan Glen Close NW, Calgary AB T3K 2C3
Tel: 403-274-5811; *Fax:* 403-295-7753
jim@agcofcanada.com
Mission: Promotion of biblical health and vitality in AGC churches through preaching, consultation, encouragment, leadership training, analysis and problem solving.
Member of: Associated Gospel Churches
Chief Officer(s):
Jim Houston, Superintendent

Quebec Office
c/o Rev. Del Gibbons, Eglise Evangelique Associee de Verdun, 350, av Woodland, Verdun QC H4H 1V6
Tél: 514-768-8446
del@agcofcanada.com
Membre de: Associated Gospel Churches
Chief Officer(s):
Del Gibbons, Director

Associated Manitoba Arts Festivals, Inc. (AMAF)
79C St. Anne's Rd., Winnipeg MB R2M 2Y6
Tel: 204-231-4507; *Fax:* 204-231-4510
amaf@mymts.net
www.amaf.mb.ca
Overview: A medium-sized provincial charitable organization founded in 1977 overseen by Federation of Canadian Music Festivals
Mission: To promote & encourage participation in growth & development of & appreciation for creative & performing arts in partnership with local festivals
Chief Officer(s):
Judy Urbonas, President
urbonas@shaw.ca
William Gordon, Vice-President
gordonw@brandonu.ca
Claire DuBois, Treasurer
claire.dubois@shawlink.ca
Finances: *Annual Operating Budget:* $100,000-$250,000; *Funding Sources:* Government; fundraising; program revenue
Staff Member(s): 3; 4000 volunteer(s)
Membership: 120 individual + 28 festivals + 10 affiliate; *Fees:* $30 individual; *Committees:* Program; Finance; Fundraising; Public Relations; Syllabus; Board of Directors
Activities: Provincial Music & Speech Finals Competition; Provincial Syllabus Annual Conference; Rising Stars program; *Awareness Events:* Festival Awareness Week; *Library:* Arts Resource Library

Associated Medical Services Inc. (AMS)
#228, 162 Cumberland St., Toronto ON M5R 3N5
Tel: 416-924-3368; *Fax:* 416-323-3338
info@ams-inc.on.ca
php.ams-inc.on.ca
Overview: A small local charitable organization founded in 1937
Mission: To sponsor programs in the history of medicine, medical education & bioethics; to facilitate education, research & other initiatives which promote the development & understanding of those human & social values that are fundamental to health
Affliation(s): Thomas Fisher Rare Book Library, University of Toronto; Association of Faculties of Medicine of Canada; Canadian Association for the History of Nursing; Canadian Institutes of Health Research; Canadian Society for the History of Medicine; College of Family Physicians of Canada; McGill University Faculty of Medicine; McGill-Queen's University Press; McMaster University; Queen's University; Royal Society of Canada; University of Calgary; University of Ottawa; University of Toronto; University of Western Ontario
Chief Officer(s):
Gail Paech, CEO
Dorothy Pringle, Chair/President

Activities: Hannah Institute for the History of Medicine Program; Bioethics Program; Education Program; Special Awards;

Associated Research Centres for the Urban Underground Space (ACUUS) / Association des Centres de recherche sur l'Utilisation Urbaine du Sous-sol (ACLUS)

ACUUS Secrétariat, 34, rue Seville, Montréal QC H9B 2S5
e-mail: info@acuus.qc.ca
www.acuus.qc.ca
www.linkedin.com/groups/Interested-involved-in-urban-undergro und-42046
Overview: A small international organization founded in 1996
Mission: To enhance the international co-operation & exchange amongst the world community of planners, researchers, builders, investors, decision-makers & other parties involved in the use & development of the urban underground space
Chief Officer(s):
Ray Sterling, President
Jacques Besner, General Manager
Finances: *Annual Operating Budget:* Less than $50,000; *Funding Sources:* Public & private
Staff Member(s): 1
Membership: 10; *Member Profile:* Organizations & individuals interested in furthering the objectives of the ACUUS in regard to urban underground space
Activities: Co-ordination of international events; creation of international directory of urban underground planning data; promotion of strategies & actions for the integrated planning & management of urban underground spaces;; *Library* by appointment

Associated Senior Executives of Canada Ltd. (ASE)

450 The West Mall, Toronto ON M9C 1E9
Tel: 416-695-2435
contactus@a-s-e.ca
www.a-s-e.ca
Previous Name: Associated Business Executives of Canada
Overview: A small national organization founded in 1963
Mission: To offer practical business advice
Membership: *Member Profile:* Retired executives with experience in a wide variety of corporate areas

Association acadienne des artistes professionnel.le.s du Nouveau-Brunswick inc. (AAAPNB)

#29, 140, rue Botsford, Moncton NB E1C 4X5
Tél: 506-852-3313
info@aaapnb.ca
www.aaapnb.ca
www.facebook.com/aaapnb
twitter.com/AAAPNB
www.youtube.com/AAAPNB
Aperçu: *Dimension:* petite; *Envergure:* provinciale; Organisme sans but lucratif; fondée en 1990
Mission: Promouvoir et défendre les droits et les intérêts des artistes. A titre de porte-parole officiel, représente ses membres auprès des instances gouvernementales, travaille au développement des secteurs artistiques et offre des services d'information, de publication et de promotion
Membre de: Fédération culturelle canadienne-française (FCCF); Conférence canadienne des arts
Membre(s) du bureau directeur:
Carmen Gibbs, Directrice générale
carmen.gibbs@aaapnb.ca
Membre(s) du personnel: 10
Membre: *Montant de la cotisation:* 50$ artiste professionnel; 25$ artiste stagiaire/ami des arts; *Critères d'admissibilite:* Artistes acadiens et acadiennes de profession
Activités: *Bibliothèque:* Centre de ressources des arts et de la culture

Association accréditée du personnel non enseignant de l'université McGill *See* McGill University Non Academic Certified Association

Association albertaine des parents francophones *Voir* Fédération des parents francophones de l'Alberta

Association amateur des sports des sourds du Québec; Fédération sportive des sourds du Québec inc. *Voir* Association sportive des sourds du Québec inc.

Association Aquacole du Canada *See* Aquaculture Association of Canada

Association Atlantique du Sport Collegial *See* Atlantic Collegiate Athletic Association

Association botanique du Canada *See* Canadian Botanical Association

Association canadienne des interprètes de conférence (AIIC Canada) / Canadian Association of Conference Interpreters (CACI)

c/o Susan Asselin, 11 Woodbrook Rd. SW, Calgary AB T2W 4M5
www.aiic.ca
Aperçu: *Dimension:* petite; *Envergure:* internationale; fondée en 1953
Mission: Fournir des conseils aux organisateurs de conférences en ce qui concerne les services d'interprétation; l'AIIC est la seule association internationale professionnelle d'interprètes de conférence
Affiliation(s): Centre du Commerce Mondial
Membre(s) du bureau directeur:
Susan Asselin, Membre du conseil, 403-698-2012, Fax: 403-454-5500
s.asselin@aiic.net
Gabriela Rangel, Secrétaire régional, 613-863-2843, Fax: 613-821-3134
g.rangel@aiic.net
Aisbel Guerrero, Trésorier régional, 613-841-4934, Fax: 613-818-3957
aisbelguerrero@rogers.com
Linda Ballantyne, Membre du Bureau régional, 514-286-4310, Fax: 514-281-5581
linda.ballantyne@sympatico.ca
Wendy Greene, Membre du Bureau régional, 416-545-1470, Fax: 416-545-0581
wgreene@dialogueinterpreters.ca
Membre: 100-499; *Montant de la cotisation:* Barème; *Critères d'admissibilite:* Diplôme post-universitaire; expérience; parrainage par les pairs; *Comités:* Technique; Santé; Formation; Associations internationales; Secteur privé; Relations publiques; Interprètes permanents
Activités: *Service de conférenciers:* Oui

Association canadienne aide aux victimes *See* Canadian Association for Victim Assistance

L'Association canadienne Angus *See* Canadian Angus Association

Association canadienne d'Accès Vasculaire *See* Canadian Vascular Access Association

Association canadienne d'acoustique *See* Canadian Acoustical Association

Association canadienne d'administrateurs de recherche universitaire *See* Canadian Association of University Research Administrators

Association canadienne d'anatomie, de neurobiologie et de biologie cellulaire *See* Canadian Association for Anatomy, Neurobiology, & Cell Biology

L'Association canadienne d'art photographique *See* Canadian Association for Photographic Art

L'association canadienne d'art thérapie *See* Canadian Art Therapy Association

Association canadienne d'articles de sport *See* Canadian Sporting Goods Association

Association canadienne d'assurance nucléaire *See* Nuclear Insurance Association of Canada

L'Association canadienne d'auto-distribution *See* Canadian Automatic Merchandising Association

Association canadienne d'aviron amateur *See* Rowing Canada Aviron

Association canadienne d'économique *See* Canadian Economics Association

Association canadienne d'éducation *See* Canadian Education Association

Association canadienne d'éducation de langue française (ACELF)

#303, 265, rue de la Couronne, Québec QC G1K 6E1
Tél: 418-681-4661; *Téléc:* 418-681-3389
info@acelf.ca
www.acelf.ca
www.facebook.com/acelf.ca
www.twitter.com/_ACELF
www.youtube.com/acelfcanada
Aperçu: *Dimension:* grande; *Envergure:* nationale; Organisme sans but lucratif; fondée en 1947
Mission: L'ACELF inspire et soutient le développement et l'action des institutions éducatives francophones du Canada
Affiliation(s): UNESCO
Membre(s) du bureau directeur:
Yves St-Maurice, Président
Richard Lacombe, Direction générale
lacombe@acelf.ca
Finances: *Budget de fonctionnement annuel:* $500,000-$1.5 Million
Membre(s) du personnel: 8
Membre: 450; *Montant de la cotisation:* 62,08$ individu; *Critères d'admissibilite:* Doit être une personne, un organisme, une institution ou une association de langue française qui souscrit aux objectifs généraux de l'ACELF et reconnu comme tel par le conseil d'administration; *Comités:* Stages de perfectionnement; thématique du congrès; Semaine nationale de la francophonie; Échanges francophones; Outils d'intervention
Activités: Échanges d'élèves; Congrès annuel; outils pédagogiques; *Evénements de sensibilisation:* Semaine nationale de la francophonie, mars; *Listes de destinataires:* Oui

Association canadienne d'énergie éolienne *See* Canadian Wind Energy Association Inc.

Association canadienne d'énergie fluide *See* Canadian Fluid Power Association

Association canadienne d'équitation thérapeutique *See* Canadian Therapeutic Riding Association

L'Association canadienne d'ergonomie *See* Association of Canadian Ergonomists

Association canadienne d'esperanto *See* Esperanto Association of Canada

Association canadienne d'ethnologie et de folklore *See* Folklore Studies Association of Canada

L'Association canadienne d'études du développement international *See* Canadian Association for the Study of International Development

Association canadienne d'études en loisir *See* Canadian Association for Leisure Studies

Association canadienne d'études environnementales *See* Environmental Studies Association of Canada

Association canadienne d'experts-conseils en patrimoine *See* Canadian Association of Heritage Professionals

Association canadienne d'habitation et de rénovation urbaine *See* Canadian Housing & Renewal Association

L'Association canadienne d'histoire de l'éducation *See* Canadian History of Education Association

Association canadienne d'histoire ferroviaire *See* Canadian Railroad Historical Association

Association canadienne d'hydrographie *See* Canadian Hydrographic Association

Association canadienne d'investissement dans des fiducies de revenu *See* Canadian Association of Income Trusts Investors

Association Canadienne d'oncologie psychosociale *See* Canadian Association of Psychosocial Oncology

Association canadienne d'orthopédie *See* Canadian Orthopaedic Association

Association canadienne de basketball en fauteuil roulant *See* Canadian Wheelchair Basketball Association

Association canadienne de boxe amateur *See* Canadian Amateur Boxing Association

Association canadienne de cadeaux *See* Canadian Gift Association

Association canadienne de cardiologie d'intervention *See* Canadian Association of Interventional Cardiology

Association canadienne de cartographie *See* Canadian Cartographic Association

Association canadienne de caution *See* Surety Association of Canada

Association canadienne de communication *See* Canadian Communication Association

Association canadienne de compagnies de traductions et d'interpretation *See* Association of Canadian Corporations in Translation & Interpretation

L'Association canadienne de counseling et de psychothérapie *See* Canadian Counselling & Psychotherapy Association

Association canadienne de counseling universitaire et collégial *See* Canadian University & College Counselling Association

Association canadienne de crosse *See* Canadian Lacrosse Association

Association canadienne de curling *See* Canadian Curling Association

Association canadienne de dermatologie *See* Canadian Dermatology Association

Association canadienne de développement économique *See* Economic Developers Association of Canada

Association canadienne de documentation professionnelle *See* Canadian Career Information Association

Association canadienne de droit et société *See* Canadian Law & Society Association

Association canadienne de droit maritime *See* Canadian Maritime Law Association

Association Canadienne de educateurs en radiodiffusion *See* Broadcast Educators Association of Canada

Association canadienne de fabricants d'armoires de cuisine *See* Canadian Kitchen Cabinet Association

Association canadienne de fabricants des arômes *See* Flavour Manufacturers Association of Canada

L'association canadienne de fabry *See* Canadian Fabry Association

Association canadienne de financement et de location *See* Canadian Finance & Leasing Association

Association canadienne de fournisseurs de laboratoire *See* Canadian Laboratory Suppliers Association

Association canadienne de gastroentérologie *See* Canadian Association of Gastroenterology

Association canadienne de gérontologie *See* Canadian Association on Gerontology

Association canadienne de gestion du fret *See* Freight Management Association of Canada

Association Canadienne de Golf des Sourds *See* Canadian Deaf Golf Association

Association canadienne de hockey-balle *See* Canadian Ball Hockey Association

Association canadienne de justice pénale *See* Canadian Criminal Justice Association

Association canadienne de l'assurance comptes clients *See* Receivables Insurance Association of Canada

Association Canadienne de l'Ataxie de Friedreich *Voir* Association canadienne des ataxies familiales

Association canadienne de l'aviation d'affaires *See* Canadian Business Aviation Association

Association canadienne de l'éducation en génie *See* Canadian Engineering Education Association

Association canadienne de l'électricité *See* Canadian Electricity Association

Association canadienne de l'emballage *See* Packaging Association of Canada

Association canadienne de l'enseigne *See* Sign Association of Canada

Association canadienne de l'enseignement coopératif *See* Canadian Association for Co-operative Education

Association canadienne de l'hydroélectricité *See* Canadian Hydropower Association

Association canadienne de l'immeuble *See* The Canadian Real Estate Association

Association canadienne de l'imprimerie *See* Canadian Printing Industries Association

Association canadienne de l'industrie de l'imagerie *See* Canadian Imaging Trade Association

Association canadienne de l'industrie de la clôture *See* Canadian Fence Industry Association

Association canadienne de l'industrie de la peinture et du revêtement *See* Canadian Paint & Coatings Association

Association canadienne de l'industrie des plastiques *See* Canadian Plastics Industry Association

Association canadienne de l'industrie du vélo *See* Bicycle Trade Association of Canada

L'Association canadienne de l'informatique *See* Canadian Information Processing Society

Association canadienne de la boulangerie *See* Baking Association of Canada

Association canadienne de la construction *See* Canadian Construction Association

Association canadienne de la courtepointe *See* Canadian Quilters' Association

Association canadienne de la distribution de fruits et légumes *See* Canadian Produce Marketing Association

Association canadienne de la dyslexie *See* Canadian Dyslexia Association

Association canadienne de la formation professionnelle *See* Canadian Vocational Association

Association canadienne de la franchise *See* Canadian Franchise Association

Association Canadienne de la Gestion de Créances Inc. *See* Receivables Management Association of Canada Inc.

Association canadienne de la gestion de l'approvisionnement pharmaceutique *See* Canadian Association for Pharmacy Distribution Management

Association canadienne de la gestion de l'innovation *See* Innovation Management Association of Canada

Association canadienne de la gestion parasitaire *See* Canadian Pest Management Association

L'Association canadienne de la maladie coeliaque *See* Canadian Celiac Association

Association canadienne de la médecine du travail et de l'environnement *See* Occupational & Environmental Medical Association of Canada

L'Association canadienne de la paie *See* Canadian Payroll Association

Association canadienne de la poésie *See* Canadian Poetry Association

Association canadienne de la presse syndicale *See* Canadian Association of Labour Media

Association canadienne de la recherche théâtrale *See* Canadian Association for Theatre Research

L'Association canadienne de la sécurité *See* Canadian Security Association

L'association canadienne de la Suisse Brune et de la Braunvieh *See* Canadian Brown Swiss & Braunvieh Association

Association canadienne de la surdicécité (Bureau National) *See* Canadian Deafblind Association (National)

Association canadienne de la technologie de l'information *See* Information Technology Association of Canada

Association canadienne de la technologie des cartes à mémoire *See* Advanced Card Technology Association of Canada

Association canadienne de linguistique *See* Canadian Linguistic Association

Association canadienne de littérature comparée *See* Canadian Comparative Literature Association

Association canadienne de luge *See* Canadian Luge Association

Association canadienne de lutte amateur *See* Canadian Amateur Wrestling Association

Association canadienne de méchanique des roches *See* Canadian Rock Mechanics Association

L'association canadienne de médecine esthétique *See* Canadian Association of Aesthetic Medicine

Association canadienne de médecine nucléaire *See* Canadian Association of Nuclear Medicine

Association canadienne de médecine physique et de réadaptation *See* Canadian Association of Physical Medicine & Rehabilitation

Association canadienne de microbiologie clinique et des maladies contagieuses *See* Canadian Association for Clinical Microbiology & Infectious Diseases

Association Canadienne de myélite transverse *See* Canadian Transverse Myelitis Association

L'Association canadienne de neurologie pédiatrique *See* Canadian Association of Child Neurology

Association canadienne de neuropathologistes *See* Canadian Association of Neuropathologists

L'Association canadienne de pharmacie en oncologie *See* Canadian Association of Pharmacy in Oncology

Association canadienne de philosophie *See* Canadian Philosophical Association

Association canadienne de photographes et illustrateurs de publicité *See* Canadian Association of Professional Image Creators

L'Association canadienne de physiothérapie *See* Canadian Physiotherapy Association

Association canadienne de pipelines d'énergie *See* Canadian Energy Pipeline Association

Association canadienne de planification et de recherche institutionnelles *See* Canadian Institutional Research & Planning Association

Association canadienne de protection médicale *See* The Canadian Medical Protective Association

Association canadienne de radio-oncologie *See* Canadian Association of Radiation Oncology

Association canadienne de radioprotection *See* Canadian Radiation Protection Association

Association canadienne de réadaptation cardiaque *See* Canadian Association of Cardiac Rehabilitation

L'Association Canadienne de recherche sur le HIV *See* The Canadian Association for HIV Research

Association canadienne de recherches dentaires *See* Canadian Association for Dental Research

Association canadienne de rédactologie *See* Canadian Association for the Study of Discourse & Writing

Association canadienne de réflexologie *See* Reflexology Association of Canada

Association canadienne de réhabilitation des sites dégradés *See* Canadian Land Reclamation Association

Association canadienne de santé dentaire publique *See* Canadian Association of Public Health Dentistry

Association canadienne de santé publique *See* Canadian Public Health Association

Association canadienne de science économique des affaires *See* Canadian Association for Business Economics

Association canadienne de science politique *See* Canadian Political Science Association

Association canadienne de sécurité agricole *See* Canadian Agricultural Safety Association

Association canadienne de sensibilisation à l'infertilité *See* Infertility Awareness Association of Canada

Association canadienne de ski acrobatique *See* Canadian Freestyle Ski Association

Association canadienne de soccer *See* Canadian Soccer Association

Association canadienne de soccer *See* Canadian Soccer Association

Association canadienne de soins et services à domicile *See* Canadian Home Care Association

Association canadienne de soins palliatifs *See* Canadian Hospice Palliative Care Association

Association canadienne de soins spirituels *See* Canadian Association for Spiritual Care

Association canadienne de spécialistes en chirurgie buccale et maxillo-faciale *See* Canadian Association of Oral & Maxillofacial Surgeons

Association canadienne de sport pour paralytiques cérébraux *See* Canadian Cerebral Palsy Sports Association

Association canadienne de taxe foncière, inc *See* Canadian Property Tax Association, Inc.

Association canadienne de technologie de pointe *See* Canadian Advanced Technology Alliance

Association canadienne de terrazzo, tuile et marbre *See* Terrazzo Tile & Marble Association of Canada

Association canadienne de traductologie (ACT) / Canadian Association for Translation Studies (CATS)

a/s École de traduction et d'interprétation, Université d'Ottawa, 70, av Laurier est, Ottawa ON K1N 6N5
www.act-cats.ca
Overview: A small national organization founded in 1987
Mission: Société savante qui regroupe des chercheurs, des professeurs et des praticiens qui se consacrent ou s'intéressent à l'étude ou à l'enseignement de la traduction et des disciplines apparentées
Member of: Canadian Federation for the Humanities & Social Science
Chief Officer(s):
Marco Fiola, Président
mfiola@ryerson.ca
Denise Nevo, Vice-présidente
denise.nevo@msvu.ca
Membership: *Fees:* 30$ étudiants; 45$ retraités; 90$ individuel
Publications:
• ACT / CATS
Type: Newsletter/Bulletin; *Editor:* Denise Nevo *ISSN:* 0835-8435
• TRR: Translation Terminology Writing
Type: Journal; *Editor:* Natalia Teplova *ISSN:* 0835-8443

Association canadienne de traitement d'images et de reconnaissance des formes *See* Canadian Image Processing & Pattern Recognition Society

Association canadienne de traumatologie *See* Trauma Association of Canada

L'Association canadienne de vérification *See* Auditing Association of Canada

Association canadienne de vexillologie *See* Canadian Flag Association

Association canadienne de vol à voile *See* Soaring Association of Canada

Association canadienne de vol libre *See* Hang Gliding & Paragliding Association of Canada

Association canadienne des administrateurs de la législation ouvrière *See* Canadian Association of Administrators of Labour Legislation

Association canadienne des administrateurs de régimes de retraite *See* Association of Canadian Pension Management

Association canadienne des administrateurs et des administratrices scolaires *See* Canadian Association of School System Administrators

Association canadienne des agences de voyages *See* Association of Canadian Travel Agencies

Association canadienne des agents de communication en éducation *See* Canadian Association of Communicators in Education

Association canadienne des agents financiers *See* Association of Canadian Financial Officers

Association canadienne des agronomes-conseils *See* Canadian Consulting Agrologists Association

Association canadienne des aliments de santé *See* Canadian Health Food Association

Association canadienne des annonceurs *See* Association of Canadian Advertisers Inc.

Association canadienne des annonceurs inc.

#925, 2015, rue Peel, Montréal QC H3A 1t8
Tél: 514-842-6422; *Téléc:* 514-964-0771
Ligne sans frais: 800-565-0109
www.acaweb.ca
www.linkedin.com/company/2553878
twitter.com/aca_tweets
Aperçu: *Dimension:* petite; *Envergure:* nationale surveillé par Association of Canadian Advertisers Inc.
Mission: Pour représenter les intérêts des entreprises de publicité et de marketing au Canada
Membre(s) du bureau directeur:
Ron Lund, Président/Chef de la direction
rlund@ACAweb.ca
Membre(s) du personnel: 8
Membre: *Comités:* Médias; Marketing Numérique; Gestion Financière des Communications Marketing et des Achats

Association canadienne des archivistes *See* Association of Canadian Archivists

Association canadienne des assistants(es) dentaires *See* Canadian Dental Assistants Association

Association canadienne des ataxies familiales (ACAF) / Canadian Association for Familial Ataxias (CAFA)

#110, 3800, rue Radisson, Montréal QC H1M 1X6
Tél: 514-321-8684
Ligne sans frais: 855-321-8684
ataxie@lacaf.org
www.lacaf.org
fr-fr.facebook.com/acaf.cafa.5
twitter.com/ataxiecanada
www.youtube.com/user/LACAF2010
Également appelé: Fondation Claude St-Jean
Nom précédent: Association Canadienne de l'Ataxie de Friedreich
Aperçu: *Dimension:* petite; *Envergure:* nationale; Organisme sans but lucratif; fondée en 1972
Mission: Recueillir des dons du public pour financer les recherches médicales qui se font sur l'Ataxie familial ainsi que d'améliorer la condition de vie des personnes ataxiques (personnes qui sont affligées par la maladie de l'Ataxie de Friedreich)
Membre de: Confédération des organismes de personnes handicapées du Québec
Membre(s) du bureau directeur:
Isabelle Pinet, Présidente
Samuel Camirand, Vice-Présidente
Finances: *Budget de fonctionnement annuel:* $100,000-$250,000
Membre(s) du personnel: 4
Membre: 1 500; *Montant de la cotisation:* 10 $ membre canadien; 15 $ membre États-Unis; 20 $ membre international; *Critères d'admissibilite:* Une personne atteinte de la maladie de l'Ataxie de Friedreich
Activités: Loisirs organisés par notre bureau des services sociaux; *Evénements de sensibilisation:* Campagne de financement annuelle; Banquet-Bénéfice
Publications:
• Eldorado
Type: Journal
Profile: Describes current research on familial ataxia

CAFA Central
ON
central@lacaf.org
central.lacaf.org
www.facebook.com/CAFAcentral
twitter.com/CAFAcentral
Mission: Represents CAFA in Ontario & Manitoba
Membre(s) du bureau directeur:
Roger Foley, President
Pam Shortt, Vice-President

CAFA Maritimes
NS
maritimes@lacaf.org
maritimes.lacaf.org
www.facebook.com/CAFAmaritimes
twitter.com/CAFAmaritimes
Mission: Represents CAFA in Nova Scotia, New Brunswick, Newfoundland & Labrador & Prince Edward Island
Membre(s) du bureau directeur:
Natalie Denny, Branch Founder

CAFA West
Vancouver BC
west@lacaf.org
west.lacaf.org
www.facebook.com/cafa.west
Mission: Represents CAFA in Saskatchewan, Alberta & British Columbia
Membre(s) du bureau directeur:
Brenda Dixon, President
Fiona Jackson, Vice-President

Association canadienne des automobilistes *See* Canadian Automobile Association

Association canadienne des barrages *See* Canadian Dam Association

Association canadienne des bègues *See* Canadian Stuttering Association

Association canadienne des bibliothèques *See* Canadian Library Association

Association canadienne des bibliothèques de droit *See* Canadian Association of Law Libraries

Association canadienne des bibliothèques, archives et centres de documentation musicaux inc. *See* Canadian Association of Music Libraries, Archives & Documentation Centres

Association canadienne des boissons *See* Canadian Beverage Association

Association canadienne des carburants *See* Canadian Fuels Association

Association canadienne des carburants renouvelables *See* Canadian Renewable Fuels Association

Association canadienne des centres contre les agressions à caractère sexuel *See* Canadian Association of Sexual Assault Centres

Association canadienne des centres de santé pédiatriques *See* Canadian Association of Paediatric Health Centres

L'Association canadienne des centres de sciences *See* Canadian Association of Science Centres

Association canadienne des chefs de police *See* Canadian Association of Chiefs of Police

Association canadienne des chefs de pompiers *See* Canadian Association of Fire Chiefs

Association canadienne des chefs de tirage *See* Circulation Management Association of Canada

Association canadienne des chirurgiens généraux *See* Canadian Association of General Surgeons

Association canadienne des chirurgiens thoraciques *See* Canadian Association of Thoracic Surgeons

Association canadienne des cinq quilles *See* Canadian 5 Pin Bowlers' Association

Association canadienne des commissaires d'écoles catholique *See* Canadian Catholic School Trustees' Association

Association canadienne des commissions de police *See* Canadian Association of Police Governance

Association canadienne des commissions et conseil des droits de la personne ***See*** Canadian Association of Statutory Human Rights Agencies

Association canadienne des commissions/conseils scolaires ***See*** Canadian School Boards Association

Association canadienne des compagnies d'assurance mutuelles ***See*** Canadian Association of Mutual Insurance Companies

Association canadienne des compagnies d'assurance titres ***See*** Title Insurance Industry Association of Canada

Association canadienne des compagnies d'assurances de personnes inc. ***See*** Canadian Life & Health Insurance Association Inc.

Association canadienne des comptables en assurance ***See*** Canadian Insurance Accountants Association

Association Canadienne des conseillers en génétique ***See*** Canadian Association of Genetic Counsellors

Association canadienne des conseillers en management ***See*** Canadian Association of Management Consultants

Association canadienne des conseillers hypothécaires accrédités ***See*** Canadian Association of Accredited Mortgage Professionals

L'Association canadienne des conseillers juridiques d'entreprises ***See*** The Canadian Corporate Counsel Association

Association Canadienne des Conseillers Professionnels en Immigration ***See*** Canadian Association of Professional Immigration Consultants

Association canadienne des constructeurs d'habitations ***See*** Canadian Home Builders' Association

Association canadienne des constructeurs d'habitations - Nouveau-Brunswick ***See*** Canadian Home Builders' Association - New Brunswick

Association canadienne des constructeurs de véhicules ***See*** Canadian Vehicle Manufacturers' Association

Association canadienne des consultantes en lactation ***See*** Canadian Lactation Consultant Association

Association Canadienne des Consultants en Radito-télédiffusion ***See*** Canadian Association of Broadcast Consultants

Association canadienne des cosmétiques, produit de toilette et parfums ***See*** Canadian Cosmetic, Toiletry & Fragrance Association

Association canadienne des courtiers de fonds mutuels ***See*** Mutual Fund Dealers Association of Canada

Association Canadienne des Croix Bleue ***See*** Canadian Association of Blue Cross Plans

Association canadienne des déménageurs ***See*** Canadian Association of Movers

Association Canadienne des dépanneurs en alimentation ***See*** Canadian Convenience Stores Association

Association canadienne des directeurs d'école ***See*** Canadian Association of Principals

Association canadienne des directeurs d'expositions ***See*** Canadian Association of Exposition Management

Association canadienne des directeurs de l'information en radio-télévision ***See*** Radio Television News Directors' Association (Canada)

Association Canadienne des Directeurs Médicaux en Assurance-Vie ***See*** Canadian Life Insurance Medical Officers Association

Association canadienne des distributeurs de produits chimiques ***See*** Canadian Association of Chemical Distributors

Association canadienne des distributeurs et exportateurs de films ***See*** Canadian Association of Film Distributors & Exporters

Association canadienne des docteurs en naturopathie ***See*** The Canadian Association of Naturopathic Doctors

Association Canadienne des Doyens et Doyennes d'Éducation ***See*** Association of Canadian Deans of Education

Association canadienne des eaux potables et usées ***See*** Canadian Water & Wastewater Association

Association canadienne des eaux souterraines ***See*** Canadian Ground Water Association

L'Association canadienne des échecs par correspondance ***See*** Canadian Correspondence Chess Association

Association canadienne des écoles de sciences infirmières ***See*** Canadian Association of Schools of Nursing

Association canadienne des éducateurs de musique ***See*** Canadian Music Educators' Association

L'Association canadienne des éleveurs de porcs ***See*** Canadian Swine Breeders' Association

Association canadienne des embouteilleurs d'eau ***See*** Canadian Bottled Water Association

Association canadienne des employés professionnels ***See*** Canadian Association of Professional Employees

Association Canadienne des Enseignantes et des Enseignants Retraités ***See*** Canadian Association of Retired Teachers

Association canadienne des enterprises familiales ***See*** Canadian Association of Family Enterprise

Association canadienne des entraîneurs ***See*** Coaching Association of Canada

Association canadienne des entrepreneurs électriciens ***See*** Canadian Electrical Contractors Association

Association canadienne des entrepreneurs en couverture ***See*** Canadian Roofing Contractors' Association

Association canadienne des entrepreneurs en mousse de polyuréthane ***See*** Canadian Urethane Foam Contractors Association

Association canadienne des entreprises de géomatique ***See*** Geomatics Industry Association of Canada

Association canadienne des épices ***See*** Canadian Spice Association

Association canadienne des ergothérapeutes ***See*** Canadian Association of Occupational Therapists

Association canadienne des études asiatiques ***See*** Canadian Asian Studies Association

Association canadienne des études cinématographiques ***See*** Film Studies Association of Canada

Association canadienne des études hongroises ***See*** Hungarian Studies Association of Canada

Association canadienne des études latino-américaines et caraïbes ***See*** Canadian Association for Latin American & Caribbean Studies

Association canadienne des études patristiques ***See*** Canadian Society of Patristic Studies

L'Association canadienne des études sur l'alimentation ***See*** Canadian Association for Food Studies

Association canadienne des étudiants et internes en pharmacie ***See*** Canadian Association of Pharmacy Students & Interns

Association canadienne des évaluateurs de capacités de travail société ***See*** Canadian Assessment, Vocational Evaluation & Work Adjustment Society

L'Association canadienne des ex-parlementaires ***See*** Canadian Association of Former Parliamentarians

Association canadienne des experts indépendants ***See*** Canadian Independent Adjusters' Association

Association canadienne des exportateurs d'équipement et services miniers ***See*** Canadian Association of Mining Equipment & Services for Export

Association canadienne des fabricants de confiseries ***See*** Confectionery Manufacturers Association of Canada

Association canadienne des fabricants de fermes de bois ***See*** Canadian Wood Truss Association

Association canadienne des fabricants de produits de quincaillerie et d'articles ménagers ***See*** Canadian Hardware & Housewares Manufacturers' Association

Association canadienne des fabricants de tuyaux de béton ***See*** Canadian Concrete Pipe Association

Association canadienne des fabricants des grignotines ***See*** Canadian Snack Food Association

Association canadienne des femmes cadres et entrepreneurs ***See*** Canadian Association of Women Executives & Entrepreneurs

Association canadienne des femmes d'assurance ***See*** Canadian Association of Insurance Women

Association canadienne des femmes en communication ***See*** Canadian Women in Communications

Association canadienne des foires et expositions ***See*** Canadian Association of Fairs & Exhibitions

Association canadienne des fondements de l'éducation ***See*** Canadian Association of Foundations of Education

Association canadienne des fournisseurs de chemins de fer ***See*** Canadian Association of Railway Suppliers

Association canadienne des fournisseurs de produits sanitaires ***See*** Canadian Sanitation Supply Association

Association canadienne des fournisseurs internet ***See*** Canadian Association of Internet Providers

Association canadienne des géographes ***See*** Canadian Association of Geographers

Association canadienne des gestionnaires de fonds de retraite ***See*** Pension Investment Association of Canada

Association canadienne des greffes ***See*** Canadian Transplant Association

Association canadienne des harmonies ***See*** Canadian Band Association

Association canadienne des hygiénistes dentaires ***See*** Canadian Dental Hygienists Association

Association canadienne des importateurs & exportateurs ***See*** Canadian Association of Importers & Exporters

Association canadienne des importateurs règlementés ***See*** Canadian Association of Regulated Importers

Association canadienne des industries de la musique ***See*** Music Industries Association of Canada

Association canadienne des industries du recyclage ***See*** Canadian Association of Recycling Industries

Association canadienne des infirmières en oncologie ***See*** Canadian Association of Nurses in Oncology

Association canadienne des infirmières en soins holistiques ***See*** Canadian Holistic Nurses Association

Association canadienne des infirmières et infirmiers de pratique avancée ***See*** Canadian Association of Advanced Practice Nurses

Association canadienne des infirmières et infirmiers en gérontologie ***See*** Canadian Gerontological Nursing Association

Association canadienne des infirmières et infirmiers en hépatologie ***See*** Canadian Association of Hepatology Nurses

Association canadienne des infirmières et infirmiers en orthopédie ***See*** Canadian Orthopaedic Nurses Association

Association canadienne des infirmières et infirmiers en périnatalité et en santé des femmes ***See*** Canadian Association of Perinatal & Women's Health Nurses

Association canadienne des infirmières et infirmiers en santé du travail ***See*** Canadian Occupational Health Nurses Association

Association canadienne des infirmières et infirmiers en sidologie ***See*** Canadian Association of Nurses in HIV/AIDS Care

Association canadienne des infirmières et infirmiers en soins aux brûlés *See* Canadian Association of Burn Nurses

Association canadienne des infirmières et infirmiers en soins intensifs *See* Canadian Association of Critical Care Nurses

Association canadienne des infirmières et infirmiers et technologues de néphrologie *See* Canadian Association of Nephrology Nurses & Technologists

Association Canadienne des Infirmiers et Infirmieres d'Apheresis *See* Canadian Association of Apheresis Nurses

Association canadienne des infirmiers et infirmières en sciences neurologiques *See* Canadian Association of Neuroscience Nurses

Association canadienne des inspecteur(e)s en bâtiments du Québec *Voir* Canadian Association of Home & Property Inspectors

Association canadienne des inspecteurs de biens immobiliers *See* Canadian Association of Home & Property Inspectors

Association canadienne des institutions financières en assurance *See* Canadian Association of Financial Institutions in Insurance

Association canadienne des intervenants en formation policière *See* Canadian Association of Police Educators

Association canadienne des investisseurs obligataires *See* Canadian Bond Investors' Association

L'Association canadienne des journalistes *See* Canadian Association of Journalists

Association canadienne des journaux *See* Canadian Newspaper Association

L'Association canadienne des juges de cours provinciales *See* Canadian Association of Provincial Court Judges

Association canadienne des juristes de l'État *See* Canadian Association of Crown Counsel

Association canadienne des juristes-traducteurs (ACJT) / Canadian Association of Legal Translators (CALT)

a/s OOTTIAQ, #1108, 2021 Union Ave., Montreal QC H3A 2S9
info@acjt.ca
www.acjt.ca
Aperçu: *Dimension:* petite; *Envergure:* nationale; fondée en 1988
Mission: Pour promouvoir le double qualification comme avocat (ou juriste) et comme traducteur pour la traduction de documents juridiques.
Membre(s) du bureau directeur:
Louis Fortier, President
Membre: 156

Association canadienne des laboratoires d'essais *Voir* Association des consultants et laboratoires experts

Association canadienne des lésés cérébraux *See* Brain Injury Association of Canada

Association canadienne des libertés civiles *See* Canadian Civil Liberties Association

Association canadienne des maîtres de poste et adjoints *See* Canadian Postmasters & Assistants Association

Association canadienne des maîtres en ski de fond *See* Canadian Masters Cross-Country Ski Association

Association canadienne des manufacturiers de palettes et contenants *See* Canadian Wood Pallet & Container Association

Association canadienne des marchands numismatiques *See* Canadian Association of Numismatic Dealers

Association canadienne des marchés des capitaux *See* Canadian Capital Markets Association

Association canadienne des massothérapeutes du sport *See* Canadian Sport Massage Therapists Association

Association canadienne des médecins d'urgence *See* Canadian Association of Emergency Physicians

Association canadienne des médecins vétérinaires *See* Canadian Veterinary Medical Association

Association canadienne des métiers de la truelle, section locale 100 (CTC) / Trowel Trades Canadian Association, Local 100 (CLC)

#2000, 565, rue Crémazie est, Montréal QC H2M 2V6
Tél: 514-326-3691; *Téléc:* 514-326-5562
Ligne sans frais: 888-326-3691
acmt@qc.aira.com
truellelocal100.org
www.facebook.com/pages/ACMT-Local-100/364336873624899/
Aperçu: *Dimension:* moyenne; *Envergure:* nationale
Mission: La FTQ-Construction a, bien entendu, de manière très précise le mandat de négocier les conventions collectives applicables dans les sous secteurs d'activités (industriel, commercial et institutionnel, génie civil et voirie, résidentiel) et de voir à leur application. Mais bien au-delà de ce mandat traditionnel, la FTQ-Construction veut s'assurer d'être présent dans l'ensemble des débats représentant un intérêt pour les travailleurs et les travailleuses qu'il représente.
Membre(s) du bureau directeur:
Roger Poirier, Directeur-général
Membre: 2 000 en 4 régions

Association canadienne des moniteurs de ski nordique *See* Canadian Association of Nordic Ski Instructors

Association canadienne des moniteurs de surf des neiges *See* Canadian Association of Snowboard Instructors

Association canadienne des mouleurs sous pression *See* Canadian Die Casters Association

Association canadienne des négociants en timbres-poste *See* Canadian Stamp Dealers' Association

Association Canadienne des Officiels de Football *See* Canadian Football Officials Association

Association canadienne des oncologues médicaux *See* Canadian Association of Medical Oncologists

Association canadienne des opérateurs de traversiers *See* Canadian Ferry Operators Association

Association canadienne des optométristes *See* Canadian Association of Optometrists

Association canadienne des organismes artistiques *See* Canadian Arts Presenting Association

Association canadienne des organismes de contrôle des régimes de retraite *See* Canadian Association of Pension Supervisory Authorities

Association canadienne des orthodontists *See* Canadian Association of Orthodontists

Association canadienne des paiements *See* Canadian Payments Association

Association canadienne des palynologues *See* Canadian Association of Palynologists

Association canadienne des parajuristes *See* Canadian Association of Paralegals

Association canadienne des parcs et loisirs *See* Canadian Parks & Recreation Association

Association canadienne des pathologistes *See* Canadian Association of Pathologists

Association canadienne des pensionnés et rentiers militaires *See* Armed Forces Pensioners'/Annuitants' Association of Canada

Association canadienne des physiciens et physiciennes *See* Canadian Association of Physicists

Association canadienne des pilotes d'avions ultra-légers *See* Ultralight Pilots Association of Canada

Association canadienne des policiers *See* Canadian Police Association

Association canadienne des prêteurs sur salaire *See* Canadian Payday Loan Association

Association canadienne des producteurs d'acier *See* Canadian Steel Producers Association

Association canadienne des producteurs de semences *See* Canadian Seed Growers' Association

Association canadienne des producteurs pétroliers *See* Canadian Association of Petroleum Producers

Association canadienne des professeures et professeurs d'université *See* Canadian Association of University Teachers

Association canadienne des professeurs d'immersion (ACPI) / Canadian Association of Immersion Teachers (CAIT)

#310, 176, rue Gloucester, Ottawa ON K2P 0A6
Tél: 613-230-9111; *Téléc:* 613-230-5940
bureau@acpi.ca
www.acpi.ca
Aperçu: *Dimension:* moyenne; *Envergure:* nationale; Organisme sans but lucratif; fondée en 1977
Membre(s) du bureau directeur:
Chantal Bourbonnais, Directrice générale
chantal.bourbonnais@acpi.ca
Finances: *Budget de fonctionnement annuel:* $50,000-$100,000
Membre(s) du personnel: 1
Membre: 1 400; *Montant de la cotisation:* 45$

Association canadienne des professeurs de comptabilité *See* Canadian Academic Accounting Association

Association canadienne des professeurs de danse *See* Canadian Dance Teachers' Association

Association canadienne des professeurs de langues secondes *See* Canadian Association of Second Language Teachers

Association Canadienne des Professionels de l'Apiculture *See* Canadian Association of Professional Apiculturists

Association canadienne des professionnels de l'insolvabilité et de la réorganisation *See* Canadian Association of Insolvency & Restructuring Professionals

Association canadienne des professionnels de la sécurité routière *See* Canadian Association of Road Safety Professionals

Association canadienne des professionnels de la vente *See* Canadian Professional Sales Association

Association canadienne des professionnels des services alimentaires *See* Canadian Association of Foodservice Professionals

Association canadienne des professionnels en conditionnement physique *See* The Canadian Association of Fitness Professionals

Association canadienne des professionnels en conformité *See* Association of Canadian Compliance Professionals

Association canadienne des professionnels en dons planifiés *See* Canadian Association of Gift Planners

Association canadienne des professionnels en réglementation *See* Canadian Association of Professional Regulatory Affairs

Association canadienne des programmes d'aide aux employés *See* Canadian Employee Assistance Program Association

Association canadienne des programmes de ressources pour la famille *See* Canadian Association of Family Resource Programs

Association canadienne des prospecteurs & entrepreneurs *See* Prospectors & Developers Association of Canada

Association canadienne des radiodiffuseurs *See* Canadian Association of Broadcasters

Association canadienne des radiodiffuseurs ethniques *See* Canadian Association of Ethnic (Radio) Broadcasters

L'Association canadienne des radiologistes *See* Canadian Association of Radiologists

Association canadienne des rédacteurs scientifiques *See* Canadian Science Writers' Association

Association canadienne des relations industrielles (ACRI) / Canadian Industrial Relations Association (CIRA)

Département des relations industrielles, Université Laval, #3129, 1025, av. des Sciences-Humaines, Québec QC G1V 0A6
acri-cira@rlt.ulaval.ca
www.cira-acri.ca

Aperçu: *Dimension:* moyenne; *Envergure:* nationale; Organisme sans but lucratif; fondée en 1963
Mission: Promouvoir la discussion, la recherche, et la formation dans le domaine des relations industrielles
Affiation(s): International Industrial Relations Association; Industrial Relations Research Association; La Fédération canadienne des sciences sociales
Membre(s) du bureau directeur:
Kelly Williams Whitt, Président
kelly.williams@uleth.ca
Étienne Cantin, Secrétaire
etienne.cantin@rlt.ulaval.ca
Finances: *Budget de fonctionnement annuel:* Moins de $50,000
Membre(s) du personnel: 1
Membre: 400; *Montant de la cotisation:* 120$ régulier; 60$ étudiant/retraité; 160$ institutionnel; *Critères d'admissibilite:* Ouverte à toute personne ou organisation qui s'intéresse aux relations industrielles, par exemple aux relations patronales-syndicales, au droit du travail, aux problèmes de main-d'oeuvre et à la gestion des ressources humaines; parmi les membres actuels de l'Association, on retrouve des avocats, des économistes, des sociologues, des syndicalistes, des gestionnaires; quatre catégories de membres - régulier, institutionnel, étudiant, à la retraite
Activités: Congrès annuel; *Listes de destinataires:* Oui
Prix, Bouses:
• Le prix Allen Ponak (Prix)
Eligibility: Étudiant aux études supérieures *Amount:* 500$
• Prix Gérard Dion (Prix)
Eligibility: Personne our organisation qui s'est démarquée dans sa discipline
• Prix H.D. Woods (Prix)
Eligibility: Praticien ou praticienne ou une personne du milieu académique du domaine des relations industrielles
Meetings/Conferences: • Association canadienne des relations industrielles 2015 Conférence, May, 2015, HEC Montréal, Montréal, QC
Scope: National

Association canadienne des représentants de ventes en gros ***See*** Canadian Association of Wholesale Sales Representatives

L'Association Canadienne des Residents en Orthopédie ***See*** Canadian Orthopaedic Residents Association

Association canadienne des ressources hydriques ***See*** Canadian Water Resources Association

Association canadienne des restaurateurs professionnels ***See*** Canadian Association of Professional Conservators

Association canadienne des réviseurs ***See*** Editors' Association of Canada

Association canadienne des revues savantes ***See*** Canadian Association of Learned Journals

L'Association canadienne des sages-femmes ***See*** Canadian Association of Midwives

Association canadienne des sciences de l'information ***See*** Canadian Association for Information Science

Association canadienne des sciences géomatiques ***See*** Canadian Institute of Geomatics

Association canadienne des sciences régionales (ACSR) / Canadian Regional Science Association (CRSA)

a/s INRS-Urbanisation, 3465, rue Durocher, Montréal QC H2X 2C6
Tél: 514-499-4052; *Téléc:* 514-499-4065
geog.utm.utoronto.ca/crsa-acsr
Aperçu: *Dimension:* petite; *Envergure:* nationale; fondée en 1977
Mission: Favoriser la circulation des idées et promouvoir les études canadiennes portant sur les régions en se servant d'instruments, de méthodes et de cadres théoriques; propos aux sciences régionales comme ceux mis en avant par les diverses sciences, sociales ou autres
Membre de: Humanities & Social Sciences Federation of Canada
Membre(s) du bureau directeur:
Bill Anderson, Président
bander@uwindsor.ca
Richard Shearmur, Vice-président
richard.shearmur@ucs.inrs.ca
Pierre-Marcel Desjardins, Directeur exécutif
pierre-marcel.desjardins@umoncton.ca
Finances: *Budget de fonctionnement annuel:* Moins de $50,000
Membre: 245; *Montant de la cotisation:* 60$ individuel; 25$ étudiant/sans emploi
Activités: *Listes de destinataires:* Oui

Association canadienne des slavistes ***See*** Canadian Association of Slavists

Association canadienne des Snowbirds ***See*** Canadian Snowbird Association

Association canadienne des sociétés Elizabeth Fry ***See*** Canadian Association of Elizabeth Fry Societies

Association canadienne des sociétés fraternelles ***See*** Canadian Fraternal Association

Association canadienne des spécialistes en emploi et des employeurs ***See*** Canadian Association of Career Educators & Employers

L'Association canadienne des sports d'hiver ***See*** Canadian Snowsports Association

Association canadienne des sports en fauteuil roulant ***See*** Canadian Wheelchair Sports Association

Association canadienne des sports pour amputés ***See*** Canadian Amputee Sports Association

Association canadienne des sports pour aveugles inc. ***See*** Canadian Blind Sports Association Inc.

Association canadienne des stomathérapeutes ***See*** Canadian Association for Enterostomal Therapy

Association canadienne des surintendants de golf ***See*** Canadian Golf Superintendents Association

Association canadienne des techniciens en explosif ***See*** Canadian Explosives Technicians' Association

Association canadienne des techniciens et technologistes en santé animale ***See*** Canadian Association of Animal Health Technologists & Technicians

Association canadienne des technologues en electroneurophysiologie inc. ***See*** Canadian Association of Electroneurophysiology Technologists Inc.

Association canadienne des technologues en radiation médicale ***See*** Canadian Association of Medical Radiation Technologists

Association canadienne des télécommunications sans fil ***See*** Canadian Wireless Telecommunications Association

Association canadienne des thérapeutes du sport ***See*** Canadian Athletic Therapists Association

Association canadienne des travailleurs sociaux ***See*** Canadian Association of Social Workers

Association canadienne des travaux publics ***See*** Canadian Public Works Association

Association Canadienne des Troubles Anxieux ***See*** Anxiety Disorders Association of Canada

L'association Canadienne des troubles d'apprentissage ***See*** Learning Disabilities Association of Canada

Association canadienne des tunnels ***See*** Tunnelling Association of Canada

Association canadienne des utilisateurs SAS ***See*** Canadian Association of SAS Users

Association canadienne des vétérans de la Corée ***See*** Korea Veterans Association of Canada Inc., Heritage Unit

Association Canadienne des Vétérans des Forces de la Paix pour les Nations Unies ***See*** Canadian Association of Veterans in United Nations Peacekeeping

Association Canadienne des Vétérinaires Porcins ***See*** Canadian Association of Swine Veterinarians

Association canadienne des victimes de la thalidomide ***See*** Thalidomide Victims Association of Canada

Association canadienne du béton préparé ***See*** Canadian Ready Mixed Concrete Association

Association canadienne du bison ***See*** Canadian Bison Association

Association canadienne du camionnage d'entreprise ***See*** Private Motor Truck Council of Canada

Association canadienne du capital de risque et d'investissement ***See*** Canada's Venture Capital & Private Equity Association

Association canadienne du cartonnage ondulé et du carton-caisse ***See*** Canadian Corrugated Containerboard Association

Association canadienne du cheval Percheron ***See*** Canadian Percheron Association

Association canadienne du ciment ***See*** Cement Association of Canada

Association canadienne du commerce des semences ***See*** Canadian Seed Trade Association

Association canadienne du commerce des valeurs mobilières ***See*** Investment Industry Association of Canada

Association canadienne du Contreplaqué et de Placages de bois dur ***See*** Canadian Hardwood Plywood & Veneer Association

Association canadienne du contrôle du trafic aérien ***See*** Canadian Air Traffic Control Association

Association canadienne du diabète ***See*** Canadian Diabetes Association

Association canadienne du droit de l'environnement ***See*** Canadian Environmental Law Association

Association canadienne du droit des technologies de l'information ***See*** Canadian IT Law Association

Association canadienne du gaz ***See*** Canadian Gas Association

L'Association canadienne du Jouet ***See*** Canadian Toy Association / Canadian Toy & Hobby Fair

Association canadienne du marketing ***See*** Canadian Marketing Association

L'Association canadienne du médicament générique ***See*** Canadian Generic Pharmaceutical Association

Association canadienne du parachutisme sportif ***See*** Canadian Sport Parachuting Association

Association canadienne du personnel administratif universitaire ***See*** Canadian Association of University Business Officers

Association canadienne du plongeon amateur Inc. ***See*** Diving Plongeon Canada

L'Association canadienne du pneu et du caoutchouc ***See*** Tire and Rubber Association of Canada

Association canadienne du propane ***See*** Canadian Propane Association

Association canadienne du soin des plaies ***See*** Canadian Association of Wound Care

Association canadienne du sport collégial ***See*** Canadian Collegiate Athletic Association

Association canadienne du téléphone indépendant ***See*** Canadian Independent Telephone Association

Association canadienne du transport urbain ***See*** Canadian Urban Transit Association

Association canadienne du véhicule récréatif ***See*** Canadian Recreational Vehicle Association

Association canadienne en prothéses et orthéses ***See*** Canadian Association of Prosthetics & Orthotics

L'association Canadienne en psychopedagogie ***See*** Canadian Association for Educational Psychology

Association canadienne en vibrations de machines ***See*** Canadian Machinery Vibration Association

Association canadienne française pour l'avancement des sciences ***Voir*** Association francophone pour le savoir

Association canadienne Hereford *See* Canadian Hereford Association

Association canadienne pour l'avancement des études néerlandaises *See* Canadian Association for the Advancement of Netherlandic Studies

Association canadienne pour l'avancement des femmes du sport et de l'activité physique *See* Canadian Association for the Advancement of Women & Sport & Physical Activity

Association canadienne pour l'éducation médicale *See* Canadian Association for Medical Education

Association canadienne pour l'étude de l'éducation des adultes *See* Canadian Association for the Study of Adult Education

Association canadienne pour l'etude de l'education des autochtones *See* Canadian Association for the Study of Indigenous Education

Association canadienne pour l'étude des langues et de la littérature du Commonwealth *See* Canadian Association for Commonwealth Literature & Language Studies

Association canadienne pour l'étude du foie *See* Canadian Association for the Study of the Liver

Association canadienne pour l'étude du Quaternaire *See* Canadian Quaternary Association

Association canadienne pour l'histoire du nursing *See* Canadian Association for the History of Nursing

Association canadienne pour l'intégration communautaire *See* Canadian Association for Community Living

Association canadienne pour l'obtention des services aux personnes autistiques *See* Autism Treatment Services of Canada

Association canadienne pour la conservation et la restauration des biens culturels *See* Canadian Association for Conservation of Cultural Property

Association canadienne pour la formation des enseignants *See* Canadian Association for Teacher Education

Association canadienne pour la formation en travail social *See* Canadian Association for Social Work Education

Association canadienne pour la prévention de la discrimination et ou harcèlement en milieu d'enseignement supérieur *See* Canadian Association for the Prevention of Discrimination & Harassment in Higher Education

L'Association canadienne pour la prévention du suicide *See* Canadian Association for Suicide Prevention

Association canadienne pour la promotion des services de garde à l'enfance *See* Child Care Advocacy Association of Canada

Association canadienne pour la recherche infirmière *See* Canadian Association for Nursing Research

Association canadienne pour la recherche sur les services et les politiques de la santé *See* Canadian Association for Health Services & Policy Research

L'Association canadienne pour la reconnaissance des acquis *See* Canadian Association for Prior Learning Assesment

Association canadienne pour la santé des adolescents *See* Canadian Association of Adolescent Health

Association canadienne pour la santé mentale *See* Canadian Mental Health Association

Association canadienne pour la science des animaux de laboratoire *See* Canadian Association for Laboratory Animal Science

Association canadienne pour les énergies renouvelables *See* Canadian Association for Renewable Energies

Association canadienne pour les études de renseignement et de sécurité *See* Canadian Association for Security & Intelligence Studies

L'Association canadienne pour les études irlandaises *See* Canadian Association for Irish Studies

Association canadienne pour les études supérieures *See* Canadian Association for Graduate Studies

Association canadienne pour les études sur la coopération *See* Canadian Association for Studies in Co-operation

Association canadienne pour les jeunes enfants *See* Canadian Association for Young Children

Association canadienne pour les Nations Unies *See* United Nations Association in Canada

Association Canadienne pour les Plantes Fourragères *See* Canadian Forage & Grassland Association

Association canadienne pour les skieurs handicapés *See* Canadian Association for Disabled Skiing

Association canadienne pour les structures et matériaux composites *See* Canadian Association for Composite Structures & Materials

Association canadienne pour une étude pratique de la loi dans le système éducatif *See* Canadian Association for the Practical Study of Law in Education

Association canadienne sur la qualité de l'eau *See* Canadian Association on Water Quality

Association canadienne Tourbe de Sphaigne *See* Canadian Sphagnum Peat Moss Association

Association canadienne-française de l'Alberta (ACFA)

#303, Pav. II, 8627, rue Marie-Anne-Gaboury, Edmonton AB T6C 3N1
Tél: 780-466-1680; *Téléc:* 780-465-6773
acfa@acfa.ab.ca
www.acfa.ab.ca
www.facebook.com/acfaab
www.youtube.com/user/acfaab
Aperçu: *Dimension:* moyenne; *Envergure:* provinciale; Organisme sans but lucratif; fondée en 1926 surveillé par Fédération des communautés francophones et acadienne du Canada
Mission: Représenter la population francophone de l'Alberta; promouvoir le bien-être intellectuel, culturel et social des francophones de l'Alberta; encourager, faciliter et développer l'enseignement en français; entretenir des relations amicales avec les groupes de différentes origines ethniques et anglophones dans la province
Membre de: Association canadienne d'éducation de langue française
Affiliation(s): Fédération culturelle canadienne-française
Membre(s) du bureau directeur:
Isabelle Laurin, Directeur général (par intérim)
i.laurin@acfa.ab.ca
Membre(s) du personnel: 11
Membre: 13 associations régionales
Activités: *Service de conférenciers:* Oui; *Bibliothèque* rendez-vous

Association canadienne-française de l'Ontario (ACFO) *Voir* Association canadienne-française de l'Ontario, Mille-îles

Association canadienne-française de l'Ontario, Mille-îles (ACFOMI)

Kingston ON
Tél: 613-546-7863; *Téléc:* 613-507-7794
www.acfomi.org/acfo
Nom précédent: Association canadienne-française de l'Ontario (ACFO)
Aperçu: *Dimension:* moyenne; *Envergure:* provinciale surveillé par Fédération des communautés francophones et acadienne du Canada
Mission: Appuyer le développement communautaire; rassembler les forces vives de la communauté franco-ontarienne; faire des représentations politiques
Membre(s) du bureau directeur:
Lucie Mercier, Directrice générale
Membre: 1-99; *Critères d'admissibilite:* Quiconque de langue ou de culture française résident en Ontario

Association canadienne-française de Régina (ACFR)

#100, 3850, rue Hillsdale, Regina SK S4S 7J5
Tél: 306-545-4533
acfr.admin@gmail.com
www.acfr.ca
www.facebook.com/acfr.deregina
Aperçu: *Dimension:* petite; *Envergure:* provinciale; fondée en 1965
Mission: Assurer une concertation entre les associations francophones de Régina; assurer la visibilité des francophones de Régina; promouvoir l'épanouissement de la langue française dans les secteurs ci-haut mentionnés; assurer l'accès à des services répondant aux besoins de la communauté francophone de Régina; défendre et promouvoir les droits et les intérêts des francophones de Régina; offrir aux associations communautaires des services d'information
Membre de: Association culturelle franco-canadienne de la Saskatchewan
Affiliation(s): Commission culturelle fransaskoise; Regina Multicultural Council
Membre(s) du bureau directeur:
Jessica Chartier, Directrice générale
direction.acfr@gmail.com
Siriki Diabagaté, Président
Jean-Marie Allard, Vice-président
Isabelle Nkapnang, Trésorière
Membre(s) du personnel: 3
Membre: *Critères d'admissibilite:* Francophones et francophiles; *Comités:* Comité culturel
Activités: Activités sociales, culturelles, éducatives et sportives; vente de produits français

Association Carrefour Famille Montcalm (ACFM)

197, rue Industrielle, Saint-Lin-Laurentides QC J5M 2S9
Tél: 450-439-2669; *Téléc:* 450-439-8763
Ligne sans frais: 877-439-2669
info@acfm-qc.org
www.acfmqc.org
www.facebook.com/293704847321436
Également appelé: Maison de la Famille Montcalm
Nom précédent: Association des familles monoparentales et recomposées de Montcalm
Aperçu: *Dimension:* petite; *Envergure:* locale; Organisme sans but lucratif; fondée en 1986
Mission: Le but premier de l'association est d'améliorer la qualité de vie de toutes les familles qui résident dans le comté de Montcalm en leur apportant les ressources et les outils nécessaires
Membre de: Familles de Montcalm
Affiliation(s): Fédération des associations de familles monoparentales du Québec; Fédération québécoise des organismes communautaires Famille; Carrefour Jeunesse Emploi; Les Filandières; Centre Jeunesse; Le Tremplin; Régie régionale de la Santé et des Services sociaux des Laurentides; Centraide; Santé Canada; Le Réseau; Centre local de services communautaires
Membre(s) du bureau directeur:
Henri Thibodeau, Directeur général
henri.thibodeau@acfm-qc.org
Nathalie Tessier, Présidente
Jennifer Mojor, Vice-présidente par intérim
Finances: *Fonds:* Gouvernement régional
Membre(s) du personnel: 20
Membre: *Montant de la cotisation:* Gratuite; *Critères d'admissibilite:* Familles
Activités: Acceuil, écoute et références; journal mensuel; ateliers; relation d'aide; sorties familiales; rencontres avec intervenants; alphabétisation; café; rencontres; toxicomanie; transport accompagnement; Halte-garderie; conferences; location sieges d'auto; Programme d'Aide Personnelle, Familiale, et Communautaire; Programme d'action communautaire pour les enfants; *Stagiaires:* Oui; *Service de conférenciers:* Oui

Association catholique franco-canadienne de la Saskatchewan; Association culturelle franco-canadienne de la Saskatchewan *Voir* Assemblée communautaire fransaskoise

Association catholique manitobaine de la santé *See* Catholic Health Association of Manitoba

Association CFA Montréal / Montreal CFA Society

#408, 3131 boul de la Concorde est, Montréal QC H7E 4W4
Tél: 514-990-3772; *Téléc:* 514-990-3772
info@cfamontreal.org
www.cfamontreal.org
Également appelé: Association des analystes financiers de Montréal
Aperçu: *Dimension:* petite; *Envergure:* locale; fondée en 1950
Mission: Faire respecter le code de déontologie et les règles de comportement professionnel élaboré par le CFA Institute à l'intention des professionnels de l'industrie de l'analyse financière de manière à assurer la qualité et la perception de

notre profession auprès du public. Appuyer ses membres dans leurs efforts de perfectionnement et de formation par le biais de: conférences avec un grand contenu formatif, de nature pratique ou théorique; cours de préparation à l'examen du CFA Institute; la promotion du programme d'accréditation du CFA Institute pour les membres possédant déjà le titre de CFA
Membre(s) du bureau directeur:
Suzie Éthier, Directrice à l'administration
suzie.ethier@cfamontreal.org
Jacques Lussier, Président
Membre: 1275; *Comités:* Programmes; adhésions; communications; relations universitaires; éthique; gouvernance; relations avec les employeurs
Activités: *Événements de sensibilisation:* Soirée bénéfice annuelle

Association chasse & pêche de Chibougamau
CP 171, Chibougamau QC G8P 2K6
Tél: 418-748-2021
info@acpcchibougamau.com
www.acpcchibougamau.com
Aperçu: *Dimension:* petite; *Envergure:* locale
Mission: Favoriser et développer parmi les membres l'esprit sportif en préservant la conservation des richesses naturelles
Membre(s) du bureau directeur:
Serge Picard, Président

Association chasse et pêche du Lac Brébeuf
247, ch du Lac Brébeuf, Saint-Félix-d'Otis QC G0V 1M0
Tél: 418-544-4884; *Téléc:* 418-544-7456
Aperçu: *Dimension:* petite; *Envergure:* locale
Mission: S'occupe de ce territoire protégé et contrôlé de chasse, de pêche et de villégiature
Affliation(s): Regroupement régional de gestionnaires de Zec
Finances: *Fonds:* Gouvernement provincial

Association chiropratique canadienne ***See*** Canadian Chiropractic Association

Association chiropratique de l'Ontario ***See*** Ontario Chiropractic Association

Association chrétienne du travail du Canada ***See*** Christian Labour Association of Canada

Association Cinématographique - Canada ***See*** Motion Picture Association - Canada

L'Association commerciale Hong Kong-Canada ***See*** Hong Kong-Canada Business Association

L'Association communautaire francophone de St-Jean (ACFSJ) / St. John's Francophone Community Association
#245, 65, rue Ridge, St. John's NL A1B 4P5
Tél: 709-726-4900
bonjour@acfsj.ca
www.acfsj.ca
Également appelé: Association francophone de St-Jean
Aperçu: *Dimension:* petite; *Envergure:* locale; fondée en 2003
Mission: Inspirer et soutenir le développement et l'action de la communauté francophone de St-Jean par le biais du centre scolaire et communautaire des Grands-Vents
Membre de: Le Fédération des francophones de Terre-Neuve et du Labrador
Membre(s) du bureau directeur:
Adrienne Pratt, Directrice générale
Membre(s) du personnel: 4
Membre: *Montant de la cotisation:* 20$ individu; 40$ famille; 15$ étudiant
Activités: Programmation socio-culturelle; *Bibliothèque:* Centre de ressources Centre scolaire et communautaire des Grands-; Bibliothèque publique

Association continentale pour l'automatisation des bâtiments ***See*** Continental Automated Buildings Association

Association coopérative d'économie familiale - Abitibi-Témiscamingue
CP 514, Rouyn-Noranda QC J9X 3C6
Tél: 819-279-5721
acef.at@gmail.com
Également appelé: ACEF - Abitibi-Témiscamingue
Aperçu: *Dimension:* petite; *Envergure:* locale; Organisme sans but lucratif
Mission: Défendre les droits des consommateurs; éducation et prévention en matière de budget, crédit, endettement
Membre de: Fédération des ACEF du Québec
Activités: Consultation budgétaire, cours sur le budget - service aux consommateurs

Association coopérative d'économie familiale - Amiante, Beauce, Etchemins
1176, rue Notre-Dame est, Thetford Mines QC G6G 1J1
Tél: 418-338-4755; *Téléc:* 418-338-6234
Ligne sans frais: 888-338-4755
info@acef-abe.org
www.acef-abe.org
www.facebook.com/ACEF.ABE
Également appelé: ACEF - Amiante-Beauce-Etchemins
Nom précédent: Association coopérative d'économie familiale - Thetford Mines
Aperçu: *Dimension:* petite; *Envergure:* locale; Organisme sans but lucratif; fondée en 1967
Mission: Intervenir dans les domaines du budget, du crédit, de l'endettement et de la protection des consommateurs; défendre les droits des personnes assistées sociales
Membre de: Coalition des associations de Consommateurs
Membre(s) du personnel: 4
Membre: *Montant de la cotisation:* $10

Association coopérative d'économie familiale - Basses Laurentides
42B, rue Turgeon, Sainte-Thérèse QC J7E 3H4
Tél: 450-430-2228
acefbl@consommateur.qc.ca
acefbl.org
Également appelé: ACEF - Basses Laurentides
Aperçu: *Dimension:* petite; *Envergure:* locale; Organisme sans but lucratif
Mission: Viser la protection, la défense et la représentation des consommateurs et consommatrices de la région des Basses-Laurentides
Membre de: Coalition des associations des consommateurs de Quebec (CACQ)
Affliation(s): Ligue des droits et libertés; Regroupement des organismes communautaires des Laurentides (ROCL)
Membre(s) du bureau directeur:
Sylvie Perron, Coordonnatrice
coordination-acefbl@b2b2c.ca
Membre(s) du personnel: 4
Membre: *Montant de la cotisation:* 10$
Activités: Consultations budgétaires; ateliers d'éducation populaire

Association coopérative d'économie familiale - Bois-Francs
#230, 59, rue Monfette, Victoriaville QC G6P 1J8
Tél: 819-752-5855
acefbf@cdcbf.qc.ca
cacq.ca/ACEF-des-Bois-Francs
Également appelé: ACEF des Bois-Francs
Aperçu: *Dimension:* petite; *Envergure:* locale; Organisme sans but lucratif

Association coopérative d'économie familiale - Estrie
#202, 187, rue Laurier, Sherbrooke QC J1H 4Z4
Tél: 819-563-8144
acefestrie@consommateur.qc.ca
www.acefestrie.ca
Également appelé: ACEF - Estrie
Aperçu: *Dimension:* petite; *Envergure:* locale; Organisme sans but lucratif; fondée en 1972
Mission: De défendre et de promouvoir des droits des consommatrices et consommateurs
Membre de: Union des consommateurs
Affliation(s): Table d'action contre l'appauvrissement Estrie; Solidarité populaire Estrie
Finances: *Fonds:* Agence de l'efficacité énergétique; Secrétariat à l'action communautaire autonome du Québec (SACA)
Membre: *Montant de la cotisation:* 10$ individuel; 5$ personne à faible revenu; 25$ organisme; 100$ syndicat; *Critères d'admissibilite:* Individus; organismes; syndicats; caisses populaires
Activités: Rencontre d'information; service aux consommateurs; *Bibliothèque:* Centre de documentation

Association coopérative d'économie familiale - Granby ***Voir*** Association coopérative d'économie familiale - Montérégie-est

Association coopérative d'économie familiale - Grand-Portage
5, rue Iberville, Rivière-du-Loup QC G5R 1G5
Tél: 418-867-8545; *Téléc:* 418-867-8546
Ligne sans frais: 866-762-0269
acefgp@videotron.ca
www.acefgp.ca
www.facebook.com/profile.php?id=100001677523200
Également appelé: ACEF du Grand-Portage
Aperçu: *Dimension:* petite; *Envergure:* locale; fondée en 1990
Membre de: Fédération des associations d'économie familiale
Membre(s) du bureau directeur:
Jean-Philippe Nadeau, Président
Finances: *Budget de fonctionnement annuel:* Moins de $50,000

Association coopérative d'économie familiale - Haut-Saint-Laurent
#111, 28, rue Saint-Paul, Salaberry-de-Valleyfield QC J6S 4A8
Tél: 450-371-3470; *Téléc:* 450-371-3425
acefhsl@rocler.com
Également appelé: ACEF du Haut-Saint-Laurent
Aperçu: *Dimension:* petite; *Envergure:* locale
Membre de: Fédération des associations coopératifs d'économie familiale
Membre(s) du bureau directeur:
Carole Gadoua, Coordonnatrice

Association coopérative d'économie familiale - Ile-Jésus
#103, 1686, boul des Laurentides, Vimont QC H7M 2P4
Tél: 450-662-9428
aceflav@mediom.com
aceflav.wordpress.com
Également appelé: ACEF - Ile Jésus
Aperçu: *Dimension:* petite; *Envergure:* locale; fondée en 1997
Mission: D'offrir des services facilitant l'atteinte de l'équilibre du budget familial ou personnel.

Association coopérative d'économie familiale - Lanaudière
#124, 200, rue de Salaberry, Joliette QC J6E 4G1
Tél: 450-756-1333
Ligne sans frais: 866-414-1333
aceflanaudiere@consommateur.qc.ca
www.consommateur.qc.ca/acef-lan
www.facebook.com/314361095272708
Également appelé: ACEF - Lanaudière
Aperçu: *Dimension:* petite; *Envergure:* locale; Organisme sans but lucratif; fondée en 1974
Membre de: L'Union des consommateurs
Finances: *Budget de fonctionnement annuel:* $100,000-$250,000
Membre(s) du personnel: 7
Membre: 100-499; *Montant de la cotisation:* 10-35/an; *Critères d'admissibilite:* Individus, coopératives, OSBL
Activités: Consultation budgétaire; cours en budget et consommation; ateliers thématiques; conseils en crédit, budget familial, endettement et consommation;

Association coopérative d'économie familiale - Mauricie ***Voir*** Centre d'intervention budgétaire et sociale de la Mauricie

Association coopérative d'économie familiale - Montérégie-est
162, rue St-Charles Sud, Granby QC J2G 7A4
Tél: 450-375-1443; *Téléc:* 450-375-2449
Ligne sans frais: 888-375-1443
acefme@videotron.ca
www.acefmonteregie-est.com
Également appelé: ACEF - Montérégie-est
Nom précédent: Association coopérative d'économie familiale - Granby
Aperçu: *Dimension:* petite; *Envergure:* locale; Organisme sans but lucratif; fondée en 1974
Mission: Promouvoir et à défendre les intérêts des consommateurs à faibles et moyens revenus.
Membre de: Union des consommateurs
Membre(s) du bureau directeur:
Roger Lafrance, Coordinateur
coordo.acefme@videotron.ca
Membre(s) du personnel: 6
Membre: *Critères d'admissibilite:* Individus et syndicats
Activités: Consultations budgétaires; rencontres éducatives sur le budget et sur la loi de la protection du consommateur; cours sur le budget; service de référence et d'aide en consommation; *Stagiaires:* Oui; *Service de conférenciers:* Oui
Prix, Bourses:
• Office de la protection du consommateur (Prix)

Association coopérative d'économie familiale - Montréal (Centre) *Voir* Option consommateurs

Association coopérative d'économie familiale - Montréal (Rive-Sud) (ACEF)
2010, ch de Chambly, Longueuil QC J4J 3Y2
Tél: 450-677-6394; *Téléc:* 450-677-0101
Ligne sans frais: 877-677-6394
acefrsm@consommateur.qc.ca
www.acefrsm.com
Aperçu: *Dimension:* petite; *Envergure:* locale; fondée en 1973
Mission: Pour fournir des conseils financiers aux gens pour qu'ils puissent devenir stable financière
Membre de: Fédérations nationale des associations de consommateurs du Québec
Membre(s) du bureau directeur:
Marie-Edith Trudel, Coordonnatrice
Membre: *Montant de la cotisation:* Barème

Association coopérative d'économie familiale - Québec (Rive-sud)
33, rue Carrier, Lévis QC G6V 5N5
Tél: 418-835-6633; *Téléc:* 418-835-5818
Ligne sans frais: 877-835-6633
acef@acefrsq.com
www.acefrsq.com
www.facebook.com/218767461471174
twitter.com/acefrsq
www.youtube.com/user/acefrsq
Également appelé: ACEF Rive-sud
Aperçu: *Dimension:* petite; *Envergure:* locale; Organisme sans but lucratif; fondée en 1987
Mission: L'Association coopérative d'économie familiale (ACEF) Rive-Sud est un organisme à but non lucratif d'aide, d'éducation et d'intervention dans les domaines du budget, de l'endettement et de la consommation. L'ACEF travaille à défendre les droits des consommatrices et consommateurs
Membre de: Union des Consommateurs
Membre(s) du bureau directeur:
Denise Lavallée, Présidente
Daniel Lemay, Vice-président
Édith St-Hilaire, Coordonnatrice
Finances: *Budget de fonctionnement annuel:* $100,000-$250,000
Membre(s) du personnel: 87; 20 bénévole(s)
Membre: 40; *Montant de la cotisation:* 20$ individuel; 30$ organisme à but non lucratif; 65$ autres types d'organismes
Activités: *Stagiaires:* Oui; *Service de conférenciers:* Oui; *Bibliothèque* Bibliothèque publique

Association coopérative d'économie familiale - Thetford Mines *Voir* Association coopérative d'économie familiale - Amiante, Beauce, Etchemins

Association coopérative d'économie familiale de l'est de Montréal
5955, rue de Marseille, Montréal QC H1N 1K6
Tél: 514-257-6622; *Téléc:* 514-257-7998
acefest@consommateur.qc.ca
www.consommateur.qc.ca/acefest
Également appelé: ACEF de l'est
Aperçu: *Dimension:* petite; *Envergure:* locale; Organisme sans but lucratif; fondée en 1983
Mission: Informer le consommateur pour le réhabiliter dans son fonctionnement budgétaire, économique et social; travailler à l'émancipation économique du consommateur, dans l'intérêt de la famille
Membre de: Coalition des associations de consommateurs du Québec
Membre(s) du bureau directeur:
Maryse Bouchard, Coordonnatrice
Membre(s) du personnel: 5
Activités: Conférences publiques sur la consommation; consultations budgétaires; *Service de conférenciers:* Oui

Association coopérative d'économie familiale de l'Outaouais (ACEF)
109, rue Wright, Gatineau QC J8X 2G7
Tél: 819-770-4911
Ligne sans frais: 866-770-4911
acefoutaouais@videotron.ca
acefo.com
Aperçu: *Dimension:* petite; *Envergure:* locale; fondée en 1966
Mission: Association de défense des consommateurs et consommatrices; offre des services de consultation budgétaire, cours sur le budget, informations téléphoniques et aide aux consommateurs. Champs d'activités: endettement et consommation
Affiliation(s): Coalition des associations consommateurs du Québec
Finances: *Fonds:* Gouvernement provincial
Membre(s) du personnel: 3; 20 bénévole(s)
Membre: 30 institutionnel; 200 individu; *Montant de la cotisation:* 10$

Association coopérative d'économie familiale du Nord de Montréal
7500, av Chateaubriand, Montréal QC H2R 2M1
Tél: 514-277-7959; *Téléc:* 514-277-7730
www.acefnord.org
Également appelé: ACEF du Nord de Montréal
Aperçu: *Dimension:* petite; *Envergure:* locale; fondée en 1974
Mission: Offrir des services de consultation budgétaire, d'aide aux consommateurs, des cours sur le budget, des sessions sur le budget, crédit, endettement
Membre de: Union des consommateurs
Finances: *Budget de fonctionnement annuel:* $100,000-$250,000
Membre: 100-499; *Montant de la cotisation:* 5$ individu; 50$ organisme
Activités: Consultations budgétaires; cours sur le budget; soirées de l'ACEF; rencontres d'information; service d'aide aux consommateurs; *Service de conférenciers:* Oui; *Bibliothèque:* Centre de documentation; Bibliothèque publique rendez-vous
Publications:
• Consomm'action
Type: Newsletter

Association coopérative d'économie familiale du Sud-Ouest de Montréal (ACEF)
6734, boul Monk, Montréal QC H4E 3J1
Tél: 514-362-1771; *Téléc:* 514-362-0660
acefsom@consommateur.qc.ca
consommateur.qc.ca/acef-som
Aperçu: *Dimension:* petite; *Envergure:* locale; Organisme sans but lucratif; fondée en 1984
Mission: Défendre des droits des consommateurs, individuels et collectifs dans le domaine de la consommation, de la formation en gestion des finances personnelles, de la prévention de l'endettement aux solutions du surendettement
Membre de: Coalition des associations de consommateurs du Québec
Membre(s) du bureau directeur:
Marie-Claude Desjardins, Coordonnatrice
Membre: 100-499; *Montant de la cotisation:* 10$ régulier; 2$ personne à faible revenu
Activités: Cours sur le budget; ateliers sur finances personnelles et solutions à l'endettement; projets d'animation de milieu; *Bibliothèque* rendez-vous

Association coopérative d'économie familiale Rimouski-Neigette et Mitis (ACEF)
CP 504, #306, 124, rue Sainte-Marie, Rimouski QC G5L 7C5
Tél: 418-723-0744; *Téléc:* 418-723-7972
acefriki@globetrotter.net
www.consommateur.qc.ca/acef-m/index.htm
Aperçu: *Dimension:* petite; *Envergure:* locale; Organisme sans but lucratif; fondée en 1993
Mission: Aider les personnes à moyens et faibles revenus, qui éprouvent des difficultés dans les domaines du budget et de la consommation; travailler à la défense des intérêts des consommateurs dans le but de promouvoir une plus grande justice sociale
Membre de: Coalition des associations de consommateurs du Québec
Finances: *Budget de fonctionnement annuel:* $50,000-$100,000
Membre(s) du personnel: 2; 13 bénévole(s)
Membre: 101; *Montant de la cotisation:* 10$ individu; *Critères d'admissibilite:* Consommateurs et organismes qui souscrivent aux objectifs de l'organisme; *Comités:* Logement; Promotion
Activités: Consultation budgétaire; rencontres de groupes; cours sur budget; aide en consommation; *Événements de sensibilisation:* Concours Endettement: Prudence!; *Service de conférenciers:* Oui; *Bibliothèque:* Centre de documentation

Association coopérative d'économie famillale de Québec (ACEF)
570, rue du Roi, Québec QC G1K 2X2
Tél: 418-522-1568; *Téléc:* 418-522-7023
acefque@mediom.qc.ca
www.acefdequebec.org
Également appelé: Association Coopérative d'économie sociale de Québec
Nom précédent: Association d'économie familiale du Québec; Association québécoise d'économie familiale
Aperçu: *Dimension:* moyenne; *Envergure:* provinciale
Membre(s) du bureau directeur:
Réjeanne Cyr-Reid, Coordonnatrice
Ulla Gunst, Secrétaire
Publications:
• L'Intercom

Association coopérative des pêcheurs de l'île Itée (ACPI) / Island Fishermen Cooperative Association Ltd. (IFCA)
90, rue principale, Lamèque NB E8T 1M8
Tél: 506-344-2204; *Téléc:* 506-344-0413
www.acpi-ifca.com
Aperçu: *Dimension:* petite; *Envergure:* locale; fondée en 1943
Membre(s) du bureau directeur:
Paul-Orel Chiasson, Directeur général

Association culturelle du Haut Saint-Jean inc.
165, rue Bellevue, Edmundston NB E3V 2E2
Tél: 506-735-7073
Aperçu: *Dimension:* petite; *Envergure:* locale
Mission: Favoriser le développement culturel communautaire francophone dans la région du Nord
Membre de: Conseil provincial des sociétés culturelles
Membre(s) du bureau directeur:
Hélène Desjardins, Contact
hedesjardins@gmail.com
Membre: *Critères d'admissibilite:* Comunauté de langue française de la région
Activités: Rencontres; concerts; ateliers; formation;

Association Culturelle Latino Canadienne *See* Latino Canadian Cultural Association

Association Culturelle Recréative Portugaise de Lasalle *Voir* Associaça Portuguesa de LaSalle

Association cycliste ontarienne *See* Ontario Cycling Association

L'Association d'Action Communautaire Bénévole du Restigouche *See* Restigouche County Volunteer Action Association Inc.

Association d'Acupuncture du Québec *Voir* Association des Acupuncteurs du Québec

Association d'archéologie canadienne *See* Canadian Archaeological Association

Association d'art des universités du Canada *See* Universities Art Association of Canada

Association d'assurances des juristes canadiens *See* Canadian Lawyers Insurance Association

Association d'économie familiale du Québec; Association québécoise d'économie familiale *Voir* Association coopérative d'économie famillale de Québec

Association d'éducation juridique communautaire (Manitoba) inc. *See* Community Legal Education Association (Manitoba) Inc.

Association d'éducation préscolaire du Québec (AÉPQ)
CP 99039, Succ. CSP Du Tremblay, Longueuil QC J4N 0A5
Tél: 514-343-6111
aepq@aepq.ca
www.aepq.ca
www.pinterest.com/aepq
Aperçu: *Dimension:* moyenne; *Envergure:* provinciale; Organisme sans but lucratif; fondée en 1976
Mission: Défendre la qualité de vie des enfants d'éducation préscolaire
Membre de: Conseil pédagogique interdisciplinaire du Québec (CPIQ)
Membre(s) du bureau directeur:
Maryse Rondeau, Présidente
Raymonde Hébert, Vice-Présidente
Véronique Chaloux, Trésorière
Membre: 1,000+; *Critères d'admissibilite:* Personnes intéressées à l'éducation préscolaire (enseignantes, éducatrices, cadres, conseillers pédagogiques, parents, chercheurs, professeurs)
Activités: Congrès; formation; *Service de conférenciers:* Oui
Prix, Bouses:
• Prix Monique-Vaillancourt-Antippa (Prix)

Avoir contribué à la promotion et à l'amélioration de la qualité de l'éducation préscolaire par un projet original et pertinent ayant un impact dans le milieu préscolaire

Association d'églises baptistes évangéliques au québec

9780, rue Sherbrooke est, Montréal QC H1L 6N6
Tél: 514-337-2555; *Téléc:* 514-337-8892
www.aebeq.qc.ca
Aperçu: *Dimension:* moyenne; *Envergure:* nationale; fondée en 1971 surveillé par Canadian Baptist Ministries
Mission: Aider les églises à communiquer l'évangile de Jésus-Christ à tous les Québécois; former des disciples et des leaders; devenir plus solides et se reproduire
Membre de: Fellowship of Evangelical Baptist Churches in Canada
Affliation(s): Camp des Bouleaux, Camp Patmos, Aujourd'hui l'Espoir, Organisme Renaissance Autochtone
Membre(s) du bureau directeur:
Michel M. Habbib, Secrétaire général
Gilles Lapierre, Directeur général
Membre: 65 000
Activités: Camps de jeunes; retraites; congrès; cohortes; *Stagiaires:* Oui; *Service de conférenciers:* Oui

Association d'élocution et des débats de la Saskatchewan ***See*** Saskatchewan Elocution & Debate Association

Association d'entraide des avocats de Montréal / Montreal Advocates' Mutual Assistance Assocation

#980, 1, rue Notre-Dame Est, Montréal QC H2Y 1B6
Tél: 514-866-9392; *Téléc:* 514-866-1488
aeam@barreaudemontreal.qc.ca
www.barreaudemontreal.qc.ca
Nom précédent: Association de bienfaisance des avocats de Montréal
Aperçu: *Dimension:* petite; *Envergure:* locale; fondée en 1938
Mission: Pour aider financièrement les membres du Barreau de Montréal dans leurs moments de besoin
Membre(s) du bureau directeur:
Jeffrey Boro, Président, Conseil d'administration
10 bénévole(s)
Membre: *Montant de la cotisation:* 25$

Association d'entraide Le Chaînon inc.

4373, rue de l'Esplanade, Montréal QC H2W 1T2
Tél: 514-845-0151; *Téléc:* 514-844-4180
info@lechainon.org
www.lechainon.org
www.facebook.com/lechainonmontreal
twitter.com/LeChainonMTL
Également appelé: Le Chaînon
Aperçu: *Dimension:* petite; *Envergure:* provinciale; Organisme sans but lucratif; fondée en 1932
Mission: Quatre programmes d'hébergement: A des femmes, momentanément sans logement et sans moyen financier/l'unité accueil de nuit (18 ans et plus) (16 places) et l'unité court terme (18 ans et plus) (20 places) offre un chez-soi temporaire avec présence attentionnée, support, consultation et orientation; A des femmes de 18 ans et plus en besoin d'un milieu de vie et en difficulté d'autonomie, l'unité transition (16 places) offre un chez-soi à moyen terme (durée maximale d'un an) avec accompagnement intensif. A des femmes d'un âge avancé et en perte d'autonomie, la maison Yvonne-Maisonneuve (maison de chambres supervisée avec services) (15 places) offre un chez-soi autonome à long terme
Affliation(s): Fédération de ressources d'hébergement pour femmes violentées et en difficulté du Québec
Membre(s) du bureau directeur:
Marcèle Lamarche, Directeur général
300 bénévole(s)

Association d'épilepsie de Calgary ***See*** Epilepsy Association of Calgary

Association d'équipement de transport du canada ***See*** Canadian Transportation Equipment Association

Association d'équitation thérapeutique Windsor-Essex ***See*** Windsor-Essex Therapeutic Riding Association

Association d'escrime de l'Ontario ***See*** Ontario Fencing Association

Association d'escrime de la Nouvelle-Écosse ***See*** Fencing Association of Nova Scotia

Association d'études américaines au Canada ***See*** Canadian Association for American Studies

Association d'études Baha'is ***See*** Association for Baha'i Studies

Association d'études canadiennes ***See*** Association for Canadian Studies

Association d'études juives canadiennes ***See*** Association for Canadian Jewish Studies

Association d'hospitalisation Canassurance ***See*** Canadian Association of Blue Cross Plans

Association d'iléostomie et colostomie de Montréal ***See*** Ileostomy & Colostomy Association of Montréal

Association d'informations en logements et immeubles adaptés (AILIA)

#213, 150 rue Grant, Longueuil QC J4H 3H6
Tél: 450-646-4343; *Téléc:* 450-646-6446
ailia@qc.aira.com
ailia.info
Aperçu: *Dimension:* petite; *Envergure:* locale; fondée en 1986
Mission: Encourager les personnes handicapées à vivre de façon autonome et à réformer les normes de construction résidentielle ainsi que tous les bâtiments sont accessibles aux personnes handicapées
Membre de: Groupement des personnes handicapées de la rive-sud de Montréal; Confédération des organismes de personnes handicapées du Québec; Habitations communautaires Longueuil; Logis des Aulniers
Membre(s) du bureau directeur:
Lloyd Feeney, Président, Conseil d'administration
Membre: *Comités:* Ville de Longueuil sur le Plan d'intervention des personnes handicapées; Bâtiments de la Ville de Longueuil sur le Plan d'intervention des personnes handicapées; Coordination de la Table des personnes handicapées de la Rive-Sud; Ressources résidentielles de la TPHRS; Environnement bâti et aménagement public
Activités: Rencontres; Conférences

Association d'isolation du Québec (AIQ)

#102, 4099, boul St-Jean-Baptiste, Montréal QC H1B 5V3
Tél: 514-354-9877; *Téléc:* 514-354-7401
Ligne sans frais: 800-711-2381
info@isolation-aiq.ca
www.isolation-aiq.ca
Nom précédent: Association des entrepreneurs en isolation de la Province de Québec
Aperçu: *Dimension:* petite; *Envergure:* provinciale; fondée en 1959
Mission: L'AIQ fait la promotion du respect des règles de l'art du métier et de l'utilisation de l'isolation dans les secteurs commerciaux, industriels et institutionnels.
Membre(s) du bureau directeur:
Linda Wilson, Directrice générale
linda.wilson@isolation-aiq.ca
Membre: *Montant de la cotisation:* 700 $ - 1 073.24 $; *Critères d'admissibilite:* Entrepreneurs; fabricants; distributeurs

Association d'orthopédie du Québec

Tour de L'Est, CP 216, Succ. Desjardins, 2, Complexe Desjardins, 30e étage, Montréal QC H5B 1G8
Tél: 514-844-0803; *Téléc:* 514-844-6786
aoq@fmsq.org
www.orthoquebec.ca
Aperçu: *Dimension:* moyenne; *Envergure:* provinciale surveillé par Fédération des médecins spécialistes du Québec
Mission: Valoriser le statut professionnel de ses membres; promouvoir leurs intérêts économiques; contribuer au développement de la chirurgie orthopédique et de la traumatologie par le biais d'activités de formation médicale continue
Membre(s) du bureau directeur:
Louis Bellemare, Président
Louise Leclaire, Secrétariat
Membre: 354; *Comités:* Exécutif; Développement professionnel continu; Affaires économiques; Exercice Professionnel et normes de pratique

Association d'oto-rhino-laryngologie et de chirurgie cervico-faciale du Québec

#3000, 2, Complexe Desjardins, Montréal QC H5B 1G8
Tél: 514-350-5125; *Téléc:* 514-350-5165
assorl@fmsq.org
www.orlquebec.org
Aperçu: *Dimension:* petite; *Envergure:* provinciale; Organisme sans but lucratif; fondée en 1959 surveillé par Fédération des médecins spécialistes du Québec
Mission: Valoriser le statut professionnel de ses membres, promouvoir leurs intérêts scientifiques, économiques et professionnels, et contribuer au développement de l'oto-rhino-laryngologie
Membre(s) du bureau directeur:
Frédéric Hélie, Secrétaire
Yanick Larivée, Président
Membre: 200

Association de balle des jeunes handicapés de Laval-Laurentides-Lanaudière (ABJHLLL)

2020, rue Laplante, Laval QC H7S 1E7
Tél: 450-689-4668
abjhl@hotmail.ca
Également appelé: Association de balle des jeunes handicapés de Laval/ABJHL
Aperçu: *Dimension:* petite; *Envergure:* locale; Organisme sans but lucratif; fondée en 1995
Mission: Etablir et opérer des équipes de balle pour la détente de l'esprit et du corps de jeunes handicapés physiques et/ou intellectuels, garçons et filles, principalement des régions de Laval, Laurentides et Lanaudière. Organiser et maintenir toute autre activités social, sportive et culturelle connexe pour promouvoir les buts de la corporations
Membre de: La petite ligue de baseball du Québec (Division Challenger)
Membre(s) du bureau directeur:
Tony Condello
Finances: *Budget de fonctionnement annuel:* Moins de $50,000
30 bénévole(s)
Membre: 91; *Montant de la cotisation:* 50$; *Critères d'admissibilite:* Fille ou garçon 6 à 18 ans, déficient physique et/ou intellectuel et ses père et mère
Activités: *Stagiaires:* Oui; *Service de conférenciers:* Oui

Association de bienfaisance des avocats de Montréal ***Voir*** Association d'entraide des avocats de Montréal

Association de bienfaisance et de retraite des policiers de la communauté urbaine de Montréal ***Voir*** Association de bienfaisance et de retraite des policiers et policières de la ville de Montréal

Association de bienfaisance et de retraite des policiers et policières de la ville de Montréal

#200, 480, rue Gilford, Montréal QC H2J 1N3
Tél: 514-527-8061; *Téléc:* 514-522-7736
info@caisse-abr.com
caisse-abr.com
Nom précédent: Association de bienfaisance et de retraite des policiers de la communauté urbaine de Montréal
Aperçu: *Dimension:* petite; *Envergure:* locale
Membre(s) du bureau directeur:
Louis Monette, Président/Directeur général

Association de chasse et pêche nordique, inc.

148, rue St-Marcellin Ouest, Les Escoumins QC G0T 1K0
Tél: 418-233-3062; *Téléc:* 418-233-3083
Aperçu: *Dimension:* petite; *Envergure:* locale; fondée en 1978
Affliation(s): Fédération québécoise des gestionnaires de Zec
Membre(s) du bureau directeur:
Donald Tremblay, Responsable
Finances: *Budget de fonctionnement annuel:* $100,000-$250,000; *Fonds:* Gouvernement régional
Membre: 600; *Montant de la cotisation:* 12$

Association de Curling des Sourdes du Canada ***See*** Canadian Deaf Curling Association

Association de Curling du Nouveau-Brunswick ***See*** New Brunswick Curling Association

Association de Dards du Québec inc. (ADQDA) / Québec Dart Association Inc.

#3, 3177, rue Notre Dame, Lachine QC H8S 2H4
Tél: 514-637-2858; *Téléc:* 514-637-9054
www.adqda.com
Aperçu: *Dimension:* moyenne; *Envergure:* provinciale; Organisme sans but lucratif; fondée en 1978 surveillé par National Darts Federation of Canada
Mission: L'A.D.Q. est la seule et unique Association de dards qui représente la Fédération de dards du Canada et aussi la seule qui est reconnue par la Fédération de Dards mondiale (World Darts Federation)
Membre de: National Darts Federation of Canada
Membre(s) du bureau directeur:
Maggie LeBlanc, Présidente
maggieleblanc417@hotmail.com

Membre: 700; *Montant de la cotisation:* 20$

Association de droit Lord Reading *See* Lord Reading Law Society

L'Association de gestion d'information de la santé du nouveau-brunswick *See* New Brunswick Health Information Management Association

Association de golf du nouveau brunswick *See* New Brunswick Golf Association

Association de golf du Québec *Voir* Fédération de golf du Québec

Association de Hearst et de la région pour l'intégration communautaire *See* Hearst & Area Association for Community Living

Association de hockey amateur de la Colombie-Britannique *See* British Columbia Amateur Hockey Association

Association de hockey de la Saskatchewan *See* Saskatchewan Hockey Association

Association de hockey de Terre-Neuve et Labrador *See* Hockey Newfoundland & Labrador

Association de hockey féminin de l'Ontario *See* Ontario Women's Hockey Association

Association de Hockey-Balle du Québec *See* Québec Ball Hockey Association

Association de joueurs de bridge de Boucherville

780, rue Pierre Viger, Boucherville QC J4B 3V5
ajbb2009.tripod.com
Aperçu: *Dimension:* petite; *Envergure:* locale
Membre(s) du bureau directeur:
Mary Ann Shtym, Contact, 450-465-7476
mash2810@hotmail.com
Activités: Bridge;

Association de l'Agricotourism et du Tourisme Gourmand

4545, av Pierre-de Coubertin, Montréal QC H1V 0B2
Tél: 514-252-3138; *Téléc:* 514-252-3173
info@terroiretsaveurs.com
www.terroiretsaveurs.com
www.facebook.com/terroirsaveurs
twitter.com/terroirsaveurs
www.youtube.com/user/terroiretsaveurs
Nom précédent: Fédération des Agricotours du Québec
Aperçu: *Dimension:* moyenne; *Envergure:* provinciale; fondée en 1976
Mission: La Fédération développe et fait la promotion du tourisme au Québec en maison privée de style Bed & Breakfast
Membre(s) du bureau directeur:
Odette Chaput, Directrice générale

Association de l'aluminium du Canada *Voir* Aluminium Association of Canada

Association de l'éducation coopérative de l'Ontario *See* Ontario Cooperative Education Association

L'Association de l'efficacité énergétique du Canada *See* Canadian Energy Efficiency Alliance

Association de l'exploration minière de Québec (AEMQ) / Quebec Mineral Exploration Assocation (QMEA)

#203, 132, av du Lac, Rouyn-Noranda QC J9X 4N5
Tél: 819-762-1599; *Téléc:* 819-762-1522
info@aemq.org
www.aemq.org
www.linkedin.com/company/association-de-l%27exploration-mini-re-du-qu-
www.facebook.com/AEMQ1975
twitter.com/AEMQ_
Nom précédent: Association des prospecteurs du Québec
Aperçu: *Dimension:* moyenne; *Envergure:* provinciale; fondée en 1975
Mission: Développer, défendre et promouvoir l'exploration minière au Québec
Membre(s) du bureau directeur:
Philippe Cloutier, Président
Valerie Fillion, Directrice générale, 819-762-1599 Ext. 224
dg@aemq.org
Finances: *Budget de fonctionnement annuel:* $100,000-$250,000
Membre(s) du personnel: 5; 20 bénévole(s)
Membre: 2000 membres individuels; plus de 250 corporatifs; *Montant de la cotisation:* 20$ étudiant - 2 000$ entreprises; *Critères d'admissibilite:* Oeuvrer en exploration minière
Activités: *Evénements de sensibilisation:* Événements Explo-Abiti; *Service de conférenciers:* Oui
Meetings/Conferences: • Congrès de l'exploration minière du Québec, octobre, 2015
Attendance: 1500+
Description: Prospecteurs, géologues, investisseurs, fournisseurs, conférenciers et futurs diplômés pourront débattre des questions qui entourent l'industrie minérale. Les activités comprennent des ateliers, des conférences, une réception de réseautage et une foire commerciale.
Contact Information: Numéro de téléphone: 819-762-1599; numéro sans frais: 1-877-762-1599; courriel: info@aemq.org

Association de l'industrie de la langue *See* Language Industry Association

Association de l'industrie des technologies de la santé *See* Canada's Medical Technology Companies

Association de l'industrie électrique du Québec (AIEQ)

#320, 2000, rue Mansfield, Montréal QC H3A 2Y9
Tél: 514-281-0615; *Téléc:* 514-281-7965
info@aieq.net
www.aieq.net
www.linkedin.com/groups/AIEQ-4314122?trk=myg_ugrp_ovr
www.facebook.com/AIEQuebec
twitter.com/_AIEQ
www.youtube.com/user/aiequebec
Nom précédent: Club d'électricité du Québec inc.
Aperçu: *Dimension:* moyenne; *Envergure:* provinciale; Organisme sans but lucratif; fondée en 1916
Mission: Etre porte parole de l'industrie 'électrique au Québec; favoriser la circulation de toute information et intérêt pour les membres et l'industrie électrique en général; contribuer au développement de nos membres et à la promotion de leurs intérêts par des initiatives de concertation et de représentation; encourager l'utilisation rationnelle des ressources dans une perspective de développement
Affliation(s): ABB; AECOM; ALSTOM; DESSAU; SNC-LAVALIN; VOITH; BPR: Brookfield; Mitsubishi Electric Power Products, Inc.; Qualitas
Membre(s) du bureau directeur:
Jean-François Samray, Président et directeur général
Finances: *Budget de fonctionnement annuel:* $500,000-$1.5 Million
Membre(s) du personnel: 7
Membre: 121; *Montant de la cotisation:* Selon le nombre d'employés au Québec; *Critères d'admissibilite:* Membres industriels; *Comités:* Consultatif; Finances; Services aux membres; Promotion; Débats projects
Activités: Déjeuners; conférences; activités sociales; *Service de conférenciers:* Oui

Association de l'industrie touristique du Canada *See* Tourism Industry Association of Canada

Association de l'industrie touristique du Nouveau-Brunswick inc. *See* Tourism Industry Association of New Brunswick Inc.

Association de l'Ontario des officers en bâtiment inc. *See* Ontario Building Officials Association Inc.

Association de l'opéra de vancouver *See* Vancouver Opera

Association de la banque canadienne de grains inc. *See* Canadian Foodgrains Bank Association Inc.

Association de la boulimie et d'anorexie mentale *See* Bulimia Anorexia Nervosa Association

Association de la chirurgie infantile canadienne *See* Canadian Association of Paediatric Surgeons

Association de la communauté du service extérieur *See* Foreign Service Community Association

L'Association de la construction d'Ottawa *See* Ottawa Construction Association

Association de la construction du Québec (ACQ) / Construction Association of Québec

9200, boul Métropolitain est, Anjou QC H1K 4L2
Tél: 514-354-0609; *Téléc:* 514-354-8292
Ligne sans frais: 888-868-3424
info@prov.acq.org
www.acq.org
www.linkedin.com/company/association-de-la-construction-du-qu-bec
www.facebook.com/ACQprovinciale
twitter.com/ACQprovinciale
www.youtube.com/user/ACQprovinciale
Aperçu: *Dimension:* grande; *Envergure:* provinciale; fondée en 1989 surveillé par Canadian Construction Association
Mission: Promotion et défense des intérêts des entreprises de construction, de gestionnaire de plans de garantie des bâtiments résidentiels neufs (Qualité Habitation) et d'agent patronal négociateur pour tous les employeurs des secteurs institutionnel/commercial et industriel (IC/I)
Membre(s) du bureau directeur:
Jean Pouliot, Président
Manon Bertrand, Vice-présidente, IC/I
Marc Dugré, Vice-président, Finances
René Hamel, Vice-président, Habitation
Laberge Yvan, Vice-président, Régions
Membre: 15 000 entreprises; 12 associations affiliées; *Montant de la cotisation:* 175$ et plus; *Critères d'admissibilite:* Entrepreneur en construction; *Comités:* Exécutif; Finances; Mises en nomination et élection; Déontologie; Relations du travail
Activités: Qualification professionnelle des entreprises; Lobbying gouvernemental; Services professionnels aux entrepreneurs; Relations de travail pour les secteurs institutionnel-commercial et industriel; Olans de garantie, salles de plans; *Bibliothèque:* Centre de documentation; Bibliothèque publique
Meetings/Conferences: • Association de la construction du Québec 2015 congrès annuel, D'autres conférences en 2015, 2015, QC
Scope: Provincial

Région Bas-St-Laurent - Gaspésie - Les Iles
424, 2e rue est, 2e étage, Rimouski QC G5M 1S6
Tél: 418-724-4044; *Téléc:* 418-724-0673
acqbsl@globetrotter.net
Membre(s) du bureau directeur:
David Redmond, Agent de promotion

Région de l'Ouest du Québec
#10-A, 85, rue Gamble ouest, Rouyn-Noranda QC J9X 2R5
Tél: 819-797-1222; *Téléc:* 819-797-1222

Région de l'Outaouais
170, boul. Maisonneuve, Gatineau QC J8X 3N4
Tél: 819-770-1818; *Téléc:* 819-770-8272
acq-outaouais@acq.org
www.acq.org/outaouais
Membre(s) du bureau directeur:
Sylvie Leblond, Directrice générale
leblonds@acq.org

Région de la Côte Nord
#231, 700, boul Laure, Sept-ILes QC G4R 1Y1
Tél: 418-968-5420; *Téléc:* 418-968-5421
bsdqspt@bsdq.org

Région de la Mauricie - Bois-Francs - Lanaudière - Centre-du-Québec
#100, 2575, rue de l'Industrie, Trois-Rivières QC G8Z 4T1
Tél: 819-374-1465; *Téléc:* 819-374-5757
Ligne sans frais: 800-785-7519
Membre(s) du bureau directeur:
Bernard Lavallee, Directeur général

Région de Québec
#100, 375, rue de Verdun, Québec QC G1N 3N8
Tél: 418-687-4121; *Téléc:* 418-687-3026
Membre(s) du bureau directeur:
Nicole Bourque, Directrice générale

Région Estrie
2925, rue Hertel, Sherbrooke QC J1L 1Y3
Tél: 819-566-7077; *Téléc:* 819-566-2440
Ligne sans frais: 866-893-7077
acq.estrie@videotron.ca
Membre(s) du bureau directeur:
Pauline Garand, Directrice générale

Région Laval / Laurentides
#113, 50, rue Sicard, Sainte-Thérèse QC J7E R51
Tél: 450-420-9240; *Téléc:* 450-420-9242
info@acqlavallaurentides.org
www.acq.org

Région Manicouagan
#102, 1, place Lasalle, Baie-Comeau QC G7Z 1J8
Tél: 418-296-8894; *Téléc:* 418-296-8815
acqmanicouagan@globetrotter.net

Région Métropolitaine
#302, 433, rue Chabanel ouest, Montréal QC H2N 2J4
Tél: 514-355-3245; *Téléc:* 514-351-7490
Région Montérégie
#200, 1085, boul du Séminaire Nord, Saint-Jean-sur-Richelieu QC J3A 1R2
Tél: 450-348-6114; *Téléc:* 450-348-0057
Ligne sans frais: 514-877-4988
acqmonteregie@videotron.ca
Membre(s) du bureau directeur:
Suzie Bessette, Directrice générale
Région Montérégie - Bureau de Ste-Julie
#17, 1999, boul Nobel, Sainte-Julie QC J3E 1Z7
Tél: 450-649-3004; *Téléc:* 450-649-0087
acqmonteregie.j@videotron.ca
Région Saguenay / Lac St-Jean
2496, rue Dubose, Jonquière QC G7S 1B4
Tél: 418-548-4678; *Téléc:* 418-548-9218
acq-saglac@videotron.ca
Membre(s) du bureau directeur:
Claire Grenon, Directrice Générale

Association de la construction navale du Canada *See* Shipbuilding Association of Canada

Association de la Construction Richelieu Yamaska (ACRY)
1190, rue Dessaules, Saint-Hyacinthe QC J2S 7X8
Tél: 450-773-0166; *Téléc:* 450-773-9148
Ligne sans frais: 877-743-0166
info@acry.qc.ca
acry.qc.ca
Nom précédent: Regroupement des professionnels de la construction Richelieu Yamaska
Aperçu: *Dimension:* petite; *Envergure:* locale; Organisme sans but lucratif; fondée en 1957
Mission: Promotion et défense des droits et intérêts des entrepreneurs en construction
Membre de: Fédération des Associations et Corporations en Construction du Québec
Affiliation(s): Fédération des Associations et Corporations en Construction du Québec (FACCQ)
Membre(s) du bureau directeur:
Marco Gaudette, Président
mgaudette@ntic.qc.ca
Bruno Bazinet, Vice-président
bruno2012@cgocable.ca
Jacqueline Rainville, Directrice générale
Finances: *Budget de fonctionnement annuel:* $100,000-$250,000
Membre(s) du personnel: 3
Membre: 260; *Montant de la cotisation:* 430$; *Critères d'admissibilite:* Entrepreneur de construction; *Comités:* Activités sociales

Association de la déficience intellectuelle de la région de Sorel (ADIRS)
#210, 189, rue Prince, Sorel-Tracy QC J3P 4K6
Tél: 450-743-0664; *Téléc:* 450-743-1769
adirs@videotron.ca
adirs.e-monsite.com
www.facebook.com/adirs.sorel
Aperçu: *Dimension:* petite; *Envergure:* locale
Affiliation(s): Association du Québec pour l'intégration sociale
Membre(s) du bureau directeur:
Julie Trudeau, Directrice générale
Membre(s) du personnel: 8

Association de la fibromyalgie de la Montérégie
#202, 150 rue Grant, Longueuil QC J4H 3H6
Tél: 450-928-1261; *Téléc:* 450-679-8784
Ligne sans frais: 888-928-1261
info@fibromyalgiemonteregie.ca
fibromyalgiemonteregie.ca
Aperçu: *Dimension:* petite; *Envergure:* locale
Mission: Fournir des informations et des soutien pour des personnes atteintes de fibromyalgie
Membre(s) du bureau directeur:
Annie Proulx, Directrice/Coordinatrice

Association de la Fibromyalgie des Laurentides
366, rue Laviolette, Saint-Jérôme QC J7Y 2S9
Tél: 450-569-7766; *Téléc:* 450-569-7769
Ligne sans frais: 877-705-7766
afl@videotron.ca
www.fibromyalgie-des-laurentides.ca
www.facebook.com/376578422426237
twitter.com/FibromyaLaurent
Aperçu: *Dimension:* moyenne; *Envergure:* locale; Organisme sans but lucratif; fondée en 1995
Membre de: Fédération québécoise de la fibromyalgie; Regroupement des Organismes communautaires des Laurentides; Réseau de concertation pour les personnes handicapées des Laurentides
Membre(s) du bureau directeur:
Lise Cloutier, Directrice et coordinatrice, 450-569-7766
Membre(s) du personnel: 2
Membre: *Montant de la cotisation:* 20$ membre fibromyalgique; 20$ membres accompangnateur; *Critères d'admissibilite:* Personnes des Laurentides atteintes de fibromyalgie et des gens qui assistent les personnes atteintes de fibromyalgie

Association de la fibromyalgie du Québec *Voir* Association québécoise de la fibromyalgie

Association de la gendarmerie royale de Terre-Neuve *See* Royal Newfoundland Constabulary Association

Association de la gestion de la chaîne d'approvisionnement *See* Supply Chain Management Association

Association de la librairie ancienne du Canada *See* Antiquarian Booksellers' Association of Canada

Association de la musique country canadienne *See* Canadian Country Music Association

Association de la musique de la côte est *See* East Coast Music Association

L'Association de la Neurofibromatose du Québec (ANFQ)
CP 150, Succ. St-Michel, Montréal QC H2A 3B0
Tél: 514-385-6702; *Téléc:* 514-385-1420
Ligne sans frais: 888-385-6702
www.anfq.org
Aperçu: *Dimension:* petite; *Envergure:* provinciale; Organisme sans but lucratif; fondée en 1989
Mission: Regrouper les membres et leurs familles; diffuser l'information sur la NF auprès des membres et des professionnels de la santé et de l'éducation; favoriser la recherche
Membre de: Confédération des organismes de personnes handicapées; National Neurofibromatosis Foundation; Association québécoise pour les troubles d'apprentissage; NF Canada
Membre(s) du bureau directeur:
Louise L'Africain, Chair
Finances: *Fonds:* Provincial
12 bénévole(s)
Membre: 200; *Montant de la cotisation:* 20$; *Critères d'admissibilite:* Personne atteinte de la NF et leur famille ou ami; intervenants en santé et en éducation
Activités: Rencontres; conférences de professionnels; informations; soutien téléphonique; levées de fonds (concert-bénéfice); sensibilisation; *Événements de sensibilisation:* Journée mondiale de la Neurofibromatose mai

Association de la police d'Edmonton *See* Edmonton Police Association

Association de la police de Belleville *See* Belleville Police Association

Association de la police de Cornwall *See* Cornwall Police Association

Association de la police de Guelph inc. *See* Guelph Police Association Inc.

Association de la police de Hamilton *See* Hamilton Police Association

Association de la police de Kingston *See* Kingston Police Association

Association de la police de la région de Niagara *See* Niagara Region Police Association

Association de la police de la ville de Brandon *See* Brandon Police Association

Association de la police de la ville de Saskatoon *See* Saskatoon City Police Association

Association de la police de London *See* London Police Association

Association de la police de Peterborough *See* Peterborough Police Association

Association de la police de Sault-Ste-Marie *See* Sault Ste Marie Police Association

Association de la police de Thunder Bay *See* Thunder Bay Police Association

Association de la police de Toronto *See* Toronto Police Association

Association de la police de Waterloo *See* Waterloo Regional Police Association

Association de la police de Windsor *See* Windsor Police Association

Association de la police de Winnipeg *See* Winnipeg Police Association

Association de la presse francophone (APF) / Association of Francophone Newspapers
267, rue Dalhousie, Ottawa ON K1N 7E3
Tél: 613-241-1017; *Téléc:* 613-241-6313
apf@apf.ca
www.apf.ca
Aperçu: *Dimension:* moyenne; *Envergure:* nationale; Organisme sans but lucratif; fondée en 1976
Mission: Promouvoir l'existence d'une presse communautaire écrite en langue française aussi vigoureuse et aussi répandue que possible dans les communautés de langue française à l'extérieur du Québec; Contribuer à l'amélioration de sa qualité et de son rayonnement; défendre énergiquement les principes de la liberté de parole et de la presse écrite
Membre(s) du bureau directeur:
Francis Potié, Directeur général
dg@apf.ca
Geneviève Gazaille, Directrice, Communications et des relations gouvernementales
communications@apf.ca
Michelle Laliberté, Gestionnaire, Opérations financières
admin@apf.ca
Pascale Castonguay, Coordonnatrice, Service de nouvelles
journaliste@apf.ca
Finances: *Fonds:* Fonds des communicateurs (de la Fondation Donatien Frémont)
Membre: 26; *Montant de la cotisation:* 750$ ou 1 500$ + 5% des ventes
Activités: *Stagiaires:* Oui; *Service de conférenciers:* Oui

L'Association de la recherche et de l'intelligence marketing *See* Marketing Research & Intelligence Association

Association de la recherche industrielle du Québec (ADRIQ)
#1120, 555, boul. René-Lévesque Ouest, Montréal QC H2Z 1B1
Tél: 514-337-3001; *Téléc:* 514-337-2229
adriq@adriq.com
www.adriq.com
www.linkedin.com/groups?gid=2999463
twitter.com/ADRIQ_RCTi
Nom précédent: Association des directeurs de recherche industrielle du Québec
Aperçu: *Dimension:* moyenne; *Envergure:* provinciale; Organisme sans but lucratif; fondée en 1978
Mission: De promouvoir les nouvelles technologies afin d'accroître le commerce concurrentiel au Québec et à l'étranger
Membre(s) du bureau directeur:
Jean-Louis Legault, Président-directeur général

Association de la Rivière Ste-Marguerite Inc. (ARSM)
CP 326, 160, rue Principale, Sacré-Coeur QC G0T 1Y0
Tél: 418-236-4604
Ligne sans frais: 877-236-4604
info@rivieresainte-marguerite.com
www.rivieresainte-marguerite.com
www.facebook.com/rivieresaintemarguerite
www.youtube.com/user/RivSainteMarguerite
Aperçu: *Dimension:* petite; *Envergure:* locale; Organisme sans but lucratif; fondée en 1980
Membre(s) du bureau directeur:
Richard Perron, Président
Nicole Gauthier, Directrice générale
Finances: *Budget de fonctionnement annuel:* $100,000-$250,000
Membre: 100-499; *Montant de la cotisation:* 23$

Canadian Associations

Activités: Pêche au saumon; pêche à la truite de mer; fête vallée du Saumon; cours d'initiation à la pêche à la morue; interprétation saumon atlantique

Association de la Sainte Face ***See*** Holy Face Association

Association de la santé et de la sécurité des pâtes et papiers et des industries de la forêt du Québec (ASSIFQ-ASSPPQ)

Place Iberville II, #210, 1175, av Lavigerie, Québec QC G1V 4P1
Tél: 418-657-2267; *Téléc:* 418-651-4622
Ligne sans frais: 888-632-9326
info@santesecurite.org
www.santesecurite.org
Aperçu: *Dimension:* moyenne; *Envergure:* provinciale; fondée en 2010
Mission: De soutenir et d'accompagner les entreprises dans l'amélioration continue de la santé et de la sécurité du travail
Affliation(s): Association des entrepreneurs en travaux sylvicoles du Québec; Association des fabricants des meubles du Québec; Association des manufacturiers de palettes et contenants du Québec; Conseil de l'industrie forestière du Québec; Fédération québécoise des coopératives forestières; Regroupement des sociétés d'aménagement du Québec; Commission de la santé et de la sécurité du travail
Membre(s) du bureau directeur:
Jacques Laroche, Président-directeur général
jlaroche@santesecurite.org
Suzanne Lavoie, Adjointe administrative
slavoie@santesecurite.org
Membre(s) du personnel: 27
Membre: 600 entreprises; *Montant de la cotisation:* Barème; *Critères d'admissibilite:* Oeuvrer dans le domaine des industries de la forêt ou des pâtes et papiers
Activités: Information; formation; expertise-conseil et impartition; mutuelles de prévention; activités régionales; *Stagiaires:* Oui; *Bibliothèque*

Association de la sécurité de l'information du Québec (ASIQ)

CP 9772, Succ. Ste-Foy, Québec QC G1V 4C3
Tél: 418-621-0464; *Téléc:* 418-621-0464
administration@asiq.org
www.asiq.org
www.linkedin.com/groups?gid=1934860
www.facebook.com/AssociationASIQ
twitter.com/ASIQCQSI
www.youtube.com/asiqvideos
Nom précédent: Association de sécurité de l'information de la région de Québec
Aperçu: *Dimension:* petite; *Envergure:* provinciale; Organisme sans but lucratif; fondée en 1983
Mission: Promouvoir la sécurité de l'information; regouper les personnes qui s'intéressent à la sécurité; favoriser les échanges entre les membres; diffuser de l'information pour permettre aux membres de suivre l'évolution dans le domaine de la sécurité de l'information
Membre(s) du bureau directeur:
Alex Bédard, Président
Finances: *Budget de fonctionnement annuel:* Moins de $50,000
10 bénévole(s)
Membre: 200+; *Montant de la cotisation:* 85$ étudiant; 170$ individuel; 250$ corporatif (de base - 1 membre), 125$ membres supplémentaires; *Comités:* Travail (pour répartir les tâches à réaliser)
Activités: Conférences, colloque annuel, ateliers

Association de la Vallée-du-Richelieu pour la déficience intellectuelle (AVRDI)

625, rue Lechasseur, Beloeil QC J3G 2L3
Tél: 450-467-8644
infos@avrdi.org
www.avrdi.org
Nom précédent: Association de la Vallée-du-Richelieu pour les déficients mentaux
Aperçu: *Dimension:* petite; *Envergure:* locale
Mission: D'aider les familles à l'intégration des personnes vivant avec une déficience intellectuelle. L'organisme offre des activités pour stimuler talents et intérets, et informe et dirige les familles vers les différents recours disponible dans la région
Affliation(s): Association du Québec pour l'intégration sociale
Membre(s) du bureau directeur:
Jocelyn Chauveau, Président
Joelichauveau@yahoo.ca
Membre(s) du personnel: 10

Association de la Vallée-du-Richelieu pour les déficients mentaux ***Voir*** Association de la Vallée-du-Richelieu pour la déficience intellectuelle

Association de Laval pour la déficience intellectuelle (ALDI)

73, boul Saint-Elzéar Ouest, Laval QC H7W 1E7
Tél: 450-972-1010; *Téléc:* 450-972-1515
secretariat@aldi1959.com
www.aldi1959.com
www.facebook.com/381062655279547
Aperçu: *Dimension:* petite; *Envergure:* locale; fondée en 1959
Mission: L'association a pour mission de permettre aux personnes ayant une déficience intellectuelle de vivre de la façon la plus normale possible en sus itant le développement de conditions facilitantes favorisant l'intégration et l'adaptation sociale
Affliation(s): Association du Québec pour l'intégration sociale
Membre(s) du bureau directeur:
France Locas, Présidente
Claude Bonneville, Vice-Président
Johanne Lefebvre, Trésorière
Membre: *Montant de la cotisation:* 10$ personne vivant avec une déficience; 20$ membre de la famille élargie; 25$ les tuteurs et responsable de résidence; 50$ organismes et associés

Association de le communauté noire de Côte-des-Neiges inc. / Côte-des-Neiges Black Community Association Inc.

#30, 6999, Côte-des-Neiges, Montréal QC H3S 2B6
Tél: 514-737-8321; *Téléc:* 514-737-6893
www.cdnbca.org
www.facebook.com/245257718844085
Aperçu: *Dimension:* petite; *Envergure:* locale
Mission: Cultural, recreational & social activities for youth & adults; after-school tutorials; summer camp; Teen Leadership Program; adult classes & sports activities
Membre(s) du bureau directeur:
John Cruickshank, Chairperson

Association de linguistique des provinces atlantiques ***See*** Atlantic Provinces Linguistic Association

Association de location du Canada ***See*** Canadian Rental Association

Association de logistique des soins personnels et pharmaceutiques ***See*** Pharmaceutical & Personal Care Logistics Association

Association de loisirs pour personnes handicapées psychiques de Laval (ALPHPL)

6600, av 29e, Laval QC H7R 3M3
Tél: 450-627-4370; *Téléc:* 450-627-4370
alphpl@videotron.ca
www.alphpl.org
Aperçu: *Dimension:* petite; *Envergure:* locale; Organisme sans but lucratif; fondée en 1983
Mission: Promouvoir l'évolution sociale des personnes handicapées psychiques en stimulant leurs intérêts pour des activités physiques, socio-culturelles et des loisirs; les soutenir dans leur apprentissage, l'entraînement et l'utilisation des ressources et équipments socio-communautaires; créer un sentiment d'appartenance du participant dans son milieu
Membre de: Association régionale pour personnes handicapées des Laurentides; Association québécoise pour la réadaptation psychosociale; Regroupement des ressources alternatives en santé mentale du Québec; l'Association canadienne pour la santé mentale
Membre(s) du bureau directeur:
François Bullock, Directeur général
Finances: *Budget de fonctionnement annuel:* $100,000-$250,000
Membre(s) du personnel: 7; 4 bénévole(s)
Membre: 100-499; *Montant de la cotisation:* 50-250
Activités: Expositions des travaux des bénéficiaires

Association de lutte contre l'Ambrosia (ALCA Québec)

#208, 3781, rue Le Marié, Sainte-Foy QC G1X 4V7
Tél: 418-658-7459
gmorency@globetrotter.qc.ca
Aperçu: *Dimension:* petite; *Envergure:* provinciale; Organisme sans but lucratif; fondée en 1989
Mission: Sensibiliser la population, les dirigeants et gouvernements aux problèmes de l'herbe à poux
Membre de: Table québécoise sur l'herbe à poux

Membre: 100; *Montant de la cotisation:* 10$ individuel; 15$ associations; *Critères d'admissibilite:* Individus; associations; municipalités

Association de maison de transition atlantique ***See*** Atlantic Halfway House Association

Association de medecine naturapathique du Québec ***See*** Québec Association of Naturopathic Medicine

Association de médiation familiale du Québec (AMFQ)

4800, ch Queen Mary, Montréal QC H3W 1W9
Tél: 514-990-4011; *Téléc:* 514-733-9081
Ligne sans frais: 800-667-7559
info@mediationquebec.ca
www.mediationquebec.ca
www.facebook.com/669501183095454
twitter.com/Amfqinfo
Aperçu: *Dimension:* petite; *Envergure:* provinciale; fondée en 1985
Mission: L'Association de médiation familiale du Québec a pour mission de développer et promouvoir la médiation familiale et les médiateurs familiaux accrédités, au Québec et à l'étranger.
Affliation(s): Family Mediation Canada
Membre(s) du bureau directeur:
Jean-François Chabot, Présidente
Gerald Schoel, Trésorier
José Mongeau, Secrétaire
Membre: 244+
Activités: Formation; colloque annuel; distribution de publications; écoute et soutien

Association de Montréal pour la déficience intellectuelle (AMDI) / Montreal Association for the Intellectually Handicapped (MAIH)

#100, 633, boul Crémazie Est, Montréal QC H2M 1L9
Tél: 514-381-2300; *Téléc:* 514-381-0454
info@amdi.info
www.amdi.info
www.facebook.com/181368175217004
Aperçu: *Dimension:* moyenne; *Envergure:* locale; Organisme sans but lucratif; fondée en 1935
Mission: De promouvoir et défendre les droits et intérêts des personnes présentant une déficience intellectuelle et ceux de leur famille
Membre de: Centraide
Affliation(s): Association du Québec pour l'intégration sociale
Membre(s) du bureau directeur:
Patricia Tonelli, Présidente
Nadia Bastien, Directrice générale
Finances: *Budget de fonctionnement annuel:* $500,000-$1.5 Million; *Fonds:* Gouvernement provincial et municipaux
Membre(s) du personnel: 8; 60 bénévole(s)
Membre: 1,244; *Critères d'admissibilite:* Parents; personnes présentant une déficience intellectuelle
Activités: Service de références; fin de semaine de plein air; camps familiaux; voyages organisés; accompagnements; gardiennage; *Bibliothèque:* Centre Allen Hanley; rendez-vous

Association de musicothérapie du Canada ***See*** Canadian Association for Music Therapy

Association de neurochirurgie du Québec (ANCQ)

CP 216, Succ. Desjardins, #3000, 2, Complexe Desjardins, Montréal QC H5B 1G8
Tél: 514-350-5120; *Téléc:* 514-350-5100
ancq@fmsq.org
www.ancq.net
Aperçu: *Dimension:* petite; *Envergure:* provinciale; fondée en 1965 surveillé par Fédération des médecins spécialistes du Québec
Mission: Pour représenter les médecins spécialistes et de promouvoir leurs intérêts
Membre de: Fédération des Médecins Spécialistes de Québec (FMSQ)
Membre(s) du bureau directeur:
Alain Bouthillier, Président
David Mathieu, Secrétaire
Publications:
• Interneurone
Type: Newsletter

Association de nutrition animale du Canada ***See*** Animal Nutrition Association of Canada

Association de paralysie cérébrale du Québec (APCQ) / Québec Cerebral Palsy Association

CP 1781, Sherbrooke QC J1H 5N8
Tél: 819-829-1144; *Téléc:* 819-829-1144
Ligne sans frais: 800-311-3770
info@paralysiecerebrale.com
www.paralysiecerebrale.com
Aperçu: *Dimension:* petite; *Envergure:* provinciale; fondée en 1949
Mission: Favoriser l'amélioration de la qualité de vie et l'intégration sociale des personnes vivant avec une paralysie cérébrale ou toutes autres déficiences; défendre leurs droits; sensibiliser et informer la population, les organismes et les gouvernements; encourager la recherche et découverte de nouvelles thérapies
Membre(s) du bureau directeur:
Joseph Khoury, Président
Michel Larochelle, Directeur général
m.larochelle@paralysiecerebrale.com
Activités: Orientation; information; prêt d'équipements spécialisés; aide financière

Bureau de Granby
CP 653, 170, rue St-Antoine Nord, Granby QC J2G 8W7
Tél: 450-777-2907; *Téléc:* 450-777-2907
Ligne sans frais: 800-311-3770
d.ares@paralysiecerebrale.com

Bureau de Montréal
3800, rue Radisson, Montréal QC H1M 1X6
Tél: 514-253-9444
Ligne sans frais: 800-311-3770
montreal@paralysiecerebrale.com

Bureau de Saint-Jean-sur-Richelieu
#1.01, 870, rue Curé St-Georges, Iberville QC J2X 2Z8
Tél: 450-357-2740
Ligne sans frais: 866-849-2740
p.jolivet@paralysiecerebrale.com

Association de parents d'enfant trisomique-21 de Lanaudière

245, ch des Anglais, Mascouche QC J7L 3P3
Tél: 450-477-4116; *Téléc:* 560-477-3534
www.apetl.org
www.facebook.com/199268050113168
Aperçu: *Dimension:* petite; *Envergure:* locale; fondée en 1990
Affliation(s): Association du Québec pour l'intégration sociale
Membre(s) du bureau directeur:
Chantal Lamarre, Directrice générale
Membre(s) du personnel: 6; 50 bénévole(s)
Membre: *Montant de la cotisation:* 20$ actif; 15$ souscripteurs; 35$ associé

Association de Parents de Jumeaux et de Triplés de la région de Montréal (APJTM)

CP 52, Succ. Du Parc, Montréal QC H2S 3K6
Tél: 514-990-6165
apjtm@apjtm.com
www.apjtm.com
Aperçu: *Dimension:* petite; *Envergure:* locale; Organisme sans but lucratif; fondée en 1961
Mission: Support et informations aux familles ayant des jumeaux, triplés, quadruplés ou en attentes de naissances multiples
Membre: *Critères d'admissibilite:* Parents d'enfants de naissances multiples
Activités: Réunions mensuelles avec conférenciers; pique-Nique; cabane à sucre; fête de Noël; bazar; marraines d'allaitemen; parrainage; casting; téléphones du mois; bibliothèque, joujouthèque, vidéothèque; *Bibliothèque:* BJV

Association de parents pour l'adoption québécoise (APAQ)

#112, 921, boul du Séminaire Nord, Saint-Jean-sur-Richelieu QC J3A 1B6
Tél: 514-990-9144
apaq@quebecadoption.net
apaq.quebecadoption.net
Aperçu: *Dimension:* petite; *Envergure:* provinciale; fondée en 1996
Mission: Promouvoir l'adoption d'enfants québécois; en faisant connaître les réalités particulières des enfants du Québec adoptés ou en voie de l'être; en faisant connaître la situation de l'adoption des enfants du Québec et ses principaux enjeux actuels; favoriser l'entraide, le partage et le soutien mutuel entre les parents qui vivent l'adoption; vous faire profiter de rabais de 25-30% sur des ouvrages de références et livres d'enfants
Membre(s) du bureau directeur:
Kathleen Neault, Présidente
Membre: *Montant de la cotisation:* 35$ famille

Association de planification fiscale et financière (APFF) / Fiscal & Financial Planning Association

#660, 1100, boul. René-Lévesque ouest, Montréal QC H3B 4N4
Tél: 514-866-2733; *Téléc:* 514-866-0113
Ligne sans frais: 877-866-0113
Autres numéros: Télécopier sans frais: 877-866-0113
apff@apff.org
www.apff.org
www.linkedin.com/groups/Association-planification-fiscale-financière-A
Aperçu: *Dimension:* moyenne; *Envergure:* provinciale; Organisme sans but lucratif; fondée en 1976
Mission: Regrouper les personnes intéressées à la planification fiscale successorale et financière; publier et diffuser l'information dans ces domaines; favoriser la recherche
Membre(s) du bureau directeur:
Maurice Mongrain, Président et directeur général
mongrainm@apff.org
Finances: *Budget de fonctionnement annuel:* $1.5 Million-$3 Million
Membre(s) du personnel: 14; 300 bénévole(s)
Membre: 2,500+; *Montant de la cotisation:* 330$; *Critères d'admissibilite:* Avocats, notaires, comptables agréés, comptables en management accrédités, comptables généraux accrédités, conseillers en sécurité financière, planificateurs financiers, gestionnaires de patrimoines, actuaires, conseillers en placements, économistes, chercheurs universitaires, enseignants et étudiants.; *Comités:* Activités régionales; colloques; Congrès annuel; cours de formation continue; études fiscales; Flash Fiscal; golf; marketing et développement; planification financière; Revue; stratège; symposium des taxes
Activités: 5 à 8 colloques d'une journée par année sur des thèmes spécifiques avec publication intégrale des textes de conférences; *Evénements de sensibilisation:* Congrès annuel; Tournoi de golf annuel; *Bibliothèque:* Centre d'information

Association de protection des épargnants et investisseurs du Québec *Voir* Mouvement d'éducation et de défense des actionnaires

Association de Ringuette Chutes Chaudière

CP 1807, Saint-Rédempteur QC G6K 1N6
arcc_equipements@hotmail.ca
www.ringuettearcc.ca
www.facebook.com/273644039403446
Aperçu: *Dimension:* petite; *Envergure:* provinciale surveillé par Ringuette-Québec
Membre de: Ringuette-Québec
Membre(s) du bureau directeur:
Tanya Moore, Présidente
arcc_presidente@hotmail.ca
Membre: 12 équipes

Association de ringuette de Colombie-Britannique *See* British Columbia Ringette Association

Association de ringuette de l'Ontario *See* Ontario Ringette Association

Association de Ringuette de Longueuil

710, rue Riverin, Longueuil QC J4L 3E4
Tél: 438-884-9437
ringuettelongueuil@gmail.com
www.ringuettelongueuil.com
Aperçu: *Dimension:* petite; *Envergure:* provinciale surveillé par Ringuette-Québec
Membre de: Ringuette-Québec
Membre(s) du bureau directeur:
Valérie Clément, Présidente
vclement.valerie@gmail.com
Membre: *Montant de la cotisation:* Barème

Association de ringuette de Lotbinière

c/o Marie-Noël Duclos, 412, rue Belanger, Saint-Narcisse-de-Beaurivage QC G0S 1W0
Tél: 418-475-4125
pages.globetrotter.net
Aperçu: *Dimension:* petite; *Envergure:* provinciale surveillé par Ringuette-Québec
Membre de: Ringuette-Québec
Membre(s) du bureau directeur:
Caroline Fortier, Présidente, 418-728-5508
lemay4@videotron.ca
Membre: 7 équipes; *Montant de la cotisation:* Barème

Association de Ringuette de Sainte-Marie

QC
ringuette.ste-marie@hotmail.com
www.ringuettestemarie.com
www.facebook.com/181771528541007
twitter.com/Les_Valkyries
Aperçu: *Dimension:* petite; *Envergure:* provinciale; fondée en 1983 surveillé par Ringuette-Québec
Membre de: Ringuette-Québec
Membre(s) du bureau directeur:
Maryse Jacques, Présidente, 418-386-2869

Association de Ringuette de Ste-Julie

CP 85, Succ. Chef, Ste-Julie QC J3E 1X5
communications@ringuettestejulie.com
www.ringuettestejulie.com
Aperçu: *Dimension:* petite; *Envergure:* provinciale surveillé par Ringuette-Québec
Membre de: Ringuette-Québec
Membre(s) du bureau directeur:
Marie-Claude Bérubé, Présidente
president@ringuettestejulie.com
Stéphane Lemay, Directeur, Communications
Membre: 12 équipes

Association de ringuette de Saskatchewan *See* Ringette Association of Saskatchewan

Association de Ringuette de Sept-Iles

QC
www.ringuettesept-iles.org
fr.facebook.com/228073003907401
Aperçu: *Dimension:* petite; *Envergure:* provinciale surveillé par Ringuette-Québec
Membre de: Ringuette-Québec
Membre(s) du bureau directeur:
Alain Cajolet, Président, 418-962-4491
alain.cajolet@cegep-sept-iles.qc.ca
Membre: 7 équipes;

Association de Ringuette de Thetford

555 St-Alphonse Nord, Thetford Mines QC G6G 3X1
Tél: 418-338-3729
www.ringuettethetford.com
Aperçu: *Dimension:* petite; *Envergure:* provinciale surveillé par Ringuette-Québec
Membre de: Ringuette-Québec
Membre(s) du bureau directeur:
Dany Harvey, Président
dharvey27@hotmail.ca
Membre: 6 équipes

Association de Ringuette de Vallée-du-Richelieu

CP 85113, 345, boul. Sir-Wilfrid-Laurier, Mont-Saint-Hilaire QC J3H 5W1
vdrringuette@hotmail.com
www.ringuettevdr.com
www.facebook.com/145272202165165
www.youtube.com/user/VDRringuette
Aperçu: *Dimension:* petite; *Envergure:* provinciale surveillé par Ringuette-Québec
Membre de: Ringuette-Québec
Membre(s) du bureau directeur:
Patrick Beauchemin, Président

Association de Ringuette des Moulins

840, rue Brien, Mascouche QC J7K 2X3
Tél: 450-474-6558
admin@ringuettedesmoulins.com
www.ringuettedesmoulins.com
www.facebook.com/217093858329471?ref=hl
Aperçu: *Dimension:* petite; *Envergure:* provinciale surveillé par Ringuette-Québec
Membre de: Ringuette-Québec
Membre(s) du bureau directeur:
Claude Hogue, Président, 514-886-3158
hogueclaude@hotmail.com
Membre: 3 équipes

Association de ringuette du Manitoba *See* Manitoba Ringette Association

Association de Ringuette Repentigny

435, boul. Iberville, Repentigny QC J6A 2B6
Tél: 450-582-2309
ringuette.repentigny@videotron.ca
www.ringuetterepentigny.com

Aperçu: *Dimension:* petite; *Envergure:* provinciale surveillé par Ringuette-Québec
Membre de: Ringuette-Québec
Membre(s) du bureau directeur:
Gordon Britton, Président
ringuette.repentigny@videotron.ca
Membre: 7 équipes

Association de ringuette Roussillon
CP 164, Saint-Constant QC J5A 2G2
communications@ringuetteroussillon.ca
www.ringuetteroussillon.ca
www.facebook.com/ARRoussillon
twitter.com/ARRoussillon
Aperçu: *Dimension:* petite; *Envergure:* provinciale surveillé par Ringuette-Québec
Membre de: Ringuette-Québec
Membre(s) du bureau directeur:
Patrick Henri, Président

Association de sécurité de l'information de la région de Québec ***Voir*** Association de la sécurité de l'information du Québec

Association de Sherbrooke pour la déficience intellectuelle (ASDI)
2065, rue Belvédère Sud, Sherbrooke QC J1H 5R8
Tél: 819-346-2227; *Téléc:* 819-346-8752
info@asdi-org.qc.ca
asdi-org.qc.ca
Aperçu: *Dimension:* petite; *Envergure:* locale; Organisme sans but lucratif; fondée en 1965
Mission: Promouvoir l'intégration sociale; favoriser le bien-être; défendre les droits des personnes ayant une déficience intellectuelle
Affliation(s): Association du Québec pour l'intégration sociale
Membre(s) du bureau directeur:
Denis Crête, Directeur général
Chantal Charland, Présidente
Membre(s) du personnel: 6
Membre: *Montant de la cotisation:* 20$
Activités: *Stagiaires:* Oui; *Bibliothèque* Bibliothèque publique rendez-vous

Association de spina-bifida et d'hydrocephalie du Canada ***See*** Spina Bifida & Hydrocephalus Association of Canada

L'Association de spina-bifida et d'hydrocéphalie du Québec (ASBHQ)
#542, 3333, ch. Queen-Mary, Montréal QC H3V 1A2
Tél: 514-340-9019; *Téléc:* 514-340-9109
Ligne sans frais: 800-567-1788
info@spina.qc.ca
www.spina.qc.ca
twitter.com/ASBHQ
Aperçu: *Dimension:* moyenne; *Envergure:* provinciale; Organisme sans but lucratif; fondée en 1975 surveillé par Spina Bifida & Hydrocephalus Association of Canada
Mission: Promouvoir et défendre les droits, les intérêts et le bien-être des personnes ayant le spina-bifida et l'hydrocéphalie; sensibiliser le public à la nature du spina-bifida et de l'hydrocéphalie ainsi qu'aux besoins des personnes ayant ces malformations; favoriser et soutenir la recherche sur les causes, les nouveaux traitements et les techniques de prévention du spina-bifida et de l'hydrocéphalie
Membre de: Confédération des organismes provinciaux de personnes handicappées du Québec
Affliation(s): Institut de réadaptation en déficience physique de Québec; Hôpital Shriners, Centre de réadaptation Constance-Lethbridge, Centre de réadaptation en déficience physique Chaudière-Appalaches
Membre(s) du bureau directeur:
Marc Picard, Président
Finances: *Budget de fonctionnement annuel:* $100,000-$250,000; *Fonds:* MSSS; diverses activités de levées de fonds; individuels et corporatifs
Membre(s) du personnel: 2; 206 bénévole(s)
Membre: 100-499; *Montant de la cotisation:* 20$ associé; *Comités:* Promotion; Rédaction; Prévention; Financement; Colloque
Activités: Organiser des colloques permettant aux membres une mise à jour avec des professionnels de la santé, de l'éducation et des services sociaux; recueillir, traduire, réorganiser et distribuer la documentation; une attention particulière est portée aux personnes qui habitent dans les régions éloignées des grands centres médicaux afin de leur prêter un appui moral et technique nécessaire à leur intégration et à leur épanouissement; *Evénements de sensibilisation:* Campagne de prévention du spina-bifida; *Service de conférenciers:* Oui; *Bibliothèque* rendez-vous

A.S.B.H. Région Estrie
928, rue Fédéral, Sherbrooke QC J1H 5A7
Tél: 819-822-3772; *Téléc:* 819-822-4529
asbhestrie@hotmail.com
www.spina.qc.ca/estrie
Membre(s) du bureau directeur:
René Labonté, Président
Aline Nault, Coordonnatrice

A.S.B.H. Région Montréal
#448, 14115, Prince-Arthur, Montréal QC H1A 1A8
Tél: 514-739-5515; *Téléc:* 514-739-5505
asbhrm@mainbourg.org
www.spina.qc.ca
www.facebook.com/asbhq.quebec
twitter.com/ASBHQ
Membre(s) du bureau directeur:
André Bougie, Président

Association de taekwondo du Québec
4545, av Pierre-de Coubertin, Montréal QC H1V 3R2
Tél: 514-252-3198; *Téléc:* 514-254-7075
Ligne sans frais: 800-762-9565
info@taekwondo-quebec.ca
www.taekwondo-quebec.ca
www.facebook.com/115348592723
Également appelé: Taekwondo Québec
Aperçu: *Dimension:* moyenne; *Envergure:* provinciale
Mission: Favoriser le développement du taekwondo québécois
Membre(s) du bureau directeur:
Jean Faucher, Président
jfaucher@taekwondo-quebec.ca
Martin Desjardins, Vice-président
mdesjardins@taekwondo-quebec.ca
Abdel Ilah Es Sabbar, Directeur exécutif
essabbar@taekwondo-quebec.ca

Association de TED du Canada ***See*** EFILE Association of Canada

Association de tir de la province de Québec ***See*** Province of Québec Rifle Association

L'Association de tir dominion du canada ***See*** Dominion of Canada Rifle Association

Association de ventes directes du Canada ***See*** Direct Sellers Association of Canada

Association de vitrerie et fenestrations du Québec (AVFQ)
#216, 2065, rue Frank-Carrel, Québec QC G1N 2G1
Tél: 418-688-1256; *Téléc:* 418-688-2460
Ligne sans frais: 800-263-4032
info@avfq.ca
www.avfq.ca
www.linkedin.com/groups?home=&gid=5142613
www.facebook.com/1383936025162152
Nom précédent: L'Association des industries de produits verriers et de fenestration du Québec; L'Association des industries de portes et fenêtres du Québec
Aperçu: *Dimension:* moyenne; *Envergure:* provinciale; Organisme sans but lucratif; fondée en 1964
Mission: Promouvoir et défendre les intérêts des membres; regrouper et représenter toutes les entreprises de produits verriers, de portes et fenêtres du Québec
Affliation(s): Association canadienne des manufacturiers de portes et fenêtres du Canada
Membre(s) du bureau directeur:
Gilbert Lemay, Vice-président à la direction
glemay@avfq.ca
Marc Bilodeau, Président, 450-681-0483, Fax: 450-681-8432
marcbilodeau@vitreco.ca
Membre(s) du personnel: 3
Membre: 200+; *Critères d'admissibilite:* Fournisseurs de composants et manufacturiers; *Comités:* Bourses d'Études; Commercial; Congrès; Contrats; Développement; Formation; Gala; Golf; Hydro-Québec; Innovation Bois; Technique
Activités: Séminaires; congrès; salon; *Service de conférenciers:* Oui

Association de voile de l'Ontario ***See*** Ontario Sailing

Association de vol à voile Champlain
10, 745 de Martigny, Montréal QC H2B 2N1
Tél: 450-771-0500
info@avvc.qc.ca
www.avvc.qc.ca
Aperçu: *Dimension:* petite; *Envergure:* locale; Organisme sans but lucratif
Mission: Former des pilotes de planeur et les amener au niveau du vol voyage; répondre aux attentes de ses membres actifs
Membre de: Soaring Association of Canada
Membre: *Montant de la cotisation:* 620$

L'Association de water polo d'Ontario ***See*** Ontario Water Polo Association Incorporated

L'Association dentaire canadienne ***See*** Canadian Dental Association

Association des accidentés cérébro-vasculaires et traumatisés crâniens de l'Estrie (ACTE)
68, boul Jacques-Cartier Nord, Sherbrooke QC J1J 2Z8
Tél: 819-821-2799; *Téléc:* 819-821-4599
www.acteestrie.com
Aperçu: *Dimension:* petite; *Envergure:* locale; fondée en 1984
Mission: Pour aider les personnes de la région de l'Estrie du Québec qui ont subi un accident vasculaire cérébral ou un traumatisme crânien
Membre de: Regroupement des associations de personnes traumatisées craniocérébrales du Québec / Coalition of Associations of Craniocerebral Trauma in Quebec
Membre(s) du bureau directeur:
Denis Veilleux, Directeur général, 819-821-2799 Ext. 223
denis.veilleux@acteestrie.com
Membre(s) du personnel: 9
Membre: *Critères d'admissibilite:* Personnes de la région de l'Estrie, Québec qui ont survécu à un accident vasculaire cérébral (AVC) ou d'un traumatisme crânien; Membres de la famille des personnes qui ont survécu à un accident vasculaire cérébral
Activités: La sensibilisation du public et la diffusion d'informations sur les accidents vasculaires cérébraux ou un traumatisme crânien; Défendre les droits et intérêts des personnes qui ont survécu à un accident vasculaire cérébral; Aider les personnes à maintenir leurs capacités et développer les intérêts, en organisant des ateliers sur des sujets tels que l'art et loisirs de plein air; Offrir un soutien psychosocial, à travers des réunions de groupe de soutien aux victimes, aux familles, et amis
Publications:
• L'Actif
ISSN: 1488-4453
Profile: Executive reports & association activities

Association des actuaires I.A.R.D.
QC
Autres numéros: Alt. courriel: babillard@aaiard.com
commentaire@aaiard.com
www.aaiard.com
Aperçu: *Dimension:* petite; *Envergure:* provinciale
Mission: Promouvoir la connaissance de la science actuarielle appliquée aux situations d'assurance I.A.R.D. et domaines connexes
Membre(s) du bureau directeur:
Sébastien Vachon, Président
president@aaiard.com
Frédérick Guillot, Vice-président
vicepresident@aaiard.com

Association des Acupuncteurs du Québec (L'AAQ)
#203, 1453, rue Beaubien Est, Montréal QC H2G 3C6
Tél: 514-564-5115
Ligne sans frais: 844-564-5115
info@acupuncture-quebec.com
www.acupuncture-quebec.com
fr-ca.facebook.com/128162563939912
Nom précédent: Association d'Acupuncture du Québec
Aperçu: *Dimension:* petite; *Envergure:* provinciale; Organisme sans but lucratif; fondée en 2000
Mission: Promouvoir la médecine traditionnelle chinoise et l'acupuncture; défendre les intérets de ses membres
Affliation(s): Ordre des acupuncteurs du Québec; Département d'acupuncture: Collège de Rosemont; Distributeurs de l'AAQ
Membre(s) du bureau directeur:
Julie Dorval, Présidente
8 bénévole(s)
Membre: *Montant de la cotisation:* 200$ actif; 150$ nouveau gradué; 100$ congé parental; 75$ retraité ou inactif; 50$ sympathisant

Activités: Échanges professionnels; séminaires; symposiums; recherches; matériel promotionnel

Association des adjoints administratifs *See* Association of Administrative Assistants

Association des administrateurs des écoles anglaises du Québec *See* Association of Administrators of English Schools of Québec

Association des administrateurs municipaux du Nouveau-Brunswick *See* Association of Municipal Administrators of New Brunswick

Association des affaires publiques du Canada *See* The Public Affairs Association of Canada

Association des agences d'agrément du Canada *See* Association of Accrediting Agencies of Canada

Association des agences de publicité du Québec (AAPQ) / Association of Québec Advertising Agencies

#925, 2015, rue Peel, Montréal QC H3A 1T8
Tél: 514-848-1732; *Téléc:* 514-848-1950
Ligne sans frais: 877-878-1732
aapq@aapq.ca
www.aapq.ca
Aperçu: *Dimension:* moyenne; *Envergure:* provinciale; Organisme sans but lucratif; fondée en 1988
Mission: Promouvoir et défendre les intérêts des agences membres
Membre(s) du bureau directeur:
Dominique Villeneuve, Directrice générale
d.villeneuve@aapq.ca
Membre(s) du personnel: 5
Membre: 70 agences membres; *Montant de la cotisation:* Barème

Association des agents de police de la ville de Regina *See* Regina Policemen Association Inc.

Association des agents de services au public de Winnipeg *See* Winnipeg Association of Public Service Officers

Association des agents de voyages du Québec *Voir* Association of Canadian Travel Agents - Québec

Association des agents des immeubles du Nouveau-Brunswick *See* New Brunswick Real Estate Association

Association des Allergologues et Immunologues du Québec

CP 216, Succ. Desjardins, #3000, 2, Complexe Desjardins, Montréal QC H5B 1G8
Tél: 514-350-5101
aaiq@fmsq.org
www.allerg.qc.ca
Aperçu: *Dimension:* moyenne; *Envergure:* provinciale surveillé par Fédération des médecins spécialistes du Québec
Membre de: Fédération des medecins spéialistes du Québec

Association des alternatives en santé mentale de la Montérégie (AASMM)

#304-B, 279, rue Principale, Granby QC J2G 2W1
Tél: 450-375-5868; *Téléc:* 450-375-8828
info@aasmm.com
www.aasmm.com
Aperçu: *Dimension:* petite; *Envergure:* locale; Organisme sans but lucratif; fondée en 1986
Mission: Promouvoir la vie associative par des action concrètes; promouvoir les expertises de ses ressources membres; soutenir et défendre les intérêts de ses ressources membres; promouvoir l'idéologie alternative en santé mentale auprès de ses ressources membres et auprès des communautés
Membre(s) du bureau directeur:
Sylvie Tétreault, Présidente
Nicole Malo, Vice Présidente

Association des Aménagistes Régionaux du Québec (AARQ)

#204, 870, av de Salaberry, Québec QC G1R 2T9
Tél: 418-524-4666
administration@aarq.qc.ca
www.aarq.qc.ca
www.facebook.com/160531930681615
Aperçu: *Dimension:* petite; *Envergure:* provinciale; Organisme sans but lucratif; fondée en 1984
Membre(s) du bureau directeur:
François Lestage, Président
Membre: *Critères d'admissibilite:* Aménagiste travaillant au sein d'une M.R.C.; *Comités:* Vigie; répresentation; évaluation; opérations
Activités: Lieu d'échange entre les professionnels de l'aménagement du territoire oeuvrant au sein des municipalités régionales de comté (M.R.C.)

Association des amis canadiens de l'Université Hébraïque *See* Canadian Friends of the Hebrew University

Association des Amis d'ATD Quart-Monde *Voir* Mouvement ATD Quart Monde Canada

L'Association des Anciens Combattants de la marine marchande canadienne Inc. *See* Canadian Merchant Navy Veterans Association Inc.

Association des anciens de la Gendarmerie royale du Canada *See* Royal Canadian Mounted Police Veterans' Association

Association des anciens élèves du collège Sainte-Marie

www.saintemarie.ca
Aperçu: *Dimension:* petite; *Envergure:* locale; fondée en 1882
Membre(s) du bureau directeur:
Richard L'Heureux, Président, 514-482-0095
richard.lheureux@videotron.ca
Jacques D. Girard, Contact, 514-485-8114
jacques.girard@saintemarie.ca
Membre: *Montant de la cotisation:* 35$

Association des archéologues du Québec (AAQ)

CP 322, Succ. Haute-Ville, Québec QC G1R 4P8
info@archeologie.qc.ca
www.archeologie.qc.ca
Également appelé: AAQ
Aperçu: *Dimension:* moyenne; *Envergure:* provinciale; Organisme sans but lucratif; fondée en 1979 surveillé par Canadian Archaeological Association
Mission: Définir les standards de la profession; veiller à la saine gestion et la mise en valeur du patrimoine archéologique à cause d'une éthique exemplaire et de la qualité de ses membres; agir comme interlocuteur privilégié pour tout ce qui regarde la question archéologique auprès des gouvernements et des organismes, privés ou publics, qui ont à coeur la préservation de notre patrimoine collectif
Membre de: 'éseau-Archéo; Fédération des sociétés d'histoire du Québec
Finances: *Fonds:* Ministère de la Culture et des communications du Québec
Membre: *Montant de la cotisation:* 125$ régulier; 60$ associé; $30 étudiant; *Critères d'admissibilite:* Archéologue professionel
Activités: Colloque annuel; publications; prises de position;

Association des architectes du Nouveau-Brunswick *See* Architects' Association of New Brunswick

Association des Architectes en pratique privée du Québec (AAPPQ) / Association of Architects in Private Practice of Québec

#302, 420, rue McGill, Montréal QC H2Y 2G1
Tél: 514-937-4140; *Téléc:* 514-937-2329
aappq@aappq.qc.ca
www.aappq.qc.ca
Aperçu: *Dimension:* moyenne; *Envergure:* provinciale; fondée en 1977
Membre(s) du personnel: 2; 20 bénévole(s)
Membre: 400 sociétés; *Montant de la cotisation:* Barème; *Critères d'admissibilite:* Il faut être architecte et avoir un bureau d'architecte à son compte; *Comités:* Comité de formation continue et de recherche; Comité honoraires, conditions d'engagement et de pratique; Comité de liaisons; Comité de relations publiques
Activités: Formation; Marketing; Médiation; Qualité-totale

Association des architectes paysagistes du Canada *See* Canadian Society of Landscape Architects

Association des architectes paysagistes du Québec (AAPQ)

#406, 420, rue McGill, Montréal QC H2Y 2G1
Tél: 514-526-6385; *Téléc:* 514-526-6385
info@aapq.org
www.aapq.org
www.facebook.com/pageaapq
twitter.com/AAPQ_paysages
Aperçu: *Dimension:* petite; *Envergure:* provinciale; fondée en 1965
Mission: Promouvoir la création et la valorisation du paysage en milieu naturel et construit dans le but de constituer un cadre de vie sain, fonctionnel, esthétique, axé sur les besoins de la population et répondant aux exigences écologiques
Affliation(s): Association des Architectes Paysagistes du Canada
Membre(s) du bureau directeur:
Édith Normandeau, Directrice générale par intérim
dg@aapq.org
Membre: *Montant de la cotisation:* Barème

L'Association des archives de l'Ontario *See* Archives Association of Ontario

Association des archivistes du Québec (AAQ)

CP 9768, Succ. Sainte-Foy, Québec QC G1V 4C3
Tél: 418-652-2357; *Téléc:* 418-646-0868
infoaaq@archivistes.qc.ca
www.archivistes.qc.ca
www.linkedin.com/groups/Association-archivistes-Québec-2311475
www.facebook.com/ArchivistesQc
twitter.com/archivistesQc
Aperçu: *Dimension:* moyenne; *Envergure:* nationale; Organisme sans but lucratif; fondée en 1967
Mission: Regrouper les personnes qui offrent aux organisations et à leurs clientèles des services liés à la gestion de leur information organique et consignée; offrir à ses membres des services en français et propres à assurer le développement, l'enrichissement et la promotion de leur profession et de leur discipline; assurer aux membres les services susceptibles de favoriser et d'accroître les échanges et la communication internes et externes des idées et des connaissances; promouvoir le développement professionnel des membres en s'impliquant activement au plan de la formation et du perfectionnement, en favorisant la recherche et le développement et en assurant une représentation adéquate de la profession au sein de la société et auprès des corps politiques
Membre de: Conseil canadien des archives
Membre(s) du bureau directeur:
André Gareau, Président
Andrée Gingras, Directrice générale, 416-652-2357, Fax: 418-646-0868
dg.infoaaq@archivistes.qc.ca
Finances: *Budget de fonctionnement annuel:* $100,000-$250,000; *Fonds:* Cotisation, Congrès
Membre(s) du personnel: 2; 108 bénévole(s)
Membre: 670; *Montant de la cotisation:* Basé sur le revenu; *Critères d'admissibilite:* Professionnel ou technicien; *Comités:* Revue Archives; La Chronique; Prix annuels; Congrès annuel; Certification; Affaire professionnelles; Communications; Formation et de perfectionnement
Activités: Formation; banque de consultants; congrès; *Service de conférenciers:* Oui
Meetings/Conferences: • 44e Congrès de l'Association des archivistes du Québec, mai, 2015, Hôtel Tadoussac, Tadoussac, QC
Contact Information: Maude Leclerc, Courriel: congres2015@archivistes.qc.ca
Publications:
• Archives: La revue de l'Association des archivistes du Québec
Type: Revue; *Number of Pages:* 175 *ISSN:* 0044-9423; *Price:* Membre: 29$; Non-membre: 54$
Profile: Présente des articles sur la gestion des archives, traditionnelle et électronique des archives
• La chronique
Type: Bulletin; *Frequency:* 10 fois par ans *ISSN:* 0706-3431
Profile: Bulletin d'information sur les événements de l'association: colloques; nouvelles des professionnels et du conseil d'administration

Association des Arénas du Québec *Voir* Association québécoise des arénas et des installations récréatives et sportives

Association des armateurs canadiens *See* Canadian Shipowners Association

Association des armateurs du Saint-Laurent inc.; Association des opérateurs de navires du Saint-Laurent *Voir* Armateurs du Saint-Laurent

Association des arpenteurs des terres du Canada *See* Association of Canada Lands Surveyors

Canadian Associations

Association des arpenteurs-géomètres du Nouveau-Brunswick *See* Association of New Brunswick Land Surveyors

L'Association des artistes Baltes à Montréal (AAB) / Baltic Artists' Association - Montréal

Overview: A small local organization
Mission: To support Baltic artists in the Montréal area
Chief Officer(s):
Ann Kallaste-Kruzelecky, President
Mara Rudzitis, Vice-President
Dzintra Palejs, Secretary
Aleksandras Piesena, Treasurer
John Vazalinskas, Contact, Newsletter/Membership
Finances: *Annual Operating Budget:* Less than $50,000
6 volunteer(s)
Membership: *Member Profile:* Visual artists, photographers & makers of handcrafts
Activities: Meetings; workshops; annual exhibitions

Association des artistes en arts visuels de Saint-Jérôme (AAAV)

101, pl du Curé Labelle, Saint-Jérôme QC J7Z 1X6
courrier@aaavsj.com
aaavsj.com
Aperçu: *Dimension:* petite; *Envergure:* locale; Organisme sans but lucratif; fondée en 1990
Mission: Promouvoir l'art dans la région; aider chacun des membres dans son cheminement personnel; demeurer accessible à tous; créer une dynamique de groupe pour favoriser l'émulation et les échanges
Affliation(s): Conseil québécois de l'Estampe; Conseil de la sculpture du Québec; Conseil des arts textiles du Québec; Conseil des artistes peintres du Québec; Association des illustrateurs et illustratrices du Québec
Membre(s) du bureau directeur:
Lorraine Bergeron, Présidente
Finances: *Budget de fonctionnement annuel:* Moins de $50,000
20 bénévole(s)
Membre: 140 à 180 chaque année; *Montant de la cotisation:* 25$ membres; 20$ amis de l'Art; *Critères d'admissibilité:* Artistes peintre-sculpteur (reliés aux arts)
Activités: Réunions mensuelles; expositions; ateliers; *Evénements de sensibilisation:* Exposition annuelle nov. Galeries Laurentides

Association des artistes peintres affiliés de la Rive-Sud (AAPARS)

PO Box 261, Saint-Bruno-de-Montarville QC J3V 4P9
aapars.com
Overview: A small local organization
Mission: Promouvoir de nouveaux artistes avec l'aide d'artistes établis
Chief Officer(s):
Jacques Landry, Président, Conseil d'administration, 450-461-3796
famille_landry00@sympatico.ca

Association des artistes peintres de Longueuil

CP 55083, Succ. Vieux Longueuil, Longueuil QC J4H 0A2
Tél: 450-646-8450
laapl@hotmail.com
laapl.blogspot.ca
Aperçu: *Dimension:* petite; *Envergure:* locale; fondée en 1989
Mission: Pour encourager les gens à développer leurs compétences artistiques
Membre(s) du bureau directeur:
Claude Charter, Présidente, Conseil d'administration
Activités: Des expositions; des ateliers

Association des arts thérapeutes du Québec (AATQ)

#307B, 911, rue Jean-Talon Est, Montréal QC H2R 1V5
Tél: 514-990-5415
info@aatq.org
aatq.org
Aperçu: *Dimension:* petite; *Envergure:* provinciale; fondée en 1981
Membre(s) du bureau directeur:
Sylvie Goyette, Président
Membre: *Montant de la cotisation:* 100$ professionnels/alliés; 45$ étudiants; 80$ affiliés spéciaux; 95$ affiliés étrangers/bienfaiteurs affilié; 45$ étudiants affiliés

Association des assistant(e)s-dentaires du Québec (CDAA/AADQ)

#410, 7400, boul. Les Galeries d'Anjou, Montréal QC H1M 3M2
Tél: 514-722-9900; *Téléc:* 514-355-4159
aadq@spg.qc.ca
www.aadq.ca
Aperçu: *Dimension:* petite; *Envergure:* provinciale; fondée en 1973 surveillé par Canadian Dental Assistants Association
Mission: Aider ses membres à parfaire leurs connaissances par des cours pratiques et théoriques; moderniser le domaine dentaire; règlementer les assistants-dentaires
Membre(s) du bureau directeur:
Denise Longpré, Présidente
Membre: *Montant de la cotisation:* 50$ étudiant; 80$ enseignant; 150$ régulier; *Critères d'admissibilite:* Hygiénistes dentaires, des étudiants et des professeurs

Association des Assistantes Dentaires du Nouveau-Brunswick *See* New Brunswick Dental Assistants Association

Association des auteures et des auteurs de l'Ontario français (AAOF)

335B, rue Cumberland, Ottawa ON K1N 7J3
Tél: 613-744-0902; *Téléc:* 613-744-6915
dg@aaof.ca
www.aaof.ca
Aperçu: *Dimension:* moyenne; *Envergure:* provinciale; Organisme sans but lucratif; fondée en 1988
Mission: Promotion et diffusion de la littérature d'expression française en Ontario; Promotion des auteurs/es membres et de leurs oeuvres; Services professionnels aux membres; Représentation des intérêts des membres auprès d'intervenants publics
Affliation(s): Alliance culturelle de l'Ontario
Membre(s) du bureau directeur:
Yves Turbide, Directeur général, 613-744-0902
8 bénévole(s)
Membre: 125; *Montant de la cotisation:* 75$; *Critères d'admissibilite:* Écrivaines et écrivains; *Comités:* Bulletin; Librairie; CREHP
Activités: *Evénements de sensibilisation:* Journée mondiale du livre et du droit d'auteur, 23 avril; *Bibliothèque:* Centre de resources pour écrivains/es en herbe et professionnels/; Bibliothèque publique

Association des auteurs-compositeurs canadiens *See* Songwriters Association of Canada

L'Association des autocaristes Canadiens *See* Motor Coach Canada

L'association des auxiliaires bénévoles des soins de santé du Canada *See* Canadian Association of Healthcare Auxiliaries

Association des Aviateurs et Pilotes de Brousse du Québec (APBQ)

#207, 3509, boul de la Concorde Est, Laval QC H7E 2C6
Tél: 514-255-9998; *Téléc:* 450-436-4411
Ligne sans frais: 877-317-2727
secretariat@apbq.com
www.apbq.com
Nom précédent: Association des pilotes de brousse du Québec
Aperçu: *Dimension:* moyenne; *Envergure:* provinciale; Organisme sans but lucratif; fondée en 1979
Mission: Regrouper et représenter les aviateurs du Québec; promouvoir l'aviation récréative et le vol de brousse; protéger le droit de voler; favoriser l'accessibilité et la sécurité du vol; faciliter l'échange entre les membres; donner accès à des ressources d'aide, de formation et d'information
Membre(s) du bureau directeur:
Bernard Gervais, Président
Finances: *Fonds:* Cotisations; vente de publicité sur le web; ristournes; petites annonces
Membre: *Montant de la cotisation:* Barème
Activités: Assemblée générale; soirées techniques; programme de formation

Association des avocats de la défense de Montréal (AADM)

#300, 402, rue Notre-Dame est, Montréal QC H2Y 1C8
Tél: 514-687-4924; *Téléc:* 514-687-4923
info@aadm.ca
aadm.ca
twitter.com/aadm_expo
Aperçu: *Dimension:* petite; *Envergure:* locale
Mission: Association d'avocats de la défense en droit criminel et pénal pratiquant essentiellement à Montréal. Sa mission comporte deux volets principaux: la défense des intérêts de ses membres et la promotion des droits et libertés individuels au sein du système judiciaire
Membre(s) du bureau directeur:
Richard F. Prihoda, Président
rprihoda@yourdefence.ca
Alexandre Bergevin, Vice-présidente
abergevin@aadm.ca
Membre: 475; *Montant de la cotisation:* Basé sur le statut d'avocat
Activités: Journée d'étude; Symposium; Formation

Association des avocats en droit de la jeunesse

Tél: 514-278-1738
Aperçu: *Dimension:* petite; *Envergure:* provinciale
Membre(s) du bureau directeur:
Anne-Suzie Guercin, Contact

Association des avocats et avocates de la région de Moncton *See* Moncton Area Lawyers' Association

Association des avocats et avocates de province (AAP)

2097, rue Casson, Trois-Rivières QC G8Y 7E8
Tél: 450-516-4800
secretaire@avocatsdeprovince.qc.ca
www.avocatsdeprovince.qc.ca
Aperçu: *Dimension:* moyenne; *Envergure:* provinciale
Mission: Pour réunir des juristes qui partagent des expériences et conseils avec l'autre
Membre(s) du bureau directeur:
Daniel Kimpton, Directeur général et secrétaire
secretaire@avocatsdeprovince.qc.ca
Caroline Blache, Présidente
cblache@cjll.qc.ca

Association des avocats et avocates représentant les bénéficiaires des régimes d'indemnisation publics (AAARBRIP)

445, boul. Saint-Laurent, Montréal QC H2Y 3T8
Tél: 514-954-3471; *Téléc:* 517-954-3451
Ligne sans frais: 800-361-8495
www.aaarbrip.com
Aperçu: *Dimension:* petite; *Envergure:* locale
Mission: Protéger ceux qui reçoivent des prestations du Régime des rentes du Québec et de créer une communauté de juristes qui défendent leurs droits
Membre(s) du bureau directeur:
André Laporte, Président, Conseil d'administration
Membre: *Montant de la cotisation:* 75$

Association des avocats et avovates en droit familial du Québec (AAADFQ)

445, boul St-Laurent, 5e étage, Montréal QC H2Y 3T8
Tél: 514-954-3471
Ligne sans frais: 800-361-8495
info@aaadfq.ca
www.aaadfq.ca
Aperçu: *Dimension:* petite; *Envergure:* locale; fondée en 1985
Mission: Pour aider à rendre la pratique du droit de la famille plus pratique et plus efficace et de créer une communauté parmi ses membres
Membre(s) du bureau directeur:
Marie Annik Walsh, Présidente, Conseil d'administration
Membre: *Montant de la cotisation:* 45$ Avocat stagiaire; 70$ Moins de 5 ans de pratique; 90$ 5 ans et plus de pratique

L'Association des Avocats Noirs du Canada *See* Canadian Association of Black Lawyers

Association des banques alimentaires du Nouveau-Brunswick *See* New Brunswick Association of Food Banks

Association des banquiers canadiens *See* Canadian Bankers Association

Association des bibliotechniciens de l'Ontario *See* Ontario Association of Library Technicians

Association des bibliothécaires du Québec (ABQLA) / Québec Library Association (QLA)

CP 26717, Succ. Beaconsfield, Beaconsfield QC H9W 6G7
Tél: 514-697-0146; *Téléc:* 514-697-0146
abqla@abqla.qc.ca
www.abqla.qc.ca
www.facebook.com/124766477552846
Aperçu: *Dimension:* moyenne; *Envergure:* provinciale; fondée en 1932
Membre(s) du bureau directeur:

Luigina Vileno, Présidente
Luigina.Vileno@concordia.ca
Membre(s) du personnel: 1
Membre: 500-999; *Montant de la cotisation:* Personal $30-$105, salary dependent; $140 institutional; $155 commercial; *Comités:* Archives; By-Laws; Communications
Meetings/Conferences: • 83e Congrès annuel de l'Association des bibliothécaires du Québec 2015, May, 2015, Centre de Conférence Gelber, Montréal, QC
Scope: Provincial
• 84e Congrès annuel de l'Association des bibliothécaires du Québec 2016, 2016, QC
Scope: Provincial
Publications:
• ABQLA Bulletin
Type: Journal; *Frequency:* 3 pa; *Editor:* Rosarie Coughlan; Michelle Lake *ISSN:* 0380-7150
Profile: Book reviews, library-related issues, new technologies

Association des bibliothécaires francophones de l'Ontario (ABFO)
c/o Ontario Library Association, 2 Toronto St., 3rd Fl., Toronto ON M5C 2B6
Tél: 416-363-3388; *Téléc:* 416-941-9581
Ligne sans frais: 866-873-9867
Aperçu: *Dimension:* petite; *Envergure:* provinciale; fondée en 1996
Mission: L'ABFO est l'Association des Bibliothécaires Francophones de l'Ontario qui oeuvrent dans le domaine public, collégial, universitaire ou scolaire et qui ont à coeur la culture francophone.
Membre(s) du bureau directeur:
Julie Desmarais, Présidente
julie.desmarais@biblioottawalibrary.ca

Association des bibliothécaires professionnel(le)s du Nouveau-Brunswick (ABPNB) / Association of Professional Librarians of New Brunswick (APLNB)
PO Box 423, Stn. A, Fredericton NB E3B 4Z9
e-mail: info@abpnb-aplnb.ca
www.abpnb-aplnb.ca
Overview: A medium-sized provincial organization founded in 1992
Mission: Promouvoir les bibliothécaires et les services de bibliothèques au Nouveau-Brunswick
Chief Officer(s):
Johanne Jacob, Présidente
johanne.jacob@gnb.ca
Christin Sheridan, Secrétaire
Anne LePage, Trésorier
Membership: *Fees:* 30$; *Committees:* Adhésion; Hackmatack; Information et de publicité; Bulletin de nouvelles; Bibliothèques scolaires; Alphabétisation
Activities: *Rents Mailing List:* Yes

Association des bibliothécaires, des professeures et professeurs de l'Université de Moncton (ABPPUM)
Université de Moncton, Pavillon Pierre-A.-Landry, #234, Moncton NB E1A 3E9
Tél: 506-858-4509; *Téléc:* 506-858-4559
abppum@umoncton.ca
www.caut.ca/abppum
Aperçu: *Dimension:* petite; *Envergure:* locale; fondée en 1976
Mission: Prendre toutes mesures susceptibles de sauvegarder et promouvoir le bien-être et les intérêts de l'association et de ses membres; se livrer aux activités d'enseignement et de recherche jugées utiles et nécessaires; agir de façon à promouvoir les meilleurs intérêts de l'Université de Moncton
Affliation(s): Association canadienne des professeures et professeurs d'université; Fédération des associations des professeures et professeurs d'université du Nouveau-Brunswick
Membre(s) du bureau directeur:
Michel Cardin, Présidente
Membre(s) du personnel: 2
Membre: 300; *Montant de la cotisation:* Barème; *Critères d'admissibilité:* Ouvert à toute personne employée à plein temps par le campus de Moncton de l'Université de Moncton à titre de professeure ou professeur ou de bibliothécaire
Activités: *Stagiaires:* Oui

Association des bibliothèques de droit de Montréal (ABDM) / Montréal Association of Law Libraries (MALL)
CP 482, 800, carre Victoria, Montréal QC H4Z 1J7
Aperçu: *Dimension:* petite; *Envergure:* locale; Organisme sans but lucratif; fondée en 1987
Mission: Vise à permettre aux gens qui travaillent dans les bibliothèques de droit et qui exercent des fonctions connexes de communiquer et d'échanger des idées; d'encourager l'avancement de la profession; de maintenir et d'accroître l'utilité des bibliothèques de droit; promouvoir la coopération
Membre(s) du bureau directeur:
Maryvon Coté, Présidente
maryvon.cote@mcgill.ca
Finances: *Budget de fonctionnement annuel:* Moins de $50,000
Membre *Montant de la cotisation:* 20$ étudiant; 45$ membre actif; 100$ membre associé
Activités: Réunions mensuelles sous forme de conférence avec conférencier et table ronde des membres; *Stagiaires:* Oui

Association des bibliothèques de l'Ontario-Franco
c/o Ontario Library Association, #201, 50 Wellington St. East, Toronto ON M5E 1C8
www.accessola.com/abfo/
Also Known As: ABO-Franco
Overview: A medium-sized provincial organization
Chief Officer(s):
Claire Dionne, Présidente
claire.dionne@russellbiblio.com

Association des bibliothèques de la région de la capitale nationale *See* Library Association of the National Capital Region

Association des bibliothèques de la santé affiliées à l'Université de Montréal (ABSAUM)
a/s Bibliothèque de la santé, Université de Montréal, CP 6128, Succ. Centre-Ville, Montréal QC H3C 3J7
Tél: 514-343-6111; *Téléc:* 514-343-6457
www.bib.umontreal.ca/absaum
Aperçu: *Dimension:* petite; *Envergure:* locale; fondée en 1978
Mission: Favoriser les rencontres entre les membres et promouvoir l'étude des problèmes communs; mettre de l'avant des projets d'intérêt commun; faire des recommandations auprès des autorités ou organismes concernés
Affliation(s): Université de Montréal
Membre(s) du bureau directeur:
Audrey Attia, President, 514-340-2800 Ext. 326
Finances: *Budget de fonctionnement annuel:* Moins de $50,000
Membre: 15; *Montant de la cotisation:* 50$; *Critères d'admissibilite:* Bibliothécaire
Activités: 3 réunions par an

Association des bibliothèques de la santé des Maritimes *See* Maritimes Health Libraries Association

Association des bibliothèques de la santé du Canada *See* Canadian Health Libraries Association

Association des bibliothèques de recherche du Canada *See* Canadian Association of Research Libraries

Association des bibliothèques de santé de la Vallée d'Outaouais *See* Ottawa Valley Health Libraries Association

Association des bibliothèques parlementaires au Canada *See* Association of Parliamentary Libraries in Canada

Association des bibliothèques publiques de l'Estrie (ABIPE)
1002, av J.-A.-Bombardier, Valcourt QC J0E 2L0
Tél: 450-532-1532; *Téléc:* 450-532-5807
www.bpq-estrie.qc.ca
Aperçu: *Dimension:* petite; *Envergure:* locale; fondée en 1990
Mission: Regrouper les bibliothèques publiques d'Estrie pour en favoriser le développement; informer les membres et échanger sur toute question pertinente au dossier des bibliothèques; représenter les intérêts des bibliothèques membres de la région 05 en étant leur porte-parole officiel auprès des instances gouvernementales et autres; organiser et réaliser des activités d'animation culturelle; sensibiliser le milieu au rôle et à l'importance de la bibliothèque publique dans la communauté
Membre(s) du bureau directeur:
Karine Corbeil, Présidente
k.corbeil@fjab.qc.ca
Patrick Falardeau, Vice-président
Membre: 11 bibliothèques

Association des bibliothèques publiques de la Montérégie
620, rue Richelieu, Beloeil QC J3G 5E8
Tel: 450-467-7872; *Fax:* 450-467-3257
tanguayy@mediatheque.qc.ca
www.abpq.ca/fr/monteregie
Overview: A small local organization
Chief Officer(s):
Parent Marie-Hélène, Présidente
Membership: 40

Association des bibliothèques publiques du Québec (ABPQ)
1453, rue Beaubien est, ste. 215, Montréal QC H2G 3C6
Tél: 514-886-7779; *Téléc:* 514-845-1618
info@abpq.ca
www.abpq.ca
Nom précédent: Les bibliothèques publiques du Québec; Association des directeurs de bibliothèques publiques du Québec
Aperçu: *Dimension:* moyenne; *Envergure:* provinciale; Organisme sans but lucratif; fondée en 1984
Mission: Agit à titre de représentant officiel des bibliothèques publiques du Québec
Membre(s) du bureau directeur:
Eve Lagacé, Directrice générale
eve.lagace@bibliothequespubliquesduquebec.ca
Membre(s) du personnel: 3
Activités: *Evénements de sensibilisation:* Semaine des Bibliothèques publiques du Québec

Association des bleuets sauvages de l'Amérique du Nord *See* Wild Blueberry Association of North America

Association des Boulangers Artisans du Québec (ABAQC)
2436, rue de Châteauguay, Montréal QC H3K 1L1
info@abaqc.com
www.apaqweb.com
www.linkedin.com/company/association-des-boulangers-artisans-du-qu-bec
www.facebook.com/ABAQc
twitter.com/BoulangersArtis
Aperçu: *Dimension:* petite; *Envergure:* provinciale
Mission: De promouvoir la cuisson comme une profession; pour créer camaraderie entre ses membres
Membre(s) du bureau directeur:
Bonraisin Guy, Président
Membre: *Montant de la cotisation:* Barème

L'Association des brasseurs du Canada *See* Brewers Association of Canada

Association des brasseurs du Québec (ABQ) / Québec Brewers Association
#888, 2000, rue Peel, Montréal QC H3A 2W5
Tél: 514-284-9199; *Téléc:* 514-284-0817
Ligne sans frais: 800-854-9199
asbq@brasseurs.qc.ca
brasseurs.qc.ca
Aperçu: *Dimension:* moyenne; *Envergure:* provinciale; fondée en 1943
Mission: De représenter les intérêts de ses membres à des organismes et des intervenants govenment
Membre de: Brewers Association of Canada
Membre(s) du bureau directeur:
Philippe Batani, Directeur général
p.batani@brasseurs.qc.ca
Membre(s) du personnel: 3
Membre: 3; *Critères d'admissibilite:* Brasseurs en Québec et participants en l'industrie; *Comités:* Communications

Association des cadres de la santé et des services sociaux du Québec *Voir* APER Santé et services sociaux

Association des cadres municipaux de Montréal (ACMM)
2e étage, 281, rue St-Paul, Montréal QC H2Y 1H1
Tél: 514-499-1130; *Téléc:* 514-499-1737
acmm@acmm.qc.ca
www.acmm.qc.ca
Aperçu: *Dimension:* petite; *Envergure:* provinciale
Mission: A pour objet l'établissement de relations ordonnées entre l'employeur et les membres ainsi que l'étude, la défense et le développement des intérêts économiques sociaux, moraux et professionnels de ces derniers
Membre(s) du bureau directeur:
Pascale Tremblay, Président

Association des cadres scolaires du Québec
#170, 1195, av Lavigerie, Québec QC G1V 4N3
Tél: 418-654-0014; *Téléc:* 418-654-1719
acsq@acsq.qc.ca
www.acsq.qc.ca

Aperçu: *Dimension:* moyenne; *Envergure:* provinciale; Organisme sans but lucratif; fondée en 1972
Mission: Valoriser le statut professionnel de ses membres et promouvoir leurs intérêts professionnels et éconimiques; Collaborer avec les autorités gouvernementales et les organismes intéressés, au développement ordonné du système scolaire, par une participation constante et adéquate à l'élaboration et à la mise en oeuvre des politiques relatives à l'éducation
Affliation(s): Table nationale de lutte contre l'homophobie du réseau scolaire; Success for Youth Foundation; Olympiades Réussite Jeunesse; Grand défi Pierre Lavoie; Québec Entrepreneurship Contest; Provincial Issue Table on Violence, Youth & the School Environment; Allô prof; Le Point en administration de l'éducation
Membre(s) du bureau directeur:
Lucie Godbout, Directrice général, 418-654-0014 Ext. 222
lgodbout@acsq.qc.ca
Lucie Demers, Présidente
lucie_demers@csmv.qc.ca
Mario Vachon, Vice-Président
mario.vachon@eco.csaffluents.qc.ca
Jean-François Lussier, Secrétaire-trésorier
ilussier@csdp.gc.ca
Membre(s) du personnel: 13
Membre: Over 50,000; *Critères d'admissibilite:* Personnel d'encadrement de l'éducation
Activités: *Bibliothèque* rendez-vous
Publications:
• L'En Bloc
Type: Bulletin
• Réussir
Type: Bulletin

Association des cadres supérieurs de la santé et des services sociaux du Québec (ACSSSS)
#1494, rue Victoria, Greenfield Park QC J4V 1M2
Tél: 450-465-0360; *Téléc:* 450-465-0444
cadres.superieurs@acssss.qc.ca
www.acssss.qc.ca
www.linkedin.com/company/association-des-cadres-supérieurs-de-la-santé
www.facebook.com/1438926259719098
www.youtube.com/user/ACSSSSQC
Aperçu: *Dimension:* petite; *Envergure:* provinciale; fondée en 1959
Affliation(s): La Coalition de l'encadrement en matière de retraite d'assurance; Commission administrative des régimes de retraite et d'assurances; Commission administrative des régimes de retraite et d'assurances Québec
Membre(s) du bureau directeur:
Carole Trempe, Directrice générale
carole.trempe.acssss@ssss.gouv.qc.ca

Association des camps du Canada See Canadian Camping Association

Association des camps du Québec inc. (ACQ) / Québec Camping Association
CP 1000, Succ. M, 4545, av Pierre-de Coubertin, Montréal QC H1V 3R2
Tél: 514-252-3113; *Téléc:* 514-252-1650
Ligne sans frais: 800-361-3586
info@camps.qc.ca
www.camps.qc.ca
www.facebook.com/130062375961
Aperçu: *Dimension:* moyenne; *Envergure:* provinciale; Organisme sans but lucratif; fondée en 1950 surveillé par Canadian Camping Association
Mission: Assurer le développement, la promotion et la qualité des camps de vacances; s'assurer de la formation du personnel des camps
Affliation(s): Regroupement loisir Québec; Association des camps du Canada
Membre(s) du bureau directeur:
Eric Beauchemin, Directeur
ericbeauchemin@camps.qc.ca
Finances: *Budget de fonctionnement annuel:* $250,000-$500,000; *Fonds:* Secrétariat au loisir et au sport du Québec
Membre(s) du personnel: 6; 25 bénévole(s)
Membre: 120 camp; 60 individu; *Montant de la cotisation:* 575 camp; 40$ individu; *Critères d'admissibilite:* Camp de vacances accredité par l'ACQ ou membre individuel; *Comités:* Ressources Humaines; Communications; Membership
Activités: *Stagiaires:* Oui; *Listes de destinataires:* Oui

Association des capitaines propriétaires de Gaspésie inc (ACPG)
CP 9, 1, rue de la Langevin, Gaspé QC G4X 5G4
Tél: 418-269-7701; *Téléc:* 418-269-3278
jpc-acpg@cgocable.ca
www.acpgaspesie.com
Aperçu: *Dimension:* petite; *Envergure:* locale; fondée en 1983
Membre(s) du bureau directeur:
Vincent Dupuis, Président
Jean-Pierre Couillard, Directeur général

Association des cardiologues du Québec (ACQ)
#3000, 2, Complexe Desjardins, Montréal QC H5B 1G8
Tél: 514-350-5106; *Téléc:* 514-350-5156
acq@fmsq.org
Aperçu: *Dimension:* petite; *Envergure:* provinciale surveillé par Fédération des médecins spécialistes du Québec
Membre(s) du bureau directeur:
Gilles O'Hara, Président
Louise Girard, Directrice

Association des cartothèques et archives cartographiques du Canada *See* Association of Canadian Map Libraries & Archives

L'Association des CBDC du Nouveau-Brunswick *See* New Brunswick Association of Community Business Development Corporations

Association des Centres de recherche sur l'Utilisation Urbaine du Sous-sol *See* Associated Research Centres for the Urban Underground Space

Association des centres de santé de l'Ontario *See* Association of Ontario Health Centres

Association des centres hospitaliers et centres d'accueil privés du Québec *Voir* Association des établissements privés conventionnés - santé services sociaux

Association des centres jeunesse du Québec (ACJQ)
#410, 1001, boul de Maisonneuve Ouest, Montréal QC H3A 3C8
Tél: 514-842-5181; *Téléc:* 514-842-4834
info.acjq@ssss.gouv.qc.ca
www.acjq.qc.ca
Aperçu: *Dimension:* moyenne; *Envergure:* provinciale; fondée en 1992
Mission: Concertation, coordination et représentation des Centres Jeunesse du Québec
Membre(s) du bureau directeur:
Alain St-Pierre, Directeur général par intérim
Finances: *Fonds:* Fundraising; donations

Association des centres pour aînés de l'Ontario *See* Older Adult Centres' Association of Ontario

Association des cercles canadiens *See* Association of Canadian Clubs

Association des chefs de services d'incendie du Québec *Voir* Association des chefs en sécurité incendie du Québec

Association des chefs en sécurité incendie du Québec (ACSIQ) / Québec Association of Fire Chiefs
5, rue Dupré, Beloeil QC J3G 3J7
Tél: 450-464-6413; *Téléc:* 450-467-6297
Ligne sans frais: 888-464-6413
administration@acsiq.qc.ca
www.acsiq.qc.ca
Nom précédent: Association des chefs de services d'incendie du Québec
Aperçu: *Dimension:* moyenne; *Envergure:* provinciale; Organisme sans but lucratif; fondée en 1968
Mission: Regrouper les personnes détanant un poste de commande dans le domaine de la prévention et de la lutte contre les incendies
Membre(s) du bureau directeur:
Daniel Brazeau, Président
Membre: *Montant de la cotisation:* 230$; *Critères d'admissibilite:* Chefs de service incendie de municipalités ou de brigade en industries; *Comités:* Mise en candidature; Vérification des politiques; Évaluation du rendement du directeur général; Finances; Consultatif; Reconnaissances; Développement et de stratégie de l'ACSIQ; Stratégique avec le MSP; Stratégique MSP; Prévention de l'ACSIQ; Réduction des alarmes non-fondées; Consultatif sur la législation du gaz propane; Guide de prévention; Certification des résidences pour personnes âgées; Consultatif sur l'Éducation du public; Consultatif provincial sur le code de construction du Québec; Les foyers à l'éthanol; Le code de sécurité; Les résidences pour personnes âgées autonomes

L'Association des chemins de fer du Canada *See* Railway Association of Canada

Association des chercheurs et chercheures étudiants en médecine (ACCEM)
Pavillon Ferdinand-Vandry, Faculté de médecine, Université Laval, #4645, 1050, av de la Médecine, Québec QC G1V 0A6
accem@asso.ulaval.ca
www.fmed.ulaval.ca/ACCEM
www.facebook.com/accemulaval
twitter.com/ACCEMulaval
Aperçu: *Dimension:* petite; *Envergure:* locale
Membre(s) du bureau directeur:
Jean-Philippe Pialasse, Président
Membre: *Critères d'admissibilite:* Chercheurs étudiant à la faculté de médecine de l'Université Laval

Association des chevaux Morgan canadien inc. *See* Canadian Morgan Horse Association

Association des chiropraticiens du Nouveau-Brunswick *See* New Brunswick Chiropractors' Association

Association des chiropraticiens du Québec
7960, boul Métropolitain est, Montréal QC H1K 1A1
Tél: 514-355-0557; *Téléc:* 514-355-0070
Ligne sans frais: 866-292-4476
acq@chiropratique.com
www.chiropratique.com
Aperçu: *Dimension:* moyenne; *Envergure:* provinciale; fondée en 1966 surveillé par Canadian Chiropractic Association
Mission: Défendre les intérêts professionnels, sociaux et économiques de ses membres
Membre(s) du bureau directeur:
Richard Giguère, Président
Marie-Hélène Boivin, Secrétaire
Claude Pilon, Trésorier
Membre: 530

Association des chirurgiens dentistes du Québec (ACDQ)
#1425, 425, boul de Maisonneuve ouest, Montréal QC H3A 3G5
Tél: 514-282-1425; *Téléc:* 514-282-0255
Ligne sans frais: 800-361-3794
info@acdq.qc.ca
www.acdq.qc.ca
Aperçu: *Dimension:* moyenne; *Envergure:* provinciale; Organisme de réglementation; fondée en 1966 surveillé par Canadian Dental Association
Mission: L'Association a pour objet l'étude, la défense et le développement des intérêts économiques, sociaux et moraux de ses membres.
Membre(s) du bureau directeur:
Serge Langlois, DDS, Président

Association des chirurgiens généraux du Québec *Voir* Association Québécoise de chirurgie

Association des cinémas parallèles du Québec (ACPQ)
4545, av Pierre-de Coubertin, Montréal QC H1V 0B2
Tél: 514-252-3021; *Téléc:* 514-252-3063
www.cinemasparalleles.qc.ca
www.facebook.com/CinemasParalleles
Également appelé: L'oeil cinéma réseau plus
Aperçu: *Dimension:* petite; *Envergure:* provinciale; fondée en 1979
Mission: Regrouper les organisations du cinéma non commercial du Québec dans le but de promouvoir auprès des Québécois la culture cinématographique et de développer une activité de loisir cinématographique diversifiée et de qualité.
Membre de: SODEP; CQL; RLSQ; CQRHC
Membre(s) du bureau directeur:
Martine Mauroy, Directrice générale
m.mauroy@cinemasparalleles.qc.ca
Finances: *Budget de fonctionnement annuel:* $500,000-$1.5 Million; *Fonds:* Financement du gouvernement; Financement privé; Vente de services
Membre(s) du personnel: 5
Membre: 57; *Montant de la cotisation:* 80$
Activités: Conférences; Ateliers; *Stagiaires:* Oui; *Service de conférenciers:* Oui

Association des citoyennes averties Alma *Voir* Maison de Campagne & d'Entraide Communautaire du Lac

Association des clubs d'entrepreneurs étudiants du Québec

1510, rue Jean-Berchmans-Michaud, Drummondville QC J2C 7V3
Tél: 819-850-7573
info@acee.qc.ca
www.acee.qc.ca
Également appelé: ACEE du Québec
Aperçu: *Dimension:* petite; *Envergure:* provinciale; Organisme sans but lucratif; fondée en 1991
Mission: Organisme de dépistage du profil entrepreneurial à travers la francophonie et de mise en réseautage
Membre(s) du bureau directeur:
Nicolas Duval-Mace, Président
Pierre Touzel, Directeur général
touzelp@acee.qc.ca
Finances: *Budget de fonctionnement annuel:* $500,000-$1.5 Million
Membre(s) du personnel: 6; 60 bénévole(s)
Membre: 2 500; *Montant de la cotisation:* 50$; *Critères d'admissibilité:* Étudiant de tout champ d'études
Activités: Colloque annuel

Association des clubs de Biathlon du Québec (ACBQ)

172, rue Louis-Bureau, Sherbrooke QC J1E 3Z7
Tel: 819-820-4330
www.acbq.qc.ca
www.facebook.com/acbq.qc.ca
Overview: A small provincial organization founded in 2005 overseen by Biathlon Canada
Member of: Biathlon Canada
Chief Officer(s):
Érika Charron, Président, 819-348-0523
dan10eri@abacom.com
Sandrine Charron, Directrice, Haute performance
charrons@globetrotter.net

Association des collections d'entreprises (ACE) / Corporate Art Collectors Association

QC
info@ace-cca.ca
ace-cca.ca
Aperçu: *Dimension:* moyenne; *Envergure:* nationale; Organisme sans but lucratif; fondée en 1985
Mission: Réunir les conservateurs et les propriétaires de collections corporatives; favoriser l'échange d'information, d'idées, d'expériences, d'expertise, de systèmes ou de services; représenter de façon générale les intérêts de ses membres; favoriser la diffusion de l'art au Québec
Membre(s) du bureau directeur:
Jo-Ann Kane, Présidente et secrétaire
jkane@ace-cca.ca
François Rochon, Trèsorier
Kimberlee Clarke, Responsable, Logistique
kclarke@ace-cca.ca
3 bénévole(s)
Membre: 20 sociétés; *Critères d'admissibilité:* Sociétés ayant des collections d'art ou désirant devenir collectionneurs
Activités: Réunions; séminaires; attribution de subventions occasionnelles à des organismes artistiques

Association des collèges communautaires du Canada *See* Colleges and Institutes Canada

Association des collèges privés du Québec (ACPQ)

1940, boul Henri-Bourassa est, Montréal QC H2B 1S2
Tél: 514-381-8891; *Téléc:* 514-381-4086
Ligne sans frais: 888-381-8891
acpq@cadre.qc.ca
www.acpq.net
Aperçu: *Dimension:* moyenne; *Envergure:* provinciale; Organisme sans but lucratif; fondée en 1968
Mission: Défendre les intérêts de ses collèges membres et contribuer au développement de l'enseignement collégial privé au Québec
Membre de: Conseil du Patronat du Québec
Membre(s) du bureau directeur:
Guy Forgues, Directeur général, 514-381-8891 Ext. 325
Lucie Leduc, Adjointe administrative, 514-381-8891 Ext. 326
Finances: *Budget de fonctionnement annuel:* $250,000-$500,000
Membre(s) du personnel: 2
Membre: 24 institutions d'enseignement; *Montant de la cotisation:* Barème

Association des commerçants de véhicules récréatifs du Canada *See* Recreation Vehicle Dealers Association of Canada

Association des commerçants de véhicules récréatifs du Québec (ACVRQ) / RVDA of Québec

#100, 4360, av Pierre-de Coubertin, Montréal QC H1V 1A6
Tél: 514-338-1471; *Téléc:* 514-335-6250
Ligne sans frais: 866-338-1471
info@acvrq.org
www.acvrq.com
Aperçu: *Dimension:* petite; *Envergure:* provinciale; fondée en 1988
Mission: L'Association des Commerçants de Véhicules Récréatifs du Québec représente les principales entreprises ouvrant dans l'industrie du Véhicule Récréatif. L'A.C.V.R.Q. est une compagnie sans but lucratif constituée en vertu de la Partie III de la Loi sur les Compagnies du Québec, aux fins de venir en aide à ses membres relativement à la promotion et au développement de l'industrie des véhicules récréatifs et à l'harmonisation des relations entre les consommateurs et les commerçants
Membre(s) du bureau directeur:
Danielle Godbout, Directrice générale
dgodbout@acvrq.org
Jean-François Lussier, Président
Finances: *Budget de fonctionnement annuel:* $500,000-$1.5 Million
Membre(s) du personnel: 2
Membre: 119; *Montant de la cotisation:* Barème
Activités: Participation aux salons des véhicules récréatifs; *Evénements de sensibilisation:* Salons des VR, mars/avril

Association des commissaires d'écoles de Colombie-Britannique *See* British Columbia School Trustees Association

Association des commissaires de bibliothèque du Nouveau-Brunswick, inc. *See* New Brunswick Library Trustees' Association

Association des commissaires industriels du Québec (ACIQ) *Voir* Association des professionnels en développement économique du Québec

Association des commissions des accidents du travail du Canada *See* Association of Workers' Compensation Boards of Canada

Association des commissions scolaires anglophones du Québec *See* Québec English School Boards Association

Association des communautés chorales canadiennes *See* Association of Canadian Choral Communities

Association des compagnies de théâtre (ACT)

605, rue Prospect, Sherbrooke QC J1H 1B1
Téléc: 866-499-5587
Ligne sans frais: 866-348-8960
info@act-theatre.ca
www.act-theatre.ca
www.facebook.com/118684904872068
Aperçu: *Dimension:* petite; *Envergure:* provinciale; fondée en 1989
Membre(s) du bureau directeur:
Jacques Jobin, Coordonnateur
Mélanie St-Laurent, Présidente
info@petittheatredunord.com
Étienne Langlois, Vice-président
elanglois@theatresdf.com
Membre: *Montant de la cotisation:* 20$ l'ouverture de dossier; 25$ nouveaux membres; 200$ membre actif; 100$ par production & 50$ par une première production; 200$ corporation

L'association des compositeurs d'Edmonton *See* Edmonton Composers' Concert Society

Association des comptables généraux accrédités du Nouveau-Brunswick *See* Certified General Accountants Association of New Brunswick

Association des concessionnaires Ford du Québec

16, rue Marguerite-Bourgeoys, Boucherville QC J4B 2H3
Tél: 450-655-2090
Aperçu: *Dimension:* petite; *Envergure:* provinciale; Organisme sans but lucratif

Association des conseils des médecins, dentistes et pharmaciens du Québec (ACMDP) / Association of Councils of Physicians, Dentists & Pharmacist of Québec

#212, 560, boul Henri-Bourassa ouest, Montréal QC H3L 1P4
Tél: 514-858-5885; *Téléc:* 514-858-6767
acmdp@acmdp.qc.ca
www.acmdp.qc.ca
Aperçu: *Dimension:* moyenne; *Envergure:* provinciale; Organisme sans but lucratif; fondée en 1946
Mission: Offrir l'information, la motivation, et la formation médico-administrative nécessaire aux Conseils des médecins, dentistes, et pharmaciens membres afin qu'ils accomplissent adéquatement leurs tâches
Membre(s) du bureau directeur:
Annick Lavoie, Directrice générale
Membre(s) du personnel: 4
Membre: 154; *Montant de la cotisation:* Barème; *Critères d'admissibilité:* Conseils de médecins, dentistes et pharmaciens des établissements de santé du Québec
Activités: *Bibliothèque*

Association des conseils en gestion linguistique Inc. (ACGL) / Association of Linguistic Services Managerse (ALSM)

#403, 2030, boul Pie-IX, Montréal QC H1V 2C8
Tél: 514-355-8001; *Téléc:* 514-355-4159
acgl@spg.qc.ca
www.lacgl.org
Aperçu: *Dimension:* petite; *Envergure:* provinciale
Mission: Apporter une aide concrète et efficace aux responsables de services linguistiques; Permettre aux membres d'échanger des expériences pratiques; Informer ses membres des nouvelles techniques en usage dans les professions langagières; Offrir à ses membres des possibilités de perfectionnement; Favoriser la concertation entre les universités et les employeurs.
Membre(s) du bureau directeur:
François Chartrand, Président
francois.chartrand@textualis.com
Finances: *Fonds:* individual and corporate members
Membre: *Montant de la cotisation:* 350$ individuel; 525$ enterprise
Activités: Organization has seminars, committees, publications and training and development

Association des conseils scolaires de la Nouvelle-Écosse *See* Nova Scotia School Boards Association

Association des consommateurs du Canada *See* Consumers' Association of Canada

Association des consommateurs industriels de gaz *See* Industrial Gas Users Association Inc.

Association des constructeurs de routes et grands travaux du Québec (ACRGTQ) / Québec Road Builders & Heavy Construction Association

435, av Grande-Allée est, Québec QC G1R 2J5
Tél: 418-529-2949; *Téléc:* 418-529-5139
Ligne sans frais: 800-463-4672
acrgtq@acrgtq.qc.ca
www.acrgtq.qc.ca
Aperçu: *Dimension:* grande; *Envergure:* provinciale; Organisme sans but lucratif; fondée en 1944 surveillé par Canadian Construction Association
Mission: Défendre les intérêts des entrepreneurs en génie civil et voirie du Québec
Membre(s) du bureau directeur:
Michel Giroux, Président
François Lefebvre, Trésorier
Gisèle Bourque, Directrice générale
Membre: 600; *Montant de la cotisation:* 536.93$ - 7 884.99$; *Critères d'admissibilité:* Entrepreneurs génie civil et voirie et fournisseurs de services; *Comités:* Camionnage; Événements spéciaux; Chaussées en béton; Entrepreneurs en transport d'énergie; ISO-Construction; Ouvrages d'art; Terrassement et assainissement des eaux; Travaux municipaux; Entrepreneurs en déneigement du Québec; Professionnel des exploitants de centrales d'enrobage; Professionnel des producteurs de granulat; Négociation; Patronal de santé et sécurité du travail; Relations du travail; Négociation
Publications:
• CONSTAS [a publication of the Association des constructeurs de routes et grands travaux du Québec]
Type: Magazine; *Frequency:* q.

Bureau à la Romaine
Tél: 418-538-7676
Membre(s) du bureau directeur:
Denis Houle, Contact, 418-538-0708
Bureau de Montréal
#100, 7905, boul Louis-Hippolyte-Lafontaine, Montréal QC H1K 4E4
Tél: 514-354-1362; *Téléc:* 514-354-1301
Ligne sans frais: 877-903-1362

Association des consultants et conseillers en santé mentale, psychométriciens, et psychothérapeutes de l'Ontario *See* Ontario Association of Consultants, Counsellors, Psychometrists & Psychotherapists

Association des consultants et laboratoires experts (ACLE)
#211, 6360, rue Jean-Talon est, Saint-Léonard QC H1S 1M8
Tél: 514-253-2878; *Téléc:* 514-253-6825
info@acle.qc.ca
www.acle.qc.ca
Nom précédent: Association canadienne des laboratoires d'essais
Aperçu: *Dimension:* moyenne; *Envergure:* nationale; Organisme sans but lucratif; fondée en 1959
Mission: Développer, promouvoir et sauvegarder les intérêts techniques et commerciaux communs des membres et de leurs clients.
Membre(s) du bureau directeur:
Ghislain Houde, Président
ghoude@groupesm.com
Membre(s) du personnel: 1
Membre: 100; *Critères d'admissibilite:* Entreprises indépendantes réparties en trois divisions - Ingénierie des Sols et Matériaux; Services Analytiques et Environnement; Toiture et Étanchéité

Association des coopératives du Canada *See* Canadian Co-operative Association

Association des coordonnateurs de congrès des universités et des collèges du Canada *See* Canadian University & College Conference Organizers Association

Association des cordes de la Rive-Sud *Voir* Association des orchestres de jeunes de la Montérégie

Association des courtiers d'assurances de la Province de Québec *Voir* Chambre de l'assurance de dommages

Association des courtiers d'assurances du Canada *See* Insurance Brokers Association of Canada

Association des courtiers d'assurances du Nouveau-Brunswick *See* Insurance Brokers Association of New Brunswick

Association des critiques de théâtre du Canada *See* Canadian Theatre Critics Association

l'Association des déchets solides du Nouveau-Brunswick *See* New Brunswick Solid Waste Association

Association des démographes du Québec (ADQ)
CP 49532, Succ. du Musée, Montréal QC H3T 2A5
www.demographesqc.org
Aperçu: *Dimension:* petite; *Envergure:* provinciale; fondée en 1971
Mission: Resserrer les liens entre les démographes; faire connaître la démographie sur le marché du travail; diffuser les connaissances d'ordre démographique
Membre(s) du bureau directeur:
Marc Tremblay, Président
marc_tremblay@uqac.ca
Julien Bérard-Chagnon, Vice-président
Julien.Berard-Chagnon@statcan.gc.ca
Rufteen Shumanty, Trésorière
rufteen.shumanty@stat.gouv.qc.ca
Membre: 160; *Montant de la cotisation:* Barème
Activités: Colloque annuel de démographie dans le cadre du colloque de l'Association canadienne française pour l'avancement des sciences;

Association des denturologistes du Canada *See* Denturist Association of Canada

Association des denturologistes du Québec (ADQ)
#230, 8150, boul Métropolitain Est, Anjour QC H1K 1A1
Tél: 514-252-0270; *Téléc:* 514-252-0392
Ligne sans frais: 800-563-6273
denturo@adq-qc.com
www.adq-qc.com
www.facebook.com/denturo
Aperçu: *Dimension:* moyenne; *Envergure:* provinciale; fondée en 1971
Mission: Protéger et développer les intérêts professionnels, moraux, sociaux et économiques de ses membres
Membre de: Association des denturologistes du Canada; Fédération internationale de denturologie
Membre(s) du bureau directeur:
Marie-France Brisson, Directrice générale
marie-france.brisson@adq-qc.com
Membre(s) du personnel: 4
Membre: *Montant de la cotisation:* 528,89$; *Comités:* Exécutif

Association des dermatologistes du Québec (ADQ) / Association of Dermatologists of Québec
CP 216, Succ. Succ. Desjardins, #3000, 2, Complexe Desjardins, Montréal QC H5B 1G8
Tél: 514-350-5111; *Téléc:* 514-350-5161
www.adq.org
Aperçu: *Dimension:* moyenne; *Envergure:* provinciale; Organisme sans but lucratif; fondée en 1950 surveillé par Fédération des médecins spécialistes du Québec
Mission: Syndicat professionnel: assure la défense des intérêts économiques, professionnels et scientifiques de ses membres
Affiliation(s): Fédération des médecins spécialistes du Québec
Membre(s) du bureau directeur:
Chantal Bolduc, Présidente
Finances: *Budget de fonctionnement annuel:* $100,000-$250,000
Membre(s) du personnel: 1
Membre: 180

Association des designers d'intérieur immatriculés du Nouveau-Brunswick *See* Association of Registered Interior Designers of New Brunswick

Association des designers industriels du Canada *See* Association of Canadian Industrial Designers

Association des designers industriels du Québec (ADIQ)
CP 182, Succ. Rosemont, Montréal QC H1X 3B7
Tél: 514-287-6531; *Téléc:* 514-278-3049
info@adiq.ca
www.adiq.ca
www.facebook.com/adiquebec
Aperçu: *Dimension:* moyenne; *Envergure:* provinciale; fondée en 1984 surveillé par Association of Canadian Industrial Designers
Mission: De soutenir, de représenter et de promourvoir les membres professionels et de mettre en valeur la profession.
Membre de: Forum Design Montréal
Membre(s) du bureau directeur:
Mario Gagnon, Président
Membre: 398; *Comités:* Services; Communication
Activités: Forum annuel; séminaires techniques/juridiques

Association des détaillants de matériaux de construction du Québec *Voir* Association québécoise de la quincaillerie et des matériaux de construction

Association des détaillants en alimentation du Québec (ADA) / Québec Food Retailers' Association
#900, 2120, rue Sherbrooke Est, Montréal QC H2K 1C3
Tél: 514-982-0104; *Téléc:* 514-849-3021
Ligne sans frais: 800-363-3923
info@adaq.qc.ca
www.adaq.qc.ca
www.facebook.com/ADAQuebec
twitter.com/ADAquebec
vimeo.com/adaquebec
Aperçu: *Dimension:* moyenne; *Envergure:* provinciale; fondée en 1955
Mission: Représenter et défendre les intérêts professionnels, socio-politiques et économiques de tous les détaillants du Québec, et ce, quels que soient leur bannière et le type de surface qu'ils opèrent
Membre de: Centre de promotion de l'industrie alimentaire du Québec; Éco Entreprises Québec
Membre(s) du bureau directeur:
Daniel Choquette, Président
Florent Gravel, Président-directeur général
Membre(s) du personnel: 7
Membre: *Montant de la cotisation:* Barème; *Critères d'admissibilite:* Propriétaire-détaillants en alimentation
Activités: *Stagiaires:* Oui; *Listes de destinataires:* Oui

Association des devenus sourds et des malentendants du Québec (ADSMQ)
#001, 1951, boul de Maisonneuve est, Montréal QC H2K 2C9
Tél: 514-278-9633; *Téléc:* 514-278-9075; *TTY:* 514-278-9636
adsmq@videotron.ca
www.adsmq.org
www.facebook.com/pages/Adsmq/127319074076568
twitter.com/adsmq
Aperçu: *Dimension:* petite; *Envergure:* provinciale; fondée en 1982
Mission: Défense des droits; intégration des personnes avec problèmes auditifs; assistance à la recherche sur la surdité; assistance pour l'obtention des aides techniques aux personnes ayant un handicap auditif
Membre(s) du bureau directeur:
Michel Nadeau, Président
Gilles Lauzon, Coordonnateur
Finances: *Budget de fonctionnement annuel:* $50,000-$100,000; *Fonds:* Ministère de la santé et des services sociaux du Québec
Membre(s) du personnel: 1; 50 bénévole(s)
Membre: 350; *Montant de la cotisation:* 25$; *Critères d'admissibilite:* Devenus sourds; malentendants
Activités: Support moral pour personnes malentendantes; Cours d'ordinateur

Association des diététistes du Nouveau-Brunswick *See* New Brunswick Association of Dietitians

Association des diffuseurs culturels de l'Ile de Montréal (ADICIM)
176, ch du Bord-du-Lac, Pointe-Claire QC H9S 4J7
Tél: 514-630-1220; *Téléc:* 514-630-1259
info@adicim.ca
www.adicim.ca
Nom précédent: Association des diffuseurs culturels des arrondissements de Montréal; Association des diffuseurs culturels des banlieues de Montréal
Aperçu: *Dimension:* petite; *Envergure:* locale
Mission: De promouvoir et développer des activités artistiques sur l'île de Montréal
Membre de: Réseau indépendant des diffuseurs d'événements artistiques unis
Membre(s) du bureau directeur:
Micheline Bélanger, Présidente, 514-630-1220 Ext. 1773
belangerm@ville.pointe-claire.qc.ca
Virginia Elliot, Vice-présidente, 514-989-5265
10 bénévole(s)
Membre: 10

Association des diffuseurs culturels des arrondissements de Montréal; Association des diffuseurs culturels des banlieues de Montréal *Voir* Association des diffuseurs culturels de l'Ile de Montréal

Association des diplômés de l'École des hautes Études commerciales *Voir* Réseau HEC Montréal

Association des Diplômés de Polytechnique
CP 6079, Succ. Centre-Ville, Montréal QC H3C 3A7
Tél: 514-340-4764; *Téléc:* 514-340-4472
Ligne sans frais: 866-452-3296
adp@polymtl.ca
www.adp.polymtl.ca
www.linkedin.com/groups/Association-Diplômés-Polytechnique-Montréal-Gr
Aperçu: *Dimension:* moyenne; *Envergure:* provinciale; fondée en 1910
Mission: Établir des relations amicales entre les membres; défendre et promouvoir leurs intérêts
Affiliation(s): Roche, Gestion Férique, TD, Hydro Québec, Banque Nationale Group Financier, Rio Tinto Alcan
Membre(s) du bureau directeur:
Martin Choinière, Président
Diane de Champlain, Directrice générale, 514-340-3225, Fax: 514-340-4472
Stéphanie Oscarson, Directrice, des opérations
Membre(s) du personnel: 5
Membre: 29,000+; *Comités:* Communications; Jeunes Diplômés; Relations avec les étudiants; Prix Mérite; Matins ADP; Soirée Retrouvailles; Golf; Technologie; Partie d'huîtres; Sections; Activité familiale; Ambassadeurs; Événements spéciaux

Association des directeurs d'école de Montréal *Voir* Association montréalaise des directions d'établissement scolaire

Association des directeurs de recherche industrielle du Québec *Voir* Association de la recherche industrielle du Québec

Association des directeurs généraux des commissions scolaires du Québec (ADIGECS)

a/s Directeur exécutif, #212, 195 ch de Chambly, Longueuil QC J4H 3L3
Tél: 450-674-6700; *Téléc:* 450-674-7337
adigecs.qc.ca
Aperçu: *Dimension:* petite; *Envergure:* provinciale; fondée en 1972
Mission: Contribuer à l'avancement de l'éducation au Québec; protéger les intérêts de ses membres notamment au chapitre des conditions de travail
Affiliation(s): Ministère de l'éducation, loisir et sport; Fédération des commissions scolaires du Québec
Membre(s) du bureau directeur:
Raynald Thibeault, Président
Serge Lefebvre, Directeur exécutif
Membre: 163
Activités: Programmes d'aide; bourses d'études; *Événements de sensibilisation:* Colloque ADIGECS (novembre); Congrès ADIGECS (mai); *Service de conférenciers:* Oui

Association des directeurs généraux des municipalités du Québec

#470, 43, rue de Buade, Québec QC G1R 4A2
Tél: 418-660-7591; *Téléc:* 418-660-0848
adgmq@adgmq.qc.ca
adgmq.qc.ca
Aperçu: *Dimension:* moyenne; *Envergure:* provinciale; fondée en 1973
Mission: Permettre l'amélioration des connaissances et du statut de ses membres et la promotion de la formule de gestion conseil/directeur général
Membre(s) du bureau directeur:
Jack Benzaquen, Président
Martine Lévesque, Directrice génerale
martine.levesque@adgmq.qc.ca
Membre(s) du personnel: 3
Membre: 200; *Montant de la cotisation:* 365$; *Critères d'admissibilite:* Directeur général d'une municipalité gérée par la loi des cités et villes

Association des directeurs généraux des services de santé et des services sociaux du Québec (ADGSSSQ) / Association of Executive Directors of Québec Health & Social Services

#B-10, 425, boul. de Maisonneuve Ouest, Montréal QC H3A 3G5
Tél: 514-281-1896; *Téléc:* 514-281-5054
courriel@adgsssq.qc.ca
www.adgsssq.qc.ca
Aperçu: *Dimension:* moyenne; *Envergure:* provinciale; Organisme de réglementation; fondée en 1973
Mission: L'Association des directeurs généraux des services de santé et des services sociaux du Québec est une société dont l'objet premier est ® l'étude, la défense et le développement des intérêts économiques, sociaux et moraux de ses membres
Membre(s) du bureau directeur:
Camil Picard, Présidente
Finances: *Budget de fonctionnement annuel:* $100,000-$250,000
Membre(s) du personnel: 3
Membre: 426; *Montant de la cotisation:* 750$

Association des directeurs généraux, secrétaires et trésoriers municipaux de l'Ontario *See* Association of Municipal Managers, Clerks & Treasurers of Ontario

Association des directeurs municipaux du Québec (ADMQ)

Hall Est, #535, 400, boul. Jean-Lesage, Québec QC G1K 8W1
Tél: 418-647-4518; *Téléc:* 418-647-4115
admq@admq.qc.ca
admq.qc.ca
Aperçu: *Dimension:* moyenne; *Envergure:* provinciale; Organisme sans but lucratif; fondée en 1939
Mission: De voir à la promotion et à la défense des membres en plus d'offrir un soutien professionnel constant au niveau des outils de formation et de communication
Membre(s) du bureau directeur:
Charles Ricard, Président
Marc Laflamme, Directeur général
mlaflamme@admq.qc.ca
Membre(s) du personnel: 7
Membre: 1 100; *Montant de la cotisation:* 395$; *Comités:* Internes; Direction

Association des distillateurs canadiens *See* Association of Canadian Distillers

Association des distributeurs exclusifs de livres en langue française inc. (ADELF)

47, av Wicksteed, Ville Mont-Royal QC H3P 1P9
Tél: 514-739-2220; *Téléc:* 514-739-8307
adelf@videotron.ca
www.adelf.qc.ca
Aperçu: *Dimension:* petite; *Envergure:* locale; Organisme sans but lucratif; fondée en 1978
Mission: Promotion et défense des intérêts des diffuseurs d'éditeurs de langue française; soutenir la diffusion et la distribution de livres en français et leurs produits dérivés; établir entre ses membres des rapports de confraternité; promouvoir la lecture
Affiliation(s): Société de développement du livre et du périodique
Membre(s) du bureau directeur:
Pascal Chamaillard, Président
Benoit Prieur, Directeur général
Finances: *Fonds:* Ministère du Patrimoine canadien; Société de développement des entreprises culturelles
Membre(s) du personnel: 1
Membre: 24
Activités: *Listes de destinataires:* Oui

Association des doyens de pharmacie du Canada *See* Association of Deans of Pharmacy of Canada

Association des eaux souterraines du Québec *Voir* Association des enterprises spécialiseés en eau du Québec

Association des écoles forestières universitaires du Canada *See* Association of University Forestry Schools of Canada

Association des écoles juives *See* Association of Jewish Day Schools

Association des écoles privées du Québec *See* Québec Association of Independent Schools

Association des économistes québécois (ASDÉQ)

#7118, 385, rue Sherbrooke Est, Montréal QC H2X 1E3
Tél: 514-342-7537; *Téléc:* 514-342-3967
Ligne sans frais: 866-342-7537
info@economistesquebecois.com
www.economistesquebecois.com
www.linkedin.com/groups/Association-économistes-québécois-3809359
www.facebook.com/127117010671812
twitter.com/EconomistesQc
Aperçu: *Dimension:* moyenne; *Envergure:* provinciale; Organisme sans but lucratif; fondée en 1975
Mission: Assurer la promotion professionnelle des économistes
Membre(s) du bureau directeur:
Bernard Barrucco, Directeur général
bernardbarrucco@economistesquebecois.com
Membre(s) du personnel: 4
Membre: *Critères d'admissibilite:* Économistes; tout intervenant intéressé par les questions économiques; *Comités:* Développement; Politiques Publiques
Activités: Congrès; colloques; prix de journalisme; ateliers de formation; déjeuners causeries; *Service de conférenciers:* Oui

Association des éditeurs canadiens *See* Association of Canadian Publishers

Association des éditeurs de langue anglaise du Québec *See* Association of English Language Publishers of Québec

Association des Éditeurs de périodiques culturels québécois *Voir* Société de développement des périodiques culturels québécois

Association des éducateurs professionnels du Nouveau-Brunswick *See* Association of New Brunswick Professional Educators

Association des églises chrétiennes du Manitoba *See* Association of Christian Churches in Manitoba

Association des églises évangéliques *See* Associated Gospel Churches

Association des électrolystes du Québec *Voir* Association des électrolystes et esthéticiennes du Québec

Association des électrolystes et esthéticiennes du Québec (AEEQ)

3381, rue des Récollets, Québec QC G2A 2S7
Tél: 418-407-4454; *Téléc:* 418-407-4452
Ligne sans frais: 800-363-9009
www.aeeq.ca
Nom précédent: Association des électrolystes du Québec
Aperçu: *Dimension:* petite; *Envergure:* provinciale; Organisme sans but lucratif; fondée en 1976
Mission: Regrouper le plus d'électrolystes possible au Québec; informer et former ses membres de concert avec les intervenants concernés et promouvoir les intérêts de ses membres
Membre(s) du bureau directeur:
Sylvianne Bouchard, Présidente
Finances: *Budget de fonctionnement annuel:* $50,000-$100,000
Membre(s) du personnel: 1; 15 bénévole(s)
Membre: 500; *Montant de la cotisation:* 185$
Activités: Congrès annuel; soupers-rencontre; cours de perfectionnement

Association des éleveurs de chevaux Belge du Québec / Breeders of Belgian Horses Association of Québec

#1025, Rang 4, Saint-Cyrille-de-Wendover QC J1Z 1T8
Tél: 819-397-4693; *Téléc:* 819-397-5057
fr-fr.facebook.com/201986326506407
Aperçu: *Dimension:* moyenne; *Envergure:* provinciale; Organisme sans but lucratif; fondée en 1905
Mission: Promouvoir l'élevage de chevaux de race pure de grande qualité et aider les éleveurs à améliorer leur cheptel chevalin à travers la province au moyen de concours et d'expositions
Membre(s) du bureau directeur:
Simon Janelle, contact
Finances: *Budget de fonctionnement annuel:* Moins de $50,000
Membre: 88; *Montant de la cotisation:* Barème; *Critères d'admissibilite:* Avoir un intérêt aux choses agricoles et spécialement en ce qui regarde la production chevaline et une race en particulier et se conformer au règlement général de l'association

Association des embouteilleurs d'eau du Québec (AEEQ) / Québec Water Bottlers' Association

a/s CTAC, #102, 200, rue MacDonald, Saint-Jean-sur-Richelieu QC J3B 8J6
Tél: 450-349-1521; *Téléc:* 450-349-6923
info@conseiltac.com
www.aeeq.org
Aperçu: *Dimension:* moyenne; *Envergure:* provinciale; fondée en 1975
Mission: L'association des embouteilleurs d'eau du Québec (AEEQ) est le porte-parole de l'industrie québécoise de l'embouteillage de l'eau de source et de l'eau minérale
Membre de: Canadian Bottled Water Federation
Membre(s) du bureau directeur:
Benoit Grégoire, Président
Nicole Lelièvre, Vice-présidente
Membre: *Critères d'admissibilite:* Entreprises spécialisées dans le commerce de l'eau embouteillée; fournisseurs de services et d'équipments

Association des employées et employés du gouvernement du Québec (AEGQ)

700, boul. René-Lévesque Est, 2e étage, Québec QC G1R 5H1
Tél: 418-643-4020; *Téléc:* 418-643-4064
association@aegq.qc.ca
www.aegq.qc.ca
Aperçu: *Dimension:* grande; *Envergure:* provinciale; Organisme sans but lucratif; fondée en 1925
Mission: Défendre les intérêts professionnels des employés de la fonction publique; club social
Membre(s) du bureau directeur:
Gérald Germain, Président & Directeur général
Finances: *Budget de fonctionnement annuel:* $100,000-$250,000
Membre(s) du personnel: 3; 6 bénévole(s)
Membre: 500; *Montant de la cotisation:* 52$; *Critères d'admissibilite:* Fonctionnaires provinciaux
Publications:
• Le Journal [a publication of the Association des employées et employés du gouvernement du Québec]
Type: Newspaper

Association des employés de bureau de Schneider (FCNSI) *See* Schneider Office Employees' Association

Association des employés de Charlotte Seafood *See* Charlotte Seafood Employees Association

Association des employés de l'Université de Moncton (AEUM) / Moncton University Employees Association

Université de Moncton, Moncton NB E1A 3E9
Tél: 506-858-4050; *Téléc:* 506-858-4166
Ligne sans frais: 800-363-8336
Aperçu: *Dimension:* petite; *Envergure:* locale; Organisme de réglementation; fondée en 1969
Mission: Négocier la convention collective des membres et organiser les relations ouvrières entre les employés et l'Université de Moncton; améliorer les conditions de vie et de travail des employés
Membre(s) du bureau directeur:
Denis Malliet, Président
Juliette Belliveau, Secrétaire, 506-858-4443
Membre(s) du personnel: 5
Membre: 182

Association des employés de Milltronics (FCNSI) *See* Employees Association of Milltronics - CNFIU Local 3005

Association des employés de Schneider (ind.) *See* Schneider Employees' Association (Ind.)

Association des employés du conseil de recherches (ind.) *See* Research Council Employees' Association (Ind.)

Association des employés du Service de sécurité de la Chambre des communes *See* House of Commons Security Services Employees Association

Association des employés du Service de sécurité du Sénate *See* Senate Protective Service Employees Association

Association des employés et employées gestionnaires, administratifs et professionnels de la Couronne de l'Ontario *See* Association of Management, Administrative & Professional Crown Employees of Ontario

Association des employés municipaux de Vancouver-Ouest *See* West Vancouver Municipal Employees' Association

Association des employés non enseignants de Winnipeg *See* Winnipeg Association of Non-Teaching Employees

Association des employés non enseignants du Manitoba *See* Manitoba Association of Non-Teaching Employees

Association des employés professionnels (ind.) *See* Professional Employees Association (Ind.)

Association des employés, l'Hôpital Saint Mary's of the Lake (FCNSI) *See* Employees' Union of St. Mary's of the Lake Hospital - CNFIU Local 3001

Association des enseignant(e)s des Appalaches *See* Appalachian Teachers' Association

Association des enseignantes et des enseignants du Yukon *See* Yukon Teachers' Association

Association des enseignantes et des enseignants franco-ontariens (AEFO) / Franco-Ontarian Teachers' Association

#801, 1420, place Blair, Ottawa ON K1J 9L8
Tél: 613-244-2336; *Téléc:* 613-563-7718
Ligne sans frais: 800-267-4217
aefo@aefo.on.ca
www.aefo.on.ca
www.facebook.com/155281931200167
twitter.com/AEFO_ON_CA
Aperçu: *Dimension:* moyenne; *Envergure:* provinciale; Organisme sans but lucratif; fondée en 1939
Mission: De regrouper les travailleuses et les travailleurs au service des établissements publics et privés francophones en Ontario
Membre de: Fédération canadienne des enseignantes et des enseignants
Affliation(s): Ontario Teachers' Federation
Membre(s) du bureau directeur:
Pierre Léonard, Directeur général
pleonard@aefo.on.ca
Nicole Beauchamp, Responsable des communications
nbeauchamp@aefo.on.ca
Membre: 7,855
Activités: *Bibliothèque*

Association des enseignantes et des enseignants francophones du Nouveau-Brunswick (AEFNB)

CP 712, 650, rue Montgomery, Fredericton NB E3B 5B4
Tél: 506-452-8921; *Téléc:* 506-452-1838
www.aefnb.ca
www.facebook.com/pages/A-E-F-N-B/134963956559270
Aperçu: *Dimension:* moyenne; *Envergure:* provinciale; fondée en 1970 surveillé par Canadian Teachers' Federation
Mission: Représenter les intérêts des enseignantes et des enseignants francophones de la province; favoriser et maintenir au Nouveau-Brunswick des services éducatifs de langue française de première qualité
Membre(s) du bureau directeur:
Suzanne Bourgeois, Présidente
Louise Landry, Directrice générale
louise.landry@aefnb.ca
Finances: *Budget de fonctionnement annuel:* $500,000-$1.5 Million
Membre(s) du personnel: 8
Membre: 2 500; *Montant de la cotisation:* 58$ associé; *Critères d'admissibilite:* Enseignant ou enseignante
Activités: *Stagiaires:* Oui; *Bibliothèque:* Centre d'information

Association des enseignants de l'Université du Nouveau-Brunswick *See* Association of University of New Brunswick Teachers

Association des enseignants de Terre-Neuve *See* Newfoundland & Labrador Teachers' Association

Association des enseignants du collège régional de Grande Prairie *See* Grande Prairie Regional College Academic Staff Association

Association des enseignants en imprimerie du Québec (AEIQ)

Centre 24 Juin, 639, rue du 24 Juin, Fleurimont QC J1E 1H1
Tél: 819-822-6853; *Téléc:* 819-822-6847
webmestre.aeiq@gmail.com
www.aeiq.info
Aperçu: *Dimension:* petite; *Envergure:* provinciale; Organisme sans but lucratif; fondée en 1982
Mission: De regrouper les enseignants, les industriels ainsi que toutes les personnes qui ont un intérêt dans l'enseignement et l'industrie des arts graphiques au Québec.
Membre de: Conseil pédagogique interdisciplinaire du Québec
Membre(s) du bureau directeur:
René Tétreault, Président
Finances: *Budget de fonctionnement annuel:* Moins de $50,000
Membre(s) du personnel: 7; 7 bénévole(s)
Membre: 70
Activités: *Listes de destinataires:* Oui

Association des enterprises spécialiseés en eau du Québec

5930, boul Louis-H. Lafontaine, Montréal QC H1M 1S7
Tél: 514-353-9960; *Téléc:* 514-352-5259
Ligne sans frais: 800-468-8160
contact@aeseq.com
www.aeseq.com
Nom précédent: Association des eaux souterraines du Québec
Aperçu: *Dimension:* moyenne; *Envergure:* provinciale surveillé par Canadian Ground Water Association
Mission: Regrouper les entrepreneurs de construction oeuvrant dans tous les secteurs du cycle de l'eau décentralisé au Québec
Membre(s) du bureau directeur:
Daniel Schanck, Directeur général
Membre(s) du personnel: 3
Membre: *Critères d'admissibilite:* Entrepreneurs puisatiers; entrepreneurs en installation de pompe, ou en assainissement autonome, ou en traitement d'eau potable; fournisseurs d'équipement et de matériaux; consultants; organismes publics et parapublics

Association des entomologistes amateurs du Québec inc. (AEAQ)

302, rue Gabrielle Roy, Varennes QC J3X 1L8
info@aeaq.ca
www.aeaq.ca
www.facebook.com/114179175276983
Aperçu: *Dimension:* petite; *Envergure:* provinciale; Organisme sans but lucratif; fondée en 1973
Mission: Promouvoir l'entomologie comme loisir scientifique; favoriser l'échange d'informations entre les membres lors des réunions; publier les travaux et les observations entomologiques des membres; veiller à la protection et à la conservation de l'entomofaune et du patrimoine entomologique du Québec; initier les nouveaux membres à l'étude des insectes à l'aide de séances d'identification, d'excursions et de rencontres avec des spécialistes
Affliation(s): Société d'entomologie du Québec; Corporation Entomofaune du Québec; Amis de l'Insectarium de Montréal
Membre(s) du bureau directeur:
Claude Chantal, Président
Membre: *Montant de la cotisation:* 30$ régulière; 35$ familiale; 50$ de soutien; 35$ institutions Canadien

Association des entrepreneurs de systèmes intérieurs du Québec

#227, 3221, Autoroute 440 ouest, Laval QC H7P 5P2
Tél: 450-978-2666; *Téléc:* 450-978-1833
www.aesiq.org
Aperçu: *Dimension:* petite; *Envergure:* provinciale
Mission: Promouvoir et défendre les intérêts de nos membres et de l'industrie des systèmes intérieurs au Québec

Association des entrepreneurs en construction du Québec (AECQ) / Association of Building Contractors of Québec (ABCQ)

#101, 7905, boul Louis-H. Lafontaine, Anjou QC H1K 4E4
Tél: 514-353-5151; *Téléc:* 514-353-6689
Ligne sans frais: 800-361-4304
info@aecq.org
www.aecq.org
Aperçu: *Dimension:* grande; *Envergure:* provinciale; fondée en 1976
Mission: Étudier, promouvoir, protéger et défendre les intérêts des employeurs en matière de relations de travail; négocier les clauses du tronc commun à chacune des quatre conventions collectives sectorielles
Affliation(s): Canadian Construction Association
Membre(s) du bureau directeur:
Pierre Dion, Directeur général
Finances: *Budget de fonctionnement annuel:* $500,000-$1.5 Million
Membre(s) du personnel: 4
Membre: 25 000
Activités: *Service de conférenciers:* Oui

Association des entrepreneurs en couverture du Nouveau-Brunswick *See* New Brunswick Roofing Contractors Association, Inc.

Association des entrepreneurs en isolation de la Province de Québec *Voir* Association d'isolation du Québec

Association des entrepreneurs en maçonnerie du Québec (AEMQ)

#101, 4097 boul St-Jean-Baptiste, Montréal QC H1B 5V3
Tél: 514-645-1113; *Téléc:* 514-645-1114
Ligne sans frais: 866-645-1113
aemg@aemg.com
www.aemq.com
www.facebook.com/group.php?gid=171902572902949
Aperçu: *Dimension:* petite; *Envergure:* provinciale; fondée en 1984
Mission: Faire la promotion du métier de maçon et s'assurer que tous travaillent à promouvoir davantage le marché de la maçonnerie
Membre de: Institut de la maçonnerie
Affliation(s): Association des entrepreneurs en construction du Québec; Association de la construction du Québec
Membre(s) du bureau directeur:
Normand Turenne, Président
Marco Tommasel, Vice-Président
Finances: *Budget de fonctionnement annuel:* Moins de $50,000
Membre: 225; *Montant de la cotisation:* 688,85 $ corporatif et affilié; 344,93 $ professionnel
Activités: Offre des produits et services à tous les entrepreneurs ou organismes dont les activités commerciales sont reliées à l'industrie de la maçonnerie

Association des entrepreneurs en mécanique d'Ottawa *See* Mechanical Contractors Association of Ottawa

Association des entrepreneurs en mécanique du Canada *See* Mechanical Contractors Association of Canada

Association des entrepreneurs en mécanique du N.-B. *See* Mechanical Contractors Association of New Brunswick

Association des entreprises métallurgiques du Nouveau-Brunswick *See* The Metal Working Association of New Brunswick

Association des ergothérapeutes du Nouveau-Brunswick *See* New Brunswick Association of Occupational Therapists

Association des Estimateurs et Économistes en Construction du Québec *Voir* Insitut canadien des économistes en construction - Québec

Association des établissements de réadaptation en déficience physique du Québec (AERDPQ) / Quebec Rehabilitation Centres Association (QRCA)

#430, 1001, boul de Maisonneuve ouest, Montréel QC H3A 3C8
Tél: 514-282-4205; *Téléc:* 514-847-9473
info@aerdpq.org
aerdpq.org
Aperçu: *Dimension:* moyenne; *Envergure:* provinciale; fondée en 1974
Mission: L'Association des établissements de réadaptation en déficience physique du Québec (AERDPQ) regroupe les 21 établissements du réseau de la santé et des services sociaux, répartis en 108 points de services sur l'ensemble du territoire québécois
Affliation(s): Centres de réadaptation en déficience physique du Québec (CRDP)
Membre(s) du bureau directeur:
Anne Lauzon, Directrice générale, 514-282-4205 Ext. 222
lguilbea@ssss.gouv.qc.ca
Marie-Josée Boivin, Directrice, Ressources humaines, 514-282-4205 Ext. 228
marie-josee.boivin.aerdpq@ssss.gouv.qc.ca
Finances: *Budget de fonctionnement annuel:* $1.5 Million-$3 Million

Association des établissements privés conventionnés - santé services sociaux (AEPC)

#200, 204, rue Notre-Dame ouest, Montréal QC H2Y 1T3
Tél: 514-499-3630; *Téléc:* 514-873-7063
info@aepc.qc.ca
www.aepc.qc.ca
Nom précédent: Association des centres hospitaliers et centres d'accueil privés du Québec
Aperçu: *Dimension:* moyenne; *Envergure:* nationale; Organisme sans but lucratif; fondée en 1979
Mission: Promouvoir l'amélioration continue de la qualité des soins et des services donnés au sein des entreprises membres; protéger et promouvoir l'entreprise privée dans le domaine de la santé et du bien-être
Membre(s) du bureau directeur:
Jean Hébert, Directeur Général
j.hebert@aepc.qc.ca
Finances: *Budget de fonctionnement annuel:* $100,000-$250,000
Membre(s) du personnel: 9
Membre: 67 établissements; *Critères d'admissibilité:* Détenir un permis d'établissement privé conventionné du Ministère de la santé et des services sociaux du Québec

Association des étudiantes infirmières du Canada *See* Canadian Nursing Students' Association

Association des Étudiants de Science Politique du Canada *See* Canadian Political Science Students' Association

L'Association des etudiants noirs en droit du Canada *See* Black Law Students' Association of Canada

Association des évaluateurs immobiliers du Nouveau-Brunswick *See* New Brunswick Association of Real Estate Appraisers

Association des experts en sinistre indépendants du Québec inc (AESIQ)

n/a Claude Nadeau, Cunningham Lindsey Canada Claims Services Ltd., #1000, 1250, rue Guy, Montréal QC H3H 2T4
www.ciaa-adjusters.ca
Aperçu: *Dimension:* petite; *Envergure:* provinciale; fondée en 1942 surveillé par Canadian Independent Adjusters' Association
Affiliation(s): Association canadienne des experts indépendants/Canadian Independent Adjusters' Association
Membre(s) du bureau directeur:
Claude Nadeau, Président, 514-938-1570, Fax: 514-938-5445
cnadeau@cl-na.com
Finances: *Budget de fonctionnement annuel:* $100,000-$250,000
Membre(s) du personnel: 1; 8 bénévole(s)
Membre: 300; *Montant de la cotisation:* 215$; *Critères d'admissibilite:* Détenteur d'un certificat d'expert en sinistre du B.S.F.

Association des expositions agricoles du Québec (AEAQ)

#223, 1173 boul Charest ouest, Québec QC G1N 2C9
Tél: 418-527-1196; *Téléc:* 418-527-6954
info@expoduquebec.com
expoduquebec.com
www.facebook.com/203811642990737
Aperçu: *Dimension:* petite; *Envergure:* provinciale; fondée en 1940
Mission: D'offrir aux agriculteurs et aux éleveurs des événements professionnels spécialisés et bien organisés; et de présenter au grand public des événements populaires, éducatifs, divertissants et sécuritaires.
Membre(s) du bureau directeur:
François Brunet, Directeur général
direction@expoduquebec.com

Association des fabricants d'aliments pour animaux familiers du Canada *See* Pet Food Association of Canada

Association des fabricants de béton préparé des provinces atlantiques *See* Atlantic Provinces Ready-Mixed Concrete Association

Association des fabricants de meubles du Québec inc. (AFMQ) / Québec Furniture Manufacturers Association Inc.

#101, 1111, rue St-Urbain, Montréal QC H2Z 1Y6
Tél: 514-866-3631; *Téléc:* 514-871-9900
Ligne sans frais: 800-363-6681
info@afmq.com
www.afmq.com
Aperçu: *Dimension:* moyenne; *Envergure:* provinciale; Organisme sans but lucratif; fondée en 1942
Mission: Participer activement au développement de l'industrie du meuble du Québec
Membre de: Canadian Council of Furniture Manufacturers
Membre(s) du bureau directeur:
Pierre Richard, Président/Directeur général
prichard@afmq.com
Anne Marie Byrnes, Coordonnatrice, Communications et marketing
abyrnes@afmq.com
Membre(s) du personnel: 9
Membre: 150; *Critères d'admissibilite:* Fabricants de meubles, de composantes et fournisseurs de l'industrie

Association des fabricants et détaillants de l'industrie de la cuisine du Québec (AFDICQ)

841, rue des Oeillets, Saint-Jean-Chrysostome QC G6Z 3B7
Tél: 418-834-0200; *Téléc:* 418-834-7924
info@afdicq.ca
www.afdicq.ca
www.facebook.com/Afdicq
Aperçu: *Dimension:* moyenne; *Envergure:* provinciale; fondée en 1981
Mission: L'AFDICQ regroupe des fabricants et des distributeurs d'armoires de cuisine et de salle de bains, de meubles sur mesure et d'ébénisterie architecturale. Services: programme hors-série, la licence RBQ, mutuelles de prévention, assurance collective, représentation auprès du gouvernement, opportunité d'établir des contacts d'affaires, sécurité et main d'oeuvre, et le Bulletin.
Membre(s) du bureau directeur:
Simon Bouchard, Président
Membre: 157; *Critères d'admissibilite:* Manufacturiers et distributeurs d'armoires de cuisine et de salle de bains, de meubles sur mesure et d'ébénisterie architecturale

Association des fabricants internationaux d'automobiles du Canada *See* Association of International Automobile Manufacturers of Canada

L'Association des facultés de médecine du Canada *See* Association of Faculties of Medicine of Canada

Association des facultés de pharmacie du Canada *See* Association of Faculties of Pharmacy of Canada

Association des facultés dentaires du Canada *See* Association of Canadian Faculties of Dentistry

Association des faculty du universitaire du Cap-Breton *See* Cape Breton University Faculty Association

Association des familialistes de Québec

#RC-21, 300, boul. Jean Lesage, Québec QC G1K 8K6
Tél: 418-529-0301
www.barreaudequebec.ca
Aperçu: *Dimension:* moyenne; *Envergure:* provinciale; fondée en 1994
Mission: Pour représenter les intérêts de ses membres avec les différents organismes et à assurer la formation de ses membres
Membre(s) du bureau directeur:
Isabelle Perreault, Présidente, Conseil d'administration, 418-627-2442, Fax: 418-627-6656
Membre: *Montant de la cotisation:* 50$ Membre du Barreau depuis moins de 5 ans; 65$ Membre du Barreau depius plus de 5 ans
Activités: Les conférences; Activités sociales

Association des familles Gosselin, Inc.

1647, ch Royal, Saint-Laurent d'Orléans QC G0A 3Z0
Tél: 418-828-2896; *Téléc:* 418-828-0149
associationfamillesgosselin@hotmail.com
www.genealogie.org/famille/gosselin
Aperçu: *Dimension:* petite; *Envergure:* locale; fondée en 1979
Mission: Informer et guider les recherches en généalogie sur le patronyme Gosselin; faire connaître le résultat des recherches sur tout ce qui touche le patronyme Gosselin; faciliter la communication et les échanges entre les cousins Gosselin
Membre(s) du bureau directeur:
Jacques Gosselin, Président
lac-gosselin@hotmail.com
William Gosselin, Vice-président
7 bénévole(s)
Membre: 200; *Montant de la cotisation:* 20$
Activités: Assemblemt annuel des familles Gosselin; recherches en généalogie; basse de données

Association des familles monoparentales et recomposées de l'Outaouais (AFMRO)

584, rue Guizot Est, Montréal QC H2P 1N3
Tél: 514-729-6666; *Téléc:* 514-729-6746
fafmrq.info@videotron.ca
www.fafmrq.org
www.facebook.com/215273325165435
twitter.com/FAFMRQ
Aperçu: *Dimension:* petite; *Envergure:* locale
Mission: Aider les chefs de famille monoparentale démunis à acquérir l'autonomie financière, sociale, personnelle et familiale. Etre un centre de consultation, de support, d'évaluation, de formation et d'éducation en matière de rupture et de réorganisation familiale.
Affliation(s): Fédération des associations de familles monoparentales et recomposées du Québec
Membre(s) du bureau directeur:
Sylvie Lévesque, Directrice générale
fafmrq.sylvie@videotron.ca
Finances: *Fonds:* Gouvernement régional
Membre(s) du personnel: 3
Membre: *Montant de la cotisation:* 45$ individuelle; 150$ associé; 50$ actif moins de 50 000$/année; 100$ actif entre 50 000$ et 99 999$/année; 150$ actif 100 000$ et plus/année

Association des familles monoparentales et recomposées de Montcalm *Voir* Association Carrefour Famille Montcalm

Association des familles Rioux d'Amérique inc. (AFRA)

CP 7141, Trois-Pistoles QC G0L 4K0
Tél: 418-851-2599
www.famillesriou-x.com
Aperçu: *Dimension:* petite; *Envergure:* nationale; Organisme sans but lucratif; fondée en 1984
Mission: Regrouper dans une même grande famille tous les Riou-x d'Amérique et d'ailleurs issus de Jean Riou et de Catherine Leblond; faire connaître l'histoire des ancêtres et de leurs descendants
Membre de: Fédération des familles-souches québécoises inc.
Membre(s) du bureau directeur:
Jean-Jacques Rioux, Président
jari.jama@sympatico.ca
Louise Morissette Garon, Vice-président, 418-877-2881
ggaron@oricom.ca
Finances: *Budget de fonctionnement annuel:* Moins de $50,000
10 bénévole(s)
Membre: 450; *Montant de la cotisation:* 25$; *Critères d'admissibilite:* Agé de 50 ans et plus
Activités: Assemblée générale; organiser des rencontres des familles Rioux

Association des familles unies de la rue Walkley *See* Walkley Centre

Association des familles uniparentales du Canada *See* One Parent Families Association of Canada

Association des femmes acadiennes en marche de la région de Richmond *Voir* La Fédération des femmes acadiennes de la Nouvelle-Écosse

L'Association des femmes autochtones du Canada *See* Native Women's Association of Canada

L'Association des femmes compositeurs canadiennes *See* Association of Canadian Women Composers

Association des femmes d'assurance de Montréal (AFAM) / Montréal Association of Insurance Women

Montréal QC
info@afam-maiw.com
www.afam-maiw.com
Aperçu: *Dimension:* petite; *Envergure:* locale; fondée en 1963
Mission: Promouvoir et coordonner des programmes pratiques et éducatifs afin d'encourager ses membres à rechercher le plus haut niveau de connaissances en matière d'assurance ainsi que dans la conduite des affaires; Encourager une franche loyalté et entretenir des relations amicales entre membres; Sensibiliser ses membres aux besoins et necessités de leurs collègues.
Membre de: Canadian Association of Insurance Women
Membre(s) du bureau directeur:
Josée Loyer, Présidente, 450-452-4043, Fax: 450-452-2310
jloyer@impactauto.ca
Membre: 300+; *Montant de la cotisation:* 60$/adhèsion; *Comités:* Exécutif; Programme et éducation; Bulletin; Accueil; Adhésion et recrutement; Archiviste; Communication; Légisaltion; Constitution et règlement; Levée de fonds; Prix réalisations première générale; Prix éducation encan d'auto impact; Golf; Site internet; Traduction; Projets spéciaux; Vérificateurs externes; Relais pour la vie
Prix, Bouses:
• Mildred Jones Award - Insurance Woman of the Year (Prix)

Association des fermières de l'Ontario (AFO)

CP 190, Saint-Eugène ON K0B 1P0
Tél: 613-674-2035; *Téléc:* 613-674-1176
fermieres@cacseo.ca
Aperçu: *Dimension:* moyenne; *Envergure:* provinciale; Organisme sans but lucratif; fondée en 1969
Mission: Travailler aux intérêts des femmes et jeunes filles dans les paroisses, en artisanat, au progrès spirituel, social, culturel, économique et technique
Affliation(s): Association canadienne-française de l'Ontario
Membre(s) du bureau directeur:
Rachèle St-Denis-Lachaîne, Présidente
Louise Myler, Sec.-trés.
Membre: *Critères d'admissibilite:* Femme de 20 ans (en moyenne) et plus, interessée à sa santé, bien-être, culture (artisanat), connaissances générales, économie, loi etc.
Activités: Exposition artisanale annuelle; *Service de conférenciers:* Oui

L'Association des firmes d'ingénieurs-conseils - Canada *See* Association of Consulting Engineering Companies - Canada

Association des flûtistes d'Ottawa *See* Ottawa Flute Association

Association des fondations d'établissements de santé du Québec (AFÉSAQ)

#A301, 455, boul Base-de-Roc, Joliette QC J6E 5P3
Tél: 450-760-2325; *Téléc:* 450-760-2326
Ligne sans frais: 888-760-2325
www.afesaq.qc.ca
Aperçu: *Dimension:* petite; *Envergure:* provinciale
Mission: Pour représenter les intérêts des associations de soins de santé et les associations de services sociaux
Membre(s) du bureau directeur:
Roland Granger, Président-directeur général
rgranger@afesaq.qc.ca
Membre: 100+; *Critères d'admissibilite:* Fondations provenant du réseau de la santé; *Comités:* Directeurs généraux; Gouvernance; Nomination et des ressources humaines; Relations éstablissement/fondation; Consultatif colloque

Association des fonderies canadiennes *See* Canadian Foundry Association

L'Association des forces aériennes du Canada *See* Air Force Association of Canada

Association des forestiers agréés du Nouveau-Brunswick *See* Association of Registered Professional Foresters of New Brunswick

Association des fournisseurs d'hôtels et restaurants inc. (AFHR) / Hotel & Restaurant Suppliers Association Inc. (HRSA)

#230, 9300, boul Henri-Bourassa ouest, Saint-Laurent QC H4S 1L5
Tel: 514-334-3404; *Fax:* 514-334-1279
info@afhr.com
www.afhr.com
Overview: A medium-sized local charitable organization founded in 1936
Mission: Informer et parfaire les connaissances des professionnels de l'industrie; offrir une vitrine aux fournisseurs par le biais du site web de l'association; centre d'information pour les hôtels, restaurants and institutions à la recherche de fournisseurs; programme d'escomptes pour les membres sur divers services; l'AFHR organise le Salon Rendez-vous HRI
Member of: Association canadienne des professionnels de la vente
Chief Officer(s):
Victor Francoeur, President & CEO
vfrancoeur@afhr.com
Isabelle Julien, Operation Manager
ijulien@afhr.com
Hughes Moisan, Vice-President, Business Development
hmoisan@afhr.com
Staff Member(s): 3; 12 volunteer(s)
Membership: 100 companies; *Fees:* 350-500$; *Member Profile:* Fournisseurs de produits et de services dans les secteurs de la restauration et de l'hébergement; *Committees:* Activités sociales; Bourses; Exposition; Guide d'achats; Inscription; Publicité; Services aux membres
Activities: Expositions de fournisseurs de produits alimentaires et équipments pour hôtels, restaurants institutions; *Awareness Events:* Exposition Campagnes de recrutement/assemblées

Association des foyers de soins du Nouveau-Brunswick, inc. *See* New Brunswick Association of Nursing Homes, Inc.

Association des francophone du Nunavut (AFN)

CP 880, Iqaluit NU X0A 0H0
Tél: 867-979-4606; *Téléc:* 867-979-0800
cuerrier@nunafranc.ca
Aperçu: *Dimension:* moyenne; *Envergure:* provinciale; fondée en 1981 surveillé par Fédération des communautés francophones et acadienne du Canada
Mission: Pour représenter la communauté française et l'aider à développer
Affiliation(s): Coopérative de tourisme Odyssée limitée; Conseil de coopération du Nunavut; Société immobilière Franco-Nunavut; CFRT; la Nunavoix; Commission scolaire francophone du Nunavut; Défi Nunavut; Réseau de développement économique et d'employabilité Nunavut; SAFRAN; Toit du monde
Membre(s) du bureau directeur:
Éric Corneau, Président

Association des francophones de Fort Smith (AFFS)

212, ch McDougal, Fort Smith NT X0E OPO
Tél: 867-872-2338; *Téléc:* 867-872-5710
affs@northwestel.net
www.associationfrancophonesfortsmith.ca
Aperçu: *Dimension:* petite; *Envergure:* locale; fondée en 1984 surveillé par Fédération franco-ténoise
Mission: Afin de préserver et de développer la communauté francophone de Fort Smith
Membre(s) du bureau directeur:
Marie-Christine Aubrey, Présidente

Association des francophones du delta du Mackenzie Association des francophones du delta du Mackenzie (AFDM)

CP 2845, Inuvik NT X0E OTO
Tél: 867-678-2661; *Téléc:* 867-777-2799
afdm@hotmail.ca
www.afdm.ca
Aperçu: *Dimension:* petite; *Envergure:* locale surveillé par Fédération franco-ténoise
Mission: Pour représenter les intérêts et les droits de la communauté francophone de delta du Mackenzie
Membre(s) du bureau directeur:
André Church, Président

Association des francophones du nord-ouest de l'Ontario (AFNOO)

#200, 292, rue Court sud, Thunder Bay ON P7B 6C6
Tél: 807-684-1951; *Téléc:* 807-343-5780
Ligne sans frais: 888-229-5845
admin@afnoo.org
www.afnoo.org
Aperçu: *Dimension:* moyenne; *Envergure:* locale; Organisme sans but lucratif; fondée en 1977
Mission: Vise la promotion et la valorisation de la communauté francophone dans le Nord-Ouest de l'Ontario afin de célébrer la richesse et la valeur ajoutée qu'elle représente pour les communautés, la région, la société ontarienne, et pour l'ensemble du pays
Membre de: La Coopérative du regroupement des organismes francophones de Thunder Bay Inc.
Affliation(s): Assemblée de la Francophonie de l'Ontario
Membre(s) du bureau directeur:
Chantal Brochu, Présidente
Claudette Gleeson, Vice-présidente
Claire Drainville, Secrétaire
Rose Viel, Trésorière
Finances: *Budget de fonctionnement annuel:* l0l
35 bénévole(s)
Membre: 23 groupes; *Montant de la cotisation:* 75$; 25$ pour groupes de jeunes; *Critères d'admissibilite:* Agences et groupes francophones du Nord-Ouest de l'Ontario
Activités: *Bibliothèque* rendez-vous

L'Association des fruiticulteurs et des maraîchers de l'Ontario *See* Ontario Fruit & Vegetable Growers' Association

L'Association des gais, lesbiennes et bisexuel(le)s du Québec *Voir* GRIS-Mauricie/Centre-du-Québec

Association des garderies privées du Québec (AGPQ)

#230, 5115, av Trans Island, Montréal QC H3W 2Z9
Tél: 514-485-2221
Ligne sans frais: 888-655-6060
correspondance@agpq.ca
www.agpq.ca
www.facebook.com/agpq.quebec
Aperçu: *Dimension:* petite; *Envergure:* provinciale; fondée en 1973
Mission: Promouvoir, favoriser, développer et améliorer la qualité des services de garde éducatifs pour les enfants et les familles; assurer le libre choix des parents et la pérennité du réseau; protéger, défendre et représenter les droits des membres; informer les membres, formuler des recommandations et les promouvoir auprès des instances gouvernementales et organismes partenaires; valoriser le perfectionnement et le développement du personnel en milieu de garde
Membre(s) du bureau directeur:
Sylvain Lévesque, Président
Samir Alahmad, Vice-Président
5 bénévole(s)
Activités: *Evénements de sensibilisation:* Semaine des services de garde du Québec

Association des gastro-entérologues du Québec (AGEQ)

CP 216, Succ. Desjardins, 2, Complexe Desjardins, Montréal QC H5B 1G8
Tél: 514-350-5112; *Téléc:* 514-350-5146
www.ageq.qc.ca
Aperçu: *Dimension:* petite; *Envergure:* !E!; fondée en 1965 surveillé par Fédération des médecins spécialistes du Québec
Mission: D'informer et de formations aux médecins de première ligne, aux patients souffrant de pathologies gastro-intestinales et aux autres médecins intéressés par la gastro-entérologie; de créer des liens avec la communauté médicale internationale.
Membre(s) du bureau directeur:
Josée Parent, Président

Association des gens d'affaires & professionnels italo-canadiens *See* Canadian Italian Business & Professional Association

Association des Gestionnaires de l'information de la santé du Québec (AGISQ)

#104, 5104, boul Bourque, Sherbrooke QC J1N 2K7
Tél: 819-823-6670; *Téléc:* 819-823-0799
info@agisq-québec.ca
www.agisq-quebec.ca
www.facebook.com/pages/Agisq/392680864114521

Nom précédent: Association québécoise des archivistes médicales; Association des archivistes médicales de la province de Québec
Aperçu: *Dimension:* moyenne; *Envergure:* provinciale; Organisme sans but lucratif; fondée en 1960
Mission: Promouvoir les connaissances scientifiques, techniques, professionnelles, morales, sociales et légales se rattachant directement ou indirectement à la profession d'archiviste médicale; promouvoir la formation et le perfectionnement des membres; promouvoir la profession dans les différents établissements de santé, organismes gouvernementaux, paragouvernementaux et privés; favoriser les échanges et les communications entre les membres; offrir des services-conseils; accomplir toute activité qui peut être nécessaire à l'atteinte des objectifs fixés
Membre(s) du bureau directeur:
Lise Chagnon, Directrice générale (par intérim)
Alexandre Allard, Président
Matthew Audet, Vice-Président
Marie-Eve Sirois, Trésorière
Membre: 1000; *Montant de la cotisation:* 209,25$ régulier ou affilié; 34,49$ étudiant; *Critères d'admissibilité:* Avant complété ses études en archives médicales dans une école reconnue par le ministère de l'Éducation du Québec et posséder son diplôme d'études collégiales ou être certifié de la CHIMA; *Comités:* Archivistes médicaux en milieu psychiatrique; Éducation; Gestion de l'information; Information; Organisation; Promotion de la confidentialité; Régionaux; Registraires en oncologie; Registraires en traumatologie; Site Internet et forum de discussion
Activités: Journée de perfectionnement; formation continue; *Evénements de sensibilisation:* Semaine de sensibilisation à la confidentialité aux 2 ans (nov); *Stagiaires:* Oui

Association des gestionnaires de ressources bénévoles du Québec (AGRBQ)

7000, rue Sherbrooke Ouest, Montréal QC H4B 1R3
Tél: 514-489-8201; *Téléc:* 514-489-3477
jcollette.hlhl@ssss.gouv.qc.ca
www.agrbq.com
Aperçu: *Dimension:* petite; *Envergure:* provinciale; fondée en 1958
Mission: L'Association permet la mise en commun d'idées, d'expériences et de recherches afin d'avoir une vision plus contemporaine et plus globale de l'action bénévole
Membre de: Canadian Administrators of Volunteer Resources
Membre(s) du bureau directeur:
Lise Pettigrew, Présidente
Membre: *Montant de la cotisation:* 135$

Association des Gestionnaires de Risques et d'Assurance du Québec *Voir* Risk & Insurance Management Society Inc.

Association des gestionnaires des établissements de santé et des services sociaux (AGESSS) / Association for Manager of Health Facilities & Social Services

#101, 601, boul Adoncour, Longueuil QC J4G 2M6
Tél: 450-651-6000; *Téléc:* 450-651-9750
Ligne sans frais: 800-361-6526
reception@agesss.qc.ca
www.agesss.qc.ca
Aperçu: *Dimension:* moyenne; *Envergure:* provinciale; fondée en 1969
Mission: Représenter ses membres; promouvoir et défendre l'intérêt de ses membres; tenir ses membres informés; gérer ses biens pour assurer sa survie et l'efficacité de son action
Affiliation(s): Desjardins Sécurité financière; laPersonelle; RACAR; La Capitale; Le Point
Membre(s) du bureau directeur:
François Jean, Président-directeur général, 450-651-6000 Ext. 2022
direction@agesss.qc.ca
Yves Bolduc, Vice-Président
Louise Verville, Trésorière
Finances: *Budget de fonctionnement annuel:* $1.5 Million-$3 Million
Membre(s) du personnel: 18
Membre: 5 000+; *Critères d'admissibilité:* Cadre intermédiaire d'établissements de santé et de services sociaux; *Comités:* Comité des conditions de travail; comité de renumération et fonctions types; comité sur l'équité salariale; comité sur l'assurance et la retraite; comité de développement professionnel; comité des finances; comité de coordination des communications; comité des retraités

Prix, Bouses:
• Prix d'excellence du réseau de la santé et des services sociaux (Prix)

Association des goélands de Longueuil

150, rue Grant, 2e étage, Longueuil QC J4H 1C6
Tél: 450-674-3490
Aperçu: *Dimension:* petite; *Envergure:* locale
Mission: Pour réunir des personnes ayant des handicaps physiques et de leur fournir des services de loisirs et de l'information

Association des golfeurs professionnels du Canada *See* Professional Golfers' Association of Canada

Association des golfeurs professionnels du Québec (AGP)

435, boul Saint-Luc, Saint-Jean-sur-Richelieu QC J2W 1E7
Tél: 450-349-5525; *Téléc:* 450-349-6640
agpinfo@agp.qc.ca
www.agp.qc.ca
www.facebook.com/384893361542645
twitter.com/AGPduQuebec
/www.youtube.com/user/AGPduQuebec
Aperçu: *Dimension:* petite; *Envergure:* provinciale; fondée en 1927
Mission: Vouée à la promotion et à l'évolution du golf
Membre(s) du bureau directeur:
Jean Châtelain, Président
Jean Trudeau, Directeur général
jtrudeau@agp.qc.ca
Membre(s) du personnel: 21
Membre: 500; *Comités:* Finance-vérification; Formation/éducation; Discipline et administrateur; Gouvernance; Ressources humaines; Assistance aux membres; Discipline

Association des Grands Frères et Grandes Soeurs de Québec (GFGS) / Big Brothers & Big Sisters of Québec

#201, 2380, av du Mont-Thabor, Québec QC G1J 3W7
Tél: 418-624-3304; *Téléc:* 418-624-4013
gfgsquebec@videotron.ca
www.gfgs.qc.ca
Aperçu: *Dimension:* moyenne; *Envergure:* provinciale; Organisme sans but lucratif; fondée en 1981
Mission: Favoriser l'épanouissement de jeunes âgés de 6 à 16 ans privés de la presence d'un de leurs parents en les jumelant avec un adulte mature, qui s'engage à le rencontrer 3-4 heures par semaine pour échanger et faire des activités, selon leurs goûts réciproques
Membre de: Big Brothers/Big Sisters of Canada
Finances: *Budget de fonctionnement annuel:* $50,000-$100,000; *Fonds:* Gouvernement provincial
Membre(s) du personnel: 2; 15 bénévole(s)
Membre: 20; *Critères d'admissibilité:* Agence locale au Québec; *Comités:* Marketing; Communications
Activités: *Service de conférenciers:* Oui

Abitibi Ouest
CP 460, 6, 8 av est, La Sarre QC J9Z 3J3
Tél: 819-333-9132; *Téléc:* 819-333-9525
gfgsao@ad.com
www.bigbrothersbigsisters.ca/abitibi
Membre(s) du bureau directeur:
Solange Bordeleau

Domaine du Roy
CP 182, 869, rue Arthur, Roberval QC G8H 2N6
Tél: 418-275-0483; *Téléc:* 418-275-0483
gfgsddr@destination.ca
www.gfgsddr.ca
Membre(s) du bureau directeur:
Pierre Donaldson

Estrie
2634, rue Galt Ouest, Sherbrooke QC J1K 2X2
Tél: 819-822-3243; *Téléc:* 819-652-6952
Ligne sans frais: 866-922-3243
gfgsestrie@gfgsestrie.ca
www.gfgsestrie.ca
Membre(s) du bureau directeur:
Lisanne Bujold

Lac St-Jean Nord
#106, 1461, boul Wallberg, Dolbeau-Mistassini QC G8L 1H4
Tél: 418-276-8297; *Téléc:* 418-276-8297
gfgslsjn@bellnet.ca
www.gfgslsjn.ca
Membre(s) du bureau directeur:
Audrey Noël

Lanaudière
144, St-Joseph, Joliette QC J6E 5C4
Tél: 450-759-2654; *Téléc:* 450-760-3586
Ligne sans frais: 888-759-2654
gfgslan@aol.com
Membre(s) du bureau directeur:
Isabelle Emery

Montréal
#300, 3740, rue Berri, Montréal QC H2L 4G9
Tél: 514-842-9715; *Téléc:* 514-842-2454
info@gfgsmtl.qc.ca
www.gfgsmtl.qc.ca
Membre(s) du bureau directeur:
Ginette Sauvé

Ouest de l'Ile
#265, 267 av Dorval, Dorval QC H9S 3H5
Tél: 514-538-6100; *Téléc:* 514-538-4625
bbbsofwi@aol.com
www.bbbsofwi.org
Membre(s) du bureau directeur:
Gloria Coulter

Outaouais
379 B, boul. Alexandre-Taché, Gatineau QC J9A 1M4
Tél: 819-778-0101; *Téléc:* 819-778-3750
info@gfgso.com
www.gfgso.com
Membre(s) du bureau directeur:
Denis Quinn

Porte du Nord
770, rue Labelle, Saint-Jérôme QC J7Z 5M3
Tél: 450-565-4562; *Téléc:* 450-436-9735
gfgspn@aol.com
www.payerausuivant.com
Membre(s) du bureau directeur:
Carole Dionne

Québec
2380, av Mont-Thabor, Québec QC G1J 3W7
Tél: 418-624-3304; *Téléc:* 418-624-4013
gfgsquebec@videotron.ca
www.gfgs.qc.ca/quebec
Membre(s) du bureau directeur:
France Tremblay

Région Amiante
#101-A, 733, boul. Frontenac Ouest, Thetford Mines QC G6G 7X9
Tél: 418-335-7404; *Téléc:* 418-335-0937
caroline.gagne@gfgsamiante.com
www.gfgsamiante.com
Membre(s) du bureau directeur:
Elaine Vachon

Rouyn-Noranda
#225, 380, av Richard, Rouyn-Noranda QC J9X 4L3
Tél: 819-762-0167; *Téléc:* 819-762-9967
gfgsrn@cablevision.qc.ca
www.bigbrothersbigsisters.ca/rouynnoranda
Membre(s) du bureau directeur:
Liliane Cyr

St-Hyacinthe
#204, 1195, rue Saint-Antoine, Saint-Hyacinthe QC J2S 3K6
Tél: 450-774-8723; *Téléc:* 450-261-0983
Ligne sans frais: 866-464-6188
www.gfgssth.org
Membre(s) du bureau directeur:
Sébastien Royez, Président
Nancy Duval, Vice-Président

Val-d'Or
1011, 6e rue, Val-d'Or QC J9P 3W4
Tél: 819-825-2802; *Téléc:* 819-825-7155
gfgsvd@lino.com
www.bigbrothersbigsisters.ca/valdor
Membre(s) du bureau directeur:
Cecilia Lessard

Association des Grands Frères/Grands Soeurs du Québec *Voir* Less Grands Frères et Grandes Soeurs de L'Abitibi Ouest

Association des grands-parents du Québec

3, rue Fatima, Beaupré QC G0A 1E0
Tél: 514-745-6110; *Téléc:* 514-745-6110
Ligne sans frais: 866-745-6110
Autres numéros: Téléphone de Québec: 418-529-2355; Télécopier: 418-529-2355
agp@grands-parents.qc.ca
www.grands-parents.qc.ca
twitter.com/grandsparents

Aperçu: *Dimension:* petite; *Envergure:* provinciale
Mission: Aider des grands-parents et des petits-enfants préserver leur lien et lutter contre la maltraitance des personnes âgées
Activités: *Evénements de sensibilisation:* Journée des grands-parents (septembre)

Association des groupes d'intervention en défense de droits en santé mentale du Québec (AGIDD-SMQ)

#210, 4837, rue Boyer, Montréal QC H2J 3E6
Tél: 514-523-3443; *Téléc:* 514-523-0797
Ligne sans frais: 866-523-3443
info@agidd.org
www.agidd.org
Aperçu: *Dimension:* moyenne; *Envergure:* provinciale; fondée en 1990
Mission: Au service des personnes qui ont des problèmes et qui ont besoin d'aide et de soutien pour exercer et faire valoir leurs droits

Association des guides de montagne canadiens ***See*** Association of Canadian Mountain Guides

Association des guides touristiques de Québec (AGTQ)

CP 17, 755, ch St-Louis, Québec QC G1S 1C1
Tél: 418-683-2104; *Téléc:* 418-624-0450
Aperçu: *Dimension:* petite; *Envergure:* provinciale; fondée en 1993
Mission: L'Association des guides touristiques de Québec (AGTQ) vise à assurer une formation continue à ses membres, à protéger leurs droits, à valoriser cette fonction auprès des intervenants et, d'une manière générale, à contribuer au développement touristique dans la région de Québec
Membre: 170

Association des handicapées de Charlevoix ***Voir*** Association des personnes handicapées de Charlevoix inc.

Association des handicapés adultes de la Côte-Nord / Association of Disabled Adults on the North Shore (AHACNI)

#103, 859, rue Bossé, Baie-Comeau QC G5C 3P8
Tél: 418-589-2393; *Téléc:* 418-589-2953
www.ahacn.org
Aperçu: *Dimension:* petite; *Envergure:* locale; fondée en 1978
Mission: Pour répondre aux besoins des personnes handicapées et une lésion cérébrale traumatique, et leurs familles, sur la Rive-Nord de Québec
Membre de: Regroupement des associations de personnes traumatisées craniocérébrales du Québec / Coalition of Associations of Craniocerebral Trauma in Quebec
Membre(s) du bureau directeur:
Stéphanie Jourdain, Directrice générale
Membre(s) du personnel: 3
Membre: *Critères d'admissibilite:* Les personnes handicapées et les lésions cérébrales traumatiques de Tadoussac à Blanc-Sablon et sur l'île d'Anticosti au Québec
Activités: Promouvoir et protéger les droits des personnes ayant une lésion traumatique du cerveau et handicapées; L'organisation de groupes de soutien; Offrir un soutien psychosocial; Offrant des activités de loisirs, pour éviter l'isolement; Offrant des services d'accompagnement

Association des handicapés adultes de la Mauricie (AHAM)

1322, rue Ste-Julie, Trois-Rivières QC G9A 1Y6
Tél: 819-374-9566; *Téléc:* 819-374-2230
aham1322@yahoo.com
www.ahamauricie.org
Aperçu: *Dimension:* petite; *Envergure:* locale; fondée en 1951
Mission: Promouvoir et sauvegarder les droits et privilèges des personnes handicapées; offrir également des services de prêt de fauteuils roulants, de béquilles, et de marchettes
Membre(s) du bureau directeur:
Francois Dubois, Président
Stephane Drolet, Vice-Président
Finances: *Budget de fonctionnement annuel:* $100,000-$250,000; *Fonds:* Agence de santé et des services sociaux de la Maurice et Centre-du-Québec
Membre(s) du personnel: 4; 35 bénévole(s)
Membre: 178 handicapés; 20 affiliés; *Montant de la cotisation:* 10$; *Critères d'admissibilite:* Personnes adultes vivant avec un handicap permanent, et limitations physiques
Activités: Activités culturelles et récréatives; voyages; visites guidées; soirées; rencontres d'informations;

Association des herboristes de la province de Québec

CP 80, 7, av 70e ouest, Blainville QC J7C 1R7
Tél: 450-435-2979
herbesunivers@bellnet.ca
Aperçu: *Dimension:* petite; *Envergure:* provinciale
Membre: 100-499

Association des hôteliers du Québec (AHQ) / Hotel Association of Québec

#100, 450, ch. de Chambly, Longueuil QC J4H 3L7
Tél: 579-721-6215; *Téléc:* 579-721-3663
Ligne sans frais: 877-769-9776
info@hoteliersquebec.org
www.hoteliers-quebec.org
www.facebook.com/HoteliersQuebecAHQ
Aperçu: *Dimension:* moyenne; *Envergure:* provinciale; Organisme sans but lucratif; fondée en 1949 surveillé par Hotel Association of Canada Inc.
Mission: Regrouper les établissements hôteliers pour les représenter, défendre leurs intérêts et leurs fournir des services et ce, tout en collaborant au développement de la qualité de la profession hôtelière et de l'industrie touristique en général
Membre de: Chambre de commerce du Québec; Hotel Association of Canada
Membre(s) du bureau directeur:
Danielle Chayer, Présidente/Directrice générale
dchayer@hoteliersquebec.org
Finances: *Budget de fonctionnement annuel:* $250,000-$500,000
Membre(s) du personnel: 3
Membre: 540; *Critères d'admissibilite:* Hôtelier/associés

Association des hôtels du Canada ***See*** Hotel Association of Canada Inc.

Association des hypnologues du Québec

8206, rue Berri, Montréal QC H2P 2E9
Tél: 514-939-3780; *Téléc:* 514-846-1601
info@hypno-quebec.com
www.hypno-quebec.com
Aperçu: *Dimension:* petite; *Envergure:* provinciale; fondée en 1977
Mission: Promouvoir les bienfaits de l'hypnose auprès des utilisateurs et de faire respecter les règles de conduite définies par le code de déontologie
Membre de: Ordre canadien des practiciens de naturopathie et des naturotherapies
Membre(s) du personnel: 1; 5 bénévole(s)
Membre: *Montant de la cotisation:* 200$; *Critères d'admissibilite:* Hypnologue clinicien; *Comités:* Discipline
Activités: Conférences; groupes de discussion

Association des Illustrateurs et Illustratrices du Québec (AIIQ)

#123, 372, Ste-Catherine ouest, Montréal QC H3B 1A2
Tél: 514-522-2040; *Téléc:* 514-521-0297
Ligne sans frais: 888-522-2040
info@illustrationquebec.com
www.illustrationquebec.com
Aperçu: *Dimension:* petite; *Envergure:* provinciale; Organisme sans but lucratif; fondée en 1983
Mission: Promouvoir l'art de l'illustration et faire en sorte que la profession se pratique dans les meilleures conditions possibles
Membre(s) du bureau directeur:
Yves Dumont, Président, 514-799-4573
yvesushi@gmail.com
Finances: *Budget de fonctionnement annuel:* $50,000-$100,000; *Fonds:* Gouvernement provincial
Membre(s) du personnel: 1
Membre: 100-499; *Montant de la cotisation:* Barème
Activités: Répertoire annuel destiné aux clients des communications graphiques autant au Canada, aux Etats-Unis et au niveau international; exposition annuelle intitulée 'Salon de l'illustration québécoise'; soirées; portefeuilles; bulletin; cours d'infographie; participation à divers salons du livre ou congrès touchant de près ou de loin le domaine de l'illustration;

Association des implantés cochléaires du Québec (AICQ)

#130, 5100, rue des Tournelles, Québec QC G2J 1E4
Tél: 418-623-7417; *Téléc:* 418-623-7462
aicq@bellnet.ca
www.aicq-implant.org
Aperçu: *Dimension:* petite; *Envergure:* provinciale; Organisme sans but lucratif; fondée en 1995
Mission: Promouvoir l'implant cochléaire; supporter le patient et sa famille; offrir des activités
Membre(s) du bureau directeur:
Martin Girard, Président
Membre(s) du personnel: 1; 30 bénévole(s)
Membre: 100-499; *Montant de la cotisation:* 25$; *Comités:* Acceuil et hébergement; Comité de Montréal; Comité de Québec; Promotion et sollicitation; Comité du journal
Activités: *Evénements de sensibilisation:* Journée nationale de l'implant cochléaire - 17 mai

Association des industries aérospatiales du Canada ***See*** Aerospace Industries Association of Canada

Association des industries canadiennes de défense et de sécurité ***See*** Canadian Association of Defence & Security Industries

Association des industries CANDU ***See*** Organization of CANDU Industries

Association des industries de l'automobile du Canada ***See*** Automotive Industries Association of Canada

L'Association des industries de produits verriers et de fenestration du Québec; L'Association des industries de portes et fenêtres du Québec ***Voir*** Association de vitrerie et fenestrations du Québec

L'Association des Infirmier(ère)s Auxiliares Autorisé(e)s du Nouveau-Brunswick ***See*** Association of New Brunswick Licensed Practical Nurses

Association des infirmières et infirmiers autochtones du Canada ***See*** Aboriginal Nurses Association of Canada

L'Association des infirmières et infirmiers autorisés de l'Ontario ***See*** Registered Nurses' Association of Ontario

Association des infirmières et infirmiers de l'Ontario ***See*** Ontario Nurses' Association

Association des infirmières et infirmiers de salles d'opération du Canada ***See*** Operating Room Nurses Association of Canada

Association des infirmières et infirmiers du Canada ***See*** Canadian Nurses Association

Association des infirmières et infirmiers du Nouveau-Brunswick ***See*** Nurses Association of New Brunswick

Association des infirmières et infirmiers en santé du travail du Québec (AIISTQ)

1370, rue Notre-Dame ouest, Montréal QC H3C 1K8
Tél: 514-282-4231; *Téléc:* 514-282-4292
admin@aiistq.qc.ca
www.aiistq.qc.ca
Aperçu: *Dimension:* moyenne; *Envergure:* provinciale; Organisme sans but lucratif; fondée en 1978
Mission: Assurer la protection du statut; consolider l'autonomie professionnelle et définir les besoins de ses membres; promouvoir et maintenir la qualité des services professionnels dispensés; favoriser l'actualisation des connaissances dans un contexte de constante évolution; intensifier le lien entre ses membres et la santé et sécurité au travail
Membre de: Association canadienne des infirmiers et infirmières en santé du travail
Membre(s) du bureau directeur:
Diane LaBonté, Président
Richard Matte, Vice-président
Finances: *Budget de fonctionnement annuel:* $100,000-$250,000
Membre: 221; *Montant de la cotisation:* 135$
Activités: Déjeuners causerie; sessions de formation et de perfectionnement; congrès; colloque; *Service de conférenciers:* Oui

Association des ingénieurs et géoscientifiques du Nouveau-Brunswick ***See*** Association of Professional Engineers & Geoscientists of New Brunswick

Association des ingénieurs municipaux du Québec (AIMQ) / Association of Québec Municipal Engineers

CP 792, Succ. B, Montréal QC H3B 3K5
Tél: 514-845-5303
admin@aimq.net
www.aimq.net
Aperçu: *Dimension:* moyenne; *Envergure:* provinciale; fondée en 1963

Mission: Améliorer les connaissances et le statut de l'ingénieur municipal par l'échange d'information, la coopération entre ingénieurs municipaux et avec d'autres associations professionnelles et la promotion des intérêts communs des membres de l'Association
Membre(s) du bureau directeur:
Mathieu Richard, Directeur général
dg@aimq.net
Richard Lamarche, Adjoint administratif
aimq.rlamarche@videotron.ca
Finances: *Budget de fonctionnement annuel:* $100,000-$250,000
Membre(s) du personnel: 3; 15 bénévole(s)
Membre: 200; *Montant de la cotisation:* 225.75$; *Critères d'admissibilite:* Membre de l'Ordre des ingénieurs du Québec; employé d'une administration municipale ou régionale
Activités: Séminaire de formation annuel; *Listes de destinataires:* Oui

Association des ingénieurs-conseils du Québec (AICQ) / Consulting Engineers of Québec

#930, 1440, rue Ste-Catherine ouest, Montréal QC H3G 1R8
Tél: 514-871-2229; *Téléc:* 514-871-9903
info@aicq.qc.ca
www.aicq.qc.ca
www.linkedin.com/company/association-des-ing-nieurs-conseils-du-qu-bec
www.facebook.com/forumAICQ
www.youtube.com/aicqtv
Aperçu: *Dimension:* grande; *Envergure:* provinciale; fondée en 1974 surveillé par Association of Consulting Engineering Companies - Canada
Mission: Promouvoir et développer l'industrie du génie-conseil en regroupant des membres qui offrent des services de qualité
Membre(s) du bureau directeur:
Marc Tremblay, ing., Président du Conseil
Johanne Desrochers, Présidente-directrice générale, 514-871-2229
jdesrochers@aicq.qc.ca
Pierre Nadeau, Directeur, Communications, 514-871-0589 Ext. 28
pnadeau@aicq.qc.ca
Membre(s) du personnel: 5; 100 bénévole(s)
Membre: 280 bureaux; *Comités:* Bâtiment; Énergie; Environnement; Industrie; Municipal; Télécommunications et nouvelles technologies; Transport
Activités: *Listes de destinataires:* Oui; *Bibliothèque* rendez-vous

Association des ingénieurs-professeurs des sciences appliquées (AIPSA)

c/o Université de Sherbrooke, 2500, boul Université, Sherbrooke QC J1K 2R1
Tél: 819-821-7929; *Téléc:* 819-821-7955
aipsa@usherbrooke.ca
pages.usherbrooke.ca/aipsa/
Aperçu: *Dimension:* petite; *Envergure:* locale; Organisme sans but lucratif; fondée en 1970
Mission: Négocier la convention collective des ingénieur-professeurs; représenter les ingénieur-professeurs au sens du code du travail
Membre(s) du bureau directeur:
François Boone, Président
aipsa@usherbrooke.ca
Finances: *Budget de fonctionnement annuel:* Moins de $50,000
Membre(s) du personnel: 6
Membre: 95; *Montant de la cotisation:* 0.75% du salaire régulier annuel; *Critères d'admissibilite:* Membre de l'ordre des ingénieurs du QC; salarié affecté à une tâche d'enseignement ou de recherche à l'Université de Sherbrooke

Association des institutions d'enseignement secondaire; Association québécoise des Écoles secondaires privées *Voir* Fédération des établissements d'enseignement privés

Association des intermédiaires en assurance de personnes du Québec *Voir* Chambre de la sécurité financière

Association des interprètes en langage visuel du Canada *See* Association of Visual Language Interpreters of Canada

Association des intervenantes et des intervenants en soins spirituels du Québec (AIISSQ)

6910, rue St-Denis, Montréal QC H2S 2S0
Tél: 514-259-9229; *Téléc:* 514-259-3741
secretariat@aiissq.org
www.aiissq.org
Nom précédent: Association québécoise de la pastorale de la santé
Aperçu: *Dimension:* petite; *Envergure:* provinciale; Organisme sans but lucratif; fondée en 2005
Mission: Formation professionnelle des membres et promotion de leurs intérêts spirituels et professionnels; représentation des membres auprès d'instances civiles et religieuses reconnues
Membre de: Association canadienne des périodiques catholiques
Affiliation(s): Association canadienne pour la pratique et l'éducation pastorale; Association catholique canadienne de la santé; Carrefour Humanisation - Santé
Membre(s) du bureau directeur:
Lorraine Rooke, Présidente
presidence@aiissq.org
Fernand Patry, Vice-président
vice-presidence@aiissq.org
Finances: *Budget de fonctionnement annuel:* $50,000-$100,000
Membre(s) du personnel: 1
Membre: 200; *Montant de la cotisation:* 275$; 70$ par jour; *Critères d'admissibilite:* Animateur(trice) de pastorale dans un établissement de santé; *Comités:* Pastorale pratique; pastorale en santé mentale
Activités: Congrès annuel; colloques; sessions de formation; *Stagiaires:* Oui; *Listes de destinataires:* Oui

Association des intervenants en toxicomanie du Québec inc. (AITQ)

505, rue Ste-Hélène, 2e étage, Longueuil QC J4K 3R5
Tél: 450-646-3271; *Téléc:* 450-646-3275
info@aitq.com
www.aitq.com
Aperçu: *Dimension:* moyenne; *Envergure:* provinciale; Organisme sans but lucratif; fondée en 1977
Mission: Regrouper les intervenants professionnels et bénévoles oeuvrant dans le domaine de la toxicomanie et du jeu excessif
Membre(s) du bureau directeur:
Carmen Trottier, Directrice générale
ctrottier@aitq.com
Membre(s) du personnel: 3; 32 bénévole(s)
Membre: 350 individus; 94 corporatif; *Montant de la cotisation:* 40$ étudiant; 75$ individu; 275$ corporatif
Activités: Journées de formation; colloque annuel
Prix, Bouses:
• Rose des Sables (Prix)

Association des jardins du Québec / Québec Gardens Association

82, Grande-Allée ouest, Québec QC G1R 2G6
Tél: 418-692-0886
www.jardinsduquebec.com
www.facebook.com/9180555411
Aperçu: *Dimension:* petite; *Envergure:* provinciale
Mission: L'Association des jardins du Québec a comme mission de regrouper en corporation les jardins du Québec ouverts au public afin d'aider à leur développement et à leur promotion et de souligner leur apport à la culture et au patrimoine québécois
Membre(s) du bureau directeur:
Geneviève David, Chargée de projet en communication
gdavid@tapagecreation.com
Membre: 20;

Association des jeunes Barreaux du Québec (AJBQ)

445, boul. St-Laurent, Montréal QC H2Y 3T8
Tél: 514-954-3471; *Téléc:* 514-954-3451
Ligne sans frais: 800-361-8495
Autres numéros: AJBQ.Info@gmail.com
info@votreavocate.com
ajbq.net
www.facebook.com/553959894636970
twitter.com/AJBQInfo
Aperçu: *Dimension:* moyenne; *Envergure:* provinciale
Mission: Pour représenter les intérêts des avocats qui ont moins de dix ans d'expérience et de créer un réseau d'avocats à travers le Québec
Membre(s) du bureau directeur:
Marie-Eve Landreville, Présidente, Conseil d'administration
Membre: *Comités:* Législation; Communications; Financement

Association des jeunes bègues de Québec (AJBQ)

#R304, 10780, rue Laverdure, Montréal QC H3L 2L9
Tél: 514-388-8455
Ligne sans frais: 800-661-2348
info@ajbq.qc.ca
www.ajbq.qc.ca
www.facebook.com/153236978042793
Aperçu: *Dimension:* petite; *Envergure:* provinciale; Organisme sans but lucratif; fondée en 1993
Mission: Contrer la méconnaissance de la société à l'égard du bégaiement; offrir du soutien aux jeunes bègues de 2 à 25 ans; promouvoir les services qui leur sont accessibles ainsi qu'à leurs parents
Membre(s) du bureau directeur:
Julie Tanguy, Présidente
Chantale Baillargeon, Directrice générale
Finances: *Budget de fonctionnement annuel:* $50,000-$100,000
Membre(s) du personnel: 1; 60 bénévole(s)
Membre: 250; *Montant de la cotisation:* 30$; *Critères d'admissibilite:* Parents, professionnels; jeunes adultes
Activités: Soutien, information, conseils aux jeunes bègues et leurs familles; activités de regroupement; thérapies; programmes de sensibilisation dans les écoles et auprès du grand public; *Evénements de sensibilisation:* Journée mondiale du bégaiement 22 oct.; *Bibliothèque:* AJBQ; rendez-vous

Association des jeunes femmes chrétiennes du Canada *See* YWCA Canada

Association des jeunes ruraux du Québec (AJRQ)

65, rang 3 est, Princeville QC G6L 4B9
Tél: 819-364-5606; *Téléc:* 819-364-5006
info@ajrq.qc.ca
www.ajrq.qc.ca
Aperçu: *Dimension:* moyenne; *Envergure:* provinciale; fondée en 1974
Mission: Promouvoir la formation auprès de nos membres; soutenir leur sentiment d'appartenance au milieu rural
Membre de: Regroupement Loisir Québec
Affliation(s): Conseil des 4-H du Canada
Membre(s) du bureau directeur:
Cindy Jaton, Présidente
cindyjaton15@hotmail.com
Annie Chabot, Directrice générale
Activités: *Stagiaires:* Oui; *Listes de destinataires:* Oui

Association des jeunes travailleurs et travailleuses de Montréal inc

3565, ch du lac Legault, Sainte-Lucie-des-Laurentides QC J0T 2J0
Tél: 819-326-4069; *Téléc:* 819-326-0837
info@interval.qc.ca
interval.qc.ca
www.facebook.com/group.php?gid=6136488588
Également appelé: L'Interval base de plein-air
Aperçu: *Dimension:* petite; *Envergure:* locale; Organisme sans but lucratif; fondée en 1971
Mission: Accès aux vacances dans la nature
Membre de: Association touristique des Laurentides
Affliation(s): Mouvement Québécois des camps familiaux; Éducation, Loisir et Sport Québec; Patrouille canadienne de ski; Tourisme Laurentides; Bonjour Quebec
Membre(s) du bureau directeur:
Cloée La Rocque, Directrice générale
dg@interval.qc.ca
Finances: *Budget de fonctionnement annuel:* $500,000-$1.5 Million; *Fonds:* Provincial government
Membre(s) du personnel: 26; 80 bénévole(s)
Membre: 1-99; *Montant de la cotisation:* 6$
Activités: Séjours en milieu naturel

Association des joueurs de la ligue de football canadienne *See* Canadian Football League Players' Association

Association des journalistes automobile du Canada *See* Automobile Journalists Association of Canada

Association des journalistes indépendants du Québec (AJIQ) / Québec Association of Independent Journalists

#12, 1124, rue Marie-Anne Est, Montréal QC H2J 2B7
Tél: 514-529-3105
info@ajiq.qc.ca
www.ajiq.qc.ca
www.facebook.com/lajiq
twitter.com/ajiq
Aperçu: *Dimension:* moyenne; *Envergure:* provinciale; fondée en 1988
Mission: Défendre les droits des journalistes à statut précaire: les pigistes, les contractuels et les surnuméraires
Affiliation(s): Fédération nationale des communications(FNC); Confédération des syndicats nationaux(CSN)
Membre(s) du bureau directeur:
Simon Van Vliet, Vice-président

Sara-Emmanuelle Dichesne, Vice-présidente
Marie-Eve Cloutier, Vice-présidente
Membre: *Montant de la cotisation:* 130$ régulier; 95$ associé; 90$ bénévole; 65$ étudiant; 100$ sympathisant; *Comités:* Recrutement
Activités: *Service de conférenciers:* Oui
Prix, Bouses:
• Bourse AJIQ-Le Devoir (Brouse)
Gagnant du concours passera un stage de 4 mois au quotidien le Devoir

Association des journaux régionaux du Québec *See* Québec Community Newspaper Association

Association des juristes d'expression française de l'Ontario (AJEFO)

#201, 214 ch Montréal, Ottawa ON K1L 8L8
Tél: 613-842-7462; *Téléc:* 613-842-8389
bureau@ajefo.ca
www.ajefo.ca
www.facebook.com/group.php?gid=6848134959
Aperçu: *Dimension:* petite; *Envergure:* provinciale; Organisme sans but lucratif; fondée en 1980
Mission: Représenter les intérêts des avocates, des avocats, des juges, des fonctionnaires de la justice, des professeures, des professeurs, des étudiantes et des étudiants en droit, et des autres participants et participantes du monde juridique, qui travaillent à la promotion des services juridiques en français sur le territoire de l'Ontario; viser à assurer un accès égal à la justice, sans pénalité, délai, obstacle ou hésitation à l'utilisation du français par l'appareil judiciaire, les membres du Barreau ou la population francophone de notre province
Membre(s) du bureau directeur:
Paul Le Vay, Président
Danielle Manton, Directrice générale
Finances: *Budget de fonctionnement annuel:* $50,000-$100,000
Membre(s) du personnel: 1
Membre: 650; *Montant de la cotisation:* 30-125; *Critères d'admissibilite:* Étudiants en droit, avocats, juges, professeurs, et autres juristes

Association des juristes d'expression française de la Saskatchewan (AJEFS) / French Jurists Association of Saskatchewan

#219, 1440, 9e av Nord, Regina SK S4R 8B1
Tél: 306-924-8543; *Téléc:* 306-781-7916
Ligne sans frais: 800-991-1912
ajefs@sasktel.net
www.ajefs.ca
www.facebook.com/ajefs.saskatchewan
twitter.com/AJEFS1
Aperçu: *Dimension:* petite; *Envergure:* provinciale; Organisme sans but lucratif; fondée en 1989
Mission: Développer et promouvoir les droits et services en français auprès des instances juridiques et gouvernementales; informer et sensibiliser la population fransaskoise sur la vulgarisation des lois et l'utilisation des services juridiques en français
Membre(s) du bureau directeur:
Francis Poulin, Président
fpoulin@millerthomson.com
Membre: *Critères d'admissibilite:* Avocats, juges, traducteurs, greffiers; professeurs; étudiants en droit
Activités: Services d'information légale en français; documentation légale en français; ateliers; conférences; cours de perfectionnement; *Service de conférenciers:* Oui; *Listes de destinataires:* Oui; *Bibliothèque*
Prix, Bouses:
• Prix Turgeon (Prix)
Décerné à un juriste francophone qui a contribué à l'avancement des droits des francophones

Association des juristes d'expression française du Manitoba inc. (AJEFM)

177-B, rue Eugénie, Winnipeg MB R2H 0X9
Tél: 204-415-7526; *Téléc:* 204-415-4482
reception@ajefm.ca
www.mondroitmonchoix.com
Aperçu: *Dimension:* petite; *Envergure:* provinciale; Organisme sans but lucratif; fondée en 1988
Mission: Promouvoir et protéger les droits linguistiques des membres de la communauté francophone du Manitoba; assurer une plus grande offre de services en français dans l'administration de la justice au Manitoba
Membre de: Fédération des associations de juristes d'expression française de common law inc.
Membre(s) du bureau directeur:
Robert Tétrault, Président
Philippe Richer, Directeur général
dg@ajefm.ca
Paulette Desaulniers, Directrice adjointe
direction@ajefm.ca
Finances: *Budget de fonctionnement annuel:* $50,000-$100,000
Membre(s) du personnel: 2
Membre: 99; *Montant de la cotisation:* 35$; *Critères d'admissibilite:* Juristes d'expression française du Manitoba; *Comités:* Groupe de travail sur l'amélioration des services en langue française au sein du système judiciaire au Manitoba; Table ronde - Gendarmerie royale au Canada
Activités: Comités; suivis de rapports; interventions visés vers l'accèss à la justice en français; ateliers; activités de sensibilisation; *Service de conférenciers:* Oui

Association des juristes d'expression française du Nouveau-Brunswick (AJEFNB)

Pavillon A.-J. Cormier, Université de Moncton, 18, av Antonine-Maillet, Moncton NB E1A 3E9
Tél: 506-853-4151; *Téléc:* 506-853-4152
association@ajefnb.nb.ca
www.ajefnb.nb.ca
Aperçu: *Dimension:* petite; *Envergure:* provinciale; Organisme sans but lucratif; fondée en 1987
Mission: Continue à oeuvrer pour l'avancement des droits linguistiques dans la province du Nouveau-Brunswick; travaille avec ténacité à accroître l'exercise de la pratique du droit en français et à concrétiser et faciliter l'accès aux tribunaux néo-brunswickois, dans toutes ses facettes, dans les deux langues officielles
Membre de: Fédération des associations de juristes d'expression française de common law
Membre(s) du bureau directeur:
Julie Emond-McCarthy, Présidente, 506-384-7978, Fax: 506-384-4787
julie@jcem.ca
Euclide LeBouthillier, Vice-présidente
euclide.dllb@nb.aibn.com
France Levesque, Secrétaire/Trésorière
france@mcintyrefinn.com
Lise Mazerolle, Directrice générale, 506-853-4154
directiongenerale@ajefnb.nb.ca
Finances: *Budget de fonctionnement annuel:* $50,000-$100,000
Membre(s) du personnel: 2; 20 bénévole(s)
Membre: 260; *Montant de la cotisation:* 50-80

Bathurst - Chaleur
Robichaud Theriault Riordon Arseneault, #300, 270, av Douglas, Bathurst NB E2A 1M9
Tél: 506-548-8822; *Téléc:* 506-548-5297
Membre(s) du bureau directeur:
Florian Arsenault, Contact
farseno@nb.aibn.com

Campbellton - Restigouche
Étude légale, CP 127, 87, rue Roseberry, Campbellton NB E3N 3G1
Tél: 506-753-3681; *Téléc:* 506-753-3683
Membre(s) du bureau directeur:
Prisca Levesque, Contact
prisca@nb.sympatico.ca

Drummond - Victoria-Carleton
1318, ch Tobique, Drummond NB E3Y 2N7
Tél: 506-473-7253; *Téléc:* 506-473-5802
Membre(s) du bureau directeur:
Tina Lagacé-Rivard, Contact
tlagacerivard@nb.aibn.com

Edmunston - Madawaska
64, av Fraser, Edmunston NB E3V 2B5
Tél: 506-473-7620; *Téléc:* 506-473-7621
Membre(s) du bureau directeur:
Mélanie Tremblay, Contact
melanie.tremblay@live.ca

Fredericton
Foster & Company, #100, 564, rue Prospect ouest, Fredericton NB E3B 9M3
Tél: 506-462-4000; *Téléc:* 506-462-4001
Membre(s) du bureau directeur:
Tammy Moreau, Contact
tmoreau@fandclaw.com

Miramichi-Kent

Moncton - Westmorland
Actus Droit, 900, rue Main, 2e étage, Moncton NB E1C 1G4
Tél: 506-854-4040; *Téléc:* 506-854-4044
Membre(s) du bureau directeur:
Adèle Savoie, Contact
adele@actuslaw.com

Tracadie-Sheila - Péninsule acadienne
Doiron LeBouthillier Boudreau Allain, CP 3010, Succ. Bureau-Chef, Tracadie-Sheila NB E1X 1G5
Tél: 506-395-0044; *Téléc:* 506-395-0050
Membre(s) du bureau directeur:
Mireille Saulnier, Contact
mireille.dllb@nb.aibn.com

Association des juristes pour l'avancement de la vie artistique (AJAVA)

445, boul. Saint-Laurent, Montréal QC H2Y 3T8
Tél: 514-954-3471; *Téléc:* 514-954-3451
Ligne sans frais: 800-361-8495
lajava@barreau.qc.ca
www.lajava.org
Aperçu: *Dimension:* petite; *Envergure:* locale; fondée en 1997
Mission: Pour sensibiliser les membres sur le droit du divertissement et de créer un réseau de professionnels qui travaillent dans l'industrie du divertissement
Membre(s) du bureau directeur:
Martin Lavallée, Président, Conseil d'administration
Membre: *Montant de la cotisation:* 50$; *Critères d'admissibilite:* Les avocats qui de droit de divertissement pratique; les personnes qui travaillent dans l'industrie du divertissement

Association des laryngectomisés de Montréal *Voir* Fédération québécoise des laryngectomisés

Association des lesbiennes et des gais sur Internet (ALGI)

CP 476, Succ. C, Montréal QC H2L 4K4
Tél: 514-528-8424
info@algi.qc.ca
www.algi.qc.ca
www.facebook.com/algi.qc.ca
Aperçu: *Dimension:* petite; *Envergure:* provinciale
Mission: Favoriser l'expression des lesbiennes et des gais au moyen de l'Internet; favoriser l'échange entre les individus et les organismes de la communauté gaie et lesbienne dans un esprit d'entraide
Membre: *Montant de la cotisation:* 20$

Association des libraires du Québec (ALQ)

#801, 407, boul St-Laurent, Montréal QC H2Y 2Y5
Tél: 514-526-3349; *Téléc:* 514-526-3340
info@alq.qc.ca
www.alq.qc.ca
Aperçu: *Dimension:* moyenne; *Envergure:* provinciale; Organisme sans but lucratif; fondée en 1969
Mission: Regrouper, pour leur bénéfice mutuel, les libraires engagées dans la vente au détail au Québec et celles engagées dans la vente du livre en langue française au Canada; fournir des services, faire des études, fournir de l'information, tenir des réunions et des rencontres et contribuer à des programmes pour le bénéfice et l'amélioration de ses membres; encourager la vente au détail du livre au Québec; encourager la communication et la collaboration entre les éditeurs, les distributeurs et les autres participants de l'industrie du livre; aider les libraires à encourager la lecture; lutter contre toute forme de censure
Membre(s) du bureau directeur:
Katherine Fafard, Directrice générale, 514-526-3349 Ext. 21
kfafard@alq.qc.ca
Membre(s) du personnel: 6
Membre: 115 libraires; *Critères d'admissibilite:* Être un libraire agréé (agrément délivré par le ministère québécois de la culture); *Comités:* Formation; Prix des libraires; Prix Jeunesse des libraires du Québec; Prix réglementé; Loi 51; Pratiques commerciales
Activités: Gestion des programmes de subventions accessibles aux libraires; protocole d'entente avec les fournisseurs; service de recherche; participation, gestion, élaboration et promotion de la Banque de données (BTLF); rencontres, colloques, ateliers; *Bibliothèque*

L'Association des littératures canadiennes et québécoise *See* Association for Canadian & Québec Literatures

Association des locataires de l'Ile-des-Soeurs (ALIS/NITA) / Nuns' Island Tenants Association

CP 63008, 40, Place du Commerce, Verdun QC H3E 1V6
Tél: 514-767-1003
Aperçu: *Dimension:* petite; *Envergure:* locale; fondée en 1993
Mission: Défense des droits des locataires

Association des maisons de commerce extérieur du Québec (AMCEQ) / Québec Association of Export Trading Houses (QAETH)
643, av Grosvenor, Westmount QC H3Y 2S9
Tél: 514-486-5308
www.amceq.org
Aperçu: *Dimension:* petite; *Envergure:* internationale; fondée en 1985
Mission: Développer des maisons de commerce, la promotion des intérêts, du rôle et de l'importance des Maisons de commerce, l'augmentation des exportations par l'intégration systématique de maisons de commerce dans la stratégie de marketing international de l'industrie Québécoise, le rapprochement entre maisons de commerce et PME manufacturières; la reconnaissance et la valorisation de la profession de trader; la formation de traders qualifiés
Membre de: Alliance of Manufacturers & Exporters Canada; Forum Francophone des Affaires
Affliation(s): Manufacturiers et Exportateurs du Québec
Membre(s) du bureau directeur:
Claude Tardif, Administrateur
claude@interunion.ca
Membre: *Montant de la cotisation:* 225$ membre associé; 400$ membre affilié ou accrédité
Activités: Formation; *Stagiaires:* Oui; *Service de conférenciers:* Oui

Association des maîtres couvreurs du Québec (AMCQ) / Québec Master Roofers Association
3001, boul Tessier, Laval QC H7S 2M1
Tél: 450-973-2322; *Téléc:* 450-973-2321
Ligne sans frais: 888-973-2322
amcq@amcq.qc.ca
www.amcq.qc.ca
Aperçu: *Dimension:* petite; *Envergure:* provinciale; Organisme sans but lucratif; fondée en 1967 surveillé par Canadian Roofing Contractors' Association
Mission: Promouvoir les intérêts généraux des entreprises de couvertures et ceux de diverses entreprises des secteurs connexes dans la province de Québec; promouvoir la hausse de la qualité des travaux de couvertures
Finances: *Fonds:* Comm. santé, sécurité du travail du Québec, promotion sécurité
Membre: 163
Activités: *Bibliothèque:* Centre de documentation; Bibliothèque publique rendez-vous

Association des malentendants canadiens *See* Canadian Hard of Hearing Association

Association des malentendants Québécois (AMQ)
7260, boul Cloutier, Charlesbourg QC G1H 3E8
Tél: 418-623-5080; *Téléc:* 418-623-8936
info@amq1985.org
www.amq1985.org
Aperçu: *Dimension:* moyenne; *Envergure:* locale; Organisme sans but lucratif; fondée en 1985
Mission: Offrir un service d'accueil, d'écoute, d'informations, de références aux personnes vivant avec la surdité afin d'améliorer leur réalité quotidienne, et de développer un réseau d'entraide et de support
Membre de: Centre québecois de la déficience auditive, Centre d'action bénévole de Québec; Regroupement des organismes de promotion region D3
Membre(s) du bureau directeur:
Gilles Nolet, Président
gilles.nolet2@sympatico.ca
Finances: *Budget de fonctionnement annuel:* $50,000-$100,000
Membre(s) du personnel: 2; 20 bénévole(s)
Membre: 130; *Montant de la cotisation:* 10$ étudiants; 25$ adultes; 35$ organisme; *Critères d'admissibilite:* Personnes sourdes congénitale, devenues sourdes ou malentendantes
Activités: Information, formation, sensibisation, défense des droits, entraide, écoute, support et activités sociales

Association des manufacturiers de bois de sciage de l'Ontario *See* Ontario Lumber Manufacturers' Association

Association des manufacturiers de bois de sciage du Québec *Voir* Conseil de l'industrie forestière du Québec

Association des manufacturiers de chaussures du Canada *See* Shoe Manufacturers' Association of Canada

Association des manufacturiers de produits alimentaires de Saskatchewan *See* Saskatchewan Food Processors Association

Association des manufacturiers de produits alimentaires du Québec *Voir* Conseil de la transformation agroalimentaire et des produits de consommation

Association des marchands d'art du Canada *See* Art Dealers Association of Canada Inc.

Association des marchands de machines aratoires de la province de Québec (AMMAQ)
7, rue Bernier, Bedford QC J0J 1A0
Tél: 450-248-7946; *Téléc:* 450-248-3264
info@ammaq.ca
www.ammaq.ca
Aperçu: *Dimension:* petite; *Envergure:* provinciale; Organisme sans but lucratif; fondée en 1949
Mission: Aider et regrouper tous les concessionnaires de machineries agricoles de toute la province; compiler des statistiques et des renseignements sur la vente de machines aratoires dans la province du Québec; obtenir une plus grande coopération entre les marchands de machines aratoires des diverses régions de la province; promouvoir la vente et l'utilisation des machines aratoires
Membre(s) du bureau directeur:
Peter Maurice, Directeur général, 450-248-7946
Activités: Congrès annuel; tournoi de golf annuel; rencontre régionale; matériel de support

Association des marchands de voitures d'occasion du Manitoba *See* Used Car Dealers Association of Manitoba

Association des marchands dépanneurs et épiciers du Québec (AMDEQ)
#229, 3075, boul W-Hamel, Québec QC G1P 4C6
Tél: 418-654-3232; *Téléc:* 418-654-3222
Ligne sans frais: 877-227-6045
info@amdeq.ca
www.amdeq.ca
www.facebook.com/205891622815182
Nom précédent: Association des marchands détaillants de l'est du Québec
Aperçu: *Dimension:* moyenne; *Envergure:* provinciale
Mission: Représenter et défendre les intérêts socio-économiques des membres; négocier des ristournes supplémentaires, des rabais ou de meilleurs prix auprès des fournisseurs; informer les détaillants-membres sur les sujets pertinents à la bonne gestion de leur commerce
Affliation(s): RDEI
Membre(s) du bureau directeur:
Yves Servais, Directeur général
Membre(s) du personnel: 9
Membre: 1,000-4,999
Activités: Congrès annuel; cours de formation; rencontres régionales; *Evénements de sensibilisation:* Conférence de Presse - Lutte contre la contrebande du tabac; Tournée sur la contrebande - Réduire a 10%

Association des marchands détaillants de l'est du Québec *Voir* Association des marchands dépanneurs et épiciers du Québec

Association des marchés financiers du Canada *See* Financial Markets Association of Canada

Association des marchés financiers du Canada *See* Canadian Association of Direct Response Insurers

Association des massologues et techniciens en massage du Canada - Association des massothérapeutes professionnels du Québec
#200, 5967, rue Jean-Talon est, Saint-Léonard QC H1S 1M5
Tél: 514-727-5444; *Téléc:* 514-727-6555
Ligne sans frais: 888-434-6914
admin@amtmc-ampq.qc.ca
www.amtmc-ampq.qc.ca
Aperçu: *Dimension:* moyenne; *Envergure:* provinciale; Organisme sans but lucratif; fondée en 1984
Membre(s) du bureau directeur:
Jean-Claude Bleau, Président
jcbleau@amtmc-ampq.qc.ca
Léon Gauthier, Vice-président
lgauthier@amtmc-ampq.qc.ca
Luisa Carlisi, Secretaire-tresorière
Membre(s) du personnel: 3
Membre: 1,650; *Montant de la cotisation:* 182.50$; *Critères d'admissibilite:* Technicien ou étudiant en massage; Massothérapeute

Association des massothérapeutes du Nouveau-Brunswick *See* New Brunswick Massotherapy Association

Association des MBA du Québec (AMBAQ)
1970, rue Notre-Dame Ouest, Montréal QC H3C 1K8
Tél: 514-323-8480; *Téléc:* 514-282-4292
info@ambaq.com
www.ambaq.com
www.linkedin.com/groups/Association-MBA-Québec-78306
www.facebook.com/ambaq
twitter.com/AMBAQ
Aperçu: *Dimension:* moyenne; *Envergure:* provinciale; fondée en 1974
Mission: Òtre le porte-parole des MBA du Québec; constituer un réseau actif de diplômés et étudiants MBA; favoriser le développement personnel et professionnel des membres; valoriser et promouvoir le diplôme MBA
Membre(s) du bureau directeur:
Ivan Roy, Directeur général, 514-282-2731
iroy@ambaq.com
Membre: 1,300; *Montant de la cotisation:* Barème; *Critères d'admissibilite:* Diplômé de maîtrise en administration des affaires; *Comités:* Gala MBA; Classique de golf; Midis-conférences; Échanges et découvertes; Cercles d'échange; Publications; Région de Québec; Membership et fidélisation; Région de Gatineau-Ottawa; Région de Sherbrooke; Webinaires; Relations universitaires; Activités du 40e anniversaire; Réseaux sociaux
Activités: Ateliers; conférences; tournois de golf; déjeuners-rencontres

Association des médecins biochimistes du Canada *See* Canadian Association of Medical Biochemists

Association des médecins biochimistes du Québec (AMBQ)
#3000, 2, Complexe Desjardins, Montréal QC H5B 1G8
Tél: 514-350-5105; *Téléc:* 514-350-5151
ambq@fmsq.org
www.ambq.med.usherbrooke.ca
Aperçu: *Dimension:* petite; *Envergure:* provinciale surveillé par Fédération des médecins spécialistes du Québec
Mission: Promouvoir l'utilisation optimale des tests de laboratoire au Québec en offrant, au professionnel de la santé et au patient, les meilleurs services de diagnostic et de dépistage de maladies grâce à des techniques biochimiques et immunologiques
Membre(s) du bureau directeur:
Elaine Letendre, Présidente

Association des médecins cliniciens enseignants de Laval (AMCEL)
c/o Hôpital Laval, Département de chirurgie, 2725, ch Ste-Foy, Québec QC G1V 4G5
Tél: 418-656-4810; *Téléc:* 418-656-4865
amcel@criucpq.ulaval.ca
Aperçu: *Dimension:* petite; *Envergure:* locale; fondée en 1975
Mission: Défense des intérêts de ses membres (médecins-professeurs à l'Université Laval)
Finances: *Budget de fonctionnement annuel:* Moins de $50,000
Membre: 130; *Montant de la cotisation:* 0.40%

Association des médecins cliniciens enseignants de Montréal (AMCEM)
a/s Dr. Jean Wilkins, Le CHU Sainte-Justine, 3175, ch de la Côte-Ste-Catherine, Montréal QC H3T 1C5
Aperçu: *Dimension:* petite; *Envergure:* locale; fondée en 1969
Membre(s) du bureau directeur:
Jean Wilkins, Responsable
Membre: 100-499; *Critères d'admissibilite:* Médicins professeurs à la Faculté de Médecine Université de Montréal

Association des médecins de langue française du Canada *Voir* Médecins francophones du Canada

Association des médecins endocrinologues du Québec
CP 216, Succ. Desjardins, #3000, 2, Complexe Desjardins, Montréal QC H5B 1G8
Tél: 514-350-5135; *Téléc:* 514-350-5049
Ligne sans frais: 800-561-0703
ameq@fmsq.org
www.ameq.qc.ca
Aperçu: *Dimension:* petite; *Envergure:* provinciale surveillé par Fédération des médecins spécialistes du Québec
Mission: L'Association est un porte-parole des endocrinologues; elle favorise les intérêts scientifiques de ses membres et

organise plusieurs réunions afin de permettre une formation médicale continue des endocrinologues
Activités: Programmation éducative, expositions

Association des médecins généticiens du Québec
#300, 2, Complexe Desjardins, Montréal QC H5B 1G8
Tél: 514-350-5141; *Téléc:* 514-350-5116
Aperçu: *Dimension:* petite; *Envergure:* provinciale surveillé par Fédération des médecins spécialistes du Québec
Membre(s) du bureau directeur:
Bruno Maranda, M.D., Présidente
Sandrine Guillot, Directrice
sguillot@fmsq.org

Association des médecins gériatres du Québec
CP 216, Succ. Desjardins, #3000, 2, Complexe Desjardins, Montréal QC H5B 1G8
Tél: 514-350-5145
info@amgq.ca
www.amgq.ca
Aperçu: *Dimension:* petite; *Envergure:* provinciale surveillé par Fédération des médecins spécialistes du Québec
Affiliation(s): Fédération des médecins spécialistes du Québec
Membre(s) du bureau directeur:
Maurice St-Laurent, Président
Membre: 60+

Association des médecins hématologistes-oncologistes du Québec (AMHOQ)
CP 216, Succ. Desjardins, 2, Complexe Desjardins, Montréal QC H5B 1G8
Tél: 514-350-5121; *Téléc:* 514-350-5126
info@amhoq.org
amhoq.org
Aperçu: *Dimension:* petite; *Envergure:* provinciale; Organisme sans but lucratif surveillé par Fédération des médecins spécialistes du Québec
Membre(s) du bureau directeur:
Daniel Bélanger, Président
Nathalie Latendresse, Adjointe de direction
Finances: *Budget de fonctionnement annuel:* $50,000-$100,000
Membre(s) du personnel: 1
Membre: 100-499;

Association des médecins microbiologistes-infectiologues du Québec (AMMIQ)
#3000, 2, Complexe Desjardins, Montréal QC H5B 1G8
Tél: 514-350-5104; *Téléc:* 514-350-5144
info@ammiq.org
www.ammiq.org
Aperçu: *Dimension:* petite; *Envergure:* provinciale surveillé par Fédération des médecins spécialistes du Québec
Mission: L'Association regroupe des médecins (de laboratoire et dans le diagnostic clinique) spécialisés dans l'épidémiologie, le traitement et la prévention des maladies infectieuses
Membre(s) du bureau directeur:
Karl Weiss, Président
Membre: 210
Activités: Formation; réunions

Association des médecins omnipraticiens de Montréal (AMOM)
#1000, 1440, rue Ste-Catherine Ouest, Montréal QC H3G 1R8
Tél: 514-878-1911; *Téléc:* 514-878-2608
info@amom.net
www.amom.net
Aperçu: *Dimension:* petite; *Envergure:* locale
Mission: L'AMOM représente plus de 1900 médecins généralistes oeuvrant dans les différentes sphères de l'omnipratique, de l'urgentologie à la gériatrie en passant par la médecine familiale
Affiliation(s): Fédération des médecins omnipraticiens du Québec
Membre(s) du bureau directeur:
Marc-André Asselin, Président
Membre: 1 900

Association des médecins ophtalmologistes du Québec (AMOQ)
CP 216, Succ. Desjardins, 2, Complexe Desjardins, Montréal QC H5B 1G8
Tél: 514-350-5124; *Téléc:* 514-350-5174
amoq@fmsq.org
www.amoq.org
Aperçu: *Dimension:* petite; *Envergure:* provinciale; Organisme sans but lucratif; fondée en 1955 surveillé par Fédération des médecins spécialistes du Québec
Mission: Promouvoir les intérêts professionnels et économiques de ses membres; se préoccuper du maintien de la compétence; susciter et appuier des activités scientifiques susceptibles de favoriser l'avancement de l'ophtalmologie; se préoccuper de l'accessibilité aux soins ophtalmologiques
Membre(s) du bureau directeur:
Côme Fortin, Président
Membre: *Critères d'admissibilite:* Médecins ophtalmologistes

Association des médecins rhumatologues du Québec (AMRQ)
CP 216, Succ. Desjardins, Montréal QC H5B 1G8
Tél: 514-350-5136; *Téléc:* 514-350-5029
Ligne sans frais: 800-561-0703
info@rhumatologie.org
www.rhumatologie.org
Aperçu: *Dimension:* petite; *Envergure:* provinciale surveillé par Fédération des médecins spécialistes du Québec
Mission: La rhumatologie se consacre au diagnostic et au traitement des pathologies qui touchent les articulations, les os, les muscles et tendons et parfois tout organe dans le cadre de maladies systémiques. Ceci regroupe au-delà de 100 conditions pouvant aller de l'arthrite rhumatoïde au lupus érythémateux disséminé en passant par l'arthrose, les vasculites et l'ostéoporose.
Membre de: Fédération des Médecins Spécialistes de Québec (FMSQ)
Membre(s) du bureau directeur:
Frédéric Morin, Président

Association des médecins spécialistes en médecine nucléaire du Québec (AMSMNQ)
CP 216, Succ. Desjardins, #3000, 2, Complexe Desjardins, Montréal QC H5B 1G8
Tél: 514-350-5133; *Téléc:* 514-350-5151
Ligne sans frais: 800-561-0703
amsmnq@fmsq.org
www.medecinenucleaire.com
Aperçu: *Dimension:* petite; *Envergure:* provinciale surveillé par Fédération des médecins spécialistes du Québec
Mission: Pour former ses membres et maintenir un haut niveau de professionnalisme
Membre(s) du bureau directeur:
François Lamoureux, Président
Jean Guimond, Vice-président
Membre: *Comités:* Développement Professionnel Continu; Exercice professionnel; Radioprotection; Tarification; Site Internet

Association des médecins spécialistes en santé communautaire du Québec (AMSSCQ)
#3000, 2, Complexe Desjardins, Montréal QC H5B 1G8
Tél: 514-350-5138; *Téléc:* 514-350-5151
amsscq@fmsq.org
www.amsscq.org
Aperçu: *Dimension:* petite; *Envergure:* provinciale; fondée en 1982 surveillé par Fédération des médecins spécialistes du Québec
Mission: De promouvoir les intérêts professionnels et économiques de ses membres
Membre(s) du bureau directeur:
Yv Bonnier Viger, Président
Michelle Laviolette, Directrice
Membre: 173

Association des médecins vétérinaires du Nouveau-Brunswick *See* New Brunswick Veterinary Medical Association

Association des médecins vétérinaires praticiens du Québec (AMVPQ)
#4500, 2336, ch Ste-Foy, Québec QC G1V 1S5
Tél: 418-651-0477; *Téléc:* 450-261-9435
amvpq@amvpq.org
www.amvpq.org
www.facebook.com/amvpq
Aperçu: *Dimension:* petite; *Envergure:* provinciale; Organisme sans but lucratif; fondée en 1969
Membre de: Canadian Veterinary Medical Association
Membre(s) du bureau directeur:
Michel Savard, Directeur général
Finances: *Fonds:* Cotisations syndicales
Membre(s) du personnel: 2
Membre: 480+; *Critères d'admissibilite:* Médecins vétérinaires practiciens
Activités: Formation continue; étude et défense des membres; promotion; développement
Meetings/Conferences: • Congrès Association des médecins vétérinaires praticiens du Québec 2015, 2015, QC
Scope: Provincial

Association des médecins-psychiatres du Québec (AMPQ) / Québec Psychiatrists' Association
CP 216, Succ. Desjardins, 2, complexe Desjardins, Tour de l'Est, 30e étage, Montréal QC H5B 1G8
Tél: 514-350-5128; *Téléc:* 514-350-5198
ampq@fmsq.org
www.ampq.org
Aperçu: *Dimension:* moyenne; *Envergure:* provinciale; fondée en 1953
Mission: Promouvoir les intérêts professionnels et économiques de ses membres
Membre(s) du bureau directeur:
Brian G. Bexton, Président, Administration
Gérard Cournoyer, Secrétaire
Finances: *Budget de fonctionnement annuel:* $500,000-$1.5 Million
Membre(s) du personnel: 3
Membre: 1,000-4,999; *Montant de la cotisation:* 500$; *Critères d'admissibilite:* Médecins-psychiatres

Association des médias écrits communautaires du Québec (AMECQ)
140 rue Fleury ouest, Montréal QC H3L 1T4
Tél: 514-383-8533; *Téléc:* 514-383-8976
Ligne sans frais: 800-867-8533
medias@amecq.ca
www.amecq.ca/
www.facebook.com/JournauxAmecq
twitter.com/AmecqMedias
Aperçu: *Dimension:* moyenne; *Envergure:* provinciale; Organisme sans but lucratif; fondée en 1981
Mission: Fournir des services de soutien et de formation à ses journaux communautaires membres; les regrouper et les représenter pour que ceux-ci puissent remplir leur rôle et leur mission fondamentale.
Membre(s) du bureau directeur:
Yvan Noé Girouard, Directeur général
medias@amecq.ca
Kristina Jensen, Présidente
kristinajensen@gmail.com
Finances: *Budget de fonctionnement annuel:* $100,000-$250,000
Membre(s) du personnel: 2
Membre: 90; *Montant de la cotisation:* 75$; *Critères d'admissibilite:* Journaux communautaires
Activités: *Evénements de sensibilisation:* Mois de la presse communautaire, avril; Le Congrès annuel de L'AMECQ; *Bibliothèque:* Centre de documentation et d'archives; rendez-vous

Association des microbiologistes du Québec (AMQ)
5094A, av. Charlemagne, Montréal QC H1X 3P3
Tél: 514-728-1087; *Téléc:* 514-374-3988
amq@microbiologistes.ca
www.microbiologistes.ca
www.facebook.com/AssociationDesMicrobiologistesDuQuebec
Aperçu: *Dimension:* moyenne; *Envergure:* provinciale; fondée en 1975
Mission: De regrouper les microbiologistes du Québec oeuvrant principalment en environnement, en alimentaire et en pharmaceutique; d'étudier, de protéger et de développer les intérêts économiques, sociaux et professionnels des microbiologistes et de promouvoir l'essor de la microbiologie en général
Membre(s) du bureau directeur:
Patrick D. Paquette, Président
patrick.d.paquette@microbiologistes.ca
Membre: *Montant de la cotisation:* Barème; *Critères d'admissibilite:* 30 crédits universitaires en microbiologie; *Comités:* Statut professionnel; Inspection professionnelle; Risques biologiques; Sélection; Affaires académiques; Communications

Association des mines de métaux du Québec inc. *Voir* Association minière du Québec

Association des motocyclistes gais du Québec (AMGQ)
CP 36, Succ. C, Montréal QC H2L 4J7
info.amgq@gmail.com
www.amgq.org
Aperçu: *Dimension:* petite; *Envergure:* provinciale; Organisme sans but lucratif; fondée en 1989
Mission: L'AMGQ est une association apolitique qui répond aux intérêts, aux goûts et aux besoins de ses membres par des activités et des services dans le domaine du motocyclisme.
Membre de: Alliance Motocycliste Métropolitaine; Fédération Motocycliste du Québec; Association des lesbiennes et des gais sur Internet; Table de concertation des lesbiennes et des gais du Québec; Égale Canada
Membre(s) du bureau directeur:
Coquille St-Jacques, Président
James Connolly, Vice-président
Dan Grondin, Trésorier
Membre: *Montant de la cotisation:* 65$; *Critères d'admissibilité:* Gai (homme) et propriétaire de moto
Activités: Balades, soupers mensuels, brunchs; *Bibliothèque*

Association des municipalités bilingues du Manitoba ***Voir*** Conseil de développement économique des municipalités bilingues du Manitoba

Association des municipalités du Nouveau-Brunswick ***Voir*** Association francophone des municipalités du Nouveau-Brunswick Inc.

Association des musées canadiens ***See*** Canadian Museums Association

Association des musées de l'Ontario ***See*** Ontario Museum Association

Association des musées de la province de Québec (1973) ***Voir*** Société des musées québécois

Association des musées du Nouveau-Brunswick ***See*** Association Museums New Brunswick

Association des naturopathes professionnels du Québec (ANPQ)
27, rue Béliveau, Laval QC H7B 1A7
Tél: 450-720-0560
anm.anpq@videotron.ca
www.anpq.qc.ca
Aperçu: *Dimension:* petite; *Envergure:* provinciale; fondée en 1971
Mission: Association à but non lucratif et à charte provinciale qui regroupe des praticiens en naturopathie dûment qualifiés
Membre: 100-499; *Montant de la cotisation:* 180$

Association des néphrologues du Québec
CP 216, Succ. Desjardins, #3000, 2, Complexe Desjardins, Montréal QC H5B 1G8
Tél: 514-350-5134; *Téléc:* 514-350-5151
nephrologie@fmsq.org
Aperçu: *Dimension:* petite; *Envergure:* provinciale surveillé par Fédération des médecins spécialistes du Québec
Membre(s) du bureau directeur:
Robert Charbonneau, Président
Lillian Plasse, Directrice

Association des neurologues du Québec (ANQ)
CP 216, Succ. Desjardins, #3000, 2, Complexe Desjardins, Montréal QC H5B 1G8
Tél: 514-350-5122; *Téléc:* 514-350-5172
anq@fmsq.org
www.anq.qc.ca
Aperçu: *Dimension:* petite; *Envergure:* provinciale surveillé par Fédération des médecins spécialistes du Québec
Mission: Représenter des médecins spécialistes qui diagnostique et traite les maladies affectant le système nerveux central ainsi que le système nerveux périphérique
Membre(s) du bureau directeur:
Ginette Guilbeault, Directrice
J. Marc Girard, Président
Anne Lortie, Secrétaire
Membre: *Comités:* Développement professional continu; Effectifs médicaux; Neurophysiologie clinique; Rémunération; Relations avec les médias

Association des neurotraumatisés de l'Outaouais (ANO)
#1, 115 boul Sacré-Coeur, Gatineau QC J8X 1C5
Tél: 819-770-8804; *Téléc:* 819-770-5863
ano@ano.ca
www.ano.ca
Aperçu: *Dimension:* petite; *Envergure:* locale; fondée en 1990
Mission: Pour aider les personnes dans la région québécoise de l'Outaouais qui ont subi un traumatisme crânien ou un AVC
Membre de: Regroupement des associations de personnes traumatisées craniocérébrals du Québec; Regroupement des associations de personnes handicapées de l'Outaouais; CDC Rond Point
Membre(s) du bureau directeur:
Johanne Chaussé, Directrice
Anne Karine Gauthier, Présidente
Julie Larochelle, Secrétaire
Gary Leonard, Trésorier
Finances: *Budget de fonctionnement annuel:* $100,000-$250,000; *Fonds:* Agence de la santé; agence des services sociaux; SAAQ; LSO
Membre(s) du personnel: 3; 40 bénévole(s)
Membre: 140; *Montant de la cotisation:* 10$; *Critères d'admissibilite:* Les survivants de lésions cérébrales et accidents vasculaires cérébraux, et leurs familles, dans la région de l'Outaouais au Québec
Activités: Fournir des informations sur les blessures et accidents vasculaires cérébraux traumatiques au cerveau; Offrir un soutien psychosocial aux membres; Offrant des activités pour favoriser la réinsertion sociale des victimes de la blessure et accident vasculaire cérébral traumatique
Publications:
• Le Mieux Etre
Type: Newsletter; *Frequency:* 3 pa
Profile: Information about health & social services & leisure activities for members of Association des neurotraumatisés de l'Outaouais

L'association des nouveaux Canadiens ***See*** Association for New Canadians

Association des Numismates et des Philatélistes de Boucherville
CP 111, Boucherville QC J4B 5E6
Tél: 450-655-4433
anpb.net
Aperçu: *Dimension:* petite; *Envergure:* locale; fondée en 1967
Mission: Promouvoir l'activité de collecte de pièces et les timbres

Association des obstétriciens et gynécologues du Québec (AOGQ)
#3000, 2, Complexe Desjardins, Montréal QC H5B 1G8
Tél: 514-849-4969; *Téléc:* 514-849-5011
info@gynecoquebec.com
www.gynecoquebec.com
Aperçu: *Dimension:* petite; *Envergure:* provinciale; fondée en 1966
Mission: Promouvoir l'intérêt professionnel scientifique et économique de ses membres
Affiliation(s): Fédération des médecins spécialistes du Québec
Membre(s) du bureau directeur:
Isabelle Girard, Présidente
Membre: *Critères d'admissibilite:* Obstétriciens, gynécologues certifiés

Association des offices municipaux d'habitation du Québec ***Voir*** Regroupement des offices d'habitation du Québec

L'Association des officiels de la construction du Nouveau-Brunswick ***See*** New Brunswick Building Officials Association

L'Association des officiers de la marine du Canada ***See*** The Naval Officers' Association of Canada

Association des optométristes du Nouveau-Brunswick ***See*** New Brunswick Association of Optometrists

Association des optométristes du Québec (AOQ) / Québec Optometric Association
#740, 1265, rue Berri, Montréal QC H2L 4X4
Tél: 514-288-6272; *Téléc:* 514-288-7071
info@aoqnet.qc.ca
www.aoqnet.qc.ca
www.facebook.com/109631962406806
Aperçu: *Dimension:* moyenne; *Envergure:* provinciale; fondée en 1973 surveillé par Canadian Association of Optometrists
Mission: De développer meilleures conditions de pratique économiques et professionnelles pour les optométristes du Québec
Membre(s) du bureau directeur:
Maryse Nolin, Directeur général
Steven Carrier, Président
Membre(s) du personnel: 10
Membre: 1,447; *Critères d'admissibilite:* Optométriste en pratique privée; *Comités:* Gouvernance; Réflexion sur l'avenir de la pratique optométrique; Négociation; Services aux membres; Relations publiques; AOQnet, le portail Internet; Réglementation et formation professionnelles; A.C.O. et affaires fédérales; Relations gouvernementales; Assurances et Placements A.O.Q.; C.P.R.O.; Guide des lentilles ophtalmiques progressives; Vision des enfants; Information-communication; Optométrie sportive
Activités: Service aux membres; information au public; relation gouvernementale; *Service de conférenciers:* Oui

Association des orchestres de jeunes de la Montérégie (AOJM)
CP 36573, 58, rue Victoria, Saint-Lambert QC J4P 3S8
Tél: 450-923-3733
courrier@aojm.org
www.aojm.org
www.facebook.com/349656105067547
Également appelé: Orchestre symphonique des jeunes de la Montérégie
Nom précédent: Association des cordes de la Rive-Sud
Aperçu: *Dimension:* petite; *Envergure:* locale; fondée en 1974 surveillé par Orchestras Canada
Mission: De promouvoir le développement et la formation de jeunes musiciens
Membre de: Association des orchestres de jeunes de Québec
Membre(s) du bureau directeur:
Normand Doyon, Président
Membre(s) du personnel: 11
Membre: 75;

Association des orchestres de jeunes du Québec inc. (AOJQ)
901, rue Saint-Louis, Terrbonne QC J6W 1K1
Tél: 514-899-1150; *Téléc:* 514-658-1603
info@aojq.qc.ca
www.aojq.qc.ca
www.facebook.com/AOJQuebec
www.youtube.com/user/AOJQuebec
Aperçu: *Dimension:* petite; *Envergure:* provinciale; fondée en 1979
Mission: De regrouper les orchestres de jeunes dûment incorporés pour offrir aux cadres bénévoles un soutien administratif et aux jeunes musiciens en formation des activités de perfectionnement
Membre(s) du bureau directeur:
Louise Richard, Présidente
lrichard@aojq.qc.ca
Membre: 8; *Critères d'admissibilite:* Orchestre de jeunes de 14-25 ans
Activités: Concerts

L'Association des organistes liturgiques du Canada ***Voir*** LAUDEM, L'Association des musiciens liturgiques du Canada

Association des orthésistes et prothésistes du Québec (AOPQ)
715-A, ch des Pères, Magog QC J1X 5R9
Tél: 514-396-9303; *Téléc:* 514-396-9304
Ligne sans frais: 888-323-8834
info@aopq.ca
www.aopq.ca
Nom précédent: Association nationale des orthésistes du pied
Aperçu: *Dimension:* petite; *Envergure:* provinciale
Mission: • protéger et à développer des intérêts professionnels, moraux, sociaux et économiques des membres

L'Association des orthopédagogues du Québec inc. (ADOQ)
#410, 7400, boul. les Galeries d'Anjou, Montréal QC H1M 3M2
Tél: 514-374-5883; *Téléc:* 514-355-4159
Ligne sans frais: 888-444-0222
info@ladoq.ca
www.adoq.ca
Aperçu: *Dimension:* petite; *Envergure:* provinciale; Organisme sans but lucratif; fondée en 1988
Mission: Promouvoir les services d'orthopédagogie, assurer un programme de formation continue de grande qualité
Membre(s) du bureau directeur:
Christine Pruneau, Présidente
Jacynthe Turgeon, Vice-présidente
Finances: *Budget de fonctionnement annuel:* $50,000-$100,000
8 bénévole(s)

Canadian Associations

Membre: 760; *Montant de la cotisation:* 100$ membre actif; 50$ étudiant; *Comités:* Conseil d'administration; Comités de section (situés dans différentes régions au Québec); Visibilité et Publicité; Formation continue; Site web; Revue
Activités: Colloque annuel; programme de formation continue comprenant de nombreuses activités; café-rencontre; code de déontologie et revue semestrielle remis gratuitement aux membres; publicité; annuaire offert aux membres; références pour la pratique privée; service de secrétariat; *Bibliothèque:* Centre de ressources didactiques; rendez-vous

Association des orthophonistes et des audiologistes du Manitoba *See* Manitoba Speech & Hearing Association

Association des orthophonistes et des audiologistes du Nouveau-Brunswick *See* New Brunswick Association of Speech-Language Pathologists & Audiologists

Association des otpiciens du Nouveau-Brunswick *See* Opticians Association of New Brunswick

L'Association des paramédics du Nouveau-Brunswick *See* Paramedic Association of New Brunswick

Association des parents ayants droit de Yellowknife (APADY)

CP 2103, Yellowknife NT X1A 2P5
Tél: 867-446-8285
apady@franco-nord.com
www.apady.ca
Aperçu: *Dimension:* petite; *Envergure:* locale; fondée en 1989 surveillé par Fédération franco-ténoise
Mission: Pour promouvoir l'éducation de la langue française à Yellowknife
Membre(s) du bureau directeur:
Jacques Lamarche, Président, 867-446-8285
Membre: *Montant de la cotisation:* 5$; *Critères d'admissibilite:* Parents de l'ecole Allain St-Cyr et de la garderie Plein Soleil

Association des parents ayants droit de Yellowknife (APADY)

CP 2103, Yellowknife NT X1A 2P7
Tél: 867-446-8285
apady@franco-nord.com
apady.ca
Nom précédent: Association des parents francophones de Yellowknife
Aperçu: *Dimension:* petite; *Envergure:* provinciale
Mission: Les parents ayants droit de Yellowknife interviennent pour mettre en place toutes les conditions indispensables à la prestation de services d'éducation de qualité en français favorisant l'épanouissement de leurs enfants et la transmission de l'identité canadienne-française
Affliation(s): Commission nationale des parents francophones; La Fédération Franco-TéNOise
Membre(s) du bureau directeur:
Jacques Lamarche, Président
Membre: *Montant de la cotisation:* 5$

Association des parents catholiques du Québec (APCQ)

5425 - 5e av, Montréal QC H1Y 2S8
Tél: 514-276-8068; *Téléc:* 514-948-2595
apcq406@bellnet.ca
www.apcqc.net
Aperçu: *Dimension:* grande; *Envergure:* provinciale; Organisme sans but lucratif; fondée en 1966
Mission: Regroupe des parents catholiques pour promouvoir et défendre leurs droits et leurs intérêts selon les valeurs catholiques en matière d'éducation, de famille, et de culture par l'information et la représentation de ses membres auprès de la population et des autorités civiles et religieuses
Membre de: Regroupement Inter-Organismes pour une politique familiale au Québec
Affliation(s): Organisation internationale de l'enseignement catholique (OIEC)
Membre(s) du bureau directeur:
Diane Joyal, Présidente
Finances: *Budget de fonctionnement annuel:* $50,000-$100,000
25 bénévole(s)
Membre: 4 000; *Montant de la cotisation:* 12$; *Critères d'admissibilite:* Familles; *Comités:* Éducation de la foi; comité provincial d'enseignement privé; carrefour famille-Québec
Activités: Secrétariat permanent; Périodique; Colloques; Conférences; Cours; Congrès parents-jeunes; Pétitions; Rédactions de mémoires; *Service de conférenciers:* Oui
Publications:
• Famille Québec [a publication of the Association des parents catholiques du Québec]
Type: Journal

Association des parents d'enfants handicapés du Témiscamingue inc.

#1, 3, rue Industrielle, Ville-Marie QC JV9 1S3
Tél: 819-622-1126; *Téléc:* 819-622-0021
apeht@cablevision.qc.ca
Aperçu: *Dimension:* petite; *Envergure:* locale
Mission: Offrir des services d'aide aux personnes vivant avec un handicap physique et intellectuel ainsi qu'à leurs familles.
Affliation(s): Association du Québec pour l'intégration sociale

Association des parents et amis de la personne atteinte de maladie mentale Rive-Sud (APAMM-RS)

#206, 10, boul Churchill, Greenfield Park QC J4V 2L7
Tél: 450-776-0524; *Crisis Hot-Line:* 450-679-8689
apammrs.org
www.facebook.com/apammrs
Aperçu: *Dimension:* petite; *Envergure:* locale; Organisme sans but lucratif
Mission: Aide des familles qui sont touchées par la maladie mentale et soutient des recherches sur les maladies mentales
Membre(s) du bureau directeur:
Patricia Arnaud, Directrice Générale
Guy Savoy, Président, Conseil d'administration
Membre(s) du personnel: 5
Membre: *Montant de la cotisation:* 20$ par membres; $35 par famille

Association des parents et des handicapés de la Rive-Sud métropolitaine (APHRSM)

#200, 2545, rue De Lorimier, Longueuil QC J4K 3P7
Tél: 450-674-5224; *Téléc:* 450-674-8594
aphrsm@hotmail.com
www.aphrsm.org
Aperçu: *Dimension:* petite; *Envergure:* locale
Mission: Pour offrir aux personnes souffrant de handicaps mentaux et physiques à des activités récréatives et d'éviter l'isolement
Membre(s) du bureau directeur:
Stephanie Coutellier, Directrice générale
Membre: *Critères d'admissibilite:* Toutes personne qui a un handicap physique ou mental
Activités: Sports; Chorale; Vacances; Ateliers; *Evénements de sensibilisation:* Semaine québécoise de la déficience intellectuelle (mars)

Association des parents francophones de la Colombie-Britannique *Voir* Fédération des parents francophones de Colombie-Britannique

Association des parents francophones de Yellowknife *Voir* Association des parents ayants droit de Yellowknife

Association des parents fransaskois (APF) / Fransaskois Parents Association

910, 5, rue est, Saskatoon SK S7N 2C6
Tél: 306-653-7444; *Téléc:* 306-653-7001
Ligne sans frais: 855-653-7444
apf.direction@sasktel.net
www.parentsfransaskois.ca
www.facebook.com/148583571881687
Nom précédent: Association provinciale des parents fransaskois
Aperçu: *Dimension:* moyenne; *Envergure:* provinciale; fondée en 1982
Mission: Assurer la mise sur pied et le développement d'un système scolaire complet de qualité, conforme au Projet éducatif de la communauté des familles fransaskoises
Membre de: Commission nationale des parents francophones
Membre(s) du bureau directeur:
Danielle Raymond, Directrice générale
Brigitte Chassé, Agente à la petite enfance
apf.info@sasktel.net
Finances: *Budget de fonctionnement annuel:* $250,000-$500,000
Membre(s) du personnel: 5; 50 bénévole(s)
Membre: 1200; *Montant de la cotisation:* 5 $ par famille; *Critères d'admissibilite:* Parents francophones d'enfants d'âge préscolaire & scolaire
Activités: Projet éducatif fransaskois; intégration culturelle; *Bibliothèque:* Centre de ressources éducatives à la petite enfance (CREPE); Bibliothèque publique

Association des pathologistes du Québec (APQ)

CP 216, Succ. Desjardins, #3000, 2, Complexe Desjardins, Montréal QC H5B 1G8
Tél: 514-350-5102; *Téléc:* 514-350-5152
Ligne sans frais: 800-561-0703
patho@fmsq.org
www.apq.qc.ca
Aperçu: *Dimension:* petite; *Envergure:* provinciale surveillé par Fédération des médecins spécialistes du Québec
Membre de: Fédération des médecins spécialistes du Québec
Membre(s) du bureau directeur:
Danielle Joncas, Directrice
Activités: Le Prix Pierre-Masson
Prix, Bouses:
• Prix Pierre-Masson (Prix)

Association des Pêcheurs de Longueuil

1895, rue Adoncour, Longueuil QC J4J 5G8
Tél: 514-726-1786
info@assopechelongueuil.ca
assopechelongueuil.ca
Aperçu: *Dimension:* petite; *Envergure:* locale; fondée en 2004
Mission: De promouvoir la pêche dans Longueuil
Membre(s) du bureau directeur:
Sylvain Latulippe, Président, Conseil d'administration
Membre: *Montant de la cotisation:* 15$
Activités: Tournois de pêche

Association des pédiatres du Québec

CP 216, Succ. Desjardins, #3000, 2, Complexe Desjardins, Montréal QC H5B 1G8
Tél: 514-350-5000; *Téléc:* 514-350-5100
Ligne sans frais: 800-561-0703
www.fmsq.org
www.facebook.com/laFMSQ
twitter.com/FMSQ
www.youtube.com/user/LaFMSQ
Aperçu: *Dimension:* moyenne; *Envergure:* provinciale surveillé par Fédération des médecins spécialistes du Québec
Membre de: Fédération des Médcins Spécialistes du Québec (FMSQ)
Affliation(s): Association des allergologues et immunologues du Québec; Association des anesthésiologistes du Québec; Association des médecins biochimistes du Québec; Association des cardiologues du Québec; Association des chirurgiens cardio-vasculaires et thoraciques du Québec; Association québécoise de chirurgie; Association des chirurgiens vasculaires du Québec; Association des spécialistes en chirurgie plastique et esthétique du Québec; Association des dermatologistes du Québec; Association des médecins endocrinologues du Québec; Association des gastro-entérologues du Québec
Membre(s) du bureau directeur:
Gaétan Barrette, Président
Membre: 35 associations

Association des pères gais de Montréal inc. (APGM) / Gay Fathers of Montréal Inc.

4245, rue Laval, Montréal QC H2W 2J6
Tél: 514-528-8424; *Téléc:* 514-528-9708
peresgais@gmail.com
www.algi.qc.ca/asso/apgm/
Aperçu: *Dimension:* petite; *Envergure:* locale; Organisme sans but lucratif; fondée en 1984
Mission: Regrouper les hommes qui sont à la fois pères et gais; offrir support et aide aux hommes gais soucieux d'éduquer leurs enfants; permettre au père gai de se situer face à la condition de vie au moyen d'échanges, de discussion et d'information; promouvoir la condition des pères gais et la défense de leurs intérêts communs
Membre: *Montant de la cotisation:* 20$; *Critères d'admissibilite:* Etre père d'enfant naturel ou adoptif; se reconnaissant gai
Activités: Rencontres hebdomadaires;

Association des Perfusionnistes du Québec Inc. (APQI)

CP 65, Succ. Jean-Talon, Montréal QC H1S 2Z1
www.apqi.com
Aperçu: *Dimension:* petite; *Envergure:* provinciale
Membre(s) du bureau directeur:
Julie Gagnon, Présidente, 514-413-0617
Alina Parapuf, Vice-Présidente, 514-415-7622
Marie-Eve Dufort, Trésorière
Catherine Derome, Secrétaire

Association des personnes accidentées cérébro-vasculaires, aphasiques et traumatisées crânio-cérébrales du Bas-Saint-Laurent (ACVA-TCC du BSL)

391, boul Jessop, Rimouski QC G5L 1M9

Tel: 418-723-2345; *Fax:* 418-723-2220
Toll-Free: 888-302-2282
acvatcc@globetrotter.net
www.acvatcc.com
Overview: A small local organization founded in 1991
Mission: To support persons in the Bas-Saint-Laurent region who have been affected by brain injury, stroke, or aphasia
Member of: Regroupement des associations de personnes traumatisées craniocérébrales du Québec / Coalition of Associations of Craniocerebral Trauma in Quebec
Chief Officer(s):
Grazuela Ramassamy, Coordinatrice
Membership: *Member Profile:* Persons in the Bas-Saint-Laurent area of Québec who have experience a traumatic brain injury, a stroke, or who are aphasic; Family members of person living with brian injury, stroke, or aphasia
Activities: Informing the public about brain injury, stroke, & aphasia; Advocating on behalf of persons affected by brain injury, stroke, & aphasia; Offering support groups; Engaging in advocacy activities

Association des personnes en perte d'autonomie de Chibougamau inc. & Jardin des aînés

101, av du Parc, Chibougamau QC G8P 3A5
Tél: 418-748-4411
jardindesaines@tlb.sympatico.ca
Aperçu: *Dimension:* petite; *Envergure:* locale
Membre(s) du bureau directeur:
Chantal Lessard, Directrice générale

Association des personnes handicapées de Charlevoix inc. (APHC)

342, Rte 138, Saint-Hilarion QC G0A 3V0
Tél: 418-457-3760; *Téléc:* 418-457-3901
info@aphcharlevoix.com
www.aphcharlevoix.com
Nom précédent: Association des handicapées de Charlevoix
Aperçu: *Dimension:* petite; *Envergure:* locale; fondée en 1978
Mission: Regrouper régionalement les personnes handicapées du Comté de Charlevoix afin de permettre leur intégration pleine et entière à la collectivité dans toutes les sphères d'activités du milieu, et à tous les niveaux
Membre(s) du bureau directeur:
Robert Thivierge, Président
Finances: *Budget de fonctionnement annuel:* $50,000-$100,000
Membre(s) du personnel: 2; 50 bénévole(s)
Membre: 215; *Montant de la cotisation:* 5$ pour 1 an; 12$ pour 3 ans; *Critères d'admissibilite:* Personnes handicapées physiques

Association des personnes handicapées de la Rive-Sud Ouest (APHRSO)

100, rue Ste-Marie, La Prairie QC J5R 1E8
Tél: 450-659-6519; *Téléc:* 450-659-6510
info@aphrso.org
www.aphrso.org
www.facebook.com/aphrso
Aperçu: *Dimension:* petite; *Envergure:* locale; Organisme sans but lucratif; fondée en 1980
Mission: Promotion, intégration et défense des droits des personnes handicapées
Affliation(s): Groupement des Associations personnes handicapées Rive-Sud Montréal
Membre(s) du bureau directeur:
Priscille Arel, Présidente
Nancy Côté, Directrice
Finances: *Fonds:* ASSM; Centraide; EEC (emploi été); revenue des membres; SQPH; Municipalités; Autres
Membre: 219; *Critères d'admissibilite:* Personnes handicapées
Activités: Loisirs pour personnes handicapées; *Bibliothèque* rendez-vous

Association des personnes handicapées physiques et sensorielles du secteur Joliette (APHPSSJ)

200, rue de Salaberry, Local 134, Joliette QC J6E 4G1
Tel: 450-759-3322; *Fax:* 450-759-8749
Toll-Free: 888-756-3322
APHPSSJ@cepap.ca
www.aphpssj.com
Previous Name: Association of Physically Disabled Joliette - L'Assomption; Association of People with Physical Disabilities Joliette
Overview: A small local organization founded in 1977
Mission: To promote the rights of people with physical & sensory disabilities in the Joliette region; To encourage social intergration of disabled people
Member of: Regroupement des associations de personnes traumatisées craniocérébrales du Québec / Coalition of Associations of Craniocerebral Trauma in Quebec
Chief Officer(s):
Jocelyn Picard, Président
Jacynthe Arseneau, 1ère Vice-président
Michel Lacourse, 2e Vice-président
François Gagnon, Secretaire
Murielle Desrosiers, Trèsorière
Finances: *Funding Sources:* Membership fees; Grants; Fundraising
Staff Member(s): 6; 60 volunteer(s)
Membership: 300; *Member Profile:* People with physical & sensory disabilities in Joliette, St-Felix-de-Valois, St. Ligouri, Saint-Esprit, St-Jacques, St-Alexis Ste-Marie-Salome, & Lanaudière, Québec
Activities: Advocating on behalf of persons with physical & sensory disabilities; Offering home support services; Organizing recreational activities; Providing psychosocial services; Offering information services; Providing accompaniment for disabled persons to various activities; Coordinating support groups, for persons with aphasia, Parkinson's disease, & brian injury
Publications:
• Dynamic Player
Type: Newsletter
Profile: Association updates, announcements, & forthcoming activities

Association des personnes handicapés visuels de l'Estrie, inc (AHVEI)

838, rue St-Charles, Sherbrooke QC J1H 4Z2
Tél: 819-566-4848; *Téléc:* 819-566-5913
aphve@cooptel.qc.ca
www.aphve.com
Aperçu: *Dimension:* petite; *Envergure:* locale; Organisme sans but lucratif; fondée en 1991
Mission: Favoriser l'intégration sociale des personnes handicapées visuelles; promouvoir les droits et intérêts des personnes handicapées visuelles; sensibiliser la population à la problématique du handicap visuel
Affliation(s): Regroupement des aveugles et amblyopes du Québec
Membre(s) du bureau directeur:
Denis Barrette, Président
Finances: *Budget de fonctionnement annuel:* Moins de $50,000; *Fonds:* Gouvernement provincial
Membre(s) du personnel: 1; 10 bénévole(s)
Membre: 115; *Montant de la cotisation:* $5; *Critères d'admissibilite:* Personnes hancicapées visuelles
Activités: conférences; entrevues; émissions de radio et télévision; animation de groupes de personnes âgées handicapées visuelles; rencontres d'information; *Bibliothèque*
Publications:
• Journal Nouveau Regard
Type: Newsletter; *Frequency:* Quarterly; *Editor:* Marie Claude Guay, Hélène Dubois

Association des personnes hanicapées de la Vallée du Richelieu (APHVR)

221, rue Brunelle, Beloeil QC J3G 2M9
Tél: 450-464-7445; *Téléc:* 450-464-6049
aphvr.org
Aperçu: *Dimension:* petite; *Envergure:* locale; fondée en 1981
Mission: Aider ses membres à accroître leur qualité de vie et informer le public sur les problèmes rencontrés par les personnes handicapées

Association des personnes intéressées à l'aphasie *Voir* Association des personnes intéressées à l'aphasie et à l'accident vasculaire cérébral

Association des personnes intéressées à l'aphasie et à l'accident vasculaire cérébral (APIA)

#A07, 525, boul Wilfrid-Hamel, Québec QC G1M 2S8
Tél: 418-647-3684; *Téléc:* 418-647-1925
apia-avc@bellnet.ca
www.apia-avc.org
Nom précédent: Association des personnes intéressées à l'aphasie
Aperçu: *Dimension:* petite; *Envergure:* provinciale; Organisme sans but lucratif; fondée en 1985
Mission: Répondre à toute demande d'information sur l'aphasie; sensibiliser le public à la problématique de l'aphasie; promouvoir et défendre les droits des personnes aphasiques; améliorer la qualité de vie des personnes aphasiques et de leurs proches
Membre(s) du bureau directeur:
Claude Hébert, Co-Présidente
Claudia-Lynn Pelletier, Co-Présidente
Membre(s) du personnel: 2
Activités: *Service de conférenciers:* Oui

L'Association des Personnes Seules de Montréal *See* Single Persons Association of Montréal

Association des personnes traumatisées cranio-cérébrales de la Gaspésie et des Iles-de-la-Madeleine inc. *Voir* Association des TCC (le traumatisme cranio-cérébral) et ACV (un accident vasculaire cérébral) de la Gaspésie et des Iles-de-la-Madeleine Inc.

Association des pharmaciens des établissements de santé du Québec (APES)

#320, 4050, rue Molson, Montréal QC H1Y 3N1
Tél: 514-286-0776; *Téléc:* 514-286-1081
info@apesquebec.org
www.apesquebec.org
Aperçu: *Dimension:* moyenne; *Envergure:* provinciale; fondée en 1963
Membre(s) du bureau directeur:
Linda Vaillant, Directrice générale
France Boucher, Directrice générale adjointe
Finances: *Budget de fonctionnement annuel:* $500,000-$1.5 Million
Membre(s) du personnel: 5; 100 bénévole(s)
Membre: 1 300; *Montant de la cotisation:* 1.3% du salaire hebdomadaire de base

L'Association des pharmaciens des établissements du Québec *See* Canadian Society of Hospital Pharmacists

Association des pharmaciens du Canada *See* Canadian Pharmacists Association

Association des pharmaciens du Nouveau-Brunswick *See* New Brunswick Pharmacists' Association

Association des physiatres du Québec (APQ)

CP 216, Succ. Desjardins, #3000, 2, Complexe Desjardins, Montréal QC H5B 1G8
Tél: 514-350-5119; *Téléc:* 514-350-5147
apq@fmsq.org
www.fmsq.org
Aperçu: *Dimension:* petite; *Envergure:* provinciale surveillé par Fédération des médecins spécialistes du Québec
Mission: Pour ouvrer à la prévention, au diagnostic et au traitement médical des douleurs et des troubles de l'appareil locomoteur (la colonne vertébrale, les os, les muscles, les tendons, les articulations, les vaisseaux et le cerveau)
Membre de: Féderation des Médecins Spécialistes du Québec (FMSQ)
Membre(s) du bureau directeur:
Claude Bouthillier, Président
Membre: 66

Association des physiciens et ingénieurs biomédicaux du Québec (APIBQ)

1817, boul des Laurentides, Laval QC H7M 2P7
www.apibq.ca
Aperçu: *Dimension:* petite; *Envergure:* provinciale; fondée en 1971
Mission: Promouvoir la production et la diffusion de connaissances en lien avec la technologie médicale; assurer l'utilisation sécuritaire de celle-ci pour le bénéfice de la population; favoriser la synergie entre ses membres
Membre(s) du bureau directeur:
Claude Pérusse, Président
claude.perusse.agence16@ssss.gouv.qc.ca
Membre: *Critères d'admissibilite:* Ingénieurs, physiciens et autres professionnels oeuvrant dans le domaine de la santé; *Comités:* Étudiant; Radioprotection; Sécurité électrique; Terminologie; Bonnes pratiques en génie biomédical; Certification; Formation continue; Mentorat

Association des Physiques Québécois (APQ)

529, rue Delorme, Granby QC J2J 2C9
Tél: 450-991-1174; *Téléc:* 450-991-1184
www.apquebec.com
Aperçu: *Dimension:* petite; *Envergure:* provinciale surveillé par Canadian Bodybuilding Federation
Membre de: Canadian Bodybuilding Federation; International Federation of Bodybuilding
Membre(s) du bureau directeur:
Yves Desbiens, Director technique
photoyd@videotron.ca
Joe Spinello, Directeur des juges
spinellojoe@hotmail.com

L'Association des pilotes d'Air Canada *See* Air Canada Pilots Association

Association des pilotes de brousse du Québec *Voir* Association des Aviateurs et Pilotes de Brousse du Québec

Association des pilotes fédéraux du Canada *See* Canadian Federal Pilots Association

Association des pilotes maritimes du Canada *See* Canadian Marine Pilots' Association

Association des planificateurs de retraite du Canada *See* Retirement Planning Association of Canada

Association des plongeurs de Chibougamau

535, 4e Rue, Chibougamau QC G8P 1S4
Aperçu: *Dimension:* petite; *Envergure:* locale

Association des pneumologues de la province de Québec (APPQ)

#3000, 2, Complexe Desjardins, Montréal QC H5B 1G8
Tél: 514-350-5117; *Téléc:* 514-350-5153
appq@fmsq.org
www.fmsq.org
Aperçu: *Dimension:* petite; *Envergure:* provinciale surveillé par Fédération des médecins spécialistes du Québec
Mission: Promouvoir les intérêts professionnels et économiques de ses membres; se préoccuper du maintien de leur compétence; se prononcer sur les problématiques de la pneumologie dans les meilleurs intérêts de la population
Membre(s) du bureau directeur:
Dionne Raymonde, Directrice
Alain Beaupré, Président
Membre: 240

Association des policières et policiers provinciaux du Québec (ind.) (APPQ) / Québec Provincial Police Association (Ind.)

1981, rue Léonard-De Vinci, Sainte-Julie QC J3E 1Y9
Tél: 450-922-5414; *Téléc:* 450-922-5417
www.appq-sq.qc.ca
www.youtube.com/watch?v=2AWQQrHbx20
Aperçu: *Dimension:* moyenne; *Envergure:* provinciale; Organisme sans but lucratif; fondée en 1966
Mission: Promouvoir le bien-être de ses membres et voir à leurs intérêts sociaux, moraux et culturels
Membre(s) du bureau directeur:
Pierre Veilleux, Président
Jocelyn Boucher, Vice-président, Ressources humaines
Luc Fournier, Vice-président, Finances
Jacques Painchaud, Vice-président, Discipline et déontologie
Pierre Lemay, Vice-président, Griefs et formation
Daniel Rolland, Vice-président, Ress. matérielles et santé et sécurité du travail
Finances: *Budget de fonctionnement annuel:* $1.5 Million-$3 Million
Membre(s) du personnel: 18
Membre: 4 812; *Montant de la cotisation:* 746.20$
Activités: *Bibliothèque*

Association des policiers de Fredericton *See* Fredericton Police Association

Association des policiers de l'Ontario *See* Police Association of Ontario

Association des policiers de la Nouvelle-Écosse *See* Police Association of Nova Scotia

Association des policiers de la région de Peel *See* Peel Regional Police Association

Association des policiers de Medicine Hat *See* Medicine Hat Police Association

Association des policiers des chemins de fer nationaux du Canada (ind.) *See* Canadian National Railways Police Association (Ind.)

Association des pompiers autochtones de Canada *See* Aboriginal Firefighters Association of Canada

Association des pompiers de Laval

374, boul Cartier Ouest, Laval QC H7N 2K2
Tél: 450-663-3025; *Téléc:* 450-663-3037
info@pompierslaval.org
www.apl.tel
Aperçu: *Dimension:* petite; *Envergure:* locale; fondée en 1979
Mission: Rassembler les membres en un groupement qui les représente et parle en leur nom; revaloriser les membres sur le plan physique, moral et intellectuel; promouvoir et défendre les intérets économiques, sociaux et moraux des membres.
Membre(s) du bureau directeur:
Richard Carpentier, Président
r.carpentier@pompierslaval.org
Luc Gauthier, Vice-Président, Santé Sécurité
l.gauthier@pompierslaval.org
Hugo Lamarche, Vice-Président, Griefs et Secrétariat
h.lamarche@pompierslaval.org
Claude Gagné, Vice-Président, Finances et Activités Sociales
c.gagne@pompierslaval.org

Association des Pompiers de Montréal inc. (APM) / Montréal Firefighters' Association Inc.

2655, place Chassé 2e étage, Montréal QC H1Y 2C3
Tél: 514-527-9691; *Téléc:* 514-527-8119
info@adpm.qc.ca
adpm.qc.ca
Aperçu: *Dimension:* moyenne; *Envergure:* locale; Organisme sans but lucratif; fondée en 1920
Membre(s) du bureau directeur:
Ronald Martin, Président
rmartin@adpm.qc.ca
Chris Ross, Vice-président
Finances: *Budget de fonctionnement annuel:* $1.5 Million-$3 Million
Membre: 2290; *Montant de la cotisation:* 754$
Activités: Syndicales; *Stagiaires:* Oui

Association des pompiers professionnels de l'Ontario (ind.) *See* Ontario Professional Fire Fighters Association

Association des Poneys Welsh & Cob au Québec / Québec Welsh Pony & Cob Association

a/s Diane Belhumeur, 354, rang 3, Kingsey Falls QC J0A 1B0
Tel: 819-358-5495; *Fax:* 819-358-5435
welshquebec@hotmail.com
www.apwcq.com
www.facebook.com/APWCQ
Overview: A small provincial organization overseen by Welsh Pony & Cob Society of Canada
Mission: Pour promouvoir et développer la race de poney Welsh au Québec
Chief Officer(s):
Michel Bougie, Président
boogie@telwarwick.net
Diane Belhumeur, Secrétaire
Membership: 31; *Member Profile:* Personnes impliquées dans la race de poney Welsh au Québec

Association des Praticiens de la santé naturelle du Canada *See* Natural Health Practitioners of Canada Association

Association des praticiens en éthique du Canada *See* Ethics Practitioners' Association of Canada

Association des presses universitaires canadiennes *See* Association of Canadian University Presses

Association des procureurs de cours municipales du Québec (APCMQ)

700, av Hôtel-de-ville, Saint-Hyacinthe QC J2S 5B2
Tél: 450-778-8316; *Téléc:* 450-778-2514
www.apcmq.com
Aperçu: *Dimension:* moyenne; *Envergure:* provinciale; fondée en 1998
Mission: Pour défendre les intérêts des avocats qui travaillent dans les tribunaux municipaux
Membre(s) du bureau directeur:
Normand Sauvageau, Président, Conseil d'administration
n.sauvageau@ville.laval.qc.ca
Membre: 68; *Montant de la cotisation:* 85$ Membre officiel; 60$ Membre honoraire; *Critères d'admissibilité:* Tout procureur agissant en poursuite devant une cour municipale
Activités: Réunions; Formations

Association des procureurs de la couronne de l'Ontario *See* Ontario Crown Attorneys Association

Association des producteurs de films et de télévision du Québec (APFTQ)

Edifice City Centre, #1030, 1450, rue City Councillors, Montréal QC H3A 2E6
Tél: 514-397-8600; *Téléc:* 514-392-0232
info@apftq.qc.ca
www.apftq.qc.ca
Aperçu: *Dimension:* moyenne; *Envergure:* provinciale; Organisme sans but lucratif; fondée en 1966
Mission: Représente ses membres auprès des gouvernements et organismes et encourage la coopération étroite entre tous les intervenants de l'industrie cinématographique et télévisuelle
Membre(s) du bureau directeur:
Claire Samson, President and CEO
Membre(s) du personnel: 12
Membre: 130 corporations; *Critères d'admissibilite:* Entreprise de production independante; *Comités:* Finances; Relations de travail
Activités: Représentation, relations de travail, communications; *Stagiaires:* Oui

Association des producteurs maraîchers du Québec (APMQ) / Québec Produce Growers Association (QPGA)

905, rue du Marché-Central, Montréal QC H4N 1K2
Tél: 514-387-8319
Autres numéros: www.mangezquebec.com
apmq@apmquebec.com
www.apmquebec.com
Aperçu: *Dimension:* petite; *Envergure:* provinciale
Mission: Favorise le développement du secteur horticole québécois et veille à la promotion des fruits et légumes cultivés au Québec, sur le marché local et sur les marchés extérieurs.
Membre: 450

Association des produits forestiers du Canada *See* Forest Products Association of Canada

L'Association des produits forestiers du Nouveau-Brunswick *See* New Brunswick Forest Products Association Inc.

Association des professeur(e)s à temps partiel de l'Université d'Ottawa (APTPUO) / Association of Part-Time Professors of the University of Ottawa

#124, 85 University St., Ottawa ON K1N 6N5
Tél: 613-562-5800; *Téléc:* 613-562-5153
info@aptpuo.ca
www.aptpuo.ca
twitter.com/APTPUO
Aperçu: *Dimension:* petite; *Envergure:* locale; fondée en 1986
Mission: promouvoir et protéger les droits et privilèges des professeurs à temps partiel travaillant sur les campus de l'Université d'Ottawa.
Membre(s) du bureau directeur:
Greer Knox, Président
Lawrence Harris, Vice-Président
Susan L'Heureux, Vice-Présidente
Membre(s) du personnel: 1
Membre: 2,500; *Comités:* Comités Mixtes: Harcèlement sexuel, Régime de retraite, Santé et sécurité; Sécurité sur le campus; Services alimentaires; Stationnement; Enseignement
Prix, Bouses:
• Prix d'excellence (Prix)
Décerné à un professeur à temps partiel pour l'excellence en enseignement, les activités de recherche et la participation à la vie universitaire.

Association des professeures et professeurs à temps partiel de l'Université Concordia *See* Concordia University Part-time Faculty Association

Association des professeures et professeurs de la Faculté de médecine de l'Université de Sherbrooke (APPFMUS)

Faculté de médecine, 3001, 12e av nord, Sherbrooke QC J1H 5N4
Tél: 819-564-5257; *Téléc:* 819-564-5394
appfmus-med@USherbrooke.ca
www.usherbrooke.ca/appfmus/
Aperçu: *Dimension:* petite; *Envergure:* locale; fondée en 1974
Mission: Représente plus de 300 professeures et professeurs oeuvrant en Médecine, en Sciences fondamentales ou en Sciences infirmières à la Faculté de médecine de l'Université de Sherbrooke
Membre de: Fédération québécoise des professeures et professeurs des universités du Québec
Affliation(s): Association canadienne des professeurs et professeures d'universités
Membre(s) du bureau directeur:
Yves Patenaude, Président
Finances: *Budget de fonctionnement annuel:* $50,000-$100,000
Membre(s) du personnel: 1
Membre: 300
Activités: Voir à l'application du protocole d'entente et défendre les intérêts des membres;

Disponible sous forme de listes ou d'étiquettes:
416-644-6479, ou Ligne sans frais: 1-866-433-4739

L'Association des professeurs d'allemand des universités canadiennes ***See*** Canadian Association of University Teachers of German

Association des professeurs d'anglais du Québec ***See*** Association of Teachers of English in Quebec

Association des professeurs de Campus Notre-Dame-de-Foy

5000, rue Clément-Lockquell, Saint-Augustin-de-Desmaures QC G3A 1B3
Tél: 418-877-3217; *Téléc:* 418-872-3448
Aperçu: *Dimension:* petite; *Envergure:* locale
Membre de: Fédération autonome du collégial
Finances: *Budget de fonctionnement annuel:* Moins de $50,000
Membre: 400; *Montant de la cotisation:* .95% du salaire brut; *Critères d'admissibilité:* Professeurs au cégep

Association des professeurs de Collège Communautaire de Vancouver ***See*** Vancouver Community College Faculty Association

Association des professeurs de Dalhousie ***See*** Dalhousie Faculty Association

Association des professeurs de français des universités et collèges canadiens (APFUCC) / Canadian Association of University & College Teachers of French (CAUCTF)

Département de Françaises, Université de Simon Fraser, 8888 University Dr., Burnaby BC V5A 1S6
www.apfucc.net
Aperçu: *Dimension:* moyenne; *Envergure:* nationale; fondée en 1958
Mission: Constitue sur le plan national un lieu de recontre destiné à présentation de recherches individuelles ou collectives portant sur la langue français, les littératures et les civilisations de la francophonie; collabore avec des organismes ayant des objectifs similaires
Membre de: La Fédération canadienne des études humaines; La Fédération internationale des professeurs de français
Membre(s) du bureau directeur:
Jorge Calderon, Président
calderon@sfu.ca
Membre: *Montant de la cotisation:* 55$ professeur à plein temps; 25$ étudiant ou autre/professeur à la retraite
Prix, Bouses:
• Le Prix de l'APFUCC (Prix)
Décerné chaque année au meilleur ouvrage et au meilleur article publiés au cours de l'année précédente par les membres de l'APFUCC
Meetings/Conferences: • Congrès 2015 de l'Association des professeurs de français des universités et collèges canadiens, Mai, 2015, Université d'Ottawa, Ottawa, ON

Association des professeurs de Kwantlen ***See*** Kwantlen Faculty Association

Association des professeurs de l'École Polytechnique de Montréal (APEP)

CP 6079, Succ. Centre-Ville, Montréal QC H3C 3A7
Tél: 514-340-4979; *Téléc:* 514-340-5215
apep@polymtl.ca
www.apep.polymtl.ca
Aperçu: *Dimension:* petite; *Envergure:* locale
Membre(s) du bureau directeur:
Christian Mascle, Président

Association des professeurs de l'Université Acadia ***See*** Acadia University Faculty Association

Association des professeurs de l'Université Bishop ***See*** Association of Professors of Bishop's University

Association des professeurs de l'Université Brock ***See*** Brock University Faculty Association

Association des professeurs de l'Université Concordia ***See*** Concordia University Faculty Association

Association des professeurs de l'Université d'Athabasca ***See*** Athabasca University Faculty Association

Association des professeurs de l'université d'Ottawa (APUO) / Association of Professors of the University of Ottawa

#348, Centre Universitaire, Ottawa ON K1N 6N5
Tél: 613-562-5800; *Téléc:* 613-562-5197
apuo@uottawa.ca
www.apuo.ca
Aperçu: *Dimension:* moyenne; *Envergure:* locale; fondée en 1976
Mission: L'association est l'agent négociateur exclusif de tous les 1130 employés qui font partie de l'unité de négociation qu'elle représente. L'unité comprend les professeurs (autres que les professeurs invités), les professeurs de langue, les conseillers, les bibliothécaires et certains chercheurs boursiers
Membre(s) du bureau directeur:
Christian Rouillard, Président, Études Politiques
Membre: 1130

Association des professeurs de l'Université de Brandon ***See*** Brandon University Faculty Association

Association des professeurs de l'Université de Calgary ***See*** University of Calgary Faculty Association

Association des professeurs de l'Université de l'Ile-du-Prince-Edouard ***See*** University of Prince Edward Island Faculty Association

Association des professeurs de l'Université de la Colombie-Britannique ***See*** University of British Columbia Faculty Association

Association des professeurs de l'Université de la Saskatchewan ***See*** University of Saskatchewan Faculty Association

Association des professeurs de l'Université de Lethbridge ***See*** University of Lethbridge Faculty Association

Association des professeurs de l'Université de Regina ***See*** University of Regina Faculty Association

Association des professeurs de l'Université de Toronto ***See*** University of Toronto Faculty Association

Association des professeurs de l'Université de Victoria ***See*** University of Victoria Faculty Association

Association des professeurs de l'Université de Winnipeg ***See*** University of Winnipeg Faculty Association

Association des professeurs de l'Université du Manitoba ***See*** University of Manitoba Faculty Association

Association des professeurs de l'Université Lakehead ***See*** Lakehead University Faculty Association

Association des professeurs de l'Université Laurentienne ***See*** Laurentian University Faculty Association

Association des professeurs de l'Université McMaster ***See*** McMaster University Faculty Association

Association des professeurs de l'Université Mount Saint Vincent ***See*** Mount Saint Vincent University Faculty Association

Association des professeurs de l'Université Queen's ***See*** Queen's University Faculty Association

Association des professeurs de l'Université Saint-François-Xavier ***See*** Saint Francis Xavier Association of University Teachers

Association des professeurs de l'Université Saint-Thomas ***See*** Faculty Association of University of Saint Thomas

Association des professeurs de l'Université Simon Fraser ***See*** Simon Fraser University Faculty Association

Association des professeurs de l'Université Trent ***See*** Trent University Faculty Association

Association des professeurs de l'Université Wilfrid-Laurier ***See*** Wilfrid Laurier University Faculty Association

Association des professeurs de l'Université Windsor ***See*** Windsor University Faculty Association

Association des professeurs de l'Université York ***See*** York University Faculty Association

Association des professeurs de Langara ***See*** Langara Faculty Association

Association des professeurs de Mount Allison ***See*** Mount Allison Faculty Association

Association des professeurs de musique enregistrés de l'Ontario ***See*** Ontario Registered Music Teachers' Association

Association des professeurs de Ryerson ***See*** Ryerson Faculty Association

Association des professeurs de sciences de l'Ontario ***See*** Science Teachers' Association of Ontario

Association des professeurs de sciences de Québec ***Voir*** Association pour l'enseignement de la science et de la technologie au Québec

Association des professeurs du Collège Camosun ***See*** Camosun College Faculty Association

Association des professeurs du Collège de Lakeland ***See*** Lakeland College Faculty Association

Association des professeurs du Collège de Medicine Hat ***See*** Faculty Association of Medicine Hat College

Association des professeurs du Collège de New Caledonia ***See*** Faculty Association of the College of New Caledonia

Association des professeurs du Collège Douglas ***See*** Douglas College Faculty Association

Association des professeurs du Collège Grant MacEwan ***See*** Grant MacEwan College Faculty Association

Association des professeurs du Collège Keyano ***See*** Keyano College Faculty Association

Association des professeurs du Collège Olds ***See*** Olds College Faculty Association

Association des professeurs du Collège Red Deer ***See*** Faculty Association of Red Deer College

Association des professeurs du SAIT ***See*** SAIT Academic Faculty Association

Association des professeurs(es) des collèges militaires du Canada ***See*** Canadian Military Colleges Faculty Association

Association des professionnels de la chanson et de la musique (APCM)

#401, 450 rue Rideau, Ottawa ON K1N 5Z4
Tél: 613-745-5642; *Téléc:* 613-745-9715
Ligne sans frais: 800-465-2726
communications@apcm.ca
www.apcm.ca
www.facebook.com/MusiqueAPCM
Aperçu: *Dimension:* petite; *Envergure:* provinciale; Organisme sans but lucratif; fondée en 1990
Mission: Afin de promouvoir et distribuer de la musique et des artistes francophones de l'Ontario et ailleurs au Canada
Membre de: Alliance Nationale de l'industrie musicale
Affliation(s): Alliance culturelle de l'Ontario
Membre(s) du bureau directeur:
Daniel Sauvé, Président
Anique Granger, Vice-Présidente
Membre(s) du personnel: 7
Membre: *Montant de la cotisation:* 50$ amis/associés; 75$ renouvèlement; 100$ toute nouvelle adhésion; 150$ groupe; *Critères d'admissibilité:* Auteurs, compositeurs et chanteurs francophones
Activités: Gala de la chanson et et la musique franco-ontariennes, semestriellement; Vendredis de la chanson francophone, chaque année; *Service de conférenciers:* Oui; *Bibliothèque:* Bibliothèque; Bibliothèque publique rendez-vous

Association des professionnels de la santé du Manitoba ***See*** Manitoba Association of Health Care Professionals

Association des professionnels des arts de la scène du Québec (APASQ)

#014, 2065, rue Pathenais, Montréal QC H2K 3T1
Tél: 514-523-4221; *Téléc:* 514-523-4418
Ligne sans frais: 877-523-4221
info@apasq.org
www.apasq.org
Aperçu: *Dimension:* petite; *Envergure:* provinciale; Organisme sans but lucratif; fondée en 1984
Mission: A pour mandat l'étude, la défense et le développement des intérêts économiques, sociaux, moraux et professionnels de ses membres; négocie des ententes avec les associations de producteurs; promeut et difffuse la scènographie québécoise. Incorporée sous la loi des syndicats professionnels et reconnue en vertu de la loi sur le statut professionnel et des conditions d'engagement des artistes de la scène, du disque et du cinéma
Membre de: L'Académie québécoise du théâtre
Affliation(s): Fédération nationale des communications (FNC)

Membre(s) du bureau directeur:
Michel Beauchemin, Directeur général
mbeauchemin@apasq.org
Claude Accolas, Président
Mathieu Marcil, Vice-président
Finances: *Fonds:* Emploi-Québec; Conseil des arts et des lettres du Québec; Conseil des arts du Canada
Membre(s) du personnel: 5
Membre: *Montant de la cotisation:* 25$ membre associé; 50$ membre adhérent; 100$ membre actif; *Critères d'admissibilité:* Artiste concepteur de tous les aspects des arts de la scène
Activités: Expositions; colloques; tables rondes; *Service de conférenciers:* Oui

Association des professionnels du chauffage (APC)

CP 37303, Succ. Beaubien, 1465, rue Jean-Talon est, Montréal QC H2E 3B5
Tél: 514-270-4944; *Téléc:* 514-270-5488
apc@poelesfoyers.ca
www.poelesfoyers.ca
Aperçu: *Dimension:* moyenne; *Envergure:* provinciale; fondée en 1983
Mission: Représenter l'industrie du chauffage d'appoint auprès des diverses instances et servir de centre d'informations aux consommateurs
Membre(s) du bureau directeur:
Ghislain Bélanger, Directeur général
Membre: *Montant de la cotisation:* Barème
Activités: Cours de formation

Association des professionnels en développement économique du Québec (APDEQ) / Economic Development Professionals Association of Québec

CP 297, Magog QC J1X 3W8
Tél: 819-868-9778; *Téléc:* 819-868-9907
Ligne sans frais: 800-361-8470
info@apdeq.qc.ca
www.apdeq.qc.ca
www.linkedin.com/companies/111964
twitter.com/apdeq
Nom précédent: Association des commissaires industriels du Québec (ACIQ)
Aperçu: *Dimension:* moyenne; *Envergure:* provinciale; fondée en 1959
Mission: Pour aider les artisans du Développement économique à acquérir des compétences et de la formation afin de les aider à réussir
Membre(s) du bureau directeur:
Patrice Gagnon, Directeur général
pgagnon@apdeq.qc.ca
Membre(s) du personnel: 3
Membre: 695; *Montant de la cotisation:* 450$ individuelle; 795$ multimembres; *Comités:* Formation; Communication; Services aux membres; Congrès; Activité printanière
Activités: *Stagiaires:* Oui

Association des professionnels en exposition du Québec (APEQ)

868, rue Brisette, Sainte-Julie QC J3E 2B1
Tél: 514-990-0224; *Téléc:* 450-922-7238
info@apeq.org
www.apeq.org
Aperçu: *Dimension:* moyenne; *Envergure:* provinciale; fondée en 1991
Mission: Faire reconnaître le rôle vital de l'industrie des expositions dans la vie économique, industrielle, culturelle et sociale au Québec; promouvoir, auprès du monde des affaires, l'efficacité des expositions comme moyen de promotion, de commercialisation et de communication; favoriser l'éducation de ses membres
Membre(s) du bureau directeur:
Jacques Perreault, Directeur général, 514-990-0224
info@apeq.org
Finances: *Budget de fonctionnement annuel:* $50,000-$100,000
Membre: 130; *Montant de la cotisation:* 395$; *Critères d'admissibilité:* Membres directeurs - directeurs, promoteurs d'expositions commerciales, professionnelles, industrielles ou publiques; membres fournisseurs - fournisseurs d'équipements et services; halls d'expositions, hôtels et autres sites de réunion; décorateurs et accessoiristes; fabricants de signalisation; spécialistes en logistique et services techniques; communicateurs; spécialistes en douanes et transport; service de personnel; autres services reliés à l'industrie; *Comités:* Activités; Congrès
Activités: *Listes de destinataires:* Oui

Association des professionnels en gestion philanthropique (APGP)

CP 22124, Succ. Iberville, 2505, boul. Rosemont, Montréal QC H1Y 3K8
Tél: 514-529-6865; *Téléc:* 800-217-1562
Ligne sans frais: 866-545-2747
apgp@apgp.com
www.apgp.com
www.facebook.com/apgpqc
twitter.com/APGP_
www.youtube.com/APGPphilanthropie
Aperçu: *Dimension:* petite; *Envergure:* locale; Organisme sans but lucratif; fondée en 1988
Mission: Promouvoir et développer la profession de gestionnaire en philanthropie
Membre(s) du bureau directeur:
Isabelle Morin, Présidente
France Locas, Vice-présidente
Maryse Beaulieu, Directrice générale
Finances: *Budget de fonctionnement annuel:* $100,000-$250,000
Membre: 380; *Montant de la cotisation:* 100$ étudiant; 150$ membre certifié; 300$ corporatif; *Critères d'admissibilité:* Professionnel en gestion philanthropique; consultant
Activités: Déjeuners-causeries

Association des professionnels en ressources humaines du Québec *Voir* Ordre des conseillers en ressources humaines agréés

Association des professionnels en SGRH *See* HRMS Professionals Association

Association des professionnels et superviseurs de Radio-Canada (APS SRC) / Association of Professionals & Supervisors of the Canadian Broadcasting Corporation (APS CBC)

1212, rue Panet, Montréal QC H2L 2Y7
Tél: 514-845-0411; *Téléc:* 450-687-2761
aps@apscbcsrc.org
www.apscbcsrc.org
Aperçu: *Dimension:* moyenne; *Envergure:* nationale
Membre(s) du bureau directeur:
Mario Poudrier, Président, 514-597-7214
Claude Beausoleil, Directeur général, 514-845-0411
beausoleil_claude@videotron.ca
Emilio D'Orazio, Secrétaire général, 418-205-2238
Hervé Lamarre, Trésorier, 514-597-3856
Gisèle Perron, Administratrice, 514-845-0411
aps@apscbcsrc.org
Membre: 6700; *Montant de la cotisation:* 5$; *Critères d'admissibilité:* Toutes les personnes de supervision de la Société Radio-Canada dont les tâches principales comportent la surveillance d'autres employés

Association des professionnels unis de la santé: Terre-Neuve et Labrador (ind.) *See* Association of Allied Health Professionals: Newfoundland & Labrador (Ind.)

Association des Projets charitables Islamiques (AICP) / Association of Islamic Charitable Projects

6691, av du Parc, Montréal QC H2V 4J1
Tel: 514-274-6194; *Fax:* 514-274-0011
www.aicp.ca
www.facebook.com/AicpCanada
twitter.com/AICP_CANADA
www.youtube.com/user/aicpmultimediamtl
Overview: A small local organization
Mission: Dénonce tout acte de terrorisme et promouvoit le support envers la communauté musulmane
Activities: Yearly pilgrimage trip; Madih group; marriage contracts; funerary services

Association des propriétaires canins de Prévost (APCP)

CP 604, Prévost QC J0R 1T0
Tél: 450 224-800
apcp_wouf@yahoo.ca
www.wouflaurentides.org
www.facebook.com/145223315575911
Aperçu: *Dimension:* petite; *Envergure:* locale
Membre: *Montant de la cotisation:* Cotisation annuelle de 5$

Association des propriétaires d'autobus du Québec (APAQ)

#107, 225, boul Charest est, Québec QC G1K 3G9
Tél: 418-522-7131; *Téléc:* 418-522-6455
apaq@apaq.qc.ca
www.apaq.qc.ca
Aperçu: *Dimension:* moyenne; *Envergure:* provinciale; Organisme sans but lucratif; fondée en 1926
Mission Défendre les intérêts des enterprises offrant des services de transport collectif de personnes par autobus et autocars
Membre de: Association de l'industrie touristique du Canada
Membre(s) du bureau directeur:
Sylvain Langis, Directeur général par intérim
sylvainlangis@apaq.qc.ca
Martin Bureau, Directeur, Communications & Marketing
martinbureau@apaq.qc.ca
Geneviève Frenette, Conseillère, Entreprises
genevievefrenette@apaq.qc.ca
Sophie Guay, Coordonnatrice, Comptabilité
sophieguay@apaq.qc.ca
Membre: 471 sociétés; *Montant de la cotisation:* Barème (entre 240$ et 8 000$); *Critères d'admissibilité:* Transportateurs par autocars; Vendeurs de produits touristiques pour les groupes; *Comités:* Scolaire; Interurbain/urbain/périurbain; Nolise-touristique; Spécialisé (aéroportuaire, abommement, médical, adapté)

Association des propriétaires de cinémas du Québec (APCQ)

5744, rue De Contrecoeur, Montréal QC H1K OE2
Tél: 514-493-9898; *Téléc:* 514-493-4848
Ligne sans frais: 877-540-1900
info@apcq.ca
www.apcq.com
www.linkedin.com/groups?gid=4416873
www.youtube.com/channel/UC7-iriaaDjcuw7i7fqIxiLg
Aperçu: *Dimension:* petite; *Envergure:* provinciale; Organisme sans but lucratif; fondée en 1932
Mission: Promouvoir et protéger les intérêts des propriétaires de cinémas au Québec
Membre de: Association cinématographique - Canada
Membre(s) du bureau directeur:
Carole Boudreault, Directrice générale
Vincent Guzzo, Président
Finances: *Budget de fonctionnement annuel:* $50,000-$100,000; *Fonds:* Cotisations des membres
Membre(s) du personnel: 1
Membre: 1-99; *Montant de la cotisation:* Barème

Association des propriétaires de machinerie lourde du Québec inc. (APMLQ)

Plaza Laval, #259, 2750, ch Ste-Foy, Sainte-Foy QC G1V 1V6
Tél: 418-650-1877; *Téléc:* 418-650-3361
Ligne sans frais: 800-268-7318
info@apmlq.com
www.apmlq.com
Aperçu: *Dimension:* moyenne; *Envergure:* provinciale; fondée en 1966
Mission: Informer et instruire ses membres au moyen de publications; maintenir un secrétariat permanent dans un but de liaison entre les membres et de contact avec différentes autorités; négocier avec les autorités publiques toutes ententes susceptibles de promouvoir les buts de l'Association et ceux de ses membres
Membre de: Conseil du Patronat du Québec
Affliation(s): Association des entrepreneurs en forage du Québec; Association des propriétaires de grues du Québec; Association des propriétaires de pompes à béton du Québec; Association des transporteurs épandeurs de pierre à chaux agricole du Québec; Regroupement des loueurs de véhicules du Québec
Membre(s) du bureau directeur:
Jacques Guimond, Président
Yvan Grenier, Directeur général
Membre(s) du personnel: 3
Membre: 500 individu; 108 associé; *Montant de la cotisation:* Barème

Association des propriétaires de Saint-Bruno

CP 81, Saint-Bruno-sur-Richelieu QC J3V 4P8
Tél: 450-461-0445
info@apsb.ca
apsb.ca
Aperçu: *Dimension:* petite; *Envergure:* locale
Mission: Fournir un voix pour les habitants de Saint-Bruno
Membre(s) du bureau directeur:
Claude Lamarre, Président, Conseil d'administration, 450-461-0445

Association des propriétaires du Québec inc. (APQ) / Quebec Landlords Association (QLA)
10720, boul St-Laurent, Montréal QC H3L 2P7
Tél: 514-382-9670; *Téléc:* 514-382-9676
Ligne sans frais: 888-382-9670
www.apq.org
www.facebook.com/141154527095
www.youtube.com/user/assoproprietaires
Aperçu: *Dimension:* moyenne; *Envergure:* provinciale; fondée en 1984
Mission: Défendre les droits et les intérêts des propriétaires de logements locatifs du Québec
Membre: 8,000

Association des propriétaires et administrateurs d'immeubles du Québec *Voir* BOMA Québec

Association des prospecteurs du Québec *Voir* Association de l'exploration minière de Québec

Association des psychiatres du Canada *See* Canadian Psychiatric Association

Association des psychologues du Manitoba *See* Psychological Association of Manitoba

Association des psychothérapeutes pastoraux du Canada (APPC) / Association of Pastoral Psychotherapists of Canada
892, rue Bernard Pilon, McMasterville QC J3G 5W8
Tél: 450-446-9058; *Téléc:* 450-446-9058
Aperçu: *Dimension:* petite; *Envergure:* nationale; fondée en 1985
Mission: Regrouper tous les psychothérapeutes pastoraux qui s'intéressent à la dimension pastorale en relation d'aide; assurer la spécificité de la psychothérapie pastorale afin d'empêcher tout empiètement dans les domaines connexes, et de sauvegarder ainsi l'autonomie de chaque profession concernée par la relation d'aide; veiller de manière efficace à la compétence vérifiée des psychothérapeutes pastoraux membres de l'Association pour éviter les dangers du charlatanisme; promouvoir la psychothérapie pastorale étant donnée son importance pour assurer le respect réel de la personne totale dans la relation d'aide
Activités: *Service de conférenciers:* Oui

Association des psychothérapeutes psychanalytiques du Québec
#310, 911, rue Jean-Talon Est, Montréal QC H2R 1V5
Tel: 514-383-1240
info@appq.com
www.appq.com
Overview: A small provincial organization founded in 1985
Mission: Développer chez ses membres un sentiment d'appartenance à un groupe partageant des vues théoriques et thérapeutiques communes basées sur la pensée psychanalytique
Chief Officer(s):
Thérèse Nadeau, Présidente
Marie Gauthier, Trésorière
Membership: 140; *Fees:* 55$; *Member Profile:* Détenir un diplôme de premier cycle en sciences humaines ou de la santé; posséder une solide culture psychanalytique
Activities: Journées cliniques; séminaires; colloques; soirées cinéma

Association des puéricultrices de la province de Québec
CP 464, Succ. Ahuntsic, Montréal QC H3L 3P1
Tél: 514-856-9130; *Téléc:* 514-856-0823
riopfq.com/membres/puericultrice.html
Nom précédent: Association des puéricultrices du Québec
Aperçu: *Dimension:* petite; *Envergure:* provinciale; fondée en 1948
Mission: Promouvoir, maintenir et défendre l'intérêt de ses membres et de la profession auprès d'autorités responsables

Association des puéricultrices du Québec *Voir* Association des puéricultrices de la province de Québec

Association des radiodiffuseurs communautaires du Québec (ARCQ)
#202, 2, rue Sainte-catherine Est, Montréal QC H2X 1K4
Tél: 514-287-9094; *Téléc:* 514-285-2814
radiovision.ca/arq/
Aperçu: *Dimension:* petite; *Envergure:* provinciale; Organisme sans but lucratif; fondée en 1979
Mission: Contribuer au progrès et à la renomée de la radiophonie communautaire
Membre(s) du bureau directeur:
Martin Bougie, Directeur général

Association des radiologistes du Québec
CP 216, Succ. Desjardins, Montréal QC H5B 1G8
Tél: 514-350-5129; *Téléc:* 514-350-5179
bureau@arq.qc.ca
www.arq.qc.ca
ww.facebook.com/496349387128403
twitter.com/SCFRQuebec
Aperçu: *Dimension:* petite; *Envergure:* provinciale surveillé par Fédération des médecins spécialistes du Québec
Mission: Regrouper les médecins spécialisés en radiologie; défendre leurs intérêts et promouvoir leur spécialité
Membre(s) du bureau directeur:
André Constantin, Président
Membre: 592

Association des radio-oncologues du Québec (AROQ)
CP 216, Succ. Desjardins, #3000, 2, Complexe Desjardins, Montréal QC H5B 1G8
Tél: 514-350-5130; *Téléc:* 514-350-5126
aroq@fmsq.org
www.aroq.ca
Aperçu: *Dimension:* petite; *Envergure:* provinciale surveillé par Fédération des médecins spécialistes du Québec
Mission: De fournir un forum où ses membres peuvent échanger des idées afin d'aider à améliorer leurs méthodes de traitement
Membre(s) du bureau directeur:
Khalil Sultanem, Président
Membre: 121

Association des réalisateurs et réalisatrices de Télé-Québec (ARRTQ)
1000, rue Fullum, Montréal QC H2K 3L7
Tél: 514-521-2424
Aperçu: *Dimension:* petite; *Envergure:* provinciale surveillé par Centrale des syndicats du Québec
Affiliation(s): Centrale des syndicats du Québec
Membre(s) du bureau directeur:
Rachel Archambault, Coordonnatrice
rarchambault@sympatico.ca
Membre: *Critères d'admissibilite:* Tout réalisateur ayant signé un contrat avec la Société Télé-Québec

Association des réalisateurs et réalisatrices du Québec (ARRQ)
5154, rue St-Hubert, Montréal QC H2J 2Y3
Tél: 514-842-7373; *Téléc:* 514-842-6789
realiser@arrq.qc.ca
www.arrq.qc.ca
Nom précédent: Association québécoise des réalisateurs et réalisatrices de cinéma et de télévision
Aperçu: *Dimension:* petite; *Envergure:* provinciale; fondée en 1973
Mission: Défendre les intérêts et les droits professionnels, économiques, culturels, sociaux et moraux des réalisateurs pigistes membres, travaillant principalement dans les domaines du cinéma et de la télévision
Membre de: Fédération professionnelle des réalisateurs et réalisatrices de cinéma et de télévision du Québec
Affiliation(s): Coalition des créateurs et titulaires de droits d'auteur; Association littéraire et artistique internationale
Membre(s) du bureau directeur:
Caroline Fortier, Directrice générale
cfortier@arrq.qc.ca
Membre(s) du personnel: 4
Membre: 670 réalisateurs/réalisatrices pigistes; *Montant de la cotisation:* 150$ professionnel; 75$ stagiaire; *Critères d'admissibilite:* Réalisateurs de longs, courts moyens métrages, téléfilms, vidéoclips, films publicitaires
Activités: Programmes d'aide financière, droits d'auteur, politiques de diffusion, promotion du statut professionnel, etc.; *Service de conférenciers:* Oui; *Listes de destinataires:* Oui
Prix, Bouses:
• Prix lumières (Prix)

Association des recycleurs de pièces d'autos et de camions (ARPAC) / Association of Auto Part Recyclers
#101, 37, rue de la Gare, St-Jérôme QC J7Z 2B7
Tel: 450-504-8315; *Fax:* 450-504-8313
Toll-Free: 855-504-8315
info@arpac.org
arpac.org
www.facebook.com/pages/ARPAC/106847846016208
www.youtube.com/user/ARPACpiecesvertes
Overview: A medium-sized provincial organization
Member of: Automotive Recyclers of Canada
Chief Officer(s):
Simon Matte, Président-directeur général
Membership: 88
Meetings/Conferences: • 2015 Association des recycleurs de pièces d'autos et de camions Congress, September, 2015, Cacouna, Rivière-du-Loup, QC
Scope: Provincial

Association des registraires des universités et collèges du Canada *See* Association of Registrars of the Universities & Colleges of Canada

Association des relations publiques des organismes de la santé *See* Health Care Public Relations Association

Association des résidents du Lac Echo (ARLEQ)
CP 343, St-Hippolyte QC J8A 3P6
Tél: 450-224-4338
Aperçu: *Dimension:* petite; *Envergure:* locale
Membre(s) du bureau directeur:
Michel Lamontagne, Contact

Association des résidents du Lac Renaud
Prévost QC J0R 1T0
www.lacrenaud.org
Aperçu: *Dimension:* petite; *Envergure:* locale
Membre(s) du bureau directeur:
Marcelle Théoret, Présidente
Marcelle.Theoret@LacRenaud.org
Gilles Tourigny, Administrateur
Gilles.Tourigny@LacRenaud.org

Association des ressources humaines du Nouveau-Brunswick *See* Human Resources Association of New Brunswick

Association des ressources intervenant auprès des hommes ayant des comportement violent *Voir* A Coeur d'Homme

Association des restaurateurs du Québec (ARQ) / Québec Restaurant Association
6880, boul Louis-H.-La Fontaine, Montréal QC H1M 2T2
Tél: 514-527-9801; *Téléc:* 514-527-3066
Ligne sans frais: 800-463-4237
arqc@arqc.qc.ca
www.restaurateurs.ca
www.facebook.com/167396323369138
twitter.com/ARQ_resto
Aperçu: *Dimension:* petite; *Envergure:* provinciale; Organisme sans but lucratif; fondée en 1938
Mission: Fournir à l'ensemble des restaurateurs du Québec des services complets d'information, de formation, d'escomptes, d'assurances et de représentation gouvernementale
Membre de: Conseil du Patronat; Conseil québécois des ressources humaines en tourisme
Membre(s) du bureau directeur:
Bernard Fortin, Président directeur général
dirgen@arqc.qc.ca
Membre(s) du personnel: 26
Membre: 4,500; *Montant de la cotisation:* 385$ restaurant/hôtel/brasserie; 235$ saisonnier; 185$ service; *Critères d'admissibilite:* Restaurateurs, fournisseurs
Activités: Volet économique - rabais sur frais d'administration de cartes de crédit, d'achat d'essence et d'approvisionnements; réduction de la cotisation à la Commission de la santé et de la sécurité du travail; assurances; volet politique - représentation gouvernementale; information (règlementation et statistiques); programmes de formation - séminaires de perfectionnement, santé et sécurité au travail; conférences; programme d'ateliers de formation accréditée
Prix, Bouses:
• Prix Coup de Chapeau (Prix)
Remis annuellement à des restaurateurs pour leur contribution au rayonnement de l'industrie de la restauration

Association des sages-femmes de l'Ontario *See* Association of Ontario Midwives

Association des sciences administratives du Canada *See* Administrative Sciences Association of Canada

Association des sciences de la santé de l'Alberta (ind.) *See* Health Sciences Association of Alberta

Association des sciences de la santé de la Saskatchewan (ind.) *See* Health Sciences Association of Saskatchewan

Association des Scouts du Canada

7331, rue St-Denis, Montréal QC H2R 2E5
Tél: 514-252-3011; *Téléc:* 514-254-1946
Ligne sans frais: 866-297-2688
infoscout@scoutsducanada.ca
www.scoutsducanada.ca
www.facebook.com/125583680848884
Également appelé: Les Scouts du Québec
Nom précédent: Fédération québécoise du scoutisme
Aperçu: *Dimension:* moyenne; *Envergure:* internationale; Organisme sans but lucratif; fondée en 1980
Mission: Assurer la qualité, la permanence et la croissance du scoutisme francophone au Canada; elle détermine les orientations, objectifs, moyens et politiques pour répondre aux besoins de ses membres; elle développe aussi les processus de planification stratégique, réalise, analyse des recherches, des scénarios de l'environnement; elle agit comme porte parole du scoutisme au Québec
Membre de: Association des scouts du Canada
Affliation(s): Organisation Mondiale du Mouvement Scout
Membre(s) du bureau directeur:
Robert Nowlan, Commissaire national/Chef de la direction
commissaire.national@scoutsducanada.ca
Jean-François Champagne, Président
president@scoutsducanada.ca
Christian Perreault, Vice-président
christian.perreault@scoutsducanada.ca
Finances: *Budget de fonctionnement annuel:* $1.5 Million-$3 Million
Membre(s) du personnel: 8; 30 bénévole(s)
Membre: 35 000; *Montant de la cotisation:* 22$; *Critères d'admissibilite:* Jeune (7-21 ans); adulte (18 ans et plus)
Activités: *Stagiaires:* Oui; *Service de conférenciers:* Oui; *Bibliothèque:* La Référence; rendez-vous

Association des services aux étudiants des universités et collèges du Canada *See* Canadian Association of College & University Student Services

Association des services de garde à l'enfance de la Nouvelle-Écosse *See* Nova Scotia Child Care Association

Association des services de réhabilitation sociale du Québec inc. (ASRSQ) / Association of Social Rehabilitation Agencies of Québec Inc.

2000, boul St-Joseph est, Montréal QC H2H 1E4
Tél: 514-521-3733; *Téléc:* 514-521-3753
info@asrsq.ca
www.asrsq.ca
Aperçu: *Dimension:* moyenne; *Envergure:* nationale; Organisme sans but lucratif; fondée en 1962
Mission: Promouvoir la participation des citoyens dans l'administration de la justice, la prévention du crime et la réhabilitation des délinquants adultes
Membre(s) du bureau directeur:
Josée Rioux, Présidente
Philippe Létourneau, Vice-présidente
Ruth Gagnon, Secrétaire
Serge Arel, Trésorier
12 bénévole(s)
Membre: 50 corporations; 109 points de services
Activités: Semaine de la justice réparatrice; *Service de conférenciers:* Oui; *Bibliothèque* Bibliothèque publique rendez-vous
Prix, Bouses:
• Prix Reneault-Tremblay (Prix)
Décerné tous les deux ans à une personne ou un organisme communautaire en reconnaissance de son apport unique et exceptionnel à l'action communautaire en justice pénale, à la prévention du crime et à la réhabilitation sociale des personnes contrevenantes adultes

L'Association des services funéraires du Canada *See* Funeral Service Association of Canada

Association des services sociaux des municipalités de l'Ontario *See* Ontario Municipal Social Services Association

Association des sexologues du Québec (ASQ)

#709, 1100, boul Crémazie Est, Montréal QC H2P 2X2
Tél: 514-270-9289; *Téléc:* 514-270-6351
info@associationdessexologues.com
www.associationdessexologues.com
Aperçu: *Dimension:* petite; *Envergure:* provinciale; fondée en 1978
Mission: Susciter auprès du public une meilleure connaissance de la sexologie et du rôle du sexologue, en favorisant et en maintenant les normes scientifiques et professionnelles les plus élevées dans l'exercice de la sexologie et dans la formation des sexologues
Membre de: Sex Information & Education Council of Canada; World Association of Sexology
Membre: 200+; *Montant de la cotisation:* 350$ régulier; 45$ étudiant; 210$ réguliers MA (candidat); *Critères d'admissibilite:* Maîtrise ou étudiant à la maîtrise en sexologie clinique
Activités: *Service de conférenciers:* Oui; *Listes de destinataires:* Oui; *Bibliothèque* rendez-vous

Association des Sociétés d'aide au développement des collectivités de l'Ontario *See* Ontario Association of Community Futures Development Corporations

Association des Sourds de Beauce *Voir* Regroupement des Sourds de Chaudière-Appalaches

Association des Sourds de l'Estrie Inc. (ASE)

#100, 359, rue King est, Sherbrooke QC J1G 1B3
Tél: 819-563-1186; *Téléc:* 819-563-3476; *TTY:* 819-563-1186
sourdestrie@videotron.ca
www.sourdestrie.com
www.facebook.com/sourdestrie
Aperçu: *Dimension:* petite; *Envergure:* locale; Organisme sans but lucratif; fondée en 1968
Mission: Briser l'isolement des sourds; sensibilisation des intervenants et de la population en général sur la surdité
Membre de: Centre québécois de la déficience auditive; Regroupement québécois pour le sous-titrage inc.
Affiliation(s): Coalition Sida des sourds de Québec; Regroupement Canadien des Enseignants et Enseignantes Sourds en Langue des Signes Québécois
Membre(s) du bureau directeur:
Céline Martineau, Directrice
Alain Ouellette, Adjoint administratif
Finances: *Budget de fonctionnement annuel:* $100,000-$250,000; *Fonds:* Agence de la Santé et services sociaux de l'Estrie, Centraide, Emploi été Canada, Communautique, dons
Membre(s) du personnel: 1; 15 bénévole(s)
Membre: 120; *Montant de la cotisation:* 20$ individuel; 25$ couple/organisme; *Critères d'admissibilite:* Sourd, malentendant, entendant connaissant la langue des signes québécois; *Comités:* Comité de poches baseball, 50e anniversaire, histoire
Activités: Activités de loisirs; conférences; information; accueil; St-Valentin; Noël; fêtes pour enfants; café internet; cours de Langue des Signes Québécois; journal d'information; *Evénements de sensibilisation:* Journée Mondiale des Sourds; *Stagiaires:* Oui; *Service de conférenciers:* Oui; *Bibliothèque:* Bibliothèque
Publications:
• Nouvellestrie [a publication of Association des Sourds de l'Estrie inc.]
Type: Journal; *Frequency:* Trimestriel

Association des Sourds de Lanaudière

200, rue de Salaberry, local 312, Joliette QC J6E 4G1
Tel: 450-752-1426; *TTY:* 450-752-1426
asl@cepap.ca
www.asljoliette.org
www.facebook.com/ASLanaudiere
Overview: A small local organization
Chief Officer(s):
Richard Geoffroy, Président

Association des Sourds de Québec inc.

765, boul Charest est, Québec QC G1K 3J6
Tél: 418-640-9258; *Téléc:* 418-640-9258
Ligne sans frais: 800-855-0511
asq1964@hotmail.com
Aperçu: *Dimension:* petite; *Envergure:* locale; Organisme sans but lucratif; fondée en 1964
Membre(s) du bureau directeur:
Richard Dagenault, Président
25 bénévole(s)
Membre: 100-499

Association des sourds du Canada *See* Canadian Association of the Deaf

Association des Sourds du Haut-Richelieu *Voir* Association montérégienne de la surdité inc.

Association des spécialistes du pneus et Mécanique du Québec (ASPQ)

CP 1033, Drummondville QC J2A 0B1
Tél: 514-461-1035; *Téléc:* 514-461-1035
Ligne sans frais: 866-454-0477
info@aspmq.ca
www.aspq.ca/aspq
Aperçu: *Dimension:* moyenne; *Envergure:* provinciale; fondée en 1969
Membre(s) du bureau directeur:
Daniel Dubuc, Président, 450-923-4656, Fax: 450-923-9669
ddubuc@videotron.qc.ca
Danny Houle, Vice-président, 819-357-2494, Fax: 819-357-9442
dhoule@droletpneusmecanique.com
Wendy Allain, Directrice éxécutive, 514-461-1035, Fax: 514-657-2176
info@aspmq.ca
Membre: 150

Association des spécialistes en chirurgie plastique et esthétique du Québec (ASCPEQ)

CP 216, Succ. Desjardins, 2, Complexe Desjardins, Montréal QC H5B 1G8
Tél: 514-350-5109; *Téléc:* 514-350-5246
ascpeq@fmsq.org
www.ascpeq.org
Aperçu: *Dimension:* petite; *Envergure:* provinciale surveillé par Fédération des médecins spécialistes du Québec
Mission: L'Association entend se consacrer essentiellement au développement continu de l'art et de la science de la chirurgie plastique et esthétique, entre autres par la diffusion de renseignements pertinents auprès du public, par la promotion d'une relation médecin-patient fondée sur la communication, la compréhension et le respect mutuel, ainsi que par une contribution active aux programmes d'éducation et de formation continue et par une participation critique aux débats relatifs au rôle et à la place des professionnels de la santé au sein de la société québécoise
Affliation(s): La Société canadienne des chirurgiens plasticiens, The Toronto Aesthetic Meeting, The Toronto Breast Symposium, La Société canadienne de chirurgie plastique esthétique, The Canadian Association for Accreditation of Ambulatory Surgical Facilities
Membre(s) du bureau directeur:
Éric Bensimon, Président

Association des spécialistes en extermination du Québec *Voir* Association québécoise de la gestion parasitaire

Association des spécialistes en médecine d'urgence du Québec

Tour de l'Est, #3000, 2, Complexe Desjardins, Montréal QC H5B 1G8
Tél: 514-350-5115; *Téléc:* 514-350-5116
www.asmuq.org/
Aperçu: *Dimension:* moyenne; *Envergure:* provinciale surveillé par Fédération des médecins spécialistes du Québec
Membre(s) du bureau directeur:
François Dufresne, Président

Association des spécialistes en médecine interne du Québec

CP 216, Succ. Desjardins, #3000, 2, Complexe Desjardins, Montréal QC H5B 1G8
Tél: 514-350-5118; *Téléc:* 514-350-5168
med.interne@fmsq.org
Aperçu: *Dimension:* moyenne; *Envergure:* provinciale; Organisme sans but lucratif
Membre de: Fédération des médecins spécialistes du Québec
Membre(s) du bureau directeur:
Patrick Chagnon, Président

Association des sports des sourds du Canada *See* Canadian Deaf Sports Association

Association des sports pour aveugles de Montréal (ASAM)

4545, av Pierre-de Coubertin, Montréal QC H1V 0B2
Tél: 514-252-3178
infoasam@sportsaveugles.qc.ca
www.sportsaveugles.qc.ca/asam
www.facebook.com/ASAMONTREAL
Aperçu: *Dimension:* petite; *Envergure:* locale; Organisme sans but lucratif; fondée en 1983

Mission: Promouvoir l'accessibilité et la pratique des sports et loisirs aux personnes handicapées visuelles; organiser et structurer les différentes activités sportives; recruter et former des bénévoles accompagnateurs
Affiliation(s): Association sportive des aveugles du Québec
Membre(s) du bureau directeur:
Caroline Bouchard, Directrice générale
cbouchard@sportsaveugles.qc.ca
Finances: *Budget de fonctionnement annuel:* $50,000-$100,000
Membre(s) du personnel: 1; 75 bénévole(s)
Membre: 175 individu; 2 associées; *Montant de la cotisation:* 20$ individuel; 30$ membre affilié; *Critères d'admissibilité:* Personne ayant un handicap visuel
Activités: Goalball; conditionnement physique; aqua forme; tandem; ski alpin et ski de fond; tai-chi; activités ponctuelles: équitation, escalade, canot, randonnée pédestre; *Evénements de sensibilisation:* Tournoi de golf, sept.

Association des stations de ski du Québec (ASSQ)

1347, rue Nationale, Terrebonne QC J6W 6H8
Tél: 450-765-2012; *Téléc:* 450-765-2025
media@assq.qc.ca
www.quebecskisurf.com
www.facebook.com/skiqc
twitter.com/assq_maneige
Aperçu: *Dimension:* moyenne; *Envergure:* provinciale; Organisme sans but lucratif; fondée en 1979
Mission: Représenter et défendre les intérêts des membres; favoriser la pratique du ski alpin; améliorer la qualité du produit ainsi que la performance des stations
Membre(s) du bureau directeur:
Yves Juneau, Président-directeur général
ski@assq.qc.ca
Membre(s) du personnel: 16
Membre: 75 stations de ski
Activités: *Listes de destinataires:* Oui

Association des statisticiennes et statisticiens du Québec (ASSQ)

3340, rue de La Pérade, 3e étage, Québec QC G1X 2L7
assq@association-assq.qc.ca
www.association-assq.qc.ca
Aperçu: *Dimension:* petite; *Envergure:* provinciale
Mission: Regrouper les statisticiennes et statisticiens en vue de promouvoir la statistique et d'en favoriser la bonne utilisation
Membre(s) du bureau directeur:
Christian Genest, President
Membre: *Montant de la cotisation:* $10

Association des surintendants de golf du Québec (ASGQ) / Québec Golf Superintendents Association (QSGA)

1370, rue Notre-Dame ouest, Montréal QC H3C 1K8
Tél: 514-285-4874; *Téléc:* 514-282-4292
info@asgq.org
www.asgq.org
Aperçu: *Dimension:* petite; *Envergure:* provinciale; Organisme sans but lucratif; fondée en 1964
Mission: Dédiée à la promotion des intérêts des surintendants; offre à ses membres des avantages, informations et défense des intérêts des surintendants
Membre(s) du bureau directeur:
Jacques Lessard, Président
Finances: *Budget de fonctionnement annuel:* $50,000-$100,000
Membre(s) du personnel: 1; 12 bénévole(s)
Membre: 400; *Critères d'admissibilité:* Surintendant; adjoint; aspirant
Activités: Tournois de golf; salon exposition; *Service de conférenciers:* Oui

Association des syndicalistes retraités du Canada ***See*** Congress of Union Retirees Canada

Association des syndicats de copropriété du Québec (ASCQ) / Syndicates of Co-Ownership Association of Québec

#1800, 1010, rue Sherbrooke Ouest, Montréal QC H3A 2R7
Tél: 514-866-3557; *Téléc:* 514-866-4149
Ligne sans frais: 800-568-5512
ascq@ascq.qc.ca
www.ascq.qc.ca
Aperçu: *Dimension:* grande; *Envergure:* provinciale; Organisme sans but lucratif; fondée en 1976
Mission: Former, informer, aider à la gestion les syndicats de copropriété membres
Membre de: Centre patronal santé sécurité au travail
Membre(s) du bureau directeur:
Michel G. Charlebois, Président
michel.charlebois@ascq.qc.ca
Michèle Bérard, Vice-président
michel.charlebois@ascq.qc.ca
Membre(s) du personnel: 4
Membre: *Critères d'admissibilité:* Syndicat de copropriété
Activités: Sessions formation colloques, séminaires; *Stagiaires:* Oui
Publications:
• Bulletin de la Copropriété Plus [a publication of the Association des syndicats de copropriété du Québec]
Type: Bulletin

Association des TCC (le traumatisme cranio-cérébral) et ACV (un accident vasculaire cérébral) de la Gaspésie et des Iles-de-la-Madeleine Inc.

CP 308, Maria QC G0C 1Y0
Tél: 418-759-5120; *Téléc:* 418-759-8188
Ligne sans frais: 888-278-2280
tccacv@globetrotter.net
www.tccacvgim.org
Nom précédent: Association des personnes traumatisées cranio-cérébrales de la Gaspésie et des Iles-de-la-Madeleine inc.
Aperçu: *Dimension:* petite; *Envergure:* locale; fondée en 1993
Mission: Pour informer et aider les personnes cranio-cérébral, traumatisme et leurs familles, en Gaspésie et les Iles de la Madeleine
Membre de: Regroupement des associations de personnes traumatisées craniocérébrales du Québec / Coalition of Associations of Craniocerebral Trauma in Quebec
Membre: *Critères d'admissibilité:* Les survivants de traumatisme crânien cérébral-des îles de la Madeleine et Gaspésie
Activités: S'engager dans des activités de plaidoyer; Fournir un soutien psychosocial; Se référant victimes et les familles vers les ressources appropriées; Organiser des réunions et des groupes de discussion
Publications:
• La Bulle
Type: Newsletter; *Frequency:* Quarterly
Profile: Association activities

Association des techniciennes et techniciens en diététique du Québec ***Voir*** Société des technologues en nutrition

Association des techniciens en santé animale du Québec (ATSAQ)

#240, 2300, 54e av, Montréal QC H8T 3R2
Tél: 514-324-5202
Ligne sans frais: 800-463-8555
atsaq@atsaq.org
www.atsaq.org
Aperçu: *Dimension:* petite; *Envergure:* provinciale; fondée en 1979
Membre de: Canadian Association of Animal Health Technologists & Technicians
Membre(s) du bureau directeur:
Élisabeth Lebeau, Directrice générale
atsaq@atsaq.org
Danny Ménard, Président
Laurence Santerre-Bélec, Vice-Président
Brigitte Couturier, Trésorière

Association des technologistes agro-alimentaires inc. ***Voir*** Association des technologues en agroalimentaire

Association des technologistes de laboratoire médical du Nouveau-Brunswick ***See*** New Brunswick Society of Medical Laboratory Technologists

Association des technologues en agroalimentaire (ATA) / Agricultural Technologists Association Inc.

a/s Ordre des technologues professionnels du Québec, #720, 1265, rue Berri, Montréal QC H2L 4X4
Tél: 514-845-3247; *Téléc:* 514-845-3643
Ligne sans frais: 800-561-3459
www.otpq.qc.ca
Nom précédent: Association des technologistes agro-alimentaires inc.
Aperçu: *Dimension:* moyenne; *Envergure:* provinciale; Organisme sans but lucratif; fondée en 1964
Mission: Défendre les intérêts professionnels; promouvoir la profession et le perfectionnement des membres
Membre de: Ordre des technologues professionnels du Québec
Membre(s) du bureau directeur:
Alain Bernier, Président
alain.bernier@collegeahuntsic.qc.ca
Denis Beauchamp, Directeur général
dbeauchamp@otpq.qc.ca
Membre(s) du personnel: 8
Membre: 4,000; *Montant de la cotisation:* 25,23$ étudiante/affilié; 75$ régulier

Association des théâtres francophones du Canada (ATFC)

#404, 450, rue Rideau, Ottawa ON K1N 5Z4
Tél: 613-562-2233; *Téléc:* 613-241-6064
Ligne sans frais: 866-821-2233
info@atfc.ca
www.atfc.ca
www.facebook.com/183284631764569
Aperçu: *Dimension:* petite; *Envergure:* nationale; fondée en 1984
Mission: Défendre les intérêts et à assurer le développement et la promotion des théâtres francophones professionnels oeuvrant dans les régions canadiennes où les francophones sont minoritaires
Membre(s) du bureau directeur:
Marcia Bibineau, Présidente
Alain Jean, Directeur général
ajean@atfc.ca
Membre: *Critères d'admissibilité:* 14 compagnies de théâtre francophones professionnelles; *Comités:* Programmation; Politiques; Formation; Mises en nomination

Association des Therapeuets de Sport des Provinces Altantique ***See*** Atlantic Provinces Athletic Therapists Association

L'Association des thérapeutes respiratoires du Manitoba, inc. ***See*** Manitoba Association of Registered Respiratory Therapists, Inc.

L'Association des thérapeutes respiratoires du Nouveau-Brunswick inc. ***See*** The New Brunswick Association of Respiratory Therapists Inc.

Association des Townshippers ***See*** Townshippers' Association

Association des traducteurs et interprètes de l'Alberta ***See*** Association of Translators & Interpreters of Alberta

Association des traducteurs et interprètes de l'Ontario ***See*** Association of Translators & Interpreters of Ontario

Association des traducteurs et interprètes de la nouvelle-écosse ***See*** Association of Translators & Interpreters of Nova Scotia

Association des traducteurs et interprètes de la Saskatchewan ***See*** Association of Translators & Interpreters of Saskatchewan

Association des traducteurs et interprètes judiciares ***See*** Association of Legal Court Interpreters & Translators

Association des traducteurs et traductrices littéraires du Canada ***See*** Literary Translators' Association of Canada

Association des traducteurs, terminologues et des interprètes du Manitoba ***See*** Association of Translators, Terminologists & Interpreters of Manitoba

Association des transitaires internationaux canadiens, inc. ***See*** Canadian International Freight Forwarders Association, Inc.

Association des transports du Canada ***See*** Transportation Association of Canada

Association des transports du Canada ***See*** The Association of School Transportation Services of British Columbia

Association des traumatisés crâniens de l'Abitibi-Témiscamingue (Le Pilier)

3, 9e rue, Rouyn-Noranda QC J9X 2A9
Tél: 819-762-7478; *Téléc:* 819-797-8313
pilieratcat@cablevision.qc.ca
www.pilieratcat.qc.ca
Aperçu: *Dimension:* petite; *Envergure:* locale
Mission: Pour fournir des services de soutien aux personnes qui ont subi une lésion cérébrale acquise, et leurs familles, dans la région de l'Abitibi-Témiscamingue du Québec
Membre de: Regroupement des associations de personnes traumatisées craniocérébrales du Québec / Coalition of Associations of Craniocerebral Trauma in Quebec

Membre(s) du bureau directeur:
Francine Chalifoux, Directrice générale et responsable clinique, 819-762-7478 Ext. 47421
Finances: *Fonds:* Les frais d'adhésion; Collecte de fonds
Membre(s) du personnel: 5
Membre: *Montant de la cotisation:* $10
Activités: Offrir des programmes de soutien psychosocial aux personnes de la région de l'Abitibi-Témiscamingue qui ont subi un traumatisme cranio-cérébral; Fournir des activités sociales, culturelles, et de loisirs; Plaidoyer en faveur des victimes de traumatisme crânien;

Association des Traumatisés cranio-cérébraux de la Montérégie (ATCCM)

#D-131, 308, rue Montsabré, Beloeil QC J3G 2H5
Tél: 450-446-1111; *Téléc:* 450-446-6405
Ligne sans frais: 877-661-2822
atcc@atccmonteregie.qc.ca
www.atccmonteregie.qc.ca
Aperçu: *Dimension:* petite; *Envergure:* locale; fondée en 1994
Mission: Pour fournir des services de soutien aux personnes de la région de la Montérégie du Québec qui ont subi une lésion cérébrale traumatique ou un accident vasculaire cérébral; Pour favoriser la réinsertion et les expériences d'apprentissage
Membre de: Regroupement des associations de personnes traumatisées craniocérébrales du Québec / Coalition of Associations of Craniocerebral Trauma in Quebec
Membre(s) du bureau directeur:
Chantal Bourguignon, Directrice générale
c.bourguignon@atccmonteregie.qc.ca
Membre(s) du personnel: 6
Membre: *Critères d'admissibilite:* Les survivants de traumatisme crânien ou accident vasculaire cérébral, et leurs familles, dans la région de la Montérégie au Québec
Activités: Création d'opportunités de partager des expériences avec d'autres personnes qui ont subi une lésion cérébrale traumatique dans la région de la Montérégie; L'animation de groupes de soutien; Offrant des services psychosociaux; Offrir une éducation; Promouvoir la prévention des lésions cérébrales

Association des traumatisés cranio-cérébraux des deux rives (Québec-Chaudière-Appalaches)

Territoire de Québec et de Chaudiere-Appalaches, 14, rue Saint-Amand, Loretteville QC G2A 2K9
Tel: 418-842-8421; *Fax:* 418-842-9616
Toll-Free: 866-844-8421
tcc2rives@oricom.ca
www.tcc2rives.qc.ca
Overview: A small local organization founded in 1989
Mission: To assist victims, parents, friends, & professionals affected by traumatic brain injury in the Quebec's Chaudiere-Appalaches area
Member of: Regroupement des associations de personnes traumatisées craniocérébrales du Québec / Coalition of Associations of Craniocerebral Trauma in Quebec
Chief Officer(s):
Nathalie Laroche, Executive Director
Caroline Tremblay, President
Patrick Guillemette, Vice-President
Michele Gauthier, Secretary
Christine Pineau, Treasurer
Finances: *Annual Operating Budget:* $500,000-$1.5 Million; *Funding Sources:* SAAQ; Agence de la sante et des services sociaux
Staff Member(s): 11; 50 volunteer(s)
Membership: 500-999; *Fees:* 10% an; *Committees:* Loisir, Bênevole
Activities: Helping persons reintegrate after rehabilitation from traumatic brain injury; Offering psychosocial support groups; Providing education about traumatic brain injury, such as lectures; *Speaker Service:* Yes
Publications:
• L'En Tête
Type: Newspaper; *Frequency:* Quarterly
Profile: Information about the association's services

Association des traumatisés cranio-cérébraux Mauricie-Centre-du-Québec (ATCC)

39, rue Bellerive, Trois-Rivières QC G8T 6J4
Tél: 819-372-4993
atcc@assotcc.org
www.associationtcc.org
www.facebook.com/381058281920939
Aperçu: *Dimension:* petite; *Envergure:* locale
Mission: Pour soutenir les personnes touchées par une lésion cérébrale traumatique en Mauricie-Centre-du-Québec
Membre de: Regroupement des associations de personnes traumatisées craniocérébrales du Québec / Coalition of Associations of Craniocerebral Trauma in Quebec
Activités: Plaidoyer en faveur des personnes qui ont subi une lésion cérébrale traumatique; L'organisation de groupes de soutien pour aider les victimes et leurs familles; Offrant des activités sociales pour les membres;

Association des travailleurs sociaux de l'Alberta *See* Alberta College of Social Workers

Association des travailleurs sociaux de l'Ile-du-Prince-Édouard *See* Prince Edward Island Association of Social Workers

Association des travailleurs sociaux de la Colombie-Britannique *See* British Columbia Association of Social Workers

Association des travailleurs sociaux de la Nouvelle-Écosse *See* Nova Scotia Association of Social Workers

Association des travailleurs sociaux de la Saskatchewan *See* Saskatchewan Association of Social Workers

Association des travailleurs sociaux de Terre-Neuve et Labrador *See* Newfoundland & Labrador Association of Social Workers

L'Association des travailleurs sociaux du Nord canadien *See* The Association of Social Workers of Northern Canada

Association des travailleurs sociaux du Nouveau-Brunswick *See* New Brunswick Association of Social Workers

Association des travailleuses et travailleurs sociaux de l'Ontario *See* Ontario Association of Social Workers

Association des Troubles Alimentaires du Canada *See* Eating Disorder Association of Canada

Association des universités de l'Atlantique *See* Association of Atlantic Universities

Association des universités de la francophonie canadienne (AUFC)

#400, 260, rue Dalhousie, Ottawa ON K1N 7E4
Tél: 613-244-7837; *Téléc:* 613-244-0699
Ligne sans frais: 866-551-2637
info@aufc.ca
www.aufc.ca
Nom précédent: Regroupement des universités de la francophonie Hors-Québec
Aperçu: *Dimension:* petite; *Envergure:* nationale; Organisme sans but lucratif; fondée en 1990
Mission: Promouvoir l'enseignement universitaire en milieu minoritaire francophone au Canada par la consultation et la collaboration des établissements membres, chacun d'eux constituant un outil privilégié de développement culturel, social, et économique dans la communauté qu'il dessert; représenter les établissements membres auprès des instances gouvernementales du Canada
Affliation(s): Association of Universities & Colleges of Canada; Association des universités partiellement ou entièrement de langue française
Membre(s) du bureau directeur:
Marc Arnal, Président
Jocelyne Lalonde, Directrice générale
jolalonde@aufc.ca
Finances: *Budget de fonctionnement annuel:* $100,000-$250,000
Membre(s) du personnel: 3
Membre: 13 universités

Association des universités et collèges du Canada *See* Association of Universities & Colleges of Canada

Association des universités partiellement ou entièrement de langue française *Voir* Agence universitaire de la Francophonie

Association des urologues du Canada *See* Canadian Urological Association

Association des urologues du Québec (AUQ) / Quebec Urological Association (QUA)

#3000, 2, Complexe Desjardins, 32e étage, Montréal QC H5B 1G8
Tél: 514-350-5131; *Téléc:* 514-350-5181
info@auq.org
www.auq.org
Aperçu: *Dimension:* petite; *Envergure:* provinciale surveillé par Fédération des médecins spécialistes du Québec
Membre(s) du bureau directeur:
Steven P. Lapointe, Président
Liliane Verret, Secrétariat
Membre: 100-499
Meetings/Conferences: • Association des urologues du Québec 40e Congrès annuel, 2015, QC
Scope: Provincial

Association des usagers du transport adapté de Longueuil (AUTAL)

#211, 150, rue Grant, Longueuil QC J4H 3H6
Tél: 450-646-2224
Aperçu: *Dimension:* petite; *Envergure:* locale; fondée en 1981
Mission: Défendre les droits des personnes handicapées qui utilisent le système de transport aménagé à Longueuil

Association des vétérans et amis du bataillon Mackenzie-Papineau, Brigades internationales en Espagne *See* Association of Veterans & Friends of the Mackenzie-Papineau Battalion, International Brigades in Spain

Association des veuves de Montréal inc.

120, boul St-Joseph ouest, Montréal QC H2T 2P6
Tél: 514-276-3911
Aperçu: *Dimension:* petite; *Envergure:* locale; fondée en 1959
Mission: Est une maison qui accueille toutes les dames seules dans le but de briser leur isolement
Membre: 500; *Critères d'admissibilite:* Dames cherchant à briser l'isolement
Activités: Parties de cartes; bridge; dîners; voyages; conférences

Association des vietnamiens de Sherbrooke (AVS)

1604, rue Simard, Sherbrooke QC J1J 4A5
Tél: 819-346-1042; *Téléc:* 819-346-1042
Aperçu: *Dimension:* petite; *Envergure:* nationale; Organisme sans but lucratif; fondée en 1975
Mission: La plus vieille des associations vietnamiennes au Canada
Membre de: Vietnamese Canadian Federation
Membre(s) du bureau directeur:
Van-Nha Tran, Président
Finances: *Budget de fonctionnement annuel:* Moins de $50,000
Membre: 300; *Critères d'admissibilite:* Tous les viêtnamiens du Sherbrooke métropolitain
Activités: *Evénements de sensibilisation:* Fête de la mi-automne pour les enfants (oct.); Fête du jour l'an (fév.)

L'Association des vignerons du Canada *See* Canadian Vintners Association

Association des zoos et aquariums du Canada *See* Canadian Association of Zoos & Aquariums

Association du barreau canadien *See* Canadian Bar Association

L'association du barreau de l'Ontario *See* Canadian Bar Association

Association du barreau du comté de Carleton *See* Carleton County Law Association

Association du barreau du Manitoba *See* Manitoba Bar Association

Association du café du Canada *See* Coffee Association of Canada

Association du camionnage du Québec inc. (ACQ) / Québec Trucking Association Inc.

#200, 6450, rue Notre Dame ouest, Montréal QC H4C 1V4
Tél: 514-932-0377; *Téléc:* 514-932-1358
info@carrefour-acq.org
www.carrefour-acq.org
Aperçu: *Dimension:* moyenne; *Envergure:* provinciale; Organisme sans but lucratif; fondée en 1951 surveillé par Canadian Trucking Alliance
Mission: Favoriser l'amélioration des normes de sécurité, d'efficacité et d'éthique dans l'industrie du camionnage; maintenir un contact avec l'autorité gouvernementale, les usagers des services de camionnage et le public en général; soutenir le perfectionnement professionnel; soutenir les entreprises dans la défense de leurs intérêts.
Affiliation(s): Union Internationale des Transports Routiers - Genève; American Trucking Association - Washington, DC
Membre(s) du bureau directeur:
Bernard Boutin, Président

Marc Cadieux, Président-directeur général
mcadieux@carrefour-acq.org
Finances: *Budget de fonctionnement annuel:* $500,000-$1.5 Million
Membre(s) du personnel: 13
Membre: 500 entreprises; *Critères d'admissibilite:* Transporteurs et locateurs publics & privés
Activités: *Stagiaires:* Oui

Association du Diabète du Québec *Voir* Diabète Québec

Association du génie électronique et mécanique *See* Electrical & Mechanical Engineering Association

Association du jeune barreau de Montréal (AJBM) / Young Bar Association of Montréal (YBAM)

#RC-03, 445, boul. St-Laurent, Montréal QC H2Y 3T8
Tél: 514-954-3450; *Téléc:* 514-954-3496
info@ajbm.qc.ca
www.ajbm.qc.ca
www.linkedin.com/groups?gid=93709
www.facebook.com/308197005868434
twitter.com/AJBM_YBAM
Aperçu: *Dimension:* petite; *Envergure:* locale; fondée en 1898
Mission: Pour défendre les intérêts des avocats qui ont moins de dix ans d'expérience qui sont enregistrés dans la région de Montréal
Membre(s) du bureau directeur:
Catherine Ouimet, Directrice générale
couimet@ajbm.qc.ca
Marie-Noël Bouchard, Coordonnatrice aux communications et finance
mnbouchard@ajbm.qc.ca
Andréanne Malacket, Présidente, Conseil d'administration
Membre(s) du personnel: 4; 15 bénévole(s)
Membre: 4200+; *Critères d'admissibilite:* Avocats inscrits dans la région de Montréal qui ont pratiqué le droit pendant au moins dix ans; *Comités:* Activités socioculturelles et sportives; Affaires publiques; Communications; Congrès - Gala; Développement international et professionnel; Diversité ethnoculturelle; ÉcoComité; Financement; Formation; Recherche et législation; Relations avec les membres; Services juridiques pro bono; Technologies de l'information
Meetings/Conferences: • Congrès annuel de Association du jeune barreau de Montréal 2015, May, 2015, Palais des congrès de Montréal, Montréal, QC
Scope: Provincial
Publications:
• L'extrajudiciaire
Type: Bulletin; *Frequency:* 6 fois par ans; *Accepts Advertising*; *Editor:* Marie-Noël Bouchard
Profile: Articles sur des sujets juridiques que les membres de l'association d'intérêt, ainsi que des informations sur les services que l'association propose

Association du Nouveau-Brunswick pour l'intégration communautaire *See* New Brunswick Association for Community Living

Association du patrimoine d'Aylmer *See* Aylmer Heritage Association

Association du personnel administratif et professionnel de l'Université de Moncton (APAPUM)

Local B1503, Centre étudiant, Campus de Moncton, Université de Moncton, 19, av Antonine-Maillet, Moncton NB E1A 3E9
apapum@umoncton.ca
web.umoncton.ca/umcm-apapum
Aperçu: *Dimension:* petite; *Envergure:* locale; Organisme sans but lucratif; fondée en 1976
Membre de: Fédération du personnel professionnel des universités et de la recherche (FPPU)
Membre(s) du bureau directeur:
Chantal DeGrâce, Présidente, 506-858-3716
chantal.degrace@umoncton.ca
Conrad Melanson, Vice-président, 506-858-4163
Hélène Savoie, Secrétaire, 506-858-4797
Mélissa Kate Lelièvre, Trésorière, 506-858-4588
Membre: 80+; *Critères d'admissibilite:* Personnel administatif et professionnel de l'universté de Moncton; *Comités:* Comité d'équité en matière d'emploi; Comité d'étude de plaintes en matière de harcèlement sexuel et sexiste; Comité de harcèlement et gestion de conflits; Comité paritaire sur la classification des postes; Comité de liaison; Comité de perfectionnement professionnel; Comité de retraite; Comité de santé et sécurité au travail; Comité des bourses; Comité des circonstances spéciales; Comité du régime d'assurance en soins de santé; Comité de travail pour les négociations; Comité aviseur du mieux-être universitaire; Comité de l'assurance invalidité de longue durée

Association du personnel de l'Université York *See* York University Staff Association

Association du personnel enseignant de l'Université Carleton *See* Carleton University Academic Staff Association

Association du personnel enseignant de l'Université de l'Alberta *See* Association of Academic Staff - University of Alberta

Association du personnel professionelle de l'Université de Guelph *See* University of Guelph Professional Staff Association

L'Association du Québec de l'Institut canadien des évaluateurs (AQICE) / Québec Association of the Appraisal Institute of Canada

587, ch Rhéaume, Saint-Michel QC J0L 2J0
Tél: 613-234-6533
Ligne sans frais: 866-726-5916
aqice@aicanada.ca
www.aicanada.ca
Aperçu: *Dimension:* petite; *Envergure:* provinciale; fondée en 1995 surveillé par Appraisal Institute of Canada
Mission: La mission de l'Institut canadien des évaluateurs est de protéger l'intérêt du public en s'assurant que ses membres offrent des services d'expert-conseil selon des normes élevées de pratique professionnelle
Membre(s) du bureau directeur:
George Semine, President
george.semine@sympatico.ca
Membre: *Montant de la cotisation:* 115,03$

Association du Québec pour enfants avec problèmes auditifs (AQEPA)

3700, rue Berri, #A-446, Montréal QC H2L 4G9
Tél: 514-842-8706; *Téléc:* 514-842-4006
Ligne sans frais: 877-842-4006
info@aqepa.org
www.aqepa.org
www.facebook.com/AQEPA
Aperçu: *Dimension:* moyenne; *Envergure:* provinciale; Organisme sans but lucratif; fondée en 1969
Mission: Regrouper les parents d'enfants sourds et malentendants; informer et sensibiliser les parents et le public
Membre: *Montant de la cotisation:* 20$ étudiant; 40$ parents/individu; 70$ institutionnel; *Critères d'admissibilite:* Parents, sympathisants, professionnels, institutions
Activités: *Bibliothèque:* Centre d'information; rendez-vous

AQEPA Abitibi-Témiscamingue
CP 583, Amos QC J9T 3X2
aqepa.abitibi-temiscamingue@aqepa.org
www.facebook.com/groups/aqepaabitibi/
Membre(s) du bureau directeur:
Benoit Bergeron, Président

AQEPA Bas-Saint-Laurent
CP 53, Rimouski QC G5L 7B7
aqepa.bas-st-laurent@aqepa.org
Membre(s) du bureau directeur:
François Jean, Président

AQEPA Côte-Nord
a/s Secrétariat provincial, #A-446, 3700, rue Berri, Montréal QC H2L 4G9
Téléc: 514-842-4006
Ligne sans frais: 877-842-4006
aqepa.cote-nord@aqepa.org

AQEPA Estrie
435, rue Wellington sud, Sherbrooke QC J1H 5E2
Tél: 819-929-2737
aqepa.estrie@aqepa.org
Membre(s) du bureau directeur:
Almir Omercevic, Président

AQEPA Gaspésie - Iles-de-la-Madeleine
a/s Secrétariat provincial, #A-446, 3700, rue Berri, Montréal QC H2L 4G9
Téléc: 514-842-4006
Ligne sans frais: 877-842-4006
aqepa.gaspesie-iles-de-la-madeleine@aqepa.org

AQEPA Lac-Saint-Jean
CP 174, Roberval QC G8H 2N6
aqepa.lac-st-jean@aqepa.org
Membre(s) du bureau directeur:
Nataly Joncas, Président

AQEPA Mauricie/Centre du Québec
#212, 3550, rue Cherbourg, Trois-Rivières QC G8Y 6S6
Tél: 819-370-3558; *Téléc:* 819-370-1413
aqepa.mauricie-centre-du-quebec@aqepa.org
Membre(s) du bureau directeur:
Johanne Fournier, Présidente

AQEPA Montréal Régional
#A-436, 3700, rue Berri, Montréal QC H2L 4G9
Tél: 514-842-3926; *Téléc:* 514-842-4006
aqepa.montreal@aqepa.org
www.aqepa-mtl.org
Membre(s) du bureau directeur:
Pierre Lazure, Présidente

AQEPA Outaouais
117, rue des Manoirs, Gatineau QC J9J 2N2
aqepa.outaouais@aqepa.org

AQEPA Québec Métro
#330, 6780, 1ere av, Québec QC G1H 2W8
Tél: 418-623-3232
aqepa.quebec-metro@aqepa.org
www.facebook.com/lunik0312
Membre(s) du bureau directeur:
Caroline Émond, Président

AQEPA Saguenay
205, rue Lacordaire, Chicoutimi QC G7G 3Y8
aqepa.saguenay@aqepa.org
Membre(s) du bureau directeur:
Sylvie Tremblay, Président

Association du Québec pour l'intégration sociale / Institut québécois de la déficience intellectuelle (AQIS-IQDI) / Québec Association for Community Living / Québec Institute for Intellectual Disability

3958, rue Dandurand, Montréal QC H1X 1P7
Tél: 514-725-7245; *Téléc:* 514-725-2796
Autres numéros: IQDI, Tél: 514-725-2387
info@aqis-iqdi.qc.ca
www.aqis-iqdi.qc.ca
www.facebook.com/151177351568742
Aperçu: *Dimension:* moyenne; *Envergure:* provinciale; fondée en 1951 surveillé par Canadian Association for Community Living
Mission: Défendre les droits et promouvoir les intérêts des personnes ayant une déficience intellectuelle
Membre de: Canadian Association for Community Living
Membre(s) du bureau directeur:
Jacqueline Babin, Présidente
Diane Milliard, Directrice générale
dmilliard@aqis-iqdi.qc.ca
Finances: *Budget de fonctionnement annuel:* $500,000-$1.5 Million
Membre: 73 associations; *Critères d'admissibilite:* Association locale de parents
Activités: *Événements de sensibilisation:* Semaine québécoise de la déficience intellectuelle; *Bibliothèque:* Centre de documentation; Bibliothèque publique rendez-vous

L'Association du saumon Nepisiguit *See* Nepisiguit Salmon Association

Association du syndrome de Down de L'Estrie (ASDE)

836, rue St-Charles, Sherbrooke QC J1H 4Z2
Tél: 819-569-8112; *Téléc:* 819-569-5144
Ligne sans frais: 877-569-8112
asde_t21@hotmail.com
pages.videotron.com/trisomie
Aperçu: *Dimension:* petite; *Envergure:* locale; Organisme sans but lucratif; fondée en 1987
Mission: Promotion et la défense des enfants et adultes atteint de la Trisomie 21 ou Syndrome de Down
Membre de: Association canadienne du Syndrome de Down; Assn. régionale loisir personnes handicapées Estrie; Trisomie Québec; Action Handicap Estrie
Affliation(s): Association du Québec pour l'intégration sociale
Membre(s) du bureau directeur:
France St-Pierre, Directrice générale
Maryse Martel, Présidente
Henriette Racicot, Vice-présidente
Finances: *Budget de fonctionnement annuel:* Moins de $50,000
Membre(s) du personnel: 5; 76 bénévole(s)
Membre: 182; *Montant de la cotisation:* 10$; *Critères d'admissibilite:* Famille

Association du syndrome de Marfan *See* Canadian Marfan Association

Association du Syndrome de Sjogren, Inc / Sjögren's Syndrome Association
#001, 3155 Hochelaga, Montréal QC H1W 1G4
Tel: 514-934-3666; *Fax:* 514-934-1241
Toll-Free: 877-934-3666
sjogren.montreal@qc.aira.com
www.sjogrens.ca
Overview: A small national charitable organization
Mission: To work to draw the attention of medical world to Sjogren's Syndrome & the urgent need to discover a cause & cure; to provide support & education to patients & information to the medical community
Finances: *Funding Sources:* Donations

Association du Syndrome de Turner du Québec
1908-14, rue du Caribou, Montréal QC J4N 2R2
Tél: 450-448-9009
Ligne sans frais: 888-988-7637
turnerquinfo@syndrometurnerquebec.com
www.syndrometurnerquebec.com
Aperçu: *Dimension:* petite; *Envergure:* provinciale; Organisme sans but lucratif; fondée en 1984
Mission: Faire connaître les personnes atteintes du S.T.; faire circuler l'information médicale; créer des nouveaux contacts
Membre(s) du bureau directeur:
Mélanie Boivin, Co-présidente
Annie Hébert, Co-présidente
Membre: *Montant de la cotisation:* 25$ (personne atteinte); 30$ famille; 50$ professionnel(le) de la santé
Activités: Écoute téléphonique; information de base; Info Cassette; articles médicaux

Association du thé du Canada *See* Tea Association of Canada

Association du transport aérien du Canada *See* Air Transport Association of Canada

Association du transport aérien international *See* International Air Transport Association

Association du transport écolier du Québec (ATEQ)
#300, 5300, boul des Galeries, Québec QC G2K 2A2
Tél: 418-622-6544; *Téléc:* 418-622-6595
courrier@ateq.qc.ca
www.ateq.qc.ca
Aperçu: *Dimension:* moyenne; *Envergure:* provinciale; fondée en 1962
Mission: De promouvoir les intérêts de ses membres et créer une haute qualité, un service de transport fiable
Membre(s) du bureau directeur:
Luc Lafrance, Directeur général
llafrance@ateq.qc.ca
Membre(s) du personnel: 9
Membre: 625 transporteurs scolaires; *Montant de la cotisation:* Barème

Association du transport urbain du Québec (ATUQ) / Quebec Urban Transit Association
#8090, 800, rue de la Gauchetière, Montréal QC H5A 1J6
Tél: 514-280-4640; *Téléc:* 514-280-7053
info@atuq.com
www.atuq.com
www.linkedin.com/company/association-du-transport-urbain-du-quebec-atu
Aperçu: *Dimension:* moyenne; *Envergure:* provinciale; fondée en 1983
Mission: Organisme de concertation et de représentation politique qui a pour mandat d'assurer la promotion du transport en commun et la défense des intérêts de ses membres auprès des partenaires de l'industrie et des différentes instances gouvernementales
Membre(s) du bureau directeur:
Patrice Martin, Président
France Vézina, Directrice générale
Valèrie Leclerc, Responsable de communications, 514-280-8167
valerie.leclerc@atuq.com
Membre(s) du personnel: 6
Membre: 9; *Critères d'admissibilite:* Sociétés de transport en commun du Québec
Activités: *Bibliothèque* Bibliothèque publique

Association du verre d'art du Canada *See* Glass Art Association of Canada

Association échecs et maths *See* Chess & Math Association

Association Évangile & Enfance *Voir* Child Evangelism Fellowship of Canada

Association fédérale des représentants de la sécurité *See* Federal Association of Security Officials

Association féline Canadienne *See* Canadian Cat Association

Association féminine d'éducation et d'action sociale (AFEAS) / Feminine Association for Education & Social Action
5999, rue de Marseille, Montréal QC H1N 1K6
Tél: 514-251-1636; *Téléc:* 514-251-9023
info@afeas.qc.ca
www.afeas.qc.ca
www.facebook.com/pages/Afeas/181581728519026
twitter.com/afeas1966
www.youtube.com/results?search_query=afeas&aq=f
Aperçu: *Dimension:* moyenne; *Envergure:* provinciale; fondée en 1966
Mission: Avec ses Activités femmes d'ici organisées sur tout le territoire québécois, l'Afeas informe ses membres, suscite des échanges et des débats et les incite à participer davantage aux différentes structures de la société
Affliation(s): Union mondiale des organisations féminines catholiques (UMOFC)
Membre: 14 000; *Montant de la cotisation:* 23$
Activités: *Bibliothèque*

Saguenay-Lac-St-Jean-Chibougamau
208, rue Dequen, St-Gédéon QC G0W 2P0
Tél: 418-345-8324; *Téléc:* 418-345-8289
afeas02@hotmail.com
www.afeas.qc.ca
Membre(s) du bureau directeur:
France Morissette, Responsable

Association for Awareness & Networking around Disordered Eating *See* Jessie's Hope Society

Association for Baha'i Studies (ABS) / Association d'études Baha'is
34 Copernicus St., Ottawa ON K1N 7K4
Tel: 613-233-1903; *Fax:* 613-233-3644
www.bahai-studies.ca
www.facebook.com/331784303733
Previous Name: Canadian Association for Studies in the Baha'i Faith
Overview: A medium-sized international charitable organization founded in 1975
Mission: To foster Baha'i scholarship & to demonstrate the value of this scholarly approach; to promote courses of study on the Baha'i faith; to foster relationships with various leaders of thought & persons of capacity; to publish scholarly materials examining the Baha'i faith, especially on its application to the concerns & needs of humanity; to organize annual meetings & develop chapters of the Association around the world
Finances: *Annual Operating Budget:* $100,000-$250,000; *Funding Sources:* Grants; Conference & Literature revenue; Membership fees
Staff Member(s): 2
Membership: 2,000; *Fees:* $50 adult; $60 couple; $25 student/senior; $60 institution; $999 individual life
Activities: *Library* Open to public by appointment
Awards:
• Awards for Distinguished Scholarship
Eligibility: Scholarship advancing our collective understanding of Baha'i teachings; two awards: 1) published research study; 2) graduate thesis.
Meetings/Conferences: • Annual Conference, Association for Baha'i Studies, August

Association for Bright Children (Ontario) (ABC Ontario) / Société pour enfants doués et surdoués (Ontario)
c/o 135 Brant St., Oakville ON L6K 2Z8
Tel: 416-925-6136
abcinfo@abcontario.ca
www.abcontario.ca
Overview: A small provincial charitable organization founded in 1975
Mission: To provide information & support to parents of bright & gifted children; to increase the understanding & acceptance of bright & gifted children/youth at home, at school & in the community & encourages society to nurture them that they may reach their full potential.
Chief Officer(s):
David Croome, President
president@abcontario.ca
Claire Collins, Executive Director
director@abcontario.ca
Pascale Lapointe-Antunes, Secretary-Treasurer
finance@abcontario.ca
Finances: *Funding Sources:* Membership fees; donations
Membership: *Fees:* Free; *Member Profile:* Anyone interested in special needs of bright & gifted children; *Committees:* Finance; Advocacy; Research & Support; Business Development

Association for Canadian & Québec Literatures (ACQL) / L'Association des littératures canadiennes et québécoise (ALCQ)
c/o Steven Urquhart, Dept. Modern Languages, University of Lethbridge, 4401 University Dr., Lethbridge AB T1K 3M4
www.alcq-acql.ca
Overview: A small national organization founded in 1973
Mission: To promote research, theory, & literary criticism about the literature of Canada & Québec
Chief Officer(s):
Lucie Hotte, President
lhotte@uottawa.ca
Steven Urquhart, Treasurer
steven.urquhart@uleth.ca
Membership: *Fees:* $25 students; $50 regular membership; $350 lifetime membership
Activities: Encouraging scholarly conversation among persons studying & researching the literature of Canada & Québec in English & French
Awards:
• Priz Gabrielle Roy Prize (Award)
To hounour the best works of Canadian literary criticism in English & French *Contact:* Maité Snauwaer; Cynthia Sugars, E-mail: snauwaer@ualberta.ca; csugars@uottawa.ca
• Barbara Godard Emerging Scholar Prize (Award)
To honour the best paper by an emerging scholar

Association for Canadian Educational Resources (ACER)
#44, 3665 Flamewood Dr., Mississauga ON L4Y 3P5
Tel: 905-275-7685; *Fax:* 905-275-9420
acerinfo@rogers.com
www.acer-acre.org
www.facebook.com/pages/ACER/113442745413630
twitter.com/AcerAcre
Overview: A small national organization founded in 1991
Mission: To promote & to help create Canadian materials for classroom life early learners
Chief Officer(s):
Alice Casselman, President
Ana Maria Martinez, Program Coordinator
Finances: *Annual Operating Budget:* Less than $50,000; *Funding Sources:* Membership fees; donations; grants
Staff Member(s): 1; 30 volunteer(s)
Membership: 50; *Fees:* $30 adult; $20 retired person; $10 student; *Member Profile:* Volunteers from all sectors especially retired educators
Activities: Schools, community groups volunteer as part of Environment Canada delivery of mentoring system; community outreach; training workshops; displays at conferences

Association for Canadian Jewish Studies (ACJS) / Association d'études juives canadiennes (AEJC)
Dept. of Religion, Concordia University, 1455, rue de Maisonneuve ouest, Montréal QC H3G 1M8
Tel: 514-848-2424; *Fax:* 514-848-4541
secretary@acjs-aejc.ca
acjs-aejc.ca
Overview: A small national charitable organization founded in 1974
Mission: To encourage interdisciplinary study of the Canadian Jewish experience
Member of: Canadian Jewish Congress
Chief Officer(s):
Randal F. Schnoor, President
Robin Bergart, Treasurer
Finances: *Annual Operating Budget:* Less than $50,000; *Funding Sources:* Foundations
Staff Member(s): 1; 38 volunteer(s)
Membership: 28 institutional; 20 student; 150 individual; *Fees:* $180 institutional; $25 student/senior; $50 individual; *Member Profile:* Open to anyone; *Committees:* Journal; Bulletin; Membership; Community Archives; Conference Program; Fundraising

Activities: Hosting an annual conference; Publishing a bulletin & journal; Sponsoring local workshops & activities; Facilitating an online discussion group
Awards:
• ACJS/AEJC Distinguished Service Award (Award)
Publications:
• Canadian Jewish Studies
Profile: Annual academic journal

Association for Canadian Registered Safety Professionals *See* Board of Canadian Registered Safety Professionals

Association for Canadian Studies (ACS) / Association d'études canadiennes (AEC)
1822A, rue Sherbooke ouest, Montréal QC H3H 1E4
Tel: 514-925-3099; *Fax:* 514-925-3095
general@acs-aec.ca
www.acs-aec.ca
www.facebook.com/acs.aec.canadianstudies
twitter.com/Canadianstudies
plus.google.com/113769569781539301984?prsrc=3
Overview: A large national charitable organization founded in 1973
Mission: To initiate & supports activities in the areas of research, teaching, communications, & the training of students in the field of Canadian studies, especially in interdisciplinary & multidisciplinary perspectives; To strive to raise public awareness of Canadian issues; To provide the Canadian Studies community, principally within Canada, with a wide range of activities & programs
Member of: International Council for Canadian Studies; Humanities & Social Sciences Federation of Canada
Chief Officer(s):
Jack Jedwab, Executive Director
James Ondrick, Director, Programs & Administration
Finances: *Annual Operating Budget:* $500,000-$1.5 Million; *Funding Sources:* Federal government; Membership dues
Staff Member(s): 5; 25 volunteer(s)
Membership: 130 institutional + 350 individual; *Fees:* $55-$125 regular; $90-$160 institutional; $25-$95 student/retired
Activities: Publications; national programs for students (graduate scholarship; aid for conferences); international programs (Chinese faculty meet & greet program; foreign speakers program); annual meeting of Canadian Studies program administrators; *Rents Mailing List:* Yes; *Library:* Documentation Centre
Awards:
• Award of Merit (Award)
Meetings/Conferences: • 17th National Metropolis Conference: Broadening the Conversation: Policy and Practice in Immigration, Settlement and Diversity, March, 2015, Sheraton Wall Centre, Vancouver, BC
Scope: National
Contact Information: URL: www.metropolisconference.ca

Association for Canadian Theatre History *See* Canadian Association for Theatre Research

Association for Community Living - Manitoba *See* Community Living Manitoba

Association for Corporate Growth, Toronto Chapter (ACG)
#202, 720 Spadina Ave, Toronto ON M5S 2T9
Tel: 416-868-1881; *Fax:* 416-292-5256
acgtoronto@managingmatters.com
www.acg.org/toronto
Also Known As: ACG Toronto
Previous Name: Canadian Association for Corporate Growth
Overview: A medium-sized national organization founded in 1973
Mission: To foster sound corporate growth by providing its members with an opportunity to gain new ideas from speakers, seminars & discussions with people working in the field of corporate growth; to develop additional skills & techniques which will contribute to the growth of their respective organizations; to meet other corporate growth professionals who can provide counsel & valuable contacts
Member of: Association for Corporate Growth, Chicago USA
Chief Officer(s):
Stephen B. Smith, President
Finances: *Annual Operating Budget:* Less than $50,000; *Funding Sources:* Membership dues; events
Staff Member(s): 1
Membership: 14,000 worldwide; *Fees:* $406.80; $960 corporate; *Member Profile:* Granted on an individual basis only to those involved in corporate growth; approximately 2/3 membership drawn from the industrial & consumer product fields, & the balance from accounting firms, financial intermediaries, & related service businesses; *Committees:* Nominations; Programming; Membership; Social

Association for Democracy in Romania *See* Romanian Children's Relief

Association for Financial Professionals - Calgary (AFPC)
PO Box 20177, Stn. Bow Valley, Calgary AB T2P 4L2
afpc-calgary.ca
Also Known As: AFP - Calgary
Overview: A small local organization overseen by Association for Financial Professionals
Mission: To enhance members' expertise in the field of treasury management
Member of: Association for Financial Professionals
Chief Officer(s):
Rhian Silvennoinen, President
Membership: *Fees:* $350 corporate; *Member Profile:* Local treasury professionals
Activities: Networking & career development opportunities

Association for Financial Professionals - Ottawa
PO Box 889, Stn. B, Ottawa ON K1P 5P9
www.afpc-ottawa.ca
Also Known As: AFP - Ottawa
Overview: A small local organization overseen by Association for Financial Professionals
Mission: To exchange knowledge, ideas & solutions for challenges facing the industry
Member of: Association for Financial Professionals
Chief Officer(s):
Anju Malhotra, President
anju.malhotra@scotiabank.com
Membership: *Fees:* $125 individual; $325 corporate; $600 large corporate; *Member Profile:* Treasury, risk & financial professionals in Ottawa; *Committees:* Program; Event; Membership; Publicity/Sponsorship
Activities: Networking & speaker events;

Association for Financial Professionals - Vancouver
c/o Scotiabank, Global Transaction Banking, PO Box 11502, #305, 650 West Georgia St., Vancouver BC V6B 4P6
Other Communication: Toll-Free Fax: 1-888-593-8166
info@afpcvancouver.com
www.afpc-vancouver.ca
Also Known As: AFP - Vancouver
Previous Name: Treasury Management Association of Canada - British Columbia
Overview: A small local organization founded in 2010 overseen by Association for Financial Professionals
Mission: To promote & facilitate high standards of professional development & conduct in treasury management
Member of: Association for Financial Professionals
Chief Officer(s):
Rory Langran, President
Paula Merrier, Director, Membership
Membership: *Fees:* $50-$125 regular & associate; $50 student; *Member Profile:* Treasury professionals from mid-market corporations, crown corporations, banks, investment dealers, finance & trust companies, software vendors, management consultants & government organizations
Activities: Networking & career development opportunities

Association for German Education in Calgary (AGEC)
Bowcroft Elementary School, 3940 - 73 St. NW, Calgary AB T3B 2L9
Tel: 403-777-6020
germaneducationcalgary@gmail.com
www.germaneducationcalgary.ca
www.facebook.com/AssociationForGermanEducationInCalgary
Overview: A small local organization founded in 2001
Mission: To promote bilingual German-English education from kindergarten to grade 6 in Calgary
Membership: *Fees:* $10

Association for Healthcare Philanthropy (Canada)
c/o Stratford General Hospital Foundation, 46 General Hospital Dr., Stratford ON N5A 2Y8
Tel: 519-272-8210; *Fax:* 519-272-8238
www.ahp.org
Also Known As: AHP Canada
Overview: A small national organization
Mission: Educational organization and advocacy body for health care fundraising professionals in Canada.
Member of: Association for Healthcare Philathropy
Chief Officer(s):
Mitze Mourinho, Campaign Director
Membership: 400
Activities: Education & accreditation opportunities for members through conferences & roundtables
Awards:
• Culture of Philanthropy Award (Award)
• Best Practices Award (Award)
• Mentoring Award (Award)
• Leadership Award (Award)
• AHP Canada Regional Conference Bursaries (Scholarship)
Amount: $1,200 (2)
Meetings/Conferences: • 2015 Association for Healthcare Philanthropy Convene Canada, April, 2015, Sheraton Wall Centre Hotel., Vancouver, BC
Scope: National

Association for Image & Information Management International - 1st Canadian Chapter (AIIM Canada)
Toronto ON
www.aiim.org/Community/Chapters/First-Canadian
Previous Name: Canadian Micrographic Society; Canadian Information & Image Management Society
Overview: A medium-sized international organization founded in 2000
Mission: To connect users & suppliers of e-business technologies & services
Affiliation(s): Association for Information & Image Management
Chief Officer(s):
Winnie Tsang, President
winnie.tsang@teranet.ca
Finances: *Funding Sources:* Membership fees; conference

Association for Literature, Environment, & Culture in Canada (ALECC) / Association pour la littérature, l'environnement et la culture au Canada
c/o Department of English, University of Calgary, 2500 University Dr. NW, 11th Fl., Calgary AB T2N 1N4
e-mail: contactus@alecc.ca
www.alecc.ca
Overview: A small national organization founded in 2005
Mission: To promote and support artistic, critical and cultural studies work on a wide range of environmental issues.
Chief Officer(s):
Robert Boschman, President
rboschman@mtroyal.ca
Membership: *Fees:* $25-$40
Meetings/Conferences: • Association for Literature, Environment, & Culture in Canada 2016 Biennial Conference, 2016
Scope: National

Association for Manager of Health Facilities & Social Services *Voir* Association des gestionnaires des établissements de santé et des services sociaux

Association for Manitoba Archives (AMA)
PO Box 26005, Stn. Maryland, Winnipeg MB R3G 3R3
Tel: 204-942-3491; *Fax:* 204-942-3492
ama1@mts.net
mbarchives.ca
Previous Name: Manitoba Council of Archives
Overview: A medium-sized provincial organization founded in 1992 overseen by Canadian Council of Archives
Mission: To promote understanding & awareness of the role & use of archives; to promote standards, procedures & practices in the management of archives; to provide assistance & education to persons seeking to improve their skills in the development, management or operation of archives
Affliation(s): Association of Canadian Archivists
Chief Officer(s):
Christy Henry, Chair
Finances: *Annual Operating Budget:* $100,000-$250,000; *Funding Sources:* Government grants; membership fees
Staff Member(s): 1
Membership: 36 institutions + 100 individual; *Committees:* Education Advisory Services; Information & Outreach
Publications:
• AMA Newsletter
Editor: Joan Sinclair *ISSN:* 1193-9958
Profile: Informs members of association activities, events & news.

Association for Media Literacy (AML)
Toronto ON
e-mail: associationformedialiteracy@gmail.com
www.aml.ca
twitter.com/A_M_L_
www.youtube.com/user/AssociationMediaLit
Overview: A medium-sized international organization founded in 1978
Mission: Made up of teachers, librarians, consultants, parents, cultural workers, and media professionals concerned about the impact of the mass media on contemporary culture.
Chief Officer(s):
Neil Anderson, President

Association for Mineral Exploration British Columbia (AMEBC)
#800, 889 West Pender St., Vancouver BC V6C 3B2
Tel: 604-689-5271; *Fax:* 604-681-2363
info@amebc.ca
www.amebc.ca
Previous Name: British Columbia & Yukon Chamber of Mines
Overview: A medium-sized provincial organization founded in 1912
Mission: To promote & assist development & growth of mining of mineral exploration in BC
Affliation(s): Mining Association of Canada; Mining Association of BC
Chief Officer(s):
Gavin C. Dirom, President & CEO
Finances: *Annual Operating Budget:* $250,000-$500,000; *Funding Sources:* Membership dues
Staff Member(s): 6
Membership: 3,605 individual + 179 corporate; *Fees:* $50 individual; *Member Profile:* Member of mining community; *Committees:* Many-Land Use; Mining Law; Safety
Activities: *Library:* Charles S. Ney Library; Open to public
Meetings/Conferences: • Mineral Exploration Roundup 2015, January, 2015, BC
Scope: Provincial

Association for Mountain Parks Protection & Enjoyment (AMPPE)
PO Box 2999, Banff AB T1L 1C7
Tel: 403-762-3800; *Fax:* 403-762-3828
info@amppe.org
www.amppe.org
www.facebook.com/158883817584661
twitter.com/amppe
Overview: A small provincial organization founded in 1994
Mission: To champion & promote sustainable tourism, a vibrant mountain economy, & responsible human use in mountain parks
Chief Officer(s):
Monica Andreeff, Executive Director
Membership: *Fees:* $50

Association for Native Development in the Performing & Visual Arts (ANDPVA)
#10, 610 Baldwin St., Toronto ON M5T 3K7
Tel: 416-535-4567; *Fax:* 416-535-9331
info@andpva.com
www.andpva.com
Overview: A medium-sized national organization founded in 1974
Mission: To coordinate & develop programs that will encourage Indigenous peoples & communities to become more actively involved in the arts; to act as liaison for Native groups & individuals who are seeking funds for specific arts projects
Chief Officer(s):
Millie Knapp, Executive Director
millie.andpva@gmail.com
Finances: *Funding Sources:* Government
Staff Member(s): 3
Membership: 300; *Fees:* $25 - $75; *Committees:* Music Advisory; Writers & Storytellers; Visual Arts
Activities: *Internships:* Yes; *Speaker Service:* Yes; *Rents Mailing List:* Yes

Association for New Canadians (ANC) / L'association des nouveaux Canadiens (ANC)
Head Office & Settlement Services, PO Box 2031, Stn. C, 144 Military Rd., St. John's NL A1C 5R6
Tel: 709-722-9680; *Fax:* 709-754-4407
settlement@nfld.net
www.ancnl.ca
Overview: A small provincial organization founded in 1979
Mission: To provide full service immigrant settlement programs & services to the newcomer community in Newfoundland & Labrador; To support integration, & cross cultural understanding
Finances: *Funding Sources:* Citizenship & Immigration Canada; HRSDC; Service Canada; Canadian Hertiage; ACOA; Government of Newfoundland & Labrador; United Way
100 volunteer(s)
Activities: Providing ESL adult training, career services, life skills training, diversity & organizational change training, an immigrant settlement adaptation program, integration programs, a resettlement assistance program, a settlement workers in the schools program, programming for children, youth, & women, & public education activities

Association for Operations Management (APICS)
#300, 1370 Don Mills Rd., Toronto ON M3B 3N7
Tel: 416-366-5388; *Fax:* 416-381-4054
info@apics.ca
www.apics.ca
Previous Name: Canadian Association for Production & Inventory Control; American Production & Inventory Control Society
Overview: A medium-sized national licensing organization founded in 1962
Mission: To offer programs & materials on business management techniques; To promotes education in resource management
Chief Officer(s):
Shari Bricks, Executive Director
shari.bricks@apics.ca
Lina DeMatteo, Manager, Events
events@apics.ca
Anthony Nijmeh, Manager, Technical Support
anthony.nijmeh@apics.ca
Greg Mulroney, Coordinator, Membership Support
info@apics.ca
9 volunteer(s)
Membership: 3,000; *Fees:* Schedule available; *Member Profile:* Professional operations managers; *Committees:* Specific Interest Groups: Aerospace & Defence; Process Industry; Remanufacturing; Repetitive Manufacturing Group; Small Manufacturing; Textile & Apparel
Activities: Administering courses for CPIM (Certified in Production & Inventory Management) & CIRM (Certified in Integrated Resource Management) certifications; *Speaker Service:* Yes; *Rents Mailing List:* Yes

Association for Persons with Physical Disabilities of Windsor & Essex County *See* Assisted Living Southwestern Ontario

Association for Science & Reason (ASR)
Toronto ON
www.scienceandreason.ca
Previous Name: Skeptics Canada
Overview: A small national organization
Mission: To promote the understanding and application of critical thinking skills and scientific methodology in the explanation of human experience - from the seemingly mundane to the alleged paranormal.

Association for the Advancement of Scandinavian Studies in Canada (AASSC) / L'association pour l'avancement des études scandinaves au Canada
c/o Dr. Ingrid Urberg, Augustana Campus, University of Alberta, #4901, 46th Ave., Camrose AB T4V 2R3
Tel: 780-679-1573; *Fax:* 780-679-1590
aassc.com
www.facebook.com/groups/6426106974/
Overview: A small national organization founded in 1982
Mission: AASSC is an association for research in Canada on all aspects of life in the Scandinavian societies. It provides a multi-disciplinary forum for the presentation of papers on all matters relevant to Scandinavia.
Member of: Canadian Federation for the Humanities & Social Sciences
Chief Officer(s):
Ingrid Urberg, President, 780-679-1573
iurberg@augustana.ca
Mads Bunch, Vice President/Programming Chair
mads.bunch@gmail.com
Brigitta Wallace, Treasurer, 902-443-5281
birwallace@eastlink.ca
Susan Gold Smith, Secretary, 519-253-3000 Ext. 2845
sgold@uwindsor.ca
Finances: *Annual Operating Budget:* Less than $50,000; *Funding Sources:* Membership fees, donations, Canadian Institute of Nordic Studies
Membership: 150; *Fees:* $40 regular; $40 institutional; $20 retired; $15 student; *Member Profile:* Academics; students; interested members of the community
Activities: Scholarly research of Scandinavian topics & dissemination of its results
Publications:
• Association for the Advancement of Scandanavian Studies in Canada
Type: Newsletter; *Editor:* Erin McGuire; *Price:* Free for members
Profile: Eighteen volumes, available in digital format from vol. 15 on, in a searchable database
• Scandinavian-Canandian Studies
Type: journal; *Price:* Free for members
Profile: Eighteen volumes, available in digital format from vol. 15 on, in a searchable database

Association for the Export of Canadian Books *See* Livres Canada Books

Association for the Hearing Handicapped *See* Connect Society - D.E.A.F. Services

Association for the Rehabilitation of the Brain Injured (ARBI)
3412 Spruce Dr. SW, Calgary AB T3C 3A4
Tel: 403-242-7116; *Fax:* 403-242-7478
info@arbi.ca
arbi.ca
www.facebook.com/associationfortherehabilitationofthebraininjured
twitter.com/arbi_ca
Overview: A medium-sized provincial charitable organization founded in 1972
Mission: To improve the quality of life of individuals with severe acquired brain injury through long-term personalized rehabilitation
Chief Officer(s):
Mary Ellen Neilson, Executive Director
MaryEllenNeilson@arbi.ca
Bruce Murray, President
Finances: *Funding Sources:* United Way; Calgary Health Region; service clubs; foundations; individual donations
Activities: Volleyball tournament; golf tournament; *Awareness Events:* Brain Injury Awareness Week, June; *Speaker Service:* Yes

The Association for the Soldiers of Israel (ASI)
#201, 788 Marlee Ave., Toronto ON M6B 3K1
Tel: 416-783-3053; *Fax:* 416-787-7496
Toll-Free: 800-433-6226
info@asicanada.org
asicanada.org
Also Known As: ASI Canada
Overview: A small international organization founded in 1971
Mission: To support the well-being of Israeli soldiers on active duty; to fund social, spiritual & recreational programs & facilities to ease the burden faced by young soldiers defending the Jewish homeland
Chief Officer(s):
Talia Klein Leighton, Administrator
talia.klein@asicanada.org
Membership: 500-999
Activities: Mobile clubrooms; fitness rooms; synagogues on IDF bases; Spirit Program; Dignity Program; Lone Soliders program; Soliders in Transit program;

Association for the Study of Nationalities (ASN)
c/o Harriman Institute, Columbia University, 420 West 118th St., 12th Fl., New York NY 10027 USA
www.nationalities.org
www.facebook.com/Nationalities
twitter.com/ASN_Org
Overview: A small international organization
Mission: The Association for the Study of Nationalities (ASN) is the only scholarly association devoted to the study of ethnicity and nationalism from Europe to Eurasia.
Chief Officer(s):
Zsuzsa Csergo, President
csergo@queensu.ca
Ryan Kreider, Executive Director
rk2780@columbia.edu
Membership: *Fees:* US$70 individual; US$40 student; *Committees:* Program

Association for Vaccine Damaged Children
c/o Mary James, 67 Shier Dr., Winnipeg MB R3R 2H2
Overview: A small national organization founded in 1986
Mission: To inform parents of the risks of immunization; To support parents in any challenging situation with public health authorities
Chief Officer(s):
Mary James, Contact, 204-895-9192
tjames4@shaw.ca

Association for Women's Residential Facilities ***See*** Adsum for Women & Children

Association forestière canadienne ***See*** Canadian Forestry Association

Association forestière canadienne du Nouveau-Brunswick ***See*** Canadian Forestry Association of New Brunswick

L'Association française des municipalités de l'Ontario / Francophone Association of Municipalities of Ontario
#310, 1173, rue Cyrville, Ottawa ON K1J 7S6
Tél: 613-746-7707; *Téléc:* 613-746-8187
admin@afmo.on.ca
www.afmo.on.ca
Aperçu: *Dimension:* petite; *Envergure:* provinciale; fondée en 1989
Mission: De revendiquer le maintien et l'amélioration de la gouvernance et de la prestation des services municipaux en français et en anglais dans les régions de l'Ontario désignées en vertu de la Loi sur les services en français de l'Ontario.
Membre(s) du bureau directeur:
Jacqueline Noiseux, Directrice générale
dg@afmo.on.ca
Membre(s) du personnel: 2
Membre: 35 corporations, 47 membres associés

Association franco-culturelle de Hay River
CP 4482, 77A, rue Woodland, Hay River NT XOE 1G2
Tél: 867-674-3171
afchr.ca
www.facebook.com/AssociationFrancoCulturelleDeHayRiver
Aperçu: *Dimension:* petite; *Envergure:* locale; fondée en 1987 surveillé par Fédération franco-ténoise
Mission: Pour représenter la communauté francophone de Hay River et de défendre leurs droits
Membre(s) du bureau directeur:
Christian Girard, Président

Association Franco-culturelle de Yellowknife (AFCY)
CP 1586, Succ. Principale, 5016, 48 rue, Yellowknife NT X1A 2P2
Tél: 867-873-3292; *Téléc:* 867-873-2158
dgafcy@franco-nord.com
afcy.info
www.facebook.com/afcy.yellowknife
twitter.com/AFCYTNO
Aperçu: *Dimension:* petite; *Envergure:* locale; fondée en 1985 surveillé par Fédération franco-ténoise
Membre(s) du bureau directeur:
Pascaline Gréau, Direction générale
Membre(s) du personnel: 2
Membre: *Montant de la cotisation:* 20$ individuel; 30$ famille
Activités: Musique; théâtre; arts visuels; événements communautaires

Association francophone à l'éducation des services à l'enfance de l'Ontario (AFÉSEO)
#222. 135, rue Alice, Ottawa ON K1L 7X5
Tél: 613-741-5107; *Téléc:* 613-746-6140
communications@afeseo.ca
afeseo.ca
www.facebook.com/245498925585517
Aperçu: *Dimension:* moyenne; *Envergure:* provinciale; fondée en 1991
Mission: Pour aider les personnes en Ontario qui ont un intérêt dans l'éducation de la petite enfance
Membre de: Canadian Child Care Federation
Membre(s) du bureau directeur:
Martine St-Engo, Directrice générale
Bianca Nugent, Agente en communications
Membre: *Montant de la cotisation:* $25 étudiant; $75 individuel; $175 corporatif

Association francophone des municipalités du Nouveau-Brunswick Inc. (AFMNB)
#322, 702, rue Principale, Petit-Rocher NB E8J 1V1
Tél: 506-542-2622; *Téléc:* 506-542-2618
Ligne sans frais: 888-236-2622
afmnb@afmnb.org
www.afmnb.org
Nom précédent: Association des municipalités du Nouveau-Brunswick
Aperçu: *Dimension:* moyenne; *Envergure:* provinciale; fondée en 1989
Mission: Promouvoir le développement des municipalités francophones du Nouveau-Brunswick
Affliation(s): Association internationale des maires et responsables des capitales et métropoles partiellement ou entièrement francophones; Fédération canadienne des municipalités; Union des municipalités régionales de comté et des municipalités locales du Québec
Membre(s) du bureau directeur:
Frédérick Dion, Directeur général
direction@afmnb.org
Roger Doiron, Président
Finances: *Budget de fonctionnement annuel:* $50,000-$100,000
Membre(s) du personnel: 3
Membre: 48 municipalités; *Montant de la cotisation:* 750$ - 3,500$; *Comités:* Formation et spéciaux
Activités: Relations gouvernementales; porteur de dossiers contribuant au développement des municipalités francophones du Nouveau-Brunswick; *Stagiaires:* Oui; *Listes de destinataires:* Oui; *Bibliothèque:* Centre de documentation; Bibliothèque publique

Association francophone des parents du Nouveau-Brunswick (AFPNB)
421, av Acadie, Dieppe NB E1A 1H4
Tél: 506-859-8107; *Téléc:* 506-859-7191
Ligne sans frais: 888-369-9955
afpnb@nb.aibn.com
www.afpnb.ca
Nom précédent: Comité de parents du Nouveau-Brunswick
Aperçu: *Dimension:* petite; *Envergure:* provinciale; Organisme sans but lucratif; fondée en 1988
Mission: Est l'organisme porte-parole des parents acadiens et francophones du NB sur toutes les questions concernant le mieux-être de ses enfants et de la jeunesse
Membre de: Commission nationale des parents francophones
Affliation(s): Forum de concertation des organismes acadiens
Membre(s) du bureau directeur:
Madeleine Vachon, Présidente
Denyse LeBouthillier, Directrice générale
Finances: *Budget de fonctionnement annuel:* $250,000-$500,000; *Fonds:* Min. de l'Éducation; Patrimoine canadien; Min. des Affaires intergouvernementales
Membre(s) du personnel: 3; 15 bénévole(s)
Membre: 1 000; *Critères d'admissibilite:* Parents et autres personnes intéressés par l'éducation et la petite enfance
Activités: *Evénements de sensibilisation:* Semaine d'appréciation de l'éducation fév.
Prix, Bouses:
• Prix des Parents (Prix)
Décerné à une personne ou un groupe de personnes qui par leurs actions quotidiennes perpétuent une meilleure qualité de vie en milieu francophone
• Prix de la Commission nationale des parents francophones (Prix)
Reconnaît une personne qui a oeuvré au sein des comit‚s de parents; pour encourager et renforcer l'engagement et la solidarité des parents et de la communauté; pour permettre l'épanouissement de l'enfant et de sa famille; pour promouvoir la langue et la culture française

Association francophone pour le savoir (ACFAS)
425, rue de la Gauchetière est, Montréal QC H2L 2M7
Tél: 514-849-0045; *Téléc:* 514-849-5558
www.acfas.ca
linkedin.com/company/acfas---association-francophone-pour-le-savoir
www.facebook.com/33532707807
twitter.com/_Acfas
Nom précédent: Association canadienne française pour l'avancement des sciences
Aperçu: *Dimension:* moyenne; *Envergure:* nationale; fondée en 1923
Mission: Promouvoir et soutenir la science et la technologie pour encourager le développement culturel et économique de la société
Membre(s) du bureau directeur:
Esther Gaudreault, Directrice générale, 514-849-0045 Ext. 232
esther.gaudreault@acfas.ca
Finances: *Budget de fonctionnement annuel:* $500,000-$1.5 Million
Membre(s) du personnel: 8
Membre: 8 000 individu; 40 institutionnel; *Montant de la cotisation:* 45$
Prix, Bouses:
• Prix J.-Armand-Bombardier (Bourse d études)
Award for technological innovation *Amount:* $2,500
• Prix Léo-Pariseau (Bourse d études)
Award for biological or health sciences *Amount:* $2,500
• Prix Marcel-Vincent (Bourse d études)
Award for social sciences; sponsored by Bell Canada *Amount:* $2,500
• Prix Urgel-Archambault (Bourse d études)
Award for physics, mathematics or engineering; sponsored by Alcan *Amount:* $2,500
• Prix Desjardins d'excellence étudiants-chercheurs (Bourse d études)
For master's or doctoral students; sponsored by the Fondation Desjardins *Amount:* Three awards of $2,500
• Prix Bernard-Belleau (Bourse d études)
Award for doctoral student in health or pharmaceuticals *Amount:* $2,500
• Prix Michel-Jurdant (Bourse d études)
Award recognizes research in environmental sciences; sponsored by Hydro-Québec *Amount:* $2,500

Association franco-yukonnaise (AFY)
302, rue Strickland, Whitehorse YT Y1A 2K1
Tél: 867-668-2663; *Téléc:* 867-663-3511
afy@afy.yk.ca
www.afy.yk.ca
www.facebook.com/AFY.Yukon
Aperçu: *Dimension:* petite; *Envergure:* provinciale; Organisme sans but lucratif; fondée en 1982 surveillé par Fédération des communautés francophones et acadienne du Canada
Mission: D'offrir plusieurs activités sociales, culturelles et artistiques.
Membre de: Fédération culturelle canadienne-française; Fédération canadienne pour l'alphabétisation en français; Fédération de la jeunesse canadienne-française
Affliation(s): Chambre de commerce du Yukon et de Whitehorse
Membre(s) du bureau directeur:
Isabelle Salesse, Codirectrice générale
isalesse@afy.yk.ca
Finances: *Fonds:* Bureau des services en français; Développement des ressources humaines du Canada; sports et récréati
Membre(s) du personnel: 22
Activités: *Service de conférenciers:* Oui

Association Frontière Hors Taxes ***See*** Frontier Duty Free Association

Association Gaspé-Jersey & Guernesey
CP 6004, Gaspé QC G4X 1A0
gaspejga@gogaspe.com
www.gogaspe.com/gcis
Aperçu: *Dimension:* petite; *Envergure:* locale; fondée en 2002
Membre(s) du bureau directeur:
Suzanne Mauger, Présidente
Membre: *Montant de la cotisation:* 15$
Publications:
• L'Anglo-Normand
Type: Newsletter

Association généalogique de la Nouvelle-Écosse ***See*** Genealogical Association of Nova Scotia

Association générale des insuffisants rénaux (AGIR)
4865, boul. Gouin Est, Montréal QC H1G 1A1
Tél: 514-852-9297; *Téléc:* 514-323-1231
Ligne sans frais: 888-852-9297
reins@bellnet.ca
www.agir.qc.ca
Aperçu: *Dimension:* moyenne; *Envergure:* provinciale; fondée en 1979
Mission: Pour soutenir les personnes atteintes de maladies rénales et qui ont eu des greffes de rein et pour aider à améliorer leur vie
Membre de: Office des personnes handicapées du Québec
Membre(s) du bureau directeur:
Bertha Martin, Directrice générale
Membre: *Critères d'admissibilite:* Professionels de la santé, insuffisant rénal, sympathisants; *Comités:* Bien-être des patients; Levées de fonds; Activités sociales; Bon d'organes

Association géologique du Canada ***See*** Geological Association of Canada

Association G.R.A.N.D.
#1, 12, Place du Parc, Westmount QC H3Z 2K5
Tél: 514-846-0574
Aperçu: *Dimension:* petite; *Envergure:* locale
Mission: Aider des grands-parents et des petits-enfants créent et se maintiennenet un lien

Association gymnastique du Nouveau-Brunswick ***See*** New Brunswick Gymnastics Association

Association Hereford du Québec
162, rue des Érables, Ste-Catharine-de-la-Jacques-Cartier QC G3N 1A7
Tél: 418-875-2343
CCRBQ@hotmail.com
www.herefordquebec.ca
Aperçu: *Dimension:* petite; *Envergure:* provinciale; fondée en 1950
Membre de: Canadian Hereford Association
Membre(s) du bureau directeur:
Lori Power, Contact
Membre: 250; *Montant de la cotisation:* 85$

Association historique de Westmount ***See*** Westmount Historical Association

Association indépendante des employés de soutien ***See*** Independent Association of Support Staff

Association industrielle de l'est de Montréal
#412, 11370, rue Notre-Dame Est, Montréal QC H1B 2W6
Tél: 514-645-8111
www.aiem.qc.ca
Aperçu: *Dimension:* petite; *Envergure:* locale; fondée en 1960
Mission: Contribuer à l'harmonisation des activités industrielles de ses membres avec leur environnement physique et communautaire
Membre: 13; *Critères d'admissibilite:* Entreprises de l'est de l'Ile de Montréal qui sont actives dans les secteurs industriels du raffinage de pétrole, de la pétrochimie et de la métallurgie

L'Association Interac ***See*** Interac Association

Association internationale d'orientation scolaire et professionnelle ***See*** International Association for Educational & Vocational Guidance

Association internationale de communicateurs professionels ***See*** International Association of Business Communicators

Association internationale de science politique ***See*** International Political Science Association

Association Internationale des Avocats de la Défense ***See*** International Criminal Defence Attorneys Association

L'Association internationale des machinistes et des travailleurs et travailleuses de l'aérospatiale ***See*** International Association of Machinists & Aerospace Workers

Association internationale des maires francophones - Bureau à Québec (AIMF)
CP 700, Succ. Haute-Ville, #312, 2, rue des Jardins, Québec QC G1R 4S9
Tél: 418-641-6188; *Téléc:* 418-641-6437
Aperçu: *Dimension:* moyenne; *Envergure:* internationale; Organisme sans but lucratif
Mission: Favoriser les échanges et la coopérations entre les villes membres
Finances: *Budget de fonctionnement annuel:* $3 Million-$5 Million
Membre: 1-99

Association Jeannoise pour l'intégration sociale inc. (AJIS)
CP 53, Roberval QC G8H 2N4
Tél: 418-275-1360
ajis53@hotmail.com
Aperçu: *Dimension:* petite; *Envergure:* locale
Affliation(s): Association du Québec pour l'intégration sociale
Membre(s) du bureau directeur:
Marie-Claude Dallaire, Responsable

Association jeunesse fransaskoise (AJF) / Saskatchewan Francophone Youth Association
2320 av Louise, Saskatoon SK S7J 3M7
Tél: 306-653-7447; *Téléc:* 306-653-7448
Ligne sans frais: 855-253-1225
info@ajf.ca
www.ajf.ca
www.facebook.com/AJFransaskoise
www.flickr.com/photos/ajfhardis/collections
Aperçu: *Dimension:* petite; *Envergure:* nationale; Organisme sans but lucratif; fondée en 1977
Mission: L'Association jeunesse fransaskoise est l'organisme voué à l'épanouissement de la jeunesse, au développement du leadership et de l'identité fransaskois
Membre de: Fédération de la jeunesse canadienne-française inc.
Membre(s) du bureau directeur:
Lilian Nguema-Emane, Directeur général
direction@ajf.ca
Finances: *Budget de fonctionnement annuel:* $250,000-$500,000
Membre(s) du personnel: 8; 40 bénévole(s)
Membre: 400; *Critères d'admissibilite:* Jeunes fransaskois(es) entre 14 et 25 ans; *Comités:* Conseil d'administration
Activités: Parlement jeunesse fransaskois; parlement franco-canadien du Nord et de l'Ouest; équipe Saskatchewan; jeux fransaskois; sports et loisirs

Association littéraire et artistique canadienne inc. ***See*** Canadian Literary & Artistic Association

Association longueuilloise des photographes amateurs (ALPA)
Centre Culturel Jacques-Ferron, 100, boul. St-Laurent Ouest, Longueuil QC J4H 1M1
Tél: 450-463-9699
info@alpaphoto.ca
alpaphoto.ca
www.facebook.com/alpaphoto
twitter.com/alpaphoto
Aperçu: *Dimension:* petite; *Envergure:* locale
Mission: D'inspirer de nouveaux artistes et de partager leur travail avec les personnes ainsi que d'accroître les connaissances de la photographie
Membre(s) du bureau directeur:
Mario Paquet, Président, Conseil d'administration
president@alpaphoto.ca
Membre: *Montant de la cotisation:* 80$
Activités: Conférences de photographes; concours de photo; ateliers

Association manitobaine des conseillers d'Orientation ***See*** Manitoba School Counsellors' Association

Association Marie-Reine de Chibougamau
CP 295, Chibougamau QC G8P 2K7
Tél: 418-748-4760
Aperçu: *Dimension:* petite; *Envergure:* locale
Mission: Aider les femmes & les enfants victimes de violence
Membre(s) du bureau directeur:
Marie-Paule Lévesque, Présidente

Association maritime du Québec (AMQ)
#200, 621, rue Stravinski, Brossard QC J4X 1Y7
Tél: 450-466-1777; *Téléc:* 450-466-6056
Ligne sans frais: 877-560-1777
info@nautismequebec.com
www.nautismequebec.com
Aperçu: *Dimension:* moyenne; *Envergure:* provinciale; Organisme sans but lucratif; fondée en 1996
Mission: Promouvoir la sécurité nautique; organiser des représentations et des séances d'information auprès des instances gouvernementales et de différents regroupements canadiens et américains
Membre(s) du bureau directeur:
Yves Paquette, Directeur général
ypc@videotron.ca
Béatrice Launay, Directrice, Québec Stations Nautiques
blaunay@nautismequebec.com
Finances: *Budget de fonctionnement annuel:* $250,000-$500,000
Membre(s) du personnel: 6; 7 bénévole(s)
Membre: 3 500; *Montant de la cotisation:* 30$ plaisanciers; 300$ corporatif; *Critères d'admissibilite:* Propriétaires de bateaux de plaisance et industrie nautique
Activités: Salon du bateau

Association marketing canadienne de l'affichage ***See*** Out-of-Home Marketing Association of Canada

Association Marocaine de Toronto ***See*** Moroccan Association of Toronto

Association mathématique du Québec (AMQ)
a/s Département de didactique, Université de Montréal, CP 6128, Succ. Centre-ville, Montréal QC H3C 3J7
Tél: 514-278-4263; *Téléc:* 514-343-7286
info@amq.math.ca
archimede.mat.ulaval.ca/amq
Aperçu: *Dimension:* moyenne; *Envergure:* internationale; Organisme sans but lucratif; fondée en 1958
Membre(s) du bureau directeur:
France Caron, Présidente
france.caron@umontreal.ca
Membre: *Montant de la cotisation:* 68,99$ régulier; 40,24$ étudiant; 40,24$ retraité; 229,95$ institutoin; 86,23$ domiciliés à l'étranger; *Critères d'admissibilite:* Professeurs de mathématiques

Association médicale canadienne ***See*** Canadian Medical Association

Association médicale du Québec (AMQ) / Québec Medical Association (QMA)
#3200, 380, rue Saint-Antoine ouest, Montréal QC H2Y 3X7
Tél: 514-866-0660; *Téléc:* 514-866-0670
Ligne sans frais: 800-363-3932
admin@amq.ca
www.amq.ca
www.facebook.com/Association.medicale.du.Quebec
Aperçu: *Dimension:* moyenne; *Envergure:* provinciale; Organisme sans but lucratif; fondée en 1922 surveillé par Canadian Medical Association
Mission: Rassembler et soutenir les médecins du Québec afin de garantir à la population québécoise des conditions et des soins de santé de qualité
Membre(s) du bureau directeur:
Claudette Duclos, Directrice générale
Membre(s) du personnel: 10; 50 bénévole(s)
Membre: 8 500; *Montant de la cotisation:* 136-765, schedule; *Critères d'admissibilite:* Etre médecin et être membre de la Corporation professionnelle des médecins du Québec; *Comités:* Soins et promotion de la santé; Économique et politique de la santé; Éducation; Éthique; Mises en candidatures; Finances

Association médicale podiatrique canadienne ***See*** Canadian Podiatric Medical Association

Association minéralogique du Canada ***See*** Mineralogical Association of Canada

Association minière du Canada ***See*** Mining Association of Canada

Association minière du Québec (AMQ) / Québec Mining Association (QMA)
Place de la Cité - Tour Belle Cour, #720, 2590, boul Laurier, Québec QC G1V 4M6
Tél: 418-657-2016; *Téléc:* 418-657-2154
mines@amq-inc.com
www.amq-inc.com
Nom précédent: Association des mines de métaux du Québec inc.
Aperçu: *Dimension:* grande; *Envergure:* provinciale; Organisme sans but lucratif; fondée en 1936 surveillé par Mining Association of Canada
Mission: Promouvoir le développement de l'industrie des mines, de la métallurgie et des industries connexes; défendre les intérêts généraux de ses membres; soutenir les efforts de ses membres quant au bien-être, à la sécurité et à la prévention des accidents au travail
Membre(s) du bureau directeur:
Dan Tolgyesi, Président
dtolgyesi@amq-inc.com
Josée Méthot, Présidente-directrice générale
jmethot@amq-inc.com
Finances: *Budget de fonctionnement annuel:* $500,000-$1.5 Million
Membre(s) du personnel: 9
Membre: 1-99; *Critères d'admissibilite:* Toutes les compagnies opérant dans le secteur minier ou dans un secteur connexe; *Comités:* Environnement; Prévention des accidents; Santé; Relations publiques; Fiscalité; Contrôle de terrain; Sauvetage minier (catamine); Entretien

Association mondiale pour la communication ***See*** World Association for Christian Communication

Association montérégienne de la surdité inc. (AMS)
CP 201, #11, 125, rue Jacques-Cartier, Saint-Jean-sur-Richelieu QC J3B 6S6
Tél: 450-346-6029; *Téléc:* 450-895-1010
amsinc2@hotmail.com
Nom précédent: Association des Sourds du Haut-Richelieu
Aperçu: *Dimension:* petite; *Envergure:* locale; Organisme sans but lucratif
Mission: Aider les personnes, de Montérégie, vivant avec une surdité et leurs proches; offrir des services pour briser l'isolement; promouvoir les droits de ces personnes; sensibiliser la population
Membre(s) du bureau directeur:
Julie Boulais, Contact
Lucie Bourassa, Contact
Finances: *Budget de fonctionnement annuel:* Moins de $50,000
Membre: 1-99
Activités: Rencontres mensuelles sociales

Association montréalaise de science-fiction et de fantastique *See* Montréal Science Fiction & Fantasy Association

Association montréalaise des directions d'établissement scolaire (AMDES)
3751, rue Fleury Est, Montréal QC H1H 2T2
Tél: 514-328-6990; *Téléc:* 514-328-9324
amdes@amdes.qc.ca
www.amdes.qc.ca
Nom précédent: Association des directeurs d'école de Montréal
Aperçu: *Dimension:* petite; *Envergure:* locale; fondée en 1942
Mission: Promouvoir et défendre les droits et les intérêts des membres; assurer le développement professionnel des membres; apporter une contribution significative à l'éducation
Membre(s) du bureau directeur:
Hélène Bourdages, Présidente
Membre(s) du personnel: 4

Association montréalaise pour les aveugles *See* Montréal Association for the Blind

Association motocycliste canadienne *See* Canadian Motorcycle Association

Association mototocycliste Chibougamau Chapais
CP 580, Chibougamau QC G8P 2Y8
Tél: 418-745-3765
amcc.e-monsite.com
Aperçu: *Dimension:* petite; *Envergure:* locale
Membre(s) du bureau directeur:
Jean-Paul Mercier, President
jpomercier@hotmail.com

Association multiculturelle de Fredericton Inc. *See* Multicultural Association of Fredericton

Association multiculturelle de la Nouvelle-Écosse *See* Multicultural Association of Nova Scotia

Association multiculturelle, Grand Moncton *See* Multicultural Association of the Greater Moncton Area

Association multi-ethnique pour l'intégration des personnes handicapées (AMEIPH) / Multi-Ethnic Association for the Integration of Persons with Disabilities
6462, boul St-Laurent, Montréal QC H2S 3C4
Tél: 514-272-0680; *Téléc:* 514-272-8530
ameiph@ameiph.com
www.ameiph.com
Aperçu: *Dimension:* moyenne; *Envergure:* provinciale; Organisme sans but lucratif; fondée en 1981
Mission: Intervenir pour faciliter l'intégration et l'amélioration de la qualité de vie des personnes handicapées issues de l'immigration et des communautés ethnoculturelles, ainsi que les membres de leur famille, à travers l'intervention directe, la promotion des droits et la défense des intérêts et la concertation avec les différents organismes partenaires
Membre(s) du bureau directeur:
Luciana Soave, Directrice générale
Caddeo Caddeo, Director of Services
icaddeo@ameiph.com
Finances: *Budget de fonctionnement annuel:* $250,000-$500,000
Membre(s) du personnel: 10; 50+ bénévole(s)
Membre: 450; *Montant de la cotisation:* 5$ personnes handicapées et famille; 7$ associé; 25$ corporatif; 50$ de soutien; *Critères d'admissibilite:* Personnes handicapées d'origine ethnoculturelle
Activités: Journée Minorité inVISIBLE; *Événements de sensibilisation:* Journée 'Minorité inVISIBLE'; *Stagiaires:* Oui; *Service de conférenciers:* Oui

Association Museums New Brunswick (AMNB) / Association des musées du Nouveau-Brunswick
668 Brunswick St., Fredericton NB E3B 1H6
Tel: 506-454-3561; *Fax:* 506-462-7687
info@amnb.ca
www.amnb.ca
www.facebook.com/AMNB2012
Overview: A medium-sized provincial charitable organization founded in 1974
Mission: To preserve New Brunswick's heritage by uniting, promoting & advancing our heritage workers, supporters & organizations
Member of: Canadian Museums Association
Affliation(s): Canadian Heritage Information Network
Chief Officer(s):
David Desjardins, President
Chantal Brideau, Administrative Officer
Finances: *Annual Operating Budget:* $100,000-$250,000; *Funding Sources:* Provincial & federal governments; membership dues; donations & foundations
Staff Member(s): 2; 16 volunteer(s)
Membership: 126 individual + 70 corporate + 11 honorary + 84 museums; *Fees:* $35 institution; $25 individual; $20 associate; *Committees:* Advocacy; Awards; Membership; Professional Development
Activities: *Awareness Events:* New Brunswick Day Initiative; Heritage Week; *Library:* Resource Centre/Centre de documentation; by appointment
Awards:
- Certificate of Distinction (Award)
- Recognition of Achievement (Award)
- Award of Merit (Award)

Association nationale de la femme et du droit *See* National Association of Women & the Law

Association nationale des camionneurs artisans inc. (ANCAI)
#235, 670, rue Bouvier, Québec QC G2J 1A7
Tél: 418-623-7923; *Téléc:* 418-623-0448
infos@ancai.com
www.ancai.com
Aperçu: *Dimension:* moyenne; *Envergure:* provinciale; fondée en 1966
Mission: Défendre les intérêts des transporteurs en vrac (gravier et forêts) auprès des gouvernements, organismes patronaux et entreprises privées
Membre(s) du bureau directeur:
Guy Laplante, Président
g.laplante@ancai.com
Gaétan Légaré, Directeur général
g.legare@ancai.com
Membre(s) du personnel: 16
Membre: 5,000; *Montant de la cotisation:* $205; *Critères d'admissibilite:* Camionneur propriétaire de son véhicule; *Comités:* Négociations
Activités: Congrès annuel; Tirage camion

Association nationale des Canadiens d'origine indienne *See* National Association of Canadians of Origin in India

Association nationale des centres d'amitié *See* National Association of Friendship Centres

Association nationale des collèges de carrières *See* National Association of Career Colleges

Association nationale des distributeurs aux petites surfaces alimentaires (ANDPSA) / National Convenience Stores Distributors Association (NACDA)
#410, 1695, boul Laval, Laval QC H7S 2M2
Tel: 450-967-3858; *Fax:* 450-967-8839
Toll-Free: 800-686-2823
nacda@nacda.ca
www.nacda.ca
Previous Name: Association nationale des distributeurs de tabac et de confiserie
Overview: A medium-sized national charitable organization founded in 1955
Mission: Promouvoir le bien-être et les intérêts de nos membres distributeurs-grossistes ainsi que de l'industrie
Chief Officer(s):
Raymond Bouchard, Président du conseil d'administration
raymond.bouchard@metro.ca
Finances: *Annual Operating Budget:* $500,000-$1.5 Million
Staff Member(s): 6
Membership: 1-99; *Fees:* 550$ - 1 650$; *Member Profile:* Grossistes-distributeurs et manufacturiers; *Committees:* Exécutif; Developpement des Affaires

Association nationale des distributeurs de tabac et de confiserie *See* Association nationale des distributeurs aux petites surfaces alimentaires

Association nationale des éditeurs de livres (ANEL)
2514, boul Rosemont, Montréal QC H1Y 1K4
Tél: 514-273-8130; *Téléc:* 514-273-9657
Ligne sans frais: 866-900-2635
info@anel.qc.ca
anel.qc.ca
www.facebook.com/61084204798
twitter.com/ANEL_QE
anel.qc.ca/blogue
Aperçu: *Dimension:* moyenne; *Envergure:* nationale; fondée en 1992
Mission: Soutenir le développement d'une industrie nationale de l'édition québécoise et canadienne de langue française; établir entre ses membres des rapports de bonne confraternité; étudier et défendre les intérêts tant généraux que politiques et économiques de ses membres; étudier toute question relative à la profession et diffuser l'information auprès de ses membres; constituer une représentation réelle et efficace de la profession à toute les instances pertinentes
Membre de: Union internationale des éditeurs (UIE)
Membre(s) du bureau directeur:
Jean-François Bouchard, Président
Richard Prieur, Directeur général
Finances: *Budget de fonctionnement annuel:* $250,000-$500,000
Membre(s) du personnel: 9
Membre: 125 maisons d'éditions; *Montant de la cotisation:* 412,50$ - 4 290$; *Critères d'admissibilite:* 10 titres au catalogue minimum; propriété 100% canadienne; *Comités:* Finances; médiation; formation et services aux membres; promotion du livre; édition scolaire; Québec Édition
Activités: *Stagiaires:* Oui; *Service de conférenciers:* Oui; *Bibliothèque* rendez-vous

Association nationale des entreprises en recrutement et placement de personnel *See* Association of Canadian Search, Employment & Staffing Services

Association nationale des étudiant(e)s handicapé(e)s au niveau postsecondaire *See* National Educational Association of Disabled Students

Association nationale des ferblantiers et couvreurs, section locale 2020 *Voir* Syndicat interprovincial des ferblantiers et couvreurs, la section locale 2016

Association nationale des ferblantiers et couvreurs, section locale 2020 (CTC) *Voir* Syndicat interprovincial des ferblantiers et couvreurs, la section locale 2016 à la FTQ-Construction

Association nationale des gestionnaires des terres autochones *See* National Aboriginal Lands Managers Association

Association nationale des grands usagers postaux inc. *See* National Association of Major Mail Users, Inc.

Association nationale des organismes de réglementation de la pharmacie *See* National Association of Pharmacy Regulatory Authorities

Association nationale des orthésistes du pied *Voir* Association des orthésistes et prothésistes du Québec

Association nationale des peintres et métiers connexes, section locale 99 (CTC) (ANPMC) / National Association of Painters & Allied Trades, Local 99 (CLC)
#200, 5275, rue Jean-Talon est, Saint-Léonard QC H1S 1L2
Tél: 514-593-5413; *Téléc:* 514-727-8331
Aperçu: *Dimension:* moyenne; *Envergure:* provinciale; Organisme sans but lucratif; fondée en 1984
Mission: Aider nos membres dans leur métier; faire respecter les conventions collectives sur les chantiers
Affiliation(s): Fédération des travailleuses et travailleurs du Québec - Construction

Membre(s) du personnel: 3
Membre: 1 756; *Critères d'admissibilite:* Peintre en bâtiment

L'Association nationale des propriétaires de terrains de golf du Canada *See* National Golf Course Owners Association Canada

Association nationale des radio étudiantes et communautaires *See* National Campus & Community Radio Association

L'Association nationale des retraités fédéraux *See* National Association of Federal Retirees

Association nationale des revêtements de sol *See* National Floor Covering Association

Association nationale pour la conservation de l'énergie *See* National Energy Conservation Association Inc.

L'association néo-brunswickoise de massothérapeutes *See* Association of New Brunswick Massage Therapists

Association nucléaire canadienne *See* Canadian Nuclear Association

Association of Academic Staff - University of Alberta (AAS-UA) / Association du personnel enseignant de l'Université de l'Alberta

University of Alberta, 1600 College Plaza, 8215 - 112 St., Edmonton AB T6G 2C8
Tel: 780-492-5321; *Fax:* 780-492-7449
reception@ualberta.ca
www.aasua.ca
Overview: A small local organization founded in 1950
Mission: To act as the negotiating & administering body for contract agreements between its members & the university governors
Affliation(s): Canadian Association of University Teachers
Chief Officer(s):
Kevin Kane, President
kevin.kane@ualberta.ca
Brygeda Renke, Executive Director
brygeda.renke@aasua.ca
Finances: *Funding Sources:* Membership dues
Staff Member(s): 8
Membership: 4,429 individual; *Committees:* Economic Benefits; Equity; Finance; Governance; Members' Advisory; Personnel; Research & Scholarly Activity; Salary; Teaching & Learning; Academic Faculty; Academic Librarians; Administrative & Professional Officers; Contract Academic Staff: Teaching; Faculty Service Officers; Sessionals & Other Temporary Staff; Trust/Research Academic Staff; Copyright; Other Intellectual Property; Nominating; Renaissance

Association of Accrediting Agencies of Canada (AAAC) / Association des agences d'agrément du Canada (AAAC)

PO Box 370, #3, 247 Barr St., Renfrew ON K7V 1J6
Tel: 613-432-9491; *Fax:* 613-432-6840
info@aaac.ca
www.aaac.ca
Overview: A small national organization
Mission: Pursues excellence in standards and processes of accreditation to foster the highest quality of professional education.
Chief Officer(s):
Bob Cross, Executive Director
bobcross@aaac.ca
Membership: *Fees:* $750 for all member agencies

Association of Administrative & Professional Staff - University of British Columbia (AAPS-UBC)

Tef III Building, #208, 6190 Agronomy Rd., Vancouver BC V6T 1Z3
Tel: 604-822-9025; *Fax:* 604-922-4699
aaps.office@ubc.ca
www.aaps.ubc.ca
Overview: A small local organization founded in 1977
Mission: To negotiate terms & conditions of employment on behalf of its members with the university administration.
Chief Officer(s):
Isabella Losinger, President, 604-827-4169
isabella.losinger@midwifery.ubc.ca
Michael Conlon, Executive Director, 604-822-8230
michael.conlon@ubc.ca
Staff Member(s): 5
Membership: 3,700+; *Member Profile:* Administrative & professional staff at UBC; *Committees:* Advocacy; Communications; Professional Development; Bargaining; Finance; Member Engangement

Association of Administrative Assistants (AAA) / Association des adjoints administratifs

c/o 11110 - 108 St., Edmonton AB T5G 2T2
Tel: 780-423-2929; *Fax:* 780-407-3340
registrar@aaa.ca
www.aaa.ca
www.linkedin.com/pub/association-of-administrative-assistants/3a/356/4
Overview: A medium-sized national organization founded in 1951
Mission: To establish a national standard of qualifications for an administrative assistant; to help assistants to reach this standard by providing opportunities for advanced education; to make management aware of the value of the fully-qualified administrative assistant
Chief Officer(s):
Doris Kurtz, Director
doris.kurtz@ualberta.ca
Finances: *Annual Operating Budget:* Less than $50,000; *Funding Sources:* Membership fees; branch-level fundraising
Membership: 200+; *Fees:* $144; *Member Profile:* Persons with appropriate experience & education as administrative assistants, coordinators, office administrators & senior secretaries
Activities: Q.A.A. (Qualified Administrative Assistant) Program offered at universities across Canada

Association of Administrators of English Schools of Québec (AAESQ) / Association des administrateurs des écoles anglaises du Québec

#5, 17035, boul Brunswick, Montréal QC H9H 5G6
Tel: 514-426-5110; *Fax:* 514-426-5109
www.aaesq.ca
Overview: A small provincial charitable organization founded in 1998
Mission: To act as the negotiating body, on behalf of its members, with educational authorities regarding salary, working conditions & fringe benefits. It also a regluating body, maintaining adequate qualifications & training in educational administration.
Affliation(s): Canadian Association of Principals; Canadian Association of School Administrators
Chief Officer(s):
Jim Jordan, President
Ron Silverstone, Executive Director
Staff Member(s): 5
Membership: 475; *Member Profile:* Board-level administrators; in-school administrators
Activities: *Internships:* Yes

Association of Alberta Agricultural Fieldmen (AAAF)

c/o Municipal District of Rocky View, 911 - 32nd Ave. NE, Calgary AB T2E 6X6
Tel: 403-230-1401
info@aaaf.ab.ca
www.aaaf.ab.ca
www.facebook.com/175905085771203
twitter.com/aaafieldmen
Overview: A small provincial organization
Mission: Committed to the enhancement, promotion & protection of the agricultural resources of Alberta
Chief Officer(s):
Jason Storch, President, 403-526-2888
Stephen Majek, Secretary-Treasurer, 780-352-3321
Finances: *Annual Operating Budget:* Less than $50,000
Membership: 107; *Fees:* $125; *Member Profile:* Agricultural fieldmen develop, implement, and control programs that adhere to the priorities and policies set by the Agricultural Service Board across the province.; *Committees:* Education; Policy; Soils; Weed Control

Association of Alberta Coordinated Action for Recycling Enterprises

5212 - 49 St., Leduc AB T9E 7H5
Tel: 780-980-0035; *Fax:* 780-980-0232
Toll-Free: 866-818-2273
www.albertacare.org
Also Known As: Alberta CARE
Overview: A medium-sized provincial organization founded in 2010
Mission: To support waste management & recycling activities at the community level in Alberta
Chief Officer(s):
Linda McDonald, Executive Director
executivedirector@albertacare.org
Membership: *Fees:* $52.50 associate, non-voting membership; $105 non-profit; $262.50 corporate; $272 goverment; $105-$525 municipality, based on population; *Member Profile:* Non-profit organizations; Governments; Municipalities; Businesses
Activities: Organizing partnerships; Establishing & operating programs such as Electronic Waste Recycling, Regional Concrete & Asphalt Crushing, Regional Scrap Metals Recycling, Alberta CARE Ink Recycle, Paper Fibre Recycling, Fluorescent Tube Recycling, Wood Waste Grinding
Publications:
- Reuse / Recycle Directory

Type: Directory; *Number of Pages:* 122
Profile: A list of organizations & companies that offer alternatives to throwing garbage in landfills

Association of Allied Health Professionals: Newfoundland & Labrador (Ind.) (AAHP) / Association des professionnels unis de la santé: Terre-Neuve et Labrador (ind.)

6 Mount Carson Ave., Mount Pearl NL A1N 3K4
Tel: 709-722-3353; *Fax:* 709-722-0987
Toll-Free: 800-728-2247
info@aahp.nf.ca
www.aahp.nf.ca
Overview: A small provincial organization founded in 1975

Association of Applied Geochemists (AEG)

PO Box 26099, 72 Robertson Rd., Nepean ON K2H 9R0
Tel: 613-828-0199; *Fax:* 613-828-9288
office@appliedgeochemists.org
www.appliedgeochemists.org
Previous Name: Association of Exploration Geochemists
Overview: A medium-sized international organization founded in 1970
Mission: To promote interest in the applications of geochemistry to mineral & petroleum exploration, resource evaluation & related fields
Affliation(s): International Union of Geological Sciences (IUGS)
Chief Officer(s):
David R. Cohen, President
Betty Arseneault, Business Manager
Finances: *Annual Operating Budget:* $50,000-$100,000; *Funding Sources:* Membership dues; publisher rebates
Staff Member(s): 2; 70 volunteer(s)
Membership: 650; *Fees:* US$100; *Committees:* New Membership; Admissions; Awards and Medals; Education; Symposia
Activities: *Speaker Service:* Yes

Association of Architects in Private Practice of Québec *Voir* Association des Architectes en pratique privée du Québec

Association of Architectural Technologists of Ontario (AATO)

#38, 2355 Derry Rd. East, Mississauga ON L5S 1V6
Tel: 905-405-0840; *Fax:* 905-405-9882
Toll-Free: 866-805-2286
aato@bellnet.ca
aato.on.ca
Overview: A medium-sized provincial organization founded in 1969
Mission: To maintain the standard of professional conduct of its members, as well as advocates to all levels of government on behalf of them & the industry.
Chief Officer(s):
Sharon Creasor, President
Finances: *Funding Sources:* Membership fees; advertisements
Membership: *Fees:* $220 accredited; $190 interns; $35 students; *Member Profile:* Architectural technologists & technicians; building technologists & technicians in Ontario; *Committees:* Annual General Meeting; Board of Examiners; By-law Review, Ethics & Professional Practice; Certification Board; Education; External Affiliations; Membership Services; Newsletter; Private Practice; Student Membership; Web Site
Activities: Chapter meetings; accreditation exams; information seminars; networking; referral services; professional recognition; advocacy; *Internships:* Yes; *Speaker Service:* Yes
Awards:
- Recognition Awards (Award)
- Chapter Chair Awards (Award)
- AATO Student Awards Program (Award)

Hamilton-Niagara Chapter
Hamilton ON
e-mail: aato_hamilton_niagara@yahoo.ca
Chief Officer(s):
Greg Cherwaty, Contact

London Chapter
PO Box 733, Stn. B, London ON N6A 4Y8
Tel: 519-439-6262; *Fax:* 519-439-7376
Chief Officer(s):
Dan Doneff, Contact
design@edenhall.ca

Ottawa Chapter
#1, 306 Savard Ave., Ottawa ON K1L 7S2
Tel: 613-748-8260
www.aato-ottawa.ca
Chief Officer(s):
Herb Lagois, chair

Sudbury Chapter
Sudbury ON P3C 4B3
Chief Officer(s):
Leo Chaloux, Chair

Thousand Islands Chapter
c/o Mill & Ross Architects, 382 King St E., Kingston ON K7K 2Y2
Tel: 613-549-1403; *Fax:* 613-549-5997
Chief Officer(s):
Michael Paquette, Contact
sixpaq@1000island.net

Toronto Central Chapter
Toronto ON
Chief Officer(s):
Denis Heroux, Interim Secretary

Toronto East Chapter
Toronto ON
Chief Officer(s):
Martin Paivio, Chair

Toronto West Chapter
Toronto ON
Chief Officer(s):
Sam Pasquale, Chair

Association of Atlantic Universities (AAU) / Association des universités de l'Atlantique
#403, 5657 Spring Garden Rd., Halifax NS B3J 3R4
Tel: 902-425-4230; *Fax:* 902-425-4233
info@atlanticuniversities.ca
www.atlanticuniversities.ca
Overview: A medium-sized provincial organization founded in 1964 overseen by Association of Universities & Colleges of Canada
Mission: To assist in assuring the quality & coordination of higher education in Atlantic Provinces; to provide a forum for university administrators to discuss & coordinate their views, interests & concerns in support of higher education in the Atlantic provinces
Chief Officer(s):
Peter Halpin, Executive Director, 902-425-4238
Finances: *Funding Sources:* Membership fees
Staff Member(s): 3
Membership: 18; *Member Profile:* Universities & colleges; *Committees:* Faculty Development

Association of Auto Part Recyclers *See* Association des recycleurs de pièces d'autos et de camions

Association of Battlefords Realtors
PO Box 611, North Battleford SK S9A 2Y7
Tel: 306-445-6300; *Fax:* 306-445-9020
bfords.realestate@sasktel.net
Overview: A small local organization overseen by Saskatchewan Real Estate Association
Mission: To advance & promote interest of those engaged in real estate as brokers, agents, valuators, examiners, & experts; To increase public confidence in & respect for those engaged in real estate
Member of: The Canadian Real Estate Association
Chief Officer(s):
Rick Cann, Executive Officer
Finances: *Annual Operating Budget:* $50,000-$100,000
Membership: 33 individual

Association of BC Drama Educators (ABCDE)
c/o BC Teachers' Federation, #100, #550 West 6 Ave., Vancouver BC V5Z 4P2
Tel: 604-871-2283; *Fax:* 604-871-2286
Toll-Free: 800-663-9163
www.bcdramateachers.com
twitter.com/BCDRAMATEACHERS
Overview: A small provincial organization
Mission: To provide help drama teachers with guidance, resources & communication
Member of: BC Teachers' Federation
Chief Officer(s):
Lana O'Brien, President
lobrien@sd22.bc.ca
Christine Knight, Director, Communications
christine.knight@sd72.bc.ca
Meetings/Conferences: • Association of BC Drama Educators 2015 Spring Conference, 2015, BC
Scope: Provincial

Association of BC First Nations Treatment Programs
PO Box 325, Invermere BC V0A 1K0
Tel: 778-526-2501; *Fax:* 778-526-2505
director@healingisajourney.com
firstnationstreatment.org
Overview: A small provincial organization
Mission: To provide a forum that promotes culturally relevant practices to enhance & advance the continuum of care in addressing addictions among First Nations peoples

Association of Book Publishers of British Columbia (ABPBC)
#600, 402 West Pender St., Vancouver BC V6B 1T6
Tel: 604-684-0228; *Fax:* 604-684-5788
admin@books.bc.ca
books.bc.ca
Overview: A medium-sized provincial organization founded in 1974
Mission: To encourage writing, publishing, distribution & promotion of books written by BC & Canadian authors; to cooperate with other associations & organizations to further the reading & studying of books; to work for the development & maintenance of strong competitive book publishing houses owned & controlled in BC & Canada; to further professional training for individuals engaged in book publishing
Affiliation(s): Association of Canadian Publishers
Chief Officer(s):
Ruth Linka, President
Margaret Reynolds, Executive Director
Finances: *Annual Operating Budget:* $100,000-$250,000; *Funding Sources:* Canada Council; Dept. of Canadian Heritage
Staff Member(s): 2
Membership: 26 active + 2 associate + 6 supporting; *Fees:* $350 Active, Associates & Supporting; *Member Profile:* Active - 7 titles in print, 2 per year; associate - 2 titles in print, published in previous 3 years; supporting - 1 title published in previous 3 years
Activities: *Awareness Events:* BC Book & Magazine Week, April; *Rents Mailing List:* Yes; *Library* by appointment

Association of British Columbia Forest Professionals (ABCFP)
#330 - 321 Water St., Vancouver BC V6B 1B8
Tel: 604-687-8027; *Fax:* 604-687-3264
info@abcfp.ca
www.abcfp.ca
www.facebook.com/79659811198
twitter.com/abcfp
www.youtube.com/user/TheABCFP
Previous Name: Association of British Columbia Professional Foresters
Overview: A medium-sized provincial licensing organization founded in 1947
Mission: To protect the public interest in the practice of professional forestry by ensuring the competence, independence & integrity of its members; to ensure that every person practising professional forestry is accountable to the association & to the public
Member of: Canadian Federation of Professional Foresters Association
Chief Officer(s):
Sharon Glover, Chief Executive Officer, 604-331-2323
sglover@abcfp.ca
Finances: *Annual Operating Budget:* $500,000-$1.5 Million; *Funding Sources:* Membership dues
Staff Member(s): 12; 300 volunteer(s)
Membership: 5,300; *Fees:* $300-330 + GST; *Member Profile:* Individual - membership is mandatory for all who practise professional forestry in the province of British Columbia; *Committees:* ABCFP Forestrust
Activities: Policy review seminars; Professional Foresters' Network; Forest Capital of BC
Awards:
• Honorary Membership (Award)
Non-members, nominated by the membership
• Distinguished Forest Professional Award (Award)
Eligibility: BC registered professional foresters, nominated by their peers
• Forester of the Year Award (Award)
Eligibility: BC registered professional foresters, nominated by their peers
Meetings/Conferences: • Annual Forestry Conference and AGM 2015, February, 2015, Vancouver Island Conference Centre, Nanaimo, BC
Scope: Provincial

Association of British Columbia Grape Growers *See* British Columbia Grapegrowers' Association

Association of British Columbia Land Surveyors (ABCLS)
#301, 2400 Bevan Ave., Sidney BC V8L 1W1
Tel: 250-655-7222; *Fax:* 250-655-7223
Toll-Free: 800-332-1193
office@abcls.ca
www.abcls.ca
Also Known As: Association of BC Land Surveyors
Previous Name: Corporation of BC Land Surveyors
Overview: A medium-sized provincial licensing organization founded in 1905 overseen by Professional Surveyors Canada
Mission: To protect the public interest & the integrity of the survey system in British Columbia by regulating & governing the practice of land surveying in the province.
Member of: Professional Surveyors Canada
Affiliation(s): Canadian Society of Association Executives
Chief Officer(s):
R. Chad Rintoul, Chief Administrative Officer
crintoul@abcls.ca
Ian Lloyd, President
Chuck Salmon, Secretary & Treasurer
csalmon@abcls.ca
Finances: *Annual Operating Budget:* $500,000-$1.5 Million; *Funding Sources:* Membership dues; Electronic Checklist Registry
Staff Member(s): 7
Membership: 600; *Fees:* Various; *Member Profile:* Land Surveyors
Activities: Conducting examining for admission; Performing legal surveys in British Columbia; Providing professional development opportunities; *Internships:* Yes; *Library:* BC Land Surveyors Foundation Anna Papove Memorial; Open to public by appointment
Meetings/Conferences: • Association of British Columbia Land Surveyors 2015 110th Annual General Meeting, March, 2015, Penticton Lakeside Resort, Penticton, BC
Scope: Provincial
Contact Information: Board & Administrative Coordinator, Vicki Pettigrew, E-mail: office@abcls.ca
Publications:
• The Land Surveyor
Type: Newsletter; *Editor:* Janice Henshaw
Profile: Articles about land surveying in British Columbia
• The Link
Type: Magazine; *Frequency:* 3 pa; *Accepts Advertising*; *Editor:* Dave Morton, BCLS
Profile: Articles & news relevant to British Columbia land surveyors

Association of British Columbia Professional Foresters *See* Association of British Columbia Forest Professionals

Association of British Columbia Teachers of English as an Additional Language (B.C. TEAL)
#206, 640 West Broadway, Vancouver BC V5Z 1G4
Tel: 604-736-6330; *Fax:* 604-736-6306
admin@bcteal.org
www.bcteal.org
Overview: A medium-sized provincial charitable organization founded in 1967
Mission: To foster & promote effective instruction in English as a second language in BC; to raise the professional status of BC ESL teachers; to promote communication among BC ESL professionals
Member of: TESL Canada; TESOL International
Affiliation(s): Affiliation of Multicultural Societies & Service Agencies of B.C., TESL Canada, TESOL, and ELSA Net
Chief Officer(s):
Shawna Williams, President
Finances: *Funding Sources:* Membership dues; conferences

Staff Member(s): 1
Membership: 800; *Fees:* Schedule available; *Member Profile:* ESL teacher; *Committees:* Awards; Action; Policy; Certification; Newsletter
Activities: *Rents Mailing List:* Yes

Association of Building Contractors of Québec *Voir* Association des entrepreneurs en construction du Québec

Association of Canada Lands Surveyors / Association des arpenteurs des terres du Canada

100E, 900 Dynes Rd., Ottawa ON K2C 3L6
Tel: 613-723-9200; *Fax:* 613-723-5558
www.acls-aatc.ca
Previous Name: Canadian Institute of Surveying
Overview: A medium-sized national organization
Mission: To establish & maintain standards of qualification for Canada Lands Surveyors; to regulate Canada Lands Surveyors; To establish & maintain standards of conduct, knowledge & skill among members of the Association & permit holders; to govern the activities of members of the Association & permit holders; To cooperate with other organizations for the advancement of surveying; To perform the duties & exercise the powers that are imposed or conferred on the Association by the Act
Chief Officer(s):
Jean-Claude Tétreault, Executive Director
jctetreault@acls-aatc.ca
Meetings/Conferences: • Association of Canada Lands Surveyors 2015 11th National Surveyor's Conference, May, 2015, Fairmont Winnipeg, Winnipeg, MB
Scope: National
Description: Topics include the Code of Ethics, risk management, social media, & geodetic information, plus business meetings, award presentations, & networking opportunities
Contact Information: Administrator, Communications & Membership Services: Martha Reeve, Phone: 613-723-9200

Association of Canadian Advertisers Inc. (ACA) / Association canadienne des annonceurs

#1103, 95 St. Clair Ave. West, Toronto ON M4V 1N6
Tel: 416-964-3805; *Fax:* 416-964-0771
Toll-Free: 800-565-0109
www.acaweb.ca
www.linkedin.com/company/2553878
twitter.com/aca_tweets
Overview: A medium-sized national organization founded in 1914
Mission: To promote the common interests of advertisers & to provide expertise, education & information
Member of: The World Federation of Advertisers
Chief Officer(s):
Ronald S. Lund, President & CEO
rlund@ACAweb.ca
Susan Charles, Vice President, Member Services
scharles@ACAweb.ca
Staff Member(s): 8
Membership: 200 corporate; *Member Profile:* Advertiser of a product or service in Canada; *Committees:* Media; Marcom Financial Management & Procurement; Digital Marketing
Awards:
• ACA Gold Medal (Award)
Established in 1941 to encourage high standards of personal achievement in advertising - for introducing new concepts or techniques, for significantly improving existing practices, or for enhancing the stature of advertising

Association of Canadian Archivists (ACA) / Association canadienne des archivistes

PO Box 2596, Stn. D, Ottawa ON K1P 5W6
Tel: 613-234-6977; *Fax:* 613-234-8500
aca@archivists.ca
www.archivists.ca
www.linkedin.com/groups?home=&gid=3704759
www.facebook.com/AssociationofCanadianArchivists
twitter.com/archivistsdotca
Previous Name: Canadian Historical Association, Archives Section
Overview: A medium-sized national organization founded in 1975
Mission: To ensure the preservation & accessibility of Canada's documentary heritage; To provide professional leadership among persons engaged in the discipline & practice of archival science; To promote the development of archives & archivists in Canada; To encourage cooperation of archivists with all those interested in the preservation & use of documents of human experience
Chief Officer(s):
Duncan Grant, Executive Director, 613-234-6977 Ext. 2, Fax: 613-234-8500
ExecDir@archivists.ca
Loryl MacDonald, President
loryl.macdonald@utoronto.ca
Finances: *Funding Sources:* Membership fees
Staff Member(s): 2
Membership: 600+; *Fees:* $52 students; Fee for individual membership based upon income; Fee for institutional membership based upon number of employees involved in archives; *Member Profile:* Practising archivists; Institutions with archival collections; Archival students; Individuals with an interest in archival activities; *Committees:* Communications; Outreach; Professional Learning; Membership Development; Governance; Ethics
Activities: Organizing professional development events; Engaging in advocacy activities; Increasing appreciation for Canada's archival heritage; Offering networking opportunities;
Meetings/Conferences: • Association of Canadian Archivists 2015 40th Annual Conference & Annual General Meeting, June, 2015, Radisson Plaza, Hotel Saskatchewan, Regina, SK
Scope: National
Description: A meeting occurring in May or June each year, for archivists from across Canada, featuring educational presentations, trade show exhibits, networking opportunities, as well as workshops immediately prior or following conference sessions
Contact Information: Association of Canadian Archivists Board or Office, E-mail: aca@archivists.ca
• Association of Canadian Archivists 2016 41st Annual Conference & Annual General Meeting, June, 2016, Marriott Chateau Champlain, Montréal, QC
Scope: National
Description: A meeting occurring in May or June each year, for archivists from across Canada, featuring educational presentations, trade show exhibits, networking opportunities, as well as workshops immediately prior or following conference sessions
Contact Information: Association of Canadian Archivists Board or Office, E-mail: aca@archivists.ca
• Association of Canadian Archivists 2017 42nd Annual Conference & Annual General Meeting, June, 2017, Ottawa Marriott Hotel, Ottawa, ON
Scope: National
Description: A meeting occurring in May or June each year, for archivists from across Canada, featuring educational presentations, trade show exhibits, networking opportunities, as well as workshops immediately prior or following conference sessions
Contact Information: Association of Canadian Archivists Board or Office, E-mail: aca@archivists.ca
• Association of Canadian Archivists 2018 43rd Annual Conference & Annual General Meeting, 2018
Scope: National
Description: A meeting occurring in May or June each year, for archivists from across Canada, featuring educational presentations, trade show exhibits, networking opportunities, as well as workshops immediately prior or following conference sessions
Contact Information: Association of Canadian Archivists Board or Office, E-mail: aca@archivists.ca
Publications:
• The ACA Bulletin
Type: Newsletter; *Frequency:* Quarterly; *Accepts Advertising*; *Editor:* Amanada Tomé *ISSN:* 0709-4604
Profile: Association activities & professional news, such as conferences, workshops, archival developments, & publications
• The Archival Imagination: Essays in Honour of Hugh Taylor
Type: Book; *Number of Pages:* 263; *Editor:* Barbara L. Craig; *ISBN:* 1-895382-06-8
Profile: A collection of eleven essays
• Archivaria: The Journal of the Association of Canadian Archivists
Type: Journal; *Frequency:* Semiannually; *Accepts Advertising*; *Editor:* Jean Dryden *ISSN:* 0318-6954
Profile: A scholarly journal, with feature articles, book & exhibition reviews, & material related to the archivalcommunity in Canada & internationally
• Association of Canadian Archivists Membership Directory
Type: Directory; *Frequency:* Annually; *Accepts Advertising*
Profile: An annual spring publication for more than 600 individual & institutional members, containing contact information as well as key association documents
• Association of Canadian Archivists Conference Program
Frequency: Annually; *Accepts Advertising*
Profile: A detailed description of the annual conference's sessions & social events
• Canadian Archival Studies & the Rediscovery of Provenance
Editor: Tom Nesmith
Profile: A joint publication with the Society of American Archivists
• Imagining Archives: Essays & Reflections by Hugh A. Taylor
Type: Book; *Number of Pages:* 254; *Editor:* Terry Cook; Gordon Dodds; *ISBN:* 0-8108-4771-X
Profile: A collection of fifteen essays
• The Monetary Appraisal of Archival Documents in Canada
Type: Book; *Number of Pages:* 21; *Author:* S.D. Hanson; *ISBN:* 1-895382-04-1
Profile: Information about establishing the fair market value of archival documents
• The Power and Passion of Archives: A Festschrift in Honour of Kent Haworth
Type: Book; *Number of Pages:* 269; *Editor:* R. Ware; M. Beyea, C. Avery; *ISBN:* 1-895382-26-2
Profile: A collection of fifteen essays
• Preparing for Monetary Appraisals: A Guide for Canadian Archival Institutions
Type: Book; *Number of Pages:* 18; *Author:* Brock Silversides; *ISBN:* 1-895382-22-X
Profile: A practical guide featuring a bibliography & a information checklist
• Promoting Archives: A Handbook
Type: Handbook; *Number of Pages:* 26; *Author:* Anne ten Cate; *ISBN:* 1-895382-08-4

Association of Canadian Choral Communities (ACCC) / Association des communautés chorales canadiennes

A-1422 Bayview Ave., Toronto ON M4G 3A7
Tel: 416-519-1165
accc@choralcanada.org
www.choralcanada.org
www.facebook.com/111037998913858?sk=wall&filter=1
choralbytes.blogspot.ca
Overview: A small national organization founded in 1980
Mission: To promote choral music, particularly Canadian works, in schools, post-secondary institutions, churches & communities throughout Canada
Affliation(s): Canadian Conference of the Arts; International Federation for Choral Music
Chief Officer(s):
Jeff Joudrey, President
Marta McCarthy, President Elect
Marta McCarthy, President Elect
Ki Hawn, Secretary Treasurer
Finances: *Annual Operating Budget:* Less than $50,000; *Funding Sources:* Membership fees; donations; advertising
Staff Member(s): 1; 25 volunteer(s)
Membership: 500; *Fees:* $90 individual/institutional; $40 student; $150 industry; *Committees:* Advocacy; Communications; Professional Development; Financial
Activities: National Youth Choir of Canada; Podium (biennial National Conference) choral composition competition; National Choral Awards; NYC Conducting Apprenticeship Program; Canadian Choral Foundation; *Awareness Events:* National Competition for Canadian Amateur Choirs; Choralscapes Podium; Competition for Choral Writing
Awards:
• National Choral Awards / Prix nationaux de chant choral (Award)

Association of Canadian Clubs / Association des cercles canadiens

#211, 2415 Holly Lane, Ottawa ON K1V 2P2
Tel: 613-236-8288; *Fax:* 613-236-8299
support@istcl.com
www.canadianclub.ca
Overview: A medium-sized national organization founded in 1909
Mission: To promote Canadian identity; to encourage Canadian unity; to foster throughout Canada an interest in public affairs; to cultivate attachment to Canadian institutions
Chief Officer(s):
Lyn Goldman, National President
Christine Merrikin, Executive Secretary
Jim Waters, Regional Director, British Columbia
Marjorie Nickerson, Regional Director, Alberta
Maura Gillis-Cipywnyk, Regional Director, Saskatchewan
Jacqui Blanchard, Regional Director, Manitoba
Allan Mutart, Regional Director, Southern Ontario

Clara Edwardson, Regional Director, Eastern & Northern Ontario
Cynthia Dinsmore, Regional Director, Québec
Finances: *Annual Operating Budget:* $100,000-$250,000; *Funding Sources:* Membership fees
Staff Member(s): 2; 20 volunteer(s)
Membership: 12,000 individual; *Fees:* Schedule available
Activities: Provides a National Speakers Program for clubs across Canada; *Speaker Service:* Yes

Association of Canadian College & University Teachers of English (ACCUTE)

c/o Department of English, Dalhousie University, PO Box 15000, 6135 University Ave., Dalhousie NS B3H 4R2
Tel: 902-494-6901; *Fax:* 902-494-2176
info.accute@gmail.com
www.accute.ca
twitter.com/ACCUTEnglish
Overview: A small national organization founded in 1957
Mission: To represent faculty teaching English in Canadian universities & colleges, & students studying English at the graduate level; to act as the lobbying body at the provincial & federal levels; to encourage the dissemination & exchange of research.
Member of: Canadian Federation for the Humanities & Social Sciences
Affiliation(s): Congress of Learned Societies
Chief Officer(s):
Jason Haslam, President
Finances: *Funding Sources:* Membership fees
Membership: *Fees:* Schedule available dependant on yearly earnings of the member
Activities: *Rents Mailing List:* Yes
Awards:
• F.E.L Priestley Prize (Award)
Awarded annually for an outstanding essay published in English Studies in Canada & service to ACCUTE

Association of Canadian Compliance Professionals / Association canadienne des professionnels en conformité

c/o Hub Capital Inc., #1001, 3700 Steeles Ave. West, Woodbridge ON L4L 8M9
e-mail: info@complianceprofessionals.ca
www.complianceprofessionals.ca
Also Known As: Association of Compliance Professionals
Overview: A small national organization founded in 2000
Mission: To represent individuals in the field of compliance, who are dedicated to improving compliance operations within the mutual fund & exempt market dealer communities
Chief Officer(s):
Manny DaSilva, Chair
Cheryl Hamilton, Treasurer, 905-264-1634 Ext. 2075
Kathleen Black, Executive Director, 403-796-8298
Membership: 100+; *Fees:* $300 individual; $150 per subsequent person (corporate); *Member Profile:* Compliance professionals working with the following: mutual fund dealers, exempt market dealers, mutual fund companies, insurance companies & MGAs, as well as industry service providers including legal, technology & independent consultants
Activities: Job center; events; educational programs;

Association of Canadian Corporations in Translation & Interpretation (ACCTI) / Association canadienne de compagnies de traductions et d'interpretation

#306, 421 Bloor St. East, Toronto ON M4W 3T1
Tel: 416-975-5000; *Fax:* 416-975-0505
Other Communication: info_francais@accti.org
english_info@accti.org
www.accti.org
Overview: A medium-sized national organization founded in 2003
Mission: To unite the Canadian translation industry, providing a quality standard to protect the public & service providers alike; to arrange for arbitration in the event of a dispute; to operate in the best interest of members
Member of: American Translator's Association, Translation Companies; Association of Hungarian Translation Companies; Association of Language Companies; Association of Translation Companies; European Union Association of Translation Companies
Chief Officer(s):
Paul Penzo, President
Maryse M. Benhoff, Vice-President, 514-376-7919, Fax: 514-376-4486
Finances: *Funding Sources:* Membership fees, sponsors
Staff Member(s): 3
Membership: *Fees:* Non-voting $500; Associate $1,000; Voting $1,500; Cost per specialty $2,000; *Member Profile:* Non-voting, all parties interested in being involved with Canadian corporations providing translation & interpreting services; Voting, Canadian corporations whose core business is in traditional translation &/or interpretation services, which adere to the ACCTI Code of Professional Conduct, Ethics & Business Practices.; *Committees:* Executive; Membership; R&D
Activities: Keeps members abreast of developments, new technologies & opportunities within the industry through website postings, newsletters & annual conferences; arranges for preferred pricing from interested vendors

Association of Canadian Deans of Education (ACDE) / Association Canadienne des Doyens et Doyennes d'Éducation

ACDE Secretariat, c/o 1144 Skana Dr., Delta BC V4M 2L4
Tel: 604-943-6374
acde@telus.net
www.csse-scee.ca/acde
Overview: A medium-sized national organization
Mission: To advance knowledge & inform practice in educational settings
Chief Officer(s):
Blye Frank, President
blyefrank@ubc.ca
Katy Ellsworth, Executive Director
Finances: *Funding Sources:* Primarily by the fees of individual & institutional members & a small subsidy from the Social Sciences & Humanities Research Council of Canada
Publications:
• Canadian Journal of Education
Type: Journal; *Frequency:* Quarterly; *Editor:* Dr. Julia Ellis

Association of Canadian Distillers (ACD) / Association des distillateurs canadiens

#704, 255 Albert St., Ottawa ON K1P 6A9
Tel: 613-238-8444; *Fax:* 613-238-3411
www.acd.ca
Also Known As: Spirits Canada
Overview: A large national organization founded in 1947
Mission: To protect & advance the interests of its members; To promote & protect, both nationally & internationally, the well-being & viability of the Canadian distilling industry; To foster responsible attitudes toward the consumption of distilled spirits (gin, vodka, rum, Canadian Whisky) in Canada; To aggressively pursue & enhance the recognition of the name & positive reputation of Canadian Whisky as Canada's unique appellation distilled spirits product; To preserve & protect the integrity & standards of all distilled products
Membership: *Member Profile:* Canadian licensed manufacturers & marketers of distilled spirits products
Activities: *Library*

Association of Canadian Ergonomists (ACE) / L'Association canadienne d'ergonomie

#1003, 105-150 Crowfoot Cres. NW, Calgary AB T3G 3T2
Tel: 403-219-4001; *Fax:* 403-451-1503
Toll-Free: 888-432-2223
info@ace-ergocanada.ca
www.ace-ergocanada.ca
Previous Name: Human Factors Association of Canada
Overview: A small national organization founded in 1968
Mission: To advance human factors/ergonomics through encouraging a high quality of practice, education & research; To facilitate communication among members; To represent the discipline; To increase awareness of human factors/ergonomics; To identify resources
Member of: International Ergonomics Association
Chief Officer(s):
Margo Fraser, Executive Director
margo@ace-ergocanada.ca
Brenda Mallat, President
Finances: *Annual Operating Budget:* $100,000-$250,000; *Funding Sources:* Membership dues; annual conference
Staff Member(s): 2
Membership: 600 individuals; *Fees:* $150 full; $75 affiliate; $34 student; *Member Profile:* Engineers; medical practitioners; safety specialists; research scientists; architects; designers; educators; managers; consultants; kinesiologists; psychologists; ergonomists
Activities: *Speaker Service:* Yes
Awards:
• Student Paper Awards
Amount: $250
Meetings/Conferences: • Association of Canadian Ergonomists 46th Annual Conference, 2015
Scope: National

Association of Canadian Faculties of Dentistry (ACFD) / Association des facultés dentaires du Canada (AFDC)

#350, 2194 Health Sciences Mall, Vancouver BC V6T 1Z3
Tel: 604-827-1083; *Fax:* 604-822-4532
admin@acfd.ca
www.acfd.ca
Overview: A medium-sized national organization founded in 1968 overseen by Association of Universities & Colleges of Canada
Mission: To assure the quality of dental education & research in Canada. It also strives to keep its members informed of issues regarding University-based dental education and promote communication between its members.
Member of: Canadian Dental Association; Canadian Dental Hygienist Association; Canadian Dental Assistants Association; National Dental Examining Board of Canada; Royal College of Dentists of Canada; American Association of Dental Schools; American Dental Education Association
Chief Officer(s):
Daniel Haas, President
daniel.haas@utoronto.ca
Tom Boran, Vice-President & Treasurer
tom.boran@dal.ca
Finances: *Annual Operating Budget:* $50,000-$100,000
Staff Member(s): 1
Membership: 400; *Member Profile:* Canadian University-based Faculty, School, or other entity that offers an undergraduate dental program leading to the DDS/DMD degree.; *Committees:* Deans' Committee; Academic Affairs; Clinical Affairs; Research Affairs
Awards:
• ACFD Distinguished Service Award (Award)
Recognizes individuals or groups who have made significant contributions to dental education in Canada.
• Bisco National Dental Teaching Award (Award)
Recognizes a faculty member who has displayed the qualities of an outstanding dental educator. *Amount:* $2,500

Association of Canadian Film Craftspeople

Local 2020 Communications, Energy & Paperworkers Union of Canada, #108, 3993 Henning Dr., Burnaby BC V5C 6P7
Tel: 604-299-2232; *Fax:* 604-299-2243
info@acfcwest.com
www.acfcwest.com
Also Known As: ACFC West, Local 2020 CEP
Overview: A medium-sized national organization
Chief Officer(s):
Benoit Lamarche, President
president@acfcwest.com
Richard Chilton, Ssecretary/Treasurer
secretarytreasurer@acfcwest.com
Greg Chambers, Business Manager

Association of Canadian Financial Officers (ACFO) / Association canadienne des agents financiers (ACAF)

#400, 2725 Queensview Dr., Ottawa ON K2B 0A1
Tel: 613-728-0695; *Fax:* 613-761-9568
Toll-Free: 877-728-0695
information@acfo-acaf.com
www.acfo-acaf.com
Previous Name: Association of Public Service Financial Administrators (Ind.)/Association des gestionnaires financiers de la fonction publique (Ind.)
Overview: A medium-sized national organization founded in 1989
Mission: To unite in a democratic organization all public service financial administrators for which the association becomes or applies to become a bargaining agent; to serve the welfare of its members through effective collective bargaining with their employers; to obtain for members the best levels of compensation for services rendered to their employers & the best terms & conditions of employment; to protect the rights & interests of all members in all matters upon their employment or upon their relationship with their employers; to seek to maintain high professional standards & promote their professional development; to affiliate as appropriate with other associations, unions or labour organizations for the purpose of enhancing the interests of members in the attainment of their professional & bargaining goals
Chief Officer(s):

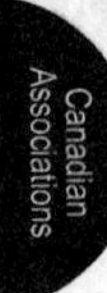

Milt Isaacs, President & Chair
misaacs@acfo-acaf.com
Karen Hall, Executive Vice-President
khall@acfo-acaf.com
Raoul Andersen, Vice-President
randersen@acfo-acaf.com
Tony Bourque, Vice-President
tbourque@acfo-acaf.com
Rob Hawkins, Vice-President
rhawkinks@acfo-acaf.com
Nicole Bishop-Tempke, Vice-President
nbishoptempke@acfo-acaf.com
Dany Richard, Vice-President
drichard@acfo-acaf.com
Finances: *Annual Operating Budget:* $250,000-$500,000
Staff Member(s): 10
Membership: 3,000; *Fees:* $28 per month; *Member Profile:* Financial Administrators; *Committees:* Collective Bargaining; Executive; Finance; Honourarium; Nominations; Representative
Activities: *Library*

Association of Canadian Franchisors ***See*** Canadian Franchise Association

Association of Canadian Industrial Designers (ACID) / Association des designers industriels du Canada

#251, 157 Adelaide St. West, Toronto ON M5H 4E7
e-mail: info@designcanada.org
www.designcanada.org
Overview: A medium-sized national organization founded in 1948
Mission: To represent Canadian industrial designers throughout world. The ACID represents the collective interests of designers and is dedicated to increasing the knowledge, skill and proficiency of its members through networking, discussion forums, seminars and trade events
Affliation(s): International Council of Societies of Industrial Design - Helsinki, Finland
Finances: *Annual Operating Budget:* Less than $50,000
Membership: 3 corporate, & members-at-large; *Fees:* $50 annually; *Member Profile:* Graduate of recognized design institution; minimum of 2 years experience in design field; portfolio of work to be presented
Activities: *Speaker Service:* Yes; *Rents Mailing List:* Yes

Association of Canadian Knights of the Sovereign Military Order of Malta ***See*** Sovereign Military Hospitaller Order of St-John of Jerusalem of Rhodes & of Malta - Canadian Association

Association of Canadian Map Libraries & Archives (ACMLA) / Association des cartothèques et archives cartographiques du Canada (ACACC)

c/o Legal Deposit, Maps, Published Heritage, Library & Archives Canada, 550, boul de la Cité, Gatineau ON K1N 0N4
e-mail: membership@acmla.org
www.acmla-acacc.ca
Overview: A medium-sized national organization founded in 1967
Mission: To represent Canadian map librarians & cartographic archivists, as well as others who are interested in geographic information; To develop professional standards & international cataloguing rules for the management & access to geographic information; To promote the contributions of map libraries & cartographic archives
Chief Officer(s):
Andrew Nicholson, President, 905-828-3886
president@acmla.org
Dan Duda, First Vice-President, 709-737-3198
vice.president1@acmla.org
Wenonah Van Heyst, Second Vice-President, 204-727-7466
vice.president2@acmla.org
Susan McKee, Secretary, 403-220-5090
secretary@acmla.org
Susan Greaves, Treasurer, 613-533-6952
treasurer@acmla.org
Membership: *Fees:* $20 students; $45 individuals & associates; $65 institutions; *Member Profile:* Individuals, libraries, archives, & other organizations with an interest in maps & geographic data; *Committees:* Archives; Awards; Bibliographic Control; Copyright; Geospatial Data Access; Historical Maps; Membership; Nominations & Elections; Social Science & Humanities Research Council (SSHRC); Web; Conference; Map Users' Advisory; Directory
Activities: Offering a mentoring program; Disseminating information to members; Facilitating the exchange of ideas through the member ACMLA- ACACC-L Listserv; Organizing professional development activities; Publishing maps, including the ACMLA Facsimile Map Series & historical maps of Canada
Meetings/Conferences: • Association of Canadian Map Libraries & Archives 2015 Annual Conference, June, 2015, Carleton University & University of Ottawa, Ottawa, ON
Scope: National
Description: A yearly gathering of map librarians & archivists & other individuals with an interest in maps & geographic data who support the objectives of the association
Contact Information: First Vice-President Siobhan Hanratty, E-mail: vice.president1@acmla.org
• Association of Canadian Map Libraries & Archives 2016 Annual Conference, 2016
Scope: National
Description: A yearly gathering of map librarians & archivists & other individuals with an interest in maps & geographic data who support the objectives of the association
Publications:
• ACMLA Bulletin
Type: Journal; *Frequency:* 3 pa; *Editor:* Cathy Moulder *ISSN:* 0840-9331; *Price:* Free withmembership in the Association of Canadian Map Libraries & Archives
Profile: Content reflecting the goals, interests, & values of the Association of Canadian Map Libraries & Archives of interest to the Canadian cartographic & geographic communities

Association of Canadian Medical Colleges ***See*** Association of Faculties of Medicine of Canada

Association of Canadian Mountain Guides (ACMG) / Association des guides de montagne canadiens

PO Box 8341, Canmore AB T1W 2V1
Tel: 403-678-2885; *Fax:* 403-609-0070
acmg@acmg.ca
www.acmg.ca
www.facebook.com/ACMG.ca
twitter.com/ACMGca
Overview: A small national organization founded in 1963
Mission: To represent mountain guides in dealing with both public & private official bodies; to maintain standards of guiding & acts as a public relations body to promote the sport in a safe & educational manner.
Member of: International Federation of Mountain Guides Associations
Chief Officer(s):
Marc Ledwidge, President, 403-762-4129
pres@acmg.ca
Peter Tucker, Executive Director, 403-949-3587
ed@acmg.ca
Finances: *Funding Sources:* Membership fees
Membership: 904; *Fees:* Schedule available; *Member Profile:* Personal membership is open exclusively to trained/certified professional guides & instructors.
Activities: Training & Certification Program

Association of Canadian Pension Management (ACPM) / Association canadienne des administrateurs de régimes de retraite

#304, 1255 Bay St., Toronto ON M5R 2A9
Tel: 416-964-1260; *Fax:* 416-964-0567
info@acpm.com
www.acpm.com
Overview: A medium-sized national organization founded in 1976
Mission: To act as the voice of Canada's pension industry; To foster the growth of the the national retirement income system
Chief Officer(s):
Christopher Brown, President
Bryan Hocking, Chief Executive Officer, 416-964-1260 Ext. 225
Bryan.Hocking@acpm.com
Diane Bélanger, Director, Member & Stakeholder Relations, 416-964-1260 Ext. 226
Diane.Belanger@acpm.com
Ric Marrero, Director, Marketing & Communications, 416-964-1260 Ext. 223
Ric.Marrero@acpm.com
Becky J. West, Secretary, Communications, 416-964-1260 Ext. 223
Vanessa.Wilson@acpm.com
Membership: *Fees:* $25 students; $50 retired persons; $455 individuals engaged in the industry; *Member Profile:* Individuals in the pension & benefit industry from across Canada; Retired persons; Students; *Committees:* Advocacy & Government Relations; Strategic Communications; National Conference Planning; Financial Resources
Activities: Liaising with govenments; Advocating for an effective & sustainable retirement income system
Meetings/Conferences: • Association of Canadian Pension Management 2015 National Conference, September, 2015, Delta Grand Okanagan, Kelowna, BC
Scope: National
Contact Information: Member Loginrketing, Communications & Membership: Ric Marrero, Phone: 416-964-1260, ext. 223, E-mail: Ric.Marrero@acpm.com
Publications:
• ACPM Education Initiative Report
Type: Booklet; *Number of Pages:* 35
Profile: Roundtable discussions, case studies, & resources
• Association of Canadian Pension Management Newsletter
Type: Newsletter
Profile: Information for members only
• Association of Canadian Pension Management Member Directory
Type: Directory
Profile: Contact information for members
• Back from the Brink: Securing the Future of Defined Benefit Pension Plan
Type: Report; *Number of Pages:* 40
Profile: Issues related to the funding of defined benefit pension plans
• Delivering the Potential of DC Retirement Savings Plans
Type: Booklet; *Number of Pages:* 33
Profile: Information about improving the retirement saving plan system
• Dependence or Self-reliance: Which way fo Canada's Retirement Income System?
Type: Booklet; *Number of Pages:* 36
Profile: Overview & recommendations
• Improving Retirement Income Coverage in Canada: The ACPM Five-Point Plan
Type: Booklet; *Number of Pages:* 9
• Retirement Income Strategy for Canada: Creating the Best Retirement Income System in the World
Type: Booklet; *Number of Pages:* 39
Profile: Overview & recommendations

Association of Canadian Port Authorities (ACPA)

#1006, 75 Albert St., Ottawa ON K1P 5E7
Tel: 613-232-2036; *Fax:* 613-232-9554
www.acpa-ports.net
twitter.com/ACPA_AAPC
Previous Name: Canadian Port & Harbour Association
Overview: A medium-sized national organization founded in 1958
Mission: To encourage, mentor & stimulate the development of excellence within Canadian ports
Affliation(s): American Association of Port Authorities
Chief Officer(s):
Wendy Zatylny, Executive Director
wzatylny@acpa-ports.net
Finances: *Funding Sources:* Membership fees; seminars
Staff Member(s): 2
Membership: 18 corporate + 37 supporters; *Fees:* $750 associate/supporters; $100 individual; *Committees:* Finance & Administration; National Operations; Execuitve; Audit; Governance; Enviroment; Law
Activities: Annual conferences where papers are given by experts in the field of port operations & where members inspect the host port's dock & industrial facilities; port-related research; special seminars; *Speaker Service:* Yes

Association of Canadian Publishers (ACP) / Association des éditeurs canadiens

#306, 174 Spadina Ave., Toronto ON M5T 2C2
Tel: 416-487-6116; *Fax:* 416-487-8815
admin@canbook.org
www.publishers.ca
Overview: A large national organization founded in 1972
Mission: To encourage writing, publishing, distribution & promotion of books written by Canadian authors in particular, & reading & study of books in general; To represent the members at international book fairs; To facilitate the exchange of information & professional expertise among members
Affliation(s): Association of Book Publishers of British Columbia; Book Publishers Association of Alberta; Saskatchewan Publishers Group; Association of Manitoba Book Publishers; Ontario Publishers Group; Association des editeurs anglophones du Québec; Atlantic Publishers Association; The Literary Press Group of Canada
Chief Officer(s):

Bill Harnum, President
bill.harnum@gmail.com
Carolyn Wood, Executive Director, 416-487-6116 Ext. 222
carolyn_wood@canbook.org
Kate Edwards, Manager, Programs, 416-487-6116 Ext. 234
kate_edwards@canbook.org
Staff Member(s): 7
Membership: 135 corporate members; *Fees:* Sliding scale; *Member Profile:* Canadian-owned & controlled firms which engage in every major type of book publishing - educational, scholarly, & the full range of trade publications; *Committees:* Canada Council; Copyright; Export; Supply Chain; Children's Publishers; Education
Activities: Book fairs; conferences; seminars; professional development programs; workshops; Top Grade: CanLit for the Classroom; eBOUND Canada; National reading Campaign; The 49th Shelf; BNC Buying Groups; Writers' Coalition Benefits Program; *Rents Mailing List:* Yes
Meetings/Conferences: • Association of Canadian Publishers 2015 Mid-Winter PD & Meeting, January, 2015, Hyatt Regency Hotel, Toronto, ON
Scope: National
Description: Themes include copyright law & the digital marketplace at an event featuring guest speakers, roundtables, & committee meetings
Contact Information: Meeting Contact: Inna Shepelska, Fax: 416-487-8815, E-mail: inna_shepelska@canbook.org
• Association of Canadian Publishers 2015 Annual General Meeting, June, 2015, Toronto Reference Library, Toronto, ON
Scope: National
Description: An event featuring plenary sessions, professional development seminars, presentations, as well as committee meetings & reports
Contact Information: Program Manager: Kate Edwards, Phone: 416-487-6116, ext 234, E-mail: kate_edwards@canbook.org
Publications:
• ACP [Association of Canadian Publishers] Update
Type: Newsletter

Association of Canadian Search, Employment & Staffing Services (ACSESS) / Association nationale des entreprises en recrutement et placement de personnel

#100, 2233 Argentia Rd., Mississauga ON L5N 2X7
Tel: 905-826-6869; *Fax:* 905-826-4873
Toll-Free: 888-232-4962
acsess@acsess.org
www.acsess.org
www.linkedin.com/company/281336
twitter.com/ACSESS_
www.youtube.com/user/acsess123
Previous Name: Federation of Temporary Help Services
Merged from: Association of Professional Placement Agencies & Consultants; Employment & Staffing Services Associa
Overview: A medium-sized national organization founded in 1998
Mission: To promote the advancement & growth of the employment & staffing services industry in Canada
Chief Officer(s):
Neil Smith, National President
neil.smith@ctsna.ca
Amanda Curtis, Executive Director
acurtis@acsess.org
Finances: *Funding Sources:* Membership dues; member services
Staff Member(s): 3
Membership: *Committees:* Executive; Nominating; Ethics; Government Relations; Public Relations & Communications; Certification & Education; Awards; National Conference; Chapter Presidents' Committee Mandate
Meetings/Conferences: • Association of Canadian Search, Employment & Staffing Services National Conference 2015, May, 2015, Marriott Ch†teau Champlain, Montréal, QC
Scope: National

Association of Canadian Television & Radio Artists *See* Alliance of Canadian Cinema, Television & Radio Artists

Association of Canadian Travel Agencies (ACTA) / Association canadienne des agences de voyages

#328, 2560 Matheson Blvd. East, Mississauga ON L4W 4Y9
Tel: 905-282-9294; *Fax:* 905-282-9826
Toll-Free: 866-725-2282
actacan@acta.travel
www.acta.ca
Previous Name: Association of Canadian Travel Agents; Alliance of Canadian Travel Associations
Overview: A large national organization founded in 1977
Mission: To provide leadership for the retail travel professional
Affiliation(s): Universal Federation of Travel Agency Associations
Chief Officer(s):
David McCaig, President & COO
DMcCaig@ACTA.ca
Finances: *Annual Operating Budget:* $1.5 Million-$3 Million
Staff Member(s): 16; 20 volunteer(s)
Membership: 3,000 corporate; *Fees:* $185-500 allied; $220-3,750 retail; *Member Profile:* Membership includes travel agencies, tour operators, travel wholesalers, national & international travel service suppliers such as airlines, hotels, tourist boards, cruise lines, railways, car rental companies & other members of the travel industry; *Committees:* Board of Directors
Activities: ACTA's Education Program has made available 4 different courses which are taught by experienced personnel: Financial Management Course; Staff Management Course; Senior Counsellor's Course; ACCESS (ACTA/CITC Canadian Educational Standards System) with a mandate to standardize education & training & to certify travel counsellors & managers across Canada, is designed to benefit those entering the industry as well as those already working as travel counsellors & managers; ACTA Marketing Services;

Association of Canadian Travel Agencies - Atlantic

PO Box 21007, Quispamsis NB E2E 4Z4
Tel: 888-257-2282; *Fax:* 855-349-0658
actaatlantic@acta.ca
www.acta.ca
Also Known As: ACTA - Atlantic
Overview: A medium-sized provincial organization founded in 1976 overseen by Association of Canadian Travel Agencies
Mission: To represent & defend the interests of the retail travel services industry; To serve as the focal point for the retail travel services industry, where ideas & resources are pooled into initiatives designed to create & maintain a healthly business & legislative environment
Chief Officer(s):
Lorie Cohen Hackett, Regional Manager
Membership: *Fees:* Schedule available
Activities: *Rents Mailing List:* Yes

Association of Canadian Travel Agents - Alberta & NWT

PO Box 21058, Stn. Terwilligar, Edmonton AB T6R 2V4
Tel: 780-437-2555; *Fax:* 855-349-0658
Toll-Free: 888-257-2282
www.acta.ca
Also Known As: ACTA - Alberta & NWT
Overview: A medium-sized provincial organization founded in 1977 overseen by Association of Canadian Travel Agencies
Mission: To represent the retail travel sector of Canada's tourism industy, with a focus on Albertan travel agents
Chief Officer(s):
Doug Boyd, Regional Chair
Barbara Sutherland, Regional Manager
bsutherland@ACTA.ca
Membership: *Fees:* Schedule available; *Member Profile:* Travel agencies

Association of Canadian Travel Agents - British Columbia/Yukon

#213, 5760 Minoru Blvd., Richmond BC V6X 2A9
Tel: 604-231-0544; *Fax:* 604-231-6020
Also Known As: ACTA - BC/Yukon
Previous Name: Association of Travel Agents of British Columbia
Overview: A medium-sized provincial organization overseen by Association of Canadian Travel Agencies
Chief Officer(s):
David McCaig, President & CEO
dmccaig@acta.ca
Membership: *Fees:* Schedule available based on # of travel personnel. $190-$2,850

Association of Canadian Travel Agents - Manitoba

#700, 177 Lombard Ave., Winnipeg MB R3B 0W5
Tel: 204-831-0831; *Fax:* 204-925-8000
actambsk@acta.ca
Also Known As: ACTA - Manitoba
Overview: A medium-sized provincial charitable organization founded in 1978 overseen by Association of Canadian Travel Agencies
Chief Officer(s):
Shelley Morris, Regional Manager
Finances: *Annual Operating Budget:* $50,000-$100,000
Staff Member(s): 1; 20 volunteer(s)
Membership: 155; *Fees:* $195-295; *Committees:* Trade Show; Golf; Executive
Activities: Manitoba Travel Marketplace;

Association of Canadian Travel Agents - Ontario

#226, 2560 Matheson Blvd. East, Mississauga ON L4W 4Y9
Tel: 905-282-9294; *Fax:* 905-282-9826
Toll-Free: 888-257-2282
www.acta.ca
Also Known As: ACTA - Ontario
Overview: A medium-sized provincial organization founded in 1974 overseen by Association of Canadian Travel Agencies
Mission: To represent the retail travel sector of Canada's tourism industry, with a focus on Ontario travel agents
Chief Officer(s):
Fiona Bowen, Regional Manager
fbowen@acta.ca
Mike Foster, Regional Chair
Finances: *Funding Sources:* Membership dues; fundraising
Membership: *Fees:* Schedule available; *Member Profile:* Travel agency owners; tour operators; travel suppliers

Association of Canadian Travel Agents - Québec / Association des agents de voyages du Québec

CP 50043, Succ. Dagenais, Laval QC H7M 0A1
Tél: 450-933-4802; *Téléc:* 450-933-4803
Également appelé: ACTA - Québec
Aperçu: *Dimension:* moyenne; *Envergure:* provinciale; fondée en 1972 surveillé par Association of Canadian Travel Agencies
Mission: Défense des droits et intérêts de l'industrie du voyage
Membre(s) du bureau directeur:
Jean Luc Beauchemin, Directeur régional
jean-luc.beauchemin@videotron.ca
Finances: *Budget de fonctionnement annuel:* $100,000-$250,000
Membre(s) du personnel: 5; 100 bénévole(s)
Membre: 500
Activités: *Stagiaires:* Oui; *Listes de destinataires:* Oui; *Bibliothèque* Bibliothèque publique

Association of Canadian Travel Agents; Alliance of Canadian Travel Associations *See* Association of Canadian Travel Agencies

Association of Canadian Universities for Northern Studies (ACUNS) / Association universitaire canadienne d'études nordiques

PO Box 321, Stn. A, Ottawa ON K1N 8V3
Tel: 613-669-8162
office@acuns.ca
www.acuns.ca
www.facebook.com/110949402264676
twitter.com/acunsaucen
Overview: A small national charitable organization founded in 1977 overseen by Association of Universities & Colleges of Canada
Mission: To encourage the government & private sector to support polar scholarship, which fosters programs to increase public awareness of polar sciences & research; to represent its member universities & colleges, encouraging the establishment of funds & resources to ensure a network of trained researchers, regional managers & educators.
Chief Officer(s):
Peter Geller, President
Monique Bernier, Vice-President
Gary Wilson, Secretary-Treasurer
Heather Cayouette, Program Manager
Finances: *Funding Sources:* University dues
Membership: 45 universities/colleges
Activities: Maintaining a network of circumpolar contacts; providing education & public awareness programs; triennial Student Conference on Northern Studies;
Awards:
• Caribou Research Award (Award)
Awarded to students enrolled in a recognized Canadian community college or university pursuing studies that will contribute to the understanding of the Beverly & Qamanirjuaq Barren Ground Caribou (& their habitat) in Canada*Deadline:* January 31 *Amount:* Up to $1,500
• Studentships in Northern Studies (Scholarship)
Research culminating in a thesis or similar document involving direct northern experience; for students enrolled in graduate & undergraduate degree programs or other courses of study

recognized at a Canadian university with special relevance to Canada's northern territories & adjacent regions*Deadline:* January 31 *Amount:* $10,000
• Cooperative Award (Award)
Awarded to a student whose studies will contribute to the understanding & development of cooperatives in NWT; applicants who are not northern residents must be full-time students at the Cooperative College of Canada, a recognized Canadian community college, or a Canadian university*Deadline:* January 31 *Amount:* $2,000
• Research Support Opportunity in Arctic Environmental Studies (Award)
Preference is given to environmental research proposals in the physical &/or biological sciences for which location at the High Arctic Weather Stations would be advantageous; graduate level studies*Deadline:* January 31 *Amount:* Logistical support
• Canadian Northern Studies Polar Commission Scholarship (Award)

Association of Canadian University Presses (ACUP) / Association des presses universitaires canadiennes (APUC)

#700, 10 St. Mary St., Toronto ON M4Y 2W8
Tel: 416-978-2239; *Fax:* 416-978-4738
www.acup.ca
Overview: A medium-sized national organization founded in 1965
Mission: To support scholarly publishing by university presses in Canada
Chief Officer(s):
Charley LaRose, Contact
clarose@utpress.utoronto.ca
Finances: *Annual Operating Budget:* Less than $50,000; *Funding Sources:* Membership dues
Staff Member(s): 1
Membership: 16 presses; *Fees:* Schedule available
Activities: *Rents Mailing List:* Yes
Publications:
• Association of Canadian University Presses Directory of Members
Type: Directory; *Price:* Free download from website

Association of Canadian Women Composers (ACWC) / L'Association des femmes compositeurs canadiennes (AFCC)

c/o Canadian Music Centre, 20 St. Joseph St., Toronto ON M4Y 1J9
e-mail: acwcafcc@gmail.com
www.acwc.ca
www.facebook.com/215231155239835
Overview: A small national organization founded in 1980
Mission: To promote the music of Canadian women composers through concerts, commissions, publications, recordings, etc.
Affliation(s): Fondezione Adkins Chiti: Donne in Musica, Italy; Women in Music Foundation
Chief Officer(s):
Joanna Estelle, Chair
vivestarmusic@yahoo.com
Finances: *Funding Sources:* Membership fees; Canada Council; SOCAN
Membership: 40; *Fees:* $25 student; $35 associate/affiliate; $40 individual; *Member Profile:* Women only; professional composer active - Canadian citizen/landed immigrant; professional composer affiliate - other nationality; associate - performer, teacher, non-composer; student composer

Association of Certified Engineering Technicians & Technologists of Prince Edward Island (ACETTPEI)

PO Box 1436, 92 Queen St., Charlottetown PE C1A 7N1
Tel: 902-892-8324
info@acettpei.ca
www.techpei.ca
Previous Name: Prince Edward Island Society of Certified Engineering Technologists
Overview: A small provincial organization founded in 1972 overseen by Canadian Council of Technicians & Technologists
Mission: To benefit society by advancing the professions of applied science & engineering technology in Prince Edward Island
Affliation(s): Island Technology Professionals
Chief Officer(s):
Trent Collicutt, President
Alan Robison, Vice-President
Delbert Reeves, Treasurer
Tom MacDonald, Registrar
Activities: Certifying engineering / applied science technicians & technologists; Conferring the designations C.Tech., C.E.T., & A.Sc.T.; *Awareness Events:* Career Options Day, November; National Skilled Trades Day, November; National Technology Week, November
Publications:
• AtlanTECH News
Type: Newsletter
Profile: Information for technology professionals in New Brunswick, Prince Edward Island, & Newfoundland & Labrador

Association of Certified Forensic Investigators of Canada (ACFI)

4 Iris St., Huntsville ON P1H 1L8
Tel: 416-226-3018
Toll-Free: 877-552-5585
info@acfi.ca
www.acfi.ca
Overview: A small national organization founded in 1998
Mission: To act as a governing body for professionals who provide forensic investivations for governments, the public, & employers; To promote high standards in the field for the benefit of the public
Chief Officer(s):
Alan M. Langley, Executive Director & Officer, Information
Membership: *Fees:* $245 regular members; $100 associate members; *Member Profile:* Individuals with expertise in fraud prevention, detection, & investigation; Candidates for membership must demonstrate their competency through education, examination, & experience
Activities: Accrediting forensic investigators; Promoting the Certified Forensic Investigator (CFI) designation; Providing continuing education opportunities

Association of Certified Fraud Examiners - Toronto Chapter

PO Box 1408, 3230 Yonge St., Toronto ON M4N 3P6
Tel: 416-480-9475; *Fax:* 416-480-1813
acfe.toronto@sympatico.ca
acfetoronto.ca
ca.linkedin.com/pub/acfe-toronto-chapter/25/971/329
facebook.com/acfeto
twitter.com/ACFETO
Also Known As: ACFE Toronto
Overview: A small national organization
Chief Officer(s):
Toby Bishop, CFE, CPA, FCA, President
Astra Williamson, CPA, CGA, CFE, Vice-President
Tom Eby, MBA, CPA, CA, Secretary
William Vasiliou, CGA, CFE, CCRA, Treasurer
Penny Hill, Administrator
Membership: *Fees:* $85 individuals; $22 students; *Member Profile:* Individuals who offer investigative, forensic, & security services to the public; *Committees:* Canada Chapter Development; Conference; Educational Outreach; Membership; Newsletter; Training
Activities: Education, training, seminars, conferences, networking, & outreach presentations; *Library:* Association of Certified Fraud Examiner Library
Publications:
• ACFE [Association of Certified Fraud Examiners] Toronto Newsletter
Type: Newsletter; *Editor:* Eric Bettencourt

Association of Chartered Industrial Designers of Ontario (ACIDO)

PO Box 1009, Stn. K, 2384 Yonge St., Toronto ON M4P 2H3
Tel: 905-475-1385
info@acido.info
acido.info/wordpress
Overview: A small provincial organization overseen by Association of Canadian Industrial Designers
Mission: To develop & promote the industrial design profession in Ontario; To act as the voice of Ontario's industrial design profession
Affliation(s): International Council of Societies of Industrial Design (ICSID)
Chief Officer(s):
Jonathan Loudon, President, 416-564-9780
jonathan@swavestudios.com
Tim Poupore, Vice-President, Standards, 416-932-8505
standards@acido.info
Membership: *Fees:* $25 students; $125 Rocket members; $150 associate & affiliate members; $300 professional & international members; $1200 corporate members; *Member Profile:* Accredited Ontario industrial designers
Activities: Promoting common standards throughout Ontario; Providing networking opportunities; Increasing public awareness of the profession's benefit to society; Offering continuing education opportunities; *Awareness Events:* Rocket: ACIDO's Annual Industrial Design Graduation Show & Competition
Publications:
• "O"
Type: Newsletter
Profile: Association activities, members' views, & profiles of products & individuals
• Association of Chartered Industrial Designers of Ontario Membership Directory
Type: Directory
Profile: Names, addresses, telephone numbers, & membership status of all ACIDO members

Association of Christian Churches in Manitoba (ACCM) / Association des églises chrétiennes du Manitoba

151 de la Cathedrale Ave., Winnipeg MB R2H 0H6
Tel: 204-237-9851
Previous Name: Ecumenical Committee of Manitoba
Overview: A medium-sized provincial organization founded in 1990
Mission: To bring Christian churches into living encounter with one another; to provide a network of news & events which can help member churches act together in all matters except those in which deep differences compel us to act separately; to act as common Christian voice & media contact on issues of spiritual & social concern in the Province
Finances: *Annual Operating Budget:* Less than $50,000

Association of Colleges of Applied Arts & Technology of Ontario *See* Colleges Ontario

Association of Commercial & Industrial Contractors of PEI

PO Box 1685, Charlottetown PE C1A 7N4
Tel: 902-566-3456; *Fax:* 902-368-2754
wmm@wmm93.pe.ca
Overview: A small provincial organization overseen by Mechanical Contractors Association of Canada
Chief Officer(s):
Mary MacDonald, Contact

Association of Complementary & Integrative Physicians of BC (ACIPBC)

PO Box 526, #185, 911 Yates St., Victoria BC V8V 4Y9
Tel: 250-382-6356; *Fax:* 250-483-1507
info@acpbc.org
www.acpbc.org
Overview: A small provincial organization founded in 1995
Mission: Society for doctors with expertise or interest in complementary health care or integrative medicine
Affliation(s): Canadian Complementary Medical Association
Chief Officer(s):
Janet Ray, President
Membership: *Fees:* $100; $30 student/resident/retired
Publications:
• ACIPBC Newsletter
Type: Newsletter; *Frequency:* Quarterly

Association of Condominium Managers of Ontario (ACMO)

#100, 2233 Argentia Rd., Mississauga ON L5N 2X7
Tel: 905-826-6890; *Fax:* 905-826-4873
Toll-Free: 800-265-3263
www.acmo.org
www.linkedin.com/groups/ACMOnews-3782859
www.facebook.com/pages/ACMOnews/163609167022080
twitter.com/ACMOnews
Overview: A medium-sized provincial organization founded in 1977
Mission: To enhance the quality performance of condominium property managers & management companies in Ontario
Chief Officer(s):
Steven Christodoulou, R.C.M., President
Finances: *Annual Operating Budget:* $250,000-$500,000; *Funding Sources:* Membership dues; advertising
10 volunteer(s)
Membership: 534 R.C.M.s + 132 candidates + 47 corporate + 14 affiliate + 331 associate; *Fees:* 106.00 individual; $270 general; $450-550 corporate; *Member Profile:* Any person in a full-time capacity in the managment of condominiums in Ontario may become a member of the Association and must agree to meet all of the criteria to be eligble to write and pass the R.C.M.

examiniation with a further six months. A Candidate Membership shall not be renewed after the fourth year.
Activities: Educational certification designation - Registered Condominium Manager RCM; *Speaker Service:* Yes; *Library* by appointment

Association of Consulting Engineering Companies - Canada (ACEC) / L'Association des firmes d'ingénieurs-conseils - Canada (AFIC)

#420, 130 Albert St., Ottawa ON K1P 5G4
Tel: 613-236-0569; *Fax:* 613-236-6193
Toll-Free: 800-565-0569
info@acec.ca
www.acec.ca
twitter.com/ACECCanada
Previous Name: Association of Consulting Engineers of Canada
Overview: A large national organization founded in 1925
Mission: To assist in promoting satisfactory business relations between its Member Firms & their clients; To promote cordial relations among the various consulting engineering firms in Canada & to foster the interchange of professional, management & business experience & information among them; To safeguard the interest of the consulting engineer; To further the maintenance of high professional standards in the consulting engineering profession
Member of: International Federation of Consulting Engineers
Chief Officer(s):
Murray Thompson, Chair
murray.thompson@urs.com
John D. Gamble, CET, P.Eng., President
jgamble@acec.ca
Jean-Marc Carrière, Vice-President, Finance & Administration, 613-236-0569 Ext. 209
jmcarriere@acec.ca
Susie Grynol, CAE, Vice-President, Policy & Public Affairs, 613-236-0569 Ext. 203
sgrynol@acec.ca
35 volunteer(s)
Membership: 600 independent consulting engineering companies & 11 provincial and territorial member organizations; *Fees:* Based on annual revenue; *Member Profile:* Firms which have passed a thorough membership screening process: proven technical capability, necessary experience as consultants, adherence to rules of ethical practice & professional responsibility; membership is voluntary & is limited to those firms primarily engaged in providing independent consulting engineering services to the public; *Committees:* Executive Directors' Coordination; Member Organization Chairs; Budget & Finance; General Reserve Investment; International; Federal/Industry Real Property Advisory Council; DND/DCC Liaison; Student Outreach Advisory Group; Canadian Engineering Leadership Forum; Contracts; Allen D. Williams Scholarship Foundation; Public-Private Partnerships (P3) Task Force
Activities: Federal government lobbying on major public policy issues; Negotiations with government departments re: contracting-out of public work, selection of consultants & remuneration; Negotiations with other industry organizations re: establishment of guidelines for contracts; International market development; *Awareness Events:* National Engineering Month; *Speaker Service:* Yes; *Rents Mailing List:* Yes; *Library* Open to public
Awards:
• Public Service Awards (Award), Canadian Consulting Engineering Awards
• Shreyer Award (Award), Canadian Consulting Engineering Awards
• Awards of Excellence & Merit (Award), Canadian Consulting Engineering Awards
• Allen D. Williams Scholarship (Scholarship)
Meetings/Conferences: • Association of Consulting Engineering Companies Leadership Summit 2015, June, 2015, Niagara Falls, ON
Scope: National
Contact Information: registration@unconventionalplanning.com
Publications:
• Concept [a publication of the Association of Consulting Engineering Companies - Canada]
Number of Pages: 4
• Source [a publication of the Association of Consulting Engineering Companies - Canada]
Type: Newsletter; *Frequency:* Monthly
• Source Express [a publication of the Association of Consulting Engineering Companies - Canada]
Type: Newsletter

Association of Consulting Engineering Companies - New Brunswick (ACEC-NB)

183 Hanwell Rd., Fredericton NB E3B 2R2
Tel: 506-470-9211; *Fax:* 506-451-9629
info@acec-nb.ca
www.acec-nb.ca
Overview: A medium-sized provincial organization founded in 1983 overseen by Association of Consulting Engineering Companies - Canada
Mission: To develop & support member firms; To improve the business environment for member firms & their clients; To further the professional standards of the consulting engineering profession
Chief Officer(s):
John Fudge, Executive Director
David McAllister, President
Christy Cunningham, Secretary
Karen Robichaud, Treasurer
Activities: Advocating for consulting engineering companies in New Brunswick; Providing training opportunities;
Awards:
• CENB Showcase Awards (Award)
Includes the following awards: Benefit to Society Award, Innovation Award, Technical Excellence Award, & Sustainability Award
Meetings/Conferences: • Association of Consulting Engineering Companies - New Brunswick 2015 17th Annual General Meeting, Trade Show, Conference, & Awards Gala, 2015, NB
Scope: Provincial
Description: Featuring a business meeting, speakers, conference seminars, exhibits, & the presentation of awards
Contact Information: E-mail: info@acec-nb.ca
Publications:
• CE [Consulting Engineers] News
Type: Newsletter; *Frequency:* Bimonthly
Profile: Information for Association of Consulting Engineering Companies - New Brunswick members

Association of Consulting Engineers of Canada *See* Association of Consulting Engineering Companies - Canada

Association of Consulting Engineers of Saskatchewan *See* Consulting Engineers of Saskatchewan

Association of Corporate Travel Executives Inc. Canada

PO Box 85020, Stittsville ON K2S 1X6
Tel: 613-836-7652; *Fax:* 613-836-0619
canada@acte.org
www.acte.org/regions/canada/index.php
Also Known As: ACTE Canada
Overview: A medium-sized national organization
Chief Officer(s):
Pauline Valiquette, ACTE Regional Chair, Canada
pauline.valiquette@cbc.ca
Membership: *Member Profile:* Travel management companies; Corporate buyers; Suppliers; Students
Activities: Offering educational events; Providing professional networking opportunities
Awards:
• Association of Corporate Travel Executives Inc. Canada Hospitality, Hotel, & Tourism Scholarships (Scholarship)
Eligibility: College & university students *Amount:* $2,500
Publications:
• ACTE / Conference Board of Canada Canadian Business Travel Outlook
• ACTE Global Business Journal
Frequency: Quarterly
Profile: Travel industry best practices & management strategies
• ACTE Membership Directory
Type: Directory
Profile: Listings of travel managers & industry suppliers
• Environmental Checklist for Canadian Corporate Travel Managers
Editor: ACTE & Hotel Association of Canada

Association of Councils of Physicians, Dentists & Pharmacists of Québec *Voir* Association des conseils des médecins, dentistes et pharmaciens du Québec

Association of Day Care Operators of Ontario (ADCO)

6 Davidson St., St. Catharines ON L2R 2V4
Fax: 705-733-2154
www.adco-o.on.ca
Overview: A medium-sized provincial organization founded in 1977
Mission: To promote the growth of private & independent (non-profit) licensed child care programs & safeguard the interests of the providers of this service in Ontario through public education, advocacy, professional (management) development & advisory activities locally & provincially
Finances: *Annual Operating Budget:* $100,000-$250,000; *Funding Sources:* Membership dues
Staff Member(s): 3
Membership: 350+; *Fees:* Schedule available
Activities: Centre of the Year Competition; conferences; luncheons; management training seminars; extensive insurance program; *Awareness Events:* Kids Helping Kids Walkathon, May; *Speaker Service:* Yes; *Library:* Resource Centre; by appointment

Association of Deans of Pharmacy of Canada (ADPC) / Association des doyens de pharmacie du Canada (ADPC)

c/o College of Pharmacy & Nutrition, University of Saskatchewan, 110 Science Pl., Saskatoon SK S7N 5C9
Tel: 306-966-6328; *Fax:* 306-966-6377
www.afpc.info/deans
Overview: A medium-sized national organization overseen by Association of Universities & Colleges of Canada
Chief Officer(s):
Harold Lopatka, Executive Director
hlopatka@telus.net
David Hill, Treasurer
david.hill@usask.ca
Finances: *Annual Operating Budget:* Less than $50,000; *Funding Sources:* Membership dues
Membership: 10; *Fees:* $250; *Member Profile:* Faculty of Pharmacy Deans in Canada

Association of Dental Technologists of Ontario (ADTO)

#235, 7181 Woodbine Ave., Markham ON L3R 1A3
Tel: 416-742-2386; *Fax:* 416-742-2386
Toll-Free: 877-788-8668
info@adto.org
www.adto.org
Overview: A small provincial organization
Mission: To pursue the advancement of the profession through education, communication amongst members & liaison with external agencies; to encourage excellence in the provision of dental technology services
Chief Officer(s):
Jason Robson, President
constantinos Nedinis, Vice-President
Frank Parada, Secretary
Irene Tamblyn, Treasurer & Education
Veronica Ng, Administrator, 416-742-2384
Finances: *Funding Sources:* Membership dues & events revenue
Staff Member(s): 1
Membership: 500-999; *Fees:* $670; *Member Profile:* Registered dental technologists practicing in Ontario
Activities: Continuing education; social events
Publications:
• The Ontario Report
Type: Newsletter; *Frequency:* Quarterly
Profile: Keeps members informed of the activities of the ADTO

Association of Dermatologists of Québec *Voir* Association des dermatologistes du Québec

Association of Disabled Adults on the North Shore *Voir* Association des handicapés adultes de la Côte-Nord

Association of Early Childhood Educators of Newfoundland & Labrador (AECENL)

PO Box 8657, #19, 50 Pippy Pl., St. John's NL A1B 3T1
Tel: 709-579-3028; *Fax:* 709-579-0217
Toll-Free: 877-579-3028
Other Communication: aecenlpd@nfld.net
aecenl@nfld.net
www.aecenl.ca
Overview: A small provincial organization founded in 1989
Mission: To promote professionalism in the field of early childhood education; To improve working conditions for early childhood educators in Newfoundland & Labrador; To ensure quality child care & education for young children in the province
Affiliation(s): Canadian Child Care Federation (CCCF)
Chief Officer(s):
Mary Walsh, Chair

Mary Goss-Prowse, Registrar, Child Care Services Certification, 709-579-3004, Fax: 877-579-0217
Skye Crawford Taylor, Director, Professional Development, 709-579-3028, Fax: 877-579-0217
Lori Dalton, Secretary
Leslie Hardy, Treasurer
Staff Member(s): 3; 12 volunteer(s)
Membership: *Fees:* $20 students; $30 individuals; $75 associations; *Member Profile:* Early childhood educators; Students; Associate member, such as associations or agencies
Activities: Providing the Child Care Services Certification service; Supporting orientation courses to achieve certification; Offering professional development workshops; Advocating for early childhood educators in Newfoundland & Labrador; Liaising with the Government of Newfoundland & Labrador & related organizations; Promoting awareness of quality child care; *Awareness Events:* NL Early Childhood Educators Week, last week of May; National Child Day, November 20th
Publications:
• Association of Early Childhood Educators of Newfoundland & Labrador Newsletter
Type: Newsletter; *Price:* Free with Assn. of Early Childhood Educators of Newfoundland & Labrador membership

Association of Early Childhood Educators of Quebec (AECEQ)

1001 Lenoir St., #A2-10, Montreal QC H4C 2Z6
e-mail: membership@aeceq.ca
www.aeceq.ca
Previous Name: Nursery School Teachers Association
Overview: A medium-sized provincial organization founded in 1946
Mission: To improve the quality of early childhood education in Quebec
Member of: Canadian Child Care Federation
Chief Officer(s):
Julie Butler, Contact
Membership: *Fees:* $35; *Member Profile:* Early childhood educators

Association of Early Childhood Educators Ontario (AECEO)

#211, 40 Orchard View Blvd., Toronto ON M4R 1B9
Tel: 416-487-3157; *Fax:* 416-487-3758
Toll-Free: 866-932-3236
info@aeceo.ca
www.aeceo.ca
www.facebook.com/189978994376068
twitter.com/AECEO
Overview: A medium-sized provincial charitable organization founded in 1950
Mission: To support early childhood educators throughout Ontario
Affliation(s): Canadian Child Care Federation
Chief Officer(s):
Rachel Langford, President
Eduarda Sousa, Executive Director
esousa@aeceo.ca
Lena DaCosta, Coordinator, Professional Development, Marketing & Advertising
ldacosta@aeceo.ca
Sue Parker, Coordinator, Membership Services & Office Manager
membership@aeceo.ca
Goranka Vukelich, Secretary
Gaby Chauvet, Treasurer
Finances: *Funding Sources:* Membership fees; Advertising; Sponsorships
Membership: *Fees:* $60-$125; *Member Profile:* Early childhood educators in Ontario; Students enrolled in an Ontario College of Applied Arts & Technology or an Ontario university leading to a diploma or degree in early childhood education; Individuals interested in the field of early childhood education
Activities: Advocating on behalf of early childhood educators across Ontario; Disseminating research; Providing professional development opportunities; Offering networking events for persons interested in early childhood education & care; Educating the public about the quality of early childhood education; *Awareness Events:* Week of the Child, October
Awards:
• Children's Service Award (Award)
An annual award to recognize two persons who have made significant contributions toward young people
Meetings/Conferences: • Association of Early Childhood Educators Ontario 2015 65th Annual Provincial Conference, 2015, ON
Scope: Provincial
Description: A conference & exhibits for delegates from across Ontario
Contact Information: Professional Development, Marketing & Advertising: Lena DaCosta, E-mail: ldacosta@aeceo.ca
Publications:
• Association of Early Childhood Educators Ontario Annual Report
Type: Yearbook; *Frequency:* Annually
• Association of Early Childhood Educators Ontario e-Bulletin
Type: Newsletter; *Frequency:* Weekly
Profile: Current events of the association & child care updates
• eceLINK
Type: Newsletter; *Frequency:* Quarterly; *Accepts Advertising*
Profile: A publication for members of the Association of Early Childhood Educators Ontario, affiliate organizations, & ministry contacts

Association of Educational Research Officers of Ontario
See Association of Educational Researchers of Ontario

Association of Educational Researchers of Ontario (AERO) / Association ontarienne des chercheurs et chercheuse en éducation

c/o Research & Information Services, Toronto District School Board, 1 Civic Centre Court, Lower Level, Toronto ON M9C 2B3
Tel: 416-394-4929; *Fax:* 416-394-4946
info@aero-aoce.org
www.aero-aoce.org
Previous Name: Association of Educational Research Officers of Ontario
Overview: A small provincial organization founded in 1972
Mission: To promote & improve research, education, planning & development pertaining to education in the Ontario school system
Affliation(s): American Educational Research Association
Chief Officer(s):
Terry Spencer, President
tspencer@office.ldcsb.on.ca
Finances: *Funding Sources:* Membership fees
Membership: *Fees:* $40; *Member Profile:* Active - based on current employment & training in research, supervisory responsibility, past employment or interest in goals of the Association; *Committees:* Fall & Spring Professional Learning; Communications & Partnerships; Research & Resources
Activities: *Speaker Service:* Yes

Association of Educators of Gifted, Talented & Creative Children in BC

c/o British Columbia Teachers' Federation, #100, 550 West 6th Ave., Vancouver BC V5Z 4P2
Tel: 604-871-2283
Toll-Free: 800-663-9163
psac63@bctf.ca
aegtccbc.ca
Overview: A small provincial organization founded in 1979
Mission: To advocate the special needs of gifted children in the province.
Affliation(s): Council for Exceptional Children
Chief Officer(s):
Elizabeth Ensing, Contact
conference@aegtccbc.ca
Membership: *Member Profile:* Member of British Columbia Teachers' Federation
Activities: *Speaker Service:* Yes; *Rents Mailing List:* Yes; *Library* by appointment

Association of Electromyography Technologists of Canada (AETC)

www.aetc.ca
Overview: A small national organization founded in 1976
Mission: To further the standards and education of persons engaged in the practice of electromyography (EMG) technology.
Chief Officer(s):
Geoff Whelan, President
Geoff.Whelan@easternhealth.ca
Nancy Verreault, Secretary-Treasurer
nverreault@Ottawahospital.on.ca

Association of Employees Supporting Education Services (AESES)

#102, 900 Harrow St. East, Winnipeg MB R3M 3Y7
Tel: 204-949-5200; *Fax:* 204-949-5215
aeses@aeses.ca
www.aeses.ca
Overview: A small local organization founded in 1972
Mission: To act as the certified bargaining agent for the support staff at the University of Manitoba, the University of Winnipeg, & St. Andrew's College, as well as the University of Manitoba's security services staff; To represent the interests of members; To maintain the welfare of members; To foster & maintain communication & goodwill between employers & employees
Chief Officer(s):
Lisa McKendry, Office Manager
lmckendry@aeses.ca
Alice Foster, Secretary
Membership: 2,000+; *Member Profile:* Support staff & security services employees at the University of Manitoba; Support staff at the University of Winnipeg & St. Andrew's College
Activities: Securing appropriate working conditions for the support staff employees of the University of Manitoba, St. Andrew's College, & the University of Winnipeg, plus the University of Manitoba's security services staff; Educating members about collective bargaining; Providing fellowship opportunities
Publications:
• Inside AESES
Type: Newsletter; *Frequency:* 5 pa
Profile: Association happenings

Association of Engineering Technicians & Technologists of Newfoundland & Labrador (AETTNL)

Donovan's Industrial Park, PO Box 790, 22 Sagona Ave., Mount Pearl NL A1N 2Y2
Tel: 709-747-2868; *Fax:* 709-747-2869
Toll-Free: 888-238-8600
aettnl@aettnl.com
www.aettnl.com
Overview: A small provincial organization founded in 1968 overseen by Canadian Council of Technicians & Technologists
Mission: To advance the profession of Applied Science/Engineering Technology & the professional recognition of Certified Technicians & Technologists.
Chief Officer(s):
Newton Pritchett, President
Donna Parsons, Registrar
Membership: 1279; *Fees:* $165 certified; $110 associate; $50 student; $82.20 retired/unemployed; *Committees:* Certification/Registration Board; Act; Public Relations; Consitution By-laws; Accreditation; AETTNL/PEGNL; AETTNL/ALBNL-NLAA; Ethics-Disciplinary; Nominations; Professional Ethics Exam

Association of English Language Publishers of Québec (AELAQ) / Association des éditeurs de langue anglaise du Québec

#3, 1200 Atwater Ave., Montréal QC H3Z 1X4
Tel: 514-932-5633
admin@aelaq.org
www.aelaq.org
Previous Name: AEAQ Inc.
Overview: A small provincial organization founded in 1990 overseen by Association of Canadian Publishers
Mission: To raise the profile of English-language books published in Québec
Chief Officer(s):
Julia Kater, Executive Director
Finances: *Funding Sources:* Canada Council for the ARts; Dept. of Canadian Heritage; SODEC; Conseil des arts de Montréal
Membership: 21 publishers; *Member Profile:* Membership is open to any firm, partnership, indivdual proprietorships or institutions which; has its chief office of business in Québec; Is at least 80 % owned by persons who are Canadian citizens or landed immigrants; Is effectively controlled by persons who are residents in Quebec and are Canadian citizens or landed immigrants; Publishes original Canadian books as an important and substantial part of its business; Has in print not less than five original Canadian titles and an on-going publishing program of not less than one title a year, and has been in operation for at least two years from the date of publication of its first title; Has no more than 25 % of its books written by its principals; Is a member of ACP or other national organization.
Activities: Professional development; public awareness; promotion of English-language literature from Québec; book of the month

Association of Equipment Manufacturers - Canada (AEM-Canada)

World Exchange Plaza, PO Box 81067, #880, 111 Albert St., Ottawa ON K1P 1B1

Tel: 613-566-4568; *Fax:* 613-566-2026
www.aem.org
Previous Name: Canadian Farm & Industrial Equipment Institute
Overview: A small national organization founded in 1966
Mission: To act as a voice for its members to the public & on a governmental level. It is also a regulatory body setting standars for safety, offering a variety of educational programs & seminars.
Chief Officer(s):
Dennis Slater, President, 414-298-4140
dslater@aem.org
Howard Mains, Canada Consultant, Public Policy
hmains@aem.org
Membership: *Member Profile:* Manufacturers & distributors of equipment, & those who offer services, in the agriculture, construction, forestry, mining & utility industries.

Association of Executive Directors of Québec Health & Social Services ***Voir*** Association des directeurs généraux des services de santé et des services sociaux du Québec

Association of Exploration Geochemists ***See*** Association of Applied Geochemists

Association of Faculties of Medicine of Canada (AFMC) / L'Association des facultés de médecine du Canada (AFMC)

#800, 265 Carling Ave., Ottawa ON K1S 2E1
Tel: 613-730-0687; *Fax:* 613-730-1196
www.afmc.ca
twitter.com/afmc_e
Previous Name: Association of Canadian Medical Colleges
Overview: A medium-sized national charitable organization founded in 1943
Mission: To represent the interests of members in medical research policy formulation; to promote & advance academic medicine through the review & development of standards for medical education, through the development of national policies appropriate to the aims & purposes of Canadian faculties of medicine, through the fostering of research, & through representation of Canadian faculties of medicine to professional associations & governments
Affliation(s): Canadian Medical Association; Association of Universities & Colleges of Canada
Chief Officer(s):
Genevieve Moineau, President & CEO
gmoineau@afmc.ca
Finances: *Annual Operating Budget:* $500,000-$1.5 Million; *Funding Sources:* Membership fees; annual meeting; research contracts; sale of publications
Staff Member(s): 6
Membership: 17 Canadian Faculties of Medicine; *Fees:* Fixed fee per school & a capitation fee based on first-time undergraduate enrollment; *Member Profile:* Accredited Canadian Faculties of Medicine; *Committees:* Special Resource Committee on Medical School Libraries; Executive; Accreditation of Canadian Medical Schools; Admissions & Student Affairs; Undergraduate, Postgraduate & Continuing Medical Education; Research & Graduate Studies; Gender & Equity Issues; Research in Medical Education; Informatics

Association of Faculties of Pharmacy of Canada (AFPC) / Association des facultés de pharmacie du Canada

14612 - 64 Ave., Edmonton AB T6H 1T8
Tel: 780-868-5530
www.afpc.info
Previous Name: Canadian Conference of Pharmaceutical Faculties
Overview: A medium-sized national charitable organization founded in 1944
Mission: To develop & implement policies & programs which will provide a forum for exchange of ideas, ensure a liaison with other organizations; to foster & promote excellence in pharmaceutical education & research in Canada
Member of: Canadian Council on Continuing Education in Pharmacy
Affliation(s): Canadian Pharmacists Association
Chief Officer(s):
Harold Lopatka, Executive Director
hlopatka@telus.net
Finances: *Annual Operating Budget:* $100,000-$250,000
18 volunteer(s)
Membership: 30 associate + 250 individual; *Fees:* Schedule available; *Member Profile:* Full - member of teaching faculty of Canadian Faculty of Pharmacy; associate - interested in goals of the association; *Committees:* Pharmaceutical Research; Pharmaceutical Education; Professional Liaison

Association of Faculties of Veterinary Medicine in Canada ***See*** Canadian Faculties of Agriculture & Veterinary Medicine

Association of Family Health Teams of Ontario (AFHTO)

#800, 60 St. Clair Ave. East, Toronto ON M4T 1N5
Tel: 647-234-8605
info@afhto.ca
www.afhto.ca
www.facebook.com/159561464069422
Overview: A medium-sized provincial organization
Mission: The Association of Family Health Teams of Ontario (AFHTO) provides leadership to promote the expansion of high-quality, comprehensive, well-integrated interprofessional primary care for the benefit of all Ontarians.
Chief Officer(s):
Angie Heydon, Executive Director
angie.heydon@afhto.ca
Meetings/Conferences: • Association of Family Health Teams of Ontario 2015 Conference, October, 2015, Westin Harbour Castle, Toronto, ON
Scope: Provincial
Contact Information: Saleemeh Abdolzahraei, Membership and Conference Coordinator; saleemeh@afhto.ca

Association of Filipino Canadian Accountants (AFCA)

PO Box 55554, Stn. Cedar Heights, Toronto ON M1H 3G7
www.afcatoronto.org
Overview: A small national organization founded in 1978 overseen by National Council of Philippine American Canadian Accountants
Mission: To promote the continuing education of Filipino Canadian accountants; To promote high professional standards; To liaise with other international organizations
Member of: National Council of Philippine American Canadian Accountants (NCPACA)
Chief Officer(s):
Mercedita Gonzales, President
president@afcatoronto.com
Ramon Guanzon, Executive Vice-President
Imelda Bautista, Vice-President, External Affairs
Rodel Acoba, Vice-President, Internal Affairs
Nimfa Santos, Secretary
Leonora Salvador, Treasurer
Nechane Vitales, Officer, Public Relations
Finances: *Funding Sources:* Membership fees; Sponsorships; Fundraising
Membership: 400; *Fees:* $30 individuals; $50 couples; *Member Profile:* Filipino designated accounting professionals; Filipino students, who are pursuing a career in accounting; *Committees:* Scholarship
Activities: Presenting professional development activities, such as career options seminars, tax preparation training, & accounting software training; Helping new immigrant members evaluate their credentials & qualifications with Canadian accounting bodies; Facilitating members' assimilation in Canada; Assisting with job placements; Organizing an AFCA toastmasters club; Arranging social & recreational activities; Engaging in community services, such as the free income tax preparation program
Awards:
• AFCA Scholarship (Scholarship)
To provide financial assistance to Filipino Canadian students in Ontario who are pursuing a career in accounting
Publications:
• Association of Filipino Canadian Accountants Members' Directory
Type: Directory
• Spreadsheet [a publication of the Association of Filipino Canadian Accountants]
Type: Newsletter; *Frequency:* Quarterly; *Editor:* Ramon Guanzon
Profile: Association of Filipino Canadian Accountants' achievements & activities, plus important events

Association of Filipino Canadian Accountants in British Columbia (AFCA-BC)

BC
Other Communication: Library E-mail: library@afca-bc.org
information@afca-bc.org
www.afca-bc.org
twitter.com/AFCABC
Overview: A small provincial organization founded in 2008 overseen by National Council of Philippine American Canadian Accountants
Member of: National Council of Philippine American Canadian Accountants (NCPACA)
Chief Officer(s):
Eloisa Peralta, President
Mary Anthonette Tecson, Vice-President
Marilyn Aceja-Uy, Secretary
Paolo Sanchez, Treasurer
Finances: *Funding Sources:* Membership fees; Sponsorships; Fundraising
Membership: *Member Profile:* Filipino designated accounting professionals; Filipino students, who are pursuing a career in accounting; *Committees:* Finance & Fundraising; Membership & Recruitment; Mentorship Program Coordinator; Nomination & Election; Professional Development & Education; Public Relations & Communications; Social & Community Relations; Values & Ethics; Web Development Team
Activities: Workshops; professional development activities; *Library:* AFCA-BC Library
Awards:
• AFCA-BC Scholarship (Scholarship)

Association of First Nations' Women; West Coast Professional Native Women's Association ***See*** Pacific Association of First Nations' Women

Association of Food Banks & CVAs for New Brunswick ***See*** New Brunswick Association of Food Banks

Association of Francophone Newspapers ***Voir*** Association de la presse francophone

Association of Hearing Instrument Practitioners of Ontario (AHIP)

#211, 55 Mary St. West, Lindsay ON K9V 5Z6
Tel: 705-328-0907; *Fax:* 705-878-4110
Toll-Free: 888-745-2447
office@ahip.ca
www.helpmehear.ca
Overview: A small provincial organization
Mission: AHIP is a non-profit organization that serves as a regulatory & lobbying body for it membership of hearing healthcare professoinals. It ensures education requirements, a code of ethics, & ultimately an improvement of services by its members to the public.
Chief Officer(s):
B. Maggie Arzani, President
Joanne Sproule, Executive Director
Staff Member(s): 3
Membership: *Fees:* $790 full; $60 student
Activities: Symposiums; *Internships:* Yes

Association of Hemophilia Clinic Directors of Canada (AHCDC)

70 Bond St., Toronto ON M5B 1X3
Tel: 416-864-5042; *Fax:* 416-864-5251
ahcdc@smh.ca
www.ahcdc.ca
Overview: A small national organization founded in 1994
Mission: To improve the treatment of people with hemophilia
Affiliation(s): Canadian Hemophilia Society
Chief Officer(s):
Annie Kaplan, Contact
Membership: 83; *Member Profile:* Directors of Hemophilia Clinics; *Committees:* Executive; Membership & Nominating; CHR & CHARMS; Research; Inhibitor; Privacy; FIX

Association of Heritage Consultants ***See*** Canadian Association of Heritage Professionals

Association of Home Appliance Manufacturers Canada Council (AHAM)

PO Box 45560, Stn. Chapman Mills, 3151 Strandherd Dr., Ottawa ON K2J 5N1
Tel: 613-823-3223
info@ahamcanada.ca
www.ahamcanada.ca
Merged from: The Canadian Appliance Manufacturers Association
Overview: A small national organization
Mission: To represent member interests in the establishment of product standards & in environmental legislation; To advocate the safe removal of mercury & other ozone depleting substances from older appliances; To support the development of energy efficient products
Chief Officer(s):

Steve Caldow, Chair
Membership: 1-99; *Member Profile:* Canadian manufacturers of major, portable, & floor care appliances
Activities: Conducting industry research projects; Identifying & communicating issues of members; Providing information required to operate in the Canadian market

Association of Image Consultants International Canada (AICI Canada)

c/o Mihaela Ciocan, ImagePro International Institute, PO Box 16079, 1199 Lynn Valley Rd., North Vancouver BC V7J 3H2
www.aicicanada.com
Overview: A small local organization founded in 1994
Mission: To advance professionalism within the field of image consultants
Chief Officer(s):
Mihaela Ciocan, President, 778-861-5776
mihaela.ciocan@image-pro.ca
Carol Robichaud, Treasurer, 905-278-1472
kcrimage@eol.ca
Mirella Zanatta, Vice-President, Communications, 519-473-2396
mz@firstimpressionsimageconsulting.com
Membership: 110+; *Member Profile:* Image professionals who specialize in visual appearance, & verbal & non-verbal communication, such as media trainers, career coaches, cosmetic & skin care specialists, colour & wardrobe consultants, & etiquette experts
Activities: Providing networking opportunities; Offering certification levels for members; Upgrading technical knowledge through continuing professional development; Liaising with related organizations
Publications:
• Association of Image Consultants International Membership Directory
Type: Directory
• Image Insights
Type: Newsletter; *Frequency:* Quarterly; *Editor:* Porcia Blake, AICI FLC; *Price:* Free with AICI Canada membership

Association of Independent Consultants (AIC)

145 Thornway Ave., Thornhill ON L4J 7Z3
Tel: 416-410-8163; *Fax:* 905-669-5233
info1@aiconsult.ca
www.aiconsult.ca
Overview: A small national charitable organization founded in 1989
Affliation(s): Society of Internet Professionals (SIP); Canadian Association of Professional Speakers (CAPS); XL Results Canada Inc.; The Mississauga Technology Association (MTA)
Chief Officer(s):
Lawrence Fox, President
president1@aiconsult.ca
Paul Marcus, Vice-President, Membership Services
membership1@aiconsult.ca
Finances: *Funding Sources:* Sponsorships
Membership: *Fees:* $149 full membership; $55 remote membership; *Member Profile:* Canadian individuals who run their own consulting businesses
Activities: Providing networking opportunities; Offering professional development activities; Assisting people to hire a consultant in many fields; *Speaker Service:* Yes
Publications:
• Association of Independent Consultants Newsletter
Type: Newsletter; *Frequency:* Monthly
• Marketing Tip of the Month [a publication of the Association of Independent Consultants]
Frequency: Monthly; *Price:* Free with Association of Independent Consultants membership
Profile: Information for Canadian consultants & entrepreneurs

Association of Independent Corrugated Converters

PO Box 73063, Stn. White Shields, 2300 Lawrence Ave. East, Toronto ON M1P 4Z5
Tel: 905-727-9405; *Fax:* 905-727-1061
info@aicc11.com
aiccbox.ca
www.linkedin.com/company/aicc-canada
Also Known As: AICC Canada
Overview: A small national organization founded in 1975
Mission: To provide a forum for the independent corrugated converter on legitimate matters of mutual interest; To enhance the level of professionalism of the independent converter in the operation of his/her business; To implement democratically determined goals on matters civil & governmental which have a positive effect on all independent corrugated converters
Member of: AICC International
Chief Officer(s):
Jana Marmei, Executive Director
Finances: *Funding Sources:* Membership fees
Membership: *Fees:* Levels based on gross sales or total number of staff; *Member Profile:* Sheet plant owners & associated members; *Committees:* Golf; Christmas

Association of Independent Schools & Colleges in Alberta (AISCA)

#201, 11830 - 111 Ave., Edmonton AB T5X 5Y3
Tel: 780-469-9868; *Fax:* 780-469-9880
office@aisca.ab.ca
www.aisca.ab.ca
Overview: A medium-sized provincial organization founded in 1958 overseen by Federation of Independent Schools in Canada
Mission: To defend & promote the right of parents to determine the context for their children's education; to create a positive social, fiscal & political environment in which independent schools are free to maintain their identity as they serve the public interest; to support & encourage independent schools in providing significant educational choices for parents & their children; to foster public understanding & appreciation of independent schools & their services
Chief Officer(s):
Duane Plantinga, Executive Director
Finances: *Annual Operating Budget:* $100,000-$250,000; *Funding Sources:* Membership fees; grants
Staff Member(s): 5
Membership: 200 schools & private ECS operators; *Member Profile:* Independent schools in Alberta

Association of Interior Designers of Nova Scotia (IDNS)

PO Box 2042, Halifax NS B3J 3B4
Tel: 902-425-4367
idns.ca
Overview: A small provincial charitable organization founded in 1975 overseen by Interior Designers of Canada
Mission: To promote the profession; to serve both the interests of public and the interior design industry.
Affliation(s): Interior Designers of Canada
Chief Officer(s):
Fran Underwood, President
Membership: 37; *Member Profile:* Registered; Intern; Inactive; Allied; Non-Resident Registered; Sudent; Retired; Honorary; Fellow.

Association of International Automobile Manufacturers of Canada (AIAMC) / Association des fabricants internationaux d'automobiles du Canada

PO Box 5, #1804, 2 Bloor St. West, Toronto ON M4W 3E2
Tel: 416-595-8251; *Fax:* 416-595-2864
auto@aiamc.com
www.aiamc.com
Previous Name: Automobile Importers of Canada
Overview: A medium-sized national organization founded in 1973 overseen by The Canadian Association of Importers & Exporters
Mission: To represent before federal, provincial, & territorial governments the interests of members engaged in the manufacturing, importation, distribution, & servicing of light-duty vehicles
Chief Officer(s):
David C. Adams, President
Mary Hogarth, Director, Policy Development & Corporate Affairs
Andrew Morin, Director, Technical & Regulatory Affairs
Finances: *Funding Sources:* Membership dues
100 volunteer(s)
Membership: 25; *Committees:* Executive; Consumer Relations; Custom; Finance & Taxation; Financial Services; Government Relations; Legal; Logistics; Parts; Show Exhibitors; Statistical; Technical
Activities: *Library* Open to public

Association of International Physicians & Surgeons of Ontario (AIPSO)

#850, 36 Toronto St., Toronto ON M5C 2C5
e-mail: imdontario@yahoo.ca
aipso.webs.com
Overview: A small provincial organization founded in 1998
Mission: To assist internationally trained physicians & surgeons by facilitating access to the licensing process in Canada; To ensure effective & equitable integration into the Canadian health care system for internationally trained physicians & surgeons
Chief Officer(s):
Amin Lakhani, President
Membership: 2,000+ registered physicians from 105 countries in AIPSO & its local affiliates; *Fees:* Free; *Member Profile:* Physicians & surgeons trained & licensed in jurisdictions outside Canada
Activities: Developing orientation, upgrading & integration programs, plus assessment, for internationally trained physicians; Providing information to members; Offering networking opportunities; Liaising with regulatory & government bodies; Engaging in advocacy activities
Publications:
• Association of International Physicians & Surgeons of Ontario Members Directory
Type: Directory

Association of Internet Marketing & Sales (AIMS)

#650, 99 Spadina Ave., Toronto ON M5V 3P8
e-mail: admin@aimscanada.com
www.aimscanada.com
Overview: A medium-sized national organization founded in 1996
Mission: To assist business professionals to leverage the internet in their daily business
Chief Officer(s):
Bruce Powell, Member, Executive Board
Finances: *Funding Sources:* Sponsorships
Membership: 5,000+; *Fees:* $195 premium members; $95 virtual members; free for basic members; *Member Profile:* Business professionals, including developers, designers, salespeople, marketers, & executives
Activities: Providing networking opportunities; Offering learning activities
Publications:
• AIMS Newsletter
Type: Newsletter; *Price:* Free with Association of Internet Marketing & Sales membership
• Association of Internet Marketing & Sales Member Directory
Type: Directory

Association of Investigators & Guard Agencies of Ontario Inc. *See* Council of Private Investigators - Ontario

Association of Iroquois & Allied Indians

387 Princess Ave., London ON N6B 2A7
Tel: 519-434-2761; *Fax:* 519-675-1053
Toll-Free: 888-269-9593
www.aiai.on.ca
Overview: A medium-sized local organization founded in 1969
Mission: To advocate for the political interests of eight member nations in Ontario
Chief Officer(s):
Geoff Stonefish, Office Manager
gstonefish@aiai.on.ca
Staff Member(s): 17
Membership: 20,000+; *Member Profile:* Member of Batchewana First Nation, Caldwell First Nation, Delaware Nation, Hiawatha First Nation, Oneida Nation of the Thames, Mississaugas of the New Credit, Mohawks of the Bay of Quinte, or Wahta Mohawks

Association of Islamic Charitable Projects *See* Association des Projets charitables Islamiques

Association of Islamic Community Gazi Husrev-Beg *See* Bosnian Islamic Association

Association of Italian Canadian Writers (AICW)

PO Box 41, Montréal QC H1M 2Y2
e-mail: info@aicw.ca
www.aicw.ca
www.facebook.com/151311478238844
twitter.com/aicwcanada
www.youtube.com/user/AICWCanada
Overview: A small international organization founded in 1986
Mission: To promote Italian Canadian literature & culture; To implement education toward the understanding of heritage in a diversified society
Chief Officer(s):
Licia Canton, President
Joseph Pivato, Vice-President
vp@aicw.ca
Michael Mirolla, Treasurer
Venara Fazio, Secretary
sec@aicw.ca
Membership: 100+; *Member Profile:* Writers; Critics; Academics; Artists
Publications:
• Association of Italian Canadian Writers Newsletter / Bollettino dell'ASSIC / Bulletin d' AEIC

Type: Newsletter; *Frequency:* 3 pa; *Editor:* Frank Giorno
Profile: Information about AICW readings, author updates, book launches, contest winners, & conferences

Association of Jewish Chaplains of Ontario
c/o Beth Emeth Bais Yehuda Synagogue, 100 Elder St., Toronto ON M3H 5G7
Tel: 416-633-3838; *Fax:* 416-633-3153
info@beby.org
www.beby.org
www.facebook.com/BEBY.Toronto
twitter.com/BethEmeth
Overview: A small local organization
Mission: To draw together those who are active in pastoral care of Jewish people & their families, for fellowship, mutual support & education; to facilitate the understanding of the role & function that a professional performs in the pastoral care of Jewish people in hospitals, seniors' homes, correctional institutions, synagogues & schools; to develop & define standards for Jewish pastoral care providers; to develop & provide training & ensure the availability of competent pastor care where needed
Affiliation(s): Toronto Board of Rabbis
Chief Officer(s):
Bernard Schwartz, President
Pearl Grundland, Executive Director
Finances: *Funding Sources:* Membership fees; donations
Membership: *Committees:* Cantor Edwards Mentoring; Greening; Golf; Investment; Nomination; Rabbi Lipson Advisory
Activities: Public lectures; *Speaker Service:* Yes

Association of Jewish Day Schools (AJDS) / Association des écoles juives
1, carré Cummings, Montréal QC H3W 1M6
Tel: 514-345-2615; *Fax:* 514-345-6415
Overview: A small provincial organization founded in 1976
Mission: To act as the central body for Montreal's Jewish day schools; to represent the interests and educational needs of its members to governments and outside public and private bodies.
Activities: Liason with the Québec Ministry of Education & schools' associations;

Association of Jewish Seniors (AJS)
#401, 4211 Yonge St., Toronto ON M2P 2A9
Tel: 416-635-2900; *Fax:* 416-635-1692
ajs@circleofcare.com
www.circleofcare.com
Overview: A medium-sized local organization
Mission: To act as a ollective voice for affiliated organizations & members-at-large; To address issues of concern to older persons
Member of: Circle of Care
Chief Officer(s):
Tammy Parker, Coordinator
Membership: *Fees:* $15 individual; $25 couple

Association of Kootenay & Boundary Local Governments (AKBLG)
c/o Arlene Parkinson, 790 Shakespeare St., Trail BC V1R 2B4
Tel: 250-368-8650
akblg@shaw.ca
www.akblg.ca
Overview: A small local organization
Mission: To serve communities by ensuring effective local government that engages citizens & helps communities
Chief Officer(s):
Andy Shadrack, President
Christina Benty, Vice-President
Arlene Parkinson, Secretary-Treasurer
Membership: *Member Profile:* Community leaders from regional governments of the Kootenay & Boundary area
Activities: Liaising with municipal, provincial, & federal governments
Meetings/Conferences: • Association of Kootenay Boundary Local Governments 2015 Annual General Meeting, April, 2015, Nakusp, BC
Scope: Local

Association of Korean Canadian Scientists & Engineers (AKCSE)
#206, 1133 Leslie St., Toronto ON M3C 2J6
Tel: 416-449-5204; *Fax:* 416-449-2875
info@akcse.org
www.akcse.org
Overview: A small national organization founded in 1986
Mission: To contribute to the advancement of science & technology
Affiliation(s): Korean Federation of Science & Technology Societies (KOFST)
Chief Officer(s):
Chi-Guhn Lee, President
Gap Soo Chang, Vice-President, External
Sun Hee Cho, Vice-President, Internal
Youn Young Shim, Secretary General
Haloo Choi, Treasurer
Membership: *Fees:* $10 undergraduate student; $20 graduate student; $30 regular; $100 foreign; *Member Profile:* Korean Canadian scientists & engineers; Science & engineering university undergraduate & graduate students
Activities: Organizing seminars; Facilitating cooperative networking opportunities; Participating in the Young Generation Forum
Awards:
• AKCSE Annual Service Award (Award)
• AKCSE Annual Best Chapter Award (Award)
• AKCSE Annual Student Award (Award)
Meetings/Conferences: • Canada-Korea Conference on Science & Technology, 2015
Description: Organized by the Association of Korean-Canadian Scientists and Engineers & Korean Federation of Science and Technology Societies, the conference is an opportunity for scientists to showcase their research results, projects & innovations
Contact Information: URL: ckc.akcse.org
Publications:
• AKCSE Newsletter
Type: Newsletter
Profile: Information about upcoming events, reviews of past events, & scholarship & award application information

Association of Large School Boards of Ontario ***See*** Ontario Public School Boards Association

Association of Latvian Craftsmen in Canada / Latviesu Dailamatnieku Savieniba
Latvian Canadian Cultural Centre, 4 Credit Union Dr., Toronto ON M4A 2N8
Tel: 416-759-4900; *Fax:* 416-759-9311
Overview: A small national organization founded in 1953
Affiliation(s): Canadian-Latvian Cultural Centre
30 volunteer(s)
Membership: 1-99; *Committees:* Display; Sales; Research; Heritage

Association of Learning Disabled Adults ***See*** Adult Learning Development Association

Association of Legal Court Interpreters & Translators (ALCIT) / Association des traducteurs et interprètes judiciares (ATIJ)
483, rue St-Antoine est, Montréal QC H2Y 1A5
Tel: 514-845-3113; *Fax:* 514-845-3006
admin@atij.ca
www.atij.ca
Overview: A medium-sized national organization founded in 1972
Mission: To provide translation & interpretation services, mainly for the Municipal Court of Montréal and the City of Montréal Police Department
Staff Member(s): 15
Membership: 1,300 individual

Association of Lesbians, Gays & Bisexuals of Ottawa ***See*** Pink Triangle Services

Association of Licensed Nursing Homes (ALNH); Associated Homes for Special Care (AHSC) ***See*** Continuing Care Association of Nova Scotia

Association of Linguistic Services Managerse ***Voir*** Association des conseils en gestion linguistique Inc.

Association of Little People of Quebec ***Voir*** Association québécoise des personnes de petite taille

Association of Local Official Health Agencies (ALOHA) ***See*** Association of Local Public Health Agencies

Association of Local Public Health Agencies (ALPHA)
#1306, 2 Carlton St., Toronto ON M5G 1T6
Tel: 416-595-0006; *Fax:* 416-595-0030
info@alphaweb.org
www.alphaweb.org
Previous Name: Association of Local Official Health Agencies (ALOHA)
Overview: A medium-sized provincial organization founded in 1986
Mission: To provide leadership in public health management to health units in Ontario; To assist local public health units in the provision of efficient & effective services
Affiliation(s): ANDSOOHA - Public Health Nursing Management; Association of Ontario Public Health Business Administrators; Association of Public Health Epidemiologists in Ontario; Association of Supervisors of Public Health Inspectors of Ontario; Health Promotion Ontario; Ontario Association of Public Health Dentistry; Ontario Society of Nutrition Professionals in Public Health
Chief Officer(s):
Linda Stewart, Executive Director
linda@alphaweb.org
Gordon Fleming, Manager, Public Health Issues
gordon@alphaweb.org
Tannisha Lambert, Manager, Administrative & Association Services
tannisha@alphaweb.org
Membership: 36 health units; *Member Profile:* Board of health members of health units in Ontario; Medical & associate medical officers of health; *Committees:* Advocacy
Activities: Advocating for public health policies, programs, & services
Meetings/Conferences: • Association of Local Public Health Agencies 2015 Annual General Meeting & Conference, June, 2015, Ottawa, ON
Scope: Provincial
Publications:
• Public Health Pulse
Type: Newsletter; *Frequency:* Quarterly; *Editor:* Tannisha Lambert
Profile: Association activities, affiliate information, conference highlights, & upcoming events

Association of Major Power Consumers in Ontario (AMPCO)
Thomson Bldg., #1510, 65 Queen St. West, Toronto ON M5H 2M5
Tel: 416-260-0280; *Fax:* 416-260-0442
www.ampco.org
www.linkedin.com/profile/view?id=11277536
twitter.com/powerconsumer
Overview: A large provincial organization founded in 1975
Mission: To represent Ontario's electricity-intensive companies; To ensure reliability of power supply to support the economy of Ontario; To advocate a fair & equitable pricing system for electricity; To present views on energy matters to such groups as the Ontario Energy Board, the Ontario Government, Ontario Hydro, the news media, & the general public; To provide decision makers with recommendations on resolving issues
Chief Officer(s):
Adam White, President
awhite@ampco.org
Fareeda Heeralal, Contact
Finances: *Funding Sources:* Membership fees
Membership: 44; *Fees:* Based on electrical energy usage; *Member Profile:* Companies that are major manufacturers, employers, & power consumers (represents key industries - mining, pulp & paper, automobile manufacturing, petro-chemicals, metals, consumer products, steel, etc.)
Publications:
• AMPCO [Association of Major Power Consumers in Ontario] Bulletins
Type: Newsletter

Association of Management, Administrative & Professional Crown Employees of Ontario (AMAPCEO) / Association des employés et employées gestionnaires, administratifs et professionnels de la Couronne de l'Ontario
PO Box 72, #2310, 1 Dundas St. West, Toronto ON M5G 1Z3
Tel: 416-595-9000; *Fax:* 416-340-6461
Toll-Free: 888-262-7326
amapceo@amapceo.on.ca
www.amapceo.on.ca
twitter.com/AMAPCEONews
Overview: A medium-sized provincial organization founded in 1992
Mission: To represent the interests of Ontario Public Service employees
Affliation(s): Professional Employees Network
Chief Officer(s):

Gary Gannage, President & CEO
gannage@amapceo.on.ca
Staff Member(s): 41
Membership: 12,000; *Member Profile:* Middle managers & professional employees of the Ontario public service
Activities: Collective bargaining; workplace advocacy

Association of Manitoba Book Publishers (AMBP)

#404, 100 Arthur St., Winnipeg MB R3B 1H3
Tel: 204-947-3335; *Fax:* 204-956-4689
Overview: A medium-sized provincial organization founded in 1979 overseen by Association of Canadian Publishers
Mission: To promote Manitoba publishing industry
Chief Officer(s):
Michelle Peters, Executive Director
Activities: *Awareness Events:* Manitoba Book Week (April)
Awards:
• Manitoba Book Awards (Award)

Association of Manitoba Hydro Staff & Supervisory Employees (AMHSSE)

PO Box 353, 905 Corydon Ave., Winnipeg MB R3M 3V3
Tel: 204-482-2559
tesmith@hydro.mb.ca
Overview: A small provincial organization
Chief Officer(s):
Gord Kirk, President
gdkirk@hydro.mb.ca
Membership: 415

Association of Manitoba Land Surveyors

#202, 83 Gary St., Winnipeg MB R3C 4J9
Tel: 204-943-6972; *Fax:* 204-957-7602
www.amls.ca
Overview: A medium-sized provincial licensing organization founded in 1881 overseen by Professional Surveyors Canada
Mission: To license qualified persons becoming commissioned land surveyors; To protect public interests concerning land boundary matters
Affliation(s): Canadian Institute of Surveying & Mapping; Western Canadian Board of Examiners for Land Surveyors
Chief Officer(s):
Lori McKietiuk, Executive Director
Finances: *Funding Sources:* Membership fees
Membership: *Fees:* Schedule available; *Member Profile:* Commissioned land surveyor in Manitoba; *Committees:* Professional Association Liaison; Annual General Mtg Planning; AMLS Annual Golf Tournament; Nominating; Red River College Advisory; Canadian Board of Examiners for Professional Surveyors; Bylaw Rewrite; Public Awareness/Website; Professional Standards & Ethics; Unauthorized Practice; Manual of Good Practice; Professional Practice Review; Professional Development; Complaint/Discipline Investigation
Activities: *Internships:* Yes; *Speaker Service:* Yes; *Rents Mailing List:* Yes; *Library* Open to public by appointment

Association of Manitoba Municipalities (AMM)

1910 Saskatchewan Ave. West, Portage la Prairie MB R1N 0P1
Tel: 204-857-8666; *Fax:* 204-856-2370
amm@amm.mb.ca
www.amm.mb.ca
www.facebook.com/124665930946719
twitter.com/AMMManitoba
Merged from: Union of Manitoba Municipalities; Manitoba Association of Urban Municipalities
Overview: A medium-sized provincial organization founded in 1905
Mission: To provide communications link between municipalities; to lobby for municipal governments with senior levels of government
Member of: Federation of Canadian Municipalities
Chief Officer(s):
Joe Masi, Executive Director, 204-856-2360
Doug Dobrowolski, President
Finances: *Annual Operating Budget:* $500,000-$1.5 Million; *Funding Sources:* Membership fees
Staff Member(s): 6
Membership: 165 municipalities
Activities: *Library*
Meetings/Conferences: • Association of Manitoba Municipalities 17th Annual Convention, November, 2015, Brandon Keystone Centre, Brandon, MB
• Association of Manitoba Municipalities 18th Annual Convention, November, 2016, RBC Convention Centre, Winnipeg, MB
Attendance: 600
• Association of Manitoba Municipalities 19th Annual Convention, 2017, Brandon, MB

Association of Manitoba Museums (AMM)

#1040, 555 Main St., Winnipeg MB R3B 1C3
Tel: 204-947-1782; *Fax:* 204-942-3749
www.museumsmanitoba.com
Overview: A medium-sized provincial charitable organization founded in 1972
Mission: To strengthen the museum community by promoting excellence in preserving & presenting Manitoba's heritage; To improve the AMM's ability to communicate with its members; To continue a training program
Member of: Canadian Museums Association; American Museums Association
Chief Officer(s):
Monique Brandt, Executive Director
director@museumsmanitoba.com
Beryth Strong, Coordinator, Training
training@museumsmanitoba.com
Jame Dalley, Conservator, Cultural Stewardship Program
conservator@museumsmanitoba.com
Finances: *Annual Operating Budget:* $100,000-$250,000; *Funding Sources:* Federal & provincial government; membership fees; registration fees
Staff Member(s): 3
Membership: 248; *Fees:* $30 individual; $40 family; $20 student; $40 associate; institutional based on organization's budget; *Member Profile:* Museums; heritage organizations; families; students; individuals; *Committees:* Advocacy; Exhibits; Membership Services; Publications; Standards; Training
Activities: *Library:* AMM Resource Library
Meetings/Conferences: • Association of Manitoba Museums Conference 2015, 2015, MB
Scope: Provincial

Association of Marine Underwriters of British Columbia *See* Marine Insurance Association of British Columbia

The Association of Maritime Arbitrators of Canada (AMAC) / Les Arbitres Maritimes Associés du Canada

c/o Fednav Limitée, #3500, 1000, rue de la Gauchetière ouest, Montréal QC H3B 4W5
Tel: 514-878-6439; *Fax:* 514-878-7670
Overview: A small national organization founded in 1986
Mission: To promote & provide arbitration facilities for all types of maritime disputes whether in or outside Canada
Chief Officer(s):
Donald Pinkerton, Secretary-Treasurer
dpinkerton@fednav.com
John Weale, President, 514-878-6676, Fax: 514-878-6508
j.weale@fednav.com
Finances: *Annual Operating Budget:* Less than $50,000
Membership: 100-499; *Fees:* $50; *Member Profile:* Shipping, transport & maritime corporations; law firms, surveyors, adjusters & insurers

Association of Massage Therapists & Wholistic Practitioners *See* Natural Health Practitioners of Canada

Association of Mature Canadians (AMC)

366 Bay St., 7th Fl., Toronto ON M5H 4B2
Tel: 416-601-0429
Toll-Free: 800-667-0429
service@maturecanadians.ca
www.maturecanadians.ca
Overview: A medium-sized national organization
Chief Officer(s):
Robert Bruce, Executive Director
rbruce@maturecanadians.ca
Membership: *Fees:* $15

Association of Medical Microbiology & Infectious Disease Canada (AMMI Canada) / Association pour la microbiologie médicale et l'infectiologie Canada

#101, 298 Elgin St., Ottawa ON K2P 1M3
Tel: 613-260-3233; *Fax:* 613-260-3235
Other Communication: Alternate e-mail: communications@ammi.ca; manager@ammi.ca
info@ammi.ca
www.ammi.ca
Previous Name: Canadian Infectious Disease Society
Overview: A small national charitable organization founded in 1978
Mission: To represent the broad interests of researchers & physicians who specialize in the fields of infectious diseases & medical microbiology in Canada; To contribute to the health of people at risk of, or affected by, infectious diseases; To promote & facilitate research; To develop policies for the prevention, diagnosis, & management of infectious diseases
Chief Officer(s):
Lynn Johnston, President
Brett Filson, Executive Director
director@ammi.ca
Riccarda Galioto, Office Manager & Coordinator, Special Events
manager@ammi.ca
Sarah Forgie, Secretary
Mel Krajden, Treasurer
Kimberley Wannamaker, Administrative Assistant, Membership
info@ammi.ca
Gwen Lovagi, Contact, Communications
communications@ammi.ca
Membership: *Fees:* $43.38 + applicable taxes in province of residence for associates; $191.30 + applicable taxes for active members; $1,695.65 for sustaining members; *Member Profile:* Professionals dealing with human microbiology & infectious disease in Canada; Infectious disease or medical microbiology trainees in accredited training programs; Post-graduate trainees in related disciplines; Organizations & corporations interested in the objectives of Association of Medical Microbiology & Infectious Disease Canada; *Committees:* Associate; Guidelines; Canadian Hospital Epidemiology; Nominations; Education / Continuing Professional Development; Grants & Awards; Program Planning; Communications & Public Relations; Antimicrobial Stewardship & Resistance; Finance; Nominations
Activities: Offering opportunities for communication among members; Engaging in advocacy activities; Communicating with other organizations with common interests; Encouraging excellence in infectious disease & medical microbiology professional training; Providing professional development opportunities; Protecting & educating the public; Communicating issues to the medical community & the public; Promoting ethical behaviour of members; Providing access to information about research grants, awards, & career opportunities
Awards:
• Association of Medical Microbiology & Infectious Disease Canada / Pfizer Post Residency Fellowship (Grant)
• Canadian Journal of Infectious Diseases & Medical Microbiology Trainee Review Article Award (Award)
• Association of Medical Microbiology & Infectious Disease Canada Distinguished Service Award (Award)
• Association of Medical Microbiology & Infectious Disease Canada Lifetime Achievement Award (Award)
• Association of Medical Microbiology & Infectious Disease Canada Honorary Membership (Award)
• Association of Medical Microbiology & Infectious Disease Canada / Astellas Post Residency Fellowship (Grant)
Meetings/Conferences: • Association of Medical Microbiology & Infectious Disease Canada 2015 Annual Conference, April, 2015, Delta Prince Edward Island & PEI Convention Centre, Charlottetown, PE
Scope: National
Description: A yearly meeting presenting the latest information in the fields of infectious diseases and microbiology for microbiologists, physicians, researchers, laboratory technologists, & students in the areas of medical microbiology & infectious diseases
Publications:
• Association of Medical Microbiology & Infectious Disease Canada Annual Report
Type: Yearbook; *Frequency:* Annually
• Association of Medical Microbiology & Infectious Disease Canada Membership Directory
Type: Directory
• Canadian Journal of Infectious Disease & Medical Microbiology
Type: Journal; *Price:* Free with membership in the Association of Medical Microbiology & Infectious Disease
• Members Connect [a publication of the Association of Medical Microbiology & Infectious Disease Canada]
Type: Newsletter; *Price:* Free with membership in theAssociation of Medical Microbiology & Infectious Disease
Profile: The newsletter of the Association of Medical Microbiology & Infectious Disease Canada

Association of Midwives of Newfoundland & Labrador (AMNL)

Southcott Hall, Centre for Nursing Studies, #1017, 100 Forest Rd., St. John's NL A1A 1E5
Tel: 709-777-8140
www.ucs.mun.ca/~pherbert
Overview: A small provincial organization founded in 1983

Mission: To promote midwifery in Newfoundland & Labrador
Membership: *Member Profile:* Midwives in Newfoundland & Labrador
Activities: Creating information sharing opportunities for midwives; Advocating for the practice of midwives; Offering continuing education through workshops & publications; Liaising with other professional & special interest groups; Establishing & maintaining a code of ethics for midwives in the province;

Association of Millwrighting Contractors of Ontario Inc. (AMCO)

#218, 290 North Queen St., Toronto ON M9C 5L2
Tel: 416-620-8558; *Fax:* 416-620-1293
amco@amcontario.ca
www.amcontario.ca
Overview: A small provincial organization founded in 1959
Mission: Established to further the aims and objectives of its members with particular reference to Labour Relations and related activities including Collective Bargaining & Administration
Affliation(s): Council of Ontario Construction Association; Construction Employers Coordinating Council of Ontario; Construction Safety Associan of Ontario; Provincial Labour Management Health & Safety Committee; Ontario Construction Secretariat
Chief Officer(s):
R.H. LeChien, General Manager
Staff Member(s): 1; 20 volunteer(s)
Membership: 51; *Fees:* $262.50; *Member Profile:* Millwrighting contractors; *Committees:* Finance; Apprenticeship; Millwright Trust Fund; Labour/Management Health & Safetty; Commuting Trust Fund; Construction Millwright Apprenticeship Provincial Advisory; Labour Management Relations; Scholarship; Negotiation; Nominating

Association of Municipal Administrators of New Brunswick (AMANB) / Association des administrateurs municipaux du Nouveau-Brunswick (AAMNB)

20 Courtney St., Douglas NB E3G 8A1
Tel: 506-453-4229; *Fax:* 506-444-5452
amanb@nb.aibn.com
www.amanb-aamnb.ca
Overview: A medium-sized provincial organization founded in 1977
Mission: To promote & advance status of persons employed in field of municipal administration; to advance quality of administration of municipal services; to encourage closer official & personal relationship among members to facilitate interchange of ideas & experience; to establish & maintain standards of performance for members; to assist in provision of formal training & educational facilities
Chief Officer(s):
Cynthia Geldart, President, 506-451-3333
Danielle Charron, Executive Director
Finances: *Annual Operating Budget:* Less than $50,000
Staff Member(s): 1
Membership: 226 municipal + 23 associate; *Committees:* Legislation; Education; Membership
Meetings/Conferences: • Association of Municipal Administrators of New Brunswick 2015 Annual Conference and Annual General Meeeting, 2015, NB
Scope: Provincial

Association of Municipal Administrators, Nova Scotia (AMANS)

CIBC Building, #1106, 1809 Barrington St., Halifax NS B3J 3K8
Tel: 902-423-2215; *Fax:* 902-425-5592
amans@eastlink.ca
www.amans.ca
Overview: A medium-sized provincial organization founded in 1970
Mission: To improve the quality of local government in Nova Scotia through the development of educational programs; To provide a forum for the exchange of ideas; to provide a resource to municipal officials; To provide service to members to improve their professional capabilities
Chief Officer(s):
Janice Wentzell, Executive Director, 902-423-8323, Fax: 902-425-5592
jwentzell@amans.ca
Kristy Hardie, Administrative Assistant, 902-423-2215, Fax: 902-425-5592
khardie@amans.ca
Finances: *Funding Sources:* Membership dues; Conference surplus
Membership: 165; *Fees:* $175

Association of Municipal Clerks & Treasurers of Ontario
See Association of Municipal Managers, Clerks & Treasurers of Ontario

Association of Municipal Managers, Clerks & Treasurers of Ontario (AMCTO) / Association des directeurs généraux, secrétaires et trésoriers municipaux de l'Ontario (ASTMO)

#610, 2680 Skymark Ave., Mississauga ON L4W 5L6
Tel: 905-602-4294; *Fax:* 905-602-4295
amcto@amcto.com
www.amcto.com
Previous Name: Association of Municipal Clerks & Treasurers of Ontario
Overview: A medium-sized provincial organization founded in 1938
Mission: To foster administrative excellence in local government; to identify & meet training & education needs in local government; to be an influential voice for local government; to provide an effective communication forum for local government; to promote public awareness of & confidence in local government; to facilitate change within AMCTO
Affliation(s): Association of Municipalities of Ontario; International Institute of Municipal Clerks; Municipal Information Systems Association
Chief Officer(s):
Andy Koopmans, Executive Director
akoopmans@amcto.com
Nadeem Dean, Manager, Finance & Administration
ndean@amcto.com
Finances: *Annual Operating Budget:* $500,000-$1.5 Million; *Funding Sources:* Membership fees; program fees; products
Staff Member(s): 13
Membership: 2,200; *Fees:* Schedule available; *Member Profile:* Accreditation program in Canada for those involved in municipal government.; *Committees:* Legislative & Policy Advisory
Activities: Education & training; software; reference surveys
Awards:
• E.A. Danby Award (Award)
Meetings/Conferences: • Association of Municipal Managers, Clerks & Treasurers of Ontario Annual Conference 2015, June, 2015, Thunder Bay, ON
Scope: Provincial

Association of Municipal Recycling Coordinators *See* Municipal Waste Association

Association of Municipal Tax Collectors of Ontario *See* Ontario Municipal Tax & Revenue Association

Association of Municipalities of Ontario (AMO)

#801, 200 University Ave., Toronto ON M5H 3C6
Tel: 416-971-9856; *Fax:* 416-971-6191
Toll-Free: 877-426-6527
amo@amo.on.ca
www.amo.on.ca
Overview: A medium-sized provincial organization founded in 1899
Mission: To support & enhance strong & effective municipal government in Ontario; To represent almost all of Ontario's 444 municipal governments
Member of: Federation of Canadian Municipalities
Chief Officer(s):
Pat Vanini, Executive Director, 416-971-9856 Ext. 316
pvanini@amo.on.ca
Nancy Plumridge, Director, Administration & Business Development
NPlumridge@amo.on.ca
Monika Turner, Director, Policy
MTurner@amo.on.ca
Finances: *Funding Sources:* Membership fees; Sales of services & products; Sponsorships
Membership: 100-499; *Member Profile:* Ontario municipalities; Related non-profit organizations & private corporations
Activities: Developing policy positions; Reporting on issues; Liaising with the Ontario provincial government; Informing & educating the media & the public; Marketing services to the municipal sector
Meetings/Conferences: • Association of Municipalities of Ontario 2015 Annual Conference, August, 2015, Scotiabank Conference Centre, Niagara Falls, ON
Scope: Provincial
Description: A yearly gathering of municipal government officials to discuss current issues.
Contact Information: Special Events & Business Development Coordinator: Navneet Dhaliwal, Phone: 416-971-9856, ext. 330, Fax: 416-971-6191, E-mail: ndhaliwal@amo.on.ca

Publications:
• AMO Watch File e-Newstter
Type: Newsletter
• Association of Municipalities of Ontario Annual Report
Type: Yearbook; *Frequency:* Annually

Association of Naturopathic Physicians of British Columbia
See College of Naturopathic Physicians of British Columbia

Association of Neighbourhood Houses BC (ANH)

#203, 3102 Main St., Vancouver BC V5T 3G7
Tel: 604-875-9111; *Fax:* 604-875-1256
central@anhbc.org
www.anhbc.org
www.facebook.com/148894038481998
twitter.com/anhbc
Previous Name: Association of Neighbourhood Houses of Greater Vancouver; Alexandra Neighbourhood House
Overview: A small local charitable organization founded in 1894 overseen by United Way of the Lower Mainland
Mission: A volunteer driven community based organization committed to enhancing neighbourhoods; to enable people to enhance their lives & strengthen their communities; to work with communities to develop innovative programs & services that meet the changing needs of a diverse population
Member of: International Federation of Settlement & Neighbourhood Centres
Affliation(s): Multicultural Societies
Chief Officer(s):
Terry Stanway, President
Mamie Hutt-Temoana, CEO
Finances: *Annual Operating Budget:* $1.5 Million-$3 Million; *Funding Sources:* 3 levels of government; United Way; fundraising; endowment funds
Staff Member(s): 400; 2000 volunteer(s)
Membership: 1-99; *Committees:* Finance; Personnel; Executive; Board Development
Activities: Good Neighbour Award, Nov.; *Awareness Events:* Celebration of Good Neighbour, 3rd Thu. in Nov.
Awards:
• Good Neighbour Award - House/Unit (Award)
• Good Neighbour Award - Youth (Award)
• Good Neighbour Award - Lower Mainland (Award)
• Good Neighbour Award - Corporate (Award)

Alexandra
2916 McBride Ave., Crescent Beach BC V4A 3G2
Tel: 604-535-0015; *Fax:* 604-535-2720
info@alexhouse.net
www.alexhouse.net
twitter.com/AlexHouseBC
Chief Officer(s):
Susan Vanin, House Representative

Cedar Cottage
4065 Victoria Dr., Vancouver BC V5N 4M9
Tel: 604-874-4231; *Fax:* 604-874-7169
ccnh@cedarcottage.org
www.cedarcottage.org
Chief Officer(s):
Carol Macpherson, House Representative

Frog Hollow
2131 Renfrew St., Vancouver BC V5M 4M5
Tel: 604-251-1225; *Fax:* 604-254-3764
contact@froghollow.bc.ca
www.froghollow.bc.ca
Chief Officer(s):
Daryl Wong, House Representative

Gordon House
1019 Broughton St., Vancouver BC V6G 2A7
Tel: 604-683-2554; *Fax:* 604-683-4486
www.gnh.vcn.bc.ca
www.facebook.com/gordonhse
Chief Officer(s):
John Lucas, Executive Director
jlucas@gordonhouse.org

Kitsilano House
3683 4th Ave. West, Vancouver BC V6R 4N6
Tel: 604-736-3588; *Fax:* 604-736-3640
frontdesk@kitshouse.org
www.kitshouse.org
www.facebook.com/KitsilanoNeighbourhoodHouse
twitter.com/kitshouse
www.youtube.com/user/KitsHouseCommunity
Chief Officer(s):
Catherine Leach, Executive Director
catherine@kitshouse.org

Mount Pleasant
800 East Broadway, Vancouver BC V5T 1Y1
Tel: 604-879-8208; *Fax:* 604-879-4136
info@mpnh.org
www.mpnh.org
www.facebook.com/mountpleasantneighbourhoodhouse
twitter.com/mountpleasantnh
Chief Officer(s):
Sarah Farina, House Representative

Sasamat Outdoor Centre
3302 Senkler Rd., Belcarra BC V3H 4S3
Tel: 604-939-2268; *Fax:* 604-939-3522
info@sasamat.org
www.sasamat.org
www.facebook.com/SasamatOutdoorCentreOfficial
Chief Officer(s):
Bronco Cathcart, Executive Director
bronco@sasamat.org

South Vancouver
6470 Victoria Dr., Vancouver BC V5P 3X7
Tel: 604-324-6212; *Fax:* 604-324-6116
svnh@southvan.org
www.southvan.org
www.facebook.com/southvanNH
Chief Officer(s):
Karen Larcombe, Executive Director
karen@southvan.org

Association of Neighbourhood Houses of Greater Vancouver; Alexandra Neighbourhood House *See* Association of Neighbourhood Houses BC

Association of New Brunswick Land Surveyors (ANBLS) / Association des arpenteurs-géomètres du Nouveau-Brunswick (AA-GN-B)

#312, 212, Queen St., Fredericton NB E3B 1A8
Tel: 506-458-8266; *Fax:* 506-458-8267
anbls@nb.aibn.com
www.anbls.nb.ca
Overview: A small provincial licensing organization founded in 1954 overseen by Professional Surveyors Canada
Mission: To regulate & govern the practice of land surveying in New Brunswick; To develop & maintain standards of knowledge, skill, & professional ethics
Chief Officer(s):
Doug Morgan, Executive Director
dmorgan@nb.aibn.com
Staff Member(s): 2
Membership: 140; *Member Profile:* Individuals who comply with the requirements as specified in the New Brunswick Land Surveyors Act, 1986, & By-Laws
Activities: Increasing public awareness of the role of the association; Liaising with other professional organizations
Meetings/Conferences: • Association of New Brunswick Land Surveyors 2015 Annual General Meeting, 2015, NB
Scope: Provincial
Publications:
• Surveyor-In-Training Manual
Type: Manual

Association of New Brunswick Licensed Practical Nurses (ANBLPN) / L'Association des Infirmier(ère)s Auxiliares Autorisé(e)s du Nouveau-Brunswick (AIAANB)

384 Smythe St., Fredericton NB E3B 3E4
Tel: 506-453-0747; *Fax:* 506-459-0503
Toll-Free: 800-942-0222
www.anblpn.ca
Overview: A medium-sized provincial organization founded in 1965
Mission: To ensure the public's right to quality ethical care by regulating & enhancing the profession of practical nursing
Chief Officer(s):
JoAnne Graham, Executive Director & Registrar
execdir@anblpn.ca
Awards:
• LPN Bursary (Grant)
Eligibility: Students enrolled in continuing education programs
• Audrey D. Galbraith Excellence in Practice Award (Award)
To honour those who demonstrate excellence in nursing practice
• The Foster Greenlaw Scholarship (Scholarship)
Eligibility: A person enrolled in the Practical Nurse program who is he child, grandchild or someone in the guardianship of a Licensed Practical Nurse
• The Inez Smith Scholarship (Scholarship)
Eligibility: A person enrolled in any post-secondary education program who is the child, grandchild, or someone in the guardianship of an LPN
Meetings/Conferences: • Association of New Brunswick Licensed Practical Nurses 2015 Annual General Meeting, 2015, NB
Scope: Provincial
Attendance: 200+
Contact Information: Executive Director/Registrar: JoAnne Graham, LPN, E-mail: execdir@anblpn.ca
Publications:
• The Blue Band
Type: Newsletter; *Frequency:* Semiannually; *Editor:* JoAnne Graham
Profile: Messages from the president & executive director, educational articles, meeting reviews, & upcoming events
• Care of the Patient Receiving IV Therapy Manual
Type: Manual; *Price:* $15
Profile: A manual used for the Association of New Brunswick Licensed Practical Nurses' workshop
• Catheterization Manual
Type: Manual; *Price:* $10
Profile: A manual used for the Association of New Brunswick Licensed Practical Nurses' catheterization workshop
• Dressings Manual
Type: Manual; *Price:* $40
Profile: A manual used for the Association of New Brunswick Licensed Practical Nurses' self-learning module
• Feeding Tubes & Medication Administration by the Enteral Route for Licensed Practical Nurses Manual
Type: Manual; *Price:* $15
Profile: A manual used for the Association of New Brunswick Licensed Practical Nurses' workshop
• Insulin Administration for Licensed Practical Nurses Manual
Type: Manual; *Price:* $25
Profile: A manual used for the Association of New Brunswick Licensed Practical Nurses' course
• Intramuscular Injection Manual
Type: Manual; *Price:* $15
Profile: A manual used for the Association of New Brunswick Licensed Practical Nurses' self-learning module

Association of New Brunswick Massage Therapists (ANBMT) / L'association néo-brunswickoise de massothérapeutes (ANBMT)

PO Box 323, Stn. A, Fredericton NB E3B 4Y9
Tel: 506-452-6972; *Fax:* 506-451-8173
anbmt@anbmt.ca
www.anbmt.ca
Overview: A small provincial organization founded in 1994
Mission: To represent massage therapists in New Brunswick; To ensure members provide safe & effective massage therapy
Chief Officer(s):
Coralie Hopkins-Hashey, Executive Director
Membership: *Member Profile:* Massage therapists in New Brunswick, with training accepted by the CMTO; Members must graduate from a school with a provincially accepted curriculum & with provincially legislated standards for practice; All active members must carry Professional Liability Insurance
Activities: Encouraging high standards of practice in massage therapy; Upholding a code of ethics; Promoting massage therapy; Representing members before governmental & regulatory bodies; Offering a mentoring program
Publications:
• ANBMT Newsletter
Type: Newsletter; *Frequency:* Quarterly; *Price:* Free with ANBMT membership

Association of New Brunswick Professional Educators (ANBPE) / Association des éducateurs professionnels du Nouveau-Brunswick

c/o Wayne Milner, Counselling Services, NBCC Moncton, #1101A, 1234 Mountain Rd., Moncton NB E1C 8H9
Overview: A small provincial organization
Mission: To operate as a bargaining unit of the New Brunswick Union of Public & Private Employees (NBUPPE / NUPGE)
Chief Officer(s):
Wayne Milner, President & Director, 506-856-2742
wayne.milner@gnb.ca
Membership: 99; *Member Profile:* Members of the New Brunswick Community College system

Association of Newfoundland & Labrador Archives (ANLA)

PO Box 23155, St. John's NL A1B 4J9
Tel: 709-726-2867; *Fax:* 709-722-9035
anla@nf.aibn.com
www.anla.nf.ca
Merged from: Newfoundland & Labrador Council of Archives
Overview: A medium-sized provincial charitable organization founded in 1982 overseen by Canadian Council of Archives
Mission: To provide professional leadership among persons engaged in practice of archival science; to promote development of archives & archivists in Newfoundland & Labrador; to encourage cooperation of archivists with all those interested in preservation & use of documents of human experience
Chief Officer(s):
Jenny Seeman, President
Mary Ellen Wright, Officer, Professional Development & Outreach
Finances: *Funding Sources:* Dept. of Canadian Heritage; Province of Newfoundland & Labrador; membership fees
Staff Member(s): 1
Membership: 90 institutional members; *Fees:* $25; *Committees:* Education; Publications; Information Technology; Outreach; Grants
Activities: *Speaker Service:* Yes; *Library* by appointment

Association of Newfoundland Land Surveyors

#203, 62-64 Pippy Pl., St. John's NL A1B 4H7
Tel: 709-722-2031; *Fax:* 709-722-4104
www.surveyors.nf.ca
Overview: A small provincial licensing organization founded in 1953 overseen by Professional Surveyors Canada
Mission: To establish & maintain standards of knowledge, skill, & professional conduct in the practice of land surveying, in order to serve & protect the public interest in Newfoundland; to regulate & govern the practice of land surveying in the province
Chief Officer(s):
Robert Way, President
r.way@nf.sympatico.ca
Paula Baggs, Executive Director
paulabaggs@anls.ca
Staff Member(s): 2
Membership: 100; *Committees:* Archives; Board of Examiners; Discipline; Liaison; Nominating; Continuing Professional Development; Executive; Act & Manual of Practice; AGM; By-laws & Regulations; Quality Assurance; Finance
Activities: Advancing & protecting the interests of members; Improving the knowledge & skill of members; Liaising with other professional organizations

Association of Newfoundland Psychologists (ANP) *See* Association of Psychology in Newfoundland & Labrador

Association of Nigerians in Nova Scotia (ANNS)

17 Sovereign Cres., Dartmouth NS
Tel: 902-482-2473
secretary@nigeriansinnovascotia.org
www.nigeriansinnovascotia.org
Previous Name: Nigerian Students Association
Overview: A small provincial organization founded in 1983
Mission: To foster Canadians' awareness of Nigeria; to encourage Nigerians to participate in economic & social activities in Canada
Membership: *Member Profile:* Nigerians who have immigrated to Canada
Activities: Liaising with similar organizations

Association of Northwest Territories Speech Language Pathologists & Audiologists (ANTSLPA)

PO Box 982, Yellowknife NT X1A 2N7
Overview: A small provincial organization
Mission: Supports and represents the professional needs of speech-language pathologists, audiologists and supportive personnel inclusively within one organization.

Association of Nova Scotia Land Surveyors (ANSLS)

325A Prince Albert Rd., Dartmouth NS B2Y 1N5
Tel: 902-469-7962; *Fax:* 902-469-7963
ansls@accesswave.ca
www.ansls.ca
Overview: A medium-sized provincial licensing organization founded in 1951 overseen by Professional Surveyors Canada
Mission: To establish & maintain standards of professional ethics among its members, student members & holders of a certificate of authorization, in order that the public interest may be served & protected; & knowledge & skills among its members, student members & holders of a certificate of authorization; to regulate the practice of professional land

surveying & govern the profession in accordance with the Act, the regulations & the by-laws; & to communicate & cooperate with other professional organizations for the advancement of the best interests of the surveying profession
Chief Officer(s):
Fred Hutchinson, Executive Director
Finances: *Funding Sources:* Membership dues
Membership: 174 regular + 17 student; *Member Profile:* Examinations & apprenticeship; licensed professionals; *Committees:* Legislative Review; Life & Honourary Membership; MCE Evaluation Group; Administrative Review; AGM; PSC; Nominating; NS Board of Examiners; Continuing Education; Public Awareness; Discipline; SRD Advisory; Strategic Planning; Governance; Unauthorized Practice; Wetlands
Activities: *Internships:* Yes; *Speaker Service:* Yes
Awards:
• J.E.R. March Prize (Award)
• J.A.H. Church Prize (Award)
• G.T. Bates Scholarship (Scholarship)

Association of Nova Scotia Museums (ANSM)
1113 Marginal Rd., Halifax NS B3H 4P7
Tel: 902-423-4677; *Fax:* 902-422-0881
Toll-Free: 800-355-6873
admin@ansm.ns.ca
ansm.ns.ca
www.facebook.com/113166268748419
Previous Name: Federation of Nova Scotian Heritage
Overview: A medium-sized provincial organization founded in 1976
Mission: The Association of Nova Scotia Museums, using a consultative regional representative model, proactively champions museums through education, outreach, networking and advocacy to achieve excellence.
Affliation(s): Heritage Canada; Canadian Museums Association; Association for State & Local History
Chief Officer(s):
Anita Price, Managing Director
director@ansm.ns.ca
Membership: 50 organizational + 25 individual + 1 student + 2 lifetime; *Fees:* $50 organizational; $25 individual; $15 student
Activities: Training & Education Program; Heritage Studies Certificate; applied learning workshops; seminars
Awards:
• President's Award (Award)
• Dr. Phyllis R. Blakeley Lifetime Achievement Award (Award)
• Outstanding Exhibit Award/Outstanding Promotion Award (Award)

Association of Nurses of Prince Edward Island *See*
Association of Registered Nurses of Prince Edward Island

Association of Occupational Health Nurses of Newfoundland & Labrador (AOHNNL)
c/o ARNNL, 55 Military Rd., St. John's NL A1C 2C5
Tel: 709-722-7676; *Fax:* 709-722-6029
www.aohnnl.net63.net
Overview: A small provincial organization founded in 1981
Mission: To promote and maintain the physical, social and psychological well-being of all individuals in working as Occupational Health Nurses.
Affliation(s): Association of Registered Nurses of Newfoundland & Labrador
Chief Officer(s):
Pamela Weels, President
pamela.wells@easternhealth.ca
Membership: *Fees:* $25

Association of Occupational Therapists of Manitoba *See*
College of Occupational Therapists of Manitoba

Association of Ontario Health Centres (AOHC) / Association des centres de santé de l'Ontario (ACSO)
#500, 907 Lawrence Ave. West, Toronto ON M6A 3B6
Tel: 416-236-2539; *Fax:* 416-236-0431
mail@aohc.org
www.aohc.org
Overview: A medium-sized provincial charitable organization founded in 1982
Mission: To promote community based primary care, health promotion, & illness prevention services, focusing on the broader determinants of health such as education, employment, poverty, isolation, & housing
Member of: Canadian Alliance of Community Health Centre Associations; Ontario Health Providers Alliance; Ontario Public Health Association
Affliation(s): Healthy Communities; Ontario Rural Council; Health Determinants Partnership; Canadian Health Network
Chief Officer(s):
Adrianna Tetley, Executive Director
adrianna@aohc.org
Sophie Bart, Manager, Membership & Organizational Health
sophie@aohc.org
Mary MacNutt, Manager, Strategic Communications & Campaigns
marym@aohc.org
Anjali Misra, Manager, Performance Management
anjali@aohc.org
Carolyn Poplak, Manager, Education & Capacity Building
carolyn@aohc.org
Finances: *Funding Sources:* Membership fees; Grants; Fundraising
100 volunteer(s)
Membership: 86 institutional; *Fees:* Schedule available; *Member Profile:* Community Health Centres (CHC); Aboriginal Health Access Centres (AHAC) & Community Health Service Organizations (CHSO); associates; *Committees:* Conference Planning; Executive; Information Systems Coordinating; Membership Secretariat; Nominations; Public Relations; Resolutions
Activities: *Awareness Events:* Community Health Day, April; *Speaker Service:* Yes; *Library:* Resource Centre
Awards:
• EPIC Award (Award)
• AOHC Award (Award)
• Health is a Community Affair Award (Award)
Meetings/Conferences: • Association of Ontario Health Centres 2015 32nd Annual Conference & General Meeting, June, 2015, Sheraton Parkway Toronto North, Richmond Hill, ON
Scope: Provincial
Description: The theme of this year's conference will be Shift the Conversation: Community Health & Wellbeing
Contact Information: Event Coordinator: John Boggan, E-mail: john.boggan@aohc.org

Association of Ontario Land Economists
#205, 555 St. Clair Ave. West, Toronto ON M4V 2Y7
Tel: 416-283-0440; *Fax:* 866-401-3665
admin@aole.org
www.aole.org
Overview: A medium-sized provincial organization founded in 1962
Mission: To continue attracting membership-quality professionals engaged in land economics pursuits; To broaden & enrich the professional development of members; To promote & maintain high ethical work standards throughout our membership; To make submissions to government for improvements in law & public administration bearing on land economics
Chief Officer(s):
Andrea Calla, President, 416-736-2610
acalla@tridel.com
John Blackburn, Vice-President & Secretary, 416-948-6969
johnblackburn@brightstarcorp.ca
Naomi Irizawa, Treasurer, 416-283-0440
naomiiriz@yahoo.ca
Membership: *Fees:* $197; *Member Profile:* Architects; Certified Property Managers; Economists; Land Use Planners; Management Consultants; Mortgage Brokers; Municipal Assessors; Ontario Land Surveyors; Engineers; Property Tax Agents; Quantity Surveyors; Real Estate Brokers; Real Property Appraisers

Association of Ontario Land Surveyors (AOLS)
1043 McNicoll Ave., Toronto ON M1W 3W6
Tel: 416-491-9020; *Fax:* 416-491-2576
Toll-Free: 800-268-0718
info@aols.org
www.aols.org
www.linkedin.com/groups/Association-Ontario-Land-Surveyors-AOLS-408320
www.facebook.com/288456831275733
twitter.com/_AOLS
www.youtube.com/user/AOLSTUBE
Overview: A medium-sized provincial licensing organization founded in 1892 overseen by Professional Surveyors Canada
Mission: To be responsible for the licensing and governance of professional land surveyors, in accordance with the Surveyors Act.
Chief Officer(s):
Blain W. Martin, Executive Director
blain@aols.org
William D. Buck, Registrar
bill@aols.org
Finances: *Funding Sources:* Membership fees
Staff Member(s): 12
Membership: 245; *Fees:* $155 associate; *Member Profile:* Individuals with a degree in Geomatics from an accredited university program, followed bu a term of articles & professional examinations
Activities: Providing continuing education; *Speaker Service:* Yes
Meetings/Conferences: • Association of Ontario Land Surveyors 2015 Annual General Meeting, February, 2015, Deerhurst Resort, Huntsville, ON
Scope: Provincial
Description: The theme is "Building Our Geospatial Future"
Contact Information: Lena Kassabian; lena@aols.org; Phone: 416-491-9020 ext. 25
• Association of Ontario Land Surveyors 2016 Annual General Meeting, February, 2016, London Convention Centre & London Hilton, London, ON
Scope: Provincial
Contact Information: Lena Kassabian; lena@aols.org; Phone: 416-491-9020 ext. 25
• Association of Ontario Land Surveyors 2017 Annual General Meeting, March, 2017, Ottawa Convention Centre & Westin Ottawa, Ottawa, ON
Scope: Provincial
Contact Information: Lena Kassabian; lena@aols.org; Phone: 416-491-9020 ext. 25
• Association of Ontario Land Surveyors 2018 Annual General Meeting, February, 2018, Sheraton On The Falls Hotel, Niagara Falls, ON
Scope: Provincial
Contact Information: Lena Kassabian; lena@aols.org; Phone: 416-491-9020 ext. 25

The Association of Ontario Locksmiths (TAOL)
#106, 2220 Midland Ave., Toronto ON M1P 3E6
Tel: 416-321-2219; *Fax:* 416-321-5115
office@taol.net
www.taol.net
Overview: A medium-sized provincial organization founded in 1973
Chief Officer(s):
Steve Kischak, President, 416-258-5490
president@taol.net
Dennis Mailloux, Treasurer, 705-389-2908
dennis@taol.net
Finances: *Funding Sources:* Membership dues
14 volunteer(s)
Membership: 400; *Fees:* $160; *Member Profile:* Locksmiths; Security-related personnel; Manufacturers; Suppliers; *Committees:* Finance; Membership; Trade Legislation; Education; Ethics; By-Laws; Publications; Public Relations; Fundraising; Convention
Activities: *Speaker Service:* Yes
Publications:
• The Ontario Locksmith Magazine
Type: Magazine; *Accepts Advertising*; *Editor:* Howard Kerr

Association of Ontario Midwives (AOM) / Association des sages-femmes de l'Ontario
#301, 365 Bloor St. E., Toronto ON M3W 3L4
Tel: 416-425-9974; *Fax:* 416-425-6905
Toll-Free: 866-418-3773
admin@aom.on.ca
www.aom.on.ca
Previous Name: Ontario Association of Midwives
Overview: A small provincial organization founded in 1985
Mission: To represent midwives & the practice of midwifery in Ontario
Chief Officer(s):
Kelly Stadelbauer, Executive Director
executivedirector@aom.on.ca
Finances: *Annual Operating Budget:* $250,000-$500,000; *Funding Sources:* Membership fees
Staff Member(s): 3
Membership: 500; *Member Profile:* Midwives, student midwives & supporting members
Activities: *Library:* AOM Resource Centre; by appointment
Meetings/Conferences: • Association of Ontario Midwives 2015 Annual General Meeting & Conference, May, 2015, Delta Toronto East, Toronto, ON
Scope: Provincial

Association of Ontario Road Supervisors (AORS)

PO Box 129, 160 King St., Thorndale ON N0M 2P0
Tel: 519-461-1271; *Fax:* 519-461-1343
admin@aors.on.ca
www.aors.on.ca
Overview: A medium-sized provincial organization founded in 1961
Mission: To promote the exchange of ideas & information concerning public works among municipalities
Chief Officer(s):
John Maheu, Executive Director
Finances: *Annual Operating Budget:* $250,000-$500,000; *Funding Sources:* Membership dues; certification; publication; trade show
Staff Member(s): 2; 30 volunteer(s)
Membership: 1,719 municipal, supplier, honourary & individual members; *Fees:* $40

Association of Ontario Snowboarders (AOS)

#203, 4 - 115 First St., Collingwood ON L9Y 4W3
Tel: 705-446-1488
aosadmin@ontariosnowboarders.ca
www.ontariosnowboarders.ca
Also Known As: Snowboard Ontario (SO)
Overview: A small provincial organization founded in 1998 overseen by Canadian Snowboard Federation
Mission: To be the governing body for the sport of competitive snowboarding in Ontario.
Member of: Canadian Snowboard Federation
Chief Officer(s):
Mary Frances Carter, President
maryfrances@ontariosnowboarders.ca
Janet Richter, Manager, Administration

Association of Parent Support Groups in Ontario Inc. (APSGO)

PO Box 27581, Stn. Yorkdale, Toronto ON M6A 3B8
Tel: 416-223-7444
Toll-Free: 800-488-5666
mail@apsgo.ca
www.apsgo.ca
Overview: A small provincial charitable organization founded in 1985
Mission: To enable parents to develop strategies to deal with their children's disruptive behaviour
Finances: *Funding Sources:* Donations; Fundraising
Membership: *Member Profile:* Parents of disruptive youth
Activities: Supporting parents to deal with their disruptive youth; Offering weekly meetings; Providing seminars & workshops; Disseminating resources to parents & professionals; Operating an information line; *Speaker Service:* Yes
Publications:
• Parent to Parent
Type: Newsletter; *Editor:* Sue Kranz

Association of Parliamentary Libraries in Canada (APLIC) / Association des bibliothèques parlementaires au Canada (ABPAC)

c/o Vicki Whitmell, Ontario Legislative Library, Queen's Park, Toronto ON M7A 1A9
Tel: 416-325-3939; *Fax:* 416-325-3925
www.aplic-abpac.ca
Overview: A small national organization founded in 1975
Mission: To improve parliamentary library service in Canada; To encourage cooperation with related officials & organizations
Chief Officer(s):
Vicki Whitmell, President
vicki_whitmell@ontla.ola.org
Membership: 13; *Member Profile:* Parliamentary / legislature libraries in Canada; Chief executive officers of the library of each jurisdiction are the voting members in the association
Activities: Identifying research areas; Facilitating communication among members; Highlighting best practices to support members' work
Publications:
• APLIC Bulletin
Type: Newsletter
Profile: Information available only for members of The Association of Parliamentary Libraries in Canada
• APLIC Directory
Type: Directory
Profile: Directory information for librarians at parliamentary / legislature libraries

Association of Part-Time Professors of the University of Ottawa *Voir* Association des professeur(e)s à temps partiel de l'Université d'Ottawa

Association of Pastoral Psychotherapists of Canada *Voir* Association des psychothérapeutes pastoraux du Canada

Association of Physically Disabled Joliette - L'Assomption; Association of People with Physical Disabilities Joliette *See* Association des personnes handicapées physiques et sensorielles du secteur Joliette

Association of Polish Engineers in Canada

206 Beverly St., Toronto ON M5T 1Z3
Tel: 416-977-7723; *Fax:* 416-977-3996
webmaster@polisheng.ca
www.polisheng.ca
www.facebook.com/polisheng
Overview: A medium-sized national organization founded in 1941
Mission: To represent the Polish Canadian engineering community; to provide assistance & contribute to social life
Member of: Canadian Polish Congress
Chief Officer(s):
Jerome Teresinski, President, 416-497-9810
hieronim@interlog.com
Finances: *Funding Sources:* Membership fees
Membership: *Member Profile:* Engineers
Activities: Monthly meetings; lectures; annual ball; help with immigration; advice regarding Canadian life & its engineering aspects; submissions to federal & provincial governments

Edmonton Branch
1332 - 116 St. NW, Edmonton AB T6J 7B3
Tel: 780-450-9367
ajedrych@shaw.ca
edmonton.polisheng.ca
Chief Officer(s):
Andrzej Jedrych, Contact

Hamilton Branch
263 Wellington St., Brantford ON N3S 3Z8
Tel: 905-578-6584
andrzej.felinczak@sympatico.ca
www.hamilton.polisheng.ca
Chief Officer(s):
Ryszard Murynowicz, Contact

Kitchener Branch
#2, 285 Sandowne Dr., Kitchener ON N2K 2C1
Tel: 519-747-1402
bulik@sympatico.ca
kitchener.polisheng.ca
Chief Officer(s):
Jerzy Bulik, Contact

London Branch
80 Ann St., London ON N6A 1G9
e-mail: sip.london.ca@gmail.com
london.polisheng.ca
Chief Officer(s):
Bartek Froncisz, President

Mississauga Branch
c/o Cyclone MFG. Inc., 7300 Rapistan Crt., Mississauga ON L5N 5S1
Tel: 905-578-6584
slawomir.basiukiewicz@polisheng.ca
mississauga.polisheng.ca
Chief Officer(s):
Slawomir Basiukiewicz, Contact

Montréal Branch
63 Prince Arthur East, Montréal QC H2X 1B4
Tel: 514-996-9723
bella97@videotron.ca
montreal.polisheng.ca
Chief Officer(s):
Lech Bilinski, Contact
Lech Bilinski, President

Ottawa Branch
1945 South Lavant Rd., Poland ON K0G 1K0
Tel: 613-259-5015
sip@kpk-ottawa.org
www.kpk-ottawa.org/sip
Chief Officer(s):
Bogdan Gajewski, Contact

Toronto Branch
206 Beverley St., Toronto ON M5T 1Z3
Tel: 416-486-7346
toronto.polisheng.ca
Chief Officer(s):
Krystyna Sroczynska, Contact

Association of Power Producers of Ontario (APPrO)

PO Box 1084, Stn. F, #1602, 25 Adelaide St. East, Toronto ON M5C 3A1
Tel: 416-322-6549; *Fax:* 416-481-5785
Other Communication: marketing@appro.org
appro@appro.org
www.appro.org
Previous Name: Independent Power Producers Society of Ontario (IPPSO)
Overview: A medium-sized provincial organization founded in 1986
Mission: To act as the voice of electricity generators in Ontario; To support a reliable & secure electricity supply in Ontario
Chief Officer(s):
Jake Brooks, Executive Director
jake.brooks@appro.org
David Butters, President
david.butters@appro.org
Carole Kielly, Manager, Sales & Marketing, 416-322-6549 Ext. 222
carole.kielly@appro.org
Soraya Rivera, Manager, Registration & Data
soraya.rivera@appro.org
Karla Martinez, Manager, Office
karla.martinez@appro.org
Membership: 100+; *Member Profile:* Companies involved in the generation of electricity in Ontario, including suppliers of services & consulting services
Activities: Advocating for generators; Offering resources to assist business, government, utilities, & researchers; Organizing educational programs
Meetings/Conferences: • Association of Power Producers of Ontario 2015: 27th Annual Canadian Power Conference & Power Networking Centre, November, 2015, ON
Scope: Provincial
Description: An annual event held in the autumn, featuring speakers, educational sessions, exhibits, & a student program
Contact Information: E-mail: appro@appro.org
• Association of Power Producers of Ontario 2016: 28th Annual Canadian Power Conference & Power Networking Centre, 2016, ON
Scope: Provincial
Description: An annual event held in the autumn, featuring speakers, educational sessions, exhibits, & a student program
Contact Information: E-mail: appro@appro.org
Publications:
• APPrO [Association of Power Producers of Ontario] Conference Proceedings
Type: Yearbook; *Frequency:* Annually; *Price:* $40
• Canadian Power Directory
Type: Directory
Profile: Contact information for organizations involved in all aspects of electricity generation in Canada, such as developers, equipment & service suppliers, utilities, & resource groups
• IPPSO FACTO: Magazine of the Association of Power Producers of Ontario
Type: Magazine; *Frequency:* Bimonthly; *Accepts Advertising*; *Price:* Free with Association of Power Producers of Ontario membership
Profile: Ontario, national, international, & regulatory news

Association of Prince Edward Island Land Surveyors (APEILS)

PO Box 20100, Charlottetown PE C1A 9E3
Tel: 902-394-3121
info@apeils.ca
www.apeils.ca
Overview: A small provincial licensing organization overseen by Professional Surveyors Canada
Mission: To regulate the practice of land surveying in PEI
Chief Officer(s):
Serge Bernard, Secretary-Treasurer
bernardsurvey@gmail.com
John Mantha, President
Membership: 27

The Association of Professional Accounting & Tax Consultants Inc. (APATC)

#310, 4025 Dorchester Rd., Niagara Falls ON L2E 7K8
Tel: 905-354-1856; *Fax:* 905-374-0600
Toll-Free: 888-621-1005
www.apatcinc.com
www.linkedin.com/groups?gid=2112088
Overview: A small national organization founded in 1981
Mission: To represent professionals involved in accounting, bookkeeping & tax

Membership: *Fees:* $386.25 affiliated; $283.25 associate; $35 application fee
Activities: Continuing education; seminars; Group Errors & Omissions Insurance Plan for members

Association of Professional Biology (APB)

#300, 1095 McKenzie Ave., Victoria BC V8P 2L5
Tel: 250-483-4283; *Fax:* 250-483-3439
www.apbbc.bc.ca
Overview: A medium-sized provincial organization founded in 1980
Mission: To promote & assist professional practitioners of applied biology
Chief Officer(s):
Megan Hanacek, Managing Director & Registrar
managingdirector@apbbc.bc.ca; registrar@apbbc.bc.ca
Gerry Leering, President
Linda Stordeur, Registrar
registrar@apbbc.bc.ca
Linda Michaluk, Executive Director
executivedirector@apbbc.bc.ca
Membership: *Committees:* Constitution & By-law; Legislation & Policy; Nominations; Communications & Networking; Mentorship; Awards & Scholarships; Conference; AGM Resolutions; Practice Advisory
Activities: Providing continuing education
Awards:
• Ian McTaggart-Cowan Award for Excellence in Biology (Award)
To recognize significant contribution to the biological sciences in British Columbia *Contact:* Debbi Stanyer, R.P.Bio., Chair, Awards, #300, 1095 McKenzie Ave., Victoria, BC, V8P 2L5
• W. Young Award for Integrated Resource Management (Award)
Sponsored jointly with the Association of BC Forest Professionals *Contact:* Debbi Stanyer, R.P.Bio., Chair, Awards, #300, 1095 McKenzie Ave., Victoria, BC, V8P 2L5
• Biology Professional of the Year Award (Award)
To honour contributions to biological science & the application of biology in a local or regional area *Contact:* Debbi Stanyer, R.P.Bio., Chair, Awards, #300, 1095 McKenzie Ave., Victoria, BC, V8P 2L5
• Meritorious Service Awards (Award)
To recognize members of the Association of Professional Biology for outstanding contributions to the association *Contact:* Debbi Stanyer, R.P.Bio., Chair, Awards, #300, 1095 McKenzie Ave., Victoria, BC, V8P 2L5
• Fellowship in Association of Professional Biology (Award)
A designation reserved for members who bring distinction to the profession through inspiration & mentorship to others *Contact:* Association of Professional Biology Office, Phone: 250-483-4283, Fax: 250-483-3439, E-mail: apbbc@apbbc.bc.ca
Meetings/Conferences: • Association of Professional Biology 2015 10th Annual Professional Biology Conference, 2015
Scope: Provincial
Description: Part of the event is the annual general meeting, featuring reports from the association executive & committee chairs, the auditor's report & financial statement, resolutions, & new business
Contact Information: Managing Director & Registrar: Megan Hanacek, E-mail: managingdirector@apbbc.bc.ca
Publications:
• Advisory Practice Bulletins [publications of the Association of Professional Biology]
Profile: Topics include principles of stewardship, professional behaviour, & the code of ethics interpretive notes
• BioNews [a publication of the Association of Professional Biology]
Type: Newsletter; *Frequency:* Quarterly; *Editor:* Megan Hanacek; Barb Faggetter
Profile: Featuring a summary of the meetings of the association's board of directors & other information of interest to members

Association of Professional Community Planners of Saskatchewan *See* Saskatchewan Professional Planners Institute

Association of Professional Computer Consultants - Canada (APCC)

#700, 2200 Yonge St., Toronto ON M4S 2C6
Tel: 416-545-5275
Toll-Free: 800-487-2722
information@apcconline.com
www.apcconline.com
www.linkedin.com/groups?home=&gid=3768080
www.facebook.com/APCCOnline
twitter.com/APCC_Canada
Overview: A medium-sized provincial organization founded in 1997
Mission: To promote the interests of independent computer consultants; to provide cost-saving services to members; to provide members with a forum for interaction & exchange
Chief Officer(s):
Frank McCrea, President
Finances: *Funding Sources:* Membership fees
Membership: *Fees:* $22.60 general; $90.40 gold; *Member Profile:* Independent computer consultant

Association of Professional Economists of British Columbia (APEBC)

#102, 211 Columbia St., Vancouver BC V6A 2R5
Tel: 604-689-1455; *Fax:* 604-681-4545
info@apebc.ca
www.apebc.ca
Overview: A small provincial organization founded in 1967 overseen by Canadian Association for Business Economics
Mission: To encourage a high standard of professional competence; To foster continuing education
Member of: Canadian Association for Business Economics
Chief Officer(s):
Bryan Yu, President
Membership: *Fees:* $125 Full & affiliate; $60 Associate; $35 Student
Activities: Speaker program

Association of Professional Engineers & Geoscientists of British Columbia (APEGBC)

#200, 4010 Regent St., Burnaby BC V5C 6N2
Tel: 604-430-8035; *Fax:* 604-430-8085
Toll-Free: 888-430-8035
apeginfo@apeg.bc.ca
www.apeg.bc.ca
twitter.com/APEGBC
Overview: A large provincial licensing organization founded in 1920 overseen by Engineers Canada
Mission: To protect the public interest in matters related to geoscience & engineering; To regulate & govern the professions of professional engineers & geoscientists in British Columbia, according to the Engineers & Geoscientists Act; To strive for professional excellence, by establishing academic, experience, & professional practice standards
Member of: Engineers Canada
Chief Officer(s):
Michael Isaacson, P.Eng., PhD, President
president@apeg.bc.ca
Ann English, P.Eng., CEO & Registrar, 604-412-4850 Ext. 4850
aenglish@apeg.bc.ca
Tony Chong, P.Eng., Chief Regulatory Officer & Deputy Registrar, 604-412-6058 Ext. 6058
tchong@apeg.bc.ca
Janet Sinclair, COO, 604-412-4874 Ext. 4874
jsinclair@apeg.bc.ca
Jennifer Cho, CGA, Director, Finance & Administration, 604-412-4870 Ext. 4870
jcho@apeg.bc.ca
Peter Mitchell, P.Eng., Director, Professional Practice, Standards, & Development, 604-412-4853 Ext. 4853
pmitchell@apeg.bc.ca
Gillian Pichler, P.Eng., Director, Registration, 604-412-4857 Ext. 4857
gpichler@apeg.bc.ca
Geoff Thiele, LLB, Director, Legislation, Ethics & Compliance, 604-412-4852 Ext. 4852
gthiele@apeg.bc.ca
Megan Archibald, Associate Director, Communications & Stakeholder Engagement, 604-412-4883 Ext. 4883
marchibald@apeg.bc.ca
Don Gamble, Associate Director, Information Systems, 604-412-4867 Ext. 4867
dgamble@apeg.bc.ca.ca
Deesh Olychick, Associate Director, Member Services, 604-412-4882 Ext. 4882
dolychick@apeg.bc.ca
Membership: *Committees:* Audit; Branches; Discipline; Executive; Geoscience; Registration; Structural Qualifications Bd.; Applications; Bd. of Examiners; Registration Task Force; Professional Renewal Task Force; ABCPF/APEGBC Joint Practice Bd.; Building Codes; Building Enclosure; Consulting Practice; Environment; Investigation; Practice Review; Sustainability; Continuing Professional Dev.; Editorial Bd.; Mentoring; Standing Awards; Div. for Advancement of Woman in Engineering & Geoscience; Div. of Engineers & Geoscientists in the Resource Sector; Municipal Engineers Div.; and others...
Activities: Maintaining practice standards; Upholding the code of ethics; Publishing brochures, position papers, & other association documents; Promoting the professions; Protecting members' interests; Establishing the Engineers Benevolent Fund to assist members; Setting up Foundation Trustees to support education through scholarships & bursaries & to promote professional development opportunities
Awards:
• President's Awards (Award)
• Environmental Awards (Award)
• Sustainability Awards (Award)
• Mentor of the Year Award (Award)
• Forest Engineering Award of Excellence (Award)
Meetings/Conferences: • Association of Professional Engineers & Geoscientists of British Columbia 2015 Conference & Annual General Meeting, 2015, BC
Scope: Provincial
Attendance: 700+
Description: A chance to learn & network with colleagues & suppliers during business & technical sessions, a trade exhibition, & social events
Contact Information: Sponsorship Information: Maria-Carmen Kelly, mckelly@apeg.bc.ca; Exhibtor Booth Information: Tim Verigin, tverigin@apeg.bc.ca
Publications:
• APEGBC [Association of Professional Engineers & Geoscientists of British Columbia] Membership Directory
Type: Directory
Profile: Rosters of professional engineers & professional geoscientists with contact information & scope of practice
• APEGBC [Association of Professional Engineers & Geoscientists of British Columbia] Professional Practice Guidelines
Type: Guides
Profile: Examples of guidelines are as follows: APEGBC/CEBC Budget Guidelines for Engineering Services; Guidelinesfor Terrain Stability Assessments in the Forest Sector; & Guidelines for Legislated Landslide Assessments for Proposed Residential Development in British Columbia
• Association of Professional Engineers & Geoscientists of British Columbia Compensation Survey
Profile: Information on APEGBC members' compensation & benefits
• Association of Professional Engineers & Geoscientists of British Columbia Annual Report
Type: Yearbook; *Frequency:* Annually
Profile: A yearly review, featuring reports from the association's executive director & president, as well as the auditor
• Association of Professional Engineers & Geoscientists of British Columbia Technical Bulletins
Type: Bulletins
Profile: Examples of technical bulletins are as follows: Assessment of Seismic Slope Stability; Engineering Modifications to FireTested & Listed Assemblies; & Addressing Smoke & CO Control in Elevator Machine Rooms
• Bylaws of the Association [a publication of the Association of Professional Engineers & Geoscientists of British Columbia]
Type: Booklet
Profile: Information about items such as conduct of meetings, election of council, finances, & membership
• Connections E-news [a publication of the Association of Professional Engineers & Geoscientists of British Columbia]
Type: Newsletter; *Frequency:* Monthly
Profile: Currents happenings in the association & in the professions of engineers & geoscientists in BritishColumbia
• Innovation [a publication of the Association of Professional Engineers & Geoscientists of British Columbia]
Type: Magazine; *Frequency:* Bimonthly; *Accepts Advertising*; *Editor:* Melinda Lau
Profile: Information circulated to more than 26,000 British Columbia registered professionalengineers & geoscientists, industry & government reporesentatives, educational institutions, as well as the general public

Burnaby/New West Branch
e-mail: bn@apeg.bc.ca
apeg.bc.ca/services/branches/bn.html
Chief Officer(s):
Mike Samilski, P.Eng, Chair

Central Interior Branch
e-mail: ci@apeg.bc.ca
apeg.bc.ca/services/branches/ci.html
Chief Officer(s):

Brendon Masson, P.Eng, Chair, 250-561-2229
bmasson@mcelhanney.com

East Kootenay Branch
e-mail: ek@apeg.bc.ca
apeg.bc.ca/services/branches/ek.html
Chief Officer(s):
Sean Abram, Chair, 250-489-8188
sean@abramcs.com

Fraser Valley Branch
e-mail: fv@apeg.bc.ca
apeg.bc.ca/services/branches/fv.html
Chief Officer(s):
Bernadette Currie, P.Eng, Chair
daweg.past.chair.fv.exec@gmail.com

Northern Branch
e-mail: no@apeg.bc.ca
apeg.bc.ca/services/branches/no.html
Chief Officer(s):
Anatasia Ledwon, P.Geo., Chair

Okanagan Branch
e-mail: ok@apeg.bc.ca
apeg.bc.ca/services/branches/ok.html

Peace River Branch
e-mail: pr@apeg.bc.ca
apeg.bc.ca/services/branches/pr.html
Chief Officer(s):
Adel Morhart, EIT, Chair

Richmond/Delta Branch
e-mail: rd@apeg.bc.ca
apeg.bc.ca/services/branches/rd.html
Chief Officer(s):
Ravee Ramakrishnan, MBA, P.Eng, Chair

Sea-to-Sky Branch
e-mail: ss@apeg.bc.ca
apeg.bc.ca/services/branches/seatosky/index.html
Chief Officer(s):
Piotr Mazur, P.Eng, Chair

South Central Branch
e-mail: sc@apeg.bc.ca
apeg.bc.ca/services/branches/sc.html
Chief Officer(s):
Eric Sears, EIT, Chair
sc@apeg.bc.ca

Tri-City Branch
e-mail: tc@apeg.bc.ca
apeg.bc.ca/services/branches/tc/index.html
Chief Officer(s):
Stella Chiu, P.Eng, Chair

Vancouver Branch
e-mail: van@apeg.bc.ca
apeg.bc.ca/services/branches/van/index.html
Chief Officer(s):
Ben Skillings, P.Eng., Chair

Vancouver Island Branch
e-mail: vi@apeg.bc.ca
apeg.bc.ca/services/branches/vi.html
Chief Officer(s):
Lee Rowley, P.Eng, Chair, 250-751-8558
lrowley@HeroldEngineering.com

Victoria Branch
e-mail: vic@apeg.bc.ca
apeg.bc.ca/services/branches/vic.html
Chief Officer(s):
Richard Summers, P.Eng, Chair
Richard.Summers@forces.gc.ca

West Kootenay Branch
e-mail: wk@apeg.bc.ca
apeg.bc.ca/services/branches/wk.html
Chief Officer(s):
Mark Sirges, P.Eng, Chair & Treasurer, 250-365-4230
msirges@telus.net

Association of Professional Engineers & Geoscientists of British Columbia Foundation

#200, 4010 Regent St., Burnaby BC V5C 6N2
Tel: 604-430-8035; *Fax:* 604-430-8085
Toll-Free: 888-430-8035
www.apeg.bc.ca/services/foundation.html
Also Known As: APEGBC Foundation
Overview: A medium-sized provincial charitable organization founded in 1994
Mission: To operate at arms-length from the APEGBC & to promote education in engineering & geoscience through the granting of bursaries & scholarships

Association of Professional Engineers & Geoscientists of Manitoba (APEGM)

870 Pembina Hwy., Winnipeg MB R3M 2M7
Tel: 204-474-2736; *Fax:* 204-474-5960
Toll-Free: 866-227-9600
Other Communication: volunteer@apegm.mb.ca; events@apegm.mb.ca
apegm@apegm.mb.ca
www.apegm.mb.ca
Overview: A large provincial organization founded in 1920 overseen by Engineers Canada
Mission: To serve & protect the public interest by governing & advancing the practice of engineering in accordance with the Engineering Profession Act of Manitoba
Member of: Engineers Canada
Chief Officer(s):
Grant Koropatnick, P.Eng., Executive Director & Registrar, 204-474-2736 Ext. 234
GKoropatnick@apegm.mb.ca
Sharon E. Sankar, Director, Admissions, 204-474-2736 Ext. 229
SSankar@apegm.mb.ca
Michael Gregoire, P.Eng., Officer, Professional Standards, 204-474-2736 Ext. 225
MGregoire@apegm.mb.ca
William C. Boyce, Manager, Operations & Finance, 204-474-2736 Ext. 231
WBoyce@apegm.mb.ca
Lorraine Dupas, Coordinator, Admissions, 204-474-2736 Ext. 228
LDupas@apegm.mb.ca
Angela Moore, Coordinator, Events & Communications, 204-474-2736 Ext. 233
AMoore@apegm.mb.ca
Diana Vander Aa, Coordinator, Volunteers, 204-474-2736 Ext. 233
Volunteer@apegm.mb.ca
Finances: *Annual Operating Budget:* $500,000-$1.5 Million
Membership: 3,500; *Fees:* $218

Association of Professional Engineers & Geoscientists of New Brunswick (APEGNB) / Association des ingénieurs et géoscientifiques du Nouveau-Brunswick (AINB)

183 Hanwell Rd., Fredericton NB E3B 2R2
Tel: 506-458-8083; *Fax:* 506-451-9629
Toll-Free: 888-458-8083
info@apegnb.com
www.apegnb.com
twitter.com/APEGNB
Also Known As: Engineers & Geoscientists New Brunswick
Overview: A large provincial licensing organization founded in 1920 overseen by Engineers Canada
Mission: To establish, maintain & develop standards of knowledge & skill, qualification & practice, & professional ethics; To promote public awareness of the role of the association
Member of: Engineers Canada
Chief Officer(s):
Mark Bellefleur, P.Eng., President
Christine Plourde, P.Eng., Vice-President
Andrew McLeod, FEC (Hon.), CEO
mcleod@apegnb.com
Finances: *Funding Sources:* Membership fees
Membership: 5,500; *Fees:* Schedule available; *Committees:* Council; Admissions; Board of Examiners; Discipline; Internship; Legislation; Nominating; Professional Conduct; Annual Meeting; Awards; Association Affairs; Continuing Competency Assurance; Lay Councillor Appointment; Scrutineers
Awards:
- C.C. Kirby Award (Award)
- L.W. Bailey Award (Award)
- Individual Award for Technical Excellence (Award)
- Corporate Award of Excellence (Award)
- Citizenship Award (Award)
- Honorary Membership (Award)
- Service to the Profession Award (Award)
- Support of Women in Engineering Award (Award)
- Outstanding Educator Award (Award)
- Outstanding Student Award (Award)
- Young Professional Achievement Award (Award)
- Volunteer Award (Award)

Meetings/Conferences: • 95th Association of Professional Engineers & Geoscientists of New Brunswick Annual Meeting, 2015, NB
Scope: Provincial

Publications:
- APEGNB [Association of Professional Engineers & Geoscientists of New Brunswick] Annual Meeting Magazine
Type: Magazine; *Frequency:* Annual; *Editor:* Melissa Mertz
- Association of Professional Engineers & Geoscientists of New Brunswick Annual Report
Type: Yearbook; *Frequency:* Annual
- Engenuity [a publication of the Association of Professional Engineers & Geoscientists of New Brunswick]
Type: Newsletter; *Frequency:* 3 pa; *Editor:* Melissa Mertz
- Member Salary Survey [Association of Professional Engineers & Geoscientists of New Brunswick]
Type: Report; *Frequency:* Annual

Fredericton Branch
engineersfredericton.ca
Chief Officer(s):
Bill Lamey, P.Eng, Chair

Moncton Branch
Chief Officer(s):
Tina Levesque, MIT, Chair
tina.levesque@canadapost.ca
Julie Thériault, P.Eng., Contact, Communications & Website
julie.theriault@roche.ca

Northeastern Branch
c/o Kevin Gallant, 1907 Water St., Miramichi NB E1N 1B2
Tel: 506-773-7873; *Fax:* 506-778-6001
Chief Officer(s):
Claude Mallet, P.Eng., Chair, 506-546-4484
claude.mallet@grouperoy.com
Kevin Gallant, P.Eng., Contact, Communications, 506-773-7873
kevin.gallant@gnb.ca

Northwestern Branch
Chief Officer(s):
Karine Savoie, Chair
karine.savoie@gnb.ca

Saint John Branch
Chief Officer(s):
Lisa Frazee, P.Eng, Chair
frazee.lisa@oceansteel.com
Jeremy Stuart, P.Eng, Communications Officer
jstuart@nbpower.com

Association of Professional Engineers & Geoscientists of Newfoundland *See* Professional Engineers & Geoscientists Newfoundland & Labrador

Association of Professional Engineers & Geoscientists of Saskatchewan (APEGS)

#104, 2255 - 13 Ave., Regina SK S4P 0V6
Tel: 306-525-9547; *Fax:* 306-525-0851
Toll-Free: 800-500-9547
apegs@apegs.sk.ca
www.apegs.sk.ca
Overview: A large provincial licensing organization founded in 1930 overseen by Engineers Canada
Mission: To achieve a safe & prosperous future through engineering & geoscience
Member of: Engineers Canada
Chief Officer(s):
Leon C. Botham, P.Eng., President
Dennis Paddock, P.Eng., FEC, Executive Director & Registrar
dkpaddock@apegs.sk.ca
Patti Kindred, P.Eng., FEC, Director, Education & Compliance
pkindred@apegs.sk.ca
Barb Miller, Director, Finance & Operations
barbmiller@apegs.sk.ca
Kate MacLachlan, Ph.D., P.Geo., Director, Academic Review
katem@apegs.sk.ca
Tina Maki, P.Eng., FEC, Director, Registration
tmaki@apegs.sk.ca
Bob McDonald, P.Eng., FEC, LL, Director, Membership & Legal Services
rhmcdonald@apegs.sk.ca
Chris Wimmer, P.Eng., Director, Professional Standards
cwimmer@apegs.sk.ca
Finances: *Funding Sources:* Membership dues
125 volunteer(s)
Membership: 3,070; *Fees:* Schedule available; *Committees:* Education Board (Professional Development, Student Development, K-12, Environment & Sustainability); Governance Board (Academic Review, Experience Review, Professional Practice Exam, Licensee Admissions, Registrar's Advisory); Image & Identity Board (Awards, Communications & Public

Relations, Connection & Involvement, Professional Edge, Equality & Divserity); Discipline; Investigation; Executive
Activities: *Internships:* Yes; *Speaker Service:* Yes
Awards:
• Outstanding Achievement Award (Award)
• Promising Member Award (Award)
• McCannel Award (Award)
• Brian Eckel Distinguished Service Award (Award)
• Environmental Excellence Award (Award)
• Exceptional Engineering/Geoscience Project Award (Award)
Publications:
• APEGS [Association of Professional Engineers & Geoscientists of Saskatchewan] Salary Survey
Type: Report
• Association of Professional Engineers & Geoscientists of Saskatchewan Annual Report
Type: Yearbook; *Frequency:* Annual
• The Professional Edge [a publication of the Association of Professional Engineers & Geoscientists of Saskatchewan]
Type: Magazine; *Accepts Advertising*; *Editor:* Lyle Hewitt

Association of Professional Engineers of Ontario ***See*** Professional Engineers Ontario

Association of Professional Engineers of Prince Edward Island (APEPEI)
135 Water St., Charlottetown PE C1A 1A8
Tel: 902-566-1268; *Fax:* 902-566-5551
www.engineerspei.com
twitter.com/EngineersPEI
Also Known As: Engineers PEI
Overview: A small provincial licensing charitable organization founded in 1955 overseen by Engineers Canada
Mission: To regulate the practice of professional engineering in the province, with authority over members, licensees, engineers-in-training, & holders of certificates of authorization.
Member of: Engineers Canada
Chief Officer(s):
Richard MacEwan, President
Jim Landrigan, Executive Director/Registrar
Finances: *Funding Sources:* Membership dues
Staff Member(s): 2
Membership: *Fees:* $300; *Member Profile:* Open to those with B.Sc. (Engineering) from an accredited institution & four years acceptable engineering experience; *Committees:* Act Enforcement; Advocacy; Annual Meeting; Awards; Construction & Consulting; Discipline; Environment; Finance; Experience Reivew Board & EIT; Engineering Qualifications; Nominating; Student Outreach; Professional Development & Continuing Education; Social; Women in Engineering
Activities: Bridge Building Contest for students, grades 5-12; *Awareness Events:* National Engineering Month, March; *Internships:* Yes
Awards:
• Friend of the Profession Award (Award)
• Honorary Life Members (Award)
• Engineering Award for Excellence (Award)
• Young Engineer Achievement Award (Award)
• Community Service Award (Award)
• The Ralph L. Woodside Memorial Award for Service to the Profession (Award)

Association of Professional Engineers of the Government of Québec (Ind.) ***Voir*** Association professionnelle des ingénieurs du gouvernement du Québec (ind.)

Association of Professional Engineers of Yukon (APEY)
312B Hanson St., Whitehorse YT Y1A 1Y6
Tel: 867-667-6727; *Fax:* 867-668-2142
staff@apey.yk.ca
www.apey.yk.ca
Overview: A medium-sized provincial licensing organization founded in 1955 overseen by Engineers Canada
Mission: To establish, maintain & develop standards of knowledge & skill, standards of qualification & practice & standards of professional ethics; to promote public awareness of the role of the association
Member of: Engineers Canada
Finances: *Funding Sources:* Membership fees
Membership: *Fees:* $252; *Member Profile:* Persons with a degree in engineering from an accredited university & with 4 years of experience
Activities: Annual Bridge Building Competition; Professional development; National Secondary Professional Liability Insurance Program; *Awareness Events:* Engineering Week
Awards:
• APEY Educational Award (Scholarship)
Publications:
• Association of Professional Engineers of Yukon Newsletter
Type: Newsletter; *Frequency:* 3 pa

Association of Professional Executives of the Public Service of Canada (APEX) / L'Association professionnelle des cadres de la fonction publique du Canada
#508, 75 Albert St., Ottawa ON K1P 5E7
Tel: 613-995-6252; *Fax:* 613-943-8919
info@apex.gc.ca
www.apex.gc.ca
Overview: A medium-sized national organization founded in 1984
Mission: The association focuses on issues such as compensation, the work environment and public service management reform.
Chief Officer(s):
Nadir Patel, Chair
Nadir.Patel@international.gc.ca
Lisanne Lacroix, Chief Executive Officer, 613-995-6252
lisannel@apex.gc.ca
Finances: *Annual Operating Budget:* $250,000-$500,000
Staff Member(s): 4; 120 volunteer(s)
Membership: 1,000+; *Fees:* $95

Association of Professional Geoscientists of Nova Scotia (APGNS)
PO Box 232, 53 Queen St., Dartmouth NS B2Y 1C2
Tel: 902-420-9928; *Fax:* 902-463-1419
info@geoscientistsns.ca
www.apgns.ns.ca
Overview: A small provincial organization
Mission: To ensure high standards of practice within the geoscience community; To promote & advance the profession; To work with associated organizations across Canada to facilitate the registration of APGNS members in other provinces
Chief Officer(s):
David C. Carter, Executive Director & Registrar
exec.director@geoscientistsns.ca
Membership: *Fees:* $200 Member-in-Training; $400 License to Practice; $450 Member

Association of Professional Geoscientists of Ontario (APGO)
#1100, 25 Adelaide St. East, Toronto ON M5C 3A1
Tel: 416-203-2746; *Fax:* 416-203-6181
Toll-Free: 877-557-2746
info@apgo.net
www.apgo.net
www.linkedin.com/groups?gid=4495029&trk=myg_ugrp_ovr
www.facebook.com/489636501070336
Overview: A small provincial organization founded in 2000
Mission: To govern the practice of professional geoscience in Ontario, in accordance with The Professional Geoscientists Act, 2000, in order to protect the public & investors; To develop standards of knowledge & skills for association members
Affiliation(s): Canadian Council of Professional Geoscientists; Canadian Geoscience Standards Board; National Professional Practice & Ethics Exam Advisory Committee; CCPG Licensure Compliance Committee
Chief Officer(s):
Gord White, CEO
gwhite@apgo.net
Ian Macdonald, President
imac@wesa.ca
Andrew Cheatle, Vice-President
amcheatle@mac.com
Finances: *Funding Sources:* Sponsorships
Membership: 1,389 practising members + 12 temporary members + 10 limited members + 12 non-practising members + 60 geoscientists in training + 24 student members; *Committees:* Discipline; Complaints; Registration; Executive; Finance; Nomination; Non-Member Appointment; Insurance Advisory; Governance; Professional Practice; Enforcement & Compliance; Communications & Public Awareness
Activities: Reporting to Ontario's Minister of Northern Development & Mines; Accepting registration for the licensure to practice professional geoscience in Ontario; Disciplining members for professional misconduct; Organizing continuing professional development programs
Publications:
• Association of Professional Geoscientists of Ontario Annual Report
Type: Yearbook; *Frequency:* Annually
• Field Notes: Association of Professional Geoscientists of Ontario Newsletter
Type: Newsletter; *Frequency:* Bimonthly; *Editor:* Wendy Diaz, M.Sc., P.Geo.
Profile: Association reports, meetings, awards, & news for all APGO members

Association of Professional Librarians of New Brunswick ***See*** Association des bibliothécaires professionnel(le)s du Nouveau-Brunswick

Association of Professional Recruiters of Canada
#2210, 1081 Ambleside Dr., Ottawa ON K2B 8C8
Tel: 613-721-5957; *Fax:* 613-721-5850
Toll-Free: 888-421-0000
www.workplace.ca/resources/aprc_assoc.html
www.facebook.com/InstituteofProfessionalManagement
Previous Name: Canadian Recruiters Guild
Overview: A medium-sized national licensing organization founded in 1984
Mission: To establish standards & practices for the recruitment & selection of human resources in Canada & to provide members with the tools to practice at the highest professional levels
Member of: Institute of Professional Management
30 volunteer(s)
Membership: 800; *Fees:* $175; *Member Profile:* Senior human resources & management professionals
Activities: Chapter meetings; regional & national conferences; *Speaker Service:* Yes; *Library:* Online Workplace Library

Association of Professional Researchers for Advancement - Canada
c/o Valerie Moore, Manager, Research & Prospect Mgmt, BC Children's H, 938 West, 28th Ave, Vancouver BC V5Z 4H4
Tel: 604-875-2444; *Fax:* 604-875-2596
www.apracanada.ca
Also Known As: APRA - Canada
Overview: A medium-sized national organization
Chief Officer(s):
Valery Moore, President
vmoore@cw.bc.ca
Marcia Steeves, Vice-President & Secretary
Mark Neilans, Treasurer
Membership: *Fees:* $40 + $2 GST; *Member Profile:* Canadian researchers; Front-line fundraisers; Individuals interested in advancement research
Activities: Providing networking opportunities; Offering professional development days; Mentoring activities
Publications:
• APRA Canada Newsletter
Type: Newsletter; *Frequency:* Quarterly; *Price:* Free with APRA-Canada membership
• Association of Professional Researchers for Advancement - Canada Membership Directory
Type: Directory; *Price:* Free with APRA-Canada membership

Association of Professionals & Supervisors of the Canadian Broadcasting Corporation ***Voir*** Association des professionnels et superviseurs de Radio-Canada

Association of Professors of Bishop's University (APBU) / Association des professeurs de l'Université Bishop
McGreer Hall, Bishop's University, #304, 2600 College St., Sherbrooke QC J1M 1Z7
Tel: 819-822-9600; *Fax:* 819-822-9727
apbuoffice@ubishops.ca
apbu.ca
Overview: A small local organization founded in 1975
Mission: To promote their members' interests in negotiations with the university regarding employment
Member of: Féderation québecoise des professeures et professeurs d'université; Canadian Association of University Teachers
Chief Officer(s):
Virginia Stroeher, President
virginia.stroeher@ubishops.ca
Membership: *Member Profile:* University professors; professional librarians; contract academic staff; non-academic staff; *Committees:* Faculty Joint; Staff Joint; Staff Council Executive; Staff Stewards
Activities: Bursaries & scholarships made available to Bishop's students contributes to crisis fund for students in dire financial need

Association of Professors of the University of Ottawa *Voir* Association des professeurs de l'université d'Ottawa

Association of Psychologists of Nova Scotia (APNS)
#435, 5991 Spring Garden Rd., Halifax NS B3H 1Y6
Tel: 902-422-9183; *Fax:* 902-462-9801
apns@apns.ca
www.apns.ca
Overview: A small provincial organization founded in 1965
Mission: To represent psychology in Nova Scotia; to establish professional guidelines; to promote psychology as a science & a profession for human welfare
Affliation(s): Council of Provincial Associations of Psychology; Canadian Psychological Association (CPAP); Canadian Register of Health Service Providers in Psychology (CRHSPP); American Psychological Association (APA).
Chief Officer(s):
Susan Marsh, Executive Director
Lynne Robinson, President
Marc Blumberg, President-Elect
Stilman Jacquard, Treasurer
Membership: *Fees:* Schedule available; *Member Profile:* Psychology professionals in Nova Scotia; *Committees:* Advocacy; Continuing Education; Convention; Elections; Membership; Private Practice, ad hoc; Post Trauma Services; Psychology Month Advisory; Publications; Archivist
Activities: Providing professional development activities; Engaging in advocacy activities; Liaising with government; Presenting awards; *Awareness Events:* Psychology Month, Feb.
Publications:
• The APNS Private Practice Directory
Type: Directory
• The Nova Scotia Psychologist
Type: Journal; *Frequency:* 3 pa; *Accepts Advertising*; *Editor:* Susan Marsh; *Price:* Free for association members & affiliates; $25 for non-members
Profile: APNS activities, articles, book & test reviews, continuing education, & employment opportunities

Association of Psychologists of the Northwest Territories
PO Box 1320, Yellowknife NT X1A 2L9
Tel: 867-920-8058
psych@theedge.ca
Overview: A small provincial organization
Affliation(s): Canadian Provincial Association of Psychologists (CPAP)
Chief Officer(s):
Robert O'Rourke, President

Association of Psychology in Newfoundland & Labrador (APNL)
PO Box 26061, Stn. LeMarchant Rd., St. John's NL A1E 0A5
Tel: 709-739-5405
admin@nlpsych.ca
www.nlpsych.ca
Previous Name: Association of Newfoundland Psychologists (ANP)
Overview: A small provincial organization founded in 1976
Mission: To promote all areas of professional psychology in Newfoundland & Labrador
Member of: Canadian Psychological Association
Chief Officer(s):
Dayle Denney, President
dayledenney@esdnl.ca
Membership: 200; *Fees:* Schedule available; *Member Profile:* Registered psychologists, working in healthcare, education, or in private practice in Newfoundland & Labrador; Psychology graduate students; *Committees:* Archives; Constitution; Continuing Education; Finance; Membership; Information Technology; Advocacy
Activities: Upholding the Canadian Psychological Association's Code of Ethics & Practice Guidelines, & the Newfoundland & Labrador Psychology Board's Standards of Professional Conduct for psychologists; Supporting the profession of psychology; Promoting continuing education of psychologists; Engaging in advocacy activities; Providing information to the public; *Awareness Events:* Psychology Month, Feb.
Publications:
• Association of Psychology in Newfoundland & Labrador e-Newsletter
Type: Newsletter; *Price:* Free with APNL membership

Association of Public Service Financial Administrators (Ind.)/Association des gestionnaires financiers de la fonction publique (Ind.) *See* Association of Canadian Financial Officers

Association of Quantity Surveyors of Alberta (AQSA)
Kingsway Mall, PO Box 34062, Edmonton AB T5G 3G4
Tel: 780-628-7324
info@aqsa.ca
www.aqsa.ca
Overview: A small provincial organization founded in 1979
Mission: To promote & advance the professional status of quantity surveyors & certified cost estimators; To establish & maintain high standards of professional competence
Member of: International Cost Engineering Council; Pacific Association of Quantity Surveyors
Affliation(s): Canadian Institute of Quantity Surveyors (CIQS); Australian Institute of Quantity Surveyors (Reciprocal Agreement); Canadian Construction Association (Reciprocal Agreement); Appraisal Institute of Canada (Memoranda of Understanding); Royal Institution of Chartered Surveyors - Canada (Memoranda of Understanding)
Chief Officer(s):
Dave Burns, President
president@aqsa.ca
Dave Moller, Vice-President
vicepresident@aqsa.ca
Doug Eastwell, Registrar
registrar@aqsa.ca
Membership: *Member Profile:* Professional Quantity Surveyors (PQS) & Construction Estimator Certifieds (CEC), from areas such as construction companies, private practice, & government organizations, in the provinces of Alberta, Saskatchewan, & Manitoba, as well as the Northwest Territories & Nunavut
Activities: Offering continuing professional development programs; Facilitating networking opportunities & the exchange of knowledge; Providing professional costing, value, & estimating advice; Disciplining members; Collaborating with other organizations
Publications:
• Association of Quantity Surveyors of Alberta Newsletter
Type: Newsletter; *Price:* Free with association membership
Profile: Association reports, chapter news, forthcoming events, & Canadian Institute of Quantity Surveyors (CIQS) updates
• Consultants Directory [a publication of the Association of Quantity Surveyors of Alberta]
Type: Directory
Profile: Listing of firms, with one or more principals who are Professional Quantity Surveyors (PQS) &, which are operating in privatepractice in Alberta, Saskatchewan, Manitoba, the Northwest Territories, or Nunavut

Association of Québec Advertising Agencies *Voir* Association des agences de publicité du Québec

Association of Québec Municipal Engineers *Voir* Association des ingénieurs municipaux du Québec

Association of Québec Regional English Media *See* Québec Community Newspaper Association

Association of Records Managers & Administrators *See* ARMA Canada

Association of Regina Realtors Inc.
1854 McIntyre St., Regina SK S4P 2P9
Tel: 306-791-2700; *Fax:* 306-781-7940
www.reginarealtors.com
www.facebook.com/ReginaREALTORS
twitter.com/ReginaREALTORS
Overview: A small local organization founded in 1912 overseen by Saskatchewan Real Estate Association
Member of: The Canadian Real Estate Association
Chief Officer(s):
Mike Duggleby, President
mikeduggleby@royallepage.ca
Stacy Svendsen, President-Elect
ssvendsen@sasktel.net
Finances: *Annual Operating Budget:* $500,000-$1.5 Million
Staff Member(s): 7
Membership: 400+

Association of Registered Graphic Designers of Ontario
#210, 96 Spadina Ave., Toronto ON M5V 2J6
Tel: 416-367-8819
Toll-Free: 888-274-3668
info@rgdontario.com
www.rgdontario.com
www.linkedin.com/groups/RGD-Association-Registered-Graphic-Designers-1
www.facebook.com/RGDhub
twitter.com/rgdontario
instagram.com/rgdhub
Also Known As: RGD Ontario
Overview: A small provincial organization founded in 1996
Mission: To act as the voice of graphic design in Ontario; to improve standards of education in the industry; to establish standards of knowledge, skills, & ethics for the profession
Member of: International Council of Graphic Design Associations (ICOGRADA)
Chief Officer(s):
Hilary Ashworth, Executive Director, 416-367-8819 Ext. 23
execdir@rgd.ca
Heidi Veri, Chief Operating Officer & Director, Membership, 416-367-8819 Ext. 22
Finances: *Funding Sources:* Advertising; Sponsorships
Staff Member(s): 8
Membership: *Member Profile:* Professional graphic designers, managers, educators, & students in Ontario; *Committees:* Communications; Education; Ethics; Membership; PR; Provisional; Student
Activities: Granting those who qualify the right to use the designation Registered Graphic Designer (R.G.D.); Organizing professional development events; Facilitating the exchange of ideas & information; Disseminating information about the industry; Increasing public recognition of the R.G.D. designation; Promoting the value of graphic design in business; Lobbying government & business; Presenting student awards; Mentoring; *Speaker Service:* Yes
Publications:
• E-Flash: Email Newsletter of the Association of Registered Graphic Designers of Ontario
Type: Newsletter; *Frequency:* Biweekly; *Accepts Advertising*
Profile: Announcements, upcoming RGD & design-related events, member news, industry updates, & employment opportunities
• RGD Ontario Membership Directory
Type: Directory
Profile: Listing of RGD Ontario members distributed to more than 1,000 marketing & adverising executives
• RGD Review
Type: Newsletter; *Frequency:* Bimonthly
Profile: Articles, RGD presentations, members news, & book reviews

Association of Registered Interior Designers of New Brunswick (ARIDNB) / Association des designers d'intérieur immatriculés du Nouveau-Brunswick (ADIINB)
PO Box 1541, Fredericton NB E3B 5G2
Tel: 506-459-3014
info@aridnb.ca
www.aridnb.ca
Previous Name: Interior Designers of New Brunswick
Overview: A small provincial licensing organization founded in 1987 overseen by Interior Designers of Canada
Mission: To establish & maintain standards of knowledge, skill, & professional ethics among association members; To serve the public interest by governing the practice of interior design in New Brunswick
Member of: Interior Designers of Canada (IDC)
Chief Officer(s):
Rachel Mitton, President
Lyn Van Tassel, Vice-President
Chrystalla Wilde, Treasurer & Registrar
Ginette Fougère, Secretary
Membership: *Member Profile:* Registered interior design practitioners in New Brunswick; Interns; Students; Trade affiliates
Activities: Increasing public awareness of quality interior design; Disciplining members of the association

Association of Registered Interior Designers of Ontario (ARIDO)
43 Hanna Ave., #C536, Toronto ON M6K 1X1
Tel: 416-921-2127; *Fax:* 416-921-3660
Toll-Free: 800-334-1180
adminoffice@arido.ca
www.arido.ca
Previous Name: Interior Designers of Ontario (IDO)
Overview: A medium-sized provincial organization founded in 1984 overseen by Interior Designers of Canada
Mission: To govern the conduct & professional standards of members; To increase awareness of the profession & ensure rights of interior designers & the public they serve
Affliation(s): Interior Designers Educators Council; National

Council for Interior Design Education; American Society of Interior Designers; Foundation for Interior Design Education; International Federation of Interior Designers
Chief Officer(s):
Sharon Portelli, Registrar
sportelli@arido.ca
Finances: *Funding Sources:* Membership dues
Staff Member(s): 4
Membership: 3,300+; *Fees:* $25 student; $280 educator; $295.50 intern; $654.50 registered; *Member Profile:* Registered - fully accredited members who are interior designers; intern - graduate interior designers with recognized interior design degree/diploma working towards registered member status; resource alliance - manufacturers &/or suppliers of goods & services for interior design industry; affiliate - allied professionals, media, educators & individuals interested in the advancement of interior design; student - students presently enrolled in recognized interior design program
Activities: *Internships:* Yes

Association of Registered Nurses of Prince Edward Island (ARNPEI)

53 Grafton St., Charlottetown PE C1A 1K8
Tel: 902-368-3764; *Fax:* 902-628-1430
info@arnpei.ca
www.arnpei.ca
Previous Name: Association of Nurses of Prince Edward Island
Overview: A medium-sized provincial licensing organization founded in 1922 overseen by Canadian Nurses Association
Mission: Professional Association for Registered Nurses in P.E.I.
Chief Officer(s):
Becky Gosbee, Executive Director
bgosbee@arnpei.ca
Paul Boudreau, Coordinator, Regulatory Services
pboudreau@arnpei.ca
Finances: *Annual Operating Budget:* $500,000-$1.5 Million
Staff Member(s): 3
Membership: 1,700; *Fees:* $350; *Member Profile:* Registered nurses practicing in Prince Edward Island

Association of Registered Professional Foresters of New Brunswick (ARPFNB) / Association des forestiers agréés du Nouveau-Brunswick (AFANB)

#221, 1350 Regent St., Fredericton NB E3C 2G6
Tel: 506-452-6933; *Fax:* 506-450-3128
arpf@nbnet.nb.ca
www.arpfnb.ca
Overview: A small provincial organization founded in 1937
Mission: To manage the forest resources of New Brunswick for the sustained development of these resources; To assure the proficiency & competency of Registered Professional Foresters in New Brunswick
Affliation(s): Canadian Federation of Professional Foresters Association (CFPFA)
Chief Officer(s):
Edward Czerwinski, Executive Director
Steven Spears, President
Jasen Golding, Secretary-Treasurer
Membership: 300; *Member Profile:* Registered Professional Foresters eligible to practice Forestry in New Brunswick, including forestry consultants, & federal & provincial public servants
Activities: Improving forestry practice in New Brunswick; Increasing understanding of forestry issues; Promoting the knowledge & skill of association members
Meetings/Conferences: • Association of Registered Professional Foresters of New Brunswick Annual General Meeting 2015, 2015, NB
Scope: Provincial

Association of Registrars of the Universities & Colleges of Canada (ARUCC) / Association des registraires des universités et collèges du Canada

c/o Angelique Saweczko, Thompson Rivers University, 900 McGill Rd., Kamloops BC V2C 0C8
Tel: 250-828-5019
www.arucc.ca
Overview: A medium-sized national organization founded in 1964 overseen by Association of Universities & Colleges of Canada
Mission: ARUCC was developed in response to the professional needs of student administrative services personnel in universities.
Chief Officer(s):
Hans Rouleau, President, 819-822-9600 Ext. 2217
hrouleau@ubishops.ca
Finances: *Annual Operating Budget:* Less than $50,000; *Funding Sources:* Membership fees
Staff Member(s): 4; 4 volunteer(s)
Membership: 139 institutional + 23 associate + 6 corporate + 718 individual; *Fees:* Based on budget of each institution; *Member Profile:* Member of AUCC & Association of Canadian Community Colleges
Activities: *Rents Mailing List:* Yes
Meetings/Conferences: • ARUCC 2015 Conference, 2015
Scope: National

Association of Regular Baptist Churches (Canada) (ARBC)

130 Gerrard St. East, Toronto ON M5A 3T4
Tel: 416-925-3261; *Fax:* 416-925-8305
Overview: A small national organization founded in 1957
Membership: 10 churches, 1500 members

Association of Saskatchewan Forestry Professionals (ASFP)

#102C, 1061 Central Ave., Prince Albert SK S6V 4V4
Tel: 306-922-4655; *Fax:* 306-764-7461
registrar@asfp.ca
www.asfp.ca
Overview: A small provincial organization founded in 2006
Mission: To promote the profession of forestry & its members; to satisfy the public demand for competent & ethical management of the province's forests
Chief Officer(s):
Roman Ornyik, Registrar
David Stevenson, Vice-President
Finances: *Annual Operating Budget:* Less than $50,000; *Funding Sources:* Membership dues
Membership: 166; *Member Profile:* Registered Professional Foresters & Forest Technologists; Foresters-in-training & forest technologists-in-training; *Committees:* Admissions; Finance; Continuing Competence; Professional Conduct; Discipline

Association of Saskatchewan Home Economists (ASHE)

c/o Gayleen Turner, President, 270 Battleford Trail, Swift Current SK S9H 4J5
Tel: 306-773-2574
www.homefamily.info
Overview: A small provincial organization founded in 1958
Mission: To provide professional support to members & persons in allied professions in managing personal & public resources to meet the needs of individuals & families as they strive to achieve a desirable quality of life
Chief Officer(s):
Gayleen Turner, President
Beverley Dinnell, Registrar
beverley.dinnell@spiritsd.ca
Membership: *Member Profile:* Home economists

Association of Saskatchewan Realtors (ASR)

2811 Estey Dr., Saskatoon SK S7J 2V8
Tel: 306-373-3350; *Fax:* 306-373-5377
Toll-Free: 877-306-7732
info@saskatchewanrealestate.com
www.saskatchewanrealestate.com
www.facebook.com/69418510914
twitter.com/saskREALTORS
Previous Name: Saskatchewan Real Estate Association
Overview: A medium-sized provincial organization founded in 1949
Mission: Represents real estate boards & their realtor members on government affairs & provincial issues; develops standards of professional practice; administers training; provides information to members, governments & the public; provides support services to members; registers brokers & salespeople; develops special projects for the educational benefit of all registrants in Saskatchewan
Member of: The Canadian Real Estate Association
Chief Officer(s):
Bill Madder, Executive Vice President
bmadder@saskatchewanrealestate.com
Patty Kalytuk, Director, Communication & Administration
patty@saskatchewanrealestate.com
Arvid Kuhnle, Director, Professional Development
education@saskatchewanrealestate.com
Linda Minor, Member Services Coordinator
Staff Member(s): 7
Membership: 1,300
Activities: *Library*

Association of Saskatchewan Taxpayers; Resolution One Association of Alberta *See* Canadian Taxpayers Federation

Association of School Business Officials of Alberta (ASBOA)

#1200, 9925 - 109 St., Edmonton AB T5K 2J8
Tel: 780-451-7103; *Fax:* 780-482-5659
www.asboa.ab.ca
www.linkedin.com/company/association-of-school-business-officials-of-a
www.facebook.com/220709328072097
twitter.com/ASBOA_
Overview: A small provincial organization founded in 1939
Mission: To promote the highest standards of school business management in all aspects & the status, competency, leadership qualities & ethical standards of school business officials at all levels
Affliation(s): Association of School Business Officials International
Chief Officer(s):
Susan Lang, Executive Director
Finances: *Funding Sources:* Membership fees
Staff Member(s): 1
Membership: *Committees:* Communications; Discipline; Information Reporting; Leadership Development; Legislative; Practice Review; Professional Development; Registration
Meetings/Conferences: • Association of School Business Officials of Alberta 2015 Annual Conference and Trade Show, May, 2015, DoubleTree by Hilton, Edmonton, AB
Scope: Provincial

The Association of School Transportation Services of British Columbia (ASTSBC) / Association des transports du Canada

BC
Tel: 250-804-7892; *Fax:* 250-832-2584
info@astsbc.org
www.astsbc.org
Overview: A large provincial organization
Mission: Dedicated to the promotion of safe transportation and encourages those associated with it to do likewise.
Chief Officer(s):
Robyn Stephenson, President
Membership: *Fees:* $85 associate; $175 full
Meetings/Conferences: • Association of School Transportation Services of British Columbia 50th Annual Convention and Trade Show, July, 2015, Sun Peaks Grand Hotel and Conference Centre, Sun Peaks, BC
Scope: Provincial

Association of Science & Engineering Technology Professionals of Alberta (ASET)

Phipps-McKinnon Building, #1630, 10020 - 101A Ave. NW, Edmonton AB T5J 3G2
Tel: 780-425-0626; *Fax:* 780-424-5053
Toll-Free: 800-272-5619
www.aset.ab.ca
Previous Name: Alberta Society of Engineering Technologists
Overview: A large provincial organization founded in 1963 overseen by Canadian Council of Technicians & Technologists
Mission: To benefit the public & the profession by regulating & promoting safe, high quality, professional technology practice; To focus on the engineering technology, applied science, & information technology fields; To issue credentials to qualified individuals; To accredit training programs. There are 9 chapters across the province
Member of: Canadian Council of Technicians & Technologists
Chief Officer(s):
Norman Kyle, R.E.T., P.L.(En, President
Barry Cavanaugh, CEO & General Counsel
Jennifer McNeil Betrand, BA, Director, Education & Special Projects
Russifer Medvedev, MA, Director, Communications & Member Benefits
Heather Shewchuk, B.Comm., Director, Corporate & Government Relations
Norman Viegas, CMA, CAE, Director, Finance & Administration
Membership: 16,500
Activities: Awarding Engineering Technology Scholarship Foundation of Alberta (ETSFA) scholarships; *Speaker Service:* Yes
Awards:
• Tech of the Year Award (Award)
• Tech Employer of the Year (Award)
• Technical Excellence (Award)
• Technical Instruction (Award)

• Volunteer of the Year (Award)
• Certificate of Achievement (Award)
• Certificate of Appreciation (Award)
• Certificate of Recognition (Award)
• Award of Merit (Award)
• Honourary Membership (Award)
• Honourary Life Membership (Award)
• Years of Membership Pins (Award)
• College & Institute Scholarships & Bursaries (Scholarship)
• Dale Tufts Memorial Scholarship (Scholarship)
• Don Stirling Memorial Bursary (Scholarship)
• TD Insurance Meloche Monnex Technology Scholarship (Scholarship)
• Women in Technology Scholarship (Scholarship)
Publications:
• Salary Survey [a publication of the Association of Science & Engineering Technology Professionals of Alberta]
• Technology Alberta [a publication of the Association of Science & Engineering Technology Professionals of Alberta]
Frequency: 5 pa

Association of Seafood Producers
Fort William Place, #103, Baine Johnston Centre, St. John's NL A1C 1K4
Tel: 709-726-3730; *Fax:* 709-726-3731
info@seafoodproducers.org
www.seafoodproducers.org
Overview: A small provincial organization
Mission: To represent the interests of seafood producers in Newfoundland & Labrador
Chief Officer(s):
Derek Butler, Executive Director
dbutler@seafoodproducers.org
Sherry Day, Executive Secretary
sday@seafoodproducers.org
Roger Hollahan, Coordinator, Programs
rhollahan@seafoodproducers.org
Membership: *Member Profile:* Seafood producers in the Newfoundland & Labrador
Activities: Liaising with government at all levels; Promoting the industry

Association of Service Providers for Employability & Career Training (ASPECT)
975 Alston St., Victoria BC V9A 3S5
Tel: 250-382-9675; *Fax:* 250-382-9677
Toll-Free: 888-287-4957
info@aspect.bc.ca
www.aspect.bc.ca
twitter.com/aspectbc
Overview: A small provincial organization
Mission: To represent & promote the interests & activities of members; To strengthen members' capacity to provide services to people with barriers to employment
Affliation(s): Canadian Coalition for Community Based Employability Training; Canada Career Consortium; National Headquarters for Human Resources & Skills Development Canada; Canadian Counselling Association; Career Management Association; Canadian Community Economic Development Network; BC Career Information Partnership; BC Workinfonet
Chief Officer(s):
Norma Strachan, CEO
nstrachan@aspect.bc.ca
Membership: *Fees:* $100 for all members
Publications:
• Association of Service Providers for Employability & Career Training Newsletter
Type: Newsletter; *Accepts Advertising*

Association of Sign Language Interpreters of Alberta (ASLIA)
6240 - 113 St., Edmonton AB T6H 3L2
Tel: 780-438-2319
aslia@aslia.ca
www.aslia.ca
Previous Name: Alberta Chapter of the Registry of Interpreters for the Deaf, Inc.
Overview: A small provincial organization founded in 1978 overseen by Association of Visual Language Interpreters of Canada
Mission: To uphold the Code of Ethics for professional conduct within the profession; To maintain national standards; To ensure the provision of quality services
Chief Officer(s):
Deb Flaig, President
president@aslia.ca
Robyn Sauks, Treasurer
treasurer@alisa.ca
Finances: *Funding Sources:* Donations; Fundraising
Membership: *Fees:* Schedule available; *Member Profile:* Professional sign language interpreters; Deaf & hard of hearing persons; Interested individuals who support the goals of the organization
Activities: Providing professional development opportunities
Awards:
• Donna Korpiniski Mentorship Award (Award)
• Greg Douglas Bursary (Award)
Amount: $500
• Community Spirit Award (Award)
• Volunteer Award (Award)
• President's Award (Award)
Publications:
• ACRID Express
Type: Newsletter; *Frequency:* 3 pa; *Editor:* Karen Sheets
Profile: ACRID activities, meeting minute summaries, upcoming events, & awards
• Alberta Chapter of the Registry of Interpreters for the Deaf Directory
Type: Directory
Profile: Listings of interpreters & services

Association of Social Rehabilitation Agencies of Québec Inc. *Voir* Association des services de réhabilitation sociale du Québec inc.

The Association of Social Workers of Northern Canada (ASWNC) / L'Association des travailleurs sociaux du Nord canadien (ATSNC)
PO Box 2963, Yellowknife NT X1A 2R2
Tel: 867-699-7964
ed@socialworknorth.com
www.socialworknorth.com
Overview: A small provincial organization founded in 1974
Mission: The ASWNC represents social workers practicing in Canada's three Territories in the far north - Nunavut, the Northwest Territories, and the Yukon Territory.
Member of: Canadian Association of Social Workers
Chief Officer(s):
Dana Jennejohn, President

Association of Strategic Alliance Professionals - Toronto Chapter
Tel: 416-734-1011
www.asaptoronto.com
Also Known As: ASAP Toronto Chapter
Overview: A medium-sized local organization
Chief Officer(s):
Phil Hogg, President
phil.hogg@moneris.com
Activities: Networking; professional development; member programs; *Awareness Events:* Seminar & Golf Event, June; Global Alliance Summit

Association of Summer Theatres 'Round Ontario (ASTRO)
c/o Theatre Ontario, #350, 401 Richmond St. West, Toronto ON M5V 3A8
Tel: 416-408-4556; *Fax:* 416-408-3402
info@summertheatre.org
www.summertheatre.org
twitter.com/summer_theatre
Also Known As: Summer Theatre Ontario
Overview: A small provincial organization founded in 1985
Mission: To act as an information & resource network for its members; to support the professional development of its members; to act as a liaison for its membership with arts & business organizations, the media & the community; to advocate for its membership with government, government agencies & other organizations; to undertake projects to increase awareness of the activities of its membership among the general public
Chief Officer(s):
Derek Ritschel, President
Finances: *Funding Sources:* Membership fees
Membership: 21 theatres; *Member Profile:* Professional summer theatres
Activities: Promotion of summer theatres in Ontario;

Association of Teachers of English in Quebec (ATEQ) / Association des professeurs d'anglais du Québec
PO Box 46547, Stn. Comptoire Newman, LaSalle QC H8N 3G3
e-mail: info@ateq.org
www.ateq.org
www.linkedin.com/groups?gid=6543092
www.facebook.com/ateqorg
twitter.com/ATEQc
pinterest.com/quebecteach
Overview: A small provincial organization
Mission: To provide leadership in the development of teaching theory, practice & resources; to strengthen communicaion between English language educators through a sharing of resources & language arts conferences.
Affliation(s): Canadian Council of Teachers of English Language Arts; Conseil pédagogique interdisciplinaire du Québec; National Council of Teachers of English
Chief Officer(s):
Anne Beamish, President
Judy Brebner, Administrative Assistant
Membership: *Fees:* $25
Activities: Springboards, an annual conference; workshops; site-based project grants

Association of the Chemical Profession of Alberta (ACPA)
PO Box 21017, Edmonton AB T6R 2V4
Tel: 780-413-0004; *Fax:* 780-413-0076
www.pchem.ca
www.linkedin.com/groups/Association-Chemical-Profession-Alberta-415151
www.facebook.com/?ref=tn_tnmn#!/groups/312651632085514/
Overview: A small provincial organization founded in 1992
Mission: To provides a legal definition of chemistry; To promote & increase the knowledge, skills, & proficiency of members in all things relating to chemistry
Chief Officer(s):
Maurice Shevalier, President
Kathy Janzen, Executive Director
Membership: *Fees:* $150 Professional Chemist; $75 Chemist-in-Training; $50 Retired Member. Associate Member; Student Members free; *Committees:* Awards; Discipline; Legislative; Practice Review; Registration; Technical Seminar
Awards:
• Frank W. Bachelor Award (Award)
This award recognizes outstanding volunteer contributions to the chemical profession in Alberta.
• ACPA Undergraduate Scholarship in Chemistry (Scholarship)
Awarded annually to a student who is registered in a full-time undergraduate chemistry program at a university in the province of Alberta. Eligibility: Applicant must be registered in a program accredited by the Canadian Society for Chemistry (CSC)
Amount: $1000
• Arthur Bollo-Kamara Graduate Scholarship (Scholarship)
Awarded annually to a student registered in a graduate chemistry program at a university in the province of Alberta. *Deadline:* March 31 *Amount:* $1000
Meetings/Conferences: • Association of the Chemical Profession of Alberta 2015 Annual General Meeting, 2015
Scope: Provincial
Publications:
• Association of the Chemical Profession of Alberta Newsletter
Type: Newsletter; *Frequency:* Irregular

Association of the Chemical Profession of Ontario (ACPO)
#1801, 1 Yonge St., Toronto ON M5E 1W7
Tel: 416-364-4609; *Fax:* 416-369-0515
Toll-Free: 800-260-0992
Other Communication: executivedirector@acpo.on.ca
info@acpo.on.ca
www.acpo.on.ca
Overview: A medium-sized provincial organization founded in 1958
Mission: To promote & increase the knowledge, skills & proficiency of its members in all things relating to chemistry & to establish standards of chemical practice for its members; provides a legal definition of chemistry & of those practising chemistry in Ontario
Chief Officer(s):
T. Obal, President
Finances: *Annual Operating Budget:* Less than $50,000
Membership: 1,200; *Fees:* $40-$140; *Member Profile:* Honours degree with work experience deemed acceptable by the association; 3-year chemistry degree with 5 years experience; 6 years experience & written examinations set by the association; *Committees:* Professional Affairs; Membership; Environmental
Activities: *Speaker Service:* Yes

Association of Trade & Consumer Exhibitions *See* Canadian Association of Exposition Management

Association of Translators & Interpreters of Alberta (ATIA) / Association des traducteurs et interprètes de l'Alberta

PO Box 546, Stn. Main, Edmonton AB T5J 2K8
Tel: 780-434-8384
www.atia.ab.ca
Overview: A small provincial organization founded in 1979 overseen by Canadian Translators, Terminologists & Interpreters Council
Mission: To protect the interests of their members
Member of: International Federation of Translators
Chief Officer(s):
Hellen Martinez, President
info@etstranslations.com
Finances: *Funding Sources:* Membership dues; exam revenues
Membership: 151; *Fees:* $150 associate; $200 certified
Activities: *Speaker Service:* Yes

Association of Translators & Interpreters of Nova Scotia (ATINS) / Association des traducteurs et interprètes de la nouvelle-écosse

PO Box 372, Halifax NS B3J 2P8
e-mail: info@atins.org
www.atins.org
Overview: A small provincial organization founded in 1990 overseen by Canadian Translators, Terminologists & Interpreters Council
Mission: To ensure that clients have access to a body of qualified professionals; to promote the profession & the development of its members
Affliation(s): Fédération internationale des traducteurs (FIT)
Chief Officer(s):
Bassima Jurdak O'Brien, President
Membership: *Fees:* $110 associate; $140 certified

Association of Translators & Interpreters of Ontario (ATIO) / Association des traducteurs et interprètes de l'Ontario

#1202, 1 Nicholas St., Ottawa ON K1N 7B7
Tel: 613-241-2846; *Fax:* 613-241-4098
Toll-Free: 800-234-5030
info@atio.on.ca
www.atio.on.ca
Overview: A medium-sized provincial licensing organization founded in 1921 overseen by Canadian Translators, Terminologists & Interpreters Council
Mission: To promote a high degree of professionalism & to protect the interest of those who use the language services provided by its members; to organize professional development activities & to encourage exchanges among its members
Member of: Fédération internationale des traducteurs (FIT)
Chief Officer(s):
Catherine Bertholet-Schweizer, Executive Director
cbertholet@atio.on.ca
Barbara Collishaw, President
bcollishaw@rogers.com
Finances: *Funding Sources:* Membership dues; services
Staff Member(s): 3
Membership: 859; *Fees:* $378.55 certified; $189.27 senior; $62.15 retired; $124.30 special circumstances; $343.52 candidate for certification; $0 student; *Member Profile:* Associate; translator; interpreter & terminologist
Activities: *Speaker Service:* Yes

Association of Translators & Interpreters of Saskatchewan (ATIS) / Association des traducteurs et interprètes de la Saskatchewan

50 Harvard Cres., Regina SK S7H 3R1
www.atis-sk.ca
www.facebook.com/ATIS.SK.CA
Overview: A medium-sized provincial organization founded in 1980 overseen by Canadian Translators, Terminologists & Interpreters Council
Mission: To provide a collective voice for members; to ensure that members exercise the profession in accordance with their code of ethics; to administer admission procedures of national certification examination; to provide a list of current certified members
Affliation(s): Canadian Translators & Interpreters Council, Regional Center for North America (USA, Canada, Mexico); Fédération internationale des traducteurs
Chief Officer(s):
Robert Jerrett, President
Estelle Bonetto, Vice-President
Finances: *Funding Sources:* Membership fees
Membership: 70; *Fees:* $125 certified; $85 associate/affiliate; *Member Profile:* Must pass national certification examination

Association of Translators, Terminologists & Interpreters of Manitoba (ATIM) / Association des traducteurs, terminologues et des interprètes du Manitoba

PO Box 83, 200 Cathédrale Ave., Winnipeg MB R2H 0H7
Tel: 204-797-3247
info@atim.mb.ca
www.atim.mb.ca
Overview: A small provincial organization founded in 1980 overseen by Canadian Translators, Terminologists & Interpreters Council
Mission: To provide a collective voice for its members, ensure that members exercise their profession in accordance with its Code of Ethics, & protect the public interest by ensuring the quality of the services rendered by its members.
Affliation(s): Canadian Translators & Interpreters Council (CTIC)
Membership: 49 individuals

Association of Travel Agents of British Columbia *See* Association of Canadian Travel Agents - British Columbia/Yukon

Association of Treatment Centres of Ontario *See* Ontario Association of Children's Rehabilitation Services

Association of Unity Churches Canada

2631 Kingsway Dr., Kitchener ON N2C 1A7
Tel: 519-894-0810
info@unitycanada.org
www.unitycanada.org
www.facebook.com/beunity
Also Known As: Unity
Overview: A small national charitable organization founded in 1978
Mission: Unity is a Christian association asserting that reunion with God in mind brings certain fulfillment in life. It is a registered charity, BN: 118794544RR0001.
Affliation(s): Association of Unity Churches USA
Chief Officer(s):
Doris Lewis, President
president@unitycanada.org
David Durksen, Judicatory Representative
ucjr@unitycanada.org
Finances: *Annual Operating Budget:* $50,000-$100,000
Membership: 20 churches
Activities: *Internships:* Yes; *Speaker Service:* Yes

Association of Universities & Colleges of Canada (AUCC) / Association des universités et collèges du Canada

#600, 350 Albert St., Ottawa ON K1R 1B1
Tel: 613-563-1236; *Fax:* 613-563-9745
info@aucc.ca
www.aucc.ca
Overview: A large national charitable organization founded in 1911
Mission: To foster & promote the interests of higher education
Chief Officer(s):
Paul Davidson, President/CEO
president@aucc.ca
Stephen Toope, Chair
Finances: *Annual Operating Budget:* Greater than $5 Million; *Funding Sources:* Membership dues; contract administration; publication sales
Staff Member(s): 85
Membership: 94 institutional; *Member Profile:* Degree granting colleges & universities
Activities: Government relations; research; international cooperation; publications & communications; scholarship contract; administration; *Library:* Information Centre
Awards:
• Paul Sargent Memorial Linguistic Scholarship Program (Scholarship)
Translation of an Oriental, Middle East or Eastern European language at the Masters level *Amount:* Two $12,000 scholarships
• TD Canada Trust Scholarship for Outstanding Community Leadership (Scholarship)
All disciplines, undergraduate degrees *Amount:* 20 renewable scholarships for $5,000 living stipend, plus tuition, compulsory fees and summmer job
• Department of National Defence Security & Defence Forum (Scholarship)
Eight $8,000 (master's), four $16,000 (doctorate) scholarships & two $35,000 (post-doctoral) fellowships in studies relating to current & future Canadian natural security & defence issues. Three internships of up to 12 months worth $32,000 to help recent MA graduates obtain work experience in security & defence studies by working in this field in the non-governmental or private sectors.
• Canadian Wireless Telecommunications Association Graduate Scholarship (Scholarship)
Scholarships open to graduate level studies related to wireless communications, including engineering or business *Amount:* Up to 10 $10,000 available per year
• MDS Nordion Corporate Scholarship (Scholarship)
Scholarship open to students of pure, applied or health sciences, engineering & related disciplines *Amount:* $2,000
• Queen Elizabeth Silver Jubilee Endowment Fund for Study in a Second Official Language Award Program (Award)
Scholarships open to all disciplines, except translations, for students studying in their second language *Amount:* Three $5,000 (plus travel costs)
• Frank Knox Memorial Fellowship Program (Scholarship)
Awards, plus tuition fees & health insurance for Canadian citizens or permanent residents who have graduated from a AUCC member institution before Sept. 2005 & wish to study at Harvard in the following disciplines: arts & sciences (including engineering), business administration, design, divinity studies, education, law, public administration, medicine, dental medicine & public health; applications for students currently studying in the US will not be considered *Amount:* Up to three US$18,500
• Public Safety & Emergency Preparedness Canada Research Fellowship (Scholarship)
For research in the area of disaster/emergency research & planning; preference is given to applicants who hold a Master's degree & who are planning research in the following fields: Urban & Regional Planning, Economics, Earth Sciences, Risk Analysis & Management, Systems Science, Social Sciences, Business Administration & Health Administration *Amount:* Eight up to $19,250
• CIBC Youthvision Scholarship (Scholarship)
Must be enrolled in Big Brothers/Big Sisters of Canada *Amount:* 30 scholarships: $4,000 or actual tuition fees, plus paid summer employment with YMCA Canada
• Imperial Tobacco Canada Limited Scholarship Fund for Disabled Students (Scholarship)
Disabled undergraduate students, following a degree program or college university program *Amount:* 10 $5,000 scholarships
• Mattinson Endowment Fund Scholarship for Disabled Students (Scholarship)
For undergraduate study, all disciplines *Amount:* $2,500
• Bowater Maritimes Scholarship Program (Scholarship)
Scholarships open to grade 12 New Brunswick students *Amount:* Three $1,500 for undergraduate studies
• Cable Telecommunications Research Fellowship (Canadian Cable Telecommunications Association) (Scholarship)
Scholarship awarded annually to students pursuing a master's degree in any discipline directly related to the development & delivery of cable in Canada *Amount:* $5,000
• Fairfax Financial Holdings Limited Program (Scholarship)
Undergraduate students of all disciplines *Amount:* 36 university undergraduate scholarships of $5,000; 24 college diploma scholarships of $3,500
• C.D. Howe Scholarship Program (Scholarship)
Scholarships open to all disciplines but for students from Thunder Bay or the following school boards: Lakehead, Lakehead District R.C., Lake Superior, North of Superior District R.C., Geraldton, Geraldton District R.C., Nipigon-Red Rock, & Hornepayne *Amount:* Two $5,500
• C.D. Howe Memorial Foundation Engineering Awards (Scholarship)
(One male, one female) for students who have completed the first year of an engineering program *Amount:* Two $7,500 scholarships
• Fessenden-Trott Awards (Scholarship)
Scholarships open to all disciplines; restricted to Ontario in 2005 *Amount:* Four $9,000
• Cement Association of Canada Environmental Scholarship Program (Scholarship)
Open to students in Alberta, British Columbia, Newfoundland, Nova Scotia, Ontario & Quebec who have fully completed the two years of course work in an environmental science or environmental engineering program that is required to continue a third year of their eligible program *Amount:* Six $2,000
• The Serbian Educational Foundation of Ontario Scholarship (Scholarship)
Candidates must be of Serbian descent enrolled at an Ontario

university & have completed the first year of their undergraduate degree, open to all disciplines *Amount:* Five $1,000

Association of University Forestry Schools of Canada (AUFSC) / Association des écoles forestières universitaires du Canada

c/o Faculty of Agric., Life & Environ. Sciences, University of Alberta, 751 General Services Building, Edmonton AC T6G 1H1
Tel: 780-492-6722
www.aefuc-aufsc.ca
Overview: A medium-sized national organization overseen by Association of Universities & Colleges of Canada
Chief Officer(s):
Vic Lieffers, Chair
Victor.Lieffers@ualberta.ca
Membership: 8 organizations; *Member Profile:* Forest education and research organizations in Canada.

Association of University of New Brunswick Teachers (AUNBT) / Association des enseignants de l'Université du Nouveau-Brunswick

University Of New Brunswick, PO Box 4400, Fredericton NB E3B 5A3
Tel: 506-453-4661; *Fax:* 506-453-3514
aunbt@aunbt.ca
aunbtweb.wordpress.com
www.linkedin.com/company/association-of-university-of-new-brunswick-te
www.facebook.com/211900002197182
twitter.com/AUNBTweeter
www.youtube.com/AUNBT
Overview: A medium-sized local organization founded in 1956
Mission: To stimulate research, instruction, cooperative relations; to promote professional interests of instructors, faculty & librarians; to protect freedom of expression, thought & research within the university; to act as a bargaining agent; to cooperate with like-minded organizations; to seek full representation of all members in academic operations of the University
Member of: Canadian Association of University Teachers; Federation of New Brunswick Faculty Associations
Chief Officer(s):
Miriam Jones, President, 506-453-4661, Fax: 506-453-3514
miriamjones@aunbt.ca
Juan Carretero, Secretary
jcarrete@unb.ca
Staff Member(s): 2
Membership: 1000+; *Committees:* Collective Bargaining; Grievance; Negotiating; Status of Women; Investment; Pension; Personnel; Accessibility & Accommodation; Adjustment; Economic Adjustment; Employment Equity; Fringe Benefits; Impact of Technology; Joint Health & Safety; Joint Liaison; Assessment of Teaching Competence; Credit in Rank Anomalies; External Partners; Graduate Training & Supervision; Harassment Policy; Pre-Retirement Benefit; Teaching Apprenticeships

Association of Vancouver Island Coastal Communities (AVICC)

Local Government House, 525 Government St., Victoria BC V8W 0A8
Tel: 250-356-5122; *Fax:* 250-356-5119
www.avicc.ca
Overview: A small local organization
Mission: To represent & provide a unified voice for the coastal communities of Vancouver Island
Chief Officer(s):
Joe Stanhope, President
Larry Cross, First Vice-President
Cindy Solda, Second Vice-President
Iris Hesketh-Boles, Contact
iheskethboles@ubcm.ca
Membership: *Member Profile:* Municipalities & regional districts of Vancouver Island
Activities: Providing information to its member municipalities & regional districts; Liaising with the provincial & federal governments
Meetings/Conferences: • Association of Vancouver Island Coastal Communities 2015 Annual General Meeting & Convention, April, 2015, Courtenay, BC
Scope: Local
Contact Information: Contact: Iris Hesketh-Boles, E-mail: iheskethboles@ubcm.ca
• Association of Vancouver Island Coastal Communities 2016 Annual General Meeting & Convention, April, 2016, Nanaimo, BC
Scope: Local
Contact Information: Contact: Iris Hesketh-Boles, E-mail: iheskethboles@ubcm.ca
• Association of Vancouver Island Coastal Communities 2017 Annual General Meeting & Convention, 2017
Scope: Local
Publications:
• Association of Vancouver Island Coastal Communities Annual Report
Type: Yearbook; *Frequency:* Annually
• AVICC Newsletter
Type: Newsletter

Association of Veterans & Friends of the Mackenzie-Papineau Battalion, International Brigades in Spain / Association des vétérans et amis du bataillon Mackenzie-Papineau, Brigades internationales en Espagne

c/o S. Skup, 56 Riverwood Terrace, Bolton ON L7E 1S4
Tel: 905-951-8499; *Fax:* 905-951-7629
www.macpapbattalion.ca
Also Known As: Mac-Paps
Overview: A small national charitable organization founded in 1990
Mission: To promote programs & activities to inform the public on the role of the Mackenzie-Papineau Battalion of the International Brigades in Spain in 1936-1939
Affliation(s): Canadian Peace Alliance
Activities: Mackenzie-Papineau Memorial Fund; *Speaker Service:* Yes

Association of Visual Language Interpreters of Canada (AVLIC) / Association des interprètes en langage visuel du Canada

#110, 39012 Discovery Way, Squamish BC V8B 0E5
Tel: 604-617-8502; *Fax:* 604-567-8502
avlic@avlic.ca
www.avlic.ca
www.facebook.com/AVLIC
www.youtube.com/user/TheAVLIC
Overview: A small national organization founded in 1979
Mission: To represent interpreters whose working languages are English & American Sign Language (ASL); To promote high standards & uniformity within the profession of interpreting
Chief Officer(s):
Christie Reaume, President
president@avlic.ca
Caroline Tetreault, Secretary
secretary@avlic.ca
Cindy Haner, Treasurer
treasurer@avlic.ca
Jane Pannell, Administrative Manager
Membership: *Member Profile:* Providers of visual language interpreting services; Students; Organizations of visual language interpreters; *Committees:* Awards; Board & Committee Development; Dispute Resolution; Educational Interpreting Issues; Evaluations; Health & Safety; Member Services; Public Relations; Publications; Website; Interpreting in Legal Settings Document Review; Use of the Term "Certified Interpreter"; 2012 & 2014 Biennial Conference Planning
Activities: Implementing accreditation of visual language interpreters; Providing professional development opportunities
Meetings/Conferences: • Association of Visual Language Interpreters of Canada Summer 2016 Biennial Conference: Interpreters & Human Rights, July, 2016, Fredericton Convention Centre, Fredericton, NB
Scope: National
Contact Information: Web Site: www.avlic2016.com; Co-Chair: Becky Schirato, E-mail: chairperson@avlic2016.com
• Association of Visual Language Interpreters of Canada Summer 2018 Biennial Conference, 2018, SK
Scope: National
Publications:
• AVLIC Directory
Type: Directory
Profile: Interpreters in Canada & the United States
• AVLIC News
Type: Newsletter; *Frequency:* 3 pa; *Accepts Advertising*; *Editor:* Miriam West; *Price:* Free with Association of Visual Language Interpreters of Canada membership
Profile: Articles & information about interpreting, plus association activities

Association of Visual Language Interpreters of New Brunswick (AVLI-NB)

324 Duke St. West, Saint John NB E2M 1V2
e-mail: avli_nb@hotmail.com
Overview: A small provincial organization founded in 1998 overseen by Association of Visual Language Interpreters of Canada
Mission: To ensure confidentiality, impartiality, & integrity of visual language interpreters in New Brunswick
Member of: Association of Visual Language Interpreters of Canada (AVLIC)
Affliation(s): Maritime Association of Professional Sign Language Interpreters (MAPSLI)
Membership: *Member Profile:* Visual language interpreters in New Brunswick

Association of Women in Finance (AWF)

#142, 757 West Hastings St., Vancouver BC V6C 1A1
Tel: 604-765-2850
admin@womeninfinance.ca
womeninfinance.ca
www.linkedin.com/company/association-of-women-in-finance
Overview: A small provincial organization founded in 1996
Mission: To promote women in finance-related industries by encouraging their advancement, development & involvement in the business community; to acknowledge accomplished women who have achieved excellence in their field
Chief Officer(s):
Sandra Abley, President & Director, 604-659-7487
Sandra.abley@td.com
Sandra Tetzlaff, Treasurer, 604-731-3798
stetzlaff@heavertetzlaff.com
Finances: *Annual Operating Budget:* Less than $50,000
Staff Member(s): 2
Membership: 106; *Member Profile:* Women in finance industry in B.C.; *Committees:* PEAK Nominations; PEAK Judging
Activities: Monthly networking events; Aug. & Dec. social; Annual PEAK Awards Gala;
Awards:
• Lifetime Achievement Award (Award), PEAK Awards
• Performance & Excellence Award (Award), PEAK Awards
• Knowledge & Leadership Award (Award), PEAK Awards

Association of Women of India in Canada *See* AWIC Community & Social Services

Association of Women's Health, Obstetric & Neonatal Nurses Canada *See* Canadian Association of Perinatal & Women's Health Nurses

Association of Workers' Compensation Boards of Canada (AWCBC) / Association des commissions des accidents du travail du Canada

6551B Mississauga Rd., Mississauga ON L5N 1A6
Tel: 905-542-3633; *Fax:* 905-542-0039
Toll-Free: 855-282-9222
contact@awcbc.org
www.awcbc.org
Overview: A medium-sized national organization founded in 1919
Mission: To facilitate cooperation among Canadian Boards & Commissions; To foster greater public understanding or dialogue about workplace health & safety & workers' compensation
Member of: Canadian Society of Association Executives
Chief Officer(s):
Cheryl Tucker, Executive Director
Membership: 12 provincial & territorial workers' compensation jurisdictions; *Fees:* $400 associate; *Member Profile:* Full - restricted to the 12 Canadian Workers' Compensation Boards & Commissions; associate - offered to any regional, national or international organization having adjudicative or policy-making responsibilities in administration of workers' compensation laws; *Committees:* Financial Comparability; College Advisory; Research; Communications

Association of Yukon Communities (AYC)

#15, 1114 - 1st Ave., Whitehorse YT Y1A 1A3
Tel: 867-668-4388; *Fax:* 867-668-7574
www.ayc-yk.ca
Previous Name: Association of Yukon Municipalities
Overview: A medium-sized provincial organization founded in 1974
Mission: To further the establishment of responsible government at the community level; To provide a united approach to issues affecting local governments; To advance ambitions & goals of member communities by developing a shared common vision of the future; To represent members in matters affecting them & the welfare of their communities; To provide programs & services of common interest & benefit to

members
Affliation(s): Federation of Canadian Municipalities
Chief Officer(s):
John Pattimore, Executive Director
ayced@northwestel.net
Finances: *Funding Sources:* Membership dues; Government
Membership: 52; *Fees:* Schedule available; *Member Profile:* Yukon communities & elected officials; *Committees:* Energy; Municipal Act Review

Association of Yukon Municipalities *See* Association of Yukon Communities

Association ontarienne d'équitation thérapeutique *See* Ontario Therapeutic Riding Association

Association ontarienne d'espéranto *See* Ontaria Esperanto-Asocio

Association ontarienne de gérontologie *See* Ontario Gerontology Association

Association ontarienne de soutien communautaire *See* Ontario Community Support Association

Association ontarienne des chercheurs et chercheuse en éducation *See* Association of Educational Researchers of Ontario

L'Association ontarienne des conseilliers à l'enfance et à la jeunesse *See* Ontario Association of Child & Youth Counsellors

Association ontarienne des ex-parlementaires *See* Ontario Association of Former Parliamentarians

Association ontarienne des services de réhabilitation pour enfants *See* Ontario Association of Children's Rehabilitation Services

Association ontarienne des sociétés de l'aide à l'enfance *See* Ontario Association of Children's Aid Societies

Association ontarienne des Sourd(e)s francophones (AOSF)

3349, ch Navan, Orléans ON K4B 1H9
www.aosf-ontario.ca
www.facebook.com/aosfontario
vimeo.com/aosfontario
Aperçu: *Dimension:* petite; *Envergure:* provinciale; fondée en 1995
Mission: L'AOSF est un organisme sans but lucratif qui favorise le regroupement des personnes franco-ontariennes vivant avec une surdité afin de répondre à leurs besoins et à leurs aspirations. Son but est de permettre à la communauté sourde de s'épanouir et de se développer.
Membre(s) du bureau directeur:
Michael McGuire, Président
mmcguire.aosf@hotmail.com

Association Ontario Danse *See* Dance Ontario Association

Association paritaire pour la santé et la sécurité du travail - Administration provinciale

#10, 1220, boul Lebourgneuf, Québec QC G2K 2G4
Tél: 418-624-4801; *Téléc:* 418-624-4858
apssap@apssap.qc.ca
apssap.qc.ca
Aperçu: *Dimension:* moyenne; *Envergure:* provinciale
Mission: Supporter la prise en charge paritaire de la prévention en matière de santé, de sécurité et d'intégrité physique des personnes du secteur de l'Administration provinciale
Membre(s) du bureau directeur:
Colette Trudel, Directrice générale
ctrudel@apssap.qc.ca
Sylvie Bédard, Technicienne, Administration
sbedard@apssap.qc.ca

Association paritaire pour la santé et la sécurité du travail - Affaires sociales

#950, 5100, rue Sherbrooke Est, Montréal QC H1V 3R9
Tél: 514-253-6871; *Téléc:* 514-253-1443
Ligne sans frais: 800-361-4528
info@asstsas.qc.ca
www.asstsas.qc.ca
ca.linkedin.com/in/asstsas
www.facebook.com/305696879444973
twitter.com/InfosASSTSAS
Aperçu: *Dimension:* moyenne; *Envergure:* provinciale
Mission: Pour promouvoir la santé et la sécurité et à assurer la formation et l'information du public
Membre(s) du bureau directeur:
Diane Parent, Directrice générale
dparent@asstsas.qc.ca
Membre(s) du personnel: 30
Membre: 14 associations;

Association paritaire pour la santé et la sécurité du travail - Habillement *Voir* ASPHME

Association paritaire pour la santé et la sécurité du travail - Imprimerie et activités connexes

#450, 7450, boul Galeries d'Anjou, Anjou QC H1M 3M3
Tél: 514-355-8282; *Téléc:* 514-355-6818
info@aspimprimerie.qc.ca
www.aspimprimerie.qc.ca
Également appelé: ASP Inprimerie
Aperçu: *Dimension:* moyenne; *Envergure:* provinciale; Organisme sans but lucratif; fondée en 1983
Mission: Fournir aux employeurs et aux travailleurs du secteur imprimerie et activités connexes des services d'information, de formation, de conseil et de recherche pour favoriser la prise en charge de la prévention dans les entreprises
Membre(s) du bureau directeur:
Marie Ménard, Directrice générale
mmenard@aspimprimerie.qc.ca
Finances: *Budget de fonctionnement annuel:* $500,000-$1.5 Million
Membre(s) du personnel: 8
Membre: 1-99
Activités: Formations de groupe: Action sur les machines; Évacuation en cas d'incendie; Introduction à la prévention; Superviser avec diligence; Enquête accident; Formateur chariot; Formation de formateurs SIMDUT; *Stagiaires:* Oui; *Bibliothèque* rendez-vous

Association paritaire pour la santé et la sécurité du travail - Produits en métal et électriques

#301, 2271, boul Fernand-Lafontaine, Longueuil QC J4G 2R7
Tél: 450-442-7763; *Téléc:* 450-442-2332
jarsenault@aspme.org
www.aspme.org
Aperçu: *Dimension:* moyenne; *Envergure:* provinciale
Membre(s) du bureau directeur:
Jocelyne Arsenault, Conseillère en gestion
jarsenault@asphme.org
Éric Bélanger, Conseiller technique

Association paritaire pour la santé et la sécurité du travail - Secteur Affaires municipales (APSAM)

#710, 715, rue du Square-Victoria, Montréal QC H2Y 2H7
Tél: 514-849-8373; *Téléc:* 514-849-8873
Ligne sans frais: 800-465-1754
Autres numéros: www.apsam.com/blogue
info@apsam.com
www.apsam.com
www.facebook.com/apsamsst
twitter.com/APSAM
plus.google.com/+apsam
Aperçu: *Dimension:* moyenne; *Envergure:* provinciale; fondée en 1986
Membre(s) du bureau directeur:
Denise Soucy, Directrice générale
dsoucy@apsam.com
Guylaine Chevalier, Agente de bureau, Comptabilité
gchevalier@apsam.com
Steve Langlois, Technicien, Informatique
slanglois@apsam.com
Finances: *Budget de fonctionnement annuel:* $500,000-$1.5 Million
Membre: 100; *Montant de la cotisation:* .13$/100$ de masse salariale
Publications:
• L'APSAM
Type: Revue; *Frequency:* Trimestriel

Association paritaire pour la santé et la sécurité du travail - Textiles primaires *Voir* Préventex - Association paritaire du textile

Association patronale des entreprises en construction du Québec (APECQ)

#6550, ch de la Côte-de-Liesse, 2e étage, Saint-Laurent QC H4T 1E3
Tél: 514-739-2381; *Téléc:* 514-341-1216
Ligne sans frais: 800-371-2381
info@apecq.org
www.apecq.org
www.linkedin.com/groups/APECQ-Association-patronale-entreprises-constr
www.facebook.com/516728745061135
twitter.com/APECQ
www.youtube.com/user/APECQ2002
Aperçu: *Dimension:* moyenne; *Envergure:* provinciale; fondée en 1897
Mission: Défendre et promouvoir les intérêts de ses entreprises membres et de leur offrir des services de qualité pour soutenir le développement de leurs affaires
Membre de: Association des gens d'affaires et professionnels du Québec; Conseil du Patronat; Chambre de Commerce
Membre(s) du bureau directeur:
Linda Marchand, Directrice générale
linda.marchand@apecq.org
Christian Thériault, President
Finances: *Fonds:* Cotisations; commandites
Membre(s) du personnel: 22
Membre: *Montant de la cotisation:* Barème; *Comités:* Activités; Finances; Formation; Interventions politiques; Mutuelle; Rémunération et Ressources humaines; Salle de plans
Activités: Colloques; séminaires; congrès; tournoi de golf; partie d'huîtres

Association pétrolière et gazière du Québec (APGQ) / Quebec Oil and Gas Association (QOGA)

#200, 140, Grande Allée est, Québec QC G1R 5P7
Tél: 418-261-2941
info@apgq-qoga.com
www.apgq-qoga.com
Aperçu: *Dimension:* grande; *Envergure:* provinciale
Mission: L'APGQ a été créée afin d'encourager le dialogue sur le potentiel d'une nouvelle industrie au Québec :
Meetings/Conferences: • Association pétrolière et gazière du Québec 2015 Conférence Annuelle, 2015, QC
Scope: Provincial
Contact Information: conference@apgq-qoga.com

Association Portugaise De L'Ile De L'Ouest *Voir* Associaça Portuguesa do West Island

Association Portugaise De Sainte-Thérèse *Voir* Associaça Portuguesa de Ste-Thérèse

Association Portugaise du Saint-Esprit *Voir* Associaça Portuguesa Espirito Santo

Association pour aînés résidant à Laval (APARL)

#110, 4901, rue St-Joseph, Laval QC H7C 1H6
Tél: 450-661-5252; *Téléc:* 450-661-2497
information@aparl.org
www.aparl.org
Nom précédent: Aide aux personnes âgées en résidence à Laval inc
Aperçu: *Dimension:* petite; *Envergure:* locale; Organisme sans but lucratif; fondée en 1974
Mission: Offir aux aînés l'intégration sociale, les services et les ressources nécessaires qui brisent leur isolement afin de conserver leur autonomie et leur maintien à domicile; favoriser la participation; encourager
Membre de: Table de concertation; Centre local de services communautaires; Corporation de Développement Communautaire
Membre(s) du bureau directeur:
Luc Dominic Massé, Directeur Général
Finances: *Budget de fonctionnement annuel:* $250,000-$500,000
Membre(s) du personnel: 9; 90 bénévole(s)
Membre: 390; *Montant de la cotisation:* 10$; *Critères d'admissibilite:* Ainés actifs et en perte d'autonomie; *Comités:* Journal
Activités: Cours; ateliers; café-causerie; Pignon sur rue; *Stagiaires:* Oui; *Service de conférenciers:* Oui

Association pour l'amélioration des sols et des récoltes de l'Ontario *See* Ontario Soil & Crop Improvement Association

Association pour l'amélioration du sol et des cultures du Nouveau-Brunswick *See* New Brunswick Soil & Crop Improvement Association

Association pour l'asthme et l'allergie alimentaire du Québec *Voir* Asthme et allergies Québec

L'association pour l'avancement des études scandinaves au Canada *See* Association for the Advancement of Scandinavian Studies in Canada

Association pour l'avancement des sciences et des techniques de la documentation (ASTED)

#387, 2065, rue Parthenais, Montréal QC H2K 3T1
Tél: 514-281-5012; *Téléc:* 514-281-8219
info@asted.org
www.asted.org
Aperçu: *Dimension:* moyenne; *Envergure:* provinciale; fondée en 1973
Mission: Promouvoir l'excellence des services documentaires et de leur personnel; inspirer la législation et promouvoir les intérêts des services documentaires et d'information; exercer au sein de la francophonie nord-américaine le leadership documentaire
Membre(s) du bureau directeur:
Jacqueline Labelle, Présidente
Suzanne Morin, Directrice générale
Membre(s) du personnel: 4
Membre: *Montant de la cotisation:* Barème; *Critères d'admissibilite:* Spécialistes et technicien(ne)s oeuvrant dans les centres de documentation, les bibliothèques universitaires, publiques et scolaires tant au Québec qu'au Canada français; *Comités:* Comité des règlements et règles administratives; Comité des résolutions; Comité des élections; Comité des publications; Comité de rédaction de Documentation et bibliothèques; Comité du bulletin Les Nouvelles de l'ASTED; Comité de formation continue; Comité sur le droit d'auteur; Comité sur les normes des bibliothèques publiques; Comité du Fonds de recherche et de développement Hubert-Perron; Comité du Prix Alvine-Bélisle; Comité sur la création d'un OBNL; Comité canadien de catalogage; Comité canadien du MARC; Comité éditorial de la traduction française de la classification décimale Dewey
Activités: Activités de perfectionnement et de formation
Prix, Bouses:
• Bourse Françoise-Jobin (Bourse d études)
Bourse pour les etudiants en techniques de documentation au niveau collegial (CÉGEP)
• Prix d'excellence de l'ASTED (Prix)
Leadership et innovation en gestion de l'information; Bénévole de l'année
Publications:
• Documentation et bibliothèques
Type: Revue; *Frequency:* 4 fois par ans *ISSN:* 0315-2340; *Price:* 65$
Profile: Une des deux plus importantes publications en français concernant les activités reliées à la bibliothéconomie

Association pour l'éducation permanente dans les universités du Canada *See* Canadian Association for University Continuing Education

Association pour l'enseignement de la géographie et de l'environnement en Ontario *See* Ontario Association for Geographic & Environmental Education

Association pour l'enseignement de la science et de la technologie au Québec (AESTQ)

9601, rue Colbert, Anjou QC H1J 1Z9
Tél: 514-948-6422; *Téléc:* 514-948-6423
info@aestq.org
www.aestq.org
Nom précédent: Association des professeurs de sciences de Québec
Aperçu: *Dimension:* moyenne; *Envergure:* provinciale; fondée en 1964
Mission: Avancement de l'enseignement des sciences et des technologies
Membre(s) du bureau directeur:
Pablo Desfossés, Président
Sylvie Tremblay, Administratrice
Finances: *Budget de fonctionnement annuel:* $250,000-$500,000
Membre(s) du personnel: 2; 50 bénévole(s)
Membre: 600+; *Montant de la cotisation:* $65 tarif régulier; $35 tarif étudiant ou personne retraitée

Association pour l'histoire de la science et de la technologie au Canada *See* Canadian Science & Technology Historical Association

Association pour l'intégration communautaire de l'Outaouais (APICO)

405, boul. Maloney E., Gatineau QC J8P 6Z8
Tél: 819-669-6219; *Téléc:* 819-669-7967
apico@bellnet.ca
www.apico.ca
www.facebook.com/403660446331598
twitter.com/APICO1957
Aperçu: *Dimension:* petite; *Envergure:* locale; Organisme sans but lucratif; fondée en 1957
Mission: Faciliter l'intégration sociale et communautaire des personnes ayant une déficience intellectuelle
Affliation(s): Association du Québec pour l'intégration sociale
Membre(s) du bureau directeur:
Stéphane Viau, Directeur général, 819-669-6219 Ext. 212
stephane.viau.apico@bellnet.ca
Membre: 350; *Montant de la cotisation:* 10$ individuel; 15$ famille
Activités: Service de répit (Programmes défis); conférences; boules de Noël; soirées; sorties

Association pour l'intégration sociale - Région Beauce-Sartigan

12625, 1re av, Saint-Georges QC G5Y 2E4
Tél: 418-228-5021
ais.rbs@aisrbs.com
www.aisrbs.com
Également appelé: L'A.I.S. Beauce-Sartigan
Aperçu: *Dimension:* petite; *Envergure:* locale; Organisme sans but lucratif; fondée en 1988
Mission: Promouvoir l'intégration sociale; travailler à la défense des droits des personnes ayant une déficience intellectuelle; soutenir les familles en offrant du répit; informer la population en général et la sensibiliser
Membre de: Regroupement des Associations de personnes handicapées région Chaudière-Appalaches
Affliation(s): Association du Québec pour l'intégration sociale
Membre(s) du bureau directeur:
Valérie Poulin, Directrice générale
direction@aisrbs.com
Membre(s) du personnel: 3
Membre: *Critères d'admissibilite:* Personnes ayant une déficience intellectuelle et/ou un trouble envahissant du développement
Activités: *Evénements de sensibilisation:* La semaine québécoise de la déficience intellectuelle; *Stagiaires:* Oui

Association pour l'intégration sociale (Région de Québec) (AISQ)

5225, av 3e ouest, Charlesbourg QC G1H 6G6
Tél: 418-622-4290; *Téléc:* 418-622-1683
aisq@aisq.org
www.aisq.org
www.facebook.com/aisqc
Aperçu: *Dimension:* petite; *Envergure:* locale; fondée en 1961
Mission: Soutenir et informer les familles de personnes vivant avec une déficience intellectuelle ainsi que les personnes elles-mêmes, et ce, tout en faisant la promotion et la défense de leurs droits.
Membre de: Association canadienne pour l'intégration communautaire; Association du Québec pour l'intégration sociale
Membre(s) du bureau directeur:
Marie Boulanger-Lemieux, Directrice générale
mblemieux@aisq.org
Finances: *Budget de fonctionnement annuel:* $100,000-$250,000; *Fonds:* Principales sources : Centraide et Agence de la Santé et des Services sociaux de la Capitale-Nationale
Membre(s) du personnel: 5; 115 bénévole(s)
Membre: 321; *Montant de la cotisation:* 15 $ / année; *Critères d'admissibilite:* Parents d'un enfant présentant une déficience intellectuelle; professionnels; organismes; amis, frères, soeurs, grands parents; *Comités:* Prents-Soutien; Scolaire; Transition école-vieactive; Travail; Ressources résidentielles; Planifier l'avenir; Fratrie
Activités: Intervention communautaire; Soutien et accompagnement; Ateliers de langage (orthophonie); Ateliers frères-soeurs; Guides et outils de référence; Projet résidentiel APPART'enance; Promotion et campagnes de sensibilisation du grand public; *Evénements de sensibilisation:* Semaine québécoise de la déficiance intellectuelle, mars; *Stagiaires:* Oui; *Bibliothèque:* Centre de documentation; rendez-vous

Association pour l'intégration sociale (Région des Bois-Francs)

#105, 59, rue Monfette, Victoriaville QC G6P 1J8
Tél: 819-758-0574; *Téléc:* 819-758-8270
ais.bf@cdcbf.qc.ca
www.cdcbf.qc.ca
Également appelé: AIS Bois-Francs
Aperçu: *Dimension:* petite; *Envergure:* locale; fondée en 1981
Mission: Aider et soutenir les personnes ayant une déficience intellectuelle afin de leur permettre de vivre comme des citoyens et des citoyennes à part entière et de permettre à leur famille de s'épanouir de façon harmonieuse
Affliation(s): Association du Québec pour l'intégration sociale
Membre(s) du bureau directeur:
Chantal Charest, Directrice Générale
chantal@cdcbf.qc.ca
Francine Tardif, Responsable, Informatique
tactic@cdcbf.qc.ca
Activités: Accompagnement; café-rencontre; camp du jour; club jeunesse; soutien aux familles

Association pour l'intégration sociale (Rouyn-Noranda) inc. (AIS)

1249, av Granada, Rouyn-Noranda QC J9Y 1G8
Tél: 819-797-9587; *Téléc:* 819-797-9553
administration@aisrn.com
www.aisrn.com
Aperçu: *Dimension:* petite; *Envergure:* locale; Organisme sans but lucratif; fondée en 1981
Mission: Promotion des intérêts et défense de droits des personnes vivant avec un handicap; promotion de l'integration sociale, culturelle, scolaire et professionelle; aide, entraide; service aux familles vivant avec une personne handicapée
Membre(s) du bureau directeur:
Mélanie Vachon, Directrice générale
melanievachon@aisrn.com
Membre(s) du personnel: 3
Membre: *Critères d'admissibilite:* Parent d'enfant vivant avec une déficience intellectuelle et/ou physique
Activités: Camp de jour estival pour enfants (5-18 ans) vivant avec une déficience physique et/ou intellectuelle

Association pour l'intégration sociale d'Ottawa (AISO)

235, rue Donald, Ottawa ON K1K 1N1
Tél: 613-744-2241; *Téléc:* 613-744-4898
info@aiso.org
www.aiso.org
Nom précédent: Association pour l'Intégration sociale d'Ottawa-Carleton
Aperçu: *Dimension:* grande; *Envergure:* locale; Organisme sans but lucratif; fondée en 1991
Mission: Favoriser l'autonomie et promouvoir l'intégration de la personne francophone intellectuellement handicapée au sein de la communauté franco-ontarienne d'Ottawa
Membre de: Association pour l'intégration communautaire de l'Ontario; Association canadienne pour l'intégration communautaire
Membre(s) du bureau directeur:
Patricia Dostie, Directrice générale
pdostie@aiso.org
Suzanne Rydzik, Présidente
Maryse Bermingham, Vice-présidente
Finances: *Budget de fonctionnement annuel:* $3 Million-$5 Million; *Fonds:* Centraide; Fondation Trillium
Membre(s) du personnel: 95; 10 bénévole(s)
Membre: 130; *Montant de la cotisation:* $10; *Critères d'admissibilite:* Familles, partenaires, intervenants; *Comités:* Exécutif; Finance
Activités: Tournoi de golf; expositions d'oeuvres d'art; *Service de conférenciers:* Oui

Association pour l'intégration sociale d'Ottawa-Carleton *Voir* Association pour l'intégration sociale d'Ottawa

Association pour la coordination des fréquences *See* Frequency Co-ordination System Association

Association pour la littérature, l'environnement et la culture au Canada *See* Association for Literature, Environment, & Culture in Canada

Association pour la microbiologie médicale et l'infectiologie Canada *See* Association of Medical Microbiology & Infectious Disease Canada

Association pour la prévention de la contamination de l'air et du sol (APCAS) / Air Waste Management Association - Québec Section

CP 49527, 5122, Côte des Neiges, Montréal QC H3T 2A5

Tél: 514-355-2675; *Téléc:* 514-355-4159
apcas@apcas.qc.ca
www.apcas.qc.ca
www.linkedin.com/groups/APCAS-Association-prévention-contamination-lai
Aperçu: *Dimension:* petite; *Envergure:* provinciale
Mission: Pour informer et d'éduquer dans les domaines de la gestion des déchets et l'assainissement de l'air, ainsi que de créer des occasions de réseautage pour ses membres
Membre(s) du bureau directeur:
Pierre Carabin, Président
Finances: *Budget de fonctionnement annuel:* Moins de $50,000
10 bénévole(s)
Membre: 100; *Montant de la cotisation:* 50$

Association pour la prévention des infections à l'hôpital et dans la communauté - Canada ***See*** Community & Hospital Infection Control Association Canada

Association pour la promotion des droits des personnes handicapées

CP 814, 2435, rue Saint-Jean-Bâptiste, Jonquière QC G7X 7W6
Tél: 418-548-5832; *Téléc:* 418-548-5291
apdph@videotron.ca
Aperçu: *Dimension:* petite; *Envergure:* locale; Organisme sans but lucratif; fondée en 1972
Mission: Trouver des solutions et des moyens aux problèmes rencontrés relatifs à la santé, à l'éducation, aux loisirs et à l'intégration sociale des personnes handicapées; sensibiliser la population; informer et assister les parents et les personnes handicapées et offrir des activités de loisirs adaptés aux besoins des personnes handicapées
Affiliation(s): Association du Québec pour l'intégration sociale
Membre(s) du bureau directeur:
Geneviève Siméon, Directrice générale
Finances: *Budget de fonctionnement annuel:* $100,000-$250,000
Membre: 100-499; *Montant de la cotisation:* 75$; *Critères d'admissibilite:* Personne handicapée
Activités: Diverses activités récréatives et sociocommunautaires; arts plastiques; terrain de jeux; chorale; danse; discothèque; ligue de quilles

Association pour la promotion des services documentaires scolaires (APSDS)

#5, 7870, rue Madeleine-Huguenin, Montréal QC H1L 6M7
Tél: 514-588-9400
apsds@bibliothequesscolaires.qc.ca
apsds.org
facebook.com/APSDS.QC
twitter.com/apsds_
Aperçu: *Dimension:* moyenne; *Envergure:* provinciale; fondée en 1989
Mission: APSDS est une association professionnelle qui contribue au développement des services documentaires dans les commissions scolaires du Québec, dans les écoles primaires et secondaires, publiques et privées, et qui en assure la promotion.
Membre(s) du bureau directeur:
Marie-Hélène Charest, Présidente
pres@aspds.org

Association pour la protection automobile ***See*** Automobile Protection Association

Association pour la protection des intérêts des consommateurs de la Côte-Nord

872, rue de Puyjalon St., 2e étage, Baie-Comeau QC G5C 1N1
Tél: 418-589-7324; *Téléc:* 418-589-7088
apic@globetrotter.net
Également appelé: APIC Côte-Nord
Aperçu: *Dimension:* petite; *Envergure:* locale; Organisme sans but lucratif; fondée en 1978
Mission: Promouvoir les intérêts des consommateurs dans tous les aspects de la consommation; grouper les consommateurs de la région Côte-Nord
Membre de: Coalition des associations de consommateurs du Québec
Membre(s) du bureau directeur:
Colette Savard, Responsable
Finances: *Budget de fonctionnement annuel:* $50,000-$100,000
Membre(s) du personnel: 2; 12 bénévole(s)
Membre: 1199; *Montant de la cotisation:* 5$ individu
Activités: Aide de planification budgétaire; ateliers; centre de documentation; traitement des plaintes; informations; *Bibliothèque*

Association pour la recherche au collégial (ARC)

a/s Cégep du Vieux Montréal, #A7.76, 255, rue Ontario Est, Montréal QC H2X 1X6
Tél: 514-843-8491; *Téléc:* 514-982-3448
arc@cvm.qc.ca
vega.cvm.qc.ca/arc
Aperçu: *Dimension:* petite; *Envergure:* provinciale; fondée en 1988
Mission: Promouvoir le développement de la recherche au collegial
Membre(s) du bureau directeur:
Lynn Lapostolle, Directice générale
Membre(s) du personnel: 7
Activités: Belle Rencontres; colloques; remise de prix

Association pour la santé environnementale du Québec (ASEQ) / Environmental Health Association of Québec (EHA Québec)

CP 364, Saint-Sauveur QC J0R 1R0
Tél: 450-240-5700; *Téléc:* 450-227-9648
office@aseq-ehaq.ca
www.aeha-quebec.ca
www.facebook.com/184591904921401
twitter.com/aseq_ehaq
www.youtube.com/channel/UCEya4qkkW0xkPoxpxzLUIVQ
Aperçu: *Dimension:* petite; *Envergure:* locale
Mission: La mission de l'ASEQ est la protection de l'environnement et la santé humaine au plan individuel et collectif en sensibilisant, soutenant et éduquant la population en regard les produits toxiques et les pesticides. Numéro d'enregistrement d'organisme de bienfaisance: BN 810116624RR0001.
Affiliation(s): EHA Nova Scotia; EHA Ontario; EHA Alberta; EHA BC
Membre(s) du bureau directeur:
Rohini Peris, Président
Membre: *Montant de la cotisation:* $5

Association pour la santé publique de l'Ontario ***See*** Ontario Public Health Association

Association pour la santé publique du Québec (ASPQ) / Québec Public Health Association

#102, 4529, rue Clark, Montréal QC H2T 2T3
Tél: 514-528-5811; *Téléc:* 514-528-5590
info@aspq.org
www.aspq.org
fr-ca.facebook.com/AssociationPourLaSantePubliqueDuQuebec
aspq
twitter.com/ASPQuebec
Aperçu: *Dimension:* moyenne; *Envergure:* provinciale; Organisme sans but lucratif; fondée en 1943 surveillé par Canadian Public Health Association
Mission: Favoriser un regard critique sur les enjeux de santé publique au Québec en constituant un regroupement volontaire, autonome, multidisciplinaire et multisectoriel de personnes et d'organisations provenant des milieux tant institutionnels et professionnels que communautaires. L'Association constitue un forum qui offre un espace à ses membres pour développer des prises de position communes ou concertées, appuyer des politiques favorables à la santé et au bien-être et développer des coalitions et des projets en collaboration avec d'autres partenaires de santé publique ou du milieu.
Membre(s) du bureau directeur:
Lucie Granger, Directrice Générale, 514-528-5811 Ext. 225
Lilianne Bertrand, Présidente
Membre(s) du personnel: 17
Membre: 36 membres institutionnels; 172 membres individuels; *Montant de la cotisation:* 46$ pour un an; *Comités:* Finances, comptabilité et vérification; Gouvernance et mise en candidature; Vie associative; Ressources humaines; Appréciation de la contribution de la DG
Prix, Bouses:
- Prix Jean-Pierre Bélanger (Prix)

Association pour la sécurité des bébés et des tout petits ***See*** Infant & Toddler Safety Association

Association pour le commerce des produits biologiques ***See*** Canada Organic Trade Association

Association pour le développement de la personne handicapée intellectuelle du Saguenay (ADHIS)

766, rue du Cénacle, Chicoutimi QC G7H 2J2
Tél: 418-543-0093; *Téléc:* 866-896-0820
adhis@bellnet.ca
www.adhis.ca
Aperçu: *Dimension:* petite; *Envergure:* locale; fondée en 1976
Mission: Travailler à la défense des droits des personnes vivant avec une déficience intellectuelle, apporter du support aux parents et voir à l'amélioration de la qualité de vie des personnes
Affiliation(s): Association du Québec pour l'intégration sociale
Membre(s) du bureau directeur:
Sylvie Jean, Directrice générale
Membre(s) du personnel: 20
Membre: *Montant de la cotisation:* 5$ régulier; 10$ soutien/famille; *Critères d'admissibilite:* Parent, personne handicapée; ami
Activités: Brunch annuel, semaine québécoise de la déficience intellectuelle; loisirs samedi; intégration en terrain de jeux; sensibilisation dans les écoles; camps; discothèque

Association pour les applications pédagogiques de l'ordinateur au postsecondaire (APOP)

1660, boul de l'Entente, Québec QC G1S 4S3
Tél: 418-688-8310
info@apop.qc.ca
apop.qc.ca
Aperçu: *Dimension:* moyenne; *Envergure:* provinciale
Mission: Regroupe des professeurs, des professionnels et des cadres des collèges du Québec qui s'intéressent à l'utilisation pédagogique des nouvelles technologies et de l'ordinateur
Membre(s) du bureau directeur:
Hélène Martineau, Coordonnatrice
Finances: *Budget de fonctionnement annuel:* Moins de $50,000
Membre(s) du personnel: 1; 100 bénévole(s)
Membre: 500; *Montant de la cotisation:* 20$
Activités: *Service de conférenciers:* Oui

Association pour les droits des non-fumeurs ***See*** Non-Smokers' Rights Association

Association pour les neurinomes acoustiques du Canada ***See*** Acoustic Neuroma Association of Canada

L'Association professionnelle des agents du service extérieur (ind.) ***See*** Professional Association of Foreign Service Officers (Ind.)

L'Association professionnelle des cadres de la fonction publique du Canada ***See*** Association of Professional Executives of the Public Service of Canada

Association professionnelle des designers d'intérieur du Québec (APDIQ)

#101, 465, rue Saint-Jean, Montréal QC H2Y 2R6
Tél: 514-284-6263
www.apdiq.com
Nom précédent: Société des designers d'intérieurs du Québec
Aperçu: *Dimension:* moyenne; *Envergure:* provinciale; Organisme sans but lucratif; fondée en 1935 surveillé par Interior Designers of Canada
Mission: Promouvoir la reconnaissance des designers d'intérieur comme ordre professionnel; assurer la qualité de leurs services; les regrouper pour faire évoluer leur profession; veiller aux intérêts du public; édicter et assurer le respect des règles d'éthique professionnelle
Membre(s) du bureau directeur:
André Lapointe, Président
Finances: *Budget de fonctionnement annuel:* $100,000-$250,000
Membre(s) du personnel: 3
Membre: 700; *Montant de la cotisation:* Barème; *Critères d'admissibilite:* Designer d'interieur
Activités: *Listes de destinataires:* Oui

Association professionnelle des écrivains de la Sagamie-Côte-Nord (APES)

#304, 240, rue Bossé, Chicoutimi QC G7J 1L9
Tél: 418-698-1176
apescn@hotmail.com
www.apescn.org
Aperçu: *Dimension:* petite; *Envergure:* provinciale; Organisme sans but lucratif; fondée en 1994
Mission: L'association se consacre: à la création individuelle et collective (publication de textes dans des recueils et organes de communications régionaux); au développement d'échanges créateurs avec les membres des autres communautés artistiques au Saguenay-Lac Saint-Jean et dans d'autres régions du Québec; au développement de l'intérêt du public pour l'écriture et pour la lecture; à la promotion et à la diffusion des ouvrages de ses membres; à la défense des intérêts socio-économiques et moraux de ses membres; à la représentation de ses membres auprès des pouvoirs publics

Membre(s) du bureau directeur:
Yvon Paré, Président
Membre: 29
Activités: *Bibliothèque:* Centre de documentation

Association professionnelle des enseignantes et enseignants en commerce (APEC)

a/s Stéphanie Dubois, 1455, boul Casavant Est, Saint-Hyacinthe QC J2S 8S8
www.profapec.com
www.facebook.com/apec.commerce
Nom précédent: Association provinciale de l'enseignement commercial
Aperçu: *Dimension:* petite; *Envergure:* provinciale; Organisme sans but lucratif; fondée en 1970
Mission: Informer le milieu enseignant en Administration Commerce et informatique de tout ce qui se fait, se dit sur les programmes de notre secteur, surtout les aspects pédagogiques de notre métier; être agent de liaison entre les enseignants de la Province
Membre de: Conseil pédagogique interdisciplinaire du Québec (CPIQ)
Membre(s) du bureau directeur:
Stéphanie Dubois, Présidente
stephanie.dubois@epsh.qc.ca

Association professionnelle des informaticiens et informaticiennes du Québec (APIIQ)

#17, 3107, av des Hôtels, Sainte-Foy QC G1W 4W5
Tél: 418-659-1216; *Téléc:* 418-659-3317
Ligne sans frais: 800-897-1216
apiiq@apiiq.qc.ca
www.apiiq.qc.ca
Aperçu: *Dimension:* moyenne; *Envergure:* provinciale; Organisme sans but lucratif; fondée en 1986
Mission: Établir les critères d'excellence et les règles d'éthique pour les professionnel(le)s de l'informatique afin d'assurer à la société des services efficaces, sécuritaires et de qualité
Membre(s) du bureau directeur:
Alexandre Lalancette, Président
Finances: *Budget de fonctionnement annuel:* $50,000-$100,000
Membre(s) du personnel: 1; 7 bénévole(s)
Membre: 400; *Montant de la cotisation:* 130$ régulier; 20$ étudiant; *Critères d'admissibilite:* Diplôme en informatique universitaire

Association professionnelle des ingénieurs du gouvernement du Québec (ind.) (APIGQ) / Association of Professional Engineers of the Government of Québec (Ind.)

Complexe Iberville Trois, #218, 2960, boul. Laurier, Québec QC G1V 4S1
Tél: 418-683-3633; *Téléc:* 418-683-6878
info@apigq.qc.ca
www.apigq.qc.ca
Aperçu: *Dimension:* moyenne; *Envergure:* provinciale; fondée en 1986
Mission: Pour représenter les intérêts de leurs membres
Membre(s) du bureau directeur:
Michel Gagnon, Président
Membre: 10 sections; *Critères d'admissibilite:* Ingénieur; *Comités:* Exécutif; Surveillance; Classification; Ministériel des relations professionnelles; Négociation; Organisateur du Colloque des ingénieurs de l'État; Équité salariale; Assurances; Déontologie et du champ de pratique exclusif; Griefs; Révision des griefs; Statuts et réglements; Stratégie, d'action et d'information; Suffrage universel

Association professionnelle des inhalothérapeutes du Québec (ind.) / Professional Association of Inhalation Therapists of Québec (Ind.)

#201, 4101, rue Molson, Montréal QC H1Y 3L1
Tél: 514-251-8050; *Téléc:* 514-259-8084
Aperçu: *Dimension:* moyenne; *Envergure:* provinciale
Mission: négocier une convention collective adaptée aux besions des membres; voir à l'application de la convention collective; défendre et promouvoir les intérêts sociaux économiques des membres; améliorer les conditions de travail des membres; faciliter des relations de travail harmonieuses au niveau local grâce à la tenue de comités de relations professionnelles (CRP); adapter les conditions de travail des membres au vécu et aux impératifs du milieu; promourvoir une vie syndicale active.
Membre: 1 890

Association professionnelle des internes et résidents de la Saskatchewan (ind.) *See* Professional Association of Interns & Residents of Saskatchewan

Association professionnelle des internes et résidents de Terre-Neuve *See* Professional Association of Internes & Residents of Newfoundland

Association professionnelle des pharmaciens salariés du Québec (APPSQ)

3560, rue la Verendrye, Sherbrooke QC J1L 1Z6
Tél: 819-563-6464; *Téléc:* 819-563-6464
Ligne sans frais: 877-565-6464
appsq@hotmail.com
Aperçu: *Dimension:* moyenne; *Envergure:* provinciale
Mission: De defendre des intérêts des pharmaciens salariés du Québec

Association professionnelle des résidents de l'Alberta *See* Professional Association of Residents of Alberta

Association professionnelle des résidents de la Colombie-Britannique *See* Professional Association of Residents of British Columbia

Association professionnelle des résidents des provinces maritimes *See* Professional Association of Residents in the Maritime Provinces

Association professionnelle des résidents et internes du Manitoba *See* Professional Association of Residents & Interns of Manitoba

Association professionnelle des techniciennes et techniciens en documentation du Québec (APTDQ)

594, rue des Érables, Québec QC G0A 2R0
Tél: 418-909-0608; *Téléc:* 418-909-0608
info@aptdq.org
www.aptdq.org
www.facebook.com/aptdq
twitter.com/aptdq
Nom précédent: Association professionnelle des techniciens en documentation du Québec
Aperçu: *Dimension:* moyenne; *Envergure:* provinciale; Organisme sans but lucratif; fondée en 1988
Mission: Regrouper les techniciens en documentation; promouvoir auprès des employeurs le caractère professionnel de ce travail; défendre les intérêts de ses membres auprès des employeurs et de l'État; fournir des services de toute nature en relation avec les buts de l'association; favoriser le développement de la profession; développer les échanges entre professionnels
Membre(s) du bureau directeur:
Cynthia St-Pierre, Présidente
Danielle Gilbert, Vice-Présidente
Membre(s) du personnel: 1
Membre: 200; *Montant de la cotisation:* 25-65; *Critères d'admissibilite:* Technicien/technicienne en documentation du Québec; *Comités:* Congrès; formation et perfectionnement; publications; recrutement; régionales; aide à l'emploi
Activités: Formation; service d'aide à l'emploi
Prix, Bouses:
• Prix Manon-Bourget (Prix)
Avoir contribué de façon exceptionnelle au prestige de la profession

Association professionnelle des techniciens en documentation du Québec *Voir* Association professionnelle des techniciennes et techniciens en documentation du Québec

Association professionnelle des technologistes médicaux du Québec (ind.) / Québec Professional Association of Medical Technologists (Ind.)

1595, rue St-Hubert, 3e étage, Montréal QC H2L 3Z2
Tél: 514-524-3734; *Téléc:* 514-524-7863
Aperçu: *Dimension:* moyenne; *Envergure:* provinciale; Organisme sans but lucratif; fondée en 1955
Mission: L'étude, la sauvegarde et le développement des intérêts économiques, sociaux, moraux, éducatifs et professionnels de ses membres et particulièrement la négotiation et l'application de la convention collective
Membre(s) du personnel: 14
Membre: 4 341 individus; 1 section locale
Activités: *Service de conférenciers:* Oui; *Bibliothèque* rendez-vous

Association provinciale de l'enseignement commercial *Voir* Association professionnelle des enseignantes et enseignants en commerce

Association provinciale des constructeurs d'habitations du Québec inc. (APCHQ) / Provincial Association of Home Builders of Québec

5930, boul Louis-H.-Lafontaine, Anjou QC H1M 1S7
Tél: 514-353-9960; *Téléc:* 514-353-4825
Ligne sans frais: 800-468-8160
www.apchq.com
www.linkedin.com/company/apchq/
www.facebook.com/apchq
twitter.com/APCHQ
www.youtube.com/APCHQinc/
Aperçu: *Dimension:* moyenne; *Envergure:* provinciale; fondée en 1961
Mission: Depuis 1997, l'APCHQ est la plus importante gestionnaire de mutuelles de prévention du domaine de la construction. Étant le seul agent négociateur patronal des relations de travail dans le secteur résidentiel, elle défend les intérêts de quelque 12 000 employeurs et 25 000 travailleurs
Membre(s) du bureau directeur:
Marc Savard, Directeur général
nsavard@apchqmontreal.ca
Frédéric Birtz, Directeur des opérations
fbirtz@apchqmontreal.ca
Membre: 3 600

Abitibi-Témiscamingue
5930, boul Louis-H.-Lafontaine, Montréal QC H1M 1S7
Tél: 514-353-9960; *Téléc:* 514-353-4825
Ligne sans frais: 800-468-8160
www.apchq.com

Beauce-Appalaches
505, 90e rue, Saint-Georges QC G5Y 3L1
Tél: 418-228-8393; *Téléc:* 418-227-8000
www.apchq.com/beauceappalaches
Membre(s) du bureau directeur:
Maxime Tanguay, Directeur général
mtanguay@apchq-ba.com

Bois-Francs
CP 737, Victoriaville QC G6P 7W7
Tél: 819-758-5741; *Téléc:* 819-758-6007
apchq@apchqboisfrancs.com
www.apchq.com/boisfrancs
www.facebook.com/apchq.boisfrancs
Mission: Adresse civique: #200, 1097, rue Notre-Dame Ouest, Victoriaville
Membre(s) du bureau directeur:
Robert Jutras, Directeur général régional

Centre du Quebec
1051, boul St-Joseph, Drummondville QC J2C 2C4
Tél: 819-477-3638; *Téléc:* 819-477-1711
Ligne sans frais: 888-771-1155
apchq.cdq@cgocable.ca
www.apchq.com/centreduquebec
Membre(s) du bureau directeur:
Denis Sauvageau, Directeur général

Côte-Nord
5930, boul Louis-H.-Lafontaine, Montréal QC H1M 1S7
Tél: 514-353-9960; *Téléc:* 514-353-4825
Ligne sans frais: 800-468-8160
www.apchq.com

Est-du-Quebec
243, rue Saint-Germain Est, Rimouski QC G5L 1B6
Tél: 418-722-6622; *Téléc:* 418-725-4362
Ligne sans frais: 800-463-9004
apchq@apchqestduquebec.com
www.apchq.com/estduquebec
Membre(s) du bureau directeur:
Alain Bernier, Directeur général

Estrie
#300, 100, rue Belvédère Sud, Sherbrooke QC J1H 4B5
Tél: 819-563-9643; *Téléc:* 819-563-0000
Ligne sans frais: 888-563-9335
apchq@apchq-estrie.com
www.apchq.com/estrie
www.facebook.com/ApchqEstrie
Membre(s) du bureau directeur:
Sylvain Mathieu, Directeur général
smathieu@apchq-estrie.com

Haute-Yamaska
1380, rue Denison ouest, Saint-Alphonse de Granby QC J0E 2A0
Tél: 450-777-3177; *Téléc:* 450-777-8399
Ligne sans frais: 800-989-3177
info@apchqhauteyamaska.com
www.apchq.com/hauteyamaska

Membre(s) du bureau directeur:
Édith Rivard, Directrice générale
Mauricie-Lanaudière
Centre de services Mauricie, 4800, rue Raymond-Bellemare, Trois-Rivières QC G9B 0G3
Tél: 819-376-5634; *Téléc:* 819-376-5445
Ligne sans frais: 877-376-5634
apchq@apchqmauricielanaudiere.com
www.apchq.com/mauricie
Membre(s) du bureau directeur:
Maxime Rodrigue, Directeur général
mrodrigue@apchq-ml.com
Montérégie-Suroît
#200, 21, boul de la Cité-des-Jeunes Est, Vaudreuil-Dorion QC J7V 0N3
Tél: 450-371-1363; *Téléc:* 450-510-3003
info@apchqmonteregie-suroit.com
www.apchq.com
Membre(s) du bureau directeur:
Nathalie Brière, Directrice générale
nbriere@apchqmonteregie-suroit.com
Montréal métropolitain
5800, boul Louis-H.-Lafontaine, Anjou QC H1M 1S7
Tél: 514-354-8722; *Téléc:* 514-355-7777
Ligne sans frais: 877-354-8722
info@apchqmontreal.ca
www.apchq.com/montreal
www.facebook.com/APCHQMtlMetro
twitter.com/apchqmm
Membre(s) du bureau directeur:
Marc Savard, Directeur général
msavard@apchqmontreal.ca
Outaouais
149, ch de la Savane, Gatineau QC J8T 5C1
Tél: 819-561-7000; *Téléc:* 819-561-0186
Ligne sans frais: 800-561-7001
www.apchq.com/outaouais
www.facebook.com/pages/APCHQ-OUTAOUAIS/143106429090222
twitter.com/APCHQOutaouais
Membre(s) du bureau directeur:
Benoît Mottard, Directeur général régional
bmottard@apchqoutaouais.com
Québec
1720, boul Père-Lelièvre, Québec QC G1M 3J6
Tél: 418-682-3353; *Téléc:* 418-682-3851
Ligne sans frais: 877-775-3353
apchqquebec@apchqquebec.ca
www.apchq.com/quebec
Membre(s) du bureau directeur:
Martine Savard, Directrice générale
Saguenay
1479, boul Saint-Paul, Chicoutimi QC G7J 3Y3
Tél: 418-549-8046; *Téléc:* 418-549-3409
apchq.sag@bellnet.ca
www.apchq.com
Membre(s) du bureau directeur:
Marie-Josée Bouchard, Directrice générale

Association provinciale des enseignantes et enseignants du Québec (APEQ) / Québec Provincial Association of Teachers (QPAT)

#1, 17035, boul Brunswick, Kirkland QC H9H 5G6
Tél: 514-694-9777; *Téléc:* 514-694-0189
Ligne sans frais: 800-361-9870
reception@qpat-apeq.qc.ca
www.qpat-apeq.qc.ca
www.facebook.com/pages/Kirkland-QC/QPATAPEQ/243536577025
Aperçu: *Dimension:* moyenne; *Envergure:* provinciale surveillé par Canadian Teachers' Federation
Membre(s) du bureau directeur:
Richard Goldfinch, Executive Director
Membre: *Comités:* Adult Education; Finance & Budget; Human Rights & Social Justice; Membership Plans; New Teachers; Nominations; Vocational Education
Meetings/Conferences: • Association provinciale des enseignantes et enseignants du Québec Congrès Annuel 2015, 2015, QC
Scope: Provincial

Association provinciale des parents fransaskois *Voir* Association des parents fransaskois

Association Provinciale des Professeurs d'Immersion et du Programme Francophone (APPIPF) / Provincial French Immersion & Francophone Programme Teachers' Association

a/s Conseil scolaire de Coquitlam, 1100, av Winslow, Coquitlam BC V3J 2G3
Tél: 604-937-6392; *Téléc:* 604-936-6129
Nom précédent: Association provinciale des professeurs de l'immersion et du program-cadre BC
Aperçu: *Dimension:* petite; *Envergure:* provinciale
Mission: Promouvoir et améliorer tous les aspects de l'enseignement au programme d'immersion et au programme francophone.
Membre de: BC Teachers' Federation
Membre(s) du bureau directeur:
Sophie Bergeron, Présidente
sbergeron@sd43.bc.ca

Association provinciale des professeurs de l'immersion et du program-cadre BC *Voir* Association Provinciale des Professeurs d'Immersion et du Programme Francophone

Association pulmonaire du Canada *See* Canadian Lung Association

Association pulmonaire du Nouveau-Brunswick *See* New Brunswick Lung Association

Association pulmonaire du Québec *See* Québec Lung Association

Association Québec Snowboard (AQS) / Québec Snowboard Association

4545, av Pierre-de Coubertin, Montréal QC H1V 0B2
Tél: 581-995-0615
quebecsnowboard.ca
www.facebook.com/AssociationQuebecSnowboard
twitter.com/aqsnowboard
Aperçu: *Dimension:* petite; *Envergure:* provinciale surveillé par Canadian Snowboard Federation
Membre de: Canadian Snowboard Federation
Membre(s) du bureau directeur:
Patrick Lussier, Président

Association Québec-France (AQF)

Maison Fornel, 9, Place Royale, Québec QC G1K 4G2
Tél: 418-643-1616; *Téléc:* 418-643-3053
Ligne sans frais: 877-236-5856
www.quebecfrance.qc.ca
www.facebook.com/369206759890
twitter.com/Quebec_France
www.youtube.com/user/Quebecfrance
Également appelé: Québec-France
Aperçu: *Dimension:* moyenne; *Envergure:* internationale; fondée en 1971
Mission: Faire connaître, comprendre et apprécier la France aux Québécois et le Québec en France; participer au développement de l'amitié et de la coopération entre les deux principales communautés francophones du monde
Affiliation(s): Association France-Québec
Membre(s) du bureau directeur:
Pierre Provost, Président
pierreprovost@hotmail.com
Finances: *Budget de fonctionnement annuel:* $250,000-$500,000
Membre(s) du personnel: 5
Membre: 3 500; *Montant de la cotisation:* 10$ membre de 18 à 25 ans; 30$ membre individuel; 40$ couple/famille; 60$ organisation; 100$ membre bienfaiteur
Activités: *Stagiaires:* Oui; *Bibliothèque* Bibliothèque publique

Association québécoise d'aviron (AQA)

CP 1000, Succ. M, 4545, av Pierre-de Coubertin, Montréal QC H1V 3R2
Tél: 514-252-3191
info@avironquebec.ca
www.avironquebec.ca
Aperçu: *Dimension:* moyenne; *Envergure:* nationale; fondée en 1981 surveillé par Rowing Canada Aviron
Membre de: Rowing Canada Aviron
Membre(s) du bureau directeur:
Daniel Aucoin, Président

Association québécoise d'établissements de santé et de services sociaux (AQESSS) (AQESS) / Québec Hospital Association

#400, 505, boul de Maisonneuve Ouest, Montréal QC H3A 3C2
Tél: 514-842-4861; *Téléc:* 514-282-4271
Ligne sans frais: 800-361-4661
www.aqesss.qc.ca
twitter.com/aqesss
Aperçu: *Dimension:* moyenne; *Envergure:* provinciale; Organisme sans but lucratif; fondée en 1963 surveillé par Canadian Healthcare Association
Mission: Représenter et promouvoir les intérêts de ses membres et leur fournir des services qui répondent à leurs besoins
Membre de: Canadian Society of Association Executives
Membre(s) du bureau directeur:
Diane Lavallée, Directrice générale
diane.lavallee@aqesss.qc.ca
Membre(s) du personnel: 96
Membre: 125; *Critères d'admissibilité:* Établissements offrant des services et des soins médicaux, infirmiers, pharmaceutiques, psychosociaux et de réadaptation; *Comités:* Exécutif; Vérification et de gestion des risques; Pérennité et le financement du système de santé; Gouvernance; Vieillissement; Ressources humaines; Qualité et la performance
Activités: *Bibliothèque:* Centre de documentation

Association québécoise d'information scolaire et professionnelle (AQISEP)

801, rue des Agates, Québec QC G2L 2N4
Tél: 418-847-1781; *Téléc:* 418-634-0566
aqisep@bellnet.ca
www.aqisep.qc.ca
Aperçu: *Dimension:* petite; *Envergure:* provinciale; fondée en 1963
Mission: Offrir aux membres un service d'information, de soutien et d'accompagnement dans leurs interventions professionnelles; assurer le développement continu de leurs compétences; développer et promouvoir l'information scolaire et professionnelle
Membre(s) du bureau directeur:
Gaston Leclerc, Président
Membre: *Montant de la cotisation:* Barème; *Critères d'admissibilité:* Professionnels des réseaux de l'éducation et de la main-d'oeuvre

Association québécoise d'interprétation du patrimoine (AQIP)

CP 11003, Succ. Le Plateau, Gatineau QC J9A 0B6
Tél: 819-595-2190
aqip@aqip.ca
www.aqip.ca
Aperçu: *Dimension:* moyenne; *Envergure:* provinciale; Organisme sans but lucratif; fondée en 1977
Mission: Stimuler la communication entre les individus et les organismes intéressés à l'interprétation du patrimoine naturel, culturel, historique et industriel; promouvoir l'interprétation du patrimoine québécois auprès des gouvernements, des organismes, des médias et du public en général; stimuler l'acquisition de connaissances et la recherche liée à l'interprétation du patrimoine
Membre(s) du bureau directeur:
Denis Lavoie, Président
Finances: *Budget de fonctionnement annuel:* Moins de $50,000
Membre: 150; *Montant de la cotisation:* 10$ étudiant; 35$ individuel; 100$ affilié
Activités: Séminaire de formation et de perfectionnement; congrès thématique
Prix, Bouses:
• Prix du mérite en interprétation du patrimoine (Prix)

Association québécoise d'urbanisme (AQU)

CP 27, Montréal QC H3C 1C5
Tél: 514-277-0228; *Téléc:* 514-277-0093
info@aqu.qc.ca
www.aqu.qc.ca
Aperçu: *Dimension:* petite; *Envergure:* provinciale; Organisme sans but lucratif; fondée en 1978
Mission: La promotion de l'urbanisme et de l'aménagement du territoire
Membre(s) du bureau directeur:
Pierre Dauphinais, Président
Finances: *Budget de fonctionnement annuel:* Moins de $50,000
Membre(s) du personnel: 1; 1 bénévole(s)
Membre: 700; *Montant de la cotisation:* 35$ étudiant; 100$ individuel; 370$ collectif

Association québécoise de canoë-kayak de vitesse (AQCKV)

4545, av Pierre-de-Coubertin, Montréal QC H1V 0B2

Tél: 514-252-3086
canoekayakquebec.com
www.facebook.com/100275890167157
Également appelé: Canoë Kayak Québec
Aperçu: *Dimension:* moyenne; *Envergure:* provinciale; Organisme sans but lucratif; fondée en 1979 surveillé par CanoeKayak Canada
Mission: Promouvoir les activités de canoë-kayak de vitesse au Québec
Membre de: CanoeKayak Canada
Membre(s) du bureau directeur:
Jean-François Meunier, Président
jfmeunier@jfactory.net
Jean-Guy Lahie, Directeur technique
jg.lahaie@canoekayakquebec.com
Finances: *Budget de fonctionnement annuel:* $50,000-$100,000
Membre: 2 000; *Montant de la cotisation:* 600$
Activités: *Stagiaires:* Oui; *Bibliothèque* rendez-vous

Association Québécoise de chirurgie
#3000, 2, Complexe Desjardins, Montréal QC H5B 1G8
Tél: 514-350-5107; *Téléc:* 514-350-5157
aqc-dpc@fmsq.org
www.chirurgiequebec.ca
Nom précédent: Association des chirurgiens généraux du Québec
Aperçu: *Dimension:* moyenne; *Envergure:* provinciale surveillé par Fédération des médecins spécialistes du Québec
Mission: Objectifs sont la protection et défense des intérêts professionnels collectifs des chirurgiens et l'enseignement chirurgical continu
Membre(s) du bureau directeur:
Richard Ratelle, Président
Membre(s) du personnel: 1

Association québécoise de commercialisation de poissons et de fruits de mer (AQCMER) / Quebec Fish and Seafood Marketing Association
CP 43050, 1859, boul René-Laennec, Laval QC H7M 6A1
Tél: 450-973-3388; *Téléc:* 450-973-3381
info@aqcmer.org
www.aqcmer.com
Aperçu: *Dimension:* petite; *Envergure:* provinciale; Organisme sans but lucratif; fondée en 1989
Mission: Promouvoir et accroître la commercialisation des poissons et fruits de mer tout en maintenant des liens étroits avec les différentes associations de l'industrie des pêches, de l'aquaculture en eau douce et de la mariculture
Membre de: Réseau Pêches du Québec
Membre: 34; *Critères d'admissibilite:* Distributeur; chaînes alimentaires; transformateurs

Association québécoise de défense des droits des personnes retraitées et préretraitées (AQDR)
#10, 1620, ave. de la Salle, Montréal QC H1V 2J8
Tél: 514-935-1551; *Téléc:* 514-937-7371
Ligne sans frais: 877-935-1551
bureaunational@aqdr.org
www.aqdr.org
www.facebook.com/pages/ADQR-NATIONALE/112808388818843
twitter.com/ADQRnationale
Aperçu: *Dimension:* moyenne; *Envergure:* provinciale; fondée en 1979
Mission: Défense des droits culturels, économiques et sociaux des personnes retraitées et pré-retraitées
Membre(s) du bureau directeur:
Serge Séguin, Directeur General
Louis Plamandon, Président
Finances: *Budget de fonctionnement annuel:* $250,000-$500,000
Membre(s) du personnel: 3; 9 bénévole(s)
Membre: 36 000 individuels; 20 000 associés; *Montant de la cotisation:* 10 à 20 $; *Critères d'admissibilite:* 50 ans et plus
Activités: AGA; Assemblée des présidents; Colloques; *Service de conférenciers:* Oui; *Listes de destinataires:* Oui; *Bibliothèque:* Centre de documentation; Bibliothèque publique rendez-vous
Prix, Bouses:
• Prix Yvette Brunet (Prix)
Décerné à la section reconnue annuellement comme la plus active dans son milieu pour la défense des droits de ses concitoyens

Association québécoise de doit comparé (AQDC) / Quebec Society of Comparitive Law
a/s Université d'Ottawa, Faculté de droit, #308, 57, rue Louis Pasteur, Ottawa ON K1N 6N5
Tél: 613-562-5800; *Téléc:* 613-562-5121
www.aqdc.qc.ca
Aperçu: *Dimension:* petite; *Envergure:* provinciale; fondée en 1960
Mission: Pour sensibiliser le public aux problèmes et des défauts dans le droit comparé
Membre(s) du bureau directeur:
Michelle Giroux, Présidente par intérim, Conseil d'administration
Nathalie Vézina, Présidente (en congé), Conseil d'administraion
Membre: *Montant de la cotisation:* 35$ Adultes; 15$ Étdiants aux cycles supérierus à temps plein
Activités: Colloques; Concours; Ateliers

Association québécoise de doit constitutionel (AQDC)
Faculté de droit, Université Laval, 1030, av des Sciences-Humaines, QuéBec QC G1V 0A6
Tél: 418-656-2131; *Téléc:* 418-656-7230
info@aqdc.org
www.aqdc.org
Aperçu: *Dimension:* moyenne; *Envergure:* provinciale; fondée en 2005
Mission: Pour diffuser les connaissances sur le droit constitutionnel au Québec
Membre(s) du bureau directeur:
Daniel Turp, Président, Conseil d'administraion
d@nielturpqc.org
Membre: *Montant de la cotisation:* 50$ Adultes; 20$ Étudiants
Activités: Congès

Association québécoise de gérontologie (AQG)
#100.3, 7225 Durocher St., Montréal QC H3N 2Y3
Tél: 514-387-3612; *Téléc:* 514-387-0352
Ligne sans frais: 888-387-3612
info@aqg-quebec.org
www.aqg-quebec.org
Aperçu: *Dimension:* moyenne; *Envergure:* provinciale; Organisme sans but lucratif; fondée en 1978
Mission: Promouvoir la qualité des services offerts aux personnes âgées, ainsi que la formation du personnel oeuvrant dans le domaine de la gérontologie; favoriser la recherche; analyser, inspirer et critiquer les politiques et les législations gouvernementales; favoriser la circulation de l'information et provoquer des échanges entre personnes et groupes s'intéressant au vieillissement; sensibiliser la collectivité et les individus à leur vieillissement personnel ainsi qu'au phénomène du vieillissement
Membre de: Association canadienne de gérontologie
Affiliation(s): Association canadienne-française pour l'avancement des sciences
Membre(s) du bureau directeur:
Ledoux André, Secrétaire générale
Finances: *Budget de fonctionnement annuel:* $50,000-$100,000
Membre(s) du personnel: 1; 50 bénévole(s)
Membre: 450; *Montant de la cotisation:* 70$; *Comités:* Formation; Politiques sociales; Colloques
Activités: Congrès annuel; *Bibliothèque* rendez-vous

Association québécoise de joueirs d'échechs handicapeés visuels (AQJEHV)
2495, rue De Lorimier, Longueuil QC J4K 3P5
Tél: 514-447-2792
Ligne sans frais: 855-283-8453
info@aqjehy.org
aqjehv.org
Aperçu: *Dimension:* petite; *Envergure:* locale; fondée en 2009
Mission: Encourager les personnes ayant une déficience visuelle de pratiquer les échecs et développer des compétences qui peuvent être utilisés à l'intérieur et en dehors du jeu
Membre(s) du bureau directeur:
Emile Ouellet, Président, Conseil d'administration
Membre: *Critères d'admissibilite:* Toute personne vivant au Québec qui est aveugle et qui veut jouer d'échecs; des gens et des organisme qui croient aux buts et objectifs de l'association
Activités: *Evénements de sensibilisation:* Tournoi d'échechs invitation Jean-Marie Lebel (novembre)

Association québécoise de l'épilepsie
#204, 1650, boul de Maisonneuve Ouest, Montréal QC H3H 2P3
Tél: 514-875-5595; *Téléc:* 514-875-6734
aqe@cooptel.qc.ca
www.associationquebecoiseepilepsie.com
Aperçu: *Dimension:* moyenne; *Envergure:* provinciale; Organisme sans but lucratif; fondée en 1960
Mission: Veiller au mieux-être des personnes épileptiques et à leurs familles; promouvoir les droits des personnes épileptiques; sensibiliser le public à l'épilepsie; promouvoir l'intégration scolaire et au travail
Membre: 10 association régionale

Épilepsie - Section de Québec
1411, boulevard Père-Lelièvre, Québec QC G1M 1N7
Tél: 418-524-8752; *Téléc:* 418-524-5882
epilepsiequebec@megaquebec.net
www.epilepsiequebec.com
Mission: Un organisme à but non lucratif qui a sa charte depuis 1960 et qui a porté jusqu'en 1990 le nom de La Ligue de l'Épilepsie du Québec. Sa mission est de veiller au mieux-être des personnes épileptiques à travers la province.
Membre(s) du bureau directeur:
Nicole Bélanger, Directrice générale

Épilepsie Abitibi-Témiscamingue
115, rue du Terminus ouest, Rouyn-Noranda QC J9X 2P7
Tél: 819-279-7992
epilepsieat@yahoo.fr
www.ae-at.qc.ca
Mission: Un organisme à but non lucratif qui a sa charte depuis 1960 et qui a porté jusqu'en 1990 le nom de La Ligue de l'Épilepsie du Québec. Sa mission est de veiller au mieux-être des personnes épileptiques à travers la province.
Membre(s) du bureau directeur:
Jacques Bouffard, Président

Épilepsie Côte-Nord
652, av Dequen, Sept-Iles QC G4R 2R5
Tél: 418-968-2507
Ligne sans frais: 866-968-2507
epilepsiecn@globetrotter.net
Mission: Un organisme à but non lucratif qui a sa charte depuis 1960 et qui a porté jusqu'en 1990 le nom de La Ligue de l'Épilepsie du Québec. Sa mission est de veiller au mieux-être des personnes épileptiques à travers la province.
Membre de: Epilepsy Canada

Épilepsie Gaspésie-sud
176, boul. Gérard D. Lévesque Ouest, Paspébiac QC G0C 2K0
Tél: 418-752-6819; *Téléc:* 418-752-5959
info@epilepsiegaspesiesud.com
www.epilepsiegaspesiesud.com
Membre de: Epilepsy Canada
Membre(s) du bureau directeur:
Gilles Aspirot, Président

Épilepsie Granby et régions
17, boul. Mountain nord, 2e étage, Granby QC J2G 9M5
Tél: 450-378-8876
Ligne sans frais: 866-374-5377
info@epilepsiegranby.com
www.epilepsiegranby.com
Mission: Un organisme à but non lucratif qui a sa charte depuis 1960 et qui a porté jusqu'en 1990 le nom de La Ligue de l'Épilepsie du Québec. Sa mission est de veiller au mieux-être des personnes épileptiques à travers la province.
Membre de: Epilepsy Canada
Membre(s) du bureau directeur:
Anne Roy, Coordonnatrice, Membres
anie@epilepsiegranby.com

Épilepsie Outaouais
#111, 115, boul Sacré-Coeur, Gatineau QC J8X 1C5
Tél: 819-595-3331; *Téléc:* 819-771-3286
EpilepsieOutaouais@videotron.ca
www.epilepsieoutaouais.org
Mission: De soutenir les personnes atteintes d'épilepsie et leurs familles et d'interpréter auprès du public leurs besoins dans tous les domaines.
Membre de: Epilepsy Canada
Membre(s) du bureau directeur:
Roger Hébert, Directeur général

Épilepsie régionale pour personnes épileptiques de la région 02
CP 1633, 371, rue Racine est, Chicoutimi QC G7H 6Z5
Tél: 418-549-9888; *Téléc:* 418-549-3547
arpe@bellnet.ca
Mission: Un organisme à but non lucratif qui a sa charte depuis 1960 et qui a porté jusqu'en 1990 le nom de La Ligue de l'Épilepsie du Québec. Sa mission est de veiller au mieux-être des personnes épileptiques à travers la province.
Membre de: Epislepsy Canada
Membre(s) du bureau directeur:
Nicole Bouchard, Coordonnatrice

Association québécoise de l'industrie de la pêche (AQIP) / Québec Fish Processors Association
#860, 2600, boul Laurier, Sainte-Foy QC G1V 4W2

Tél: 418-654-1831; *Téléc:* 418-654-1376
aqip@globetrotter.net
www.quebecweb.com/aqip
Aperçu: *Dimension:* moyenne; *Envergure:* provinciale; fondée en 1978
Mission: Défendre les intérêts professionnels des industries québécoises de la transformation des produits marins; travailler au développement des services; aider à l'amélioration de la productivité en usines
Membre de: CRCD Gaspésie des Iles
Finances: *Budget de fonctionnement annuel:* $250,000-$500,000
Membre: 40 industriels; *Montant de la cotisation:* 1 000-3 000$; *Comités:* Comité sur la rationnalisation des usines; Comité sur les approvisionnements extérieurs; Comité sur le transport des produits marins
Activités: Négociations des plans conjoints

Association québécoise de l'industrie de la peinture (AQIP)
#103, 9900, boul Cavendish, Saint-Laurent QC H4M 2V2
Tél: 514-745-2611; *Téléc:* 514-745-2031
Aperçu: *Dimension:* petite; *Envergure:* provinciale

Association québécoise de l'industrie du disque, du spectacle et de la vidéo (ADISQ)
6420, rue Saint-Denis, Montréal QC H2S 2R7
Tél: 514-842-5147; *Téléc:* 514-842-7762
info@adisq.com
www.adisq.com
www.facebook.com/galaadisq
twitter.com/ADISQ_
Aperçu: *Dimension:* moyenne; *Envergure:* provinciale; fondée en 1978
Mission: Promouvoir les intérêts des producteurs de disques, spectacles et vidéos
Membre(s) du bureau directeur:
Solange Drouin, Directrice générale, 514-842-5147 Ext. 228
sdrouin@adisq.com
Membre: 250; *Montant de la cotisation:* Barème; *Critères d'admissibilite:* Entreprises oeuvrant dans le milieu de la production d'enregistrements sonores, de spectacles ou de vidéos
Activités: *Service de conférenciers:* Oui; *Listes de destinataires:* Oui; *Bibliothèque*
Prix, Bouses:
• ADISQ Awards (Prix)
The event honours the best musical achievement produced in Québec during the past year

Association québécoise de la distribution de fruits et légumes (AQDFL) / Québec Produce Marketing Association (QPMA)
6020 rue Jean-Talon est, Saint-Léonard QC H1S 3B1
Tél: 514-355-4330; *Téléc:* 514-355-9876
info@aqdfl.ca
www.aqdfl.ca
www.facebook.com/pages/AQDFL/113881425290921
Aperçu: *Dimension:* moyenne; *Envergure:* provinciale; Organisme sans but lucratif; fondée en 1948
Mission: Créer un environnement propice à la commercialisation des fruits et légumes au Québec
Membre(s) du bureau directeur:
Sophie Perreault, Executive Director
sperreault@aqdfl.ca
Finances: *Budget de fonctionnement annuel:* $500,000-$1.5 Million
Membre(s) du personnel: 5
Membre: 500+; *Montant de la cotisation:* 450$ membre actif; *Critères d'admissibilite:* Individus ou entreprises reliés de près ou de loin à l'industrie des fruits et légumes
Activités: Activités de reseautage; Campagne de promotion de la consommation de fruits et légumes ("J'aime 5 à 10 portions par jour."); *Événements de sensibilisation:* Congrès; Tournoi Golf; Partie d'huîtres; Tournoi de Poker

Association québécoise de la dysphasie
3958 Dandurand, Montréal QC H1X 1P7
Tél: 514-495-4118; *Téléc:* 514-495-8637
Ligne sans frais: 800-495-4118
aqea@aqea.qc.ca
www.aqea.qc.ca
Nom précédent: Association québécoise pour les enfants atteints d'audimutité
Aperçu: *Dimension:* moyenne; *Envergure:* provinciale; fondée en 1986
Mission: Regrouper les parents d'enfants dysphasiques ou atteints d'audimutité; sensibiliser la communauté à la réalité que vivent ces enfants; informer les parents de leurs droits et des divers services dont ils peuvent bénéficier; identifier leurs besoins; susciter la création de nouveaux services; colliger et encourager les recherches faites sur les dysphasies et l'audimutité
Membre(s) du bureau directeur:
Lise Bertrand, Directrice générale, Région Montérégie
direction@dysphasiemonteregie.qc.ca
Membre: 1 400; *Montant de la cotisation:* 25$ membre régulier; 50$ membre corporatif; *Critères d'admissibilite:* Parents d'enfants dysphasiques; professionnels
Activités: Ateliers; conférences; congrès; symposium; formation pour parents ou professionnels

Association québécoise de la fibromyalgie (AQF)
#208, 333, boul Lacombe, LeGardeur QC J5Z 1N2
Tél: 450-582-3075; *Téléc:* 450-582-0674
Ligne sans frais: 866-582-3075
aqf@aqf.ca
www.aqf.ca
Nom précédent: Association de la fibromyalgie du Québec
Aperçu: *Dimension:* moyenne; *Envergure:* provinciale; fondée en 1989
Mission: Sensibiliser la population face à la maladie par la défense des droits des personnes atteintes dans les différentes régions du Québec
Membre(s) du bureau directeur:
Carole Sirois, Présidente par intérim
Membre: 1 300; *Montant de la cotisation:* 20$ membre actif; 10$ membre auxiliaire

Association québécoise de la fibrose kystique (AQFK) *Voir* Fibrose kystique Québec

Association québécoise de la gestion parasitaire (AQGP)
#403, 2030, boul Pie-IX, Montréal QC H1V 2C8
Tél: 514-355-3757; *Téléc:* 514-355-4159
Ligne sans frais: 800-663-2730
aqgp@spg.qc.ca
www.aqgp.ca
Nom précédent: Association des spécialistes en extermination du Québec
Aperçu: *Dimension:* petite; *Envergure:* provinciale; fondée en 1968
Mission: Promouvoir le professionnalisme de ses membres - en les représentant auprès des instances régissant l'industrie de l'extermination et du public en général; en s'assurant de la conformité de ses membres par l'élaboration de normes et de règlements spécifiques; en contribuant à l'accroissement de leurs connaissances techniques et scientifiques par l'accès à l'information et l'élaboration de programmes de formation adaptés
Membre de: Canadian Pest Management Association
Membre(s) du bureau directeur:
Jean-Pierre Lamy, Président
André Maheu, Vice-président
Membre: 125

Association québécoise de la pastorale de la santé *Voir* Association des intervenantes et des intervenants en soins spirituels du Québec

Association québécoise de la quincaillerie et des matériaux de construction (AQMAT) / The Building Materials Retailers Association of Québec
#200, 476, rue Jean-Neveu, Longueuil QC J4G 1N8
Tél: 450-646-5842; *Téléc:* 450-646-6171
www.aqmat.org
Nom précédent: Association des détaillants de matériaux de construction du Québec
Aperçu: *Dimension:* moyenne; *Envergure:* provinciale; Organisme sans but lucratif; fondée en 1940
Mission: Promouvoir l'intérêt général de ses membres-clients engagés dans la vente au détail de matériaux de construction et de quincaillerie, en leur offrant une panoplie de produits et services visant à faciliter la gestion de leurs commerces, des Québécois et la rénovation
Affliation(s): Conseil québécois du commerce de détail
Membre(s) du bureau directeur:
Richard Darveau, Président-directeur général
rdarveau@aqmat.org
Membre: 720; *Montant de la cotisation:* 375$ fournisseurs et associés; 325$ détaillants
Activités: Assurances collectives; cours; quatres réunions du Conseil d'Administration; mémoires aux instances gouvernementales; Opération Ratios (tous les deux ans); participation aux Congrès des Associations-Soeurs; programme de recrutement et de formation; rencontres régionales; deux tournois de golf annuels; taux préférentiel MasterCard et Visa; programme de réduction sur carburant; mutuelle de prévention; lois et règlements abrégés; guide de référence et de bonnes pratiques sur l'étiquetage et l'exactitude des prix

Association québécoise de la schizophrénie *Voir* Société québécoise de la schizophrénie

Association québécoise de lutte contre la pollution atmosphérique (AQLPA)
484, rte 277, Saint-Léon-de-Standon QC G0R 4L0
Tél: 418-642-1322; *Téléc:* 418-642-1323
Ligne sans frais: 855-702-7572
info@aqlpa.com
www.aqlpa.com
www.facebook.com/aqlpa
twitter.com/AQLPA
Aperçu: *Dimension:* petite; *Envergure:* provinciale; fondée en 1982
Mission: L'Association québécoise de lutte contre la pollution atmosphérique (AQLPA) est un organisme qui s'est donnée pour mandat de contribuer à la protection de l'air et de l'atmosphère entourant notre planète, à la fois pour la santé des humains et des écosystèmes qu'elle abrite
Membre(s) du bureau directeur:
André Belisle, Président, 418-642-1322 Ext. 223
andre.belisle@aqlpa.com
Bernard Roy, Directeur général, 418-642-1322 Ext. 235
bernard.roy@aqlpa.com
Membre: 415
Meetings/Conferences: • Association québécoise de lutte contre la pollution atmosphérique Coquetel bénéfice 2015, d'autres conférences en 2015, 2015
Scope: Provincial

Association québécoise de pédagogie collégiale (AQPC)
Cégep marie-victorin, 7000, rue Marie-Victorin, Montréal QC H2G 1J6
Tél: 514-328-3805; *Téléc:* 514-328-3824
info@aqpc.qc.ca
www.aqpc.qc.ca
Aperçu: *Dimension:* moyenne; *Envergure:* provinciale; Organisme sans but lucratif; fondée en 1981
Mission: Alimenter la réflexion sur la pédagogie collégiale et promouvoir le développement pédagogique dans le réseau collégial québécois
Membre(s) du bureau directeur:
Fanny Kingsbury, Directeur général
dg@aqpc.qc.ca
Finances: *Budget de fonctionnement annuel:* $250,000-$500,000
Membre(s) du personnel: 3
Membre: 1000; *Montant de la cotisation:* 50$; *Critères d'admissibilite:* Enseignants; professionnels & cadres de l'éducation collégiale
Activités: Colloque annuel; publication d'ouvrages pédagogiques; stages
Meetings/Conferences: • Association québécoise de pédagogie collégiale 35e colloque annuel, juin, 2015, Hôtel Le Montagnais, Saguenay, QC
Scope: National

Association québécoise de promotion du tourisme socioculturel (AQPTSC)
CP 1000, Succ. M, 4545, av Pierre-de Coubertin, Montréal QC H1V 3R2
Tél: 514-252-3139; *Téléc:* 514-254-9464
aqptsc@sympatico.ca
Aperçu: *Dimension:* moyenne; *Envergure:* provinciale
Mission: Association appuyant les groupes associatifs et favorisant le tourisme thématique et les échanges culturels
Membre(s) du bureau directeur:
Guy Lefebvre, Directeur général

Association québécoise de racquetball (AQR) / Quebec Racquetball Association
4545, av Pierre-de-Coubertin, Montréal QC H1V 0B2
Tél: 514-252-3062
info@sports-4murs.qc.ca
www.racquetball.qc.ca
www.facebook.com/427582940621028

Aperçu: *Dimension:* petite; *Envergure:* provinciale surveillé par Racquetball Canada
Mission: Promouvoir le développement du racquetball au Québec en offrant différentes opportunités aux adeptes, tout en encourageant la participation sportive à travers un ensemble de services et de programmes
Membre de: Racquetball Canada; Sports-Québec; Regroupement Loisir Québec
Membre(s) du bureau directeur:
Michel Gagnon, Président
michelgagnoncoach@sympatico.ca
Finances: *Budget de fonctionnement annuel:* $50,000-$100,000; *Fonds:* Éducation, Loisir et Sport Québec
Membre(s) du personnel: 4
Membre: 10 000; *Montant de la cotisation:* 15$
Activités: Tournois; championnats; formation d'arbitres et d'entraîneurs; *Stagiaires:* Oui

Association québécoise de sports pour paralytiques cérébraux (AQSPC)

4545, av Pierre-de Coubertin, Montréal QC H1V 0B2
Tél: 514-252-3143; *Téléc:* 514-254-1069
secadmin@sportpc.qc.ca
www.sportpc.qc.ca
www.facebook.com/189413534433667
Aperçu: *Dimension:* petite; *Envergure:* provinciale surveillé par Canadian Cerebral Palsy Sports Association
Membre de: Canadian Cerebral Palsy Sports Association
Membre(s) du bureau directeur:
Jo-ann Arvey, Directrice générale

Association québécoise de Vol Libre (AQVL)

CP 321, Succ. St-Paul D'abbotsford, Québec QC J0E 1A0
info@aqvl.qc.ca
aqvl.qc.ca
Aperçu: *Dimension:* petite; *Envergure:* locale; fondée en 1978
Mission: Promouvoir l'activité du Vol Libre au Québec; intermédiaire entre l'association canadienne et les membres québécois; publier le Survol Québec
Affliation(s): Association Canadienne de Vol Libre
Membre(s) du bureau directeur:
Christian Grenier, Président
president@aqvl.qc.ca
Patrick Dupuis, Secrétaire
Finances: *Budget de fonctionnement annuel:* Moins de $50,000
10 bénévole(s)
Membre: 240; *Montant de la cotisation:* 150$; *Critères d'admissibilite:* Pilote de parapente ou de delta-plane
Activités: *Listes de destinataires:* Oui

Association québécoise des allergies alimentaires (AQAA)

6020, rue Jean Talon Est, St-Léonard QC H1S 3B1
Tél: 514-990-2575
Ligne sans frais: 800-990-2575
allergies-alimentaires.org
Aperçu: *Dimension:* petite; *Envergure:* provinciale; fondée en 1990
Mission: A pour mission d'offrir du support et de l'information, de promouvoir l'éducation et la prévention, ainsi que d'encourager la recherche sur les allergies alimentaires et l'anaphylaxie
Membre de: Food Allergy & Anaphylaxis Alliance
Membre(s) du bureau directeur:
Daniel Lapointe, Directeur général
dlapointe@aqaa.qc.ca
Membre(s) du personnel: 7
Membre: *Comités:* Scientifique
Activités: Journée annuelle; ateliers de formation; consultations par professionnels; support téléphonique; *Stagiaires:* Oui; *Service de conférenciers:* Oui

Association québécoise des archivistes médicales; Association des archivistes médicales de la province de Québec *Voir* Association des Gestionnaires de l'information de la santé du Québec

Association québécoise des arénas et des installations récréatives et sportives (AQAIRS)

4545, av Pierre-de-Coubertin, Montréal QC H1V 0B2
Tél: 514-252-5244; *Téléc:* 514-252-5220
info@aqairs.ca
www.aqairs.ca
Nom précédent: Association des Arénas du Québec
Aperçu: *Dimension:* moyenne; *Envergure:* provinciale; fondée en 1979
Mission: Contribuer au respect et à l'amélioration des normes visant les arénas et des installations récréatives et sportives au profit des participants aux activités qui s'y déroulent
Membre(s) du bureau directeur:
Gaston Boisvert, Président
arenacb@videotron.ca
Luc Toupin, Directeur général, 514-252-5244 Ext. 3
Membre: 400 membres réguliers; 100 membres affaires; *Montant de la cotisation:* Barème
Activités: Sessions de formation; publication

Association québécoise des auteurs dramatiques (AQAD)

187, rue Sainte-Catherine Est, 3e étage, Montréal QC H2X 1K8
Tél: 514-596-3705; *Téléc:* 514-596-2953
info@aqad.qc.ca
www.aqad.qc.ca
Aperçu: *Dimension:* petite; *Envergure:* nationale; fondée en 1990
Mission: Défendre les droits et les intérêts moraux, sociaux, économiques et professionnels des auteurs dramatiques, des librettistes, des adaptateurs et des traducteurs francophones, québécois et canadiens
Membre(s) du bureau directeur:
Marie-Eve Gagnon, Directrice par intérim
megagnon@aqad.qc.ca
Finances: *Fonds:* Conseil des arts et des lettres du Québec
Membre(s) du personnel: 4
Membre: *Montant de la cotisation:* 80$
Activités: Librairie virtuelle ADEL; ateliers de formation; laboratoires; bureau de consultation

Association québécoise des avocats et avocates de la défense (AQAAD)

445, boul. Saint-Laurent, Montréal QC H2Y 3T8
Tél: 514-954-3426; *Téléc:* 514-954-3451
Ligne sans frais: 800-361-8495
info@aqaad.com
www.aqaad.com
Aperçu: *Dimension:* petite; *Envergure:* provinciale; fondée en 1995
Mission: Défendre les droits et intérêts des avocats qui pratiquent le droit pénal
Membre(s) du bureau directeur:
Joëlle Roy, Présidente, Conseil d'administration, 450-530-3202, Fax: 450-530-2511
gagne_roy@videotron.ca
Membre: 800; *Montant de la cotisation:* 57,49$; *Comités:* Relations avec le Barreau du Québec; Relations avec la magistrature; Relations et intervention auprès du gouvernement du Québec; Relations et intervention auprès du gouvernement fédéral; Relations avec la Commission des services juridiques; Relations avec les médias; Relations avec l'A.A.D.M. et l'A.A.D.Q.; Finances et trésorerie; Règlements de l'AQAAD; Agenda annuel; C-10; Colloque annuel; Prix de l'AQAAD; Relations avec les associations canadiennes de défense; C-2; Jurisprudence; Pratique privée; Service de recherches et relations avec les universités; Demandes d'intervention

Association québécoise des avocats et avocates en droit de l'immigration (AQAADI)

#500, 445, boul. Saint-Laurent, Montréal QC H2Y 3T8
Tél: 514-954-3471; *Téléc:* 514-954-3451
Ligne sans frais: 800-361-8495
www.aqaadi.com
Aperçu: *Dimension:* petite; *Envergure:* provinciale; fondée en 1991
Mission: Pour informer les avocats de l'immigration des modifications apportées aux lois sur l'immigration, et de créer une communauté d'avocats en immigration qui peuvent partager leurs expériences et s'entraider
Membre(s) du bureau directeur:
Jean-Sébastien Boudreault, Président, Conseil d'administration
jsboudreault@gmail.com
Membre: 190; *Comités:* Qualité des services; Comité de formation; AQAADI pour les femmes et les enfants

Association québécoise des banques alimentaires et des Moissons (AQBAM)

262, rue Bellevue, Pincourt QC J7V 4A8
Tél: 514-453-6257; *Téléc:* 514-453-6736
cbec@videotron.ca
Nom précédent: Fédération des Moissons du Québec inc.
Aperçu: *Dimension:* moyenne; *Envergure:* provinciale; Organisme sans but lucratif; fondée en 1988
Mission: Regrouper les banques alimentaires et les moissons du Québec; maintenir et développer un réseau d'échanges et de partage des savoirs, savoirs-faire et des savoirs-être au niveau de l'intervention régionale dans la lutte contre la pauvreté; concerter les membres et coordonner des actions de représentation politique, de sensibilisation populaire, de recherche et de développement des pratiques alternatives pour mieux favoriser la prise en main et l'autonomie des bénéficiaires de l'aide alimentaire
Membre de: Canadian Association of Food Banks
Membre(s) du bureau directeur:
Clément Bergeron, Directeur général
Finances: *Budget de fonctionnement annuel:* $50,000-$100,000
Membre(s) du personnel: 1; 1000 bénévole(s)
Membre: 1,000; *Montant de la cotisation:* barème
Activités: Cuisines collectives, jardins communautaires, groupes d'achat, coopératives de ventes; *Service de conférenciers:* Oui

Association québécoise des centres de la petite enfance (AQCPE)

#200, 6611, rue Jarry est, Montréal QC H1P 1W5
Tél: 514-326-8008; *Téléc:* 514-326-3322
Ligne sans frais: 888-326-8008
info@aqcpe.com
www.aqcpe.com
Aperçu: *Dimension:* moyenne; *Envergure:* provinciale; fondée en 2003
Mission: A pour mandat la concertation des acteurs du réseau, la représentation politique de ses membres et la promotion des centres de la petite enfance, et services de soutien; représente les employeurs du secteur des CPE à l'occasion de négociations, en matière de relations du travail et de main-d'oeuvre; l'AQCPE est reconnue par le Min. de la Famille et des Aînés pour les négociations provinciales.
Affliation(s): Association des services de garde en milieu scolaire du Québec; Carrefour action municipal et famille; Centrale des syndicats du Québec; Fédération canadienne des services de garde à l'enfance; Fédération des femmes du Québec; Fédération des travailleurs et travailleuses du Québec; Fédération québécoise des organismes communautaires famille; Réseau de la santé et des services sociaux
Membre(s) du bureau directeur:
Louis Senécal, Directeur général
Viriya Thach, Responsable des communications
Membre(s) du personnel: 24
Membre: 13 associations;

Association québécoise des critiques de cinéma (AQCC)

a/s Cinémathèque québécoise des critiques de cinéma, 335, boul. De Maisonneuve Est, Montréal QC H2X 1K1
aqcc.ca
Aperçu: *Dimension:* petite; *Envergure:* provinciale; Organisme sans but lucratif; fondée en 1973
Mission: Regrouper l'ensemble des personnes reconnues par l'Association comme oeuvrant au Québec dans le domaine de la critique cinématographique
Membre: *Montant de la cotisation:* 40$; *Critères d'admissibilite:* Oeuvrer dans le domaine de la critique cinématographique au Québec
Activités: Remise de prix cinématographiques; composition de jurys

Association québécoise des cyclothymiques *Voir* Revivre - Association Québécoise de soutien aux personnes souffrant de troubles anxieux, dépressifs ou bipolaires

Association Québécoise des dépanneurs en alimentation (AQDA)

#501, 1, av Holiday, Montréal QC H9R 5N3
Tél: 514-240-3934; *Téléc:* 514-630-6989
info@acda-aqda.ca
www.acda-aqda.ca
Aperçu: *Dimension:* moyenne; *Envergure:* provinciale surveillé par Canadian Convenience Stores Association
Affliation(s): Canadian Convenience Stores Association; Western Convenience Stores Association; Ontario Convenience Stores Association; Atlantic Convenience Stores Association
Membre(s) du bureau directeur:
Michel Gadbois, Président
mgadbois@depanneurscanada.ca

Association québécoise des directeurs et directrices d'établissement d'enseignement retraités

#100, 7855, boul Louis-H.-Lafontaine, Anjou QC H1K 4E4
Tél: 514-353-3254
info@aqder.ca

www.aqder.ca
twitter.com/AQDER_National
Également appelé: AQDER
Aperçu: *Dimension:* moyenne; *Envergure:* provinciale; fondée en 1976
Mission: Développer les services nécessaires pour que les membres puissent vivre une retraite de qualité.
Membre(s) du bureau directeur:
Guy Lessard, Président

Association québécoise des directeurs et directrices du loisir municipal ***Voir*** Association québécoise du loisir municipal

Association québécoise des écoles de français langue étrangère (AQEFLE)

a/s Collège de Jonquière, 2505, rue St-Hubert, Jonquière QC G7X 7W2
Tél: 418-542-0352; *Téléc:* 418-542-3536
Ligne sans frais: 800-622-0352
www.aqefle.com
Aperçu: *Dimension:* moyenne; *Envergure:* provinciale
Mission: Fournir à des jeunes adultes et des adultes professionnels une compétence en français langue seconde
Membre(s) du bureau directeur:
Pierre Lincourt, Président
pierre_lincourt@uqac.ca
Finances: *Budget de fonctionnement annuel:* Moins de $50,000
Membre(s) du personnel: 4; 3 bénévole(s)
Membre: 7 écoles; *Critères d'admissibilite:* Etre une institution collégiale ou universitaire reconnue par le ministère de l'Éducation du Québec; offrir des cours de français langue seconde; être agréée par les membres de l'association

Association québécoise des éditeurs de magazines (AQEM)

a/s Félix Maltais, 4475, rue Frontenac, Montréal QC H2H 2S2
Tél: 514-844-2111
info@magazinesquebec.com
www.magazinesquebec.com
Aperçu: *Dimension:* petite; *Envergure:* provinciale; Organisme sans but lucratif; fondée en 1991
Mission: De promouvoir le développement de l'industrie du magazine dans son ensemble et défendre les intérêts de ses membres.
Membre(s) du bureau directeur:
Robert Goyette, Président
Membre: 44; *Montant de la cotisation:* Barème dépendent des ventes; *Critères d'admissibilite:* Éditeurs de magazines

Association québécoise des Éducateurs du primaire ***Voir*** Association québécoise des enseignantes et des enseignants du primaire

Association québécoise des éducatrices et éducateurs spécialisés en arts plastiques (AQÉSAP)

c/o Laurence Borys, Secrétaire Exécutive de l'AQÉSAP, 2761, Route 125 Nord, Saint-Donat-de-Montcalm QC J0T 2C0
Tél: 819-323-6537
info@aqesap.org
www.aqesap.org
www.facebook.com/AQESAP.org
twitter.com/AQESAP
Aperçu: *Dimension:* petite; *Envergure:* provinciale; fondée en 1967
Mission: De promouvoir et de défendre la qualité de l'enseignement des arts, de stimuler la recherche et de favoriser le partage d'expériences pédagogiques par le biais de formations, de colloques, de congrès et de sa revue Vision.
Membre(s) du bureau directeur:
Michel Lemieux, Président
presidence@aqesap.org
Membre: *Montant de la cotisation:* 75$ individu; 37.50$ étudiant/retraité; 175$ entreprise; *Comités:* Gouvernance; Finances; Site web; Base de données et inscription en ligne

Association québécoise des enseignantes et des enseignants du primaire (AQEP)

90, av Vincent-d'Indy, bureau C-559, Montréal QC H2V 2S9
Téléc: 866-941-2737
Ligne sans frais: 866-940-2737
aqep@aqep.org
www.aqep.org
www.facebook.com/AQEP.ORG
Nom précédent: Association québécoise des Éducateurs du primaire
Aperçu: *Dimension:* moyenne; *Envergure:* provinciale
Mission: Promouvoir et valoriser la profession d'enseignantes et d'enseignants; créer, organiser, administrer et développer un fond pour promouvoir l'avancement de la pédagogie; acquérir et développer des compétences au regard de la profession; favoriser l'excellence de l'acte d'enseigner; collaborer avec tout organisme poursuivant des buts similaires; être la source de référence et de ralliement pour la communauté enseignante primaire dans le but de favoriser l'avancement et l'excellence afin de promouvoir et valoriser l'acte d'enseigner. Notre contribution fera en sorte que la communauté enseignante du primaire puisse permettre à chaque personne la composant de se réaliser professionnellement, dans le plaisir, en faisant preuve d'innovation et de créativité
Membre(s) du bureau directeur:
Stéphan Lenoir, Président
slenoir@aqep.org
Membre: 1000; *Montant de la cotisation:* 30$
Activités: Enseignement primaire; formation continue; organisation d'un congrès annuel; publication de Vivre le primaire; *Service de conférenciers:* Oui

Association québécoise des enseignants de français langue seconde (AQEFLS) / Québec Association of Teachers of French as a Second Language

#228, 7400, boul Saint-Laurent, Montréal QC H2R 2Y1
Tél: 514-276-6470; *Téléc:* 514-276-3350
info@aqefls.org
www.aqefls.org
twitter.com/AQEFLS
Aperçu: *Dimension:* moyenne; *Envergure:* provinciale; fondée en 1979
Mission: Promouvoir l'enseignement du français langue seconde et les aspects qui s'y rattachent; coordonner et encourager les recherches d'ordre pratique dans le domaine de la pédagogie et dans tout autre domaine touchant l'enseignement du français langue seconde; permettre la diffusion des derniers développements de la recherche et les techniques dans le domaine de l'enseignement du français langue seconde
Affiliation(s): Fédération internationale des professeurs de français
Membre(s) du bureau directeur:
Carlos Carmona, Président
Membre(s) du personnel: 1; 10 bénévole(s)
Membre: 500+; *Critères d'admissibilite:* L'Association réunit des enseignants qui oeuvrent dans les secteurs public et privé, de la maternelle à l'université, qu'il s'agisse d'organismes à vocation éducative ou d'entreprises industrielles ou commerciales; les secteurs du régulier, de l'immersion, et de l'accueil y sont représentés

L'association québécoise des fournisseurs de services pétroliers et gaziers du Québec (AFSPC) / Oil & Gas Services Association of Québec (OGSAQ)

QC
Tél: 514-284-3069
info@afspg.com
www.afspg.com
www.facebook.com/Afspg
Aperçu: *Dimension:* petite; *Envergure:* provinciale; fondée en 2011
Mission: L'AFSPG a été créé dans le but de pouvoir développer le gaz de schiste au Québec et surtout, de pouvoir améliorer le présent mais, avant tout, l'avenir de chaque Québécois. Dans les prochaines années, l'AFSPG souhaite être en mesure de créer plus de deux cents puits par année au Québec, où l'on retrouve des sources de gaz schiste. Pour ce faire, ils utiliseront les plus grandes mesures de sécurité lors de l'extraction des gaz, limitant les chances de contaminations des sols environnants.
Membre(s) du bureau directeur:
Mario Lévesque, Directrice générale
Membre: 60

Association québécoise des groupes d'ornithologues ***Voir*** Regroupement QuébecOiseaux

Association québécoise des industries de nutrition animale et céréalière (AQINAC)

#200, 4790, rue Martineau, Saint-Hyacinthe QC J2R 1V1
Tél: 450-799-2440; *Téléc:* 450-799-2445
info@aqinac.com
www.aqinac.com
www.facebook.com/group.php?gid=13695606643991
twitter.com/AQINAC
Aperçu: *Dimension:* grande; *Envergure:* provinciale; fondée en 1963
Membre(s) du bureau directeur:
Yvan Lacroix, Président-directeur général
yvan.lacroix@aqinac.com
Cynthia Vallée, Agente, Communication/Événements
cynthia.vallee@aqinac.com
Membre(s) du personnel: 8
Membre: 225+ sociétés; *Montant de la cotisation:* 900$ minimum; *Critères d'admissibilite:* Produits et/ou services en agro-alimentaire

Association Québécoise des Industries de Nutrition Animale et Céréalières ***Voir*** Animal Nutrition Association of Canada

Association québécoise des infirmières et des infirmiers en recherche clinique (AQIIRC)

4200, rue Molson, Montréal QC H1Y 4V4
Tél: 514-935-2501; *Téléc:* 514-935-1799
info@aqiirc.qc.ca
aqiirc.qc.ca
www.facebook.com/aqiirc.asso?sk=wall
Aperçu: *Dimension:* petite; *Envergure:* provinciale; Organisme sans but lucratif; fondée en 1991
Mission: Regrouper les infirmières et infirmiers qui travaillent dans tous les domaines de la recherche clinique et promouvoir leurs rôles; soutenir la participation active des membres dans l'élaboration et la réalisation d'études cliniques; créer un réseau de sources d'information et d'entraide pour les membres et favoriser leur perfectionnement
Membre(s) du bureau directeur:
Lucie Tremblay, Présidente
Finances: *Budget de fonctionnement annuel:* Moins de $50,000
Membre: 300; *Montant de la cotisation:* 90$; *Critères d'admissibilite:* Infirmiers et infimières licenciés; *Comités:* Adhésion; Journal; Site web; Congrès; Réseau de ressources en recherche
Activités: Séances de formation; congrès; conférences;
Meetings/Conferences: • Association québécoise des infirmières et des infirmiers en recherche clinique Congrès 2015, April, 2015, Québec, QC
Scope: Provincial
Publications:
• Portail infOIIQ
Type: Portail internet; *Editor:* Lauréanne Marceau
Profile: Portail d'actualités officiel de l'Ordre des infirmières et infirmiers du Québec

Association québécoise des infirmières et infirmiers en urologie (AQIIU)

342, rue Morin, Laval QC H7L 4V2
Tél: 450-625-0214
infoaqiiu@gmail.com
www.aqiiu.com
Aperçu: *Dimension:* moyenne; *Envergure:* provinciale
Membre(s) du bureau directeur:
Annie Taillefer, Présidente

Association québécoise des informaticiennes et informaticiens indépendants (AQIII) / Québec Association for ICT Freelancers

#974, rue Michelin, Laval QC H7L 5B6
Tél: 514-388-6147; *Téléc:* 514-388-7249
Ligne sans frais: 888-858-7777
aqiii@aqiii.org
www.aqiii.org
www.linked.in/company/691970
www.facebook.com/pages/AQIII/45009582564
twitter.com/aqiii
Aperçu: *Dimension:* moyenne; *Envergure:* provinciale; fondée en 1993
Mission: Réunir le maximum de consultants autonomes et d'expérience en TI afin de bénéficier des avantages d'un réseau solide tout en préservant la liberté du travail indépendant. L'association favorise l'obtention de mandats en TI, le réseautage, le partage d'information entre informaticiens ainsi que les économies d'échelle chez des fournisseurs ciblés
Membre(s) du bureau directeur:
Sylvie Racine, Directrice générale par intérim
sracine@aqiii.org
Finances: *Fonds:* Commanditaires, subventions, tarifs
Membre(s) du personnel: 7
Membre: 1700; *Montant de la cotisation:* $215
Activités: *Service de conférenciers:* Oui

Association québécoise des joueurs de dames (AQJD)
4545, av Pierre-de Coubertin, Montréal QC H1V 3R2
Tél: 514-252-3032
dames@fqjr.qc.ca
dames.quebecjeux.org
Aperçu: *Dimension:* petite; *Envergure:* provinciale; fondée en 1973
Mission: Favoriser le développement et la promotion du jeu de dames
Membre de: Fédération Canadienne des Jeux de Dames
Membre(s) du bureau directeur:
Mario Bélanger, Président
Membre: *Montant de la cotisation:* 5$
Activités: Championnat provincial annuel; compétitions; jeux électroniques; logiciels; système de cote-classement

Association Québécoise des Loisirs Folkloriques (AQLF)
471, chemin de l'Église, Sainte-Barbe QC J0S 1P0
Tél: 450-373-5577; *Téléc:* 450-373-5577
info@quebecfolklore.qc.ca
www.quebecfolklore.qc.ca
Aperçu: *Dimension:* moyenne; *Envergure:* provinciale; fondée en 1975
Mission: Préserver et promouvoir le folklore québécois
Membre(s) du bureau directeur:
Gérald Cyr, Président
Michel Mallette, Sec.-trés.
Membre(s) du personnel: 3
Membre: *Montant de la cotisation:* 20$ individuel; 30$ familial; 50$ groupe; 100$ associatif; *Critères d'admissibilite:* Musiciens; chanteurs; danseurs; adepts
Activités: Gala Folklorique; compétition; soirée folklorique; *Service de conférenciers:* Oui

Association québécoise des marionnettistes (AQM)
Centre UNIMA-CANADA (section Québec), #300, 7755, boul Saint-Laurent, Montréal QC H2R 1X1
Tél: 514-522-1919
info@aqm.ca
www.aqm.ca
www.facebook.com/175003799226012
twitter.com/AQMarionnette
Également appelé: Union internationale de la marionnette - Canada
Aperçu: *Dimension:* petite; *Envergure:* provinciale; fondée en 1981
Mission: Représenter ses membres et créer un terrain propice aux échanges, aux actions communes et à la réflexion sur la pratique de l'art de la marionnette
Membre de: Conseil québécois du théatre; Académie québécoise du théatre
Membre(s) du bureau directeur:
Hélène Ducharme, Présidente
Membre: 150+; *Montant de la cotisation:* 42$ ami; 60$ organise culturel; 66$ artiste professionel; 120$ compagnie artistique professionnelle; *Critères d'admissibilite:* Professionnel de la marionnette; *Comités:* Animation du milieu; AQM-UNIMA; Communications Web; Revue Marionnettes; Formation
Activités: Renseigne ses membres sur tout ce qui touche la marionnette au Québec et à l'étranger; organise des rencontres, des débats, des expositions, des colloques qui suscitent des échanges entre les diverses pratiques artistiques; *Stagiaires:* Oui; *Listes de destinataires:* Oui; *Bibliothèque:* Centre de documentation

Association québécoise des organismes de coopération internationale (AQOCI) / Québec Association of International Cooperation
#540, 1001, rue Sherbrooke Est, Montréal QC H2L 1L3
Tél: 514-871-1086; *Téléc:* 514-871-9866
aqoci@aqoci.qc.ca
www.aqoci.qc.ca
www.facebook.com/aqoci
twitter.com/aqoci
www.youtube.com/aqoci
Aperçu: *Dimension:* moyenne; *Envergure:* internationale; fondée en 1976
Mission: Soutenir le travail des membres afin de permettre leur développement en s'inspirant des principes de solidarité et de coopération; favoriser l'échange pour mieux coordonner les actions communautaires; regrouper des organismes de coopération et d'éducation à la solidarité oeuvrant au Québec
Membre de: Canadian Council for International Cooperation; Conseil canadien pour la coopération internationale.
Affiliation(s): Réseau québécois sur l'intégration continentale; Conseil canadien pour la coopération internationale
Membre(s) du bureau directeur:
Gervais L'Heureux, Directeur général, 514-871-1086 Ext. 202
glheureux@aqoci.qc.ca
Denis Labelle, Président
Finances: *Budget de fonctionnement annuel:* $500,000-$1.5 Million
Membre(s) du personnel: 9
Membre: 69; *Critères d'admissibilite:* Regroupements d'organismes de coopération internationale
Activités: *Stagiaires:* Oui; *Service de conférenciers:* Oui

Association québécoise des orthophonistes et des audiologistes (AQOA)
#102, 7229 rue St-Denis, Montréal QC H2R Ee3
Tél: 514-369-8929
admin@aqoa.qc.ca
www.aqoa.qc.ca
Aperçu: *Dimension:* petite; *Envergure:* provinciale; Organisme sans but lucratif; fondée en 1996
Mission: Défendre les droits et les intérêts des orthophonistes et audiologistes du Québec auprès de diverses instances, gouvernementales, syndicales, etc.
Affiliation(s): Ordre des orthophonistes et audiologistes du Québec, Mouvement pour l'adhésion aux traitements, Orthophonie et audiologie Canada, Association des jeunes bègues du Québec
Membre(s) du bureau directeur:
Philippe Fournier, Président
Finances: *Budget de fonctionnement annuel:* Moins de $50,000
Membre: *Critères d'admissibilite:* Orthophonistes et audiologistes québécois; *Comités:* Pratique privée
Prix, Bouses:
• Prix Phénix (Prix)
Eligibility: C'est un prix pour un membre de l'AQOA qui est un exemple d'excellence dans sa profession.

Association québécoise des parents d'enfants handicapés visuels (AQPEHV) / Quebec Association for Parents of Visually Impaired Children (QAPVIC)
#203, 10, boul Churchill, Greenfield Park QC J4V 2L7
Tél: 450-465-7225; *Téléc:* 450-465-5129
Ligne sans frais: 888-849-8729
www.aqpehv.qc.ca
Aperçu: *Dimension:* petite; *Envergure:* provinciale; fondée en 2004
Membre(s) du bureau directeur:
Roland Savard, Directeur général
direction.generale@aqpehv.qc.ca
Finances: *Fonds:* Ministère de la Santé et des Services sociaux du Québec
Membre: *Critères d'admissibilite:* Les parents d'enfants (0 à 21 ans) ayant une déficience visuelle.

Association québécoise des personnes de petite taille (AQPPT) / Association of Little People of Quebec
#308, 6300, av du Parc, Montréal QC H2V 4H8
Tél: 514-521-9671; *Téléc:* 514-521-3369
info@aqppt.org
www.aqppt.org
www.facebook.com/AQPPT
Aperçu: *Dimension:* petite; *Envergure:* provinciale; Organisme sans but lucratif; fondée en 1976
Mission: Promouvoir des intérêts et défendre les droits des personnes de petite taille et faciliter leur intégration scolaire, sociale et professionnelle.
Membre(s) du bureau directeur:
Normande Gagnon, Co-fondatrice
direction@aqppt.org
Finances: *Budget de fonctionnement annuel:* $100,000-$250,000
Membre(s) du personnel: 3; 47 bénévole(s)
Membre: 397; *Montant de la cotisation:* 25-50 famille; 25$ soutien; 50$ organisme; *Critères d'admissibilite:* Etre une personne de petite taille, ou un parent, ou membre soutien
Activités: Information médicale; soutien aux membres; sensibilisation auprès de la population et dans les écoles; concertation et actions sur des dossiers comme l'accessibilité, le transport adapté, l'intégration au travail; promotion et défense des droits des personnes de petite taille; *Service de conférenciers:* Oui; *Bibliothèque:* Centre de documentation

Association québécoise des pharmaciens propriétaires (AQPP) / Québec Association of Pharmacy Owners
4378, av Pierre-de Coubertin, Montréal QC H1V 1A6
Tél: 514-254-0676; *Téléc:* 514-254-1288
Ligne sans frais: 800-361-7765
info@aqpp.qc.ca
www.aqpp.qc.ca
twitter.com/VotrePharmacien
www.youtube.com/user/VotrePharmacien
Aperçu: *Dimension:* moyenne; *Envergure:* provinciale; fondée en 1970
Mission: Assurer l'étude, la défense et le développement des intérêts économiques, sociaux et professionnels de ses membres.
Membre(s) du bureau directeur:
Normand Cadieux, Vice-président exécutif et directeur général
Membre(s) du personnel: 12
Membre: 1 930
Activités: *Service de conférenciers:* Oui; *Listes de destinataires:* Oui

Association québécoise des phytothérapeutes (AQP)
3805, rue Bélair, Montréal QC H2A 2C1
Tél: 514-722-8888; *Téléc:* 514-722-5164
Ligne sans frais: 800-268-5878
info@aqp-annspq.org
www.aqp-annspq.ca
Également appelé: Association des naturopathes et naturothérapeutes spécialisés en phytothérapie
Aperçu: *Dimension:* moyenne; *Envergure:* provinciale; Organisme sans but lucratif; fondée en 1969
Mission: Regrouper les phytothérapeutes; favoriser l'atteinte d'un niveau de compétence supérieure; assurer la protection du public; contribuer à l'avancement de la phytothérapie
Membre: 500+; *Critères d'admissibilite:* Phytothérapeutes; naturopathes; naturothérapeutes; étudiants

Association Québécoise des Pompiers Volontaires et Permanents *Voir* Fédération Québécoise des Intervenants en Sécurité Incendie

Association québécoise des professeures et professeurs de français *Voir* Association québécoise des professeurs de français

Association québécoise des professeurs de français (AQPF)
773, rue Sainte-Hélène, Longueuil QC J4K 3R5
Tél: 450-332-5885; *Téléc:* 450-332-5888
Ligne sans frais: 800-267-0947
info@aqpf.qc.ca
www.aqpf.qc.ca
Nom précédent: Association québécoise des professeures et professeurs de français
Aperçu: *Dimension:* moyenne; *Envergure:* nationale; Organisme sans but lucratif; fondée en 1967
Mission: Les principaux champs d'intervention sont - la didactique et l'enseignement du français langue maternelle du préscolaire à l'université; l'enseignement du français aux adultes; l'alphabétisation; l'enseignement du français langue seconde; promotion de la langue française, de la culture québécoise et de la francophonie
Affiliation(s): Fédération internationale des professeurs de français
Membre(s) du bureau directeur:
Érick Falardeau, Président, Section de Québec-et-Est-du-Québec
Erick.Falardeau@fse.ulaval.ca
Danielle Lefebvre, Présidente, Section Centre du Québec
danielef@cgocable.ca
Geneviève Messier, Présidente, Section de Montréal-et-Ouest-du-Québec
Suzanne Richard, Présidente
Suzanne.Richard@USherbrooke.ca
Isabelle Péladeau, Directrice générale
dg@aqpf.qc.ca
Finances: *Budget de fonctionnement annuel:* $50,000-$100,000
Membre(s) du personnel: 2; 30 bénévole(s)
Membre: 600; *Montant de la cotisation:* 10-50; *Critères d'admissibilite:* Enseignants, professeurs, chercheurs, conseilleurs pédagogiques, cadres, éditeurs; *Comités:* Congrès annuel; Ateliers de littérature; activités pédagogiques
Activités: Rencontres pédagogiques, sociales, culturelles; commission pédagogique; commission linguistique; *Service de conférenciers:* Oui

Association québécoise des professionnels d'insolvabilité *See* Quebec Association of Insolvency & Restructuring Professionals

Association québécoise des professionnels de la rèorganisation et de l'insolvabilité *See* Quebec Association of Insolvency & Restructuring Professionals

Association québécoise des réalisateurs et réalisatrices de cinéma et de télévision *Voir* Association des réalisateurs et réalisatrices du Québec

Association québécoise des salons du livre (AQSL)

#100, 60, rue St-Antoine, Trois-Rivières QC G9A 0C4
Téléc: 819-376-4222
Ligne sans frais: 888-542-2075
info@aqsl.org
www.aqsl.org
Aperçu: *Dimension:* moyenne; *Envergure:* provinciale; fondée en 1978
Mission: De promouvoir du livre, du périodique et de la lecture; De défendre les intérêts des Salons membres et favorise la recherche, la documentation, les contacts professionnels, la création et la diffusion du livre
Membre de: Société de développment des entreprises culturelles.
Membre(s) du bureau directeur:
Julie Brosseau, Présidente
direction@sltr.qc.ca
Membre: 9; *Critères d'admissibilite:* Salon du livre au Québec

Abitibi-Témiscamingue
150, av du Lac, Rouyn-Noranda QC J9X 4N5
Tél: 819-797-4610; *Téléc:* 819-764-6375
info@slat.qc.ca
www.slat.qc.ca
Membre(s) du bureau directeur:
Ginette Vézina, Presidente
ginettevc@hotmail.com

Côte-Nord
#12, 652, av de Quen, Sept-Iles QC G4R 2R5
Tél: 418-968-4634; *Téléc:* 418-962-3684
slcn@cgocable.ca
www.salondulivrecotenord.com
Membre(s) du bureau directeur:
Mélanie Devost, Directrice générale

Estrie
#104, 138, rue Wellington nord, Sherbrooke QC J1H 5C5
Tél: 819-563-0744; *Téléc:* 819-563-3630
salondulivredelestrie@bellnet.ca
www.salondulivredelestrie.com
Membre(s) du bureau directeur:
Ghislaine Thibault, Directrice générale
Lucie Nicol, Présidente
lunic2@videotron.ca

Montréal
#430, 300 rue Saint-Sacrement, Montréal QC H2Y 1X4
Tél: 514-845-2365; *Téléc:* 514-845-7119
slm.info@videotron.ca
www.salondulivredemontreal.com
Membre(s) du bureau directeur:
Francine Bois, Directrice générale

Outaouais
CP 7, #301, 115, rue Principale, Gatineau QC J9H 3M2
Tél: 819-775-4873; *Téléc:* 819-775-3812
info@slo.qc.ca
www.slo.qc.ca
Membre(s) du bureau directeur:
Anne-Marie Trudel, Directrice générale
amtrudel@slo.qc.ca

Québec
26, rue St-Pierre, Québec QC G1K 8A3
Tél: 418-692-0010; *Téléc:* 418-692-0029
info@silq.ca
www.silq.ca
Membre(s) du bureau directeur:
Philippe Sauvageau, Président/Directeur général
psauvageau@silq.ca

Rimouski
CP 353, #105, 110, rue de l'Évêche est, Rimouski QC G5L 7C3
Tél: 418-723-7456; *Téléc:* 418-725-4543
slrinfo@globetrotter.net
www.salondulivrederimouski.ca
Membre(s) du bureau directeur:
Robin Doucet, Directeur général

Saguenay-Lac-St-Jean
2675, boul du Royaume, Jonquière QC G7X 7W4
Tél: 418-542-7294; *Téléc:* 418-542-3525
info@salondulivre.ca
www.salondulivre.ca
Membre(s) du bureau directeur:
Sylvie Marcoux, Directrice générale
marcoux.syl@videotron.ca

Trois-Rivières
#100, 60, rue St-Antoine, Trois-Rivières QC G9A 0C4
Tél: 819-376-5308; *Téléc:* 819-376-4222
info@sltr.qc.ca
www.sltr.qc.ca
Membre(s) du bureau directeur:
Julie Brosseau, Directrice générale
direction@sltr.qc.ca

Association québécoise des sports en fauteuil roulants *Voir* Parasports Québec

Association québécoise des techniques de l'environnement *Voir* Réseau environnement

Association québécoise des technologies (AQT) / Quebec Technology Association (QTA)

32, rue des Soeurs-Grises, Montréal QC H3C 2P8
Tél: 514-874-2667; *Téléc:* 514-874-1568
info@aqt.ca
www.aqt.ca
www.linkedin.com/groups/AQT-Association-qu%C3%A9b%C3%A9coise-technolog
twitter.com/aqtech
www.youtube.com/user/AQTechno/videos?view=0
Nom précédent: Centre de promotion du logiciel québécois; Réseau inter logiQ
Aperçu: *Dimension:* moyenne; *Envergure:* provinciale; fondée en 1990
Mission: Aider et soutenir les entrepreneurs en logiciel et multi média du Québec dans le développement de leur entreprise sur les scènes locales et internationale
Membre de: Canadian Advanced Technology Association; Information Technology Association of Canada; Fédération de l'Informatique du Québec
Membre(s) du bureau directeur:
Nicole Martel, Présidente directrice générale, 514-874-2667 Ext. 105
nmartel@aqt.ca
Finances: *Budget de fonctionnement annuel:* $500,000-$1.5 Million
Membre(s) du personnel: 14
Membre: 500; *Montant de la cotisation:* 325$ à 1250$ selon le nombre d'employés et le statut de l'entreprise; *Critères d'admissibilite:* Développeurs de logiciels du Québec
Activités: *Service de conférenciers:* Oui; *Listes de destinataires:* Oui

Association québécoise des traumatisés crâniens (AQTC)

#106, 911, rue Jean-Talon Est, Montréal QC H2R 1V5
Tél: 514-274-7447; *Téléc:* 514-274-1717
www.aqtc.ca
www.facebook.com/AQTC.montreal.laval
Aperçu: *Dimension:* petite; *Envergure:* locale; fondée en 1989
Mission: Accompagner les victimes de lésions cérébrales traumatiques en fournissant des loisirs activites, ateliers de groupe, et des informations
Membre de: Regroupement des associations de personnes traumatisées craniocérébrals du Québec / Coalition of Associations of Craniocerebral Trauma in Quebec
Membre(s) du bureau directeur:
Pierre Mitchell, Executive Director, 514-274-7447 Ext. 224
Manon Beaudoin, Présidente
Céline Martel, Vice-présidente
Denyse Rousselet, Secrétaire
Nathalie Boucher, Intervenante psychosociale, 514-274-7447 Ext. 222
Membre(s) du personnel: 11
Membre: *Critères d'admissibilite:* Personnes du Québec qui ont survécu à une blessure traumatique du cerveau, de leurs familles, et amis; Toute personne intéressée à en apprendre davantage sur les lésions cérébrales traumatiques
Activités: Des activités de loisirs par des professionnels formés à la psychologie et la récréologie, afin d'aider ceux qui ont souffert d'une lésion cérébrale traumatique; Organiser des ateliers de groupe qui mettent l'accent sur ??l'intégration pour les victimes de lésions cérébrales; Sensibiliser le public aux lésions cérébrales; Se référant à des personnes ressources appropriées; Fournir de l'information sur les blessures traumatiques au cerveau; Collaborer avec d'autres organismes communautaires; *Service de conférenciers:* Oui
Publications:
• Association québécoise des traumatisés crâniens rapport annuel
Type: Yearbook; *Frequency:* Annually
• Phoenix
Type: Newspaper; *Frequency:* Quarterly
Profile: Reports & photographs of association happenings

Association québécoise des traumatisés craniens (AQTC)

#106, 911, rue Jean-Talon est, Montréal QC H2R 1V5
Tél: 514-274-7447; *Téléc:* 514-274-1717
www.aqtc.ca
www.facebook.com/AQTC.montreal.laval
Aperçu: *Dimension:* moyenne; *Envergure:* provinciale; Organisme sans but lucratif; fondée en 1986
Mission: Organisme sans but lucratif; a pour mission de défendre et promouvoir les droits et les intérêts des personnes traumatisés cranio-cérébrales et de leurs familles et de favoriser le maintien ou l'amélioration de la qualité de vie. AQTC Laval: 220, av du Parc, (450) 629-9911.
Membre(s) du bureau directeur:
Pierre Mitchell, Directeur général
Pascal Brodeur, Adjoint à la direction, 514-274-7447 Ext. 233
Finances: *Fonds:* Gouvernement provincial - SAAQ
Membre(s) du personnel: 11; 68 bénévole(s)
Membre: 427; *Critères d'admissibilite:* Personnes ayant subi un traumatisme cranio cérébral; les proches et les professionnels
Activités: Camp de vacances; activités; ateliers; services pour les proches; bénévolat interne et externe

Association québécoise des troubles d'apprentissage (AQETA) / Learning Disabilities Association of Québec (LDAQ)

#502, 740, rue Saint-Maurice, Montréal QC H3C 1L5
Tél: 514-847-1324; *Téléc:* 514-281-5187
info@aqeta.qc.ca
www.aqeta.qc.ca
www.facebook.com/aqeta.provinciale
twitter.com/AQDRnationale
Aperçu: *Dimension:* moyenne; *Envergure:* provinciale; Organisme sans but lucratif; fondée en 1966 surveillé par Learning Disabilities Association of Canada
Mission: Faire connaître les troubles d'apprentissage; faire la promotion des besoins et des droits collectifs des enfants et des adultes qui vivent avec des troubles d'apprentissage
Membre de: Learning Disabilities Association of Canada
Membre(s) du bureau directeur:
Lise Bibaud, Directrice générale, 514-847-1324
Finances: *Budget de fonctionnement annuel:* $250,000-$500,000; *Fonds:* Provinciaux; fédéraux
Membre(s) du personnel: 8; 1 bénévole(s)
Membre: 1 300; *Montant de la cotisation:* 30$; *Comités:* Administration; Congrès; Communications et Collecte de Fonds
Activités: Informer les parents; travailler avec les intervenants; recruter et former des bénévoles; développer un partenariat avec le monde des affaires et les centres d'emploi pour favoriser l'intégration des jeunes; représentation; informer les intervenants en éducation et santé; *Service de conférenciers:* Oui; *Bibliothèque:* Centre de ressources; rendez-vous

Association québécoise des troubles d'apprentissage - section Outaouais

#203, 109, rue Wright, Gatineau QC J8X 2G7
Tél: 819-777-3126; *Téléc:* 819-777-5423
info@aqetaoutaouais.qc.ca
www.aqetaoutaouais.qc.ca
Aperçu: *Dimension:* petite; *Envergure:* locale; Organisme sans but lucratif; fondée en 1978
Mission: Répond aux besoins des personnes ayant des troubles d'apprentissage pour ainsi promouvoir l'intégration au niveau de l'éducation et de la vie communautaire en Outaouais.
Membre de: Troubles d'apprentissage - association Canadienne
Membre(s) du bureau directeur:
Josée Lavigne, Présidente
Paul Morin, Directeur général
aqetaoutaouais@videotron.ca
Finances: *Fonds:* Centraide; Agence de dévelop. de réseaux locaux de services de santé et de services sociaux
Membre(s) du personnel: 4

Membre: *Montant de la cotisation:* 20$ étudiant; 40$ régulier 100$ institution; *Critères d'admissibilite:* Adultes et enfants de 6 à 12 ans ayant des troubles d'apprentissage
Activités: Camp du samedi; camp d'été; écoute active; références; *Stagiaires:* Oui; *Service de conférenciers:* Oui; *Bibliothèque:* La découverte; rendez-vous

Association québécoise des utilisateurs de l'ordinateur au primaire-secondaire (AQUOPS)

#1, 6818, boul Saint-Denis, Montréal QC H2S 2S2
Tél: 514-948-1234; *Téléc:* 514-948-1231
accueil@aquops.qc.ca
www.aquops.qc.ca
Aperçu: *Dimension:* moyenne; *Envergure:* provinciale
Mission: Grouper en association les utilisateurs de l'ordinateur ainsi que les personnes intéressées au développement et à l'utilisation des technologies de l'information et des communications dans l'enseignement primaire et secondaire
Membre(s) du bureau directeur:
Mario Morin, Président & Directeur général
mario.morin@aquops.qc.ca
Membre(s) du personnel: 11; 11 bénévole(s)
Membre: 1,000-4,999
Activités: Ateliers; colloques; journées thématiques
Prix, Bouses:
• CHAPO (Prix)
Décerné à des personnes ou groupes du monde scolaire, culturel ou commercial afin de souligner la qualité de leur engagement et de leur travail dans le domaine de l'intégration des technologies de l'information et de la communication (TIC)

Association québécoise du chauffage au mazout (AQCM) / Quebec Oil Heating Association

#202, 2, Place du Commerce, Île-des-Soeurs QC H3E 1A1
Tél: 514-285-1150
info@petcommunication.ca
www.lemazout.org
Aperçu: *Dimension:* moyenne; *Envergure:* provinciale; fondée en 1957
Mission Pour protéger les intérêts des utilisateurs, ainsi que le public; de promouvoir les avantages de l'huile de chauffage auprès des consommateurs; pour représenter et défendre les intérêts de ses membres au sein de l'industrie.
Membre: 18; *Critères d'admissibilite:* Entreprises qui commercialisent et fabriquent pétrole

Association québécoise du loisir municipal (AQLM)

4545, av Pierre-de Coubertin, Montréal QC H1V 0B2
Tél: 514-252-5244; *Téléc:* 514-252-5220
infoaqlm@loisirmunicipal.qc.ca
www.loisirmunicipal.qc.ca
Nom précédent: Association québécoise des directeurs et directrices du loisir municipal
Aperçu: *Dimension:* moyenne; *Envergure:* provinciale; Organisme sans but lucratif; fondée en 1999
Mission: Intégrer le domaine de vie communautaire au mandat de loisir; Affirmer la maîtrise d'oeuvre de la municipalité en loisir; faire valoir le service municipal de loisir comme partenaire du réseau des organisations locales (institutionnelles et associatives); Promouvoir l'expertise des professionnels du loisir; démontrer l'utilité et les bénéfices du loisir; Développer des pratiques professionnelles en loisir
Membre de: Regroupement loisir Québec
Membre(s) du bureau directeur:
Luc Toupin, Directeur général
dg@loisirmunicipal.qc.ca
Pierre Waters, Directeur, Services aux membres associés
p.watters@loisirmunicipal.qc.ca
Joëlle Derulle, Conseillère, Formations et développement
jderulle@loisirmunicipal.qc.ca
Finances: *Fonds:* Ponctuelles pour projets de recherches
15 bénévole(s)
Membre: 700 actif + 90 associés + 12 étudiants; *Montant de la cotisation:* 172-700; *Critères d'admissibilite:* Professionnel en loisir
Activités: *Service de conférenciers:* Oui

Association Québécoise du Lymphoedème (AQL) / Lymphedema Association of Québec (LAQ)

6565 St. Hubert, Montréal QC H2S 2M5
Tél: 514-979-2463
aql@infolympho.ca
www.infolympho.ca
www.facebook.com/AQL.LAQ
Aperçu: *Dimension:* moyenne; *Envergure:* provinciale; Organisme sans but lucratif
Meetings/Conferences: • 11e Congrès annuel de l'Association québécoise du lymphoedème, 2015, QC
Scope: Provincial

Association québécoise du personnel de direction des écoles (AQPDE)

#235, 3291, ch Ste-Foy, Québec QC G1X 3V2
Tél: 418-781-0700; *Téléc:* 418-781-0276
info@aqpde.ca
www.aqpde.ca
Aperçu: *Dimension:* moyenne; *Envergure:* provinciale; fondée en 1967
Mission: Défendre et promouvoir les intérêts professionnels, sociaux et économiques des membres, favoriser leur participation et établir une concertation avec les autres organismes du réseau de l'éducation pour assurer les meilleures conditions de ses membres
Membre de: AFIDES International
Membre(s) du bureau directeur:
Danielle Boucher, Présidente
Finances: *Budget de fonctionnement annuel:* $250,000-$500,000
Membre(s) du personnel: 3
Membre: 500; *Montant de la cotisation:* 1.2% du salaire; *Critères d'admissibilite:* Cadre des établissements scolaires
Activités: Congrès au 2 ans

Association québécoise du théâtre amateur inc. *Voir* Fédération québécoise du théâtre amateur

Association québécoise du transport aérien (AQTA)

Aéroport international Jean-Lesage, 600, 6e av de l'Aéroport, Québec QC G2G 2T5
Tél: 418-871-4635; *Téléc:* 418-871-8189
aqta@aqta.ca
www.aqta.ca
www.linkedin.com/groups?home=&gid=2588987
www.facebook.com/group.php?gid=119190028092054
Aperçu: *Dimension:* moyenne; *Envergure:* provinciale; Organisme sans but lucratif; fondée en 1975
Mission: Voué à la défense et la promotion des intérêts de tous les secteurs du transport aérien
Membre(s) du bureau directeur:
Éric Lippé, Président-directeur général
Membre(s) du personnel: 2
Membre: 135; *Montant de la cotisation:* Barème; *Critères d'admissibilite:* Transporteurs aériens et fournisseurs de produits et services liés à l'aviation

Association québécoise du transport et des routes inc. (AQTR)

Bureau de Montréal, #200, 1255, rue University, Montréal QC H3B 3B2
Tél: 514-523-6444; *Téléc:* 514-523-2666
www.aqtr.qc.ca
www.facebook.com/AQTransports
www.twitter.com/AQTransports
Aperçu: *Dimension:* grande; *Envergure:* provinciale; fondée en 1965
Mission: Assumer un leadership technique; définir des règles en matière de sécurité et d'environnement; Favoriser l'échange international des expertises; promouvoir la recherche et le développement des expertises et des produits en transport; promouvoir la formation dans le domaine des transports; Assumer la représentativité de l'AQTR par la participation aux principaux forums sur les transports; Contribuer à servir la société par l'éducation et l'information du grand public
Membre(s) du bureau directeur:
Jean Mastropietro, Président
Dominique Lacoste, Présidente-directrice générale
Mathieu Charbonneau, Directeur général adjoint
Finances: *Budget de fonctionnement annuel:* $500,000-$1.5 Million
Membre(s) du personnel: 7; 100 bénévole(s)
Membre: 950; *Montant de la cotisation:* 270 $; *Critères d'admissibilite:* Secteur privé - Ingénieur conseils; Entrepreneurs; Fournisseurs et manufacturiers; Laboratoires; Transporteurs; Architectes et urbanistes; Étudiants; Spécialistes en environnement; Secteur public et parapublic - Ministères; Municipalités; Maisons d'enseignement; Sociétés de transport; Autres sociétés, départements et services publics; *Comités:* Directions techniques - Infrastructures de transport; Transport des personnes; Circulation; Sécurité dans les transports; Transport aérien; Recherche et développement; Comités - Transport des marchandises; Environnement; Revue; Congrès; Activités municipales
Activités: Regrouper les personnes impliquées dans les techniques du transport; Encourager les échanges multidisciplinaires et favoriser la collaboration entre différents secteurs; Recommander toute mesure permettant de développer des techniques du transport; *Listes de destinataires:* Oui
Prix, Bouses:
• Grands prix d'excellence en transport (Prix)
• Prix Josef-Hode-Keyser (Prix)
• Prix Guy-Paré (Prix), Reconnaissance aux bénévoles
• Prix du Président (Prix), Reconnaissance aux bénévoles
• Prix Meilleure conférence (Prix), Reconnaissance aux bénévoles
• Programme de bourses d'études de l'AQTr (Bourse d études)
• Concours de mémoire AIPCR-Québec (Prix)
Meetings/Conferences: • Le 50e Congrès annuel de l'Association québécoise du transport et des routes inc., mars, 2015, Palais des congrès de Montréal, Montréal, QC
Scope: National
Contact Information: Responsable: Ôve Arcand, téléphone: 514-523-6444 ext. 325, courriel: congres@aqtr.qc.ca
Publications:
• Routes et Transports [a publication of Association québécoise du transport et des routes inc.]
Type: Revue

Bureau de Québec
#505, 580, rue Grande-Allée est, Québec QC G1R 2K2
Tél: 418-948-8850; *Téléc:* 418-948-8854

Association québécoise Plaidoyer-Victimes (AQPV)

#201, 4305, rue d'Iberville, Montréal QC H2H 2L5
Tél: 514-526-9037; *Téléc:* 514-526-9951
aqpv@aqpv.ca
www.aqpv.ca
Également appelé: Plaidoyer-Victimes
Aperçu: *Dimension:* petite; *Envergure:* provinciale; Organisme sans but lucratif; fondée en 1984
Mission: Défense des droits et des intérêts des victimes d'actes criminels par la discussion, la sensibilisation, la formation, la concertation et la recherche
Membre(s) du bureau directeur:
Marie-Hélène Blanc, Directrice générale
Membre(s) du personnel: 3
Membre: 242; *Montant de la cotisation:* 55$ individu; 65$ associatif; 130$ partenaire; *Critères d'admissibilite:* Toutes personnes ou organismes s'intéressant à la problématique des victimes d'actes criminels
Activités: *Stagiaires:* Oui; *Service de conférenciers:* Oui; *Listes de destinataires:* Oui

Association québécoise pour l'évaluation d'impacts (AQEI)

CP 785, Succ. Place d'Armes, Montréal QC H2Y 3J2
Tél: 514-990-2193
mondorf@aqei.qc.ca
www.aqei.qc.ca
Aperçu: *Dimension:* moyenne; *Envergure:* provinciale
Mission: Regrouper toute personne, professionnelle ou non, intéressée par l'évaluation d'impacts et à son utilisation dans le processus de planification et de prise de décision
Affliation(s): International Association for Impact Assessment
Membre(s) du bureau directeur:
Eric Giroux, Président
Membre: *Montant de la cotisation:* Barème

Association québécoise pour l'hygiène, la santé et la sécurité du travail (AQHSST)

CP 52, 89, boul de Bromont, Bromont QC J2L 1A9
Tél: 450-776-2169
Ligne sans frais: 888-355-3830
info@aqhsst.qc.ca
www.aqhsst.qc.ca
www.linkedin.com/pub/aqhsst-ca/37/9b0/30b
www.facebook.com/pages/AQHSST/118417061527266
twitter.com/AQHSST
www.youtube.com/channel/UCXPB11tZPC7yEyBkfQPjvTg
Aperçu: *Dimension:* moyenne; *Envergure:* provinciale; Organisme sans but lucratif; fondée en 1978
Mission: Promouvoir les connaissances relatives à l'hygiène industrielle par l'échange et la vulgarisation de l'information; Faire la promotion des connaissances dans des domaines connexes pouvant avoir un impact sur la santé et la sécurité du travail tels la sécurité, l'ergonomie et l'environnement; étudier les législations pertinentes et toute action gouvernementale relatives à ses champs d'activités et faire les représentations qu'elle juge à propos; Encourager la reconnaissance de la compétence de ses membres

Membre(s) du bureau directeur:
Nicolas Perron, Président, 450-774-9131, Fax: 450-261-2107
Amélie Trudel, Vice-présidente, 514-849-8373, Fax: 514-849-8873
France de Repentigny, Secrétaire, 514-982-2553, Fax: 514-283-6737
Christine Venditto, Trésorière
Finances: *Budget de fonctionnement annuel:* $100,000-$250,000
Membre(s) du personnel: 2; 20 bénévole(s)
Membre: 475; *Montant de la cotisation:* 30$ membre étudiant; 125$ membre individuel; 325$ membre corporatif; *Comités:* Comité de formation; Comité des communications et du service à la clientèle
Activités: Congrès annuel; Formations; Activités associatives; regroupement de professionnels; *Bibliothèque:* UNF Library; Bibliothèque publique
Prix, Bouses:
- Prix Antoine-Aumont de l'AQHSST (Prix)
- Prix Méritas (Prix)
- Bourse 3M (Brouse)
- Bourse Levitt sécurité Ltée (Brouse)

Meetings/Conferences: • Congrès annuel de l'Association québécoise pour l'hygiène, la santé et la sécurité du travail 2015, May, 2015, Manoir Saint-Sauveur, St-Sauveur, QC
Scope: Provincial

Association québécoise pour la maîtrise de l'énergie (AQME) / Québec Association of Energy Managers (QAEM)

#750, 255, boul. Crémazie Est, Montréal QC H2M 1L5
Tél: 514-866-5584; *Téléc:* 514-874-1272
info@aqme.org
www.aqme.org
twitter.com/MaitriseEnergie
www.youtube.com/user/2729AQME
Aperçu: *Dimension:* moyenne; *Envergure:* provinciale; Organisme sans but lucratif; fondée en 1985
Mission: Contribuer à la promotion de la maîtrise de l'énergie au Québec pour une utilisation et une exploitation optimale des ressources et pour le respect de l'environnement
Membre(s) du bureau directeur:
Jean Lacroix, Président/directeur général, 514-866-5584 Ext. 225
jlacroix@aqme.org
Membre(s) du personnel: 14
Membre: 800; *Montant de la cotisation:* Barème; *Critères d'admissibilite:* Utilisateur ou fournisseur d'énergie; *Comités:* Bâtiment; Industriel; Organisateur de la Soirée de crustacés et moules annuelle; Organisateur de la Soirée de homards annuelle; Organisateur du congrès annuel; Organisateurs des Classiques de golf annuelles; Relève; Technique et jury du Concours Énergia; Transport; Exécutif
Activités: Congrès annuel, concours Énergia, party homards, tournois de golf; *Stagiaires:* Oui

Association Québécoise pour la Santé Mentale des Nourrisson (AQSMN)

CP 10009, St-Jean-sur-Richelieu QC J2W 0G6
Tél: 514-598-8413
info@aqsmn.org
www.aqsmn.org
Aperçu: *Dimension:* petite; *Envergure:* provinciale
Mission: De promouvoir la recherche dans les domaines de la santé et le développement mental du nourrisson; pour étudier la santé mentale des parents.
Membre(s) du bureau directeur:
Alain Lebel, Président
Membre: *Montant de la cotisation:* 20$ étudiant; 60$ individu; 100$ organisme; *Critères d'admissibilite:* Cliniciens et de chercheurs

Association québécoise pour la thérapie conjugale et familiale *See* Québec Association of Marriage & Family Therapy

Association québécoise pour le loisir des personnes handicapées (AQLPH)

CP 1000, Succ. M, 4545, av Pierre-de Coubertin, Montréal QC H1V 3R2
Tél: 514-252-3144
info@aqlph.qc.ca
www.aqlph.qc.ca
Aperçu: *Dimension:* moyenne; *Envergure:* provinciale; fondée en 1978
Mission: Promouvoir le droit à un loisir de qualité (éducatif, sécuritaire, valorisant et de détente); promouvoir la participation et la libre expression de la personne face à son loisir; promouvoir l'accès à tous les champs d'application du loisir (tourisme, plein air, sport et activité physique, loisir scientifique, socio-éducatif et socioculturel) pour toutes les personnes handicapées du Québec sans restriction d'âge, de sexe, ni de type d'handicap
Membre de: Alliance de vie active pour les canadiens; Canadiennes ayant un handicap
Membre(s) du bureau directeur:
Guylaine Laforest, Directrce générale
Membre: 14; *Critères d'admissibilite:* Associations régionales
Activités: "Destination Loisirs": une rencontre sportive, récréative et culturelle d'envergure provinciale de type participative où on y retrouve des activités sportives, de loisirs, touristiques et sociales pratiquées dans la plupart des régions tels le hockey-balle, le mini-golf, les quilles, etc.; *Bibliothèque:* Centre de documentation AQLPH; rendez-vous

AlterGo
#340, 525, rue Dominion, Montréal QC H3J 2B4
Tél: 514-933-2739; *Téléc:* 514-933-9384
info@altergo.net
www.altergo.net
Membre(s) du bureau directeur:
Sylvain Gamache, Président

ARLPH Abitibi-Témiscamingue
330, rue Perreault est, Rouyn-Noranda QC J9X 3C6
Tel: 819-762-8121; *Fax:* 819-762-0707
arlphat@ulsat.qc.ca
www.ulsat.qc.ca/templates/arlphat/
Membre(s) du bureau directeur:
Yvon Falardeau, Président

ARLPH Centre du Québec
La Place Rita St-Pierre, #236, 59, rue Monfette, Victoriaville QC G6P 1J8
Tél: 819-758-5464; *Téléc:* 819-758-4375
arlphcq@cdcbf.qc.ca
www.arlphcq.com

ARLPH Chaudière-Appalaches
5515, rue St-Georges, Lévis QC G6V 4M7
Tél: 418-833-4495; *Téléc:* 418-833-7214
arlphca@videotron.ca
www.arlphca.com
Membre(s) du bureau directeur:
Marie-Claude Hardy, Président

ARLPH Côte-Nord
#218, 859, rue Bossé, Baie-Comeau QC G5C 3P8
Tél: 418-589-5220; *Téléc:* 418-589-4612
info@urlscn.qc.ca
www.urlscn.qc.ca
Membre(s) du bureau directeur:
Noëlla Ouellet, Président

ARLPH de la Capitale-Nationale
CP 1000, Succ. M, 4545, av Pierre-De Coubertin, Montréal QC H1V 3R2
Tél: 514-252-3144
info@aqlph.qc.ca
www.aqlph.qc.ca
Membre(s) du bureau directeur:
Guylaine Laforest, Directrice

ARLPH Estrie
5182, boul Bourque, Sherbrooke QC J1N 1H4
Tél: 819-864-0864; *Téléc:* 819-864-1864
arlpphe@abacom.com
www.csle.qc.ca/fr/arlpphe
Membre(s) du bureau directeur:
Brigitte Blanchard, Président

ARLPH Lanaudière
200, rue de Salaberry, Joliette QC J6E 4G1
Tél: 450-752-2586; *Téléc:* 450-759-8749
arlphl@cepap.ca
Membre(s) du bureau directeur:
Paulette Goulet, Présidente

ARLPH Laurentides
#100, 300, rue Longpré, Saint-Jérôme QC J7Y 3B9
Tél: 450-431-3388; *Téléc:* 450-436-2277
arlphl@videotron.ca
www.arlphl.org
Membre(s) du bureau directeur:
Kevin Hoskin, Président

ARLPH Laval
#215A, 387, boul. des Prairies, Laval QC H7N 2W4
Tél: 450-668-2354; *Téléc:* 450-668-2226
info@arlphl.qc.ca
www.arlphl.qc.ca
Membre(s) du bureau directeur:
Rachid Ababou, Président

ARLPH Saguenay/Lac St-Jean
138, rue Price ouest, Chicoutimi QC G7H 1J8
Tél: 418-545-4132; *Téléc:* 418-545-7271
arlph@cybernaute.com
www.lavilla.ca/arlph
Membre(s) du bureau directeur:
Francine Vigneault, Présidente

URLS Bas St-Laurent
#304, 38, rue St-Germain est, Rimouski QC G5L 1A2
Tél: 418-723-5036; *Téléc:* 418-722-8906
lisearsenault@globetrotter.net
www.urls-bsl.qc.ca
Membre(s) du bureau directeur:
Émilien Nadeau, Président

URLS Gaspésie/Iles de la Madeleine
CP 99, 8, boul. Perron Est, Caplan QC G0C 1H0
Tél: 418-388-2121; *Téléc:* 418-388-2133
informations@urlsgim.com
www.urlsgim.com
Membre(s) du bureau directeur:
Gérald Arsenault, Président

URLS Mauricie
260, rue Dessureault, Trois-Rivières QC G8T 9T9
Tél: 819-691-3075; *Téléc:* 819-373-6046
urls@urlsmauricie.com
www.urlsmauricie.com
Membre(s) du bureau directeur:
Pierre Tremblay, Président

URLS Outaouais
#102, 394, boul. Maloney ouest, Gatineau QC J8P 7Z5
Tél: 819-663-2575; *Téléc:* 819-663-5568
info@loisirsportoutaouais.com
www.urlso.qc.ca
Membre(s) du bureau directeur:
Lise Waters, Présidente

Zone loisir Montérégie
3800, boul Casavant Ouest, Saint-Hyacinthe QC J2S 8E3
Tél: 450-771-0707
infozlm@zlm.qc.ca
www.zlm.qc.ca
Membre(s) du bureau directeur:
Vincent Robichaud, Présidente

Association québécoise pour le tourisme équestre et l'équitation de loisir du Québec

1025, ch du Plan-Bouchard, Blainville QC J7C 4K7
Tél: 450-434-1433; *Téléc:* 450-434-8826
quebec@cheval.qc.ca
www.cheval.qc.ca
Également appelé: Québec à cheval
Aperçu: *Dimension:* moyenne; *Envergure:* provinciale; fondée en 1980
Mission: Assurer le développement de la randonnée équestre dans ses dimensions de plein air et de tourisme; inventorier et soutenir le développement de sentiers équestres; promouvoir par tous les moyens la randonnée et le tourisme équestres; sensibiliser les adeptes de l'équitation à une pratique sécuritaire de l'activité
Membre(s) du bureau directeur:
Julie Villeneuve, Directeur général
Membre(s) du personnel: 6
Membre: 50 institutionnel; 7,000 individu
Activités: Stages et cliniques de formation; Équi-Livres; *Stagiaires:* Oui; *Service de conférenciers:* Oui

Association québécoise pour les enfants atteints d'audimutité *Voir* Association québécoise de la dysphasie

L'Association récréative *See* The Recreation Association

Association régionale de la communauté francophone de Saint-Jean inc. (ARCf)

125 Prince William St., Saint John NB E2L 2B4
Tél: 506-658-4600; *Téléc:* 506-643-7880
arcf@arcf-sj.org
www.arcf-sj.org
www.facebook.com/arcfsaintjean?ref=name
twitter.com/ARCfdeSaintJean
Nom précédent: Conseil communautaire Samuel-de-Champlain
Aperçu: *Dimension:* moyenne; *Envergure:* locale; Organisme sans but lucratif; fondée en 1985
Mission: Donner aux francophones du Saint-Jean métropolitain le meilleur milieu de vie au Nouveau-Brunswick
Membre de: Conseil provincial des sociétés culturelles; Chambre de commerce de Saint John; Société canadienne des

directeurs d'association
Affiliation(s): Chevaliers de colomb; Scouts et guides; Association sportive
Membre(s) du bureau directeur:
Michel Côté, Directeur général
Finances: *Budget de fonctionnement annuel:* $1.5 Million-$3 Million; *Fonds:* Subventions gouvernementales; commandites; activités-bénéfices et commerciales
Membre(s) du personnel: 30; 350 bénévole(s)
Membre: 100-499; *Critères d'admissibilite:* Appuie le développement de la communauté francophone
Activités: *Bibliothèque:* Bibliothèque Le Cormoran

Association régionale de la police de York ***See*** York Regional Police Association

Association régionale de ringuette Laval
3235, boul, St-Martin Est, Laval QC H7E 5G8
Tél: 450-664-1917
info@ringuettelaval.org
ringuettelaval.org
Aperçu: *Dimension:* petite; *Envergure:* provinciale surveillé par Ringuette-Québec
Membre de: Ringuette-Québec
Membre(s) du bureau directeur:
Nathalie Trudel, Présidente

Association Régionale de Ringuette Richelieu Yamaska
QC
info@rery.ca
www.rery.ca
Aperçu: *Dimension:* petite; *Envergure:* provinciale surveillé par Ringuette-Québec
Membre de: Ringuette-Québec
Membre(s) du bureau directeur:
Nathalie Babineau, Présidente, 514-812-4633

Association régionale des maisons de transition ***See*** Regional Halfway House Association

Association régionale du sport étudiant de l'Abitibi-Témiscamingue ***Voir*** Réseau du sport étudiant du Québec Abitibi-Témiscamingue

Association régionale du sport étudiant de l'Est du Québec ***Voir*** Réseau du sport étudiant du Québec Est-du-Québec

Association régionale du sport étudiant de la Côte-Nord ***Voir*** Réseau du sport étudiant du Québec Côte-Nord

Association régionale du sport étudiant de la Mauricie ***Voir*** Réseau du sport étudiant du Québec, secteur Mauricie

Association régionale du sport étudiant de Montréal ***Voir*** Réseau du sport étudiant du Québec Montréal

Association régionale du sport étudiant de Québec et Chaudière-Appalaches ***Voir*** Réseau du sport étudiant du Québec Chaudière-Appalaches

Association régionale du sport étudiant du Saguenay-Lac St-Jean ***Voir*** Réseau du sport étudiant du Québec Saguenay-Lac St-Jean

Association régionale du sport étudiant Lac Saint-Louis ***Voir*** Réseau du sport étudiant du Québec Lac Saint-Louis

Association régionale du sport étudiant Laurentides-Lanaudière ***Voir*** Réseau du sport étudiant du Québec Laurentides-Lanaudière

Association régionale du sport scolaire ***See*** Greater Montreal Athletic Association

Association Renaissance de la région de l'Amiante
76, rue Saint-Joseph nord, Thetford Mines QC G6G 3N8
Tél: 418-335-5636
as.ren@bellnet.ca
Aperçu: *Dimension:* petite; *Envergure:* locale
Mission: Défendre les droits des personnes ayant une déficience intellectuelle et de leur famille; faciliter l'intégration sociale de ces personnes
Affliation(s): Association du Québec pour l'intégration sociale
Membre(s) du bureau directeur:
Johanne Lessard, Coordonnatrice
Finances: *Budget de fonctionnement annuel:* Moins de $50,000
Membre: *Montant de la cotisation:* 7$ membre actif; 15$ bénévole ou intervenant; 25$ établissement; *Critères d'admissibilite:* Personne vivant avec une déficience intellectuelle ou un trouble envahissant du développement et sa famille
Activités: Information; orientation; activités éducatives; parrainage; activités sociales; samedi-répit; camp de vacances pour enfants; groupes d'entraide pour parents et pour personnes intégrées au marché du travail

Association renaissance des personnes traumatisées crâniennes du Saguenay-Lac-Saint-Jean (ARPTC)
2223, boul du Saguenay, Jonquière QC G7S 4H5
Tél: 418-548-9366; *Téléc:* 418-548-9369
Ligne sans frais: 855-548-9366
arptc@arptc.org
www.arptc.org
Aperçu: *Dimension:* petite; *Envergure:* locale; fondée en 1995
Mission: Pour aider les personnes dans la région du Saguenay-Lac-Saint-Jean du Québec qui ont été touchés par les conséquences de lésions cérébrales; Pour aider les membres de la famille des personnes qui ont subi une lésion cérébrale
Membre de: Regroupement des associations de personnes traumatisées craniocérébrales du Québec / Coalition of Associations of Craniocerebral Trauma in Quebec
Membre(s) du bureau directeur:
Jonathan Jean-Vézina, Directeur général
direction@arptc.org
Membre(s) du personnel: 9
Activités: Protéger les droits des personnes souffrant de lésions cérébrales; Accroître la sensibilisation et fournir des informations sur les lésions cérébrales; Offrir un soutien psychosocial

Association royale de golf du Canada ***See*** Royal Canadian Golf Association

Association salers du Canada ***See*** Salers Association of Canada

Association scientifique canadienne de la viande ***See*** Canadian Meat Science Association

Association Sclérose en Plaques Rive-Sud (ASPRS)
3825, rue Windsor, Saint-Hubert QC J4T 2Z6
Tél: 450-926-5210; *Téléc:* 450-926-5215
asprs.qc.ca
Aperçu: *Dimension:* petite; *Envergure:* locale; fondée en 1976
Mission: Aider des gens qui a sclérose en plaques de surmonter avec leur maladie en s'engageant dans des activités sociales
Membre(s) du bureau directeur:
Nancy Caron, Directrice générale
nancy.caron@asprs.qc.ca
Membre(s) du personnel: 10
Membre: *Critères d'admissibilite:* Toute personne avec de sclérose en plaques et leurs parents

Association SeCan ***See*** SeCan Association

Association sectorielle - Fabrication d'équipement de transport et de machines (ASFETM) / Sectorial Association - Transportation Equipment & Machinery Manufacturing (SATEMM)
#202, 3565, rue Jarry est, Montréal QC H1Z 4K6
Tél: 514-729-6961; *Téléc:* 514-729-8628
Ligne sans frais: 888-527-3386
info@asfetm.com
www.asfetm.com
Aperçu: *Dimension:* grande; *Envergure:* provinciale; Organisme sans but lucratif; fondée en 1983
Mission: Aider les employeurs et les travailleurs à prévenir les accidents du travail et les maladies professionnelles, en faisant pour eux de la recherche, en leur dispensant de l'information, de la formation et de l'assistance technique qui visent essentiellement à rendre impossibles les accidents et les maladies au travail, et en privilégiant, à cette fin, l'élimination de cette possibilité à sa source même selon un processus de participation paritaire
Membre de: National Safety Council (USA); Association du camionnage du Québec
Membre(s) du bureau directeur:
Arnold Dugas, Directeur général
adugas@asfetm.com
Suzanne Ready, Chargée de l'information
sready@asfetm.com
Finances: *Budget de fonctionnement annuel:* $500,000-$1.5 Million
Membre(s) du personnel: 20
Membre: 8 groupes corporatifs - 3 patronaux + 5 syndicaux; *Critères d'admissibilite:* Etre une association patronale ou syndicale du secteur
Activités: Programme d'action annuel (30 projets); journées de sessions et de formation; colloques; *Service de conférenciers:* Oui
Publications:
- Fiches techniques [a publication of Association sectorielle - Fabrication d'équipement de transport et de machines]
- Santé + Sécurité [a publication of Association sectorielle - Fabrication d'équipement de transport et de machines]
Type: Magazine

Association sectorielle services automobiles
#150, 8, rue de la Place-du-Commerce, Brossard QC J4W 3H2
Tél: 450-672-9330; *Téléc:* 450-672-4835
Ligne sans frais: 800-363-2344
info@autoprevention.qc.ca
autoprevention.qc.ca
twitter.com/AutoPrevention
www.youtube.com/autoprevention
Également appelé: Auto Prévention
Aperçu: *Dimension:* moyenne; *Envergure:* provinciale
Mission: Aider les travailleurs et les employeurs du secteur des services automobiles à prendre en charge la santé et la sécurité au travail, afin d'éliminer les risques d'accidents et de maladies professionnelles
Membre(s) du bureau directeur:
Jean-Guy Trottier, Directeur général
trottier@autoprevention.qc.ca
Diane Gareau, Adjointe à la direction
gareau@autoprevention.qc.ca
Publications:
- AUTO Prévention
Type: Journal; *Frequency:* Trimestriel

Association Sépharade Francophone ***Voir*** Communauté sépharade unifiée du Québec

Association Simmental du Québec ***See*** Québec Simmental Association

Association Sportive de Ringuette Brossard
CP 210, 8000, boul Leduc, Brossard QC J4Y 0E9
communications@ringuetteroussillon.ca
www.ringuettebrossard.com
www.facebook.com/AssociationSportiveDeRinguetteDeBrossard
twitter.com/ARRoussillon
Aperçu: *Dimension:* petite; *Envergure:* provinciale surveillé par Ringuette-Québec
Membre de: Ringuette-Québec
Membre(s) du bureau directeur:
Sylvain Lebel, President, 450-926-1497
slebel1@sympatico.ca

Association sportive des aveugles du Québec inc. (ASAQ)
4545, av Pierre-de Coubertin, Montréal QC H1V 3R2
Tél: 514-252-3178
infoasaq@sportsaveugles.qc.ca
www.sportsaveugles.qc.ca
Aperçu: *Dimension:* petite; *Envergure:* provinciale; fondée en 1979 surveillé par Canadian Blind Sports Association Inc.
Mission: Promouvoir la pratique du sport amateur auprès des personnes handicapées de la vue et de favoriser ainsi leur intégration
Membre(s) du bureau directeur:
Nathalie Chartrand, Directrice générale
nchartrand@sportsaveugles.qc.ca
Membre(s) du personnel: 5
Membre: 135; *Montant de la cotisation:* 15$
Activités: *Service de conférenciers:* Oui

Association sportive des sourds du Québec inc. (ASSQ)
CP 1000, Succ. M, 4545, av Pierre-de Coubertin, Montréal QC H1V 3R2
Téléc: 514-252-3049
www.assq.org
Nom précédent: Association amateur des sports des sourds du Québec; Fédération sportive des sourds du Québec inc.
Aperçu: *Dimension:* moyenne; *Envergure:* provinciale; fondée en 1968 surveillé par Canadian Deaf Sports Association
Mission: Promouvoir le sport, les loisirs et l'activité physique chez les personnes sourdes et malentendantes du Québec
Membre de: Canadian Deaf Sports Association
Membre(s) du bureau directeur:

Françis Roussel, Président
froussel@assq.org
Suzanne Laforest, Coordonnatrice à l'administration
slaforest@assq.org

Association sportive et communautaire du Centre-Sud (ASCCS)

2093, rue de la Visitation, Montréal QC H2X 3C9
Tél: 514-522-2246; *Téléc:* 514-522-6702
centre@asccs.qc.ca
asccs.qc.ca
www.linkedin.com/groups/Association-sportive-communautaire-CentreSud-3
www.facebook.com/103895026361019
twitter.com/ASCCSMontreal
Aperçu: *Dimension:* petite; *Envergure:* locale; fondée en 1974
Mission: Pour améliorer la qualité de vie des résidents de la région en offrant des activités de loisirs abordables
Membre(s) du bureau directeur:
Stéphane Proulx, Directeur adjoint, 514-522-2246 Ext. 223
sproulx@asccs.qc.ca
Membre: *Montant de la cotisation:* 15$ Adultes; 7$ Jeunes; 10$ Aînés
Activités: Sports; Activités d'arts et culture; Activités aquatiques

L'Association St.Vincent et Grenadines de Montréal Inc. ***See*** St. Vincent & the Grenadines Association of Montreal Inc.

Association syndicale des employées de production et de service (ASEPS)

CP 1063, Saint-Lazare QC J7T 2Z7
Tél: 450-455-8346; *Téléc:* 450-455-9731
Ligne sans frais: 877-455-8346
aseps@aseps.qc.ca
aseps.qc.ca
Aperçu: *Dimension:* petite; *Envergure:* locale; fondée en 1996
Mission: Hausser le statut économique et social de ses membres; appuyer les personnes qui la recherche; promouvoir le plein-emploi, les activités éducatives, législatives et politiques
Membre(s) du bureau directeur:
Donald A. Caron, Président
dcaron@aseps.qc.ca
Guillaume Caron, Vice-Président
guicaron@aseps.qc.ca
Paul-André Gagnon, Vice-Président, 819-269-3359
Daniel Guénette, Secrétaire
Jean-Claude Gobeil, Vice-Président
Finances: *Budget de fonctionnement annuel:* Moins de $50,000
Membre(s) du personnel: 2
Membre: 850; *Montant de la cotisation:* 5-8/semaine; *Critères d'admissibilite:* Salariés

Association technique canadienne du bitume ***See*** Canadian Technical Asphalt Association

Association technique des pâtes et papiers du Canada ***See*** Pulp & Paper Technical Association of Canada

Association to Reunite Grandparents & Families ***See*** CANGRANDS Kinship Support

Association touristique Chaudière-Appalaches ***Voir*** Tourisme Chaudière-Appalaches

Association touristique des Iles-de-la-Madeleine ***Voir*** Tourisme Iles de la Madeleine

Association touristique des Laurentides (ATL) / Laurentian Tourist Association

14 142, rue de la Chapelle, Mirabel QC J7J 2C8
Tél: 450-436-8532; *Téléc:* 450-436-5309
Ligne sans frais: 800-561-6673
info-tourisme@laurentides.com
www.laurentides.com
www.facebook.com/TourismeLaurentides
www.youtube.com/notredecor
Aperçu: *Dimension:* moyenne; *Envergure:* locale; Organisme sans but lucratif; fondée en 1975 surveillé par Associations touristiques régionales associées du Québec
Mission: Unir tous les agents, corporations, corps publics et municipaux, associations et organismes, entreprises, oeuvrant dans le domaine touristique dans la région nord de Montréal; orienter et favoriser le développement et l'activité touristique régionale dans le meilleur intérêt régional; obtenir au nom de toute la région des interventions gouvernementales ou autres propres à favoriser son développement touristique
Membre de: Association de l'industrie touristique du Canada; National Tour Association
Finances: *Budget de fonctionnement annuel:* $1.5 Million-$3 Million
Membre(s) du personnel: 16
Membre: 752; *Montant de la cotisation:* 275$-2 900$; *Critères d'admissibilite:* Industrie touristique
Activités: Promotion et développement touristique regional; service d'accueil; information; reservation

Association touristique du Saguenay-Lac-Saint-Jean ***Voir*** Association touristique régionale du Saguenay-Lac-Saint-Jean

Association touristique régionale de Charlevoix

495, boul de Comporté, La Malbaie QC G5A 3G3
Tél: 418-665-4454; *Téléc:* 418-665-3811
Ligne sans frais: 800-667-2276
info@tourisme-charlevoix.com
www.tourisme-charlevoix.com
www.facebook.com/tourismecharlevoix
twitter.com/gocharlevoix
www.youtube.com/user/TourismeCharlevoix
Également appelé: Tourisme Charlevoix
Aperçu: *Dimension:* moyenne; *Envergure:* locale; Organisme sans but lucratif surveillé par Associations touristiques régionales associées du Québec
Mission: Acceuil, promotion, développement de Charlevoix en tourisme
Finances: *Budget de fonctionnement annuel:* $1.5 Million-$3 Million

Association touristique régionale de Duplessis (ATRD)

312, av Brochu, Sept-Iles QC G4R 2W6
Tél: 418-962-0808; *Téléc:* 418-962-6518
Ligne sans frais: 888-463-0808
info@tourismeduplessis.com
www.tourismeduplessis.com
Aperçu: *Dimension:* moyenne; *Envergure:* locale; Organisme sans but lucratif; fondée en 1979 surveillé par Associations touristiques régionales associées du Québec
Mission: Regrouper efficacement, sur une base géographique et sectorielle, les diverses entreprises touristiques de la région; proposer un plan d'action annuel dans lequel sont déterminés les priorités, les programmes et les services offerts à ses membres
Membre(s) du bureau directeur:
Marie-Soleil Vigneault, Directrice générale
msvigneault@tourismeduplessis.com
Danys Jomphe, Président
Finances: *Budget de fonctionnement annuel:* $250,000-$500,000
Membre(s) du personnel: 6
Membre: 220; *Comités:* Communication; Commercialisation

Association touristique régionale du Saguenay-Lac-Saint-Jean

#100, 412, boul. Saguenay Est, Chicoutimi QC G7H 7Y8
Tél: 418-543-3536; *Téléc:* 418-543-1805
Ligne sans frais: 855-253-8387
admin@tourismesaglac.net
www.saguenaylacsaintjean.ca
www.linkedin.com/tourisme-saguenay-lac-saint-jean
www.facebook.com/TourismeSaguenayLacSaintJean
twitter.com/Saguenay_Lac
www.youtube.com/SaguenayLacStJean
Également appelé: Tourisme Saguenay-Lac-Saint-Jean; ATR Saguenay-Lac-Saint-Jean
Nom précédent: Association touristique du Saguenay-Lac-Saint-Jean
Aperçu: *Dimension:* moyenne; *Envergure:* locale; Organisme sans but lucratif; fondée en 1977 surveillé par Associations touristiques régionales associées du Québec
Mission: Au service et à l'écoute de ses membres et de l'industrie touristique régionale dans son ensemble, elle est une organisation de concertation dont les principales activités visent à promouvoir à développer la qualité de l'expérience touristique, à assurer l'accueil et l'information et la mise en marché
Membre de: l'Association des ATR Associées du Québec
Membre(s) du bureau directeur:
Julie Dubord, Directrice générale
jdubord@tourismesaglac.net
Sylvianne Dufour, Adjointe à la direction générale
directiongenerale@tourismesaglac.net
Finances: *Budget de fonctionnement annuel:* $1.5 Million-$3 Million
Membre(s) du personnel: 16
Membre: 612; *Critères d'admissibilite:* Tourisme
Activités: *Evénements de sensibilisation:* Lancement de saison; Grands Prix du tourisme québécois

Association touristique régionale Manicouagan

#304, 337, boul LaSalle, Baie-Comeau QC G4Z 2Z1
Tél: 418-294-2876; *Téléc:* 418-294-2345
Ligne sans frais: 888-463-5319
info@cotenord-manicouagan.com
www.tourismemanicouagan.com/fr/
www.facebook.com/manicouagancotenord
Aperçu: *Dimension:* petite; *Envergure:* locale; Organisme sans but lucratif; fondée en 1971 surveillé par Associations touristiques régionales associées du Québec
Mission: Promouvoir la région comme destination touristique et mettre en valeur ses attraits
Membre(s) du bureau directeur:
Grétha Fougèrers, Directrice générale, 418-294-2876 Ext. 224
ww.facebook.com/manicouagancotenord
Finances: *Budget de fonctionnement annuel:* $500,000-$1.5 Million
Membre(s) du personnel: 10
Membre: 400; *Critères d'admissibilite:* Intervenants touristiques
Activités: Soutien technique; accueil et information; centres Infotouristes; programmes de publicité; colloque; outils promotionnels
Prix, Bouses:
• Grand Prix du tourisme (Prix)

Association Trot & Amble du Québec (ATAQ) / Québec Trotting & Pacing Society

#216, 5375, rue Paré, Montréal QC H4P 1P7
Tél: 514-731-9484
Ligne sans frais: 800-731-9484
courses@qc.aira.com
www.trotetamble.ca
Aperçu: *Dimension:* moyenne; *Envergure:* provinciale
Mission: Coopérer avec les promoteurs afin de s'assurer de la bonne conduite des programmes de courses aux différents hippodromes du Québec; améliorer les lois et règlements en vue de favoriser le sport des courses sous harnais; représenter et aider tous les members; encourager et promouvoir les courses d'élevage québécois et les courses régulières; collaborer avec les différents organismes afin d'établir un juste équilibre pour le bien-être de l'industrie
Membre(s) du bureau directeur:
Marc Camirand, Président
Gilles Fortier, Secrétaire général, 514-731-9484
Membre: *Montant de la cotisation:* Barème
Activités: Service d'assurances; activités sociales; promotion

Association universitaire canadienne d'études nordiques ***See*** Association of Canadian Universities for Northern Studies

Association Zoroastrianne de Québec (AZQ) / Zoroastrian Associaton of Québec (ZAQ)

PO Box 35, Stn. Beaconsfield, Beaconsfield QC H9W 5T6
Tel: 514-426-9929
quebeczoroastrians@gmail.com
zaq.org
www.facebook.com/www.zaq.org?ref=hl
twitter.com/ZAQGROUP
www.youtube.com/channel/UCH_sL1HiIlPUnPgg9kt1yew
Overview: A small provincial charitable organization founded in 1984
Affliation(s): Federation of North American Zoroastrian Associations
Chief Officer(s):
Dolly Dastoor, President
dollydastoor@sympatico.ca

Association ®Et si c'était moi

#106, 386, rue De Gentilly Ouest, Longueuil QC J4H 2A2
Tél: 450-651-2006
Aperçu: *Dimension:* petite; *Envergure:* locale
Mission: Aider les gens à surmonter les angoisses sociales avec l'art

Association/Troubles Anxieux du Québec (ATAQ)

CP 49018, Montréal QC H1N 3T6
Tél: 514-251-0083
info@ataq.org
www.ataq.org
Aperçu: *Dimension:* petite; *Envergure:* provinciale; Organisme sans but lucratif; fondée en 1991 surveillé par Anxiety Disorders Association of Cnada
Mission: Formée par un groupe de professionnels oeuvrant dans le domaine des troubles anxieux et de ses comorbidités

avec pour but de collaborer au niveau des soins, de l'enseignement, de la recherche, de la formation médicale et de l'information du public
Membre(s) du bureau directeur:
Stéphane Bouchard
Membre: 24; *Critères d'admissibilité:* Psychiatres; psychologues; omnipraticiens; professionnels de la sant, mentale
Activités: Information; recherche; conférences; émissions pour télévision

Associations de retraités des universités et collèges du Canada ***See*** College & University Retiree Associations of Canada

Associations touristiques régionales associées du Québec (ATRAQ) / Québec Regional Tourist Associations Inc.
#330, 1575, boul de l'Avenir, Laval QC H7S 2N5
Tél: 450-686-8358; *Téléc:* 450-686-9630
Ligne sans frais: 877-686-8358
information@atrassociees.com
www.atrassociees.com
www.facebook.com/ATRassociees
twitter.com/atrassociees
www.youtube.com/user/ATRassociees
Aperçu: *Dimension:* moyenne; *Envergure:* provinciale; Organisme sans but lucratif; fondée en 1981
Mission: Regrouper l'ensemble des associations touristiques régionales oeuvrant au Québec en vue de les représenter et défendre leurs intérêts collectifs; les promouvoir et leur offrir des services; contribuer ainsi au développement de l'industrie touristique québécoise
Membre(s) du bureau directeur:
François-G. Chevrier, Président-Directeur général
francoisgchevrier@atrassociees.com
Membre(s) du personnel: 10
Membre: 21 ATR; *Critères d'admissibilite:* Etre une association touristique régionale reconnue par le ministère du tourisme du Québec
Activités: Grands Prix du Tourisme Québécois; Bourse des Médias

L'Associaton des éleveurs Ayrshire du Canada ***See*** Ayrshire Breeders Association of Canada

Associés bénévoles qualifiés au service des jeunes (ABQSJ)
#8146, rue Drolet, Montréal QC H2P 2H5
Tél: 514-948-6180
info@abqsj.org
www.abqsj.org
www.facebook.com/pages/ABQSJ/132550216834026
Aperçu: *Dimension:* petite; *Envergure:* provinciale; Organisme sans but lucratif
Mission: Former des bénévoles qui viennent en aide aux jeunes en difficulté
Membre(s) du bureau directeur:
Sandra Murphy, Présidente
Ginette Charron-Matte, Vice-présidente
Membre(s) du personnel: 2
Membre: *Comités:* Coordination des stages; Bulletin; Publicité et levées de fonds; Chaîne téléphonique
Activités: *Service de conférenciers:* Oui

Assyrian Association ***See*** Welfare Committee for the Assyrian Community in Canada

Asthma Society of Canada (ASC) / Société canadienne de l'asthme
#401, 124 Merton St., Toronto ON M4S 2Z2
Tel: 416-787-4050; *Fax:* 416-787-5807
Toll-Free: 866-787-4050
info@asthma.ca
www.asthma.ca
www.facebook.com/AsthmaSocietyofCanada
twitter.com/AsthmaSociety
Overview: A medium-sized national charitable organization founded in 1974
Mission: To optimize the health of people with asthma through education and asthma awareness.
Member of: Canadian Network for Asthma Care
Affliation(s): Family Physicians Asthma Group of Canada; Health Canada Laboratory Centre for Disease Control's National Asthma Control Task Force
Chief Officer(s):
Robert Oliphant, President & CEO, 416-787-4050 Ext. 109
roboliphant@asthma.ca
Noah Farber, Director, Communications & Government Relations, 416-787-4050 Ext. 100
noah@asthma.ca
Finances: *Annual Operating Budget:* $500,000-$1.5 Million; *Funding Sources:* Donations; special events; partnerships & sponsorships
Staff Member(s): 5
Membership: *Fees:* Schedule available; *Committees:* Executive; Nominations; Medical & Scientific Advisory; Finance; Program Development; Communications; Financial Development; Education
Activities: Research funding; national education website; toll-free Asthma Infoline; educational brochures & print materials; newsletter & magazine; annual fundraising; public awareness events; *Awareness Events:* National Asthma Awareness Month, May; *Speaker Service:* Yes; *Library* Open to public

Asthme et allergies Québec
#225, 2590, boul. Laurier, Québec QC G1V 4M6
Tél: 418-627-3141; *Téléc:* 418-627-8716
Ligne sans frais: 877-627-3141
info@asthmeallergies.com
asthmeallergies.com
www.facebook.com/171652556213925
Également appelé: Asthmédia
Nom précédent: Association pour l'asthme et l'allergie alimentaire du Québec
Aperçu: *Dimension:* petite; *Envergure:* provinciale; fondée en 1986
Mission: Informer les personnes souffrant d'asthme et d'allergie alimentaire sur leur problème de santé et sur les difficultés vécues par ces dernières dans leur vie quotidienne
Affliation(s): Desjardins: Caisse populaire de Chalesbourg, GlaxoSmithKline, Sanofi, Paladin
Membre(s) du bureau directeur:
Gervais Bélanger, Directeur général
Membre: *Montant de la cotisation:* $20
Activités: Ligne d'écoute; camps d'été; camps familiaux; conférences; centre de documentation; journées thématiques provinciales

Ataxia of Charlevoix-Saguenay Foundation ***Voir*** Fondation de l'Ataxie Charlevoix-Saguenay

ATD Fourth World Movement Canada ***Voir*** Mouvement ATD Quart Monde Canada

Atelier d'histoire Hochelaga-Maisonneuve
2929, av Jeanne-d'Arc, Montréal QC H1W 3W2
Tél: 514-899-9979; *Téléc:* 514-259-6466
videosepmedia@videotron.ca
Aperçu: *Dimension:* petite; *Envergure:* locale; Organisme sans but lucratif; fondée en 1978
Mission: Promouvoir l'intérêt pour l'histoire; utiliser tout processus d'animation pour oeuvrer au sein de la collectivité, des milieux populaires et scolaires; mettre en valeur les églises historiques d'Hochelaga-Maisonneuve
Membre(s) du bureau directeur:
Paul Labonne, Directeur
Finances: *Budget de fonctionnement annuel:* $50,000-$100,000
Membre(s) du personnel: 5; 5 bénévole(s)
Membre: 20; *Montant de la cotisation:* 10$
Activités: Expositions de photos anciennes; visites dans les écoles; visites guidées d'églises et bâtiments patrimoniaux de Montréal; *Bibliothèque:* Centre de documentation; Bibliothèque publique

L'Atelier De Clare
PO Box 126, Church Point NS B0W 1M0
Tel: 902-769-3253; *Fax:* 902-769-0002
caclclare@eastlink.ca
www.swwd.ca/atelier
Overview: A small local organization
Mission: To help members become productive members of society through work placements & the development of life skills
Member of: DIRECTIONS Council for Vocational Services Society; Canadian Association for Community Living - Clare Branch
Chief Officer(s):
Kathy Jacques, Executive Director/Manager

Atelier de Formation Socioprofessionnelle de la Petite-Nation
358, rue Rossy, Saint-André-Avellin QC J0V 1W0
Tél: 819-983-6373; *Téléc:* 819-983-6368
atelier@afspn.qc.ca
www.atelierfspn.org
www.facebook.com/LAtelierFspn
Également appelé: Atelier FSPN
Aperçu: *Dimension:* petite; *Envergure:* locale; fondée en 1987
Mission: Pour aider les personnes handicapées physiques et mentales à trouver un emploi
Membre(s) du bureau directeur:
Katherine Provost, Directrice générale
Membre(s) du personnel: 15

L'Atelier des lettres
1710, rue Beaudry, MontréAl QC H2L 3E7
Tél: 514-524-0507; *Téléc:* 514-524-0222
latelier@qc.aira.com
www.atelierdeslettres.org
Aperçu: *Dimension:* petite; *Envergure:* locale
Mission: Pour réduire le degré d'analphabétisme entre les adultes vivant dans la région Centre-Sud, ainsi que pour améliorer la vie des gens qui sont analphabètes et à sensibiliser la population à l'analphabétisme
Membre(s) du bureau directeur:
Francine Lefebvre, Coordinatrice
coordination@qc.aira.com
Membre(s) du personnel: 3
Membre: *Montant de la cotisation:* Gratuit

Atelier habitation Montréal
#206, 55, av Mont-Royal Ouest, Montréal QC H2T 2S6
Tél: 514-270-8488; *Téléc:* 514-270-6728
info@atelierhabitationmontreal.org
atelierhabitationmontreal.org
Aperçu: *Dimension:* petite; *Envergure:* locale; fondée en 1978
Mission: Pour offrir un soutien et des connaissances à ceux qui souhaitent créer des logements communautaires
Membre(s) du bureau directeur:
Robert Manningham, Directeur général
r.manningham@atelierhabitationmontreal.org
Membre(s) du personnel: 9

Atelier RADO Inc. (RADO)
CP 432, 325, rue St-François, Edmundston NB E3V 3L1
Tél: 506-735-6313; *Téléc:* 506-735-5803
rado@nb.aibn.com
www.nb-shopping.com/rado.htm
Aperçu: *Dimension:* petite; *Envergure:* locale; Organisme sans but lucratif; fondée en 1983
Mission: Alléger le fardeau de la pauvreté au sein des personnes à faibles revenus dans le comté du Madawaska
Membre de: Association of Food Banks & C.V.A.'s for New Brunswick; Canadian Association of Food Banks
Membre(s) du bureau directeur:
David Couturier, Personne ressource
Finances: *Budget de fonctionnement annuel:* $250,000-$500,000
Membre(s) du personnel: 6; 10 bénévole(s)
Membre: 1-99
Activités: Banque alimentaire; cuisine communautaire; comptoir vestimentaire; services d'urgence

Athabasca & District Chamber of Commerce (ADCofC)
PO Box 3074, Athabasca AB T9S 2B9
Tel: 780-675-5378
www.athabasca-chamber.org
Overview: A small local organization founded in 1976
Member of: Alberta Chamber of Commerce
Affliation(s): Canadian Chambers of Commerce
Chief Officer(s):
Joanne Peckham, President
Michael Neville, Secretary
Finances: *Annual Operating Budget:* Less than $50,000; *Funding Sources:* Membership fees
85 volunteer(s)
Membership: 79; *Fees:* $50-$275; *Committees:* Retail; Membership; Welcome Neighbour; Maintenance; Promotion & Marketing; Canada Day; Tourism
Activities: Canada Day; Customer Appreciation Day, 3rd Friday in July
Awards:
• High School Graduation Math Award (Award)

Athabasca Native Friendship Centre Society
4919 - 53 St., Athabasca AB T9S 1L1

Tel: 780-675-3086; *Fax:* 780-675-3063
anfcs@telusplanet.net
anfca.com/friendship-centres/athabasca
Overview: A small local organization founded in 1988 overseen by Alberta Native Friendship Centres Association
Mission: The Society is a non-profit, social services agency administering programs & services to meet the needs of all Aboriginal people of the region, both transient & resident.
Member of: Alberta Native Friendship Centres Association (ANFCA)
Activities: Offering a comprehensive range of services, such as diabetes initiative, summer & after-school programs for children, court liaison, job training, housing consultation, language/literacy classes, recreational activities, health-related programs, low-cost clothing distriubtion

Athabasca University Faculty Association (AUFA) / Association des professeurs de l'Université d'Athabasca

#219, 1 University Dr., Athabasca AB T9S 3A3
Tel: 780-675-6282; *Fax:* 780-675-6182
Toll-Free: 800-788-9041
aufahq@athabascau.ca
aufa.ab.ca
twitter.com/aufacultyassoc
Overview: A small local organization founded in 1973
Mission: To protect, enhance & improve salaries, benefits & working conditions of the AUFA membership
Member of: Canadian Association of University Teachers; Confederation of Alberta Faculty Associations
Affliation(s): Alberta Federation of Labour; Canadian Labour Congress
Chief Officer(s):
Colleen Powell, Executive Director
colleenp@athabascau.ca
Finances: *Annual Operating Budget:* Less than $50,000
Staff Member(s): 2; 14 volunteer(s)
Membership: 400; *Member Profile:* All Athabasca University academic and professional staff are members of AUFA by legislation under Alberta's Post-secondary Learning Act.; *Committees:* Social Development; Equity; Communications
Activities: Collective bargaining

Athabasca University Students' Association ***See*** Athabasca University Students' Union

Athabasca University Students' Union (AUSU)

Energy Sqaure, #500, 10109 - 106th St. NW, Edmonton AB T5J 3L7
Tel: 780-497-7000; *Fax:* 780-497-7003
Toll-Free: 855-497-7003
ausu@ausu.org
www.ausu.org
www.facebook.com/AthaUSU
twitter.com/AthabascaUSU
Previous Name: Athabasca University Students' Association
Overview: A small local organization founded in 1992
Mission: To advocate on behalf of its student members by lobbying the provincial & federal governments for funding, & by approaching the University regarding such concerns as course problems or fees.
Chief Officer(s):
Toni Fox, President
Tamra Ross, Executive Director
executivedirector@ausu.org
Finances: *Funding Sources:* Student fees
Staff Member(s): 3; 9 volunteer(s)
Membership: *Member Profile:* All undergraduate Athasbasca University Students
Publications:
• The Voice
Type: Magazine; *Frequency:* Weekly

The Athletes Association of Canada ***See*** AthletesCAN

Athletes International

#2702, 3550 Jeanne Mauce, Montréal QC H2X 3P7
Tel: 514-982-9989; *Fax:* 514-982-0111
Toll-Free: 800-344-1810
info@athletes-int.com
www.athletes-int.com
twitter.com/athletesint
Overview: A small national organization
Mission: To promote a sense of community & sharing in Canadian sport; To offer discounted products & services, to members of the Canadian sport community, through partners
Chief Officer(s):
Peter Schleicher, President
pschleicher@athletes-int.com
Membership: *Member Profile:* Canadian sport community
Activities: Offering benefits in areas such as airfare, travel insurance, & hotel reservations

AthletesCAN

PO Box 60039, Stn. Findlay Creek, Ottawa ON K1T 0K9
Tel: 613-526-4025; *Fax:* 613-526-9735
Toll-Free: 888-832-4222
info@athletescan.com
www.athletescan.com
www.facebook.com/AthletesCAN
twitter.com/AthletesCAN
Also Known As: The Association of Canada's National Team Athletes
Previous Name: The Athletes Association of Canada
Overview: A medium-sized national organization founded in 1992
Mission: To work with others in leadership, advocacy & education to ensure a fair, responsive & supportive sport system for athletes
Chief Officer(s):
Jasmine Northcott, Executive Director
jnorthcott@athletescan.com
Ashley LaBrie, Director, Athlete Relations & Strategic Partnerships
alabrie@athletescan.com
Staff Member(s): 3
Membership: 3,000+
Awards:
• AthletesCAN Leadership Award

Athletic Therapists' Association of British Columbia ***See*** Athletic Therapy Association of British Columbia

Athletic Therapy Association of British Columbia (ATABC)

#200, 4170 Still Creek Dr., Burnaby BC V5C 6C6
Tel: 604-918-5077
info@athletictherapybc.ca
www.athletictherapybc.ca
www.facebook.com/264629906893091
twitter.com/ATABC
Previous Name: Athletic Therapists' Association of British Columbia
Overview: A small provincial organization founded in 1994
Mission: ATABC is a non-profit organization that represents athletic therapists in the province. It ensures that all of its members are in good standing with the Canadian Athletic Therapists Association. It promotes injury prevention, immediate care & rehabilition of musculoskeletal injuries.
Member of: Canadian Athletic Therapists Association
Chief Officer(s):
Sandy Zinkowski, President
5 volunteer(s)
Membership: 1-99; *Member Profile:* Certified athletic therapists & certification candidates
Activities: Sports medical coverage throughout BC; *Speaker Service:* Yes
Meetings/Conferences: • Athletic Therapists Association for British Columbia 10th Annual General Meeting, 2015
Scope: Provincial

Athletics Alberta

Percy Page Centre, 11759 Groat Rd., Edmonton AB T5M 3K6
Tel: 780-427-8792; *Fax:* 780-427-8899
Other Communication: www.flickr.com/photos/athleticsalberta
info@athleticsalberta.com
www.athleticsalberta.com
www.linkedin.com/groups/Athletics-Alberta-1997317
www.facebook.com/AthleticsAlberta
twitter.com/athleticsAB
www.youtube.com/user/AthleticsAB
Previous Name: Alberta Track & Field Association
Overview: A medium-sized provincial organization founded in 1969 overseen by Athletics Canada
Mission: To encourage participation & development of excellence in athletics (track & field, cross-country, & road-running)
Member of: Athletics Canada
Chief Officer(s):
Linda Blade, President
Peter Ogilvie, Executive Director
peterogilvie@athleticsalberta.com
Sheryl Mack, Office Manager
sherylmack@athleticsalberta.com
Finances: *Funding Sources:* Lottery dollars; fundraising; membership fees
Staff Member(s): 3
Membership: *Committees:* Administration; Programs; Personnel; Executive; Marketing

Athletics Canada / Athlétisme Canada

#B1-110, 2445 St-Laurent Blvd., Ottawa ON K1G 6C3
Tel: 613-260-5580; *Fax:* 613-260-0341
Other Communication: www.flickr.com/photos/athleticscanada
athcan@athletics.ca
www.athletics.ca
www.facebook.com/Canadatrackandfield
twitter.com/athleticscanada
www.youtube.com/AthleticsCanada
Previous Name: Canadian Track & Field Association
Overview: A large national organization
Mission: To promote & encourage participation via competitions from the grass roots level through to the very highest level of proficiency; To assist coaches, officials & executives in fulfilling their goals through courses, conferences & clinics; To provide regular communication lines with members; To continually review & update technical programs; To assist in the research & investigation of potential new facilities; To engender more public awareness, interest & acceptance of the sport of track & field
Member of: International Association of Athletics Federations
Affliation(s): International Amateur Athletic Federation
Chief Officer(s):
Gordon Orlikow, Chair
gordon.orlikow@kornferry.com
Rob Guy, CEO
rguy@athletics.ca
Sally Clare, Director, Finance
sclare@athletics.ca
Mathieu Gentès, Director, Public Relations & Corporate Services
mgentes@athletics.ca
Kristine Deacon, Coordinator, National Team Programs
kdeacon@athletics.ca
Staff Member(s): 20
Membership: *Committees:* Athlete Development Program; Competitions; Finance; International; Masters; National Officials; National Team; Personnel; Planning; Rules & Awards; Run Canada; Para-Athletics
Activities: Offering national team events
Awards:
• Athletics Canada Annual Awards (Award)
• Run Canada Division Awards Program (Award)

Athletics Manitoba

#416, 145 Pacific Ave., Winnipeg MB R3B 2Z6
Tel: 204-925-5745
www.athleticsmanitoba.com
Overview: A medium-sized provincial organization founded in 1978 overseen by Athletics Canada
Mission: The governing and sanctioning organization for Track and field, Road Running and Cross Country in the province of Manitoba.
Member of: Athletics Canada; Sport Manitoba
Chief Officer(s):
Grant Mitchell, President
Chris Belof, Manager, Competition & Program
chris.belof@athleticsmanitoba.com
Awards:
• Athletics Manitoba Awards (Award)

Athletics New Brunswick (ANB) / Athlétisme du Nouveau-Brunswick

66 Belle Foret St., Dieppe NB E1A 8X9
Tel: 506-855-5003; *Fax:* 506-855-5011
anb@anb.ca
www.anb.ca
www.facebook.com/AthNB
twitter.com/AthNB
Overview: A medium-sized provincial organization founded in 1968 overseen by Athletics Canada
Mission: To act as the provincial sports organization for the sports of track & field & cross-country running
Member of: Athletics Canada
Chief Officer(s):
Bill MacMackin, President
Bill.MacMackin@anb.ca
Germain Landry, Vice-President
Germain.Landry@anb.ca
Gabriel (Gabe) LeBlanc, Director, Technical
anb@anb.ca

Camilla MacDougall, Registrar
Camilla.MacDougall@anb.ca
Membership: *Fees:* Schedule available
Activities: *Speaker Service:* Yes; *Rents Mailing List:* Yes

Athletics Nova Scotia
5516 Spring Garden Rd, 4th Fl., Halifax NS B3J 1G6
Tel: 902-425-5450; *Fax:* 902-425-5606
www.athleticsnovascotia.ca
Overview: A small provincial organization overseen by Athletics Canada
Mission: The Association is a non-profit, amateur sport governing body that develops, coordinates & promotes track & field, road running & cross-country running in Nova Scotia.
Member of: Athletics Canada
Chief Officer(s):
Anitra Stevens, Executive Director
Joanthan Doucette, Manager, Coaching & Officiating
Staff Member(s): 2
Membership: *Fees:* $60 club athlete; $75 independent athelete; $30 independent coach; $20 Run Jump Throw athlete; *Member Profile:* Track & field clubs
Awards:
• Athletics Nova Scotia Awards (Award)

Athletics Ontario
#211, 3 Concorde Gate, Toronto ON M3C 3N7
Tel: 416-426-7215; *Fax:* 416-426-7358
www.athleticsontario.ca
www.facebook.com/135196239850966
twitter.com/athleticsont
Previous Name: Ontario Track & Field Association
Overview: A medium-sized provincial organization founded in 1974 overseen by Athletics Canada
Mission: To promote & encourage participation via competitions from the grass roots level through to the very highest level of proficiency; To assist coaches, officials & executives in fulfilling their goals through courses, conferences & clinics; to provide regular communication lines with members; To continually review & update technical programs; To assist in the research & investigation of potential new facilities; To engender more public awareness, interest, & acceptance of the sport of track & field
Member of: Athletics Canada
Chief Officer(s):
John Craig, Managing Director
Roman Olszewski, Director, Technical Services
roman.otfa@cogeco.ca
Anthony Biggar, Manager, Communications & Public Relations
anthonybiggar@athleticsontario.ca
Staff Member(s): 8
Publications:
• Athletics Magazine
Type: Magazine; *Accepts Advertising*; *Editor:* Cecil Smith; Hazel North
Profile: Articles, event highlights, conference information, & athlete profiles

Athletics PEI
PO Box 302, Charlottetown PE C1A 7K7
www.athleticspei.ca
Overview: A small provincial organization
Member of: Athletics Canada
Chief Officer(s):
Gordon Sobey, President
gordonsobey@bellaliant.net

Athletics Yukon
4061 - 4th Ave., Whitehorse YT Y1A 1H1
e-mail: athleticsyukon@gmail.com
www.athleticsyukon.ca
www.facebook.com/pages/Athletics-Yukon/149557131815078
Overview: A small provincial organization overseen by Athletics Canada
Mission: To promote & encourage athletics as a life-long pursuit
Member of: Athletics Canada; Sport Yukon
Affliation(s): Boreal Adventure Running Association; Mount Lorne Mis-Adventure Race, Run Dawson
Chief Officer(s):
Ben Yu Schott, President
Membership: *Fees:* $15 youth & senior; $30 regular; $60 family
Activities: Administering the sports of: Road Racing; Cross Country Running; Track & Field; Snowshoeing; & Race Walking

Athlétisme Canada *See* Athletics Canada

Athlétisme du Nouveau-Brunswick *See* Athletics New Brunswick

Atikokan & District Association for the Developmental Services *See* Community Living Atikokan

Atikokan Chamber of Commerce
PO Box 997, 214 Main St. West, Atikokan ON P0T 1C0
Tel: 807-597-1599; *Fax:* 807-597-2726
Toll-Free: 888-334-2332
info@atikokanchamber.com
www.atikokanchamber.com
Overview: A small local charitable organization founded in 1952
Mission: To fairly represent the business & community concerns of Atikokan; To provide educational services to the business community & interested public
Member of: Sunset Country Travel Association; Northwestern Ontario Associated Chambers of Commerce
Affliation(s): Canadian Chamber of Commerce
Chief Officer(s):
Michael McKinnon, President
Jolene Wood, Office Manager
Finances: *Annual Operating Budget:* Less than $50,000; *Funding Sources:* Membership dues
Staff Member(s): 1; 20 volunteer(s)
Membership: 47; *Fees:* $35 individual; $80-340 business; $80 non-profit groups; *Committees:* Social; Retail; Tourism; Membership; Special Events
Activities: Annual general meeting; Business awards; Contests with Atikokan Auto, Home & Leisure Show; *Awareness Events:* Small Business Week; *Speaker Service:* Yes; *Rents Mailing List:* Yes

Atikokan Native Friendship Centre
PO Box 1510, #307, 309 Main St., Atikokan ON P0T 1C0
Tel: 807-597-1213; *Fax:* 807-597-1473
nativefriend@bellnet.ca
www.atikokannativefriendshipcentre.ca
Overview: A small local charitable organization founded in 1983
Mission: To serve as a meeting place for urban, Aboriginal people and also community members regardless of nationality; to provide an Aboriginal Family Support program for families with children up to 6 years old (includes parent relief/ mom/dads & tots, prenatal and postnatal support); to provide health outreach services, healing & wellness services, family violence initiatives, crisis intervention services, seniors care support services, cultural events, educational assistance, food bank, resource library, community support &d assistance for newcomers & community referral services.
Member of: Ontario Federation of Indian Friendship Centres
Chief Officer(s):
Deloris Veran, Executive Director
Finances: *Funding Sources:* Heritage Canada
Membership: 7; *Fees:* $2 single; $3 family
Activities: Drop in Centre; clothing depot; Ashandiwin Food Bank; arts & crafts; recreation programs; referrals; family intervention; support services; job search skills; dabber bingo; *Library* Open to public

Atlantic Alliance of Family Resource Centres *See* Valley Family Resource Centre Inc.

The Atlantic Alliance of Family Resource Centres
#1, 110 Richmond St, Woodstock NB E7M 2N9
Tel: 506-325-2299; *Fax:* 506-328-8896
anna.hayes@frc-crf.com
Overview: A medium-sized local organization
Member of: Canadian Association of Family Resource Programs (FRP Canada)
Chief Officer(s):
Anna-Marie Hayes, Contact

Atlantic Association of Applied Economists (AAAE)
1701 Hollis St., 13th Fl., Halifax NS B3J 3M8
Tel: 902-420-4601
www.cabe.ca/jmv3/index.php/cabe-chapters/aaae
Overview: A medium-sized provincial organization overseen by Canadian Association for Business Economics
Mission: To provide forums for current economic & public policy issues
Member of: Canadian Association for Business Economics
Chief Officer(s):
Thomas Storring, President, 902-424-2410
storrith@gov.ns.ca
Tara Ainsworth, Treasurer, 902-420-4601
tainsworth@bankofcanada.ca
Finances: *Annual Operating Budget:* Less than $50,000; *Funding Sources:* Membership
Membership: 1-99; *Fees:* $160 regular; $75 local; $20 student; $35 retiree

Atlantic Association of CBDCs
PO Box 40, 54 Loggie St., Mulgrave NS B0E 2G0
Tel: 902-747-2232; *Fax:* 902-747-2019
info@cbdc.ca
www.cbdc.nf.ca
www.youtube.com/user/AtlanticCBDCs
www.facebook.com/AACBDC
twitter.com/CBDCatlantic
Previous Name: Provincial Association of CBDCs
Overview: A small provincial organization
Mission: To oversee Community Business Development Corporations in Atlantic Canada
Affliation(s): Pan Canadian Community Futures Network
Chief Officer(s):
Roseanne Leonard, Managing Director
roseanne.leonard@cbdc.ca
Finances: *Funding Sources:* Atlantic Canada Opportunities Agency

Atlantic Association of Community Business Development Corporations
PO Box 40, 54 Loggie St., Mulgrave NS B0E 2G0
Tel: 902-747-2232; *Fax:* 902-747-2019
Toll-Free: 888-303-2232
info@cbdc.ca
www.cbdc.ca
www.facebook.com/AACBDC
twitter.com/CBDCatlantic
www.youtube.com/user/AtlanticCBDCs
Also Known As: Atlantic Association of CBDCs
Overview: A medium-sized local organization
Mission: To promote the development of small business & job creation
Affliation(s): Pan Canadian Community Futures Network
Chief Officer(s):
Basil Ryan, Chief Operating Officer
Membership: 41;

Atlantic Association of Prosthetists & Orthotists
c/o Canadian Association for Prosthetics & Orthotics, #605, 294 Portage Ave., Winnipeg MB R3C 0B9
Overview: A small provincial organization overseen by Canadian Association for Prosthetics & Orthotics
Mission: To promote quality patient care & a high standard of professionalism in the prosthetic & orthotic profession in the Atlantic region
Chief Officer(s):
Elizabeth Harris, President
Chantelle Dooley, Vice-President
Gerald Cadigan, Secretary/Treasurer
Membership: *Member Profile:* Certified prosthetic & orthotic practitioners & registered technicians in the Atlantic provinces; Allied health professionals & suppliers; Students in the prosthetic & orthotic field; Retired individuals
Activities: Encouraging continuing education

Atlantic Building Supply Dealers Association (ABSDA)
70 Englehart St., Dieppe NB E1A 8H3
Tel: 506-858-0700; *Fax:* 506-859-0064
www.absda.ca
twitter.com/absdadealers
Previous Name: Maritime Lumber Dealers Association
Overview: A medium-sized local organization founded in 1955
Mission: To keep membership informed of new trends & developments in the industry; to provide a forum to discuss mutual problems & ideas; to provide continuing education programs for members
Chief Officer(s):
Don Sherwood, President
sherwood@absda.ca
Brian Warr, Chair
Staff Member(s): 3
Membership: 625; *Member Profile:* Properly established lumber & building materials retailers
Activities: *Library*

Atlantic Canada Centre for Environmental Science (ACCES)
Saint Mary's University, 923 Robie St., Halifax NS B3H 3C3
Tel: 902-496-8234; *Fax:* 902-420-5261
www.smu.ca
Overview: A medium-sized local organization founded in 1991
Mission: To foster interdisciplinary research related to the environment
Membership: *Member Profile:* Saint Mary's University faculty members; Professionals interested in environmental science

Atlantic Canada Cruise Association (ACCA)
PO Box 1, Chester Basin NS B0J 1K0
Tel: 902-273-3330; *Fax:* 902-273-3331
info@atlanticcanadacruise.com
www.atlanticcanadacruise.com
Overview: A medium-sized provincial organization
Mission: To have Atlantic Canada as a preferred cruise destination in North America and lead the growth and development of the cruise industry in Atlantic Canada.
Chief Officer(s):
Corryn Morrissey, Chair
cmorrissey@chaipei.com
Membership: 10 ports + 14 organizations;

Atlantic Canada Fish Farmers Association (ACFFA)
226 Limekiln Rd., Letang NB E5C 2A8
Tel: 506-755-3526; *Fax:* 506-755-6237
info@atlanticfishfarmers.com
atlanticfishfarmers.com
www.facebook.com/150506105026651
twitter.com/AtlFishFarmers
www.youtube.com/user/acffavideos
Previous Name: New Brunswick Salmon Growers Association
Overview: A small provincial organization founded in 1987
Mission: To act as the voice of Atlantic Canada's salmon farming industry; To implement fish health initiatives to produce high-quality finfish
Affliation(s): Atlantic Canada Aquaculture Industry Research & Development Network (ACAIRDN)
Chief Officer(s):
Pamela Parker, Executive Director
Tobi Taylor, Manager, Operations
Betty House, Coordinator, Research & Development
Jim Hanley, Manager, Wharf
Staff Member(s): 7
Membership: 25; *Fees:* Schedule available; *Member Profile:* Salmon farming producers in New Brunswick; Companies & organizations that support the industry
Activities: Liaising with governments; Promoting fish health & welfare & social responsibility; Developing training programs; Fostering a positive image for finfish aquaculture in Atlantic Canada; Participating in management & research initiatives with related organizations, such as the Aquaculture Association of Canada, the National Fish Health Working Group, the Bay of Fundy Marine Resource Planning, & the Musquash Marine Protected Area Steering Committee

Atlantic Canada Pipe Band Association (ACPBA)
75 Donaldson Ave., Halifax NS B3M 3B6
Tel: 902-443-6570
Overview: A small local charitable organization founded in 1965
Chief Officer(s):
Lorna MacIsaac, President
Kelly MacKellar, Secretary
Finances: *Annual Operating Budget:* Less than $50,000
Membership: 250

Atlantic Canada Trail Riding Association (ACTRA)
c/o Pat Rideout, 3540 Rte. 890, Hillgrove NB E4Z 5W6
www.ac-tra.ca
Overview: A small local organization founded in 1980 overseen by Canadian Long Distance Riding Association
Mission: To promote safe horsemanship & friendly competition in the long distance trail competition
Member of: Canadian Long Distance Riding Association
Membership: *Fees:* $17.50
Awards:
• ACTRA Award (Award)
• Mileage Awards (Award)
Publications:
• ACTRA [Atlantic Canada Trail Riding Association] Newsletter
Type: Newsletter; *Frequency:* 5 pa.

Atlantic Canada Water & Wastewater Association (ACWWA)
PO Box 41002, Dartmouth NS B2Y 4P7
Tel: 902-434-6002; *Fax:* 902-435-7796
acwwa@hfx.andara.com
www.acwwa.ca
Overview: A medium-sized local organization
Mission: To improve drinking water in Atlantic Canada
Member of: American Water Works Association (AWWA); Water Environment Federation (WEF)
Chief Officer(s):
Ensor Nicholson, Chair
ensor.nicholson@moncton.org
Willard D'Eon, Secretary-Treasurer
willardd@cbcl.ca
Darrell Fisher, Director, Communications
dfisher@adi.ca
Membership: 430+; *Member Profile:* Water professionals in Atlantic Canada, from areas such as service provision, contracting, utility management, operations, system design, consulting, & academia; *Committees:* Education; Membership; Newsletter; Technical Papers; CWWA & CAC; Cross Connection Control; Young Professionals; Water for People; Government Affairs; Conference; Operator Involvement; Volunteers; Website
Activities: Providing training & information about the water & wastewater industry to members; Enhancing government relations; Offering networking opportunities
Meetings/Conferences: • Atlantic Canada Water & Wastewater Association 2015 68th Annual Conference, October, 2015
Scope: Provincial
Attendance: 260-340
Description: The association's annual general meeting & the election of its executive committee, plus a trade show, educational events, & networking occasions
Contact Information: Technical Director: Jennie Rand
• Atlantic Canada Water & Wastewater Association 2016 69th Annual Conference, 2016
Scope: Provincial
Description: A trade show, plus educational sessions & networking opportunities for Atlantic Canada's water professionals
Contact Information: Technical Director: Jennie Rand
Publications:
• ACWWA [Atlantic Canada Water & Wastewater Association] Newsletter
Type: Newsletter
Profile: Association activities
• AWWA Wastewater Operator Field Guide
Type: Booklet; *Price:* $55
Profile: Information used daily by wastewater system operators
• AWWA Water Operator Field Guide
Type: Booklet; *Price:* $55
Profile: Information for water treatment plant operators & water distribution operators
• Operator Certification Study Guide [a publication of the Atlantic Canada Water & Wastewater Association]
Type: Booklet; *Price:* $75
Profile: Information for water treatment & water distribution operators
• Wastewater Operator Certification Study Guide
Type: Booklet; *Price:* $75
Profile: Sample questions & answer for wastewater operator certification exams

Atlantic Canadian Anti-Sealing Coalition
e-mail: contact@antisealingcoalition.ca
www.antisealingcoalition.ca
www.facebook.com/260618610812
www.twitter.com/GreySealHugger
Overview: A medium-sized provincial organization
Mission: The Atlantic Canadian Anti-Sealing Coalition is a collection of individuals and groups from across the Atlantic Region working to end the commercial seal hunt by peaceful and legal means.
Membership: 285 individual; 10 organizations;

Atlantic Canadian Organic Regional Network (ACORN) / Réseau régional du l'industrie biologique du Canada atlantique
PO Box 6343, Sackville NB E4L 1G6
Toll-Free: 866-322-2676
admin@acornorganic.org
www.acornorganic.org
www.facebook.com/group.php?gid=153617164641
twitter.com/acornorganic
Overview: A medium-sized local organization founded in 2000
Mission: To act as the voice of organics in Atlantic Canada
Member of: Volunteer Canada; Organic Materials Review Institute
Affliation(s): Canadian Organic Growers
Chief Officer(s):
Beth McMahon, Executive Director
Staff Member(s): 1; 100 volunteer(s)
Membership: 300; *Fees:* $30

Atlantic Chamber of Commerce (ACC) / La Chambre de commerce de l'Atlantique
PO Box 2291, Windsor NS B0N 2T0
Tel: 902-698-0265; *Fax:* 902-678-7420
contact@apcc.ca
apcc.ca
www.facebook.com/122204667965417
Previous Name: Maritime Board of Traide; Atlantic Provinces Chamber of Commerce
Overview: A small provincial organization founded in 1896
Mission: To promote commerce in Atlantic Canada & to provide support for its members
Chief Officer(s):
Pierre Cadieux, President & CEO, 506-292-1033
pierre@apcc.ca
Staff Member(s): 3
Membership: 16,000; *Member Profile:* Corporations & individual business men & women; *Committees:* Provincial Division Advisory

Atlantic Collegiate Athletic Association (ACAA) / Association Atlantique du Sport Collegial (AASC)
PO Box 95, Hubbards NS B0J 1T0
Tel: 902-857-0592
acaa@eastlink.ca
acaa.ca
Previous Name: Nova Scotia College Conference
Overview: A small provincial organization founded in 1967
Mission: To govern intercollegiate sports in the Atlantic provinces
Member of: Canadian Collegiate Athletic Association
Affliation(s): Pacific Western Athletic Association; Alberta Colleges Athletic Conference; Réseau du sport étudiant du Québec; Ontario Colleges Athletic Association
Chief Officer(s):
Ron O'Flaherty, Chair
Activities: Soccer; volleyball; badminton; basketball; golf; cross country

Atlantic Community Newspapers Association *See* Newspapers Atlantic

Atlantic Conference of Independent Schools (ACIS)
708 Main St., Wolfville NS B4P 1G4
Tel: 902-542-2237
gmitchell@landmarkeast.org
Overview: A small local organization
Mission: To promote the role of independent school education in the Maritime provinces; To coordinate educational, sporting & other activities of mutual interest to member schools
Affliation(s): Canadian Association of Independent Schools

Atlantic Convenience Store Association (ACSA)
#B, 100 Ilsley Ave., Dartmouth NB B3B 1L3
Tel: 902-880-9733
theacsa.ca
Overview: A medium-sized provincial organization founded in 2008 overseen by Canadian Convenience Store Association
Mission: To represent convenience store retailers in the Atlantic provinces
Affliation(s): Canadian Convenience Stores Association; Western Convenience Stores Association; Association Québécoise des dépanneurs en alimentation; Ontario Convenience Stores Association
Chief Officer(s):
Mike Hammoud, President
hammoud@conveniencestores.ca
Finances: *Funding Sources:* Membership fees
Membership: *Member Profile:* Major convenience store companies; independent owners; food retailers; suppliers & wholesalers; oil companies; gasoline & automotive product vendors

Atlantic Council of Canada (ACC) / Conseil atlantique du Canada (CAC)
#102, 165 University Ave., Toronto ON M5H 3B8
Tel: 416-979-1875; *Fax:* 416-979-0825
info@atlantic-council.ca
www.atlantic-council.ca
www.linkedin.com/company/atlantic-council-of-canada
www.facebook.com/TheAtlanticCouncilOfCanada
twitter.com/NATOCanada
www.youtube.com/user/TheAtlanticCouncil
Previous Name: Canadian Atlantic Coordinating Committee
Overview: A medium-sized international charitable organization founded in 1966
Mission: To inform Canadians of the purpose & benefits of Canada's membership in the Atlantic Alliance & NATO.
Affliation(s): NATO; Atlantic Treaty Association - Paris, France
Chief Officer(s):

Julie Lindhout, President
Hugh Segal, Chair
Membership: *Fees:* $125 2 people; $75 regular; $50 young professionals/senior; $25 student
Activities: *Internships:* Yes; *Speaker Service:* Yes

Atlantic Dairy Council (ADC)
PO Box 9410, Stn. A, #700, 6009 Quinpool Rd., Halifax NS B3K 5S3
Tel: 902-425-2445; *Fax:* 902-425-2441
info@adcrecycles.com
www.adcrecycles.com
Overview: A medium-sized local organization
Mission: To maintain good relations among those engaged in dairy processing & distribution industries; to provide opportunities for industry training courses; & to enable united action on any matter concerning the welfare of the dairy trade
Chief Officer(s):
John K. Sutherland, Executive Secretary
15 volunteer(s)
Membership: 80

Atlantic Division, CanoeKayak Canada (ADCKC)
PO Box 295, 34 Boathouse Lane, Dartmouth NS B2Y 3Y3
Tel: 902-425-5450; *Fax:* 902-425-5606
www.adckc.ca
www.facebook.com/196999566862
twitter.com/ADCKC
www.youtube.com/user/TheADCKC
Previous Name: CanoeKayak Canada - Atlantic Division
Overview: A small local organization overseen by CanoeKayak Canada
Member of: CanoeKayak Canada; Sport Nova Scotia
Chief Officer(s):
Tracy White, General Manager
gm@adckc.ca
Jeff Houser, Regional Coach
regionalcoach@adckc.ca

Atlantic Episcopal Assembly (AEA) / Assemblée des évêques de l'Atlantique
3 Oakley Ave., Halifax NS B3M 3G6
Tel: 902-443-9325
Overview: A small local organization founded in 1967 overseen by Canadian Conference of Catholic Bishops
Mission: Proposer l'évangile de Jésus Christ dans les diverses situations de la vie ainsi que ses implications pratiques de notre temps; echange d'information pour les évêques
Chief Officer(s):
Gérald LeBlanc, Secretary-Treasurer
geraldleblanc@eastlink.ca
François Thibodeau, President
Terrence Prendergast
Finances: *Annual Operating Budget:* Less than $50,000
Membership: 12; *Committees:* Executive; Social Affairs

Atlantic Federation of Musicians, Local 571 (AFM, Local 571)
32B St. Margaret's Bay Rd., Halifax NS B3N 1J7
Tel: 902-479-3200; *Fax:* 902-479-1312
Toll-Free: 866-240-4809
571@bellaliant.com
www.cfm571.ca
Overview: A small provincial organization founded in 1953
Affliation(s): American Federation of Musicians of the United States & Canada
Chief Officer(s):
Varun Vyas, Secretary-Treasurer, 902-479-3200
varun@cfm571.ca
Finances: *Funding Sources:* Membership fees
Staff Member(s): 2
Membership: 500; *Fees:* $162; *Member Profile:* Professional musicians united through the American Federation of Musicians

The Atlantic Film Festival Association (AFFA)
PO Box 36139, Halifax NS B3J 3S9
Tel: 902-422-3456; *Fax:* 902-422-4006
festival@atlanticfilm.com
www.atlanticfilm.com
Previous Name: ScreenScene-Film & Television for Young People
Overview: A medium-sized international charitable organization founded in 1981
Mission: To promote & to build a strong film industry in Atlantic Canada
Member of: Atlantic Film Festival Association
Chief Officer(s):
Wayne Carter, Executive Director
Staff Member(s): 10
Activities: A 10-day celebration of film & video from around the world, Atlantic Film Festival, Sept.; Strategic Partners, an international co-production market focusing on film & TV and early stage projects, Sept.; The ViewFinders: International Film Festival for Youth, a 5-day event in the spring; AlFresco filmFesto, the AFFA's outdoor summer film series, held on the Halifax waterfront.;

Atlantic Filmmakers Cooperative (AFCOOP)
PO Box 2043, Stn. M, Halifax NS B3J 2Z1
Tel: 902-405-4474; *Fax:* 902-405-4485
membership@afcoop.ca
afcoop.ca
www.facebook.com/117025119810
twitter.com/afcoop
www.youtube.com/afcoophalifax
Overview: A small local organization founded in 1973
Mission: To provide a space where media artists can meet & produce films; to give members access to production equipment & facilities
Member of: Cooperative Associations of Nova Scotia
Affliation(s): Independent Film & Video Alliance; Academy of Canadian Cinema & TV; Linda Joy Busby Media Arts Foundation; Atlantic Independent Media; Atlantic Film Festival
Chief Officer(s):
Martha Cooley, Executive Director
director@afcoop.ca
Finances: *Funding Sources:* Canada Council; NS Dept. of Tourism, Culture & Heritage; NFB; NS Film Development Corp.
Staff Member(s): 3
Membership: *Fees:* $70 full; $40 associate; $180 production; *Member Profile:* Participation in making of film; taken film-related courses; demonstrate interest in co-op & function in community
Activities: Super 8, super 16 & 35mm film class; equipment workshop; animation classes; self-made films; five, three, one minute film program; *Library:* AFCOOP Video & Film Library; Open to public

Atlantic Fishing Industry Alliance
#10, 3045 Robie St., Halifax NS B3K 4P6
Tel: 902-446-4477
Overview: A medium-sized provincial organization founded in 1999
Mission: To represent organizations in the harvesting, processing and marketing sectors of the commercial fishing industry in the Maritime Provinces.

Atlantic Floorcovering Association (AFA)
PO Box 251, 1246 Rocky Lake Dr., Waverley NS B0N 2S0
Tel: 902-861-1889; *Fax:* 902-861-1910
info@atlanticfloorcovering.ca
Overview: A small provincial organization founded in 1987
Member of: National Floorcovering Association
Chief Officer(s):
Cathy Cochrane, Executive Director
Darryl Johnson, President
9 volunteer(s)
Membership: 65; *Fees:* $200-$400 dealer/retailer; $250 distributor/manufacturer; $75 installer
Awards:
• Educational Grants "Floor Knowledge" (Grant)

Atlantic Food & Beverage Processors Association
500 St. George St., Moncton NB E1C 1Y3
Tel: 506-389-7892; *Fax:* 506-854-5850
info@atlanticfood.ca
www.atlanticfood.ca
Overview: A medium-sized national organization
Mission: To actively support the food processors in the region in their efforts to operate efficiently and profitably.
Chief Officer(s):
Don Newman, Executive Director
Membership: 400;

Atlantic Halfway House Association (AHHA) / Association de maison de transition atlantique (AMTA)
c/o Stacey Dort, 3170 Romans Ave., Halifax NS B3L 3W9
halfwayhouses.ca/en/region/ahha
Overview: A small provincial organization overseen by Regional Halfway House Association
Mission: To help offenders reintegrate themselves into society
Member of: Regional Halfway House Association

Atlantic Health Promotion Research Centre (AHPRC)
City Centre Atlantic, Dalhousie University, #209, 1535 Dresden Row, Halifax NS B3J 3T1
Tel: 902-494-2240; *Fax:* 902-494-3594
ahprc@dal.ca
www.ahprc.dal.ca
Overview: A medium-sized local organization founded in 1993
Affliation(s): Canadian Consortium for Health Promotion Research
Chief Officer(s):
Sandra J. Crowell, Managing Director
sandra.crowell@dal.ca
Finances: *Annual Operating Budget:* $100,000-$250,000
Staff Member(s): 3

Atlantic Institute for Market Studies (AIMS)
Park West Centre, #204, 287 Lacewood Dr., Halifax NS B3M 3Y7
Tel: 902-429-1143
aims@aims.ca
www.aims.ca
www.facebook.com/AtlanticInstituteforMarketStudies
twitter.com/AIMST
www.youtube.com/user/AtlanticInstMarkStud
Overview: A small local charitable organization founded in 1994
Mission: To conduct research regarding economic & social issues that are relevant to Canadians.
Chief Officer(s):
Marco Navarro-Genie, President & CEO
marco.navarro-genie@aims.ca
Staff Member(s): 4
Activities: Promotes practical research in areas of employment insurance, social welfare & the impact of free trade on the region; *Speaker Service:* Yes

The Atlantic Jewish Council
#508, 5670 Spring Garden Rd., Halifax NS B3J 1H6
Tel: 902-422-7491; *Fax:* 902-425-3722
atlanticjewishcouncil@theajc.ns.ca
theajc.ns.ca
Overview: A medium-sized local organization
Member of: The Centre for Israel & Jewish Affairs
Chief Officer(s):
Jon M. Goldberg, Executive Director

Atlantic Marksmen Association
PO Box 181, Stn. Dartmouth Main, Dartmouth NS B2Y 3Y3
Tel: 902-469-2062
boudreau@chebucto.ns.ca
www.atlanticmarksmen.ca
Overview: A small local organization founded in 1954
Member of: Shooting Federation of Canada
Chief Officer(s):
Sean Hansen, President
schansen@hfx.eastlink.ca
Membership: 200; *Fees:* Sr. $150; Jr. $30, plus induction fee of $100
Activities: Owns & operates two range facilities;

Atlantic Mission Society (AMS)
ams.pccatlantic.ca
Overview: A medium-sized national organization founded in 1976 overseen by Presbyterian Church in Canada
Mission: To support missions with prayer, study & service
Member of: Presbyterian Church in Canada
Chief Officer(s):
Jennifer Whitfield, President
ajwhitfield@nl.rogers.com
Publications:
• The Presbyterian Message [a publication of the Atlantic Mission Society]
Type: Magazine

Atlantic Motion Picture Exhibitors Association
c/o Empire Theatres Ltd., 190 Chain Lake Dr., Halifax NS B3S 1C5
Tel: 902-876-4848
Overview: A small local organization
Member of: The Motion Picture Theatre Associations of Canada

Atlantic Pest Management Association (APMO)
51 Duke St., Bedford NS B4A 2Z2
Tel: 902-835-2304; *Fax:* 902-835-0953
pestworldapma.net/apma/
Overview: A small local organization
Member of: Canadian Pest Management Association
Chief Officer(s):

Don McCarthy, President
microkil@ns.sympatico.ca

Atlantic Planners Institute (API) / Institut des Urbanistes de l'atlantique (IVA)

35 Ascot Ct., Fredericton NB E3B 6C4
Tel: 506-455-7203; *Fax:* 506-455-1113
apiexecutivedirector@gmail.com
www.atlanticplanners.org
Overview: A medium-sized provincial organization overseen by Canadian Institute of Planners
Mission: To represent professional planners in New Brunswick, Prince Edward Island, Nova Scotia, Newfoundland & Labrador.
Affiliation(s): Canadian Institute of Planners
Chief Officer(s):
Jennifer Griffiths, Executive Director
Finances: *Funding Sources:* Membership fees
Membership: *Fees:* $170; *Member Profile:* Professional planner in the four Atlantic Provinces of Canada; New Brunswick, Newfoundland and Labrador, Nova Scotia, and Prince Edward Island.; *Committees:* Membership; Professional Practice Review; Continuous Professional Learning
Meetings/Conferences: • 2015 Canadian Institute of Planners and Atlantic Planners Institute Annual Conference, 2015
Scope: Provincial

Atlantic Provinces Art Gallery Association (APAGA)

c/o MSVU Art Gallery, 166 Bedford Hwy., Halifax NS B3M 2J6
Tel: 902-457-6160; *Fax:* 902-457-2447
info@apaga.com
Overview: A small local organization founded in 1975
Mission: To pursue & promote high standards of excellence in care & presentation of works of art in public art galleries in the Atlantic region; To encourage the closest possible cooperation between art galleries, museums & artists; To serve as an advisory body in matters of professional interest
Affiliation(s): Canadian Museums Association
Chief Officer(s):
Ingrid Jenkner, Director
Membership: 25 institutional; *Member Profile:* Open to art galleries in Atlantic region supported at least in part by public funds; registered as charitable organization (gallery or its umbrella organization); at least one full-time paid professionally qualified staff member

Atlantic Provinces Association of Landscape Architects (APALA)

PO Box 653, Stn. Halifax CRO, Halifax NS B3J 2Z1
e-mail: info@apala.ca
www.apala.ca
Overview: A medium-sized local organization
Mission: To promote, improve & advance the profession; to maintain standards of professional practice & conduct consistent with the need to serve & to protect the public interest; to support improvement &/or conservation of the natural, cultural, social & built environment
Member of: Canadian Society of Landscape Architects
Chief Officer(s):
Angela Morin, Secretary-Treasurer
angela@sagehousedesign.ca
Daniel Glenn, President
dkg@glenngroup.ca
Membership: 83; *Member Profile:* Individuals in the process of completing or having completed a program in landscape architecture & organizations involved in the landscape business

Atlantic Provinces Athletic Therapists Association (APATA) / Association des Therapeuets de Sport des Provinces Altantique (ATSPA)

c/o Memorial University, PO Box 4200, 2300 Elizabeth Ave., St. John's NL A1C 5S7
Tel: 709-737-3442
info@apata.ca
www.apata.ca
Overview: A small local organization
Member of: Canadian Athletic Therapists Association
Chief Officer(s):
Colin King, President
colin.king@acadiau.ca
Membership: *Committees:* Ethics; Insurance Billing
Awards:
• Diane Webster Memorial Award

Atlantic Provinces Chambers of Commerce (APCC) / Chambres de commerce des provinces de l'Atlantique

PO Box 832, Kentville NS B4N 4H8
Tel: 902-678-6284; *Fax:* 902-678-7420
www.apcc.ca
Overview: A large provincial organization founded in 1896
Mission: To create an environment in which Chambers & Boards of Trade in Atlantic Canada can achieve their full potential & represent the business community in a unified & effective manner
Chief Officer(s):
Bill Denyar, President & CEO
Staff Member(s): 2
Membership: 300; *Member Profile:* New Brunswick Chamber of Commerce; Nova Scotia Chamber of Commerce; Newfoundland & Labrador Chamber of Commerce; PEI Chamber of Commerce
Awards:
• Dr. Stuart Peters (Award)
• Harvey Webber's Award (Award)
• President's Award (Award)
• Golden Chamber Pot (Award)

Fredericton
270 Rookwood Ave., Fredericton NB E3B 4Y9
Tel: 902-678-6284
Chief Officer(s):
Pierre Cadieux, President & Chief Executive Officer
Pierre@apcc.ca

Moncton
PO Box 481, Moncton NB E1C 1H0
Tel: 506-857-3980
Chief Officer(s):
Valerie Roy, Vice-President, Chamber & Member Services
valerie@apcc.ca

Atlantic Provinces Council on the Sciences; Atlantic Provinces Inter-University Committee on the Sciences *See* Science Atlantic

Atlantic Provinces Economic Council (APEC) / Conseil économique des provinces de l'Atlantique

#500, 5121 Sackville St., Halifax NS B3J 1K1
Tel: 902-422-6516; *Fax:* 902-429-6803
info@apec-econ.ca
www.apec-econ.ca
twitter.com/APECatlantic
Overview: A medium-sized local organization founded in 1954
Mission: To be the leading advocate for the economic development of the Atlantic region and accomplishes this by: monitoring and analysing current and emerging economic trends and policies; communicating the results of this analysis to its mbmers on a regular basis; consulting with a wide audience; dissminating its research and policy analysis to business, gov't, and the community at large; advocating the appropriate public and private sector policy responses.
Chief Officer(s):
Elizabeth Beale, President & CEO
elizabeth.beale@apec-econ.ca
Staff Member(s): 9
Membership: *Fees:* Schedule available
Activities: *Speaker Service:* Yes; *Library* by appointment

Atlantic Provinces Education Foundation *See* Council of Atlantic Ministers of Education & Training

Atlantic Provinces Library Association (APLA)

c/o School of Information Management, Kenneth C. Rowe Management Bldg., 6100 University Ave., Halifax NS B3H 3J5
e-mail: executive@yahoo.ca
www.apla.ca
www.facebook.com/group.php?gid=10792140537
twitter.com/APLAcontact
Previous Name: Maritime Library Association
Overview: A medium-sized local organization founded in 1918
Mission: To promote library & information service & workers throughout the Atlantic region; To represent & support the interests of persons who work in libraries in the Atlantic provinces; To cooperate with other library associations & similar organizations; To develop & offer effective continuing education programs
Chief Officer(s):
Jocelyne Thompson, President, 506-458-7053
jlt@unb.ca
Lou Duggan, Vice-President, 902-420-5534
lou.duggan@smu.ca
Jocelyne Thompson, Vice-President, 506-458-7053
jlt@unb.ca
Ann Smith, Vice-President, Membership, 902-585-1378
apla_executive@yahoo.ca
Debbie Costelo, Secretary, 902-491-1031
debbie.costelo@nscc.ca
Bill Slauenwhite, Treasurer, 902-453-2461
bill.slauenwhite@novanet.ns.ca
Membership: *Fees:* Free, students enrolled in an accredited library program; $25 library support staff, trustees, & retired persons; $55 professional librarians; *Member Profile:* Students, individuals, & institutions engaged in library study or services in the provinces of New Brunswick, Nova Scotia, Prince Edward Island, & Newfoundland & Labrador; *Committees:* Communications - Public Relations; Memorial Awards
Activities: Establishing the following interest groups: Collections Development, Computers & Connectivity, Conservation of Library Materials, Continuing Education, Francophone, Information Literacy, Library Technicians, New Librarians & Information Specialists, Trustees, & Youth Services
Awards:
• Carin Alma E. Somers Scholarship (Scholarship)
Annual scholarship to assist a Canadian citizen, who is an Atlantic Provinces resident, needing financial assistance to undertake or complete a Library & Information Science degree *Amount:* $2,000 *Contact:* Jocelyne Thompson, University of NB, Phone: 506-458-7053; E-mail: jlt@unb.ca
• Memorial Trust (Grant)
Financial assistance is available for study & research *Amount:* 1,000 *Contact:* Erin Alcock, Convener, Award Committee, Phone: 709-737-7427; E-mail: ekalcock@mun.ca
• First Timer's Conference Grant (Grant)
Grants are allocated to members of APLA, residing in Atlantic Canada, to attend his or her first APLA annual conference *Contact:* Sarah Gladwell, St John Free Public Library, Phone: 506-643-7224; E-mail: sarah.gladwell@gnb.ca
• Merit Award (Award)
To honour an individual who has made an outstanding contribution to library services in the Atlantic Provinces *Contact:* Donald Moses, Librarian, UPEI, Phone: 902-566-0479; E-mail: dmoses@upei.ca
• General Activities Fund Grant (Grant)
Provision of funds for projects that will further the aims of the APLA *Contact:* Sarah Gladwell, St John Free Public Library, Phone: 506-643-7224; E-mail: sarah.gladwell@gnb.ca
Meetings/Conferences: • Atlantic Provinces Library Association 2015 Annual Conference, June, 2015, Memorial University, St. John's, NL
Scope: Provincial
Description: An educational program to support the interests & concerns of the library community in the Atlantic provinces
Contact Information: Conference coordinator: Kathryn Rose, 2015apla@gmail.com; URL: apla2015.wordpress.com
• Atlantic Provinces Library Association 2016 Annual Conference, 2016
Scope: Provincial
Description: An educational program to support the interests & concerns of the library community in the Atlantic provinces
• Atlantic Provinces Library Association 2017 Annual Conference, 2017
Scope: Provincial
Description: An educational program to support the interests & concerns of the library community in the Atlantic provinces
Publications:
• APLA Bulletin
Type: Journal; *Frequency:* 5 pa; *Accepts Advertising*; *Editor:* Ron Rooth; Corinne Gilroy *ISSN:* 0001-2203
Profile: Happenings in all sectors of librarianship in the Atlantic provinces

Atlantic Provinces Linguistic Association (APLA) / Association de linguistique des provinces atlantiques (ALPA)

c/o Saint Mary's University, Dept. of Modern Languages & Classics, Halifax NB B3H 3C3
www.unb.ca/apla-alpa
Overview: A small local organization founded in 1977
Mission: To promote the study of languages & linguistics in Atlantic Canada
Chief Officer(s):
Raymond Mopoho, President
Raymond Mopoho, President
Egor Tsedryk, Treasurer
egor.tsedryk@smu.ca
Finances: *Annual Operating Budget:* Less than $50,000; *Funding Sources:* Membership dues; national government
Membership: 7 institutional; *Fees:* $30 individual; $15 student; $50 institution

Publications:
• Linguistica Atlantica
Editor: Prof. Catherine Borin
Profile: Annual academic journal

Atlantic Provinces Numismatic Association (APNA)
c/o Dartmouth Seniors' Service Centre, 45 Ochterloney St., Dartmouth NS B2Y 4M7
Overview: A medium-sized provincial organization founded in 1958
Member of: Royal Canadian Numismatic Association

Atlantic Provinces Ready-Mixed Concrete Association (APRMCA) / Association des fabricants de béton préparé des provinces atlantiques
c/o Mary Macaulay, #301, 3845 Joseph Howe Dr., Halifax NS B3L 4H9
Tel: 902-443-4456; *Fax:* 902-404-8074
info@atlanticconcrete.ca
www.aprmca.com
Overview: A medium-sized local organization founded in 1966 overseen by Canadian Ready Mixed Concrete Association
Mission: To promote the use of ready-mixed concrete while providing leadership to the industry through the exchange of ideas & information.
Member of: Road Builders Association of New Brunswick; Canadian Poured Concrete Wall Association; Construction Associations in NB, NS, & PEI
Affliation(s): Canadian Portland Cement Association
Chief Officer(s):
Mary Macaulay, Executive Director
Finances: *Funding Sources:* Membership fees
Staff Member(s): 1
Membership: *Fees:* Schedule available; *Member Profile:* Ready mixed concrete firms; related firms; *Committees:* Marketing; Technical & Plant Certification; Membership; Executive; Quality & Professional Affairs; Environment; Safety; Annual Golf Tournament

Atlantic Provinces Special Education Authority / Commission d'enseignement spécial des provinces de l'Atlantique
5940 South St., Halifax NS B3H 1S6
Tel: 902-424-8500; *Fax:* 902-424-0543; *TTY:* 902-424-8500
apsea@apsea.ca
www.apsea.ca
Overview: A small provincial organization founded in 1975
Mission: To provide educational services to children & youth who are visually impaired & hard of hearing
Chief Officer(s):
Bertram Tulk, Superintendent, 902-424-7765
tulkb@apsea.ca
Activities: *Library:* APSEA Library

Atlantic Provinces Trial Lawyers Association (APTLA)
PO Box 2618, Central RPO, Halifax NS B3J 3N5
Tel: 902-446-4446; *Fax:* 902-425-9552
Toll-Free: 866-314-4446
www.aptla.ca
Overview: A medium-sized provincial organization
Mission: The Atlantic Provinces Trial Lawyers Association is a plaintiff-oriented organization dedicated to obtaining legal redress for those who have suffered injury or injustice, and to preserving the rights of the injured to full and fair compensation.
Chief Officer(s):
David Gauthier, President
dgg@gauthierlaw.ca
Elizabeth Ann (Libby) Kinghorne, Executive Director
libbykinghorne@aptla.ca
Staff Member(s): 6
Membership: *Member Profile:* Trial lawyers
Meetings/Conferences: • Atlantic Provinces Trial Lawyers Association's Specialty MCPD Education Conference 2015, November, 2015, Delta Halifax, Halifax, NS
Scope: Provincial
• Atlantic Provinces Trial Lawyers Association Annual Spring Plaintiff Pracetice Conference 2015, May, 2015, Inverary Inn, Baddeck, NS
Scope: Provincial
• Atlantic Provinces Trial Lawyers Association 14th Annual Plaintiff Pracetice Conference 2015, November, 2015, Delta Halifax, Halifax, NS
Scope: Provincial

Atlantic Provinces Trucking Association (APTA)
#800, 105 Englehart St., Dieppe NB E1A 8K2
Tel: 506-855-2782; *Fax:* 506-853-7424
Toll-Free: 866-866-1679
www.apta.ca
www.linkedin.com/groups/Atlantic-Provinces-Trucking-Association-481142
twitter.com/APTA_Trucking
Overview: A medium-sized local organization founded in 1950 overseen by Canadian Trucking Alliance
Mission: To promote an efficient, safe & environmentally sound trucking industry in Atlantic Canada.
PUBLICATIONS: Atlantic Trucking Magazine (quaterly); Atlantic Report Newsletter (monthly) (only to members).
Chief Officer(s):
Donnie Fillmore, Chair
Jean Marc Picard, Executive Director
jmpicard@apta.ca
Danielle Hébert, Coordinator, Marketing
dhebert@apta.ca
Staff Member(s): 4
Membership: 325+; *Fees:* Schedule available; *Member Profile:* Open to anyone having an interest in the trucking industry in Atlantic Canada, including common carriers, owner-operators & private fleets; *Committees:* Associated Trades Council; Safety Council; Charity; Human Resource & Education; Marine; Legislative; Future Leaders
Activities: Infrastructure improvements; complete twinning of the highway between Halifax & Saint John; elimination of motor carrier plates & fees; simplification of multiple registration & other tax collection systems in North America to allow for "one-stop shipping"; establishment of training programs; Annual Meeting & Convention; Atlantic Truck Show; Spring Maintenance Seminar; *Rents Mailing List:* Yes
Awards:
• Safety to Motor Transporation (Award)
Sponsored by Laurentian General Insurance Company; presented to an individual actively involved in promoting road & safety in the trucking industry
• Service to Industry Award (Award)
Sponsored by Trailmobile Canada; awarded to the person who has made the greatest contribution to the industry in the past year
• Atlantic Driver of the Year (Award)
Sponsored by Volvo GM Canada Heavy Truck Corporation; recognizes all-round distinction in driving, courtesy, safety & community activity

Atlantic Publisher Association *See* Atlantic Publishers Marketing Association

Atlantic Publishers Marketing Association (APMA)
1484 Carlton St., Halifax NS B3H 3B7
Tel: 902-420-0711; *Fax:* 902-423-4302
apma.admin@atlanticpublishers.ca
www.atlanticpublishers.ca
Previous Name: Atlantic Publisher Association
Overview: A medium-sized provincial organization founded in 1980 overseen by Association of Canadian Publishers
Mission: To promote the growth & development of Canadian-owned publishing houses based in Atlantic Canada
Chief Officer(s):
Carolyn Guy, Executive Director
cguy@atlanticpublishers.ca
Terrilee Bulger, President
Mike Hunter, Vice-President
Jim Lorimer, Treasurer
Beverely Rach, Secretary
Staff Member(s): 3
Membership: 25 publishers; *Fees:* Schedule available; *Member Profile:* Publishers & those interested in publishing
Activities: Books for the summer for Atlantic Canada; various marketing projects

Atlantic Recreation Vehicle Dealers' Association (ARVDA)
PO Box 9410, Stn. A, Halifax NS B3K 5S3
Tel: 902-425-2445; *Fax:* 902-425-2441
www.arvda.ca
Also Known As: Atlantic RVDA
Overview: A small local organization overseen by Recreation Vehicle Dealers Association of Canada
Chief Officer(s):
George Goodrick, President, 902-434-0227, Fax: 902-462-7583
adventure@adventuresportsrv.com
John K. Sutherland, Executive Director
jsutherland@pathfinder-group.com
15 volunteer(s)
Membership: 1-99
Activities: Annual RV shows in Halifax & Moncton

Atlantic Region Aboriginal Lands Association
c/o Joe Sabattis, 77 French Village Rd., Kingsclear NB E3E 1K3
Tel: 506-363-3028
Overview: A small provincial organization founded in 2000 overseen by National Aboriginal Lands Managers Association
Chief Officer(s):
Joe Sabattis, Chair
joesabattis@kingsclear.ca
Staff Member(s): 1

Atlantic Salmon Federation (ASF) / Fédération du saumon atlantique
PO Box 5200, St. Andrews NB E5B 3S8
Tel: 506-529-4581; *Fax:* 506-529-1070
Toll-Free: 800-565-5666
savesalmon@asf.ca
www.asf.ca
www.facebook.com/pages/Atlantic-Salmon-Federation/143596265564
twitter.com/SalmonNews
www.youtube.com/user/ASFatlanticsalmon
Overview: A large international charitable organization founded in 1948
Mission: To protect, conserve & restore wild Atlantic salmon & their ecosystems
Chief Officer(s):
Bill Taylor, President & Chief Executive Officer, 506-529-1034
btaylor@asf.ca
Todd Dupuis, Executive Director, Regional Programs, 902-628-4349
tdupuis@upei.ca
Jonathan Carr, Director, Research & Environment, 506-529-1385
jcarr@asf.ca
Bill Mallory, Executive Vice-President & CFO, 506-529-1386
wmallory@asf.ca
Rob Beatty, Vice-President, Development, 506-529-1031
rbeatty@asf.ca
Sue Ann Scott, Vice-President, Communications, 506-529-1027
sscott@asf.ca
Muriel Ferguson, Manager, Public Information, 506-529-1033
mferguson@asf.ca
Martin Silverstone, Editor, Atlantic Salmon Journal, 514-457-8737
martinsilverstone@videotron.ca
Finances: *Annual Operating Budget:* Greater than $5 Million; *Funding Sources:* Donations from individuals, corporations, & foundations
Staff Member(s): 25; 40,0 volunteer(s)
Membership: 8,000; *Fees:* Schedule available
Activities: Sharing knowledge with adults & children about wild Atlantic salmon; Conducting scientific research; *Internships:* Yes; *Library:* Interpretive Centre (summer)
Awards:
• Olin Fellowships (Scholarship)
Presented annually to individuals who seek to improve their knowledge & skills while searching for solutions to challenges in Atlantic salmon biology, conservation, & management*Deadline:* March 15 *Amount:* $1,000-3,000 *Contact:* Olin Fellowships, Atlantic Salmon Federation, PO Box 5200, St. Andrews, NB, EOG 2X0
• T.B. (Happy) Fraser Award (Award)
Presented annually to an individual who has made outstanding contributions to wild Atlantic salmon conservation at a regional or national level
• Lee Wulff Conservation Award (Award)
Presented annually to an individual who has made outstanding contributions to wild Atlantic salmon conservation
• Atlantic Salmon Federation Roll Of Honor (Award)
Presented annually to individuals who demonstrate outstanding commitment to wild Atlantic salmon conservation at the grass-roots level
• Affiliate of the Year Award (Award)
To recognize outstanding leadership in wild Atlantic salmon conservation within the Atlantic Salmon Federation's affiliate structure
Publications:
• Atlantic Salmon Federation Annual Report
Type: Yearbook; *Frequency:* Annually
Profile: Information about the federation's current projects that impact Atlantic salmon restoration plus future strategies

- Atlantic Salmon Federation Newsletter
Type: Newsletter
Profile: Updates on activities of the Federation
- Atlantic Salmon Journal
Type: Journal; *Accepts Advertising*; *Editor:* Martin Silverstone
Profile: Issues surrounding wild Atlantic salmon, including protection of the species
- Incidence & Impacts of Escaped Farmed Atlantic Salmon "Salmo Salar" in Nature
Type: Report; *Number of Pages:* 114; *Author:* Eva B. Thorstad et al.
Profile: The impacts of escaped farmed salmon
- Prince Edward Island Nitrate Report
Type: Report
Profile: The problem of nitrates entering streams & lakes
- State of the Population - Atlantic Salmon
Type: Report
Profile: A backgrounder on the Atlantic salmon population, featuring statistics, tables, & graphs

Atlantic Standardbred Breeders Association
c/o Lynne MacLennan, PO Box 65, Port Hood NS B0E 2W0
Tel: 902-787-2869; *Fax:* 902-787-2214
Overview: A small local organization
Mission: To promote the breeding of standardbred horses in the Atlantic provinces
Member of: Prince Edward Island Harness Racing Industry Association
Chief Officer(s):
Lynne MacLennan, Contact
the.maclennans@ns.sympatico.ca
Activities: Sponsoring the Atlantic Sires Stakes program

Atlantic Standardbred Breeders Association (ASBA)
PO Box 65, Port Hood NS B0E 2W0
Tel: 902-787-2869; *Fax:* 902-787-2214
the.maclennans@ns.sympatico.ca
www.atlanticsiresstakes.ca/contact.html
Overview: A small local organization
Mission: To promote the breeding of standardbred horses in the Atlantic provinces
Chief Officer(s):
Lynne MacLennan, Executive Director/Manager
Staff Member(s): 1; 10 volunteer(s)
Membership: 700 individual
Activities: Sponsoring the Atlantic Sires Stakes program

Atlantic Therapeutic Touch Network (ATTN) / Le réseau Toucher Thérapeutique de l'Atlantique
PO Box 24073, 21 MicMac Blvd., Dartmouth NS B3A 4T4
Tel: 902-454-2919
Toll-Free: 888-339-1224
info@atlanticttn.com
www.atlanticttn.com
www.facebook.com/groups/157670450965143/
Overview: A small local organization founded in 1996
Chief Officer(s):
Judy Donovan-Whitty, Coordinator

Atlantic Tire Dealers Association (ATDA)
93 Henderson St., Riverview NB E1B 4B6
Tel: 506-386-4306; *Fax:* 506-387-3987
www.atda.ca
Overview: A medium-sized local organization founded in 1960
Chief Officer(s):
Frank Connor, Executive Director
fconnor@nbnet.nb.ca
Membership: 126;

Atlantic Turfgrass Research Foundation (ATRC)
Nova Scotia Agricultural College, 20 Rock Garden Rd., Truro NS B2N 5E3
Tel: 902-456-8571
Overview: A small provincial organization founded in 1992
Mission: To advance the turfgrass industry in Atlantic Canada
Chief Officer(s):
David Davey, President
Kevin Wentzell, Secretary
Activities: Researching turfgrass systems, in areas such as irrigation efficiency & water conservation & management

Atlantic Universities Athletic Association ***See*** Atlantic University Sport Association

Atlantic University Sport Association (AUS)
#403, 5657 Spring Garden Rd., Halifax NS B3J 3R4
Tel: 902-425-4235; *Fax:* 902-425-7825
www.atlanticuniversitysport.com
www.facebook.com/AtlanticUniversitySport
twitter.com/AUS_SUA
www.youtube.com/ATLuniversitysport
Also Known As: Atlantic University Sport
Previous Name: Atlantic Universities Athletic Association
Overview: A medium-sized local organization founded in 1974
Mission: To advance student athletes & university sport
Member of: Canadian Interuniversity Sport Association
Chief Officer(s):
Philip M. Currie, Executive Director
pcurrie@atlanticuniversitysport.com
Finances: *Funding Sources:* Memberships; Partners
Staff Member(s): 4
Membership: 11 institutional, 2,000 individuals; *Fees:* Schedule available; *Member Profile:* Institutions of higher learning

Atlantic Wildlife Institute
220 Cookville Rd., Cookville NB E4L 1Z8
Tel: 506-364-1902
www.atlanticwildlife.ca
www.facebook.com/AtlanticWildlife
twitter.com/atlanticwild
Overview: A small local organization
Chief Officer(s):
Barry Rothfuss, Co-Founder/Executive Director
Pam Novak, Co-Founder

Atlaz Sheltered Workshop ***See*** JVS of Greater Toronto

Atlin Board of Trade
PO Box 106, Atlin BC V0W 1A0
Tel: 250-651-7717
bookies-r-us@atlin.net
Overview: A small local organization founded in 1904
Mission: To promote & improve trade, commerce & the economic, civic & social welfare of the district
Affiliation(s): Yukon Chamber of Commerce; BC Chamber of Commerce
Chief Officer(s):
George Holman, President
Finances: *Annual Operating Budget:* Less than $50,000; *Funding Sources:* Membership fees; donations
12 volunteer(s)
Membership: 40; *Fees:* $40

ATM Industry Association Canada Region (ATMIA)
c/o Curt Binns, Executive Director, #218, 10520 Yonge St., Unit 35B, Richmond Hill ON L4C 3C7
Tel: 416-970-7954; *Fax:* 905-770-6230
www.atmia.com/regions/canada
www.linkedin.com/company/atm-industry-association
Overview: A large international organization
Mission: To promote ATM convenience, growth, & usage worldwide; to protect the ATM industry's assets, interests, & reputation; to provide education, networking opportunities, & best practices
Chief Officer(s):
Curt Binns, Executive Director, Canada
curt.binns@atmia.com
Membership: 5,000 worldwide; *Fees:* Schedule available
Activities: Consulting; training; networking; newsletters; conferences
Publications:
- ATMIA [ATM Industry Association Canada] Canada E-Newsletter
Type: Newsletter

Attractions Ontario
#504, 344 Bloor St. West, Toronto ON M5S 3A7
Tel: 416-868-4386; *Fax:* 416-868-0386
Toll-Free: 877-557-3386
www.attractionsontario.ca
www.facebook.com/attractionsontario
twitter.com/AttractionsOnt
Overview: A small provincial organization founded in 1983
Mission: To develop effective marketing programs that increase attendance for members' attractions.
Chief Officer(s):
Tamara Russell, President
Troy Young, Executive Director
tyoung@attractionsontario.ca
Staff Member(s): 5
Membership: *Fees:* Schedule available dependant on annual admissions or attendance; *Member Profile:* Public & privately owned attractions in such categories as amusement parks, historical sites, cultural activities, arts & entertainment & adventure

Au bas de l'échelle (ABE)
#305, 6839A, rue Drolet, Montréal QC H2S 2T1
Tél: 514-270-7878; *Téléc:* 514-270-7726
abe@aubasdelechelle.ca
www.aubasdelechelle.ca
Aperçu: *Dimension:* petite; *Envergure:* provinciale; Organisme sans but lucratif; fondée en 1975
Mission: Défense des droits des non syndiqué(e)s; service d'information sur les lois du travail; information sur les droits des personnes non-syndiquées
Finances: *Budget de fonctionnement annuel:* $100,000-$250,000; *Fonds:* Gouvernement régional, provincial, fédéral, membres, dons etc.
Membre(s) du personnel: 6; 40 bénévole(s)
Membre: 200 individu; *Montant de la cotisation:* 5$ sans emploi; 12$ individu; *Critères d'admissibilite:* Travailleuses et travailleurs non-syndiqués
Activités: *Stagiaires:* Oui; *Service de conférenciers:* Oui

Au Coup de pouce Centre-Sud inc.
2338, rue Ontario est, Montréal QC H2K 1W1
Tél: 514-521-2439; *Téléc:* 514-521-5763
admin@aucoupdepouce.qc.ca
www.aucoupdepouce.qc.ca
Aperçu: *Dimension:* petite; *Envergure:* locale; fondée en 1973
Mission: Pour habiliter l'individu ainsi que l'intégration économique et sociale des personnes démunies; identifier les besoins prioritaires en éducation populaire aux gens du quartier Sainte-Marie; alphabétisation, accès à l'internet, initiation à l'informatique, ateliers, clubs, babillard d'emploi
Affiliation(s): Centraide du Grand Montréal
Membre(s) du bureau directeur:
Gisèle Caron, Coordinatrice
gisele@aucoupdepouce.qc.ca
Membre(s) du personnel: 2
Membre: *Comités:* Journal; Événements

Auctioneers Association of Alberta
RR#1, Red Deer AB T4N 5E1
Tel: 403-340-2070; *Fax:* 403-340-2019
www.albertaauctioneers.com
Overview: A small provincial organization founded in 1934
Mission: To develop standards of ethics for the profession; to help member become bonded; to lobby governments on laws & issues which affect the industry & keeps its members abreast of any news.
Chief Officer(s):
Don Montgomery, President, 403-350-0523
Membership: *Committees:* AMVIC & Automotive; Archives; Education; Membership & Nominating; Legislative; Surety; Convention; All Around Canadian Championships; Finance & Investment; Communications
Activities: Annual conference; trade fairs
Publications:
- The Alberta Auctioneer
Type: newsletter; *Frequency:* 3 pa

Auctioneers Association of Ontario
30959 Wyatt Rd., RR#6, Strathroy ON N7G 3H7
Tel: 519-232-4138; *Fax:* 519-232-9166
execdir@auctioneersassociation.com
www.auctioneersassociation.com
www.facebook.com/AuctioneersAssociationOntario
Overview: A small provincial organization
Chief Officer(s):
Rick Rittenhouse, President
salesrit@mergetel.com

Audio Engineering Society (AES)
AES Toronto Section, PO Box 292, #32E, 223 Pioneer Dr., Kitchner ON N2P 1L9
Tel: 519-894-5308
torontoaes@torontoaes.org
www.torontoaes.org
www.linkedin.com/groups?mostPopular=&gid=2023730
Overview: A small national organization
Mission: Dedicated to audio technology.
Chief Officer(s):
Blair Francey, Chair
Karl Machat, Secretary
Frank Lockwood, Vice Chair

Audit Bureau of Circulations ***See*** Alliance for Audited Media

Auditing Association of Canada (AAC) / L'Association canadienne de vérification
9 Forest Rd., Whitby ON L1N 3N7

Tel: 905-404-9511
admin@auditingcanada.com
www.auditingcanada.com
Previous Name: Canadian Environmental Auditing Association
Overview: A medium-sized international organization
Mission: To represent & promote the auditing profession; To advance public interest by enabling members to provide quality services
Chief Officer(s):
Don Fraser, Executive Director
Sue Keane, President
Membership: *Fees:* $30 plus GST student members; $230 plus GST general members; *Member Profile:* Auditors in environmental, health & safety, & related areas from across Canada, such as ISO 14001 & OHSAS 18001 registration auditors; Students who are interested in environmental & health & safety auditing; Corporations that support association activities
Activities: Certifying auditors; Upholding a code of ethics; Offering educational programs; Providing opportunities to network with colleagues; Offering information about government legislation & activities; Partnering with similar organizations
Meetings/Conferences: • 2015 Auditing Canada Annual Conference, 2015, Halifax, NS
Scope: National
Contact Information: Brenda Macdonald; Brenda.MacDonald@nspower.ca
Publications:
• Auditing Association of Canada Membership Directory
Type: Directory

Augustines de la Miséricorde de Jésus

2655, rue Guillaume - Le Pelletier, Québec QC G1C 3X7
Tél: 418-628-8860
secretaire@augustines.org
www.augustines.org
Aperçu: *Dimension:* petite; *Envergure:* locale
Mission: Les trois dimensions de la vie spirituelle des Augustines d'hier et de demain sont: communion fraternelle; louange et intercession; et miséricorde
Membre(s) du bureau directeur:
Claire Gagnon, Supérieure générale

Aurora & District Historical Society, Inc. *See* Aurora Historical Society, Inc.

Aurora Chamber of Commerce

#321, 6 - 14845 Yonge St., Aurora ON L4G 6H8
Tel: 905-727-7262; *Fax:* 905-841-6217
info@aurorachamber.on.ca
www.aurorachamber.on.ca
twitter.com/ChamberinAurora
Overview: A small local organization
Member of: Ontario Chamber of Commerce; Canadian Chamber of Commerce
Chief Officer(s):
Judy Marshall, Executive Director, 905-727-7262 Ext. 33
j.marshall@aurorachamber.on.ca
Staff Member(s): 4; 14 volunteer(s)
Membership: 700 corporate; *Fees:* $75-$915

Aurora Historical Society, Inc.

Hillary House, National Historic Site, 15372 Yonge St., Aurora ON L4G 1N8
Tel: 905-727-8991
ahs@aurorahs.com
aurorahistoricalsociety.ca
www.facebook.com/HillaryHouseNHS
www.youtube.com/user/HillaryHouseNHS
Previous Name: Aurora & District Historical Society, Inc.
Overview: A small local charitable organization founded in 1963
Mission: To promote local awareness of & committment to heritage matters
Member of: Ontario Historical Society; Canadian Museums Association; Ontario Museum Association
Chief Officer(s):
John McIntyre, President
Staff Member(s): 2
Membership: *Fees:* $10 student; $20 individual; $35 family; $75 corporate; $200 life; *Committees:* Restoration; Fundraising; Finance
Activities: Operates Aurora Museum & Hillary House; *Library* Open to public

Aurora House

PO Box 3779, The Pas MB R9A 1S4
Tel: 204-623-7427; *Fax:* 204-623-3901
Toll-Free: 877-977-0007; *Crisis Hot-Line:* 204-623-5497
auroratp@mts.net
www.aurorahouse-sharethecare.com
www.facebook.com/pages/Aurora-House/187177044629222
Also Known As: The Pas Committee for Women in Crisis Inc.; My Sister's House
Overview: A small local charitable organization founded in 1982
Mission: To address the issue of domestic violence; whether a woman & her children require a safe haven from an immediate abusive situation, or the woman is seeking to create change in her life, Aurora House & My Sister's House exist to empower the woman, providing programs & resources that promote & facilitate growth, self-esteem & understanding of the personal power to independently make choices; offers safe haven, education, information & resources that women & children require
Member of: Manitoba Association of Women's Shelters
Chief Officer(s):
Dawna Pritchard, Executive Director
Activities: Crisis line operation; residential services for women fleeing abusive relationships; walk-in follow up service; child support; Victims First Cell Phone; Second Stage Housing; presentations to schools, worksites; information booths at public events; tollfree number to nearest shelter 1-877-977-0007 (collect calls accepted); *Internships:* Yes; *Speaker Service:* Yes; *Library* Open to public by appointment

Ausable Bayfield Conservation Foundation

71108 Morrison Line, RR#3, Exeter ON N0M 1S5
Tel: 519-235-2610; *Fax:* 519-235-1963
Toll-Free: 888-286-2610
info@abca.on.ca
www.abca.on.ca
Overview: A small local organization founded in 1974
Mission: Raising funds for conservation, preservation & protection of the natural landscapes of the Ausable River, Bayfield River & Packhill Creek watersheds
Chief Officer(s):
Tom Prout, General Manager/Sec.-Treas., 519-235-261 Ext. 234
Finances: *Annual Operating Budget:* Less than $50,000
Staff Member(s): 2; 9 volunteer(s)
Membership: 1-99
Activities: Conservation Dinner Auction

Australian Cattle Dog Rescue of Ontario (ACDRO)

PO Box 249, 762 Upper James St., Hamilton ON L9C 3A2
Tel: 905-973-6687
Overview: A small provincial organization
Mission: To provides for the rescue, care, and adoption of needy Australian Cattle Dogs
Chief Officer(s):
Sarah Mombourquette, Director
sarahm@acdro.com
Activities: Trio Kennel Club Show, Cowtown; booths at various pet shows

Australian Football League Ontario (AFLO)

The Exchange Tower, PO Box 99, #3680, 130 King St. West, Toronto ON M5X 1B1
Tel: 416-304-0032
exec@aflontario.com
www.aflontario.com
www.facebook.com/AFLOntario
twitter.com/AFLOntario
www.youtube.com/channel/UC0FrzrNpBBtFdZAVYjKxbTA
Also Known As: AFL Ontario
Overview: A medium-sized provincial organization founded in 1989
Mission: To organize amateur Australian football competitions in Ontario & Québec.
Member of: AFL Canada
Chief Officer(s):
Martin Walter, President
Membership: 11 clubs

Australian Wine Society of Toronto (AWS)

c/o 39 Sierra Ct., Maple ON L6A 2E5
e-mail: info@aws.ca
www.aws.ca
Overview: A small local organization founded in 1985
Mission: To encourage a greater awareness of the varietals, diversity & styles of Australian wines.
Chief Officer(s):
Malcolm Cocks, Chair
Membership: *Fees:* $35 single; $60 couple
Activities: Australian wine fair; monthly tastings & dinners

Australia-New Zealand Association (ANZA)

3 West 8 Ave., Vancouver BC V5Y 1M8
Tel: 604-876-7128
info@anzaclub.org
www.anzaclub.org
www.facebook.com/anzaclubvancouver
twitter.com/anzaclub
Also Known As: The ANZA Club
Overview: A medium-sized international organization founded in 1935
Mission: To foster friendly relations between British Columbia, Canada, Australia & New Zealand
Finances: *Funding Sources:* Membership dues; hall rentals; pub
Membership: *Fees:* $10
Activities: *Library*
Awards:
• Member of the Year (Award)
• Board Member of the Year (Award)

Austrian Canadian Edelweiss Club of Regina Inc

320 Maxwell Cres., Regina SK S4N 5Y1
Tel: 306-721-6388; *Fax:* 306-721-9980
austrianclubregina@gmail.com
www.austrianclubregina.ca
Also Known As: Austrian Club
Overview: A small local organization founded in 1974
Mission: To promote Austrian culture within the community of Regina; to provide social, educational, recreational & athletic programs, projects & gatherings; to assist newcomers of Austrian origin to establish themselves in Canada; to learn & advance within Canadian culture & citizenship
Affliation(s): Canadian German Congress; Saskatchewan German Council; Austrian Canadian Council
Chief Officer(s):
John Josst, President

Autism Calgary Association

#174, 3359 - 27th St. NE, Calgary AB T1Y 5E4
Tel: 403-250-5033; *Fax:* 403-250-2625
info@autismcalgary.com
www.autismcalgary.com
www.facebook.com/autismcalgary
twitter.com/autismcalgary
Overview: A small local organization
Mission: Provides support, information and education to families
Chief Officer(s):
Lyndon Parakin, Executive Director, 403-250-5033 Ext. 223
lyndon@autismcalgary.com
Staff Member(s): 5
Membership: *Fees:* Free
Publications:
• The Autism Echo
Type: Newsletter; *Frequency:* Quarterly

Autism Northwest Territories

4904 Matonabee St., Yellowknife NT X1A 1X8
Tel: 867-920-4206
autism.nwt@hotmail.com
Overview: A small provincial organization overseen by Autism Society Canada
Chief Officer(s):
Lynn Elkin, Contact
lynnelkin@hotmail.com
Activities: Support & information groups

Autism Nova Scotia (ANS)

1456 Brenton St., Halifax NS B3J 2K7
Tel: 902-446-4995; *Fax:* 902-446-4997
Toll-Free: 877-544-4495
info@autismns.ca
www.autismnovascotia.ca
Previous Name: The Provincial Autism Centre
Overview: A small provincial charitable organization founded in 2002 overseen by Autism Society Canada
Mission: To advocate for, educate the public about, & provide support to, persons with autism/pervasive developmental disorders & their families
Affliation(s): Society for Treatment of Autism
Finances: *Funding Sources:* Fundraising
8 volunteer(s)
Membership: *Fees:* $10 individual
Activities: *Awareness Events:* Walk the Walk for Autism; Autism Golf Ball, October; *Speaker Service:* Yes; *Rents Mailing List:* Yes; *Library* Open to public
Publications:
• Autistics Aloud
Type: Newsletter; *Frequency:* Quarterly

Profile: Displays the many talents amongst the autistic community, explores relavant issues and provides vital insight into autistic life.

Autism Ontario

#004, 1179 King St. West, Toronto ON M6K 3C5
Tel: 416-246-9592; *Fax:* 416-246-9417
Toll-Free: 800-472-7789
mail@autismontario.com
www.autismontario.com
www.facebook.com/autismontarioprovincial
twitter.com/AutismONT
Also Known As: Autism Society Ontario
Previous Name: Ontario Society for Autistic Citizens
Overview: A medium-sized provincial organization founded in 1973 overseen by Autism Society Canada
Mission: To ensure that each individual with autism spectrum disorders is provided the means to achieve quality of life as a respected member of society
Chief Officer(s):
Marg Spuelstra, Executive Director
marg@autismontario.com
Finances: *Funding Sources:* Membership dues; fundraising
Membership: *Fees:* $50 individual/family; $90 professional/researcher; $250 group; $500 lifetime individual/family; *Member Profile:* Anyone with an interest in autism: parents, friends, family, professionals
Activities: *Speaker Service:* Yes

Autism Society Alberta (ASA)

#101, 11720 Kingsway Ave., Edmonton AB T5G 0X5
Tel: 780-453-3971; *Fax:* 780-447-4948
autism@autismedmonton.org
www.autismedmonton.org
www.facebook.com/autismedmonton
twitter.com/AutismEdmonton
Also Known As: Edmonton Autism Society
Overview: A medium-sized provincial organization founded in 1972 overseen by Autism Society Canada
Mission: To improve the understanding of autism throughout Alberta by the dissemination of information to parents, health care workers, educators, government, private agencies & the public
Affliation(s): Edmonton Autism Society; Autism Calgary Association; Autism Society Central Alberta
Chief Officer(s):
Shane Lynch, President
Jenni Schwetz, Secretary
Finances: *Funding Sources:* Donations; membership fees
Membership: *Fees:* $50 family; $100 group; *Member Profile:* Parents of autistic individuals; groups
Activities: Summer recreational program; Christmas Party; support groups; hosting guest lecturers; *Speaker Service:* Yes

Autism Society Canada (ASC) / Société canadienne d'autisme

PO Box 22017, 1670 Heron Rd., Ottawa ON K1V 0W2
Tel: 613-789-8943
Toll-Free: 866-476-8440
info@autismsocietycanada.ca
www.autismsocietycanada.ca
Overview: A medium-sized national charitable organization founded in 1976
Mission: To provide support on a national basis to people affected by autism & related conditions through the collective efforts of Canadian provincial & territorial autism societies; to provide information & general referrals to the public regarding autism & related conditions; to promote public awareness of autism & related conditions; to encourage research in fields related or relevant to autism & related conditions; to communicate with government, agencies, & other organizations on behalf of persons affected by autism & related conditions; to promote actions to ensure people with autism & related conditions live in an environment that supports their well-being & enables them to reach their full potential; to promote & encourage the convening of conferences focused on autism & related conditions
Member of: Autism Society Ontario; World Autism Organization
Chief Officer(s):
Michael Lewis, President
michael.lewis@telus.net
Richard Burelle, Executive Director
richard@autismsocietycanada.ca
Finances: *Annual Operating Budget:* $100,000-$250,000
Staff Member(s): 2
Membership: 3,000
Activities: ICare4Autism Conference, July

Autism Society Manitoba

825 Sherbrook St., 2nd Fl., Winnipeg MB R3A 1M5
Tel: 204-783-9563; *Fax:* 204-975-3027
Toll-Free: 888-444-9563
info@autismmanitoba.com
www.autismmanitoba.com
www.facebook.com/AutismSocietyOfManitoba
twitter.com/manitobaautism
Overview: A small provincial charitable organization founded in 1977 overseen by Autism Society Canada
Mission: To promote the quality of life for people with Pervasive Developmental Disorder/Autism & their families; to promote full inclusion, dignity & development of personal skills & abilities for our members
Membership: *Fees:* $25
Activities: Educational resources; advocacy; structured social opportunities; *Speaker Service:* Yes; *Library* Open to public

Autism Society Newfoundland & Labrador (ASNL)

PO Box 14078, St. John's NL A1B 4G8
Tel: 709-722-2803; *Fax:* 709-722-4926
info@autism.nf.net
www.autism.nf.net
twitter.com/AutismSocietyNL
Overview: A medium-sized provincial charitable organization founded in 1987 overseen by Autism Society Canada
Mission: To promote the diagnosis, treatment, education & integration into the community of all autistic persons; to provide information about autism; to promote research; to promote integrated care for autistic persons; to encourage the formation of parent support groups around the province
Chief Officer(s):
Scott Crocker, Executive Director
scrocker@autism.nf.net
Finances: *Funding Sources:* Donations; government employment grants
Staff Member(s): 25
Membership: 600
Activities: Parent Support Meetings; Summer Leisure Time & Recreation; *Speaker Service:* Yes

Autism Society of British Columbia

#303, 3701 East Hastings St., Burnaby BC V5C 2H6
Tel: 604-434-0880; *Fax:* 604-434-0801
Toll-Free: 888-437-0880
info@autismbc.ca
www.autismbc.ca
www.facebook.com/autismbc
twitter.com/AutismSocietyBC
Overview: A small provincial charitable organization founded in 1975 overseen by Autism Society Canada
Mission: To promote awareness of autism & the needs of families with a child or adult with autism; to provide advocacy, resources, & referrals to families of people with autism in BC
Chief Officer(s):
Michael Lewis, President
mlewis@autismbc.ca
Staff Member(s): 8
Membership: 300 families; *Fees:* Adult client, student $5; family, professional $25; $100 institution/school/business; Lifetime $500; *Member Profile:* Parents of children with autism & professionals working in the autism field
Activities: *Library*

Nanaimo Branch
PO Box 180, Stn. A, Nanaimo BC V9R 5K9
Tel: 250-714-0801; *Fax:* 250-714-0802
www.autismbc.ca/nanaimo.php
twitter.com/autismbcvanisle
Chief Officer(s):
Alexandria Stuart, Coordinator
astuart@autismbc.ca

Prince George Branch
13950 Athabasca Rd., Prince George BC V2N 5X9
Tel: 250-963-0803; *Fax:* 250-963-0804
www.autismbc.ca/prince_george.php
Chief Officer(s):
Heather Borland, Coordinator
hborland@autismbc.ca

Autism Society of PEI

PO Box 3243, Charlottetown PE C1A 8W5
Tel: 902-566-4844
Toll-Free: 888-360-8681
www.autismsociety.pe.ca
www.facebook.com/autismsocietypei
twitter.com/AutismSocietyPE
Overview: A small provincial organization overseen by Autism Society Canada
Mission: To provide austim resources to families in PEI
Chief Officer(s):
Nathalie Walsh, Executive Director
nathalie@autismsociety.pe.ca
Membership: *Fees:* $10 family; $50 professional

Autism Speaks Canada

2450 Victoria Park Ave., Toronto ON M2J 4A2
Tel: 416-362-6227; *Fax:* 416-362-6228
Toll-Free: 888-362-6227
Other Communication:
canadianfamilyservices@autismspeaks.org
autismspeakscanada@autismspeaks.org
www.autismspeaks.ca
www.facebook.com/AutismSpeaksCanada
twitter.com/autismspeaksCAN
Previous Name: National Alliance for Autism Research
Overview: A medium-sized national organization
Mission: To fund & accelerate biomedical research focusing on autism spectrum disorders
Chief Officer(s):
Frank P. Viti, President & CEO
Activities: *Awareness Events:* World Autism Awareness Day, April 2

Autism Treatment Services of Canada (ATSC) / Association canadienne pour l'obtention des services aux personnes autistiques

404 - 94 Ave. SE, Calgary AB T2J 0E8
Tel: 403-253-2291; *Fax:* 403-253-6974
Toll-Free: 888-301-2872
autismtreatment@sta-ab.com
www.autism.ca
Previous Name: Society for the Treatment of Autism
Overview: A medium-sized national charitable organization founded in 1988
Mission: To ensure that a comprehensive range of services exists across Canada to meet the needs of individuals with autism & their families, & that autistic people are given the opportunity to achieve maximum independence & productivity within the community.
Chief Officer(s):
Peter Johnson, Chair
Dave Mikkelsen, Executive Director
Activities: Supports existing service providing organizations; assists in the development of such groups; initiates & develops services independently when necessary; acts as an ongoing resource for those with an interest in autism & related disorders

British Columbia - Society for Treatment of Autism
Kamloops BC V1C 2L6
Tel: 250-377-4956
lmdawson51@hotmail.com
Mission: Provides treatment, educational, management and consultative services to people with autism and related disorders across British Columbia.
Chief Officer(s):
Leah Dawson, Contact

Manitoba - Autism Treatment Services
c/o 142 Renfrew St., Winnipeg MB R3N 1J4
Tel: 204-487-6606
tward@gatewest.net
Mission: Provides treatment, educational, management and consultative services to people with autism and related disorders across Manitoba.
Chief Officer(s):
Tracy Ward, Contact

Nova Scotia - Society for Treatment of Autism
PO Box 392, 541 Charlotte St., Sydney NS B1P 6H2
Tel: 902-567-6441; *Fax:* 902-567-0425
autism@ns.sympatico.ca
www.nsnet.org/autismns
Chief Officer(s):
Marlene Weaver, Director

Ontario - Autism Treatment Services
Centre for Family Therapy, 9 Emily St., Carleton Place ON K7C 1R9
Tel: 613-253-0032
tekirkp@sympatico.ca
Chief Officer(s):
Terry Kirkpatrick, Director

Québec - Association canadienne pour l'obtention de services aux personnes autistiques
a/s 4290, ave Powell, Montréal QC H4P 1E4
Tél: 514-738-6169
airsan@videotron.ca
Mission: Provides treatment, educational, management and consultative services to people with autism and related disorders across Quebec.
Chief Officer(s):
Sandra Aird, Contact

Saskatchewan - Autism Services
609 - 25th St. East, Saskatoon SK S7K 0L7
Tel: 306-665-7013; *Fax:* 306-665-7011
admin@autismservices.ca
www.autismservices.ca
Mission: Provides treatment, educational, management and consultative services to people with autism and related disorders across Saskatchewan
Chief Officer(s):
Faye Davis, Executive Director

Autism Treatment Services of Saskatchewan *See* Autism Treatment Services of Canada

Autism Yukon

503B Steele St., Whitehorse YT Y1A 2E1
Tel: 867-667-6406; *Fax:* 867-667-6408
executive@autismyukon.org
www.autismyukon.org
www.facebook.com/162869033819118
Overview: A small provincial organization overseen by Autism Society Canada
Membership: *Fees:* $5 friend; $15 family; $10 individual; $25 business

Auto Sport Québec (ASQ)

CP 1000, Succ. M, 4545, av Pierre-de Coubertin, Montréal QC H1V 3R2
Tél: 514-252-3052; *Téléc:* 514-254-5369
info@lasq.ca
lasq.ca
Nom précédent: Fédération Auto-Québec
Aperçu: *Dimension:* moyenne; *Envergure:* provinciale; fondée en 1973
Mission: Pour représenter les responsables du sport automobile
Membre(s) du bureau directeur:
Gilles Villeneuve, Président et Directeur Général
Membre(s) du personnel: 8
Activités: *Stagiaires:* Oui; *Listes de destinataires:* Oui

AUTO21 - The Automobile of the 21st Century *See* AUTO21 Network of Centres of Excellence

AUTO21 Network of Centres of Excellence

401 Sunset Ave., Windsor ON N9B 3P4
Tel: 519-253-3000; *Fax:* 519-971-3626
info@auto21.ca
www.auto21.ca
www.linkedin.com/groups?about=&gid=2804256&trk=anet_ug_grppro
www.facebook.com/AUTO21
twitter.com/auto21nce
www.youtube.com/user/AUTO21NCE
Also Known As: AUTO21
Previous Name: AUTO21 - The Automobile of the 21st Century
Overview: A medium-sized national organization founded in 2001
Mission: To partner the public & private secotrs in applied automotive R&D
Member of: Networks of Centres of Excellence
Chief Officer(s):
Peter Frise, CEO & Scientific Director
Michelle Watters, COO & Executive Director
Stephanie Campeau, Director, Public Affairs & Communications
Finances: *Annual Operating Budget:* Greater than $5 Million; *Funding Sources:* Federal government; Private sector
Staff Member(s): 11
Membership: 200 researchers + 120 industry & government partners
Activities: Automotive research; *Internships:* Yes
Meetings/Conferences: • AUTO21 Annual Conference 2015, May, 2015, Westin Ottawa, Ottawa, ON
Scope: National
Attendance: 350
Description: Theme: A Legacy of Collaborative Innovation

Automobile et touring club du Québec *Voir* CAA-Québec

Automobile Importers of Canada *See* Association of International Automobile Manufacturers of Canada

Automobile Journalists Association of Canada (AJAC) / Association des journalistes automobile du Canada

PO Box 398, Stn. Main, Cobourg ON K9A 4L1
Tel: 519-563-8417
www.ajac.ca
Overview: A small national organization founded in 1981
Mission: To report on new vehicles & new industry trends in various print and broadcast media.
Chief Officer(s):
Siobhan Duffield, Event Coordinator
siobhan@ajac.ca
Membership: *Fees:* Schedule available; *Member Profile:* Working automobile journalists & automotive industry public relations representatives
Activities: Art of the Automobile Competition; *Rents Mailing List:* Yes
Awards:
• Car of the Year Awards (Award)

Automobile Protection Association (APA) / Association pour la protection automobile

292, boul St. Joseph ouest, Montréal QC H2V 2N7
Tel: 514-272-5555; *Fax:* 514-273-0797
apamontreal@apa.ca
www.apa.ca
Overview: A medium-sized national organization founded in 1969
Mission: To inform & represent the public on major automobile-related issues
Finances: *Annual Operating Budget:* $500,000-$1.5 Million
Staff Member(s): 15
Membership: 10,000; *Fees:* $77+ tax
Activities: *Internships:* Yes; *Speaker Service:* Yes; *Library* by appointment

Toronto Office
#1319, 2 Carlton St., Toronto ON M5B 1J3
Tel: 416-204-1444; *Fax:* 416-204-1985
apatoronto@apa.ca
www.apa.ca

Automotive Aftermarket Retailers of Ontario

#10, 5100 South Service Rd., Burlington ON L7L 6A5
Tel: 905-634-4040; *Fax:* 905-634-6274
Toll-Free: 800-268-5400
aaro@aaro.ca
www.aaro.ca
Overview: A medium-sized provincial organization
Mission: To advance the Interests of the Independent Sector of the Automotive Service Industry.
Chief Officer(s):
Rudy Graf, President
grafauto@on.aibn.com
Diane Freeman, Executive Director
execdirector@aaro.ca

Automotive Industries Association of Canada (AIAC) / Association des industries de l'automobile du Canada

1272 Wellington St. West, Ottawa ON K1Y 3A7
Fax: 613-728-6021
Toll-Free: 800-808-2920
info@aia@aiacanada.com
www.aiacanada.com
www.facebook.com/AIAofCanada
Overview: A large national organization founded in 1964
Mission: To represent the automotive aftermarket industry in Canada; To promote, educate, & represent members
Chief Officer(s):
John P. MacDonald, Chair
john.macdonald@aiacanada.com
Marc Brazeau, President & CEO
marc.brazeau@aiacanada.com
Therese Santostefano, Director, Operations & Finance
therese.santostefano@aiacanada.com
Andrew Shepherd, Director, Collision Training
andrew.shepherd@aiacanada.com
Patty Kettles, Manager, Marketing & Communications
patty.kettles@aiacanada.com
Finances: *Funding Sources:* Membership dues
300 volunteer(s)
Membership: 1,400 organizations; *Fees:* Dues based on the confirmed sales volumes of the individual members; *Member Profile:* Open to wholesalers, warehouse distributors, mass merchandizers, specialty groups & oil company headquarters, manufacturers, rebuilders, national distributors, manufacturers' agents, international exporters, allied organizations that supply goods &/or services to members of the association not for resale to warehouse distributors or wholesalers; *Committees:* Government Relations; Market Research; Audit & Finance; Paint, Body & Equipment; Yobe Car Care Aware Advisory
Activities: Offering correspondence courses (parts specialist training; sales training; jobber management; dangerous goods, WHMIS & hazardous waste); Providing insurance services (benefits & pensions); government relations; *Awareness Events:* Car Care Month, May; Car Safety Month, October; *Speaker Service:* Yes
Awards:
• AIA & the Global Automotive Aftermarket Symposium (GAAS) Scholarship Program (Scholarship)
For students in secondary education *Amount:* $1,000
• Hans McCorriston Motive Power Machinist Grant Program (Scholarship)
For students in a motive power machinist course *Amount:* $500
• The Arthur Paulin Automotive Aftermarket Scholarship Award (Scholarship)
For students in an automotive program *Amount:* $700

Atlantic Division
c/o David Vaughan, Eastern Automotive Warehousing, 50 Whiting Rd., Fredericton NB E3B 4Y2
Tel: 506-453-1663
Chief Officer(s):
David Vaughan, Chair
frontline@automachinery.ca

Automotive Parts Manufacturers' Association (APMA)

#801, 10 Four Seasons Pl., Toronto ON M9B 6H7
Tel: 416-620-4220; *Fax:* 416-620-9730
info@apma.ca
www.apma.ca
www.linkedin.com/groups?home=&gid=2654454
www.facebook.com/APMACanada
twitter.com/APMACanada
Overview: A large national organization founded in 1952
Mission: To promote the manufacture in Canada of automotive parts, systems, components, materials, tools, equipment & supplies, & also the provision of services used in the automotive industry & in particular for the original equipment market; To engage in activities in support of the welfare of the members of the Association
Chief Officer(s):
Keith Henry, Chair
Steve Rodgers, President
Vincent Guglielmo, Vice-President, 416-620-4220 Ext. 233
Shaun Cott, Manager, Marketing, 416-620-4220 Ext. 224
Staff Member(s): 4
Membership: 400+ corporate; *Fees:* Schedule available; *Member Profile:* Canadian producers of parts, components, systems, tools, equipment & services for the automotive & truck manufacturing industries worldwide; 3 categories: Regular - manufacturers in Canada independent of vehicle companies; Canadian manufacturers which are divisions or affiliates of vehicle companies; International associates - manufacturers outside Canada interested or involved in the Canadian market & industry; Other associates - not manufacturers but interested in keeping in touch with industry trends & developments; *Committees:* Annual Conference; Environment, Energy, Health & Safety; Human Resources Development; Innovation & Technology; Marketing & Strategic Initiatives; Strategic Purchasing
Activities: Conducting an emissions survey
Meetings/Conferences: • Automotive Parts Manufacturers' Association 2015 19th Annual Automotive Outlook Conference, 2015
Scope: National
Contact Information: Dongi Pranaitis, 905-940-2800 x404. DongiP@autoshow.ca
Publications:
• APMA [Automotive Parts Manufacturers' Association] Bulletins
Type: Bulletin
Profile: Information on issues, opportunities, & events
• APMA [Automotive Parts Manufacturers' Association] eNews Brief
Type: Newsletter
Profile: APMA activities, issues & news delivered electronically

Automotive Recyclers Association of Atlantic Canada (ARAAC)
Tel: 519-858-8761
araac@execulink.com
araac.ca
twitter.com/autorecyclersCA
Previous Name: Maritime Auto Wreckers Association
Overview: A medium-sized provincial organization founded in 1972
Mission: ARAAC is the forum for channeling information, establishing the highest ethical and environmental standards of its membership, and is the official representative in the Atlantic Provinces for the Automotive Recyclers of Canada
Member of: Automotive Recyclers of Canada
Chief Officer(s):
Brian Green, President, 506-458-9234
bgreen@greensautoparts.com
Membership: *Member Profile:* Automotive recyclers (wholesale and retail recycled auto parts dealers); Suppliers of end-of-life vehicles to provincial shredding facilities; *Committees:* Government Affairs; Group Buying; Meetings Committee; Membership; Transportation; Budget and Audit; Nominations
Meetings/Conferences: • Automotive Recyclers Association of Atlantic Canada 2015 Mid-Year Meeting, May, 2015, Crowne Plaza Fredericton Lord Beaverbrook Hotel, Fredericton, NB
Scope: Provincial
• Automotive Recyclers Association of Atlantic Canada 2015 Annual General Meeting, October, 2015, Radisson Suite Hotel Halifax, Halifax, NS
Scope: Provincial

Automotive Recyclers Association of Manitoba (ARM)
PO Box 43049, Stn. Kildonan Place, Winnipeg MB R2C 5G5
Tel: 204-667-7882
info@arm.mb.ca
www.arm.mb.ca
Overview: A medium-sized provincial organization
Mission: To provide quality recycled auto parts; To serve its customers & communities; To help the environment
Member of: Automotive Recyclers of Canada
Chief Officer(s):
Alec Gilman, President, 204-633-2540, Fax: 204-633-0723
Membership: *Member Profile:* Automotive recyclers (wholesale and retail recycled auto parts dealers); Suppliers of end-of-life vehicles to provincial shredding facilities

Automotive Recyclers of Canada (ARC)
134 Langarth St. East, London ON N6C 1Z5
Tel: 519-858-8761
info@autorecyclers.ca
autorecyclers.ca
twitter.com/autorecyclersCA
www.youtube.com/watch?v=wlmtDORQeOw&feature=youtu.be
Overview: A large national organization founded in 1997
Mission: To act as the national voice for provincial member automotive recycling associations
Chief Officer(s):
Steve Fletcher, Managing Director
Membership: 7 associations; *Member Profile:* Automotive recycling associations
Publications:
• Canadian Auto Recyclers [a publication of Automotive Recyclers of Canada]
Type: Magazine; *Frequency:* Annually; *Editor:* Mike Raine

Automotive Retailers Association of British Columbia
#1, 8980 Fraserwood Ct., Burnaby BC V5J 5H7
Tel: 604-432-7987; *Fax:* 604-432-1756
reception@ara.bc.ca
www.ara.bc.ca
www.facebook.com/autoretailers
twitter.com/autoretailers
Overview: A medium-sized provincial organization founded in 1951
Mission: To enhance the image & competitive status of association members throughout BC & ensure high quality service to protect the road safety of the motoring public
Member of: Automotive Recyclers of Canada
Chief Officer(s):
Ken McCormack, President
Finances: *Funding Sources:* Membership dues
Membership: 1,000+; *Fees:* $525 associate; $656.25 full member; $262.50 branch/cross-divisional; *Member Profile:* Automotive aftermarket industry

Autonomous Federation of Collegial Staff (Ind.) *Voir* Fédération autonome du collégial (ind.)

Autorité des marchés financiers (AMF)
Place de la Cité, tour Cominar, #400, 2640, boul Laurier, Quebéc QC G1V 5C1
Tél: 418-525-0337; *Téléc:* 418-525-9512
Ligne sans frais: 877-525-0337
www.lautorite.qc.ca
www.linkedin.com/company/1128549
www.facebook.com/Bonnesquestions
twitter.com/lautorite
Aperçu: *Dimension:* moyenne; *Envergure:* provinciale; fondée en 2004 surveillé par Canadian Securities Administrators
Membre de: Canadian Securities Administrators
Membre(s) du bureau directeur:
Bernard Motulsky, Président
Michel Lespérance, Secrétaire
Publications:
• Bulletin de l'Autorité des marchés financiers
Type: Newsletter; *Frequency:* hebdomadaire
• L'Info-Autorité
Type: Newsletter; *Frequency:* au 2 mois
• Rapport annuel de gestion de l'Autorité des marchés financiers
Type: Report; *Frequency:* annuel
Montréal
Tour de la Bourse, CP 246, 800, rue du Square-Victoria, 22e étage, Montréal QC H4Z 1G3
Tél: 514-395-0337; *Téléc:* 514-873-3090

Autorités canadiennes en valeurs mobilières *See* Canadian Securities Administrators

Aux Prismes Plein air et culture
CP 476, Succ. C, Montréal QC H2L 4K4
Tél: 514-990-7674
info@auxprismes.qc.ca
www.auxprismes.qc.ca
Aperçu: *Dimension:* petite; *Envergure:* locale
Mission: Association sans but lucratif pour gais, lesbiennes et amis/amies - tous les âges, sexes et orientations sexuelles; activités sociales, culturelles, sportives
Membre: *Montant de la cotisation:* 15$

Auxiliaires bénévoles de l'Hôpital de Chibougamau
51, 3e Rue, Chibougamau QC G8P 1N1
Tél: 418-748-2676
Aperçu: *Dimension:* petite; *Envergure:* locale
Membre(s) du bureau directeur:
Priscilla Ratthé, Présidente, 418-748-6453

Avataq Cultural Institute
#360, 4150, rue Sainte-Catherine Ouest, Montréal QC H3Z 2Y5
Tel: 514-989-9031; *Fax:* 514-989-8789
Toll-Free: 800-361-5029
avataq@avataq.qc.ca
www.avataq.qc.ca
Overview: A small provincial organization founded in 1980
Mission: To promote & protect the Inuit language & culture in Nunavik
Chief Officer(s):
Charlie Arngaq, President
Activities: *Library* Open to public by appointment

The Avian Preservation Foundation (APF)
PO Box 123, Chemainus BC V0R 1K0
Tel: 250-246-4803; *Fax:* 250-246-4912
exec@aacc.ca
www.aacc.ca/apf.htm
Overview: A medium-sized national charitable organization
Mission: To support recognized expert aviculturists who are endeavouring to breed rare & endangered avian species; to establish a Canadian breeding centre for rare & endangered avian species; to establish a monitoring body for captive avian stocks in Canada through surveys & computer software; to create & maintain a breeding program throughout Canada for avian species currently listed as endangered; to create a captive preservation program for rare & endangered species within zoos, bird parks & sanctuaries where re-introduction into the natural habitat is not possible or practical
Member of: Avicultural Advancement Council of Canada
Chief Officer(s):
Mark S. Curtis, Executive Director
Finances: *Annual Operating Budget:* Less than $50,000
12 volunteer(s)
Membership: 250; *Fees:* $35

Aviation Alberta (AVA)
Edmonton International Airport, 3715 - 56th Ave. East, Edmonton AB TYE 0V4
Tel: 780-890-0006
aviationalberta@gmail.com
www.aviationalberta.com
Previous Name: Alberta Aerospace Association
Overview: A small provincial organization founded in 2004
Mission: To be a catalyst for industry growth & the recognized voice of aerospace, airport & aviation interests in Alberta; To serve its membership & promote the growth & prosperity of aerospace, airports & aviation in Alberta through collaboration, communication, training, education, research & advocacy
Affliation(s): Aeropsace Industries Association of Canada; Aerospace Industry Association of British Columbia; Air Transport Association of Canada; Association for Unmanned Vehicles International; Association for Unmanned Vehicles International-Canada; Canada Aviation Museum; Canada's Aviation Hall of Fame; Canadian Airports Council; Canadian Association of Defence & Security Industries; Canadian Aviation Maintenance Council; Canadian Business Aircraft Association; Canadian Owners & Pilots Association; Civil Air Search & Rescue Association of Canada; Manitoba Aerospace Association; UVSI-Canada
Chief Officer(s):
Bram Tilroe, Acting Chair
Membership: 226; *Fees:* $40-$1,650; *Member Profile:* Aircraft/airline operators; aerospace; airport operators & uvs (unmanned vehicle systems)
Awards:
• President's Award (Award)
• Airport Operator Award (Award)
• Private Pilot Advanced Training (Scholarship)
• Commercial Pilot Advanced Training (Scholarship)
• AME or Avionics Technology (Scholarship)
• UVS Robotics Technology (Scholarship)
• Reilly Memorial Award (Award)

Avicultural Advancement Council of Canada (AACC)
28 Greene Dr., Brampton ON L6V 2R6
www.aacc.ca
Overview: A medium-sized national licensing organization founded in 1972
Mission: To establish & maintain a national association of interested societies & individuals to promote the advancement of aviculture in Canada; To represent the Canadian avicultural community internationally; To disseminate information; to support recognized expert aviculturalists; To assist all levels of government in preparing informed legislation & policy relating to aviculture; To establish standards for the exhibition of birds in Canada; To provide a national identification leg band registry; To establish an avian species preservation program in Canada
Affliation(s): American Singer Canary Club of Canada; Assoc. des amateurs d'oiseaux de la Mauricie; Assoc. des éléveurs d'oiseaux de Montréal; BC Avicultural Society; BC Exotic Bird Society; Budgerigar & Foreign Bird Society; Cage Bird Society of Hamilton; Calgary Canary Club; Canadian Dove Assoc.; Canadian Gloster Club; Cowichan Valley & Upper Island Cage Bird Club; Durham Avicultural Society; Edmonton Avicultural Association; Essex-Kent Cage Bird Society; Feather Fanciers Club; Golden Triangle Parrot Club; Kamloops Aviculturalist Society; London & District Cage Bird Society; Manitoba Canary & Finch Club
Chief Officer(s):
Dunstan H. Browne, President
hdbrowne@shaw.ca
Denise Antler, Ring Registrar
antler3795@rogers.com
Roslynne Webb, Secretary
rozwebb@telus.net
Finances: *Annual Operating Budget:* Less than $50,000; *Funding Sources:* Membership dues; Donations
12 volunteer(s)
Membership: 300 individual + 40 institutional; *Fees:* $30 individual; $70 club; *Member Profile:* Breeders, exhibitors & fanciers of birds; Clubs thaa subscribe to the principles of association
Activities: *Library*

Avocats en faveur d'une conscience sociale *See* Lawyers for Social Responsibility

Avocats Hors Québec (AHQ) / Quebec Lawyers Abroad
445, boul. St-Laurent, Montréal QC H2Y 3T8
www.avocatshorsquebec.org

Aperçu: *Dimension:* moyenne; *Envergure:* provinciale
Mission: Pour défendre les intérêts des membres du Barreau du Québec qui travaillent à l'étranger
Membre(s) du bureau directeur:
Lucie Laplante, Présidente, Conseil d'administration
Membre: *Critères d'admissibilite:* Membres du Barreau du Québec

Avocats sans frontières Canada (ASFC) / Lawyers Without Borders Canada (LWBC)

#230, 825, rue St-Joseph Est, Québec QC G1K 3C8
Tel: 418-907-2607; *Fax:* 418-948-2241
info@asfcanada.ca
www.asfcanada.ca
Also Known As: Abogados sin fronteras
Overview: A large national organization
Mission: Pour aider à défendre les droits humains dans les endroits où ils sont le plus négligés
Chief Officer(s):
Migues Baz, Président, Conseil d'administration
Membership: *Fees:* 15$
Activities: Conférences; séminaires; *Internships:* Yes

Avon River Chamber of Commerce

PO Box 2188, Windsor NS B0N 2T0
Tel: 902-472-7200
info@whcc.ca
www.whcc.ca
www.facebook.com/theAvonChamber
twitter.com/avonchamber
Previous Name: West Hants Chamber of Commerce; Windsor Board of Trade
Overview: A small local organization founded in 1972
Mission: Working to improve the business climate for members by increasing awareness, being proactive in public policy & providing workshops, seminars & information session
Chief Officer(s):
Scott Geddes, President
Andrew Bauchman, Vice-President
Membership: 82; *Fees:* $57.50

The Avon Trail

PO Box 21148, Stratford ON N5A 7V4
e-mail: info@avontrail.ca
www.avontrail.ca
Overview: A small local charitable organization founded in 1975
Mission: To promote an interest in hiking & maintain hiking trails
Member of: Hike Ontario
Chief Officer(s):
Karen Hill, President
Membership: *Fees:* $30 family; $20 individual/organization/youth; $15 student; *Committees:* Conservancy
Activities: Trail winds through river valleys, farm lands & festival country of Southern Ontario, from the Grand Valley to the Thames Valley Trail (100 km); guided hikes year round

AWIC Community & Social Services (AWIC)

1761 Sheppard Ave., Toronto ON M2J 0A5
Tel: 416-499-4144; *Fax:* 416-499-4077
awic@bellnet.ca
www.awic.info
www.facebook.com/185101574859967
Previous Name: Association of Women of India in Canada
Overview: A small local organization
Mission: To assist newcomers to achieve full integration & participation in Canadian life while maintaining their culture & heritage
Chief Officer(s):
Chitra Sunder, President
Vanita Pais, Director
Membership: *Fees:* One year: $5; Five year: $20
Publications:
• AWIC Newsletter

Awo Taan Healing Lodge Society

PO Box 6084, Stn. A, Calgary AB T2H 2L3
Tel: 403-531-1970; *Fax:* 403-531-1977; *Crisis Hot-Line:* 403-531-1972
www.awotaan.org
www.facebook.com/awotaan
twitter.com/AwoTaan1
www.youtube.com/user/awotaan
Previous Name: Calgary Native Women's Shelter Society
Overview: A small local organization founded in 1992
Mission: To offer safe accommmodation, a full-service emergency shelter, counselling, support, & referrals to women & their children who consider themselves to be physically, emotionally, or sexually abused.
Member of: Calgary Regional Shelter Directors Network; Associaton of Directors & Volunteer Resources: Volunteer Calgary; Volunteer Collective
Affiliation(s): Alberta Council of Women's Shelters
Chief Officer(s):
Josie Nepinak, Executive Director
Finances: *Funding Sources:* Provincial, municipal government; United Way
Membership: *Fees:* $5
Activities: Gala Dinner; Golf Tournament

Aylmer Heritage Association (AHA) / Association du patrimoine d'Aylmer (APA)

PO Box 476, Aylmer QC J9H 5E7
Tel: 819-684-6809; *Fax:* 819-684-6480
heritage.aylmer@videotron.ca
www.facebook.com/PatrimoineAylmerHeritage
Overview: A small local organization founded in 1974
Mission: To promote the preservation & protection of Aylmer's heritage, including its buildings, landmarks, natural environment, history & culture.
Member of: Heritage Canada; Féderation des sociétés d'histoire du Québec
Chief Officer(s):
Mary Duggan, Contact
Finances: *Funding Sources:* Fundraising events; municipal & provincial grants
Membership: *Fees:* $10 senior/student; $15 individual; $20 family; $50 corporate/group
Activities: Publications; walking tours; genealogy; town planning; *Speaker Service:* Yes; *Library:* Aylmer Heritage Association Archives; Open to public
Publications:
• The Aylmer Road - an illustrated history
Type: guide; *Author:* Diane Aldred; *Price:* $25
Profile: The history of the region's last remaining heritage highway, its mansions and private clubs
• Aylmer, Quebec: Its heritage, son patrimoine
Type: guide; *Author:* Diane Aldred; *Price:* $15
Profile: A bilingual, 200-page book with photos & illustrations on Aylmer's history & houses
• Discover Aylmer's Heritage
Type: guide; *Author:* Enid Page & Lyne St-Jacques; *Price:* $7
Profile: An account of early settlement, with a walk along the town's main street; suitable for children
• From Conroy's Inn to the British Hotel
Type: guide; *Author:* Richard M. Bégin; *Price:* $10
Profile: 150 years in the life of Canada's oldest surviving hotel & tavern west of Montreal

Aylsham & District Board of Trade

PO Box 21, Aylsham SK S0E 0C0
Tel: 306-862-4849; *Fax:* 306-862-4506
mgbritton@sasktel.net
Overview: A small local organization
Chief Officer(s):
Glen Gray, President, 306-862-3028
Marlene Britton, Secretary, 306-862-4849
Richard Archer, Treasurer, 306-862-9432
Staff Member(s): 9; 200 volunteer(s)

Ayrshire Breeders Association of Canada (ABAC) / L'Associaton des éleveurs Ayrshire du Canada

4865, boul Laurier ouest, Saint-Hyacinthe QC J2S 3V4
Tel: 450-778-3535; *Fax:* 450-778-3531
info@ayrshire-canada.com
www.ayrshire-canada.com
www.facebook.com/profile.php?id=100000928371239
Also Known As: Ayrshire Canada
Overview: A large national organization
Mission: To bring Ayrshire breeders together for the purpose of cooperating in their efforts to further the interests of the breed; promote the breeding of purebred Ayrshire cattle in Canada; establish breeding standards; cooperate with industry partners to enhance programs; program services in English & French
Chief Officer(s):
Linda Ness, Executive Director
Chad McKell, Registrar
Finances: *Annual Operating Budget:* $500,000-$1.5 Million
Staff Member(s): 5
Membership: 1,200; *Committees:* Executive; Budget; Breed Improvement; Marketing
Activities: *Speaker Service:* Yes; *Rents Mailing List:* Yes
Awards:
• Award of Merit (Award)
• Master Breeder (Award)

The Azorean House of Toronto *See* Casa dos Acores (Toronto) Inc

B'nai Brith Canada (BBC)

15 Hove St., Toronto ON M3H 4Y8
Tel: 416-633-6224; *Fax:* 416-630-2159
communications@bnaibrith.ca
www.bnaibrith.ca
www.facebook.com/bnaibrithcanada
Also Known As: Children of the Covenant
Overview: A large national charitable organization founded in 1875
Mission: To bring men & women of the Jewish faith together in fellowship to serve the Jewish community through combating anti-Semitism, bigotry & racism in Canada & abroad; carrying out & supporting activities which ensure the security & survival of the State of Israel & Jewish communities worldwide; community service through various volunteer activities, cultivation of leadership, charitable work, advocacy & government relations
Affiliation(s): B'nai Brith International
Chief Officer(s):
Eric Bissell, President
Frank Dimant, Executive Vice President
Finances: *Annual Operating Budget:* $1.5 Million-$3 Million; *Funding Sources:* Private donations; membership dues
Staff Member(s): 35
Membership: 20,000 families; *Fees:* Schedule available; *Member Profile:* Open to individuals 18 years of age & of Jewish faith; *Committees:* Affordable Housing Program; Centre for Community Action; Department of Government Relations; The League for Human Rights; Institute for International Affairs
Activities: Educational programs; community volunteer projects; leadership development programs; government relations; Anti-Hate Hotline: 1-800-892-2624; *Awareness Events:* Annual Golf Tournament; Award of Merit Dinner; *Internships:* Yes; *Speaker Service:* Yes; *Rents Mailing List:* Yes; *Library* Open to public by appointment
Awards:
• Award of Merit & Humanitarian Awards (Award)
Established 1981; presented annually at gala events in major communities across Canada*Eligibility:* Selection of honourees based on outstanding achievement in their chosen fields as well as personal commitment to the overall betterment of Canadian society *Contact:* Sharon Anisman

Midwest Region
#C403, 123 Doncaster St., Winnipeg MB R3N 2B2
Tel: 204-487-9623; *Fax:* 204-487-9648
wbb@bnaibrith.ca
www.bnaibrith.ca
Chief Officer(s):
Maria Medina, Contact

Ontario Region
15 Hove St., Toronto ON M3H 4Y8
Tel: 416-633-6224; *Fax:* 416-630-2159
bnb@bnaibrith.ca
www.bnaibrith.ca

Québec Region
#202, 7155 Côte St. Luc Rd., Montréal QC H4V 1J2
Tel: 514-733-5377; *Fax:* 514-342-9632
Chief Officer(s):
Harvey Levine, Regional Director
hlevine@bnaibrith.ca

Western Region
PO Box 67306, Stn. Hawkstone R.P.O., Edmonton AB T6M 0J5
Tel: 780-483-6939
bnaibrith.westcan@shaw.ca
www.bnaibrith.ca

B'nai Brith Canada Institute for International Affairs

15 Hove St., Toronto ON M3H 4Y8
Tel: 416-633-6224; *Fax:* 416-630-2159
bnb@bnaibrith.ca
www.bnaibrith.ca/institute.html
Overview: A small international organization
Mission: To identify & fight human rights abuses throughout the world, with special emphasis on Jewish communities worldwide
Chief Officer(s):
Eric Bissell, President
Frank Dimant, Executive Vice-President
Staff Member(s): 2; 3 volunteer(s)
Membership: 100

Activities: Advocacy & community mobilization; public education; media liaison; fact finding missions; briefs & consultations with government & non-government; organizations; publications

B'nai Brith Women of Eastern Canada; Jewish Women International of Canada ***See*** Act To End Violence Against Women

B2ten
Westmount QC
b2ten.ca
twitter.com/B2ten
www.youtube.com/user/B2ten
Overview: A small national charitable organization founded in 2005
Mission: To help Canadian athletes achieve success in the sporting world, particularly in an international context.
Chief Officer(s):
Dominick Gauthier, Co-Founder
Jennifer Heil, Co-Founder
J.D. Miller, Co-Founder
Finances: *Funding Sources:* Donations

Baccalieu Trail Board of Trade Inc.
College of the North Atlantic, 22 Goff Ave., Carbonear NL A1Y 1A7
Tel: 709-596-4525; *Fax:* 709-596-4555
Overview: A small local organization
Chief Officer(s):
Ron Delaney, Chair
Trish Baker, Contact
Membership: 100-499

Bach Elgar Choir
86 Homewood St., Hamilton ON L8P 2M4
Tel: 905-527-5995; *Fax:* 905-527-0555
bachelgar@gmail.com
www.bachelgar.com
www.facebook.com/bachelgar
Overview: A medium-sized local charitable organization founded in 1905
Mission: To provide choral music of excellent quality & broad-based appeal to the community; To act as a cultural & educational resource
Affliation(s): Ontario Choral Federation; Hamilton & Region Arts Council; Council for Business & the Arts in Canada; Canadian Conference of the Arts
Chief Officer(s):
Alexander Cann, Artistic Director
Finances: *Funding Sources:* Municipal & provincial governments; foundation; fundraising; ticket sales
Staff Member(s): 2
Membership: *Member Profile:* Admittance to choir by audition
Activities: *Rents Mailing List:* Yes

Back Country Horsemen of British Columbia (BCHBC)
c/o Carol Creasy, Comp. 6, Site 10, RR#1, Sorrento BC V0E 2W0
Tel: 250-835-8587
ccreasy07@gmail.com
www.bchorsemen.org
Overview: A small provincial organization
Mission: To preserve & enhance public lands for use by equestrians; To offer a safe learning atmosphere for persons interested in trail riding & the wilderness experience; To act as a voice for members in dealing with provincial & municipal governing agencies on matters of concern to trail riders
Chief Officer(s):
Ybo Plante, President, 250-743-3356
president@bchorsemen.org
Brian Wallace, Vice-President, 250-569-2324
hbwally@gmail.com
Sharon Pickthorne, Treasurer, 250-337-1818
oneonone@telus.net
Finances: *Funding Sources:* Membership fees
Membership: 584; *Fees:* $35; *Member Profile:* Equestrians of any age interested in trail riding & the back country of British Columbia; *Committees:* Trails; Chapter Communications; Education
Activities: Providing information about trails; Offering educational clinics about trail riding; Organizing monthly meetings; Collaborating with other groups, such as Scouts Canada, to work on projects such as bridge building; Increasing public awareness of the association
Publications:
• Back Country Horsemen of British Columbia Provincial Newsletter
Type: Newsletter
Profile: Association information, such as upcoming events & meetings

Alberni Valley Chapter
alberni valley BC
Tel: 250-720-1298
Mission: To inform & educate members about trail riding & British Columbia's back country
Chief Officer(s):
Melody Francoeur, Contact
melodyfrancoeur@shaw.ca

Aldergrove Chapter
aldergrove BC
Tel: 604-856-4433
Mission: To provide education to equestrians about trail riding in British Columbia's back country
Chief Officer(s):
Brian Harder, Contact, 604-941-9888
bharder@usw.ca
Carleigh Paterson, Vice-Chair, 604-308-1962

Kamloops Chapter
Kamloops BC
Tel: 778-469-0041
Mission: To inform & educate equestrians in the Kamloops area
Chief Officer(s):
Wendy Harris, Contact
alwendyharris@shaw.ca
• Back Country Horsemen of British Columbia Kamloops Chapter Newsletter
Type: Newsletter; *Accepts Advertising; Editor:* Rick Weik
Profile: Information & announcements about the Kamloops chapter

Kootenay Chapter
kootenay BC
Tel: 250-367-9834
Mission: To offer a safe learning environment for persons interested in trail riding & the wilderness experience
Chief Officer(s):
Rick Fillmore, Contact
ricof@direct.ca

Northwest Chapter
BC
Tel: 250-846-9251
Mission: To preserve, protect, & ride the trails of northwestern British Columbia; To educate equestrians through clinics
Chief Officer(s):
Floyd Kennedy, Contact
• Back Country Horsemen of British Columbia Northwest Chapter Newsletter
Type: Newsletter; *Author:* Eileen Shorter

Okanagan Chapter
okanagan BC
Tel: 250-763-3962
Mission: To offer educational clinics to equestrians in the Okanagan area
Chief Officer(s):
Joanne Poole, Contact
• Back Country Horsemen of British Columbia Okanagan Chapter Newsletter
Type: Newsletter; *Editor:* Anne Smith
Profile: Updates & announcements from the Okanagan Chapter

Powell River Chapter
Powell River BC
Tel: 604-487-1337
Mission: To provide a learning environment for persons interested in trail riding & the wilderness experience
Chief Officer(s):
Lynn Whittle, Contact
lynn.w@shaw.ca

Robson Valley Chapter
BC
Tel: 250-569-2324
Chief Officer(s):
Brian Wallace, Contact
hbwally@gmail.com

Shuswap Chapter
Shuswap BC
Tel: 778-257-7700
Affliation(s): Horse Council of British Columbia
Chief Officer(s):
Linda Buchanan, Contact
lindaturtlevalley@gmail.com
• Back Country Horsemen of British Columbia Shuswap Chapter Newsletter
Type: Newsletter; *Editor:* Susan Noltner
Profile: Shuswp chapter updates & announcements

South Cariboo Chapter
Cariboo BC
Tel: 250-395-6492
Mission: To enhance & preserve public lands for use by equestrians
Chief Officer(s):
Peter Reid, Contact
peterreid99@hotmail.com

South Vancouver Island Chapter
BC
Tel: 250-361-6290
Mission: To preserve & enhance public lands for use by equestrians; To provide a safe atmosphere to learn about trail riding
Chief Officer(s):
Ybo Plante, Contact
farmgirlbc@gmail.com
Liza Sprang, Vice-Chair
Nancy Lane, Secretary, 250-743-1268
nancylane@shaw.ca
Rhonda Hittinger, Treasurer

Vancouver Island - North Chapter
BC
Tel: 250-337-1818
Mission: To enhance & improve public lands for use by equestrians; To provide educational clinics for members
Chief Officer(s):
Sharon Pickthorne, Contact
oneonone@telus.net

Vancouver Island Chapter
BC
Tel: 250-245-4204
Mission: To provide educational clinics in trail riding, including safety, courtesy & environmental awareness, for persons on Vancouver Island; To preserve & enhance public lands for use by equestrians; To ensure Canadians maintain access to use horses & mules on public lands
Chief Officer(s):
Lynn deVries, Contact

Yarrow Chapter
Yarrow BC
Tel: 604-854-1245
Mission: To provide educational clinics in trail riding for person in the Yarrow area; To preserve & enhance public lands for use by equestrians; To offer a voice for members on issues related to the back country
Chief Officer(s):
Rose Schroeder, Contact
milkmaid@shaw.ca
John Gardener, Vice-Chair, Membership, 604-794-7272
Karin Smith, Secretary, 604-792-3902
Linda Kuhr, Treasurer, 604-823-7456
Peter Kuhr, Coordinator, Education, 604-823-7456
Gene Peters, Coordinator, Work Bee, 604-823-4672
Rose Schroeder, Coordinator, Trails, 604-854-1245
• Back Country Horsemen of British Columbia Yarrow Chapter Newsletter
Type: Newsletter; *Editor:* Kelly Hawes
Profile: Information & announcements from the Yarrow chapter

Badlands Historical Centre
335 - 1st St. East, Drumheller AB T0J 0Y0
Tel: 403-823-2593
landsbad@telus.net
Previous Name: Drumheller Museum Society
Overview: A small local organization
Mission: The Centre displays exhibits on the history of Drumheller Valley from the age of dinosaurs, up through the ice ages & into modern times.

Badminton Alberta
c/o Alberta Badminton Centre, 60 Patterson Blvd. SW, Calgary AB T3H 2E1
Tel: 403-297-2722; *Fax:* 403-297-2706
Toll-Free: 888-397-2722
members@badmintonalberta.ca

www.badmintonalberta.ca
www.facebook.com/170234779702176
Previous Name: Alberta Badminton Association
Overview: A medium-sized provincial organization founded in 1928 overseen by Badminton Canada
Mission: To promote the sport of badminton
Member of: Badminton Canada; International Badminton Federation
Chief Officer(s):
Jeff Bell, Executive Director
jbell@badmintonalberta.ca
Finances: *Funding Sources:* Alberta Sport Recreation Parks & Wildlife Foundation
Staff Member(s): 4
Membership: 7000 members; 350 affliated clubs; *Fees:* Schedule available; *Member Profile:* Athlets, clubs, coaches, officials; *Committees:* Executive

Badminton BC

#110, 12761 - 16 Ave., Surrey BC V4A 1N2
Tel: 604-385-3595
info@badmintonbc.com
www.badmintonbc.com
www.facebook.com/badmintonbc
twitter.com/b2dmintonbc
instagram.com/badminton_bc
Overview: A medium-sized provincial organization founded in 1925 overseen by Badminton Canada
Mission: To provide leadership to develop & promote badminton in BC by increasing the membership base, facilitating a higher standard of participation through competitive & development opportunities for players, coaches, officials & volunteers
Member of: Sport BC; International Badminton Federation
Chief Officer(s):
Phil Weier, Executive Director, 604-333-3599
philw@badmintonbc.com
Finances: *Funding Sources:* Government grants; fundraising; sponsorships
Staff Member(s): 5
Membership: *Fees:* $15; *Member Profile:* Recreational & competitive players; coaches & officials; age 6 to 60; *Committees:* Executive; Nominations; Governance Review; Risk Management; Finance & Audit; Regional/Sport Development; Membership; Performance; Competitions; Officials; Coaches; Judicial
Activities: Tournaments; athlete training; coaching; *Speaker Service:* Yes; *Library:* Badminton Resource Library; Open to public

Badminton Canada

#401, 700 Industrial Ave., Ottawa ON K1G 0Y9
Tel: 613-569-2424; *Fax:* 613-748-5724
badminton@badminton.ca
www.badminton.ca
www.facebook.com/BadmintonCanada
twitter.com/BdmintonCanada
Previous Name: Canadian Badminton Association
Overview: A medium-sized national organization
Mission: To provide centralized support, &/or leadership in furthering member association objectives, act as custodian of the laws of badminton & to foster outstanding player development; to act for its members in helping to assure national & international class competition for Canada's outstanding badminton players, & to establish Canada as a leading participant in international badminton
Affliation(s): International Badminton Federation
Chief Officer(s):
Kyle Hunter, Executive Director
khunter@badminton.ca
Staff Member(s): 3

Badminton New Brunswick *See* Badminton New Nouveau Brunswick 2008 Inc.

Badminton New Nouveau Brunswick 2008 Inc. (BNNB)

NB
e-mail: webmaster@bnnb.ca
www.bnnb.ca
www.facebook.com/bnnb.ca
Previous Name: Badminton New Brunswick
Overview: A small provincial organization overseen by Badminton Canada
Mission: Badminton NB is a registered, non-profit organization which organizes junior & senior badminton tournaments.
Member of: Badminton Canada
Chief Officer(s):
Eric Fortin, President
Jerry Zhang, Regional Director, Capital
Membership: *Fees:* $15

Badminton Newfoundland & Labrador Inc. (BNL)

1296A Kenmount Rd., Paradise NL A1L 1N3
Tel: 709-576-7606; *Fax:* 709-576-7493
badminton@sportnl.ca
www.badmintonnl.ca
www.facebook.com/285446971492858
www.youtube.com/user/NLBadminton
Overview: A small provincial organization founded in 1969 overseen by Badminton Canada
Mission: BNL is the non-profit, volunteer, sports governing body for badminton in Newfoundland & Labrador.
Member of: Sport Newfoundland & Labrador
Chief Officer(s):
John Gillam, President
Jeff Milley, Director, Labrador
Geoff Robinson, Director, Eastern
Finances: *Annual Operating Budget:* $50,000-$100,000
Membership: 1-99; *Member Profile:* School & community badminton clubs for recreational, competitive junior & senior players
Activities: Sanctioned tournaments & events

Badminton Ontario (BON)

#209, 3 Concorde Gate, Toronto ON M3C 3N7
Tel: 416-426-7195; *Fax:* 416-426-7346
info@badmintonontario.ca
www.badmintonontario.ca
www.facebook.com/cweculture
twitter.com/cweculture
www.youtube.com/cweculture
Previous Name: Ontario Badminton Association
Overview: A medium-sized provincial organization founded in 1925 overseen by Badminton Canada
Mission: To provide an organized, structured environment for the activity of badminton
Member of: Badminton Canada
Affliation(s): Badminton Canada; Badminton World Federation
Chief Officer(s):
Stephane Cadieux, Technical Director
stephane.cadieux@badmintonontario.ca
Jolande Amoraal, Marketing Director
jolande.amoraal@badmintonontario.ca
Finances: *Annual Operating Budget:* $50,000-$100,000; *Funding Sources:* Ministry of Citizenship, Culture & Recreation
Staff Member(s): 1; 60 volunteer(s)
Membership: 1,000; *Fees:* Schedule available; *Member Profile:* Badminton players; clubs; coaches; officials
Activities: *Awareness Events:* Provincial Championships

Badminton Québec

4940, rue Hochelaga est, Montréal QC H1V 1E7
Tél: 514-252-3066; *Téléc:* 514-252-3175
badmintonquebec@videotron.ca
www.badmintonquebec.com
www.facebook.com/190220224436587
twitter.combadquebec
www.youtube.com/user/badmintonqc/videos
Également appelé: Fédération québécoise de badminton inc.
Aperçu: *Dimension:* grande; *Envergure:* provinciale; fondée en 1929 surveillé par Badminton Canada
Mission: Promouvoir et développer le sport sur tout le territoire québécois en regroupant tous ses membres, les personnes et associations intéressées au rayonnement de notre discipline
Membre de: Fédération internationale de badminton; Badminton Canada
Membre(s) du bureau directeur:
Claude Tessier, Président
Chantal Brouillard, Directrice générale
chantal.brouillard@badmintonquebec.com
Christian Guibourt, Directeur technique
christian.guibourt@badmintonquebec.com
Alexandre Grosleau, Coordonnateur des services aux membres
alexandre.grosleau@badmintonquebec.com
Activités: *Stagiaires:* Oui
Publications:
• La Plume [a publication of Badminton Québec]
Type: Infolettre

Baffin Regional Chamber of Commerce (BRCC)

Building 607, PO Box 59, Iqaluit NU X0A 0H0
Tel: 867-979-4654; *Fax:* 867-979-2929
www.baffinchamber.ca
Overview: A small local organization founded in 1987
Mission: The non-partisan organization fosters, promotes & improves business development throughout the Baffin Region & Canada.
Chief Officer(s):
Chris West, Executive Director
execdir@baffinchamber.ca
Ike Hauli, President
ihaulli@aol.com
Finances: *Funding Sources:* Membership fees; project management & administration fees; profits from the annual Nunavut Trade Show & Conference
Membership: *Fees:* $25-$150; *Member Profile:* Baffin businesses & professionals; *Committees:* Communications Committee; Chamber Relations Committee; Trade Show Committee
Activities: *Awareness Events:* Community Economic Development Weeks

Baha'i Community of Ottawa

211 McArthur Ave., Ottawa ON K1L 6P6
Tel: 613-297-9406
Toll-Free: 800-433-3284
www.bahai-ottawa.org
twitter.com/OttawaBahais
Overview: A small local organization
Mission: To support the development of the Baha'i Faith Community in Ottawa, Ontario.
Membership: 9 sectors;

The Bahá'í Community of Canada / La communauté bahá'íe du Canada

Baha'i National Centre, 7200 Leslie St., Thornhill ON L3T 6L8
Tel: 905-889-8168; *Fax:* 905-889-8184
Other Communication: www.bahainews.ca
secretariat@cdnbnc.org
ca.bahai.org
www.facebook.com/Bahai.Community.of.Canada
www.flickr.com/photos/103796735@N05
Overview: A large national charitable organization founded in 1844
Mission: To teach the oneness of humanity, the common divine source of all the great religions, equality of the sexes & harmony of science & religion; headquarters in Haifa, Israel; 5-6 million adherents in 214 countries & territories; Canada's 36,000 Baha'is are located in some 1,500 centres, 261 of which elect local governing councils called Spiritual Assemblies; National Spiritual Assembly of Baha'is of Canada incorporated by Act of Parliament in 1949
Member of: Bahá'í International Community
Affliation(s): Baha'i International Community
Chief Officer(s):
Gerald Filson, Director, External Affairs, 416-587-0632
externalaffairs@cdnbnc.org
Susanne E. Tamás, Director, Government Relations, 613-233-3712
ogr@bcc-cbc.org
Finances: *Annual Operating Budget:* Greater than $5 Million; *Funding Sources:* Contributions from members
Staff Member(s): 30
Membership: 36,000
Activities: Study circles; Devotional gatherings; Junior youth spiritual empowerment program; Children's classes; *Awareness Events:* Unity in Diversity Week, Nov.; *Speaker Service:* Yes; *Library* by appointment

Baie Verte & Area Chamber of Commerce

PO Box 578, Baie Verte NL A0K 1B0
Tel: 709-532-4204; *Fax:* 709-532-4252
bvachamber@nf.aibn.com
www.bvachamber.com
Overview: A small local organization
Chief Officer(s):
Vacant, President
Celia Dicks, Chamber Coordinator
Membership: 44; *Fees:* $45.20-$90.40; *Committees:* Mining Conference; Craft, Trade & Homo Show

Bakery Council of Canada *See* Baking Association of Canada

Baking Association of Canada (BAC) / Association canadienne de la boulangerie

#202, 7895 Tranmere Dr., Mississauga ON L5S 1V9
Tel: 905-405-0288; *Fax:* 905-405-0993
Toll-Free: 888-674-2253
info@baking.ca
www.baking.ca
Previous Name: Bakery Council of Canada

Overview: A medium-sized national organization founded in 1947
Mission: To further the interests of Canadian retail, in-store, & wholesale bakers, through advocacy & effective programs at the regional & national level
Member of: Retailer's Bakery Association; Conseil de la Boulangerie du Québec
Membership: 2,500; *Fees:* Schedule available; *Member Profile:* Retail bakers; In-store bakers; Commercial bakers; suppliers; *Committees:* Education; Technical; Food Safety
Activities: *Library*
Meetings/Conferences: • Bakery Showcase 2015 Trade Show & Conference, May, 2015, Palais des congrès de Montréal, Montréal, QC
Scope: National
Publications:
• The Bulletin [a publication of the Baking Association of Canada]
Type: Newsletter
Profile: Industry information & forthcoming events

BALANCE for Blind Adults
#302, 4920 Dundas St. West, Toronto ON M9A 1B7
Tel: 416-236-1796; *Fax:* 416-236-4280
info@balancefba.org
www.balancefba.org
Overview: A medium-sized local charitable organization founded in 1986
Mission: To provide instruction & support to individuals with visual impairment to enable them to live independently & confidently in their community; To promote independence, decision making, & self-fulfillment
Chief Officer(s):
Susan Archibald, Executive Director, 416-236-1796 Ext. 22
s.archibald@balancefba.org
Laura Antal, Coordinator, Office, 416-236-1796 Ext. 0
l.antal@balancefba.org
David Kopman, Coordinator, Volunteers, 416-236-1796 Ext. 30
d.kopman@balancefba.org
Doug Poirier, Coordinator, Programs, 416-236-1796 Ext. 24
d.poirierd@balancefba.org
5 volunteer(s)
Membership: 10 board + 9 staff + 210 participants; *Fees:* $10 individual; $15 family; $25 organization; *Member Profile:* Application assessment process & must be responsible adult 18 years of age & older, self motivated to enhance his/her independence, able to live alone without supervision, & have sufficient resources to cover living expenses
Activities: Teaching daily living skills, orientation & mobility, community access & awareness, & life skills

Balle au mur Québec (BAMQ) / Québec Handball Association
CP 1000, Succ. M, 4545, av Pierre-de Coubertin, Montréal QC H1V 3R2
Tél: 514-252-3062; *Téléc:* 514-252-3103
info@sports-4murs.qc.ca
www.balleaumur.qc.ca
Aperçu: *Dimension:* moyenne; *Envergure:* provinciale; fondée en 1971
Affliation(s): Association canadienned de Balle au mur
Membre(s) du bureau directeur:
Étienne Pélissier, Président
pelo3@hotmail.com
Finances: *Budget de fonctionnement annuel:* $50,000-$100,000; *Fonds:* Gouvernement provincial
Membre(s) du personnel: 2; 10 bénévole(s)
Membre: 10 institutionnel; 1 000 individu

Ballet British Columbia
677 Davie St., 6th Fl., Vancouver BC V6G 2B6
Tel: 604-732-5003; *Fax:* 604-732-4417
info@balletbc.com
www.balletbc.com
www.facebook.com/BalletBC
twitter.com/BalletBC
www.youtube.com/user/BalletBC1
Overview: A medium-sized provincial charitable organization founded in 1986
Mission: To commission & perform a balanced repertoire rooted in classical technique, which encompasses the best new ballets & late 20th century classics
Member of: Vancouver Cultural Alliance
Chief Officer(s):
Branislav Henselmann, Executive Director
bhenselmann@balletbc.com
Finances: *Funding Sources:* Government; corporate & private donations
Staff Member(s): 17
Activities: *Internships:* Yes; *Speaker Service:* Yes

Ballet Creole
61 Primrose Ave., Toronto ON M6H 3V2
Tel: 416-960-0350; *Fax:* 416-960-2067
info@balletcreole.org
www.balletcreole.org
www.facebook.com/ballet.creole
Overview: A small local charitable organization founded in 1990
Mission: Preserves and perpetuates traditional and contemporary African culture and increases awareness of the rich African culture that exists in Canada. Establishes a dynamic new Canadian artistic tradition based on a fusion of diverse dance and music traditions. Promotes multicultural understanding through education and quality entertainment to national and international audiences.
Chief Officer(s):
Patrick Parson, Artistic Director
patrick@balletcreole.org
Finances: *Funding Sources:* Ontario Ministry of Culture; Toronto Arts Council; Ontario Arts Council; private donations

Ballet Jörgen
c/o George Brown College, Casa Loma Campus, Building C, #126, 160 Kendal Ave., Toronto ON M5R 1M3
Tel: 416-961-4725; *Fax:* 416-415-2865
info@balletjorgen.ca
www.balletjorgen.ca
www.facebook.com/balletjorgencanada
twitter.com/balletjorgenca
Overview: A small local charitable organization founded in 1987
Mission: To operate exclusively as a charitable organization to administer & employ its property, assets & rights for the purpose of raising the public's awareness of ballet as an art form by establishing, maintaining & operating a ballet company; to advance knowledge & increase public recognition of ballet by developing a repertoire of original dance productions for performance, film & video for the benefit of the community at large; to advance artistic appreciation & education of the general public of choreography as a distinctive art form by commissioning & making available to the public presentations by a variety of choreographers
Affliation(s): George Brown Dance
Chief Officer(s):
Bengt Jörgen, Artistic Director & CEO
artisticdirector@balletjorgen.ca
Finances: *Funding Sources:* Individuals; government; corporate
Membership: *Committees:* Finance & Audit
Activities: Professional ballet company currently performing across North America

Ballet Ouest *See* Ballet West

Ballet West / Ballet Ouest
#218, 269, boul St. Jean, Pointe-Claire QC H9R 3J1
Tel: 514-783-1245
reception@balletouest.com
www.balletouest.com
www.facebook.com/pages/Ballet-Ouest-de-Montréal/256063904541184
twitter.com/BalletOuest
www.youtube.com/user/balletouest
Overview: A small local organization founded in 1984
Mission: To provide a milieu that encourages young dancers to express themselves through dance & to move from amateur to professional status; educate & develop audiences; present an alternative view to counteract the mass culture that is being fed to our youth
Member of: RQD
Chief Officer(s):
Claude Caron, Artistic Director
Finances: *Funding Sources:* Ticket sales
Membership: *Member Profile:* Parents of dancers, dancers 18 & older
Activities: Ballet performances

Les ballets de la jeunesse Saskatchewan *See* Youth Ballet & Contemporary Dance of Saskatchewan Inc.

Les Ballets Jazz de Montréal (BJM)
1210, rue Sherbrooke est, Montréal QC H2L 1L9
Tél: 514-982-6771; *Téléc:* 514-982-9145
info@bjmdanse.ca
www.bjmdanse.ca
www.facebook.com/LESBALLETSJAZZDEMONTREAL
twitter.com/BJMDANSE
vimeo.com/balletsjazzmontreal
Aperçu: *Dimension:* petite; *Envergure:* locale; Organisme sans but lucratif; fondée en 1972
Mission: Crée, produit et diffuse à l'échelle nationale et internationale des spectacles de danse contemporaine; offre à ses danseurs un entraînement professionnel; permet aux chorégraphes invités et aux danseurs de développer leur propre recherche; génère un répertoire exclusif et conserve l'esprit novateur qui anime la compagnie de puis sa création
Membre de: Canadian Association of Professional Dance Organizations; Regroupement québécois de la danse; Conseil International de la Danse (UNESCO)
Membre(s) du bureau directeur:
Louis Robitaille, Directeur artistique
Céline Cassone, Coordinatrice, Artistique et répétitrice
Finances: *Budget de fonctionnement annuel:* $1.5 Million-$3 Million
Membre(s) du personnel: 22; 20 bénévole(s)
Membre: 1-99; *Comités:* Levée de fonds
Activités: *Événements de sensibilisation:* Nuit magique, Mai, 1er vendredi du mois; *Stagiaires:* Oui

Ballon sur glace Broomball Canada
145 Pacific Ave., Winnipeg MB R3B 2Z6
Tel: 204-925-5656; *Fax:* 204-925-5792
cbfbroomball@shaw.ca
www.broomball.ca
Previous Name: Broomball Canada Federation
Overview: A medium-sized national charitable organization founded in 1976
Chief Officer(s):
George Brown, President
president@broomball.ca
Membership: 30,000 provincial; *Fees:* $1,000 annual affiliation fee/association
Activities: *Library* by appointment

Baltic Artists' Association - Montréal *See* L'Association des artistes Baltes à Montréal

Baltic Federation in Canada
c/o Andris Kesteris, 1754 Turnberry Rd., Orléans ON K1E 3T7
Tel: 416-755-2352
www.balticfederation.ca
Overview: A medium-sized national organization founded in 1949
Mission: To provide political representation for its member organizations of Estonian, Latvian & Lithuanian Canadians
Chief Officer(s):
Andris Kesteris, President, 613-837-4928
akestr0542@rogers.com
Membership: *Member Profile:* The Estonian Central Council in Canada; The Latvian National Federation in Canada; The Lithuanian-Canadian Community

Bamfield Chamber of Commerce
Bamfield BC V0R 1B0
Tel: 250-728-3006
info@bamfieldchamber.com
www.bamfieldchamber.com
Overview: A small local organization
Mission: To improve & promote trade, commerce, the economic, civil & social welfare of the district
Member of: BC Chamber of Commerce
Affliation(s): Pacific Rim Tourism Association
Finances: *Annual Operating Budget:* $50,000-$100,000; *Funding Sources:* Membership dues; government
43 volunteer(s)
Membership: 43; *Fees:* $80

Bamfield Marine Sciences Centre
100 Pachena Rd., Bamfield BC V0R 1B0
Tel: 250-728-3301; *Fax:* 250-728-3452
info@bms.bc.ca
www.bms.bc.ca
Overview: A small local organization founded in 1970
Mission: University level instruction; core research facility for marine biologists; public education in marine biology
Member of: Western Universities Marine Biological Society
Chief Officer(s):
Brad Anholt, Director/Professor
director@bms.bc.ca
Finances: *Annual Operating Budget:* $3 Million-$5 Million; *Funding Sources:* Provincial government; national government
Staff Member(s): 25; 3 volunteer(s)

Membership: 5; *Member Profile:* University of British Columbia; University of Alberta; University of Calgary; Simon Fraser University; University of Victoria
Activities: *Library:* Devonian Library; Open to public

Bancroft & District Chamber of Commerce, Tourism & Information Centre
PO Box 539, 8 Hastings Heritage Way, Bancroft ON K0L 1C0
Tel: 613-332-1513; *Fax:* 613-332-2119
Toll-Free: 888-443-9999
chamber@bancroftdistrict.com
www.bancroftdistrict.com
www.facebook.com/bancroftdistrict.ofcommerce
Overview: A small local organization founded in 1960
Mission: To develop & promote Bancroft & district as a great place to live, work & visit
Member of: Ontario Chamber of Commerce
Chief Officer(s):
Greg Webb, General Manager
gregwebb@bancroftdistrict.com
Staff Member(s): 4
Membership: 311; *Fees:* $231.65; *Member Profile:* Businesses & tourism organizations
Activities: *Library* Open to public

Bancroft District Real Estate Board
PO Box 1522, 69 Hastings St. North, Bancroft ON K0L 1C0
Tel: 613-332-3842; *Fax:* 613-332-3842
www.bancroftrealestate.on.ca
Overview: A small local organization overseen by Ontario Real Estate Association
Member of: The Canadian Real Estate Association
Membership: 8

Bancroft Gem & Mineral Club
PO Box 1749, Bancroft ON K0L 1C0
Overview: A small local charitable organization
Mission: To foster an interest in the earth sciences & related lapidary arts
Member of: Central Canadian Federation of Mineralogical Societies
Chief Officer(s):
Frank Melanson, President, 613-332-1032
wfmelanson@sympatico.ca
Finances: *Funding Sources:* Gem & Mineral Club Show admission; Donations
Activities: Hosting monthly meetings (except August & December); Organizing field trips; Presenting displays; *Awareness Events:* Bancroft Gem & Mineral Club Annual Gem & Mineral Show

Banda de nossa Senhora dos Milagres / Bande de Notre-Dame des Miracles
6024, rue Hochelaga, Montréal QC H1N 1X6
bdnsdm@gmail.com
www.bdnsdm.com
Également appelé: Our Lady of Miracles Band
Aperçu: *Dimension:* petite; *Envergure:* locale; fondée en 1996
Mission: Jouer de la musique et offrir des cours de musique
Membre(s) du bureau directeur:
Décio Cardoso, Président, Conseil d'administration
Activités: Concerts

Bande de Notre-Dame des Miracles *Voir* Banda de nossa Senhora dos Milagres

Banff & Lake Louise Tourism
Cascade Plaza, PO Box 1298, 375 Banff Ave., Banff AB T1L 1B3
Tel: 403-762-8421; *Fax:* 403-762-8163
info@banfflakelouise.com
www.banfflakelouise.com
twitter.com/banff_squirrel
www.youtube.com/user/banfflakelouise2;
www.flickr.com/groups/banff
Overview: A medium-sized local organization founded in 1991
Chief Officer(s):
Julie Canning, President/CEO
julie@banfflakelouise.com
Wendy Beard, Manager, Brand & Member Services
wendy@banfflakelouise.com
Finances: *Annual Operating Budget:* $500,000-$1.5 Million
Staff Member(s): 12
Membership: 800
Activities: Convention & visitors' bureau

The Banff Centre
PO Box 1020, Banff AB T1L 1H5
Tel: 403-762-6100; *Fax:* 403-762-6444
communications@banffcentre.ca
www.banffcentre.ca
Overview: A medium-sized local organization
Mission: To offer educational activities, performances, exhibitions, & special events
Chief Officer(s):
Jeff Melanson, President

Banff Food Bank Association
PO Box 4373, Banff AB T1L 1E7
Tel: 403-762-1060
Overview: A small local charitable organization overseen by Alberta Food Bank Network Association
Member of: Canadian Association of Food Banks

Banff International String Quartet Competition (BISQC)
The Banff Centre, PO Box 1020, Stn. 23, 107 Tunnel Mountain Dr., Banff AB T1L 1H5
Tel: 403-762-6188; *Fax:* 403-762-6338
Toll-Free: 800-565-9989
bisqc@banffcentre.ca
www.banffcentre.ca/bisqc
www.facebook.com/thebanffcentre
twitter.com/thebanffcentre
www.youtube.com/thebanffcentre
Overview: A small international organization founded in 1983
Mission: Triennial competition open to string quartets whose members are under 35 years of age
Member of: World Federation of International Music Competitions (WFIMC)/Fédération mondiale des concours internationaux de musique
Chief Officer(s):
Barry Shiffman, Director
Activities: *Internships:* Yes; *Library:* Paul P. Fleck Library & Archives; Open to public

Banff Television Foundation *See* Banff World Television Festival Foundation

Banff World Television Festival Foundation
c/o Achilles Media Ltd., #202, 102 Boulder Cres., Canmore AB T1W 1L2
Tel: 403-678-1216; *Fax:* 403-678-3357
info@achillesmedia.com
www.btvf.com
www.linkedin.com/groups?gid=1863732&trk=myg_ugrp_ovr
www.facebook.com/BanffMedia
twitter.com/banffmedia
www.youtube.com/user/banffmediafest?feature=watch
Previous Name: Banff Television Foundation
Overview: A medium-sized national charitable organization founded in 1979
Mission: To inspire innovation in content creation, celebrate excellence, & provide learning & business opportunities for creators & other industry professionals in television & new media
Finances: *Annual Operating Budget:* $1.5 Million-$3 Million; *Funding Sources:* International government
Staff Member(s): 30; 25 volunteer(s)
Activities: Categories: Animation Programs; Arts Documentaries; Children's Programs; Comedies; Continuing Series; History & Biography Programs; Information Programs; Made-for-TV-Movies; Mini-Series; Performance Programs; Popular Science & Natural History; Short Dramas; Social & Political Documentaries; Sports Programs
Awards:
• Banff World Television Awards (Award)
Meetings/Conferences: • Banff World Media Festival 2015, June, 2015, Fairmont Banff Springs Hotel, Banff, AB
Scope: National

La banque d'alimentation d'Ottawa *See* Ottawa Food Bank

Banque d'yeux nationale inc.
2705, boul Laurier, Sainte-Foy QC G1V 4G2
Tél: 418-654-2702; *Téléc:* 418-654-2247
Aperçu: *Dimension:* petite; *Envergure:* nationale; fondée en 1970
Membre(s) du bureau directeur:
Céline Lemay, Coordonnatrice
Activités: *Service de conférenciers:* Oui

Banques alimentaires Canada *See* Food Banks Canada

Baptist Convention of Ontario & Québec *See* Canadian Baptists of Ontario & Quebec

Baptist Foundation, Alberta, Saskatchewan & the Territories, Inc. (B-FAST)
PO Box 168, 11525 23 Ave., Edmonton AB T6J 4T3
Tel: 780-451-4878; *Fax:* 780-436-4871
febcast@shaw.ca
www.fellowshipprairies.ca
Overview: A small local organization founded in 1982
Mission: Funding capital projects for Fellowship of Evangelical Baptist Churches in Alberta, Saskatchewan & the Territories
Chief Officer(s):
Laurie Kennedy, Regional Director
15 volunteer(s)
Membership: 15 individual;

Baptist General Conference of Canada (BGCC)
#205, 15824 - 131 Ave., Edmonton AB T5V 1J4
Tel: 780-438-9127; *Fax:* 780-435-2478
office@bgc.ca
www.bgc.ca
Overview: A large national charitable organization founded in 1981
Mission: To unite churches in a fellowship that is scriptual in doctrine, evangelical in character & irenic (peaceful) in spirit, & seeking to fulfil the Great Commission of Christ (Mt.28: 19-20) in Canada & abroad
Member of: Evangelical Fellowship of Canada
Chief Officer(s):
Jamey McDonald, Executive Director, 780-438-9127 Ext. 22
Diane Wiebe, Administrator, Global Ministries, 780-438-9127 Ext. 24
Finances: *Funding Sources:* Churches; individuals; BGC Stewardship Foundation
Staff Member(s): 5; 12 volunteer(s)
Membership: 7,000+ individuals + 106 churches; *Member Profile:* Agreement with our Affirmation of Faith, Distinctives & ministry goals; *Committees:* Global Ministries; Equipping Ministries; Women; Youth; Regents - Canadian Baptist Seminary; Finance
Activities: Global Ministries; new church development; leadership training; youth programs; women's ministries; international development consulting; *Library:* BGC Canada Archives; by appointment

Baptist General Conference - Eastern Expansion
2148, rue de Romagne, Laval QC H7M 5R1
Tel: 450-629-5173
Scott@BGCCeast.ca
bgcceast.ca
Chief Officer(s):
Scott Campbell, Field Supervisor

Baptist General Conference in Alberta
11525 - 23 Ave., Edmonton AB T6J 4T3
Tel: 780-438-9126; *Fax:* 780-434-9170
info@bgcalberta.ca
www.bgcalberta.ca
www.facebook.com/pages/BGC-Alberta/144543022275737
www.twitter.com/bgcalberta
Affliation(s): Baptist General Conference of Canada; Canadian Baptist Seminary; Lone Prairie Camp
Chief Officer(s):
Roger Helland, Executive Coach, 403-975-8927
roger@bgcalberta.ca

Baptist General Conference in Saskatchewan
c/o Martensville Baptist Church, PO Box 389, Martensville SK S0K 2T0
Tel: 306-931-2688
bgccoach@gmail.com
Chief Officer(s):
Harvey Sawatzky, District Coach
martensvillebaptist@sasktel.net

Baptist General Conference of Central Canada
877 Wilkes Ave., Winnipeg MB R3P 1B8
Tel: 204-479-9071; *Fax:* 204-452-1799
bgccoach@gmail.com
www.bgc-cc.com
Chief Officer(s):
Lorne Meisner, District Coach
efmanitoba@hotmail.com

British Columbia Baptist Conference
20581 - 36 Ave., Langley BC V3A 4Y3
Tel: 604-888-2246; *Fax:* 604-539-2247
info@bcbc.ca
www.bcbc.ca
Mission: The BCBC is a group of churches in B.C. with common theological convictions who share resources and work in strategic alliance in order to achieve together more

than what can be achieved along.
Member of: Baptist General Conference of Canada
Chief Officer(s):
Bernard Mukwavi, District Minister
bernard.mukwavi@bcbc.ca

The Baptist Union of Western Canada ***See*** Canadian Baptists of Western Canada

Bar of Montréal ***Voir*** Barreau de Montréal

Barbados Cultural Association of British Columbia
PO Box 33504, Surrey BC V3T 5R5
Tel: 604-275-8617
info@barbadosbcassoc.com
Overview: A small provincial organization founded in 1994
Mission: To maintain communicative links with Barbadians elsewhere; act as a liaison between Barbadians in BC & the High Commissioner's office in Ottawa; extend benevolence to the needy at home & abroad
Affliation(s): National Council of Barbadian Association of Canada
Chief Officer(s):
Eric Drayton, Contact
Membership: *Fees:* $15 student; $25 individual/senior; $35 couple; $50 family

Barbados Ottawa Association
PO Box 55101, 240 Sparks St., Ottawa ON K1P 1A1
Tel: 613-843-1448
info@barbadosottawaassoc.com
www.barbadosottawaassoc.com
Overview: A small local organization founded in 1966
Mission: To keep culture of Barbados active in community
Affliation(s): National Council of Barbadian Associations in Canada
Chief Officer(s):
Sandra Asgill, President
Membership: *Fees:* $20
Activities: Monthly meetings, dances, dinners, trips

The Barbra Schlifer Commemorative Clinic (BSCC)
#503, 489 College St., Toronto ON M6G 1A5
Tel: 416-323-9149; *Fax:* 416-323-9107; *TTY:* 416-323-1361
www.schliferclinic.com
www.facebook.com/BarbraSchliferCommemorativeClinic
twitter.com/schliferclinic
Overview: A small local charitable organization founded in 1981
Mission: To provide legal counsellling & interpreter services for women who are victims of violence including partner assault, incest, sexual assault; we also engage in public education & advocacy on issues related to violence against women
Chief Officer(s):
Amanda Dale, Executive Director
adale@schliferclinic.com
Finances: *Annual Operating Budget:* $1.5 Million-$3 Million
Staff Member(s): 26; 150 volunteer(s)
Membership: 1-99; *Fees:* $10
Activities: *Internships:* Yes; *Speaker Service:* Yes

Bard on the Beach Theatre Society
#203, 456 West Broadway, Vancouver BC V5Y 1R3
Tel: 604-737-0625; *Fax:* 604-737-0425
info@bardonthebeach.org
www.bardonthebeach.org
www.facebook.com/bardonthebeach
twitter.com/bardonthebeach
www.youtube.com/user/bardonthebeachfest
Overview: A small local charitable organization founded in 1990
Mission: To provide Vancouver residents & visitors with affordable, accessible Shakespearean productions of the finest quality
Member of: Shakespeare Theatre Association of America
Chief Officer(s):
Christopher Gaze, Artistic Director
Claire Sakaki, Managing Director
Staff Member(s): 18
Membership: *Fees:* $25-$9,999
Activities: *Speaker Service:* Yes

The Barnard-Boecker Centre Foundation (BBCF)
1022 McGregor Ave., Victoria BC V8S 3T9
Tel: 250-595-7519; *Fax:* 250-595-7519
bbcf@bbcf.ca
www.bbcf.ca
Overview: A small local organization founded in 1996
Mission: To create, to develop, & to encourage programs that promote social justice, peace, sustainability, diversity & community, through research, writing, film & art; to organize public events that will contribute, globally & locally, to knowledge & awareness
Chief Officer(s):
Theresa Wolfwood, Director

Baron de Hirsch Hebrew Benevolent Society
1480 Oxford St., Halifax NS B3H 3Y8
Tel: 902-422-1301; *Fax:* 902-422-7251
info@thebethisrael.com
www.jewishhalifax.com
www.facebook.com/thebethisrael
Overview: A small local organization founded in 1894
Chief Officer(s):
Steven Zatzman, President
Membership: 180 families
Activities: Beth Israel Synagogue; Hebrew school; kosher supervision; gift shop
Publications:
• The Beth
Frequency: Quarterly

Barreau de Montréal / Bar of Montréal
Palais de Justice, #980, 1, rue Notre Dame est, Montréal QC H2Y 1B6
Tél: 514-866-9392; *Téléc:* 514-866-1488
info@barreaudemontreal.qc.ca
www.barreaudemontreal.qc.ca
Aperçu: *Dimension:* moyenne; *Envergure:* locale; Organisme sans but lucratif; fondée en 1849
Mission: Administrer une corporation professionnelle
Membre(s) du bureau directeur:
Doris Larrivée, Directrice générale
dlarrivee@barreaudemontreal.qc.ca
Gislaine Dufault, Directrice des communications
gdufault@barreaudemontreal.qc.ca
Finances: *Budget de fonctionnement annuel:* $500,000-$1.5 Million
Membre(s) du personnel: 8; 300 bénévole(s)
Membre: 11 500; *Montant de la cotisation:* 50-200; *Critères d'admissibilite:* Avocat
Activités: Dîners; Conféderences; Colloques; Tournoi de golf; Tournoi de tennis; Tournoi de badminton; *Evénements de sensibilisation:* Salon Visez Droit; *Service de conférenciers:* Oui

Le Barreau des Territoires du Nord-Ouest ***See*** Law Society of the Northwest Territories

Barreau du Haut-Canada ***See*** Law Society of Upper Canada

Barreau du Nouveau-Brunswick ***See*** Law Society of New Brunswick

Barrhead Animal Rescue Society (BARS)
c/o Terry Colborne, PO Box 4702, Barrhead AB T7N 1A5
Tel: 780-307-6590
www.barrheadanimalrescue.org
www.facebook.com/BarrheadAnimalRescueSociety
Overview: A medium-sized local charitable organization founded in 2010
Mission: Dedicated to ensuring the humane treatment of all animals in the Town of Barrhead, the County of Barrhead and surrounding areas.
Chief Officer(s):
Terry Colbourne, President
Finances: *Funding Sources:* Private donations

Barrhead Association for Community Living (BACL)
4815 - 51 Ave., Barrhead AB T7N 1M1
Tel: 780-674-5051; *Fax:* 780-674-5023
Overview: A small local charitable organization founded in 1973
Mission: To promote the welfare of people with handicaps & their families; To promote a community that embraces all people
Member of: Alberta Association for Community Living
Finances: *Annual Operating Budget:* $50,000-$100,000
Staff Member(s): 2; 40 volunteer(s)
Membership: 50; *Fees:* $10
Activities: *Internships:* Yes; *Speaker Service:* Yes

Barrhead Chamber of Commerce
PO Box 4524, Barrhead AB T7N 1A4
e-mail: admin@barrheadchamberofcommerce.com
barrheadchamberofcommerce.com
Overview: A small local organization
Mission: To enhance the development of business by providing a liaison between local business & the rest of the community
Member of: Alberta Chamber of Commerce
Finances: *Annual Operating Budget:* Less than $50,000; *Funding Sources:* Membership fee
Membership: 69
Activities: Promotion of local shopping; educational speakers & seminars; tourist promotions; town & country beautification; farming community promotion support; *Library* Open to public

Barrhead Gem Seekers
c/o Laura Tywoniuk, 5508 - 58 Ave., Barrhead AB T7N 1C7
Tel: 780-674-4341
Overview: A small local organization founded in 1978
Mission: To promote & encourage interest in gem & mineral hobby
Member of: Alberta Federation of Rock Clubs
Chief Officer(s):
Laura Tywoniuk, Contact

Barrie & District Real Estate Board Inc.
30 Mary St., Barrie ON L4N 1S8
Tel: 705-739-4650; *Fax:* 780-721-9101
info@barrie.mls.ca
www.barrie.mls.ca
www.facebook.com/BDARInc
Overview: A small local organization overseen by Ontario Real Estate Association
Mission: To provide continuing education, Multiple Listing Service (MLS), statistical information and many other services to its members.
Member of: The Canadian Real Estate Association (CREA) and the Ontario Real Estate Association (OREA)
Chief Officer(s):
Wendy Elzner, President
wendy@wendyelzner.ca
Frances Clarke, Executive Officer
Membership: 800; *Member Profile:* Real estate sales agents

Barrie Agricultural Society
PO Box 217, #3, 199 Essa Rd., Barrie ON L4M 4T2
Tel: 705-737-3670; *Fax:* 705-737-2581
info@essaagriplex.ca
www.eventcentre.ca
www.facebook.com/pages/Barrie-Fair/122250804475473
Also Known As: Event Centre
Overview: A small local charitable organization founded in 1853
Mission: To encourage an awareness of agriculture; To promote improvements in the quality of life for persons living in our community, rural & urban; To organize & operate the Barrie Fair & other similar events; To provide a venue where exhibitors can showcase, compete & market their products, crops or livestock
Chief Officer(s):
Henry VanderWielen, President
Wayne Hawke, Executive Director
Cindy Vecchiarelli, Administrator
cindy@essagriplex.ca
Finances: *Annual Operating Budget:* $250,000-$500,000; *Funding Sources:* Sponsors; Rental revenue; Barrie Fair
Staff Member(s): 4; 150 volunteer(s)
Membership: 1,000-4,999; *Fees:* $5

Barrie Gem & Mineral Society Inc.
PO Box 143, Barrie ON L4M 4S9
Overview: A small local organization
Mission: To foster an interest in the earth sciences & related lapidary arts
Member of: Central Canadian Federation of Mineralogical Societies

Barrie Literacy Council
#244, 80 Bradford St., Barrie ON L4N 6S7
Tel: 705-728-7323; *Fax:* 705-728-7155
barrie_literacy@on.aibn.com
www.barrieliteracy.ca
www.facebook.com/BarrieLiteracyCouncil
Overview: A small local charitable organization founded in 1979
Mission: To help adults improve their basic reading, writing & math skills to reach their goals & improve their self-esteem
Member of: Laubach Literacy of Canada, Ontario
Affliation(s): Community Literacy of Ontario; Learning Disabilities Association of Ontario; Simcoe/Muskoka Literacy Network
Chief Officer(s):
Judy DesRoches, Executive Director
Finances: *Funding Sources:* Donations; Ministry of Training, Colleges & Universities
Staff Member(s): 6; 89 volunteer(s)

Membership: 150; *Committees:* Public Relations; Tutor Training; Finance; Planning & Evaluation; Social; Internal Communications; Fundraising; Volunteer Management; Student Liasion; Members-at-Large
Activities: Training adults in basic reading, writing, math; training tutors; *Speaker Service:* Yes

Barrie Native Friendship Centre (BNFC)
175 Bayfield St., Barrie ON L4M 3B4
Tel: 705-721-7689; *Fax:* 705-721-7418
www.barrienativefriendshipcentre.com
twitter.com/BNFC2014
Overview: A small local charitable organization founded in 1987
Mission: To promote social activities, community awareness, culture-language, information/resources, employment/education/staffing, children's programs; to assist urban Natives; to work in cooperation with non-Native community
Member of: Ontario Federation of Indian Friendship Centres
Membership: *Fees:* Free seniors; $10 adult; $20 family; *Member Profile:* Native & non-native membership
Activities: Culture-based Native programming; youth, family support, employment & training; healing & wellness; monthly meetings

Barrie Parents of Twins and More *See* Simcoe County Parents of Multiples

Barrie Post Polio Association
57 Henry St., Barrie ON L4N 1C6
Overview: A small local charitable organization
Mission: A self help group working with Ontario March of Dimes for those suffering from the late effects of poliomyelitis & for any other interested persons
Chief Officer(s):
Pauline Berry, Contact
pberry@marchofdimes.ca
Membership: *Fees:* $10

Barriere & District Chamber of Commerce
PO Box 1190, #3, 4353 Conner Rd., Barriere BC V0E 1E0
Tel: 250-672-9221
bcoc@telus.net
www.barrieredistrict.com
Overview: A small local organization
Affliation(s): Canadian Chamber of Commerce
Chief Officer(s):
Scott Kershaw, President
Finances: *Annual Operating Budget:* Less than $50,000; *Funding Sources:* Membership dues; fundraising
Membership: 25; *Fees:* $60

Barriere & District Food Bank Society
4748 Gilbert Rd., Barriere BC V0E 1E0
Tel: 250-672-0029
Overview: A small local organization overseen by Food Banks British Columbia
Member of: Food Banks British Columbia
Membership: *Fees:* $2

Barrington & Area Chamber of Commerce
PO Box 110, Barrington NS B0W 1E0
Tel: 902-745-1655
barringtoncofc@eastlink.ca
www.barrington-chamberofcommerce.com
Overview: A small local organization founded in 1990
Chief Officer(s):
Gary Thomas, President
Bobbi Jo Symonds, Coordinator
Membership: 65; *Fees:* $50-$175; *Member Profile:* Individuals, corporations, businesses or firms in the Municipality of Barrington or the Town of Clark's Harbour

Barrow Bay & District Sports Fishing Association (BB&DSFA)
PO Box 987, Lions Head ON N0H 1W0
Fax: 519-793-3363
barrowbayfishing@hotmail.com
www.bltg.com/bbdsfa/
Overview: A small local organization founded in 1993
Member of: Ontario Federation of Anglers & Hunters
Finances: *Annual Operating Budget:* $50,000-$100,000; *Funding Sources:* Membership dues; fundraising; government grants
35 volunteer(s)
Membership: 92; *Member Profile:* Local sport fishers & environmentalists
Publications:
• Barrow Bay & District Sports Fishing Association Newsletter *Type:* Newsletter

Barth Syndrome Foundation of Canada
#115, 162 Guelph St., Georgetown ON L7G 5X7
Tel: 905-873-2391; *Fax:* 905-877-5952
Toll-Free: 888-732-9458
www.barthsyndrome.ca
Overview: A medium-sized national charitable organization
Mission: To find research grants into the cause, treatments & cure for Barth Syndrome; to assist Canadian families & physicians dealing with the disease.
Affliation(s): Barth Syndrome Foundation Inc.
Chief Officer(s):
Lynn Elwood, President
Finances: *Funding Sources:* Donations

Base Borden Soaring (BBSG)
PO Box 286, Borden ON L0M 1C0
Tel: 705-424-1200
ourplace@csolve.net
users.csolve.net/~ourplace/contents.htm
Overview: A small local organization founded in 1974
Member of: Soaring Association of Canada
Chief Officer(s):
Ray Leiska
Membership: *Fees:* $50

Baseball Alberta (BA)
Percy Page Centre, 11759 Groat Rd., Edmonton AB T5M 3K6
Tel: 780-427-8943; *Fax:* 780-427-9032
registrar@baseballalberta.com
www.baseballalberta.com
www.facebook.com/pages/Baseball-Alberta/130042917037092
twitter.com/BaseballAlberta
Also Known As: Alberta Baseball Association
Overview: A large provincial organization founded in 1967 overseen by Baseball Canada
Mission: To promote & develop Baseball in Alberta; to provide life & leadership skills for all genders through Baseball; to encourage fun & fair play
Member of: Western Canada Baseball Association; Edmonton International Baseball Foundation
Affliation(s): Alberta Amateur Baseball Council
Chief Officer(s):
Don Paulencu, President
dpaulencu@deloitte.ca
Darren Dekinder, Registrar & Office Manager, 780-427-9014
registrar@baseballalberta.com
Finances: *Funding Sources:* Membership dues; government; corporate
Staff Member(s): 3
Membership: *Fees:* Schedule available
Activities: Programs include: Rally Cap; Winterball; Reaching Baseball Ideals; Long Term Athlete Development; Canadian Sport for Life; National Coaching Certification Program; programs for girls & women;
Awards:
• Baseball Alberta Life Members (Award)
• Ted Rudd Minor Coach Award (Award)
• Presidents Award (Award)
• Wally A. Footz Builders Award (Award)
• Aurora Baseball Association Coach of the Year Award (Award)
• Murray Service Umpire of the Year Award (Award)
• Baseball Alberta Umpire Hall of Fame Award (Award)
• Junior Umpire of the Year Award (Award)
• Baseball Alberta Players of the Year (Award)
• Baseball Alberta Associations of the Year (Award)
• EIBF Bill Chmiliar Award of Merit (Award)

Baseball BC
#310, 15225 - 104th Ave., Surrey BC V3R 6Y8
Tel: 604-586-3310; *Fax:* 604-586-3311
info1@baseball.bc.ca
www.baseball.bc.ca
www.facebook.com/pages/Baseball-BC/233202485008
twitter.com/Baseball_BC
Previous Name: BC Amateur Baseball Association
Overview: A medium-sized provincial organization overseen by Baseball Canada
Mission: To support the development of baseball & the aspirations of its members; To offer oppourtunities & setting procedures, standards, & policies
Chief Officer(s):
David Laing, Executive Director, 604-586-3312
davidlaing@baseball.bc.ca
Finances: *Funding Sources:* Government of B.C., Legacies Now, Rawlings Sporting Goods, Prostock Athletic Supply, Toronto Blue Jays, All Sport Insurance, Gatorade, Sport B.C.
Membership: 4,500

Baseball Canada / Fédération canadienne de baseball amateur
#A7, 2212 Gladwin Cres., Ottawa ON K1B 5N1
Tel: 613-748-5606; *Fax:* 613-748-5767
info@baseball.ca
www.baseball.ca
www.facebook.com/baseballcanada
twitter.com/baseballcanada
Also Known As: Canadian Federation of Amateur Baseball
Overview: A large national charitable organization founded in 1964
Mission: To promote the development of baseball across Canada through support of provincial organizations & design of programs, including athletes, coaches, events, umpires & partner groups
Member of: International Baseball Association; Confederation of PanAmerican Baseball
Affliation(s): Canadian Olympic Association
Chief Officer(s):
Ray Carter, President
Jason Dickson, Vice-President
Holly LaPierre, Treasurer
Jim Baba, Director General
jbaba@baseball.ca
Finances: *Funding Sources:* Federal government; membership fees; sponsors; sales; program revenues
Staff Member(s): 7
Activities: Hosts seven national championships; selects three national teams for international competition; National Skill Competition; Coach & Umpire Certification; Baseball Canada Cup; Honda Hit-Run-Throw; *Internships:* Yes; *Library* by appointment

Baseball New Brunswick (BNB) / Baseball Nouveau-Brunswick
#13, 900 Hanwell Rd., Fredericton NB E3B 6A2
Tel: 506-451-1329; *Fax:* 506-451-1325
director@baseballnb.ca
www.baseballnb.ca
www.facebook.com/pages/Baseball-NB/87671406193
twitter.com/NB_Selects
Overview: A medium-sized provincial organization founded in 1989 overseen by Baseball Canada
Mission: To promote & govern baseball in New Brunswick.
Affliation(s): Sport New Brunswick; Baseball Atlantic
Chief Officer(s):
David Watling, President
bnbwatling@rogers.com
David Dion, Executive Director
Finances: *Funding Sources:* Provincial government
Staff Member(s): 1
Membership: 5841; *Member Profile:* Baseball players, coaches, officials, volunteers & administrators.; *Committees:* Financial; High Performance; Hall of Fame; Personnel; Linguistics

Baseball Nouveau-Brunswick *See* Baseball New Brunswick

Baseball Nova Scotia (BNS)
5516 Spring Garden Rd., 4th Fl., Halifax NS B3J 1G6
Tel: 902-425-5454
baseball@sportnovascotia.ca
www.baseballnovascotia.com
www.facebook.com/baseballnovascotia
twitter.com/baseball_ns
Overview: A medium-sized provincial organization overseen by Baseball Canada
Mission: To represent baseball teams & leagues under the jurisdiction of BaseballCanada.
Member of: Canadian Federation of Amateur Baseball
Chief Officer(s):
Brandon Guenette, Executive Director

Baseball Ontario
#3, 131 Sheldon Dr., Cambridge ON N1R 6S2
Tel: 519-740-3900; *Fax:* 519-740-6311
baseball@baseballontario.com
www.baseballontario.com
Overview: A medium-sized provincial organization founded in 1918 overseen by Baseball Canada
Member of: CSAE
Affliation(s): Little League Ontario
Chief Officer(s):

Mary-Ann Smith, Administrative Director
maryann@baseballontario.com
Finances: *Annual Operating Budget:* $500,000-$1.5 Million
Staff Member(s): 2
Membership: 18 organizations
Activities: Coaching; Umpiring; Elite Player Development; Insurance; Tournaments; Communications; *Awareness Events:* Spring Break Camp; AGM

Baseball PEI
PO Box 302, 40 Enman Cres., Charlottetown PE C1A 7K7
Tel: 902-569-0583; *Fax:* 902-368-4548
Toll-Free: 800-247-6712
baseball@sportpei.pe.ca
www.baseballpei.ca
www.facebook.com/BaseballPEI
Previous Name: Prince Edward Island Amateur Baseball Association
Overview: A medium-sized provincial organization founded in 1967 overseen by Baseball Canada
Mission: To promote & develop minor & amateur baseball in PEI
Chief Officer(s):
Don LeClair, President
donleclair@eastlink.ca
Jacob Smith, Executive Director
Finances: *Annual Operating Budget:* Less than $50,000
Membership: *Fees:* Schedule available
Activities: Tournments including Bantam, Pee Wee, and Midget levels.

Bashaw Chamber of Commerce
PO Box 645, 5020 - 52nd St., Bashaw AB T0B 0H0
Tel: 780-372-3923
admin@enjoybashaw.com
enjoybashaw.com
Overview: A small local organization
Chief Officer(s):
Ryan Hewitt, President
president@enjoybashaw.com

Basketball Alberta
Percy Page Centre, 11759 Groat Rd., 2nd Fl., Edmonton AB T5M 3K6
Tel: 780-427-9044; *Fax:* 780-427-9124
www.basketballalberta.ca
www.facebook.com/BasketballAlberta
twitter.com/BasketballAB
Overview: A medium-sized provincial organization founded in 1975 overseen by Canada Basketball
Mission: To be premier facilitators of participation, development, and excellence in basketball. To champion the sport of basketball as a game for life by inspiring unity facilitating development and delivering superior value.
Chief Officer(s):
Bob Mitchell, President
bmitchell@basketballalberta.ab.ca
Paul Sir, Executive Director
psir@basketballalberta.ab.ca
Finances: *Funding Sources:* Provincial government; self-generated
Staff Member(s): 6
Membership: *Fees:* $11 per athlete

Basketball BC
#210, 7888 - 200th St., Langley BC V2Y 3J4
Tel: 604-888-8088; *Fax:* 604-888-8323
info@basketball.bc.ca
www.basketball.bc.ca
www.facebook.com/basketballbc
twitter.com/BasketballBC
Overview: A medium-sized provincial organization overseen by Canada Basketball
Mission: To be British Columbia's leading resource for basketball; To build the game of basketball
Member of: Sport BC
Chief Officer(s):
Lawrie Johns, Executive Director, 604-455-2812
ljohns@basketball.bc.ca
Finances: *Funding Sources:* Government grant; fundraising; membership dues
Staff Member(s): 7
Membership: *Fees:* $15

Basketball Manitoba
145 Pacific Ave., Winnipeg MB R3B 2Z6
Tel: 204-925-5775; *Fax:* 204-925-5929
info@basketball.mb.ca
www.basketball.mb.ca
www.linkedin.com/company/basketball-manitoba
www.facebook.com/basketballmanitoba
twitter.com/basketballmb
www.youtube.com/user/baskmanbaskman
Overview: A medium-sized provincial organization founded in 1976 overseen by Canada Basketball
Mission: To operate as the provincial sport governing body for basketball in Manitoba; To ensure all Manitobians have access to the programs run by the association & that the game of basketball is enjoyed by as many people as possible
Chief Officer(s):
Adam Wedlake, Executive Director
awedlake@basketball.mb.ca
Staff Member(s): 4
Membership: *Committees:* Technical

Basketball New Brunswick (BNB) / Basketball Nouveau-Brunswick
#13, 900 Hanwell Rd., Fredericton NB E2E 6A2
Tel: 506-472-4667; *Fax:* 506-451-1325
info@basketball.nb.ca
www.basketball.nb.ca
Overview: A large provincial organization founded in 1973 overseen by Canada Basketball
Mission: To promote, develop & encourage sport & recreation aspects of basketball in New Brunswick; To assist in establishment of basketball clubs throughout New Brunswick; To liaise with government & private agencies interested in promoting & supporting basketball
Affliation(s): New Brunswick Association of Approved Basketball Officials; New Brunswick Interscholastic Athletic Association
Chief Officer(s):
Mike Lavigne, President
Carolyn Peppin, Executive Director
carolyn.peppin@basketball.nb.ca
Kim Flemming, Office Administrator
kim.flemming@basketball.nb.ca
Finances: *Funding Sources:* Membership dues; Provincial government; Programs
Staff Member(s): 3
Membership: *Member Profile:* All players competing in provincial championships; minor association members
Activities: Offering National Coaching Certification, an Elite Development Program, & junior officials development; *Library:* Training Film Library
Awards:
- Service Awards (Award)
- Play Fair Awards (Award)

Basketball Newfoundland *See* Newfoundland & Labrador Basketball Association

Basketball Nouveau-Brunswick *See* Basketball New Brunswick

Basketball Nova Scotia
5516 Spring Garden Rd., 4th Fl., Halifax NS B3J 1G6
Tel: 902-425-5450; *Fax:* 902-425-5606
bnsadmin@basketball.ns.ca
www.basketball.ns.ca
www.facebook.com/BasketballNovaScotia
twitter.com/BasketballNS
Overview: A small provincial organization overseen by Canada Basketball
Mission: To promote & encourage the game of basketball throughout the province
Member of: Sport Canada
Affliation(s): Sport Nova Scotia
Chief Officer(s):
Brad Lawlor, Executive Director
blawlor@basketball.ns.ca
Finances: *Annual Operating Budget:* $250,000-$500,000; *Funding Sources:* Government grants; membership fees; special events
Staff Member(s): 3; 12 volunteer(s)
Membership: 4,000; *Fees:* Schedule available
Activities: National Coaching Certificate Program; Coaches Club; elite development programs; referees; provincial club championships; tournaments; player development camps

Basketball NWT
PO Box 44, Yellowknife NT X1A 2N1
e-mail: info@bnwt.ca
www.bnwt.ca
www.facebook.com/bnwt.ca
Overview: A medium-sized provincial organization overseen by Canada Basketball
Mission: The Association encourages participation in basketball, develops athletes, & provides opportunities for cultural & social interchange among all involved in the sport
Affliation(s): Steve Nash Youth Basketball; Sport North; Arctic Winter Games
Chief Officer(s):
Damien Healy, President & Executive Director

Basketball PEI
#101, 40 Enman Cres., Charlottetown PE C1E 1E6
Tel: 902-368-4208; *Fax:* 902-368-4208
Toll-Free: 800-247-6712
Other Communication: Toll-Free Fax: 1-800-235-5687
info@basketballpei.ca
www.basketballpei.ca
www.facebook.com/104347713005329
twitter.com/basketballpei
Overview: A medium-sized provincial organization overseen by Canada Basketball
Mission: To develop basketball in the province of Prince Edward Island in a fun environment
Chief Officer(s):
Stephen Marchbank, Executive Director
smarchbank@basketballpei.ca
Activities: Developing the skills needed to play basketball successfully

Basketball Saskatchewan (BSI)
2205 Victoria Ave., Regina SK S4P 0S4
Fax: 306-525-4009
basketball@basketballsask.com
www.basketballsask.com
www.facebook.com/basketballsask
twitter.com/basketballsask
Previous Name: Saskatchewan Basketball
Overview: A medium-sized provincial licensing charitable organization founded in 1988 overseen by Canada Basketball
Mission: To support & improve basketball opportunities in Saskatchewan
Affliation(s): Sask Sport
Chief Officer(s):
Greg Lucas, Executive Director, 306-780-9264
glucas@basketballsask.com
Dave Werry, Coordinator, High Performance, 306-780-9249
dwerry@basketballsask.com
Finances: *Funding Sources:* Sask Sport; Fundraising
Staff Member(s): 2
Membership: 12,000; *Fees:* $35 active; $12 associate; $3.50 affiliate; *Member Profile:* Ages 9 to 60
Activities: *Speaker Service:* Yes; *Library* Open to public

Basketball Yukon
4061 - 4th Ave., Whitehorse YT Y1A 1H1
Tel: 867-456-7874
bballyukon@klondiker.com
www.basketballyukon.ca
Overview: A medium-sized provincial organization overseen by Canada Basketball
Mission: To assist in player & coaching development in the North; to lead the territory's basketball community through programs & services benefitting all levels of play
Affliation(s): Sport Yukon, Canada Basketball
Chief Officer(s):
Jeff Cressman, President
Tim Brady, Technical Director
Membership: *Fees:* $30 affiliate; $5 individual

Bateau-Dragon Canada *See* Dragon Boat Canada

Bathurst & District Labour Council
PO Box 114, Bathurst NB E2A 3Z1
Overview: A small local organization
Member of: New Brunswick Federation of Labour
Chief Officer(s):
John Gagnon, Contact, 506-545-0651
gagnonj@nb.sympatico.ca

Bathurst Jewish Community Centre *See* Prosserman Jewish Community Centre

Bathurst Volunteer Centre de Bénévolat Inc. (BVC)
464 King Ave., Bathurst NB E2A 1P6

Tel: 506-549-5955; *Fax:* 506-549-5866
info@bvc-cbb.ca
www.bvc-cbb.ca
Overview: A small local charitable organization founded in 1981
Mission: To provide basic needs to families in Chaleur who are unable to provide for themselves
Member of: Canadian Association of Food Banks; New Brunswick Association of Food Banks
Chief Officer(s):
Michel Godin, Manager
manager@bvc-cbb.ca
Staff Member(s): 3
Activities: clothing exchange; food action programs; meals-on-wheels

Bâtiments Durables Canada *See* Sustainable Buildings Canada

Baton New Brunswick (BNB)
20 Adams St., Tide Head NB E3N 4T3
Tel: 506-759-7113
www.batonnb.ca
Overview: A small provincial organization overseen by Canadian Baton Twirling Federation
Mission: To govern baton twirling in New Brunswick
Member of: Canadian Baton Twirling Federation
Chief Officer(s):
Nadine LeBelle-Déjario, President
Membership: *Committees:* Technical; Membership

Baton Twirling Association of British Columbia (BTABC)
22411 Westminster Hwy., Richmond BC V6V 1B6
Tel: 604-722-1595
btabc@shaw.ca
batontwirlingbc.com
www.facebook.com/groups/107064568832
Overview: A small provincial organization overseen by Canadian Baton Twirling Federation
Mission: To promote the sport of baton twirling in British Columbia.
Member of: Canadian Baton Twirling Federation
Chief Officer(s):
Denise DeWolff, Chair
Shannon Webster, Membership Officer
greataunty@operamail.com
Activities: Competitions; training

Batshaw Youth & Family Centres
5 Weredale Pk., Westmount QC H3Z 1Y5
Tel: 514-989-1885
www.batshaw.ca
Overview: A small local organization founded in 1992
Mission: To intervene with children and families in situations of abuse, neglect, abandonment & when youth have serious behaviour problems, providing psychosocial, rehabilitation & social integration services.
Chief Officer(s):
Judy Martin, President
Lesley Hill, Executive Director
Staff Member(s): 719
Membership: *Committees:* Executive; Governance & Ethics; Verifitication; Service Quality & Vigilance; Human Resources
Activities: *Library:* Centre de documentation

Battle River Historical Society
PO Box 2936, 1001 - 1st Ave., Wainwright AB T9W 1S9
Tel: 780-842-3115
battleriverhs@gmail.com
Overview: A small local charitable organization founded in 1983
Mission: To preserve past & present history of Wainwright & district; to promote interest in history; to collect historical materials
Member of: Alberta Museums Association; Canadian Council for Railway Heritage
Finances: *Funding Sources:* Donations; grants
Activities: The Wainwright & District Museum

Battle River Research Group (BRRG)
PO Box 339, 4804 - 43 Ave., Forestburg AB T0B 1N0
Tel: 780-582-7308; *Fax:* 780-582-7312
Toll-Free: 866-828-6774
brrg@cciwireless.ca
www.areca.ab.ca/brrghome.html
Overview: A small local organization overseen by Agricultural Research & Extension Council of Alberta
Mission: To support agricultural research, in order to make agriculture more sustainable
Member of: Agricultural Research & Extension Council of Alberta
Chief Officer(s):
Alvin Eyolfson, P.Ag., Manager & Agrologist
brrgmgr@cciwireless.ca
Vicki Heidt, Agrologist, Forage & Livestock
brrgfl@cciwireless.ca
Membership: *Fees:* $20 individual (annual); $50 individual (3 years); $100 corporate
Publications:
• Over the Fence [a publication of the Battle River Research Group]
Type: Newsletter

Battle River Soccer Association
PO Box 5558, Leduc AB T9E 2A1
Tel: 780-362-0798
admin@battleriversoccer.com
www.fmyouthsoccer.com
Overview: A small local organization founded in 1983 overseen by Alberta Soccer Association
Member of: Alberta Soccer Association; Federation Internationale de Football Association; Canada Soccer Association
Affliation(s): Breton Soccer Association; Calmar Soccer Association; Devon Soccer Association; Leduc Soccer Association; Millet Soccer Association; New Sarepta Soccer Association; Pigeon Lake Soccer Association; Thorsby Soccer Association; Warburg Soccer Association; Wetaskiwin Soccer Association
Chief Officer(s):
Tom Siermachesky, President
president@battleriversoccer.com
Kristen Eliasson, Officer Administrator
Membership: 3,000 players in 10 associations; *Committees:* Human Resources; Bylaw Reviewl Financial Policy; IT

Battlefords Agricultural Society (BAS)
PO Box 668, North Battleford SK S9A 2Y9
Tel: 306-445-2024; *Fax:* 306-445-3352
b.exhibition@sasktel.net
agsociety.com
www.facebook.com/113736988690080
twitter.com/BfordsAg
Previous Name: Battlefords Exhibition Association
Overview: A small local charitable organization founded in 1884
Mission: To promote improvements in agriculture & community development; to provide facilities for educational & leisure programs
Member of: Saskatchewan Association of Agricultural Societies & Exhibitions
Chief Officer(s):
Dana Alexander, President
Jocelyn Ritchie, General Manager
Staff Member(s): 4
Membership: *Fees:* $40; *Member Profile:* Families, ages 16-85
Activities: Trade shows, quarter horse shows, raffles, chuckwagon races, 4H Regional Show, children's festival

Battlefords Chamber of Commerce
Hwy. 16 & 40 East, North Battleford SK S9A 3E6
Tel: 306-445-6226; *Fax:* 306-445-6633
b.chamber@sasktel.net
www.battlefordschamber.com
www.facebook.com/battlefordschamber
Previous Name: North Battleford Chamber of Commerce
Overview: A small local organization founded in 1905
Member of: Canadian Chamber of Commerce; Saskatchewan Chamber of Commerce
Affliation(s): Institution of Association Executives; Tourism Industry Association of Saskatchewan
Chief Officer(s):
Pat Smith, President
Linda Machniak, Executive Director
lindamachniak@sasktel.net
Finances: *Annual Operating Budget:* $100,000-$250,000; *Funding Sources:* Membership dues
Staff Member(s): 3
Membership: 340; *Fees:* $75-$550; *Committees:* Civic Affairs; Economic Development; Membership; Promotion

Battlefords Dance Festival Association *See* Svoboda Dance Festival Association

Battlefords Exhibition Association *See* Battlefords Agricultural Society

Battlefords Friendship Centre (BFC)
960 - 103 St., North Battleford SK S9A 1K2
Tel: 306-445-8216
Also Known As: Battlefords Indian & Metis Friendship Centre
Overview: A small local charitable organization founded in 1960
Member of: Aboriginal Friendship Centres of Saskatchewan
Membership: *Member Profile:* Aboriginal people

Battlefords Interval House Society
2092 - 102 St., North Battleford SK S9A 1H7
Tel: 306-445-2742; *Fax:* 306-446-2520; *Crisis Hot-Line:* 306-445-2742
Overview: A small local charitable organization founded in 1980
Mission: Provides 16-bed shelter; transportation; education/health promotion on anti-violence; life skills training advocate; court work advocate; partnership with agencies of justice, education, social services, health
Member of: Partnership Promoting Violence-Free Communities
Affliation(s): Provincial Association of Transition Houses (PATHS)
Chief Officer(s):
Ann McArthur, Executive Director
a.mcarthur@sasktel.net
Cheryl Cook, Chair, 306-445-3414
Finances: *Funding Sources:* Provincial government
Staff Member(s): 14; 3 volunteer(s)
Membership: 30 individual; *Fees:* $5

The Battlefords Music Festival
PO Box 1301, North Battleford SK S9A 3L8
Tel: 306-445-0437
t.iverson@loccsd.ca
Overview: A small local organization
Affliation(s): Saskatchewan Music Festival Association
Chief Officer(s):
Kelly Waters, President
25 volunteer(s)
Membership: 30 individual

Battlefords United Way Inc.
#203, 891 - 99th St., North Battleford SK S9A 0N8
Tel: 306-445-1717
buw@sasktel.net
www.battlefordsunitedway.ca
Overview: A small local charitable organization founded in 1967 overseen by United Way of Canada - Centraide Canada
Mission: To improve lives & build community by engaging individuals & mobilizing collective action
Chief Officer(s):
Brendon Boothman, Chair
Jana Blais, Treasurer
Finances: *Funding Sources:* Donations
Activities: *Library* by appointment

Bay of Islands SPCA; Bay of Islands Society for the Prevention of Cruelty to Animals *See* NL West SPCA

Bay of Quinte Dental Society (BQDS)
c/o John Marinovich, 257 Dundas St. East, Trenton ON K8V 1M1
Tel: 613-392-3939; *Crisis Hot-Line:* 613-961-0033
quintedentists.com
Overview: A small local organization overseen by Canadian Dental Association
Mission: To provide direction & education for dentistry within the Bay of Quinte region; To provide dental treatment & education for people in the community
Member of: Ontario Dental Association (ODA)
Chief Officer(s):
John Marinovich, President
john@marinovichgroup.com
Membership: 62; *Member Profile:* Dentists & Dental Specialists

Bay St. George Artists Association
PO Box 14, Stephenville Crossing NL A0N 2C0
Tel: 709-643-9395
info@bsgartists.ca
www.bsgartists.ca
Overview: A small local organization founded in 1973
Chief Officer(s):
Chrissie Kerr, President
Paul O'Keefe, Treasurer, 709-643-9590
Membership: 25

Bay St. George Chamber of Commerce
35 Carolina Ave., Stephenville NL A2N 3P8
Tel: 709-643-5854; *Fax:* 709-643-6398
bsgcoc@wec-center.nl.ca
www.bsgcc.org
Previous Name: Stephenville Chamber of Commerce
Overview: A small local organization founded in 1955
Mission: To promote & enhance economic growth towards a viable community
Chief Officer(s):
Sheila Hawco, Executive Director
Cynthia Downey, President
Finances: *Annual Operating Budget:* Less than $50,000
Membership: 102; *Fees:* $10 student; $25 retired; $55 individual; $85-$500 business; *Committees:* Business/Community Liaison; Government Liaison; Airport; Oil & Gas; Hospital

Baycrest Foundation
3560 Bathurst St., 2nd Fl., Toronto ON M6A 2E1
Tel: 416-785-2875; *Fax:* 416-785-4296
donations@baycrest.org
www.baycrest.org
Overview: A small local charitable organization founded in 1979
Mission: To raise money on behalf of the Baycrest Centre, which helps funds research for age related diseases
Chief Officer(s):
Garry Foster, President & CEO
gfoster@baycrest.org
Finances: *Annual Operating Budget:* Less than $50,000

Bayfield & Area Chamber of Commerce
PO Box 2065, Bayfield ON N0M 1G0
Tel: 519-565-2499
Toll-Free: 800-565-2499
info@villageofbayfield.com
cc.villageofbayfield.com
Overview: A small local organization
Chief Officer(s):
Janet Snider, President
Membership: 1-99
Activities: *Awareness Events:* Sail & Canvas, 3rd weekend in June

BBM Bureau of Measurement; Bureau of Broadcast Measurement; BBM Canada ***See*** Numeris

BC & Yukon Heart Foundation ***See*** Heart & Stroke Foundation of British Columbia & Yukon

BC Aboriginal Mine Training Association ***See*** Aboriginal Mentoring & Training Association

BC Adaptive Snowsports (BCAS)
780 Marine Dr. SW, Vancouver BC V6P 5Y7
Tel: 604-333-3630
info@bcadaptive.com
www.disabledskiingbc.com
www.facebook.com/206245376114584
twitter.com/DisabledSkiBC
Previous Name: Disabled Skiers Association of BC
Overview: A medium-sized provincial charitable organization founded in 1973 overseen by Canadian Association for Disabled Skiing
Mission: To contribute to the quality of life by promoting the sport of skiing for disabled persons
Member of: BC Disability Sports; Canadian Association for Disabled Skiing
Chief Officer(s):
Kay Fulford, President
kay@bcadaptive.com
Jim Dixon, Executive Director
jim@bcadaptive.com
Finances: *Annual Operating Budget:* $100,000-$250,000
Staff Member(s): 2; 700 volunteer(s)
Membership: 1,326; *Fees:* $40-45
Activities: Learn to Ski programs; BC Winter Games; Provincial Championships; Ski Improvement; Building Our Best; *Awareness Events:* Challenge Cup; *Speaker Service:* Yes

BC Amateur Baseball Association ***See*** Baseball BC

BC Artificial Insemination Centre ***See*** Westgen

BC Assocation for Crane Safety (BCACS)
PO Box 48883, Stn. Bentall, 595 Burrard St., Vancouver BC V7X 1A8
Tel: 604-336-4699; *Fax:* 604-339-4510
info@bcacs.ca
bcacs.ca
Overview: A small provincial organization founded in 2005
Mission: To create a safer workplace for those in the crane hoisting industry as well as to promote the industry
Chief Officer(s):
Ron Karras, Chair, Board of Directors

BC Association for Individualized Technology and Supports (BCITS)
#103, 366 East Kent Ave. South, Vancouver BC V5X 4N6
Fax: 604-326-0176
Toll-Free: 866-326-1245
prop@bcits.org
www.bcits.org
Overview: A medium-sized provincial charitable organization
Mission: BCITS is committed to enabling people with severe disabilities, who need assistive technologies, respiratory services and supports, to meet their needs while living in the community.
Activities: Provincial Respiratory Outreach Program; Technology for Independent Living; Discharge Planning

BC Association of Counsellors of Abusive Men ***See*** Ending Relationship Abuse Society of British Columbia

BC Association of Legal Assistants ***See*** British Columbia Paralegal Association

BC Association of Performing Arts Festivals ***See*** Performing Arts BC

BC Athlete Voice (BCAV)
#227, 3820 Cessna Dr., Richmond BC V7B 0A2
Tel: 604-345-1615
info@bcathletevoice.ca
www.bcathletevoice.ca
www.facebook.com/BCAthleteVoice
twitter.com/BCAthleteVoice
www.youtube.com/user/BCAthleteVoice;
flickr.com/photos/72052636@N04
Overview: A medium-sized provincial organization
Mission: To offer athletes in British Columbia leadership, education & advocacy programming.
Chief Officer(s):
Callum Ng, Executive Director
callum@bcathletevoice.ca
Activities: Funding & sponsoring athletes

BC Biotech ***See*** LifeSciences British Columbia

BC Cheerleading Association (BCCA)
BC
www.bccheerleading.ca
Overview: A small provincial organization overseen by Cheer Canada
Mission: To maintain athleticism & safety in cheerleading in British Columbia.
Member of: Cheer Canada
Chief Officer(s):
Robyn Dyk, Co-Chair
Jodi Yorston, Co-Chair

BC Community Connectivity Consortium ***See*** The British Columbia Community Connectivity Cooperative

BC Construction Safety Alliance (BCCSA)
#400, 625 Agnes St., New Westminster BC V3M 5Y4
Tel: 604-636-3675; *Fax:* 604-636-3676
Toll-Free: 877-860-3675
www.bccsa.ca
www.facebook.com/SafetyInConstruction
twitter.com/BCCSABeSafe
Previous Name: Construction Safety Network
Overview: A small provincial organization founded in 2001
Mission: To partner with WorkSafeBC to promote a positive occupational health & safety culture for the construction industry
Chief Officer(s):
Mike McKenna, Executive Director
mmckenna@bccsa.ca
Staff Member(s): 9

BC Disc Sports Society ***See*** Disc BC

BC Egg Producers ***See*** British Columbia Egg Marketing Board

BC English Teachers' Association ***See*** British Columbia Teachers of English Language Arts

BC Federation of School Athletic Associations ***See*** BC School Sports

BC First Party
PO Box 95037, 370 East Broadway, Vancouver BC V5T 4T8
Tel: 604-564-0288
Toll-Free: 855-223-4778
www.bcfirst.ca
www.facebook.com/bcfirst
Also Known As: BC First
Overview: A small provincial organization
Chief Officer(s):
Salvatore Vetro, Party Leader
sal@bcfirst.ca
Membership: *Fees:* $10 individual; $20 family

BC Floorball Federation (BCFF)
3183 Edgemont Blvd., North Vancouver BC V7R 2N8
Tel: 778-385-7825
info@bcfloorball.com
www.bcfloorball.com
www.facebook.com/BCFloorball
twitter.com/bcfloorball
Overview: A small provincial organization overseen by Floorball Canada
Mission: To be the provincial governing body for the sport of floorball in British Columbia.
Member of: Floorball Canada
Chief Officer(s):
Blair Zimmerman, President

BC Freestyle Ski Association
#327, 3104 - 30th Ave., Vernon BC V1T 9M9
Tel: 604-637-7270
info@bcfreestyle.com
bcfreestyle.com
www.facebook.com/BCFreestyleSkiAssociation
Overview: A small provincial organization overseen by Canadian Freestyle Ski Association
Mission: To develop, promote & coordinate the sport of freestyle skiing in British Columbia.
Member of: Canadian Freestyle Ski Association
Chief Officer(s):
Camille Douglas, Executive Director
camille@bcfreestyle.com

BC Friends of Schizophrenics ***See*** British Columbia Schizophrenia Society

BC Games Society
#200, 990 Fort St., Victoria BC V8V 3K2
Tel: 250-387-1375; *Fax:* 250-387-4489
info@bcgames.org
www.bcgames.org
www.facebook.com/BCGamesSociety
twitter.com/BCGames1
www.youtube.com/user/BCGamesSociety;
flickr.com/photos/bcgames
Previous Name: British Columbia Games Society
Overview: A small provincial organization
Mission: To provide event management leadership in the creation of development opportunities for individuals, sport organizations & host communities
Chief Officer(s):
Kelly Mann, President & CEO
kellym@bcgames.org
Staff Member(s): 8

BC Hands & Voices
1965 Rodger Ave., Port Coquitlam BC V3C 1B8
e-mail: info@bchandsandvoices.com
www.bchandsandvoices.com
Overview: A small provincial charitable organization
Mission: BC Hands & Voices supports families with children who are deaf or hard of hearing.
Membership: *Fees:* $15 individual; $25 agency

BC Helicopter & Snowcat Skiing Operators Association ***See*** HeliCat Canada

B.C. Horseshoe Association
c/o Sam Tomasevic, 7987 Graham Ave., Burnaby BC V3N 1V8
Tel: 604-525-2186
administrator@bchorseshoe.com
www.bchorseshoe.com
Overview: A small provincial organization overseen by Horseshoe Canada

Mission: To promote the sport of horseshoe pitching in British Columbia.
Member of: Horseshoe Canada
Chief Officer(s):
Sam Tomasevic, President
samtom@telus.net
Membership: 346

BC Institute on Family Violence ***See*** British Columbia Institute Against Family Violence

BC Lacrosse Association (BCLA)
#101, 7382 Winston St., Burnaby BC V5A 2G9
Tel: 604-421-9755; *Fax:* 604-421-9775
info@bclacrosse.com
www.bclacrosse.com
www.facebook.com/481524661862119
twitter.com/BCLacrosse
www.youtube.com/user/BCLacrosseA
Overview: A medium-sized provincial organization overseen by Canadian Lacrosse Association
Mission: Promotes and regulates the sport of lacrosse in British Columbia
Member of: Canadian Lacrosse Association
Chief Officer(s):
Rochelle Winterton, Executive Director
rochelle@bclacrosse.com
Staff Member(s): 5

BC Lymphedema Association (BCLA)
#215, 5589 Byrne Rd., Burnaby BC V5J 3J1
Toll-Free: 866-991-2252
info@bclymph.org
www.bclymph.org
Overview: A medium-sized provincial charitable organization founded in 2006
Mission: To raise awareness about lymphedema & to represent & support lymphedema patients
Chief Officer(s):
Lucette Wesley, Presdient
Membership: *Fees:* $25 individual; $50 professional; $100 corporate; *Member Profile:* Lymphedema patients & professionals; *Committees:* Healthcare Advisory; Executive; Fundraising & Development; Marting & Communications; Program

BC Motels, Campgrounds, Resorts Association ***See*** British Columbia Lodging & Campgrounds Association

BC Motor Transport Association ***See*** British Columbia Trucking Association

BC Northern Real Estate Association
2609 Queensway, Prince George BC V2L 1N3
Tel: 250-563-1236; *Fax:* 250-563-3637
inquiries@bcnreb.bc.ca
Overview: A medium-sized local organization founded in 1966 overseen by British Columbia Real Estate Association
Member of: The Canadian Real Estate Association
Chief Officer(s):
Alexandra Goseltine, Executive Director
agoseltine@bcnreb.bc.ca

BC Parents in Crisis Society ***See*** Parent Support Services Society of BC

BC Rural & Small Schools Teachers' Association (BCRSSTA)
www.bcruralteachers.org
Previous Name: British Columbia Rural Teachers' Association
Overview: A small provincial organization founded in 1982
Mission: To support teachers of multi-grade classrooms who live & teach in small communities
Affliation(s): British Columbia Teachers Federation
Chief Officer(s):
Virginia Ivey, President
vcivey@xplornet.com
Christina McDonald, Treasurer
cgmac11@telus.net
Susan J. Hay, Secretary
shay@sd81.bc.ca
Finances: *Annual Operating Budget:* Less than $50,000
Membership: 1-99; *Fees:* $20; *Member Profile:* BC teachers working/living in rural areas
Awards:
• Lottie Bowron Memorial Bursary (Scholarship)
• Professional Development Travel Grants (Grant)
Publications:
• The Rural Root [a publication of the BC Rural & Small Schools Teachers' Association]
Type: Newsletter; *Frequency:* 2-3 pa; *Editor:* Erika Momeyer

BC Sailing Association
#195, 3820 Cessna Dr., Richmond BC V7B 0A2
Tel: 604-333-3628; *Fax:* 604-333-3626
crew@bcsailing.bc.ca
www.bcsailing.bc.ca
www.facebook.com/bcsailing
Also Known As: BC Sailing
Overview: A medium-sized provincial organization overseen by Sail Canada
Mission: The provincial sport authority for sailing
Member of: Sail Canada; Sport BC
Affliation(s): International Sailing Federation
Chief Officer(s):
Tine Moberg-Parker, Executive Director
tmpsailing@shaw.ca
Finances: *Funding Sources:* Provincial government; membership fees; programs
Staff Member(s): 2
Membership: 5,000; *Fees:* $22

BC School Sports (BCSS)
Sydney Landing, #2003A, 3713 Kensington Ave., Burnaby BC V5B 0A7
Tel: 604-477-1488; *Fax:* 604-477-1484
info@bcschoolsports.ca
www.bcschoolsports.ca
www.facebook.com/224539464369947
twitter.com/bcschoolsports
www.youtube.com/channel/UCbaiTGzwF92qYAk7lClkS6Q
Previous Name: BC Federation of School Athletic Associations
Overview: A medium-sized provincial charitable organization founded in 1968 overseen by School Sport Canada
Mission: To encourage student participation in extra-curricular athletics, assist schools in the development & delivery of their programs & provide governance for interschool competition
Member of: School Sport Canada; Sport BC
Affliation(s): USA National Federation of State High Schools
Chief Officer(s):
Deb Whitten, President
dwhitten@sd61.bc.ca
Christine Bradstock, Executive Director
cbradstock@bcschoolsports.ca
Finances: *Annual Operating Budget:* $500,000-$1.5 Million; *Funding Sources:* Membership fees; government; sponsors; advertising
Staff Member(s): 3; 6 volunteer(s)
Membership: 400; *Fees:* Schedule available; *Member Profile:* Accredited secondary school in British Columbia; *Committees:* Administrators; Coaching Development; Competitive Standards; Disciplinary; Eligibility; Scholarship & Awards
Activities: Provincial championships; advocacy; regulatory services; fundraising services; coaching conference; leadership camp; *Awareness Events:* Milk Run; Spirit Week; National School Sports Week, Oct.
Awards:
• Two Provincial Student/Athlete of the Year (Scholarship)
• Six BCSS Scholarships (Scholarship)

BC Smallbore Rifle Association ***See*** British Columbia Target Sports Association

BC Snowboard Association
PO Box 2040, Kelowna BC V1X 4K5
Tel: 250-491-7626
Other Communication: Alt. E-mail: info@bcsnowboard.com
admin@bcsnowboard.com
bcsnowboard.com
www.facebook.com/BCSnowboardAssociation
Overview: A small provincial organization overseen by Canadian Snowboard Federation
Mission: To support snowboard athletes, coaches & officials in the province of British Columbia.
Member of: Canadian Snowboard Federation
Chief Officer(s):
Cathy Astofooroff, Executive Director
cathy@bcsnowboard.com

BC Soccer Referee Association
8130 Selkirk St., Vancouver BC V6P 4H7
e-mail: bcreferees@gmail.com
www.bcsra.com
www.facebook.com/BcSoccerRefereesAssociation
Overview: A small provincial organization
Mission: To support referees in the province of British Columbia.
Chief Officer(s):
Nick Hawley, President
nickhawley@shaw.ca

BC Society of Transition Houses (BCSTH)
#325, 119 West Pender St., Vancouver BC V6B 1S5
Tel: 604-669-6943; *Fax:* 604-682-6962
Toll-Free: 800-661-1040
info@bcsth.ca
bcsth.ca
www.facebook.com/BCSTH
twitter.com/BCSTH
www.youtube.com/BCYSTH
Overview: A small provincial organization
Mission: To educate, promote & advocate on issues of violence against women; to support an organization that provides or seeks to provide shelter &/or services to women & their children who experience violence
Chief Officer(s):
Shabna Ali, Executive Director
Finances: *Funding Sources:* Government; members; fundraising
Membership: *Fees:* $75 individual; $150 agency; $300 full member; *Member Profile:* Shelters for abused women & their children
Activities: *Library:* BCSTH Library

BC Summer Swimming Association (BCSSA)
#205, 2323 Boundary Rd., Vancouver BC V5M 4V8
Tel: 604-473-9447; *Fax:* 604-473-9660
office@bcsummerswimming.com
www.bcsummerswimming.com
www.facebook.com/bcsummerswimming
twitter.com/BCSSAstaff
Overview: A medium-sized provincial organization founded in 1958
Mission: To provide summer swimming opportunities to children across British Colubia through member clubs.
Membership: 60 clubs + 5,000 athletes
Activities: Speed swimming; diving; water polo; synchronized swimming

BC Taekwondo Association
6560 - 188th St., Surrey BC V3S 8V1
www.bctaekwondo.org
Overview: A small provincial organization founded in 1994
Mission: To govern the sport of Tae Kwon Do in British Columbia.
Chief Officer(s):
Michael Smith, President
westsidetkd@shaw.ca

BC Track & Field Association ***See*** British Columbia Athletics

BC Trappers' Association (BCTA)
c/o Alana Leclerc, PO Box 1063, Prince George BC V2L 4V2
Tel: 250-962-5452; *Fax:* 250-962-5462
info@bctrappers.bc.ca
bctrappers.bc.ca
Overview: A small provincial organization
Chief Officer(s):
Brian Dack, President
Membership: *Member Profile:* Licensed trappers in British Columbia
Meetings/Conferences: • 70th BC Trappers' AssociationAnnual General Meeting & Convention, April, 2015, 100 Mile House Curling Club, 100 Mile House, BC
Scope: Provincial

BC Water Ski Association ***See*** Water Ski & Wakeboard British Columbia

BCADA - The New Car Dealers of BC
#70, 10551 Shellbridge Way, Richmond BC V6X 2W9
Tel: 604-214-9964; *Fax:* 604-214-9965
info@newcardealers.ca
www.newcardealers.ca
Previous Name: Motor Dealers' Association of BC; BC Automobile Dealers' Association
Overview: A medium-sized provincial organization founded in 1942
Mission: To promote benefits & heighten awareness of issues of interest to members
Member of: Canadian Automobile Dealers' Association
Chief Officer(s):

Blair Qualey, President & CEO
bqualey@newcardealers.ca
Staff Member(s): 7
Membership: 345 dealerships; *Fees:* Schedule available; *Member Profile:* New vehicle franchise - car & truck

Beach Hebrew Institute
109 Kenilworth Ave., Toronto ON M4L 3S4
Tel: 416-757-8393
info@beachsynagogue.com
www.beachhebrewinstitute.ca
Overview: A small local organization
Chief Officer(s):
Arie Nerman, President
president@beachhebrewinstitute.ca
Membership: *Fees:* $400 individual; $650 family
Publications:
• The Weekly Huddle [a publication of Beach Hebrew Institute]
Type: Newsletter; *Frequency:* Weekly

Beachville District Historical Society
PO Box 220, 584367 Beachville Rd., Beachville ON N0J 1A0
Tel: 519-423-6497; *Fax:* 519-423-6935
bmchin@execulink.com
www.beachvilledistrictmuseum.ca
Overview: A small local organization founded in 1973
Member of: Ontario Historical Society
Chief Officer(s):
Carl MacDonald, Contact
Membership: 56; *Fees:* $10 husband & wife; $5 per person
Activities: Beachville District Museum

Bear River Board of Trade
c/o Bear River Visitor Information Centre, PO Box 235, Bear River NS B0S 1B0
Tel: 902-467-3200; *Fax:* 902-467-0901
info@churchillmansion.com
www.bearriver.ca
Overview: A small local organization founded in 1905
Chief Officer(s):
Larry Knox, President
larryknox.ns@gmail.com
Membership: *Committees:* Fundraiser & Events; Operations; Public Relations; Waterfront & Greenspaces; Transportation; Bylaws

Bear River Historical Society
PO Box 182, Bear River NS B0S 1B0
e-mail: BearRiverHistory@gmail.com
bearrivermuseum.wordpress.com
www.facebook.com/133976233381746
Overview: A small local charitable organization founded in 1987
Chief Officer(s):
Rosamond McCue, President
Bonnie MacLeod, Secretary & Communications Contact
Activities: Operates community museum & archives
Publications:
• Bear River Tributary
Type: newsletter

Beaton Institute
Cape Breton University, PO Box 5300, 1250 Grand Lake Rd., Sydney NS B1P 6L2
Tel: 902-563-1329; *Fax:* 902-562-8899
beaton@cbu.ca
www.cbu.ca/beaton
Previous Name: Beaton Institute of Cape Breton Studies
Overview: A small local charitable organization founded in 1957
Mission: To collect & conserve the social, economic, political & cultural history of Cape Breton Island
Affliation(s): Council of Nova Scotia Archives; Iona Connection Co-operative Limited; Cape Breton Genealogical Association; Association of Canadian Archivists; Society of American Archivists
Chief Officer(s):
Catherine Arseneau, BA, MA, Manager, 902-563-1326
catherine_arseneau@cbu.ca
Finances: *Annual Operating Budget:* $100,000-$250,000
Staff Member(s): 5
Activities: *Library* Open to public

Beaton Institute of Cape Breton Studies *See* Beaton Institute

Beaumont Coin Discovery Group
c/o Ron Darbyshire, 4907 - 114 St., Edmonton AB T6H 3L5
Tel: 780-436-4335
coinguy@telus.net
Overview: A small local organization
Chief Officer(s):
Ron Darbyshire, Director

Beausejour & District Chamber of Commerce
PO Box 224, Beausejour MB R0E 0C0
Tel: 204-268-3502
beausejourchamber@ourhomeyourhome.ca
ourhomeyourhome.ca
Overview: A small local organization founded in 1939
Mission: To serve commerce & community; to promote the economic, civic, educational & cultural interests of the town of Beausejour & area
Chief Officer(s):
Kerryleegh Hilderbandtt, President
Sherri Garrity, Executive Director
Finances: *Annual Operating Budget:* Less than $50,000; *Funding Sources:* Membership dues
Staff Member(s): 1; 10 volunteer(s)
Membership: 87

BeautyCouncil (BC)
899 West 8th Ave., Vancouver BC V5Z 1E3
Tel: 604-871-0222; *Fax:* 604-871-0299
Toll-Free: 800-663-9283
info@beautycouncil.ca
beautycouncil.ca
www.facebook.com/beautycouncilwesterncanada
twitter.com/beautycouncil
www.pinterest.com/beautycouncil
Previous Name: Cosmetologists' Association of British Columbia; Cosmetology Industry Association of British Columbia
Overview: A small provincial licensing organization founded in 1929
Mission: To strive for the highest standards of excellence in professional cosmetology services through its member enhancement programs & to service the public through education & knowledge.
Chief Officer(s):
Bill Moreland, Chair
Debbie Nickel, Executive Director
debbie.nickel@beautycouncil.ca
Finances: *Funding Sources:* Licence fees
Staff Member(s): 5
Membership: *Fees:* $30 honoree/trainee; $65 individual; $100 company; $150 company & individual; *Member Profile:* Licenced in hair, esthetics, nail technology or barbering
Activities: Regional shows; *Library*
Awards:
• Hazel Kinnon Award (Award)
• Achievement Award (Award)

Beaverhill Bird Observatory (BBO)
PO Box 1418, Edmonton AB T5J 2N5
www.beaverhillbirds.com
Overview: A small local charitable organization
Mission: To promote study of resident & migratory birds & other aspects of natural history at Beaverhill Lake & elsewhere
Chief Officer(s):
Charles Priestley, Chair
charles@ualberta.ca
Lisa Takats Priestley, Executive Director
lisa@beaverhillbirds.com
Membership: *Fees:* $10 one year; $20 two year; $25 family/club; *Member Profile:* Biologists; Nature lovers
Activities: Documenting & monitoring changes in the avian species that utilize the Beaverhill area; Promoting an interest in the conservation of birds; Encouraging nature activities
Publications:
• The Willet [a publication of the Beaverhill Bird Observatory]
Type: Newsletter

Beaverlodge Chamber of Commerce
PO Box 303, Beaverlodge AB T0H 0C0
Tel: 780-354-8785
Overview: A small local organization
Member of: Alberta Chamber of Commerce
Chief Officer(s):
Judy Olson, Treasurer
Membership: 50

Beaverlodge Food Bank
PO Box 1154, Beaverlodge AB T0H 0C0
Tel: 780-354-8069; *Fax:* 780-354-4187
beaverlodgenrc.ca/foodbank.html
Overview: A small local charitable organization founded in 1989 overseen by Alberta Food Bank Network Association
Activities: Christmas Hamper program

Beaverton District Chamber of Commerce
PO Box 29, Beaverton ON L0K 1A0
Tel: 705-426-2051
chamber@beavertononlakesimcoe.com
www.beavertononlakesimcoe.com
Overview: A small local organization founded in 1989
Affliation(s): Ontario Chamber of Commerce
Chief Officer(s):
Ted McCollum, President, 705-426-5972
revted@mac.com
Finances: *Funding Sources:* Membership fee
7 volunteer(s)
Membership: 1-99; *Fees:* $80

Beaverton Thorah Eldon Historical Society
PO Box 314, 284 Simcoe St., Beaverton ON L0K 1A0
Tel: 705-426-9641
bte.hist.soc@bellnet.ca
www.btehs.com
Overview: A small local charitable organization founded in 1976
Mission: To depict the history of the communities of Beaverton, Thorah, & Eldon; To provide genealogical & history resources, such as local newspapers, census information, church registers, & assessment rolls
Chief Officer(s):
Donna Richardson, President
Jane Veale, Curator
Ken Alsop, Archivist
Finances: *Funding Sources:* Donations; Fundraising; Grants
Membership: *Fees:* $20 / year; *Committees:* History; Antique Show; Education; Program; Museum Gift Shop; Membership; Genealogy; Property; House Tour
Activities: Operating the Beaver River Museum, which consists of a log house, a brick house (c. 1900), & a mid 19th century stone jail; Hosting history meetings
Publications:
• The Beaverton Story: Harvest of Dreams
Type: Book; *Price:* $30
• Continuing Dreams: The Second Beaverton Story
Type: Book; *Price:* $30

Bechtel Foundation of Canada
#350, 1981 McGill College Ave., Montréal QC H3A 3A8
Tel: 514-871-1711; *Fax:* 514-871-1392
www.bechtel.com
Overview: A small provincial organization founded in 1949
Mission: To finance educational activities in engineering & the support of community & national health, welfare & cultural organizations
Chief Officer(s):
Russell Barrettal, General Manager
rjbarret@bechtel.com
Staff Member(s): 165

Bed & Breakfast Association of the Yukon (BBAY)
PO Box 31518, Whitehorse YT Y1A 6K8
e-mail: info@yukonbandb.org
www.yukonbandb.org
Overview: A small provincial organization
Mission: To support and promote both the individual members and the B&B industry, to broaden public awareness, understanding and appreciation of the B&B industry in the Yukon, & to represent the B&B industry where a unified voice is needed and appropriate.
Chief Officer(s):
Mo Hartigan, President

Bedeque Bay Environmental Management Association (BBEMA)
PO Box 8310, 1929 Nodd Rd., Emerald PE C0B 1M0
Tel: 902-886-3211
www.bbema.ca
www.facebook.com/140016226032255
Overview: A small local organization founded in 1992
Mission: To provide a framework for citizen-based education and action that reduced soil erosion, maintained water quality and improved the ecosystem.
Membership: *Fees:* $20 single; $25 family; $10 student; $50-$250 corporate

Beef Cattle Research Council (BCRC)
#180, 6815 - 8th St. NE, Calgary AB T2E 7H7
Tel: 403-275-8558; *Fax:* 403-274-5686
info@beefresearch.ca
www.beefresearch.ca
www.facebook.com/BeefResearch

twitter.com/BeefResearch
www.youtube.com/beefresearch
Overview: A medium-sized national organization founded in 1997
Mission: Canada's national industry-led funding agency for beef research.
Affliation(s): Canadian Cattlemen's Association (CCA)
Chief Officer(s):
Andrea Brocklebank, Research Manager
brocklebanka@beefresearch.ca
Reynold Bergen, Science Director
Finances: *Funding Sources:* Producer-paid national levy; government funding

Beef Farmers of Ontario (BFO)

130 Malcolm Rd., Guelph ON N1K 1B1
Tel: 519-824-0334; *Fax:* 519-824-9101
info@ontariobeef.com
www.ontariobeef.com
www.facebook.com/BeefFarmersofOntario
twitter.com/OntarioBeef
Previous Name: Ontario Beef Improvement Association; Ontario Cattlemen's Association
Overview: A medium-sized provincial organization founded in 1963
Mission: To foster a sustainable & profitable beef industry in Ontario; To provide programs & serivces to support local cattlemen's associations & provincial cattlemen in general; To lobby on issues at the provincial & national level
Member of: Canadian Cattlemen's Association
Chief Officer(s):
Dave Stewart, Executive Director
Paul Stiles, Assistant Manager
Lianne Appleby, Manager, Communications
Jamie Thomas, Coordinator, Market Information
Lisa Turney, Coordinator, Research & Projects
Jen Snively, Policy Advisor
Staff Member(s): 13
Membership: *Member Profile:* Cattle producers in Ontario; *Committees:* Cow / Calf; Feedlot; Research
Activities: Providing education & information to Ontario cattlemen; Engaging in advocacy activities on behalf of the Ontario beef industry; Liaising with government; Initiating studies, programs, & reviews; Encouraging economically sustainable production methods; Promoting Quality Starts Here programs to beef producers across Ontario; Developing domestic & export markets Promoting beef
Awards:
• The Environmental Stewardship Award (Award)
Meetings/Conferences: • 2015 Beef Farmers of Ontario Annual General Meeting, February, 2015, International Plaza Hotel, Toronto, ON
Scope: Provincial
Description: An opportunity for Ontario Cattlemen's Association members to help set policy direction on cattle industry issues
Contact Information: Communications Manager: Lianne Wuermli, E-mail: leaanne@ontariobeef.com
Publications:
• OCA [Ontario Cattlemen's Association] Weekly Update
Type: Newsletter; *Frequency:* Weekly; *Editor:* Lianne Appleby
• Ontario Beef
Type: Magazine; *Frequency:* 5 pa; *Accepts Advertising*; *Editor:* Lianne Appleby; *Price:* Free for members of the OntarioCattlemen's Association
Profile: Information for producers, featuring articles of interest in the beef industry, research, market information, producer profiles, & current policy issues
• Ontario Cattlemen's Association Production Guides
Type: Guide
Profile: Production information of a wide variety of topics
• The Ontario Steakholder
Type: Newsletter; *Frequency:* Irregular; *Editor:* Lianne Appleby
Profile: A timely publication for Ontario's MPs & MPPs to connect them with Ontario's beef farmers

Beef Improvement Ontario (BIO)

#205, 660 Speedvale Ave. West, Guelph ON N1K 1E5
Tel: 519-767-2665; *Fax:* 519-767-2502
Toll-Free: 855-246-2333
info@biobeef.com
www.biobeef.com
Overview: A small provincial organization
Mission: To provide genetic & management products & services to breeders & feeders of beef cattle & enhance the competitive position of the Ontario beef industry
Affliation(s): Agricultural Adaptation Council; Canadian Dairy Network; Centre of Genetic Improvement of Livestock; Igenity; Ontario Cattlemen's Association
Chief Officer(s):
Mike Buis, President
Mike McMorris, General Manager
mmcmorris@bridgingintelligence.com
Staff Member(s): 11

Beehive Adult Service Centre, Inc.

PO Box 98, 1119 Station St., Aylesford NS B0P 1C0
Tel: 902-847-9696; *Fax:* 902-847-9189
beehiveasc@eastlink.ca
Overview: A small local organization
Member of: DIRECTIONS Council for Vocational Services Society
Chief Officer(s):
Cora Auclair, Executive Director/Manager

Beehive Support Services Association

PO Box 6007, 5225 - 55A St., Drayton Valley AB T7A 1R6
Tel: 780-542-3113; *Fax:* 780-542-3115
bsupport@telus.net
www.beehivesupportservices.com
Previous Name: Drayton Valley Association for Community Living
Overview: A small local charitable organization founded in 1975
Mission: To support and promote the welfare of people with disabilities.
Member of: Alberta Association for Community Living; Alberta Association of Rehabilitation Centres
Chief Officer(s):
Dwayne Henley, Executive Director, 780-542-3113 Ext. 221
Staff Member(s): 30; 8 volunteer(s)
Membership: 30; *Fees:* $1
Activities: Supporting the community through recycling initiatives like the Drayton Valley Bottle Depot.

Beekeepers' Association of Niagara Region

St Catharines ON
Tel: 905-934-4913
Overview: A small local organization
Mission: To offer education on beekeeping skills to person in the Niagara area
Member of: Ontario Beekeepers' Association
Chief Officer(s):
George Dubanow, President, 905-934-4913
panosmarg@gmail.com
Membership: *Member Profile:* Beekeepers of the Niagara region
Activities: Organizing monthly meetings at the Niagara Regional Police Station Community Room in Welland to share information about beekeeping & association business; Providing networking opportunities for local beekeepers; Assisting beekeepers in handling issues in the beekeeping industry

Beiseker & District Chamber of Commerce

PO Box 277, Beiseker AB T0M 0G0
Tel: 403-947-3920
Overview: A small local organization
Member of: Alberta Chamber of Commerce
Chief Officer(s):
Balson Iris, Contact
Membership: *Member Profile:* Business owners & the public

Beiseker & District Chamber of Commerce

PO Box 277, Beiseker AB T0M 0G0
Overview: A small local organization
Chief Officer(s):
Iris Balson, Contact, 403-947-3920

Belgian Canadian Business Association ***See*** Belgian Canadian Business Chamber

Belgian Canadian Business Chamber (BCBC)

PO Box 508, 161 Bay St., 27th Fl., Toronto ON M5J 2S1
Tel: 416-816-9154
info@belgiumconnect.com
www.belgiumconnect.com
www.linkedin.com/company/belgian-canadian-business-chamber
www.facebook.com/BelgiumConnect
twitter.com/Belgiumconnect
Previous Name: Belgian Canadian Business Association
Overview: A small international organization founded in 1988
Mission: The Belgian Canadian Business Chamber (BCBC) is based in Toronto and works to foster contacts and relationships for our members who share an interest in developing business and trade opportunities between Canada and Belgium.members who share an interest in developing business & trade opportunities between Canada & Belgium.
Member of: European Chambers of Commerce in Toronto (EUCOCIT)
Chief Officer(s):
Dominiek Arnout, President & Chief Executive Officer
Christian Frayssignes, Vice-President & EUCOCIT Representative
André van der Heyden, Vice-President & Chief Operating Officer
Klaus Koeppen, Treasurer & Chief Financial Officer
Idalia Obregón, Executive Director
Lionel Tarin, Membership Secretary
Sébastien Dillien, Events Director
Membership: *Fees:* Individuals: $60, Corporate: $300-$3,000; *Member Profile:* Membership is open to anyone interested in developing or expanding their business relationship with Belgium.
Activities: Business seminars, Business with Belgium, Belgians in Canada, networking events, Frites Night, joint events with other European chambers

Belgo-Canadian Association (BCA)

121 Chillery Ave., Toronto ON M1K 4T5
Tel: 416-261-4603
www.belgo-canadian.com
Overview: A small national organization founded in 1948
Finances: *Funding Sources:* Membership dues
Membership: 250-300

The Belinda Stronach Foundation (TBSF)

#310, 150 Bloor St. West, Toronto ON M5S 2X9
Tel: 416-531-1919; *Fax:* 416-531-1918
info@tbsf.ca
www.tbsf.ca
twitter.com/@GW_TBSF
www.youtube.com/user/TheTBSFChannel
Overview: A small national charitable organization founded in 2008
Mission: Assists girls and women and Aboriginal youth in Canada and youth in developing nations to achieve a better life through the provision of programs that enhance basic health and education, improve economic and political independence and that promote civic involvement.
Chief Officer(s):
Belinda Stronach, President & CEO
Activities: Spread the Net campaign

Bell Aliant Pioneers

PO Box 1430, Saint John NB E2L 4K2
Toll-Free: 800-565-1436
www.bellaliantpioneers.com
Overview: A large provincial organization overseen by TelecomPioneers of Canada
Mission: The Bell Aliant Pioneer Volunteers is the largest corporate based volunteer organization in Atlantic Canada and is comprised of current and former Bell Aliant employees and its predecessor companies.
Chief Officer(s):
Sandra King, President, 506-853-3766
Membership: 9000

Prince Edward Island
PO Box 820, Charlottetown PE C1A 7M1
Tel: 902-629-5250
Chief Officer(s):
Joseph Rowledge, Contact
joseph.rowledge@bellaliant.ca

Newfoundland and Labrador
PO Box 25, Mount Pearl NL A1N 2C1
Tel: 709-758-6323
Chief Officer(s):
Bernie Molloy, President, Metro Club
bernie.molloy@bellaliant.ca

Nova Scotia
PO Box 880, Halifax NS S4P 3Y2

Belleville & District Chamber of Commerce (BCC)

PO Box 726, 5 Moira St., Belleville ON K8N 5B3
Tel: 613-962-4597; *Fax:* 613-962-3911
Toll-Free: 888-852-9992
info@bellevillechamber.ca
www.bellevillechamber.ca
www.facebook.com/126461154084001
twitter.com/@BCC1864
Overview: A small local organization founded in 1864
Mission: To be recognized as the voice of business in promoting & nurturing a prosperous Belleville & district community: To act as a strong advocate of business in ensuring

sound government policies which will create sustainable economic growth; To promote tourism & by developing partnership in education, training & the environment; To provide a means of networking amongst members to enable both business & personal development opportunities
Member of: Ontario Chamber of Commerce; Canadian Chamber of Commerce
Chief Officer(s):
Ray Dassylva, President
Bill Saunders, CEO
bill@bellevillechamber.ca
Finances: *Annual Operating Budget:* $100,000-$250,000; *Funding Sources:* Fundraising; tourism promotion revenue; membership fees
Staff Member(s): 4; 16 volunteer(s)
Membership: 600+; *Fees:* $118.79-$2,627.25

Belleville Police Association / Association de la police de Belleville
93 Dundas St. East, Belleville ON K8N 1C2
Tel: 613-966-0882; *Fax:* 613-966-1834
Overview: A small local organization
Chief Officer(s):
Peter Goulah, President

Benedictine Sisters of Manitoba (OSB)
225 Masters Ave., Winnipeg MB R4A 2A1
Tel: 204-338-4601; *Fax:* 204-339-8775
stbens@mts.net
www.stbens.ca
Also Known As: Sisters of the Order of St. Benedict
Overview: A small provincial charitable organization founded in 1912
Mission: To witness Jesus Christ, through community life & prayer, contemplative living, hospitality, service to the people of God & stewardship of all God's gifts
Member of: Federation of St. Gertrude
Chief Officer(s):
Virginia Evard, Prioress
Finances: *Funding Sources:* Donations
Staff Member(s): 35; 30 volunteer(s)
Membership: 33
Activities: Programs in spirituality, personal growth & a variety of retreats; *Library:* St. Benedict's Monastery Library; by appointment

Benevolent & Protective Order of Elks of Canada
#100, 2629 - 29 Ave., Regina SK S4S 2N9
Tel: 306-359-9010; *Fax:* 306-565-2860
Toll-Free: 888-843-3557
grandlodge@elks-canada.org
www.elks-canada.org
Also Known As: Elks of Canada
Overview: A medium-sized national licensing charitable organization founded in 1913
Mission: To promote & support community needs, through volunteer efforts of local lodges
Chief Officer(s):
Bill Blake, National Executive Director
bblake@elks-canada.org
Sebastian Merk, Manager, Finance & Administration
smerk@elks-canada.org
Finances: *Annual Operating Budget:* $1.5 Million-$3 Million; *Funding Sources:* Membership dues
Staff Member(s): 8
Membership: 20,000; *Fees:* $42

Benevolent Irish Society of Prince Edward Island (BIS)
Benevolent Irish Society Hall, PO Box 34, 582 North River Rd., Charlottetown PE C1A 7K4
Tel: 902-892-2367
Overview: A small provincial organization founded in 1825
Mission: To enhance & preserve Irish heritage & culture; To assist the poor & indigent of all denominations; To promote friendship & unity among Irish people & their descendants for mutual benefit
Member of: Canadian Association of Irish Studies; Festivals & Events PEI
Chief Officer(s):
David Corrigan, President
Finances: *Annual Operating Budget:* Less than $50,000; *Funding Sources:* Membership; special events
50 volunteer(s)
Membership: 160; *Fees:* $20; *Member Profile:* Men & women of Irish descent; *Committees:* Charitable; Culture; Finance; Heritage; Newsletter; Property; Social
Activities: Ceilidh at the Irish Hall; lecture series; St. Patrick's Parade; pub nights; Irish dance lessons;

Bénévoles Canada *See* Volunteer Canada

Benfica House of Toronto *See* Casa do Benfica

Bengough Agricultural Society
PO Box 411, Bengough SK S0C 0K0
Tel: 306-268-2855
Overview: A small local charitable organization founded in 1915
Mission: To improve agriculture & the quality of life in the community by educating members & the community; to provide a community forum for discussing agricultural issues; to foster community development & community spirit; to help provide markets for Saskatchewan products; to encourage conservation of natural resources, including soil conservation, reforestation, rural & urban beautification
Member of: Saskatchewan Association of Agricultural Societies & Exhibitions
Chief Officer(s):
Rocky Kaufman, President, 306-268-4248
Membership: *Member Profile:* Area residents striving to promote our community through education & entertainment
Activities: Horse show & fair; trade show; farmers market
Awards:
• Bengough Agricultural Society Agricultural Scholarship (Scholarship)
To any Bengough high school student for post-secondary education studying agriculture *Amount:* $200

Bennington Heights Community Orchestra; East York Symphony Orchestra *See* Orchestra Toronto

Le Berceau de Kamouraska inc.
4, rue Lauzier, Route 132 Est, Kamouraska QC G0L 1M0
Tél: 418-492-5099
Aperçu: *Dimension:* petite; *Envergure:* locale; fondée en 1993
Mission: Préservation et conservation d'un lieu historique et parc commémoratif racontant l'histoire du Berceau de Kamouraska.

Bereaved Families of Ontario (BFO)
PO Box 10015, Stn. Watline, Mississauga ON L4Z 4G5
e-mail: info@bereavedfamilies.net
www.bereavedfamilies.net
Overview: A medium-sized provincial charitable organization founded in 1978
Mission: To create programs, services & resources to support bereaved families; committed to self-help & mutual aid; focus is on families who have experienced the death of a child
Member of: Ontario Self-Help Network
Chief Officer(s):
Carolyn Baltaz, Chair
Finances: *Funding Sources:* Individual & corporate solicitations; foundations
1000 volunteer(s)
Membership: 12 affiliates; *Member Profile:* Bereaved parents, bereaved young people & others who wish to support
Activities: Telephone support; One-to-One support; group sessions; family nights; training for volunteers; workshops for health professionals & others; *Speaker Service:* Yes; *Library:* Resource Centre

Cornwall
216 Montreal Rd., Cornwall ON K6H 1B4
Tel: 613-936-1455; *Fax:* 613-936-9689
bfcornwall@on.aibn.com
bfocornwall.ca
www.facebook.com/bfo.cornwall

Durham Region
1050 Simcoe St. North, Oshawa ON L1G 4W5
Tel: 905-579-4293; *Fax:* 905-579-7403
Toll-Free: 800-387-4870
admin@bfodurham.net
www.bfodurham.net
Chief Officer(s):
Gary Goswell, Chair

Halton/Peel
#610, 33 City Centre Dr., Mississauga ON L5B 2N5
Tel: 905-848-4337; *Fax:* 905-848-4338
Toll-Free: 877-826-3566
info@bereavedfamilies.ca
www.bereavedfamilies.ca
Chief Officer(s):
Gay Routhier-Paige, Executive Director
gay.routhier-paige@bereavedfamilies.ca

Hamilton/Burlington
#118, 293 Wellington St. North, Hamilton ON L8L 8E7
Tel: 905-318-0070; *Fax:* 905-318-9181
community@bfo-hamiltonburlington.on.ca
bfo-hamiltonburlington.on.ca
www.facebook.com/147021168642545
twitter.com/bfohb
Chief Officer(s):
Lisa Lesnicki-Young, Executive Director

Kingston
435 Davis Dr., Kingston ON K7M 8L9
Tel: 613-634-1230
bfo@kingston.net
www.bfo-kingston.ca
twitter.com/BFOKingston
Chief Officer(s):
Jenn Fowler, Executive Administrator

Kitchener-Waterloo
PO Box 25017, Kitchener ON N2A 4A5
Tel: 519-603-0196; *Fax:* 519-603-0198
support@bfomidwest.org
www.bfomidwest.org
www.facebook.com/BFOMR
twitter.com/BFOMR
www.pinterest.com/BFOMR
Chief Officer(s):
Rose Greensides, Executive Director
rose@bfomidwest.org

London
#4, 571 Wharncliffe Rd. South, London ON N6J 2N6
Tel: 416-686-1573; *Fax:* 416-686-1573
bflondon@rogers.com
bfolondon.ca
www.facebook.com/bfosw/timeline
Chief Officer(s):
Cathy Walsh, Executive Director

Ottawa Region
#308, 211 Bronson Ave., Ottawa ON K1R 6H5
Tel: 613-567-4278
office@bfo-ottawa.org
www.bfo-ottawa.org
Chief Officer(s):
Deborah Krogan, Program Coordinator

Peterborough
916 Elmdale Cres., Peterborough ON K9H 6G3
Tel: 705-743-7233
Toll-Free: 866-887-2912
bfoptbo@gmail.com
Chief Officer(s):
Gary Beamish, Chair

Toronto
80 Woodlawn Ave. East, Toronto ON M4T 1W6
Tel: 416-440-0290
info@bfotoronto.ca
www.bfotoronto.ca
www.facebook.com/bfotoronto
twitter.com/bfotoronto
www.youtube.com/user/BFOToronto
Chief Officer(s):
Aruna Ogale, Executive Director
aogale@bfotoronto.ca

York Region
#203, 17070 Yonge St., Newmarket ON L3Y 8Z4
Tel: 905-898-6265; *Fax:* 905-898-5870
Toll-Free: 800-969-6904
bfoyr@bellnet.ca
www.bfoyr.com
Chief Officer(s):
Mary Beatson, Executive Director

Bereavement Ontario Network (BON)
174 Oxford St., Woodstock ON N4S 6B1
Tel: 519-266-4747
info@BereavementOntarioNetwork.ca
www.bereavementontarionetwork.ca
Overview: A medium-sized provincial organization
Mission: Bereavement Ontario Network is a diverse group of organizations and individuals throughout the province that work in the field of grief, bereavement, and mourning as professionals and volunteers.
Chief Officer(s):
Janet Devine, Chair, 905-354-2446
ddevine17@cogeco.ca

Meetings/Conferences: • Bereavement Ontario Network 2015 25th Annual Fall Conference, 2015, ON
Scope: Provincial

Bernard Betel Centre for Creative Living
1003 Steeles Ave. West, Toronto ON M2R 3T6
Tel: 416-225-2112; *Fax:* 416-225-2097
reception@betelcentre.org
www.betelcentre.org
Also Known As: Betel Centre
Overview: A small local charitable organization founded in 1965
Mission: To maximize the quality of life for seniors in the community & reflecting Jewish values
Member of: Ontario Community Support Association; Older Adult Centres of Ontario; Association of Ontario Health Centres
Chief Officer(s):
Adam Silver, Executive Director
adams@betelcentre.org
400 volunteer(s)
Membership: 2,000; *Fees:* $18 community; $40 complete; *Member Profile:* Seniors living in the community
Activities: Over 50 recreational, educational & health promotion programs; wellness screening clinics; community support services; kosher meals; *Internships:* Yes

Bertie Historical Society (BHS)
c/o Fort Erie Historical Museum, PO Box 339, Ridgeway ON L0S 1N0
Tel: 905-894-5322; *Fax:* 905-894-6851
museum@forterie.on.ca
Overview: A small local organization founded in 1969
Mission: To operate the Fort Erie Historical Museum
Chief Officer(s):
Earl Plato, Past President, 905-894-5322
earlplato@enoreo.on.ca
Activities: Monthly speakers; annual trip; supports local museum; *Speaker Service:* Yes

Berwick & District Ringette Association
NS
ringette.wordpress.com
Overview: A small local organization overseen by Ringette Nova Scotia
Member of: Ringette Nova Scotia
Chief Officer(s):
Marlene Connell, President
ron.connell@ns.sympatico.ca

Berwick Food Bank
100 South St., Berwick NS B0P 1E0
Tel: 902-538-1996
Overview: A small local organization
Member of: Nova Scotia Food Bank Association; Atlantic Alliance of Food Banks & C.V.A.'s

Berwyn & District Chamber of Commerce
PO Box 144, Berwyn AB T0H 0E0
Tel: 780-338-3668; *Fax:* 780-336-2100
berwynchamber@gmail.com
Overview: A small local organization
Member of: Alberta Chamber of Commerce

Best Buddies Canada (BBC) / Vrais Copains
#923, 1243 Islington Ave., Toronto ON M8X 1Y9
Tel: 416-531-0003; *Fax:* 416-531-0325
Toll-Free: 888-779-0061
info@bestbuddies.ca
www.bestbuddies.ca
www.facebook.com/BestBuddiesCanada
twitter.com/BestBuddiesCND
Overview: A medium-sized national charitable organization founded in 1995
Mission: To enhance our communities through one-to-one friendships between students & people with intellectual disabilities
Member of: Best Buddies International
Chief Officer(s):
Stephon Pinnock, Executive Director, 416-531-0003
sp@bestbuddies.ca
Emily Bolyea-Kyere, Director, Program & Special Events
emily@bestbuddies.ca
Finances: *Funding Sources:* Corporate & individual donations; foundation grants
Staff Member(s): 9
Membership: 80 chapters; 2,000 participants; *Committees:* Fundraising; Program; Gala; Strategic Planning
Activities: Annual gala; *Speaker Service:* Yes

Better Business Bureau of Central & Northern Alberta
16102 - 100 Ave. NW, Edmonton AB T5P 0P3
Tel: 780-482-2341; *Fax:* 780-482-1150
Toll-Free: 800-232-7298
info@edmonton.bbb.org
edmonton.bbb.org
www.facebook.com/BBBCentralandNorthernAlberta
twitter.com/EdmontonBBB
Overview: A medium-sized local organization founded in 1957 overseen by Canadian Council of Better Business Bureaus
Mission: To handle inquiries & complaints; To provide an ad review program; To educate the public
Chief Officer(s):
Chris Lawrence, President & CEO
chris@edmonton.bbb.org
Finances: *Funding Sources:* Membership fees
Staff Member(s): 14
Membership: 3,200; *Fees:* Based on number of employees
Activities: *Speaker Service:* Yes

Better Business Bureau of Eastern & Northern Ontario & the Outaouais / Bureau d'éthique commerciale de l'Est et Nord de l'Ontario et l'Outaouais
#505, 700 Industrial Ave., Ottawa ON K1G 0Y9
Tel: 613-237-4856; *Fax:* 613-237-4878
info@ottawa.bbb.org
ottawa.bbb.org
Overview: A medium-sized local organization founded in 1937 overseen by Canadian Council of Better Business Bureaus
Mission: To promote & foster the highest ethical relationship between business & the public through voluntary self regulation, consumer & business education, & service excellence
Chief Officer(s):
Spencer Nimmons, Vice-President, Business Relations
Finances: *Funding Sources:* Membership fees
Membership: 2,100; *Fees:* $230-850; *Committees:* Governance; Marketing; HR; Finance; Membership
Awards:
• Annual Torch Awards for Marketplace Ethics (Award)

Better Business Bureau of Mainland BC
#404, 788 Beatty St., Vancouver BC V6B 2M1
Tel: 604-682-2711; *Fax:* 604-681-1544
Toll-Free: 888-803-1222
contactus@mbc.bbb.org
mbc.bbb.org
www.linkedin.com/groups?gid=1323147
www.facebook.com/BBBmainlandBC
twitter.com/BBB_BC
Overview: A medium-sized local organization founded in 1939 overseen by Canadian Council of Better Business Bureaus
Mission: To promote, develop & encourage an ethical marketplace
Finances: *Annual Operating Budget:* $500,000-$1.5 Million; *Funding Sources:* Membership dues
Staff Member(s): 20; 24 volunteer(s)
Membership: 4,000; *Fees:* $310+
Activities: *Awareness Events:* Annual "Scam Jam"; *Speaker Service:* Yes

Better Business Bureau of Manitoba & Northwest Ontario
1030B Empress St., Winnipeg MB R3G 3H4
Tel: 204-989-9010; *Fax:* 204-989-9016
Toll-Free: 800-385-3074
Other Communication: Complaints, E-mail: complaints@bbbmb.ca
ceo@bbbmb.ca
manitoba.bbb.org
www.facebook.com/197313847036123
Previous Name: Better Business Bureau of Winnipeg & Manitoba
Overview: A medium-sized provincial organization founded in 1930 overseen by Canadian Council of Better Business Bureaus
Mission: To encourage ethical business practices through self-regulation in Manitoba.
Finances: *Annual Operating Budget:* $250,000-$500,000; *Funding Sources:* Business memberships
Staff Member(s): 6
Membership: 1,000 corporate; *Fees:* $220-$2,000; *Member Profile:* Satisfactory performance as per Better Business Bureau; *Committees:* Executive; Finance; Human Resources; Membership; Public Service

Activities: Business performing reporting; complaint handling; business & consumer information; *Speaker Service:* Yes

Better Business Bureau of Mid-Western & Central Ontario
354 Charles St., Kitchener ON N2G 4L5
Tel: 519-579-3080; *Fax:* 519-570-0072
Toll-Free: 800-459-8875
mwco.bbb.org
www.facebook.com/234049259942145
Previous Name: Better Business Bureau of Mid-Western Ontario
Overview: A medium-sized local organization founded in 1976 overseen by Canadian Council of Better Business Bureaus
Mission: To encourage ethical business practices through self-regulation in Mid-Western Ontario.
Chief Officer(s):
Ric Borski, President
Finances: *Funding Sources:* Membership fees
Staff Member(s): 10
Membership: 2,600; *Fees:* $300 - $800; *Member Profile:* Businesses

Better Business Bureau of Mid-Western Ontario *See* Better Business Bureau of Mid-Western & Central Ontario

Better Business Bureau of Newfoundland *See* Better Business Bureau Serving the Atlantic Provinces

Better Business Bureau of Saskatchewan
980 Albert St., Regina SK S4R 2P7
Tel: 306-352-7601; *Fax:* 306-565-6236
Toll-Free: 888-352-7601
info@bbbsask.com
sask.bbb.org
twitter.com/BBBSask
Also Known As: BBB Serving Saskatchewan
Overview: A medium-sized provincial organization founded in 1981 overseen by Canadian Council of Better Business Bureaus
Mission: To promote & foster high ethical relationships between business & the public through voluntary self-regulation, consumer & business education, & service excellence
Member of: Council of Better Business Bureaus
Chief Officer(s):
Patrick Heffernan, Chief Executive Officer
pheffernan@bbbsask.com
Staff Member(s): 4
Membership: 1100; *Committees:* Governance, Executive, Audit, Accreditation
Activities: Alternative dispute resolution services; Advertising review; Investigation of marketplace practices; Public education about scams & frauds; *Speaker Service:* Yes
Awards:
• Torch Awards (Award)
Given to businesses that show ethical leadership through ongoing social responsibility*Eligibility:* Registered businesses operating in Saskatchewan for 1 year or more*Deadline:* January

Better Business Bureau of Southern Alberta *See* Better Business Bureau Serving Southern Alberta & East Kootenay

Better Business Bureau of the Maritime Provinces; Better Business Bureau of Nova Scotia *See* Better Business Bureau Serving the Atlantic Provinces

Better Business Bureau of Vancouver Island
#220, 1175 Cook St., Victoria BC V8V 4A1
Tel: 250-386-6348; *Fax:* 250-386-2367
Toll-Free: 877-826-4222
Other Communication: Complaints, E-mail: complaints@vi.bbb.org
info@vi.bbb.org
vi.bbb.org
www.linkedin.com/company/better-business-bureau-of-vancouver-island
www.facebook.com/BBBVancouverIsland
twitter.com/VIBBB
www.youtube.com/user/BBBVancouverIsland
Overview: A small local organization founded in 1962 overseen by Canadian Council of Better Business Bureaus
Mission: Committed to the principle that fair dealing is good business for both buyer & seller & the majority of buyers & sellers are honest & responsible
Member of: Council of Better Business Bureaus Virginia
Chief Officer(s):
Vern Fischer, President
Rosalind Scott, Executive Director

Finances: *Annual Operating Budget:* $250,000-$500,000; *Funding Sources:* Membership dues
Staff Member(s): 10; 2 volunteer(s)
Membership: 2,000; *Fees:* $395-895
Activities: Reliability reports; fraud warnings; reliability reports on charitable organizations; arbitration between members & customer(s) involved; *Speaker Service:* Yes

Better Business Bureau of Western Ontario
PO Box 2153, #308, 200 Queens Ave., London ON N6A 4E3
Tel: 519-673-3222
Toll-Free: 877-283-9222
Other Communication: Complaints, E-mail: complaints@westernontario.bbb.org
info@westernontario.bbb.org
westernontario.bbb.org
www.facebook.com/BBBWesternOnt
twitter.com/BBB_Western_Ont
Overview: A medium-sized local licensing organization founded in 1983 overseen by Canadian Council of Better Business Bureaus
Mission: To promote the vitality of the free enterprise system & ethical business practices; To serve the concerns of business & the consuming public
Chief Officer(s):
Jan Delaney, President
jdelaney@westernontario.bbb.org
Chris Lavoie, Manager, Operations
chris@westernontario.bbb.org
Marlene Aquilina-Bock, Coordinator, Business Development
marlene@london.bbb.org
Finances: *Annual Operating Budget:* $250,000-$500,000; *Funding Sources:* Membership dues
Staff Member(s): 6; 18 volunteer(s)
Membership: 1,284; *Fees:* Based on company size; *Member Profile:* For profit business; *Committees:* Membership; Marketing; Executive; Finance; Charitable Review
Activities: *Speaker Service:* Yes
Awards:
• Business Integrity Award (Scholarship)
Includes $2,500 scholarship for post-secondary education to be awarded by the winning company

Better Business Bureau of Windsor & Southwestern Ontario *See* IntegrityLink

Better Business Bureau of Winnipeg & Manitoba *See* Better Business Bureau of Manitoba & Northwest Ontario

Better Business Bureau Serving Southern Alberta & East Kootenay
#350, 7330 Fisher St. SE, Calgary AB T2H 2H8
Tel: 403-531-8784; *Fax:* 403-640-2514
Other Communication: Complaints, E-mail: complaints@calgary.bbb.org
info@calgary.bbb.org
calgary.bbb.org
www.facebook.com/CalgaryBBB
twitter.com/calgarybbb
www.youtube.com/user/BBBServingSouthernAB
Previous Name: Better Business Bureau of Southern Alberta
Overview: A medium-sized local organization founded in 1955 overseen by Canadian Council of Better Business Bureaus
Mission: To promote & encourage ethical practices in retail market for goods & services through provision of a wide range of consultative, informative & conciliatory arbitration services for businesses & consumers.
Finances: *Annual Operating Budget:* $500,000-$1.5 Million; *Funding Sources:* Membership fees
Staff Member(s): 20; 10 volunteer(s)
Membership: 3,000; *Fees:* $395 base fee; *Member Profile:* Company free of legal or ethical transgressions; *Committees:* Executive; Board of Directors
Activities: Ethics Award; *Speaker Service:* Yes
Awards:
• Ethics Awards (Award)

Better Business Bureau Serving the Atlantic Provinces
#303, 1888 Brunswick St., Halifax NS B3J 3J8
Tel: 902-422-6581; *Fax:* 902-429-6457
Toll-Free: 877-663-2363
info@ap.bbb.org
atlanticprovinces.bbb.org
Previous Name: Better Business Bureau of Newfoundland
Overview: A medium-sized provincial organization overseen by Canadian Council of Better Business Bureaus
Mission: To promote and foster the highest ethical relationships between business and the public through voluntary self-regulation, consumer and business education and service excellence
Member of: BBB
Chief Officer(s):
J. Colin Dodds, Chair
Staff Member(s): 2

Better Business Bureau Serving the Atlantic Provinces
#303, 1888 Brunswick St., Halifax NS B3J 3J8
Tel: 902-422-6581; *Fax:* 902-429-6457
Toll-Free: 877-663-2363
info@ap.bbb.org
atlanticprovinces.bbb.org
www.facebook.com/300802543311820
twitter.com/BBBAtlantic
Previous Name: Better Business Bureau of the Maritime Provinces; Better Business Bureau of Nova Scotia
Overview: A medium-sized provincial organization founded in 1949 overseen by Canadian Council of Better Business Bureaus
Mission: To provide mutually beneficial relationships between buyer & seller based on responsible business practices
Chief Officer(s):
Don MacKinnon, President
Finances: *Annual Operating Budget:* $250,000-$500,000; *Funding Sources:* Membership dues
Staff Member(s): 13; 75 volunteer(s)
Membership: 1,400

Bi Unité Montréal (BUM)
CP 476, Succ. C, Montréal QC H2L 4K4
info@biunitemontreal.org
www.algi.qc.ca/asso/bum/
Aperçu: *Dimension:* petite; *Envergure:* locale
Mission: Association à but non lucratif; a pour mission de fair connaître la bisexualité et de rassembler les bisexuel(le)s dans un lieu commun pour qu'ils/qu'elles puissent s'informer, se divertir, et se supporter.

Biathlon Alberta
Bob Niven Training Centre, #102, 88 Canada Olympic Rd. SW, Calgary AB T3B 5R5
Tel: 403-202-6548
info@biathlon.ca
www.biathlon.ca
www.facebook.com/588814881135031
Overview: A small provincial organization founded in 1980 overseen by Biathlon Canada
Mission: To promote, develop & maintain biathlon in Alberta
Member of: Biathlon Canada; Alberta Ski & Snowboard Association
Chief Officer(s):
Ken Davies, President
Andy Holmwood, Executive Director
andy@biathlon.ca
Finances: *Annual Operating Budget:* $100,000-$250,000
Staff Member(s): 2; 300 volunteer(s)
Membership: 12 clubs + 357 individual; *Fees:* $55 Junior; $90 Senior

Biathlon BC
PO Box 2922, Garibaldi Highlands BC V0N 1T0
biathlonbc.ca
Overview: A small provincial organization overseen by Biathlon Canada
Mission: To promote Biathlon throughout British Columbia as a recreational & competitive sport.
Member of: Biathlon Canada
Membership: *Fees:* Schedule available

Biathlon Canada
#111, 2197 Riverside Dr., Ottawa ON K1H 7X3
Tel: 613-748-5608; *Fax:* 613-748-5762
info@biathloncanada.ca
www.biathloncanada.ca
www.facebook.com/BiathlonCanada
twitter.com/biathloncanada
Overview: A medium-sized national charitable organization founded in 1976
Mission: To act as the governing body for the sport of biathlon in Canada
Affiliation(s): International Biathlon Union; Canadian Olympic Committee
Chief Officer(s):
Joanne Thomson, Executive Director
jthomson@biathloncanada.ca
Finances: *Funding Sources:* Sport Canada; Canadian Olympic Committee (COC); International Biathlon Union (IBU); Coaching Association of Canada (CAC)
Staff Member(s): 8
Membership: *Fees:* Schedule available; *Committees:* Human Resources & Compensation; Finance & Audit; Biathlon Canada Officials; Biathlon Canada Coaching

Biathlon Manitoba
Sport for Life Centre, 145 Pacific Ave., Winnipeg MB R3B 2Z6
Tel: 204-925-5687
biathlon@sportmanitoba.ca
biathlonmanitoba.ca
www.facebook.com/biathlonmanitoba
twitter.com/BiathlonMB
Overview: A small provincial organization overseen by Biathlon Canada
Mission: To promote the sport of biathlon in Manitoba.
Member of: Biathlon Canada
Chief Officer(s):
Brian Walters, Executive Director

Biathlon Newfoundland & Labrador
Mount Pearl NL
e-mail: info@biathlonnl.ca
www.biathlonnl.ca
www.facebook.com/biathlonnl
twitter.com/biathlonnl
Overview: A small provincial organization overseen by Biathlon Canada
Mission: To govern the sport of biathlon in Newfoundland & Labrador, both competitively & recreationally.
Member of: Biathlon Canada
Chief Officer(s):
Gary Dawson, Contact
Membership: 3 clubs; *Fees:* Schedule available

Biathlon Nouveau-New Brunswick
11051 Hwy. 430, Trout Brook NB E9E 1R5
Tel: 506-627-6437
biathlon@biathlonnb.ca
www.biathlonnb.ca
Also Known As: Biathlon NB
Overview: A small provincial organization overseen by Biathlon Canada
Mission: To govern the sport of biathlon in New Brunswick.
Member of: Biathlon Canada
Chief Officer(s):
Ray Kokkonen, President
kokkonen@nbnet.nb.ca
Lisa Belliveau, Secretary, 506-854-0524
ddsally@yahoo.com
Paula Septon, Treasurer, 506-622-8047
Membership: *Fees:* Schedule available; *Committees:* Marketing & Fundraising; Coaching Development; Membership; Officials

Biathlon Nova Scotia
c/o Sport Nova Scotia, 5516 Spring Garden Rd., Halifax NS B3J 1G6
Tel: 902-425-5454; *Fax:* 902-425-5606
admin@biathlonns.ca
www.biathlonns.ca
www.facebook.com/biathlonns
Overview: A small provincial organization overseen by Biathlon Canada
Mission: To govern the sport of biathlon in Nova Scotia.
Member of: Biathlon Canada
Chief Officer(s):
Bruce Jarvis, President
Membership: *Fees:* Schedule available; *Committees:* Marketing; Fundraising; Technical; Officials

Biathlon Ontario
61 Kayla Cres., Collingwood ON L9Y 5K8
www.biathlonontario.ca
Also Known As: BiON
Overview: A small provincial organization overseen by Biathlon Canada
Mission: To govern the sport of biathlon in the Northwest Territories; to encourage physical activity & community through sport
Member of: Biathlon Canada
Chief Officer(s):
Mike Scholte, President
mikescholte@rogers.com

Greg Dalton, Vice-President, Member & Club Relations
gdalton@tribsys.com
Daniel Guay, Secretary
dsguay@lakesuperiorbiathlon.com
Membership: 7 clubs

Biathlon PEI
2759 Glasgow Rd., Hunter River PE C0A 1N0
Tel: 902-964-3294
Other Communication: Alt. Phone: 902-314-2587
biathlonpei@gmail.com
www.biathlonpei.com
Overview: A small provincial organization founded in 2005 overseen by Biathlon Canada
Mission: To govern the sport of biathlon in Prince Edward Island.
Member of: Biathlon Canada; Sport PEI Inc.
Chief Officer(s):
Bob Bentley, President
Steve Woodman, Secretary, 902-566-8003
steven.woodman@vac-acc.gc.ca
Activities: Programs for athletes of all levels

Biathlon Saskatchewan
1860 Lorne St., Regina SK S4P 2L7
Tel: 306-780-9236; *Fax:* 306-780-9462
sask.ski@sasktel.net
biathlon.sasktelwebhosting.com
Overview: A small provincial organization founded in 2005 overseen by Biathlon Canada
Mission: To govern the sport of biathlon in Saskatchewan.
Member of: Biathlon Canada
Chief Officer(s):
Alana Ottenbreit, Contact
Membership: 6 clubs

Biathlon Yukon
PO Box 31673, Whitehorse YT Y1A 6L3
Tel: 867-633-5717
biathlonyukon@gmail.com
www.biathlonyukon.org
Overview: A small provincial organization overseen by Biathlon Canada
Mission: To enhance opportunities for all Yukon persons in their pursuit of excellence & in their enjoyment of participation in biathlon
Member of: Biathlon Canada; Sport Yukon
Chief Officer(s):
Bill Curtis, President
Membership: *Fees:* $50

The Bible Holiness Mission *See* The Bible Holiness Movement

The Bible Holiness Movement / Mouvement de sainteté biblique
PO Box 223, Stn. A, Vancouver BC V6C 2M3
Tel: 250-492-3376
www.bible-holiness-movement.com
Previous Name: The Bible Holiness Mission
Overview: A medium-sized international charitable organization founded in 1949
Mission: To emphasize the original Methodist faith of salvation & scriptural holiness, with principles of discipline, non-conformity, & non-resistance, & to administer overseas indigenous missionary centres in West Africa, the Philippines, East Africa, & the West Indies; South Korea, India
Member of: Christian Holiness Partnership; National Black Evangelical Association; Anti-Slavery International
Affliation(s): Religious Freedom of Council of Christian Minorities; Christians Concerned for Racial Equality
Chief Officer(s):
Wesley H. Wakefield, Bishop-General
Finances: *Annual Operating Budget:* $100,000-$250,000; *Funding Sources:* Unsolicited gifts from Christian believers
Staff Member(s): 16; 6 volunteer(s)
Membership: 93,658 worldwide in 89 countries; 954 Canadian; *Fees:* None
Activities: *Internships:* Yes; *Speaker Service:* Yes; *Library* by appointment
Publications:
• Hallelujah Magazine
Type: Magazine; *Frequency:* Bimonthly; *Editor:* Wesley H. Wakefield

The Bible League of Canada / Société canadienne pour la distribution de la Bible
PO Box 368, 399 Main Street West, Grimsby ON L3M 4H8
Tel: 905-319-9500; *Fax:* 905-319-0484
Toll-Free: 800-363-9673
www.bibleleague.ca
www.facebook.com/140398061327
www.twitter.com/BibleLeagueCan
Previous Name: World Home Bible League
Overview: A large international charitable organization founded in 1949
Mission: To introduce people to Jesus Christ; to spread God's Word worldwide
Member of: Canadian Council of Christian Charities; International Association of Bible Leagues
Affliation(s): The Bible League
Chief Officer(s):
Paul Richardson, President
Finances: *Annual Operating Budget:* $3 Million-$5 Million; *Funding Sources:* Donations
Staff Member(s): 15
Activities: *Speaker Service:* Yes
Awards:
• Bible League Canada Grants (Grant)
Bible League Canada Grants for Canadians are awarded primarily based on a needs criteria and the completion of a grant application form. Eligibility: Needs-based criteria & completion of a grant application form.
Publications:
• Joy Report
Type: Newsletter; *Frequency:* Quarterly

Bibles & Literature in French Canada (BLF)
256, Marc-Aurele-Fortin, Lachute QC J8H 3W7
Tél: 450-562-7859; *Téléc:* 450-562-7859
info@blfcanada.org
www.blfcanada.org
Également appelé: BLF Canada
Aperçu: *Dimension:* petite; *Envergure:* nationale
Mission: BLF Canada distribue une littérature de qualité afin de permettre de présenter, à ces millions de Canadiens, celui qui seul peut leur apporter la vraie vie.
Membre(s) du bureau directeur:
Toe-Blake Roy, Director
toeblake@blfcanada.org

Bibles for Missions Foundation (BFM)
Head Office, 45515 Knight Rd., Chilliwack BC V2R 5L2
Tel: 604-858-4980; *Fax:* 604-858-4334
Toll-Free: 855-204-4980
admin@bfmthriftstores.ca
www.bfmthriftstores.ca
www.facebook.com/279261462189925
twitter.com/bfmfred
Overview: A large international charitable organization founded in 1989
Mission: To operates thrift stores across Canada to generate funds for Bible League Canada
Member of: The Bible League of Canada (TBLC)
Chief Officer(s):
Casey Langbroek, Executive Director
Finances: *Funding Sources:* Donations

Bibliographical Society of Canada (BSC) / Société bibliographique du Canada (SBC)
PO Box 19035, Stn. Walmer, 360 Bloor St. West, Toronto ON M5S 3C9
e-mail: secretary@bsc-sbc.ca
www.bsc-sbc.ca
www.facebook.com/207539352655326
Overview: A small national organization founded in 1946
Mission: To encourage the learning & practice of bibliography; To further the study, research & publication of book history & print culture; To promote preservation & conservation of archival & published materials
Chief Officer(s):
Janet Friskney, President
Greta Golick, Secretary
secretary@bsc-sbc.ca
Membership: *Fees:* $80; *Member Profile:* Support & participate in bibliographical research & publication; *Committees:* Communications; Awards; Fellowships
Meetings/Conferences: • Bibliographical Society of Canada 2015 Annual General Meeting, July, 2015, Montreal, QC
Scope: National
• Bibliographical Society of Canada 2016 Annual General Meeting, May, 2016, University of Calgary, Calgary, AB
Scope: National
• Bibliographical Society of Canada 2017 Annual General Meeting, May, 2017, Ryerson University, Toronto, ON
Scope: National
Publications:
• Bulletin
Type: Newsletter; *Frequency:* Twice annually; *Editor:* John Shoesmith *ISSN:* 0709-3756
Profile: Society news
• Papers of the Bibliographical Society of Canada
Type: Journal; *Frequency:* Semi-annually *ISSN:* 0067-6896
Profile: Papers submitted by any scholar studying bibliography

Les bibliothèques publiques des régions de Québec et Chaudière-Appalaches
4705, rue de la Promenade-des-Soeurs, Cap-Rouge QC G1Y 2W2
Tél: 418-641-6143; *Téléc:* 418-650-7795
www.bibliotheques.qc.ca
Aperçu: *Dimension:* moyenne; *Envergure:* locale; Organisme sans but lucratif; fondée en 1989
Mission: Regrouper les responsables des bibliothèques publiques de ces régions; promouvoir et défendre les intérêts de ces bibliothèques; représenter le secteur des bibliothèques publiques des ces régions au sein des organismes à caractères culturel et social.
Membre de: Bibliothèques publiques du Québec
Membre(s) du bureau directeur:
Suzanne Rochefort, Présidente
srochefort@ville.levis.qc.ca
Finances: *Budget de fonctionnement annuel:* Moins de $50,000
5 bénévole(s)
Membre: 9; *Montant de la cotisation:* 85$; *Critères d'admissibilite:* Bibliothèques publiques du Québec; *Comités:* Catalogue collectif régional sur l'Internet

Bibliothèques publiques du Bas-Saint-Laurent
67, Du Rocher, Rivière-du-Loup QC G5R 1J8
Tél: 418-862-4252; *Téléc:* 418-862-3478
yves.savard@ville.riviere-du-loup.qc.ca
Aperçu: *Dimension:* moyenne; *Envergure:* locale
Mission: Défense des intérêts des bibliothèques publiques; promotion de la lecture
Membre(s) du bureau directeur:
Cadieux Geneviève, Président
genevieve.cadieux@ville.riviere-du-loup.qc.ca
Marie Côté, Sec.-trés.
Finances: *Budget de fonctionnement annuel:* Moins de $50,000
Membre: 6 bibliothèques; *Montant de la cotisation:* 100$

Les bibliothèques publiques du Québec; Association des directeurs de bibliothèques publiques du Québec *Voir* Association des bibliothèques publiques du Québec

Bicycle Newfoundland & Labrador
NL
Tel: 709-576-3397
admin@bnl.nf.ca
www.bnl.nf.ca
www.facebook.com/BicycleNL
twitter.com/BicycleNL
Overview: A small provincial organization overseen by Cycling Canada Cyclisme
Chief Officer(s):
Scott Humber, President
president@bnl.nf.ca
Natelle Tulk, Executive Director
Membership: *Fees:* $30 general; $50 under-17 racing; $70 adult racing license

Bicycle Nova Scotia (BNS)
5516 Spring Garden Rd., 4th Fl., Halifax NS B3J 1G6
Tel: 902-425-5454; *Fax:* 902-425-5606
staff@bicycle.ns.ca
www.bicycle.ns.ca
www.facebook.com/181794321832620
twitter.com/bicyclens
Overview: A small provincial organization overseen by Cycling Canada Cyclisme
Mission: To act as the governmnent body for cycling in Nova Scotia & to advocate for on & off road cycling
Member of: Canadian Cycling Association
Chief Officer(s):
Jamie Lamb, President
president@bicycle.ns.ca
Membership: *Fees:* $15 supporting; $30 general; $110 club
Activities: All aspects of cycling in Nova Scotia;

Bicycle Trade Association of Canada (BTAC) / Association canadienne de l'industrie du vélo (ACIV)
PO Box 72, 202 Church St., Keswick ON L4P 3E1
Fax: 866-898-3320
Toll-Free: 866-528-2822
info@btac.org
www.btac.org
www.facebook.com/BTACanada
twitter.com/BTACanada
Overview: A small national organization founded in 2001
Mission: To represent its members & their interests at various levels of the government
Chief Officer(s):
Bill Yetman, Executive Director, 416-427-2870
byetman@btac.org
Finances: *Annual Operating Budget:* $500,000-$1.5 Million; *Funding Sources:* Membership fees; Trade show revenue; Publications revenue
Staff Member(s): 3
Membership: *Fees:* $300 associate; $197.75 retail; $425-$1550 supplier; *Member Profile:* Retailers & suppliers
Activities: *Rents Mailing List:* Yes
Awards:
• BTAC Grant (Grant)
Gives priority to projects that advance BTAC's mission *Contact:* Bill Yetman, byetman@btac.org
Publications:
• Bike Connexions
Type: Magazine; *Frequency:* Quarterly

Bicycling Association of BC *See* Cycling British Columbia

Bide Awhile Animal Shelter Society
PO Box 50029, Stn. Southdale, 67 Neptune Cres., Dartmouth NS B2Y 4S2
Tel: 902-469-9578; *Fax:* 902-463-6173
bideawhile@bideawhile.org
www.bideawhile.org
www.facebook.com/bideawhile
twitter.com/bideawhile
Overview: A small local charitable organization founded in 1969
Mission: To rescue & care for abandoned animals with the hope of rehoming them; to promote spaying & neutering; to cultivate respect for animals through outreach.
Member of: Canadian Federation of Humane Societies
Chief Officer(s):
Nancy Mansfield, President
nancy.mansfield@bellaliant.net
Darrold Gould, Executive Director
darroldgould@bideawhile.org
Finances: *Funding Sources:* Donations; small businesses; calendar sales
Membership: 500-999; *Fees:* $10 student/senior; $25 individual; $45 family; $135 patron; $200 bronze; $400 silver; $600 gold
Activities: Spook's Memorial Kitty Fund; Pet of the Day Contest

La Biennale de Montréal
460, rue Sainte-Catherine Ouest, Bureau 304, Montréal QC H3B 1A7
Tél: 514-521-7340
info@biennalemontreal.org
www.biennalemontreal.org
Aperçu: *Dimension:* petite; *Envergure:* locale
Mission: D'analyser la relation que existe entre les pratiques en art contemporain et les discours historiques sur le futur, d'une part, et nos modes de projection actuels dans l'avenir.
Membre(s) du bureau directeur:
Lydie Bochatay, Adjointe à la direction
lydie.bochatay@biennalemontreal.org

Big Brothers & Big Sisters of Québec *Voir* Association des Grands Frères et Grandes Soeurs de Québec

Big Brothers & Big Sisters of Toronto
#501, 2345 Yonge St., Toronto ON M4P 2E5
Tel: 416-925-8981; *Fax:* 416-925-4671
www.bbbst.com
www.linkedin.com/company/big-brothers-big-sisters-of-toronto
www.facebook.com/BigBrothersBigSistersToronto
twitter.com/BBBSToronto
www.youtube.com/user/bike4tykes
Overview: A small local charitable organization founded in 1920
Mission: To promote positive growth in children & youths with distinct needs, by matching them one-to-one with mature, caring adult volunteers.
Affliation(s): Big Brothers Big Sisters of Canada; Big Sisters Association of Ontario
Chief Officer(s):
David Sturdee, Chair
Cathy Denyer, President & CEO
cathy.denyer@bigbrothersbigsisters.ca
Finances: *Annual Operating Budget:* $3 Million-$5 Million; *Funding Sources:* United Way; special events; corporate foundations; individuals
Staff Member(s): 34
Membership: *Member Profile:* Active volunteers
Activities: Bowl for Kids' Sake; The Big Ski; Volunteer Recognition Night; Gourmet Dinner; Media Dimensions Golf Tournament; Iron Man Golf; Soap Box Derby; Corporate Recognition Night; Celebrity Rally; Ultimate Pro Am; Littles Holiday Party; E-mentoring; In-School Mentoring Program; Co-op Program; In-School Newcomer Program; Group Program; Original Program; *Awareness Events:* Bay Street Hoops, Mar.; Molson Indy Remote Car Race, July; BBBS Day at the Blue Jays, Aug; Recruitment Month, Sept.; BBBS Day at the Raptors, April; *Internships:* Yes; *Speaker Service:* Yes

Big Brothers & Sisters of Kings & Annapolis Counties *See* Big Brothers Sisters of Annapolis County

Big Brothers Big Sisters Edmonton & Area
10135 - 89 St., Edmonton AB T5H 1P6
Tel: 780-424-8181; *Fax:* 780-426-6689
Toll-Free: 855-424-8181
general@bgcbigs.ca
bgcbigs.ca
www.facebook.com/BGCBigs
twitter.com/BGCBigs
Overview: A small local charitable organization
Mission: To ensure the healthy development of children and their families through professionally supported volunteer mentoring relationships
Affliation(s): Big Brothers Big Sisters of Canada; United Way, Alberta Capital Region; Boys & Girls Clubs of Edmonton & Area
Chief Officer(s):
Kelly Micetich, President
Finances: *Funding Sources:* provincial government; school boards; charitable foundations, local businesses
Activities: Summer camp; golf tournaments

Big Brothers Big Sisters of Antigonish
PO Box 781, New Glasgow NS B2H 5G2
Tel: 902-863-5332; *Fax:* 902-752-6262
bigbrothers@eastlink.ca
www.bbbsofanti.com
www.facebook.com/BigBrothersBigSistersPictouCounty
twitter.com/bbbspc
Overview: A small local organization
Affliation(s): Big Brothers Big Sisters of Canada
Chief Officer(s):
George Cameron, President
Margie Grant-Walsh, Executive Director
margie.grantwalsh@bigbrothersbigsisters.ca
Staff Member(s): 3

Big Brothers Big Sisters of Barrie & District
PO Box 261, 168 Bayfield St., Barrie ON L4M 4T2
Tel: 705-728-0515; *Fax:* 705-728-2965
mentor@bbbsbarrie.com
www.bigbrothersbigsisters.ca/barrie
www.facebook.com/216393495057704
twitter.com/BBBSBarrie
Previous Name: Big Sisters Association of Barrie & District
Overview: A small local organization founded in 1975
Mission: To provide the children ages 6-16 the chance to experience fun & friendship through mentoring relationships with adult volunteers
Affliation(s): Big Brothers Big Sisters of Canada
Chief Officer(s):
Brian Kennedy, President
Marianne Arbour, Executive Director
marianne.arbour@bigbrothersbigsisters.ca
Finances: *Funding Sources:* Regional government
Staff Member(s): 5
Activities: Bowl, Curl & Golf for Kids' Sake; *Rents Mailing List:* Yes

Big Brothers Big Sisters of Calgary & Area
5945 Centre St. SW, Calgary AB T2H 0C2
Tel: 403-777-3535; *Fax:* 403-777-3525
bbbs.calgary@bigbrothersbigsisters.ca
www.bbbscalgary.com
www.facebook.com/BBBSCalgary
twitter.com/BBBSCalgary
Overview: A small local charitable organization founded in 1994
Mission: To enrich the lives of children in need through mentoring
Affliation(s): Big Brothers Big Sisters of Canada
Chief Officer(s):
Richard Brown, Chair
Trish Bronsch, President & CEO
Finances: *Annual Operating Budget:* $3 Million-$5 Million
2359 volunteer(s)
Membership: *Member Profile:* Volunteers; in-school mentors; parents; members of Canadian Progress Clubs of Calgary
Activities: Bowl 4 Kids; provincial lottery; Quarterback Luncheon

Big Brothers Big Sisters of Canada (BBBSC) / Les Grands Frères Grandes Soeurs du Canada
#113E, 3228 South Service Rd., Burlington ON L7N 3H8
Tel: 905-639-0461; *Fax:* 905-639-0124
Toll-Free: 800-263-9133
www.bigbrothersbigsisters.ca
www.facebook.com/bigbrothersbigsistersofcanada
twitter.com/bbbsc
www.youtube.com/bbbscanada
Overview: A medium-sized national charitable organization founded in 1981
Mission: To provide leadership to member agencies as they develop programs to meet the changing needs of young people
Chief Officer(s):
Bruce MacDonald, President & CEP
bruce.macdonald@bigbrothersbigsisters.ca
Finances: *Funding Sources:* Private corporations; public donations
Membership: 118 agencies
Activities: *Library:* Resource Centre; by appointment

Big Brothers Big Sisters of Chatham-Kent
137 Queen St., Chatham ON N7M 1G7
Tel: 519-351-1582; *Fax:* 519-351-1621
www.bigbrothersbigsistersofchatham-kent.com
www.facebook.com/bbbsck
twitter.com/bbbsck
Previous Name: Chatham-Kent Big Sisters Association Inc.
Overview: A small local organization
Mission: To match girls and boys between the ages of 6 & 16 with volunteers at least 19 years of age to provide a special friend and mentor
Affliation(s): Big Brothers Big Sisters of Canada; United Way; Goodlife Kids Foundation
Chief Officer(s):
Tammy Mungar, President
Nan Stuckey, Executive Director
nan.stuckey@bigbrothersbigsisters.ca
Staff Member(s): 5

Big Brothers Big Sisters of Eastern Newfoundland
The Village Shopping Centre, PO Box 10, 430 Topsail Rd., St. John's NL A1E 4N1
Tel: 709-368-5437; *Fax:* 709-368-5477
Toll-Free: 877-513-5437
info@helpingkids.ca
www.helpingkids.ca
Previous Name: Big Brothers/Big Sisters of St. John's Mount Pearl
Overview: A small local charitable organization founded in 1975
Mission: To provide quality mentoring programs to children & youth
Affliation(s): Big Brothers Big Sisters of Canada
Chief Officer(s):
Peter Ringrose, Chair
Kelly Leach, Executive Director
kelly@helpingkids.ca
Staff Member(s): 8
Membership: 100-499
Activities: *Awareness Events:* Bowl for Kids' Sake; Rally for the Kids; *Internships:* Yes; *Speaker Service:* Yes

Big Brothers Big Sisters of Greater Halifax
PO Box 307, 86 Ochterloney St., Dartmouth NS B2Y 3Y5
Tel: 902-466-5437; *Fax:* 902-465-4281
halifax@bigbrothersbigsisters.ca
www.bigbrothersbigsistershalifax.ca
www.facebook.com/BBBSHalifax
twitter.com/bbbshalifax
www.youtube.com/user/BBBSHalifax
Overview: A small local charitable organization founded in 1967

Mission: To pair children with adult mentors for friendship, support & guidance
Affliation(s): Big Brothers Big Sisters of Canada
Chief Officer(s):
Chris Lydon, Chair
Carol Goddard, Executive Director
carol.goddard@bigbrothersbigsisters.ca
Staff Member(s): 18
Activities: Bowl for Kids' Sake; Golf Classic; auctions, BBQs

Big Brothers Big Sisters of Miramichi
115 Maher St., Miramichi NB E1N 4B4
Tel: 506-778-2444; *Fax:* 506-778-1855
yvillage@nbnet.nb.ca
www.bbbsmiramichi.com
www.facebook.com/miramichibbbs
Overview: A small local charitable organization
Affliation(s): Big Brothers Big Sisters Canada
Chief Officer(s):
Greg MacDonald, Chair
Sheree A. Allison, Executive Director
Finances: *Annual Operating Budget:* $500,000-$1.5 Million
Staff Member(s): 2

Big Brothers Big Sisters of Moncton
20 Brandon St., Moncton NB E1C 7E6
Tel: 506-857-3047; *Fax:* 506-857-0929
www.bigbrothersbigsisters.ca/moncton
www.facebook.com/BigBrothersBigSistersMoncton
www.pinterest.com/MonctonBBBS
Overview: A small local charitable organization
Mission: To pair children with adult mentors for friendship, support & guidance
Affliation(s): Big Brothers Big Sisters of Canada
Chief Officer(s):
Brett Murphy, President
Peter MacDonald, Executive Director
peter.macdonald@bigbrothersbigsisters.ca
Staff Member(s): 4
Activities: Bowl for Kids' Sake, Cruise to the Bay, golf, magic show

Big Brothers Big Sisters of Morden-Winkler
ALG Professional Centre, PO Box 450, 309 Main St., Winkler MB R6W 4A6
Tel: 204-325-9707; *Fax:* 204-326-6308
www.bigbrothersbigsisters.ca/mordenwinkler
Overview: A small local charitable organization
Affliation(s): Big Brothers Big Sisters of Canada
Chief Officer(s):
Michael Penner, Executive Director
michael.penner@bigbrothersbigsisters.ca
Activities: Bowl for Kids Sake Campaign; Golf for Kids' Sake

Big Brothers Big Sisters of Pictou County
PO Box 781, 74 Stellarton Rd., New Glasgow NS B2H 5G2
Tel: 902-752-6260; *Fax:* 902-752-6262
bigbrothers@eastlink.ca
www.bbbsofpc.com
Overview: A small local organization founded in 1980
Mission: To provide professional services for children primarily of single-parent families
Affliation(s): Big Brothers Big Sisters of Canada; Atlantic Staff Association
Chief Officer(s):
George Cameron, President
Margie Grant-Walsh, Executive Director
margie.grantwalsh@bigbrothersbigsisters.ca
Finances: *Annual Operating Budget:* $100,000-$250,000; *Funding Sources:* Provincial government
Staff Member(s): 3

Big Brothers Big Sisters of Portage la Prairie
234 Princess Ave., Portage la Prairie MB R1N 0R1
Tel: 204-857-4397
www.bigbrothersbigsisters.ca/portage
Overview: A small local charitable organization founded in 1974
Mission: To foster one to one relationships between adults & children 6-18 years old who live in single-parent homes. To develop friendship & mentoring through the companionship of one or more adults
Affliation(s): Big Brothers Big Sisters of Canada
Chief Officer(s):
Jan Halmarson, President
Dawn Froese, Executive Director
Finances: *Annual Operating Budget:* $100,000-$250,000; *Funding Sources:* Provincial government; United Way; fundraising
Staff Member(s): 2
Membership: *Committees:* Finance; Organizational; Programming
Activities: Bowl for Kids; *Awareness Events:* Bowl for Kids' Sake, Mar.; *Speaker Service:* Yes

Big Brothers Big Sisters of Prince Edward Island
2 St. Peters Rd., Charlottetown PE C1A 5N2
Tel: 902-569-5437; *Fax:* 902-892-5593
Toll-Free: 877-411-3729
www.bigbrothersbigsisterspei.org
www.linkedin.com/company/big-brothers-big-sisters-of-prince-edward-isl
www.facebook.com/pages/Big-Brothers-Big-Sisters-PEI/148802489018
twitter.com/BBBSPEI
www.pinterest.com/bbbspei
Overview: A medium-sized provincial organization founded in 1975
Affliation(s): Big Brothers Big Sisters of Canada
Chief Officer(s):
Peter Russell, Chair
Myron Yates, Executive Director
myron.yates@bigbrothersbigsisters.ca
Staff Member(s): 6

Big Brothers Big Sisters of Prince George
777 Kinsmen Pl., Prince George BC V2M 6Y7
Tel: 250-563-7410; *Fax:* 250-564-5217
reception@bbbspg.ca
www.bbbspg.ca
www.facebook.com/bbbspg
twitter.com/bbbspg
instagram.com/bbbspg
Overview: A small local organization founded in 1968
Mission: To enhance the resiliency of children, of families & of our community
Affliation(s): Big Brothers Big Sisters of Canada
Chief Officer(s):
Wende Bracklow, President
Tim Bennett, Executive Director
Finances: *Funding Sources:* Municipal government; provincial government; fundraising
Staff Member(s): 12

Big Brothers Big Sisters of Saskatoon
182 Wall St., Saskatoon SK S7K 1N4
Tel: 306-244-8197; *Fax:* 306-244-4171
office@bbbssaskatoon.org
www.bbbssaskatoon.org
www.facebook.com/BBBSSaskatoon
twitter.com/BBBSSaskatoon
Overview: A small local charitable organization
Mission: To match adult volteer mentors with children & youth in the Saskatoon, Saskatchewan area
Member of: Big Brothers Big Sisters of Canada; United Way of Saskatoon
Staff Member(s): 12
Activities: *Internships:* Yes; *Speaker Service:* Yes

Big Brothers Big Sisters of South Niagara
Seaway Mall, Upper Level, 800 Niagara St., Welland ON L3C 5Z4
Tel: 905-735-0570; *Fax:* 905-735-2122
admin.southniagara@bigbrothersbigsisters.ca
www.bbbsinniagara.ca
www.facebook.com/bigbrothersbigsistersn
twitter.com/BBBS_SNiagara
Overview: A small local organization founded in 1964
Mission: To provide friendship & guidance for children 6 to 18 years of age, through matching them with volunteer adults to act as role models & mentors
Affliation(s): Big Brothers Big Sisters of Canada; United Way
Chief Officer(s):
Barb Van Der Heyden, Executive Director
barb.vanderheyden@bigbrothersbigsisters.ca
Staff Member(s): 5

Big Brothers Big Sisters of the Okanagan
#102, 151 Commercial Dr., Kelowna BC V1X 7W2
Tel: 250-765-2661
Toll-Free: 800-404-4483
www.bigs.bc.ca
www.facebook.com/BigBrothersBigSistersOkanagan
twitter.com/BBBSOkanagan
Overview: A small local charitable organization
Mission: To help children reach their potential and become self sufficient members of society through professionally supported, one-to-one relationships with mentors; communities served include: Kelowna, Osoyoos, Salmon Arm, Vernon, Enderby
Affliation(s): Big Brothers Big Sisters of Canada
Chief Officer(s):
Bryn Gilbert, President
Lisa Hobson, Executive Director
lisa.hobson@bigbrothersbigsisters.ca
Staff Member(s): 4

Big Brothers Big Sisters of Thunder Bay
559 South Syndicate Ave., Thunder Bay ON P7E 1E6
Tel: 807-623-1112; *Fax:* 807-622-5244
bbbsa@tbaytel.net
www.thunderbaybigbrotherbigsister.ca
www.facebook.com/bigbrothersbigsistersofthunderbay
twitter.com/BBBSThunderBay
Overview: A small local charitable organization founded in 1970
Mission: To pair children with adult mentors for friendship, support & guidance
Affliation(s): Big Brothers Big Sisters of Canada
Chief Officer(s):
Jennifer Bencharski, President
Casey Farrell, Interim Executive Director
Staff Member(s): 4
Activities: Bowl for Kids' Sake

Big Brothers Big Sisters of Victoria
230 Bay St., Victoria BC V9A 3K5
Tel: 250-475-1117; *Fax:* 250-475-1197
Toll-Free: 877-475-1114
reception.victoria@bigbrothersbigsisters.ca
www.bbbsvictoria.com
www.facebook.com/bbbsvictoria
twitter.com/bbbs_victoria
pinterest.com/bbbsvictoria
Overview: A small local organization
Mission: To build confidence, resiliency and self-esteem in children by pairing them with adult mentors
Affliation(s): Big Brothers Big Sisters of Canada; United Way
Chief Officer(s):
Sheila Elworthy, President
Rhonda Brown, Executive Director
rhonda.brown@bigbrothersbigsisters.ca
Finances: *Funding Sources:* BC Gaming; fundraising; donations; grants; subsidies; United Way
Staff Member(s): 15

Big Brothers Big Sisters of Winnipeg
765 Portage Ave., Winnipeg MB R3G 0N2
Tel: 204-988-9200; *Fax:* 204-988-9208
main@bigwinnipeg.com
www.bigwinnipeg.com
www.facebook.com/189313732189
twitter.com/BBBSWpg
Overview: A small local charitable organization founded in 1969
Mission: To pair children with adult mentors for friendship, support & guidance.
Affliation(s): Big Brothers Big Sisters of Canada; United Way of Winnipeg
Chief Officer(s):
Ian Coupland, President
Greg Unger, Executive Director
greg.unger@bigbrothersbigsisters.ca
Finances: *Annual Operating Budget:* $500,000-$1.5 Million; *Funding Sources:* Government; United Way; fundraising; foundations; individuals
Staff Member(s): 13; 468 volunteer(s)
Membership: *Member Profile:* Positive adults who enjoy children
Activities: Fundraising; recreational; *Speaker Service:* Yes

Big Brothers Big Sisters of Yukon
305 Wood St., Whitehorse YT Y1A 2E7
Tel: 867-668-7911
bbbsyukon@gmail.com
www.bbbsofyukon.ca
www.facebook.com/BigBrothersBigSistersOfYukon
Overview: A small local organization
Affliation(s): Big Brothers Big Sisters of Canada
Chief Officer(s):
Harold Sher, Executive Director
Staff Member(s): 2

Activities: Bowl for Dollars; Soap Box Derby; volunteer appreciation

Big Brothers Big Sisters Ottawa (BBBSO) / Grands Frères Grandes Soeurs d'Ottawa
39 Camelot Dr., Ottawa ON K2G 5W6
Tel: 613-247-4776; *Fax:* 613-247-2240
info@bbbso.ca
www.bbbso.ca
www.linkedin.com/company/318325
www.facebook.com/BBBSO
twitter.com/BBBSO
Overview: A small local charitable organization founded in 1970
Mission: To foster, facilitate & support volunteer based mentoring programs for children in need
Member of: United Way/Centraide Ottawa
Affliation(s): Big Brothers Big Sisters of Canada
Chief Officer(s):
Linda Graupner, President
Kathleen Provost, Executive Director
Finances: *Annual Operating Budget:* $500,000-$1.5 Million
Staff Member(s): 11; 1000 volunteer(s)
Membership: 100-499; *Fees:* $25
Activities: *Speaker Service:* Yes
Awards:
- Special Friend Award (Award)
- Robert Allen in School Mentoring Achievement Award (Award)

Big Brothers of Greater Vancouver
#102, 1193 Kingsway, Vancouver BC V5V 3C9
Tel: 604-876-2447; *Fax:* 604-876-2446
www.bigbrothersvancouver.com
www.facebook.com/bigbrothersvancouver
twitter.com/bigbrosonline
Overview: A small local charitable organization founded in 1957
Mission: To enhance the resiliency & well-being of children by involving them in high quality prevention-focused mentoring programs & by actively seeking to positively influence policies & programs that affect children's social & emotional development; Serving the communities of: Sunshine Coast, Darcy, Squamish, Whistler, Pemberton, Surrey, Coquitlam, Vancouver & the Sea-to-Sky Corridor
Affliation(s): Big Brothers Big Sister of Canada; United Way of the Lower Mainland
Chief Officer(s):
Kathi Irvine, Chair
Valerie Lambert, Executive Director
valerie.lambert@bigbrothersbigsisters.ca
Finances: *Annual Operating Budget:* $1.5 Million-$3 Million
Staff Member(s): 52
Membership: *Committees:* Ambassardors; Bowl for Big Brothers Classic
Activities: *Speaker Service:* Yes

Big Brothers of Regina
#100, 2150 Scarth St., Regina SK S4P 0X5
Tel: 306-757-3900; *Fax:* 306-206-1255
www.bigbrothersofregina.com
www.facebook.com/BigBrothersRegina
twitter.com/BigBroRegina
Overview: A small local charitable organization
Mission: To encourage children to make good life choices by matching them with positive adult role models for a mentor relationship
Affliation(s): Big Brothers Big Sisters of Canada
Chief Officer(s):
Ash Nouredin, Executive Director
executivedir@accesscomm.ca
Staff Member(s): 5
Activities: Bowl for Kids, dinner & auction, swimming, biking, camping, BBQ

Big Brothers Sisters of Annapolis County
136 Exhibition St., Kentville NS B4N 4E5
Tel: 902-678-8641
annapolis.valley@bigbrothersbigsisters.ca
www.bbbsannapolisvalley.ca
www.facebook.com/bbbsav
Previous Name: Big Brothers & Sisters of Kings & Annapolis Counties
Overview: A small local charitable organization founded in 1975
Mission: To match Big Brothers & Sisters (volunteers 19 years of age & older) with Little Brothers & Sisters (children 8 to 16 years of age, from single-parent families); to provide the children with friendship & positive role models
Affliation(s): Big Brothers Big Sisters of Canada
Chief Officer(s):
Jonathan Leard, Program Manager
jonathan.leard@bigbrothersbigsisters.ca
Finances: *Funding Sources:* Regional government
Staff Member(s): 3
Activities: *Speaker Service:* Yes

Big Brothers Sisters of Red Deer
c/o Youth & Volunteer Centre, 4633 - 49th St., Red Deer AB T4N 1T4
Tel: 403-342-6500; *Fax:* 403-342-7734
www.bbbsreddeer.ca
www.facebook.com/BigBrothersBigSistersofRedDeerandDistrict
Overview: A small local charitable organization founded in 1976
Mission: To provide youth programming through mentoring
Affliation(s): Big Brothers Big Sisters of Canada; United Way of Central Alberta
Chief Officer(s):
Dawn Flanagan, Program Director
dawnf@yvc.ca
Brianna Berthiaume, Program Coordinator
Finances: *Funding Sources:* Municipal government
Staff Member(s): 4
Activities: Mentors matched with mentees; programs for children 5-15 yrs. of age

Big Brothers/Big Sisters of St. John's Mount Pearl *See* Big Brothers Big Sisters of Eastern Newfoundland

Big Rideau Lake Association (BRLA)
PO Box 93, Portland ON K0G 1V0
Tel: 613-272-3629
brla@brla.on.ca
www.brla.on.ca
Overview: A medium-sized local organization founded in 1911
Mission: To protect & conserve Big Rideau Lake and share its resources.
Chief Officer(s):
Doug Good, President
president@brla.on.ca
Membership: *Fees:* $60 individual; $180 corporate

Big River Chamber of Commerce
PO Box 159, Big River SK S0J 0E0
Tel: 306-469-2124; *Fax:* 306-469-4409
Overview: A small local organization
Chief Officer(s):
Jeanette Wicinski-Dunn, President
Linda McKenzie, Secretary
Membership: 45; *Fees:* $50
Activities: *Rents Mailing List:* Yes

Big Salmon River Anglers Association
Saint John NB
Tel: 506-634-1679; *Fax:* 506-653-7072
Overview: A small local organization
Member of: Atlantic Salmon Federation; New Brunswick Wildlife Federation
Affliation(s): Moncton Fish and Game Association; Northumberland Salmon Protection Association; Atlantic Salmon For Northern Maine
Chief Officer(s):
Paul P. Elson, Contact
pelson@nbnet.nb.ca

Big Sisters Association of Barrie & District *See* Big Brothers Big Sisters of Barrie & District

Biggar & District Agricultural Society
PO Box 1116, Biggar SK S0K 0M0
Tel: 306-948-2563
Overview: A small local charitable organization
Mission: To promote improvement of agriculture & improve the quality of life in the community; To provide a community forum for discussion of agricultural issues; To encourage conservation of natural resources
Member of: Saskatchewan Association of Agricultural Societies & Exhibitions
Affliation(s): Saskatchewan Provincial Association of Fairs
Chief Officer(s):
Lisa Haynes, Contact
100 volunteer(s)
Membership: 20; *Fees:* $5; *Member Profile:* Resident of Biggar; *Committees:* Advertising
Activities: Biggar Rodeo Days

Biggar & District Arts Council
Majestic Theatre, 322 Main St., Biggar SK S0K 0M0
e-mail: biggardistrictartscouncil@yahoo.ca
www.facebook.com/16279732308
www.myspace.com/biggardistrictartscouncil
Overview: A small local organization
Mission: To provide the opportunity for local residents to experience quality professional performances & visual art exhibits within their own community
Member of: Organization of Saskatchewan Arts Councils
Chief Officer(s):
Jan Phillip, President

Biggar & District Chamber of Commerce
PO Box 327, Biggar SK S0K 0M0
Tel: 306-948-2295; *Fax:* 306-948-5050
townofbiggar.com
Overview: A small local charitable organization
Mission: To support & promote economic growth for the business, community & its residents
Member of: Saskatchewan Chamber of Commerce
Finances: *Annual Operating Budget:* Less than $50,000; *Funding Sources:* Membership dues
Membership: 1-99; *Fees:* $50-150

Bikes Without Borders (BWB)
25 Havelock St., Toronto ON M6H 3B3
Tel: 416-432-4801
info@bikeswithoutborders.org
bikeswithoutborders.org
www.facebook.com/bikeswithoutborders
twitter.com/BWB_Canada
www.youtube.com/user/bikeswithoutborders/videos
Overview: A small international charitable organization founded in 2008
Mission: Uses bikes and bike-related solutions as a tool for development in marginalized communities.
Chief Officer(s):
Tanya Smith, Executive Director
Tanya@bikeswithoutborders.org
Activities: The Bicycle Ambulance; Pedal Powered Hope Project

Bilingual Exchange Secretariat & Visites interprovinciales *See* Society for Educational Visits & Exchanges in Canada

Billy Graham Evangelistic Association of Canada (BGEAC)
20 Hopewell Ave. NE, Calgary AB T3J 5H5
Tel: 403-219-2300; *Fax:* 403-250-6567
Toll-Free: 800-293-3717
info@bgea.ca
www.billygraham.ca
www.facebook.com/BillyGrahamEvangelisticAssociationOfCanada
twitter.com/BGEAnews
Also Known As: BGEA of Canada
Overview: A small national charitable organization founded in 1968
Mission: To expose those who are searching to the message of Christ; To help edify the Christian body in Canada
Affliation(s): Bill Graham Evangelistic Association USA
Chief Officer(s):
Fred Weiss, Executive Director
fweiss@samaritan.ca
Ken Forbes, Senior Director, Ministry Support
kforbes@samaritan.ca
Adams Jeff, Director, Communications
jadams@samaritan.ca
Finances: *Annual Operating Budget:* Greater than $5 Million; *Funding Sources:* Donations
Staff Member(s): 30
Activities: Television & radio broadcasts; schools of evangelism; evangelistic crusades; teaching seminars

The Bimetallic Question
Stock Exchange Tower, PO Box 883, Montréal QC H4Z 1K2
e-mail: info@bimetallicquestion.org
www.bimetallicquestion.org
Also Known As: The Sherlock Holmes Society of Montréal
Overview: A small local organization founded in 1979
Mission: To bring together those people who enjoy Sherlock Holmes & the Victorian world in which he flourished
Membership: 35; *Fees:* $20

Bimose Tribal Council
598 Lakeview Dr., Kenora ON P9N 3P7

Tel: 807-468-5551; *Fax:* 807-468-3908
reception@bimose.ca
www.bimose.ca
Overview: A small local organization
Mission: Council services include: assisting communities to establish & maintain effective & efficient financial systems; helping communities & individuals access economic development opportunities, & develop sustainable businesses; educational counseling, assistance with tuition, advice to educational authorities & Boards; technical advisory services.
Chief Officer(s):
Allan Luby, Executive Director
aluby@bimose.ca
Staff Member(s): 28
Membership: *Member Profile:* Membership services are provided for the following First Nations:Asubpeeschewagong Netum Anishinabek; Eagle Lake; Iskatewizaagegan # 39; Lac Des Mille Lacs; Naotkamegwanning; Obashkaandagaang; Ochiichagwe'Babigo'Ining; Shoal Lake # 40; Wabaseemoong Independent Nations; Wabauskang; Wabigoon Lake Ojibway

Binbrook Agricultural Society (BAS)
PO Box 244, 2600, RR #56, Binbrook ON L0R 1C0
Tel: 905-692-4003; *Fax:* 905-692-1434
Other Communication: President, e-mail: president@binbrookagriculturalsociety.org
info@binbrookagriculturalsociety.org
www.binbrookagriculturalsociety.org
twitter.com/BinbrookFair
Overview: A small local organization founded in 1854
Affliation(s): Ontario Association of Agricultural Societies; Canadian Association of Exhibitions
Finances: *Annual Operating Budget:* Less than $50,000; *Funding Sources:* Regional government
Staff Member(s): 1; 140 volunteer(s)
Membership: 175 individual; 18 associate; *Fees:* $5 individual; $5 associate
Activities: Annual Fall Fair; agricultural education & awareness programs

Bio-dynamic Agricultural Society of British Columbia
2478 East 23rd Ave., Vancouver BC V5R 1A2
Tel: 778-869-4060
bdcertification@yahoo.ca
Overview: A small provincial licensing organization
Affliation(s): Certified Organic Associations of BC
Chief Officer(s):
Doug Helmer, Treasurer
Grant Watson, Administrator

Biogas Association
#900, 275 Slater St., Ottawa ON K1P 5H9
Tel: 613-822-1004
jgreen@biogasassociation.ca
www.biogasassociation.ca
www.linkedin.com/e/-ykkigj-gm1520gc-3z/vgh/3854330/eml-grp-sub/
www.facebook.com/168782246502009
www.twitter.com/BiogasOntario
Previous Name: Agrienergy Producers' Association of Ontario
Overview: A medium-sized provincial organization founded in 2008
Mission: The Biogas Association is the collective voice of the biogas industry.
Membership: *Fees:* $500 small business; $1500 large business
Activities: Advancing policy and regulatory developments; supporting research; outreach events

BioNova
#124, 1344 Summer St., Halifax NS B3H 0A8
Tel: 902-421-5705; *Fax:* 902-421-2733
info@bionova.ca
www.bionova.ca
www.facebook.com/10990488574179б
twitter.com/NSLifeSciences
www.youtube.com/user/NSLifeSciences
Also Known As: Nova Scotia Biotechnology & Life Sciences
Overview: A small provincial organization
Mission: To advocate for Nova Scotia's life sciences industry; to educate by telling positive news stories related to the life sciences industries; to build the life sciences community within the province; to provide member companies with support & resources to allow them to grow & be more prosperous
Chief Officer(s):
Robert Cervelli, Chair
Marli MacNeil, CEO
mmacneil@bionova.ca
Membership: 46 organizations; *Fees:* Schedule available; *Member Profile:* Companies working in pharmaceuticals/vaccines, medical technologies, natural health products/nutraceuticals, bio IT & bioproducts; research organizations; service providers
Activities: *Awareness Events:* National Biotechnology Week, Sept.; Biotech & Beer, Nov.

Biophysical Society of Canada (BSC) / La société de biophysique du Canada
a/s Dept. de chimie, Univ. Laval, 1045 Avenue de la médecine, Québec QC G1V 0A6
Tel: 418-656-3393; *Fax:* 418-656-7916
info@biophysicalsociety.ca
www.biophysicalsociety.ca
Overview: A medium-sized national organization founded in 1985 overseen by Canadian Federation of Biological Societies
Mission: To promote biophysical research & education; to encourage cross-feeding of ideas between the physical & biological sciences; to foster & support scientific meetings, workshops & discussions in biophysics; to represent Canadian biophysics & biophysicists
Chief Officer(s):
Bruce C. Hill, President
Finances: *Annual Operating Budget:* Less than $50,000; *Funding Sources:* Membership dues
10 volunteer(s)
Membership: 80; *Fees:* $84.20
Activities: *Speaker Service:* Yes
Awards:
• Student Poster Award (Award)

BIOQuébec / Québec Bio-Industries Business Network
#120, 500, Boul Cartier ouest, Laval QC H7V 5B7
Tél: 450-781-3965; *Téléc:* 450-781-3966
info@bioquebec.com
www.bioquebec.com
Nom précédent: Conseil des bio-industries du Québec; Association québécoise des bio-industries
Aperçu: *Dimension:* moyenne; *Envergure:* provinciale; Organisme sans but lucratif; fondée en 1997
Mission: Ôtre le porte-parole des entreprises biotechnologiques du Québec; favoriser le développement et la mise en valeur des biotechnologies et des bioindustries québécoises, et ce au bénéfice de ses membres; To promote the development & the upgrading of biotechnologies; to supply strategic information of technical & economical content as well as carry out projects, events & activities; to stimulate collaboration between private industry, governments & universities; to stimulate the growth of structuring economical activities in this field; to act as a spokesman for the bio-industry in Québec
Membre(s) du bureau directeur:
Gilles R. Gagnon, Président
Mario Lebrun, Directeur général
brun@bioquebec.com
Finances: *Budget de fonctionnement annuel:* $500,000-$1.5 Million; *Fonds:* Federal Office of Regional Development - Québec; membership fees; Laval Technopole
Membre(s) du personnel: 1; 4 bénévole(s)
Membre: 240 companies; *Montant de la cotisation:* 385$ (corporatif 1-5 employés); *Comités:* Environnement d'affaires; Conseil de l'innovation biopharmaceutique
Activités: Colloques, conférences, expositions
Prix, Bouses:
• Genesis Awards (Prix)

BioTalent Canada
#300, 130 Slater St., Ottawa ON K1P 6E2
Tel: 613-235-1402; *Fax:* 613-233-7541
Toll-Free: 866-243-2472
corporate@biotalent.ca
www.biotalent.ca
www.linkedin.com/in/biotalentcanada
www.facebook.com/biotalentcanada
twitter.com/BioTalentCanada
www.youtube.com/biotalentcanada
Previous Name: Biotechnology Human Resource Council
Overview: A small national organization founded in 1997
Mission: Help Canadian companies & academia develop the highly skilled staff necessary for commercial success; facilitate industry involvement in skills training & knowledge upgrading for employees; help the Canadian biotechnology sector strategically manage its workforce with human resource tools & HR intelligence services; facilitate the entry of new workers to the biotech sector through the communication of job opportunities to a broad audience
Member of: Global Bioscience Partnership; The Alliance of Sector Councils; Bio (Biotechnology Industry Organization)
Chief Officer(s):
Rob Henderson, President & CEO
François Schubert, Chair
Norma K. Biln, Vice-Chair
Reg Joseph, Treasurer
Staff Member(s): 5

BIOTECanada
#600, 1 Nicholas St., Ottawa ON K1N 7B7
Tel: 613-230-5585; *Fax:* 613-563-8850
info@biotech.ca
www.biotech.ca
www.linkedin.com/company/biotecanada
twitter.com/biotecanada
Previous Name: Canadian Institute of Biotechnology; Industrial Biotechnology Association of Canada
Overview: A medium-sized national organization founded in 1987
Mission: To provide a unified voice fostering an environment that responds to the needs of the biotechnology industry & research community, both nationally & internationally
Chief Officer(s):
Brad Thompson, Chair
Andrew Casey, President & CEO, 613-230-5585 Ext. 229
andrew.casey@biotech.ca
Finances: *Annual Operating Budget:* $1.5 Million-$3 Million; *Funding Sources:* Membership dues; government; sponsorship
Staff Member(s): 10
Membership: 250 institutional; *Fees:* Schedule available; *Member Profile:* Biotechnology industry & regional groups; *Committees:* Agriculture; Human Health Care; Environment; Finance; Intellectual Property; Ethics; Communications; Government Relations; Science
Activities: Policy & regulatory advocacy; communications; human resources; *Rents Mailing List:* Yes

Biotechnology Human Resource Council *See* BioTalent Canada

Birchmount Bluffs Neighbourhood Centre (BBNC)
93 Birchmount Rd., Toronto ON M1N 3J7
Tel: 416-396-4310; *Fax:* 416-396-4314
contact@bbnc.ca
www.bbnc.ca
www.facebook.com/birchmountbluffs
twitter.com/bbncentre
Overview: A medium-sized local charitable organization
Mission: To provide programs and supports and foster social inclusion within the community, with a focus on individuals that face a barrier to service.
Chief Officer(s):
Enrique Robert, Executive Director
enrique@bbnc.ca
Finances: *Annual Operating Budget:* $1.5 Million-$3 Million; *Funding Sources:* Government, United Way, Donations
750 volunteer(s)
Membership: *Fees:* Youth free; $15 individual; $40 family; *Committees:* Executive; Personnel; Finance; Fundraising; Access & Equity; Nominations

Bird Studies Canada (BSC)
PO Box 160, 115 Front St., Port Rowan ON N0E 1M0
Fax: 519-586-3532
Toll-Free: 888-448-2473
generalinfo@birdscanada.org
www.bsc-eoc.org
www.facebook.com/birdscanada
twitter.com/BirdStudiesCan
Previous Name: Long Point Bird Observatory
Overview: A small provincial charitable organization founded in 1960
Mission: To advance the understanding, appreciation & conservation of wild birds & their habitats, in Canada & elsewhere, through studies that engage the skills, enthusiasm, & support of its members volunteers, staff & the interested public
Member of: Federation of Ontario Naturalists
Affliation(s): Bird Life International; Partners in Flight; Ontario Bird Banding Association; James L. Baillie Memorial Fund; Newfoundland and Labrador Murre Conservation Fund
Chief Officer(s):
David Love, Chair

Finances: *Annual Operating Budget:* $1.5 Million-$3 Million; *Funding Sources:* Corporate sponsors; general donations; membership fees
Staff Member(s): 45
Membership: 5,000-14,999; *Fees:* $25 student; $35 individual; $50 household; $100 contributing; $175 sustaining; $1000 lifetime; $2,500 patron; *Committees:* Long Point Bird Observatory (LPBO) Committee; National Science Advisory Council
Activities: Monitoring several species as part of the requirement of the Species at Risk Act (SARA); Implementing international training in order to foster good conservation and research in Latin America; *Internships:* Yes; *Rents Mailing List:* Yes; *Library* by appointment
Awards:
• Baillie Fund Regular Grant (Grant), Baillie Fund Grant Program
Eligibility: Non-profit organizations*Deadline:* December *Amount:* $1,000-5,000 *Contact:* Andrew Coughlan, Phone: 866-518-0212; E-mail: acoughlan@birdscanada.org
• Baillie Fund Small Grant (Grant), Baillie Fund Grant Program
Eligibility: Individuals or organizations*Deadline:* January *Amount:* $250-1,000 *Contact:* Andrew Coughlan, Phone: 866-518-0212; E-mail: acoughlan@birdscanada.org
• Baillie Fund Student Research Award (Grant), Baillie Fund Grant Program
Eligibility: Graduate students*Deadline:* February *Amount:* $1,000 *Contact:* Andrew Coughlan, Phone: 866-518-0212; E-mail: acoughlan@birdscanada.org
• Murre Conservation Fund Grant (Grant)
Eligibility: Eligible recipients are Canadian & include: non-profit organizations; aboriginal organizations; associations & wildlife management boards; research, academic & educational institutions; for profit organizations such as small businesses, companies, corporations, & industry associations; local organizations such as community associations & groups, seniors' & youth groups, & service clubs; & provincial, territorial, municipal & local governments*Deadline:* November *Contact:* Becky Stewart, E-mail: bstewart@birdscanada.org
• Doug Tarry Bird Study Award (Award)
To foster the development of ornithological interests in Canadian tennagers*Eligibility:* Canadian teenagers ranging in age from 13-17 years old*Deadline:* April

Birks Family Foundation / Fondation de la famille Birks
#1200, 615 boul. René-Lévesque ouest, Montréal QC H3B 1P5
Tel: 514-397-2567; *Fax:* 514-397-1121
secretarytreasurer@birksfamilyfoundation.ca
www.birksfamilyfoundation.ca
Overview: A small local charitable organization founded in 1961
Chief Officer(s):
G. Drummond Birks, Chairman & Executive Director
Staff Member(s): 2
Awards:
• Birks Family Foundation Grant (Grant)
Eligibility: Registered charity; in support of Canadian universities, hospitals, health care, social services or the development of Canadian culture.

Birth Control & Venereal Disease Information Centre
#403, 960 Lawrence Ave West, Toronto ON M6A 3B5
Tel: 416-789-4541; *Fax:* 416-789-0762
info@BirthControlVD.org
www.birthcontrolvd.org
Overview: A small provincial organization founded in 1972
Mission: To help maintain sexual health with an emphasis on education & prevention. To provide patient-centred service in a caring, non-judgmental manner.

Birthright International / Accueil Grossesse
777 Coxwell Ave., Toronto ON M4C 3C6
Tel: 416-469-4789; *Fax:* 416-469-1772; *Crisis Hot-Line:* 800-550-4900
info@birthright.org
www.birthright.org
Overview: A medium-sized international charitable organization founded in 1968
Mission: To provide non-judgmental support to women facing an unplanned pregnancy, helping them carry their baby to term.
Chief Officer(s):
Louise R. Summerhill, Co-President & Founder
Mary Berney, Co-President
Finances: *Funding Sources:* Donations
Membership: 300 chapters
Activities: Counselling; *Speaker Service:* Yes

Drummondville Chapter
1190, rue Goupil, Drummondville QC J2B 4Z7
Tel: 819-478-7474

Halifax Chapter
#201-2, 1521 Grafton St., Halifax NS B3J 2B9
Tel: 902-422-3400
Toll-Free: 800-550-4900

Lethbridge Chapter
#503, 740 - 7 Ave. South, Lethbridge AB T1J 0N9
Tel: 403-320-1003
Toll-Free: 800-550-4900

Moncton Chapter
#107, 236 St. George St., Moncton NB E1C 1W1
Tel: 506-382-2227
Toll-Free: 800-550-4900

Ottawa Chapter
#302, 200 Isabella St., Ottawa ON K1S 1V7
Tel: 613-231-5683
Toll-Free: 800-550-4900

Regina Chapter
#202, 1771 Rose St., Regina SK S4P 1Z4
Tel: 306-359-1862

Vancouver Chapter
#1107, 207 West Hastings St., Vancouver BC V6B 1H7
Tel: 604-687-7223
Toll-Free: 800-550-4900

Birtle & District Chamber of Commerce
PO Box 278, Birtle MB R0M 0C0
Tel: 204-842-3234
Overview: A small local organization
Finances: *Funding Sources:* Membership fees
Membership: *Member Profile:* Business owners & private individuals

Bison Producers of Alberta
501 - 11 Ave., Nisku AB T9E 7N5
Tel: 780-955-1995; *Fax:* 780-955-1990
info@bisoncentre.com
bisoncentre.com
Merged from: Alberta Bison Commission; Alberta Bison Association; Peace Country Bison Association
Overview: A small local organization
Member of: Canadian Bison Association
Membership: *Fees:* $236.25

Black Academic Scholarship Fund (BASF) / Fonds d'études académiques pour les Noirs
3270, rue Prince-Charles, St. Hubert QC J3Y 4X4
Other Communication: Scholarship Information, E-mail: scholarship@basfund.ca
info@basfund.ca
www.basfund.ca
Overview: A small local charitable organization founded in 1991
Mission: To enhance the economic status of visible minorities by providing educational opportunities
Finances: *Funding Sources:* Donations; Sponsorships; Fundraising
Activities: Promoting entrepreneurship & professional excellence; Offering career counselling services; Providing financial support to young people who are studying at accredited institutions; Sponsoring youth programs; *Awareness Events:* Jackie Robinson International Golf Tournament (golf@basfund.ca)

Black Artists Network of Nova Scotia (BANNS)
NS
Tel: 902-430-3560
admin@banns.ca
www.banns.ca
Overview: A small provincial organization founded in 1991
Mission: BANNS is a non-profit, multi-disciplinary arts association that seeks to develop the African Nova Scotian arts community.
Activities: B Space Gallery & Arts Centre; Preston Cultural Festival; Voices Black Theatre Ensemble; African Nova Scotian Quiltmakers Initiative

Black Business & Professional Association (BBPA)
#210, 675 King St. West, Toronto ON M5V 1M9
Tel: 416-504-4097; *Fax:* 416-504-7343
information@bbpa.org
www.bbpa.org
www.facebook.com/thebbpa
twitter.com/thebbpa
www.youtube.com/user/TheOfficialBBPA
Overview: A medium-sized national organization founded in 1983
Mission: To address discrimination in business, employment, education, housing, policing, political representation & immigration; to encourage entrepreneurship; to identify & reward excellence & achievement; to cooperate with other organizations with similar purposes to influence public opinion & public policy on matters of social & economic justice
Chief Officer(s):
Pauline Christian, President
Membership: *Fees:* $25 student/senior; $50 under 30; $100 regular; $175 family; $300 business
Awards:
• Harry Jerome Scholarships (Scholarship)
Aimed at helping young people who may lack resources for further education *Amount:* Five $2,000 annual awards

Black Business Initiative (BBI)
Centennial Bldg., #1201, 1660 Hollis St., Halifax NS B3J 1V7
Tel: 902-426-2224; *Fax:* 902-426-8699
Toll-Free: 888-664-9333
bbi@bbi.ns.ca
www.bbi.ca
Overview: A small provincial organization
Mission: To grow the Black presence in business sectors including high-tech, manufacturing, tourism & culture
Chief Officer(s):
Greg Browning, Chair
Michael Wyse, CEO
Membership: *Committees:* Executive; Finance; Lending; Governance; BBI Site; Services
Activities: Operating the Black Business Centre; strategic planning; regional business development; loan fund
Awards:
• The Black Business Initiative Society's Entrepreneur of the Year (Award)
• The Hector Jacques Award of Business Excellence (Award)
Publications:
• Annual Business Directory [a publication of the Black Business Initiative]
Type: Directory; *Frequency:* Annual
Profile: Black business listings & community resource information
• Black to Business [a publication of the Black Business Initiative]
Type: Magazine; *Frequency:* q.

Black Coalition for AIDS Prevention
20 Victoria St., 4th Fl., Toronto ON M5C 2N8
Tel: 416-977-9955; *Fax:* 416-977-7664
info@black-cap.com
www.black-cap.com
www.facebook.com/264852343610058
Also Known As: Black CAP
Overview: A medium-sized national organization founded in 1987 overseen by Canadian AIDS Society
Mission: To reduce the spread of HIV infection in the Black communities & to enhance the quality of life for Black people living with or affected by HIV/AIDS
Member of: Ontario AIDS Network
Chief Officer(s):
Shannon Thomas Ryan, Executive Director
s.ryan@black-cap.com
Finances: *Annual Operating Budget:* $250,000-$500,000; *Funding Sources:* Ontario Ministry of Health & Long-Term Care; Health Canada; Toronto Public Health; private donations
Staff Member(s): 6; 60 volunteer(s)
Membership: 40; *Fees:* $10 & up
Activities: Community workshops & forums; training of community professionals & volunteers; development of culturally specific education materials; support & counselling; *Speaker Service:* Yes

Black Coalition of Québec / La Ligue des Noirs du Québec
5201, boul Decarie, Montréal QC H3W 3C2
Tel: 514-489-3830
info@liguedesnoirs.org
www.liguedesnoirs.org
Overview: A small local organization
Mission: The Coalition speaks for the Black community in the defence of individual human rights and against all forms of discrimination
Chief Officer(s):
Peterson Frederick, President

Canadian Associations

Black Community Resource Centre (BCRC)
#497, 6767, ch de la Côte-des-Neiges, Montréal QC H3S 2T6
Tel: 514-342-2247; *Fax:* 514-342-2283
bcrc@qc.aira.com
www.bcrcmontreal.com/bcrc
Overview: A medium-sized local organization
Mission: BCRC is a resource-based organization committed to helping English-speaking visible minority youth rekindle their dreams and achieve their full potential. The Centre takes a comprehensive approach, with a strategy that is progressive, multi-interventionist and holistic; emphasis is on infrastructure support and training, prevention and empowerment, community-building, collaboration, and an inclusive perspective. BCRC has a mandate to provide support services to individuals, communities, para-public and public organizations, and develops and implements health, education, socio-cultural and economic development programs.
Activities: Information & referral; support to schools; conference, meeting & workshop support; Documentation Centre; document translation; web design; workshops for adults & youth; Mini-Poste project; Expressing Life project
Publications:
• Semaji
Type: Newsletter; *Frequency:* Q

Black Creek Conservation Project
PO Box 98552, 873 Jane St., Toronto ON M6N 5A6
Tel: 416-661-6600; *Fax:* 416-661-6898
bccp@rogers.com
www.bccp.ca
Previous Name: Black Creek Project of Toronto Inc.
Overview: A small local organization founded in 1982
Mission: To preserve & rehabilitate the Black Creek watershed; To support a healthy, diverse, & sustainable ecosystem
Member of: Federation of Ontario Naturalists
Chief Officer(s):
Gaspar Horvath, President and Director
ghorvath@trca.on.ca
Finances: *Annual Operating Budget:* $50,000-$100,000; *Funding Sources:* Government; private
Staff Member(s): 5; 2500 volunteer(s)
Membership: 45; *Fees:* $20/year general membership; $35/year group membership; $10/year youth membership
Activities: Tree planting; garbage clean-up; environmental lectures; erosion control; wetland creation; *Awareness Events:* Clean Toronto Together Event, April; Black Creek Earth Day Event, April; *Rents Mailing List:* Yes
Meetings/Conferences: • Black Creek Conservation Project Regular Monthly Meeting, Third Wednesday of the month, Royal Canadian Legion, Branch 31, Toronto, ON
Scope: Local
Publications:
• Kingfisher Newsletter
Type: Newsletter; *Frequency:* irregular

Black Creek Project of Toronto Inc. *See* Black Creek Conservation Project

Black Cultural Society for Nova Scotia
10 Cherry Brook Rd., Cherry Brook NS B2Z 1A8
Tel: 902-434-6223; *Fax:* 902-434-2306
Toll-Free: 800-465-0767
contact@bccns.com
www.bccns.com
www.facebook.com/188265867860941
Overview: A medium-sized provincial charitable organization founded in 1977
Mission: To create among members of the Black community an awareness of their past, their heritage & identity; to provide programs & activities to explore, learn about, understand & appreciate Black history, achievements & experiences in Canadian life.
Member of: Multicultural Association of Nova Scotia
Chief Officer(s):
Leslie Oliver, President
Membership: *Fees:* $15 student/senior; $25 individual; $50 family/group; $100 corporate
Activities: Operates the Black Cultural centre for Nova Scotia; *Speaker Service:* Yes; *Library* Open to public

Black Educators Association of Nova Scotia (BEA)
2136 Gottingen St., Halifax NS B3K 3B3
Tel: 902-424-7036; *Fax:* 902-424-0636
Toll-Free: 800-565-3398
info@theblackeducators.ca
www.theblackeducators.ca
Overview: A medium-sized provincial organization founded in 1969
Mission: To monitor and ensure the development of an equitable education system, so that African Nova Scotians are able to achieve their maximum potential.
Chief Officer(s):
Robert Upshaw, Executive Director

Black Educators Association of Nova Scotia (BEA)
2136 Gottingen St., Halifax NS B3K 3B3
Tel: 902-424-7036; *Fax:* 902-424-0636
Toll-Free: 800-565-3398
info@theblackeducators.ca
www.theblackeducators.ca
Overview: A small provincial charitable organization founded in 1969
Mission: To monitor & ensure the development of an equitable education system, so that African Nova Scotians are able to achieve their maximum potential
Affliation(s): National Council of Black Educators of Canada
Chief Officer(s):
Ken Fells, President
Robert Upshaw, Executive Director
Finances: *Funding Sources:* Department of Canadian Heritage
Membership: *Fees:* $30 regular; $20 associate; $15 member at large; $10 student; $100 organization; *Committees:* Operations; Community Involvement; Curriculum; Professional Involvement; Membership; Personnel
Activities: Community workshops; provincial conferences

Black Law Students' Association of Canada (BLSA) / L'Association des etudiants noirs en droit du Canada
e-mail: Admin@blsacanada.com
www.blsacanada.com
www.facebook.com/blsacanada
twitter.com/BLSAC
Overview: A small national organization founded in 1991
Mission: A national organization committed to supporting and enhancing academic and professional opportunities for black law students in both official languages.
Chief Officer(s):
Moses Gashirabake, President
President@blsacanada.com
Meetings/Conferences: • Black Law Students' Association of Canada 23rd Annual National Conference, 2015
Scope: National
Contact Information: Conference@blsacanada.com

Black Loyalist Heritage Society (BLHS)
PO Box 1194, 98 Birchtown Rd., Shelburne NS B0T 1W0
Tel: 902-875-1310; *Fax:* 902-875-1352
Toll-Free: 888-354-0772
blackloyalist@blackloyalist.com
www.blackloyalist.com
www.facebook.com/111527972216141
Overview: A small local organization
Mission: To promote the history of Black Loyalists
Chief Officer(s):
Beverly Cox, Site Manager, 902-875-1606
beverly@blackloyalist.com
Staff Member(s): 3
Membership: *Fees:* $20 individual; $25 family; $40 organization/business

Black River-Matheson Chamber of Commerce
PO Box 518, Matheson ON P0K 1N0
e-mail: chamber@brmchamberofcommerce.org
www.brmchamberofcommerce.org
Also Known As: BRM Chamber of Commerce
Overview: A small local organization
Mission: To promote commerce in the community
Member of: Canadian Chamber of Commerce
Membership: 53; *Fees:* $40 private; $95 non-profit; $95 1-11 employees; $175 12-50 employees; $275 51+ employees

Black Star Big Brothers Big Sisters of Montréal
#12, 6870 rue Terrebone, Montréal QC H4B 1C5
Tel: 514-485-9737; *Fax:* 514-485-9712
Overview: A small local organization founded in 1995
Mission: To serve Visible Minority male & female youth between the ages of 6 & 16 from single-parent homes; Visible Minority adult volunteers are matched with youth to provide positive role models & mentoring
Affliation(s): Big Brothers Big Sisters of Canada

Black Studies Centre (BSC)
1968 boul. de Maosonneuve Ouest, Montréal QC H3H 1K5
Tel: 514-933-0798
www.blackstudies.ca
Overview: A medium-sized local organization founded in 1970
Mission: The Black Studies Centre (BSC) has been providing a wide range of services to the Montreal community and to its various institutions. The BSC is committed to the continued educational development of Montreal's Black community and to the recognition of the contributions they have made in helping Montreal to grow as a city.
Chief Officer(s):
Clarence S. Bayne, President

Black Theatre Workshop (BTW)
#432, 3680, Jeanne-Mance, Montréal QC H2X 2K5
Tel: 514-932-1104; *Fax:* 514-932-6311
www.blacktheatreworkshop.ca
Overview: A medium-sized national organization founded in 1972
Mission: To encourage & promote the development of a Black & Canadian theatre, rooted in a literature that reflects the creative will of Black Canadian writers & artists, & the creative collaborations between Black & other artists; To strive to create a greater cross-cultural understanding by its presence & the intrinsic value of its work
Chief Officer(s):
Quincy Armorer, Artistic Director
ad@blacktheatreworkshop.ca
Jacklin Webb, President

Blackfalds & District Chamber of Commerce
PO Box 249, Blackfalds AB T0M 0J0
Tel: 403-885-2386; *Fax:* 403-885-2386
info@blackfaldslive.ca
ww.blackfaldslive.ca
Overview: A small local organization
Chief Officer(s):
Shirley Johnson, President, 403-885-5001

Bladder Cancer Canada (BCC) / Cancer de la vessie Canada
#1000, 4936 Yonge St., Toronto ON M2N 6S3
Toll-Free: 866-674-8889
Other Communication: media@bladdercancercanada.org
info@bladdercancercanada.org
www.bladdercancercanada.org
www.linkedin.com/company/2599127?trk=NUS_CMPY_TWIT
www.facebook.com/BladderCancerCanada
twitter.com/BladderCancerCA
www.youtube.com/user/BladderCancerCA
Overview: A medium-sized national charitable organization founded in 2009
Mission: Bladder Cancer Canada aims to improve patient support by having a patient to patient support system in place; be a source of information about available treatment options and create greater awareness of bladder cancer.
Chief Officer(s):
David Guttman, CHair
Tammy Udall, Executive Director
Finances: *Annual Operating Budget:* $50,000-$100,000; *Funding Sources:* Private donations; fundraisers

Blaine Lake & District Chamber of Commerce
PO Box 178, Blaine Lake SK S0J 0J0
Tel: 306-226-4646; *Fax:* 306-497-2402
blainelakecofc@sasktel.net
www.blainelake.ca/business/chamber.html
Overview: A small local organization
Mission: To unite the efforts of business & community to ensure economic health & social well being of Blaine Lake & District
Member of: Saskatchewan Chamber of Commerce, SaskTourism
Chief Officer(s):
Vivian Nemish, President
Finances: *Annual Oporating Budget:* Less than $50,000; *Funding Sources:* Annual silent auction; Membership fees
Membership: 58; *Fees:* $10 - $50; *Member Profile:* Business
Activities: Annual Banquet; Community Candle Service; Cabin Drop; community events; community bulletin board; Community Contribution Awards

Blairmore Board of Trade *See* Crowsnest Pass Chamber of Commerce

Blankets for Canada Society Inc.
#217, 210A - 12A St. North, Lethbridge AB T1H 2J1

Tel: 403-329-6586; *Fax:* 403-381-8668
www.blankets4canada.ca
Also Known As: B4C
Overview: A small national charitable organization founded in 1998
Mission: To create blankets for those Canadians who are without shelter or in need of warmth; To support organizations who care for these people
Chief Officer(s):
Nancy Panting, Founder
nancy@blankets4canada.ca
Gwennie Simpson, President
Finances: *Annual Operating Budget:* Less than $50,000
250 volunteer(s)
Membership: 23; *Fees:* $20
Activities: Knit, crochet, quilt blankets for distribution
Publications:
• The Joiner
Type: Newsletter

Blenheim & District Chamber of Commerce
PO Box 1353, Blenheim ON N0P 1A0
Tel: 519-676-6555
blenheimontario.com/chamber-of-commerce
Overview: A small local organization founded in 1977
Chief Officer(s):
Frank Vercouteren, President
Betty Russell, Secretary, 519-676-8090
Finances: *Annual Operating Budget:* Less than $50,000
2 volunteer(s)
Membership: 51

Blind Bowls Association of Canada (BBAC)
Regina SK
bbacanada.org
Overview: A small national organization
Mission: To govern the sport of bowls in Canada; to promote the interests of visually impaired lawn bowlers in Canada & around the world.
Chief Officer(s):
Vivian Berkeley, President
vberkeley@sympatico.ca
Shirley Ahern, Secretary
shirice@sympatico.ca

Blind River Chamber of Commerce (BRCC)
PO Box 998, 243 Causley St., Blind River ON P0R 1B0
Tel: 705-356-2555; *Fax:* 705-356-3911
Toll-Free: 800-563-8719
chamber@brchamber.ca
www.brchamber.ca
Overview: A small local organization founded in 1951
Mission: To be the recognized voice of business committed to the enhancement of economic prosperity in our area
Member of: Ontario Chamber of Commerce; Northeastern Chamber of Commerce
Affliation(s): Algoma Kinniwabi Travel Association
Chief Officer(s):
Louise Demers, President, 705-356-2685
Betty-Ann Dunbar, Treasurer, 705-356-7553
Finances: *Annual Operating Budget:* Less than $50,000
Staff Member(s): 1; 13 volunteer(s)
Membership: 92; *Fees:* $95-$425; *Committees:* Travel Centre; Small Business Week; Golf
Activities: Moonlight madness & summer sidewalk sale; retail events; Chamber Golf Classic

Blind Sailing Association of Canada (BSAC)
17 Boustead Ave., Toronto ON M6R 1Y7
Tel: 416-489-2433
info@blindsailing.ca
www.blindsailing.ca
www.facebook.com/385889524843037
twitter.com/blindcansail
Overview: A small national organization founded in 2002
Mission: To provide opportunities for the blind to learn to sail, thus boosting skills, confidence & self-esteem
Member of: Ontario Sailing Association; Sail Canada
Membership: *Fees:* $40

Blind Sports Nova Scotia
4 Avon Cres., Halifax NS B3R 2E3
e-mail: info@blindsportsnovascotia.ca
www.blindsportsnovascotia.ca
twitter.com/blindsportsns
Overview: A small provincial organization overseen by Canadian Blind Sports Association Inc.
Mission: Blind Sports Nova Scotia is an organization that presents sport & recreational activities for visually impaired athletes in Nova Scotia.
Member of: Canadian Blind Sport Association; Sport Nova Scotia
Chief Officer(s):
Jennifer MacNeil, President
Membership: *Fees:* $15/yr.; *Member Profile:* Adults, age 19+ (but 14+ are welcome, too)

Blissymbolics Communication International (BCI)
#425, 1210 Don Mills Rd., Toronto ON M3B 3N9
www.blissymbolics.ca
Overview: A small international charitable organization founded in 1975
Mission: BCI is a non-profit, charitable organization that has the license for the use and publication of Blissymbols designed for persons with communication, language, & learning difficulties, severe speech & physical impairments.
Affliation(s): Ontario Federation for Cerebral Palsy
Chief Officer(s):
Shirley McNaughton, Co-Chair
Finances: *Funding Sources:* Federal & provincial governments, Ontario Crippled Children's Centre, Easter Seal society, charitable foundations, donations
Activities: BCI trains professionals, assists users, offers consultation, continues technology & software development.; *Internships:* Yes; *Speaker Service:* Yes; *Library* Open to public

Bloc British Columbia Party *See* Progressive Nationalist Party of British Columbia

Bloc québécois (BQ)
3750, boul Crémazie est, 4e étage, Montréal QC H2A 1B4
Tél: 514-526-3000; *Téléc:* 514-526-2868
www.blocquebecois.org
www.facebook.com/blocquebecois
twitter.com/blocquebecois
www.youtube.com/user/blocquebecois?feature=results_main
Aperçu: *Dimension:* moyenne; *Envergure:* provinciale; fondée en 1990
Membre(s) du bureau directeur:
Daniel Paillé, Chef
Xavier Barsalou Duval, Président
Finances: *Budget de fonctionnement annuel:* $500,000-$1.5 Million
Membre(s) du personnel: 8; 1500 bénévole(s)
Membre: 110 000; *Montant de la cotisation:* 5$

Block Parent Program of Canada Inc. (BPPCI) / Programme Parents-Secours du Canada inc.
PO Box 7, 50 Dunlop St. East, Lower Level, Barrie ON L4N 6S7
Tel: 705-792-4245; *Fax:* 705-792-4245
Toll-Free: 800-663-1134
info@blockparent.ca
www.blockparent.ca
Overview: A large national charitable organization founded in 1968
Mission: To provide immediate assistance through a safety network; to offer supporting community education programs
Chief Officer(s):
Linda Patterson, President
Finances: *Annual Operating Budget:* $100,000-$250,000; *Funding Sources:* Federal grants; corporate sponsor
Staff Member(s): 2
Membership: 12 provincial & territorial programs; 900+ community members; *Fees:* $1,500 to set up a program in a neighbourhood with 25,000 students & three elementary schools
Activities: *Awareness Events:* National Block Parent Week, Oct.; *Library:* Safety Video Library;
Awards:
• National Block Parent Award (Award)
Publications:
• Block Parent Program of Canada Inc. Communiqué
Type: Newsletter

Block Parent Program of Winnipeg Inc.
466 Gertrude Ave., Winnipeg MB R3L 0M8
Tel: 204-284-7562
bppw@mts.net
www.winnipegblockparents.mb.ca
Previous Name: Manitoba Block Parent Program
Overview: A small provincial organization overseen by Block Parent Program of Canada Inc.
Mission: To provide a network of police-screened, easily recognizable, safe places for the members of the community, primarily children.
Member of: Block Parent Program of Canada Inc.
Chief Officer(s):
George Jarvis, President

Block Rosary Group of Ontario
22 Norman Ross Dr., Markham ON L3S 3E8
Tel: 905-472-3194
Also Known As: The Block Rosary Crusaders
Overview: A small provincial charitable organization founded in 1982
Mission: To encourage families & friends to pray the Holy Rosary together; To pray for the ill, the deceased, & those in need of help spiritually & otherwise; To pray for peace & unity in families, communities, & the world
Affliation(s): Archdiocese of Toronto
Chief Officer(s):
Jaime Marasigan, Contact
jmarasigan@sympatico.ca
Finances: *Funding Sources:* Donations
Membership: 10 groups, with 500+ families & 80 coordinators; *Member Profile:* Catholic families in Durham Region, York Region & Metro Toronto, Ontario; *Committees:* Picnic; Carey Ohio; Anniversary; Living Rosary; Christmas Party
Activities: Organizing pilgrimages to Carey, Ohio, the Shrine of Our Lady of Fatima in Youngstown, New York & Midland, Ontario; Providing faith instruction; Offering prayer groups; Hosting social events such as summer picnics, anniversary dances & family Christmas parties

Block Watch Society of British Columbia (BCBPS)
#120, 12414 - 82nd Ave., Surrey BC V3W 3E9
Tel: 604-418-3827; *Fax:* 604-501-2509
Toll-Free: 877-602-3358
blockwatch@blockwatch.com
blockwatch.com
Overview: A small provincial charitable organization founded in 1986
Mission: To build safe neighbourhoods across British Columbia; To encourage bonds among local residents & businesses to create a crime free area through community participation; To assist in the reduction of crime; To improve relations between police & communities
Chief Officer(s):
Colleen Staresina, President, 604-502-6287, Fax: 604-502-6539
colleen.staresina@rcmp-grc.gc.ca
Gary O'Brien, Vice-President, 250-754-2345
Gary.OBrien@rcmp-grc.gc.ca
Jenniffer Sanford, Secretary, 604-529-2494, Fax: 604-529-2422
Blockwatch@nwpolice.org
Michelle Wulff, Treasurer, 604-393-3000, Fax: 604-819-0865
michelle.wulff@rcmp-grc.gc.ca
Membership: 88 societies; *Member Profile:* Members who watch for suspicious activity in their neighbourhoods
Activities: Partnering with police; Supporting Block Watch programs throughout British Columbia; Increasing crime awareness; Sharing knowledge of security measures, through the provision of resource materials; Training captains & co-captains;
Awards:
• Safe Communities Grant (Grant)
• Crime Prevention Award (Award)
Publications:
• Block Watch Society of British Columbia Newsletter
Type: Newsletter
Profile: Information about crime trends, security, & society events

Blomidon Naturalists Society (BNS)
PO Box 2350, Wolfville NS B4P 2N5
e-mail: members@blomidonnaturalists.ca
blomidonnaturalists.ca
Overview: A small local charitable organization founded in 1974
Mission: To encourage & develop an understanding & appreciation of nature
Member of: Nature Nova Scotia, Nature Canada
Chief Officer(s):
John Owen, President
john.owen@ns.sympatico.ca
Helen Archibald, Secretary
hfarchibald@ns.sympatico.ca
Finances: *Annual Operating Budget:* $50,000-$100,000; *Funding Sources:* Membership dues
15 volunteer(s)
Membership: 250; *Fees:* $20 adult, family; $1 Junior

Activities: Monthly meetings; field trips; bird counts; astronomy sessions
Awards:
• Robie Tufts Young Naturalist Award (Award)
Publications:
• Blomidon Naturalists Society Newsletter
Type: Newsletter; *Frequency:* Quarterly; *Number of Pages:* 48
Profile: Published once every season of the year around the equinoxes & solstices.

Blonde d'Aquitaine du Québec
1395, Rte. 122, Notre-Dame-du-Bon-Conseil QC J0C 1A0
Tel: 819-336-3966; *Fax:* 819-336-2883
www.blondaquitaineqc.com
Overview: A small provincial organization
Member of: Canadian Blonde d'Aquitaine Association
Chief Officer(s):
Clemency Landry, President
Maureen Landry, Secretary

Blood Ties Four Directions Centre
307 Strickland St., Whitehorse YT Y1A 2J9
Tel: 867-633-2437; *Fax:* 867-633-2447
Toll-Free: 877-333-2437
bloodties@klondiker.com
www.bloodties.ca
Previous Name: AIDS Yukon Alliance
Overview: A small provincial charitable organization founded in 1988 overseen by Canadian AIDS Society
Mission: To acts as an information & support centre; to promote public awareness of AIDS/AIDS & hepatitis C and aid in their prevention; to assist people living with HIV/AIDS & hep C.
Member of: Pacific AIDS Network
Chief Officer(s):
Patricia Bacon, Executive Director
executivedirector@bloodties.ca
Finances: *Funding Sources:* Government grants
Staff Member(s): 6
Membership: *Member Profile:* PHA's, families, friends, interested parties
Activities: Support group; treatment information; outreach; *Speaker Service:* Yes; *Library:* Resource Library; Open to public

Blue Line Racing Association
Edmonton AB
e-mail: bluelineracing@live.ca
bluelineracing.ca
www.facebook.com/214136468679819
Overview: A small local charitable organization founded in 1996
Mission: To promote safe & legal alternatives to street racing in Edmonton
Chief Officer(s):
Mike Wynnyk, Constable, Contact
Finances: *Funding Sources:* Donations
5 volunteer(s)

Blue Mountain Foundation for the Arts (BMFA)
PO Box 581, 163 Hurontario St., Collingwood ON L9Y 4E8
Tel: 705-445-3430; *Fax:* 705-445-0840
admin@bmfa.on.ca
www.bmfa.on.ca
Overview: A medium-sized local organization founded in 1975
Mission: To make the arts an integral part of life in southern Georgian Bay community; To develop talent & broaden appreciation of the arts; To nurture excellence in the arts; To work with other community groups; To foster wide variety of opportunities for creative expression; To broaden range of quality programs which are offered to increase public participation & fundraising
Chief Officer(s):
Deborah Mobbs, Executive Director
Susan Cook, Adminstrator, 705-445-3430
admin@bmfa.on.ca
Staff Member(s): 1; 100 volunteer(s)
Membership: 375; *Fees:* Schedule available; *Committees:* Performing Arts; Performing Arts for Youth; Publications; Visual Arts; Policy; Planning; Finance

Blue Mountains Chamber of Commerce
PO Box 477, Thornbury ON N0H 2P0
Tel: 519-599-1200; *Fax:* 519-599-2567
info@bluemountainschamber.ca
www.bluemountainschamber.ca
Previous Name: Thornbury & District Chamber of Commerce
Overview: A small local organization
Chief Officer(s):
Jim Farmilo, President, 519-599-3859
akfarmilo2@sympatico.ca
Membership: 131; *Fees:* $55 non-profit; $155 business; $120 banner ad; *Committees:* Executive; Membership; Events; Finance; Nominating; Economic Development; Chamber Building; Community Watch; Sparc Competition
Awards:
• Business of the Year Award (Award)
• Entrepreneur of the Year Award (Award)
• Carol Kordts Customer Service Award (Award)
• Site Improvement Award (Award)
• Special Merit Award for Business (Award)
• Merit Award for Individuals (Award)

Blue Water Chamber of Commerce
PO Box 204, St Georges MB R0E 1V0
Tel: 204-367-2762; *Fax:* 204-367-4030
bluewaterchamber@hotmail.com
Overview: A small local organization
Member of: Manitoba Chamber of Commerce
Chief Officer(s):
Diane Dube, President
cdc@granite.mb.ca

Bluegrass Music Association of Canada (BMAC)
c/o Secretary, 339 Wellington St. N, Woodstock ON N4S 6S6
Tel: 519-539-8967
bluegrasscanada.ca
www.facebook.com/bluegrassmusicassociationofcanada.ca
Overview: A small national organization
Mission: The Bluegrass Music Association is dedicated to the preservation and promotion of Bluegrass and Old-time music throughout Canada. The BMAC works to support individuals, groups and organizations involved in bluegrass and old-time music and provide leadership and promote education among fans, clubs, bands and artists.
Affliation(s): International Bluegrass Music Association; Canadian Country Music Association; The Ontario Council of Folk Festivals; Northern Ontario Country Music Association
Chief Officer(s):
Denis Chadbourn, President
Membership: *Fees:* $20 individual

Bluewater Recycling Association (BRA)
415 Canada Ave., Huron Park ON N0M 1Y0
Tel: 519-228-6678; *Fax:* 519-228-6656
info@bra.org
www.bra.org
Overview: A small local organization founded in 1989
Mission: To provide ethical, innovative, effective resource-management services; To carry out our mission efficiently, safely & in an environmentally responsible manner, ultimately enabling our members to meet their environmental commitments
Finances: *Annual Operating Budget:* Greater than $5 Million
Staff Member(s): 55
Membership: 21; *Fees:* Schedule available; *Member Profile:* Municipalities
Activities: *Speaker Service:* Yes
Publications:
• Bluewater Recycling Newsletter
Type: Newsletter

Bluffton & District Chamber of Commerce
PO Box 38, Bluffton AB T0C 0M0
Tel: 403-843-6805; *Fax:* 403-843-3392
Overview: A small local organization
Chief Officer(s):
Peter Broere, Director
petercanada@hotmail.com

BMW Club of Canada *See* BMW Clubs Canada

BMW Club of Regina *See* BMW Clubs Canada

BMW Clubs Canada (BMWCC) / Le Club BMW du Canada
c/o National Secretary, 4635 Doherty Ave., Montréal QC H4B 2B2
e-mail: info@bmwclub.ca
www.bmwclub.ca
www.facebook.com/BMW.Canada
Previous Name: BMW Club of Canada
Overview: A medium-sized national organization founded in 1973
Mission: The umbrella organization is comprised of regional chapter clubs that actively provide a variety of events to promote the enjoyment & sharing of good will & fellowship derived from owning a BMW automobile or motorcycle.
Member of: International Council of BMW Clubs
Chief Officer(s):
Phil Abrami, President
Finances: *Annual Operating Budget:* $100,000-$250,000; *Funding Sources:* Membership dues
Membership: 800; *Fees:* $40-$60 (depending on local chapter)
Activities: Driving schools; motorsport; social activities; technical information; *Speaker Service:* Yes
Awards:
• Participation Trophy (Award)
• Competition Trophy (Award)

Atlantic Canada Chapter
#607, 105 Dunbrack St., Halifax NS B3M 3G7
Tel: 902-443-6369
info@bmwclubatlantic.ca
bmwclubatlantic.ca
twitter.com/BMWClubAtlantic
www.flickr.com/photos/55144543@N08

BMW Car Club of BC
PO Box 3452, 349 West Georgia St., Vancouver BC V6B 3Y4
e-mail: info@bmwccbc.org
www.bmwccbc.org
Chief Officer(s):
David Gray, President
david@bmwccbc.org

BMW Car Club of Ottawa
PO Box 23179, Ottawa ON K2A 4E2
e-mail: info@bmwccottawa.org
bmwccottawa.org
Chief Officer(s):
Chris Pawlowicz, President, Webmaster
chris@pawlowicz.ca

BMW Club of Manitoba
2071 Portage Ave., Winnipeg MB R3J 0K9
e-mail: info@bmwpower.ca
bmwclubmanitoba.com
twitter.com/BMWclubMB
Chief Officer(s):
Jeremy Choy, Contact

BMW Club of Québec
4535, av du Parc, Montréal QC H2V 4E4
e-mail: info@bmwquebec.ca
bmwquebec.ca

BMW Club of Saskatchewan
3655 Wetmore Cres., Regina SK S4V 2C2
e-mail: hello@bmwsask.com
bmwsask.com
www.facebook.com/bmwsask
twitter.com/bmwsask

Northern Alberta BMW Club
PO Box 52024, Edmonton AB T6G 2T5
e-mail: info@nabmwclub.ca
www.nabmwclub.ca
www.facebook.com/NorthernAlbertaBmwClub
twitter.com/NABMWyeg
Chief Officer(s):
Vince Paniak, President
vpaniak@nabmwclub.ca

Southern Alberta BMW Club
3 Canova Rd. SW, Calgary AB T2W 2K5
Fax: 403-281-4463
email@bmwcsa.ca
www.bmwcsa.ca
Chief Officer(s):
Brian Deboeck, President
president@bmwcsa.ca

Trillium Chapter
#530, 4936 Yonge St., Toronto ON M2N 6S3
Fax: 866-801-9185
trillium@bmwclub.ca
www.trillium-bmwclub.ca
Chief Officer(s):
Jennifer Venditti, President
jennifer.venditti@trillium-bmwclub.ca

Vancouver Island BMW Club
PO Box 30181, Stn. Saanich Centre, Victoria BC V8X 5E1
e-mail: island@bmwclub.ca
www.bmwccvi.ca

Board of Canadian Registered Safety Professionals (BCRSP) / Conseil canadien des professionnels en securité agréés
6519B Mississauga Rd., Mississauga ON L5N 1A6

Tel: 905-567-7198; *Fax:* 905-567-7191
Toll-Free: 888-279-2777
info@bcrsp.ca
www.bcrsp.ca
Previous Name: Association for Canadian Registered Safety Professionals
Overview: A medium-sized national licensing organization founded in 1976
Mission: To protect & promote occupational health & safety, environmental safety, & public safety, through the registration of qualified health & safety professionals committed to a code of ethics
Chief Officer(s):
Ron Durdle, Chair
Nicola Wright, Executive Director
Finances: *Annual Operating Budget:* $250,000-$500,000; *Funding Sources:* Membership dues
Staff Member(s): 5; 130 volunteer(s)
Membership: 2,000; *Fees:* $125; *Member Profile:* Successfully completed high school or equivalency; three years of continuous safety experience & current employment of at least 50% in a safety practitioners role
Activities: CRSP designation (the Board evaluates qualifications of candidates & members against established standards);

Board of Directors of Drugless Therapy, Naturopathy (Ontario) (BDDT-N)
112 Adelaide St. East, Toronto ON M5C 1K9
Tel: 416-866-8383; *Fax:* 416-866-2175
Toll-Free: 877-361-1925
office@bddtn.on.ca
www.bddtn.on.ca
Also Known As: Board of Naturopathy
Previous Name: Ontario Board of Directors, Drugless Therapy/Naturopathy
Overview: A small provincial licensing organization founded in 1925
Mission: To register & regulate Naturopathic Doctors in Ontario; To investigate complaints from patients & the public
Member of: Federation of Health Regulatory Colleges of Ontario
Affliation(s): North American Board of Naturopathic Examiners; Ontario Association of Naturopathic Doctors
Chief Officer(s):
Patricia J. Rennie, ND, Chair
Angela M. Moore, ND, Executive Director
Finances: *Annual Operating Budget:* $250,000-$500,000
Staff Member(s): 3
Membership: 810 total; 669 active NDs in Ontario; 140 inactive or out or province; *Fees:* $250 inactive; $900 active; *Committees:* Continuing Education; Examinations; Parenteral Therapy; Complaints Review; Policy Development

Board of Examiners in Optometry in B.C. *See* College of Optometrists of BC

Board of Funeral Services Ontario
PO Box 117, #2810, 777 Bay St., Toronto ON M5G 2C8
Tel: 416-979-5450; *Fax:* 416-979-0384
Toll-Free: 800-387-4458
info@funeralboard.com
www.funeralboard.com
Also Known As: Ontario Board of Funeral Services
Overview: A medium-sized provincial licensing organization founded in 1976
Chief Officer(s):
Peter M. Jordan, Acting Registrar, 416-979-5450 Ext. 29
peterjordan@funeralboard.com
Susan J. Beck, Manager, Licensing, 416-979-5450 Ext. 23
susanb@funeralboard.com
Finances: *Annual Operating Budget:* $1.5 Million-$3 Million; *Funding Sources:* License fees; Examination fees; Professional development; Investment revenue
Staff Member(s): 10; 26 volunteer(s)
Membership: 3,200; *Member Profile:* Funeral Directors & Funeral Establishments; *Committees:* Executive; Licensing; Complaints; Discipline; Compensation Fund; Audit, Finance & Risk; Communications & Long Range Planning
Publications:
• Board of Funeral Services Annual Report
Type: Annual Report; *Frequency:* a.
Profile: The board's year in review
• Board of Funeral Services Newsletter
Type: Newsletter
Profile: Technical information for licensees
• Professional Competency Profile: Ontario Funeral Director
Type: Guide; *Number of Pages:* 25
Profile: Description of a position & the associated duties to aid in education and professional development
• Review of the Goals & Objectives of Funeral Service Education in the Province of Ontario 2001
Type: Report; *Number of Pages:* 73
Profile: A report to identify necessary changes to funeral service education in Ontario

Board of Registration for Social Workers in B.C. *See* British Columbia College of Social Workers

Board of Trade of Metropolitan Montréal *Voir* Chambre de commerce du Montréal métropolitain

Boating Ontario
15 Laurier Rd., Penetanguishene ON L9M 1G8
Tel: 705-549-1667; *Fax:* 705-549-1670
Toll-Free: 888-547-6662
info@boatingontario.ca
www.boatingontario.ca
Previous Name: Ontario Marine Operators Association
Overview: A medium-sized provincial organization founded in 1967
Mission: To promote recreational boating throughout Ontario
Chief Officer(s):
Dick Peever, President, 519-524-4409, Fax: 519-524-2301
Graham Lacey, Vice-President, 705-383-2295, Fax: 705-383-2243
Al Donaldson, Executive Director, 705-549-1667, Fax: 705-549-1670
Ed Leeman, Secretary, 613-583-7973
Bob Eaton, Director, Environmental Services, 705-326-9359, Fax: 705-326-3827
Membership: 460+ individual marinas + 160 trade members; *Member Profile:* Ontario marinas; Yacht clubs; Marine dealers; Associated companies
Activities: Lobbying on behalf of the industry; Providing information; Encouraging safe boating; Participating in boat shows; Offering workshops
Publications:
• Boating Ontario: Marinas & Destination Guide
Type: Directory; *Frequency:* Annually
Profile: A guide to more than 450 marina members of the Ontario Marine Operators Association, with information about their facilities & services
• Enviro Boater
Type: Manual
Profile: Suggestions for environment-friendly boating, produced by the Ontario Marine Operators Association, the Canadian Power & Sail Squadrons, & other interested organizations
• Marina News
Type: Newsletter; *Frequency:* 8 pa; *Price:* Free with membership in the Ontario Marine Operators Association
Profile: Business suggestions & industry news, for members of the Ontario Marine Operators Association

The Bob Rumball Centre for the Deaf (BRCD)
2395 Bayview Ave., Toronto ON M2L 1A2
Tel: 416-449-9651; *Fax:* 416-449-8881; *TTY:* 416-449-2728
info@bobrumball.org
www.bobrumball.org
www.facebook.com/86097284911
Overview: A large local organization founded in 1979
Mission: To provide opportunities for a higher quality of life for deaf people while preserving & promoting their language & culture; to foster & develop good relations with the community at large & actively promote the Centre; to work closely with the various ministries of the provincial government & related agencies.
Member of: Ontario Mission of the Deaf
Chief Officer(s):
Alistair M. Fraser, Chairman
Finances: *Annual Operating Budget:* $3 Million-$5 Million; *Funding Sources:* Government; user fees; private & public donations
Staff Member(s): 75; 200 volunteer(s)
Activities: Adult education and residential program; Day and early years programs; Preschool program; Progressive independent living; Senior Supportive Housing; Sign language services; Volunteer services.; *Internships:* Yes; *Speaker Service:* Yes

Bob Rumball Foundation for the Deaf
2395 Bayview Ave., Toronto ON M2L 1A2
Tel: 416-449-9651; *Fax:* 416-449-8881; *TTY:* 416-449-2728
fundraising@bobrumball.org
www.bobrumball.org
www.facebook.com/86097284911
Previous Name: Ontario Mission of the Deaf
Overview: A small local organization founded in 1872
Mission: To meet the social, recreational, educational & spiritual needs of the deaf community & raise funds for The Bob Rumball Centre for the Deaf in Toronto, The Bob Rumball Associations for the Deaf in Milton, The Bob Rumball Long Term Care Home for the Deaf in Barrie & The Bob Rumball Camp for the Deaf in Parry Sound.
Chief Officer(s):
Derek Rumball, Executive Director

Bobcaygeon & Area Chamber of Commerce
PO Box 388, 21 Canal St. East, Bobcaygeon ON K0M 1A0
Tel: 705-738-2202; *Fax:* 705-738-1534
Toll-Free: 800-318-6173
chamber@bobcaygeon.org
www.bobcaygeon.org
Overview: A small local organization
Mission: To promote Bobcaygeon as a tourist area; To promote business in the area
Member of: Ontario Chamber of Commerce
Affliation(s): Kawartha Lakes Associated Chambers of Commerce
Chief Officer(s):
Jim DeClute, President
Finances: *Annual Operating Budget:* Less than $50,000; *Funding Sources:* Membership dues; Ministry of Transportation
Staff Member(s): 3; 14 volunteer(s)
Membership: 200; *Fees:* $145

Bobsleigh Canada Skeleton
c/o Canada Olympic Park, #329, 151 Canada Olympic Rd. SW, Calgary AB T3B 6B7
Tel: 403-247-5950; *Fax:* 403-202-6561
info@bobsleigh.ca
www.bobsleigh.ca
www.facebook.com/BobsleighCanadaSkeleton
twitter.com/BobsleighCAN
Overview: A medium-sized national charitable organization founded in 1990
Mission: To strive to create Olympic & world champions
Member of: Canadian Olympic Association
Affliation(s): Fédération internationale de bobsleigh et de tobogganing
Chief Officer(s):
Don Wilson, CEO
Finances: *Funding Sources:* Government & corporate sponsorship
Staff Member(s): 8
Activities: Operating national teams in men's & women's bobsleigh & skeleton; Hosting national & international events

Boissevain & District Chamber of Commerce
c/o Municipal Office, PO Box 490, 420 South Railway St., Boissevain MB R0K 0E0
Tel: 204-534-2433; *Fax:* 204-534-3710
admin@boissevain.ca
www.boissevain.ca
Overview: A small local organization
Mission: To promote the business of Boissevain & area.
Chief Officer(s):
Bill Dougall, President, 204-534-2411
Rhonda Coupland, Secretary, 204-534-2010
60 volunteer(s)
Membership: 60+; *Fees:* $20-150; *Committees:* Tourism; Agriculture; Beautification

Boîte à science - Conseil du loisir scientifique du Québec
4274 rue Saint-Felix, Québec QC G1Y 1X5
Tél: 418-658-1426; *Téléc:* 418-658-1012
info@boiteascience.com
www.boiteascience.com
Nom précédent: Conseil du loisir scientifique de Québec
Aperçu: *Dimension:* moyenne; *Envergure:* locale; Organisme sans but lucratif; fondée en 1981
Mission: Éveiller, prioritairement chez les jeunes, leur interêt pour les science et la technologie
Membre(s) du bureau directeur:
Manon Théberge, Directrice générale
Alain Madgin, Président

Finances: *Budget de fonctionnement annuel:* $500,000-$1.5 Million; *Fonds:* Gouvernement; autofinancement; levées de fonds
Membre(s) du personnel: 8; 250 bénévole(s)
Membre: 8
Activités: Club des Débrouillards; Expo-sciences régionale; Aventure scientifique; Innovateur à l'école; Salle de découvertes; Défi apprenti-génie; Voilà Science!; Centres de table scientifiques; la Science dans ma classe; Pop science; *Stagiaires:* Oui; *Service de conférenciers:* Oui

Les Bolides
3350, rue Ontario Est, Montréal QC H1W 1P7
Tél: 514-522-7773
info@lesbolides.org
www.lesbolides.org
Aperçu: *Dimension:* petite; *Envergure:* locale
Mission: Ligue de quilles

BOMA Québec
#900, 500, rue Sherbrooke ouest, Montréal QC H3A 3C6
Tél: 514-282-3826; *Téléc:* 514-844-7556
Ligne sans frais: 855-682-3826
boma@boma-quebec.org
www.boma-quebec.org
www.linkedin.com/groups/BOMA-Québec-Association-propriétaires-gestionn
twitter.com/BOMAQc
Nom précédent: Association des propriétaires et administrateurs d'immeubles du Québec
Aperçu: *Dimension:* moyenne; *Envergure:* provinciale; fondée en 1927
Mission: Représenter les intérêts des propriétaires et des gérants d'édifices commerciaux et à bureaux au Québec
Membre de: Building Owners & Managers Association of Canada
Membre(s) du bureau directeur:
Anne Marie Guèvremont, Président
Linda Carbone, Directrice générale
Membre: 228; *Montant de la cotisation:* Barème; *Comités:* Affairs gouvernementales; conseil Québec métropolitan; communications; énergie et gestion technique; envrionnement; fête de Noël et activités sociales; formation; gestion des immeubles; golf; golf Québec métropolitan; membres affaires; normes et réglementations; recrutement; recrutement Québec métropolitan; relève; sécurité et mesures d'urgence
Activités: Déjeuner-causerie; cours de formation

Bon Accord Food Bank
PO Box 886, Bon Accord AB T0A 0K0
Tel: 780-923-2344; *Fax:* 780-923-3691
bbnimmo@telus.net
Previous Name: Bon Accord/Gibbon Food Bank
Overview: A small local organization overseen by Alberta Food Bank Network Association
Mission: A registered charity, BN: 118813328RR0001
Chief Officer(s):
Evelyn Orsten, Contact

Bon Accord/Gibbon Food Bank *See* Bon Accord Food Bank

Le Bon Pilote inc.
#511, 445, rue Jean-Talon ouest, Montréal QC H3N 1R1
Tél: 514-593-5454; *Téléc:* 514-419-6954
lebonpilote@videotron.ca
www.lebonpilote.com
www.linkedin.com/company/2609230
twitter.com/lebonpilote
Aperçu: *Dimension:* petite; *Envergure:* locale
Mission: Pour aider les personnes ayant une déficience visuelle en leur fournissant des services et en développant de nouveaux services pour faire avancer leur cause
Affliation(s): Institut Nazareth & Louis-Braille; MAB-Mackay; Agence de la santé et des services sociaux de Montréal; Agence de la santé et des services sociaux de la Montérégie; Les BusBoys.com, site pour les employés / retraités de la STM
Membre(s) du bureau directeur:
John D. Gill, Directeur général, 514-531-5330
johngill@videotron.ca
Membre: *Montant de la cotisation:* Barème; *Critères d'admissibilite:* Les personnes ayant une déficience visuelle ou amblyope

Bonavista Area Chamber of Commerce (BACC)
PO Box 280, Bonavista NL A0C 1B0
Fax: 709-468-2495
info@bacc.ca
www.bacc.ca
Overview: A small local organization founded in 2002
Mission: To create a business climate of competitiveness, profitability & job creation for all businesses on the northern section of the Bonavista Peninsula; To improve the general civic & social welfare of the region
Chief Officer(s):
Diane Thorpe, Secretary
Finances: *Annual Operating Budget:* Less than $50,000
10 volunteer(s)
Membership: 1-99
Awards:
• Order of the Bonavista Area Chamber of Commerce
• Long Service Awards

Bonavista Historic Townscape Foundation (BHTF)
PO Box 10, Bonavista NL A0C 1B0
Tel: 709-468-2880; *Fax:* 709-468-7253
Other Communication: Alternate Phone: 709-468-7547; e-mail: info@garricktheatre.ca
garrickboxoffice@nf.aibn.com
www.garricktheatre.ca
www.facebook.com/garricktheatre
twitter.com/Garrick_Theatre
Overview: A small local organization founded in 1998
Chief Officer(s):
Ray Troke, Manager
David Bradley, Contact, 709-737-8232
Finances: *Annual Operating Budget:* Less than $50,000
Staff Member(s): 5; 20 volunteer(s)
Membership: 1-99
Activities: Operating the Garrick Theatre;

Bonnechere Soaring Club
PO Box 1081, Deep River ON K0J 1P0
Tel: 613-584-4636
Overview: A small local organization
Member of: Soaring Association of Canada
Chief Officer(s):
Erik Hagberg, Contact
hagberg@sympatico.ca

Bonnyville & District Chamber of Commerce
PO Box 6054, Hwy. 28 West, Bonnyville AB T9N 2G7
Tel: 780-826-3252; *Fax:* 780-826-4525
www.bonnyvillechamber.com
ca.linkedin.com/pub/bonnyville-chamber-of-commerce/91/356/212
Overview: A small local organization
Mission: To act as the voice of local business
Member of: Alberta Chamber of Commerce; Canadian Chamber of Commerce
Chief Officer(s):
Megan Naylor, Contact
Finances: *Funding Sources:* Membership dues
Membership: *Fees:* Schedule available based on number of employees
Activities: Rodeo; Small Business Seminars; Golf Scramble; Business of the Year

Bonnyville & District Fine Arts Society
PO Box 5086, 4900 - 49 St., Bonnyville AB T9N 2G3
Tel: 780-826-3986; *Fax:* 780-826-2959
Overview: A small local organization
Mission: To encourage & facilitate appreciation & involvement in the arts in Bonnyville & district
Member of: Alberta Municipal Association for Culture
Chief Officer(s):
Patricia Perry, President
Finances: *Funding Sources:* Fees; donations; Alberta Community Development Grants; fundraising bingos & performances
Activities: "Touch of Class" Performance Series

Bonnyville Canadian Native Friendship Centre
PO Box 5399, 4711 - 50 Ave., Bonnyville AB T9N 2G5
Tel: 780-826-3374; *Fax:* 780-826-2540
bcnfced@incentre.net
www.bcnfc.com
Overview: A small local organization founded in 1971 overseen by Alberta Native Friendship Centres Association
Mission: To create a healthy, productive community through innovative & cultural services
Member of: Alberta Native Friendship Centres Association
Finances: *Funding Sources:* Membership dues
Membership: *Fees:* $5-10

Book & Periodical Council (BPC)
#107, 192 Spadina Ave., Toronto ON M5T 2C2
Tel: 416-975-9366; *Fax:* 416-975-1839
info@thebpc.ca
www.thebpc.ca
Overview: A medium-sized national organization founded in 1975
Mission: To increase the level of awareness & the use of Canadian materials by the general public & in educational systems at all levels; To ensure the public has an adequate & representative range of Canadian books & periodicals in sales outlets, library systems & educational institutions; To strengthen book & periodical distribution systems; To support the development of new & existing Canadian-owned companies & encourage their growth & expansion; To improve market conditions & contractual arrangements as well as promotion & publicity given to Canadian writers & their work; To encourage the development of writing & publishing projects of social & cultural importance; To improve the cultural & economic climate in which the Canadian book & periodical industries exist; To discourage expansion of foreign ownership in all sectors of the book & periodical publishing industries
Member of: Canadian Conference of the Arts
Chief Officer(s):
Anita Purcell, Chair
Finances: *Funding Sources:* Membership fees
100 volunteer(s)
Membership: 12 full + 15 associate associations + 5 affiliates; *Fees:* Schedule available; *Committees:* Freedom of Expression; Freight; Appointed Task Forces
Activities: *Awareness Events:* Freedom to Read Week, February
Meetings/Conferences: • Book & Periodical Council's 2015 Book Summit, 2015
Scope: National
Description: An annual one day professional development conference, featuring workshops, panel discussions, & keynote speakers
Contact Information: Web Site: www.booksummit.ca; E-mail: publicity@theBPC.ca

Book Publishers Association of Alberta (BPAA)
10523 - 100 Ave., Edmonton AB T5J 0A8
Tel: 780-424-5060; *Fax:* 780-424-7943
info@bookpublishers.ab.ca
www.bookpublishers.ab.ca
Previous Name: Alberta Publishers Association
Overview: A medium-sized provincial organization founded in 1975 overseen by Association of Canadian Publishers
Mission: To work for maintenance & growth of strong book publishing houses owned & controlled in Alberta; to speak for common interests of constituent members; to liaise & cooperate with other associations for the good of the Canadian publishing industry
Member of: Canadian Booksellers Association; Alberta Library Association; Edmonton Arts Council; Access Copyright; Book & Periodical Council; Edmonton Small Press Association; Alberta Cultural Industries Association
Affliation(s): Publishers Association of the West
Chief Officer(s):
Kieran Leblanc, Executive Director
Finances: *Annual Operating Budget:* $100,000-$250,000; *Funding Sources:* Membership fees; grants; project
Staff Member(s): 2
Membership: 35 publishers; *Fees:* $250 Supporting; $500 Associate; $750; Full
Activities: Displays; promotion; seminars; liaison; resource; professional development; *Awareness Events:* Alberta Book Fair
Awards:
• Alberta Book Awards (Award)
To recognize outstanding achievements in Alberta publishing; nine awards are given - Alberta Publisher of the Year, Alberta Trade Book of the Year, Alberta Book Design Award, Alberta Book Cover Design Award, Alberta Educational Book of the Year, Alberta Childrens' Book of the Year, Alberta Book Illustration Award, Alberta Scholarly Book, Alberta Emerging Publisher of the Year *Amount:* Stone carvings by Brian Clark are presented & kept by the winner in the award year

Boot'n Bonnet British Car Club
c/o Brian & Linda Thomas, RR#1, Wolfe Island ON K0H 2Y0
Tel: 613-385-1947
www.bootnbonnet.ca
Overview: A small national organization founded in 1990

Member of: British Car Council of Canada
Chief Officer(s):
Jamie Berry, President, 613-968-6990
j_berry@xplornet.ca
Finances: *Annual Operating Budget:* Less than $50,000; *Funding Sources:* Membership dues; events
10 volunteer(s)
Membership: 250+; *Fees:* $30
Activities: Car tours; meetings; barbeques; *Awareness Events:* British Car Day, Aug.; Autojumble
Publications:
• The Spanner [a pubication of the Boot'n Bonnet British Car Club]
Type: Newsletter; *Frequency:* q.; *Editor:* Ken Law

Border Boosters Square & Round Dance Association (BBSRDA)
Toll-Free: 866-206-6696
www.borderboosters.qc.ca
Previous Name: Québec Square & Round Dance Clubs
Overview: A medium-sized local organization founded in 1952 overseen by Canadian Square & Round Dance Society
Mission: To promote square & round dancing in the Québec, eastern Ontario & northern New York area
Chief Officer(s):
Ruth Cunningham, President
Membership: 14 clubs
Activities: Supports member clubs & holds two dances a year

Border Cities Real Estate Board *See* Windsor-Essex County Real Estate Board

Boreal Institute for Northern Studies (1960-1990) *See* Canadian Circumpolar Institute

Bosnian Canadian Relief Association (BCRA)
122 North Queen St., Toronto ON M8Z 2E4
Tel: 416-236-9411; *Fax:* 416-237-0656
bosnianrelief.org
www.facebook.com/BosnianCanadianReliefAssociation
Also Known As: Bosnian Islamic Association Gazi Husrev-Beg
Overview: A small international organization founded in 1992
Mission: To provide humanitarian aid for the victims in Bosnia & Herzegovina
Affliation(s): Bosnian Canadian Community Association
Finances: *Funding Sources:* Provincial grant; private donations
Activities: *Speaker Service:* Yes; *Library:* Documentation Centre; Open to public by appointment

Bosnian Islamic Association (BIAGH)
122 North Queen St., Toronto ON M8Z 2E4
Tel: 416-233-5967
www.biaghb.com
www.facebook.com/BosnianIslamicAssociationGaziHusrevBeg
Also Known As: Gazi Husrev-Beg
Previous Name: Association of Islamic Community Gazi Husrev-Beg
Overview: A small local organization founded in 1977
Mission: To respond to the religious needs of the Bosnian Islamic community
Chief Officer(s):

Membership: *Member Profile:* Bosnian Canadians
Activities: Providing classes, lectures, & workshops in Islamic education & national folklore for children, youth, & adults; Offering recreational activities, such as soccer & karate; Hosting special programs to observe religious holidays; Performing marriage ceremonies by the Imam; Providing counselling for individuals & families; Offering assistance with wills & Janazah; Cooperating with other Bosnian organizations

Bothwell-Zone & District Historical Society
PO Box 271, Bothwell ON N0P 1C0
Tel: 519-695-3619
historicbothwell@hotmail.com
www.historicbothwell.ca
Also Known As: Bothwell-Zone Oil Museum
Overview: A small local charitable organization founded in 1990
Mission: To establish & maintain the Bothwell-Zone Oil Museum to depict & preserve the history, production methods, & equipment of primitive oil technology used in the 19th & 20th century as the world was striving to find a product to light their homes
Affliation(s): Ontario Historical Society
Finances: *Annual Operating Budget:* Less than $50,000
Activities: Black Gold Days; Bothwell-Zone Oil Museum; *Speaker Service:* Yes; *Library* by appointment

Bouctouche Chamber of Commerce / Chambre de commerce de Bouctouche
PO Box 2104, Bouctouche NB E4S 2J2
Tel: 506-743-2411; *Fax:* 506-743-8991
chambouc@nb.aibn.com
www.bouctouche.ca/site/CDC/
Overview: A small local organization founded in 1947
Mission: To be the spokesperson for the businesses of the region; To help develop economic growth & a better quality of life in Bouctouche
Member of: Atlantic Chamber of Commerce; New Brunswick Chamber of Commerce; Chambre de Commerce du Canada
Chief Officer(s):
Claude LeBlanc, President
Carole Léger, Staff
Finances: *Annual Operating Budget:* Less than $50,000; *Funding Sources:* Bingo; golf tournament
Staff Member(s): 1
Membership: 120; *Fees:* Schedule available; *Committees:* Funding; Programs & Services; Promotion
Activities: *Rents Mailing List:* Yes

Bouffe pour tous/Moisson Longueuil
911, boul Roalnd-Therrien, Longueuil QC J4J 4L3
Tél: 450-970-5449
www.bouffepourtous.org
Aperçu: *Dimension:* petite; *Envergure:* locale
Mission: Faciliter l'approvisionnement en d'enrées alimentaires aux familles démunies et personnes seules depuis plus de 12 ans; familles monoparentales, gens sans emploi, gens aux prises avec des problèmes de drogues ou de violence
Membre: 1,200; *Critères d'admissibilite:* Les familles et les personnes dans le besoin

Boundary Country Regional Chamber of Commerce
PO Box 2942, 1647 Central Ave., Grand Forks BC V0H 1H0
Tel: 250-442-2722; *Fax:* 250-442-5311
info@boundarychamber.com
www.boundarychamber.com
Previous Name: Chamber of Commerce of the City of Grand Forks, Grand Forks Board of Trade
Overview: A small local organization founded in 1899
Mission: To improve the economic growth & well-being of our community.
Member of: Canadian Chamber of Commerce; BC Chamber of Commerce
Chief Officer(s):
Todd Benson, President
Finances: *Annual Operating Budget:* $50,000-$100,000; *Funding Sources:* Membership fees; municipal & provincial fees for service
Staff Member(s): 2; 12 volunteer(s)
Membership: 142; *Fees:* $85-$345
Activities: Visitor Info Centre & Business Information Centre; Chamberlink - a direct electronic link to all BC chambers; *Library:* Business Resource Library

Boundary District Arts Council (BDAC)
PO Box 2636, Grand Forks BC V0H 1E0
e-mail: boundaryarts@yahoo.ca
boundaryarts.org
www.facebook.com/108200982601187
Overview: A small local organization founded in 1976
Mission: To promote art in the Boundary area by investing in various artistic productions
Member of: Assembly of BC Arts Councils
Chief Officer(s):
Michele Garrison, President
michele.shellygarrison@gmail.com
Membership: 19; *Fees:* $20; *Member Profile:* Arts groups

Boundary Organic Producers Association (BOPA)
PO Box 675, Grand Forks BC V0H 1H0
Tel: 250-442-5840
Overview: A small local licensing organization
Affliation(s): Certified Organic Associations of BC
Chief Officer(s):
Karl Lilgert, President
Christine Carlson, Administrator
christine@slowkettle.org
Finances: *Annual Operating Budget:* Less than $50,000
Staff Member(s): 1
Membership: 10-15 certified organic operators & associate members; *Fees:* $25; *Member Profile:* Organic producers & processors; *Committees:* Certification
Activities: Organic certification of producers & processors

Boundless Adventures Association
7513 River Rd., RR#1, Palmer Rapids ON K0J 2E0
Tel: 416-658-7059; *Fax:* 613-758-2196
office@theboundlessschool.com
www.theboundlessschool.com
www.facebook.com/theboundlessschool
www.flickr.com/photos/boundlesshighschool
Also Known As: The Boundless School
Overview: A small local charitable organization founded in 1984
Mission: To improve the lives of marginalized youth, adults & children at risk through counselling, social rehabilitation, alternative education and outdoor adventure.
Chief Officer(s):
Steven Gottlieb, Executive Director

Bow Island / Burdett District Chamber of Commerce
PO Box 1001, 116 North Railway Ave. West, Bow Island AB T0K 0G0
Tel: 403-545-6222; *Fax:* 403-545-6042
chamber@bowislandchamber.com
www.bowislandchamber.com
Overview: A small local organization founded in 1951
Mission: To present various events & promotions
Member of: Alberta Chamber of Commerce; Red Coat Trail Association
Chief Officer(s):
Nan Maclean, President, 403-545-2991
Ron Thomson, Vice-President, 403-545-6242
drron@shaw.ca
Finances: *Annual Operating Budget:* Less than $50,000; *Funding Sources:* Trade fair; Las Vegas Days; Rentals; Membership dues
3 volunteer(s)
Membership: 147; *Fees:* $50/yr.; *Member Profile:* Businesses; Farmers; *Committees:* Business Awards; Trade Fair; Las Vegas; Christmas; Rodeo
Activities: Organizing an annual trade fair, Las Vegas Days, & a rodeo barbecue

Bow Valley Food Bank
PO Box 8071, 20 Sandstone Terrace, Camore AB T1W 2T8
Tel: 403-678-9488; *Fax:* 403-678-2694
admin@bowvalleyfoodbank.ca
www.bowvalleyfoodbank.ca
Overview: A small local charitable organization founded in 1994 overseen by Alberta Food Bank Network Association
Mission: Providing a supply of emergency food in crisis situations; Building partnerships with other community organizations dedicated to fighting hunger; Raising the awareness of hunger everywhere
Member of: Food Banks Canada

Bowden Historical Society
PO Box 576, Bowden AB T0M 0K0
Tel: 403-224-2122
2201@shawbiz.ca
www.bowdenpioneermuseum.com
Overview: A small local charitable organization founded in 1976
Mission: To create appreciation of our community & identity through the collection & preservation of historical artifacts & stories from Bowden.
Affliation(s): Alberta Museums Associations
Chief Officer(s):
Syd Cannings, President
Finances: *Funding Sources:* Grants; membership dues; donations; fundraising
Membership: *Fees:* $10
Activities: Operates Bowden Pioneer Museum

Bowen Island Arts Council (BIAC)
PO Box 211, Bowen Island BC V0N 1G0
Tel: 604-947-2454; *Fax:* 604-947-2460
admin@biac.ca
www.biac.ca
Overview: A small local charitable organization founded in 1988
Mission: To support & promote art & culture on Bowen Island through direct support to artists & performing groups; to operate a gallery & performance space on Bowen Island
Affliation(s): Assembly of BC Arts Councils
Chief Officer(s):
Carol Cram, President
Jacqueline M. Massey, Executive Director
Karen Watson, Gallery Coordinator/Curator
Finances: *Funding Sources:* Local grant; provincial grant; membership fees; donations
Staff Member(s): 2

Membership: *Fees:* $25 individual; $35 family; $45 organization; *Committees:* Gallery; Cultural Development; Communications; Community Hall & Arts Centre
Activities: Operates the multi-purpose gallery at Artesan Square for Bowen's Arts Council; sponsors performances & exhibits; links more specialized arts groups on Bowen Island; organizes the Bowen Art Walk, Studio Tours, & BC Cultural Crawl; produces the Classical Concert Series; *Speaker Service:* Yes

Bowen Island Chamber of Commerce
PO Box 199, 432 Cardena Rd., Bowen Island BC V0N 1G0
Tel: 604-947-9024; *Fax:* 604-947-0633
info@bowenisland.org
www.bowenisland.org
Overview: A small local organization
Chief Officer(s):
Tim Rhodes, President
Alison Morse, Administrator
Mary McGregor, Manager

Bowen Nature Club
RR#1, CL-27, Bowen Island BC V0N 1G0
Tel: 604-947-9562
bowennatureclub@gmail.com
bowennatureclub.blogspot.ca
Overview: A small local organization founded in 1985
Mission: To promote the enjoyment of nature through environmental appreciation & conservation; To encourage wise use & conservation of natural resources & environmental protection
Member of: Federation of BC Naturalists
Membership: *Fees:* $18 individual; $22 family

Bowling Federation of Alberta
11759 Groat Rd., Edmonton AB T5M 3K6
Tel: 780-422-8251
bowlfedab.ca
Overview: A small provincial organization
Mission: To promote competitive & noncompetitive bowling in Alberta.
Chief Officer(s):
Annette Bruneau, President
Grady Long, Executie Director
gradyed@bowlfedab.ca
Membership: 5 associations

Bowling Federation of Canada / Fédération des quilles du Canada
250 Shields Ct., #10A, Markham ON L3R 9W7
Tel: 905-479-1560
info@canadabowls.ca
www.canadabowls.ca
Overview: A medium-sized national organization
Mission: To promote & foster the sport of bowling in Canada; To promote among the recognized national organizations in Canada, sportmanship, good fellowhsip, & the continued interest in the future development of bowling throughout Canada
Affliation(s): Bowling Proprietors Association of Canada; Canadian 5-pin Bowlers Association; Canadian Tenpin Federation.
Chief Officer(s):
Bob Randall, President, 604-533-2695
brandall@shaw.ca
Sheila Carr, Administrator, 613-744-5090
c5pba@c5pba.ca

Bowling Federation of Saskatchewan
#101, 1805 - 8th Ave., Regina SK S4R 1E8
Tel: 306-780-9412; *Fax:* 306-780-9455
bowling@sasktel.net
saskbowl.com
twitter.com/SaskBowl
Overview: A medium-sized provincial organization founded in 1984
Mission: Working together through cooperation & harmonization to access & allocate funding for our members programs & services in order to enhance the sport of bowling
Member of: Sask Sport; Bowling Federation of Canada
Chief Officer(s):
Rhonda Sereda, Executive Director
Finances: *Funding Sources:* Sask Lotteries; sponsorship; fundraising

Bowling Proprietors' Association of BC
#209, 332 Columbia St., New Westminster BC V3L 1A6
Tel: 604-522-2990; *Fax:* 604-522-2055
bowl4fun@bowlbc.com
www.bowlbc.com
www.facebook.com/BowlBc
Also Known As: Bowl BC
Overview: A small provincial organization founded in 1954
Mission: To provide opportunities for people to bowl at their individual level
Chief Officer(s):
Ken Clarke, President
Activities: Adult, youth & seniors tournaments

Bowling Proprietors' Association of Canada (BPAC)
#10A, 250 Shields Ct., Markham ON L3R 9W7
Tel: 905-479-1560; *Fax:* 905-479-8613
info@bowlcanada.ca
www.bowlcanada.ca
Also Known As: Bowl Canada
Overview: A small national organization
Mission: The aim of this association is to improve general conditions in the bowling industry, to promote to the general public the benefits of bowling, to create a better relationship between the many bowling establishments across Canada and to encourage any and all practices which are in the best interests of the game.
Chief Officer(s):
Paul Oliveira, Executive Director
paul@bowlcanada.ca
Membership: 500 bowling centres
Activities: Youth Bowling Canada (YBC); Sunshine Bowlers; Club 55+.

Bowling Proprietors' Association of Ontario (BPAO)
#202, 500 Alden Rd., Markham ON L3R 5H5
Tel: 905-940-8200; *Fax:* 905-940-8201
info@bowlontario.ca
www.bowlontario.ca
Also Known As: Bowl Ontario
Overview: A medium-sized provincial organization founded in 1953
Mission: To improve conditions in bowling industry; To protect members from unreasonable legislation; To bring attention to the pleasures of bowling
Affliation(s): Bowling Proprietors' Association of Canada
Membership: 124 bowling centres; *Member Profile:* Bowling centre ownership
Awards:
• Annual Director's Service Award (Award)
• Player Award for Perfect Game (Award)
• Volunteer 5, 10, 20, 25 Year Service Awards (Award)
• Member of the Year Award (Award)

Bowls British Columbia
c/o Jackie West, 2168 Stirling Cres., Courtenay BC V9N 9X1
e-mail: info@bowlsbc.com
bowlsbc.com
twitter.com/bowlsbc
Also Known As: Bowls BC
Overview: A medium-sized provincial organization founded in 1925 overseen by Bowls Canada Boulingrin
Mission: To foster & promote the game of Lawn Bowls; To make the game available to all in accordance within the Canadian Human Rights Code within the Province of British Columbia
Affliation(s): World Bowls Board; World Indoor Bowls Board
Chief Officer(s):
Jim Aitken, President, 604-904-8834
bowlsbc.prez@yahoo.ca
Harry Carruthers, Vice-President, 604-985-2241
hcarruthers@telus.net
Diane Fulton, Secretary
pacu@shaw.ca
Carolle Allen, Treasurer
cjallen@live.ca
Activities: *Library:* BBC Library at Pacific Indoor Bowls Club
Awards:
• Bowls BC Volunteer Awards (Award)
Publications:
• Bowls British Columbia Newsletter
Type: Newsletter; *Editor:* Marueen Johston
Profile: Timely information for members

Bowls Canada Boulingrin (BCB)
#207, 720 Belfast Rd., Ottawa ON K1G 0Z5
Tel: 613-244-0021; *Fax:* 613-244-0041
Toll-Free: 800-567-2695
info@bowlscanada.com
www.bowlscanada.com
www.facebook.com/BCBOfficial
twitter.com/BCBBowls
Previous Name: Lawn Bowls Canada Boulingrin
Overview: A medium-sized national charitable organization founded in 1902
Mission: To promote, foster & safeguard the sport of indoor & outdoor lawn bowling in all its forms in Canada, through events & programs
Member of: World Bowls Board; International Women's Bowls Board; World Indoor Bowls Council
Affliation(s): Commonwealth Games Association of Canada
Chief Officer(s):
Anna Mees, Executive Director
amees@bowlscanada.com
Finances: *Annual Operating Budget:* $250,000-$500,000; *Funding Sources:* Membership dues; marketing; advertising; merchandising; donations
Staff Member(s): 4; 100 volunteer(s)
Membership: 15,000; 252 clubs; *Fees:* $11; *Committees:* International Competition; Domestic Competition; Athlete Development; Sport Development
Activities: Canadian championships; Canadian Senior Triples; Canadian Junior Championships; Under 25 World Junior Cup Qualifier; Canadian Mixed Pairs Championships; Canadian Indoor Singles.

Bowls Manitoba
145 Pacific Ave., Winnipeg MB R3B 2Z6
Tel: 204-925-5694; *Fax:* 204-925-5792
bowls@shawbiz.ca
www.bowls.mb.ca
www.facebook.com/BowlsMBInc
twitter.com/BowlsManitoba
Previous Name: Manitoba Lawn Bowling Association
Overview: A medium-sized provincial organization overseen by Bowls Canada Boulingrin
Mission: To promote lawnbowling in the province of Manitoba; To host various lawnbowling events
Member of: Sport Manitoba
Affliation(s): Bowls Canada Boulingrin; World Bowls Ltd
Chief Officer(s):
Cathy Derewianchuk, Executive Director, 204-925-5694

Bowls Saskatchewan Inc.
#102, 1860 Lorne St., Regina SK S4P 2L7
Tel: 306-780-9426; *Fax:* 306-781-6021
bowlsask@sasktel.net
www.bowls.sk.ca
Also Known As: Saskatchewan Lawn Bowling Association
Overview: A medium-sized provincial organization founded in 1991 overseen by Bowls Canada Boulingrin
Mission: To promote & expand the sport of bowls, which contains programs that accommodate/challenge all those interested, with the result that bowls becomes a high profile sport
Chief Officer(s):
Jordan St. Onge, Executive Director
Jean Roney, President
Finances: *Annual Operating Budget:* $50,000-$100,000; *Funding Sources:* Saskatchewan lotteries
Staff Member(s): 1
Membership: 503 in 9 clubs; *Fees:* $125 club membership; *Committees:* Executive; Officiating; Coaching; Sport for All
Activities: Learn to Bowl; Junior; Clinics; summer & fall tournaments; Regina Mixed Pairs Open Tournament

Boxing Alberta
Percy Page Centre, 11759 Groat Rd., Edmonton AB T5M 3K6
Tel: 780-427-6515; *Fax:* 780-427-1205
www.boxingalberta.com
Previous Name: Alberta Amateur Boxing Association
Overview: A small provincial organization overseen by Canadian Amateur Boxing Association
Member of: Canadian Amateur Boxing Association
Chief Officer(s):
Jim Titley, President
mjtcon@telus.net
Dennis Belair, Executive Director
dbelair@telus.net
Staff Member(s): 2
Membership: 46 clubs

Boxing BC Association
481 - 23rd St. NE, Salmon Arm BC V1E 1Y8
Tel: 250-832-7759; *Fax:* 250-832-7769
boxingbc@telus.net

www.boxing.bc.ca
www.facebook.com/489238011141309
Previous Name: British Columbia Amateur Boxing Association
Overview: A small provincial organization founded in 1985 overseen by Canadian Amateur Boxing Association
Mission: To provide all citizens of British Columbia access to & participation in the opportunities, programs & activities
Member of: Canadian Amateur Boxing Association
Finances: *Annual Operating Budget:* $100,000-$250,000
Staff Member(s): 1; 150 volunteer(s)
Membership: 1,100 in 42 clubs; *Fees:* $27.50 recreational; $38.50 cadets; $55 others; *Member Profile:* Competitors, coaches, officials, associated volunteers
Activities: Club shows, tournament highlights & provincial championships & Golden Gloves tournaments; *Awareness Events:* Golden Gloves, March; *Internships:* Yes

Boxing Manitoba

#421, 145 Pacific Ave., Winnipeg MB R3B 2Z6
Tel: 204-925-5658; *Fax:* 204-925-5792
info@boxingmanitoba.com
www.boxingmanitoba.com
www.facebook.com/groups/boxingmanitoba
Previous Name: Manitoba Amateur Boxing Association
Overview: A small provincial organization overseen by Canadian Amateur Boxing Association
Mission: To govern the sport of boxing in Manitoba.
Member of: Canadian Amateur Boxing Association
Chief Officer(s):
Mark Collins, President, 204-586-1992
allianceboxing@shaw.ca
Nancy MacPherson, Office Manager

Boxing New Brunswick Boxe

413 Millidge Ave., Saint John NB E2K 2N3
Tel: 506-652-8251
nbref@yahoo.ca
boxingnb.com
www.facebook.com/100624973327745
Also Known As: Boxing NB Boxe
Overview: A small provincial organization overseen by Canadian Amateur Boxing Association
Mission: To govern the sport of boxing in New Brunswick.
Member of: Canadian Amateur Boxing Association
Chief Officer(s):
Ed Blanchard, President
Kevin Watson, Executive Director
k-watson@bellaliant.net

Boxing Newfoundland & Labrador

17 Brixham Cres., Torbay NL A1K 1N6
Tel: 709-754-5356; *Fax:* 709-576-0858
www.boxingnewfoundlandandlabrador.ca
Overview: A small provincial organization overseen by Canadian Amateur Boxing Association
Mission: To govern the sport of boxing in Newfoundland & Labrador.
Member of: Canadian Amateur Boxing Association; Sport NL
Chief Officer(s):
Mike Summers, President
mgsone@hotmail.com

Boxing Nova Scotia

PO Box 3010, Stn. Park Lane Centre, 5516 Spring Garden Rd., Halifax NS B3J 3G6
Tel: 902-425-5450; *Fax:* 902-425-5606
www.boxingnovascotia.com
www.facebook.com/BoxingNovaScotia
Overview: A small provincial organization overseen by Canadian Amateur Boxing Association
Mission: To govern the sport of boxing in Nova Scotia.
Member of: Canadian Amateur Boxing Association
Affliation(s): Sport Nova Scotia; Nova Scotia Health Promotion & Protection
Membership: *Fees:* Schedule available

Boxing Ontario

#202, 3 Concorde Gate, Toronto ON M3C 3N7
Tel: 416-426-7250; *Fax:* 416-426-7367
info@boxingontario.com
www.boxingontario.com
www.facebook.com/boxingontario
twitter.com/BoxingOntario
Overview: A small provincial licensing organization founded in 1972 overseen by Canadian Amateur Boxing Association
Mission: This is the only governing body for amateur boxing in Ontario. It aims to organize, promote, develop interest & participation in the sport in the province.
Member of: Canadian Amateur Boxing Association
Affliation(s): Association International de Boxe Amateur (AIBA); Ontario Ministry of Health Promotion
Chief Officer(s):
Mike Power, President
bigmikepower@sympatico.ca
Matt Kennedy, Executive Director
mkennedy@boxingontario.com
Finances: *Annual Operating Budget:* $250,000-$500,000; *Funding Sources:* membership, fundraising, Ministry of Tourism and Recreation
Staff Member(s): 3
Membership: 80 clubs; *Fees:* $40-50; $5 fans
Activities: Governing amateur boxing; sanctioning amateur events;

Boxing Saskatchewan

PO Box 4711, Regina SK S4P 3Y3
Tel: 306-789-1271; *Fax:* 306-789-2149
skboxing@accesscomm.ca
www.boxingsask.com
Also Known As: Saskatchewan Amateur Boxing Association
Overview: A small provincial organization overseen by Canadian Amateur Boxing Association
Mission: This is a non-profit society that enforces rules & regulations governing amateur boxing in the province. It also promotes the formation of new clubs.
Member of: Canadian Amateur Boxing Association
Affliation(s): Canadian Amateur Boxing Association
Chief Officer(s):
George Goff, President
georgegoff@yahoo.com
Jordan St. Onge, Executive Director
boxingsask@sasktel.net
Finances: *Funding Sources:* Sask Sport
Membership: 23 clubs

The Boy Scouts Association - Canadian General Council
See Scouts Canada

Boyle & Community Food & Clothing Bank

PO Box 728, Boyle AB T0A 0M0
Overview: A small local charitable organization overseen by Alberta Food Bank Network Association

Boyle & District Chamber of Commerce

PO Box 9, 5010, 3rd St., Boyle AB T0A 0M0
e-mail: boylechamber@gmail.com
boylechamber.blogspot.ca
Overview: A small local organization
Mission: The Boyle & District Chamber of Commerce is very active in the affairs of the community and recognizes the importance of effective promotion and sustainable industry.
Chief Officer(s):
Bill Goodwin, President
Membership: 25

Boys & Girls Clubs of Canada (BGCC) / Clubs garçons & filles du Canada

National Office, #400, 2005 Sheppard Ave. East, Toronto ON M2J 5B4
Tel: 905-477-7272; *Fax:* 416-640-5331
info@bgccan.com
www.bgccan.com
www.facebook.com/groups/2233316912
twitter.com/BGCCAN
www.youtube.com/user/bgccan
Overview: A large national charitable organization founded in 1947
Mission: To provide safe, supportive place where children & youth can experience new opportunities, overcome barriers, build positive relationships, & develop confidence & skills for life
Member of: Coalition of National Voluntary Organizations; Coalition for the Rights of Children
Chief Officer(s):
Robert Livingston, Chair
Pam Jolliffe, President & CEO
Marlene Deboisbriand, Vice-President, Member Services
Susan Bower, CMA, Vice-President, Business Operations
Sue Sheridan, Director, Resource Development
Denise Silverstone, Director, National Programs
Mary O'Connell, Manager, Communications Services
Karen McCullagh, Western Region Director, 403-936-0899
kmccullagh@bgccan.com
Sandra Morris, Central Region Director, 416-535-9675
smorris@bgccan.com
Jennifer Bessell, Newfoundland & Labrador Region Director
jbessell@bgccan.com
Debbie Cooper, Maritime Region Director
dcooper@bgccan.com
Michèle Fournier, Québec Region Director
mfournier@bgccan.com
Carrie Wagner-Miller, Pacific Regional Director, 250-762-3989 Ext. 124
cwmiller@bgccan.com
Finances: *Funding Sources:* Private sector donations
40 volunteer(s)
Membership: 200,000 individuals; 99 Clubs nationally; *Member Profile:* Children & youth, ages 0-21
Activities: Offering national programs, such as Active Living & Stay in School; Providing residential & day camping experiences; Offering street youth outreach; *Library*
Meetings/Conferences: • Boys and Girls Clubs of Canada Pacific / Western Regional Conference 2015, April, 2015, Saskatoon, SK
Scope: National
• Boys and Girls Clubs of Canada National Youth Forum 2015, May, 2015, University of Manitoba, Winnipeg, MB
Scope: National
• Boys and Girls Clubs of Canada 13th Annual ED Symposium, May, 2015, Intercontinental Toronto Centre, Toronto, ON
Scope: National
Publications:
• Boys & Girls Clubs of Canada Newsletter
Type: Newsletter

Boys & Girls Clubs of Canada - Central Region

ON
Tel: 416-535-9675
Overview: A medium-sized provincial organization overseen by Boys & Girls Clubs of Canada
Chief Officer(s):
Sandra Morris, Regional Director
smorris@bgccan.com
Serena Surujbali, Program Coordinator
ssurujbali@bgccan.com

Albion Neighbourhood Services Boys & Girls Club
#10, 86 Guided Crt., Toronto ON M9V 4K6
Tel: 416-740-3704; *Fax:* 416-740-7124
filomena@albionservices.ca
Chief Officer(s):
Filomena Ferlisi, Executive Director

Boys & Girls Club of Kingston & Area
559 Bagot St., Kingston ON K7K 3E1
Tel: 613-542-3306; *Fax:* 613-542-7964
bgclub@kingston.net
Chief Officer(s):
Harold Parsons, Executive Director

Boys & Girls Club of London
184 Horton St., London ON N6B 1K8
Tel: 519-434-9114; *Fax:* 519-432-9306
info@bgclondon.ca
www.bgclondon.ca
Chief Officer(s):
Peter McConnell, President

Boys & Girls Club of Niagara
6681 Culp St., Niagara Falls ON L2G 2C5
Tel: 905-357-2444; *Fax:* 905-357-7401
boysgirlsclubnia@on.aibn.com
www.boysandgirlsclubniagara.org
Chief Officer(s):
JoAnne Hett, Executive Director

Boys & Girls Club of North Simcoe
PO Box 194, 525 Dominion Ave., Midland ON L4R 4K6
Tel: 705-526-4007; *Fax:* 705-526-3844
davearew@yahoo.ca
Chief Officer(s):
Carrie Courts, Contact

Boys & Girls Club of Ottawa
2825 DuMaurier Ave., Ottawa ON K2B 7W3
Tel: 613-232-0925; *Fax:* 613-230-0891
sbradford@bgcottawa.org
www.bgcottawa.org
www.facebook.com/group.php?gid=5556823122
Chief Officer(s):
Scott Bradford, Executive Director

Boys & Girls Club of Peel
#11, 315 Traders Blvd., Mississauga ON L4Z 3E4
Tel: 905-712-1789; *Fax:* 905-451-9014
bgcpeel4@on.aibn.com
Chief Officer(s):

Debbie Smith, Executive Director

Boys & Girls Club of Sarnia/Lambton
180 North College Ave., Sarnia ON N7T 7X2
Tel: 519-337-3651; *Fax:* 519-337-7281
boysandgirls@cogeco.net
Chief Officer(s):
Diane MacLeod-Hummel, Executive Director
dmhummel@cogeco.net

Boys & Girls Club of Windsor
#109, 647 Ouellette St., Windsor ON N9A 4J4
Tel: 519-254-8145; *Fax:* 519-974-9933
bgcwec@hotmail.com
www.bgcwindsor.com
Chief Officer(s):
Kenny Gbadebo, Executive Director
kgbyouth@mnsi.net

Boys & Girls Clubs of Brantford
2 Edge St., Brantford ON N3T 6H1
Tel: 519-752-2964; *Fax:* 519-752-6530
bgcrecep@teksavvy.com
www.bgcbrant.ca
Chief Officer(s):
Deanna Searle, Executive Director
bgced@teksavvy.com

Boys & Girls Clubs of Kawarth Lakes
107 Lindsay St. South, Lindsay ON K9V 2M5
Tel: 705-324-4493; *Fax:* 705-878-8605
srobertson@bgckawarthalakes.com
www.bgckawarthalakes.com
Chief Officer(s):
Scott Robertson, Executive Director

Boys & Girls Clubs of Pembroke
PO Box 1354, Pembroke ON K8A 6Y6
Tel: 613-735-1933; *Fax:* 613-735-1730
pembgclub@bellnet.ca
www.boysandgirlsclubofpembroke.com
Chief Officer(s):
Crystal Peoples, Executive Director

Boys & Girls Clubs of York Region
c/o York Region Neighbourhood Services, #202, 17705 Leslie St., Newmarket ON L3Y 3E3
Tel: 905-895-0809; *Fax:* 905-953-8241
yns@socialenterprise.ca
Chief Officer(s):
Patricia Robertson, Executive Director
patricia.robertson@socialenterprise.ca

Braeburn Boys & Girls Club
#108, 75 Tandridge Cres., Toronto ON M9W 2N9
Tel: 416-745-3113; *Fax:* 416-745-9108
sadore@braeburn.net
Chief Officer(s):
Shobha Adore, Executive Director

Dovercourt Boys & Girls Club
180 Westmoreland Ave., Toronto ON M6H 3A2
Tel: 416-536-4102; *Fax:* 416-536-2015
antonio@radiant.net
www.dovercourtkids.com
Chief Officer(s):
Tony Puopolo, Executive Director

East Scarborough Boys & Girls Club
100 Galloway Rd., Toronto ON M1E 1W7
Tel: 416-281-0262; *Fax:* 416-281-0458
info@esbgc.org
www.esbgc.org
Chief Officer(s):
Ron Rock, Executive Director
rrock@esbgc.org

Eastview (Toronto) Boys & Girls Club
c/o Eastview Neighbourhood Community Centre, 86 Blake St., Toronto ON M4J 3C9
Tel: 416-392-1750; *Fax:* 416-392-1175
info@eastviewcentre.com
www.eastviewcentre.com
Chief Officer(s):
Susan Neal, Executive Director
susanneal@eastviewcentre.com

Eastview Boys & Girls Club (Oshawa)
433 Eulalie Ave., Oshawa ON L1H 2C6
Tel: 905-728-5121; *Fax:* 905-728-5126
eastviewbgc@eastviewbgc.com
www.eastviewbgc.com
Chief Officer(s):
Lisa McNee-Baker, Executive Director
lmcneebaker@eastviewbgc.com

Hamilton East Kiwanis Boys & Girls Club
45 Ellis Ave., Hamilton ON L8H 4L8
Tel: 905-549-2814; *Fax:* 905-549-2313
glenn@kboysandgirlsclub.com
www.kboysandgirlsclub.com
Chief Officer(s):
Glenn Harkness, Executive Director

St. Alban's Boys & Girls Club
843 Palmerston Ave., Toronto ON M6G 2R8
Tel: 416-534-8461; *Fax:* 416-534-8860
info@stalbansclub.ca
www.stalbansclub.ca
Chief Officer(s):
Chris Foster, Executive Director
chris@stalbansclub.ca

Thunder Bay Boys & Girls Club
270 Windsor St., Thunder Bay ON P7B 1V6
Tel: 807-623-0354; *Fax:* 807-622-5000
tbbgc@tbaytel.net
www.tbayboysandgirlsclub.org
www.facebook.com/group.php?gid=218875750860
Chief Officer(s):
Albert Aiello, Executive Director

Toronto Kiwanis Boys & Girls Clubs - Gerrard Unit
101 Spruce St., Toronto ON M5A 2J3
Tel: 416-925-2243; *Fax:* 416-925-9885
admin@believeinkids.ca
www.believeinkids.ca
Chief Officer(s):
Ian Edward, Executive Director
ianedward@believeinkids.ca

West Scarborough Boys & Girls Club
313 Pharmacy Ave., Toronto ON M1L 3E7
Tel: 416-755-9215; *Fax:* 416-755-7521
cdumont@wsncc.on.ca
Chief Officer(s):
Cynthia duMont, Executive Director

Boys & Girls Clubs of Canada - Maritime Region

NS
Overview: A medium-sized provincial organization overseen by Boys & Girls Clubs of Canada
Chief Officer(s):
Debbie Cooper, Regional Director
dcooper@bgccan.com

Boys & Girls Club of Cole Harbour
1237 Cole Harbour Rd., Dartmouth NS B2V 1N1
Tel: 902-462-7148
Chief Officer(s):
Ryan Rutledge, Team Lead

Boys & Girls Club of Dartmouth
60 Farrell St., Dartmouth NS B3A 4B3
Tel: 902-463-1210

Boys & Girls Club of Greater Halifax
50 Caledonia Rd., Dartmouth NS B2X 1K8
Tel: 902-435-3204
info@bgcgh.ca
www.bgcgh.ca
www.linkedin.com/company/boys-&-girls-club-of-greater-halifax
www.facebook.com/edbgc
twitter.com/BGCGreaterHfx
Chief Officer(s):
John Burton, Executive Director
executivedirector@edbgc.ca

Boys & Girls Club of Preston
180 Lower Partridge River Rd., East Preston NS B2Z 1G8
Tel: 902-829-2665; *Fax:* 902-435-2397
prestonbgclub@eastlink.ca
Chief Officer(s):
Margaret Fraser, Executive Director

Boys & Girls Club of Sackville
Sackville Heights Community Centre, 45 Connolly Rd., Lower Sackville NS B4E 1S6
Tel: 902-865-5010; *Fax:* 902-865-2563
boysandgirlsclubofsackville@gmail.com
www.bgcsackville.ca
Chief Officer(s):
Trevor Brown, Executive Director

Boys & Girls Club of Spryfield
11 Aldergrove Dr., Halifax NS B3R 1M6
Tel: 902-477-9840; *Fax:* 902-477-0436
bgcspryfield.ca
twitter.com/bgcspryfield
Chief Officer(s):
Darlene MacLean, Executive Director
director@bgcspryfield.org

Boys & Girls Club of Truro And Colchester
175 Victoria St., Truro NS B2N 1Z5
Tel: 902-895-5008; *Fax:* 902-893-1171
www.bgctc.ca
www.facebook.com/BoysAndGirlsClubOfTruroAndColchester
twitter.com/BGCTC2013
Chief Officer(s):
Amanda McNea, Acting Director of Operations
amcnea@bgctc.ca

Boys & Girls Club of Yarmouth
11 Bond St., Yarmouth NS B5A 1P6
Tel: 902-742-9103; *Fax:* 902-742-5915
bgcydirector@hotmail.com
Chief Officer(s):
Jodie Pothier, Executive Director

Boys & Girls Clubs of Canada - Newfoundland & Labrador Region

c/o Boys and Girls Clubs of Canada, #400, 2005 Sheppard Ave. East, Toronto ON M2J 5B4
Tel: 905-477-7272; *Fax:* 416-640-5331
Overview: A medium-sized provincial organization overseen by Boys & Girls Clubs of Canada
Member of: Boys & Girls Clubs of Canada
Chief Officer(s):
Jennifer Bessell, Regional Director
jbessell@bgccan.com

Botwood Boys & Girls Club Inc.
PO Box 1049, Botwood NL A0H 1E0
Tel: 709-257-3191; *Fax:* 709-257-4293
bbgclub@nf.aibn.com
www.facebook.com/boysgirlsclub.botwood
Chief Officer(s):
Colleen Hayter, Executive Director

Gander Boys & Girls Club
PO Box 124, Gander NL A1V 1W5
Tel: 709-256-7803; *Fax:* 709-256-7040
www.ganderboysandgirlsclub.com
Chief Officer(s):
Brenda Paul, Executive Director
brenda.paul@nfld.net

James Hornell Boys & Girls Club
1 Williams Turnpike, Buchans NL A0H 1G0
Tel: 709-672-3342; *Fax:* 709-672-3345
jhbgc@nf.aibn.com
www.facebook.com/196125310411519
Chief Officer(s):
Gary Noftle, Executive Director

Norris Arm Boys & Girls Club
95 Citizen's Dr., Norris Arm NL A0G 3M0
Tel: 709-653-2225; *Fax:* 709-653-2227
naboysandgirlsclub@hotmail.com
Chief Officer(s):
Betty Saunders, Executive Director

St. Anthony & Area Boys & Girls Club
272 West St., St Anthony NL A0K 4S0
Tel: 709-454-2582; *Fax:* 709-454-2052
stanthonybgclub.com
www.facebook.com/StAnthonyAreaBoysGirlsClub
Chief Officer(s):
Colleen Loder, Executive Director
colleen@stanthonybgclub.com

St. John's Boys & Girls Club
PO Box 5012, St. John's NL A1C 5V3
Tel: 709-579-0181; *Fax:* 709-579-0182
www.bgclub.ca
www.facebook.com/bgcstjohns
twitter.com/BGC_of_StJohns
Chief Officer(s):
Jason Fleming, Club Manager
jfleming@bgcstjohns.ca

Upper Island Cove Boys & Girls Club
PO Box 190, Stn. Conception Bay, Upper Island Cove NL A0A 4E0
Tel: 709-589-2943; *Fax:* 709-589-2943
Chief Officer(s):
Mose Drover, President

Wabana Boys & Girls Club
PO Box 539, Bell Island NL A0A 4H0
Tel: 709-488-2288; *Fax:* 709-488-2226
Chief Officer(s):

Joe Somerton, Acting Executive Director

Boys & Girls Clubs of Canada - Pacific Region
PO Box 20222, Kelowna BC V1Y 9H2
Tel: 250-762-3989
Overview: A medium-sized provincial organization overseen by Boys & Girls Clubs of Canada
Member of: Boys and Girls Clubs of Canada
Chief Officer(s):
Carrie Wagner-Miller, Regional Director
cwmiller@bgccan.com
Membership: *Member Profile:* Includes clubs in BC & the Yukon
Activities: Traditional recreation programs; child care; camping services; drug & alcohol counselling; services for teen mothers; programs for street youth, parents; & activities aimed at preparing youth for employment environments;

Boys & Girls Club Community Services of Delta/Richmond
11861 - 88th Ave., 3rd Fl., Delta BC V4C 3C6
Tel: 604-591-9262; *Fax:* 604-591-8971
info@bgcbc.ca
www.bgcbc.ca
Chief Officer(s):
Carolyn Tuckwell, President & CEO

Boys & Girls Club of Kamloops
PO Box 885, Stn. Main, Kamloops BC V2C 5M8
Tel: 250-554-5437; *Fax:* 250-554-2756
admin@bgckamloops.com
www.bgckamloops.com
www.facebook.com/bgckamloops
twitter.com/BGCKamloops
Chief Officer(s):
Traci Anderson, Executive Director
exdir@bgckamloops.com

Boys & Girls Club of Williams Lake & District
51 South 4th Ave., Williams Lake BC V2G 1J6
Tel: 250-392-5730; *Fax:* 250-392-5743
www.bgcwilliamslake.com
Chief Officer(s):
Matt Neufeld, Executive Director
execdir@bgcwilliamslake.com

Boys & Girls Club Services of Greater Victoria
#301, 1195 Esquimalt Rd., Victoria BC V8A 3N6
Tel: 250-384-9133; *Fax:* 250-384-9136
info@bgcvic.org
www.bgcvic.org
www.facebook.com/bgcvic
Chief Officer(s):
Dalyce Dixon, Executive Director
DDixon@bgcvic.org

Boys & Girls Clubs of Central Vancouver Island
20 - 5th St., Nanaimo BC V9R 1M7
Tel: 250-754-3215; *Fax:* 250-754-4771
reception@bgccvi.com
www.bgccvi.com
Chief Officer(s):
Ian Kalina, Executive Director
ikalina@bgccvi.com

Boys & Girls Clubs of South Coast BC
2875 St. George St., Vancouver BC V5T 3R8
Tel: 604-879-6554; *Fax:* 604-879-6525
info@bgcbc.ca
www.bgcbc.ca
Chief Officer(s):
Carolyn Tuckwell, President & CEO
ctuckwell@bgcbc.ca

Comox Valley Boys & Girls Club
367 - 11 St., Courtenay BC V9N 1S4
Tel: 250-338-7582; *Fax:* 250-338-7592
comoxvalley@bgccvi.com
ww.bgccvi.com
Chief Officer(s):
Ian Kalina, Executive Director
ikalina@bgccvi.com

Cranbrook Boys & Girls Club
1404 - 2nd St. North, Cranbrook BC V1C 3L2
Tel: 250-426-3830; *Fax:* 250-426-3036
Chief Officer(s):
Lori McNeill, Executive Director

Okanagan Boys & Girls Clubs
PO Box 20222, 1434 Graham St., Kelowna BC V1Y 9H2
Tel: 250-762-3914; *Fax:* 250-762-6562
www.boysandgirlsclub.ca
www.facebook.com/group.php?gid=2340713121
Chief Officer(s):
Craig Monley, CEO

Boys & Girls Clubs of Canada - Québec Region
c/o Boys & Girls Clubs of Canada National Office, #400, 2005 Sheppard Ave. East, Toronto ON M5J 5B4
Tél: 905-477-7272; *Téléc:* 416-640-5331
Aperçu: *Dimension:* moyenne; *Envergure:* provinciale surveillé par Boys & Girls Clubs of Canada
Membre de: Boys & Girls Clubs of Canada
Membre(s) du bureau directeur:
Marlene Deboisbriand, Vice-President, Member Services
mdeboisbriand@bgccan.com

Boys & Girls Club of LaSalle
8600, rue Hardy, LaSalle QC H8N 2P5
Tel: 514-364-4661; *Fax:* 514-364-3907
info@bgclasalle.com
www.bgclasalle.com
Membre(s) du bureau directeur:
Mark Branch, Executive Director

Boys & Girls Clubs of Canada - Western Region
AB
Tel: 780-415-1734
Overview: A medium-sized provincial organization overseen by Boys & Girls Clubs of Canada
Member of: Boys & Girls Clubs of Canada
Chief Officer(s):
Karen McCullagh, Regional Director, 403-936-0899
KMcCullagh@bgccan.com
Pearl Kapitzke, Regional Services Coordinator
pkapitzke@bgccan.com
Staff Member(s): 2
Membership: 47,000

Boys & Girls Club of Airdrie
1003 Allen St., Airdrie AB T4B 1B3
Tel: 403-948-3331; *Fax:* 403-948-5132
info@bgcairdrie.com
www.bgcairdrie.com
Chief Officer(s):
Karen MacDonald, Executive Director
kmacdonald@bgcairdrie.com

Boys & Girls Club of Bonnyville
PO Box 1006, Bonnyville AB T9N 2J7
Tel: 780-826-3037; *Fax:* 780-826-6488
byc@town.bonnyville.ab.ca
Chief Officer(s):
Rhonda Miron, Acting Executive Director
flepfcss@town.bonnyville.ab.ca

Boys & Girls Club of Bruderheim
PO Box 511, Bruderheim AB T0B 0S0
Tel: 780-796-3630; *Fax:* 780-796-3639
bgcexecdir@shaw.ca
Chief Officer(s):
Sandi Offenberger, Executive Director

Boys & Girls Club of Calgary
731 - 13 Ave. NE, Calgary AB T2E 1C8
Tel: 403-276-9981; *Fax:* 403-276-9988
info@bgcc.ab.ca
www.calgaryboysandgirlsclub.ca
Chief Officer(s):
Cheryl Doherty, Executive Director
cdoherty@bgcc.ab.ca

Boys & Girls Club of Cochrane and Area
PO Box 1554, 111 - 5th Ave. West, Cochrane AB T4C 1B5
Tel: 403-932-4747; *Fax:* 403-851-0167
info@cochraneyouth.org
www.cochraneyouth.org
Chief Officer(s):
Dylan Oosterveld, Executive Director
dylan.oosterveld@cochraneyouth.org

Boys & Girls Club of Hinton
222 Pembina Ave., Hinton AB T7V 2B4
Tel: 780-865-3208; *Fax:* 780-865-4038
bandg1@telusplanet.net
Chief Officer(s):
Sheryl Nein, Executive Director

Boys & Girls Club of Leduc
#102, 4330 Black Gold Dr., Leduc AB T9E 3C3
Tel: 780-986-3121; *Fax:* 780-986-3137
edbgleduc@shaw.ca
www.leducboysandgirls.com
Chief Officer(s):
John Norton, Executive Director

Boys & Girls Club of Lethbridge
1405 - 8th Ave. North, Lethbridge AB T1H 6N9
Tel: 403-327-6423; *Fax:* 403-327-1711
laura@bgclethbridge.com
www.bgclethbridge.com
Chief Officer(s):
Trever Broadhead, Executive Director
trever@bgclethbridge.com

Boys & Girls Club of Red Deer & District
4633 - 49th St., Red Deer AB T4N 1T4
Tel: 403-342-6500; *Fax:* 403-342-7734
info@yvc.ca
www.yvc.ca
Chief Officer(s):
David Murphy, Executive Director
davidm@yvc.ca

Boys & Girls Club of St. Paul & District
PO Box 1009, St Paul AB T0A 3A0
Tel: 780-645-6769; *Fax:* 780-645-3650
rising.starchildcare@live.com
Chief Officer(s):
Sylvie Proteau, Interim Executive Director

Boys & Girls Club of Slave Lake
PO Box 232, Slave Lake AB T0G 2A2
Tel: 780-805-1778
bgclub.slavelake@gmail.com
Chief Officer(s):
Inga Lanctot, Executive Director

Boys & Girls Club of Strathcona County
3 Spruce Ave., Sherwood Park AB T8A 2B6
Tel: 780-416-1500; *Fax:* 780-416-2901
info@scbgc.com
www.scbgc.com
Chief Officer(s):
Tyler Roed, Program Coordinator
tyler@scbgc.com

Boys & Girls Club of Wetaskiwin
5109 - 51 St., Wetaskiwin AB T9A 2A5
Tel: 780-352-4643; *Fax:* 780-352-7780
info@wetaskiwinyouth.ca
www.wetaskiwinyouth.ca
Chief Officer(s):
Dana Badke, Executive Director
dana@wetaskiwinyouth.ca

Boys & Girls Club of Whitecourt
PO Box 2053, 5011 - 52 Ave., Whitecourt AB T7S 1P7
Tel: 780-778-6696; *Fax:* 780-778-3464
bgclub@telus.net
Chief Officer(s):
Kirstie Greenshields, Executive Director
director@whitecourtbgc.org

Boys & Girls Clubs of Edmonton
9425 - 109A Ave., Edmonton AB T5H 1G1
Tel: 780-422-6038; *Fax:* 780-426-6216
info@bgce.ca
www.boysandgirls.ab.ca
Chief Officer(s):
Ross Tyson, Executive Director
rtyson@bgce.ca

Camrose & District Boys & Girls Club
4516 - 54th St., Camrose AB T4V 4W7
Tel: 780-672-8004; *Fax:* 780-672-8002
rjames@brsd.ab.ca
Chief Officer(s):
Rees James, Executive Director

Clearwater Boys & Girls Club
PO Box 1467, Rocky Mountain House AB T4T 1B1
Tel: 403-844-2165; *Fax:* 403-845-5704
yesrocky@hotmail.com
www.clearwaterboysandgirlsclub.com
Chief Officer(s):
Warren Fay, Executive Director

Crowsnest Pass Boys & Girls Club
PO Box 68, Bellevue AB T0K 0C0
Tel: 403-562-8664; *Fax:* 403-562-8664
treeshemp@hotmail.com
Chief Officer(s):
Teresa MacGarva, Program Coordinator
treeshemp@hotmail.com

Diamond Valley & District Boys & Girls Club
PO Box 904, Black Diamond AB T0L 0H0
Tel: 403-933-4066; *Fax:* 403-933-4068
dvdbgc@telus.net
bgcdvd-com.registerit.ca

Chief Officer(s):
Shirley Puttock, Executive Director
exdirect@telus.net

Edson & District Boys & Girls Club
Griffiths Park Centre, PO Box 6032, 5414 - 6th Ave., Edson AB T7E 1T6
Tel: 780-723-7240; *Fax:* 780-723-7240
theclub8@telus.net
www.bgcedson.com
Chief Officer(s):
Barbara Quiring, Executive Director

Fort McMurray Boys & Girls Club
20 Riedel St., Fort McMurray AB T9H 3E1
Tel: 780-791-7775; *Fax:* 780-743-9359
www.fmbgc.ca
www.facebook.com/168574413161299
twitter.com/FMBGC
Chief Officer(s):
Veronica Doleman, President
Nicole Dion, Executive Director
prodirector@shaw.ca

Fort Saskatchewan Boys & Girls Club
PO Box 3201, 9923 - 103 St., Fort Saskatchewan AB T8L 2T2
Tel: 780-992-0103; *Fax:* 780-998-0405
wserink@telusplanet.net
Chief Officer(s):
Wendy Serink, Executive Director

Plamondon & Wandering River Boys & Girls Club
PO Box 149, Wandering River AB T0A 3M0
Tel: 780-771-2400; *Fax:* 780-771-2375
pwresource@telus.net
Chief Officer(s):
Maureen Hagan, Contact
maureenhagan343@hotmail.com

Saddle Lake Boys & Girls Club
PO Box 220, Saddle Lake AB T0A 3T0
Tel: 780-726-2178; *Fax:* 780-726-3754
slbgclub@mcsnet.ab.ca
Chief Officer(s):
Natalie Cardinal, Executive Director

Stettler & District Boys & Girls Club
PO Box 876, 4702 - 50 Ave., Stettler AB T0C 2L0
Tel: 403-742-5437; *Fax:* 403-742-4700
hystett@telus.net
Chief Officer(s):
Winnie Bissett, Executive Director

Boys & Girls Clubs of Canada Foundation / Fondation des Clubs Garçons et Filles du Canada

Boys and Girls Clubs of Canada, #400, 2005 Sheppard Ave. East, Toronto ON M2J 5B4
Tel: 905-477-7272; *Fax:* 416-640-5331
www.bgccan.com/en/AboutUs/BGCCFoundation/Pages/default.aspx
Overview: A large national organization founded in 1995
Mission: To support the Boys & Girls Clubs of Canada
Chief Officer(s):
Peter Wallace, Chair
Finances: *Annual Operating Budget:* $1.5 Million-$3 Million; *Funding Sources:* Donations

Boys & Girls Clubs of Manitoba

Central Region, #204, 7100 Woodbine Ave., Markham ON L3R 5J2
Tel: 416-535-9675; *Fax:* 905-477-2056
www.bgccan.com/clubresults.asp?l=e&location=mb
Overview: A medium-sized provincial organization overseen by Boys & Girls Clubs of Canada
Mission: The Clubs offer educational, recreational & skills development programs & services to children from pre-school to young adulthood. Activities are scheduled after school, evenings & weekends, providinge a safe, supportive place where children & youth can build positive relationships, & develop confidence & skills.
Member of: Boys & Girls Clubs of Canada
Activities: Counselling; conflict resolution training; street safety

Boys & Girls Clubs of Winnipeg
#300, 61 Juno St., Winnipeg MB R3A 1T1
Tel: 204-982-4940; *Fax:* 204-982-4950
reception@wbgc.mb.ca
www.wbgc.mb.ca
www.facebook.com/bgcwinnipeg
twitter.com/BGCWinnipeg
vimeo.com/user16185899
Chief Officer(s):
Ron Brown, President & CEO
brown@wbgc.mb.ca

Thompson Boys & Girls Club
PO Box 484, Thompson MB R8N 1N2
Tel: 204-778-1945; *Fax:* 204-778-1942
bgclub@mts.net
Chief Officer(s):
Kim Hickes, Executive Director
Ron Dearman, President
Contois Howard, Treasurer

Boys & Girls Clubs of Yukon

6209 - 6th Ave., Whitehorse YT Y1A 1P1
Tel: 867-393-2824; *Fax:* 867-667-2108
info@bgcyukon.com
www.bgcyukon.com
www.facebook.com/pages/Boys-and-Girls-Club-of-Yukon/352893081482275
Overview: A small local organization
Chief Officer(s):
Dave Blottner, Executive Director
ed@bgcyukon.com
Kate Mechan, Chair
chair@bgcyukon.com

Bracebridge Chamber of Commerce

#1, 1 Manitoba St., Bracebridge ON P1L 2A8
Tel: 705-645-5231; *Fax:* 705-645-7592
chamber@bracebridgechamber.com
www.bracebridgechamber.com
www.facebook.com/265998763428556
twitter.com/BracebridgeCofC
Overview: A small local organization founded in 1952
Mission: To promote the commercial, industrial, agricultural & civic welfare of Bracebridge & the surrounding district
Member of: Canadian Chamber of Commerce
Chief Officer(s):
John Crawley, General Manager
jcrawley@bracebridgechamber.com
Finances: *Annual Operating Budget:* $100,000-$250,000; *Funding Sources:* Membership dues; fee for service to operate Visitor Centre; federal & provincial governments
Staff Member(s): 5; 12 volunteer(s)
Membership: 412; *Fees:* $95 associate; $195 regular; *Committees:* Business Enhancement; Membership; Events & Networking; Executive
Activities: Business/educational seminars; Festival of Lights; Golf Tourney; Public Relations; Visitors Information Centre
Awards:
• Business Achievement Awards (Award)

Bracebridge Historical Society

PO Box 376, Bracebridge ON P1L 1T7
Tel: 705-645-5501; *Fax:* 705-645-0385
info@octagonalhouse.com
www.octagonalhouse.com
Also Known As: Woodchester Villa
Overview: A small local charitable organization founded in 1978
Mission: To operate & maintain historical sites & museums in Bracebridge
Finances: *Funding Sources:* Town of Bracebridge; provincial government

Bradford Board of Trade

PO Box 1713, 61 Holland St. East, Bradford ON L3Z 2B9
Tel: 905-778-8727
info@bradfordboardoftrade.com
www.bradfordboardoftrade.com
www.facebook.com/BBTVoice
twitter.com/BBTVoice
Overview: A small local organization
Mission: To sustain & promote local businesses
Chief Officer(s):
Cliff Ngai, President, 905-775-2323
president@bradfordboardoftrade.com
Rebecca Davis, Office Administrator
administration@bradfordboardoftrade.com

Bragg Creek Chamber of Commerce

PO Box 216, Bragg Creek AB T0L 0K0
Tel: 403-949-0004
info@visitbraggcreek.com
visitbraggcreek.com
Overview: A small local organization
Mission: To work together to increase development; To foster improvements that benefit the whole community
Chief Officer(s):
Louise-Marie Eager, President
lm@braggcreekchamber.com
Marcella Campbell, Secretary
marcella@braggcreekchamber.com
Membership: 220+; *Fees:* $130; *Member Profile:* Business owners & professionals who are committed to the promotion & improvement of trade & commerce, as well as the economic, civic, & social welfare of the area of Bragg Creek

Braille Literacy Canada (BLC)

c/o CNIB Library, 1929 Bayview Ave., Toronto ON M4G 3E8
Tel: 416-480-7522; *Fax:* 416-480-7700
info@blc-lbc.ca
www.canadianbrailleauthority.ca
www.linkedin.com/company/3502741?trk=tyah&trkInfo=tas%3Abraille%20lite
www.facebook.com/brailleliteracycanada
twitter.com/@brllitcan
Previous Name: Canadian Braille Authority
Overview: A small national organization founded in 1990
Mission: To promote braille as a primary medium for persons who are blind; To enables all Canadians who require braille to access information to have braille literacy; To sets up systems that allow blind persons to access print information in braille
Chief Officer(s):
Jen Goulden, President
Membership: *Fees:* $20; $200 life; $250 corporate; *Committees:* UEB Implementation; Web Site; Transactional Documents; Teaching and Learning; French Braille; Braille Promotion; Grants

Brain Care Centre (BCC)

Royal Alex Place, #229, 10106 - 111th Ave., Edmonton AB T5G 0B4
Tel: 780-477-7575; *Fax:* 780-474-4415
Toll-Free: 800-425-5552
admin@braincarecentre.com
www.braincarecentre.com
www.facebook.com/pages/Brain-Care-Centre/291605290917593
twitter.com/BrainCareCentre
Previous Name: Northern Alberta Brain Injury Society
Overview: A small local charitable organization founded in 1983
Mission: To support people affected by acquired brain injury in northern Alberta
Chief Officer(s):
Garnet Cummings, Executive Director
Stephanie Boldt, President
Finances: *Funding Sources:* Membership fees; Donations; Fundraising
Membership: *Fees:* $10 brain injury survivors; $30 individuals; $60 families; $75 non-profit organizations; $200 corporate members; *Member Profile:* Persons in northern Alberta who are affected by brain injury; Families of individuals affected by brain injury
Activities: Coordinating services for people affected by acquired brain injury in northern Alberta; Providing information & referrals, through programs such as the information line 780-479-1757, ext. 34; Advocating on behalf of persons affected by acquired brain injury; Offering leisure & recreational activities; Providing one to one supportive counselling & support groups; Organizing educational workshops, such as Understanding Brain Injury; Liaising with the community to increase awareness about brain injury services; *Awareness Events:* Kick-off to Brain Injury Awareness Month Breakfast, early June; *Library:* Northern Alberta Brain Injury Society Library Resource Centre
Awards:
• Ginny Awards (Award)
• Patrick Hirschi Lifetime Achievement Award (Award)
Meetings/Conferences: • Brain Care Centre 2015 Defying Limitations Gala, February, 2015, DoubleTree by Hilton Hotel West Edmonton, Edmonton, AB
Scope: Provincial
Publications:
• NABIS News
Type: Newsletter; *Frequency:* Quarterly; *Price:* Free with membership in the Northern Alberta Brain Injury Society

Brain Injury Association of Alberta (BIAA)

4916 - 50th St., Red Deer AB T4N 1X7
Tel: 403-309-0866; *Fax:* 403-342-3880
Toll-Free: 888-533-5355
biac-aclc.ca/alberta
Overview: A small provincial organization founded in 1986 overseen by Brain Injury Association of Canada

Mission: To support acquired brain injury survivors, their families, caregivers, & professionals in Alberta; To provide information for individuals & organizations working with brain injury communities
Chief Officer(s):
Meloni Lyon, President
Shelly Wieser, Secretary
Finances: *Funding Sources:* Fundraising
Membership: *Fees:* Free, courtesy membership for brain injury survivors; $10 individuals; $15 families; $20 professionals & organizations
Activities: Promoting prevention of acquired brain injury; Raising awareness of acquired brain injury; Engaging in advocacy activities; Developing partnerships; Providing education

Brain Injury Association of Canada (BIAC) / Association canadienne des lésés cérébraux
#200, 440 Laurier Ave. West, Ottawa ON K1R 7X6
Tel: 613-762-1222; *Fax:* 613-236-5208
Toll-Free: 866-977-2492
info@biac-aclc.ca
www.biac-aclc.ca
www.facebook.com/143123439082446
twitter.com/BIACACLC
www.youtube.com/user/BrainInjuryCanada
Overview: A medium-sized national organization founded in 2003
Mission: To improve the quality of life for persons affected by acquired brain injury; To promote the prevention of brain injuries, through legislation & education in Canada
Chief Officer(s):
Harry Zarins, Executive Director
Shirley Johnson, President
Larry Carlson, Vice-President, Internal Affairs
Barb Butler, Secretary
Marion Barfurth, Treasurer
Finances: *Funding Sources:* Donations; Fundraising
Activities: Raising awareness of acquired brain injury; Providing education; Facilitating research; Engaging in advocacy activities; *Awareness Events:* Brain Injury Awareness Month, June
Meetings/Conferences: • Brain Injury Association of Canada 2015 Annual Conference, April, 2015, Halifax, NS
Scope: National
Publications:
• Brain Injury Association of Canada Annual Report
Type: Yearbook
• Impact: Pathways Ahead
Type: Newsletter; *Editor:* Barb Butler
Profile: Happenings at the Brain Injury Association of Canada, plus news from across Canada

Brain Injury Association of Nova Scotia (BIANS)
13th Fl., Victoria Bldg., QEII Health Sciences Centre, PO Box 8804, Halifax NS B3K 5M4
Tel: 902-473-7301; *Fax:* 902-473-7302
bians1@ns.sympatico.ca
www3.ns.sympatico.ca/bians1
Previous Name: Nova Scotia Head Injury Association
Overview: A small provincial organization founded in 1988 overseen by Brain Injury Association of Canada
Mission: To promote an environment throughout Nova Scotia that is responsive to the lifelong needs of persons affected by acquired brain injury
Chief Officer(s):
Margo Dauphinee, Executive Director
Don Sullivan, President
Connie Wheatley, Vice-President
Alberte LeBlanc, Secretary
Tracy MacIntyre, Treasurer
Finances: *Funding Sources:* Donations; Fundraising
Membership: *Fees:* $10 individuals; $15 families; $20 business members
Activities: Promoting the prevention of acquired brain injury in Nova Scotia; Increasing public awareness of acquired brain injury; Providing a framework for self-help for people with acquired brain injuries in the province; Lobbying on behalf of people with acquired brain injury; Liaising with both regional & provincial governments; Promoting research, quality care, & rehabilitation; Offering education, such as information; Providing support, such as peer support; Offering referrals; *Speaker Service:* Yes
Publications:
• BIANS News
Type: Newsletter; *Accepts Advertising; Editor:* Mary Bourgeois
Profile: Association happenings, such as upcoming events & chapter news, plus articles & profiles

Brain Injury Coalition of Prince Edward Island (BICPEI)
#5, 81 Prince St., Charlottetown PE C1A 4R3
Tel: 902-314-4228
info@biapei.com
www.bicpei.com
www.facebook.com/243812565693892
Overview: A small provincial organization overseen by Brain Injury Association of Canada
Mission: To contribute to an environment that is responsive to the needs of peoples affected with a brain injury in Prince Edward Island; To promote brain injury prevention
Finances: *Funding Sources:* Fundraising
Membership: *Member Profile:* Persons with brian injury & their families in Prince Edward Island
Activities: Promoting public awareness of the causes & consequences of brain injuries in Prince Edward Island; Education persons about brain injuries & their prevention; Providing information to individuals & organizations which serve the brain injury community; Offering advocacy services for persons with brain injury & their families; Promoting enhanced rehabilitation programs & facilities in Prince Edward Island; Liaising with other brain injury organizations & related groups; *Library:* Brain Injury Coalition of Prince Edward Island Resource Centre;

Brain Tumour Foundation of Canada (BTFC) / La Fondation canadienne sur les tumeurs cérébrales
#301, 620 Colborne St., London ON N6B 3R9
Tel: 519-642-7755; *Fax:* 519-642-7192
Toll-Free: 800-265-5106
braintumour@braintumour.ca
www.braintumour.ca
www.facebook.com/BrainTumourFoundationofCanada
twitter.com/BrainTumourFdn
www.youtube.com/BrainTumourFdn
Overview: A small national charitable organization founded in 1982
Mission: To find a cure for brain tumors & to improve the quality of life for those affected; To fund brain tumor research; to provide patient & family support services; To educate the public
Member of: North American Brain Tumor Coalition; Canadian Alliance of Brain Tumor Organizations
Chief Officer(s):
Susan D. Marshall, Executive Director
Finances: *Annual Operating Budget:* $500,000-$1.5 Million; *Funding Sources:* Group, individual, corporations & organization donations; fundraising events
Staff Member(s): 7; 200 volunteer(s)
Membership: 13; *Fees:* $5; *Committees:* Research; Fundraising; Information; Support Services; Finance & Audit
Activities: Support the Brain Tumor Tissue Bank; resource handbooks; pamphlets; books & videos dealing with brain tumors; support groups; national telephone support system; education & awareness; information displays in healthcare facilities; children's storybooks; *Awareness Events:* Brain Tumour Foundation of Canada Information Days; Brain Tumour Awareness Month, Oct.
Publications:
• BrainStorm
Type: Newsletter

Bramalea Stamp Club
PO Box 92531, Brampton ON L6W 4R1
Tel: 905-452-8343
bramstampclub@hotmail.com
Overview: A small local organization founded in 1975
Member of: Royal Philatelic Society of Canada; Grand River Valley Philatelic Association; Greater Toronto Area Philatelic Association
Chief Officer(s):
Robert Thorne, President, 905-792-3526
Ingo G. Nessel, Treasurer
Finances: *Funding Sources:* Membership dues; fundraising; show
Membership: 45; *Fees:* $15 individual; $20 family; *Member Profile:* Stamp collectors & philatelists

Brampton Arts Council (BAC)
24A Alexander St., Brampton ON L6V 1H6
Tel: 905-874-2919; *Fax:* 905-874-2921
info@artsbrampton.ca
www.artsbrampton.ca
www.facebook.com/pages/Brampton-Arts-Council/56347506618
www.youtube.com/bactalkbac
Overview: A small local charitable organization founded in 1978
Mission: To foster & promote arts within the City of Brampton; To educate public in the arts by providing various artistic presentations designed to raise level of aesthetic appreciation
Affiliation(s): Community Arts Ontario; Canadian Conference of the Arts; Brampton Board of Trade; Ontario Arts Council; Arts West
Chief Officer(s):
Marnie Richards, Executive Director
mrichards@artsbrampton.ca
Staff Member(s): 2; 50 volunteer(s)
Membership: 43 corporate + 4 student + 90 individual; *Fees:* Schedule available; *Committees:* Finance & Administration; Planning; Publicity; Bi-Consultative; Bingo; Policy
Activities: Artists' Alley; Studio Tour; *Library* Open to public
Awards:
• Arts Person of the Year (Award)
• BAC/Royal Bank School Artistic Achievement Awards (Award)

The Brampton Board of Trade (BBOT)
#101, 36 Queen St. East, Brampton ON L6V 1A2
Tel: 905-451-1122
admin@bramptonbot.com
www.bramptonbot.com
www.linkedin.com/company/2087561
www.facebook.com/BramptonBOT
twitter.com/BramptonBOT
www.youtube.com/user/BramptonBoT
Overview: A small local organization founded in 1887
Mission: To represent & actively promote the interests of Brampton business, members & the private enterprise system
Member of: Ontario Chamber of Commerce; Canadian Chamber of Commerce
Chief Officer(s):
Steve Sheils, Chief Executive Officer
ssheils@bramptonbot.com
Carrie Andrews, Operations Manager
candrews@bramptonbot.com
Glenn Williams, Chair
Membership: 883; *Fees:* Schedule available

Brampton Caledon Community Living (BCCL)
34 Church St. West, Brampton ON L6X 1H3
Tel: 905-453-8841; *Fax:* 905-453-8853
info@bramptoncaledoncl.ca
www.bcclnet.com
www.facebook.com/BramptonCaledonCommunityLiving
Overview: A small local organization founded in 1958
Mission: To support people with a developmental disability in partnership with their families and the community, to help them lead enriched and meaningful lives.
Member of: Community Living Ontario; Ontario Agencies Supporting Individuals with Special Needs; Advocacy Resource Centre for the Handicapped
Chief Officer(s):
Sean Travis, President
Jim Triantafilou, Executive Director
jimt@bramptoncaledoncl.ca
Finances: *Funding Sources:* Ministry of Community of Social Services; Region of Peel; United Way; the Trillium Foundation; fundraising

Brampton Horticultural Society
PO Box 92546, 160 Main St. South, Brampton ON L6W 4R1
e-mail: bramhort@hotmail.com
bramptonhort.org
Overview: A small local charitable organization founded in 1895
Member of: Ontario Horticultural Association
Chief Officer(s):
Fran Caldwell, President
Wendy Lovegrove, Secretary
Membership: *Fees:* $19 single; $26 family; $14 senior single; $20 senior family; $2.50 junior

Brampton Office *See* Heart & Stroke Foundation of Ontario

Brampton Real Estate Board (BREB)
#401, 60 Gillingham Dr., Brampton ON L6X 0Z9
Tel: 905-791-9913; *Fax:* 905-791-9430
info@breb.org
www.breb.org
www.facebook.com/theBREB
twitter.com/thebreb
www.youtube.com/user/TheBREBTV

Overview: A small local organization founded in 1955 overseen by Ontario Real Estate Association
Mission: To help members achieve their real estate related goals.
Member of: The Canadian Real Estate Association; Brampton Board of Trade
Chief Officer(s):
Denise Dilbey, President
ddilbey@royallepage.ca
Gerry Verdone, Executive Officer
eo@breb.org
Staff Member(s): 7
Activities: Realtor Expo; Annual Charity Golf Tournament

Brampton Rock & Mineral Club
#61, 46 Dearbourne Cres., Bramalea ON L6T 1J7
Overview: A small local organization
Mission: To share knowledge about collecting rocks & minerals
Member of: Central Canadian Federation of Mineralogical Societies
Chief Officer(s):
Gord Major, Contact
gordmajor@rogers.com
Membership: *Fees:* $15 students; $20 individuals; $25 families
Activities: Hosting monthly meetings from September to June; Organizing field trips

Brampton Symphony Orchestra
PO Box 93091, Stn. Brampton South, 499 Main St. South, Brampton ON L6Y 4V8
e-mail: info@bramptonsymphony.com
www.bramptonsymphony.com
Overview: A small local charitable organization overseen by Orchestras Canada
Activities: *Rents Mailing List:* Yes; *Library:* Music Library; by appointment

Brampton-Mississauga & District Labour Council (BMDLC)
PO Box 173, Stn. A, #403, 989 Derry Rd. East, Mississauga ON L5T 2J8
Tel: 905-696-8882; *Fax:* 905-696-7355
support@bmdlc.ca
www.bmdlc.ca
Overview: A small local organization founded in 1962 overseen by Ontario Federation of Labour
Member of: Canadian Labour Congress
Chief Officer(s):
Motilall Sarjoo, President
Finances: *Annual Operating Budget:* Less than $50,000; *Funding Sources:* Per capita tax from affiliates
12 volunteer(s)
Membership: 25,000; *Member Profile:* Affiliated local unions; *Committees:* Political Action; Affiliation; Events/Education
Activities: Labour Community Services, 905/696-7444; Monthly membership meetings; *Awareness Events:* Day of Mourning, April 28; Labour Day, Sept. 1

Brandon AIDS Support Inc. *See* AIDS Brandon Inc.

Brandon Chamber of Commerce
1043 Rosser Ave., Brandon MB R7A 0L5
Tel: 204-571-5340; *Fax:* 204-571-5347
Overview: A medium-sized local organization
Mission: To encourage growth in the Brandon community by fostering a progressive business environment, favourable to enhancing existing & attracting new business
Member of: Manitoba Chambers of Commerce; Canadian Chamber of Commerce
Chief Officer(s):
Randy Brown, President
Marnie McGregor, General Manager
gm@brandonchamber.ca
Finances: *Annual Operating Budget:* $100,000-$250,000
Staff Member(s): 4; 60 volunteer(s)
Membership: 900

Brandon Economic Development Board *See* Economic Development Brandon

Brandon Friendship Centre
836 Lorne Ave., Brandon MB R7A 0T8
Tel: 204-727-1407; *Fax:* 204-726-0902
bfcinc@mts.net
brandonfriendshipcentre.net
Overview: A small local charitable organization
Mission: To provide services to the community with an emphasis on Aboriginal culture.
Chief Officer(s):
Darlene Paquette, President
Gail Cullen, Executive Director
Staff Member(s): 55
Activities: Services include: Brandon Aboriginal Youth Activity Centre; Parent Child Centre Program; Portage Aboriginal HeadStart Program; Brandon Friendship Centre Housing Authority; Kokum's Little Friends Daycare

Brandon Humane Society
2200 - 17 St. East, Brandon MB R7A 7M6
www.brandonhumanesociety.ca
Also Known As: Brandon Society for the Prevention of Cruelty to Animals
Overview: A small local organization founded in 1946 overseen by Canadian Federation of Humane Societies
Mission: To provide care for & homes for abused companion animals; to educate the public about the value of humane treatment of animals.
Member of: Canadian Federation of Humane Societies
Chief Officer(s):
Darren Creighton, President
Tracy Munn, Shelter Manager
75 volunteer(s)
Membership: *Fees:* $10 individual; $20 family
Activities: Info booths in local malls, television, Access TV;

Brandon Police Association (BPA) / Association de la police de la ville de Brandon
c/o Brandon Police Service, 1020 Victoria Ave., Brandon MB R7A 1A9
Tel: 204-729-2345; *Fax:* 204-726-1323
police.brandon.ca
Overview: A small local licensing organization founded in 1956
Mission: The Association represents the city police employees, negotiating a collective agreement with the city on their behalf.
Affiliation(s): Manitoba Police Association; Canadian Police Association
Chief Officer(s):
Kevin Loewen, President
Membership: 125; *Member Profile:* Member/employee of Brandon Police
Activities: *Internships:* Yes

Brandon Real Estate Board (BREB)
857 - 18 St., Unit B, Brandon MB R7A 5B8
Tel: 204-727-4672; *Fax:* 204-727-8331
info@breb.mb.ca
www.breb.mb.ca
Overview: A small local organization overseen by Manitoba Real Estate Association
Mission: To provide real estate support for Realtors in Brandon.
Member of: The Canadian Real Estate Association
Chief Officer(s):
Cam Toews, President
Annette Wiebe, Executive Officer
eo@breb.mb.ca
Staff Member(s): 3

Brandon University Faculty Association (BUFA) / Association des professeurs de l'Université de Brandon
Clark Hall, Brandon University, #333, 270 - 18th St., Brandon MB R7A 6A9
Tel: 204-727-7347
www.bufa.org
Overview: A small local organization founded in 1978
Mission: To represent the faculty members in negotiating collective agreements
Member of: Canadian Association of University Teachers; Manitoba Organization of Faculty Associations
Chief Officer(s):
Todd Fugleberg, President, 204-571-8577
Maureen Barrett, Administrator
barrett@brandonu.ca
Staff Member(s): 1

Brandon University School of Music
270 - 18th St., Brandon MB R7A 6A9
Tel: 204-728-9631; *Fax:* 204-728-6839
music@brandonu.ca
www.brandonu.ca/music/
www.facebook.com/group.php?gid=31991706716
Overview: A small local organization

Brant Community Social Planning Council
Brantford ON
Tel: 519-754-1081
Overview: A small local organization founded in 1989
Mission: To enhance the quality of life for all citizens in Brant County by facilitating effective planning in conjunction with an informed & involved community

Brant Historical Society (BHS)
57 Charlotte St., Brantford ON N3T 2W6
Tel: 519-752-2483
www.brantmuseums.ca
www.facebook.com/BrantMuseums
twitter.com/Branthistorical
www.youtube.com/user/branthistorical
Overview: A small local charitable organization founded in 1908
Mission: To collect, preserve & share the history & heritage of Brantford/Brant County & Six Nations/New Credit
Member of: Ontario Historical Society; Ontario Museums Association
Chief Officer(s):
Lana Jobe, Executive Director
Membership: *Fees:* $20 student; $25 individual; $40 family
Activities: Operates Brant Museum & Archives; Publication of local history for Brantford/Brant County; Lecture series; *Speaker Service:* Yes; *Library* Open to public

Brant United Way (BUW)
125 Morrell St., Brantford ON N3T 4J9
Tel: 519-752-7848; *Fax:* 519-752-7913
info@brantunitedway.org
www.brantunitedway.org
www.facebook.com/pages/Brant-United-Way/33874902961
twitter.com/brantunitedway
Overview: A small local charitable organization founded in 1953 overseen by United Way of Canada - Centraide Canada
Mission: To help people in their time of need
Chief Officer(s):
Kristin Pass, Executive Director
Finances: *Funding Sources:* Campaigns; donations
Staff Member(s): 3; 300 volunteer(s)
Activities: *Speaker Service:* Yes

Brantford & District Association for Community Living *See* Community Living Brantford

Brantford & District Labour Council
PO Box 8, #201, 1100 Clarence St. South, Box 8, Brantford ON N3S 7N8
Tel: 519-753-9142; *Fax:* 519-753-9747
labour@brantfordlabourcouncil.ca
www.brantfordlabourcouncil.ca
Overview: A small local organization overseen by Ontario Federation of Labour
Member of: Ontario Federation of Labour
Chief Officer(s):
Garry Mac Donald, President
Roxanne Bond, Recording Secretary

Brantford CADORA *See* CADORA Ontario Association Inc.

Brantford Lapidary & Mineral Society Inc. (BLMS)
1 Sherwood Dr., Brantford ON N3T 1N3
e-mail: brantfordlapclub@live.ca
www.brantfordlapidarymineral.ca
Overview: A small local organization founded in 1964
Mission: To increase interest in the earth sciences & related lapidary arts
Chief Officer(s):
Ernie Edmonds, President, 519-583-9457
John Moons, Vice-President, 519-752-9756
Campbell.moons@silomail.com
Kim LeBlanc, Secretary, 519-442-7372
marcell@execulink.com
Darren Gage, Treasurer, 519-758-8426
darren_gage@hotmail.com
Russ McCrory, Librarian, 905-389-6526
russelldavid.mccrory@sympatico.ca
Membership: *Fees:* $15 single membership; $18 family
Activities: Offering lapidary training; Providing equipment access; Organizing monthly meetings; Arranging field trips; *Library:* Brantford Lapidary & Mineral Society Library
Awards:
• Brantford Lapidary and Mineral Society Inc. Awards (Award)
Eligibility: Presented annually to students enrolled in an Earth Sciences program in the Faculty of Science at the University of Waterloo who have achieved a minimum overall average of 75%
Amount: $1,000 each

Publications:
• The Telephone City Crystal [a publication of the Brantford Lapidary & Mineral Society, Inc.]
Type: Newsletter; *Editor:* Marcel LeBlanc
Profile: Information about lapidary & minerals, equipment advice, & forthcoming events

Brantford Musicians' Association (BMA)
101 Chatham St., Brantford ON N3T 2P3
Tel: 519-752-7973; *Fax:* 519-752-7973
Toll-Free: 800-463-6333
musicians@bellnet.ca
www.brantfordmusicians.org
Also Known As: AFM Local 467
Overview: A small local organization founded in 1907
Mission: To unite professional musicians; to secure improved wages, hours & working conditions for professional musicians; To promote live music in the community
Member of: American Federation of Musicians
Chief Officer(s):
Rusty James, President
Marg Conway, Secretary
Finances: *Annual Operating Budget:* Less than $50,000; *Funding Sources:* Membership fees
Staff Member(s): 1; 8 volunteer(s)
Membership: 202; *Fees:* $125; *Member Profile:* Professional musicians
Activities: Annual showcase of talent; annual "Bring Your Axe Night"

Brantford Numismatic Society
PO Box 28015, Stn. North Park Plaza, Brantford ON N3R 7K5
Tel: 519-759-5137
Overview: A small local organization
Member of: Ontario Numismatic Association
Chief Officer(s):
Len Trakalo, Contact
ltrakalo@rogers.com

Brantford Police Association (BPA)
344 Elgin St., Brantford ON N3S 7P6
Tel: 519-756-6621
Overview: A small local organization founded in 1946
Mission: To represent its members during collective bargaining negotiations.
Member of: Police Association of Ontario
Membership: *Member Profile:* Brantford Police officers and staff

Brantford Regional Chamber of Commerce ***See*** Chamber of Commerce of Brantford & Brant

Brantford Regional Real Estate Association Inc. (BRREA)
106 George St., Brantford ON N3T 2Y4
Tel: 519-753-0308; *Fax:* 519-753-8638
brantfordreb@rogers.com
www.brrea.com
www.facebook.com/BrantfordRegionalRealEstateAssociation
twitter.com/_BRREA
www.youtube.com/BRREAssociation
Overview: A small local organization overseen by Ontario Real Estate Association
Mission: To provide real estate support for realtors working in Brantford.
Member of: The Canadian Real Estate Association
Chief Officer(s):
Julia Price-Greig, Executive Officer
Staff Member(s): 4
Membership: 300 relators in 24 organizations; *Committees:* Political Affairs; Community Awareness; Education; MLS/Technology

Brantford Stamp Club
c/o Pamela Kilpin, PO Box 25003, Stn. West Brant, Brantford ON N3T 6K5
Tel: 519-754-1305
www.brantfordstamp.org
Overview: A small local organization founded in 1937
Member of: Royal Philatelic Society of Canada; Grand River Valley Philatelic Association
Chief Officer(s):
Paul James, President, 519-751-3513
pjames@execulink.com
Pamela Kilpin, Secretary
Finances: *Funding Sources:* Membership dues; annual stamp show
Membership: 50; *Fees:* $15 single; $20 family; $3 children; $7 associate; *Member Profile:* Those interested in postage stamps & postal history; *Committees:* Executive; Annual Stamp Show
Activities: *Awareness Events:* Brantford Stamp Club Annual Show

Brantford Symphony Orchestra Association Inc.
PO Box 24012, 185 King George Rd., Brantford ON N3R 7X3
Tel: 519-759-8781; *Fax:* 519-759-0842
administrator@brantfordsymphony.ca
www.brantfordsymphony.ca
www.facebook.com/Brantford.Symphony
twitter.com/bsobrant
Overview: A small local charitable organization overseen by Orchestras Canada
Mission: To provide enduring access to the best symphonic entertainment, giving people of all ages opportunities for musical growth & education
Chief Officer(s):
Maureen Wills, Vice-President
Philip Sarabura, Conductor/Music Director
Staff Member(s): 3; 40 volunteer(s)
Membership: 100-499
Activities: *Awareness Events:* Annual Book Fair, April; *Speaker Service:* Yes; *Library* by appointment

Brantford Tourism & Convention Services ***See*** Tourism Brantford

Brantwood Foundation
25 Bell Lane, Brantford ON N3T 1E1
Tel: 519-753-2658
www.brantwood.ca/brantwood-foundation
Overview: A small local charitable organization founded in 1982
Mission: To raise funds for the Brantrwood Centre, a facility that provides services to challenged individuals in Brantford and Brant County.
Chief Officer(s):
Emilie Brown, Coordinator, Public Relations & Fundraising
publicrelations@brantwood.ca
Finances: *Funding Sources:* Provincial government; Brant United Way; private sector
Activities: Golf tournament; fundraising for Brantwood Centre

Break Open Ticket Program Management Alliance (BOTPMA)
142 Springfield Blvd., Ancaster ON L9K 1H8
Tel: 613-292-4102
www.botpma.com
Overview: A small provincial organization founded in 1992
Mission: Entrepreneurs whose members provide fundraising products, services & leadership for the charitable gaming industry in Ontario
Chief Officer(s):
Garry T. Jacob, President
gtjacob@rogers.com
Membership: *Fees:* $500; *Member Profile:* Registered suppliers of Break Open Tickets & services to Ontario's charitable sector

Breakfast Cereals Canada (BCC)
#600, 100 Sheppard Ave. East, Toronto ON M2N 6N5
Tel: 416-510-8024; *Fax:* 416-510-8043
breakfastcereals.ca
Overview: A medium-sized national organization founded in 1983
Mission: To provide a forum for members to review issues of significance to the breakfast industry; to represent industry with government
Affliation(s): Food & Consumer Products Manufacturers of Canada
Chief Officer(s):
Kathryn Fitzwilliam, Contact
kathrynf@fcpc.ca
Membership: 4; *Member Profile:* Cereal manufacturers only: General Mills Canada Corporation, Kellogg Canada Inc., Post Foods Canada Corporation & Quaker

Breast Cancer Action (BCA) / Sensibilisation au cancer du sein
#301, 1390 Prince of Wales Dr., Ottawa ON K2C 3N6
Tel: 613-736-5921; *Fax:* 613-736-8422
info@bcaott.ca
www.bcaott.ca
www.facebook.com/106397202723177
twitter.com/bcaott
Overview: A medium-sized local charitable organization founded in 1993
Mission: To advocate establishment of a national resource office, directed by women affected by breast cancer, to serve as clearinghouse for information about treatment, legislative action, access to treatments & support services; to advocate for a designated centre for excellence to accelerate research; to advocate greater emphasis on developing earlier detection; to promote increased survivor participation in cancer care planning & policy making; to promote better education of family physicians & women in early detection & follow-up
Chief Officer(s):
Karen Graszat, Executive Director
executivedirector@bcaott.ca
Finances: *Funding Sources:* Private donations; fundraisers
Staff Member(s): 2
Membership: *Fees:* $40
Activities: *Awareness Events:* Annual Walk/Fun Run, June; *Library* Open to public

Breast Cancer Action Nova Scotia (BCANS)
#205, 967 Bedford Hwy., Bedford NS B4A 1A9
Tel: 902-465-2685; *Fax:* 902-484-6436
bcans@bca.ns.ca
www.bcans.ca
www.facebook.com/group.php?gid=168336816529386
twitter.com/BCANSBedford
Overview: A medium-sized provincial charitable organization founded in 1994
Mission: To address the obstacles faced by those living with breast cancer; To provide information; To create a support network for those with breast cancer
Affliation(s): Keller Williams Realty (Harold Shea)
Finances: *Annual Operating Budget:* $100,000-$250,000; *Funding Sources:* Donations
Membership: *Fees:* $10; *Committees:* Education; Advocacy; Web; Funding; Network; Library
Activities: Monthly educational talks; *Awareness Events:* Pink Spring Celebration Dinner, Dance, Fashion Show & Auction, Spring; *Library:* Rosanna Bechtel Memorial Library
Meetings/Conferences: • Breast Cancer Action Nova Scotia 2015 Annual General Meeting, 2015, NS
Scope: Provincial
Description: A business meeting for members, featuring reports from committee chairs
Contact Information: E-mail (general information): bcans@bcans.ca
Publications:
• Atlantic Breast Cancer Net E-Newsletter
Type: Newsletter; *Price:* Free with membership in Breast Cancer Action Nova Scotia

Breast Cancer Society of Canada / Société du cancer du sein du Canada
420 East St. North, Sarnia ON N7T 6Y5
Tel: 519-336-0746; *Fax:* 519-336-5725
Toll-Free: 800-567-8767
bcsc@bcsc.ca
www.bcsc.ca
www.facebook.com/breastcancersocietyofcanada
twitter.com/bcsctweet
www.youtube.com/user/BreastCancerSociety
Overview: A large national charitable organization founded in 1991
Mission: To support research into the prevention, detection, & treatment of breast cancer
Chief Officer(s):
Marsha Davidson, Executive Director
mdavidson@bcsc.ca
Dawn Hamilton, Coordinator, Fund Development
dhamilton@bcsc.ca
Bunny Caughlin, Officer, Operations
bcaughlin@bcsc.ca
Johanne Deschamps, Officer, Communications
jdeschamps@bcsc.ca
Finances: *Funding Sources:* Donations; Fundraising
Activities: Bosom Buddy program; Caring Kids Corner; golf tournament; fundraising events; *Awareness Events:* Dress for the Cause, October; Pam Greenaway-Kohlmeier Memorial Golf Tournament; Mother's Day Walk
Publications:
• Breast Cancer Society of Canada Newsletter
Type: Newsletter
Profile: Recent information about the society & research endeavours

Breeders of Belgian Horses Association of Québec ***Voir*** Association des éleveurs de chevaux Belge du Québec

Brereton Field Naturalists' Club Inc. (BFN)
PO Box 1084, Barrie ON L4M 5E1
bfnclub.org
www.facebook.com/groups/1470726149815044/
Overview: A small local charitable organization founded in 1951
Mission: To acquire & disseminate knowledge of natural history; to protect & preserve wildlife; to stimulate public interest in nature & its preservation
Affiliation(s): Federation of Ontario Naturalists
Chief Officer(s):
Brian Gibbon, Contact, 705-726-8969
bwg@backland.net
Finances: *Annual Operating Budget:* Less than $50,000; *Funding Sources:* Membership fees
95 volunteer(s)
Membership: 125; *Fees:* $10 student; $15 corresponding; $25 individual; $30 family; *Committees:* Conservation; Education; Field Trips; Newsletter; Program
Activities: Bird-watching outings; nature strolls; lunches; *Speaker Service:* Yes; *Library:* BFN Library; by appointment
Publications:
• The Blue Heron
Type: Newsletter; *Frequency:* Annually

Brethren in Christ (BIC)
2700 Bristol Circle, Oakville ON L6H 6EH
Tel: 905-339-2335; *Fax:* 905-337-2120
office@canadianbic.ca
www.canadianbic.ca
www.facebook.com/BICCanada
twitter.com/BICCanada
Overview: A medium-sized international charitable organization founded in 1788
Member of: Evangelical Fellowship of Canada
Affliation(s): Mennonite Central Committee; Canadian Holiness Federation
Chief Officer(s):
Brad Fisher, Treasurer
Trish Hogg, Secretary
Darrell Winger, Executive Director
darrell.winger@canadianbic.ca
Finances: *Annual Operating Budget:* $500,000-$1.5 Million; *Funding Sources:* Congregational giving
Staff Member(s): 8
Membership: 3,450 + 43 congregations in Canada; *Member Profile:* North American membership is about 20,000 with significant churches in other countries including India, Japan, Zambia, Zimbabwe, Nicaragua, Cuba, Venezuela, Columbia, South Africa
Activities: *Speaker Service:* Yes; *Rents Mailing List:* Yes

Breton & District Chamber of Commerce
PO Box 364, Breton AB T0C 0P0
Tel: 780-696-2557; *Fax:* 780-696-2557
bretonchamber@gmail.com
Overview: A small local organization

Breton & District Historical Society
PO Box 696, 4711 - 51 St., Breton AB T0C 0P0
Tel: 780-696-2551
bretonmuse@yahoo.com
Overview: A small local charitable organization founded in 1978
Mission: To present information & exhibits about Black history, community development, agriculture, & lumbering in Breton, Alberta
Chief Officer(s):
Allan Goddard, Contact
Finances: *Funding Sources:* Donations; Fundraising; Sponsorships
Activities: Operating the Breton & District Historical Museum; Restoring the Keystone Cemetery & honouring Black families who settled in the area

Brewers Association of Canada / L'Association des brasseurs du Canada
#650, 45 O'Connor St., Ottawa ON K1P 1A4
Tel: 613-232-9601; *Fax:* 613-232-2283
info@beercanada.com
www.beercanada.com
www.linkedin.com/company/beer-canada
twitter.com/beercanada
Also Known As: Beer Canada
Overview: A large national organization founded in 1943
Mission: To represent brewing companies operating in Canada; to collect information & statistics about the brewing industry; to provide information about the industry to the public
Chief Officer(s):
John Sleeman, Chair
André Forin, Director, Public & Government Affairs, 613-286-8974
Edwin P. Gregory, Director, Policy & Research, 613-286-8978
Linda Andrusek, Executive Assistant & Manager, Administrative Services, 613-232-9601
Peter A.B. MacPhail, Accountant, 613-232-9601
Membership: 24 brewers
Activities: Promoting the responsible use of alchohol; BrewStats feature on website; *Library*

Brewery, Winery & Distillery Workers Union - Local 300
7128 Gilley Ave., Burnaby BC V5J 4X2
Tel: 604-434-5155; *Fax:* 604-434-7333
brew300@telus.net
www.brew300.ca
Overview: A small provincial organization founded in 1925
Member of: National Union of Public and General Employees
Affliation(s): BC Government & Service Employees' Union
Chief Officer(s):
Roy Graham, President
Finances: *Annual Operating Budget:* $500,000-$1.5 Million
Staff Member(s): 3
Membership: 880; *Fees:* 1.5% of gross

Brewing & Malting Barley Research Institute (BMBRI) / Institut de recherche - brassage et orge de maltage
PO Box 1497, Stn. Main, Winnipeg MB R3C 2Z4
Tel: 204-927-1407
info@bmbri.ca
www.bmbri.ca
Overview: A medium-sized national organization founded in 1948
Mission: To support the development & evaluation of new malting barley varieties in Canada
Chief Officer(s):
Michael Brophy, President & CEO, 204-927-1401
mbrophy@bmbri.ca
Staff Member(s): 2
Membership: 8 corporate; *Fees:* Schedule available; *Member Profile:* Commercial brewing or malting companies

Brian Webb Dance Co.
PO Box 53092, Edmonton AB T5N 48A
Tel: 780-452-3282
webbcdf@shaw.ca
www.bwdc.ca
www.facebook.com/pages/Brian-Webb-Dance-Company/104046922978344
twitter.com/BrianWebbDance
pinterest.com/brianwebbdance
Overview: A small local charitable organization founded in 1979
Mission: To produce & present contemporary dance; to build work through collaboration
Chief Officer(s):
Brian Webb, Artistic Director
Staff Member(s): 5

Bricklayers, Masons Independent Union of Canada (CLC) / Syndicat indépendant des briqueteurs et des maçons du Canada (CTC)
PO Box 105, #307, 1263 Wilson Ave., Toronto ON M3M 3G3
Tel: 416-247-9841; *Fax:* 416-241-9636
localone.ca
Overview: A medium-sized national organization
Chief Officer(s):
Fernando Da Cunha, Vice President
John Meiorin, Secretary-Treasurer
Membership: 1,500 + 1 local

Bridge Adult Service Society
16 Station St., Amherst NS B4H 0C2
Tel: 902-667-8433; *Fax:* 902-667-8433
b.workshop@ns.sympatico.ca
Overview: A small local organization
Member of: DIRECTIONS Council for Vocational Services Society
Chief Officer(s):
Susan Thibodeau, Executive Director/Manager

Bridges
#2, 670 Prince St., Truro NS B2N 1G6
Tel: 902-897-6665; *Fax:* 902-897-0569
bridges@bridgesinstitute.org
bridgesinstitute.org
Overview: A small local organization founded in 1991
Mission: To help to end men's violence against women
Chief Officer(s):
Tod Augusta-Scott
tod@bridgesinstitute.org

Bridges Family Programs Association
477 - 3rd St. SE, Medicine Hat AB T1A 0G8
Tel: 403-526-7473; *Fax:* 403-504-2459
bridgesfamilyprograms.com
Also Known As: BRIDGES
Previous Name: Parents of the Handicapped of Southeastern Alberta
Overview: A small local charitable organization founded in 1977
Mission: To work with families by building on their strengths, providing support, information & advocacy to make a positive difference in the lives of each person, family & community; families are able to access information & support which will assist them to meet their needs & enjoy safe, loving, healthy relationships & environments
Chief Officer(s):
Lauren Fourriere, Executive Director
Sylvia March, President
Finances: *Annual Operating Budget:* $500,000-$1.5 Million; *Funding Sources:* Provincial Government
Staff Member(s): 20
Membership: 30; *Fees:* $10 institutional; $10 individual
Activities: Summer Program - Camp Wannacombac; Bridges Program; Healthy Start; Building Blocks; Best Babies; *Library:* Resource Centre; by appointment

Bridgetown & Area Chamber of Commerce (BACC)
PO Box 467, Bridgetown NS B0S 1C0
Tel: 902-665-4679; *Fax:* 902-665-4747
info@bridgetownareachamber.com
www.bridgetownareachamber.com
www.facebook.com/baccsociety?sk=wall
Overview: A small local organization
Chief Officer(s):
Andrew Kerr, President
Marion Tanner, Secretary

Bridgetown & Area Historical Society
PO Box 645, 12 Queen St., Bridgetown NS B0S 1C0
Tel: 902-665-4530
Also Known As: James House Museum
Overview: A small local charitable organization founded in 1979
Mission: To promote interest in local history of Bridgetown & area
Member of: Federation of Nova Scotia Heritage
Affliation(s): Nova Scotia Museum - Halifax
10 volunteer(s)
Membership: 65 lifetime + 50 individual; *Fees:* $10 individual yearly; $20 family yearly; $100 lifetime; *Member Profile:* Interest in museum & history & archives; *Committees:* Maintenence; Special Events; Tea Room; Victoria Garden
Activities: Operates seasonal museum; *Library* by appointment

Bridgewater & Area Chamber of Commerce (BACC)
373 King St., Bridgewater NS B4V 1B1
Tel: 902-543-4263; *Fax:* 902-527-1156
www.bridgewaterchamber.com
www.facebook.com/group.php?gid=100619843315571
Overview: A small local organization founded in 1899
Mission: To act as the voice of the business community in Bridgewater, Nova Scotia & the surrounding area
Chief Officer(s):
Ann O'Connell, Executive Director
Membership: *Fees:* Schedule available based on number of employees; *Member Profile:* Any individual, business, or organization in Bridgewater, Nova Scotia & the surrounding region
Activities: Advocating on behalf of businesses to all levels of government; Partnering with other business associations & community organizations; Hosting community events; Providing training; Offering networking opportunities
Awards:
• Entrepreneurship Scholarship (Scholarship)
• Business Excellence Awards: Entrepreneur, Small Business, Large Business, President's Award (Award)
Publications:
• BACC [Bridgewater & Area Chamber of Commerce] Buzz
Type: Newsletter; *Price:* Free

Brier Island Chamber of Commerce
PO Box 74, Westport NS B0V 1H0
Tel: 902-839-2347; *Fax:* 902-839-2006

Overview: A small local organization
Chief Officer(s):
Harold Graham, President
Joan Riday, Secretary

Brighton & District Chamber of Commerce
PO Box 880, 74 Main Street, Brighton ON K0K 1H0
Tel: 613-475-2775; *Fax:* 613-475-3777
Toll-Free: 877-475-2775
info@brightonchamber.ca
www.brightonchamber.ca
www.facebook.com/BrightonandDistrictChamberofCommerce
Previous Name: AppleRoute Country Chamber of Commerce
Overview: A small local organization founded in 1994
Member of: Ontario Chamber of Commerce
Chief Officer(s):
Don Parks, President
Finances: *Annual Operating Budget:* $50,000-$100,000; *Funding Sources:* Membership fees; Fund raising
Staff Member(s): 1; 10 volunteer(s)
Membership: 150; *Fees:* $125; *Member Profile:* Local business owners; *Committees:* Economic; Membership; Tourism
Activities: Business breakfasts; tourism information; economic strategy; visitor enquiries; business referrals

Britiish Columbia Veterinary Technologists Association (BCVTA)
101 Todd Rd., Kamloops BC V5C 5A9
Tel: 250-319-0027; *Fax:* 866-319-1929
bcvta.com
Previous Name: Animal Health Technologists Association of BC
Overview: A small provincial organization founded in 1980
Mission: To promote, encourage & maintain the knowledge, ability & competence of members of the Association in the area of animal care; to establish minimum standards of training for members of the Association; to participate in the development of a standard level of provincial recognition as a profession
Member of: Canadian Association of Animal Health Technologists & Technicians
Chief Officer(s):
Christine Watson, Executive Director
ed@bcvta.com
Lindsay Ramage, President
lindsaybcvta@yahoo.ca
Finances: *Annual Operating Budget:* Less than $50,000; *Funding Sources:* Membership fees
Staff Member(s): 6
Membership: 310; *Fees:* $110 regular; $40 student; $15 non-resident; $100 renewal; *Member Profile:* Graduates of CVMA-accredited 2-year AHT program
Activities: *Awareness Events:* Animal Health Technologists Week, Oct.
Meetings/Conferences: • Britiish Columbia Veterinary Technologists Association 2015 Conference, 2015, BC
Scope: Provincial

British Canadian Chamber of Trade & Commerce
Dominion Centre, Royal Trust Tower, 2401, 77 King St., Toronto ON M5K 1G8
Tel: 416-816-9154; *Fax:* 647-435-3436
central@bcctc.ca
www.bcctc.ca
twitter.com/bcctc
Overview: A medium-sized international organization
Mission: To foster reciprocal trading between Canada & the U.K.
Chief Officer(s):
Thomas O'Carroll, Vice-President, Central
tocarroll@bcctc.ca
Liam J. Hopkins, Vice President, Western
ljhopkins@telus.net
John Hoblyn, Contact, Eastern
Membership: *Fees:* Schedule available

British Columbia & Yukon Chamber of Mines *See* Association for Mineral Exploration British Columbia

British Columbia & Yukon Community Newspapers Association (BCYCNA)
9 West Broadway, Vancouver BC V5Y 1P1
Tel: 604-669-9222; *Fax:* 604-684-4713
Toll-Free: 866-669-9222
info@bccommunitynews.com
www.bccommunitynews.com
www.linkedin.com/company/220705?goback=%2Efcs
Overview: A medium-sized local organization founded in 1922 overseen by Canadian Community Newspapers Association
Mission: To encourage excellence in the publishing of community newspapers
Chief Officer(s):
George Affleck, General Manager
gm@bccommunitynews.com
Kerry Slater, Manager, Special Projects
kerry@bccommunitynews.com
Connor Barnsley, Manager, Communications & Member Services
Cora Schupp, Accounting Manager
accounting@bccommunitynews.com
Staff Member(s): 5
Membership: 125; *Committees:* Finance; Marketing/Community classifieds; Membership; CCNA; Awards Gala/Professional Development; Scholarships; Government Relations; Press Council; Independents; Stewardship
Activities: *Rents Mailing List:* Yes

British Columbia Aboriginal Child Care Society (ACCS)
#102, 100 Park Royal South, West Vancouver BC V7T 1A2
Tel: 604-913-9128; *Fax:* 604-913-9129
reception@acc-society.bc.ca
www.acc-society.bc.ca
www.facebook.com/aboriginal.childcare
Overview: A small provincial organization
Mission: To develop & provide quality Aboriginal child care services in British Columbia; To support community-based child care services to ensure children develop as First Nations with a distinct language & culture
Affliation(s): Canadian Child Care Federation
Chief Officer(s):
Mary Teegee, President
Karen Isaac, Executive Director
karen@acc-society.bc.ca
Mary Burgaretta, Advisor, Aboriginal Child Care
mary@acc-society.bc.ca
Kirsten Bevelander, Advisor, Child Care
kirsten@acc-society.bc.ca
Pepper Brewster, Resource Librarian
library@acc-society.bc.ca
Dawn Westlands, Program Coordinator, Singing Frog Aboriginal Head Start Preschool
coordinator@sf.acc-society.bc.ca
Dawn Westlands, Program Coordinator, Eagle's Nest Aboriginal Head Start Preschool
coordinator@en.acc-society.bc.ca
Finances: *Funding Sources:* British Columbia Ministry of Children & Family Development; Membership fees; Donations
Staff Member(s): 7
Membership: *Fees:* $15 student; $25 individuals; $100 organizations & centres; $200 associate members; *Member Profile:* Organizations & centres, such as early childhood, preschool, & out-of-school care programs that serve Aboriginal families throughout British Columbia; Individuals, such as administrators in Aboriginal child care, early childhood educators who are Aboriginal or who work with Aboriginal children, elders, parents of Aboriginal children, & Aboriginal students enrolled in ECE or ECD; Associate members who are interested in the objectives of the society
Activities: Initiating research on Aboriginal child care issues; Providing research reports; Presenting training workshops in various communities; Offering networking activities; *Library:* British Columbia Aboriginal Child Care Society Resource Library
Awards:
• British Columbia Aboriginal Child Care Society Aboriginal Child Care Recognition Award (Award)
Presented to an early childhood educator or caregiver for their contribution to the well-being of Aboriginal children in British Columbia *Contact:* Awards Committee, Fax: 604-913-9129
Publications:
• Caring For Our Children
Type: Newsletter; *Frequency:* Quarterly; *Editor:* David Wu; *Price:* Free with British Columbia Aboriginal Child Care Societymembership
Profile: Articles & information about the British Columbia Aboriginal Child Care Society's policies, library, training, events, & funding

British Columbia Aboriginal Lands Managers (BCALM)
c/o Shuswap First Nation, PO Box 2847, #3A-492, Arrow Rd., Invermere BC V0A 1K0
Tel: 250-349-5281; *Fax:* 250-342-6301
Overview: A small provincial organization founded in 2012 overseen by National Aboriginal Lands Managers Association
Chief Officer(s):
Latrica (Terry) Nicholas, Chair
latricanic@gmail.com
Staff Member(s): 1

British Columbia Aboriginal Network on Disability Society (BCANDS)
1179 Kosapsum Cres., Victoria BC V9A 7K7
Tel: 250-381-7303; *Fax:* 250-381-7312
Toll-Free: 888-815-5511
bcands@bcands.bc.ca
www.bcands.bc.ca
Overview: A small provincial charitable organization founded in 1991
Mission: To promote the betterment of Aboriginal people with disabilities
Chief Officer(s):
Frazer Smith, President
Ruby Reid, Secretary-Treasurer
Finances: *Annual Operating Budget:* $250,000-$500,000
Staff Member(s): 9; 2 volunteer(s)
Membership: 6,100; *Member Profile:* Aboriginal people with disabilities
Activities: Advocacy; *Speaker Service:* Yes; *Library:* BCANDS Aboriginal Health Resource Centre

British Columbia Agriculture Council
#230, 32160 South Fraser Way, Abbotsford BC V2T 1W5
Tel: 604-854-4454; *Fax:* 604-854-4485
Toll-Free: 866-522-3477
info@bcac.bc.ca
www.bcac.bc.ca
twitter.com/bcagcouncil
Overview: A medium-sized provincial organization founded in 1997 overseen by Canadian Federation of Agriculture
Mission: To provide leadership in representing, promoting, & advocating the collective interests of all agriculture producers in the province of British Colombia; To foster cooperation & a collective response to matters affecting the future of agriculture in the province; To facilitate programs & service delivery for a number of programs that benefit the industry
Chief Officer(s):
Reg Ens, Executive Director
Staff Member(s): 3
Membership: 27; *Committees:* Agriculture Environment Initiatives; Climate Action Advisory; Finance; Labour; Wild Predator Loss Prevention; Agriculture Environment Partnership; Growing Forward Advisory; Provincial Risk Management Advisory

British Columbia Alliance of Information & Referral Services (BC-AIRS)
#201, Capilano Mall, 935 Marine Dr., North Vancouver BC V7P 1S3
Tel: 604-985-7138; *Fax:* 604-985-0645
nscr@nscr.bc.ca
www.nscr.bc.ca
Overview: A medium-sized provincial organization
Mission: To develop & maintain a high quality, coordinated information & referral network for the province of British Columbia
Chief Officer(s):
Klassen Suzanne, Vice President
s.klassen@shaw.org
Membership: *Fees:* $25-30

British Columbia Alpine Ski Association
#403, 1788 West Broadway, Vancouver BC V6J 1Y1
Tel: 604-678-3070; *Fax:* 604-678-8073
office@bcalpine.com
www.bcalpine.com
Overview: A small local organization
Mission: To promote the sport of alpine skiing in British Columbia
Chief Officer(s):
Bruce Goldsmid, CEO
bruceg@bcalpine.com
Staff Member(s): 8
Membership: 35 ski clubs; *Fees:* Schedule available
Awards:
• Dave Murray Ski Foundation Bursary (Grant)
Eligibility: Financial need; athletic ability; sportsmanship; leadership *Amount:* $750
• Bob Parsons' Memorial Fund Bursary (Grant)
Eligibility: Leadership, dedication to sport, financial need, recommendation *Amount:* $1000

• Ski Canada Magazine Bursary (Grant)
Eligibility: K2 level athlete, financial need, potential *Amount:* $1000
• RTA Nancy Greene Ski League Bursary (Grant)
Eligibility: Member of the RTA NGSL program, financial need, sportsmanship*Deadline:* January 31 *Amount:* Four $100 bursaries

British Columbia Alternate Education Association (BCAEA)

c/o British columbia Teachers' Federation, #100, 550 West 6th Ave., Vancouver BC V5Z 4P2
Tel: 604-871-2283; *Fax:* 604-871-2286
Toll-Free: 800-663-9163
www.bctf.ca/bcaea
Overview: A small provincial organization
Mission: To help at-risk youth who are unsuccessful in the main stream educational system; to promote alternative education throughout the province and makes recommendations to the BC Teachers' Federation; to distribute $6500 in bursaries each year.
Affliation(s): BC Teacher's Federation
Chief Officer(s):
Mike Shaw, President, 250-768-3253, Fax: 778-476-5939
mike.shaw@telus.net
Membership: *Fees:* $15 student/retired; $30 BCTF member; $50 non-BCTF member
Activities: Annual conference, Jan.;
Awards:
• Student Bursary (Grant)
Eligibility: Graduate student continuing at post-secondary institution*Deadline:* March 15 *Amount:* Five $500 awards
• Student Achievement Award (Grant)
Eligibility: Student who shows responsibility, motivation, mastery skills*Deadline:* March 15 *Amount:* Fifteen $100 awards
• Kathi Hughes Innovative Programming Award (Grant)
Eligibility: Teacher who shares unique program at Annual Conference*Deadline:* March 15 *Amount:* $500

British Columbia Amateur Bodybuilding Association (BCABBA)

PO Box 84020, 2844 Bainbridge Ave., Burnaby BC V5A 4T9
e-mail: bcabbainfo@hotmail.com
www.bcabba.org
Overview: A small provincial organization overseen by Canadian Bodybuilding Federation
Mission: To govern the sport of amateur bodybuilding, fitness & figure in British Columbia.
Member of: Canadian Bodybuilding Federation; International Federation of Bodybuilding
Chief Officer(s):
Sandra Wickham, President
Tamara Knight, Coordinator, Membership
tzonefitness@telus.net
Membership: *Fees:* $75 competitive

British Columbia Amateur Boxing Association ***See*** Boxing BC Association

British Columbia Amateur Hockey Association (BCAHA) / Association de hockey amateur de la Colombie-Britannique

6671 Oldfield Rd., Saanichton BC V8M 2A1
Tel: 250-652-2978; *Fax:* 250-652-4536
info@bchockey.net
www.bchockey.net
twitter.com/BCHockey_Source
Also Known As: BC Hockey
Overview: A medium-sized provincial organization founded in 1919 overseen by Hockey Canada
Mission: To foster, improve & perpetuate amateur hockey in BC.
Member of: Hockey Canada
Chief Officer(s):
Wilf Liefke, President
wliefke@bchockey.net
Finances: *Annual Operating Budget:* $500,000-$1.5 Million
Staff Member(s): 7; 2000 volunteer(s)
Membership: 60,000 individual + 4,500 referees; *Fees:* Schedule available; *Member Profile:* Amateur hockey teams/leagues/associations; referees' organizations

British Columbia Amateur Softball Association (BCASA)

PO Box 45570, Stn. Sunnyside Mall, 2201 - 148th St., Surrey BC V4A 9N3
Tel: 604-531-0044; *Fax:* 604-531-8831
info@softball.bc.ca
www.softball.bc.ca
www.facebook.com/softball.bc
Also Known As: Softball BC
Overview: A medium-sized provincial organization overseen by Canadian Amateur Softball Association
Mission: To promote, govern & build the sport of Softball in British Columbia
Member of: Canadian Amateur Softball Association
Chief Officer(s):
Rick Benson, President
Membership: *Fees:* schedule; $8-$22/person; *Member Profile:* Softball players, coaches, umpires

British Columbia Amateur Wrestling Association ***See*** British Columbia Wrestling Association

British Columbia Angus Association

#15, 3805 Patten Dr., Armstrong BC V0E 1B2
Tel: 250-249-5469; *Fax:* 250-249-5469
www.bcangus.ca
Overview: A small provincial organization
Member of: Canadian Angus Association
Affliation(s): B.C. Junior Angus Association
Chief Officer(s):
Tom de Waal, President
tom@harvestholsteins.com
Lorraine Sanford, National Director
alsanford@hotmail.com
Membership: 253; *Fees:* #50 regular; $7.50 junior

British Columbia Apartment Owners & Managers Association (BCAOMA)

#203, 1847 West Broadway, Vancouver BC V6J 1Y6
Tel: 604-733-9440; *Fax:* 604-733-9420
Toll-Free: 877-700-9440
questions@bcaoma.com
www.bcapartmentowners.com
www.facebook.com/BCAOMA
twitter.com/BCAOMA
pinterest.com/bcaoma
Previous Name: Greater Vancouver Apartment Owners Association
Overview: A medium-sized provincial organization founded in 1964
Mission: To promote & sustain with a unified voice, residential rental housing in the province of British Columbia
Chief Officer(s):
Valerie MacLean, CEO
Finances: *Funding Sources:* Membership fees
Staff Member(s): 6
Membership: 1,200; *Fees:* Schedule available; *Member Profile:* Must own or manage residential rental property in BC
Activities: Education; practical advice & assistance; employee benefits program; recommended trades & suppliers; tenancy agreements/applications & other forms & stationery; garbage disposal; advertising vacancies; credit checks
Awards:
• Building Manager Graduate Scholarship (Scholarship)
Awarded each year to the top Building Manager graduate from the Building Manager Certificate Program offered by the Vancouver Community College of Continuing Education

British Columbia Archery Association (BCAA)

c/o Samantha Wright, 4683 Ten Mile Lake Rd., Quesnel BC V2J 6X1
Tel: 250-992-5586
www.archeryassociation.bc.ca
Overview: A small provincial organization overseen by Archery Canada Tir à l'Arc
Mission: To be the governing body for the sport of archery in British Columbia.
Member of: Archery Canada Tir à l'Arc; Sport BC
Affliation(s): World Archery Federation
Chief Officer(s):
Ron Ostermeier, President, 250-468-3205
rono@justthatsimple.com
Samantha Wright, Secretary
samantha.wright@westfraser.com
Linda Price, Treasurer, 604-826-4906
price.falk@shaw.ca
Finances: *Funding Sources:* Ministry of Community, Sport & Cultural Development; Sport BC

British Columbia Art Teachers' Association (BCATA)

c/o B.C. Teachers' Federation, #100, 550 West 6th Ave., Vancouver BC V5Z 4P2
Tel: 250-248-4662; *Fax:* 250-248-4628
Toll-Free: 800-663-9163
psac41@bctf.ca
bcata.ca
twitter.com/BCArtTeachers
Also Known As: BC Art Teachers' Association
Overview: A small provincial organization
Mission: To support & promote quality art education for all British Columbia students; to provide a network for art educators at the Primary, Intermediate & Graduation levels, & provides opportunities for professional development & collaboration.
Affliation(s): B.C. Teachers' Federation; Canadian Society for Education through Art (CSEA); National Art Education Association (NAEA)
Chief Officer(s):
Regan Rasmussen, Co-President, 250-478-5548, Fax: 250-472-2349
rrasmussen@shaw.ca
Eileen Ryan, Co-President, 604-576-4138
ryan_e@surreyschools.ca
Membership: *Fees:* $57.75 non-BCTF members; $35 BCTF member; $20 BCTF retired member/student
Meetings/Conferences: • 2015 British Columbia Art Teachers' Association Annual Conference, February, 2015, Vancouver, BC
Scope: Provincial
Publications:
• BCATA Journal for Art Teachers
Type: journal; *Price:* $10 members; $15 non-members
Profile: Members share their experiences in art education.
• Visually Speaking
Type: newsletter

British Columbia Art Therapy Association (BCATA)

#101, 1001 West Broadway, Dept. 123, Vancouver BC V6H 4E4
Tel: 604-878-6393
Other Communication: admin@bcarttherapy.com
info@bcarttherapy.com
www.bcarttherapy.com
Overview: A small provincial organization founded in 1978
Mission: To foster the professional development of art therapy in British Columbia; To govern the standards & practice of the profession of art therapy & its practitioners; To uphold the British Columbia Art Therapy Association Code of Ethics
Chief Officer(s):
Michelle Oucharek-Deo, President
president@bcarttherapy.com
Frances Bryant-Scott, Vice-President
vp@bcarttherapy.com
Carolyn Simpson, Corresponding Secretary
corresponding@bcarttherapy.com
Jodi Murphy, Treasurer
treasurer@bcarttherapy.com
Morgan Broadhurst, Chair, Membership
membership@bcarttherapy.com
Membership: *Fees:* $20 students; $40 retired members; $60 associate members; $100 professional & registered members; *Member Profile:* Any person who is interested in the therapeutic use of art
Activities: Offering professional registration for art therapists in British Columbia; Hosting professional development programs; Promoting research
Publications:
• BCATA [British Columbia Art Therapy Association] Newsletter
Type: Newsletter; *Frequency:* Quarterly; *Editor:* Geri Nolan Hilfiker
Profile: Information about professional development workshops, book reviews, updates about the association, & regionalnews for art therapists in British Columbia & western Canada

British Columbia Association for Behaviour Analysis (BC-ABA)

PO Box 64743, Stn. Sunwood Square, Coquitlam BC V3B 6S0
e-mail: info@bc-aba.org
bc-aba.org
Overview: A small provincial organization
Membership: *Fees:* $25 student; $30 full

British Columbia Association for Charitable Gaming

#401, 151 - 10090 152nd St., Surrey BC V3R 8X8
Tel: 604-568-8649; *Fax:* 250-627-1200
Toll-Free: 888-672-2224
bcacg.com
www.facebook.com/167363223281218
twitter.com/bcacg
Overview: A large provincial organization founded in 1997

Mission: A non-profit society representing charities' interests in British Columbia by addressing the concerns of charities with licensing and access to gaming revenue.
Chief Officer(s):
David Sheach, Executive Director
executivedirector@bcacg.com
Meetings/Conferences: • British Columbia Association for Charitable Gaming 2015 Symposium, 2015, BC
Scope: Provincial

British Columbia Association for Community Living; British Columbians for Mentally Handicapped People ***See*** Inclusion BC

British Columbia Association for Marriage & Family Therapy (BCAMFT)

PO Box 3958, Stn. Main, 349 West Georgia St., Vancouver BC V6B 3Z4
Tel: 604-687-6131
info@bcamft.bc.ca
www.bcamft.bc.ca
www.facebook.com/BCAMFT
Overview: A small provincial organization
Mission: To support family well-being through preventative programs & social actions, promotes education & training for therapists & provides a province-wide, professional network.
Member of: American Association for Marriage & Family Therapy
Chief Officer(s):
Janey Komm, President
janey.cunningham@gmail.com
Finances: *Funding Sources:* Membership dues
Membership: *Fees:* $291 clinical/independent; $175 associate/pre-clinical; $206 affiliate; $67 student

British Columbia Association for Regenerative Agriculture (BCARA)

PO Box 1601, Aldergrove BC V4W 2V1
Tel: 778-240-8746
bcara.admin@gmail.com
newcity.ca/Pages/regener_agricult.html
Overview: A small provincial organization
Affliation(s): Certified Organic Associations of BC
Chief Officer(s):
Sarah Davidson, Administrator
Susan Davidson, President
Membership: 100-499;

British Columbia Association of Aboriginal Friendship Centres (BCAAFC)

551 Chatham St., Victoria BC V8T 1E1
Tel: 250-388-5522; *Fax:* 250-388-5502
Toll-Free: 800-990-2432
admin@bcaafc.com
www.bcaafc.com
www.facebook.com/group.php?gid=160027657353593
Overview: A medium-sized provincial organization overseen by National Association of Friendship Centres
Mission: To promote the betterment of Aboriginal Friendship Centres in British Columbia by acting as a unifying body for the Centres; To establish & maintain communications between Aboriginal Friendship Centres, other associations, & government
Chief Officer(s):
Annette Morgan, President, 250-847-5211
Barb Ward-Burkitt, Vice-President, 250-534-3568, Fax: 250-563-7533
Christopher Phillips, Treasurer, 250-376-1228, Fax: 250-376-2275
Richard Samuel, Second Vice-President
Paul Lacerte, Executive Director
placerte@bcaafc.com
Staff Member(s): 20
Membership: 23 friendship centres; *Member Profile:* Friendship Centres in British Columbia
Activities: Advising government on programs & services to assist Aboriginal Friendship Centres
Meetings/Conferences: • Aboriginal Youth 2015 13th Annual Gathering Our Voices Conference, March, 2015, Prince George Civic Centre, Prince George, BC
Scope: Provincial
Description: Hosted by the British Columbia Association of Aboriginal Friendship Centres & Ooknakane Friendship Centre. For Aboriginal youth aged 14 to 24.
Contact Information: Youth Conference Coordinator: Della Preston, Phone: 250-388-5522, Toll-Free Phone: 1-800-990-2432, Fax: 250-388-5502, E-mail: dpreston@bcaafc.com
Publications:
• British Columbia Association of Aboriginal Friendship Centres Newsletter
Type: Newsletter; *Editor:* Jamin Zuroski
Profile: Association activities, campaigns, events, & local news
• The Drumbeat: Newsletter of BC Aboriginal Friendship Centre Youth
Type: Newsletter
Profile: Conceived & developed by Aboriginal youth from Friendship Centres within British Columbia, featuring their stories, ideas, wisdom,challenges, opinions, & creativity
• Off-Reserve Aboriginal Action Plan
Type: Report; *Number of Pages:* 13
Profile: A business case to close the socioeconomic gaps for off-reserve Aboriginal people in British Columbia

British Columbia Association of Agricultural Fairs & Exhibitions (BCAAFE)

18231 - 60th Ave., Surrey BC V3S 1V7
Tel: 778-574-4082
info@bcfairs.ca
www.bcfairs.ca
www.facebook.com/BCFairs
twitter.com/BCFairs
Also Known As: BC Fairs
Previous Name: The Provincial Agricultural Fairs Association
Overview: A small provincial organization founded in 1910
Mission: To celebrate the importance of agriculture in British Columbia; To represent agricultural fairs, exhibitions, & related events throughout British Columbia
Chief Officer(s):
Janine Saw, Executive Director
jbsaw@bcfairs.ca
Leah North Hryko, President, 250-338-0165
lhryko@shaw.ca
Pamela Brenner, Chair, Finance, 604-823-2109, Fax: 604-852-6631
pamela.agrifair@telus.net
Finances: *Funding Sources:* Fundraising; Sponsorships
Membership: *Committees:* Agriculture Awareness & Education; Annual Awards Program; B.C. 4-H Liaison; BCAAFE Annual Scholarship; By-laws, Constitution, & Board Policies; Conference & Annual General Meeting; Evaluation Program; Finance; Fundraising & Sponsorship; Government & Corporate Relations; Media & Public Relations; Nominating; Membership
Activities: Educating the public about the importance of agriculture; Offering resources & services to agricultural exhibitions & fairs; Providing networking opportunities
Meetings/Conferences: • 2015 BC Fairs Conference, 2015, BC
Scope: Provincial
Publications:
• BC Fairs LiveWire
Type: Newsletter; *Frequency:* Quarterly; *Accepts Advertising*
Profile: Developments on the agricultural fair circuit across British Columbia

British Columbia Association of Broadcasters (BCAB)

BC
www.bcab.ca
www.facebook.com/126523200745913
twitter.com/bcabinfo
Overview: A medium-sized provincial organization
Mission: To unify the broadcasting community in British Columbia
Chief Officer(s):
James Stewart, President
james.stuart@bellmedia.ca
Membership: *Member Profile:* Private broadcasters in radio & television; associate members in the advertising & business communities
Activities: Community programs; annual conference
Awards:
• Humanitarian Award (Award)
Meetings/Conferences: • British Columbia Association of Broadcasters 68th Annual Conference, May, 2015, Penticton, BC
Scope: Provincial

British Columbia Association of Clinical Counsellors (BCACC)

#14, 2544 Dunlevy St., Victoria BC V8R 5Z2
Tel: 250-595-4448; *Fax:* 250-595-2926
Toll-Free: 800-909-6303
hoffice@bc-counsellors.org
www.bc-counsellors.org
www.linkedin.com/company/bc-association-of-clinical-counsellors
www.facebook.com/196801843685705
twitter.com/bccounsellors
Overview: A small provincial organization founded in 1988
Mission: To promote and regulate the practice of Registered Clinical Counsellors in BC and beyond
Membership: *Fees:* $436 active; $218 student; *Member Profile:* Registered Clinical Counsellors
Activities: *Rents Mailing List:* Yes
Publications:
• Insights
Editor: Diane Payette
Profile: Magazine, three issues published annually

British Columbia Association of Family Resource Programs

#203, 2590 Granville St., Vancouver BC V6H 3H1
Tel: 604-738-0068; *Fax:* 604-738-0568
info@frpbc.ca
www.frpbc.ca
Also Known As: FRP-BC
Overview: A small provincial organization founded in 1989
Member of: Canadian Association of Family Resource Programs (FRP Canada)
Chief Officer(s):
Mimi Hudson, President
mhudson@familyservices.bc.ca
Nicky Logins, Vice-President
nlogins@sfrs.ca
Finances: *Annual Operating Budget:* $100,000-$250,000
Staff Member(s): 3
Membership: 150; *Fees:* $25-$40

British Columbia Association of Insolvency & Restructuring Professionals (BCAIRP)

c/o Boale, Wood & Company Ltd., #410, 800 West Pender St., Vancouver BC V6C 2V6
Tel: 604-605-3335; *Fax:* 604-605-3359
directors@bcairp.ca
www.bcairp.ca
Previous Name: British Columbia Insolvency Practitioners Association
Overview: A small provincial organization founded in 1979 overseen by Canadian Association of Insolvency & Restructuring Professionals
Member of: Canadian Association of Insolvency & Restructuring Professionals
Affliation(s): Canadian Institute of Chartered Accountants
Chief Officer(s):
Jennifer Dawn McCracken, President
jmccracken@csvan.com
7 volunteer(s)
Membership: 1-99; *Fees:* $85; *Member Profile:* Licensed trustees in bankruptcy
Activities: *Internships:* Yes; *Speaker Service:* Yes

British Columbia Association of Kinesiologists (BCAK)

#102, 211 Columbia St., Vancouver BC V6A 2R5
Tel: 604-601-5100; *Fax:* 604-681-4545
office@bcak.bc.ca
www.bcak.bc.ca
www.linkedin.com/groups/BCAK-British-Columbia-Association-Kinesiologis
www.facebook.com/groups/BCAssociationofKinesiologists
twitter.com/BCKinesiology
Overview: A small provincial organization founded in 1991
Mission: To uphold the standards of the profession of kinesiology; to promote the applications of kinesiology to other professionals & to the community; to assist in professional development; to encourage the exchange of ideas
Chief Officer(s):
Bassam Khaleel, President
Happy Jhaj, Vice-President
Craig Aspinall, Treasurer
Edwards Reynolds, Executive Director
Finances: *Funding Sources:* Membership dues & services
Membership: *Fees:* $50 student & academic; $175 associate; $175 non-practicing member; $300 practicing member; *Member Profile:* Registered kinesiologists; Students in kinesiology programs; *Committees:* Membership

British Columbia Association of Laboratory Physicians (BCALP)

BC
www.bcalp.ca

Overview: A small provincial organization
Chief Officer(s):
Christopher Sherlock, President, 604-806-8422
csherloc@mail.ubc.ca

British Columbia Association of Mathematics Teachers (BCAMT)
c/o British Columbia Teachers' Federation, #100, 550 West 6th Ave., Vancouver BC V5Z 4P2
Tel: 604-871-2283
Toll-Free: 800-663-9163
www.bcamt.ca
Overview: A small provincial organization
Member of: BC Teachers' Federation
Chief Officer(s):
Ron Coleborn, President
ron.coleborn@sd41.bc.ca
Michael Pruner, Vice-President
mpruner@nvsd44.bc.ca
Debbie Loo, Treasurer
debbie.loo@sd41.bc.ca
Membership: *Fees:* $40 BCTF members; $20 students & retired teachers; $58.50 non-BCTF members
Meetings/Conferences: • 54th Annual Northwest Math Conference, October, 2015, Whistler, BC
Scope: Provincial

British Columbia Association of Medical Radiation Technologists (BCAMRT)
Central Office, #102, 211 Columbia St., Vancouver BC V6A 2R5
Tel: 604-682-8171; *Fax:* 604-681-4545
Toll-Free: 800-990-7090
office@bcamrt.bc.ca
www.bcamrt.bc.ca
Overview: A medium-sized provincial organization founded in 1951 overseen by Canadian Association of Medical Radiation Technologists
Mission: To manage the professional affairs of medical radiation technologists in British Columbia; To advocate for the profession of medical radiation technology across the province
Chief Officer(s):
Louise Kallhood, President
louise.kallhood@shaw.ca
Lori Rowe, Vice-President
lrowe@bccancer.bc.ca
Darlene Hyde, Executive Director
darlenehyde@shaw.ca
Membership: 2,000; *Member Profile:* Medical radiation technologists throughout British Columbia
Activities: Upholding the Canadian Association of Medical Radiation Technologists code of ethics; Communicating with stakeholders; Offering information about radiography, nuclear medicine, magnetic resonance imaging, & radiation therapy; Providing continuing education programs
Awards:
• WQ Stirling Award (Award)
• Bracco Diagnostics' Paragon Award (Award)
• Membership Recognition Awards (Award)
Meetings/Conferences: • British Columbia Association of Medical Radiation Technologists 2015 Annual General Conference & Annual General Meeting, April, 2015, Executive Plaza Hotel, Coquitlam, BC
Scope: Provincial
Description: Speakers present on a variety of educational topics as well as tips for the workplace and health and wellness.
Publications:
• Board Room News
Type: Newsletter; *Frequency:* Annually; *Price:* Free with membership in the B.C. Association of Medical Radiation Technologists
• Radiaction
Type: Newsletter; *Frequency:* Semiannually; *Accepts Advertising*; *Price:* Free with membership in the B.C. Association of Medical Radiation Technologists

The British Columbia Association of Optometrists (BCAO)
#610, 2525 Willow St., Vancouver BC V5Z 3N8
Tel: 604-737-9907; *Fax:* 604-737-9967
Toll-Free: 888-393-2226
info@optometrists.bc.ca
www.optometrists.bc.ca
www.facebook.com/AskaDoctorofOptometry
www.youtube.com/BCDoctorsofOptometry
Overview: A medium-sized provincial organization founded in 1921 overseen by Canadian Association of Optometrists
Mission: To maintain standards; to represent membership to government & other health care professions; to raise public levels of awareness about optometry, good vision & eye care.
Chief Officer(s):
Cheryl Williams, CEO
Sherman Tung, President
Finances: *Funding Sources:* Membership dues
Staff Member(s): 6
Membership: *Member Profile:* Licensed by board of examiners; practising optometrists
Activities: *Speaker Service:* Yes; *Library* Open to public by appointment
Awards:
• OD of the Year (Award)
• President's Award (Award)
• Scholarships (2) (Scholarship)

British Columbia Association of People Who Stutter (BCAPS)
8582 Flowering Pl., Burnaby BC V5A 4B4
Fax: 888-301-2227
Toll-Free: 888-301-2227
info@bcaps.ca
www.bcaps.ca
www.facebook.com/bcaps123
twitter.com/BCAPS1
Overview: A small provincial organization
Mission: To encourage & assist local support groups for people who stutter
Chief Officer(s):
Kim Block, President
Membership: *Fees:* $10 individual; $15 family
Publications:
• B.C. Blockbuster
Type: Newsletter; *Frequency:* Quarterly

British Columbia Association of Professionals with Disabilities
714 Warder Place, Victoria BC V9A 7H6
Tel: 250-361-9697
info@bcprofessionals.org
www.bcprofessionals.org
Overview: A small provincial organization founded in 2003
Mission: Provincially incorporated non-profit association dedicated to maximizing the inclusion, job retention, and advancement of current and future professionals with disabilities
Affliation(s): Canadian Association of Professionals with Disabilities

British Columbia Association of School Business Officials (BCASBO)
#208, 1118 Homer St., Vancouver BC V6B 6L5
Tel: 604-687-0595; *Fax:* 604-687-8118
executivedirector@bcasbo.ca
www.bcasbo.ca
Previous Name: British Columbia School District Secretary-Treasurers' Association
Overview: A small provincial organization
Mission: To uphold professional standards of ethics, competence, & leadership in British Columbia's school district corporate & business administration
Chief Officer(s):
Greg Frank, President, 604-296-6900 Ext. 661004, Fax: 604-296-6910
president@bcasbo.ca
Lyle Boyce, Executive Director, 778-420-4210, Fax: 604-687-8118
executivedirector@bcasbo.ca
Allan Reed, Secretary-Treasurer, 250-561-6800, Fax: 250-561-6889
SecretaryTreasurer@bcasbo.ca
Membership: *Fees:* $1000 first member from a school district; $700 second & subsequent members from a school district; *Member Profile:* British Columbia business officials who work in school districts, such as secretary-treasurers, assistant secretary-treasurers, accountants, payroll supervisors, comptrollers, benefits supervisors, human resources managers, & information systems managers; *Committees:* Executive; Annual General Meeting; Strategic Planning; Accounting Advisory; BCeSIS Steering; Audit Program Advisory; Carbon Neutral; Capital Advisory; Education Advisory; Education Resource Acquisition; Leadership Development; Membership; Payroll & Benefits Advisory; PLNet Steering; School District Telecommunications Advisory; Shared Practice Working; Technical Review; Transportation; Web Site Content Management; Work Force Planning Steering
Activities: Providing professional development opportunities; Facilitating the exchange of ideas & concerns; Liaising with the province's Ministry of Education
Meetings/Conferences: • 2015 British Columbia Association of School Business Officials Annual General Meeting, May, 2015, Penticton, BC
Scope: Provincial
• 2016 British Columbia Association of School Business Officials Annual General Meeting, May, 2016, Penticton, BC
Scope: Provincial
Publications:
• School Business: Newsletter of the British Columbia Association of School Business Officials
Type: Newsletter; *Editor:* Alba Urban
Profile: BCASBO meeting minutes, upcoming events, reports, member news, & articles

British Columbia Association of School Psychologists (BCASP)
#562, 162 - 2025 Corydon Ave., Winnipeg MB R3P 0N5
e-mail: executives@bcasp.ca
www.bcasp.ca
Overview: A small provincial organization
Mission: To represent the interests of school psychologists and to further the standards of school psychology practice in order to promote effective service to all students and their families.
Chief Officer(s):
Douglas Agar, President
president@bcasp.ca
Meetings/Conferences: • 27th Annual British Columbia Association of School Psychologists Conference, 2015, BC
Scope: Provincial

British Columbia Association of Social Workers (BCASW) / Association des travailleurs sociaux de la Colombie-Britannique
#402, 1755 West Broadway, Vancouver BC V6J 4S5
Tel: 604-730-9111; *Fax:* 604-730-9112
Toll-Free: 800-665-4747
bcasw@bcasw.org
www.bcasw.org
Overview: A medium-sized provincial organization founded in 1956
Mission: Represents member concerns regarding the practice of social work in BC, professional education & regulation.
Member of: Canadian Association of Social Workers
Affliation(s): End Legislated Poverty; End the Arms Race Coalition; BC Human Rights Coalition
Chief Officer(s):
Dianne Heath, Executive Director
dheath@bcasw.org
Jocelyn Chee, Manager, Member Services & Administration
Finances: *Annual Operating Budget:* $100,000-$250,000; *Funding Sources:* Membership fees
Staff Member(s): 2
Membership: 800; *Fees:* $288; *Committees:* Editorial; Ethics; Membership; Multicultural Concerns; Perspectives; Private Practice; Social Work Education
Activities: *Speaker Service:* Yes
Meetings/Conferences: • British Columbia Association of Social Workers Conference 2015, 2015, BC
Scope: Provincial

British Columbia Association of Specialized Victim Assistance & Counselling Programs *See* Ending Violence Association of British Columbia

British Columbia Association of Speech-Language Pathologists & Audiologists (BCASLPA)
#402, 1755 Broadway West, Vancouver BC V6J 4S5
Tel: 604-420-2222; *Fax:* 604-736-5606
Toll-Free: 877-222-7572
bcaslpa@telus.net
www.bcaslpa.ca
www.facebook.com/61200960963
Overview: A small provincial charitable organization founded in 1957
Mission: BCASLPA is a non-profit body that connects people with language, swallowing & hearing disorders with professionals in BC. It represents speech & hearing professionals and provides information about disorders & treatments.
Member of: Pan-Canadian Alliance of Speech-Language Pathology and Audiology Associations
Affliation(s): Canadian Association of Speech Language Pathologists & Audiologists
Chief Officer(s):

Marlene Lewis, President
president@bcaslpa.ca
Finances: *Annual Operating Budget:* $100,000-$250,000
Staff Member(s): 2; 25 volunteer(s)
Membership: 800; *Fees:* $174; *Committees:* Government Affairs; School Affairs; Audiology; Speech Language Pathology; Private Practice; Continuing Education
Activities: Continuing education; research; standards of practice; *Awareness Events:* Speech & Hearing Month, May; *Internships:* Yes; *Speaker Service:* Yes; *Library* by appointment
Meetings/Conferences: • British Columbia Association of Speech-Language Pathologists & Audiologists 2015 Conference, 2015, BC
Scope: Provincial

British Columbia Association of Teachers of Modern Languages (BCATML)

c/o BC Teachers' Federation, #100, 550 West 6th Ave., Vancouver BC V5Z 4P2
Tel: 604-871-2283; *Fax:* 604-871-2286
psac51@bctf.ca
www.bcatml.org
www.facebook.com/bcatml
twitter.com/bcatml
Overview: A small provincial organization
Mission: To promote & advance the teaching of modern languages throughout BC.
Member of: BC Teachers' Federation
Affliation(s): Canadian Assoc. of Second Language Teachers
Chief Officer(s):
Rome Lavrencic, President
rlavrenc@sd40.bc.ca
Membership: *Fees:* $40 BCTF member; $63 non BCTF member/institution; $15 retired teacher/student
Activities: annual conference
Meetings/Conferences: • British Columbia Association of Teachers of Modern Languages 2015 Conference, October, 2015, Delta Burnaby Hotel and Conference Centre, Burnaby, BC
Scope: Provincial

British Columbia Association of the Appraisal Institute of Canada (BCAAIC)

#210, 10451 Shellbridge Way, Richmond BC V6X 2W8
Tel: 604-284-5515; *Fax:* 604-284-5514
Toll-Free: 888-707-8287
info@appraisal.bc.ca
www.appraisal.bc.ca
Overview: A medium-sized provincial organization overseen by Appraisal Institute of Canada
Mission: To represent, promote & support members as leaders in the counselling, analysis & evaluation of real property.
Chapters: Fraser Valley, Nanaimo, Okanagan, Vancouver, Kamloops, The North, Victoria, & Kootenay.
Chief Officer(s):
Douglas Janzen, President
Janice P. O'Brien, Executive Director
janice@appraisal.bc.ca
Finances: *Annual Operating Budget:* $100,000-$250,000; *Funding Sources:* Membership dues
Staff Member(s): 2
Membership: 1,000; *Fees:* Schedule available
Activities: *Speaker Service:* Yes

British Columbia Athletics

#2001, 3713 Kensington Ave., B. Oslo Landing, Burnaby BC V5B 0A7
Tel: 604-333-3550; *Fax:* 604-333-3551
bcathletics@bcathletics.org
www.bcathletics.org
www.facebook.com/BCAthletics1
twitter.com/bc_athletics
Also Known As: BC Amateur Athletics Association
Previous Name: BC Track & Field Association
Overview: A medium-sized provincial licensing organization overseen by Athletics Canada
Mission: To promote, encourage & develop excellence by creating opportunities in athletics (track & field, road-running & cross-country running)
Member of: Athletics Canada; Sport BC
Chief Officer(s):
Brian McCalder, President & CEO
brian.mccalder@bcathletics.org
Staff Member(s): 9
Membership: *Fees:* Schedule available; *Committees:* Track & Field; Road Running; Cross Country; Masters; Junior Development; Masters
Activities: *Internships:* Yes; *Speaker Service:* Yes; *Rents Mailing List:* Yes; *Library* Open to public

British Columbia Automobile Association (BCAA)

4567 Canada Way, Burnaby BC V5G 4T1
Toll-Free: 877-325-8888; *Crisis Hot-Line:* 800-222-4357
www.bcaa.com
Overview: A large provincial organization founded in 1906 overseen by Canadian Automobile Association
Mission: To provide motoring, travel, & insurance services to members in British Columbia & the Yukon
Member of: Canadian Automobile Association (CAA); American Automobile Association (AAA)
Chief Officer(s):
Timothy J. Condon, President & CEO
Brenda Lowden, Senior Vice-President, People & Community
Collin MacKinnon, Senior Vice-President & Chief Risk Officer
Ken Ontko, Senior Vice-President & CIO
Greg Oyhenart, Sr. VP & Chief Member Experience Officer
Heidi Worthington, Sr. Vice-President & Chief Marketing Officer
Finances: *Annual Operating Budget:* Greater than $5 Million; *Funding Sources:* Membership fees
Staff Member(s): 1000
Membership: 790,000; *Committees:* Human Resources; Finance & Investment; Audit; Governance
Activities: *Internships:* Yes
Publications:
• BCAA [British Columbia Automobile Association] Newsletter
Type: Newsletter

Abbotsford Branch
33338 South Fraser Way, Abbotsford BC V2S 2B4
Tel: 604-870-3850; *Fax:* 604-870-3899

Chilliwack Branch
#1, 45609 Luckakuck Way, Chilliwack BC V2R 1A3
Tel: 604-824-2720; *Fax:* 604-824-2749

Coquitlam Branch
#50, 2773 Barnet Hwy., Coquitlam BC V3B 1C2
Tel: 604-268-5750; *Fax:* 604-268-5799

Courtenay
#17, 1599 Cliffe Ave., Courtenay BC V9N 2K6
Tel: 250-703-2328; *Fax:* 250-703-2329

Delta Branch
7343 - 120 St., Delta BC V4C 6P5
Tel: 604-268-5900; *Fax:* 604-268-5949

Kamloops Branch
#400, 500 Notre Dame Dr., Kamloops BC V2C 6T6
Tel: 250-852-4600; *Fax:* 250-852-4637

Kelowna Branch
Burtch Plaza, #18, 1470 Harvey Ave., Kelowna BC V1Y 9K8
Tel: 250-870-4900; *Fax:* 250-870-4937

Langley Branch
#10, 20190 Langley ByPass, Langley BC V3A 9J9
Tel: 604-268-5950; *Fax:* 604-268-5999

Maple Ridge
#500, 20395 Lougheed Hwy., Maple Ridge BC V2X 2P9
Tel: 604-205-1200; *Fax:* 604-205-1249

Nanaimo Branch
Metral Place, #400, 6581 Aulds Rd., Nanaimo BC V9T 6J6
Tel: 250-390-7700; *Fax:* 250-390-7739

Nelson Branch
596 Baker St., Nelson BC V1L 4H9
Tel: 250-505-1720; *Fax:* 250-505-1749

New Westminster Branch
501 - 6th St., New Westminster BC V3L 3B9
Tel: 604-268-5700; *Fax:* 604-268-5749

North Vancouver
1527 Lonsdale Ave., North Vancouver BC V7M 2J2
Tel: 604-205-1050; *Fax:* 604-990-1547

Penticton Branch
#100, 2100 Main St., Penticton BC V2A 5H7
Tel: 250-487-2450; *Fax:* 250-487-2479

Prince George Branch
River Point Shopping Centre, #100, 2324 Ferry Ave., Prince George BC V2N 0B1
Tel: 250-649-2399; *Fax:* 250-649-2397

Richmond Branch
Lansdowne Centre, #618, 5300 No. 3 Rd., Richmond BC V6X 2X9
Tel: 604-268-5850; *Fax:* 604-268-5899

Surrey
#D1, 15251 - 101 Ave., Surrey BC V3R 9V8
Tel: 604-205-1000; *Fax:* 604-205-1049

Vancouver - Broadway Branch
999 West Broadway, Vancouver BC V5Z 1K5
Tel: 604-268-5600; *Fax:* 604-268-5647

Vancouver - Kerrisdale Branch
2347 West 41st Ave., Vancouver BC V6M 2A3
Tel: 604-268-5800; *Fax:* 604-268-5848

Vernon Branch
Vernon Square, #103, 5710 - 24th St., Vernon BC V1T 9T3
Tel: 250-550-2400; *Fax:* 250-550-2429

Victoria - Broadmead Branch
#120, 777 Royal Oak Dr., Victoria BC V8X 4V1
Tel: 250-704-1750; *Fax:* 250-704-1789

Victoria - Downtown Branch
1262 Quadra St., Victoria BC V8W 2K7
Tel: 250-414-8320; *Fax:* 250-414-8369

West Vancouver Branch
#710, 2002 Park Royal South, West Vancouver BC V7T 2W4
Tel: 604-268-5650; *Fax:* 604-268-5699

British Columbia Aviation Council (BCAC)

PO Box 31040, RPO Thunderbird, Langley BC V1M 0A9
Tel: 604-278-9330; *Fax:* 604-278-8210
info@bcaviationcouncil.org
www.bcaviationcouncil.org
twitter.com/bcac1938
www.flickr.com/photos/63124160@N08/
Also Known As: BC Aviation Council
Overview: A small provincial organization founded in 1936
Mission: A self-sustaining organization with the mission to "promote the safe and orderly development of aviation and aviation services to the province of British Columiba."
Chief Officer(s):
Mike Matthews, Chair
mmatthews@bcaviationcouncil.org
Donna Farquar, Executive Administrator
Finances: *Funding Sources:* Membership fees
Membership: *Committees:* Airport
Awards:
• Silver Wings Awards (Award)
• BC Aviation Council Scholarship (Scholarship)
Eligibility: Students pursuing studies in the fields of commercial piloting, aviation maintenance, airport operations or private piloting *Amount:* $1000-$3000

British Columbia Bailiffs Association (BCBA)

c/o Accurate Effective Bailiffs, 6139 Trapp Ave., Burnaby BC V3N 2V3
Tel: 604-526-3737
Overview: A small provincial organization
Mission: To assist members to develop their professional expertise
Membership: 1-99; *Member Profile:* British Columbia recovery & liquidation experts

British Columbia Ball Hockey Association (BCBHA)

9107 Norum Rd., Delta BC V4C 3H9
Tel: 604-998-1410
www.bcbha.com
Overview: A small provincial organization founded in 1980
Mission: To govern the sport of ball hockey in British Columbia; To establish bylaws & regulations, in order to ensure a safe & fun activity; To uphold the rules& regulations of ball hockey
Affiliation(s): Canadian Ball Hockey Association
Chief Officer(s):
Mike Schweighardt, President
Kris Little, Vice-President
Rob Moxness, Secretary
Roger Sidhu, Treasurer
Finances: *Funding Sources:* Sponsorships
Membership: *Fees:* $300 full members; $200 associate members; $100 affiliate members; $70 referee registration; *Member Profile:* Ball hockey leagues in British Columbia which follow the rules & regulations of the British Columbia Ball Hockey Association & the Canadian Ball Hockey Association
Activities: Promoting ball hockey in British Columbia; Assisting in the establishment of ball hockey leagues in the province; Disseminating rulebooks; Organizing provincial championships; Providing certification programs for officials; Resolving disputes

British Columbia Bed & Breakfast Innkeepers Guild

#305, 1845 Bellevue Ave., North Vancouver BC V7V 1B2
e-mail: info@bcinnkeepers.com
www.bcsbestbnbs.com
www.facebook.com/BCBandBInnkeepersGuild
pinterest.com/bcinnkeepers
Previous Name: Western Canada B&B Innkeepers Association

Overview: A medium-sized provincial licensing organization founded in 1993
Mission: To increase the awareness of an optional accommodation for visitors & business travellers
Chief Officer(s):
Dennis Cyr, Secretary/Treasurer
Membership: *Fees:* Schedule available; *Member Profile:* Bed & Breakfast Innkeepers in British Columbia; *Committees:* Membership; Website; Brochure; Moyra Turner Award; Policy & Procedures; Communications; Standards & Ethics

British Columbia Bee Breeders' Association (BCBBA)
c/o Brenda Jager, 948 Harrison Way, Gabriola BC V0R 1X2
Tel: 250-755-5834
dencor.ca/BCBBA
Overview: A small provincial organization founded in 1987
Mission: Promoting and encouraging bee breeding in British Columbia.
Chief Officer(s):
Barry Denluck, President, 250-900-5159
President@BCBeeBreeders.ca
Axel Krause, Secretary, 250-608-7397
secretary@BCBeeBreeders.ca

British Columbia Bison Association
c/o Bill Bouffioux, President, RR#1, Site 1, Comp 1, Fort St. John BC V1J 4M6
Tel: 250-785-4183
xybison@pris.ca
www.bcbuffalo.ca
Previous Name: British Columbia Interior Bison Association
Overview: A small provincial organization
Mission: To promote the bison industry as a economically & environmentally sustainable business
Member of: Canadian Bison Association
Chief Officer(s):
Bill Bouffioux, President
Isobel Vere, Secretary
ttonka@ttonka.ca
Membership: 60; *Fees:* $150

British Columbia Blind Sports & Recreation Association (BCBSRA)
#330, 5055 Joyce St., Vancouver BC V5R 6B2
Tel: 604-325-8638; *Fax:* 604-325-1638
Toll-Free: 877-604-8638
info@bcblindsports.bc.ca
www.bcblindsports.bc.ca
Also Known As: BC Blind Sports
Overview: A medium-sized provincial charitable organization founded in 1975 overseen by Canadian Blind Sports Association Inc.
Mission: To provide sports, physical recreation & fitness activities & programs for persons of all ages who are blind/visually impaired; to alleviate isolating & inhibiting effects of blindness/visual impairment; to improve physical capabilities & self-image of blind/visually impaired individuals by providing opportunities for them to learn; to encourage, promote & maintain interest in & cooperation with all such amateur sports & recreation organizations.
Chief Officer(s):
Brian Cowie, President
Tami Grenon, Vice-President
Finances: *Funding Sources:* Private donations; provincial government
Membership: *Fees:* $15 athlete; $5 supporting; *Member Profile:* Legally blind athletes; sighted guides; coaches; parents whose children are blind
Activities: Operates in nine regions: Kootenays, Thompson/Okanagan, Fraser Valley, Cariboo/North East, Vancouver/Squamish; Vancouver Island/South, Vancouver Island/North, North West, Fraser River/Delta; fundraisers; trade shows; workshops; *Speaker Service:* Yes

British Columbia Blueberry Council
#275, 32160 South Fraser Way, Abbotsford BC V2T 1W5
Tel: 604-864-2117; *Fax:* 604-864-2197
info@bcblueberry.com
www.bcblueberry.com
Also Known As: BC Blueberries
Overview: A small provincial organization
Mission: To use promotion, research, industry education & relationship building to enhance the development of the blueberry industry
Chief Officer(s):
Mike Makara, Chair
Membership: 800+; *Committees:* Finance; Promotions; Industry Relations; Research; ED Support; Bird Management

British Columbia Bottle Depot Association (BCBDA)
9850 King George Hwy., Surrey BC V3T 4Y3
Tel: 604-930-0003; *Fax:* 604-930-0060
Other Communication: www.mydepot.ca
bcbda@telus.net
www.bcbda.com
Overview: A small provincial organization founded in 1997
Mission: To further the interests of association members through representation; To support a healthy environment by promoting recycling programs
Chief Officer(s):
Corinne Atwood, Executive Director
Grant Robertson, Chair
grobertson@bcbda.com
Kulbir Rana, Secretary-Treasurer
krana@bcbda.com
Finances: *Funding Sources:* Membership fees
Membership: *Member Profile:* Bottle depots in British Columbia
Activities: Liaising with government & industry partners; Assisting the public by maintaining a website with information about depot locations, sales, & what each depot accepts for recycling

British Columbia Brain Injury Association (BCBIA)
PO Box 143, 11948 - 207 St., Maple Ridge BC V2X 1X7
Tel: 604-465-1783; *Fax:* 888-429-0656
Toll-Free: 877-858-1788
info@bcbraininjuryassociation.com
www.bcbraininjuryassociation.com
twitter.com/stop_ABI
www.youtube.com/user/bcbraininjury
Overview: A small provincial organization overseen by Brain Injury Association of Canada
Mission: To promote a better quality of life for those living with acquired brain injury om British Columbia
Chief Officer(s):
Julia Zarudzka, President
Finances: *Funding Sources:* Membership fees; Ministry of Children & Families; Donations; Sponsorships
Membership: *Fees:* $10 individuals; $25 families; $50 professional; $100 non-profit associations; $150 corporate; 200 diamond executive memberships
Activities: Promoting prevention of acquired brain injury throughout British Columbia; Providing education, resources, & referrals; Lobbying on behalf of persons affected by acquired brain injury; Supporting survivors of acquired brain injury, their families, & caregivers
Publications:
• The Synaptic Post
Type: Newsletter; *Frequency:* Quarterly

British Columbia Broadband Association (BCBA)
248 Reid St., Quesnel BC V2J 2M2
e-mail: info@bcba.ca
bcba.ca
Overview: A medium-sized provincial organization
Mission: To be the principal voice of the telecommunications & service provider industry in British Columbia
Chief Officer(s):
Bob Allen, President
Membership: 39; *Fees:* $250
Meetings/Conferences: • 11th Annual BC Broadband Conference - BCBC 2015, April, 2015, Radisson Hotel Vancouver Airport, Richmond, BC
Scope: Provincial
Publications:
• British Columbia Broadband Association Newsletter
Type: Newsletter

British Columbia Broiler Hatching Egg Producers' Association (BCBHEC)
PO Box 191, Abbotsford BC V4X 3R2
Tel: 604-864-7556
association@bcbhec.com
www.bcbhec.com
Also Known As: BC Hatching Eggs
Overview: A small provincial licensing organization founded in 1963
Mission: To establish a better understanding & appreciation with the public & other interested parties regarding the industry; to stimulate & encourage improvements related to sales & scientific development in the field; to promote the exchange of ideas in an effort to find solutions to problems in the broiler hatching egg industry; to encourage economical plans to assists producers; & to provide better contact with hatcheries, feed suppliers, processors, & broiler growers.
Affliation(s): BC Broiler Hatching Egg Commission; Sustainable Poultry Farming Group; British Columbia Agriculture Council; British Columbia Poultry Association; Environmental Farm Planning
Chief Officer(s):
Bryan Brandsma, President
Membership: *Committees:* Biosecurity Committee; Emergency Response Committee

British Columbia Broomball Society (BCBS)
BC
Tel: 250-361-1249
info@bcbroomball.ca
www.bcbroomball.ca
Overview: A small provincial organization overseen by Ballon sur glace Broomball Canada
Member of: Ballon sur glace Broomball Canada
Chief Officer(s):
Rick Przybysz, President
president@broomballbc.com
Bruce MacRae, Secretary-Treasurer
secretary@bcbroomball.ca

British Columbia Business Educators Association (BCBEA)
c/o BC Teachers Federation, #100, 550 West 6th Ave., Vancouver BC B5Z 4P2
Tel: 604-871-2283; *Fax:* 604-871-2286
Toll-Free: 800-663-9163
bcbea.ca@gmail.com
bcbea.ca
www.facebook.com/bcbea.ca
twitter.com/bcbea
Overview: A small provincial organization
Mission: To support business education teachers at elementary, middle, & secondary schools who teach courses in business education & related fields.
Member of: BC Teachers' Federation
Chief Officer(s):
Harmale Sangha, President
sangha_h@sd36.bc.ca
Membership: *Fees:* $23 student/retired; $35 BCTF member; $59.92 Non-BCTF member
Activities: Representation at regional, provincial & international conferences

British Columbia Call Centre Association *See* British Columbia Contact Centre Association

British Columbia Camping Association
c/o Camp Luther, 9311 Shook Rd., Mission BC V2V 7M2
bccamping.org
Overview: A medium-sized provincial organization overseen by Canadian Camping Association
Mission: To facilitate the development of organized camping in order to provide educational, character-building & constructive recreational experiences for all people; to develop awareness & appreciation of the natural environment
Chief Officer(s):
Luke Ferris, President
Membership: 55; *Fees:* $30 individual; $230 camp
Activities: *Rents Mailing List:* Yes
Meetings/Conferences: • British Columbia Camping Association 2015 Conference, 2015, BC
Scope: Provincial

British Columbia Cancer Foundation (BCCF)
#150, 686 West Broadway, Vancouver BC V5Z 1G1
Tel: 604-877-6040; *Fax:* 604-877-6161
Toll-Free: 888-906-2873
bccfinfo@bccancer.bc.ca
www.bccancerfoundation.com
www.facebook.com/BCCancerFoundation
twitter.com/bccancer
Overview: A medium-sized provincial charitable organization founded in 1935
Mission: To reduce the incidence of cancer, reduce the mortality rate from cancer, & improve the quality of life for those living with cancer, through the acquisition, development, & stewardship of resources
Affliation(s): British Columbia Cancer Research Centre; British Columbia Cancer Agency
Chief Officer(s):
Douglas Nelson, President & Chief Executive Officer
Luigi (Lou) Del Gobbo, Chief Financial Officer & Vice-President

Patsy Worrall, Vice-President, Marketing & Communications
Cindy Dopson, MBA, CHRP, Director, Human Resources
Membership: 150; *Fees:* $25

British Columbia Captive Insurance Association *See* Canadian Captive Insurance Association

British Columbia Care Providers Association (BCCPA)

#301, 1338 West Broadway, Vancouver BC V6H 1H2
Tel: 604-736-4233; *Fax:* 604-736-4266
info@bccare.ca
www.bccare.ca
Also Known As: Care Online
Overview: A small provincial organization founded in 1977 overseen by Canadian Alliance for Long Term Care
Mission: To provide the best possible care for seniors by supporting change, & promoting the growth & success of the association's members
Member of: Canadian Alliance for Long Term Care
Chief Officer(s):
Mary McDougall, President
Ed Helfrich, CEO, 604-736-4233 Ext. 229
ehelfrich@bccare.ca
Membership: *Fees:* Schedule available; *Member Profile:* Long term care providers & home support agencies in British Columbia
Meetings/Conferences: • 38th British Columbia Care Providers Association Annual Conference, May, 2015, The Fairmont Chateau Whistler Resort, Whistler, BC
Scope: Provincial

British Columbia Career College Association (BCCCA)

PO Box 40528, #11, 200 Burrard, Vancouver BC V6C 3L0
Tel: 604-874-4419; *Fax:* 604-874-4420
thebccca@gmail.com
www.bccca.com
www.linkedin.com/pub/bc-career-colleges-association/89/95/31b
www.facebook.com/pages/BC-Career-Colleges-Association/370318143114942
twitter.com/@thebccca
Also Known As: BC Career College Association
Overview: A medium-sized provincial organization founded in 1977
Mission: This association's aim is to promote and support post secondary schools, stakeholders, students and all interested parties involved in private post-secondary education and training in BC.
Chief Officer(s):
Amanda Steele, Executive Director, 604-874-4419, Fax: 604-874-4420
Jeremy Sabell, President
Membership: *Member Profile:* Private career colleges in British Columbia; *Committees:* Advocacy; Conference Planning; SABC; Financial Viability; Membership Value; Nominations
Awards:
• Outstanding Graduate (Award)
• Outstanding Educator (Award)
Meetings/Conferences: • British Columbia Career College Association Annual Conference 2015, 2015, BC
Scope: Provincial

British Columbia Career Development Association (BCCDA)

#728, 510 West Hastings St., Vancouver BC V6B 1L8
Tel: 604-684-3638
www.bccda.org
www.linkedin.com/groups?home=&gid=2106147
www.youtube.com/user/BCCDA
Previous Name: Career Management Association of BC; Labour Market & Career Information Association of British Columbia
Merged from: CMA & ENET
Overview: A small provincial organization founded in 1996
Mission: To advance the interests of practitioners & organizations in British Columbia, who are affected by career development & management
Affliation(s): BC Career Information Partnership (BCCIP); National Integrated Delivery Strategy (NIDS); Canadian Standards & Guidelines National Stakeholder Committee
Chief Officer(s):
Michael Yue, M.Ed., President
myue@vcc.ca
Gordon MacDonald, Treasurer & Interim Registrar
Donna Brendon, General Manager
Finances: *Funding Sources:* Sponsorships
Membership: *Fees:* $25-$100; *Committees:* Professional Development; Certification; Membership
Activities: Consulting with & surveying members
Meetings/Conferences: • Career Development Conference (CDC) 2015: Raising the Bar: In Practice and in Community, March, 2015, Executive Airport Plaza Hotel & Conference Centre, Richmond, BC
Scope: Provincial
Publications:
• The Career Manager Connection
Type: Newsletter; *Frequency:* Quarterly; *Price:* Free with CMA membership
Profile: Articles & resources about current issues

British Columbia Carpenters Union *See* Construction Maintenance & Allied Workers

British Columbia Cattlemen's Association (BCCA)

#4, 10145 Dallas Dr., Kamloops BC V2C 6T4
Tel: 250-573-3611; *Fax:* 250-573-5155
info@cattlemen.bc.ca
www.cattlemen.bc.ca
Also Known As: BC Cattlemen
Overview: A medium-sized provincial organization founded in 1929
Mission: To develop & protect the cattle industry in British Columbia; To act as the official voice of the beef cattle industry in British Columbia; To act in an environmentally responsible manner; To provide quality beef products to consumers
Affliation(s): Canadian Cattlemen's Association
Chief Officer(s):
David Haywood-Farmer, President
Kevin Boon, General Manager
bccattle@cattlemen.bc.ca
Elaine Stovin, Coordinator, Communications
elaine@cattlemen.bc.ca
Finances: *Funding Sources:* Sponsorships
Staff Member(s): 7
Membership: 1,200; *Fees:* $101 regular; $150 direct; $35 silver; $250 associate; *Member Profile:* Cattle producers in British Columbia
Activities: Providing input on government regulations related to ranching; Advocating for cattle producers; Liaising with local, provincial, & federal government officials; Sponsoring courses at the Rangeland Management School; Providing industry information; Increasing awarenss of the beef industry & its issues; Offering various programs, such as the Dam Inspection Program & the BC Highways Fencing Program; Researching; Collaborating with the Canadian Beef Export Federation to expand foreign markets; Protecting landowner rights
Awards:
• Environmental Stewardship Award (Award)
To recognize a ranching family for outstanding commitment to environmental stewardship
• Brigadier W.N. Bostock Memorial Research Grant (Grant)
To recognize those whose research benefits the beef cattle industry in British Columbia *Amount:* $2,000
• Martin Riedemann Annual Bursary (Grant)
To assist worthy students, especially those from rural areas *Amount:* $1,000
• Gung Loy Jim Scholarships (Scholarship)
To assist worthy students from British Columbia, especially those from rural areas *Amount:* $2,000
• RBC Dominion Securities Bursary (Grant)
To assist worthy students, especially those from rural areas *Amount:* $1,000
• British Columbia Cattlemen's Association Bursary (Grant)
Eligibility: Applicants must be a child or grandchild of a British Columbia Cattlemen's Association member *Amount:* $1,000
Meetings/Conferences: • 87th Annual BC Cattlemen's Association Convention & AGM Trade Show, May, 2015, Merritt, BC
Scope: Provincial
Publications:
• Beef In BC
Type: Magazine; *Frequency:* 7 pa; *Accepts Advertising*; *Editor:* Diane Edstrom; *Price:* $24 Canada; $34 USA
Profile: Association reports & articles about issues important to the cattle production industry
• British Columbia Cattlemen's Association Newsletter
Type: Newsletter; *Frequency:* Monthly

British Columbia Centre for Ability

2805 Kingsway, Vancouver BC V5R 5H9
Tel: 604-451-5511; *Fax:* 604-451-5651
info@bc-cfa.org
www.bc-cfa.org
twitter.com/bccfa
www.youtube.com/user/TheBCCFA
Previous Name: Neurolodical Centre & Children's Centre for Ability; Vancouver Neurological Association
Overview: A small local charitable organization founded in 1969
Mission: To enhance the quality of life for children, youth & adults with disabilities & their families in ways that build on their potential & promotes inclusion in all aspects of social life
Member of: United Way
Chief Officer(s):
Jason Campbell, Contact
Jason.campbell@bc-cfa.org
Activities: Physiotherapy, occupational therapy, speech-language therapy, brain injury program, employment resource centre, transitional employment program, consultation, assessment, counselling; *Awareness Events:* Dining for Dreams, May; BC Centre FORE Ability Golf Tournament, Sept.; *Library:* Play & Therapeutic Toy Libraries & Family Resource Centre; by appointment

British Columbia Centre for Ability Association (BCCFA)

2805 Kingsway, Vancouver BC V5R 5H9
Tel: 604-451-5511; *Fax:* 604-451-5651
info@bc-cfa.org
bc-cfa.org
www.facebook.com/sharer.php
twitter.com/bccfa
Previous Name: Children's Rehabilitation & Cerebral Palsy Association; Children's Centre for Ability
Overview: A medium-sized provincial charitable organization founded in 1970
Mission: To provide community-based services that enhance the quality of life for children, youth & adults with disabilities & their families in ways that facilitate & build competencies & foster inclusion in all aspects of life
Member of: United Way
Chief Officer(s):
Jennifer Baumbusch, President
Finances: *Annual Operating Budget:* Greater than $5 Million; *Funding Sources:* Provincial & federal governments; fundraising; donations
Staff Member(s): 139
Membership: 1-99; *Fees:* $15
Activities: Endeavour Gala Dinner & Auction; Dining for Dreams; Breakfast with the Easter Bunny; *Library:* Equipment Lending Library; Toy Lending Library; Book & Video Reso

British Columbia Centre of Excellence for Women's Health (BCCEWH)

c/o British Columbia Women's Hospital & Health Centre, PO Box 48, #311E, 4500 Oak St., Vancouver BC V6H 3E1
Tel: 604-875-2633; *Fax:* 604-875-3716
Toll-Free: 888-300-3088
bccewh@cw.bc.ca
www.bccewh.bc.ca
Overview: A small provincial charitable organization founded in 1995
Mission: To ensure that women's health & wellness are considered by clinicians & policy makers
Chief Officer(s):
Lorraine Greaves, Executive Director
lgreaves@cw.bc.ca
Ann Pederson, Manager, Research & Policy
apederson@cw.bc.ca
Membership: *Member Profile:* Individuals interested in improving women's health & advancing health policy
Activities: Promoting a women-centred approach to health; Developing women-centred programs & practices; Liaising with organizations at all levels to exchange knowledge & conduct research; Producing scientific & technical reports; Providing training & education; *Speaker Service:* Yes
Publications:
• British Columbia Centre of Excellence for Women's Health Research Bulletin
Profile: Research findings produced by the four Centres of Excellence for Women's Health
• Women-Health eNews
Type: Newsletter
Profile: Information for researchers, policy makers, & activists

British Columbia Chamber of Commerce

#1201, 750 West Pender St., Vancouver BC V6C 2T8
Tel: 604-683-0700; *Fax:* 604-683-0416
Other Communication: www.flickr.com/photos/43089524@N08

bccc@bcchamber.org
www.bcchamber.org
www.linkedin.com/company/1134700
www.facebook.com/bcchamber
twitter.com/bcchamberofcom
www.youtube.com/user/bcchamberofcom
Overview: A large provincial organization founded in 1951
Mission: To make British Columbia a great place to do business; to be the leadership voice of B.C. business; to build a strong Chamber of Commerce network
Chief Officer(s):
Maureen Kirkbride, Chair
John Winter, President & CEO, 604-638-8110
jwinter@bcchamber.org
Staff Member(s): 7
Membership: 23,000+; *Fees:* $11 individual; $300-$1,000 business
Activities: *Rents Mailing List:* Yes
Publications:
• Insight [a publication of British Columbia Chamber of Commerce]
Type: Newsletter; *Frequency:* Monthly
• Legislative Watch [a publication of British Columbia Chamber of Commerce]
Type: Newsletter
• Public Affairs Update [a publication of British Columbia Chamber of Commerce]
Type: Newsletter; *Frequency:* Weekly

British Columbia Charolais Association
PO Box 44, Brisco BC V0A 1B0
Tel: 250-346-3227; *Fax:* 250-346-3227
brisco@redshift.bc.ca
Overview: A small provincial organization
Member of: Canadian Charolais Association

British Columbia Chess Federation
c/o Treasurer, PO Box 15548, 1012 Spiritwood Pl., Victoria BC V8Y 1C6
www.chess.bc.ca
Overview: A small provincial organization founded in 1987
Mission: To foster interest in chess throughout British Columbia; To manage chess events throughout British Columbia.
Member of: Chess Federation of Canada
Chief Officer(s):
Roger Patterson, President
bccf.president@gmail.com
Lyle Craver, Secretary, 250-624-2937
jniksic@citytel.net
Staff Member(s): 11
Membership: *Fees:* Membership is obtained by playing in BCCF sanctioned tournaments; *Member Profile:* BC residents

British Columbia Chicken Growers' Association (BCCGA)
PO Box 581, Abbotsford BC V2T 6Z8
Tel: 604-859-9332; *Fax:* 604-853-4808
bccga@telus.net
www.bcchicken.ca
Overview: A small provincial organization founded in 1957
Mission: To represent chicken producers in British Columbia; To work towards a stable industry
Affliation(s): BC Chicken Marketing Board; BC Agriculture Council; BC Poultry Association; BC Sustainable Poultry Farming Group
Chief Officer(s):
Ravi Bathe, President
Margret Duin, Administrator
Membership: 340; *Member Profile:* Commercial chicken growers in British Columbia
Activities: Distributing information to chicken growers; Engaging in lobbying activities; Developing a Poultry in Motion mobile barn in partnership with the BC Broiler Hatching Egg Producers' Association to educate consumers & raise public awareness

British Columbia Chiropractic Association (BCCA)
#125, 3751 Shell Rd., Richmond BC V6X 2W2
Tel: 604-270-1332; *Fax:* 604-278-0093
Toll-Free: 866-256-1474
info@bcchiro.com
www.bcchiro.com
twitter.com/bcchiro
www.youtube.com/bcchiropractic
Overview: A medium-sized provincial organization founded in 1934 overseen by Canadian Chiropractic Association
Mission: To represent BC chiropractors in matters relating to health policy, public relations & health authorities
Chief Officer(s):
Jay Robinson, President
Membership: *Committees:* WorkSafeBC; Insurance - ICBC; CCA; Membership
Activities: *Speaker Service:* Yes; *Rents Mailing List:* Yes

British Columbia Choral Federation (BCCF)
PO Box 4397, Vancouver BC V6B 3Z8
Tel: 604-733-9687; *Fax:* 604-738-3215
Toll-Free: 877-733-9688
bccf@bcchoralfed.com
www.bcchoralfed.com
Overview: A medium-sized provincial organization founded in 1978
Mission: To promote & encourage choral activity throughout British Columbia; to strengthen public & governmental awareness of choral plans & achievements
Member of: Canadian Conference of the Arts; International Federation for Choral Music
Affliation(s): BC Education & Arts; BC Music Educators Association; Association of Canadian Choral Conductors
Chief Officer(s):
Willi Zwozdesky, Executive Director
willi_zwozdesky@telus.net
Finances: *Funding Sources:* Membership dues; provincial government; BC Gaming
Staff Member(s): 3
Membership: *Fees:* $50 choir; $2 youth; $25 choir singer; $30 solo singer; $500 lifetime; *Member Profile:* Interest in choral music; individuals; choirs
Awards:
• Herbert Drost Award (Award)
• Herbert Kent Award (Award)
• Amy Fergusen Award (Award)

British Columbia Civil Liberties Association (BCCLA)
900 Helmcken St., 2nd Fl., Vancouver BC V6Z 1B3
Tel: 604-687-2919; *Fax:* 604-687-3045
info@bccla.org
www.bccla.org
www.facebook.com/pages/BC-Civil-Liberties-Association/884126 3601
twitter.com/bccla
www.youtube.com/user/BCCivilLiberties
Overview: A medium-sized provincial charitable organization founded in 1962
Mission: To protect & enhance civil liberties & human rights in British Columbia
Chief Officer(s):
David Eby, Executive Director
david@bccla.org
Michael Vonn, Policy Director
micheal@bccla.org
Finances: *Annual Operating Budget:* $100,000-$250,000
Staff Member(s): 10; 40 volunteer(s)
Membership: 1,000-4,999
Activities: *Speaker Service:* Yes

British Columbia Coalition of People with Disabilities (BCCPD)
#204, 456 West Broadway, Vancouver BC V5Y 1R3
Tel: 604-875-0188; *Fax:* 604-875-9227
Toll-Free: 800-663-1278; *TTY:* 604-875-8835
feedback@bccpd.bc.ca
www.bccpd.bc.ca
Overview: A medium-sized provincial organization founded in 1977
Mission: To raise public & political awareness of issues concerning people with disabilities; to facilitate full participation of disabled people in society by promoting independence & the self-help model; to lobby government on policies & attitudes which affect people with disabilities
Affliation(s): Council of Canadians with Disabilities
Chief Officer(s):
Pat Danforth, President
Finances: *Annual Operating Budget:* $500,000-$1.5 Million
Staff Member(s): 23
Membership: 1,200 groups/individual; *Fees:* $15; *Committees:* Transportation; Physical Access
Activities: Advocacy Access Program; AIDS & Disability Action Program; Individualized Funding Community Development Project; Community & Residents Mentors Associatin Project; Wellness & Disability Initiative; Health Literacy Network; Kids on the Block; *Speaker Service:* Yes; *Library:* BCCPD Library; Open to public

British Columbia Coalition to Eliminate Abuse of Seniors (BCCEAS)
#370, 1199 West Pender St., Vancouver BC V6E 2R1
Tel: 604-688-1927
Toll-Free: 866-437-1940
www.bcceas.ca
twitter.com/bcceas
Also Known As: BC Centre for Elder Advocacy Support
Overview: A small provincial organization founded in 1994
Mission: To assist & support elderly individuals who are abused or at risk of abuse, or whose rights have been violated
Chief Officer(s):
Leah Sandhu, President
Martha Jane Lewis, Executive Director
Finances: *Funding Sources:* Provincial government; Law Foundation of British Columbia; TD Financial Literacy Grant; Human Resources & Skills Development Canada
Staff Member(s): 10; 25 volunteer(s)
Membership: 180; *Fees:* $5 senior; $10 individual; $20 organization; *Member Profile:* Seniors' advocates; community agencies; government
Activities: Advocate for abused seniors; education & training materials; workshops; training; research; projects for prevention of abuse; videos; public education; legal advocacy line for seniors & community;

British Columbia College of Chiropractors *See* College of Chiropractors of British Columbia

British Columbia College of Social Workers
#302, 1765 West 8th Ave., Vancouver BC V6J 5C6
Tel: 604-737-4916; *Fax:* 604-737-6809
Other Communication: registration@bccsw.ca
info@bccsw.bc.ca
www.bccollegeofsocialworkers.ca
Previous Name: Board of Registration for Social Workers in B.C.
Overview: A medium-sized provincial organization
Mission: To operate as the regulatory body for the practice of social work in British Columbia; To protect the public from preventable harm
Affliation(s): British Columbia Association of Social Workers
Chief Officer(s):
John Mayr, Registrar
john.mayr@bccsw.ca
Sheila Begg, Director, Registration
sheila.begg@bccsw.ca
Staff Member(s): 4
Membership: *Member Profile:* Only individuals who are registered with the British Columbia College of Social Workers or are employed as social workers by one of the exempt employers under Section 18(2) of the Social Workers Act may represent themselves as social workers in British Columbia. It is an offence to represent themselves as social workers.
Meetings/Conferences: • British Columbia College of Social Workers 2015 Annual Meeting, 2015, BC
Scope: Provincial
Description: A business meeting featuring an election of social workers to the board
Contact Information: Office Coordinator: Christeen Young, E-mail: christeen.young@bccsw.ca
Publications:
• British Columbia College of Social Workers Annual Report
Type: Yearbook; *Frequency:* Annually
Profile: The year of the college in review, including registration, complaints, public inquiries, the election & annual meeting, & committee reports
• College Conversation: The Newsletter of the British Columbia College of Social Workers
Type: Newsletter; *Frequency:* Semiannually; *Editor:* Mark Budgen
Profile: Reports from the chair & registrar, educational articles, & information about meetings

British Columbia College of Teachers *See* British Columbia Teacher Regulation Branch

British Columbia Colleges Athletics Association *See* Pacific Western Athletic Association

The British Columbia Community Connectivity Cooperative (BC3)
www.bc3.ca
Previous Name: BC Community Connectivity Consortium
Overview: A medium-sized provincial organization founded in 2004

Mission: To assist communities across British Columbia with setting up local broadband networks
Chief Officer(s):
Bob Carter, Chair
bcarter@bc3.ca
Arvo Koppel, Vice-Chair
sysop@pris.ca
Penny A.P. Anderson, Board Member
pennyap@telus.net

British Columbia Competitive Trail Riders Association (BCCTRA)
c/o Kay Klippenstein, PO Box 99, Bridge Lake BC V0K 1E0
Tel: 250-593-4022; *Fax:* 250-593-4022
bcctra@shaw.ca
www.bcctra.ca
Overview: A small provincial organization founded in 1983
Mission: To promote & improve the rapidly growing sport of competitive trail riding in BC
Member of: Canadian Long Distance Riding Association
Chief Officer(s):
Tammy Mercer, President, 250-335-3390
ridingforfreedomranch@shaw.ca
Kay Klippenstein, Secretary-Treasurer
Membership: *Fees:* $60 family; $30 senior; $25 senior plus; $25 junior; $300 lifetime; $20 supporter; *Member Profile:* Senior & junior riders
Activities: Two yearly meetings
Awards:
- Year End Awards (Award)

British Columbia Confederation of Parent Advisory Councils (BCCPAC)
#200, 4170 Still Creek Dr., Burnaby BC V5C 6C6
Tel: 604-687-4433; *Fax:* 604-687-4488
Toll-Free: 866-529-4397
info@bccpac.bc.ca
www.bccpac.bc.ca
www.facebook.com/153750724696021
twitter.com/bccpac
Previous Name: British Columbia Parent-Teacher (Home & School) Federation
Overview: A medium-sized provincial charitable organization founded in 1922 overseen by Canadian Home & School Federation
Mission: To advance the public school education & well-being of children in British Columbia
Chief Officer(s):
Terry Berting, President
terryberting@bccpac.bc.ca
Carla Giles, COO
Finances: *Annual Operating Budget:* $500,000-$1.5 Million; *Funding Sources:* Ministry of Education; membership dues
Staff Member(s): 6; 40 volunteer(s)
Membership: 1,036; *Fees:* $65; *Member Profile:* Parent advisory council of BC public school/school district
Activities: *Speaker Service:* Yes
Awards:
- George Matthews Award (Award)
- Bev Hosker Motivational Award (Award)
- BCCPAC Educational Award (Award)
Amount: $500

British Columbia Conservation Foundation (BCCF)
#206, 17564 - 56A Ave., Surrey BC V3S 1G3
Tel: 604-576-1433; *Fax:* 604-576-1482
hoffice@bccf.com
www.bccf.com
Overview: A medium-sized provincial organization founded in 1969
Mission: To contribute significantly to the perpetuation and expansion of fish and wildlife populations through the efficient implementation of projects in the field.
Chief Officer(s):
Deborah Gibson, Executive Director
Staff Member(s): 3
Activities: Four regional offices

British Columbia Conservative Party
PO Box 30065, RPO Parkgate Vlg., North Vancouver BC V7H 1Y8
Toll-Free: 866-800-9025
conservatives@bcconservative.ca
www.bcconservative.ca
www.youtube.com/bcconservativeparty
Also Known As: BC Conservative Party
Overview: A small provincial organization
Chief Officer(s):
John Brooks, President
Membership: *Fees:* $10

British Columbia Construction Association (BCCA)
#401, 655 Tyee Rd., Victoria BC V9A 6X5
Tel: 250-475-1077; *Fax:* 250-475-1078
www.bccassn.com
www.facebook.com/WeBuildBC
twitter.com/WeBuildBC
www.youtube.com/user/BCCASSN
Overview: A large provincial organization founded in 1969 overseen by Canadian Construction Association
Mission: To provide excellence in the representation of & service to British Columbia's construction industry
Chief Officer(s):
Manley McLachlan, President & CEO
Abigail Fulton, Vice-President, Government Relations
Warren Perks, Vice-President & Director, Industry Practices
Jen Reid, Coordinator, Marketing & Communications
Finances: *Funding Sources:* Membership dues; Group benefit plan; Industry forms; Publications
13 volunteer(s)
Membership: 2,000 companies + 4 regional associations
Publications:
- British Columbia Construction Association Member Bulletin
Type: Bulletin
- Construction File [a publication of the British Columbia Construction Association]
Type: Newsletter
- Green Building Market Update [a publication of the British Columbia Construction Association]
Type: Newsletter
- Issue Update [a publication of the British Columbia Construction Association]
Type: Newsletter

British Columbia Construction Association - North (BCCA-N)
3851 - 18 Ave., Prince George BC V2N 1B1
Tel: 250-563-1744; *Fax:* 250-563-1107
www.bccanorth.ca
Previous Name: Northern British Columbia Construction Association
Overview: A medium-sized local charitable organization founded in 1969 overseen by Canadian Construction Association
Mission: To act as a united voice on behalf of all sectors of the construction industry on concerns of the industry; To promote education, training, safety, standard practices, high standards, & investment in the construction industry of northern British Columbia
Affiliation(s): British Columbia Construction Association; Canadian Construction Association; Local British Columbia construction associations in Dawson Creek, Bulkley Valley-Lakes District, Fort St. John, Prince George; Terrace-Kitimat; Williams Lake, & Quesnel
Chief Officer(s):
Rosalind Thorn, President
Ken Morland, Chair
kmorland@sterlingcrane.com
Lee Bedell, Secretary
lbedell@dgsastro.bc.ca
Bonnie Griffith, Treasurer
bonnie@burgessphe.com
Staff Member(s): 5
Membership: 249; *Member Profile:* Manufacturers; General & trade contractors; Suppliers; Allied service firms
Activities: Liaising with government, design authorities, & the public; Providing educational opportunities

British Columbia Contact Centre Association (BC CCA)
#102, 211 Columbia St., Vancouver BC V6A 2R5
Tel: 604-682-0296; *Fax:* 604-681-4545
info@bccontactcentre.com
www.bccallcentre.com
Previous Name: British Columbia Call Centre Association
Overview: A small provincial organization
Mission: To connect call centre employees & users with suppliers & government representatives
Chief Officer(s):
Jean Mitchell, President, 604-622-7839
jean_mitchell@bcit.ca
Finances: *Funding Sources:* Sponsorships
Membership: 100+; *Member Profile:* Call centre educators, managers, supervisors, consultants, & vendor suppliers; *Committees:* Finance; Programs; Marketing & Communications; Sponsorship; Membership
Activities: Promoting growth of the contact centre industry; Conducting "boot camps" for those wishing to gain employment in customer service & sales; Exchanging best practices; Offering networking opportunities; Providing information sessions
Awards:
- Vendor of the Year (Award)
- Community Spirit Award (Award)
- Employee of the Year (Award)
- Contact Centre of the Year (Award)
Publications:
- British Columbia Contact Centre Association Newsletter
Type: Newsletter

British Columbia Contract Cleaner's Association (BCCCA)
PO Box 75346, White Rock BC V4B 5L5
e-mail: info@bccca.ca
www.bccca.ca
Overview: A small provincial organization
Mission: To advance the interests of contract cleaners in the province of British Columbia
Chief Officer(s):
Iain Hunt, President
Membership: *Fees:* $170 primary; $195 associate; *Member Profile:* Organizations engaged in the contract cleaning industry

British Columbia Co-operative Association (BCCA)
#212, 1737 - 3rd Ave. West, Vancouver BC V6J 1K7
Tel: 604-662-3906; *Fax:* 604-662-3968
general@bcca.coop
www.bcca.coop
www.facebook.com/bc.cooperativeassociation
twitter.com/bc_coop
Overview: A medium-sized provincial organization
Mission: To promote & develop the co-operative economy in British Columbia
Chief Officer(s):
Carol Murray, Executive Director
murray@bcca.coop
Finances: *Annual Operating Budget:* $500,000-$1.5 Million
Membership: 47; *Fees:* Sliding scale; *Member Profile:* Co-operatives; credit unions; non profit organizations
Activities: Promotion & development of co-operatives in BC; *Internships:* Yes

British Columbia Cooperative Learning Provincial Specialist Association
c/o British Columbia Teachers' Federation, #100, 550 West 6th Ave., Vancouver BC V5Z 4P2
Tel: 604-871-2283
bccla.weebly.com
Overview: A small provincial organization
Mission: To foster and promote cooperative learning and cooperative schools in British Columbia.
Chief Officer(s):
Mike Galliford, President
mgalliford@sd43.bc.ca
Membership: *Fees:* $25 BCTF member; $10 student

British Columbia Council for Families (BCCF)
#208, 1600 West 6th Ave., Vancouver BC V6J 1R3
Tel: 604-678-8884; *Fax:* 604-678-8886
bccf@bccf.ca
www.bccf.ca
www.linkedin.com/company/bc-council-for-families
www.facebook.com/BCFamilies
twitter.com/BC_Families
Also Known As: The Council
Overview: A medium-sized provincial charitable organization founded in 1977
Mission: To strengthen, encourage & support families through information, education, research & advocacy
Chief Officer(s):
Sylvia Tremblay, President
Joel B. Kaplan, Executive Director, 604-678-8884 Ext. 102, Fax: 604-678-8886
joelk@bccf.ca
Tina Albrecht, Manager, Communications
tinaa@bccf.ca
Finances: *Annual Operating Budget:* $500,000-$1.5 Million; *Funding Sources:* Membership fees; sale of publications; government; foundations
Staff Member(s): 5; 12-2 volunteer(s)

Membership: 515; *Fees:* $25 student; $35 individual & family; $55 group; $150 corporate; *Member Profile:* Organizations & individuals interested in family well-being
Activities: *Awareness Events:* National Family Week; Intergenerational Week; Intl. Family Day - Connect with Kindness; *Internships:* Yes; *Speaker Service:* Yes
Awards:
• Distinguished Service to Families Award (Award)

British Columbia Courthouse Library Society
800 Smithe St., Vancouver BC V6Z 2E1
Tel: 604-660-2841; *Fax:* 604-660-9418
Toll-Free: 800-665-2570
librarian@courthouselibrary.ca
www.bccls.bc.ca
Overview: A medium-sized provincial organization
Chief Officer(s):
Johanne Blenkin, Executive Director, 604-660-2409
Activities: *Library:* Vancouver Courthouse Library

British Columbia Cranberry Marketing Commission (BCCMC)
PO Box 162, Stn. A, Abbotsford BC V2T 6Z5
Tel: 604-897-9252
cranberries@telus.net
www.bccranberries.com
www.facebook.com/bccranberries
twitter.com/BCcranberries
instagram.com/bccranberries
Overview: A small provincial organization founded in 1968
Mission: To regulate cranberry farming in BC

British Columbia Cricket Association *See* British Columbia Mainland Cricket League

British Columbia Crime Prevention Association (BCCPA)
#120, 12414 - 82nd Ave., Surrey BC V3W 3E9
Tel: 604-501-9222; *Fax:* 604-501-2261
Toll-Free: 888-405-2288
info@bccpa.org
www.bccpa.org
www.facebook.com/pages/BC-Crime-Prevention-Association/25 5950554446178
twitter.com/crimeprevention
Overview: A medium-sized provincial charitable organization founded in 1978
Mission: To promote active community participation in crime prevention initiatives through awareness & education
Member of: Better Business Bureau; Canadian Security Association
Chief Officer(s):
Rob Smith, President
Shelley Cole, First Vice-President
Pat Patterson, Second Vice-President
Colleen Staresina, Treasurer
12 volunteer(s)
Membership: 377; *Fees:* $50 individual; $70 non-profit; $125 police; $250 corporate; $125 small business; $125 municipal; *Member Profile:* All who are concerned about crime; *Committees:* Education - Awareness; Development - Innovation; Administration - Management; Financial - Funding Management
Activities: *Awareness Events:* Golf Tournament & Silent Auction, June; *Speaker Service:* Yes; *Library* Open to public
Awards:
• Brian G. Jones Business of the Year (Award)
• Citizens Patrol Innovation (Award)
• Outstanding Patroller (Award)
Meetings/Conferences: • 2015 British Columbia Crime Prevention Association Training Symposium, November, 2015, BC
Scope: Provincial

British Columbia Criminal Justice Association (BCCJA)
PO Box 405, 104 Columbia St., New Westminster BC V3M 6V3
www.bccja.com
Overview: A small provincial organization
Mission: To promote cooperation concerning the problems of crime & its consequences
Member of: Canadian Criminal Justice Association
Chief Officer(s):
Chris Thomson, Contact, 604-528-5842
cthomson@bccja.com
Activities: Providing education & information on criminal justice issues; Encouraging professional networking opportunities; Promoting debate on issues within the criminal justice system; Fostering study of problems in the field; Providing advocacy
Publications:
• Sources & Resources
Type: Newsletter; *Editor:* Tim Stiles; Art Gordon
Profile: Information for criminal justice & related professionals in British Columbia

British Columbia Culinary Arts Specialist Association
c/o British Columbia Teachers' Federation, #100, 550 West 6th Ave., Vancouver BC V5Z 4P2
bccasa.ca
twitter.com/BCCASAchef
Overview: A small provincial organization founded in 2000
Mission: To run culinary classes for students in British Columbia
Member of: BC Teachers' Federation
Chief Officer(s):
Eric MacNeill, President, 250-751-3409
emacneil@sd68.bc.ca

British Columbia Dairy Association
3236 Beta Ave., Burnaby BC V5G 4K4
Tel: 604-294-3775; *Fax:* 604-294-8199
Toll-Free: 800-242-6455
contactus@bcdairy.ca
www.bcdairyfoundation.ca
www.linkedin.com/company/bcdairy
www.facebook.com/bcdairy
twitter.com/bcmilk
www.youtube.com/MustDrinkMoreMilkTV
Merged from: BC Dairy Foundation; BC Milk Producers Association
Overview: A small provincial organization founded in 2011
Mission: To coordinate, plan, produce & administer dairy products promotion, education & public relations programs best suited to meet the needs of the dairy industry in British Columbia.
Chief Officer(s):
Dave Eto, Executive Director
Activities: The Cold Crew; Dairy Farm Tours.;

British Columbia Dance Educators' Association (BCDEA)
c/o BC Teachers' Federation, #100, 550 West 6th Ave., Vancouver BC V5Z 4P2
Tel: 604-871-2283
Toll-Free: 800-663-9163
psac73@bctf.ca
www.bcdea.ca
www.twitter.com/BCDanceEd
Overview: A small provincial organization
Mission: Organization for teachers of dance in BC public schools.
Member of: BC Teachers' Federation
Chief Officer(s):
Kim Wolski, President
Meetings/Conferences: • British Columbia Dance Educators' Association 2015 Conference, 2015, BC
Scope: Provincial

British Columbia Deaf Sports Federation (BCDSF)
#4, 320 Columbia St., new westminster BC V3L 1A6
Tel: 604-333-3606; *Fax:* 604-333-3450; *TTY:* 604-526-5010
info@bcdeafsports.bc.ca
www.bcdeafsports.bc.ca
www.facebook.com/139556792849947
twitter.com/bcdeafsports
Overview: A medium-sized provincial charitable organization founded in 1975 overseen by Canadian Deaf Sports Association
Mission: To provide & support the development of competitive sporting events in BC among deaf & hard of hearing athletes; to encourage training for deaf coaches; to provide financial assistance to deaf athletes to participate in local, provincial & national competitions
Member of: Canadian Deaf Sports Association
Affliation(s): BC Sport & Fitness Council for the Disabled
Chief Officer(s):
Jamie Finley, Vice-President
jfinley@bcdeafsports.bc.ca
Leonor Johnson, Administrator
info@bcdeafsports.bc.ca
Finances: *Annual Operating Budget:* $100,000-$250,000; *Funding Sources:* Grants; gaming; membership fees; donations
Staff Member(s): 1
Membership: 300; *Fees:* $20 club

British Columbia Dental Association
#400, 1765 - 8th Ave. West, Vancouver BC V6J 5C6
Tel: 604-736-7202; *Fax:* 604-736-7588
Toll-Free: 888-396-9888
post@bcdental.org
www.bcdental.org
Overview: A medium-sized provincial organization founded in 1998 overseen by Canadian Dental Association
Mission: To act as the voice of dentistry in British Columbia; To prevent oral disease
Membership: 2,900+; *Member Profile:* All dentists licensed to practise in British Columbia; Retired dentists & dentists unable to practise because of disability; Dentists who reside outside British Columbia; Students
Activities: Advocating for access to dental care for everyone in British Columbia; Raising public awareness of oral health; *Awareness Events:* Oral Health Month, April
Meetings/Conferences: • Pacific Dental Conference 2015, March, 2015, Vancouver, BC
Scope: Provincial
Attendance: 12,000+
Description: An opportunity for dental professionals to obtain continuing education credits
Contact Information: Address: Pacific Dental Conference, #305, 1505 West 2nd Ave., Vancouver, BC V6H 3Y4; Phone: 604-736-3781; E-mail: info@pdconf.com; URL: www.pdconf.com
• Pacific Dental Conference 2016, March, 2016, Vancouver, BC
Scope: Provincial
Attendance: 12,000+
Contact Information: Address: Pacific Dental Conference, #305, 1505 West 2nd Ave., Vancouver, BC V6H 3Y4; Phone: 604-736-3781; E-mail: info@pdconf.com, exhibits@pdconf.com
• Pacific Dental Conference 2017, March, 2017, Vancouver, BC
Scope: Provincial
Attendance: 12,000+
Contact Information: Address: Pacific Dental Conference, #305, 1505 West 2nd Ave., Vancouver, BC V6H 3Y4; Phone: 604-736-3781; E-mail: info@pdconf.com, exhibits@pdconf.com
• Pacific Dental Conference 2018, 2018
Scope: Provincial
Contact Information: Address: Pacific Dental Conference, #305, 1505 West 2nd Ave., Vancouver, BC V6H 3Y4; Phone: 604-736-3781; E-mail: info@pdconf.com; URL: www.pdconf.com
• Pacific Dental Conference 2019, 2019, BC
Scope: Provincial
Contact Information: Address: Pacific Dental Conference, #305, 1505 West 2nd Ave., Vancouver, BC V6H 3Y4; Phone: 604-736-3781; E-mail: info@pdconf.com; URL: www.pdconf.com
Publications:
• the bridge [a publication of the British Columbia Dental Association]
Type: Magazine; *Frequency:* Bimonthly; *Accepts Advertising*
Profile: Issues that affect dentists in British Columbia
• British Columbia Dental Association Annual Fee Guide
Type: Guide; *Frequency:* Annually; *Accepts Advertising*
Profile: A reference published for dentists each January

British Columbia Dental Hygienists' Association (BCDHA)
#307, 9600 Cameron St., Burnaby BC V3J 7N3
Tel: 604-415-4559; *Fax:* 604-415-4579
Toll-Free: 888-305-3338
info@bcdha.bc.ca
www.bcdha.bc.ca
www.facebook.com/101954289892034
twitter.com/BCDHA
Overview: A small provincial organization founded in 1964
Mission: To promote the profession in British Columbia; To advocate on behalf of dental hygienists
Member of: Canadian Dental Hygienists' Association (CDHA)
Chief Officer(s):
Brenda Morris, Chair
upperislanddirector@bcdha.bc.ca
Jodi Noble, Vice-Chair
victoriadirector@bcdha.bc.ca
Cindy Fletcher, Executive Director
cfletcher@bcdha.bc.ca
Staff Member(s): 5
Membership: 3,000; *Member Profile:* Dental hygienists in British Columbia
Activities: Offering continuing education; Providing information about career opportunities for dental hygienists
Publications:
• Outlook

Type: Newsletter; *Frequency:* 3 pa; *Accepts Advertising*
Profile: Educational articles & association updates

British Columbia Diving

#114, 15272 Croydon Dr., Surrey BC V3S 0Z5
Tel: 604-531-5576; *Fax:* 604-542-0387
www.bcdiving.ca
Also Known As: British Columbia Diving Association
Previous Name: Dive B.C.
Overview: A small provincial charitable organization founded in 1986
Mission: To develop and promote diving throughout British Columbia by encouraging participation, growth and personal success for everyone.
Member of: Diving Plongeon Canada
Chief Officer(s):
Jayne McDonald, Executive Director
jayne@bcdiving.ca
Beverley Boys, Technical Director
bevboys@shaw.ca
Finances: *Funding Sources:* Province of British Columbia through the Ministry of Community, Sport and Cultural Development
Staff Member(s): 3
Membership: *Fees:* Schedule available; *Member Profile:* Divers, associations, coaches, officials

British Columbia Drama Association

Old Courthouse Cultural Centre, 7 Seymour St. West, Kamloops BC V2C 1E4
Tel: 778-471-5620; *Fax:* 778-471-5639
Toll-Free: 888-202-2913
info@theatrebc.org
www.theatrebc.org
www.facebook.com/291432170918438
twitter.com/Theatre_BC
Also Known As: Theatre BC
Previous Name: British Columbia Festival Association
Overview: A medium-sized provincial charitable organization founded in 1933
Mission: To promote the development of theatre in BC & Canada through a wide range of programs, services, activities, competitions, festivals & events
Member of: Greater Nanaimo Chamber of Commerce
Affliation(s): Centre for the Arts Nanaimo
Chief Officer(s):
Vance Schneider, Executive Director
vance.schneider@theatrebc.org
Glen Miller, President
glen.miller@theatrebc.org
Membership: *Fees:* Schedule available; *Member Profile:* Membership includes clubs, individuals, talent banks, family members, family youth members, & youth members.
Activities: MAINSTAGE features the productions of Theatre BC's 10 preceding Zone Festivals; Zone Festivals celebrate regional community theatre; Annual Canadian National Playwriting Competition; Backstage annual provincial workshop; Talent bank referrals; Professional instruction; Club card program; *Awareness Events:* ACToberfest, Oct.; Zone Festivals, March - June; *Library:* Script Library
Awards:
• Theatre BC Diamond of the Year Award (Award)
Awarded to a Theatre BC member who, in the past year, worked toward furthering the association's mission statement
• Eric Hamber Award (Award)
Presented annually at MAINSTAGE to a person, member club or institution having made an outstanding contribution to community theatre in BC over a long period of time
• Zone Recognition Awards (Award)
Given at the Zone Festival annually to a person or member club having made an outstanding contribution to his or her Zone
• Jessie L. Richardson & Sid Williams Memorial Scholarships (Scholarship)
Awarded to two student applicants accepted by a post-secondary theatre program at a recognized Canadian institution to further their training *Amount:* $1,000
Publications:
• Theatre BC News
Frequency: Quarterly; *Accepts Advertising*
Profile: Updates on the Club Card Program, freelance opportunities for Talent Bank members, MAINSTAGE updates, competition announcements, postings, festival results, event features, & Curtain Call listing of professionaland member club productions around B.C.

British Columbia Drug & Poison Information Centre (DPIC)

BC Centre for Disease Control, #0063, 655 West 12th Ave., Vancouver BC V5Z 4R4
Tel: 604-707-2789; *Fax:* 604-707-2807; *Crisis Hot-Line:* 800-567-8911
info@dpic.org
www.dpic.org
www.facebook.com/231889396821389
twitter.com/BCDPIC
Overview: A small provincial organization founded in 1975
Mission: To support healthcare providers in British Columbia, by providing a consultative service
Activities: Supporting the safe & effective use of medicines; Providing drug information to healthcare professionals; *Awareness Events:* Poison Prevention Week, March
Publications:
• Drug Information Perspectives
Type: Newsletter; *Editor:* Barbara Cadario
Profile: Issues on topics such as Dementia Therapy, Rivastigmine, Rasagiline, & Varenicline
• Drug Information Reference
Price: $65
Profile: Basic clinical facts. evaluations of commonly used drugs, investigational uses, nursing instructions, & clinical trial summaries

British Columbia Economic Development Association (BCEDA)

#102, 9300 Nowell St., Chilliwack BC V2P 4V7
Tel: 604-858-7199; *Fax:* 604-795-7118
info@bceda.ca
www.bceda.ca
www.linkedin.com/groups/BC-Economic-Development-Association-3948865
www.facebook.com/EconomicDevBC
twitter.com/economicdevBC
Previous Name: Economic Development Association of British Columbia
Overview: A small provincial organization founded in 1987
Mission: To serve members from economic, community, & employment development practice in a strategic manner through raising the profile & understanding of economic development & its practitioners; To act as an advisory resource contact point, regarding economic development; To broaden the opportunities for professional development, skills enhancement, & education for the members & member employers; To build & expand upon the associations' capabilities & portfolio of services; To increase the participation, services, & ownership of members
Affliation(s): Futurpreneur Canada; Applied Science Technologists & Technicians of BC; International Council of Shopping Centers; Small Business BC
Chief Officer(s):
Dale Wheeldon, President & CEO, 604-858-7199 Ext. 1
dwheeldon@bceda.ca
Finances: *Annual Operating Budget:* $50,000-$100,000
Membership: 420+; *Fees:* $65 student; $100 international/retired/elected official; $225 international organization; $305 regular; $595 organizational
Activities: Providing education & training opportunities
Awards:
• Marketing Award (Award)
• Community Project Award (Award)
Meetings/Conferences: • 2015 BC Economic Summit, April, 2015, Sheraton Vancouver Airport Hotel, Richmond, BC
Scope: Provincial
Publications:
• The Pulse
Type: Newsletter; *Frequency:* Monthly
Profile: Activities, community news, economic development articles.

British Columbia Educators for Distributed Learning Provincial Specialist Association *See* Educators for Distributed Learning PSA (British Columbia)

British Columbia Egg Marketing Board

#250, 32160 South Fraser Way, Abbotsford BC V2T 1W5
Tel: 604-556-3348; *Fax:* 604-556-3410
bcemb@bcegg.com
www.bcegg.com
www.facebook.com/bcegg
twitter.com/bceggs
www.youtube.com/user/BCEggProducers
Previous Name: BC Egg Producers
Overview: A small provincial organization founded in 1967
Mission: To regulate British Columbia's egg farming industry
Chief Officer(s):
Richard King, Chair
Finances: *Annual Operating Budget:* Greater than $5 Million; *Funding Sources:* Levy system for registered producers
Membership: *Committees:* Production Management; Finance

British Columbia Electrical Association (BCEA)

#224, 3989 Henning Dr., Burnaby BC V5C 6N5
Tel: 604-291-7708; *Fax:* 604-291-7795
www.bcea.bc.ca
www.linkedin.com/groups/BC-Electrical-Association-2154444
Overview: A small provincial organization founded in 1924
Mission: To act as a voice for the industry; To assist members & the electrical industry achieve success
Chief Officer(s):
John Baron, Chair
Wade Emmons, Vice-Chair
Kelly Hanson, Treasurer & 2nd Vice-Chair
Barbette Ishii, CAE, Executive Director
Membership: 158 corporate members; *Fees:* Schedule available; *Member Profile:* All segments of the electrical industry in British Columbia, including industrial plants, electrical engineers, electrical contractors, electrical distributors, electrical manufacturers, electrical testing labs, & utilities; *Committees:* Executive; Education; Careers; Membership; Social; Communications; Advocacy
Activities: Promoting British Columbia's electrical industry; Providing networking opportunities; Offering courses in areas such as basic electricity, sales & marketing, & materials handling & logistics
Meetings/Conferences: • British Columbia Electrical Association 2015 Conference, 2015, BC
Scope: Provincial
Publications:
• British Columbia Electrical Association Member Directory
Type: Directory
Profile: Listing of BCEA members
• The Connector
Type: Newsletter; *Frequency:* Quarterly; *Accepts Advertising*
Profile: Coverage & commentary on the electrical industry in British Columbia, distributed to 6,000 people involved in the industry

British Columbia Environment Industry Association (BCEIA)

#400, 602 West Hastings St., Vancouver BC V6B 1P2
Tel: 604-683-2751; *Fax:* 604-677-5960
info@bceia.com
www.bceia.com
twitter.com/BCEIA_
Previous Name: Canadian Environment Industry Association - British Columbia Chapter
Overview: A medium-sized provincial organization founded in 1992
Mission: To develop the environmental industry in British Columbia; To promote technological development
Chief Officer(s):
Frank Came, President
frank.came@bceia.com
Charles Bois, Secretary-Treasurer
Membership: *Member Profile:* Engineering & environmental service companies; Research organizations; Technology providers; Disaster response organizations; Environmental law firms; Environmental analysts & consultants; Government agencies; *Committees:* Contaminated sites & Brownfields; Hazardous waste; Executive; Energy conservation & efficiency; Eduction & professional development; First Nations; International affairs; Business development; Task forces
Activities: Networking within the environmental industry; Engaging in advocacy activities; Providing market & regulatory information; Offering professional development seminars on environmental related topics
Publications:
• British Columbia Environment Industry Association Newsletter
Type: Newsletter; *Frequency:* Weekly; *Price:* Free with British Columbia Environment Industry Association membership
Profile: Association announcements & upcoming events
• Environmental Product & Services Directory
Type: Directory; *Accepts Advertising*
Profile: Comprehensive listings available to British Columbia Environment Industry Association members

British Columbia Environmental Network (BCEN)

PO Box 1209, Mile House BC V0K 2G0

Tel: 604-515-1969
www.ecobc.org
Overview: A medium-sized provincial organization founded in 1979 overseen by Canadian Environmental Network
Mission: To facilitate communication among environmental groups & individuals so that ecological sustainability & economic stability prevail, & biological diversity & human health remain viable
Chief Officer(s):
Dave Stevens, Chair
geek@uniserve.com
Rod Marining, Coordinator, Communications, 604-219-3424
Membership: 425 groups; *Fees:* schedule; *Member Profile:* Open to non-profit environmental groups promoting environmental integrity
Activities: *Speaker Service:* Yes; *Rents Mailing List:* Yes

British Columbia Epilepsy Society (BCES)

#2500, 900 West 8 Ave., Vancouver BC V5Z 1E5
Tel: 604-875-6704; *Fax:* 604-875-0617
info@bcepilepsy.com
www.bcepilepsy.com
www.facebook.com/265298573586670
twitter.com/BCEpilepsy
www.youtube.com/BCEpilepsySociety
Also Known As: BC Epilepsy
Overview: A medium-sized provincial charitable organization founded in 1959
Mission: To serve the well-being of people living with epilepsy; to provide & promote services & education to those with epilepsy; to advance awareness, understanding & acceptance of epilepsy in British Columbia
Member of: Canadian Epilepsy Alliance
Chief Officer(s):
Shawn Laari, Executive Director
laari@bcepilepsy.com
Finances: *Funding Sources:* Foundations; corporations; government; United Way; gaming; general donations
Staff Member(s): 5
Membership: *Fees:* $10 individual; $50 organization; *Member Profile:* Individuals/families living with epilepsy; *Committees:* Professional Advisory
Activities: *Speaker Service:* Yes; *Library:* Dr. Norman Auckland Library; Open to public

British Columbia Family Child Care Association (BCFCCA)

#100, 6878 King George Blvd., Surrey BC V3W 4Z9
Tel: 604-590-1497; *Fax:* 604-590-1427
Toll-Free: 800-686-6685
office@bcfcca.ca
www.bcfcca.ca
www.facebook.com/1433767050225700
twitter.com/BCFCCA
Previous Name: Western Canada Family Child Care Association of British Columbia (WCFCCA)
Overview: A medium-sized provincial organization founded in 1981
Mission: To act as a voice for family child care providers in British Columbia; To promote awareness of professionalism in family child care
Affliation(s): Canadian Child Care Federation
Chief Officer(s):
Janeen Fowler, Administrator
Finances: *Funding Sources:* Membership fees; Online store sales
Staff Member(s): 1
Membership: *Fees:* $45; *Member Profile:* Family child care providers throughout British Columbia; Persons undertaking a family child care training program; Individuals involved in family child care, such as parents or staff of a related organization; Organizations, stakeholders, or partnering agencies
Activities: Advocating for family child care providers; Liaising with government; Cooperating with other agencies that deliver education & resources to child care programs; Developing & implementing workshops; Providing information about family child care homes, such as regulations for British Columbia, & training inforamtion; Offering peer support
Publications:
• Caregiver Connection
Type: Newsletter
Profile: Information for British Columbia Family Child Care Association members about child care issues, resources, & professional development opportunities

British Columbia Farm Industry Review Board (BCFIRB)

PO Box 9129, Stn. Prov. Govt., 1007 Fort St., 3rd Fl., Victoria BC V8W 9B5
Tel: 250-356-8945; *Fax:* 250-356-5131
firb@gov.bc.ca
www.firb.gov.bc.ca
Previous Name: British Columbia Marketing Board (BCMB)
Merged from: British Columbia Marketing Board (BCMB) & The Farm Practices Board (FPB)
Overview: A medium-sized provincial organization founded in 1934
Mission: To act in accordance with the Natural Products Marketing (BC) Act, the Agricultural Produce Grading Act, & the Farm Practices Protection (Right to Farm) Act; To supervise regulated marketing boards; To hear complaints regarding agriculture or aquaculture operations; To hear appeals from those who have had grading licenses refused, suspended, or revoked; To serve & protect the public interest
Chief Officer(s):
Jim Collins, Executive Director
Ron Kilmury, Chair
Shane Ford, Manager, Issues & Planning
Activities: Studying & reporting on farm practices in British Columbia; Promoting cooperation between urban & agricultural interests; Meeting regularly with commodity boards
Publications:
• British Columbia Farm Industry Review Board Strategic Plan

British Columbia Farm Machinery & Agriculture Museum Association

9131 King St., Fort Langley BC V1M 2R9
Tel: 604-888-2273
bcfm@telus.net
www.bcfma.com
Also Known As: BC Farm Museum
Overview: A small provincial charitable organization founded in 1958
Member of: British Columbia Museums Association
Chief Officer(s):
Syd Pickerell, P.Ag (Ret)., President
Membership: *Fees:* $10
Activities: Operating a museum with a collection of farm artifacts, such as carriages, wagons, & tractors, a sawmill, & a blacksmith shop; *Library:* British Columbia Farm Machinery & Agriculture Museum Library; Open to public

British Columbia Federation of Foster Parent Associations (BCFFPA)

#207, 22561 Dewdney Truck Rd., Maple Ridge BC V2X 3K1
Tel: 604-466-7487; *Fax:* 604-466-7490
Toll-Free: 800-663-9999
office@bcfosterparents.ca
www.bcfosterparents.ca
Overview: A medium-sized provincial charitable organization founded in 1967
Mission: To be the collective voice for all foster parents & to promote fostering; to act as a channel of communication between authorized child welfare agencies & foster parents concerning children & foster children in particular
Member of: Canadian Foster Parent Association
Chief Officer(s):
Heather Bayes, President
Sheila Davis, Secretary
Finances: *Annual Operating Budget:* $250,000-$500,000
Staff Member(s): 4
Membership: 131 associate + 2,203 voting; *Fees:* $30 individual; $35 couple; *Member Profile:* Foster parent - foster home agreement with MSS & H; associate - interested in child welfare
Activities: *Speaker Service:* Yes; *Rents Mailing List:* Yes; *Library* Open to public

British Columbia Federation of Foster Parent Associations (BCFFPA)

#207, 22561 Dewdney Truck Rd., Burnaby BC V2X 3K1
Tel: 604-466-7487; *Fax:* 604-466-7490
Toll-Free: 800-663-9999
office@bcfosterparents.ca
www.bcfosterparents.ca
www.facebook.com/group.php?gid=128343287224587
Overview: A medium-sized provincial organization
Mission: To bring together foster parents, social workers, & other interested people working to improve the standard of care for children in British Columbia; To provide opportunities for education, training, & professional development as well as support & assistance for the Foster Parents of British Columbia
Chief Officer(s):
Melanie Filiatrault, President
Heather Bayes, Vice-President
Les Toth, Treasurer
Lea Ann Bryant, Interim Executive Director
Staff Member(s): 3
Membership: *Fees:* individual $30 1 yr., $50 2 yrs.; couple $35 1 yr., $60 2 yrs.
Awards:
• Maurice Graydon, Author, Bursaries (Grant)
Eligibility: Youth currently & formerly in care who wish to continue their education*Deadline:* January *Amount:* $500
Contact: BC Federation of Foster Parent Associations, #207, 22561 Dewdney Trunk Rd, Maple Ridge, BC V2X 3K1
• Maurice & Carson Graydon, Navy Vets, Bursary (Grant)
Eligibility: Youth currently & formerly in care who wish to continue their education*Deadline:* January *Amount:* $500
Contact: BC Federation of Foster Parent Associations, #207, 22561 Dewdney Trunk Rd, Maple Ridge, BC V2X 3K1
• Maurice & Maureen Graydon Bursary (Grant)
Eligibility: Youth currently & formerly in care who wish to continue their education*Deadline:* January *Amount:* $500
Contact: BC Federation of Foster Parent Associations, #207, 22561 Dewdney Trunk Rd, Maple Ridge, BC V2X 3K1
Meetings/Conferences: • British Columbia Federation of Foster Parent Associations 2015 Conference & Annual General Meeting, May, 2015, Hilton Whistler Resort & Spa, Whistler, BC
Scope: Provincial
Description: Workshops & a business meeting of the federation for members from all regions of British Columbia
Contact Information: E-mail (general information): office@bcfosterparents.ca
Publications:
• British Columbia Federation of Foster Parent Associations Policies & Procedures Manual
Type: Manual; *Number of Pages:* 31
Profile: Contents include membership, association structure, the annual general meeting, financial policy, in camera meetings, resolution ofboard conflicts, conflicts of interest, accountability, delegates to the CFFA, & the library
• British Columbia Federation of Foster Parent Associations Organizational Handbook
Type: Handbook; *Number of Pages:* 21
Profile: Assistance for organization & effectiveness of macro & regional councils
• British Columbia Federation of Foster Parent Associations Fosterline BC
Type: Newsletter; *Frequency:* Quarterly; *Accepts Advertising*
Profile: Previously entitled "InfoLetter", the newsletter offers statistics, guidelines, reports, resources, membershipinformation, & news

British Columbia Federation of Labour (BCFL) / Fédération du travail de la Colombie-Britannique

#200, 5118 Joyce St., Vancouver BC V5R 4H1
Tel: 604-430-1421; *Fax:* 604-430-5917
Other Communication: admin@bcfed.ca
bcfed@bcfed.ca
www.bcfed.com
www.facebook.com/bcfed
twitter.com/bcfed
Overview: A large provincial organization founded in 1956 overseen by Canadian Labour Congress
Mission: To promote the interests of affiliated unions & their members; To advance the economic & social welfare of the workers of British Columbia; To act as the single voice for workers' rights in British Columbia
Affliation(s): 50+ unions
Chief Officer(s):
Jim Sinclair, President
exec@bcfed.ca
Jim Chorostecki, Executive Director
jchorostecki@bcfed.ca
Gord Lechner, Director, Occupational Health & Safety Education Centre
glechner@bcfed.ca
Summer McFadyen, Director, Political Action
smcfadyen@bcfed.ca
Nina Hansen, Director, Occupational Health & Safety
ohs@bcfed.ca
Kassandra Cordero, Director, Young Workers
kcordero@bcfed.ca

Michael Gardiner, Director, Communications
mgardiner@bcfed.ca
Jessie Uppal, Director, Human Rights
juppal@bcfed.ca
John Weir, Director, Organizing
jweir@bcfed.ca
Membership: 500,000+; *Member Profile:* British Columbia workers from affiliated unions in over 800 locals
Activities: Promoting the rights of working people; Providing educational opportunities; Publishing reports; Engaging in political, social, & community action; Promoting occupational health & safety; Organizing campaigns around issues such as minimum wage, working alone, & childcare; Supporting affiliated unions during labour disputes
Meetings/Conferences: • British Columbia Federation of Labour 2015 Policy Convention: The 59th Convention of the British Columbia Federation of Labour, 2015, BC
Scope: Provincial
Attendance: 800
Description: A policy conference held every other year for delegates from British Columbia's local unions, branches, lodges, & labour councils
Contact Information: E-mail: admin@bcfed.ca
• British Columbia Federation of Labour 2016 Convention: The 60th Convention of the British Columbia Federation of Labour, 2016, Vancouver, BC
Scope: Provincial
Attendance: 1,000+
Description: A meeting held every two years to set the direction of the labour movement in British Columbia, attended by rank & file trade union members
Contact Information: E-mail: admin@bcfed.ca
• British Columbia Federation of Labour 2017 Convention: The 61st Convention of the British Columbia Federation of Labour, 2017
Scope: Provincial
Attendance: 1,000+
Description: A meeting for trade union members from throughout British Columbia to set the direction for the labour movement

British Columbia Federation of Police Officers ***See*** British Columbia Police Association

British Columbia Fencing Association (BCFA)
#15, 12900 Jack Bell Dr., Richmond BC V6V 2V8
www.fencing.bc.ca
Also Known As: Fencing BC
Overview: A small provincial organization overseen by Canadian Fencing Federation
Mission: BCFA is a non-profit, provincial sports organization & governing body, charged with promoting the sport of fencing in the province. It is managed by volunteers & is responsible for setting policies & procedures which govern programs & events.
Member of: Canadian Fencing Federation
Chief Officer(s):
John French, President
president.bcfa@gmail.com
Membership: 15; *Fees:* $40 individual; $65 club

British Columbia Ferry & Marine Workers' Union (CLC) (BCFMWU) / Syndicat des travailleurs marins et de bacs de la Colombie-Britannique (CTC)
1511 Stewart Ave., Nanaimo BC V9S 4E3
Tel: 250-716-3454; *Fax:* 250-716-3455
Toll-Free: 800-663-7009
mailroom@bcfmwu.com
www.bcfmwu.com
twitter.com/BCFMWU
Also Known As: Ferry Workers' Union
Overview: A medium-sized provincial organization founded in 1977
Mission: To unite in the Union all workers eligible for membership; to seek the best possible wage standards & improvements in the conditions of employment for these workers & to represent members in protecting & maintaining their rights; to act as the representative of the membership; to establish free child day care for all individuals; to engage in educational, legislative, political, civic, social, welfare, community & other activities to safeguard & promote economic & social benefits & justice for all workers, unionized & non-unionized.
Member of: National Union of Public and General Employees
Affiliation(s): BC Federation of Labour; National Union of Public & General Employees (NUPGE)
Chief Officer(s):
Kevin Lee, Sec.-Treas.
kevinlee@bcfmwu.com
Chris Abbott, President
chrisabbott@bcfmwu.com
Finances: *Annual Operating Budget:* $1.5 Million-$3 Million; *Funding Sources:* Union dues
Staff Member(s): 9
Membership: 4,400; *Fees:* $60 initiation fee; 1.5% of gross monthly income; *Committees:* Asbestos; Apprenticeship; Communications; Convention; Education; Finance; Hours of Work; Human Rights; Occupational Health and Safety; Solidarity; Young Workers

British Columbia Festival Association ***See*** British Columbia Drama Association

British Columbia Fishing Resorts & Outfitters Association (BCFROA)
PO Box 3301, Kamloops BC V2C 6B9
Tel: 250-374-6836; *Fax:* 250-374-6640
Toll-Free: 800-374-6836
bcfroa@bcfroa.ca
www.bcfroa.ca
www.facebook.com/pages/Fish-British-Columbia/222148681226223
twitter.com/Fish_BC
www.youtube.com/user/BCFROA
Overview: A small provincial organization founded in 1974
Mission: Works with the public & private sector to protect areas currently in use; to preserve the wildlife experience in BC for the enjoyment of future generations; a lobby group whose members are dedicated to providing a quality outdoor experience
Member of: Outdoor Recreation Council of British Columbia
Chief Officer(s):
Jan Lingford, Executive Director
Finances: *Annual Operating Budget:* $100,000-$250,000; *Funding Sources:* Membership dues; funding programs; promotions; sponsorships
Staff Member(s): 2; 10 volunteer(s)
Membership: 170; *Fees:* $344.50-$524.70; *Member Profile:* Resort owner or angling & hunting guide
Activities: Marketing; lobbying; advocacy

British Columbia Floor Covering Association (BCFCA)
#2-19299 - 94 Ave., Surrey BC V4N 4E6
Tel: 604-881-4944; *Fax:* 604-881-4744
Toll-Free: 866-575-9928
info@bcfca.com
www.bcfca.com
Overview: A small provincial organization overseen by National Floor Covering Association
Mission: To communicate standards & codes to its members & to encourage industry development by offering training seminars & disseminating current information related to the industry; to act as the public voice of the provincial floor covering industry, & lobbies on its behalf.
Chief Officer(s):
Scott Rust, President
Membership: 140; *Fees:* $550 dealers; $650 distributors; *Member Profile:* Manufacturers, distributors, retail stores, installers of flooring products; *Committees:* Grievance; Social; Membership; Education

British Columbia Folklore Society (BCFS)
7345 Seabrook Rd., Central Saanich BC V8M 1M9
Tel: 250-652-7614
info@folklore.bc.ca
www.folklore.bc.ca
Overview: A small provincial charitable organization founded in 1994
Mission: To collect and preserve the traditional and contemporary folklife and folklore of the people of British Columbia.
Member of: BC Heritage Society
Activities: *Library:* British Columbia Folklore Society Reference Library; by appointment

British Columbia Food Technolgists (BCTF)
c/o Nilmini Wijewickreme, SGS Canada, 50-655 West Kent Ave. North, Vancouver BC V6P 6T7
Other Communication: membership@bcft.ca; employment@bcft.ca
info@bcft.ca
www.bcft.ca
www.facebook.com/group.php?gid=180485308680605
twitter.com/bcfoodtech
Overview: A small provincial organization overseen by Canadian Institute of Food Science & Technology
Mission: To advance food science & technology in British Columbia
Member of: Canadian Institute of Food Science & Technology; Institute of Food Technologists
Affiliation(s): Packaging Association of British Columbia; British Columbia Food Protection Association; British Columbia Nutraceutical Network
Chief Officer(s):
Reena Mistry, Chair
chair@bcft.ca
Jenny Li, Secretary
jli@shafer-haggart.com
Thu Pham, Treasurer
Erin Friesen, Chair, Membership
membership@bcft.ca
Peter Taylor, Chair, Program, Banquet, & Suppliers' Night Committee
taylor58@telus.net
Nilmini Wijewickreme, Chair, Advertising
nilmini_wijewickreme@sgs.com
Membership: *Member Profile:* Scientists & technologists from government, academia, & industry; *Committees:* Advertising; Banquet; Membership; Program
Activities: Engaging in advocacy activities; Offering networking opportunities
Meetings/Conferences: • British Columbia Food Technologists 2015 Annual Suppliers' Night, February, 2015, Delta Burnaby Hotel & Conference Centre, Burnaby, BC
Scope: Provincial
Description: A learning event featuring over 100 supplier exhibits of interest to food scientists, research & development technologists, & senior managers & purchasers from food & beverage companies
Contact Information: Chair, Program Committee: Emilie Le Bihan, E-mail: elebihan@metaromneotech.com
• British Columbia Food Technologists 2015 Annual Speaker's Night, 2015
Scope: Provincial
Publications:
• Tech Talk: The British Columbia Food Technolgists Newsletter
Type: Newsletter; *Frequency:* Monthly; *Accepts Advertising*; *Editor:* Brian Jang; *Price:* Free with membership in British Columbia Food Technolgists
Profile: Association information, meetings, & food-related activities on the local & international scene, for persons involved in areas suchas food processing, research, product development, quality control, sales, & management

British Columbia Freedom of Information & Privacy Association (FIPA-BC)
#103, 1093 West Broadway, Vancouver BC V6H 1E2
Tel: 604-739-9788
fipa@fipa.bc.ca
www.fipa.bc.ca
twitter.com/bcfipa
Overview: A small provincial organization founded in 1990
Mission: To defend & improve public access to information in a world where quality of information & speed of access equals power; to defend personal privacy in a world where our personal information travels at the speed of light & its use is increasingly beyond our control
Chief Officer(s):
Richard Rosenberg, President
Vincent Gogolek, Executive Director
Staff Member(s): 2; 10 volunteer(s)
Membership: 150; *Fees:* $10 student/senior; $25 individual; $250 organization
Activities: Law reform; public legal education; public assistance; legal & policy research; legal & administrative interventions; legislation; freedom of information & privacy awards/seminars; *Speaker Service:* Yes; *Library* by appointment
Awards:
• Freedom of Information & Privacy Awards (Award)
Publications:
• The Privacy Handbook: A practical Guide to Your Privacy Rights in British Columbia and How to Protect Them
Number of Pages: 183; *Price:* $15

British Columbia Fruit Growers' Association
1473 Water St., Kelowna BC V1Y 1J6
Tel: 250-762-5226; *Fax:* 250-861-9089
info@bcfga.com
www.bcfga.com
www.facebook.com/pages/BC-Fruit-Growers-Association/208331935875260
Overview: A medium-sized provincial organization

Mission: To represent fruit growers' interests in British Columbia
Chief Officer(s):
Joe Sardinha, President
Membership: *Member Profile:* Fruit growers in British Columbia
Activities: Lobbying the government for positive change to risk management programs, such as crop insurance & the Net Income Stablization Program; Providing services & products to growers
Meetings/Conferences: • BC Fruit Growers Association 126th Annual General Meeting 2015, February, 2015, Penticton, BC
Scope: Provincial
Contact Information: info@bcfga.com

British Columbia Fuchsia & Begonia Society
c/o #17, 910 Fort Fraser Rise, Port Coquitlam BC V3C 6K3
e-mail: info@bcfuchsiasociety.com
www.bcfuchsiasociety.com
Overview: A small provincial organization founded in 1961
Mission: The Society encourages the cultivation & promotion of fuchsias, begonias, ferns, gesneriads & all other shade-loving plants.
Member of: BC Council of Garden Clubs
Chief Officer(s):
Fran Carter, President
fccarter@hotmail.ca
Lorna Herchenson, Int'l Corresponding Secretary
lherchenson@telus.net
Finances: *Annual Operating Budget:* Less than $50,000; *Funding Sources:* Membership dues; plant sales; raffles
185 volunteer(s)
Membership: 185; *Fees:* $20 single; $25 family
Activities: Meetings; workshops; plant sales; speaking to the community & other garden clubs; *Awareness Events:* Annual Show & Competition; *Speaker Service:* Yes

British Columbia Funeral Association (BCFA)
#211, 2187 Oak Bay Ave., Victoria BC V8R 1G1
Tel: 250-592-3213; *Fax:* 250-592-4362
Toll-Free: 800-665-3899
info@bcfunerals.com
www.bcfunerals.com
Also Known As: BC Funeral Association
Overview: A medium-sized provincial organization founded in 1912
Mission: To promote, through education, communication, & leadership, the highest standards of ethics & service in the funeral profession
Chief Officer(s):
Ryan McLane, President
Finances: *Funding Sources:* Membership dues; Sponsorships
Membership: *Member Profile:* Licensed funeral providers
Activities: Liaising with government representatives about legislation, regulations, & policies; Providing a province-wide toll-free line for information & referral; Offering continuing education programs; Organizing conferences & seminars; Providing Funeral Service Apprenticeship Training for British Columbia; Increasing public awareness;
Meetings/Conferences: • 2015 BC Funeral Association Exhibitors' Showcase and Conference, April, 2015, Delta Grand Okanagan Resort & Conference Centre, Okanagan, BC
Scope: Provincial

British Columbia Games Society *See* BC Games Society

British Columbia Genealogical Society (BCGS)
PO Box 88054, Stn. Lansdowne Mall, Richmond BC V6X 3T6
Tel: 604-502-9119; *Fax:* 604-502-9119
bcgs@bcgs.ca
www.bcgs.ca
Overview: A medium-sized provincial charitable organization founded in 1971
Mission: To perpetuate the heritage of BC; to collect, preserve & publish material relevant to promotion of ethical principles, scientific methods & effective techniques in genealogical & historical research
Member of: Canadian Federation of Genealogical & Family History Societies
Affliation(s): Richmond Heritage
Chief Officer(s):
Lorraine Irving, President
Finances: *Annual Operating Budget:* Less than $50,000; *Funding Sources:* Membership dues; donations; miscellaneous fundraising
50 volunteer(s)
Membership: 650+; *Fees:* $45 indivdual; $10 family associate; $22.50 student; $45 Affiliate society; *Member Profile:* Individuals interested in genealogy & related fields of local history, biography, heraldry & other aspects of historical research; *Committees:* British Columbia Research; Publications
Activities: Records of BC cemeteries; publishes & sells transcripts; exchange of journals with other societies all over the world; research of various countries; *Library:* BCGS Walter Draycott Library & Resource Centre; Open to public

British Columbia Golf Association (BCGA)
#2110, 13700 Mayfield Pl., Richmond BC V6V 2E4
Tel: 604-279-2580; *Fax:* 604-207-9535
Toll-Free: 888-833-2242
info@britishcolumbiagolf.org
www.britishcolumbiagolf.org
www.facebook.com/BritishColumbiaGolf
twitter.com/bc_golfer
Also Known As: British Columbia Golf
Overview: A large provincial licensing organization founded in 1922 overseen by Royal Canadian Golf Association
Mission: To promote interest in golf in BC; To protect the mutual interests of member clubs & their members; To establish & enforce uniformity in the rules of the game; To establish, control, & conduct amateur championships, matches & competitions; To interest & develop junior golfers; To select all teams to represent BC in national & international matches
Affliation(s): Canadian Golf Foundation; Professional Golf Association of BC; Canadian Ladies Golf Association of BC; Golf Course Superintendents Association of BC; International Association of Golf Administrators; National Golf Foundation; Pacific Coast Golf Association; Pacific Northwest Golf Association
Chief Officer(s):
Kris Jonasson, Executive Director
kris@britishcolumbiagolf.org
Deborah Pyne, Managing Director, Player Development
debbie@britishcolumbiagolf.org
Andy Fung, Director, Finance & Administration
andy@britishcolumbiagolf.org
Kathy Gook, Director, School Golf
kathy@britishcolumbiagolf.org
Shirley Simmons-Doyle, Manager, Membership
shirley@britishcolumbiagolf.org
Finances: *Funding Sources:* Government; Sponsorship; Membership
Staff Member(s): 10
Membership: *Fees:* $46
Activities: *Rents Mailing List:* Yes; *Library* Open to public

British Columbia Golf Superintendents Association (BCGSA)
PO Box 807, Lake Cowichan BC V0R 2G0
Tel: 250-749-6703; *Fax:* 250-749-6702
admin@bcgsa.com
www.bcgsa.com
Overview: A small provincial organization founded in 1995
Mission: To promote the professional recognition of golf course superintendents; To uphold the association's code of ethics
Chief Officer(s):
Ginny Tromp, Executive Administrator
Dean Piller, President, 250-658-4445
dpiller@telus.net
Mike Ferdinandi, Secretary/Treasurer
mike.ferdinandi@vancouver.ca
Membership: 300+; *Member Profile:* Turfgrass professionals involved in golf course maintenance & the science of turf management
Activities: Participating in turfgrass research; Exchanging knowledge related to golf course care; Sponsoring educational opportunities to benefit members
Publications:
• BCGSA Newsletter
Type: Newsletter

British Columbia Government & Service Employees' Union (BCGEU) / Syndicat des fonctionnaires provinciaux et de service de la Colombie-Britannique
4911 Canada Way, Burnaby BC V5G 3W3
Tel: 604-291-9611; *Fax:* 604-291-6030
Toll-Free: 800-663-1674
www.bcgeu.ca
Previous Name: British Columbia Government Employees' Union
Overview: A medium-sized provincial organization
Member of: National Union of Public and General Employees
Affliation(s): BC Federation of Labour; Canadian Labour Congress
Chief Officer(s):
Judi Filion, Treasurer
Darryl Walker, President
Finances: *Annual Operating Budget:* Greater than $5 Million; *Funding Sources:* Membership dues
Staff Member(s): 170
Membership: 67,000; *Member Profile:* Persons who work in direct government services, including the protection of children, the provision of financial assistance to the poor, the protection of the environment, the management of natural resources, the care of the mentally ill in institutions, the staffing of provincial correctional facilities, the fighting of forest fires, & the provision of the government's technical & clerical services

British Columbia Government Employees' Union *See* British Columbia Government & Service Employees' Union

British Columbia Grapegrowers' Association (BCGA)
451 Atwood Rd., Grand Forks BC V0H 1H9
Tel: 877-762-4652; *Fax:* 250-442-4076
Toll-Free: 877-762-4652
www.grapegrowers.bc.ca
Previous Name: Association of British Columbia Grape Growers
Overview: A medium-sized provincial organization founded in 1960
Mission: The Association represents all commercial Columbia on agricultural issues and concerns. It works with other industry organizations, with procincial and federal agricultural organizations and all levels of government to represent, promote and advance the interests of all grapegrowers in British Columbia.
Chief Officer(s):
Manfred Freese, President
Finances: *Annual Operating Budget:* Less than $50,000; *Funding Sources:* Membership dues
Staff Member(s): 1; 10 volunteer(s)
Membership: 250; *Fees:* $150 minimum; *Committees:* Viticulture; Crop Insurance

British Columbia Ground Water Association (BCGWA)
1708 - 197A St., Langley BC V2Z 1K2
Tel: 604-530-8934; *Fax:* 604-530-8934
secretary@bcgwa.org
www.bcgwa.org
Overview: A small provincial organization overseen by Canadian Ground Water Association
Affliation(s): Canadian Ground Water Association
Chief Officer(s):
Joan Perry, Secretary
Staff Member(s): 2
Membership: *Member Profile:* Corporations that employ persons who work in water well contracting, manufacturing, or supplying materials & equipment; Individuals employed by a company or who belong to an association affiliated with the ground water industry
Activities: Offering workshops & seminars; Promoting research & standards in water well construction; Liaising with government agencies
Publications:
• British Columbia Ground Water Association Newsletter
Type: Newsletter; *Frequency:* Quarterly

British Columbia Hang Gliding & Paragliding Association (BCHPA)
BC
www.bchpa.ca
Previous Name: Hang Gliding Association of British Columbia
Overview: A small provincial organization
Mission: To protect, maintain & improve flying sites throughout the province.
Chief Officer(s):
Margit Nance, President
margitnance@show.ca

British Columbia Herb Growers Association (BCHGA)
998 Skeena Dr., Kelowna BC V1V 2K7
Tel: 604-824-2833
Overview: A small provincial organization founded in 1997
Mission: To promote & enhance herb growing in British Columbia; To represent herb growers
Finances: *Funding Sources:* Sponsorships
Membership: 50; *Fees:* $50 individuals; $75 foreign memberships; $125 corporations; *Member Profile:* Individuals &

corporations involved in the herb business, such asresearchers, educators, growers, manufacturers, processors, buyers, distributors, retailers, & service providers
Activities: Facilitating research; Providing networking opportunities; Offering market information; Organizing workshops; Supporting herb marketing
Publications:
• BCHGA [British Columbia Herb Growers Association] Newsletter
Type: Newsletter; *Frequency:* Quarterly; *Accepts Advertising*
Profile: Upcoming meetings, trade shows, & educational opportunities, association reports, & articles
• British Columbia Herb Growers Association Annual Report
Type: Yearbook; *Frequency:* Annually
• British Columbia Herb Growers Association Directory
Type: Directory
Profile: Listing of association members with contact information

British Columbia Hereford Association (BCHA)
c/o Vic Redekop, 25440 - 16th Ave., Aldergrove BC V4W 2R7
Tel: 250-557-4348; *Fax:* 250-557-4468
www.bchereford.ca
Overview: A small provincial organization founded in 1921
Mission: To produce Hereford seedstock to meet the demands of the commercial cattle industry
Chief Officer(s):
Daryl Kirton, President
3-d-l@telus.net
Darlene Borrow, Secretary
dborrow@xplornet.com
Membership: 170; *Member Profile:* Purebred Hereford breeders in British Columbia
Activities: Organizing field days, shows, & sales; *Awareness Events:* Hereford Week In Canada, August
Publications:
• BC Bulletin
Type: Newsletter

British Columbia Heritage Party *See* Christian Heritage Party of British Columbia

British Columbia Historical Federation (BCHF)
PO Box 5254, Stn. B, Victoria BC V8R 6N4
e-mail: info@bchistory.ca
www.bchistory.ca
Overview: A medium-sized provincial charitable organization founded in 1922
Mission: To offer assistance to writers of BC history; to disburse loans for publishing to members only; to offer a scholarship for undergraduate history major; to sponsor an annual competition for writers of BC history; to stimulate public interest & to encourage historical research in BC history
Member of: Heritage Council of British Columbia
Chief Officer(s):
Barb Hynek, President, 604-535-9090
president@bchistory.ca
Jean Wilson, Secretary, 604-222-2230
secretary@bchistory.ca
Kerri Gibson, Treasurer, 250-386-3405, Fax: 250-361-3188
treasurer@bchistory.ca
Finances: *Annual Operating Budget:* Less than $50,000; *Funding Sources:* Individual societies - Heritage Trust of BC
100+ volunteer(s)
Membership: 134 member societies, 40 affiliate members, 218 associate members, 6 corporate members; *Fees:* $25-$75; *Member Profile:* Historic societies; Museums; Archives; Historic sites; *Committees:* Writing Competition; Scholarship; Historic Trails & Sites; Publications Assistance
Awards:
• Lieutenant-Governor's Medal for Historical Writing (Award)
Established 1983; Lieutenant-Governor's Medal for Historical Writing, three Certificates of Merit, & cash awards given annually to authors of best books on any facet of BC history*Eligibility:* Book about B.C. history, published within the competition year*Deadline:* December 31 *Amount:* $600 *Contact:* William R. Morrison
• W. Kaye Lamb Essay Scholarships (Scholarship)
Essay must be between 1500 and 5000 words, on a topic related to B.C. history*Eligibility:* Essay written by a student registered in university/college in B.C. *Amount:* $750-1000
Contact: Marie Elliot
• Anne & Philip Yandle Best Article Award (Award)
Eligibility: Article that has appeared in the journal "British Columbia History" *Amount:* $250
• Historic Website Competition (Award)
The site must have existed for 12 months or more before the competition & be currently active*Eligibility:* Volunteer work in creating a website about B.C. history*Deadline:* December 31 *Amount:* $250
Meetings/Conferences: • British Columbia Historical Federation 2015 Conference: Journey to the Cariboo, May, 2015, Quesnel, BC
Scope: Provincial
Description: Informative lectures & presentations by local historians

British Columbia Hog Marketing Commission
PO Box 8000-280, Abbotsford BC V2S 6H1
Tel: 604-287-4647; *Fax:* 604-820-6647
info@bcpork.ca
bcpork.ca
Also Known As: BC Pork
Overview: A small provincial organization founded in 1980
Chief Officer(s):
Geraldine Auston, Contact

British Columbia Honey Producers Association (BCHPA)
PO Box 1650, Comox BC V9M 8A2
www.bcbeekeepers.com
Overview: A small provincial organization founded in 1920
Mission: To promote the keeping of bees in British Columbia, using the most suitable methods; To represent the interest of beekeepers in British Columbia
Member of: Canadian Honey Council
Finances: *Funding Sources:* Membership fees; Donations
Membership: *Fees:* $40, 0-25 hives; $50, 26-50 hives; $60, 51-150 hives; $70, 151-300 hives; $120, 301-500 hives; $130, 501-1,000 hives; $200, more than 1,000 hives; *Member Profile:* Honey producers in British Columbia
Activities: Engaging in advocacy activities; Liaising with both the provincial & federal government & the media; Providing education & information, through symposiums & the association website; Offering group liability insurance; Educating the public, through instructional programs & exhibitions; Facilitating networking opportunities for infomation exchange
Meetings/Conferences: • British Columbia Honey Producers 2015 Annual General Meeting, Convention & Trade Show, October, 2015, Courtney, BC
Scope: Provincial
Publications:
• BeesCene
Type: Newsletter; *Frequency:* Quarterly; *Price:* Free with membership in the British Columbia Honey Producers Association

British Columbia Hospice Palliative Care Association (BCHPCA)
#1100, 1200 West 73rd Ave., Vancouver BC V6P 6G5
Tel: 604-267-7026; *Fax:* 604-267-7026
Toll-Free: 877-410-6297
office@hospicebc.org
www.bchpca.org
www.facebook.com/group.php?gid=220848977957203
twitter.com/BCHPCA
Overview: A medium-sized provincial charitable organization
Mission: To ensure the quality of life for all British Columbians affected by life-limiting illness, death, & bereavement; To act as a collective voice in British Columbia, advocating for hospice palliative care at all levels
Member of: Canadian Hospice Palliative Care Association
Chief Officer(s):
Carolyn Marshall, President
sleepydoc@telus.net
Barb Henham, Treasurer
barb.henham@crossroadshospice.bc.ca
Finances: *Annual Operating Budget:* $250,000-$500,000; *Funding Sources:* Grants
Membership: 100-499; *Fees:* Schedule available based on an organization's annual budget; *Member Profile:* Member organizations & individuals from British Columbia & the Yukon provide a range of services to patients, families, caregivers, & communities.
Activities: Encouraging the study of hospice & palliative care & providing educational resources; Increasing public awareness & support of programs; Promoting recognized standards of care; Providing communication networks;
Awards:
• British Columbia Hospice Palliative Care Association Award of Excellence (Award)
To honour achievement in the field of hospice palliative care in British Columbia, in either a paid or volunteer position*Deadline:* April
• British Columbia Hospice Palliative Care Association Research Prize in Honour of Michael Downing (Award)
• Awards Recognizing Enhanced End-of-Life Care for British Columbians (Award)
Funded by the Sovereign Order of St. John of Jerusalem, Knights Hospitaller, & administered by the British Columbia Hospice Palliative Care Association*Deadline:* April *Amount:* $5,000
• British Columbia Hospice Palliative Care Association Volunteer Award in Recognition of Shara-Lee (Award)
To recognize personal achievements of volunteers working in the field of hospice palliative care in British Columbia*Deadline:* April
Meetings/Conferences: • British Columbia Hospice Palliative Care Association 2015 Conference, 2015, BC
Scope: Provincial
Description: An annual meeting of members, with guest speakers, exhibits, regional meetings, the presentation of awards, & networking sessions
Contact Information: E-mail: office@hospicebc.org
Publications:
• British Columbia Hospice Palliative Care Association Facilitators Guide
Type: Guide
• British Columbia Hospice Palliative Care Association Annual Report
Type: Yearbook; *Frequency:* Annually
Profile: The year's happenings
• Full Circle: The Voice of Hospice Palliative Care in British Columbia
Type: Newsletter
Profile: Issues related to hospice palliative care & the activities of the British Columbia Hospice Palliative Care Association

British Columbia Hotel Association (BCHA)
#200, 948 Howe St., Vancouver BC V6Z 1N9
Tel: 604-681-7164; *Fax:* 604-681-7649
Toll-Free: 800-663-3153
www.bchotelassociation.com
twitter.com/bchotelassoc
Overview: A small provincial organization founded in 1917
Mission: To promote excellence & professionalism in the accommodation & hospitality industry of British Columbia; To advocate for the interests of British Columbia's hotel industry; To improve & increase the tourism & hospitality industry in British Columbia; To enhance the financial viability of members
Chief Officer(s):
David Wetsch, President
Al McCreary, Treasurer
James Chase, Chief Executive Officer
james@bchotelassociation.com
Cailey Murphy, Coordinator, Communications, 604-443-4751
cailey@bchotelassociation.com
Louise Thompson, Coordinator, Member Services
Membership: 650 hotel members + 200 associate members
Activities: Providing educational & training opportunities; Offering marketing services; Liaising with government organizations & regulatory authorities; Recommending improvements in law
Publications:
• InnFocus
Type: Magazine; *Frequency:* Quarterly; *Accepts Advertising*; *Editor:* Cailey Murphy
Profile: Feature articles about British Columbia's hotel industry, plus association reports
• InnTouch
Type: Newsletter; *Frequency:* Bi-weekly; *Editor:* Cailey Murphy
Profile: Current information about British Columbia's hospitality industry

British Columbia Human Resources Management Association (BC HRMA)
#1101, 1111 West Hastings St., Vancouver BC V5E 2J3
Tel: 604-684-7228; *Fax:* 604-684-3225
Toll-Free: 800-665-1961
Other Communication: hrma@bchrma.org
info@bchrma.org
www.bchrma.org
www.linkedin.com/company/bc-human-resources-management-association
www.facebook.com/BCHRMA
twitter.com/BCHRMA
Overview: A medium-sized provincial organization founded in 1942

Mission: To uphold industry standards; To advance professional people practices
Member of: Canadian Council of Human Resource Associations
Chief Officer(s):
Mike Cass, President
hrma@bchrma.org
Simon Evans, CEO, 604-694-6937
sevans@bchrma.org
Ian J. Cook, Director, Research & Learning, 604-694-6938
ijcook@bchrma.org
Staff Member(s): 26
Membership: 4,000+; *Fees:* $380 general; $60 student plus provincial tax, where applicable; 65.00 plus provincial tax, where applicable, outside B.C.; *Member Profile:* Members include CEOs, directors of human resources, consultants, educators, students, human resources generalists, & small-business owners; *Committees:* Awards; CHRP Audit; Recertification; Conference Steering.
Activities: Providing human resources information & services; Partnering with post-secondary academic institutions & education providers; Providing networking opportunities
Awards:
• Rising Star Award (Award)
For HR practitioners within the first five years of their career
• Award of Excellence (Award)
BC HRMA's highest honour for established HR practitioners
• BC HRMA Annual Scholarships (Scholarship)
Three scholarships awarded annually to one student enrolled at each of the following three schools: BCIT, SFU, & UBC
Meetings/Conferences: • British Columbia Human Resources Management Association 2015 53rd Annual Conference & Tradeshow, April, 2015, Vancouver Convention Centre, Vancouver, BC
Scope: Provincial
Description: A human resources professional development event, with guest speakers, educational sessions, exhibits, the presentation of awards, & networking events
Contact Information: Manager, Conference & Events: Erin Roddie, Phone: 604-694-6933, E-mail: eroddie@hrma.ca
Publications:
• PeopleTalk
Type: Magazine; *Frequency:* Weekly; *Accepts Advertising*
Profile: Each issue focuses on a topical human resources theme, plus labour relations, books & websites, health & wellness, CHRP certification, international news, & technology services for humanresources

British Columbia Human Rights Coalition (BCHRC)
#1202, 510 West Hastings St., Vancouver BC V6B 1L8
Tel: 604-689-8474; *Fax:* 604-689-7511
Toll-Free: 877-689-8474
info@bchrcoalition.org
www.bchrcoalition.org
Overview: A small provincial organization
Mission: Promotes and strengthens human rights throughout BC and Canada.
Finances: *Annual Operating Budget:* Less than $50,000
4 volunteer(s)
Membership: 100+; *Fees:* $20
Activities: *Internships:* Yes; *Speaker Service:* Yes
Awards:
• Renate Shearer Award

British Columbia Industrial Designer Association (BCID)
PO Box 33943, Vancouver BC V6J 4L7
Tel: 604-608-3204; *Fax:* 604-608-3204
email@bcid.com
www.bcid.com
Overview: A small provincial organization overseen by Association Of Canadian Industrial Designers
Mission: To act as the public voice for its members; to represent their interests nationally; to maintain a set of standards to preserve the integrity of the profession; to keep a register of professional industrial designers in the province.
Membership: *Member Profile:* Available to any permanent, legal resident of B.C., Alberta, or Sask. who has obtained at least an undergraduate degree, with a major in industrial design, and whose primary professional responsibility as a practioner or educator is with industrial design.

British Columbia Insolvency Practitioners Association *See* British Columbia Association of Insolvency & Restructuring Professionals

British Columbia Institute Against Family Violence (BCIFV)
74640 Kitsilano RPO, Vancouver BC V6K 4P4
Tel: 604-669-7055; *Fax:* 604-669-7054
Toll-Free: 877-755-7055
resource@bcifv.org
www.bcifv.org
Previous Name: BC Institute on Family Violence
Overview: A small provincial charitable organization founded in 1989
Mission: To work to eliminate family violence through public awareness; education for professionals; research; assisting community organizations & developing & distributing information
Finances: *Annual Operating Budget:* $250,000-$500,000
Staff Member(s): 5
Membership: 13; *Fees:* $40
Activities: Prevention education; information & referral research; training; conferences; publications; resource centre; *Library* Open to public

British Columbia Institute of Agrologists (BCIA)
2777 Claude Rd., Victoria BC V9B 3T7
Tel: 250-380-9292; *Fax:* 250-380-9233
Toll-Free: 877-855-9291
p.ag@bcia.com
www.bcia.com
Overview: A medium-sized provincial licensing organization founded in 1947 overseen by Agricultural Institute of Canada
Chief Officer(s):
Kelly McLaughlin, Financial Officer
Robert Moody, Executive Director
Finances: *Annual Operating Budget:* $250,000-$500,000; *Funding Sources:* Membership dues
Staff Member(s): 2; 20 volunteer(s)
Membership: 950; *Fees:* $150; *Member Profile:* Professional agrologists
Activities: *Internships:* Yes
Meetings/Conferences: • British Columbia Institute of Agrologists 68th Annual General Meeting & Conference 2015, May, 2015, Coast Capri Hotel & Laurel Packinghouse, Kelowna, BC
Scope: Provincial

British Columbia Institute of Technology Faculty & Staff Association (BCIT FSA)
#SE16-116, 3700 Willingdon Ave., Burnaby BC V5G 3H2
Tel: 604-432-8695; *Fax:* 604-432-8348
fsa@bcit.ca
www.bcitfsa.ca
Overview: A medium-sized provincial organization founded in 1974
Mission: To defend & advance the employment interests of members, through representation; To improve employment conditions for members
Chief Officer(s):
Paul Reniers, Executive Director, 604-432-8696
Paul_Reniers@bcit.ca
Amy Fell, President, 604-432-8569
Amy_Fell@bcit.ca
Activities: Engaging in collective bargaining & advocacy activities; Liaising with government & the community; Promoting the association & its members
Publications:
• British Columbia Institute of Technology Faculty & Staff Association Newsletter
Type: Newsletter
Profile: Association reports & activities, plus articles about employment issues

British Columbia Institute of the Purchasing Management Association of Canada *See* Supply Chain Management Association - British Columbia

British Columbia Interior Bison Association *See* British Columbia Bison Association

British Columbia International Commercial Arbitration Centre (BCICAC)
#348, 1275 West 6th Ave., Vancouver BC V6H 1A6
Tel: 604-684-2821; *Fax:* 604-736-9233
Toll-Free: 877-684-2821
admin@bcicac.com
www.bcicac.com
Overview: A medium-sized international organization founded in 1986
Mission: To provide effective alternative dispute resolution services to our clients
Chief Officer(s):
Patrick Williams, President & Director
Membership: *Member Profile:* Arbitrators & mediators

British Columbia Investment Agriculture Foundation (IAF)
PO Box 8248, 808 Douglas Victoria, 3rd Fl., Victoria BC V8W 2Z7
Tel: 250-356-1662; *Fax:* 250-953-5162
Other Communication: Funding Inquiries e-mail: funding@iafbc.ca
info@iafbc.ca
www.iafbc.ca
Also Known As: Investment Agriculture Foundation of BC
Overview: A medium-sized provincial organization founded in 1996
Mission: To encourage growth & innovation in the agriculture & agri-food industry across British Columbia
Chief Officer(s):
Peter Levelton, Chair
Peter Donkers, Executive Director, 250-356-6654
pdonkers@iafbc.ca
Finances: *Funding Sources:* Federal & provincial government
Awards:
• Award of Excellence for Innovation in Agriculture & Agri-Food (Award)
Publications:
• Growing Tomorrow [a publication of British Columbia Investment Agriculture Foundation]
Type: Newsletter; *Frequency:* 3 pa

British Columbia Katahdin Sheep Association
c/o Christopher & Christine Page, Venner Brook Farm, 9166 Chemainus Rd., Chemainus BC V0R 1K0
Tel: 250-246-4140
vennerbrookfarm@hotmail.com
www.katahdinsheep.com
Overview: A small provincial organization overseen by Canadian Katahdin Sheep Association Inc.
Mission: To develop British Columbia's Katahdin sheep industry
Chief Officer(s):
Hans Bissig, Contact, 250-428-3365
bissigl@hotmail.com
Membership: 1-99; *Member Profile:* Katahdin sheep breeders in British Columbia

British Columbia Landscape & Nursery Association (BCLNA)
#102, 5783 - 176A St., Surrey BC V3S 6S6
Tel: 604-575-3500; *Fax:* 604-574-7773
Toll-Free: 800-421-7963
www.bclna.com
www.linkedin.com/groups?home=&gid=2387526&trk=anet_ug_hm
www.facebook.com/bclna
twitter.com/bclna
Previous Name: British Columbia Nursery Trades Association
Overview: A medium-sized provincial organization founded in 1953 overseen by Canadian Nursery Landscape Association
Mission: To work together to improve quality & standards of the industry
Member of: BC Agriculture Council
Chief Officer(s):
Lesley Tannen, Executive Director
ltannen@bclna.com
Finances: *Annual Operating Budget:* $1.5 Million-$3 Million; *Funding Sources:* Membership dues; CanWest Horticultural Show
Staff Member(s): 10
Membership: 800; *Fees:* $370-$980, based on gross sales; *Member Profile:* Nurserymen, garden centre operators, landscape & maintenance contractors, sod growers, arborists & suppliers from across British Columbia
Activities: Educational seminars; certification programs

British Columbia Law Institute (BCLI)
University of British Columbia, 1822 East Mall, Vancouver BC V6T 1Z1
Tel: 604-822-0142; *Fax:* 604-822-0144
Toll-Free: 800-565-5297
bcli@bcli.org
www.bcli.org
Overview: A small provincial organization founded in 1997
Mission: A not-for-profit law reform agency that performs research & studies to change & modernize British Columbian law.
Chief Officer(s):

D. Peter Ramsay, Q.C., Chair
R.C. (Tino) DiBella, Vice-Chair
W. James Emmerton, Executive Director, 604-822-0145
jemmerton@bcli.org
Krista James, National Director, 604-822-0564
kjames@bcli.org
Staff Member(s): 4
Activities: *Awareness Events:* GREATdebate

British Columbia Liberal Party

PO Box 21014, Stn. Waterfront Ctr., Vancouver BC V6C 3K3
Tel: 604-606-6000; *Fax:* 604-632-0253
Toll-Free: 800-567-2257
contact@bcliberals.com
www.bcliberals.com
www.facebook.com/ChristyClarkForBC
twitter.com/christyclarkbc
www.youtube.com/user/BCLiberals
Also Known As: BC Liberal Party
Overview: A small provincial organization
Chief Officer(s):
Sharon White, Party President
Christy Clark, Leader of the Party

British Columbia Libertarian Party (BCLP)

#703, 1180 Falcon Dr., Coquitlam BC V3E 2K7
Tel: 604-944-2845
info@libertarian.bc.ca
www.libertarian.bc.ca
Overview: A small provincial organization founded in 1986 overseen by The Libertarian Party of Canada
Mission: BCLP holds the principle that no individual or group shall initiate the use of force or fraud against any other, as a means of achieving political or social gains. It also holds that owning private property is essential to the preservation of human liberty. The Party advocates drug legalization, the end of coercive taxation, & works to elect candidates to the BC Legislature.
Affliation(s): Foundation for Research on Economics & the Environment
Chief Officer(s):
Paul Geddes, President
gedswest@shaw.ca
Membership: *Fees:* $5
Activities: *Speaker Service:* Yes

British Columbia Library Association (BCLA)

#150, 900 Howe St., Vancouver BC V6Z 2M4
Tel: 604-683-5354; *Fax:* 604-609-0707
Toll-Free: 888-683-5354
office@bcla.bc.ca
www.bcla.bc.ca
twitter.com/bclibassoc
Overview: A large provincial licensing charitable organization founded in 1911
Mission: To encourage library development throughout British Columbia; To coordinate library services to various parts of the province; To promote cooperation between libraries; To advance the mutual interests of libraries & library personnel
Chief Officer(s):
Annette DeFaveri, Executive Director
execdir@bcla.bc.ca
Gwen Bird, President
Heather Buzzell, Vice-President/President Elect
Myron Groover, Second Vice-President
Carla Graebner, Treasurer
Allie Douglas, Office Manager
office@bcla.bc.ca
Finances: *Funding Sources:* Membership dues; Donations; Sponsorships
Membership: 700+; *Fees:* Schedule available; *Member Profile:* Individuals in the library profession in British Columbia; Library trustees; Supporters of libraries in British Columbia; Libraries; Governments; Companies & organizations providing products or services to libraries; *Committees:* Continuing Education; Copyright; Diversity & Multicultural Services; Fund Development; Information Policy; Intellectual Freedom; Resolutions; Interest Groups: Acquisitions & Collection Development; Cataloguing & Technical Services (BCCATS); First Nations; LGBTQ; Libraries Across Borders; Literacy; Public Librarians; Special Needs; Vancouver Island; Sections: Academic Librarians in Public Service; Library Technicians & Assistants; Young Adults & Children's
Activities: Coordinating projects to improve library services & information access; Providing workshops & seminars; Preparing briefs to government; Sponsoring scholarships & awards; Providing an online job posting service; Liaising with similar organizations across Canada; Co-hosting the British Columbia Library Conference, with the British Columbia Library Trustees' Association & the Health Libraries Association of British Columbia, featuring educational sessions, speakers, meetings, social events, & a trade show
Awards:
• Helen Gordon Stewart Award (Award)
Amount: Plaque; life membership in the association
• Honourary Life Membership (Award)
Amount: Plaque; life membership in the association
• Achievement in Library Service (Award)
Amount: Plaque
• Keith Sacré Library Champion Award (Award)
Amount: Invitation to awards banquet
• BCLA President's Award (Award)
• Merit Awards (Award)
• Ken Haycock Student Conference Award (Award)
Amount: $300; conference registration
• Alice Bacon Continuing Education Scholarship (Scholarship)
Amount: No less than $100
• Harry Newsom Memorial Award (Award)
Amount: Varies
• Virginia Chisholm Memorial Award (Award)
Amount: $250; basic conference registration
• Academic Librarians in Public Service Award for Outstanding Service (Award)
Amount: Plaque
• Young Adult & Children's Services Section Award (Award)
Amount: Plaque
Meetings/Conferences: • British Columbia Library Association 2015 Conference, May, 2015, Sheraton Vancouver Airport Hotel, Richmond, BC
Scope: Provincial
• British Columbia Library Association 2016 Conference, 2016, BC
Scope: Provincial
Publications:
• BCLA Browser: Linking the Library Landscape
Type: Newsletter; *Frequency:* Quarterly; *Editor:* Sandra Wong
Profile: Library news & information from British Columbia
• YAACING: Newsletter of the Young Adult & Children's Services Section of BCLA
Type: Newsletter; *Frequency:* Quarterly; *Editor:* April Ens; Alicia Cheng
Profile: Section's newsletter with information of interest to personnel in British Columbia who providelibrary services to youth; Available with membership in YAACS

British Columbia Library Trustees' Association (BCLTA)

432 - 3 St., Vancouver BC V3L 2S2
Tel: 604-913-1424; *Fax:* 604-913-1413
Toll-Free: 888-206-1245
admin@bclta.ca
www.bclta.org
www.facebook.com/392761817401045
twitter.com/BCLTA
Overview: A small provincial charitable organization founded in 1977
Mission: To develop & support library trustees who govern local public libraries in British Columbia; To advance public library service in the province
Affliation(s): British Columbia Library Association
Chief Officer(s):
Paul Tutsch, President
pjtutsch@telus.net
Peter Kafka, Vice-President
peterkafka@shaw.ca
Erfan Kazemi, Secretary-Treasurer
ekazemi@sandstormltd.com
Lauren Wolf, Executive Director
laurenwolf@bclta.ca
Finances: *Funding Sources:* Grants; Sponsorships
Staff Member(s): 2
Membership: 71 library boards, with 700+ library trustees; *Fees:* Institutional membership based upon annual operating expenditures; $100 associate membership; *Member Profile:* Institutional membership for library boards, featuring general membership privileges for each individual trustee; Associate membership for library systems or persons interested in libraries
Activities: Promoting literacy & library services; Engaging in advocacy activities; Liaising with the provincial government's Public Library Services Branch; Providing educational opportunities for members; Offering networking opportunities
Awards:
• Nancy Bennett Merit Award (Award)
• Super Trustee Award (Award)
• Library Advocate Award (Award)
Meetings/Conferences: • British Columbia Library Trustees' Association 2015 Annual General Meeting, 2015, BC
Scope: Provincial
Contact Information: Administrative Assistant, British Columbia Library Trustees' Association: Jan Thomas, Phone: 604-913-1424, Fax: 604-913-1413, E-mail: admin@bclta.ca
• British Columbia Library Trustees' Association 2015 Annual General Meeting, 2016
Scope: Provincial
Publications:
• BCLTA Bulletin
Type: Newsletter; *Price:* Free with British Columbia Library Trustees' Association membership
Profile: Current issues & events for trustees, plus BCLTA board activities & initiatives
• The Board Chair
Type: Handbook; *Price:* Free with British Columbia Library Trustees' Association membership
Profile: Educational resource for British Columbia public library board chairs
• British Columbia Library Trustees' Association Annual Report
Type: Yearbook; *Frequency:* Annually
• The Effective Board Member
Type: Handbook; *Price:* Free with British Columbia Library Trustees' Association membership
Profile: A British Columbia public library trustee educational resource
• Open Door
Type: Newsletter; *Frequency:* Semiannually; *Accepts Advertising*; *Price:* Free with British Columbia Library Trustees' Association membership
Profile: Updates on provincial & federal issues, trustee education programs, event announcements, resource reviews, & trustee contributions

British Columbia Lions Society for Children with Disabilities (BCLS)

3981 Oak St., Vancouver BC V6H 4H5
Tel: 604-873-1865; *Fax:* 604-873-0166
Toll-Free: 800-818-4483
info@lionsbc.ca
www.lionsbc.ca
www.facebook.com/125279254193295?fref=ts
twitter.com/LionsBC
Also Known As: Lions Society of BC; Easter Seals; BC Lions Foundation for Children with Disabilities
Overview: A large provincial charitable organization founded in 1952
Mission: To provide as many services as possible to children with disabilities; to enhance the lives of children with special needs; to continue building, not only specialized services & facilities, but challenging young hearts & minds as well; giving children with disabilities self-esteem, self-confidence & a sense of independence
Member of: Easter Seals Canada
Affliation(s): Easter Seal House Society; 24 HR Relay Society
Chief Officer(s):
Stephen J. Miller, President
Nirm Blatchford, Contact
nblatchford@lionsbc.ca
Finances: *Annual Operating Budget:* Greater than $5 Million; *Funding Sources:* Appeals & lotteries; events; donations from Lions Clubs; estates & gifts to societies; foundations
Staff Member(s): 36
Membership: 5,000-14,999
Activities: Camping Programs - three camps, to any child between the age of 6 & 18 with a disability, free of charge; Patient Care Grants - offers financial assistance for some medical treatments not covered by BC Med; Easter Seal Houses - three houses for families to stay while their sick child is in for medical treatment; *Awareness Events:* Snowarama, Jan.-April; Paper Eggs, March; 24-Hour Relay for the Kids, June; Drop-Zone, September; Scotiabank Easter Seals Regatta, July; Timmy's Christmas Telethon, December; *Rents Mailing List:* Yes

Victoria Office
2095 Granite St., Victoria BC V8S 3G5
Tel: 250-370-0518; *Fax:* 250-370-5098
Toll-Free: 888-868-2822
info@forthekidsbc.org

British Columbia Literacy Council (BCLCIRA)
c/o Sir Wilfred Grenfell Elementary School, 3323 Wellington Ave., Vancouver BC V5R 4Y3
Tel: 604-713-4844; *Fax:* 604-713-4846
www.readingbc.ca
Also Known As: Council No: CF300
Overview: A small provincial organization overseen by International Reading Association
Chief Officer(s):
Dianna Mezzarobba, Coordinator

British Columbia Lodging & Campgrounds Association (BCLCA)
#209, 3003 St. John's St., Port Moody BC V3H 2C4
Tel: 778-383-1037; *Fax:* 604-945-7606
www.bclca.com
www.facebook.com/TravellinginBritishColumbia
twitter.com/TravellinginBC
Previous Name: BC Motels, Campgrounds, Resorts Association
Overview: A medium-sized provincial organization founded in 1944
Mission: To promote the public's utilization of member lodging & campground businesses; to monitor & make representation to governments on legislation affecting the interests of British Columbia's lodging & campground businesses; to speak for the membership on matters of general or specific interest; to encourage members to strive for excellence in accommodation & service
Chief Officer(s):
Joss Penny, Executive Director
jpenny@bclca.com
Finances: *Annual Operating Budget:* $250,000-$500,000
Staff Member(s): 3
Membership: 625; *Fees:* $280; *Member Profile:* Motels; resorts; campgrounds
Activities: Marketing & promotion; group purchasing discounts; lobbying; education & industry standards

British Columbia Lung Association (BCLA)
2675 Oak St., Vancouver BC V6H 2K2
Tel: 604-731-5864; *Fax:* 604-731-5810
Toll-Free: 800-665-5864
info@bc.lung.ca
www.bc.lung.ca
www.facebook.com/home.php?#!/BCLungAssociation
Previous Name: Anti-Tuberculosis Society
Overview: A medium-sized provincial charitable organization founded in 1906 overseen by Canadian Lung Association
Mission: To support lung health research, education, prevention, & advocacy; To help people manage respiratory diseases, including asthma, COPD (chronic bronchitis and emphysema), lung cancer, sleep apnea, & tuberculosis
Chief Officer(s):
Scott McDonald, Executive Director
Kelly Ablog-Morrant, Director, Health Education & Program Services
Chris Lam, Manager, Development
Katrina van Bylandt, Manager, Communications
Debora Wong, Manager, Finance & Administration
Marissa McFadyen, Coordinator, Specia Events
Finances: *Funding Sources:* Donations; Sponsorships; Fundraising
Membership: *Committees:* Executive; Medical Advisory
Activities: Providing money to physicians & scientists doing research in British Columbia on lung diseases; Offering breathing test events; *Awareness Events:* The Stairclimb for Clean Air, February; The Bicycle Trek for Life & Breath, September
Meetings/Conferences: • British Columbia Lung Association 2015 12th Annual Air Quality & Health Workshop, 2015
Scope: Provincial
• British Columbia Lung Association 2015 Annual General Meeting, 2015, BC
Scope: Provincial
Description: An annual meeting to determine the association's direction during the coming year
Contact Information: Phone: 604-731-5864; Toll-Free Phone: 1-800-665-5864
Publications:
• British Columbia Lung Association Annual Report
Type: Yearbook; *Frequency:* Annually
• Your Health
Type: Magazine; *Frequency:* Semiannually; *Editor:* Katrina van Bylandt; Destin Haynes
Profile: Health information for medical & health promoters, educators, donors to the Lung Association, & persons interested in respiratory health

British Columbia Lupus Society (BCLS)
#329, 720 - 6th St., New Westminster BC V3L 5T9
Tel: 604-714-5564
Toll-Free: 866-585-8787
info@bclupus.org
www.bclupus.org
Also Known As: BC Lupus Society
Overview: A medium-sized provincial organization founded in 1978 overseen by Lupus Canada
Mission: To provide education & support to Lupus patients & their friends & families; to increase public awareness of lupus
Chief Officer(s):
Michael Hinman, President
Val Bishop, Office Administrator, 604-714-5564
val@bclupus.org
Finances: *Annual Operating Budget:* $50,000-$100,000
Staff Member(s): 1; 25 volunteer(s)
Membership: 400; *Fees:* $20 individual; $25 family
Activities: *Awareness Events:* Lupus Awareness Month, Oct.; World Lupus Day, May 10

British Columbia Mainland Cricket League (BCMCL)
PO Box 100, 12886 - 96th Ave., Surrey BC V3V 6A8
Fax: 604-909-2669
info@bcmcl.ca
www.bcmcl.org
www.facebook.com/129601080392424
twitter.com/bcmcl
www.youtube.com/thebcmcl
Previous Name: British Columbia Cricket Association
Overview: A small provincial organization overseen by Cricket Canada
Member of: Cricket Canada
Chief Officer(s):
Alex Turko, President, 778-229-7858
president@bcmcl.ca
Adnan Ali, Secretary

British Columbia Marijuana Party
303 Hastings St. West, Vancouver BC V6B 1H6
Tel: 604-632-1750
www.bcmarijuanaparty.com
Also Known As: BC Marijuana Party
Overview: A small provincial organization
Chief Officer(s):
Mark Emery, Party Leader
Publications:
• Cannabis Culture Magazine
Type: Magazine; *Frequency:* Every 2 months; *Editor:* Jeremiah Vandermeer

British Columbia Marine Trades Association (BCMTA)
#300, 1275 West 6th Ave., Vancouver BC V6H 1A6
Tel: 604-683-5191; *Fax:* 604-893-8808
info@bcmta.com
www.bcmta.com
Overview: A medium-sized provincial organization
Mission: To act as the voice of the BC recreational marine industry
Chief Officer(s):
Alan Stovell, President
stovell@westernmarine.com
Kim Barbero, Executive Director, 604-683-5191, Fax: 604-893-8808
kim@bcmta.com
Chris Goulder, Treasurer, 604-872-7511, Fax: 604-872-4606
christopher.goulder@volvo.com
Finances: *Annual Operating Budget:* $50,000-$100,000
Membership: 300 corporate; *Fees:* $295-395

British Columbia Maritime Employers Association (BCMEA)
349 Railway St., Vancouver BC V6A 1A4
Tel: 604-688-1155; *Fax:* 604-684-2397
www.bcmea.com
Overview: A medium-sized local organization founded in 1963
Chief Officer(s):
Andy Smith, President & Chief Executive Officer
John Beckett, Vice-President, Training, Safety, & Recruitment, 604-688-1155
jbeckett@bcmea.com
Terry Duggan, Vice-President, Finance & Secretary, 604-688-1155
tduggan@bcmea.com
Mike Leonard, Vice-President, Labour Relations, 604-688-1155 Ext. 513
mleonard@bcmea.com
Eleanor Marynuik, Vice-President, Human Resources, 614-688-1155 Ext. 511
emarynuik@bcmea.com
Greg Vurdela, Vice-President, Marketing & Information Services, 604-688-1155
gvurdela@bcmea.com
Membership: 69 organizations

British Columbia Marketing Board (BCMB) *See* British Columbia Farm Industry Review Board

British Columbia Medical Association *See* Doctors of BC

British Columbia Milk Marketing Board
#200, 32160 South Fraser Way, Abbotsford BC V2T 1W5
Tel: 604-556-3444; *Fax:* 604-556-7717
info@milk-bc.com
www.milk-bc.com
Overview: A small provincial organization
Mission: To promote, control and regulate the production, transportation, packing, storing and marketing of milk, fluid milk and manufactured milk products within British Columbia
Chief Officer(s):
Bob Ingratta, Chief Executive Officer
bingratta@milk-bc.com
Jim Byrne, Chair
jbyrne@milk-bc.com
Staff Member(s): 13

British Columbia Miniature Horse Club (BCMHC)
1620 Baldy Mountain Rd., Shawnigan Lake BC V0R 2W2
Tel: 250-743-1183
pipb@shaw.ca
www.bcminiaturehorseclubs.com
Overview: A small provincial organization founded in 1978
Mission: To share information about the miniature horse breed
Chief Officer(s):
Jason Walmsley, President, 604-856-1419
Jazbo@telus.net
Marie O'Neill, Vice-President, 604-514-1467
omarie@telus.net
Jo Anne Barnhill, Secretary, 604-856-7812
barnhill@uniserve.com
Heather Ward, Treasurer, 604-858-9650
sunnyvalehjward@telus.net
Rebecca Bermudez, Editor, Newsletter, 604-316-5060
bec@pipsqueakpaddocks.com
Lavon Read, Show Secretary, 360-659-1711
Membership: *Fees:* $5 youth members; $25 individuals; $35 families; *Member Profile:* Adults & youth, in British Columbia, who are interested in the miniature horse breed; Members do not have to be horse owners
Activities: Organizing educational clinics to help members with their show skills; Hosting shows for miniature horses; Presenting demonstrations at equine functions; Participating in parades to increase awareness of the miniature horse breed; Providing networking opportunities for the exchange of information
Publications:
• British Columbia Miniature Horse Club Newsletter
Type: Newsletter; *Editor:* Rebecca Bermudez
Profile: Club news & announcements

British Columbia Mountaineering Club
PO Box 20042, Vancouver BC V5Z 0C1
Tel: 604-268-9502
info@bcmc.ca
www.bcmc.ca
Overview: A small provincial organization founded in 1907
Mission: BCMC is a group of active individuals who organize mountaineering & skiing trips throughout the year. The primary mode of locomotion is pedestrian to allow appreciation of the mountains with least environmental impact. The Club is also active in conservation, trail & hut construction, trail maintenance, mountain safety & education.
Affliation(s): Federation of Mountain Clubs of BC
Chief Officer(s):
David Scanlon, President
16 volunteer(s)
Membership: 500 individual; *Fees:* $45 individual; $68 couple; $23 youth/senior; $800 lifetime; *Committees:* Conservation

Activities: Hiking; climbing; mountaineering; backcountry skiing; snowshoeing; hiking, backpacking; *Library* by appointment

British Columbia Municipal Safety Association (BCMSA)

20430 Fraser Hwy., Langley BC V3A 4G2
Fax: 778-278-0029
www.bcmsa.ca
www.facebook.com/167587416635419?sk=wall
Overview: A small provincial organization
Mission: The central purpose of the BC Municipal Safety Association is to improve worker health and safety through the sharing of knowledge and resources within local government.
Chief Officer(s):
Cathy Cook, Executive Director, 778-278-3486
ccook@bcmsa.ca
Meetings/Conferences: • BC Municipal OH&S Conference, June, 2015, BC
Scope: Provincial

British Columbia Museums Association (BCMA)

675 Belleville St., Victoria BC V8W 9W2
Tel: 250-356-5700; *Fax:* 250-387-1251
bcma@museumsassn.bc.ca
museumsassn.bc.ca
Also Known As: BC Museums Association
Overview: A medium-sized provincial charitable organization founded in 1957
Mission: To promote the protection & preservation of the objects, specimens, records & sites significant to the natural, creative & human history of British Columbia; to aid in the improvement of museums & galleries as educational institutions; to assist in the development of the museum profession.
Member of: Heritage Council of British Columbia; Forum of Association of Museums; Canadian Museums Association
Chief Officer(s):
Peter Ord, President
president@museumsassn.bc.ca
Theresa Mackay, Executive Director, 250-356-5694
tmackay@museumsassn.bc.ca
Heather Jeliazkov, Manager, Marketing and Membership Services, 250-356-5700
members@museumsassn.bc.ca
Finances: *Annual Operating Budget:* $50,000-$100,000; *Funding Sources:* Government; membership fees; services fees; sponsorships; donations
Staff Member(s): 2
Membership: 400+; *Fees:* $50 individual; $30 student; $80-550 institutional; $100 affiliate; $36 Round-up Newsletter subscription only; *Member Profile:* Individual/institution subscribing to the aims of the BCMA; *Committees:* Publications; Training Advisory; Awards; Advocacy; Member Services; 50th Anniversary
Activities: Technology services; advocacy; training/conferences; *Internships:* Yes; *Speaker Service:* Yes; *Library* Open to public
Awards:
• Corporate Service Award (Award)
• Award of Merit (Award)
• Distinguished Service Award (Award)
• Hardcastle Bursary (Scholarship)
• Joe Nagel Technology Bursary (Scholarship)
Meetings/Conferences: • British Columbia Museums Association Conference 2015, October, 2015, New Westminster, BC
Scope: Provincial

British Columbia Music Educators' Association (BCMEA)

c/o British Columbia Teachers' Federation, #100, 550 West 6th Ave., Vancouver BC V5Z 4P2
www.bctf.ca/bcmea
Overview: A small provincial organization founded in 1957
Mission: To promote excellence in music education in British Columbia schools; To advocate for music education in British Columbia; To foster music appreciation
Member of: British Columbia Teachers' Federation
Chief Officer(s):
Mark Reid, President, 604-713-8215, Fax: 604-713-8214
bcmusiced@gmail.com
Cindy Lewis, Secretary, 250-477-6945, Fax: 250-721-1960
cindylewis@shaw.ca
Michael Doogan-Smith, Treasurer, 250-847-2231 Ext. 133, Fax: 250-847-2165
mdoogansmith@sd54.bc.ca
Membership: *Fees:* $36 retired persons & students; $60 British Columbia Teachers' Federation members; $87.92 non-BCTF members; *Member Profile:* Music educators in British Columbia; Persons interested in music education; Retired educators; Students
Activities: Promoting music education in British Columbia schools; Providing professional development activities; Liaising with partner organizations; Offering networking opportunities
Meetings/Conferences: • British Columbia Music Educators' Association 2015 Annual Conference, October, 2015, BC
Scope: Provincial
Description: Professional development activities & exhibits for British Columbia teachers
Contact Information: Alia Chua, Conference Co-chair, alianicolechua@gmail.com; URL: www.bcmeaconference.com
Publications:
• The BC Music Educator
Type: Journal; *Frequency:* Quarterly; *Accepts Advertising*; *Editor:* Jody Paul (Layout Editor)
Profile: Articles, plus music ourse, festival, & conference offerings

British Columbia Muslim Association (BCMA)

12300 Blundell Rd., Richmond BC V6W 1B3
Tel: 604-270-2522; *Fax:* 604-244-9750
bcma@shawcable.com
www.thebcma.com
Overview: A large provincial organization founded in 1966
Mission: To represent Sunni Muslims in British Columbia; To promote the interests of the Muslim community
Chief Officer(s):
Musa Ismail, President
president@thebcma.com
Imtiaz Asin, Vice-President, Youth Services
youth@thebcma.com
Mohammed Asin Bakridi, Vice-President, Burial
burial@thebcma.com
Faisal Abdul Aziz, Vice-President, Education Services
education@thebcma.com
Shawkat Hasan, Vice-President, Social Services
social@thebcma.com
Azhar Syed, Vice-President, Religious Services
religious@thebcma.com
Abdul Rahiman, Vice-President, Planning & Development
planning@thebcma.com
David Ali, Vice-President, Public Relations & Communication
media@thebcma.com
Alex Housil, Vice-President, Sports & Recreation
sports@thebcma.com
Mohammed Ayub Khairati, General Secretary
secretary@thebcma.com
Afzal Khan, General Treasurer
treasurer@thebcma.com
Finances: *Funding Sources:* Donations; Fundraising
Membership: 40,000; *Member Profile:* Sunni Muslims throughout British Columbia
Activities: Developing & maintaining religious, cultural, & educational facilities; Owning & operating Mosques; Providing funeral & burial facilities; Providing locations for prayers; Operating the British Columbia Muslim School Richmond & the Surrey Muslim School; Offering educational opportunities; Providing social services to youth, adults, & seniors; Organizing social & recreational activities; Cooperating with other Muslim organizations; Promoting community awareness about Islam; Disseminating information about Islam
Publications:
• BCMA Gazette
Type: Newsletter; *Frequency:* Irregular; *Accepts Advertising*
Profile: Association reports & announcements & articles of interest to members

Abbotsford Branch
1980 Salton Rd., Abbotsford BC V2S 3W7
Tel: 778-552-1354
abbotsford@thebcma.com
abbotsford.thebcma.com
Mission: To serve the Muslim community in Abbotsford & the surrounding areas
Chief Officer(s):
Amir Zeb, Chair, 778-240-0133
Yaqoob Shah, Secretary
Nabeek Akhtar, Treasurer, 604-308-4972

Burnaby Branch
5060 Canada Way, Burnaby BC V5E 3N2
Tel: 604-294-2824; *Fax:* 604-244-9750
www.bcmaburnaby.org
Mission: To provide guidance & learning to the Muslim community in Burnaby, British Columbia; To promote unity & Islamic values
Chief Officer(s):
Hazra Ismail, Chair
hazra7866@yahoo.ca
Khatoon Nisha Zuber, Secretary
nishazuber@hotmail.com
Tazul Ali, Treasurer

Kelowna Branch
1120 Hwy. 33N, Kelowna BC V1X 1Z2
Tel: 250-979-1370
kelowna@thebcma.com
kelowna.thebcma.com
Mission: To provide worship, education, & service to the Muslim population in the Kelowna area of British Columbia
Chief Officer(s):
Mostafa Shoranick, Chair

Nanaimo Branch
Islamic Centre of Nanaimo, 905 Hecate St., Nanaimo BC V9R 4K7
Tel: 250-754-3471
Nanaimo@thebcma.com
nanaimo.thebcma.com
Mission: To meet the needs of the Muslim population from Duncan to Tofino on Vancouver Island; To serve the religious & community needs of Muslim foreign students, who attend the Vancouver Island University, Nanaimo
Chief Officer(s):
Ghazi Farooq, Chair
ghazi_farooq@hotmail.com

North Shore Branch
2300 Kirkstone Rd., North Vancouver BC V7J 3M3
Tel: 604-980-4613
northshore@thebcma.com
northshore.thebcma.com
Mission: To serve the needs of the Muslim population in British Columbia's North Shore region
Chief Officer(s):
Mohammad Rahamatulla, Chair
raham9@yahoo.com

Prince George Branch
PO Box 23025, Stn. College Heights, Prince George BC V2N 6Z2
Tel: 250-277-1791; *Fax:* 604-244-9750
bcma.pgchapter@gmail.com
pg.thebcma.com
Mission: To assist the Muslims of Prince George & region in their practice of Islam; To help the Muslim student population at the University of Northern British Columbia in Prince George; To promote understanding between Muslims & non-Muslims
Chief Officer(s):
Mostafa Mohammed, Chair, 250-564-5412
dr.mm_201210@yahoo.ca
Hassan Tahir, Secretary
Khalid Bashir, Treasurer, 250-612-7384
kbashir10@gmail.com

Richmond Branch
12300 Blundell Rd., Richmond BC V6W 1B3
Tel: 604-244-9750
richmond@thebcma.com
Richmond.thebcma.com
Mission: To serve the Muslim community of Richmond, British Columbia & the surrounding area
Chief Officer(s):
Syed Tariq Kamal, Chair, 604-716-3510
Asif R. Butt, Secretary
Abdul Fayun Khan, Treasurer
Mohammed Gul, Director, Social Services
Mohsin Chaudhry, Director, Youth
Mahmood Awan, Director, Membership
Shahzad Mansoory, Director, Sports
Ismail Patel, Director, Education

Surrey Delta Branch
12407 - 72nd Ave., Surrey BC V3W 2M5
Tel: 604-596-7834
surreydelta@thebcma.com
surrey.thebcma.com
Mission: To serve the Muslim population in the Surrey Delta region of British Columbia

Surrey East Branch
13585 - 62nd Ave., Surrey BC V6X 2J3

Tel: 604-597-7863
surreyeast@thebcma.com
surreyeast.thebcma.com
Mission: To serve the needs of the Muslim community in the Surrey east region of British Columbia
Chief Officer(s):
Iltaf Sahib, Chair
iltafsahib@gmail.com
Vancouver Branch
4162 Welwyn St., Vancouver BC V5N 3Z2
Tel: 604-873-1787
vancouver@thebcma.com
vancouver.thebcma.com
Mission: To serve the Muslim community of Vancouver
Chief Officer(s):
Hakim Mohammed, Chair
Victoria Branch
2218 Quadra St., Victoria BC V8T 4C6
Tel: 250-995-1422
bcmavictoria@gmail.com
www.masjidal-iman.com
Mission: To serve the quickly growing Muslim community of Victoria, British Columbia
Chief Officer(s):
Belkacem Chergui, Chair

British Columbia Native Women's Society

4213 Alexis Park Dr., Vernon BC V1T 7T8
Overview: A medium-sized provincial organization overseen by Native Women's Association of Canada
Chief Officer(s):
Barb Morin

British Columbia Nature (Federation of British Columbia Naturalists) (FBCN)

c/o Parks Heritage Centre, 1620 Mount Seymour Rd., North Vancouver BC V7G 2R9
Tel: 604-985-3057
manager@bcnature.ca
www.bcnature.ca
Previous Name: Nature Council of British Columbia
Overview: A medium-sized provincial organization founded in 1969
Mission: To protect biodiversity, species at risk, & natural areas throughout British Columbia; To present a unified voice on conservation & environmental issues
Chief Officer(s):
Betty Davison, Office Manager, 604-985-3057
manager@bcnature.ca
Bev Ramey, President
bevramey@telus.net
Rosemary Fox, Chair, Conservation
foxikrj@bulkley.net
Elisa Kreller, Treasurer
elisakreller@shaw.ca
Maria Hamann, Office Manager
Joan Snyder, Chair, Education
snowdance@columbiawireless.ca
Pat Westheuser, Chair, Awards
hughwest@shaw.ca
Finances: *Funding Sources:* Membership fees; Donations; Fundraising
Membership: 50+ local nature clubs; *Fees:* $20; *Member Profile:* Naturalists, biologists, academics, environmentalists, nature experts, local natural history groups, & nature clubs throughout British Columbia; *Committees:* Conservation; Education; Awards
Activities: Providing educational opportunities; Coordinating stewardship projects
Meetings/Conferences: • British Columbia Nature (Federation of British Columbia Naturalists) 2015 Nature Conference & Annual General Meeting, May, 2015, Salt Spring, BC
Scope: Provincial
Description: An annual meeting of naturalists, environmentalists, biologists, & academics who are members of British Columbia Nature
Contact Information: Office Manager: Betty Davison, E-mail: manager@bcnature.ca
Publications:
• BC Nature Magazine
Type: Magazine; *Frequency:* Quarterly; *Accepts Advertising*; *Price:* Free with membership in the British Columbia Nature (Federation of BC Naturalists)
Profile: Club news, conservation information, & book reviews

British Columbia Naturopathic Association (BCNA)

2238 Pine St., Vancouver BC V6J 5G4
Tel: 604-736-6646; *Fax:* 604-736-6048
Toll-Free: 800-277-1128
bcna@bcna.ca
www.bcna.ca
www.facebook.com/BCNaturopathicAssociation
twitter.com/BCnaturopath
www.youtube.com/user/BCNaturopathicAssoc
Overview: A small provincial organization founded in 1993 overseen by The Canadian Association of Naturopathic Doctors
Mission: To act on behalf of the naturopathic profession in British Columbia; To advance the welfare of members of the profession
Affliation(s): Canadian Association of Naturopathic Doctors
Chief Officer(s):
Victor Chan, Co-President
Loreen Dawson, Co-President
Tonia Mitchell, Treasurer
Membership: *Fees:* $155.33 doctors; $25 public members; *Member Profile:* Licensed NDs (naturopathic physicians) in British Columbia, specializing in disease prevention & clinical nutrition; Public members
Activities: Promoting services provided by the naturopathic profession; Offering referrals; Engaging in collective bargaining & advocacy activities; Providing educational opportunities; *Awareness Events:* Naturopathic Medicine Week, first week of May
Publications:
• Your Health
Type: Newsletter; *Frequency:* Quarterly
Profile: Research & articles

British Columbia Netball Association

3468 Triumph St., Vancouver BC V5K 1T8
Tel: 604-293-1820
info@netball.ca
bcnetball.ca
Also Known As: BC Netball
Overview: A small provincial organization overseen by Netball Canada
Mission: To oversee the sport of netball in British Columbia.
Member of: Netball Canada
Affliation(s): International Federation of Netball Associations
Chief Officer(s):
Ann Willcocks, President

British Columbia Neurofibromatosis Foundation (BCNF)

PO Box 5339, Victoria BC V8R 6S4
Toll-Free: 800-385-2263
info@bcnf.bc.ca
www.bcnf.bc.ca
www.facebook.com/10150157765325565
twitter.com/BC_NF
Overview: A small provincial charitable organization founded in 1984
Mission: To empower individuals with NF & their families to reach their full potential by providing support, education & research funding to find a cure
Member of: INFA - International NF Association
Affliation(s): National NF Foundation
Chief Officer(s):
Desirée Sher, Executive Director
Finances: *Funding Sources:* Grants; fundraising events; membership dues; donations
Staff Member(s): 2
Membership: *Member Profile:* Individuals with neurofibro materials
Activities: Physician awareness campaign & various community awareness events; *Library* Open to public

British Columbia Non-Profit Housing Association (BCNPHA)

#303, 3680 East Hastings St., Vancouver BC V5K 2A9
Tel: 604-291-2600; *Fax:* 604-291-2636
Toll-Free: 800-494-8859
admin@bcnpha.ca
www.bcnpha.ca
Also Known As: BC Non-Profit Housing Association
Overview: A small provincial organization founded in 1993
Mission: To support non-profit housing providers in British Columbia, by offering services; to strive towards safe & affordable housing for tenants in the province; to encourage excellence, through best practices
Affliation(s): BC Housing; Canada Mortgage & Housing Corporation
Chief Officer(s):
Karen Stone, Executive Director
karen@bcnpha.ca
Kathy Stinson, Chair
Shelagh Turner, Secretary
shelagh.turner@cmha.bc.ca
Dick Visser, Treasurer
divsser@cmhakootenays.org
Kate Nielsen, Program Coordinator, Education & Communications
kate@bcnpha.ca
Finances: *Funding Sources:* CMHC; Sponsorships
Membership: *Fees:* $70-$500; *Member Profile:* Individuals; Non-profit housing societies; Non-profit organizational associations; For-profit service organizations
Activities: Offering core courses, workshops, & seminars led by BCNPHA-certified instructors; Engaging in advocacy activities at both the provincial & national levels; Liaising with public, private, & non profit sectors; Participating in policy development
Publications:
• BCNPHA eNews
Type: Newsletter; *Price:* Free
• British Columbia Non-Profit Housing Association Membership Directory
Type: Directory; *Frequency:* Annually
• British Columbia Non-Profit Housing Association Annual Report
Type: Yearbook; *Frequency:* Annually
• InfoLink
Type: Newsletter; *Frequency:* Bimonthly; *Accepts Advertising*; *Editor:* Karen Stone; *Price:* Free with British Columbia Non-Profit Housing Association membership; $20 non-members
Profile: News updates, resources, & articles related to British Columbia's non-profit housing sector
• Supplier Directory
Type: Directory
Profile: Listings of British Columbia Non-Profit Housing Association associate members, who offer professional services or products, & suppliers, recommended by non-profit housing providers

British Columbia Northern Real Estate Board

2609 Queensway, Prince George BC V2L 1N3
Tel: 250-563-1236; *Fax:* 250-563-3637
inquiries@bcnreb.bc.ca
boards.mls.ca/bcnreb
Overview: A small local organization overseen by British Columbia Real Estate Association
Chief Officer(s):
Dorothy Friesen, President

British Columbia Nurse Practitioner Association (BCNPA)

27656 - 110th AVe., Maple Ridge BC V2W 1P6
e-mail: info@bcnpa.org
www.bcnpa.org
www.linkedin.com/profile/view?id=183647207
www.facebook.com/164024656963424
twitter.com/BCNPA2012
Overview: A small provincial organization
Mission: To represent nurse practitioners on a variety of issues with stakeholders, such as British Columbia's health authorities & the British Columbia Ministry of Health; To develop a professional environment in which nurse practitioners can provide accessible, efficient, & effective healthcare; To foster the role of nurse practitioners as an autonomous healthcare providers
Chief Officer(s):
Rosemary Graham, President
Membership: *Fees:* $50 / year, associate members & students; $200 / year, active members; *Member Profile:* Nurse practitioners from across British Columbia; Nurses interested in the nurse practitioner practice; Nurse practitioner students
Activities: Advancing the professional interests of nurse practitioners in British Columbia; Providing educational resources; Sponsoring clinical education by healthcare experts; Liaising with government & other health disciplines; Offering networking opportunities; Promoting awareness of the role of nurse practitioners
Meetings/Conferences: • 10th Annual British Columbia Nurse Practitioner Association Conference, June, 2015, Hyatt Regency Hotel, Vancouver, BC
Scope: Provincial

British Columbia Nursery Trades Association *See* British Columbia Landscape & Nursery Association

British Columbia Nurses' Union (BCNU) / Syndicat des infirmières de la Colombie-Britannique
4060 Regent St., Burnaby BC V5C 6P5
Tel: 604-433-2268; *Fax:* 604-433-7945
Toll-Free: 800-663-9991
contactbcnu@bcnu.org
www.bcnu.org
www.facebook.com/groups/85552225865
www.youtube.com/user/TheBCNursesUnion?ob=0
Overview: A large provincial organization founded in 1981
Mission: BCNU regulates contract administration, protects contract rights and speaks out to protect public, non-for-profit healthcare.
Member of: Canadian Federation of Nurses' Union
Chief Officer(s):
Debra McPherson, President, 604-209-4253
dmcpherson@bcnu.org
Finances: *Annual Operating Budget:* Greater than $5 Million; *Funding Sources:* Membership fees
Staff Member(s): 60
Membership: 40,000
Activities: *Rents Mailing List:* Yes
Awards:
• BCNU Members Education Bursary (Scholarship)
• Retraining Fund for Displaced RNs/RPNs (Scholarship)
• Student Nurse Education Bursary (Scholarship)
Meetings/Conferences: • British Columbia Nurses' Union Convention 2015, February, 2015, Hyatt Regency Vancouver, Vancouver, BC
Scope: Provincial

British Columbia Occupational Health Nurses Professional Practice Group *See* Occupational Nurses' Specialty Association of British Columbia

British Columbia Oyster Growers' Association *See* British Columbia Shellfish Growers Association

British Columbia Paint Manufacturers' Association (BCPMA)
c/o Cloverdale Paint Inc., 6950 King George Blvd., Surrey BC V3W 4Z1
Tel: 604-596-6261; *Fax:* 604-597-2677
helpdesk@cloverdalepaint.com
Overview: A small provincial organization founded in 1933
Mission: To act as the voice of paint manufacturers in British Columbia; To promote the welfare of association members
Chief Officer(s):
Ed Linton, President, 604-596-6261, Fax: 604-597-2677
Ron Vanderdrift, Vice-President, 604-521-7779, Fax: 604-521-2323
Deryk Pawsey, Secretary, 604-541-2569
Yvon Poitras, Treasurer, 604-575-3188, Fax: 604-575-3184
Membership: 1-99; *Member Profile:* Paint manufacturing companies in British Columbia
Activities: Engaging in advocacy activities related to the paint manufacturing industry in British Columbia; Liaising with various levels of government;

British Columbia Paleontological Alliance (BCPA)
c/o THe Exploration Place, PO Box 1779, Prince George BC V2L 4V7
www.bcfossils.ca
Overview: A small provincial organization
Mission: To advance the science of paleontology in the province by fostering public awareness, scientific collecting and education & by promoting communication among all those interested in fossils
Chief Officer(s):
Tom Cockburn, Chair
Membership: 5 regional societies; *Member Profile:* Paleontology organizations

British Columbia Paralegal Association (BCPA)
PO Box 75561, RPO Edgemont Village, North Vancouver BC V7R 4X1
e-mail: info@bcparalegalassociation.com
www.bcparalegalassociation.com
www.linkedin.com/groups?gid=2710823&goback=.anp_2710823_1348602183661_
www.facebook.com/pages/BC-Paralegal-Association/157974147624118
Previous Name: BC Association of Legal Assistants
Overview: A small provincial organization founded in 1979
Mission: To promote the use of academically trained legal assistants within the legal community
Chief Officer(s):
Samantha Kuypers, President
Yves Moisan, Vice-President
Lisa Evenson, Treasurer
Janet Crnkovic, Vice-President, Education & Certification
Finances: *Funding Sources:* Membership fees
10 volunteer(s)
Membership: 700; *Fees:* $25 student; $75 voting/associate; $125 corporate; *Member Profile:* An educational background sufficient to satisfy Directors of Proficiency as LA; *Committees:* Education; Membership; Program; Newsletter
Activities: Educational seminars; meetings

British Columbia Paraplegic Association; Canadian Paraplegic Association *See* Spinal Cord Injury British Columbia

British Columbia Parent-Teacher (Home & School) Federation *See* British Columbia Confederation of Parent Advisory Councils

British Columbia Party
7665 Sapperton Ave., Burnaby BC V3N 4C9
Tel: 604-526-8909
ggiffy@telus.net
Also Known As: BC Party
Overview: A small provincial organization founded in 1998
Chief Officer(s):
Graham Gifford, President

British Columbia Persons with AIDS Society *See* Positive Living BC

British Columbia Pharmacy Association (BCPhA)
#1530, 1200 West 73rd Ave., Vancouver BC V6P 6G5
Tel: 604-261-2092; *Fax:* 604-261-2097
Toll-Free: 800-663-2840
info@bcpharmacy.ca
www.bcpharmacy.ca
Overview: A medium-sized provincial organization founded in 1968
Mission: To support & advance the economic & professional well-being of members, with the goal that they will provide improved health care in British Columbia
Chief Officer(s):
Marnie Mitchell, Chief Executive Officer
marnie.mitchell@bcpharmacy.ca
Parkash Ragsdale, Deputy Chief Executive Officer & Director, Professional Services
parkash.ragsdale@bcpharmacy.ca
Kate Hunter, Director, Communications
kate.hunter@bcpharmacy.ca
Cyril Lopez, Director, Member & Corporate Services
cyril.lopez@bcpharmacy.ca
Finances: *Funding Sources:* Membership fees
Membership: 2,200 pharmacists + 700 pharmacies; *Member Profile:* Pharmacists registered with the College of Pharmacists of British Columbia; Pharmacies licensed by the College of Pharmacists of British Columbia; Persons with an interest in pharmacy who are not registerd with the College of Pharmacists of British Columbia; Pharmacy students; Persons retired from active pharmacy
Activities: Communicating with other groups, agencies, & governments; Developing & maintaining education for members; Promoting ethical & competent professional activities of members
Meetings/Conferences: • British Columbia Pharmacy Association 2015 Conference, May, 2015, Delta Victoria Ocean Pointe Resort and Spa, Victoria, BC
Scope: Provincial
Description: Information & exhibits related to pharmacy in British Columbia
Contact Information: Chief Operating Officer, Member & Corporate Services: Cyril Lopez, Phone: 604-269-2869, E-mail: cyril.lopez@bcpharmacy.ca
Publications:
• The Tablet
Type: Magazine; *Frequency:* Bimonthly; *Accepts Advertising*; *Editor:* Simon Briault; *Price:* Free with membership in the British Columbia Pharmacy Association
Profile: News, comment, & analysis of topics important to pharmacists in British Columbia

British Columbia Philatelic Society
Grosvenor Bldg., PO Box 40, 1040 West Georgia St., Vancouver BC V6E 4H1
Tel: 604-694-0014
mermfabu45@hotmail.com
www.bcphilatelic.org
Overview: A medium-sized provincial organization founded in 1919
Mission: To publicize the hobby of philately
Affliation(s): Royal Philatelic Society of Canada; American Philatelic Society; Northwest Federation of Stamp Clubs
Chief Officer(s):
Duff Malkin, President, 604-738-7979
edm@telus.net
Trevor Larden, Vice-President, 604-224-5836
nanbellcan@netscape.net
Martine Mercier, Secretary, 604-929-8167
mermfabu45@hotmail.com
Finances: *Funding Sources:* Membership dues; Gerald E. Wellburn Philatelic Foundation
Membership: 80; *Fees:* $7.50 students under age 18; $20 individuals; $30 families; *Member Profile:* Stamp & postal-history collectors in British Columbia
Activities: Conducting weekly meetings at West Burnaby United Church; Hosting montly auctions, "Swap & Shop Socials" & exhibitions; Liaising with clubs across North America & abroad; *Library:* British Columbia Philatelic Society Philatelic Library
Publications:
• British Columbia Philatelic Society Newsletter
Type: Newsletter; *Frequency:* 3 pa; *Editor:* Keith Lowe
Profile: Information distributed to society members
• Greater Victoria & Vancouver Area Stamp Show & Bourse Listing of Events & Stamp Directory
Type: Directory; *Editor:* Bill Bartlett
Profile: Listings of dealers, stores, clubs, & local shows

British Columbia Physical Education Provincial Specialist Association *See* Physical Education in British Columbia

British Columbia Play Therapy Association (BCPTA)
#335, 2818 Main St., Vancouver BC V5T 0C1
Tel: 778-710-7529
bcplaytherapy.ca
www.facebook.com/196439843813637
Overview: A small provincial organization founded in 1993
Mission: To promote the status of play therapy in British Columbia, encourage sound play therapy principles; promote high standards of professional and ethical conduct; and nurture the professional development of play therapists within a supportive association.
Membership: 120; *Fees:* $50 annual; $30 student; *Member Profile:* Professionals who work with children, youth, adults and family members; *Committees:* Education; E-newsletter; Membership; Website
Meetings/Conferences: • British Columbia Play Therapy Association 2015 Annual General Meeting & Workshops, May, 2015, Vancouver Public Library, Vancouver, BC
Scope: Provincial

British Columbia Podiatric Medical Association (BCPMA)
#725, 1155 West Pender St., Vancouver BC V6E 2P4
Tel: 604-682-2767; *Fax:* 604-682-2766
info@bcpodiatrists.ca
www.foothealth.ca
Overview: A small provincial organization
Activities: Providing a list of podiatrists who are licensed & registered with the College of Podiatric Surgeons of British Columbia; Offering information about foot care to British Columbians; Hosting & participating in health events for the public; *Speaker Service:* Yes

British Columbia Police Association
#202, 190 Alexander St., Vancouver BC V6A 1B5
Tel: 604-685-6486; *Fax:* 604-685-5228
contact@bc-pa.ca
www.bc-pa.ca
Previous Name: British Columbia Federation of Police Officers
Overview: A medium-sized provincial organization
Mission: To represent the interests of its members
Member of: Canadian Police Association
Chief Officer(s):
Tom Stamatakis, President
Membership: 2,500

British Columbia Powerlifting Association (BCPA)
#222, 12085 - 228 St., Maple Ridge BC V2X 6M2

bc-powerlifting.com
www.facebook.com/291376977556248
Overview: A small provincial organization founded in 2011 overseen by Canadian Powerlifting Union
Mission: To promote powerlifting throughout British Columbia
Member of: Canadian Powerlifting Union; International Powerlifting Federation
Chief Officer(s):
Joe Oliveira, President, 604-734-2932
olivejoe1969@gmail.com
Membership: *Fees:* $60 first time; $85 general; $60 special olympics; $25 associaite

British Columbia Prader-Willi Syndrome Association (BCPWSA)
2133 Chilcotin Cres., Kelowna BC V1V 2N9
www.bcpwsa.com
www.facebook.com/bcpwsa
Overview: A small provincial charitable organization founded in 1982
Mission: To provide an understanding & awareness of PWS by supporting those who have the syndrome, their families & all who come in contact with PWS
Chief Officer(s):
Heather Beach, President
president@bcpwsa.com
Cheryl Gagne, Treasurer
treasurer@bcpwsa.com
Frances Robinson, Secretary
secretary@bcpwsa.com
3 volunteer(s)
Membership: *Fees:* $25 individual

British Columbia Press Council
201 Selby St., Nanaimo BC V9R 2R2
Tel: 250-245-1051
Toll-Free: 888-687-2213
council@bcpresscouncil.org
www.bcpresscouncil.org
Overview: A small provincial organization founded in 1983
Mission: To preserve the established freedom of the press; to serve as a medium of understanding between the public & the press; To encourage the highest professional & commercial standards of journalism; to consider complaints from the public about the conduct of the press; To review & report attempts to restrict access of information of public interest; To make representations to governments on matters relating to press council objectives; To publish reports recording Council work; To exchange information with other press councils
Affliation(s): Canadian Conference of Press Councils
Chief Officer(s):
Rollie Rose, Executive Director
Vern Slanley, Chair
Finances: *Annual Operating Budget:* $50,000-$100,000; *Funding Sources:* BC Newspapers
Membership: *Member Profile:* Newspapers published in British Columbia

British Columbia Primary Teachers Association (BCPTA)
#C27, RR#2, S120, Rock Creek BC V0H 1Y0
Tel: 250-446-2198; *Fax:* 250-446-2198
www.bcpta.ca
www.facebook.com/340793353262?fref=ts
twitter.com/BCprimaryteach
Overview: A small provincial organization founded in 1958
Mission: To foster & promote the cause of early childhood education in British Columbia; To provide leadership in professional development; To provide BCTF with a source of consultation on matters affecting early childhood education & primary teachers in British Columbia
Member of: BC Teachers' Federation
Chief Officer(s):
Janine Fraser, President
janine.fraser@sd51.bc.ca
Finances: *Annual Operating Budget:* $100,000-$250,000
15 volunteer(s)
Membership: 60; *Fees:* $45 full; $22.50 student; $65 subscription
Activities: *Speaker Service:* Yes
Meetings/Conferences: • British Columbia Primary Teachers Association Conference & AGM 2015, 2015, BC
Scope: Provincial
• British Columbia Primary Teachers Association Spring Event 2015, 2015, BC
Scope: Provincial

British Columbia Principals & Vice-Principals Association (BCPVPA)
#200, 525 - 10 Ave. West, Vancouver BC V5Z 1K9
Tel: 604-689-3399; *Fax:* 604-877-5380
Toll-Free: 800-663-0432
www.bcpvpa.bc.ca
twitter.com/bcpvpa
www.youtube.com/user/BCPVPAVideos
Overview: A medium-sized provincial organization founded in 1988
Mission: To provide legal and contractual services advice, organize student leadership activities, and provide professional development programs
Member of: Canadian Society of Association Executives
Chief Officer(s):
Shelley Green, President
sgreen@bcpvpa.bc.ca
Kit Krieger, Executive Director
kkrieger@bcpvpa.bc.ca
Meetings/Conferences: • British Columbia Principals & Vice-Principals Association Annual Conference 2015, May, 2015, Fairmont Chateau Whistler, Whistler, BC
Scope: Provincial

British Columbia Printing & Imaging Association (BCPIA)
PO Box 75218, Stn. White Rock, Surrey BC V4A 0B1
Tel: 604-542-0902
www.bcpia.org
Previous Name: British Columbia Printing Industries Association
Overview: A medium-sized provincial organization
Mission: To be the voice of the BC printing industry & its employees; to provide services & benefits which encourage fellowship, education, community involvement & high standards in business conduct.
Member of: Canadian Printing Industries Association
Affliation(s): Printing Industries of America
Chief Officer(s):
Marilynn Knoch, Executive Director
mknoch@bcpia.org
Membership: 60 companies; *Fees:* Schedule available
Activities: *Library:* Industry Reference Library

British Columbia Printing Industries Association *See* British Columbia Printing & Imaging Association

British Columbia Professional Fire Fighters' Burn Fund
#463, 4800 Kingsway, Burnaby BC V5H 4J2
Tel: 604-436-5617; *Fax:* 604-436-3057
info@burnfund.org
www.burnfund.org
Overview: A small provincial charitable organization founded in 1978
Mission: The charitable arm of the BC Professional Fire Fighters Association; Helps with burn prevention programs; help burn survivors
Affliation(s): BC Professional Fire Fighters Association
Chief Officer(s):
Tony Burke, Executive Director
tj@burnfund.org
Finances: *Funding Sources:* Donations; BC Professional Fire Fighters Association

British Columbia Professional Golfers Association *See* Professional Golfers' Association of British Columbia

British Columbia Provincial Renal Agency (BCPRA)
#700, 1380 Burrard St., Vancouver BC V6Z 2H3
Tel: 604-875-7340
bcpra@bcpra.ca
www.bcrenalagency.ca
www.facebook.com/BCRenalAgency
twitter.com/BCRenalAgency
Overview: A large provincial organization founded in 1997
Mission: To make BC a leader in kidney care delivery in Canada, through enhancing the network of kidney care, providing a coordinated patient-focused information system & monitoring & maintaining quality & standards of care
Finances: *Annual Operating Budget:* Greater than $5 Million; *Funding Sources:* Provincial government
Membership: *Committees:* Executive; Medical Advisory; Pharmacy & Formulary; Facilities & equipment planning; Independent Hemodialysis; Information Management Council; Provincial Vascular Access; PD Clinicians; End of Life Leadership Group; BC Renal Educators Group; Professional groups
Activities: Planning & monitoring province-wide kidney care services; Developing province-wide clinical standards & guidelines; Developing funding models; Measuring & reporting on patient & system results; Supporting research & development
Meetings/Conferences: • Western Canada 24th Annual PD Days 2015, April, 2015, Renaissance Vancouver Hotel Harbourside, Vancouver, BC
Scope: Provincial
Description: A showcase of approaches to the delivery of peritoneal dialysis
Contact Information: E-mail: westernpddays@bcpra.ca
• BC Kidney Days 2015, October, 2015, Vancouver Renaissance Harbourside Hotel, Vancouver, BC
Scope: Provincial
Description: Brings together clinicians & administrators from across BC & other parts of Canada & the United States to discuss current research, trends, clinical treatment & surgical breakthroughs in renal patient care.
Contact Information: Kidney Days Contact: Stephanie Allan, E-mail: sallan2@bcpra.ca
Publications:
• PROMIS UpDate
Type: Newsletter
Profile: Up-to-date information about projects & system features, distributed every eight to ten weeks
• Renal News
Type: Newsletter; *Frequency:* Quarterly
Profile: Information about projects & practices across British Columbia's renal network

British Columbia Psychogeriatric Association (BCPGA)
PO Box 47028, 1030 Denman St., Vancouver BC V6G 3E1
Fax: 888-835-2451
www.bcpga.com
www.facebook.com/pages/BC-Psychogeriatric-Association/1388698178027128
twitter.com/BCPGA1
Overview: A small provincial organization founded in 1997
Mission: A professional association of clinicians working in the field of mental health and older adults.
Chief Officer(s):
Nancy Jokinen, Co-President, 250-960-5111
jokinenn@unbc.ca
Dawn Hemingway, Co-President, 250-960-5694
Dawn.Hemingway@unbc.ca
Meetings/Conferences: • British Columbia Psychogeriatric Association 2015 Conference, 2015, BC
Scope: Provincial

British Columbia Psychological Association (BCPA)
#402, 1177 West Broadway, Vancouver BC V6H 1G3
Tel: 604-730-0501; *Fax:* 604-730-0502
Toll-Free: 800-730-0522
www.psychologists.bc.ca
Overview: A medium-sized provincial organization
Mission: Provides leadership for the advancement and promotion of the profession and science of psychology to serve our membership and the people of British Columbia
Staff Member(s): 1

British Columbia Public Interest Advocacy Centre (BCPIAC)
#208, 1090 West Pender St., Vancouver BC V6E 2N7
Tel: 604-687-3063; *Fax:* 604-682-7896
bcpiac@bcpiac.com
www.bcpiac.com
Overview: A small provincial organization founded in 1981
Mission: BCPIAC is a non-profit, public interest law office that advances the interests of groups that are generally unrepresented or underrepresented in issues of major public concern, such as welfare, disability, human, farmworkers & consumers rights.
Chief Officer(s):
Tannis Braithwaite, Executive Director
Targol Salehi, Administrative Staff
targol@bcpiac.com
Finances: *Funding Sources:* Law Foundation of BC
Staff Member(s): 7

British Columbia Purebred Sheep Breeders' Association (BCPSBA)
c/o Jan Carter, 3606 Ferguson Rd., Port Alberni BC V9Y 8L4

Tel: 250-723-8214
cottonwoodfarm@telus.net
www.bcsheep.com
Overview: A small provincial organization
Mission: To encourage a general & constant improvement in sheep breeding & a better organization of the interests of purebred sheep breeders of the province; to advance the interests of its members through cooperation with other industry organizations, & the governments, provincial & federal.
Member of: British Columbia Sheep Federation; Canadian Sheep Breeders Association
Chief Officer(s):
Anna Green, President, 250-546-6545
anna@otterlakefarm.ca
Finances: *Funding Sources:* Membership dues; fundraising
Membership: 83; *Fees:* $20; $10 junior
Activities: Sheep shows; fair displays & events

British Columbia Racquetball Association (BCRA)
BC
e-mail: info@racquetballbc.ca
www.racquetballbc.ca
twitter.com/bcracquetball
Overview: A medium-sized provincial charitable organization founded in 1970 overseen by Racquetball Canada
Member of: Racquetball Canada
Chief Officer(s):
Rick Mattson, President, 604-986-7934
rickmattson@telus.net
Cal Smith, Vice-President, Officiating, 604-931-4944
cdsmithh@shaw.ca
Debbie Goodhope, Treasurer & General Contact, 604-522-8932
goodhope@telus.net
Finances: *Funding Sources:* Fundraising; SportsFunder Lottery; Sponsorships
Membership: *Fees:* $25
Activities: Supporting tournaments; Providing rules, skills, & junior development clinics; Hosting school programs
Publications:
• Racquetball Matters
Type: Newsletter; *Editor:* Sandra Nielsen
Profile: Association reports & tournament & championship results

British Columbia Railway Historical Association (BCRHA)
1148 Balmoral Rd., Victoria BC V8T 1B1
e-mail: bcrha@shaw.ca
www.trainweb.org/bcrha
Overview: A small provincial charitable organization founded in 1961
Mission: To preserve railway exhibits, manuscripts & film of BC railways
Member of: Heritage Society of BC
Finances: *Funding Sources:* Donations; book sales; membership dues
Membership: *Fees:* $15 full; *Member Profile:* Interest in BC railway history
Activities: Research & publication of books on BC railway history; *Library*

British Columbia Raspberry Industry Council *See* Raspberry Industry Development Council

British Columbia Ready Mixed Concrete Association
26162 - 30A Ave., Aldergrove BC V4W 2W5
Tel: 604-626-4141; *Fax:* 604-626-4143
info@bcrmca.ca
www.bcrmca.ca
Overview: A medium-sized provincial organization overseen by Canadian Ready Mixed Concrete Association
Mission: To work cooperatively with all levels of government to ensure the ready-mix concrete industry operates with a focus on the communities & the environment
Chief Officer(s):
Charles Kelly, President
ckelly@bcrmca.ca
Staff Member(s): 3
Membership: 266; *Fees:* Schedule available

British Columbia Real Estate Association (BCREA)
#1420, 701 Georgia St. West, Vancouver BC V7Y 1C6
Tel: 604-683-7702; *Fax:* 604-683-8601
bcrea@bcrea.bc.ca
www.bcrea.bc.ca
Overview: A large provincial organization founded in 1976
Mission: To promote the interests of & advocate for the real estate profession; To secure public support & trust in the profession; To promote property rights & real estate related issues; To ensure high standards of ethics & professionalism through ongoing education of realtors
Member of: The Canadian Real Estate Association
Affliation(s): National Association of Realtors - USA
Chief Officer(s):
Robert Laing, Chief Executive Officer, 604-742-2787
rlaing@bcrea.bc.ca
Melinda Entwistle, Chief Operating Officer, 604-742-2798
mentistle@bcrea.bc.ca
Cameron Muir, Chief Economist, 604-742-2780
cmuir@bcrea.bc.ca
Marla Gerein, Director, Education, 604-909-1132
mgerein@bcrea.bc.ca
Borg Jorgensen, Director, Finance & Systems, 604-742-2790
bjorgensen@bcrea.bc.ca
Damian Stathonikos, Director, Communications, 604-742-2793
dstathonikos@bcreas.bc.ca
Finances: *Funding Sources:* Membership fees; Education programs
13 volunteer(s)
Membership: 12 member real estate boards; *Fees:* $113; *Member Profile:* Board or association of realtors in British Columbia; *Committees:* Audit; Legislative; Education; Standard Forms; Government Relations
Activities: Offering the Applied Real Estate Course & continuing professional education seminars; *Library* by appointment
Publications:
• The Bulletin
Type: Newsletter; *Frequency:* Quarterly
• Legally Speaking
Type: Newsletter; *Frequency:* 8 pa; *Author:* J. Clee; M. Mangan; B. Taylor

British Columbia Recreation & Parks Association (BCRPA)
#101, 4664 Lougheed Hwy., Burnaby BC V5C 5T5
Tel: 604-629-0965; *Fax:* 604-629-2651
Toll-Free: 866-929-0965
Other Communication: registration@bcrpa.bc.ca
bcrpa@bcrpa.bc.ca
www.bcrpa.bc.ca
Overview: A medium-sized provincial charitable organization founded in 1958 overseen by Canadian Parks & Recreation Association
Mission: To establish & sustain healthy lifestyles & communities in British Columbia
Chief Officer(s):
Dean Gibson, President
Suzanne Allard Strutt, Chief Executive Officer
sstrutt@bcrpa.bc.ca
Holly-Ann Burrows, Manager, Communication
hburrows@bcrpa.bc.ca
Sandra Couto, Manager, Finance
scouto@bcrpa.bc.ca
Kara Misra, Manager, Parks & Recreation
kmisra@bcrpa.bc.ca
Misty Thomas, Manager, Fitness Program
mthomas@bcrpa.bc.ca
Finances: *Funding Sources:* Membership fees; Donations
Membership: *Fees:* Free, 1st year students; $60 individual goverment members; $245 individual independent members; Schedule based on population for local governments; *Member Profile:* Local governments, such as municipalities & regional districts; Corporations or commercial organizations; Not-for-profit organizations & educational institutions, connected to park, recreation, & cultural sectors; Individuals who work for or who are connected to a local government member; Students
Activities: Advocating accessibility & inclusiveness to recreation & physical activity; Providing training & resources; Distributing manuals on topics such as fitness theory, aquatic fitness group fitness, weight training, & yoga fitness
Meetings/Conferences: • British Columbia Recreation & Parks Association 2015 In Your Face Youth Workers' Conference, November, 2015, BC
Scope: Provincial
Contact Information: Programs & Initiatives Coordinator: Natalie Korsovetski, Phone: 604-629-0965, ext. 229, E-mail: nkorsovetski@bcrpa.bc.ca
• British Columbia Recreation & Parks Association 2015 38th Annual ProvincialParks & Grounds Spring Training Conference, February, 2015, The Anvil Centre, New Westminster, BC
Scope: Provincial
Description: Continuing education sessions that cover a wide range of interests for parks & grounds professionals
Contact Information: Programs & Initiatives Coordinator: Natalie Korsovetski, Phone: 604-629-0965, ext. 229, E-mail: nkorsovetski@bcrpa.bc.ca
• British Columbia Recreation & Parks Association 2015 Symposium, May, 2015, Victoria, BC
Scope: Provincial
Attendance: 400+
Description: An annual meeting of interest to parks & recreation professionals & volunteers, as well as elected officials from across British Columbia
Contact Information: Corporate Account Coordinator: Matt Anderson, Phone: 604-629-0965, ext. 239, E-mail: corpsales@bcrpa.bc.ca
• British Columbia Recreation & Parks Association 2015 Provincial Ripple Effects Aquatics Conference, October, 2015, Pinnacle North Vancouver, Vancouver, BC
Scope: Provincial
Description: A two-day conference which occurs every two years, presenting operations, programming, & best practices for aquatics professionals
Contact Information: Parks & Recreation Program Coordinator: Natalie Korsovetski, Phone: 604-629-0965, ext. 229; E-mail: nkorsovetski@bcrpa.bc.ca
Publications:
• British Columbia Recreation & Parks Association Annual Report
Type: Yearbook
• Recreation & Parks BC
Type: Magazine; *Frequency:* Quarterly
Profile: Happenings in the parks & recreation sector

British Columbia Refederation Party
#573, 7360 - 137 St., Surrey BC V3W 1A3
Tel: 604-593-4833
info.bcr@bcrefed.com
www.refedbc.com
Also Known As: BC Refed
Previous Name: Western Refederation Party of BC; Western Independence Party of BC
Overview: A small provincial organization founded in 2000
Mission: Advocates direct democracy and reform to Canadian federalism.
Chief Officer(s):
Dale Marcell, President

British Columbia Registered Music Teachers' Association (BCRMTA)
c/o Registrar, PO Box 45537, Stn. Sunnyside, Surrey BC V4A 9N3
e-mail: registrar@bcrmta.bc.ca
www.bcrmta.bc.ca
Overview: A medium-sized provincial organization founded in 1947
Mission: To raise the standard of the profession of music teaching in British Columbia; to promote the interests of music teachers in British Columbia
Chief Officer(s):
Cynthia Taylor, President
president@bcrmta.bc.ca
Susan Olsen, Registrar
Membership: 1,000+ individual; *Committees:* Canada Music Week; Standing Rules & By-Laws; Archives; Website; Professional Development; Young Artists Tour & BC Piano Competition
Activities: 22 branches in BC

Abbotsford Branch
Abbotsford BC
Tel: 604-850-9224
info@abbotsfordmusicteachers.com
www.abbotsfordmusicteachers.com
Chief Officer(s):
Jean Ritter, President
jeanacademy@gmail.com

Chilliwack Branch
Chilliwack BC
Tel: 604-847-9915
bcrmta.bc.ca/chilliwack-branch
Chief Officer(s):
Sherrie Van Akker, Contact
vanakker@telus.net

Coquitlam/Maple Ridge Branch
BC

Tel: 604-941-0109
bcrmta.bc.ca/coquitlammaple-ridge-2
Chief Officer(s):
Sandra Lee, President
sandrabraathenlee@hotmail.com
East Kootenay Branch
BC
Tel: 250-426-0165
cmw@caraspiano.ca
bcrmta.bc.ca/east-kootenay
Chief Officer(s):
Cara Webb, Contact
Kelowna Branch
Kelowna BC
Tel: 250-763-5873
www.kelownabcrmta.com
Chief Officer(s):
Deborah Batycki, Contact
batycki@telus.net
Mid-Island Branch
BC
Tel: 250-248-2249
makingmelodies@hotmail.com
www.musicnanaimo.com
Chief Officer(s):
Dianne Bohn, President
bdbohn@shaw.ca
Mission Branch
Mission BC
Tel: 604-826-3312
www.bcrmta.bc.ca/mission
Chief Officer(s):
Florence Graham, Contact
Nelson Branch
Nelson BC
Tel: 250-352-7625
acmacd@shaw.ca
www.bcrmta.bc.ca/nelson
Chief Officer(s):
Anne McDonald, President
North Island Branch
BC
Tel: 250-923-3731
bcrmta.bc.ca/north-island
Chief Officer(s):
Cynthia Taylor, Contact
cindytaylormusic@gmail.com
North Shore Branch
BC
Tel: 604-921-7204
bcrmta.bc.ca/north-shore
Chief Officer(s):
Valerie Cook, President
valeriecook@shaw.ca
Prince George Branch
Prince George BC
Tel: 250-963-7001
bcrmta.bc.ca/prince-george
Chief Officer(s):
Louise Phillips, Contact
louisephillips@hotmail.com
Richmond Branch
PO Box 39502, Stn. Broadmoor, Richmond BC V7A 5G9
Tel: 604-268-9559
info@bcrmta.com
www.bcrmta.com
Chief Officer(s):
Mimi Ho, President
Shuswap Branch
BC
bcrmta.bc.ca/shuswap
Chief Officer(s):
Jane Hein, President
janehein@telus.net
South Fraser (Surrey, North Delta, White Rock, Langley) Branch
BC
www.southfrasermusic.com
South Okanagan Branch
BC
Tel: 250-494-0871
bcrmta.bc.ca/south-okanagan
Chief Officer(s):
Anita Perry, Contact
apaf@shaw.ca
Sunshine Coast Branch
Gibsons BC
Tel: 604-885-6756
bcrmta.bc.ca/sunshine-coast
Chief Officer(s):
Val Anderson, Contact
valand@uniserve.com
Trail/Castlegar Branch
BC
Tel: 250-362-9526
bcrmta.bc.ca/trailcastlegar
Chief Officer(s):
Dawna Kavanagh, President
kavanagh@telus.net
Vancouver Branch
Vancouver BC
e-mail: bcrmta@bcrmta.org
www.bcrmta.org
Chief Officer(s):
Toni Meyer, President
tmeyerkeys@gmail.com
Vernon Branch
Vernon BC
Tel: 250-542-5873
bcrmta.bc.ca/vernon
Chief Officer(s):
Carol Stromberg, Contact
kcstromberg@yahoo.com
Victoria Branch
Victoria BC
Tel: 250-370-2551
bcrmtavictoria.webs.com
Chief Officer(s):
Patricia Williamson, President
pwilliamson@shaw.ca

British Columbia Restaurant & Foodservices Association (BCRFA)
#2, 2246 Spruce St., Vancouver BC V6H 2P3
Tel: 604-669-2239; *Fax:* 604-669-6175
Toll-Free: 877-669-2239
info@bcrfa.com
www.bcrfa.com
www.linkedin.com/company/bc-restaurant-&-foodservices-association-bcrf
www.facebook.com/BCRFA
twitter.com/BCRFA
Overview: A medium-sized provincial organization founded in 1977
Mission: To be the voice of the hospitality industry in British Columbia; the advocat of the restaurant industry.
Chief Officer(s):
Ian Tostenson, President & CEO
itostenson@bcrfa.com
Staff Member(s): 5
Membership: 3,000; *Fees:* $185 education; $325 restaurant-licenced; $275 restaurant-non licensed; $350 supplier; *Member Profile:* Restaurateurs, foodservice retailers, suppliers & educators.
Activities: *Speaker Service:* Yes

British Columbia Rhythmic Sportive Gymnastics Federation (BCRSGF)
#268, 828 West 8th Ave., Vancouver BC V5Z 1E2
Tel: 604-333-3485; *Fax:* 604-909-1749
bcrsgf@rhythmicsbc.com
www.rhythmicsbc.com
www.facebook.com/Rhythmicsbc
www.youtube.com/user/bcrsgf
Also Known As: BC Rhythmic Gymnastics Federation
Overview: A small provincial organization
Mission: To be the governing body of the sport of rhythmic gymnastics in British Columbia, including special olympics, Aethetic Group Gymnastics & men's rhythmic gymnastics.
Chief Officer(s):
Sashka Gitcheva, Program Coordinator

British Columbia Rifle Association (BCRA)
PO Box 2418, Stn. Sardis Main, Chilliwack BC V2R 1A7
e-mail: contact@bcrifle.org
www.bcrifle.org
Overview: A medium-sized provincial organization founded in 1874
Mission: To create a public sentiment for the encouragement of marksmanship in all its trades among citizens of British Columbia, both as a sport & as a definite contribution to the defence of Canada
Member of: Dominion of Canada Rifle Association
Membership: *Fees:* Schedule available
Activities: BC Marksmanship Championships in 7 different shooting sports;

British Columbia Ringette Association (BCRA) / Association de ringuette de Colombie-Britannique
#420, 789 West Pender St., Vancouver BC V6C 1H2
Tel: 604-629-4583
info@bcringette.org
www.bcringette.org
www.facebook.com/pages/BC-Ringette-Association/388774601776
twitter.com/bcringette
www.youtube.com/user/ringettebc
Overview: A small provincial organization founded in 1976 overseen by Ringette Canada
Mission: To promote ringette & allow for opportunities for people in British Columbia to play ringette.
Chief Officer(s):
Colin Ensworth, Manager, Sports Operations
manager@bcringette.org
Rob Tait, Chair
chair@bcringette.org
Staff Member(s): 2
Membership: *Committees:* High Performance; Canada Winter Games; Officiating Development; Audit & Finance; Sport & Athlete Development; Coaching Development; House Provincials & Tournaments; Strategic Planning; Nomination & Sucession; Risk Management; Human Resources
Awards:
• BCRA Scholarship

British Columbia Road Builders & Heavy Construction Association (BCRB&HCA)
#307, 8678 Greenall Ave., Burnaby BC V5J 3M6
Tel: 604-436-0220; *Fax:* 604-436-2627
info@roadbuilders.bc.ca
www.roadbuilders.bc.ca
Overview: A medium-sized provincial organization founded in 1965 overseen by Canadian Construction Association
Mission: To represent the interests of member companies to government, media, other organizations, & the public
Member of: British Columbia Business Council; British Columbia Chamber of Commerce
Affliation(s): Western Canada Roadbuilders Association; Canadian Construction Association
Chief Officer(s):
Jack W. Davidson, President
jack@roadbuilders.bc.ca
Jackson Yu, Administrator
jackson@roadbuilders.bc.ca
Kate Cockerill, Manager, Communications & Membership
kate@roadbuilders.bc.ca
Finances: *Funding Sources:* Membership fees; Events
Membership: 100-499; *Fees:* Schedule available; *Member Profile:* Firms involved in asphalt & concrete manufacturing, grading, paving, blasting, road & bridge building & maintenance, utility construction, & the supply of related goods & services; *Committees:* Construction; Maintenance; Service & Supply
Activities: Advocating for balanced, safe transportation systems & infrastructure development that promotes provincial economic growth; Conducting research; Providing networking opportunities; *Speaker Service:* Yes
Meetings/Conferences: • British Columbia Road Builders & Heavy Construction Association 2015 Annual General Meeting & Convention, February, 2015, Westin Resort & Spa, Los Cabos
Scope: Provincial
Contact Information: Manager, Communications & Membership: Parveen Parhar, E-mail: parveen@roadbuilders.bc.ca
Publications:
• Blue Book Equipment Rental Rate Guide
Frequency: Annually; *Accepts Advertising*
Profile: Published by the BC Road Builders & Heavy Construction Association, in partnership with the provincial Ministry of Transportation
• The Voice
Type: Newsletter; *Frequency:* Bimonthly
Profile: Association activities, member profiles, industry news, & forthcoming events for British Columbia Road Builders & Heavy Construction Association members & industry partners

British Columbia Rugby Union
#203, 210 West Broadway, Vancouver BC V5Y 3W2
Tel: 604-737-3065; *Fax:* 604-737-3916
bcrugby@telus.net
www.bcrugby.com
www.facebook.com/bcrugbyunion
twitter.com/bcrugbyunion
www.youtube.com/bcrugbyunion
Also Known As: BC Rugby
Overview: A medium-sized provincial organization founded in 1889 overseen by Rugby Canada
Mission: To promote, sustain & manage the game of rugby in BC in a manner that will ensure wide participation & the continuous development in a safe & responsible manner
Member of: Rugby Canada
Chief Officer(s):
Jim Dixon, Chief Executive Officer, 604-737-3021
jdixon@bcrugby.com
Louise Wheeler, Manager, Member Services
lwheeler@bcrugby.com
Staff Member(s): 4
Membership: 14,000; *Fees:* $1,056 per team; *Committees:* Competition; Discipline; Youth; Medical Science; Appeal
Activities: *Library* Open to public

British Columbia Rural Teachers' Association *See* BC Rural & Small Schools Teachers' Association

British Columbia Safety Authority
#200, 505-6th St, New Westminster BC V3L 0E1
Tel: 778-396-2000; *Fax:* 778-396-2064
Toll-Free: 866-566-7233
info@safetyauthority.ca
www.safetyauthority.ca
Overview: A medium-sized provincial organization
Mission: Protects the residents of BC by ensuring the safety of mechanical systems, products, equipment & work practices
Chief Officer(s):
Catherine Roome, President & CEO

British Columbia Salmon Farmers Association (BCSFA)
#201, 909 Island Hwy., Campbell River BC V9W 2C2
Tel: 250-286-1636
Toll-Free: 800-661-7256
info@salmonfarmers.org
www.salmonfarmers.org
www.facebook.com/SalmonFarmers?ref=ts
twitter.com/BCSalmonFarmers
www.youtube.com/bcsalmonfarmers;
pinterest.com/bcsalmonfarmers
Overview: A small provincial organization founded in 1984
Mission: To act as the voice of British Columbia's farmed salmon industry; To advance the competitiveness & sustainable growth of the salmon farming industry
Chief Officer(s):
Mary Ellen Walling, Executive Director
mwalling@salmonfarmers.org
Colleen Dane, Manager, Communications, 250-286-1636 Ext. 225
colleen.dane@telus.net
Valerie Lamirande, Coordinator, Events
valerie.lamirande@telus.net
David Minato, Coordinator, Community & Member Relations, 250-286-1636 Ext. 224
david.minato@telus.net
Membership: *Member Profile:* Salmon farmers from British Columbia; Supply & service companies that support the salmon farming industry
Activities: Liaising with government; Educating the public
Publications:
• Catch! [a publication of the British Columbia Salmon Farmers Association]
Type: Newsletter; *Frequency:* Quarterly
Profile: Information for members & forthcoming events

British Columbia Saw Filers Association (BCSFA)
6521 Orchard Hill Rd., Vernon BC V1H 1B6
Tel: 250-546-2234; *Fax:* 604-585-4014
info@bcsawfilers.com
www.bcsawfilers.com
Overview: A small provincial organization
Chief Officer(s):
Bruce Doroshuk, President
bruce.doroshuk@tolko.com
Meetings/Conferences: • 2015 British Columbia Saw Filers Association Annual General Meeting, Supplier's Fair & Conference, 2015, BC
Scope: Provincial

British Columbia Schizophrenia Society
#201, 6011 Westminster Hwy., Richmond BC V7C 4V4
Tel: 604-270-7841; *Fax:* 604-270-9861
Toll-Free: 888-888-0029
bcss.prov@telus.net
www.bcss.org
www.facebook.com/BCSchizophreniaSociety
twitter.com/BCSchizophrenia
www.youtube.com/user/bcssprov
Previous Name: BC Friends of Schizophrenics
Overview: A small provincial charitable organization founded in 1982 overseen by Schizophrenia Society of Canada
Mission: To alleviate the suffering caused by schizophrenia; provide support and education; increase public awareness and understanding of schizophrenia and other persistent mental illness; promote research into the causes, treatment and cure of schizophrenia
Member of: Schizophrenia Society of Canada
Chief Officer(s):
Jane Duval, Executive Director
Staff Member(s): 24
Activities: 30 branches in British Columbia; *Library* Open to public

British Columbia School Counsellors' Association
PO Box 858, Terrace BC V8G 4R1
www.bcschoolcounsellor.com
Overview: A small provincial organization
Member of: BC Teachers' Federation
Chief Officer(s):
Jim Hooper, President
jhooper.bcsca@gmail.com

British Columbia School District Secretary-Treasurers' Association *See* British Columbia Association of School Business Officials

British Columbia School Superintendents Association (BCSSA)
#208, 1118 Homer St., Vancouver BC V6B 6L5
Tel: 604-687-0590
info@bcssa.org
www.bcssa.org
Overview: A small provincial organization
Mission: To provide equity & excellence in student learning; To develop competent, ethical, & visionary leaders
Chief Officer(s):
Keven Elder, President
keven_elder@sd63.bc.ca
Wendy Lee, Executive Director
wlee@bcssa.org
Steve Cardwell, Vice President
scardwell@deltasd.bc.ca
Juleen McElgunn, Secretary-Treasurer
jmcelgunn@sd53.bc.ca
Steve Carlton, Chair, Membership Services Committee
steve_carlton@sd34.bc.ca
Charlie Etchell, Chair, Professional Development Committee
cetchell@sd35.bc.ca
Lisa Aspinall, Manager, Communications
laspinall@bcssa.org
Membership: 250+; *Member Profile:* Superintendents, assistant superintendents, directors of instruction, & other senior executives from British Columbia's sixty school districts
Activities: Supporting professional development activities; Advocating for high quality public education; Providing networking opportunities
Meetings/Conferences: • British Columbia School Superintendents Association 2015 Spring Forum, April, 2015, Westin Bayshore, Vancouver, BC
Scope: Provincial
Description: Topics related to the British Columbia School Superintendents Association's Dimensions of Practice, featuring innovative & successful models of leadership
Contact Information: Professional Development Coordinator: Kim Young, E-mail: kimyoung@bcssa.org
• British Columbia School Superintendents Association 2015 Summer Leadership Academy, August, 2015, Delta Grand Okanagan, Kelowna, BC
Scope: Provincial
Contact Information: Professional Development Coordinator: Kim Young, E-mail: kimyoung@bcssa.org
• British Columbia School Superintendents Association 2015 Fall Conference & Annual General Meeting, 2015, BC
Scope: Provincial
Description: Themes include leadership, school effectiveness, & improvement
Contact Information: Professional Development Coordinator: Kim Young, E-mail: kimyoung@bcssa.org
• British Columbia School Superintendents Association 2015 Winter Conference, 2015, BC
Scope: Provincial
Contact Information: Professional Development Coordinator: Kim Young, E-mail: kimyoung@bcssa.org
Publications:
• Leadergram
Type: Newsletter
Profile: Information for BCSSA members

British Columbia School Trustees Association (BCSTA) / Association des commissaires d'écoles de Colombie-Britannique
1580 West Broadway, 4th Fl., Vancouver BC V6J 5K9
Tel: 604-734-2721; *Fax:* 604-732-4559
bcsta@bcsta.org
www.bcsta.org
www.linkedin.com/company/bc-school-trustees-association
www.facebook.com/pages/BC-School-Trustees-Association
twitter.com/bc_sta
Overview: A medium-sized provincial organization founded in 1905 overseen by Canadian School Boards Association
Mission: To promote effective boards of public school trustees working together for BC students. It is a non-profit, voluntary organization dedicated to assisting school boards in their key work; improving student achievement through community engagement.
Member of: School Boards Association (CSBA)
Chief Officer(s):
Stephen Hansen, Executive Director
shansen@bcsta.org
Jodi Olstead, Director, Finance & Human Resources
jolstead@bcsta.org
Mike P. Gagel, Director, Information & Education Technology
mgagel@bcsta.org
Staff Member(s): 12
Membership: 60 boards + 420 trustees; *Fees:* Based on enrolment; *Committees:* Education; Finance; Aboriginal Education

British Columbia Science Teachers' Association (BCScTA)
c/o Ashcroft Secondary School, PO Box 669, Ashcroft BC V0K 1A0
Tel: 250-453-9144; *Fax:* 250-453-2368
bcscta@gmail.com
www.bcscta.ca
Overview: A medium-sized provincial organization
Member of: BC Teachers' Federation
Chief Officer(s):
Grahame Rainey, President
Tim McCracken, 1st Vice-President
Membership: *Fees:* $35 BCTF member; $10 Student/Retiree/TOC
Meetings/Conferences: • British Columbia Science Teachers' Association Catalyst Conference 2015, 2015, BC
Scope: Provincial
Contact Information: catalyst.bcscta.ca

British Columbia Scientific Cryptozoology Club (BCSCC)
BC
e-mail: bcscc@bcscc.ca
bcscc.ca
Overview: A small provincial organization founded in 1989
Mission: To research & preserve the databases of cryptozoological animals internationally
Chief Officer(s):
Paul H. Leblond, Chairman & Founder
John Kirk, President & Founder
Membership: *Fees:* $30 Canadian residents; $30 USD international residents; *Member Profile:* People involved with cryptozoological

British Columbia Seafood Alliance (BCSA)
#1100, 1200 West 73rd Ave., Vancouver BC V6P 6G5
Tel: 604-377-9213; *Fax:* 604-683-4510
www.bcseafoodalliance.com
Overview: A medium-sized provincial organization
Mission: To represent the interests & values of a majority of BC's seafood industries to the federal & provincial governments & to the general public; to promote the conservation &

environmentally sustainable use & production of seafood resources in BC; to foster an economically viable & internationally competitive seafood industry
Chief Officer(s):
Christina Burridge, Executive Director
cburridge@telus.net
Gina McKay, Coordinator, Safety & Assistance, 604-261-9700
gina@fishsafebc.com
Membership: 18

British Columbia Securities Commission (BCSC)
PO Box 10142, Stn. Pacific Centre, 701 West Georgia St., 12th Fl., Vancouver BC V7Y 1L2
Tel: 604-899-6500; *Fax:* 604-899-6506
Toll-Free: 800-373-6393
inquiries@bcsc.bc.ca
www.bcsc.bc.ca
Overview: A medium-sized provincial organization overseen by Canadian Securities Administrators
Mission: To regulate securities trading in British Columbia, through the administration of the Securities Act; To report to the Legislature, through the minister responsible for the administration of the Securities Act; To foster a fair & competitive securities market; To protect investors & market integrity
Member of: Canadian Securities Administrators
Chief Officer(s):
Brenda Leong, Chair & Chief Executive Officer
Brent Aiken, Vice-Chair
Nigel P. Cave, Vice-Chair
Paul C. Bourque, Executive Director
Finances: *Annual Operating Budget:* Greater than $5 Million; *Funding Sources:* Fees collected from market participants under the legislation
Staff Member(s): 190
Membership: *Committees:* Governance; Audit; Human Resources
Activities: Education investors & market participants; Monitoring compliance & demanding corrective action
Publications:
• British Columbia Securities Commission Ethics & Conduct Policy
Number of Pages: 12
• British Columbia Securities Commission Governance Policy
Number of Pages: 22
• British Columbia Securities Commission Service Plan
• British Columbia Securities Commission Plain Language Style Guide
Type: Guide; *Number of Pages:* 63
• British Columbia Securities Commission Annual Report
Type: Yearbook; *Frequency:* Annually
• Governance Manual
Type: Manual
Profile: A description of the commission's governance structure & the practices used by the board

British Columbia Seniors Living Association (BCSLA)
#300, 3665 Kingsway, Vancouver BC V5R 5W2
Tel: 604-689-5949; *Fax:* 604-689-5946
Toll-Free: 888-402-2722
membership@bcsla.ca
www.bcsla.ca
Overview: A small provincial organization
Chief Officer(s):
Marlene Williams, Executive Director
executivedirector@bcsla.ca
Stuart Bowden, Vice-President, Finance
Meetings/Conferences: • British Columbia Seniors Living Association 2015 Conference, 2015, BC
Scope: Provincial

British Columbia Shake & Shingle Association
33017 - 14th Ave., Mission BC V2V 2P3
Tel: 604-826-7185
enquiries@bcshakeshingle.com
www.bcshakeshingle.com
Overview: A small provincial charitable organization founded in 1979
Mission: To coordinate the efforts of the member mills & associates with the objective of protecting & increasing the viability of the BC wood shake & shingle manufacturing industry
Affiliation(s): Cedar Shake & Shingle Bureau
Finances: *Funding Sources:* Membership fees; government
Membership: 18; *Member Profile:* Direct involvement in the shake & shingle industry
Activities: *Internships:* Yes; *Rents Mailing List:* Yes

British Columbia Sheet Metal Association (SMACNA-BC)
#315, 15225 - 104 Ave., Surrey BC V3R 6Y8
Tel: 604-585-4641; *Fax:* 604-584-9304
smacnabc@smacna-bc.org
www.smacna-bc.org
twitter.com/smacnabc
Also Known As: Sheet Metal & Air Conditioning Contractors National Association - BC Division
Overview: A medium-sized provincial organization founded in 1969
Mission: To promote financial stability in the sheet metal industry as well as to improve working conditions for their members
Chief Officer(s):
Bruce E. Sychuk, Executive Director
Membership: 69; *Member Profile:* Unionized sheet metal contractors throughout British Columbia (exluding Vancouver Island); Suppliers to the industry

British Columbia Shellfish Growers Association (BCSGA)
2002 Comox Ave., Unit F, Comox BC V9M 3M6
Tel: 250-890-7561; *Fax:* 250-890-7563
www.bcsga.ca
Previous Name: British Columbia Oyster Growers' Association
Overview: A small provincial organization founded in 1949
Mission: Advancing the sustainable growth & prosperity of the BC shellfish industry in a global economy by providing leadership & advocacy to members & stakeholders while maintaining the integrity of the marine environment
Member of: Canadian Aquaculture Industry Alliance; Aquaculture Association of Canada
Chief Officer(s):
Roberta Stevenson, Executive Director
roberta@bcsga.ca
Finances: *Annual Operating Budget:* $100,000-$250,000; *Funding Sources:* Membership fees
Staff Member(s): 2
Membership: 181; *Fees:* $500
Activities: Advocacy; research & development; marketing; member services; *Library*

British Columbia Shorthand Reporters Association (BCSRA)
PO Box 130, 1027 Davie St., Vancouver BC V6E 4L2
Tel: 604-734-5311; *Fax:* 604-642-5177
Toll-Free: 866-207-2222
bcsra@bcsra.net
www.bcsra.net
Overview: A small provincial organization founded in 1975
Mission: To support the court reporting community & related fields in British Columbia; To uphold the professional standards & ethics of court reporters, broadcast captioners, & CART providers in the province
Chief Officer(s):
Debra Collos, President
Finances: *Funding Sources:* Membership dues
Membership: *Fees:* $15 students; $35 associates/affiliates; $85 new graduates; $170 full members; *Member Profile:* Court / realtime reporters, broadcast captioners, & CART (communication acess realtime translation) providers in British Columbia
Activities: Engaging in advocacy activities on behalf of the profession; Providing public relations services;

British Columbia Shorthorn Association
16951 - 12 Ave., Surrey BC V3S 9M3
Tel: 604-536-2800; *Fax:* 604-538-6760
semiahmooshorthorns@shaw.ca
www.facebook.com/222735927770671
Overview: A small provincial organization
Mission: To raise shorthorn cattle
Member of: Canadian Shorthorn Association
Chief Officer(s):
Gary Wood, President
Membership: 49

British Columbia Simmental Association *See* Simmental Association of British Columbia

British Columbia Snowmobile Federation (BCSF)
PO Box 277, 18 - 1st St., Keremeos BC V0X 1N0
Tel: 250-499-5117; *Fax:* 250-499-2103
Toll-Free: 877-537-8716
office@bcsf.org
www.bcsf.org
Overview: A medium-sized provincial organization founded in 1965
Mission: To encourage & promote the sport of operating snowmobiles in BC by enhancing cooperation & communication between & among snowmobile clubs, recreation industry & racing divisions, the provincial government, other motorized recreational organizations & groups supportive of snowmobiling
Member of: Outdoor Recreation Council of British Columbia; Wilderness Tourism Association; BC Avalanche Association
Affliation(s): International Snowmobile Council; Canadian Council of Snowmobile Organizations
Chief Officer(s):
Erin Hart, President
president@bcsf.org
Donegal Wilson, Contact, Office
Finances: *Annual Operating Budget:* $50,000-$100,000; *Funding Sources:* Membership fees
Staff Member(s): 1; 70 volunteer(s)
Membership: 6,000 individual + 70 clubs; *Fees:* $17.50; *Committees:* Trails; Charities; Safety; Environment; Government Relations; Snow Show
Activities: Tread Lightly Program; Safety Training Program; SnoVision 2000 Program; Exemplary Service Recognition Program; *Awareness Events:* Snowarama (charity ride); *Speaker Service:* Yes; *Rents Mailing List:* Yes
Awards:
• Snowmobile Family of the Year (Award)
• Snowmobile Charity Award (Award)
• Snowmobiler of the Year (Award)

British Columbia Soccer Association
#250, 3410 Lougheed Hwy., Vancouver BC V5M 2A4
Tel: 604-299-6401; *Fax:* 604-299-9610
info@bcsoccer.net
www.bcsoccer.net
www.facebook.com/bcsoccerassociation
twitter.com/1bcsoccer
Overview: A medium-sized provincial organization founded in 1907 overseen by Canadian Soccer Association
Mission: To promote & develop the sport of soccer in British Columbia
Member of: Canadian Soccer Association
Chief Officer(s):
Paul Mullen, Executive Director
paulmullen@bcsoccer.net
Staff Member(s): 18

British Columbia Social Studies Teachers Association (BCSSTA)
c/o BC Teachers' Federation, #100, 550 West 6th Ave., Vancouver BC V5Z 4P2
Tel: 604-871-2283; *Fax:* 604-871-2286
Toll-Free: 800-663-9163
bcssta@gmail.com
bcssta.wordpress.com
twitter.com/bcssta
Overview: A small provincial organization
Mission: To support & improve the teaching of social studies
Member of: BC Teachers' Federation
Chief Officer(s):
Dale Martelli, President
Membership: *Fees:* Schedule available
Meetings/Conferences: • British Columbia Social Studies Teachers Association 2015 Annual Conference, 2015, BC
Scope: Provincial

British Columbia Society for Male Survivors of Sexual Abuse (BCSMSSA)
#202, 1252 Burrard St., Vancouver BC V6Z 1Z1
Tel: 604-682-6482; *Fax:* 604-684-8883
bcsmssa@hotmail.com
www.bc-malesurvivors.com
Merged from: Vancouver Society for Male Survivors of Sexual Abuse; Victoria Male Survivors of Sexual Assault Soc.
Overview: A small provincial charitable organization founded in 1990
Mission: To provide treatment & support services to male survivors of sexual abuse & support for their families & partners; to acquire & develop education material re: male survivors & gather statistics; to establish new programs for male survivors within British Columbia or assist other agencies in setting up programs through training & consultation; to advocate for male survivors with government & the general population
Member of: British Columbia Association of Specialized Victim Assistance & Counselling Programs

Chief Officer(s):
Don Wright, Executive Director
Finances: *Annual Operating Budget:* $250,000-$500,000; *Funding Sources:* Provincial government, donations, foundation grants; client paid fees; client compensation program
Staff Member(s): 13; 5 volunteer(s)
Activities: Individual & group therapy; guidance & support through legal processes; education through training programs; video & manual production & sale; *Awareness Events:* Male Surviviors of Sexual Abuse Awareness Month, Apr.; *Internships:* Yes; *Speaker Service:* Yes

British Columbia Society for the Prevention of Cruelty to Animals

1245 East 7th Ave., Vancouver BC V5T 1R1
Tel: 604-681-7271
Toll-Free: 800-665-1868
info@spca.bc.ca
www.spca.bc.ca
www.facebook.com/bcspca
twitter.com/BC_SPCA
www.youtube.com/user/bcspcabc
Also Known As: BC SPCA
Overview: A medium-sized provincial charitable organization founded in 1895 overseen by Canadian Federation of Humane Societies
Mission: To protect & enhance the quality of life for domestic, farm, & wild animals in British Columbia
Member of: Canadian Federation of Humane Societies
Chief Officer(s):
Craig Daniell, Chief Executive Officer
4000 volunteer(s)
Membership: *Fees:* $25 regular; $15 senior; $100 associate/corporate; $250 lifetime

British Columbia Society of Electroneurophysiology Technologists (BCSET)

c/o EEG Department, Penticton Regional Hospital, 550 Carmi Ave., Penticton BC V2A 3G6
Tel: 250-492-1000; *Fax:* 250-492-9037
webmaster@bcset.org
www.bcset.org
Overview: A small provincial organization
Mission: A professional non-profit association dedicated to fostering excellence in diagnostic electroneurophysiology, furthering education and providing a forum for discussion and interaction.
Affliation(s): Canadian Association of Electroneurophysiology Technologists
Chief Officer(s):
Tara Cassidy, President
3 volunteer(s)
Membership: 1-99; *Member Profile:* Electroneurophysiology technologists in British Columbia

British Columbia Society of Laboratory Science (BCSLS)

#720, 999 West Broadway, Vancouver BC V5Z 1K5
Tel: 604-714-1760; *Fax:* 604-738-4080
Toll-Free: 800-304-0033
bcsls@bcsls.net
www.bcsls.net
Previous Name: British Columbia Society of Medical Technologists
Overview: A medium-sized provincial organization founded in 1969 overseen by Canadian Society for Medical Laboratory Science
Mission: To provide the members with representation, education, fellowship & leadership
Chief Officer(s):
Malcolm Ashford, Executive Director
malcolm@bcsls.net
Erica Meredith, President
ericajp.meredith@gmail.com
Finances: *Funding Sources:* Membership dues; education programs
Staff Member(s): 2
Membership: *Member Profile:* Medical laboratory technologists & assistants in British Columbia; *Committees:* Congress; MLA Education Day
Activities: Fall Congress; *Awareness Events:* National Medical Laboratory Week, April; *Internships:* Yes; *Speaker Service:* Yes

British Columbia Society of Landscape Architects (BCSLA)

#110, 355 Burrard St., Vancouver BC V6C 2G8
Tel: 604-682-5610; *Fax:* 604-681-3394
admin@bcsla.org
www.bcsla.org
www.linkedin.com/groups/BC-Society-Landscape-Architects-507 4296
www.facebook.com/BCSocietyofLandscapeArchitects
twitter.com/BCSLA
Overview: A medium-sized provincial licensing organization founded in 1964
Mission: To promote, improve & advance the profession; to maintain standards of professional practice & conduct consistent with the need to serve & protect the public interest; to support the improvement &/or conservation of the natural, cultural, social & built environment.
Member of: Canadian Society of Landscape Architects
Chief Officer(s):
Robert Evans, President
Finances: *Funding Sources:* Membership dues; special events; sponsors
Membership: *Fees:* $623 landscape architect; $180 associate/intern; $42 student; $263 affiliate; $106 inactive; *Member Profile:* Must have university degree in landscape architecture followed by two years experience working for registered landscape architect; must complete series of exams.; *Committees:* Bylaws & Standards; Public & Professional Relations; Nominations; Finance; Credentials
Activities: *Internships:* Yes

British Columbia Society of Medical Technologists *See* British Columbia Society of Laboratory Science

British Columbia Society of Prosthodontists (BCSP)

#220, 2425 Oak St., Vancouver BC V6H 3S7
Tel: 604-734-1232; *Fax:* 604-732-1719
www.bcprosthodontists.org
Overview: A small provincial organization
Mission: A non-profit organization made up of certified specialists in Prosthodontics.
Chief Officer(s):
Alec Cheng, President
Membership: 30; *Member Profile:* Certified specialists in Prosthodontics in the province of British Columbia.

British Columbia Society of Respiratory Therapists (BCSRT)

PO Box 4760, Vancouver BC V6B 4A4
Tel: 604-623-2227
www.bcsrt.ca
Overview: A medium-sized provincial organization founded in 1977
Mission: To represent the interests of the respiratory therapy profession in British Columbia; To promote best practices within the occupation; To uphold the British Columbia Society of Respiratory Therapists Standards for Professional Conduct, Code of Ethics, & Standards of Practice
Chief Officer(s):
Elizabeth Goodfellow, President
preselect.bcsrt@gmail.com
Membership: *Fees:* Free, for first & second year students; $15 third year students; $20 associate & affiliate members; $75 corporate members; $85 active members; *Member Profile:* Registered respiratory therapists of British Columbia; Non-practicing individuals; Students; Corporations
Activities: Promoting the role of registered respiratory therapists (RTs); Providing continuing educational oppotunities in respiratory care; Awarding grants; Liaisinig with regulators & national professional associations; Reviewing & revising standards of practice
Meetings/Conferences: • 2015 Annual Meeting of the British Columbia Society of Respiratory Therapists, 2015, BC
Scope: Provincial

British Columbia Spaces for Nature

PO Box 673, Gibsons BC V0N 1V0
e-mail: info@spacesfornature.org
www.spacesfornature.org
Overview: A medium-sized provincial charitable organization founded in 1989
Mission: To protect British Columbia's wilderness resource
Chief Officer(s):
Robert Ballantyne, Executive Member
Chloe O'Loughlin, Executive Member
Loretta Woodcock, Executive Member
Activities: Leading campaigns to protect wilderness areas throughout British Columbia; *Library:* British Columbia Spaces for Nature Library
Publications:
• Jobs & Environment: Moving British Columbia into the 21st Century
Type: Report; *Number of Pages:* 74
Profile: Policy options & recommendations for British Columbia's future
• Keeping the Special in Special Management Zones: A Citizens Guide [a publication of British Columbia Spaces for Nature]
Type: Report; *Number of Pages:* 143
Profile: Information about special management zones, or government designated land use planning areas, whereconservation is emphasized in management decisions
• Klinaklini Resource Analysis [a publication of British Columbia Spaces for Nature]
Type: Report; *Number of Pages:* 87
Profile: Suggestions for safeguarding the biodiversity of this interior-to-coastal watershed
• West Chilcotin Demonstration Project [a publication of British Columbia Spaces for Nature]
Type: Report; *Number of Pages:* 73
Profile: Collaboration between First Nations, the local community, the tourism industry, & the forest industry to create a sustainablefuture for the West Chilcotin

British Columbia Special Olympics *See* Special Olympics BC

British Columbia Speed Skating Association

PO Box 2023, Stn. A, #202, 2306 McCallum Rd., Abbotsford BC V2T 3T8
Tel: 604-746-4349; *Fax:* 604-746-4549
lorna@speed-skating.bc.ca
www.speed-skating.bc.ca
Overview: A small provincial organization overseen by Speed Skating Canada
Mission: The organization wishes to foster the growth & development of Speed Skating in B.C. by providing quality services & support programs to all members in their pursuit of a healthy lifestyle while encouraging challenges & promoting excellence.
Member of: Speed Skating Canada
Chief Officer(s):
Ted Houghton, Executive Director
ted.houghton@telus.net

British Columbia Sporthorse - Sport Pony Breeders Group

c/o Shelley Fraser, 2547 - 208th St., Langley BC V2Z 2B1
Tel: 604-533-1228
www.bcsporthorses.com
Overview: A small provincial organization
Mission: To promote the breeding of sporthorses & sportponies in British Columbia; To organize shows for owners & breeders of sporthorses & sportponies to show their stock; To improve the breeding program
Chief Officer(s):
Ulli Dargel, Entry Secretary, 604-421-6681
actionfilm@telus.net
Shelley Fraser, Entry Secretary, 604-534-8782
tiwi@telus.net
Membership: *Fees:* $25 senior (19 years & older); $15 junior (18 years & under); $35 family (parents & children 18 years & under); *Member Profile:* Owners & breeders of sporthorses & sportponies in British Columbia
Activities: Providing educational seminars & clinics about sporthorses & sportponies; Marketing British Columbia bred sporthorses & sportponies; Offering networking opportunities

British Columbia Sports Hall of Fame & Museum

Gate A, BC Place Stadium, 777 Pacific Blvd. South, Vancouver BC V6B 4Y8
Tel: 604-687-5520; *Fax:* 604-687-5510
sportsinfo@bcsportshalloffame.com
www.bcsportshalloffame.com
www.facebook.com/bcsportshall
twitter.com/BCSportsHall
Overview: A medium-sized provincial charitable organization founded in 1966
Mission: To collect, preserve & display sports artifacts from BC's sporting history; to provide an exciting & educational environment for sports history
Member of: Canadian Museums Association; BC Museums Association
Affliation(s): International Association of Sports Museums & Halls of Fame
Chief Officer(s):
Allison Mailer, Executive Director
allison.mailer@bcsportshalloffame.com

Jason Beck, Curator
jason.beck@bcsportshalloffame.com
Finances: *Funding Sources:* Corporate & private
Staff Member(s): 5; 50 volunteer(s)
Membership: 1-99
Activities: Champions Banquet & Tournament of Champions; *Awareness Events:* Banquet of Champions, Induction Ceremonies; *Internships:* Yes; *Library* by appointment

British Columbia Square & Round Dance Federation

c/o President, 1459 Claudia Pl., Port Coquitlam BC V3C 2V5
Tel: 604-941-6392
Toll-Free: 800-335-9433
www.squaredance.bc.ca
twitter.com/bcfeddancenews
Overview: A medium-sized provincial charitable organization overseen by Canadian Square & Round Dance Society
Mission: To provide healthy recreation at the community level for an affordable cost
Chief Officer(s):
Ken Crisp, President
kcrisp@shaw.ca
Membership: *Member Profile:* Leaders; dancers; volunteers
Activities: Square dancing; round dancing; country dancing; clogging; wheelchair dancing; *Library:* BC Federation Library

British Columbia Stone, Sand & Gravel Association (BCSSGA)

c/o Paul Allard, PO Box 36065, Stn. Hillcrest Village, Surrey BC V3S 7Y4
Tel: 778-571-2670; *Fax:* 778-571-2680
gravelbc@telus.net
www.gravelbc.ca
Previous Name: Aggregate Producers Association of BC
Overview: A medium-sized provincial organization founded in 1988
Mission: To represent the aggregate industry in British Columbia, at all levels of government & in the community
Chief Officer(s):
Bob Esau, President
Paul Allard, Executive Director
Membership: *Fees:* Schedule available; *Member Profile:* Companies & organizations working in or involved with the aggregate industry in British Columbia
Activities: Networking for members; lessons for elementary children on the use of aggregate
Awards:
• BCSSGA Annual Awards (Award)

British Columbia Supercargoes' Association

#206, 3711 Delbrook Ave., North Vancouver BC V7N 3Z4
Tel: 604-878-1258; *Fax:* 604-904-6545
president@supercargoes.bc.ca
www.supercargoes.bc.ca
Overview: A medium-sized provincial organization founded in 1952
Mission: To provide expert marine cargo planning & onsite management & supervision of shiploading & discharge of all types of cargoes & vessels on the west coast of North America
Chief Officer(s):
Terry Stuart, President
Finances: *Funding Sources:* Membership dues
Membership: 9; *Member Profile:* Marine professionals in the shipping industry

British Columbia Surgical Society (BCSS)

#115, 1665 West Broadway, Vancouver BC V6J 5A4
Tel: 604-638-2843; *Fax:* 604-638-2938
athomas@bcma.bc.ca
www.bcss.ca
Overview: A small provincial organization founded in 1947
Mission: To further the teaching, practice, & science of the branches of surgery; to advance patient care
Chief Officer(s):
Diane Wong, Contact
Finances: *Funding Sources:* Sponsorships
Membership: *Fees:* $100
Activities: Promoting continuous learning; Facilitating the exchange of information among surgeons
Meetings/Conferences: • 2015 BC Surgical Society Annual Spring Meeting, April, 2015, Fairmont Chateau Whistler, Whistler, BC
Scope: Provincial

British Columbia Sustainable Energy Association (BCSEA)

PO Box 44104, Stn. Gorge Plaza, 2947 Tillicum Rd., Victoria BC V9A 7K1
Tel: 250-744-2720
info@bcsea.org
www.bcsea.org
www.facebook.com/BCSEA
twitter.com/bcsea
www.youtube.com/BCSEA
Overview: A medium-sized provincial organization founded in 2004
Mission: To empower British Columbians to build a clean, renewable energy future
Affliation(s): Canadian Renewable Energy Association; Canadian Solar Industries Association; Canadian Wind Energy Association; Climate Action Network Canada; KyotoPLUS; Livable Region Coalition; NorthWest Energy Coalition; Oil Free Coast Alliance; Organizing for Change: Priorities for Environmental Leadership
Chief Officer(s):
Nigel Protter, CEO & Executive Director
Finances: *Funding Sources:* Donations
Membership: *Fees:* Schedule available; *Member Profile:* Individuals & organizations
Activities: Providing education through programs & webinars
Meetings/Conferences: • British Columbia Sustainable Energy Association Annual General Meeting 2015, 2015, BC
Scope: National
Contact Information: watershow@shaw.ca; Website: www.watershow.ca; Phone: 778-432-2120

British Columbia Table Tennis Association (BCTTA)

#208, 5760 Minoru Blvd., Richmond BC V6X 2A9
Tel: 604-270-3393
bctta@lightspeed.ca
www.bctta.ca
Overview: A small provincial organization overseen by Table Tennis Canada
Member of: Table Tennis Canada; Sport BC
Affliation(s): International Table Tennis Federation
Chief Officer(s):
Amelia Ho, President
Membership: 200+; *Fees:* $15 junior; $25 adult; $15 senior

British Columbia Target Sports Association

PO Box 496, Kamloops BC V2C 5L2
e-mail: targetsports@bctsa.bc.ca
www.bctsa.bc.ca
Previous Name: BC Smallbore Rifle Association
Overview: A small provincial organization
Mission: To promote target rifle sports in British Columbia
Member of: Shooting Federation of Canada
Finances: *Funding Sources:* Membership dues; donations; sports grants; entry fees
Membership: *Fees:* $25 family/senior; $10 junior; $10 associate; $25 club
Activities: Provincial/national championships;

British Columbia Teacher Regulation Branch (BCCT)

#400, 2025 West Broadway, Vancouver BC V6J 1Z6
Tel: 604-660-6060; *Fax:* 604-775-4859
Toll-Free: 800-555-3684
www.bcteacherregulation.ca
Previous Name: British Columbia College of Teachers
Overview: A medium-sized provincial organization founded in 1987
Mission: To establish standards for the education, professional responsibility & competence of its members; To certify educators
Chief Officer(s):
Alison Hougham, Media Relations Contact
alison.hougham@gov.bc.ca
Finances: *Funding Sources:* Application & membership fees
Staff Member(s): 22
Membership: 68,000+; *Fees:* $80; *Member Profile:* Certified educators in British Columbia; *Committees:* Finance; Discipline; Qualifications; Teacher Education Programs

British Columbia Teacher-Librarians' Association (BCTLA)

c/o British Columbia Teachers' Federation, #100, 550 West 6th Ave., Vancouver BC V5Z 4P2
Tel: 604-871-2283; *Fax:* 604-871-2286
Toll-Free: 800-663-9163
bctlamembership@gmail.com
www.bctf.ca/bctla
twitter.com/bctla
Overview: A medium-sized provincial organization
Mission: To promote the essential role of teacher-librarians within British Columbia's education community; To improve the learning & working condition in school library resource centres
Member of: British Columbia Teachers' Federation (BCTLA is a provincial specialist association of the BCTF)
Chief Officer(s):
Heather Daly, President, 604-937-6380
Lindsay Ross, Vice-President, Chapter Relations, 250-386-3591
Jeff Yasinchuk, Vice-President, Advocacy
jyasinchuk@gmail.com
Amanda Hufton, Chair, Working & Learning Conditions, 604-668-6269
kaela2@shaw.ca
Finances: *Annual Operating Budget:* Less than $50,000
Membership: *Fees:* $15 Students, TTOCs, Retired; $40 BCTF Members; *Member Profile:* Teacher-librarians throughout British Columbia
Activities: Supporting resource-based learning & cooperative planning & teaching; Encouraging professional development; Advocating for strong school libraries
Meetings/Conferences: • British Columbia Teacher-Librarians' Association 2015 Provincial Conference, 2015, BC
Scope: Provincial
Description: A gathering of British Columbia's teacher-librarians for workshops, keynote presentations, & social events
Contact Information: Conference Chair: Sylvia Zubke, Phone: 604-713-4985, E-mail: szubke@gmail.com
• British Columbia Teacher-Librarians' Association 2016 Provincial Conference, 2016, BC
Scope: Provincial
Description: A gathering of British Columbia's teacher-librarians for workshops, keynote presentations, & social events
Contact Information: Conference Chair: Sylvia Zubke, Phone: 604-713-4985, E-mail: szubke@gmail.com
Publications:
• The Bookmark
Type: Journal; *Frequency:* Quarterly *ISSN:* 0381-6028
Profile: Developments in the field of teacher-librarianship, information about learning resources in British Columbia, & the promotion of literature appreciation

British Columbia Teachers for Peace & Global Education (PAGE)

c/o BC Teachers' Federation, #100, 550 West 6th Ave., Vancouver BC V5Z 4P2
Tel: 604-871-2283; *Fax:* 604-871-2286
Toll-Free: 800-663-9163
www.pagebc.ca
www.facebook.com/PAGEBC.CA
twitter.com/PAGE_BC
Overview: A small provincial organization founded in 1985
Mission: To maintain a network of teachers who support both local & international initiatives to make the world a more equitable & sustainable one; to foster awareness raising, professional development & activism, & encourage students to demonstrate humanitarian concern.
Affliation(s): British Columbia Teachers' Federation
Chief Officer(s):
Greg van Vugt, President
gvanvugt@hotmail.com
Finances: *Funding Sources:* Grant; membership fees
Membership: *Fees:* $10 student/retired; $25 BCTF member; $45 non-BCTF member
Publications:
• The Global Educator
Type: journal

British Columbia Teachers of English Language Arts

c/o B.C. Teachers' Federation, #100, 550 West 6th Ave., Vancouver BC V5Z 4P2
Tel: 604-871-1848
Toll-Free: 800-663-9163
www.bctela.ca
Previous Name: BC English Teachers' Association
Overview: A medium-sized provincial organization
Member of: BC Teachers' Federation
Membership: *Fees:* $50; *Member Profile:* English Language Arts teachers from British Columbia & Yukon

British Columbia Teachers' Federation (BCTF) / Fédération des enseignants de la Colombie-Britannique

#100, 550 - 6th Ave. West, Vancouver BC V5Z 4P2

Tel: 604-871-2283; *Fax:* 604-871-2293
Toll-Free: 800-663-9163
benefits@bctf.ca
www.bctf.ca
www.facebook.com/BCTeachersFederation
twitter.com/bctf
www.youtube.com/bctfvids
Overview: A large provincial organization founded in 1917 overseen by Canadian Teachers' Federation
Mission: To represent 41,000 public school teachers in the province of British Columbia; To support 33 provincial specialist associations, such as the British Columbia Teacher-Librarians' Association & the British Columbia Music Educators' Association; To advocate for the professional, economic, & social goals of teachers
Member of: Canadian Labour Congress; British Columbia Federation of Labour
Chief Officer(s):
Susan Lambert, President
presidentsoffice@bctf.ca
Jim Iker, First Vice-President
jiker@bctf.ca
Membership: 41,000; *Member Profile:* Public school teachers in the province of British Columbia
Activities: Offering workshops & programs for members; Publishing research reports; Promoting a quality pluralistic public school system; Engaging in collective bargaining
Meetings/Conferences: • British Columbia Teachers' Federation 2015 Summer Leadershipo Conference, August, 2015, BC
Scope: Provincial
• British Columbia Teachers' Federation 2015 99th Annual General Meeting, March, 2015
Scope: Provincial
Description: A meeting to set the future directions of the Federation
• British Columbia Teachers' Federation 2015 Provincial Specialist Associations Day, October, 2015, BC
Scope: Provincial
Description: An annual professional development day, offering a wide range of workshops for teachers across British Columbia
Contact Information: British Columbia Teachers' Federation Media Relations Officer: Rich Overgaard, E-mail: rovergaard@bctf.ca
Publications:
• BCTF [British Columbia Teachers' Federation] Services Handbook
Type: Handbook
Profile: Featuring the British Columbia Teachers' Federation staff directory, plus information about opportunities to develop leadership skills
• BCTF [British Columbia Teachers' Federation] Members' Guide
Type: Guide
Profile: Federation constitution, bylaws, policies, procedures, & the code of ethics
• BCTF [British Columbia Teachers' Federation] News
Type: Newsletter; *Frequency:* Monthly
Profile: Significant issues for staff & PD representatives throughout British Columbia
• BCTF [British Columbia Teachers' Federation] Handbook for TOCs & New Teachers: The Practice of Teaching
Type: Handbook; *Number of Pages:* 64
Profile: Practical information, such as reporting requirements, classroom management, working with parents, & sources foraid for new teachers
• Issue Alert [a publication of the British Columbia Teachers' Federation]
Type: Newsletter
Profile: Important issues for all British Columbia Teachers' Federation members
• PSA Guidebook [a publication of the British Columbia Teachers' Federation]
Type: Guide
Profile: Information about operations & activities for officers of British Columbia Teachers' Federation's provincial specialist associations
• Public Education Advocates
Type: Newsletter; *Frequency:* Semimonthly
Profile: A review of current education issues
• School Staff Alert
Type: Newsletter; *Frequency:* Irregular
Profile: Alerts from the British Columbia Teachers' Federation faxed to schools throughout British Columbia
• Teacher Inquirer
Type: Newsletter
Profile: Reports by British Columbia's public school teachers on teacher inquiries
• Teacher Newsmagazine
Type: Magazine; *Frequency:* 7 pa; *Accepts Advertising*
Profile: Circulating to 57,000 public school teachers, student teachers, retired teachers, teacher affiliates, parent advisory councils, & university personnel in British Columbia

British Columbia Team Handball Federation (BCTHF)

Vancouver BC
e-mail: bchandball@gmail.com
bchandball.wix.com/bchandball
www.facebook.com/BCHandball
twitter.com/van_handball
Overview: A small provincial organization founded in 2003
Mission: To act as the governing body for handball in BC
Member of: Canadian Team Handball Federation
Chief Officer(s):
David Lee, Executive Director
Membership: *Fees:* Schedule available

British Columbia Technology Education Association

c/o L.V. Rogers Secondary School, 1004 Cottonwood St., Nelson BC V1L 3W2
Tel: 250-352-5538; *Fax:* 250-352-3119
info@bctea.org
www.bctea.org
Overview: A medium-sized provincial organization
Mission: To promote technology education in British Columbia schools
Member of: BC Teachers' Federation; Provincial Specialist Association
Chief Officer(s):
Mike Howard, President
mhoward@telus.net
Membership: *Fees:* Schedule available

British Columbia Technology Industries Association (BCTIA)

#900, 1188 West Georgia St., Vancouver BC V6E 4A2
Tel: 604-683-6159
info@bctia.org
www.bctia.org
www.linkedin.com/groupInvitation?gid=112219
www.facebook.com/bctia.org
twitter.com/bctia
www.youtube.com/user/bctiaTV
Also Known As: BC Technology Industries Association
Merged from: Electronic Manufacturers' Association of BC & the Information Technology Assn of Canada, BC Chapter
Overview: A medium-sized provincial organization founded in 1993
Mission: To support the growth of a strong knowledge economy in British Columbia; To act as the voice of the technology industry
Chief Officer(s):
Bill Tam, President & Chief Executive Officer, 604-602-5230
btam@bctia.org
Cindy Pearson, Vice-President & Chief Operating Officer, 604-602-5234
cpearson@bctia.org
Peter Payne, Executive in Residence
Staff Member(s): 11
Membership: *Fees:* Schedule available; *Member Profile:* Companies of all sizes, from all sectors
Activities: Offering professional development activities; Delivering programs, such as Xcelerate, an executive education program & PODIUM, an industry promotion program; Advocating on behalf of the industry; Facilitating partnerships; Increasing public awareness

British Columbia Tennis Association *See* Tennis BC

British Columbia Tenpin Bowling Association

Nanaimo BC
www.bctenpin.com
Overview: A small provincial organization overseen by Canadian Tenpin Federation, Inc.
Mission: To oversee the sport of tenpin bowling in British Columbia.
Member of: Canadian Tenpin Federation, Inc.
Chief Officer(s):
Jennifer Park, President
president@bctenpin.com
Mark Westerberg, Vice-President
vicepresident@bctenpin.com
MaryAnne Madsen, Secretary
secretary@bctenpin.com
Miriam Reid, Treasurer
bowlermommy@hotmail.com

British Columbia Therapeutic Recreation Association (BCTRA)

PO Box 54569, 7155 Kingsway, Burnaby BC V5E 4J6
e-mail: info@bctra.org
www.bctra.org
Overview: A small provincial organization founded in 1991
Mission: To represent Therapeutic Recreation Professionals & their practice within BC
Chief Officer(s):
Jasmine Jagpal-Balson, President
president@bctra.org
Membership: *Fees:* $210; $110 supporting; $50 student

British Columbia Therapeutic Riding Association (BCTRA)

3885B - 96th St., Delta BC V4K 3N3
Tel: 604-590-0897
ponypalstra@yahoo.ca
www.vcn.bc.ca/bctra
Overview: A small provincial charitable organization founded in 1986
Mission: To adhance the quality of life of people with disabilities
Member of: Canadian Therapeutic Riding Association; Horse Council of British Columbia
Affliation(s): Horse Council BC; Sports & Fitness Council for the Disabled
Chief Officer(s):
Candice Miller, President
Finances: *Funding Sources:* Membership dues; donations
Membership: *Fees:* $30 group/centre; $10 individual; *Member Profile:* Therapeutic riding centres/individuals
Activities: *Speaker Service:* Yes

British Columbia Transplant Society (BCTS)

West Tower, 555 West 12th Ave., 3rd Fl., Vancouver BC V5Z 3X7
Tel: 604-877-2240; *Fax:* 604-877-2111
Toll-Free: 800-663-6189
BCTS_Webmaster@bcts.hnet.bc.ca
www.transplant.bc.ca
www.facebook.com/BCTransplant
twitter.com/bc_transplant
Overview: A medium-sized provincial organization founded in 1986
Mission: To lead & coordinate all activities related to organ transplantation & donation, ensuring high standards of quality & efficient management.
Affliation(s): University of British Columbia
Finances: *Funding Sources:* Provincial government; donations; private funding
Activities: Organ transplant services & research; *Speaker Service:* Yes

British Columbia Trucking Association (BCTA)

#100, 20111 - 93A Ave., Langley BC V1M 4A9
Tel: 604-888-5319
bcta@bctrucking.com
www.bctrucking.com
Previous Name: BC Motor Transport Association
Overview: A large provincial organization founded in 1913 overseen by Canadian Trucking Alliance
Mission: To act as the recognised voice of the commercial road transportation industry in British Columbia, by consulting & communicating with the industry, government, & the public; To promote a prosperous, safe, efficient & responsible road transportation industry; To provide programs & services to members
Chief Officer(s):
Louise Yako, President & Chief Executive Officer
Trace Acres, Vice-President
Greg Kolesniak, Director, Policy
Michele Nicol, Director, Business Operations
Veena Nanubhai, Coordinator, Accounting
Sandra Stashuk, Coordinator, Member Services
Shelley McGuinness, Specialist, Communications
Finances: *Funding Sources:* Membership dues
Membership: 1,000 corporate; *Fees:* $325-$400; *Member Profile:* Trucking company operating in BC; Supplier to trucking industry; *Committees:* Convention; Insurance; International; Labour; Freight Claims & Hazardous Goods; Safety; Truxpo; Vehicle Standards

Activities: *Speaker Service:* Yes; *Rents Mailing List:* Yes; *Library* by appointment
Meetings/Conferences: • British Columbia Trucking Association 2015 102nd Annual General Meeting & Management Conference, 2015, BC
Scope: Provincial
Description: A meeting of members of the British Columbia motor carrier association
Contact Information: Administrative Coordinator: Jennifer Cameron, E-mail: bcta@bctrucking.com

British Columbia Turkey Marketing Board
#106, 19329 Enterprise Way, Surrey BC V3S 6J8
Tel: 604-534-5644; *Fax:* 604-534-3651
info@bcturkey.com
www.bcturkey.com
Overview: A small provincial organization founded in 1966
Member of: British Columbia Turkey Association
Chief Officer(s):
Michel Benoit, General Manager
Ron Charles, Chair
Finances: *Funding Sources:* Grower levy
Staff Member(s): 5
Membership: 65; *Member Profile:* Turkey grower

British Columbia Ultrasonographers' Society (BCUS)
127 - 62nd Ave. East, Vancouver BC V5X 2E7
www.bcus.org
Overview: A small provincial organization founded in 1981
Mission: To promote & encourage the science & art of diagnostic medical sonography; provide a forum to promote the discussion of matters affecting the field; provide a place for professional growth
Chief Officer(s):
Vickie Lessoway, Executive Director
Membership: 1-99; *Fees:* $15 active/associate; $0 student

British Columbia Vegetable Marketing Commission (BCVMC)
#207, 15252- 32nd Ave., Surrey BC V3S 0R7
Tel: 604-542-9734; *Fax:* 604-542-9735
tom@bcveg.com
www.bcveg.com
Overview: A small provincial licensing organization
Chief Officer(s):
Tom Demma, General Manager
tom@bcveg.com
David Taylor, Chair
Staff Member(s): 5

British Columbia Veterinary Medical Association *See* College of Veterinarians of British Columbia

British Columbia Video Relay Services Committee
c/o WIDHH, 2125 West 7th Ave., Vancouver BC V6K 1X9
e-mail: bcvrsc@gmail.com
bcvrs.ca
www.facebook.com/bcvrs
twitter.com/BCVRS
Also Known As: BCVRS Committee
Overview: A small provincial organization founded in 2008
Mission: To represent the deaf community's view on Video Relay Services
Chief Officer(s):
Lisa Anderson-Kellett, Communications Officer
lisa@bcvrs.ca

British Columbia Wall & Ceiling Association
#112, 18663 - 52nd Ave., Surrey BC V3S 8E5
Tel: 604-575-0511; *Fax:* 604-575-0544
info@bcwca.org
www.bcwca.org
Overview: A small provincial organization overseen by Northwest Wall & Ceiling Bureau
Mission: To represent British Columbia chapters of the Northwest Wall & Ceiling Bureau on issues related to the wall & ceiling industry; To improve & promote industry apprenticeship & training; To uphold a Code of Ethics
Chief Officer(s):
Cathy LaPointe, President
Leesa Matwick, Executive Director
Finances: *Funding Sources:* Membership fees; Sponsorships
Membership: *Fees:* $800 contractors/associate members; $1,800 per chapter for suppliers/dealers' $2,000-$7,500 manufactuers; *Member Profile:* Professional from British Columbia's wall & ceiling industry, such as manufacturers, suppliers, & drywall & stucco contractors
Activities: Providing technical resources & educational seminars for members; Offering networking opportunities; *Library:* British Columbia Wall & Ceiling Association Resource Library
Publications:
• The Trowel
Type: Magazine; *Frequency:* Bimonthly; *Accepts Advertising*; *Editor:* Jessica Krippendorf; *Price:* Free with membership in the British Columbia Wall & Ceiling Association
Profile: Information for BC Wall & Ceiling Association members & other construction professionals throughout western Canada

British Columbia Wall & Ceiling Association (BCWCA)
#112, 18663 - 52nd Ave., Surrey BC V3S 8E5
Tel: 604-575-0511; *Fax:* 604-575-0544
info@bcwca.org
www.bcwca.org
twitter.com/BCWCA
Overview: A small provincial organization
Chief Officer(s):
Murray Corey, Executive Director
Eric Brown, President

British Columbia Water & Waste Association (BCWWA)
#221, 8678 Greenall Ave., Burnaby BC V5J 3M6
Tel: 604-433-4389; *Fax:* 604-433-9859
Toll-Free: 877-433-4389
contact@bcwwa.org
www.bcwwa.org
www.facebook.com/group.php?gid=21435804125
Overview: A medium-sized provincial organization founded in 1964
Mission: To safeguard public health & the environment through the sharing of skills, knowledge, experience & education; To provide a voice for the water & waste community in British Columbia & the Yukon
Member of: American Water Works Association (AWWA); Water Environment Federation (WEF); Canadian Water & Wastewater Association (CWWA)
Chief Officer(s):
Daisy Foster, Chief Executive Officer, 604-433-7824
dfoster@bcwwa.org
David Icharia, Director, Operations, 604-433-0093
dicharia@bcwwa.org
Judy Zhang, Manager, Finance, 604-433-6941
jzhang@bcwwa.org
Sarah Vaughan, Manager, Communications, 604-630-0011
svaughan@bcwwa.org
Kimberly Perreault, Coordinator, Member Services, 604-433-4389
kperreault@bcwwa.org
TBA, Coordinator, Education & Technology
Finances: *Funding Sources:* Membership fees; Courses; Seminars; Annual conference
Membership: *Fees:* $25 students; $35 operators; $60 full members; *Member Profile:* British Columbia & Yukon professionals & students in the water & wastewater fields; *Committees:* Young Professionals; Climate Change; Cross Connection Control; Decentralized Wastewater Management; Drinking Water; Energy Management; Infrastructure Management; Residuals Management; Small Water Systems; SCADA & Information Technology; Vancouver Island; Wastewater Collection; Wastewater Management; Wastewater Source Control; Water Sustainability; Watershed (Stormwater) Management; Yukon; Small Wastewater Systems; Small Water Systems; Wastewater Treatment; Water Distribution; Water Treatment; Awards; Elections; Governance; Nominations; Leadership Council
Activities: Promoting dialogue & information dissemination on environmental matters; Offering operator education & training opportunities (online training now available); Providing networking opportunities such as our Annual Conference; Certifying backflow assembly testers in British Columbia & Yukon through our Cross Connection Control program; Creating awareness of the value of water through Drinking Water Week, which occurs annually in May.; *Awareness Events:* Drinking Water Week, May; *Library:* British Columbia Water & Waste Association Library
Awards:
• Stanley S. Copp Award (Award)
• Personal Recognition Award (Award)
• Corporate Recognition Award (Award)
• Bridge Building Award (Award)
• Small Water Systems Award (Award)
• Victor M. Terry Award (Award)
• Water for People Kenneth J. Miller Award (Award)
• Okanagan College Bursary (Grant)
• UBC Bursary (Grant)
Meetings/Conferences: • British Columbia Water & Waste Association 2015 43rd Annual Conference & Trade Show, May, 2015, Kelowna, BC
Scope: Provincial
Attendance: 1,250
Description: A four day conference, including technical sessions & the chance to view current products at the trade show
Contact Information: Manager, Conferences & Events: Carlie Thauvette, Phone: 604-630-0011, E-mail: cthauvette@bcwwa.org
• British Columbia Water & Waste Association 2016 44th Annual Conference & Trade Show, 2016, BC
Scope: Provincial
Attendance: 1,250
Description: A four day conference, including technical sessions & the chance to view current products at the trade show
Contact Information: Manager, Conferences & Events: Carlie Thauvette, Phone: 604-630-0011, E-mail: cthauvette@bcwwa.org
Publications:
• Watermark
Type: Magazine; *Frequency:* Quarterly; *Accepts Advertising*; *Editor:* Carol Campbell
Profile: Calendar of events, product listings, new member listings, employment opportunities, informative articles, & reports on the annual conference, technical seminars & symposia

British Columbia Water Polo Association
#2002B, 3713 Kensington Ave., Burnaby BC V5B 0A7
Tel: 604-333-3480; *Fax:* 604-333-3450
Other Communication: Alt. Phone: 604-200-8635
office@bcwaterpolo.ca
www.bcwaterpolo.ca
www.facebook.com/BCWPA
twitter.com/bcwaterpolo
Also Known As: BC Water Polo
Overview: A medium-sized provincial organization founded in 1975 overseen by Water Polo Canada
Mission: To develop water polo in BC; to train provincal team & national team athletes
Member of: Water Polo Canada
Chief Officer(s):
Dave Soul, Executive Director, 778-237-3601
dsoul@telus.net
Finances: *Funding Sources:* Direct access funding; sponsorshp; government grant; membership fees
Staff Member(s): 1; 300 volunteer(s)
Membership: 1,000; *Fees:* Schedule available; *Committees:* Technical Advisory
Activities: *Library* Open to public

British Columbia Waterfowl Society
5191 Robertson Rd., RR#1, Delta BC V4K 3N2
Tel: 604-946-6980
www.reifelbirdsanctuary.com/bcws2.html
Also Known As: Reifel Bird Sanctuary
Overview: A medium-sized provincial charitable organization founded in 1963
Mission: To encourage conservation of wetlands; to spur public awareness on importance of conservation of estuaries; to operate George C. Reifel Migratory Bird Sanctuary.
Chief Officer(s):
Kathleen Fry, Manager
Jack Bates, President
Finances: *Annual Operating Budget:* $100,000-$250,000
Staff Member(s): 6; 40 volunteer(s)
Membership: 2,000; *Fees:* $20 single; $40 family; $500 life; *Committees:* Conservation; Publicity & Promotion; Operations; Membership Services
Activities: *Awareness Events:* Snow Goose Festival, Nov.; *Speaker Service:* Yes

British Columbia Weightlifting Association (BCWA)
5698 - 9A Ave., Delta BC V4L 1B7
e-mail: info@bcweightlifting.ca
www.bcweightlifting.ca
www.facebook.com/bcweightlifting
twitter.com/bcweightlifting
www.flickr.com/photos/bcwa
Also Known As: BC Weightlifting Association

Overview: A small provincial organization founded in 1969
Mission: To promote the sport of Olympic weightlifting in British Columbia
Affiliation(s): Canadian Weightlifting Federation
Finances: *Funding Sources:* Membership fees; Donations; Sponsorships
Membership: *Fees:* $10 volunteers; $24 youth athletes; $36 student athletes & officials; $48 senior & master athletes & coaches; $90 households; *Member Profile:* Coaches; Officials: Youth (age 12 & under), student, senior, & master (age 35 & over) athletes; Volunteers
Activities: Providing information about champtionships

British Columbia Welsh Pony & Cob Association

c/o Debbie Miyashita, 11075 Hynes St., Whonnock BC V2W 1P5
Tel: 604-462-7166
www.bcwelshponyandcob.com
Overview: A small provincial organization overseen by Welsh Pony & Cob Society of Canada
Mission: To promote the Welsh pony breed in British Columbia
Chief Officer(s):
Jan Systad, President, 604-533-3392
jsystad@bc-alter.net
Kathy Stanley, Vice-President, 250-456-7462
stanley_k@telus.net
Debbie Miyashita, Secretary, 604-462-7166
debbiem8@shaw.ca
Dennis Huber, Treasurer, 250-456-6050
hubersx3@telus.net
Moya Petznick, Newsletter Editor, 250-833-5711
petznick@telus.net
Lesley Flint, Contact, Membership, 250-846-5833
dhelps@mail.bulkey.net
Membership: 1-99; *Member Profile:* Persons in British Columbia who are involved with the Welsh pony breed; *Committees:* Northern; Interior; Fraser Valley
Activities: Offering networking opportunities for club members; Providing information about the Welsh breed to the public; Organizing the annual All Pony Show each July at Maple Ridge
Awards:
• Presidents Award (Award)
To recognize an outstanding contribution in the promotion of the Welsh pony breed
Meetings/Conferences: • British Columbia Welsh Pony & Cob Association 2015 Annual General Meeting, 2015, BC
Scope: Provincial
Publications:
• BC on the Move
Type: Newsletter; *Frequency:* Bimonthly; *Accepts Advertising*; *Editor:* Moya Petznick
Profile: Association activities, articles, & forthcoming events

Vancouver Island Region
c/o Philip Towell, 6033 Kellow Rd., Port Alberni BC V9Y 7L5
Tel: 250-724-1176
Mission: To promote the Welsh pony breed on Vancouver Island
Chief Officer(s):
Philip Towell, Contact, 250-724-1176

British Columbia Wheelchair Sports Association (BCWSA)

780 Southwest Marine Dr., Vancouver BC V6P 5Y7
Tel: 604-333-3520; *Fax:* 604-333-3450
Toll-Free: 877-737-3090
info@bcwheelchairsports.com
www.bcwheelchairsports.com
Overview: A medium-sized provincial charitable organization
Mission: To promote & develop wheelchair sport opportunities for British Columbians with physical disabilities
Member of: Canadian Wheelchair Sports Association
Chief Officer(s):
Gail Hamamoto, Executive Director
gail@bcwheelchairsports.com
Staff Member(s): 10
Membership: *Fees:* $10; *Member Profile:* Individuals with a disability & able bodied individuals
Activities: *Awareness Events:* Rick Hansen Wheels in Motion Event, June; *Speaker Service:* Yes
Awards:
• Most Improved Athlete of the Year (Award)
• Female Athlete of the Year (Award)
• Male Athlete of the Year (Award)
• Community Support Award (Award)
• Junior Athlete of the Year (Award)
• Spirit of Sport Award (Award)
• Volunteer of the Year (Award)
• Coach of the Year (Award)

British Columbia Wine Institute (BCWI)

#107, 1726 Dolphin Ave., Kelowna BC V1Y 9R9
Tel: 250-762-9744; *Fax:* 250-762-9788
Toll-Free: 800-661-2294
info@winebc.com
www.winebc.org
twitter.com/winebcdotcom
Overview: A medium-sized provincial organization founded in 1990
Chief Officer(s):
Josie Tyabji, Chairman
Staff Member(s): 6
Membership: 119

British Columbia Women's Institutes (BCWI)

#203B, 750 Cottonwood Ave., Kamloops BC V2B 3X2
Tel: 250-554-5406; *Fax:* 250-554-5406
info@bcwi.org
www.bcwi.org
Overview: A medium-sized provincial charitable organization founded in 1909 overseen by Federated Women's Institutes of Canada
Mission: To help discover, stimulate & develop leadership among women; to assist, encourage & support women to become knowledgeable & responsible citizens; to ensure basic human rights for women & to work towards their equality; to be a strong voice through which matters of utmost concern can reach the decision makers; to network with organizations sharing similar objectives; to promote the improvement of agricultural & other rural communities & to safeguard the environment
Member of: Associated Country Women of the World
Affiliation(s): BC Federation of Agriculture
Finances: *Annual Operating Budget:* $50,000-$100,000; *Funding Sources:* Membership dues; grants
Staff Member(s): 1
Membership: 1,800; *Fees:* $15
Activities: *Awareness Events:* Women's Institutes Week, Feb.; *Speaker Service:* Yes; *Library* Open to public by appointment

British Columbia Wood Specialities Group Association

#200, 9292 - 200th St., Langley BC V1M 3A6
Tel: 604-882-7100; *Fax:* 604-882-7300
Toll-Free: 877-422-9663
info@bcwood.com
www.bcwood.com
twitter.com/BC_Wood
Also Known As: BC Wood
Overview: A medium-sized provincial charitable organization founded in 1989
Mission: To assist BC manufacturers of value-added products achieve global competitiveness by providing essential marketing services to capitalize on new market opportunities
Chief Officer(s):
Brian Hawrysh, CEO Ext. 244
Finances: *Annual Operating Budget:* $1.5 Million-$3 Million; *Funding Sources:* Membership dues; provincial government; federal government
Staff Member(s): 12
Membership: 260; *Fees:* $500-$2,000; *Member Profile:* Manufacturers of value-added wood products in BC; *Committees:* Marketing
Activities: *Speaker Service:* Yes; *Library:* BC Wood Resource Library; by appointment

British Columbia Wrestling Association (BCWA)

3333 Ardingley Ave., Burnaby BC V5B 4A5
Tel: 604-737-3092; *Fax:* 604-737-6043
info@bcwrestling.com
www.bcwrestling.com
www.facebook.com/bcwrestling
twitter.com/wrestlingBC
Also Known As: Wrestling BC
Previous Name: British Columbia Amateur Wrestling Association
Overview: A small provincial organization founded in 1979 overseen by Canadian Amateur Wrestling Association
Mission: To promote & enhance the well-being of young people through their participation in wrestling
Member of: Sport BC
Affiliation(s): BC School Sports
Chief Officer(s):
Phil Cizmic, President, 250-923-0735
philip.cizmic@sd72.bc.ca
Staff Member(s): 2; 300 volunteer(s)
Membership: 2,200; *Member Profile:* Wrestlers, coaches, and officials
Activities: Camps; clinics; tournaments

British Columbia's Children's Hospital Foundation (BCCHF)

938 West 28th Ave., Vancouver BC V5Z 4H4
Tel: 604-875-2444; *Fax:* 604-875-2596
Toll-Free: 888-663-3033
info@bcchf.ca
www.bcchf.ca
www.facebook.com/BCChildrens
twitter.com/BCCHF
www.youtube.com/user/bcchf
Overview: A small provincial charitable organization
Mission: To make positive differences in the lives of children by supporting excellence at British Columbia's Children's Hospital & its related health partners
Member of: Children's & Women's Health Centre of British Columbia
Chief Officer(s):
Kevin Bent, Chair
Teri Nicholas, President & CEO
Finances: *Annual Operating Budget:* $500,000-$1.5 Million
Staff Member(s): 35
Activities: *Awareness Events:* CMN Telethon, June 2-3

British Columbian Francophone Youth Council *Voir* Conseil jeunesse francophone de la Colombie-Britannique

British Columbia-Yukon Halfway House Association (BCYHHA)

763 Kingsway, Vancouver BC V5V 3C2
e-mail: contact@bcyhha.org
www.bcyhha.org
Overview: A small provincial organization overseen by Regional Halfway House Association
Mission: To help offenders with their reintegration into society
Member of: Regional Halfway House Association

British Columia Patriot Party (PPC)

#206, 3407 - 39 Ave., Vernon BC V1T 3E3
Tel: 250-545-9057; *Fax:* 250-545-9157
Also Known As: BC Patriot Party
Overview: A small provincial organization founded in 2001
Mission: The party's political goal is to empower citizens to govern themselves by converting the provincial government into a republic with an upper house made up of citizen selected at random and based on merit.
Chief Officer(s):
Lillian Stokes, Party Leader
Arthur Carrier, Contact
acarrier@telus.net

British Council - Canada

#2800, 777 Bay St., Toronto ON M5G 2G2
e-mail: educatioinfo@ca.britishcouncil.org
www.britishcouncil.org/canada
www.linkedin.com/company/british-council
www.facebook.com/BritishCouncilCanada
twitter.com/britishcouncil
www.youtube.com/user/britishcouncilcanada
Overview: A small international charitable organization
Mission: To encourage cultural, scientific, technological & educational cooperation between Britain & Canada
Staff Member(s): 5
Activities: Education, arts, science & information
Awards:
• Arts Grants (Grant)
• UK/Canada Collaborative Programme (Scholarship)
• British Chevening Scholarships (Award)
One year's postgraduate study at a British university in disciplines including: environmental studies, science, international relations, engineering

Montréal Office
#1940, 2000, av McGill College, Montréal QC H3A 3H3
Tel: 514-866-5863; *Fax:* 514-866-5322
info@ca.britishcouncil.org
Chief Officer(s):
Sarah Dawbarn, Director

British Exservicemen's Association

1143 Kingsway Ave., Vancouver BC V5V 3C9
Tel: 604-874-6510
britexassoc@shawbiz.ca
britishex.ca
Overview: A small local organization founded in 1958

Chief Officer(s):
Carolyn Crompton, President
Membership: *Member Profile:* Exservices & associates

British Isles Family History Society of Greater Ottawa (BIFHSGO)
PO Box 38026, Ottawa ON K2C 3Y7
Tel: 613-234-2520
queries@bifhsgo.ca
www.bifhsgo.ca
Overview: A small local charitable organization founded in 1994
Mission: To promote & encourage research & publishing of Canadian family histories by descendants of British Isles emigrants
Member of: Federation of Geneological Societies; Federation of Family History Societies
Chief Officer(s):
Glenn Wright, President
president@bifhsgo.ca
Finances: *Annual Operating Budget:* Less than $50,000; *Funding Sources:* Membership dues; conference fees
49 volunteer(s)
Membership: 515; *Fees:* $40 individual; $50 family; $40 institution; *Member Profile:* Interest in family history of descendants of ancestors who migrated from British Isles
Activities: Annual conference held in Sept.; *Library:* Brian O'Regan Family History Library; Open to public
Meetings/Conferences: • British Isles Family History Society of Greater Ottawa 2015 21st Annual Family History Conference, September, 2015, Ottawa, ON
Scope: Provincial
Publications:
• Anglo-Celtic Roots
Type: Journal; *Editor:* Jean Kitchen
Profile: Presents articles on Canadian and British Isles family and social history, as well as genealogical research techniques and practices

British Israel World Federation (Canada) Inc. (BIWF)
313 Sherbourne St., Toronto ON M5A 2S3
Tel: 416-921-5996; *Fax:* 416-921-9511
info@british-israel-world-fed.ca
www.british-israel-world-fed.ca
Overview: A small international charitable organization founded in 1929
Mission: To proclaim the Gospel of the Kingdom of God as contained in the Holy Bible
Staff Member(s): 2
Membership: 1,200; *Fees:* $10
Activities: Meetings; *Speaker Service:* Yes
Publications:
• The Kingdom Herald
Profile: Magazine, 10 issues published annually

The British Methodist Episcopal Church of Canada (BME)
460 Shaw St., Toronto ON M6G 3L3
Tel: 416-534-3831; *Fax:* 416-298-2276
Overview: A medium-sized national organization
Affliation(s): African Methodist Episcopal Church
Membership: 130 churches

British North America Philatelic Society Ltd. (BNAPS)
c/o David G. Jones, 184 Larkin Dr., Ottawa ON K2J 1H9
www.bnaps.org
Overview: A small international charitable organization founded in 1943
Mission: To collect stamps from pre-confederation Canada
Chief Officer(s):
Norris R. Dyer, President
nrdyer@comcast.net
David G. Jones, Secretary
shibumi.management@gmail.com
Membership: *Fees:* $35; *Member Profile:* Individuals & families in Canada, the United States, & the United Kingdom who are interested in the hobby of collecting BNA philately; *Committees:* Convention; Elections; Ethics; Finance; On-line Resources & Exhibits; Publications; Admissions; Ballot; Catalog; Education; Handbook; Judging; Library; Membership; Nominations; Resolutions; Rules & Bylaws; Yearbook
Activities: Offering 21 study groups & 14 regional groups; Providing financial grants for activities to encourage young people to pursue a hobby in philately; *Speaker Service:* Yes; *Library:* The Horace W. Harrison Library
Publications:
• BNA Topics
Type: Journal; *Frequency:* Quarterly; *Number of Pages:* 80; *Editor:* Robert Lemire & Mike Street
Profile: Articles about BNA philately, as well as philatelic news, bood reviews, & postal history
• BNAPortraitS: The People's Publication of BNAPS
Type: Newsletter; *Frequency:* Quarterly; *Accepts Advertising*; *Editor:* Victor Willson
Profile: Society activities, study group & regional group news, awards, & membership information
• Canadian Philately - an Outline
Author: J. Burnett; F. Scrimgeour; V Wilson

Broadcast Educators Association of Canada (BEAC) / Association Canadienne de educateurs en radiodiffusion
beac.ca
www.facebook.com/BEACanada
twitter.com/BEACanada
www.flickr.com/photos/beacanada; vimeo.com/user6518105
Overview: A large national organization
Mission: To be dedicated to the professional development of staff, faculty & administrators of provincially accredited colleges & universities throughout Canada that specialize in radio, television, broadcast journalism & new media programs.
Chief Officer(s):
Dan Pihlainen, President
pihlaid@algonquincollege.com
Anna Rodrigues, Vice-President
anna.rodrigues@durhamcollege.ca
Michelle Grimes, Secretary
mgrimes@loyalistc.on.ca
Stephen Melanson, Treasurer
yvonne.colbert@cbc.ca
Awards:
• BEAC National Awards (Award)

Broadcast Executives Society (BES)
PO Box 75150, 20 Bloor St. East, Toronto ON M4W 3T3
Tel: 416-899-0370
www.bes.ca
Overview: A medium-sized national organization founded in 1961
Mission: To serve as forum for the broadcast industry.
Chief Officer(s):
John Tucker, Administrator
Membership: 300+; *Fees:* $169.50 GTA resident; $113 non-resident; *Member Profile:* Broadcasters, broadcast representatives, advertising agency personnel, advertisers, film producers, distributors & other parties interested in the business of broadcasting

Broadcast Research Council of Canada (BRC)
#1005, 160 Bloor St. East, Toronto ON M4W 1B9
Tel: 416-413-3864; *Fax:* 416-413-3879
brc@tvb.ca
www.brc.ca
ca.linkedin.com/pub/brc-broadcast-research-council-of-canada/24/462/11
www.facebook.com/117260268358077
twitter.com/BroadcastBRC
Overview: A medium-sized national organization
Mission: To provide a forum for presentations relating to the broadcast advertising business; to provide awards to the most promising students at colleges that train people to enter the advertising business.
Chief Officer(s):
Robert DaSilva, President
Membership: *Member Profile:* Membership in the BRC is open to advertisers, advertising agencies, media, media representatives, research companies, and organizations, and to students active in the field of research.

Brock Information Centre *See* Information Brock

Brock University Faculty Association (BUFA) / Association des professeurs de l'Université Brock
Mackenzie-Chown Complex, Brock University, 500 Glenridge Ave., #D402, St Catharines ON L2S 3A1
Tel: 905-688-5550; *Fax:* 905-688-8256
bufa@brocku.ca
www.bufa.ca
www.facebook.com/212515592101908
twitter.com/BUFABrock
Overview: A small local organization founded in 1996
Mission: To influence conditions of employment, including promotion, tenure, pensions, sabbaticals & research grants.
Affliation(s): Canadian Association of University Teachers; Ontario Confederation of University Faculty Associations
Chief Officer(s):
Linda Rose-Krasnor, President
linda.rose-krasnor@brocku.ca
Shannon Lever, Administrative Assistant
slever@brocku.ca
Finances: *Funding Sources:* Membership dues
Staff Member(s): 3
Membership: *Member Profile:* Brock University faculty & professional librarians; *Committees:* Negotiating; Academic & Professional Awards; Collective Agreement; Grievance Panel; Hiring Advice; Occupational Health & Safety; Pension; Communications; Social Justice; Status of Women

Brockville & District Association for Community Involvement (BDACI)
#4, 2495 Parkedale Ave., Brockville ON K6V 3H2
Tel: 613-345-4092; *Fax:* 613-345-7469
bdaci@ripnet.com
Previous Name: Brockville & District Association for Community Living; Brockville & District Association for the Mentally Retarded
Overview: A medium-sized local charitable organization founded in 1956
Mission: To support people with intellectual disabilities & their families; To promote their full participation, as equal citizens, in community life
Member of: Community Living Ontario
Chief Officer(s):
Beth French, Executive Director
Activities: *Speaker Service:* Yes

Brockville & District Association for Community Living; Brockville & District Association for the Mentally Retarded
See Brockville & District Association for Community Involvement

Brockville & District Chamber of Commerce
#1, 3 Market St. West, Brockville ON K6V 7L2
Tel: 613-342-6553; *Fax:* 613-342-6849
info@brockvillechamber.com
www.brockvillechamber.com
www.linkedin.com/groups/Brockville-District-Chamber-Commerce-4074940
www.facebook.com/brockvillechamber
twitter.com/brockvillechamb
Overview: A small local organization founded in 1906
Mission: To foster a competitive business environment in the Brockville region that benefits the people of this region through the growth of jobs, wealth & quality of life.
Member of: Ontario Chamber of Commerce; Canadian Chamber of Commerce
Chief Officer(s):
Heather Halladay, President, 613-342-0240
heather_halladay@scotiamcleod.com
Anne MacDonald, Executive Director
anne@brockvillechamber.com
Finances: *Annual Operating Budget:* $50,000-$100,000; *Funding Sources:* Membership dues
Staff Member(s): 5; 15 volunteer(s)
Membership: 560+; *Fees:* Schedule available; *Committees:* Advocacy; Economic Development; Tourism; Membership; Programs
Awards:
• Awards of Excellence (Award)

Brockville & District Multicultural Council Inc.
PO Box 1757, Brockville ON K6V 6K8
Tel: 613-342-1469
brkMulticulturalCommittee@yahoo.ca
www.brockvillemulticulturalfestival.com
Overview: A small local charitable organization founded in 1981
Mission: To preserve, maintain, & stimulate the creative expression of all cultures & folk art heritages through community interaction; to promote multiculturalism in Leeds & Gronville Counties; to offer assistance to newcomers & other Canadians in maintaining & nurturing their cultural heritage.
Affliation(s): Ministry of Citizenship & Culture
Chief Officer(s):
Bea Singh, Contact
Membership: *Member Profile:* Any cultural individual or group
Activities: Annual community festival; annual wine & cheese party; monthly meetings, 3rd Tuesday of each month; provides entertainment &/or cultural displays at various community functions

Brome County Historical Society (BCHS) / La Société historique du Comté de Brome
130 chemin Lakeside, Knowlton QC J0E 1V0
Tel: 450-243-6782
bchs@endirect.qc.ca
bromemuseum.com
Overview: A small local charitable organization founded in 1897
Member of: Federation of Québec Historical Societies
Chief Officer(s):
Arlene Royea, Managing Director
Finances: *Annual Operating Budget:* $50,000-$100,000; *Funding Sources:* Admissions; book sales; donations; memberships; fundraising
Staff Member(s): 2; 5 volunteer(s)
Membership: 600; *Fees:* $50 libraries/organizations; $30 family; $15 single; $3 junior; *Committees:* Building; Finance; Fundraising; Heritage
Activities: Operates Brome County Historical Museum: Old Fire Hall, Marion L. Phelps Building, Centennial Building, County Court House & Tibbits Hill Pioneer School; offers historical lectures; *Library*

The Bronte Society
7 West Rivers St., Oakville ON L6L 6N9
Tel: 905-825-5552
brontehistoricalsociety@bellnet.ca
www.brontehistoricalsociety.ca
Overview: A small international charitable organization founded in 1893
Mission: To bring closer together all who honour the Brontë sisters; to act as the guardian of such letters, writings & personal belongings as could be acquired for the Museum; to dispel legend & false sentiments regarding the Brontë story
Chief Officer(s):
Judith Watkins, Canadian Representative
Finances: *Funding Sources:* Membership fees; donations; museum fees
Activities: General meetings, member gathering and fundraising events; *Speaker Service:* Yes

Brooks & District Chamber of Commerce
PO Box 400, 403 - 2 Ave. West, Brooks AB T1R 1B4
Tel: 403-362-7641; *Fax:* 403-362-6893
manager@brookschamber.ab.ca
www.brookschamber.ab.ca
www.facebook.com/BrooksandDistrictChamberofCommerce
twitter.com/BrooksChamber
Overview: A small local organization founded in 1947
Member of: Alberta Chamber of Commerce; Canadian Chamber of Commerce
Chief Officer(s):
Tracy Acorn, Manager
Eric Barstad, Communications Coordinator
assistant@brookschamber.ab.ca
Finances: *Funding Sources:* Sponsorship; trade show; membership fees; educational events
Staff Member(s): 1; 16 volunteer(s)
Membership: 300; *Fees:* $130-370; *Member Profile:* Businesses; *Committees:* Policy; Trade Show; Executive; Speaker Series
Activities: Luncheons monthly; *Internships:* Yes; *Speaker Service:* Yes
Awards:
- Business of the Year
- New Business of the Year
- Customer Service Excellence Award

Broomball Canada Federation *See* Ballon sur glace Broomball Canada

Broomball Federation of Ontario *See* Federation of Broomball Associations of Ontario

Broomball Newfoundland & Labrador
734 Birch St., Labrador City NL A2V 1C8
Tel: 709-944-5780; *Fax:* 709-944-5780
Overview: A small provincial organization overseen by Ballon sur glace Broomball Canada
Member of: Ballon sur glace Broomball Canada
Chief Officer(s):
Harold Clarke, President
clarkep@nf.sympatico.ca

Brotherhood of Locomotive Engineers *See* Teamsters Canada Rail Conference

Brothers of Our Lady of Mercy *Voir* Frères de Notre-Dame de la Miséricorde

Bruce Children's Aid Society *See* Bruce Grey Child & Family Services

Bruce County Historical Society
c/o Marvin Doran, 15 Birch Trail, Southampton ON N0H 2L0
www.brucecountyhistory.on.ca
Overview: A small local charitable organization founded in 1957
Mission: To bring together people concerned with the preservation of Bruce County's heritage; To collect & preserve historical items, accounts, manuscripts, books, etc.
Affliation(s): Ontario Historical Society
Chief Officer(s):
Audrey Underwood, President
aumelrosefarm@bmts.com
Marvin Doran, Secretary
mdoran@bmts.com
Catharine McKeeman, Membership Coordinator
jrich@wightman.ca
30 volunteer(s)
Membership: 420; *Fees:* $20 annual; $500 lifetime

Bruce Grey Child & Family Services (BGCFS)
1290 - 3rd Ave. East, Owen Sound ON N4K 2L5
Tel: 519-371-4453; *Fax:* 519-376-8934
Toll-Free: 855-322-4453; *Crisis Hot-Line:* 855-322-4453
inquiries@bgcfs.ca
www.bgcfs.ca
Previous Name: Bruce Children's Aid Society
Merged from: The Children's Aid Societies of Bruce & Grey Counties
Overview: A small local organization founded in 1898 overseen by Ontario Association of Children's Aid Societies
Mission: To protect children by providing supportive services to children & families through partnerships
Chief Officer(s):
Gary Harron, Chair
Melissa Mockler-Wunderlich, Secretary
Finances: *Annual Operating Budget:* Greater than $5 Million
Staff Member(s): 170
Membership: *Fees:* Schedule available

Bruce House
#402, 251 Bank St., Ottawa ON K2P 1X3
Tel: 613-729-0911; *Fax:* 613-729-0959
admin@brucehouse.org
www.brucehouse.org
www.facebook.com/MoreThanAHouse
twitter.com/MoreThanAHouse
Overview: A small local charitable organization founded in 1988 overseen by Canadian AIDS Society
Mission: To provide housing, compassionate care & support in Ottawa-Carleton for people living with HIV/AIDS, believing that everyone has the right to live & die with dignity; to operate a 7-bed residence staffed 24-hours a day for people who require extensive support & 34 rent-to-income apartment units for those able to live independently.
Member of: Ontario AIDS Network; Ontario Non-Profit Housing Association
Affliation(s): City of Ottawa, Province of Ontario, government of Canada, a network of community centers & agencies, local hospitals, physicians, social service agencies, other local charitable agencies & organizations
Finances: *Funding Sources:* Ministry of Health; donations; RMOC; United Way

Bruce Peninsula Association for Community Living
314 George St., Wiarton ON N0H 2T0
Tel: 519-534-0553; *Fax:* 519-534-2739
www.communitylivingbp.org
Previous Name: Community Living Wiarton & District
Overview: A medium-sized local organization
Mission: To help people with disabilities fully participate in all aspects of society
Member of: Community Living Ontario

Bruce Peninsula Environment Group (BPEG)
PO Box 1072, Lions Head ON N0H 1W0
e-mail: info@bpeg.ca
www.bpeg.ca
Overview: A small local organization founded in 1989
Mission: BPEG is a group of people concerned about the environment & committed to preserving the unique ecology of the Bruce Peninsula. It promotes awareness of the region's diverse flora, fauna, geology & cultural history, & monitors human impact on them. It has planted trees, helped with water quality issues on farmland, encouraged wildlife with habitat improvement, & has been active in legislating for better forestry practices.
Member of: Great Lakes United; Ontario Environment Network; Durham Nuclear Awareness; Canadian Environmental Network; Grey-Bruce Power Council
Chief Officer(s):
Jim Kuellmer, Chair
Finances: *Annual Operating Budget:* Less than $50,000; *Funding Sources:* Membership fees; donations
8 volunteer(s)
Membership: 125; *Fees:* $25 family, $15 single; *Member Profile:* Residents of the Bruce Peninsula; *Committees:* Alternate Energy; Dark Sky; Media; Recycling; Sustainable Forestry
Activities: Earth Day; energy tour; monthly meetings; tree planting; road clean-ups; recycling; environmental awards; *Awareness Events:* Energy Tour, June 4; *Library* by appointment
Awards:
- Bruce Peninsula Environment Group Award for Excellence (Award)

The Bruce Trail Association *See* The Bruce Trail Conservancy

The Bruce Trail Conservancy
PO Box 857, Hamilton ON L8N 3N9
Tel: 905-529-6821; *Fax:* 905-529-6823
Toll-Free: 800-665-4453
info@brucetrail.org
www.brucetrail.org
www.facebook.com/TheBruceTrailConservancy
Previous Name: The Bruce Trail Association
Overview: A medium-sized provincial charitable organization founded in 1963
Mission: To secure, develop & manage the Bruce Trail as a public footpath along the Niagara Escarpment from Queenston to Tobermory, thereby promoting preservation of the escarpment's ecological & cultural integrity & fostering an appreciation of its natural beauty. The Bruce Trail, designated as a UNESCO World Biosphere Reserve, is Canada's oldest and longest footpath.
Member of: Hike Ontario
Affliation(s): Ontario Trails Council; Coalition on the Niagara Escarpment; Federation of Ontario Naturalists; Hike Ontario
Chief Officer(s):
Beth Gilhespy, Executive Director
bgilhespy@brucetrail.org
Finances: *Funding Sources:* Memberships; donations; sales
Staff Member(s): 15; 1250 volunteer(s)
Membership: 8,500; *Fees:* $50; $125 organization
Activities: Land conservation; trail management & development; environmental hikes; *Speaker Service:* Yes; *Library* by appointment

Beaver Valley
PO Box 3251, Meaford ON N4L 1A5
www.beavervalleybrucetrail.org
www.facebook.com/pages/Beaver-Valley-Bruce-Trail-Club/132342103543346
Chief Officer(s):
Ros Rossetti, President, 519-538-1866
rosamundr@aol.com

Blue Mountains
PO Box 91, Collingwood ON L9Y 3Z4
e-mail: hart@bmbtc.org
www.bmbtc.org
Chief Officer(s):
Herman Ohrt, President, 705-446-1440
hermanohrt@sympatico.ca

Caledon Hills
PO Box 65, Stn. Caledon Village, Caledon ON L7K 3L3
e-mail: info@caledonbrucetrail.org
www.caledonbrucetrail.org
www.facebook.com/CaledonHillsBruceTrailClub

Dufferin Hi-Land
PO Box 698, Alliston ON L9R 2V9
www.dufferinbrucetrailclub.org
Chief Officer(s):
Carl Alexander, President
carlwalexander@gmail.com

Iroquoia
ON
e-mail: info@iroquoia.on.ca
www.iroquoia.on.ca
www.facebook.com/IroquoiaBruceTrailClub
twitter.com/IroquoiaBruceTr
Chief Officer(s):
Cathie Mills, President

Niagara
PO Box 176, Niagara-on-the-Lake ON L0S 1J0
e-mail: niagarabrucetrailclub@gmail.com
www.niagarabrucetrail.org
www.facebook.com/pages/Niagara-Bruce-Trail-Club/156401064406469
Chief Officer(s):
Barbara Henderson, President
barb.a.henderson@gmail.com

Peninsula
PO Box 2, Tobermory ON N0H 2R0
e-mail: peninsulabrucetrailclub@gmail.com
www.pbtc.ca
www.facebook.com/pages/Peninsula-Bruce-Trail-Club/154060254652464
Chief Officer(s):
John Whitworth, President
ajwhitworth@rogers.com

Sydenham
PO Box 431, Owen Sound ON N4K 5P7
e-mail: info@sydenhambrucetrail.ca
www.sydenhambrucetrail.ca
www.facebook.com/sydenhambrucetrailclub
Chief Officer(s):
Bob Knapp, President, 519-371-1255
rmknapp@yahoo.com

Toronto
PO Box 857, Hamilton ON L8N 3N9
Tel: 905-529-6821; *Fax:* 905-529-6823
Toll-Free: 800-665-4453
info@brucetrail.org
www.torontobrucetrailclub.org
Affliation(s): Halton Hills Chapter
Chief Officer(s):
Todd Bardes, President

Buckskinners Muzzleloading Association, Limited
PO Box 4127, Stn. Champlain Place, 2493 Route 490, Dieppe NB E1A 6E8
Tel: 506-576-1959; *Fax:* 506-859-1249
buckskinnersweb@yahoo.com
buckskinnersweb.weebly.com
Overview: A small local organization founded in 1978
Mission: To promote good & safe blackpowder shooting, marksmanship & sportsmanship; to encourage & promote buckskinning knowledge & skills
Affliation(s): New Brunswick Wildlife Federation
Chief Officer(s):
Shirley Stuart, Contact
Finances: *Annual Operating Budget:* Less than $50,000
36 volunteer(s)
Membership: 36; *Fees:* $20 single; $35 family; *Member Profile:* Buckskinners, Civil War & pre-1840 re-enactors
Activities: Winter Rendezvous, Feb.; Summer Rendezvous, June

Buddhist Association of Canada - Cham Shan Temple
7254 Bayview Ave., Toronto ON L3T 2R6
Tel: 905-886-1522
www.chamshantemple.org/en
Overview: A small national organization founded in 1973
Mission: In addition to the main worship hall & 2 congregation halls, the Buddhist temple also includes a Dharma seminary for the Chinese community to learn Buddhism.
Chief Officer(s):
Dayi Shi, President & Abbot
Activities: Seminars, sutra reading groups, meditation retreats; *Library*

Buddhist Churches of Canada *See* Jodo Shinshu Buddhist Temples of Canada

Buddies in Bad Times Theatre
12 Alexander St., Toronto ON M4Y 1B4
Tel: 416-975-9130
buddiesinbadtimes.com
www.facebook.com/buddiesinbadtimes
twitter.com/yyzbuddies
www.youtube.com/BIBTTV
Overview: A medium-sized local organization founded in 1979
Mission: To promote gay, lesbian, & queer theatrical expression
Chief Officer(s):
Brendan Healy, Artistic Director
Finances: *Funding Sources:* Government; foundations
Staff Member(s): 18

Buffalo Lake Naturalists Club
PO Box 1802, Stettler AB T0C 2L0
e-mail: BuffaloLakeNC@gmail.com
www.buffalolakenature.com
www.facebook.com/BuffaloLakeNaturalists
Overview: A small local organization founded in 1973
Mission: To promote the enjoyment of nature through environmental appreciation & conservation; To encourage wise use & conservation of natural resources & environmental protection
Member of: Federation of Alberta Naturalists
Finances: *Funding Sources:* Membership fees
Membership: *Fees:* $10 single; $20 family
Activities: Bird, plant & butterfly identification field trips; community projects; park planning & cleanup; *Library*

Buffalo Narrows Chamber of Commerce
PO Box 504, Buffalo Narrows SK S0M 0J0
Tel: 306-235-4485; *Fax:* 306-235-4416
Overview: A small local organization

Buffalo Narrows Friendship Centre
PO Box 189, 351 Buffalo St., Buffalo Narrows SK S0M 0J0
Tel: 306-235-4633; *Fax:* 306-235-4544
Overview: A small local organization
Chief Officer(s):
Brenda Chartier, Executive Director

Building Energy Management Manitoba (BEMM)
#309, 23 - 845 Dakota St., Winnipeg MB R2M 5M3
Tel: 204-452-2098
info@bemm.ca
www.bemm.ca
Overview: A medium-sized provincial organization
Mission: To promote energy efficiency & management in the various building sectors
Chief Officer(s):
Monica Samuda Poitras, Chair, 204-261-0718
monica@samudaenergy.com
Robert Bisson, Treasurer, 204-945-8452
robert.bisson@gov.mb.ca
Kent Glenday, Contact, Membership, 204-669-3346, Fax: 204-669-3350
kent.glenday@philips.com
Membership: *Fees:* $125; *Member Profile:* Engineers, architects, property managers, contractors & energy management professionals; government, school boards, hospitals & utility representatives
Meetings/Conferences: • Building Energy Management Manitoba 2015 Better Buildings Conference, 2015
Scope: Provincial
Contact Information: URL: www.betterbuildingsconference.com

Building Envelope Council of Ottawa Region (BECOR)
PO Box 7328, Stn. Vanier, Ottawa ON K1L 8E4
Tel: 819-956-3401; *Fax:* 819-956-3400
info@becor.org
www.becor.org
Overview: A small local charitable organization founded in 1988
Mission: To promote the pursuit of excellence in the design, construction & performance of the building envelope
Member of: National Building Envelope Council
Chief Officer(s):
Hélène Roche, President
helene.roche@nrc-cnrc.gc.ca
Peter Fridgen, Treasurer
fridgen@fridgen.ca
Finances: *Annual Operating Budget:* Less than $50,000
Membership: 100-499; *Fees:* $75; $25 student; $300 corporate
Activities: Seminars, conferences; *Speaker Service:* Yes

Building Industry & Land Development Association (BILD)
#100, 20 Upjohn Rd., Toronto ON M3B 2V9
Tel: 416-391-3445; *Fax:* 416-391-2118
info@gthba.ca
www.newhomes.org
Merged from: Greater Toronto Home Builders' Association; Urban Development Institute/Ontario
Overview: A medium-sized local organization overseen by Canadian Home Builders' Association
Mission: To represent the land development & renovation industry in the Greater Toronto Area
Chief Officer(s):
Stephen E. Dupuis, President & CEO

Membership: 1,500 corporate; *Member Profile:* Home builders; Land developers; Renovators; Land use & environmental planners; Sub-contractors; Manufacturers; Lawyers; Surveyors; Architects; Suppliers; Representatives of service, professional and financial institutions

The Building Materials Retailers Association of Québec *Voir* Association québécoise de la quincaillerie et des matériaux de construction

Building Officials' Association of British Columbia (BOABC)
#205, 3740 Chatham Street, Richmond BC V7E 2Z3
Tel: 604-270-9516; *Fax:* 604-270-9488
info@boabc.org
www.boabc.org
Overview: A small provincial organization founded in 1954
Mission: To serve the public interest in building safety, health & welfare by advancing high, consistent standards of building official practice through the professional competence of its members
Chief Officer(s):
Richard Bushey, Executive Director
richard@boabc.org
Staff Member(s): 2
Membership: 633; *Fees:* $183.75 regular; $183.75-210 associate; $36.75 student/retired; *Member Profile:* Local government building officials & those involved in building design, construction, testing & research
Activities: Education seminars

Building Owners & Managers Association - Atlantic *See* Building Owners & Managers Association - Nova Scotia

Building Owners & Managers Association - Canada
PO Box 61, #1801, 1 Dundas St. West, Toronto ON M5G 1Z3
Tel: 416-214-1912; *Fax:* 416-214-1284
info@bomacanada.ca
www.bomacanada.ca
www.linkedin.com/groups/BOMA-Canada-3958628?gid=3958628&mostPopular=&t
www.facebook.com/pages/BOMA-Canada/107613392698316
twitter.com/BOMA_CAN
Also Known As: BOMA Canada
Overview: A medium-sized national organization
Mission: To represent the Canadian commerical real estate industry on matters of national concern; To develop a strong communications network between local associations; To promote professionalism of members through education programs & effective public relations activity
Affliation(s): BOMA International
Chief Officer(s):
Benjamin L, Shinewald, President/CEO
Membership: 2,000
Meetings/Conferences: • Building Owners & Managers Association 2015 Conference, September, 2015, Québec, QC
Scope: National
• Building Owners & Managers Association 2016 Conference, September, 2016, Regina, SK
Scope: National
• Building Owners & Managers Association 2017 Conference, 2017, Toronto, ON
Scope: National

Building Owners & Managers Association - Nova Scotia
PO Box 1597, Halifax NS B3J 2Y3
Tel: 902-425-3717; *Fax:* 902-431-7220
info@bomanovascotia.com
www.bomanovascotia.com
Also Known As: BOMA Nova Scotia
Previous Name: Building Owners & Managers Association - Atlantic
Overview: A medium-sized local organization
Mission: To actively represent our members, through education, networking & lobbying in matters affecting the ownership, management & operation of commercial properties
Member of: Building Owners & Managers Association of Canada
Chief Officer(s):
Rod Winters, President
Membership: *Member Profile:* Owners, managers and suppliers of the commercial real estate industry

Building Owners & Managers Association of British Columbia
#556, 409 Granville St., Vancouver BC V6C 1T2

Tel: 604-684-3916; *Fax:* 604-684-4876
bomabc@boma.bc.ca
www.boma.bc.ca
twitter.com/bomaEnergyXpres
Also Known As: BOMA BC
Overview: A medium-sized provincial organization founded in 1911
Mission: To represent the interests & concerns of building owners & managers in the commercial & office space industry in British Columbia
Member of: Building Owners & Managers Association of Canada; BOMA International
Affliation(s): Heritage Canada; Vancouver Board of Trade; CSAE
Chief Officer(s):
Colin Murray, President
cmurray@buk.ca
Paul Labranche, Executive Vice President
pdl@boma.bc.ca
Lorina Keery, Manager, Energy & Environment
lorina@boma.bc.ca
Kiomi Lutz, Manager, Member Services
kiomi@boma.bc.ca
Membership: 300; *Fees:* $850-$2,700 Corporate real estate; $215-$1,500 Corporate business; *Member Profile:* Corporate real estate & corporate business; *Committees:* Evaluation, emergency response, environment & energy, health & safety, recycling, taxation, transportation & traffic
Awards:
- Earth Award (Award)
- Toby Award (Award)
- Leasing Deal of the Year (Award)
- Tenant Improvement of the Year (Award)
- Supplier/Contractor of the Year

Building Owners & Managers Association of Edmonton

Standard Life Centre, #390, 10405 Jasper Ave., Edmonton AB T5J 3N4
Tel: 780-428-0419; *Fax:* 780-426-6882
www.bomaedmonton.org
Also Known As: BOMA Edmonton
Overview: A medium-sized local organization founded in 1958 overseen by Building Owners & Managers Association International
Mission: To represent the interests & concerns of building owners & managers in the commercial & office space industry in Edmonton
Member of: euilding Owners & Managers Association of Canada
Chief Officer(s):
Percy J. Woods, President & Chief Staff Officer
pwoods@bomaedm.ca
Finances: *Funding Sources:* Membership dues; education programs; advertising
Staff Member(s): 2
Membership: *Fees:* Schedule available; *Member Profile:* Building owner/manager or service company to property management industry
Activities: *Library* by appointment

Building Owners & Managers Association of Manitoba

PO Box 3107, Winnipeg MB R3C 4E6
Tel: 204-777-2662; *Fax:* 204-777-0326
bomamanitoba.ca
www.linkedin.com/company/boma-manitoba
www.facebook.com/308490885833086
twitter.com/bomamanitoba
Also Known As: BOMA Manitoba
Overview: A medium-sized provincial organization founded in 1982
Mission: To represent the interests & concerns of building owners & managers in the commercial real estate industry in Manitoba
Member of: Building Owners & Managers Association of Canada; Building Owners & Managers Association International
Chief Officer(s):
Tom Thiessen, Executive Director
tom@bomamanitoba.ca
Staff Member(s): 2
Membership: 250+; *Fees:* $895; *Member Profile:* Companies involved in commercial real estate ownership, development & management; *Committees:* Awards of Excellence; Education; Marketing & Development; Membership; Golf Tournament; Government Affairs/Advocacy; Building Operators & Engineers Group; Codes & Standards; Energy & Environment
Awards:
- Awards of Excellence (Award)

Building Owners & Managers Association of Ottawa

#1005, 141 Laurier Ave. West, Ottawa ON K1P 5J3
Tel: 613-232-1875; *Fax:* 613-563-3908
administration@bomaottawa.org
www.BOMAOTTAWA.org
twitter.com/boma_ottawa
Also Known As: BOMA Ottawa
Overview: A small local organization founded in 1971
Member of: BOMA International
Chief Officer(s):
Dean Karakasis, Executive Director
executivedirector@bomaottawa.org
Finances: *Annual Operating Budget:* $500,000-$1.5 Million; *Funding Sources:* Membership dues
Membership: 450; *Fees:* Schedule available; *Committees:* Marketing; Membership; Planning & Policy; Awards; Education; Government Affairs; Security & Life Safety; Curling; Spring Golf; Fall Golf; Lunch; Ski

Building Owners & Managers Association Toronto

#1800, 1 Dundas St. West, Toronto ON M5G 1Z3
Tel: 416-596-8065; *Fax:* 416-596-1085
info@bomatoronto.org
www.bomatoronto.org
www.linkedin.com/company/boma-toronto
www.facebook.com/bomatoronto
twitter.com/bomatoronto
www.youtube.com/user/BOMAtoronto
Also Known As: BOMA Toronto
Overview: A large local organization
Mission: To represent the interests & concerns of building owners & managers in the commercial & office space industry in the Greater Toronto Area
Member of: BOMA International
Chief Officer(s):
Neil Lacheur, Chair
Chris Conway, President & Chief Staff Officer
cconway@bomatoronto.org
Shahla Defileh, Director, Finance, Administration & Information Technology, 416-596-8065 Ext. 225, Fax: 416-596-1085
sdefileh@bomatoronto.org
Robyn Fremeth, Manager, Events & Education, 416-596-8065 Ext. 223
rfremeth@bomatoronto.org
Kirsten Martin, Manager, Marketing & Communication, 416-596-8065 Ext. 222
kmartin@bomatoronto.org
Thomas Catania, Consultant, Sales & Sponsorship, 416-596-8065 Ext. 226
tcatania@bomatoronto.org
400 volunteer(s)
Membership: 700; *Committees:* Executive; Awards & Certifications; Building Operations; Emergency Management; Energy & Environment; Regulatory Affairs; BOMA CDM Oversight; Marketing & Communications; Membership; Professional Development & Education; Program Coordination, Networking & Sponsorship
Awards:
- Certificate of Excellence (Award)
- The Outstanding Building of the Year (TOBY) Award (Award)
- Earth Award (Award)
- Pinnacle Award (Award)
- Chair's Award (Award)

Building Owners & Managers Institute of Canada

#1201, 55 York St., Toronto ON M5J 1R7
Tel: 416-977-8700; *Fax:* 416-977-8800
Toll-Free: 888-821-9319
admin@bomicanada.com
www.bomicanada.com
Also Known As: BOMI Canada
Overview: A small national organization founded in 1974
Mission: Provides education for members of the commercial property industry, including certification for property managers, facilities professionals, systems personnel and systems supervisors
Chief Officer(s):
Jim Preece, President
jpreece@bomicanada.com

Building Supply Industry Association of British Columbia (BSIA of BC)

#2, 19299 - 94th Ave., Surrey BC V4N 4E6
Tel: 604-513-2205; *Fax:* 604-513-2206
Toll-Free: 888-711-5656
www.bsiabc.ca
Overview: A medium-sized provincial organization founded in 1938
Mission: To act as the official voice of the building supply industry in British Columbia; To provide services to members
Chief Officer(s):
Thomas Foreman, President
thomas@bsiabc.ca
Marijoel Chamberlain, Coordinator, Member Services, & Manager, Trade Show
marijoel@bsiabc.ca
Jackie Trafton, Administrator
jackie@bsiabc.ca
Membership: *Fees:* $169 wholesale branches; $199 retail stores & manufacturer's agents; $399 associates & retail & wholesale head offices; *Member Profile:* Manufacturers; Wholesalers; Suppliers; Retailers who operate lumber yards, hardware stores, & home centres
Activities: Promoting the building supply industry in British Columbia; Liaising with government; Addressing concerns within the industry; Providing information to members; Hosting product knowledge evenings at the BSIA office
Meetings/Conferences: • Westcoast Building & Hardware Trade Show & Conference 2015, March, 2015, Cloverdale, BC
Scope: Provincial
Description: A trade show for members of the building supply industry, presenting educational opportunities & new & innovative products & services
Contact Information: Registration & Sponsorship Information, Phone: 604-513-2205, E-mail: info@bsiabc.ca
Publications:
- BSIA e-news
Type: Newsletter; *Frequency:* Monthly; *Accepts Advertising*; *Price:* Free with membership in the Building Supply Industry Association of British Columbia
Profile: Industry & association news
- BSIA News Magazine
Type: Magazine; *Frequency:* 5 pa; *Accepts Advertising*; *Price:* Free with membership in the Building Supply Industry Association of British Columbia
Profile: A 40 to 60 page magazine, featuring association activities & in-depth articles for building supply dealers & suppliers throughout British Columbia, who retail a wide range of home improvement supplies& materials
- Building Supply Industry Association of British Columbia Directory
Type: Directory; *Frequency:* Annually; *Accepts Advertising*; *Price:* Free with membership in the Building SupplyIndustry Association of British Columbia
Profile: An alphabetical & city listing of British Columbia's building material & hardware retailers & suppliers
- Building Supply Industry Association of British Columbia Retail Product Buying Guide
Type: Guide; *Frequency:* Annually; *Accepts Advertising*; *Price:* Free with membership in the Building Supply Industry Association of BritishColumbia
Profile: Information about industry related vendors & suppliers
- Occupational Health & Safety Policy & Procedures Manual
Type: Manual; *Price:* Free with membership in the BSIA of British Columbia; $19.95 non-members
Profile: A generic guide to the development of a specific manual for each business
- Retail Job Descriptions Handbook
Type: Handbook

Bukas Loob sa Diyos Covenant Community / "Open in Spirit to God"

2565 Bathurst Street, Toronto ON M6B 2Z3
Tel: 416-787-7003; *Fax:* 416-787-6677
BLD_Toronto_Secretariat@googlegroups.com
www.bldtoronto.org
Also Known As: BLD Toronto
Overview: A small local charitable organization
Mission: To be witnesses to the Word that others may hear & understand; To be counsellors with the Spirit, that others may have healing & wholeness; to be defenders in Christ of those who suffer injustice & oppression; To be charismatic in activities; to be faithful to the Magisterium of the Church; To ensure that all activities & teachings of a BLD district are in accordance with official doctrines & dogmas of the Church, through ecclesial

Canadian Associations

authority of the local Archdiocese over each BLD district; To ensure that the activities of each BLD member are the pastoral responsibilities of the Spiritual Director, who is under the ecclesial authority of the Archdiocese of Manila; To ensure the structure of each BLD consists of one couple to act as Community Shepherd of the local district, & five district counsellor couples who, through prayer & discernment, listen to God's will on the BLD's direction
Affliation(s): Archdiocese of Toronto
Chief Officer(s):
Pat Canlas, Contact
prcanlas316@rogers.com
Finances: *Funding Sources:* Donations
Activities: Providing faith instruction; Offering programs for couples, singles, & youth, such as renewal programs & encounters; Organizing prayer groups, Living Word groups, & First Friday devotions; Conducting services for apostolic & pastoral groups, families, communities, married couples, missions, the separated, widowed & divorced, solo parents, & youth & children; Conducting teachings, praise, worship, & seminars, such as Life in the Spirit seminars

Bulimia Anorexia Nervosa Association (BANA) / Association de la boulimie et d'anorexie mentale
#100, 1500 Ouellette Ave., Windsor ON N8X 1K7
Tel: 519-969-2112; *Fax:* 519-969-0227
info@bana.ca
www.bana.ca
www.linkedin.com/groups/Bulimia-Anorexia-Nervosa-Association-2223288
www.facebook.com/277063735753721
twitter.com/BANAWindsor
banawindsor.tumblr.com
Overview: A medium-sized local charitable organization founded in 1982
Mission: To reduce the incidence of bulimia & anorexia nervosa with preventative programs; To offer services in the form of group, family & individual counselling; To provide a hotline for the community; to maintain a library for community use; To provide an educational, preventative curriculum
Chief Officer(s):
Luciana Rosu Sieza, Interim Executive Director
luciana@bana.ca
Finances: *Annual Operating Budget:* $500,000-$1.5 Million; *Funding Sources:* Provincial government
Staff Member(s): 8; 30 volunteer(s)
Membership: 300
Activities: *Awareness Events:* Eating Disorder Awareness Week, early Feb.; *Internships:* Yes; *Speaker Service:* Yes; *Library* Open to public

Bulkley Valley Community Arts Council
PO Box 3971, Smithers BC V0J 2N0
Tel: 250-847-8022
info@bvartscouncil.com
www.bvartscouncil.com
www.facebook.com/bvartscouncil
Overview: A small local organization
Member of: Assembly of BC Arts Councils
Chief Officer(s):
Tristan Jones, President & Treasurer
Ken Eng, Vice President
Sue Brookes, Secretary
Staff Member(s): 6

Bulkley Valley Naturalists (BVN)
15087 H. Kerr Rd., Telkwa BC V0J 2X2
www.bvnaturalists.ca
Overview: A small local organization founded in 1979
Mission: To promote the enjoyment of nature through environmental appreciation & conservation; To encourage wise use & conservation of natural resources & environmental protection.
Member of: Federation of BC Naturalists
Affliation(s): Federation of BC Naturalists.
Membership: *Fees:* $20 individual; $25 family
Activities: Participating in Christmas bird count and midwinter Bald Eagle count; participating on advisory committees on land use; developing nature education programs, field trips for schools;

Bully B'Ware
6 Beddingfield St., Port Moody BC V3H 3N1
Tel: 604-936-8000; *Fax:* 604-936-8000
Toll-Free: 888-552-8559
bully@direct.ca
www.bullybeware.com
Overview: A small international organization
Chief Officer(s):
Cindi Seddon, Contact
Alyson McLellan, Contact
Gesele Lajoie, Contact
Finances: *Annual Operating Budget:* Less than $50,000
Membership: 1-99
Activities: *Speaker Service:* Yes

Bullying.org Canada Inc.
159 Riverview Circle, Cochrane AB T4C 1K9
Tel: 403-932-1748
help@bullying.org
www.bullying.org
www.facebook.com/pages/Bullyingorg/150593625003962
twitter.com/Bullying_org
Overview: A small national organization
Mission: To eliminate bullying in our society by supporting individuals & organizations to take positive actions against bullying through the sharing of resources; To guide & champion individuals & organization in creating non-violent solutions to the challenges & problems associated with bullying; To increase the awareness of, & the problems associated with, bullying; To prevent, resolve & eliminate bullying in society
Chief Officer(s):
Bill Belsey, President
Activities: *Awareness Events:* Bullying Awareness Week, November

Bund Deutscher Karnevalsgesellschaften Kanada *See* German-Canadian Mardi Gras Association Inc.

Bureau canadien d'agrément en foresterie *See* Canadian Forestry Accreditation Board

Bureau canadien de l'éducation internationale *See* Canadian Bureau for International Education

Bureau canadien de reconnaissance professionnelle des spécialistes de l'environnement *See* Canadian Environmental Certification Approvals Board

Bureau canadien de soudage *See* Canadian Welding Bureau

Bureau canadien des ressources humaines en technologie *See* Canadian Technology Human Resources Board

Bureau d'assurance du Canada *See* Insurance Bureau of Canada

Bureau d'éthique commerciale de l'Est et Nord de l'Ontario et l'Outaouais *See* Better Business Bureau of Eastern & Northern Ontario & the Outaouais

Bureau de bois de sciage des Maritimes *See* Maritime Lumber Bureau

Bureau de la télévision du Canada *See* Television Bureau of Canada, Inc.

Bureau de promotion du commerce Canada *See* Trade Facilitation Office Canada

Bureau de tourisme et de congrès de Saint John *See* Tourism Saint John

Le Bureau des examinateurs en pharmacie du Canada *See* The Pharmacy Examining Board of Canada

Bureau des regroupements des artistes visuels de l'Ontario (BRAVO)
CP 53004, Succ. Rideau, Ottawa ON K1N 1C5
Tél: 819-457-1892
Ligne sans frais: 800-611-4789
info@bravoart.org
bravoart.org
www.facebook.com/pages/Bravo-Art/125741824103363
twitter.com/BRAVOmembres
www.youtube.com/user/dgbravo1
Aperçu: *Dimension:* petite; *Envergure:* provinciale; fondée en 1991
Mission: BRAVO est voué à la défense des intérêts individuels et collectifs de ses membres et ses activités répondent à ses besoins de communication, de représentation, de formation, de promotion et d'appui à la diffusion des arts visuels. Bref, BRAVO vise la dynamisation des arts visuels et médiatiques non seulement chez ses artistes, mais aussi dans toutes les communautés de l'Ontario.
Membre(s) du bureau directeur:
Yves Larocque, Directeur général et artistique
Membre(s) du personnel: 2
Membre: 135; *Montant de la cotisation:* 15$ étudiant; 40$ associé; 50$ statutaire; 75$ institutionnel; *Critères d'admissibilite:* Artistes professionnels

Bureau local d'intervention traitant du SIDA (BLITS)
#116, 59, rue Monfette, Victoriaville QC G6P 1J8
Tél: 819-758-2662; *Téléc:* 819-758-8270
Ligne sans frais: 866-758-2662
blits@cdcbf.qc.ca
www.blits.ca
Aperçu: *Dimension:* petite; *Envergure:* locale; Organisme sans but lucratif; fondée en 1989
Membre(s) du bureau directeur:
Gabrielle Bergeron, Présidente
Maryse Laroche, Coordonnatrice
blitscoordo@cdcbf.qc.ca
Claire Lefebvre, Agente de bureau
Véronique Vanier, Agente d'éducation
blitsprojet@cdcbf.qc.ca
Membre: *Montant de la cotisation:* 5$ annuellement
Activités: *Bibliothèque* Bibliothèque publique

Bureau national d'examen d'assistance dentaire *See* National Dental Assisting Examining Board

Le bureau national d'examen dentaire du Canada *See* National Dental Examining Board of Canada

Bureau régional d'action sida (Outaouais) (BRAS)
109, rue Wright, bur 03, Gatineau QC J8X 2G7
Tél: 819-776-2727; *Téléc:* 819-776-2001
Ligne sans frais: 877-376-2727
info@lebras.qc.ca
www.lebras.qc.ca
Aperçu: *Dimension:* petite; *Envergure:* locale; fondée en 1991
Mission: Développer et promouvoir des actions communautaires vizant l'amelioration de la qualité de vie de la population de l'Outaonais face au VIH/sida
Membre de: Réseau juridique canadien du VIH/Sida; Coalition des organismes communautaires québécois de lutte contre le sida; CATIE, TROCAO, CRIO
Membre(s) du bureau directeur:
Sylvain Laflamme, Directeur général
dg@lebras.qc.ca
Finances: *Budget de fonctionnement annuel:* $500,000-$1.5 Million
Membre(s) du personnel: 25; 70 bénévole(s)
Membre: 55; *Montant de la cotisation:* 5$; *Comités:* Groupe d'actions positives (par et pour les PVVIH)
Activités: Soutien; éducation à la prévention; promotion et concertation; *Evénements de sensibilisation:* Journée mondiale de lutte contre le sida, ateliers VIH;Dèmystification de l'homosexualité; Realités de larue Journie de lutte à l'homophobie
Prix, Bouses:
• Prix Lemieux-Tremblay (Prix)

Burford Township Historical Society
141 Harley Rd., Harley ON N0E 1E0
Tel: 519-449-4658
info@BurfordTownshipMuseum.ca
burfordtownshipmuseum.ca
twitter.com/BurfordTHS
Overview: A small local charitable organization founded in 1986
Mission: To promote interest in the history of Burford Township; to preserve artifacts for the use of the public; Operation of the Burford Township Museum
Affliation(s): Ontario Historical Society
Chief Officer(s):
Gary Jermy, Archivist
Linda Robbins, President
Activities: Heritage Week events for school children; Strawberry Social & Garden Party; Old Fashioned Christmas Concert

Burgess Shale Geoscience Foundation
PO Box 148, Field BC V0A 1G0
Tel. 250-343-6006; *Fax:* 250-343-6426
Toll-Free: 800-343-3006
info@burgess-shale.bc.ca
www.burgess-shale.bc.ca
www.facebook.com/BurgessShale
Overview: A small local organization founded in 1993
Mission: To increase the exposure of the genereal public to the earth sciences & in particular, to promote interest in geology & paleantology
Chief Officer(s):
Randle Robertson, Executive Director

Jim Abbott, Chair
Activities: Earth Science Guided Hikes Program; High School Research Project; Burgess Shale Learning Centre; Burgess Shale Discovery Centre

Burin Peninsula Chamber of Commerce
PO Box 728, Marystown NL A0E 2M0
Tel: 709-279-2080; *Fax:* 709-279-4492
administration@bpchamber.ca
burinpeninsulachamber.com
www.facebook.com/BurinPeninsulaChamberOfCommerce
Overview: A small local organization founded in 1991
Mission: To promote local businesses & help them grow
Member of: Canadian Chamber of Commerce; Atlantic Provinces Chamber of Commerce
Chief Officer(s):
Don MacBeath, President
Lisa MacLeod, Business Manager
Staff Member(s): 6
Membership: *Fees:* Schedule available based on number of employees
Activities: *Speaker Service:* Yes; *Library* Open to public

Burke Mountain Naturalists
PO Box 52540, RPO Coquitlam Centre, Coquitlam BC V3B 7J4
Tel: 604-937-3483; *Fax:* 604-937-3483
burkemtnnats@gmail.com
www.bmn.bc.ca
www.facebook.com/BurkeMountainNaturalists
twitter.com/BurkeMtnNats
Overview: A small local charitable organization founded in 1989
Mission: The group is a non-profit society that promotes the enjoyment of nature through environmental appreciation & conservation. It advocates accessibility & maintenance of natural areas, particularly local ones. It is a registered charity, BN: 873847966RR0001.
Member of: BC Nature
Chief Officer(s):
Ian McArthur, President, 604-939-4039
imcart@telus.net
Carole Edwards, Treasurer, 604-461-3864
caroleedwards@shaw.ca
Membership: 450; *Fees:* $25 single; $30 family/group
Activities: Monthly meetings; field trips & hikes; recording bird/flora sightings; preparing natural history brochures

Burlington Association for Nuclear Disarmament (BAND)
278 Linden Ave., Burlington ON L7L 2P5
Tel: 905-624-4774
band@cogeco.ca
Overview: A small international organization founded in 1983
Mission: To educate Canadians about the consequences of the nuclear arms race; To support the broader peace movement
Member of: Canadian Peace Alliance
Affliation(s): November 16 Coalition; Abolition 2000; Halton Peace Network
Chief Officer(s):
Doug W. Brown, Chair
Finances: *Annual Operating Budget:* Less than $50,000; *Funding Sources:* Membership fees; donations
Membership: 60 individual; *Fees:* $10; *Committees:* Letter Writing
Activities: Forum on Missile Defence; public forums on peace issues; *Speaker Service:* Yes

Burlington Chamber of Commerce
#201, 414 Locust St., Burlington ON L7S 1T7
Tel: 905-639-0174; *Fax:* 905-333-3956
info@burlingtonchamber.com
www.burlingtonchamber.com
www.facebook.com/burlington.chamber
twitter.com/burlingtoncofc
www.youtube.com/user/BurlingtonChamber
Overview: A medium-sized local organization founded in 1947
Mission: To be the focus for business in Burlington; to encourage & promote a strong Burlington business community through sound practices that support social & economic development
Member of: Ontario Chamber of Commerce; Canadian Chamber of Commerce; Ontario Association of Marketing Directors; Ontario Chamber of Commerce Executives; Chamber of Commerce Executives of Canada
Chief Officer(s):
Tamar Fahmi, Chair
Finances: *Annual Operating Budget:* $250,000-$500,000; *Funding Sources:* Membership dues; programming
Staff Member(s): 5
Membership: 950; *Fees:* $185 & up; *Committees:* Membership Management; Marketing & Communication; Education; Programs; Political Action
Activities: *Speaker Service:* Yes; *Rents Mailing List:* Yes

Burlington Historical Society (BHS)
PO Box 93164, 1450 Headon Rd., Burlington ON L7M 4A3
e-mail: info@burlingtonhistorical.ca
www.burlingtonhistorical.ca
Overview: A small local charitable organization founded in 1961
Mission: To bring together those people interested in the history of Burlington and district, and to stimulate public awareness in its local heritage.
Member of: Ontario Historical Society
Chief Officer(s):
Alan Harrington, President
Membership: *Fees:* $30 individual; $25 seniors; $40 family; *Member Profile:* Interest in local history
Activities: Sales tables at heritage events; monthly meetings; Heritage Week activities; Joseph Brant Day; *Library:* Galloway Room, Burlington Central Library; by appointment

Burlington Telecare Distress Line
PO Box 62041, Stn. Burlington Mall, Burlington ON L7R 4K2
Tel: 905-681-1488
www.telecareburlington.com
Overview: A small local organization founded in 1976 overseen by Distress Centres Ontario
Mission: To provide confidential care & contact to those in need
Member of: Telecare Teleministries
Finances: *Funding Sources:* Inter-Church Council; Halton Region; Donations
Activities: 24 hours, 7 days a week, confidential listening service; support services to those who are disadvantaged, isolated & in need of non-judgemental caring & listening; *Speaker Service:* Yes

BurlingtonGreen Environmental Association
3281 Myers Lane, Burlington ON L7N 1K6
Tel: 905-466-2171
www.burlingtongreen.org
www.facebook.com/burlington.green.environment
twitter.com/burlingtongreen
Overview: A medium-sized local organization
Mission: To advocate for local environmental issues
Chief Officer(s):
Amy Schnurr, Executive Director
Finances: *Funding Sources:* Membership fees; Donations
Membership: *Fees:* $5 students; $20 individuals; $25 families; *Member Profile:* Citizens for a greener community
Activities: Establishing the BurlingtonGreen Youth Network which meets monthly; *Awareness Events:* BurlingtonGreen Eco-Film Festival
Publications:
• BurlingtonGreen Environmental Association Newsletter
Type: Newsletter; *Frequency:* Annually
Profile: Information, eco-event listings, stories, & special bulletins
• BurlingtonGreen Youth Network Bulletin
Type: Newsletter
Profile: Information about volunteering, events, competitions, & scholarships
• Greening Tips
Type: Newsletter; *Frequency:* Monthly

Burn Survivors Association
c/o Camp BUCKO, #15549, 265 Port Union Rd., Toronto ON M1C 4Z7
Tel: 647-343-2267
Toll-Free: 877-272-8256
info@campbucko.ca
www.campbucko.ca
www.facebook.com/groups/2466350290
twitter.com/camp_bucko
Also Known As: Camp BUCKO
Overview: A small local charitable organization founded in 1979
Mission: To provide support & information for burn survivors & their families; To offer a safe & caring camp program for children, from ages 7 to 17, with burn injuries
Finances: *Funding Sources:* Donations; Fundraising
Membership: *Member Profile:* Burn survivors; Families & friends of burn survivors; Interested individuals
Activities: Operating Camp BUCKO summer camp for young burn survivors, featuring recreational & therapeutic activities; Offering volunteer camp positions to adult burn survivors
Publications:
• Survivor
Type: Newsletter
Profile: Information & reviews of Camp BUCKO experiences

Burnaby Arts Council (BAC)
6584 Deer Lake Ave., Burnaby BC V5G 3T7
Tel: 604-298-7322; *Fax:* 604-298-9465
info@burnabyartscouncil.org
www.burnabyartscouncil.org
Overview: A small local charitable organization founded in 1967
Mission: To promote artists in the community; To encourage access to the arts; to increase & broaden the opportunities for public enjoyment of & participation in cultural activities
Member of: Assembly of BC Arts Councils
Chief Officer(s):
Brian Daniel, President
Bill Thomson, Vice-President
Finances: *Annual Operating Budget:* $50,000-$100,000
Staff Member(s): 7; 13 volunteer(s)
Membership: 14 corporate + 125 individual; *Member Profile:* Engaged in arts or related activity; *Committees:* Administration; Communication; Executive; Gallery; Program
Activities: Christmas Craft Fair; Cavalcade of Stars; Artwalk; Summer Theatre; Members Showcase; *Library* Open to public

Burnaby Association for Community Inclusion (BACI)
2702 Norland Ave., Burnaby BC V5B 3A6
Tel: 604-299-7851; *Fax:* 604-299-5921; *TTY:* 604-563-2579
reception@gobaci.com
www.gobaci.com
www.facebook.com/gobaci
twitter.com/gobaci/
Overview: A small local organization founded in 1956
Mission: Support services for people with developmental disabilities
Chief Officer(s):
Tanya Sather, Co-Executive Director, 604-292-1292
tanya.sather@gobaci.com
Richard Faucher, Co-Executive Director
richard.faucher@gobaci.com
Membership: *Committees:* Accreditation; Advocacy; Board Governance Review; Burnaby Association of Self Advocates; Committee on Seniors' Issues; Events & Hospitality; Audit; Employee Wellness; Labour Management; Occupational Health & Safety; Quality Assurance

Burnaby Board of Trade (BBOT)
#201, 4555 Kingsway, Burnaby BC V5H 4T8
Tel: 604-412-0100; *Fax:* 604-412-0102
admin@bbot.ca
www.bbot.ca
www.linkedin.com/company/burnaby-board-of-trade
www.facebook.com/burnabyboardoftrade
twitter.com/burnabybot
Also Known As: Burnaby Chamber of Commerce
Overview: A medium-sized local organization founded in 1910
Mission: To make Burnaby a better place to live & do business
Member of: Canadian Chamber of Commerce
Chief Officer(s):
Paul Holden, CEO Ext. 4
Finances: *Annual Operating Budget:* $250,000-$500,000; *Funding Sources:* Membership dues; fundraising
Staff Member(s): 5
Membership: 550; *Fees:* Schedule available; *Member Profile:* Burnaby businesses from a large variety of industries
Activities: International Trade Mission; Education; Tourism Management; Lobbyist; *Rents Mailing List:* Yes
Awards:
• Business Innovation (Award)
For ingenuity & innovation in business activities
• Entrepreneurial Spirit (Award)
For having demonstrated a highly entrepreneurial approach to launching a successful new business or new initiative
• Newsmaker of the Year (Award)
For having been widely recognized in the press for achievements as a Burnaby based business; helping to promote the city as a dynamic business location
• Business of the Year: Small Business (Award)
For a Burnaby business with less than 50 employees with annual revenues of up to 5 million, which has made an outstanding contribution in the combined area of business success, innovation & community service
• Burnaby Hall of Fame (Award)
For a Burnaby business which has demonstrated outstanding

success over many years & had a positive & significant impact on the community
• Community Spirit Award (Award)
For an exceptional contribution promoting Burnaby through its community festivals, events or programs & business activities
• Community Service (Award)
For the strong support of local service agencies, businesses, civic projects, positive business/community relations & promotion of the arts
• Business Person of the Year (Award)
For a local business person who is an outstanding role model for business development & excellence
• Business of the Year (Award)
For a Burnaby business that has made an outstanding contribution in the areas of business success, innovation & community service

Burnaby Laphounds Club

3051 Aires Place, Burnaby BC V3J 7G1
Tel: 604-444-4464
Overview: A small local organization founded in 1957
Member of: Lapidary, Rock & Mineral Society of British Columbia
Chief Officer(s):
Nancy Dickson, Contact
nancyandallan@telus.net

Burnaby Multicultural Society (BMS)

6255 Nelson Ave., Burnaby BC V5H 4T5
Tel: 604-431-4131
info@thebms.ca
www.thebms.ca
Overview: A small local charitable organization founded in 1984
Mission: To raise awareness & appreciation of gender, racial, ethnic & cultural diversity in Canada
Member of: Affiliation of Multicultural Societies & Service Agencies of BC
Chief Officer(s):
Ruminder Sadhra, President
bms.chair@shaw.ca
Rana Dhatt, Executive Director
rana.dhatt@thebms.ca
Activities: Immigrant settlement & integration; Public education; Seniors programs; English classes; *Library* Open to public by appointment

Burnaby Volunteer Centre Society

#203, 2101 Holdom Ave., Burnaby BC V5B 0A4
Tel: 604-294-5533
www.volunteerburnaby.ca
www.facebook.com/volunteerburnaby
twitter.com/volunteerbby
Also Known As: Volunteer Burnaby
Overview: A small local organization founded in 1979
Mission: To encourage volunteerism in local communities which in turn helps support non-profit organizations & neighbourhood events
Member of: Volunteer BC; Volunteer Canada
Chief Officer(s):
Dave Baspaly, Executive Director
dave@volunteerburnaby.ca
Finances: *Funding Sources:* All levels of government; donations; United Way
Staff Member(s): 4
Membership: 53; *Fees:* Schedule available based on budget for organizations; *Member Profile:* Agencies in need of volunteers; volunteers

Burnaby Writers' Society

Burnaby BC
Tel: 604-421-4931
info@bws.bc.ca
www.burnabywritersnews.blogspot.ca
Overview: A small local charitable organization founded in 1967
Mission: A community-oriented writers' group, dedicated to mutual support & encouragement of local talent; with a strong emphasis on skill development, marketing, & a professional approach to writing
Member of: Burnaby Arts Council
Finances: *Funding Sources:* Municipal Government
Membership: *Member Profile:* Membership ranges from novice writers to full-time professionals; from poets, short story writers & journalists to authors of science fiction, fantasy, mystery & romance novels

Burns Lake & District Chamber of Commerce

Heritage Centre, PO Box 339, 540 Hwy. 16, Burns Lake BC V0J 1E0
Tel: 250-692-3773; *Fax:* 250-692-3701
info@burnslakechamber.com
burnslakechamber.com
www.facebook.com/327936400553227
twitter.com/BurnsLakeBiz
Overview: A small local organization founded in 1927
Mission: To have a vibrant business community; To serve & connect our members by providing the tools & information to grow, enhance & develop existing & new business
Member of: BC Chamber of Commerce; Canadian Chamber of Commerce; Northern BC Tourism Association
Chief Officer(s):
Rise Johansen, President
Finances: *Annual Operating Budget:* $50,000-$100,000; *Funding Sources:* Membership dues
Staff Member(s): 2
Membership: 156; *Fees:* $150-450; *Committees:* Retail
Activities: *Library:* Business Information Centre

Burns Lake Christian Supportive Society

PO Box 1142, Burns Lake BC V0J 1E0
Tel: 250-692-7809; *Fax:* 250-692-7809
Overview: A small local organization
Mission: To provide services to special-needs citizens, their family, &/or advocates
Member of: British Columbia Association for Community Living
Chief Officer(s):
Kathy Janzen, Executive Director
kwjanzen@telus.net
Staff Member(s): 1
Membership: 150; *Fees:* Schedule available
Activities: *Internships:* Yes

Burrard Inlet Environmental Action Program & Fraser River Estuary Management Program (BIEAP/FREMP)

#501, 5945 Kathleen Ave., Burnaby BC V5H 4J7
Tel: 604-775-5756; *Fax:* 604-775-5198
info@bieapfremp.org
www.bieapfremp.org
Overview: A small local organization founded in 1985
Mission: To establish a management framework to facilitate activities to protect & improve the environmental quality of Burrard Inlet & the Fraser River Estuary; To promote the balance between the environment & the economy
Chief Officer(s):
Annemarie De Andrade, Program Manager, 604-775-5755
manager@bieapfremp.org
Michelle Gaudry, Policy Coordinator, 604-775-5195
mgaudry@bieapfremp.org
Finances: *Funding Sources:* Federal, provincial & regional government
Staff Member(s): 3

Burrows Trail Arts Council (BTAC)

PO Box 29, McCreary MB R0J 1B0
Tel: 204-835-2192
btac@mts.net
www.mts.net/~btac
Overview: A small local charitable organization founded in 1986
Member of: Manitoba Association of Community Arts Councils Inc.
Chief Officer(s):
Joyce Wiebe, President
Membership: *Fees:* $5 annually
Activities: *Library* Open to public

Bus History Association, Inc. (BHA)

c/o Bernie Drouillard, 965 McEwan Ave., Windsor ON N9B 2G1
www.bus-history.org
Overview: A medium-sized national organization founded in 1963
Mission: To preserve & record data, information & other related materials of the bus industry, both within North America & worldwide
Member of: Canadian Transit Heritage Foundation
Chief Officer(s):
Paul A. Leger, Chair
Bernard Drouillard, Secretary-Treasurer
bdrouillard3@cogeco.ca
6 volunteer(s)
Membership: *Fees:* $35 Canadian resident; US$25 US resident; US$35 international; *Member Profile:* Persons interested in bus industry

Business Council of British Columbia

#810, 1050 Pender St. West, Vancouver BC V6E 3S7
Tel: 604-684-3384; *Fax:* 888-488-5376
Other Communication: Media Contact Phone: 604-696-6582
info@bcbc.com
www.bcbc.com
www.linkedin.com/company/business-council-of-british-columbia
twitter.com/BizCouncilBC
Previous Name: Employers' Council of BC
Overview: A large provincial organization founded in 1966
Mission: To build a competitive & growing economy that provides opportunities for all who invest, work, & live in British Columbia
Chief Officer(s):
Hank Ketcham, Chair
Greg D'Avignon, President & CEO
greg.davignon@bcbc.com
Jock Finlayson, Executive VP & Chief Policy Officer
jock.finlayson@bcbc.com
Herb Eibensteiner, COO & Vice-President, Membership
herb.eibensteiner@bcbc.com
Ken Peacock, Chief Economist & Vice-President
ken.peacock@bcbc.com
Finances: *Funding Sources:* Membership fees
Membership: 260 organizations; *Fees:* Schedule available; *Committees:* Environment; Employee Relations; Membership; Competitiveness; Innovation; Energy Policy; Human Capital; Aboriginal Affairs
Publications:
• BC Economic Index [a publication of Business Council of British Columbia]
Frequency: q.
• BC Economic Review & Outlook [a publication of Business Council of British Columbia]
• Environment & Energy Bulletin [a publication of Business Council of British Columbia]
Type: Bulletin
• Human Capital Law & Policy [a publication of Business Council of British Columbia]
• Industrial Relations Bulletin [a publication of Business Council of British Columbia]
Type: Bulletin
• Policy Perspectives [a publication of Business Council of British Columbia]
Type: Newsletter

Business Council on National Issues *See* Canadian Council of Chief Executives

Business Development Centre (Toronto)

#900, 1 Yonge St., Toronto ON M5E 1E5
Tel: 416-345-9437; *Fax:* 416-345-9044
torbiz@tbdc.com
www.tbdc.com
www.linkedin.com/groups?homeNewMember=&gid=2847142
www.facebook.com/TorontoBusinessDevelopmentCentre
twitter.com/theTBDC
Overview: A medium-sized international organization founded in 1990
Mission: To assist people in business (non-profit); to provide regular seminars on import/export; entrepreneurial training; community programs
Affliation(s): Canadian Industrial Innovation Centre
Membership: *Member Profile:* Small business people; entrepreneurs
Activities: *Speaker Service:* Yes; *Library* Open to public

Business Development Centre of Greater Fort Erie *See* Business Success & Laon Centre Fort Erie

Business for the Arts / Affairs pour les arts

174 Avenue Rd., Toronto ON M5R 2J1
Tel: 416-869-3016; *Fax:* 416-869-0435
www.businessforthearts.org
www.linkedin.com/company/businessforthearts
www.facebook.com/businessforthearts
twitter.com/businessftarts
www.flickr.com/photos/businessforthearts
Overview: A medium-sized national organization founded in 1974
Mission: To make the partnership between business & the arts more effective in supporting the nation's creative minds.
Chief Officer(s):
James D. Fleck, Chair
Nichole Anderson, President & CEO
n_anderson@businessforthearts.org

Finances: *Funding Sources:* Membership fees; special project sponsorships
Staff Member(s): 8
Membership: 36 corporate; *Fees:* $6500
Activities: artsVest; boardLink; artsScene; BFTA Annual Awards
Awards:
• John P. Fisher Award for Media Support of the Arts (Award)
Created by CBAC & Southam Inc. in honour of the late John P. Fisher, who was CBAC's Chairman from 1991-1996 and was also CEO of Southam Inc.; to recognize newspapers that combine a mixture of quality arts journalism with significant contributions of advertising, in-kind & volunteer support
• Edmund C. Bovey Award (Award)
To recognize individual members of the business community who contribute leadership, time, money & expertise to the arts
Amount: A sculpture to the winner & $20,000 distributed to the arts in a way specified by the winner
• National Post Awards for Business in the Arts (Award)
Created in 1979 to encourage the corporate sector's involvement with the visual & performing arts in Canada & to recognize this involvement

Business Practices & Consumer Protection Authority of British Columbia *See* Consumer Protection BC

Business Professional Association of Canada (BPA Canada)
Tel: 905-619-3601; *Fax:* 647-317-3990
Toll-Free: 877-619-3601
www.bpacanada.com
Overview: A large national organization
Mission: To give members quality referrals while helping them build their client relationships. Chapters located in Ajax, Markham, Oshawa & Whitby
Chief Officer(s):
Mike Hurley, HRM, Director
Mike@BPACanada.com
Chuck Trumphour, HRM, Director
Membership: *Member Profile:* Business professionals
Activities: Weekly meetings; E-newsletter; social networking events; seminars & workshops

Ajax Chapter
c/o Darryl Glover, 562 Kingston Rd. West, Ajax ON L1T 3A2
Tel: 905-619-3700; *Fax:* 905-619-0022
ajax@bpacanada.com
Chief Officer(s):
Darryl Glover, President

Markham Corporate Chapter
c/o Phil Richardson, #400, 3601 Hwy. 7 East, Markham ON L4R 0M3
Tel: 905-881-0959; *Fax:* 905-294-6676
markham@bpacanada.com
Chief Officer(s):
Phil Richardson, President

Oshawa Chapter
c/o Richard Atkinson, 1600 Champlain Ave., Whitby ON L1N 9B2
Tel: 905-433-9999
oshawa@bpacanada.com
Chief Officer(s):
Richard Atkinson, President, 647-248-2862

Whitby Chapter
e-mail: whitby@bpacanada.com
Chief Officer(s):
Marshall Spencer, President, 905-430-0552

Business Success & Laon Centre Fort Erie (BSL)
45 Jarvis St., Fort Erie ON L2A 2S3
Tel: 905-871-7331; *Fax:* 905-871-5284
bslft@niagara.com
www.bslft.com
Previous Name: Business Development Centre of Greater Fort Erie
Overview: A small provincial organization founded in 1985
Mission: To provide loans to small businesses & entrepreneurs to start & maintain businesses, or to finance growth for existing companies & start-up businesses; To administer the Ontario Self-Employment Benefit program for eligible individuals
Member of: Ontario Association of Community Development Corporations
Affliation(s): Human Resources Development Canada; Ministry of Training, College, & Universities
Chief Officer(s):
Larry Graber, Manager
larrygraber@niagara.com
Joseph Katz, Coordinator, Self-Employment Benefit
jkatz@niagara.com
Finances: *Annual Operating Budget:* $100,000-$250,000
Staff Member(s): 3; 11 volunteer(s)
Activities: Assisting in the development of a business plan; Providing ongoing monitoring & training; Offering coaching & evaluation of progress during the first year of a new business; *Speaker Service:* Yes; *Library:* BSL Reference Library; Open to public

Business Women's Networking Association (BWNA)
Aurora ON
Tel: 289-466-6100
www.bwna.ca
Overview: A small local organization
Mission: To offer support & exchange information on issues unique to women in business.
Chief Officer(s):
Elina Bagshaw, President, Aurora Chapter
Membership: *Fees:* $120; *Member Profile:* Entrepreneurial women in professional & service occupations who are self-employed and/or small business owners
Activities: Monthly meetings & lunches with speakers

King Chapter
King City ON
Tel: 905-939-8025
Chief Officer(s):
Jane Cameron, President

Buy-Side Investment Management Association (BIMA)
c/o Zzeem, Inc., PO Box 38179, Toronto ON M5N 1B6
e-mail: info@bima.ca
www.bima.ca
Overview: A small national organization founded in 2005
Mission: To help members reach & maintain a high level of success
Chief Officer(s):
Justin Lord, President
Membership: 1-99
Activities: Networking opportunities; educational opportunities; representing member interests; semi-annual conferences

Bytown Railway Society (BRS)
PO Box 47076, Ottawa ON K1B 5P9
Tel: 613-745-1201; *Fax:* 613-745-1201
info@bytownrailwaysociety.ca
www.bytownrailwaysociety.ca
Overview: A medium-sized national charitable organization founded in 1969
Mission: To promote an interest in railways & railway history, with particular emphasis on Canadian railways.
Finances: *Funding Sources:* Publications sale; memberships
Activities: Restoration/preservation of owned railway equipment; *Library* Open to public by appointment

CAA Manitoba
870 Empress St., Winnipeg MB R3C 2Z3
Tel: 204-262-6100
contact@caamanitoba.com
www.caamanitoba.com
www.facebook.com/caamanitoba
twitter.com/caamanitoba
Overview: A medium-sized provincial organization overseen by Canadian Automobile Association
Chief Officer(s):
Bohdan (Bud) V. Halkewycz, Chair
Michael R. Mager, President & Chief Executive Officer
Membership: 160,000 individual

Caanadian Society of Presbyterian History
c/o Burns Presbyterian Church, 765 Myrtle Rd. West, Ashburn ON L0B 1A0
Tel: 905-655-8509
www.csph.ca
Overview: A small local organization founded in 1975
Mission: To study Presbyterian & Reformed history
Chief Officer(s):
A. Donald MacLeod, President
adonaldmacleod@gmail.com

CAA-Québec
444, rue Bouvier, Québec QC G2J 1E3
Tél: 418-624-2424
Ligne sans frais: 800-686-9243; *Crisis Hot-Line:* 800-222-4357
info@caa-quebec.qc.ca
www.caaquebec.com
Nom précédent: Automobile et touring club du Québec
Aperçu: *Dimension:* grande; *Envergure:* provinciale; fondée en 1904 surveillé par Canadian Automobile Association
Mission: Veut assurer la sécurité et paix d'esprit à chacun de ses membres ainsi qu'à ses clients en leur offrant des services et des produits de très haute qualité dans les domaines de l'automobile, du voyage, de l'habitation et des services financiers
Affliation(s): Alliance internationale du Tourisme; Fédération internationale de l'automobile
Membre(s) du bureau directeur:
Sophie Gagnon, Vice-présidente adjointe, Relations publiques et gouvernementales de CAA-Québec, 418-624-2424 Ext. 2324
sogagnon@caaquebec.com
Philippe St-Pierre, Conseiller en communication, 418-624-2424 Ext. 2418
pstpierre@caaquebec.com
Membre: 1 000 000; *Montant de la cotisation:* Schedule available
Activités: Services routiers; Services aux voyageurs - Agences de voyages et Auto-Touring; Assurances et services financiers; Services techniques; Services habitation
Publications:
• Touring [a publication of CAA-Québec]
Type: Magazine; *Frequency:* 4 fois par an

Boisbriand
2715, rue d'Annemasse, Boisbriand QC J7H 0A5
Tél: 450-435-3636

Brossard
#20, 8940, boul Leduc, Brossard QC J4Y 0G4
Tél: 450-465-0620

Gatineau
960, boul Maloney Ouest, Gatineau QC J8T 3R6
Tél: 819-778-2225

Laval
#100, 3131, boul St-Martin Ouest, Laval QC H7T 2Z5
Tél: 450-682-8100

Montréal
#100, 1180, rue Drummond, Montréal QC H3G 2R7
Tél: 514-861-5111

Pointe-Claire
1000, boul St-Jean, Pointe-Claire QC H9R 5P1
Tél: 514-426-2760

Québec
#202, 500, rue Bouvier, Québec QC G2J 1E3
Tél: 418-624-8222

Québec (Place de la Cité)
#133, 2600, boul Laurier, Québec QC G1V 4T3
Tél: 418-653-9200

Saguenay
#1100, 1700, boul Talbot, Saguenay QC G7H 7Y1
Tél: 418-545-8686

Saint-Léonard
7178, boul Langelier, Saint-Léonard QC H1S 2X6
Tél: 514-255-3560

Sherbrooke
2990, rue King Ouest, Sherbrooke QC J1L 1Y7
Tél: 819-566-5132

Terrebonne
302, montée des Pionniers, Terrebonne QC J6V 1S6
Tél: 450-585-9797

Trois-Rivières
4085, boul des Récollets, Trois-Rivières QC G9A 6M1
Tél: 819-376-9393

Cabbagetown Community Arts Centre (CCAC)
422 Parliament St., Toronto ON M5A 2A2
Tel: 416-925-7222; *Fax:* 416-928-1741
theccac@yahoo.com
www.cabbagetownarts.org
Overview: A small local charitable organization founded in 1979
Mission: To provide underpriviledged children with the opportunity to learn music & art
Chief Officer(s):
Sarah Patrick, Executive Director
Staff Member(s): 9

Cabbagetown Preservation Association (CPA)
PO Box 82808, Stn. Cabbagetown, 467 Parliament St., Toronto ON M5A 3Y2
Tel: 416-964-8004
cpa@cabbagetownpa.ca
www.cabbagetownpa.ca
www.facebook.com/338478909574779
Overview: A small local charitable organization founded in 1989

Mission: To preserve the architectural integrity of the Cabbagetown neighbourhood
Member of: Metro Area Heritage Group; Toronto Historical Association
Affliation(s): Ontario Historical Association
Chief Officer(s):
David Pretlove, Chair
Mary Martin, Treasurer
Sue McMurtry, Secretary
Finances: *Annual Operating Budget:* Less than $50,000; *Funding Sources:* Membership dues; sale of t-shirts, book & postcards; provincial & corporate grants
100 volunteer(s)
Membership: 442; *Member Profile:* Members live in or are interested in this area of Toronto; *Committees:* Heritage Issues; Riverdale Farm & Riverdale Park Issues; Walking Tours; Tour of Homes; Cabbagetown People Program; Hidden Gardens & Private Spaces Tour
Activities: Walking tours; tea; public meetings, Nov. & Feb.; Historic Plaque Program; *Awareness Events:* Forsythia Festival, 1st Sunday in May; Cabbagetown Festival, 2nd weekend in Sept.; *Speaker Service:* Yes; *Library* by appointment
Awards:
• Streetscape in Bloom Award (Award)
• The Peggy Kurtin Award for Excellence in Restoration (Award)
Publications:
• The CPA [Cabbagetown Preservation Association] Newsletter
Type: Newsletter; *Frequency:* Quarterly

Cable in the Classroom (CITC) / La Câblo-éducation

#1450, 45 O'Connor St., Ottawa ON K1P 1A4
Tel: 613-233-3033; *Fax:* 613-233-7650
Toll-Free: 800-244-9049
www.facebook.com/CableintheClassroom
twitter.com/CableClassroom
Previous Name: Canadian Cable in the Classroom Association
Overview: A medium-sized national organization founded in 1993
Mission: To provide free, copyright-cleared, commercial-free, educationally relevant, French & English-language television programming free to elementary & secondary schools across Canada
Chief Officer(s):
Frank Gallagher, Executive Director
Finances: *Annual Operating Budget:* $250,000-$500,000
Membership: 1-99; *Member Profile:* Canadian cable companies; television networks licenced in Canada & the USA
Activities: Educational television programming; CITC listings online; *Speaker Service:* Yes

La Câblo-éducation *See* Cable in the Classroom

Cache Creek Chamber of Commerce

PO Box 460, Cache Creek BC V0K 1H0
Tel: 250-457-9668; *Fax:* 250-457-9669
Toll-Free: 888-457-7661
admin@cachecreek.info
www.cachecreekvillage.com
Overview: A small local organization
Chief Officer(s):
Gordon Daily, President

CADORA British Columbia

PO Box 31120, RPO University Heights, Victoria BC V8N 6J3
Tel: 250-722-4791
www.cadorabc.com
Also Known As: Canadian Dressage Owners & Riders Association, Pacific Chapter
Overview: A small provincial organization overseen by Canadian Dressage Owners & Riders Association
Mission: To act as a unified voice on dressage issues in British Columbia; To develop & promote dressage in British Columbia
Chief Officer(s):
Courtenay Fraser, President, 778-232-1664
courtenay@courtenayfraser.com
Megan Andersen, Vice-President, 604-533-3130
admin@jctraining.ca
Stephanie Sutton, Secretary, 604-535-7477
Pamela Williams, Treasurer, 250-722-4791
pamw@shaw.ca
Membership: *Fees:* $10 senior members; $5 non-riding family members; $2.50 junior members; *Member Profile:* Junior & senior dressage riders & their non-riding family members from across British Columbia
Activities: Liaising with regulatory bodies on dressage issues; Encouraging participation in competitions & demonstrations; Offering awards, scholarships, & travel assistance programs; Increasing knowledge of good horsemanship; Presenting the CADORA BC Provincial Dressage Program, with educational clinics, seminars, & symposia throughout British Columbia

Country CADORA Chapter
c/o Linda Dieno, PO Box 10091, Aldergrove BC V4W 3Z5
Tel: 604-882-0120
cassabyrne@shaw.ca
Mission: To develop & promote dressage in the Surrey region of British Columbia
Chief Officer(s):
Linda Dieno, Contact
cassabyrne@shaw.ca

Courtenay CADORA Chapter
c/o Christal Quinn, 4722 Condensory Rd., Courtenay BC V9J 1R6
Tel: 250-334-2306
Mission: To develop dressage in the Courtenay area of British Columbia
Isobell Springett, Contact, 250-338-9834
isobell@mars.ark.com

Mid-Island CADORA Chapter
c/o Pam Williams, 2711 Ritten Rd., Nanaimo BC V9X 1W4
Tel: 250-722-4791
pamw@shaw.ca
Chief Officer(s):
Pam Williams, Contact, 250-722-4791
pamw@shaw.ca

North Central - Skeena CADORA Chapter
c/o Cindy Thiele, 1420 PG Pulpmill Rd., Prince George BC V2K 5P4
Tel: 250-563-2933
Mission: To promote dressage in British Columbia's North Central - Skeena area
Chief Officer(s):
Jodie Kennedy-Baker, Contact, 250-963-6866
jobaker@sd57.bc.ca
Cindy Thiele, Contact, 250-563-2933
thiele@mailscar.ca

Okanagan CADORA Chapter
c/o Suzanne Wallace, 7069 Nakiska Dr., Vernon BC V1B 3M5
Tel: 250-545-5573
suwallace@shaw.ca
Mission: To promote interest in dressage riding as in the Okanagan
Chief Officer(s):
Suzanne Wallace, Contact, 250-545-5573
suwallace@shaw.ca

Saltspring CADORA Chapter
c/o Barb Murphy, 166 Lakefair Dr., Saltspring Island BC V8K 1C7
Tel: 250-537-8470
bj55murphy@telus.net
Mission: To develop dressage on Saltspring Island
Chief Officer(s):
Barb Murphy, Contact, 250-537-8470
bj55murphy@telus.net

Vancouver - Richmond CADORA Chapter
c/o Sarah T. Simpson, 7273 Balaclava St., Vancouver BC V6N 1M7
Tel: 604-266-9202
stsimpson@shaw.ca
Mission: To develop & promote dressage in British Columbia's Vancouver - Richmond region
Anki Sjoholm, Contact, 604-274-8735
ankisjoholm@shaw.ca

Victoria - Saanich CADORA Chapter
c/o Ann Brouwer, 1513 San Juan Ave., Victoria BC V8N 2L4
Tel: 250-477-3607
ann.brouwer@shaw.ca
www.vscadora.com
Mission: To develop dressage in the Victoria - Saanich area of British Columbia
Chief Officer(s):
Ann Brouwer, President, 250-477-3607
ann.brouwer@shaw.ca
Ilona Rule, Secretary, 250-652-6384
ilonarule@telus.net
Jill Rogers, Treasurer, 250-383-5126
jillrogers@shaw.ca
• The Extension: The Victoria - Saanich CADORA Newsletter
Type: Newsletter; *Frequency:* Bimonthly; *Accepts Advertising*; *Editor:* Lisa Bricknell
Profile: Chapter information, such as event reports, rule changes, & upcoming shows & clinics

CADORA Ontario Association Inc.

c/o Don Barnes, #13, 1475 Upper Gage Ave., Hamilton ON L8W 1E6
Tel: 905-387-2031
www.cadora.ca/cadora-ontario
www.facebook.com/CadoraOntario?fref=ts
Also Known As: Canadian Dressage Owners & Riders Association, Eastern Chapter
Overview: A small provincial organization overseen by Canadian Dressage Owners & Riders Association
Mission: To develop the talent, the art, & the sport of dressage in Ontario
Chief Officer(s):
Don Barnes, President, 905-387-2031
Dressagegames@aol.com
Membership: *Member Profile:* Ontario dressage enthusiasts
Activities: Disseminating information to members about dressage; Presenting championships
Awards:
• CADORA Ontario Riding Scholarship (Scholarship)
To recognize the highest scoring champion at each level as determined at the Silver Dressage Championships
• Year-End Bronze Competitor Awards (Award)
To recognize the highest-placing competitor at all levels (training through fourth level)
• Ontario Provincial Sport Horse Dressage Award (Award)
To recognize the highest-placing competitor at all levels (training through fourth level) *Contact:* Susan Johnson, Phone: 905-549-4491; E-mail: suej99@hotmail.com
Publications:
• CADORA [Canadian Dressage Owners & Riders Association] Ontario Association Newsletter
Type: Newsletter; *Frequency:* Semiannually; *Editor:* Don Barnes
Profile: Association contact information, lists of members, application forms, championship results, meeting notices, & articles

Caledon CADORA Chapter
c/o Lynne Poole, PO Box 415, Schomberg ON L0G 1T0
www.caledondressage.com
Mission: To foster interest in the sport of dressage in Ontario's Caledon region
Affliation(s): Dressage Canada; Equine-Hippeque Canada; Ontario Equestrian Federation; Toronto CADORA
Chief Officer(s):
Kristy Nahirniak, President & Show Secretary, 519-925-6256
knahirniak@sympatico.ca
Nina Barker, Vice-President & Treasurer, 705-534-2717
nbarker@csolve.net
Sean Antonello, Secretary & Sponsorship, 519-404-3852

Conestoga CADORA Chapter
c/o Philip Parkes, RR#2, Listowel ON N4W 3G8
www.conestogacadora.ca
Mission: To promote ownership of dressage horses; To foster participation in dressage riding
Affliation(s): Equine Canada; Dressage Canada; Ontario Equestrian Federation
Chief Officer(s):
Philip Parkes, President, 519-588-8768
Philip@philipparkesequestrian.com
Chris Henderson, Secretary, 519-744-6319
chenders@uwaterloo.ca
Jane MacIntosh, Treasurer, 519-653-8290
jmacintosh@bellnet.ca
Karen Carter, Show Coordinator, 519-570-2375
randkcarter@sympatico.ca
Trish Faucette, Show Coordinator, 519-634-8147
jweber@golden.net
• Conestoga CADORA Newsletter
Type: Newsletter; *Editor:* Philip Parkes; *Price:* Free with membership in Conestoga CADORA
Profile: Chapter activities & announcements

Dressage Niagara Chapter
PO Box 231, Fonthill ON L0S 1E0
Tel: 905-468-8534
www.dressageniagara.com
www.facebook.com/pages/Dressage-Niagara/166396176766652?ref=stream
Mission: To promote the sport of dressage in the Niagara Region of Ontario; To encourage participation in competitions
Affliation(s): Equine Canada
Chief Officer(s):

Jane Langdon, President, 905-468-8534
info@winecountrycooking.com
Kait Whittle, Vice-President, 905-957-9061
k_80kat@hotmail.com
Jen Goul, Secretary, 905-371-5451
jen.goul@gmail.com
Linda Warrell, Treasurer, 905-682-7333
garlin131@sympatico.ca
Kelly Dolynski, Coordinator, Membership & Volunteers, 905-329-8529
DressageNiagara@live.ca
Janet Henderson, Coordinator, Clinic, 905-228-3091
rivendel@lastmilenet.ca
Louise Kennedy, Coordinator, Show, 905-892-3470
redloui@yahoo.com
Sue Wyrcimaga, Coordinator, Communications, 905-563-1888
ronandsue@talkwireless.ca

• Annual Dressage Niagara Competition Handbook
Type: Yearbook; *Frequency:* Annually; *Accepts Advertising*
• Dressage Niagara Membership Directory
Type: Directory
• Dressage Niagara Newsletter
Type: Newsletter; *Frequency:* Quarterly; *Price:* Free with membership in Dressage Niagara
Profile: Club information

Glanbrook CADORA Chapter
c/o Judith Wanner, 828 King Rd., Burlington ON L7T 3K9
Tel: 905-333-5481; *Fax:* 905-333-0582
dwanner@sympatico.ca
www.glanbrook.com
Mission: To encourage ownership of dressage horses in the Glanbrook area of Ontario; To foster interest in the sport of dressage riding; To increase knowlege of good horsemanship
Affliation(s): Dressage Canada; Equine Canada; Ontario Equestrian Federation
Chief Officer(s):
Judy Wanner, Area Representative, 905-333-5481
judithwanner@sympatico.ca
Susan Anderson, Treasurer, 519-821-4435
susan114@sympatico.ca

• Glanbrook CADORA Newsletter
Type: Newsletter; *Price:* Free with Glanbrook CADORA membership
Profile: Chapter activities & announcments

Greater Sudbury Chapter
c/o Ashley Czerkas, 4028 Regional Rd. 15, Chelmsford ON P0M 1L0
Tel: 705-855-2254
gsda@persona.ca
www.gsda.info
www.facebook.com/402568493165315
Mission: To promote the sport of dressage in the Greater Sudbury region; To increase understanding of good horsemanship
Affliation(s): Equine-Hippique Canada; Dressage Canada
Chief Officer(s):
Connie Czerkas, President
connie_czerkas@personainternet.com
Vanessa Catto, Vice-President
vancatt@hotmail.com
Donna Keller, 1st Secretary
Ashley Czerkas, 2nd Secretary
ashley.czerkas@personainternet.com

Kawartha Lakes Dressage Chapter
c/o Lisa Hossack-Scott, 2833 Hwy. 28, RR#1, Duro ON K0L 1S0
Tel: 705-749-9726
klda@klda.ca
www.klda.ca
www.facebook.com/groups/53381682734/
Mission: To foster the sport of dressage in the Kawartha Lakes area of Ontario
Affliation(s): Dressage Canada
Chief Officer(s):
Miranda Trudeau, President
Lynne Milford, Secretary, Membership
Lisa Hossack-Scott, Treasurer
Jennifer Plumbtree, Communications

• The Centre Line
Type: Newsletter; *Accepts Advertising*; *Editor:* Jennifer Plumbtree
Profile: Chapter activities, such as meeting reports & show information

London Chapter
c/o Tara Young, 1430 Windemere, Sarnia ON N7S 3M2
londondressage.com
Mission: To encourage the ownership of dressage horses; To foster interest & participation in dressage riding
Affliation(s): Dressage Canada; Equine-Hippique Canada
Chief Officer(s):
Lynn Young, Chair, 519-542-1326
ryoung1@cogeco.ca
Gail Lamb, Secretary, 519-227-0582
gail@gailelamb.com
Stephanie Murdoch-Tosh, Treasurer, 519-649-8248
stephanie-murdoch@hotmail.com

• London Dressage Association Newsletter
Type: Newsletter; *Price:* Free with membership in the London Dressage Association
Profile: Club activities

Ottawa Area CADORA Chapter
c/o Cathy Gordon, 819 Drummond Rd., R.R. 1, Carleton Place ON K7C 3P1
Tel: 613-257-5145
www.ottawadressage.ca
www.facebook.com/pages/OADG-Ottawa-Area-Dressage-Group/187355987992852
Mission: To develop the sport of dressage in the Ottawa area
Affliation(s): Dressage Canada
Chief Officer(s):
Pierre Paquette, President, 613-821-6206
president@ottawadressage.ca
Laura-Lee Brenneman, Secretary/Treasurer, 613-421-1741
treasurer@ottawadressage.ca
Cathy Gordon, Director, Membership, 613-257-5145
membership@ottawadressage.ca
Peggy McQuaid, Coordinator, Education, 613-831-2692
education@ottawadressage.ca
Catherine Maguire, Director, Awards, 613-256-2725
awards@ottawadressage.ca

• Ottawa Area Dressage Group Newsletter
Type: Newsletter; *Frequency:* 8 pa; *Accepts Advertising*; *Editor:* Diana Bayer; *Price:* Free with Ottawa Area DressageGroup membership
Profile: Chapter activities, including show schedules, results, awards, forthcoming clinics & meetings, & updates on rules & regulations

Quinte St. Lawrence CADORA Chapter
c/o Sharrie Lynch, 4027 Shannonville Rd., Roslin ON K0K 2Y0
e-mail: qslbinfo@gmail.com
www.qslb.ca
www.facebook.com/QSLBCadora
Mission: To encourage interest in the sport of dressage riding in the Quinte St. Lawrence region of Ontario; To increase understanding of good horsemanship
Affliation(s): Dressage Canada
Chief Officer(s):
Micky Colton, President
mccolton@sympatico.ca
Shari Clark, Vice-President
sclark@kos.net
Jane Casson, Secretary/Treasurer
tjcasson@sympatico.ca

• Quinte St. Lawrence Branch Newsletter
Type: Newsletter; *Editor:* Alicia Finan
Profile: QSLB activities & announcements

Toronto CADORA Chapter
#1206, 15 Michael Power Pl., Toronto ON M9A 5G4
Tel: 905-640-1720
tcinfo@torontocadora.com
www.torontocadora.com
www.facebook.com/pages/TC-Youth/159168527875
twitter.com/torontocadora
Mission: To promote the sport & art of dressage in the Toronto area; To nurture good horsemanship; To offer an education-focused & horse-friendly atmosphere
Chief Officer(s):
Sue Saunders, President
Mary Chamberlain, Secretary, Membership
mchamberlain@sympatico.ca
Sue Pallotta, Treasurer

• Track Right
Type: Newsletter; *Editor:* Andrea Wetzel; *Price:* Free with membership in the Toronto CADORA Chapter
Profile: Club activities

Windsor - Essex CADORA Chapter
c/o Sarah Reaume, 184 Texas Rd., Amherstburg ON N9V 2R7
windsoressexcadora.weebly.com
Mission: To foster participation in the sport of dressage riding in Ontario's Windsor - Essex region; To increase awareness of the sport of dressage riding
Affliation(s): Equine Canada; Dressage Canada
Chief Officer(s):
Jenn Bauermann, President
Andrea Bingham, Treasurer
Jen Ingratta, Secretary

• Windsor - Essex Canadian Dressage Owners & Riders Association Members' Farm Directory
Type: Directory
• Windsor - Essex Canadian Dressage Owners & Riders Association Omnibus
Type: Handbook
Profile: Rules, regulations, & requirements for Windsor - Essex club awards

---

CAE Basses-Laurentides inc. ***Voir*** Réseau des SADC et CAE

CAE de la Rive-Sud inc. ***Voir*** Réseau des SADC et CAE

CAEO Québec

PO Box 55505, Stn. Maisonneuve, Montréal QC H1W 0A1
e-mail: info@caeoquebec.org
www.caeoquebec.org
www.facebook.com/CAEOquebec
twitter.com/CAEOquebec
Previous Name: Gay Line
Overview: A small local charitable organization founded in 1976
Mission: To provide a listening & information telephone service for English-speaking gays, lesbians, bisexuals & transgendered people in Québec.
Affliation(s): Gai Écoute
Chief Officer(s):
Nick Frate, Founder
Membership: *Member Profile:* Lesbian; gay; bisexual; transgendered
Activities: *Speaker Service:* Yes; *Library:* Gay Line Resource Library

---

La Caisse des acteurs du Canada inc. ***See*** The Actors' Fund of Canada

---

Caisse Financial Group ***Voir*** Caisse Groupe Financier

Caisse Groupe Financier / Caisse Financial Group

#400, 205 Provencher Blvd., Winnipeg MB R2H 0G4
Tél: 204-237-8988; *Téléc:* 204-233-6405
Ligne sans frais: 866-926-0706
info@caisse.biz
www.caisse.biz
Merged from: Fédération des Caisses populaires du Manitoba
Aperçu: *Dimension:* grande; *Envergure:* provinciale; fondée en 2010
Mission: Contribuer à l'essor économique et socio-culturel des manitobains en poursuivant le développement des services et du réseau financiers dont les avoirs sont gérés, administrés et contrôlés par des francophones
Affliation(s): Mouvement Desjardins
Membre(s) du bureau directeur:
Réal Déquier, President
Joël Rondeau, Chief Executive Officer
Membre: *Critères d'admissibilite:* Résidant ou entreprise du Manitoba

---

Caledon Chamber of Commerce

PO Box 626, 12598 Hwy. 50 South, Bolton ON L7E 5T5
Tel: 905-857-7393; *Fax:* 905-857-7405
info@caledonchamber.com
www.caledonchamber.com
www.facebook.com/caledon.chamber
Overview: A small local organization founded in 1985
Mission: To promote, encourage & represent local business; To be the "voice of business" committed to the economic, social & environmental health of Caledon
Affliation(s): Canadian Chamber of Commerce; Ontario Chamber of Commerce
Chief Officer(s):
Steve Owen, Chair
Kelly Darnley, President & CEO
kelly@caledonchamber.com
Finances: *Annual Operating Budget:* $100,000-$250,000; *Funding Sources:* Membership dues; programs; trade show

14 volunteer(s)
Membership: 250; *Fees:* $217.35-$569.25; *Committees:* Programs; Events; Advocacy/Policy; Marketing & Communication; Membership Development
Activities: Caledon Home Show; Headwaters Golf Classic; Caledon Women's Christmas Dinner; meetings; networking; *Library* Open to public
Awards:
- Business of the Year (Award)
- Property Improvement Awards (Award)
- Caledon Woman of the Year Recognition (Award)

Caledon Community Services (CCS)
Royal Cortyards, Upper Level, 18 King St. East, Bolton ON L7E 1E8
Tel: 905-584-2300; *Fax:* 905-951-2303
Toll-Free: 800-985-2471
info@ccs4u.org
www.ccs4u.org
www.facebook.com/pages/Caledon-Community-Services/17402 1567360
twitter.com/CaledonCS
www.youtube.com/user/CaledonCServices
Overview: A small local charitable organization founded in 1971 overseen by InformOntario
Mission: CCS is a health & social service organization with volunteer-delivered programs to provide the Caledon community with support in times of difficulty & change.
Member of: Ontario Community Support Association; Association of Community Information Centres in Ontario
Affliation(s): Social Planning Council of Peel; Volunteer Centre of Peel
Chief Officer(s):
Monty Laskin, Chief Executive Officer
mlaskin@ccs4u.org
Finances: *Annual Operating Budget:* $500,000-$1.5 Million; *Funding Sources:* United Way; Donations
Staff Member(s): 64; 336 volunteer(s)
Membership: *Member Profile:* Caledon residents
Activities: Community information; family & individual counselling; crisis support; support for seniors; housing; respite caregivers; Ontario Works Jobs Development; employment services; training; ESL classes

Caledon East & District Historical Society
PO Box 37, Caledon East ON L7C 3L8
Tel: 905-584-0352
www.cedhs.ca
Overview: A small local organization founded in 1984
Mission: To promote & maintain the history of the Caledon East area
Member of: Ontario Historical Society
Chief Officer(s):
Donna Davies, President
donnadavies@rogers.com
Finances: *Funding Sources:* Membership fees; publications sales
Membership: 70; *Fees:* $10
Activities: Archives; tours
Publications:
- Settling the Hills
Type: book; *Number of Pages:* 224; *Editor:* Ken Weber, Donna Davies; *Price:* $24.95
Profile: An early history of the area of Caledon East, with 160 b/w photos

Caledon Institute of Social Policy
1354 Wellington Street West, 3rd Fl., Ottawa ON K1Y 3C3
Tel: 613-729-3340; *Fax:* 613-729-3896
caledon@caledoninst.org
www.caledoninst.org
www.twitter.com/CaledonINST
Overview: A small national charitable organization founded in 1992
Mission: Researches & analyzes public policy; seeks to inform & influence public opinion & foster discussion on poverty & social policy
Chief Officer(s):
Ken Battle, President/Founder
battle@caledoninst.org
Finances: *Funding Sources:* Maytree Foundation; Donations

The Caledon Institute of Social Policy
1354 Wellington St. West, 3rd Fl., Ottawa ON K1Y 3C3
Tel: 613-729-3340; *Fax:* 613-729-3340
caledon@caledoninst.org
www.caledoninst.org
www.twitter.com/CaledonINST
Overview: A small international charitable organization founded in 1992
Mission: Social policy research, analysis & public education; focuses on areas such as income security, taxation, social spending, employment & poverty analysis
Affliation(s): Avona Capital Corp.
Chief Officer(s):
Ken Battle, President
battle@caledoninst.org
Staff Member(s): 5

Caledonia Regional Chamber of Commerce
PO Box 2035, 1 Grand Trunk Lane, Caledonia ON N3W 2G6
Tel: 905-765-0377
caledoniachamber@shaw.ca
www.caledonia-ontario.com
Overview: A small local organization
Chief Officer(s):
Suzanne Athanasiou, President, 905-765-1100
Barb Martindale, Executive Director

Calgary & Area Medical Staff Society (CAPA)
c/o Alberta Medical Association, 350, 708 - 11 Ave. SW, Calgary AB T2R 0E4
Tel: 403-205-2093
audrey.harlow@albertadoctors.org
www.camss.ca
Previous Name: Calgary & Area Physician's Association
Overview: A small local organization
Mission: Represents physicians working in the Calgary Health Region in hospitals or in the community
Chief Officer(s):
Dave Lowery, Communications Director
Steve Patterson, President
steve.patterson@albertahealthservices.ca
Finances: *Funding Sources:* Membership dues
Membership: *Fees:* $275; *Member Profile:* All physicians working for the Calgary Health Region
Publications:
- Vital Signs
Type: Magazine; *Frequency:* Monthly; *Editor:* Dave Lowery

Calgary & Area Physician's Association *See* Calgary & Area Medical Staff Society

Calgary & District Labour Council (CDLC)
#321, 3132 - 26 St. NE, Calgary AB T1Y 6Z1
Tel: 403-262-2390; *Fax:* 403-262-2408
cdlc@telusplanet.net
www.thecdlc.ca
Overview: A large provincial organization founded in 1905 overseen by Alberta Federation of Labour
Mission: To maintain, strengthen & protect Calgary's public & social institutions & programs
Affliation(s): Canadian Labour Congress; Alberta Federation of Labour
Staff Member(s): 1
Membership: 60 unions representing 30,000 workers; *Member Profile:* Affiliated union locals; *Committees:* Political Action; Strike Support; Education; Website; Education; Finance; Labour Day BBQ; May Day Arts Festival; S'ean Gillen Memorial Scholarship; United Way Partnership
Activities: *Awareness Events:* Labour Day BBQ, Sept.; May Day Arts Festival
Awards:
- S'ean Gillen Memorial Scholarship (Scholarship)

Calgary & District Target Shooters Association (CDTSA)
AB
Tel: 403-275-3257
www.cdtsa.ca
Overview: A small local organization founded in 1981
Affliation(s): Alberta Federation of Shooting Sports; Alberta Fish & Game Association; Alberta Black Powder Association; Alberta Metallic Silhouette Association
Finances: *Annual Operating Budget:* Less than $50,000
12 volunteer(s)
Membership: *Fees:* Schedule available

Calgary Aboriginal Arts Awareness Society (CAAAS)
#202B, 351 - 11 Ave. SW, Calgary AB T2R 0C7
Tel: 403-296-2227
c_a_a_a_s@yahoo.ca
www.freewebs.com/caaas
Previous Name: Calgary Aboriginal Awareness Society
Overview: A small local charitable organization founded in 1988
Mission: To celebrate positive reinforcement, communication & outreach of the cultural continuum of traditional & contemporary practice of Aboriginal Professional Artists
Finances: *Annual Operating Budget:* $50,000-$100,000
Staff Member(s): 2; 40 volunteer(s)
Membership: 40; *Member Profile:* Calgary & area aboriginals & non-aboriginals
Activities: Art exhibition; theatre productions; literary & media arts; *Awareness Events:* Aboriginal Awareness Week, 3rd week June; *Speaker Service:* Yes

Calgary Aboriginal Awareness Society *See* Calgary Aboriginal Arts Awareness Society

Calgary Alpha House Society
203 - 15 Ave. SE, Calgary AB T2G 1G4
Tel: 403-237-8341; *Fax:* 403-237-8361
alphahousecalgary.com
Also Known As: Alpha House
Overview: A small local organization founded in 1981
Mission: Provides drop-in/overnight shelter & short-term detoxification for males & females with alcohol &/or drug abuse issues
Chief Officer(s):
Kathy Christiansen, Executive Director
kathy@alphahousecalgary.com
Staff Member(s): 22

Calgary Association of Self Help
1019 - 7th Ave. SW, Calgary AB T2P 1A8
Tel: 403-266-8711; *Fax:* 403-266-2478
info@calgaryselfhelp.com
calgaryselfhelp.com
www.facebook.com/CalgaryAssociationofSelfHelp
twitter.com/yycselfhelp
Overview: A medium-sized local charitable organization founded in 1973
Mission: To provide client-centred, flexible services promoting the abilities of adults with mental illness through rehabilitation, counselling & social/leisure programs
Chief Officer(s):
Marion McGrath, Chief Executive Officer
Samuel Peter Mckenzie, Chair
Finances: *Funding Sources:* Provincial government; fundraising
Staff Member(s): 24

Calgary Association of the Deaf (CgyAD)
#512, 3545 - 32nd St. NE, Calgary AB T1Y 6M6
TTY: 403-236-1498
contact@cgyad.ca
www.cgyad.ca
www.facebook.com/groups/28180396051
Overview: A small local organization
Affliation(s): Alberta Association of the Deaf
Chief Officer(s):
Dean Stuber, President
deanstuber@shaw.ca

Calgary Birth Control Association *See* Calgary Sexual Health Centre

Calgary Boxing & Wrestling Commission *See* Calgary Combative Sports Commission

Calgary Caribbean Cultural Association *See* Caribbean Community Council of Calgary

Calgary Catholic Immigration Society (CCIS)
1111 - 11 Ave. SW, 5th Fl., Calgary AB T2R 0G5
Tel: 403-262-2006; *Fax:* 403-262-2033
contact@ccis-calgary.ab.ca
www.ccis-calgary.ab.ca
www.facebook.com/298577383506539
www.youtube.com/user/CCISTV
Overview: A small international organization
Mission: CCIS is a non-profit organization which provides settlement & integration services to immigrants & refugees in Southern Alberta.
Chief Officer(s):
Fariborz Birjandian, Executive Director
Staff Member(s): 110; 2000 volunteer(s)

Activities: Pre-employment training & counseling; community outreach for families & seniors; temporary accommodation facility; Integrated Resettlement Program;

Brooks & County Immigration Services
PO Box 844, 500 Cassils Rd., Bay 2, Brooks AB T1R 1B5
Tel: 403-362-0404; *Fax:* 403-362-0435
info@bcis-brooks.ca
Mission: Provides settlement and integration services to all immigrants, refugees and temporary foreign workers.

Foothills Community Immigrant Services
PO Box 45043, 609 Centre St., 2nd Fl., High River AB T1V 1R7
Tel: 403-652-5325; *Fax:* 403-652-5350
highriver@ccis-calgary.ab.ca
Mission: Provides comprehensive settlement and integration services throughout the Municipal District of Foothills and Southern Alberta.

Margaret Chisholm Resettlement Centre
23 McDougall Ct. NE, Calgary AB T2E 8R3
Tel: 403-262-8132
mcrc@ccis-calgary.ab.ca
Mission: Margaret Chisholm Resettlement Centre provides temporary accommodation to newcomers as they begin the resettlement process in Calgary.
Chief Officer(s):
Margaret Styczynska, Manager, 403-262-2006
mstyczynska@ccis-calgary.ab.ca.

Calgary Chamber of Commerce
#600, 237 - 8th Ave. SE, Calgary AB T2G 5C3
Tel: 403-750-0400
www.calgarychamber.com
www.linkedin.com/company/calgary-chamber-of-commerce
www.facebook.com/CalgaryChamber
twitter.com/calgarychamber
Overview: A medium-sized local organization founded in 1891
Mission: To lead & serve the Calgary business community valuing its diversity
Chief Officer(s):
David Sprague, Chair
Adam Legge, President & CEO
Ginny Hunter, Manager, Member Services, 403-750-0440
ghunter@calgarychamber.com
Finances: *Annual Operating Budget:* $1.5 Million-$3 Million
Staff Member(s): 23; 450 volunteer(s)
Membership: 1,000-4,999

Calgary Chamber of Voluntary Organizations (CCVO)
#1070, 105 - 12 Ave. SE, Calgary AB T2G 1A1
Tel: 403-261-6655; *Fax:* 403-261-6602
info@calgarycvo.org
www.calgarycvo.org
www.facebook.com/nonprofitvoice
twitter.com/nonprofitvoice
Overview: A small local organization
Mission: To strengthen Calgary's voluntary sector & provide leadership on policy matters impacting the sector as a whole
Chief Officer(s):
Katherine von Kooy, President & CEO, 403-261-6655 Ext. 224
kvk@calgarycvo.org
Membership: *Fees:* $50-$500 voting member; $100 associate
Meetings/Conferences: • 2015 Calgary Chamber of Voluntary Organizations Connections Conference, April, 2015, Mount Royal University, Ross Glen Hall, Calgary, AB
Scope: Local

Calgary Children's Foundation
#105, 630 - 3rd Ave. SW, Calgary AB T2P 4L4
Tel: 403-263-5437; *Fax:* 403-254-2684
Overview: A small local organization
Mission: To promote the mental & physical health & welfare of children & certain adults who are disadvantaged & reside within Alberta
Finances: *Annual Operating Budget:* $50,000-$100,000; *Funding Sources:* Donations
Staff Member(s): 1; 9 volunteer(s)
Membership: 10
Activities: Pledge day; luncheon; golf tournament; *Awareness Events:* Pledge Day

Calgary Chinese Cultural Society (CCCS)
#201, 116 - Ave. SW, Calgary AB T2P 0B9
Tel: 403-263-8830
Overview: A small provincial organization founded in 1975
Mission: To contribute to multiculturalism by promoting mutual understanding & cultural interaction between the Chinese community & fellow Canadians; to promote the construction of a multi-purpose cultural & educational centre in Chinatown; to contribute to charitable & community service; to promote cultural exchange & friendship between Canada & China
Member of: Alberta Chinese Community Congress; National Congress of Chinese Canadians
Activities: Operates Chinese language school

Calgary Civil Liberties Association ***See*** Alberta Civil Liberties Research Centre

Calgary Combative Sports Commission
c/o Development & Building Approvals, City of Calgary, PO Box 2100, Stn. M #8043, Calgary AB T2P 2M5
Tel: 403-268-5591; *Fax:* 403-268-2291
combativesportscommission@calgary.ca
www.calgary.ca
Previous Name: Calgary Boxing & Wrestling Commission
Overview: A small local licensing organization founded in 2007 overseen by Canadian Professional Boxing Federation
Mission: The commission acts as a regulation body for professional combative sports within the City of Calgary.
Member of: Canadian Professional Boxing Federation
Chief Officer(s):
Shirley Stunzi, Chair, 403-710-6148
Shirley.Stunzi@calgary.ca
Kent Pallister, Chief Licence Inspector, City of Calgary
Membership: 1-99

Calgary Community Living Society (CCLS)
#211, 4014 Macleod Trail South, Calgary AB T2G 2R7
Tel: 403-245-4665; *Fax:* 403-228-2132
ccls@telus.net
www.cclscalgary.com
Overview: A small local charitable organization founded in 1984
Mission: To empower families, through advocacy & education & support to create meaningful & inclusive community lives for their family members & friends with devleopmental disabiblities
Member of: Alberta Association for Community Living
Finances: *Annual Operating Budget:* $50,000-$100,000; *Funding Sources:* Grants; private donations; fundraising
Staff Member(s): 2; 60 volunteer(s)
Membership: 70; *Fees:* $20; *Member Profile:* Persons with development disabilities, their families & friends; *Committees:* Fundraising; Communications; Personnel
Activities: Calgary Family Network; Family Connection meetings; Coffee Talk meetings; referrals & resources; summer picnic; Christmas party; *Library:* CCLS Resource Library; Open to public

Calgary Construction Association (CCA)
2725 - 12 St. NE, Calgary AB T2E 7J2
Tel: 403-291-3350; *Fax:* 403-250-1607
www.cca.cc
Overview: A medium-sized local organization founded in 1944
Mission: To create opportunities; To deliver the best leading edge services; To be the effective voice for the local construction industry
Affliation(s): Alberta Construction Association; Canadian Construction Association
Chief Officer(s):
Jim Clement, President
jimcl@graham.ca
Staff Member(s): 5; 35 volunteer(s)
Membership: 500 companies; *Fees:* $1,350-$2,500

Calgary Co-operative Memorial Society (CCMS)
#204A, 223 - 12th Ave. SW, Calgary AB T2R 0G9
Tel: 403-248-2044
Toll-Free: 800-566-9959
admin@calgarymemorial.com
www.calgarymemorial.com
www.facebook.com/calgarycooperativememorialsociety
Also Known As: Calgary Memorial Society
Previous Name: Memorial Society of Calgary
Overview: A small local organization founded in 1966
Mission: To negotiate on behalf of members for funeral plans with contracted funeral providers to ensure dignified funerals as economically as possible.
Chief Officer(s):
Tony Kasper, Chair
tonykasper@shaw.ca
Membership: *Fees:* $22.15; *Committees:* Governance; Service Provider; Presentations; Advertising; Legislative Watch; Nominating & AGM; Giving
Activities: *Speaker Service:* Yes

Calgary Danish Businessmen's Association
c/o Danish Canadian Club, 727 - 11 Ave. SW, Calgary AB T2R 0E3
Tel: 403-261-9774; *Fax:* 403-261-6631
Overview: A small local organization founded in 1980
Mission: To encorage networking, friendship & the promotion of business knowledge in a social setting.
Member of: Federation of Danish Associations in Canada
Chief Officer(s):
Vaughn Schuler, Contact, 403-207-3126
vschuler@devry.edu
Activities: Meetings with guest speaker, discussions on current business issues, & dinners

Calgary Exhibition & Stampede
PO Box 1060, Stn. M, 1410 Olympic Way SE, Calgary AB T2P 2K8
Tel: 403-261-0101; *Fax:* 403-265-7197
Toll-Free: 800-661-1260
Other Communication: www.flickr.com/photos/calgarystampede
info@calgarystampede.com
www.calgarystampede.com
www.facebook.com/calgarystampede
twitter.com/calgarystampede
www.youtube.com/calgarystampede
Also Known As: Calgary Stampede
Overview: A large local organization founded in 1912
Mission: To preserve & promote Western heritage & values
Member of: Canadian Association of Exhibitions
Chief Officer(s):
Michael Casey, President & Chair
Vern Kimball, CEO
Finances: *Annual Operating Budget:* $3 Million-$5 Million
Staff Member(s): 1200; 1700 volunteer(s)
Activities: Presenting year-round events; *Internships:* Yes; *Speaker Service:* Yes

Calgary Faceter's Guild
c/o Dave Biro, PO Box 395, Blackfalds AB T0M 0J0
www.afrc.ca/calgaryfacetersguild.htm
Overview: A small local organization
Mission: To promote and support the development of faceting and related activities, and to aid in the education of its members.
Member of: Alberta Federation of Rock Clubs; Gem & Mineral Federation of Canada.
Chief Officer(s):
Dave Biro, Contact
dbiroret@telus.net
Finances: *Funding Sources:* Membership

Calgary Field Naturalists' Society (CFNS)
PO Box 981, Stn. M, Calgary AB T2P 2K4
Tel: 403-239-6444
naturecalgary@cfns.fanweb.ca
www.naturecalgary.com
www.facebook.com/naturecalgary
Also Known As: Nature Calgary
Overview: A small local charitable organization founded in 1955 overseen by Federation of Alberta Naturalists
Mission: To promote enjoyment of nature through environmental appreciation & conservation; To encourage wise use & conservation of natural resources & environmental protection
Member of: Calgary Area Outdoor Council; Alberta Environmental Network
Chief Officer(s):
Jamie Noakes, Contact, 403-243-7232
Hart Andrew, Contact, 403-279-5209
Finances: *Annual Operating Budget:* Less than $50,000; *Funding Sources:* Membership dues; donations; publications sale
185 volunteer(s)
Membership: 100-499; *Fees:* $20 regular; $25 family; *Committees:* Bird Study; Botany & Fungi Study; Nature Photography; Endangered Species; Natural Areas
Activities: 35 slide shows/presentations & over 100 field trips a year; *Speaker Service:* Yes; *Library* by appointment
Awards:
• President's Award, Honorary Life Memberships (Award)

Calgary Firefighters Burn Treatment Society (CFFBTS)
2234 - 30 Ave. NE, Calgary AB T2E 7K9
Tel: 403-701-2876; *Fax:* 403-271-0744
info@cfbts.org

cfbts.org
www.facebook.com/hotstuffcalgary
twitter.com/hotstuffcalgary
plus.google.com/118136276895313278395
Overview: A medium-sized local charitable organization founded in 1978
Mission: To raise funds for burn victims in burn units throughout Calgary & Southern Alberta
Chief Officer(s):
Ray Musukak, President
president@cfbts.org
Finances: *Funding Sources:* Calendar sales; fundraisers; public donations; special events
Membership: 1,000

Calgary Folk Club

#85, 305 - 4625 Varisty Dr. NW, Calgary AB T3A 0Z9
Tel: 403-286-5651; *Fax:* 403-286-6534
manager@calgaryfolkclub.com
www.calgaryfolkclub.com
www.facebook.com/CalgaryFolkClub
twitter.com/calgfolkclub
Overview: A small local organization founded in 1972
Mission: To present 13 concerts from September to April featuring internationally touring folk artists
Chief Officer(s):
Donna McTaggart, Manager
donnamc@kaos-consulting.com
Suze Casey, Artistic Director
suze@beliefrepatterning.com
Finances: *Funding Sources:* Provincial government; local Arts Council
30 volunteer(s)
Membership: 200 individual; 350 associate; *Fees:* $195 individual

The Calgary Foundation

#700, 999 - 8 St. SW, Calgary AB T2R 1J5
Tel: 403-802-7700; *Fax:* 403-802-7701
info@thecalgaryfoundation.org
thecalgaryfoundation.org
www.facebook.com/TheCalgaryFoundation
twitter.com/CalgFoundation
Overview: A small local charitable organization founded in 1955
Mission: To act as a catalyst & a convener; To provide a meeting place, fostering partnerships, engaging citizens, & addressing needs; To promotes & facilitate philanthropy for the long term benefit of Calgary & area; To operate as a community builder, applying its resources, expertise, & leadership, in partnership with others, to identify needs, address community issues, & build a stronger community for the benefit of Calgary & area citizens; To strengthen the charitable sector to be better able to serve the existing & emerging needs of the Calgary & area community
Member of: Community Foundations of Canada; Council on Foundations
Chief Officer(s):
Eva Friesen, President & CEO
efriesen@thecalgaryfoundation.org
Gerald M. Deyell, Chair
Finances: *Annual Operating Budget:* $3 Million-$5 Million; *Funding Sources:* Private donations
Staff Member(s): 18; 110 volunteer(s)
Activities: Friends of the Foundation Annual Celeration

Calgary Horticultural Society (CHS)

208 - 50 Ave. SW, Calgary AB T2S 2S1
Tel: 403-287-3469; *Fax:* 403-287-6986
office@calhort.org
www.calhort.org
www.facebook.com/calhort
twitter.com/yycgardening
Overview: A medium-sized provincial organization founded in 1907
Mission: To educate, promote & encourage gardening in the Calgary area
Affiliation(s): Royal Horticultural Society
Chief Officer(s):
Kenna Burima, President
Elizabeth Jolicoeur, Executive Director
Finances: *Funding Sources:* Membership fees; committee activities
Staff Member(s): 6
Membership: 5,000+; *Fees:* $25 students/seniors; $35 senior family; $45 individual/affiliate; $55 family; $245 corporate
Activities: Gardeners Fair; garden competition; plant exchanges; *Speaker Service:* Yes

Calgary Humane Society

4455 - 110 Ave. SE, Calgary AB T2C 2T7
Tel: 403-205-4455; *Fax:* 403-723-6050
general.inquiries@calgaryhumane.ca
www.calgaryhumane.ca
www.facebook.com/CalgaryHumaneSociety
twitter.com/CalgaryHumane
www.youtube.com/user/CalgaryHumaneSociety
Overview: A medium-sized provincial charitable organization founded in 1922 overseen by Canadian Federation of Humane Societies
Mission: To foster humane treatment of animals & to promote values which demonstrate respect for animals.
Member of: Alberta SPCA; Canadian Federation of Humane Societies
Chief Officer(s):
Carrie Fritz, Executive Director
Finances: *Funding Sources:* Donations; memberships; bequests; services; planned giving.
Staff Member(s): 19
Membership: *Fees:* $10 senior; $15 youth; $40 individual; $250 lifetime
Activities: *Library:* Resource Centre; by appointment

Calgary Immigrant Aid Society ***See*** Immigrant Services Calgary

Calgary Immigrant Women's Association (CIWA)

#200, 138 - 4th Ave. SE, Calgary AB T2G 4Z6
Tel: 403-263-4414; *Fax:* 403-264-3914
reception@ciwa-online.com
www.ciwa-online.com
Overview: A medium-sized local charitable organization founded in 1982
Mission: To promote & support the integration of immigrant women into the community & the larger Canadian society
Affiliation(s): Alberta/NWT Network of Immigrant Women; Alberta Association of Immigrant Serving Agencies
Chief Officer(s):
Beba Svigir, Executive Director, 403-444-1755
bebas@ciwa-online.com
Finances: *Annual Operating Budget:* $1.5 Million-$3 Million; *Funding Sources:* All levels of government; corporate; individuals
Staff Member(s): 137; 696 volunteer(s)
Membership: 175; *Fees:* $10 individual; $25 associate; *Committees:* Fund Development; Public Relations; Finance; Personnel
Activities: CIWA Conference; youth program; new friends & neighbourhood groups; cross-cultural parenting program; family conflict program; skills training & employment program; volunteer program (off-site at Connaught School); language instruction for newcomers to Canada; Pebbles in the Sand; intake, settlement & referral services; integration project; women & youth safety program; childcare; baby club; accent reduction; Lifting the Bar; *Library:* Toy & Interactive Book Bag Library; Open to public

Calgary Insurance Women ***See*** Insurance Professionals of Calgary

Calgary Interfaith Food Bank

5000 - 11 St. SE, Calgary AB T2H 2Y5
Tel: 403-253-2059; *Fax:* 403-259-4240
info@calgaryfoodbank.com
www.calgaryfoodbank.com
www.linkedin.com/company/calgary-food-bank
www.facebook.com/calgaryfoodbank
twitter.com/CalgaryFoodBank
www.youtube.com/yycfoodbank
Also Known As: Calgary Food Bank
Overview: A small local charitable organization overseen by Alberta Food Bank Network Association
Mission: To gather & distribute quality emergency food to those in need

Calgary Japanese Community Association (CJCA)

2236 - 29th St. SW, Calgary AB T3E 2K2
Tel: 403-242-4143
cjcamain@shaw.ca
www.calgaryjca.com
Overview: A small local organization
Member of: National Association of Japanese Canadians
Chief Officer(s):
Joanne Planidin, President
Membership: *Committees:* Advertising; Communications; Community & Seniors Foundation; Cultural; Fundraising; Membership; Social Events; Special Projects
Publications:
• CJCA [Calgary Japanese Community Association] Q-Newsletter
Type: Newsletter; *Frequency:* Quarterly

Calgary Jewish Community Council ***See*** The Centre for Israel & Jewish Affairs

Calgary Law Library Group (CLLG)

c/o Law Society Library, Calgary Courts Centre, #501N, 601 - 5th St. SW, Calgary AB T2P 5P7
www.cllg.ca
Overview: A small local organization
Mission: To promote the services of law librarians & legal information professionals; To represent the interests of law librarians & legal information professionals in Calgary & the surrounding area; To offer continuing education to members
Chief Officer(s):
Nadine Hoffman, Chair
nadine.hoffman@ucalgary.ca
Kim Clarke, Secretary
kim.clarke@ucalgary.ca
Bonnie Heumann, Treasurer
bheumann@telus.net
Membership: 60; *Fees:* Free, students; $40 individuals; *Member Profile:* Persons in Alberta who provide services to libraries disseminating legal information; Individuals interested in legal information libraries; MLIS & Library Technician students; *Committees:* Program; Student; Travel Grant
Activities: Facilitating networking opportunities with other professionals in many areas of librarianship; Providing professional development activities; Cooperating with other organizations
Meetings/Conferences: • Calgary Law Library Group 2015 Annual General Meeting, 2015, Calgary, AB
Scope: Local
Description: An annual meeting of legal information professionals & law librarians from Calgary & the surrounding area
Publications:
• Calgary Law Library Group Directory of Members
Type: Directory; *Editor:* Tracey Cote & Susan Spady

Calgary Marching Showband Association

Calgary Stampede, PO Box 1060, Stn. M, Calgary AB T2P 2K8
Tel: 403-261-9318; *Fax:* 403-233-7245
info@stampedeshowband.com
www.stampedeshowband.com
www.facebook.com/calgarystampede
twitter.com/calgarystampede
Also Known As: Calgary Stampede Showband
Overview: A small local organization
Chief Officer(s):
Michelle Fior, Chair
mfior@calgarystampede.com
Mike Jewitt, Director, Bands
mjewitt@calgarystampede.com
Scott A. Grant, General Contact
sgrant@calgarystampede.com

Calgary Meals on Wheels

3610 Macleod Trail SE, Calgary AB T2G 2P9
Tel: 403-243-2834; *Fax:* 403-243-8438
info@mealsonwheels.com
www.mealsonwheels.com
www.facebook.com/calgarymealsonwheels
twitter.com/MealsOnWheelsca
Overview: A small local charitable organization founded in 1965
Mission: To provide nutritious meals as a preventative health measure to individuals in the city of Calgary, to the elderly, to the disabled & to short term convalescents without regard to race, creed or financial status
Chief Officer(s):
Janice Curtis, Executive Director
jcurtis@mealsonwheels.com
Finances: *Funding Sources:* Provincial government 20%; United Way 10%; clients 55%; donations 15%
Staff Member(s): 7; 750 volunteer(s)
Membership: 195; *Fees:* $10 institutional; $5 individual; *Member Profile:* Anyone who supports our mission; *Committees:* Capital Project; Operations; Finance & Audit; Governance; Marketing; Capital Campaign
Activities: *Awareness Events:* Meals on Wheels Awareness Week; *Internships:* Yes; *Speaker Service:* Yes

Awards:
• Pat Bourne Award (Award)

Calgary Mennonite Centre for Newcomers Society

#1010, 999 - 36 St. NE, Calgary AB T2A 7X6
Tel: 403-569-3325; *Fax:* 403-248-5041
newcomer@centrefornewcomers.ca
www.centrefornewcomers.ca
Overview: A small local organization founded in 1988
Mission: The Society is a not-for-profit, registered charity that operates the Centre for Newcomers, assisting refugees & immigrants arriving in Calgary to meet their settlement needs.
Affliation(s): Canadian Red Cross
Chief Officer(s):
Dale Taylor, Executive Director, Centre for Newcomers, 403-537-8800
Membership: *Member Profile:* Members beyond the Mennonite constituency is enoucraged.
Activities: Calgary Career Show for immigrant youth; preschool activities for immigrant children; employment preparation courses; anti-bullying workshop; EthniCity Catering Program; ESL classes

Calgary Minor Soccer Association (CSMA)

#7, 6991 - 48 St. SE, Calgary AB T2C 5A4
Tel: 403-279-8686; *Fax:* 403-236-3669
info@calgaryminorsoccer.com
calgaryminorsoccer.com
Overview: A small local organization overseen by Alberta Soccer Association
Member of: Alberta Soccer Association
Chief Officer(s):
Daryl Leinweber, Executive Director
execdirector@calgaryminorsoccer.com
Staff Member(s): 12

Calgary Motor Dealers Association (CMDA)

#101, 7309 Flint Rd. SE, Calgary AB T2H 1G3
Tel: 403-974-0707; *Fax:* 403-974-0711
Toll-Free: 866-318-2632
www.calgarymotordealers.com
Overview: A small local organization founded in 1951
Affliation(s): Motor Dealers Association of Alberta
Chief Officer(s):
Jack Thompson, Executive Director
Staff Member(s): 2; 25 volunteer(s)
Membership: 70; *Member Profile:* Franchised new vehicle dealers in Calgary

Calgary Musicians Association

#5, 606 Meredith Rd. NE, Calgary AB T2E 5A8
Tel: 403-264-6610; *Fax:* 403-264-6610
Toll-Free: 888-796-8742
info@calgarymusicians.org
calgarymusicians.org
www.facebook.com/CalgaryMusiciansAssociation
twitter.com/YYCmusicians
Overview: A medium-sized local organization founded in 1938
Mission: To establish & maintain working standards in the music industry, as well as to provide support to & to promote their members
Member of: American Federation of Musicians of the United States & Canada
Chief Officer(s):
Allistair Elliott, President
Finances: *Annual Operating Budget:* $100,000-$250,000; *Funding Sources:* Membership dues
Staff Member(s): 1
Membership: 700; *Fees:* $185; $115 initiation fee
Activities: Improving wages & working conditions of musicians; collective bargaining; promotion of musicians; referral service; *Speaker Service:* Yes

Calgary Native Women's Shelter Society *See* Awo Taan Healing Lodge Society

Calgary Numismatic Society (CNS)

PO Box 633, Calgary AB T2P 2J3
Tel: 403-461-2663
info@calgarynumismaticsociety.org
www.calgarynumismaticsociety.org
Overview: A small local organization founded in 1950
Member of: Canadian Numismatic Association
Chief Officer(s):
Robert Albrecht, President
wargamer@shaw.ca
Finances: *Annual Operating Budget:* Less than $50,000; *Funding Sources:* Membership dues; special events
Membership: 75; *Fees:* $10 senior; $14 family; $2 junior
Activities: *Awareness Events:* Annual Spring Coin Show; Canada's Money Collector Show, July
Publications:
• CNS [Calgary Numismatic Society] Bulletin
Type: Newsletter; *Editor:* Neil Probert

Calgary Olympic Development Association *See* WinSport Canada

Calgary Opera Association

Arrata Opera Centre, 1315 - 7 St. SW, Calgary AB T2R 1A5
Tel: 403-262-7286; *Fax:* 403-263-5428
info@calgaryopera.com
www.calgaryopera.com
www.facebook.com/pages/Calgary-Opera/18782898651
twitter.com/CalgaryOpera
Overview: A small local organization founded in 1972
Mission: To enrich the cultural life of the community by celebrating musical art through the performance of professional opera
Member of: Opera America
Affliation(s): Actors Equity Association
Chief Officer(s):
W.R. (Bob) McPhee, General Director & CEO
Finances: *Funding Sources:* Government; corporate; individual
Staff Member(s): 21

Calgary Parents of Multiple Births Association *See* Twins, Triplets & More Association of Calgary

Calgary Philatelic Society (CPS)

PO Box 1478, Calgary AB T2P 2L6
e-mail: calphilso@calgaryphilatelicsociety.com
www.calgaryphilatelicsociety.com
Overview: A small local organization founded in 1922
Mission: To provide a meeting place for local stamp collectors to get together and share their interest in stamps and postal history.
Member of: Royal Philatelic Society of Canada; American Philatelic Society; American Topical Association
Affliation(s): British North America Philatelic Society
Chief Officer(s):
Peter Fleck, President
president@calgaryphilatelicsociety.com
Finances: *Funding Sources:* Membership fees
Membership: *Member Profile:* Stamp collectors; exhibitors; accumulators; *Committees:* Archives; Caltapex Show; Circuit Books; Dealer Bourse; Exhibits; Library; Life Members; Membership; Private Treaty Books; Programmes; Regular Auction; Sergeant-at-Arms; Silent Auction; Spring Show
Activities: Stamp collecting, auctions, shows & presentations; *Library*
Awards:
• Founder's Award (Award)
• Life Membership Award (Award)
• Bob Monilaws Award (Award)
Publications:
• The Calgary Philatelist
Price: Free for members

Calgary Philharmonic Society (CPO)

#205, 8 Ave. SE, Calgary AB T2G 0K9
Tel: 403-571-0270; *Fax:* 403-294-7424
info@cpo-live.com
www.cpo-live.com
www.facebook.com/group.php?gid=39456269313
twitter.com/calgaryphil
www.youtube.com/CalgaryPhilharmonic
Also Known As: Calgary Philharmonic Orchestra
Overview: A large local charitable organization founded in 1955 overseen by Orchestras Canada
Mission: To provide our audience with a rich, diverse & unequalled symphonic musical experience which earns broad community support
Member of: Calgary Chamber of Commerce
Affliation(s): American Symphony Orchestra League
Chief Officer(s):
Ann Lewis-Luppino, President & CEO
alewis@cpo-live.com
Finances: *Annual Operating Budget:* Greater than $5 Million; *Funding Sources:* Federal, provincial & city grants; corporate & individual donations; sponsorships
Staff Member(s): 90; 80 volunteer(s)
Membership: 1-99; *Member Profile:* Must be over 18; current subscriber or Amadeus patron; *Committees:* Governance; Finance; Audit
Activities: *Awareness Events:* Mozart on the Mountain; Beethoven in the Badlands; *Internships:* Yes; *Library:* Music Library

Calgary Police Association (CPA)

Calgary AB
www.backtheblue.ca
Overview: A small local organization
Mission: To lobby government to influence the criminal justice systen & promote the interests of the citizens of Calgary & the members; to bargain for improved wages, working conditions & benefits; to help members being investigated or charged with offences
Chief Officer(s):
Howard Burns, President
Mike Baker, Vice-President, Finance
Staff Member(s): 2
Membership: 1,800+; *Member Profile:* Members of Calgary police

Calgary Power Employees Association; TransAlta Employees' Association *See* United Utility Workers' Association

Calgary Real Estate Board Cooperative Limited (CREB)

300 Manning Rd. NE, Calgary AB T2E 8K4
Tel: 403-263-0530; *Fax:* 403-218-3688
info@creb.com
www.creb.com
Overview: A medium-sized local organization overseen by Alberta Real Estate Association
Member of: Alberta Real Estate Association; The Canadian Real Estate Association
Chief Officer(s):
Alan Tennant, CEO, 403-781-1359
alan.tennant@creb.ca
Staff Member(s): 70
Membership: 1,000-4,999;

Calgary Residential Rental Association (CRRA)

4653 Macleod Trail SW, Calgary AB T2G 0A6
Tel: 403-265-6055; *Fax:* 403-265-9696
info@crra.ca
www.crra.ca
www.facebook.com/www.crra.ca
twitter.com/crra_ca
Overview: A small local organization founded in 1959
Mission: To provide representation & networking for the residential rental industry.
Chief Officer(s):
Gerry Baxter, Executive Director
gerry@crra.ca
Finances: *Funding Sources:* Membership dues
Staff Member(s): 4
Membership: 1,000+; *Fees:* Schedule available dependant on number of units owned; *Member Profile:* Owners, managers and companies that service residential rental units in Calgary
Activities: Courses & seminars on educating landlords; annual trade show

Calgary Rock & Lapidary Club

110 Lissington Dr. SW, Calgary AB T3E 5E3
Tel: 403-287-1570
martintm@shaw.ca
www.crlc.ca
www.facebook.com/CalgaryRockandLapidaryClub
twitter.com/CRLCrockhounds
Overview: A small local organization founded in 1959
Mission: The club encourages interest in the study of rocks, minerals, gems, fossils & artifacts in Alberta & elsewhere. The hobby is promoted to all ages groups. Appreciation & conservation of natural resources are encouraged.
Member of: Alberta Federation of Rock Clubs
Affliation(s): Gem & Mineral Federation of Canada
Chief Officer(s):
Kelly Jackson, President Ext. \
kellyjackson236@msn.com
Membership: 250; *Fees:* $20 adult; $18 senior; $2 under age 17 & full-time students; *Member Profile:* Persons with a common interest in the lapidary arts & earth sciences
Activities: Collecting, working & exhibiting finished gemstones & geological specimens public display; Organizing field trips for collecting lapidary materials; Offering study groups with

hands-on sessions for children;; *Library:* Calgary Rock and Lapidary Club Library
Publications:
• The Calgary Lapidary Journal
Type: Newsletter; *Frequency:* 8 pa; *Editor:* Shelley Gibbins

Calgary Round-Up Band Association (CRUB)
PO Box 787, Stn. T, Calgary AB T2H 2H3
Tel: 403-259-3120
info@roundupband.org
www.roundupband.org
www.facebook.com/pages/Calgary-Round-Up-Band/107043849317344
Overview: A small international charitable organization founded in 1956
Mission: To provide instruction, discipline & social activities for junior high school-aged musicians
Affliation(s): Calgary Stampede Show Band; Calgary Stetson Show Band
Chief Officer(s):
Manuel Macias, President
msmacias@gmail.com
Amy Hensch, Vice-President
amy.hensch@gmail.com
Staff Member(s): 4; 290 volunteer(s)
Membership: 300 associates; 100 students; *Fees:* $750; *Member Profile:* Enrolled in music program; *Committees:* Recruiting; Publicity; Uniforming
Activities: Marching & Show Band Performances

Calgary Seniors' Resource Society
#3639, 26 St. NE, Calgary AB T1Y 5E1
Tel: 403-266-6200; *Fax:* 403-269-5183
info@calgaryseniors.org
www.calgaryseniors.org
www.facebook.com/CalgarySeniors
twitter.com/Calgary_Seniors
Previous Name: Senior Citizens' Central Council of Calgary
Overview: A medium-sized local charitable organization founded in 1995
Mission: To enhance the quality of life & human dignity of seniors by supporting their independence through home services & community based programs
Member of: Alberta Council on Aging; Alberta Association on Gerontology
Affliation(s): Calgary Homeless Foundation
Chief Officer(s):
Lori Paine, Executive Director
lpaine@calgaryseniors.org
Priscilla Feng, Administrative Assistant
pfeng@calgaryseniors.org
Annastasia Sommer, Volunteer Team Leader
asommer@calgaryseniors.org
Finances: *Annual Operating Budget:* Less than $50,000; *Funding Sources:* Family & Community Support Services; donations
Staff Member(s): 16; 155 volunteer(s)
Membership: 1-99; *Member Profile:* Individuals 55 years of age or over
Activities: Information, referral & advice; outreach services; escorted transportation; friendly visiting; ABCs' Fraud Awareness program; SeniorConnect program

Calgary Sexual Health Centre
#304, 301 - 14 St. NW, Calgary AB T2N 2A1
Tel: 403-283-5580; *Fax:* 403-270-3209
generalmail@calgarysexualhealth.ca
www.calgarysexualhealth.ca
www.facebook.com/182324198460359
twitter.com/yycsexualhealth
Previous Name: Calgary Birth Control Association
Overview: A small local organization founded in 1972
Mission: To offer counselling & education services to help people consider their sexual & reproductive choices in informed & responsible ways.
Member of: Planned Parenthood Alberta; Planned Parenthood Federation of Canada
Chief Officer(s):
Pam Krause, Executive Director
pkrause@calgarysexualhealth.ca
Activities: Pregnancy options; birth control; referrals; support groups; pregnancy tests; wontgetweird.com program; Resource Centre with books, pamphlets, tools, kits, & DVDs for sale; Training Centre with professional development programs; *Speaker Service:* Yes; *Library* Open to public

Awards:
• Dr. Maria Eriksen Scholarship (Scholarship)
Eligibility: Applicant must be enrolled in post-secondary institution full-time; be a Canadian citizen or landed immigrant; submit essay on how to forward feminism; support the values of the Centre *Amount:* $2,500

Calgary Sledge Hockey Association
Calgary AB
e-mail: info@calgarysledgehockey.ca
calgarysledgehockey.ca
www.facebook.com/CalgarySledgeHockey
Overview: A small local charitable organization
Affliation(s): Hockey Alberta; Hockey Canada
Chief Officer(s):
Dave TAylor, Director of Marketing, 403-891-9295
Membership: 3 teams

Calgary Soccer Federation
Subway Soccer Centre, 7000 - 48 St. SE, Calgary AB T2C 4E1
Tel: 403-279-8453; *Fax:* 403-279-8796
www.calgarysoccerfederation.com
www.facebook.com/calgarysoccerfederation
Overview: A small local organization overseen by Alberta Soccer Association
Member of: Alberta Soccer Association

Calgary Society for the Investigation of Child Sexual Abuse *See* Canadian Society for the Investigation of Child Abuse

Calgary Society of Independent Filmmakers (CSIF)
CommunityWise Resource Centre, #103, 223 - 12 Ave. SW, Calgary AB T2R 0G9
Tel: 403-205-4747
communications@csif.org
www.csif.org
twitter.com/CSIF
Overview: A small local organization founded in 1975
Mission: To promote film making as art, reflecting & challenging the changing cultural landscape through production & exhibition of films.
Chief Officer(s):
Leah Nicholson, President
Bobbie Todd, Operations Coordinator
Finances: *Funding Sources:* Canada Council; Alberta Foundation for the Arts; Calgary Arts Development; Nat'l Film Board; AMAA; IMAA
Staff Member(s): 5
Membership: *Fees:* $40 associate; $60 production B; $15 library; *Committees:* Membership; Finance; Production; HR; Facilities; Programming; Communications; Strategic Planning; Policy
Activities: *Speaker Service:* Yes

Calgary Society of Organists
6311 Crowchild Trail SW, Calgary AB T3E 5R6
Tel: 403-249-0764
cso@shaw.ca
members.shaw.ca/cso
Overview: A small local charitable organization
Mission: To promote and appreciate organ music in and around the Calgary area.
Chief Officer(s):
Howard Janzen, Treasurer
janzenh@shaw.ca
Membership: 150; *Fees:* $15

Calgary Stampede Foundation (CSF)
Calgary Stampede Headquarters, PO Box 1060, Stn. M, 1410 Olympic Way SE, Calgary AB T2P 2K8
Tel: 403-261-9155; *Fax:* 403-261-9390
CSF_Administration@calgarystampede.com
www.stampedefoundation.com
Overview: A medium-sized local charitable organization founded in 1994
Mission: To generate income to support the development of youth in Southern Alberta
Chief Officer(s):
Ann McCaig, Chair
Sarah Hayes, Executive Director, 403-261-0349
shayes@calgarystampede.com
Bianca von Nagy, Foundation Manager, 403-261-9176
bvonnagy@calgarystampede.com
Activities: *Awareness Events:* Stampede Volunteer & Friends Divot Classic Golf Tournament, Aug.

Calgary Stetson Show Band (CSSB)
PO Box 30031, RPO Chinook, Calgary AB T2H 2V8
Tel: 403-258-0889
office@stetsonband.org
www.stetsonband.org
Overview: A small local organization
Mission: A marching show band for Calgary and area Senior High School students offering opportunities for personal development, advanced musicianship, performance, and travel.
Chief Officer(s):
Earl Paddock, Executive Director
epaddock@stetsonband.org
Membership: *Fees:* $750

Calgary Tourist & Convention Bureau *See* Tourism Calgary

Calgary United Soccer Association
#183, 2880 Glenmore Trail SE, Calgary AB T2C 2E7
Tel: 403-270-0363; *Fax:* 403-270-0573
info@cusa.ab.ca
www.cusa.ab.ca
www.facebook.com/CalgaryUnitedSoccerAssociation
Overview: A small local organization overseen by Alberta Soccer Association
Member of: Alberta Soccer Association
Chief Officer(s):
Pearl Doupe, Executive Director, 403-648-0861
pearl@cusa.ab.ca
Staff Member(s): 5

Calgary Urban Project Society (CUPS)
1001 - 10 Ave. SW, Calgary AB T2R 0B7
Tel: 403-221-8780; *Fax:* 403-221-8791
info@cupscalgary.com
cupscalgary.com
www.facebook.com/CUPSCalgary
twitter.com/CUPSCalgaryAB
www.youtube.com/user/CUPSCalgary1989
Also Known As: CUPS Community Health Centre
Overview: A small local charitable organization founded in 1988
Mission: To advance the quality of life & affirm the worth of all persons through a compassionate, Christ-centred, & holistic healing ministry directed especially to persons who have rejected or who have been rejected or neglected by society
Chief Officer(s):
Carlene Donnelly, Executive Director
carlened@cupscalgary.com
Finances: *Annual Operating Budget:* Greater than $5 Million; *Funding Sources:* Corporations; individual donors; foundations; government
Staff Member(s): 180; 564 volunteer(s)
Activities: *Awareness Events:* Christmas Wreath Campaign, Dec.

Calgary Vietnamese Canadian Association
#317, 4909 - 17 Ave. SE, Calgary AB T2A 0V5
Tel: 403-272-4668; *Fax:* 403-207-4633
Overview: A small local organization

Calgary Wildlife Rehabilitation Society (CWRS)
11555 - 85th St. NW, Calgary AB T3R 1J3
Tel: 403-266-2282; *Fax:* 403-266-2449
Other Communication: Wildlife Rescue e-mail: wildlife@calgarywildlife.org
admin@calgarywildlife.org
calgarywildlife.org
www.facebook.com/calgarywildlife
twitter.com/calgarywildlife
Overview: A small local organization founded in 1993
Mission: To rescue, rehabilitate & release injured wild animals
Chief Officer(s):
Garry Nielsen, President
Nicola Murphy, Manager
Site & Wildlife

Calgary Women's Emergency Shelter Association (CWES)
#201, 2616 - 18 St. NE, Calgary AB T2E 7R1
Tel: 403-213-5166; *Crisis Hot-Line:* 403-234-7233
info@cwes.ca
www.calgarywomensshelter.com
www.facebook.com/calgarywomenemergencyshelter
twitter.com/end_abuse
www.youtube.com/user/CalgaryWomensShelter
Overview: A small local charitable organization founded in 1974
Mission: To end abuse & violence in the lives of women & their families through empowerment, advocacy, education & the mobilization of community action
Member of: Alberta Association of Services for Children &

Families; Calgary Coalition Against Family Violence
Affiliation(s): Alberta Council of Womens Shelters
Chief Officer(s):
Rob Carpenter, President
Finances: *Funding Sources:* Regional government; United Way; Alberta Mental Health Board; City of Calgary; charitable donations
Activities: Turning Points Dinner; *Speaker Service:* Yes

Calgary Women's Soccer Association (CWSA)
#206, 4441 - 76 Ave. SE, Calgary AB T2C 2G8
Tel: 403-720-6692; *Fax:* 403-720-6693
office@mycwsa.ca
www.womensoccer.ab.ca
www.facebook.com/124525960988252
Overview: A small local organization overseen by Alberta Soccer Association
Member of: Alberta Soccer Association
Chief Officer(s):
Madeleine Loughery, Manager
madeleine@mycwsa.ca
Staff Member(s): 5

Calgary Youth Orchestra
c/o Mount Royal College Conservatory, 4825 Mount Royal Gate SW, Calgary AB T3E 6K6
Tel: 403-440-5978; *Fax:* 403-440-6594
cyo@mtroyal.ca
www.cyo.ab.ca
Overview: A small local organization overseen by Orchestras Canada
Mission: To provide the best possible musical experience for the talented young musicians of the Calgary region, in an art form that is considered one of the highest forms of expression
Chief Officer(s):
George Fenwick, Orchestra Manager
Activities: Rehearsals; workshops; concerts; tours

Calgary Zoological Society
1300 Zoo Rd. NE, Calgary AB T2E 7V6
Tel: 403-232-9300; *Fax:* 403-237-7582
Toll-Free: 800-588-9993
comments@calgaryzoo.ab.ca
www.calgaryzoo.org
www.facebook.com/thecalgaryzoo
www.youtube.com/calgaryzoo1
Overview: A large provincial charitable organization founded in 1929
Mission: To operate the Calgary Zoo, Botanical Garden & Prehistoric Park; to advocate on behalf of animals
Member of: Canadian Association of Zoos & Aquariums (CAZA); Association of Zoos & Aquariums (AZA)
Affiliation(s): Amphibian Ark; Tourism Calgary
Chief Officer(s):
Greg Turnbull, Chair
Clément Lanthier, President & CEO
Finances: *Annual Operating Budget:* $100,000-$250,000; *Funding Sources:* Donations; Sponsorships; Admission
Activities: Offering educational programs; Providing the Calgary Zoo's Endangered Species Reintroduction Research program;

Meetings/Conferences: • Calgary Zoological Society 2015 Annual General Meeting, 2015, AB
Scope: Provincial
Description: Members of the society receive voting rights at the annual meeting
Contact Information: Manager, Communications: Laurie Skene, E-mail: lauries@calgaryzoo.com
Publications:
• Calgary Zoological Society eMagazine
Frequency: Quarterly

Call2Recycle Canada, Inc.
#606, 4576 Yonge St., Toronto ON M2N 6N4
Toll-Free: 888-224-9746
www.call2recycle.ca
www.linkedin.com/company/call2recycle
www.facebook.com/Call2Recycle
twitter.com/Call2Recycle
plus.google.com/109631060180236144576
Previous Name: Canadian Household Battery Association; Rechargeable Battery Recycling Corporation Canada
Overview: A small international organization
Mission: To recycle rechargeable battery & cell phones; to conduct public education campaigns & recycling programs
Finances: *Funding Sources:* Manufacturers & marketers of portable rechargeable batteries & products
Activities: *Awareness Events:* Waste Reduction Week, Oct.

Calypso Association of Manitoba
474 Gilmore Ave., Winnipeg MB R2G 2G6
Tel: 204-669-3439
Overview: A small provincial organization founded in 1982
Mission: To demonstrate the versatility & adaptability of Calypso

Cambrian Youth Orchestra *See* Sudbury Youth Orchestra Inc.

Cambridge Association for the Mentally Handicapped *See* Community Living Cambridge

Cambridge Association of Realtors
2040 Eagle St. North, Cambridge ON N3H 0A1
Tel: 519-623-3660; *Fax:* 519-623-8253
cambridge-admin@rogers.com
cambridgeassociationofrealtors.com
www.facebook.com/CambridgeAssociationOfRealtors
twitter.com/CamRealtors
Previous Name: Galt and District Real Estate Board; Real Estate Board of Cambridge
Overview: A small local organization founded in 1953 overseen by Ontario Real Estate Association
Member of: The Canadian Real Estate Association
Membership: 382

Cambridge Chamber of Commerce
750 Hespler Rd., Cambridge ON N3H 5L8
Tel: 519-622-2221; *Fax:* 519-622-0177
cchamber@cambridgechamber.com
www.cambridgechamber.com
ca.linkedin.com/in/cambridgechamber
twitter.com/My_Chamber
Overview: A medium-sized local organization founded in 1973
Member of: Canadian Chamber of Commerce; Ontario Chamber of Commerce
Chief Officer(s):
Greg Durocher, General Manager, 519-622-2221 Ext. 2223
greg@cambridgechamber.com
Finances: *Annual Operating Budget:* $250,000-$500,000; *Funding Sources:* Membership fees
Staff Member(s): 6; 150 volunteer(s)
Membership: 850; *Fees:* Starts at $170; based on number of employees
Activities: Operates Cambridge Visitor & Convention Bureau; Business Outlook dinner; Business After Hours; *Speaker Service:* Yes; *Rents Mailing List:* Yes

Cambridge Literacy Council; Literacy Council of Kitchener-Waterloo *See* The Literacy Group of Waterloo Region

Cambridge Multicultural Centre *See* YMCA Immigrant & Community Services

Cambridge Self-Help Food Bank
54 Ainslie St. South, Cambridge ON N1R 3K3
Tel: 519-622-6550; *Fax:* 519-622-9076
www.cambridgefoodbank.on.ca
www.facebook.com/CambridgeFoodBank
twitter.com/CambFoodBank
Overview: A small local charitable organization
Mission: To distribute food to underpriviledged people; to provide programs that help people in need become self-sufficient
Chief Officer(s):
Pat Singleton, Executive Director
Staff Member(s): 20

Cambridge Tourism
750 Hespeler Rd., Cambridge ON N3H 5L8
Tel: 519-622-2336; *Fax:* 519-622-0177
Toll-Free: 800-749-7560
visit@cambridgechamber.com
www.cambridgetourism.com
www.facebook.com/pages/Visit-Cambridge-Ontario/249977815059176
www.pinterest.com/cambridgeon
Also Known As: Cambridge Visitor & Convention Bureau
Overview: A small local charitable organization founded in 1981
Mission: To develop tourism initiatives & build partnerships that pool ideas & resources to promote Cambridge as a viable travel destination, generating greater economic impact for the city & other tourism stakeholders.
Member of: Cambridge Chamber of Commerce; City of Cambridge
Affliation(s): Ontario Motor Coach Association; Grand River County; Tourism Toronto; Southern Ontario Travel Organization; Canadian Society of Associations Executives
Finances: *Funding Sources:* 50% municipal government + 50% private sector
Membership: *Member Profile:* Private sector tourism organizations
Activities: Marketing; visitor services; tourism awareness; Annual Tourism Awards; *Library:* Tourist Information Resource Centre; Open to public

Cameco Capitol Arts Centre
20 Queen St., Port Hope ON L1A 3Z4
Tel: 905-885-1071; *Fax:* 905-885-9714
Toll-Free: 800-434-5092
boxoffice@capitoltheatre.com
www.capitoltheatre.com
www.facebook.com/CapitolTheatrePortHope
Overview: A medium-sized local organization founded in 1993
Mission: To provide the Northumberland County Area with the best in professional & community theatre music & dance & provide educational community & theatre arts program
Chief Officer(s):
Uwe Meyer, Managing & Artistic Director
capitol@eagle.ca
Jacob Hamayda, Technical Director
jhamayda@capitoltheatre.com
Cindy Fortner, Manager, Office
cfortner@capitoltheatre.com
180 volunteer(s)
Membership: 500; *Fees:* $25

CAMH Foundation
Bell Gateway Building, 100 Stokes St., 5th Fl., Toronto ON M6J 1H4
Tel: 416-979-6909; *Fax:* 416-979-6910
Toll-Free: 800-414-0471
foundation@camh.ca
www.supportcamh.ca
www.facebook.com/end.stigma
twitter.com/endstigma
www.youtube.com/user/CAMHFoundation
Also Known As: Centre for Addiction & Mental Health Foundation
Overview: A small local charitable organization
Mission: To raise money on behalf of CAMH in order to improve the services provided to patients & to fund research
Chief Officer(s):
Darrell Gregersen, President & CEO
Staff Member(s): 40

Camosun College Faculty Association (CCFA) / Association des professeurs du Collège Camosun
Camosun College, #221, 3100 Foul Bay Rd., Victoria BC V8P 5J2
Tel: 250-370-3655; *Fax:* 250-370-3641
willcox@camosun.bc.ca
www.camosunfaculty.ca
Overview: A small local organization
Chief Officer(s):
Kelly Pitman, President, 250-370-3594
pitman@camosun.bc.ca
Membership: 350 continuing, 150 term; *Committees:* Code of Ethics; Contract Management; Contract Negotiating; Professional Development

Camp Norway Foundation
c/o The Royal Norwegian Consulate, #206, 11 Morris Dr., Dartmouth NS B3B 1M2
Tel: 902-468-1330
cnf@nfsl.ca
Overview: A small provincial charitable organization
Mission: To raise awareness of the contributions of allied merchant fleets during World War II; To promote the study of maritime subjects
Activities: Accepting donations to the Camp Norway Scholarship Fund, for students who study World War II or maritime history; Sponsoring the writing & translation of a book about Camp Norway

Campaign for Nuclear Phaseout (CNP)
#412, 1 Nicholas St., Ottawa ON K1N 7B7
www.cnp.ca
Overview: A small national organization
Mission: The Campaign for Nuclear Phaseout (CNP) represents a coalition of Canadian public interest organizations concerned with the environmental consequences of nuclear power generation.

Affliation(s): Canadian Coalition for Nuclear Responsibility; Concerned Citizens of Renfrew County and Area; Energy Probe; Greenpeace Canada; Sierra Club of Canada

Campaign Life Coalition (CLC)
#300, 104 Bond St., Toronto ON M5B 1X9
Tel: 416-204-9749; *Fax:* 416-204-1027
Toll-Free: 800-730-5358
clc@campaignlifecoalition.com
www.campaignlifecoalition.com
twitter.com/CampaignLife
Previous Name: Coalition for the Protection of Human Life
Overview: A medium-sized national organization
Mission: To protect human life from conception to natural death; to maintain representatives on Parliament Hill; to foster respect for life through adequate legal protection from abortion, infanticide, euthanasia & other life-threatening social & moral trends
Member of: Campaign Life Coalition of Canada
Chief Officer(s):
Jim Hughes, President

Campbell River & Area Multicultural & Immigrant Services Association *See* Campbell River Multicutural Society

Campbell River & Courtenay District Labour Council
#2, 830 - 14th Ave., Campbell River BC V9W 4H4
Tel: 250-287-3884
Overview: A small local organization overseen by British Columbia Federation of Labour
Mission: To promote the interests of affiliates in the Campbell River British Columbia area; To advance the economic & social welfare of workers
Affliation(s): Canadian Labour Congress (CLC)
Chief Officer(s):
Anne Davis, President
annerdavis@gmail.com
John Fitzpatrick, First Vice-President
johnjfitzpatrick@msn.com
Dave Wills, Second Vice-President
Andrea Craddock, Secretary
randyc5@telus.net
Brian Clark, Treasurer
bas-clark@telus.net
Membership: *Committees:* Membership; Miners' Memorial Day; Political Action; Labour History Conference; Labour Day Event
Activities: Offering educational opportunities; Lobbying local elected officials for the rights of workers; Conducting campaigns around labour issues, such as pensions; Taking part in a ceremony on the annual Day of Mourning to remember workers who have died or been injured while at work; Participating in the Annual Miners' Memorial Day; Supporting community organizations; Hosting monthly meetings to discuss council business & to hear union reports

Campbell River & District Association for Community Living
1153 Greenwood St., Campbell River BC V9W 3C5
Tel: 250-286-0391; *Fax:* 250-286-3732
www.cradacl.bc.ca
Overview: A small local organization
Mission: Provides advocates for local services to support people of all ages with special needs, their families and caregivers.
Chief Officer(s):
Greg Hill, Executive Director
Winna Mitchell, President
Membership: *Fees:* $5

Campbell River & District Chamber of Commerce
PO Box 400, 900 Alder St., Campbell River BC V9W 5B6
Tel: 250-287-4636; *Fax:* 250-286-6490
admin@campbellriverchamber.ca
www.campbellriverchamber.ca
Overview: A medium-sized local organization founded in 1931
Member of: BC Chamber of Commerce
Chief Officer(s):
Colleen Evans, Executive Director, 250-287-4513
colleen.evans@campbellriverchamber.ca
Finances: *Annual Operating Budget:* $100,000-$250,000; *Funding Sources:* Membership dues
Staff Member(s): 2
Membership: 600

Campbell River & District Food Bank
1393 Marwalk Cres., Campbell River BC V9W 5V9
Tel: 250-286-3226; *Fax:* 250-286-3296
campbellriverfoodbank@gmail.com
Overview: A small local charitable organization overseen by Food Banks British Columbia
Mission: The agency provides food to those in need in the Campbell River area.
Member of: Food Banks British Columbia
Chief Officer(s):
Debbie Willis, Contact

Campbell River & District United Way
PO Box 135, Campbell River BC V9W 5A7
Tel: 250-702-2911
bvbayly@uwcnvi.ca
Overview: A small local organization overseen by United Way of Canada - Centraide Canada
Mission: A non-profit organization that raises and distributes funds to member agencies that are providing support and services to residents in the Campbell River area. They are committed to building a strong and healthy community for all. The role of the United Way is to match the resources (and fundraising campaign) to those areas of greatest need.
Member of: United Way of Canada
Chief Officer(s):
Brad Bayly, Community Development Coordinator
Activities: Awareness campaign starts in September.

Campbell River Multicutural Society (MISA)
#A114, 740 Robron Rd., Campbell River BC V9W 6J7
Tel: 250-830-0171; *Fax:* 250-830-1010
www.immigrantwelcome.ca
www.facebook.com/157900677578942
Also Known As: Immigrant Welcome Centre of Campbell River
Previous Name: Campbell River & Area Multicultural & Immigrant Services Association
Overview: A small local organization founded in 1992
Mission: To develop services & programs which provide an on-going opportunity for immigrants & their families to learn skills to adapt to Canadian society; To sponsor opportunities to celebrate cultural diversity & learn about the issues of cultural acceptance, network & support other agencies as the provide services to the multicultural community
Member of: Affiliation of Multicultural Societies & Service Agencies of BC
Finances: *Funding Sources:* Government; bingo
Staff Member(s): 4
Membership: 90; *Fees:* $5 youth; $10 individual; $20 family; $30 organization
Activities: ESL; Intercultural Friendship Program; Multicultural Settlement; Community Kitchen; Multicultural & Anti-Racism workshop; interpreter; referral; drop-in centre; crisis counselling; citizenship classes; Youth 4 Diversity; Family Night; Seniors Group; Women's Group; Diversity Health Fair; Inclusive Leadership Adventure; Meaningful Media Night; *Speaker Service:* Yes; *Library:* Video & Resource Library

Campbell River Museum & Archives Society
PO Box 70, Stn. A, Campbell River BC V9W 4Z9
Tel: 250-287-3103; *Fax:* 250-286-0109
general.inquiries@crmuseum.ca
www.crmuseum.ca
twitter.com/crmuseum
Also Known As: Museum at Campbell River
Overview: A small local charitable organization founded in 1958
Mission: To operate the museum, a 21,000-sq. ft. facility sitting on a 7-acre wooded lot; to exhibit a First Nations Gallery showing a coastal lifestyle with such themes as logging, floathouse & the salmon industry.
Member of: Canadian Museums Association; BC Museums Association; Association of Cultural Executives
Chief Officer(s):
Bruce Izard, President
Sandra Parrish, Executive Director
sandra.parrish@crmuseum.ca
Finances: *Funding Sources:* All levels of government
Staff Member(s): 9
Membership: *Fees:* $30 individual; $40 family; $25 senior; $20 student; $45 business
Activities: Public & school programs; special exhibits; family events; field trips; guided tours; museum shop; *Library* Open to public

Campbellford & District Association for Community Living *See* Community Living Campbellford/Brighton

Campbellford/Seymour Heritage Society
PO Box 1294, 113 Front St. North, Campbellford ON K0L 1L0
Tel: 705-653-2634
csheritage@persona.ca
www.csheritage.org
Overview: A small local charitable organization founded in 1983
Member of: Ontario Historical Society
Affliation(s): Ontario Historical Society
Chief Officer(s):
Ian McCulloch, President
Finances: *Annual Operating Budget:* Less than $50,000; *Funding Sources:* Fundraising; government grants
25 volunteer(s)
Membership: 50; *Fees:* $10 single; $5 under 18; $25 corporate; $15 family; $25 sponsor/patron; $20 model railroad club; *Committees:* Collections; publicity; computer; building; membership; publications; garden displays
Activities: *Library:* Archives
Publications:
- Campbellford Memorial Hospital: 50 Years of Care Beyond Compare
Number of Pages: 103; *Editor:* Ann Rowe; *Price:* $20
- Gleanings: A History of Campbellford-Seymour
Number of Pages: 559; *Editor:* Margaret Crothers, Ann Rowe et al.; *Price:* $40
- A Walk Down Memory Lane: 150 Years of the Campbellford-Seymour Agricultural Society, 1854-2004
Number of Pages: 142; *Editor:* Ann Rowe; *Price:* $20

Campbellford-Seymour Chamber of Commerce *See* Trent Hills & District Chamber of Commerce

Campbellton Regional Chamber of Commerce / Chambre de commerce régional de Campbellton
PO Box 236, 18 Water St., Campbellton NB E3N 3G4
Tel: 506-759-7856; *Fax:* 506-759-7557
crcc@nbnet.nb.ca
www.campbelltonregionalchamber.ca
Overview: A small local organization founded in 1985
Member of: Industrial Commission of Restigouche; NB Chamber of Commerce; Atlantic Provinces Chamber of Commerce; NB Economic Council
Affliation(s): NB Chamber of Commerce; Atlantic Chamber of Commerce
Chief Officer(s):
Melissa Beaullieu, Secretary
Colleen Donnahee, Executive Director
Eric Comeau, President
comeaujewellery@nb.aibn.com
Membership: 200+ businesses; *Fees:* $110

Campground Owners Association of Nova Scotia (COANS)
c/o Tourism Industry Association of Nova Scotia, 2089 Maitland St., Halifax NS B3K 2Z8
Tel: 902-496-7474
www.campingnovascotia.com
Previous Name: Camping Association of Nova Scotia
Overview: A medium-sized provincial organization founded in 1941 overseen by Canadian Camping Association
Mission: To provide the best camping experience possible throughout our diverse province; to improve standards at all the province's campgrounds; to provide leadership to this important segment of the provincial economy.
Chief Officer(s):
Jennifer Falkenham, Manager, Membership
jennifer@tourism.ca
Finances: *Funding Sources:* Membership dues; conferences; government grants
Awards:
- Betty Campbell Camper Award (Award)

Camping Association of Nova Scotia *See* Campground Owners Association of Nova Scotia

Camping Association of Nova Scotia
PO Box 33039, Halifax NS B3L 4T6
Tel: 902-425-5454
info@campingns.ca
www.campingns.ca
Overview: A medium-sized provincial organization founded in 1941
Mission: The Camping Association of Nova Scotia, or CANS, is a not-for-profit organization supported by the provincial government of Nova Scotia and is dedicated to supporting and serving the residential camps of Nova Scotia and Prince Edward Island.

Chief Officer(s):
Mike LeDuc, President
Finances: *Funding Sources:* Nova Scotia Sport and Recreation Commission
Membership: *Fees:* $15 individual; $10 student; $100 commercial; $50 camp; $25 agency

Camping in Ontario
#6, 1915 Clements Rd., Pickering ON L1W 3V1
Tel: 289-660-2192; *Fax:* 289-660-2146
Toll-Free: 877-672-2226
Other Communication: Tollfree Fax: 877-905-2714
info@campinginontario.ca
www.campinginontario.ca
www.facebook.com/pages/Camping-In-Ontario/119145788133338
twitter.com/CampInOntario
plus.google.com/+CampinginontarioCanada
Also Known As: Ontario Private Campground Association (OPCA)
Overview: A medium-sized provincial organization founded in 1969
Mission: To support & improve the operation of private campgrounds in Ontario by establishing standards, disseminating information & by representation in the tourist industry & at all levels of government
Member of: Tourism Industry Association of Canada; Tourism Federation of Ontario
Affliation(s): Campgrounds Campings Canada; Go RVing Canada
Chief Officer(s):
Alexandra Anderson, Executive Director
opca@campinginontario.ca
Finances: *Funding Sources:* Member dues; sponsorship; educational activities
Staff Member(s): 4
Membership: 400+; *Fees:* Schedule available dependant on number of sites; *Member Profile:* Active - private campground operators who have legal authority to operate, have paid current annual dues & all other outstanding accounts owed to the association; Associate - person, firms, companies or organizations which provide products or services to the association or membership, & have paid current annual dues & all other outstanding accounts owed to the association; Affiliate - non-private parks, persons, firms, companies or organizations which do not provide products or services to the association or membership
Activities: Member education; marketing; advocacy; *Library*

Camping Québec
#700, 2001, rue de la Métropole, Longueuil QC J4G 1S9
Tél: 450-651-7396; *Téléc:* 450-651-7397
Ligne sans frais: 800-363-0457
www.campingquebec.com
Également appelé: Association des terrains de camping du Québec
Aperçu: *Dimension:* moyenne; *Envergure:* provinciale; fondée en 1962
Mission: Défendre les intérêts de nos membres; offrir des services de publications et promotion, des activitées, des escomptes sur achats et programmes divers.
Membre(s) du bureau directeur:
Natasha Bouchard, Présidente
Membre: *Critères d'admissibilite:* Exploitants de terrains de camping
Prix, Bouses:
• Prix de l'Excellence (Prix)

Campus Gay Club (University of Manitoba) *See* Rainbow Resource Centre

CAMPUT, Canada's Energy & Utility Regulators (CAMPUT)
#646, 200 North Service Rd. West, Oakville ON L6M 2Y1
Tel: 905-827-5139; *Fax:* 905-827-3260
info@camput.org
www.camput.org
Previous Name: Canadian Association of Members of Public Utility Tribunals / Association canadienne des membres des tribunaux d'utilité publique
Overview: A small national organization founded in 1976
Mission: To improve public utility regulation in Canada
Affiliation(s): National Association of Regulatory Utility Commissioners (NARUC)
Chief Officer(s):
Terry Rochefort, Executive Director, 905-827-5139
rochefort@camput.org
Ken Quesnelle, Chair, 416-440-7731
ken.quesnelle@ontarioenergyboard.ca
Régis Gosselin, Secretary-Treasurer, 204-945-2460
regis.gosselin@gov.mb.ca
Membership: 14 member boards and commissions, and 7 associate member boards and commissions; *Member Profile:* Any Canadian tribunal, board, commission, or agency that is responsible for the economic regulation of utilities; Any Canadian energy tribunal, board, commission, or agency that makes binding decisions through adjudicative or quasi-judicial processes; *Committees:* Regulatory Affairs; Education
Activities: Educating & training commissioners & staff of public utility tribunals; Communicating with members; Liaising with parallel regulatory organizations
Meetings/Conferences: • CAMPUT, Canada's Energy & Utility Regulators 2015 Annual General Meeting, September, 2015, Chartlottetown, PE
Scope: National
Description: A meeting held each August or September to deal with the administration of the association
• CAMPUT, Canada's Energy & Utility Regulators 2015 Conference, May, 2015, Hyatt Regency Hotel, Calgary, AB
Scope: National
Description: An annual event to address current regulatory issues & energy related subjects
Contact Information: E-mail: info@camput.org
• CAMPUT, Canada's Energy & Utility Regulators 2016 Conference, 2015
Scope: National
Description: An annual event to address current regulatory issues & energy related subjects
Contact Information: E-mail: info@camput.org

Camrose & District Food Bank
PO Box 1936, 4524 - 54 St., Camrose AB T4V 1X8
Tel: 780-679-3220; *Fax:* 780-679-3221
nbaid@cable-lynx.net
Also Known As: Neighbourlink
Overview: A small local charitable organization founded in 1979 overseen by Alberta Food Bank Network Association
Mission: To provide food to those in need
Member of: World Vision
Finances: *Funding Sources:* Donations
Staff Member(s): 2; 500 volunteer(s)

Camrose Arts Society
Chuck MacLean Arts Centre, 4809 - 52 St., Camrose AB T4V 1T9
Tel: 780-672-9949; *Fax:* 780-608-8740
www.camrose.com
Overview: A small local charitable organization founded in 1979
Mission: To help people understand & value culture & the arts as integral to life
Member of: Alberta Municipal Association for Culture
Chief Officer(s):
Jane Cherry-Lemire, Arts Director
jcherry@camrose.com
Membership: *Fees:* Schedule available
Activities: Art auction; Arts Fest; Camrose arts & rec program; creative arts summer school; Christmas craft sale; teen/kids dances; *Library* Open to public

Camrose Association for Community Living (CAFCL)
Burgess Building, 4604 - 57 St., Camrose AB T4V 2E7
Tel: 780-672-0257; *Fax:* 780-672-7484
www.cafcl.org
www.facebook.com/137368986301614
Overview: A medium-sized local charitable organization founded in 1962
Mission: To assist people to live in the community; a community that values & embraces all people
Member of: Alberta Association for Community Living; Alberta Association of Rehabilitation Centres
Chief Officer(s):
Esther McDonald, CEO
Finances: *Annual Operating Budget:* $3 Million-$5 Million
Staff Member(s): 100; 100 volunteer(s)
Membership: 15; *Fees:* $5
Activities: Adult Residences; Adult Outreach; Respite Care; Skill Development; Rose Club - Drop In Centre; Fundraising; Sexuality Relationship; Parenting Support; Day Options Program; *Awareness Events:* Community Living Awareness Month
Awards:
• Donor of the Year
• Volunteer of the Year

Camrose Chamber of Commerce
5402 - 48 Ave., Camrose AB T4V 0J7
Tel: 780-672-4217; *Fax:* 780-672-1059
camcham@telusplanet.net
www.camrosechamber.ca
www.facebook.com/pages/Camrose-Chamber-of-Commerce/139252349446748
Overview: A small local organization founded in 1908
Mission: To promote & maintain a proud & prosperous business community
Member of: Alberta Chamber of Commerce; Canadian Chamber of Commerce
Chief Officer(s):
Sharon Anderson, Executive Director
Dawn Anderson, President
Finances: *Annual Operating Budget:* $100,000-$250,000; *Funding Sources:* Membership dues; designated projects
Staff Member(s): 2
Membership: 380; *Fees:* Schedule available; *Committees:* Agriculture; Ambassadors Club; Better Business; Corporate; Economic Development; Education; Finance; Government Affairs; Jaywalkers; Membership; Nominating; Personal; Programs; Parade; Small Business Week; Tourism; Transportation; Ways & Means
Awards:
• Jessie Burgess Memorial Award (Scholarship)

Canada - Albania Business Council (CABC) / Conseil Commercial Canada - Albanie
#701, 165 University Ave., Toronto ON M5H 3B8
Tel: 416-979-1875; *Fax:* 416-979-0825
canadaalbaniabusinesscouncil.ca
Overview: A small local organization founded in 2010
Mission: To help encourage businesses to invest in & trade with Albania
Chief Officer(s):
Robert Baines, Executive Director
robert.baines@CanadaAlbaniaBusinessCouncil.ca
Abby Badwi, Chairman, Board of Directors
Membership: *Fees:* $113 - $16,950; *Member Profile:* Corporations who support bilateral trade between Canada & Albania
Activities: Forums;

Canada - Newfoundland & Labrador Offshore Petroleum Board (C-NLOPB)
TD Place, 140 Water St., 5th Fl., St. John's NL A1C 6H6
Tel: 709-778-1400; *Fax:* 709-778-1473
information@cnlopb.nl.ca
www.cnlopb.nl.ca
twitter.com/CNLOPB
Mission: To apply the provisions of the *Atlantic Accord* & the *Atlantic Accord Implementation Acts*; To regulate the oil & gas industry for the Newfoundland & Labrador Offshore Area
Chief Officer(s):
Scott Tessier, Chair & CEO
Ed Williams, Vice-Chair
John P. Andrews, Director, Legal, Regulatory & Public Affairs
Mike Baker, Director, Administration & Industrial Benefits
Dave Burley, Director, Environmental Affairs
Craig Rowe, Director, Exploration
Daniel B. Chicoyne, Director & Chief Safety Officer, Safety
Sean Kelly, Manager, Public Relations, 709-778-1418, Fax: 709-689-0713
skelly@cnlopb.nl.ca
Jeff O'Keefe, Director & Chief Conservation Officer, Resource Management
Jeffrey M. Bugden, Director, Operations
Activities: Facilitating the exploration for & development of hydrocarbon resources
Publications:
• Canada - Newfoundland & Labrador Offshore Petroleum Board Annual Report
Type: Yearbook; *Frequency:* Annually
Profile: Contents include the board's role, objectives, & financial statements

Canada - Nova Scotia Offshore Petroleum Board (CNSOPB)
TD Centre, 1791 Barrington St., 8th Fl., Halifax NS B3J 3K9
Tel: 902-422-5588; *Fax:* 902-422-1799
info@cnsopb.ns.ca
www.cnsopb.ns.ca
twitter.com/CNSOPB

Mission: To regulate petroleum activities in the Nova Scotia Offshore Area
Chief Officer(s):
Stuart Pinks, P.Eng., Chief Executive Officer, 902-496-3206
spinks@cnsopb.ns.ca
Carl Makrides, Director, Resources, 902-496-0747
cmakrides@cnsopb.ns.ca
Christine Bonnell-Eisnor, Director, Regulatory Affairs & Finance, 902-496-0734
cbonnell@cnsopb.ns.ca
Shanti Dogra, General Counsel, 902-496-0736
sdogra@cnsopb.ns.ca
Troy MacDonald, Director, Information Services, 902-496-0734
tmacdonald@cnsopb.ns.ca
Kathleen Funke, Advisor, Communications, 902-496-0750
Activities: Issuing licences for offshore exploration & development; Collecting & distributing data
Publications:
• Canada - Nova Scotia Offshore Petroleum Board Annual Report
Type: Yearbook; *Frequency:* Annually
Profile: A summary of offshore activities, healthy & safety initiatives, environmental protection, information services, & financial statements

Canada Bandy
Winnipeg MB
e-mail: canadabandy@gmail.com
www.canadabandy.ca
twitter.com/canadabandy
Overview: A small national organization
Mission: To govern the sport of bandy in Canada
Chief Officer(s):
Morris Glimcher, President
morris@mhsaa.ca

Canada Basketball
#11, 1 Westside Dr., Toronto ON M9C 1B2
Tel: 416-614-8037; *Fax:* 416-614-9570
info@basketball.ca
www.basketball.ca
www.facebook.com/CanadaBasketball
twitter.com/CanBball
www.youtube.com/user/CanadaBasketball08
Also Known As: Canadian Basketball Association
Overview: A large national charitable organization founded in 1972
Mission: Basketball Canada is the national sport governing body for amateur basketball in Canada; to develop the sport of basketball domestically & to contribute to the development of basketball internationally
Member of: International Basketball Federation
Affliation(s): 10 provincial + 2 territorial associations; Canadian Interuniversity Athletic Union; Canadian Colleges Athletic Association; Canadian School Sports Federation; Toronto Raptors; Canadian Wheelchair Basketball Association; Canadian Association of Basketball Officials; National Association of Basketball Coaches of Canada; Women's Basketball Coaches Association
Chief Officer(s):
Wayne Parrish, President & CEO
Michele O'Keefe, Executive Director
mokeefe@basketball.ca
Staff Member(s): 32
Activities: National Teams; coaching programs; championships; direct mail; licensing; youth basketball programs; *Internships:* Yes

Canada Beef Inc.
Plaza 4, #101, 2000 Argentia Rd., Mississauga ON L5N 1W1
Tel: 905-821-4900; *Fax:* 905-821-4915
Toll-Free: 888-248-2333
info@canadabeef.ca
www.canadabeef.ca
www.facebook.com/ILoveCanadianBeef
twitter.com/canadianbeef
www.youtube.com/user/LoveCDNBeef
Overview: A medium-sized national organization
Mission: To build consumer demand for beef
Member of: Market development division of the Canadian Cattlemen's Association
Activities: *Speaker Service:* Yes
Alberta Office
#310, 6715 - 8th St. NE, Calgary AB T2E 7H7
Tel: 403-275-5890; *Fax:* 403-275-9288

Canada BIM Council Inc.
PO Box 28006, Stn. Oakridge, London ON N6H 5E1
Toll-Free: 877-778-5194
admin@canbim.com
www.canbim.com
www.facebook.com/125791377505468
twitter.com/CanBIM
Also Known As: CanBIM
Overview: A small national organization
Mission: To serve & benefit members who work with Building Information Modeling (BIM) technologies in the fields of architecture, engineering, construction, building ownership & facility management, construction law & education
Chief Officer(s):
Allan Partridge, President
Al Prowse, Executive Director
Membership: 53; *Committees:* Designers; Education & Research; Marketing; General Contractors

Canada China Business Council (CCBC) / Conseil commercial Canada Chine
#1501, 330 Bay St., Toronto ON M5H 2S8
Tel: 416-954-3800; *Fax:* 416-954-3806
ccbc@ccbc.com
www.ccbc.com
Previous Name: Canada-China Trade Council
Overview: A medium-sized international organization founded in 1978
Mission: To build business success in China & Canada by offering service & support, from direct operational support in China, to trade & investment advocacy on its members' behalf
Chief Officer(s):
Peter Kruyt, Chair
Sarah Kutulakos, Executive Director, 416-954-3800 Ext. 311
sarah@ccbc.com
Eumie Leung, Director, Operations
eumieleung@ccbc.com
Finances: *Funding Sources:* Corporations; member dues
Membership: 200 Cdn. companies & organizations; *Fees:* Based on annual gross revenue; *Member Profile:* Companies, universities, non-profit corporations, government agencies; sectors ranging from agri-food, energy & manufacturing to business, legal & financial services, education & health care.
Activities: Advice on export marketing; business consulting; joint venture negotiation; trade promotion; research; translation & interpretation; *Internships:* Yes
Montréal Office
759, Square Victoria, Montréal QC H2Y 2K3
Tel: 514-880-3807; *Fax:* 514-846-3427
chenail@ccbc.com
Chief Officer(s):
André-Philippe Chenail, Manager
chenail@ccbc.com
Vancouver Office
#600, 890 West Pender St., Vancouver BC V6C 1J9
Tel: 604-281-8838; *Fax:* 604-281-8831
ccbcvan@ccbc.com
Chief Officer(s):
Wei Liu, Chapter Manager
weiliu@ccbc.com

Canada Chinese Computer Association (CCCA)
PO Box 64510, Stn. Unionville Postal Outlet, 4721 Hwy. 7 East, Unionville ON L3R 0M9
Tel: 905-294-8891; *Fax:* 905-294-8908
ccca@theccca.com
www.theccca.com
Overview: A small national organization founded in 1993
Mission: To promote & protect member interests
Affliation(s): CCCA Charitable Foundation
Chief Officer(s):
Gordon Chan, President
Paul Ling, Vice-President
Raymond Au, Treasurer
Finances: *Funding Sources:* Membership fees; Income from events & services
Membership: *Fees:* $300 sponsors & directors; $50 voting members & media; *Member Profile:* Chinese computer business community in Canada
Activities: Communicating with members; Providing networking opportunities

Canada Cricket Umpires Association (CCUA)
c/o Basdeo Dookhie, 38 Windbreak Cres., Whitby ON L1P 1P9
Tel: 905-430-3844
www.ccua.ca
twitter.com/WDBUA
Overview: A small national organization
Mission: To promote & advance cricket umpires throughout Canada.
Member of: West Indies Cricket Umpires Association
Chief Officer(s):
Basdeo Dookhie, President
b.dookhie@hotmail.com

Canada Czech Republic Chamber of Commerce (CNACC)
Stn. A, 115 George St, Oakville ON L6J 0A2
Tel: 905-845-9606
admin@ccrcc.net
www.ccrcc.net
Overview: A medium-sized international organization founded in 1994
Mission: To provide a forum for members to discuss ideas; To promote business; To liaise with Canadian & Czech government agencies, such as CzechTrade, to further the interests of members; To cooperate with Czech cultural organizations on programs; To inform & support members
Chief Officer(s):
Miroslav Princ, Chamber President
miroslav.princ@ccrcc.net
Membership: *Member Profile:* Businesses, entrepreneurs, & professionals with economic, social, or historical ties with the Czech Republic
Activities: Implementation of programs

Canada Dance Festival Society
PO Box 1376, Stn. B, Ottawa ON K1P 5R4
Tel: 613-947-7000
cdffdc@nac-cna.ca
www.canadadance.ca
www.facebook.com/Canadadancefest
twitter.com/canadadancefest
www.youtube.com/user/canadadancefestival
Overview: A small local charitable organization
Mission: To hold a festival of dance every two years
Chief Officer(s):
Jeanne Holmes, Artistic Director
jholmes@nac-cna.ca
Sébastien Audette, President
Staff Member(s): 2

Canada DanceSport (CDS)
www.dancesport.ca
Previous Name: Canadian Amateur DanceSport Association
Overview: A medium-sized national organization founded in 1978
Member of: World DanceSport Federation
Chief Officer(s):
Sandy Brittain, President

Canada East Equipment Dealers' Association (CEEDA)
580 Bryne Dr, #C1, Barrie ON L4N 9P6
Tel: 705-726-2100; *Fax:* 705-726-2187
www.ceeda.ca
www.linkedin.com/groups/Canada-East-Equipment-Dealers-Association-3210
www.facebook.com/189673951062605
twitter.com/@ceedaCanadaEast
Previous Name: Ontario Retail Farm Equipment Dealers' Association
Overview: A medium-sized provincial organization founded in 1945
Mission: To promote the welfare of equipment trade retailers in the Maritimes & Ontario; To represent dealer interests in government legislation & regulation; To foster cooperation among manufacturers & distributors; To promote high standards for the retail equipment industry
Affliation(s): North American Equipment Dealers' Association (NAEDA)
Chief Officer(s):
Craig Smith, Chair, 905-572-6714
oneils@mountaincable.net
Keith Stoltz, 1st Vice-Chair, 519-291-2151
keith@stoltzsales.com
Beverly J. Leavitt, President & CEO, 905-841-6888
bev@ceeda.ca
Carol Schoen, Secretary-Treasurer, 519-638-3317
cschoen2003@yahoo.com

Membership: *Member Profile:* Farmstead, agricultural, powersport, & outdoor power equipment dealers from Ontario & the Maritimes
Activities: Liaising with educational institutions, equipment manufacturers, & provincial & federal governments; Providing training seminars; Collecting industry statistics; Disseminating timely information; Offering insurance counselling; Promoting safety
Meetings/Conferences: • Canada East Equipment Dealers' Association 2015 Annual Meeting & Convention, 2015
Scope: Provincial

Canada Employment & Immigration Union (CEIU) / Syndicat de l'emploi et de l'immigration du Canada (SEIC)

#1004, 233 Gilmour St., Ottawa ON K2P 0P2
Tel: 613-236-9634; *Fax:* 613-236-7871
courchs@ceiu-seic.ca
ceiu-seic.ca
Overview: A large national organization founded in 1977 overseen by Public Service Alliance of Canada (CLC)
Mission: To unite all the union members in the Canada Employment & Immigration Commission, the Department of Employment & Immigration & the Immigration Appeal Board, & anyone who wishes to join in a single union acting on their behalf by processing appeals & grievances; To unite all members by fostering an understanding of the fundamental differences between the interests of the members & those of the employer; To assure a union presence at the workplace through collective strength of membership
Chief Officer(s):
Don Rogers, National President
rogersd@ceiu-seic.ca
Steve McCuaig, National Executive Vice-President
mccuais@ceiu-seic.ca
Membership: 21,702 + 279 locals; *Member Profile:* Co-workers in Canada Employment & Immigration Commission; Immigration Refugee Board; *Committees:* Call Centres'; Human Rights/Race Relations; Immigration & Refugee Board; Citizenship & Immigration Advisory
Awards:
• CEIU National Scholarships (Award)

British Columbia & Yukon Regional Office
#530, 789 West Pender St., Vancouver BC V6C 1H2
Tel: 604-436-3120; *Fax:* 604-436-3108
Toll-Free: 800-663-3151
Chief Officer(s):
Julie Paul, National Union Representative
paulj@ceiu-seic.ca
Kathy Sand, National Union Representative
sandk@ceiu-seic.ca

Bureaux régionaux du Québec
#405, 1255, rue Carré Philips, Montréal QC H3B 3G1
Tél: 514-861-7342; *Téléc:* 514-861-7343
Ligne sans frais: 800-361-2871
Guy Boulanger, Représentant syndical sénior
boulang@ceiu-seic.ca
Sylvain Archambault, Représentant syndical national
archams@ceiu-seic.ca
André Julien, Représentant syndical national
juliena@ceiu-seic.ca

Manitoba & Saskatchewan Regional Office
Melton Bldg., #301, 10310 Jasper Ave., Edmonton AB T5J 2W4
Tel: 780-426-7934; *Fax:* 780-425-2225
Toll-Free: 888-426-7934
Chief Officer(s):
Robert Strang, National Union Representative
strangr@ceiu-seic.ca

New Brunswick Regional Office
#201, 96 Norwood Ave., Moncton NB E1C 6L9
Tel: 506-857-2220; *Fax:* 506-857-0848
Toll-Free: 888-441-5022
Chief Officer(s):
Mona Daigle, National Union Representative (Mentoree)
daiglem@ceiu-seic.ca
Jérémie Leblanc, Administrative Assistant, NB, NS & NL
leblanj@ceiu-seic.ca

Newfoundland & Labrador Regional Office
PO Box 3123, Paradise NL A1L 3W3
Tel: 709-782-2622; *Fax:* 709-782-2644
Toll-Free: 866-782-2622
Chief Officer(s):
Denise Richey, National Union Representative, 709-728-1866
richeyd@ceiu-seic.ca

Nova Scotia & Prince Edward Island Regional Office
PO Box 46052, Stn. Novalea, Halifax NS B3K 5V8
Tel: 902-455-7085; *Fax:* 902-455-2128
Toll-Free: 877-498-0277
Chief Officer(s):
Sharon Barbour, National Union Representative
barbous@ceiu-seic.ca

Ontario Regional Office
#1720, 2 Carlton St., Toronto ON M5B 1J3
Tel: 416-488-3000; *Fax:* 416-488-8319
Toll-Free: 800-268-8809
Chief Officer(s):
Ian Thompson, Senior Union Representative
thompsi@ceiu-seic.ca
Todd Ferguson, National Union Representative
fergust@ceiu-seic.ca
Patricia Homonnay, National Union Representative
homonnp@ceiu-seic.ca
Ram Sivapalan, National Union Representative
sivapar@ceiu-seic.ca

Canada Eurasia Russia Business Association (CERBA)

c/o Heenan Blaikie LLP, #2900, 333 Bay St., Toronto ON M5H 2T4
Tel: 416-360-2299; *Fax:* 416-360-8425
www.cerbanet.org
Overview: A medium-sized international organization founded in 1997
Mission: To enhance & support trade, investment, & good relations between Canada, Russia, & Eurasia; To act as the voice of Canadian business in Russia & Eurasia; to expand Canadian business activity in Eurasia
Chief Officer(s):
Piers Cumberlege, National Chair
Katherine Balabanova, Regional Director, Toronto
Finances: *Funding Sources:* Sponsors
Membership: 200+; *Member Profile:* Corporations; Individuals
Activities: Promoting bilateral business growth; Advocating & lobbying on government policy; Offering trade missions to & from Canada, Russia, & Eurasia; Providing networking opportunities; Offering seminars, conferences, & roundtables; Providing market intelligence & marketing; Partnering with organizations; *Awareness Events:* Annual Charity Auction
Publications:
• CERBA [Canada Eurasia Russia Business Association] Newsletter
Type: Newsletter; *Frequency:* Quarterly; *Editor:* Elena Settles
Profile: CERBA events & news

Canada Fitness Survey (1985) ***See*** Canadian Fitness & Lifestyle Research Institute

Canada Foundation for Innovation (CFI) / Fondation canadienne pour l'innovation (FCI)

#450, 230 Queen St., Ottawa ON K1P 5E4
Tel: 613-947-6496; *Fax:* 613-943-0923
feedback@innovation.ca
www.innovation.ca
www.facebook.com/innovationcanada
twitter.com/innovationca
www.youtube.com/user/InnovationCanada
Overview: A small local organization founded in 1997
Mission: To fund research infrastructure; To strengthen the capacity of Canadian universities, colleges, research hospitals, & non-profit research institutions to carry out world-class research & technology development to benefit Canadians
Chief Officer(s):
Gilles G. Patry, President/CEO, 613-947-7260
gilles.patry@innovation.ca
Robert Davidson, Vice-President, Programs & Planning, 613-996-3109
robert.davidson@innovation.ca
Manon Harvey, Vice-President, Finance & Corporate Services, 613-947-6497
manon.harvey@innovation.ca
Pierre Normand, Vice-President, External Relations & Communications, 613-943-0211
pierre.normand@innovation.ca
Staff Member(s): 71
Activities: *Speaker Service:* Yes
Publications:
• Canada Foundation for Innovation / Fondation canadienne pour l'innovation Annual Report
Type: Yearbook; *Frequency:* Annually *ISSN:* 1712-0608; *ISBN:* 978-0-9784394-1-5

Canada Fox Breeders' Association

c/o Melanie Williams, 30 Tanya Cres., Moncton NB E1E 4W5
Tel: 506-388-2087
cfba@nb.sympatico.ca
www.clrc.ca/foxes.shtml
Overview: A small national organization founded in 1920
Mission: To improve, advance, & protect the Canadian ranched fox industry; To assist breeders & producers of foxes in Canada
Affliation(s): Canadian Livestock Records Corporation
Chief Officer(s):
Melanie Williams, Secretary-Treasurer
Lorna Woolsey, Registrar, Canadian Livestock Records Corporation, 613-731-7110 Ext. 306
lorna.woolsey@clrc.ca
Membership: *Fees:* $15 / year; *Member Profile:* Applicants for membership must own at least one ranch fox; *Committees:* Executive; Registration; Finance; Marketing & Promotion; Research & Development
Activities: Keeping a record of the breeding & origin of all purebred foxes bred in captivity; Promoting fox pelts; Assisting members with marketing

Canada Games Council (CGC) / Conseil des jeux du Canada

#701, 2197 Riverside Dr., Ottawa ON K1H 7X3
Tel: 613-526-2320; *Fax:* 613-526-4068
canada.games@canadagames.ca
www.canadagames.ca
www.facebook.com/CanadaGames
twitter.com/CanadaGames
Overview: A medium-sized national organization founded in 1967
Mission: The Canada Games Council is a well-established, national organization that fosters on-going partnerships with organizations at the municipal, provincial and national levels. It allocates resources in support of the following mission and strategic directions.
Chief Officer(s):
Luc Fournier, Chief Executive Officer
Lynn Blouin, Deputy CEO, Communications & Human Resources
Finances: *Annual Operating Budget:* $250,000-$500,000; *Funding Sources:* Federal Government (operation costs); Federal Government, Provincial Government & host city (capital).
Staff Member(s): 9; 5000 volunteer(s)
Membership: *Committees:* Sport; Marketing; Communications; Operations
Activities: *Internships:* Yes

Canada Grains Council (CGC)

#1215, 220 Portage Ave., Winnipeg MB R3C 0A5
Tel: 204-925-2130; *Fax:* 204-925-2132
office@canadagrainscouncil.ca
www.canadagrainscouncil.ca
Overview: A large national organization founded in 1969
Mission: To be the primary networking group for those involved in the grain industry
Chief Officer(s):
Chantelle Donahue, Chair
Patti Miller, Vice-Chair
Membership: 30 organizations; *Committees:* Executive; Finance; Membership
Meetings/Conferences: • Canada Grains Council's Second Annual Canadian Global Crops Symposium, April, 2015, Saskatoon, SK
Scope: National

Canada Green Building Council (CaGBC) / Conseil du bâtiment durable du Canada (CBDCa)

#202, 47 Clarence St., Ottawa ON K1N 9K1
Tel: 613-241-1184; *Fax:* 613-241-4782
Toll-Free: 866-941-1184
info@cagbc.org
www.cagbc.org
www.linkedin.com/groups?mostPopular=&gid=1333997
www.facebook.com/pages/CaGBC/168202776539520
twitter.com/CaGBC
www.youtube.com/user/CaGBC
Overview: A small national organization founded in 2002
Mission: To create buildings, homes, & communities across Canada that are environmentally responsible & high-performing; To advocate for green buildings
Chief Officer(s):
Lisa Bate, Chair
Joanne Weir, Secretary

Anthony Exposti, Treasurer
Finances: *Funding Sources:* Sponsorships
Activities: Developing best design practices; Providing educational materials for members
Meetings/Conferences: • Canada Green Building Council 2015 Annual General Meeting, 2015
Scope: National
Description: Presentations of the financial report & the president's report, & a guest speaker
Contact Information: E-mail: info@cagbc.org
• Canada Green Building Council 2015 National Conference & Expo, June, 2015, Vancouver, BC
Scope: International
Description: Educational sessions & exhibits devoted to green building.
Contact Information: General Inquiries, E-mail: info@greenbuildexpo.org

Canada Health Infoway / Inforoute Santé du Canada

#1200, 1000, rue Sherbrooke ouest, Montréal QC H3A 3G4
Tel: 514-868-0550; *Fax:* 514-868-1120
Toll-Free: 866-868-0550
info@infoway-inforoute.ca
www.infoway-inforoute.ca
www.linkedin.com/company/canada-health-infoway
www.facebook.com/CanadaHealthInfoway
twitter.com/infoway
www.youtube.com/user/InfowayInforoute
Overview: A medium-sized national organization founded in 2001
Mission: To accelerate the development of compatible electronic health information systems, which provide healthcare professionals with rapid access to complete & accurate patient information, enabling better decisions about diagnosis & treatment.
Chief Officer(s):
Richard C. Alvarez, President & CEO
Finances: *Funding Sources:* Federal funding
Membership: *Member Profile:* Federal, provincial & territorial deputy ministers of health.
Activities: Active in accelerating the implementation of electonic health record (EHR).

Halifax
#125, 200 Waterfront Dr., Bedford NS B4A 4J4
Tel: 902-832-0876; *Fax:* 902-835-4719
Toll-Free: 877-832-0876
www.infoway-inforoute.ca
Mission: To foster and accelerate the development and adoption of electronic health information systems with compatible standards and communications technologies on a pan-Canadian basis, with tangible benefits to Canadians; and to build on existing initiatives.
Chief Officer(s):
Michael Green, President & CEO

Toronto
#1300, 150 King St. West, Toronto ON M5H 1J9
Tel: 416-979-4606; *Fax:* 416-593-5911
Toll-Free: 888-733-6462
www.infoway-inforoute.ca
Mission: To foster and accelerate the development and adoption of electronic health information systems with compatible standards and communications technologies on a pan-Canadian basis, with tangible benefits to Canadians; and to build on existing initiatives.
Chief Officer(s):
Michael Green, President & CEO

Vancouver
Commerce Place, #1120, 400 Burrard St., Vancouver BC V6C 3A6
Tel: 604-682-0420; *Fax:* 604-682-8034
Toll-Free: 877-682-0420
www.infoway-inforoute.ca
Mission: To foster and accelerate the development and adoption of electronic health information systems with compatible standards and communications technologies on a pan-Canadian basis, with tangible benefits to Canadians; and to build on existing initiatives.
Chief Officer(s):
Michael Green, President & CEO

Canada Hippique *See* Equine Canada

Canada India Village Aid Association (CIVA)

1822 West 2nd Ave., Vancouver BC V6J 1H9
e-mail: projects@civaid.ca
www.civaid.ca
Overview: A small international charitable organization founded in 1981
Mission: To raise funds to support anti-poverty projects benefiting the peoples of rural India; to foster self-help & self-reliance, particularly through sustainable development & women's empowerment, collaborating with Indian non-profit agencies & organizations in various fields of development, education, health care, & environmental concern.
Chief Officer(s):
Ashok Kotwal, Contact
50 volunteer(s)
Activities: Health training programs; irrigation projects

Canada Israel Experience Centre (CIEC)

#220, 4600 Bathurst St., Toronto ON M2R 3V3
Tel: 416-398-6931; *Fax:* 416-631-6373
Toll-Free: 800-567-4772
ciec@ujafed.org
www.canadaisraelexperience.com
Overview: A small national organization
Mission: To maximize the number of young Canadian Jews participating in formal & informal educational experiences in Israel; to provide information on summer tours, kibbutz programs, Israel-related community activities, accredited programs & long-term stays in Israel
Affliation(s): United Israel Appeal of Canada; CRB Foundation
Activities: Israel summer programs for youth; referrals to other programs with other organizations

Canada Korea Business Association (CKBA)

#2900, 550 Burrard St., Vancouver BC V6C 0A3
Tel: 604-631-3217; *Fax:* 604-631-3232
info@ckba.org
ckba.org
www.facebook.com/ckba.org
twitter.com/CkbaOrg
Overview: A small international organization founded in 1972
Mission: To increase understanding between business communities in Canada & Korea; To promote trade & capital investment between Canada & Korea
Chief Officer(s):
John C.H. Kim, President & Secretary
Richard Hall, Vice-President
Jay Oh, Chief Financial Officer
Finances: *Funding Sources:* Membership fees; Sponsorships; Donations
Staff Member(s): 13
Membership: *Fees:* $30 student; $110 individual; $350 corporate; *Member Profile:* Canadian companies that sell goods & services to Korea; Korean companies with branch offices in Canada; Service organizations, such as financial & legal organizations; Cultural organizations
Activities: Promoting technical cooperation & cultural educational relationships between Canada & Korea; Organizing a delegation visit to Korea each autumn; Hosting delegations from Korea in the areas of investment & trade; Arranging guest speakers, such as ambassadors, politicians, & business leaders; Donating to Korea related charities
Awards:
• Canada Korea Business Association Scholarship (Scholarship) To assist university students in British Columbia, who are studying Korean language & culture

Canada Media Fund (CMF)

#4, 50 Wellington St. East, Toronto ON M5E 1C8
Tel: 416-214-4400; *Fax:* 416-214-4420
Toll-Free: 877-975-0766
info@cmf-fmc.ca
www.cmf-fmc.ca
www.facebook.com/cmf.fmc
twitter.com/cmf_fmc
Overview: A medium-sized national organization
Mission: To provide funding to Canada's television & digital media industries through the following two streams: Experimental & Convergent.
Chief Officer(s):
Louis L. Roquet, Chair
Valerie Creighton, President & CEO
Stéphane Cardin, Vice-President, Industry & Public Affairs
Sandra Collins, Vice-President & CFO, Operations

Canada Nature *See* Nature Canada

Canada Organic Trade Association (COTA) / Association pour le commerce des produits biologiques (ACPB)

PO Box 13, Stn. A, Ottawa ON kKN 8V1
Tel: 613-482-1717; *Fax:* 613-236-0743
www.ota.com/canada-ota
www.linkedin.com/company/organic-trade-association
www.facebook.com/OrganicTrade
twitter.com/OrganicTrade
Overview: A large national organization founded in 1985
Mission: To promote & protect the growth of organic trade in Canada; to benefit organic farmers, consumers, the environment & the economy; to provide information on ingredients, sourcing, certification, marketing, imports & exports, & a range of other concerns
Chief Officer(s):
Matthew Holmes, Executive Director, 613-482-1717
mholmes@ota.com
Matthew Holmes, Executive Director, 613-482-1717
mholmes@ota.com
Membership: *Fees:* Schedule available; *Member Profile:* Businesses engaged in the production, distribution, certification & promotion of organic products, including growers, shippers, importers & exporters, consultants, retailers & others supportive of organic agriculture & trade; *Committees:* COTA Advisory
Activities: *Awareness Events:* Parliament Day

Canada Porc International *See* Canada Pork International

Canada Pork International (CPI) / Canada Porc International

#900, 220 Laurier Ave. West, Ottawa ON K1P 5Z9
Tel: 613-236-9886; *Fax:* 613-236-6658
cpi@canadapork.com
www.canadapork.com
Overview: A medium-sized international organization founded in 1991
Mission: To carry out its responsibilities as the export development agency of the Canadian pork industry; To develop & implement international promotional efforts
Affliation(s): Canadian Meat Council; Canadian Pork Council
Chief Officer(s):
Jacques Pomerleau, President
Martin Charron, Vice-Presidemt, Market Access & Trade Development (Asia, Europe, Agrica)
César Urias, Director, Latin America & Government Programs Management
Amélie Chabot, Coordinator, Communications & Events Planning
Activities: Providing information to foreign customers about Canadian pork products; to liaise with the federal government & trading partners in matters of foreign market access issues; Informing the Canadian industry about changes in export markets

Canada Romania Business Council

c/o DEPAG Deposit Agency of Canada Inc., #1402, 67 Yonge St., Toronto ON M5E 1J8
Tel: 416-364-4112; *Fax:* 416-364-4074
Overview: A medium-sized international organization founded in 1990
Mission: To increase awareness of opportunities in trade, exchange of technology, & investments among members
Member of: Federation of Export Clubs Canada
Chief Officer(s):
Charles Janthur, Executive Director

Canada Safety Council (CSC) / Conseil canadien de la sécurité (CCS)

1020 Thomas Spratt Pl., Ottawa ON K1G 5L5
Tel: 613-739-1535; *Fax:* 613-739-1566
csc@safety-council.org
www.canadasafetycouncil.org
www.facebook.com/canada.safety
twitter.com/CanadaSafetyCSC
Overview: A large national charitable organization founded in 1968
Chief Officer(s):
Jack Smith, President
jack.smith@safety-council.org
Raynard Marchand, General Manager
raynald.marchand@safety-council.org
Publications:
• Famille Avertie
Frequency: Quarterly
• Living Safety
Type: Magazine; *Frequency:* Quarterly; *Price:* $11.25
Profile: CSC news, CSC initiatives, & traffic, occupational & public safety

Canada Sans Pauvreté *See* Canada Without Poverty

Canada Saut à Ski *See* Ski Jumping Canada

Canada Sheep Council *See* Canadian Sheep Federation

Canada Taiwan Trade Association (CTTA)
#450, 1090 West Georgia St., Vancouver BC V6E 3V7
Tel: 604-682-2848; *Fax:* 604-285-3601
ctta@intergate.ca
Overview: A small international organization founded in 1988
Mission: To establish an active network of business contacts to develop trade and investment opportunities between Tawainese investors & local business communities; to promote a mutual understanding & an exchanging of business and cultural information between the various business broups of Canada & Taiwan.
Activities: Meetings; trade mission; trade show; golf tournament

Canada Tibet Committee (CTC)
PO Box 217, Stn. Place du Parc 2 Station, Montréal QC H2X 4A4
Tel: 514-487-0665; *Fax:* 514-487-7825
ctcoffice@tibet.ca
www.tibet.ca
www.facebook.com/groups/31692752904
twitter.com/canadatibetcomm
www.youtube.com/tibetchannel
Overview: A large national organization founded in 1987
Mission: To create a structure where concerned Canadians can work together with their Tibetan friends to develop increased awareness in Canada.
Finances: *Funding Sources:* Member fees, donations, fundraising events
Membership: *Fees:* $25 individual; $35 family; $50 organization; $500 life
Activities: *Library:* Dharma Resource Centre

Canada West Equipment Dealers Association (CWEDA)
2435 Pegasus Rd. NE, Calgary AB T2E 8C3
Tel: 403-250-7581; *Fax:* 403-291-5138
info@cweda.ca
www.cweda.ca
www.linkedin.com/groups/Canada-West-Equipment-Dealers-Association
twitter.com/cweda
www.youtube.com/user/CWEDA1
Also Known As: Canada West
Overview: A small provincial organization founded in 1941
Mission: To represent equipment dealers in Manitoba, Saskatchewan, Alberta & British Columbia; to provide its members with industry intelligence, business support, & acts as their voice in industry & manufacturer relations.
Member of: North American Equipment Dealers Association
Chief Officer(s):
Cameron Bode, President
bodecameron@southcountry.ca
John Schmeiser, Executive Vice-President & CEO
Finances: *Funding Sources:* Membership fees; association services
Staff Member(s): 5
Membership: *Fees:* $500 dealer; $600 associate; *Member Profile:* Farm, industrial & outdoor power equipment dealers
Awards:
- Merit Award (Dealer of the Year) (Award)
- Safety & Loss Control Award (Award)
- Outstanding Dealership Award (Award)

Canada West Foundation (CWF)
#900, 105 - 12th Ave. SE, Calgary AB T2G 5A5
Tel: 403-264-9535
Toll-Free: 888-825-5293
cwf@cwf.ca
www.cwf.ca
www.linkedin.com/groups?home=&gid=2343545
www.facebook.com/canadawestfoundation?ref=ts
twitter.com/CanadaWestFdn
Overview: A medium-sized local charitable organization founded in 1971
Mission: A leading source of strategic insight, conducting and communicating non-partisan economic and public policy research of importance to the four western provinces and all Canadians.
Chief Officer(s):
Dylan Jones, President & Chief Executive Officer, 403-264-9535
djones@cwf.ca
Shawna Stirrett, Interim Vice-President, Operations
Robert Roach, Vice-President, Research, 403-538-7354
roach@cwf.ca
Barry Spencer, Director, Finance
Doug Firby, Director, Communications, 403-538-7357
firby@cwf.ca
Finances: *Annual Operating Budget:* $1.5 Million-$3 Million; *Funding Sources:* Individuals; Corporations; Foundations; Governments
Staff Member(s): 18
Membership: 26 Board Members; *Fees:* $200 annual; $50 friends
Activities: Conducting research projects; *Internships:* Yes; *Speaker Service:* Yes
Publications:
- Currents

Type: Bulletin; *Frequency:* Monthly; *Editor:* Doug Firby
Profile: Currents is a quarterly update on the state of the economy in Canada's four western provinces.It is sponsored by Canadian Western Bank.
- Window on the West

Type: Magazine; *Frequency:* Quarterly
Profile: Western economic issues & policies

Canada West Universities Athletic Association
PO Box 78090, Stn. Northside, Port Coquitlam BC V3B 7H5
Tel: 604-475-1213; *Fax:* 604-475-1997
sportsinfo@canadawest.org
www.canadawest.org
Overview: A small local organization
Mission: To organize inter-collegiate sporting events between members
Chief Officer(s):
Diane St. Denis, Executive Director
dstdenis@canadawest.org
Staff Member(s): 4
Membership: 17 universities; *Member Profile:* Western Canadian universities

Canada Without Poverty / Canada Sans Pauvreté
251 Bank St., 2nd Fl., Ottawa ON K2P 1X3
Tel: 613-789-0096; *Fax:* 613-566-3449
Toll-Free: 800-810-1076
info@cwp-csp.ca
www.cwp-csp.ca
www.facebook.com/106633876058589
twitter.com/CWP_CSP
Previous Name: National Anti-Poverty Organization
Overview: A medium-sized national charitable organization founded in 1971
Mission: To eradicate poverty in Canada by promoting income and social security for all Canadians, and by promoting poverty eradication as a human rights obligation.
Affliation(s): Citizens for Public Justice; Public Interest Law Centre; Amnesty International Canada; Assembly of First Nations; Canadian Association of Social Workers; Canadian Co-operative Association; Canadian Council on Social Development; Canadian Labour Congress & a number of labour unions/organizations
Chief Officer(s):
Leilani Farha, Executive Director
Megan Yarema, Director, Education & Outreach
Staff Member(s): 2
Activities: Dignity for All: The Campaign for a Poverty-free Canada; *Speaker Service:* Yes; *Library:* Resource Centre; Open to public by appointment

Canada World Youth (CWY) / Jeunesse Canada Monde (JCM)
#300, 2330, rue Notre-Dame ouest, Montréal QC H3J 1N4
Tel: 514-931-3526; *Fax:* 514-939-2621
Toll-Free: 800-605-3526
info@cwy-jcm.org
www.canadaworldyouth.org
www.facebook.com/group.php?gid=6244934985
twitter.com/cwyjcm
Overview: A large international charitable organization founded in 1971
Mission: To increase people's ability to participate actively in the development of just, harmonious & sustainable societies; To create exceptional learning opportunities for communities, groups & individuals wishing to acquire skills & explore new ideas.
Member of: Canadian Council for International Cooperation; Youth Net International
Affliation(s): World Assembly of Youth
Chief Officer(s):
Louis Moubarak, President & CEO
Finances: *Annual Operating Budget:* Greater than $5 Million; *Funding Sources:* CIDA, fundraising activities; diversification programs.
Staff Member(s): 160; 3950 volunteer(s)
Activities: Youth Exchange Program (ages 17-20); Work Partner Program (ages 18-29); Customized Program; Joint Ventures Program; Other services include human resource development; north-south cooperation; educational exchanges; leadership & intercultural training; development education; group travel.; *Internships:* Yes
Awards:
- Outstanding Canadian CWY Alumni Award (Award)

Amount: $3,000
- Youth Innovation Award (Award)

Amount: $3,000
- Outstanding Overseas CWY Alumni Award (Award)

Amount: $3,000

Toronto Office
#602, 130 Spadina Ave., Toronto ON M5V 2L4
Toll-Free: 800-605-3526

Canada's Advanced Internet Development Organization (CANARIE)
#500, 45 O'Connor St., Ottawa ON K1P 1A4
Tel: 613-943-5454; *Fax:* 613-943-5443
info@canarie.ca
www.canarie.ca
www.linkedin.com/groups?mostPopular=&gid=3712846
www.facebook.com/CanarieInc
twitter.com/CANARIE_Inc
Overview: A medium-sized national organization founded in 1993
Mission: Canada's advanced internet development organization; to facilitate & promote the development of Canada's communications infrastructure; to stimulate next-generation products, applications & services; to communicate the benefits of an information-based society. CANARIE also intends to act as a catalyst and partner with governments, industry and the research community to increase overall IT awareness, ensure continuing promotion of Canadian technological excellence and ultimately, foster long-term productivity and improvement of living standards.
Chief Officer(s):
Jim Ghadbane, President & CEO, 613-944-5603
jim.ghadbane@canarie.ca
Nancy E. Carter, Chief Financial Officer, 613-943-5437
nancy.carter@canarie.ca
Finances: *Funding Sources:* Government
Staff Member(s): 22
Membership: 100
Activities: Core programs: Advanced Networks; E-Business; E-Content; E-Health; E-Learning; *Speaker Service:* Yes
Awards:
- CANARIE IWAY Awards (Award)

Canada's Aviation Hall of Fame (CAHF)
PO Box 6090, Wetaskiwin AB T9A 2G1
Tel: 780-361-1351; *Fax:* 780-361-1239
Toll-Free: 800-661-4726
cahf2@telus.net
www.cahf.ca
www.facebook.com/pages/Canadas-Aviation-Hall-of-Fame/7078424647
www.youtube.com/user/cahf1973
Overview: A small national charitable organization founded in 1973
Mission: To preserve & publicize the names & deeds of those who have made a significant contribution to Canadian aviation; to house an extensive collection of personal items & memorabilia, as well as a library of about 2,500 books & over 12,000 periodicals.
Member of: Canadian Museums Association; Alberta Museums Association; Canadian Aeronautical Preservation Association
Chief Officer(s):
Tom Appleton, Chair
Membership: *Committees:* Operations
Activities: Annual induction ceremonies, May/June; *Library:* Documentation Centre; Open to public by appointment
Awards:
- Belt of Orion (Award)

Eligibility: An organization, group, society or association who has made an outstanding contribution to the advancement of aviation in Canada

Canada's History / Histoire Canada
Bryce Hall, 515 Portage Ave., Main Fl., Winnipeg MB R3B 2E9
Tel: 204-988-9300; *Fax:* 204-988-9309
Toll-Free: 866-952-3444
Other Communication: www.flickr.com/photos/canadas_history
memberservices@canadashistory.ca
www.canadashistory.ca
www.facebook.com/CanadasHistory
twitter.com/canadashistory
www.youtube.com/canadashistory
Previous Name: Canada's National History Society
Overview: A large national charitable organization founded in 1995
Mission: To promote greater popular interest in Canadian history
Chief Officer(s):
Deborah Morrison, Publisher, President & CEO
dmorrison@canadashistory.ca
Finances: *Annual Operating Budget:* $1.5 Million-$3 Million; *Funding Sources:* Subscriptions; grants; corporate & individual support
Staff Member(s): 12
Membership: 47,004; *Fees:* $29.95
Activities: *Rents Mailing List:* Yes; *Library* by appointment
Awards:
• Governor General's History Award for Community Programming (Award)
Awarded to volunteer-led community organizations for creating innovating programming to commemorate Canadian heritage*Deadline:* August 14*Amount:* 2 awards of $2,500 (English & French)
• Governor General's History Award for Museums (Award)
• Governor General's History Award for Popular Media (Award)
Awarded to individuals who introduced historical Canadian characters & events to the national & international public
Amount: $5,000 & a medal
• Governor General's History Award for Scholarly Research (Award)
Awarded for a non-fiction work of Canadian history published in the last year that made the most significant contribution to an understanding of the Canadian past*Amount:* $5,000
• Governor General's History Awards for Excellence in Teaching (Award)
Deadline: April 1 *Amount:* 6 prizes of $2,500 & the recipient's school will also receive $1,000
• Kayak Kids' Illustrated History Challenge (Award), Student Awards
Eligibility: Ages 10-14
• Begbie Canadian History Contest (Award), Student Awards
Eligibility: Grades 11-12
• Canadian Aboriginal Writing & Arts Challenge (Award), Student Awards
Eligibility: Ages 14-29
Publications:
• 100 Days That Changed Canada
Type: Book; *Price:* $29.70 (Hardcover); $19.79 (Softcover)
• 100 Photos That Changed Canada
Type: Book; *Price:* $45 (Hardcover); $19.79 (Softcover)
• Canada's History
Type: Magazine; *Frequency:* 6 pa; *Accepts Advertising*; *Price:* $32.95
• Kayak: Canada's History Magazine for Kids
Type: Magazine; *Frequency:* 6 pa
Profile: For children from ages 7 to 11

Canada's Medical Technology Companies / Les Sociétés Canadiennes de Technologies Médicales
#900, 405 The West Mall, Toronto ON M9C 5J1
Tel: 416-620-1915
Toll-Free: 866-586-3332
www.medec.org
Also Known As: MEDEC
Previous Name: Association de l'industrie des technologies de la santé
Overview: A large national organization founded in 1987
Mission: To advocate for the adoption & use of medical technology by healthcare systems in Canada
Chief Officer(s):
Peter Robertson, Chair
Brian Lewis, President & CEO
ceo@medec.org
Membership: *Committees:* Cardiac; Diabetes Care; Diagnostic; Vision Care; Orthopaedic; Medical Imaging; Wound Care; Ontario; Québec; Western Canada; Federal Affairs; Human resources; Policy & Issues; Procurement; Regulatory Affairs; Value of Technology; Code of Conduct
Publications:
• ePULSE [a publication of Canada's Medical Technology Companies]
Type: Newsletter; *Frequency:* Weekly
• PULSE [a publication of Canada's Medical Technology Companies]
Type: Newsletter; *Frequency:* Weekly
Québec Office
#1515-A, 740, rue Notre-Dame ouest, Montréal QC H3C 3X6
Tél: 514-871-8096
Chief Officer(s):
Diane Côté, Vice-présidente, 514-871-8096 Ext. 36
Western Office
Vancouver BC
Tel: 604-353-5233
Chief Officer(s):
Robert Rauscher, Executive Director
rrauscher@medec.org

Canada's National Bible Hour (CNBH)
c/o Global Outreach Mission, PO Box 1210, St Catharines ON L2R 7A7
Tel: 905-684-1401; *Fax:* 905-684-3069
www.missiongo-radio.org/cnbh/
Overview: A small national organization founded in 1925
Mission: The Hour is a bible-teaching ministry, & Canada's oldest religious broadcast, heard from coast to coast. It is sponsored by Global Outreach Mission (GOM), an organization dedicated to evangelism & missions.
Member of: Global Outreach Mission
Chief Officer(s):
Brian Albrecht, President, GOM
Len Lane, Contact
len@missiongo.org

Canada's National Firearms Association (NFA)
PO Box 49090, Edmonton AB T6E 6H4
Tel: 780-439-1394; *Fax:* 780-439-4091
Toll-Free: 877-818-0393
Other Communication: Membership e-mail: membership@nfa.ca; Legal e-mail: legal@nfa.ca
info@nfa.ca
nfa.ca
www.facebook.com/NFACANADA
Previous Name: National Firearms Association
Overview: A large national organization founded in 1984
Mission: To support hunting & sport shooting rights in Canada
Chief Officer(s):
Sheldon Clare, President
Finances: *Annual Operating Budget:* $500,000-$1.5 Million; *Funding Sources:* Membership fees; donations
Staff Member(s): 1
Membership: 100,000+; *Fees:* $30 senior; $35 individual; $45 family; $60 business; $850 lifetime; $600 lifetime (senior)
Activities: Speeches & presentations; political action; *Speaker Service:* Yes; *Library:* NFA Resources
Meetings/Conferences: • 2015 Annual General Meeting of Canada's National Firearms Association, 2015
Scope: National
Publications:
• Bulletin Français [a publication of Canada's National Firearms Association]
Type: Newsletter
Profile: The association's French-language newsletter
• Canadian Firearms Journal [a publication of Canada's National Firearms Association]
Type: Journal

Canada's National History Society *See* Canada's History

Canada's Public Policy Forum / Forum des politiques publiques du Canada
#1405, 130 Albert St., Ottawa ON K1P 5G4
Tel: 613-238-7160; *Fax:* 613-238-7990
mail@ppforum.ca
www.ppforum.com
www.facebook.com/publicpolicyforum
twitter.com/ppforumca
www.youtube.com/user/PublicPolicyForum;
flickr.com/photos/ppforumdotca
Overview: A small national organization founded in 1988
Mission: To promote better public policy & better public management through dialogue among leaders from the public, private, labour & voluntary sectors
Chief Officer(s):
Larry Murray, Chair
David J. Mitchell, President & CEO
Julie Cafley, Vice-President
julie.cafley@ppforum.ca
Natasha Gauthier, Director, Communications
natasha.gauthier@ppforum.ca
Finances: *Annual Operating Budget:* $3 Million-$5 Million; *Funding Sources:* Private sector, government, academia
Staff Member(s): 25
Membership: 180; *Fees:* $1,130-$19,210

Canada's Research-Based Pharmaceutical Companies (Rx&D) / Les companies de recherche pharmaceutique du Canada
#1220, 55 Metcalfe St., Ottawa ON K1P 6L5
Tel: 613-236-0455
Toll-Free: 800-363-0203
info@canadapharma.org
www.canadapharma.org
Previous Name: Pharmaceutical Manufacturers Association of Canada
Overview: A medium-sized national organization founded in 1914
Mission: To discover new medicines that improve the quality of health care available for every Canadian
Member of: Canadian Institute of Biotechnology
Chief Officer(s):
Philip Blake, Chair
Russell Williams, President
Staff Member(s): 35
Membership: 23,000 Canadians who work for 54 companies
Activities: Administers Rx&D Health Research Foundation
Awards:
• Post-Doctoral Fellowships in Pharmacy (Scholarship), PMAC Health Research Foundation
Provides highly-qualified individuals the opportunity to undertake post-graduate research & research training in the area of therapeutics or drug evaluation; the four annual awards are tenable only at Canadian faculties of pharmacy for two years
• Research Career Awards in Medicine (Scholarship), PMAC Health Research Foundation
Provides protected time for independent investigators in the fields of clinical pharmacology, therapeutics or drug evaluation; tenable for a five-year period
• Research Studentships in Pharmacology (Scholarship), PMAC Health Research Foundation
Provides the opportunity for students to undertake research in either basic or clinical pharmacology; tenable only at the faculties of medicine at the University of Calgary & McMaster University
• Summer Student Research Scholarships in Pharmacy (Scholarship), PMAC Health Research Foundation
Provides the opportunity for students to undertake research in the fields of medicine & therapeutics during the summer; tenable only at Canadian faculties of pharmacy; two scholarships per faculty are available
• Graduate Research Scholarships in Pharmacy (Scholarship), PMAC Health Research Foundation
Provides the opportunity for graduate students to undertake research training in the fields of medicine & therapeutics; tenable only at Canadian schools of pharmacy for two years
• Summer Student Research Scholarships in Medicine (Scholarship), PMAC Health Research Foundation
Provides promising students the opportunity to undertake research in either basic or clinical pharmacology during the summer; tenable only at Canadian faculties of medicine (the University of Calgary & McMaster University excepted)
• Medal of Honour (Award)
Established 1945; awarded periodically when an individual has made an invaluable contribution to the advancement of science

Canada's Sports Hall of Fame / Temple de la renommée des sports du Canada
169 Canada Olympic Rd. SW, Calgary AB T3B 6B7
Tel: 403-776-1040
info@cshof.ca
www.sportshall.ca
www.facebook.com/CANsportshall
twitter.com/CANsportshall
Overview: A medium-sized national organization founded in 1955

Mission: To inspire Canadian identity & national pride by telling the compelling stories of those outstanding achievements that make up Canada's sports history.
Chief Officer(s):
Mario Siciliano, President & CEO
msiciliano@cshof.ca
Janice Smith, Director, Exhibits & Programming
jsmith@cshof.ca
Membership: 100-499

Canada's Venture Capital & Private Equity Association (CVCA) / Association canadienne du capital de risque et d'investissement (ACCR)
Heritage Bldg., MaRS Centre, #120J, 101 College St., Toronto ON M5G 1L7
Tel: 416-487-0519; *Fax:* 416-487-5899
cvca@cvca.ca
www.cvca.ca
www.linkedin.com/company/cvca
twitter.com/cvcacanada
Previous Name: Canadian Venture Capital Association
Overview: A small national organization
Mission: To provide advocacy, networking, information & professional development for venture capital & private equity professionals.
Chief Officer(s):
Gregory Smith, Chair
Peter van der Velden, President
Finances: *Funding Sources:* Membership dues, Sponsorship
Membership: 2,000+; *Fees:* Schedule available; *Member Profile:* Members include Canadian venture capital & private equity companies.; *Committees:* Executive; Nominating; Tax Policy; Government Relations; Membership; Professional Development; Regulatory, Reporting & Valuation; Finance; Conference; Awards; Golf Tournament; Young Private Capitalists; Communications & Research; Corporate Venturing; Canadian Women in Private Equity; Aboriginal Liaison
Activities: Researching; Encouraging investment from the Canadian institutional sector; Fostering international investment in Canadian venture capital & private equity funds
Awards:
• Entrepreneur of the Year Award (Award)
• Deal of the Year Award (Award)
Meetings/Conferences: • Canada's Venture Capital & Private Equity Association 2015 Annual Conference, May, 2015, Westin Bayshore, Vancouver, BC
• Canada's Venture Capital & Private Equity Association 2016 Annual Conference, May, 2016, Halifax Convention Centre, Halifax, NS
Attendance: 600
Publications:
• Canada's Venture Capital & Private Equity Association Members' Weekly Update
Type: Newsletter; *Frequency:* Weekly
Profile: CVCA events, investment statistics, press releases, special discounts to industry events, & industry happenings

Canada-Arab Business Council (CABC) / Conseil de commerce canado-arabe (CCCA)
#702, 116 Albert St., Toronto ON K1P 5G3
Tel: 613-680-3888; *Fax:* 613-565-3013
info@canada-arabbusiness.org
www.canada-arabbusiness.org
www.facebook.com/216689288352215
twitter.com/CABC1983
Previous Name: Canadian-Arab Business Council
Overview: A medium-sized international organization founded in 1983
Mission: To promote trade investment with Arab countries
Affliation(s): Canadian Chamber of Commerce
Chief Officer(s):
Hugh O'Donnell, Chairman & CEO
Finances: *Annual Operating Budget:* $500,000-$1.5 Million
Membership: 60

Canada-China Bilateral Cooperation Association (CCBCA)
Oceanic Business Centre, #2300, 1066 West Hastings St., Vancouver BC V6E 3X2
Tel: 604-726-7669; *Fax:* 604-304-5566
tour2010@gmail.com
www.ccbca.ca
Overview: A medium-sized international organization
Mission: To promote trade between Canada & China

Canada-China Trade Council *See* Canada China Business Council

Canada-Cuba Sports & Cultural Festivals (CCS&CF)
#3, 221 Trowers Rd., 2nd Fl., Woodbridge ON L4L 6A2
Tel: 905-850-0999; *Fax:* 905-850-0997
admin@canadacuba.com
canadacuba.com
www.youtube.com/user/CanadaCubaEvents
Overview: A medium-sized international organization founded in 1988
Mission: To represent Cuban organizations operating in sport, recreation, education & culture
Affliation(s): Cuban Sports Federation; Institute of Music; Ministry of Culture; Havana Convention Centre; Casa del Caribe; Casa de las Americas
Chief Officer(s):
Jonathan Watts, President

Canada-Finland Chamber of Commerce
c/o Finnish Credit Union, 191 Eglinton Ave. East, Toronto ON M4P 1K1
Tel: 416-486-1533; *Fax:* 416-486-1592
info@canadafinlandcc.com
www.canadafinlandcc.com
www.facebook.com/?sk=2361831622
Overview: A medium-sized international organization founded in 1971
Chief Officer(s):
Peter Auvien, 416-595-8162
pauvien@millerthomson.com
11 volunteer(s)
Membership: 55; *Fees:* $25-$75

Canada-India Business Council (C-IBC) / Conseil de commerce Canada-Inde
#302, 1 St. Clair Ave. East, Toronto ON M4T 2V7
Tel: 416-214-5947; *Fax:* 416-214-9081
info@canada-indiabusiness.ca
www.canada-indiabusiness.ca
Overview: A small international organization founded in 1982
Mission: To promote trade & investment between Canada & India by fostering direct contacts between Canadian & Indian business people; To advise the Canadian government with respect to policies & programs affecting Canada's relations with India; To serve as a forum for exchange of information & views between business executives of Canada & India on issues of importance to both countries; To provide information & advice to companies of both countries with respect to trade & investment matters in either country.
Chief Officer(s):
Don Stewart, Chair
Peter Sutherland, President & Executive Director
Finances: *Funding Sources:* Membership & consulting fees.
Staff Member(s): 2
Membership: 103; *Fees:* Schedule available; *Member Profile:* Entrepreneurs & corporations; *Committees:* Cleantech; Energy-Resources; Infrastructure; Education; Trade Policy
Activities: Development of trade, investment & services; trade missions, seminars & networking events.; *Speaker Service:* Yes

Canada-Indonesia Business Council (CIBC)
PO Box 11-C, #110, 260 Adelaide St. East, Toronto ON M5A 1N1
Tel: 416-366-8490; *Fax:* 416-947-1534
Overview: A small international organization
Mission: To promote trade & investment between Canada & Indonesia
Chief Officer(s):
Peter J. Dawes, Chair
Membership: 100-499

Canada-Israel Cultural Foundation (CICF) / Fondation culturelle Canada-Israël
4700 Bathurst St., 2nd Fl., Toronto ON M2R 1W8
Tel: 416-932-2260
cicf@bellnet.ca
www.cicfweb.ca
Overview: A small international charitable organization founded in 1963
Mission: To act as a cultural bridge between Canada and Israel, promoting and supporting intercultural exchange with a special focus on young artists, and developing artistic life by awarding scholarships and grants
Chief Officer(s):
Cheryl Wetstein, Executive Director
Staff Member(s): 2
Membership: *Fees:* $50 regular; $100 spondor; $500 patron
Activities: Bringing Israeli performers & artists to Canada

Ottawa Chapter
73 Loch Isle Rd., Nepean ON K2H 8G7
Tel: 613-726-0713; *Fax:* 613-728-3497

The Canada-Japan Society of British Columbia
PO Box 47071, #15, 555 West 12th Ave., Vancouver BC V5Z 3X0
canadajapansociety.bc.ca
Overview: A small provincial organization
Mission: To encourage & to increase the opportunities in British Columbia for the extension of friendship & understanding between the people of Canada & the people of Japan
Membership: *Fees:* $325 corporate; $100 individual; $35 retired/student

Canada-Japan Society of Montréal *Voir* Société Canada-Japon de Montréal

Canada-Japan Society of Toronto
Toronto ON
www.canadajapansociety.blogspot.com
www.linkedin.com/company/canada-japan-society
twitter.com/canadajapansoc
Overview: A small local organization
Mission: To provide opportunities to enhance understanding of Japan, Canada & Canada-Japan relations
Member of: Japanese and Canadian Community Network
Chief Officer(s):
Lisa Houston, Communications Director
Activities: *Awareness Events:* Bonenkai, December

Canada-Pakistan Association of the National Capital Region (Ottawa-Hull) (CPA-NCR)
PO Box 400, #2, 2026 Lanthier Dr., Ottawa ON K4A 0N6
Tel: 613-899-2610
info@pcpa-ncr.org
www.cpa-ncr.org
www.facebook.com/cpa.ncr.ottawa
twitter.com/CPANCR
Overview: A small local organization
Mission: To help and establish the Pakistani community in Canada.
Member of: National Federation of Pakistani Canadians Inc.
Affliation(s): National Association of Pakistani Canadians
Chief Officer(s):
Anis Rehman, President
Membership: *Fees:* $10 individual; $25 family

Canada-Poland Chamber of Commerce of Toronto
77 Stoneham Rd., Toronto ON M9C 4Y7
Tel: 416-621-2032; *Fax:* 416-621-2472
info@canada-poland.com
www.canada-poland.com
Overview: A small international organization
Mission: To promote, develop & expand business, trade & investment opportunities between Canada & Poland.
Chief Officer(s):
Jack Smagala, President
Activities: Polish-Cup Golf Tournament; *Library*

Canada-Singapore Business Association
c/o Edwards, Kenny & Bray, #1900, 1040 West Georgia St., Vancouver BC V6E 4H3
Tel: 604-464-0019; *Fax:* 604-464-0872
info@csba.ca
www.csba.ca
Overview: A small international organization founded in 1995
Mission: To promote the development of commerce between Singapore & Canada; to liaise with government & keeps it members abreast of related government programs; to serve as a forum in Canada for individuals & companies with mutual interest to exchange ideas & information.
Affliation(s): CSBA Singapore; Vancouver Singapore Club
Chief Officer(s):
Brian M. Cole, Chair
colebm@telus.net
Finances: *Funding Sources:* Membership dues
Membership: *Fees:* $75 individual; $150 corporate
Activities: Meetings; seminars; workshops; networking; *Library* Open to public

Canada-Sri Lanka Business Council (CSLSC)
PO Box 309, #6A, 170 The Donway West, Toronto ON M3C 2E8
Tel: 416-445-5390; *Fax:* 416-363-4601
info@cslbcbiz.com
www.cslbcbiz.com
Overview: A medium-sized international organization founded in 1990

Mission: To promote trade, investment, technological exchange, tourism, & industrial cooperation between Canada & Sri Lanka
Chief Officer(s):
Upali Obeyesekere, President
Mohan Perera, General Secretary
Activities: Networking; providing business information; annual President's Awards Gala
Awards:
• President's Award (Award)
Publications:
• CSLBC [Canada-Sri Lanka Business Council] Newsletter
Type: Newsletter

Canada-Yukon Business Service Centre / Centre de services aux entreprises Canada-Yukon (CYBSC)

#101, 307 Jarvis St., Whitehorse YT Y1A 2H3
Tel: 867-633-6257; *Fax:* 867-667-2001
Toll-Free: 800-661-0543; *TTY:* 800-457-8466
yukon@cbsc.ic.gc.ca
Overview: A small provincial organization founded in 1997
Mission: To provide access to information & resources on federal & territorial government business services, programs, & regulations
Member of: Canada Business Network
Activities: Offering workshops; *Library:* Canada-Yukon Business Service Centre Reference Library; Open to public

Canadian & American Reformed Churches

607 Dynes Rd., Burlington ON L7N 3T9
Tel: 905-333-3555
comments@canrc.org
canrc.org
Also Known As: Canadian Reformed Churches
Overview: A large national organization
Mission: Federation of churches that are rooted in the Great Reformation of the sixteenth century. They aim is to exalt the Triune God by faithfully proclaiming the gospel of Jesus Christ.
Membership: 50+ organizations

Canadian 4-H Council / Conseil des 4-H du Canada

Central Experimental Farm, #26, 960 Carling Ave., Ottawa ON K1A 0C6
Tel: 613-234-4448; *Fax:* 613-234-1112
www.4-H-canada.ca
www.facebook.com/4HCanada
twitter.com/4HCanada
www.youtube.com/4hcanada
Previous Name: Canadian Council on 4-H Clubs
Overview: A large national charitable organization founded in 1933
Mission: To inspire youth across Canada to become contributing leaders in their communities; To support the development of Canada's rural youth
Chief Officer(s):
Shannon Benner, Chief Executive Officer
Tammy Oswick-Kearney, Officer, Special Projects
Finances: *Funding Sources:* Memberhip fees; Sponsorships; Donations; Wills & Bequests
Membership: *Committees:* Youth Advisory
Activities: Offering exchanges & scholarships which focus on citizenship; Providing leadership development opportunities;
Awards:
• 4-H AgriVenture Scholarship Opportunity (Scholarship)
Awarded to one student nationally, to be used toward an AgriVenture travel and work program. *Amount:* $3,000
• CIBC 4-H Post-Secondary Education Scholarship (Scholarship)
Funding may be used for tuition, books and/or lodging. Eligibility: 4-H members in their last year of high school or CEGEP *Amount:* $2,500 (3)
• TD 4-H Agriculture Scholarship (Scholarship)
Eligibility: 4-H members in their last year of high school who are planning to enroll in post-secondary education in an agriculture or agri-business related discipline *Amount:* $2,500 (10)
• Co-operators/4-H National Volunteer Leader of the Year Award (Award)
A volunteer leader is selected from each province, and a grand prize winner is selected from that group. *Amount:* $1,100
• Sears in Your Community 4-H Club Grants Program (Grant)
Provides funding support to 4-H groups that provide after-school programs so youth can have fun while developing leadership skills, citizenship, and life skills in a positive and safe environment. Eligibility: Available for any 4-H club in Canada *Amount:* $1,000
• Agrium 4-H Youth Leadership Initiative (Grant)
Challenges 4-H members to enhance their local communities by actively participating and practicing their leadership skills. Eligibility: Available for any 4-H club in Canada *Amount:* $50,000
Publications:
• L'avantage 4-H Advantage
Type: Magazine; *Frequency:* Semiannually; *Price:* Free
Profile: Coverage of national programs & 4-H activities across Canada
• Canadian 4-H Council Annual Report
Type: Yearbook; *Frequency:* Annually
Profile: Annual Report of the Canadian 4-H Council & Canadian 4-H Foundation

Alberta - Airdrie Office
Airdrie Office, 97 East Lake Ramp NE, Airdrie AB T4A 0C3
Tel: 403-948-8510; *Fax:* 403-948-2069
www.4h.ab.ca
Mission: To provide a place for youth to learn & grow; To organize outings, achievement days, & fundraiers; To participate in various activities in the community which meet the interests of youth, increase their knowledge, & develop life skills
Member of: Canadian 4-H Council
Chief Officer(s):
Margarite Stark, Head
margarite.stark@gov.ab.ca

British Columbia
2741 - 30 St., Vernon BC V1T 5C6
Tel: 250-545-0336; *Fax:* 250-545-0399
Toll-Free: 866-776-0373
mail@bc4h.bc.ca
www.bc4h.bc.ca
www.facebook.com/472654772849933
Mission: To provide young people with an oppourtunity to learn how to become productive, self-assured adults who can make their community and country a good place in which to live.
Chief Officer(s):
Kevin Rothwell, Interim Manager
manager@bc4h.bc.ca

Manitoba
1129 Queens Ave, Brandon MB R7A 1L9
Tel: 204-726-6412; *Fax:* 204-726-6260
4hdirector@mymts.net
www.4h.mb.ca
Chief Officer(s):
Clayton Robins, Executive Director

New Brunswick
#5, 267 Connell St., Woodstock NB E7M 1L2
Tel: 506-324-6244; *Fax:* 506-325-9266
nb4h@aernet.ca
www.nb4h.com
www.facebook.com/358222067633135?success=1
twitter.com/4HNB
Mission: To learn to do by doing

Newfoundland
PO Box 23047, St. John's NL A1B 4J9
Tel: 709-722-2112
www.4hnl.ca
Gerry Sullivan, President
gerry@4hnl.ca

Nova Scotia
PO Box 550, 157 College Rd., Truro NS B2N 5E3
Tel: 902-893-6587; *Fax:* 902-893-2757
pickaa@gov.ns.ca
www.gov.ns.ca/agri/4h
Mission: Part of the 4-H Club which operates for youth between the ages of 7-21 and which offers various projects from livestock to scrapebooking.
Chief Officer(s):
Arthur Pick, Acting Manager

Ontario
PO Box 212, 111 Main St. North, Rockwood ON N0B 2K0
Tel: 519-856-0992; *Fax:* 519-856-0515
Toll-Free: 877-410-6748
inquiries@4-hontario.ca
www.4-hontario.ca
www.facebook.com/4hontario
twitter.com/4hontario
Mission: To work with Members to develop leadership and life skills that equip them with tools to reach their full potential and become conscious and contributing citizens; To look at the big picture: youth need to see beyond themselves and focus on how their actions affect personal relationships, their community, the environment & society as a whole.
Member of: Canadian 4-H Council
Chief Officer(s):
John denHaan, President
Wraychel Horne, Executive Director

Prince Edward Island
PO Box 2000, Charlottetown PE C1A 7N8
Tel: 902-368-4833; *Fax:* 902-368-6289
pei4h@gov.pe.ca
www.pei4h.pe.ca
Chief Officer(s):
Robert Holmes, Administrative Director
rmholmes@gov.pe.ca

Saskatchewan
Rural Service Centre, 3830 Thatcher Ave., Saskatoon SK S7K 2H6
Tel: 306-933-7727; *Fax:* 306-933-7730
webmaster@4-h.sk.ca
www.4-h.sk.ca
Chief Officer(s):
Valerie Pearson, Executive Director, 306-933-7729
valerieAT4-h.sk.ca

Canadian 5 Pin Bowlers' Association (C5PBA) / Association canadienne des cinq quilles (AC5Q)

#206, 720 Belfast Rd., Ottawa ON K1G 0Z5
Tel: 613-744-5090; *Fax:* 613-744-2217
c5pba@c5pba.ca
www.c5pba.ca
www.facebook.com/117638274967514
Previous Name: Canadian Bowling Congress
Overview: A medium-sized national licensing charitable organization founded in 1978
Mission: The sports organization of male & female 5 pin bowlers provides programs & services to its members for their participation in organized 5-pin bowling. It also regulates bowling systems to standardize the sport.
Affliation(s): Bowling Federation of Canada
Chief Officer(s):
Dave Post, President
Sheila Carr, Executive Director
Finances: *Funding Sources:* Membership fees; government; sponsors
Membership: 150,000; *Fees:* $7; *Member Profile:* Male & female 5 pin bowlers
Activities: Awards Program; *Library*

Canadian Abilities Foundation

#803, 255 Duncan Mill Rd., Toronto ON M3B 3H9
Tel: 416-421-7944; *Fax:* 416-421-8418
abilities@bcsgroup.com
www.abilities.ca
twitter.com/abilitiescanada
Overview: A small national charitable organization founded in 1988
Mission: To provide information, inspiration & opportunity to Canadians with disabilities
Chief Officer(s):
Cameron Graham, Chair
Activities: *Internships:* Yes; *Speaker Service:* Yes; *Rents Mailing List:* Yes
Publications:
• Abilities
Type: Magazine; *Frequency:* Quarterly; *Accepts Advertising*
Profile: For people with disabilities, their families, friends, & professionals

Canadian Aboriginal & Minority Supplier Council (CAMSC)

95 Berkeley St., Toronto ON M5A 2W8
Tel: 416-941-0004; *Fax:* 416-941-9282
info@camsc.ca
www.camsc.ca
Overview: A small national organization
Mission: Dedicated to the economic empowerment of Aboriginal & visible minority communities through business development & employment; to identify & certify Aboriginal & minority-owned businesses, & to integrate them into the supply chain of major corporations in Canada.
Chief Officer(s):
Cassandra Dorrington, President
Activities: CAMCS Business Achievement Awards; Aboriginal & Minority Supplier Procurement Fair.

Canadian Aboriginal AIDS Network (CAAN)

6520 Salish Dr., Vancouver BC V6N 2C7
Tel: 604-266-7616; *Fax:* 604-266-7612
www.caan.ca

www.facebook.com/CAAN.ca
twitter.com/caan_says
Overview: A medium-sized national organization
Mission: To provide support & advocacy for Aboriginal people living with or affected by HIV/AIDS
Chief Officer(s):
Emma Palmantier, Chair
Peetanacoot Nenakawekapo, Vice-Chair
Ken Clement, CEO, 604-244-7616 Ext. 227
Staff Member(s): 10
Membership: 26 organizations; *Fees:* $50 full organization; $25 associate organizations; *Member Profile:* Aboriginal groups & associations; Aboriginals with AIDS; Associate organizations & individuals
Activities: *Awareness Events:* Aboriginal AIDS awareness week, December
Publications:
• Canadian Journal of Aboriginal Community-Based HIV/AIDS Research (CJACBR)
Type: Journal; *Frequency:* Annually; *Editor:* Renee Masching et al.
Profile: A peer-reviewed journal directed toward Aboriginal HIV/AIDS service organizations, Aboriginal people living with HIV/AIDS,community leaders, policy & decision-makers, & anyone with an interest in HIV/AIDS

Canadian Aboriginal Minerals Association (CAMA)

#404, 1910 Yonge St., Toronto ON M4S 3B2
Tel: 416-925-0866
Toll-Free: 800-443-6452
ginal.mine@xplornet.com
www.aboriginalminerals.com
twitter.com/aboriginalmine
Overview: A small national organization founded in 1992
Mission: To increase the understanding of the minerals industry & the Aboriginal communities' interests in lands & resources; to advance economic development, environmental protection, & mineral resource management in the Aboriginal community
Chief Officer(s):
Hans Matthews, President
P. Jerry Asp, Vice-President
Finances: *Funding Sources:* Sponsors
Activities: Providing networking opportunities between First Nations communities & industry; Advocating in Aboriginal community, land, & resource development; Presenting workshops across Canada

Canadian Aboriginal Veterans & Serving Members Association (CAV)

34 Kingham Pl., Victoria BC V9B 1L8
Tel: 250-900-5768
national-president@nationalalliance.ca
canadianaboriginalveterans.ca
Overview: A small national organization

Canadian Academic Accounting Association (CAAA) / Association canadienne des professeurs de comptabilité (ACPC)

245 Fairview Mall Dr., Toronto ON M2J 4T1
Tel: 416-486-5361; *Fax:* 416-486-6158
admin@caaa.ca
www.caaa.ca
twitter.com/caaa_acpc
Overview: A medium-sized national organization founded in 1976
Mission: To promote excellence in accounting education & research in Canada with particular reference to Canadian post-secondary accounting programs & Canadian issues
Chief Officer(s):
Alan J. Richardson, President
pres@caaa.ca
Jamison Aldcorn, Vice-President, Colleges
vpcolleges@caaa.ca
Sarah Gumpinger, Vice-President
vpatlarge@caaa.ca
Chi Ho Ng, Treasurer
treasurer@caaa.ca
Gina Létourneau, Secretary
secretary@caaa.ca
Membership: 100-499; *Fees:* $74-$185; *Committees:* Annual Conference; Education; George Baxter; Haim Falk; L.S. Rosen; Membership; Nominating; Research
Activities: *Rents Mailing List:* Yes
Meetings/Conferences: • 2015 Canadian Academic Accounting Association Annual Conference, May, 2015, Hilton Toronto Hotel, Toronto, ON
Scope: National
Contact Information: Ron Baker, Chair, CAAA Annual Conference 2015; annualconfchair@caaa.ca
Publications:
• Accounting Perspectives
Type: Journal; *Frequency:* Quarterly; *Editor:* J. Efrim Boritz
Profile: Applied research on the discipline & practice of accounting
• Canadian Accounting Education & Research News (CAERN)
Type: Newsletter; *Frequency:* 3 pa
Profile: CAAA events, relations with granting agencies, research opportunities, professional activities, & announcements involving members & their associates
• Contemporary Accounting Research (CAR)
Type: Journal; *Frequency:* Quarterly
Profile: Academic research of interest to the Canadian accounting community

Canadian Academic Institute in Athens *See* Canadian Institute in Greece

Canadian Academies of Science *See* Council of Canadian Academies

Canadian Academy of Audiology (CAA) / Académie canadienne d'audiologie (ACA)

PO Box 62117, 777 Guelph Line, Burlington ON L7R 4K2
Tel: 905-633-7114; *Fax:* 905-633-9113
Toll-Free: 800-264-5106
caa@canadianaudiology.ca
www.canadianaudiology.ca
www.facebook.com/170049173048398
Overview: A medium-sized national organization founded in 1996
Mission: To represent the audiological community in Canada; To provide quality hearing health care & education to persons with, or at risk for, hearing or vestibular disorders; To maintain & advance ethical standards of practice
Chief Officer(s):
Susan Nelson Oxford, President
Petra Smith, President-Elect
Membership: *Fees:* $35 student; $95 retired/international; $140 affiliate; $195 full; *Member Profile:* Audiologists from across Canada
Activities: Encouraging & facilitating research; Promoting & enhancing the profession of audiology; *Awareness Events:* Speech & Hearing Awarenss Month, May; National Audiology Week, Nov.
Meetings/Conferences: • Canadian Academy of Audiology 2015 18th Annual Conference & Exhibition, October, 2015, Niagara Falls, ON
Scope: National
Description: Annual general meeting, educational sessions, speaker presentations, exhibits, & networking opportunities
Contact Information: Phone: 1-800-264-5106; Fax: 905-633-9113; E-mail: conference@canadianaudiology.ca

Canadian Academy of Child & Adolescent Psychiatry (CACAP) / Académie canadienne de psychiatrie de l'enfant et de l'adolescent

#701, 141 Laurier Ave. West, Ottawa ON KIP 5J3
Tel: 613-288-0408; *Fax:* 613-234-9857
info@cacap-acpea.org
www.cacap-acpea.org
Previous Name: Canadian Academy of Child Psychiatry
Overview: A small national charitable organization founded in 1980
Mission: To advance the mental health of children, youth, & families; To promote the highest standards of patient care & service to children, youth, & families, incorporating a psychological, social, & biological approach
Chief Officer(s):
Wade Junek, President
Elizabeth Waite, Executive Director
Alexa Bagnell, Secretary-Treasurer
Membership: *Fees:* $325 full; $195 associate; $195 affiliate; $260 international; *Member Profile:* Psychiatrists, specializing in the treatment of children & adolescents, & other professionals in Canada; *Committees:* Advocacy; Education; Fees & Tariffs; Industry Relations; Professional Standards; Research & Scientific; Website; Awards; Budget; Constitution; Credentials; Elections
Activities: Engaging in advocacy activities related to the mental health of children, youth, & families; Collaborating with other professional disciplines; Promoting research; Furthering the continuing education of practicing child & adolescent psychiatrists;
Awards:
• Paul D. Steinhauer Advocacy Award (Award)
To recognize a member of the Canadian Academy of Child & Adolescent Psychiatry who has advocated for children, adolescents, & their families
• Naomi Rae-Grant Award (Award)
To recognize a member of the Canadian Academy of Child & Adolescent Psychiatry who has done innovative work on an aspect of consultation, community intervention, or prevention
• Excellence in Education Award (Award)
To recognize a psychiatric educator who has made a significant contribution in undergraduate, postgraduate, continuing professional education, public education in child & adolescent mental health
Meetings/Conferences: • Canadian Academy of Child and Adolescent Psychiatry 35th Annual Meeting, October, 2015, Quebec, QC
Scope: National
• International Association for Child & Adolescent Psychiatry & Allied Professions / Canadian Academy of Child and Adolescent Psychiatry Conference 2016, September, 2016, Calgary TELUS Convention Centre, Calgary, AB
Scope: International
Contact Information: URL: www.iacapap2016.org
Publications:
• Journal of the Canadian Academy of Child & Adolescent Psychiatry
Type: Journal; *Frequency:* Quarterly; *Accepts Advertising*; *Editor:* Normand Carrey *ISSN:* 1719-8429
Profile: Featuring original articles, clinical perspectives, & book reviews

Canadian Academy of Child Psychiatry *See* Canadian Academy of Child & Adolescent Psychiatry

Canadian Academy of Endodontics / L'Académie canadienne d'endodontie

c/o Wayne Maillet, #301, 400 St. Mary Ave., Winnipeg MB R3C 4K5
e-mail: info@caendo.ca
www.caendo.ca
Overview: A small national organization founded in 1964
Mission: To advance the art & science of endodontics by providing learning experiences through lectures, providing teachers of endodontics a forum for interaction, providing information & acting as a resource to dental governing bodies, & ultimately to improving the health of the public.
Affiliation(s): Canadian Dental Association
Chief Officer(s):
Douglas Conn, President
docconn@oakridgeendo.com
Wayne Maillet, Executive Secretary
w.maillet@dal.ca
Finances: *Funding Sources:* Membership dues; fees; convention; newsletter ads
Membership: *Fees:* $300 active; $250 associate; $200 academic; $15 retired/student; *Committees:* Standards of Practice; Scientific Advisory; Membership; Public Relations; Nominating; Communications

The Canadian Academy of Engineering (CAE) / L'Académie canadienne du génie (ACG)

#1402, 180 Elgin St., Ottawa ON K2P 2K3
Tel: 613-235-9056; *Fax:* 613-235-6861
info@acad-eng-gen.ca
www.acad-eng-gen.ca
Overview: A medium-sized national charitable organization founded in 1987
Mission: To ensure that Canadian engineering expertise is applied to the benefit of all Canadians
Member of: International Council of Academies of Engineering & Technological Sciences (CAETS)
Chief Officer(s):
Kevin Goheen, Executive Director
Finances: *Funding Sources:* Sponsorships
Staff Member(s): 2
Membership: 584; *Member Profile:* Accomplished engineers, nominated & elected by their peers; *Committees:* Fellowship; Honours & Awards; Finance; Investment
Activities: Increasing awareness of engineering in society; Promoting industrial competitiveness & environmental preservation; Advising on engineering education, research, & innovation; Developing relations with other professional engineering organizations;
Publications:
• Canadian Academy of Engineering Newsletter / Communiqué

Type: Newsletter; *Frequency:* Quarterly
Profile: Reports, updates, upcoming events, & activities of the Academy & its Fellows

Canadian Academy of Facial Plastic & Reconstructive Surgery (CAFPRS)

Mount Sinai Hospital, #401, 600 University Ave., Toronto ON M5G 1X5
Tel: 905-569-6965
Toll-Free: 800-545-8864
www.cafprs.com
Overview: A small national organization
Chief Officer(s):
Corey Moore, President
Membership: 60

Canadian Academy of Geriatric Psychiatry (CAGP)

#255, 55 St. Clair Ave. West, Toronto ON M4V 2Y7
Tel: 416-921-5443; *Fax:* 416-967-6320
info@cagp.ca
www.cagp.ca
www.facebook.com/CanadianAcademyofGeriatricPsychiatry
Also Known As: L'Académie canadienne de psychiatrie gériatrique
Overview: A small national organization
Mission: To promote mental health for elderly people in Canada
Member of: Council of Academies of the Canadian Psychiatric Association
Chief Officer(s):
Kiran Rabheru, President
Marlene Smart, Treasurer & Secretary
Stuart Sanders, Chair, Communications
stuart.sanders@calgaryhealthregion.ca
Membership: 200
Activities: Encouraging education & research of members; Advocating for seniors' mental health; Developing guidelines for training in geriatric psychiatry; Providing networking opportunities; Promoting exchange of knowledge; Initiating the Canadian Coalition for Seniors Mental Health to implement research, education, & partnership development
Awards:
• Fellowship Award
• Resident Award
• Outstanding Contributions to Geriatric Psychiatry in Canada
• Lifetime Achievement in Geriatric Psychiatry
Publications:
• CAGP [Canadian Academy of Geriatric Psychiatry] E-newsletter
Type: Newsletter; *Frequency:* Quarterly
Profile: CAGP reports, meetings, awards, & statistics
• Canadian Journal of Geriatric Medicine & Psychiatry
Type: Journal
Profile: Peer-reviewed original research on the health & care of older adults, co-sponsored by the Canadian Academy of Geriatric Psychiatry & the Canadian Geriatrics Society

Canadian Academy of Periodontology (CAP) / Académie canadienne de parodontologie (ACP)

#201, 1815 Alta Vista Dr., Ottawa ON K1G 3Y6
Tel: 613-523-9800; *Fax:* 613-523-1968
info@cap-acp.ca
www.cap-acp.ca
Overview: A small national organization founded in 1958 overseen by Canadian Dental Association
Mission: To act as the national voice of periodontists; To promote excellence in the practice of periodontics; To establish standards of care & guidelines for therapy; To advance public knowledge & awareness of periodontal health
Affliation(s): American Academy of Periodontology
Chief Officer(s):
Todd Jones, President
drj@perio.ca
Claire D'Amour, Executive Secretary
Finances: *Funding Sources:* Sponsors
Membership: *Fees:* $250; *Member Profile:* Periodontists; *Committees:* CDSA; Mentorship program; Periodontal Education; RCDC; Web Site

Canadian Academy of Psychiatry & the Law (CAPL) / L'Académie canadienne de psychiatrie et droit (ACPD)

c/o M. Bordeleau, Canadian Psychiatric Association, #701, 141 Laurier Ave., Ottawa ON K1P 5J3
Tel: 613-234-2815; *Fax:* 613-234-9857
www.capl-acpd.org
Overview: A small national organization founded in 1995 overseen by Canadian Psychiatric Association
Mission: To advance the science & practice of medicine in the specialty of forensic psychiatry; To promote high standards of patient care & professional practice; To advocate on issues related to forensic psychiatry
Chief Officer(s):
Gary Chaimowitz, MB, ChB, MBA, F, President, 905-388-2511
chaimow@mcmaster.ca
Marie Bordeleau, Contact
mbordeleau@cpa-apc.org
Finances: *Funding Sources:* Sponsors
Membership: *Fees:* $200 full, affiliate, & associate members; $75 members in training; *Member Profile:* Members of the Royal College of Physicians & Surgeons of Canada, or an equivalent organization; Psychiatrists with an interest in psychiatry & the law
Activities: Furthering the continuing education of practising forensic psychiatrists; Encouraging research in forensic psychiatry; Providing information to the public related to psychiatry & law
Awards:
• Bruno Cormier Award (Award)
• The CAPL Fellowship Award (Award)
Meetings/Conferences: • Canadian Academy of Psychiatry & the Law 20th Annual Conference, March, 2015, Fairmont Château Frontenac, Quebec, QC
Scope: National
Description: Information for psychiatrists working in law & psychiatry, & for any physicians interested in furthering their knowledge of this field
Publications:
• CAPL [Canadian Academy of Psychiatry & the Law] Newsletter
Type: Newsletter
Profile: Review of meeting presentations for CAPL members

Canadian Academy of Recording Arts & Sciences (CARAS) / Académie canadienne des arts et des sciences de l'enregistrement (ACASE)

345 Adelaide St. West, 2nd fl., Toronto ON M5V 1J6
Tel: 416-485-3135; *Fax:* 416-485-4978
Toll-Free: 888-440-5866
info@carasonline.ca
carasonline.ca
Overview: A medium-sized national charitable organization founded in 1975
Mission: To promote Canadian artists and music; To identify & reward the achievements of Canadian artists
Chief Officer(s):
Ed Robinson, Chair
Melanie Berry, President & Chief Executive Officer, CARAS & MusiCounts
Meghan McCabe, Senior Manager, Communications
meghan@junoawards.ca
Membership: *Fees:* $75 regular; $25 student; *Member Profile:* Individuals & artists who work in the Canadian music industry; Persons must hold a Canadian birth certificate or passport, or they must be a Canadian Landed Immigrant, with residency in Canada
Activities: Voting for the JUNO Awards; *Awareness Events:* JUNO Awards
Awards:
• JUNO Fan Choice Award (Award)
• JUNO Award: Single of the Year (Award)
• JUNO Award: International Album of the Year (Award)
• JUNO Award: Album of the Year (Award)
• JUNO Award: Artist of the Year (Award)
• JUNO Award: Group of the Year (Award)
• JUNO Award: New Artist of the Year (Award)
• JUNO Award: New Group of the Year (Award)
• JUNO Award: Songwriter of the Year (Award)
• JUNO Award: Country Album of the Year (Award)
• JUNO Award: Adult Alternative Album of the Year (Award)
• JUNO Award: Alternative Album of the Year (Award)
• JUNO Award: Pop Album of the Year (Award)
• JUNO Award: Rock Album of the Year (Award)
• JUNO Award: Vocal Jazz Album of the Year (Award)
• JUNO Award: Contemporary Jazz Album of the Year (Award)
• JUNO Award: Traditional Jazz Album of the Year (Award)
• JUNO Award: Instrumental Album of the Year (Award)
• JUNO Award: Francophone Album of the Year (Award)
• JUNO Award: Children's Album of the Year (Award)
• JUNO Award: Classical Album of the Year - Solo or Chamber Ensemble (Award)
• JUNO Award: Classical Album of the Year - Large Ensemble or Soloist(s) With Large Ensemble Accompaniment (Award)
• JUNO Award: Classical Album of the Year - Vocal or Choral Performance (Award)
• JUNO Award: Classical Composition of the Year (Award)
• JUNO Award: Rap Recording of the Year (Award)
• JUNO Award: Dance Recording of the Year (Award)
• JUNO Award: R&B / Soul Recording of the Year (Award)
• JUNO Award: Reggae Recording of the Year (Award)
• JUNO Award: Aboriginal Album of the Year (Award)
• JUNO Award: Roots & Traditional Album of the Year - Solo (Award)
• JUNO Award: Roots & Traditional Album of the Year - Group (Award)
• JUNO Award: Blues Album of the Year (Award)
• JUNO Award: Contemporary Christian / Gospel Album of the Year (Award)
• JUNO Award: World Music Album of the Year (Award)
• JUNO Award: Jack Richardson Producer of the Year (Award)
• JUNO Award: Recording Engineer of the Year (Award)
• JUNO Award: Recording Package of the Year (Award)
• JUNO Award: Video of the Year (Award)
• JUNO Award: Music DVD of the Year (Award)
Publications:
• CARAS [Canadian Academy of Recording Arts & Sciences] News
Type: Newsletter; *Frequency:* 3 pa; *Price:* Free with Canadian Academy of Recording Arts & Sciences membership
Profile: Music industry happenings, MusiCounts updates, & JUNO Award news
• MusiCounts News
Type: Newsletter; *Frequency:* 3 pa; *Price:* Free with Canadian Academy of Recording Arts & Sciences membership
Profile: JUNO Award news, music industry happenings, & MusiCounts updates

Canadian Academy of Sport Medicine (CASM) / Académie canadienne de médecine du sport (ACMS)

#1400, 180 Elgin St., Ottawa ON K2P 2K3
Tel: 613-748-5851; *Fax:* 613-231-3739
Toll-Free: 877-585-2394
bfalardeau@casem-acmse.org
www.casm-acms.org
www.facebook.com/groups/3990849665
twitter.com/CASEMACMSE
Overview: A medium-sized national charitable organization founded in 1970
Mission: To promote excellence in the practice of medicine, as it applies to physical activity; To advance the art & science of sport medicine
Affliation(s): World Federation of Sport Medicine
Chief Officer(s):
Dawn Haworth, Executive Director
dhaworth@casem-acmse.org
Finances: *Funding Sources:* Membership fees; Donations
Membership: *Member Profile:* All medical doctors; Residents & fellows; Medical students with an interest in sport medicine; *Committees:* Athletes with a Disabilty; Annual Symposium; Clinical Journal of Sport Medicine; Credentials (Diploma); Communications, Marketing & Membership; Fellowship; Official Languages; Paediatric Sport & Exercise Medicine; Timely Topics; Publications; Research; Selection; Sport Safety; Team Physician; Team Physician Development; Women's Issues in Sport Medicine; Interest Groups
Activities: Conducting research; Offering continuing medical education; Providing current information; Creating networking opportunities
Publications:
• Canadian Academy of Sport Medicine Newsletter
Type: Newsletter; *Frequency:* Quarterly; *Price:* Free with membership in the Canadian Academy of Sport Medicine
• Clinical Journal of Sport Medicine
Type: Journal; *Price:* Free with regular membership in the Canadian Academy of Sport Medicine

Canadian Academy of the History of Pharmacy (CAHP) / Académie canadienne d'histoire de la pharmacie

4714 - 174 St., Edmonton AB T6H 5E7
www.cahp.ca
Overview: A small national organization founded in 1945
Mission: To provide research & information on the historical & social aspects of pharmacy in Canada
Chief Officer(s):
Gary Cavanagh, President
John Bachynsky, Secretary/Treasurer
jbachynsky@pharmacy.ualberta.ca

Membership: 54 members + 10 schools of pharmacy; *Fees:* $10 individuals; $20 institutions
Activities: Collecting, publishing, & distributing historical information about pharmacy in Canada;

Canadian Accredited Independent Schools (CAIS)
PO Box 3013, 2 Ridley Rd., St Catharines ON L2R 7C3
Tel: 905-683-5658; *Fax:* 905-684-5057
director@cais.ca
www.cais.ca
Previous Name: Canadian Association of Independent Schools
Overview: A small national organization founded in 1979
Chief Officer(s):
Anne-Marie Kee, Executive Director
akee@cais.ca
Membership: 90 schools; *Fees:* $1000 + $17.35 per student; *Member Profile:* Independent schools which meet certain requirements, such as teaching a curriculum on a K-12 continuum & operating for at least five years
Activities: Fostering leadership in education
Publications:
• CAIS [Canadian Association of Independent Schools] e-Newsletter
Type: Newsletter; *Frequency:* 11 pa; *Editor:* Lindsay Ireland
Profile: Conference, course, & workshop information, upcoming events, & reports

Canadian Accredited Independent Schools (CAIS)
PO Box 3013, 2 Ridley Rd., St Catharines ON L2R 7C3
Tel: 905-684-5658; *Fax:* 905-684-5057
www.cais.ca
Previous Name: Canadian Educational Standards Institute
Overview: A medium-sized national charitable organization founded in 1986
Mission: To develop & promote educational standards & to foster compliance with those standards related to independent elementary & secondary school education.
Member of: National Staff Development Council; Canadian Education Association; Canadian Evaluation Society; Teachers for Excellence in Education; National Association of Independent Schools.
Chief Officer(s):
Anne-Marie Kee, Executive Director
akee@cais.ca
Finances: *Funding Sources:* Membership dues; evaluation fees
Staff Member(s): 14
Membership: 90+; *Fees:* $17.35 per student
Activities: *Library* by appointment

Canadian Accredited Independent Schools Advancement Professionals (CAISAP)
e-mail: communications@caisap.ca
www.caisap.ca
www.linkedin.com/groups?gid=2071818
www.facebook.com/CAISap.ca
twitter.com/CAISap
Overview: A medium-sized national organization founded in 1981
Mission: The Canadian Accredited Independent Schools Advancement Professionals is an association of development and advancement directors and officers.
Affliation(s): Canadian Accredited Independent Schools
Chief Officer(s):
Laura Edwards, President
ledwards@yorkhouse.ca
Membership: 340; *Member Profile:* Canadian independent school advancement professionals employed in development, alumni/ae relations, major gift fundraising, planned giving, event management, advancement support services, prospect researching, database management and communications
Awards:
• Rising Star Award (Award)
• Mary Birt Award for Mentorship (Award)
• Sam Heaman Award (Award)
• Distinguished Award for Advancement Support Staff (Award)

Meetings/Conferences: • Canadian Accredited Independent Schools Advancement Professionals Biennial National Confernece 2015, January, 2015, Le Place d'Armes Hôtel & Suites, Montreal, QC
Scope: National

Canadian Acoustical Association (CAA) / Association canadienne d'acoustique (ACA)
c/o C. Laroche, Faculty of Health Sciences, University of Ottawa, #3062, 451 Smyth Rd., Ottawa ON K1H 8M5
Tel: 613-562-5800; *Fax:* 613-562-5248
www.caa-aca.ca
Overview: A large national charitable organization
Mission: To foster communication among people working in all areas of acoustics in Canada; To promote the growth & practical application of knowledge in acoustics; To encourage education, research, & employment in acoustics
Chief Officer(s):
Christian Giguère, President
president@caa-aca.ca
Dalila Giusti, Treasurer
treasurer@caa-aca.ca
Chantal Laroche, Executive Secretary
secretary@caa-aca.ca
Finances: *Funding Sources:* Membership; Subscriptions; Conference fees
20 volunteer(s)
Membership: 300 individuals + 80 organizations; *Fees:* $90 individual; $40 student; *Member Profile:* Individuals with an interest in acoustics, including students, professors, consultants & government
Activities: *Awareness Events:* Canadian Acoustics Week, October
Awards:
• Student Presentation Awards (Scholarship)
Awarded annually to undergraduate or graduate students making the best presentations during the technical sessions of Canadian Acoustics Week*Eligibility:* Application must be made at the time of submission of the abstract *Amount:* Three awards of $500 each
• Bell Student Prize in Speech Communication & Hearing (Scholarship)
Eligibility: For a graduate student enrolled in a Canadian academic institution & conducting research in the field of speech communication or behavioural acoustics; applicants must submit an application form & supporting documentation before the end of February of the year the award is to be made *Amount:* $500
• Fessenden Student Prize in Underwater Acoustics (Scholarship)
Awarded every two years*Eligibility:* For a graduate student enrolled at a Canadian university & conducting research in underwater acoustics or in a branch of science closely connected to underwater acoustics; applicants must submit an application & supporting documentation before the end of February of the year the award is to be made *Amount:* $500
• Eckel Student Prize in Noise Control (Scholarship)
Awarded annually for a graduate student pursuing studies in any discipline of acoustics & conducting research related to the advancement of the practice of noise control*Amount:* $500
• Directors' Awards (Award)
Eligibility: The first author must study or work in Canada; all papers reporting new results, as well as review & tutorial papers are eligible; technical notes are not eligible *Amount:* $250 for best student paper; $250 for best member paper published in Canadian Acoustics *Contact:* Chantal Laroche
• Shaw Postdoctoral Prize in Acoustics (Scholarship)
Eligibility: For full-time research for 12 months for a highly qualified candidate holding a Ph.D. degree or the equivalent, who has completed all formal academic research training & who wishes to acquire up to two years supervised research training in an established setting; the proposed research must be related to some area of acoustics, psychoacoustics, speech communication or noise; applicants must submit an application form & supporting documentation *Amount:* $3,000
• Student Prize in Psychological Acoustics (Scholarship)
Amount: $500
• Student Prize in Architectural & Room Acoustics (Scholarship)
Amount: $500
• Hétu Prize in Acoustics (Scholarship)
Amount: A book about acoustics & one-year subscription to Canadian Acoustics
• Canada-Wide Science Fair Award in Acoustics (Scholarship)
Amount: $1,000
• Student Travel Subsidies (Scholarship)
Amount: Travel to the CAA Conference
• Underwater Acoustics & Signal Processing Student Travel Award (Scholarship)
Amount: One $500 or two $250
Meetings/Conferences: • Canadian Acoustical Association / Association canadienne d'acoustique Annual Conference, 2015
Scope: National
Contact Information: Technical Coordinator, Tim Kelsall, Phone: 905-403-3932, Fax: 905-855-8270, E-Mail: conference@caa-aca.ca
Publications:
• Canadian Acoustics Journal [a publication of the Canadian Acoustical Journal]
Type: Journal; *Frequency:* Quarterly; *Editor:* Frank Russo; *Price:* Free to CAAmembers
Profile: Refereed articles, research, reviews, activities, new products, & news about acoustics & vibration

Canadian Acquirer's Association (CAA)
#1400, 2000, rue Mansfield, Montréal QC M3A 3A2
Tel: 514-842-0886
contact@acquirers.ca
www.acquirers.ca
Overview: A small national organization founded in 2008
Mission: To bring together payment professionals in Canada
Chief Officer(s):
Adam Atlas, Founding President
atlas@adamatlas.com
Membership: *Member Profile:* Entrepreneurs in the field of electronic payments (credit, debit, gift card, EFT & other)

Canadian Action Party (CAP)
333 Sockeye Creek St., Terrace BC V8G 0G5
Tel: 250-638-0011
www.canadianactionparty.ca
Overview: A small national organization founded in 1997
Chief Officer(s):
Jason Chase, Leader

Canadian Actors' Equity Association (CLC) (CAEA)
44 Victoria St., 12th Fl., Toronto ON M5C 3C4
Tel: 416-867-9165; *Fax:* 416-867-9246
Other Communication: membership@caea.com
info@caea.com
www.caea.com
Also Known As: Actors' Equity
Overview: A medium-sized national organization founded in 1976
Mission: To negotiate & administer collective agreements, provides benefit plans, information & support; to act as an advocate for its membership.
Chief Officer(s):
Allan Teichman, President
president@caea.com
Arden R. Ryshpan, Executive Director
execdir@caea.com
Lynn McQueen, Director, Communications
editor@caea.com
Membership: 6,000; *Fees:* $180; *Member Profile:* Performers, directors, choreographers, fight directors, & stage managers involved in live performance in theatre, opera, & dance in English Canada; *Committees:* Honours; Directors, Choreographers, & Fight Directors; Atlantic; Council Renewal; Diversity; Equity Independent & Small-Scale Theatre Resource; Member Communications & Education; Opera; Stage Management
Publications:
• EQ
Type: Newsletter; *Frequency:* Quarterly; *Editor:* Barb Farwell
Profile: Information for equity members

Western Office
#510, 736 Granville St., Vancouver BC V6Z 1G3
Tel: 604-682-6173; *Fax:* 604-682-6174
woffice@caea.com
Chief Officer(s):
Jennifer Riedle, Business Representative
jennifer@caea.com

Canadian Addiction Counsellors Certification Board *See* Canadian Addiction Counsellors Certification Federation

Canadian Addiction Counsellors Certification Federation (CACCF) / Fédération canadienne d'agrément des conseillers en toxicomanie
81 Bruce St., #C, Kitchener ON N2B 1Y7
Tel: 519-772-0533; *Fax:* 519-772-0535
Toll-Free: 866-624-1911
info@caccf.ca
www.caccf.ca
twitter.com/CACCF_Canada
Previous Name: Canadian Addiction Counsellors Certification Board
Overview: A medium-sized national organization
Mission: To offer credible certifications to all addiction specific counsellors in Canada; To promote & monitor the competency of addiction specific counsellors in Canada

Member of: International Certification & Reciprocity Consortium / Alcohol & Other Drug Abuse (IC&RC/AODA)
Chief Officer(s):
Tom Tuppenney, President & Chair
Membership: 900+
Publications:
• The Beacon
Type: Newsletter; *Frequency:* Semiannually

The Canadian Addison Society / La Société canadienne d'Addison

193 Elgin Ave. West, Goderich ON N7A 2E7
Toll-Free: 888-550-5582
Other Communication: newsletter@addisonsociety.ca
liaisonsecretary@addisonsociety.ca
www.addisonsociety.ca
Overview: A small national charitable organization founded in 1990
Mission: To offer information about Addison's Disease; To assist in the education of the medical society & the public about Addison's Disease
Chief Officer(s):
Harold Smith, President
president@addisonsociety.ca
Roger Steinmann, Vice-President
vicepresident@addisonsociety.ca
Rick Burpee, Secretary-Treasurer
Treasurer@addisonsociety.ca
Finances: *Funding Sources:* Donations
Membership: 111; *Fees:* $25
Activities: Providing support, through various groups
Meetings/Conferences: • The Canadian Addison Society Annual General Meeting 2015, 2015
Scope: National
Publications:
• The Canadian Addison Society Newsletter
Type: Newsletter; *Frequency:* Quarterly; *Editor:* Patricia Hehner
Profile: Society updates & current information regarding Addison's Disease

Canadian ADHD Resource Alliance (CADDRA)

#604, 3950 - 14th Ave., Markham ON L3R 0A9
Tel: 416-637-8583; *Fax:* 416-385-3232
info@caddra.ca
www.caddra.ca
Also Known As: Canadian Attention Deficit Hyperactivity Disorder Resource Alliance
Overview: A small national organization
Mission: To take a leadership role in ADHD research in Canada; to develop the Canadian ADHD Practice Guidelines (CAP-G); to facilitate development & implementation of training standards & guidelines; to share information amongst all stakeholder groups; to advocate to governments, teaching environments & employment organizations on ADHD
Chief Officer(s):
Niamh McGarry, Executive Director
niamh.mcgarry@caddra.ca
Membership: *Fees:* $200 full; $170 international/associate; $60 resident; *Member Profile:* Doctors who support patients & their families, who suffer from ADHD
Meetings/Conferences: • 11th Annual Canadian ADHD Resource Alliance Conference, October, 2015, Vancouver, BC
Scope: National

Canadian Administrative Housekeepers Association *See* Canadian Association of Environmental Management

Canadian Administrators of Volunteer Resources (CAVR) / Administrateurs canadiens des ressources bénévoles (ACRB)

381 Seven Oaks Ave, Winnipeg MB R2V 0L5
e-mail: info@cavrcanada.org
www.cavrcanada.org
Overview: A medium-sized national organization
Mission: To offer certification in the field of volunteer resources management
Affiliation(s): Administrators of Volunteer Resources - British Columbia (AVRBC); Association des gestionnaires de ressources bénévoles du Québec (AGRBQ); Manitoba Association for Volunteer Administration (MAVA); Newfoundland & Labrador Association of Volunteer Resources (NLAVR); Professional Administrators of Volunteer Resources - Ontario (PAVR-O); Volunteer Management Group - Edmonton, Alberta (VMG-Edmonton); Community Council on Volunteerism - Montreal, Qubec; Volunteer Management Group - Saskatoon, Saskatchewan (VMG-Saskatoon)
Chief Officer(s):
Suzie Matenchuk, President
President@cavrcanada.org
Gwenda Templeton, Secretary
Secretary@cavrcanada.org
Membership: *Committees:* Professional Development; Professional Standards; Certification; Communications; Membership; Advocacy
Activities: Promoting the profession of & continuing education standards for the administration of volunteer resources; Collaborating with other organizations; *Awareness Events:* National Volunteer Week, April

Canadian Adult Congenital Heart Network (CACH)

c/o BB&C, #100, 2233 Argentia Rd., Mississauga ON L5N 2K7
Tel: 905-826-6665; *Fax:* 905-826-4873
news@cachnet.org
www.cachnet.org
Overview: A small national organization
Mission: To promote the interests of Canadians born with heart defects
Affiliation(s): Toronto Congenital Cardiac Centre for Adults; Adult Congenital Heart Council
Chief Officer(s):
Erwin Oechslin, President
erwin.oechslin@cachnet.org
Finances: *Funding Sources:* Donations
Membership: *Fees:* $100
Publications:
• The Beat
Type: Newsletter; *Editor:* Laura-Lee Walter
Profile: Stories, overviews, & clinic updates

Canadian Adult Recreational Hockey Association (CARHA)

#610, 1420 Blair Pl., Ottawa ON K1J 9L8
Tel: 613-244-1989; *Fax:* 613-244-0451
Toll-Free: 800-267-1854
hockey@carhahockey.ca
www.carhahockey.ca
www.facebook.com/carhahockey
twitter.com/CARHAHockey
Also Known As: CARHA Hockey
Previous Name: Canadian Oldtimers' Hockey Association
Overview: A medium-sized national charitable organization founded in 1975
Mission: To develop & provide a wide range of innovative hockey benefits & solutions to customers; To build & retain relationships among the adult recreational hockey community across Canada
Chief Officer(s):
Michael S. Peski, President
mpeski@carhahockey.ca
Lori Lopez, Director, Business Operations
llopez@carhahockey.ca
Karen Hodgson, Manager, Member Services
kHodgson@carhahockey.ca
Laurie Snider, Coordinator, Member Services & Special Projects
lsnider@carhahockey.ca
Finances: *Funding Sources:* Membership; Sponsorship
Membership: *Fees:* $23; *Member Profile:* Men & women, 19 years of age or older
Activities: *Internships:* Yes
Publications:
• Ice Chips
Type: Newsletter; *Frequency:* Quarterly

Canadian Advanced Technology Alliance (CATA Alliance) / Association canadienne de technologie de pointe

National Headquarters, #416, 207 Bank St., Ottawa ON K2P 2N2
Tel: 613-236-6550
info@cata.ca
www.cata.ca
www.facebook.com/groups/5391503953
twitter.com/CATAAlliance
Overview: A large national organization founded in 1978
Mission: To provide members with a network to establish partnerships, to match up with global business opportunities; To offer communication & advocacy services, notably in dealing with the government; To work to ensure that policies are favourable to Canadian technology companies; To maintain a research repository where members can access information to advance their agendas
Affiliation(s): Canadian Association of Internet Providers (CAIP)
Chief Officer(s):
John Reid, President & CEO
jreid@cata.ca
Barry Gander, Executive Vice-President, 613-340-0701
bgander@cata.ca
Charles Duffet, Senior Vice-Presient & CIO Advisor
cduffett@cata.ca
Russ Roberts, Senior Vice-President, Tax & Finance
roberts-bishop@sympatico.ca
Kevin Wennekes, Vice-President, Research
kwennekes@cata.ca
Membership: *Member Profile:* Corporations with Canadian offices, engaged in research & development activities; International corporations in a collaboration with CATA; User industries; Service companies
Activities: Engaging in advocacy activities; Providing original & timely information for members & stakeholders; Supporting research projects
Awards:
• Innovation & Leadership Awards (Award)
To recognize expertise, innovation, & leadership in the Canadian high-technology sector
• Sara Kirke Award (Award)
To recognize woman entrepreneurship, including outstanding technological innovation & corporate leadership
Meetings/Conferences: • Canadian Advanced Technology Alliance National Public Alerting Summit, February, 2015, Edmonton, AB
Scope: National

CATA Québec/ADRIQ
#514, 1155, rue University, Montréal QC H3B 3A7
Tél: 514-337-3001; *Téléc:* 514-337-2229
adriq@adriq.com
adriq.com
www.linkedin.com/groups/ADRIQ-Association-développement-recherche-linn
twitter.com/adriq_rcti
www.youtube.com/user/TheADRIQ
Chief Officer(s):
Jean-Louis Legault, Président
jean.louis.legault@adriq.com

Operations Office
Telfer School of Management, Desmarais Bldg., #6119, 55 Laurier East, Ottawa ON K1N 6N5
Tél: 514-337-3001; *Téléc:* 514-337-2229
adriq@adriq.com
adriq.com

Canadian Adventist Teachers Network

c/o Seventh-day Adventist Church in Canada, 1148 King St. East, Oshawa ON L1H 1H8
Tel: 905-433-0011; *Fax:* 905-433-0982
education@adventist.ca
catnet.sdacc.org
Also Known As: CAT-net
Overview: A small national organization
Mission: Dedicated to promoting excellence in Christian education by helping facilitate communication and the exchange of ideas among Adventist educators.
Affliation(s): Seventh-day Adventist Church in Canada
Chief Officer(s):
Dennis Marshall, Director
marshall.dennis@adventist.ca

Canadian Advertising Research Foundation (CARF) / Fondation canadienne de recherche en publicité (FCRP)

#1005, 160 Bloor St. East, Toronto ON M4W 1B9
Tel: 416-413-3864; *Fax:* 416-413-3879
tkormann@tvb.ca
www.carf.ca
Overview: A medium-sized national organization founded in 1949
Mission: To promote greater effectiveness in advertising & marketing through completely impartial & objective research; to further, through the fostering of research, scientific practices in advertising & marketing
Affiliation(s): Advertising Research Foundation, New York
Chief Officer(s):
Tiffany James, Administrator, 416-413-3864
TJames@tvb.ca
Lisa Eaton, Co-Chair
LEaton@bbm.ca
Membership: 115 organizations; *Fees:* $440-$585 based on number of employees; *Member Profile:* Open to companies & individuals in companies using advertising, advertising agencies, media, research companies & other persons or companies

interested in furthering CARF's objectives; government & educational organizations may become associate members
Activities: CARF offers full consulting & advisory services for both media & advertising research; conducts comprehensive appraisals of media & advertising research projects; organizes an annual Advertising Research Seminar & periodic workshops dealing with specific aspects of advertising research; has published a set of Media Research Standards to help promote the best possible media research in Canada
Awards:
• Arnold Action Award (Award)
Publications:
• CARF [Canadian Advertising Research Foundation] Newsletter
Type: Newsletter
Profile: Developments in advertising research in Canada & internationally, for CARF members only

Canadian Aerial Applicators Association (CAAA)
#202, 4505 - 99 St., Edmonton AB T6E 3N8
Tel: 780-413-0078; *Fax:* 780-413-0076
caaa@telusplanet.net
www.canadianaerialapplicators.com
Overview: A small national organization founded in 1986
Mission: To promote safety & continuing education within the industry, & to support professionalism amongst its members; to lobby federal & provincial government agencies to design policies; to advise regulatory agencies on the safe & efficient aerial application of pesticides & other crop inputs.
Affliation(s): Bayer CropScience Canada Co.; BASF Canada, Inc.; Syngenta Crop Protection Canada, Inc.
Chief Officer(s):
Paul O'Carroll, President
Jill Lane, Executive Director
director@canadianaerialapplicators.com
Staff Member(s): 5
Membership: 172; *Fees:* Schedule available dependant on number of aircrafts & staff
Activities: Mentorship Program; training from ground crews to pilots; conference & tradeshow; *Internships:* Yes

Canadian Aeronautical Institute (CAI) *See* Canadian Aeronautics & Space Institute

Canadian Aeronautics & Space Institute (CASI) / Institut aéronautique et spatial du Canada
#104, 350 Terry Fox Dr., Ottawa ON K2K 2W5
Tel: 613-591-8787; *Fax:* 613-591-7291
Other Communication: membership@casi.ca
casi@casi.ca
www.casi.ca
Previous Name: Canadian Aeronautical Institute (CAI)
Merged from: Institute of Aircraft Technicians; Ottawa Aeronautical Society; US Institute of Aeronautical Science
Overview: A medium-sized national licensing organization founded in 1954
Mission: To advance the art, science, engineering, & applications of aeronautics & associated technologies in Canada; To promote Canadian competence & international competitiveness
Affliation(s): Canadian Air Cushion Technology Society; Canadian Navigation Society; Canadian Remote Sensing Society
Chief Officer(s):
Geoff Languedoc, Executive Director
April Duffy, Coordinator, Publications, Information & Membership Services
Membership: 1,600; *Fees:* $36.75 juniors; $63 seniors; $94.50 associates & individuals
Activities: Facilitating communications among the Canadian aeronautics & space community; Developing members' skills
Awards:
• Trans-Canada (McKee) Trophy (Award)
• The McCurdy Award (Award)
To recognize outstanding achievement in the science & creative aspects of engineering
• The C.D. Howe Award (Award)
To honour achievements in the fields of planning & policy making, plus leadership
• The Romeo Vachon Award (Award)
To recognize an outstanding display of initiative & practical skills in the solution of a particular problem
• The Alouette Award (Scholarship)
To celebrate an outstanding contribution to advancement in space technology, science, engingeering, & application
Meetings/Conferences: • Canadian Aeronautics & Space Institute 62nd Aeronautics Conference & Annual General Meeting 2015, April, 2015, Fairmont The Queen Elizabeth Hotel, Montréal, QC
Scope: International
Publications:
• Canadian Aeronautics & Space Journal (CASJ)
Type: Journal; *Frequency:* 4 pa; *Accepts Advertising*; *Editor:* Dr. Steven Zan; *Price:* Free to members & corporate
Profile: Fundamental & applied research, new technologies, & developments in the aerospace sciences & related fields
• Canadian Journal of Remote Sensing (CJRS)
Type: Journal; *Frequency:* 6 pa; *Accepts Advertising*; *Editor:* Nicholas Coops; *Price:* Free to members & corporatepartners
Profile: Technical research articles, notes, & review papers on topics such as information processing methods, data acquisition, & applications
• CASI [Canadian Aeronautics & Space Institute] Clipper
Frequency: Bimonthly
Profile: Information about the aeronautics, space, & remote sensing communities, produced & distributed to members & corporate partners
• CASI [Canadian Aeronautics & Space Institute] Log
Type: Newsletter
Profile: Information about events & branches, produced & distributed to members & corporate partners

Canadian Aerophilatelic Society (CAS) / La société canadienne d'aérophilatélie (SCA)
203A Woodfield Dr., Nepean ON K2G 4P2
www.aerophilately.ca
Overview: A small national organization founded in 1984
Mission: To represent Canadian aerophilatelists nationally & internationally
Chief Officer(s):
Steve Johnson, President
steverman@rogers.com
Brian Wolfenden, Secretary-Treasurer
bjnepean@trytel.com
Membership: *Fees:* $20 members in Canada; $22 US residents; $25 members outside Canada; *Member Profile:* Canadians who are interested in world-wide aerophilately; Collectors throughout the world who are interested in Canadian aerophilately
Activities: Facilitating the exchange of information; Providing information about air mail stamps & covers; Selling covers; *Library:* Canadian Aerophilatelic Society Library
Publications:
• The Canadian Aerophilatelist
Type: Newsletter; *Frequency:* Quarterly; *Editor:* Chris Hargreaves

Canadian Agencies Practicing Marketing Activation (CAPMA)
#107, 1 Eva Rd., Toronto ON M9C 4Z5
e-mail: info@capma.org
www.capma.org
Overview: A medium-sized national organization
Mission: To raise the profile of the industry
Chief Officer(s):
Christine Ross, Executive Director
Mike Armstrong, President
Matthew Diamond, Vice-President
Chad Grenier, Secretary
Rick Takamatsu, Treasurer
Membership: *Fees:* Based upon number of employees
Activities: Developing networking opportunities

Canadian Agency for Drugs & Technologies in Health (CADTH) / Agence canadienne des médicaments et des technologies de la santé (ACMTS)
#600, 865 Carling Ave., Ottawa ON K1S 5S8
Tel: 613-226-2553; *Fax:* 613-226-5392
Toll-Free: 866-988-1444
requests@cadth.ca
www.cadth.ca
www.linkedin.com/company/canadian-agency-for-drugs-and-technologies-in
twitter.com/CADTH_ACMTS
www.youtube.com/user/CADTHACMTS
Previous Name: Canadian Coordinating Office for Health Technology Assessment
Overview: A medium-sized national organization founded in 1989
Mission: To offer evidence-based information & impartial advice to health care decision makers about the effectiveness of drugs & other health technologies
Chief Officer(s):
Brian O'Rourke, President & CEO
Finances: *Funding Sources:* Canadian federal, provincial, & territorial governments
Membership: *Member Profile:* Canadian health care decision makers
Activities: Assessing drugs & health technologies; Conducting drug reviews; Identifying optimal drug therapy
Awards:
• Canadian Agency for Drugs & Technologies in Health Award of Excellence (Award)
To recognize individuals whose achievements have advanced the fields of health technology assessment, evidence-based drug reviews, or optimal technology utilization in Canada *Contact:* Peter Chinneck, #600, 865 Carling Ave., Ottawa, ON K1S 5S8
Meetings/Conferences: • 2015 Canadian Agency for Drugs & Technologies in Health Symposium, April, 2015, Saskatoon, SK
Scope: National
Publications:
• Canadian Agency for Drugs & Technologies in Health Annual Report
Type: Yearbook; *Frequency:* Annually
• Canadian Agency for Drugs & Technologies in Health Technology Reports
Profile: Peer reviewed assessments of health care technologies & services
• CDR [Common Drug Review] Update
Type: Bulletin; *Price:* Free
Profile: Common Drug Review program initiatives & activities
• COMPUS [Canadian Optimal Medication Prescribing & Utilization Service] Communiqué
Type: Newsletter; *Price:* Free
Profile: Activities of the Canadian Optimal Medication Prescribing & Utilization Service
• Connection [a publication of the Canadian Agency for Drugs & Technologies in Health]
Type: Newsletter
Profile: Corporate newsletter of the Canadian Agency for Drugs & Technologies in Health
• Health Technology Update
Type: Newsletter; *Frequency:* 3 pa *ISSN:* 1715-5568
Profile: Articles about new medical devices, procedures, & health systems
• Issues in Emerging Health Technologies
Type: Bulletin
Profile: Drug & non-drug technologies that are not yet used, or widely diffused, in Canada

Canadian Agricultural Economics & Farm Management Society *See* Canadian Agricultural Economics Society

Canadian Agricultural Economics Society (CAES) / Société canadienne d'agroéconomie (SCAE)
University Of Victoria, PO Box 1700, Stn. CSC, Rm. 360, Business & Economics Bldg., Victoria BC V8W 2Y2
Fax: 866-543-7613
caes.usask.ca
www.facebook.com/CanadianAgriculturalEconomicsSociety
twitter.com/CAES_AgEcon
Previous Name: Canadian Agricultural Economics & Farm Management Society
Overview: A medium-sized national organization
Mission: To address problems related to the economics of food production & marketing & the quality of rural life through extension, research, teaching, & policy making in government & private industry
Affliation(s): Agricultural Institute of Canada
Chief Officer(s):
Valerie Johnson, Executive Director
valcaes@telus.net
Membership: 488; *Fees:* $125 regular; $30 student; $65 senior; $75 early career; *Member Profile:* Individuals with interest in agricultural economics
Awards:
• Excellence in Farm Business Management (Award)
• Outstanding Ph.D. Thesis Award (Award)
• Outstanding Master's Thesis Award (Award)
• Outstanding Agribusiness Master's Project Award (Award)
• Outstanding Journal Article Award (Award)
• Publication of Enduring Quality Award (Award)
• Undergraduate Book Prize Award (Award)
Publications:
• Canadian Agricultural Economics Society Newsletter
Type: Newsletter
Profile: CAES news & activities

• Canadian Journal of Agricultural Economics / Revue Canadienne d'Agroéconomie
Type: Journal; *Frequency:* 4 pa; *Price:* Free to members
Profile: International peer-reviewed journal about agricultural & resource economics

Canadian Agricultural Safety Association (CASA) / Association canadienne de sécurité agricole (ACSA)

3325-C Pembina Hwy., Winnipeg MB R3V 0A2
Tel: 204-452-2272; *Fax:* 204-261-5004
Toll-Free: 877-452-2272
info@casa-acsa.ca
www.casa-acsa.ca
www.linkedin.com/company/canadian-agricultural-safety-association
www.facebook.com/group.php?gid=161720997195550
twitter.com/planfarmsafety
www.youtube.com/planfarmsafety
Overview: A medium-sized national organization founded in 1993
Mission: To address problems of illness, injuries & accidental death in farmers, their families & agricultural workers; To improve health & safety conditions of those that live or work on Canadian farms
Chief Officer(s):
Marcel L. Hacault, Executive Director
Denis Bilodeau, Chair
denisbilodeau@upa.qc.ca
Dean Anderson, Vice-Chair
dean.anderson@wsps.ca
Lauranne Sanderson, Treasurer
Finances: *Annual Operating Budget:* $1.5 Million-$3 Million
Staff Member(s): 4
Membership: *Fees:* $100 personal, not-profit; $300 academia, producer, government, service/supply industry
Activities: *Library* Open to public
Meetings/Conferences: • Canadian Agricultural Safety Association's Conference & AGM 2015, 2015
Scope: National
Description: A forum for members, supporters, researchers and innovators to network, share, and learn about important trends and developments in agricultural safety.
Contact Information: CASA Conference Coordinator: Diane Wreford, Phone: 204-930-4612; Emil: dwreford@casa-acsa.ca
Publications:
• CASA [Canadian Agricultural Safety Association] / ACSA [Association canadienne de sécurité agricole] Liaison
Type: Newsletter; *Frequency:* Monthly
Profile: News for members & interested individuals
• CASA [Canadian Agricultural Safety Association] Annual Report
Type: Yearbook; *Frequency:* Annually
Profile: Long term objectives of the association & financial statements

Canadian Agri-Marketing Association (CAMA)

22 Guyers Dr., RR#3, Port Elgin ON N0H 2C7
Tel: 519-389-6552
info@cama.org
www.cama.org
Overview: A medium-sized national organization founded in 1966
Mission: To promote the exchange & application of agricultural marketing ideas; To encourage high professional standards of agricultural marketing in Ontario
Affliation(s): National Agri-Marketing Association (Canadian Agri-Marketing Association's USA counterpart)
Chief Officer(s):
Mary Thornley, Executive Director, 519-389-6552
Membership: *Member Profile:* Agribusiness marketing professionals from across Ontario, such as manufacturers, agencies, retailers, & associations
Activities: Encouraging professional development; Creating networking opportunities with others in the industry in Ontario; Promoting interest in agri-marketing as a career
Publications:
• Agri-Marketing
Type: Newsletter; *Price:* Free with membership in the Canadian Agri-Marketing Association
• Canadian Agri-Marketing Association Membership Directory
Type: Directory; *Price:* Free with membership in the Canadian Agri-Marketing Association
Profile: A national directory of CAMA members

Canadian Agri-Marketing Association (Alberta) (CAMA)

c/o CAMA, 22 Guyers Dr., RR#3, Port Elgin ON N0H 2C7
e-mail: Alberta@cama.org
www.cama.org/alberta/AlbertaHome.aspx
Also Known As: CAMA Alberta
Overview: A medium-sized provincial organization founded in 1978 overseen by Canadian Agri-Marketing Association
Mission: To increase knowledge of ideas related to agri-marketing; To promote high professional standards of agricultural marketing
Affliation(s): National Agri-Marketing Association (NAMA); CAMA Saskatchewan; CAMA Manitoba; CAMA Ontario; CAMA Québec
Chief Officer(s):
Jenn Norrie, CAMA AB Treasurer
Membership: *Fees:* $140
Activities: Offering professional development seminars; Providing networking opportunities
Publications:
• CAMA [Canadian Agri-Marketing Association] Membership Directory
Type: Directory
Profile: Contact information for CAMA members throughout Canada
• MarketNews [a publication of the Canadian Agri-Marketing Association]
Type: Newsletter; *Frequency:* 5 pa
Profile: Association events & industry information for members

Canadian Agri-Marketing Association (Manitoba)

210 - 1600 Kenaston Blvd., Winnipeg MB R3P 0Y4
Tel: 204-799-2019; *Fax:* 204-257-5651
camamb@mts.net
www.cama.org/manitoba/ManitobaHome.aspx
Also Known As: CAMA Manitoba
Overview: A small provincial organization founded in 1985 overseen by Canadian Agri-Marketing Association
Mission: To promote excellence in agrimarketing
Affliation(s): CAMA Ontario; CAMA Alberta; CAMA Saskatchewan
Chief Officer(s):
Barbara Chabih, President
Finances: *Annual Operating Budget:* Less than $50,000
Staff Member(s): 1; 12 volunteer(s)
Membership: 125 individual; *Fees:* $100 individual; $25 student

Canadian Agri-Marketing Association (Saskatchewan)

PO Box 4005, Regina SK S4P 3R9
Tel: 303-262-0733
camask@sasktel.net
www.cama.org/saskatchewan/saskatchewanHome.aspx
Also Known As: CAMA Saskatchewan
Overview: A medium-sized provincial organization overseen by Canadian Agri-Marketing Association
Mission: To operate as a networking organization for all sectors of Saskatchewan's agricultural industry
Chief Officer(s):
Lesley Kelly, President
Membership: *Committees:* Events & Programs; Membership; Membership Communications; Promotions / Public Relations; Website

Canadian AIDS Society (CAS) / Société canadienne du sida (SCS)

#100, 190 O'Connor St., Ottawa ON K2P 2R3
Tel: 613-230-3580; *Fax:* 613-563-4998
Toll-Free: 800-499-1986
casinfo@cdnaids.ca
www.cdnaids.ca
www.facebook.com/aidsida
twitter.com/CDNAIDS
Overview: A medium-sized national charitable organization founded in 1988
Mission: To strengthen the response to HIV/AIDS across Canada; To enrich the lives of people living with HIV/AIDS
Chief Officer(s):
Albert McNutt, Chair
albertm@cdnaids.ca
Jim Kane, Vice-Chair
jimk@cdnaids.ca
Monique Doolittle-Romas, Chief Executive Officer
moniquedr@cdnaids.ca
Simonne LeBlanc, Secretary
simonnel@cdnaids.ca
Gary Lacasse, Treasurer
garyl@cdnaids.ca
Ahmed Bechir, Director, Youth
ahmedh@cdnaids.ca
Finances: *Funding Sources:* Membership fees; Sponsorships; Fundraising
Membership: 120+ organizations; *Fees:* Schedule available; *Member Profile:* Community-based AIDS organizations across Canada
Activities: Promoting awareness & education; Offering information; Advocating on federal public policy; Establishing networking groups; *Awareness Events:* AIDS Walk for Life; Annual World AIDS Day, December 1; *Speaker Service:* Yes
Awards:
• Canadian AIDS Society Leadership Award (Award)
National contribuitions made in the fight again HIV/AIDS
Publications:
• Canadian AIDS Society Annual Report
Type: Yearbook; *Frequency:* Annually
Profile: Society's achievements, finances, supporters, & volunteers
• InfoCAS
Type: Newsletter; *Frequency:* Quarterly; *Price:* Free
Profile: HIV/AIDS national policy, governmental news, & activities of member groups
• InFocus
Type: Newsletter; *Frequency:* Semiannually
Profile: Examination of HIV/AIDS issues, ideas, & information

Canadian AIDS Treatment Information Exchange (CATIE) / Réseau canadien d'info-traitements sida

PO Box 1104, #505, 555 Richmond St. West, Toronto ON M5V 3B1
Tel: 416-203-7122; *Fax:* 416-203-8284
Toll-Free: 800-263-1638
questions@catie.ca
www.catie.ca
www.facebook.com/CATIEInfo
twitter.com/CATIEInfo
www.youtube.com/catieinfo
Previous Name: Community AIDS Treatment Information Exchange
Overview: A small national charitable organization founded in 1989
Mission: To improve the health & quality of life of all people living with HIV/AIDS (PHAs) in Canada; to provide HIV/AIDS treatment information to PHAs, caregivers & AIDS service organizations who are encouraged to be active partners in achieving informed decision-making & optimal health care
Member of: Canadian AIDS Society; Ontario AIDS Network; Ontario Hospital Association
Chief Officer(s):
Laurie Edmiston, Executive Director
ledmiston@catie.ca
Finances: *Annual Operating Budget:* Greater than $5 Million
Staff Member(s): 40
Membership: 2,300+; *Member Profile:* HIV+ individuals; allied health care professionals; community health organizations
Activities: Current & confidential treatment information; print publications; extensive website; *Awareness Events:* World AIDS Day, Dec. 1; *Speaker Service:* Yes; *Library:* CATIE Resources; by appointment
Meetings/Conferences: • Canadian AIDS Treatment Information Exchange Forum 2015, October, 2015, Toronto, ON
Scope: National

Canadian Air Cushion Technology Society (CACTS)

c/o Canadian Aeronautics & Space Institute, #104, 350 Terry Fox Dr., Kanata ON K2K 2W5
Tel: 613-591-8787; *Fax:* 613-591-7291
www.casi.ca/canadian-air-cushion-tech-soc
Overview: A small national organization overseen by Canadian Aeronautics & Space Institute
Mission: To serve the air cushion technology (hovercraft) community throughout Canada; To advance the science, technologies, & applications of air cushion technology
Chief Officer(s):
Jacques Laframboise, Society Chair
malina1@vif.com
Activities: Providing air cushion technology information; Liaising with other organizations interested in hovercraft;

Canadian Air Line Pilots Association *See* Air Line Pilots Association, International - Canada

Canadian Air Traffic Control Association (CATCA) / Association canadienne du contrôle du trafic aérien (ACCTA)
#304, 265 Carling Ave., Ottawa ON K1S 2E1
Tel: 613-225-3553; *Fax:* 613-225-8448
catca@catca.ca
www.catca.ca
www.facebook.com/CATCA5454
twitter.com/CATCA5454
Overview: A medium-sized national organization founded in 1959
Mission: To represent the air traffic controllers of Canada
Chief Officer(s):
Peter Duffey, President
Doug Best, Executive Vice-President
Membership: *Committees:* Convention; Contract; Election; Occupational Health & Safety
Meetings/Conferences: • Canadian Air Traffic Control Association 2016 Convention, April 2016, 2016, Halifax, NS
Scope: National
Description: A biennial convention attended by delegates from regions across Canada

Canadian Airports Council (CAC) / Conseil des aéroports du Canada
#600, 116 Lisgar St., Ottawa ON K2P 0C2
Tel: 613-560-9302; *Fax:* 613-560-6599
www.cacairports.ca
Overview: A medium-sized national organization founded in 1991
Mission: To act as the voice for Canadian airports on a great range of important issues
Member of: Airports Council International - North America (ACI-NA)
Affliation(s): Air Transport Association of Canada (ATAC); Canadian International Freight Forwarders Association (CIFFA); Canadian Chamber of Commerce; Canadian Tourism Commission; Tourism Industry Association of Canada (TIAC)
Chief Officer(s):
Daniel-Robert Gooch, President, 613-560-9302 Ext. 16
daniel.gooch@cacairports.ca
Nicole Larocque, Administrative Assistant, 613-560-9302 Ext. 14
nicole.larocque@cacairports.ca
Finances: *Funding Sources:* Sponsorships
Membership: 48; *Member Profile:* Canadian airports (CAC members are also members of Airports Council International - North America)
Activities: Preparing submissions to governmental bodies & agencies
Publications:
• The Airport Voice: News & Views
Type: Newsletter
Profile: National & international news affecting Canadian airports
• The Canadian Airports Council Annual Report
Type: Yearbook; *Frequency:* Annually
Profile: Significant developments at the CAC & in the industry during the year

Canadian Alarm & Security Association ***See*** Canadian Security Association

Canadian Albacore Association (CAA)
PO Box 98093, 970 Queen St. East, Toronto ON M4M 1J8
www.albacore.ca
www.facebook.com/pages/Canadian-Albacore-Association/160940480620584
twitter.com/AlbacoreSailCan
Overview: A small national organization founded in 1961
Mission: To promote & support the development of the Albacore fleet
Chief Officer(s):
Mary Neumann, Commodore
John Cawthorne, Treasurer
Membership: *Fees:* $60 full member; $27 associate member; $21 youth member; *Member Profile:* Canadian owners & sailors of Albacore dinghies
Activities: Sharing news & information about Canadian Albacore sailing; Sponsoring events & regattas
Publications:
• Shackles & Cringles
Type: Newsletter; *Frequency:* Quarterly; *Editor:* Jelena Balic; *Price:* Free to members

Canadian Alliance for Long Term Care (CALTC)
e-mail: info@caltc.ca
www.caltc.ca
Overview: A medium-sized national organization
Mission: To ensure the delivery fo quality care to vulnerable citizens of Canada
Chief Officer(s):
Gail Paech, Contact & CEO, Ontario Long Term Care Association
gpaech@oltca.com
Membership: *Member Profile:* Provincial associations & publicly funded long term care providers

Canadian Alliance for the Safe & Effective Use of Medications in Pregnancy & Breastfeeding
4 Innovation Dr., Dundas ON L9H 7P3
Tel: 905-689-3980; *Fax:* 905-689-1465
info@pregmedic.org
www.pregmedic.org
Also Known As: Pregmedic
Overview: A small national organization
Mission: To advocate for maternal, fetal, & neonatal health, especially with regard to the safety of medications during pregnancy & breastfeeding; To ensure that health care professionals & patients have access to current & reliable information about the safety & efficacy of medications used during pregnancy & breastfeeding
Chief Officer(s):
David Knoppert, Chair, Pregmedic
dknoppert@pregmedic.org
Karen Laurriston, Executive Director
klauriston@pregmedic.org
Membership: 1-99; *Member Profile:* Health professionals, health care policy experts, academia, & industry individuals who address issues related to the use of medications during pregnancy & breastfeeding
Activities: Developing the best knowledge & information possible regarding the use of drugs during pregnancy or breastfeeding & their potential effects upon vulnerable populations; Liaising with Health Canada, the medical community, & the pharmaceutical industry; Advocating for the development of patient registries & follow-up for the use of medications during pregnancy & breastfeeding in Canada
Publications:
• CaseMed-Pregnancy Resource Newsletter
Type: Newsletter
Profile: Recent resources about the use of medications during pregnancy & breastfeeding

Canadian Alliance of British Pensioners (CABP)
#202, 4800 Dundas St. West, Toronto ON M9A 1B1
Tel: 416-253-6402
Toll-Free: 888-591-3964
info@britishpensions.com
www.britishpensions.com
www.facebook.com/131267116913840
twitter.com/CABP_News
www.youtube.com/user/ICBPandCABP
Overview: A medium-sized national organization
Mission: To campaign politically to cease the freezing of British state pensions paid in certain countries
Member of: International Consortium of British Pensioners
Chief Officer(s):
Sheila Telford, Chair
Finances: *Funding Sources:* Membership fees; Campaigning
Membership: *Fees:* $25; $40 international; *Member Profile:* Current & soon to be expatriate British pensioners in Canada
Activities: Providing information & advice to members about British state pensions; Organizing public information meetings about the legal challenge against the United Kingdom government's pension-freezing policy;
Publications:
• Justice
Type: Magazine; *Frequency:* Quarterly; *Price:* Free with membership in the Canadian Alliance of British Pensioners
Profile: Current information about pension issues & the Alliance's campaign to end pension discrimination

British Pensioners Association of Western Canada
211 Fonda Way SE, Calgary AB T2A 4Z7
Tel: 403-730-0525
expats@britishpensioners.com
www.britishpensioners.com
Chief Officer(s):
Jonathan Macfarland, President

Canadian Alliance of Community Health Centre Associations (CACHCA) / Regroupement canadien des associations de centres communautaires de santé
c/o North End Community Health Centre, 2165 Gottingen St, Halifax NS B3K 3B5
Tel: 613-238-8210; *Fax:* 613-238-7595
cachca@sympatico.ca
www.cachca.ca
www.facebook.com/CACHCA.RCACCS
twitter.com/CACHCA_RCACCS
Overview: A medium-sized national organization founded in 1995
Mission: To support provincially-based community health centre organizations in Canada; to represent community health centre organizations nationally; to improve health services in Canadian communities; to promote community health centre organizations for the delivery of primary health care
Chief Officer(s):
Scott Wolfe, Federal Coordinator
Jane Moloney, Chair
Jack McCarthy, Treasurer

Canadian Alliance of Physiotherapy Regulators / Alliance canadienne des organismes de réglementation de la physiothérapie
#501, 1243 Islington Ave., Toronto ON M8X 1Y9
Tel: 416-234-8800; *Fax:* 416-234-8820
email@alliancept.org
www.alliancept.org
Overview: A large national organization founded in 1987
Mission: To facilitate the sharing of information & build consensus on national regulatory issues in order to assist member regulators in fulfilling their mandate of protecting the public interest
Chief Officer(s):
Katya Duvalko, Chief Executive Officer, 416-234-8800 Ext. 224
Finances: *Annual Operating Budget:* $500,000-$1.5 Million
Staff Member(s): 8
Membership: 11 provincial physiotherapy regulators; *Fees:* Schedule available; *Member Profile:* Member boards must have provincial regulation respecting physiotherapists; *Committees:* CEO Review Committee; Governance and Nominations Committee; Evaluation Services Committee; Registrars' Committee
Activities: Credentialling; examinations
Publications:
• Canadian Alliance of Physiotherapy Regulators Annual Report
Type: Yearbook; *Frequency:* Annually

Canadian Alliance of Student Associations (CASA) / Alliance canadienne des associations étudiantes (ACAE)
130 Slater St., Ottawa ON K1P 6E2
Tel: 613-236-3457; *Fax:* 613-236-2386
www.casa-acae.com
www.facebook.com/casa.acae
twitter.com/casadaily
www.youtube.com/user/CASAACAE;
www.flickr.com/photos/casa-acae
Overview: A medium-sized national organization founded in 1995
Chief Officer(s):
Chris Saulnier, Chair, 902-494-1277
chair@casa.ca
Zach Dayler, National Director, 613-236-3457 Ext. 222
casand@casa.ca
Michael McDonald, Manager, Stakeholder Relations, 613-236-3457 Ext. 227
members@casa.ca
Matthew McMillan, Secretary, 403-220-3910
secretary@casa.ca
Ghislain LeBlanc, Treasurer, 506-858-4818
treasurer@casa.ca
Finances: *Funding Sources:* Membership dues
Membership: 27; *Member Profile:* Student associations & student unions from across Canada

Canadian Alliance on Mental Illness & Mental Health (CAMIMH)
#702, 141 Laurier Ave. West, Ottawa ON K1P 5J3
Tel: 613-237-2144; *Fax:* 613-237-1674
www.facebook.com/FaceMentalIllness
www.twitter.com/miawcanada
www.flickr.com/photos/45033589@N02
Overview: A medium-sized national organization founded in 1998

Mission: An alliance of mental health organizations comprised of health care providers and organizations representing persons with mental illness and their families and caregivers.
Activities: *Awareness Events:* Mental Illness Awareness Week

Canadian Alopecia Areata Foundation (CANAAF)
316 Kirkvalley Cres., Aurora ON L4G 7S1
e-mail: info@canaaf.org
canaaf.org
Overview: A medium-sized national charitable organization founded in 2009
Mission: To give support to people suffering from Alopecia Areata
Chief Officer(s):
Colleen Butler, President
colleen@canaaf.org

Canadian Amateur Bobsleigh & Luge Association *See* Canadian Luge Association

Canadian Amateur Boxing Association (CABA) / Association canadienne de boxe amateur (ACBA)
888 Belfast Rd., Ottawa ON K1G 0Z6
Tel: 613-238-7700; *Fax:* 613-238-1600
caba@boxing.ca
www.boxing.ca
www.facebook.com/BoxingCa
twitter.com/boxing_canada
Also Known As: Boxing Canada
Overview: A medium-sized national organization founded in 1969
Mission: To develop & maintain uniform rules & regulations to govern amateur boxing competitions in Canada; To develop coaches & officials; To organize national team programs, including development, training, & competition
Affliation(s): International Amateur Boxing Association
Chief Officer(s):
Robert G. Crête, Executive Director
robert.crete@boxing.ca
Daniel Trépanier, Director, High Performance
robert.crete@boxing.ca
Lynn Levis, Registrar
lynn@boxing.ca
Activities: Providing news & results about the sport;
Awards:
- Male Rookie of the Year (Award)
- Female Rookie of the Year (Award)
- Male Boxer of the Year (Award)
- Female Boxer of the Year (Award)
- Most Courageous Boxer (Award)

The Canadian Amateur Brewers Association
#749, 2255B Queen St. East, Toronto ON M4E 1G3
e-mail: homebrewer@sympatico.ca
www.homebrewers.ca
Overview: A small national organization founded in 1964
Mission: To promote homebrewing & to educate home brewers through seminars, workshops & publications
Chief Officer(s):
Kevin Tighe, President
Membership: *Fees:* $10

Canadian Amateur DanceSport Association *See* Canada DanceSport

Canadian Amateur Musicians (CAMMAC) / Musiciens amateurs du Canada
85 Cammac Rd., Harrington QC J8G 2T2
Tel: 819-687-3938; *Fax:* 819-687-3323
Toll-Free: 888-622-8755
national@cammac.ca
www.cammac.ca
www.linkedin.com/company/centre-musical-du-lac-macdonald-cammac-lake-m
www.facebook.com/cammacmusic
twitter.com/CAMMACMUSIC
www.youtube.com/user/MusicCentreLakeMacDo
Overview: A medium-sized national charitable organization founded in 1953
Mission: To create opportunities for musicians of all levels & ages to play music in a non-competitive environment
Chief Officer(s):
Raymond Vies, President
rvles@vles.ca
Caroline Rider, Secretary
caroline.rider@yahoo.com
Urseula Kobel, Treasurer
ukobel@gmail.com
Margaret Little, Executive Director
mlittle@cammac.ca
Patricia Abbott, Artistic Director
abbottpat@uniserve.com
Jacques Turner, Controller
j.turner@cammac.ca
Finances: *Funding Sources:* Membership fees; Donations
Staff Member(s): 10; 50 volunteer(s)
Membership: 2,200; *Fees:* $30 students & seniors; $35 individuals; $55 families; $200 groups; *Member Profile:* Amateur musicians from across Canada & other countries
Activities: Offering a music library with over 10,000 scores; Maintaining the Lake MacDonald Music Centre site; Organizing summer musical programs; Developing school & community programs; *Internships:* Yes; *Library:* CAMMAC Music Library;
Publications:
- The Amateur Musician
Type: Journal; *Frequency:* Semiannually; *Accepts Advertising*; *Editor:* Peter Lowensteyn; Madeleine Little *ISSN:* 0227-4310
Profile: Articles & news for amateur musicians

Montréal Region
Montréal QC
www.cammac.ca
Mission: To offer music making activities in the Montréal area
Chief Officer(s):
David Bernard, President, 514-487-1957
dn_bernard@yahoo.ca
François Marcotte, Secretary, 514-658-0828
frs.marcotte@videotron.ca
Sally Campbell, Co-Treasurer, 514-842-3011
sally.campbell@mcgill.ca
Sean McCutcheon, Co-Treasurer, 514-842-3011
montrealsean@gmail.com
- Express
Type: Newsletter; *Frequency:* 5 pa; *Editor:* Peter Lowensteyn
ISSN: 1493-0129
Profile: Musical activities & happening in the Montréal area for members of Canadian Amateur Musicians, Montréal Region

Ottawa-Gatineau Region
309 Olmstead St., Ottawa ON K1L 7K2
Tel: 613-860-1751
ottawagatineau@cammac.ca
www.cammac.ca
Mission: To offer musical activities for amateur musicians in the Ottawa-Gatineau region
Chief Officer(s):
Janet Stevens, President
Diana Winninger, Secretary
Daniela Planka, Treasurer
- Canadian Amateur Musicians, Ottawa-Gatineau Region Newsletter
Type: Newsletter; *Frequency:* Quarterly; *Accepts Advertising*; *Editor:* Susan Isaac
Profile: News items, announcements, & event reports for members of the Canadian Amateur Musicians Ottawa-Gatineau region

Québec Region
Québec QC
Tel: 418-659-7344
cammac.quebec@gmail.com.
Mission: To provide music making opportunities for amateur musicians in the Québec City area
Chief Officer(s):
Mireille Barry, President
Marie Garon, Secretary

Toronto Region
83 Bellefair Ave., Toronto ON M4L 3T7
Tel: 416-421-0779
toronto@cammac.ca
Chief Officer(s):
Tim Moody, President
tim@timmoody.com
- CAMMAC [Canadian Amateur Musicians] Toronto Region Newsletter
Type: Newsletter; *Frequency:* 5 pa; *Accepts Advertising*; *Editor:* Riccarda Balogh; *Price:* Free with Canadian Amateur Musicians Toronto Regionmembership
Profile: Local CAMMAC Toronto news, articles, & information about forthcoming events

Canadian Amateur Radio Federation *See* Radio Amateurs of Canada Inc.

Canadian Amateur Softball Association
#212, 223 Colonnade Rd., Ottawa ON K2E 7K3
Tel: 613-523-3386; *Fax:* 613-523-5761
info@softball.ca
www.softball.ca
www.facebook.com/SoftballCanadaNSO
twitter.com/softballcanada
Also Known As: Softball Canada
Overview: A medium-sized national organization founded in 1965
Mission: To develop & promote softball in Canada
Chief Officer(s):
Kevin Quinn, President
kevin.quinn1@pei.sympatico.ca
Hugh Mitchener, CEO
hmitchener@softball.ca
Staff Member(s): 8
Membership: 13 provincial/territorial associations

Canadian Amateur Synchronized Swimming Association *See* Synchro Canada

Canadian Amateur Synchronized Swimming Association (Manitoba Section) *See* Synchro Manitoba

Canadian Amateur Wrestling Association (CAWA) / Association canadienne de lutte amateur
#7, 5370 Canotek Rd., Gloucester ON K1J 9E6
Tel: 613-748-5686; *Fax:* 613-748-5756
info@wrestling.ca
www.wrestling.ca
Also Known As: Wrestling Canada Lutte
Overview: A medium-sized national organization founded in 1970
Mission: To operate as the national sport governing body for Olympic style wrestling in Canada; To implement a long term athlete development model; To develop coaches, officials, & administrators; To achieve podium finishes for Canadian wrestlers at World Championships & Olympic Games
Chief Officer(s):
Tamara Medwidsky, Executive Director
Doug Cox, President
Clint Kingsbury, Manager, Domestic Development
Dave Mair, Manager, High Performance
Dave McKay, National Coach, Senior Men
Leigh Vierling, National Coach, Senior Women
Finances: *Funding Sources:* Sponsorships
Membership: *Committees:* Executive; High Performance; Coaching Education & Certification; Science & Medical; International Team; Development; Marketing; Hall of Fame
Activities: Encouraging participation in Olympic wrestling in Canada; Liaising with provincial sport governing bodies; Selecting & preparing Canada's teams which compete at the world championships & multi-sport events, such as the Olympic Games; Overseeing three national championships & one international cup on an annual basis
Meetings/Conferences: • Canadian Amateur Wrestling Association / Association canadienne de lutte amateur 2015 Annual General Meeting, 2015
Scope: National

Canadian Amputee Golf Association (CAGA)
PO Box 6091, Stn. A, Calgary AB T2H 2L4
e-mail: canamps@caga.ca
www.caga.ca
Overview: A small national organization founded in 2000
Mission: To provide support for amputees both before & after amputation; To raise awareness to the general population on the effects of amputation; To offer rehabilitation, through teaching amputees golf; To run amputee golf tournaments
Chief Officer(s):
Gwen Davies, President
Membership: *Fees:* $25; $150 lifetime

Canadian Amputee Sports Association (CASA) / Association canadienne des sports pour amputés
c/o Dale Murphy, 1126 Millcove Rd., RR#1, Mount Stewart PE C0A 1T0
www.canadianamputeesports.ca
Overview: A medium-sized national charitable organization founded in 1977
Mission: To promote & organize amateur sport competitions in Canada for persons who are without a limb or part of a limb; To promote research in prosthetic devices for sport activities; To select a Canadian national team for participation in international sports events for amputees
Affliation(s): Canadian Paralympic Committee; Hockey Canada

Chief Officer(s):
James Reilly, President
jf.reilly@hotmail.com
Dale Murphy, Secretary
dj.murphy@pei.sympatico.ca
Wayne Epp, Treasurer
wepp@telus.net
Finances: *Funding Sources:* Membership dues
10 volunteer(s)
Membership: *Member Profile:* Amputees & other athletes

Canadian Andropause Society *See* Canadian Society for the Study of the Aging Male

Canadian Anesthesiologists' Society (CAS) / Société canadienne des anesthésiologistes (SCA)

#208, One Eglinton Ave. East, Toronto ON M4P 3A1
Tel: 416-480-0602; *Fax:* 416-480-0320
anesthesia@cas.ca
www.cas.ca
twitter.com/CASUpdate
Overview: A large national organization founded in 1943
Mission: To advance the medical practice of anesthesia throughout Canada
Affliation(s): Canadian Anesthesia Research Foundation (CARF); CAS International Education Foundation (CAS IEF)
Chief Officer(s):
Richard Chisholm, President
Richard Chisholm, Vice-President
Stanley Mandarich, Executive Director
director@cas.ca
Patricia Houston, Secretary
Susan O'Leary, Treasurer
Membership: *Fees:* $575 active; $510 associate; $460 associate, not residing in Canada; *Member Profile:* Canadian anesthesiologists; *Committees:* Allied Health Professions; Annual Meeting; Local Arrangements; Scientific Affairs; Archivist; By-Law & Constitution; Continuing Education & Professional Development; Ethics; Finance; Medical Economics; Membership Services; Nominations; Patient Safety; Physician Resources; Research; Standards
Activities: Presenting professional development opportunities; Promoting excellent patient care; Supporting research
Awards:
• The Gold Medal (Award)
The highest award of the Canadian Anesthesiologists' Society for an individual who has made a significant contribution to anesthesia in Canada
• Clinical Teacher Award (Award)
To recognize excellence in the teaching of clinical anesthesia
• Clinical Practitioner Award (Award)
To recognize excellence in clinical anesthesia practice
• John Bradley Young Educator Award (Award)
To recognize excellence & effectiveness in education in anesthesia
• Research Recognition Awardr Award (Award)
To recognize a senior investigator who has sustained major contributions in anesthesia research in Canada
• Medical Student Prize (Award)
Eligibility: Full-time medical students in any Canadian medical school
• CAS Career Scientist Award in Anesthesia (Award)
• New Investigator Operating Grants (Grant)
• Subspecialty Operating Grants (Grant)
• Open Operating Grants (Grant)
Meetings/Conferences: • Canadian Anesthesiologists' Society 2015 71st Annual Meeting, June, 2015, Ottawa Convention Centre, Ottawa, ON
Scope: National
Description: A convention, with an exhibition pharmaceutical companies & equipment manufacturers
• Canadian Anesthesiologists' Society 2016 72nd Annual Meeting, June, 2016, Vancouver Convention Centre, Vancouver, BC
Scope: National
Description: A convention, with an exhibition pharmaceutical companies & equipment manufacturers
• Canadian Anesthesiologists' Society 2017 73rd Annual Meeting, June, 2017, Scotiabank Convention Centre, Niagara Falls, ON
Scope: National
Description: A convention, with an exhibition pharmaceutical companies & equipment manufacturers
• Canadian Anesthesiologists' Society 2018 74th Annual Meeting, June, 2018, Palais de Congrès, Montreal, QC
Scope: National
Description: A convention, with an exhibition pharmaceutical companies & equipment manufacturers
• Canadian Anesthesiologists' Society 2019 75th Annual Meeting, June, 2019, Telus Convention Centre, Calgary, AB
Scope: National
Description: A convention, with an exhibition pharmaceutical companies & equipment manufacturers
Publications:
• Anesthesia News
Type: Newsletter; *Frequency:* Quarterly; *Editor:* Dr. Patricia Houston
Profile: Society updates, including events, prizes, & research
• Canadian Anesthesiologists' Society Annual Report
Type: Yearbook; *Frequency:* Annually
• Canadian Journal of Anesthesia / Journal canadien d'anesthésie
Type: Journal; *Frequency:* Monthly; *Editor:* Donald R. Miller, MD, FRCPC *ISSN:* 0832-610X
Profile: Peer-reviewed clinical research, basic research, & expert reviews & opinions to assist anesthesiologists
• Guidelines to the Practice of Anesthesia
Price: $25

Canadian Angelman Syndrome Society (CASS) / Société canadienne du syndrome d'Angelman (SCSA)

PO Box 37, Priddis AB T0L 1W0
Tel: 403-931-2415; *Fax:* 403-931-4237
info@angelmancanada.org
www.angelmancanada.org
Overview: A small national organization
Mission: To educate concerned families, medical & educational communities & the general public about Angelman Syndrome; to establish & maintain support systems; to promote research activities on the diagnosis, treatment, management & prevention of Angelman syndrome; to fundraise
Chief Officer(s):
John Carscallen, Secretary-Treasurer
cass@davincibb.net
13 volunteer(s)
Membership: 1-99

Canadian Angus Association (CAA) / L'Association canadienne Angus

#142, 6715 - 8 St. NE, Calgary AB T2E 7H7
Tel: 403-571-3580; *Fax:* 403-571-3599
Toll-Free: 888-571-3580
www.cdnangus.ca
www.facebook.com/CanadianAngusAssociation
www.youtube.com/user/CanadianAngusAssoc/videos
Also Known As: Canadian Aberdeen Angus Association
Overview: A small national organization founded in 1906
Mission: To offer services to enhance the growth & position of the Angus breed; To maintain breed purity
Member of: Canadian Beef Breeds Council
Chief Officer(s):
Doug Fee, Chief Executive Officer
Bob Switzer, President
Sharmayne Byrgesen, Registrar
Membership: *Fees:* $50 individuals, partnerships, & corporations; $10 juniors; *Member Profile:* Individuals; Partnerships; Incorporated companies
Activities: Maintaining breed registry
Publications:
• Aberdeen Angus World
Type: Magazine; *Frequency:* 5 pa; *Editor:* Dave Callaway; *Price:* $25 Canadian; $35 USA; $50 Foreign
• CAA [Canadian Angus Association] Newsletter
Type: Newsletter
Profile: Angus news & events

Canadian Animal Health Institute (CAHI) / Institut canadien de la santé animale (ICSA)

#102, 160 Research Lane, Guelph ON N1G 5B2
Tel: 519-763-7777; *Fax:* 519-763-7407
cahi@cahi-icsa.ca
www.cahi-icsa.ca
Overview: A medium-sized national organization founded in 1968
Mission: To work closely with allied industry groups for the betterment of Canadian agriculture; To foster & maintain a regulatory & legislative climate which will encourage member companies to develop & market useful animal health products & services; To promote the proper use of animal health & nutrition products by livestock & poultry farmers through user education information programs; To develop a public information program which enhances appreciation of the contributions the animal health & nutrition industry makes to the economy & society
Chief Officer(s):
Jean Szkotnicki, President
Tracey Firth, Director, Programs
Finances: *Funding Sources:* Membership dues
Staff Member(s): 3
Membership: 60 organizations
Awards:
• Industry Leadership Award (Award)
Meetings/Conferences: • Canadian Animal Health Institute 2015 Annual Meeting, 2015
Scope: National
Description: An exploration of predictions in the industry, plus strategies to prepare for change. The Board of Directors is elected annually.
Publications:
• CAHI [Canadian Animal Health Institute] Resource Directory
Type: Directory; *Frequency:* Biennially
Profile: Listings of CAHI members, veterinary associations, government agencies related to animal health, commodity organizations, & CAHI's foreign sisterorganizations
• Inforum [a publication of the Canadian Animal Health Institute]
Type: Newsletter; *Frequency:* 4 pa
Profile: Distributed to Canadian veterinarians in the Canadian Veterinary Journal

Canadian Anthropology Society (CASCA) / Société canadienne d'Anthropologie

c/o Department of Sociology & Anthropology, Carleton University, 1125 Colonel By Dr., Ottawa ON K1S 5B6
Other Communication: membership@anthropologica.ca
www.cas-sca.ca
Overview: A small national organization
Mission: To promote anthropology in Canada
Member of: World Council of Anthropological Associations
Chief Officer(s):
Regna Darnell, President
rdarnell@uwo.ca
Robert Adlam, Treasurer
radlam@mta.ca
Activities: Supporting anthropological research; Sharing anthropological knowledge with the academic community & the public; *Awareness Events:* Third Annual Anthropology Film Festival
Publications:
• Anthropologica
Type: Journal; *Frequency:* Semiannually; *Editor:* Andrew Lyons; *Price:* Free to CASCA members
Profile: Peer-reviewed articles about social & cultural issues
• Culture: The Newsletter for the Canadian Anthropology Society
Type: Newsletter; *Editor:* Daphne Winlan & Karine Vanthuyne
Profile: News, book notes

Canadian Anti-Counterfeiting Network (CACN)

#300, 180 Attwell Dr., Toronto ON M9W 6A9
Tel: 647-260-3090; *Fax:* 416-679-9234
cacn@electrofed.com
www.cacn.ca
twitter.com/BuyTheRealThing
Overview: A small national organization
Mission: The Canadian Anti-Counterfeiting Network (CACN) is a coalition of individuals, companies firms and associations that have united in the fight against product counterfeiting and copyright piracy in Canada and Internationally.
Chief Officer(s):
Wayne Edwards, Chair
wedwards@electrofed.com
Membership: *Fees:* $1,500

Canadian Anti-Money Laundering Institute (CAMLI)

PO Box 427, 629 St. Lawrence St., Merrickville ON K0G 1N0
Tel: 613-269-2619; *Fax:* 613-526-9384
contactus@camli.org
www.camli.org
www.linkedin.com/company/canadian-anti-money-laundering-institute-caml
www.twitter.com/CAMLIorg
Overview: A small national organization
Mission: CAMLI is an education and resource forum for anti-money laundering compliance professionals.
Membership: *Fees:* Two-year general membership: $400 + HST; *Member Profile:* Canadian-based and international compliance professionals
Activities: Training Programs

Meetings/Conferences: • Money Laundering in Canada 2015 Conference, September, 2015, Banff Springs Hotel, Banff, AB
Scope: National

Canadian Antique Phonograph Society (CAPS)
122 Major St., Toronto ON M5S 2L2
e-mail: info@capsnews.org
www.capsnews.org
Overview: A small national organization founded in 1970
Mission: To share information about phonographs, gramophones, all types of sound recordings of historical importance, ephemera & related memorabilia with emphasis on the history of the phonograph & recorded sound in Canada.
Chief Officer(s):
Mike Bryan, President
Bill Pratt, Treasurer
Membership: 225+; *Fees:* $35
Activities: 8 meetings with presentations annually

Canadian Apheresis Group (CAG) / Groupe canadien d'aphérèse
#199, 435 St. Laurent Blvd., Ottawa ON K1K 2Z8
Tel: 613-748-9613; *Fax:* 613-748-6392
cag@ca.inter.net
www.apheresis.ca
Overview: A small national organization founded in 1980
Mission: To provide a forum for information exchange among apheresis practioners in Canada; To promote clinical research in apheresis
Chief Officer(s):
Gail Rock, Chair
Membership: Representatives from 42 apheresis units in 19 medical centers in Canada; *Member Profile:* Physicians; Nurses
Activities: Collecting & reviewing information on apheresis procedures;

Canadian Apparel Federation (CAF) / Fédération canadienne du vêtement
#708, 151 Slater St., Ottawa ON K1P 5H3
Tel: 613-231-3220; *Fax:* 613-231-2305
info@apparel.ca
www.apparel.ca
www.linkedin.com/company/canadian-apparel-federation
www.facebook.com/102242196491712
twitter.com/caf_apparel
Previous Name: Canadian Apparel Manufacturers Institute
Overview: A large national organization
Mission: To provide a forum for provincial apparel associations representing the vast majority of the country's manufacturers; To exercise leadership in relations with government, suppliers & the general public
Chief Officer(s):
Bob Kirke, Executive Director
bkirke@apparel.ca
Finances: *Funding Sources:* Membership fees; sponsorship
Membership: *Fees:* Schedule available; *Member Profile:* Canadian firms engaged in apparel manufacture or marketing, & suppliers to the apparel industry
Activities: Industry information & resources
Publications:
• Apparel Directory
Type: Directory; *Editor:* editor@apparel.ca
Profile: Listings of manufacturers, importers, & designers in all apparel categories
• CAF/FCV [Canadian Apparel Federation/Fédération canadienne du vêtement] Bulletin
Type: Newsletter; *Editor:* editor@apparel.ca
• Directory of Suppliers to the Apparel Industry
Type: Directory; *Editor:* editor@apparel.ca
Profile: Listings of suppliers of textiles, trimmings, technology, & services

Canadian Apparel Manufacturers Institute ***See*** Canadian Apparel Federation

Canadian Applied & Industrial Mathematics Society (CAIMS) / Société canadienne de mathématiques appliquées et industrielles (SCMAI)
c/o Prof. Sharene Bungay, Dept. of Comp. Science, Memorial University, St. John's NL A1B 3X5
www.caims.ca
Overview: A small national organization
Chief Officer(s):
Jianhong Wu, President
wujh@mathstat.yorku.ca
Publications:
• Canadian Applied & Industrial Mathematics Society Newsletter
Type: Newsletter; *Frequency:* Quarterly
• Canadian Applied Mathematics Quarterly
Type: Journal; *Frequency:* Quarterly; *Editor:* Jack W. Macki; T. Bryant Moodie

Canadian Apprenticeship Forum (CAF) / Forum canadien sur l'apprentissage
#404, 2197 Riverside Dr., Ottawa ON K1H 7X3
Tel: 613-235-4004
www.caf-fca.org
www.linkedin.com/company/2231800
www.facebook.com/cafapprenticeship
twitter.com/CAF_FCA
www.youtube.com/user/cafapprenticeship
Overview: A small national organization
Mission: To bring together the key participants who make up the Canadian apprenticeship community
Chief Officer(s):
Sarah Watts-Rynard, Executive Director
Staff Member(s): 6
Membership: *Fees:* $100 contributer; $1,000 supporter; $3,000 patron; $5,000 champion
Activities: Promotion of apprenticeship; inventory/information project; accessibility & barriers to apprenticeship; common core;

Canadian Aquaculture Industry Alliance (CAIA) / Alliance de l'industrie canadienne de l'aquiculture
PO Box 81100, Stn. World Exchange Plaza, #705, 116 Albert St., Ottawa ON K1P 1B1
Tel: 613-239-0612; *Fax:* 613-239-0619
info@aquaculture.ca
www.aquaculture.ca
www.facebook.com/155794491097836
twitter.com/CDNaquaculture
www.youtube.com/channel/UCgg1cyvyiLcDP8lF81oHAWg
Overview: A medium-sized national organization founded in 1987
Mission: To represent the interests of aquaculture operators, feed companies, suppliers, & provincial finfish & shellfish aquaculture associations on both the national & international scenes; To ensure the international competitiveness of the Canadian aquaculture industry
Chief Officer(s):
Ruth Salmon, Executive Director, 613-239-0612, Fax: 613-239-0619
ruth.salmon@aquaculture.ca
Clare Backman, President
Membership: *Member Profile:* Aquaculture operators; Feed companies; Suppliers; Provincial shellfish & finfish aquaculture associations
Activities: Advocating for Canadian aquaculture issues; Fostering cooperation among various aquaculture interests; Promoting a positive image of the Canadian aquaculture industry; Encouraging the consumption of aquaculture products from Canada

Canadian Arab Federation (CAF) / La Fédération Canado-Arabe
1057 McNicoll Ave., Toronto ON M1W 3W6
Tel: 416-493-8635; *Fax:* 416-493-9239
Toll-Free: 866-886-4675
info@caf.ca
www.caf.ca
Overview: A medium-sized national organization founded in 1967
Mission: To represent Canadian Arabs on issues related to public policy; To protect civil liberties & the equality of human rights
Chief Officer(s):
Farid Ayad, President
Abdallah Alkrunz, Vice-President, East
Mohamed El Rashidy, Vice-President, West
Finances: *Funding Sources:* Donations
Membership: 40+ organizations; *Member Profile:* Arab-Canadian associations throughout Canada
Activities: Providing educational opportunities; Increasing public awareness; Liaising with all levels of government on issues important to Canadian Arabs; Handling media relations; Encouraging community empowerment, through civic participation; Promoting Arab & Muslim culture; Combatting racism; Fundraising; Offering networking opportunities; Providing job search workshops; Offering meeting rooms; Providing Arabic classes; *Speaker Service:* Yes; *Library:* Canadian Arab Federation Community Resource Library; Open to public
Publications:
• CAF [Canadian Arab Federation] Weekly Bulletin
Type: Newsletter; *Frequency:* Weekly
Profile: Current events, articles, & event announcements

Canadian Arab Horse Association ***See*** Canadian Arabian Horse Registry

Canadian Arabian Horse Registry
#113, 37 Athabascan Ave., Sherwood Park AB T8A 4H3
Tel: 780-416-4990; *Fax:* 780-416-4860
cahr@cahr.ca
www.cahr.ca
Previous Name: Canadian Arab Horse Association
Overview: A small national organization founded in 1958
Mission: To register purebred Arabian horses in Canada; to establish standards of breeding practices; To serve the needs of Arabian horse owners
Affliation(s): Canadian Equestrian Federation
Chief Officer(s):
Christine Tribe, Registrar
Marcia Friesen, President
Robert Sproule, Secretary-Treasurer
Membership: *Fees:* $68.25 Canadian residents; $78.75 international residents; *Member Profile:* Owners of Arabian horses
Activities: Encouraging the development of Arabian horses in Canada; Maintaining efficient inspection; Developing Arabian horse show rules in Canada
Publications:
• The CAHR [Canadian Arabian Horse Registry] Members' Directory
Type: Directory; *Frequency:* Annually
• Canadian Arabian Horse News
Type: Magazine; *Accepts Advertising; Editor:* Christina Weese; *Price:* $31.50 Canada; $40 International
Profile: Features include Canadian show results

Canadian Archaeological Association (CAA) / Association d'archéologie canadienne
c/o William Ross, 189 Peter St., Thunder Bay ON P7A 5H8
Tel: 807-345-2733
www.canadianarchaeology.com
Overview: A small national charitable organization founded in 1968
Mission: To publish & disseminate archaeological knowledge in Canada; To encourage archaeological research & conservation efforts; To promote cooperation among archaeological societies & agencies
Chief Officer(s):
William Ross, President, 807-345-2733
wiross@tbaytel.net
Jennifer Birch, Vice-President
jabirch@uga.edu
Jeff Hunston, Secretary-Treasurer, 867-667-5363
keeperaustraliamt@klondiker.com
Membership: *Fees:* $35 students; $75 regular; $100 institutional & supporting; *Member Profile:* Professional, avocational, & student archaeologists; General public; *Committees:* Heritage & Legislation Policy; Aboriginal Heritage; Student's; Membership; Cultural Resource Management; Financial Advisory; Public Communication Awards; Comité du Prix Weetaluktuk Award; James & Margaret Pendergast Award; Smith-Wintemberg Award
Activities: Fostering cooperation with aboriginal groups; Promoting activities advantageous to archaeology; Advocating nationally
Awards:
• Public Communication Awards (Award)
• Comité du Prix Weetaluktuk Award (Award)
• James & Margaret Pendergast Award (Award)
• Smith-Wintemberg Award (Award)
Meetings/Conferences: • Canadian Archaeological Association Annual Meeting 2015, April, 2015, St. John's, NL
Scope: National
Contact Information: Amanda Crompton, Conference Chair; caa2015aca@gmail.com
Publications:
• CAA [Canadian Archaeological Association] Newsletter / Bulletin de l'ACA [Association d'archéologie canadienne
Type: Newsletter; *Frequency:* Semiannually; *Editor:* Karen Ryan; *Price:* Free with membership in the CanadianArchaeological Association
Profile: A spring & fall publication

• Canadian Journal of Archaeology / Journal canadien d'archéologie
Type: Journal; *Frequency:* Semiannually; *Editor:* Dr. Gerry Oetelaar; *Price:* Free with membership in the Canadian ArchaeologicalAssociation
Profile: Documents the processes & results of Canadian archaeology

Canadian Architectural Certification Board (CACB) / Conseil canadien de certification en architecture (CCCA)

#710, 1 Nicholas St., Ottawa ON K1N 7B7
Tel: 613-241-8399; *Fax:* 613-241-7991
info@cacb.ca
www.cacb.ca
Overview: A medium-sized national licensing organization founded in 1976
Mission: The Canadian Architectural Certification Board fulfills two seperate but related mandates: 1- Administer a program of accreditation of the Canadaian schools of architecture in accordance with "Conditions and Procedures for Accreditation" approved by the CCAC and the CCUSA and 2- Administer a program of certification of the educational qualifications of indivdual applicants in accordance withe criteria contained within the "Education Standard" approved by the CCAC.
Chief Officer(s):
Branko Kolarevic, President
Myriam Blais, Vice-President
Finances: *Annual Operating Budget:* $100,000-$250,000; *Funding Sources:* Collateral organizations
Staff Member(s): 3; 100 volunteer(s)
Membership: *Member Profile:* Professional associations; university schools of architecture
Activities: Certification of educational qualifications for architects; accreditation of Canadian University Schools of Architecture

Canadian Arctic Resources Committee

488 Gladstone Ave., Ottawa ON K1N 8V4
Tel: 613-759-4284; *Fax:* 613-237-3845
Toll-Free: 866-949-9006
davidg@carc.org
www.carc.org
www.facebook.com/168782596508551
Overview: A medium-sized national organization
Mission: The Canadian Arctic Resources Committee (CARC) is a citizens' organization dedicated to the long-term environmental and social well being of northern Canada and its peoples.
Chief Officer(s):
Ben McDonald, Acting Chair

Canadian Arm Wrestling Federation (CAWF)

c/o Lise Blanchard, Secretary-Treasurer, 1216 Campeau Cres., Rockland ON K4K 1B4
Tel: 613-446-4685; *Fax:* 613-446-4685
www.cawf.ca
Overview: A medium-sized national organization
Mission: To oversee & promote the sport of arm wrestling in Canada.
Member of: World Arm Wrestling Federation
Chief Officer(s):
Fred Roy, President
fred.roy@sympatico.ca
Joey Costello, Vice-President
joeycostello@vianet.ca
Lise Blanchard, Secretary-Treasurer
Anthony Dall'Antonia, Director, Communications
vancouverarm@hotmail.com
Membership: 3,500; *Fees:* $20
Awards:
• The John Miazdzyk Award (Award)
For dedication to the sport of arm wrestling.

Canadian Armenian Business Council Inc. (CABC) / Conseil commercial canadien-arménien inc.

#102, 2425 de Salaberry, Montréal QC H3M 1L2
Tel: 514-333-7655; *Fax:* 514-333-7280
info@cabc.ca
www.cabc.ca
Overview: A small national organization founded in 1985
Mission: To promote & serve the Armenian business community; To act as a marketing tool for North American Armenian businesses
Chief Officer(s):
Paul Nahabedian, President, 514-878-5111, Fax: 514-878-5070
paul.nahabedian@rbc.com
Membership: *Fees:* $60 individuals; $100 corporations; $25 students; *Committees:* Membership; Events; Publications; Recognition of Excellence; Youth; Inter-trade; Sponsorships & Grants; Public Relations
Activities: Increasing communication & cooperation between Armenians in business; Providing business courses; Conducting market research; Promoting trade & investments; Participating in international trade missions
Publications:
• CABC [Canadian Armenian Business Council Inc.] Business Directory
Type: Directory

The Canadian Art Foundation

#320, 215 Spadina Ave., Toronto ON M5T 2C7
Tel: 416-368-8854; *Fax:* 416-368-6135
Toll-Free: 800-222-4762
info@canadianart.ca
www.canadianart.ca
www.facebook.com/canadianart
twitter.com/canartca
vimeo.com/channels/canadianart; canadianart.tumblr.com
Overview: A medium-sized national charitable organization founded in 1991
Mission: To foster & support the visual arts in Canada & to celebrate artists & their creativity with a program of events, lectures, competitions, publications & educational initiatives.
Member of: Canadian Magazine Publishers Association
Chief Officer(s):
Ann Webb, Executive Director
Romina Tina Fontana, Director, Marketing & Communications
Ann Webb, Publisher, Canadian Art
Richard Rhodes, Editor, Canadian Art
rhodes@canadianart.ca
Finances: *Annual Operating Budget:* $500,000-$1.5 Million; *Funding Sources:* Government grants; ad sales; circulation; private
Staff Member(s): 5; 1 volunteer(s)
Activities: Programs include: Gallery Events; Film Festival; International Speaker Series; Tours; Writing Prize; Anne Lind International Program; RBC Canadian Painting Competition; Editorial Residency; & School Hop.; *Internships:* Yes; *Rents Mailing List:* Yes
Publications:
• Canadian Art
Type: Magazine; *Frequency:* Quarterly; *Accepts Advertising*; *Editor:* Richard Rhodes *ISSN:* 0825-3854; *Price:* $24 Canada; $34 USA; $42 International - plus applicable taxes

Canadian Art Therapy Association (CATA) / L'association canadienne d'art thérapie

26 Earl Grey Rd., Toronto ON M4J 3L2
www.catainfo.ca
Overview: A small national organization founded in 1977
Mission: To promote the development & maintenance of professional standards of art therapy training, registration, research, & practice in Canada; To heighten awareness of art therapy as an important mental health discipline
Chief Officer(s):
Nick Zwaagstra, President
Lori Boyko, Registrar
Marie Alexander, Chair, Ethics
Olena Darewych, Chair, Membership
Membership: *Fees:* $25 students; $50 associate members; $70 professional members; $95 registered members; *Member Profile:* Art therapists, who have a R.C.A.T.,or equivalent; Art therapists, who have finished professional post-graduate training & are active in the field; Individuals interested in the promotion of art therapy may be associate members; Students, who are enrolled in a Canadian graduate art therapy program
Activities: Facilitating the exchange & collaboration of art therapists, students, & professionals in related fields; Fostering research; Organizing educational opportunities, such as lectures, seminars, & workshops
Awards:
• Art Therapy Student Bursary (Scholarship)
Amount: $1,000
• Research Award for an Art Therapy Student (Scholarship)
Amount: $1,000
• Research Award for a Registered Art Therapist (Scholarship)
Amount: $1,000
Publications:
• Canadian Art Therapy Association Directory
Type: Directory
Profile: Listings of professional & registered art therapists, who are members of the Canadian Art Therapy Association & who chose to be listed in the directory
• Canadian Art Therapy Association Journal
Type: Journal; *Frequency:* Semiannually; *Editor:* Helene Burt *ISSN:* 0832-2473; *Price:* Free with membership CATA; $30 non-members in Canada; $35 in the U.S.A.; $40 intl.
• Canadian Art Therapy Association Newsletter
Type: Newsletter; *Frequency:* 3 pa; *Editor:* Marilyn Magnuson

Canadian Arthritis & Rheumatism Society *See* Arthritis Society

Canadian Arthritis Network (CAN) / Le Réseau canadien de l'arthrite

#1002, 522 University Ave., Toronto ON M5T 1W7
Tel: 416-586-4770; *Fax:* 416-586-8395
can@arthritisnetwork.ca
www.arthritisnetwork.ca
www.facebook.com/102841629761794
twitter.com/commcan
Overview: A medium-sized national organization founded in 1998
Mission: To improve the quality of life for people with arthritis; To support integrated, trans-disciplinary research & development, with a focus upon inflammatory joint diseases, osteoarthritis, & bioengineering for restoration of joint function
Member of: Networks of Centres of Excellence
Affliation(s): The Arthritis Society; Canadian Institute of Health Research Institute of Musculoskeletal Health & Arthritis
Chief Officer(s):
Robin Armstrong, Chair
John Riley, Managing Director, 416-586-3167
jriley@mtsinai.on.ca
Claire Bombardier, Co-Scientific Director
Monique Gignac, Co-Scientific Director
Kate Lee, Director, Research & Development, 416-586-4800 Ext. 4117
klee2@mtsinai.on.ca
Everdina Carter, Administrative Assistant, 416-586-4800 Ext. 4461
ecarter@mtsinai.on.ca
Finances: *Funding Sources:* Grants; Federal government
Membership: 200 researchers; 45 institutions; *Member Profile:* Canadian arthritis researchers & clinicians; Canadian academic institutions; *Committees:* Research Management; Partnerships & Sustainability; Training & Education; Consumer Advisory Council; Scientific & Medical Advisory Council
Activities: Partnering with clinicians, academics, government, industry, voluntary agencies, & consumers; Facilitating the commercialization of new discoveries
Publications:
• Annual Report of the Canadian Arthritis Network
Type: Yearbook; *Frequency:* Annually
• Arthritis in Canada
Type: Report
Profile: Impacts of arthritis on Canadians, plus information about ambulatory care, prescription medications, & hospital services
• Research Excellence at the Canadian Arthritis Network
Type: Report; *Number of Pages:* 20

Canadian Artists Representation Copyright Collective Inc. (CARCC) / Société des droits d'auteur du Front des artistes canadiens inc

214 Barclay Rd., Ottawa ON K1K 3C2
Tel: 613-232-3818; *Fax:* 613-232-8384
carcc@carcc.ca
www.carcc.ca
Overview: A large national organization founded in 1990
Mission: Operating as a coyright collecting society
Affliation(s): Société des droits d'auteur du Front des artistes canadiens inc
Chief Officer(s):
Janice Seline, Executive Director
Staff Member(s): 1
Membership: *Fees:* Schedule available; *Member Profile:* Artists living in Canada & Canadian artists living outside Canada

Canadian Artists' Representation (CARFAC) / Le Front des artistes canadiens

#250, 2 Daly Ave., Ottawa ON K1N 6E2
Tel: 613-233-6161; *Fax:* 613-233-6162
Toll-Free: 866-344-6161
www.carfac.ca
www.facebook.com/155665580277
twitter.com/carfacnational
Overview: A large national organization founded in 1968

Mission: To act as a national voice for Canada's professional visual artists; To promote a socio-economic climate that is conducive to the production of visual arts
Member of: Canadian Conference of the Arts (CCA); International Association of Artists; Coalition for Cultural Diversity
Affliation(s): Creators Rights Alliance (CRA); Access Copyright
Chief Officer(s):
Grant McConnell, National President & Spokesperson
Deirdre Logue, Vice-President
Barbara Gamble, Secretary
Julie McIntyre, Treasurer
April Britski, Executive Director
Taylor Norris, Coordinator, Membership
Melissa Gruber, Director, Advocacy & Communications
Finances: *Funding Sources:* Donations
Membership: *Member Profile:* Canadian professional visual artists
Activities: Defending artists' economic & legal rights; Conducting research; Educating the public about dealing fairly with artists
Publications:
• Calendar [a publication of Canadian Artists' Representation]
Type: Newsletter; *Frequency:* s-a.; *Editor:* Melissa Gruber; April Britski *ISSN:* 1495-558X
Profile: Information for professional artists & association news

Canadian Artists' Representation British Columbia
#100, 938 Howe St., Vancouver BC V6Z 1N9
Tel: 604-519-4669
bc@carfac.ca
www.carfacbc.org
www.linkedin.com/company/carfac-bc
www.facebook.com/carfacbc
twitter.com/Carfacbc
www.youtube.com/user/carfacbc
Overview: A medium-sized provincial organization overseen by Canadian Artists' Representation
Mission: To assist BC visual artists to advance their professional status & economic potential; to provide informational services to assist in the development of the visual artist & the visual arts as a profession; to research, publish & otherwise provide educational information for the development of the visual arts professional & for the benefit of all Canadians interested in the visual arts; to advocate the role & value of the visual arts in BC & beyond; to assist & encourage members of the visual arts profession to make individual & group contributions to the growth & development of the visual arts in Canada
Chief Officer(s):
Julie McIntyre, President
Membership: 181

Canadian Artists' Representation Manitoba / Le Front des artistes canadiens de Manitoba
#407, 100 Arthur St., Winnipeg MB R3B 1H3
Tel: 204-943-7211; *Fax:* 204-942-1555
carfac-mbcontact@mts.net
Also Known As: CARFAC Manitoba
Overview: A small provincial organization founded in 1981 overseen by Canadian Artists' Representation
Mission: To protect & promote the social economic interests of practising visual artists in Manitoba; to lobby the government on issues related to the field, including copyright issues; to provide artists & the public with current information on such events as exhibitions, workshops & art classes.
Member of: Canadian Artists' Representation
Activities: Workshops; *Internships:* Yes; *Library* Open to public

Canadian Artists' Representation Maritimes
2575 Elm St., Halifax NS B3L 2Y5
Tel: 516-454-3285
Other Communication: membership.carfac@gmail.com
elmstreetstudio@ns.sympatico.ca
www.carfacmaritimes.org
www.facebook.com/groups/8081097018/
Overview: A medium-sized local organization founded in 2003 overseen by Canadian Artists' Representation
Mission: To defend artists' economic & legal rights in the Maritime provinces; To educate the public on fair dealing with artists
Chief Officer(s):
Susan Tooke, President
Membership: *Fees:* $20 student; $40 professional artist & individual associate; $60 professional artist couple; $80 institutional associate; $250 sustaining member; *Member Profile:* Professional visual artists living & working in Nova Scotia, New Brunswick, & Prince Edward Island
Activities: Engaging in advocacy activities; Facilitating communications among artists; Providing information to members
Publications:
• The / Le Studio
Type: Newsletter; *Frequency:* Monthly
Profile: Updates about the organization for members

Canadian Artists' Representation Ontario / Le Front des artistes canadiens de l'Ontario
#440, 401 Richmond St. West, Toronto ON M5V 3A8
Tel: 416-340-8850; *Fax:* 416-340-7653
Toll-Free: 877-890-8850
carfacontario@carfacontario.ca
www.carfacontario.ca
Also Known As: CARFAC Ontario
Overview: A medium-sized provincial organization founded in 1968 overseen by Canadian Artists' Representation
Mission: To improve legal & economic issues facing visual artists; To develop policies & services to help artists, curators, art patrons, galleries, & other stakeholders
Member of: Canadian Artists Representation/Front des artistes canadiens
Chief Officer(s):
Kristian Clarke, Executive Director
Susan Gold, President
Finances: *Funding Sources:* Donations
Membership: *Fees:* Schedule available; *Member Profile:* Professional visual & media artists
Activities: Offering professional development courses
Publications:
• Dispatch: CARFAC Ontario Newsletter
Type: Newsletter; *Frequency:* Quarterly; *Accepts Advertising*
Profile: Business & artistic resource for CARFAC members

Canadian Artists' Representation Saskatchewan
1734A Dewdney Ave., Regina SK S4R 1G6
Tel: 306-522-9788; *Fax:* 306-522-9783
programs@carfac.sk.ca
www.carfac.sk.ca
www.facebook.com/pages/CARFAC-SASK/120312261258
Also Known As: CARFAC SASK
Overview: A medium-sized provincial organization overseen by Canadian Artists' Representation
Mission: To improve the status of Saskatchewan visual artists; To advocate on behalf of practising visual artists in Saskatchewan
Affliation(s): CARFAC National; CARFAC Copyright Collective; International Association of Art
Chief Officer(s):
Jennifer McRorie, Executive Director
director@carfac.sk.ca
Finances: *Funding Sources:* Donations
Membership: *Fees:* Schedule available; *Member Profile:* Visual artists in Saskatchewan
Activities: Providing education & resources to visual artists; Conducting research; Consulting with arts & cultural organizations & other provincial agencies; *Library:* CARFAC SASK Resource Centre
Publications:
• CARFAC SASK [Canadian Artists' Representation Saskatchewan] Newsletter
Type: Newsletter; *Frequency:* 10 pa; *Price:* Free for CARFAC SASK members
Profile: CARFAC SASK & CARFAC National news, events & exhibitions, educational opportunities, grant information, cultural developments, research, & articlesfor visual artists
• The Saskatchewan Gallery Survey
Frequency: Triennially; *Price:* Free to CARFAC SASK members
Profile: A guide to the galleries of Saskatchewan
• Visual Arts Handbook
Frequency: Triennially; *Price:* Free to Saskatchewan residents
Profile: A guide for artists, art gallery personnel, art dealers, collectors, librarians, & educators in the visual arts in Saskatchewan

Saskatoon Office
#203, 416 - 21st St. East, Saskatoon SK S7K 0C2
Tel: 306-933-3206; *Fax:* 306-933-2053
membership@carfac.sk.ca

Canadian Arts Presenting Association (CAPACOA) / Association canadienne des organismes artistiques
#200, 17 York St., Ottawa ON K1N 9J6
Tel: 613-562-3515; *Fax:* 613-562-4005
mail@capacoa.ca
www.capacoa.ca
www.facebook.com/CAPACOA
twitter.com/capacoa
Overview: A large national charitable organization founded in 1985
Mission: To promote the development of the presentation of the arts in Canada; to promote & encourage greater knowledge & appreciation of the presentation of the performing arts; To encourage touring of artists & attractions throughout all regions of Canada; To provide information on artists & attractions touring regionally & nationally; To assist presenters of the arts in Canada with coordination of bookings; To provide opportunities for professional development of presenters in Canada; To promote communication & understanding between presenters of the arts in Canada; To provide forum for exchange of views concerning presentation of the performing arts generally; To provide information on regional & federal policies which relate to presentation of the arts; To provide the opportunity to make contacts nationwide
Chief Officer(s):
Phyllis Stenson, President
phyllis@harrisonfestival.com
Erin Benjamin, Executive Director
erin.benjamin@capacoa.ca
Mélanie Bureau, Operations Manager
melanie.bureau@capacoa.ca
Finances: *Annual Operating Budget:* $100,000-$250,000
Staff Member(s): 2
Membership: 186 organizations; *Fees:* Schedule available
Activities: Training Initiatives Program in Tour Organization & Presenting (TIP TOP) - a mentorship program for those entering or in transition in the touring performing arts sector; *Rents Mailing List:* Yes
Meetings/Conferences: • Canadian Arts Presenting Association / Association canadienne des organismes artistiques 2015 27th Annual Conference, January, 2015, Marriott Harbourfront Hotel, Halifax, NS
Scope: National
• Canadian Arts Presenting Association / Association canadienne des organismes artistiques 2016 28th Annual Conference, 2016
Scope: National

Canadian Asian Studies Association (CASA) / Association canadienne des études asiatiques (ACEA)
c/o Dept. of Geography, Université du Québec à Montréal, PO Box 8888, Stn. Centre Ville, Pavillon Hubert Aquin Local A-4310, Montréal QC H3C 3P8
Tel: 514-848-2280; *Fax:* 514-848-4514
casa_acea@yahoo.ca
www.casa-acea.ca
Overview: A medium-sized national organization founded in 1968
Mission: To expand & disseminate knowledge about Asia in Canada
Chief Officer(s):
André Laliberté, Secretary
andre.laliberte@uottawa.ca
Prashant Keshavmurthy, Treasurer
prashant.keshavmurthy@mcgill.ca
Finances: *Funding Sources:* Sponsorships
Membership: *Fees:* $35 students; $45 unwaged or retired members; $60 regular members; $75 families; $100 institutions; $250 corporate sustaining members
Activities: Publishing monographs, such as South Asia Between Turmoil & Hope
Awards:
• Best Canadian Dissertation on East Asia Award Competition (Award)
• Chiang Ching-Kuo Foundation Fellowship Award (Award)
Amount: $10,000 each, for up to 2 doctoral fellowships; $22,000, for 1 post-doctoral fellowship

Canadian Assembly of Narcotics Anonymous (CANA)
PO Box 25073 RPO West Kildonan, Winnipeg MB R2V 4C7
www.canaacna.org
Previous Name: Narcotics Anonymous
Overview: A small national organization founded in 1989
Mission: To help the addict who suffers from the disease of addiction
Membership: *Member Profile:* Anyone regardless of age, race, religion, sexual identity or preference

Activities: *Speaker Service:* Yes; *Library* Open to public by appointment

British Columbia Region
PO Box 1695, Stn. A, Vancouver BC V6C 2P7
Tel: 604-873-1018
www.bcrna.ca

Canada Atlantic Region
PO Box 26025, 407 Westmorland Rd., Saint John NB E2J 4M3
Toll-Free: 800-564-0228
contact.us@carna.ca
www.carna.ca

Golden Triangle Area
#311, 23-500 Fairway Rd. South, Kitchener ON N2C 1X3
Tel: 519-651-1121
Toll-Free: 866-311-1611
www.gtascna.org

Hamilton Area
PO Box 57067, Stn. Jackson, 2 King St. West, Hamilton ON L8P 4W9
Tel: 905-522-0332; *Crisis Hot-Line:* 888-811-3887
www.nahamilton.org

Narcotiques Anonymes
5496 rue Notre-Dame est, Montréal QC H1N 2C4
Ligne sans frais: 855-544-6362
info@naquebec.org
www.naquebec.org

Ontario Region
PO Box 5939, Stn. A, Toronto ON M5W 1P3
www.orscna.org

Canadian Assessment, Vocational Evaluation & Work Adjustment Society (CAVEWAS) / Association canadienne des évaluateurs de capacités de travail société (ACECTS)

#310, 4 Cataraqui St., Kingston ON K7K 1Z7
Tel: 613-531-9210
Toll-Free: 866-560-3838
www.cavewas.com
Previous Name: Canadian Association for Vocational Evaluation & Work Adjustment
Overview: A small national organization
Mission: To identify & resolve issues relevant to vocational rehabilitation & career transition services
Chief Officer(s):
Phillip W. Boswell, President
pwboswell@telus.net
Activities: Certified Vocational Evaluator (CVE) Designation

Canadian Associated Air Balance Council (CAABC)

Tel: 905-886-6513; *Fax:* 905-886-6513
mail@designtest.ca
www.caabc.org
Overview: A small national organization founded in 1970
Mission: To promote independent testing & balancing of mechanical systems; to produce standards to advance the industry
Affiliation(s): Associated Air Balance Council
Chief Officer(s):
Surrinder S. Sahota, President
Finances: *Funding Sources:* Membership fees
Staff Member(s): 1; 18 volunteer(s)
Membership: 20; *Fees:* $3,000; *Committees:* Membership; Technical; Standards

Canadian Associates of Ben-Gurion University of the Negev

National & Toronto Office, #506, 1000 Finch Ave. West, Toronto ON M3J 2V5
Tel: 416-665-8054; *Fax:* 416-665-8055
bgutoronto@bengurion.ca
www.bengurion.ca
www.facebook.com/119559301437197
twitter.com/BenGurionCanada
www.youtube.com/user/BenGurionUniversity
Overview: A small international charitable organization founded in 1975
Mission: To raise funds for needy & worthy students, for scholarships, to attend Ben-Gurion University
Chief Officer(s):
Mark Mendelson, Chief Executive Officer
markmendelson@bengurion.ca
Activities: *Speaker Service:* Yes

Montréal Office
#400, 4950 Queen Mary Rd., Montréal QC H3W 1X3
Tel: 514-937-8927; *Fax:* 514-937-8920
bgumontreal@sympatico.ca
Chief Officer(s):
Agar Grinberg, Executive Director
agargrinberg@bengurion.ca

Winnipeg Office
#C309, 123 Doncaster St., Winnipeg MB R3N 2B2
Tel: 204-942-7347; *Fax:* 204-944-8041
bguwinnipeg@bengurion.ca
Chief Officer(s):
Ariel Karabelnicoff, Executive Director
arielkarabelnicoff@bengurion.ca

Canadian Association Against Sexual Harassment in Higher Education *See* Canadian Association for the Prevention of Discrimination & Harassment in Higher Education

Canadian Association for American Studies (CAAS) / Association d'études américaines au Canada (AEAC)

c/o Jennifer Harris, Assoc. Prof., Mount Allison University, 63D York St., Sackville NB E4L 1G9
e-mail: webmaster@american-studies.ca
www.american-studies.ca
twitter.com/CAASCanada
Overview: A small national organization founded in 1964
Mission: To encourage study & research concerning the United States; To examine the implications of American studies for Canada & the world
Chief Officer(s):
Jennifer Harris, President
jharris@mta.ca
Jason Haslam, Vice-President
jason.haslam@dal.ca
Jennifer Harris, Secretary
jharris@mta.ca
Percy Walton, Treasurer
pwalton@ccs.carleton.ca
Publications:
• Canadian Review of American Studies
Type: Journal; *Frequency:* 3 pa; *Accepts Advertising*; *Editor:* Percy Walton; *Price:* Free with membership in the Canadian Association for American Studies
Profile: Published with the support of Carleton University, the journal features essays & reviews related to the culture of the United States & relations between the United States &Canada

Canadian Association for Anatomy, Neurobiology, & Cell Biology (CAANCB) / Association canadienne d'anatomie, de neurobiologie et de biologie cellulaire (ACANBC)

Dr. W.H. Baldridge, Department of Anatomy, Faculty of Medicine, Dalhousie University, Halifax BC B3H 4H7
Tel: 613-533-2864; *Fax:* 613-533-2566
www.caancb.blogspot.com
Previous Name: Canadian Association of Anatomists / Association Canadienne d'Anatomie
Overview: A small national organization founded in 1956 overseen by Canadian Federation of Biological Societies
Mission: To advance knowledge of anatomy; To represent anatomical sciences throughout Canada
Chief Officer(s):
William H. Baldridge, Secretary, 902-494-6305, Fax: 902-494-6309
William.Baldridge@dal.ca
Finances: *Funding Sources:* Membership fees
Membership: *Member Profile:* Elected members are individuals who have contributed to the development of the science; Associate members are persons who are interested in the discipline; Graduate students; Retired persons (emeritus members)
Awards:
• Murray L. Barr Junior Scientist Award (Award)
• J.C.B. Grant Award (Award)
• C.P. Leblond Research Presentation Award (2) (Award)
Amount: $400
• Research Publication Award of the CAANCB / ACANBC Chairs (Award)
Amount: $250
• Arthur W. Ham Graduate Student Award (Award)
• Travel / Meeting Awards (2) (Award)
Publications:
• CAANCB [Canadian Association for Anatomy, Neurobiology, & Cell Biology] Anchor
Type: Newsletter; *Editor:* Michelle Black, Dalhousie U.

Canadian Association for Business Economics (CABE) / Association canadienne de science économique des affaires

PO Box 898, Stn. B, Ottawa ON K1P 5P9
Fax: 613-238-7698
Toll-Free: 855-222-3321
www.cabe.ca
www.facebook.com/CABEconomics
twitter.com/CABE_Economics
Overview: A medium-sized national organization founded in 1975
Mission: To represent the interests of business economists in Canada; To enhance the professionalism of business economists
Affliation(s): International Federation of Associations of Business Economists; National Association of Business Economists (Canadian Association for Business Economics's sister organization in the United States)
Chief Officer(s):
Paul Jacobson, President
pmj@jciconsult.com
Membership: 900+; *Fees:* Schedule available; *Member Profile:* Canadian professionals in the field of business economics, including economists in businesses, governments, associations, & other organizations
Activities: Creating a network with other other applied economists to discuss business economics & related subjects; Promoting the study of business economics in Canada; Liaising with other national & international organizations of business economists; Offering professional development activities, such as workshops
Publications:
• CABE [Canadian Association for Business Economics, Inc.] Membership Directory
Type: Directory; *Price:* Free with membership in Canadian Association for Business Economics
• CABE [Canadian Association for Business Economics, Inc.] News
Type: Newsletter; *Price:* Free with membership in Canadian Association for Business Economics
• Canadian Business Economics
Type: Journal; *Price:* Free with membership in Canadian Association for Business Economics

Canadian Association for Child & Play Therapy

24 Hayes Ave., Guelph ON N1E 5V5
Tel: 519-827-1506; *Fax:* 519-827-1825
membership@cacpt.com
www.cacpt.com
Overview: A small national organization
Mission: To offer certification as a child psychotherapist & play therapist (CPT) & play therapist associate (CPTA); To offer training & insurance for members
Chief Officer(s):
Elizabeth A. Sharpe, Executive Director
Elizabeth@cacpt.com
Membership: *Fees:* $40 student; $60 general; $75 professional; $140 certified; $200 agency; *Member Profile:* Professional association for the field of child psychotherapy & play therapy in Canada
Publications:
• Playground Magazine
Type: Magazine; *Frequency:* Quarterly; *Accepts Advertising*; *Editor:* Donika Budd
Profile: Information on Play Therapy; Association information & upcoming events

Canadian Association for Clinical Microbiology & Infectious Diseases (CACMID) / Association canadienne de microbiologie clinique et des maladies contagieuses

c/o Heather Adam, Dept of Medical Microbiology & Infectious Diseases, University of Manitoba, MS675F-820 Sherbrook St., Winnipeg MB R3A 1R9
Tel: 204-787-8678; *Fax:* 204-787-4699
www.cacmid.ca
www.facebook.com/CACMID
twitter.com/cacmid
Overview: A small national charitable organization founded in 1932
Mission: To enhance the cooperation of professionals specializing in clinical microbiology & infectious disease; To act as the voice for clinical microbiology & infectious disease professionals; To develop standards in the field of clinical microbiology
Chief Officer(s):

Heather Adam, President
hadam@dsmanitoba.ca
Matthew W. Gilmour, Secretary-Treasurer
Matthew.Gilmour@phac-aspc.gc.ca
Membership: *Fees:* $50 regular member; $20 student & retired members; $800 sustaining member; *Member Profile:* Medical & clinical microbiologists; Infectious disease physicians; Medical technologists; Laboratory scientists & managers; Research technologists
Activities: Promoting education & research
Meetings/Conferences: • Canadian Association for Clinical Microbiology and Infectious Diseases Annual Conference 2015, April, 2015, Prince Edward Island Convention Centre, Charlottetown, PE
Scope: National
Publications:
• CACMID [Canadian Association for Clinical Microbiology & Infectious Diseases] Membership Directory
Type: Directory

Canadian Association for Commonwealth Literature & Language Studies (CACLALS) / Association canadienne pour l'étude des langues et de la littérature du Commonwealth

c/o Kristina Fagan, Department of English, University of Saskatchewan, 9 Campus Dr., Saskatoon SK S7N 5A5
www.caclals.ca
Overview: A small international organization founded in 1973
Mission: To promote the study of Commonwealth literature in Canada; To encourage the reading of Canadian literature abroad
Affliation(s): Association for Commonwealth Literature & Language Studies (ACLALS)
Chief Officer(s):
Susan Gingell, President
Kristina Fagan, Secretary-Treasurer
Neil ten Kortenaar, Editor, Chimo
kortenaar@utsc.utoronto.ca
Membership: *Fees:* $20 students & unwaged persons; $50 regular members; *Member Profile:* Teachers, scholars, writers, & students who are interested in Commonwealth & postcolonial literature
Meetings/Conferences: • Canadian Association for Commonwealth Literature & Language Studies 2015 Annual Conference, May, 2015, University of Ottawa, Ottawa, ON
Scope: National
Description: Keynote speakers, roundtables, sessions, & readings
Publications:
• Chimo: The Newsjournal of the Canadian Association for Commonwealth Literature & Language Studies
Type: Newsletter; *Frequency:* Semiannually; *Editor:* Neil ten Kortenaar
Profile: Association activities, conference information, & member news

Canadian Association for Commonwealth Literature & Language Studies (CACLALS)

c/o Surrey Campus, Kwantlen Univ. College, 12666 - 72 Ave., Surrey BC V3W 2M8
Tel: 604-599-2187; *Fax:* 604-599-2068
www.caclals.ca
Overview: A small international organization founded in 1964
Mission: To promote Commonwealth Literature Studies, organize seminars & workshops, arrange lectures by writers & scholars; to disseminate knowledge
Member of: The Commonwealth
Affliation(s): Commonwealth Consortium of Education; International Federation for Modern Languages & Literatures
Chief Officer(s):
Geoffrey V. Davis, Chair
Susan Gingell, President
Finances: *Annual Operating Budget:* Less than $50,000
30 volunteer(s)
Membership: 1,600; *Member Profile:* Professors; researchers; practitioners; students; public; *Committees:* Conference, Afrikan Participation; First Nations; Indigenous & Dalit; South Asian
Activities: Chapters in Canada, Europe, India, Malaysia, South Africa, Sri Lanka, South Pacific, West Indies & USA

Canadian Association for Community Living (CACL) / Association canadienne pour l'intégration communautaire

Kinsmen Building, York University, 4700 Keele St., Toronto ON M3J 1P3
Tel: 416-661-9611; *Fax:* 416-661-5701
inform@cacl.ca
www.cacl.ca
www.facebook.com/canadianacl
twitter.com/cacl_acic
www.youtube.com/canadianacl
Previous Name: Canadian Association for the Mentally Retarded
Overview: A large national charitable organization founded in 1958
Mission: To ensure the following for people with intellectual disabilities: the same rights, & access to choice, services, & supports as others; the same opportunities to live in freedom & dignity with the necessary supports to do so; & the ability to articulate & realize their rights & aspirations
Member of: Inclusion International
Affliation(s): People First of Canada; Council of Canadians with Disabilities (CCD); National Alliance for Children & Youth; Active Living Alliance; Canadian Council on Social Development (CCSD); Canadian Coalition for the Rights of Children (CCRC); Canadian Institute of Child Health (CICH); Canadian Caregiver Coalition; Canadian Down Syndrome Society (CDSS); Family Service Canada; DisAbled Women's Network Canada (DAWN)
Chief Officer(s):
Laurie Larson, President
Michael Bach, Executive Vice-President
mbach@cacl.ca
John Cairns, Director, Finance & Administration
jcairns@cacl.ca
Cam Crawford, Director, Research & Knowledge Management
cameronc@cacl.ca
Doris Rajan, Director, Social Development & Public Education
d.rajan@rogers.com
Neil Wiernik, Manager, Online Community & Communications
nwiernik@cacl.ca
Finances: *Funding Sources:* Government of Canada; Assessments from provincial & territorial associations; Fundraising; Donations; Sponsorships
Membership: 10 provincial associations + 3 territorial associations (consisting of 400 local associations & 40,000+ members); *Member Profile:* Family members & others who work for the benefit of people with an intellectual disability
Activities: Defending the rights & advocating for the interests of individuals with intellectual disabilities; Promoting research; Engaging with governments; Raising awareness of inclusion; *Speaker Service:* Yes; *Library:* Canadian Association for Community Living Resource Centre; Open to public by appointment
Meetings/Conferences: • Canadian Association for Community Living 2015 National Family Conference, 2015
Scope: National
Attendance: 500+
Description: A discussion of issues that impact families, professionals, & self-advocates who help people with intellectual disabilities
Publications:
• Coming Together [a publication of the Canadian Association for Community Living]
Type: Newsletter
Profile: The Canadian Association for Community Living's family newsletter, featuring stories of families
• Education Watch [a publication of the Canadian Association for Community Living]
Type: Newsletter; *Frequency:* Quarterly
Profile: Inclusive education across Canada
• INFO@ [a publication of the Canadian Association for Community Living]
Type: Newsletter; *Frequency:* Bimonthly
Profile: Up-to-date topics & issues within the Canadian Association for Community Living & its members & affiliates
• Institution Watch [a publication of the Canadian Association for Community Living]
Type: Newsletter
Profile: Produced by the People First of Canada - CACL Joint Task Force on Deinstitutionalization
• Invisible No More [a publication of the Canadian Association for Community Living]
Type: Book; *Number of Pages:* 160; *Author:* Vincenzo Pietropaolo
Profile: A photography book chronicling the lives of individuals with intellectual disabilities
• National Report Card on Inclusion [a publication of the Canadian Association for Community Living]
Type: Report; *Frequency:* Annual
Profile: The purpose is to track the progress of inclusion in Canadian society
• Povery Watch [a publication of the Canadian Association for Community Living]
Type: Newsletter; *Frequency:* Quarterly
Profile: A publication from the Canadian Association for Community Living's National Action Committee on Disability Supports, Income, & Employment

Canadian Association for Community Living - Antigonish

83 Kirk St., Antigonish NS B2G 1Y7
Tel: 902-863-5024; *Fax:* 902-863-0090
cacl@ns.sympatico.ca
Also Known As: CACL - Antigonish
Overview: A small local organization overseen by Nova Scotia Association for Community Living
Member of: DIRECTIONS Council for Vocational Services Society; Nova Scotia Association for Community Living
Chief Officer(s):
Jeff Teasdale, Executive Director/Manager

Canadian Association for Composite Structures & Materials (CACSMA) / Association canadienne pour les structures et matériaux composites (ACSMAC)

c/o J. Denault, Industrial Materials Institute, Ntl. Research Council, 75 Mortange Blvd., Boucherville QC J4B 6Y4
Tel: 450-641-5149; *Fax:* 450-641-5105
www.cacsma.ca
Overview: A medium-sized national organization founded in 1988
Mission: To support composites companies in Canada; To promote Canadian composites capabilities; To encourage the application of composites in all sectors
Chief Officer(s):
Suong V. Hoa, President, 514-848-2424 Ext. 3139, Fax: 514-848-3178
hoasuon@alcor.concordia.ca
Mehdi Hojjati, Secretary, 514-283-9209, Fax: 514-283-9445
Mehdi.Hojjati@nrc-cnrc.gc.ca
Johanne Denault, Treasurer, 450-641-5149, Fax: 450-641-5105
Johanne.Denault@imi.cnrc-nrc.gc.ca
Membership: *Fees:* $20 students; $60 individuals; $250 corporate members; *Member Profile:* Canadian individuals & corporate members, such as government employees, teachers, researchers, research centers, consultants, technologists, materials specialists, fabricators, equipment manufacturers, suppliers, & distributors
Activities: Informing members of scientific & technological developments in the composites industry; Liaising with government; Fostering research & development alliances; Creating networking opportunities with other national & international materials organizations

Canadian Association for Conservation of Cultural Property (CAC) / Association canadienne pour la conservation et la restauration des biens culturels (ACCR)

c/o Danielle Allard, #419, 207 Bank St., Ottawa ON K2P 2N2
Tel: 613-231-3977; *Fax:* 613-231-4406
coordinator@cac-accr.com
www.cac-accr.ca
www.facebook.com/289264431135291
Previous Name: Canadian Association for Conservation; International Institute for Conservation of Historic & Artistic Works - Canadian Group
Overview: A small national organization founded in 1974
Mission: To promote conservation of Canadian cultural property
Chief Officer(s):
Cindy Colford, President
president@cac-accr.ca
Jessica Lafrance, Vice-President
jessca.lafrance@live.ca
Susannah Kendall, Secretary
sookendall@yahoo.com
Michael Harrington, Treasurer
mharrington@jhgconsulting.com
Finances: *Funding Sources:* Membership fees; Sponsorships
Membership: *Member Profile:* Persons interested in the field of conservation, such as professional conservation practitioners & individual & institutional collectors; *Committees:* Communication; Translations; CAC Grants & Awards; Membership; Job Descriptions; Bulletin; Journal; Conference Planning; Central Conference; Training; Workplace Issues; Fundraising; Marketing, Sales & Promotions; Emerging Conservators

Activities: Disseminating information to conservators about technical advances; Offering professional development activities; Providing networking opportunities
Awards:
• Charles Mervyn Ruggles Award (Award)
• Training Activity Grant (Grant)
• Professional Development Grant to Attend a Conservation Conference, Workshop or Seminar (Grant)
• Professional Development Grant to Attend the Annual CAC Conference &/or Workshop (Grant)
Meetings/Conferences: • Canadian Association for Conservation 2015 41st Annual Conference & Workshop, May, 2015, Edmonton, AB
Scope: National
Description: Educational sessions & a tradeshow
Contact Information: Conference Chair: Kateri Morin, E-mail: kateri.morin@mcc.gouv.qc.ca
Publications:
• Canadian Association for Conservation Bulletin
Type: Newsletter; *Frequency:* Quarterly
Profile: Association activities
• Canadian Association for Conservation Conference Program & Abstracts
Type: Abstracts; *Frequency:* Annually
Profile: Abstracts from the association's annual conference
• Canadian Association for Conservation Directory of Members
Type: Directory; *Frequency:* Annually; *Accepts Advertising*; *Editor:* Anne Sinclair
Profile: Contact information for association members
• Code of Ethics & Guidance for Practice
Price: $10
• The Journal of the Canadian Association for Conservation
Type: Journal; *Frequency:* Annually; *Editor:* Irene Karsten; Carole Dignard
Profile: Peer reviewed articles about the conservation of cultural property, including treatments & research
• Selecting & Employing a Conservator in Canada
Profile: Assistance to select a conservator to preserve, repair, & restore objects

Canadian Association for Conservation; International Institute for Conservation of Historic & Artistic Works - Canadian Group *See* Canadian Association for Conservation of Cultural Property

Canadian Association for Co-operative Education (CAFCE) / Association canadienne de l'enseignement coopératif

#202, 720 Spadina Ave., Toronto ON M5S 2T9
Tel: 416-929-5256
cafce@cafce.ca
www.cafce.ca
Overview: A medium-sized national organization founded in 1973
Mission: To act as the voice for post-secondary co-operative education in Canada; To advance post-secondary co-operative education throughout the country; To establish national standards
Affliation(s): World Association for Cooperative Education (WACE)
Chief Officer(s):
Christine Arsenault, President
president@cafce.ca
Daniela Attard, Director, Operations, 416-483-3311 Ext. 224
danielaa@cafce.ca
Shane Phillipe, Treasurer
treasurer@cafce.ca
Finances: *Funding Sources:* Membership fees; Sponsorships
Membership: *Fees:* Schedule available; *Member Profile:* Organizations & persons with a professional interest in co-operative education; *Committees:* Co-op Student of the Year Awards Selection; Fundraising; International Co-op Work Experiences; Membership; National Co-operative Education Week; Nominations & Awards; Professional Development; Public Relations; Research; CAFCE Accreditation Council
Activities: Promoting co-operative education & accreditation; Offering mentorship for institutions considering accreditation; Providing opportunities for professional development; Offering networking opportunities for sharing best practices; Increasing national & government awareness; Presenting annual awards; *Awareness Events:* National Co-operative Education Week, March
Awards:
• Albert S. Barber Award (Award)
Recognizes outstanding contributions to the advancement of the philosophy and practice of Co-operative Education in Canada. Eligibility: Member of CAFCE; must have made an outstanding contribution to the association*Deadline:* June
• Dr. Graham Branton Research Award (Award)
Recognizes outstanding contributions to the advancement of the philosophy and practice of Co-operative Education in Canada. Eligibility: Member of CAFCE; must have made an outstanding contribution to the association*Deadline:* June
• Co-op Students of the Year Award (Award)
This award recognizes a wide variety of achievements — job performance, academic performance and responsibility, and particular contributions to their co-op employer, to Co-operative Education, and the community-at-large. Eligibility: College and a university Co-operative Education student*Deadline:* June
Amount: Certificate and $500
Meetings/Conferences: • Canadian Association for Co-operative Education (CAFCE) 2016 Conference, 2016
Scope: National
Publications:
• CAFCE [Canadian Association for Co-operative Education] News
Type: Newletter
• Canadian Association for Co-operative Education Annual Report
Type: Yearbook; *Frequency:* Annually
• Co-operative Education Directory
Type: Directory
Profile: Listings of post-secondary co-operative education programs offered by CAFCE member institutions
• Co-operative Education Manual
Type: Manual; *Number of Pages:* 62
Profile: A guide to planning & implementing co-operative education programs in post-secondary institutions
• National Co-op Statistics

Canadian Association for Corporate Growth *See* Association for Corporate Growth, Toronto Chapter

Canadian Association for Curriculum Studies (CACS)

#204, 250 Dalhousie St., Ottawa ON K1N 7E4
Tel: 613-241-0018; *Fax:* 613-241-0019
csse-scee@csse.ca
www.csse.ca/CACS
www.facebook.com/csse.scee
twitter.com/CSSESCEE
Overview: A small national organization
Mission: Supports inquiries into and discussions of curricula that are of interest to Canadian educators.
Member of: Canadian Society for the Study of Education
Chief Officer(s):
Victor Glickman, President

Canadian Association for Dental Research (CADR) / Association canadienne de recherches dentaires (ACRD)

c/o Dr. C. Birek, Faculty of Dentistry, University of Manitoba, 780 Bannatyne Ave., Winnipeg MB R3E 0W2
Tel: 204-789-3256; *Fax:* 204-789-3913
birek@ms.umanitoba.ca
www.cadr-acrd.ca
Overview: A medium-sized national organization
Mission: To advance research & increase knowledge in order to improve oral health in Canada; To support & represent Canadian oral health researchers
Member of: International Association for Dental Research
Chief Officer(s):
Edward Putnins, President, 604-822-1734
putnins@interchange.ubc.ca
Michael Greene, President, CADR Student Research Group
umgre222@cc.umanitoba.ca
Debora Matthews, Vice-President, 902-494-1419
debora.matthews@dal.ca
Catalena Birek, Secretary-Treasurer, 204-789-3256
birek@ms.umanitoba.ca
Membership: *Member Profile:* Oral health researchers in Canada, who are interested in the furtherance of research in fields related to dental science; Persons interested in the latest reserach (affiliate members); Students interested in dental research; Retired persons who have been members of the association
Activities: Communicating & applying research findings; Presenting awards & scholarships
Meetings/Conferences: • Canadian Association for Dental Research 39th Annual Meeting, March, 2015, Boston, MA
Scope: International
Description: In conjunction with the 44th Annual Meeting of the American Association of Dental Research & the 93rd General Session & Exhibition of the International Association for Dental Research
• Canadian Association for Dental Research 40th Annual Meeting, March, 2016, Los Angeles, CA
Scope: International
Description: In conjunction with the 45th Annual Meeting of the American Association of Dental Research & the 94th General Session & Exhibition of the International Association for Dental Research
• Canadian Association for Dental Research 41st Annual Meeting, March, 2017, San Francisco, CA
Scope: International
Description: In conjunction with the 46th Annual Meeting of the American Association of Dental Research & the 95th General Session & Exhibition of the International Association for Dental Research
• Canadian Association for Dental Research 42nd Annual Meeting, March, 2018, Fort Lauderdale, FL
Scope: International
Description: In conjunction with the 47th Annual Meeting of the American Association of Dental Research & the 96th General Session & Exhibition of the International Association for Dental Research
Publications:
• CADR [Canadian Association for Dental Research]/ACRD [Association canadienne de recherches dentaires] Division Annual Report
Type: Yearbook; *Frequency:* Annually

Canadian Association for Disabled Skiing (CADS) / Association canadienne pour les skieurs handicapés (ACSH)

791 Strathcona Dr. SW, Calgary AB T3H 1N8
Tel: 587-315-5870; *Fax:* 866-531-9644
disabledskiing.ca
Overview: A medium-sized national charitable organization founded in 1976
Mission: To assist individuals with a disability to participate in recreational & competitive snow skiing & snowboarding
Chief Officer(s):
Maureen O'Hara-Leman, Executive Director
executive.director@disabledskiing.ca
Finances: *Funding Sources:* Sponsorships; Donations
1900 volunteer(s)
Membership: 1,130 disabled members; *Fees:* $25
Activities: Ensuring that programs are delivered at an appropriate level of expertise, through the work of a technical committee; Providing information about adaptive equipment; *Awareness Events:* CADS Ski Improvement & Race Development Festival, March
Publications:
• The Perspective: CADS National Newsletter
Type: Newsletter; *Editor:* Karen Elliott
Profile: Reports from the Canadian Association for Disabled Skiing, plus programming & forthcoming events

Canadian Association for Disabled Skiing - Alberta (CADS Alberta)

11759 Groat Rd., Edmonton AB T5M 3K6
Tel: 780-427-8104; *Fax:* 780-427-0524
info@cadsalberta.ca
www.cadsalberta.ca
www.facebook.com/CADSAB
twitter.com/CADSAlberta
Overview: A small provincial charitable organization founded in 1961 overseen by Canadian Association for Disabled Skiing
Mission: CADS Alberta is a volunteer-based organization assisting individuals with a disability to lead fuller lives through active participation in recreational & competitive snow skiing & snowboarding. It is a registered charity, BN: 133967406RR0001.
Member of: Canadian Association for Disabled Skiing
Affliation(s): Canadian Ski Instructors' Alliance (CSIA), Canadian Association of Snowboard Instructors (CASI)
Chief Officer(s):
John Stone, President
president@cadsalberta.ca
Allyson Szafranski, Executive Coordinator
Finances: *Annual Operating Budget:* $50,000-$100,000
500 volunteer(s)
Membership: 800+; *Fees:* $40

Calgary Zone
CADS Calgary, Canada Olympic Park, 88 Canada Olympic Rd. SW, Calgary AB T3B 5R5

Tel: 403-286-8050
info@cadscalgary.ca
www.cadscalgary.ca
Chief Officer(s):
Rick Logan, Chair
chairperson@cadscalgary.ca
Edmonton Zone
CADS Edmonton, PO Box 35073, 10818 Jasper Ave., Edmonton AB T5J 0B7
Tel: 780-669-3856
info@cadsedmonton.ca
www.cadsedmonton.ca
Chief Officer(s):
Dale Loyer, President
Lethbridge Zone
Castle Mountain, PO Box 610, Pincher Creek AB T0K 1W0
Tel: 403-627-5101; *Fax:* 403-627-3515
Toll-Free: 888-754-8667
info@skicastle.ca
www.skicastle.ca
Rocky Mountain Zone
Rocky Mountain Adaptive Sport Center, #2, 201 Carey, Canmore AB T1W 2R7
Tel: 403-675-9000
info@rmasc.ca
www.rmasc.ca
Chief Officer(s):
Ian Hipkins, Director
ian@rmasc.ca

Canadian Association for Disabled Skiing - National Capital Division (CADS-NCD)

1216 Bordeau Grove, Ottawa ON K1C 2M7
Tel: 819-827-4378
cads-ncd.ca
Overview: A medium-sized provincial charitable organization overseen by Canadian Association for Disabled Skiing
Member of: Canadian Association for Disabled Skiing
Chief Officer(s):
Bernie Simpson, President
berniesimpson@sympatico.ca
Membership: *Committees:* Technical

Canadian Association for Disabled Skiing - New Brunswick

35 Bloomfield Station Rd., Bloomfield Station NB E5N 4M5
Tel: 506-832-1104
www.facebook.com/CADSNB
Overview: A medium-sized provincial charitable organization overseen by Canadian Association for Disabled Skiing
Member of: Canadian Association for Disabled Skiing
Chief Officer(s):
Jim Bowland, Contact
jimbowland.cadsnb@nb.sympatico.ca

Canadian Association for Disabled Skiing - Newfoundland & Labrador Division

6 Albany Pl., St. John's NL A1E 1Y2
Tel: 709-753-3625; *Fax:* 709-777-4884
disabledskiing.ca/?page_id=123
Also Known As: CADS Newfoundland/Labrador
Overview: A small provincial organization overseen by Canadian Association for Disabled Skiing
Member of: Canadian Association for Disabled Skiing
Chief Officer(s):
Marg Tibbo, Representative
margaret.tibbo@easternhealth.ca

Canadian Association for Disabled Skiing - Nova Scotia

c/o Alpine Ski Nova Scotia, 5516 Spring Garden Rd., Halifax NS B3J 1G6
Tel: 902-425-5450; *Fax:* 902-425-5606
alpinens@sportnovascotia.ca
www.alpineskinovascotia.ca
Also Known As: CADS Nova Scotia
Overview: A medium-sized provincial organization overseen by Canadian Association for Disabled Skiing
Member of: Alpine Canada Alpin; Canadian Association for Disabled Skiing
Chief Officer(s):
Lorraine Burch, Executive Director
Finances: *Annual Operating Budget:* $250,000-$500,000
Staff Member(s): 1; 5 volunteer(s)
Membership: 1-99; *Fees:* $20

Canadian Association for Disabled Skiing - Ontario

c/o Hennum, 1481 Jalna Ave., Mississauga ON L5J 1S6
www.disabledskiingontario.com
twitter.com/cads_ontario
Also Known As: CADS Ontario
Overview: A medium-sized provincial organization overseen by Canadian Association for Disabled Skiing
Member of: Canadian Association for Disabled Skiing
Chief Officer(s):
Carl Hennum, President
carl@disabledskiingontario.com

Canadian Association for Distance Education (CADE); Association for Media & Technology in Education in Canada (AMTEC) ***See*** Canadian Network for Innovation in Education

Canadian Association for Educational Psychology (CAEP) / L'association Canadienne en psychopedagogie (ACP)

C/O Nancy Perry, University Of British Columbia, 2125 Main Mall, Vancouver BC V6T 1Z4
Tel: 604-822-6410
caepacp.wordpress.com
www.facebook.com/CAEP.ACP
Overview: A small national organization founded in 1997
Mission: To research, discuss, & encourage the study of educational psychology
Member of: Canadian Society for Studies in Education
Chief Officer(s):
Sylvie Cartier, Co-President
sylvie.cartier@umontreal.ca
Deborah Butler, Co-President
deborah.butler@ubc.ca
Membership: *Fees:* $10
Publications:
• Canadian Association for Educational Psychology Newsletter
Type: Newsletter; *Frequency:* Semiannually

Canadian Association for Enterostomal Therapy (CAET) / Association canadienne des stomathérapeutes

66 Leopolds Dr., Ottawa ON K1V 7E3
Fax: 613-834-6351
Toll-Free: 888-739-5072
office@caet.ca
www.caet.ca
Overview: A small national charitable organization founded in 1981
Mission: To promote high standards for nursing practice in the area of enterostomal therapy
Chief Officer(s):
Paulo DaRosa, President
paulo_darosa@rogers.com
Elise Rodd-Nielsen, Treasurer
eliserodd@hotmail.com
Catherine Harley, Executive Director
catherine.harley@sympatico.ca
Membership: 350+; *Member Profile:* Nurses specializing in the care of patients with challenges in wound, ostomy, & continence; *Committees:* National Conference Planning; Political Action; Professional Development and Practice; Informatics and Research; Marketing
Activities: Promoting education & research; Providing networking opportunities
Awards:
• President's Award (Award)
Eligibility: Awarded for excellence in ET Nursing.
Meetings/Conferences: • Canadian Association for Enterostomal Therapy National Conference 2015, May, 2015, Halifax Marriott Harbourfront Hotel, Halifax, NS
Scope: National
• Canadian Association for Enterostomal Therapy National Conference 2016, June, 2016, Palais Congres, Montreal, QC
Scope: National
Description: In partnership with Wound, Ostomy Continence Nurses Society (WOCN).
Publications:
• CAET [Canadian Association for Enterostomal Therapy] Membership Directory
Type: Directory
• The Link: The Official Publication of the CAET [Canadian Association for Enterostomal Therapy]
Type: Newsletter; *Frequency:* 3 pa; *Accepts Advertising*; *Price:* Free to CAET members
Profile: Reports, research projects, clinical papers, review articles, & industry news

Canadian Association for Familial Ataxias ***Voir*** Association canadienne des ataxies familiales

Canadian Association for Food Studies (CAFS) / L'Association canadienne des études sur l'alimentation

c/o Centre for Studies in Food Security, Ryerson University, 350 Victoria St., Toronto ON M5B 2K3
Tel: 416-979-5000; *Fax:* 416-979-5362
cafsadmin@foodstudies.ca
cafs.landfood.ubc.ca
www.linkedin.com/groups/Canadian-Association-Food-Studies-3916447?home
www.facebook.com/CAFSpage
twitter.com/CAFSfoodstudies
Overview: A small national organization founded in 2005
Mission: Aims to allow researchers from diverse disciplines working at universities as well as public and community based organizations to meet regularly to identify research priorities and to share research findings on diverse issues dealing with food security concerns.
Membership: *Fees:* $75 regualr; $30 student
Meetings/Conferences: • Canadian Association for Food Studies 10th Annual Assembly: Capital Ideas - Nourishing Debates, Minds and Bodies, May, 2015, University of Ottawa, Ottawa, ON
Scope: National

Canadian Association for Free Expression (CAFE)

PO Box 332, Stn. B, Toronto ON M9W 5L3
Tel: 905-897-7221; *Fax:* 905-277-3914
cafe@canadafirst.net
www.canadianfreespeech.com
Overview: A small national organization founded in 1981
Mission: To protect Canadian civil liberties; To promote free speech & discussion as essential parts to a functioning democracy
Activities: Researching threats to freedom of speech; Informing media of concerns about threats to freedom of speech & freedom of belief; Engaging in lobbying activities & court interventions
Publications:
• The Free Speech Monitor
Frequency: 10 pa; *Price:* $15
Profile: CAFE research on threats to freedom of speech

Canadian Association for Graduate Studies (CAGS) / Association canadienne pour les études supérieures (ACES)

#301, 260 St. Patrick St., Ottawa ON K1N 5K5
Tel: 613-562-0949; *Fax:* 613-562-9009
info@cags.ca
www.cags.ca
Overview: A medium-sized national charitable organization founded in 1962
Mission: To promote excellence in graduate education; To foster research, scholarship, & creative activity; To provide a nationwide link for the exchange of information between graduate schools & granting councils, research, business, & industrial sectors, & all levels of government; To hold meetings & conferences; To publish materials to advance graduate education; To develop & maintain national standards for graduate degree programs; To support the regular external evaluation of these standards; To deal with other matters of concern to Deans & Associate Deans of graduate studies
Member of: Canadian Consortium for Research; Association of Universities & Colleges of Canada
Chief Officer(s):
Sally Rutherford, Executive Director
sally.rutherford@cags.ca
John Doering, President, 204-474-9887
jay_doering@umanitoba.ca
Gary Slater, Vice-President, 613-562-5800 Ext. 1234
deangrad@uottawa.ca
Sue Horton, Sec.-Treas., 519-888-4567 Ext. 33439
sehorton@uwaterloo.ca
Finances: *Annual Operating Budget:* $250,000-$500,000; *Funding Sources:* Subscriptions
Staff Member(s): 2
Membership: 58 Canadian universities with graduate programs + 2 national graduate student associations + 3 federal research-granting agencies & organizations; *Fees:* Schedule available; *Member Profile:* Institutional members are Canadian universities with graduate programs & which are members of the

Association of Universities & Colleges of Canada. Graduate student association members are national associations with objectives consistent with CAGS. Corresponding members are related national & international organizations & Canadian institutions with plans for graduate programs. Sustaining members are nonprofit and for-profit organizations which provide services to graduate studies & research. Federal research-granting agency membership is open to federal research-granting agencies.
Awards:
• CAGS [Canadian Association for Graduate Studies] / UMI [University Microfilms International] Distinguished Dissertation Awards (Award)
To honour doctoral students whose dissertations make an unique contribution to the areas of engineering, medical sciences, & natural sciences or fine arts, humanities, & social sciences
• CAGS [Canadian Association for Graduate Studies] / ETS Educational Testing Service] Award for Excellence & Innovation (Award)
Presented to a member institution or one its graduate programs for excellence & innovation in enhancing the graduate student experience
Meetings/Conferences: • Canadian Association for Graduate Studies 2015 Annual General Meeting & Conference, October, 2015, Hyatt Regency - Calgary, Calgary, AB
Scope: National
Description: A yearly conference held at the end of October or the beginning of November, including plenary & breakout sessions, workshops, the presentation of awards, & the Killam Lecture related to graduate studies
Publications:
• Canadian Association for Graduate Studies Statistical Report
Type: Yearbook; *Frequency:* Annually
Profile: A report on registration in graduate studies at Canadian universities for association members only

Canadian Association for Health Services & Policy Research (CAHSPR) / Association canadienne pour la recherche sur les services et les politiques de la santé (ACRSPS)

292 Somerset St. West, Ottawa ON K2P 0J6
Tel: 613-288-9239; *Fax:* 613-599-7805
info@cahspr.ca
www.cahspr.ca
www.facebook.com/CAHSPR
twitter.com/CAHSPR
www.youtube.com/CAHSPR
Previous Name: Canadian Health Economics Research Association
Overview: A small national organization founded in 1983
Mission: To provide a multidisciplinary association fostering and supporting linkages between researchers and decision makers; knowledge translation and exchange; education and training; and advocacy for research and its more effective use in planning, practice and policy-making.
Chief Officer(s):
Steve Morgan, President
Adalsteinn (Steini) Brown, President-Elect
Finances: *Funding Sources:* Membership dues
Membership: 450; *Fees:* $175 individual; $75 student; *Member Profile:* Health services & policy researchers; Decision makers; Practitioners; Students; Users of research from organizations & industry; Representatives from sponsor organizations; *Committees:* Collaborative Healthcare Improvement Partnerships; Cancer; Health and Human Resources; Maternal and Child Health; Mental Health; Primary Health Care; Student Working Group
Meetings/Conferences: • Canadian Association for Health Services and Polivc ResearchConference 2015, May, 2015, Hilton Bonaventure, Montreal, QC
Scope: National
Publications:
• CAHSPR [Canadian Association for Health Services & Policy Research] Newsletter
Type: Newsletter; *Frequency:* Weekly
Profile: CAHSPR activities & upcoming events, career opportunities, links to course materials for student members, research & policy items ofinterest to members
• Healthcare Policy
Type: Journal; *Frequency:* Quarterly

The Canadian Association for HIV Research (CAHR) / L'Association Canadienne de recherche sur le HIV (ACRV)

#1105, 1 Nicholas St., Ottawa ON K1N 7B7
Tel: 613-241-5785
info@cahr-acrv.ca
www.cahr-acrv.ca
Overview: A medium-sized national charitable organization founded in 1991
Mission: Focuses on HIV/AIDS research & education
Chief Officer(s):
Jonathan Angel, President
Carol Strike, Secretary
Curtis Cooper, Treasurer
Andrew Matejcic, Executive Director
Erin Love, Project Coordinator
Shelley Mineavet, Project Coordinator
Staff Member(s): 3
Meetings/Conferences: • 24th Annual Canadian Conference on HIV/AIDS Research - Canadian Association for HIV Research 2015, April, 2015, Metro Toronto Convention Centre, Toronto, ON
Scope: National

Canadian Association for Humane Trapping (CAHT)

PO Box 7115, Stn. Maplehurst, Burlington ON L7T 4J8
e-mail: caht1@cogeco.ca
www.caht.ca
Overview: A medium-sized national charitable organization founded in 1954
Mission: To reduce & eliminate suffering of animals trapped for whatever reason; To work with governments, trappers, the commercial fur industry, animal welfare organizations & the public-at-large to bring about actual trapping improvements
Member of: World Conservation Union; Fur Institute of Canada; World Wildlife Fund; Canadian Nature Federation; Canadian Federation of Humane Societies
Chief Officer(s):
James H. Bandow, Executive Director
Donald Mitton, Project Director
Donna Bandow, Coordinator, Grants & Fundraising
Finances: *Funding Sources:* Membership fees; Bequests; Donations
Membership: 750; *Fees:* $10; *Committees:* Trap research & development
Activities: *Speaker Service:* Yes
Publications:
• The CAHT [Canadian Association for Humane Trapping] Bulletin
Type: Newsletter; *Number of Pages:* 16

Canadian Association for Information Science (CAIS) / Association canadienne des sciences de l'information (ACSI)

c/o Nadia Caidi, Faculty of Information, #335, 45 Willcocks St., Toronto ON M5S 1C7
Tel: 416-978-4664
nadia.caidi@utoronto.ca
www.cais-acsi.ca
Overview: A small national organization founded in 1970
Mission: To advance information science in Canada by encouraging & facilitating the exchange of information on the use, access, retrieval, organization, management, & dissemination of information
Chief Officer(s):
Nadia Caidi, President
nadia.caidi@utoronto.ca
Siobhan Stevenson, Vice-President
siobhan.stevenson@utoronto.ca
Heather Hill, Director, Membership
hhill6@uwo.ca
Dinesh Rathi, Director, Communications
drathi@ualberta.ca
Heather O'Brien, Secretary
hlobrien@interchange.ubc.ca
Ali Shiri, Treasurer
ali.shiri@ualberta.ca
Membership: *Member Profile:* Information scientists, librarians, archivists, computer scientists, educators, journalists, documentalists, economists & others who support the objectives of the Canadian Association for Information Science
Meetings/Conferences: • Canadian Association for Information Science / Association canadienne des sciences de l'information 2015 43rd Annual Conference, June, 2015, University of Ottawa, Ottawa, ON
Scope: National
Description: Held in conjunction with the Congress of the Humanities & Social Sciences; Canadian information scientists & professionals have met to discuss the access, retrieval, production, value, use, & management of information.
Contact Information: Conference Co-Chair: Eric Meyers, Phone: 604-827-3945, E-mail: Eric.Meyers@ubc.ca; Conference Co-Chair: Heather O'Brien, Phone: 604-822-6365, E-mail: h.obrien@ubc.ca
• Canadian Association for Information Science / Association canadienne des sciences de l'information 2016 44th Annual Conference, 2016
Scope: National
Description: Held in conjunction with the Congress of the Humanities & Social Sciences; Canadian information scientists & professionals have met to discuss the access, retrieval, production, value, use, & management of information.
Contact Information: Conference Co-Chair: Eric Meyers, Phone: 604-827-3945, E-mail: Eric.Meyers@ubc.ca; Conference Co-Chair: Heather O'Brien, Phone: 604-822-6365, E-mail: h.obrien@ubc.ca
Publications:
• Canadian Journal of Information & Library Science
Type: Journal; *Frequency:* Quarterly; *Accepts Advertising*; *Editor:* H Julien (heidi.julien@ualberta.ca) *ISSN:* 1195-096X; *Price:* Free for personal or institutional members of CAIS;$95 Canada; $110 other countries
Profile: Research, reviews of books, software & technology, & letters to the editor

Canadian Association for Integrative and Energy Therapies (CAIET)

Tel: 416-221-5639; *Fax:* 416-221-7126
www.caiet.org
www.facebook.com/119293418135544
twitter.com/CEPConference
Overview: A small national organization
Mission: A Canadian nonprofit organization of licensed mental health professionals and related energy and integrative health practitioners promoting knowledge and understanding of Energy Psychology and related fields.
Chief Officer(s):
Sharon Cass-Toole, President & Executive Director
Membership: *Fees:* $75 regular; $250 corporate
Meetings/Conferences: • Energy Psychology Conference 2015, 2015
Scope: National

Canadian Association for Interpretation ***See*** Interpretation Canada - A Professional Association for Heritage Interpretation

Canadian Association for Irish Studies (CAIS) / L'Association canadienne pour les études irlandaises

c/o Andrea Walisser, Dept. of History, Simon Fraser University, 8888 University Dr., Burnaby BC V5A 1S6
e-mail: info@irishstudies.ca
www.irishstudies.ca
Overview: A small international charitable organization founded in 1974
Mission: To encourage the study of Irish culture in Canada
Chief Officer(s):
Michele Holmgren, President
mholmgren@mtroyal.ca
Andrea Walisser, Secretary-Treasurer
awalisse@sfu.ca
Jean Talman, Communications Officer
jean.talman@utoronto.ca
Membership: *Fees:* $35 students; $75 regular & senior members; $110 family; *Member Profile:* Individuals in Canada & throughout the world who are interested in the promotion of Irish culture in Canada
Activities: Supporting discussions of current issues in Irish studies
Publications:
• CAIS [Canadian Association for Irish Studies] Newsletter
Type: Newsletter; *Frequency:* Semiannually; *Editor:* Michael Quigley; *Price:* Free for CAIS members
Profile: Announcements & information from the association
• The Canadian Journal of Irish Studies (CJIS) / Revue canadienne d'études irlandaises (RCÉI)
Type: Journal; *Frequency:* Semiannually; *Editor:* Rhona Richman Kenneally; *Price:* Free for CAIS members
Profile: Research, book reviews, & general interest writing about aspects of the life ofIreland, especially work with a Canadian dimension

Canadian Association for Israel Philately (CAFIP)

11 Evening Side Rd., Thornhill ON L3T 4K1
Tel: 416-879-4298
Overview: A small international organization founded in 1952

Mission: To promote the study of postage stamps & the postal history of Israel
Affliation(s): Society of Israel Philately; World Philatelic Congress; Royal Philatelic Society of Canada; American Philately Society
Chief Officer(s):
Morty Wagman, Contact
Membership: *Member Profile:* Interest in Israel, Judaica & Holy Land philatelics
Activities: Meets second Wed. of each month at Bet Joseph Lubavitch, 44 Edinburgh St. E. Toronto; *Library*

Canadian Association for Japanese Language Education (CAJLE)

PO Box 75133, 20 Bloor St. East, Toronto ON M4W 3T3
e-mail: cajle.pr@gmail.com
www.cajle.info
Overview: A small national organization founded in 1988
Mission: Promotes Japanese language education in Canada.
Chief Officer(s):
Ikuko Komuro-Lee, President
Membership: 200; *Fees:* $45 regular; $30 student; $120 institutional
Activities: Annual conference, lectures, workshops, publication of academic journals and newsletters
Meetings/Conferences: • Canadian Association for Japanese Language Education 2015 Annual Conference, 2015
Scope: National

Canadian Association for Laboratory Accreditation Inc. (CALA)

#310, 1565 Carling Ave., Ottawa ON K1Z 8R1
Tel: 613-233-5300; *Fax:* 613-233-5501
www.cala.ca
www.linkedin.com/company/canadian-association-for-laboratory-accredita
www.facebook.com/161209647296775
Overview: A medium-sized national organization founded in 1989
Mission: To provide internationally-recognized accreditation services; To assist laboratories in the achievement of high levels of scientific & management excellence; To improve environmental quality & public health & safety
Member of: Asia Pacific Laboratory Accreditation Cooperation; International Laboratory Accreditation Cooperation
Chief Officer(s):
Charlie Brimley, President & CEO
cbrimley@cala.ca
Brenda Dashney, Chief Financial Officer
bdashney@cala.ca
Tim Delaney, Chair
Ken Middlebrook, Manager, Proficiency Testing
kmiddlebrook@cala.ca
Andrew Morris, Manager, Data & Information
amorris@cala.ca
Staff Member(s): 15
Membership: *Member Profile:* Individuals, consultants, institutions, industrial organizations, regulatory agencies, laboratory equipment suppliers, & user groups interested in the work of environmental analytical laboratories; *Committees:* Accreditation Council; Advisory Panel; Program
Activities: Advocating for change in protecting public health & safety; Educating the public & raising awareness of laboratory accreditation; Offering training opportunities, such as workshops & web-based education; Conducting site audits & proficiency testing to evaluate the performance of laboratories; Granting accreditation to laboratories, based on decisions of the CALA Accreditation Council;
Meetings/Conferences: • Canadian Association for Laboratory Accreditation 2015 Annual General Meeting, 2015, Winnipeg, MB
Scope: National
Publications:
• Canadian Association for Laboratory Accreditation Inc. Annual Report
Type: Yearbook; *Frequency:* Annually

Canadian Association for Laboratory Animal Science (CALAS) / Association canadienne pour la science des animaux de laboratoire (ACSAL)

#640, 144 Front St., Toronto ON M5J 2L7
Tel: 416-593-0268; *Fax:* 416-979-1819
Other Communication: membership@calas-acsal.org
office@calas-acsal.org
calas-acsal.org
Overview: A small national organization founded in 1961
Mission: To elevate standards of laboratory animal science; To promote excellence in research; To eliminate inhumane & unnecessary use of animals in research; To enhance animal welfare
Chief Officer(s):
Jacqui Sullivan, Board Liaison
jacqui@calas-acsal.org
Khadijah Hewitt, Contact, Membership & Registry Relations
khadijah@calas-acsal.org
Wendy Ansell, Registrar, Symposium
wendy@calas-acsal.org
Alysone Will, Contact, Finance
alysone@calas-acsal.org
Khadijah Hewitt, Coordinator, Membership & Registry
Finances: *Funding Sources:* Membership fees; Sponsorships
Membership: 1,000; *Member Profile:* Veterinarians; Physicians; Researchers; Technicians; Administrators; Students; Institutions; *Committees:* Awards; Marketing; Membership; Educational; Regional Chapter; Symposium; Continuing Education
Activities: Providing information about the animal science industry; Offering networking opportunities; Providing continuing education to advance the knowledge & skills of persons who work with laboratory animals
Publications:
• Canadian Association for Laboratory Animal Science Members' Magazine
Type: Magazine; *Frequency:* Bimonthly; *Price:* Free with membership in the Canadian Association for Laboratory Animal Science

Canadian Association for Latin American & Caribbean Studies (CALACS) / Association canadienne des études latino-américaines et caraïbes (ACELAC)

c/o Juan Pablo Crespo Vasquez, York Research Tower, York University, #8-17, 4700 Keele St., Toronto ON M3J 1P3
Tel: 416-736-2100; *Fax:* 519-971-3610
calacs@yorku.ca
www.can-latam.org
Overview: A medium-sized national organization founded in 1969
Mission: To facilitate networking & the exchange of information among those engaged in teaching & research on Latin America & the Caribbean in Canada & abroad; To foster throughout Canada, especially within the universities, colleges, & other centres of higher education, the expansion of information on & interest in Latin America & the Caribbean; To represent the academic & professional interest of Canadian Latin Americanists
Member of: Canadian Council of Area Studies Learned Societies
Chief Officer(s):
Pablo Crespo Vasquez Juan, Contact, Administration
Steven Palmer, Secretary-Treasurer, 519-253-3000 Ext. 2329
spalmer@uwindsor.ca
Finances: *Funding Sources:* International Development Research Council
Membership: 350; *Fees:* $80 regular; $23 student; $90 institution; *Member Profile:* Academics; Students; NGO officers; Government officials; *Committees:* Advisory; Organizing
Meetings/Conferences: • Canadian Association for Latin American & Caribbean Studies 2015 44th Congress, 2015
Scope: National
Description: Theme: Environments, Socieities Imaginaries: The Americas in Motion
Contact Information: Communications Contact: James Gaede, E-mail: admin@can-latam.org
Publications:
• CALACS [Canadian Association for Latin American & Caribbean Studies] Bulletin
Type: Newsletter
Profile: Information & announcements for members about the activities of the association
• Canadian Journal of Latin American and Caribbean Studies (CJLACS)
Type: Journal; *Frequency:* Semiannually; *Accepts Advertising*; *Editor:* Catherine Krull
Profile: Articles, research, debates, & reviews of recent publications on Latin America & the Caribbean

Canadian Association for Leisure Studies (CALS) / Association canadienne d'études en loisir

c/o Recreation & Leisure Studies, Faculty of Applied Health Sciences, University of Waterloo, Waterloo ON N2L 3G1
www.cals.uwaterloo.ca
Overview: A small national organization founded in 1981
Chief Officer(s):
Heather Mair, President
hmair@uwaterloo.ca
Dawn Trussell, Vice-President & Treasurer
Karen Gallant, Secretary
Membership: *Member Profile:* Canadian & international practitioners & scholars with an interest in recreation & leisure services & research
Activities: Establishing the Research Group on Leisure & Aging
Meetings/Conferences: • Canadian Association for Leisure Studies Canadian Congress on Leisure 2017, May 2017, 2017, University of Waterloo, Waterloo, ON
Scope: National
Description: A triennial meeting at the Canadian Congress on Leisure Research. The theme in 2017 is Engaging Legacies, which will involve discussions focused on inclusive communities
Publications:
• Leisure / Loisir
Type: Journal; *Frequency:* Quarterly *ISSN:* 1492-7713
Profile: Scholarly papers in the field of leisure, recreation, sport, parks, tourism, & the arts

Canadian Association for Medical Education (CAME) / Association canadienne pour l'éducation médicale (ACÉM)

#800, 265 Carling Ave., Ottawa ON K1S 2E1
Tel: 613-730-0687; *Fax:* 613-730-1196
came@afmc.ca
www.came-acem.ca
Overview: A medium-sized national organization founded in 1987
Mission: To improve medical education in Canada; To promote excellence & scholarship in medical education; To support educational development; To encourage research in medical education
Chief Officer(s):
Glen Bandiera, President, 416-864-5095
bandierag@smh.toronto.on.ca
Jerry Maniate, Secretary, 416-340-3079
jerry.maniate@utoronto.ca
François Goulet, Treasurer, 514-933-4441 Ext. 237
goulet.cmq@sympatico.ca
Derek Puddester, Coordinator, 613-737-7600 Ext. 2703
drpuddester@me.com
Stéphanie Mutschler, Development Officer
smutschler@afmc.ca
Finances: *Annual Operating Budget:* $100,000-$250,000
Staff Member(s): 1; 40 volunteer(s)
Membership: 680; *Fees:* $10 students; $25 residents; $150 regular membership; *Member Profile:* Medical educators in Canada; Faculty members; Residents; Students; *Committees:* Executive; Finance; Awards; Nominating
Activities: Advocating for medical education & medical educators; Offering networking opportunities; Providing professional development activities, such as workshops
Awards:
• CAME Ian Hart Award for Distinguished Contribution to Medical Education (Award)
To recognize senior faculty who have made an exceptional contribution to medical education *Contact:* Stéphanie Mutschler, smutschler@afmc.ca
• CAME New Educator's Award (Award)
To recognize persons in the first phase of their professional career *Contact:* Stéphanie Mutschler, E-mail: smutschler@afmc.ca
Meetings/Conferences: • Canadian Association for Medical Education / Association canadienne pour l'éducation médicale 2015 Canadian Conference on Medical Education, April, 2015, Fairmont Vancouver & Hyatt Regency Vancouver, Vancouver, BC
Scope: National
Contact Information: Social Media: www.facebook.com/CanadianConferenceOnMedicalEducation; twitter.com/MedEdConference; Web Site: www.mededconference.ca
Publications:
• CAME [Canadian Association for Medical Education] Newsletter
Type: Newsletter; *Editor:* Marcel D'Eon
Profile: Articles & commentaries of interest to Canadian medical educators
• CAME [Canadian Association for Medical Education] E-Bulletin
Type: Newsletter; *Frequency:* Monthly
Profile: Current association information, such as announcements, upcoming meetings, grant opportunities, & career postings

Canadian Association for Mine & Explosive Ordnance Security (CAMEO)

1009 Oak Cres., Cornwall ON K6J 2N2
Tel: 613-937-0686; *Fax:* 613-937-4643
www.cameo.org
Also Known As: CAMEO Landmine Clearance
Overview: A small international charitable organization
Mission: To engage in humanitarian mine clearance; to engage in humanitarian explosive ordnance disposal; to engage in live-firing area clearance & environmental clean-up; to engage in land mine & explosive ordnance awareness training; to engage in land mine & battle area surveys; to provide training & assistance to others in the carrying out of all of the above activities
Affliation(s): Gurkha Security Guards' EOD Trust; Defence Remediation Incorporated; Canadian Landmine Research Network; Operation Save Innocent Lives - Sudan; Wolf's Flat Ordnance Disposal Corporation; Sécuriplus; AGRA Inc.; Somali-Canadian Aid; Christian Council of Mozambique; New Sudan Council of Churches; Igreja Evangélica Unida - Comunhao Anglicana em Angola
Chief Officer(s):
James D. McGill, Executive Director, President & CEO
megill@cameo.org
Activities: Landmine clearance in Southern Sudan; *Speaker Service:* Yes

Canadian Association for Music Therapy (CAMT) / Association de musicothérapie du Canada (AMC)

#320, 110 Cumberland St., Toronto ON M5R 3V5
Tel: 416-944-0421; *Fax:* 416-944-0431
Toll-Free: 800-996-2268
camt@musictherapy.ca
www.musictherapy.ca
Overview: A medium-sized national licensing organization founded in 1974
Mission: To promote excellence in music therapy practice & education in Canadian clinical, educational, & community settings
Affliation(s): World Federation of Music Therapy
Chief Officer(s):
Guylaine Vaillancourt, President
Finances: *Funding Sources:* Membership; Book sales; Conference fees
Staff Member(s): 1
Membership: 650; *Fees:* $60 students, interns, & retired & inactive therapists; $75 graduate students; $125 associate members; $175 accredited therapists; $330 corporate; *Member Profile:* Accredited music therapists; Unaccredited graduates of a CAMT recognized music therapy training program; Students; Individuals who support the music therapy profession & its aims; Corporate members
Activities: Accrediting music therapists; Setting standards for music therapy training; Increasing awareness of music therapy; Providing guidance & information to members; Representing members in matters related to practice & government legislation; *Awareness Events:* National Music Therapy Week; *Internships:* Yes; *Library:* Canadian Association for Music Therapy Library; by appointment
Awards:
• Norma Sharpe Award (Award)
Awarded to an MTA who has made an outstanding contribution to the field of music therapy in Canada
• Peer Recognition Award (Award)
Meetings/Conferences: • Canadian Association for Music Therapy 2015 Conference, May, 2015, Calgary, AB
Scope: National
Publications:
• CAMT [Canadian Association for Music Therapy] Newsletter
Type: Newsletter; *Frequency:* Quarterly
• Canadian Association for Music Therapy Conference Proceedings
Frequency: Annually
Profile: Proceedings from each CAMT national conference
• The Canadian Association for Music Therapy Member Sourcebook
Type: Directory
• The Canadian Journal of Music Therapy
Type: Journal; *Frequency:* Annually; *Accepts Advertising*; *Editor:* Kevin Kirkland
Profile: Peer-reviewed papers about music therapy knowledge & practice

Music Therapy Association of British Columbia
c/o Capilano College, 2055 Purcell Way, North Vancouver BC V7N 3H5
Tel: 604-924-0046; *Fax:* 604-983-7559
Toll-Free: 800-424-0556
info@mtabc.com
www.mtabc.com
www.facebook.com/141974696573
twitter.com/musictherapybc
www.youtube.com/channel/UCiLiJ0Aj_3TLcmCatxASwBg
Mission: To advocate for music therapists in matters related to standards of professional practice, salary scales, ethics, and promotion of the field with other organizations, government agencies, unions and employer groups.
Chief Officer(s):
Gemma Isaac, President
president@mtabc.com

Canadian Association for Neuroscience (CAN)

can-acn.org
Overview: A large national organization
Mission: To promote communication amongst Canadian neuroscientists & encourage research related to the nervous system; To educate about current neuroscience research
Meetings/Conferences: • 9th Annual Canadian Neuroscience Meeting, May, 2015, Westin Bayshore, Vancouver, BC
Scope: National
Description: Neuroscientists meet to discuss neuroscience research in Canada.
• 10th Annual Canadian Neuroscience Meeting, 2016
Scope: National
Description: Neuroscientists meet to discuss neuroscience research in Canada.

Canadian Association for Nursing Research (CANR) / Association canadienne pour la recherche infirmière

c/o Caroline Park, Athabasca University, Faculty of Health Disciplines, 1 University Dr., Athabasca AB T9S 3A3
www.canr.ca
Overview: A medium-sized national organization
Mission: To foster practice-based nursing research & research-based nursing practice across Canada
Member of: Canadian Nursing Association
Chief Officer(s):
Caroline Park, President, 866-500-2928
clpark@athabascau.ca
Pam Hawranik, Secretary, 780-675-6550, Fax: 780-675-6431
phawranik@athabascau.ca
Riek van den Berg, Treasurer, 613-737-8439
riekvandenberg@gmail.com
Membership: *Fees:* $20 students & retired persons; $35 regular members; $65 students & retired persons (includes CJNR); $100 regular members (includes CJNR); *Member Profile:* Nurses; Students; Persons committed to the association's purposes
Activities: Providing information about research & funding; Educating professionals & the public about nursing research & its link to practice; Advocating for members' interests; Liaising with governments & other nursing organizations
Awards:
• Outstanding New Investigator Award (Award)
• Promotion of Research Based Practice Award (Award)
• Practitioner-Researcher Award (Award)
• Nurse Researcher Award (Award)

Canadian Association for Pastoral Practice & Education *See* Canadian Association for Spiritual Care

Canadian Association for People Who Stutter (CAPS) *See* Canadian Stuttering Association

Canadian Association for Pharmacy Distribution Management (CAPDM) / Association canadienne de la gestion de l'approvisionnement pharmaceutique (ACGAP)

#301A, 3800 Steeles Ave. West, Woodbridge ON L4L 4G9
Tel: 905-265-1706; *Fax:* 905-265-9372
www.capdm.ca
ca.linkedin.com/company/canadian-association-for-pharmacy-distribution
www.facebook.com/group.php?gid=182173808506667
Previous Name: Canadian Wholesale Drug Association
Overview: A large national organization founded in 1964
Mission: To act as a resource & an advocacy voice for its members to advance the pharmacy distribution system as an effective, efficient, & safe delivery system for patient health care in Canada
Chief Officer(s):
Brent Teulon, Chair
David W. Johnston, President & CEO
david@capdm.ca
Allan Reynolds, Vice-President, Industry & Member Relations
allan@capdm.ca
Allison Chan, Manager, Member Services & Events
allison@capdm.ca
Finances: *Funding Sources:* Membership dues; Conference fees
Staff Member(s): 4
Membership: 1-99; *Fees:* Schedule available; *Member Profile:* Pharmacy supply chain industry trading partners, including full consolidated distributors, allied distributors, self-distributing pharmacy chains, manufacturers, & service providers; *Committees:* Customer Service; Electronic Signature; Government Relations; Pandemic Preparedness; Member Services; Safe & Secure Supply Chain
Activities: *Library*
Meetings/Conferences: • Canadian Association for Pharmacy Distribution Management 2015 Executive Conference, January, 2015, Montréal Airport Marriott Inn, Dorval, QC
Scope: National
• Canadian Association for Pharmacy Distribution Management 2015 Annual Conference, May, 2015, Omni Scottsdale Resort & Spa at Montelucia, Paradise Valley, AZ
Scope: National
Description: Information for pharmacy supply chain industry professionals
Contact Information: Canadian Association for Pharmacy Distribution Management, Phone: 905-265-1706
• Canadian Association for Pharmacy Distribution Management 2015 Annual September Member Forum, September, 2015
Scope: National
Description: An educational & social event for pharmacy supply chain industry professionals
Contact Information: Canadian Association for Pharmacy Distribution Management, Phone: 905-265-1706
• Canadian Association for Pharmacy Distribution Management 2016 Executive Conference, 2016
Scope: National
Contact Information: Canadian Association for Pharmacy Distribution Management, Phone: 905-265-1706
• Canadian Association for Pharmacy Distribution Management 2016 Annual Conference, 2016
Scope: National
Description: A meeting of pharmacy supply chain industry professionals, featuring presentations by experts on timely & important topics for the industry
Contact Information: Canadian Association for Pharmacy Distribution Management, Phone: 905-265-1706
• Canadian Association for Pharmacy Distribution Management 2016 September Member Forum, 2016
Scope: National
Contact Information: Allison Chan, Phone: 905-265-1706, ext. 223, allison@capdm.ca
Publications:
• Guidebook on Government Prescription Drug Reimbursement Plans & Related Programs
Price: $75 for members; $125 for non-members
Profile: Details on each provincial drug benefit program
• Industry Trends Reports
Price: Free for members; $49.95 for non-members
Profile: Statistics & highlights information related to the distribution & consumption of health care goods & services in Canada
• Pharmacy Who's Who
Type: Directory; *Price:* $180
Profile: Lists retail chains, banners & franchises, manufacturers, distributors, goods & service suppliers, pharmacy associations, top retailers, & post-graduate educational programs

Canadian Association for Photographic Art (CAPA) / L'Association canadienne d'art photographique

PO Box 357, Logan Lake BC V0K 1W0
Tel: 604-523-2378; *Fax:* 604-523-2333
capa@capacanada.ca
capacanada.ca
www.facebook.com/TheCanadianAssociationForPhotographicArt
Merged from: National Association for Photographic Art; Colour Photographic Association of Canada
Overview: A medium-sized national organization founded in 1998
Mission: To promote the advancement of photography as an art form in Canada
Affliation(s): Fédération Internationale de l'Art Photographique
Chief Officer(s):

Canadian Associations

Jacques S. Mailloux, President
president@capacanada.ca
Finances: *Funding Sources:* Membership dues
Membership: *Fees:* Schedule available
Activities: Exhibitions, seminars, workshops, & field trips; sponsors Camera Canada College, an annual summer weekend of field trips, seminars, & camaraderie held in a different city each year
Publications:
• Canadian Camera
Type: Magazine; *Frequency:* Quarterly; *Number of Pages:* 40+; *Price:* Subscription with membership
Profile: Articles about photography, photography tips, photographs from competitions, CAPA news, & profiles of member clubs

Canadian Association for Population Therapeutics (CAPT)

CHU - Ste-Justine, Research Center, 3175, Cote-Ste-Catherine, Montréal QC H3T 1C5
Tel: 514-345-4931; *Fax:* 514-345-4801
www.capt-actp.com
Overview: A small national organization founded in 1996
Mission: To advance the sound development of population-based studies of therapeutic interventions & to provide a forum for the reporting, scientific discussion & dissemination of the data derived from such studies, as an information resource for medical decision-making in the best interests of the individual patient & the public well-being
Chief Officer(s):
Nicole Mittmann, President
nicole.mittmann@sunnybrook.ca
Membership: 100-499; *Fees:* $75; $25 students
Meetings/Conferences: • Canadian Association for Population Therapeutics Annual Conference 2015, 2015
Scope: National

Canadian Association for Prior Learning Assesment (CAPLA) / L'Association canadienne pour la reconnaissance des acquis

PO Box 56001, RPO Minto Place, Ottawa ON K1R 7Z1
Tel: 613-860-1747
info@capla.ca
www.capla.ca
Overview: A small national organization founded in 1994
Mission: Provides the expertise, advocacy and support for the development of prior learning assessment in Canada through its workshops, quarterly newsletter and education and training activities.
Chief Officer(s):
Bonnie Kennedy, Executive Director
b.kennedy@quicklinks.on.ca

Canadian Association for Production & Inventory Control; American Production & Inventory Control Society *See* Association for Operations Management

Canadian Association for Prosthetics & Orthotics (CAPO)

#217, 294 Portage Ave., Winnipeg MB R3C 0B9
Tel: 204-949-4970; *Fax:* 204-947-3627
capo@mts.net
www.prostheticsandorthotics.ca
www.youtube.com/user/PandOCanada?feature=watch
Overview: A medium-sized national organization founded in 1955
Mission: To promote high standards of patient care & professionalism in the prosthetic & orthotic profession throughout Canada; To represent members with government, related organizations, & the general public
Chief Officer(s):
Leslie Pardoe, President
Paul E. Osborne, Secretary-Treasurer
Kathy Kostycz, Association Manager
Membership: 350+; *Member Profile:* Canadian certified prosthetic & orthotic practitioners; Registered technical members; Associate members, such as suppliers, allied health professionals, or people associated with the prosthetic & orthotic field; Students; Retired persons
Activities: Encouraging continuing education, such as lectures & seminars; Providing educational materials, such as up-to-date medical research
Meetings/Conferences: • Canadian Association for Prosthetics and Orthotics 2015 Conference, 2015
Scope: National
Publications:
• Alignment
Editor: Jeff Tiessen
• Canadian Association for Prosthetics & Orthotics Newsletter
Type: Newsletter; *Editor:* Mary Miller

Canadian Association for Renewable Energies (CARE) / Association canadienne pour les énergies renouvelables

7885 Jock Trail, Ottawa ON K0A 2Z0
Tel: 613-663-5400; *Fax:* 613-822-4987
www.renewables.ca
twitter.com/renewablesca
Also Known As: we c.a.r.e
Overview: A small national organization founded in 1998
Mission: To promote feasible applications of renewable energies
Chief Officer(s):
Bill Eggertson, Executive Director
eggertson@renewables.ca
Finances: *Annual Operating Budget:* Less than $50,000; *Funding Sources:* Membership fees
Staff Member(s): 1
Membership: *Member Profile:* Supporters of renewable energies
Activities: Undertaking research to optimize renewable energy technologies; *Speaker Service:* Yes
Publications:
• Refocus Weekly [a publication of the Canadian Association for Renewable Energies]
Type: Newsletter; *Frequency:* Weekly; *Accepts Advertising*
Profile: News, reports, & events from around the world
• Renewable Energy Focus
Type: Magazine; *Accepts Advertising*
Profile: Debate & dialogue between industry, research, government agencies, & financial organizations throughout the world on topics such as biomass, biogass, hydroelectricity, wind, waves, solararchitecture, & fuel cells

Canadian Association for Sandplay Therapy (CAST)

c/o Dave Rogers, Treasurer, #232, 220 Century Rd., Spruce Grove AB T7X 3X7
www.sandplay.ca
Overview: A small national organization founded in 1993
Mission: To promote the development of sandplay in Canada by providing training, offering opportunities for professional exchange, and maintaining guidelines for professional practice.
Member of: International Society for Sandplay Therapy (ISST)
Chief Officer(s):
Barbara Dalziel, President
Activities: Training program; workshops & information meetings
Meetings/Conferences: • Canadian Association for Sandplay Therapy 2015 Conference, 2015
Scope: National

Canadian Association for School Health (CASH)

16629 - 62A Ave., Surrey BC V3S 9L5
Tel: 604-575-3199
info@cash-aces.ca
www.cash-aces.ca
Overview: A small national organization
Mission: Provincial/area coalitions who promote the health of youth through a school-related health program called Comprehensive School Health (CSH); to develop & implements projects, activities & services that follow the CSH approach. This approach helps community agencies, parents, educators, & health professionals work together.
Member of: International School Health Network
Activities: *Library:* Canadian Centre on Community & School Health

Canadian Association for Scottish Studies (CASS)

Dept. of History, Centre for Scottish Studies, University of Guelph, 1008 MacKinnon Ext., Guelph ON N1G 2W1
Tel: 519-824-4120; *Fax:* 519-766-9516
scottish@uoguelph.ca
www.uoguelph.ca/scottish
www.facebook.com/scottishstudies
twitter.com/ScottishStudies
Overview: A small national organization founded in 1971
Mission: To promote interest in Scottish history, literature, & culture
Affiliation(s): Scottish Studies Foundation
Chief Officer(s):
Graeme Morton, General Editor, IRSS, 519-824-4120 Ext. 52255
gmorton@uoguelph.ca
Publications:
• International Review of Scottish Studies
Type: Journal; *Frequency:* Annually; *Editor:* Dr. Graeme Morton
ISSN: 0703-1580; *Price:* Free to members
Profile: Articles & reviews related to Scottish history & culture

Canadian Association for Security & Intelligence Studies (CASIS) / Association canadienne pour les études de renseignement et de sécurité (ACERS)

PO Box 71007, RPO L'Esplanade, Ottawa ON K2P 2L9
e-mail: ecretariat@casis.ca
www.casis.ca
Overview: A small national organization founded in 1985
Mission: To provide informed debate in Canada on security & intelligence issues; To facilitate awareness & understandingof the intelligence & security community
Chief Officer(s):
Greg Fyffe, President
Sarah Jane Corke, Vice-President
Robert Crawhall, Treasurer
Membership: *Fees:* $75 general member; $40 student; *Member Profile:* Academics; Government officials; Lawyers; Journalists; Concerned citizens
Activities: Encouraging research & fostering accumulation of knowledge

Canadian Association for Size Acceptance (CASA)

#511, 99 Dalhousie St., Toronto ON M5B 2N2
Tel: 416-861-0217; *Fax:* 416-861-1668
Overview: A small local organization founded in 1997
Mission: To lobby against & raises awareness of discrimination towards people of size.
Member of: International Size Acceptance Association; National Association to Advance Fat Acceptance
Activities: Conducts media interviews; educates children, teachers, medical professionals & public about the dangers & health effects of dieting; maintains database of plus size services

Canadian Association for Social Work Education (CASWE) / Association canadienne pour la formation en travail social (ACFTS)

#410, 383 Parkdale Ave., Ottawa ON K1Y 4R4
Tel: 613-792-1953
Toll-Free: 888-342-6522
admin@caswe-acfts.ca
caswe-acfts.ca
Previous Name: National Committee of Schools of Social Work; Canadian Association of Schools of Social Work (CASSW)
Overview: A small national charitable organization founded in 1967
Mission: To advance university education for the profession of social work; To accredit professional social work educational programs, based on high educational standards; To increase understanding of the nature & role of social work practice & social welfare
Chief Officer(s):
Carolyn Campbell, President, -, 902-494-1188
Carolyn.Campbell@dal.ca
Sylvie Renaud, Coordinator, Accreditation
accred@caswe-acfts.ca
Sheri McConnell, Vice-President
smcconne@mun.ca
John Flynn, Treasurer
jflyn033@uottawa.ca
Sharon Leslie, Office Administrator, 613-792-1953 Ext. 221
admin@caswe-acfts.ca
Alexandra Wright, PhD, Executive Director
awright@caswe-acfts.ca
Membership: 38 university departments or schools of social work; *Fees:* $30 unwaged persons; $35 retired faculty; $40 students; $60 field & sessional instructors & admin; $80 faculty; $100 - $5000 Insitutions; *Member Profile:* University faculties, schools, & departments offering professional education in social work at the undergraduate, graduate, & post-graduate levels, & accredited by the CASWE / ACFTS Board of Accreditation; University departments or schools planning to operatie programs in social work; Individuals, such as university social work current or retired teachers, field instructors, administrators, alumni or students; *Committees:* Nominating; Educational Policy; International Affairs; Student; Field Education; Social Policy & Advocacy; Francophone Social Work in Linguistic Minority Contexts; Diversity
Activities: Formulating educational policies; Promoting research related to social work practice; Exchanging information & ideas with other national & international social work associations;

Meetings/Conferences: • Canadian Association for Social Work Education 2015 Annual Conference, June, 2015, University of Ottawa, Ottawa, ON
Scope: National
Description: A forum for the exchange of scientific & professional practice ideas. The theme is Le travail social à la croisée des idées, des langues et des cultures / Social Work at the Intersection of Ideas, Languages and Cultures
Contact Information: Phone: 613-792-1953, ext 221; E-mail: admin@caswe-acfts.ca
Publications:
• Canadian Association for Social Work Education Directory of Schools
Type: Directory; *Price:* Free with membership in the Canadian Association for Social Work Education
• Canadian Social Work Review / Revue canadienne de service social
Type: Journal; *Frequency:* Semiannually; *Editor:* David Este; *Price:* Free with membership in the Canadian Association for Social Work Education
Profile: A peer-reviewed journal, featuring original research, critical analyses, & debates that affect social work educators,practitioners, & students

Canadian Association for Spiritual Care (CASC) / Association canadienne de soins spirituels (ACSS)

#27, 1267 Dorval Dr., Oakville ON L6M 3Z4
Tel: 289-837-2272; *Fax:* 289-837-4800
Toll-Free: 866-442-2773
www.spiritualcare.ca
Previous Name: Canadian Association for Pastoral Practice & Education
Overview: A medium-sized national organization founded in 1965
Mission: A national multifaith organization committed to the professional education, certification & support of people involved in pastoral care & pastoral counselling.
Chief Officer(s):
Tony Sedfawi, Executive Director
office@spiritualcare.ca
Kathy Greig, Manager
kathy@spiritualcare.ca
Finances: *Funding Sources:* Membership dues
Membership: *Fees:* $185 associate members, with any amount of CPE or PCE training, & corporate members; $395 certified specialists or teaching supervisors; *Member Profile:* Persons involved in a variety of ministries, in settings such as parishes, prisons & correctional facilities, pastoral counselling centres, health care facilities & industrial facilities
Activities: Offering educational programs for both clergy & lay persons; Providing certification for supervisors & specialists; Creating networking opportunities
Meetings/Conferences: • Annual CASC/ACSS Conference
Scope: National
Publications:
• Canadian Association for Pastoral Practice & Education Handbook
Type: Handbook
Profile: Information about accreditation, certification, & practice
• CAPPE [Canadian Association for Pastoral Practice & Education] / ACPEP National E-Newsletter
Type: Newsletter; *Price:* Free with membership in the Canadian Association for Pastoral Practice & Education
• CAPPE [Canadian Association for Pastoral Practice & Education] / ACPEP Annual Report
Type: Yearbook; *Frequency:* Annually; *Price:* Free with membership in the Canadian Association for Pastoral Practice & Education

Canadian Association for Student Robotics *See* FIRST Robotics Canada

Canadian Association for Studies in Co-operation (CASC) / Association canadienne pour les études sur la coopération (ACEC)

c/o Centre for the Study of Co-operatives, University of Saskatchewan, 101 Diefenbaker Pl., Saskatoon SK S7N 5B8
Tel: 306-966-8509; *Fax:* 306-966-8517
casc.acec@usask.ca
www.coopresearch.coop
Overview: A small national organization founded in 2000
Mission: To promote research on co-operatives in Canada
Chief Officer(s):
Darryl Reed, President
Monica Adler, Vice-President
Membership: *Member Profile:* Researchers, scholars, & practitioners working in the area of co-operatives
Awards:
• Lemaire Co-operative Studies Award (Scholarship)
Postgraduate & undergraduate awards to encourage students to undertake studies which will help them to contribute to the development of co-operatives in Canada or elsewhere; disciplines include: housing, planning, environmental studies, engineering, geography, science, architecture *Amount:* $1,000 - $3,000
• Alexander Fraser Laidlaw Fellowship (Scholarship)
Postgraduate award for students in: housing, environmental studies, planning, geography, science, architecture, civil engineering, engineering; the fellowship is awarded on the basis of the applicant's academic record & the importance of the proposed research activities to the development of the co-operative movement in Canada or elsewhere *Amount:* $1,000
• Amy & Tim Dauphinee Scholarships for Studies in Co-operation (Scholarship)
For graduate students in the following disciplines: cooperatives, housing, planning, environmental studies, geography, science, architecture, civil engineering, engineering; awards based on the applicant's academic records & on the importance of the proposed research activities to the development of the co-operative movement in Canada or abroad *Amount:* $3,000
Meetings/Conferences: • 2015 Canadian Association for Studies in Co-operation Conference, June, 2015, Ottawa, ON
Scope: National
Publications:
• CASC [Canadian Association for Studies in Co-operation] Newsletter
Type: Newsletter

Canadian Association for Studies in the Baha'i Faith *See* Association for Baha'i Studies

Canadian Association for Suicide Prevention (CASP) / L'Association canadienne pour la prévention du suicide (ACPS)

870 Portage Ave., Winnipeg MB R3G 0P1
Tel: 204-784-4073
casp@casp-acps.ca
www.suicideprevention.ca
Overview: A small national charitable organization founded in 1985
Mission: To reduce the suicide rate; To minimize the harmful consequences of suicide
Chief Officer(s):
Dammy Damstrom Albach, President
Renée Ouimet, Vice-President
Yvonne Bergmans, Secretary
Ian Ross, Treasurer
Tim Wall, Executive Director
Finances: *Funding Sources:* Donations; Memoriams; Fundraising
Membership: *Fees:* $30 students; $50 individuals; $150 agencies
Activities: Advocating for policy development; Liaising with provincial, territorial, & federal governments; Providing educational services; Offering information & resources to communities; Facilitating research; Developing the Sharing the Healing Fund & the Network Fund to increase the availability of grief groups; *Awareness Events:* World Suicide Prevention Day, September
Publications:
• Canadian Association for Suicide Prevention Newsletter
Type: Newsletter
Profile: Association issues & information about suicide prevention

Canadian Association for Supported Employment (CASE)

c/o AiMHi Prince George Association for Community Living, 950 Kerry St., Prince George BC V2M 5A3
Tel: 250-564-6408; *Fax:* 250-564-6801
info@supportedemployment.ca
www.supportedemployment.ca
www.facebook.com/CanadianAssocSupportedEmployment
twitter.com/casecanada
Overview: A medium-sized national organization
Mission: CASE is a national organization that promotes workplace inclusion for Canadians with disabilities through supported employment.
Chief Officer(s):
Tracy Williams, President
Membership: *Fees:* $25 individual; $100 organization; *Member Profile:* Individuals and organizations that are interested in working towards full employment for all members of our community.
Meetings/Conferences: • Canadian Association for Supported Employment 2015 Conference, June, 2015, Victoria, BC
Scope: National

Canadian Association for Teacher Education (CATE) / Association canadienne pour la formation des enseignants (ACFE)

c/o The Canadian Society for the Study of Education, #204, 260 Dalhousie St., Ottawa ON K1N 7E4
Tel: 613-241-0018; *Fax:* 613-241-0019
www.csse-scee.ca/cate
Overview: A medium-sized national charitable organization founded in 1978
Mission: To encourage scholarly study & research in education, with special emphasis on teacher education; to provide for the membership a national forum for the presentation & discussion of significant studies in education, with special emphasis on teacher education
Member of: Canadian Society for the Study of Education
Affliation(s): Canadian Association for Research in Early Childhood/Association canadienne pour la recherche préscolaire; Association of Business Teacher Educators of Canada/Association des professeurs en enseignement commercial au Canada
Chief Officer(s):
Lynn Thomas, President
lynn.thomas@usherbrooke.ca
Finances: *Annual Operating Budget:* Less than $50,000; *Funding Sources:* Membership dues; grants
Membership: 300; *Fees:* $10; *Member Profile:* Open to faculty in education departments & students researching & developing teacher education; *Committees:* Awards

Canadian Association for the Advancement of Music & the Arts (CAAMA)

PO Box 42293, 128 Queen St. South, Mississauga ON L3R 4B8
Tel: 905-858-3298
info@caama.org
www.caama.org
Overview: A large national organization founded in 1991
Mission: To further the independent music industry, in Canada & abroad; to ensure that laws regarding the music industry are favourable to members
Chief Officer(s):
Patti Jannetta, President
Membership: *Fees:* $50
Awards:
• The Indie Awards (Award)

Canadian Association for the Advancement of Netherlandic Studies (CAANS) / Association canadienne pour l'avancement des études néerlandaises (ACAEN)

c/o Secretary, 613 Huycks Point Rd., Wellington ON K0K 3L0
www.caans-acaen.ca
www.facebook.com/29784957106215
Overview: A small national organization founded in 1971
Mission: To stimulate awareness & interest in & to promote the study of Netherlandic languages (Dutch, Flemish, Afrikaans), as well as Netherlandic literature, history & culture; to provide a forum for discussion in these areas, hold an annual conference, publish research & sponsor relevant cultural & scholarly activities such as meetings, presentations, lectures & discussions
Affliation(s): Congress of the Social Sciences and Humanities
Chief Officer(s):
Michiel Horn, President
schuhhorn@sympatico.ca
Paul de Laat, Secretary-Treasurer
pgdelaat@gmail.com
Finances: *Funding Sources:* Membership fees; University of Windsor subsidies; Netherlandic Language Union
Membership: *Fees:* $30 individuals & institutions; $25 seniors; $20 students
Publications:
• CAAN [Canadian Association for the Advancement of Netherlandic Studies] Newsletter / Bulletin de l'ACAEN
Type: Newsletter; *Frequency:* 3 pa; *Editor:* Mary Eggermont-Molenaar
• Canadian Journal of Netherlandic Studies / Revue canadienne d'études néerlandaises
Type: Journal; *Frequency:* Semiannually; *Editor:* Basil D. Kingstone *ISSN:* 0225-0500

Canadian Association for the Advancement of Women & Sport & Physical Activity (CAAWS) / Association canadienne pour l'avancement des femmes du sport et de l'activité physique (ACAFS)

#202N, 801 King Edward Ave., Ottawa ON K1N 6N5
Tel: 613-562-5667; *Fax:* 613-562-5668
caaws@caaws.ca
www.caaws.ca
www.facebook.com/CAAWS
twitter.com/caaws
Overview: A medium-sized national organization founded in 1981
Mission: To promote an equitable sport & physical activity system, in which girls & women are participants & leaders; To foster equitable support & diverse opportunities, in sport & physical activity for females across Canada
Chief Officer(s):
Karin Lofstrom, Executive Director
klofstrom@caaws.ca
Sydney Millar, Manager, National Program
snmillar@caaws.ca
Stéphanie Parker, Manager, Marketing & Projects
slegault@caaws.ca
Finances: *Funding Sources:* Donations
Activities: Fostering positive experiences for women in sport & physical activitythroughout Canada; Providing education on issues related to female participation in sport & physical activity; Creating community awareness about the value of an equitable sport & physical activity system; Collaborating with related organizations to foster an equitable system; Presenting awards, grants, & scholarships
Awards:
• Breakthrough Awards (Award)
Presented annually to outstanding nominees who have used innovative ideas & alternative approaches to encourage & enable more girls & women to participate/lead/coach in sport & physical activity *Contact:* Karin Lofstrom
• Girls@Play Nike Youth Award (Award)
• CAAWS/Nike Girls@Play MVP Grant (Award)
Monthly grant awarded to a female athlete, coach, official or sport/recreation organization to help make their sporting goals & dreams *Contact:* www.caaws.ca/girlsatplay/grants/index.html
• Stacey Levitt Scholarships (Scholarship)
Eligibility: Awarded each year on behalf of the Levitt family & in memory of Stacey Levitt, who was killed while jogging in 1995 after being hit by a car *Amount:* $500 & a copy of "I am a Rose"
Publications:
• Health Benefits of Physical Activity for Girls & Women
Profile: A research project on the topic of health benefits & risks of physical activity for girls & women
• In Her Voice: An Exploration of Young Women's Sport & Physical Activity Experiences
Profile: A report, based on group conversations with women, from the ages of 13 to 17, from diverse communities across Canada
• Including Transitioned & Transitioning Athletes in Sport - Issues, Facts, & Perspectives
Profile: Information about gender transition & sport participation
• Making the Most of Your Opportunities: A Media Guide for Athletes & Their Coaches
Price: $15
Profile: Information about effective self-promotion
• On the Move
Type: Handbook
Profile: A practical guide for programmers, coaches teachers, volunteers, & parents to create a female-only program
• Seeing the Invisible, Speaking about the Unspoken: A Position Paper on Homophobia in Sport
Number of Pages: 11
• Sex Discrimination in Sport - An Update
Type: Report; *Number of Pages:* 20; *Author:* Hilary Findlay
• Success Stories: Increasing Opportunities for Girls & Women in National & Multi-Sport Organizations
Number of Pages: 25
• Women on Boards: A Guide to Getting Involved
Number of Pages: 72
Profile: Information for women on governing boards & in senior roles of organizations

Canadian Association for the History of Nursing (CAHN) / Association canadienne pour l'histoire du nursing

c/o Jayne Elliot, School of Nursing, University of Ottawa, 451 Smyth Rd., Ottawa ON K1H 8M5
www.cahn-achn.ca
Overview: A small national charitable organization founded in 1987
Mission: To promote interest in the history of nursing; To develop scholarship in the field
Member of: Canadian Nurses Association
Affliation(s): Canadian Nurses Association
Chief Officer(s):
Margaret Scaia, President
president@cahn-achn.ca
Lydia Wytenbroek, Vice-President
lydia.wytenbroek@gmail.com
Finances: *Funding Sources:* Memberships; Donations
Membership: *Fees:* $60 registered nurses; $30 retired nurses, students & associate members
Activities: Promoting the preservation of historical nursing materials; Hosting forums; Supporting innovations in teaching nursing history; Advancing historical research
Awards:
• The Dr. Margaret Allemang Scholarship for the History of Nursing (Scholarship)
• Vera Roberts Endowment Fund for Nursing Research (Grant)
Meetings/Conferences: • Canadian Society for the History of Medicine & Canadian Association for the History of Nursing 2015 Annual Conference, May, 2015, University of Ottawa, Ottawa, ON
Description: The theme of the conference is "Capital Ideas," asking attendees to consider the different ways ideas affect society
Publications:
• CAHN [Canadian Association for the History of Nursing] / ACHN [Association canadienne pour l'histoire du nursing] Newsletter
Type: Newsletter; *Frequency:* Semiannually; *Editor:* Marilyn Beaton; Jeanette Walsh
Profile: Reports, articles, book reviews, research items, announcements,& letters to the editor

Canadian Association for the Mentally Retarded *See* Canadian Association for Community Living

Canadian Association for the Practical Study of Law in Education (CAPSLE) / Association canadienne pour une étude pratique de la loi dans le système éducatif

c/o Lori Pollock, 37 Moultrey Cres., Georgetown ON L7G 4N4
Tel: 905-702-1710; *Fax:* 905-873-0662
info@capsle.ca
capsle.ca
Overview: A small national organization founded in 1989
Mission: To provide an open forum for the practical study of legal issues affecting education
Chief Officer(s):
Robert Weir, President
president@capsle.ca
Membership: *Fees:* $35 student; $95 regular; $275 corporate; *Member Profile:* Teachers, administrators, board members, trustees, unions, school board associations, educators, academics, students, government & lawyers

The Canadian Association for the Prevention of Consumption & Other Forms of Tuberculosis; The Canadian Tuberculosis & Respiratory Disease Associa *See* Canadian Lung Association

Canadian Association for the Prevention of Discrimination & Harassment in Higher Education (CAPDHHE) / Association canadienne pour la prévention de la discrimination et ou harcèlement en milieu d'enseignement supérieur (ACPDHMES)

c/o University of British Columbia, Vancouver BC V6T 1Z2
Tel: 604-822-4859; *Fax:* 604-822-3260
amlong@ubc.ca
www.capdhhe.org
Previous Name: Canadian Association Against Sexual Harassment in Higher Education
Overview: A medium-sized national organization founded in 1985
Mission: To provide professional development for individuals employed at colleges & universities in the area of discrimination & harassment, including harassment as identified under human rights law
Chief Officer(s):
Anne-Marie Long, President
amlong@ubc.ca
Membership: 150
Meetings/Conferences: • Canadian Association for the Prevention of Discrimination and Harassment in Higher Education 2015 Conference, May, 2015, Toronto, ON
Scope: National

Canadian Association for the Study of Adult Education (CASAE) / Association canadienne pour l'étude de l'éducation des adultes (ACÉÉA)

#204, 260 Dalhousie St., Ottawa ON K1N 7E4
Tel: 613-241-0018; *Fax:* 613-241-0019
casae.aceea@csse.ca
www.casae-aceea.ca
Overview: A small national charitable organization founded in 1981
Mission: To promote the study of adult education; To facilitate research; to share knowledge in adult education
Chief Officer(s):
Shauna Butterwick, Co-President
shauna.butterwick@ubc.ca
Carole Roy, Co-President
croy@stfx.ca
Membership: *Fees:* $100 regular; $40 student, retired, & unwaged members; *Member Profile:* Individuals, institutions & agencies interested in the study of adult education; *Committees:* Constitutional; Archives; Peer Review Committee for Canadian and International Papers
Meetings/Conferences: • Canadian Association for the Study of Adult Education (CASAE) 2015 Annual National Conference, June, 2015, Université de Montréal, Montréal, QC
Scope: National
Contact Information: URL: www.casaeconference.ca
Publications:
• Canadian Journal for the Study of Adult Education (CJSAE) / Revue canadienne pour l'étude de l'éducation des adultes (RCÉÉA)
Type: Journal; *Editor:* Tom Nesbit
Profile: Reports of research, reviews of literature, & essays about issues in adult & continuingeducation
• CASAE [Canadian Association for the Study of Adult Education] / ACÉÉA Directory
Type: Directory
Profile: Listings of all CASAE / ACÉÉA members & faculty engaged in adult education
• The Learning Edge / La Fine pointe [a publication of the Canadian Association for the Study of Adult Education]
Type: Newsletter
Profile: Newsletter / Bulletin of the Canadian Association for the Study of Adult Education / Association Canadiennepour l' Étude de l' Éducation des Adults on research projects, regional developments, publications, new programs, & institutional reports

Canadian Association for the Study of Discourse & Writing (CASDW) / Association canadienne de rédactologie (ACR)

c/o W. Brock MacDonald, Woodsworth College, University of Toronto, 119 St. George St., Toronto ON M5S 1A9
www.cs.umanitoba.ca/~casdw
Previous Name: Canadian Association of Teachers of Technical Writing (CATTW)/L'Association canadienne de professeurs de rédaction technique et scientifique (ACPRTS)
Overview: A small national organization
Mission: To advance the study & teaching of discourse, writing, & communication in both academic & nonacademic settings
Member of: Canadian Federation for the Humanities & Social Sciences (CFHSS)
Chief Officer(s):
W. Brock MacDonald, Treasurer, Membership, 416-978-0246, Fax: 416-978-6111
wb.macdonald@utoronto.cagill.ca
Finances: *Funding Sources:* Membership dues
Membership: *Fees:* $25 retirees & students; $40 regular members; $50 institutions; *Member Profile:* Researchers, teachers, & practitioners who study & teach written & oral communication
Activities: Supporting writing in digital environments; Providing networking opportunities
Meetings/Conferences: • 3rd Annual Canadian Writing Centres Conference, May, 2015, University of Ottawa, Ottawa, ON
Scope: National
Publications:
• Canadian Journal for Studies in Discourse & Writing (formerly Technostyle)
Type: Journal; *Editor:* Rick Gooding; Katharine Patterson; *Price:* Free with membership inthe Canadian Association for the Study of Discourse & Writing
Profile: Peer-reviewed journal with articles & reviews for teachers, practitioners, & researchers

Canadian Association for the Study of Indigenous Education (CASIE) / Association canadienne pour l'etude de l'education des autochtones (ACÉFÉ)
c/o Canadian Society for the Study of Education, #204, 260 Dalhousie St., Ottawa ON K1N 7E4
Overview: A medium-sized national organization founded in 2008 overseen by Canadian Society for the Study of Education
Chief Officer(s):
Dwayne Donald, President, 780-492-5639
dwayne.donald@ualberta.ca

Canadian Association for the Study of International Development (CASID) / L'Association canadienne d'études du développement international (ACEDI)
c/o The Canadian Federation for the Humanities & Social Sciences, #300, 275 Bank St., Ottawa ON K2P 2L6
Tel: 613-238-6112; *Fax:* 613-238-6114
info@ideas-idees.ca
ideas-idees.ca
Overview: A medium-sized national organization
Mission: National, bilingual, interdisciplinary & pluralistic association devoted to the study of international development in all parts of the world
Member of: Social Science Federation of Canada
Chief Officer(s):
Ann Miller, Contact
amiller@fedcan.ca
Finances: *Annual Operating Budget:* $100,000-$250,000; *Funding Sources:* International Development Research Centre
Membership: 182; *Fees:* $65; $35 students
Activities: Annual conferences; cross-Canada tours of development specialists; facilitates networking among students, academics, researchers & policymakers involved in international development; provides a limited amount of travel grants to assist graduate students & others to participate in the annual conference
Publications:
• Canadian Journal of Development Studies / Revue canadienne d'études du développement
Type: Journal; *Frequency:* Quarterly; *Editor:* Henry Rempel & Scott Simon *ISSN:* 0225-5189; *Price:* $110 institutions; $65 individuals; $35 students
Profile: International & interdisciplinary journal about development issues, with contributions from allcountries of the developing world
• CASID [Canadian Association for the Study of International Development] / ACÉDI Bulletin
Type: Newletter
Profile: News, publications, announcements, & events

Canadian Association for the Study of the Liver (CASL) / Association canadienne pour l'étude du foie
c/o BUKSA Strategic Conference Services, #307, 10328 - 81st Ave., Edmonton AB T6E 1X2
Tel: 780-436-0983; *Fax:* 780-437-5984
casl@hepatology.ca
www.hepatology.ca
Overview: A small national organization
Mission: To eliminate liver disease
Affliation(s): International Association for the Study of the Liver (IASL)
Chief Officer(s):
Winnie Wong, President
Robert Bailey, Secretary-Treasurer
Eric Yoshida, President-Elect
Membership: *Fees:* Free for students & trainees; $50 associatie members; $200 regular & international members; *Member Profile:* Scientists & healthcare professionals with a interest in liver diseases, such as gastroenterologists, hepatologists, transplant surgeons, radiologists, & pediatricians; Undergraduates & post-graduate students, residents, fellows, & trainees; *Committees:* Education; Membership; Research
Activities: Engaging in advocacy activities; Promoting education & research
Meetings/Conferences: • Canadian Digestive Diseases Week (CDDW) & the 2015 Annual Canadian Association for the Study of the Liver (CASL) Winter Meeting, February, 2015, Banff, AB
Scope: National
Description: A February or March scientific conference of the Canadian Association of Gastroenterology (CAG) & the Canadian Association for the Study of the Liver (CASL), featuring lectures, symposia, small group sessions, exhibits, & opportunities for networking
• Canadian Digestive Diseases Week (CDDW) & the 2016 Annual Canadian Association for the Study of the Liver (CASL) Winter Meeting, February, 2016, Montreal, QC
Scope: National
Description: A February or March scientific conference of the Canadian Association of Gastroenterology (CAG) & the Canadian Association for the Study of the Liver (CASL), featuring lectures, symposia, small group sessions, exhibits, & opportunities for networking
• Canadian Digestive Diseases Week (CDDW) & the 2017 Annual Canadian Association for the Study of the Liver (CASL) Winter Meeting, February, 2017, Banff, AB
Scope: National
Description: A February or March scientific conference of the Canadian Association of Gastroenterology (CAG) & the Canadian Association for the Study of the Liver (CASL), featuring lectures, symposia, small group sessions, exhibits, & opportunities for networking
Publications:
• Canadian Journal of Gastroenterology: The Official Journal of the Canadian Association for the Study of the Liver (CASL)
Type: Journal; *Price:* Free with membership in the Canadian Association for the Study of the Liver

Canadian Association for the Teachers of French as a First Language *Voir* Alliance canadienne des responsables et enseignants en français (langue maternelle)

Canadian Association for Theatre Research (CATR) / Association canadienne de la recherche théâtrale (ACRT)
c/o Peter Kuling, #2507, 140 Erskine Ave., Toronto ON M4P 1Z2
Tel: 416-303-0441; *Fax:* 647-344-6198
catr.membership@gmail.com
www.catr-acrt.ca
Previous Name: Association for Canadian Theatre History
Overview: A small national organization founded in 1976
Mission: To focus on theatre, drama, & performance in a Canadian context, including acting, directing, practical matters of theatre, historiography, & the teaching, reception, theory, & literary criticism of drama
Member of: Humanities & Social Sciences Federation of Canada; Canadian Conference of the Arts; International Federation for Theatre Research
Chief Officer(s):
Jenn Stephenson, Secretary
jenn.stephenson@queensu.ca
Stephen Johnson, President
stephen.johnson@utoronto.ca
James Dugan, Treasurer
jdugan@ucalgary.ca
Finances: *Funding Sources:* Membership dues
Membership: *Fees:* $40 students & retired persons; $100 full members; *Member Profile:* Academics; Students; Libraries; *Committees:* McCallum Scholarship; Saddlemyer; Godin; Plant; O'Neill; CATR
Activities: *Library:* Graduate Centre for Study of Drama; by appointment
Awards:
• McCallum Scholarship (Scholarship)
Meetings/Conferences: • Canadian Association for Theatre Research 2015 Conference: "Capital Ideas", May, 2015, Ottawa, ON
Scope: National

Canadian Association for Translation Studies *See* Association canadienne de traductologie

Canadian Association for University Continuing Education (CAUCE) / Association pour l'éducation permanente dans les universités du Canada (AEPUC)
c/o Centre for Continuing & Distance Education, U. of Saskatchewan, #464, 221 Cumberland Ave. North, Saskatoon SK S7N 1M3
Tel: 306-966-5604; *Fax:* 306-966-5590
cauce.secratariat@usask.ca
www.cauce-aepuc.ca
Overview: A medium-sized national charitable organization founded in 1974
Mission: To enlarge the quality & scope of educational opportunities for adults at the university level
Chief Officer(s):
Cathy Kelly, President, 519-888-4873, Fax: 519-746-4607
cathy.kelly@uwaterloo.ca
Membership: *Fees:* Schedule available; *Member Profile:* Deans, practitioners, & senior administrative personnel with careers in university continuing education in Canada; *Committees:* Executive; Professional Development; Communications & Publications; Conference Development; Marketing Awards; Membership; Nominations; Program Awards; Research & Information
Activities: Offering professional development activities, such as a teleconference series
Awards:
• Marketing Awards (Award)
To recognize marketing work in continuing education*Deadline:* March *Contact:* Marilou Cruz, m1cruz@ryerson.ca
• Program Awards (Award)
To recognize excellence in continuing education programs*Deadline:* March *Contact:* Heather Stamp-Nunes, hstampnunes@mun.ca
Meetings/Conferences: • CAUCE 2015: The 62nd Annual Conference & General Meeting of the Canadian Association for University Continuing Education, May, 2015, University of Manitoba, Winnipeg, MB
Scope: National
• CAUCE 2016: The 63rd Annual Conference & General Meeting of the Canadian Association for University Continuing Education, 2016, University of Waterloo, Waterloo, ON
Scope: National
• CAUCE 2017: The 64th Annual Conference & General Meeting of the Canadian Association for University Continuing Education, 2017, Simon Fraser University, Burnaby, BC
Scope: National
• CAUCE 2018: The 65th Annual Conference & General Meeting of the Canadian Association for University Continuing Education, 2018
Scope: National
Publications:
• The Bulletin
Type: Newsletter
Profile: Current information for Canadian Association for University Continuing Education members

Canadian Association for Victim Assistance (CAVA) / Association canadienne aide aux victimes (ACAV)
e-mail: info@infocava.ca
www.infocava.ca
Overview: A small national organization founded in 2004
Mission: To promote justice for victims of crime & tragedy; To act as a referral for victims, Canadian victim assistance organizations, & the general public
Chief Officer(s):
Carolyn Sinclair, President
Annamaria Collopy, Vice-President
Membership: *Fees:* $50 individuals; $25 students & seniors; $100 organizations
Activities: Providing information on victim rights, criminal justice, & laws & legislation; Offering professional development & networking opportunities; *Awareness Events:* Canada's National Victims of Crime Awareness Week, April
Publications:
• CAVA [Canadian Association for Victim Assistance] Newsletter
Type: Newsletter

Canadian Association for Vocational Evaluation & Work Adjustment *See* Canadian Assessment, Vocational Evaluation & Work Adjustment Society

Canadian Association for Williams Syndrome (CAWS)
19 Pereverzoff Pl., Prince Albert SK S6X 1A8
Tel: 306-922-3230; *Fax:* 306-922-3457
caws.sasktelwebhosting.com
Overview: A small national charitable organization founded in 1984
Mission: To support William syndrome individuals & their families; To advance education, research, & knowledge of the genetic disorder known as Williams Syndrome
Chief Officer(s):
Gloria Manhussier, Editor/Secretary
mahussier.m@sasktel.net
Finances: *Funding Sources:* Donations; Fundraising
Activities: Supporting research; Increasing awareness of Williams Syndrome; Sharing information; *Library:* Canadian Association for Williams Syndrome Resource Centre
Publications:
• Canadian Association for Williams Syndrome Newsletter
Type: Newsletter; *Frequency:* Quarterly
Profile: News, resources, & medical & educational information from across Canada

CAWS - Alberta
c/o Mary Kueller, 10733 St. Gabriel Rd., Edmonton AB T6A 3S7

Chief Officer(s):
Misty Kuefler, Chairperson
MKuefler@vsm.ab.ca

CAWS - British Columbia
c/o Cindy Sanford, PO Box 26206, Richmond BC V6Y 3V3
Chief Officer(s):
Cindy Sanford, Provincial Contact, 604-564-7779
cawsbc@yahoo.com

CAWS - Manitoba
c/o Coralee Crowe, 27 Regis Dr., Winnipeg MB R2N 1J9
Chief Officer(s):
Coralee Crowe, Vice Chair, 204-479-7734
dcrowe@mymts.net

CAWS - New Brunswick
c/o Michelle Dobbin, 28 West Ave., Sackville NB E4L 4P1
Chief Officer(s):
Michelle Dobbin, Provincial Contact, 506-536-0821
dobbinwm@gmail.com

CAWS - Newfoundland
c/o April Williams, 1680 A. Torbay Rd., Torbay Rd. NL A1K 1H2
Chief Officer(s):
April Williams, Provincial Contact
aprildswilliams@hotmail.com

CAWS - Nova Scotia
c/o Christena Cote, NS
Tel: 902-422-8670

CAWS - Ontario
c/o Monique & John Plessas, 163 Wolverleigh Blvd., Toronto ON M4C 1S1
Tel: 416-269-7030
Chief Officer(s):
Monique Plessas, Toronto Contact
John Plessas, Toronto Contact
momslilangel@rogers.com

CAWS - Québec
c/o Jocelyne Z'Graggen, 108, av 59ème, Saint-Hippolyte QC J8A 1N9
Chief Officer(s):
Jocelyne Z'Graggen, Provincial Contact, 450-563-3574
coeurachanter@bellnet.ca

CAWS - Saskatchewan
c/o Gloria Mahussier, 19 Pereverzoff Pl., Prince Albert SK S6X 1A8
Chief Officer(s):
Kelly Fraser, Provincial Contact
schmister@hotmail.com

Canadian Association for Young Children (CAYC) / Association canadienne pour les jeunes enfants (ACJE)

c/o Vicki Brown, 356B Prospect Bay Rd., Prospect Bay NS B3T 1Z7
www.cayc.ca
Overview: A medium-sized national charitable organization founded in 1974
Mission: To influence policies & programs affecting critical issues related to the education & welfare of Canadian young children from birth through age nine
Chief Officer(s):
Margaret Fair, President
margaret.fair@cayc.ca
Iris Berger, Chair, Publications
publications@cayc.ca
Vicki Brown, Contact, Membership Dervice
membership@cayc.ca
Finances: *Funding Sources:* Membership fees
Membership: *Fees:* $25 students & seniors; $40 regular; $85 associations & institutions; $80 international; *Member Profile:* Parents; Teachers; Caregivers; Administrators; Students
Activities: Promoting & providing professional development opportunities
Awards:
• Friends of Children Award (Award)
Publications:
• Canadian Children: Journal of the Canadian Association for Young Children
Type: Journal; *Frequency:* Semiannually; *Accepts Advertising*; *Editor:* Mabel Higgins
Profile: For CAYC members & professionals concerned with early childhood development & primary education

Alberta/North West Territories
c/o Linda O'Donoghue, Bow Valley College, 345 - 6th Ave. SE, Calgary AB T2G 4V1
Chief Officer(s):
Becky Kelley, Co-Director
becky.kelley@cayc.ca
Linda O'Donoghue, Co-Director
linda.odonoghue@cayc.ca
• CAYC [Canadian Association for Young Children]: Alberta / NWT Newsletter
Type: Newsletter; *Editor:* Jayne Clarke & Elizabeth Ashton
Profile: Upcoming events, new regulations, book reviews, website resources, & information

British Columbia/Yukon
c/o Kathleen Kummen, Capilano University, #374, 2055 Purcell Way, North Vancouver BC V8B 0B1
Tel: 604-986-1911
Chief Officer(s):
Kathleen Kummen, Provincial Director
kathleen.kummen@cayc.ca

Manitoba/Nunavut
Chief Officer(s):
Joanna Malkiewicz, Provincial Director
joanna.malkiewicz@cayc.ca

New Brunswick, Prince Edward Island & Nova Scotia
Chief Officer(s):
Sherry Riggs, Provincial Director
sherry.riggs@cayc.ca

Newfoundland & Labrador
Chief Officer(s):
Margaret Fair, CAYC President & Provincial Contact
margaret.fair@cayc.ca

Ontario
c/o Anne Marie Coughlin, London Bridge Child Care Services, 550 Fanshawe Park Rd., London ON N5X 1L1
Chief Officer(s):
Anne Marie Coughlin, Provincial Director
annemarie.coughlin@cayc.ca

Québec
c/o Fiona Rowlands, Dept. of Education, Concordia University, #LB-579, 1455, boul de Maisonneuve ouest, Montréal QC H3G 1M8
Tel: 514-848-2424
Chief Officer(s):
Fiona Rowlands, Provincial Director
fiona.rowlands@cayc.ca

Saskatchewan
Chief Officer(s):
Kari Nagel, Provincial Director
kari.nagel@cayc.ca
• CAYC [Canadian Association for Young Children] Saskatchewan Newsletter
Type: Newsletter; *Frequency:* Semiannually
Profile: Information & forthcoming events

Canadian Association of Accredited Mortgage Professionals (CAAMP) / Association canadienne des conseillers hypothécaires accrédités (ACCHA)

Atria II, #1401, 2235 Sheppard Ave. East, Toronto ON M2J 5B5
Tel: 416-385-2333; *Fax:* 416-385-1177
Toll-Free: 888-442-4625
Other Communication: communications@caamp.org
info@caamp.org
www.caamp.org
Previous Name: Canadian Institute of Mortgage Brokers & Lenders / Institut canadien des courtiers et des prêteurs hypothécaires
Overview: A medium-sized national organization founded in 1994
Mission: To act as the voice of the mortgage industry with legislators, government, & the media; To increase the level of professionalism in the mortgage industry through the creation of the Accredited Mortgage Professional (AMP) designation
Chief Officer(s):
Jim Murphy, President/CEO
jmurphy@caamp.org
Samir Asusa, Vice-President, Finance & Administration
sasusa@caamp.org
Mark Webb, Vice-President, Education & Professional Affairs
mwebb@caamp.org
Membership: 12,000+; *Member Profile:* Mortgage professionals, including mortgage brokers, lenders, insurers, & other stakeholders in the industry; *Committees:* Communications; Constitution & By-laws; Education; Government Relations; Membership; National Ethics; NEC Appeals; Nominating; Past Presidents; Professional Standards; Special Events
Activities: Promoting professional development
Meetings/Conferences: • Canadian Association of Accredited Mortgage Professionals 2015 Ontario Regional Symposium & Trade Show, March, 2015, Toronto, ON
Scope: Provincial
Contact Information: E-mail: events@caamp.org
• Canadian Association of Accredited Mortgage Professionals 2015 Saskatchewan Regional Symposium & Trade Show, March, 2015, Saskatoon, SK
Scope: Provincial
Contact Information: E-mail: events@caamp.org
• Canadian Association of Accredited Mortgage Professionals 2015 Manitoba Regional Symposium & Trade Show, March, 2015, Winnipeg, MB
Scope: Provincial
Contact Information: E-mail: events@caamp.org
• Canadian Association of Accredited Mortgage Professionals 2015 Québec Regional Symposium & Trade Show, May, 2015, Montréal, QC
Scope: Provincial
Contact Information: E-mail: events@caamp.org
• Canadian Association of Accredited Mortgage Professionals 2015 Alberta Regional Symposium & Trade Show, April, 2015, Calgary, AB
Scope: Provincial
Contact Information: E-mail: events@caamp.org
• Canadian Association of Accredited Mortgage Professionals 2015 British Columbia Regional Symposium & Trade Show, June, 2015, Vancouver, BC
Scope: Provincial
Contact Information: E-mail: events@caamp.org
• Canadian Association of Accredited Mortgage Professionals 2015 Atlantic Regional Symposium & Trade Show, June, 2015, Halifax, NS
Scope: Provincial
Contact Information: E-mail: events@caamp.org
• Canadian Association of Accredited Mortgage Professionals 2015 Annual General Meeting, November, 2015, Toronto, ON
Scope: Provincial
Contact Information: E-mail: events@caamp.org
• Canadian Association of Accredited Mortgage Professionals Mortgage Forum 2015, 2015
Scope: Provincial
Contact Information: E-mail: events@caamp.org
Publications:
• CAAMP [Canadian Association of Accredited Mortgage Professionals] Update
Type: Newsletter; *Frequency:* Monthly
Profile: Review of CAAMP activities & issues that affect the mortgage industry
• Canadian Association of Accredited Mortgage Professionals Annual Report
Type: Yearbook; *Frequency:* Annually
• Mortgage Journal hypothécaire
Type: Magazine
Profile: CAAMP / ACCHA news, member information, conference reports, upcoming events, & articles related to the industry

Canadian Association of Acupuncture & Traditional Chinese Medicine (CAACTM)

c/o Chinese Medicine & Acupuncture Clinic of Toronto, 3195 Sheppard Ave. East, 2nd Fl., Toronto ON M1T 3K1
Tel: 416-493-8447; *Fax:* 416-493-9450
Toll-Free: 888-299-9799
info@caatcm.com
www.caatcm.com
Overview: A small national organization founded in 1994
Mission: To promote & improve the practice of traditional Chinese medicine & acupuncture in the prevention & treatment of diseases, & the restoration & maintenance of health; To implement acceptable standards of practice within the profession
Chief Officer(s):
James X.N. Yuan, Chair
Membership: 2,366; *Fees:* $185 first year; $100 renewal; *Member Profile:* Graduates of a traditional Chinese medicine university & acupuncturists with knowledge of traditional Chinese medicine with at least 5 years of experience; students of traditional Chinese medicine & acupuncture

Canadian Association of Administrators of Labour Legislation (CAALL) / Association canadienne des administrateurs de la législation ouvrière (ACALO)

CAALL Secretariat, Phase II, Place du Portage, 165, rue Hôtel-de-Ville, 8e étage, Gatineau QC K1A 0J2

Tel: 819-934-7814; *Fax:* 819-953-9779
CAALL-secretariat@hrsdc-rhdsc.gc.ca
www.caall-acalo.org/en
Overview: A small national organization founded in 1938
Mission: To provide a forum for federal, provincial, & territorial senior officials; to develop agenda, background papers, & logistics for meetings of Ministers responsible for Labour; To follow-up on issues as directed by Ministers
Chief Officer(s):
Margaret MacDonald, President
Debra Young, Secretary
Sandy Jones, Acting Manager, Intergovernmental Relations & Social Dialogue
Nina Chretien, Officer, Research & Project, Intergovernmental Relations & Social Dialogue
Membership: *Member Profile:* Federal, provincial, & territorial departments of labour; Heads of occupational safety & health agencies; *Committees:* International Labour Affairs; Conciliation & Mediation; Labour Standards; Occupational Health & Safety; Research & Policy
Activities: *Library:* CAALL Resource Library
Publications:
• CAALL [Canadian Association of Administrators of Labour Legislation] Monthly Bulletin
Type: Newsletter; *Frequency:* Monthly
Profile: National & international articles

Canadian Association of Adolescent Health (CAAH) / Association canadienne pour la santé des adolescents (ACSA)

c/o Section Médecine de l'Adolescence, Sainte-Justine Hospital, 3175, ch Côte Ste-Catherine, 7e étage, Montréal QC H3T 1C5
Tel: 514-345-9959; *Fax:* 514-345-4778
acsacaah@globetrotter.net
www.acsa-caah.ca
twitter.com/youngandhealthy
Overview: A small national organization founded in 1993
Mission: To promote health & well-being of adolescents, from ages 10 to 19; to set standards in healthcare & services for adolescents
Chief Officer(s):
Romaric Durand, Coordinator, Marketing & Communications
Finances: *Funding Sources:* Donations
Membership: 900+; *Fees:* $90 individual; $20 student; $295 group/institution; *Member Profile:* Heathcare professionals
Activities: Promoting cooperation between healthcare professionals & organizations; Disseminating knowledge & new practices;
Publications:
• Pro-Teen / Pro-Ado [a publication of the Canadian Association for Adolescent Health]
Type: Journal; *Frequency:* 2-3 pa; *Number of Pages:* 90
Profile: Association news, articles, scientific events, publications, ethics & laws, research, & clinical practices

Canadian Association of Advanced Practice Nurses (CAAPN) / Association canadienne des infirmières et infirmiers de pratique avancée (ACIIPA)

PO Box 117, 153 Frederick St., Kitchener ON N2H 2M2
Tel: 519-579-1096; *Fax:* 519-578-9185
adminassist@caapn-aciipa.org
caapn-aciipa.org
www.facebook.com/CanadianAssociationofAdvancedPracticeNurses
Overview: A medium-sized national organization
Mission: To represent advanced practice nurses from across Canada
Member of: Canadian Nurses Association (CNA)
Chief Officer(s):
Maureen Klenk, President
president@caapn-aciipa.org
Jacquelyn (Jackie) Gerlach, Executive Director
executivedirector@caapn-aciipa.org
Membership: 500+; *Fees:* $60 associate non-voting members; $80 regular members, with full voting privileges; *Member Profile:* Advanced practice nurses (also known as clinical nurse specialists, acute care nurse practitioners, & primary health care nurse practitioners) throughout Canada, with a wide range of specialties; Students of advanced practice programs
Activities: Liaising with other professional nursing organizations; Facilitating local, provincial, national, & international discussions of advanced practice nursing issues; Offering networking opportunities
Meetings/Conferences: • Canadian Association of Advanced Practice Nurses Conference & Biennial General Meeting, September, 2015, Winnipeg, MB
Scope: National
• Canadian Association of Advanced Practice Nurses Conference & Biennial General Meeting 2017, 2017
Scope: National

Canadian Association of Aerial Surveyors *See* Geomatics Industry Association of Canada

Canadian Association of Aesthetic Medicine (CAAM) / L'association canadienne de médecine esthétique

#220, 445 Mountain Hwy., North Vancouver BC V7J 2L1
Tel: 604-988-0450; *Fax:* 604-929-0871
info@caam.ca
www.csa-sce.ca
Overview: A small national organization founded in 2003
Mission: CAAM is the face of aesthetic medicine in Canada, comprising of a multidisciplinary group of aesthetic physicians from various backgrounds and interests.
Chief Officer(s):
Susan Roberts, Executive Director
s.roberts@caam.ca
Activities: *Library:* CAAM Library
Meetings/Conferences: • Canadian Association of Aesthetic Medicine 12th Annual Conference, November, 2015, The Westin Prince Hotel, Toronto, ON
Scope: National

Canadian Association of Agri-Retailers (CAAR)

#628, 70 Arthur St., Winnipeg MB R3B 1G7
Tel: 204-989-9300; *Fax:* 204-989-9306
Toll-Free: 800-463-9323
info@caar.org
www.caar.org
www.facebook.com/group.php?gid=142300712530309
Previous Name: Western Fertilizer & Chemical Dealers Association
Overview: A medium-sized national organization founded in 1978
Mission: To represent & protect the interests of Canadian agricultural retailers
Chief Officer(s):
Delaney Ross, Manager, Communications & Marketing, 204-989-9305
delaney@caar.org
Irene O'Dell, Office Coordinator, 204-989-9300
irene@caar.org
Lynda Nicol, Coordinator, Communications & Research, 204-989-9304
lynda@caar.org
Staff Member(s): 6
Membership: *Member Profile:* Canadian agricultural retailer members, who provide farmers with the products & services required for agricultural production; Canadian suppliers, who manufacture the products sold by retailers; *Committees:* Executive Council; Finance; Membership Development & Services; Facility & Transport Logistics; Convention; Communication & Public Relations; Stewardship & Agronomy; Government Affairs & Industry Relations
Activities: Liaising with provincial & national governments; Engaging in advocacy actitivities; Offering networking opportunities for agricultural suppliers & retailers; Providing information & training events
Awards:
• Agronomist of the Year (Award)
To honour agronomic knowledge, customer satisfaction, commitment to continuing education, & community & industry leadership*Deadline:* December
• Retailer of the Year (Award)
To recognize a retailer who provides exceptional customer service, plus environmental stewardship & community & industry leadership*Deadline:* December *Amount:* $2,000
• Retailer Hall of Fame (Award)
A lifetime achievement award in the agri-retail industry*Deadline:* December *Amount:* $2,000
Meetings/Conferences: • Canadian Association of Agri-Retailers 2015 20th Annual Convention & Trade Show, February, 2015, Delta Grand Okanagan Resort, Kelowna, BC
Scope: National
Description: A conference & exhibition featuring the annual general meeting, educational workshops, guest speaker sessions, the presentation of awards, & networking events
Contact Information: Canadian Association of Agri-Retailers, Phone: 1-800-463-9323, E-mail: info@caar.org
Publications:
• CAAR [Canadian Association of Agri-Retailers] Communicator
Type: Magazine; *Frequency:* 5 pa; *Accepts Advertising*
Profile: Information about government regulations, industry initiatives, & new technology for recipients throughout Canada & the United States
• CAAR [Canadian Association of Agri-Retailers] Roster
Type: Directory
Profile: A networking tool with hundreds of listings of businesses & organizations, as well as the Supplier's Guide & the CAARPerk$ Guide (formerly the Member BenefitsGuide)
• CCA [Certified Crop Advisors] Examiner
Type: Newsletter; *Frequency:* Quarterly
Profile: Distributed with the Canadian Association of Agri-Retailers Input newsletter
• Fast Facts [a publication of the Canadian Association of Agri-Retailers]
Type: Newsletter; *Frequency:* Monthly
Profile: Events, services, & information for association members
• Input [a publication of the Canadian Association of Agri-Retailers]
Type: Newsletter; *Frequency:* Quarterly
Profile: Information about the association & the industry for members only
• Retail Compensation Survey [a publication of the Canadian Association of Agri-Retailers]
Type: Newsletter

The Canadian Association of Amateur Oarsmen *See* Rowing Canada Aviron

Canadian Association of Ambulatory Care (CAAC)

#B602, 2075 Bayview Ave., Ontario ON M4N 3M5
e-mail: canadianambulatorycare@gmail.com
www.canadianambulatorycare.com
www.facebook.com/ambulatory.care
twitter.com/ambulatorycare
Overview: A small national organization founded in 2012
Mission: To enhance the ambulatory care field in Canada
Chief Officer(s):
Denyse Henry, President
caacpresident@gmail.com
Julie Young, Interim Treasurer
caactreasurer1@gmail.com
Ania Janik, Secretary
caacsecretary@gmail.com
Membership: *Fees:* $45
Meetings/Conferences: • Canadian Association of Ambulatory Care 2015 Conference, 2015, Westin Prince Hotel, Toronto, ON
Scope: National

Canadian Association of Anatomists / Association Canadienne d'Anatomie *See* Canadian Association for Anatomy, Neurobiology, & Cell Biology

Canadian Association of Animal Health Technologists & Technicians (CAAHTT) / Association canadienne des techniciens et technologistes en santé animale (ACTTSA)

339 Booth St., Ottawa ON K1R 7K1
Tel: 800-567-2862
info@caahtt-acttsa.ca
www.caahtt-acttsa.ca
Overview: A medium-sized national organization founded in 1989
Mission: To provide coordination & resources to support members in the delivery of animal health care services
Member of: International Veterinary Nurses & Technicians Association (IVNTA)
Affliation(s): Canadian Veterinary Medical Association; National Association of Veterinary Technicians in America (NAVTA)
Chief Officer(s):
Phyllis Mierau, Executive Director
Michele Moroz, President
Chantal Cormier, Vice-President
Finances: *Funding Sources:* Provincial association fees; Corporate sponsorship
Membership: *Committees:* Professional Development; Veterinary Technician Testing; CVMA Animal Health Technology / Veterinary Technician Program Accreditation; CVMA Professional Development
Activities: Facilitating communication links; Providing informational updates; Lobbying to protect & promote the profession; Coordinating national & provincial activities; Promoting Doggone Safe, a national dog bit prevention program; *Awareness Events:* Veterinary Technician Week; Animal Health Week
Awards:
• Canadian AHT/VT of the Year Award (Award)

Awarded to a technician who exemplifies the definition of an outstanding individual in the profession of AHT/VT
• CAAHTT/ACTTSA Recognition Award: "Making a Difference" (Award)
Formally recognizes the contribution of an individual AHT/VT & their contribution to their national association
Meetings/Conferences: • Canadian Association of Animal Health Technologists & Technicians 2015 26th Annual General Meeting, 2015
Scope: National
Description: A meeting usually held in partnership with the Canadian Veterinary Medical Association Convention, featuring full inclusion of technicians in the scientific program
Contact Information: Conventions & Special Programs Assistant: Sarah M. Cunningham, Phone: 613-236-1162, ext. 121, Fax: 613-236-9681, E-mail: scunningham@cvma-acmv.org
Publications:
• Canadian Association of Animal Health Technologists & Technicians Annual Report
Type: Yearbook; *Frequency:* Annually
• TechLife [a publication of the Canadian Association of Animal Health Technologists & Technicians]
Type: Journal
Profile: Continuing education publication for animal health technicians

Canadian Association of Apheresis Nurses (CAAN) / Association Canadienne des Infirmiers et Infirmieres d'Apheresis

#199, 435 St. Laurent Blvd., Ottawa ON K1K 2Z8
Tel: 613-748-9613; *Fax:* 613-748-6392
cag@ca.inter.net
www.apheresis.ca
Overview: A small national organization founded in 1980
Mission: Involved in the organization and direction of many randomized, controlled studies of plasma exchange; acts as a registry by collecting information on all apheresis procedures including plasma exchange, cytapheresis, photopheresis and stem cell collection.
Member of: World Apheresis Association
Affliation(s): Canadian Apheresis Group; Canadian Nurses Association
Membership: *Member Profile:* Professional nurses
Activities: Offering regional education days
Publications:
• Canadian Association of Apheresis Nurses
Type: Newsletter

Canadian Association of Apiculturists *See* Canadian Association of Professional Apiculturists

Canadian Association of Aquarium Clubs (CAOAC)

#223, 1717 60th St. SE, Calgary AB T2A 7Y7
e-mail: amtowell@shaw.ca
www.caoac.ca
Overview: A medium-sized national organization founded in 1959
Mission: A non-profit corporation and are composed of member aquarium, reptile & amphibian, pond & water garden, and similar clubs or societies from across Canada and the Northeast United States.
Chief Officer(s):
Ron Bishop, President
ron.bishop2@sympatico.ca
Meetings/Conferences: • 2015 Canadian Association of Aquarium Clubs Convention, May, 2015, Burlington Holiday Inn & Conference Centre, Burlington, ON
Scope: National

Canadian Association of Black Journalists

42 Charles St. East, Toronto ON M4Y 1T4
cabj.wordpress.com
www.linkedin.com/groups/Canadian-Association-Black-Journalists-Communi
www.facebook.com/186302344752083
Overview: A small national organization founded in 1996
Mission: Dedicated to both diversifying Canada's newsrooms, and promoting journalism as a viable career for African-Canadian youth.
Member of: National Black Alliance
Membership: *Fees:* $65 full; $50 associate; $40 supporting; $20 student; *Member Profile:* Committed to building relationships among Black journalists & other media communicators; welcomes everyone who supports goals & values; encourages people of colour to enter the industry; students welcome
Activities: Professional development
Awards:
• Scholarships (Scholarship)
Two scholarships awarded yearly to second year journalism or radio/television arts students *Amount:* $1,000

Canadian Association of Black Lawyers (CABL) / L'Association des Avocats Noirs du Canada

#300, 20 Toronto St., Toronto ON M5C 2B8
www.cabl.ca
Overview: A medium-sized national organization founded in 1996
Chief Officer(s):
Andrew Alleyne, President

British Columbia Chatper
BC
www.cabl.ca/chapters/bc-chapter

Canadian Association of Blue Cross Plans (CABCP) / Association Canadienne des Croix Bleue (ACCB)

PO Box 2005, #610, 185 The West Mall, Toronto ON M9C 5P1
Toll-Free: 866-732-2583
www.bluecross.ca
Also Known As: Blue Cross Canada
Overview: A small national licensing organization founded in 1955
Mission: To maintain & monitor standards of performance by association members; to ensure members manage effectively supplementary health, dental, life insurance, & disability income products on an individual and group basis
Affiliation(s): Blue Cross (USA); Blue Shield (USA); International Federation of Health Funds
Membership: *Member Profile:* Independent Blue Cross Member Plans in Canada

Alberta Blue Cross
Blue Cross Place, 10009 - 108th St. NW, Edmonton AB T5J 3C5
Tel: 780-498-8100; *Fax:* 780-425-4627
Toll-Free: 800-661-6995
www.ab.bluecross.ca
Mission: To provide supplementary health care & related benefit programs & services
Chief Officer(s):
Ron W. Malin, President/CEO
• Alberta Blue Cross Annual Report
Type: Yearbook; *Frequency:* Annually

Manitoba Blue Cross
PO Box 1046, Stn. Main, 599 Empress St., Winnipeg MB R3C 2X7
Tel: 204-775-0151; *Fax:* 204-786-5965
Toll-Free: 800-873-2583
www.mb.bluecross.ca
Mission: To offer services within the supplementary health care & travel benefit fields to all Manitobans

Medavie Blue Cross/Atlantic Blue Cross Care/Service Croix Bleue de l'Atlantique
PO Box 220, 644 Main St., Moncton NB E1C 8L3
Tel: 506-853-1811; *Fax:* 506-867-4651
Toll-Free: 800-667-4511
www.medavie.bluecross.ca
Chief Officer(s):
Pierre-Yves Julien, President/CEO

Ontario Blue Cross
#610, 185 The West Mall, Toronto ON M9C 5P1
Fax: 800-893-0997
Toll-Free: 866-732-2583
bco.indhealth@ont.bluecross.ca
www.useblue.com
Mission: To provide health & travel insurance in Ontario
• Ontario Blue Cross Annual Report
Type: Yearbook; *Frequency:* Annually

Pacific Blue Cross
c/o British Columbia Life & Casualty Company (BC Life), PO Box 7000, Vancouver BC V6B 4E1
Tel: 604-419-2000; *Fax:* 604-419-2990
Toll-Free: 888-275-4672
www.pac.bluecross.ca
Mission: To provide extended health & dental benefits
Chief Officer(s):
Kenneth G. Martin, President/CEO
H. James Rhodes, Chair
• Pacific Blue Cross Annual Report
Type: Yearboook; *Frequency:* Annually

Québec Blue Cross/Croix Bleue du Québec
#9B, 550, rue Sherbrooke ouest, Montréal QC H3A 1B9
Fax: 866-286-8358
Toll-Free: 877-909-7686
info@qc.croixbleue.ca
www.qc.croixbleue.ca
Mission: To offer health & travel insurance in Québec
• Québec Blue Cross Annual Report
Type: Yearbook; *Frequency:* Annually

Saskatchewan Blue Cross
PO Box 4030, 516 - 2nd Ave. North, Saskatoon SK S7K 2C5
Tel: 306-244-1192; *Fax:* 306-652-5751
Toll-Free: 800-873-2583
www.sk.bluecross.ca
Chief Officer(s):
G.N. (Arnie) Arnott, President/CEO

Canadian Association of Broadcast Consultants (CABC) / Association Canadienne des Consultants en Radito-télédiffusion (ACCR)

c/o D.E.M. Allen & Associates Ltd., 130 Cree Cres., Winnipeg MB R3J 3W1
Tel: 204-889-9202; *Fax:* 204-831-6650
www.cabc-accr.ca
Overview: A medium-sized national organization
Chief Officer(s):
Joseph Sadoun, President, 514-934-3024
jsadoun@yrh.com
Kerry Pelser, Secretary-Treasurer, 204-889-9202
kpelser@dema.mb.ca
Membership: 14

Canadian Association of Broadcasters (CAB) / Association canadienne des radiodiffuseurs (ACR)

#770, 45 O'Connor St., Ottawa ON K1P 1A4
Tel: 613-233-4035; *Fax:* 613-233-6961
www.cab-acr.ca
Overview: A medium-sized national organization founded in 1926
Mission: To act as the national voice of Canada's private broadcasters
Member of: Radio Starmaker Fund
Chief Officer(s):
Sylvie Bissonnette, CFO & Vice-President, Finance, 613-233-4035 Ext. 221
sbissonnette@cab-acr.ca
Finances: *Funding Sources:* Membership fees
Membership: 80+; *Member Profile:* Private broadcasters from the radio, television, & specialty sectors
Activities: Engaging in copyright advocacy
Awards:
• Astral Media Scholarship (Scholarship)
Established in 1975 by Astral Media with the association; awarded annually to French Canadian students with broadcasting experience who are enrolled in, or wish to begin or complete a program of studies in communications at the university level *Amount:* $5,000
• Ruth Hancock Memorial Scholarships (Scholarship)
Award established jointly in 1975 by the association, the Broadcast Executives Society & Canadian Association of Broadcast Representatives; presented annually to three Canadian students enrolled in recognized communications courses *Amount:* $1,500 (x3)
Publications:
• CAB [Canadian Association of Broadcasters] Update
Type: Newsletter; *Frequency:* Weekly
Profile: CAB activities & priorities

Canadian Association of Burn Nurses (CABN) / Association canadienne des infirmières et infirmiers en soins aux brûlés

c/o Shannon Bonn, IWK Health Centre, PO Box 9700, 5850-5980 University Ave., Halifax NS B3K 6R8
e-mail: shannon.bonn@iwk.nshealth.ca
www.cabn.ca
Overview: A small national organization
Mission: To provide education related to burn care; To research & develop national burn standards; To promote & support nurses & other care providers
Affiliation(s): Canadian Nurses Association
Chief Officer(s):
Shannon Bonn, President
Amelia Potter, Vice-President
pottera@shaw.ca
Judy Sleith, Treasurer
jjsleith@telusplanet.net

Membership: *Member Profile:* Registered Nurses involved with burn nursing; Individuals practicing in a related discipline, or with an interest in burn nursing
Meetings/Conferences: • Canadian Association of Burn Nurses 14th Biennial Conference, September, 2015, Moncton, NB
Scope: National
Contact Information: Sharon Brown; sharon.brown@horizonnb.ca
Publications:
• CABN [Canadian Association of Burn Nurses] Newsletter
Type: Newsletter; *Editor:* Debbie Kruz
Profile: For CABN members

Canadian Association of Business Incubation (CABI)
#2002A, 1 Yonge St., Toronto ON M5E 1E5
Tel: 416-345-9937; *Fax:* 416-345-9044
info@cabi.ca
www.cabi.ca
twitter.com/cabimember
Previous Name: Canadian Association of Business Incubators
Overview: A small national organization
Mission: The Canadian Association of Business Incubation, (CABI) is a national organization of member organizations whose members are dedicated to creating employment and economic activity through the development of enterprises supported by the business incubation industry.
Chief Officer(s):
Gail Gillian-Bain, President & COO
ggillian@cabi.ca
Membership: *Fees:* $425
Meetings/Conferences: • Canadian Association of Business Incubation Leadership Summit 2015, March, 2015, Waterloo, ON
Scope: National

Canadian Association of Business Incubators *See* Canadian Association of Business Incubation

Canadian Association of Business Valuators (CABV) *See* Canadian Institute of Chartered Business Valuators

Canadian Association of Cardiac Rehabilitation (CACR) / Association canadienne de réadaptation cardiaque
1390 Taylor Ave., Winnipeg MB R3M 3V8
Tel: 204-488-5854; *Fax:* 204-928-7873
info@cacr.ca
www.cacr.ca
www.facebook.com/226258394069313
Overview: A small national organization founded in 1991
Mission: To provide research & advocacy in cardiovascular disease prevention & rehabilitation
Chief Officer(s):
Marilyn J. Thomas, Executive Director
mthomas@cacr.ca
Robert D. Reid, President
Membership: *Member Profile:* Health professionals in cardiac rehabilitation; *Committees:* Finance & Marketing; Membership; Guidelines; CACR Registry Project; Research; Nominations; Professional & Career Development
Activities: *Awareness Events:* Walk of Life for Cardiac Rehabilitation
Awards:
• Canadian Cardiac Rehabilitation Foundation Graduate Scholarship Awards (Scholarship)
To recognize the research of graduate students in the area of cardiac rehabilitation & to reflect CACR's support of their educational endeavours in this area *Amount:* Four awards of $3,000 each
Publications:
• Current Issues in Cardiac Rehabilitation & Prevention (CICRP)
Type: Newsletter; *Frequency:* Semiannually; *Editor:* Scott Lear; *Price:* Free to members
Profile: Articles, research, reviews, national news, & events
• Journal of Cardiopulmonary Rehabilitation & Prevention (JCRP)
Type: Journal; *Price:* Free for members; $263 non-members

Canadian Association of Cardio-Pulmonary Technologists (CACPT)
PO Box 848, Stn. A, Toronto ON M5W 1G3
e-mail: contactus@cacpt.ca
www.cacpt.ca
Overview: A small national organization founded in 1970
Mission: To establish maintain high standards for Registered Cardio-Pulmonary Technologists
Affiliation(s): Canadian Cardiovascular Society; Canadian Cardiovascular Congress
Chief Officer(s):
David Hu, Head, Pulmonary
davidyhu@ican.net
Mike Stevenson, Head, Cardiac
fmws@yahoo.com
Membership: *Member Profile:* Technologists employed in the Heart Catheterization Laboratories &/or Pulmonary Function Laboratories; *Committees:* Education; Pulmonary; Cardiac

Canadian Association of Career Educators & Employers (CACEE) / Association canadienne des spécialistes en emploi et des employeurs (ACSEE)
#202, 720 Spadina Ave., Toronto ON M5S 2T9
Tel: 416-929-5156
Toll-Free: 866-922-3303
www.cacee.com
www.linkedin.com/groups?home=&gid=882447
twitter.com/followCACEE
Previous Name: ACCIS - The Graduate Workforce Professionals
Overview: A medium-sized national organization founded in 1946
Mission: To facilitate the process of matching graduates with employment; a partnership of employer recruiters & career educators providing information, advice & services to students, employers & career centre personnel in the areas of career planning & student recruitment
Member of: International Network of Graduate Recruitment & Development Associations
Chief Officer(s):
Paul Smith, Executive Director
pauls@cacee.com
Jennifer McCleary, President
jmcclea@mcmaster.ca
Staff Member(s): 6
Membership: *Fees:* Schedule available; *Member Profile:* Career services professionals and employers; *Committees:* Executive; Awards & Recognition; Communications; Diversity; Education; Elections; Ethics; Performance; Business School Working Group; Membership
Meetings/Conferences: • 2015 Canadian Association of Career Educators & Employers National Conference, June, 2015, The Westin Ottawa, Ottawa, ON
Scope: National

Canadian Association of Centres for the Management of Hereditary Metabolic Diseases
c/o London Health Sciences Centre, 800 Commissioners Rd. East, London ON N6C 2V5
Tel: 519-685-8140
www.garrod.ca
Also Known As: GARROD Association
Overview: A small national organization
Mission: To coordinate of the management of inherited metabolic disorders; to provide a forum for the exchange of information & develops guidelines for the investigation & treatment of the diseases.
Affiliation(s): Western Group of Investigators of Inborn Errors of Metabolism; Canadian Paediatric Society; Canadian Dietetic Association; Canadian Society for Metabolic Diseases; CORD (Canadian Organization of Rare Disorders); Canadian College of Medical Geneticists (CCMG); SIMD; National Food Distribution Centre for the Treatment of Hereditary Metabolic Diseases
Chief Officer(s):
Chitra Prasad, Chair
chitra.prasad@lhsc.on.ca
Pierre Allard, Secretary-Treasurer, 514-345-4931
pierre.allard.hsj@ssss.gouv.qc.ca
Membership: 16; *Fees:* $15; *Member Profile:* Hereditary metabolic disease centres in Canada

Canadian Association of Certified Planning Technicians (CACPT)
PO Box 69006, 1900 King St. East, Hamilton ON L8K 6R4
Tel: 905-578-4681; *Fax:* 905-578-9581
director@cacpt.org
www.cacpt.org
Overview: A small national licensing organization founded in 1979
Mission: To maintain high standards for Planning Technicians & other related planning professionals
Chief Officer(s):
Danielle Stevens, President
Norman Pearson, Registrar
Diane LeBreton, CPT, MCIP, RPP, Executive Director
Membership: *Fees:* $30 full member; $20 associate member; *Committees:* Budget; Outreach/Promotional; Website; Professional Development Conference; Newsletter; Registration; Awards
Awards:
• CACPT Student Merit Awards (Award)
Presented annually to a student in each recognized college training program
• CACPT Merit Awards (Award)
Publications:
• Techtalk
Type: Newsletter; *Editor:* Rebecca Dahl

Canadian Association of Chemical Distributors (CACD) / Association canadienne des distributeurs de produits chimiques (ACDPC)
349 Davis Rd., #A, Oakville ON L6J 2X2
Tel: 905-844-9140; *Fax:* 905-844-5706
www.cacd.ca
www.linkedin.com/company/canadian-association-of-chemical-distributors
www.facebook.com/group.php?gid=339092806129805
www.youtube.com/user/CatherineCACD
Overview: A medium-sized national organization founded in 1986
Chief Officer(s):
Cathy Campbell, President, 905-844-9140 Ext. 21
ccampbell@cacd.ca
Staff Member(s): 5; 180 volunteer(s)
Membership: 46 companies; *Fees:* Schedule available based on sales; *Member Profile:* Chemical distributing companies; *Committees:* Financial Reporting; Health & Safety; Montréal Chapter; Operation & Logistics; Regulatory Affairs; Responsible Distribution; Western Chapter; You be The Chemist
Activities: Collaborating with government to establish policies;
Meetings/Conferences: • Canadian Association of Chemical Distributors 2015 29th Annual General Meeting, 2015
Scope: National
Description: An event featuring keynote speakers
Contact Information: Manager, Communications & Member Services: Catherine Wieckowska, Phone: 905-844-9140, E-mail: catherine@cacd.ca
Publications:
• The Chemunicator
Type: Magazine; *Frequency:* 3 pa; *Accepts Advertising*; *Editor:* Catherine Wieckowska
Profile: Canadian Association of Chemical Distributors reports, plus news & information for the chemical distribution industry

Canadian Association of Chiefs of Police (CACP) / Association canadienne des chefs de police (ACCP)
#100, 300 Terry Fox Dr., Kanata ON K2K 0E3
Tel: 613-595-1101; *Fax:* 613-383-0372
cacp@cacp.ca
www.cacp.ca
Overview: A medium-sized national organization founded in 1905
Mission: To encourage & develop cooperation among all Canadian police organizations & members in pursuit & attainment of common objects to create & develop the highest standards of efficiency in law enforcement through the fostering & encouragement of police training, education & research; To promote & maintain a high standard of ethics, integrity, honour & conduct in profession of law enforcement; To encourage & advance the study of modern & progressive practices in prevention & detection of crime; To foster uniformity of police practices & cooperation for the protection & security of the people of Canada
Member of: Canadian Society of Association Executives; International Association of Chiefs of Police
Chief Officer(s):
Dale McFee, O.O.M., President
Finances: *Annual Operating Budget:* $500,000-$1.5 Million; *Funding Sources:* Federal & provincial government sustaining grants; Membership fees; Publications
Staff Member(s): 7
Membership: 766 active & associate; *Fees:* $375; *Member Profile:* Police executives; corporate executives; *Committees:* Crime Prevention/Community Policing; Drug Abuse; Electronic Crime; Human Resources; Informatics; Law Amendments; National Police Service; Organized Crime; POLIS; Policing with Aboriginal Peoples; Private Sector Liaison; National Security
Activities: *Library*
Meetings/Conferences: • Canadian Association of Chiefs of Police 2015 110th Annual Conference, August, 2015, Québec,

QC
Scope: National
Description: Conference sessions & exhibits
• Canadian Association of Chiefs of Police 2015 SMILE Conference, 2015
Scope: National
Description: Participants gain technical hands-on skills & practical knowledge about social media
• Canadian Association of Chiefs of Police 2016 111th Annual Conference, 2016
Scope: National
Description: Conference sessions & exhibits
• Canadian Association of Chiefs of Police 2017 112th Annual Conference, July, 2017, Palais des congrès de Montréal, Montréal, QC
Scope: National
Description: Conference sessions & exhibits

Canadian Association of Child Neurology (CACN) / L'Association canadienne de neurologie pédiatrique (ACNP)

#709, 7015 Macleod Trail SW, Calgary AB T2H 2K6
Tel: 403-229-9544; *Fax:* 403-229-1661
www.cnsfederation.org
Overview: A small national organization founded in 1991 overseen by Canadian Neurological Sciences Federation
Mission: To advance knowledge about the development of the nervous system from conception, as well as the diseases of the nervous system in children; To improve treatment of young people with neurological handicaps
Membership: 100; *Fees:* $80 junior members; $250 associate members; $440 active members; *Member Profile:* Pediatric neurologists in Canada
Activities: Engaging in advocacy activities
Awards:
• President's Prize (Award)
Awarded for the best paper in pediatric neuroscience by a resident or fellow *Contact:* Marika Fitzgerald, E-mail: marika-fitzgerald@cnsfederation.org
Publications:
• Canadian Association of Child Neurology Membership Directory
Type: Directory

Canadian Association of College & University Student Services (CACUSS) / Association des services aux étudiants des universités et collèges du Canada (ASEUCC)

#202, 720 Spadina Ave., Toronto ON M5S 2T9
Tel: 647-345-1116
contact@cacuss.ca
www.cacuss.ca
www.facebook.com/cacuss
twitter.com/cacusstweets
Overview: A medium-sized national organization founded in 1977 overseen by Association of Universities & Colleges of Canada
Mission: To represent & serve persons who work in Canadian post-secondary institutions in student affairs & services; To offer advocacy & assistance on issues that affect the quality of student life on Canadian university & college campuses
Member of: Association of Universities and Colleges of Canada; Council for the Advancement of Standards in Higher Education
Chief Officer(s):
Janet Mee, President
David Newman, President-Elect
Jennifer Hamilton, Executive Director, 416-889-7650
cacuss-ed@cacuss.ca
Membership: *Fees:* Schedule available; *Member Profile:* Individuals who work in Canadian post-secondary institutions in student affairs & services; Institutions; Students
Activities: Providing professional development services & programs for members
Awards:
• CACUSS Award of Honour (Award)
To honour a distinguished contribution to the development & promotion of student services *Contact:* Corinna Fitzgerald, E-mail: cfitzger@stfx.ca
• CACUSS Life Membership Award (Award)
Eligibility: A retired member recommended by a divisional president*Deadline:* February *Contact:* Corinna Fitzgerald, E-mail: cfitzger@stfx.ca
• Special Projects Fund (Grant)
To support projects that will have value to Canadian Association of College & University Student Services members*Eligibility:* Any current member of the Canadain Association of College & University Student Services *Contact:* Corinna Fitzgerald, E-mail: cfitzger@stfx.ca
Meetings/Conferences: • Canadian Association of College & University Student Services 2015 Annual Conference, 2015
Scope: National
Contact Information: conference@cacuss.ca
Publications:
• CACUSS [Canadian Association of College & University Student Services] Member Directory
Type: Directory
Profile: For members only
• Campus Crime: University Liability for Failure to Protect Its Students
Type: Monograph; *Author:* D.R.R. DuPlessis
• Canadian Association of College & University Student Services Communiqué
Type: Newsletter; *Frequency:* 3 pa; *Accepts Advertising*; *Price:* Free with membership; $64.20 individual non-members
Profile: News, articles, updates, opinion pieces, letters to the editor, artwork, & photographs related to college & university student services inCanada
• Growing Together in Service
Type: Monograph; *Author:* W.A. Stewart
• Making the Connection: Civic Leadership Development on Post Secondary Campuses through Community Service Learning
Type: Monograph; *Author:* Cheryl Rose
• Procedural Fairness for University & College Students
Type: Monograph; *Author:* Lynn M. Smith
• Suicide Risk Management on the Post-Seconday Campus
Type: Monograph; *Author:* Judy Murphy

Canadian Association of Communicators in Education (CACE) / Association canadienne des agents de communication en éducation

2490 Don Reid Dr., Ottawa ON K1H 1E1
e-mail: info@cace-acace.org
www.cace-acace.org
www.facebook.com/cace.acace
Overview: A medium-sized national organization founded in 1984
Mission: To support teaching & learning through effective communication strategies
Chief Officer(s):
Kim Hamilton, President
Catherine Shedden, Treasurer
Membership: *Fees:* $150 associate; $195 full; *Member Profile:* Educational marketing & communications professionals in Canada
Activities: Offering regional workshops & networking opportunities; Increasing awareness of the role of communicators in education
Meetings/Conferences: • Canadian Association of Communicators in Education Conference 2015, October, 2015, Charlottetown, PE
Scope: National
Description: Theme: "Sharing our Stories"
Publications:
• CACE [Canadian Association of Communicators in Education] Membership Directory
Type: Directory
• CACE [Canadian Association of Communicators in Education] Annual Report
Type: Yearbook; *Frequency:* Annually

Canadian Association of Community Financial Service Providers *See* Canadian Payday Loan Association

Canadian Association of Conference Interpreters *Voir* Association camadienne des interprètes de conférence

Canadian Association of Credit Counselling Services (CACCS)

PO Box 189, Grimsby ON L3M 4G3
Toll-Free: 800-263-0260
info@caccs.ca
www.caccs.ca
www.facebook.com/195249373845789
twitter.com/finfitscore
Overview: A medium-sized national charitable organization
Mission: The Canadian Association of Credit Counselling Services (CACCS) represents a Canada-wide network of accredited, not-for-profit agencies & affiliates offering preventative education & confidential services to clients experiencing financial difficulties. With a focus on financial counselling education, accreditation of agencies & certification of Financial Counsellors, CACCS is also committed to national research & policy initiatives concerning personal finance & industry advocacy.
Chief Officer(s):
Henrietta Ross, CEO

Canadian Association of Critical Care Nurses (CACCN) / Association canadienne des infirmières et infirmiers en soins intensifs (ACIISI)

PO Box 25322, London ON N6C 6B1
Tel: 519-649-5284; *Fax:* 519-649-1458
Toll-Free: 866-477-9077
caccn@caccn.ca
www.caccn.ca
www.facebook.com/121001477977759
twitter.com/CACCNI
blog.caccn.ca/wordpress
Previous Name: National Society of Critical Care Nurses
Overview: A medium-sized national organization founded in 1983
Mission: To maintain & enhance the quality of patient- & family-centred care throughout Canada; To develop standards of critical care nursing practice
Member of: CNA Network; WFCCN; WFPICCS
Chief Officer(s):
Christine Halfkenny-Zellas, Chief Operating Officer
Finances: *Funding Sources:* Membership; advertising revenue; conference registration
Staff Member(s): 1
Membership: 1,200; *Fees:* $50 students; $75 / year or $140 / 2 years, regular & associate members; *Member Profile:* Canadian critical care nurses who work in, or have an interest in, the care of neonatal, paediatric or adult patients; International members; Students
Activities: Advocating for critical care nurses across Canada; Responding to the educational needs of critical care nurses; Presenting educational funds & awards; Offering networking opportunities; Publishing position statements on topics of significance to the critical care nursing profession
Meetings/Conferences: • Dynamics 2015: The Annual National Convention & Product Exhibition of the Canadian Association of Critical Care Nurses, September, 2015, RBC Convention Centre Winnipeg, Winnipeg, MB
Scope: National
Description: Featuring programming to enhance education, clinical practice, research, & leadership.
Contact Information: Toll-Free Phone: 1-866-477-9077; E-mail: caccn@caccn.ca
• Dynamics 2016: The Annual National Convention & Product Exhibition of the Canadian Association of Critical Care Nurses, September, 2016, Charlottetown, PE
Scope: National
Description: Featuring programming to enhance education, clinical practice, research, & leadership.
Contact Information: Toll-Free Phone: 1-866-477-9077; E-mail: caccn@caccn.ca
• Dynamics 2017: The Annual National Convention & Product Exhibition of the Canadian Association of Critical Care Nurses, September, 2017, Toronto, ON
Scope: National
Description: Featuring programming to enhance education, clinical practice, research, & leadership.
Contact Information: Toll-Free Phone: 1-866-477-9077; E-mail: caccn@caccn.ca
Publications:
• CACCN [Canadian Association of Critical Care Nurses] Standards for Critical Care Nursing Practice
Price: Free with membership in the Canadian Association ofCritical Care Nurses
Profile: A resource for nurses, administrators, & other health care professionals
• CACCN [Canadian Association of Critical Care Nurses] Annual Report
Type: Yearbook; *Frequency:* Annually; *Price:* Free with membership in the Canadian Association of Critical Care Nurses
• Dynamics [a publication of the Canadian Association of Critical Care Nurses]
Type: Journal; *Frequency:* Quarterly; *Accepts Advertising*; *Editor:* Paula Price, RN PhD; *Price:* Free with membership in the Canadian Association of Critical Care Nurses
Profile: A peer reviewed critical care nursing journal

British Columbia Chapter
Vancouver BC
e-mail: bclm@caccn.ca
www.caccn.ca

Mission: To support critical care nurses in British Columbia to provide the best possible care to critically ill patients
Chief Officer(s):
Vena Camenzuli, Contact

Greater Edmonton Chapter
PO Box 52191, Edmonton AB T6G 2C5
e-mail: greateredmonton@caccn.ca
www.caccn.ca
Mission: To foster the best possible nursing care in the greater Edmonton district
Liane Manz, President

• Canadian Association of Critical Care Nurses, Greater Edmonton Chapter, Newsletter
Type: Newsletter; *Editor:* Sara Pretzlaff
Profile: Chapter activities, conference reviews, & future plans

London Regional Chapter
ON
e-mail: londonregional@caccn.ca
www.caccn.ca
Mission: To represent critical care nurses in the London & southwestern Ontario area
Chief Officer(s):
Alison Rowlands, President
alison.rowlands@lhsc.on.ca
Jane Moore, Secretary
jpm@golden.net
Dianne Morley, Treasurer
diane.morley@lhsc.on.ca
Denise Geroux, Contact, Education
denise.geroux@lhsc.on.ca
Janet Taylor, Contact, Newsletter
janet.taylor@lhsc.on.ca

• Canadian Association of Critical Care Nurses, London Regional Chapter, Newsletter
Type: Newsletter; *Editor:* Janet Taylor; *Price:* Free with membership in the CACCN London regional chapter
• Canadian Association of Critical Care Nurses, London Regional Chapter, Annual Report
Type: Yearbook; *Frequency:* Annually; *Price:* Free with membership in the CACCN London regional chapter

Manitoba Chapter
MB
e-mail: manitoba@caccn.ca
www.caccn.ca
Mission: To promote & advance critical care nursing in Manitoba
Chief Officer(s):
Tannis Sidloski, President, 204-235-3493
tsidloski@sbgh.mb.ca
Sara Unrau, Chair, Publicity & Newsletter
sunrau@sbgh.mb.ca

• Canadian Association of Critical Care Nurses, Manitoba Chapter, Newsletter
Type: Newsletter; *Frequency:* Semiannually; *Editor:* Sara Unrau
Profile: Chapter initiatives, executive reports, awards, current events, professional development information, & upcoming educationalopportunities

Montréal Chapter
Montréal QC
e-mail: montreal@caccn.ca
www.caccn.ca
Mission: To support critical care nurses in the Montréal area to attain excellence in their nursing practice; To implement standards of critical care nursing practice; To address political & professional issues
Chief Officer(s):
Christine Echegaray-Benites, Co-President
Mélanie Gauthier, Co-President

New Brunswick Chapter
NB
e-mail: newbrunswick@caccn.ca
www.caccn.ca
www.facebook.com/482650845176504
Mission: To promote critical care nursing across New Brunswick
Chief Officer(s):
Joe Carr, President, New Brunswick

Nova Scotia Chapter
NS
e-mail: novascotia@caccn.ca
www.caccn.ca
Mission: To act as the voice of critical care nursing in Nova Scotia
Chief Officer(s):
Ashley Mowatt, President
Barb Fagan, BOD Liaison

Ottawa Regional Chapter
Ottawa ON
e-mail: ottawaregional@caccn.ca
www.caccn.ca
Mission: To work as the voice of critical care nurses in Ottawa & the surrounding region
Chief Officer(s):
Marilyn White, President

• Canadian Association of Critical Care Nurses, Ottawa Regional Chapter, Newsletter
Type: Newsletter
Profile: Chapter information for members

Saskatchewan Chapter
SK
e-mail: saskatchewan@caccn.ca
www.caccn.ca
Mission: To support critical care nurses in Saskatchewans
Chief Officer(s):
Jennifer Graf, President, 306-535-1960
jengarf@gmail.com
Jennifer Graf, Vice-President

• Canadian Association of Critical Care Nurses, Saskatchewan Chapter, Newsletter
Type: Newsletter; *Editor:* Shelley Anderson
Profile: Chapter activities, executive reports, conference reviews, & forthcoming events

Southern Alberta
Calgary AB
e-mail: calgary@caccn.ca
www.caccn.ca
www.facebook.com/caccn.southernalberta
Chief Officer(s):
Tricia Bray, President
Ashley Altenbeck, Secretary
Susan Gerritsen, Treasurer

• Canadian Association of Critical Care Nurses, Calgary Chapter, Annual Report
Type: Yearbook; *Frequency:* Annually

Toronto Chapter
PO Box 79660, 1995 Weston Rd., Toronto ON M9N 3W9
e-mail: caccn.executive@gmail.com
www.torontocaccn.ca
Chief Officer(s):
Ingrid Daley, President
Jo-Ann Fernando, Secretary
Natalia Lavrencic, Treasurer
Alicia Jones-Harmer, Coordinator, Education
Primrose Mharapara, Contact, Membership

• Critical Connections
Type: Newsletter; *Accepts Advertising; Editor:* Teresa Robitaille
Profile: Executive reports, articles, & forthcoming events

Canadian Association of Crown Counsel (CACC) / Association canadienne des juristes de l'État (ACJE)

PO Box 30, #1015, 180 Dundas St. West, Toronto ON M5G 1Z8
Tel: 416-260-4888; *Fax:* 416-977-1460
info@cacc-acje.ca
www.cacc-acje.ca
Overview: A small national organization
Mission: To represent the collective interests of its members on a national level
Chief Officer(s):
Rick Woodburn, President, 902-424-7670
Membership: *Member Profile:* Crown prosecutors & Crown lawyers

Canadian Association of Customs Brokers *See* Canadian Society of Customs Brokers

Canadian Association of Defence & Security Industries (CADSI) / Association des industries canadiennes de défense et de sécurité (AICDS)

#300, 251 Laurier Ave. West', Ottawa ON K1P 5J6
Tel: 613-235-5337; *Fax:* 613-235-0784
cadsi@defenceandsecurity.ca
www.defenceandsecurity.ca
Previous Name: Canadian Defence Industries Association
Overview: A medium-sized national organization founded in 1985
Mission: To represent Canadian defence & security industries domestically & internationally
Chief Officer(s):
Christyn Cianfarani, President
christyn.cianfarani@defenceandsecurity.ca
Janet Thorsteinson, Vice-President, Policy & Government Relations
janet@defenceandsecurity.ca
Andrea Walton, Manager, Operations & Administration
andrea@defenceandsecurity.ca
Stefanie van Duynhoven, Manager, Communications & Membership
stefanie@defenceandsecurity.ca
Brian Berube, Director, Communications & Marketing
Brian@defenceandsecurity.ca
Membership: *Fees:* Schedule available, based on number of defence & security employees; *Member Profile:* Registered, legal, private-sector companies with Canadian operations & whose business interests include defence & / or security; Canadian non-commercial organizations or companies which have an interest in defence & security; *Committees:* Small Medium Enterprise; Events; Government Relations; International; Contracts & Business
Activities: Engaging in advocacy activities; Offering business development information & activities to members; Organizing educational events; Providing networking opportunities;
Meetings/Conferences: • Canadian Association of Defence & Security Industries 2015 Trade Show, May, 2015
Scope: National
Attendance: 11,000+
Publications:
• Canadian Defence & Security Directory
Type: Directory; *Frequency:* Annually; *Price:* Free
Profile: An inventory of member firms' capabilities, plus information on Canadian government departments & agencies that work with defence & security industries, prepared for members,government departments, foreign embassies, Canadian trade commissioners, & military attaches abroad
• ENews Bulletin
Type: Newsletter; *Frequency:* Weekly
Profile: Recent developments in the defence & security sectors, & Canadian Association of Defence & Security Industries events & activities

Canadian Association of Direct Response Insurers (CADRI) / Association des marchés financiers du Canada

#301, 250 Consumers Rd., Toronto ON M2J 4V6
Tel: 416-773-0101; *Fax:* 416-495-8723
cadri@cadri.com
www.cadri.com
Overview: A medium-sized national organization
Mission: To support & represent direct response insurers to benefit consumers
Chief Officer(s):
Alain Thibault, President
Ruth Abrahamson, Association Manager
manager@cadri.com
Membership: *Member Profile:* Insurers who are involved in the sales & servicing of property & casualty insurance products in Canada, through direct response marketing & distribution
Activities: Researching t support advocacy; Providing information on direct response insurance

Canadian Association of Drilling Engineers (CADE)

#560, 400 - 5 Ave. SW, Calgary AB T2P 0L2
Tel: 403-532-0220; *Fax:* 403-263-2722
info@cade.ca
www.cade.ca
twitter.com/cade_can
Overview: A medium-sized national organization founded in 1974
Mission: To provide a forum for the exchange of technical drilling knowledge & expertise
Affliation(s): Canadian Association of Oilwell Drilling Contractors
Chief Officer(s):
Eric Schmelzl, President, 403-862-0870
Jeff Arvidson, Chair, Technical, 403-232-7478
Mike Buker, Chair, Education, 403-213-3615
John Burnell, Chair, Membership, 403-265-4973
Graham Evans, Chair, Information Technology
Finances: *Funding Sources:* Membership dues
11 volunteer(s)
Membership: 620 corporate + 2 institutional + 8 student + 8 senior/lifetime; *Fees:* $10 student; $47.50 retiree; $95 full member; *Member Profile:* Open to those who work in the petroleum industry

Publications:
• CADEnews [a publication of the Canadian Association of Drilling Engineers]
Type: Newsletter; *Editor:* Glenn Mencer

Canadian Association of Electroneurophysiology Technologists Inc. (CAET) / Association canadienne des technologues en electroneurophysiologie inc. (ACTE)

c/o University of Alberta Hospital, 8440 - 112 St. NW, Edmonton AB T6G 2B7
Tel: 780-407-8822
www.caet.org
Overview: A small national organization founded in 1951
Mission: To advance the the knowledge, science, & technology of electroneurophysiology in Canada
Affliation(s): Canadian Board of Registration of Electroencephalograph Technologists Inc. (CBRET)
Chief Officer(s):
Tony Card, President
tony.card@caet.org
Joanne Nikkel, Vice-President
joanne.nikkel@caet.org
Bruce Goddard, Director
bruce.goddard@caet.org
Finances: *Funding Sources:* Membership fees; Sponsorships
Membership: *Fees:* $60 regular; $50 associate; $65 new regular; $55 new associate; *Committees:* Nomination/Accreditation/Training Standards; Education/Scientific Committee/Technical Standards; By-Laws
Activities: Promoting technical standards of electroneurophysiology
Meetings/Conferences: • Canadian Association of Electroneurophysiology Technologists 2015 Annual General Meeting, 2015
Scope: National
Publications:
• Canadian Association of Electroneurophysiology Technologists Inc. Membership Directory
Type: Directory

Canadian Association of Elizabeth Fry Societies (CAEFS) / Association canadienne des sociétés Elizabeth Fry (ACSEF)

#701, 151 Slater St., Ottawa ON K1P 5H3
Tel: 613-238-2422; *Fax:* 613-232-7130
Toll-Free: 800-637-4606
admin@caefs.ca
www.elizabethfry.ca
www.facebook.com/138252919680859
twitter.com/CAEFS
www.youtube.com/user/CAEFSElizabethFry
Overview: A medium-sized national charitable organization founded in 1978
Mission: To work with & on behalf of women & girls involved with the justice system, in particular criminalized women; to offer services & programs to women in need, advocating for reforms & offering fora within which the public may be informed about & participate in all aspects of the justice system as it affects women
Affliation(s): Canadian Association of Sexual Assault Centres; Congress of Black Women; National Anti-Poverty Organization; Equality for Gays & Lesbians Everywhere; National Associations Active in Criminal Justice; National Action Committee on the Status of Women; National Association of Women & the Law; National Organization of Immigrant & Visible Minority Women of Canada; National Voluntary Organizations; Native Women's Association of Canada; Pauktuutit, the Inuit Women's Association; Women's Legal Education & Action Fund; National Council of Women of Canada; United Way National Agencies Committee
Chief Officer(s):
Cathie Penny, President
Finances: *Funding Sources:* Dept. of Solicitor General; corporate & individual donations
Membership: 24 societies
Activities: *Internships:* Yes; *Speaker Service:* Yes; *Library* Open to public by appointment

Central Okanagan Elizabeth Fry Society
#104, 347 Leon Ave., Kelowna BC V1Y 8C7
Tel: 250-763-4613; *Fax:* 250-763-4272
www.empowerific.com
www.facebook.com/empowerific
twitter.com/empowerific
Chief Officer(s):
Michelle Novakowski, Executive Director

Council of Elizabeth Fry Societies of Ontario
c/o Canadian Association of Elizabeth Fry Societies, #701, 151 Slater St., Ottawa ON K1P 5H3
Toll-Free: 800-637-4606
info@cefso.ca
www.cefso.ca
Chief Officer(s):
Bryonie Baxter, President
president@cefso.ca

Elizabeth Fry Society for the Regional Municipality of Waterloo
58 Queen St. South, Kitchener ON N2G 1V6
Tel: 519-579-6732; *Fax:* 519-579-6367
e.f.society@gmail.com
www.cefso.ca/waterloo.html
Mission: Believes in helping to create a caring, egalitarian society which respects and supports women. The organization tries to address the needs and circumstances of women of all ages who are, have been or are at risk of coming into conflict with the law. It promotes and provides community-based alternatives to incarceration. Their purpose is to create choices for women, act as a liaison between women and existing services and to promote community awareness.
Chief Officer(s):
Patrice Butts, Manager

Elizabeth Fry Society of Calgary
1730 - 10 Ave. SW, Calgary AB T3C 0K1
Tel: 403-294-0737; *Fax:* 403-262-0285
Toll-Free: 877-398-3656
reception@elizabethfry.ab.ca
www.elizabethfrycalgary.ca
www.facebook.com/232422026837022
Mission: To offer pathways to healing for women involved in the criminal justice system, by providing programming, support, & advocacy; To work with girls & women in conflict with the law, by offering information & support through the court process, the term of sentence, & re-integration into society; To provide programs & services to people in conflict or contact with the law, which acknowledge the economic, social, & psychological realities of their lives
Chief Officer(s):
Barbara Hagen, Executive Director

Elizabeth Fry Society of Cape Breton
16C Levatte Cres., Sydney NS B1N 3K3
Tel: 902-539-6165; *Fax:* 902-539-1683
efrycb@eastlink.ca
Chief Officer(s):
Darlene McEachern, Executive Director

Elizabeth Fry Society of Edmonton
10523 - 100th Ave., Edmonton AB T5J 0A8
Tel: 780-421-1175; *Fax:* 780-425-8989
Toll-Free: 866-421-1175
admin@efryedmonton.ab.ca
www.efryedmonton.ab.ca
www.facebook.com/EFryEdmonton
twitter.com/EFryEdmonton
Mission: To foster the dignity & worth of women of all ages who come into contact with the legal system; to work with girls & women in conflict with the law by offering information & support through the court process, the term of sentence, and re-integration into society; to provide programs & services to people in conflict or contact with the law which acknowledge the economic, social & psychological realities of their lives; to monitor, participate in, & advocate for fairness & equality within the justice system; to cooperate with other organizations which share its commitment to equality & fairness for girls & women; to encourage & provide opportunities for the community to be informed of and involved in the Society's activities; to raise community awareness of social & economic disadvantages & of systemic inequalities.
Chief Officer(s):
Toni Sinclair, Executive Director
director@elizabethfry.ab.ca

Elizabeth Fry Society of Greater Vancouver
237 East Columbia St., New Westminster BC V3L 3W4
Tel: 604-520-1166; *Fax:* 604-520-1169
Toll-Free: 888-879-9593
info@elizabethfry.com
www.elizabethfry.com
www.facebook.com/EFryVancouver
twitter.com/EFryVancouver
Chief Officer(s):
Shawn Bayes, Executive Director

Elizabeth Fry Society of Hamilton
85 Holton Ave. South, Hamilton ON L8M 2L4
Tel: 905-527-3097; *Fax:* 905-527-4278
Toll-Free: 866-216-3379
www.efryhamilton.org
Chief Officer(s):
Leanne Kilby, Executive Director
lkilby@efryhamilton.org

Elizabeth Fry Society of Kingston
127 Charles St., Kingston ON K7K 1V8
Tel: 613-544-1744
Toll-Free: 888-560-3379
info@efrykingston.ca
efrykingston.ca
Chief Officer(s):
Trish Crawford, Executive Director

Elizabeth Fry Society of Mainland Nova Scotia
1 Tulip St., Dartmouth NS B3A 2S3
Tel: 902-454-5041; *Fax:* 902-455-5913
Toll-Free: 877-619-1354
www.efrynovascotia.com
Chief Officer(s):
Nicole Farmer, Contact
nefarmer@efrynovascotia.com

Elizabeth Fry Society of Manitoba
544 Selkirk Ave., Winnipeg MB R2W 2M9
Tel: 204-589-7335; *Fax:* 204-589-7338
Toll-Free: 800-582-5655
administration@efsmanitoba.org
www.efsmanitoba.org
Chief Officer(s):
Tracy Booth, Executive Director
executivedirector@efsmanitoba.org

Elizabeth Fry Society of Northwestern Ontario
217 South Algoma St., Thunder Bay ON P7B 3C3
Tel: 807-623-1319
www.cefso.ca
Chief Officer(s):
Erin Bellavance, Coordinator

Elizabeth Fry Society of Ottawa
#309, 211 Bronson Ave., Ottawa ON K1R 6H5
Tel: 613-237-7427; *Fax:* 613-237-8312
Toll-Free: 800-611-4755
info@efryottawa.com
www.efryottawa.com
Chief Officer(s):
Bryonie Baxter, Executive Director
bryonie.baxter@efryottawa.com

Elizabeth Fry Society of Peel Halton
#LL-01, 24 Queen St. East, Brampton ON L6V 1A3
Tel: 905-459-1315; *Fax:* 905-459-1322
efry@efrypeelhalton.ca
www.efrypeelhalton.ca
Chief Officer(s):
Deborah Riddle, Executive Director

Elizabeth Fry Society of Peterborough
223C Aylmer St. North, Peterborough ON K9J 3K3
Tel: 705-749-6809; *Fax:* 705-749-6818
Toll-Free: 800-820-7384
info@efryptbo.org
www.efryptbo.org
www.facebook.com/ElizabethFrySocietyOfPeterborough
twitter.com/Efry_society
Chief Officer(s):
Lesley Hamilton, President

Elizabeth Fry Society of Saint John
PO Box 23012, Saint John NB E2J 4M1
Tel: 506-635-8851; *Fax:* 506-635-8851
Toll-Free: 866-301-8800
efry@nb.aibn.com
www.facebook.com/173421546050588
Chief Officer(s):
Marianna Stack, President

Elizabeth Fry Society of Saskatchewan
#600, 245 - 3 Ave. South, Saskatoon SK S7M 1M4
Tel: 306-934-4606; *Fax:* 306-652-2933
Toll-Free: 888-934-4606
info@elizabethfrysask.org
www.elizabethfrysask.org
Chief Officer(s):
Sue Delanoy, Executive Director
executivedirector@elizabethfrysask.org

Elizabeth Fry Society of Simcoe County
102 Maple Ave., Barrie ON L4N 1S4
Tel: 705-725-0613
www.elizabethfrysociety.com
Chief Officer(s):
Tracy Wood, Executive Director
tracyw@elizabethfrysociety.com

Elizabeth Fry Society of Sudbury
204 Elm St. West, Sudbury ON P3C 1V3
Tel: 705-673-1364; *Fax:* 705-673-2159
mlepage@on.aibn.com
Mission: Offers pathways to healing for women involved in the criminal justice system by providing programming, support and advocacy. The organization works with girls and women in conflict with the law by offering information and support through the court process, the term of sentence, and re-integration into society; provides programs and services to people in conflict or contact with the law which acknowledge the economic, social, and psychological realities of their lives; monitors, participates in, and advocates for fairness and equality within the justice system; cooperates with other organizations which share its commitment to equality and fairness for girls and women; encourages and provides opportunities for the community to be informed of and involved in the Society's activities; and raises community awareness of social and economic disadvantages and of systemic inequalities.
Chief Officer(s):
Maureen Schizkoske, Executive Director
mschizkoske@efrysudbury.com

Kamloops & District Elizabeth Fry Society
827 Seymour St., Kamloops BC V2C 2H6
Tel: 250-374-2119
admin@kamloopsefry.com
www.kamloopsefry.com
www.facebook.com/KamloopsEFry
Chief Officer(s):
Jennifer Murphy, President

Prince George & District Elizabeth Fry Society
1575 - 5th Ave., Prince George BC V2L 3L9
Tel: 250-563-1113; *Fax:* 250-563-8765
www.pgefry.bc.ca
Chief Officer(s):
Kathi Heim, Executive Director
kathi@pgefry.bc.ca

Société Elizabeth Fry du Québec
5105, ch de la Côte St-Antoine, Montréal QC H4A 1N8
Tél: 514-489-2116; *Téléc:* 514-489-2598
elizabethfry@qc.aira.com
www.elizabethfry.qc.ca
www.facebook.com/elizabethfry.duquebec
Mission: De créer des services pour les femmes ayant des démêlés avec la justice afin de faciliter leur intégration dans la communauté.
Chief Officer(s):
Ruth Gagnon, Directrice générale
ruthgagnon.efry@qc.aira.com

South Cariboo Elizabeth Fry Society
PO Box 603, 601 Bancroft St., Ashcroft BC V0K 1A0
Tel: 250-453-9656; *Fax:* 250-453-2034

Toronto Elizabeth Fry Society
215 Wellesley St. East, Toronto ON M4X 1G1
Tel: 416-924-3708
Toll-Free: 855-924-3708
info@efrytoronto.org
www.efrytoronto.org
www.linkedin.com/groups?gid=3384615
www.facebook.com/elizabethfrytoronto
twitter.com/efry_toronto
Chief Officer(s):
Gemma Napoli, Executive Director
gnapoli@efrytoronto.org

Canadian Association of Emergency Physicians (CAEP) / Association canadienne des médecins d'urgence (ACMU)

#808, 180 Elgin St., Ottawa ON K2P 2K3
Tel: 613-523-3343; *Fax:* 613-523-0190
Toll-Free: 800-463-1158
admin@caep.ca
www.caep.ca
ca.linkedin.com/pub/canadian-assoc-of-emergency-physicians/22/b06/4a5
www.facebook.com/275451855826447
twitter.com/CAEP_Docs
Overview: A medium-sized national charitable organization founded in 1978
Mission: To act as the national voice of emergency medicine; To empower physicians to provide excellent emergency care, through leadership, continuing education, & advocacy
Chief Officer(s):
Vera Klein, Executive Director
vklein@caep.ca
Bruce McLeod, President
president@caep.ca
Paul Pageau, Treasurer
board@caep.ca
Janice MacIsaac, Manager, CME
jmacisaac@caep.ca
Lee Arbon, Manager, Communications & Marketing
larbon@caep.ca
Finances: *Funding Sources:* Membership fees; Grants
Staff Member(s): 10
Membership: *Fees:* Schedule available; *Member Profile:* Emergency physicians; Researchers; Residents; Spouses; Students; *Committees:* Bylaws; CJEM-CAEP Liaison; Continuing Medical Education; Financial Audit; Canadian Triage and Acuity Scale; Membership; Nominating; Public Affairs; Research; Standards; Bioethics; Critical Care; Disaster; Emergency Medical Services; Emergency Targeted Ultrasound; International Emergency Medicine; Interprovincial EM Practice; Medical Students Subsection; Medical Toxicology; Patient Safety; Rural & Small Urban; Stroke; Trauma, Illness & Injury Prevention; Undergraduate Education; Women in Emergency Medicine
Activities: Providing networking opportunities; Liaising with governments, policy makers, & other stakeholders
Awards:
• President's Award (Award)
• Research Grants (Grant)
• Resident Abstract Award (Award)
• CCFP(EM) & FRCPC Resident Leadership Award (Award)
• Resident Teacher of the Year Award (Award)
Meetings/Conferences: • Canadian Association of Emergency Physicians (CAEP) 2015 Annual Conference, May, 2015, Shaw Conference Centre, Edmonton, AB
Scope: National
• Canadian Association of Emergency Physicians (CAEP) 2016 Annual Conference, June, 2016, Quebec City Convention Centre, Quebec City, QC
Scope: National
• Canadian Association of Emergency Physicians (CAEP) 2017 Annual Conference, 2017, Whistler Conference Centre, Whistler, BC
Scope: National
Publications:
• Canadian Journal of Emergency Medicine
Type: Journal; *Frequency:* Bimonthly; *Accepts Advertising*; *Editor:* James Ducharme, MD; *Price:* $225 Canadian individuals; $399 Canadianinstitutions; $254 international individuals
Profile: A peer-reviewed journal, featuring articles of interest to emergency care providers in rural, urban, or academic settings

Canadian Association of Environmental Law Societies (CAELS)

e-mail: info@caels.org
caels.org
facebook.com/CAELSorg
www.twitter.com/CAELSorg
Overview: A medium-sized national organization
Mission: The Canadian Association of Environmental Law Societies (CAELS) is a networking project connecting environmental law students across the country. CAELS will allow law students to interact with their peers and professors, practitioners and environmental professionals.
1 volunteer(s)
Meetings/Conferences: • Canadian Association of Environmental Law Societies 2015 Conference, February, 2015, Univeristy of Calgary, Calgary, AB
Scope: National

Canadian Association of Environmental Management

c/o Homewood Health Centre, 150 Delhi St., Guelph ON N1E 6K9
Tel: 519-824-1010; *Fax:* 519-824-1827
www.caenvironmentalmanagement.com
Previous Name: Canadian Administrative Housekeepers Association
Overview: A small national organization founded in 1972
Mission: To promote the professional growth & development of its members & help them improve the environmental & housekeeping services they offer.
Chief Officer(s):
Keith Sopha, President
sophkeit@homewood.org
Finances: *Funding Sources:* Advertising; membership dues
Membership: *Fees:* $80 individual; $140 organization; $40 additional member; *Member Profile:* Managers, supervisors, self-employed people, corporate & associate members involved in the environmental services field
Activities: Conference & trade shows; *Speaker Service:* Yes

Canadian Association of Ethnic (Radio) Broadcasters (CAEB) / Association canadienne des radiodiffuseurs ethniques

c/o CHIN Radio, #400, 622 College St., Toronto ON M6G 1B6
Tel: 416-531-9991; *Fax:* 416-531-5274
info@chinradio.com
www.chinradio.com
www.facebook.com/pages/CHIN-Radio-Canada/109552875750238
twitter.com/chinradiocanada
Overview: A small national organization founded in 1981
Mission: To foster & promote the development of multilingual / multicultural radio broadcasting in Canada
Chief Officer(s):
Lenny Lombardi, President
Membership: *Member Profile:* Ethnic radio stations in Canada

Canadian Association of Exposition Management (CAEM) / Association canadienne des directeurs d'expositions

PO Box 218, #2219, 160 Tycos Dr., Toronto ON M6B 1W8
Tel: 416-787-9377; *Fax:* 416-596-1808
Toll-Free: 866-441-9377
info@caem.ca
www.caem.ca
Previous Name: Association of Trade & Consumer Exhibitions
Overview: A medium-sized national organization founded in 1983
Mission: To represent & improve the exposition & trade show industry in Canada
Chief Officer(s):
Serge Micheli, Executive Director, 416-787-9377 Ext. 224
smicheli@caem.ca
Lisa McDonald, President
Sherry Kirkpatrick, 1st Vice-President
Catherine MacNutt, 2nd Vice-President
Jennifer Allaby, Secretary
Mike Russell, Treasurer
Michael Dargavel, Office Manager, 416-787-9377 Ext. 225
Finances: *Funding Sources:* Membership fees; Sponsorships
Membership: *Member Profile:* Professional trade & consumer show producers & managers, & industry suppliers
Activities: Promoting Canada's exposition & trade show industry; Offering networking opportunities; Providing professional development sessions

Canadian Association of Fairs & Exhibitions (CAFE) / Association canadienne des foires et expositions

PO Box 13161, Ottawa ON K2K 1X4
Tel: 613-233-0012; *Fax:* 613-233-1154
Toll-Free: 800-663-1714
info@canadian-fairs.ca
www.canadian-fairs.ca
Overview: A large national charitable organization founded in 1924
Mission: To provide leadership in the development of the Canadian Fair Industry; To represent the Canadian fairs & exhibitions sector at the national level
Member of: Imagine Canada
Affiliation(s): International Association of Fairs & Exhibitions; Provincial Associations of Agricultural Societies; Outdoor Amusement Business Association; Showmens League of Canada; Canadian 4H Council
Chief Officer(s):
Harry Emmott, President
hemmott@sympatico.ca
Mavis Hanna, Executive Director, 613-233-0012 Ext. 222
Finances: *Funding Sources:* Membership fees
300 volunteer(s)
Membership: 225 corporate; *Fees:* Schedule available; *Member Profile:* Recognized fair or exhibition established under Provincial Act; firms & organizations which derive significant percentage of annual income from providing products & services

to fair organizations; *Committees:* Government Relations; Communications; Programs & Services
Activities: Workshops; CAFE Learning Forums; insurance program
Awards:
• Best of Show Award (Award)
• CAFE Volunteer of the Year Award (Award)
• Service Member of the Year (Award)
• Roll of Honour (Award)
• Poster Competition (Award)
• Fun Doniker (Award)
A humorous award presented to an organization or individual for whom an event or program did not go as planned
Meetings/Conferences: • Canadian Association of Fairs & Exhibitions Annual Convention 2015, 2015
Scope: National
Publications:
• Canadian Fair & Exhibition National Industry Directory [a publication of the Canadian Association of Fairs & Exhibitions]
Frequency: Annually
Profile: Listings of CAFE members & fair dates
• Canadian Fair News [a publication of the Canadian Association of Fairs & Exhibitions]
Frequency: Quarterly; *Editor:* Hannah Service
Profile: Industry information including agricultural issues, government programs & regulations, trends, & association programs

Canadian Association of Family Enterprise (CAFE) / Association canadienne des enterprises familiales

#112, 465 Morden Rd., Oakville ON L6K 3W6
Tel: 905-337-8375; *Fax:* 905-337-0572
Toll-Free: 866-849-0099
info@cafecanada.ca
www.cafecanada.ca
www.linkedin.com/groups?home=&gid=1883375
www.facebook.com/fambizsupport
twitter.com/CAFECanada
www.youtube.com/user/CAFECanada1
Also Known As: CAFE Canada
Overview: A medium-sized national licensing organization founded in 1983
Mission: To improve succession statistics for family businesses across Canada where Canadian family businesses connect with peers & resources for success.
Affliation(s): Family Enterprise Foundation
Chief Officer(s):
Paul MacDonald, Executive Director, 905-337-8375 Ext. 223
paul@cafecanada.ca
Lorraine Bauer, Managing Director, 905-337-8375 Ext. 224
lorraine@cafecanada.ca
Simms Sheila, Office Administrator, 905-337-8375 Ext. 221
sheila@cafecanada.ca
Finances: *Annual Operating Budget:* $500,000-$1.5 Million; *Funding Sources:* Membership fees
Staff Member(s): 15; 100+ volunteer(s)
Membership: 800; *Fees:* Schedule available based on chapter; *Member Profile:* Families in business
Activities: Monthly meetings, workshops, seminars, networking events in chapters across Canada; *Speaker Service:* Yes; *Library:* Canadian Association of Family Enterprise Library; by appointment
Awards:
• CAFE Award for Family Enterprise of the Year (Award)
Established to recognize the importance of family enterprise; looks at: job creation, technological advancement, environment, innovation & entrepeneurial success; open to any family enterprise, private or publicly owned*Deadline:* March
Meetings/Conferences: • 2015 CAFE Family Business Symposium, May 2015, 2015, Westin Harbour Castle, Toronto, ON

CAFE Calgary
PO Box 16055, Stn. Lower Mount Royal, Calgary AB T2T 1A0
Fax: 905-337-0572
Toll-Free: 866-849-0099
calgary@cafecanada.ca
www.cafecanada.ca/calgary
Chief Officer(s):
Todd Coleman, President

CAFE Central Ontario
#112, 465 Morden Rd., Oakville ON L6K 3W6
Tel: 905-337-8375; *Fax:* 905-337-0572
Toll-Free: 866-886-0982
centralontario@cafecanada.ca
www.cafecanada.ca/chapters/central-ontario
Chief Officer(s):
Allen Taylor, President

CAFE Edmonton
PO Box 22015, Stn. Pollard Meadows, Edmonton AB T6L 0A1
Tel: 780-953-7047
edmonton@cafecanada.ca
www.cafecanada.ca/edmonton
Chief Officer(s):
Ray Zadrey, President
ray@zadrey.ca

CAFE Manitoba
PO Box 45081, RPO Kildonan Place, Winnipeg MB R2C 5G5
Tel: 204-918-6170
manitoba@cafecanada.ca
www.cafecanada.ca/manitoba
Chief Officer(s):
Bob Spriggs, President

CAFE Nova Scotia
65 Celtic Dr., Dartmouth NS B2Y 3G5
Tel: 902-465-2535; *Fax:* 902-463-6308
novascotia@cafecanada.ca
www.cafecanada.ca/chapters/nova-scotia
Chief Officer(s):
Michelle LaVigne, Executive Director

CAFE Okanagan
#300, 1674 Bertram St., Kelowna BC V1Y 9G4
Tel: 250-764-0638
okanagan@cafecanada.ca
www.cafecanada.ca/chapters/okanagan
Chief Officer(s):
Carolyn Reimer, Managing Director

CAFE Ottawa
PO Box 8096, Stn. T, Ottawa ON K1G 3H6
Tel: 613-232-2233; *Fax:* 613-247-7584
ottawa@cafecanada.ca
www.cafecanada.ca/ottawa
Chief Officer(s):
Kim McWaters, Managing Director

CAFE Regina
PO Box 37228, Regina SK S4S 7K4
Toll-Free: 866-578-0978
regina@cafecanada.ca
www.cafecanada.ca/regina
Chief Officer(s):
Petra Coutts, Managing Director

CAFE Saskatoon
Norplex Business Centre, 2366 Ave. C North, Saskatoon SK S7L 5X5
Tel: 306-292-7838
saskatoon@cafecanada.ca
www.cafecanada.ca/chapters/saskatoon
Chief Officer(s):
Paula Simon, Executive Director

CAFE Southwestern Ontario
PO Box 23034, London ON N6A 5N9
Tel: 519-642-4349; *Fax:* 519-642-2873
southwesternontario@cafecanada.ca
www.cafecanada.ca/swo
twitter.com/CAFE_SWO
Chief Officer(s):
Tamelynda Lux, Executive Director

CAFE Vancouver Island
PO Box 8482, 706 Yates St., Victoria BC V8W 3S1
Tel: 250-532-2402
vancouverisland@cafecanada.ca
www.cafecanada.ca/chapters/vancouver-island
Chief Officer(s):
Bernadine Rudichuk, Managing Director

CAFE Vancouver Region
#200, 375 Water St., Vancouver BC V6B 5C6
Tel: 604-721-1241
vancouver@cafecanada.ca
www.cafecanada.ca/chapters/vancouver-region
Chief Officer(s):
Jane O'Connor, Executive Director

Canadian Association of Family Resource Programs / Association canadienne des programmes de ressources pour la famille

#707, 331 Cooper St., Ottawa ON K2P 0G5
Tel: 613-237-7667; *Fax:* 613-237-8515
Toll-Free: 866-637-7226
Other Communication: www.parentsmatter.ca
info@frp.ca
www.frp.ca
www.facebook.com/frpcanada
twitter.com/frpcanada
Also Known As: FRP Canada
Previous Name: Canadian Association of Toy Libraries
Overview: A medium-sized national charitable organization founded in 1976
Mission: To promote the well-being of families, through provision of leadership, consultation, & resources to organizations which care for children & support families; To act as the national voice for family resource programs; To advance social policy, research, resource development, & training for those who support the capacity of families to raise their children
Member of: National Alliance for Children & Youth
Chief Officer(s):
Janice MacAulay, Executive Director
macaulay@frp.ca
Trish Plant, President
trishp@lampchc.org
Jackie Collins, Vice-President
c-jcollins@hotmail.com
Laura Graham, Secretary
laurafamilyplace@eastlink.ca
Stéphane Rivest, Treasurer
stephane.rivest@oag-bvg.gc.ca
Jill Heckman, Director, Operations
jheckman@frp.ca
Finances: *Annual Operating Budget:* $500,000-$1.5 Million; *Funding Sources:* Donations; Membership fees; Grants
Staff Member(s): 5; 27 volunteer(s)
Membership: 500+ organizations; *Fees:* $150/year; *Member Profile:* Canadian community-based family resource programs
Activities: Offering training in areas such as child development, literacy, & early learning; Researching topics, such as family development, to assist family resource programs; Providing a network for family resource programs; Promoting family support programs to communities; Publishing numerous resources, such as newcomer resources; *Awareness Events:* National Family Week
Meetings/Conferences: • FRP Canada 2015 National Conference, March, 2015, Sheraton Hamilton Hotel, Hamilton, ON
Scope: National
Description: A biennial conference, presenting a keynote speaker, a panel discussion, workshops, & exhibits
Contact Information: Phone: 613-237-7667, ext. 231; E-mail: conference@frp.ca
Publications:
• Canadian Association of Family Resource Programs Annual Report
Type: Yearbook; *Frequency:* Annually
• Discovering Our Capacities
Type: Study; *Editor:* Deborah Sullivan; *Price:* $12 members; $15 non-members
Profile: The philosophies & perspectives of informal community support systems & more formal service delivery systems
• The Evaluation of Family Resource Programs: Challenges & Promising Approaches
Editor: Peter Gabor; *Price:* $15 members; $18 non-members
Profile: Ideas to improve evaluation of family resource programs
• e-Valuation: Building Evaluation Capacity in the Family Resource Sector
Type: Report; *Editor:* Peter Gabor; *Price:* $15 members; $18 non-members
Profile: A detailed guide to employing the evaluation system & tools developed for family resource programs
• Finding Our Way: A Participatory Evaluation Method for Family Resource Programs
Type: Manual; *Number of Pages:* 200; *Editor:* Diana Ellis; *Price:* $28 members; $32non-members
Profile: A guide for family resource programs, featuring a glossary, samply tools, & an annotated bibliography
• FRP Canada Member Directory
Type: Directory
Profile: A listing of more than 500 family resource programs throughout Canada, such as Ontario Early Years Centres & Certified Canadian Family Educators
• Improving Facilities: Innovative Approaches for Community Programs
Type: Guide; *Editor:* Patrick Chen; Janice MacAulay; *Price:* $24 members; $28 non-members

Profile: Tips to improve facilities, including checklists, forms, & a bibliography
• Making Choices: Parenting Program Inventory
Price: $20 members; $25 non-members
Profile: Information for practitioners & parents
• Play & Parenting Connections
Type: Newsletter; *Frequency:* Quarterly; *Price:* Free with membership in the Canadian Association of Family Resource Programs
• Responsibility & Accountability: What Community-Based Programs Need to Know
Type: Book; *Number of Pages:* 64; *Price:* $15 members; $18 non-members
Profile: Liability for community organizations
• Supporting Fathers
Type: Handbook; *Editor:* B. Beauregard; F. Brown; K. Kidder; *Price:* $22 members; $27 non-members
Profile: A guide for program staff to improve their programs for fathers
• Synergy: Integrated Approaches in Family Support
Type: Report; *Price:* $27 members; $32 non-members
Profile: Experiences surrounding the provision of comprehensive services for families in Canada
• Tensions & Possibilities: Forging Better Links Between Family Resource Programs & Child Welfare
Type: Report; *Number of Pages:* 104; *Editor:* Janice MacAulay; *Price:* $20 members; $25 non-members
Profile: Practices for family resource programs in relation to child welfare issues, featuring charts & checklists
• Weaving Literacy into Family & Community Life
Editor: Suzanne Smythe; Lee Weinstein; *Price:* $25 members; $30 non-members
Profile: A resource featuring the following booklets: Book 1-Literacy in our Lives; Book 2-Creating Learning Environments for Children; Book 3-Community-BasedFamily Literacy Partnerships - 3 Case Studies; Book 4-Literacy Initiatives in Family Resource Programs; & Book 5: A Literacy Workers' Guide to FRPs
• Working With Parent Groups: A Handbook for Facilitators
Type: Handbook; *Editor:* Betsy Mann; *Price:* $25 members; $29 non-members
Profile: Ideas & a list of resources for strengthening parents' ability to fill their role

Canadian Association of Farm Advisors (CAFA)

PO Box 578, Blaine Lake SK S0J 0J0
Tel: 306-466-2294; *Fax:* 306-466-2297
Toll-Free: 877-474-2871
info@cafanet.com
www.cafanet.com
ca.linkedin.com/company/canadian-association-of-farm-advisors
twitter.com/CAFANET
www.youtube.com/watch?v=xQnYKyJVTk0
Overview: A medium-sized national organization founded in 2001
Mission: To assist farm producers & agribusinesses by improving the advice provided to them; to improve the education & professionalism of farm advisors; to represent farm advisors on issues of concern
Chief Officer(s):
Don Roberts, Chair
Liz Robertson, Executive Director
Finances: *Funding Sources:* Sponsorships
Staff Member(s): 1
Membership: *Fees:* $350 regular; $130 associate; $100 student; *Member Profile:* Agribusinesses; Agricultural economists; Agrologists; Agronomists; Farm producers; Educators; Appraisers; Bankers, accountants, commodity traders, financial planners, trust officers, & insurance agents; Lawyers; Consultants; Marketing representatives; Media members; & Veterinarians
Activities: Increasing the skills & knowledge of farm advisors; Providing better access to farm advice; Offering networking opportunities; *Awareness Events:* Regional Conferences; *Speaker Service:* Yes; *Library:* CAFA Library
Meetings/Conferences: • Canadian Association of Farm Advisors 2015 Conference, January, 2015, Saskatoon, SK
Scope: National
Description: Joint conference with SK Young Ag Entrepreneurs to maximize learning, engagement and networking.
Publications:
• AgVisor
Type: Newsletter
Profile: For producers & their families about planning considerations
• Cultivating Business
Type: Newsletter; *Number of Pages:* q.
Profile: CAFA news & events from across Canada for farmers & their advisors
• Farm Business Advisor Manual
Editor: Howard L. Morry & Donna M. Hastings; *Price:* $150members; $295 non-members
Profile: Technical & human resource information about farming basics, farm management, financing, legislation family law, taxation, & estate & succession planning

Canadian Association of Film Distributors & Exporters (CAFDE) / Association canadienne des distributeurs et exportateurs de films (ACDEF)

#1605, 85 Albert St., Ottawa ON K1P 6A4
Tel: 613-238-3557
info@CAFDE.ca
cafde.ca
Previous Name: National Association of Canadian Film & Video Distributors
Overview: A medium-sized national organization founded in 1991
Mission: To foster & promote the health of the Canadian motion picture industry by strengthening the Canadian owned & controlled distribution/export sector
Affliation(s): Association des producteurs de films et de television du Québec
Chief Officer(s):
Hussain Amarshi, President
Finances: *Funding Sources:* Membership dues
Membership: 9; *Member Profile:* Canadian owned & controlled film & television distributors; *Committees:* Copyright; Inter-Provincial Restrictions; Classification & Censorship; Theatrical; Home Video; Television & Airlines; Cable Fund; Export Issues; Festivals

Canadian Association of Financial Institutions in Insurance (CAFII) / Association canadienne des institutions financières en assurance (ACIFA)

#255, 55 St. Clair Ave. West, Toronto ON M4V 2Y7
Tel: 416-494-9224; *Fax:* 416-967-6320
info@cafii.com
www.cafii.com
Overview: A small national organization founded in 1997
Mission: To develop an efficient & effective, open & flexible insurance marketplace; to provide a voice for financial institutions that sell insurance through a range of distribution methods
Chief Officer(s):
Brendan Wycks, Executive Director
Finances: *Funding Sources:* Annual fees of members
Membership: *Member Profile:* Organizations that sell insurance through a variety of methods, such as agents & brokers, travel agents, call centres, direct mail, DTIs, & the Internet; Organizations that sell insurance in all major lines of business
Activities: Working with governments & regulators to develop a legislative & regulatory framework for the insurance sector; Monitoring. analyzing, & offering information & advice to members; Communicating with consumers & the media; Supporting training & professional development; Researching to support association objectives
Publications:
• CAFII [Canadian Association of Financial Institutions in Insurance] Monthly Newsletter
Type: Newsletter; *Frequency:* Monthly; *Editor:* Lawrie Savage & Associates
Profile: Updates for CAFII members
• Regulatory Updates [a publication of the Canadian Association of Financial Institutions in Insurance]
Type: Newsletter; *Frequency:* Monthly
Profile: Information for CAFII members

Canadian Association of Fire Chiefs (CAFC) / Association canadienne des chefs de pompiers (ACCP)

#702, 280 Albert St., Ottawa ON K1P 5G8
Tel: 613-270-9138
Toll-Free: 800-775-5189
www.cafc.ca
ca.linkedin.com/pub/canadian-association-of-fire-chiefs/2a/a05/82b
twitter.com/cafc2
Overview: A medium-sized national organization
Mission: To lead & represent the Canadian Fire Service on public safety issues with the vision of being nationally recognized as the fire service voice of authority
Affliation(s): International Association of Fire Chiefs
Chief Officer(s):
Robert Simonds, President
Pierre Voisine, Secretary
Lee Grant, Treasurer
Membership: 1,000; *Fees:* $190 + GST
Activities: *Rents Mailing List:* Yes; *Library:* Fire Services Resource Centre; Open to public
Meetings/Conferences: • Canadian Association of Fire Chiefs 2015 Fire Rescue Canada Conference, September, 2015, Victoria Conference Centre, Victoria, BC
Scope: International
Description: Speaker presentations, seminars, & workshops for the fire & emergency services community from across Canada & the United States
• Canadian Association of Fire Chiefs 2016 Conference, 2016
Scope: International
Description: Speaker presentations, seminars, & workshops for the fire & emergency services community from across Canada & the United States
Publications:
• Canadian Association of Fire Chiefs Directory of Members
Type: Directory; *Frequency:* Annually
Profile: Includes CAFC leadership listings & updated bylaws
• Fire Chief Magazine
Type: Magazine; *Frequency:* Quarterly
Profile: Important issues about fire services

The Canadian Association of Fitness Professionals / Association canadienne des professionnels en conditionnement physique

#110, 225 Select Ave., Toronto ON M1X 0B5
Tel: 416-493-3515; *Fax:* 416-493-1756
Toll-Free: 800-667-5622
info@canfitpro.com
www.canfitpro.com
www.linkedin.com/groups?gid=1773770&trk=hb_side_g
www.facebook.com/group.php?gid=2524100816
twitter.com/canfitpro
www.youtube.com/user/canfitpro/featured
Also Known As: Can-Fit-Pro
Overview: A medium-sized national licensing organization founded in 1993
Mission: Can-Fit-Pro takes today's fitness professionals' challenges & creates tomorrow's solutions through ongoing relative knowledge & personal enrichment
Member of: National Fitness Leadership Advisory Committee
Chief Officer(s):
Maureen Hagan, Executive Director
Kathy Ash, Contact, Administration
Finances: *Annual Operating Budget:* $1.5 Million-$3 Million; *Funding Sources:* Sponsorship; private; membership dues; courses
Staff Member(s): 10; 400 volunteer(s)
Membership: 30,000; *Member Profile:* Interest in fitness industry
Activities: Certification & standards for fitness instructors & personal trainers, who work at private & public fitness facilities; continuing education; events & six conferences a year

Canadian Association of Food Banks *See* Food Banks Canada

Canadian Association of Foodservice Professionals (CAFP) / Association canadienne des professionnels des services alimentaires

CAFP National Office, #130, 10691 Shellbridge Way, Richmond BC V6X 2W8
Tel: 604-248-0215; *Fax:* 604-270-3644
Toll-Free: 877-599-2237
national@cafp.com
www.cafp.com
twitter.com/wearecafp
Previous Name: Canadian Food Service Executives Association
Overview: A large national organization founded in 1901
Mission: To enhance the prestige of the food service profession through improving standards of service; To promote education in the industry & to provide increased opportunity for youth to train for the food service profession; to promote research in food service & nutrition; To work for food service regulation & legislation in the public interest; To promote through good fellowship & personal association new opportunities for increased management efficiency & exchange of professional information

Chief Officer(s):
Andrea Gillespie, National President
Leslie Smith, Vice-President, Membership
Dwayne Botchar, Secretary-Treasurer
Staff Member(s): 1; 22 volunteer(s)
Membership: 1,121
Meetings/Conferences: • 2015 Canadian Association of Foodservice Professionals National Conference, May, 2015, Delta Fredricton, Fredericton, NB
Scope: National
Publications:
• Food Bites [a publication of the Canadian Association of Foodservice Professionals]
Type: Newsletter
• Quick Bites [a publication of the Canadian Association of Foodservice Professionals]
Type: Newsletter

Calgary Branch
Chief Officer(s):
Helen Scott, President
hscott@burlodgeca.com
Ken Upton, National Director/Past President
Hunter Hobbs, Contact
hhobbs@gfscanada.com

Division de Montréal
Chief Officer(s):
Béatrice Martin, Présidente
beatrice.martin@berthelet.com

Edmonton Branch
e-mail: CAFPedmonton@gmail.com
Chief Officer(s):
Marc Haine, President
Darrell Lindstrom, CFE, National Director

Halifax/Dartmouth Branch
Chief Officer(s):
Lisa Slauenwhite, President
Delores Smith, CFE, National Director/Vice-President, Public Relations & Recruitment
dasmith@accesswave.ca

London Branch
Chief Officer(s):
Lin Yuan-Su, President
0610@hotmail.com
Tammy Latta, Vice-President, Membership
tlatta@nms.on.ca

New Brunswick Branch
Chief Officer(s):
Jeff Williams, President
Esther Archibald, CFE, National Director

Northumberland Branch
Chief Officer(s):
David Breen, President
breen.dave@hfx.sysco.ca

Ottawa Branch
Chief Officer(s):
Frances Furmankiewicz, President
Leesa Franklin, CFE, National Director/Past President
Chantal Cheff, Vice-President, Membership
chantal.cheff@leisureworld.ca

Toronto Branch
e-mail: toronto@cafp.com
Chief Officer(s):
Nancy Hewittlo, President
Rosie Maclean, National Director/Sargeant-at-Arms

Vancouver Branch
Chief Officer(s):
Simon Tse, President
tosimontse@gmail.com
Susan Cox, National Director/Past President
Lezlie Smith, Vice-President, Membership
lezlie.smith@telus.net

Canadian Association of Foot Care Nurses (CAFCN)

c/o Pat MacDonald, President, 110 Linden Park Bay, Winnipeg MB R2R 1Y3
www.cafcn.ca
Previous Name: Foot Care Canada
Overview: A large national organization founded in 2005
Mission: To advance the practice of foot care through a collaborative and networking process for all individuals providing foot care.
Chief Officer(s):
Pat MacDonald, President
president@cafcn.ca
Membership: *Committees:* Education; Policy; Conference; Website; Newsletter; Nominations; Public Relations; Bylaw
Meetings/Conferences: • The 6th Canadian Association of Foot Care Nurses 2015 Annual General Meeting & Conference, May, 2015, Winnipeg, MB
Contact Information: conference@cafcn.ca

Canadian Association of Former Parliamentarians (CAFP) / L'Association canadienne des ex-parlementaires (ACEP)

House of Commons, PO Box 1, 131 Queen St., Ottawa ON K1A 0A6
Tel: 613-947-1690; *Fax:* 613-947-1764
Toll-Free: 888-567-4764
exparl@parl.gc.ca
www.exparl.ca
Overview: A small national organization founded in 1987
Mission: To provide support to the government, fostering good relations between Senate, House of Commons & former parliamentarians; to raise funds to promote the knowledge, education & experience of the principles & operation of democratic & parliamentary procedure.
Chief Officer(s):
Andy Mitchell, President
Finances: *Funding Sources:* Membership dues; grant
Staff Member(s): 3
Membership: *Fees:* $125; *Member Profile:* Former Senators & Members of the House of Commons
Publications:
• Beyond the Hill
Type: Magazine; *Frequency:* Quarterly; *Editor:* Dorothy Dobbie

Canadian Association of Foundations of Education (CAFE) / Association canadienne des fondements de l'éducation (ACFE)

c/o The Canadian Society for the Study of Education, #204, 260 Dalhousie St., Ottawa ON K1N 7E4
Tel: 613-241-0018; *Fax:* 613-241-0019
csse-scee@csse.ca
www.csse-scee.ca/cafe
Overview: A medium-sized national organization founded in 1971
Mission: To provide a forum for discussing the contribution of the social sciences & humanities (eg. history of education, philosophy of education, sociology of education) to educational theory, research & practice
Member of: Canadian Society for the Study of Education
Affliation(s): Canadian Philosophy of Education Society; Canadian History of Education Society; Sociology in Education Network (SOCINET)
Chief Officer(s):
Michael O'Sullivan, President
mosullivan@brocku.ca
Finances: *Annual Operating Budget:* Less than $50,000; *Funding Sources:* Membership fees
12 volunteer(s)
Membership: 160; *Fees:* $90 Regular, $45 Student/Retired/Low Income, $48 Intern; *Member Profile:* Professors & graduate students in education foundations; *Committees:* Executive; Programme; Publication Awards; Distinguished Service Awards
Activities: Given annually by CAFE to recognize, celebrate and promote the achievements of Canadian family businesses and the considerable contribution they make to both their local communities and our national economy.
Awards:
• Statistics Canada Award (Award)
Presented to a pre-service student who completes a project of paper involving the application of Statistics Canada material *Amount:* $500 cash prize; nation-wide publication of article; opportunity to present paper
• Award for Edited Collections & Authored Monographs (Award)
To recognize scholarly books & monographs that make a major contribution to knowledge in the disciplines & areas that come under the rubric of the foundations of education
• Service Award (Award)
Recognizes individuals who made major contributions through teaching, research &/or professional service to the disciplines & areas that come under the rubric of foundations of education
Publications:
• Canadian Journal of Education / Revue canadienne de l'éducation
Type: Journal; *Editor:* Julia Ellis & Stéphane Allaire *ISSN:* 0380-2361; *Price:* Included with CSSE membership; $100 non-members
Profile: Articles & book reviews for a well-read general readership
• CSSE [Canadian Association of Foundations of Education] News
Type: Newsletter; *Frequency:* Monthly
Profile: CSSE news, post-secondary education

Canadian Association of Freediving & Apnea (CAFA)

19640 - 34A Ave., Lengley BC V3A 7W6
Other Communication: Board, E-mail: board@freedivecanada.com
www.freedivecanada.com
Overview: A small national organization
Mission: To further the sport of freediving in Canada & abroad.
Chief Officer(s):
Andrew Hogan, President
president@freedivecanada.com
Membership: *Fees:* $25 full; $50 associate

Canadian Association of Gastroenterology / Association canadienne de gastroentérologie

#224, 1540 Cornwall Rd., Oakville ON L6J 7W5
Tel: 905-829-2504; *Fax:* 905-829-0242
Toll-Free: 888-780-0007
general@cag-acg.org
www.cag-acg.org
Overview: A small national organization founded in 1962
Mission: To support & engage in the study of gastroenterology; to promote patient care, research, teaching and professional development in the field; to promote and maintain the highest ethical standards of practice.
Affliation(s): Canadian Medical Association; World Organization of Gastroenterology
Chief Officer(s):
Paul Sinclair, Executive Director
Staff Member(s): 6
Membership: 1,100; *Fees:* schedule; *Member Profile:* Doctors, scientists; health care providers; *Committees:* Administrative Affairs; Education Affairs; Clinical Affiars; Research Affairs; Nominations; Operations
Meetings/Conferences: • Canadian Digestive Diseases Week: Canadian Association of Gastroenterology Annual Scientific Conference 2015, February, 2015, Fairmont Banff Springs, Banff, AB
Scope: National
• Canadian Digestive Diseases Week: Canadian Association of Gastroenterology Annual Scientific Conference 2016, February, 2016, Montreal, QC
Scope: National
• Canadian Digestive Diseases Week: Canadian Association of Gastroenterology Annual Scientific Conference 2017, February, 2017, Banff, AB
Scope: National

Canadian Association of General Surgeons (CAGS) / Association canadienne des chirurgiens généraux (ACCG)

PO Box 1428, Stn. B, Ottawa ON K1P 5R4
Tel: 613-882-6510
cags@cags-accg.ca
www.cags-accg.ca
Overview: A medium-sized national charitable organization founded in 1977
Mission: To assist all general surgeons with continuing education; facilitate & promote surgical research; develop policies & new ideas in the areas of clinical care, education & research
Affliation(s): Canadian Medical Association; Royal College of Physicians & Surgeons of Canada
Chief Officer(s):
Susan Reid, President
Finances: *Funding Sources:* Membership fees; Corporate funding
Staff Member(s): 1
Membership: 1,600; *Fees:* $275; $16 Associate; *Member Profile:* General surgeons
Meetings/Conferences: • 2015 Canadian Surgery Forum, September, 2015, Quebec, QC
Scope: National
Publications:
• CAGS [Canadian Association of General Surgeons] Newsletter
Type: Newsletter
Profile: Association news, conference highlights, & research

Canadian Association of Genetic Counsellors (CAGC) / Association Canadienne des conseillers en génétique (ACCG)

PO Box 52083, Oakville ON L6J 7N5

Tel: 905-847-1363; *Fax:* 905-847-3855
Other Communication: president@cagc-accg.ca
CAGCOffice@cagc-accg.ca
www.cagc-accg.ca
Overview: A small national organization
Mission: To promote high standards of practice; To encourage professional growth; To increase public awareness of the profession; To offer certification in genetic counselling
Membership: 1-99; *Fees:* $100 full, associate; $50 student; *Member Profile:* Genetic counsellors
Meetings/Conferences: • Canadian Association of Genetic Counsellors Annual Conference 2015, September, 2015, The Westin Ottawa, Ottawa, ON
Scope: National

Canadian Association of Geographers (CAG) / Association canadienne des géographes

Department of Geography, McGill University, #425, 805, rue Sherbrooke ouest, Montréal QC H3A 2K6
Tel: 514-398-4946; *Fax:* 514-398-7437
valerie.shoffey@cag-acg.ca
www.cag-acg.ca
Overview: A medium-sized national organization founded in 1951
Mission: To promote the discipline of geography in Canada & internationally
Member of: Humanities & Social Science Federation of Canada; Canadian Federation of Earth Sciences; International Geographical Union
Affliation(s): L'l'association professionelle des géographes du Québec; Association of American Geographers; Institute of British Geographers
Chief Officer(s):
Anne Godlewska, President
anne.godlewska@queensu.ca
Mary-Louise Byrne, Secretary-Treasurer
mlbyrne@wlu.ca
Ian MacLachlan, Editor, The Canadian Geographer
TCG.editor@cag-acg.ca
Valerie Shoffey, Editor, The CAG Newsletter
valerie.shoffey@cag-acg.ca
Membership: *Member Profile:* Practicing geographers from the public & private sectors & universities across Canada & internationally; Students
Activities: Promoting geographic education; Disseminating geographic research; Collaborating with other national & international geographic organizations;
Meetings/Conferences: • Canadian Association of Geographers 2015 Annual Meeting & Conference, June, 2015, Simon Fraser University, Vancouver, BC
Scope: National
Description: A business meeting & educational conference for geographers & students, featuring the presentation of papers & posters, plus exhibits, & social activities
• Canadian Association of Geographers 2016 Annual Meeting & Conference, 2016, Halifax, NS
Scope: National
Description: A business meeting & educational conference for geographers & students, featuring the presentation of papers & posters, plus exhibits, & social activities
• Canadian Association of Geographers 2017 Annual Meeting & Conference, 2017, York University, Toronto, ON
Scope: National
Description: A business meeting & educational conference for geographers & students, featuring the presentation of papers & posters, plus exhibits, & social activities
Publications:
• The CAG [Canadian Association of Geographers] Newsletter
Type: Newsletter; *Frequency:* Quarterly; *Editor:* Valerie Shoffey; *Price:* Free with membership in the Canadian Association of Geographers
Profile: News about members, employment opportunities & announcements, technical features, Statistics Canada news, research highlights, & studentinformation
• The CAG [Canadian Association of Geographers] Annual Directory
Type: Directory; *Frequency:* Annually; *Editor:* Kim Falcigno (kimfalcigno@shaw.ca); *Price:* Free with membership in the Canadian Association of Geographers
Profile: Listings of CAG members, academic staff, research activities, & current publications of Canadian university geographydepartments & government agencies
• The Canadian Geographer (TCG) / Le Géographe canadien (LGC)
Type: Journal; *Frequency:* Quarterly; *Editor:* Ian MacLachlan; *Price:* Free with membership in theCanadian Association of Geographers
Profile: Philosophical, theoretical, & methodological subjects of interest to scholars & geographers in Canada & worldwide

Atlantic Division
c/o James Boxall, GIS Centre, Killam Library, Dalhousie University, 6225 University Ave., Halifax NS B3H 4H8
community.smu.ca/acag
Mission: To promote the study, research, & application of geography throughout the Atlantic provinces; To serve geographers who reside in Newfoundland & Labrador, Prince Edward Island, Nova Scotia, & New Brunswick
Chief Officer(s):
Colin Laroque, President
claroque@mta.ca
James Boxall, Secretary-Treasurer
James.Boxall@Dal.ca
• Canadian Association of Geographers, Atlantic Division Annual Report
Type: Yearbook; *Frequency:* Annually

Ontario Division
c/o Wayne Forsythe, Dept. of Geography, Ryerson University, Toronto ON M5B 2K3
www.geography.ryerson.ca/cagont
Mission: To promote the study, teaching, research, & application of geography, especially in Ontario
Chief Officer(s):
Wayne Forsythe, President, 416-979-5000 Ext. 7141
forsythe@geography.ryerson.ca
Peter Kedron, Vice-President, 416-979-5000 Ext. 7147
pkedron@ryerson.ca

Prairie Division
c/o D. Eberts, J.R. Brodie Science Ctr., Dept of Geography, Brandon U., #4-09, 270 - 18th St., Brandon MB R7A 6A9
pcag.uwinnipeg.ca
Mission: To encourage geographic study, research, & applications in Saskatchewan, Manitoba, & North Dakota
Chief Officer(s):
Dirk de Boer, President
dirk.deboer@usask.ca
Derrek Eberts, Secretary-Treasurer
ebertsd@BrandonU.ca
• Prairie Perspectives: Geographical Essays
Type: Yearbook; *Frequency:* Annually
Profile: Proceedings of the prairie division's annual meeting

Western Division
c/o H. Jiskoot, Water & Environmental Science Bldg., U. of Lethbridge, 4401 University Dr., Lethbridge AB T1K 3M4
www.geog.uvic.ca/dept/wcag
Mission: To promote geographic education & research in Alberta, British Columbia, Yukon, & the Northwest Territories
Theresa Garvin, President
Theresa.Garvin@ualberta.ca
Craig Coburn, Secretary-Treasurer
hester.jiskoot@uleth.ca
• Canadian Association of Geographers Western Division Newsletter
Type: Newsletter; *Frequency:* Semiannually; *Editor:* C. Beaney (claire.beaney@ufv.ca)
Profile: Updates distributed to members
• Occasional Papers in Geography of the Canadian Assn of Geographers, Western Division: Proceedings of the Annual Conference
Type: Yearbook; *Frequency:* Annually
• Western Geography
Type: Journal; *Editor:* Neil Hanlon (hanlon@unbc.ca)
Profile: Original scholarly work on geographical themes, focussing on western Canada & its surrounding regions

Canadian Association of Geophysical Contractors (CAGC)

#1045, 1015 - 4 St. SW, Calgary AB T2R 1J4
Tel: 403-265-0045; *Fax:* 403-265-0025
info@cagc.ca
www.cagc.ca
www.linkedin.com/groups?gid=3696242
www.facebook.com/166335486730528
Overview: A small national organization founded in 1977
Mission: To act as the voice of business in the Canadian seismic industry; To promote the Canadian geophysical industry
Chief Officer(s):
Cam Moore, Chair
cam@cossackland.ca
Mike Doyle, President
mjd@cagc.ca
Membership: 600; *Committees:* Source Magazine; Chainsaw Certification; Buried Facilities; Blasters Harmonization; Seismic Blasters; Seismic Permit Agent
Activities: Working with governments, stakeholders, & communities; Promoting hight ethical standards throughout the geophysical industry; Providing health & safety training
Publications:
• The Source: The Voice of Business in the Canadian Seismic Industry
Type: Magazine; *Frequency:* Quarterly
Profile: Canadian Association of Geophysical Contractors membership news, awards, & upcoming events

Canadian Association of Gift Planners (CAGP) / Association canadienne des professionnels en dons planifiés (ACPDP)

#201, 1188 Wellington St. West, Ottawa ON K1Y 2Z5
Tel: 613-232-7991; *Fax:* 613-232-7286
Toll-Free: 888-430-9494
communications@cagp-acpdp.org
www.cagp-acpdp.org
twitter.com/CAGP_ACPDP
Overview: A medium-sized national organization founded in 1992
Mission: To advance the work of professionals in gift planning; To ensure professionals adhere to the CAGP-ACPDP code of ethics; To advocate for a favourable legislative regime for philanthropy
Chief Officer(s):
Ruth MacKenzie, Executive Director, 613-232-7991 Ext. 223
rmackenzie@cagp-acpdp.org
Nancy Shore, Coordinator, Membership, 613-232-7991 Ext. 227
nshore@cagp-acpdp.org
Jean-Marie Niangoran, Coordinator, Accounting & Finance, 613-232-7991 Ext. 221
jmniangoran@cagp-acpdp.org
Finances: *Funding Sources:* Membership fees; Sponsorships
Membership: 1,350; *Fees:* $290 individual; $85 student; *Member Profile:* Individuals involved in the gift planning process of registered charitable organizations or foundations, as well as fundraising consultants, lawyers, accountants, financial planners, life insurance representatives, trust officers, & other professionals
Activities: Fostering the development & growth of gift planning; Developing strategic partnerships; Creating awareness of charitable giving; Providing education opportunities; Offering networking opportunities; *Library*
Awards:
• Friend of CAGP / Ami de l'ACPDP (Award)
Individuals & organizations which exemplify the spirit & vision of CAGP *Contact:* Coordinator, Programs: Sharyon Smith, E-mail: education@cagp-acpdp.org
Meetings/Conferences: • Canadian Association of Gift Planners 2015 Conference, April, 2015, Halifax, NS
Scope: National
Description: An annual spring meeting, featuring educational workshops, experienced speakers, & exhibits
Contact Information: URL: www.cagpconference.org; conference@cagp-acpdp.org
Publications:
• The Planner
Type: Newsletter
Profile: CAGP-ACPDP news, statistics, education updates, & career information

Canadian Association of Healthcare Auxiliaries (CAHA) / L'association des auxiliaires bénévoles des soins de santé du Canada

c/o Canadian Healthcare Assn., #100, 17 York St., Ottawa ON K1N 9J6
Tel: 613-236-9364; *Fax:* 613-236-9350
caha.office@rogers.com
www.caha.freeservers.com
Previous Name: Canadian Association of Hospital Auxiliaries; Canadian Association of Health-Care Auxiliaries
Overview: A medium-sized national charitable organization founded in 1951
Mission: To assist provincial members in providing support to local auxiliaries through leadership, education, advocacy, communication & representation
Member of: Canadian Healthcare Association
Finances: *Annual Operating Budget:* $50,000-$100,000; *Funding Sources:* Membership fees; product line; convention
Staff Member(s): 1; 16 volunteer(s)

Membership: 8 provincial associations; *Fees:* $1 per auxilian in each provincial association; *Member Profile:* Healthcare auxiliary volunteers across Canada
Activities: Providing support, education, advocacy & leadership for healthcare auxilians across Canada; *Awareness Events:* Canada Health Auxiliary Week

Canadian Association of Hepatology Nurses (CAHN) / Association canadienne des infirmières et infirmiers en hépatologie

c/o Dawn King, 1 Campbell Ave., St. Johns NL A1E 2Z1
www.livernurses.org
Overview: A small national organization
Mission: To represent & support hepatology nurses throughout Canada; To encourage liver health & to prevent illness; To improve the standards of practice in hepatology nursing; To promote the excellent care of persons with liver related health problems & disorders
Affiliation(s): Canadian Nurses Association (CNA); Canadian Association for the Study of Liver Disease (CASL); Canadian Liver Foundation (CLF)
Chief Officer(s):
Cheryl Dale, President
cheryl.dale@lhsc.on.ca
Kathy Poldre, Vice-President
kathy.poldre@uhn.on.ca
Kathy Dallaire, Secretary
kathy.dallaire@regional.niagara.on.ca
Suzanne Sumner, Treasurer
suzanne.sumner@capitalhealth.ca
Geri Hirsch, Chair, Newsletter, Policy, & Nominations Committee
geri.hirsch@cdha.nshealth.ca
Sharon Bojarski, Co-Director, Education
sharonbojarski@hotmail.com
Stephanie Eiloart, Co-Director, Education
stephanieeiloart@hotmail.com
Membership: *Member Profile:* Nurses in Canada who practice hepatology; *Committees:* Executive; Conference; Newsletter; Website; Standards; Policy; Nomination; CAHN Awards
Activities: Establishing Hepatology Nursing Standards of Practice; Promoting research in hepatology nursing; Sharing information about hepatology; Providing continuing education for professionals in hepatology & clients; Engaging in advocacy activities; Offering networking opportunities
Meetings/Conferences: • Canadian Association of Hepatology Nurses 2015 Annual National Education Conference, February, 2015, Banff, AB
Scope: National
Contact Information: Co-Chair, Conference Committee: Sharon Bojarski, E-mail: sharonbojarski@hotmail.com; Co-Chair, Conference Committee: Sandi Mitchell, E-mail: sandi.mitchell@bccdc.ca
• Canadian Association of Hepatology Nurses 2016 Annual National Education Conference, 2016
Scope: National
Contact Information: Co-Chair, Conference Committee: Sharon Bojarski, E-mail: sharonbojarski@hotmail.com; Co-Chair, Conference Committee: Sandi Mitchell, E-mail: sandi.mitchell@bccdc.ca
Publications:
• Canadian Association of Hepatology Nurses Newsletter
Type: Newsletter; *Frequency:* Quarterly; *Editor:* Geri Hirsch & Marie Raymond
Profile: Updates on issues affecting hepatology nurses, forthcoming educational opportunities, award information, & association membership news

Canadian Association of Heritage Professionals (CAPHC) / Association canadienne d'experts-conseils en patrimoine (ACECP)

190 Bronson Ave., Ottawa ON K1R 6H4
Tel: 613-569-7455
admin@cahp-acecp.ca
www.caphc.ca
www.facebook.com/pages/CAHP-Acecp/121466461265655
Previous Name: Association of Heritage Consultants
Overview: A medium-sized national organization founded in 1987
Mission: To represent & further the professional interests of heritage consultants active in both the private & public sectors; To establish & maintain principles & standards of practice for heritage consultants; To enhance awareness & appreciation of heritage resources, & the contribution of heritage consultants; To foster communication among private practitioners, public agencies, & the public at large in matters related to heritage conservation
Affliation(s): ICOMOS International (International Council on Monuments & Sites); ICOMOS Canada - English-Speaking Committee
Chief Officer(s):
Jill Taylor, President
Julie Harris, Secretary
Membership: *Fees:* $25 student; $50 subscriber/retired; $180 intern; $290 professional; *Member Profile:* Practitioners active in either private or public sector in fields allied to heritage conservation; *Committees:* Advocacy; Annual General Meeting & Nominations; Business Development; Communications; Conference & Awards; Corporate Planning; Education; Ethics & Conduct; Governance; Government Liaison; Membership
Activities: Offering the following range of services by members: archaeology, anthropology, conservation, curation, design & planning, education, heritage administration, landscape design, photography, illustration & recording, & restoration
Publications:
• Canadian Association of Professional Heritage Consultants Forum
Type: Newsletter; *Accepts Advertising*
Profile: Articles on conservation, CAPHC / ACECP news & events
• CAPHC [Canadian Association of Professional Heritage Consultants] Membership Directory
Type: Directory; *Accepts Advertising*

Canadian Association of Home & Property Inspectors (CAHPI) / Association canadienne des inspecteurs de biens immobiliers

PO Box 13715, Ottawa ON K2K 1X6
Fax: 866-876-9877
Toll-Free: 888-748-2244
info@cahpi.ca
www.cahpi.ca
Previous Name: Canadian Association of Home Inspectors
Overview: A small national organization founded in 1982
Mission: To promote & enhance the professionalism & competency of professional home & property inspectors
Affiliation(s): American Association of Home Inspectors (ASHI)
Chief Officer(s):
Blaine Swan, President, 902-890-0710
president@cahpi.ca
Brian Hutchinson, Treasurer, 902-452-8858
treasurer@cahpi.ca
Sharry Featherston, Executive Director
sharry@cahpi.ca
Membership: *Committees:* Executive; Bylaw & Policy; CAHPI Conference; CAHPI Liaison to ASHI; Ethics; CHI Magazine; CAHPI National Website Administration
Activities: Establishing & maintaining a national standard for the education, certification, & professional practice of Canadian home & property inspectors; Enabling transferability of certification within all Canadian home & property inspector provincial organizations
Awards:
• Stephen Greenford Award (Award)
Presented to an individual who has furthered the development of the Home Inspection profession nationally
• President's Award (Award)
Presented to an individual who has furthered the development of the Home Inspection profession in his/her Provincial/Regional Association
• Michael Ludolph Memorial Award (Award)
• Tropea / Hipperson Memorial Award (Award)
Meetings/Conferences: • National Home Inspectors' 2015 22nd Annual National Conference, 2015
Scope: National
Contact Information: Conference Chair: Terry Gordon, E-mail: tegordon@ns.sympatico.ca
Publications:
• The Canadian Home Inspector Magazine
Type: Magazine; *Accepts Advertising*; *Price:* Free with CAHPI membership
Profile: Information on the home inspection profession for CAHPI provincial & regional members

Alberta Chapter
PO Box 27039, Stn. Tuscany, Calgary AB T3L 2Y1
Tel: 403-248-6893; *Fax:* 888-812-4249
Toll-Free: 800-351-9993
cahpi@telus.net
cahpi-alberta.com
Mission: To support & regulate the home inspection profession in Alberta
Chief Officer(s):
Bill Baird, President
Joanne Albertson, Administrator

Association des inspecteurs en bâtiments du Québec (AIBQ)
#008, 7777, boul Louis H. Lafontaine, Anjou QC H1K 4E4
Tél: 514-352-2427; *Téléc:* 514-355-8248
Ligne sans frais: 877-644-2427
aibq.qc.ca
Mission: To ensure a proper control of the building inspection practice in Québec
Chief Officer(s):
Denys Aubert, President
Cynthia Laforte, Vice-President
Normand René, Treasurer

Atlantic Chapter
c/o Brian Hutchinson, #257, 3045 Robie St., Halifax NS B3K 4P6
e-mail: info@cahpi-atl.com
www.cahpi-atl.com
Mission: To define the qualifications & performance requirements of Registered Home Inspectors; to regulate members; to grant the designation, Registered Home Inspector, to qualified practitioners in Nova Scotia, New Brunswick, Newfoundland, & Price Edward Island
Chief Officer(s):
Brian Hutchinson, President
Terry Gordon, Vice-President
Manzer Young, Treasurer

British Columbia Chapter
#5, 3304 Appaloosa rd., Kelowna BC V1V 2W5
Tel: 250-491-3979; *Fax:* 250-491-2285
Toll-Free: 800-610-5665
executivedirector@cahpi.bc.ca
www.cahpi.bc.ca
www.linkedin.com/company/2647618?trk=tyah
Mission: To protect consumers in British Columbia, through membership requirements, a Standards of Practice & Code of Ethics, & mandatory ongoing training programs for home & property inspectors
Chief Officer(s):
Craig Hostland, President
Helene T. Barton, Executive Director
executivedirector@cahpi.bc.ca

Manitoba Chapter
PO Box 91, 287 Tache Ave., Winnipeg MB R2H 3B8
Tel: 204-724-2911
info@cahpi.mb.ca
www.cahpi.mb.ca
Mission: To promote the professional pre-purchase home inspection industry in Manitoba; To provide continuing educational opportunities to member inspectors in Manitoba
Chief Officer(s):
Ari Marantz, President, 204-291-5358
trainedeye@iname.com
Leonard Borbridge, Vice-President, 204-771-3453
pillar2post@shaw.ca

Ontario Association of Home Inspectors (OAHI)
#205, 1515 Matheson Blvd., Mississauga ON L4W 2P5
Tel: 416-256-0960; *Fax:* 905-624-4360
Toll-Free: 800-744-6244
www.oahi.com
www.linkedin.com/groups?gid=2398169
www.facebook.com/203366866398648
Mission: To enhance the technical skills & professional practice of home inspectors in Ontario; To educate & discipline in order to maintain high professional standards
Chief Officer(s):
Pam Sayne, RHI, President

Saskatchewan Chapter
PO Box 20045, Stn. Cornwall Centre, Regina SK S4P 4J7
Toll-Free: 866-546-7888
cahpi-sk.ca
Mission: To maintain & regulate national standards in home inspections in Saskatchewan
Chief Officer(s):
Jim Nichols, Contact, Membership

Canadian Association of Home Inspectors *See* Canadian Association of Home & Property Inspectors

Canadian Association of Hospital Auxiliaries; Canadian Association of Health-Care Auxiliaries *See* Canadian Association of Healthcare Auxiliaries

Canadian Association of Immersion Teachers *Voir* Association canadienne des professeurs d'immersion

Canadian Association of Immunohematologists *See* Canadian Society for Transfusion Medicine

Canadian Association of Importers & Exporters / Association canadienne des importateurs & exportateurs

#200, 10 St. Mary St., Toronto ON M4Y 1P9
Tel: 416-595-5333
info@iecanada.com
www.iecanada.com
Also Known As: IE Canada
Previous Name: Canadian Importers Association Inc.
Overview: A large national organization founded in 1932
Mission: To act as the voice of Canadian importers & exporters; To support Canadian importers & exporters so that they remain profitable & competitive in a global market
Chief Officer(s):
Joy Nott, CCS, P.Log, President
jnott@iecanada.com
Keith Mussar, VP, Regulatory Affairs & Co-Chair, Food Committee
kmussar@iecanada.com
Carol Osmond, Vice-President, Policy
cosmond@iecanada.com
Amesika Baeta, Director, Member Relations & Development
abaeta@iecanada.com
Andrea MacDonald, Contact, Media Inquiries, I.E. Now, & Special Publications
amacdonald@iecanada.com
Finances: *Funding Sources:* Membership fees; Sponsorships
Membership: *Fees:* $500 small businesses (fewer than 5 employess & less than $2 million in annual sales) & individuals members; $995 corporate members; *Member Profile:* Importers; Exporters; Distributors; Agents; *Committees:* Customs & Legislation; Textiles & Apparel; Export; Trade Security; Canadian Meat Importers & Exporters;Food, Electronic Import
Activities: Providing information about Canadian customs & trade policy; Liaisinig with government
Awards:
• Trade Compliance Leadership Award (Award)
To recognize a Canadian customs compliance and trade professional who has been providing leadership, innovation and advocacy on behalf of their own company and other importers and exporters in Canada.
• Best Practices in Trade Compliance Processes Award (Award)
To recognize the corporate accomplishment of implementing new processes intended to improve trade efficiencies or trade compliance.
• Greening the Supply Chain Award (Award)
To recognize a Canadian company that has initiated, implemented and proven corporate commitment to the greening of the supply chain and reducing their carbon footprint.
• Beth Travis Memorial I.E. Canada Member of the Year Award (Award)
To recognize an outstanding I.E.Canada member who represents the spirit of the Association: to be the leading voice of the Canadian trade community and to represent and advocate on behalf of importers and exporters to influence change.
Meetings/Conferences: • Canadian Association of Importers & Exporters 2015 12th Annual Western Canada Conference, 2015
Scope: National
Description: A yearly educational opportunity for presidents, general managers, directors of operations, controllers, customs specialists, & logistics managers
Contact Information: Western Region Coordinator: Paulette Niedermier, Phone: 403-808-2451, E-mail: pniedermier@iecanada.com
• Canadian Association of Importers & Exporters 2015 83rd Annual Conference & Tradeshow, 2015
Scope: National
Description: Sessions & workshops addressing current topics relevant to trade practitioners
Contact Information: General E-mail: conference@iecanada.com
Publications:
• Canadian Association of Importers & Exporters Membership Directory
Type: Directory; *Price:* Free with membership in the Canadian Association of Importers & Exporters
Profile: A source for establishing contacts in international trade
• I.E. Now
Type: Newsletter; *Frequency:* Monthly; *Editor:* Andrea Macdonald; *Price:* Free with membership in the Canadian Association of Importers & Exporters
Profile: Articles about international trade & customs
• I.E. Today
Type: Newsletter; *Frequency:* Daily; *Accepts Advertising; Editor:* M. Weaver (mweaver@iecanada.com); *Price:* Free with membership in the Canadian Association of Importers & Exporters
Profile: News about trade & customs issues, plus activities of the Canadian Association of Importers & Exporters, including the presentation of awards, educational opportunities, &previews & reviews of conferences
• Importing into Canada
Type: Guide; *Price:* $49.95
Profile: Information about how to establish an importing business, including current rules & regulations for bringing goods into the country
• Mon I.E.
Type: Newsletter; *Frequency:* Monthly; *Editor:* C. Sivière (csiviere@iecanada.com); *Price:* Free with membership in the Canadian Association of Importers & Exporters
Profile: Customs & international trade articles

Canadian Association of Income Trusts Investors (CAITI) / Association canadienne d'investissement dans des fiducies de revenu

#1062, 1930 Yonge St., Toronto ON M4S 1Z4
Tel: 647-505-2224
contact@caiti.info
www.caiti.info
Overview: A small national organization
Mission: Mission is to preserve the viability and sustainability of the Canadian income trust market, for the benefit of Canadians saving for retirement now and in the future
Chief Officer(s):
Brent D. Fullard, President & CEO

Canadian Association of Independent Credit Counselling Agencies (CAICCA)

#306, 15225 - 104th Ave., Surrey BC V3R 6Y8
Tel: 604-588-9491; *Fax:* 604-588-9007
Toll-Free: 877-588-9491
info@caicca.org
www.caicca.ca
Overview: A small national organization
Mission: To maintain a Code of Ethics for the independent credit counselling industry; to liaise with appropriate provincial regulatory bodies; to promote & educate consumers & the credit granting industry on services provided by the association
Chief Officer(s):
Margaret Johnson, President
Finances: *Annual Operating Budget:* $100,000-$250,000
Membership: 7; *Fees:* $100

Canadian Association of Independent Life Brokerage Agencies (CAILBA)

105 King St. East, Toronto ON M5C 1G6
Tel: 416-548-4223; *Fax:* 416-340-9977
info@cailba.com
www.cailba.com
Overview: A large national organization
Mission: To lobby provincial & federal governments on legislative issues affecting the life & health insurance brokerage industry; to provide a forum for networking & relationship building among members, insurance companies & industry vendors
Affiliation(s): The National Association of Independent Life Brokerage Agencies (NAILBA); IFB Independent Financial Brokers; Canadian Life and Health Insurance Association (CLHIA); Advocis, The Financial Advisors Association of Canada
Chief Officer(s):
Michael Williams, President
mwilliams@bfgon.com
Bob Ferguson, Executive Director
bobferg2000@yahoo.com
Membership: *Fees:* $1,250 independent/corporate; $3,125 industry supplier; $3,125 industry solution provider; *Member Profile:* Life & health insurance brokerage agencies; *Committees:* Business in Force; CAILBA Compliance Toolbox; Carrier Contract Review; Legislative Affairs; Membership; Publicity; Regulatory Affairs; Technology
Activities: Monthly Board Meetings; CAILBA Information Series (teleconferences)
Meetings/Conferences: • CAILBA 2015 Annual General Meeting, June, 2015, Westin Prince Hotel Toronto, Toronto, ON
Scope: National

Canadian Association of Independent Living Centres *See* Independent Living Canada

Canadian Association of Independent Schools *See* Canadian Accredited Independent Schools

Canadian Association of Insolvency & Restructuring Professionals (CAIRP) / Association canadienne des professionnels de l'insolvabilité et de la réorganisation (ACPIR)

277 Wellington St. West, Toronto ON M5V 3H2
Tel: 416-204-3242; *Fax:* 416-204-3410
info@cairp.ca
www.cairp.ca
Previous Name: Canadian Insolvency Practitioners Association
Overview: A medium-sized national organization founded in 1979
Mission: To develop, educate, support & give value to members; To foster the provision of insolvency, business recovery service with integrity, objectivity & competence, in a manner that instils the highest degree of public trust; To advocate for a fair, transparent, & effective system of insolvency/business recovery administration throughout Canada
Member of: Insol International
Affliation(s): The Canadian Institute of Chartered Accountants
Chief Officer(s):
Mark Yakabuski, President
mark.yakabusk@cairp.ca
Bea Casey, Director, CAIRP Education Programs
bea.casey@cairp.ca
Ali R. Hemani, Director, Finance & Administration
ali.hemani@cairp.ca
Joshua Katchen, Manager, Events
joshua.katchen@cairp.ca
Finances: *Funding Sources:* Membership dues
Membership: 1,441; *Fees:* $210-610, depending on category; *Member Profile:* Completion of National Insolvency Qualification Program (NIQP) offered jointly by CAIRP & the Superintendent of Bankruptcy; *Committees:* Conference; Communications; Continuing education; Corporate practice; Discipline; Executive; Finance; Honours & awards
Activities: Working with the federal government on joint committees concerning policy, legislation, education programs & Oral Boards for trustee licence candidates; Providing education programs; *Speaker Service:* Yes
Meetings/Conferences: • Canadian Association of Insolvency & Restructuring Professionals 2015 Annual Conference, August, 2015, Fairmont Château Whistler, Whistler, BC
Scope: National
Description: Technical sessions plus networking opportunities & social events
Contact Information: Events Manager: Cristina Contesti, Phone: 416-204-3242, ext. 3245; cristina.contesti@cairp.ca
Publications:
• Chair's Newsletter
Type: Newsletter
Profile: CAIRP news
• Rebuilding Success
Type: Magazine; *Frequency:* Semiannually; *Accepts Advertising; Editor:* Jon Waldman
Profile: CAIRP information, articles, & buyer's guide

Canadian Association of Insurance Women (CAIW) / Association canadienne des femmes d'assurance (ACFA)

c/o Sovereign General Insurance Co., 1718 Argyle St., 4th Fl., Halifax NS B3J 3N6
Tel: 902-492-4970; *Fax:* 902-492-0440
www.caiw-acfa.com
www.linkedin.com/groups/CAIW-ACFA-Canadian-Association-Insurance-42542
Overview: A medium-sized national organization founded in 1966
Mission: To enhance the value of member associations
Chief Officer(s):
Laura Greening, President
laura.greening@sovgen.com
Cheryl Morton, Treasurer
cmortoncaiw@gmail.com
Finances: *Funding Sources:* Sponsorships
Activities: Providing education & networking opportunities

Canadian Association of Internes & Residents (CAIR)

#412, 151 Slater St., Ottawa ON K1P 5H3
Tel: 613-234-6448
cair@cair.ca
www.cair.ca
www.linkedin.com/company/the-canadian-association-of-interne

s-and-resi
www.facebook.com/CAIRACMR
twitter.com/ResidentsCAIR
Overview: A medium-sized national organization founded in 1973
Mission: To improve the quality of medical education & professionalism for resident physicians in Canada
Affliation(s): Royal College of Physicians & Surgeons of Canada; College of Family Physicians of Canada; Canadian Medical Association; Federation of Medical Licensing Authorities of Canada
Chief Officer(s):
Noor Amin, Executive President
namin@cair.ca
Jillian Schwartz, Executive Vice-President
jschwartz@cair.ca
Adelaine Wong, Executive Secretary
awong@cair.ca
Henry Conter, Executive Treasurer
hconter@cair.ca
Membership: 7,500; *Member Profile:* Resident physicians in Newfoundland & Labrador, the Maritime provinces, Ontario, Manitoba, Saskatchewan, Alberta, & British Columbia; *Committees:* Advocacy & Policy; Education & Professionalism; Finance, Audit & Risk; Member Outreach; Awards; Executive; Governance & Nominating; Human Resources; Regional Networking; Sub-Committee on Professionalism
Activities: Collaborating with other national health organizations; Developing national policies
Meetings/Conferences: • Canadian Association of Internes and Residents 2015 Annual General Meeting, 2015
Scope: National
Publications:
• Canadian Association of Internes & Residents Annual Report
Type: Report; *Frequency:* Annually

Canadian Association of Internet Providers *See* Canadian Association of Internet Providers

Canadian Association of Internet Providers (CAIP) / Association canadienne des fournisseurs internet (ACFI)

#416, 207 Bank St., Ottawa ON K2P 2N2
Tel: 613-236-6550; *Fax:* 613-236-8189
info@cata.ca
www.caip.ca
Previous Name: Canadian Association of Internet Providers
Overview: A small national organization founded in 1996
Mission: To foster the growth of a healthy & competitive Internet service industry in Canada through collective & cooperative action on issues of mutual interest.
Member of: Canadian Advanced Technology Alliance (CATAAlliance)
Chief Officer(s):
Tom Copeland, Chair
Cathi Malette, Manager, Member Services
cmalette@cata.ca
Finances: *Annual Operating Budget:* $250,000-$500,000
Staff Member(s): 4
Membership: 100; *Fees:* Schedule available; *Member Profile:* Internet service providers; suppliers to the internet industry

Canadian Association of Interventional Cardiology (CAIC) / Association canadienne de cardiologie d'intervention

3, boul Lakeview, Beaconsfield QC H9W 4P8
Toll-Free: 877-990-9044
info@caic-acci.org
www.caic-acci.org
Overview: A small national organization
Mission: To advance the discipline, development, & implementation of interventional cardiology
Member of: Canadian Cardiology Society
Chief Officer(s):
Eric Cohen, President
Kevin McKenzie, Executive Director
Warren J. Cantor, Treasurer
Membership: 100+; *Member Profile:* Members Canadian Cardiovascular Society; Cardiologists who specialize in hemodynamic interventions; Trainees in Cardiology (or Fellows in interventional cardiology) may apply for Affiliate-in-Training membership

Canadian Association of Journalists (CAJ) / L'Association canadienne des journalistes

PO Box 280, Brantford N3T 5M8
Tel: 519-756-2020
www.caj.ca
Previous Name: Centre for Investigative Journalism
Overview: A medium-sized national organization founded in 1978
Mission: To promote excellence in journalism; to encourage & promote investigative journalism
Chief Officer(s):
Hugo Rodrigues, National Director
Finances: *Funding Sources:* Membership fees; media corporations; advertising
Membership: *Fees:* $20 student; $45 first time; $75 regular; $120 couple; $100 associate; $65 retired
Activities: *Internships:* Yes; *Speaker Service:* Yes; *Rents Mailing List:* Yes
Awards:
• Award for Journalistic Excellence in Conflict Analysis (Award)
• CAJ/Canada NewsWire Student Award of Excellence in Journalism (Award)
• The CAJ Awards (Award)
Awards presented for the top investigative report published or broadcast in the following media: Newspaper/Newswire (open category), Newspaper (circulation under 25,000), Magazine, TV, Radio, Faith & Spirituality, Photojournalism, Computer assisting reporting & the Don McGillivray award for Best Investigative Report*Deadline:* January *Amount:* $1,000 *Contact:* John Dickins
Meetings/Conferences: • Canadian Association of Journalists 2015 Annual Conference, June, 2015, Atlantica Hotel, Halifax, NS
Scope: National
Publications:
• Media
Type: Magazine; *Frequency:* 3 pa; *Accepts Advertising*; *Number of Pages:* 32; *Editor:* David McKie; *Price:* Free with CAJ membership; $14.98/yr
Profile: Investigative stories as well as analytical pieces about the practice of journalism in Canada
• The Wire
Type: Newsletter; *Frequency:* Quarterly
Profile: CAJ news & activities, articles, & profiles

Canadian Association of Labour Media (CALM) / Association canadienne de la presse syndicale (ACPS)

PO Box 10624, Stn. Bloorcourt, Toronto ON M6H 4H9
Tel: 581-983-4397; *Fax:* 581-983-4397
editor@calm.ca
www.calm.ca
www.facebook.com/canadian.association.of.labour.media
twitter.com/CanLabourMedia
Overview: A medium-sized national organization founded in 1976
Mission: To provide training, labour-friendly news, & graphics for labour communicators
Affliation(s): Canadian Labour Congress
Chief Officer(s):
Chris Lawson, President
Martin Lukacs, Executive Editor
Nora Loreto, Executive Editor
Staff Member(s): 4
Membership: 300+; *Fees:* Schedule available; *Member Profile:* Union publication editors
Activities: Producing stories & graphics for members to use in their newsletters; Organizing training sessions
Awards:
• Best Overall Publication (Award)
• Excellence in Layout & Design (Award)
• Excellence in Writing (Award)
• Best Photograph (Award)
• Best Cartoon (Award)
• Best Illustration (Award)
• Ed Finn Award (Award)
• Morden Lazarus Prize (Award)
• Cliff Scotton Prize (Award)
• Breaking Barriers Award (Award)
• Muckraking Award (Award)
• Best Audio-Visual Production (Award)
• Best Public Advocacy Audio-Visual Production (Award)
• Best Commercial Television Ad (Award)
• Best Commercial Radio Ad (Award)
• Best Poster (Award)
• Best Print Ad (Award)
• Best Moving Billboard (Award)
• Best Flyer or Brochure (Award)
• Dennis McGann Stroke-of-Genius Award (Award)
• Best Overall Website (Award)
• Best Website Content (Award)
• Best Website Design (Award)
• Best Cyberunion (Award)
Meetings/Conferences: • 2015 Canadian Association of Labour Media Conference, June, 2015, Victoria, BC
Publications:
• CALMideas [a publication of the Canadian Association of Labour Media]
Type: Newsletter
Profile: Information for editors about how to compile a newsletter
• Union Editor's Handbook / Rédacteurs en chef syndicaux [a publication of the Canadian Association of Labour Media]
Type: Handbook; *Number of Pages:* 28; *Price:* $7
Profile: A guide for union editors
• What is Copyright?
Type: Booklet; *Number of Pages:* 8; *Price:* $5
• What's Libel?: Say What You Want Without Getting Sued
Type: Booklet; *Number of Pages:* 16; *Price:* $5

Canadian Association of Law Libraries (CALL) / Association canadienne des bibliothèques de droit (ACBD)

PO Box 1570, #310, 4 Cataraqui St., Kingston ON K7L 5C8
Tel: 613-531-9338; *Fax:* 613-531-0626
office@callacbd.ca
www.callacbd.ca
Overview: A medium-sized national organization founded in 1963
Mission: To promote law librarianship; To develop Canadian law libraries; To promote access to legal information
Chief Officer(s):
Elizabeth Hooper, National Officer
Cyndi Murphy, President
Annette Demers, Vice-President
Shaunna Mireau, Secretary
Barbara Campbell, Treasurer
Membership: 500; *Member Profile:* Individuals who represent a variety of law libary interests; *Committees:* Archives; By-Laws; Hugh Lawford Award for Excellence in Legal Publishing; CanLII Advisory; Conference Planning; Copyright; Education; Elections; Eunice Beeson Memorial Bursary; Financial Advisory; Government Relations; KF Modified Classification; Law Library Statistics; Nominations; CALL/ACBD First-Timers Program; Preservation Needs of Law Libraries; Promote Research; Public Relations; Scholarships & Awards; Vendors' Liaison; CALL/ACBD Website
Activities: Fostering cooperation among Canadian law libraries; Encouraging professional development; Creating networking opportunities for persons engaged in or interested in law library work; Cooperating with related organizations; Conducting surveys; Organizing special interest groups, such as academic law libraries, access services & resource sharing, courthouse & law society libraries, Department of Justice / Attorney General libraries, knowledge management, prison library, & private law libraries
Awards:
• Hugh Lawford Award for Excellence in Legal Publishing (Award)
An annual award to recognize excellence in legal publishing.*Deadline:* February 15, 2013 *Contact:* Rosalie Fox, Rosalie.Fox@SCC-CSC.GC.CA
• Denis Marshall Memorial Award for Excellence in Law Librarianship (Award)
This award is an honour bestowed upon a current member of CALL/ACBD who has provided outstanding service to the Association AND/OR enhanced the profession of law librarianship in the recent past. *Amount:* $3,000 *Contact:* Ann Marie Melvie, amelvie@sasklawcourts.ca
• Canadian Law Library Review Feature Article Award (Award)
Given annually to the author of a feature length article published in Canadian Law Library Review / Revue canadienne des bibliothèques de droit. *Amount:* $500
• Diana M. Priestly Memorial Scholarship (Scholarship)
To support professional development in the field.*Deadline:* February 1, 2013 *Amount:* $2,500 *Contact:* Ann Marie Melvie, amelvie@sasklawcourts.ca
• James D. Lang Memorial Scholarship (Scholarship)
The scholarship is designed to support attendance at a continuing education program, be it a workshop, certificate program or other similar activity deemed appropriate by the CALL/ACBD Scholarships and Awards Committee.*Deadline:* Mar. 15, June 15, Sept 15 *Contact:* Ann Marie Melvie, amelvie@sasklawcourts.ca

Meetings/Conferences: • Canadian Association of Law Libraries Annual General Meeting, 2015, May, 2015, Moncton, NB
Scope: National
• Canadian Association of Law Libraries Annual General Meeting, 2016, May, 2016, Vancouver, BC
Scope: National
Publications:
• Canadian Law Library Review
Type: Journal; *Frequency:* Quarterly; *Price:* Members free; Non-Members $90
Profile: Yearly subscription; Canadian Law Library Review is the official journal of the Canadian Association of Law Libraries.
• Law Reporting and Legal Publishing in Canada: A History
Type: Book; *Price:* Members $26; Non-Members $35
• Guide to KF Modified Classification
Type: Book; *Author:* Janet Moss; *Price:* Members $100; Non-Members $100
• KF Modified Schedule
Type: Book; *Price:* New subscriber $225; Quarterly updates $100
• Canadian Law Library Review / Revue canadienne des bibliothèques de droit
Type: Journal; *Frequency:* 5 pa; *Accepts Advertising*; *Editor:* Lenore Rapkin; *Price:* $90
Profile: Articles on all aspects of law librarianship, book reviews, & regular columns about the field of legal information in Canada
• Law Reporting & Legal Publishing in Canada: A History
Type: Book
Profile: A collection of CALL's essays for persons interested in publishing & legal history
• Canadian Courthouse & Law Society Library Stadards
Number of Pages: 23
• CALL [Canadian Association of Law Libraries] / ACBD [Association canadienne des bibliothèques de droit] Annual Directory
Type: Directory; *Frequency:* Annually; *Price:* Free withmembership in the Canadian Association of Law Libraries
Profile: Listings of CALL members, officers, & committee & special interest group chairs

Canadian Association of Learned Journals (CALJ) / Association canadienne des revues savantes (ACRS)

PO Box 20304, Stn. Rideau East, Ottawa ON K1N 1A3
e-mail: info@calj-acrs.ca
www.calj-acrs.ca
Overview: A small national organization founded in 1990
Mission: To ensure the well-being of learned journals in Canada, through promotion, education, & lobbying
Chief Officer(s):
Frits Pannekoek, President
Michael Eberle-Sinatra, Secretary-Treasurer
michael.eberle.sinatra@umontreal.ca
Ellen Henderson, Executive Director
Membership: 100+; *Fees:* Schedule available; *Member Profile:* Canadian journals of scholarly work in the humanities & social sciences
Publications:
• Best Practices Guide to Scholarly Journal Publishing
Type: Handbook; *Price:* $40 non-member journals & Canadian & international research libraries

Canadian Association of Legal Translators *Voir* Association canadienne des juristes-traducteurs

Canadian Association of Management Consultants (CMC-Canada) / Association canadienne des conseillers en management

#2004, 401 Bay St., Toronto ON M5H 2Y4
Tel: 416-860-1515; *Fax:* 416-860-1535
Toll-Free: 800-268-1148
consulting@cmc-canada.ca
www.cmc-canada.ca
www.linkedin.com/groups?mostPopular=&gid=80782
www.facebook.com/153670124764294
twitter.com/CMCCanada1
cmc-yonemitsu.blogspot.ca;
ww.youtube.com/user/CMCCanada1
Previous Name: Institute of Certified Management Consultants of Canada
Overview: A medium-sized national licensing organization founded in 1963
Mission: To foster excellence & integrity in the management consulting profession; To administer the Certified Management Consultant (CMC) designation in Canada; To advance the practice & profile of the profession of management consulting in Canada; To promote ethical standards
Member of: International Council of Management Consulting Institutes (ICMCI)
Chief Officer(s):
Glenn Yonemitsu, Chief Executive Officer
gyonemitsu@cmc-canada.ca
Lynn Bennett, Vice Chair, 416-929-6653
Glenn Yonemitsu, Chief Executive Officer, 519-673-7397
gyonemitsu@cmc-canada.ca
Mary Blair, Managing Director
mblair@cmc-canada.ca
Finances: *Annual Operating Budget:* $1.5 Million-$3 Million
Staff Member(s): 10; 200 volunteer(s)
Membership: 3,100; *Fees:* $499; *Member Profile:* Persons in the business of management consulting across Canada; *Committees:* National Certification; National Advocacy; Professional Development Operations; Marketing & Communications; Operations Review; Insight Editorial Board
Activities: Advocating for the profession in both government & public settings; Providing education; Offering networking opportunities through events & seminars; *Library:* Knowledge Centre
Publications:
• CMC [Canadian Association of Management Consultants] Annual Report
Type: Yearbook; *Frequency:* Annually
• Consult
Type: Magazine; *Frequency:* s-a; *Editor:* Andrea Vandenberg
Profile: Magazine dedicated to management consulting, including industry insights & profiles on industry professionals.
• Management Consulting Industry Study
Type: Research report; *Price:* $50 members & non-members
• Management Consulting: An Introduction to the Methodologies, Tools & Techniques of the Profession
Price: $100 members; $200 non-members

Canadian Association of Manufacturers of Medical Devices; Canada's Medical Device Technology Companies *See* Medical Devices Canada

Canadian Association of Medical Biochemists (CAMB) / Association des médecins biochimistes du Canada (AMBC)

774 Echo Dr., Ottawa ON K1S 5N8
Tel: 613-730-8177; *Fax:* 613-730-1116
Toll-Free: 800-668-3740
camb@rcpsc.edu
www.camb-ambc.ca
Overview: A small national organization founded in 1975
Chief Officer(s):
Danièle Saintonge, Association Manager
Membership: *Fees:* $100 ordinary members; $15 emeritus & student members

Canadian Association of Medical Device Reprocessing (CAMDR)

147 Parkside Dr., Oak Bluff MB R4G 0A6
e-mail: info@camdr.ca
www.camdr.ca
Overview: A small national organization
Mission: CAMDR seeks to address numerous issues including patient safety, infection prevention & control, technology assessments, vendor relations, organizational management, and education.
Chief Officer(s):
Abdool Karim, President
Membership: *Fees:* $50
Meetings/Conferences: • Canadian Association of Medical Device Reprocessing 2015 Conference, 2015
Scope: National

Canadian Association of Medical Oncologists (CAMO) / Association canadienne des oncologues médicaux (ACOM)

774 Echo Dr., Ottawa ON K1S 5N8
Tel: 613-730-6284; *Fax:* 613-730-1116
camo@royalcollege.ca
www.cos.ca/camo
Overview: A small national organization
Chief Officer(s):
Kara Laing, President
kara.laing@easternhealth.ca
Alexi Campbell, Association Manager
Hal Hirte, Secretary-Treasurer
hal.hirte@jcc.hhsc.ca
Membership: *Fees:* no charge for residents, associate members, & emeritus; $50 corresponding & senior members; $250 active members
Activities: Providing continuing professional development opportunities; Facilitating communication among medical oncologists
Publications:
• Canadian Association of Medical Oncologists Membership Directory
Type: Directory
Profile: Offers access to medical oncologists throughout Canada

Canadian Association of Medical Radiation Technologists (CAMRT) / Association canadienne des technologues en radiation médicale (ACTRM)

#1000, 85 Albert St., Ottawa ON K1P 6A4
Tel: 613-234-0012; *Fax:* 613-234-1097
Toll-Free: 800-463-9729
editorialoffice@camrt.ca
www.camrt.ca
Overview: A medium-sized national licensing organization founded in 1942
Mission: To act as the certifying body for medical radiation technologists & therapists throughout Canada
Member of: International Society of Radiographers & Radiological Technologists
Chief Officer(s):
Charles Shields, Chief Executive Officer
Michelle Charest, Director, Finance & Administration
Elaine Dever, Director, Education
Mark Given, Director, Professional Practice
Leacy O'Callaghan O'Brien, Director, Advocacy, Communications, & Events
Membership: 10 provincial associations, sharing a membership of approximately 12,000; *Member Profile:* Persons from the disciplines of radiological technology, magnetic resonance, nuclear medicine, & radiation therapy
Activities: Administering national certification exams for the disciplines of radiological technology, magnetic resonance, nuclear medicine, & radiation therapy; Offering continuing education; *Awareness Events:* MRT Week, November
Awards:
• Dr. Petrie Memorial Award (Award)
An essay competition award
• L.J. Cartwright Student Award (Award)
An essay competition award
• E.I. Hood Award (Award)
An essay competition award
• Sister Mary Arthur "Sharing the Light" Award (Award)
An essay competition award
• CR/PACS Technology Award (Award)
An essay competition award
• Bayer MR Award (Award)
An essay competition award
• George Reason Memorial Award (Award)
An exhibit competition award
• Philips Award (Award)
An exhibit competition award
• Dr. Marshall Mallett Student Award (Award)
An exhibit competition award
• Bracco Diagnostics Canada MR Poster Award (Award)
An exhibit competition aaward
• Dr. Marshall Mallett "Lamp of Knowledge" Award (Award)
A CAMRT honorary award
• Welch Memorial Lecture (Award)
A CAMRT honorary award
• Life Membership Award (Award)
A CAMRT honorary award
• Honorary Life Membership Award (Award)
A CAMRT honorary award
• Award for Early Professional Achievement (Award)
A CAMRT honorary award
Meetings/Conferences: • 2015 Joint Congress on Medical Imaging and Radiation Sciences, May, 2015, Palais des congrès de Montréal, Montréal, QC
Scope: National
Publications:
• CAMRT [Canadian Association of Medical Radiation Technologists] News
Frequency: 5 pa; *Accepts Advertising*; *Editor:* Tammy McCausland
Profile: Canadian Association of Medical Radiation Technologists articles, education activities, & events

• Canadian Association of Medical Radiation Technologists Annual Report
Type: Yearbook; *Frequency:* Annually
• Journal of Medical Imaging & Radiation Sciences
Type: Journal; *Frequency:* Quarterly; *Accepts Advertising*; *Editor:* John French
Profile: A peer-reviewed journal of articles on recent research, professional practices, new technology, & book reviews

Canadian Association of Medical Teams Abroad (CAMTA)

103 Laurier Dr., Edmonton AB T5R 5P6
Tel: 780-486-7161; *Fax:* 403-223-9020
info@camta.com
camta.com
www.facebook.com/237638586268756
twitter.com/#!/camta
Overview: A small national charitable organization founded in 2001
Mission: CAMTA provides orthopedic surgeries to pediatric and adult patients in Ecuador.
Chief Officer(s):
Marc Moreau, President
Jim Raso, Secretary
Sandra Muchekeza, Administrator
Finances: *Annual Operating Budget:* $250,000-$500,000
Membership: *Member Profile:* Edmonton-based health care practitioners and lay people.

Canadian Association of Members of Public Utility Tribunals / Association canadienne des membres des tribunaux d'utilité publique *See* CAMPUT, Canada's Energy & Utility Regulators

Canadian Association of Message Exchanges, Inc. *See* Canadian Call Management Association

Canadian Association of Midwives (CAM) / L'Association canadienne des sages-femmes (ACSF)

59 Riverview, Montréal QC H8R 3R9
Tel: 514-807-3668; *Fax:* 514-738-0370
admin@canadianmidwives.org
www.canadianmidwives.org
www.facebook.com/CanadianMidwives
Overview: A medium-sized national organization
Mission: Promotion, support and uniting of the proffession of midwifery in Canada
Chief Officer(s):
Tonia Occhionero, Executive Director
Membership: 882; *Fees:* $100; *Committees:* CAM International; National Working Group for the Emergency Skills Workshop for Midwives (ESW); Ghislaine Francoeur Fund; Canadian Journal of Midwifery Research and Practic; CAM Conference Program; Scientific Abstract Review; Insurance/Risk Management
Meetings/Conferences: • Canadian Association of Midwives 15th Annual Conference & Exhibit, 2015
Scope: National

Canadian Association of Mining Equipment & Services for Export (CAMESE) / Association canadienne des exportateurs d'équipement et services miniers

#101, 345 Renfrew Dr., Markham ON L3R 9S9
Tel: 905-513-0046; *Fax:* 905-513-1834
minesupply@camese.org
www.camese.org
www.facebook.com/pages/CAMESE/137206069649085
twitter.com/miningsuppliers
Overview: A medium-sized international organization founded in 1981
Member of: Prospectors & Developers Association of Canada (PDAC); Canadian Institute of Mining, Metallurgy & Petroleum (CIM); Mining Association of Canada (MAC)
Chief Officer(s):
Jon Baird, Managing Director
baird@camese.org
Roy Jakola, Director, Business Development
jakola@camese.org
Spencer Ramshaw, Director, Information & Communication
ramshaw@camese.org
Linda Collins, Manager, Office
collins@camese.org
Dolores Wharton, Manager, Exhibition
wharton@camese.org
Finances: *Funding Sources:* Memnbership dues; Special projects
Staff Member(s): 7; 10 volunteer(s)
Membership: 300; *Fees:* Schedule available; *Member Profile:* Organizations, with an office or employee in Canada, that seek to export goods & services to the global mining industry; Organizations that assist others to export goods & services; *Committees:* Membership; Finance
Activities: Providing selling advice to members; Participating in international mining trade exhibitions; Networking with other firms in the mining sector; Researching target makets for member firms
Publications:
• CAMESE [Canadian Association of Mining Equipment & Services for Export] Bulletin
Type: Newsletter; *Frequency:* Semimonthly
Profile: Market conditions, export sales opportunities, & upcoming events in the mining sector
• Compendium of Canadian Mining Suppliers
Type: Yearbook; *Frequency:* Annually; *Editor:* Bonnie Toews

Canadian Association of Mobile Entertainers & Operators (CAMEO) *See* Canadian Professional DJ Association Inc.

Canadian Association of Moldmakers (CAMM)

c/o St. Clair College (FCEM), PO Box 16, 2000 Talbot Rd. West, Windsor ON N9A 6S4
Tel: 519-255-7863; *Fax:* 519-255-9446
info@camm.ca
www.camm.ca
Previous Name: Windsor Association of Moldmakers
Overview: A small national licensing organization founded in 1981
Mission: To address the concerns of Canadian mould making companies & to present a united voice on legislative issues to provincial & federal governments
Chief Officer(s):
Dan Moynahan, President
dmono@platinum-tool.com
Diane Deslippe, Executive Director, Office
diane@camm.ca
Finances: *Funding Sources:* Corporate sponsorships
Staff Member(s): 1
Membership: *Fees:* $850; *Member Profile:* Mould makers & their mould making network
Activities: Supporting training & education of mould makers; Conducting an annual wage & fringe benefit survey; Offering networking opportunities
Publications:
• CAMM [Canadian Association of Mould Makers] Newsletter
Type: Newsletter
Profile: Industry news & technical information
• Canadian Association of Mould Makers Membership Directory
Type: Directory
Profile: Listing of member companies

Canadian Association of Montessori Teachers (CAMT)

312 Oakwood Crt., Newmarket ON L3Y 3C8
Tel: 416-755-7184; *Fax:* 866-328-7974
info@camt100.ca
www.camt100.ca
Overview: A small national organization
Mission: To advance the standards of Montessori teaching to improve the quality of Montessori education throughout Canada; To promote the interests of Montessori teachers
Chief Officer(s):
Barton Graff, President
Shaza Tehseen, Vice-President
Activities: Promoting excellence in teaching; Organizing workshops
Meetings/Conferences: • Canadian Association of Montessori Teachers 2015 Annual Conference, 2015
Scope: National

Canadian Association of Movers (CAM) / Association canadienne des déménageurs (ACD)

PO Box 30039, Stn. New Westminster, Thornhill ON L4J 0C6
Tel: 905-848-6579; *Fax:* 905-756-1115
Toll-Free: 866-860-0065
admin@mover.net
www.mover.net
Overview: A small national organization
Mission: To further the interests of the owner-managed moving & storage companies by providing for its members leadership, motivation, research, education, programs of mutual benefit, consultation & technical advice
Affliation(s): American Moving & Storage Association; British Association of Removers; International Association of Movers
Chief Officer(s):
Ted LeLacheur, Chair
ted@westernmoving.com
John Levi, President
jlevi@mover.net
Membership: 400
Activities: Government & political affairs; membership development; volunteer participation & recognition; van lines; public affairs & publications; research & development; education & training; professional ethics & standards; organizational competency

Canadian Association of Municipal Administrators (CAMA)

PO Box 128, Stn. A, Fredericton NB E3B 4Y2
Tel: 866-771-2262
admin@camacam.ca
www.camacam.ca
Overview: A small national organization
Mission: To advance excellence in municipal management throughout Canada
Affliation(s): Local Government Managers Australia (LGMA); New Zealand Society of Local Government Managers (SOLGM); Society of Local Authority Chief Executives (SOLACE); International City / County Management Association (ICMA)
Chief Officer(s):
Jacques Des Ormeaux, President, 450-534-2021
Ron Shaw, Treasurer, 519-271-0250 Ext. 233
Finances: *Funding Sources:* Memberships fees; Sponsorships
Membership: 462; *Fees:* Schedule available, based on population of municipality; *Member Profile:* Senior managers from Canadian municipalities, such as city managers, chief administrative officers, & commissioners; Affiliate members are those who work closely with municipal administrators
Activities: Providing professional development in municipal management; Offering networking opportunities
Meetings/Conferences: • Canadian Association of Municipal Administrators 2015 44th Annual Conference & Annual General Meeting, June, 2015, Fairmont Jasper Park Lodge, Jasper, AB
Scope: National
Description: Information & a trade show for senior managers from Canadian municipalities throughout Canada
Contact Information: E-mail: admin@camacam.ca
• Canadian Association of Municipal Administrators 2016 45th Annual Conference & Annual General Meeting, May, 2016, Winnipeg, MB
Scope: National
Description: Information & a trade show for senior managers from Canadian municipalities throughout Canada
Contact Information: E-mail: admin@camacam.ca
• Canadian Association of Municipal Administrators 2017 46th Annual Conference & Annual General Meeting, May, 2017, Gatineau, QC
Scope: National
Description: Information & a trade show for senior managers from Canadian municipalities throughout Canada
Contact Information: E-mail: admin@camacam.ca
• Canadian Association of Municipal Administrators 2018 47th Annual Conference & Annual General Meeting, 2018
Scope: National
Description: Information & a trade show for senior managers from Canadian municipalities throughout Canada
Contact Information: E-mail: admin@camacam.ca
Publications:
• Canadian Association of Municipal Administrators e-Brief
Type: Newsletter; *Frequency:* Semimonthly
Profile: Association happenings, including conference information, workshops, & membership news

Canadian Association of Music Libraries, Archives & Documentation Centres (CAML) / Association canadienne des bibliothèques, archives et centres de documentation musicaux inc. (ACBM)

c/o Music Section, Library & Archives Canada, 395 Wellington St., Ottawa ON K1A 0N4
caml.info.yorku.ca
Previous Name: Canadian Music Library Association
Overview: A small national organization founded in 1971
Mission: To represent librarians, researchers, & archivists in the field of music
Affliation(s): Canadian University Music Society (CUMS); International Association of Music Libaries (IAML); Library & Archives Canada
Chief Officer(s):
Janneka L. Guise, President

Rob van der Bliek, Treasurer, 416-736-2100 Ext. 33694
bliek@yorku.ca
Laura Snyder, Secretary, 780-492-0598, Fax: 780-492-5083
laura.snyder@ualberta.ca
Kyla Jemison, Membership Secretary, 403-762-6221
kyla_jemison@banffcentre.ca
Stacy Allison-Cassin, Officer, Communications, 416-736-2100 Ext. 20461
sacassin@yorku.ca
Membership: 100 individuals & institutions; *Member Profile:* Librarians, archivists, researchers, & institutions in the field of music; Any person interested in the collection, preservation, organization, & study of music
Activities: Providing information to members; Arranging networking opportunities
Awards:
• Helmut Kallmann Award for Distinguished Service (Award)
To recognize excellence in music librarianship & archives work or outstanding contributions to other areas related to music in Canada
Meetings/Conferences: • Canadian Association of Music Libraries, Archives & Documentation Centres 2015 Conference, 2015
Scope: National
Description: A national meeting covering issues & information of interest to music librarians, archivists, & researchers
Contact Information: Contact: Brian McMillan, E-mail: brian.mcmillan@mcgill.ca.
Publications:
• CAML [Canadian Association of Music Libraries, Archives & Documentation Centres] Review / Revue de l'ACBM
Type: Journal; *Frequency:* 3 pa; *Editor:* Cathy Martin *ISSN:* 1496-9963; *Price:* Free with membership in the Canadian Association of Music Libraries
Profile: Information of interest to members of the Canadian Association of Music Libraries, Archives &Documentation Centres, including conference reports, articles, & book & CD reviews
• Directory of Music Collections in Canada
Type: Directory; *Editor:* Carol Ohlers
Profile: An up-to-date listing of major music collections in Canadian institutions

Canadian Association of Mutual Insurance Companies (CAMIC) / Association canadienne des compagnies d'assurance mutuelles (ACCAM)

#205, 311 McArthur Ave., Ottawa ON K1L 6P1
Tel: 613-789-6851; *Fax:* 613-789-7665
agervais@camic.ca
www.camic.ca
Overview: A small national organization founded in 1980
Mission: To provide information, research, advocacy to its members in areas of general concerns & to negotiate supply agreements for goods & services of common needs. Objectives: to promote a strong, health and competitive insurance market; to support regulatory efficiency and legislative change; to inform member companies on matters affecting the industry and to build consensus on action plans; to promote self-regulation for the property and casualty insurance industry
Member of: International Cooperative & Mutual Insurance Federation; National Association of Mutual Insurance Companies
Chief Officer(s):
Normand Lafrenière, President
nlafreniere@camic.ca
Finances: *Annual Operating Budget:* $250,000-$500,000; *Funding Sources:* Membership fees; conventions; commissions
Staff Member(s): 2
Membership: 94 corporate; *Fees:* Schedule available; *Member Profile:* Mutual insurance company; mutual reinsurance company or subsidiary of mutual insurance company

The Canadian Association of Naturopathic Doctors (CAND) / Association canadienne des docteurs en naturopathie

#200, 20 Holly St., Toronto ON M2S 3B1
Tel: 416-496-8633; *Fax:* 416-496-8634
Toll-Free: 800-551-4381
www.cand.ca
www.facebook.com/NaturopathicDrs
twitter.com/naturopathicdrs
Previous Name: Canadian Naturopathic Association
Overview: A medium-sized national organization founded in 1955
Mission: CAND is a not-for-profit professional organization that promotes naturopathic medicine to the public, insurance companies & corporations. CAND encourages professional, educational & networking activities among its members, & standardization of educational requirements for practitioners
Chief Officer(s):
Shawn O'Reilly, Executive Director
Alex McKenna, Marketing Director
Staff Member(s): 3; 2 volunteer(s)
Membership: 1,000 individuals; *Fees:* $25-$500; *Member Profile:* Naturopathic doctors; students of naturopathic medicine; suppliers; *Committees:* Government Relations; Internal Communications; External Communications
Activities: Advocacy, education; *Awareness Events:* Naturopathic Medicine Week, May

Canadian Association of Nephrology Nurses & Technologists (CANNT) / Association canadienne des infirmières et infirmiers et technologues de néphrologie (ACITN)

#322, 336 Yonge St., Barrie ON L4N 4C8
Tel: 705-720-2819; *Fax:* 705-720-1451
Toll-Free: 877-720-2819
cannt@cannt.ca
www.cannt.ca
www.facebook.com/160999717295820
twitter.com/CANNT1
Overview: A small national organization founded in 1968
Mission: To improve the care of renal patients through support of educational opportunities for association members; To evaluate the performance & competence of nephrology nurses & technologists against the CANNT Standards of Practice
Affiliation(s): Kidney Foundation of Canada; Canadian Nurses Association
Chief Officer(s):
Marilyn Muir, RN, CNeph(C), President, 204-787-3611
mrmuir@hsc.mb.ca
Florence (Elyn) Holder, Treasurer & Coordinator, Website
fmelyn@hotmail.com
Finances: *Funding Sources:* Sponsorships; Fundraising
Membership: *Fees:* $68.25; *Member Profile:* Individuals involved in the care of patients with renal disease
Activities: Disseminating knowledge; Promoting excellence in practice & quality care; Participating in exam development activities with the CNA;
Publications:
• CANNT [Canadian Association of Nephrology Nurses & Technologists] Journal / Journal ACITN
Type: Journal; *Frequency:* Quarterly; *Editor:* Gillian Brunier; *Price:* Free with CANNT membership

Canadian Association of Neuropathologists (CANP) / Association canadienne de neuropathologistes

c/o Department of Pathology, Vancouver General Hospital, 855 West 12th Ave., Vancouver BC V5Z 1M9
Tel: 604-875-4111; *Fax:* 604-875-4988
canp.medical.org
Overview: A small national charitable organization founded in 1960
Mission: To organize the annual scientific meeting; to promote the professional & educational objectives of neuropathologists.
Affliation(s): International Society of Neuropathology
Chief Officer(s):
Ian MacKenzie, President
ian.mackenzie@vch.ca
Peter Gould, Secretary-Treasurer
Peter.Gould@fmed.ulaval.ca
Finances: *Funding Sources:* Membership dues
Membership: *Member Profile:* Devote majority of time to neuropathology

Canadian Association of Neuroscience Nurses (CANN) / Association canadienne des infirmiers et infirmières en sciences neurologiques (ACIISN)

c/o Aline Mayer, Membership Chairperson, CANN, 30 Chantilly Gate, Stittsville ON K2S 2B1
e-mail: canninfo@cann.ca
www.cann.ca
www.facebook.com/groups/180078122050006
Overview: A small national organization founded in 1969
Mission: To prevent illness & to improve health outcomes for people with, or at risk for, neurological disorders; To establish standards of practice for neuroscience nurses
Member of: World Federation of Neuroscience Nurses
Affiliation(s): Canadian Nurses Association; Canadian Congress of Neurological Sciences; Canadian Brain & Nerve Health Coalition (CBANHC); Canadian Council on Donation and Transplantation (CCDT); National Stroke Leadership Group; Canadian Association of Brain Tumor Coalition (CABTO); Think First
Chief Officer(s):
Sandra Bérubé, President
president@cann.ca
Deb Holtom, Vice-President & Secretary
vice.president@cann.ca
Mark Bonin, Treasurer
treasurer@cann.ca
Aline Mayer, Chair, Membership
membership@cann.ca
Membership: *Fees:* $75; *Member Profile:* Registered nurses, who are licensed to practise in Canada & are working in neurological or neurosurgical nursing; Registered nurses, who live outside Canada, are associate members; Individuals practising in a related discipline in the neurosciences; Registered nurses, with an interest in neuroscience nursing; Students; *Committees:* Program; Scientific; Communications & Marketing; Legislation & Bylaws; Membership; Professional Practice; Research; Translation
Activities: Offering continuing education opportunities; Providing networking possibilities; Promoting research; Facilitating access to recent research; Collaborating, to prevent illness & to improve health outcomes
Meetings/Conferences: • Canadian Association of Neuroscience Nurses 2015 46th Annual Meeting & Scientific Sessions: Generating the Flow of Knowledge, June, 2015, Sheraton Hotel Newfoundland, St. John's, NL
Scope: National
Description: Scientific sessions offering professional development for neuroscience nurses.
Contact Information: Canadian Association of Neuroscience Nurses Professional Practice Chair (for information about the certification review workshop, held each year in conjunction with the annual scientific meeting), Newfoundland Scientific Chair, Jenny Slade, jenny.slade@easternhealth.ca
Publications:
• Canadian Journal of Neuroscience Nursing (CJNN) / Le journal canadien des infirmiers et infirmières en sciences neurologiques
Type: Journal; *Frequency:* Quarterly; *Accepts Advertising*; *Editor:* Theresa Green, RN, PhD; *Price:* Free with membership in the Canadian Association of Neuroscience Nurses
Profile: A peer reviewed journal, distributed to neuroscience nurses & medicallibraries

Canadian Association of Nordic Ski Instructors (CANSI) / Association canadienne des moniteurs de ski nordique

c/o Secrétariat, 164 Adrien-Robert St., Gatineau QC J8Y 3S2
Tel: 819-360-6700; *Fax:* 819-778-0017
office@cansi.ca
www.cansi.ca
www.facebook.com/162657427089855
Overview: A small national organization founded in 1976
Mission: To promote & advance cross-country & Telemark skiing in Canada, establishing standards, & offering levels of certification in technique & training.
Chief Officer(s):
Jeff Hampshire, President
president@cansi.ca
Françoise Chatenoud, Office Coordinator
Membership: *Fees:* $70 professional; $50 associate; $20 affiliate; *Member Profile:* Completed Level I Cross Country or Telemark course; *Committees:* Technical
Activities: Providing resources to instuctors; liaising nationally & internationally with the Nordic disciplines; coordinating national level courses
Publications:
• XCitation
Type: Newsletter; *Frequency:* Quarterly; *Editor:* Karla Wikjord
Profile: Articles, teaching tips & updates

Atlantic Region
c/o 3 Westview Ave., Corner Brook NL A2H 3B7
Tel: 709-634-9962
info@atlantic.cansi.ca
Chief Officer(s):
Keith Payne, Regional Representative

Central Region - MB, NU, & SK
c/o Jeff Hampshire, #46, 3420 Vialoux Dr., Winnipeg MB R3R 0A4
Tel: 204-510-0395
info@central.cansi.ca
Chief Officer(s):
Jeff Hampshire, Regional Representative

Mountain Region - AB & NT
c/o 9519 - 92 St., Edmonton AB T6C 3S2
e-mail: info@mountain.cansi.ca
Chief Officer(s):
Henry Madsen, Regional Representative
Ontario Region
Toll-Free: 888-226-7446
info@ontario.cansi.ca
Chief Officer(s):
Garry Almond, Regional Representative
Joseph Ferri, Director, Finance
finance-dir@ontario.cansi.ca
Pacific Region - BC & YT
c/o Canada West Mountain School, 47 West Broadway, Vancouver BC V5Y 1P1
e-mail: pacific@cansi.ca
Chief Officer(s):
Jamie Sterling, Coordinator, Communications
Québec Region
QC
info@quebec.cansi.ca
www.cansi-quebec.ca
Chief Officer(s):
Guy Lavoie, Président
Carmen Archambault, Secretary-Treasurer
Jean-Sébastien Thibault, Coordinator, XC Course
skidefond@quebec.cansi.ca
Robert Lesage, Coordinator, Telemark Course
telemark@quebec.cansi.ca

Canadian Association of Nuclear Medicine (CANM) / Association canadienne de médecine nucléaire (ACMN)

PO Box 4383, Stn. E, Ottawa ON K1S 2L0
Tel: 613-882-5097
canm@canm-acmn.ca
www.canm-acmn.ca
Overview: A small national organization founded in 1971
Affiliation(s): Canadian Medical Association; Society of Nuclear Medicine - USA; Canadian Association of Radiation Protection
Chief Officer(s):
Norman Laurin, President
Finances: *Funding Sources:* Membership dues
Membership: *Fees:* $300 regular; $0 resident; *Member Profile:* Physicians who have received certification in nuclear medicine; Scientists associated with nuclear medicine; Medical radiation technologists; Medically qualified practitioners working in the discipline of nuclear medicine; Trainees
Meetings/Conferences: • Canadian Association of Nuclear Medicine Annual Scientific Meeting 2015, January, 2015, Hotel Omni Mont-Royal, Montréal, QC
Scope: National
Description: A day of dedicated nuclear medicine technologist sessions.
Publications:
• Photon
Type: Newsletter; *Frequency:* Semiannually; *Editor:* Sandor Demeter, MD

Canadian Association of Numismatic Dealers (CAND) / Association canadienne des marchands numismatiques

c/o Jo-Anne Simpson, Executive Secretary, PO Box 10272, Stn. Winona, Stoney Creek ON L8E 5R1
Tel: 905-643-4988; *Fax:* 905-643-6329
email@cand.org
www.cand.org
Overview: A small national organization founded in 1975
Mission: To ensure professionalism by members of the association
Chief Officer(s):
Michael Findlay, President
ccdn@bconnex.net
Paul Koolhaas, Vice-President
paul.koolhaas@sympatico.ca
Wendy Hoare, Secretary-Treasurer
jhoare@jeffreyhoare.on.ca
Membership: *Member Profile:* Persons engaged in the retail numismatic trade, such as coin dealers, foreign exchange dealers, bullion dealers, & paper money dealers
Activities: Upholding the Code of Ethics;
Meetings/Conferences: • Canadian Association of Numismatic Dealers 2015 Annual Convention, January, 2015, Sheraton Hamilton Hotel, Hamilton, ON
Scope: National
Contact Information: Contact: Tom Kennedy, Phone: 519-271-8825, E-mail: cand@cogeco.ca

Canadian Association of Nurses in HIV/AIDS Care (CANAC) / Association canadienne des infirmières et infirmiers en sidologie

St. Paul's Hospital, #B552, 1081 Burrard St., Vancouver BC V6Z 1Y6
e-mail: admin@canac.org
www.canac.org
Overview: A small national charitable organization founded in 1991
Mission: The Canadian Association of Nurses in AIDS Care (CANAC) is a national professional nursing organization committed to fostering excellence in HIV/AIDS nursing, promoting the health, rights and dignity of persons affected by HIV/AIDS and to preventing the spread of HIV infection.
Affliation(s): Canadian Nurses Association
Chief Officer(s):
Janna Campbell, Executive Assistant
Finances: *Funding Sources:* Membership dues; fundraising; special projects
Membership: *Fees:* $40 associate/student; $50 regular; *Member Profile:* Nurses; support mission of CANAC; corporate & associate
Meetings/Conferences: • Canadian Association of Nurses in HIV/AIDS Care Conference 2015, May, 2015, Ottawa, ON
Scope: National
Contact Information: canac2015@gmail.com
Publications:
• Connection: The Newsletter of the Canadian Association of Nurses in AIDS Care
Type: Newsletter; *Frequency:* 3 pa; *Editor:* Jennifer Shaw
Profile: CANAD / ACIIS news & reports, conference information, events, resources, & employment opportunities

Canadian Association of Nurses in Oncology (CANO) / Association canadienne des infirmières en oncologie (ACIO)

#201, 375 West 5th Ave., Vancouver BC V5Y 1J6
Tel: 604-874-4322; *Fax:* 604-874-4378
cano@malachite-mgmt.com
www.cano-acio.ca
www.facebook.com/336467099484
twitter.com/CANO_ACIO
www.youtube.com/user/CANOACIO
Overview: A medium-sized national organization founded in 1984
Mission: To advocate for improved cancer care for all Canadians.
Affiliation(s): Canadian Nurses Association; International Society of Cancer Nurses; Canadian Oncology Societies
Chief Officer(s):
Barbara Fitzgerald, President
Ana Torres, Executive Director
ana.torres@malachite-mgmt.com
Finances: *Funding Sources:* Membership dues; sponsorships
Staff Member(s): 4
Membership: *Fees:* $100 regular/associate/affiliate; $50 student/non-working; *Member Profile:* Registered Nurses involved in or interested in cancer nursing; *Committees:* Recognition of Excellence; Research; Chapter Grant Review; CANO/ACIO Connections; Industry Relations
Meetings/Conferences: • Canadian Association of Nurses in Oncology 2015 Conference, October, 2015, Fairmont Royal York Hotel, Toronto, ON
Scope: National
Description: The conference theme is People, Purpose, Passion
Publications:
• Canadian Oncology Nursing Journal
Type: Journal; *Frequency:* Quarterly; *Editor:* Heather Porter, RN, PhD
• CANO [Canadian Association of Nurses in Oncology] Connections
Type: Newsletter

Canadian Association of Occupational Therapists (CAOT) / Association canadlenne des ergothérapeutes (ACE)

CTTC Building, #3400, 1125 Colonel By Dr., Ottawa ON K1S 5R1
Tel: 613-523-2268; *Fax:* 613-523-2552
Toll-Free: 800-434-2268
insurance@caot.ca
www.caot.ca
www.facebook.com/CAOT.ca
Overview: A large national organization founded in 1926
Mission: To develop & promote the profession of occupational therapy in Canada & abroad; To assist occupational therapists achieve excellence in their professional practice by offering services, products, events, & networking opportunities
Affliation(s): World Federation of Occupational Therapists
Chief Officer(s):
Paulette Guitard, Preisdent
guitardp@uottawa.ca
Mike Brennan, COO
mbrennan@caot.ca
Claudia von Zweck, Executive Director
cvonzweck@caot.ca
Sangita Kamblé, Executive Director, Canadian Occupational Therapy Foundation
skamble@cotfcanada.org
Membership: 12,000+; *Fees:* Schedule available; *Member Profile:* A full-time member is an occupational therapist who has graduated from an occupational therapy program accredited by the Canadian Association of Occupational Therapists, or recognized by the World Federation of Occupational Therapists. A full-time member has also passed the national certification examination & completed 1000 hours of fieldwork education. A part-time member has completed less than 800 hours of work in a membership year. A non-practising member is an individual who is unemployed, retired, on leave, a graduate student, practising outside Canada, or employed in a position unrelated to occupational therapy. An associate member is an individual who is interested in, or involved with, occupational therapy, or a person trained in other countries & not working in Canada.
Activities: Providing access to the latest developments in occupational therapy practice & research; Offering a mentoring program; Organizing continuing education opportunities; Advocating on behalf of occupational therapists; *Rents Mailing List:* Yes
Awards:
• Fellowship Award (Award)
• Award for Leadership in Occupational Therapy (Award)
• Honorary Membership (Award)
• Award for Innovative Practice (Award)
• Muriel Driver Memorial Lectureship (Award)
• Dr. Helen P. LeVesconte Award for Volunteerism in the Canadian Association of Occupational Therapists (Award)
• Award of Merit (Award)
• Life Membership (Award)
• Citation Award (Award)
• Certificate of Appreciation (Award)
• Student Award (Award)
• Golden Quill Award (Award)
Meetings/Conferences: • Canadian Association of Occupational Therapists 2015 Annual Conference, May, 2015, Winnipeg, MB
Scope: National
Description: A scientific program & exhibits
Contact Information: Conference & Advertising Manager: Lisa Sheehan, E-mail: conference@caot.ca
Publications:
• Canadian Association of Occupational Therapists Annual Report
Type: Yearbook; *Frequency:* Annually
Profile: A review of association activities during the past year, plus financial information
• Canadian Journal of Occupational Therapy
Type: Journal; *Frequency:* 5 pa; *Accepts Advertising*; *Editor:* Helene Polatajko
Profile: Professional peer-reviewed scientific journal promoting advancement in research & education
• Enabling Occupation II: Advancing an Occupational Therapy Vision for Health, Well-being & Justice through Occupation
Author: Elizabeth Townsend, Helen Polatajko; *ISBN:* 978-1-895437-76-8
Profile: A study & practice guide, focussing on occupation-basedenablement
• Occupational Therapy Now
Type: Magazine; *Frequency:* Bimonthly; *Accepts Advertising*; *Editor:* Janna MacLachlan
Profile: Practice magazine, with clinical applications of recent research & theory, evidence-based practice, & product reviews

Canadian Association of Occupational Therapists - British Columbia (CAOT-BC)

PO Box 30042, RPO Parkgate Village, N., Vancouver BC V7H 2Y8

Fax: 613-523-2552
Toll-Free: 800-434-2268
www.caot.ca
Overview: A medium-sized provincial organization
Mission: To promote the profession of occupational therapy throughout the province & represent its members to regional health boards & government, health professional groups & the public; to foster the growth & development of the profession in BC; to provide a variety of services to its members including continuing education, reentry & participation in professional issues
Member of: Canadian Association of Occupational Therapists
Chief Officer(s):
Giovanna Boniface, Managing Director
gboniface@caot.ca
Membership: *Member Profile:* Occupational therapists; affiliate organizations; students
Activities: *Rents Mailing List:* Yes
Awards:
• British Columbia Citation Award (Award)
To acknowledge the contribution to the health & well-being of Canadians of an occupational therapist living in British Columbia
• Outstanding OT of the Year (Award)
To recognize an occupational therapist living in British Columbia who has made an outstanding contribution to the profession throughout his or her career.

Canadian Association of Oilwell Drilling Contractors (CAODC)
#2050, 717 - 7th Ave. SW, Calgary AB T2P 0Z3
Tel: 403-264-4311; *Fax:* 403-263-3796
Other Communication: Membership e-mail: membership@caodc.ca
info@caodc.ca
www.caodc.ca
twitter.com/markascholz
www.youtube.com/user/TheCAODC
Overview: A large national organization founded in 1949
Mission: To represent drilling rig contractors; to provide ongoing means of communication between drilling & well servicing contractors, governments, other industry sector participants, & the general public; To improve standards for safety & training, equipment & technical procedures; To coordinate programs between government bodies & contractors; To oversee the Rig Technician Trade & Apprenticeship Program in Alberta, British Columbia, & Saskatchewan
Chief Officer(s):
W. Ross Pickering, Chair
Wade McGowan, Vice-Chair
Membership: 44 Drilling Rig Division + 2 Atlantic Division + 73 Service Rig Division + 198 Associate Division; *Fees:* Schedule available; *Member Profile:* Upstream Canadian petroleum drilling contractors (land-based & offshore) service rig contractors & associate companies; *Committees:* Accounting & Taxation (Drilling); Engineering & Technical; Finance/Audit; Forecasting; Government & Public Relations; Health, Safety & Environment (Drilling); Human Resources & Training; Information Technology; Legal & Contract (Drilling); Manpower; Rig Technician Apprenticeship
Activities: *Library* Open to public by appointment
Awards:
• CAODC Scholarship Program (Scholarship)
• CAODC Occupational Health & Safety (OHS) Scholarship Program (Scholarship)
Publications:
• CAODC [Canadian Association of Oilwell Drilling Contractors] Oil Driller
Type: Magazine; *Frequency:* 3 pa; *Accepts Advertising*; *Editor:* Cindy Soderstrom
Profile: Reports on issues about Canada's oil industry. drilling forecasts, & CAODC committee updates
• CAODC [Canadian Association of Oilwell Drilling Contractors] Members Directory & Buyers Guide
Type: Directory; *Frequency:* Annual
Profile: Available in print & online

Canadian Association of Optometrists (CAO) / Association canadienne des optométristes (ACO)
234 Argyle Ave., Ottawa ON K2P 1B9
Tel: 613-235-7924; *Fax:* 613-235-2025
Toll-Free: 888-263-4676
info@opto.ca
www.opto.ca
Overview: A large national organization founded in 1941
Mission: To represent & assist the profession of optometry in Canada; To improve the quality, availability, & accessibility of vision & eye care
Affiliation(s): Eye Health Council of Canada
Chief Officer(s):
Paul Geneau, President
paul@evecarenanalmo.com
Laurie Clement, Executive Director, 613-235-7924
lclement@opto.ca
Lise Loyer, National Director, Optometric Assistants Course, 613-235-7924 Ext. 216
oac@opto.ca
Catherine Heinmiller, National Coordinator, Children's Vision Initiative & Member Programs, 613-235-7924 Ext. 210
diradmin@opto.ca
Doug Dean, Director, Vision Care Plans, 613-235-7924 Ext. 215
ovp@opto.ca
Leslie Laskarin, Director, Communications, 613-235-7924 Ext. 213
dircomm@opto.ca
Blaine Phillips, Director, Finance & Administation, 613-235-7924
bphillips@opto.ca
Finances: *Funding Sources:* Membership fees; Sponsorships
Membership: 4,600+; *Member Profile:* Doctors of optometry in Canada; *Committees:* Diabetes; Government Relations; Children Vision Initiative; National Public Education; Executive
Activities: Liaising with government; Engaging in advocacy activities; Providing professional development & educational opportunities; Conducting research; Offering information; Promoting ethical decision-making; *Awareness Events:* Children's Vision Month, September
Meetings/Conferences: • Canadian Association of Optometrists 2015 33rd Biennial Congress, July, 2015, Fredericton, NB
Scope: National
• Canadian Association of Optometrists Optometric Leaders' Forum 2015, January, 2015, Ottawa, ON
Scope: National
Publications:
• Canadian Journal of Optometry [a publication of the Canadian Association of Optometrists]
Type: Journal; *Frequency:* q.

Canadian Association of Oral & Maxillofacial Surgeons (CAOMS) / Association canadienne de spécialistes en chirurgie buccale et maxillo-faciale (ACSCBMF)
#100, 32 Colonnade Rd., Ottawa ON K2E 7J6
Tel: 613-721-1816; *Fax:* 613-721-3581
Toll-Free: 888-369-5641
Other Communication: executivedirector@caoms.com
caoms@caoms.com
www.caoms.com
Overview: A medium-sized national organization founded in 1953
Chief Officer(s):
Kevin McCann, Chair, Membership, 519-743-7811
Finances: *Funding Sources:* Membership fees; Sponsorships
Membership: *Fees:* Free, for honorary, retired, & student members; $250 affiliate, supporting, & life members; $500 active members; *Member Profile:* Any individual who is certified & licensed to practice the specialty of oral & maxillofacial surgery in a Canadian province or territory; Affiliate members are persons in a foreign country who hold membership in that country's national organization for oral & maxillofacial surgeons; Students enrolled full-time in an accredited program for the training of oral & maxillofacial surgeons
Activities: Providing professional development opportunities; Offering networking events
Awards:
• Distinguished Service Award (Award)
To recognize Canadian Association of Oral & Maxillofacial Surgeons members who have made a contribution to benefit the specialty of oral & maxillofacial surgery or the association

Canadian Association of Orthodontists (CAO) / Association canadienne des orthodontists (aco)
#310, 2175 Sheppard Ave. East, Toronto ON M2J 1W8
Tel: 416-491-3186; *Fax:* 416-491-1670
Toll-Free: 877-226-8800
cao@taylorenterprises.com
www.cao-aco.org
Overview: A medium-sized national organization founded in 1949
Mission: To advance the science & art of orthodontics; To promote the highest quality of orthodontic care in Canada; To act as the official voice of Canadian orthodontic specialists
Chief Officer(s):
Howard Steiman, President
Paul Major, First Vice-President
Garry A. Solomon, Second Vice-President
Michael W. Patrician, Secretary-Treasurer
Dan Pollit, Chair, Communications
dpollit@rogers.com
Finances: *Funding Sources:* Membership fees; Sponsorships
Membership: 500+; *Member Profile:* Educationally qualified orthodontic specialists, registered with a Dental Regulatory Authority; Graduate & postgraduate students enrolled in a Commission on Dental Accreditation program; Academic members who have completed a university level program in orthodontics & are employed full-time in an orthodontic program; *Committees:* Nominations; Bulletin; Communications; President - CFAO; Insurance; Membership; Policy & Procedures & By-laws; WFO - Country; National Scientific Session; New & Younger Members; Database / Directory; History, Archives, & Media; CAO / AAO; Planning & Priorities; Standards of Practice; Sponsorship; WFO; CAO / CDA; CAO Web; Eucators
Activities: Promoting standards of excellence in orthodontic education; Striving for higher standards of excellence in the practice of orthodontics; Promoting public awareness of the benefits of orthodontic health care; Protecting the rights of members
Meetings/Conferences: • Canadian Association of Orthodontists 2015 67th Annual Scientific Session, September, 2015, Fairmont Empress Hotel, Victoria, BC
Scope: National
Description: A scientific session with exhibits
Contact Information: Chair, Communications Committee: Dr. Dan Pollit, E-mail: dpollit@rogers.com
• Canadian Association of Orthodontists 2016 68th Annual Scientific Session, September, 2016, Delta Prince Edward & PEI Convention Centre, Charlottetown, PE
Scope: National
Description: A scientific session with exhibits
Publications:
• Canadian Association of Orthodontists Bulletin
Type: Newsletter; *Frequency:* Semiannually; *Editor:* Dr. Jim Posluns; *Price:* Free with membership in the Canadian Association of Orthodontists
Profile: Updates on the association & the profession
• Canadian Association of Orthodontists Directory
Type: Directory; *Frequency:* Biennially; *Editor:* Dr. Stephen Roth; *Price:* Free with membership in the Canadian Association of Orthodontists
Profile: A listing of all Canadian Association of Orthodontists members
• Canadian Association of Orthodontists Membership Manual
Type: Manual; *Price:* Free with membership in the Canadian Association of Orthodontists
Profile: Information about orthodontic practice, such as GST & insurance guidelines
• Presidential News
Type: Newsletter; *Price:* Free with membership in the Canadian Association of Orthodontists
Profile: Information from the Canadian Association of Orthodontists' president
• Recommendations on Infection Control for Orthodontic Practice
Price: Free with membership in the Canadian Association of Orthodontists

Canadian Association of Paediatric Health Centres (CAPHC) / Association canadienne des centres de santé pédiatriques
c/o Canadian Association of Paediatric Health Centres, #104, 2141 Thurston Dr., Ottawa ON K1G 6C9
Tel: 613-738-4164; *Fax:* 613-738-3247
info@caphc.org
www.caphc.org
www.facebook.com/122402857839382
twitter.com/CAPHCTweets
Previous Name: Canadian Association of Paediatric Hospitals
Overview: A medium-sized national organization founded in 1968
Mission: To improve the health of children within Canada through research activities & through advocacy with governments & health care organizations; to provide information exchange amongst members
Chief Officer(s):
Elaine Orrbine, President & Chief Executive Officer
eorrdine@cacph.org
Doug Maynard, Associate Director
dmaynard@cacph.org
Meetings/Conferences: • Canadian Association of Paediatric Health Centres Annual Conference 2015, October, 2015,

Quebec City, QC
Scope: National
• Canadian Association of Paediatric Health Centres Annual Conference 2016, October, 2016, Halifax, NS
Scope: National
• Canadian Association of Paediatric Health Centres Annual Conference 2018, October, 2018, Saskatoon, SK
Scope: National

Canadian Association of Paediatric Hospitals ***See*** Canadian Association of Paediatric Health Centres

Canadian Association of Paediatric Surgeons (CAPS) / Association de la chirurgie infantile canadienne

c/o Children's Hospital Of Winnipeg, 840 Sherbrook St., #AE401, Winnipeg MB R3A 1S1
Tel: 204-787-1246; *Fax:* 204-787-4618
www.caps.ca
Overview: A medium-sized national organization
Mission: To improve the surgical care of infants and children in Canada.
Chief Officer(s):
B.J. Hancock, Secretary Treasurer
hancock.caps@gmail.com
Finances: *Funding Sources:* Membership dues, donations.
Membership: *Member Profile:* Paediatric surgeons who are active, candidates, or honorary.

Canadian Association of Palynologists (CAP) / Association canadienne des palynologues

c/o Dr. Mary A. Vetter, Luther College, University of Regina, Regina SK S4S 0A2
www.scirpus.ca/cap/cap.shtml
Overview: A small national organization founded in 1978
Mission: To advance all aspects of palynology in Canada
Affliation(s): International Federation of Palynological Societies (IFPS)
Chief Officer(s):
Francine McCarthy, President
fmccarthy@brocku.ca
Mary A. Vetter, Secretary-Treasurer
mary.vetter@uregina.ca
Florin Pendea, Editor, CAP Newsletter
ifpendea@Lakeheadu.ca
Finances: *Funding Sources:* Membership dues
Membership: 57; *Fees:* $10; *Member Profile:* Palynologists from universities, government agencies, & industries; Persons with an interest in Canadian palynology
Activities: Promoting cooperation between palynologists & persons in related fields of study; *Library:* CAP Library
Awards:
• Canadian Association of Palynologists Annual Student Research Award (Award)
To recognize students' contributions to palynological research *Contact:* Matthew Peros, E-mail: mperos@uottawa.ca
Publications:
• CAP [Canadian Association of Palynologists] Newsletter
Type: Newsletter; *Frequency:* Semiannually; *Editor:* Dr. Terri Lacourse; *Price:* Free with membership in theCanadian Association of Palynologists
Profile: Reports about fieldwork, analytical methods, & research in Canadian palynology, plus essays & conference information

Canadian Association of Paralegals (CAO) / Association canadienne des parajuristes

a/s Mrs. Cara Subirana, 2606, av Adhémar-Raynault, L'Assomption QC J5W 0E1
e-mail: info@caplegal.ca
www.caplegal.ca
Overview: A small national organization
Mission: To promote the paralegal profession; to provide support and an exchange of ideas between colleagues and members, in order to better the skills of the paralegals; to offer continuing education, such as conferences, seminars and discussion groups; and to supply valuable information to paralegals useful in their field of practice, law firms, private businesses, Canadian public corporations and others.
Chief Officer(s):
Dominique Myner, Chair
Publications:
• Liaison [a publication of the Canadian Association of Paralegals]
Type: Newsletter; *Editor:* Tina Paliotta

Canadian Association of Pathologists (CAP) / Association canadienne des pathologistes

774 Echo Dr., Ottawa ON K1S 5N8
Tel: 613-730-6230; *Fax:* 613-730-1116
Toll-Free: 800-668-3740
cap@royalcollege.ca
cap-acp.org
Overview: A medium-sized national charitable organization
Chief Officer(s):
Lakovina Alexopoulou, President
Membership: *Committees:* Awards; Special Archives; Continuing Professional Development; Professional Affairs; Local Organizing Annual Meeting; Annual Meeting; Membership; Nominating
Activities: Providing professional development opportunities; Offering networking opportunities; Providing information about developments in laboratory medicine
Publications:
• The CAP [Canadian Association of Pathologists] Newsletter
Type: Newsletter; *Frequency:* Quarterly; *Accepts Advertising*
Profile: Available to members only
• CAP [Canadian Association of Pathologists] Membership Directory
Type: Directory; *Frequency:* Annually

Canadian Association of Pension Supervisory Authorities (CAPSA) / Association canadienne des organismes de contrôle des régimes de retraite (ACOR)

c/o CAPSA Secretariat, PO Box 85, 5160 Yonge St., 18th Fl., Toronto ON M2N 6L9
Tel: 416-590-7081; *Fax:* 416-226-7878
Toll-Free: 800-668-0128
capsa-acor@fsco.gov.on.ca
www.capsa-acor.org
Overview: A small national organization founded in 1974
Mission: To facilitate an efficient & effective pension regulatory system in Canada
Member of: Joint Forum of Financial Market Regulators
Affliation(s): National Pension Compliance Officers Association; Canadian Council of Insurance Regulators; Canadian Securities Administrators; Canadian Insurance Services Regulatory Organizations
Chief Officer(s):
Andrewian Schrumm, Manager, Policy
Membership: 12; *Member Profile:* Canadian pension supervisory authorities
Activities: Developing policies to harmonize pension law across Canada
Publications:
• CAPSA [Canadian Association of Pension Supervisory Authorities] / ACOR Communiqué
Type: Newsletter
Profile: Information for stakeholders about CAPSA's priorities & initiatives

Canadian Association of Perinatal & Women's Health Nurses (CAPWHN) / Association canadienne des infirmières et infirmiers en périnatalité et en santé des femmes

780 Echo Dr., Ottawa ON K1S 5R7
Tel: 613-730-4192; *Fax:* 613-730-4314
Toll-Free: 800-561-2416
admin@capwhn.ca
www.capwhn.ca
www.facebook.com/CAPWHN
twitter.com/CAPWHN
Previous Name: Association of Women's Health, Obstetric & Neonatal Nurses Canada
Overview: A medium-sized national organization founded in 2010
Mission: To improve the health of women & newborns; To strengthen the nursing profession in Canada
Chief Officer(s):
Nancy Watts, RN, BSN, MN, President
Catherine J. Sheffer, RN, MN, PNC(C), Treasurer
Rita Assabgui, Executive Director
Staff Member(s): 1
Membership: 500+; *Member Profile:* Women's health, obstetric & newborn nurses from across Canada; *Committees:* Advocacy & Health Policy; Membership; Research; Nominations
Activities: Promoting the health of women & newborns; Engaging in advocacy activiities; Conducting research; Disseminating information about health policy, clinical practice & management; Providing education at the local, provincial & national level; Developing a professional network to share ideas
Meetings/Conferences: • Canadian Association of Perinatal & Women's Health Nurses National Conference 2015, November, 2015, Hilton Quebec, Quebec, QC
Scope: National
Contact Information: Executive Director: Rita Assabgui, E-mail: admin@capwhn.ca
Publications:
• CAPWHN Newsletter
Type: Newsletter; *Frequency:* 3 pa; *Accepts Advertising*
Profile: Activities of CAPWHN & its chapters in the Atlantic provinces, Québec, Ontario, Manitoba & Saskatchewan, & Alberta & British Columbia
• E-News
Type: Newsletter

Canadian Association of Personal Property Appraisers (CAPPA)

463 King St. East, Toronto ON M5G 1L6
Tel: 416-364-3730
www.cpa-cappa.com
Also Known As: Canadian Professional Appraisers (CPA)
Overview: A small national organization founded in 1989
Mission: To accredit appraisers with proper experience, training, & qualifications & who subscribe to a code of ethics
Chief Officer(s):
John A. Libby, President
libbygallery@rogers.com
Daniel D. Zakaib, Vice-President, 416-987-8750
dzack@rogers.com
Membership: *Member Profile:* Qualified individuals who have at least 5 years experience in their field.

Canadian Association of Petroleum Land Administration (CAPLA)

#720, 138 - 4th Ave. SE, Calgary AB T2G 4Z6
Tel: 403-452-6497; *Fax:* 403-452-6627
office@caplacanada.org
www.caplacanada.org
www.linkedin.com/groups?home=&gid=3877780
www.facebook.com/201712263172241
twitter..com/CAPLACanada
Overview: A small local organization founded in 1993
Chief Officer(s):
T. Cathy Miller, Chief Executive Officer, 403-452-6621
cathy@caplacanada.org
Katherine Matiko, Communications Specialist
katherine@caplacanada.org
Staff Member(s): 7; 300 volunteer(s)
Membership: 2,800; *Fees:* $75 student; $175 active; $75 retired; *Committees:* Awards; Certification; Conference; Education Delivery & Facilitation; Education Development; Events; Executive; Knowledge Bank; Leadership Forum; Member Services; Mentorship; NEXUS Editorial; Social Media; Surface Stakeholder Engagement

Canadian Association of Petroleum Landmen (CAPL)

#350, 500 - 5 Ave. SW, Calgary AB T2P 3L5
Tel: 403-237-6635; *Fax:* 403-263-1620
reception@landman.ca
www.landman.ca
Overview: A medium-sized national organization founded in 1948
Mission: To enhance all facets of the land profession
Chief Officer(s):
Michelle Radomski, President
Nikki Sitch, Vice-President
Kent Gibson, Director, Member Services
Brad Reynolds, Director, Communications
Connie De Ciancio, Director, Education
Gary Richardson, Director, Public Relations
Finances: *Annual Operating Budget:* $1.5 Million-$3 Million
Membership: 1,500+
Activities: Liaising with government departments & other resource based associations; Communicating with members; Providing professional development opportunities; Offering networking events
Meetings/Conferences: • Canadian Association of Petroleum Landmen 2015 Annual Conference, 2015, St. John's, NL
Scope: National
Description: Presentations on the industry by guest speakers
Contact Information: Director, Communications: Joan Dornian, Phone: 403-531-4713
Publications:
• Canadian Association of Petroleum Landmen Membership Directory

Type: Directory; *Price:* Free access with membership in the Canadian Association of Petroleum Landmen
• CAPL [Canadian Association of Petroleum Landmen] Annual Report
Type: Yearbook; *Frequency:* Annually
• The Negotiator: The Magazine of the Canadian Association of Petroleum Landmen
Type: Magazine; *Frequency:* 10 pa; *Accepts Advertising*; *Editor:* K. Rennie, M. Innes, & J. Frese; *Price:* Free with membership in the CanadianAssociation of Petroleum Landmen
Profile: Feature articles, CAPL conference information, & CAPL news & events

Canadian Association of Petroleum Producers (CAPP) / Association canadienne des producteurs pétroliers

#2100, 350 - 7 Ave. SW, Calgary AB T2P 3N9
Tel: 403-267-1100; *Fax:* 403-261-4622
Other Communication: membership@capp.ca
communication@capp.ca
www.capp.ca
www.linkedin.com/groupRegistration?gid=2632445
www.facebook.com/OilGasCanada
twitter.com/oilgascanada
www.youtube.com/cappvideos
Merged from: Canadian Petroleum Association; Independent Petroleum Association of Canada
Overview: A large national organization founded in 1992
Mission: To represent companies that produce Canada's natural gas & crude oil; To enhance the economic sustainability of the Canadian upstream petroleum industry; To ensure work is conducted in a safe & environmentally & socially responsible manner; To work with government to develop regulatory requirements
Chief Officer(s):
Tim McMillan, President
Janet Annesley, Vice-President, Communications
janet.annesley@capp.ca
Bob Bleaney, Vice-President, External Relations
bob.bleaney@capp.ca
David Pryce, Vice-President, Operations
pryce@capp.ca
Nick Schultz, Vice-President, Pipeline Regulation and General Counsel
schultz@capp.ca
Greg Stringham, Vice-President, Oil Sands & Markets
stringham@capp.ca
Membership: 100+ producer members + 150 associate members; *Member Profile:* Producer members range from two person operations to internationally recognized corporations employing thousands; Associate members provide services, such as drilling, baniking, & computing, for Canada's oil & gas industry; *Committees:* Industry Equalization Steering Committee
Activities: Reviewing, analyzing, & recommending industry policy positions; Participating in regulatory change dialogues; Representing the industry on multi-sector international, federal, & provincial consultation bodies; Communicating with governments, regulators, stakeholders, & the public; Offering seminars & workshops; Providing industry trends, statistics, & research information; Informing members of industry standards & guidelines; Monitoring pipeline expansions; Improving coordinated land use planning processes;
Awards:
• President's Award (Award)
Meetings/Conferences: • Canadian Association of Petroleum Producers (CAPP) Scotiabank Investment Symposium 2015, April, 2015, Sheraton Centre Hotel, Toronto, ON
Scope: National
Description: High-profile speakers on energy and industry discussion panels.
Contact Information: brenda.jones@capp.ca; Phone: 403-267-1174

Canadian Association of Pharmacy in Oncology (CAPhO) / L'Association canadienne de pharmacie en oncologie (ACPhO)

c/o Sea to Sky Meeting Management Inc., #206, 201 Bewicke Ave., Winnipeg MB V7M 3M7
Tel: 778-338-4142; *Fax:* 704-984-6434
info@capho.org
www.capho.ca
www.facebook.com/109491585819684
twitter.com/CAPhO_ACPhO
Overview: A small national organization
Mission: CAPhO, the national forum for oncology pharmacy practitioners & other health care professionals, promotes the practice of oncology pharmacy in Canada, by providing educational opportunites, upholding professional practice standards, & developing the profession as a specialty area of pharmacy practice.
Chief Officer(s):
Joan Fabbro, President
president@capho.org
Mark Pasetka, President-Elect
presidentelect@capho.org
Lori Emond, Treasurer
treasurer@capho.org
Membership: *Fees:* $50 pharmacy technician & pharamacy assistant; $75 pharmacist; $67.50 joint CAPhO/ISOPP; $50 supporting; $25 student; $2500 corporate; *Member Profile:* Members include oncology pharmacy practitioners & other health care professionals interested in oncology pharmacy.; *Committees:* Awards; Communications; Education; Membership; Conference Planning; Undergraduate Pharmacy Education Task Force
Activities: Facilitating communication; Fostering the development of pharmacy-based research; Promoting occupational health & safety issues
Awards:
• Long Time Service Award (Award)
• CAPhO Distinguished Service Award (Award)
Meetings/Conferences: • Canadian Association of Pharmacy in Oncology Conference 2015, May, 2015, Delta St. John's Hotel and Conference Centre, St. John's, NL
Scope: National
Publications:
• CAPhO [Canadian Association of Pharmacy in Oncology] Newsletter
Type: Newsletter; *Frequency:* 3 pa

Canadian Association of Pharmacy Students & Interns (CAPSI) / Association canadienne des étudiants et internes en pharmacie (ACEIP)

PO Box 68552, 360A Bloor St. West, Toronto ON M5S 1X0
www.capsi.ca
Overview: A medium-sized national organization founded in 1968
Mission: To prepare members for moral, social, ethical obligations to be upheld in the profession of pharmacy; to promote high standards of pharmacy education throughout Canada; to promote means by which members may enhance their professional knowledge & skills; to promote mutual interests & liaison with international pharmacy students, interns & society at large
Affliation(s): International Pharmacy Student Foundation; Canadian Pharmaceutical Association; Academy of Students; Canadian Society of Hospital Pharmacists
Chief Officer(s):
Amber-lee Carriere, President
Finances: *Annual Operating Budget:* Less than $50,000
Membership: 3,000+ student; *Member Profile:* Pharmacy student or intern; *Committees:* Finance; Objectives
Activities: *Internships:* Yes
Awards:
• Pharmaceutical Care Poster Competition (Award)
Teams of up to 3 students compete locally by preparing a pharmaceutical care case work-up in poster form *Amount:* $250 travel subsidy to PDW; membership to Canadian Society of Hospital Pharmacists
• Compounding Competition (Award)
Students compete locally by analysing & preparing pharmacy compound *Amount:* $250 travel subsidy to PDW
• Patient Interview Competition (Award)
Individual students compete locally by conducting a 15 minute patient interview *Amount:* $250 travel subsidy to PDW; USPDI V.1-2
• Literary Challenge (Award)
Individual students compete locally by composing articles relevant to Pharmacy *Amount:* $500 travel subsidy to PDW; recognition in the Canadian Pharmaceutical Journal
Publications:
• CAPSIL [Canadian Association of Pharmacy Students & Interns] / JACEIP
Type: Newsletter; *Frequency:* 3 pa; *Editor:* Roberta DeFazio
Profile: CAPSI national updates & information about current issues in pharmacy & letters & submissions from Canadian pharmacy students

Canadian Association of Pharmacy Technicians (CAPT)

#164, 9-6975 Meadowvale Town Centre Circle, Mississauga ON L5N 2V7
Tel: 416-410-1142
Other Communication: members@capt.ca
info@capt.ca
www.capt.ca
www.facebook.com/capt.ca
Overview: A medium-sized national organization founded in 1983
Mission: To act as the voice of pharmacy assistants
Member of: Canadian Council on Continuing Education in Pharmacy
Chief Officer(s):
Mary Bozoian, President
president@capt.ca
Colleen Norris, Vice-President
vp@capt.ca
Mona Sousa, Director, Membership
internal@capt.ca
Robert Solek, Director, Promotions & Public Relations
pr@capt.ca
Lois Battcock, Director, Administration
admin@capt.ca
Membership: *Fees:* $75; *Member Profile:* Pharmacy technicians, assistants, & aides throughout Canada
Activities: Increasing awareness of the value & role of pharmacy technicians; Providing information to members
Meetings/Conferences: • Canadian Association of Pharmacy Technicians Professional Development Conference 2015, May, 2015, Delta Halifax, Halifax, NS
Scope: National
Publications:
• The Mortar
Type: Journal; *Price:* Free with membership in the Canadian Association of Pharmacy Technicians
Profile: A continuing education resource
• Tech Talk
Type: Newsletter

Canadian Association of Photographers & Illustrators in Communications *See* Canadian Association of Professional Image Creators

Canadian Association of Physical Medicine & Rehabilitation (CAPM&R) / Association canadienne de médecine physique et de réadaptation

Ottawa ON
Tel: 613-707-0483; *Fax:* 613-707-0480
info@capmr.ca
www.capmr.ca
Overview: A medium-sized national organization
Mission: The CAPM&R represents and promotes the interests of the speciality of physiatry in Canada by providing and maintaining a national forum and network. It advances and increases awareness of the specialty through strategic alliances and partnerships, public policy, and professional and practice development.
Chief Officer(s):
Jeff Blackmer, MD, FRCPC, President
Roberta Sulpher, Executive Director
Staff Member(s): 1
Membership: 315; *Fees:* $350; *Member Profile:* Active members: Certified specialists in physical medicine and rehab; Associate Members: physicians from other speciality fields such as rheumatology, orthopedic surgery, and neurosciences, medical scientists with a PhD, Residents; medical student members; Corresponding members: physiatrists, other physicians, and medical scientists residing outside Canada.
Meetings/Conferences: • CAPM&R 63rd Annual Scientific Meeting, May, 2015, Sheraton Vancouver Wall Centre, Vancouver, BC
Scope: National

Canadian Association of Physicians for the Environment (CAPE)

#301, 130 Spadina Ave., Toronto ON M5V 2L4
Tel: 416-306-2273; *Fax:* 416-960-9392
info@cape.ca
www.cape.ca
twitter.com/CAPE_Doctors
Overview: A small national organization founded in 1994
Mission: To act as a national voice of physicians on issues surrounding health & the environment; To address issues of environmental degradation to protect & promote human health
Affliation(s): International Society of Doctors for the Environment (ISDE)
Chief Officer(s):
Kapil Khatter, President

John Howard, Chair
Finances: *Funding Sources:* Membership fees; Donations
Membership: *Fees:* $100 physicians; $50 non-physicians; $25 students/retirees/limited income persons; $50 member organizations; *Member Profile:* Physicians; Health care workers; Citizens across Canada
Activities: Providing educational opportunities; Liaising with other national & international organizations; Designing the online resource, Children's Environmental Health Project; Advocating for laws, standards, & policies to promote health & protect the environment
Publications:
• CAPE [Canadian Association of Physicians for the Environment] News
Type: Newsletter
Profile: Association news & information on the health implications of environmental issues

Canadian Association of Physicians of Indian Heritage (CAPIH)

115 Charingcross St., Brantford ON N3R 2H8
Tel: 519-304-1718; *Fax:* 519-304-4635
Toll-Free: 888-982-2744
info@capih.ca
www.capih.ca
www.facebook.com/groups/capih/
Overview: A medium-sized national organization founded in 2005
Mission: To arrange continuing medical educations meetings & seminars; to provide resources, services & expertise within Canada & in the Third World as needed
Affliation(s): American Association of Physicians of Indian Origin (AAPI)
Chief Officer(s):
Kempe S. Gowda, President
Joseph Kurian, CEO
Finances: *Annual Operating Budget:* Less than $50,000; *Funding Sources:* Membership dues
1 volunteer(s)
Membership: 600; *Fees:* $100 Affiliate, General; $50 Resident, associate; $25 student; $500 corporate; *Member Profile:* Physicians; residents; medical students; *Committees:* Education; Entertainment; Community Liaison
Activities: Continuing education seminars; networking; travel seminars

Canadian Association of Physicians with Disabilities

70 Hillsdale Ave. West, Toronto ON M5P 1G1
Tel: 416-485-9461; *Fax:* 416-485-9461
feedback@capd.ca
www.capd.ca
Overview: A small national organization
Mission: CAPD provides a national forum for physicians with disabilities, opening avenues for exchange of ideas & information, particularly as these apply to clinical practice. It aims to improve the quality of care & of life for people with disabilities by influencing clinical education & research in matters pertaining to both patients & physicians with disabilities. It also acts as a vehicle to inform & educate the public at large regarding the many facets of disabilities & to be proactive in influencing policies & laws.
Affliation(s): Canadian Medical Association
Chief Officer(s):
Ophelia Lynn MacDonald, Contact
Finances: *Annual Operating Budget:* Less than $50,000
Membership: 1-99; *Member Profile:* Physicians with disabilities & those interested in disabilities

Canadian Association of Physicists (CAP) / Association canadienne des physiciens et physiciennes (ACP)

MacDonald Bldg., #112, 150 Louis Pasteur Priv., Ottawa ON K1N 6N5
Tel: 613-562-5614; *Fax:* 613-562-5615
cap@uottawa.ca
www.cap.ca
Overview: A medium-sized national organization founded in 1945
Mission: CAP is a broadly-based national network of physicists working in Canadian educational, industrial, and research settings. They are a strong advocacy group for support of, and excellence in, physics research and education.
Member of: Canadian Consortium for Research & the Partnership Group for Science & Engineering.
Affliation(s): Chemical Institute of Canada; Canadian Organization of Medical Physicists; American Physical Society; Institute of Physics; Mexican Physical Society; Brazilian Physical Society
Chief Officer(s):
Gabor Kunstatter, President
g.kunstatter@uwinnipeg.ca
Francine M. Ford, Executive Director
cap@uottawa.ca
Finances: *Funding Sources:* Membership dues; Annual congress
Staff Member(s): 3
Membership: 14 corporate + 6 institutional + 54 departmental; *Fees:* $130; *Member Profile:* Degree in physics for full membership; other categories available; *Committees:* Science Policy; Editorial Board - Physics in Canada; Membership; Awards; Annual Congress Progam; Annual Congress - Local; Secondary School Physics Competition; Nominating; Membership Campaign; Corporate Members; Physics & Society; To Encourage Women in Physics; Honorary Advisory Council of Past Presidents; Teller Committee; Committee of University Physics Department Heads; Professionalism; Undergraduate Student Affairs
Awards:
• CAP Medal for Excellence in Teaching Undergraduate Physics (Award)
• CAP Medal for Outstanding Achievement in Industrial & Applied Physics (Award)
• Herzberg Medal (Award)
• CAP Medal for Achievement in Physics (Award)
• Newport Award in Optical Sciences (Award)
• Lumonics Award (Award)
• Lloyd G. Elliott Prize (University Prize Examination) (Award)
• Canada-Wide Science Fair Physics Prizes (Award)
• High School Prize Examination (Award)
• CAP/INO Medal for Outstanding Achievement in Applied Photonics (Award)
• CAP/COMP Peter Kirkby Medal for Outstanding Service to Canadian Physics (Award)
• CAP/CRM Prize in Theoretical & Mathematical Physics (Award)
Meetings/Conferences: • 2015 Canadian Association of Physicists Congress, 2015
Scope: National

Canadian Association of Police Educators (CAPE) / Association canadienne des intervenants en formation policière (ACIFP)

c/o Wayne Jacobsen, 1430 Victoria Ave. East, Brandon MB R7A 2A9
Tel: 204-725-8700
cape.educators@gmail.com
cape-educators.ca
www.facebook.com/593948850654424
Overview: A small national organization
Mission: To promote law enforcement training & education through the guidance of research, program development, knowledge transfer, network facilitation & collaborative training initiatives; to providve advice & input on national & regional law enforcement training & educations trends/needs; to promote a commitment to training
Chief Officer(s):
Catherine Wareham, Secretary
Catherine.Wareham@GeorgianCollege.ca
Wayne Jacobsen, President
jacobsew@assiniboine.net
Membership: *Member Profile:* Police educators
Meetings/Conferences: • 2015 Canadian Association of Police Educators Conference, 2015
Scope: National
Contact Information: Wayne Jacobsen; JacobseW@assiniboine.net
Publications:
• E-Journal
Type: Electronic journal

Canadian Association of Police Governance (CAPG) / Association canadienne des commissions de police

#302, 157 Gilmour St., Ottawa ON K2P 0N8
Tel: 613-235-2272; *Fax:* 613-235-2275
capg.ca
Overview: A medium-sized national organization founded in 1989
Mission: To express views & positions of municipal governing authorities; To provide means for collection & sharing of information & discussion of matters relating to policing services; To consider matters of national interest; To comment on social, economic, cultural, & legislative questions which may affect the quality, efficiency, & costs of policing services; To promote the quality & uniformity of policing services; To educate the public on matters relating to the governance of policing services; To act as a lobbying group to liaise between federal, provincial & municipal governmental authorities, & the federal & provincial solicitors general; To provide a forum for participation by civilian governors of municipal policing services & other agencies; To promote & encourage greater cooperation to serve the interest of the public; To advance criminal justice
Chief Officer(s):
Jennifer Malloy, Executive Director
jmalloy@capg.ca
Finances: *Funding Sources:* Membership dues; Conference
Membership: *Member Profile:* Canadian police governing bodies
Activities: *Library:* Canadian Association of Police Boards Library; by appointment
Meetings/Conferences: • Canadian Association of Police Governance Conference 2015, August, 2015
Scope: National

Canadian Association of Pregnancy Support Services

#304 - 4820 Gaetz Ave., Red Deer AB T4N 4A4
Tel: 403-347-2827; *Fax:* 403-343-2847
Toll-Free: 866-845-2151
www.capss.com
www.facebook.com/CanadianAssociationOfPregnancySupportServices?ref=str
twitter.com/CAPSS_RD
Overview: A small national organization
Mission: A Christian national ministry dedicated to providing support for life and sexual health by partnering with Pregnancy Centres across Canada.
Affliation(s): Evangelical Fellowship of Canada; Canadian Council of Christian Charities
Chief Officer(s):
Lola French, Executive Director, 403-347-2827
lola@capss.com
Meetings/Conferences: • 2015 Canadian Association of Pregnancy Support Services Conference, April, 2015, Coast Plaza Hotel, Vancouver, BC
Scope: National

Canadian Association of Principals (CAP) / Association canadienne des directeurs d'école

#220, 300 Earl Grey Dr., Kanata ON K2T 1C1
Tel: 613-839-0768; *Fax:* 613-622-0258
info@cdnprincipals.org
www.cdnprincipals.org
www.facebook.com/599842980034960
twitter.com/CdnPrincipals
Overview: A medium-sized national charitable organization founded in 1977
Mission: To represent the professional perspectives of principals & vice-principals at the national level & to provide the leadership necessary to ensure quality educational opportunities for Canadian students.
Chief Officer(s):
Jill Sooley-Perley, Executive Assistant
Jameel Aziz, President
jaziz@sd73.bc.ca
Finances: *Funding Sources:* Membership fees; projects; professional development.
Membership: *Fees:* $10; *Member Profile:* Principals & vice principals
Awards:
• CAP Student Leadership Award (Award)
• Distinguished School Principal Award (Award)
• Elementary Grade School Award (Award)

Canadian Association of Private Language Schools (CAPLS)

12880 - 54A Ave., Surrey BC V3X 3C9
Tel: 604-507-2577; *Fax:* 604-502-0373
info@capls.com
Overview: A medium-sized national organization

Canadian Association of Professional Academic Librarians (CAPAL)

e-mail: capalibrarians@gmail.com
capalibrarians.org
Overview: A medium-sized national charitable organization founded in 2013
Mission: CAPAL is a national membership association representing the interests of professional academic librarians in

relation to the areas of education, standards, professional practice, ethics, and core principles.
Membership: *Fees:* Regular: $49.18; Student: $20.88; *Committees:* Steering Committee, Advocacy, Communications & Publications, Diversity & Equity, Education & Training, Mentoring, Professional Development and Scholarship
Meetings/Conferences: • Canadian Association of Professional Academic Librarians 2015 Annual Conference, May, 2015, Ottawa, ON
Scope: National
• Canadian Association of Professional Academic Librarians 2016 Annual Conference, 2016
Scope: National

Canadian Association of Professional Apiculturists (CAPA) / Association Canadienne des Professionels de l'Apiculture (ACPA)

PO Box 373, Aylesford NS B0P 1C0
www.capabees.com
Also Known As: CAPABEES
Previous Name: Canadian Association of Apiculturists
Overview: A medium-sized local organization founded in 1959
Mission: To disseminate information on the management of bees
Chief Officer(s):
Rheal Lafreniere, President, Executive Commitee
Rheal.Lafreniere@gov.mb.ca
Membership: *Member Profile:* Persons who study, educate, & administrate in the fields of apiculture & pollination, such as federal & provincial apiculturalists, extension apiculturalists, teaching or research apiculturalists, apicultural technicians, & apiary inspectors; Associate members include graduate students involved in apicultural projects, technicians associated with apicultural personnel or apicultural projects, representatives of appropriate agriculture & agri-food branches & the Canadian Honey Council, plus members of the Apiary Inspectors of America & the American Association of Professional Apiculturists
Activities: Conducting research; Liaising with the Canadian Honey Council & other professional apiculturists; Co-administering the Canadian Bee Research Fund with the Canadian Honey Council
Awards:
• Student Merit Award (Award)
Eligibility: Canadian students or international students attending Canadian universities who have contributed to the development of apiculture *Amount:* $600
Publications:
• A Guide to Managing Bees for Crop Pollination
• Honey Bee Disease & Pests

Canadian Association of Professional Art Conservators *See* Canadian Association of Professional Conservators

Canadian Association of Professional Conservators (CAPC) / Association canadienne des restaurateurs professionnels (ACRP)

c/o Canadian Museums Association, #400, 280 Metcalfe St., Ottawa ON K2P 1R7
Fax: 613-233-5438
www.capc-acrp.ca
Previous Name: Canadian Association of Professional Art Conservators
Overview: A small national organization founded in 1971
Mission: To foster high standards within the conservation profession through accreditation; To facilitate public access to professional conservators
Affliation(s): Canadian Association for the Conservation of Cultural Property (CAC)
Chief Officer(s):
Dee Stubbs-Lee, President, 506-643-2341
Dee.Stubbs-Lee@nbm-mnb.ca
Heidi Sobol, Vice-President, 416-586-5583
heidis@rom.on.ca
Anita Henry, Treasurer
aehenry@sympatico.ca
Membership: *Member Profile:* Conservators; Conservation scientists
Activities: Maintaining standards of members established in the Code of Ethics & Guidance for Practice of the Canadian Association for the Conservation of Cultural Property & of the Canadian Association of Professional Conservators
Publications:
• CAPC [Canadian Association of Professional Conservators] Information for Collectors & Custodians
Type: Brochure
Profile: Available to CAPC members
• CAPC [Canadian Association of Professional Conservators] Membership Directory
Type: Directory
Profile: Membership list of accredited CAPC members
• Code of Ethics & Guidance for Practice of the Canadian Association for Conservation of Cultural Property & the CAPC
Profile: Published jointly by the Canadian Association for Conservation of Cultural Property & the Canadian Associationof Professional Conservators
• Selecting & Employing a Conservator in Canada
Profile: Published jointly by the Canadian Association for Conservation of Cultural Property & the Canadian Association of Professional Conservators
• What is Conservation?
Profile: Published jointly by the Canadian Association for Conservation of Cultural Property & the Canadian Association of Professional Conservators

Canadian Association of Professional Employees (CAPE) / Association canadienne des employés professionnels (ACEP)

World Exchange Plaza, 100 Queen St., 4th Fl., Ottawa ON K1P 1J9
Tel: 613-236-9181; *Fax:* 613-236-6017
Toll-Free: 800-265-9181
general@acep-cape.ca
www.acep-cape.ca
Previous Name: Economists', Sociologists' & Statisticians' Association
Merged from: Canadian Union of Professional & Technical Employees; Social Science Employees Association
Overview: A medium-sized national organization founded in 1915
Mission: To negotiate & monitor collective agreement for all federal government economists, sociologists & statisticians.
Affiliation(s): International Labour Organization
Chief Officer(s):
Claude Poirier, President, 613-236-9181
cpoirier@acep-cape.ca
Finances: *Annual Operating Budget:* $500,000-$1.5 Million; *Funding Sources:* Membership dues
Staff Member(s): 19
Membership: 5,000 institutional + 50 associate; *Fees:* $35/month; *Member Profile:* Federal government employees in the ES category & research officers at the Library of Parliament.; *Committees:* Collective Bargaining; Finance; Human Rights; Pensions

Canadian Association of Professional Image Creators (CAPIC) / Association canadienne de photographes et illustrateurs de publicité

#202, 720 Spadina Ave., Toronto ON M5S 2T9
Tel: 416-462-3677; *Fax:* 416-929-5256
Toll-Free: 888-252-2742
info@capic.org
www.capic.org
ca.linkedin.com/pub/capic-national-office-bureau-national/a/a76/713
www.facebook.com/pages/CAPIC/33315648062
twitter.com/followCAPIC
Previous Name: Canadian Association of Photographers & Illustrators in Communications
Overview: A small national organization founded in 1978
Mission: To safeguard & promote the rights of photographers, illustrators, & digital artists who work in the Canadian communications industry
Affliation(s): American Society of Media Photographers (ASMP)
Chief Officer(s):
Dean Casavechia, President
dean@deancasavechia.com
Membership: 1030+
Activities: Advocating for professional photographers, illustrators, & digital artists; Working for copyright protection; Maintaining industry standards; Offering educational programs;

Canadian Association of Professional Immigration Consultants (CAPIC) / Association Canadienne des Conseillers Professionnels en Immigration (ACCPI)

#602, 245 Fairview Mall Dr., Toronto ON M2J 4T1
Tel: 416-483-7044; *Fax:* 416-309-1985
info@capic.ca
www.capic.ca
www.facebook.com/group.php?gid=104799452895463
twitter.com/capicaccpi
Merged from: Association of Immigration Counsel of Canada; Organization of Professional Immigration Consultants
Overview: A small national organization founded in 2005
Mission: To represent Certified Canadian Immigration Consultants (CCIC), or full members of the Canadian Society of Immigration Consultants (CSIC)
Chief Officer(s):
Katarina Onuschak, Executive Director, 416-483-7044 Ext. 25, Fax: 416-483-0884
executive@capic.ca
Monica Poon, National Coordinator
admin@capic.ca
Christopher Daw, Director, Lobbying, 519-342-5342
lobbying@capic.ca
Lynn Gaudet, Director, Communications, 403-229-9256, Fax: 403-262-9169
communication@capic.ca
Deepak Kohli, Director, Membership, 416-877-5264
membership@capic.ca
Tanveer Sharief, Director, Education & Training, 403-975-7530
education@capic.ca
Finances: *Funding Sources:* Membership fees; Sponsorships
Membership: *Member Profile:* Professional immigration consultants in Canada; Students; *Committees:* Executive; Governance; Finance; Membership; Communication; Education & Training; Policy; Lobbying
Activities: Lobbying; Providing information & education; Communicating by social media; Offering opportunities to network with peers

Canadian Association of Professional Pet Dog Trainers (CAPPDT)

PO Box 85, 156097 Highway 10, Shelburne ON L0N 1S0
Toll-Free: 877-748-7829
info@cappdt.ca
www.cappdt.ca
Overview: A medium-sized national organization founded in 1994
Mission: To further the concept of dog-friendly & humane training techniques; to provide forum whereby professional pet dog trainers can be educated, exchange & generate ideas & network with other professionals
Chief Officer(s):
Pat Renshaw, Chair, 519-925-9542
chair@cappdt.ca
Membership: 500; *Member Profile:* Professionals who make living in the world of dog training; hobbyists who run classes; trainers who train dogs for CKC/AKC obedience competition; trainers who work with companion animals & their families
Publications:
• CAPPDT [Canadian Association of Professional Pet Dog Trainers] Forum
Type: Newsletter; *Frequency:* Quarterly; *Accepts Advertising*
Profile: Information about training, business, legislation, & rescue

Canadian Association of Professional Regulatory Affairs (CAPRA) / Association canadienne des professionnels en réglementation (ACPR)

$795, 2425 Matheson Blvd. East, Mississauga ON L4W 5K4
Tel: 905-615-6885
administrator@capra.ca
www.capra.ca
Overview: A small national organization founded in 1982
Mission: To provide a formal professional identity & recognition for regulatory affairs professionals in the pharmaceutical/healthcare field
Chief Officer(s):
Mary Speagle, Chair, 905-690-5775
Membership: 900; *Fees:* $49; *Member Profile:* Pharmaceutical regulatory affairs professionals; *Committees:* Executive; Finance; Executive Advisory; SOP and Policy; Election; Symposium; Education Day; Dinner Meeting; AGM; Annual Face-to-Face; Marketing; Publications; Student Relations; Website; Programming; Webinar; Volunteer Recognition

Canadian Association of Professional Speakers (CAPS)

#300, 1370 Don Mills Rd., Toronto ON M3B 3N7
Tel: 416-847-3355; *Fax:* 416-441-0591
Toll-Free: 877-847-3350
info@canadianspeakers.org

www.canadianspeakers.org
www.linkedin.com/groups?gid=105645
Overview: A small national organization
Mission: To help speakers succeed through partnerships, market development & accreditation.
Affliation(s): International Federation for Professional Speakers
Finances: *Funding Sources:* Membership dues
Membership: *Fees:* $495 regular; $250 GSF dual/retired; *Member Profile:* Humourists; sports celebrities; business strategists; health experts; personal growth coaches; economists; doctors; lawyers, etc.
Activities: 10 Chapters across Canada; *Rents Mailing List:* Yes

Canadian Association of Professionals with Disabilities
714 Warder Place, Victoria BC V9A 7H6
Tel: 250-361-9697
info@canadianprofessionals.org
www.canadianprofessionals.org
Overview: A medium-sized national organization founded in 2003
Mission: To address issues affecting professionals with disabilities
Finances: *Funding Sources:* Donations
Activities: Supporting self-advocacy; Sharing knowledge; Providing mentorship opportunities

Canadian Association of Programs in Public Administration (CAPPA)
c/o Johnson-Shoyama Graduate School of Public Policy, Univ. of Regina, 3737 Wascana Pkwy., Regina SK S4S 0A2
Tel: 306-585-5463; *Fax:* 306-585-5461
www.cappa.ca
Overview: A small national organization founded in 1975
Mission: To improve methods of teaching public administration
Affliation(s): Institute of Public Administration of Canada
Chief Officer(s):
Kathy Brock, President
Membership: *Fees:* $400 programs with graduate school; $250 institutional

Canadian Association of Prosthetics & Orthotics (CAPO) / Association canadienne en prothéses et orthéses
#217, 294 Portage Ave., Winnipeg MB R3C 0B9
Tel: 204-949-4970; *Fax:* 204-947-3627
capo@mts.net
www.pando.ca
www.youtube.com/user/PandOCanada
Previous Name: Canadian Association of Prosthetists & Orthotists
Overview: A medium-sized national organization founded in 1955
Mission: To promote the prosthetic/orthotic profession in Canada & abroad
Affliation(s): Canadian Board for Certification of Prosthetists & Orthotists
Chief Officer(s):
Leslie Pardoe, President
Finances: *Funding Sources:* Membership dues; conventions
Membership: *Fees:* $70 student; $105 associate/registered technician; $224 full; *Member Profile:* Prosthetic & orthotic practitioners
Meetings/Conferences: • Canadian Association of Prosthetics & Orthotics 2015 National Conference, 2015
Scope: National

Canadian Association of Prosthetists & Orthotists ***See*** Canadian Association of Prosthetics & Orthotics

Canadian Association of Provincial Cancer Agencies (CAPCA)
#300, 1 University Ave., Toronto ON M5J 2P1
Tel: 416-619-5744; *Fax:* 416-915-9224
info@capca.ca
www.capca.ca
Overview: A small national charitable organization founded in 1998
Mission: To support the reduction of the burden of cancer, through effective leadership & collaboration between the provincial cancer agencies
Chief Officer(s):
Eshwar Kumar, Chair
Brent Schacter, Chief Executive Officer, 204-787-2128, Fax: 204-786-0196
brent.schacter@cancercare.mb.ca
Staff Member(s): 3
Membership: 10; *Member Profile:* Provincial Cancer agencies; *Committees:* Systemic Therapy Safety Committee; Primary Care Policy Advisory Committee

Canadian Association of Provincial Court Judges (CAPCJ) / L'Association canadienne des juges de cours provinciales
c/o Judge Alan T. Tufts, Nova Scotia Provincial Court, 87 Cornwallis St., Kentville NS B4N 2E5
Tel: 902-679-6070; *Fax:* 902-679-6190
capcp@judges-juges.ca
www.judges-juges.ca
Overview: A medium-sized national organization founded in 1973
Mission: To ensure the soundness of provincial & territorial courts across Canada
Chief Officer(s):
Robert Prince, President, 902-742-0500, Fax: 902-742-0678
Russell J. Otter, Executive Director, 416-325-0861, Fax: 416-325-0987
Russell.Otter@jus.gov.on.ca
Robin Finlayson, Co-Chair, National Education Committee, 204-945-3912, Fax: 204-945-0552
Ronald LeBlanc, Co-Chair, National Education Committee, 506-547-2155, Fax: 506-547-7448
David Orr, Chair, Committee on the Law, 709-729-4246, Fax: 709-729-6272
Odette Perron, Co-Chair, Provincial Judges' Journal / Journal des juges provinciaux
operron@judex.qc.ca
Robert Prince, Chair, Communications Committee, 902-742-0500, Fax: 902-742-0678
Karen Ruddy, Chair, CAPCJ Newsletter Editorial Committee
Karen.ruddy@territorialcourt.yk.ca
David C. Walker, Co-Chair, Provincial Judges' Journal / Journal des juges provinciaux
dwalker@judicom.gc.ca
Finances: *Funding Sources:* Membership dues; Federal & provincial grants
Membership: 1,000-4,999; *Member Profile:* Provincial & territorial judges throughout Canada; *Committees:* Communications; Equality & Diversity; Conference; Journal; Webmaster; National Education; Atlantic Education; Prairies & Territories Education; National Judicial Institute Representative; New Judges Education Program; Compensation; Professional Responsibility & Judicial Independence; Law; History Project; Liaison with Judicial & Legal Organizations; Judicial Counselling; Electronic Newsletter; Access to Justice; Strategic Plan Review / C.A.P.C.J. Handbook
Activities: Monitoring the status of provincially-appointed judges; Engaging in advocacy activities; Participating in law reform; Providing education; Disseminating information;
Meetings/Conferences: • Canadian Association of Provincial Court Judges 2016 National Education Meeting, 2016, Vancouver, BC
Scope: National
Publications:
• Canadian Association of Provincial Court Judges Newsletter
Type: Newsletter; *Editor:* Chief Judge Karen Ruddy
Profile: Association news, events, membership information, & legal anecdotes
• C.A.P.C.J. Handbook
Type: Handbook; *Editor:* Judge Sheila Whelan
• Provincial Judges' Journal / Journal des juges provinciaux
Type: Journal; *Frequency:* Semiannually; *Editor:* Odette Perron; David C. Walker
Profile: Association reports plus articles

Canadian Association of Psychosocial Oncology (CAPO) / Association Canadienne d'oncologie psychosociale (ACOP)
#1, 189 Queen St. East, Toronto ON M5A 1S2
Tel: 416-968-0207; *Fax:* 416-968-6818
capo@funnel.ca
www.capo.ca
Overview: A small national charitable organization founded in 1986
Mission: To promote excellence in psychosocial oncology services
Chief Officer(s):
Thomas Hack, President
thack@sbrc.ca
Deborah McLeod, Vice-President
deborahl.mcleod@cdha.nshealth.ca
Marc Hamel, Secretary
marc.hamel@muhc.mcgill.ca
Steven Simpson, Treasurer
steve.simpson@calgaryhealthregion.ca
Anthony Laycock, Association Manager
Finances: *Funding Sources:* Membership fees; Donations; Sponsorships
Membership: *Fees:* $55 affiliate, student, & retired members; $75 full members; *Member Profile:* Clinicians, researchers, educators, & others committed to treating & studying th psychological, social, spiritual, & emotions aspects of cancer
Activities: Encouraging interdisciplinary excellence in psychosocial research, education, & clinical practice; Developing standards & practice guidelines; Offering educational programs; Advocating for access to psychosocial care & services; Providing a national network for the exchange of ideas
Meetings/Conferences: • Canadian Association of Psychosocial Oncology National Annual 2015 Conference, April, 2015, Montreal, QC
Scope: National
Contact Information: Association Manager: Anthony Laycock, E-mail: capo@funnel.ca
Publications:
• The Emotional Facts of Life with Cancer: A Guide to Counselling & Support for Patients, Families, & Friends
Type: Booklet; *Number of Pages:* 32; *Editor:* Beth Kapusta
Profile: Information about professional support to help people cope with cancer
• Oncology Exchange
Type: Journal; *Price:* Free with membership in the Canadian Association of Psychosocial Oncology
Profile: A Canadian interdisciplinary journal

Canadian Association of Public Health Dentistry (CAPHD) / Association canadienne de santé dentaire publique (ACSDP)
76 Proctor Blvd., Hamilton ON L8M 2M4
Tel: 613-954-3761
info@caphd.ca
www.caphd.ca
Previous Name: Canadian Society of Public Health Dentists
Overview: A small national organization
Mission: To advocate for dental public health in order to improve the oral health of Canadians; To promote oral health
Affliation(s): Canadian Dental Association
Chief Officer(s):
Gerry Uswak, President, 780-492-8240
Maureen Connors, Secretary-Treasurer, 250-314-6732
Finances: *Funding Sources:* Membership dues
Membership: *Fees:* $250 suport; $125 full; $35 retired/student; *Member Profile:* Dentists; University professors; Dental hygienists; Dental therapists; Dental assistants; Denturists; Public health administrators

Canadian Association of Radiation Oncologists ***See*** Canadian Association of Radiation Oncology

Canadian Association of Radiation Oncology (CARO) / Association canadienne de radio-oncologie (ACRO)
774 Echo Dr., Ottawa ON K1S 5N8
Tel: 613-260-4188; *Fax:* 613-730-1116
caro-acro@rcpsc.edu
www.caro-acro.ca
Previous Name: Canadian Association of Radiation Oncologists
Overview: A small national organization founded in 1986
Mission: To act as the voice of radiation oncology in Canada; To promote high standards of patient care, radiation oncology research, & education
Affliation(s): Royal College of Physicians & Surgeons of Canada; Canadian Medical Association; Canadian Association of Medical Radiation Technologists; Canadian Organization of Medical Physicists; Canadian Association of Nurses in Oncology
Chief Officer(s):
Matthew Parliament, President
John Kim, Secretary-Treasurer
Membership: 755; *Fees:* Free for fellows, residents, & retired persons; $50 associates; $363 regular members; $1,000 corporate members; *Member Profile:* Radiation oncologists in Canada; Radiation oncology fellows & residents; *Committees:* Annual Scientific Meeting; Education; Finance; History & Archives; Manpower & Standards of Care in Radiation Oncology; Membership; Nominating; Residents & Fellows; Website; Liaison
Meetings/Conferences: • Canadian Association of Radiation Oncology 2015 Annual Scientific Meeting, September, 2015, Delta Grand Okanagan, Kelowna, BC
Scope: National

Description: Lectures, presentations, & exhibits for health professionals involved in radiation oncology
• Canadian Association of Radiation Oncology 2016 Annual Scientific Meeting, September, 2016, Fairmont Banff Springs, Banff, AB
Scope: National
Description: Lectures, presentations, & exhibits for health professionals involved in radiation oncology
Publications:
• CARO [Canadian Association of Radiation Oncology] Code of Ethics
• Physician / Industry Relationships Guidelines
Profile: Guidelines established by the Canadian Association of Radiation Oncology to assist physicians
• Radiosurgery Scope of Practice in Canada

Canadian Association of Radiologists (CAR) / L'Association canadienne des radiologistes

#310, 377 Dalhousie St., Ottawa ON K1N 9N8
Tel: 613-860-3111; *Fax:* 613-860-3112
membership@car.ca
www.car.ca
Overview: A medium-sized national organization founded in 1937
Mission: Voluntary organization representing the goals & the interests of imaging specialists; to promote the clinical, educational, research & political goals of Canadian radiology to members, organized radiology, medical associations, government & the public
Affliation(s): Canadian Medical Association
Chief Officer(s):
Adele Fifield, CEO, 613-860-3111 Ext. 200
afifield@car.ca
Finances: *Annual Operating Budget:* $500,000-$1.5 Million; *Funding Sources:* Membership dues; corporate
Staff Member(s): 7; 40 volunteer(s)
Membership: 1,934; *Fees:* $495 full; $298 foreign; $179 fellows; *Member Profile:* Radiologists & residents-in-training; *Committees:* Interventional Radiology; Accreditation Programs; Nominations; Scientific Program; Standards for Radiologic Practice; CPD; Neuroradiology; Residents-in-Training; Training & Qualifications; Pediatrics; Teleradiology
Activities: *Rents Mailing List:* Yes
Awards:
• Gold Medal & Young Radiologist Award (Award)
Meetings/Conferences: • Canadian Association of Radiologists 78th Annual Scientific Meeting, May, 2015, Palais des congrès, Montréal, QC
Scope: National
Description: The theme of the event is Collaborative Care - Imaging and Treatment
Contact Information: URL: jointcongress.ca
Publications:
• Canadian Association of Radiologists Journal / Journal de l'Association canadienne de radiologiste
Type: Journal; *Frequency:* 5 pa; *Accepts Advertising*; *Editor:* Craig Coblentz, MD, FRCPC *ISSN:* 0846-5371
Profile: Scientific review of radiology in Canada

Canadian Association of Railway Suppliers / Association canadienne des fournisseurs de chemins de fer

#901, 99 Bank St., Ottawa ON K1P 6B9
Tel: 613-237-3888; *Fax:* 613-237-4888
info@railwaysuppliers.ca
www.railwaysuppliers.ca
Previous Name: Canadian Railway & Transit Manufacturers Association
Overview: A medium-sized national organization
Mission: To provide their members with more opportunities allowing their businesses to prosper
Chief Officer(s):
Gord Patterson, Interim Executive Director
Staff Member(s): 2
Membership: 400+ companies; *Fees:* Schedule available; *Member Profile:* Companies that supply products & services to Canadian railways

Canadian Association of Recycling Industries (CARI) / Association canadienne des industries du recyclage (ACIR)

#1, 682 Monarch Ave., Ajax ON L1S 4S2
Tel: 905-426-9313; *Fax:* 905-426-9314
www.cari-acir.org
Overview: A medium-sized national organization founded in 1941
Mission: To address issues facing the recycling industry in Canada & internationally; To promote commercial recycling activities
Chief Officer(s):
Bertrand Van Dorpe, President, 450-658-2183, Fax: 450-658-1461
rouvillestation@videotron.ca
Len Shaw, Executive Director
len@cari-acir.org
Donna Turner, Association Manager, 905-426-9313, Fax: 905-426-9314
donna@cari-acir.org
Tracy Shaw, Manager, Communications & Membership
tracy@cari-acir.org
Chris Cassell, Secretary-Treasurer, 613-283-5230, Fax: 613-283-9529
chirsc@glenviewiron.ca
Membership: 260+; *Member Profile:* Canadian companies in the recycling sector, from small scrap yards to large processing plants
Activities: Providing information on government legislation, environment & safety regulations, & new technology; Organizing networking events; Working to solve scrap metal theft; Developing cost cutting services for members; *Speaker Service:* Yes
Meetings/Conferences: • Canadian Association of Recycling Industries (CARI) 2015 18th Annual Consumer's Night, 2015
Scope: National
Contact Information: Association Manager: Donna Turner, Phone: 905-426-9313
Publications:
• Canadian Association of Recycling Industries Membership Directory
Type: Directory; *Frequency:* Annually
Profile: Listings of contact information for the recycling industry
• The Prompt [a publication of the Canadian Association of Recycling Industries]
Type: Newsletter; *Accepts Advertising*
Profile: Information about business opportunities & forthcoming events
• The Pulse [a publication of the Canadian Association of Recycling Industries]
Type: Newsletter; *Frequency:* Monthly; *Accepts Advertising*
Profile: Information for CARI members & industry leaders concerning recycling industry issues & opportunities, including market trends, governmentallegislation, & technology advancements

Canadian Association of Regulated Importers (CARI) / Association canadienne des importateurs règlementés

#206, 1545 Carling Ave., Ottawa ON K1Z 8P9
Tel: 613-738-1729; *Fax:* 613-733-9501
www.carlimport.org
Overview: A medium-sized national organization founded in 1986
Mission: To ensure the right & ability for importers to do business like other businesses & to create one voice for commodities on the import control list or otherwise controlled by regulations.
Finances: *Funding Sources:* Membership dues
Membership: 60+; *Member Profile:* Import permit holder - poultry, cheese, beef
Activities: *Speaker Service:* Yes

Canadian Association of Rehabilitation Professionals *See* Vocational Rehabilitation Association of Canada

Canadian Association of Rehabilitation Professionals Inc. *See* Vocational Rehabilitation Association of Canada

Canadian Association of Research Libraries (CARL) / Association des bibliothèques de recherche du Canada (ABRC)

Morisset Library, University of Ottawa, #239, 65 University St., Ottawa ON K1N 9A5
Tel: 613-562-5385; *Fax:* 613-562-5297
carladm@uottawa.ca
www.carl-abrc.ca
Overview: A medium-sized national charitable organization founded in 1976
Mission: To provide leadership to the Canadian research library community; To address issues affecting research libraries, such as federal research policy, copyright, open access publication, & preservation; To encourage broad access to scholarly information; To seek public policy encouraging of research
Chief Officer(s):
Ernie Ingles, President
ernie.ingles@ualberta.ca
Brent Roe, Executive Director, 613-562-5800 Ext. 3652
carl@uottawa.ca
Diego Argáez, Officer, Research, 613-562-5800 Ext. 2427
carlrpo@uottawa.ca
Katherine McColgan, Coordinator, Programs, 613-562-5800 Ext. 2768
Katherine.McColgan@uOttawa.ca
Membership: 32 libraries; *Member Profile:* Academic research libraries throughout Canada, as well as Library & Archives Canada, the Library of Parliament, & the Canada Institute for Scientific & Technical Information (CISTI); *Committees:* Public Policy Committee; Research Libraries Committee; Scholarly Communication Committee; Building Capacity Subcommittee; Creating & Advocating New Models & Approaches Subcommittee; Data Management Subcommittee; Demonstrating Value Subcommittee; Institutional Repositories Subcommittee; Print Preservation Working Group
Activities: Facilitating effective scholarly communication; Engaging in advocacy activities; Encouraging research partnerships
Awards:
• CARL Award for Distinguished Service to Research Librarianship (Award)
Awarded annually to an individual who has made a substantial local, national, or international contribution to research librarianship
• CARL Award of Merit (Award)
To honour a Canadian who has made an outstanding contribution to research librarianship
• CARL Research in Librarianship Grant (Grant)
Meetings/Conferences: • Canadian Association of Research Libraries 2015 Spring Meeting, May, 2015, Toronto, ON
Scope: National
Description: A spring meeting to set the future direction of the association & Canadian research libraries
Contact Information: Program & Administrative Officer: Katherine McColgan, Phone: 613-482-9344, ext. 102, E-mail: Katherine.McColgan@carl-abrc.ca
• Canadian Association of Research Libraries 2015 Fall Meeting, October, 2015, Ottawa, ON
Scope: National
Contact Information: Program & Administrative Officer: Katherine McColgan, Phone: 613-482-9344, ext. 102, E-mail: Katherine.McColgan@carl-abrc.ca
Publications:
• CARL [Canadian Association of Research Libraries] / ABRC E-Lert / Cyberavis Weekly News Bulletin
Type: Newsletter; *Frequency:* Weekly
Profile: Coverage of scholarly communication & journals, access to published government information, innovation, copyright, &research
• CARL [Canadian Association of Research Libraries] / ABRC [Association des bibliothèques de recherche du Canada] Statistics
Frequency: Annually; *Price:* $50
• CARL [Canadian Association of Research Libraries] Annual Report
Type: Yearbook; *Frequency:* Annually
• CARL [Canadian Association of Research Libraries] Members' Handbook / Manuel des Membres
Type: Handbook; *Number of Pages:* 49
Profile: By-laws, structures, procedures, awards, policies, & plans

Canadian Association of Retired Persons *See* CARP

Canadian Association of Retired Teachers (CART) / Association Canadienne des Enseignantes et des Enseignants Retraités (ACER)

c/o Canadian Teachers' Federation, 2490 Don Reid Dr., Ottawa ON K1H 1E1
Tel: 613-232-1505; *Fax:* 613-232-1886
info@acer-cart.org
www.acer-cart.org
Overview: A small national organization
Mission: To facilitate & promote liaison & mutual assistance among its member organizations; To promote the interests of its member organizations; To develop strategies for joint action on matters of common concern to member organizations; To

cooperate with other organizations on matters of common concern
Chief Officer(s):
Norbert Bourdeau, Executive Director
boudreaun@sympatico.ca
Activities: Promoting & supporting public education
Publications:
• Canadian Association of Retired Teachers Newsletter
Type: Newsletter

Canadian Association of Rhodes Scholars (CARS)
c/o Andrew Wilkinson, McCarthy Tétrault LLP, PO Box 10424, #1300, 777 Dunsmuir St., Vancouver BC V7Y 1K2
Tel: 604-643-7994; *Fax:* 604-643-7900
www.canadianrhodes.org
Overview: A medium-sized international organization
Mission: To further higher education; To assist in the administration of the Rhodes Scholarships in Canada; To represent members' views to the Warden & the Rhodes Trust
Chief Officer(s):
Niall O'Dea, President
niallodea@gmail.com
Mark Schaan, Vice-President
mschaan@sympatico.ca
John Rayner, Treasurer
jrayner@rogers.com
Andrew Wilkinson, National Secretary, Rhodes Scholarship Trust
Membership: *Fees:* $30; *Member Profile:* Rhodes Scholars who reside in Canada; *Committees:* Mentoring; Sailing Dinner
Activities: Promoting social interaction among Rhodes Scholars
Publications:
• Canadian Association of Rhodes Scholar Newsletter
Type: Newsletter; *Frequency:* 3 pa; *Editor:* John Fraser

Canadian Association of Road Safety Professionals (CARSP) / Association canadienne des professionnels de la sécurité routière (ACPSER)
St Catharines ON
e-mail: info@casp.ca
www.carsp.ca
ca.linkedin.com/pub/canadian-association-of-road-safety-professionals/
twitter.com/CARSPInfo
Overview: A small national organization
Mission: The association preserves & shares professional experience regarding road safety. It promotes research & professional development & facilitates communication & cooperation among road safety groups & agencies.
Chief Officer(s):
Brenda Suggett, Executive Administrator
Brian Jonah, President
Jennifer Kroeker-Hall, Vice-President
Membership: *Fees:* $65 regular; $10 student; Schedule for groups; *Member Profile:* Professionals involved in the research, management & delivery of road safety in Canada; *Committees:* Membership; Marketing
Activities: Disseminating traffic safety information; Acting as an influential voice for road safety professionals to communicate information to policy-makers
Publications:
• Canadian Traffic Safety Digest
Type: Newsletter; *Frequency:* Monthly
Profile: Compilation of traffic safety information from throughout Canada
• Proceedings of Canadian Multidisciplinary Road Safety Conferences
Profile: Proceedings of past conferences hosted by the Canadian Association of Road Safety Professionals
• The Safety Network / Réseau-sécurité
Type: Newsletter; *Frequency:* Quarterly
Profile: Articles, news, & research concerning road & motor vehicle safety for CARSP members

Canadian Association of SAS Users (CASU) / Association canadienne des utilisateurs SAS (ACUS)
280 King St. East, 5th Fl., Toronto ON M5A 1K7
Tel: 416-363-4424; *Fax:* 416-363-5399
twitter.com/SASCanada
Overview: A medium-sized national organization founded in 1991
Mission: To provide support to all Canadian SAS user groups; to assist them in the most efficient & effective use of the SAS system for information delivery; to provide updates on research & development of institute software & services.
Chief Officer(s):
Carl Farrell, Executive Vice President, SAS Americas

Canadian Association of School Administrators *See* Canadian Association of School System Administrators

Canadian Association of School Social Workers & Attendance Counsellors (CASSWAC)
c/o Rolling River School Div., PO Box 1170, Minnedosa MB R0J 0P0
Tel: 204-867-2754
www.casswac.ca
Overview: A medium-sized national organization founded in 1982
Chief Officer(s):
Rebecca Gray, President
rgray@rrsd.mb.ca
Finances: *Annual Operating Budget:* Less than $50,000; *Funding Sources:* Membership dues
8 volunteer(s)
Membership: 230; *Fees:* $35; *Member Profile:* Working in school system in non-teaching counselling role
Publications:
• CASSWAC [Canadian Association of School Social Workers & Attendance Counsellors] Newsletter
Type: Newsletter
Profile: News of current trends & issues

Canadian Association of School System Administrators (CASSA) / Association canadienne des administrateurs et des administratrices scolaires (ACAS)
1123 Glenashton Dr., Oakville ON L6H 5M1
Tel: 905-845-2345; *Fax:* 905-845-2044
www.cassa-acgcs.ca
twitter.com/CASSAACGCS
Previous Name: Canadian Association of School Administrators
Overview: A medium-sized national organization founded in 1975
Mission: To promote & enhance effective administration & leadership in provision of quality education in Canada; to provide a national voice on educational matters; to promote & provide opportunity for professional development to the membership; to promote communication & liaison with national & international organizations having an interest in education; to provide a variety of services to the membership; to recognize outstanding contributions to education in Canada
Affliation(s): College of Alberta School Superintendents; Manitoba Association of School Superintendents; Ontario Catholic Supervisory Officers' Association; Ontario Public Supervisory Officials' Association; Association of Administrators of English Schools of Québec; Association of Nova Scotia Educational Administrators; School Administrators of Prince Edward Island; Newfoundland & Labrador Association of Superintendents of Education; Association of Directors General of English School Boards of Québec; New Brunswick School Superintendents Association
Chief Officer(s):
Ken Bain, Executive Director
ken_bain@cassa-acgcs.ca
Finances: *Annual Operating Budget:* $50,000-$100,000; *Funding Sources:* Affiliate sponsorship
Staff Member(s): 1; 1 volunteer(s)
Membership: 1,200; *Fees:* Schedule available; *Member Profile:* Provincial & territorial associations or a designated segment whose members hold adminstrative & leadership responsibility for a school system, region, district, division, province or territory; associate - educational administrators for whom there is no provincial or territorial association; professors of educational administration; retired administrators who are not members of provincial organizations; graduate students of educational administration; accorded all rights & privileges except the right to hold office & vote; honorary life - without the privilege of holding office may be conferred on anyone who has given outstanding service in educational leadership; *Committees:* Executive
Activities: Two annual workshops
Meetings/Conferences: • Canadian Association of School System Administrators 2015 Annual Conference, July, 2015, Montréal, QC
Scope: National
Publications:
• Leaders & Learners
Type: Newsletter; *Editor:* Tara Lee Wittchen
Profile: CASA news & events, & articles

Canadian Association of Schools of Nursing (CASN) / Association canadienne des écoles de sciences infirmières (ACESI)
7, #450, 1145 Hunt Club Rd., Ottawa ON K1V 0Y3
Tel: 613-235-3150; *Fax:* 613-235-4476
inquire@casn.ca
www.casn.ca
twitter.com/CASN43
Previous Name: Canadian Association of University Schools of Nursing
Overview: A medium-sized national charitable organization founded in 1942 overseen by Association of Universities & Colleges of Canada
Mission: CASN/ACESI represents Canadian nursing programs. The association is the national voice for nursing education & nursing research.
Member of: Association of Accrediting Agencies of Canada (AAAC); Canadian Consortium for Research; Network for the Advancement of Health Services Research
Affliation(s): Association of Universities and Colleges of Canada (AUCC)
Chief Officer(s):
Cynthia Baker, Executive Director, 613-235-3150 Ext. 26
cbaker@casn.ca
Finances: *Annual Operating Budget:* $500,000-$1.5 Million; *Funding Sources:* Membership fees; services
Membership: *Member Profile:* Universities & colleges that offer all or part of an undergraduate or graduate degree in nursing; *Committees:* Accreditation Bureau; Standing Committee on Awards & Nominations; Standing Commitee on Information Management; Standing Committee on Education; Standing Committee on Research & Scholarship; Standing Committee on Strategic Planning
Awards:
• Award for Academic Administrative Excellence (Award)
Eligibility: Any member of a CASN member school (dean, director, head, chair, vice-dean, assistant dean, etc.) who is, or has been, responsible for the administration of the school, or faculty, the undergraduate program, the graduate program, or the research program during the last three academic years.
• Ethel Johns Award (Award)
Eligibility: Any present or former faculty member of CASN member school.
• Award for Excellence in Nursing Education (Award)
Eligibility: Any professor of a CASN member school may be nominated.
• Award for Excellence in Nursing Research (Award)
Eligibility: Any faculty member of a CASN member school may be nominated.
• Wendy McBride Award for Accreditation Reviewer Excellence (Award)
Eligibility: Any current CASN reviewer who has participated in an accreditation review in the last two years. The nominee can be any participating member of the on-site review team.
Meetings/Conferences: • Canadian Nursing Education Conference Anticipating and Shaping the Future of Nursing Education, 2015
Scope: National
Publications:
• Canadian Association of Schools of Nursing NewsUpdate
Type: Newsletter

Canadian Association of Science Centres (CASC) / L'Association canadienne des centres de sciences (ACCS)
PO Box 3443, Stn. D, Ottawa OM K1P 6P4
Tel: 613-566-4247
casc.accs@gmail.com
www.canadiansciencecentres.ca
Overview: A medium-sized national organization founded in 1985
Mission: Creates synergy among Canada's science centres and science-related museums, assists in finding solutions to the challenges faced by these public institutions, and provides a single voice before government.
Chief Officer(s):
Catherine Paisley, President
David Desjardins, Treasurer
Membership: *Fees:* Based on operating budget
Meetings/Conferences: • 2015 Canadian Association of Science Centres Annual Conference, May, 2015, Edmonton, AB
Scope: National
Description: Theme: "True North"

• 2016 Canadian Association of Science Centres Annual Conference, 2016, Vancouver Aquarium, Vancouver, BC
Scope: National
• 2017 Canadian Association of Science Centres Annual Conference, 2017, Ontario Science Centre, Toronto, ON
Scope: National

Canadian Association of Second Language Teachers (CASLT) / Association canadienne des professeurs de langues secondes (ACPLS)

2490 Don Reid Dr., Ottawa ON K1H 1E1
Tel: 613-727-0994; *Fax:* 613-727-3831
Toll-Free: 877-727-0994
admin@caslt.org
www.caslt.org
twitter.com/CASLT_ACPLS
www.youtube.com/user/caslcaslt
Overview: A medium-sized national organization founded in 1970
Mission: To promote & advance nationally learning of second languages; to encourage activities & research in field of second language
Member of: Canadian Association for Japanese Language Education; Canadian Association of Applied Linguistics; Canadian Teachers' Federation; Society for Educational Visits and Exchanges in Canada; Canadian Parents for French; Canadian Association of Immersion Teachers; French for the Future
Chief Officer(s):
Guy Leclair, Executive Director
guyleclair@caslt.org
Caroline Turnbull, President
carolineturnbull1@gmail.com
Finances: *Annual Operating Budget:* $250,000-$500,000; *Funding Sources:* Government; Membership dues
Staff Member(s): 4; 10 volunteer(s)
Membership: 4,500 individual; *Fees:* $0 Students; $15 Affiliates; $45 Regular; $250 Institutions; *Member Profile:* Interest in second language education; *Committees:* Nominating Committee; Awards; Performance Appraisal; Special Initiatives Fund; Membership & Provincial Association Partnerships; Communications & Marketing; Organization Capacity Building; Policy Review & Development; Board Advisory; Ad hoc (Technology; Anglais Langue Seconde; Common Framework & Portfolio for Student Teachers of Languages)
Activities: Professional development; educational publications; networking activities; research & resource development; *Speaker Service:* Yes
Awards:
• H.H. Stern Award (Award)
Amount: $500
• Prix Robert Roy Award (Award)
Eligibility: Must have been an active member of the CASLT for at least 2 years; must have distinguished his or herself in teaching, research, or writing to the improvement of second language teaching & learning in Canada
• Lifetime Membership Award (Award)
Meetings/Conferences: • Language Without Borders, March, 2015, Sheraton on the Falls & Crowne Plaza Niagara Falls - Fallsview, Niagara Falls, ON
Publications:
• CASLT [Canadian Association of Second Language Teachers] FSL Newsletter
Type: Newsletter; *Frequency:* Monthly; *Price:* Free
Profile: CASLT activities & events, teacher tips, suggested resources & web links, & new teaching & learning materials for teachers with an interest inFrench
• CASLT [Canadian Association of Second Language Teachers] ESL & Modern Languages Newsletter
Type: Newsletter; *Frequency:* Monthly; *Price:* Free
Profile: News about teaching & learning resources & Web links, in addition to CASLT events & activities for teachers of English, Spanish,German, Chinese, Japanese & other languages
• Réflexions [a publication of the Canadian Association of Second Language Teachers]
Type: Magazine; *Frequency:* 3 pa; *Number of Pages:* 24
Profile: Articles by researchers, resource reviews, conference information, Web links, & CASLT news & projects for CASLT members

Canadian Association of Sexual Assault Centres (CASAC) / Association canadienne des centres contre les agressions à caractère sexuel (ACCCACS)

77 East 20th Ave., Vancouver BC V5V 1L7
Tel: 604-876-2622; *Fax:* 604-876-8450
casac01@shaw.ca
www.casac.ca
Overview: A medium-sized national charitable organization founded in 1977
Mission: To work for an end to violence against women & toward women's equality; to provide a national voice for anti-rape workers.
Membership: *Member Profile:* Centres that work to prevent sexual assault & provide assistance to those who have been victims of sexual assault
Activities: *Speaker Service:* Yes

Canadian Association of Slavists (CAS) / Association canadienne des slavistes

Alumni Hall, Dept. of History & Classics, University of Alberta, #2, 28 Tory Bldg., Edmonton AB T6G 2H4
Tel: 780-492-2566; *Fax:* 780-492-9125
csp@ulberta.ca
www.ualberta.ca/~csp/cas/contact.html
Overview: A medium-sized national organization founded in 1954
Mission: To operate a learned society comprising scholars & professionals with interests in the social, economic, & political life of Slavic people, in addition to their languages, cultures, & histories; To promote understanding of Slavic societies & dialogue; To disseminate information about the past & present of the Slavic world
Member of: Canadian Federation for the Humanities & Social Sciences (CFHSS)
Affiliation(s): The Canadian Association for Ukrainian Studies (CAUS)
Chief Officer(s):
Megan Swift, President, 250-721-7504, Fax: 250-721-7319
maswift@uvic.ca
R. Carter Elwood, Honorary President
relwood@ccs.carleton.ca
Bohdan Nebesio, Sec.-Treas., 905-688-5550 Ext. 5211
bnebesio@brocku.ca
Elena Baraban, Vice-President
elena_baraban@umanitoba.ca
Reid Allan, Vice-President
russky@unb.ca
Bohdan Nebesio, Sec.-Treas., 905-688-5550 Ext. 5211
bnebesio@brocku.ca
Finances: *Funding Sources:* Membership fees; Grants; Gifts
Membership: 500-999; *Fees:* $70 Cdn; $45 Cdn emeritus; $90 Cdn joint; $35 student & underemployed; $600 life; foreign $70, $45 foreign emeritus; $95 foreign joint; *Member Profile:* Members include scholars engaged in teaching & research in the area of Central & East European Studies, including university, college, & secondary school teachers & librarians. Individuals interested in the aims of CAS may join as associate members.; *Committees:* Programme; Nominating; International Relations
Activities: *Rents Mailing List:* Yes
Awards:
• Canadian Association of Slavists Undergraduate & Graduate Student Essay Awards (Award)
Best undergraduate & graduate level essays*Deadline:* September
Meetings/Conferences: • Canadian Association of Slavists 2015 Annual Conference (in conjunction with the Canadian Federation for the Humanities & Social Sciences Congress), May, 2015, University of Ottawa, Ottawa, ON
Scope: National
Description: A yearly meeting with roundtable discussions, panels, & the presentation of papers by members of the Canadian Association of Slavists
• Canadian Association of Slavists 2016 Annual Conference (in conjunction with the Canadian Federation for the Humanities & Social Sciences Congress), 2016, University of Calgary, Calgary, AB
Scope: National
Description: A yearly meeting with roundtable discussions, panels, & the presentation of papers by members of the Canadian Association of Slavists
• Canadian Association of Slavists 2017 Annual Conference (in conjunction with the Canadian Federation for the Humanities & Social Sciences Congress), 2017, Ryerson University, Toronto, ON
Scope: National
Description: A yearly meeting with roundtable discussions, panels, & the presentation of papers by members of the Canadian Association of Slavists
Publications:
• Canadian Slavonic Papers / Revue Canadienne des Slavistes: An Interdisciplinary Journal Devoted to Central and Eastern Europe
Type: Journal; *Frequency:* Quarterly; *Editor:* Heather J. Coleman; Svitlana Krys; *Price:* Free with membership in the Canadian Association of Slavists
Profile: A forum for scholars fromdisciplines such as language & linguistics, literature, history, political science, sociology, economics, anthropology, geography, & the arts
• The CAS [Canadian Association of Slavists] Newsletter
Type: Newsletter *ISSN:* 0381-6133; *Price:* Free for members of the Canadian Association of Slavists
Profile: Information about the association's activities

Canadian Association of Small University Libraries (CASUL)

The University College of the Cariboo, PO Box 3010, Kamloops BC V2C 5N3
Tel: 250-828-5313; *Fax:* 250-828-5313
Overview: A medium-sized national organization
Mission: To promote effective library & information services in & among the member institutions; to promote the exchange of information about policies, problems, technology, etc. among the members; to support the investigation of such matters as financing, collections, services, personnel, technology or other common areas of concern; &, to publish reports through electronic or other means on such projects, for the use of members in gaining support for more effective services &/or other purposes of CASUL
Chief Officer(s):
Nancy Levesque, Library Director
levesque@cariboo.bc.ca
2 volunteer(s)
Membership: 51 institutional

Canadian Association of Snowboard Instructors (CASI) / Association canadienne des moniteurs de surf des neiges (ACMS)

60 Canning Cres., Cambridge ON N1T 1X2
Tel: 519-624-6593; *Fax:* 519-624-6594
Toll-Free: 877-976-2274
Other Communication: Toll free fax: 866-471-6594
headoffice@casi-acms.com
www.casi-acms.com
www.facebook.com/CASIACMS
twitter.com/casiacms
www.youtube.com/casiacms
Overview: A medium-sized national licensing organization founded in 1994
Mission: To promote the sport of snowboarding, snowboard instruction & coaching & the professions of snowboard teaching & coaching in Canada by training & certifying snowboard instructors & coaches; to ensure that a standard of safe & efficient snowboard instruction is maintained.
Member of: Canadian Ski Council
Affliation(s): Canadian Ski Instructors Alliance; Canadian Snowboard Federation
Chief Officer(s):
Dan Genge, Executive Director
dgenge@casi-acms.com
Membership: *Fees:* $91.33 regular; $48.36 associate; $26.34 student; $142.85 affiliate; *Committees:* Technical & Educational
Activities: Instructor & coaching certification courses; *Internships:* Yes; *Speaker Service:* Yes

Canadian Association of Social Workers (CASW) / Association canadienne des travailleurs sociaux (ACTS)

#402, 383 Parkdale Ave., Ottawa ON K1Y 4R4
Tel: 613-729-6668; *Fax:* 613-729-9608
casw@casw-acts.ca
www.casw-acts.ca
www.facebook.com/Canadian.Association.of.Social.Workers
Overview: A medium-sized national organization founded in 1926
Mission: To represent Canadian professional social workers; To strengthen & advances the social work profession in Canada; To preserve excellence within the profession
Affliation(s): International Federation of Social Workers
Chief Officer(s):
Fred Phelps, Executive Director
Staff Member(s): 4
Membership: *Fees:* $50 individual affiliate; $0 individual student; *Member Profile:* British Columbia Association of Social Workers; Alberta College of Social Workers; Saskatchewan

Association of Social Workers; Manitoba Association of Social Workers; Ontario Association of Social Workers; New Brunswick Association of Social Workers; Nova Scotia Association of Social Workers; Newfoundland & Labrador Association of Social Workers; Prince Edward Island Association of Social Workers; The Association of Social Workers of Northern Canada
Activities: Promoting social justice for Canadians; Producing position papers on topics such as poverty & women's income; *Library:* Canadian Association of Social Workers Library; by appointment
Publications:
• Canadian Association of Social Workers Code of Ethics & Guidelines for Ethical Practice
• Canadian Social Work
Type: Journal; *Frequency:* Annually
Profile: Current issues of interest to the Canadian social work community
• CASW [Canadian Association of Social Workers] Bulletin
Type: Newsletter; *Frequency:* Semiannually
Profile: Canadian Association of Social Workers initiatives & activities, plus activities within the International Federation of Social Workers
• CASW [Canadian Association of Social Workers] Reporter
Type: Newsletter; *Frequency:* Monthly
Profile: Events, opportunities, & initiatives of interest to social workers

Canadian Association of Specialized Kinesiology

PO Box 45071, Vancouver BC V6S 2M6
Tel: 604-669-8481
office@canask.org
www.canask.org
www.facebook.com/pages/CanASK/219459068073143?fref=ts
twitter.com/CanASK1
Also Known As: CanASK
Overview: A small national organization
Mission: To link association members to international affiliates; To support education of health care professionals & lay people
Affliation(s): International Kinesiology College; Touch for Health Kinesiology Association (USA); The Energy Kinesiology Association (USA)
Membership: *Fees:* $65 general members; $125 practitioners & instructors; $35 students
Activities: Providing resources
Publications:
• Canadian Association of Specialized Kinesiology Membership Directory
Type: Directory; *Frequency:* Annually
Profile: Listing of instructors, practitioners, general members, & student members
• Reaching Out [a publication of the Canadian Association of Specialized Kinesiology]
Type: Newsletter; *Frequency:* Quarterly
Profile: News & information about kinesiology subjects, proposed bylaws, book reviews, reports from kinesiologists, & articles from NorthAmerican conferences

Canadian Association of Speech-Language Pathologists & Audiologists ***See*** Speech-Language & Audiology Canada

Canadian Association of Sport Sciences ***See*** Canadian Society for Exercise Physiology

Canadian Association of Staff Physician Recruiters (CASPR)

e-mail: info@caspr.ca
caspr.ca
linkd.in/sFXJUG
on.fb.me/tgfzQp
twitter.com/CanadianASPR
www.youtube.com/channel/UClYSBbnwEz0hdBMkhSwobHQ
Overview: A medium-sized national organization
Mission: The Canadian Association of Staff Physician Recruiters (CASPR) is a professional organization from across Canada whose members primary role is to recruit physicians for their communities, local hospitals and other healthcare organizations.
Chief Officer(s):
Amanda English, Development & Operations Coordinator
Membership: *Committees:* Education; Sponsorship; Communication; Membership; Barriers to Physician Recruitment; Conference
Meetings/Conferences: • 2015 Canadian Association of Staff Physician Recruiters 11th Annual Conference, April, 2015, Niagara Falls, ON
Scope: National

Canadian Association of Statutory Human Rights Agencies (CASHRA) / Association canadienne des commissions et conseil des droits de la personne (ACCCDP)

#170, 99 - 5th Ave., Ottawa ON K1P 5P5
www.cashra.ca
Overview: A medium-sized national charitable organization founded in 1972
Mission: An umbrella organization for the federal, provincial and territorial human rights commissions.
Membership: 12 organizations
Meetings/Conferences: • Canadian Association of Statutory Human Rights Agencies (CASHRA) Annual Conference 2015, 2015
Scope: National
Description: A joint initiative with The Canadian Human Rights Commission

Canadian Association of Student Activity Advisors (CASAA)

c/o Bill Conconi, 2460 Tanner Rd., Victoria BC V8Z 5R1
Tel: 250-361-5886; *Fax:* 250-652-4179
bconconi@shaw.ca
www.casaaleadership.ca
Overview: A medium-sized national organization founded in 1985
Mission: To promote & develop student leadership & activities in Canadian high schools
Chief Officer(s):
Brent Allen, President
allen01@telusplanet.net
Bill Conconi, Executive Director
Moira Pollock, Admin. Coordinator, 250-885-8796
moira.pollock@gmail.com
Finances: *Funding Sources:* Sponsorships; membership dues; resource sales
Staff Member(s): 1; 22 volunteer(s)
Membership: *Fees:* $90 Canadian; $100 international; *Member Profile:* Junior & senior high school student advisors
Activities: Sharing ideas pertaining to student activities
Publications:
• Above & Beyond [a publication of the Canadian Association of Student Activity Advisors]
Type: Newsletter; *Frequency:* 3 pa; *Price:* Free to more than 3,200 Canadian schools
Profile: Assistance, ideas, & resources for advisors
• CASAA [Canadian Association of Student Activity Advisors] e-Letter
Type: Newsletter; *Frequency:* Monthly; *Price:* Free to CASAA members
Profile: Information & resources

Canadian Association of Student Financial Aid Administrators (CASFAA)

c/o Treasurer, University of Manitoba, 422 University Centre, Winnipeg MB R3T 2N2
Tel: 204-474-9532
info@casfaa.ca
www.casfaa.ca
Overview: A medium-sized national organization founded in 1979
Mission: Represents financial aid administrators & awards officers in universities & colleges across Canada
Chief Officer(s):
John Boylan, President
john.boylan@ubc.ca
Jane Lastra, Treasurer
jane.lastra@umanitoba.ca
Membership: 100-499; *Fees:* $200 full/associate/affiliate; $25 student; $1,000 corporate
Meetings/Conferences: • Canadian Association of Student Financial Aid Administrators 2015 Annual Conference, June, 2015, Université Laval, Québec, QC
Scope: National
Contact Information: URL: www.casfaa2015.ulaval.ca

Canadian Association of Swine Veterinarians (CASV) / Association Canadienne des Vétérinaires Porcins (ACVP)

Tel: 519-273-7170
www.casv-acvp.ca
Overview: A small national organization founded in 2003
Mission: To support members; To discuss issues affecting members; To offer a nation voice on issues that affect pork production; To enhance knowledge of animal welfare, herd health management, & food safety
Chief Officer(s):
John Harding, Chair, 306-966-7070
john.harding@usask.ca
George Charbonneau, President, 519-273-7170
gcharbon@swineservices.ca
Membership: *Member Profile:* Canadian veterinarians who have a special interest in swine; Persons in industry, academia, & government
Activities: Facilitating networking opportunities; Encouraging professional development; Promoting communications among organizations with similar interests

Canadian Association of Teachers of Technical Writing (CATTW)/L'Association canadienne de professeurs de rédaction technique et scientifique (ACP ***See*** Canadian Association for the Study of Discourse & Writing

Canadian Association of the Deaf (CAD) / Association des sourds du Canada (ASC)

#303, 251 Bank St., Ottawa ON K2P 1X3
Tel: 613-565-2882; *Fax:* 613-565-1207; *TTY:* 613-565-8882
info@cad.ca
www.cad.ca
Overview: A medium-sized national charitable organization founded in 1940
Mission: To protect & promote the rights, needs, & concerns of deaf Canadians
Affiliation(s): World Federation of the Deaf; Council of Canadians with Disabilities
Chief Officer(s):
Frank Folino, President
Marie-Josée Blier, Secretary
Finances: *Funding Sources:* Government funding; Fundraising; Membership fees; Grants
Staff Member(s): 5
Membership: 300,000; *Fees:* Schedule available; *Member Profile:* Affiliated organizations at the non-national level
Activities: *Speaker Service:* Yes; *Rents Mailing List:* Yes

Canadian Association of Thoracic Surgeons (CATS) / Association canadienne des chirurgiens thoraciques

#300, 421 Gilmour St., Ottawa ON K2P 0R5
e-mail: cats@canadianthoracicsurgeons.ca
www.canadianthoracicsurgeons.ca
Overview: A medium-sized national organization
Mission: To represent thoracic surgeons across Canada
Chief Officer(s):
Richard I. Inculet, President
Sean C. Grondin, Secretary-Treasurer & Chair, Programs
Membership: *Fees:* No charge for residents; $130 full members; *Member Profile:* A medical graduate of a Canadian medical school (or equivalent), who has received full-time training in a thoracic surgery training program, accredited by the Royal College of Physicians & Surgeons of Canada; Physicians with postgraduate training in thoracic surgery engaged in a practice related to thoracic surgery; Residents in a field related to thoracic surgery; Persons who have retired from the active practice of thoracic surgery or other related professional activity; Organizations with interests compatible with the interests of the association; Physicians or scientists outside Canada; *Committees:* Executive; Research; Continuing Professional Development; Bylaws; Standards of Practice; Communication / Web
Activities: Conducting clinical & laboratory research; Participating in health care planning, such as standards of practice
Meetings/Conferences: • 18th Canadian Association of Thoracic Surgeons Annual Meeting, September, 2015, Québec, QC
Scope: National

Canadian Association of Token Collectors (CATC)

PO Box 22022, Stn. Elmwood Square, St Thomas ON N5R 6A1
www.nunetcan.net/catc/catc.htm
Overview: A small national organization founded in 1972
Mission: To provide information on token collecting, from early colonial to modern trade dollars
Affliation(s): Ontario Numismatic Association (ONA); Canadian Numismatic Association (CNA)
Chief Officer(s):
Harry N. James, President
harrynj@sympatico.ca
Membership: *Fees:* $20
Publications:
• Numismatica Canada
Type: Newsletter; *Frequency:* Quarterly

Profile: Detailed information about token collecting throughout history for CATC members

Canadian Association of Tour Operators (CATO)
#1011, 7B Pleasant Blvd., Toronto ON M4T 1K2
Tel: 416-485-8232; *Fax:* 416-485-0112
info@cato.ca
www.cato.ca
Overview: A medium-sized national organization founded in 1983
Mission: To act as a voice on behalf of tour operators in dealing with government at all levels in Canada & abroad; To maintain a high standard of ethical practice in the business of tour operators; To promote public confidence & awareness of the business of tour operators
Affliation(s): Association des Tours Opérateurs du Québec (ATOQ)
Chief Officer(s):
Pierre LePage, Executive Director
Membership: *Member Profile:* Professional outbound tour companies operating in Canada
Activities: Providing market research & industry surveys; Offering crisis management & public relations; Providing networking opportunities; Increasing knowledge & skills of members; Promoting cooperation between tour operators & suppliers;

Canadian Association of Toy Libraries *See* Canadian Association of Family Resource Programs

Canadian Association of Transplantation
774 Echo Dr., Ottawa ON K1S 5N8
Toll-Free: 800-263-2833
cst@rcpsc.edu
www.transplant.ca
Overview: A medium-sized national organization
Mission: Health professionals committed to facilitating & enhancing the transplant process
Chief Officer(s):
Jan Emerton, President
Activities: *Awareness Events:* National Organ & Tissue Donation Awareness Week, April

Canadian Association of University & College Teachers of French *Voir* Association des professeurs de français des universités et collèges canadiens

Canadian Association of University Business Officers (CAUBO) / Association canadienne du personnel administratif universitaire (ACPAU)
#320, 350 Albert St., Ottawa ON K1R 1B1
Tel: 613-230-6760; *Fax:* 613-563-7739
info@caubo.ca
www.caubo.ca
Overview: A medium-sized national charitable organization founded in 1937 overseen by Association of Universities & Colleges of Canada
Mission: To promote the professional & effective management of the administrative, financial & business affairs of higher education; to have the professional standards of its members & to strengthen the contribution of higher education to the well being of Canada
Chief Officer(s):
Nathalie Laporte, Executive Director, 613-230-6760 Ext. 268
nlaporte@caubo.ca
Finances: *Annual Operating Budget:* $1.5 Million-$3 Million; *Funding Sources:* Membership fees; training & development fees; non-due revenue
Staff Member(s): 11; 198 volunteer(s)
Membership: 143 Post secondary institutions; 60 corporate; 15 associate; *Fees:* Schedule available; *Member Profile:* Member of AUCC or federated or affiliated with member of AUCC; *Committees:* Board of Directors; Executive Committee; Academic Managers; Facilities Management; Finance; Human Resources; Internal Auditors; Procurement; Risk Management; Taxes; Treasury and Investment
Activities: Workshops; online courses; outreach programs
Awards:
• Ken Clements Award (Award)
Recognizes a university administrator who has made outstanding contributions to the activities of the organization
• CAUBO Quality & Productivity Awards (Award)
Designed to recognize, reward & share university achievements in improving the quality & reducing the cost of higher education programs & services; National & Regional categories*Eligibility:* Awards evaluated on partability, originality, quality impact, productivity impact, & involvement *Amount:* National: first prize $10,000; second prize $5,000; third prize $3,000
Meetings/Conferences: • Canadian Association of University Business Officers 2015 Annual Conference, June, 2015, University of New Brunswick, Saint John, NB
Scope: National
• Canadian Association of University Business Officers 2016 Annual Conference, June, 2016, Université du Québec, Québec, QC
Scope: National
• Canadian Association of University Business Officers 2017 Annual Conference, June, 2017, Carleton University, Ottawa, ON
Scope: National
Publications:
• Debt Management Guide
Profile: A guide for CAUBO members
• Financial Information of Universities & Colleges
Frequency: Annually
Profile: Prepared by Statistics Canada for the Canadian Association of University Business Officers
• Financial Reporting Guide
Profile: Accounting principles & standards of disclosure used in Canadian univeristy published financial statements
• A Guide for Faculty Collective Bargaining: Issues, Strategies, Communication
Profile: Assistance to university administrators in managing critical events on campus
• Investment Survey
Profile: A compilation of the Canadian Universities' Investment Survey results published by the CAUBO Treasury & Investment Committee
• A Point of No Return: The Urgent Need for Infrastructure Renewal at Canadian Universities
Profile: Survey to measure the accumulated deferred maintenance on Canadian university campuses
• University Manager
Type: Magazine; *Frequency:* Quarterly; *Accepts Advertising*; *Editor:* Craig Kelman
Profile: Promotes the effective management of administrative, financial & business affairs at universities & colleges

Canadian Association of University Research Administrators (CAURA) / Association canadienne d'administrateurs de recherche universitaire (ACARU)
c/o JPDL Quebec, 189 St. Paul Rd., Québec QC G1K 3W2
Tel: 418-692-6636; *Fax:* 418-692-5587
caura-acaru@jpdl.com
www.caura-acaru.ca
Overview: A small national organization founded in 1971 overseen by Association of Universities & Colleges of Canada
Mission: To improve the profession at educational institutions, hospitals & research facilties; to provide a forum for discussion & exchange of information on current issues & policies.
Member of: Association of Universities & Colleges of Canada; Canadian Consortium for Research
Affliation(s): National Council of University Research Administrators; Society of Research Administrators; Association of University Technology Managers; Canadian Association of University Business Officers; Canadian Association of Research Ethics Boards; Research Administrators' Group Network
Chief Officer(s):
Sarah Lampson, Executive Director, 289-442-2992
executive_director@caura-acaru.ca
Finances: *Funding Sources:* Membership fees; conference income.
Membership: *Fees:* $113; *Member Profile:* Direct or indirect involvement with university research administration
Activities: New administrators workshops; other workshops & seminars; listserve
Meetings/Conferences: • Canadian Association of University Research Administrators 2015 Annual General Meeting, May, 2015, Fairmont Royal York Hotel, Toronto, ON
Scope: National

Canadian Association of University Schools of Music *See* Canadian University Music Society

Canadian Association of University Schools of Nursing *See* Canadian Association of Schools of Nursing

Canadian Association of University Teachers (CAUT) / Association canadienne des professeures et professeurs d'université (ACPPU)
2705 Queensview Dr., Ottawa ON K2B 8K2
Tel: 613-820-2270; *Fax:* 613-820-7244
acppu@caut.ca
www.caut.ca
www.linkedin.com/company/canadian-association-of-university-teachers
www.facebook.com/CAUT.ACPPU
twitter.com/CAUT_ACPPU
Overview: A large national organization founded in 1951
Mission: To act as the national voice for academic staff; To promote academic freedom; To improve the quality & accessibility of post-secondary education in Canada
Affliation(s): Association of Canadian Community Colleges; Association of Universities & Colleges of Canada; Canadian Association for Graduate Studies; Canadian Association of University Business Officers; Canadian Education Association; Canadian Federation for the Humanities and Social Sciences & other discipline-based associations; Canadian Federation of Students; Education International; Network for Education & Academic Rights; Coalition of Contingent Academic Labour
Chief Officer(s):
James Turk, Executive Director
turk@caut.ca
David Robinson, Associate Executive Director
robinson@caut.ca
David Robinson, Associate Executive Director, Research & Advocacy
robinson@caut.ca
Peter Simpson, Assistant Executive Director, Collective Bargaining & Services
simpson@caut.ca
Finances: *Annual Operating Budget:* Greater than $5 Million; *Funding Sources:* Membership fees
Staff Member(s): 35; 250 volunteer(s)
Membership: 68,000 individuals; 120 universities/colleges; *Member Profile:* Canadian university teachers, librarians, researchers, & other academic professionals; General & contract academic staff; Retired academic staff; Graduate students; *Committees:* Academic Freedom & Tenure; Collective Bargaining & Economic Benefits; Contract Academic Staff; Equity & Diversity; Librarians & Archivists
Activities: Offering courses & workshops; Conducting research about post-secondary education in Canada; Engaging in advocacy activities; Advising member associations in dealing with health & safety issues; *Awareness Events:* Fair Employment Week, October
Awards:
• Milner Memorial Award (Award)
To recognize a distinguished contribution to the cause of academic freedom
• Sarah Shorten Award (Award)
To recognize outstanding achievements in the promotion of the advancement of women in Canadian universities
• Academic Librarians' Distinguished Service Award (Award)
To recognize outstanding service by academic librarians or faculty who have contributed to the advancement of the status &/or working conditions of academic librarians at Canadian universities
• Donald C. Savage Award (Award)
To honour & to recognize outstanding achievements in the promotion of collective bargaining in Canadian universities
• J.H. Stewart Reid Memorial Fellowship Trust (Scholarship)
Awarded annually to a student registered in a doctoral program at a Canadian university. Eligibility: PhD students*Deadline:* April 30 *Amount:* $5000
• Excellence in Education Journalism (Award)
To recognize and promote in-depth and thoughtful coverage of issues related to post-secondary education in Canada.
• Equity Award (Award)
To recognize post-secondary academic staff who have demonstrated an outstanding commitment to challenging exclusionary behaviours and practices such as racism and homophobia and by so doing have made post-secondary education in Canada more inclusive.
Meetings/Conferences: • Canadian Association of University Teachers 2015 9th Annual Forum for Presidents, January, 2015, Ottawa, ON
Scope: National
Description: Information for academic staff association presidents
• Canadian Association of University Teachers 2015 Annual Forum for Chief Negotiators, March, 2015, Ottawa, ON
Scope: National
Description: An examination of collective bargaining challenges & strategies

• Canadian Association of University Teachers 2015 Annual Workshop for New Presidents, May, 2015, Ottawa, ON
Scope: National
Description: An examination fo the role of faculty association presidents
• Canadian Association of University Teachers 2015 Annual Forum for Aboriginal Academic Staff, November, 2015, Winnipeg, MB
Scope: National
• Canadian Association of University Teachers 2015 Workshop for Senior Grievance Officers, December, 2015, Ottawa, ON
Scope: National
Publications:
• CAUT [Canadian Association of University Teachers] / ACPPU Bulletin
Frequency: 10pa; *Accepts Advertising*; *Editor:* Liza Duhaime; *Price:* $25 Canada; $35 USA; $65 International
Profile: For CAUT members, politicians, reporters, & those interested in post-secondary education
• CAUT [Canadian Association of University Teachers] Almanac of Post-Secondary Education
Frequency: Annually
Profile: Statistical information about universities & colleges for students, academic staff, journalists, & the public
• CAUT [Canadian Association of University Teachers] Education Review
Profile: Policy concerns related to post-secondary education
• CAUT [Canadian Association of University Teachers] Legal Review
Profile: Published several times yearly to address issues important to post-secondary academic staff
• CAUT [Canadian Association of University Teachers] Newswire
Type: Newsletter; *Frequency:* Monthly
Profile: Information for member association communications officers & newsletter editors
• CAUT [Canadian Association of University Teachers] Facts & Figures
Profile: Details of post-secondary sector settlements relevant to negotiators & local associations
• CAUT [Canadian Association of University Teachers] Bargaining Advisories
Profile: Collective bargaining advice
• CAUT [Canadian Association of University Teachers] Bargaining Manual
• CAUT [Canadian Association of University Teachers] Handbook for New Faculty
• CAUT [Canadian Association of University Teachers] Tax Guide
Profile: Federal tax information guide for academic staff
• Directory of University & College / Corporate Board Linkages
Type: Directory; *Frequency:* Annually
Profile: Corporate connections of university & college board members
• Equity Review [a publication of Canadian Association of University Teachers]
• Making News: A CAUT [Canadian Association of University Teachers] Guide to Media Relations
Profile: Advice for effective media strategies

Canadian Association of University Teachers of German (CAUTG) / L'Association des professeurs d'allemand des universités canadiennes (APAUC)

c/o Stephan Jaeger, Dept. of German & Slavic Studies, University of MB, #326, Fletcher Argue Building, Winnipeg MB R3T 5V5
www.cautg.org
Overview: A small national organization founded in 1961
Mission: To promote studies & research in Germanic Studies at the post-secondary level
Member of: Canadian Association of Teachers of German (CATG); Canadian Federation of the Humanities & Social Sciences
Affliation(s): Deutscher Akademischer Austauschdienst (DAAD); Goethe Institute
Chief Officer(s):
Michael Boehringer, President
mboehrin@uwaterloo.ca
Gaby Pailer, Vice-President
pailer@mail.ubc.ca
Diana Spokiene, Secretary-Treasurer
spokiene@yorku.ca
Activities: Sponsoring & organizing programs for scholars; Coordinating a summer job program for Canadian students in Germany; Sponsoring a language program abroad; Participating in an exchange of teaching assistants
Publications:
• CAUTG [Canadian Association of University Teachers of German] / APAUC Bulletin
Type: Newsletter; *Frequency:* Semiannually; *Editor:* Charlotte Schallié *ISSN:* 1193-817X
• CAUTG [Canadian Association of University Teachers of German] / APAU Directory
Type: Directory; *Frequency:* Annually; *Editor:* Charlotte Schallié
Profile: A directory of departments of German at Canadian universities & colleges
• Seminar: A Journal of Germanic Studies
Type: Journal; *Frequency:* Quarterly; *Editor:* Karin Bauer; Andrew Piper *ISSN:* 0037-1939
Profile: A scholarly publication about Germanic literature, media, & culture

Canadian Association of Veterans in United Nations Peacekeeping (CAVUNP) / Association Canadienne des Vétérans des Forces de la Paix pour les Nations Unies

PO Box PO Box 46026, RPO Beacon Hill, 2339 Ogilvie Rd., Gloucester ON K1J 9M7
Tel: 613-746-3302
cavunp@rogers.com
www.cavunp.org
Overview: A small national organization founded in 1986
Mission: To perpetuate the memories of fallen comrades; to provide assistance to serving & retired Canadian peacekeepers & their families; to provide education about peacekeeping & peacekeepers
Member of: Veterans Affairs Canada Advisory Committee on the New Veterans Charter; Veterans Affairs Canada Veterans Week Advisory Committee; Veterans Affairs Canada Pacific Region Advisory Council; The Joint Veterans Affairs & National Defence Centre for the Care of Injured and Retired Members of the CF
Chief Officer(s):
Ronald R. Griffis, National President, 902-538-3399
J. Robert O'Brien, Chair
gunkeob@yahoo.com
Paul Greensides, National Secretary-Treasurer
cavunp@rogers.com
Membership: *Member Profile:* Retired & serving Canadian military (Regular & Reserve), Royal Canadian Mounted Police, & civilian personnel who have served on United Nations Peacekeeping Missions
Activities: Cooperating with other veterans' organizations; Donating literature on Canada's participation in the United Nations Peacekeeping Forces to schools & public libraries; *Awareness Events:* Canadian Peacekeeping Day, Aug. 9; International Day of United Nations Peacekeepers, May 29
Publications:
• The Thin Blue Line / Sur la corde raide en bleu
Type: Newsletter; *Editor:* John Stuart
Profile: Association news & activities from chapters across the country

Buffalo 461 Chapter (Hamilton)
c/o Chapter President, 28 Goldwin St., Hamilton ON L9G 6V9
Tel: 905-385-8045
Chief Officer(s):
Douglas Furchner, President
retiredppcli@yahoo.ca
Paul A. Hale, Contact, Chapter Membership, 905-794-2109
cavunpbuffalo461@hotmail.com

Calgary Chapter
c/o Chapter President, 39 Cedardale Hill SW, Calgary AB T2W 5A6
Tel: 403-251-0056
www.cavunp.ab.ca
Chief Officer(s):
Robert F.M. Titus, President
rfmtitus@shaw.ca
Barry T. Wood, Contact, Chapter Membership, 403-254-2882
bwood.un@shaw.ca

Camp Maple Leaf Chapter
c/o Chapter President, 412 Court St. North, Thunder Bay ON P7A 4X1
Tel: 807-475-0803
Chief Officer(s):
Robert L. Manns, President, 807-475-0803
Sydney Bouchard, Contact, Chapter Membership, 807-475-4475

Central Ontario Chapter
c/o Chapter President, 69 Brown Wood Drive, Barrie ON L4M 6M6
Tel: 705-727-1746
Chief Officer(s):
Fernand O. Taillefer, President
taillefer1746@rogers.com
Laurette G. Bedard, Contact, Chapter Membership, 705-429-1547
mlbedard@sympatico.ca

Colonel John Gardam Chapter
c/o Chapter President, 1815 Chopin Place, Orleans ON K1C 5G1
Tel: 613-834-9274
Chief Officer(s):
Wayne R. MacCullough, President
wrmac50@rogers.com
Trevor E. Luten, Contact, Chapter Membership, 613-830-7437
trevor.luten@sympatico.ca

Dartmouth - Halifax Chapter
c/o Chapter President, 315 Bellbrook Cres., Dartmouth NS B2W 0G2
Tel: 902-434-6218
cavunp-dartmouth.tripod.com
Chief Officer(s):
Shawn E. Kennedy, President
gskennedy@ns.sympatico.ca
Al J. Simpson, Contact, Chapter Membership, 902-465-6761
jackdusty51@gmail.com

Edmonton Chapter
c/o Chapter President, #4PH, 8340 Jasper Ave., Edmonton AB T5H 4C6
Tel: 780-429-7232
Chief Officer(s):
Arthur Adamson, President
artadamson@shaw.ca

Kingston Limestone Chapter
c/o Chapter President, 69 Chesterfield Drive, Amherstview ON K7N 1M5
Tel: 613-384-8527
Chief Officer(s):
Jim (Harold) James, President
hethjim@cogeco.ca

LCpl David W. Young Chapter
c/o Chapter President, 11 Goshen St., Tillsonburg ON N4G 2T7
Tel: 519-688-9212
Chief Officer(s):
Edward J. Weil, President
e-mweil@kwic.com

LGen. R.R. Crabbe Chapter
c/o Chapter President, 212 Moorgate St., Winnipeg MB R3J 2L2
Tel: 204-888-0156
www.cavunp-winnipeg.com
Chief Officer(s):
Murdoch (Doc) T.M. Jardine, President
piperdoc@shaw.ca
Gordon A. Criggar, Contact, Chapter Membership, 204-837-1844
gcriggar@mb.sympatico.ca

MCpl Mark Isfeld Memorial Chapter
c/o Chapter President, 909 Foreshaw Road, Victoria BC V9A 6M1
Tel: 250-383-8227
Chief Officer(s):
James P. MacMillan-Murphy, President, 250-889-0944
macmurph2@shaw.ca
Scott Laird, Contact, Chapter Membership, 250-383-2808
slaird2@telus.net

MGen. Lewis W. Mackenzie Chapter
c/o Chapter President, 37 Highland Drive, George's River NS B1Y 3G3
Tel: 902-794-8908
cavunplewis.tripod.com
Chief Officer(s):
Ronald V. Clarke, President, 902-794-8908
babetootie@eastlink.ca
John R. Horvath, Contact, Chapter Membership, 902-539-9953
jhorvath@syd.eastlink.ca

Niagara Chapter
c/o Chapter President, 4525 Garden Gate Terrace, Beamsville ON L0R 1B9
Tel: 905-563-9911
Chief Officer(s):

Kevin Wadden, President
kwadden@cogeco.ca
Earle Topley, Contact, Chapter Membership, 905-574-4164
North Saskatchewan Chapter
c/o Chapter President, 307 Cowley Rd., Saskatoon SK S7N 3Z3
Tel: 306-933-9847
members.shaw.ca/nschapter
Chief Officer(s):
Michael W. Titus, President
mjtitus@shaw.ca
Kenneth W. Lowther, Contact, Chapter Membership, 306-384-8208
kwl1@shaw.ca
Peterborough Chapter
c/o Bill Steedman, #205, 811 Sherbrooke St., Peterborough ON K9J 2R2
Tel: 705-743-0115
Chief Officer(s):
Bob Ware, President
Prince Edward Island Chapter
c/o Chapter President, #11, 319 Shakespeare Dr., Stratford PE C1B 2Y4
Tel: 902-892-4403
Chief Officer(s):
Peter R. Van Iderstine, President, 902-892-4403
vanider@pei.sympatico.ca
Prince George & Northern British Columbia Chapter
c/o Branch 43, Royal Canadian Legion, 6076 Trent Drive, Prince George BC V2N 2G3
Tel: 250-964-1822
Chief Officer(s):
Bruce R. Gabriel, President
brgabriel@shaw.ca
Peter M. Engensperger, Contact, Chapter Membership, 250-981-0140
pdt@canada.com
Pte Alexander LeRue Chapter
c/o Chapter President, RR#1, Lower L'Ardoise NS B0E 1W0
Tel: 902-587-2729
Chief Officer(s):
Raymond L. Gracie, President
rlgracie@ns.sympatico.ca
Harris C. MacLean, Contact, Chapter Membership, 902-625-1366
hcmaclean@ns.sympatico.ca
South Saskatchewan Chapter
c/o Chapter President, 37 Lake St., Regina SK S4S 4A7
Tel: 306-584-7308
Chief Officer(s):
Kenneth C. Garbutt, President
kgarbutt@accesscomm.ca
Wesley D. Kopp, Contact, Chapter Membership, 306-584-0678
Spr Christopher Holopina Chapter
c/o Chapter President, 533 - 16th Street, Brandon MB R7A 4Y2
Tel: 204-728-7951
Chief Officer(s):
Yves Lacerte, President, 204-728-7951
good2sea_u@yahoo.com
Martin Haller, Contact, Chapter Membership, 204-727-5009
bdfc@mts.net
Stony Plain Chapter
c/o Chapter President, Box 17, Site 12, RR#2, Carvel AB T0E 0H0
Tel: 780-963-7768
Chief Officer(s):
Norman A. Westwell, President
njwest@telus.net
Herbert Ross Reid, Contact, Chapter Membership, 780-963-8636
hrreid@telus.net
Succursale MGén Alain R. Forand
23 rue Létourneau, Saint-Jean-sur-Richelieu QC J3W 1B3
Tél: 450-359-4776
onuforand.org
Chief Officer(s):
Robert Chouinard, Président, 450-359-4776
choufam@videotron.ca
France Gagné, Secrétaire de Succursale, 514-772-8519
gafrance@hotmail.com

Wainwright Chapter
c/o Chapter President, 1833 - 1A Street Crescent, Wainwright AB T9W 1N4
Tel: 780-842-6495
Chief Officer(s):
Ronald F. McBride, President, 780-842-6495
mcbride3@telus.net
Western Newfoundland Chapter
c/o Chapter President, 18 Hillside Road, Corner Brook NL A2H 1A6
Tel: 709-639-1163
Chief Officer(s):
Michael S. Martin, President
michaelmartin@nf.sympatico.ca
Winston Childs, Chapter Secretary, 709-634-6428
wdchilds@nl.rogers.com
William C. Hall VC, Greenwood Chapter
c/o Chapter President, PO Box 1152, 883 Carol St., Greenwood NS B0P 1N0
Tel: 902-765-6755
Chief Officer(s):
Nelson G. Mullen, President
nelbel@eastlink.ca

Canadian Association of Volunteer Bureaux Centres *See* Volunteer Canada

Canadian Association of Wholesale Sales Representatives (CAWS) / Association canadienne des représentants de ventes en gros

PO Box 70003, 1725 Avenue Rd., Toronto ON M5M 0A0
Tel: 416-782-8961; *Fax:* 416-782-5876
info@caws.ca
www.caws.ca
Overview: A medium-sized national organization founded in 1983
Mission: To represent comission sales agents on a national level. Serves as an umbrella organization for affiliate markets across Canada which are responsible for the coordination of trade shows directed towards the retail buyer.
Chief Officer(s):
Kim Crawford, President
kim-crawford@hotmail.com
Membership: *Fees:* $300; $150 associate; *Member Profile:* Commissioned sales agent selling women's &/or children's wear

Canadian Association of Women Executives & Entrepreneurs (CAWEE) / Association canadienne des femmes cadres et entrepreneurs

#1600, 401 Bay St., Toronto ON M5H 2Y4
Tel: 416-756-0000; *Fax:* 416-756-0000
contact@cawee.net
www.cawee.net
Overview: A medium-sized national organization founded in 1976
Mission: To provide an environment for successful businesswomen to grow & develop, both professionally & personally, through business & community involvement
Member of: International Alliance of Women
Chief Officer(s):
Melvine Baird, President, 416-705-3247
melvine@doctorbaird.com
Lara Bazant, Director, Policy & Administration, 416-879-6367
info@bazant.ca
Susan Quinn, Director, Sponsorship, 416-462-3084 Ext. 233
Faith Seekings, Director, Membership, 416-368-8956
faith@rapportinc.ca
Finances: *Funding Sources:* Membership dues; Sponsors
10 volunteer(s)
Membership: 200 corporate/individual; *Fees:* $250; *Member Profile:* At least two years of middle-management experience; *Committees:* Program; Business Owners; Member Communications; Public Relations; Finance & Administration; Legislative; Resources; Membership
Activities: *Speaker Service:* Yes; *Rents Mailing List:* Yes
Awards:
• ExtraOrdinary Woman (Award)
Presented to one woman each year in recognition of her dedication to herself & other women in their pursuit of personal, professional & financial achievement
Publications:
• Acclaim
Type: Newsletter; *Frequency:* Quarterly
Profile: CAWEE news, activities, & member information & articles

Canadian Association of Wooden Money Collectors (CAWMC)

c/o Norm Belsten, 86 Hamilton Dr., Newmarket ON L3Y 3E8
www.nunet.ca/cawmc
Overview: A small international organization founded in 1975
Chief Officer(s):
Norm Belsten, Contact
nbelsten@sympatico.ca
Membership: *Fees:* $5 youth; $10 Canadian & USA members; $20 international members; *Member Profile:* Collectors of Canadian wooden money, tokens, & souvenirs
Activities: Facilitating networking opportunities; Distributing information of interest to wooden money collectors; Conducting C.A.W.M.C. mail auctions
Publications:
• Timber Talk
Type: Newsletter; *Accepts Advertising*; *Price:* Free with membership in the Canadian Association of Wooden Money Collectors
Profile: Current information & articles of interest to woooden money collectors

Canadian Association of Wound Care (CAWC) / Association canadienne du soin des plaies

#608, 920 Yonge St., Toronto ON M4W 3C7
Tel: 416-485-2292; *Fax:* 416-485-2291
Toll-Free: 866-474-0125
info@cawc.net
www.cawc.net
www.facebook.com/woundcarecanada
twitter.com/WoundCareCanada
Overview: A medium-sized national organization founded in 1995
Mission: To advance wound care in Canada by focussing on public policy, clinical practice, education, research, & international communications
Chief Officer(s):
Peggy Ahearn, Executive Director
Patricia Coutts, President
Christine Pearson, Treasurer
Staff Member(s): 8
Membership: *Fees:* $100 + HST clinician & industry personnel; $75 + HST student, retiree, patient, & lay caregiver; *Member Profile:* Health care professionals, industry participants, patients & caregivers
Meetings/Conferences: • Canadian Association of Wound Care 2015 21st Annual Wound Care Conference, October, 2015, Westin Harbour Castle Hotel, Toronto, ON
Scope: National
Description: Educational components of the conference include basic clinical, advanced clinical, research, & public policy & education
Contact Information: Business Manager: David Stein, E-mail: david@cawc.net
Publications:
• Wound Care Canada: The Official Publication of the Canadian Association of Wound Care
Type: Newsletter; *Accepts Advertising*; *Editor:* Fiona Hendry
ISSN: 1708-6884
Profile: Clinical practice articles, education, & research of interest toclinicians, patients, cargivers, & industry

Canadian Association of Zoological Parks & Aquariums *See* Canadian Association of Zoos & Aquariums

Canadian Association of Zoos & Aquariums (CAZA) / Association des zoos et aquariums du Canada (AZAC)

#400, 280 Metcalfe St., Ottawa ON K2P 1R7
Tel: 613-567-0099; *Fax:* 613-233-5438
Toll-Free: 888-822-2907
info@caza.ca
www.caza.ca
Previous Name: Canadian Association of Zoological Parks & Aquariums
Overview: A medium-sized national charitable organization founded in 1975
Mission: To promote the welfare of animals; To provide input into legislative matters & government policy affecting the zoo & aquarium industry
Member of: IUCN, International Union for Conservation of Nature; The World Association of Zoos & Aquariums; Canadian Museums Association
Chief Officer(s):
Robin Hale, President
rhale@torontozoo.ca

Bill Peters, National Director, 613-567-0099 Ext. 242
bpeters@caza.ca
Greg Tarry, Manager, Special Projects
gtarry@caza.ca
Serge Lussier, Secretary-Treasurer
slussier@lionsafari.com
Finances: *Funding Sources:* Donations
Membership: *Member Profile:* Zoo & aquarium professionals; *Committees:* Executive; Nominating; Ethics; Awards; Conservation & Education; National Awareness; Policy; Accreditation; Business Development; Government Relations; Membership Services; Finance; Arctic Biodiversity; Conference
Activities: Administering the CAZA Accreditation Program; Upholding the CAZA Code of Professional Ethics; Promoting education; Offering a mentoring program for institutions
Meetings/Conferences: • Canadian Association of Zoos & Aquariums 2015 Annual Conference, 2015
Scope: National
Description: A meeting of members to vote on the business of the association.
Contact Information: Cathy Simon, Cathy.Simon@moncton.ca, Phone: 506-877-7722; Bruce Dougan, Bruce.Dougan@moncton.ca
Publications:
• Canadian Association of Zoos & Aquariums Membership Directory
Type: Directory
Profile: A listing of institutional, commercial, & affiliate members of the Canadian Association of Zoos & Aquariums
• CAZA [Canadian Association of Zoos & Aquariums] News
Type: Newsletter; *Frequency:* Bimonthly; *Editor:* G. Tarry; *Price:* Free with Canadian Association of Zoos & Aquariums membership
• CAZA [Canadian Association of Zoos & Aquariums] Annual Report
Type: Yearbook; *Frequency:* Annually
• Connecting Canadians to Nature: Strategic Plan [a publication of the Canadian Association of Zoos & Aquariums
Type: Report; *Number of Pages:* 16

Canadian Association on Gerontology (CAG) / Association canadienne de gérontologie (ACG)

#328, 263 McCaul St., Toronto ON M5T 1W7
Toll-Free: 855-224-2240
cagacg@igs.net
www.cagacg.ca
www.facebook.com/group.php?gid=187077537979477
twitter.com/cagacg
Overview: A medium-sized national charitable organization founded in 1971
Mission: To develop the theoretical & practical understanding of individual & population aging through multidisciplinary research, practice, education & policy analysis in gerontology; To seek the improvement of the conditions of life of elderly people in Canada
Member of: International Association of Gerontology
Chief Officer(s):
Neena Chappell, President
Anthony Lombardo, PhD, Executive Director
Margaret Denton, Secretary-Treasurer
Finances: *Funding Sources:* Membership dues; Annual conference; Donations; Corporate sponsorships
20 volunteer(s)
Membership: 500 individuals & organizations; *Fees:* $149 individual; $216 organization; $77 senior/student; $1,000 corporate; *Member Profile:* Academics; health care professionals
Activities: *Rents Mailing List:* Yes
Awards:
• CAG Honorary Membership (Award)
Candidate has made a significant contribution to gerontology *Amount:* Life membership
• CAG Distinguished Member Award (Award)
Recognizes a CAG member who has contributed significantly to furthering objectives & activities of the CAG
• The CAG Donald Menzies Bursary (Scholarship)
To support post-baccalaureate students registered in a program of study focused on aging or the aged *Amount:* $1,500
• The CAG Margery Boyce Bursary (Award)
To support post-baccalaureate students who have made a significant contribution to their community through volunteer activities with or on behalf of seniors & who are registered in a program of study focused on aging or the aged *Amount:* $500
• CAG Award for Contribution to Gerontology (Award)
To recognize an individual who has recently made an outstanding contribution to the field of aging *Amount:* Certificate
Meetings/Conferences: • Canadian Association on Gerontology 2015 44th Annual Scientific & Educational Meeting: Landscapes of Aging, October, 2015, Calgary, AB
Scope: National
Description: A multi-discplinary conference for persons interested in individual & population aging
Publications:
• Abuse & Neglect of Older Canadians: Strategies for Change
• CAG [Canadian Association on Gerontology] Newsletter / Bulletin d'information de l'ACG
Type: Newsletter; *Frequency:* Quarterly
Profile: Information about conferences, events, students, publications, & CAG news
• Canadian Association on Gerontology Conference Program Books
Frequency: Biennially
• Canadian Association on Gerontology Policy Statements & Issues Papers
• Canadian Journal on Aging
Frequency: Quarterly; *Accepts Advertising*; *Editor:* Mark Rosenberg, Ph.D. *ISSN:* 0714-9808; *Price:* $30 student; $71 individual; $115 institution
Profile: A refereed publication with articles about aging concerned with biology, practice, social sciences, & psychology
• National Forum on Closing the Care Gap

Canadian Association on Water Pollution Research & Control *See* Canadian Association on Water Quality

Canadian Association on Water Quality (CAWQ) / Association canadienne sur la qualité de l'eau (ACQE)

PO Box 5050, 867 Lakeshore Rd., Burlington ON L7R 4A6
Tel: 905-336-4513; *Fax:* 905-336-6444
www.cawq.ca
Also Known As: Canadian National Committee of the International Association on Water Quality
Previous Name: Canadian Association on Water Pollution Research & Control
Overview: A medium-sized national charitable organization founded in 1967
Mission: To promote research on scientific, technological, legal & administrative aspects of water pollution research & control; To further the exchange of information & the practical application of such research for public benefit
Member of: International Association on Water Quality
Chief Officer(s):
Clayton Tiedemann, President, 780-412-3830, Fax: 780-412-7679
CTiedema@epcor.ca
Yves Comeau, Secretary, 514-340-4711 Ext. 3728, Fax: 514-340-5918
yves.comeau@polymtl.ca
Peter Jones, Treasurer, 819-821-8000 Ext. 62165, Fax: 819-821-7955
peter.jones@usherbrooke.ca
Finances: *Funding Sources:* Membership fees; Subscriptions; Grants
Membership: 10 corporate + 210 individual; *Fees:* Schedule available; *Member Profile:* Joint or individual - engaged in water quality & pollution research & control; Corporate - organizations engaged in water quality & pollution research & control; Sustaining - individuals & organizations interested in support & results of water quality & pollution research & control; Joint or student - students engaged in full-time study on water quality & pollution research & control
Meetings/Conferences: • Canadian Association on Water Quality 2015 Central Canadian Symposium on Water Quality Research, February, 2015, Holiday Inn, Burlington, ON
Scope: National
Description: A gathering of people in diverse fields of water quality research to present innovations in engineering, science, & policy.
Publications:
• Canadian Association on Water Quality Annual Report
Frequency: Annually
• IWA's Water 21
Type: Newsletter; *Frequency:* Bimonthly
• Water Quality Research Journal of Canada
Type: Journal; *Frequency:* Quarterly; *Editor:* Ronnie Gehr; *Price:* Free for individual CAWQ members; $250 Canada & USA; $295 International
Profile: Peer-reviewed scholarly & review articles & original research on topics such as the impact of pollutants & contaminants on aquatic ecosystems,aquatic species at risk, water treatment & quality, conservation, & water pollution policies

Canadian Astronomical Society (CASCA) / Société canadienne d'astronomie

c/o R. Hanes, Dept. of Physics, Engineering, Physics & Astronomy, 64 Bader Lane, Stirling Hall, Queen's University, Kingston ON K7L 3N6
Tel: 613-533-6000; *Fax:* 613-533-6463
casca@astro.queensu.ca
www.casca.ca
Overview: A medium-sized national organization founded in 1971
Chief Officer(s):
Gilles Joncas, President
CASCA-President@astro.queensu.ca
Nadine Manset, Secretary
CASCA-Secretary@astro.queensu.ca
Leslie Sage, Press Officer
CASCApressofficer@gmail.com a
Finances: *Funding Sources:* Membership dues
Membership: 420; *Fees:* $60
Meetings/Conferences: • Canadian Astronomical Society 2015 Annual Meeting, May, 2015, McMaster University, Hamilton, ON
Scope: National
Description: Annual meetings are open to all interested persons, but the presentation of scientific papers is restricted to members or applicants for membership & speakers invited by the Local Organizing Committee
• Canadian Astronomical Society 2016 Annual Meeting, 2016
Scope: National
Description: Annual meetings are open to all interested persons, but the presentation of scientific papers is restricted to members or applicants for membership & speakers invited by the Local Organizing Committee
Publications:
• Cassiopeia
Type: Newsletter; *Frequency:* Quarterly; *Editor:* Brian Martin
Profile: Observatory news, meeting & departmental reports, events, & instrumentation ideas

Canadian Atherosclerosis Society *See* Canadian Society of Atherosclerosis, Thrombosis & Vascular Biology

Canadian Athletes Now Fund / Fonds des Athlétes Canadiens (FDAC)

106 Berkeley St., Toronto ON M5A 2W7
Tel: 416-487-4442; *Fax:* 416-966-3321
Toll-Free: 866-937-2012
info@canadianathletesnow.ca
www.canadianathletesnow.ca
www.facebook.com/CANFund
www.youtube.com/user/CanadianAthletesNow
Also Known As: See You In CAN Fund; CAN Fund
Overview: A medium-sized national charitable organization
Mission: To provide financial assistance to amateur athletes in Canada.
Chief Officer(s):
Jane Roos, Founder & Executive Director
Finances: *Funding Sources:* Fundraising

Canadian Athletic Therapists Association (CATA) / Association canadienne des thérapeutes du sport

#300, 400 - 5th Ave. SW, Calgary AB T2P 0L6
Tel: 403-509-2282; *Fax:* 403-509-2280
Other Communication: National office info@athletictherapy.org
info@athletictherapy.org
www.athletictherapy.org
www.facebook.com/211459688972240
twitter.com/CATA_Canada
Overview: A medium-sized national licensing organization founded in 1968
Mission: CATA is dedicated to delivery of quality care through injury prevention, emergency services & rehabilitative techniques.
Chief Officer(s):
Sandy Jespersen, Executive Director, 416-549-1682
executivedirector@athletictherapy.org
Richard DeMont, President
demont.conu@gmail.com
Staff Member(s): 2; 65 volunteer(s)
Membership: 1,000-4,999; *Fees:* $204.95; *Member Profile:* Certified Athletic Therapists; Certification candidates; *Committees:* Canadian Board of Certification for Athletic Therapy; Education; Marketing, Sponsorship & Insurance Billing; Program Accredition; Member Services; High-Performance

Providers; International Relations; Financial Advisory; Ethics; Ombudsperson; President's Committee
Activities: Monitoring of professional standards; Hosting conferences
Awards:
• Hall of Fame Award (Award)
• Special Recognition Award (Award)
• Merit Award (Award)
• Distinguished Athletic Therapy Educator Award (Award)
• Writing Award (Award)
• Outstanding SAT Award (Award)
• Evert Van Beek Award (Award)
• Volunteer Appreciation Award (Award)
• Student Leadership Award (Award)
• Research Grant (Grant)
• Larry Ashley Memorial Scholarship Award (Scholarship)
• Annual Scholarship Award (Scholarship)
Meetings/Conferences: • Canadian Athletic Therapists Association's 49th National Conference, May, 2015, Westin Nova Scotian, Halifax, NS
Scope: National
Contact Information: URL: conference.athletictherapy.org
• Canadian Athletic Therapists Association's 50th National Conference, 2016
Scope: National
Publications:
• Athletic Therapy Today
Frequency: Semiannually
• CATA [Canadian Athletic Therapists Association] Newsletter
Type: Newsletter; *Number of Pages:* 4; *Editor:* Dave Jones

Canadian Atlantic Coordinating Committee *See* Atlantic Council of Canada

Canadian Authors Association (CAA)
74 Mississaga St. East, Orillia ON L3V 1V5
Tel: 705-653-0323
Toll-Free: 866-216-6222
admin@canauthors.org
www.canauthors.org
Overview: A medium-sized national charitable organization founded in 1921
Mission: To promote & protect Canadian authors & their works; To act as a voice for writers
Affliation(s): La Société des écrivains canadiens
Chief Officer(s):
Anita Purcell, Interim Executive Director
Finances: *Funding Sources:* Membership fees; Donations
Membership: *Fees:* $50 students; $150 professional or associate members; *Member Profile:* Professional members who have had work published or performed; Associate members who do not qualify for professional membership; Full-time students
Activities: Encouraging work of artistic & literary merit; Providing networking & marketing opportunities
Awards:
• Canadian Authors Association MOSAID Technologies Inc. Award for Fiction (Award)
For a full-length novel
• Canadian Authors Association Lela Common Award for Canadian History (Award)
For historical non-fiction on a Canadian subject
• Canadian Authors Association Poetry Award (Award)
For a book of poetry by one poet
• Canadian Authors Association Carol Bolt Award for Drama (Award)
For the best English-language play for adults by an author who is a Canadian or landed immigrant
• Canadian Authors Association - BookLand Press Emerging Writer Award (Award)
For a Canadian or landed immigrant writer, under age 30, showing promise in the area of literary creation
• Allan Sangster Award (Award)
Awarded to a CAA member for extraordinary service to the association
Meetings/Conferences: • Canadian Authors Association 93rd Annual National Conference: CanWrite! 2015, June, 2015, Orillia, ON
Scope: National
Description: Educational seminars, awards, readings, & networking opportunities
Contact Information: admin@canauthors.org
Publications:
• The Canadian Writer's Guide
Type: Book; *ISBN:* 1-55041-740-1; *Price:* $36
Profile: A comprehensive resource for Canadian writers, featuring articles on topics such as book contracts, copyright, editing, as well as listings of workshops, retreats, & writing schools
• National Newsline [a publication of the Canadian Authors Association]
Type: Newsletter; *Frequency:* Quarterly; *Accepts Advertising;* *ISSN:* 0833-8558; *Price:* Free with Canadian Authors Association membership

Edmonton (Alberta Branch)
PO Box 52007, Edmonton AB T6G 2T5
e-mail: branchline@canauthorsalberta.ca
www.canauthorsalberta.ca
www.facebook.com/175817798054
twitter.com/CAAAlberta
Mission: To provide guidance & recognition to writers throughout Alberta
Chief Officer(s):
Leanne Myggland-Carter, Operations Manager & Communications Manager
• The Branch Line
Type: Newsletter; *Frequency:* 8 pa; *Number of Pages:* 8
Profile: National & branch news, as well as book reviews & forthcoming Alberta literary events

Niagara Branch
PO Box 1512, 4 Queen St., St Catharines ON L2R 3B0
www.canauthorsniagara.org
Mission: To support local writers in the Niagara region
Chief Officer(s):
Karen Gansel, President, 905-468-4010
karen@gansel.net
Charlie Schott, Chair, Membership
c.schott@sympatico.ca
Charlotte King, Secretary
gctoasties@gmail.com
Ineke Brinkman, Treasurer
ineke@brinkmantravel.com

Kelowna (Okanagan Branch)
c/o 31355 Shannon Pl., Westbank BC V4T 1L3
Mission: To assist writers in the Okanagan area of British Columbia
Chief Officer(s):
Sterling Haynes, Contact
jshaynes@shaw.ca
• Branch Echo
Type: Newsletter; *Accepts Advertising*
Profile: Okanagan branch activities

Kitchener (Waterloo-Wellington Branch)
PO Box 179, #4A, 385 Fairway Rd. South, Kitchener ON N2C 2N9
canadianauthors.org/waterloo-wellington
Mission: To encourage & protect writers in the Waterloo-Wellington region of Ontario
Chief Officer(s):
Vanessa Ricci-Thode, President
vanessariccithode@gmail.com
• The Water Well
Type: Newsletter; *Frequency:* Quarterly; *Editor:* Matthew Bin
Profile: Articles, plus news from the Waterloo-Wellington branch
• Words From Here
Type: Book
Profile: An anthology of works from the Waterloo-Wellington branch
• Literary Gifts
Type: Booklet; *Frequency:* Annually
Profile: A yearly Christmas booklet
• Stroke Of The Pen
Type: Newsletter; *Frequency:* Quarterly; *Editor:* Anne Osborne
Profile: Niagara branch activities & forthcoming events

Ottawa (National Capital Region Branch)
Ottawa ON
e-mail: cdn-authors-ncr@live.ca
www.canauthors-ottawa.org
Mission: To assist writers in Ottawa & the surrounding region; To act as a collective voice for writers in the area
Chief Officer(s):
Sharyn Heagle, President
sharyn_40@yahoo.com
Jim Moran, Vice-President, Membership
jimmoran@sympatico.ca
Carol A. Stephen, Vice-President, Regional Outreach
carolstephen2@aim.com
Sherrill Wark, Vice-President, Communications, & Editor, Byline
sherrill_caa@msn.com
Arlene Smith, Treasurer
somertonsmith@yahoo.com
• Byline
Type: Newsletter; *Frequency:* 6 pa; *Editor:* Sherrill Wark; *Price:* Free to members of the Canadian Authors Association, National Capital Region Branch
Profile: Local current events, articles, & stories of interest to writers
• Weekly Notices
Type: Newsletter; *Frequency:* Weekly
Profile: Activities of interest to writers in the National Capital Region

Peterborough (Peterborough & Area Branch)
PO Box 2412, Peterborough ON K9J 7Y8
e-mail: ptbocaa@gmail.com
www.canauthors-peterborough.ca
Mission: To help writers in Peterborough, Ontario, & the surrounding region
Chief Officer(s):
J.R. Maclean, President
president@canauthors-peterborough.ca
Amanda Fife, Vice-President
Stephen Thompson, Secretary
Val Crowley, Treasurer
• E-Line Newsletter
Type: Newsletter
Profile: Peterborough & Area Branch activities & forthcoming events
• Shoreline Reflections: A Collection of Short Stories & Poetry
Type: Book; *ISBN:* 978-0-9738308-2-8; *Price:* $14.95
Profile: Short stories & poetry, presented by members of the Canadian Authors Association Peterborough & Area Branch

Toronto Branch
Toronto ON
e-mail: caatoronto@gmail.com
www.canauthorstoronto.org
Mission: To provide assistance to writers in Toronto & the surrounding area
Chief Officer(s):
Christopher Canniff, President
president@canauthorstoronto.org
Farah Mawani, Secretary
• The Authors' Quarterly
Type: Newsletter; *Frequency:* Quarterly; *Accepts Advertising*
Profile: Toronto branch activities, member news, & announcements
• Gathered Streams: A Collection of Works by Members of the CAA Toronto Branch
Type: Book; *Editor:* Sharon Crawford & Jake Hogeterp
Profile: An anthology of literary works by writers of the Canadian Authors Association, Toronto Branch

Vancouver Branch
PO Box 45019, RPO Ocean Park, South Surrey BC V4A 9L1
Tel: 604-788-9501
vaninfo@canadianauthors.org
canadianauthors.org/vancouver
www.facebook.com/CanadianAuthorsVancouver
Mission: To assist writers in Vancouver, British Columbia
Chief Officer(s):
Margo Bates, President
Grant Brandson, Secretary
Jean Kay, Treasurer
• West Coast Writers
Type: Newsletter; *Frequency:* Quarterly; *Editor:* Carol Tulpar & Barbara Mumford
Profile: Articles, member news from Vancouver, plus forthcoming branch events

Canadian Automated Buildings Association *See* Continental Automated Buildings Association

Canadian Automatic Merchandising Association (CAMA) / L'Association canadienne d'auto-distribution
Member Services, #100, 2233 Argentia Rd., Mississauga ON L5N 2X7
Fax: 905-826-4873
Toll-Free: 888-849-2262
info@vending-cama.com
www.vending-cama.com
www.facebook.com/10047975738697
twitter.com/CAMA_Vending
Overview: A medium-sized national organization founded in 1953

Canadian Associations

Mission: To represt the intersts of Vending Operators, Machine Manufacturers, and Product and Service Suppliers in Canada.
Chief Officer(s):
Ed Kozma, President
edward.kozma@meigroup.com
Amanda Curtis, Executive Director
acurtis@vending-cama.com
Staff Member(s): 2
Membership: 156; *Fees:* Schedule available; *Member Profile:* Equipment & product suppliers & vending operators

Canadian Automatic Sprinkler Association (CASA)
#302, 335 Renfrew Dr., Markham ON L3R 9S9
Tel: 905-477-2270; *Fax:* 905-477-3611
info@casa-firesprinkler.org
www.casa-firesprinkler.org
www.linkedin.com/groups/CASA-Canadian-Automatic-Sprinkler-Association-
twitter.com/CASAFS
www.youtube.com/user/CASAFiresprinkler1?blend=1&ob=5
Overview: A medium-sized national organization founded in 1961
Mission: To advance the fire sprinkler art as applied to the conservation of life & property from fire
Chief Officer(s):
John Galt, President
jgalt@casa-firesprinkler.org
Staff Member(s): 10

Canadian Automobile Association (CAA) / Association canadienne des automobilistes
National Office, #200, 1145 Hunt Club Rd., Ottawa ON K1V 0Y3
Toll-Free: 800-564-6222
www.caa.ca
twitter.com/CAA
www.youtube.com/TheCAAChannel
Overview: A large national organization founded in 1913
Mission: To promote, develop & implement programs & information related to the rights, responsibilities, & needs of the motorist as a consumer
Affliation(s): Alliance internationale de tourisme; Fédération internationale de l'automobile; Federacion interamericana de touring y automovil-clubes; Commonwealth Motoring Conference; American Automobile Association
Chief Officer(s):
Tim Shearman, President
Jeff Walker, Vice-President & Chief Strategy Officer, Public Affairs
Ian Jack, Managing Director, Communications & Government Relations, 613-247-0117 Ext. 2007
ijack@national.caa.ca
Alayne Crawford, Manager, Public Affairs, 613-247-0117 Ext. 2006
acrawford@national.caa.ca
Finances: *Funding Sources:* Membership dues
Membership: 9 clubs serving 5,000,000+ members
Activities: Roadside assistance; driver training; insurance; travel packages; Savings & Rewards program; *Speaker Service:* Yes

Canadian Automobile Association Maritimes
Corporate Office & Saint John Member Service Centre, 378 Westmorland Rd., Saint John NB E2J 2G4
Tel: 506-634-1400; *Fax:* 506-653-9500
Toll-Free: 800-471-1611
www.caa.ca/atlantic
Also Known As: CAA Maritimes
Overview: A medium-sized provincial organization overseen by Canadian Automobile Association
Mission: To serve New Brunswick, Newfoundland & Labrador, Nova Scotia, & Prince Edward Island

Canadian Automobile Association Niagara
3271 Schmon Pkwy., Thorold ON L2V 4Y6
Tel: 905-984-8585; *Fax:* 905-688-0289
www.caa.niagara.net
Also Known As: CAA Niagara
Overview: A medium-sized local organization overseen by Canadian Automobile Association

Canadian Automobile Association North & East Ontario
Administration Centre, PO Box 8350, Stn. T CSC, Ottawa ON K1G 3T2
Tel: 613-820-1890; *Fax:* 613-820-4646
Toll-Free: 800-267-8713
Other Communication: Membership e-mail:
membership@caaneo.on.ca
contactcaa@caaneo.on.ca
caaneo.ca
www.facebook.com/CAANEO
twitter.com/CAANEO
www.youtube.com/user/TheCAANEOChannel
Also Known As: CAA North & East Ontario
Overview: A large local organization founded in 1964 overseen by Canadian Automobile Association
Mission: To deliver automotive, travel, insurance & related services to members & advocate on their behalf
Chief Officer(s):
Frances Mannarino, Chair
Tim Georgeoff, President & CEO
Membership: 257,000; *Fees:* Schedule available
Activities: Providing automotive, travel, & insurance services; *Speaker Service:* Yes

Canadian Automobile Association Saskatchewan
200 Albert St. North, Regina SK S4R 5E2
Tel: 306-791-4314; *Fax:* 306-949-4461
caa.admin@caasask.sk.ca
www.caasask.sk.ca
www.linkedin.com/company/521051
twitter.com/caasaskatchewan
www.youtube.com/caasask
Also Known As: CAA Saskatchewan
Overview: A medium-sized provincial organization overseen by Canadian Automobile Association
Mission: To guarantee excellent emergency road assistance, travel, & insurance services; To provide services, products, programs, & representations to government in order to meet the needs of members, clients, & employees
Member of: Canadian Automobile Association of Canada
Chief Officer(s):
Fred Titanich, President
Membership: 185,000; *Fees:* $33 a la carte; $77 basic; $115 plus; $144 premier; $146 plus RV; $175 premier RV

Canadian Automobile Association South Central Ontario
60 Commerce Valley Dr. East, Thornhill ON L3T 7P9
Tel: 905-771-3000; *Fax:* 905-771-3101
Toll-Free: 866-988-8878
Other Communication: blog.caasco.com
info@caasco.ca
www.caasco.com
www.facebook.com/106112779480473
twitter.com/caasco
www.youtube.com/caasouthcentralON
Also Known As: CAA South Central Ontario
Previous Name: Canadian Automobile Association Toronto
Overview: A large local organization founded in 1903 overseen by Canadian Automobile Association
Mission: To enrich the driving experience of members by providing travel, insurance & automotive services & information
Chief Officer(s):
Dina Palozzi, BA, MBA, ICD.D, Chair
Nick Parks, President & CEO
Silvana Aceto, Specialist, Media & Public Relations, 905-771-3194
sace@caasco.ca
Jeff LeMoine, Consultant, Communications, 905-771-4709
jlem@caasco.ca
Finances: *Funding Sources:* Membership fees
Membership: 800,000
Activities: Offering roadside services, CAA driver training, CAA-approved vehicle repair facilities, insurance services, & travel services;
Publications:
- CAA [Canadian Automobile Association] eLetter
Type: Newsletter; *Frequency:* Monthly
Profile: CAA programs, advice, consumer information, & membership savings
- CAA [Canadian Automobile Association] Waves
Type: Newsletter; *Frequency:* Monthly
Profile: Tavel newsletter with information such as destinations, deals, & tips
- CAA [Canadian Automobile Association South Central Ontario] Magazine
Type: Magazine; *Frequency:* Quarterly; *Editor:* Tracy Howard
Profile: Publication for members includes CAA, automotive, insurance, travel, & lifestyle information
- Extraordinary Explorations [a publication of the Canadian Automobile Association]
Frequency: Quarterly
Profile: Travel ideas & vacation experiences

Canadian Automobile Association Toronto *See* Canadian Automobile Association South Central Ontario

Canadian Automobile Association Windsor
1215 Ouellette Ave., Windsor ON N8X 1J3
Tel: 519-255-1212; *Fax:* 519-255-7379
windsor@caasco.ca
www.caa.ca/csg-gce/cgs-offices-locations-e.cfm
Also Known As: CAA Windsor
Overview: A medium-sized local organization overseen by Canadian Automobile Association

Canadian Automobile Chamber of Commerce *See* Canadian Vehicle Manufacturers' Association

Canadian Automobile Dealers' Association (CADA) / Corporation des associations de détaillants d'automobiles (CADA)
85 Renfrew Dr., Markham ON L3R 0N9
Tel: 905-940-4959; *Fax:* 905-940-6870
Toll-Free: 800-463-5289
www.cada.ca
Previous Name: Federation of Automobile Dealer Associations of Canada
Overview: A large national organization founded in 1941
Mission: To deal with issues of a national nature which affect the well-being of franchised automobile & truck dealers in Canada
Chief Officer(s):
Alex Baum, Chair
Harry Mertin, D.Litt, Secretary-Treasurer
Richard C. Gauthier, President & CEO
Membership: 3,000 corporate + 13 associations; *Member Profile:* Franchised new automobile dealers in Canada
Awards:
- Canadian Automobile Dealers' Association Business in Automotive Management Scholarship (Scholarship)
Amount: $2,000
Publications:
- Canadian Auto Dealer
Type: Magazine; *Frequency:* 8 pa; *Editor:* Gerry Malloy *ISSN:* 1715-8737; *Price:* $16.95 Canada; $29.95 USA
Profile: For dealer principals & senior managers at Canadian automobile dealerships
- Driving Canada's Future: Background Information & Statistics
- Energuide
- Turning the Lights on Leasing: Consumer Guide to Vehicle Leasing
Profile: A publication for consumers from the Canadian Automobile Dealers Association, Canadian Vehicle Manufacturers Association, Association of International AutomobileManufacturers of Canada & the Canadian Finance and Leasing Association

Ottawa Office
#300, 66 Queen St., Ottawa ON K1P 5C6
Tel: 613-230-2079; *Fax:* 613-230-2669
Toll-Free: 800-465-3054

Canadian Automobile Insurance Rate Regulators Association (CARR)
PE
www.carrorg.ca
Overview: A small national organization founded in 2008
Mission: To provide a forum for members to share best practices, identify issues & participate in educational opportunities
Chief Officer(s):
Allison MacEwen, Chair
Heather Walker, Contact, 902-892-3501, Fax: 902-566-4076
HWalker@irac.pe.ca
Kate Paisley, Administrative Coordinator, 506-643-7806
kate.paisley@nbib-canb.org
Membership: 1-99
Activities: Educational opportunities; conferences
Publications:
- CARR [Canadian Automobile Insurance Rate Regulators Association] Emissions
Type: Newsletter

Canadian Automobile Sport Clubs - Ontario Region Inc. (CASC-OR)
1100 Barmac Dr., Toronto ON M9L 2X3

Tel: 416-667-9500; *Fax:* 416-667-9555
Toll-Free: 877-667-9505
office@casc.on.ca
www.casc.on.ca
Overview: A medium-sized provincial organization founded in 1964
Mission: To provide leadership, management, advocacy & the administrative services, facilities & equipment necessary to enable members to maximize their enjoyment & participation in motorsport; to maintain controls & standards necessary for safe competition
Affiliation(s): British Automobile Racing Club; British Empire Motor Club; BMW Club of Canada; Canadian Race Communications Association; Canadian Timing Association; Canadian Volvo Club; Deutscher Automobil Club; HADA Motorsport Club; Kitchener Waterloo Rally Club; London Auto Sport Club; Motorsport Club of Ottawa; Maple Leaf Rally Club; Motorsport Marshalling Services; Mazda Sportscar Owners Club; Oshawa Motor Sport Club; Ontario Z Car Owners Association; Peterborough Motor Sports Club; Race Drivers Guild of Canada; Saab Club of Canada; St. Catharines Motor Club; St. Lawrence Automobile Club
Chief Officer(s):
Peter Jackson, Secretary
secretary@casc.on.ca
Perry Iannuzzi, President
president@casc.on.ca
Finances: *Funding Sources:* Licences; permits; event services
Membership: 30 clubs; *Member Profile:* Motorsport professionals & enthusiasts; *Committees:* Race
Activities: International Auto Show Exhibitor; Ontario Regional Driving Championships; *Speaker Service:* Yes; *Library* by appointment

Canadian Automotive Historians Association (CAHA)

c/o University of Guelph, 50 Stone Rd. East, Guelph ON N1G 2W1
Tel: 519-787-7689
ejanzen@uoguelph.ca
Overview: A small local organization founded in 1977
Mission: Purpose is to preserve, serve & be useful recording Canadian automotive history
Finances: *Annual Operating Budget:* Less than $50,000; *Funding Sources:* Membership fee; donations
Membership: 60; *Fees:* $10
Activities: *Speaker Service:* Yes

Canadian Automotive Repair & Service Council

c/o Cars Training Network, 81 Osborne Rd., Courtice ON L1E 2R3
Fax: 855-813-2111
Toll-Free: 855-813-2101
info@carstraining.net
www.carsondemand.com
Also Known As: CARS Council
Overview: A small national organization founded in 1991
Mission: To serve as a virtual gathering place to access training & education programs, to research industry issues, & to learn of new skills, technologies & trends.
Member of: Alliance of Sector Councils; Society for Applied Learning Technology; Canadian Collision Industry Forum; Automotive Industries Association of Canada; Association of Accrediting Agencies of Canada; Canadian Apprenticeship Forum
Affliation(s): CARS Institute
Membership: *Member Profile:* Employers & employees in automotive repair & service; technicians; business owners; educators
Activities: National accreditation program; workshops; *Library*

Canadian Avalanche Association (CAA)

PO Box 2759, 110 MacKenzie Ave., Revelstoke BC V0E 2S0
Tel: 250-837-2435; *Fax:* 250-837-4624
Toll-Free: 800-667-1105
info@avalanche.ca
www.avalanche.ca
Overview: A medium-sized national organization founded in 1982
Mission: To foster & support a professional environment for avalanche safety operations in Canada; To represent the avalanche community to stakeholders
Chief Officer(s):
Ian Tomm, Executive Director
itomm@avalanche.ca
Mary Clayton, Director, Communications
mclayton@avalanche.ca
Kristin Anthony-Malone, Manager, Operations
kmalone@avalanche.ca
Emily Grady, Manager, Industry Training Program
egrady@avalanche.ca
Finances: *Funding Sources:* Donations
Activities: Establishing technical standards; Providing technical training courses for professional avalanche workers, wilderness guiding operations, government programs (Parks Canada & provincial parks), & highway, railway, mining, forestry, & construction operations
Meetings/Conferences: • Canadian Avalanche Association 2015 Spring Conference & Meetings, 2015
Scope: National
Description: An introduction for technicians & supervisors from transportation & utility & resource sectors, such as forestry, mining, & railways, who manage winter operations & avalanche hazard programs
Contact Information: Interim Operations Manager & Membership Services: Stuart Smith, E-mail: ssmith@avalanche.ca
Publications:
• Avalanche Accidents in Canada
Profile: Volume 1 - 1955 to 1976; Volume 2 - 1943 to 1978; Volume 3 - 1978 to 1984; Volume 4 - 1984 to 1996; Volume 5 - 1996 to 2007
• avalanche.ca
Type: Journal; *Frequency:* Quarterly; *Accepts Advertising; Price:* $30 Canada; $40 USA; $45 international
Profile: Research, reports from alpine countries, publication & product reviews, plus techniques, tools, & tips for avalanche safety
• Guidelines for Snow Avalanche Risk Determination & Mapping in Canada
Type: Guide; *Price:* $20
Profile: A technical reference for avalanche consultants & others, featuring concepts for the determination of avalanche risks, plus guidelines for avalanchemapping & acceptable risks
• Land Managers Guide for Snow Avalanche Hazards in Canada
Type: Guide; *Price:* $20
Profile: A guide to help land managers & consultants recognize & mitigate potential snow avalanche hazards
• Observation Guidelines & Recording Standards for Weather, Snowpack, & Avalanches (OGRS)
Type: Guide
Profile: A technical guide for professional avalanche safety operations & research in Canada

Canadian Aviation Artists Association (CAAA)

3800 Jennifer Rd., Victoria BC V8P 3X2
Tel: 250-380-3876
canadianaviationartistsassoc@gmail.com
www.aviationartists.ca
www.facebook.com/167043893392787
Overview: A small local organization founded in 1997
Mission: To advance aviation art in Canada
Chief Officer(s):
Eric Mitchell, President, Board of Directors, 250-380-0876
ericmitchell@telus.net
Finances: *Annual Operating Budget:* Less than $50,000
3 volunteer(s)
Membership: 30; *Fees:* $60 Canadian artists; $65 American artists; $70 artists outside North America; *Member Profile:* All artists interested in creating aviation art
Activities: Art shows; annual conference
Publications:
• AerialViews
Type: Newsletter
Profile: CAAA news; members' gallery; artist profiles; articles on technique

Canadian Aviation Historical Society (CAHS)

PO Box 2700, Stn. D, Ottawa ON K1P 5W7
www.cahs.ca
Overview: A small national charitable organization founded in 1962
Mission: To collect & disseminate information about Canada's aviation heritage; to foster public interest in the field.
Chief Officer(s):
Gary Williams, National President, 306-543-8123
Rachel Heide, Treasurer, 613-443-9975
Jim Bell, Secretary, 204-293-5402
Finances: *Funding Sources:* Donations
Membership: *Fees:* $50 Canadian members; $60 USA; $70 overseas; *Member Profile:* Individuals with an interest in the history of aviation
Activities: Supporting research in Canadian aeronautical history
Awards:
• C. Don Long Award (Award)
• Mac McIntyre Research Award (Award)
• Doug MacRitchie Memorial Scholarship (Scholarship)
Location: Centennial College
Publications:
• Canadian Aviation Historical Society Journal
Type: Journal; *Frequency:* Quarterly; *Price:* Free with CAHS membership
Profile: Articles & news about Canadian aviation history
• The Canadian Aviation Historical Society Newsletter
Type: Newsletter
Profile: Information for CAHS members

Calgary Chapter
#1021, 3235 - 56 St. NE, Calgary AB T1Y 2X7
Tel: 403-274-3711
www.cahs.ca/chapters/calgary
Chief Officer(s):
Richard Boer, Chapter President

Manitoba Chapter
819 Ashburn St., Winnipeg MB R3G 3C8
Tel: 204-786-4809
cahsywg@cahs.ca
www.cahs.ca/chapters/manitoba
Chief Officer(s):
James A. Bell, Chapter President

Montréal Chapter
101 Oakland Rd., Beaconsfield QC H9W 5C8
Tel: 514-481-8786
www.cahs.ca/chapters/montreal
Chief Officer(s):
Don Baird, Secretary
Graham Batty, Treasurer, 514-217-5369
graham@bagpiping.com
• L'Avion
Type: Newsletter; *Frequency:* Bimonthly; *Editor:* Pat Barrett
Profile: Historical articles, chapter activities, reviews, & upcoming events

New Brunswick Chapter
c/o 346 Summit Dr., Saint John NB E2J 3M2
Tel: 506-696-2501
cahsyqm@cahs.ca
Chief Officer(s):
Jim Sulis, Chapter President
Boyd Trites, Treasurer
• Contact
Type: Newsletter; *Price:* Free for Canadian Aviation Historical Society, Turnbull Chapter members

Ottawa Chapter
c/o 728 Thicket Way, Orleans ON K4A 3B6
Tel: 613-841-6349
www.cahs.ca/chapters/ottawa
Chief Officer(s):
Timothy Dubé, Chapter President
cahsyow@cahs.ca
Rachel Lea Heide, Secretary-Treasurer
• The Observair
Type: Newsletter; *Frequency:* 8 pa; *Price:* Free for Canadian Aviation Historical Society, Ottawa Chapter members
Profile: Meeting reports, historical articles, upcoming events, & reviews of aviation books

Prince Edward Island "Carl F. Burke, MBE" Chapter
c/o #7, 11 Glen Stewart Dr., Stratford PE C1B 2R8
Tel: 902-368-8825
www.cahs.ca/chapters/prince-edward-island
Chief Officer(s):
Andy Anderson, Chapter President
anderson61@eastlink.ca
• Prince Edward Island "Carl F. Burke, MBE" Chapter Newsletter
Type: Newsletter; *Editor:* Chester MacNeill
Profile: Historical articles

Regina "Roland Groome" Chapter
526 Black Dr., Regina SK S4X 2V9
Tel: 306-543-8123
www.cahs.ca/chapters/regina
Chief Officer(s):
Gary Williams, Chapter President
president@cahs.ca

Toronto Chapter
65 Sussex Ave., Toronto ON M5S 1J8
www.cahs.ca/chapters/toronto
Chief Officer(s):

George Topple, Chapter President
george.topple@gmail.com
• Flypast
Type: Newsletter; *Frequency:* 8 pa; *Price:* Free for Canadian Aviation Historical Society, Toronto Chapter members
Profile: Chapter activities, report, & upcoming events

Vancouver Chapter
3489 Lakedale Ave., Burnaby BC V5A 3E2
Tel: 604-420-6065
www.cahs.ca/chapters/vancouver
Chief Officer(s):
J.E. (Jerry) Vernon, Chapter President

Canadian Aviation Maintenance Council *See* Canadian Council for Aviation & Aerospace

Canadian Badminton Association *See* Badminton Canada

Canadian Ball Hockey Association (CBHA) / Association canadienne de hockey-balle

9107 Norum Rd., Delta BC V4C 3H9
Tel: 604-638-1480; *Fax:* 604-998-1410
info@cbha.com
www.cbha.com
www.facebook.com/BallHockeyCanada
twitter.com/CanBallHockey
Overview: A medium-sized national organization founded in 1977
Mission: To promote the sport of ball hockey; To arrange championships
Chief Officer(s):
George Gortsos, Executive Director
Membership: *Member Profile:* Leagues, teams, players, associations

Canadian Band Association (CBA) / Association canadienne des harmonies

#305, 1820 Henderson Hwy., Winnipeg MB R2G 1P2
Tel: 204-663-1226; *Fax:* 204-663-1226
cbaband@shaw.ca
www.canadianband.ca
Overview: A medium-sized national charitable organization founded in 1934
Mission: To promote & develop the musical educational & cultural values of band & band music in Canada
Chief Officer(s):
Ken Epp, Executive Director
Finances: *Annual Operating Budget:* Less than $50,000; *Funding Sources:* Membership dues
Membership: 2,600; *Fees:* $30
Activities: Canadian Band Week; National Youth Band of Canada; *Awareness Events:* Canadian Band Week

Canadian Band Directors Association (Ontario) Inc. *See* Ontario Band Association

Canadian Bankers Association (CBA) / Association des banquiers canadiens

PO Box 348, Stn. Commerce Court West, 199 Bay St., 30th Fl., Toronto ON M5L 1G2
Tel: 416-362-6093; *Fax:* 416-362-7705
inform@cba.ca
www.cba.ca
www.linkedin.com/company/1820482
twitter.com/CdnBankers
www.youtube.com/user/cdnbankers
Overview: A large national organization founded in 1893
Mission: To advocate for policies that contribute to a beneficial banking system
Chief Officer(s):
Anatol von Hahn, Chair, Executive Council
Terry Campbell, President
Kate Payne, Manager, Media Relations, 416-362-6093 Ext. 219
kpayne@cba.ca
Membership: *Member Profile:* Domestic banks; Foreign bank subsidiaries; Foreign bank branches operating in Canada
Activities: Promoting financial literacy among Canadians

Montréal Office
#2480, 1800, av McGill College, Montréal QC H3A 3J6
Tel: 514-840-8747; *Fax:* 514-282-7551

Ottawa Office
#1421, 50 O'Connor St., Ottawa ON K1P 6L2
Tel: 613-234-4431; *Fax:* 613-234-9803

Canadian Banking Ombudsman *See* Ombudsman for Banking Services & Investments

Canadian Baptist Ministries

7185 Millcreek Dr., Mississauga ON L5N 5R4
Tel: 905-821-3533; *Fax:* 905-826-3441
communications@cbmin.org
www.cbmin.org
www.facebook.com/cbmin.org
Merged from: Canadian Baptist International Ministries; Canadian Baptist Federation
Overview: A large national organization founded in 1995
Mission: To unite, encourage & enable Canadian Baptist Churches in their national & international endeavor to fulfill the commission of our Lord Jesus Christ, in the power of the Holy Spirit, proclaiming the gospel & sharing the love of God to all people.
Member of: Canadian Council of Christian Charities
Affliation(s): Canadian Baptists of Western Canada; Canadian Baptists of Ontario & Quebec; Baptist World Alliance; Convention of Atlantic Baptist Churches; Union d'Églises Baptists Francophones au Canada; Atlantic Baptist Women; Canadian Baptist Women of Ontario & Quebec
Chief Officer(s):
Sam Chaise, Executive Director
Finances: *Annual Operating Budget:* Greater than $5 Million; *Funding Sources:* Member churches; individuals; CIDA
Staff Member(s): 112; 540 volunteer(s)
Membership: 250,000 + 1,000 churches; *Member Profile:* Members of churches affiliated with the four conventions/unions; *Committees:* Public Affairs
Activities: Partners in Mission - 75 missionaries serving in Asia, Africa, Latin America, Europe & Canada; The Sharing Way - relief & development ministries in 13 countries, working in areas of agricultural & community development, community health, etc.; Canadian Baptist Volunteers - short-term ministry opportunities; Canada Caucus - consensus building among the churches in Canada; *Library:* Daniel Global Mission Resource Room

Canadian Baptists of Ontario & Quebec (CBOQ)

#100, 304 The East Mall, Toronto ON M9B 6E2
Tel: 416-622-8600; *Fax:* 416-622-2308
cboq@baptist.ca
baptist.ca
twitter.com/cboq
vimeo.com/cboq
Previous Name: Baptist Convention of Ontario & Québec
Overview: A large local organization founded in 1889 overseen by Canadian Baptist Ministries
Mission: A family of churches building Christ's kingdom; supports & enables member churches to be healthy, mission congregations as they serve God together
Member of: Canadian Baptist Ministries
Affliation(s): Baptist Women of Ontario & Quebec; McMaster Divinity College; Canadian Council of Churches; Evangelical Fellowship of Canada; Canadian Council of Christian Charities; Convention of Atlantic Baptist Churches; Canadian Baptists of Western Canada; French Union of Baptist Churches
Chief Officer(s):
Michel Belzile, President
president@baptist.ca
Tim McCoy, Executive Minister
tmccoy@baptist.ca
Finances: *Annual Operating Budget:* $3 Million-$5 Million; *Funding Sources:* Member churches
Staff Member(s): 15
Membership: 375
Activities: *Internships:* Yes; *Library* Open to public

Canadian Baptists of Western Canada (CBWC)

#1100, 550 - 11 Ave. SW, Calgary AB T2R 1M7
Tel: 403-228-9559; *Fax:* 403-228-9048
Toll-Free: 800-820-2479
office@cbwc.ca
www.cbwc.ca
www.facebook.com/115787141838284
twitter.com/@TheCBWC
www.youtube.com/user/CanadianBaptists
Previous Name: The Baptist Union of Western Canada
Overview: A medium-sized local charitable organization founded in 1908 overseen by Canadian Baptist Ministries
Mission: The Canadian Baptists of Western Canada is a Christ-centred community of churches.
Affliation(s): Baptist World Alliance; Canadian Baptist Ministries; North American Baptist Fellowship; Evangelical Fellowship of Canada; Canadian Council Of Churches
Chief Officer(s):
Bob Weber, Director of Ministry
bwebber@cbwc.ca
Finances: *Funding Sources:* Church congregations
Staff Member(s): 12
Membership: 183 congregations representing 100,000 worshippers; *Committees:* Western Canada Missions; Evangelism; Finance; Youth
Activities: *Internships:* Yes

Alberta & NWT Regional Office
#212, 9333 - 50 St. NW, Edmonton AB T6B 2L5
Tel: 780-462-2176; *Fax:* 780-465-6078
Toll-Free: 800-474-6018
abarea@cbwc.ca
Chief Officer(s):
Dennis Stone, Area Minister
dstone@cbwc.ca

British Columbia & Yukon Regional Office
7960A Winston St., Burnaby BC V5A 2H5
Tel: 604-888-7646; *Fax:* 604-422-8696
Toll-Free: 800-596-7772
bcyarea@cbwc.ca
Chief Officer(s):
Rob Ogilvie, Area Minister
rogilvie@cbwc.ca

Heartland Regional Office
PO Box 37239, #3, 4621 Rae St., Regina SK S4S 7K4
Tel: 306-789-2900; *Fax:* 306-789-2902
Toll-Free: 866-789-2940
heartland@cbwc.ca
Chief Officer(s):
Devin Seghers, Contact
dseghers@cbwc.ca

Canadian Bar Association *Voir* Association du barreau canadien

Canadian Bar Association (CBA) / Association du barreau canadien (ABC)

#500, 865 Carling Ave., Ottawa ON K1S 5S8
Tel: 613-237-2925; *Fax:* 613-237-0185
Toll-Free: 800-267-8860
Other Communication: Alternative Phone: 613-237-1988
info@cba.org
www.cba.org
www.linkedin.com/company/canadian-bar-association
www.facebook.com/CanadianBarAssociation
twitter.com/CBA_News
www.youtube.com/user/cbaspin
Overview: A large national organization founded in 1921
Mission: To promote improvements in the law; to promote improvements in the administration of justice; to promote individual lawyer training; to advocate in the public interest; to represent the profession on a national & international level; to promote the interests of the CBA; to promote equality in the profession
Affliation(s): Canadian Association of Law Teachers; Canadian Law Information Council; Commonwealth Bar Association; Inter-American Bar Association; International Bar Association; Union internationale des avocats
Chief Officer(s):
John Hoyles, Chief Executive Officer
Fred Headon, President
Finances: *Annual Operating Budget:* Greater than $5 Million
Staff Member(s): 70
Membership: 37,000; *Member Profile:* Open to lawyers, notaries, judges, law students, persons with a recognized law degree but not licensed to practise or retired from active practice of law, law administrators; membership is voluntary in all but British Columbia & New Brunswick; *Committees:* Awards; Communications; Continuing Legal Education; Equality; Ethics & Professional Issues; International Development; Judicial Compensation & Benefits Commitee; Law Day; Legal Aid; Legislation & Law Reform; Membership; Resolutions, Constitution & ByLaws; Supreme Court of Canada
Activities: Law for the Future Fund; legal aid; law reform initiatives; insurance & financial services for members; advocacy; Canadian Bar Foundation; *Awareness Events:* National Law Day, April
Awards:
• Pro Bono Award (Award)
• Justica Award (Award)
• CBA President's Award (Award)
• The Douglas Miller Award (Award)
• The Louis St-Laurent Award of Excellence (Award)
• PAJLO Student Essay Contest (Award)

• Ramon John Hnatyshyn Award for Law (Award)
• Viscount Bennett Fellowship (Scholarship)
Meetings/Conferences: • Canadian Bar Association 2015 Annual National Environmental, Energy and Resources Law Summit, 2015
Scope: National
Description: Natural Resource and Energy Legal Developments: North and South of 60. Set against the backdrop of Canada's arctic region, join us in an engaging program designed to provide private practitioners, in-house corporate and government counsel, regulators, and other professionals with an annual update on the hottest issues in the environmental, energy and resources law field.
• Canadian Bar Association Canadian Legal Conference & Expo 2015, August, 2015, St. John's, NL
Scope: National
Description: Continuing legal education programs, sessions, & networking opportunities for legal professionals in Canada
• Canadian Bar Association Mid-Winter Meeting of Council 2015, February, 2015, Fairmont Chateau Laurier, Ottawa, ON
Scope: National
• Canadian Bar Association Mid-Winter Meeting of Council 2016, 2016
Scope: National

Alberta Branch
#1725, 311 - 6 Ave. SW, Calgary AB T2P 3H2
Tel: 403-263-3707; *Fax:* 403-265-8581
communications@cba-alberta.org
www.cba.org/alberta
www.facebook.com/cba.alberta
twitter.com/cbaalberta
Chief Officer(s):
Marian De Souza, President
mdesouza@lawyersassist.ca
Steven Mandziuk, QC, Vice-President
smandziuk@finning.ca

British Columbia Branch
845 Cambie St., 10th Fl., Vancouver BC V6B 5T3
Tel: 604-687-3404; *Fax:* 604-669-9601
Toll-Free: 888-687-3404
cba@bccba.org
www.bccba.org
Chief Officer(s):
Caroline Nevin, Executive Director
cnevin@bccba.org

Division du Québec
#1935, 500, Place d'Armes, Montréal QC H2Y 2W2
Tél: 514-393-9600; *Téléc:* 514-393-3350
Ligne sans frais: 877-393-9601
info@abcqc.qc.ca
www.abcqc.qc.ca
Chief Officer(s):
Claude Beaudoin, Directrice générale
cbeaudoin@abcqc.qc.ca

Manitoba Branch
#1020, 444 St. Mary Ave., Winnipeg MB R3C 3T1
Tel: 204-927-1210; *Fax:* 204-927-1212
admin@cba-mb.ca
www.cba.org/Manitoba
Chief Officer(s):
Scott Abel, President
sabel@patersons.ca

New Brunswick Branch
422 York St., Fredericton NB E3B 3P7
Tel: 506-452-7818; *Fax:* 506-459-7959
cbanb@cbanb.com
www.nb-cba.org
Chief Officer(s):
Denise Cameron Scott, Executive Director

Newfoundland Branch
Elizabeth Business Centre, PO Box 16, #107, 49-55 Elizabeth Ave., St. John's NL A1A 1W9
Tel: 709-579-5783; *Fax:* 709-726-4166
cba-nl@cba.org
www.cba.org/newfoundland/
Chief Officer(s):
Ashley Woodford, Executive Director

Northwest Territories
PO Box 1985, Stn. Main, Yellowknife NT X1A 2N9
Tel: 867-669-7739; *Fax:* 867-873-6344
info@cba-nt.org
www.cba.org/northwest
Pamela Naylor, Executive Director
pamela@cba-nt.org

Nova Scotia Branch
#1050, 5991 Spring Garden Rd., Halifax NS B3H 1Y6
Tel: 902-422-1905; *Fax:* 902-423-0475
cbainfo@cbans.ca
www.cba.org/ns
Chief Officer(s):
Tina Tucker, Executive Director

Ontario Bar Association
#300, 20 Toronto St., Toronto ON M5C 2B8
Tel: 416-869-1047; *Fax:* 416-869-1390
Toll-Free: 800-668-8900
info@oba.org
www.oba.org
www.facebook.com/OntarioBarAssociation
twitter.com/obatoday
Chief Officer(s):
Steve Pengelly, Executive Director, 416-869-1047 Ext. 323
spengelly@oba.org

Prince Edward Island Branch
49 Water St., Charlottetown PE C1A 1A3
Tel: 902-566-1590; *Fax:* 902-566-3352
cbapei@eastlink.ca
www.cba.org/pei/
Chief Officer(s):
Jane Smith, Executive Director

Saskatchewan Branch
Canada Building, #306, 105 - 21st St. East, Saskatoon SK S7K 0B3
Tel: 306-244-3898; *Fax:* 306-652-3977
Toll-Free: 800-242-8288
cba.sk@sasktel.net
www.cba.org/saskatchewan
Chief Officer(s):
Brenda Hesje, Executive Director

Yukon Branch
PO Box 31712, Stn. Main Street, Whitehorse YT Y1A 6L3
Tel: 867-393-4769; *Fax:* 867-393-4769
cbayukon@northwestel.net
www.cba.org/yukon/
Chief Officer(s):
Laura Davidson, Executive Director

Canadian Baton Twirling Federation (CBTF) / Fédération baton canadienne

c/o Jeff Johnson, 35 Ridge Dr., Toronto ON M4T 1B6
Fax: 416-484-1672
www.cbtf.ca
www.facebook.com/CBTFCA
twitter.com/cbtfca
Overview: A medium-sized national charitable organization founded in 1979
Member of: World Baton Twirling Federation
Chief Officer(s):
Jeff Johnson, President
Lisa Wilde, Secretary
Michelle Bretherick, Treasurer
Membership: *Committees:* Technical

Canadian Battle of Normandy Foundation *See* Canadian Battlefields Foundation

Canadian Battlefields Foundation

c/o Canadian War Museum, 1 Vimy Pl., Ottawa ON K1R 1C2
Tel: 613-731-7767
cbf.fccb@gmail.com
www.canadianbattlefieldsfoundation.ca
www.facebook.com/220483754647284?ref=ts&fref=ts
www.twitter.com/CBFFCCB
Previous Name: Canadian Battle of Normandy Foundation
Overview: A medium-sized national charitable organization founded in 1992
Mission: To act with Le Mémorial to educate the international public with respect to Canada's role in the Second World War & to educate Canadians through providing scholarships, bursaries & prizes to carry on research into military history; to raise & disburse funds to support these activities.
Chief Officer(s):
H.G. Needham, Treasurer
Charles Belzile, President
Antonio Lamer, Honorary Patron
Finances: *Annual Operating Budget:* Less than $50,000; *Funding Sources:* Grants; donations; membership fees
4 volunteer(s)
Membership: 300; *Fees:* $25 individuals; $100 associations; $200 corporations; *Committees:* Communications; Education; Executive; Finance; Trust Fund
Activities: Canadian Normandy Bursary Programme; university-accepted credit course on WW II; maintenance of Canadian Memorial Garden, Caen, France; *Speaker Service:* Yes

Canadian Beef Breeds Council (CBBC)

#320, 6715 - 8th St. NE, Calgary AB T2E 7H7
Tel: 403-730-0350; *Fax:* 403-275-8490
info@canadianbeefbreeds.com
www.canadianbeefbreeds.com
www.facebook.com/246571192096458
twitter.com/CanadianBeefBre
Overview: A medium-sized national organization founded in 1994
Mission: To represent & promote the purebred cattle sector both domestically & internationally
Chief Officer(s):
Doug Fee, Executive Vice-President
doug@canadianbeefbreeds.com
Finances: *Funding Sources:* Government; corporate sponsors
Membership: 18 breed associations + 15 associate members
Activities: Presentations; trade missions; hosts international speakers

Canadian Belgian Blue Association (CBBA)

c/o Marie Goubau, 1489 Concession 1, Lefaivre ON K0B 1J0
Tel: 613-731-7110; *Fax:* 613-731-0704
info@lagantoise.com
www.belgianblue.ca
Overview: A small national organization founded in 1986
Mission: To provide for registration of Belgian Blue in Canada; To promote the Belgian Blue
Affliation(s): Canadian Livestock Records Corporation
Chief Officer(s):
Sam Dunlop, President
ulsterbelgianblues@hotmail.com
Ken Miller, Secretary-Treasurer
kejab@sasktel.net
Membership: 1-99; *Fees:* $100 initial membership; $50 annual renewal of membership; $10 junior membership (under 18 years of age); *Member Profile:* Breeders of Belgian Blue cattle in Canada; *Committees:* Executive; Finance; Registration; Breed Improvement; Information; Nominating
Activities: Maintaining a record of ancestry & origin of Belgian Blue in Canada; Supervising breeders of Belgian Blue

Canadian Belgian Horse Association

17150 Concession 10, Schomberg ON L0G 1T0
Tel: 905-939-1186; *Fax:* 905-939-7547
cbha@csolve.net
www.canadianbelgianhorse.com
Overview: A small national organization founded in 1907
Mission: To promote the Belgian breed of horse
Chief Officer(s):
Terry Morrow, President
morrowsbelgians@sympatico.ca
Membership: 793; *Fees:* $50
Publications:
• Canadian Belgian Banner
Type: Magazine; *Accepts Advertising*; *Price:* Free with membership

Canadian Beverage Association / Association canadienne des boissons

WaterPark Place, 20 Bay St., 11th Fl., Toronto ON M5J 2N8
Tel: 416-362-2424; *Fax:* 416-362-3229
info@canadianbeverage.ca
www.canadianbeverage.ca
Previous Name: Refreshments Canada; Canadian Bottlers of Carbonated Beverages; Canadian Soft Drink Association
Overview: A medium-sized national organization founded in 1942
Mission: To represent soft drink bottlers, distributors, franchise houses & industry suppliers on a variety of issues
Chief Officer(s):
Jim Goetz, President
jim@canadianbeverage.ca
Stephanie Baxter, Senior Director, Communications
stephanie@canadianbeverage.ca
Anthony Van Heyningen, Senior Director, Research & Policy
anthony@canadianbeverage.ca
Finances: *Annual Operating Budget:* $500,000-$1.5 Million
Staff Member(s): 8
Membership: 45 organizations; *Member Profile:* Manufacturers & distributors of carbonated soft drinks & their suppliers
Activities: *Library* by appointment

Canadian Bible Society (CBS) / Société biblique canadienne
National Support Office, 10 Carnforth Rd., Toronto ON M4A 2S4
Tel: 416-757-4171; *Fax:* 416-757-3376
Toll-Free: 800-465-2425
Other Communication: Online store custserv@biblesociety.ca
info@biblesociety.ca
www.biblesociety.ca
www.facebook.com/CanadianBibleSociety
twitter.com/CanadianBible
pinterest.com/canadianbible
Overview: A large national charitable organization founded in 1904
Mission: To translate, publish, & distribute Bibles, New Testaments & other Scriptures throughout Canada & Bermuda
Member of: United Bible Societies
Chief Officer(s):
Ted Seres, National Director
tseres@biblesociety.ca
Guillaume Duvieusart, Director, National Francophone Services
gduvieusart@societebiblique.ca
Nesa Gulasekharam, Director, Finance
ngulasekharam@biblesociety.ca
Dennis Hillis, Director, Operations
dhillis@biblesociety.ca
Meggy Kwok, Director, Human Resources
mkwok@biblesociety.ca
Hart Wiens, Director, Scripture Translation
hwiens@biblesociety.ca
Finances: *Funding Sources:* Donations; Sale of gifts; Fundraising
Activities: Offering various programs to share God's Word, such as Operation Bible for the Canadian military, & welcoming newcomers to Canada with God's message
Publications:
• Canadian Bible Society Annual Report
Type: Yearbook; *Frequency:* Annually
• Canadian Bible Society e-Updates
Type: Newsletter
• Daily Bible Reading [a publication of the Canadian Bible Society]
Type: Guide
• Taste & See [a publication of the Canadian Bible Society]
Type: E-Book; *Price:* Free from website
Profile: An overview of the Bible

British Columbia District Office
700 Kingsway St., Vancouver BC V5V 3C1
Tel: 604-872-6691; *Fax:* 604-872-0562
Toll-Free: 800-661-7437
vancouver@biblesociety.ca
www.biblesociety.ca/districts/britishcolumbia
Chief Officer(s):
Amie Wiebe, District Director, Southern BC
awiebe@biblesociety.ca

Central Ontario District Office
10 Carnforth Rd., Toronto ON M4A 2S4
Tel: 416-689-3437; *Fax:* 416-757-3376
centralontario@biblesociety.ca
www.biblesociety.ca/districts/ontariocentral
Chief Officer(s):
Don Miller, Director
dmiller@biblesociety.ca

Central Ontario District Office
10 Carnforth Rd., Toronto ON M4A 2S4
Tel: 416-689-3437; *Fax:* 416-757-3376
centralontario@biblesociety.ca
www.biblesociety.ca/districts/ontariocentral
Chief Officer(s):
Don Miller, District Director
dmiller@biblesociety.ca

Eastern Ontario District Office
315 Lisgar St., Ottawa ON K2P 0E1
Tel: 613-236-3910; *Fax:* 613-236-2431
ottawa@biblesociety.ca
www.biblesociety.ca/districts/ontarioeastern
Chief Officer(s):
Don Miller, Director of Ministry Advancement

Manitoba District Office
952 St. Mary's Rd., Winnipeg MB R2M 3R8
Tel: 204-257-8835; *Fax:* 204-254-2411
winnipeg@biblesociety.ca
www.biblesociety.ca/districts/manitoba
Chief Officer(s):
Len Bachiu, District Director
lbachiu@biblesociety.ca

New Brunswick District Office
c/o Crandall University (Murray Bldg), PO Box 6004, 333 Gorge Rd., Moncton NB E1C 9L7
Tel: 506-858-1067; *Fax:* 506-858-1068
Toll-Free: 888-242-5397
www.biblesociety.ca/districts/newbrunswick
Chief Officer(s):
Lorne K. Freake, District Director
lfreake@biblesociety.ca

Newfoundland & Labrador District Office
PO Box 8113, 7 Stamp's Lane, St. John's NL A1E 3C9
Tel: 709-722-7929; *Fax:* 709-722-9105
Toll-Free: 888-242-5397
www.biblesociety.ca/districts/newfoundlandandlabrador
Chief Officer(s):
Lorne Freake, District Director
lfreake@biblesociety.ca

North Alberta District Office
8749 - 53 Ave. NW, Edmonton AB T6E 5E9
Tel: 780-439-7729; *Fax:* 780-439-1676
Toll-Free: 877-439-7729
alberta@biblesociety.ca
www.biblesociety.ca/districts/albertanorth
Chief Officer(s):
Marvin Busenius, District Director
mbusenius@biblesociety.ca

Northern Ontario District Office
315 Lisgar St., Ottawa ON K2P 0E1
Tel: 613-236-3910; *Fax:* 613-236-2431
ottawa@biblesociety.ca
www.biblesociety.ca/districts/ontarionorthern
Chief Officer(s):
Don Miller, District Director
dmiller@biblesociety.ca

Nova Scotia District Office
c/o Crandall University (Murray Bldg), PO Box 6004, 333 Gorge Rd., Moncton NB E1C 9L7
Tel: 506-858-1067; *Fax:* 506-858-1068
Toll-Free: 888-242-5397
www.biblesociety.ca/districts/nova-scotia
Chief Officer(s):
Lorne K. Freake, Director of Ministry Advancement
lfreake@biblesociety.ca

Prince Edward Island District Office
c/o Crandall University (Murray Bldg), PO Box 6004, 333 Gorge Rd., Moncton NB E1C 9L7
Tel: 506-858-1067; *Fax:* 506-858-1068
Toll-Free: 888-242-5397
www.biblesociety.ca/districts/princeedwardisland
Chief Officer(s):
Bill Dean, District Director

Québec District Office
1025, rue Saint-Jean, Québec QC G1R 1R9
Tél: 418-692-2698; *Téléc:* 418-692-4616
Ligne sans frais: 855-692-2698
quebec@biblesociety.ca
www.biblesociety.ca/districts/quebec
Chief Officer(s):
Francis Lemieux, French Ministry Promotions Officer
flemieux@societebiblique.ca

Saskatchewan District Office
PO Box 1931, Stn. Main, #201, 401 - 43rd. St. East, Saskatoon SK S7K 3S5
Tel: 306-664-2480; *Fax:* 306-664-2480
Toll-Free: 800-667-4691
saskatoon@biblesociety.ca
www.biblesociety.ca/districts/saskatchewan
Chief Officer(s):
Leonard Bachiu, District Director

South Alberta District Office
8749 - 53 Ave., NW, Edmonton AB T6E 5E9
Tel: 403-261-4827; *Fax:* 403-439-1676
Toll-Free: 877-439-7729
alberta@biblesociety.ca
www.biblesociety.ca/districts/albertasouth
Chief Officer(s):
Marvin Busenius, Director, Ministry Advancement
mbusenius@biblesociety.ca

Southwestern Ontario District Office
#206, 385 Frederick St., Kitchener ON N2H 2P2
Tel: 416-522-3485
london@biblesociety.ca
www.biblesociety.ca/districts/ontario_southwestern
Chief Officer(s):
Alana Reeve, Regional Representative
areeve@biblesociety.ca

Canadian Billiards & Snooker Association (CBSA)
www.cbsa.ca
www.facebook.com/CanadianBilliardsSnookerAssociation
Overview: A medium-sized national organization founded in 1974
Member of: Canadian Olympic Committee
Affliation(s): Cue Sports for Canada; World Pool-Billiard Association; Bill Congress of America; International Billiards & Snooker Federation
Chief Officer(s):
Steve Cooper, President
steve.cooper09@gmail.com
Kyle Richard, Treasurer
kylerichard2074@msn.com
Activities: Providing championship information

Canadian Biochemical Society *See* Canadian Society for Molecular Biosciences

Canadian Bioethics Society (CBS) / Société canadienne de bioéthique
561 Rocky Ridge Bay NW, Calgary AB T3G 4E7
Tel: 403-208-8027
info@bioethics.ca
www.bioethics.ca
www.facebook.com/groups/2393214575
Merged from: Canadian Society of Bioethic; Société canadienne de la bioéthique médicale
Overview: A small national organization founded in 1988
Mission: To facilitate knowledge sharing related to bioethics; To discover solutions to bioethical problems by promotion of research & dissemination of information
Chief Officer(s):
Susan (Sue) MacRae, President, 604-786-8043
sue.macrae@utoronto.ca
Marika Warren, Treasurer, 902-470-2764
marika.warren@dal.ca
Holly Longstaff, Officer, Communications, 778-279-4007
longstaf@exchange.ubc.ca
Finances: *Funding Sources:* Donations
Membership: 600+; *Fees:* $36 student; $127 individual; $500 supporting organization; *Member Profile:* Professional individuals & institutions interested in ethics & health research & practice
Activities: Promoting teaching of bioethics
Awards:
• CBS Distinguished Service Award (Award)
• CBS Lifetime Achievement Award (Award)
Meetings/Conferences: • 26th Annual Conference and Meeting of the Canadian Bioethics Society, May, 2015, Winnipeg, MB
Scope: National
Publications:
• Canadian Bioethics Society Newsletter
Type: Newsletter; *Accepts Advertising*; *Editor:* Stacey Page
Profile: Articles. book reviews, CBS activities, & upcoming events of interest to CBS members

Canadian Biomaterials Society (CSB) / Société canadienne des biomatériaux (SCB)
www.biomaterials.ca
www.linkedin.com/groups/Canadian-Biomaterials-Society-Societe-Canadien
www.facebook.com/home.php?sk=group_227841973908311
Overview: A small national organization overseen by International Union of Societies for Biomaterials Science & Engineering
Mission: To develop biomaterials science, technology, & education in Canadian industries, universities, & governments
Member of: International Union of Societies for Biomaterials Science & Engineering
Chief Officer(s):
Diego Mantovani, Representative, International Union of Societies - Biomaterials Science/Engineeri
Ze Zhang, Representative, International Union of Societies - Biomaterials Science/Engineeri
Rosalind Labow, Treasurer
rlabow@ottawaheart.ca
Lauren Flynn, Secretary
lauren.flynn@chee.queensu.ca
Membership: *Fees:* $100 corporate members; $50 regular members; $25 students

Meetings/Conferences: • 32nd Annual Meeting of the Canadian Biomaterials Societ 2015, May, 2015, Toronto, ON

Canadian Bison Association (CBA) / Association canadienne du bison

PO Box 3116, #200, 1660 Pasqua St., Regina SK S4P 3G7
Tel: 306-522-4766; *Fax:* 306-522-4768
cba1@sasktel.net
www.canadianbison.ca
Overview: A medium-sized national licensing charitable organization founded in 1984
Mission: To develop the bison industry; to maintain the production of bison in a natural state (no growth hormones, chemicals, feed lots, free-range management); to be the voice for commercial breeders; to assist in the formation of regulations & guidelines in commercial production & management of Canadian Plains Bison & to promote the product & awareness of the bison industry
Member of: Canadian Livestock Records Corp.
Affliation(s): National Bison Association - USA; BC Interior Bison Association; Peace Country Bison Association; Alberta, Saskatchewan, Manitoba, Ontario Bison Association; Québec Bison Union
Chief Officer(s):
Gavin Conacher, Executive Director
Finances: *Funding Sources:* Membership fees; convention; show & sale
Staff Member(s): 3; 10 volunteer(s)
Membership: 1,300 active + 100 associate; *Fees:* Schedule available; *Member Profile:* Active - own bison; associate - interest in bison industry; *Committees:* Research; Promotions; Disease; Grading; Food Safety
Activities: Bison Show & Sale; Annual Convention

Canadian Blind Sports Association Inc. (CBSA) / Association canadienne des sports pour aveugles inc.

#325, 5055 Joyce St., Vancouver BC V5R 6B2
Tel: 604-419-0480; *Fax:* 604-419-0481
Toll-Free: 866-604-0480
info@canadianblindsports.ca
www.canadianblindsports.ca
www.facebook.com/canadianblindsports
Overview: A medium-sized national charitable organization founded in 1976
Mission: To facilitate opportunities for Canadians who are legally blind to participate in amateur sport at the national/international level, & to thereby enhance a healthy lifestyle & individual well-being.
Affliation(s): International Blind Sports Association; Canadian Paralympic Committee; Active Living Alliance
Chief Officer(s):
Jane D. Blaine, CEO
jane@canadianblindsports.ca
Finances: *Annual Operating Budget:* $250,000-$500,000; *Funding Sources:* Donations; government; membership dues
Staff Member(s): 2
Activities: *Rents Mailing List:* Yes

Canadian Blonde d'Aquitaine Association

c/o Canadian Livestock Records Corp., 2417 Holly Ln., Ottawa ON K1V 0M7
Tel: 613-731-7110; *Fax:* 613-731-0704
cbda@clrc.ca
www.canadianblondeassociation.ca
Overview: A medium-sized national organization founded in 1972
Mission: To improve the practice of breeding Blonde d'Aquitaine cows
Member of: Canadian Beef Breeds Council
Chief Officer(s):
Myrna Flesch, President
westwind@telusplanet.net
Finances: *Funding Sources:* Registration of animals
Membership: 178
Publications:
• Canadian Blonde d'Aquitaine Association's Newsletter
Type: Newsletter; *Frequency:* Quarterly; *Accepts Advertising*
Profile: Articles, events, & programs for association members

Canadian Blood & Marrow Transplant Group (CBMTG) / Société Canadienne de greffe de cellules souches hematopoietiques

#400, 570 West 7th Ave., Vancouver BC V5Z 1B3
Tel: 604-874-4944; *Fax:* 604-874-4378
cbmtg@malachite-mgmt.com
www.cbmtg.org
Overview: A small national organization
Mission: To provide leadership in the field of blood & marrow transplantation (BMT); to recognize & promote advances in clinical care; to promote basic, translational & clinical research & education; to represent BMT issues to government agencies, health care organizations & the public; to collaborate with fellow organizations
Chief Officer(s):
Ana Torres, Executive Director
ana.torres@malachite-mgmt.com
Finances: *Funding Sources:* Membership dues
Membership: *Fees:* $130 physician/PhD; $110 allied health membership;$1,500 - $7,500 corporate; $400 - $1,600 organizations, based on no. of members; *Member Profile:* Those with sustained interest in blood & marrow transplantation; professionals, students & interested companies; *Committees:* Executive; Education; Laboratory
Meetings/Conferences: • 2015 Annual Conference of the Canadian Blood & Marrow Transplant Group, May, 2015, Le Centre Sheraton, Montreal, QC
Scope: National
Publications:
• CBMTG [Canadian Blood & Marrow Transplant Group] Newsletter
Type: Newsletter; *Frequency:* Quarterly; *Editor:* Nancy Henderson
Profile: Professional news; case studies; clinical papers; questions; letters to the editor; industry news

Canadian Blood Services (CBS) / Societé canadienne du sang

1800 Alta Vista Dr., Ottawa ON K1G 4J5
Tel: 613-739-2300; *Fax:* 613-731-1411
Toll-Free: 888-236-6283
feedback@blood.ca
www.bloodservices.ca
www.facebook.com/canadianbloodservices
twitter.com/itsinyoutogive
www.youtube.com/18882DONATE
Previous Name: Canadian Red Cross - Blood Services
Overview: A medium-sized national organization founded in 1998
Mission: To manage the blood supply for Canadians; to ensure blood safety in every branch of its structure & in every decision
Chief Officer(s):
Leah Hollins, Chair
Graham D. Sher, Chief Executive Officer
Finances: *Funding Sources:* Fundraising
Activities: Screening donors; Collecting & processing blood; Managing the OneMatch Stem Cell & Marrow Network; Producing publications about blood, plasma, & platelet donation
Publications:
• Bloodlines
Type: Newsletter; *Frequency:* 3 pa
Profile: Updates about the blood system in each region
• Canadian Blood Services Annual Report
Type: Yearbook; *Frequency:* Annually

Ancaster
35 Stone Church Rd., Ancaster ON L9K 1S5
Tel: 905-645-6665
hamiltonfb@blood.ca
Chief Officer(s):
Thomas Warner, Regional Representative, Ontario

Barrie
#100, 231 Bayview Dr., Barrie ON L4N 4Y5
e-mail: feedback@blood.ca

Brandon
c/o Westman Collection Site, Town Centre, 800 Rosser Ave., Brandon MB R7A 6N5
Tel: 204-571-3100
feedback@blood.ca
Chief Officer(s):
Marilyn Robinson, Regional Representative, Alberta, Saskatchewan, Manitoba, Northwest Territories, & Nunavut
Gary Glavin, Representative, Medical, Scientific, Technical, Business, & Public Health

Burlington
1250 Brant St., Burlington ON
e-mail: feedback@blood.ca

Calgary
737 - 13th Ave., Calgary AB T2R 1J1
Tel: 403-410-2650
calgaryfb@blood.ca
Chief Officer(s):
Marilyn Robinson, Regional Representative, Alberta, Saskatchewan, Manitoba, Northwest Territories, & Nunavut

Charlottetown
85 Fitzroy St., Charlottetown PE C1A 1R6
Tel: 902-892-3700
feedback@blood.ca
Chief Officer(s):
Dorothy Harris, Hospital Liaison Specialist, Atlantic (NB & PEI)
dorothy.harris@blood.ca

Corner Brook
3 Herald Ave., Corner Brook NL

Edmonton
8249 - 114th St., Edmonton AB T6G 2R8
Tel: 780-431-0202; *Fax:* 780-702-8687
Toll-Free: 877-366-6717
edmontonfb@blood.ca
Chief Officer(s):
Marilyn Robinson, Regional Representative, Alberta, Saskatchewan, Manitoba, Northwest Territories, & Nunavut
Frank D. Jones, Representatives, Medical, Scientific, Technical, Business, & Public Health

Grand Falls-Windsor
Mini Mall, 105 Lincoln Rd., Grand Falls-Windsor NL

Guelph
130 Silvercreek Pkwy. North, Guelph ON
e-mail: feedback@blood.ca

Halifax
#252, 7071 Bayers Rd., Halifax NS B3L 2C2
Tel: 902-474-8200; *Fax:* 902-474-8297
Toll-Free: 877-366-6717
halifaxfb@blood.ca
Chief Officer(s):
Kenneth Wayne Ezeard, Regional Representative, Atlantic
Lynn Gordon Mason, Representative, Medical, Scientific, Technical, Business, & Public Health

Kelowna
#103, 1865 Dilworth Dr., Kelowna BC V1Y 9T1
e-mail: feedback@blood.ca

Kingston
850 Gardiners Rd., Kingston ON
e-mail: feedback@blood.ca

Kitchener-Waterloo
94 Bridgeport Rd. East, Waterloo ON
e-mail: feedback@blood.ca

Lethbridge
Lethbridge Centre Mall, #220, 200 - 4 Ave. South, Lethbridge AB

London
840 Commissioners Rd. East, London ON N6C 2V5
Tel: 519-690-3992
londonfb@blood.ca
Chief Officer(s):
Thomas Warner, Regional Representative, Ontario

Mississauga
Service Court, Lower Level, 100 City Centre Dr., Mississauga ON L5B 2C9
e-mail: feedback@blood.ca

Moncton
500 Mapleton Rd., Moncton NB E1G 0N3
Tel: 506-388-7520

Oshawa
1300 Harmony Rd. North, Oshawa ON L1K 2B1
e-mail: feedback@blood.ca

Ottawa
1575 Carling Ave., Ottawa ON K1Z 7M3
Tel: 613-560-7440
ottawafb@blood.ca
Chief Officer(s):
Thomas Warner, Regional Representative, Ontario

Ottawa - Alta Vista Dr. - National Fundraising Office
1800 Alta Vista Dr., Ottawa ON K1G 4J5
Fax: 613-739-2141
Toll-Free: 888-236-6283
fundraising@blood.ca

Peterborough
55 George St. North, Peterborough ON
e-mail: feedback@blood.ca

Prince George
2277 Westwood Dr., Prince George BC V2N 4V6
e-mail: feedback@blood.ca

Red Deer
#5, 5020 - 68th St., Red Deer AB

Regina
2571 Broad St., Regina SK S4P 3B4
Tel: 306-347-1636
reginafb@blood.ca
Chief Officer(s):
Marilyn Robinson, Regional Representative, Alberta, Saskatchewan, Manitoba, Northwest Territories, & Nunavut

Saint John
PO Box 1259, 405 University Ave., Saint John NB E2L 4G7
Tel: 506-648-5111
Toll-Free: 888-236-6283
feedback@blood.ca
Chief Officer(s):
Dorothy Harris, Hospital Liaison Specialist, Atlantic (NB & PEI)
dorothy.harris@blood.ca

St Catharines
#395, 397 Ontario St., St Catharines ON
e-mail: feedback@blood.ca

St. John's
7 Wicklow St., St. John's NL A1B 3Z9
Tel: 709-758-5300
feedback@blood.ca
Chief Officer(s):
Dorothy Harris, Hospital Liaison Specialist, Atlantic (NS & NL)
dorothy.harris@blood.ca

Sarnia
Bayside Mall, 150 Christina St. North, Sarnia ON
e-mail: feedback@blood.ca

Saskatoon
325 - 20th St. East, Saskatoon SK S7K 0A9
Tel: 306-651-6639; *Fax:* 306-651-6605
Toll-Free: 877-366-6717
saskatoonfb@blood.ca
Chief Officer(s):
Marilyn Robinson, Regional Representative, Alberta, Saskatchewan, Manitoba, Northwest Territories, & Nunavut

Sudbury
235 Cedar St., Sudbury ON P3B 1M8
Tel: 705-674-4003
sudburyfb@blood.ca
Chief Officer(s):
Thomas Warner, Regional Representative, Ontario

Sudbury - Elm St. - National Contact Centre
300 Elm St., Sudbury ON P3C 1V4
Tel: 705-688-3300
Toll-Free: 888-236-6283

Surrey
15285 - 101 Ave., Surrey BC V3R 8X8
e-mail: feedback@blood.ca

Sydney
850 Grand Lake Rd., Sydney NS B1P 5T9
Fax: 902-474-8297

Toronto - Bay & Bloor
Manulife Centre, 55 Bloor St. West, 2nd Fl., Toronto ON
e-mail: feedback@blood.ca

Toronto - College St.
67 College St., Toronto ON M5G 2M1
Tel: 416-974-9900
torontofb@blood.ca
Chief Officer(s):
Thomas Warner, Regional Representative, Ontario
Bernadette Garvey, Representative, Medical, Scientific, Technical, Business, & Public Health

Toronto - Hillcrest
#C0018, 9350 Yonge St., Toronto ON
e-mail: feedback@blood.ca

Toronto - King Street
163 King sT. West, Main Fl., Toronto ON
e-mail: feedback@blood.ca

Vancouver - Oak Street
4750 Oak St., Vancouver BC V6H 2N9
Tel: 604-707-3400
Toll-Free: 888-236-6283
feedback@blood.ca
Chief Officer(s):
Janet Unrau, Hospital Liaison Specialist, British Columbia & Yukon, 604-707-3516
janet.unrau@blood.ca

Vancouver - Standard Life
888 Dunsmuir St., 2nd Fl., Vancouver BC V6C 3K4
e-mail: feedback@blood.ca

Victoria
3449 Saanich Rd., Victoria BC V8X 1W9
e-mail: feedback@blood.ca

Windsor
3909 Grand Marais Rd. East, Windsor ON
e-mail: feedback@blood.ca

Winnipeg
777 William Ave., Winnipeg MB R3E 3R4
Tel: 204-789-1000; *Fax:* 204-789-1172
Toll-Free: 877-366-6717
winnipegfb@blood.ca
Chief Officer(s):
Marilyn Robinson, Regional Representative, Alberta, Saskatchewan, Manitoba, Northwest Territories, & Nunavut
Michael D. Mehta, Representative, Medical, Scientific, Technical, Business, & Public Health

Canadian Board for Respiratory Care Inc. (CBRC) / Le Conseil canadien des soins respiratoires inc. (CCSR)
#103, 1083 Queen St., Halifax NS B3H 0B2
Tel: 902-492-4387; *Fax:* 902-492-0045
cbrc@cbrc.ca
www.cbrc.ca
Overview: A small national organization founded in 1989
Mission: To produce examinations used to test respiratory therapists prior to entering active practice
Chief Officer(s):
Julie Brown, Secretary/Treasurer

Canadian Board of Examiners for Professional Surveyors (CBEPS) / Le Conseil canadien des Examinateurs pour les Arpenteurs-géomètres (CCEAG)
#100E, 900 Dynes Rd., Ottawa ON K2C 3L6
Tel: 613-274-7115; *Fax:* 613-723-5558
registrar@cbeps-cceag.ca
www.cbeps-cceag.ca
Overview: A medium-sized national organization
Mission: Establishes, assesses and certifies the academic qualifications of individuals who apply to become land surveyors and/or geomatics professionals in Canada, except for Quebec.
Chief Officer(s):
Jean-Claude Tétreault, Registrar
Staff Member(s): 2

Canadian Board of Marine Underwriters (CBMU)
#100, 2233 Argentia Rd., Mississauga ON L5N 2X7
Tel: 905-826-4768; *Fax:* 905-826-4873
info@cbmu.com
www.cbmu.com
Overview: A medium-sized national organization founded in 1917
Mission: To procure & disseminate information of interest to marine underwriters & others; To facilitate the exchange of views & ideas which work to improve the marine underwriting industry & marine insurance; To promote & protect the interest of the underwriting community
Member of: International Union of Marine Insurers
Chief Officer(s):
Brent Chorney, President, 416-586-3018, Fax: 416-586-2939
brent.chorney@zurich.com
Halyna Troian, Administrator
cbmu@cbmu.com
Amanda Curtis, Secretary-Treasurer
acurtis@cbmu.com
Finances: *Funding Sources:* Membership dues
Membership: 26 corporate + 160 associate; *Fees:* $1,000 corporate; $195 associate; *Member Profile:* Marine underwriters; associate - brokers, surveyors, maritime lawyers, government representatives, members of international underwriting boards & others involved in related activities; *Committees:* Underwriting; Compulsory Insurance, Planning; Loss Prevention; Legislative; Education; Communications
Meetings/Conferences: • Canadian Board of Marine Underwriters 2015 Semi-Annual Meeting, May, 2015, Delta St. John's Hotel & Conference Centre, St. John's, NL
Scope: National
Description: A gathering of representatives from the marine insurance industry of Canada
Contact Information: Administrator: Halyna Troian, E-mail: cbmu@cbmu.com

Canadian Board of Registration of Electroencephalograph Technologists Inc. (CBRET)
c/o Clinical Neurophysiology Department, #C1100, 1403 - 29th St NW, 11th Fl., Calgary AB T2N 2T9
Tel: 403-944-8310; *Fax:* 403-270-8993
www.caet.org
www.facebook.com/home.php?sk=group_182902071750881&ap=1
twitter.com/caet_acte
Overview: A small national licensing organization overseen by Canadian Association of Electroneurophysiology Technologists, Inc.
Mission: To offer registration & certification procedures for the electroneurodiagnostic profession of electroencephalography (EEG), as regulated by the College of Physicians & Surgeons in each province & territory; To conduct written & oral-practical examinations to determine the knowledge & skills of EEG technologists
Affliation(s): Canadian Association of Electroneurophysiology Technologists (CAET)
Chief Officer(s):
Erin Phillip, Registrar
Activities: Reviewing qualifications of foreign-trained electroencephalograph technologists before they come to Canada, & advising them if they meet the prerequisites for the registration examination; Maintaining liaison with the Canadian Association of Electroneurophysiology Technologists (CAET)

Canadian Boating Federation / Fédération nautique du Canada
#330, 24 St-Louis, Salaberry DDe Valleyfield QC J6T 1M4
Tel: 450-377-4122; *Fax:* 450-377-5282
cbfnc@cbfnc.ca
www.cbfnc.ca
www.facebook.com/groups/333810007987
Overview: A small national organization
Chief Officer(s):
Derek Anderson, President
Membership: *Member Profile:* Organizations that promote boating; Racing members; Officiating members; Crew members, who maintain racing equipment; Individuals who are neither owners nor drivers in any racing class, but who are interested in racing activities, may be associate members
Activities: Coordinating races; Maintaining rules; Establishing a code of ethics; Sharing race results

Canadian Bodybuilding Federation (CBBF) / Fédération canadienne de culturisme
Regina SK
e-mail: info@cbbf.ca
www.cbbf.ca
www.facebook.com/CanadianBodybuildingFederationCBBF
twitter.com/CBBFCA
plus.google.com/114425722645221501747
Overview: A small national organization
Mission: To act as the governing body for amateur bodybuilding, fitness, & body fitness (figure) competition
Affliation(s): British Columbia Amateur Bodybuilding Association; Alberta Bodybuilding Association; Saskatchewan Amateur Bodybuilders Association (SABBA); Manitoba Amateur Bodybuilding Association; Ontario Physique Association (OPA); Association des Physiques Québécois; New Brunswick Physique & Figure Association; Nova Scotia Amateur Bodybuilders Association; Newfoundland & Labrador Amateur Bodybuilding Association
Chief Officer(s):
Mark Smishek, President
mark@cbbf.ca
Debbie Karpenko, Vice-Chair, Judging
debbie@cbbf.ca
John MacLellan, Vice-Chair, Finance & Administration
john@cbbf.ca
Activities: Qualifying competitors for the three IFBB World Championships; Posting championship results
Publications:
• Rules for Bikini Competitors
• Rules for Figure Competitors
• Rules for Fitness Competitors
• Rules for Physique Competitors

Canadian Boer Goat Association *See* Canadian Meat Goat Association

Canadian Bond Investors' Association (CBIA) / Association canadienne des investisseurs obligataires (ACIO)
#123, 20 Carlton St., Toronto ON M5B 2H5

Tel: 416-585-3000
info@bondinvestors.ca
bondinvestors.ca
Overview: A small national organization founded in 2011
Mission: To be the independent voice of Canada bond investors
Chief Officer(s):
Peter Waite, Executive Director
Membership: 30+; *Fees:* $2,000 institutional; $1,000 affiliate; *Member Profile:* Canadian fixed income institutional investor organizations
Activities: Advocating on behalf of members; providing market information & expertise; providing educational opportunities

Canadian Book Professionals Association (CanBPA)

e-mail: info@canbpa.ca
canbpa.ca
www.facebook.com/136875019696314
twitter.com/canbpa
Merged from: Book Publishing Professionals Association (BPPA); Young Publishers of Canada (YPC)
Overview: A medium-sized national organization
Mission: To foster networking, provide educational opportunities & idea sharing, & job & career information & postings for book professionals of all kinds, including publishers, librarians, booksellers & agents
Chief Officer(s):
David Ward, President
Activities: Seminars; networking, social events & other programming; career information

Canadian Book Publishers' Council; Canadian Textbook Publishers Institute *See* Canadian Publishers' Council

Canadian Bookbinders & Book Artists Guild (CBBAG) / Guilde canadienne des relieurs et des artisans du livre

#207, 80 Ward. St., Toronto ON M6H 4A6
Tel: 416-581-1071
cbbag@cbbag.ca
www.cbbag.ca
www.facebook.com/333608029995650
Overview: A medium-sized national charitable organization founded in 1983
Mission: To create a spirit of community among hand workers in the book arts & those who love books; to promote greater awareness of the book arts; to increase educational opportunities, & foster excellence through exhibitions, workshops, lectures, & publications.
Affliation(s): Ontario Crafts Council
Chief Officer(s):
Mary McIntyre, President
Finances: *Funding Sources:* Membership fees; donations; grants
Membership: *Fees:* $25 student; $60 Canadian; $70 American/overseas; $70 family/institution; $80 American families/insitutions; $35 American students; *Member Profile:* Hand workers or interest in book arts; *Committees:* Communications; Events; National Education; Membership; Publications; Volunteers
Activities: Workshops; exhibitions; program meetings; suppliers list; book art fairs; *Library* Open to public by appointment

Canadian Bookkeepers Alliance *See* Canadian Bookkeepers Association

Canadian Bookkeepers Association

#482, 283 Danforth Ave., Toronto ON M4K 1N2
Fax: 866-804-4617
Toll-Free: 866-451-2204
info@canadianbookkeepersassociation.com
www.c-b-a.ca
Previous Name: Canadian Bookkeepers Alliance
Overview: A small national organization
Mission: To promote, support, provide for & encourage Canadian bookkeepers; to promote & increase the awareness of Bookkeeping in Canada as a professional discipline; to support national, regional & local networking among Canadian Bookkeepers; to provide information on leading-edge procedures, education & technologies that enhance the industry, as well as, the Canadian bookkeeping professional; to support & encourage responsible & accurate bookkeeping practices throughout Canada
Chief Officer(s):
Guy Desmarais, President
president@canadianbookkeepersassociation.com
Membership: *Fees:* $75-$300
Activities: *Awareness Events:* Annual Conference

Canadian Booksellers Association (CBA)

#902, 1255 Bay St., Toronto ON M5R 2A9
Tel: 416-467-7883; *Fax:* 416-467-7886
Toll-Free: 866-788-0790
enquiries@cbabook.org
www.cbabook.org
Overview: A medium-sized national organization founded in 1952
Mission: To promote a high standard of business methods & ethics among members; to define & expand the role of booksellers within the Canadian publishing process; to provide professional advice to prospective & practising booksellers
Chief Officer(s):
Mark Lefebvre, President
lefebvr@mcmaster.ca
Christopher Smith, Vice-President
christopher@collected-works.com
Ellen Pickle, Treasurer
tidebook@nb.sympatico.ca
Finances: *Annual Operating Budget:* $250,000-$500,000
Staff Member(s): 4
Membership: 800; *Fees:* Schedule available; *Member Profile:* Booksellers; publishers; wholesalers; distributors; *Committees:* Membership; Research Advisory; Advocacy Policy; Communications; Campus; Supplier Relations; Technology
Activities: *Rents Mailing List:* Yes
Awards:
• Book Design of the Year (Award)
• Specialty Bookseller of the Year (Award)
• Distributor of the Year (Award)
• Editor of the Year (Award)
• Fiction Book of the Year (Award)
• Author of the Year (Award)
• Bookseller of the Year (Award)
• Campus Bookseller of the Year (Award)
• Non-Fiction Book of the Year (Award)
• Marketing Achievement of the Year (Award)
• Publisher of the Year (Award)
• Sales Rep of the Year (Award)
Publications:
• Canadian Bookseller
Type: Magazine; *Frequency:* Quarterly; *Accepts Advertising*; *Editor:* Emily Sinkins; *Price:* $24
Profile: Trade magazine with news & analysis of the book industry
• Canadian Bookselling Primer
Profile: Information for new hires in Canadian book retailing
• CBA [Canadian Booksellers Association] Membership Directory
Type: Directory
• CBA [Canadian Booksellers Association] Sourcebook
Profile: Listing of publishers, distributors, wholesalers, & suppliers
• Introduction to Bookselling
Type: Manual
Profile: Tips & tools of the bookselling trade

Canadian Botanical Association (CBA) / Association botanique du Canada (ABC)

PO Box 160, Aberdeen SK S0K 0A0
Tel: 306-253-4654; *Fax:* 306-253-4744
Toll-Free: 888-993-9990
www.cba-abc.ca
Overview: A small national organization founded in 1965
Mission: To represent Canadian Botany & botanists nationally & internationally; to respond quickly & professionally on matters that are of concern to Canadian botanists.
Affliation(s): Botanical Society of America
Chief Officer(s):
Fédéerique Guinel, President, 519-884-0710 Ext. 2230
fguinel@wlu.ca
Anne Bruneau, Vice-President, 514-343-2121
anne.bruneau@umontreal.ca
Santokh Singh, Secretary
santokh.singh@botany.ubc.ca
Jane Young, Treasurer, 250-960-5861
youngj@unbc.ca
Finances: *Funding Sources:* Membership
Membership: *Fees:* $55 regular; $25 student/retired; $1000 lifetime; $500 senior lifetime; *Member Profile:* Professional botanists; academics; research scientists; *Committees:* Conservation; Development & Membership
Activities: Ecology; Mycology; Structure & development; Systematics & phytogeography; Teaching; *Library*
Awards:
• Iain & Sylvia Taylor Award (Award)
• Mary E. Elliott Service Award (Award)
• Lionel Cinq-Mars Award (Award)
• John Macoun Travel Bursary (Scholarship)
• Undergraduate Student Regional Awards (Award)
• Lawson Medal (Award)
Publications:
• Botany
Type: Journal; *Frequency:* Monthly; *Editor:* Cecily Pearson
ISSN: 1480-3305
• CBA [Canadian Botanical Association] / ABC [Association botanique du Canada] Bulletin
Type: Bulletin; *Frequency:* 3 pa; *Editor:* Christine D. Maxwell

Canadian Botanical Conservation Network (CBCN) / Le Réseau canadien pour la conservation de la flore

c/o Science Department, Royal Botanical Gardens, PO Box 399, 680 Plains Rd., Hamilton ON L8N 3H8
Tel: 905-527-1158; *Fax:* 905-577-0375
www.rbg.ca/cbcn
www.facebook.com/pages/Royal-Botanical-Gardens/140038459379746
twitter.com/RBGCanada#
www.youtube.com/user/royalbotanicalgarden
Overview: A small national organization founded in 1994
Mission: To preserve the biological diversity of Canada's rare & endangered native plant species, wild habitats & ecosystems
Membership: *Member Profile:* Individuals & organizations with an interest in conservation of plant diversity
Activities: Promoting preservation of native plant species, wild habitats, & ecosystems through education & conservation programs; *Library:* CBCN Library
Publications:
• CBCN [Canadian Botanical Conservation Network] Newsletter
Type: Newsletter; *Frequency:* Quarterly; *Editor:* Dr. David A. Galbraith *ISSN:* 1480-8218
Profile: Plant conservation & biodiversity news, CNCN member news, & upcoming events

Canadian Bottled Water Association (CBWA) / Association canadienne des embouteilleurs d'eau

#203-1, 70 East Beaver Creek Rd., Richmond Hill ON L4B 3B2
Tel: 905-886-6928; *Fax:* 905-886-9531
info@cbwa.ca
www.cbwa.ca
Overview: A medium-sized national licensing organization founded in 1992
Mission: To represent the Canadian bottled water industry; To ensure a high standard of quality for bottled water
Member of: International Council of Bottled Water Associations
Chief Officer(s):
Elizabeth Griswold, Executive Director
griswold@cbwa.ca
Membership: *Member Profile:* Canadian bottled water companies; Equipment manufacturers; Suppliers; Distributors
Activities: Providing educational opportunities
Awards:
• Lifetime Achievement Award (Award)
Meetings/Conferences: • Canadian Bottled Water Association 2015 27th Annual Canadian Bottled Water Convention & Trade Show, 2015
Scope: National
Description: Best practices, techniques, & tools to assist persons involved in the bottled water industry in Canada
Contact Information: E-mail: info@cbwa.ca
Publications:
• WaterPower
Type: Magazine; *Frequency:* Semiannually; *Accepts Advertising*
Profile: Information & news for the bottled water industry in Canada

Canadian Bowling Congress *See* Canadian 5 Pin Bowlers' Association

Canadian Braille Authority *See* Braille Literacy Canada

Canadian Brain Tumour Consortium (CBTC)

c/o Sunnybrook Health Sciences Centre, #402A, 2075 Bayview Ave., Toronto ON M4N 3M5
Tel: 416-480-4766; *Fax:* 416-480-5054
headquarters@cbtc.ca
www.cbtc.ca
Overview: A small national organization founded in 1998
Mission: To act as a national investigator network in the treatment of pediatric & adult patients with brain tumour
Affliation(s): Canadian Congress of Neurological Sciences
Chief Officer(s):
James R Perry, Chair

Finances: *Funding Sources:* Client sponsorship agreements
Membership: 100+; *Member Profile:* Brain tumour specialists & researchers; *Committees:* Credentials; Scientific
Activities: Developing multi-centre brain tumour research projects in Canada; Liaising with industry to execute clinical trials; Influencing government policy; Disseminating knowledge

Canadian Brain Tumour Tissue Bank
London Health Sciences Centre, University of Western Ontario, 339 Windermere Rd., #C7108, London ON N6A 5A4
Tel: 519-663-3427; *Fax:* 519-663-2930
www.braintumor.ca
Also Known As: Brain Tumor Tissue Bank
Overview: A small national organization
Mission: To supply optimally collected brain tumour tissue to researchers all over the country, internationally & locally in the hopes that some day the cause of & the cure for brain tumours will be found.
Affliation(s): The Brain Tumour Foundation of Canada
Chief Officer(s):
Marcela White, Coordinator
marcela.white@lhsc.on.ca
Finances: *Funding Sources:* Brain Tumor Foundation of Canada

Canadian Breast Cancer Foundation (CBCF) / Fondation Canadienne pour le Cancer du Sein
#301, 375 University Ave., Toronto ON M5G 2J5
Tel: 416-596-6773
Toll-Free: 800-387-9816
Other Communication: Blog: findinghope.cbcf.org
connect@cbcf.org
www.cbcf.org
www.facebook.com/CanadianBreastCancerFoundation
twitter.com/cbcf_
Overview: A large national charitable organization founded in 1997
Mission: To support the advancement of breast cancer research, education, diagnosis & treatment
Chief Officer(s):
Deborah Dubenofsky, Chair
Finances: *Annual Operating Budget:* Greater than $5 Million
Staff Member(s): 18; 1700 volunteer(s)
Activities: *Awareness Events:* Breast Cancer Awareness Month, Oct.; CIBC Run for the Cure; Paddle to a Cure: Journey of Hope, July/Aug.; *Speaker Service:* Yes
Awards:
• TELUS-Canadian Breast Cancer Foundation Fellowship (Grant)
• Physician Fellowship (Grant)
• Advanced Healthcare Professional Fellowship (Grant)
Publications:
• Canadian Breast Cancer Foundation Newsletter
Type: Newsletter
• Canadian Breast Cancer Foundation Community Reports
Type: Report

Atlantic Region
#417, 5251 Duke St., Halifax NS B3J 1P3
Tel: 902-422-5520; *Fax:* 902-422-5523
Toll-Free: 866-273-2223
cbcfatl@cbcf.org
www.cbcf.org/atlantic
www.facebook.com/185215488185615
twitter.com/cbcfatlregion
www.youtube.com/cbcfatlanticregion
Chief Officer(s):
Jane Parsons, CEO

British Columbia/Yukon Region
#300, 1090 West Pender St., Vancouver BC V6E 2N7
Tel: 604-683-2873; *Fax:* 604-683-2860
Toll-Free: 800-561-6111
cbcfbc@cbcf.org
www.cbcf.org/bcyukon
www.facebook.com/CBCF.BCYukon
twitter.com/CBCF_BCYukon
www.youtube.com/cbcfbc

Ontario Region
20 Victoria St., 6th Fl., Toronto ON M5C 2N8
Tel: 416-815-1313; *Fax:* 416-815-1766
Toll-Free: 866-373-6313
www.facebook.com/CBCFOntario
twitter.com/CBCF_Ontario
www.youtube.com/user/CBCFOntario
Chief Officer(s):
Gurmit Singh, Chair

Prairies/NWT Region
#700, 10665 Jasper Ave., Edmonton AB T5J 3S9
Tel: 780-452-1166; *Fax:* 780-451-6554
Toll-Free: 866-302-2223
www.facebook.com/CBCFPrairiesNWT
twitter.com/CBCF_PNWT
www.youtube.com/user/CBCFPNWT
Chief Officer(s):
Liz Viccars, CEO

Canadian Breast Cancer Network (CBCN) / Réseau canadien du cancer du sein (RCCS)
#200, 331 Cooper St., Ottawa ON K2P 0G5
Tel: 613-230-3044; *Fax:* 613-230-4424
Toll-Free: 800-685-8820
cbcn@cbcn.ca
www.cbcn.ca
Overview: A medium-sized national organization founded in 1994
Mission: To act as the national voice of breast cancer survivors
Chief Officer(s):
Cathy Ammendolea, President
Sharon Young, Vice President
Finances: *Funding Sources:* Donations
Membership: *Member Profile:* Individuals & groups, such as health care professionals, persons affected by breast cancer, & breast cancer care groups
Activities: Promoting education & awarness; Influencing research & health care policy; Supporting individuals affected by breast cancer
Publications:
• Network News [a publication of the Canadian Breast Cancer Network]
Type: Newsletter; *Accepts Advertising*
• Outreach [a publication of the Canadian Breast Cancer Network]
Type: Newsletter

Canadian Bridge Federation (CFB) / La Fédération canadienne incorporée de bridge
2719 East Jolly Pl., Regina SK S4V 0X8
Tel: 306-761-1677; *Fax:* 306-789-4919
www.cbf.ca
www.facebook.com/Canadian.Bridge.Federation
Overview: A small national organization founded in 1960
Mission: To conduct grassroot bridge events in Canada; to select & subsidize teams to World Championships.
Affliation(s): American Contract Bridge League
Chief Officer(s):
Janice Anderson, Executive Director
jan@cbf.ca
Nader Hanna, President
zone3@cbf.ca
Finances: *Funding Sources:* Membership fees; game fees
Staff Member(s): 2
Membership: *Fees:* $12 regular; $8 students/first time members

Canadian Broadcast Standards Council (CBSC) / Conseil canadien des normes de la radiotélévision (CCNR)
PO Box 3265, Stn. D, Ottawa ON K1P 6H8
Tel: 613-233-4607; *Fax:* 613-233-4826
Toll-Free: 866-696-4718
info@cbsc.ca
www.cbsc.ca
Overview: A medium-sized national organization founded in 1990
Mission: An independent, non-governmental organization created by the Canadian Association of Broadcasters (CAB) to administer standards established by its members, Canada's private broadcasters.
Chief Officer(s):
Andrée Noël, National Chair
anoel@cbsc.ca
John MacNab, Executive Director
jmacnab@cbsc.ca
Teisha Gaylard, Director of Policy
tgaylard@cbsc.ca
Membership: 700

Canadian Broiler Hatching Egg Marketing Agency (CBHEMA) / Office canadien de commercialisation des oeufs d'incubation de poulet à chair (OCCOIPC)
21 Florence St., Ottawa ON K2O 0W6
Tel: 613-232-3023; *Fax:* 613-232-5241
info@chep-poic.ca
www.chep-poic.ca
Overview: A medium-sized national organization founded in 1986
Mission: To ensure that our members produce enough hatching eggs to meet the needs of the broiler industry
Member of: Canadian Federation of Agriculture
Chief Officer(s):
Jack Greydanus, Chair
Giuseppe Caminiti, General Manager
Membership: 300+;

Canadian Brown Swiss & Braunvieh Association / L'association canadienne de la Suisse Brune et de la Braunvieh
RR#5 5653 Hwy. 6 North, Guelph ON N1H 6J2
Tel: 519-821-2811; *Fax:* 519-763-6582
brownswiss@gencor.ca
www.browncow.ca
www.facebook.com/117089315003708
Overview: A small national organization founded in 1914
Mission: To encourage, develop & regulate breeding of Brown Swiss & Braunvieh dairy cattle.
Member of: Canadian Beef Breeds Council
Chief Officer(s):
Renald Dumas, President, 418-453-2896
renciedumas@hotmail.ca
Jessie Weir, Secretary Manager
Finances: *Funding Sources:* Membership fees
Staff Member(s): 1
Membership: *Member Profile:* Owner/operator

Alberta Braunveih Association
RR#1, Leduc AB T9E 2X1
Tel: 780-986-1726; *Fax:* 780-986-3069
swisstraditionbv@yahoo.ca
Member of: Canadian Brown Swiss Association
Chief Officer(s):
Verena Peden, Contact

Canadian Bureau for International Education (CBIE) / Bureau canadien de l'éducation internationale (BCEI)
#1550, 220 Laurier Ave. West, Ottawa ON K1P 5Z9
Tel: 613-237-4820; *Fax:* 613-237-1073
info@cbie.ca
www.cbie-bcei.ca
www.facebook.com/pages/CBIE-BCEI/347318151976441
twitter.com/cbie_bcei
www.youtube.com/user/cbiebcei
Previous Name: Canadian Service for Overseas Students & Trainees
Overview: A large international charitable organization founded in 1966
Member of: Canadian Consortium for International Education
Affliation(s): UNESCO Canada; National Consortium of Scientific & Educational Societies
Chief Officer(s):
Karen McBride, President, 613-237-4820 Ext. 222
kmcbride@cbie.ca
Basel Alashi, Vice-President, 613-237-4820 Ext. 253
balashi@cbie.ca
Margaux Béland, Vice-President, 613-237-4820 Ext. 243
mbeland@cbie.ca
Bashir Hassanali, Vice-President, 613-237-4820 Ext. 252
bhassanali@cbie.ca
Jennifer Humphries, Vice-President, 613-237-4820 Ext. 246
jhumphries@cbie.ca
Finances: *Funding Sources:* Membership dues; Government; Contracts
Staff Member(s): 80
Membership: *Fees:* Schedule available; *Member Profile:* Canadian institutions involved in international education
Activities: Promoting lifelong learning; Administering formal courses & training programs; Organizing non-formal study visits, exchanges, work attachments, & other international development experiences; Managing scholarships; Promoting research; Engaging in advocacy activities; *Awareness Events:* International Education Week, mid November; *Internships:* Yes; *Speaker Service:* Yes; *Rents Mailing List:* Yes
Awards:
• Celanese Canada Internationalist Fellowships (Scholarship)
• CIDA Awards for Canadians (Scholarship)
Up to 50 awards of up to $15,000 awarded annually
• United Nations Fellowships (Scholarship)
• Lucent Global Science Scholars (Scholarship)

Meetings/Conferences: • Canadian Bureau for International Education 2015 Annual Conference, November, 2015, Niagara Falls, ON
Scope: National
Description: The Conference features professional development workshops, concurrent sessions and networking opportunities.
• Canadian Bureau for International Education 2016 Annual Conference, November, 2016, Ottawa, ON
Scope: National
Description: The Conference features professional development workshops, concurrent sessions and networking opportunities.
• Canadian Bureau for International Education 2017 Annual Conference, 2017
Scope: National
Description: The Conference features professional development workshops, concurrent sessions and networking opportunities.

Canadian Bureau for the Advancement of Music (CBAM)

#208, 40 Wynford Dr., Toronto ON M3C 1J5
Tel: 647-352-4015
www.cbam.ca
Overview: A medium-sized national charitable organization founded in 1919
Mission: To promote music (piano) education program for elementary school students
Chief Officer(s):
Nancy Manning, CAO
nancy@cbam.ca
Staff Member(s): 2

Canadian Burn Foundation (CBF)

2051 - 47 St., Edmonton AB T6L 2V5
Tel: 780-448-9025
Toll-Free: 877-448-9025
info@canadianburnfoundation.org
www.canadianburnfoundation.org
Overview: A small national organization founded in 1998
Mission: To provide support & services to burn survivors
Chief Officer(s):
Barry Peachey, President
Stephen Williams, CEO
swilliams@canadianburnfoundation.org
Nadine Spindler, Executive Director
nadine@canadianburnfoundation.org
Finances: *Funding Sources:* Donations
Activities: Offering burn awareness & prevention programs; Supporting international development efforts; Sharing knowledge; Providing computers to burn survivors; Ensuring accessibility to burn camps & retreats for children & youth;

Canadian Burn Survivors Community (CBSC)

110 Bambrick Rd., Middle Sackville NS B4E 0J4
e-mail: info@canadianburnsurvivors.ca
www.canadianburnsurvivors.ca
www.facebook.com/298455086834875
Overview: A small national organization founded in 2006
Mission: To provide support to burn survivors
Membership: *Member Profile:* Burn victims; Fire-fighters; Burn unit staff; advisors

Canadian Business Aircraft Association Inc. ***See*** Canadian Business Aviation Association

Canadian Business Aviation Association (CBAA) / Association canadienne de l'aviation d'affaires (ACAA)

#155, 955 Green Valley Cres., Ottawa ON K2C 3V4
Tel: 613-236-5611; *Fax:* 613-236-2361
www.cbaa-acaa.ca
Previous Name: Canadian Business Aircraft Association Inc.
Overview: A medium-sized national organization founded in 1962
Mission: To act as a collective voice for the business aviation community in Canada, assisting its members in all aviation related matters, & promoting the Canadian business community globally.
Affliation(s): National Business Aviation Association; International Business Aviation Council; European Business Aircraft Association
Chief Officer(s):
Frank Burke, Chair
Rudy Toering, President & CEO
rtoering@cbaa.ca
Finances: *Funding Sources:* Membership dues; convention/tradeshow
Staff Member(s): 7
Membership: 600; *Fees:* Schedule available; *Member Profile:* Business: owns or operates a Canadian privately or state registered aircraft as an aid to conduct its business; Commercial: owns or operates Canadian commercially registered aircraft; Associate: businesses primarily concerned with aviation activities, including the manufacture of aircraft; Affiliate: owns or operates aircraft exclusively registered in a nation other than Canada
Activities: Leadership; excellence; collaboration; ethics
Chief Officer(s):
Jim Thompson, Chapter Co-Chair
Alana Kuhn, Chapter Co-Chair

Atlantic Provinces Chapter
c/o AG Aviation Ltd., PO Box 2564, Balmoral NB E8E 2W7
Tel: 506-759-4629
Chief Officer(s):
Clement Nadeau, Chapter Chair
clementnadeau@hotmail.com

Edmonton Chapter
Edmonton AB
Chief Officer(s):
Marty Hope, Chapter Co-Chair
mhope@millarwestern.com
Keith Tilley, Chapter Co-Chair
kjtilley@gmail.com

Ontario Chapter
c/o Wilson Aircraft, #353, 14845 - 6 Yonge St., Auroran ON L4G 6H8
Tel: 905-713-1059
Chief Officer(s):
Michael Payne, Chapter Co-Chair
mike@wilsonaircraft.com
Mike Casey, chapter Co-Chair
mcasey@fssalliance.com

Pacific Chapter
c/o Anderson Air, 4360 Agar Dr., Richmond BC V7B 1A3
Tel: 604-270-1588
Chief Officer(s):
Jody Maclean, Co-Chair
jody@andersonair.ca
Suli Umar, Co-Chair
suli.bizjet@gmail.com

Québec Chapter
c/o Skyservice Business Aviation, 9785 Ryan Ave., Dorval QC H9P 1A2
Tel: 514-636-5250
Chief Officer(s):
Simon Roussel, Chapter Co-Chair
simon_roussel@skyservicebas.com
Jim Leggett, Chapter Co-Chair
jleggett@acass.ca

Southern Alberta Chapter
c/o Skyplan Services, #104, 7777-10th St. NE, Calgary AB T2E 8X2
Tel: 403-275-2520
cbaa_cyyc@yahoo.ca
Chief Officer(s):
Shelby Dawson-Kohls, Chapter Co-Chair
Julie Evans, Chapter Co-Chair

Canadian Business for Social Responsiblity (CBSR)

PO Box 3538, Stn. Vancouver Main, Vancouver BC V6B 3Y6
Tel: 604-323-2714; *Fax:* 416-703-7475
info@cbsr.ca
www.cbsr.ca
www.linkedin.com/companies/canadian-business-for-social-responsibility
www.facebook.com/219350940362
twitter.com/cbsrnews
www.youtube.com/user/CBSRToronto/feed
Overview: A small national charitable organization founded in 1995
Mission: To provide comprehensive CSR expertise & counsel, allowing members to formulate powerful business decisions that improve performance & contribute to a better world
Chief Officer(s):
Steven Fish, Executive Director
Don Rolfe, Chair
Howard Bogach, Treasurer
Membership: *Member Profile:* Leading Canadian corporations interested in advancing CSR policies & practices
Activities: Offering climate consultancy services; *Speaker Service:* Yes
Publications:
• The Climate Change Guide
Type: Manual; *Price:* $35
Profile: Steps outlining responsibilities, opportunities, & risks regarding climate change
• Good Company
Type: Newsletter; *Frequency:* Quarterly; *Price:* Free with CBSR membership
Profile: CSR news, events, & resources

Toronto Office
#300, 360 Bay St., Toronto ON M5H 2V6
Tel: 416-703-7435; *Fax:* 416-703-7475
info@cbsr.ca
Chief Officer(s):
Kathrin Bohr, Director, Member Development

Canadian Business Press (CBP) / La Presse spécialisée du Canada

4195 Dundas St. West, Toronto ON M8X 1Y4
Tel: 416-239-1022
Overview: A small national organization founded in 1920
Mission: To represent the interests of Canadian business, professional & farm press. It fosters communication among members of the industry, & encourages cooperation between the private sector & the government; to serve as a prime source of information for & about the industry.
Chief Officer(s):
John Kerr, Chair
Finances: *Funding Sources:* Membership dues
Membership: *Member Profile:* Publishers of business publications in Canada
Awards:
• Kenneth R. Wilson Awards (Award)
Recognize excellence in writing & graphic design (17 categories) in specialized business/professional publications; open to all business publications, regardless of CBP membership, that are published in English &/or French; all awards, except the Harvey Southam Editorial Career Award, require an entry fee *Contact:* krwawards@cbp.ca

Canadian Cable in the Classroom Association ***See*** Cable in the Classroom

Canadian Cable Systems Alliance (CCSA)

447 Gondola Point Rd., Quispamsis NB E2E 1E1
Tel: 506-849-1334; *Fax:* 506-849-1338
info@ccsa.cable.ca
www.ccsa.cable.ca
Overview: A medium-sized national organization
Mission: To act as the voice of Canadian independent cable companies
Chief Officer(s):
Alyson Townsend, President/CEO
Finances: *Funding Sources:* Sponsorships
Membership: *Member Profile:* Canadian independent cable companies
Activities: Making representations to regulatory bodies on issues which affect members; Partnering with vendors; Offering contract administration; Providing cooperative marketing initiatives; Facilitating networking opportunities
Awards:
• Canadian Cable Systems Alliance Member of the Year Award (Award)
Publications:
• CCSA [Canadian Cable Systems Alliance] Insider
Type: Newsletter
Profile: Updates on industry issues for alliance members

Canadian Call Management Association (CAM-X)

#10, 24 Olive St., Grimsby ON L3M 2B6
Tel: 905-309-0224; *Fax:* 905-309-0225
Toll-Free: 800-896-1054
info@camx.ca
www.camx.ca
www.linkedin.com/groups/CAM-X-Canadian-Association-Message-Exchange-40
www.facebook.com/pages/CAM-X/118064931573806
twitter.com/CAM-XAssociation
Previous Name: Canadian Association of Message Exchanges, Inc.
Overview: A medium-sized national organization founded in 1964
Mission: To promote the welfare of the message-handling industry & related services through the encouragement & maintenance of high standards of ethics & services; the exchange of information & the rendering of mutual aid & assistance between member organizations.
Chief Officer(s):

Linda Osip, Executive Director
linda@camx.ca
Finances: *Annual Operating Budget:* $50,000-$100,000; *Funding Sources:* Membership dues; seminars
Staff Member(s): 1
Membership: 100; *Fees:* $150-$1,680; *Member Profile:* Call centres; TAS; teleservices; *Committees:* Development; Member Services; Public Relations; Telephone Co. Liaison
Activities: Service Level Award Program; education seminars; annual convention; mentoring program
Awards:
• Award of Excellence (Award)
Meetings/Conferences: • Canadian Call Management Association 51st Annual Convention & Trade Show, September, 2015, Doubletree Hilton, Charleston, SC
Scope: National

Canadian Camping Association (CCA) / Association des camps du Canada (ACC)

c/o Stillwood Camp & Conference Centre, 43975 Watt Rd., Lindell Beach BC V2R 4X9
Toll-Free: 877-427-6958
www.ccamping.org
www.facebook.com/CanadianCampingAssociation
twitter.com/ccampingorg
Overview: A large national charitable organization founded in 1936
Mission: To develop & promote organized camping for all populations across Canada; To further the interests & welfare of children, youth, & adults through camping; To encourage high standards in camping
Affliation(s): International Camping Fellowship; American Camp Association; Outdoor Council of Canada; Canadian Canoe Museum; SmartBoater.ca
Chief Officer(s):
Harry Edwards, President
hedwards@stillwood.ca
Finances: *Funding Sources:* Provincial Camping Associations, corporate sponsors and private contributions.
Membership: 9 provincial camping associations, representing more than 700 camps throughout Canada; *Member Profile:* Provincial camping associations
Activities: Providing information about camping developments & regulations; Engaging in advocacy activities; Guiding camping leaders
Awards:
• Ron Johnstone Lifetime Achievement Award (Award)
• Jack Pearse Award of Honour (Award)
• CCA / ACC Awards of Excellence (Award)

Canadian Cancer Society (CCS) / Société canadienne du cancer

National Office, #300, 55 St. Clair Ave. West, Toronto ON M4V 2Y7
Tel: 416-961-7223; *Fax:* 416-961-4189
Toll-Free: 888-939-3333
ccs@cancer.ca
www.cancer.ca
www.facebook.com/canadiancancersociety
twitter.com/cancersociety
www.youtube.com/user/CDNCancerSociety
Overview: A large national charitable organization founded in 1938
Mission: To collect donations to fund cancer research in Canada; to disseminate information on cancer prevention & treatments, advocating for healthy environment & lifestyle to reduce the incidence of cancer; to offer individual & group support programs for caregivers, family & friends of cancer patients
Affliation(s): Canadian Breast Cancer Research Alliance; Canadian Prostate Cancer Research Initiative; Canadian Tobacco Control Research Initiative; Canadian Strategy for Cancer Control; Chronic Disease Prevention Alliance of Canada
Chief Officer(s):
Marc Généreux, Chair
Pamela Fralick, President & CEO
Christopher Barry, Chief Operating Officer
Arlene Teti, Vice President, Human Resources
Finances: *Funding Sources:* Donations
Staff Member(s): 1200; 1700 volunteer(s)
Membership: 10 provincial & territorial divisions
Activities: Advocating for social & political change to control & reduce cancer; promoting methods of prevention; providing the Cancer Information Service; *Awareness Events:* Daffodil Month, April; Childhood, Men's, & Ovarian Cancer Awareness Month, September; Breast Cancer Awareness Month, October
Awards:
• O. Harold Warwick Prize (Award), Canadian Cancer Society Awards for Excellence in Cancer Research
Amount: $20,000 toward the recipient's research program
• Robert L. Noble Prize (Award), Canadian Cancer Society Awards for Excellence in Cancer Research
Amount: $20,000 toward the recipient's research program
• The William E. Rawls Prize (Award), Canadian Cancer Society Awards for Excellence in Cancer Research
Amount: $20,000 toward the recipient's research program
• Canadian Cancer Society Young Investigator Award (Award), Canadian Cancer Society Awards for Excellence in Cancer Research
Amount: $20,000 toward the recipient's research program
Publications:
• Canadian Cancer Statistics [a publication of Canadian Cancer Society]
Frequency: Annually
Profile: Report of cancer incidence & mortality in Canada

Alberta & Northwest Territories Division
#200, 325 Manning Rd NE, Calgary AB T2E 2P5
Tel: 403-205-3966; *Fax:* 403-205-3979
Toll-Free: 800-661-2262
info@cancer.ab.ca
www.cancer.ca
www.facebook.com/CanadianCancerSocietyABNWT
twitter.com/ccs_AlbertaNWT
Mission: To eradicate cancer & enhance the quality of life of people living with cancer. We achieve this mission by funding research on all types of cancer, providing the public with comprehensive information about cancer & risk reduction, advocating for healthy public policy, as well as offering supportive care services to cancer patients, family members & friends.
Chief Officer(s):
Robert Ascah, Chair
Dan Holinda, Executive Director
dan.holinda@cancer.ab.ca
• Believe
Type: Magazine; *Frequency:* Semiannually; *Editor:* Deanna Kraus; *Price:* Free for people living with cancer, & Canadian Cancer Society volunteers & donors
Profile: Support services, cancer information, research, supporters, advocacy, & prevention

British Columbia & Yukon Division
565 West 10 Ave, Vancouver BC V5Z 4J4
Tel: 604-872-4400; *Fax:* 604-872-4113
Toll-Free: 800-663-2524
frontdesk@bc.cancer.ca
www.facebook.com/CanadianCancerSocietyBCY
twitter.com/cancersocietybc
Chief Officer(s):
Andy Hazlewood, Chair
Barbara Kaminsky, CEO

Division du Québec
5151, boul de l'Assomption, Montréal QC H1T 4A9
Tél: 514-255-5151; *Téléc:* 514-255-2808
webmestre@quebec.cancer.ca
www.facebook.com/sccquebec
twitter.com/SCC_Quebec
Chief Officer(s):
France Descharnais, Président
Suzanne Dubois, Directrice générale
• Canadian Cancer Society's Annual Report - Québec Division
Type: Yearbook; *Frequency:* Annually
Profile: Financial report & description of society activities submitted to the delegates of the general assembly

Manitoba Division
193 Sherbrook St., Winnipeg MB R3C 2B7
Tel: 204-774-7483; *Fax:* 204-774-7500
Toll-Free: 888-532-6982
info@mb.cancer.ca
www.facebook.com/CCSManitoba
twitter.com/CancerSocietyMB
Chief Officer(s):
Dean Schinkel, President
Mark A. McDonald, Executive Director
mmcdonald@mb.cancer.ca
• Community Services Directory
Type: Directory
Profile: Listings of support programs, hair donation programs, home care, transportation, stop smoking programs, & places to find a prosthesis or wig
• Society News
Type: Newsletter
Profile: Volunteer information, upcoming events, & methods of prevention

New Brunswick Division
PO Box 2089, 133 Prince William St., Saint John NB E2L 3T5
Tel: 506-634-6272; *Fax:* 506-634-3808
ccsnb@nb.cancer.ca
www.facebook.com/CanadianCancerSocietyNB
twitter.com/CancerSocietyNB
Chief Officer(s):
Neil Russon, Chair
Anne McTiernan-Gamble, CEO

Newfoundland & Labrador Division
Daffodil Place, PO Box 8921, 70 Ropewalk Ln., St. John's NL A1B 3R9
Tel: 709-753-6520; *Fax:* 709-753-9314
Toll-Free: 888-753-6520
ccs@nl.cancer.ca
Chief Officer(s):
Cyril Abbott, Chair
Matthew Piercey, Executive Director
mpiercey@nl.cancer.ca
• Community Report
Type: Yearbook; *Frequency:* Annually

Nova Scotia Division
5826 South St., Halifax NS B3H 1S6
Tel: 902-423-6183; *Fax:* 902-429-6563
Toll-Free: 800-639-0222
ccs.ns@ns.cancer.ca
www.facebook.com/CancerSocietyNS
twitter.com/cancersocietyNS
Mission: To overcome cancer; to create healthy lives for Nova Scotians
Chief Officer(s):
Jeff Stockhausen, Chair
Barbara Stead-Coyle, CEO
• Canadian Cancer Society - Nova Scotia Division Annual Report
Type: Yearbook; *Frequency:* Annually

Ontario Division
#500, 55 St. Clair Ave. West, Toronto ON M4V 2Y7
Tel: 416-488-5400; *Fax:* 416-488-2872
webmaster@ontario.cancer.ca
Chief Officer(s):
Don Paterson, Chair
Martin Kabat, CEO
Jeffrey Gullberg, Vice President & CFO, Operations
• Hope Blooms
Type: Newsletter; *Frequency:* Monthly
Profile: Cancer research updates, tips to reduce risk of cancer, upcoming events, volunteer profiles

Prince Edward Island Division
#1, 1 Rochford St., Charlottetown PE C1A 9L2
Tel: 902-566-4007; *Fax:* 902-628-8281
info@pei.cancer.ca
www.cancer.ca/pei
www.facebook.com/CancerSocietyPE
twitter.com/CancerSocietyPE
Chief Officer(s):
Lori Barker, Executive Director
• Cancer Quarterly
Type: Newsletter; *Frequency:* Quarterly

Saskatchewan Division
1910 McIntyre St., Regina SK S4P 2R3
Tel: 306-790-5822; *Fax:* 306-569-2133
Toll-Free: 877-977-4673
ccssk@sk.cancer.ca
www.facebook.com/jointhefight.sk
twitter.com/jointhefight_sk
Chief Officer(s):
Susan Holmes, Chair
Keith Karasin, Executive Director

Canadian Cancer Society Research Institute

#300, 55 St. Clair Ave. West, Toronto ON M4V 2Y7
Tel: 416-961-7223; *Fax:* 416-961-4189
ccsri@cancer.ca
www.cancer.ca/research
Previous Name: National Cancer Institute of Canada
Overview: A medium-sized national organization founded in 2009
Mission: To act as a strong voice in the cancer research community; To support a broad range of projects that involve Canadian investigators across the spectrum of cancer research
Chief Officer(s):
Sian Bevan, Director, Research, 416-934-5308
sian.bevan@cancer.ca

Christine Williams, Vice President, Research, 416-934-5305
christine.williams@cancer.ca
Staff Member(s): 10
Activities: Funding promising cancer research; Sponsoring clinical trials to test new drugs; Offering programs to train, develop, & support cancer researchers; Establishing peer review panels to review applications to conduct studies; Presenting awards; Collaborating with other research organizations, such as the Canadian Breast Cancer Research Alliance & the Canadian Tobacco Control Research Initiative
Publications:
• Research Connection [a publication of the Canadian Cancer Society Research Institute]
Type: Newsletter
Profile: News for cancer researchers, including information about research grants

Canadian Cancer Survivor Network (CCSN)
1750 Courtwood Cres., Ottawa ON K2C 2B5
Tel: 613-898-1871
info@survivornet.ca
survivornet.ca
www.facebook.com/CanadianSurvivorNet
twitter.com/survivornetca
Overview: A large national organization
Mission: To help cancer patients & their families cope with their situation and to educate the public about the costs of cancer
Chief Officer(s):
Jackie Manthorne, President & CEO
jmanthorne@survivornet.ca
Staff Member(s): 4

Canadian Canoe Association *See* CanoeKayak Canada

Canadian Canola Growers Association (CCGA)
#400, 1661 Portage Ave., Winnipeg MB R3J 3T7
Tel: 204-788-0090; *Fax:* 204-788-0039
Toll-Free: 866-745-2256
ccga@ccga.ca
www.ccga.ca
Overview: A small national organization founded in 1984
Mission: To supprt canola producers by voicing their concerns about national & international issues
Affliation(s): Alberta Canola Prorducers Commission; Saskatchewan Canola Development Commission; Manitoba Canola Growers; BC Grain Producers Association; Ontario Canola Growers
Chief Officer(s):
Rick White, General Manager, 204-789-8810
rickw@ccga.ca
Kelly Green, Director, Communications, 204-789-8821
kellyg@ccga.ca
Staff Member(s): 12
Membership: 5; *Member Profile:* Canola growers & producer associations

Canadian Capital Markets Association (CCMA) / Association canadienne des marchés des capitaux (ACMC)
85 Richmond St. West, Toronto ON M5H 2C9
Tel: 416-410-1050
info@ccma-acmc.ca
www.ccma-acmc.ca
Overview: A medium-sized national organization founded in 2000
Mission: To make recommendations to meet the challenges & opportunities facing Canadian & international capital markets; To enhance the competitiveness of capital markets in Canada
Chief Officer(s):
Jamie Anderson, Secretary
Membership: *Committees:* Board of Directors; Sell-Side; Buy-Side; Custodian; Communications & Education Working Group; Legal / Regulatory Working Group
Publications:
• CCMA [Canadian Capital Markets Association] News
Type: Newsletter
Profile: Information about the association's current initiatives

Canadian Captive Insurance Association (CCIA)
BC
e-mail: info@canadiancaptive.com
www.canadiancaptive.com
www.linkedin.com/company/2232242
www.facebook.com/canadiancaptive
twitter.com/canadiancaptive
Previous Name: British Columbia Captive Insurance Association
Overview: A small provincial organization founded in 1992
Mission: To represent association members; to promote the captive insurance industry in British Columbia
Chief Officer(s):
Baddeley Michael, Contact, 604-608-6182 Ext. 112
michael.baddeley@integrogroup.com
Day Kevin, Contact, 888-388-1112
kevin@riskebiz.com
Neil MacLean, Contact, 604-844-5507
nmaclean@guildyule.com
Barb Murray, Contact, 604-443-2476
barb.murray@aon.ca
Membership: *Fees:* $100 new company; $25 existing company; *Member Profile:* Individuals interested in British Columbia captives
Activities: Providing professional development opportunities; Reviewing proposed legislative changes; Making recommendations to regulators regarding changes to legislation

Canadian Carbonization Research Association (CCRA)
c/o Ted Todoschuk, PO Box 2460, 1330 Burlington St. East, Hamilton ON L8N 3J5
Tel: 905-548-4796; *Fax:* 905-548-4653
www.cancarb.ca
Overview: A small national organization founded in 1965
Mission: To fund coke & coal research in Canada for benefit of member companies
Chief Officer(s):
Ted Todoschuk, Contact
ted.todoschuk@arcelormittal.com
Finances: *Funding Sources:* Membership fees
Membership: 7 corporate; *Member Profile:* Coal producer, coke producer or related to coal/coke products; *Committees:* Technical

Canadian Cardiovascular Society (CCS) / Société canadienne de cardiologie
#1403, 222 Queen St., Ottawa ON K1P 5V9
Tel: 613-569-3407; *Fax:* 613-569-6574
Toll-Free: 877-569-3407
info@ccs.ca
www.ccs.ca
Previous Name: Canadian Heart Association
Overview: A medium-sized national organization founded in 1947
Mission: To promote cardiovascular health & care through knowledge translation, dissemination of research & encouragement of best practices, professional development & leadership in health policy
Member of: World Heart Federation; Inter-American Society of Cardiology; Canadian Coalition for High Blood Pressure Prevention & Control; American Society of Cardiology
Affliation(s): Canadian Society of Clinical Perfusionists; Canadian Society of Cardiology Technologists; Canadian Association of Cardiopulmonary Technologists; Canadian Medical Association; Royal College of Physicians & Surgeons of Canada; Canadian Council of Cardiovascular Nursing
Chief Officer(s):
Blair O'Neill, President
Finances: *Funding Sources:* Membership dues; programs & activities
Staff Member(s): 8; 150 volunteer(s)
Membership: 1,200+; *Fees:* Schedule available; *Member Profile:* Physicians, surgeons or scientists, whose primary interest is in practice of cardiology & cardiovascular surgery or research in related fields; *Committees:* Scientific Program; Ethics; Medical Devices; Continuing Professional Development; Annual Meeting; Workforce Steering; Joint Organizing; Nominating; Communications Policy; Consensus Conference Working Group
Activities: Consensus conference development; continuing professional development; advocacy; *Awareness Events:* Heart on the Hill; *Rents Mailing List:* Yes
Awards:
• Annual Achievement Award (Award)
• Harold N. Segall Award of Merit (Award)
• Research Achievement Award (Award)
• Distinguished Teacher Award (Award)
• Young Investigator Award (Award)
Meetings/Conferences: • 2015 Canadian Cardiovascular Congress, 2015
Scope: National
• 2016 Canadian Cardiovascular Congress, October, 2016, Palais des congrès de Montréal, Montréal, QC
Scope: National
Publications:
• The Canadian Journal of Cardiology
Type: Journal; *Editor:* Dr. E.R. Smith; *Price:* Free with CCS membership
Profile: Research reports, health outcomes, ethics, review articles, policy, political issues, & case reports concerning cardiovascular medicine

Canadian Career Development Foundation (CCDF) / Fondation canadienne pour le développement de carrière (FCDC)
#202, 119 Ross Ave., Ottawa ON K1Y 0N6
Tel: 613-729-6164; *Fax:* 613-729-3515
Toll-Free: 877-729-6164
information@ccdf.ca
www.ccdf.ca
twitter.com/CCDFFCDC
Overview: A medium-sized national charitable organization founded in 1979
Mission: To advance the understanding & practice of career development.
Affliation(s): International Association for Educational & Vocational Guidance
Chief Officer(s):
Lynne Bezanson, Executive Director
l.bezanson@ccdf.ca
Sareena Hopkins, Co-Executive Director
s.hopkins@ccdf.ca
Finances: *Funding Sources:* Government grants; contracts; donations
Staff Member(s): 8
Activities: Expert consultation on career development issues; professional development courses; workshops on quality & accountability; clearinghouse of resources; *Speaker Service:* Yes; *Library* by appointment

Canadian Career Information Association (CCIA) / Association canadienne de documentation professionnelle (ACADOP)
e-mail: cciainquiries@gmail.com
www.ccia-acadop.ca
Overview: A small national organization founded in 1975
Mission: To promote the development & effective delivery of Canadian career information
Chief Officer(s):
Christine Colosimo, Co-Chair, 416-675-6622 Ext. 4797
christine.colosimo@humber.ca
Angella Nunes, Co-Chair, 416-675-6622 Ext. 4082
angella.nunes@humber.ca
Membership: *Fees:* $40 individual; $30 student; *Member Profile:* Libraries; Educational institutions; Government & community organizations; Businesses; Private practitioners; Students
Activities: Sharing information about resources; Liaising with other organizations concerned with career information
Publications:
• Canadian Career Information Association National Membership Directory
Type: Directory; *Price:* Free for CCIA / ACADOP members
• Developing a Career Information Centre, 5th Edition
Type: Electronic guide; *Number of Pages:* 148; *Editor:* Cathy Gollert; *ISBN:* 0-9696507-1-X; *Price:* Free
• Guidelines for Creating Career Information
Type: Brochure; *Price:* Free for CCIA / ACADOP members

Canadian Caregiver Coalition (CCC-CCAN) / Coalition canadienne des aidants et aidantes naturels
110 Argyle Ave., Ottawa ON K2P 1B4
Tel: 613-233-5694; *Fax:* 613-230-4376
Toll-Free: 888-866-2273
ccc@ccc-ccan.ca
www.ccc-ccan.ca
Overview: A medium-sized national organization
Mission: To join with caregivers, service providers, policy makers & other stakeholders to identify & respond to the needs of caregivers in Canada

Canadian Caribbean Amateur Golfers Association (CCAGA)
#718, 7305 Woodbine Ave, Markham ON L3R 3V7
Fax: 905-420-8421
info@ccaga.ca
www.ccaga.ca
Overview: A small local organization founded in 1980

Mission: A Not-For-Profit Association offering beginners and amateur golfers the opportunity to play and compete among each other
Membership: *Fees:* $150 single; $200 family; $100 associate (non-playing)

Canadian Carpet Institute / Institut canadien du tapis
#200, 435 St. Laurent Blvd., Ottawa ON K1K 2z8
Tel: 613-749-3265; *Fax:* 613-745-8753
info@canadiancarpet.org
www.canadiancarpet.org
Overview: A medium-sized national organization founded in 1963
Mission: To serve as a forum in developing industry consensus for action on common problems & opportunities; To enhance the well-being of the Canadian carpet industry by any & all means consistent with the members, & the public interest
Member of: National Floor Covering Association
Affliation(s): World Carpet & Rug Council
Chief Officer(s):
Walter Eckhardt, President
Karel Vercruyssen, Vice-President
Raymonde Lemire, Manager, Administration
Finances: *Funding Sources:* Membership dues
9 volunteer(s)
Membership: 5 mills + 6 suppliers + 1 carpet cushion; *Fees:* Based on sales; *Member Profile:* Canadian carpet manufacturers & their suppliers; *Committees:* Technical Affairs

Canadian Cartographic Association (CCA) / Association canadienne de cartographie
c/o Paul Heersink, 39 Wales Ave., Markham ON L3P 2C4
Fax: 416-446-1639
treasurer@cca-acc.org
www.cca-acc.org
Overview: A small national organization founded in 1975
Mission: To promote interest in cartographic materials; To encourage research in the field of cartography; To advance education in cartography
Affliation(s): International Cartographic Association
Chief Officer(s):
Elise Pietroniro, Secretary
secretary@cca-acc.org
Paul Heersink, Treasurer
Membership: 16; *Fees:* $45 student/retired/institution; $90 regular members; $110 family membership; $200 corporate; *Member Profile:* Individuals with an interest in mapping
Activities: Facilitating the exchange of information; Organizing a biannual exhibit of Canadian cartography; Collaborating with sister organizations
Meetings/Conferences: • Canadian Cartographic Association 2015 Annual General Conference, 2015
Scope: National
Description: In partnership with the Association of Canadian Map Libraries and Archives.
Publications:
• Cartographica
Type: Journal; *Frequency:* Quarterly *ISSN:* 0317-7173; *Price:* Free with CCA membership
Profile: Cartographica also appears as a monograph on a single topic
• Cartouche
Type: Newsletter; *Frequency:* Quarterly; *Editor:* Patricia Connor Reid; *Price:* Free with CCA membership
Profile: Association activities, forthcoming events, articles, products, & news

Canadian Carwash Association (CCA)
#340, 4195 Dundas St. West, Toronto ON M8X 1Y4
Tel: 416-239-0339; *Fax:* 416-239-1076
office@canadiancarwash.ca
www.canadiancarwash.ca
twitter.com/canadiancarwash
Overview: A small national organization founded in 1961
Mission: To promote the benefits of professional carwashing
Affliation(s): International Carwash Association
Chief Officer(s):
Scott Murray, President, 905-662-6595
Finances: *Annual Operating Budget:* Less than $50,000
Staff Member(s): 7; 20 volunteer(s)
Membership: 200; *Fees:* $210 carwash operator, manufacturer/supplier, detail shop; *Member Profile:* Carwash operators; manufacturers; suppliers to the carwash industry
Activities: Legislation & regulatory activity; auto industry communications; professionalism & increasing profitability; environmental awareness
Awards:
• Ted Snyders Memorial Award (Award)
Meetings/Conferences: • Canadian Carwash Association 2015 Annual General Meeting, 2015
Scope: National
Publications:
• Octane
Type: Magazine; *Frequency:* Quarterly; *Price:* $48 Canada
Profile: Publication about the car wash & petroleum industry, including a yearly buyer's guide & a guide to the CARWACS tradeshow
• Wash Volume Report: National Report
Frequency: Quarterly; *Price:* Free with CCA membership
Profile: Comparison of carwash performance across Canada
• Wash Volume Report: Regional Market
Frequency: Quarterly; *Price:* Free with CCA membership
Profile: Comparison of carwash performance within regions
• WASH-word
Type: Newsletter

Canadian Casting Federation
c/o Toronto Sportsmen's Association, #66, 2700 Dufferin St., Toronto ON M6B 4J3
Tel: 416-487-4477; *Fax:* 416-487-4478
info@torontosportsmens.ca
www.torontosportsmens.ca/Casting.html
Overview: A small national organization founded in 1978
Mission: To teach casting skills, covering fly, bait, & spinning
Activities: *Awareness Events:* Canadian Casting Championships

Canadian Cat Association (CCA) / Association féline Canadienne (AFC)
Bldg. 12, #102, 5045 Orbitor Dr., Mississauga ON L4W 4Y4
Tel: 905-232-3481; *Fax:* 289-232-9481
office@cca-afc.com
www.cca-afc.com
www.facebook.com/100474523335824
Overview: A small national organization founded in 1961
Mission: To improve all breeds of cats in Canada, & maintains a registry of purebred lineages; to serve as a source for cat-related news, including information on shows, & an online breeders' showcase.
Chief Officer(s):
Bob Gleason, President, 519-433-2947
robertgleason@rogers.com
Sandra Dawes, Administrator & Registrar
sandra@cca-afc.com
Staff Member(s): 2
Membership: *Fees:* $50 individual; $60 family; $15 junior; *Committees:* Benefit Shows; Legislative; Ethics; Publications; Public Relations; Standards; CCA Awards & Scoring; Technology; Website; Clerking; Board of Examiners; Membership; Fundraising
Publications:
• Chat Canada Cats
Type: Magazine; *Frequency:* Annually; *Editor:* Sylvie Lamoureux St. Mathias

Canadian Catholic Biblical Association *See* Catholic Biblical Association of Canada

Canadian Catholic Campus Ministry (CCCM)
#307, 47 Queen's Park Cres. East, Toronto ON M5S 2C3
Tel: 416-506-0183; *Fax:* 416-978-782
cccmadmin@cccm.ca
www.cccm.ca
www.facebook.com/pages/Canadian-Catholic-Campus-Ministry/252224265072
Also Known As: Canadian Catholic Students Association
Overview: A small national charitable organization
Mission: To unite Catholic students on Canadian post-secondary campuses; To nurture Christian student leadership
Affliation(s): International Movement of Catholic Students - Canada
Chief Officer(s):
Lori Neale, National Coordinator, 416-506-0183
Victoria Tuason, President & Central Representative
central.rep@cccm.ca
Maureen Callaghan, Atlantic Representative & Contact, Communications
ccsa.communications@cccm.ca
Sharayhah Ulrich, Western Representative & Contact, Social Justice
ccsa.socialjustice@cccm.ca
Finances: *Funding Sources:* Donations
Membership: *Member Profile:* Persons who support the purpose of the association
Activities: Supporting prayerful, pastoral action; *Awareness Events:* Catholic Students' Week, March

Canadian Catholic Conference *See* Canadian Conference of Catholic Bishops

Canadian Catholic Historical Association - English Section (CCHA) / Société canadienne d'histoire de l'église catholique - Section anglaise
c/o St. Michael's College, 81 St. Mary St., Toronto ON M5S 1J4
Tel: 905-893-9754; *Fax:* 416-934-3444
www.cchahistory.ca
Overview: A medium-sized national organization founded in 1933
Mission: The Association promotes interest & research in the history of the Canadian Catholic Church, its dioceses, religious communities, institutions, parishes, buildings, sites, & personalities. It is divided into English & French sections.
Chief Officer(s):
Jacqueline Gresko, President-General
jgresko@telus.net
Edward Jackman, Secretary-General
revedjackman@rogers.com
Finances: *Annual Operating Budget:* Less than $50,000; *Funding Sources:* Membership fees; donations
11 volunteer(s)
Membership: 100-499; *Fees:* $50 Canadian; US$50 American; $30 student; $60 French-English
Activities: Annual scholarly conference at the Canadian Congress
Awards:
• James F. Kenney Award (Award)
Eligibility: Awarded for the best essay on any aspect of the history of Catholicism in Canada written in a course by an undergraduate student in any university. *Amount:* $500 *Contact:* Dr. Edward MacDonald, gemacdonald@upei.ca
• G.E. Clerk Award (Award)
Eligibility: Scholars who have distinguished themselves in Catholic studies, publishing, teaching, archival work, or administration. *Contact:* Dr. Edward MacDonald, gemacdonald@upei.ca
• Paul Bator Award (Award)
This award recognizes the best article published in Historical Studies in the previous two years. *Contact:* Dr. Edward MacDonald, gemacdonald@upei.ca

History Office
#508, 10 St. Mary St., Toronto ON M4Y 1P9
Tel: 416-968-3683; *Fax:* 416-975-1588
terence.fay@utoronto.ca

Canadian Catholic Historical Association - French Section *Voir* Société canadienne d'histoire de l'Église Catholique - Section française

Canadian Catholic School Trustees' Association (CCSTA) / Association canadienne des commissaires d'écoles catholique
Catholic Education Centre, 570 West Hunt Club Rd., Nepean ON K2G 3R4
Tel: 613-224-4455; *Fax:* 613-224-3187
ccsta@ocsb.ca
www.ccsta.ca
Overview: A medium-sized national organization founded in 1960
Mission: To protect the right to Catholic education in Canada; To promote excellence in Catholic education across Canada
Member of: National Catholic Education Association (US)
Chief Officer(s):
John Stunt, Executive Director
john.stunt@ocsb.ca
Ted Paszek, President
tedp@eics.ab.ca
Mike St. Amand, Vice-President
mike@ashlycw.com
Finances: *Funding Sources:* Sponsoships
Membership: 8 associations; *Member Profile:* Provincial & territorial Catholic school trustees' associations in Canada
Activities: Promoting Catholic education; Providing professional development opportunities for trustees; Collaborating with the Canadian Conference of Catholic Bishops; Liaising with Canadian government agencies & other Catholic education organizations; *Awareness Events:* Catholic Education Week
Meetings/Conferences: • Canadian Catholic School Trustees' Association Annual General Meeting, June, 2015, St. John's, NL

Publications:
• Build Bethlehem Everywhere - A Statement on Catholic Education
Type: Book
• CCSTA [Canadian Catholic School Trustees' Association] Newsletter
Type: Newsletter
Profile: Includes CCSTA activities, conferences, & provincial reports

Canadian Cattle Breeders' Association (CCBA) / Société des éleveurs de bovins canadiens (SEBC)
4865, boul Laurier ouest, Saint-Hyacinthe QC J2S 3V4
Tel: 450-774-2775; *Fax:* 450-774-9775
info@cqrl.org
www.clrc.ca/canadiancattle.shtml
Overview: A medium-sized national organization founded in 1895
Chief Officer(s):
Angèle Hébert, Sec.-trés.
Finances: *Annual Operating Budget:* $50,000-$100,000; *Funding Sources:* Membership dues, casino
Staff Member(s): 1
Membership: 93; *Fees:* $40 regular; $15 supportive; *Committees:* Genetic Classification

Canadian Cattlemen's Association (CCA)
#310, 6715 - 8 St. NE, Calgary AB T2E 7H7
Tel: 403-275-8558; *Fax:* 403-274-5686
feedback@cattle.ca
www.cattle.ca
Overview: A large national organization founded in 1932
Mission: To act as the national voice of beef producers across Canada; To produce high-quality beef products; To maintain a profitable Canadian beef industry; To use management practices that protect the health of the animal & protect the environment
Chief Officer(s):
Martin Unrau, President
Dennis Laycraft, Executive Director
Rob McNabb, General Manager, Operations
Fawn Jackson, Manager, Environmental Affairs
Finances: *Funding Sources:* Fee assessments to provincial cattle organization members; National Check-off Agency
Membership: *Committees:* Environment; Animal Care; Animal Health & Meat Inspection; Value Creation & Competitiveness; Foreign Trade; Domestic Ag-Policy & Regulations; Convention; Executive & Finance
Activities: Collaborating with other agricultural sectors & food industries on matters of mutual concern; Providing a mentorship program
Meetings/Conferences: • Canadian Cattlemen's Association 2015 Annual General Meeting, March, 2015, Delta Ottawa, Ottawa, ON
Scope: National
Description: An opportunity for members to address industry issues & to elect officers
• Canadian Cattlemen's Association 2015 Semi-Annual Meeting & Convention, August, 2015, Winnipeg, MB
Scope: National
Description: Information sessions, policy setting, networking opportunities, & a social program
Publications:
• Canadian Cattlemen's Association By-laws
Number of Pages: 20
• Canadian Cattlemen's Association Policy Manual
Type: Manual; *Number of Pages:* 26
Profile: Topics include animal care, animal health, meat inspection, environment, finance, foreign trade, value creation, & competitiveness
• CCA [Canadian Cattlemen's Association] Monthly Report
Type: Report; *Frequency:* Monthly
Profile: CCA news & information about the beef producing industry
• CCA [Canadian Cattlemen's Association] Annual Report
Frequency: Annually
Profile: Executive, division, committee, provincial association, & financial reports
• CCA [Canadian Cattlemen's Association] News
Type: Newsletter; *Frequency:* Semimonthly; *Price:* Free
Profile: Recent association & industry information

Ottawa Office
#1207, 350 Sparks St., Ottawa ON K1R 7S8
Tel: 613-233-9375; *Fax:* 613-233-2860
Chief Officer(s):
John Masswohl, Director, Government & International Relations

Canadian Celiac Association (CCA) / L'Association canadienne de la maladic coeliaque
#400, 5025 Orbitor Dr., Bldg. 1, Mississauga ON L4W 4Y5
Tel: 905-507-6208; *Fax:* 905-507-4673
Toll-Free: 800-363-7296
info@celiac.ca
www.celiac.ca
www.facebook.com/groups/canadianceliacassociation
twitter.com/gfbri
Also Known As: Celiac Canada
Previous Name: Canadian Celiac Sprue Association
Overview: A large national charitable organization founded in 1972
Mission: To increase awareness of celiac & dermatitis herpetiformis among government institutions, health care professionals & the public; to provide information about the disease & a gluten-free diet, & encourges research through the establishment of the J.A. Campbell Research Fund
Chief Officer(s):
Brian Benwell, President
Connie M. Switzer, M.D., FRCPC, Chair
Dean Orlando, Treasurer
Peter Taylor, Executive Director
Finances: *Funding Sources:* Donations
Staff Member(s): 4
Membership: *Fees:* $75 new; $50 renewal
Activities: Providing awareness & education programs; engaging in advocacy activities; *Awareness Events:* Celiac Awareness Month, Oct.
Awards:
• J.A.Campbell Research Grant (Award)
Amount: $25,000 maximum
• J.A.Campbell Young Investigator Award (Award)
Amount: $5,000
Meetings/Conferences: • Canadian Celiac Association National Conference 2015, 2015
Scope: National
Publications:
• Acceptability of Food & Food Ingredients for the Gluten Free Diet
Type: Dictionary; *Price:* Free for new members of the Canadian Celiac Association; $10 non-members
• Celiac News
Type: Newsletter; *Frequency:* 3 pa; *Price:* Free with CCA membership
Profile: Up-to-date information about the diesease & a gluten-free diet

Belleville & Quinte Chapter
c/o Karen Y. Brooks, PO Box 293, Bloomfield ON K0K 1G0
e-mail: chapter.on.bellville.quinte@celiac.ca
Chief Officer(s):
Karen Brooks, President
karenybrooks@sympatico.ca

Calgary Chapter
231 - 37 Ave. NE, Calgary AB T2E 8J2
Tel: 403-237-0304; *Fax:* 403-269-9626
info@calgaryceliac.ca
calgaryceliac.com
www.facebook.com/155433831171925
Chief Officer(s):
Carolanne Nelson, Regional Coordinator
• Calgary Chapter Newsletter
Type: Newsletter; *Frequency:* Quarterly

Edmonton Chapter
Capilano Mall, #212, 5004 - 98 Ave. NW, Edmonton AB T6A 0A1
Tel: 780-485-2949; *Fax:* 780-485-2940
info@celiacedmonton.ca
www.celiacedmonton.ca
www.facebook.com/296692389521
twitter.com/edmontonceliac
Chief Officer(s):
Don Briggs, President
Debra Free, Treasurer
• Celiac Circular
Type: Newsletter; *Frequency:* Bimonthly; *Price:* Free for members of the Canadian Celiac Association Edmonton Chapter; $20 non-members

Fredericton Chapter
#226, 527 Beaverbrook Ct., Fredericton NB E3B 1X6
Tel: 506-454-3222
fred.celiac@gmail.com

Hamilton/Burlington Chapter
PO Box 65580, Stn. Dundas, Dundas ON L9H 6Y6
Tel: 905-572-6775
hamiltonceliacchapter@gmail.com
www.glutonfreehamilton.ca
Chief Officer(s):
Laura Harrison, President
Wendy Stewart, Treasurer
• Hamilton Celiac News
Type: Newsletter; *Frequency:* Quarterly; *Accepts Advertising*; *Editor:* Laura Harrison
Profile: Upcoming events, meeting reports, celiac friendly restaurants, & recipes

Kamloops Chapter
#69, 137 McGill Rd., Kamloops BC V2C 1L9
Tel: 250-374-6185
Chief Officer(s):
Eileen Gordon, Contact
edgordon@telus.net

Kelowna Chapter
PO Box 21031, Stn. Orchard Park, Kelowna BC V1Y 9N8
Tel: 250-763-7159
kelownaceliac.org
www.facebook.com/pages/kelowna-celiac/205146224439
twitter.com/KelownaCeliac
Chief Officer(s):
Irene Thompson, President
rithomp@telus.net
Marie Ablett, Help-line Contact
dougmarieablett1@shaw.ca

Kingston Chapter
1099 Lincoln Dr., Kingston ON K7M 4Z5
Tel: 613-539-0643
info@kingstonceliac.ca
www.kingstonceliac.ca
Chief Officer(s):
Sue Jennett, President

Kitchener/Waterloo Chapter
PO Box 118, 153 Frederick St., Kitchener ON N2H 2M3
e-mail: kwceliac@sympatico.ca
www.kwceliac.org
Chief Officer(s):
Diane Haines, Contact, Bruce-Grey Satellite Group
tdhaines@bmts.com

London Chapter
PO Box 27051, London ON N5X 3X5
Tel: 519-438-3549
info@londonceliac.org
www.londonceliac.org
Chief Officer(s):
Deb Davies, Vice President
vicepresident@londonceliac.org

Manitoba - West Chapter
#11, 83 Silverbirch Dr., Brandon MB R7B 1A8
Tel: 204-727-8445
Chief Officer(s):
Debbie Barrett, Contact
deborahb@mymts.net

Manitoba Chapter
#204, 825 Sherbrook St., Winnipeg MB R3A 1M5
Tel: 204-772-6979
office@manitobaceliac.com
www.manitobaceliac.com
www.facebook.com/176000709214214
twitter.com/manitobaceliac
Chief Officer(s):
Monique Clement, President
Neil Tarr, Treasurer
• Celi-Yak
Type: Newsletter; *Frequency:* Quarterly; *Price:* Free for Manitoba Chapter members
Profile: Food & product information, recipes & restaurants, health news, & upcoming events

Moncton Chapter
PO Box 1576, Moncton NB E1C 9X4
monctonceliacchapter.org
www.facebook.com/249496635102956
Chief Officer(s):
Jo-Anne Wilson, President
Aline Farrell, Vice-President
Dave Saunders, Treasurer
• Canadian Celiac Association Moncton Chapter Newsletter
Type: Newsletter; *Editor:* Mike Murphy

Newfoundland & Labrador Chapter
PO Box 39118, St. John's NL A1E 5Y7

Tel: 709-364-8757
www.envision.ca/webs/celiacnl
Chief Officer(s):
Geralyn Costello, Contact
geralyn.costello@gmail.com
Nova Scotia Chapter
Tacoma Plaza, #14, 50 Tacoma Dr., Dartmouth NS B2W 3E6
Tel: 902-464-9222; *Fax:* 902-435-6747
info@celiacns.ca
www.celiacns.ca
www.facebook.com/celiacns
twitter.com/ccaceliac
Chief Officer(s):
Ivy Warren, President
Nell Mallett, Treasurer
Joanne Kelly, Contact, Sydney Support Group
Kim McInnis, Contact, Pictou County Support Group
Debbie McLean, Contact, Baddeck Support Group
• Canadian Celiac Association Halifax Chapter
Type: Newsletter; *Frequency:* Quarterly
Profile: Recent issues dealing with Celiac Disease & Dermatitis Herpetiformis, chapter updates, & recipes
Ottawa Chapter
PO Box 39035, Stn. Billings Bridge, Ottawa ON K1H 1A1
Tel: 613-786-1335
info@ottawaceliac.ca
www.ottawaceliac.ca
Chief Officer(s):
June Williams, President
Simmy Ahluwalia, Treasurer
• Ottawa Chapter Newsletter
Type: Newsletter; *Editor:* Quintin Wight; *Price:* Free for Ottawa Chapter members
Profile: Upcoming events, issues, gluten-free product information, & recipes
Peterborough & Area Chapter
PO Box 272, 1054 Barnum Lake Rd., Wilberforce ON K0L 3C0
Tel: 705-448-9288
Toll-Free: 800-363-7296
www.celiacpeterborough.ca
Mission: To help celiacs & their families adjust to gluten-free living
Chief Officer(s):
Colin Turner, President
colinturner360@msn.com
• Peterborough & Area Chapter Newsletter
Type: Newsletter; *Frequency:* 3 pa; *Accepts Advertising*; *Editor:* Leslee Horton; *Price:* Free with Peterborough & Area Chapter membership
Prince Edward Island Chapter
PO Box 1921, Charlottetown PE C1A 7N5
Tel: 902-961-2066
info@celiacpei.ca
www.celiacpei.ca
Chief Officer(s):
Jean Eldershaw, President
Joanne Doughart, Vice-President
Cathy Handren, Treasurer
• Canadian Celiac Association Charlottetown Chapter
Type: Newsletter; *Editor:* Jim Hancock; Gay Hancock
Québec Chapter
Tél: 514-893-9856
info@celiacquebec.ca
Regina Chapter
PO Box 1773, Regina SK S4P 3C6
Tel: 306-731-2748
Chief Officer(s):
Audrey Webb, President
h.awebb@sasktel.net
Saint John Chapter
273 Erb Settlement Rd., Erb Settlement NB E5P 1P6
Tel: 506-433-2651
Chief Officer(s):
Heather Turnbull, Contact
theturnbulls@nb.aibn.com
St Catharines Chapter
PO Box 29003, 125 Carlton St., St Catharines ON L2R 7P9
Tel: 905-988-9475
chapter.on.st.catharines@celiac.ca
Chief Officer(s):
Lynne Turcotte, President
lturcotte@cogeco.ca
Saskatoon Chapter
PO Box 8935, Saskatoon SK S7K 6S7
Chief Officer(s):
Penny Fairbrother, President, 306-997-4833
emmaj@sasktel.net
• Celiac Digest
Type: Newsletter; *Accepts Advertising*; *Editor:* Jennifer Holmes
Sudbury Chapter
PO Box 2794, Stn. A, Sudbury ON P3A 5J3
Tel: 705-897-6608
Chief Officer(s):
Tammy Lavalle, President
Judith Buse, Treasurer
Thunder Bay Chapter
739 Harold Cr., Thunder Bay ON P7C 5H8
Tel: 807-623-5572
www.celiactbay.ca
Chief Officer(s):
Deb Paris, President
Jennifer Clace, Treasurer
• Celiac News
Type: Newsletter; *Frequency:* Y; *Editor:* A. Peat, K. Smith, & B. Knott
Profile: Information with a local emphasis to support & educate people with celiac disease
Toronto Chapter
PO Box 23056, 550 Eglinton Ave. West, Toronto ON M5N 3A8
Tel: 416-781-9140
www.torontoceliac.org
Chief Officer(s):
Alison Cazalet, President
Nadia Chychota, Contact, Halton-Peel Satellite, 647-241-2816
nadia@shelfconfidence.com
• Toronto Chapter Newsletter
Type: Newsletter; *Accepts Advertising*; *Editor:* Danny Weill & Alanna Weill
Vancouver Chapter
#306, 1385 West 8th St., Vancouver BC V6H 3V9
Tel: 604-736-2229
Toll-Free: 877-736-2240
info@vancouverceliac.ca
www.vancouverceliac.ca
twitter.com/VancouverCCA
Chief Officer(s):
Lorraine Didrikson, President
Val Vaartnou, Treasurer
• Celiac News
Type: Newsletter; *Frequency:* 3 pa; *Accepts Advertising*; *Editor:* Jane Kamimura & Joy Swaddling
Profile: Vancouver area news, recipes, restaurant reviews, & upcoming events
Victoria Chapter
PO Box 5457, Stn. B, Victoria BC V8R 6S8
Tel: 250-472-0141
victoriaceliacs@hotmail.ca
www.victoriaceliac.org
Chief Officer(s):
Nancy Adrian, President
• Victoria Celiac News
Type: Newsletter; *Frequency:* Bimonthly; *Accepts Advertising*; *Editor:* Christine Rushforth
Profile: Gluten free diet information

Canadian Celiac Sprue Association *See* Canadian Celiac Association

---

Canadian Celtic Arts Association
c/o Jean Talman, 81 St. Mary St., Toronto ON M5S 1J4
e-mail: info@canadiancelticarts.ca
www.canadiancelticarts.ca
Overview: A small national organization founded in 1979
Mission: To promote Celtic culture; To serve as a link between the diverse Celtic communities in Canada
Chief Officer(s):
Janice Chan, President
president@canadiancelticarts.ca
Donald Gillies, Treasurer
treasurer@canadiancelticarts.ca
Jean Talman, Membership Secretary & Coordinator, Programmes
membership@canadiancelticarts.ca
Finances: *Funding Sources:* Membership dues; Donations
Membership: *Fees:* $15 students & seniors; $20 families
Activities: Encouraging Celtic artistic creation, research, study, literature, music, art, & thought; Providing artistic & literary events, programs, & festivals
Publications:
• Canadian Celtic Arts Association Newsletter
Type: Newsletter; *Editor:* Leah Morrigan
Profile: Literary & artistic reviews, viewpoints, & Celtic-related events

---

Canadian Centre for Advanced Film Studies *See* Canadian Film Centre

---

Canadian Centre for Architecture (CCA) / Centre Canadien d'Architecture
1920, rue Baile, Montréal QC H3H 2S6
Tel: 514-939-7026
Other Communication: Bookstore e-mail: books@cca.qc.ca
info@cca.qc.ca
www.cca.qc.ca
www.facebook.com/cca.conversation
twitter.com/ccawire
www.youtube.com/CCAChannel
Overview: A large national licensing charitable organization founded in 1979
Mission: To advance knowledge, promote public understanding, widen thought & debate on the art of architecture, its history, theory, practice & role in society
Affliation(s): International Council of Museums (ICOM); International Confederation of Architectural Museums (ICAM); American Association of Museums (AAM); Canadian Museums Association (CMA); Société des musées québécois (SMQ); Société des directeurs des musées Montréal (SDMM); Research Library Group (RLG); Independent Research Libraries Association (IRLA); Association of Research Institutes in Art History (ARIAH); Institut de recherche en histoire de l'architecture
Finances: *Annual Operating Budget:* Greater than $5 Million; *Funding Sources:* Donors; sponsors; government
Staff Member(s): 77; 50 volunteer(s)
Membership: 1,800; *Fees:* Schedule available; *Member Profile:* Professors, students & practitioners of architecture; families; general public
Activities: International exhibitions; lectures & colloqia; film & video screenings; concerts; guided tours; school programs; research activities; CCA Bookstore; *Internships:* Yes; *Library* Open to public by appointment
Publications:
• CCA [Canadian Centre for Architecture] E-Newsletter
Type: Newsletter
• CCA [Canadian Centre for Architecture] Bookstore Newsletter
Type: Newsletter

Canadian Centre for Child Protection
615 Academy Rd., Winnipeg MB R3N 0E7
Tel: 204-945-5735; *Fax:* 204-948-2461
Toll-Free: 800-532-9135
www.protectchildren.ca
www.facebook.com/184856436064
twitter.com/CdnChildProtect
Previous Name: Child Find Manitoba
Overview: A medium-sized provincial charitable organization founded in 1985 overseen by Child Find Canada Inc.
Mission: To assist in the location & prevention of missing children; to increase the provincial awareness of issues relating to missing children & to advocate for the protection & rights of children
Chief Officer(s):
Lianna McDonald, Executive Director
Finances: *Annual Operating Budget:* $250,000-$500,000; *Funding Sources:* Private donations; fundraising
Staff Member(s): 8; 200 volunteer(s)
Membership: *Committees:* Advocacy; Fundraising; Conference; Case Management
Activities: Missing children poster distribution; fingerprinting of children; Photo ID Program; educational speaking to children, parents, businesses; advocacy; *Awareness Events:* Missing Children's Day/Week, May; Green Ribbon of Hope Campaign, May; *Internships:* Yes; *Speaker Service:* Yes; *Library* by appointment

---

Canadian Centre for Creative Technology *See* Shad Valley International

---

Canadian Centre for Energy Information / Centre info-énergie
#201, 322 - 11th Ave. SW, Calgary AB T2R 0C5

Tel: 403-263-7722; *Fax:* 403-237-6286
Toll-Free: 877-606-4636
www.centreforenergy.com
twitter.com/centreforenergy
Also Known As: Centre for Energy
Overview: A medium-sized national organization founded in 2002
Mission: To provide information about the Canadian energy system & energy-related issues
Chief Officer(s):
Pierre Alvarez, Chair
Thomas Cotter, Secretary
David Luff, Treasurer
Activities: Raising awareness & understanding about the Canadian energy system; Providing learning resources for teachers & students; *Speaker Service:* Yes
Publications:
• Energy Research & Innovation Directory
Type: Directory
Profile: Highlights of energy research projects, developed in partnership with the Department of Foreign Affairs & International Trade

Canadian Centre for Ethics in Sport (CCES) / Centre canadien pour l'éthique dans le sport
#350, 955 Green Valley Cres., Ottawa ON K2C 3V4
Tel: 613-521-3340; *Fax:* 613-521-3134
Toll-Free: 800-672-7775
info@cces.ca
www.cces.ca
www.facebook.com/CanadianCentreforEthicsinSport
twitter.com/EthicsInSport
www.youtube.com/ccesonline
Overview: A medium-sized national organization founded in 1991
Mission: Foster ethical sport for all Canadians
Affliation(s): True Sport Foundation
Chief Officer(s):
David Zussman, Chair
Paul Melia, President & CEO
pmelia@cces.ca
Staff Member(s): 50

Canadian Centre for Fisheries Innovation (CCFI) / Centre canadien d'innovations des pêches
PO Box 4920, Stn. C, Ridge Rd., St. John's NL A1C 5R3
Tel: 709-778-0517; *Fax:* 709-778-0516
ccfi@mi.mun.ca
www.ccfi.ca
Previous Name: Centre for Fisheries Innovation
Overview: A medium-sized national organization founded in 1989
Mission: To work with the fishing industry to improve productivity & profitability of fishery through science & technology
Member of: Newfoundland Ocean Industries Association; Aquaculture Association of Canada; Fisheries Council of Canada; St. John's Board of Trade
Affliation(s): Memorial University of Newfoundland; Marine Institute
Chief Officer(s):
Robert Verge, Managing Director
Robert.Verge@mi.mun.caa
Gabe Gregory, Chair
ggregory@nl.rogers.com
Staff Member(s): 6
Activities: Efforts of the Centre are concentrated in four main areas: aquaculture, harvesting, processing & equipment development; the pursuit of excellence in these areas is addressed through demonstration projects, & research & development projects which pool the expertise of industry, educational institutions & governments; the Centre plays a leading role in technology transfer & information dissemination initiatives so that the fishing industry may benefit from scientific discoveries & state-of-the-art equipment

Canadian Centre for International Studies & Cooperation
Voir Centre canadien d'étude et de coopération internationale

Canadian Centre for Investigation & Prevention of Torture
See Canadian Centre for Victims of Torture

Canadian Centre for Occupational Health & Safety (CCOHS) / Centre canadien d'hygiène et de sécurité au travail (CCHST)
135 Hunter St. East, Hamilton ON L8N 1M5
Tel: 905-572-2981; *Fax:* 905-572-2206
Toll-Free: 800-668-4284
clientservices@ccohs.ca
www.ccohs.ca
www.linkedin.com/company/canadian-centre-for-occupational-health-and-s
www.facebook.com/CCOHS
twitter.com/ccohs
Overview: A large national charitable organization founded in 1978
Mission: Promotes the total well-being—physical, psychological & mental health—of working Canadians by providing information, training, education, management systems & solutions that support health, safety, & wellness programs
Chief Officer(s):
S. Len Hong, President/CEO, 905-572-2981 Ext. 4433
Patabendi K. Abeytunga, Vice-President, 905-572-2981 Ext. 4537
Finances: *Annual Operating Budget:* Greater than $5 Million; *Funding Sources:* Government & revenue from product sales
Staff Member(s): 85
Membership: *Fees:* Optional membership packages from $25 - $500/ yr.; customized membership packages can include consulting, customized training, database development
Activities: Provides a variety of both public service initiaties at no charge to user, such as OSH Answers, Inquiry Service, Newsletters, Webinars & Podcasts. Services for specialty resources provided on a cost recovery basis include databases, publications & training & education; *Speaker Service:* Yes; *Library:* Documentation Resources; by appointment
Meetings/Conferences: • Canadian Centre for Occupational Health & Safety Forum V, February, 2016, Vancouver, BC
Scope: National
Publications:
• The Health & Safety Report
Type: Newsletter; *Frequency:* Monthly; *Price:* Free
Profile: Workplace health & safety news, plus information & tips
• Liaison [a publication of the Canadian Centre for Occupational Health & Safety]
Type: Newsletter; *Frequency:* Bimonthly
Profile: CCOHS developments, resources, & initiatives

Canadian Centre for Policy Alternatives (CCPA) / Centre canadien de politique alternative
#500, 251 Bank St., Ottawa ON K2P 1X3
Tel: 613-563-1341; *Fax:* 613-233-1458
ccpa@policyalternatives.ca
www.policyalternatives.ca
www.facebook.com/policyalternatives
twitter.com/ccpa
www.youtube.com/user/policyalternatives
Overview: A medium-sized national organization founded in 1980
Mission: To promote research on economic & social issues facing Canada; to monitor current developments in economy & study important trends that affect Canadians; to demonstrate thoughtful alternatives to the limited perspectives of business, research institutes & government agencies; to put forward research that reflects concerns of women & men, labour & business, churches, cooperatives & voluntary agencies, governments, minorities, disadvantaged & fortunate individuals
Chief Officer(s):
Bruce Campbell, Executive Director
Diane Touchette, Director, Operations
Finances: *Funding Sources:* Membership fees
Staff Member(s): 16
Membership: 12,000+; *Fees:* $1000 director's circle; $500 editor's circle; $300 sponsor; $100 supporter; $35 student/low income; *Member Profile:* Open
Activities: Publishes research reports & books; organizes public symposiums & conferences
Publications:
• The CCPA Monitor
Type: Magazine; *Frequency:* Monthly; *Price:* Free to CCPA members
Profile: Research articles
• Our Schools / Our Selves
Type: Journal; *Frequency:* Quarterly
Profile: Articles on educational issues such as social justice, action, pedagogy, & educational content

British Columbia Office
#1400, 207 West Hastings St., Vancouver BC V6B 1H7
Tel: 604-801-5121; *Fax:* 604-801-5122
ccpabc@policyalternatives.ca
www.policyalternatives.ca/offices/bc
Chief Officer(s):
Seth Klein, Director

Manitoba Office
#205, 765 Main St., Winnipeg MB R2W 3N5
Tel: 204-927-3200; *Fax:* 204-927-3201
ccpamb@policyalternatives.ca
www.policyalternatives.ca/offices/manitoba
www.facebook.com/CCPAMB
twitter.com/CCPAMB
www.youtube.com/policyalternatives
Chief Officer(s):
Molly McCracken, Director

Nova Scotia Office
PO Box 8355, Halifax NS B3K 5M1
Tel: 902-240-0926
ccpans@policyalternatives.ca
www.policyalternatives.ca/offices/nova-scotia
www.facebook.com/CCPANS
twitter.com/CCPANS
www.youtube.com/policyalternatives
Chief Officer(s):
Christine Saulnier, Director

Saskatchewan Office
2835 - 13th Ave., #G, Regina SK S4T 1N6
Tel: 306-924-3372; *Fax:* 306-586-5177
ccpasask@sasktel.net
www.policyalternatives.ca/offices/saskatchewan
Chief Officer(s):
Simon Enoch, Director

Canadian Centre for Stress & Well-Being
#1801, 1 Yonge St., Toronto ON M5E 1W7
Tel: 416-363-6204; *Fax:* 416-658-9536
smcen@yahoo.com
Also Known As: Stress Management Centre
Overview: A small national organization founded in 1982
Mission: To provide education about stress management; To increase health & wellness
Activities: Counselling; Offering resources about stress management skills

Canadian Centre for Studies in Publishing (CCSP)
Simon Fraser University at Harbour Centre, 515 West Hastings St., Vancouver BC V6B 5K3
Tel: 778-782-5242; *Fax:* 778-782-5239
ccsp-info@sfu.ca
publishing.sfu.ca
Overview: A small international charitable organization founded in 1987
Mission: Dedicated to the development of publishing in Canada & internationally
Membership: *Member Profile:* Educators; publishers; students
Activities: Teaching, research, innovation & information centre; *Internships:* Yes; *Speaker Service:* Yes; *Library:* CCSP Resource Library; by appointment

Canadian Centre for Victims of Torture (CCVT)
194 Jarvis St., 2nd Fl., Toronto ON M5B 2B7
Tel: 416-363-1066; *Fax:* 416-363-2122
www.ccvt.org
www.facebook.com/115015798517911
twitter.com/ccvt_toronto
Previous Name: Canadian Centre for Investigation & Prevention of Torture
Overview: A medium-sized national charitable organization founded in 1983
Mission: To offer support & arrange medical, legal & social care for torture victims & their families; to increase public awareness in Canada & abroad of torture & its effects upon survivors & their families
Member of: Canadian Council for Refugees; Toronto Refugee Affairs Council; Ontario Council of Agencies Serving Immigrants; Multicultural Health Association; Canadian Network for the Health of Survivors of Torture & Organized Violence
Chief Officer(s):
Mulugeta Abai, Executive Director
mabai@ccvt.org
Finances: *Annual Operating Budget:* $1.5 Million-$3 Million
Staff Member(s): 30
Membership: *Committees:* Health; Legal; Volunteer Advisory; Public Education
Activities: *Internships:* Yes; *Speaker Service:* Yes; *Rents Mailing List:* Yes; *Library:* Resource Centre; Open to public

Canadian Centre on Disability Studies (CCDS)
56 The Promenade, Winnipeg MB R3B 3H9

Tel: 204-287-8411; *Fax:* 204-284-5343; *TTY:* 204-475-6223
ccds@disabilitystudies.ca
www.disabilitystudies.ca
Overview: A small national charitable organization founded in 1995
Mission: To research, educate, & disseminate information on disability issues
Chief Officer(s):
Eleanor Chornoboy, Interim Executive Director, 204-287-8411 Ext. 31
international3@disabilitystudies.ca
Staff Member(s): 9
Membership: *Fees:* $100 business/organization; $20 individual; $10 student/senior
Publications:
• CCDS [Canadian Centre on Disability Studies] Bulletin
Type: Newsletter; *Frequency:* Quarterly

Canadian Centre on Substance Abuse (CCSA) / Centre canadien de lutte contre l'alcoolisme et les toxicomanies (CCLAT)

#300, 75 Albert St., Ottawa ON K1P 5E7
Tel: 613-235-4048; *Fax:* 613-235-8101
Toll-Free: 800-559-4514
info@ccsa.ca
www.ccsa.ca
twitter.com/CCSAcanada
www.youtube.com/user/CCSACCLAT
Overview: A medium-sized national charitable organization founded in 1988
Mission: To minimize the harm associated with addictions, including substance abuse & problem gambling
Chief Officer(s):
Michel Perron, CEO, 613-235-4048 Ext. 227
Tina Barton, Advisor, Communications, 613-235-4048 Ext. 230
Doug Beirness, Senior Analyst, Research & Policy, 613-235-4048 Ext. 247
Finances: *Annual Operating Budget:* $1.5 Million-$3 Million; *Funding Sources:* Canada's Drug Strategy
Staff Member(s): 26
Activities: Provides information on substance abuse issues; reference information; provides evidence based policy guidance to governments; shares treatment knowledge & best practices on substance abuse & addiction; *Awareness Events:* National Drug Awareness Week, Nov.; *Library:* CCSA Library Collection; by appointment
Publications:
• Action News [a publication of the Canadian Centre on Substance Abuse]
Type: Newsletter; *Frequency:* Quarterly; *Editor:* Richard Garlick
ISSN: 1701-4522
Profile: Current events related to substance abuse
• Canadian Centre on Substance Abuse Annual Report
Type: Yearbook; *Frequency:* Annually
• Directory of Fetal Alcohol Spectrum Disorder (FASD) Information & Support Services in Canada
Type: Directory *ISSN:* 1715-4197
Profile: Listings of organizations & individuals that provide an FASD related service in Canada

The Canadian Centre/International P.E.N. (PEN)

#301, 24 Ryerson Ave., Toronto ON M5T 2P3
Tel: 416-703-8448; *Fax:* 416-703-3870
queries@pencanada.ca
www.pencanada.ca
www.facebook.com/pages/PEN-Canada/141054639272034
twitter.com/PENCanada
www.youtube.com/canadapen
Also Known As: PEN Canada
Overview: A medium-sized international charitable organization founded in 1926
Mission: To foster understanding among writers of all nations; to fight for freedom of expression wherever it is endangered; to work for preservation of world's literature
Member of: Network on International Human Rights
Chief Officer(s):
Philip Slayton, President
Tasleem Thawar, Executive Director
tthawar@pencanada.ca
Finances: *Funding Sources:* Donations; events
Staff Member(s): 4
Membership: 1,000; *Fees:* $25 student; $75 regular; *Member Profile:* Poets, playwrights, essayists (including nonfiction writers), editors, novelists & journalists who have produced at least one book of substantial literary value; editors who have worked at their profession for at least five years & edited at least five books eligible under the above criteria; translators who have translated at least five eligible books; playwrights who have had at least one play produced by an Equity company; associate - those who share PEN's goals but who do not quality for membership; reduced rate of membership available to students who wish to form or join established PEN chapter at a university or community college
Activities: *Library*

Canadian Cerebral Palsy Sports Association (CCPSA) / Association canadienne de sport pour paralytiques cérébraux (ACPSA)

#104, 720 Belfast Rd., Ottawa ON K1G 0Z5
Tel: 613-748-1430
info@ccpsa.ca
www.ccpsa.ca
www.facebook.com/112866075626
Overview: A medium-sized national charitable organization founded in 1985
Mission: To act as umbrella group for all provincial cerebral palsy sport organizations; To design programs that are designed for athletes with cerebral palsy & non-progressive head injuries
Affliation(s): Cerebral Palsy International Sports & Recreation Association; International Paralympic Committee
Chief Officer(s):
Marie Dannhaeuser, Executive Director
marie@ccpsa.ca
Finances: *Annual Operating Budget:* $500,000-$1.5 Million; *Funding Sources:* Government of Canada, Dept. of Heritage; Sport Canada; donations; fundraising
Staff Member(s): 3; 11 volunteer(s)
Membership: 2,500; *Fees:* $25-200; *Committees:* Coaching; Boccia; Classification; Athletics
Activities: Programs include cycling, soccer, athletics & boccia, swimming, bowls, powerlifting

The Canadian Chamber of Commerce / La Chambre de commerce du Canada

#420, 360 Albert St., Ottawa ON K1R 7X7
Tel: 613-238-4000; *Fax:* 613-238-7643
info@chamber.ca
www.chamber.ca
www.facebook.com/CanadianChamberofCommerce
twitter.com/CdnChamberofCom
www.youtube.com/user/CdnChamberofCommerce
Overview: A large national organization founded in 1925
Mission: To create a climate for competitiveness, profitability & job creation for enterprises of all sizes in all sectors across Canada. Offices in Ottawa, Toronto, Montreal & Calgary
Member of: International Chamber of Commerce
Affliation(s): Canadian Services Coalition; Canadian Society of Association Executives; C.D. Howe Institute; Chamber of Commerce Executives of Canada; Forum for International Trade Training; International Chamber of Commerce; World Chambers Federation
Chief Officer(s):
Michael McMullen, Chair
Perrin Beatty, President & CEO
pbeatty@chamber.ca
Michel Barsalou, Executive Vice-President, Communications & Services
mbarsalou@chamber.ca
Staff Member(s): 32
Membership: 450+ chambers of commerce + 200,000 businesses across Canada; *Fees:* Schedule available; *Committees:* Competition Law & Policy; Economic Policy; Human Resources Policy; Innovations; Intellectual Property; International Affairs; Natural Resources & Environment; Ottawa Liaison; SME; Taxation; Territorial Policy; Transportation & Infrastructure
Meetings/Conferences: • Canadian Chamber of Commerce 2015 AGM and Convention, October, 2015, Westin Ottawa, Ottawa, ON
Scope: National
Contact Information: Marley Ransom, Communications and Events Specialist; mransom@chamber.ca; Phone: 613-238-4000 ext. 227

Calgary Office
PO Box 38057, Calgary AB T3K 5G9
Tel: 403-271-0595; *Fax:* 403-226-6930

Montréal Office
#709, 1155, rue Université, Montréal QC H3B 3A7
Tel: 514-866-4334; *Fax:* 514-866-7296

Toronto Office
#901, 55 University Ave., Toronto ON M5J 2H7
Tel: 416-868-6415; *Fax:* 416-868-0189

Canadian Chapter of the International Council of Community Churches *See* Christian Catholic Church Canada

Canadian Charolais Association (CCA)

2320 - 41 Ave. NE, Calgary AB T2E 6W8
Tel: 403-250-9242; *Fax:* 403-291-9324
cca@charolais.com
www.charolais.com
www.facebook.com/cdncharolais
twitter.com/canCharolais
Overview: A medium-sized national organization founded in 1958
Mission: To be leaders in predictable beef genetics; to register, record, transfer & promote Canadian Charolais; to provide services for membership
Member of: Canadian Beef Breeds Council
Chief Officer(s):
Wade Beck, President
wcbeck@sasktel.net
Finances: *Annual Operating Budget:* $500,000-$1.5 Million; *Funding Sources:* Registration & transfer of Charolais cattle
Staff Member(s): 4
Membership: 1,100; *Fees:* $42.80; *Member Profile:* Owner of registered Charolais cattle; *Committees:* Public Relations; Education; Youth & Export; Market Development; Breed Improvement; Audit; Executive

Canadian Chemical Producers' Association *See* Chemistry Industry Association of Canada

Canadian Chianina Association

c/o Barb Jack, PO Box 45, Meskanaw SK S0K 2W0
Tel: 306-864-3644; *Fax:* 306-864-2936
www.clrc.ca/chianina.shtml
Overview: A small national organization founded in 1972
Mission: To provide for registration of Chianina cattle in Canada
Affliation(s): Canadian Livestock Records Corporation
Chief Officer(s):
Barb Jack, Secretary Manager, 306-864-3644, Fax: 306-864-2936
Membership: *Fees:* $50 initiation fee; $25 annual membership; *Member Profile:* Breeders of Canadian Chianina cattle

Canadian Chicken Marketing Agency *See* Chicken Farmers of Canada

Canadian Chihuahua Rescue & Transport (CCRT)

PO Box 83023, 5899 Leslie St., Toronto ON M2H 3R9
Toll-Free: 877-783-7333
info@ccrt.net
www.ccrt.net
Overview: A small national charitable organization founded in 1999
Mission: To rescue & provide necessary veterinary care for homeless & abused Chihuahua & Chihuahua mix breed dogs throughout Canada
Finances: *Funding Sources:* Adoption fees; Sponsorships; Donations; Purchases from store
Activities: Assisting in finding homes for pets; Microchipping, spaying, neutering, & vaccinating Chihuahuas placed through the organization; Educating Chihuahua owners & the public about the breed;

Canadian Child Care Federation (CCCF) / Fédération canadienne des services de garde à l'enfance (FCSGE)

#600, 700 Industrial Ave., Ottawa ON K1G 0Y9
Tel: 613-729-5289; *Fax:* 613-729-3159
Toll-Free: 800-858-1412
info@cccf-fcsge.ca
www.cccf-fcsge.ca
www.facebook.com/groups/5657406573
twitter.com/CCCFed
www.youtube.com/user/Qualitychildcare
Previous Name: Canadian Child Day Care Federation
Overview: A large national charitable organization founded in 1987
Mission: To promote excellence in child care & early learning
Affliation(s): AB Family Child Care Assn; AB Child Care Assn; Association francophone à l'éducation des services à l'enfance de l'Ontario; Assn of Early Childhood Educators NL; Assn of Early Childhood Educators ON; Assn of Early Childhood Educators QC; BC Aboriginal Child Care Society; BC Family Child Care Assn; Certification Council of Early Childhood Educators NS; Early Childhood Care & Education NB; Early Childhood Development Assn PEI; Early Childhood Educators

BC; Home Child Care Assn ON; MB Child Care Assn; NS Child Care Assn; SK Early Childhood Assn; YK Child Care Assn; NT Liaison
Chief Officer(s):
Don Giesbrecht, President & CEO, 613-729-5289 Ext. 220
Linda Skinner, Treasurer
Claire McLaughlin, Manager, Publications & Marketing, 613-729-5289 Ext. 221
Finances: *Funding Sources:* Donations; Sponsorships
Membership: 11,000+; *Fees:* $35 student; $65 individual; $90 organization; *Member Profile:* Individuals who support the goals of the Canadian Child Care Federation, such as educators & policy makers; organizations, such as educational institutions & child care organizations
Activities: Conducting research; providing resources to enrich curriculum & to increase understanding of child development; offering professional development opportunities; promoting child health & safety; establishing partnerships; *Awareness Events:* National Child Day
Awards:
• Award for Excellence in Child Care (Award)
To honour persons who have made an outstanding contribution to the field of child care *Contact:* Award Selection Committee, Cdn Child Care Fed, Phone: 613-729-5289; E-mail: info@cccf-fcsge.ca
Meetings/Conferences: • Canadian Child Care Federation 2015 Annual General Meeting, 2015
Scope: National
Publications:
• Canadian Child Care Federation Annual Report
Type: Yearbook; *Frequency:* Annually
• Early Learning Canada
Type: Toolkit
Profile: A program to develop child health & literacy, containing a workshop leader guide, a trainer manual, resource sheets, tip cards, plus participant resources, evaluations, & certificates
• Family Child Care Training Program
Type: Manual
Profile: Program resources include training manuals for levels one, two, & three
• Foundations for Numeracy: An Evidence-based Toolkit for Early Learning Practitioners
Type: Guide; *Price:* $25 (Contact: Cate Morisset, E-mail: cmorisset@cccf-fcsge.ca)
• Foundations for Numeracy: An Evidence-based Toolkit for the Effective Mathematics Teacher
Type: Guide; *Price:* $25 (Contact: Cate Morisset, E-mail: cmorisset@cccf-fcsge.ca)
• Guide to Successful Facilitation
Type: Guide
Profile: A guide to facilitating workshops
• Interaction [a publication of Canadian Child Care Federation]
Type: Magazine; *Frequency:* Quarterly; *Accepts Advertising*; *Editor:* Claire McLaughlin; *Price:* Free with membership in the Canadian Child Care Federation; $50/year for non-members
Profile: News, opinions, current research, & practice information from across Canada on topics such as family based care, health,& best practices
• Learning Kit: Children's Environmental Health
Type: Kit; *Price:* $20
• Learning Kit: Children's Rights
Type: Kit; *Price:* $20
• Learning Kit: Leadership
Type: Kit; *Price:* $20
• Learning Through Play Resources (a three volume set, available in English, French, & Spanish)
Type: Guide; *Price:* $25 / volume (Contact: Cate Morisset, E-mail: cmorisset@cccf-fcsge.ca)
Profile: Volume 1: Curriculum Guide (with a CD insert); Volume 2: Construction & Maintenance Guide; Volume 3: Mentor & CommunityPartnerships Guide
• Meeting the Challenge: Effective Strategies for Challenging Behaviours in Early Childhood Environments
Type: Book; *Number of Pages:* 40; *Editor:* B. Kaiser; J. Sklar Rasminsky; *Price:* $18
Profile: A guide to providing effective early intervention, written for persons who work with youngchildren & their families
• Moving & Growing
Price: $7 / publication
Profile: A series to promote healthy living for children, consisting of the following publications: Physical Activities for the First Two Years; Physical Activities for Twos, Threes, & Fours; Physical Activities for Fives& Sixes; & Physical Activities for Sevens & Eights
• Nourish, Nurture Neurodevelopment: Neurodevelopmental Research: Implications for Caregiver Practice
Type: Kit; *Price:* $10
Profile: Research findings, resource sheets, & notes, designed for presentation to educators & parents
• Occupational Standards for Early Childhood Educators
Price: $15
Profile: Best practices in early childhood education & care settings
• Outdoor Play in Early Childhood Education & Care Programs
Price: $15
• Partners in Quality
Price: $15 / publication
Profile: A series to support practitioners in the child care field, consisting of the following resources: Volume 1 - Issues; Volume 2 - Relationships; Volume 3 - Infrastructure; Volume 4 - Communities; Tools forPractitioners in Child Care Settings; & Tools for Administrators in Child Care Settings

Canadian Child Day Care Federation *See* Canadian Child Care Federation

Canadian Children's Book Centre (CCBC)
#217, 40 Orchard View Blvd., Toronto ON M4R 1B9
Tel: 416-975-0010; *Fax:* 416-975-8970
info@bookcentre.ca
www.bookcentre.ca
www.facebook.com/kidsbookcentre
twitter.com/kidsbookcentre
Overview: A medium-sized national charitable organization founded in 1976
Mission: To promote the reading, writing, & illustrating of Canadian books for young readers, providing programs, publications & resources for teachers, librarians, authors, illustrators, publishers, booksellers & parents.
Affliation(s): Book & Periodical Council; Book Promoters Association of Canada; Canadian Booksellers Association; Canadian Coalition of School Libraries
Chief Officer(s):
Todd Kyle, President
Charlotte Teeple, Executive Director
charlotte@bookcentre.ca
Dawn Todd, General Manager
dawn@bookcentre.ca
Finances: *Funding Sources:* Canada Council for the Arts; Canadian Heritage; TD Bank Financial Group; Imperial Oil Foundation
Staff Member(s): 6
Membership: *Fees:* $30 senior/student; $60 individual; $135 associate; $500 corporate; $1,000 patron; *Member Profile:* Teachers, librarians, authors, illustrators, publishers, booksellers, wholesalers & parents
Activities: TD Canadian Children's Book Week; TD Grade One Book Giveaway Program; resource libraries of Canadian Children's books in Toronto, Halifax, Edmonton, Vancouver & Winnipeg; Regional Officers in Alberta, British Columbia, Manitoba & Nova Scotia; *Library* Open to public by appointment

Awards:
• The Norma Fleck Award for Non-Fiction (Award)
Rewards excellence in outstanding work of non-fiction for young people by a Canadian author, published in previous calendar year; jury members include a teacher, a librarian, a reviewer & a bookseller *Amount:* $10,000
• The Geoffrey Bilson Award for Historical Fiction (Award)
Rewards excellence in outstanding work of historical fiction for young people by a Canadian author, published in previous calendar year; judges are: a writer, bookseller, children's books specialist, historian, librarian *Amount:* $1,000
• TD Canadian Children's Literature Award (Award)
Amount: $20,000
Publications:
• Canadian Children's Book News
Type: Magazine; *Frequency:* Quarterly; *Accepts Advertising*; *Price:* Free with CCBC membership; $19.50
Profile: New Canadian children's books, industry issues, profiles of publishers & bookstores, & author & illustrator interviews
• Get Published!
Price: $16.75
Profile: Kit includes Writing & Illustrating Children's Books: A Guide to Getting Published, The Publishers List, Author & Editor: A Working Guide, as well as Canadian Children's Book News, & Our Choice
• Our Choice
Frequency: Annually; *Price:* Free with CCBC membership
Profile: Highlights the best new Canadian children's books, magazines, & audiovisual resources
• Theme Guide
Frequency: Annually
Profile: Theme guides, with over 200 book selections for reading & interest levels ranging from junior kindergarten to young adult, on a different topic each year, including adventure, mystery, sports, multiculturalism,families & friends, the environment, book illustrations, Canada & the sea

Alberta
8132 Hunterview Dr. NW, Calgary AB T4G 1A8
Tel: 403-695-7761
alberta@bookcentre.ca
Chief Officer(s):
Ginger Mullen, Regional Officer

British Columbia
c/o National Office, #101, 40 Orchard View Dr., Toronto ON M4R 1B9
Tel: 416-975-0010
bc@bookcentre.ca
Chief Officer(s):
Cynthia Nugent, Regional Officer

Manitoba
274 Mowat Rd., East St. Paul MB R2E 0L6
Tel: 204-654-3721
manitoba@bookcentre.ca
Chief Officer(s):
Gail Hamilton, Regional Officer

Nova Scotia
#110, 2070 Oxford St., Halifax NS B3L 2T2
Tel: 902-420-1471; *Fax:* 902-420-1468
ns@bookcentre.ca
Chief Officer(s):
Kathleen Martin, Regional Officer

Canadian Children's Dance Theatre (CCDT)
509 Parliament St., Toronto ON M4X 1P3
Tel: 416-924-5657; *Fax:* 416-924-4141
info@ccdt.org
www.ccdt.org
www.facebook.com/CanadianContemporaryDanceTheatre
twitter.com/CCDTdance
Overview: A small national organization founded in 1980
Mission: To promote dance theatre to young people
Chief Officer(s):
Deborah Lundmark, Artistic Director & Resident Choreographer
Michael de Coninck Smith, Co-Artistic Director & Production Manager

Canadian Children's Opera Chorus (CCOC)
227 Front St. East, Toronto ON M5A 1E8
Tel: 416-366-0467; *Fax:* 416-366-9204
info@canadianchildrensopera.com
www.canadianchildrensopera.com
www.facebook.com/110622059017962
twitter.com/OperaKidsCanada
Overview: A small national organization founded in 1968
Mission: To be the foremost children's operatic chorus in Canada & to achieve international recognition
Member of: Ontario Choral Federation; Opera for Youth Inc.; Canadian Conference for the Arts
Chief Officer(s):
Ken Hall, General Manager
Ann Cooper Gay, Executive Artistic Director
Finances: *Annual Operating Budget:* $500,000-$1.5 Million
Staff Member(s): 12
Membership: 200; *Fees:* Schedule available

Canadian Chiropractic Association (CCA) / Association chiropratique canadienne (ACC)
#6, 186 Spadina Ave., Toronto ON M5T 3B2
Tel: 416-585-7902; *Fax:* 416-585-2970
Toll-Free: 877-222-9303
www.chiropracticcanada.ca
Overview: A large national organization founded in 1943
Mission: To see every Canadian have full & equitable access to chiropractic care; To promote the integration of chiropractic into the Canadian health care system
Affliation(s): Canadian Chiropractic Examining Board; Canadian Federation of Chiropractic Regulatory & Educational Accrediting Boards; Canadian Chiropractic Historical Association; Canadian Memorial Chiropractic College; Université du Québec á Trois-Rivières Programme de Doctorat en Chiropratique; Canadian Chiropractic Protective Association;

Canadian Chiropractic Research Foundation; World Federation of Chiropractic
Chief Officer(s):
Alison Dantas, CEO
adantas@chiropracticcanada.ca
Allan Gotlib, Director, Research Programs
agotlib@chiropracticcanada.ca
Michael Heitshu, Director, Government Affairs & Policy
mheitshu@canadianchiropractic.ca
Ronda Parkes, Director, Marketing & Communications
rparkes@canadianchiropractic.ca
Ronda Parkes, Director, Operations
mpaulin@chiropracticcanada.ca
Nekeisha Mohammed, Manager, Communications
nmohammed@chiropracticcanada.ca
Finances: *Funding Sources:* Membership fees; Corporate partnerships
Membership: *Fees:* $235-$465 based on the number of years in practice; *Member Profile:* Graduates of accredited chiropractic colleges, who are licensed by their provincial licensing offices, & who are members of their provincial associations
Activities: Raising public awareness of the benefits of chiropractic care; Facilitating research; Advocating for the needs of the chiropractic profession; Communicating timely information with registered members
Meetings/Conferences: • Canadian Chiropractic Association 2015 Conference, September, 2015, Scotiabank Convention Centre, Niagara Falls, ON
Scope: National
Publications:
• Canadian Chiropractic Association Membership Directory [a publication of the Canadian Chiropractic Association]
Type: Directory; *Price:* Free with CCA membership
Profile: A listing of all associate members
• Canadian Chiropractic Association Update
Type: Newsletter
• The CCA [Canadian Chiropractic Association] Report
Type: Newsletter; *Price:* Free with CCA membership
• Journal of the Canadian Chiropractic Association (JCCA)
Frequency: Quarterly; *Accepts Advertising*; *Editor:* Dr. Allan Gotlib *ISSN:* 1715-6181; *Price:* Free with CCA membership; $30 Canadiannon-members; $74 foreign
Profile: Peer-reviewed research & communication between the CCA & its members

Canadian Chiropractic Examining Board (CCEB) / Conseil canadien des examens chiropratiques

#230, 1209 - 59th Ave. SE, Calgary AB T2H 2P6
Fax: 403-230-3321
exams@cceb.ca
www.cceb.ca
Overview: A small national organization founded in 1962
Mission: To provide high quality exams for licensure
Member of: National Certification Commission
Membership: *Member Profile:* Provincial chiropractic licensing boards
Activities: Clinical competency evaluation & cognitive skill examinations; annual general meeting

Canadian Chiropractic Research Foundation (CCRF) / La Fondation canadienne pour la recherche en chiropratique

#600, 30 St Patrick St., Toronto ON M5T 3A3
Tel: 416-585-7902
Toll-Free: 877-222-9303
www.canadianchiropracticresearchfoundation.com
Previous Name: Chiropractic Foundation for Spinal Research
Overview: A small national charitable organization founded in 1976
Mission: To fund & facilitate health services & research related to the practice of chiropractic
Affliation(s): Canadian Chiropractic Association; Canadian Institute for Health Research
Chief Officer(s):
Allan Gotlib, Executive Vice-President
agotlib@chiropracticcanada.ca
Finances: *Funding Sources:* Donations; Foundation memberships; Fundraising
Activities: Assisting doctors of chiropractic to obtain Masters & PhD degrees; Liaising with other organizations; Creating a university-based chiropractic research chair in each province

Canadian Chito-Ryu Karate-Do Association

89 Curlew Ave., Toronto ON M3A 2P8
Tel: 416-444-5310
info@canadianchitoryu.ca
www.canadianchitoryu.ca
Overview: A small national organization founded in 1991
Mission: Committed to understanding and propagating the karate-do of its founder O'Sensei Dr. Tsuyoshi Chitose.
Chief Officer(s):
David Smith, President
Derek J. Ryan, Vice-President

Canadian Christian Relief & Development Association (CCRDA)

374 North Scugog Crt., bowmanville ON L1C 3K2
Tel: 289-385-7307; *Fax:* 519-885-5225
ccrdacoordinator@gmail.com
www.ccrda.ca
Previous Name: CCCC Relief & Development Group (R&D Group).
Overview: A small national charitable organization founded in 1984
Mission: Building partnerships to effectively provide emergency relief, facilitate sustainable development, promote justice, and speak with one voice on behalf of the world's poor and disadvantaged peoples.
Membership: 41; *Fees:* $120-$1,800; *Member Profile:* Canadian Christian organizations involved in relief, development, and/or justice who are committed to integrated, transformational development.

Canadian Church Press (CCP)

8 MacDonald Ave., Hamilton ON L8P 4N5
Tel: 905-521-2240
cdnchurchpress@hotmail.com
www.canadianchurchpress.com
www.facebook.com/CanadianChurchPress
Overview: A small national organization founded in 1957
Mission: To promote high standards of religious journalism; to encourage a positive Christian influence on contemporary society
Chief Officer(s):
Ian Adnams, President
Saskia Rowley, Vice-President
Jim O'Leary, Treasurer
Finances: *Funding Sources:* Sponsorships
Membership: 56; *Fees:* Annual costs varies according to circulation numbers, from under 4,999 ($60) to over 100,000 ($215); *Member Profile:* Christian publications in Canada
Activities: Offering fellowship for members; Supporting members; Conducting professional development workshops in annual convention
Awards:
• General Canadian Church Press Awards (Award)
• A.C. Forrest Award (Award)
Meetings/Conferences: • Canadian Church Press/Association of Roman Catholic Communicators of Canada Convention
Publications:
• Canadian Church Press Membership Directory
Type: Directory
Profile: Listings of publication members, associate members, & honorary life members

The Canadian Churches' Forum for Global Ministries / Le forum des églises canadiennes pour les ministères globaux

47 Queen's Park Cres. East, Toronto ON M5S 2C3
Tel: 416-924-9351; *Fax:* 416-978-7821
www.ccforum.ca
www.facebook.com/CanadianChurchesForum
Previous Name: Ecumenical Forum of Canada
Overview: A medium-sized international charitable organization founded in 1921
Mission: To provide ecumenical orientation & re-entry programs for mission personnel; To stimulate ecumenical dialogue on issues of mission, global concerns & social justice; To prepare individuals to serve faithfully in mission in an ever-changing world
Member of: International Association for Mission Studies; Forum on International Personnel
Affliation(s): Canadian Council of Churches
Chief Officer(s):
Jonathan Schmidt, Co-director
Alice Schuda, Co-director
Finances: *Annual Operating Budget:* $100,000-$250,000; *Funding Sources:* Churches; Religious orders; Individuals
Staff Member(s): 2; 30 volunteer(s)
Membership: 1-99
Activities: Mission Personnel Programs, Jan., July & Sept.; Annual Katherine Hockin Award & Dinner; International Visitor; *Library* by appointment
Awards:
• Katharine Hockin Award for Global Mission & Ministry (Award)
Publications:
• Forum Focus [a publication of the The Canadian Churches' Forum for Global Ministries]
Type: Newsletter; *Frequency:* Annually; *Editor:* Alice Schuda; Jonathan Schmidt
Profile: Letters from overseas, information about mission personnel programs, book reviews, articles byinternational visitors, articles related to global mission, & updates on Forum staff & board members

Canadian Circulation Management Association *See* Circulation Management Association of Canada

Canadian Circulations Audit Board Inc. (CCAB) / Office canadien de vérification de la diffusion

Div. of BPA International, #800, 1 Concorde Gate, Toronto ON M3C 3N6
Tel: 416-487-2418; *Fax:* 416-487-6405
www.bpaww.com
Overview: A medium-sized national organization founded in 1937
Mission: To issue standardized statements of data reported by a member; to verify the figures shown in these statements by auditors' examination of any & all records considered by the corporation to be necessary; to disseminate these data for the benefit of any individual or company requiring such information
Chief Officer(s):
Tim Peel, Contact
mpeel@bpaww.com
Finances: *Funding Sources:* Membership fees
Membership: *Fees:* Schedule available

Canadian Circumpolar Institute (CCI) / Institut circumpolaire canadien

University of Alberta, #1-42, Pembina Hall, Edmonton AB T6G 2H8
Tel: 780-492-4512; *Fax:* 780-492-1153
www.cci.ualberta.ca
Previous Name: Boreal Institute for Northern Studies (1960-1990)
Overview: A small international organization founded in 1990
Mission: To promote & support research, education, & training related to the boreal & circumpolar regions of the Arctic & Antactica; To enhance awareness of polar environments
Member of: University of Alberta
Chief Officer(s):
Marianne S. Douglas, Director, 780-492-0055, Fax: 780-492-1153
marianne.douglas@ualberta.ca
Anita Dey Nuttall, Associate Director, Research Advancement, 780-492-9089, Fax: 780-492-1153
anitad@ualberta.ca
Lindsay Johnston, Circumpolar Librarian & Public Service Mgr, Cameron Library, 780-492-5946
lindsay.johnston@ualberta.ca
Elaine L. Maloney, Managing Editor, CCI Press, 780-492-4999, Fax: 780-492-1153
elaine.maloney@ualberta.ca
Finances: *Funding Sources:* Grants; Donations
Membership: 500-999
Activities: Developing & facilitating interdisciplinary circumpolar research & education; Facilitating communication among northern researchers; Awarding grants & scholarships; Providing outreach programs; Publishing three to five titles each year in subject areas related to the north; Disseminating information about circumpolar areas; *Library:* The Canadian Circumpolar Collection (CCC), U of Alberta Library; Open to public
Publications:
• Canadian Circumpolar Institute Occasional Publications Series
Type: Monographs; *Editor:* Elaine L. Maloney, CCI Press *ISSN:* 0068-0303
Profile: Conference proceedings & collections of papers
• Circumpolar Research Series
Type: Monographs; *Editor:* Elaine L. Maloney, CCI Press *ISSN:* 0838-133X
Profile: Scholarly research on circumpolar situations & concerns
• Northern Hunter-Gatherers Research Series
Editor: Elaine L. Maloney, CCI Press *ISSN:* 1707-522X
Profile: Interdisciplinary research about the hunting & gathering peoples of arctic, boreal, & sub-arctic regions

• Northern Reference Series [publications of the Canadian Circumpolar Institute]
Editor: Elaine L. Maloney, CCI Press *ISSN:* 1192-5620
Profile: Bibliographies, literature reviews, annotated bibliographies, & review papers
• Solstice Series [publications of the Canadian Circumpolar Institute]
Editor: Elaine L. Maloney, CCI Press *ISSN:* 1709-5824
Profile: Case studies & community-based models

Canadian Civil Liberties Association (CCLA) / Association canadienne des libertés civiles

#210, 215 Spadina Ave., Toronto ON M5T 2C7
Tel: 416-363-0321; *Fax:* 416-861-1291
mail@ccla.org
www.ccla.org
www.facebook.com/cancivlib
twitter.com/cancivlib
www.youtube.com/cancivlib
Overview: A medium-sized national organization founded in 1964
Chief Officer(s):
Sukanya Pillay, Executive Director
pillay@ccla.org
Staff Member(s): 12
Membership: *Fees:* $75
Activities: Operating as a law reform organization; *Awareness Events:* Rights Watch; Celebrating Canada Gala; *Library:* Canadian Civil Liberties Association Library
Publications:
• CCLA [Canadian Civil Liberties Association] Newsnotes
Frequency: 3 pa
Profile: News & events regarding Canadian civil liberties

Canadian Clean Power Coalition (CCPC)

c/o David Butler, 64 Chapala Heath, Calgary AB T2X 3P9
Tel: 403-606-0973; *Fax:* 403-256-0424
www.canadiancleanpowercoalition.com
Overview: A medium-sized national organization
Mission: To secure a future for coal-fired electricity generation, along with a mix of fuels such as solar, wind, hydro, & nuclear; To research & develop clean coal technology
Chief Officer(s):
David Butler, Executive Director
dave.butler@cleanerpower.ca
Membership: *Member Profile:* Canadian coal & coal-fired electricity producers
Activities: Addressing environmental issues with governments & stakeholders

Canadian Cloud Council (CCC)

#123, 370 - 5222-130 Ave. SE, Calgary AB T2Z 0G4
Toll-Free: 855-285-9774
info@canadiancloudcouncil.ca
canadiancloudcouncil.ca
www.linkedin.com/groups/Canadian-Cloud-Council-Voice-Canadian-4212639
www.facebook.com/CanadianCloudCouncil
twitter.com/Canada_Cloud
www.youtube.com/user/CanadianCloudCounci
Overview: A large national organization
Mission: To educate about cloud computing
Chief Officer(s):
Robert Hart, Founder & CEO
Membership: *Fees:* $100 non voting indiuals; $1000 non voting corporate; $1000 voting individuals; $5000 - $10000 voting corporate

The Canadian Club of Toronto

Royal York Hotel, 100 Front St. West, Fl. MM, Toronto ON M5J 1E3
Tel: 416-364-5590; *Fax:* 416-364-5676
info@canadianclub.org
www.canadianclub.org
www.facebook.com/193517383995
twitter.com/cdnclubto
Overview: A medium-sized local organization
Mission: To host speakers & leaders from politics, business, science, art & the media; programming is accessible to everyone through cable broadcasts & online webcasts.
Chief Officer(s):
Alison Loat, President
Lynn Chou, Executive Director
lchou@canadianclub.org
Finances: *Funding Sources:* Membership fees; ticket sales
Membership: *Fees:* $80 individual; $160 corporate

Canadian Coalition Against the Death Penalty (CCADP) / Coalition canadien contre la peine de mort

80 Lillington Ave., Toronto ON M1N 3K7
Tel: 416-693-9112; *Fax:* 416-693-9112
info@ccadp.org
www.ccadp.org
www.facebook.com/70610338689
www.youtube.com/ccadpmedia
Overview: A small national organization founded in 1998
Mission: To provide information about abuses of the death penalty internationally; To ensure Canada does not return to the death penalty
Chief Officer(s):
Tracy Lamourie, Director & Founder
Dave Parkinson, Director & Founder
Finances: *Funding Sources:* Donations
Activities: Raising funds for the wrongly convicted; *Speaker Service:* Yes

Canadian Coalition for Fair Digital Access (CCFDA) / Coalition canadienne pour un accès équitable à la technologie digitale (CCAETD)

c/o #1300, 100 Queen St., Ottawa ON K1P 1J9
Tel: 613-238-2090; *Fax:* 613-238-9380
information@ccfda.ca
www.ccfda.ca
Overview: A medium-sized national organization founded in 2002
Mission: The Canadian Coalition for Fair Digital Access (CCFDA) was established to advocate the concerns of Canadian businesses, consumers and individuals affected by the copyright levy regime Canada. CCFDA members include major Canadian retailers, consumer product manufacturers and technology companies.
Chief Officer(s):
Fraser Smith
Membership: 14; *Member Profile:* Major Canadian retailers; consumer product manufacturers; technology companies

Canadian Coalition for Good Governance (CCGG)

PO Box 22, #3304, 20 Queen St. West, Toronto ON M5H 3R3
Tel: 416-868-3576
www.ccgg.ca
Overview: A medium-sized national organization
Mission: To improve the performance of publicly traded corporations through the promotion of good governance practices across Canada
Chief Officer(s):
Stephen Erlichman, Executive Director
serlichman@ccgg.ca
Membership: 47; *Member Profile:* Pension funds, mutual funds & third party money managers.; *Committees:* Finance & Audit; Governance & Nominating
Awards:
• Governance Gavel Awards (Award)
Publications:
• Report on Clawback Provisions
Type: Report
• Report on Voting Results
Type: Report
• Shareholder Democracy Study
Type: Report; *Frequency:* irregular

Canadian Coalition for Immunization Awareness & Promotion *See* Immunize Canada

Canadian Coalition for Nuclear Responsibility (CCNR) / Regroupement pour la surveillance du nucléaire (RSN)

53 Dufferin Rd., Hampstead QC H3X 3T4
Tel: 514-489-5118
ccnr@web.ca
www.ccnr.org
Overview: A small national organization founded in 1975
Mission: To research all issues related to nuclear energy, whether civilian or military — including non-nuclear alternatives — especially those pertaining to Canada.
Affliation(s): Environment Liaison Centre - International; Friends of the Earth - Canada; Canadian Peace Alliance; Abolition 2000
Chief Officer(s):
Gordon Edwards, President

Canadian Coalition for Seniors Mental Health (CCSMH)

c/o Baycrest, West Wing, Old Hospital, #311, 3560 Bathurst St., Toronto ON M6A 2E1
Tel: 613-233-1619; *Fax:* 613-614-9450
www.ccsmh.ca
twitter.com/CCSMH
Overview: A small national organization founded in 2002
Mission: To promote the mental health of seniors by connecting people, ideas and resources.
Chief Officer(s):
Bonnie Schroeder, Executive Director
director@ccsmh.ca
Finances: *Funding Sources:* Public Health Agency of Canada: Population Health Fund; Canadian Institutes of Health Research: Institute of Aging

Canadian Coalition for the Rights of Children (CCRC)

c/o Justice for Children, #1203, 415 Yonge St., Toronto ON M5B 2E7
Tel: 416-920-1633; *Fax:* 416-920-5855
info@rightsofchildren.ca
rightsofchildren.ca
Overview: A small national organization founded in 1989
Mission: To promote respect for the rights of children; To implement the UN Convention on the Rights of the Child.
Chief Officer(s):
Cheryl Milne, Chair
Membership: *Fees:* $300 large organizations; $200 medium organizations; $100 small organizations; $50 individual; $5 students; $0 youth under 18

Canadian College & University Food Service Association (CCUFSA)

c/o Drew Hall, University of Guelph, Gordon St., Guelph ON N1G 2W1
Tel: 519-824-4120; *Fax:* 519-837-9302
mcollins@hrs.uoguelph.ca
www.ccufsa.on.ca
Overview: A medium-sized national organization
Mission: To enhance the quality of campus life through the growth & development of food service operations in colleges & universities
Chief Officer(s):
Lee Elkas, President, 519-885-1211 Ext. 32704
laelkas@connect.uwaterloo.ca
David Boeckner, Executive Director, 519-824-4120 Ext. 52222
boeckner@uoguelph.ca
Gerard Hayes, Secretary-Treasurer, 250-371-5660
ghayes@tru.ca
Membership: 160; *Fees:* $25-$295
Meetings/Conferences: • Canadian College & University Food Service Association 2015 Winter Workshop, March, 2015, Hyatt Regency - King St., Toronto, ON
Scope: National
Description: A workshop for institutional members & institutional members only
• Canadian College & University Food Service Association 2015 National Conference, June, 2015, Delta Grand Hotel, Kelowna, BC
Scope: National
Description: A gathering of food service directors, managers, & senior administrators from self-operated & contracted schools
Publications:
• CCUFSA [Canadian College & University Food Service Association] Magazine
Profile: Association information & articles

Canadian College of Emergency Medical Services (CCEMS)

c/o Edmonton General Hospital, 4712 - 91 Ave., Edmonton AB T6B 2L1
Tel: 780-451-4437
Toll-Free: 800-797-4437
info@ccofems.org
www.ccofems.org
twitter.com/ccofems
Overview: A medium-sized national organization founded in 1988
Mission: To provide training & education for emergency medical services professionals
Chief Officer(s):
John (Greg) Clarkes, President

Canadian College of Health Leaders (CCHL) / Collège canadien des leaders en santé
292 Somerset St. West, Ottawa ON K2P 0J6
Tel: 613-235-7218; *Fax:* 613-235-5451
Toll-Free: 800-363-9056
Other Communication: communications@cchse.org
info@cchl-ccls.ca
www.cchl-ccls.ca
www.linkedin.com/company/canadian-college-of-health-leaders
www.facebook.com/group.php?gid=154324094612698
twitter.com/CCHL_CCLS
www.youtube.com/HealthLeadersCanada
Previous Name: Canadian College of Service Executives
Overview: A large national organization founded in 1970
Mission: To advance excellence in health leadership; To act as a collective voice for the profession
Member of: Health Action Lobby; Coalition for Public Health in the 21st Century
Chief Officer(s):
Ray J. Racette, President & Chief Executive Office, 613-235-7218 Ext. 27
rracette@cchl-ccls.ca
Jaime M. Cleroux, Vice-President, Membership & Corporate Services, 613-235-7218 Ext. 35
jlariviere@cchl-ccls.ca
Sylvie M. Deliencourt, Director, LEADS Support & Certification, 613-235-7218 Ext. 33
Carolyn Farrington, CFO, 613-235-7218 Ext. 14
cfarrington@cchl-ccls.ca
Kathy Ivey, Manager, Marketing & Communications, 613-235-7218 Ext. 22
Finances: *Funding Sources:* Membership dues; Advertising; Sponsorships
Membership: 3,000 individuals + 80 corporate members; *Member Profile:* Individuals & corporations from all health sectors throughout Canada; Students; Retired members
Activities: Offering a competency-based certification program; Advocating for the profession; Providing professional development resources & opportunities; Preparing position papers on topics such as pandemic planning & patient safety; Offering a forum for the exchange of best practices
Awards:
• 3M Health Care Quality Team Awards (Award)
To recognize innovation, quality, & teamwork *Contact:* Cindy MacBride, Manager Awards & Sponsorships, Phone: 613-235-7218, ext. 13, E-mail: cmacbride@cchl-ccls.ca
• College Honorary Life Member Award (Award)
To honour longstanding College members who have contributed significantly to Canada's health system *Contact:* Cindy MacBride, Manager Awards & Sponsorships, Phone: 613-235-7218, ext. 13, E-mail: cmacbride@cchl-ccls.ca
• Chair's Award for Distinguished Service (Award)
To recognize individual or corporate members for significant contribution to the College *Contact:* Cindy MacBride, Manager Awards & Sponsorships, Phone: 613-235-7218, ext. 13, E-mail: cmacbride@cchl-ccls.ca
• Chapter Awards for Distinguished Service (Award)
To honour an individual or corporate member who has made a significant contribution to their chapter *Contact:* Cindy MacBride, Manager Awards & Sponsorships, Phone: 613-235-7218, ext. 13, E-mail: cmacbride@cchl-ccls.ca
• CHE Self-directed Learning Paper Award (Award)
An award for high quality papers submitted as a component of the Certified Health Executive (CHE) program *Contact:* Cindy MacBride, Manager Awards & Sponsorships, Phone: 613-235-7218, ext. 13, E-mail: cmacbride@cchl-ccls.ca
• Energy & Environmental Stewardship Award (Award)
Awarded to a health care organization that has implemented programs that demonstrate environmental responsibility, such as the preservation of natural resources, the reducion of energy usage, & effective waste diversion solutions *Contact:* Cindy MacBride, Manager Awards & Sponsorships, Phone: 613-235-7218, ext. 13, E-mail: cmacbride@cchl-ccls.ca
• Health Care Safety Award (Award)
To recognize individuals or teams that improve workplace & patient safety *Contact:* Cindy MacBride, Manager Awards & Sponsorships, Phone: 613-235-7218, ext. 13, E-mail: cmacbride@cchl-ccls.ca
• Innovation Award for Health Care Leadership (Award)
Awarded to a senior executive for innovation in their organization *Contact:* Cindy MacBride, Manager Awards & Sponsorships, Phone: 613-235-7218, ext. 13, E-mail: cmacbride@cchl-ccls.ca
• Mentorship Award (Award)
Presented to a leader who is committed to mentoring & inspiring health care leadership *Contact:* Cindy MacBride, Manager Awards & Sponsorships, Phone: 613-235-7218, ext. 13, E-mail: cmacbride@cchl-ccls.ca
• Nursing Leadership Award (Award)
To honour persons committed to excellence in patient centered care & leadership *Contact:* Cindy MacBride, Manager Awards & Sponsorships, Phone: 613-235-7218, ext. 13, E-mail: cmacbride@cchl-ccls.ca
• President's Award for Outstanding Corporate Membership in the College (Award)
Presented to a corporate member who has helped the College achieve its mission *Contact:* Cindy MacBride, Manager Awards & Sponsorships, Phone: 613-235-7218, ext. 13, E-mail: cmacbride@cchl-ccls.ca
• Quality of Life Award (Award)
Awarded to persons who improve the lives of patients & families & the community *Contact:* Cindy MacBride, Manager Awards & Sponsorships, Phone: 613-235-7218, ext. 13, E-mail: cmacbride@cchl-ccls.ca
• The Robert Wood Johnson Award (Award)
Awarded to one student from each of the six Canadian universities offering graduate programs in health services administration *Contact:* Cindy MacBride, Manager Awards & Sponsorships, Phone: 613-235-7218, ext. 13, E-mail: cmacbride@cchl-ccls.ca
• The Robert Zed Young Health Leader Award (Award)
To recognize a Canadian health care leader who has demonstrated leadership in improving the effectiveness & sustainability of the nation's health system *Contact:* Cindy MacBride, Manager Awards & Sponsorships, Phone: 613-235-7218, ext. 13, E-mail: cmacbride@cchl-ccls.ca
Meetings/Conferences: • National Health Leadership Conference 2015, June, 2015, Charlottetown, PE
Scope: National
Description: In partnership with HealthCareCAN.
Contact Information: Laurie Oman, Conference Services Coordinator; Phone: 613-235-7218 ext. 227; loman@cchl-ccls.ca
Publications:
• Canadian College of Health Service Executives Membership Directory
Type: Directory
• Canadian College of Health Service Executives Annual Report
Type: Yearbook; *Frequency:* Annually
• Code of Ethics for Members of the Canadian College of Health Service Executives
Price: Free with membership in the Canadian College of Health Service Executives
Profile: A guide for professional & personal behaviour
• Communiqué [a publication of the Canadian College of Health Leaders]
Type: Newsletter; *Frequency:* Monthly; *Accepts Advertising*; *Price:* Free with membership in the Canadian College of Health ServiceExecutives
Profile: College & member news, initiatives in health care, & career opportunities for members
• Healthcare Management FORUM
Type: Journal; *Frequency:* Quarterly; *Accepts Advertising*; *Editor:* Laurie Wilson (editor@sympatico.ca) *ISSN:* 0840-4704; *Price:* Free for active members of the College; $90 individualsin Canada; $175 institutions
Profile: Peer-reviewed articles about Canadian health services management issues, theory, & practice

Assiniboia (Saskatchewan) Regional Chapter
c/o C.G. Mirka, Executive Director, Health Svs., Cypress Health Region, 429 - 4th Ave. NE, Swift Current SK S9H 2J9
Tel: 306-778-4573; *Fax:* 306-773-9513
christine.mirka@cypressrha.ca
www.cchl-ccls.ca
Chief Officer(s):
Suzanne Boudreau, Provincial Director, 306-347-1713
suzanneb@saho.org
Christine G. Mirka, Secretary, 306-778-4573, Fax: 306-773-9513
christine.mirka@cypressrha.ca
Julie Johnson, Treasurer
julie.johnson@rqhealth.ca

Bluenose (Nova Scotia & Prince Edward Island) Regional Chapter
c/o C.A. Graham, Planning, Colchester East Hants Health Authority, 207 Willow St., Truro NS B2N 5A1
Tel: 902-893-5554; *Fax:* 902-895-7138
cheryl.graham@cehha.nshealth.ca
www.cchl-ccls.ca
Mission: To advance & recognize excellence in health leadership in Nova Scotia & Prince Edward Island
Chief Officer(s):
Theresa A. Fillatre, Director, 902-221-4719
theresa.fillatre@cdha.nshealth.ca
Arlene L. Gallant-Bernard, Director, 902-438-4514
algallant-bernard@gov.pe.ca
Cheryl A. Graham, Treasurer & Lead, Sponsorship Program, 902-893-5554 Ext. 2507
cheryl.graham@cehha.nshealth.ca
Daniel G. Currie, Lead, Membership Program, 902-574-3854, Fax: 902-473-7052
curried@cbdha.nshealth.ca
Margaret A. Jenkins, Co-Lead, Education Program, 902-681-3500 Ext. 3611, Fax: 902-678-2970
mjenkins@avdha.nshealth.ca
Catherine S. MacPherson, Lead, Awards, 902-444-8130
catherinemacpherson@shannex.com
Heather L. Wolfe, Lead, Communications, 902-892-5554 Ext. 2265, Fax: 902-893-1666
heather.wolfe@cehha.nshealth.ca
Brenda A. Worth, Co-Lead, Education Program, 902-438-4516, Fax: 902-438-4381
baworth@gov.pe.ca
• Canadian College of Health Service Executives, Bluenose Chapter, News Update
Type: Newsletter; *Frequency:* Quarterly
Profile: Chapter activities & upcoming events for Bluenose members
• Canadian College of Health Service Executives, Bluenose Chapter, Annual Report
Frequency: Annually
Profile: Review of chapter programs & services

British Columbia Interior Regional Chapter
c/o Mark L.M. Pugh, Clinical & Support Services Mgr., Interior Health, PO Box 627, 851 - 16th St. NE, Salmon Arm BC V1E 4N7
Tel: 250-833-3638
mark.pugh@interiorhealth.ca
www.cchl-ccls.ca
Chief Officer(s):
Mark L.M. Pugh, Secretary-Treasurer, 250-833-3638
mark.pugh@interiorhealth.ca

British Columbia Lower Mainland Regional Chapter
c/o Karen L. Baillie, Laurel Place, 9688 - 137A St., Surrey BC V3T 4H9
Tel: 604-582-6336; *Fax:* 604-582-6337
karen.baillie@laurelplace.ca
www.cchl-ccls.ca
Chief Officer(s):
David N.T. Thompson, Chair, 604-806-9540
dnthompson@providencehealth.bc.ca
Karen L. Baillie, Vice-Chair & Treasurer, 604-582-6336 Ext. 1120, Fax: 604-582-6337
karen.baillie@laurelplace.ca
Eda S. Karacabeyli, Coordinator, Sponsorship, 604-806-5324
eda.karacabeyli@gmail.com
Lisa Weger, Co-Lead, Mentorship Program, 604-806-5324
Lisa.weger@vch.ca
• Canadian College of Health Leaders British Columbia Lower Mainland Regional Chapter Executive Mentoring Program Handbook
Type: Handbook
Profile: Information for mentors & mentees

Eastern Ontario Regional Chapter
c/o Margaret E. Atkinson, Chief, Patient Care, Hôtel Dieu Hospital, 166 Brock St., Kingston ON K7L 5G2
Tel: 613-544-3400
boonies@sympatico.ca
www.cchl-ccls.ca
Chief Officer(s):
Graham M. Gaylord, Chair, 613-798-5555 Ext. 71700
ggaylord@ottawahospital.on.ca
Joane Simard, Vice-Chair
senaoj@rogers.com
Margaret E. Atkinson, Secretary, 613-544-3400 Ext. 2295
boonies@sympatico.ca
Elizabeth I. Woodbury, Treasurer, 613-562-5800 Ext. 8696, Fax: 613-521-9215
ewoodbury@sympatico.ca
Kyle T. Johansen, Chair, Communication & Membership Committee, 613-967-0196 Ext. 225, Fax: 613-967-1341
kyle.johansen@lhins.on.ca
Jonathan I. Mitchell, Chair, Professional Development Committee, 613-738-3800 Ext. 325, Fax: 613-738-7755
jonathan.mitchell@accreditation.ca

• Canadian College of Health Service Executives Eastern Ontario Chapter Newsletter
Type: Newsletter
Profile: Chapter activities & upcoming professional development events

Greater Toronto Area Regional Chapter
c/o Sean Molloy, Director Knowledge Mgmt., Quality Healthcare Network, 790 Bay St., 9th Fl., Toronto ON M5G 1N8
Tel: 416-351-3760
sean.molloy@qhn.ca
www.cchl-ccls.ca
Mission: To foster mentorship among health care leaders in the Greater Toronto Region; To engage early careerists in order to develop leadership skills; To provide information & facilitate knowledge exchange in the Greater Toronto Region
Chief Officer(s):
Sean J. Molloy, Secretary, 416-351-3760
sean.molloy@qhn.ca
Jatinder Bains, Treasurer, 416-243-3600 Ext. 2122
jatinder.bains@westpark.org

Hamilton & Area Regional Chapter
c/o Gavin Webb, Director, Financial Services, Guelph General Hospital, 115 Delhi St., Guelph ON N1E 4J4
Tel: 519-837-6440; *Fax:* 519-837-6466
gwebb@gghorg.ca
www.cchl-ccls.ca
Chief Officer(s):
Philip G. Christoff, Chair, 905-521-2100 Ext. 45143
christoff@hhsc.ca
Cheryl B. MacInnes, Vice-Chair, 519-621-2333 Ext. 2235, Fax: 519-740-4920
cmacinnes@cmh.org
Bryan W. Herechuk, Secretary, 905-522-1155, Fax: 905-308-7221
bherechu@stjoes.ca
Gavin J. Webb, Treasurer, 519-837-6440 Ext. 2217, Fax: 519-837-6466
gwebb@gghorg.ca
• Canadian College of Health Leaders Hamilton & Area Regional Chapter News
Type: Newsletter
Profile: Chpater happenings & upcoming events

Health Care Leaders' Association of British Columbia (Regional Chapter)
#105, 19 Dallas Rd., Victoria BC V8V 5A6
Tel: 250-383-4252
info@hclabc.bc.ca
www.hclabc.bc.ca
Mission: To promote excellence in health services leadership & management throughout British Columbia; To establish & maintain professional standards; To support members in the practice of their profession
Chief Officer(s):
Marc Pelletier, Chair
Dan Levitt, Secretary-Treasurer
Kate Lawrie, Office Manager, 250-383-4252
kate.lawrie@hclabc.bc.ca
• Health Care Leaders' Association of British Columbia Annual Report
Type: Annual; *Frequency:* Annually
Profile: A report presented at the organizational annual general meeting, which is held in conjunction with the annual leadership conference
• Health Care Leaders' Newsletter
Type: Newsletter
Profile: Articles, services, & forthcoming events of interest to members of the Health Care Leaders' Association of British Columbia

Manitoba Regional Chapter
c/o S.G. Webber, Dir, Rehab. Svs., Brandon Regional Health Authority, 150A - 7th St., Brandon MB R7A 7M2
Tel: 204-578-4505
webbers@brandonrha.mb.ca
www.cchl-ccls.ca
Mission: To support & assist health care leaders in Manitoba
Chief Officer(s):
Shannon G. Webber, Chair, 204-578-4505
webbers@brandonrha.mb.ca
Beverley R. Laurila, Vice-Chair, 204-632-3488, Fax: 204-697-3043
blaurila@sogh.mb.ca

Midnight Sun (Yukon, Northwest Territories, & Nunavut) Regional Chapter
c/o Donna L. Allen, Population Health, Dept. of Health & Social Svs., PO Box 1320, Yellowknife NT X1A 2L9
Tel: 867-873-7403; *Fax:* 867-873-0196
donna_allen@gov.nt.ca
www.cchl-ccls.ca
Chief Officer(s):
Dianna M. Korol, Chair, 867-872-6281, Fax: 867-872-6260
dianna_korol@gov.nt.ca
Norman P.M. Hatlevik, Secretary, 867-983-4198, Fax: 867-983-4116
nhatlevik@gov.nu.ca
Donna L. Allen, Treasurer, 867-873-7403, Fax: 867-873-0196
donna_allen@gov.nt.ca

NEON Lights (Northeastern Ontario) Regional Chapter
c/o Roger N. Walker, Sioux Lookout Meno-Ya-Win Health Centre, PO Box 909, 1 Meno Ya Win Way, Sioux Lookout ON P8T 1B4
Tel: 807-737-5130; *Fax:* 807-737-5127
rwalker@tadh.com
www.cchl-ccls.ca
Mission: To promote & recognize excellence in health care leadership in northeastern Ontario
Chief Officer(s):
Maureen A. McLelland, Chair, 705-523-7100 Ext. 4299
mmclelland@hrsrh.on.ca
Sharon M. Goodwin, Vice-Chair, 705-472-8050 Ext. 2230, Fax: 705-495-6691
sharon.goodwin@von.ca
Roger N. Walker, Secretary-Treasurer, 807-737-5130, Fax: 807-737-5127
rwalker@tadh.com
• NEON Lights Regional Chapter Chair Update
Type: Newsletter; *Frequency:* Irregular
Profile: News from the national Canadian College of Health Leaders, as well as local activities & professional development events

New Brunswick Regional Chapter
c/o M. Suzanne Jones, Hospital Operations, HSBC Pl, NB Dept. of Health, PO Box 5100, 520 King St., Fredericton NB E3B 5G8
Tel: 506-453-3967; *Fax:* 506-453-2958
suzanne.jones@gnb.ca
www.cchl-ccls.ca
Chief Officer(s):
M. Suzanne Jones, Secretary, 506-453-3967, Fax: 506-453-2958
suzanne.jones@gnb.ca
Mireille Lanouette, Treasurer, 506-862-4205, Fax: 506-862-4373
mireillel@rrsb.nb.ca
R. Kenneth McGeorge, Chair, Education Committee, 506-444-3880 Ext. 2507, Fax: 506-444-3544
ken.mcgeorge@yorkmanor.nb.ca

Newfoundland & Labrador Regional Chapter
c/o Katherine A. Walters, Dr. Walter Templeman Health Centre, PO Box 580, Wabana, Bell Island NL A0A 4H0
Tel: 709-488-2775; *Fax:* 709-488-2600
katherine.walters@easternhealth.ca
www.cchl-ccls.ca
Chief Officer(s):
Juliette Nicholas, Chair, 709-454-0120
julie.nicholas@lghealth.ca
Katherine A. Walters, Vice-Chair, 709-488-2775, Fax: 709-488-2600
katherine.walters@easternhealth.ca
Sharon Paulette Lehr, Treasurer, 709-752-4600, Fax: 709-752-4539
sharon.lehr@easternhealth.ca

Northern & Central Saskatchewan Regional Chapter
Marcel G. Nobert, Director, Medical Affairs, Saskatoon Health Region, #300, 410 - 22nd St. East, Saskatoon SK S7K 5T6
Tel: 306-655-0198; *Fax:* 306-655-3394
marcel.nobert@saskatoonhealthregion.ca
www.cchl-ccls.ca
Chief Officer(s):
Allen M. Backman, Vice-Chair, 306-966-2773, Fax: 306-966-7920
allen.backman@usask.ca
Suzanne Boudreau, Provincial Director, 306-347-1713, Fax: 306-525-1960
suzanneb@saho.org
Sandra J. Blevins, Secretary, 306-655-3310, Fax: 306-655-3394
sandra.blevins@saskatoonhealthregion.ca
Marcel G. Nobert, Treasurer, 306-655-0198, Fax: 306-655-3394
marcel.nobert@saskatoonhealthregion.ca

Northern Alberta Regional Chapter
c/o Katherine Chubbs, Health Profession Strategy, AB Health Services, 9732 - 100 Ave., Westlock AB T7P 2G3
Tel: 780-349-8705; *Fax:* 780-349-4189
katherine.chubbs@albertahealthservices.ca
www.cchl-ccls.ca
Mission: To support & promote management excellence in health services throughout northern Alberta
Chief Officer(s):
Katherine M. Chubbs, Vice-Chair, 780-349-8705 Ext. 265, Fax: 780-349-4189
katherine.chubbs@albertahealthservices.ca
Yolanda Lackie, Alberta Provincial Director, 780-427-0380, Fax: 780-422-5208
yolanda.lackie@gov.ab.ca
Donna L. Zaozirny, Secretary & Contact, Communications, 780-752-6090
donnazaozirny@shaw.ca
Corinne B. Schalm, Treasurer, Fax: 780-462-1643
cschalm@shopherdscare.org
• Leader to Leader
Type: Newsletter
Profile: Chapter information, reports, membership information, & upcoming events

Northern British Columbia Regional Chapter
c/o Michael Leisinger, VP, Health Services, Northern Health Authority, #600, 299 Victoria St., Prince George BC V2L 5B8
Tel: 250-565-2012
michael.leisinger@northernhealth.ca
www.cchl-ccls.ca
Chief Officer(s):
Michael A. Leisinger, Chair, 250-565-2012
michael.leisinger@northernhealth.ca
Michael Hoefer, Vice-Chair, 250-565-2303, Fax: 250-565-2753
michael.hoefer@northernhealth.ca
Gloria Murdock-Smith, Northwest Director, 250-633-5077, Fax: 250-633-2512
gms59@telus.net

Northwestern Ontario Regional Chapter
c/o C.M. Collinson, Executive Dir., Nipigon District Memorial Hospital, PO Box 37, 125 Hogan Rd., Nipigon ON P0T 2J0
Tel: 807-887-3026; *Fax:* 807-887-2800
ccollinson@ndmh.ca
www.cchl-ccls.ca
Chief Officer(s):
Catherine M. Collinson, Executive Contact, 807-887-3026 Ext. 224, Fax: 807-887-2800
ccollinson@ndmh.ca

Québec Regional Chapter
c/o Terrence P. Meehan, Director, Logistics, McGill U. Health Centre, 1650, av Cedar, Montréal QC H3G 1A4
Fax: 514-934-8323
terrence.meehan@muhc.mcgill.ca
www.cchl-ccls.ca
Chief Officer(s):
Terrence P. Meehan, Vice-President, 514-934-1934 Ext. 42021, Fax: 514-934-8323
terrence.meehan@muhc.mcgill.ca
Mathieu Jetté, Secretary, 514-934-1934 Ext. 43654, Fax: 514-934-8323
mathieu.jette@muhc.mcgill.ca
Renato De Castello, Treasurer, 514-934-1934 Ext. 23425, Fax: 514-412-4362
renatodecastello@hotmail.com

Southern Alberta Regional Chapter
c/o Rosmin Esmail, Director, Leading Practice, Alberta Health Services, 10101 Southport Rd. SW, Calgary AB T2W 3N2
Tel: 403-561-1748
rosmin.esmail@albertahealthservices.ca
www.cchl-ccls.ca
Chief Officer(s):
Grace E.D. Bole-Campbell, Contact, Conference Planning, 403-943-0151
gracie27@shaw.ca
Joyce R. Buzath, Contact, Membership Recruitment, 403-943-1457, Fax: 403-943-2720
joyce.buzath@albertahealthservices.ca

Rosmin Esmail, Contact, Administration, 403-561-1748
rosmin.esmail@albertahealthservices.ca
Carla L. Simon, Contact, Professional Development, 403-813-9831
carla@carlasimon.com

Southwestern Ontario Regional Chapter
c/o James C. Egan, CHE, Administrator, Extendicare Tecumseh, 2475 St. Alphonse St., Tecumseh ON N8N 2X2
Tel: 519-739-2998; *Fax:* 519-739-2815
jegan@extendicare.com
www.cchl-ccls.ca
Mission: To support & advocate for the health services profession in southwestern Ontario
Chief Officer(s):
James C. Egan, Contact, 519-739-2998, Fax: 519-739-2815
jegan@extendicare.com

• Canadian College of Health Service Executives, Southwestern Ontario Regional Chapter, Newsletter
Type: Newsletter
Profile: Chapter reports & upcoming events, plus news from the national Canadian College of Health Service Executives

Starlight (Canadian Forces Health Services Group) Regional Chapter
c/o Cdr. John Roland Young, Commanding Officer, 1 Field Ambulance, PO Box 10500, Stn. Forces, Edmonton AB T5J 4J5
Tel: 780-973-4011
roland.young2@forces.gc.ca
www.cchl-ccls.ca
Mission: To advance health leadership within the Canadian Forces Health Services Group
Chief Officer(s):
Daniel A. Farris, Vice-Chair
dan.farris45@gmail.com
Ian P. White, Secretary, 613-945-6920, Fax: 613-943-8021
white.ip@forces.gc.ca

Vancouver Island Regional Chapter
c/o Leslie J. Basham, Staff Nurse, Vancouver Island Health Authority, 1952 Bay St., Victoria BC V8R 1J8
Tel: 250-370-8351
cordava59@shaw.ca
www.cchl-ccls.ca
Chief Officer(s):
Goldie Luong, Chair, 250-370-5673
goldieluong@yahoo.ca
Leslie J. Basham, Treasurer, 250-370-8351
cordava59@shaw.ca

Canadian College of Medical Geneticists (CCMG) / Collège canadien de généticiens médicaux

774 Echo Dr., Ottawa ON K1S 5N8
Tel: 613-730-6250; *Fax:* 613-730-1116
ccmg@royalcollege.ca
www.ccmg-ccgm.org
Overview: A small national licensing charitable organization founded in 1975
Mission: To establish & maintain professional & ethical standards for medical genetics services in Canada; To certify individuals who provide medical genetics services; to encourage research activities
Affliation(s): Canadian Association of Genetic Counsellors (CAGC)
Chief Officer(s):
Marsha Speevak, President
Gail Graham, Treasurer
Finances: *Annual Operating Budget:* $100,000-$250,000
Staff Member(s): 1
Membership: 200; *Committees:* Accreditation of Centres; Annual Meeting; Awards; Biochemical Genetics; CAGC / CCMG; Clinical Practice; Constitution & Bylaws; Credentials; Cytogenetics; Education; Ethics & Public Policy; Examinations; Molecular Genetics; Nominations; PEACE; Prenatal Diagnosis; Scientific Program; Sponsorship
Activities: Ensuring a high quality of service is delivered to the public; Informing government & the public about the importance of medical genetics & advances in medical genetics; Offering continuing education; Lobbying for continued universal access to medical genetics services
Awards:
• Linda Stevens Fund Trainee Award (Award)
Meetings/Conferences: • Canadian College of Medical Geneticists 39th Annual Scientific Meeting 2015, September, 2015, The Westin, Ottawa, ON
Scope: National
Publications:
• CCMG [Canadian College of Medical Geneticists] Newsletter
Type: Newsletter
• CCMG [Canadian College of Medical Geneticists] Membership Directory
Type: Directory

The Canadian College of Naturopathic Medicine (CCNM)

1255 Sheppard Ave. East, Toronto ON M2K 1E2
Tel: 416-498-1255
Toll-Free: 866-241-2266
www.ccnm.edu
www.facebook.com/myccnm
twitter.com/myccnm
www.youtube.com/myccnm
Overview: A medium-sized national licensing organization
Mission: To promote naturopathic medicine; to educate its students & expand members' knowledge about naturopathic medicine
Chief Officer(s):
Bob Bernhardt, President and CEO

Canadian College of Neuropsychopharmacology (CCNP)

c/o Rachelle Anderson, Dept. of Psychiatry, University of Alberta, #IE7.19, 8440 - 112 St., Walter MacKenzie Centre, Edmonton AB T6G 2B7
Tel: 780-407-6543; *Fax:* 780-407-6672
Rachelle@ccnp.ca
www.ccnp.ca
Overview: A small national organization
Mission: To promote the development of neuropsychopharmacology in Canada & internationally; To encourage the quality of research & treatment in the field of neuropsychopharmacology
Chief Officer(s):
Paul Albert, President
Marco Leyton, Vice-President
Darrell Mousseau, Secretary
Lalit Srivastava, Treasurer
Membership: *Fees:* $100/yr. fellow members; $25/yr. junior & retired members; *Member Profile:* Clinical & basic science researchers; *Committees:* Awards; Nominating; Finance; Public Relations & Liaison; Membership; Clinical Affairs
Activities: Providing a forum for researchers to exchange ideas & experience in neuropsychopharmacology; Liaising with government organizations, educational institutions, industry, the public, & related scientific bodies
Meetings/Conferences: • Canadian College of Neuropsychopharmacology 2015 Annual Meeting, June, 2015, Lord Elgin Hotel, Ottawa, ON
Scope: National
Publications:
• CCNP [Canadian College of Neuropsychopharmacology] Newsletter
Type: Newsletter; *Editor:* Rachelle Anderson
Profile: College information, including meeting & membership news
• Journal of Psychiatry & Neuroscience
Type: Journal; *Frequency:* Bimonthly; *Editor:* Russell T. Joffe; Simon N. Young *ISSN:* 1180-4882
Profile: Original research & reviews in basic & clinical science, as well as emerging issues in biological & clinical psychiatry

Canadian College of Physicists in Medicine (CCPM) / Collège canadien des physiciens en médecine

PO Box 72024, Stn. Kanata North, Kanata ON K2K 2P4
Tel: 613-599-3491; *Fax:* 613-435-7257
admin@medphys.ca
www.ccpm.ca
Overview: A small national organization founded in 1979
Mission: To identify, through certification, individuals who have acquired & maintained a standard of knowledge & skill essential to the practice of medical physics, in order to serve the public
Affliation(s): Canadian Organization of Medical Physicists (COMP)
Chief Officer(s):
Nancy Barrett, Executive Director
nancy@medphys.ca
Wayne A. Beckham, CCPM Registrar
wbeckham@bccancer.bc.ca
Rasika Rajapakshe, Chair, Accreditation Committee on Physics of Mammography
rrajapak@bccancer.bc.ca
Membership: *Member Profile:* Individuals with a graduate degree in medical physics, physics, science with physics as amajor, or another field accepted by the College board; Members must have patient-related experience in physics as applied to medicine; Candidates must also pass examinations; Fellowship applicants must have made significant contributions in clinical service, education, or research related to medical physics
Awards:
• Harold E Johns Travel Award (Award)
To assist the individual to extend his or her knowledge by travelling to another centre or institution with the intent of gaining further experience in his or her chosen field, or, alternately, to embark on a new field of endeavour in medical physics. Eligibility: College member under 35 who became a member within the previous three years. *Amount:* $2000
Publications:
• InterACTIONS!
Type: Newsletter; *Frequency:* Quarterly; *Accepts Advertising*; *Editor:* Dr. Parminder Basran
Profile: News from the Canadian Organization of Medical Physicists & the Canadian College of Physicists in Medicine for members

Canadian College of Professional Counsellors & Psychotherapists (CCPCP)

PO Box 23045, Vernon BC V1T 9L8
Toll-Free: 866-704-4828
inquiry@ccpcp.ca
www.ccpcp.ca
Overview: A small national organization founded in 2006
Mission: To advocate for College members, and the public who seek Counselling and Psychotherapy services throughout Canada.
Chief Officer(s):
Amy Markin, Registrar
Membership: *Fees:* $200 for all members

Canadian College of Service Executives *See* Canadian College of Health Leaders

Canadian College of Service Executives; Canadian Forces Virtual Chapter *See* Canadian College of Health Leaders

Canadian College of Service Executives; Hospital Administrators Association *See* Canadian College of Health Leaders

Canadian Collegiate Athletic Association (CCAA) / Association canadienne du sport collégial (ACSC)

2 St. Lawrence Dr., Cornwall ON K6H 4Z1
Tel: 613-937-1508; *Fax:* 613-937-1530
sandra@ccaa.ca
www.ccaa.ca
www.facebook.com/CCAAsportsACSC
twitter.com/CCAAsportsACSC
www.youtube.com/ccaasportsacsc
Overview: A medium-sized national organization founded in 1974
Mission: To operate as the national governing body for men's & women's college sport in Canada
Affliation(s): Atlantic Colleges Athletic Association; Fédération québécoise du sport étudiant; Ontario Colleges Athletic Association; Alberta Colleges Athletic Conference; British Columbia Colleges Athletic Association
Chief Officer(s):
Sandra Murray-MacDonell, Executive Director
sandra@ccaa.ca
Staff Member(s): 1; 100 volunteer(s)
Membership: 108 institutional;

Canadian Colombian Professional Association (CCPA)

2408 Gladacres Lane, Oakville ON L6M 0G4
e-mail: treasurer@ccpassociation.com
www.ccpassociation.com
Also Known As: Canadian Coalition of Professionals from the Americas
Overview: A small local organization founded in 1952
Mission: To promote the interaction of Canadians of Hispanic descent & to strengthen the Canadian Hispanic community
Chief Officer(s):
Paula Calderon, President, Board of Directors
8 volunteer(s)
Membership: *Fees:* $30 Members; $15 Spouses; *Member Profile:* People who are born in Columbia or who are of Columbian origin & their spouses

Activities: Conferences; Networking; Mentoring

Canadian Columbian Professional Association (CCPA)
2408 Gladacres Lane, Oakville ON L6M 0G4
e-mail: info@ccpassociation.com
www.ccpassociation.com
Overview: A small national organization
Chief Officer(s):
Paula Calderon, President
President@ccpassociation.com
Adriana Santofimio, Treasurer
treasurer@ccpassociation.com

Canadian Commercial Arbitration Centre *Voir* Centre canadien d'arbitrage commercial

Canadian Commission for UNESCO / Commission canadienne pour l'UNESCO
PO Box 1047, 350 Albert St., Ottawa ON K1P 5V8
Tel: 613-566-4414; *Fax:* 613-566-4405
Toll-Free: 800-263-5588
info@unesco.ca
www.unesco.ca
Overview: A medium-sized international organization founded in 1957
Mission: An arm's length agency of the Government of Canada; to promote Canadian participation in the programmes & activities of UNESCO; to advise the government of Canada on its policies toward UNESCO; to act as a forum for Canadian civil society & government to discuss matters relating to UNESCO
Affliation(s): Network of 180 national commissions for UNESCO
Chief Officer(s):
David A. Walden, Secretary-General
david.walden@unesco.ca
Finances: *Funding Sources:* Division of the Canada Council for the Arts
Staff Member(s): 11
Membership: 200; *Member Profile:* Associations; institutions; government departments & agencies; *Committees:* Sectoral-commissions on education, natural & social sciences, culture & communication
Activities: *Rents Mailing List:* Yes
Publications:
• Contact: Bulletin of the Canadian Commission for UNESCO
Type: Newsletter; *Frequency:* Semiannually *ISSN:* 1705 7981
Profile: Commission news, events, & articles
• Share the Road
Type: Magazine; *Author:* Sheila Duggan *ISSN:* 978-0-9780369-3-5
Profile: Publication launched for International Adult Learners' Week 2008

Canadian Commission of Military History *Voir* Commission canadienne d'histoire militaire

Canadian Committee for the Theory of Machines & Mechanisms *Voir* Commission canadienne pour la théorie des machines et des mécanismes

Canadian Committee of Byzantinists
Talbot College, Univ. of Western Ontario, London ON N6A 3K7
Tel: 519-661-3045; *Fax:* 519-850-2388
Overview: A small national organization founded in 1965
Mission: To network among Canadian Byzantinists; to promote communications & exchange of information; to promote Byzantine Studies in Canada
Member of: Association internationale des études byzantines
Chief Officer(s):
Geoffrey Greatrex, President
Finances: *Annual Operating Budget:* Less than $50,000
Membership: 30; *Fees:* $15; *Member Profile:* Academic: professors & university students
Publications:
• Canadio-Byzantina
Type: Newsletter; *Frequency:* Annually
Profile: Scholarly work on Byzantium for CCB members & institutions worldwide

Canadian Committee of Lawyers & Jurists for World Jewry
c/o Raphael Barristers, #202, 1137 Centre St., Thornhill ON L4J 3M6
Tel: 416-594-1812; *Fax:* 416-594-0868
Toll-Free: 855-594-1812
braphael@raphaelbar.com
Also Known As: Jewish Civil Rights Educational Foundation of Canada
Overview: A small international organization founded in 1973
Mission: To promote the welfare of Jewish people in foreign countries whether they wish to emigrate or remain where they are; to undertake advocacy work on behalf of individuals or groups that have suffered discrimination at the hands of their government
Chief Officer(s):
Bert Raphael, President
Activities: *Speaker Service:* Yes; *Rents Mailing List:* Yes
Awards:
• Human Rights Award (Award)
• Arthur Maloney Prize for Advocacy (Award)

Canadian Committee on Cataloguing / Comité canadien de catalogage
Library & Archives Canada, 550, boul de la Cité, Gatineau QC K1A 0N4
Tel: 819-934-4388
standard@bac-lac.gc.ca
www.collectionscanada.gc.ca/cataloguing-standards
Overview: A medium-sized national organization founded in 1974
Mission: To formulate policy on questions concerning cataloguing & bibliographic control including subject analysis, referred to it by any of the organizationsrepresented on the Committee; to provide representative Canadian opinion for presentation at international meetings, committees & working groups; actively involved with the revision of the Anglo-American Cataloguing Rules.
Chief Officer(s):
Christine Oliver, Chair

Canadian Committee on Labour History (CCLH) / Comité canadien sur l'histoire du travail
c/o Canadian Committee on Labour History, Athabasca University, #1200, 10011 - 109 St., Edmonton AB T5J 3S8
e-mail: cclh@athabascau.ca
www.cclh.ca
Previous Name: Committee on Canadian Labour History
Overview: A medium-sized national organization founded in 1971
Mission: To promote & publish scholarly research in the area of Canadian labour history & related topics
Member of: Canadian Magazine Publishers Association; Canadian Association of Learned Journals
Affliation(s): International Association of Labour History Institutions; Canadian Historical Association; Conference of Historical Journals; Council of Editors of Learned Journals
Chief Officer(s):
Alvin Finkel, President
alvinf@athabascau.ca
G.S. Kealey, Treasurer
gkealey@unb.ca
Finances: *Annual Operating Budget:* $50,000-$100,000
Staff Member(s): 2
Membership: 800; *Fees:* $25
Awards:
• Forsey Prize (Award)
Publications:
• Labour / Le Travail: Journal of Canadian Labour Studies / Revue d'Études Ouvrières Canadiennes
Type: Journal; *Frequency:* Semiannually; *Number of Pages:* 350; *Editor:* Bryan D. Palmer *ISSN:* 0700-3862
Profile: Articles, reviews, documents, & reports about the historical perspective on Canadian workers, aswell as international work of interest to Canadian labour studies

Canadian Committee on MARC / Comité canadien du MARC
Standards, Strategic Office, Library & Archives Canada, 395 Wellington St., Ottawa ON K1A 0N4
Tel: 819-994-6936; *Fax:* 819-934-4388
marc@lac-bac.gc.ca
www.marc21.ca
Overview: A medium-sized national organization founded in 1976
Mission: Acts as a Canadian MARC Advisory Committee to the National Library by examining the MARC 21 communication formats & making recommendations on the formats; examines MARC 21 communication formats as a medium for the exchange of machine-readable bibliographic information in Canada; establishes procedures for receiving, evaluating & making recommendationss on proposed national & international standards for the representation in machine-readable form of bibliographic information & other related standards; maintains liaison with its constituent organizations & relevant outside agencies
Affliation(s): Library & Archives Canada
Chief Officer(s):
Leonard Bill, Secretary

The Canadian Committee to Protect Journalists *See* Canadian Journalists for Free Expression

Canadian Communication Association (CCA) / Association canadienne de communication (ACC)
c/o Department of Communication Studies, Wilfred Laurier University, 75 University Ave. West, Waterloo ON N2L 3C5
www.acc-cca.ca
Overview: A small national organization founded in 1980
Mission: To advance communication research and studies in the belief that a better understanding of communication is crucial to building a vibrant society.
Member of: Social Science Federation of Canada
Chief Officer(s):
Penelope Ironstone, President
pironstone@wlu.ca
Membership: *Fees:* $85 regular; $75 part time/sessional/retired; $30 student; $250 institutional

Canadian Communications Foundation (CCF)
Toronto ON
www.broadcasting-history.ca
Overview: A medium-sized national organization
Mission: To document the history of Canadian broadcasting on the foundation's online electronic database.
Chief Officer(s):
Pip Wedge, President
Fil Fraser, Vice-President

Canadian Community Newspapers Association (CCNA)
#200, 890 Yonge St., Toronto ON M4W 3P4
Tel: 416-923-3567; *Fax:* 416-923-7206
Toll-Free: 877-305-2262
info@newspaperscanada.ca
www.newspaperscanada.ca
Overview: A medium-sized national organization founded in 1919
Mission: To be the national voice of the community press in Canada
Chief Officer(s):
John Hinds, President & CEO
Membership: 700+ newspapers; *Member Profile:* Each regional association has its own criteria for full active membership.
Awards:
• Premier Awards (Award)
Awards are presented in the following categories: Outstanding Columnist, Local Cartoon, Editorial Writing, Community Service, Agricultural Edition, House Ad, Reporter Initiative, News Story, Environmental Writing, Best Ad Design
• Special Competition Awards (Award)
Awards are given in following areas: Best Spot News Photo, Best Feature Photo, Best Sports Photo, Best Christmas Edition, Best Sports Page, Best Special Section, Best Historical Story, Best Newspaper Promotion, Best Feature Story, Best Photo Essay, Best Feature Series, Best Agricultural Story
• General Excellence Awards (Award)
Awards are presented to newspapers for general excellence by circulation category, & include presentations to the Best All-Round Newspaper, Best Front Page, & Best Editorial Page

Canadian Community Reinvestment Coalition (CCRC)
PO Box 821, Stn. B, Ottawa ON K1P 241
Tel: 613-789-5753; *Fax:* 613-241-4758
info@cancrc.org
www.cancrc.org
Overview: A medium-sized national organization
Mission: To increase the accountability of Canada's financial institutions, increase their reinvestment in the Canadian economy, strengthen Canada's economy, strengthen community economic development efforts across Canada, & develop leadership in the Canadian financial sevices consumer movement.
Membership: 100; *Fees:* $25-$250

Canadian Comparative Literature Association (CCLA) / Association canadienne de littérature comparée (ACLC)

c/o Markus Reisenleitner, Department of Humanities, York University, 217 Vanier College, Toronto ON M3H 1P3
complit.ca
Overview: A small national organization founded in 1969
Affiliation(s): International Comparative Literature Association; Congress of the Humanities & Social Sciences
Chief Officer(s):
Karin Beeler, President
beeler@unbc.ca
Susan Ingram, Vice-President
singram@yorku.ca
Pascal Gin, Secretary
pascal_gin@carleton.ca
Markus Reisenleitner, Treasurer
mrln@yorku.ca
Membership: *Fees:* $30 students, retired, unemployed, & under employed persons; $60 regular members; $75 joint membership; $375 life membership; *Member Profile:* Scholars interested in comparative literature from across Canada
Activities: Organizing educational meetings & networking opportunities for members
Meetings/Conferences: • Canadian Comparative Literature Association 2015 Annual Meeting (in conjunction with the Congress of the Humanities & Social Sciences), May, 2015, University of Ottawa, Ottawa, ON
Scope: National
Description: Each yearly meeting of the Canadian Comparative Literature Association is held at the Congress of the Humanities & Social Sciences
Contact Information: Canadian Comparative Literature Association Treasurer: Paul D. Morris, E-mail: pdmorris@ustboniface.mb.ca
Publications:
• Canadian Review of Comparative Literature / Revue canadienne de littérature comparée
Type: Journal; *Price:* Free with joint membership in the Canadian Comparative Literature Association

Canadian Compensation Association *See* World at Work

Canadian Concrete Masonry Producers Association (CCMPA)

PO Box 1345, 1500 Avenue Rd., Toronto ON M5M 3X0
Tel: 416-495-7497; *Fax:* 416-495-8939
Toll-Free: 888-495-7497
information@ccmpa.ca
www.ccmpa.ca
Previous Name: Ontario Concrete Block Association
Overview: A medium-sized provincial organization founded in 1962
Mission: Works on behalf of concrete masonry producers to build an industry as strong and as enduring as the products it manufactures
Member of: Masonry Canada
Chief Officer(s):
Marina de Souza, Managing Director
Finances: *Annual Operating Budget:* $100,000-$250,000; *Funding Sources:* Membership dues
Staff Member(s): 2
Membership: 25 manufacturers
Activities: Marketing; professional development; research; technical

Canadian Concrete Paving Association *See* Canadian Ready Mixed Concrete Association

Canadian Concrete Pipe Association (CCPA) / Association canadienne des fabricants de tuyaux de béton (ACTB)

205 Miller Dr., Halton Hills ON L7G 6G4
Tel: 905-877-5369; *Fax:* 905-877-5369
info@ccpa.com
www.ccpa.com
www.linkedin.com/groups?gid=1920373&trk=anetsrch_name&goback=.gdr_1248
www.facebook.com/group.php?gid=106265401921
www.youtube.com/user/CanadianConcretePipe
Overview: A medium-sized national organization founded in 1992
Mission: To coordinate research & development, promotion, education & federal government relations programs pertaining to the marketing of high quality precast concrete waste water & storm drainage products in Canada.
Member of: Federation of Canadian Municipalities
Affiliation(s): Ontario Concrete Pipe Association; Tubecon; American Concrete Pipe Association
Chief Officer(s):
John Greer, Chair
Finances: *Annual Operating Budget:* Less than $50,000; *Funding Sources:* Membership dues; research grants
Staff Member(s): 2; 30 volunteer(s)
Membership: 35; *Member Profile:* Manufacturers of concrete pipes & related products; suppliers to manufacturers
Activities: Software development; product development; market research; *Speaker Service:* Yes; *Library:* Data Centre; Open to public

Canadian Condominium Institute (CCI)

#210, 2800 - 14th Ave., Markham ON L3R 0E4
Tel: 416-491-6216; *Fax:* 416-491-1670
Toll-Free: 866-491-6216
cci.national@associationconcepts.ca
www.cci.ca
Overview: A medium-sized national organization founded in 1982
Mission: To serve as a central clearinghouse & research centre on condominium issues & activities across the country; To provide objective research for practitioners & government agencies regarding all aspects of condominium operations; To offer professional assistance; To improve legislation & represent condominiums; to develop standards
Chief Officer(s):
Janice Pynn, RCM, ARP, ACCI, Chair
Jim MacKenzie, MBA, DAA, FCIP, National President
F. Diane Gaunt, Executive Director
dianeg@taylorenterprises.com
Alison Nash, Manager, Operations
alisonn@taylorenterprises.com
Peter K. Harris, C.A., ACCI, FCC, Secretary-Treasurer
24 volunteer(s)
Membership: 1,200
Activities: Providing an information hotline for instant answers to questions related to the condominium industry & condominium living
Publications:
• CCI [Canadian Condominium Institute] Newsletter
Type: Newsletter

CCI-Golden Horseshoe Chapter
#23, 920 Brant St., Burlington ON L7R 4J1
Tel: 905-631-0124; *Fax:* 866-320-5361
Toll-Free: 877-444-2496
admin@ghccci.org
www.ghcci.org
Chief Officer(s):
Karen Reynolds, President

CCI-Huronia Chapter
PO Box 95, Barrie ON L4M 4S9
Tel: 866-491-6216; *Fax:* 866-502-1670
info@ccihuronia.com
www.ccihuronia.com
Chief Officer(s):
Michele Farley, Acting President

CCI-London & Area Chapter
PO Box 51022, 1593 Adelaide St. North, London ON N5X 4P9
Tel: 519-453-0672; *Fax:* 519-642-4726
ccisw@cci-sw.on.ca
www.cci-sw.on.ca
Chief Officer(s):
Don Peter, President

CCI-Manitoba Chapter
PO Box 2517, Stn. Main, Winnipeg MB R3C 4A7
Tel: 204-794-1134
ccimanitoba@cci.ca
www.cci.ca/Manitoba
Chief Officer(s):
Pamela Pyke, President, 204-982-6515
pamela.pyke@marsh.com

CCI-New Brunswick Chapter
PO Box 363, Stn. A, Fredericton NB E3B 4Z9
Tel: 506-447-1511
ccinewbrunswick@cci.ca
www.cci.ca/NewBrunswick

CCI-Newfoundland & Labrador Chapter
Churchill Square, PO Box 23060, St. John's NL A1B 4J9
e-mail: ccinewfoundland@cci.ca
www.cci.ca/Newfoundland
Chief Officer(s):
Heather Whiffen, Administrator

CCI-North Alberta Chapter
Kingsway Business Center, #37, 11810 Kingsway Ave. NW, Edmonton AB T5G 0X5
Tel: 780-453-9004; *Fax:* 780-452-9003
info@cci-north.ab.ca
www.ccinorthalberta.com
Chief Officer(s):
Anand Sharma, President
anand@csmgmtinc.ca

CCI-North Saskatchewan Chapter
PO Box 7074, Saskatoon SK S7K 4J1
Tel: 306-652-0311; *Fax:* 306-652-0373
northsaskatchewan@cci.ca
www.cci.ca/NorthSaskatchewan
www.linkedin.com/company/cci-northsaskatchewan
www.facebook.com/ccinorthsaskatchewan
twitter.com/CCINorthSask

CCI-Northwestern Ontario Chapter
383 Mooney St., Thunder Bay ON P7B 5L5
Tel: 807-346-5690; *Fax:* 807-344-1507
ccinorthontario@shaw.ca
www.cci.ca/NWOntario
Chief Officer(s):
Douglas Steen, President

CCI-Nova Scotia Chapter
#135, #3-644 Portland St., Dartmouth NS B2W 2M3
Tel: 902-461-9855
info@ccinovascotia.ca
www.ccinovascotia.ca
Chief Officer(s):
Norma Cameron, President

CCI-Ottawa Chapter
PO Box 32001, 1386 Richmond Rd., Ottawa ON K2B 1A1
Fax: 866-502-1670
Toll-Free: 866-491-6216
cciottawa@cci.ca
www.cci.ca/Ottawa
Chief Officer(s):
Nancy Houle, President

CCI-South Alberta Chapter
PO Box 38107, Calgary AB T3K 4Y0
Tel: 403-253-9082; *Fax:* 403-220-1215
administrator@ccisouthalberta.com
www.ccisouthalberta.com
Chief Officer(s):
Janet Porteous, President, 403-247-2802
jporteous@shaw.ca

CCI-South Saskatchewan Chapter
PO Box 3784, Regina SK S4P 3N8
Toll-Free: 866-491-6216
cci-ssk@cci.ca
www.cci.ca/ssc
Chief Officer(s):
Gerry A. Cairns, President

CCI-Toronto & Area Chapter
#210, 2800 - 14th Ave., Toronto ON L3R 0E4
Tel: 416-491-6216; *Fax:* 416-491-1670
cci.toronto@taylorenterprises.com
www.ccitoronto.org
www.linkedin.com/company/canadian-condominium-institute—toronto-chap
www.facebook.com/CCIToronto
twitter.com/CCIToronto
instagram.com/ccitoronto
Chief Officer(s):
Brian Horlick, President

CCI-Vancouver Chapter
PO Box 17577, RPO The Ritz, Vancouver BC V6E 0B2
Toll-Free: 866-491-6216
contact@ccivancouver.ca
www.ccivancouver.ca
www.facebook.com/535357929822477
twitter.com/CCIVancouver
Chief Officer(s):
Jamie Bleay, President

CCI-Windsor - Essex County Chapter
PO Box 22015, 11500 Tecumseh Rd. East, Windsor ON N8N 5G6
Tel: 519-978-3237; *Fax:* 519-978-9042
cciwindsoressex@gmail.com
www.cci.ca/windsor
Chief Officer(s):
Andrea M. Thielk, President
amthielk@clarkslaw.com

Canadian Conference of Catholic Bishops (CCCB) / Conférence des évêques catholiques du Canada (CECC)

2500 Don Reid Dr., Ottawa ON K1H 2J2
Tel: 613-241-9461; *Fax:* 613-241-8117
cecc@cccb.ca
www.cccb.ca
www.facebook.com/123711474340639
twitter.com/CCCB_CECC
www.youtube.com/user/cccbadmin
Previous Name: Canadian Catholic Conference
Overview: A small national charitable organization founded in 1943
Mission: To exercise pastoral functions for Catholics in Canada
Chief Officer(s):
Patrick Powers, P.H., General Secretary, 613-241-9461 Ext. 209
gensec@cccb.ca
Staff Member(s): 40
Membership: *Member Profile:* Diocesan bishops in Canada; Coadjutor Bishops; Auxiliary Bishops; Titular Bishops of any rite within the Catholic Church
Activities: Providing aid to developing countries & Christian education; Offering a forum for bishops to share experiences & insights
Publications:
• At Home with the Word
Type: Yearbook; *Frequency:* Annually; *Price:* $9
• Children's Daily Prayer
Type: Yearbook; *Frequency:* Annually; *ISBN:* 978-1-56854-662-9; *Price:* $18
• Daily Prayer
Type: Yearbook; *Frequency:* Annually; *Price:* $15
• A Simple Guide to the Daily Mass Readings
Type: Yearbook; *Frequency:* Annually; *Price:* $3
• Sourcebook for Sundays & Seasons
Type: Yearbook; *Frequency:* Annually; *ISBN:* 978-1-56854-674-2; *Price:* $18
• Workbook for Lectors & Gospel Readers
Type: Yearbook; *Frequency:* Annually; *ISBN:* 978-0-88997-572-9; *Price:* $15

Canadian Conference of Mennonite Brethren Churches (CCMBC)

1310 Taylor Ave., Winnipeg MB R3M 3Z6
Tel: 204-669-6575; *Fax:* 204-654-1865
Toll-Free: 888-669-6575
karen.hume@mbchurches.ca
www.mbconf.ca
www.linkedin.com/company/canadian-conference-of-mennonite-brethren-chu
www.facebook.com/mbconf?fref=ts
twitter.com/CdnMBConf
Overview: A medium-sized national organization founded in 1945
Mission: To glorify God, to nurture & equip members to live the Christian life & to mobilize them for ministry
Chief Officer(s):
Willy Reimer, Executive Director, 855-256-3211
willy.reimer@mbchurches.ca
Elly Bargen, Account Administrator, 888-669-6575 Ext. 696
elly.bargen@mbchurches.ca
Laura Kalmar, Interim Director, Communications
laura.kalmar@mbchurches.ca
Ron Toews, Director, Leadership Development, 604-853-6959
ron.toews@mbchurches.ca
Norbert Bargen, Director, Human Resources, 888-669-6575 Ext. 698
norbert.bargen@mbchurches.ca
Finances: *Funding Sources:* Donations
Staff Member(s): 19
Membership: 31,264; 256 Mennonite Brethren congregations; *Committees:* Mennonite Central Committee; Mennonite Disaster Service; Manitoba Missions/Service
Activities: *Library:* Centre for MB Studies; Open to public
Publications:
• Le Lien
Frequency: Bimonthly; *Editor:* Jean Biéri *ISSN:* 1716-5016; *Price:* $16/year: Canada, $20/year: international
Profile: Written in French, the publication serves the conference's francophone churches in Québec
• MB Chinese Herald
Frequency: Bimonthly; *Editor:* Joseph Kwan *ISSN:* 1911-8783
Profile: Written in Chinese, the Herald serves the conference's Chinese community
• Mennonite Brethren Herald
Frequency: Monthly; *Accepts Advertising*; *Editor:* Laura Kalmar
ISSN: 0025-9349; *Price:* Free for Canadian MB Church members; from $25.20 to $27.60 fornon-members
Profile: Feature articles, columns, letters, news, people, & events for the Mennonite Brethren community
• Mennonite Historian
Type: Newsletter; *Frequency:* Quarterly; *Editor:* Jon Isaak; *Price:* $15/yr., $28/2 yrs., $40/3 yrs.

Canadian Conference of Pharmaceutical Faculties *See* Association of Faculties of Pharmacy of Canada

Canadian Conference of the Arts (CCA) / Conférence canadienne des arts

#406, 130 Slater St., Ottawa ON K1P 6E2
Tel: 613-238-3561; *Fax:* 613-238-4849
info@ccarts.ca
www.ccarts.ca
www.facebook.com/CanArts
twitter.com/CanadianArts
Overview: A medium-sized national charitable organization founded in 1945
Mission: To ensure the lively existence & continued growth of the arts & the cultural industries in Canada; to increase the Canadian materials (works created, produced, & performed by Canadians) available to Canadians; to improve the quality of life for all artists & arts groups; to unite members to work for interests of all artists & whole cultural community; to work closely with other arts service organizations to formulate policies & advocate their adoption by governments
Chief Officer(s):
Alain Pineau, National Director
alain.pineau@ccarts.ca
Anne-Marie Des Roches, Associate Director, Senior Policy Advisor
Finances: *Annual Operating Budget:* $500,000-$1.5 Million; *Funding Sources:* Membership fees; publication sales; conference fees; government subsidies (federal, provincial)
Staff Member(s): 7
Membership: 800; *Fees:* Schedule available; *Member Profile:* Persons from all arts disciplines, & all cultural industries; major arts institutions & festivals; regional & community arts councils; provincial & national associations in every discipline; individuals who support goals & aspirations of artists in Canada.
Activities: Has led arts community in realizing such achievements as creation of Public Lending Right, deductibility of capital expenses, Performers' Rights Day, formation of CACSA (Canadian Advisory Committee on the Status of the Artist); powerful influence in creation of arts policy, in changing perceptions of policy-makers on such issues as the status of the artist, funding, copyright, taxation, freedom of expression, arts education, arts awareness; *Library* by appointment
Awards:
• Keith Kelly Award for Cultural Leadership (Award)
• Diplôme d'honneur (Award)
Established in 1954; presented annually to Canadians who have contributed outstanding service to the arts; recipients have included Vincent Massey, Wilfrid Pelletier, Maureen Forrester, Floyd Chalmers, Gabrielle Roy, Glenn Gould, Alfred Pellan, Bill Reid, Antonine Maillet

Canadian Congress of Neurological Sciences *See* Canadian Neurological Sciences Federation

Canadian Connemara Pony Society (CCPS)

c/o Box 2, Site 20, RR#2, Sundre AB T0M 1X0
Tel: 780-638-9152
www.canadianconnemara.org
Previous Name: American Connemara Association - Western Canada
Overview: A small local organization founded in 1956
Mission: To assist & promote the breeding, registration, training, exhibition & general use of the Connemara Pony for pleasure, sport, equestrian competition, & therapeutic horsemanship in North America; to preserve the unique qualities of the Connemara through encouraging selective breeding for type & conformation as described in the Society's Standards for the Breed; to assist & promote local, national & international equestrian competition; to keep the members of the Society informed in all matters concerning the Connemara
Affliation(s): American Connemara Pony Society
Chief Officer(s):
Penny Huggons, President
cphuggons@gmail.com
Elsie Priddy, Secretary-Treasurer
elsie@elodon.ca
Membership: *Fees:* $15 junior; $20 associate & non-resident; $40 senior; *Committees:* Arbitration; Archives; Awards; Finance; HWSS; Inspections; Membership; Newsletter; Nominations; Promotions; Registrations; Website

Canadian Conservation Institute (CCI) / Institut canadien de conservation (l'ICC)

1030 Innes Rd., Ottawa ON K1B 4S7
Tel: 613-998-3721; *Fax:* 613-998-4721
Toll-Free: 866-998-3721; *TTY:* 819-997-3123
cci-icc.services@pch.gc.ca
www.cci-icc.gc.ca
www.facebook.com/cci.conservation
Overview: A medium-sized national organization founded in 1972
Mission: To promote the proper preservation & care of moveable cultural heritage in Canada; To advance the science, technology, & practice of conservation; To support the heritage community in Canada
Affliation(s): CCI is a Special Operating Agency within the Department of Canadian Heritage
Chief Officer(s):
Jeanne Inch, Director General & Chief Operating Officer
Activities: Working with Canadian heritage institutions, such as historic sites, art galleries, libraries, & museums; Conducting conservation research; Offering learning opportunities; Disseminating conservation information;; *Library:* Canadian Conservation Institute Library
Publications:
• CCI [Canadian Conservation Institute] News
Type: Newsletter; *Editor:* Barbara Patterson; Linda Leclerc
Profile: Canadian Conservation Institute services, learning opportunities, library acquisitions, & new publications

Canadian Construction Association (CCA) / Association canadienne de la construction (ACC)

#1900, 275 Slater St., Ottawa ON K1P 5H9
Tel: 613-236-9455; *Fax:* 613-236-9526
cca@cca-acc.com
www.cca-acc.com
www.linkedin.com/company/canadian-construction-association—-associati
twitter.com/ConstructionCAN
www.youtube.com/user/ConstructionCAN
Overview: A large national organization founded in 1918
Mission: To act as the national voice of the construction industry; To serve, promote, & enhance the construction industry by acting on behalf of its members in matters of national concern
Chief Officer(s):
John Schubert, Chair
Michael Atkinson, President
mikea@cca-acc.com
Pierre Boucher, COO
pierre@cca-acc.com
Eric Lee, Senior Director, Industry Practices
ericlee@cca-acc.com
Mark Belton, Director, Finance
mbelton@cca-acc.com
Bill Ferreira, Director, Government Relations & Public Affairs
bferreira@cca-acc.com
Chantal Montpetit, Director, Meetings & Conferences
chantal@cca-acc.com
Kirsi O'Connor, Director, Marketing & Communications
koconnor@cca-acc.com
Aneel Rangi, Director, Legal & Research Services
aneel@cca-acc.com
Membership: 17,000 firms + 70 partner associations; *Committees:* Executive; Governance; Standard Practices; Innovation & Technology; Business & Market Development; Industry Advocacy & Regulatory Affairs; Gold Seal; Canadian Design-Build Institute; Operations & Maintenance Council; Canadian Construction Documents; Institute for BIM in Canada
Awards:
• CCA Awards of Excellence (Award)
• CCA Awards of Recognition (Award)
• CCA Person of the Year (Award)
• CCA Excellence in Innovation Award (Award)
• CCA Environmental Achievement Award (Award)
• CCA International Business Award (Award)
• CCA National Safety Award (Award)
• CCA Partner Association Award of Excellence (Award)
• CCA Community Leader Award (Award)
• CCA Gold Seal Association Award (Award)
• CCA General Contractor Award of Recognition (Award)
• CCA Trade Contractor Award of Recognition (Award)
• CCA Civil Infrastructure Award of Recognition (Award)

• CCA Manufacturers, Suppliers & Services Award of Recognition (Award)
Meetings/Conferences: • Canadian Construction Association 97th Annual Conference 2015, March, 2015, San Antonio, TX
Scope: National
Publications:
• CCA [Canadian Construction Association] Weekly
Type: Newsletter; *Frequency:* Weekly

Canadian Construction Women (CCW)

#290, 142 - 757 West Hastings St., Vancouver BC V6C 1A1
www.constructionwomen.org
www.facebook.com/cdnconstructionwomen
twitter.com/constructionw
Overview: A small national organization
Mission: To attract & retain women in the construction industry
Chief Officer(s):
Kristina Morse, President
kmorse@dg.ca
Libby Rowe, Vice-President
lrowe@pcl.com
Farah Makani, Treasurer
fmakani@mcw.com
Finances: *Funding Sources:* Sponsorships
Membership: *Fees:* $150 corporate; $55 individuals
Activities: Supporting & mentoring members; Providing networking opportunities; Offering chances to learn
Publications:
• Canadian Construction Women Member Directory
Type: Directory
Profile: Listing of contacts representing a cross section of the industry
• Under the Hard Hat
Type: Newsletter; *Frequency:* Monthly
Profile: Publication informs members of approaching events

Canadian Consulting Agrologists Association (CCAA) / Association canadienne des agronomes-conseils

PO Box 20, 2004 - 401 Bay St., Toronto ON M5H 2Y4
Tel: 416-860-1515; *Fax:* 416-860-1535
Toll-Free: 800-268-1148
info@ccaa.bz
www.ccaa.bz
Overview: A small national organization founded in 1973
Mission: To provide excellence in agricultural consulting; To promote standards of competency; To maintain Standards of Ethical Conduct
Chief Officer(s):
Adele Buettner, Executive Director
Terry Betker, President, 204-775-4531, Fax: 204-783-8329
terry.betker@mnp.ca
Membership: *Fees:* Schedule available; *Member Profile:* Professional agrology consultants who offer consulting services to agricultural sectors around the world
Activities: Promoting certification; Offering professional development & networking opportunities; Advocating for the profession of agricultural consulting; Promoting member services to national & international agricultural sectors
Awards:
• Lifetime Achievement Award (Award)
• Distinguished Certified Agricultural Consultant (Award)
• CCAA Fellow Award (Award)
Publications:
• CCAA [Canadian Consulting Agrologists Association] Member Directory
Type: Directory
• CCAA [Canadian Consulting Agrologists Association] Newsletter
Type: Newsletter; *Frequency:* Quarterly
Profile: Current industry practices & trends & professional development

Canadian Consumer Specialty Products Association (CCSPA)

#800, 130 Albert St., Ottawa ON K1P 5G4
Tel: 613-232-6616; *Fax:* 613-233-6350
assoc@ccspa.org
www.ccspa.org
twitter.com/CCSPA_ACPCS
Previous Name: Canadian Manufacturers of Chemical Specialties Association
Overview: A medium-sized national organization founded in 1958
Mission: Represents the specialty chemical & formulated products industry; promotes the interests of member companies by providing a national voice, encouraging ethical practices, negotiating with government, & fostering industry cooperation
Chief Officer(s):
Shannon Coombs, Executive Director, 613-232-6616 Ext. 18
coombss@ccspa.org
Nancy Hitchins, Director, Administration & Member Services, 613-232-6616 Ext. 12
hitchinsn@ccspa.org
Finances: *Annual Operating Budget:* $250,000-$500,000
Staff Member(s): 6
Membership: 60+ corporate; *Committees:* Technical: Soap & Detergent; Antimicrobial Chemicals; Pest Control Products; Waxes & Polishes; Occupational Health & Safety; Pesticides; Automotive Chemicals; Aerosols; Environmental; Non-Technical: Executive; Public Relations; Membership Recruitment; Ontario Golf
Activities: *Rents Mailing List:* Yes
Awards:
• Chevaliar Award (Scholarship)
Publications:
• The Formulator [a publication of the Canadian Consumer Specialty Products Association]
Type: Magazine; *Frequency:* Annually; *Editor:* Ali Mintenko
Profile: Feature articles & CCSPA information
• Microgram [a publication of the Canadian Consumer Specialty Products Association]
Type: Newsletter; *Frequency:* Quarterly
Profile: CCSPA new for members only

The Canadian Continence Foundation / Fondation d'aide aux personnes incontinentes (Canada)

PO Box 417, Peterborough ON K9J 6Z3
Tel: 705-750-4600; *Fax:* 705-750-1770
Toll-Free: 800-265-9575
help@canadiancontinence.ca
www.canadiancontinence.ca
www.facebook.com/group.php?gid=122320727816460
twitter.com/cdncontinence
www.youtube.com/user/canadiancontinence
Previous Name: The Simon Foundation for Continence Canada
Overview: A large national charitable organization founded in 1986
Mission: To act as a source of information, education & support for incontinent individuals; to increase public awareness & influence government policy
Affliation(s): Simon Foundation-USA
Chief Officer(s):
Jacqueline Cahill, Executive Director
Thomas Alloway, President
Derek Griffiths, Vice-President
Finances: *Annual Operating Budget:* $100,000-$250,000
20 volunteer(s)
Membership: 60 institutional; 12,000 individual; 100 associate; 3,000 professionals; *Fees:* $100 organizations; $70 professional; *Member Profile:* Consumers & medical professionals
Activities: Montréal Helpline; *Awareness Events:* Incontinence Awareness Month, Nov.; *Speaker Service:* Yes
Publications:
• The Informer: Your Canadian Continence Resource
Type: Newsletter
Profile: Research, issues & foundation news

Canadian Contractors Association (CCA)

#4, 5660 - 10 St. NE, Calgary AB T2E 8W7
Tel: 403-509-3922; *Fax:* 403-270-8518
Toll-Free: 877-509-3925
chad@canadiancontractors.info
www.canadiancontractors.info
Overview: A medium-sized national organization
Mission: To provide information & services to the independant consultant & contractor market
Chief Officer(s):
Chad Pimm, COO
chad.p@rpibi.com
Michelle Hennessy, Director, Marketing
mh@michellehennessy.com
Activities: Providing insurance benefits to self-employed or independent contractors

Canadian Convenience Stores Association (CCSA) / Association Canadienne des dépanneurs en alimentation (ACDA)

#103, 220 Wyecroft Rd., Ontario ON L6K 3V1
Tel: 905-845-9339; *Fax:* 905-845-9340
Toll-Free: 877-934-3968
www.theccsa.ca
Overview: A large national organization founded in 2006
Mission: To be the industry voice for all convenience store matters; to provide a forum for concerns & issues; to educate members
Affliation(s): Western Convenience Stores Association; Ontario Convenience Stores Association; Association Québécoise des dépanneurs en alimentation; Atlantic Convenience Stores Association
Chief Officer(s):
Alex Scholten, President
ascholten@nb.aibn.com
Lynda Watson, Secretary
lynda@conveniencestores.ca
Finances: *Funding Sources:* Membership fees
Membership: 31,000; *Member Profile:* Major convenience store companies; independent owners; food retailers; suppliers & wholesalers; gasoline & automotive product vendors
Activities: Online Responsible Retail Training program; combating contraband tobacco

Canadian Convention of Southern Baptists (CCSB) / Convention canadienne des baptistes du Sud

100 Convention Way, Cochrane AB T4C 2G2
Tel: 403-932-5688; *Fax:* 403-932-4937
Toll-Free: 888-442-2272
office@ccsb.ca
www.ccsb.ca
Overview: A medium-sized national charitable organization founded in 1985
Mission: To help churches build the Kingdom of God; a church for every person across Canada & around the world
Affliation(s): Southern Baptist Convention
Chief Officer(s):
Gérald J. Taillon, Executive Director
gtaillon@cnbc.ca
Dwight Huffman, President
Finances: *Funding Sources:* Member churches
Staff Member(s): 8; 4 volunteer(s)
Membership: 10,189
Activities: *Library:* Resource Centre; Open to public
Publications:
• The Baptist Horizon
Type: Journal; *Frequency:* Bimonthly; *Editor:* Debbie Shelton
ISSN: 1195-4744
Profile: CCSB news

Canadian Co-operative Association (CCA) / Association des coopératives du Canada (ACC)

#400, 275 Bank St., Ottawa ON K2P 2L6
Tel: 613-238-6711; *Fax:* 613-567-0658
Other Communication: Alt. E-mail: international@coopscanada.coop
info@coopscanada.coop
www.coopscanada.coop
www.facebook.com/361648435712
twitter.com/CoopsCanada
www.youtube.com/user/CCAottawa
Overview: A large national organization founded in 1987
Mission: To develop co-operatives in other countries; To promote the co-operative model; To unite co-operatives from various industry sectors & regions of Canada
Affliation(s): Conseil canadien de la coopération et de la mutualité; Co-operative Development Initiative (co-managed by CCA and CCCM); Co-operative Development Foundation of Canada (CDF)
Chief Officer(s):
Bill Dobson, President
Jo-Anne Ferguson, Executive Director, 613-238-6711 Ext. 216
Julie Breuer, Director, Engagement, 613-238-6711 Ext. 215
Vijaya Venkatesh-Mannar, Director, Finance, 613-238-6711 Ext. 232
Michael Wodzicki, Director, Market Development, 613-238-6711 Ext. 247
Finances: *Funding Sources:* Donations
Membership: 2,000+ organizations; *Member Profile:* Co-operatives in Canada, which represent over nine million co-operative & credit union members
Activities: Supporting members through the provision of financial or technical resources; *Awareness Events:* Co-op Week, Oct.
Awards:
• Canadian Co-operative Achievement Award (Award)
To recognize individual contributions to the co-operative movement in Canada
• Global Co-operator Award (Award)
To honour an individual who demonstrates commitment to the

international development work of the Canadian Co-operative Association & the Co-operative Development Foundation of Canada
• Co-operative Governance Awards (Award)
To recognize credit unions & co-operatives which demonstrate excellence in governance or practices
• Alexander Fraser Laidlaw Fellowship (Scholarship), CASC Scholarships
• Amy & Tim Dauphinee Scholarship (Scholarship), CASC Scholarships
• Lemaire Co-operative Studies Award (Scholarship), CASC Scholarships
Publications:
• Canadian Co-operative Association Annual Report
Type: Yearbook; *Frequency:* Annually
Profile: A summary of the association's activities
• Co-operative News Briefs [a publication of the Canadian Co-operative Association]
Type: Newsletter; *Frequency:* Semimonthly; *Price:* Free
Profile: Information for those with an interest in co-operative sector developments in Canada & throughout the world
• Co-operatives Helping Fuel a Green Economy: A report on Canada's renewable energy sector
Type: Booklet; *Author:* Patti Giovannini; *Editor:* John Anderson
• Ethno-cultural & Immigrant Co-operatives in Canada
Type: Booklet; *Author:* Patti Giovannini; *Editor:* John Anderson; Donna Balkan
• Governance Matters [a publication of the Canadian Co-operative Association]
Type: Newsletter; *Frequency:* 8 pa
Profile: Governance issues for the co-operative leader
• International Development Digest [a publication of the Canadian Co-operative Association]
Type: Digest; *Frequency:* 3 pa
Profile: Information about international co-operative development efforts undertaken on behalf of CCA's Canadian credit union & co-operativemembers
• International Development Review [a publication of the Canadian Co-operative Association]
Type: Yearbook; *Frequency:* Annually
Profile: Annual highlights from the Canadian Co-operative Association's international development program
• International Dispatch [a publication of the Canadian Co-operative Association]
Type: Newsletter; *Frequency:* 6 pa
Profile: News & views about co-operatives & credit unions around the world & the war on poverty
• The Lay of the Land: Local Food Initiatives in Canada
Type: Booklet; *Number of Pages:* 53; *Author:* Adrian Egbers; *Editor:* Lynne Markell
Profile: Information about the area of local food, within & outside the co-operative sector
• New futures: Innovative Uses of the Co-op Model
Type: Booklet; *Number of Pages:* 30; *Author:* Brenda Heald; *Editor:* Donna Balkan; *ISBN:* 978-0-88817-102-3
Profile: Profiles of Canadian co-ops that use the co-op model
• Working Together for Local Food: Co-operative Profiles & Resource Guide
Type: Booklet; *Number of Pages:* 63; *Author:* Adrian Egbers; Stefan Epp; *Editor:* Lynne Markell; *ISBN:* 978-0-88817-103-0
Profile: Profiles of successful local food co-ops

Canadian Cooperative Credit Society *See* Credit Union Central of Canada

Canadian Co-operative Wool Growers Ltd. (CCWG)

PO Box 130, 142 Franktown Rd., Carleton Place ON K7C 3P3
Tel: 613-257-2714; *Fax:* 613-257-8896
Toll-Free: 800-488-2714
ccwghq@wool.ca
www.wool.ca
Overview: A medium-sized national organization founded in 1918
Mission: To operate as a producer-owned wool marketing cooperative; To collect, grade, & market, the majority of the Canadian wool clip to the global market; To retail farm supplies & animal health & identification products
Chief Officer(s):
Eric Bjergso, General Manager
ericb@wool.ca
Staff Member(s): 30
Membership: 1,200
Awards:
• Certificate of Merit, Commercial Wool Production in Canada (Award)
• Honorary Knights of the Golden Fleece (Award)
Meetings/Conferences: • Annual General Meeting of the Canadian Co-operative Wool Growers Ltd., 2015
Scope: National

Canadian Coordinating Office for Health Technology Assessment *See* Canadian Agency for Drugs & Technologies in Health

Canadian Copper & Brass Development Association (CCBDA)

#415, 49 The Donway West, Toronto ON M3C 3M9
Tel: 416-391-5599; *Fax:* 416-391-3823
Toll-Free: 877-640-0946
coppercanada@onramp.ca
www.coppercanada.ca
Overview: A medium-sized national organization founded in 1958
Mission: To promote, foster & stimulate use of products of Canadian copper & brass industry. To represent and support the primary producers fabricators, manufacturers, and consumers of copper and copper alloys in Canada, by increasing industry and public awareness of copper's capabilites and advantages compared to other metals and materials, and by providing technical services related to copper's use.
Affiliation(s): International Copper Association
Chief Officer(s):
Stephen A.W. Knapp, Executive Director
Finances: *Annual Operating Budget:* $250,000-$500,000
Staff Member(s): 6
Membership: 21 corporate; *Fees:* $1500+; *Member Profile:* Primary copper producers, fabricators and manufacturers
Activities: *Library* Open to public by appointment

Canadian Copyright Institute (CCI)

#107, 192 Spadina Ave., Toronto ON M5T 2C2
Tel: 416-975-1756; *Fax:* 416-975-1839
info@thecci.ca
www.canadiancopyrightinstitute.ca
Overview: A medium-sized national organization founded in 1965
Mission: To encourage a better understanding of the law of copyright on the part of members, public & users of copyright material; To engage in & foster research in copyright law
Affiliation(s): Book & Periodical Council
Chief Officer(s):
Anne McClelland, Administrator
Finances: *Funding Sources:* Membership fees
25 volunteer(s)
Membership: 45 individual + 19 corporate + 47 affiliate; *Fees:* $75 individual; *Member Profile:* Interest in copyright & concern to encourage its use in public interest
Activities: *Library* by appointment

The Canadian Corporate Counsel Association (CCCA) / L'Association canadienne des conseillers juridiques d'entreprises

#1210, 20 Toronto St., Toronto ON M5C 2B8
Tel: 416-869-0522; *Fax:* 416-869-0946
ccca@ccca-accje.org
www.ccca-accje.org
twitter.com/CCCA_News
Overview: A medium-sized national organization founded in 1987
Mission: To provide quality education, information & other services & resources of specific interest to corporate counsel in Canada, & to facilitate communication & networking among such counsel
Member of: Canadian Bar Association
Affiliation(s): Malaysian Corporate Counsel Association; Corporate Lawyers Association of South Africa; Australian Corporate Lawyers Association; Hong Kong Corporate Counsel Association; Singapore Corporate Counsel Association; Corporate Lawyers Association of New Zealand
Chief Officer(s):
Cathy Cummings, Executive Director
cathyc@ccca-cba.org
Christine Staley, Director, Professional Development
cstaley@cccs-cba.org
Finances: *Annual Operating Budget:* $250,000-$500,000
Staff Member(s): 5
Membership: 10,000; *Member Profile:* Regular - member of the Canadian Bar Association; employed by & providing legal services to any business enterprise, association, institution, non-profit organization, crown corporation, regulatory body or government agency or department providing funding or assistance programs to any of the foregoing; associate membership also available
Activities: *Speaker Service:* Yes; *Rents Mailing List:* Yes
Meetings/Conferences: • 2015 Canadian Corporate Council Association National Conference, April, 2015, Hilton Toronto, Toronto, ON
Scope: National
Description: Theme - The Business of Law: Black Letter and Beyond
Publications:
• CCCA Magazine
Type: Magazine; *Frequency:* Quarterly; *Editor:* Jordan Furlong
ISSN: 1913-0562
Profile: Publishes articles about issues regarding corporate law, as well as articles pertaining to the interests of coorporate lawyers

Canadian Corps Association

201 Niagara St., Toronto ON M5V 1C9
Tel: 416-504-6694
Overview: A small national organization founded in 1934

The Canadian Corps of Commissionaires / Le Corps Canadien des Commissionaires

National Office, #201, 100 Gloucester St., Ottawa ON K2P 0A4
Tel: 613-688-0710; *Fax:* 613-688-0719
Toll-Free: 888-688-0715
info@commissionaires.ca
www.commissionaires.ca
Also Known As: Commissionaires
Overview: A large national organization founded in 1925
Mission: To create meaningful employment opportunities for former members of the Canadian Forces, the Royal Canadian Mounted Police & others who wish to contribute to the security & well-being of Canadians
Member of: Canadian Society for Industrial Security; American Society for Industrial Security
Chief Officer(s):
W.G.S. (Bill) Sutherland, CD, Chair
J. Douglas Briscoe, OMM, CD, Executive Director, 613-688-0711
executivedirector@commissionaires.ca
Greg Richardson, Business Manager, 613-688-0713
grichardson@commissionaires.ca
Lynne Bermel, Contact, 613-688-0714
lbermel@commissionaires.ca
Finances: *Annual Operating Budget:* Greater than $5 Million; *Funding Sources:* Self-funded
Staff Member(s): 8; 20 volunteer(s)
Membership: 20,000; *Member Profile:* Armed Forces, RCMP & others (varies by Division)
Activities: Strong national federation of Divisions, working in harmony to be the preferred provider of security services
Awards:
• Commissionaires Long Service Medal (Award)
• Commissionaires Distinguished Service Medal (Award)
• Commissionaires Meritorious Service Medal (Award)

British Columbia Division
#801, 595 Howe St., Vancouver BC V6C 2T5
Tel: 604-646-3330; *Fax:* 604-681-9864
Toll-Free: 877-322-6777
info@commissionaires.bc.ca
www.commissionaires.bc.ca
Chief Officer(s):
F.A. (FRank) Richter, CGA, Chair
Dan Popowich, CPP, CEO

Division de Montréal
#400, 201, rue Laurier est, Montréal QC H2T 3E6
Tél: 514-273-8578; *Téléc:* 514-277-1922
Ligne sans frais: 877-322-6777
info@cccmtl.ca
www.commissionnairesquebec.ca
Chief Officer(s):
Mark E. Poirier, Chef de la direction

Division de Québec
#330, 3405, boul Wilfrid-Hamel, Québec QC G1P 2J3
Tél: 418-681-0609; *Téléc:* 418-682-6532
Ligne sans frais: 877-322-6777
courrier@cccque.ca
www.cccque.ca
www.linkedin.com/company/2843379
www.facebook.com/211839285575785
Chief Officer(s):
Guy Gendron, Chef de la direction

Great Lakes-Toronto Division
80 Church St., Toronto ON M5C 2G1

Tel: 416-364-4496; *Fax:* 416-364-3361
Toll-Free: 800-463-0994
toronto@commissionaires.ca
www.commissionaires-cgl.ca
Chief Officer(s):
Michael Hoare, CD, CEO
Hamilton Division
#208, 151 York Blvd., Hamilton ON L8R 3M2
Tel: 905-527-2775; *Fax:* 905-527-9948
Toll-Free: 800-241-9988
cccham@on.aibn.com
www.commissionaireshamilton.com
Chief Officer(s):
J.L. (John) Livingstone, CD, CEO
Kingston Division
737 Arlington Park Pl., Kingston ON K7M 8M8
Tel: 613-634-4432; *Fax:* 613-634-4436
Toll-Free: 877-346-0363
kingstoncorps@thecommissionaires.com
Chief Officer(s):
Michael Robert Voith, MSC, CD, PEng, CEO
Manitoba Division
290 Burnell St., Winnipeg MB R3G 2A7
Tel: 204-942-5993; *Fax:* 204-942-6702
Toll-Free: 877-322-6777
admin@commissionaires.mb.ca
www.commissionaires.mb.ca
Chief Officer(s):
Rick Linden, Chair
Tom Reimer, MMM CD, CEO
New Brunswick & Prince Edward Island Division
160 Mark Dr., Saint John NB E2J 4H5
Tel: 506-634-8000; *Fax:* 506-646-2400
Toll-Free: 877-322-6777
cccnbpei@nb.sympatico.ca
www.commissionaires.nbpei.ca
Chief Officer(s):
Peter Kramers, Chief Executive Officer
Dwight Maxan, Director, Business Development, 506-634-8000
dmaxan@cccnbpei.ca
Newfoundland & Labrador Division
207A Kenmount Rd., St. John's NL A1B 3P9
Tel: 709-754-0757; *Fax:* 709-754-0116
Toll-Free: 877-322-6777
info@commissionaires.nl.ca
www.commissionaires.nl.ca
Chief Officer(s):
Gerry Leahy, Chair
Jim Lynch, CEO
North Saskatchewan Division
1219 Idylwyld Dr. North, Saskatoon SK S7L 1A1
Tel: 306-244-6588; *Fax:* 306-244-6191
Toll-Free: 877-244-6588
ccc@commissionairesnsask.ca
www.commissionaires.sk.ca
Chief Officer(s):
Larry Wong, SBstJ, DS., Chair
Mike Cooper, CEO
Northern Alberta, Northwest Territories & Nunavut Division
10633 - 124 St., Edmonton AB T5N 1S5
Tel: 780-451-1974; *Fax:* 780-452-9389
Toll-Free: 877-322-6777
nalberta@commissionaires.ab.ca
www.commissionaires.ab.ca
Chief Officer(s):
David Cleveland, Chair
John D. Slater, MBA, CD, CEO
Nova Scotia Division
1472 Hollis St., Halifax NS B3J 1V2
Tel: 902-429-8101; *Fax:* 902-444-8590
commissionaires.ns.ca
Chief Officer(s):
Bill Brydon, Director, Operations
bbrydon@commissionaires.ns.ca
Anne James, Director, Human Resources
ajames@commissionaires.ns.ca
Ottawa Division
24 Colonnade Rd., Ottawa ON K2E 7J6
Tel: 613-231-6462; *Fax:* 613-567-1517
Toll-Free: 877-322-6777
staff@commissionaires-ottawa.on.ca
www.commissionaires-ottawa.on.ca
Chief Officer(s):
P.A. Guindon, CEO
South Saskatchewan Division
Alpine Village Mall, 122 Albert St., Regina SK S4R 2N2
Tel: 306-757-0998; *Fax:* 306-352-5494
Toll-Free: 866-757-0998
southsask@commissionaires.sk.ca
www.commissionaires.sk.ca
Chief Officer(s):
Randy Brooks, CPP, CD, CEO
Southern Alberta Division
1107 - 53 Ave. NE, Calgary AB T2E 6X9
Tel: 403-244-4664; *Fax:* 403-228-0623
Toll-Free: 877-322-6777
corps@cccsab.ca
www.cccsab.ca
Chief Officer(s):
Steve Gagnon, MEng, Interim CEO
Victoria, the Islands & Yukon Division
928 Cloverdale Ave., Victoria BC V8X 2T3
Tel: 250-727-7755; *Fax:* 250-727-7355
Toll-Free: 877-322-6777
cccvic@commissionaire-viy.biz
commissionaires-viy.biz
Chief Officer(s):
John Dewar, CEO

Canadian Correspondence Chess Association (CCCA) / L'Association canadienne des échecs par correspondance (ACEC)

c/o Manny Migicovsky, 1669 Country Rd. 4, RR#1, L'Orignal QC K0B 1K0
Tel: 613-632-3166
ccca@cogeco.ca
correspondencechess.com/ccca/index.htm
Overview: A small national charitable organization
Mission: To promote chess playing via mail & e-mail both nationally & internationally
Member of: Chess Federation of Canada
Chief Officer(s):
Manny Migicovsky, President
Membership: *Fees:* $30 regular; $27 senior/youth; $35 USA; $40 international
Publications:
• Check!
Type: Newsletter; *Editor:* Michael Egan, Games Editor

Canadian Corrugated Containerboard Association / Association canadienne du cartonnage ondulé et du carton-caisse

#3, 1995 Clark Blvd., Brampton ON L6T 4W1
Tel: 905-458-1247; *Fax:* 905-458-2052
info@cccabox.org
www.cccabox.org
Previous Name: Paper Packaging Canada
Overview: A medium-sized national organization overseen by Paper & Paperboard Packaging Environmental Council
Mission: To represent containerboard mill sites, corrugator plants, sheet plants & related industries; to work together with other players in the paper industry to develop an agenda of common concerns & issues
Chief Officer(s):
Rob Latter, Chair
John Mullinder, President & CEO, 905-458-0087
ppec@ppec-paper.com
Membership: 1-99
Activities: Networking & information sharing; seminars; conference & trade fair; annual golf tournament; *Awareness Events:* Golf Tournament, June

Canadian Cosmetic, Toiletry & Fragrance Association (CCTFA) / Association canadienne des cosmétiques, produit de toilette et parfums

#102, 420 Britannia Rd. East, Mississauga ON L4Z 3L5
Tel: 905-890-5161; *Fax:* 905-890-2607
cctfa@cctfa.ca
www.cctfa.ca
Overview: A medium-sized national organization founded in 1928
Mission: To encourage trust & confidence in the Canadian cosmetic, toiletry & fragrance industry & in the safety, efficacy & quality of its products; To be the princiapal voice of the personal care industry, including cosmetic-like drug products & cosmetic-like natural health products (NHP), interfacing on a timely basis with governemtn & elected representatives, to ensure development & effective representationof industry positions on a ll regulatory issues; to have the personal care industyr perceived by consumers at large as being socially concerned, responsible & involved with Canadian society; this will be primarily achieved through the CCTFA Foundation &;the Look Good Feel Better program.
Chief Officer(s):
Myles Robinson, Chair
Finances: *Annual Operating Budget:* $500,000-$1.5 Million
Membership: 64 active companies + 79 associate companies + 10 retail private brand companies + 14 custom manufacturer members;

Canadian Cosmetics Careers Association Inc. (CCCA)

48 Fenton Lane, Port Hope ON L1A 0A3
Tel: 416-410-9175
www.cccacosmetics.com
Overview: A small national organization
Mission: To advance professional development in the cosmetics industry; to provide opportunities for development in the Canadian cosmetics industry through accreditation
Activities: Offering the cosmetics correspondence course
Publications:
• Canadian Cosmetics Careers Association Inc. Membership Roster
Type: Directory; *Frequency:* Annually
Profile: Listing of current members for all members
• The CCCA [Canadian Cosmetics Careers Association Inc.] Newsletter
Type: Newsletter; *Frequency:* 3 pa
Profile: Information about events, new products, reviews, awards, trends in the retail environment, association news, & member profiles

Canadian Council for Aboriginal Business (CCAB) / Conseil canadien pour le commerce autochtone

#204, 250 The Esplanade, Toronto ON M5A 1J2
Tel: 416-961-8663; *Fax:* 416-961-3995
info@ccab.com
www.ccab.com
Previous Name: Canadian Council for Native Business
Overview: A medium-sized national charitable organization founded in 1984
Mission: To promote full participation of Aboriginal communities in the Canadian economy
Chief Officer(s):
J.P. Gladu, President & CEO
jpgladu@ccab.com
Finances: *Funding Sources:* Private sector
Staff Member(s): 9
Membership: 288; *Fees:* Schedule available
Activities: *Internships:* Yes; *Speaker Service:* Yes

The Canadian Council for Accreditation of Pharmacy Programs (CCAPP) / Le Conseil canadien de l'agrément des programmes de pharmacie

Leslie Dan Faculty of Pharmacy, University of Toronto, #1207, 144 College St., Toronto ON M5S 3M2
Tel: 416-946-5055; *Fax:* 416-978-8511
ccappinfo@phm.utoronto.ca
www.ccapp-accredit.ca
Overview: A medium-sized national organization founded in 1992
Chief Officer(s):
Carmen Vezina, President, 418-656-2131 Ext. 3065, Fax: 418-656-2305
Linda Suveges, Past President, 416-813-6534, Fax: 416-813-5880
Wayne Hindmarsh, Executive Director, 416-946-5055, Fax: 416-978-8511
wayne.hindmarsh@utoronto.ca
David Malian, Pharmacy Technician Coordinator, 416-946-4074, Fax: 416-978-8511
david.s.malian@utoronto.ca
Staff Member(s): 2
Publications:
• Annual Report & Directory of Accredited Programs [publication of The Canadian Council for Accreditation of Pharmacy Programs]
Frequency: Annually
Profile: Annual report features a list of approved Faculties of Pharmacy

Canadian Council for Aviation & Aerospace (CCAA) / Conseil canadien de l'aviation et de l'aérospatiale

#155, 955 Green Valley Cres., Ottawa ON K2C 3V4

Tel: 613-727-8272; *Fax:* 613-727-7018
Toll-Free: 800-448-9715
secretariat@camc.ca
www.camc.ca
Previous Name: Canadian Aviation Maintenance Council
Overview: A medium-sized national licensing organization founded in 1992
Mission: To develop occupational training standards & facilitate the implementation of a human resources strategy for the Canadian Aviation Maintenance Industry.
Chief Officer(s):
Robert Donald, Executive Director
Finances: *Annual Operating Budget:* $250,000-$500,000; *Funding Sources:* Aviation maintenance industry; Human Resources Development Canada; federal government
Membership: 1,000-4,999; *Committees:* CCAA Accreditation Board; CCAA Certification Board; CCAA National Standing Trade Advisory; Youth Internship Advisory
Activities: Certification; accreditation; training; youth programs; *Internships:* Yes

Canadian Council for Human Resources in the Environment Industry *See* Environmental Careers Organization of Canada

Canadian Council for International Co-operation (CCIC) / Conseil canadien pour la coopération internationale

#200, 450 Rideau St., Ottawa ON K1N 5Z4
Tel: 613-241-7007; *Fax:* 613-241-5302
Other Communication: www.flickr.com/photos/ccciccic
info@ccic.ca
www.ccic.ca
www.facebook.com/ccciccic
twitter.com/CCCICCIC
www.youtube.com/user/CCICable
Overview: A large national organization founded in 1968
Mission: To work globally to achieve sustainable human development; To seek to end global poverty; To promote social justice & human dignity for all
Chief Officer(s):
Jim Cornelius, Chair
Janice Hamilton, Treasurer
Julia Sánchez, President & CEO
jsanchez@ccic.ca
Anna Campos, Officer, Finance & Administration
acampos@ccic.ca
Chantal Havard, Officer, Government Relations & Communications
chavard@ccic.ca
Fraser Reilly-King, Policy Analyst, Aid & International Co-operation
freillyking@ccic.ca
Finances: *Funding Sources:* Federal government through CIDA
4 volunteer(s)
Membership: 100 organizations; *Fees:* Schedule available; *Member Profile:* Non-profit organizations working in Canada & overseas, including religious & secular development groups, professional associations, & labour unions; These work with NGOs, cooperatives, & citizens' groups in Africa, Asia, & Latin America to meet basic needs for food, shelter, education, health, & sanitation; Many groups conduct policy research & campaign with their southern partners for fair trade, global security, children's rights, biodiversity, or the forgiveness of multilateral debt; Some members work exclusively in Canada, designing education materials for use in classrooms & resource centres; All members must adhere to a Code of Ethics which governs their financial management, communications with the public, & administration
Activities: Monitoring & analyzing federal policies on foreign affairs, aid, trade, debt & defence & communicating findings to members & the public; Engaging Canadians in a collective search for development alternatives; *Internships:* Yes; *Speaker Service:* Yes
Publications:
• Au Courant [a publication of the Canadian Council for International Co-operation]
Type: Newsletter; *Frequency:* Semiannually *ISSN:* 118-604X
Profile: News, analysis, & opinion about domestic & international economic policy, development aid, & foreign policy
• Who's Who in International Development [a publication of the Canadian Council for International Co-operation]
Type: Directory
Profile: Listing of CCIC members working to end global poverty

Canadian Council for Native Business *See* Canadian Council for Aboriginal Business

The Canadian Council for Public-Private Partnerships (CCPPP) / Le Conseil canadien pour les partenariats public-privé

1 First Canadian Place, #1600, 100 King St. West, Toronto ON M5X 1G5
Tel: 416-861-0500; *Fax:* 416-862-7661
partners@pppcouncil.ca
www.pppcouncil.ca
Overview: A medium-sized national organization founded in 1993
Mission: To act as a proponent for improvements in the quality & cost of public services provided to Canadians through innovative partnerships between the public & private sectors
Affliation(s): Federation of Canadian Municipalities; Canadian Water & Wastewater Association
Chief Officer(s):
Mark Romoff, President
Finances: *Annual Operating Budget:* $250,000-$500,000; *Funding Sources:* Membership fees
Staff Member(s): 2; 23 volunteer(s)
Membership: 230; *Fees:* $350 public/non-profit; $700 corporate; $3,500 sponsor
Activities: *Library* by appointment
Publications:
• The Canadian Council for Public-Private Partnerships Directory of Members
Type: Directory
Profile: Listing of complete contact information for each member, for all Council members & sponsors
• For the Record [a publication of the The Canadian Council for Public-Private Partnerships]
Type: Newsletter
Profile: Summary of points & quotations from speakers at The Council's breakfast series & other events
• Public-Private Bulletin
Type: Newsletter; *Frequency:* Quarterly; *Price:* Free for Council members
Profile: Updates for members about events & projects

Canadian Council for Reform Judaism (CCRJ)

#301, 3845 Bathurst St., Toronto ON M3H 3N2
Tel: 416-630-0375; *Fax:* 416-630-5089
Toll-Free: 800-560-8242
ccrj@ccrj.ca
www.ccrj.ca
www.linkedin.com/groups?gid=1300517
facebook.com/reformjudaism
twitter.com/urj
www.youtube.com/urjweb
Previous Name: Canadian Council of Reform Rabbis
Overview: A medium-sized national organization
Mission: The CCRJ is the Canadian region of the Union for Reform Judasim Congregations, and serves as the umbrella organization for Reform Judaism in Canada, representing about 10,000 households in 26 affiliated congregations.
Member of: Union for Reform Judaism
Chief Officer(s):
Sharon L. Sobel, Executive Director

Canadian Council for Refugees (CCR) / Conseil canadien pour les réfugiés

#302, 6839, rue Drolet, Montréal QC H2S 2T1
Tel: 514-277-7223; *Fax:* 514-277-1447
Other Communication: media@ccrweb.ca
info@ccrweb.ca
www.ccrweb.ca
www.youtube.com/ccrwebvideos
www.facebook.com/ccrweb
twitter.com/ccrweb
Previous Name: Standing Conference of Organizations Concerned for Refugees
Overview: A medium-sized international charitable organization founded in 1977
Mission: To be committed to the rights & protection of refugees in Canada & around the world & to the settlement of refugees & immigrants in Canada
Member of: International Council of Voluntary Agencies; International Civil Liberties Monitoring; National Anti-Racism Council of Canada
Chief Officer(s):
Janet Dench, Executive Director, 514-277-7223 Ext. 2
jdench@ccrweb.ca
Marisa Berry-Méndez, Director, Settlement Policy, 514-277-7223 Ext. 5
mberrymendez@ccrweb.ca
Cynthia Beaudry, Coordinator, Youth, 514-277-7223 Ext. 3
cbeaudry@ccrweb.ca
Colleen French, Coordinator, Communications & Networking, 514-277-7223 Ext. 1
cfrench@ccrweb.ca
Finances: *Funding Sources:* Private donations; Membership; Government
40 volunteer(s)
Membership: 180 institutional + 30 individual; *Fees:* Schedule available; *Member Profile:* Canadian non-governmental organizations involved in the sponsorship & protection of refugees & settlement of refugees & immigrants; *Committees:* Anti-Racism; Refugee Protection; Overseas Protection & Sponsorship; Settlement; Gender Issues
Activities: Engaging in advocacy activities; Providing educational & networking opportunities; *Library* by appointment
Meetings/Conferences: • Canadian Council for Refugees 2015 Winter Working Group Meetings, February, 2015, Toronto, ON
Scope: National
Description: Meetings of the Overseas Protection & Sponsorship Working Group, the Immigration & Settlement Working Group, & the Inland Protection Working Group, for all Canadian Council for Refugees members, plus anyone who is interested in participating
Contact Information: E-mail: info@ccrweb.ca
• Canadian Council for Refugees 2015 Spring Consultation, May, 2015
Scope: National
Description: A meeting of refugees, immigrants, representatives of NGOs, government, academics, community workers, youth advocates, & international guests to examine issues that affect newcomers to Canada
Contact Information: E-mail: info@ccrweb.ca
• Canadian Council for Refugees 2015 Summer Working Group Meetings, 2015
Scope: National
Description: An opportunity for Canadian Council for Refugees members & other refugee & immigrant rights advocates to exchange information & develop policy positions
Contact Information: E-mail: info@ccrweb.ca
• Canadian Council for Refugees 2015 Fall Consultation, 2015
Scope: National
Description: An event featuring large plenary sessions, workshops, & working sessions that address issues that challenge refugees, immigrants, community workers, & advocates
Contact Information: E-mail: info@ccrweb.ca

Canadian Council for Small Business & Entrepreneurship (CCSBE) / Conseil canadien des PME et de l'entrepreneuriat (CCPME)

c/o Pat Sargeant, Women's Enterprise Centre of Manitoba, #100, 207 Donald St., Winnipeg MB R3C 1M5
Tel: 204-988-1873; *Fax:* 902-988-1871
ccsbesecretariat@wecm.ca
www.ccsbe.org
www.linkedin.com/groups/CCSBE-CCPME-2431087
www.facebook.com/pages/CCSBE-2011-Annual-Conference/244886798884450
twitter.com/CCSBE2013
Overview: A medium-sized national organization founded in 1979
Mission: The Canadian Council for Small Business and Entrepreneurship (CCSBE-CCPME) is a national membership-based organization promoting and advancing the developmet of small business and entreprenurship through research, education and training, networking, and dissemination of scholarly and policy-oriented information.
Affliation(s): International Council for Small Business
Chief Officer(s):
Sandra Altner, President
saltner@wecm.ca
Francine Schlosser, Secretary
fschloss@uwindsor.ca
Meetings/Conferences: • Canadian Council for Small Business & Entrepreneurship 2015 Conference, May, 2015, MacEwan University School of Business, Edmonton, AB
Scope: National

Canadian Council for the Advancement of Education (CCAE) / Le Conseil canadien pour l'avancement de l'éducation

#310, 4 Cataraqui St., Kingston ON K7K 1Z7
Tel: 613-531-9213; *Fax:* 613-531-0626
admin@ccaecanada.org
www.ccaecanada.org

www.facebook.com/group.php?gid=325169814892&ref=ts
twitter.com/CCAECanada
Overview: A medium-sized national organization founded in 1993
Mission: To promote excellence in educational advancement through networking opportunities, professional development, & mutual support
Chief Officer(s):
Mark Hazlett, Executive Director
haz@ccaecanada.org
Melana Soroka, President
Kathy Arney, Vice-President
kathy_arney@banff.centre.ca
Kathy Butler, Vice-President
kbutler@okanagan.bc.ca
Ivan Muzychka, Vice-President
ivanm@mun.ca
Finances: *Annual Operating Budget:* $500,000-$1.5 Million; *Funding Sources:* Membership fees
Membership: 1,000-4,999; *Fees:* Schedule available; *Member Profile:* Representatives of Canadian universities, colleges, institutes, & independent schools who may be employed in alumni administration, communications, fundraising, external relations, advancement services, public affairs, enrolment management, or related disciplines
Awards:
• Canadian Council for the Advancement of Education Prix D'Excellence (Award)
Deadline: March
• Canadian Council for the Advancement of Education Paul Webb Scholarship (Scholarship)
To fund professional development for a person working in the area of alumni relations*Deadline:* April *Amount:* $500
• TD Insurance Meloche Monnex Fellowships in Advancement (Scholarship)
For persons judged to be best suited to work in the field of educational advancement, based upon qualities of intellect, character, aptitude, & relelvant experience*Deadline:* January *Contact:* Terry Cockerline & Randy Paquette, Co-Chairs, E-mail: fellowships@ccaecanada.org
• Canadian Council for the Advancement of Education Ontario Regional Chapter Scholarship (Scholarship)
To promote professional development within the advancement profession*Eligibility:* Candidate must be employed by a CCAE member institution in Ontario*Location:* Ontario*Deadline:* April *Amount:* $500
• Canadian Council for the Advancement of Education Richard Lim Professional Development Scholarship (Scholarship)
To promote integration between the different areas of advancement*Eligibility:* A person employed by a Canadian Council for the Advancement of Education member institution in Ontario, who wishes to attend a professional seminar, workshop, or conference within a different stream of the advancement profession from the position presently held*Location:* Ontario*Deadline:* April *Amount:* $500
Meetings/Conferences: • Canadian Council for the Advancement of Education 2015 Annual Conference: Beyond Boundaries - Transformation, Collaboration and Trending, June, 2015, e Centre Sheraton Montreal Hotel, Montreal, QC
Scope: National
Description: An annual national gathering, with keynote speakers, plenary sessions, roundtables, & the presentation of awards
Contact Information: Executive Director: Mark Hazlett, E-mail: haz@ccaecanada.org

Canadian Council for the Americas (BCCC)

PO Box 1227, Oakville ON L6J 5C7
Tel: 416-367-4313; *Fax:* 416-595-8226
cca@iecanada.com
www.ccacanada.com
Overview: A medium-sized international organization founded in 1973
Mission: To foster stronger economic ties between Canada & Brazil
Chief Officer(s):
Kenneth Frankel, Chair
Finances: *Funding Sources:* Membership dues; events
Staff Member(s): 2
Membership: 40; *Fees:* $60-$13,210 based on company size; *Member Profile:* Members are Canadian companies, financial institutions & individuals doing business in & with Brazil, as well as Brazilian corporations & individuals with interests in Canada

Canadian Council for the Americas (CCA) / Conseil Canadien pour les Amériques

PO Box 48612, 595 Burrard St., Vancouver BC V7X 1A3
Tel: 604-868-8678; *Fax:* 604-806-6112
info@cca-bc.com
www.cca-bc.com
Overview: A medium-sized international organization founded in 1987
Mission: Principal private sector link between Canada & the countries of Latin America & the Caribbean.
Chief Officer(s):
André Nudelman, Chair
anudelman@cca-bc.com
Leon Teicher, Secretary
Staff Member(s): 4; 10 volunteer(s)
Membership: 550; *Fees:* $150-5,000

Canadian Council for Tobacco Control (CCTC) / Conseil canadien pour le contrôle du tabac

192 Bank St., Ottawa ON K2P 1W8
Tel: 613-567-3050; *Fax:* 613-567-2730
Toll-Free: 800-267-5234
infoservices@cctc.ca
www.cctc.ca
Previous Name: Canadian Council on Smoking & Health
Overview: A medium-sized national charitable organization founded in 1974
Mission: To envision a strong & effective tobacco control movement; To diminish the adverse impact to the health of Canadians caused by tobacco industry products; To increase the effectiveness & capacity of individuals & organizations involved in tobacco control, to achieve a smoke free society in Canada; To prevent tobaccco use; To persuade & help smokers to stop using tobacco products; To educate Canadians about the marketing strategies & tactics of the tobacco industry & the adverse effects tobacco products have on the health of Canadians
Chief Officer(s):
Robert Walsh, Executive Director
Jocelyne Koepke, Manager, Operations
Finances: *Annual Operating Budget:* $500,000-$1.5 Million; *Funding Sources:* Federal & provincial governments
Staff Member(s): 7
Membership: *Fees:* $40 student; $75 individual; $500 Organizational up to 10 members
Activities: *Awareness Events:* National Non-Smoking Week/Weedless Wednesday, Jan.; World No Tobacco Day, May; *Speaker Service:* Yes; *Library:* National Clearing House for Tobacco & Health
Awards:
• Award of Excellence (Award)

Canadian Council of Archives (CCA) / Conseil canadien des archives

#1201, 130 Albert St., Ottawa ON K1P 5G4
Tel: 613-565-1222; *Fax:* 613-565-5445
Toll-Free: 866-254-1403
cca@archivescanada.ca
www.cdncouncilarchives.ca
Overview: A medium-sized national charitable organization founded in 1985
Mission: To facilitate development of Canadian archival system & its coordination; to make recommendations to system's operation & financing; to develop & facilitate implementation & management of programs to assist archival community; to communicate archival needs & concerns to decision-makers, researchers & the general public.
Chief Officer(s):
Lara Wilson, Chairperson
ljwilson@uvic.ca
Leslie Latta-Guthrie, Vice-Chair
leslie.latta-guthrie@gov.ab.ca
Finances: *Annual Operating Budget:* $1.5 Million-$3 Million; *Funding Sources:* Federal government
Staff Member(s): 6
Membership: 18; *Member Profile:* National archivist & delegates from 2 national associations & provincial/territorial Council of Archives; *Committees:* Board of Directors; Archival Description; Preservation; Standards
Activities: Control of Holdings program; Professional Development & Training program; Special Projects program; Preservation Management program; Preservation Training & Information program.;

Canadian Council of Better Business Bureaus (CCBBB) / Conseil canadien des bureaux d'éthique commerciale

www.bbb.org/canada
Overview: A large national organization founded in 1966
Mission: To protect consumers & the vitality of the free enterprise system; To foster the highest standards of responsibility & probity in business practice by advocating truth in advertising, by assuring integrity in performance of business services, & by voluntary regulation & monitoring activities designed to enhance public trust & confidence in business
Affliation(s): The Council of Better Business Bureaus, USA
Chief Officer(s):
Jim Deane, Vice-Chair
David Steele, Treasurer
Spencer Nimmons, Vice-President, Business Relations
Membership: 31,000 organizations

Canadian Council of Cardiovascular Nurses (CCCN) / Conseil canadien des infirmières et infirmiers en nursing cardiovasculaire (CCINC)

#202, 300 March Rd., Ottawa ON K1P 5V9
Tel: 613-599-9210; *Fax:* 613-595-1155
info@cccn.ca
www.cccn.ca
Overview: A medium-sized national organization founded in 1973
Mission: To promote & maintain high standards of cardiovascular nursing through education, research, health promotion, strategic alliances, & advocacy
Member of: Canadian Nursing Association; Canadian Society of Association Executives
Affliation(s): Heart & Stroke Foundation of Canada; Canadian Coalition for High Blood Pressure Prevention & Control; Canadian Cardiovascular Society
Chief Officer(s):
Wes Clark, Executive Director
wclark@cccn.ca
Jocelyn Reimer-Kent, President
jocelyn.reimer-kent@fraserhealth.ca
Sandra Lauck, Sec.-Treas.
slauck@providencehealth.bc.ca
Finances: *Funding Sources:* Membership fees; sponsorships; conference registration
Staff Member(s): 2; 20 volunteer(s)
Membership: 1300; *Fees:* $75 regular; $38 RN students; *Member Profile:* Canadian nurses interested in heart health; Practicing nurses in the cardiovascular field; *Committees:* Professional Education; Research; Health Promotion; Board of Directors
Activities: Developing ongoing professional nursing education in the cardiovascular field; Promoting cardiovascular nursing research; Participating in health promotion activities; Collaborating with other organizations on issues involving cardiovascular nursing
Awards:
• Lynne Child Cardiovascular Nursing Certification Award (Award)
Deadline: August 31 *Contact:* Awards Committee, Fax: 613-595-1155; E-mail: cccn@rcpsc.edu
• Mae Gallant Cardiovascular Nursing Student Award (Award)
Deadline: August 31 *Contact:* Awards Committee, Fax: 613-595-1155; E-mail: cccn@rcpsc.edu
• Cardiovascular Nursing Clinical Excellence Award (Award)
Deadline: August 31 *Contact:* Awards Committee, Fax: 613-595-1155; E-mail: cccn@rcpsc.edu
• Cardiovascular Nursing Research Excellence Award (Award)
Deadline: August 31 *Contact:* Awards Committee, Fax: 613-595-1155; E-mail: cccn@rcpsc.edu
• Cardiovascular Nursing Leadership Excellence Award (Award)
Deadline: August 31 *Contact:* Awards Committee, Fax: 613-595-1155; E-mail: cccn@rcpsc.edu
• Cardiovascular Nursing Health Promotion & Advocacy Excellence Award (Award)
Deadline: August 31 *Contact:* Awards Committee, Fax: 613-595-1155; E-mail: cccn@rcpsc.edu
• Honorary Lifetime Member Award (Award)
Deadline: August 31 *Contact:* Awards Committee, Fax: 613-595-1155; E-mail: cccn@rcpsc.edu
Meetings/Conferences: • Canadian Council of Cardiovascular Nurses 2015 Spring Nursing Conference, May, 2015, Ottawa, ON
Scope: National
• Canadian Council of Cardiovascular Nurses 2015 Fall Conference, Annual General Meeting & Scientific Session,

October, 2015, Toronto, ON
Scope: National
Description: Plenary speakers & workshops address issues in the cardiovascular nursing field. This year's conference is a joint effort between the Canadian Cardiovascular Society, the Canadian Diabetes Association, the Heart & Stroke Foundation of Canada, & the Canadian Stroke Network.
Publications:
• Canadian Council of Cardiovascular Nurses Annual Report
Type: Yearbook; *Frequency:* Annually
Profile: A review of the council's year
• Canadian Council of Cardiovascular Nurses Newsletter
Type: Newsletter; *Frequency:* Monthly
Profile: Current events of the council, including conferences, award presentations, & members in the news
• Canadian Journal of Cardiovascular Nursing (CJCN)
Type: Journal; *Frequency:* Quarterly; *Accepts Advertising*; *Editor:* Nicole Parent; Paula Price; *Price:* Free for members of the Canadian Council of Cardiovascular Nurses; $75 non-members
Profile: The peer reviewed official publication of the Canadian Journal of Cardiovascular Nursing, featuringoriginal articles about health care issues related to cardiovascular health & illness & research information

Canadian Council of Chief Executives (CCCE) / Conseil canadien des chefs d'entreprise

#1001, 99 Bank St., Ottawa ON K1P 6B9
Tel: 613-238-3727; *Fax:* 613-238-3247
info@ceocouncil.ca
www.ceocouncil.ca
twitter.com/CdnCEOCouncil
Previous Name: Business Council on National Issues
Overview: A large national organization founded in 1976
Mission: To engage in policy work in Canada, North America, & the world
Chief Officer(s):
John Manley, P.C., O.C., President & CEO
Susan Scotti, Senior Vice-President, Planning & Operations, 613-288-3860
susan@ceocouncil.ca
John R. Dillon, Corporate Counsel & Vice-President, Policy, 613-288-3863
john@ceocouncil.ca
Ross H. Laver, Vice-President, Policy & Communications, 613-288-3862
ross@ceocouncil.ca
Nancy Wallace, Vice-President, Corporate Services, 613-288-3858
nancy@ceocouncil.ca
Sarah Reid, Communications Officer, 613-238-3727
media@ceocouncil.ca
Membership: 100-499; *Member Profile:* Business leaders from 150 Canadian corporations
Activities: Working on national issues, such as taxation, fiscal & monetary policy, corporate governance, & competitiveness; Preparing presentations & reports
Publications:
• Perspectives [a publication of the Canadian Council of Chief Executives]
Editor: Ross Laver
Profile: Articles about globalization challenges, sustainable growth, corporate responsibiliy, & strengthening Canadian competitiveness

Canadian Council of Christian Charities (CCCC)

#1, 43 Howard Ave., Elmira ON N3B 2C9
Tel: 519-669-5137; *Fax:* 519-669-3291
mail@cccc.org
www.cccc.org
Overview: A medium-sized national licensing charitable organization founded in 1972
Mission: To encourage the Canadian Christian community to a biblical stewardship of all He has entrusted to us by integrating practical concepts of administration, development & accountability with the spiritual concerns of ministry
Chief Officer(s):
John Pellowe, CEO
Finances: *Annual Operating Budget:* $500,000-$1.5 Million
Staff Member(s): 17; 56 volunteer(s)
Membership: 3,200; *Fees:* $195-$520
Activities: Education; training on legal, financial & leadership issues
Publications:
• CCCC [Canadian Council of Christian Charities] Bulletin
Type: Newsletter; *Frequency:* 5-7 pa; *Accepts Advertising*; *Editor:* Heather Hanson *ISSN:* 0838-6803; *Price:* Free with CCCC membership; $45 non-members
Profile: CCCC news & information & legislative developments for executives, administrators, & stewardship representatives of Christian charitiesoperating under Canadian law
• Charities Handbook
Price: Free with CCCC membership; $95 non-members

The Canadian Council of Churches (CCC) / Le Conseil canadien des Églises

47 Queen's Park Cres. East, 3rd Fl., Toronto ON M5S 2C3
Tel: 416-972-9494; *Fax:* 416-927-0405
Other Communication: meredith@councilofchurches.ca
info@councilofchurches.ca
www.councilofchurches.ca
www.facebook.com/CCC.CCE
twitter.com/ccc_cce
Overview: A large national charitable organization founded in 1944
Mission: To represent the following churches of Anglican, Eastern Catholic, & Roman Catholic, Eastern Orthodox & Oriental Orthodox, Evangelical & Protestant traditions: The Anglican Church of Canada; Archdiocese of Canada of the Orthodox Church in America; Armenian Holy Apostolic Church, Canadian Diocese; Atlantic Baptist Fellowship; Canadian Baptists of Ontario & Québec; Canadian Baptists of Western Canada; Canadian Conference of Catholic Bishops; Canadian Yearly Meeting of the Religious Society of Friends (Quakers); Christian Church (Disciples of Christ)in Canada; Christian Reformed Church in North America - Canada; The Coptic Orthodox Church of Canada; Ethiopian Orthodox Tewahedo Church of Canada; Evangelical Lutheran Church in Canada; Greek Orthodox Metropolis of Toronto (Canada); The Mar Thoma Syrian Church; Mennonite Church Canada; Polish National Catholic Church;Presbyterian Church in Canada; Regional Synod of Canada - Reformed Church in America; The Salvation Army; Ukrainian Catholic Church; Ukrainian Orthodox Church of Canada; The United Church of Canada
Affiliation(s): British Methodist Episcopal Church of Canada; Citizens for Public Justice; Friendship Ministries Canada; The Knowles-Woodsworth Centre for Theology & Public Policy; The Leprosy Mission Canada
Chief Officer(s):
Karen A. Hamilton, General Secretary, 416-972-9494 Ext. 22, Fax: 416-927-0405
hamilton@councilofchurches.ca
Finances: *Funding Sources:* Member churches
Staff Member(s): 6; 2 volunteer(s)
Activities: Sponsoring of Project Ploughshares; Maintaining dialogue with all faith groups

Canadian Council of Engineering Technicians and Technologists (CCETT) *See* Canadian Council of Technicians & Technologists

Canadian Council of Forest Ministers (CCFM) / Conseil canadien des ministres des forêts

c/o Policy, Economics & Industry Branch, Natural Resources Canada, 580 Booth St., 11th Fl., Ottawa ON K1A 0E4
Tel: 613-947-9099; *Fax:* 613-947-9033
www.ccfm.org
Mission: The Canadian Council of Ministers (CCFM) was established in 1985 to give sufficient attention to forest issues. CCFM stimulates the development of policies & initiatives for strengthening the forest sector, including the forest resource & its use. It provides leadership, addresses national & international issues & sets the direction for stewardship & sustainable management of Canada's forests. The CCFM is composed of the 14 federal, provincial & territorial ministers responsible for forests. The CCFM undertakes activities primarily through ad hoc fora, committees & working groups. CCFM initiatives include: International Forest Issues Working Group; International Forestry Partnerships Program; Sustainable Forest Management Working Group; Canadian Wildland Fire Strategy; National Forest Information System; National Forestry Database Program; Science & Technology Working Group; Forest Communities Working Group. The Council also cooperates with the Canadian Wildland Fire Strategy Declaration, a federal-provincial-territorial initiative to address the management of wildland fires. National Forestry Database Program: nfdp.ccfm.org/; National Forest Information System: nfis.org
Chief Officer(s):
Martine Ouellet, Minister, Natural Resources & Wildlife
ministre@mrnf.gouv.qc.ca
Mario Gibeault, Sous-ministre, Forêts
mario.gibeault@bmmb.gouv.qc.ca

Canadian Council of Human Resources Associations (CCHRA) / Conseil canadien des associations en ressources humaines (CCARH)

#603, 150 Metcalfe St., Ottawa ON K2P 1P1
Tel: 613-567-2477; *Fax:* 613-567-2478
Toll-Free: 866-560-1288
info@cchra-ccarh.ca
www.cchra-ccarh.ca
Overview: A medium-sized national organization founded in 1994
Mission: To establish national core standards for the human resources profession; to foster communications among participating associations; to be the recognized resource on equivalency for human resources qualifications across Canada; & to provide a national & international collective voice on human resources issues
Member of: North American Human Resource Management Association; World Federation of Personnel Management Associations
Chief Officer(s):
Patrick Hartling, Chair
Staff Member(s): 1
Membership: 33,000; *Committees:* Professional Standards; Independent Board of Examiners; Finance & Audit; Recertification; Federal Government Affairs; CHRP Marketing; National Forum Planning
Activities: Certified Human Resources Professional (CHRP) designation; *Awareness Events:* National Human Resources Forum, fall

Canadian Council of Independent Laboratories (CCIL) / Conseil canadien des laboratoires indépendants

PO Box 41027, Ottawa ON K1G 5K9
Tel: 613-746-3919; *Fax:* 613-746-4324
ccil@magma.ca
www.ccil.com
Overview: A medium-sized national licensing organization founded in 1993
Mission: Represents the independent testing industry in Canada.
Chief Officer(s):
Derwyn L. Reuber, Executive Director
dreuber@ccil.com
Jeffrey Pike, President
jeffrey.pike@alsglobal.com
Staff Member(s): 9
Membership: 330
Activities: *Speaker Service:* Yes

Canadian Council of Insurance Regulators *See* Financial Services Commission of Ontario

Canadian Council of Insurance Regulators (CCIR) / Conseil canadien des responsables de la réglementation d'assurance (CCRRA)

CCIR Secretariat, PO Box 85, 5160 Yonge St., Toronto ON M2N 6L9
Tel: 416-590-7290; *Fax:* 416-226-7878
ccir-ccrra@fsco.gov.on.ca
www.ccir-ccrra.org
Overview: A small national organization
Mission: To facilitate an effective regulatory system in Canada to serve the public interest; To enhance consumer protection
Chief Officer(s):
Carolyn Rogers, Chair
Patrick Déry, Vice-Chair
Philip Howell, Vice-Chair
Doug Murphy, Vice-Chair
Carol Shelvin, Policy Manager
Membership: *Member Profile:* Regulators of insurance across Canada
Activities: Working cooperatively with other financial services regulators; Developing insurance policies; Harmonizing insurance policy & regulation across jurisdictions
Publications:
• Meeting Highlights
Frequency: Semiannually
Profile: Summaries of the annual Canadian Council of Insurance Regulators Spring & Fall Meetings

Canadian Council of Ministers of the Environment (CCME) / Conseil canadien des ministres de l'environnement

#360, 123 Main St., Winnipeg MB R3C 1A3
Tel: 204-948-2090; *Fax:* 204-948-2125
Toll-Free: 800-805-3025

info@ccme.ca
www.ccme.ca
Mission: CCME is comprised of the environment ministers from the federal, provincial and territorial governments. These 14 ministers normally meet at least once a year to discuss national environmental priorities and determine work to be carried out under the auspices of CCME. The Council seeks to achieve positive environmental results, focusing on issues that are national in scope and that require collective attention by a number of governments. CCME aims to assist its members to meet their mandate of protecting Canada's environment. As with any association, each member can accomplish more by working together than by working alone. CCME serves as a principal forum for members to develop national strategies, norms, and guidelines that each environment ministry across the country can use. Since environment is constitutionally speaking an area of shared jurisdiction, it makes sense to work together to promote effective results. CCME is not another level of government regulator, but a council of government ministers holding similar responsibilities
Chief Officer(s):
James Arreak, President, 867-924-6423, Fax: 867-924-6429
jarreak@assembly.nu.ca
Michael Goeres, Executive Director, 204-948-2172
mgoeres@ccme.ca
David Akeeagok, Chair, Management & Deputy Ministers Committees
Kelvin Leary, Chair, Environmental Planning & Protection Committee
Finances: *Annual Operating Budget:* $1.5 Million-$3 Million; *Funding Sources:* Federal, provincial & territorial governments
Staff Member(s): 8
Membership: 1-99; *Committees:* Environmental Planning & Protection

Canadian Council of Montessori Administrators (CCMA)
#102, 4953 Dundas St. West, Toronto ON M9A 1B6
Tel: 416-239-1166; *Fax:* 416-239-9544
Toll-Free: 800-954-6300
ccma@bellnet.ca
www.ccma.ca
twitter.com/ccmamontessori
Overview: A medium-sized national organization
Mission: To support Montessori administrators in Canada; to offer expertise in Montessori school administration & the Montessori method of education
Chief Officer(s):
Terry Gouie
Membership: *Fees:* $300 + $6 per full-day student + $4 per half-day student; *Member Profile:* Montessori School Administrators

Canadian Council of Motor Transport Administrators (CCMTA) / Conseil canadien des administrateurs en transport motorisé (CCATM)
2323 St. Laurent Blvd., Ottawa ON K1G 4J8
Tel: 613-736-1003; *Fax:* 613-736-1395
ccmta-secretariat@ccmta.ca
www.ccmta.ca
Overview: A medium-sized national charitable organization founded in 1940
Mission: To coordinate operational matters dealing with the administration, regulation, & control of motor vehicle transportation & highway safety
Chief Officer(s):
Ward Keith, President
Methusalah Kunuk, Vice-President
Finances: *Funding Sources:* Member assessments; Special projects; Membership fees
Membership: 100-499; *Fees:* $433.50 associate; *Member Profile:* Members include representatives of provincial, territorial, & federal governments, & associate members from transportation related organizations.; *Committees:* Drivers & Vehicles; Compliance & Regulatory Affairs; Road Safety Research & Policies
Activities: Developing strategies & programs; Managing a communications network, called the Interprovincial Record Exchange system; *Rents Mailing List:* Yes
Awards:
• [CCMTA] Canadian Council of Motor Transport Administrators - Police Partnership Award (Award)
To honour achievements in police partnerships that increase awareness to make Canadian roads safe *Contact:* Valerie Todd, Programs Manager, Phone: 613-736-1003, ext. 251; E-mail: vtodd@ccmta.ca
• Associate Member of the Year Award (Award)
To recognize outstanding contributors to the Canadian Council of Motor Transport Administrators
• Jennie Howe Government Member of the Year Award (Award)
To recognize outstanding contributors to the Canadian Council of Motor Transport Administrators
Meetings/Conferences: • Canadian Council of Motor Transport Administrators 2015 Annual Meeting, June, 2015, Whitehorse, YT
Scope: National
Description: Educatioal events, an exhibition, a working forum where important decisions are made, & an excellent networking opportunity for government decision-makers & members of the private sector
Contact Information: Phone: 613-736-1003 Fax: 613-736-1395, E-mail: ccmta-secretariat@ccmta.ca
Publications:
• AAMVA / CCMTA Inspection Handbook
Type: Handbook
Profile: Recommended inspection procedures & standards for all types of vehicles in the United States & Canada
• CCMTA [Canadian Council of Motor Transport Administrators] News
Type: Newsletter; *Frequency:* Semiannually; *Editor:* Harvey Chartrand *ISSN:* 1192-747X; *Price:* Free for all government & assoicate members
Profile: Current projects & initiatives of CCMTA
• CCMTA [Canadian Council of Motor Transport Administrators] Directory
Type: Directory; *Price:* Free CD-ROM for associatemembers with membership renewal
Profile: Bilingual list of names, addresses, telephone & fax numbers, & e-mail addresses of over 600 contacts
• Commercial Vehicle Inspections in Canada
Type: Manual
Profile: An outline of Canadian commercial vehicle inspection requirements, availble in hard copy or CD-ROM
• Periodic Commercial Motor Vehicle Inspections
Type: Handbook

Canadian Council of Muslim Women (CCMW) / Conseil canadien des femmes musulmanes
PO Box 154, Gananoque ON K7G 2T7
Tel: 613-382-2847
info@ccmw.com
www.ccmw.com
www.linkedin.com/groups/Canadian-Council-Muslim-Women-6540822
www.facebook.com/CCMWNational
twitter.com/ccmwcanada
www.youtube.com/channel/UCOF-BIKxWy8jjPOL12GGY0A
Overview: A medium-sized national organization founded in 1982
Mission: To assist Muslim women in participating effectively in Canadian society;To promote mutual understanding with women of other faiths
Chief Officer(s):
Razia Jaffer, President
razia_jaffer@shaw.ca
Alia Hogben, Executive Director, 613-382-2847
hogben@kingston.net
Najet Hassan, Treasurer
Finances: *Funding Sources:* Fundraising; Public funds
20 volunteer(s)
Membership: 100-499; *Fees:* Schedule available; *Member Profile:* Practising Muslim women
Activities: *Speaker Service:* Yes
Publications:
• CCMW [Canadian Council of Muslim Women] National Newsletter
Type: Newsletter

Canadian Council of Practical Nurse Regulators (CCPNR)
c/o College of Licensed Practical Nurses of Newfoundland and Labrador, 9 Paton St., St. John's NL A1B 4S8
Tel: 709-579-3843; *Fax:* 709-579-3095
www.ccpnr.ca
Overview: A medium-sized national organization
Mission: Responsible for the safety of the public through the regulation of Licensed/Registered Practical Nurses.
Chief Officer(s):
Paul D. Fisher, Chair
chair@ccpnr.ca

Canadian Council of Professional Certification (CCPC)
1 Edenmills Dr., Toronto ON M1E 4L1
Tel: 416-724-5339; *Fax:* 416-724-0884
admin@ccpcglobal.com
www.ccpcprofessionals.com
www.linkedin.com/pub/jana-marmei/39/188/198
Also Known As: CCPC Global
Overview: A large national licensing organization
Mission: To grant certification & professional designation to qualified applicants
Membership: *Fees:* Schedule available
Activities: Offers the following courses: Alcohol & Drugs; Certified Professional Manager; Certified Nutrition Manager; Community Service Worker; Gambling; Solution-Focused Training Programs, Examiners & Supervisors; Spiritual Director/Supervisor; Train the Trainer
Awards:
• NET Institute Scholarship (Scholarship)

Calgary - Western Canada Regional Office
#3404, 3000 Somervale Ct. SW, Calgary AB T2Y 4J2
Tel: 403-201-2123; *Fax:* 403-254-8385
wco@CCPCglobal.com

Canadian Council of Professional Engineers ***See*** Engineers Canada

Canadian Council of Professional Fish Harvesters (CCPFH) / Conseil canadien des pêcheurs professionnels (CCPP)
#712, 1 Nicholas St., Ottawa ON K1N 7B7
Tel: 613-235-3474; *Fax:* 613-231-4313
www.ccpfh-ccpp.org
Overview: A medium-sized national organization founded in 1995
Mission: To represent the interests of professional fish harvesters across Canada in their dealings with the federal, provincial & territorial governments on national issues of common concern; To provide organizational structure & leadership for the development of a program of professionalization for fish harvesters in collaboration with the organizations representing professional fishers across Canada; To act as a national industry sector council to plan & implement training & adjustment programs for the fish harvesting industry in Canada
Chief Officer(s):
John Sutcliffe, Executive Director
Earle McCurdy, President
Dan Edwards, Vice-President
Ronnie Heighton, Vice-President
Daniel Landry, Secretary
O'Neil Cloutier, Treasurer
Membership: *Member Profile:* Fish harvesters; Captains & crew members
Publications:
• Canadian Council of Professional Fish Harvesters Newsletter
Type: Newsletter; *Frequency:* Quarterly
Profile: News & information from the council & industry

Canadian Council of Professional Geoscientists (CCPG) / Conseil Canadien des Géoscientifiques Professionnels (CCGP)
#200, 4010 Regent St., Burnaby BC V5C 6N2
Tel: 604-412-4888; *Fax:* 604-433-2494
info@ccpg.ca
www.ccpg.ca
Overview: A small national organization
Mission: To develop consistent high standards for licensure and practice of geoscience, facilitate national and international mobility, and promote the recognition of Canadian professional geoscientists.
Chief Officer(s):
Oliver Bonham, Chief Executive Officer
obonham@ccpg.ca

Canadian Council of Reform Rabbis ***See*** Canadian Council for Reform Judaism

Canadian Council of Snowmobile Organizations (CCSO) / Conseil canadien des organismes de motoneige (CCOM)
PO Box 21059, Thunder Bay ON P7A 8A7
Tel: 807-345-5299
ccso.ccom@tbaytel.net
www.ccso-ccom.ca
www.facebook.com/126035004176384
twitter.com/@ccsosnow

Overview: A large national organization founded in 1974
Mission: To provide leadership & support to organized snowmobiling in Canada
Chief Officer(s):
Steven McLelan, President
Dennis Burns, Executive Director
Activities: Promoting the welfare & betterment of snowmobile recreational activities; Cooperating with provincial & federal officials, other organizations, & the public on issues affecting snowbiles; Coordinating legislative activities; Promoting a code of ethics for snowmobiling; Completing the Trans-Canadian Snowmobile Trail; *Awareness Events:* National Safety Week, January; Take a Friend Snowmobiling Week, February
Awards:
• Outstanding Snowmobile Dealership (Award), CCSO Excellence Awards
• Outstanding Organized Snowmobile-related Company (Award), CCSO Excellence Awards
• Outstanding Promotion & Development of Snowmobiling (Award), CCSO Excellence Awards
• Outstanding Snowmobile Club (Award), CCSO Excellence Awards
• Outstanding Snowmobile Family (Award), CCSO Excellence Awards
• Outstanding Snowmobiler (Award), CCSO Excellence Awards
• Outstanding Snowmobile Tourism Promotion & Development (Award), CCSO Excellence Awards
• Outstanding Youth - The Pete Greenlaw Award (Award), CCSO Excellence Awards
Meetings/Conferences: • 47th International Snowmobile Congress / CCSO Annual General Meeting, June, 2015, Niagara Falls Convention Center, Niagara Falls, NY
Scope: International
Publications:
• CCSO [Canadian Council of Snowmobile Organizations] / CCOM [Conseil canadien des organismes de motoneige] News Bulletin
Type: Newsletter

Canadian Council of Teachers of English Language Arts (CCTELA)

#10, 730 River Rd., Winnipeg MB R2M 5A4
Tel: 204-255-1676; *Fax:* 204-253-2562
cctela.52@gmail.com
www.cctela.ca
Overview: A medium-sized national organization founded in 1967
Mission: To provide a national voice in education relating to English Language Arts; to serve as a forum for communication among provincial councils concerning English Language Arts; to provide a system of communication & cooperation for teachers of English Language Arts at all levels in Canada; to encourage research, experimentation & investigation in English Language Arts teaching; to sponsor, promote & lobby for programs of benefit to Canadian students.
Affliation(s): International Federation of Teachers of English
Chief Officer(s):
Linda Ferguson, Executive Director
Finances: *Annual Operating Budget:* Less than $50,000; *Funding Sources:* Membership fees; Journal subscriptions
Staff Member(s): 1; 15 volunteer(s)
Membership: 400; *Fees:* Regular: $60; Institution: $90; Undergraduate Student or Retiree: $35; *Member Profile:* Open to teachers of English & Language Arts
Activities: *Speaker Service:* Yes

Canadian Council of Technicians & Technologists (CCTT) / Conseil canadien des techniciens et technologues

#155, 955 Green Valley Cres., Ottawa ON K2C 3V4
Tel: 613-238-8123; *Fax:* 613-238-8822
Toll-Free: 800-891-1140
ccttadm@cctt.ca
www.cctt.ca
twitter.com/CCTTCanada
Previous Name: Canadian Council of Engineering Technicians and Technologists (CCETT)
Overview: A large national organization founded in 1973
Mission: To advocate on behalf of Canada's certified technicians & technologists; To establish & maintain national competency standards
Chief Officer(s):
Robert Okabe, CET, Chair
Isidore J. LeBlond, CEO
ileblond@cctt.ca
Rick Tachuk, Director, Communications & Marketing
rtachuk@cctt.ca
Valery Vidershpan, Manager, Project
vvidershpan@cctt.ca
Marisa Sosa, Coordinator, Program
msosa@cctt.ca
Activities: Government relations; accreditation; insurance services; trade mark protection; *Awareness Events:* National Technology Week, Nov.
Meetings/Conferences: • Canadian Council of Technicians & Technologists (CTTT) 2015 National Technology Conference, 2015
Scope: National
Publications:
• Innovation [a publication of the Canadian Council of Technicians & Technologists]
Type: Newsletter; *Frequency:* Monthly
Profile: News for technology professionals across Canada, including credential information, awards, & awareness activities

The Canadian Council of the Blind (CCB) / Le Conseil canadien des aveugles

#100, 20 James St., Ottawa ON K2P 0T6
Tel: 613-567-0311; *Fax:* 613-567-2728
Toll-Free: 877-304-0968
ccb@ccbnational.net
www.ccbnational.net
www.facebook.com/group.php?gid=143280866736
twitter.com/ccbnational
Overview: A medium-sized national charitable organization founded in 1945
Mission: To promote the well-being of individuals who are blind or vision-impaired through higher education, profitable employment, & social association; To create a closer relationship between blind & sighted friends; To organize a nation-wide organization of people who are blind & vision-impaired & groups of blind persons throughout Canada; To promote measures for the conservation of sight & the prevention of blindness
Affliation(s): World Blind Union
Chief Officer(s):
Louise Gillis, National President
Jim Tokos, First Vice-President
Linda Sobey, Second Vice-President
Finances: *Funding Sources:* Telemarketing; Product sales
1000 volunteer(s)
Membership: 3,000 individual; 82 clubs in Canada: BC 23; Alberta 4; Saskatchewan 3; Manitoba 3; Ontario 26; Québec 3; New Brunswick 9; NS/PEI 9; Newfoundland 2; *Fees:* $10; *Member Profile:* Registered legally blind; Persons with a condition that will lead to blindness; Deafblind persons; *Committees:* Legislation; Advocacy
Activities: Providing peer support; *Awareness Events:* White Cane Week, February; *Internships:* Yes; *Speaker Service:* Yes
Awards:
• Book of Fame Citation (Award)
The Book of Fame was donated to the Council in 1958 by the disbanded Comrades Club of Toronto; it contains the names & citations of outstanding blind Canadians selected yearly by the eight divisions & the National Board of Directors of the Council; each recipient of a citation is presented with a framed photograph of the appropriate page in the book
• Award of Merit (Award)
Established 1952; presented to a Canadian, blind or sighted, who has rendered outstanding work for the blind *Amount:* A gold medal & clasp, a specially printed & bound citation & honorary life membership in the CCB
Publications:
• Canadian Council of the Blind / Le Conseil Canadien des Aveugles Newsletter
Type: Newsletter; *Frequency:* Monthly
Profile: Available electronically or in large print format, the newsletter features articles on issues affecting the blind & visually impaired,products for the blind, competition results, & CCB updates & events
• White Cane Week Magazine
Type: Magazine; *Frequency:* Annually; *Accepts Advertising*; *Editor:* Mike Potvin
Profile: CCB news & information, White Cane Week review & events, & a resource guide for the blind & vision impaired

Canadian Council of University Physical Education & Kinesiology Administrators (CCUPEKA) / Conseil canadien des administrateurs universitaires en éducation physique et kinésiologie (CCAUEPK)

c/o Dr. J. Starkes, Department of Kinesiology, McMaster University, Hamilton ON L8S 4K1
www.ccupeka.ca
Overview: A small national organization founded in 1971 overseen by Association of Universities & Colleges of Canada
Mission: To serve as an accrediting body for physical education & kinesiology programs at universities in Canada; To offer a voice for academics, through lobbying initiatives
Chief Officer(s):
Angela Belcastro, President
Membership: *Member Profile:* Administrators of physical education & kinesiology programs at Canadian universities
Activities: Offering a forum for discussion among members

Canadian Council on 4-H Clubs *See* Canadian 4-H Council

Canadian Council on Africa

#702, 116 Albert St., Ottawa ON K1P 5G3
Tel: 613-565-3011; *Fax:* 613-565-3013
Toll-Free: 888-852-9461
www.ccafrica.ca
www.linkedin.com/groups/Canadian-Council-on-Africa-4471230
www.facebook.com/ccafrica
twitter.com/ccafrica2012
www.youtube.com/ccafrica1
Also Known As: CCAfrica
Overview: A medium-sized international organization founded in 2002
Mission: To promote trade & investment between Canada & Africa
Chief Officer(s):
Lucien Bradet, President & CEO
lucien.bradet@ccafrica.ca
Chris Kianza, Director, Communications & Member Relations
chris.kianza@ccafrica.ca
Publications:
• The Rising Africa [a publication of the Canadian Council on Africa]
Type: Magazine

Montréal - Eastern Office
52, Tour de la Bourse, Montréal ON H4Z 1J8
Tel: 514-451-9232; *Fax:* 514-387-5480
Chief Officer(s):
Karl Miville-de Chene, Vice-President
kmd@ccafrica.ca

Toronto - Central Office
161 Bay St., 27th Fl., Toronto ON M5J 2S1
Tel: 416-572-2129; *Fax:* 416-644-8893
Chief Officer(s):
Nola Kianza, Vice-President
nola.kianza@ccafrica.ca

Western Office
Tel: 403-218-4164; *Fax:* 708-915-1110
Chief Officer(s):
Frank Kense, Vice-President
frank.kense@ccafrica.ca

Canadian Council on Animal Care (CCAC) / Conseil canadien de protection des animaux (CCPA)

#1510, 130 Albert St., Ottawa ON K1P 5G4
Tel: 613-238-4031; *Fax:* 613-238-2837
ccac@ccac.ca
www.ccac.ca
Overview: A medium-sized national organization founded in 1968
Mission: To act on behalf of the people of Canada to ensure, through programs of education, assessment & persuasion, that the use of animals in Canada, where necessary for research, teaching & testing, employs physical & psychological care according to acceptable scientific standards; To promote an increased level of knowledge, awareness, & sensitivity to the relevant ethical principles
Chief Officer(s):
Clément Gauthier, Executive Director, 613-238-4031 Ext. 224
cgauthier@ccac.ca
Michael Baar, Director, Assessment & Certification Program, 613-238-4031 Ext. 226
mbaar@ccac.ca
Gilly Griffin, Director, Guidelines & Three Rs Programs, 613-238-4031 Ext. 225
ggriffin@ccac.ca
Pascale Belleau, Coordinator, Education, Training, & Communications, 613-238-4031 Ext. 234
pbelleau@ccac.ca

Emily Verlinden, Coordinator, Publications, 613-238-4031 Ext. 231
everlinden@ccac.ca
Membership: 22 organizations; *Committees:* Planning & Priorities; Finance; Guidelines; Education & Training; Assessments
Activities: *Library* Open to public by appointment
Publications:
• Canadian Council on Animal Care Workshop Proceedings
• CCAC [Canadian Council on Animal Care] Annual Report
Frequency: Annually
• CCAC [Canadian Council on Animal Care] Guidelines
Frequency: Irregular
Profile: Topics include procurement of animals used in science, laboratory animal facilities, the care and use of wildlife, antibody production, institutional animal user training,transgenic animals, & animal use protocol review
• CCAC [Canadian Council on Animal Care] Guide to the Care & Use of Experimental Animals
• Resource: The Newsletter of the Canadian Council on Animal Care (CCAC)
Type: Newsletter; *Frequency:* Semiannually; *Editor:* Clément Gauthier, PhD *ISSN:* 0700-5237
Profile: Articles about laboratory animal science; news about current issues & events related to the CCAC

The Canadian Council on Continuing Education in Pharmacy (CCCEP) / Le conseil canadien de l'éducation permanente en pharmacie

#210, 2002 Quebec Ave., Saskatoon SK S7K 1W4
Tel: 306-652-7790; *Fax:* 306-652-7795
Other Communication: Executive Director e-mail: exec.dir@cccep.ca
info@cccep.ca
www.cccep.ca
Overview: A small national licensing organization founded in 1973
Mission: To act as the national coordinating & accrediting body for continuing education in pharmacy in Canada; To enhance the quality of continuing pharmacy education; To advance pharmacy practice
Chief Officer(s):
Bev Zwicker, President
Membership: *Member Profile:* Organizations interested in promoting the quality of continuing professional development for pharmacy professionals
Activities: Establishing policy & criteria for accreditation; Accrediting continuing education programs provided to pharmacists; Promoting the standardization of continuing pharmacy education
Publications:
• The Canadian Council on Continuing Education in Pharmacy Annual Report
Type: Yearbook; *Frequency:* Annually

Canadian Council on Ecological Areas (CCEA)

c/o Environmental Stewardship Branch, Environment Canada, #3, 351, boul St. Joseph, Gatineau QC K1A 0H3
Tel: 819-934-6064; *Fax:* 819-994-4445
mark.richardson@ec.gc.ca
www.ccea.org
Overview: A small national organization founded in 1982
Mission: To facilitate the establishment of a comprehensive network of protected areas which are linked together in a system that will protect Canada's terrestrial & aquatic diversity in perpetuity
Chief Officer(s):
Mark Richardson, Sec.-Manager
mark.richardson@ec.gc.ca

Canadian Council on Health Services Accreditation; Canadian Council on Health Facilities Accreditation *See* Accreditation Canada

Canadian Council on International Law (CCIL) / Conseil canadien de droit international (CCDI)

275 Bay St., Ottawa ON K1R 5Z5
Tel: 613-235-0442; *Fax:* 613-232-8228
manager@ccil-ccdi.ca
www.ccil-ccdi.ca
Overview: A small international charitable organization founded in 1972
Mission: To bring together scholars of international law & organizations engaged in teaching & research at Canadian universities; To encourage & conduct studies in international law with a view to its progressive development & codification; To foster the study of legal aspects of Canada's international problems & to advocate their solution in accordance with existing or developing principles of international law.
Affliation(s): Société québécoise de droit international; American Society of International Law; Japanese Association of International Law
Chief Officer(s):
Craig Forcese, President
Elizabeth Macaulay, Manager
manager@ccil-ccdi.ca
Finances: *Annual Operating Budget:* $50,000-$100,000; *Funding Sources:* Membership fees, donations, government project funding
Staff Member(s): 1; 24 volunteer(s)
Membership: 400; *Fees:* $85 individual; $45 student; *Member Profile:* Leading scholars; students of international law; government & practising lawyers from both public & private sectors
Activities: Speakers series; *Speaker Service:* Yes
Awards:
• John E. Read Medal (Award)

Canadian Council on Rehabilitation & Work (CCRW) / Le Conseil canadien de la réadaptation et du travail (CCRT)

#1202, 1 Yonge St., Toronto ON M5E 1E5
Tel: 416-260-3060; *Fax:* 416-260-3093
Toll-Free: 800-664-0925; *TTY:* 416-260-9223
info@ccrw.org
www.ccrw.org
Overview: A medium-sized national charitable organization founded in 1976
Mission: To improve employment opportunities for persons with disabilities in Canada; To promote the equitable & meaningful employment of persons with disabilities
Chief Officer(s):
Carole J. Barron, President & Chief Executive Officer, 416-260-3060 Ext. 222
Venatius Babu, Chief Financial Officer, 416-260-3060 Ext. 223
Georgia Whalen, Director, Information Technology & Standards, 416-260-9223
Elizabeth Smith, Manager, Employer Consultations & Partnerships, 416-260-3060 Ext. 228
Monica Winkler, Senior Administrator, 416-260-3060 Ext. 227
Activities: Connecting employers with job seekers who have disabilities; Offering an ethno-cultural portal for youth with disabilities; Assisting workplaces, with the Job Accommodation Service; Conducting research in the area of employment for people with disabilities; Providing an employment program for employers & job seekers, known as the Workplace Essential Skills Partnership; Creating awareness of skilled trade careers for youth, by developing skilled trades information & workshops
Publications:
• Ability & Enterprise (A&E) [a publication of the Canadian Council on Rehabilitation & Work]
Type: Newsletter
Profile: CCRW news & information
• CCRW [Canadian Council on Rehabilitation & Work] Annual Report
Type: Yearbook; *Frequency:* Annually

Canadian Council on Smoking & Health *See* Canadian Council for Tobacco Control

Canadian Council on Social Development (CCSD) / Conseil canadien de développement social (CCDS)

PO Box 13713, Kanata ON K2K 1X6
Tel: 613-236-8977
council@ccsd.ca
www.ccsd.ca
Previous Name: Canadian Welfare Council
Overview: A large national charitable organization founded in 1920
Mission: To develop & promote progressive social policies, on issues such as child well-being, poverty, housing, employment, cultural diversity, & social inclusion
Chief Officer(s):
Peggy Taillon, President & CEO, 613-236-8977 Ext. 1
taillon@ccsd.ca
Katherine Scott, Vice-President, Research & Policy, 613-236-8977 Ext. 2
Michel Frojmovic, Manager, Community Data Program, 613-236-8977 Ext. 23
Tammy Williams, Manager, Operations & Special Projects, 613-236-8977 Ext. 3
Finances: *Funding Sources:* Membership fee; Donations; Sponsorships; United Way; Research contracts; Sale of publications
Membership: *Fees:* $50 students & low income persons; $95 individuals; $55 - $750 organizations, depending upon their budgets
Activities: Conducting research; Providing information; Consulting with others involved in the field; Engaging in advocacy activities; Educating the public
Publications:
• Canadian Fact Book on Poverty [a publication of the Canadian Council on Social Development]
Frequency: Irregular
• CCSD [Canadian Council on Social Development] Annual Report
Type: Yearbook; *Frequency:* Annually
• Perception [a publication of the Canadian Council on Social Development]
Type: Magazine; *Frequency:* Quarterly; *Accepts Advertising; ISSN:* 0704-5263; *Price:* Free for CCSD members
Profile: National periodical about social development issues, CCSD member events
• Personal Security Index [a publication of the Canadian Council on Social Development]
Frequency: Irregular
• Progress of Canada's Children & Youth [a publication of Canadian Council on Social Development]
Frequency: Irregular

Canadian Counselling & Psychotherapy Association (CCPA) / L'Association canadienne de counseling et de psychothérapie (ACCP)

#114, 223 Colonnade Rd. South, Ottawa ON K2E 7K3
Tel: 613-237-1099; *Fax:* 613-237-9786
Toll-Free: 877-765-5565
info@ccpa-accp.ca
www.ccpa-accp.ca
www.facebook.com/CCPA.ACCP
twitter.com/ccpa_accp
Previous Name: Canadian Counselling Association
Overview: A medium-sized national organization founded in 1965
Mission: To enhance the counselling profession in Canada; To promote policies & practices which support the provision of accessible, competent, & accountable counselling services throughout the human lifespan, & in a manner sensitive to the pluralistic nature of society.
Chief Officer(s):
Blythe Shepard, President
president@ccpa-accp.ca
Barbara MacCallum, Executive Director
bmaccallum@ccpa-accp.ca
Finances: *Funding Sources:* Membership dues
Staff Member(s): 11
Membership: 4,600; *Fees:* Schedule available; *Member Profile:* Professionally trained counsellors in fields of education, employment & career development, social work, business, industry, mental health, public service agencies, government & private practice; *Committees:* Executive; Governance; Risk Management; Quality Assurance & Sustainability; Regulation & Policy; Appeals; Ethics; Certification; Awards
Activities: Annual conference
Meetings/Conferences: • Canadian Counselling and Psychotherapy Association 2015 Annual Conference, May, 2015, Sheraton on the Falls Hotel, Niagara Falls, ON
Scope: National
• American Counseling Association / Canadian Counselling and Psychotherapy Association 2016 Annual Conference, March, 2016, Palais des congrès de Montréal, Montreal, QC
Scope: National

Alberta & Northwest Territories Chapter
AB
Chief Officer(s):
Kathy Offet Gartner, President
president@abnwtchapter.ca

British Columbia Chapter
BC
www.ccpa-accp.ca/en/chapters/britishcolumbia
Chief Officer(s):
Paul Yeung, President

Career Development Chapter
www.ccpa-accp.ca/en/chapters/careercounsellors
Chief Officer(s):
Jessica Isenor, President
jisen010@uottawa.ca

Counsellor Educators Chapter
www.ccpa-accp.ca/en/chapters/counselloreducator
Chief Officer(s):
Patrice Keats, President

Creative Arts in Counselling Chapter
www.ccpa-accp.ca/en/chapters/creativeartsincounselling
Chief Officer(s):
Amy Mackenzie, President
amy.mackenzie@gmail.com

Indigenous Circle Chapter
www.ccpa-accp.ca/en/chapters/indigenouscircle
Chief Officer(s):
Andrea Currie, President
andreacurrie@waycobah.ca

National Capital Region Chapter
Ottawa ON
Chief Officer(s):
Nicholas Renaud, President
nicholas.renaud@gmail.com

Pastoral & Spiritual Care in Counselling Chapter
www.ccpa-accp.ca/en/chapters/pastoralspiritualcare
Chief Officer(s):
Gerard Vardy, President

Private Practitioners Chapter
www.ccpa-accp.ca/en/chapters/privatepractitioners
Chief Officer(s):
Corrine Hendricken-Eldershaw, President
corrinealz@eastlink.ca

School Counsellors Chapter
www.ccpa-accp.ca/en/chapters/schoolcounsellors
Chief Officer(s):
Belinda Josephson, President
gjosephson@eastlink.ca

Social Justice Chapter
www.ccpa-accp.ca/en/chapters/socialjustice
Chief Officer(s):
Linda Wheeldon, Chair
linda.wheeldon@acadiau.ca
Andria Hill-Lehr, Chair
andrialehr@yahoo.ca

Canadian Counselling Association *See* Canadian Counselling & Psychotherapy Association

Canadian Country Music Association (CCMA) / Association de la musique country canadienne

#200, 120 Adelaide St. East, Toronto ON M5C 1K9
Tel: 416-947-1331; *Fax:* 416-947-5924
country@ccma.org
www.ccma.org
www.facebook.com/CCMAOfficial
twitter.com/ccmaofficial
Overview: A medium-sized national organization founded in 1976
Mission: The federally chartered non-profit professional organization protects the heritage, & advocates the development of Canadian country music both in Canada & worldwide.
Chief Officer(s):
Don Green, President
dgreen@ccma.org
Ted Ellis, Chair
Louis O'Reilly, Secretary-Treasurer
Finances: *Funding Sources:* Membership dues; sponsorship
Staff Member(s): 6
Membership: *Fees:* $0 fan; $33.33 associate; $166.67 corporate; $66.67 industry; *Member Profile:* Industry & corporate members have direct & substantial involvement required in country music, applicable to advertising, artists, broadcast personnel, producers, & record/video companies; Fan members
Activities: The Country Talent Development Fund to promote and develop Canadian talent; CCMA Canadian Tour Support Program to support domestic touring activities by Canadian artists; Country Music Week Showcases to increase public awareness & appreciation for Canadian country music; Songwriter's Café to offer Canadian songwriters the opportunity to share their songs; *Awareness Events:* Country Music Week, Sept.
Awards:
• CCMA Music Awards (Award)
Awards in 10 categories are presented annually to outstanding performers; 35 citations honour individuals & organizations that have made a significant contribution to country music
Publications:
• The Book: CCMA Source Guide
Type: Directory
Profile: Lists country music contacts
• The Source
Type: Newsletter; *Frequency:* Quarterly
Profile: Timely information about the country music industry

Canadian Courier & Logistics Association (CCLA)

PO Box 333, #119, 660 Eglinton Ave. East, Toronto ON M4G 2K2
Tel: 416-696-9995; *Fax:* 416-696-9993
Toll-Free: 877-766-6604
info@canadiancourier.org
www.canadiancourier.org
twitter.com/CCLA4
Previous Name: Canadian Courier Association
Overview: A medium-sized national organization founded in 1986
Mission: To serve the needs, promote the interests & concerns, & enhance the reputation of the courier industry in Canada regardless of size or type of operation
Chief Officer(s):
David Turnbull, President & CEO
dturnbull@canadiancourier.org
Staff Member(s): 2
Membership: *Fees:* $927 supplier; $1,850 resource partner; *Member Profile:* Couriers & time sensitive logistics service providers in Canada; *Committees:* Cargo Security; Customs; Courier Process; Environment & Energy; Regulatory; Urban Mobility; Weights & Measures
Activities: Luncheon seminars; golf tournament
Awards:
• Courier Executive of the Year Award (Award)

Canadian Courier Association *See* Canadian Courier & Logistics Association

Canadian Cowboys' Association (CCA)

PO Box 1027, Regina SK S4P 3B2
Tel: 306-931-2700; *Fax:* 306-721-2701
canadiancowboys@sasktel.net
www.canadiancowboys.ca
www.facebook.com/CCARodeo
twitter.com/CCA_Rodeo
www.youtube.com/user/CanadianCowboysAssn
Overview: A small national organization founded in 1963
Mission: To sanction over 50 rodeos in Western Canada; to serve as a source of competition information, maintaining schedules & records of standings & results.
Chief Officer(s):
Shylo Claypool, President

Canadian Craft & Hobby Association (CCHA)

Mono Plaza, PO Box 101, 633419 Hwy. 10 North, Orangeville ON L9W 2Z5
Tel: 519-940-5969; *Fax:* 519-941-0492
Paul.laplante@asi-tapedots.com
www.cdncraft.org
Overview: A medium-sized national organization founded in 1978
Mission: To further the success of every business engaged in Canada's craft & hobby industry by providing an arena for the discussion of goals & plans; to foster industry expansion through development & implementation of dynamic programs & activities; to provide a forum for meeting new people, learning new ideas & profiting from benefits of working together
Chief Officer(s):
Paul Laplante, President, 866-386-8853
Finances: *Annual Operating Budget:* $250,000-$500,000
Staff Member(s): 2; 15 volunteer(s)
Membership: 600; *Fees:* $125-$321; *Member Profile:* Retailers; residential retailers; craft converters; institutions; wholesaler/distributors; representatives; manufacturer/publisher (Canadian/foreign)
Activities: Two trade shows; education program; *Awareness Events:* National Craft Month; National Sewing Month

Canadian Crafts Federation (CCF) / Fédération canadienne des métiers d'art (FCMA)

PO Box 1231, Fredericton NB E3B 5C8
Tel: 506-462-9560
info@canadiancraftsfederation.ca
www.canadiancraftsfederation.ca
Overview: A medium-sized national charitable organization founded in 1998
Mission: To represent provincial & territorial crafts councils & the Canadian crafts sector; to advance & promote the vitality & excellence of Canadian crafts nationally & internationally to the benefit of Canadian craftspeople & the community at large
Affliation(s): World Crafts Council
Chief Officer(s):
Deborah Dumka, President, 604-486-7692
dumkasanford@telus.net
Finances: *Annual Operating Budget:* Less than $50,000; *Funding Sources:* Membership fees; grants
Staff Member(s): 1; 10 volunteer(s)
Membership: 10; *Fees:* $300+; *Member Profile:* Provincial crafts councils; honorary members

Canadian Credit Institute Educational Foundation (CCIEF)

#216C, 219 Dufferin St., Toronto ON M6L 3J1
Tel: 416-572-2615; *Fax:* 416-572-2619
Toll-Free: 888-447-3324
geninfo@creditedu.org
www.creditedu.org
Overview: A small national organization founded in 1967
Mission: To provide funding in support of credit initiatives to enhance performance of professionals dedicated to excellence.
Chief Officer(s):
Denis Serre, Director
dserre@mtdproducts.com
Staff Member(s): 5
Awards:
• The CCIEF Scholarship (Scholarship)
To promote education through the Credit Institute of Canada by providing financial support to students in pursuit of the CCP (Certified Credit Professional) designation. Eligibility: Financial need; at least two years experience in the credit/financial field with a long term goal in the credit or financial management field(s); Canadian resident; participates in local community or volunteer program and will provide a letter of reference *Amount:* up to $2000

Canadian Criminal Justice Association (CCJA) / Association canadienne de justice pénale (ACJP)

#101, 320 Parkdale Ave., Ottawa ON K1Y 4X9
Tel: 613-725-3715; *Fax:* 613-725-3720
ccja-acjp@rogers.com
www.ccja-acjp.ca
www.facebook.com/186547581359601
Overview: A medium-sized national charitable organization founded in 1919
Mission: To promote a humane, equitable & effective criminal justice system in Canada
Affliation(s): Alberta Criminal Justice Association; British Columbia Criminal Justice Association; Manitoba Criminal Justice Association; New Brunswick/Prince Edward Island Criminal Justice Association; Newfoundland & Labrador Criminology & Corrections Association; Nova Scotia Criminal Justice Association; Criminal Justice Association of Ontario; Saskatchewan Justice Institute; Société de criminologie du Québec
Chief Officer(s):
Roland LaHaye, President
Irving Kulik, Executive Director
Finances: *Annual Operating Budget:* $250,000-$500,000; *Funding Sources:* Government grants; publication sales; fundraising
Staff Member(s): 3; 50 volunteer(s)
Membership: 700; *Fees:* $25-$500; *Committees:* Policy Review; Awards; Initiatives; Public Awareness & Visability; Membership Strategies
Activities: *Library*
Publications:
• Canadian Journal of Criminology & Criminal Justice
Type: Journal; *Frequency:* Quarterly; *Editor:* Peter J. Carrington; *Price:* $40 student; $65 individual; $125 institutional
Profile: Peer-reviewed scientific journal with articles based on research & experimentation for researchers, practitioners, justice administrators, academics, &those interested in recent criminological findings
• CCJA [Canadian Criminal Justice Association] Newsletter
Type: Newsletter; *Frequency:* Biweekly
Profile: News from across Canada with CCJA member input
• The Directory of Services for Victims of Crime
Type: Directory
Profile: Listing of agencies & services for victims throughout Canada
• The Justice Directory of Services
Type: Directory
Profile: Listing of Canadian federal, provincial, & voluntary services in the field of criminal justice & corrections

• The Justice Report
Type: Magazine; *Frequency:* Quarterly
Profile: Opinion pieces by professional journalists, articles by partners in the criminal justice system, recent court decision reports, inmate opinions, & upcoming events

Canadian Critical Care Society (CCCS) / Société canadienne de soins intensifs

c/o Toronto General Hospital, 10 Eaton North, Room 220, 200 Elizabeth St., Toronto ON M5G 2C4
Tel: 416-340-4800; *Fax:* 416-340-4211
info@canadiancriticalcare.org
www.canadiancriticalcare.org
www.facebook.com/269898849687697
Overview: A medium-sized national organization
Mission: To promote & develop critical care medicine in Canada
Affliation(s): Canadian Medical Association; World Federation of Societies of Intensive & Critical Care Medicine
Chief Officer(s):
Claudio Martin, President
Meetings/Conferences: • 2015 12th Annual Canadian Critical Care Conference, February, 2015, Four Seasons Resort, Whistler, BC
Scope: National
Contact Information: URL: www.canadiancriticalcare.org

Canadian Crop Hail Association (CCHA)

c/o Co-operative Hail Insurance Company Ltd., 2709 - 13th Ave., Regina SK S4P 3A8
Overview: A small national organization
Mission: To represent insurers who write crop hail insurance in Alberta, Saskatchewan, & Manitoba
Chief Officer(s):
Murray Bantle, Chair, 306-522-8891
Brian Tainsh, Media Contact, Alberta, 403-782-8232
David Van Deynze, Media Contact, Manitoba, 204-239-3252
Membership: 11; *Member Profile:* Companies that sell crop hail insurance to producers in western Canada, such as Additional Municipal Hail Ltd., Agriculture Financial Services Corporation, Butler Byers Hail Insurance Ltd., Canadian Hail Agencies Inc., Co-operative Hail Insurance Company, Manitoba Agricultural Services Corporation, McQueen Agencies Ltd., Farmers Hail Insurance Agencies, Ltd., Rain & Hail Insurance Service, Ltd., Henderson Hail Agencies Ltd., & Wray Agencies Ltd.

Canadian Crossroads International (CCI) / Carrefour canadien international

#201, 49 Bathurst St., Toronto ON M5V 2P2
Tel: 416-967-1611; *Fax:* 416-967-9078
Toll-Free: 877-967-1611
info@cintl.org
www.cintl.org
www.facebook.com/CanadianCrossroads
twitter.com/Crossroads_CCI
www.youtube.com/user/CanadianCrossroads
Overview: A medium-sized international charitable organization founded in 1958
Mission: CCI is a development organization that is reducing poverty & increasing women's rights around the world. It works with local organizations in West Africa, Southern Africa & South America. Organizations in developing countries select Canadian, partner organizations working on similar issues, so that they can help develop programs & meet their development goals. CCI supports the exchange of skilled volunteers. It is a registered charity, BN: 129814570RR0001.
Member of: Canadian Council for International Cooperation
Chief Officer(s):
Darlene Bessey, Chair
Karen Takacs, Executive Director Ext. 333
Aranka Somlo, Executive Assistant Ext. 228
aranka@cciorg.ca
Finances: *Annual Operating Budget:* $100,000-$250,000; *Funding Sources:* CIDA; private donations
Staff Member(s): 24; 200 volunteer(s)
Membership: 12; *Committees:* National Program; National Alumni Association; National Fundraising; National Finance; Personnel; Executive
Activities: Sends over 200 volunteers to 26 countries worldwide; *Internships:* Yes

Québec Regional Office
#308, 3000, rue Omer-Lavallée, Montréal QC H1Y 3R8
Tél: 514-528-5363; *Téléc:* 514-528-5367
quebec@cintl.org
www.facebook.com/Carrefourcanadien
Mission: Carrefour canadien international (CCI) est un organisme sans but lucratif qui reçoit l'appui de l'Agence canadienne de développement international (ACDI), de bailleurs de fonds gouvernementaux et non gouvernementaux ainsi que de donateurs individuels provenant des quatre coins du globe.
Chief Officer(s):
Nicolas Gersdorff, Agent de communication, nouveaux média Ext. 222

Western Regional Office
#103, 119 West Pender St., Vancouver BC V6B 1S5
Tel: 604-734-4677; *Fax:* 604-734-4675
Mission: The Western Region works on projects in Bolivia. NGOs & community organizations in the country are partnered with similar organizations in the Western Region with the intent of building capacity in the southern organizations. The main vehicle for building capacity is skilled, motivated volunteer professionals who may come from the organizations involved or from the broader community.
Chief Officer(s):
Mary Pullen, Program Officer, Bolivia

Canadian Crude Quality Technical Association (CCQTA)

www.ccqta.com
Overview: A medium-sized national organization
Mission: The CCQTA facilitates the resolution of common crude oil quality issues by establishing direct lines of communications among crude oil stakeholders. Note: CCQTA does not have a permanent office location
Membership: 75; *Fees:* $1,000-$2,000; *Member Profile:* Any subscriber that is engaged in any commercial activity of the petroleum industry and who pays the initial and subsequent annual fees.
Meetings/Conferences: • Canadian Crude Quality Technical Association (CCQTA) 2015 Annual General Meeting, 2015
Scope: National
• Oil Sands and Heavy Oil Technologies Conference & Exhibition 2015, 2015
Scope: National
Description: Forum for oil sands innovation.
Contact Information: Gail Killough, Conference Manager, gailk@pennwell.com; Phone: 713-963-6251; Website: www.oilsandstechnologies.com; Twitter: twitter.com/ogjevents; registration@pennwell.com

Canadian Cue Sport Association (CCS)

87 Brightstone Gardens SE, Calgary AB T2Z 0C6
Tel: 403-271-9221
pplted@hotmail.com
www.cdnqsport.com
Overview: A small national organization founded in 2003
Mission: To manage a Canadian billiards Championship Program & to provide sanctioning of billiard leagues
Chief Officer(s):
Ted Harms, President
Membership: *Fees:* $50 individual; $20 per player in leagues, depending on league size; *Member Profile:* Leagues; Individual Players

Canadian Culinary Federation (CCFCC) / Fédération Culinaire Canadienne

c/o Roy Butterworth, National Administrator, 30 Hamilton Ct., Riverview NB E1B 3C3
Other Communication: membership@ccfcc.ca; marketing@ccfcc.ca
admin@ccfcc.ca
www.ccfcc.ca
www.facebook.com/CCFCC
twitter.com/@CdnChefs
Previous Name: Canadian Federation of Chefs & Cooks; Canadian Federation of Chefs de Cuisine
Overview: A large national organization founded in 1963
Mission: To promote a Canadian food culture both nationally & internationally; To encourage professional excellence among chefs & cooks throughout Canada
Member of: World Association of Chefs' Societies
Chief Officer(s):
Judson Simpson, Chair
chair@ccfcc.ca
Donald A. Gyurkovits, President
president@ccfcc.ca
Roy Butterworth, National Administrator
admin@ccfcc.ca
Blake Chapman, Secretary
secretary@ccfcc.ca
Robert Harrison, Treasurer
treasurer@ccfcc.ca
Tim Appleton, Chair, Junior Membership
juniormembership@ccfcc.ca
Don (Busch) Dubay, Chair, Finance
finance@ccfcc.ca
Membership: *Fees:* $100 / year + $30 initiation fee, national members & members at large; $50 / year, Canadian Forces members; $20 / year, junior members; *Member Profile:* Cook apprentices; Journeyman cooks; Professional chefs; Culinary professionals; *Committees:* Marketing; International Relations; Certification; Honour Society; Finance; Bylaws & Ethics; Culinary Team; Junior Membership
Activities: Creating learning opportunities
Awards:
• Chef of the Year (Award)
Eligibility: A chef that best exemplifies the elements of professionalism, dedication to the the craft of cooking and has applied themselves to the success of Branch work.
Meetings/Conferences: • 52nd Annual Canadian Culinary Federation 2015 National Convention, May, 2015, Sheraton St.John's, St. John's, NL
Scope: National
Publications:
• Mise en Place
Type: Newsletter; *Frequency:* Quarterly; *Accepts Advertising*; *Editor:* Eleanor Gasparik
Profile: Informative articles for members of the Canadian Culinary Federation

Brandon Branch
Brandon MB
Tel: 204-667-4647
Chief Officer(s):
Paul Lemire, President
pilot11@shaw.ca

Calgary Branch
#496, 130 - 5403 Crowchild Trail NW, Calgary AB T3B 4Z1
e-mail: president@calgarychefs.com
www.calgarychefs.com
www.facebook.com/259373817454055
Chief Officer(s):
Fred Malley, President

Chapitre Outaouais
Outaouais QC
Tél: 613-673-9295
Chief Officer(s):
Stephane Paquet, Président

Edmonton Branch
9797 Jasper Ave., Edmonton AB T5J 1N9
Tel: 780-475-2433; *Fax:* 780-426-1874
admin@edmontonchefs.ca
www.edmontonchefs.ca
Chief Officer(s):
Stanley Townsend, President
president@edmontonchefs.ca

Halifax Branch
PO Box 31457, Halifax NS B3K 5Z1
Tel: 902-433-0261; *Fax:* 902-433-0261
www.nsacc.ca
Chief Officer(s):
John St. John, President
john.stjohn@nscc.ca

Hamilton Branch
25 Roselle Pl., Stoney Creek ON L8G 1R2
e-mail: admin@ccfhamilton.ca
www.ccfhamilton.ca
twitter.com/HamiltonChefs

Kingston Branch
925 Hudson Dr., Kingston ON K7M 5V4
Tel: 613-384-1746
Chief Officer(s):
Ian Sarfin, President
isarfin@cogeco.ca

Lethbridge Branch
PO Box 1021, Lethbridge AB T1J 4A2
www.southernalbertachefs.ca
www.facebook.com/175006825913901
twitter.com/SAACmedia
Chief Officer(s):
Debbie Clause, President

London Branch
London ON
Tel: 519-615-9487
Chief Officer(s):

Mike A. Pitre, President
chefmikepitre@gmail.com
Moncton Branch
Moncton NB
Tel: 506-384-7026
Chief Officer(s):
Lana Manuge, President
chefroy@nbnet.nb.ca
Montréal Branch
Montréal QC
Tél: 450-467-5972
Chief Officer(s):
Denis Parent, Président
parent-denis@videotron.ca
Muskoka Branch
PO Box 773, Barrie ON L4M 4Y5
Tel: 705-791-2434
www.ccfmuskoka.com
www.facebook.com/302353886554323
Chief Officer(s):
Daniel Clements, President
danielclements@rogers.com
North Vancouver Island
PO Box 3156, Courtenay BC V9N 5N4
Tel: 250-897-3134
info@northvancouverislandchefs.com
www.northvancouverislandchefs.com
Chief Officer(s):
Lesley Stav, President
lesley.stav@northvancouverislandchefs.com
Okanagan Branch
PO Box 2612, Stn. Banks Center, Kelowna BC V1X 6A7
e-mail: secretary@okanaganchefs.com
www.okanaganchefs.com
www.facebook.com/okanaganchefs
twitter.com/okanaganchefs
Chief Officer(s):
Bernard Casavent, President
president@okanaganchefs.com
Ottawa Branch
Ottawa ON
Tel: 613-836-0268
www.ccfccottawa.ca
www.facebook.com/CCFCC.Ottawa.ca
twitter.com/CCFCC_Ottawa
Chief Officer(s):
Russell Weir, President, 613-238-1500
weirr@algonquincollege.com
Prince Edward Island Branch
PO Box 581, Charlottetown PE C1A 7L1
Chief Officer(s):
Jeff McCourt, President, 902-629-9445
mccourtjeff1@gmail.com
Québec
Québec QC
Tel: 418-871-8737
Chief Officer(s):
Martens Didier, Président
martdidier@hotmail.com
Regina Branch
PO Box 3162, Regina SK S4P 3G7
e-mail: ccfccregina@live.ca
www.ccfccregina.ca
www.facebook.com/ccfccregina
Chief Officer(s):
Trent Brears, President
president@ccfccregina.ca
St. John's Branch
St. John's NL
Tel: 709-437-6519
ccfccstjohnsbranch@nf.sympatico.ca
Chief Officer(s):
Andrew Hodge, President
andrew_hodge@hotmail.com
Saskatoon Branch
Saskatoon SK
Tel: 306-652-1780
askus@ccfccsaskatoonbranch.org
www.ccfccsaskatoonbranch.org
Chief Officer(s):
Anthony J. McCarthy, President
anthonym@saskatoonclub.com
Toronto Branch
PO Box 1093, Stn. A, Toronto ON M5V 1G6
e-mail: administrator@escoffiertoronto.com
www.escoffiertoronto.com
www.facebook.com/308371625923106
Chief Officer(s):
Cornelia Volino, President
president@escoffiertoronto.com
Vancouver Branch
PO Box 2007, Stn. Main, Vancouver BC V6B 3P8
www.bcchefs.com
www.facebook.com/BritishColumbiaChefsAssociation
twitter.com/BCChefs
Chief Officer(s):
Edgar Rahal, President
president@bcchefs.com
Victoria Branch
1735 Kingsberry Cres., Victoria BC V8P 2A8
Tel: 778-430-7977
info@ccfccvictoria.ca
www.ccfccvictoria.ca
www.facebook.com/174851829250060
twitter.com/CCFCCVictoria
Chief Officer(s):
Jamie Martinuea, President
president@ccfccvictoria.ca
Windsor Branch
788 South Pacific Ave., Windsor ON N8X 2X2
e-mail: info@culinaryguildofwindsor.ca
www.culinaryguildofwindsor.ca
Chief Officer(s):
Helmut Market, President
president@culinaryguildofwindsor.ca
Winnipeg Branch
PO Box 1072, Winnipeg MB R3C 2X4
www.winnipegchefs.org
Chief Officer(s):
Brent Prockert, President
chefbrent@shawbiz.ca

Canadian Cultural Society of The Deaf, Inc. (CCSD)

The Distillery Historic District, 34 Distillery Lake, Toronto ON M5A 3C4
Tel: 416-203-0343; *Fax:* 416-203-1086; *TTY:* 416-203-2294
info@deafculturecentre.ca
www.deafculturecentre.ca
Also Known As: Deaf Culture Centre
Overview: A medium-sized national charitable organization founded in 1973
Mission: To ensure that the cultural needs of deaf & hard-of-hearing people are being met; To concentrate efforts in the areas of the performing arts, sign language, deaf literature, the visual arts, & heritage resources
Chief Officer(s):
Joanne Cripps, CYW, Co-Director
jcripps@deafculturecentre.ca
Anita Small, M.Sc., Ed.D, Co-Director
asmall@deafculturecentre.ca
Staff Member(s): 3; 95 volunteer(s)
Membership: *Fees:* $100; *Member Profile:* 8 provincial cultural societies across Canada
Activities: Provides programs on culture, history, visual & performing artists (Deaf), with ongoing workshops, exhibits, school tours & virtual displays; gift shop showcasing Deaf artists' work; *Internships:* Yes

Canadian Curling Association (CCA) / Association canadienne de curling

1660 Vimont Ct., Orleans ON K4A 4J4
Tel: 613-834-2076; *Fax:* 613-834-0716
Toll-Free: 800-550-2875
Other Communication:
www.flickr.com/photos/seasonofchampions
boc@curling.ca
www.curling.ca
www.facebook.com/ccacurling
www.twitter.com/ccacurling
www.youtube.com/ccacurling
Overview: A large national organization founded in 1990
Mission: To attract, retain & advance participants to grow the sport of curling
Affliation(s): World Curling Federation
Chief Officer(s):
Hugh Avery, Chair
Greg Stremlaw, CEO, 613-834-2076 Ext. 117, Fax: 613-834-0716
gstremlaw@curling.ca
Pat Ray, COO, 613-834-2076 Ext. 154, Fax: 613-834-0716
pray@curling.ca
Warren Hansen, Director, Event Operations, 604-941-4330, Fax: 604-941-4332
whansen@curling.ca
Danny Lamoureux, Director, Championship Services & Curling Club Development, 613-834-2076 Ext. 116, Fax: 613-834-0716
dlamoureux@curling.ca
Gerry Peckham, Director, High Performance, 613-834-2076 Ext. 113, Fax: 613-834-0716
gpeckham@curling.ca
Membership: *Committees:* Finance & Audit; Governance; CEO Performance & Compensation; Appointment Suggestions; Hall of Fame & Awards; Constitutional Review
Activities: Championships; camps; programs
Awards:
• Volunteer of the Year Award (Award)
Based on contributions from the previous curling season; national volunteer of the year receives an all-expense paid weekend trip to Nokia Brier or Scott Tournament of Hearts, where they will be recognized during a playoff game
• Award of Achievement (Award)
Commemorative plaque presented in recognition of individuals who have contributed significantly to any aspect of Canadian curling operations*Deadline:* March
• Ray Kingsmith Award (Award)
Awarded to an individual who parallels the level of involvement & commitment exemplified by Ray Kingsmith*Deadline:* March
• Board of Governor's Special Recognition Award (Award)
Awarded to an individual or organization who has significantly impacted Canadian curling through their contributions or achievements*Deadline:* December 31
• Eight Ender Awards (Award)
Awarded to teams who score Eight Enders *Amount:* Pins & Certificates

Canadian Curly Horse Association

PO Box 35, Sunnybrook AB T0C 2M0
Tel: 780-789-2125
curlys@sunnybrookstables.com
www.curlyhorse.ca
Overview: A small national organization founded in 1993
Mission: To promote hypo-allergenic curly horses & to gather together owners of curly horses to share knowledge & activities
Chief Officer(s):
Maureen Ivan, President, 403-450-7213
maureen.i@rockinhorsecurlies.ca
Membership: *Fees:* $35 Canadians; $45 Americans

Canadian Cutting Horse Association (CCHA)

RR#3, Innisfail AB T4G 1T8
Tel: 403-227-4444; *Fax:* 403-227-3030
www.ccha.ca
Overview: A small national organization founded in 1953
Mission: To promote the cutting horse, a specially trained horse to isolate or cut an individual animal from large cattle herds
Chief Officer(s):
Les Timmons, President, 250-573-5350
Jamie Couilliard, Vice-President, 403-247-3563
Connie Delorme, National Administrator
Geoff Thomas, Secretary-Treasurer, 403-347-6900
Finances: *Funding Sources:* Membership fees; Sponsorships
Activities: Hosting cutting horse competitions
Awards:
• CCHA Sportsmanship Award (Award)
Eligibility: Person must be an active youth, amateur, non-pro, or open competitor, who displays a positive attitude, kindness, & helpfulness in & around shows
Publications:
• The Canadian Cutter
Type: Newsletter
British Columbia
c/o Lynn Graham, 640 Lister Rd., Kamloops BC V2H 0B8
Tel: 250-578-8244; *Fax:* 250-578-8244
Chief Officer(s):
Campbell Garrard, President
Lynn Graham, Secretary
Saskatchewan
c/o Elaine Good, PO Box 1064, Fillmore SK S0G 1N0
Tel: 306-722-3643; *Fax:* 306-722-3643
Chief Officer(s):
Les Jack, President
Elaine Good, Secretary/Treasurer

Canadian Cycling Association ***See*** Cycling Canada Cyclisme

Canadian Cystic Fibrosis Foundation ***See*** Cystic Fibrosis Canada

Canadian Cytology Council ***See*** Canadian Society of Cytology

Canadian Daily Newspaper Association ***See*** Canadian Newspaper Association

Canadian Dairy Commission (CDC) / Commission canadienne du lait (CCL)

NCC Driveway, Bldg. 55, 960 Carling Ave., Ottawa ON K1A 0Z2
Tel: 613-792-2000; *Fax:* 613-792-2009; *TTY:* 613-792-2082
carole.cyr@cdc-ccl.gc.ca
www.cdc-ccl.gc.ca
Overview: A medium-sized national organization founded in 1966
Mission: To provide efficient producers of milk & cream with the opportunity of obtaining a fair return for their labour & investment; to provide consumers of dairy products with a continuous & adequate supply of high quality dairy products
Chief Officer(s):
Carole Cyr, Communications Officer
Staff Member(s): 65
Activities: Sets support prices for butter & skim milk powder which provincial authorities use to set milk prices for the domestic markets; develops policies & programs which meet the needs of the industry
Meetings/Conferences: • Canadian Dairy Commission Annual Public Meeting 2015, 2015
Scope: National

Canadian Dam Association (CDA) / Association canadienne des barrages (ACB)

PO Box 2281, Moose Jaw SK S6TH 7W6
www.cda.ca
Merged from: Canadian National Committee on Large Dams
Overview: A small national organization founded in 1989
Mission: To monitor the technical, environmental, social, economic, legal, & administrative aspects of dams in Canada; To ensure the safe operation of dams across Canada
Member of: Society of the Engineering Institute of Canada; International Commission on Large Dams
Chief Officer(s):
Wayne Phillips, Executive Director
Finances: *Funding Sources:* Membership fees; Conferences; Advertising
Membership: *Fees:* $5 students; $40 individuals; $350 corporate members; $700 corporate sponsors; *Member Profile:* Individuals, students, & corporations with an interest in dam safety, such as dam owners, engineers, technologists, researchers, government agencies, hydro companies, & equipment manufacturers & suppliers
Activities: Promoting the adoption of regulatory policies & safety guidelines for dams & reservoirs in Canada; Fostering inter-provincial cooperation; Offering education & outreach about dams
Awards:
• Inge Anderson Award of Merit (Award)
• Gary Salmon Memorial Scholarship (Scholarship)
• Peter Halliday Award for Service (Award)
• Published Paper Award of Excellence (Award)
• Research Award (Award)
• Student Achievement Award (Award)
• Meritorious Achievement Award (Award)
Meetings/Conferences: • Canadian Dam Association 2015 Annual Conference, October, 2015, Mississauga, ON
Scope: National
Description: Featuring technical paper presentations, workshops, tours, exhibitor presentations, & a social program
• Canadian Dam Association 2016 Annual Conference, October, 2016, Halifax, NS
Scope: National
Description: Featuring technical paper presentations, workshops, tours, exhibitor presentations, & a social program
Publications:
• Canadian Dam Association Bulletin
Type: Magazine; *Frequency:* Quarterly; *Accepts Advertising*; *Editor:* A. Kirkham (allan.kirkham@opg.com); *Price:* Free with membership in the Canadian Dam Association
Profile: Information from the Canadian Dam Association to help members remain informed about the association, the board, awards, conferences, & suppliers &buyers
• Dam Safety Guidelines
Type: Guidelines; *Number of Pages:* 82; *Price:* $60 each, plus GST, for CDA members; $100 each, plus GST, for non-members
Profile: A Canadian Dam Association publication, with a companion series of English language technical bulletins (235 pages)
• Dams in Canada
Type: CD; *Price:* $60 each, plus GST, for CDA members; $100 each, plus GST, for non-members
Profile: Featuring chapters, with photographs, drawings, & text, on water resources, water supply, irrigation, hydroelectric dams, & flood control dams, plus the Dams in Canada Register, with information about over 900dams

Canadian Dance Teachers' Association (CDTA) / Association canadienne des professeurs de danse

#38, 6033 Shawson Dr., Mississauga ON L5T 1H8
Tel: 905-564-2139; *Fax:* 905-564-2211
canadiandanceteachers@bellnet.ca
www.cdtanational.ca
www.facebook.com/236169423103547
Overview: A medium-sized national licensing organization founded in 1949
Mission: To advance education in the field of dance & maintain throughout Canada an organization of qualified dance teachers; to promote friendship & the exchange of ideas & information among the dance teachers of Canada, to provide an organization to represent Canadian dance teachers internationally
Member of: World Dance & Dancesport Council
Chief Officer(s):
Sue Romeril, President
Finances: *Annual Operating Budget:* Less than $50,000
Staff Member(s): 1
Membership: 1,000-4,999; *Member Profile:* Professional dancers, owners of dance schools, professional dance teachers;
Committees: Executive; Division for each: Ballet, Ballroom, International Folk Dance, Scottish Dance Arts, Stage including Tap, Jazz, Baton & Acrobatics
Activities: Member teachers offer lessons in ballroom, ballet, tap, jazz, acrobatics, baton, Scottish dance arts, modern & national dancing

Alberta Branch
c/o President, 14 Dumas Cres., Red Deer AB T4R 2S1
Tel: 403-346-6333
albertacdta@shaw.ca
www.albertacdta.ca
Chief Officer(s):
Julie Dionne, President

British Columbia Branch
PO Box 31547, Pitt Meadows BC V3Y 2G7
e-mail: bcdta2009@gmail.com
www.cdtabc.com
Chief Officer(s):
Steve Nikleva, President
snikleva@shaw.ca

Ontario Branch
#38, 6603 Shawson Dr., Mississauga ON L5T 1H8
Tel: 905-564-2139; *Fax:* 905-564-2211
canadiandanceteachers@bellnet.ca
cdtaont.com
www.facebook.com/236169423103547
Chief Officer(s):
Sue Romeril, President

Québec Branch
QC

Saskatchewan Branch
c/o President, PO Box 1402, Humboldt SK S0K 2A0
Tel: 306-682-2635; *Fax:* 306-585-1634
cdtaskbranch@hotmail.com
www.cdtaskbranch.com
Mission: To promote interaction between dance teachers & through this exchange improve the standard for dancing & teaching
Chief Officer(s):
Paula Puetz, President

Canadian Day Care Advocacy Association ***See*** Child Care Advocacy Association of Canada

Canadian Deaf Curling Association (CDCA) / Association de Curling des Sourdes du Canada

Edmonton AB
Fax: 780-437-1808; *TTY:* 780-437-1808
Other Communication: Vancouver, TTY: 604-576-8141; Fax: 604-576-8125
www.deafcurlcanada.org
Also Known As: Deaf Curl Canada
Overview: A small national organization overseen by Canadian Deaf Sports Association
Mission: To provide deaf & hard of hearing curlers with opportunities across Canada.
Member of: Canadian Deaf Sports Association; Canadian Curling Association
Affliation(s): British Columbia Deaf Sports Federation; Alberta Deaf Curling Association; Saskatchewan Deaf Sports Association; Manitoba Deaf Curling Association; Ontario Deaf Curling Assocation; Association de Curling des Sourds du Quebec; Nova Scotia Deaf Curling Association
Chief Officer(s):
Bradford Bentley, President, 250-539-3264
president-cdca@shaw.ca
Allard Thomas, Vice-President, 306-565-8420
vice-pres-cdca@att.biz
Susanne Beriault, Secretary
cdca-secretary@gmail.com
David Pickard, Treasurer
dpickard@telus.net
Dean Sutton, Chief Technical Director
curlingtd@shaw.ca

Canadian Deaf Golf Association (CDGA) / Association Canadienne de Golf des Sourds

c/o Roger Beernink, Treasurer, 3575 Settlement Trail, London ON N6P 0A8
www.deafgolf.ca
Overview: A small national organization overseen by Canadian Deaf Sports Association
Mission: To aid in the development of leadership & golfing skills among deaf golfers across Canada.
Member of: Canadian Deaf Sports Association
Chief Officer(s):
Dana McCarthy, President
dhmccarthy@teksavvy.com
Peter Mitchell, Vice-President
pmitchell25@rogers.com
Rob Cundy, Secretary
robcundy@telus.net
Roger Beernink, Treasurer
rbeernink@sympatico.ca
Aurele Bourgeois, Director
abourgeois10@cogeco.ca
Membership: *Fees:* $10

Canadian Deaf Ice Hockey Federation (CDIHF)

c/o C. Cooper, #137, 201 Queen Victoria Dr., Hamilton ON L8W 1W7
e-mail: cdihf@rogers.com
www.cdihf.deafhockey.com
www.facebook.com/group.php?gid=152070790142
Previous Name: Canadian Hearing Impaired Hockey Association
Overview: A small national charitable organization founded in 1983 overseen by Canadian Deaf Sports Association
Mission: To offer ice hockey programs for deaf & hard of hearing participants; To administer a hockey team to represent Canada internationally
Member of: Canadian Deaf Sports Association
Affliation(s): Canadian Hockey Association; Ontario Deaf Sports Association, Inc.
Chief Officer(s):
Roy Hysen, Executive Director
Finances: *Funding Sources:* Donations; Sponsorships
Activities: Hosting training camps & hockey schools; Organizing the CDIHC Hockey Championships; Participating in the World Deaf Ice Hockey Championship;

Canadian Deaf Sports Association (CDSA) / Association des sports des sourds du Canada (ASSC)

#202A, 10217 Pie IX Blvd., Montréal QC H1H 3Z5
Tel: 514-321-8686; *Fax:* 514-321-8349; *TTY:* 514-321-2937
info@assc-cdsa.com
www.assc-cdsa.com
www.facebook.com/assc.cdsa
twitter.com/ASSC_CDSA
Overview: A medium-sized national licensing charitable organization founded in 1964
Mission: To promote & facilitate the practice of fitness, amateur sports & recreation among deaf people of all ages in Canada from the local recreational level to Olympics calibre.
Member of: Canadian Deaf & Hard of Hearing Forum; Canadian Paralympic Committee; Canadian Sports Coalition.
Affliation(s): International Committee of Sports for the Deaf
Chief Officer(s):
Craig Noonan, Chief Executive Officer

Ghysline "Gigi" Fiset, Manager, Operational Services & Events
Mark Kusiak, President
Staff Member(s): 3
Membership: *Committees:* Finance; Communications; Governance; Human Resources

Canadian Deafblind & Rubella Association (Ontario Chapter) Inc. ***See*** Canadian Deafblind Association (National)

Canadian Deafblind Association (National) (CDBA) / Association canadienne de la surdicécité (Bureau National)

2000 Appleby Line, Burlington ON L7L 7H7
Fax: 905-319-2027
Toll-Free: 866-229-5832
info@cdbanational.com
www.cdbanational.com
www.facebook.com/cdbanational
twitter.com/CDBANational
Overview: A medium-sized national charitable organization
Mission: To promote awareness, education & support for people who are deafblind, in order to enhance their well-being
Chief Officer(s):
Carolyn Monaco, President
carolyn.monaco@sympatico.ca
Tom McFadden, National Executive Director

Alberta Chapter
McKenzie Towne SE, PO Box 89006, Calgary AB T2Z 3W3
Tel: 403-248-2154; *Fax:* 403-249-0935
info@deafblindalberta.ca
www.deafblindalberta.ca
Chief Officer(s):
Allen Wayne Turnbull, President

British Columbia Chapter
227 - 6th St., New Westminster BC V3L 3A5
Tel: 604-528-6170; *Fax:* 604-528-6174
bcinfo@cdbabc.ca
www.cdbabc.ca
Chief Officer(s):
Theresa Tancock, Coordinator, Family Services
theresa@cdbabc.ca

Canadian Deafblind Association - New Brunswick Inc.
#408, 212 Queen St., Fredericton NB E3B 1A8
Tel: 506-452-1544; *Fax:* 506-451-8309
office@cdba-nb.ca
www.cdba-nb.ca
www.facebook.com/118342648217036
Chief Officer(s):
Alma Page, President

Manitoba Chapter
307 Devon St., Winnipeg MB R2G 0C4
Tel: 204-949-3730; *Fax:* 204-949-3732
operations@cdba.com
Chief Officer(s):
Sandy Owczar, Executive Director

Ontario Chapter
50 Main St., Paris ON N3L 2E2
Tel: 519-442-0463; *Fax:* 519-442-1871
Toll-Free: 877-760-7439; *TTY:* 519-442-6641
info@cdbaontario.com
www.cdbaontario.com
www.facebook.com/cdbaontario
twitter.com/CDBAOntario
Mission: Provides support and services to individuals who are deafblind and their families throughout the province.
Chief Officer(s):
Devin Shyminsky, Coordinator, Communications
dshyminsky@cdbaontario.com

Saskatchewan Chapter
83 Tucker Cres., Saskatoon SK S7H 3H7
Tel: 306-374-0022; *Fax:* 306-374-0004
cdba.sk@shaw.ca
Chief Officer(s):
Lorraine Williams, Executive Director

Canadian Deals & Coupons Association (CDCA)

Toronto ON
Toll-Free: 888-958-2948
info@canadiandealsassociation.com
www.canadiandealsassociation.com
www.linkedin.com/company/canadian-deals-association
www.facebook.com/CanadianDealsandCouponAssociation
twitter.com/DealsCouponsCAN
Overview: A large national organization founded in 2010
Mission: To provide services to companies in the retail industry, in order to promote specials & coupons.
Membership: *Member Profile:* Coupon providers; Distributors; Retailers; Manufacturers; Technology & Service providers; Industry Individuals

Canadian Defence Industries Association ***See*** Canadian Association of Defence & Security Industries

Canadian Dental Assistants Association (CDAA) / Association canadienne des assistants(es) dentaires (ACAD)

#202, 110 Clarence St., Ottawa ON K1N 5P6
Tel: 613-521-5495; *Fax:* 613-521-5572
Toll-Free: 800-345-5137
info@cdaa.ca
www.cdaa.ca
twitter.com/CDAA_ACAD
Overview: A medium-sized national organization founded in 1945
Mission: Strives to foster opportunities for growth, to be the voice for Canadian dental assistants, & to represent the interests of provincial & military dental associations
Chief Officer(s):
Calla Effa, President
Michelle Fowler, Vice-President
Finances: *Funding Sources:* Transfer fees from provincial associations
Staff Member(s): 2
Membership: 7
Activities: Government relations; Advocacy; Knowledge & Research; *Awareness Events:* Dental Assistants Week, March
Publications:
- The CDAA Journal
Type: Journal; *Frequency:* Semiannually; *Number of Pages:* 32; *Price:* $45 Canada; $50 USA; #60 international
Profile: Articles, information, & services for individuals involved in the dental assisting profession

Canadian Dental Association (CDA) / L'Association dentaire canadienne (ADC)

1815 Alta Vista Dr., Ottawa ON K1G 3Y6
Tel: 613-523-1770; *Fax:* 613-523-7736
reception@cda-adc.ca
www.cda-adc.ca
www.facebook.com/pages/Canadian-Dental-Health/2034526896 66842
twitter.com/mydentalhealth
Overview: A large national organization founded in 1902
Mission: The authoritative national voice of dentistry, dedicated to the representation & advancement of the profession, nationally & internationally, & to the achievement of optimum oral health
Affiliation(s): FDI World Dental Federation
Chief Officer(s):
Peter Doig, President
Staff Member(s): 35
Membership: 15000+; *Fees:* $512.53
Activities: *Awareness Events:* National Oral Health Month, April; *Library:* Sydney Wood Bradley Memorial Library; by appointment
Awards:
- Medal of Honour (Award)
- Honourary Membership Award (Award)
- Distinguished Service Award (Award)
- Award of Merit (Award)
- Oral Health Promotion Award (Award)
- Special Friend of Canadian Dentistry Award (Award)

Publications:
- Canadian Dental Association Member News
Type: Newsletter
- CD Alert [a publication of the Canadian Dental Association]
Type: Newsletter
Profile: Industry trends, best practices, & timely information
- Dentistry News
Type: Newsletter
- Directory of Dental Regulatory Authorities & Provincial / Territorial Associations
Type: Directory
Profile: Listing of contact information
- Highlights Reports [a publication of the Canadian Dental Association]
- Journal of the Canadian Dental Association (JCDA)
Type: Journal; *Frequency:* 11 pa; *Editor:* John O'Keefe
Profile: National, peer-reviewed, science-based, clinical practice information available in both paper & electronic format

Canadian Dental Hygienists Association (CDHA) / Association canadienne des hygiènistes dentaires

96 Centrepointe Dr., Ottawa ON K2G 6B1
Tel: 613-224-5515; *Fax:* 613-224-7283
Toll-Free: 800-267-5235
info@cdha.ca
www.cdha.ca
www.facebook.com/theCDHA
twitter.com/theCDHA
Overview: A medium-sized national licensing organization founded in 1964
Mission: To act as the collective voice of dental hygiene in Canada; to advance the profession in support of our members; to contribute to the health & well-being of the public.
Chief Officer(s):
Ondina Love, Executive Director
olove@cdha.ca
Finances: *Funding Sources:* Membership fees
Staff Member(s): 18
Membership: 17,000; *Fees:* Schedule available; *Member Profile:* Dental hygienists - academics & clinicians
Activities: National standards; education reform; code of ethics; *Library* Open to public

Canadian Dental Protective Association (CDOA)

#300, 1100 Burloak Dr., Burlington ON L7L 6B2
Tel: 416-491-5932; *Fax:* 416-239-3443
Toll-Free: 800-876-2372
info@cdpa.com
www.cdpa.com
Overview: A medium-sized national organization founded in 1994
Mission: The CDPA operates a mutual benefit Assistance Program funded entirely by membership dues and is not affiliated with any insurance carriers.
Chief Officer(s):
Rollin Matsui, Executive Director
Robert Katz, President
Harvey Taub, Treasurer
Finances: *Funding Sources:* Membership fees
Staff Member(s): 1; 6 volunteer(s)
Membership: 1,200; *Fees:* $995.20

Canadian Dental Therapists Association (CDTA)

87 Brookland St., Antigonish NS B2G 1W1
e-mail: admin@dental-therapists.com
wwww.dental-therapists.com
www.facebook.com/410493672365099
Overview: A medium-sized national organization founded in 1972
Mission: To cultivate, promote, & sustain the art & science of dental therapy; To maintain the honour & interests of the dental therapy profession; To contribute toward the improvement to the health of the public
Chief Officer(s):
Sajiev Thomas, Contact, Atlantic Canada
sajiev@dental-therapists.com
Sherri Scott, Contact, Manitoba
sherri@dental-therapists.com
Breanda Isaac, Contact, BC
brenda@dental-therapists.com

Canadian Depression Glass Association (CDGA)

PO Box 41564, Stn. HLRPO, 230 Sandalwood Pkwy., Brampton ON L6Z 4R1
Tel: 905-846-2835
www.waltztime.com/CDGA/index.html
Overview: A large international organization founded in 1976
Mission: The voice for Canadian collectors & dealers of Depression Glass; members across Canada & the U.S.
Chief Officer(s):
Walter Lemiski, Contact
walt@waltztime.com
Membership: *Fees:* $20; $50 for three years
Publications:
- Canadian Depression Glass Review
Type: Journal
Profile: Articles, dealer & shop directory, show notices, ads for buyers & sellers, glass book reviews, & member letters

Canadian Depression Research & Intervention Network (CDRIN)

The Royal Ottawa Mental Health Centre, #5412, 1145 Carling Ave., Ottawa ON K1Z 7K4
e-mail: info@cdrin.org
cdrin.org

Overview: A medium-sized national organization founded in 2013
Mission: A collaborative cross-Canada network with the mission to create and share knowledge that leads to more effective prevention, early diagnosis, and treatment of depression and depression-linked illnesses.
Affliation(s): Mood Disorders Society of Canada; Mental Health Commission of Canada
Chief Officer(s):
Zul Merali, Scientific Director, 613-722-6521 Ext. 6551, Fax: 613-792-3935
Phil Upshall, Chief Financial Officer, 519-824-5565, Fax: 519-824-9569
Finances: *Funding Sources:* Federal funding
Meetings/Conferences: • Canadian Depression Research and Intervention Network Conference 2015, February, 2015, Ottawa Convention Centre, Ottawa, ON
Scope: National
Attendance: 300

Canadian Dermatology Association (CDA) / Association canadienne de dermatologie (ACD)

#425, 1385 Bank St., Ottawa ON K1H 8N4
Tel: 613-738-1748; *Fax:* 613-738-4695
Toll-Free: 800-267-3376
info@dermatology.ca
www.dermatology.ca
www.facebook.com/CdnDermatology
twitter.com/cdndermatology
Overview: A medium-sized national organization founded in 1925
Mission: To advance the science of medicine & surgery related to the health of the skin; To support & advance patient care; To represent dermatologists in Canada
Affliation(s): Canadian Medical Association; American Academy of Dermatology
Chief Officer(s):
Gordon Searles, President
Chantal Courchesne, Executive Director
ccourchesne@dermatology.ca
Mariusz Sapijaszko, Secretary
Victoria Taraska, Treasurer
Jennifer Scott, Director, Communications
jscott@dermatology.ca
Finances: *Funding Sources:* Membership fees; Sponsorships
Staff Member(s): 10
Membership: *Fees:* Free for residents, fellows, life members, & honorary members; $200 international members; $225 associate members; $325 dematologist members; *Member Profile:* Dermatologists who have received certification from the Royal College of Physicians & Surgeons of Canada, or a diploma from the American Board of Dermatology; International members who are practicing dermatologist in any country other than Canada & the United States; Residents & fellows; Associate members who are interested in dermatology
Activities: Providing continuing medical education for members; Offering public education on diseases of the skin, hair, & nails; Increasing awareness about sun safety & other aspects of skin care (e-mail: educational.material@dermatology.ca); Presenting awards for educational & professional accomplishments (e-mail: info@dermatology.ca); *Awareness Events:* National Sun Awareness Week; *Library:* The Robert Jackson Library & Archives
Awards:
• Public Education Award (Award)
Entries accepted in the categories of not-for-profit organizations, industry, & media (print, radio, & television) *Contact:* Dr. Benjamin Barankin, Secretary & Chair, c/o CDA Awards Committee, #425, 1385 Bank St., Ottawa, ON K1H 8N4
• Edwin Brown - Canadian Dermatology Association Endowment Fund (Grant)
Awarded to a researcher *Contact:* Dr. Benjamin Barankin, Secretary & Chair, c/o CDA Awards Committee, #425, 1385 Bank St., Ottawa, ON K1H 8N4
• Award of Honour (Award)
Open to persons, who are not members of the medical profession *Contact:* Dr. Benjamin Barankin, Secretary & Chair, c/o CDA Awards Committee, #425, 1385 Bank St., Ottawa, ON K1H 8N4
• Young Dermatologists' Volunteer Award (Award)
To recognize a young Canadian Dermatology Association member, in private practice, who offers volunteer medical & dermatological services to the community *Contact:* Dr. Benjamin Barankin, Secretary & Chair, c/o CDA Awards Committee, #425, 1385 Bank St., Ottawa, ON K1H 8N4
• Barney Usher Research Award in Dermatology (Award)
To honour a Canadian Dermatology Association member who submits the best manuscript for original work relevant to dermatology *Contact:* Dr. Benjamin Barankin, Secretary & Chair, c/o CDA Awards Committee, #425, 1385 Bank St., Ottawa, ON K1H 8N4
• Award of Merit (Award)
To recognize a Canadian Dermatology Association member for excellence in leadership & excellence in contributions made to the Canadian Dermatology Association *Contact:* Dr. Benjamin Barankin, Secretary & Chair, c/o CDA Awards Committee, #425, 1385 Bank St., Ottawa, ON K1H 8N4
• President's Cup (Award)
Presented to a recipient, selected by the Canadian Dermatology Association president, in recognition of assistance to the president &/or the association *Contact:* Dr. Benjamin Barankin, Secretary & Chair, c/o CDA Awards Committee, #425, 1385 Bank St., Ottawa, ON K1H 8N4
Meetings/Conferences: • Canadian Dermatology Association 2015 90th Annual Conference, June, 2015, Vancouver, BC
Scope: National
Description: Oral & poster presentations on subjects relevant to practicing dermatologists
• Canadian Dermatology Association 2016 91st Annual Conference, 2016
Scope: National
Description: Oral & poster presentations on subjects relevant to practicing dermatologists
• Canadian Dermatology Association 2016 91st Annual Conference, 2016
Scope: National
Description: An educational experience with exhibits, networking opportunities, & the presentation of awards
Publications:
• Canadian Dermatology Association Bulletin
Type: Newsletter; *Frequency:* 3 pa; *Price:* Free with membership in the Canadian DermatologyAssociation
Profile: CDA activities, articles of personal & professional interest, political reports, & news from regional dermatologic associations
• Canadian Dermatology Association Membership & Corporate Directory
Type: Directory; *Frequency:* Annually; *Price:* Free with membership in the Canadian Dermatology Association
• Journal of Cutaneous Medicine & Surgery
Type: Journal; *Accepts Advertising*; *Editor:* Dr. Jason Rivers; *Price:* Free with membership in the Canadian Dermatology Association
Profile: Reviews, basic & clinical science articles, editorials, case reports, & letters to the editor

Canadian Dexter Cattle Association (CDCA) / Société canadienne des bovins Dexter

2417 Holly Lane, Ottawa ON K1V 0M7
Tel: 613-731-7110; *Fax:* 613-731-0704
ron.black@clrc.ca
www.dextercattle.ca
Overview: A medium-sized national organization founded in 1986
Mission: To preserve & promote the breeding of good quality Dexter cattle in Canada
Affliation(s): Canadian Livestock Records Corporation
Chief Officer(s):
Ron Black, Secretary
Glorianne Bjerland, President
gmbjerland@sasktel.net
Finances: *Annual Operating Budget:* Less than $50,000; *Funding Sources:* Membership dues; Registration fees
7 volunteer(s)
Membership: 100; *Fees:* $50; *Committees:* Marketing & Promotion; Newsletter; Classification; Constitution
Publications:
• Dexter Cattle in Canada
Frequency: Annually
Profile: A herd book of the Dexter breed

Canadian Diabetes Association (CDA) / Association canadienne du diabète

#1400, 522 University Ave., Toronto ON M5G 2R5
Tel: 416-363-3373; *Fax:* 416-363-7465
Toll-Free: 800-226-8464
Other Communication: Donations e-mail: donation@diabetes.ca
info@diabetes.ca
www.diabetes.ca
www.facebook.com/CanadianDiabetesAssociation
twitter.com/DiabetesAssoc
www.youtube.com/user/CDA1927
Overview: A large national charitable organization founded in 1953
Mission: To advance the welfare of Canadians with diabetes; to support research into the causes, complications, treatment, & cure of diabetes; To promote & strengthen services for people affected by diabetes & their families; To work with health professionals to improve standards in care the & treatment of diabetes; To develop guidelines for diabetes education in Canada; To promote the rights of Canadians affected by diabetes in an effort to bring about positive change in the areas of public awareness, government policy, health policy issues, & employment
Member of: International Diabetes Federation
Affliation(s): Association du diabète du Québec
Chief Officer(s):
Suzanne Deuel, Chair
Rick Blickstead, President & CEO
Walter Kurz, CFO & Vice-President, Organizational Excellence & Shared Services, 416-408-7010
Aileen Leo, Executive Directpr, Government Relations & Public Affairs
Aileen.Leo@diabetes.ca
Janelle Robertson, Vice-President, Business Operations, 709-747-4598
Jovita Sundaramoorthy, Vice-President, Research & Education, 416-408-7090
Finances: *Funding Sources:* Donations; Government; Services; Support from charities; National Diabetes Trust
2000 volunteer(s)
Membership: *Fees:* $100 active clinical; $90 professional regular/associate; $45 student; $29.95 classic; $25 clinical trainee; *Member Profile:* Regular membership open to anyone;Pprofessional members come from educational, research & clinical care fields
Activities: *Awareness Events:* Diabetes Month, November; *Speaker Service:* Yes; *Library:* Resource Centre; Open to public by appointment
Meetings/Conferences: • 18th Annual Canadian Diabetes Association Professional Conference & Annual Meeting 2015, 2015
Scope: National
Contact Information: Sonia Morgan; Phone: 416-408-7205; professional.conference@diabetes.ca
Publications:
• Beyond the Basics [a publication of the Canadian Diabetes Association]
Profile: Series of manuals based on CDA's clinical practice guidelines & current scientific evidence, including the Meal Planning Resource & the Healthy LifestyleResource
• Canadian Diabetes [a publication of the Canadian Diabetes Association]
Frequency: Quarterly; *Editor:* Sara Meltzer; *Price:* Free to general practitioners inCanada & members of the CDA's Professional Sections
Profile: Practical, state-of-the-art information about clinical care & diabetes management issues for family physicians
• Canadian Diabetes Clinical & Scientific Section (C&SS) Connect [a publication of the Canadian Diabetes Association]
Type: Newsletter; *Frequency:* Quarterly; *Number of Pages:* 4; *Editor:* Sara J. Meltzer
• Canadian Journal of Diabetes (CJD) [a publication of the Canadian Diabetes Association]
Frequency: Quarterly; *Editor:* David C.W. Lau; *Price:* $40
Profile: Peer-reviewed, interdisciplinary journal for diabetes healthcare professionals, including articles, news from the Clinical &Scientific Section & the Diabetes Educators Section of the Canadian Diabetes Association, & resource reviews
• CDA [Canadian Diabetes Association] Annual Report
Frequency: Annually
• The Diabetes Communicator [a publication of the Canadian Diabetes Association]
Type: Newsletter; *Number of Pages:* 16; *Editor:* Colleen Rand
Profile: Information on the Diabetes Educator Section
• Diabetes Current [a publication of the Canadian Diabetes Association]
Type: Newsletter
Profile: E-newsletter containing information on association news, research, medical breakthroughs & more
• Diabetes Dialogue [a publication of the Canadian Diabetes Association]
Type: Magazine; *Frequency:* Quarterly; *Price:* $29.95
Profile: Information about research, medical updates, nutrition, exercise, lifestyle management, & resources

• Pacesetter [a publication of the Canadian Diabetes Association]
Type: Newsletter
Profile: E-newsletter for Team Diabetes members, featuring information about upcoming marathon events, news, training & fundraising tips, & human intereststories

Calgary & District Branch
#204, 2323 - 32 Ave. NE, Calgary AB T2E 6Z3
Tel: 403-266-0620; *Fax:* 403-269-8927

Edmonton & District Branch
Royal Bank Bldg., #100, 12220 Stony Plain Rd., Edmonton AB T5N 3Y4
Tel: 780-423-1232; *Fax:* 780-423-3322
Toll-Free: 800-563-0032

GTA Regional Leadership Centre
#1400, 522 University Ave., Toronto ON M5G 2R5
Tel: 905-540-2510; *Fax:* 416-363-7465
Chief Officer(s):
Kerry Bruder, Regional Director

Manitoba & Nunavut Regional Leadership Centre
#200, 310 Broadway, Winnipeg MB R3C 0S6
Tel: 204-925-3800; *Fax:* 204-949-0266
Chief Officer(s):
Linda Berg, Regional Director

New Brunswick Region
#2, 61 Carleton St., Fredericton NB E3B 3T2
Tel: 506-452-9009; *Fax:* 506-455-4728
Toll-Free: 800-884-4232
Chief Officer(s):
Lisa Matte, Regional Director, Martimes
lisa.matte@diabetes.ca

Newfoundland & Labrador Regional Leadership Centre
#2007, 29-31 Pippy Pl., St. John's NL A1B 3X2
Tel: 709-754-0953; *Fax:* 709-754-0734
Chief Officer(s):
Carol Ann Smith, Regional Director
carolann.smith@diabetes.ca

North Saskatchewan Regional Leadership Centre
#104, 2301 Ave. C North, Saskatoon SK S7L 5Z5
Tel: 306-933-1238; *Fax:* 306-244-2012
Toll-Free: 800-996-4446

Nova Scotia Diabetes Supply Centre
#101, 137 Chain Lake Dr., Halifax NS B3S 1B3
Tel: 902-453-4232; *Fax:* 902-453-4440
Toll-Free: 800-326-7712
Chief Officer(s):
Lisa Matte, Regional Director, Martimes
lisa.matte@diabetes.ca

Ottawa & District Branch
45 Montreal Rd., Ottawa ON K1L 6E8
Tel: 613-521-1902; *Fax:* 613-521-3667

Prince Edward Island Region
Sherwood Business Centre, 161 St. Peter's Rd., Charlottetown PE C1A 5P7
Tel: 902-894-3195; *Fax:* 902-368-1928
Chief Officer(s):
Lisa Matte, Regional Director, Martimes
lisa.matte@diabetes.ca

Canadian Diamond Drilling Association (CDDA)
City Centre Building, #337, 101 Worthington St. East, North Bay ON P1B 1G5
Tel: 705-476-6992; *Fax:* 705-476-9494
office@cdda.ca
www.canadiandrilling.com
Previous Name: Canadian Drilling Association
Overview: A medium-sized national organization founded in 1938
Mission: To foster the commercial interests of members; to promote the simplifications, standardization & interchangeability of diamond drilling equipment; to recognize the safety & health of employees; to foster the protection of the natural environment; to secure the elimination of unfair or uneconomic practices within the industry & freedom from unjust or unlawful exactions; to establish & maintain uniformity & equity in the customs & commercial usages of the diamond drilling business; to acquire & disseminate valuable business information; to promote communication among those engaged in the industry
Member of: National Drilling Association; Canadian Association of Mining Equipment & Services for Export; Prospectors & Developers Association of Canada
Chief Officer(s):
Louise Lowe, Manager, 705-476-6992
Finances: *Annual Operating Budget:* $50,000-$100,000; *Funding Sources:* Membership dues
Staff Member(s): 1
Membership: 100; *Fees:* $100 individual; $500 associate; $1,000-$5,100 active member
Activities: *Rents Mailing List:* Yes

Canadian Die Casters Association (CDCA) / Association canadienne des mouleurs sous pression
#3, 247 Barr St., Renfrew ON K7V 1J6
Fax: 613-432-6840
Toll-Free: 866-809-7032
info@diecasters.ca
www.diecasters.ca
Overview: A small national organization founded in 1980
Mission: To assist die casters in dealing with governments & other organizations on industry issues; To provide a united voice for members
Chief Officer(s):
Bonnie James, Executive Director
Murray Abramovitch, President
murray@diecasters.ca
Yahia Reguieg, Vice-President
yahia@diecasters.ca
Danny Di Liello, Treasurer
dannyd@diecasters.ca
Membership: *Member Profile:* Canadian die casters
Activities: Conducting annual meetings, trade shows, & workshops
Publications:
• The Canadian Die Caster
Type: Magazine; *Frequency:* Semiannually
Profile: Information for members about the die casting industry in Canada
• Die Casting in Canada Manual & Directory
Type: Directory; *Frequency:* Biennially; *Accepts Advertising*; *Price:* $30
Profile: Profile of the die casting industry in Canada, including market services & capabilities, suppliers who support the industry, & alloy charts

Canadian Dietetic Association *See* Dietitians of Canada

Canadian Digestive Health Foundation (CDHF) / Fondation canadienne for la promotion de la santé digestive
PO Box 76059, #3, 1500 Upper Middle Rd., Oakville ON L6M 3H5
Tel: 905-829-3949
www.cdhf.ca
www.linkedin.com/company/649009
www.facebook.com/CDHFdn
twitter.com/TheCDHF
www.youtube.com/user/CDHFtube
Overview: A medium-sized national charitable organization founded in 1994 overseen by Canadian Association of Gastroenterology
Mission: To raise funds for the protection, promotion, & improvement of digestive health
Chief Officer(s):
Catherine Mulvale, Executive Director
Richard Fedorak, President
Finances: *Funding Sources:* Donations; Government funding; Corporate sponsors
Staff Member(s): 3
Publications:
• Canadian Digestive Health Foundation Newsletter
Type: Newsletter
Profile: Current information from digestive health experts across Canada

Canadian Direct Marketing Association *See* Canadian Marketing Association

Canadian Disaster Child Care Society (CDCC)
329 - 30th Ave. South, Cranbrook BC V1C 3K8
Tel: 250-489-0036; *Fax:* 250-489-0038
disasterchildcare@shaw.ca
www.members.shaw.ca/disasterchildcare
Overview: A small national organization
Mission: Trains volunteers to provide specialized childcare that focuses on using play to help children work through their feelings and regain control over their environment following a disaster
Activities: Has worked following the Montreal Ice Storm; with Kosovar children who came to Canada under Operation Parasol

Canadian Disaster Restoration Group (CDRG)
#5, 1084 Kenaston Rd., Ottawa ON K1B 3P5
Tel: 613-736-9222; *Fax:* 613-736-1002
Toll-Free: 866-736-9222
storm@cdrg.ca
www.cdrg.ca
www.linkedin.com/groups/Design-Rebuild-Rebuilding-your-Environment-120
www.facebook.com/117026655044784
twitter.com/CDRG_RedTeam
Overview: A medium-sized national organization founded in 2004
Mission: To provide disaster restoration services through their network of member companies across Canada
Chief Officer(s):
Simon Frigon, Founder & CEO
Melissa Baker, Director, Communications
Membership: 60+

The Canadian Don't Do Drugs Society
PO Box 1053, 7B Pleasant Blvd., Toronto ON M4T 1K2
Tel: 416-923-3779; *Fax:* 416-923-0083
Toll-Free: 800-883-7761
www.skddd.org
www.linkedin.com/company/2802976?trk
www.facebook.com/pages/Smart-Kids-Dont-Do-Drugs/320662668026184
twitter.com/SKDDD_SmartKidz
www.youtube.com/watch?v=4RvPwoWY_e4&feature=youtu.be
Also Known As: Smart Kids Don't Do Drugs
Overview: A small national charitable organization founded in 1994
Mission: To aide children & parents in the fight against the ravages of drugs in our society
Chief Officer(s):
Robert O'Reilly, Executive Director
robert@smartkidz.org
Finances: *Annual Operating Budget:* $100,000-$250,000
Staff Member(s): 10

Canadian Donkey & Mule Association (CDMA)
PO Box 12716, Lloydminster AB T7V 0Y4
Tel: 780-875-6362
donkeyandmule@live.ca
www.donkeyandmule.com
Overview: A small national organization founded in 1976
Mission: To operate registry for donkeys & recordation for mules; to promote use, well-being & protection of donkeys & mules; to assist in training & placing donkeys for disabled riding.
Affliation(s): American Donkey & Mule Society; British Donkey Breed Society; Breed Societies of Britain, Australia, Sweden, Holland, Germany, New Zealand
Chief Officer(s):
Chris Schlosser, Secretary
kindatinyfarms@telus.net
Kim Baerg, President
kimbaerg@hotmail.com
Finances: *Funding Sources:* Membership dues & charity auction
Membership: *Fees:* $20 junior; $40 single; $50 family; $50 foreign; *Member Profile:* Owner, breeder, manager, or supporter of donkeys & mules

The Canadian Doukhobor Society (CDS)
215 - 33 Ave. South, Creston BC V0G 1G1
Tel: 250-204-2931
spirit-wrestlers.com/CDS
Overview: A small national charitable organization founded in 1930
Mission: To promote brotherhood, universal peace & the spiritual growth of our members
Member of: Council of Doukhobors in Canada
Chief Officer(s):
Beth Terriff, Secretary-Treasurer
Alex Wishlow, President
awishlow@kootenay.com
Finances: *Funding Sources:* Membership donations
Membership: *Member Profile:* Groups & organizations who respect Doukhobor ideals & principles as stated in statute

Canadian Dove Association (CDA)
c/o John House, PO Box 135, Plattsville ON N0J 1S0
canadiandoveassociation.weebly.com
Overview: A small national organization founded in 1977
Mission: To better inform fanciers about dove & foreign pigeons of the world
Member of: Avicultural Advancement Council of Canada
Chief Officer(s):

John House, Secretary-Treasurer
David House, President
Finances: *Funding Sources:* Membership dues; donations
Membership: *Fees:* $7 junior; $25 family/senior; $40 international
Activities: Propagation to prevent extinction

Canadian Down Syndrome Society (CDSS) / Société canadienne du syndrome de Down

#103, 2003 - 14 St. NW, Calgary AB T2M 3N4
Tel: 403-270-8500; *Fax:* 403-270-8291
info@cdss.ca
www.cdss.ca
www.facebook.com/cdndownsyndrome
twitter.com/CdnDownSyndrome
Overview: A medium-sized national charitable organization founded in 1987
Mission: To ensure equitable opportunities for all Canadians with Down syndrome7
Chief Officer(s):
Kevin Whyte, Board Chair
Kirk Crowther, Executive Director
Jonathan A. Bateman, Coordinator, Event & Fund Development
Kaitlyn Pecson, Coordinator, Design & Communication
Ashlee Stone, Coordinator, Advocacy Research
Finances: *Funding Sources:* Health Canada; Grants; Donations; Membership
43 volunteer(s)
Membership: 1,400; *Fees:* $20 individual/family; $40 group; *Member Profile:* Families & individuals with Down syndrome; Educators; Medical professionals; *Committees:* Resource Council (Medical & Educational); National Funding; Public Awareness; Fund Raising; Membership; Adult Issues; Nominating
Activities: Providing information & education; Researching; Engaging in advocacy activities; Increasing public awareness; Offering family support & networking; Working in collaboration with other local groups & national organizations toward the realization of common objectives; *Awareness Events:* National Down Syndrome Awareness Week, November; *Library:* Resource Centre & Library; by appointment
Meetings/Conferences: • Canadian Down Syndrome Society 2015 28th National Conference, May, 2015, Edmonton, AB
Scope: National
Publications:
• Canadian Down Syndrome Society Newsletter
Type: Newsletter; *Frequency:* Quarterly
• CDSS Calendar
Frequency: Annually
• CDSS Information Series
Profile: Topics include Teaching Children with Down Syndrome, Toilet Training Your Child with Down Syndrome, Stubborn Behaviour, Registered Educational Savings Plan, Taxation, Wills & Trusts, Obstructive SleepApnea Syndrome, & Stop Running by Building Skills: Behavioural Approach

Canadian Dressage Owners & Riders Association

c/o Donald J. Barnes, #13, 1475 Upper Gage Ave., Hamilton ON L8T 1E6
Tel: 905-387-2031
dressagegames@aol.com
www.cadora.ca
www.facebook.com/CadoraInc
Also Known As: CADORA Inc.
Overview: A medium-sized national organization founded in 1969
Mission: To promote interest in dressage riding as a sport throughout Canada; To develop the sport consistent with the principles of the international governing body of the equestrian Olympic disciplines; To ensure progressions leading to competitive International levels
Member of: Equine Canada; Ontario Equestrian Federation
Affliation(s): Dressage Canada
Chief Officer(s):
Donald J. Barnes, President & Editor, Omnibus
Elizabeth Quigg, Coordinator, National Clinic, 905-640-1720
erobinson@jravideo.com
Finances: *Funding Sources:* Fundraising; Donations; Membership fees
Membership: *Member Profile:* Dressage riders from across Canada
Activities: Providing educational workshops & clinics; Coordinating competitions & matches; Presenting awards; Arranging demonstrations of dressage riding in all areas of Canada
Publications:
• Cadora INK
Type: Newsletter; *Frequency:* Quarterly; *Accepts Advertising*; *Editor:* Lisa Macklem
Profile: Competitions & results, workshops, clinics, events, meetings, feature articles, reviews, & regional reports
• Omnibus
Editor: Donald J. Barnes; *Price:* Free with membership in theCanadian Dressage Owners & Riders Association
Profile: Information about the CADORA National Awards Program, the Cadora L-Inc Program, the Cadora Education Sponsorship Plan, as well as EC/DC, FEI, & Cadora Inc dressage tests

Canadian Drilling Association ***See*** Canadian Diamond Drilling Association

Canadian Driving Society ***See*** Drive Canada

Canadian Drug Manufacturers Association ***See*** Canadian Generic Pharmaceutical Association

Canadian Dyslexia Association (CDA) / Association canadienne de la dyslexie

57, rue du Couvent, Gatineau QC J9H 3C8
Tel: 613-853-6539; *Fax:* 819-684-0672
info@dyslexiaassociation.ca
www.dyslexiaassociation.ca
Overview: A medium-sized national charitable organization founded in 1991
Affliation(s): Canadian Dyslexia Centre, Heritage Academy
Finances: *Annual Operating Budget:* Less than $50,000; *Funding Sources:* National Literacy Secretariat
Staff Member(s): 1; 10 volunteer(s)
Membership: 50; *Fees:* $20
Activities: *Internships:* Yes; *Speaker Service:* Yes; *Library* by appointment

Canadian Earth Energy Association ***See*** Earth Energy Society of Canada

Canadian Economics Association (CEA) / Association canadienne d'économique

Département des Sciences Économiques, Université du Québec à Montréal, PO Box 8888, Stn. Centre-Ville, Montréal QC H3C 3P8
Tel: 514-987-3000
www.economics.ca
Overview: A small national organization founded in 1967
Mission: To represent academic economists; To advance economic knowledge
Member of: Social Science Federation of Canada
Chief Officer(s):
Anne Motte, Executive Director, 514-987-3000 Ext. 8374
office@economics.ca
Victoria Zinde-Walsh, President, 514-398-4834, Fax: 514-398-4938
victoria.zinde-walsh@mcgill.ca
Georges Dionne, Vice-President
Steven Ambler, Secretary-Treasurer, 514-987-3000 Ext. 8372, Fax: 514-987-8494
ambler.steven@uqam.ca
Finances: *Funding Sources:* Membership fees
Membership: 1,500; *Fees:* $20 students & retirees; $50 regular; *Member Profile:* Academic economists in Canada & abroad; Undergraduate & graduate students at degree-granting universities; Retired members, age 65 or older
Activities: Encouraging study & research; Furthering discussion of economic questions; Listing employment opportunities
Awards:
• John Rae Prize (Award)
Presented every two years, in recognition of research excellence *Amount:* $10,000
• Doug Purvis Memorial Prize (Award)
To honour a work of excellence relating to Canadian economic policy *Amount:* $10,000
• Harry G. Johnson Prize (Award)
For the author or authors of the paper judged to be the best paper published in the Canadian Journal of Economics *Amount:* $5,000
• Robert Mundell Prize (Award)
For the young author or authors of the paper judged to be the best paper published in the Canadian Journal of Economics *Amount:* $3,000
• John Vanderkamp Prize (Award)
For the best paper published in Canadian Public Policy *Amount:* $2,000
• The Mike McCracken Award for Economic Statistics (Award)
To recognize contributions to the development or use of official economic statistics
Meetings/Conferences: • Canadian Economics Association 2015 49th Conference, 2015, Toronto, ON
Scope: National
Description: An annual conference held during the last week of May or the first week of June
Contact Information: Conference Organizer: Professor Thomas Lemieux, E-mail: cea2013@economics.ca
Publications:
• Canadian Economics Department Directory
Type: Directory
Profile: Contact information for economic departments across Canada
• Canadian Journal of Economics / Revue canadienne d'économique
Type: Journal; *Editor:* D. Green (journals@economics.ca); *Price:* Free with membership in the Canadian Economics Association
Profile: Theoretical & empirical papers in all areas of economics
• Canadian Public Policy
Type: Journal; *Frequency:* Quarterly; *Accepts Advertising*; *Editor:* Herb Emery (cpp.adp@gmail.com) *ISSN:* 0317-0861
Profile: An examination of public policy problems in Canada, written for advisers & decision makers in business organizations & governments, & policy researchers inuniversities & private institutions
• Directory of Canadian Academic Economists
Type: Directory
Profile: Rank & contact information for academic economists throughout Canada

Canadian Ecumenical Action ***See*** Multifaith Action Society

Canadian Eczema Society for Education & Research ***See*** Eczema Society of Canada

Canadian Education & Training Accreditation Commission (CETAC)

#310, 590 Queen St., Fredericton NB E3B 7H9
Tel: 613-800-0340
www.cetac.ca
Overview: A medium-sized national organization founded in 1984
Mission: To assure students & the general public of the quality of Canada's post-secondary institutions & the programs they offer; To assist the institutions in continuously improving themselves & the education provided to students

Canadian Education Association (CEA) / Association canadienne d'éducation (ACE)

#705, 119 Spadina Ave., Toronto ON M5V 2L1
Tel: 416-591-6300; *Fax:* 416-591-5345
Toll-Free: 866-803-9549
info@cea-ace.ca
www.cea-ace.ca
www.facebook.com/cea.ace
twitter.com/cea_ace
www.youtube.com/user/CdnEducAssn
Overview: A medium-sized national charitable organization founded in 1891
Member of: Magazines Canada; Imaging Canada
Chief Officer(s):
Ron Canuel, President & Chief Executive Officer
rcanuel@cea-ace.ca
Gilles Latour, Chief Operating Officer
glatour@cea-ace.ca
Max Cooke, Director, Communications
mcooke@cea-ace.ca
Cailey Crawford, Director, Strategic Partnerships
ccrawford@cea-ace.ca
Finances: *Funding Sources:* Provincial departments of education; Publication sales; Membership fees; Fees for service; Forums
Staff Member(s): 7
Membership: 350; *Fees:* $50 student; $120 individual; $360 non-profit organization; $540 corporate; $750 (plus fee based on enrolment) school district; $1,000 faculty; *Committees:* Executive; Council; Editorial Board
Activities: Providing information for school boards & organizations; Producing publications; Offering leadership courses; Providing a conversations series
Awards:
• Whitworth Award for Education Research (Award)

Canadian Education Exchange Foundation (CEEF) / Fondation canadienne des echanges educatifs
#4, 250 Bayview Dr., Barrie ON L4N 4Y8
Tel: 705-739-7596; *Fax:* 705-739-7764
www.ceef.ca
www.facebook.com/pages/CEEF-Exchanges/151307528282883
Overview: A medium-sized national organization

Canadian Educational Researchers' Association (CERA)
c/o Don Klinger, Duncan McArthur Hall, Faculty of Education, Queen's University, Kingston ON K7M 5R7
www.csse-scee.ca/cera
Overview: A small national organization overseen by Canadian Society for the Study of Education
Mission: To improve the quality & quantity of educational research; To act as the voice for the educational research community throughout Canada
Affliation(s): Canadian Society for the Study of Education (CSSE)
Chief Officer(s):
Don Klinger, President, 613-533-3028
don.klinger@queensu.ca
Marielle Simon, Treasurer
msimon@uottawa.ca
Anne MacCleave, Editor, CERA News
Anne.MacCleave@msvu.ca
Membership: *Fees:* $5 students, plus retired & low income persons; $10 national & international members; *Member Profile:* Educational researchers who are members of the Canadian Society for the Study of Education; Associate members who have an interest in educational research & who believe in the goals of the association; Graduate students
Activities: Promoting & supporting research in education; Mentoring students; Organizing networking events
Meetings/Conferences: • Canadian Educational Researchers' Association 2015 Annual Meeting & Reception, May, 2015, University of Ottawa, Ottawa, ON
Scope: National
Description: An event offering an annual review of the association's activities, plus professional interactions with other CERA members from across Canada.
Contact Information: URL: www.csse-scee.ca/conference
Publications:
• CERA News: The Newsletter of the Canadian Educational Researchers' Association
Type: Newsletter; *Editor:* Anne MacCleave
Profile: Information about association activities, such as the presentation of awards, support for students, & conference updates

Canadian Educational Resources Council (CERC)
#203, 250 Merton St., Toronto ON M4S 1B1
Tel: 416-322-7011; *Fax:* 416-322-6999
www.cerc-ca.org
Overview: A medium-sized national organization
Mission: Seeks to enhance elementary and secondary education in Canada by developing mutually beneficial relationships with the educational community that result in the development and acquisition of high quality learning resources and improved student achievement.
Member of: Canadian Education Association; Canadian Copyright Institute; Access Copyright
Chief Officer(s):
Gerry McIntyre, Executive Director

Canadian Educational Standards Institute *See* Canadian Accredited Independent Schools

Canadian Egg Marketing Agency *See* Egg Farmers of Canada

Canadian Electric Wheelchair Hockey Association (CEWHA)
#920, 200 Yorkland Blvd., Toronto ON M2J 5C1
Tel: 416-757-8544; *Fax:* 416-490-9334
info@cewha.ca
www.cewha.ca
www.facebook.com/cewha
twitter.com/canadianewha
www.youtube.com/cewhanational
Overview: A small national charitable organization founded in 1980
Mission: To provide a hockey program for persons with disabilities who have limited upper body strength & mobility
Chief Officer(s):
Bob Cassidy, Executive Director
Finances: *Funding Sources:* Donations; Sponsorships; Fundraising
Membership: 200 players + 80 volunteers; *Member Profile:* All persons with disabilities who would benefit from an electric wheelchair in competitive sport & daily living
Activities: Offering recreation & social programs; Organizing national tournaments

Canadian Electrical Contractors Association (CECA) / Association canadienne des entrepreneurs électriciens (ACEE)
#460, 170 Attwell Dr., Toronto ON M9W 5Z5
Tel: 416-675-3226; *Fax:* 416-675-7736
Toll-Free: 800-387-3226
ceca@ceca.org
www.ceca.org
Overview: A medium-sized national organization founded in 1955
Mission: To represent electrical contractors at the national level
Chief Officer(s):
Colin Campbell, President
David Mason, Vice-President
Eryl Roberts, Executive Secretary
Membership: 5,000-14,999; *Member Profile:* Provincial & territorial electrical contractor groups

Canadian Electrical Manufacturers Representatives Association (CEMRA)
#300, 180 Attwell Dr., Toronto ON M9W 6A9
Tel: 647-258-7476; *Fax:* 416-679-9234
Toll-Free: 866-602-8877
info@electrofed.com
www.electrofed.com
Overview: A medium-sized national organization founded in 1980
Mission: To represent over 300 member companies that manufacture, distribute & service electrical, electronics & telecommunications products
Member of: Electro-Federation Canada; Electrical Council
Chief Officer(s):
Jim Taggart, President & CEO
jtaggart@electrofed.com
Jeff Miller, Executive Director
jmiller@electrofed.com
Staff Member(s): 1; 5 volunteer(s)
Membership: 300+ member companies; *Member Profile:* Independent sales reps in the electrical industry

Canadian Electricity Association (CEA) / Association canadienne de l'électricité (ACE)
#1500, 275 Slater St., Ottawa ON K1P 5H9
Tel: 613-230-9263; *Fax:* 613-230-9326
info@electricity.ca
www.electricity.ca
www.linkedin.com/company/canadian-electricity-association
twitter.com/CDNElectricity
powerforthefuture.ca/blog
Overview: A medium-sized national organization founded in 1891
Mission: To ensure a safe, secure, reliable, sustainable & competitively priced supply of electricity. CEA is the voice of the Canadian electricity industry, promoting electricity as a key social, economic and environmental enabler that is essential to Canada's prosperity.
Chief Officer(s):
Jim Burpee, President & CEO, 613-230-9263
burpee@electricity.ca
Francis Bradley, Vice-President, Policy Development, 613-230-5027
bradley@electricity.ca
Sandra Schwartz, Vice-President, Policy Advocacy, 613-230-9876
schwartz@electricity.ca
Tracy Walden, Director, Communications, 613-627-4333
Angela Baker-MacLeod, Corporate Secretary, 613-230-7384
macleod@electricity.ca
Richard Lussier, Controller, 613-688-2065
Staff Member(s): 30
Membership: 31 Corporate Utility Members; 53 Corporate Partner Members; *Member Profile:* Members generate, transmit, & distribute electrical energy to residential, commercial, institutional, & industrial customers throughout Canada; *Committees:* Human Resources; Occupational Health and Safety; Technology
Activities: Analyzing national & international business issues; Providing a national forum for the electricity business; Advocating industry views; Helping companies in evolving markets; Communicating findings about concerns such as mercury emissions & electric & magnetic fields;
Publications:
• Annual Service Continuity Report on Distribution System Performance in Electrical Utilities
Type: Yearbook; *Frequency:* Annually
Profile: Produced by the Performance Excellence & Benchmarking program of the Canadian Electricity Association, the report containsinformation about industry standard metrics for electricity distribution, including system average interruption frequency index & the system average interruption duration index
• The CEA [Canadian Electricity Association] Member Directory
Type: Directory; *Frequency:* Annually; *Price:* $15 members; $65 non-members
Profile: Contact information for the Canadian electricity industry's major players, in addition to information about the operations of the Canadian ElectricityAssociation's member companies
• Electricity Annual
Type: Yearbook; *Frequency:* Annually
Profile: The Canadian Electricity Association's yearly industry review
• Forced Outage Performance of Transmission Equipment [a publication of the Canadian Electricity Association]
Type: Yearbook; *Frequency:* Annually
Profile: Produced by the Performance Excellence & Benchmarking program of the Canadian Electricity Association, thereport addresses the performance of transmission equipment in Canada
• Generation Equipment Status [a publication of the Canadian Electricity Association]
Type: Yearbook; *Frequency:* Annually
Profile: Produced by the Performance Excellence & Benchmarking program of the Canadian Electricity Association, the report features informationon the performance of electrical generating units in Canada

Canadian Employee Assistance Program Association (CEAPA) / Association canadienne des programmes d'aide aux employés (ACPAE)
1031 Portage Ave., Winnipeg MB R3G 0R8
Tel: 204-944-7063
www.ceapaonline.com
Overview: A medium-sized national organization founded in 1995
Mission: To promote the concept of Employee Assistance Programs in Canada & to provide networking opportunities for EAP practitioners & programs
Chief Officer(s):
Tony Showchuk, President
tony.showchuk@sasktel.com
Maria Besenski, Treasurer
Maria.besenski@saskatoon.ca
Finances: *Funding Sources:* Membership dues
19 volunteer(s)
Membership: 200; *Fees:* $35 individual; $100 corporate
Activities: *Speaker Service:* Yes
Awards:
• Workplace Excellence (Award)
Recognizing organiations that are committed to improving well being of employees
• EAP Union Excellence (Award)
Recognizing the contributions that Union members have brought to the field of EAP
• Individual Excellence (Award)
Recognizing individuals that contribute to the overall well being of fellow employees & families in dealing with challenges/changes

Canadian Employee Relocation Council (CERC)
#1010, 180 Dundas St. W., Toronto ON M5G 1Z8
Tel: 416-593-9812; *Fax:* 416-593-1139
Toll-Free: 866-357-2372
info@cerc.ca
www.cerc.ca
www.facebook.com_151161928253133
twitter.com/CERC_CA
Overview: A small national organization founded in 1982
Mission: To provide leadership, services & assistance to members enabling them to effectively serve relocated families by addressing issues that impact the relocation industry, domestically & internationally
Chief Officer(s):
Stephen Cryne, President/CEO
Finances: *Annual Operating Budget:* $100,000-$250,000

Staff Member(s): 2; 70 volunteer(s)
Membership: 550; *Fees:* $50 student; $155 individual; $275 associate; $475 corporate
Activities: *Library*
Meetings/Conferences: • Canadian Employee Relocation Council 2015 Annual Conference, September, 2015, Le Centre Sheraton, Montréal, QC
Scope: National
Publications:
• Bi-Annual Survey [a publication of the Canadian Employee Relocation Council]
Frequency: Semiannually; *Price:* Free for CERC members
Profile: Survey on employee relocation policies
• CERC [Canadian Employee Relocation Council] News
Type: Newsletter; *Frequency:* Monthly; *Price:* Free with CERC membership
Profile: Current industry news & information
• CERC [Canadian Employee Relocation Council] Perspectives Magazine
Type: Magazine; *Frequency:* Quarterly; *Price:* Free with CERC membership
Profile: Analysis of issues & trends in relocation
• CERC [Canadian Employee Relocation Council] Membership Roster
Type: Directory; *Price:* Free for Canadian Employee Relocation Council members
• Relocation Policies
Price: Free for CERC corporate members

Canadian Energy Efficiency Alliance (CEEA) / L'Association de l'efficacité énergétique du Canada

PO Box 30022, 478 Dundas St. West, Oakville ON L6H 7L8
Tel: 905-614-1641; *Fax:* 905-602-1197
Toll-Free: 866-614-1641
alliance@energyefficiency.org
www.energyefficiency.org
www.linkedin.com/groups?gid=4036109&trk=hb_side_g
www.facebook.com/111344902257508
twitter.com/CdnEnergyEffic
Overview: A medium-sized national organization founded in 1995
Mission: To become the leading energy efficiency advocate in Canada; To work in partnership with industry, environmental & consumer leaders to promote energy efficiency programs & policies that will move Canada toward a more sustainable future
Affliation(s): Canadian Energy Efficiency Centre
Chief Officer(s):
Elizabeth McDonald, President/CEO
elizabethmcdonald@energyefficiency.org
Finances: *Annual Operating Budget:* $250,000-$500,000; *Funding Sources:* Membership dues & projects
14 volunteer(s)
Membership: 40; *Fees:* $1,500 corporate; $15,000 leader; *Committees:* Codes & Standards; Executive; Government Relations
Activities: Establishing a National Energy Efficiency Centre to be North America's energy technology showcase; promoting/advocating energy efficiency; breakfast policy updates; annual meeting

Canadian Energy Law Foundation (CELF)

PO Box 4143, Stn. C, Calgary AB T2T 5M9
Tel: 403-237-2423
www.energylawfoundation.ca
Previous Name: Canadian Petroleum Law Foundation
Overview: A small national organization founded in 1963
Mission: To study oil & gas laws
Chief Officer(s):
Miles Pittman, President
miles.pittman@fmc-law.com
Membership: *Member Profile:* Legal practitioners from law firms, companies, governmental entities, administrative bodies, professional societies, and institutions of learning, as well as sole practitioners.

Canadian Energy Pipeline Association (CEPA) / Association canadienne de pipelines d'énergie

#200, 505 - 3rd St. SW, Calgary AB T2P 3E6
Tel: 403-221-8777; *Fax:* 403-221-8760
aboutpipelines@cepa.com
www.cepa.com
www.facebook.com/aboutpipelines
twitter.com/aboutpipelines
www.youtube.com/aboutpipelines;
www.slideshare.net/aboutpipelines
Overview: A medium-sized national organization founded in 1993
Mission: To represent Canada's transmission pipeline companies; To ensure a strong transmission pipeline industry
Chief Officer(s):
Brenda Kenny, President & Chief Executive Officer
Jim Donihee, Chief Operating Officer
Philippe Reicher, Vice-President, External Relations
Elaine Pacheco, Director, Safety
Amanda Affonso, Director, Regulatory & Financial
Alexandra Frison, Director, Communications
Staff Member(s): 14; 200 volunteer(s)
Membership: *Member Profile:* Canada's pipeline companies that transport natural gas & crude oil throughout North America; *Committees:* Damage Prevention Regulations; Emergency Security Management; Environment; Health & Safety; Land Issues Task Force; Pipeline Integrity; Aboriginal Affairs; Climate Change; Corporate Tax; Commodity Tax; Pipeline Abandonment Obligations; Pipeline Economics; Property Tax; Regulatory Accounting; Regulatory Policy
Activities: Liaising with government regarding industry practices
Awards:
• Environmental Management Award (Award)
• Environmental Achievement Award (Award)
• Spill Prevention Award (Award)

Canadian Energy Research Institute (CERI)

#150, 3512 - 33 St. NW, Calgary AB T2L 2A6
Tel: 403-282-1231; *Fax:* 403-284-4181
info@ceri.ca
www.ceri.ca
Overview: A medium-sized national organization founded in 1975
Mission: To provide the public, industry, & the government with information concerning all aspects of energy
Chief Officer(s):
Peter Howard, President & Chief Executive Officer
David McWhinney, Director, Accounting & Operations
Dinara Millington, Director, Research
Jon Rozhon, Senior Researcher
Thorn Walden, Senior Economist
Membership: 150
Activities: *Speaker Service:* Yes; *Library:* I.N. McKinnon Memorial Library
Meetings/Conferences: • Canadian Energy Research Institute 2015 Petrochemical Conference, June, 2015, Delta Lodge at Kananaskis, Kananaskis, AB
Scope: National
Contact Information: General Inquiries, E-mail: conference@ceri.ca; Contact, Sponsorship Information: Deanne Landry, Phone: 403-220-2395, E-mail: dlandry@ceri.ca
• Canadian Energy Research Institute 2015 Natural Gas Conference, March, 2015, Calgary TELUS Convention Center, Calgary, AB
Scope: National
Description: An exploration of issues facing the gas industry
Contact Information: General Inquiries, E-mail: conference@ceri.ca; Contact, Sponsorship Information: Deanne Landry, Phone: 403-220-2395, E-mail: dlandry@ceri.ca
• Canadian Energy Research Institute 2015 Oil Conference, April, 2015, The Fairmont Palliser Hotel, Calgary, AB
Scope: National
Contact Information: General Inquiries, E-mail: conference@ceri.ca; Contact, Sponsorship Information: Deanne Landry, Phone: 403-220-2395, E-mail: dlandry@ceri.ca

Canadian Energy Workers' Association (CEWA)

9908 - 106 St., Edmonton AB T5K 1C4
Tel: 780-420-7887; *Fax:* 780-420-7881
cewa@cewa.ca
www.cewa.ca
Previous Name: Canadian Utilities & Northland Utilities Employees' Association; Alberta Power Employees' Association
Overview: A small national organization founded in 1969
Mission: To represent the interests of members, by serving as a bargaining agent for matters related to working relations with employers
Chief Officer(s):
A.B. (Toni) Hawkins, Manager, Business
thawkins@cewa.ca
Laurie L. Pederson, Officer, Labour Relations
lpederson@cewa.ca
Membership: *Fees:* 2 hour's rate of pay each month
Activities: Engaging in problem solving between members & management; Creating programs for members in the areas of safety, security, & skills development; Seeking opportunities to organize & represent workers; Offering an annual bursary program

Canadian Engineering Education Association (CEEA) / Association canadienne de l'éducation en génie (ACEG)

c/o Design Engineering, University of Manitoba, E2-262 EITC, 75 Chancellors Circle, Winnipeg MB R3T 5V6
Tel: 204-474-7113; *Fax:* 204-474-7676
ceea@umanitoba.ca
ceea.ca
Overview: A medium-sized national organization
Mission: Aims to enhance the competence and relevance of graduates from Canadian Engineering schools through continuous improvement in engineering education.
Chief Officer(s):
Susan McCahan, President
Membership: *Fees:* $25 individual; $100 professional; $500 institutional/affiliate
Meetings/Conferences: • Canadian Engineering Education Association 2015 Conference, May, 2015, McMaster University, Hamilton, ON
Scope: National

Canadian Entertainment Conference *See* Canadian Organization of Campus Activities

Canadian Environment Industry Association (CEIA)

119, Concession 6 Rd., Fisherville ON NOA 1G0
Tel: 416-410-0432; *Fax:* 416-362-5231
Overview: A large national organization
Mission: To promote the interests and development of Canadian companies supplying environmental technologies, products and services.
Chief Officer(s):
Christopher Henderson, Chair
Membership: 1,500

Canadian Environment Industry Association - British Columbia Chapter *See* British Columbia Environment Industry Association

Canadian Environment Industry Association - Ontario Chapter *See* Ontario Environment Industry Association

Canadian Environmental Auditing Association *See* Auditing Association of Canada

Canadian Environmental Certification Approvals Board (CECAB) / Bureau canadien de reconnaissance professionnelle des spécialistes de l'environnement

#200, 308 - 11th Ave. SE, Calgary AB T2G 0Y2
Tel: 403-233-7484; *Fax:* 403-264-6240
certification@eco.ca
www.cecab.org
Overview: A small national licensing organization founded in 1998
Mission: CECAB is a professional autonomous body providing national certification for Canadian environmental practitioners.
Chief Officer(s):
Victor Nowicki, Chair
Finances: *Annual Operating Budget:* $250,000-$500,000; *Funding Sources:* Industry; HRDC; CCHREI
Staff Member(s): 3
Membership: 700+; *Fees:* CEDIT $50; CCEP $150-300; *Member Profile:* Environmental practitioners from all provinces & territories, representing all disciplines.; *Committees:* Certification; Discipline; Ethics; Professional Development

Canadian Environmental Defence Fund *See* Environmental Defence

Canadian Environmental Grantmakers' Network (CEGN) / Réseau canadien des subventionneurs en environnement (RCSE)

#300, 70 The Esplanade, Toronto ON M5E 1R2
Tel: 647-288-8891; *Fax:* 416-979-3936
pegi_dover@cegn.org
www.cegn.org
Overview: A medium-sized national organization founded in 1995
Mission: Works to develop an effective network of environmental grantmakers in Canada by facilitating information-sharing, collaboration, training & professional development, research, & communications
Chief Officer(s):

Pegi Dover, Executive Director
pegi_dover@cegn.org
Membership: *Member Profile:* Private, community, public & corporate foundations; government & corporate funding programs that give grants in support of Canadian environment
Meetings/Conferences: • Canadian Environmental Grantmakers' Network Annual Conference and CFC Conference 2015, June, 2015, The Old Mill, Toronto, ON
Scope: National
Contact Information: Pegi Dover; pegi_dover@cegn.org; Phone: 647-288-8891

Canadian Environmental Law Association (CELA) / Association canadienne du droit de l'environnement

#301, 130 Spadina Ave., Toronto ON M5V 2L4
Tel: 416-960-2284; *Fax:* 416-960-9392
articling@cela.ca
www.cela.ca
www.facebook.com/CanadianEnvironmentalLawAssociation
twitter.com/CanEnvLawAssn
Overview: A medium-sized national organization founded in 1970
Mission: To advocate for environmental law reform; To act in court or during hearings on behalf of citizens' groups & individuals who would otherwise be unable to afford legal assistance
Chief Officer(s):
Theresa McClenaghan, Executive Director & Counsel
theresa@cela.ca
Mary Anderson, Manager, Finance
mary@cela.ca
Tracy Tucker, Manager, Office
tracy@cela.ca
Kathleen Cooper, Senior Researcher
kcooper@cela.ca
Burgandy Dunn, Counsel, Public Legal Education
bdunn@cela.ca
Finances: *Funding Sources:* Legal Aid Ontario
1 volunteer(s)
Membership: 23
Activities: *Library:* Resource Library for the Environment & the Law; by appointment

Canadian Environmental Network (RCEN) / Réseau canadien de l'environnement

39 McArthur Ave., Level 1-1, Ottawa ON K1L 8L7
Tel: 613-728-9810; *Fax:* 613-728-2963
info@rcen.ca
rcen.ca
www.facebook.com/CanadianEnvironmentalNetwork
twitter.com/RCEN
www.youtube.com/user/RCEN1
Overview: A large national organization founded in 1977
Mission: To promote ecologically sound ways of life; To enhance members' work to restore, protect, & promote a clean & sustainable environment
Chief Officer(s):
Josh Brandon, Chair
chair@rcen.ca
Membership: *Member Profile:* Canadian non-profit, non-governmental organizations with a focus on environmental concerns
Activities: Providing communication & networking services for members
Meetings/Conferences: • Canadian Environmental Network / Réseau canadien de l'environnement 2015 Annual Conference on the Environment, 2015
Scope: National
Contact Information: E-mail: chair@rcen.ca
Publications:
• Getting Answers: A Guide to the Environmental Petitions Process
Type: Guide; *Number of Pages:* 27
• Ideas for a More Effective Environmental Movement in Canada
Number of Pages: 17; *Author:* Jerry DeMarco
• Mercury . . . A Global Toxin: Perspectives on Initiatives & Programs on Coal-Fired Power Plants & Mercury Emissions
Number of Pages: 114; *Author:* Anna Tilman
Profile: Coal-fired Power Plants - Mercury Emissions; Canada-wide Standards for Mercury Electric PowerGenerating Sector; Strategies & Control Technologies for Reducing Mercury Emissions; Mercury Emission Trading; U.S. Regulatory Action on Mercury & Coal-Fired Plants; Global Initiatives on Mercury
• Mercury . . . A Public Concern, including Analysis of Mercury Emissions from Coal-Fired Power Plants & Canada-Wide Standards
Number of Pages: 198; *Author:* Anna Tilman
Profile: Government Programs-Mercury; Canada-wide Standards for Mercury Electric Power GeneratingSector; Mercury Data from Coal-Fired Plants; Cumulative Emissions-The True Loading Picture; U.S. Regulatory Action on Mercury & Coal-Fired Plants; Recommendations for Canada-wide Standards for Mercury
• Participating in Federal Public Policy: A Guide for the Voluntary Sector
Type: Guide
Profile: A resource to assist voluntary organizations participate in the federal public policy development process
• RCEN [Canadian Environmental Network] e-Bulletin
Type: Newsletter; *Frequency:* Weekly
Profile: Up-to-date information about RCEN activities & news of interest for RECEN members
• RCEN [Canadian Environmental Network] Annual Report
Type: Yearbook; *Frequency:* Annually
Profile: A review of the network's activities & audited financial statements
• RCEN [Canadian Environmental Network] Youth Friendly Guide: Youth Guide to Policy Change for Intergenerational Partnerships
Type: Guide
Profile: A guidebook of interest to organizations wanting to make their operations youth-friendly
• RCEN [Canadian Environmental Network] Biodiversity Best Practices Handbook
Type: Handbook

Canadian Environmental Technology Advancement Corporation - West (CETAC)

3608 - 33rd St. NW, Calgary AB T2L 2A6
Tel: 403-777-9595; *Fax:* 403-777-9599
cetac@cetacwest.com
cetacwest.com
www.facebook.com/431936763529236
Also Known As: CETAC-West
Overview: A medium-sized national organization founded in 1994
Mission: Established by Environment Canada, CETAC-West is a private sector, not-for-profit corporation committed to helping small & medium-sized enterprises that are engaged in the development & commercialization of new environmental technologies. To this end, it has created a network of technology producers, industry experts, & investment sources.
Finances: *Funding Sources:* Provincial & federal government
Staff Member(s): 8
Activities: Specialist advisors provide technical research assistance, regulatory counsel & a range of consulting & referral services; focuses on technologies for natural resource conservation, pollution prevention & control, waste reductions & management, & environmental protection & remediation
Publications:
• CETAC [Canadian Environmental Technology Advancement Corporation] Focus
Type: Newsletter; *Frequency:* Quarterly

Canadian Epilepsy Alliance (CAE) / L'Alliance canadienne de l'épilepsie (ACE)

26 O'Leary Ave., St. John's NL A1B 2C7
Tel: 709-722-0502; *Fax:* 709-722-0999
www.epilepsymatters.com
Overview: A medium-sized national charitable organization founded in 1998
Mission: To promote independence & quality of life for people with epilepsy & their families, through support services, information, advocacy, & public awareness
Chief Officer(s):
Gail Dempsey, President
executivedirector@epilepsynl.com
Finances: *Annual Operating Budget:* Less than $50,000; *Funding Sources:* Membership fees; donations; grants; shared costs
30 volunteer(s)
Membership: 26; *Fees:* $50; *Member Profile:* Epilepsy organizations across Canada
Activities: *Speaker Service:* Yes
Publications:
• Epilepsy Matters: The Newsletter of the Canadian Epilepsy Alliance
Type: Newsletter; *Frequency:* 3 pa
Profile: National thematic journal about epilepsy issues for persons with epilepsy & their caregivers

Canadian Equestrian Federation *See* Equine Canada

Canadian ETF Association (CETFA)

c/o Horizons Exchange Traded Funds, #700, 26 Wellington St. East, Toronto ON M5E 1S2
www.cetfa.ca
twitter.com/cetfassn
www.youtube.com/cetfassn
Overview: A small national organization founded in 2011
Mission: To promote awareness of the Canadian exchange trade fund (ETF) industry
Chief Officer(s):
Howard Atkinson, Founding Managing Director & Chair, 416-777-5167
hatkinson@horizonsetfs.com
Membership: 6 member firms + 17 affiliate firms + 13 portfolio managers; *Fees:* $7,500; *Member Profile:* Any Canadian Exchange Traded Fund provider
Activities: Increasing ETF education for both retail & institutional investors; Providing industry statistics; Ensuring the adoption of best practice standards by the ETF industry

Canadian Ethnic Journalists' & Writers' Club *See* Canadian Ethnic Media Association

Canadian Ethnic Media Association (CEMA)

24 Tarlton Rd., Toronto ON M5P 2M4
Tel: 416-764-3081; *Fax:* 416-764-3245
webmaster@canadianethnicmedia.com
canadianethnicmedia.com
Previous Name: Canadian Ethnic Journalists' & Writers' Club
Overview: A small national organization founded in 1978
Mission: To promote & preserve the value of the ethnic media in Canada; To advance understanding of Canada's cultural diversity
Chief Officer(s):
Kiumars Rezvanifar, President
Madaine Ziniak, Chair
Gina Valle, Secretary
Irene Chu, Treasurer
Membership: *Fees:* $15-$40; *Member Profile:* Print, broadcast, & web journalists & writers; journalism students
Activities: Promoting multiculturalism; Providing opportunities for members to exchange ideas; Cooperating with similar organizations
Publications:
• Mosaic in Media
Price: $15 members
Profile: Anthology of writings by association members

Canadian Ethnic Studies Association (CESA) / Société canadienne d'études ethniques (SCEE)

c/o Dept. of Sociology, University of Calgary, 2500 University Dr. NW, Calgary AB T2N 1N4
Tel: 403-220-6502; *Fax:* 403-282-9298
cesa@uwinnipeg.ca
cesa.uwinnipeg.ca
Previous Name: Inter University Committee on Canadian Slavs (IUCCS)
Overview: A medium-sized national organization founded in 1971
Mission: To encourage scholarly debate about theoretical & practical issues in Canadian ethnic studies
Chief Officer(s):
Lloyd Wong, President
llwong@ucalgary.ca
Lori Wilkinson, Vice-President
lori_wilkinson@umanitoba.ca
Amal Madibbo, Secretary-Treasurer
amadibbo@ucalgary.ca
Activities: Promoting & supporting education in Canadian ethnic studies; Liaising with related organizations; Encouraging understanding of diverse cultural heritages; Providing networking opportunities among scholars
Awards:
• Howard Palmer Memorial Scholarship Award (Scholarship)
Publications:
• Canadian Ethnic Studies / Études ethniques au Canada
Type: Journal; *Frequency:* 3 pa; *Editor:* Natalia Aponiuk
Profile: Scholarly articles, book reviews & research notes about immigration, ethnicity, inter-group relations, & the history & cultural life of ethnic groups inCanada
• CES [Canadian Ethnic Studies Association] Bulletin
Type: Newsletter
Profile: CES announcements, awards, exhibitions, & conferences, & a list of new bulications & web resouces

Canadian Ethnocultural Council (CEC) / Conseil ethnoculturel du Canada

#205, 176 Gloucester St., Ottawa ON K2P 0A6
Tel: 613-230-3867; *Fax:* 613-230-8051
cec@web.net
www.ethnocultural.ca
www.youtube.com/user/EthnoCanada
Overview: A medium-sized national organization founded in 1980
Mission: To represent a cross-section of ethnocultural groups across Canada.
Chief Officer(s):
Lou Seulovski, President
Anna Chiappa, Executive Director
Membership: 33 national organizations
Activities: *Speaker Service:* Yes; *Library* by appointment

Canadian Evaluation Society (CES) / Société canadienne d'évaluation

1485 Laperriere Ave., Ottawa ON K1Z 7S8
Tel: 613-725-2526; *Fax:* 613-729-6206
secretariat@evaluationcanada.ca
www.evaluationcanada.ca
Overview: A medium-sized national organization founded in 1981
Mission: To advance evaluation for its members & the public; To establish & maintain CES as the recognized national organization which represents the evaluation community; To provide a forum for the advancement of theory & practice of evaluation; To develop competencies, ethics, & standards to improve the practice of evaluation; To advocate for high-quality evaluation with practitioners, local chapters, nationally & internationally; To promote the use of evaluation in society
Affiliation(s): American Evaluation Society; Australasian Evaluation Society
Chief Officer(s):
Martha McGuire, President
president@evaluationcanada.ca
Finances: *Annual Operating Budget:* $100,000-$250,000
Staff Member(s): 2
Membership: 1,900 individual; *Fees:* $95 individual; $60 senior; $35 full-time student; $125 library; *Member Profile:* Members come from a variety of work settings & backgrounds including the federal, provincial & municipal governments; social, health & service organizations; academic institutions & private firms; members represent disciplines ranging from psychology, sociology, social work, education, economics, health sciences, administration, political science & policy sciences to accounting, engineering, urban & regional planning; *Committees:* Professional Development; Member Services; Administration
Activities: *Speaker Service:* Yes; *Rents Mailing List:* Yes; *Library* Open to public by appointment
Awards:
• Award for Contribution to Evaluation in Canada (Award)
• CES Award for Service to the Society (Award)
To honour those members who have made an exemplary contribution in the service of the Society
• Student Essay Award (Award)
Given to the best student essay dealing with some aspect of evaluation *Amount:* $500 as well as travel & registration costs to attend the CES Annual Conference
Meetings/Conferences: • The Canadian Evaluation Society (CES) 2015 National Conference (C2015), May, 2015, Montréal, QC
Scope: National
Publications:
• Canadian Journal of Program Evaluation
Type: Journal; *Frequency:* Semiannually; *Editor:* J. Bradley Cousins *ISSN:* 0834-1516
Profile: Articles, book reviews, & research & practice notes about the theory & practice of program evaluation in Canada
• CES [Canadian Evaluation Society] Newsletter
Type: Newsletter; *Frequency:* Irregular
Profile: Articles related to evaluation, book reviews, dissertations, & conference presentations for CES members

Canadian Examiners in Optometry (CEO) / Examinateurs canadiens en optométrie (ECO)

#403, 37 Sandiford Dr., Stouffville ON L4A 7X5
Tel: 905-642-1373; *Fax:* 905-642-3786
administration@ceo-eco.org
www.ceo-eco.org
Overview: A medium-sized national organization
Mission: To assess the competence of individual optometrists in the practice of optometry and providing the assessment results to the individuals and to relevant regulators and provide mechanisms to evaluate the quality of practice of optometrists in Canada.
Membership: 10; *Member Profile:* Provincial optometry regulators

Canadian Executive Service Organization (CESO) / Service d'assistance canadienne aux organismes (SACO)

PO Box 328, #800, 700 Bay St., Toronto ON M5G 1Z6
Fax: 416-961-1096
Toll-Free: 800-268-9052
toronto@ceso-saco.com
www.ceso-saco.com
www.linkedin.com/groups/CESO-I-SACO-3677133
www.facebook.com/cesosaco
twitter.com/cesosaco
www.youtube.com/CESOSACO
Overview: A large international charitable organization founded in 1967
Mission: To enhance the socio-economic well-being of the peoples & the communities of Canada, developing nations & emerging market economies
Member of: Canadian Council for International Cooperation
Chief Officer(s):
Wendy Harris, President & Chief Executive Officer
wharris@ceso-saco.com
Patrick Kelly, Vice-President, National Services
pkelly@ceso-saco.com
Gale Lee, Vice-President, International Services
glee@ceso-saco.com
Michele Baptiste, Manager, Aboriginal Relations (British Columbia, Ontario & Yukon), 800-268-9052 Ext. 4084
mbaptiste@ceso-saco.com
Joeline Norgaard, Manager, Client Relations (Alberta, Saskatchewan & Manitoba), 800-268-9052 Ext. 4111
jnorgaard@ceso-saco.com
Finances: *Funding Sources:* Canadian International Development Agency; Indian & Northern Affairs Canada (INAC)
4000 volunteer(s)
Membership: 800; *Fees:* $100; *Committees:* Executive; National Development; Audit; Nominations & Governance; Finance & Administration; Compensation; Volunteer Liaison
Awards:
• CESO Award for International Development (Award)
• CESO Aboriginal Award (Award)
Publications:
• Canadian Executive Service Organization Annual Report
Frequency: Annually
• Focus
Type: Newsletter; *Frequency:* Quarterly; *Editor:* Ruth-Clair Alinas & Josie Marchese
Profile: CESO information, staff & clubs

Ottawa
323 Chapel St., 3rd Fl., Ottawa ON K1N 7Z2
Toll-Free: 800-268-9052
ottawa@ceso-saco.com
Chief Officer(s):
Ulrike Komaksiutiksak, Manager, National Services (Nunavut & NWT)

Québec
#500, 1001, rue Sherbrooke est, Montréal QC H2L 1L3
Fax: 514-875-6928
Toll-Free: 800-268-9052
Chief Officer(s):
Joanna Dupras, Manager, Client Relations (Québec & Atlantic), 800-268-9052 Ext. 6445
jdupras@ceso-saco.com
Gabrielle Tardif, Manager, Client Relations (Québec & Atlantic), 800-268-9052 Ext. 5809
gtardif@saco-ceso.com

Canadian Explosives Technicians' Association (CETA) / Association canadienne des techniciens en explosif

e-mail: info@edcon.ca
edconnews.com
www.linkedin.com/profile/view?id=80107163
Overview: A small local organization founded in 1992
Chief Officer(s):
Andy Olesen, President
andy@edcon.ca
Membership: 500; *Fees:* $100; *Member Profile:* Police & military bomb technicians throughout Canada
Activities: Offering professional development opportunities

Canadian Fabry Association / L'association canadienne de fabry

PO Box 40036, 4250 1re ave, Québec QC G1H 7J6
www.fabrycanada.com
www.facebook.com/27694413535
Overview: A medium-sized national organization
Mission: To educate the public & offer information on treatments; to encourage & support research; to increase facilities for those suffering from the disease.
Activities: *Awareness Events:* National Patient Conference, June

Canadian Faculties of Agriculture & Veterinary Medicine (CFAVM) / Facultés d'agriculture et de médecine vétérinaire du Canada

77 Townsend Dr., Nepean ON K2J 2V3
Tel: 613-825-6873
info@cfavm.ca
www.cfavm.ca
Previous Name: Association of Faculties of Veterinary Medicine in Canada
Overview: A medium-sized national organization founded in 1990 overseen by Association of Universities & Colleges of Canada
Membership: 8 faculties of agriculture + 4 faculties
Activities: Coordination of teaching, research & extension programs;

Canadian Fallen Firefighters Foundation / Fondation canadienne des pompiers morts en service

#200, 440 Laurier Ave. West, Ottawa ON K1R 7X6
Tel: 613-786-3024; *Fax:* 613-782-2228
info@cfff.ca
www.cfff.ca
www.facebook.com/CFFF.FCPMS
Overview: A small national charitable organization founded in 2003
Mission: To serve all firefighters & their families in time of need. This registered, non-profit, charitable organization is made up of members of the Canadian Fire Service and other interested citizens dedicated to honouring Canada's fallen firefighters.
Affiliation(s): Canadian Fire Service
Chief Officer(s):
Robert Kirkpatrick, President
Douglas Wylie, 1st Vice-President
Mike McKenna, 2nd Vice-President
John Clare, Treasurer
Finances: *Annual Operating Budget:* $100,000-$250,000
Staff Member(s): 3; 1000 volunteer(s)
Membership: 180,000; *Member Profile:* Firefighters & their families; *Committees:* Design of Monument; Funding; Executive
Activities: *Awareness Events:* National Memorial Ceremony, 2nd Sun. in Sept.; *Speaker Service:* Yes
Publications:
• Firefighter Life Safety
Type: Newsletter; *Frequency:* Monthly
Profile: Published in conjunction with the Everyone Goes Home program, for members of fire service, the newsletter contains steps to eliminate line-of-duty deaths & injuries, best practices collectedfrom fire departments, upcoming firefighter life safety events, & implementation of safety & survival plans

Canadian Families & Corrections Network (CFCN)

PO Box 35040, Kingston ON K7L 5S5
Tel: 613-541-0743
Toll-Free: 888-371-2326
national@cfcn-rcafd.org
www.cfcn-rcafd.org
Overview: A small national charitable organization
Mission: To assist families affected by criminal behaviour, incarceration, & community reintegration
Chief Officer(s):
Louise Leonardi, Executive Director
Finances: *Funding Sources:* Donations
Membership: *Fees:* $10 students, seniors, & underwaged persons; $30 individuals; $65 non-profit agencies; $175 corporate memberships
Activities: Offering family support; Providing orientation on restorative justice; Referring families to community resources; Providing visitor resource centres at institutions; Offering information, such as "Telling the children about incarceration" & "Maintaining a relationship with children during incarceration"
Publications:
• Child-Friendly Practices within the Prison Setting
Number of Pages: 26; *Author:* Margaret Holland

Profile: Written with Lori Ann Bevins-Yeomans & Joyce Waddell-Townsend of Children Visiting Prisons-Kingston Inc.
• Families & Corrections Journal
Type: Journal; *Price:* Free
Profile: Articles with news & information about Canadian families & corrections
• One Day at a Time: Writings on Facing the Incarceration of a Friend or Family Member
Number of Pages: 39
• Staying Involved: A Guide for Incarcerated Fathers
Type: Guide
Profile: A joint initiative of Pro Bono Queen's University & Canadian Families & Corrections Network
• Time Together & The Directory of Canadian Services to the Families of Adult Offenders
Number of Pages: 95; *Author:* Lloyd Withers
Profile: A survival guide for families & friends visiting in Canadian federal prisons
• Time's Up: A Reintegration Toolkit for families
Number of Pages: 36; *ISBN:* 0-9688923-5-3
• Waiting at the Gate: Families, Corrections, & Restorative Justice
Number of Pages: 242; *Price:* $25

Canadian Fanconi Anemia Research Fund / La Fondation canadienne de recherche de l'anémie de Fanconi

PO Box 38157, Toronto ON M5N 3A9
Tel: 416-489-6393; *Fax:* 416-489-6393
admin@fanconicanada.org
www.fanconicanada.org
Also Known As: Fanconi Canada
Overview: A small national organization
Mission: To raise money for research into finding a cure &/or treatments for Fanconi anemia; to raise awareness about the disease; to provide support to affected Canadian families
Chief Officer(s):
L. Sheldon, Contact

Canadian Farm & Industrial Equipment Institute ***See*** Association of Equipment Manufacturers - Canada

Canadian Farm Animal Care Trust

#306, 92 Caplan Ave., Barrie ON L4N 0Z7
Tel: 705-436-5776; *Fax:* 705-436-3551
www.canfact.ca
Also Known As: CANFACT
Overview: A small national charitable organization founded in 1989
Mission: To encourage the development & use of systems that subject farm animals to the minimum amount of stress, distress or injury in the rearing, transportation & slaughter of these animals
Chief Officer(s):
Tom Hughes, President
Finances: *Annual Operating Budget:* $50,000-$100,000
15 volunteer(s)
Activities: *Speaker Service:* Yes

Canadian Farm Builders Association (CFBA)

#152, 356 Ontario St., Stratford ON N5A 7X6
Tel: 519-271-0811; *Fax:* 519-273-3363
cfba@cfba.ca
www.cfba.ca
Overview: A small national organization founded in 1980
Mission: To promote & advance the construction of structurally efficient, environmentally sound, efficient farm buildings in Canada; to promote & advance the standards of farm structures through research, education & practical application
Chief Officer(s):
Mike Parker, General Manager
Finances: *Annual Operating Budget:* Less than $50,000
Staff Member(s): 1
Membership: 240; *Fees:* Schedule available

Canadian Farm Business Management Council ***See*** Farm Management Canada

Canadian Farm Writers' Federation (CFWF)

PO Box 250, Ormstown QC J0S 1K0
Fax: 450-829-2226
Toll-Free: 877-782-6456
secretariat@cfwf.ca
cfwf.wildapricot.org
Overview: A small national organization founded in 1955
Mission: To serve the interests of agricultural journalists
Affliation(s): British Columbia Farm Writers' Association (BCFWA); Alberta Farm Writers' Association (AFWA); Saskatchewan Farm Writers' Association (SFWA); Manitoba Farm Writers' & Broadcasters' Association; Eastern Canada Farm Writers' Association (ECFWA)
Chief Officer(s):
Lisa Guenther, President
Tamara Leigh, Vice-President
tamara.leigh@agr.gc.ca
Hugh Maynard, Secretary-Treasurer, 877-782-6456 Ext. 704
hugh@quanglo.ca
Christina Franc, Administrator, 877-782-6456 Ext. 706
christina@quanglo.ca
Membership: 380+; *Member Profile:* Agricultural journalists, such as editors, reporters, & broadcasters; Journalists in business & government who are responsible for agricultural communications
Activities: Providing networking opportunities; Offering professional development
Meetings/Conferences: • Canadian Farm Writers' Federation 2015 Annual General Meeting & Conference, 2015
Scope: National
Publications:
• The Farm Journalist: Newsletter of the Canadian Farm Writers' Federation
Type: Newsletter; *Frequency:* Bimonthly; *Editor:* Christina Franc
Profile: News for farm jouralists, information sources, events, launches, awards, & professional development information

Canadian Federal Pilots Association (CFPA) / Association des pilotes fédéraux du Canada (APFC)

#509, 350 Sparks St., Ottawa ON K1R 7S8
Tel: 613-230-5476; *Fax:* 613-230-2668
cfpa@cfpa-apfc.ca
www.cfpa-apfc.ca
Previous Name: Aircraft Operations Group Association (Ind.)
Overview: A medium-sized provincial charitable organization
Chief Officer(s):
Daniel Slunder, Chair
Denis Brunelle, Vice-Chair
denis.brunelle@tc.gc.ca
Michel Brulotte, Secretary-Treasurer
michel.brulotte@tc.gc.ca
Finances: *Annual Operating Budget:* Greater than $5 Million
Staff Member(s): 2
Membership: 15,000-49,999; *Member Profile:* Professional pilots employed by Transport Canada Aviation Group, Transportation Safety Board & NAV Canada; *Committees:* Professional Standards; Pay & Benefits
Activities: *Internships:* Yes

Canadian Federation for Humanities & Social Sciences (CFHSS) / Fédération canadienne des sciences humaines (FCSH)

#300, 275 Bank St., Ottawa ON K2P 2I6
Tel: 613-238-6112; *Fax:* 613-238-6114
fedcan@fedcan.ca
www.fedcan.ca
www.linkedin.com/company/canadian-federation-for-the-humanities-and-so
www.facebook.com/fedcan?ref=nf
twitter.com/fedcan
Previous Name: Humanities & Social Sciences Federation of Canada
Merged from: Social Science Federation of Canada (SSFC); Canadian Federation for the Humanities (CFH)
Overview: A large national charitable organization founded in 1996
Mission: The Federation represents the Canadian research community by working to support & advance research in the humanities & social sciences in Canada.
Affiliation(s): Canadian Federation of Students (CFS); Canadian Association of Research Libraries (CARL); Canadian Research Knowledge Network (CRKN); Association of Canadian Deans of Education (ACDE); American Council of Learned Societies (ACLS); Frontier College
Chief Officer(s):
Antonia Maioni, President
president@fedcan.ca
Jean-Marc Mangin, Executive Director, 613-238-6112 Ext. 306
jmmangin@fedcan.ca
Finances: *Annual Operating Budget:* $3 Million-$5 Million; *Funding Sources:* Membership fees; Congress revenue; Funding from SSHRC; Donations
Membership: 80 scholarly associations + 79 universities & colleges + 6 affiliates, with 85,000+ individuals; *Fees:* Schedule available, based upon size of association or institution; *Member Profile:* Scholarly associations; Universities & colleges; Practitioners; Scholars; Students
Activities: Publishing scholarly books; Conducting a series of lectures to increase awareness of humanities & social science research among policy makers
Awards:
• Canada Prize in the Humanities (Award)
To recognize scholarly manuscripts *Amount:* $2,500
• Canada Prize in the Social Sciences (Award)
To honour scholarly manuscripts that enrich intellectual, cultural, & social life *Amount:* $2,500
• Canada Prize in the Social Sciences (Award)
To honour scholarly manuscripts that enrich intellectual, cultural, & social life *Amount:* $2,500
• Awards to Scholarly Publications (Scholarship)
To help authors and academic presses publish scholarly books that make a significant original contribution to knowledge in the humanities and social sciences in Canada, but would not be published for commercial purposes. *Amount:* $8,000 (up to 180); $12,000 for the translation of scholarly works
Meetings/Conferences: • Canadian Federation for Humanities & Social Sciences' Congress of the Humanities & Social Sciences 2015, May, 2015, University of Ottawa, Ottawa, ON
Scope: International
Attendance: 6,500+
Description: Educational events, exhibits, & networking opportunities for researchers, policy makers, graduate students, & community members
Contact Information: E-mail: congress@fedcan.ca; Website: congress2015.ca
Publications:
• The Academy as Community: A Manual of Best Practices for Meeting the Needs of New Scholars
Type: Manual; *Number of Pages:* 31; *ISBN:* 0-920052-46-0
Profile: Prepared by the Canadian Federation for the Humanities & Social Sciences' Task Force on New Scholars
• Best Practice Manual: A Guide for Scholarly Associations in Canada
Type: Manual; *Number of Pages:* 61
Profile: Information to maintain & strengthen scholarly societies in Canada
• Canadian Federation for the Humanities & Social Science Annual Report
Type: Yearbook; *Frequency:* Annually
Profile: A year of the federation in review
• Communiqué [a publication of the Canadian Federation for the Humanities & Social Science]
Type: Newsletter
Profile: News, events, & opportunities for CFHSS members
• Renewing Scholarly Associations: Knowledge Networks for the Next Generation
Number of Pages: 51; *ISBN:* 0-920052-47-9
Profile: Prepared by the Canadian Federation for the Humanities & Social Sciences' Scholarly Associations Task Force

Canadian Federation for Robotics / Fédération canadienne de robotique

#301, 126 York St., Ottawa ON K1N 5T5
Overview: A medium-sized national organization founded in 1997
Mission: To promote interest in the use of & the application of robotics technologies by Canadian firms
Chief Officer(s):
Paul Johnston, Director
Finances: *Funding Sources:* Government; Industry

Canadian Federation for the Humanities & Social Sciences (CFHSS) / Fédération Canadienne des Sciences Humaines

#300, 275 Bank St., Ottawa ON K2P 2L6
Tel: 613-238-6112; *Fax:* 613-238-6114
info@ideas-idees.ca
www.ideas-idees.ca
www.linkedin.com/company/canadian-federation-for-the-humanities-and-so
www.facebook.com/ideas.idees
twitter.com/ideas_idees
www.youtube.com/user/IdeasIdees
Overview: A medium-sized national organization
Mission: Strives to support and advance Canada's research in the humanities and social science, fields which are intrinsically important to the development of social, cultural and economic understanding, thus giving society necessary tools to address the most complex of questions.
Chief Officer(s):

Jean-Marc Mangin, Executive Director
jmmangin@ideas-idees.ca
Finances: *Funding Sources:* Public and Private sponsorship, educational institutions
Staff Member(s): 16
Membership: 80 scholarly associations, 79 universities & colleges, 6 affiliates

Canadian Federation of Agriculture (CFA) / Fédération canadienne de l'agriculture (FCA)

21 Florence St., Ottawa ON K2P 0W6
Tel: 613-236-3633; *Fax:* 613-236-5749
info@cfafca.ca
www.cfa-fca.ca
www.facebook.com/cfafca
twitter.com/CFAFCA
Overview: A large national organization founded in 1935
Mission: To coordinate the efforts of agricultural producer organizations throughout Canada for the purpose of promoting their common interests through collective action; to promote & advance the social & economic conditions of those engaged in agricultural pursuits; to assist in formulating & promoting national agricultural policies to meet changing national & international conditions
Member of: International Federation of Agriculture Producers; World Farmers Organisation
Affliation(s): BC Agriculture Council; Keystone Agricultural Producers (Manitoba); Ontario Federation of Agriculture; L'Union des producteurs agricoles (Québec); Coopérative fédérée de Québec; NS Federation of Agriculture; PEI Federation of Agriculture; Agriculture Producers Assoc. of New Brunswick; Newfoundland & Labrador Federation of Agriculture; Dairy Farmers of Canada; Canadian Egg Marketing Agency; Chicken Farmers of Canada; Canadian Turkey Marketing Agency; Canadian Broiler Hatching Egg Marketing Agency; Canadian Sugar Beet Producers' Assoc.; Canadian Pork Council; Wild Rose Agricultural Producers
Chief Officer(s):
Ron Bonnett, President
president@cfafca.ca
Brigid Rivoire, Executive Director, 613-236-3633
brigid@cfafca.ca
Jessica Goodfellow, Director, Communications
communications@cfafca.ca
Finances: *Annual Operating Budget:* $500,000-$1.5 Million; *Funding Sources:* Membership fees
Staff Member(s): 8
Membership: 22 provincial farm organizations, national/regional commodity organizations; *Member Profile:* Farm organization or farmer co-op
Activities: *Awareness Events:* Food Freedom Day, Feb. 12; *Internships:* Yes; *Library* by appointment
Meetings/Conferences: • Canadian Federation of Agriculture 2015 Annual General Meeting, February, 2015, Delta Ottawa City Centre, Ottawa, On
Scope: National
Contact Information: Suzanne Lamirande; suzanne@cfafca.ca; Phone: 613-236-3633 ext: 2327

Canadian Federation of Amateur Roller Skaters *See* Roller Sports Canada

Canadian Federation of AME Associations (CFAMEA)

c/o AME Association of Ontario, PO Box 160, Stn. Toronto AMF, Mississauga ON L5P 1B1
Tel: 905-673-5681; *Fax:* 905-673-6328
www.cfamea.com
Also Known As: Aircraft Maintenance Engineers Association
Overview: A medium-sized national organization
Mission: To represent regional AME associations & to prmote the aircraft maintenance profession
Chief Officer(s):
Ole Nielsen, President, 519-870-5786
onielsen@rogers.com
Finances: *Funding Sources:* Membership dues
Membership: 5 regional associations; *Member Profile:* Canadian AME Associations
Activities: Liaison with government concerning aircraft maintenance & AME licensing

AME Association (Atlantic) Inc.
126 Gulliver Dr., Fredericton NB E3A 3C5
Tel: 506-472-0462; *Fax:* 626-452-1153
www.atlanticame.ca
www.facebook.com/pages/AME-Association-Atlantic-Inc/2406 88522801455
Chief Officer(s):
Ben L. McCarty, President
ben@cfamea.com

Central AME Association
PO Box 42055, Stn. Ferry Rd., Winnipeg MB R3J 3X7
Tel: 204-945-1974
camea@mymts.net
camea.ca
Chief Officer(s):
Kerry Bews, General Manager

Ontario AME Association
c/o Skyservice F.B.O. Inc., PO Box 160, Stn. Toronto AMF, Mississauga ON L5P 1B1
Tel: 905-673-5681; *Fax:* 905-673-6328
www.ame-ont.com
Chief Officer(s):
Warren Couch, President

Pacific AME Association
#314, 5400 Airport Rd. South, Richmond BC V7B 1B4
Tel: 604-279-9579
pamea@telus.net
www.pamea.ca

Western AME Association
PO Box 21101, Edmonton AB T6R 2V4
Tel: 780-462-1173; *Fax:* 780-413-0076
info@wamea.com
www.wamea.com
www.linkedin.com/company/wamea
www.facebook.com/pages/WAMEA/538014399618324
twitter.com/WAMEAWAMEA
Chief Officer(s):
Rod Fihser, President

Canadian Federation of Apartment Associations (CFAA) / Fédération canadienne des Associations de propriétaires immobiliers

#640, 1600 Carling Ave., Ottawa ON K1Z 1G3
Tel: 613-235-0101; *Fax:* 613-238-0101
admin@cfaa-fcapi.org
www.cfaa-fcapi.org
twitter.com/CFAAConference
Overview: A small national organization founded in 1995
Mission: To represent members on political & economic issues at the national level & to facilitate the exchange of information & materials amongst members while maintaining the highest professional & ethical standards in all activities
Chief Officer(s):
John Dickie, President
David Benes, Administrator
Finances: *Annual Operating Budget:* Less than $50,000; *Funding Sources:* Membership fees; donations
Staff Member(s): 1
Membership: 17 landlord organizations; *Fees:* Schedule available; *Committees:* Conference & AGM; Government Relations; Membership
Meetings/Conferences: • Canadian Federation of Apartment Associations Rental Housing Conference 2015, 2015
Scope: National
Publications:
• CFAA [Canadian Federation of Apartment Associations] - FCAPI Annual Report
Type: Yearbook; *Frequency:* Annually
• National Outlook [a publication of the Canadian Federation of Apartment Associations]
Type: Newsletter; *Frequency:* Quarterly
Profile: CFAA-FCAPI information & events, best practices, successful programs & legislation news from across Canada

Canadian Federation of Aromatherapists / La fédération canadienne d'aromathérapistes

110 Thorndale Pl., Waterloo ON N2L 5Y8
Tel: 519-746-1594; *Fax:* 519-746-9493
cfamanager@cfacanada.com
www.cfacanada.com
www.facebook.com/CanadianAromatherapy
twitter.com/cfaaromatherapy
Overview: A medium-sized national organization founded in 1993
Mission: To maintain a register of aromatherapy practicioners, schools, & instructors who meet established minimum standards; To act as a unified voice of the profession; To maintain the highest ethical standards of the profession
Chief Officer(s):
Monika Meulman, President
monika.cfa@healingmuse.com
Membership: *Fees:* $140; $85 affiliate; $45 student

The Canadian Federation of Business & Professional Women's Clubs (CFBPWC) / Fédération canadienne des clubs des femmes de carrières commerciales et professionnelles (FCCFCCP)

PO Box 62054, Orleans ON K1C 7H8
www.bpwcanada.com
www.ca.linkedin.com/in/bpwcanada
facebook.com/bpw.canada
twitter.com/bpwcan
Also Known As: BPW Canada
Overview: A large national organization founded in 1930
Mission: To develop & encourage women to pursue business, the professions & industry; To work toward the improvement of economic, employment & social conditions for women; To work for high standards of service in business, the professions, industry & public life; To stimulate interest in federal, provincial & municipal affairs; To encourage women to participate in the business of government at all levels; To encourage & assist women & girls to acquire further education & training
Member of: International Federation of Business & Professional Women
Chief Officer(s):
Doris Hall, President
dorish@rogers.com
Valerie Clarke, First Vice-President
valerie.clarke@bpwnorthtoronto.com
Sue Calhoun, Second Vice President
scalhoun@nbnet.nb.ca
Sheila Crook, Secretary
fcrook2@rogers.com
Karin Gorgerat, Treasurer
Karin.g@sympatico.ca
Finances: *Funding Sources:* Membership fees
Membership: 2,500; *Fees:* $30; *Member Profile:* Active - one who is actively engaged in renumerative occupation in business, profession or industry at the time of acceptance into membership; Associate - one who is not engaged in renumerative occupation & who has not been an active member of a club; Student; *Committees:* Federation Promotion; Health; International; Personal Development & Mentoring; Programs/Projects; Public Affairs; Resolutions & Briefs; Ways & Means; Young BPW
Activities: *Awareness Events:* Convention; *Internships:* Yes
Meetings/Conferences: • BPW Canada [Canadian Federation of Business & Professional Women's Clubs] 2015 National Convention, 2015
Scope: National
Description: An opportunity to educate & empower Canadian women to improve economic, political, employment, & social conditions
Contact Information: Secretary: Tammy Richmond, E-mail: tlrich37@gmail.com
Publications:
• BPW Connections - Coast to Coast / Connexions BPW - d'un océan à l'autre
Type: Newsletter; *Frequency:* Quarterly; *Editor:* Sue Calhoun & Judy Hagerman
Profile: BPW Canada news from across the country
• Handbook for Club Members

Abbotsford
34136 Alma St., Abbotsford BC V2T 5P3
e-mail: bpwabbotsford@gmail.com
www.bpwabbotsford.ca
www.linkedin.com/groups?gid=4150531&trk=myg_ugrp_ovr
www.facebook.com/bpwabbotsford
twitter.com/BPWAbbotsford
Chief Officer(s):
Maggie Reimer, President

Barrie
Barrie ON
www.bpwbarrie.com
www.facebook.com/195875163776382?sk=wall&filter=12
twitter.com/BPWBarrie

Brampton
#154, 10 George St. North, Brampton ON L6X 1R2
e-mail: contact@bpw-brampton.com
bpwbrampton.com
Chief Officer(s):
Pat Dowling, President

Calgary
#244, 1811 - 4 St. SW, Calgary AB T2S 1W2

Tel: 403-230-6042
info@bpwcalgary.com
www.bpwcalgary.com
www.linkedin.com/groups?gid=2303046&trk=hb_side_g
www.facebook.com/BPWCalgary
twitter.com/BPWCalgary
Chief Officer(s):
Barb Francis, President

Cambridge
Cambridge ON
e-mail: amy.phillips@live.com
www.bpwcambridge.org

Durham
PO Box 66126, Stn. Town Centre, 1355 Kingston Rd., Pickering ON L1V 6P7
bpwdurham.com
www.facebook.com/BPWDurham
Chief Officer(s):
Joanne Cox, President

Greater Moncton
PO Box 29162, Stn. North End, Moncton NB E1G 4R3
Tel: 506-874-0887
info@monctonbpw.com
www.monctonbpw.com
www.facebook.com/209150065818445
twitter.com/BPWmoncton
Chief Officer(s):
Jolene Barrieau, President

Greater Sudbury
PO Box 2593, Stn. A, Sudbury ON P3A 4S9
Tel: 705-671-2022
bpwgreatersudbury.com

Kitchener-Waterloo
Kitchener ON
www.bpwkw.com
Chief Officer(s):
Elaine Mortensen, President, 519-585-0186
elaine.mortensen@sunlife.com

London
5 Hart Cres., London ON N6E 3A3
e-mail: membership@bpwlondon.com
www.bpwlondon.com
ca.linkedin.com/in/bpwlondoncanada
facebook.com/bpwlondoncanada
twitter.com/bpwlondoncanada

Mission
PO Box 3232, Mission BC V2V 4J4
www.bpwmission.ca
www.facebook.com/BPWMission
twitter.com/BPWMission
Chief Officer(s):
Connie Friesen, President

Mississauga
PO Box 31, 145 Queen St. South, Streetsville ON L5M 2B7
e-mail: info@bpwmississauga.com
bpwmississauga.com
www.linkedin.com/in/bpwmississauga
www.facebook.com/BpwMississauga
www.twitter.com/BPWMiss
Chief Officer(s):
Asha Singh, President, 416-564-2742

Niagara Falls
Niagara Falls ON
www.bpwniagara.com
www.facebook.com/groups/394795933958982/?fref=ts
Chief Officer(s):
Nancy Broerse, President
nancy@infodiva.ca

North Toronto
#201, 29 Gervais Dr., Toronto ON M3C 1Y9
Tel: 416-510-8387
info@bpwnorthtoronto.com
www.bpwnorthtoronto.com
Chief Officer(s):
Linda Rice, President

Ontario
#201, Bramalea Rd., Brampton ON L6T 2W4
www.bpwontario.org
ca.linkedin.com/in/bpwontario
www.facebook.com/bpw.ontario.3
twitter.com/bpwontario
Chief Officer(s):
Linda Davis, President

Québec
www.bpwprovincialquebec.ca
Chief Officer(s):
Julie Leclerc, President

Regina
PO Box 1911, Regina SK S4P 3E1
Tel: 306-585-9177
contact@reginabpw.org
reginabpw.org
www.facebook.com/groups/132275349452/
twitter.com/BPWRegina
Chief Officer(s):
Karen Meban, President

Saskatoon
PO Box 22, Saskatoon SK S7K 3K1
www.bpwsaskatoon.com
www.linkedin.com/groups/BPW-Saskatoon-Inc-4426447/about
www.facebook.com/BPWSaskatoon
twitter.com/@BPWSaskatoonInc
Chief Officer(s):
Tammy Richmond, President
president@bpwsaskatoon.com

Toronto
Toronto ON
www.bpwtoronto.com

Victoria
Victoria BC
e-mail: info@bpwvictoria.com
www.bpwvictoria.com
Chief Officer(s):
Margo Almond, President

Winnipeg Central
34 Park Grove Dr., Winnipeg MB R2J 3L6
Tel: 204-257-0589
winnipegcentral.bpw.ca
Chief Officer(s):
Sharla Wasylyshen, President

Canadian Federation of Business School Deans (CFBSD) / Fédération canadienne des doyens des écoles d'administration (FCDEA)

3000, ch de la Côte-Sainte-Catherine, Montréal QC H3T 2A7
Tel: 514-340-7116; *Fax:* 514-340-7275
info@cfbsd.ca
www.cfbsd.ca
Previous Name: Canadian Federation of Deans of Management & Administrative Studies
Overview: A small national organization founded in 1976
Mission: To encourage the professional development of business school administrators; To promote excellence in management education; To represent management education to the government, the business community, & the media
Chief Officer(s):
Timothy Daus, Executive Director
daus@cfbsd.ca
Bahram Dadgostar, Chair
Jerry Tomberlin, Vice-Chair
Robert Mantha, Secretary-Treasurer
Membership: 60 university level business schools, representing 3,000 faculty members & 150,000 students; *Member Profile:* Deans & directors from Canadian faculties of management & business in Canada; Associate industry & international members; *Committees:* Management Education Research; Communications
Activities: Monitoring public policy; Engaging in advocacy activities; Providing research & information services; Raising the profile of management education; Assisting member institutions in the improvement of their programs

Canadian Federation of Chefs & Cooks; Canadian Federation of Chefs de Cuisine *See* Canadian Culinary Federation

Canadian Federation of Chiropractic Regulatory & Educational Accrediting Boards (CFCREAB)

39 River St., Toronto ON M5A 3P1
Tel: 416-646-1600; *Fax:* 416-646-9460
www.chirofed.ca
Previous Name: Canadian Federation of Chiropractic Regulatory Boards
Overview: A medium-sized national organization founded in 1978
Mission: To promote unified standards for the operations of all licensing & regulatory boards; to aid in problems confronting individual boards; to promote & aid cooperation between chiropractic learning boards & regulatory boards
Chief Officer(s):
Wayne Glover, Executive Director
Finances: *Annual Operating Budget:* $100,000-$250,000
Membership: 11; *Member Profile:* Provincial & territorial organizations having jurisdiction over licences, registration, testing or discipline of doctors of chiropractic

Canadian Federation of Chiropractic Regulatory Boards *See* Canadian Federation of Chiropractic Regulatory & Educational Accrediting Boards

Canadian Federation of Deans of Management & Administrative Studies *See* Canadian Federation of Business School Deans

Canadian Federation of Earth Sciences (CFES) / Fédération canadienne des sciences de la Terre

c/o Scott Swinden, 3 Crest Rd., Halifax NS B3M 2W1
Tel: 902-444-3525; *Fax:* 902-444-7802
info@swindengeoscience.ca
earthsciencescanada.com
Previous Name: Canadian Geoscience Council
Overview: A medium-sized national organization founded in 1972
Mission: To promote coordination & cooperation in activities in Canadian geoscientific education; to advise on science policy involving the earth sciences; to provide an informed opinion to the public of Canada on matters of public concern.
Chief Officer(s):
Scott Swinden, President
Finances: *Annual Operating Budget:* $100,000-$250,000; *Funding Sources:* Geological Survey of Canada; member societies
Membership: 15 organizations

Canadian Federation of Engineering Students (CFES) / Fédération canadienne des étudiants et étudiantes en génie

c/o Engineers Canada, #1100, 180 Elgin St., Ottawa ON K2P 2K3
e-mail: info@cfes.ca
www.cfes.ca
twitter.com/FCEEG_CFES
Overview: A medium-sized national organization founded in 1969
Mission: To act as a unified voice for engineering students both nationally & internationally; To assist engineering students in both personal & professional growth; To be aware of & communicate changes in society which affect the engineering profession & engineering students
Affliation(s): BEST (Board of European Students of Technology)
Chief Officer(s):
Nicolas Blanchet, CFES President
president@cfes.ca
Alexandra Dozzi, Vice-President, Finances & Administration
vpfa@cfes.ca
Lauren Brunet, Vice-President, Communications
vpcomm@cfes.ca
Finances: *Funding Sources:* Sponsorships
Membership: 60,000; *Member Profile:* Engineering students across Canada; *Committees:* Education; Official Languages; Information Technology; Outreach
Activities: Facilitating the exchange of information between members; Recognizing student achievements; Supporting an all-encompassing education for engineering students; Offering complementary education courses
Publications:
• CFES [Canadian Federation of Engineering Students] eBulletin
Type: Newsletter
Profile: Federation activities, commissioner reports, & upcoming events
• Project [a publication of the Canadian Federation of Engineering Students]
Type: Magazine; *Frequency:* Semiannually; *Accepts Advertising; Editor:* Shaunvir Sidhu; *Price:* Distributed to schools for engineering students
Profile: Relevant articles for engineering students across Canada

Canadian Federation of Friends of Museums (CFFM) / Fédération canadienne des amis de musées (FCAM)

#400, 280 Metcalfe St., Ottawa ON K2P 1R7

Tel: 613-567-0099; *Fax:* 613-233-5438
info@cffm-fcam.ca
www.cffm-fcam.ca
www.facebook.com/group.php?gid=146503988697066
Overview: A medium-sized national charitable organization founded in 1977
Mission: To serve as source of information & expertise for friends of museums; To serve as communications network & national voice for those who are dedicated to the support & promotion of museums for the benefit of all Canadians
Affiliation(s): World Federation of Friends of Museums - Mexico City; Canadian Museums Association
Chief Officer(s):
Tony Bowland, Co-President
Marie Senécal-Tremblay, Co-President
Yves Dagenais, Treasurer
Finances: *Funding Sources:* Membership dues; Donations
10 volunteer(s)
Membership: 242 individual + 140 institutions; *Fees:* $35 for individuals; $25 for institutions; *Committees:* Advisory; By-Laws; Growth & Development; Finance; Fundraising & Special Projects; Nominations; Strategic Alliance
Publications:
• CFFM [Canadian Federation of Friends of Museums] Newsletter
Type: Newsletter
• Significant Treasures / Trésors parlants
Number of Pages: 320
Profile: Organized by province, the resource presents information about Canadian museums, their significant objects, & their location on city maps

Canadian Federation of Humane Societies (CFHS) / Fédération des sociétés canadiennes d'assistance aux animaux

#102, 30 Concourse Gate, Ottawa ON K2E 7V7
Tel: 613-224-8072; *Fax:* 613-723-0252
Toll-Free: 888-678-2347
info@cfhs.ca
www.cfhs.ca
www.linkedin.com/company/canadian-federation-of-humane-societies
www.facebook.com/HumaneCanada
twitter.com/cfhs/
www.youtube.com/user/CanadianHumane
Overview: A large national charitable organization founded in 1957
Mission: As the national voice of societies and SPCAs, the CFHS supports its member animal welfare organizations across Canada in promoting respect & humane treatment toward all animals
Chief Officer(s):
Barbara Cartwright, CEO
Kim Elmslie, Communications Coordinator
Shelagh MacDonald, Program Director
Finances: *Annual Operating Budget:* $250,000-$500,000; *Funding Sources:* Donations
Staff Member(s): 6
Membership: 40 organizations; *Member Profile:* Any society devoted to the prevention of cruelty to or suffering of animals; *Committees:* Farm Animal; Companion Animal; Member Services; Bills & Legislation; Wildlife & Habitat
Activities: *Speaker Service:* Yes; *Library* Open to public by appointment
Meetings/Conferences: • 2015 Canadian Federation of Humane Societies National Animal Welfare Conference, May, 2015, River Rock Hotel, Richmond, BC
Scope: National
Publications:
• Animal Welfare in Focus
Type: Newsletter; *Frequency:* Semiannually; *Editor:* Tanya O'Callaghan; *Price:* Free for CFHS member societies, donors, & the public upon request
Profile: Up-to-date information about the CFHS & member societies, & animal welfare news from Canada & abroad
• Canadian Federation of Humane Societies Factsheets
Price: Free
Profile: Information about companion animals, wildlife, & farm animal welfare issues
• CFHS [Canadian Federation of Humane Societies] Annual Report
Type: Yearbook; *Frequency:* Annually

Canadian Federation of Independent Business (CFIB) / Fédération canadienne de l'entreprise indépendante

#401, 4141 Yonge St., Toronto ON M2P 2A6
Tel: 416-222-8022; *Fax:* 416-222-6103
Toll-Free: 888-234-2232
cfib@cfib.ca
www.cfib-fcei.ca
www.facebook.com/pages/CFIB/142739089079987
twitter.com/cfib
www.youtube.com/user/cfibdotca
Overview: A large national organization founded in 1971
Mission: To act as the voice for small businesses in Canada
Chief Officer(s):
Dan Kelly, President & CEO
public.affairs@cfib.ca
Laura Jones, Executive Vice-President
Brien Gray, Executive Vice-President
Corinne Pohlmann, Vice-President, National Affairs
Ted Mallett, Vice-President & Chief Economist
Doug Bruce, Vice-President, Research
Membership: 109,000+; *Member Profile:* Business owners of small & medium-sized businesses in every sector across Canada
Activities: Liaising with all levels of government; Advocating for better taxes, kaws, & regulations; Offering advice to help businesses grow
Publications:
• Atlantic Mandate [a publication of the Canadian Federation of Independent Business]
Type: Newsletter
Profile: Information for Atlantic members of the Canadian Federation of Independent Business
• Business Barometer
Profile: Results of business surveys to update the CFIB business barometer index
• Canadian Federation of Independent Business Research Reports
• Canadian Federation of Independent Business Survey Results
Profile: Results of special interest surveys
• Ontario Mandate [a publication of the Canadian Federation of Independent Business]
Type: Newsletter
Profile: Information for Ontario members of the Canadian Federation of Independent Business
• Québec Mandate [a publication of the Canadian Federation of Independent Business]
Type: Newsletter
Profile: Information for Québec members of the Canadian Federation of Independent Business
• Small Business Profile
Profile: Overview of Canada's small & mid-sized business sector
• West Mandate [a publication of the Canadian Federation of Independent Business]
Type: Newsletter
Profile: Information for western members of the Canadian Federation of Independent Business

Alberta & Northwest Territories Office
#410, 237 - 8 Ave. SE, Calgary AB T2G 5C3
Tel: 403-444-9290; *Fax:* 403-261-7667
msalb@cfib.ca
twitter.com/cfibab
Chief Officer(s):
Richard Truscott, Director, Provincial Affairs, Alberta

British Columbia Office
#1430, 625 Howe St., Vancouver BC V6C 2T6
Tel: 604-684-5325; *Fax:* 604-684-0529
msbc@cfib.ca
Chief Officer(s):
Mike Klassen, Director, Provincial Affairs, British Columbia
mike.klassen@cfib.ca

Bureau du Québec
#2880, 630, boul René Levesque ouest, Montréal QC H3B 1S6
Tél: 514-861-3234; *Téléc:* 514-861-1711
samque@fcei.ca
twitter.com/fceiqc
Chief Officer(s):
Martine Hébert, Vice-Président, Québec

Calgary Office
#410, 237 - 8th Ave. SE, Calgary AB T2G 5C3
Tel: 403-444-9290; *Fax:* 403-261-7667
Toll-Free: 888-234-2232
msalb@cfib.ca
Chief Officer(s):
Richard Truscott, Director, Provincial Affairs, Alberta

Manitoba & Yukon Office
#904, 294 Portage Ave., Winnipeg MB R3C 0B9
Tel: 204-982-0817; *Fax:* 204-982-0811
msman@cfib.ca
twitter.com/cfibmb
twitter.com/cfibyt
Chief Officer(s):
Elliot Sims, Director, Provincial Affairs, Manitoba

New Brunswick Office
#204, 814 Main St., Moncton NB E1C 1E6
Tel: 506-855-2526; *Fax:* 506-855-0843
Toll-Free: 888-234-2232
msnb@cfib.ca
Chief Officer(s):
Denis Robichaud, Director, Provincial Affairs

Newfoundland & Labrador Office
#302, 136 Crosbie Rd., St. John's NL A1B 3K3
Tel: 709-753-7745; *Fax:* 709-753-7743
Toll-Free: 888-234-2232
msnl@cfib.ca
Chief Officer(s):
Vaughan Hammond, Director, Provincial Affairs

Nova Scotia Office
#819, 1888 Brunswick St., Halifax NS B3J 3J8
Tel: 902-420-1997; *Fax:* 902-422-8270
Toll-Free: 888-234-2232
msns@cfib.ca
Chief Officer(s):
Jordi Morgan, Vice-President, Atlantic Region

Ontario Office
#401, 4141 Yonge St., Toronto ON M2P 2A6
Tel: 416-222-8022; *Fax:* 416-222-4337
Toll-Free: 888-234-2232
msont@cfib.ca
Chief Officer(s):
Plamen Petkov, Vice-President, Ontario

Prince Edward Island Office
87 Pownal St., Charlottetown PE C1A 3W4
Tel: 902-620-4914; *Fax:* 902-894-9757
Toll-Free: 888-234-2232
mspei@cfib.ca
Chief Officer(s):
Erin McGrath-Gaudet, Director, PEI

Saskatchewan Office
#101, 2400 College Ave., Regina SK S4P IC8
Tel: 306-757-0000; *Fax:* 306-359-7623
mssask@cfib.ca
twitter.com/cfibsk
Chief Officer(s):
Marilyn Braun-Pollon, Vice-President, Prairie & Agri-Business

Canadian Federation of Independent Grocers (CFIG) / Fédération canadienne des épiciers indépendants

#902, 2235 Sheppard Ave. East, Toronto ON M2J 5B5
Tel: 416-492-2311; *Fax:* 416-492-2347
Toll-Free: 800-661-2344
Other Communication: membership@cfig.ca; events@cfig.ca
info@cfig.ca
www.cfig.ca
www.facebook.com/CFIGFCEI
twitter.com/cfigfcei
Overview: A large national organization founded in 1962
Mission: To equip & enable independent, franchised, & specialty grocers for sustainable success; To act as a united voice for independent grocers across Canada
Chief Officer(s):
Francois Bouchard, Chair
John F.T. Scott, President & Chief Executive Officer, 416-492-2311 Ext. 229
jftscott@cfig.ca
Ward Hanlon, Vice-President, Industry Relations, 416-492-2311 Ext. 225
whanlon@cfig.ca
Fran Nielsen, Vice-President, Finance & Administration, 416-492-2311 Ext. 236
fran@cfig.ca
Gary Sands, Vice-President, Government Relations, 416-492-2311 Ext. 230
garys@cfig.ca
Sacha Lalla, Director, Member Services, 416-492-2311 Ext. 222
slalla@cfig.ca
Eden Minty, Director, Events, 416-492-2311 Ext. 224
eminty@cfig.ca

Irina Costachescu, Tradeshow Operations Manager, Expositions, 416-492-2311 Ext. 234
icostachescu@cfig.ca
Dan Leggieri, Manager, Communications, 416-492-2311 Ext. 231
dleggieri@cfig.ca
Rolster Taylor, Tradeshow Manager, Sales, 416-492-2311 Ext. 223
rtaylor@cfig.ca
Membership: 4,000+; *Member Profile:* Independent, franchised, & specialty grocery retailers throughout Canada
Activities: Providing educational & training programs; Offering information about the food industry
Awards:
• Canadian Federation of Independent Grocers Canadian Independent Grocer of the Year (Award)
To recognize an independent & franchised retailer for their consistency & creative approach to grocery retailing*Deadline:* February *Contact:* Canadian Federation of Independent Grocers, Toll-Free Phone: 1-800-661-2344; Fax: 416-492-2347
• Canadian Master Merchandiser Awards (Award)
To recognize retailers & their suppliers with the best promotions *Contact:* Irmeli Koskinen, Coordinator, Member Services, Fax: 416-492-2347; E-mail: ikoskinen@cfig.ca
• Canadian Federation of Independent Grocers National Scholarships (Scholarship)
Scholarships are awarded, on both a regional & national basis, in the high school category & in the college & university group*Eligibility:* Applicants must be sponsored by a Canadian Federation of Independent Grocers member store*Deadline:* May *Contact:* National Scholarship, CFIG, #902, 2235 Sheppard Ave. East, Toronto, ON, M2J 5B5
• Canadian Federation of Independent Grocers Canadian Best Bagger (Award)
Eligibility: Grocery store employees from across Canada compete in an annual "bag-off"*Deadline:* September *Contact:* Canadian Federation of Independent Grocers, Toll-Free Phone: 1-800-661-2344; Fax: 416-492-2347
• Canadian Federation of Independent Grocers Life Member - Retailer (Award)
To honour the lifetime achievements of a retailer who has shown commitment to the industry through work, federation activities, & community involvement *Contact:* Diana Stevenson, Facilitator, Member Services, Phone: 416-492-2311, ext. 227, E-mail: dstevenson@cfig.ca
• Canadian Federation of Independent Grocers Life Member - Industry Builder (Award)
To honour the lifetime achievements of an industry builder, such as outstanding suppliers, manufacturers, & distributors *Contact:* Diana Stevenson, Facilitator, Member Services, Phone: 416-492-2311, ext. 227, E-mail: dstevenson@cfig.ca
Meetings/Conferences: • Canadian Federation of Independent Grocers Grocery & Specialty Food West 2015, April, 2015, Vancouver Convention Centre, Vancouver, BC
Scope: National
Attendance: 4,500
Description: An annual two day event for grocery industry professionals & over 350 exhibitors, featuring innovative products & ideas
Contact Information: General Information, E-mail: events@cfig.ca
• Canadian Federation of Independent Grocers Grocery Innovations Canada 2015, September, 2015, Toronto Congress Centre, Toronto, ON
Scope: National
Attendance: 5,000
Description: An annual event, featuring the Canadian Federation of Independent Grocers' annual general meeting, keynote presentations, panel presentations, informative conference sessions, over 500 grocery exhibits, the presentation of industry awards, & networking opportunities
Contact Information: General Information, E-mail: events@cfig.ca
Publications:
• The Canadian Retail Food Safety Manual
Type: Manual
Profile: Retail food safety practices & procedures, produced in collaboration with the Canadian Council of Grocery Distributors
• CFIG [Canadian Federation of Independent Grocers] Emergency Food Recall Registry
Profile: Current food re-calls & government announcements available to CFIG members
• CFIG's [Canadian Federation of Independent Grocers] Crisis Communication & Pandemic Planning Manual
Type: Manual
• Independent Grocer Magazine
Type: Magazine; *Accepts Advertising*
Profile: CFIG programs, activities, & member achievements, & industry & government updates, for CFIG members only
• President's Notes Newsletter [a publication of the Canadian Federation of Independent Grocers]
Type: Newsletter
Profile: Headlines plus highlights of government policies, available to CFIG members
• Privacy Guide [a publication of the Canadian Federation of Independent Grocers]
Price: Free to CFIG members
Profile: Available to CFIG members

Canadian Federation of Junior Leagues (CFJL) / Fédération canadienne des jeunes ligues
4 Steeplehill Cres., Carlisle ON L0R 1H3
Tel: 905-659-9339
info@cfjl.org
www.cfjl.org
Previous Name: Federation of Junior Leagues of Canada
Overview: A medium-sized national organization
Mission: To promote effective leadership & volunteerism for the betterment of women & the community
Member of: Association of Junior Leagues International
Chief Officer(s):
Marion Goard, National Coordinator
coordinator@cfjl.org
Fiona Colangelo, Treasurer
treasurer@cfjl.org
Membership: 28,000; *Member Profile:* Women who want to better their communities

Canadian Federation of Mayors & Municipalities *See* Federation of Canadian Municipalities

Canadian Federation of Medical Students (CFMS) / Fédération des étudiants en médecine du Canada (FEMC)
#401, 267 O'Connor St., Ottawa ON K2P 1V3
Tel: 613-565-7740; *Fax:* 613-288-0524
office@cfms.org
www.cfms.org
www.facebook.com/CFMSFEMC
twitter.com/CFMSFEMC
Overview: A medium-sized national organization founded in 1979
Mission: To support medical students by representing their voices among the national organizations that direct or influence the policy environment or delivery of medical education in Canada; to provide services that support the needs of member medical students; to communicate national medical education issues of importance to individual medical students & to facilitate communication & interaction of medical students among member schools
Member of: International Federation of Medical Students' Associations
Chief Officer(s):
Rosemary Conliffe, General Manager
Staff Member(s): 1
Membership: 7,500 individual; *Member Profile:* Canadian medical students in 14 medical schools from coast to coast

Canadian Federation of Mental Health Nurses (CFMHN) / Fédération canadienne des infirmières et infirmiers en santé mentale
#109, 1 Concorde Gate, Toronto ON M3C 3N6
Tel: 416-426-7029; *Fax:* 416-426-7280
info@cfmhn.ca
www.cfmhn.ca
twitter.com/CFMHN
Overview: A medium-sized national organization
Mission: The CFMHN is a national voice for psychiatric and mental health (PMH) nursing. They wish to assure leadership in the development and application of nursing standards that inform and affect psychiatric and mental health nursing practice; examine and influence government policy, and address national issues related to mental health and mental illness; communicate and collaborate with national and international groups that share our professional interests; faciliate excellence in psychiatric and mental health nursing by providing members with educational and networking resources.
Affiliation(s): Canadian Nurses Association
Chief Officer(s):
Chris Davis, President
Finances: *Funding Sources:* Membership fees; workshops; conferences
11 volunteer(s)
Membership: 100-499; *Fees:* $40; *Member Profile:* Registered nurse or associate members: registered psychiatric nurse, nursing student
Activities: Certification in psychiatric & mental health nursing exam with CNA; *Speaker Service:* Yes

Canadian Federation of Music Teachers' Associations (CFMTA) / Fédération canadienne des associations des professeurs de musique
#302, 550 Berkshire Dr., London ON N6J 3S2
Tel: 519-471-6051
admin@cfmta.org
www.cfmta.org
Overview: A small national charitable organization founded in 1935
Mission: To promote high musical & academic qualifications among members
Chief Officer(s):
Charline Farrell, President
president@cfmta.org
Membership: *Member Profile:* Teachers must hold degree in music from university or recognized school of music;
Committees: By-Laws & Standing Rules; Finance; Public Relations & Marketing; Young Artist National; Translation; Canada Music Week; Nominations & Elections; Professional Development and Research; Awards & Competitions; Policies & Procedures; Strategic Planning
Activities: Young Artists Series gives students a chance to perform in various venues in Canada;
Meetings/Conferences: • 2015 Canadian Federation of Music Teachers' Associations Convention - "Pathways", July, 2015, Sheraton Vancouver Airport Hotel, Richmond, BC
Scope: National

Canadian Federation of Nurses Unions (CFNU) / La Fédération canadienne des syndicats d'infirmières/infirmiers
2841 Riverside Dr., Ottawa ON K1V 8X7
Tel: 613-526-4661; *Fax:* 613-526-1023
Toll-Free: 800-321-9821
www.nursesunions.ca
www.facebook.com/NursesUnions
twitter.com/CFNU
Previous Name: National Federation of Nurses' Unions
Overview: A large national organization founded in 1981
Mission: To advance the social, economic & general welfare of its members; To act on national matters of significant concern to the Federation; To promote unity among nurses' unions & other allied health care workers who share the objectives of the CFNU; To provide a national forum to promote desirable legislation on matters of national significance; To preserve free democratic unionism & collective bargaining in Canada; To support other organizations sharing the Union's objectives
Member of: Canadian Labour Congress
Affliation(s): Canadian Nursing Students Association
Chief Officer(s):
Linda Silas, President
president@nursesunions.ca
Pauline Worsfold, Secretary-Treasurer
Staff Member(s): 8
Membership: 156,000; *Fees:* Per capita
Meetings/Conferences: • Canadian Federation of Nurses Unions Convention 2015, June, 2015, Halifax, NS
Scope: National
Publications:
• Canadian Federation of Nurses Unions Research Reports
• Conversations with Champions of Medicare
Author: Ann Silversides
• Nurses' Voice
Type: Newsletter; *Frequency:* 10 pa
Profile: CFNU information, upcoming events, commentary on federal politics, news from nurses' unions across Canada, & international news

Canadian Federation of Orthotherapists (CFO) / Fédération Canadienne des Orthothérapeutes (FCO)
1778, rue Pir-Vir, Saint-Valentin QC J0J 2E0
Fax: 514-525-2167
Toll-Free: 888-330-6776
info@fco-cfo.ca
fco-cfo.ca
Overview: A large national organization founded in 1998
Mission: Maintain the integrity of the orthotherapist profession
Membership: *Member Profile:* Message therapists; kinesitherapists; orthotherapists

Canadian Federation of Pensioners (CFP) / Fédération Canadienne des Retraités (FCR)

133 Stonehome Cres., Almonte ON K0A 1A0
Other Communication: Membership E-mail:
membership@pensioners.ca
info@pensioners.ca
pensioners.ca
Overview: A small national organization founded in 2005
Mission: To advocate on defined benefit pension plan issues on behalf of pensioners
Chief Officer(s):
Mike Campbell, Media Contact, 416-948-8281
michael.campbell@pensioners.ca
Anne Clark-Stewart, Media Contact, 905-891-8220
anne.clark-stewart@pensioners.ca
Bob Farmer, Media Contact, 613-256-8130
robert.farmer@pensioners.ca
Membership: 20; *Member Profile:* Retiree groups

Canadian Federation of Podiatric Medicine (CFPM)

200 King St. South, Waterloo ON N2J 1P9
Fax: 519-888-9385
Toll-Free: 888-706-4444
cfpmexe.dir@cfpmcanada.ca
www.podiatryinfocanada.ca
Overview: A small national organization founded in 1999
Mission: To maintain, advance and promote the science and the practice of podiatry in Canada by representing the profession to government, community and other professional bodies.
Chief Officer(s):
Cindy Hartman, Executive Director

Canadian Federation of Sport Organizations for the Disabled *See* Canadian Paralympic Committee

Canadian Federation of Students (CFS) / Fédération canadienne des étudiantes et étudiants (FCEE)

338C Somerset St. West, Ottawa ON K2P 0J9
Tel: 613-232-7394; *Fax:* 613-232-0276
web@cfs-fcee.ca
www.cfs-fcee.ca
twitter.com/CFSFCEE
instagram.com/cfsfcee
Overview: A large national organization founded in 1981
Mission: To represent the collective interests of college & university students across Canada; To act as a unified voice for Canadian university & college students
Chief Officer(s):
Jessica McCormick, National Chair
Bilan Arte, National Deputy Chair
Gabe Hoogers, National Treasurer
Kevin Godbout, Representative, Graduate Students
Anne-Marie Roy, Representative, Francophone Students
Yolen Bollo-Kamara, Representative, Women
Simka Marshall, Representative, Aboriginal Students
Rajean Hoilett, Representative, Racialised Students
Finances: *Funding Sources:* Membership fees
Membership: 80+ student unions, with 500,000+ students; *Member Profile:* University & college students' unions from across Canada
Activities: Liaising with federal & provincial governments; Lobbying on issues, such as tuition fees & funding; Assisting in the pooling of resources to provide the National Student Health Network, the Student Work Abroad Program, & the International Student Identity Card
Publications:
• Students' Union Directory
Type: Directory; *Frequency:* Annually
Profile: Listing of students' unions, affiliated campus organizations, & campus media outlets throughout Canada

Canadian Federation of the Theosophical Society *See* Canadian Theosophical Association

Canadian Federation of University Women (CFUW) / Fédération canadienne des femmes diplômées des universités (FCFDU)

Head Office, #502, 331 Cooper St., Ottawa ON K2P 0G5
Tel: 613-234-8252; *Fax:* 613-234-8221
cfuwgen@rogers.com
www.cfuw.org
www.facebook.com/groups/2232370205
Overview: A large national organization founded in 1919
Mission: To pursue knowledge; to promote education; to improve the status of women & human rights; To participate actively in public affairs in a spirit of cooperation & friendship
Chief Officer(s):
Susan Murphy, President
Robin Jackson, Executive Director
cfuwed@rogers.com
Janice Pillon, Coordinator, Member Services
cfuwgen@rogers.com
Betty Dunlop, Manager, Fellowship Program
fellowships@cfuw.org
Tara Fischer, Coordinator, Advocacy
cfuwadvocacy@rogers.com
Ryszard Kowalski, Developer, Bookkeeper & Software
cfuwfin@rogers.com
Finances: *Annual Operating Budget:* $250,000-$500,000; *Funding Sources:* Membership dues
Staff Member(s): 5; 30 volunteer(s)
Membership: 9,000 individuals in 107 clubs; *Member Profile:* Women university graduates; *Committees:* Education; Fellowships; Finance; International Relations; Libraries & Creative Arts; Communication; Resolutions; Status of Women & Human Rights; Membership
Meetings/Conferences: • Canadian Federation of University Women 2015 Annual General Meeting, June, 2015, Québec City, QC
Scope: National
Publications:
• CFUW [Canadian Federation of University Women] History & Heroines
Profile: An eight volume series tracing Canadian Federation of University Women's historical highlights decade by decade
• CFUW [Canadian Federation of University Women] Women In Action
Profile: Published several times each year on select intiatives surrounding women's issues, such as employment insurance, education for all, HIV & AIDS, childcare, & security& prosperity
• CFUW [Canadian Federation of University Women]: A Year in Action
Frequency: Annually
• Communicator / La Communicatrice [a publication of the Canadian Federation of University Women]
Type: Newsletter; *Frequency:* 5 pa
Profile: CFUW's current events from across Canada

Canadian Federation of Vietnamese Associations of Canada *See* Vietnamese Canadian Federation

Canadian Feed Industry Association *See* Animal Nutrition Association of Canada

Canadian Feed The Children (CFTC)

174 Bartley Dr., Toronto ON M4A 1E1
Tel: 416-757-1220; *Fax:* 416-757-3318
Toll-Free: 800-387-1221
contact@canadianfeedthechildren.ca
www.canadianfeedthechildren.ca
www.linkedin.com/company/canadian-feed-the-children
www.facebook.com/CanadianFeedTheChildren
twitter.com/cdnfeedchildren
www.youtube.com/user/canadianfeed
Overview: A medium-sized international charitable organization founded in 1986
Mission: To alleviate the impact of poverty on children; we work with local partners overseas & in Canada to enhance the well-being of children & the self-sufficiency of their families & communities.
Member of: Canadian Council for International Cooperation
Chief Officer(s):
Debra Kerby, Executive Director
Finances: *Annual Operating Budget:* Greater than $5 Million; *Funding Sources:* Foundations; private contributions; CIDA
Staff Member(s): 13
Membership: *Committees:* Finance & Audit; Nomination & Governance
Activities: *Speaker Service:* Yes

Canadian Fence Industry Association (CFIA) / Association canadienne de l'industrie de la clôture

PO Box 516, 22 John St., Drayton ON N0G 1P0
Tel: 519-638-0101; *Fax:* 519-489-2805
info@cfia.ca
www.cfia.ca
Overview: A medium-sized national licensing organization founded in 1968
Mission: To ensure the industry maintains high standards of quality of work as well as ethics
Member of: American Fencing Association
Chief Officer(s):
Martin McCooey, President
president@cfia.ca
Bob Bignell, Executive Secretary
execsecretary@cfia.ca
Finances: *Funding Sources:* Membership dues
Membership: 170; *Fees:* $350; *Member Profile:* Residential & commercial manufacturers; retailers; installers

Ontario
c/o Medallion Fence, 10651 Keele St., Maple ON L6A 3Y9
Tel: 905-832-2922; *Fax:* 905-832-1564
Chief Officer(s):
Sid Isenberg, President
sid@medallionfence.com

Québec
a/s Clôture Solival Inc., 5274, boul Cléroux, Laval QC H7T 2E8
Tel: 450-682-1318; *Fax:* 450-682-0061
quebecpres@cfia.ca
Chief Officer(s):
Kim Raymond, President
kraymond@cloturesolival.com

Western
c/o Align Fence Inc., 11403 - 199 St., Edmonton AB T5S 2C6
Tel: 780-438-7300
westernpres@cfia.ca
Chief Officer(s):
Justin Reyolds, President

Canadian Fencing Federation (CFF) / Fédération canadienne d'escrime

10 Masterson Dr., St Catharines ON L2T 3P1
Tel: 647-476-2401; *Fax:* 647-476-2402
cff@fencing.ca
www.fencing.ca
www.facebook.com/168914029806258
twitter.com/fencingcanada
Also Known As: Fencing Canada
Overview: A medium-sized national charitable organization founded in 1971
Mission: To promote & develop the sport of fencing in Canada.
Affliation(s): Fédération internationale d'escrime
Chief Officer(s):
Brad Goldie, President
president@fencing.ca
Caroline Sharp, Executive Director
ed@fencing.ca
Finances: *Funding Sources:* Membership fees; government; Olympic Association
Staff Member(s): 3

Canadian Ferry Operators Association (CFOA) / Association canadienne des opérateurs de traversiers

c/o Mr. Serge Buy, 70 George St., 3rd Fl., Ottawa ON K1N 5V9
Tel: 613-686-3838; *Fax:* 613-482-3604
www.cfoa.ca
Overview: A small national organization founded in 1987
Mission: To establish & maintain a standard of professional & technical excellence in the operation of Canadian ferries; To promote & protect the interests of members of the association
Chief Officer(s):
Serge Buy, Executive Director
sbuy@cfoa.ca
David Miller, President, 604-467-7298, Fax: 604-463-5693
dave_miller@translink.bc.ca
Finances: *Funding Sources:* Sponsorships
Membership: 37; *Member Profile:* Major ferry owners & operators in Canada
Activities: Providing opportunities for discussion of matters of interest to members; Promoting the safety, reliability, & efficiency of Canadian ferry operators; Providing representation at regulatory forums such as CMAC
Publications:
• CFOA [Canadian Ferry Operators Association] News
Type: Newsletter
Profile: Articles of interest to the marine community

Canadian Fertility & Andrology Society (CFAS) / Société canadienne de fertilité et d'andrologie

#1107, 1255, rue University, Montréal QC H3B 3W7
Tel: 514-524-9009; *Fax:* 514-524-2163
info@cfas.ca
www.cfas.ca
Previous Name: Canadian Society for the Study of Fertility
Merged from: Canadian Andrology Society

Overview: A medium-sized national charitable organization founded in 1954
Mission: To speak on behalf of interested parties in the field of assisted reproductive technologies & research in reproductive sciences
Chief Officer(s):
Carl A. Laskin, President
Mathias Gysler, Vice-President
Agneta Holländer, Executive Director
Jeff Roberts, Director, Continuing Professional Development
Janet Fraser, Secretary-Treasurer
janet.fraser@aart.ca
Finances: *Funding Sources:* Membership fees; Sponsorships
Staff Member(s): 2
Membership: 625+; *Fees:* $25 trainees; $100 non-MDs; $150 medical doctors; *Member Profile:* Reproductive healthcare specialists & scientists, such as gynecologists, obstetricians, reproductive endocrinologists, psychologists, social workers, nurses, laboratory technicians, research scientists, ethicists, & lawyers; Medical students, interns, residents, graduate students, & fellows; *Committees:* Governance; Continuing Professional Development; Industry Liaison; Nominations & Elections; Government Relations; Finance; Membership; Communications; Awards
Activities: Establishing practice guidelines & standards; Providing continuing professional development credits, as recognized by the Royal College of Physicians & Surgeons of Canada; Offering public education
Meetings/Conferences: • Canadian Fertility & Andrology Society 2015 61st Annual Meeting, October, 2015, Marriott Harbourfront Hotel, Halifax, NS
Scope: National
Attendance: 350
Description: Educational presentations, a trade show, & networking opportunities for persons involved in the field of reproductive medicine
• Canadian Fertility & Andrology Society 2016 62nd Annual Meeting, September, 2016, Sheraton Centre, Toronto, ON
Scope: National
Description: Educational presentations, a trade show, & networking opportunities for persons involved in the field of reproductive medicine
Publications:
• CFAS [Canadian Fertility & Andrology Society] Communiqué
Type: Newsletter
Profile: CFAS information & events, plus articles
• Presidents' Annual Report [a publication of the Canadian Fertility & Andrology Society]
Type: Yearbook; *Frequency:* Annually

Canadian Fertilizer Institute (CFI) / Institut canadien des engrais
#907, 350 Sparks St., Ottawa ON K1R 7S8
Tel: 613-230-2600; *Fax:* 613-230-5142
info@cfi.ca
www.cfi.ca
Overview: A medium-sized national organization
Chief Officer(s):
Roger L. Larson, President, 613-230-2600
president@cfi.ca
Dave Finlayson, Vice-President, Science & Risk Management, 613-786-3031
dfinlayson@cfi.ca
Clyde Graham, Vice-President, Strategy & Alliances, 613-786-3033
cgraham@cfi.ca
Kristian Stephens, Senior Manager, Technical Affairs, 613-786-3035
kstephens@cfi.ca
Robert Godfrey, Manager, Policy, 613-786-3034
Catherine King, Manager, Communications, 613-786-3026
Monique MacDonald, Manager, Finance & Corporate Services, 613-786-3032
Membership: 70 organizations
Meetings/Conferences: • Canadian Fertilizer Institute 70th Annual Conference, August, 2015, The Westin, Bayshore, Vancouver, BC
Scope: National
• Canadian Fertilizer Institute 71st Annual Conference, August, 2016, Fairmont Tremblant Quebec, Mont-Tremblant, QC
Scope: National
• Canadian Fertilizer Institute 72nd Annual Conference, 2017
Scope: National

Canadian Field Hockey Association *See* Field Hockey Canada

Canadian Film & Television Production Association *See* Canadian Media Production Association

Canadian Film Centre (CFC) / Centre canadien du film
2489 Bayview Ave., Toronto ON M2L 1A8
Tel: 416-445-1446; *Fax:* 416-445-9481
info@cdnfilmcentre.com
www.cfccreates.com
www.facebook.com/cfccreates
twitter.com/cfccreates
www.youtube.com/user/CanadianFilmCentre
Previous Name: Canadian Centre for Advanced Film Studies
Overview: A medium-sized national charitable organization founded in 1988
Mission: To operate as Canada's foremost film, televion, & new media institution; To advance Canadian creative talent, content, & values worldwide, through training, production, promotion & investment
Chief Officer(s):
Slawko Klymkiw, Chief Executive Officer
Finances: *Funding Sources:* Government grants; private sector
Staff Member(s): 53

Canadian Film Institute (CFI) / Institut canadien du film (ICF)
#120, 2 Daly Ave., Ottawa ON K1N 6E2
Tel: 613-232-6727; *Fax:* 613-232-6315
info@cfi-icf.ca
www.cfi-icf.ca
Overview: A medium-sized national charitable organization founded in 1935
Mission: To promote Canadian cinema; To assist in locating sources for rental or purchase of individual films & videos; To give subject & content information on theatrical & non-theatrical films & videos from both private & public sources; To give general information on Canadian & international film, video, & television production, distribution, exhibition, & related subjects
Chief Officer(s):
Jack Horwitz, Chair
Tom McSorley, Executive Director & Secretary
Jerrett Zaret, Coordinator, Sponsorship
Michael Leong, Treasurer
Finances: *Funding Sources:* All levels of government; Sponsorships; Fundraising
Membership: 450; *Fees:* $10
Activities: Operating a cinema & information centre; Organizing festivals & conferences; *Rents Mailing List:* Yes; *Library* by appointment

Canadian Filmmakers Distribution Centre (CFMDC)
#245, 401 Richmond St. West, Toronto ON M5V 3A8
Tel: 416-588-0725
cfmdc@cfmdc.org
www.cfmdc.org
www.facebook.com/cfmdcmembers
Overview: A medium-sized national organization founded in 1967
Mission: To promote & distribute the work of independent Canadian filmmakers.
Chief Officer(s):
Lauren Howes, Executive Director
director@cfmdc.org
Staff Member(s): 8
Membership: 550 individual; *Fees:* $75 filmmaker; $35 student; $50 research; *Member Profile:* Individuals interested in independent Canadian film or production company; generally film-makers distributed by centre
Activities: *Library* Open to public by appointment

Canadian Finance & Leasing Association (CFLA) / Association canadienne de financement et de location (ACFL)
#301, 15 Toronto St., Toronto ON M5C 2E3
Tel: 416-860-1133; *Fax:* 416-860-1140
Toll-Free: 877-213-7373
info@cfla-acfl.ca
www.cfla-acfl.ca
www.linkedin.com/company/1360377
Merged from: Canadian Automotive Leasing Association; Equipment Lessors Association of Canada
Overview: A medium-sized national organization founded in 1973
Mission: To ensure an environment in Canada where asset-based financing, equipment & vehicle-leasing industry can be profitable
Chief Officer(s):
David Powell, President & CEO, 416-860-1133 Ext. 24
david.powell@cfla-acfl.ca
Matthew Poirier, Director, Policy, 416-860-1133 Ext. 26
matthew@cfla-acfl.ca
Lalita Sirnaik, Manager, Finance & Administration, 416-860-1133 Ext. 22
lalita@cfla-acfl.ca
Finances: *Annual Operating Budget:* $500,000-$1.5 Million; *Funding Sources:* Membership fees; events fees
Staff Member(s): 5; 120 volunteer(s)
Membership: 200+ companies; *Member Profile:* Represents the asset-based financing, equipment & vehicle-leasing industry in Canada, ranging from large multinationals to regional financing companies; *Committees:* Accounting; Auto Finance Working Group; Board of Directors; Education & Program; Fleet; Government Relations; Legal; Membership; Small Ticket Funders; Tax; Technology
Activities: *Speaker Service:* Yes; *Library:* Resource Centre
Meetings/Conferences: • Canadian Finance & Leasing Association 2015 Conference, 2015
Scope: National

Canadian Finnsheep Breeders' Association
Box 10, Site 10, RR#4, Stony Plain AB T7Z 1X4
Tel: 888-963-0416
info@finnsheep.ca
www.finnsheep.ca
Overview: A small national organization founded in 1969
Mission: To encourage, develop, & regulate the breeding of Finnsheep; To protect & assist Finnsheep breeders
Affliation(s): Canadian Livestock Records Corporation
Chief Officer(s):
Kathy Playdon, President, 888-963-0416
Lorna Woolsey, Registrar, 613-731-7110 Ext. 306, Fax: 613-731-0704
Laura Lee Mills, Registrar (French), 613-731-7110 Ext. 314, Fax: 613-731-0704
Membership: 1-99; *Fees:* $10 / year; *Member Profile:* Individuals, partnerships, shareholders, companies, or firms engaged in the breeding & propagation of Finnsheep across Canada; *Committees:* Executive; Registration; Special Committees
Activities: Establishing breeding standards; Maintaining records of the breeding & origin of Finnsheep; Compiling statistics of the industry; Supervising breeders of Finnsheep to prevent fraud

Canadian Fire Alarm Association (CFAA)
#3-4, 85 Citizen Ct., Markham ON L6G 1A8
Tel: 905-944-0030; *Fax:* 905-479-3639
Toll-Free: 800-529-0552
admin@cfaa.ca
www.cfaa.ca
Overview: A small national organization founded in 1973
Mission: To maximize the effectiveness and use of fire alarm systems in the protection of life and property in Canada.
Chief Officer(s):
Steve Clemens, Executive Director, 905-944-0030
sclemens@cfaa.ca
Ruth Kavanagh, Office Supervisor, 905-944-0030
Finances: *Annual Operating Budget:* $500,000-$1.5 Million; *Funding Sources:* Membership, registration and training fees
Staff Member(s): 4; 100 volunteer(s)
Membership: 400; *Fees:* $20 student; $50 associate; $225 participating; $500 sustaining; *Committees:* Education; Marketing & Communications; Industry Affairs; Revitalization & Membership; Technicians; Finance; Governance
Activities: Technician Training; Technician Registration; Authority Having Jurisdiction (AHJ) Fire Alarm Training; Building Owner/Manager Fire Alarm Training; Fire Alarm Standards and Legislation; *Internships:* Yes; *Speaker Service:* Yes
Awards:
• Fire Alarm Technology Program High Achievement (Scholarship)
Eligibility: Graduate of a Canadian Fire Alarm Technology Program*Deadline:* June 1, annually *Amount:* $500
Publications:
• Canadian Fire Alarm Association Journal
Type: Journal
Profile: Canadian Fire Alarm Industry News and Updates for AHJ's, Building Owners/Managers and those in the fire alarm manufacturing or service industry.

Canadian Fire Safety Association (CFSA)
#310, 2175 Sheppard Ave. East, Toronto ON M2J 1W8
Tel: 416-492-9417; *Fax:* 416-491-1670
cfsa@taylorenterprises.com

www.canadianfiresafety.com
twitter.com/CFSA4
Overview: A medium-sized national organization founded in 1971
Mission: To promote fire safety through seminars, safety training courses, scholarships & regular meetings.
Chief Officer(s):
Matteo Gilfillan, President
mgilfillan@rbacodes.com
Carolyne Vigon, Administrator
carolyne@taylorenterprises.com
Finances: *Funding Sources:* Membership fees
Membership: *Fees:* Schedule available; *Member Profile:* Membership represents a broad cross-section of government, business & education including architects, engineers, fire officials, building officials, fire protection consultants, manufacturers, the insurance industry, teachers & students.

Canadian Fisheries Association *See* Fisheries Council of Canada

Canadian Fitness & Lifestyle Research Institute (CFLRI) / Institut canadien de la recherche sur la condition physique et le mode de vie

#201, 185 Somerset St. West, Ottawa ON K2P 0J2
Tel: 613-233-5528; *Fax:* 613-233-5536
www.cflri.ca
Previous Name: Canada Fitness Survey (1985)
Overview: A medium-sized national charitable organization founded in 1980
Mission: To conduct research, monitor trends, & make recommendations to increase physical activity & improve health in Canada
Chief Officer(s):
Nancy Dubois, Chair
Christine Cameron, Acting President
Mathilde Costa, Senior Manager, Finance, Administration, & Human Resources
Cora Lynn Craig, Senior Researcher
Finances: *Funding Sources:* Fitness / Active Living Program Unit of Health Canada; Contracts; Grants; Publication sales; Donations
Activities: Providing education about leading active & healthy lives; Developing a aprovider-based intervention known as PACE Canada; Conducting surveys, such as The Canadian Physical Activity Levels Among Youth (CAN PLAY)
Publications:
• Capacity Study
Frequency: Annually
Profile: Information to increase physical activity in the Canadian workplace
• Kids CANPLAY
Profile: Information to encourage children to be active at home, at school, & in the community
• The Lifestyle Tips
Profile: Practical suggestions for integrating physical activity into daily life
• Physical Activity Monitor
Frequency: Irregular; *ISBN:* 1-895724-49-X
Profile: Report presents trends in physical activity among Canadian workers
• The Research File
ISSN: 1188-6641
Profile: Ongoing series of research summaries about physical activity, for professionals

Canadian Fjord Horse Association

c/o Canadian Livestock Records Corporation, 2417 Holly Ln., Ottawa ON K1V 0M7
Tel: 613-731-7110; *Fax:* 613-731-0704
directors@cfha.org
www.cfha.org
www.facebook.com/canadianfjord
twitter.com/canadianfjord
www.youtube.com/canadianfjord
Overview: A small national organization founded in 1977
Mission: To operate under the Animal Pedigree Act; To assure the success of the purebred registered Norwegian Fjord Horse in Canada
Member of: Fjord Horse International Association (FHI)
Affliation(s): Canadian Livestock Records Corporation
Chief Officer(s):
Carol Boehm, President, 250-838-7782
Lauralee Mills, CLRC Contact
lauralee.mills@clrc.ca
Membership: *Fees:* $40 regular; $25 junior/additional members; *Member Profile:* Owners & admirers of the Fjord Horse in Canada; *Committees:* Promotions; Membership; Education & Evaluation
Activities: Registering animals & keeping pedigrees; Providing education about the Norwegian Fjord Horse; Raising awareness & understanding of the breed; Encouraging members to show the Norwegian Fjord Horse
Publications:
• Canadian Fjord Horse Association Newsletter
Type: Newsletter; *Editor:* Darlene Shewfelt

Canadian Flag Association (CFA) / Association canadienne de vexillologie (ACV)

409 - 60 C Line, Orangeville ON L9W 0A9
e-mail: cfa.acv@gmail.com
cfa-acv.tripod.com
www.facebook.com/317266027131
Overview: A small national organization founded in 1985
Mission: To gather, organize & disseminate flag information with particular emphasis on flags having some association with Canada; to promote vexillology; to encourage & facilitate exchange of ideas between flag scholars, flag makers, flag collectors, flag designers & flag historians
Member of: Fédération Internationale des Associations Vexillologiques
Chief Officer(s):
Kevin Harrington, President
Finances: *Funding Sources:* Membership fees
Membership: *Member Profile:* Flag historians (vexillologists); flag collectors; flag makers; flag retailers; flag archivists
Activities: *Speaker Service:* Yes; *Rents Mailing List:* Yes; *Library* by appointment
Publications:
• Flagscan
Frequency: Quarterly; *Editor:* Kevin Harrington *ISSN:* 0833-1510

Canadian Fluid Power Association (CFPA) / Association canadienne d'énergie fluide

#310, 2175 Sheppard Ave. East, Toronto ON M2J 1W8
Tel: 416-499-1416; *Fax:* 416-491-1670
info@cfpa.ca
www.cfpa.ca
www.linkedin.com/groups?gid=4704028
twitter.com/CANADIANFPA
Overview: A medium-sized national organization founded in 1974
Mission: To build public awareness of fluid power technology; To provide a forum for the exchange of information & opinion; To represent the Canadian fluid power industry to government, educational institutions & other organizations; To ensure that members' concerns are known to those in government; To ensure that students are able to be properly prepared for careers in the fluid power industry; To ensure that members are kept abreast of the latest developments in the fluid power industry
Member of: National Fluid Power Association
Chief Officer(s):
Trish Torrance, Manager
torrance@cfpa.ca
John Lamb, Emerson, Chairman
Finances: *Funding Sources:* Membership fees; Sponsorships
10 volunteer(s)
Membership: 80 corporate; *Fees:* $588.50 large corporation; $401.25 small corporation; $160.50 individual; *Member Profile:* Open to manufacturers, distributors, assemblers, educators, consultants & designers of fluid power components, systems & services; *Committees:* Communications; Membership; Market Insights; Education; Industrial Relations; Regional Events
Activities: Representing the fluid power industry on the Canadian advisory committee with regard to the drafting of international standards; Representing the fluid power industry in the formulation of applicable national standards; *Speaker Service:* Yes
Meetings/Conferences: • Canadian Fluid Power Association 2015 Annual General Meeting, 2015
Scope: National

Canadian Food Exporters Association (CFEA)

#600, 100 Sheppard Ave. East, Toronto ON M2N 6N5
Tel: 416-445-3747; *Fax:* 416-510-8043
Toll-Free: 888-227-8848
info@cfea.com
www.cfea.com
www.linkedin.com/company/1656071
www.facebook.com/canadianfoodexportersassociation
twitter.com/cfea
Overview: A medium-sized national organization founded in 1996
Mission: To enhance export efforts in the food & beverage industry; To raise the international profile of Canadian food & beverage products; To increase the export sales of food & beverage products
Affliation(s): Food Beverage Canada (FBC)
Membership: *Member Profile:* Food & beverage manufacturers which export or wish to expand into new markets; *Committees:* Government Relations; Membership; Awards
Activities: Increasing exporting by small to medium-sized food & beverage processors & manufacturers; Providing a Central Information Clearinghouse & information network; Offering workshops; Coordinating trade shows & developing trade missions; Provding assistance in meeting technical regulations; Offering an in-house label service
Publications:
• Canadian Food Exporters Association Member Directory
Type: Directory
Profile: Contact information distributed to Canadian Food Exporters Association members & potential buyers
• CFEA [Canadian Food Exporters Association] E-News
Type: Newsletter; *Frequency:* Weekly
Profile: Canadian Food Exporters Association activities, industry trends, & market news & intelligence

Canadian Food for Children (CFFC)

40 King George Rd., Toronto ON M8X 1L3
Tel: 416-231-2817
www.canadianfoodforchildren.net
Overview: A small national charitable organization founded in 1985
Mission: To raise funds, gather goods, & purchase food for the hungry in developing countries; To collaborate with Universal Aide Society to make shipments directly to countries such as the Philippines, Ghana, Romania, Ukraine, & Nicaragua
Affliation(s): Universal Aide Society
Chief Officer(s):
Andrew Simone, Founder
Finances: *Funding Sources:* Donations; Corporate sponsoships
Membership: *Member Profile:* Individuals who care about the poor of the world, & who volunteer for the non-denominational, registered charity, which operates under the Society's Act & the guidelines of Revenue Canada
Activities: Collecting supplies that are donated by a variety of groups; Conducting tours of the Langley, British Columbia depot for school students; Issuing tax receipts for cash & "gifts in kind" tax receipts for donated materials; Operating a thrift shop; Fundraising

Canadian Food for the Hungry International

#1, 31741 Peardonville Rd., Abbotsford BC V2T 1L2
Tel: 604-853-4262; *Fax:* 604-853-4332
Toll-Free: 800-667-0605
info@fhcanada.org
www.fhcanada.org
www.facebook.com/Poverty.Revolution
twitter.com/fhcanada/
Overview: A medium-sized international charitable organization
Mission: To help developing countries overcome poverty through Christianity
Chief Officer(s):
Ben Hoogendoorn, President & CEO

Canadian Food Industry Council *See* Canadian Grocery HR Council

Canadian Food Service Executives Association *See* Canadian Association of Foodservice Professionals

Canadian Food Service Supervisors Association *See* Canadian Society of Nutrition Management

Canadian Foodgrains Bank Association Inc. (CFGB) / Association de la banque canadienne de grains inc.

PO Box 767, #400, 393 Portage Ave., Winnipeg MB R3C 2L4
Tel: 204-944-1993; *Fax:* 204-943-2597
Toll-Free: 800-665-0377
Other Communication: www.flickr.com/photos/foodgrainsbank
cfgb@foodgrainsbank.ca
foodgrainsbank.ca
www.facebook.com/CanadianFoodgrainsBank
twitter.com/FoodgrainsJames
www.youtube.com/user/foodgrainsbank

Also Known As: Foodgrains Bank
Overview: A large international charitable organization founded in 1983
Mission: To provide a Christian response to hunger; to share resources with & support hungry populations outside Canada to achieve food security; to reduce hunger in developing countries
Chief Officer(s):
Donald Peters, Chair
Jim Cornelius, Executive Director
jcornelius@foodgrainsbank.ca
Finances: *Funding Sources:* Donations; Fundraising
Membership: 15; *Member Profile:* Canadian churches & church-related agencies
Activities: Improving community development; Protecting & building sustainable economic livelihoods; Encouraging peace-building; Strengthening Canadian & international policy & action towards hunger issues; Increasing public awareness & engagement; Collecting grain & cash donations
Publications:
• Breaking Bread [a publication of Canadian Foodgrains Bank Association Inc.]
Type: Newsletter; *Frequency:* s-a.; *Number of Pages:* 6
• Canadian Foodgrains Bank Annual Report
Type: Yearbook; *Frequency:* Annually

Canadian Football Hall of Fame & Museum
58 Jackson St. West, Hamilton ON L8P 1L4
Tel: 905-528-7566; *Fax:* 905-528-9781
info@cfhof.ca
www.cfhof.ca
www.facebook.com/CFHOFandM
twitter.com/cfhof
www.youtube.com/user/CFHOFandM
Overview: A small national charitable organization founded in 1963
Mission: The Hall & Museum commemorate & promote the names & careers of those who have contributed to the development of Canadian football. Artifacts & other memorabilia that relate to the history of the sport are collected, preserved, documented, & exhibited. Education programs offered to students, grades K-8. The Hall & Museum are a non-profit, registered charity, BN: 106845993RR0001.
Chief Officer(s):
Dave Marler, Chair
Mark DeNobile, Executive Director
mark@cfhof.ca
Christopher Alfred, Curator
chris@cfhof.ca
Finances: *Annual Operating Budget:* $100,000-$250,000
Staff Member(s): 2; 70 volunteer(s)
Activities: Induction weekend; Grey Cup week; school outreach program; gift shop; collections; *Library* by appointment

Canadian Football League (CFL) / Ligue canadienne de football (LCF)
50 Wellington St. East, 3rd Fl., Toronto ON M5E 1C8
Tel: 416-322-9650; *Fax:* 416-322-9651
www.cfl.ca
www.facebook.com/CFL
twitter.com/CFL
www.youtube.com/CFL
Overview: A large national licensing organization founded in 1958
Affiliation(s): Canadian Football League Players' Association (CFLPA); Canadian Football League Alumni Association (CFLAA); Football Canada; Canadian Interuniversity Sport (CIS); Canadian Football Hall of Fame; Canadian Football Officials Association
Chief Officer(s):
Mark Cohon, Commissioner
Michael Copeland, President & COO
David Cuddy, Vice-President, Finance & Business Operations
Matt Maychak, Vice-President, Communications & Broadcast
Kevin McDonald, Vice-President, Football Operations
Membership: 9 CFL teams
Activities: *Awareness Events:* Grey Cup Championship Game; *Rents Mailing List:* Yes

Canadian Football League Alumni Association (CFLAA)
ON
Tel: 905-639-6359
Toll-Free: 877-890-7272
www.cflaa.ca
www.facebook.com/cflaa
twitter.com/CFL_Alumni
www.youtube.com/user/CFLAlumniAssociation
Overview: A large national organization
Mission: To foster a lifelong connection between the Canadian Football League & its alumni; to provide support to the alumni community
Chief Officer(s):
Hector Pothier, President
Leo Ezerins, Executive Director
leo@cflalumni.org
Finances: *Funding Sources:* Donations
Publications:
• Alumni Update [a publication of the Canadian Football League Alumni Association]
Type: Newsletter

Canadian Football League Players' Association (CFLPA) / Association des joueurs de la ligue de football canadienne
175 Barton St. East, Stoney Creek ON L8E 2K3
Tel: 905-664-0852; *Fax:* 905-664-9653
Toll-Free: 800-616-6865
admin@cflpa.com
www.cflpa.com
www.facebook.com/proplayers.cflpa
Overview: A small national organization founded in 1965
Mission: The Canadian Football League Players' Association was established in 1965 & has since that time represented the professional football players in the Canadian Football League with the objective of establishing fair & reasonable working conditions for the players.
Chief Officer(s):
Mike Morreale, President & Vice-President, Marketing & Business Development
m.morreale@cflpa.com
Jay McNeil, 1st Vice-President
Scott Flory, 2nd Vice-President
Susan Gordon, Director, Marketing
s.gordon@cflpa.com
Membership: approx. 400 + 8 locals
Publications:
• Canadian Football League Players' Association Negotiation Booklet
• Canadian Football League Players' Association Salary Survey
• CFLPA [Canadian Football League Players' Association] Newsletter
Type: Newsletter

Canadian Football Officials Association (CFOA) / Association Canadienne des Officiels de Football (ACOF)
c/o Ron Paluzzi, 648, rue Richmond, Montréal QC H3J 2R9
Tel: 450-448-3293
www.cfoa-acof.ca
Overview: A medium-sized national organization founded in 1969
Chief Officer(s):
Ron Paluzzi, Secretary-Treasurer
rpaluzzi@3macs.com

Canadian Forage & Grassland Association (CFGA) / Association Canadienne pour les Plantes Fourragères (ACPF)
125 Patterson Cres., Brandon MB R7A 6T7
Tel: 204-726-9393; *Fax:* 204-726-9703
www.canadianfga.ca
Overview: A small national organization
Mission: The CFGA/ACPF is the national voice for all sectors of the forage and grassland industry. Its main role is to uphold our robust forage industry and realize the potential of the domestic and export forage market.
Chief Officer(s):
Wayne Digby, Executive Director
w_digby@canadianfga.ca
Membership: *Fees:* $1500 overseas exporters; $250 US exporters, patrons; *Committees:* Producer/User; Forage Export & Domestic Development; Research & Extension

Canadian Forces Logistics Association - Montréal
c/o Léo Gravelle, 2093, rue Montarville, St-Bruno-de-Montarville QC J3V 3V8
Overview: A small national organization
Mission: To promote the interests of the Canadian Forces Logistics Branch & serves to exchange information between serving & retired logisticians & other interested parties.
Chief Officer(s):
Léo Gravelle, Treasurer
Membership: *Fees:* $15

Canadian Forestry Accreditation Board (CFAB) / Bureau canadien d'agrément en foresterie
18 Pommel Cres., Kanata ON K2M 1A2
Tel: 613-599-7259; *Fax:* 613-599-8107
cfab@cfab.ca
www.cfab.ca
Overview: A medium-sized national organization founded in 1989
Mission: Responsible for the accreditation of Canadian university forestry baccalaureate programs for the purpose of meeting academic requirements for professional registration.
Affiliation(s): Association of BC Forest Professionals; Association of Newfoundland-Labrador Registered Professional Foresters; Association of Registered Professional Foresters of New Brunswick; Association of Saskatchewan Forestry Professionals; College of Alberta Professional Foresters Association; Ordre des ingénieurs forestiers du Québec; Registered Professional Foresters Association of Nova Scotia; Canadian Institute of Forestry
Chief Officer(s):
Lorne F. Riley, Executive Director

Canadian Forestry Association (CFA) / Association forestière canadienne
1027 Pembroke St. East, Pembroke ON K8A 3M4
Tel: 613-732-2917; *Fax:* 613-732-3386
Toll-Free: 866-441-4006
www.canadianforestry.com
Overview: A large national charitable organization founded in 1900
Mission: To advocate for the wise use & protection of Canada's forest, water, & wildlife resources; To nurture economic & environmental health, through the management & conservation of forest resources; To provide a national voice for provincial forestry agencies
Chief Officer(s):
Barry Waito, Chair
Kathy Abusow, President & Chief Executive Officer
Finances: *Funding Sources:* Donations
Activities: Advising the federal government of forest policy; Increasing public awareness about the protection of forests; *Awareness Events:* National Forest Week, September
Publications:
• Canadian Forestry Association Teaching Kit, Volume 1: Canada's Forests - Learning from the Past, Building for the Future
Type: Kit; *Number of Pages:* 32
Profile: A tool for educators to help young people in junior to senior grades understand the importance ofprotecting & conserving forests
• Canadian Forestry Association Teaching Kit, Volume 2: Canada's Forests - A Breath of Fresh Air
Type: Booklet; *Number of Pages:* 40
Profile: An exploration of climate change & its effects on Canadian forests
• Canadian Forestry Association Teaching Kit, Volume 3: Canada's Forests - All Things Big & Small
Type: Booklet; *Number of Pages:* 40
Profile: An examination of biodiversity in Canada's forests for the junior to intermediate grade levels
• Canadian Forestry Association Teaching Kit, Volume 4: Canada's Forests - Source of Life
Type: Booklet; *Number of Pages:* 48
Profile: Information about forest sustainability for students from grade 4 to 7
• Canadian Forestry Association Teaching Kit, Volume 5: Canada's Forest - A Fine Balance
Type: Booklet; *Number of Pages:* 44
Profile: Information & activities about the decline of wildlife habitat & species at risk, for students from grade 4 to grade 12
• Canadian Forestry Association Teaching Kit, Volume 6: Canada's Forests & Wetlands - Our Natural Water Filters
Type: Booklet; *Number of Pages:* 40
Profile: Forest, wetland, & water issues presented for children in grades 5 to 8
• Canadian Forestry Association Teaching Kit, Volume 7: The Boreal Forest - A Global Legacy
Type: Booklet; *Number of Pages:* 48
Profile: A teaching kit about the boreal forest intended for students from age 5 to 18
• Canadian Forestry Association Teaching Kit, Volume 8: Canada's Boreal Forest - Tradition & Transition
Type: Booklet; *Number of Pages:* 44

Profile: An exploration of the boreal forest & the interdependence that exists between the forest & Canadians
• Canadian Forestry Association Teaching Kit User Guide
Type: Guide
Profile: Activities for the entire class, group activities, activities for partners, games, outdoor activities, research, student presentations, & activities with Aboriginalcontent

Canadian Forestry Association of BC; British Columbia Forestry Association *See* For Ed BC

Canadian Forestry Association of New Brunswick (CFANB) / Association forestière canadienne du Nouveau-Brunswick (AFCNB)

#248, 1350 Regent St., Fredericton NB E3C 2G6
Tel: 506-452-1339; *Fax:* 506-452-7950
Toll-Free: 866-405-7000
info@cfanb.ca
www.cfanb.ca
Also Known As: The Tree House
Overview: A medium-sized provincial charitable organization founded in 1939 overseen by Canadian Forestry Association
Mission: To champions trees & forests of New Brunswick; To promote environmental, commercial, recreational, & inspirational benefits; To encourages conservation & wise use of natural resources
Chief Officer(s):
Christopher Dickie, President
Valerie Archibald, Associate Director
Jennifer Geneau, Secretary
Jamie Morrison, Treasurer
Finances: *Funding Sources:* Membership fees; Government grants; Foundation support
20 volunteer(s)
Membership: 75; *Fees:* Schedule available; Individual membership $25; *Member Profile:* Open
Activities: *Awareness Events:* National Forest Week, September; Arbor Day, May

Canadian Foundation for AIDS Research (CANFAR) / Fondation canadienne de recherche sur le SIDA

#602, 200 Wellington St. West, Toronto ON M5V 3C7
Tel: 416-361-6281; *Fax:* 416-361-5736
Toll-Free: 800-563-2873
www.canfar.com
www.facebook.com/canfar
twitter.com/canfar
www.youtube.com/user/CANFAR; www.flickr.com/photos/canfar
Overview: A medium-sized national charitable organization founded in 1987
Mission: National, privately funded, charitable foundation created to raise awareness in order to fund research into all aspects of HIV infection & AIDS
Chief Officer(s):
Christopher Bunting, President & CEO, 416-361-6281 Ext. 229
cbunting@canfar.com
Finances: *Annual Operating Budget:* $500,000-$1.5 Million
Staff Member(s): 5; 70 volunteer(s)
Membership: 60; *Member Profile:* Anyone who actively participates in betterment of the Foundation; *Committees:* Scientific Advisory
Activities: Raise funds for AIDS research; *Speaker Service:* Yes
Publications:
• CANFAR [Canadian Foundation for AIDS Research] Annual Report
Frequency: Annually
• Catalyst [a publication of the Canadian Foundation for AIDS Research]
Type: Newsletter; *Editor:* Amanda O'Reilly
Profile: CANFAR's programs & fundraising events, reports on advances in HIV / AIDS, & updates on research
• Funding Leading-Edge Research: Canada's HIV/AIDS epidemic, the global HIV / AIDS crisis & CANFAR
Author: S.E. Read, R.S. Remis, J.K. Stewart

Canadian Foundation for Climate & Atmospheric Sciences (CFCAS) / Fondation canadienne pour les sciences du climat et de l'atmosphère (FCSCA)

#901, 350 Sparks St., Ottawa ON K1R 7S8
Tel: 613-238-2223; *Fax:* 613-238-2227
info@cfcas.org
www.cfcas.org
Overview: A medium-sized national charitable organization founded in 2000
Mission: To fund university-based research on climate, & atmospheric & related oceanic work in Canada
Chief Officer(s):
Dawn Conway, Executive Director
conway@cfcas.org
Denny Alexander, Officer, Communications
alexander@cfcas.org
Tim Aston, Officer, Science
aston@cfcas.org
Finances: *Annual Operating Budget:* Greater than $5 Million
Activities: Responding to national needs or scientific imperatives; Providing grants
Publications:
• CFCAS [Canadian Foundation for Climate & Atmospheric Sciences] News
Type: Newsletter
Profile: Foundation happenings, research news, & grant information

Canadian Foundation for Dietetic Research (CFDF)

#604, 480 University Ave., Toronto ON M5G 1V2
Tel: 519-267-0755; *Fax:* 416-596-0603
www.cfdr.ca
Overview: A medium-sized national charitable organization
Mission: Provides grants for research in dietetics and nutrition.
Chief Officer(s):
Isla Horvath, Executive Director
isla.horvath@cfdr.ca
Finances: *Funding Sources:* Donations

Canadian Foundation for Drug Policy

70 MacDonald St., Ottawa ON K2P 1H6
Tel: 613-236-1027; *Fax:* 613-238-2891
eoscapel@ca.inter.net
www.cfdp.ca
Overview: A small national organization founded in 1993
Mission: To examine drug policies & their effects; to act as a forum for the exchange of views in regards to drug policy reform
Chief Officer(s):
Eugene Oscapella, Contact
Finances: *Funding Sources:* Donations

Canadian Foundation for Economic Education (CFEE) / Fondation d'éducation économique

#201, 110 Eglinton Ave. West, Toronto ON M4R 1A3
Tel: 416-968-2236; *Fax:* 416-968-0488
Toll-Free: 888-570-7610
mail@cfee.org
www.cfee.org
twitter.com/cfee1
vimeo.com/cfee/videos
Overview: A medium-sized national charitable organization founded in 1974
Mission: To enhance the economic capabilities of Canadians
Affliation(s): Organisation for Economic Co-operation & Development (OECD); Child & Youth Finance International; Association of Asia Pacific Countries (APEC)
Chief Officer(s):
Gary Rabbior, President
grabbior@cfee.org
Finances: *Funding Sources:* Sponsorships; Project activity
Staff Member(s): 9
Activities: Engaging in research activities; Producing resources, such as teaching kits & student materials; Distributing resources to educators across Canada; Developing curriculum, workshops, seminars, & conferences; Providing advisory services; Collaborating with provincial ministries & departments of education; Partnering with various organizations & associations on various projects; *Awareness Events:* Talk With Our Kids About Money Day, April
Publications:
• Building Futures in Canada
Type: Online Resource
Profile: Stories of immigrants to Canada (www.buildingfuturesincanada.ca)
• Building Futures in Manitoba
Type: Teaching Resource
Profile: Seeks to integrate basic economic & financial education into the Manitoba curriculum in grades 4-10 (buildingfuturesinmanitoba.com)
• The Canadian Economy: The Big Picture
Type: Booklet
Profile: A model of the economy that reveals how the system works
• Catching the Wave: Framework for Youth Entrepreneurship Success
Type: Report
Profile: Research on factors that foster entrepreneurial initiative & success
• Classroom Edition
Type: Teaching Resource
Profile: Education news & resources for teachers (news from the Globe & Mail); custom lesson plans (classroomedition.ca)
• Dayplanner for Newcomers to Canada
Type: Online Resource
Profile: Interactive dayplanner to help newcomers to Canada settle (cfeedayplanner.com)
• Entrepreneurship: The Spirit of Adventure
Type: Teaching Resource
Profile: For those interested in learning more about entrepreneurship (cfeespiritofadventure.com)
• Managing Your Money in Canada
Type: Online Resource
Profile: Artciles on how to financially plan for various life events
• Money & Youth
Type: Book; *Number of Pages:* 125
Profile: A resource & teacher's guide to help young people learn how to take control of their financial future

Canadian Foundation for Healthcare Improvement (CFHI) / Fondation canadienne pour l'amélioration des services de santé (FCASS)

#700, 1565 Carling Ave., Ottawa ON K1Z 8R1
Tel: 613-728-2238; *Fax:* 613-728-3527
info@cfhi-fcass.ca
www.cfhi-fcass.ca
www.facebook.com/group.php?gid=107329739320566
twitter.com/cfhi_fcass
www.youtube.com/user/CHSRF
Previous Name: Canadian Health Services Research Foundation
Overview: A large national organization founded in 1996
Mission: To funds management & policy research in health services; To support applied health services & nursing researchers; To support the synthesis & dissemination of research results; To support the use of research results by decision makers in the health system
Chief Officer(s):
Brian D. Postl, Chair
Maureen O'Neil, President, 613-728-2238 Ext. 237
maureen.oneil@cfhi-fcass.ca
Nancy Quattrocchi, Vice-President, Corporate Services
nancy.quattrocchi@cfhi.fcass.ca
Stephen Samis, Vice-President, Programs
stephen.samis@cfhi-fcass.ca
Finances: *Annual Operating Budget:* Greater than $5 Million; *Funding Sources:* Government grants & endowments
Activities: Collaborating with regions, provinces, territories to improve healthcare systems; *Awareness Events:* CEO Forum; *Internships:* Yes; *Speaker Service:* Yes
Meetings/Conferences: • Canadian Foundation for Healthcare Improvement's CEO Forum 2015, 2015
Scope: National
Description: An invitation-only annual meeting for healthcare chief executive officers, senior leaders, deputy ministers, & experts to discuss issues in Canadian health services
Publications:
• @CFHI-FCASS [Canadian Foundation for Healthcare Improvement] Bulletin
Type: Newsletter; *Frequency:* Monthly
Profile: Current reports & activities from the Canadian Foundation for Healthcare Improvement
• Canadian Foundation for Healthcare Improvement Annual Report
Type: Yearbook; *Frequency:* Annually
Profile: Organizational highlights from the past year
• CFHI [Canadian Foundation for Healthcare Improvement] Strategic Directions 2009-2013
Profile: An outline of activities & initiatives
• Pass it on! [a series of publications from the Canadian Foundation for Healthcare Improvement]
Profile: Innovative approaches to successful changes in healthcare

Canadian Foundation for Masorti Judaism (CFMJ)

#508, 1000 Finch Ave. West, Toronto ON M3J 2V5
Tel: 416-667-1717
Toll-Free: 866-357-3384
info@masorti.ca
www.masorti.ca
Overview: A medium-sized international charitable organization founded in 1979

Mission: To support the Masorti (Conservative) Movement in Israel, which promotes scholarship, Zionism & religious tolerance & pluralism, within the context of modern Israeli society
Chief Officer(s):
Jennifer Gorman, Executive Director
Publications:
• Traditions
Type: Newsletter
Profile: Masorti news & programs

Canadian Foundation for Pharmacy (CFP) / Fondation canadienne pour la pharmacie

5809 Fieldon Rd., Mississauga ON L5M 5K1
Tel: 905-997-3238; *Fax:* 905-997-4264
www.cfpnet.ca
Previous Name: Canadian Foundation for the Advancement of Pharmacy
Overview: A medium-sized national charitable organization founded in 1945
Mission: To provide programs for the advancement of the pharmacy profession in Canada
Affliation(s): Canadian Phamacists Association
Chief Officer(s):
Ryan D. Itterman, President
Dayle Acorn, Executive Director
dacorn@cfpnet.ca
Finances: *Annual Operating Budget:* $100,000-$250,000; *Funding Sources:* Individual & corporate donations
Staff Member(s): 1; 30 volunteer(s)
Membership: 3,700; *Committees:* Bylaws; Finance; Nominating; Long Range Planning; Pharmaceutical Education & Research
Activities: *Library*
Awards:
• Pharmacy Research Awards (Award)
These awards are designed to give special recognition to deserving students pursuing postgraduate work in Canadian faculties of pharmacy *Amount:* Two awards of $1,000 each available for the best poster & podium presentations
• Clinical Practice (Scholarship)
• Pharmacy Administration (Scholarship)
• Professional Practice Awards (Award)
Established 1973; the purpose of these awards is to support student initiatives designed to foster public health awareness; two awards of $1,000 & $500 are given; open to pharmacy graduates on a national competition basis
• Industrial Pharmacy Awards (Award)
Established 1977; these awards are intended to honour distinguished performance of undergraduate pharmacy students participating in the PMAC Industrial Pharmacy Studentship Program; two awards of $1,000 & $500 are given; open to students registered in Canadian schools of pharmacy who have completed Industrial Pharmacy Summer Studentship Program
• Hospital Pharmacy Awards (Award)
Established 1956; the purpose of these awards is to recognize excellence of performance by students participating in an accredited hospital pharmacy residency program in Canada; two awards of $1,000 & $500 are given; open to Canadian pharmacy graduates

Canadian Foundation for Physically Disabled Persons (CFPDP)

#265, 6 Garamond Ct., Toronto ON M3C 1Z5
Tel: 416-760-7351; *Fax:* 416-760-9405
whynot@sympatico.ca
www.cfpdp.com
Overview: A small national charitable organization founded in 1984
Mission: To provide financial assistance to organizations sharing concern for physically disabled adults; to help create awareness in the public & business communities, & in government of the needs of physically disabled adults in the areas of housing, employment, education, accessibility, sports & recreation, & research.
Chief Officer(s):
Vim Kochhar, Chair
vimkochhar@sympatico.ca
Dorothy Price, Executive Director
dorothyprice@sympatico.ca
Finances: *Funding Sources:* Private fundraising
Staff Member(s): 2
Activities: Great Valentine Gala; Terry Fox Hall of Fame luncheon; Rolling Rampage 10K wheelchair race; *Speaker Service:* Yes
Awards:
• King Clancy Awards (Award)
• Corporate Awards (Award)

Canadian Foundation for the Advancement of Pharmacy *See* Canadian Foundation for Pharmacy

Canadian Foundation for the Americas (FOCAL) / Fondation canadienne pour les Amériques

#720, 1 Nicholas St., Ottawa ON K1N 7B7
Tel: 613-562-0005; *Fax:* 613-562-2525
www.focal.ca
Overview: A small international charitable organization founded in 1990
Mission: To foster informed & timely debate & dialogue on issues of importance to decision-makers throughout Canada & the Americas; to develop a greater understanding of important hemispheric issues & to help build a stronger community of the Americas
Member of: Transparency International Canada; Canadian Institute for International Affairs; Canadian Association for Latin America & Caribbean Studies; Latin American Studies Association; Society for International Development
Chief Officer(s):
Kathryn Hewlett-Jobes, Chair
Carlo Dade, Executive Director
Madeleine Bélanger, Director, Communications
Finances: *Annual Operating Budget:* $500,000-$1.5 Million; *Funding Sources:* Federal government; private sector
Staff Member(s): 14
Activities: Policy analysis; *Internships:* Yes; *Library:* David Pollock in Memoriam Library; by appointment
Publications:
• Focal Point: Canada's Spotlight on the Americas
Frequency: 10 pa; *Editor:* Rachel Schmidt *ISSN:* 1703-7964
Profile: Analytical pieces & opinion items
• Focal's Chronicle on Cuba
Type: Newsletter; *Frequency:* Monthly
Profile: Summary of news items about Cuba
• Policy Papers

Canadian Foundation for the Love of Children *See* Kids Kottage Foundation

Canadian Foundation for the Study of Infant Deaths (CFSID) / Fondation canadienne pour l'étude de la mortalité infantile

PO Box 21053, St Catharines ON L2R 7X2
Tel: 905-688-8884; *Fax:* 905-688-3300
Toll-Free: 800-363-7437
sidsinfo@sidscanada.org
www.sidscanada.org
www.facebook.com/sidscanada
twitter.com/SIDSCanada
Also Known As: SIDS Foundation
Overview: A small national charitable organization founded in 1973
Mission: To provide information & emotional support to families of infants who have died due to Sudden Infant Death Syndrome (SIDS); to carry out programs of public education & awareness; to promote & support research activities into the cause(s) of SIDS & its effects on families
Affiliation(s): SIDS International
Finances: *Funding Sources:* Individual; corporate donations
Membership: *Fees:* $25 individual; *Committees:* Medical & Research Advisory
Activities: *Speaker Service:* Yes; *Library* Open to public by appointment
Awards:
• Dr. Sydney Segal Research Grant (Grant)
Publications:
• The Baby's Breath
Type: Newsletter *ISSN:* 1192-9294
Profile: Foundation information & events, medical updates
• Sam's Story
Author: Fiona Chin-Yee
Profile: Resource for youngs SIDS siblings accompanied by a parents' guide

Canadian Foundation for Ukrainian Studies (CFUS) / Fondation canadienne des études ukrainiennes

620 Spadina Ave., Toronto ON M5S 2H4
Tel: 416-766-9630; *Fax:* 416-766-0599
Toll-Free: 877-766-9630
admin@cfus.ca
www.cfus.ca
Overview: A small national charitable organization founded in 1975
Mission: To encourage & advance university-level Ukrainian studies for the development of the Ukrainian community in Canada; To promote knowledge of Ukraine's history & culture in order to develop sound relations with Ukraine
Finances: *Funding Sources:* Fundraising; Donations; Bequests; Endowments; Government funding
Activities: Supporting Ukrainian studies, research, & publishing; Providing scholarships & awards to students; Administering endowment funds

Canadian Foundation on Compulsive Gambling (Ontario) *See* Responsible Gambling Council (Ontario)

Canadian Foundation on Fetal Alcohol Research (CFFAR) / Fondation canadienne de la recherche dur l'alcoolisation foetale (FCRAF)

#62, 2192 Queen St. East, Toronto ON M4E 1E6
e-mail: info@fasdfoundation.ca
www.fasdfoundation.ca
Overview: A medium-sized national organization founded in 2007
Mission: The Canadian Foundation on Fetal Alcohol Research (CFFAR), is an independent, non-profit foundation created to promote interest and fund research related to the short and long-term bio-medical, psychological and social effects of alcohol consumption during pregnancy, and the prevention of fetal alcohol spectrum disorders (FASD).
Chief Officer(s):
Louise Nadeau, Chair

Canadian Foundry Association (CFA) / Association des fonderies canadiennes (AFC)

#1500, 1 Nicholas St., Ottawa ON K1N 7B7
Tel: 613-789-4894; *Fax:* 613-789-5957
www.foundryassociation.ca
Overview: A medium-sized national organization founded in 1975
Mission: To assist & represent the membership in dealing with government on industry specific issues; To communicate information to the industry, which will assist its members in strengthening their own competitive position & ensuring a strong Canadian foundry industry
Member of: Canadian Society of Association Executives
Chief Officer(s):
Judith Arbour, Executive Director
judy@foundryassociation.ca
William Monaghan, Secretary-Treasurer
Membership: 50 organizations; *Fees:* Fees based on sales volume; *Member Profile:* Pour metal castings or supplier to the industry; *Committees:* Education; Environment; Membership; Occupational Health & Safety
Activities: *Rents Mailing List:* Yes
Meetings/Conferences: • Canadian Foundry Association 2015 Issues Meeting, March, 2015, The Waterfront Banquet & Conference Hall, Hamilton, ON
Scope: National
Description: Technical committees work on issues to represent members' interests
Contact Information: E-mail: info@foundryassociation.ca
• Canadian Foundry Association 2015 Annual Meeting, 2015
Scope: National
Description: A gathering of members to address issues facing the Canadian foundry industry
Contact Information: Executive Director: Judith Arbour

Canadian Franchise Association (CFA) / Association canadienne de la franchise

#116, 5399 Eglinton Ave. West, Toronto ON M9C 5K6
Tel: 416-695-2896; *Fax:* 416-695-1950
Toll-Free: 800-665-4232
info@cfa.ca
www.cfa.ca
Previous Name: Association of Canadian Franchisors
Overview: A medium-sized national organization founded in 1967
Mission: To promote & represent franchise excellence through a national association of businesses united by a common interest in ethical franchising
Chief Officer(s):
Lorraine McLachlan, President & CEO
Gary Martini-Wong, Manager, Finance & Accounting
Finances: *Annual Operating Budget:* $1.5 Million-$3 Million
Staff Member(s): 23
Membership: 400 franchisors + 100 franchise support service; *Member Profile:* Regular - franchising for at least two years in Canada as franchisor; franchise support service - provides products or services to franchisors.; *Committees:* FSS; Awards; Board of Directors; Convention; Editorial & Program; Franchise Advisory; Legal & Legislature; Membership.

Activities: *Speaker Service:* Yes
Awards:
• Award of Excellence in Franchise Relations (Award)
Meetings/Conferences: • Canadian Franchise Association 2015 National Convention, April, 2015, Niagara Falls, ON
Scope: National

Canadian Fraternal Association (CFA) / Association canadienne des sociétés fraternelles

c/o FaithLife Financial, 470 Weber St. North, Waterloo ON N2J 4G4
Tel: 519-886-4610; *Fax:* 519-886-0350
www.cfa-afc.org
Overview: A small national organization founded in 1891
Mission: To promote the general benefit welfare system by uniting fraternal benefit societies in all matters of mutual concern & public interest
Chief Officer(s):
Gordon Kennedy, Secretary-Treasurer
gkennedy@faithlifefinancial.ca
Karen Bjerland, President
Membership: *Member Profile:* Fraternal societies

Canadian Freestyle Ski Association / Association canadienne de ski acrobatique

808 Pacific St., Vancouver BC V6Z 1C2
Tel: 604-714-2233; *Fax:* 604-714-2232
Toll-Free: 877-714-2232
info@freestyleski.com
www.freestyleski.ca
www.facebook.com/CanFreestyleSki
twitter.com/canfreestyleski
Overview: A medium-sized national organization
Mission: The national governing body of the sport of freestyle skiing with a mandate to develop the sport within Canada; to represent our country internationally; to promote the safe development of the sport; to promote excellence in national & international competitions
Affliation(s): Canadian Ski & Snowboard Association
Chief Officer(s):
Peter Judge, CEO
Finances: *Annual Operating Budget:* $500,000-$1.5 Million
Membership: 2,000; *Fees:* $10
Activities: *Rents Mailing List:* Yes

Canadian Friends of Bar-Ilan University (CFBIU)

#214, 1750 Steeles Ave. West, Concord ON L4K 2L7
Tel: 905-660-3563; *Fax:* 905-660-1612
Toll-Free: 888-248-2720
admin@cfbiu.org
www.cfbiu.org
www.facebook.com/barilancanada
www.youtube.com/barilanuniversity
Overview: A small international organization
Mission: To raise money for Bar-Ilan University
Chief Officer(s):
Gabi Weisfeld, President
Finances: *Funding Sources:* Donations
Activities: Public lectures; *Speaker Service:* Yes

Eastern Region
#612, 5858 Côte-des-Neiges Rd., Montréal QC H3S 2S1
Tel: 514-731-7893

Western Region
#124, 3495 Cambie St., Vancouver BC V5Z 4R3
Toll-Free: 888-248-2720

Canadian Friends of Beth Hatefutsoth

1170, rue Peel, Montréal QC H3B 4P2
Tel: 514-878-5290
Overview: A small national organization
Mission: To raise funds for Beit Hatefutsoth through membership, & to bring travelling exhibits from Israel

Canadian Friends of Bikur Cholim Hospital

329 Joicey Blvd., Toronto ON M5N 2V8
Tel: 416-781-6960
Overview: A small international organization
Mission: To support & raise funds for Bakir Cholim Hospital in Jerusalem
Chief Officer(s):
David Kleiner, Secretary-Treasurer
dkleiner@danatrading.com

Canadian Friends of Boys Town Jerusalem

#200, 2788 Bathurst St., Toronto ON M6B 3A3
Tel: 416-789-7241; *Fax:* 416-789-1090
Toll-Free: 866-989-7241
btjcan@btjcanada.com
www.btjcanada.com
Overview: A small local organization founded in 1948
Mission: To take boys of high potential from all parts of Israel, (most of whom are needy) from junior high school, high school & colleges of mechanical & electrical engineering & expose them to a high level of technological, academic, & religious training
Chief Officer(s):
Jerry Tollinsky, National Executive Director
jerry@btjcanada.com
Jules Kronis, President

Canadian Friends of Burma (CFOB) / Les Amis canadiens de la Birmanie

#206, 145 Spruce St., Ottawa ON K1R 6P1
Tel: 613-237-8056; *Fax:* 613-563-0017
cfob@cfob.org
www.cfob.org
Overview: A medium-sized international organization founded in 1991
Mission: To promote democracy & human rights in Burma by working within the global movement, & educating & activating Canadian involvement in the struggle for peace in Burma
Member of: Burma Advisory Group; Network on International Human Rights; Canadian Council for Refugees
Affliation(s): World University Service of Canada; Canadian Asia Pacific Working Group; Peacefund Canada; Canadian Peacebuilding Coordinating Committee
Chief Officer(s):
Tin Maung Htoo, Executive Director
Toe Kyi, Director, Information Technology
Ashley Stewart, Director, Media & Community Relations
Kevin McLoed, Researcher
Finances: *Funding Sources:* International Centre for Human Rights & Democratic Development; Private foundations; Donors
3 volunteer(s)
Membership: 1,200 donor contacts; *Fees:* Suggested donation: $25 regular; $15 low income; $100 institution
Activities: *Speaker Service:* Yes; *Library:* CFOB Library; Open to public by appointment
Awards:
• Thakore Foundation Award (Award)

Canadian Friends of Peace Now (Shalom Achshav) (CFPN)

#517, 119-660 Eglinton Ave. East, Toronto ON M4G 2K2
Tel: 416-322-5559; *Fax:* 416-322-5587
Toll-Free: 866-405-5387
info@peacenowcanada.org
www.peacenowcanada.org
www.facebook.com/group.php?gid=135473589852225
Overview: A small national charitable organization founded in 1982
Mission: CFPN supports Peace Now, a peace movement in Israel that sponsors dialogue between Israelis & Palestinians, & advocates a 2-state solution for co-existence. CFPN organizes lectures in Canada & sponsors visits by Israeli & Palestinian peace activists. It is a registered charity, BN: 119147320RR0001.
Member of: Canadian Jewish Congress
Chief Officer(s):
David Brooks, Co-Chair, Ottawa
Gabriella Goliger, Co-Chair, Ottawa
Sheldon Gordon, Chair, Toronto
Stephen Scheinberg, Chair, Montréal
Finances: *Annual Operating Budget:* $50,000-$100,000; *Funding Sources:* Private donations
Staff Member(s): 1
Activities: Public lectures; *Speaker Service:* Yes

Canadian Friends of Schizophrenics *See* Schizophrenia Society of Canada

Canadian Friends of the Hebrew University (CFHU) / Association des amis canadiens de l'Université Hébraïque

PO Box 65, #3020, 3080 Yonge St., Toronto ON M4N 3N1
Tel: 416-485-8000; *Fax:* 416-485-8565
Toll-Free: 888-432-7398
info@cfhu.org
www.cfhu.org
www.facebook.com/CFHUFriendsandAlumni
twitter.com/CdnFriendsHU
www.youtube.com/user/CdnFriendsHU
Overview: A small international organization
Mission: To develop & promote awareness of, leadership in, & financial support for the Hebrew University of Jerusalem.
Chief Officer(s):
Rami Kleinmann, President & CEO
rkleinmann@cfhu.org
Miriam Pilc-Levine, National Director, Communications & Marketing
mpilc-levine@cfhu.org
Staff Member(s): 10
Activities: Sponsors educational programs

Calgary Chapter
120 - 7 Ave. SW, Calgary AB T2P 0W4
Tel: 403-297-0605; *Fax:* 403-253-1944
calgary@cfhu.org
Chief Officer(s):
Cheryl Baron, President

Edmonton Chapter
#7200, JCC - 156 St., Edmonton AB T5R 1X3
Tel: 780-444-0809; *Fax:* 780-444-4019
edmonton@cfhu.org

Montréal Chapter
#720, 1310 Greene Ave., Montréal QC H3Z 2B2
Tel: 514-932-2133; *Fax:* 514-932-3749
mtl@cfhu.org
Chief Officer(s):
Simon Bensimon, Director
sbensimon@cfhu.org

Ottawa Chapter
2430 Georgina Dr., Ottawa ON K2B 7M7
Tel: 613-829-3150; *Fax:* 613-726-0096
ott@cfhu.org
Chief Officer(s):
Shelli Kimmel, Director
skimmel@cfhu.org

Toronto Chapter
PO Box 65, #3020, 3080 Yonge St., Toronto ON M4N 3N1
Tel: 416-485-8000; *Fax:* 416-485-8565
tor@cfhu.org
Chief Officer(s):
Elan Divon, Director
edivon@cfhu.org

Vancouver Chapter
#204, 950 West 41st Ave., Vancouver BC V5Z 2N7
Tel: 604-257-5133; *Fax:* 604-257-5144
vanc@cfhu.org
Chief Officer(s):
Dina Wachtel, Western Region Director
dwachtel@cfhu.org

Winnipeg Chapter
#206, 1700 Corydon Ave., Winnipeg MB R3N 0K1
Tel: 204-942-3085; *Fax:* 204-943-6211
wpg@cfhu.org
Chief Officer(s):
Sharon Zalik, Director
szalik@cfhu.org

Canadian Friends of Ukraine (CFU)

South Building, 620 Spadina Ave., 2nd Fl., Toronto ON M5S 2H4
Tel: 416-964-6644; *Fax:* 416-964-6085
canfun@interlog.com
www.canadianfriendsofukraine.com
Overview: A small international organization founded in 1089
Mission: To strengthen Canadian-Ukrainian relations; To promote democracy & reform in Ukraine
Chief Officer(s):
Margareta Shpir, President
John Pidkowich, Vice-President
Lisa Shymko, Executive Director
Walentina Rodak, Treasurer
John Kuzyk, Chair, Canada-Ukraine Library Centres
Finances: *Funding Sources:* Donations
Activities: Providing technical assistance & support for government institutions, hospitals, libraries, & educational institutions; Promoting international awarenss to strengthen democracy; Supporting projects that encourage legislative reform, public access to information, & human rights; Opening Canadian library centres in eastern & southern Ukraine
Awards:
• Teachers Awards (Award)
To recognize teachers in Ukrainian-language schools & teachers of Ukrainian-language courses *Contact:* Jurij Darewych

Canadian Friends of Yeshiva University (CFYU)

#300, 4580 Dufferin St., Toronto ON M3H 5Y2
Tel: 416-783-6960; *Fax:* 416-783-9854
canada@yu.edu

www.yu.edu/canadian-friends
www.facebook.com/166648253367786
Overview: A small international charitable organization
Mission: To support Yeshiva University's Canadian students & alumni; to raise the University's profile in Canada; to bring our spiritual, intellectual and creative resources to Canadian Jewish communities-and to raise the funds needed to make all of this possible.
Member of: Yeshiva University
Chief Officer(s):
Stuart Haber, National Director
stuart.haber@yu.edu
Staff Member(s): 4

Canadian Friends Service Committee (CFSC) / Secours Quaker Canadien
60 Lowther Ave., Toronto ON M5R 1C7
Tel: 416-920-5213; *Fax:* 416-920-5214
cfsc@quakerservice.ca
quakerservice.ca
facebook.com/112772730148
twitter.com/CFSCQuakers
Also Known As: Religious Society of Friends (Quakers)
Overview: A medium-sized national charitable organization founded in 1931
Mission: To unify & expand the concerns of Friends (Quakers)
Member of: The Canadian Council of Churches; Kairos: Canadian Ecumenical Justice Initiatives; Project Ploughshares; Canadian Council for Refugees; War Resistors Support Campaign
Chief Officer(s):
Jane Orion Smith, General Secretary
janeorion@quakerservice.ca
Matthew Legge, Administration & Communications
matt@quakerservice.ca
Finances: *Annual Operating Budget:* $500,000-$1.5 Million; *Funding Sources:* Individuals; meetings
Staff Member(s): 7; 40 volunteer(s)
Membership: *Committees:* Quaker Aboriginal Affairs Committee; Quaker Peace & Sustainable Communities Committee; Quaker International Affairs Programme Committee; Quakers Fostering Justice
Activities: Peace & social justice work; *Internships:* Yes; *Speaker Service:* Yes; *Library:* Friends House Library
Publications:
• Quaker Concern
Type: Newsletter; *Frequency:* 3 pa
Profile: CFSC information & feature articles on CFSC concerns

Canadian Fruit Wholesalers Association ***See*** Canadian Produce Marketing Association

Canadian Fuels Association / Association canadienne des carburants
#1000, 275 Slater St., Ottawa ON K1P 5H9
Tel: 613-232-3709; *Fax:* 613-236-4280
canadianfuels.ca
Previous Name: Canadian Petroleum Products Institute
Overview: A large national organization founded in 1989
Mission: To represent its membership to governments on issues related to business, the environment, & health & safety in the petroleum products sector. CPPI ensures its own adherence to the Competition Act, & provides a competition compliance program & training sessions to all staff & members
Chief Officer(s):
Peter Boag, President
Membership: 10; *Member Profile:* Companies engaged in petroleum refining, marketing & distribution
Activities: Training & education; news releases, reports & technical documents; Driver Certification Program for petroleum transport drivers
Publications:
• Annual Review
Type: Report; *Frequency:* a.
Profile: Tough questions about the future of transportation fuels in Canada
• Fuels for Life [a publication of the Canadian Fuels Association]
Type: Report; *Number of Pages:* 60
Profile: Discussion paper on Canada's future transportation fuels choices

Eastern Canada Division
#1000, 275 Slater St., Toronto ON K1P 5H9
Tel: 514-284-7754; *Fax:* 514-284-3301
Chief Officer(s):
Carol Montreuil, Vice-President

Ontario Division
#1100, 151 Yonge St., Toronto ON M5C 2W7
Tel: 416-492-5677; *Fax:* 416-492-2514
Chief Officer(s):
Faith Goodman, Vice-President

Western Division
#2100, 350 - 7th Ave. SW, Calgary AB T2P 3N9
Tel: 403-266-7565
Chief Officer(s):
Brian Ahearn, Vice-President

The Canadian Fur Trade Development Institute
#1270, 1435, rue Saint-Alexandre, Montréal QC H3A 2G4
Tel: 514-844-1945; *Fax:* 514-844-8593
Toll-Free: 800-376-9996
Overview: A medium-sized national organization

Canadian Galloway Association (CGA) / Société canadienne Galloway
c/o CLRC, 2417 Holly Lane, Ottawa ON K1V 0M7
Tel: 613-731-7110; *Fax:* 613-731-0704
galloway@clrc.ca
www.galloway.ca
Overview: A medium-sized national organization founded in 1882
Mission: To promote & regulate the breeding of Galloways, Belted Galloways & White Galloways in Canada
Member of: Canadian Beef Breeds Council; Canadian Livestock Records Corp.
Chief Officer(s):
John Toon, President, 905-983-5967
jtooner@hotmail.com
Ron Black, Sec.-Treas.
Finances: *Annual Operating Budget:* Less than $50,000; *Funding Sources:* Registrations; memberships; donations
8 volunteer(s)
Membership: 135; *Fees:* $25-$80; *Member Profile:* Breeders of purebred Galloway cattle; *Committees:* Breed Advancement; Constitution; Promotion
Activities: Annual general meeting alternates between Eastern & Western Canada; Show & Sale at Agribition

Canadian Gaming Association (CGA)
#503, 131 Bloor St. West, Toronto ON M5S 1P7
Tel: 416-304-7800; *Fax:* 416-304-7805
info@canadiangaming.ca
www.canadiangaming.ca
Overview: A large national organization
Mission: To act as the voice of companies & organizations involved in the gaming & entertainment industry throughout Canada; To foster a greater understanding of the gaming industry
Chief Officer(s):
William P. Rutsey, President & Chief Executive Officer
Paul Burns, Vice-President, Public Affairs, 416-304-6870
pburns@canadiangaming.ca
Finances: *Funding Sources:* Membership fees; Sponsorships; Canadian Gaming Summit delegate fees
Membership: *Fees:* Schedule available, based upon annual gross corporate revenues; *Member Profile:* Representatives of the Canadian gaming industry, such as manufacturers, suppliers, & operators
Activities: Liaising with governmental agencies & industry stakeholders; Advocating for the Canadian gaming & entertainment industry; Initiating accurate industry data; Providing information about the gaming industry to elected officials, decision makers, the media, & general public; Offering networking opportunities for members
Meetings/Conferences: • Canadian Gaming Association 2015 19th Annual Canadian Gaming Summit, June, 2015, Caesars Windsor, Windsor, ON
Scope: International
Description: A conference & trade show for representatives from gaming & regulatory agencies, First Nations gaming, provincial lotteries, casinos, race tracks, & charitable gaming organizations
Contact Information: URL: www.canadiangamingsummit.com
Publications:
• Canadian Gaming Business Magazine
Type: Magazine; *Accepts Advertising*; *Price:* Free with membership in the Canadian Gaming Association
• Canadian Gaming Update
Type: Newsletter
Profile: Information about current issues & events which affect Canada's gaming industry

Canadian Gas Association (CGA) / Association canadienne du gaz
#809, 350 Sparks St., Ottawa ON K1R 7S8
Tel: 613-748-0057; *Fax:* 613-748-9078
info@cga.ca
www.cga.ca
twitter.com/GoSmartEnergy
Overview: A large national organization founded in 1907
Mission: To act as the voice of the natural gas distribution industry in Canada
Chief Officer(s):
Timothy M. Egan, President & Chief Executive Officer, 613-748-0057 Ext. 300
tegan@cga.ca
Paula Dunlop, Director, Public Affairs & Strategy, 613-748-0057 Ext. 341
pdunlop@cga.ca
Bryan Gormely, Director, Policy, Economics, & Information, 613-748-0057 Ext. 315
bgormley@cga.ca
Jim Tweedie, Director, Operations, Safety, & Integrity Management, 613-748-0057 Ext. 311
jtweedie@cga.ca
Valerie Prokop, Manager, Finance & Corporate Services, 613-748-0057 Ext. 309
vprokop@cga.ca
Membership: *Member Profile:* Equipment manufacturers; Distribution companies; Transmission companies; Service providers
Activities: Advancing policy positions with federal & provincial decision makers; Developing educational information
Meetings/Conferences: • Canadian Gas Association 2015 Operations Conference, March, 2015, Edmonton, AB
Scope: National
Contact Information: E-mail: help@canavents.com
• Canadian Gas Association 2015 Engineering Conference, April, 2015, Toronto, ON
Scope: National
Contact Information: E-mail: help@canavents.com
Publications:
• Canadian Gas Association Market Updates
Profile: Topics include natural gas markets pre-heating season, post-heating season, supply, & demographics
• Canadian Gas Association Membership Directory
Type: Directory
Profile: Available for current CGA members
• Canadian Natural Gas Magazine
Type: Magazine; *Frequency:* Semiannually; *Accepts Advertising*; *Editor:* Suzy Richardson
Profile: CGA news, feature articles, & a buyers' guide for the natural gas distribution industry in Canada

Canadian Gas Processors Association ***See*** Gas Processing Association Canada

Canadian Gay Archives ***See*** Canadian Lesbian & Gay Archives

Canadian Gelbvieh Association (CGA)
5160 Skyline Way NE, Calgary AB T2E 6V1
Tel: 403-250-8640; *Fax:* 403-291-5624
gelbvieh@gelbvieh.ca
www.gelbvieh.ca
Overview: A medium-sized national organization founded in 1972
Mission: To promote Gelbvieh cattle in Canada & their registration.
Member of: Canadian Beef Breeds Council
Chief Officer(s):
Darrell Hickman, President
darrell.hickman@lakelandc.ab.ca
Wendy Belcher, Secretary Manager
Finances: *Funding Sources:* Membership fees; Purebred cattle registrations & transfers
Staff Member(s): 1
Membership: 121; *Fees:* $125; *Member Profile:* Cattlemen & women

Canadian Gemmological Association (CGA)
#1301, 55 Queen St. East, Toronto ON M5C 1R6
Tel: 647-466-2436; *Fax:* 416-366-6519
info@canadiangemmological.com
www.canadiangemmological.com
Overview: A small national licensing organization founded in 1958
Mission: To set a standard for excellence in the practice of gemmology

Affliation(s): Gemmological Association & Gem Testing Laboratory of Great Britain
Chief Officer(s):
Duncan Parker, President
Brad Wilson, Vice-President
Glen King, Treasurer
Membership: *Fees:* Annually, $125
Activities: Providing training in gemmology; Liaising with governments to set guidelines for sales, marketing, & appraising; Offering a forum for gemmologists to share knowledge; *Library:* CGA Library
Awards:
• Dean S.M. Field Medal (Award)
• W. Donald Goodger Award (Award)
Publications:
• The Canadian Gemmologist
Type: Journal; *Frequency:* Quarterly; *Editor:* Karen Fox; *Price:* Free with CGA membership

Canadian General Standards Board (CGSB) / Office des normes générales du Canada (ONGC)

Place Du Portage III, #6B1, 11 Laurier St., Gatineau QC K1A 1G6
Tel: 819-956-0425; *Fax:* 819-956-1634
Toll-Free: 800-665-2472
ncr.cgsb-ongc@tpsgc-pwgsc.gc.ca
www.tpsgc-pwgsc.gc.ca/ongc-cgsb
Previous Name: Canadian Government Specifications Board
Overview: A medium-sized national organization founded in 1934
Mission: To develop standards, through accreditation with the Standards Council of Canada; To offer conformity assessment services, including product certification & registration of quality & environmental management systems, conforming to ISO standards
Member of: American Society for Quality; Business Forms Management Association; Canadian Safe Boating Council; Standards Engineering Society
Affliation(s): Standards Council of Canada; National Standards Authority of Ireland; Standards & Industrial Research Institute of Malaysia; Business & Institutional Furniture Manufacturers' Association; American Society for Testing & Materials; Canadian Centre for Occupational Health & Safety; Information Handling Services; Canadian International Development Agency; Canadian Society for Nondestructive Testing, Inc.; Techstreet; Provincial Territorial Committee on Building Standards; Canadian Council of Fire Marshals & Fire Commissioners
Chief Officer(s):
Begonia Lojk, Acting Director, 819-956-0383
begonia.lojk@tpsgc-pwgsc.gc.ca
Finances: *Annual Operating Budget:* $3 Million-$5 Million
Staff Member(s): 53; 5000 volunteer(s)
Membership: 1,000-4,999
Activities: *Library:* Sales Centre; Open to public

Canadian Generic Pharmaceutical Association (CGPA) / L'Association canadienne du médicament générique (ACMG)

#409, 4120 Yonge St., Toronto ON M2P 2B8
Tel: 416-223-2333; *Fax:* 416-223-2425
info@canadiangenerics.ca
www.canadiangenerics.ca
www.facebook.com/CanadianGenerics
twitter.com/CdnGenerics
Previous Name: Canadian Drug Manufacturers Association
Overview: A large national organization founded in 1984
Mission: To promote an environment which supports & enhances the provision of affordable generic & innovative medications to Canadians & patients around the world through research, development & manufacturing of pharmaceuticals & fine chemicals in Canada
Member of: International Generic Pharmaceutical Association
Chief Officer(s):
Jeff Connell, President
jim@canadiangenerics.ca
Finances: *Annual Operating Budget:* $1.5 Million-$3 Million; *Funding Sources:* Membership fees
Staff Member(s): 6
Membership: 17 corporate; *Fees:* % of sales; *Member Profile:* Generic pharmaceutical company; *Committees:* Scientific Affairs; Provincial Regulatory; Subsequent Entry Biologics; Intellectual Property; Market Growth; Political Action
Activities: *Speaker Service:* Yes; *Library* by appointment
Meetings/Conferences: • 2015 Value of Generic Drugs Symposium, 2015
Scope: International

Canadian Genetic Diseases Network (CGDN) / Réseau canadien sur les maladies génétiques (RCMG)

#201, 2150 Western Pkwy., Vancouver BC V6T 1Z4
Tel: 604-221-7300; *Fax:* 604-221-0778
www.cgdn.ca
Overview: A medium-sized national organization founded in 1990
Mission: A nation-wide consortium of Canada's top investigators & core-technology facilities in human genetics, partnered with colleagues from industry to conduct leading-edge research within an "Institute without Walls"; to achieve international competitiveness in scientific research with social & economic benefits
Chief Officer(s):
Rob Abbott, CEO
Finances: *Annual Operating Budget:* $3 Million-$5 Million; *Funding Sources:* Federal government; industry; foundations
Staff Member(s): 8; 1 volunteer(s)
Membership: 58; *Committees:* Board of Directors; Priority & Planning
Publications:
• CGDN [Canadian Genetic Diseases Network] Annual Report
Type: Yearbook; *Frequency:* Annually

Canadian GeoExchange Coalition (CGC) / Coalition canadienne de l'énergie géothermique

#304, 1030 Cherrier St., Montréal QC H2L 1H9
Tel: 514-807-7559; *Fax:* 514-807-8221
www.geo-exchange.ca
Overview: A medium-sized national organization
Mission: To develop industry standards; To expand the market for geoexchange technology in Canada
Member of: Energy Dialogue Group
Chief Officer(s):
Denis Tanguay, President & Chief Executive Officer, 514-807-7559 Ext. 24
denis.tanguay@geo-exchange.ca
Pierre Jolicoeur, Comptroller, 514-807-7559 Ext. 22
pierre.jolicoeur@geo-exchange.ca
Kaiser Zoghlami, Manager, Information Technology, 514-807-7559 Ext. 27
kaiser.zoghlami@geo-exchange.ca
Membership: 224; *Fees:* Schedule available; *Member Profile:* Organizations involved with residential & commercial heating & air conditioning; *Committees:* Training; Technology
Activities: Providing information, training, & certification; Increasing public awareness; Working with stakeholders to foster the growth of the Canadian geoexchange industry; Liaising with provincial ministries of energy in Canada
Meetings/Conferences: • Canadian GeoExchange Coalition 8th National Geoexchange Business & Policy Forum, 2015
Scope: International
• 12th International Energy Agency Heat Pump Conference, 2017
Scope: International
Description: To promote heat pumping technologies through discussions, networking, and information exchange.

Canadian Geophysical Union (CGU) / Union géophysique canadienne (UGC)

c/o Dept. of Geology & Geophysics, University of Calgary, ES #278, 2500 University Dr. NW, Calgary AB T2N 1N4
Tel: 403-220-5596; *Fax:* 403-284-0074
cgu@ucalgary.ca
www.cgu-ugc.ca
Overview: A medium-sized national organization founded in 1973
Mission: To bring together & promote the geophysical sciences; To provide a focus for geophysicists at Canadian universities, government agencies, & industry in fields of study encompassing the composition & processes of the whole earth, including hydrology, space studies, & geology
Chief Officer(s):
Gail Atkinson, President
gatkins6@uwo.ca
Jim Craven, Treasurer
Masaki Hayashi, Secretary
Finances: *Annual Operating Budget:* Less than $50,000
Staff Member(s): 1; 12 volunteer(s)
Membership: 500; *Fees:* $30 full; $15 associate
Meetings/Conferences: • 2015 Joint Assembly of the Canadian Geophysical Union, May, 2015, Palais des congrès de Montréal, Montréal, QC
Scope: Provincial
Publications:
• Elements: The Newsletter of the Canadian Geophysical Union / Le Bulletin de l'union géophysique canadienne
Type: Newsletter; *Frequency:* Semiannually; *Accepts Advertising; Editor:* Ed S. Krebes; *Price:* Free to CGUmembers
Profile: CGU information, announcements, events, awards, officers, & section & committee news

Canadian Geoscience Council *See* Canadian Federation of Earth Sciences

Canadian Geotechnical Society (CGS)

8828 Pigott Rd., Richmond BC V7A 2C4
Tel: 604-277-7527; *Fax:* 604-277-7529
Toll-Free: 800-710-9867
www.cgs.ca
Overview: A small national organization
Chief Officer(s):
Wayne Gibson, P.Eng., Administrator
cgs@cgs.ca
Victor Sowa, P.Eng., P.Geo., Secretary General
vsowacgs@dccnet.com
Membership: *Committees:* Computing; Education; Heritage; Landslides; Professional Practice; Transportation Geotechnique; Mining Geotechnique
Meetings/Conferences: • 68th Canadian Geotechnical Conference and 7th Canadian Permafrost Conference, September, 2015, Quebec City Conference Centre, Quebec City, QC
Scope: National

Canadian Geriatrics Society (CGS) / Société canadienne de gériatrie (SCG)

#6, 20 Crown Steel Dr., Markham ON L3R 9X9
Tel: 905-415-9161; *Fax:* 905-415-0071
Toll-Free: 866-247-0086
www.canadiangeriatrics.com
Previous Name: Canadian Society of Geriatric Medicine
Overview: A small national organization founded in 1981
Mission: To promote excellence in the medical care of the elderly; to promote high standards, research in geriatric medicare; to desseminate knowledge of the clinical care of the elderly
Member of: Royal College of Physicians & Surgeons of Canada
Affliation(s): Canadian Association of Gerontology
Chief Officer(s):
Frank Molnar, Communications Committee
Roger Wong, President
Membership: *Fees:* $170; *Member Profile:* Physicians with an interest in geriatrics; *Committees:* Foundation; CPD; Communications; Specialty; Membership; Awards; Education; Continuing Professional Development
Activities: Annual general meeting; advocacy
Meetings/Conferences: • Canadian Geriatrics Society 35th Annual General Meeting, April, 2015, Hilton Bonaventure, Montréal, QC
Scope: National
Contact Information: thecanadiangeriatricssociety.wildapricot.org

Canadian German Chamber of Industry & Commerce Inc. (CGCIC) / Deutsch-Kanadische Industrie- und Handelskammer

#1500, 480 University Ave., Toronto ON M5G 1V2
Tel: 416-598-3355; *Fax:* 416-598-1840
info@germanchamber.ca
kanada.ahk.de
www.facebook.com/AHKCanada
twitter.com/ahkcanada
Also Known As: German Trade Commission
Overview: A large international organization founded in 1968
Mission: To promote trade & investment between Germany & Canada; offices in Toronto, Montreal & Vancouver
Member of: Association of German Chambers of Industry & Commerce, Berlin
Chief Officer(s):
Gerd U. Wengler, Chair
Thomas Beck, President & CEO
Finances: *Annual Operating Budget:* $1.5 Million-$3 Million; *Funding Sources:* German government grants; own resources
Staff Member(s): 22
Membership: 500+ Canadian & German firms; *Fees:* $80-$5,000
Activities: German Marketing Services: market background information, identification of partners, publication packages, letters of introduction to German companies; official representative of several major Trade Fairs (Cologne, Frankfurt,

Hamburg, Stuttgart, Dusseldorf, Nuremberg); technical inspection services; refund of the German Value Added Tax (VAT); *Library* Open to public
Publications:
• Canadian German Headlines: CGCIC Newsletter [a publication of the Canadian German Chamber of Industry & Commerce Inc.]
Type: Newsletter; *Frequency:* Monthly; *Accepts Advertising*
Profile: CGCIC member news, articles concerning the Canadian & German business community, news about theCanadian & German economy, updated economic data, & Chamber & other events
• Kanada - groses Land, grose Potentiale [a publication of the Canadian German Chamber of Industry & Commerce Inc.]
Type: Brochure
Profile: First-hand experiences of Canadian subsidiaries of German companies
• Membership Directory of the Canadian German Chamber of Industry & Commerce
Type: Directory
• Opportunities for German companies in the Canadian mining sector
Type: Study
Profile: Focuses on the potential of the Canadian market for raw materials

Montréal
#200, 410 St. Nicolas St., Montréal QC H2Y 2P5
Tel: 514-844-3051; *Fax:* 514-844-1473
info.montreal@germanchamber.ca
Chief Officer(s):
Stephanie Weckend, Interim Managing Director
stephanie.weckend@germanchamber.ca

Vancouver
Tel: 604-681-4469; *Fax:* 604-681-4489
Chief Officer(s):
Sascha Bardens, Managing Director
sascha.bardens@germanchamber.ca

Canadian Gerontological Nursing Association (CGNA) / Association canadienne des infirmières et infirmiers en gérontologie

#1202, 71 Charles St. East, Toronto ON M4Y 2T3
Tel: 416-927-8654; *Fax:* 416-874-4378
cgna@malachite-mgmt.com
www.cgna.net
Overview: A medium-sized national charitable organization founded in 1984
Mission: To promote high standards of gerontological nursing practice; to promote educational programs in gerontological nursing; to participate in affairs which promote the health of elderly persons; to promote networking opportunities for nurses; to promote & disseminate gerontological nursing research; to present the views of the Association to government, education, professional & other appropriate bodies.
Affliation(s): Canadian Nurses Association
Chief Officer(s):
Lynn McCleary, RN, PhD, President
lmccleary@brocku.ca
Finances: *Annual Operating Budget:* $50,000-$100,000
5 volunteer(s)
Membership: 500-999; *Fees:* Schedule available
Activities: *Library*
Awards:
• Ann C. Beckingham Scholarship (Scholarship)
• Memorial Scholarship (Scholarship)
Meetings/Conferences: • Canadian Gerontological Nursing Association 18th Biennial Conference, May, 2015, Charlottetown, PE
Scope: National
Contact Information: URL: cgnaconference.ca; CGNA.conference@gmail.com
Publications:
• The Canadian Gerontological Nurse [a publication of the Canadian Gerontological Nursing Association]
Type: Newsletter; *Frequency:* Quarterly
• Gerontological Nursing Competencies & Standards of Practice
Type: Document; *Price:* $13 members; $16 non-members
• Perspectives [a publication of the Canadian Gerontological Nursing Association]
Type: Journal; *Frequency:* Quarterly *ISSN:* 0831-7445

Canadian Gift Association / Association canadienne de cadeaux

42 Voyager Ct. South, Toronto ON M9W 5M7
Tel: 416-679-0170; *Fax:* 416-679-0175
Toll-Free: 800-611-6100
info@cangift.org
www.cangift.org
www.linkedin.com/company/3520259
www.facebook.com/CanadianGift
twitter.com/cangift
www.youtube.com/user/cgtassoc
Also Known As: CanGift
Overview: A medium-sized national organization founded in 1976
Mission: To create & manage sales opportunities for the gift industry
Chief Officer(s):
Peter Moore, President & CEO, 416-642-1033
pmoore@cangift.org
Finances: *Funding Sources:* Membership fees; programs
Membership: 1,400; *Fees:* $850 silver; $1000 gold; *Member Profile:* Manufacturers; distributors; wholesalers
Activities: *Speaker Service:* Yes
Awards:
• Supplier & Sales Rep. of the Year (Award)
• Best Giftware of the Year (Award)
• Retailer of the Year (Award)
Meetings/Conferences: • Toronto Gift Fair, January, 2015, The International Centre & Congress Centre, Toronto, ON
Scope: Local
Attendance: 24,600
Description: The Toronto Gift Fair is Canada's largest temporary trade gift fair.
Contact Information: Karen Bassels, Vice President, Toronto Gift Fair; PHone: 416.642.1024; kbassels@cangift.org; URL: torontogiftfair.org; toronto@cangift.org
• Alberta Gift Fair, February, 2015, Edmonton Expo Centre, Northlands, Edmonton, AB
Scope: Local
Attendance: 16,000
Description: The Alberta Gift Fair contains Western Canada's most comprehensive collection of products and services, catering to the specialized needs of retailers, sales representatives and manufacturers.
Contact Information: Brenda Harrison, Show Manager; PHone: 416.642.1049; bharrison@cangift.org; URL: albertagiftfair.org; alberta@cangift.org
• Québec Gift Fair, March, 2015, Place Bonaventure, Montréal, QC
Scope: Local
Attendance: 10,000
Contact Information: Anne-Sophie Pelchat, Show Manager; PHone: 416.642.1051; apelchat@cangift.org; URL: quebecgiftfair.org; quebec@cangift.org
Publications:
• Canadian Gift & Tableware Association Research Publications
Profile: Information on opening a giftware store & developing a business plan, for members, retailers, & industry insiders
• Market Monitor [a publication of the Canadian Gift & Tableware Association]
Frequency: Semiannually
Profile: Analysis on timely & relevant topics such as internet retailing, market size, & channels of distribution related to the Canadian giftware market &industry, for CGTA members only
• MarketPulse [a publication of the Canadian Gift & Tableware Association]
Frequency: Semiannually; *Editor:* Erica Kirkland
Profile: Survey results, based on consumer retail purchase activity, to provide stakeholders information on bestselling categories & trends
• Retail News [a publication of the Canadian Gift & Tableware Association]
Profile: Business publication for gift retailers, with information on operating more profitable businesses, distributed to gift stores throughout Canada
• SalesPulse [a publication of the Canadian Gift & Tableware Association]
Frequency: Quarterly
Profile: Based on surveys of giftware retailers, information includes sales, margins, & inventories, to provide an outlook on the upcoming quarter

Canadian Girls Rodeo Association

PO Box 6152, Stn. D, Calgary AB T2P 2C8
Tel: 403-563-5212
cgraentries@gmail.com
www.cgra.ca
Overview: A small national charitable organization founded in 1957
Mission: To promote girls' rodeo sports in Canada; to organize, control, supervise & manage girls' rodeo events for the benefit, safety & protection of the cowgirls
Chief Officer(s):
Deb Hambling, President
d.hambling@hotmail.com
Finances: *Funding Sources:* Bingo; raffles; rodeos
Membership: *Fees:* $100 senior; $70 junior; $25 non-active

Canadian Global Campaign for Education

321 Chapel St., Ottawa ON K1N 7Z2
Tel: 613-232-3569; *Fax:* 613-232-7435
info@cgce.ca
www.cgce.ca
www.facebook.com/group.php?gid=6232974961
twitter.com/join1goal
Overview: A medium-sized international organization founded in 2004
Member of: Global Campaign for Education
Chief Officer(s):
Karen Mundy, Contact
Finances: *Funding Sources:* Government
Membership: 18
Activities: *Awareness Events:* Global Action Week
Meetings/Conferences: • Canadian Global Campaign for Education 2015 Annual Learning Forum, 2015
Scope: National
Description: An opportunity for policy makers, development practitioners, academics, & civil society organizations to share best practices & discuss future programming
Contact Information: E-mail: info@cgce.ca

Canadian Goat Society (CGS) / La Société canadienne des éléveurs de chèvres

2417 Holly Ln., Ottawa ON K1V 0M7
Tel: 613-731-9894; *Fax:* 613-731-0704
cangoatsoc@rogers.com
goat.softcorp.ca
Overview: A medium-sized national organization founded in 1917
Mission: To maintain the integrity of herdbooks, providing accurate evaluation programs for performance and type and promoting the responsible and humane treatment of goats.
Member of: Ontario Farm Animal Council
Chief Officer(s):
Arnold Steeves, President
arnsfarm@nb.sympatico.ca
Membership: *Fees:* $56
Activities: *Library*

Canadian Golf Foundation *See* Golf Canada Foundation

Canadian Golf Hall of Fame & Museum (CGHF) / Musée et Temple canadien de la renommée du golf

Glen Abbey Golf Club, 1333 Dorval Dr., Oakville ON L6M 4X7
Tel: 905-849-9700
cghf@golfcanada.ca
www.rcga.org
Also Known As: Canadian Golf Museum
Overview: A small national charitable organization founded in 1971 overseen by Royal Canadian Golf Association
Mission: Celebrates the outstanding individuals of Canadian golf: amateur and professional players, and others who have played a key role in the evolution of the game of golf in Canada. Open year round, with a shortened schedule during the winter months.
Member of: Ontario Museum Association; Canadian Museum Association; Ontario Archives Association; Canadian Association for Sport Heritage; International Sports Heritage Association
Chief Officer(s):
Karen Hewson, Managing Director, Heritage Services, 905-849-9700 Ext. 213
khewson@golfcanada.ca
Meggan Gardner, Curator, 905-849-9700 Ext. 412
mgardner@golfcanada.ca
Finances: *Funding Sources:* Golf Canada
Activities: *Library:* Canadian Golf Hall of Fame & Museum Library; Open to public

Canadian Golf Superintendents Association (CGSA) / Association canadienne des surintendants de golf

#205, 5520 Explorer Dr., Mississauga ON L4W 5L1
Tel: 905-602-8873; *Fax:* 905-602-1958
Toll-Free: 800-387-1056
cgsa@golfsupers.com
www.golfsupers.com

www.facebook.com/group.php?gid=151227228150
twitter.com/GolfSupers
Overview: A medium-sized national organization founded in 1966
Mission: To promote excellence in golf course management & environmental responsibility; To uphold the Canadian Golf Superintendents Association Principles Of Professional Practice & Code of Ethics & Conduct
Member of: Canadian Turfgrass Research Foundation
Chief Officer(s):
Kenneth S. Cousineau, Executive Director, 905-602-8873 Ext. 222, Fax: 905-602-1958
kcousineau@golfsupers.com
Tim Kubash, President, 250-832-8834
tkubash@salmonarmgolf.com
John Mills, Vice-President, 902-243-2119
jwmills@ns.sympatico.ca
Christian Pilon, Secretary-Treasurer, 450-653-1265
cpilon_mbcc@bellnet.ca
Finances: *Funding Sources:* Sponsorships
Membership: 1,500; *Fees:* $421 superintendents & course management; $330 assistant superintendents; $199 golf course maintenance; $179 equipment technicians; $61 students; *Member Profile:* Golf course superintendents & turfgrass specialists in Canada; *Committees:* Environment; Communications, Marketing, & Public Relations; Professional Development & Research; Conference & Events; Member Services; Equipment Technicians Advisory
Activities: Providing continuing professional development opportunities for members; Sponsoring research projects; Establishing the Master Superintendent Designation Program; Offering networking opportunities; *Awareness Events:* Canadian International Turfgrass Conference and Trade Show, annual; *Library:* CGSA Office Library
Meetings/Conferences: • Canadian International Turfgrass 2015 48th Annual Conference & Trade Show, February, 2015, Telus Convention Centre, Calgary, AB
Scope: International
Description: An international confernce & trade show featuring over 100 exhibitors
Contact Information: Manager, Member Services: Lori Micucci, E-mail: lmicucci@golfsupers.com; URL: golfsupers.com/en/calgary2015
Publications:
• CGSA [Canadian Golf Superintendents Association] Membership Directory
Type: Directory; *Frequency:* Annually; *Price:* Free with Canadian Golf Superintendents Association membership
Profile: Listings of CGSA members, members' clubs, & industry affiliates, for members only
• Environmental Management Resource Manual [a publication of the Canadian Golf Superintendents Association]
Type: Manual
• GreenMaster
Type: Magazine; *Frequency:* Bimonthly; *Price:* Free with Canadian Golf Superintendents Association membership
Profile: Informative articles of interest to golf course superintendents
• Greenmatter E-News [a publication of the Canadian Golf Superintendents Association]
Type: Newsletter; *Frequency:* Monthly
Profile: Current issues, regional news, & product information

Canadian Good Roads Association; Roads & Transportation Association of Canada *See* Transportation Association of Canada

Canadian Government Specifications Board *See* Canadian General Standards Board

Canadian Grand Masters Fiddling Association (CGMFA)
101 Centrepointe Dr., Ottawa ON K2G 5K7
Tel: 613-727-6641
Other Communication: Membership E-mail: members@canadiangrandmasters.ca
cgmfa@canadiangrandmasters.ca
www.canadiangrandmasters.ca
www.facebook.com/CanadianGrandMasters
twitter.com/CGMFA
Previous Name: Canadian Grand Masters Fiddling Championship
Overview: A small national organization founded in 1986
Mission: To preserve the rich heritage of Canadian fiddling
Chief Officer(s):
Ron Bourque, President
Randy Foster, Vice-President
Margaret Côté, Secretary
Todd Thompson, Treasurer & Chair, Finance, Corporations, & By-Laws
Activities: *Awareness Events:* Annual Canadian Grand Masters Competition; Annual Canadian Grand Master Fiddle Camp
Publications:
• Canadian Fiddler
Type: Newsletter; *Frequency:* Quarterly; *Accepts Advertising*; *Price:* Free for members
Profile: Articles about fiddlers, information about traditional fiddling, fiddling & stepdancing competitions, contest results, & upcoming events across Canada

Canadian Grand Masters Fiddling Championship *See* Canadian Grand Masters Fiddling Association

Canadian Grandparents' Rights Association (CGRA)
#207, 14980 - 104 Ave., Surrey BC V3R 1M9
Tel: 604-585-8242; *Fax:* 604-585-8241
Toll-Free: 866-585-8242
www.CanadianGrandparentsRightsAssociation.com
Overview: A medium-sized national organization founded in 1986
Mission: Promotes, supports, and assists Grandparents and their families in maintaining or re-establishing family ties and family stability where the family has been disrupted; especially those ties between grandparents and grandchildren.
Member of: Grand Parents Raising Grandchildren
Finances: *Funding Sources:* Donations; Membership fees; BC Gaming
Activities: *Speaker Service:* Yes; *Library* by appointment

Yukon
whitehorse YT
Tel: 867-821-3821
yukon-seniors-and-elders.org/gray/gray_home.htm
Mission: To assist grandparents with questions about access to or custody of their grandchildren
Chief Officer(s):
Eleanor Millard, Contact

Canadian Grocery HR Council (CGHRC) / Conseil canadien des RH du secteur de l'alimentation (CCRHSA)
#200, 2595 Skymark Ave., Mississauga ON L4W 4L5
Tel: 905-624-3060; *Fax:* 905-624-3061
Toll-Free: 888-624-3060
www.cghrc.ca
Previous Name: Canadian Food Industry Council
Overview: A medium-sized national organization founded in 2003
Mission: To represent the interests of the food retail & wholesale employers in our industry; to increase the profile of the industry & assist its stakeholders in providing training & development opportunities in the food sector
Chief Officer(s):
Patricia Parulekar, Executive Director, 905-624-3060 Ext. 25
patricia@cghrc.ca
Patti Galbraith, Project Manager, 905-624-3060 Ext. 22
patti@cghrc.ca

Canadian Ground Water Association (CGWA) / Association canadienne des eaux souterraines
#100-409, 1600 Bedford Hwy., Bedford NS B4A 1E8
Tel: 902-845-1885; *Fax:* 902-845-1886
info@cgwa.org
www.cgwa.org
Previous Name: Canadian Water Well Association
Overview: A medium-sized national organization founded in 1976
Mission: To act as the national voice of the ground water industry in Canada; To encourage the management & protection of ground water
Chief Officer(s):
Kevin Constable, President, 905-778-9888, Fax: 905-778-1999
kevinconstable@zing-net.ca
Wayne C. MacRae, Executive Director, 902-845-1885, Fax: 902-845-1886
cgwa@ns.sympatico.ca
Finances: *Funding Sources:* Sponsorships
Activities: Promoting the development of ground water guidelines & strategies; Providing education about ground water for members & the public
Publications:
• Guidelines for Water Well Construction
Profile: Construction requirements, according to provincial standards, for the construction of a water well

Canadian Group Psychotherapy Association (CGPA)
Tel: 902-473-8604; *Fax:* 902-425-9699
canadiangpa@gmail.com
www.cgpa.ca
Overview: A small national organization founded in 1990
Mission: To promote excellence in standards of training, practice, & research; To encourage & provide for the education of mental health professionals in group psychotherapy
Member of: International Association for Group Psychotherapy & Group Processes (IAGP)
Chief Officer(s):
Fern Cramer-Azima, President
Linda McFadyen, Secretary, 204-958-9644, Fax: 204-958-9618
lmcfadyen@matc.ca
Alina Isaac, Treasurer, 416-220-3428, Fax: 416-392-0645
alinatree@hotmail.com
Finances: *Funding Sources:* Sponsorships
Membership: *Fees:* $125 full members; $87.50 associated members; $50 auxiliary members; *Member Profile:* Canadian group psychotherapists; *Committees:* Budget & Finance; Constitution; Membership; Nominating; Program; Web & Public Relations; Publications; Research; Training & Education
Activities: Developing national standards for training & practice; Encouraging scientific research; Sponsoring workshops; Disseminating information about educational programs
Awards:
• Martin Fisher Training Award (Award)
• The Jackman Training Award (Award)
• CGPF Endowments Conference Scholarships (Scholarship)
Meetings/Conferences: • Canadian Group Psychotherapy Association's 35th Annual Conference, May, 2015, Toronto, ON
Scope: National
Publications:
• The Chronicle: The Newsletter of the Canadian Group Psychotherapy Association
Type: Newsletter; *Editor:* Colleen Wilkie, PhD
Profile: Articles, committee reports, section news, & Canadian Group Psychotherapy Foundation news

Canadian Guernsey Association
5653 Hwy. 6 North, RR#5, Guelph ON N1H 6J2
Tel: 519-836-2141; *Fax:* 519-763-6582
info@guernseycanada.ca
www.guernseycanada.ca
Overview: A medium-sized national organization founded in 1905
Mission: To provide services to breeders of Guernsey dairy cattle including records, awards, promotion, sales & shows.
Affliation(s): Canadian Livestock Records Corporation; Joint Classification Board; Agriculture & Agri-Food Canada; Canadian Dairy Network
Chief Officer(s):
Jesse Weir, Administrator
Finances: *Funding Sources:* Membership dues; registration fees
Membership: *Fees:* $85; *Member Profile:* Breeders & owners of Guernsey cattle
Activities: Shows; sales

Canadian Guide Dogs for the Blind (CGDB)
National Office & Training Centre, PO Box 280, 4120 Rideau Valley Dr. North, Manotick ON K4M 1A3
Tel: 613-692-7777; *Fax:* 613-692-0650
info@guidedogs.ca
www.guidedogs.ca
Overview: A medium-sized national charitable organization founded in 1984
Mission: To assist visually-impaired Canadians with their mobility by providing & training them in the use of professionally trained guide dogs
Member of: International Guide Dog Federation; Assistance Dogs International, Inc.
Chief Officer(s):
Jane Thornton, Co-Founder & Chief Operating Officer
Finances: *Funding Sources:* Donations; Fundraising; Gift Shop

Canadian Guild of Crafts / Guilde canadienne des métiers d'art
1460B, Sherbrooke St. West, Montreal QC H3G 1K4
Tel: 514-849-6091; *Fax:* 514-849-7351
Toll-Free: 866-477-6091
info@canadianguild.com
www.canadianguildofcrafts.com
www.facebook.com/187315447973358

Overview: A medium-sized national charitable organization founded in 1906
Mission: To preserve, encourage & promote Canadian crafts; to organize & sponsor exhibitions of the work of recognized & promising artists in the fields of arts & crafts; to educate interested groups about Canadian & native crafts through tours & lectures
Chief Officer(s):
Diane Labelle, Director
Finances: *Annual Operating Budget:* $250,000-$500,000; *Funding Sources:* Membership fees; sales; donations
Staff Member(s): 7
Membership: 1-99; *Fees:* $50 individual; $50 affiliated group
Activities: Temporary exhibitions; gallery; permanent collection; *Internships:* Yes; *Speaker Service:* Yes; *Library:* Archives; Open to public

Canadian Guild of Crafts (Ontario); Ontario Craft Foundation *See* Ontario Crafts Council

Canadian Gymnastics Federation *See* Gymnastics Canada Gymnastique

Canadian Hackney Society
PO Box 142, 2698 - 8 Line Rd., Metcalfe ON K0A 2P0
Tel: 613-821-2676
www.hackney.ca
Overview: A small national organization founded in 1892
Affliation(s): Canadian Equestrian Federation; Canadian Livestock Records Corporation; Ontario Hackney Association; Atlantic Hackney Association; Western Canada Hackney Association; American Hackney Horse Association
Chief Officer(s):
Christy Stewart, Executive Director
castewart@bell.net
Finances: *Funding Sources:* Membership fees; registration fees; fundraising
Membership: *Fees:* $15 junior; $25 regular; $500 lifetime
Activities: *Speaker Service:* Yes; *Rents Mailing List:* Yes; *Library* by appointment

Canadian Hadassah WIZO
#900, 1310, av Greene, Montréal QC H3Z 2B8
Tel: 514-937-9431; *Fax:* 514-933-6483
info@chw.ca
www.chw.ca
www.facebook.com/group.php?gid=190277547652411
twitter.com/CHWdotCA
www.youtube.com/user/CHWOrganization
Also Known As: Hadassah-WIZO Organization of Canada
Overview: A large national charitable organization founded in 1917
Mission: Canada's leading Jewish women's philanthropic organization extends material & moral support of Jewish women of Canada to needy individuals in Hadassah-WIZO welfare institutions in Israel; encourages Jewish & Hebrew culture in Canada; cooperates with other organizations; promotes Canadian ideals of democracy. Forty locations across Canada
Affliation(s): Canadian Jewish Congress; Canadian Zionist Federation; National Council of Women of Canada; United Nations Association; Women's International Zionist Organization; Hadassah International
Chief Officer(s):
Marla Dan, National President
Freda Ginsberg, National Executive Vice-President
Finances: *Funding Sources:* Fundraising
Staff Member(s): 10
Membership: 10,000+; *Fees:* $36; *Committees:* Fundraising; Advocacy; Programming
Activities: Fundraising, advocacy; Hadassim & Nahalal Youth Villages, schools, dorms, daycares; Hadassah Hospital & Assaf Harofeh Medical Centre; women's shelters; crisis hotlines; youth clubs & summer camps; *Awareness Events:* National Officers Meeting, Aug.; National Convention, Nov.

Canadian Haflinger Association (CHA)
RR#1, Burgessville ON N0J 1C0
Tel: 519-424-2521
mattway@execulink.com
www.haflinger.ca
Overview: A small national organization founded in 1981
Mission: To promote Haflinger horses in Canada
Chief Officer(s):
Jim Hird, President
jim_hird@yahoo.com
Mike Ready, Vice-President
never_ready@hotmail.com
Mary Sexsmith, Sec.-Treas.
Finances: *Annual Operating Budget:* Less than $50,000
Staff Member(s): 5
Membership: 150; *Fees:* $35
Publications:
• Chatter [a publication of the Canadian Haflinger Association]
Type: Newsletter; *Frequency:* Quarterly
Profile: Upcoming shows & events, articles & stories

Canadian Handball Association (CHA) / Fédération de balle au mur du Canada
Toronto ON
Tel: 416-577-3485
Other Communication: Alt. Phone: 905-683-9479
www.canadianhandball.com
Overview: A medium-sized national organization
Mission: To promote handball in Canada
Chief Officer(s):
Brian Goto, Co-President
briangoto@hotmail.com
Mike Wilson, Co-President
mikejwilson55@gmail.com
Membership: 3,000

Canadian Hard of Hearing Association (CHHA) / Association des malentendants canadiens (AMEC)
#205, 2415 Holly Lane, Ottawa ON K1V 7P2
Tel: 613-526-1584; *Fax:* 613-526-4718
Toll-Free: 800-263-8068; *TTY:* 613-526-2692
chhanational@chha.ca
www.chha.ca
www.facebook.com/144214962320170
twitter.com/CHHA_AMEC
Overview: A medium-sized national charitable organization founded in 1982
Mission: To act as the voice of all hard of hearing Canadians; To promote the integration of hard of hearing people into society
Chief Officer(s):
Robert Corbeil, Executive Director
rcorbeil@chha.ca
Myrtle Barrett, President
myrtlebarrett@nf.sympatico.ca
Finances: *Annual Operating Budget:* $250,000-$500,000; *Funding Sources:* Membership fees; Conference registration fees; Advertising; Sponsorships; Donations
Staff Member(s): 3; 300 volunteer(s)
Membership: 2000; *Fees:* $30 regular members; $50 family units; $30 Student; $300 Coporation; $120 not-for-profit organization; $350 lifetime; *Member Profile:* Any person or organization that supports the objectives of the Canadian Hard of Hearing Association, including hard of hearing individuals & family members
Activities: Raising public awareness about issues important to hard of hearing persons;
Awards:
• Bette Moulton Award (Award)
• Marilyn Dahl Award of Merit (Award)
• Charles Laszlo Award of Technical Excellence (Award)
• Winnifred C. Cory Award of Merit (Award)
• Lynn Wheadon Education Award (Award)
• Young Adult Award of Excellence (Award)
Meetings/Conferences: • Canadian Hard of Hearing Association 2015 National Conference, Annual General Meeting, & Trade Show, May, 2015, The Westin Nova Scotia, Halifax, NS
Scope: National
Description: Educational workshops & plenary sessions
Contact Information: General Conference Information, Toll-Free Phone: 1-800-263-8068, TTY: 613-526-2692, Fax: 613-526-4718, E-mail: conference@chha.ca
Publications:
• Listen / Écoute
Type: Magazine; *Frequency:* 3 pa; *Accepts Advertising*
Profile: Hearing health issues, technology, & the concerns of hard of hearing individuals

Alberta - Calgary Branch
c/o 63 Cornell Rd. NW, Calgary AB T2L 0L4
Tel: 403-284-6224; *Fax:* 403-824-6224
info@chha-calgary.ca
www.chha-calgary.ca
Chief Officer(s):
Terry Webb, President

Alberta - Edmonton Branch
#10, 9912 - 106 St., Edmonton AB T5K 1C5
Tel: 780-428-6622; *Fax:* 780-420-6661; *TTY:* 780-628-6622
chha-ed@shaw.ca
www.chha-ed.com
Chief Officer(s):
Marilyn Kingdon, President

Alberta - Lethbridge Branch
1010 - 18A St. North, Lethbridge AB T1H 3J3
Tel: 403-328-2929
Chief Officer(s):
Doreen Gyorkos, President
dgyorkos@telusplanet.net

British Columbia - BC Main Chapter
#101, 9300 Nowell St., Chilliwack BC V2P 4V7
Tel: 604-795-9238; *Fax:* 604-795-9628
Toll-Free: 866-888-2442
info@chha-bc.org
www.chha-bc.org
www.facebook.com/127952830548757
Chief Officer(s):
Marilyn Dahl, President

British Columbia - BC Parents' Branch
c/o 10150 Gillanders Rd., Chilliwack BC V2P 6H4
Tel: 604-819-5312; *Fax:* 604-794-3960
info@chhaparents.bc.ca
www.chhaparents.bc.ca
Chief Officer(s):
Willetta Les, Administrator

British Columbia - Chilliwack Branch
c/o BC Chapter, #101, 9300 Nowell St., Chilliwack BC V2P4V71
Tel: 604-795-9238
info@chha-bc.org
Chief Officer(s):
Scott Secord, President

British Columbia - Comox Valley
PO Box 433, Lazo BC V0R 2K0
Tel: 250-339-5770
Chief Officer(s):
Sarah Trotter, President
fstrotter@shaw.ca

British Columbia - HEAR Branch
#60, 5221 Oakmount Cres., Burnaby BC V5H 4R4
Tel: 604-438-2500
Chief Officer(s):
Betty MacGillivray, Acting President
bettymac@telus.net

British Columbia - North Shore Branch
600 West Queens Rd., North Vancouver BC V7N 2L3
Tel: 604-926-5222; *Fax:* 604-925-2286
chha_nsb@telus.net
www.chha-nsb.com
Chief Officer(s):
Mike Hocevar, President
mikehocevar@gmail.com

British Columbia - Vancouver Branch
c/o 2125 West 7th Ave., Vancouver BC V6K 1X9
Tel: 778-358-9955
chhavancouver@gmail.com
www.chhavancouver.ca
Chief Officer(s):
Ruth Warick, President

Manitoba Chapter
c/o SMD Self-Help Clearinghouse, 825 Sherbrook St., Winnipeg MB R3A 1M5
Tel: 204-975-3037; *Fax:* 204-975-3027
mbchha@mts.net
www.chha-mb.ca
Chief Officer(s):
Gladys Nielsen, Contact

New Brunswick - Moncton Branch
809 Bernard St., Dieppe NB E1A 5Y2
Tel: 506-855-3799
Chief Officer(s):
Rhéal Léger, President
legerrh@rogers.com

New Brunswick Chapter
74 Alvic Pl., Saint John NB E2M 5G1
Tel: 506-657-7643; *Fax:* 506-657-7643
winslow@nbnet.nb.ca
Chief Officer(s):
Ian Hamilton, President

Newfoundland - Exploits Valley Branch
576 Main St., Bishops Falls NL A0H 1C0
e-mail: chha-evb@nl.rogers.com
Chief Officer(s):
Lillian Menchenton, President

Newfoundland - Gander Branch
77 Fraser Rd., Gander NL A1V 1L1
Tel: 709-256-7935
Chief Officer(s):
Cal Carter, President
c-carter@nl.rogers.com

Newfoundland - Happy Valley Goose Bay Branch
Goose Bay NL A0P 1C0
Chief Officer(s):
Cyril Peach, President
cgpeach@hotmail.com

Newfoundland - Labrador West Branch
813 Carol Dr., Labrador City NL A2V 1S9
Tel: 709-944-5253
Chief Officer(s):
Jerome Gover, President
rgover@nf.sympatico.ca

Newfoundland - Western NL Branch
4 Ingrid Ave., Corner Brook NL A2H 6P2
Tel: 709-639-9547
Chief Officer(s):
Virginia Brake, President
vbrake@nf.sympatico.ca

Newfoundland & Labrador Chapter
1081 Topsail Rd., Mount Pearl NL A1N 5G1
Tel: 709-753-3224; *Fax:* 709-753-5640
info@chha-nl.ca
www.chha-nl.ca
Chief Officer(s):
Robert Young, President

Northwest Territories - Yellowknife Branch
Aven Court, #5A, 5710 - 50th Ave., Yellowknife NT X1A 1E9
Tel: 867-873-4735
Chief Officer(s):
Esther Braden, President
ebraden@theedge.ca

Ontario - Hamilton Branch
c/o #122, 762 Upper James St., Hamilton ON L9C 3A2
Tel: 905-575-4964
info@chha-hamilton.ca
www.chha-hamilton.ca
Chief Officer(s):
Rob Diehl, President

Ontario - Kingston Hard of Hearing Club
#517, 829 Norwest Rd., Kingston ON K7P 2N3
Tel: 613-378-2457
Chief Officer(s):
Margaret Shenton, President
mshenton@sympatico.ca

Ontario - National Capital Region
c/o #205, 2415 Holly Lane, Ottawa ON K1V 7P2
Tel: 613-526-1584; *Fax:* 613-526-4718
alena@chhancr.com
chhancr.com
Chief Officer(s):
Louise Normand, President
alena@chhancr.com

Ontario - Sudbury Branch
#101, 435 Notre Dame Ave., Sudbury ON P3C 5K6
Tel: 705-523-5695; *Fax:* 705-523-8621
Toll-Free: 866-300-2442; *TTY:* 705-523-5695
chha@vianet.ca
www.chhasudbury.com
Chief Officer(s):
Lorraine O'Brien, President

Ontario - York Branch
147 Primeau Dr., Aurora ON L4G 6Z6
www.chha-york.com
Chief Officer(s):
Dan McDonnell, President
dmac773@gmail.com

Prince Edward Island Chapter
RR#1 Augustine Cove, Borden-Carleton PE C0B 1X0
Tel: 902-855-2382; *Fax:* 902-885-3282
Chief Officer(s):
Annie Lee MacDonald, President
annmerdon@pei.sympatico.ca

Québec - Outaouais Branch
25, rue des Rapides, Gatineau QC J8T 5K2
Chief Officer(s):
Carole Willans, Interim President
cwillans@chha.ca

Québec Chapter
25, rue des Rapides, Gatineau QC J8T 5K2
Chief Officer(s):
Carole Willans, President
cwillans@chha.ca

Saskatchewan - Regina Branch
c/o 2341 Broad St., Regina SK S4P 1Y9
Tel: 306-457-3259; *Fax:* 306-757-3252
Toll-Free: 800-565-3323
Chief Officer(s):
Gloria Knous, President
glochha@sasktel.net

Canadian Hardware & Housewares Manufacturers' Association (CHHMA) / Association canadienne des fabricants de produits de quincaillerie et d'articles ménagers

#101, 1335 Morningside Ave., Toronto ON M1B 5M4
Tel: 416-282-0022; *Fax:* 416-282-0027
Toll-Free: 800-488-4792
www.chhma.ca
Overview: A large national organization founded in 1966
Mission: To assist members to sell more & do it more profitably
Chief Officer(s):
Vaughn Crofford, President, 416-282-0022 Ext. 30
crofford@chhma.ca
Maureen Hizaka, Director, Operations, 416-282-0022 Ext. 23
mhizaka@chhma.ca
Michael Jorgenson, Manager, Marketing & Communications, 416-282-0022 Ext. 34
mjorgenson@chhma.ca
Pam Winter, Coordinator, Events, 416-282-0022 Ext. 21
pwinter@chhma.ca
Finances: *Funding Sources:* Membership dues
50 volunteer(s)
Membership: 270 companies; *Fees:* Schedule available; *Member Profile:* Manufacture products; Agency representing manufacturer or service to manufacturer; *Committees:* Business Events; Communications; Representation; Social
Awards:
• The CHHMA Scholarship Awards (Scholarship)
Eligibility: Children of member company employees*Deadline:* July 15th *Amount:* 65 awards totalling $130,000
Meetings/Conferences: • CHHMA [Canadian Hardware & Housewares Manufacturers Association] Spring Conference & AGM 2015, April, 2015, International Centre (Conference Facility), Mississauga, ON
Scope: National

Canadian Hardwood Plywood & Veneer Association (CHPVA) / Association canadienne du Contreplaqué et de Placages de bois dur (ACCPBD)

89 Godfrey Ave., St. Sauveur QC J0R 1R5
Tel: 450-227-4048; *Fax:* 450-227-7827
www.chpva.com
Overview: A medium-sized national organization
Mission: To protect the interests & conserve the rights of those involved in the manufacture & distribution of hardwood veneer & plywood & their suppliers in Canada.
Chief Officer(s):
Gaëtan Lauzon, Executive Vice President
glauzon@chpva.ca
Carole Aussant, Coordinator
caussant@chpva.ca
Membership: 54; *Fees:* Schedule available; *Member Profile:* Manufacturers of hardwood plywood & vaneer; Furniture & cabinetry manufacturers; Wholesalers; Industry suppliers; *Committees:* Technical; Marketing

Canadian Harm Reduction Network

#1904, 666 Spadina Ave., Toronto ON M5S 2H8
Tel: 416-928-0279; *Fax:* 416-966-9512
Toll-Free: 800-728-1293
noharm@canadianharmreduction.com
www.canadianharmreduction.com
www.facebook.com/noharmcanada
twitter.com/noharmcanada
youtube.com/noharmcanada
Overview: A small national organization
Mission: To reduce the social, health & economic harms associated with drugs & drug policies
Affliation(s): Drug Policy Alliance

Canadian Harvard Aircraft Association (CHAA)

PO Box 175, 244411 Airport Rd., Tillsonburg ON N4G 4H5
Tel: 519-842-9922
info@harvards.com
www.harvards.com
www.facebook.com/canadianharvards
twitter.com/CdnHarvards
Overview: A small local organization founded in 1985
Mission: To restore, preserve, maintain, display & demostrate the Harvard aircraft & others associated with the RCAF.
Chief Officer(s):
Pat Hanna, President & Chair
p_hanna@harvards.com
Terry Scott, Director, Public Relations
t_scott@harvards.com
Membership: *Fees:* $50 general; $75 family; $500 lifetime; $15 18 & under; $1000 sponsor; *Committees:* Fundraising; Membership; Volunteer
Activities: Harvard & Tiger Moth ground schools; formation workshops; aircraft maintenance training
Publications:
• The Roar
Type: Newsletter; *Frequency:* Quarterly

Canadian Hays Converter Association

#201, 1600 - 15th Ave. SW, Calgary AB T3C 0Y2
Tel: 403-245-6923; *Fax:* 403-244-3128
haysconverter@shaw.ca
Overview: A small national organization
Mission: To develop & regulate the breeding of Hays Converter cattle; To establish & implement breeding & performance standards for Hays Converter cattle; To register Hays Converter cattle in cooperation with the Canadian Livestock Records Corporation; To maintain a record of the pedigrees of Hays Converter cattle
Member of: Canadian Beef Breeds Council
Affliation(s): Canadian Livestock Records Corporation
Chief Officer(s):
Terri Worms, Secretary-Manager
Lisa Hutt, Registrar, Canadian Livestock Records Corporation, 613-731-7110 Ext. 312
lisa.hutt@clrc.ca
Membership: *Fees:* $50 active & associate members; $20 junior members
Activities: Promoting the breeding & development of Hays Converter cattle in Canada; Publishing data & information on the industry; Supervising breeders of Hays Converter cattle

Canadian Health Care Anti-fraud Association (CHCAA)

#305, 120 Carlton St., Toronto ON M5A 4K2
Tel: 416-593-2633; *Fax:* 416-596-9532
Toll-Free: 866-962-4222
www.chcaa.org
twitter.com/joel_chcaa
Overview: A small national organization founded in 2000
Mission: To improve the Canadian Health Care environment by eliminating health care fraud; Educate & create awareness about issues pertaining to health care fraud; build partnerships with law enforcement agencies; provide a place for information sharing pertaining to fighting health care fraud
Chief Officer(s):
Jacinta Khan, Administrator
Joel Alleyne, Executive Director
Membership: 20 Corporate + 100+ individual; *Fees:* $5000 private/public corporate; $3000 provider-corporate; $1000 law enforcement agency; $300 provider-individual; $100 law enforcement-individual; *Member Profile:* Individuals or corporations involved in the detection, prevention & prosecutions of healthcare fraud

Canadian Health Coalition (CHC) / Coalition canadienne de la santé

#212, 251 Bank St., Ottawa ON K2P 1X3
Tel: 613-521-3400; *Fax:* 613-521-9638
info@healthcoalition.ca
www.healthcoalition.ca
www.facebook.com/groups/76610717247
twitter.com/healthcoalition
www.youtube.com/user/HealthCoalition
Overview: A large national organization founded in 1979
Mission: To create good health; To preserve & strengthen the Canada Health Act, the foundation of Medicare; To make the health care system democratic, accountable & representative; To provide a continuum of care from large institutions to the home; To protect our investment in the skills & abilities of our health care workers; To ensure fair wages for all health care providers; To eliminate profit-making from illness; To reduce

over-prescribing & make drugs affordable; to stop fee-for-service payments; To expand methods of health care & the role of non-physician health providers
Chief Officer(s):
Michael McBane, National Coordinator
mike@medicare.ca
Finances: *Funding Sources:* Donations
Membership: 2.5 million + 34 national organizations
Activities: *Speaker Service:* Yes

Canadian Health Economics Research Association *See* Canadian Association for Health Services & Policy Research

Canadian Health Food Association (CHFA) / Association canadienne des aliments de santé

#302, 235 Yorkland Blvd., Toronto ON M2J 4Y8
Tel: 416-497-6939; *Fax:* 905-479-3214
Toll-Free: 800-661-4510
info@chfa.ca
www.chfa.ca
www.facebook.com/CanadianHealthFoodAssociation
twitter.com/cdnhealthfood
instagram.com/canadianhealthfoodassociation
Previous Name: Health Food Dealers Association
Overview: A medium-sized national organization founded in 1964
Mission: To act as the voice of the natural products industry; To promote natural & organic products as an integral part of health & well-being; To ensure the growth of the natural & organic industry
Chief Officer(s):
Matthew James, Chair
Membership: 1,000+; *Member Profile:* Suppliers of natural products &/or organics; Retailers of natural health products &/or health foods; Associate members, such as farmers, organic certification providers, health practitioners, gyms, industry consultants, & media
Activities: Supporting & empowering members; Seeking scientific advice from the Expert Scientific Advisory Panel; Engaging in advocacy & outreach activities; Offering education; Providing networking opportunities; *Awareness Events:* National Health Food Month, November
Awards:
• Hall of Fame Award (Award)
Meetings/Conferences: • Canadian Health Food Association (CHFA) Expo West 2015, April, 2015, Vancouver Convention Centre, Vancouver, BC
Scope: Provincial
Description: A conference & trade show attended by owners, managers, employees, & nutrition & health care practitioners from pharmacies, health stores, grocery stores, specialty stores, & online retailers
Contact Information: Phone: 416-497-6939; Toll-Free Phone: 1-800-661-4510; E-mail: info@chfa.ca
• Canadian Health Food Association (CHFA) Expo East 2015, September, 2015, Metro Toronto Convention Centre, South Building, Toronto, ON
Scope: Provincial
Attendance: 2,900
Description: A trade event, featuring exhibits from leading suppliers, manufacturers, distributors, & brokers of natural health products & organics
Contact Information: Phone: 416-497-6939; Toll-Free Phone: 1-800-661-4510; E-mail: info@chfa.ca
• Canadian Health Food Association (CHFA) Québec 2015, February, 2015, Palais des congrès, Montreal, QC
Scope: Provincial
Attendance: 875
Description: A conference & trade show designed for owners & decision makers from both small & large establishments, such as natural & health food retail stores, specialty stores, food chains, & pharmacies
Contact Information: Phone: 416-497-6939; Toll-Free Phone: 1-800-661-4510; E-mail: info@chfa.ca
Publications:
• Canadian Health Food Association Annual Report
Type: Yearbook; *Frequency:* Annually
Profile: Activities of the association during the past year
• Canadian Health Food Association Asssociate Member Directory
Type: Directory; *Frequency:* Monthly; *Editor:* Eva Chen
Profile: A membership directory exclusively for members
• Canadian Health Food Association e-News
Type: Newsletter; *Frequency:* Weekly; *Price:* Free with membership in the Canadian Health Food Association
Profile: Latest developments in the natural health & organic products industry
• Canadian Health Food Association Member Bulletins
Type: Newsletter; *Frequency:* Irregular; *Price:* Free with membership in the Canadian Health Food Association
Profile: Recent news in the natural health & organic products industry
• Canadian Health Food Association Retail Member Directory
Type: Directory; *Frequency:* Monthly; *Editor:* Eva Chen
Profile: A listing with contact information
• Canadian Health Food Association Supplier Member Directory
Type: Directory; *Frequency:* Monthly; *Editor:* Eva Chen
Profile: A membership directory exclusively for members
• Membership that Matters! [a publication of the Canadian Health Food Association]
Type: Newsletter; *Price:* Free with membership in the Canadian Health Food Association
Profile: Information for members to help their businesses prosper
• The Natural Voice [a publication of the Canadian Health Food Association]
Type: Newsletter; *Frequency:* Quarterly; *Price:* Free with membership in the Canadian Health Food Association
Profile: Association & industry news
• Research & Your Health
Type: Newsletter; *Frequency:* Quarterly; *Number of Pages:* 8; *Price:* Free with membership in the Canadian Health Food Association
Profile: Abstracts about the value of natural health products

Canadian Health Information Management Association (CHIMA)

99 Enterprise Dr. South, London ON N6N 1B9
Tel: 519-438-6700; *Fax:* 519-438-7001
Toll-Free: 877-332-4462
www.echima.ca
Previous Name: Canadian Health Record Association
Overview: A medium-sized national organization founded in 1942
Mission: To contribute to the promotion of wellness & the provision of quality healthcare through excellence in health information management; to assure competency of practice through credentialling, standards & continuing education; to promote value of health information management professionals
Affliation(s): International Federation of Health Information Management Associations; American Health Information Management Association
Chief Officer(s):
Gail Crook, CEO & Registrar
gail.crook@echima.ca
Tasha Clipperton, Contact
tasha.clipperton@echima.ca
Finances: *Annual Operating Budget:* $500,000-$1.5 Million; *Funding Sources:* Membership & exam revenues; promotional products & services; continuing education; services & events
Staff Member(s): 11
Membership: 5,000 members; *Member Profile:* Graduate of recognized health information management program & successful challenge Canadian College of Health Information Management (CCHIM) certification examination
Activities: *Speaker Service:* Yes
Publications:
• CHIMA [Canadian Health Information Management Association] Source Newsletter
Type: Newsletter; *Frequency:* 3 pa; *Accepts Advertising*; *Editor:* Tamara Stefanits & Cathy Brooks
Profile: Timely, educational information to assist health information professionals
• The Guide to Managing Health Records in Community Care Agencies

Canadian Health Libraries Association (CHLA) / Association des bibliothèques de la santé du Canada (ABSC)

39 River St., Toronto ON M5A 3P1
Tel: 416-646-1600; *Fax:* 416-646-9460
info@chla-absc.ca
www.chla-absc.ca
www.facebook.com/CHLA.ABSC
Overview: A large national organization founded in 1976
Mission: To lead health librarians towards excellence
Chief Officer(s):
Jeff Mason, President
president@chla-absc.ca
Charlotte Beck, Vice-President
vice-president@chla-absc.ca
Jennifer McKeinnell, Director, Continuing Education
ce@chla-absc.ca
Laurie Blanchard, Director, Public Relations
pr@chla-absc.ca
Shauna-Lee Konrad, Secretary
secretary@chla-absc.ca
Membership: *Fees:* $40 students, unemployed & retired persons; $100 regular members; $200 institutions; $2,500 sustaining; *Member Profile:* Health librarian; Institutions; Students
Activities: Facilitating the transfer of knowledge in health sciences; Offering professional development events; Providing grants for members to attend continuing education events; Engaging in advocacy activities; Providing networking opportunities; *Rents Mailing List:* Yes
Meetings/Conferences: • Canadian Health Libraries Association (CHLA) / Association des bibliothèques de la santé du Canada (ABSC) 2015 39th Annual Conference, June, 2015, Vancouver, BC
Scope: National
Description: An annual May or June gathering of health science librarians to participate in continuing education courses & lectures, & to view products & services related to their work
Contact Information: Continuing Education, E-mail: ce@chla-absc.ca; Public Relations, E-mail: pr@chla-absc.ca
• Canadian Health Libraries Association (CHLA) / Association des bibliothèques de la santé du Canada (ABSC) 2016 40th Annual Conference, May, 2016, Toronto, ON
Scope: National
Description: A joint conference with the Medical Library Association
Contact Information: Continuing Education, E-mail: ce@chla-absc.ca; Public Relations, E-mail: pr@chla-absc.ca
• Canadian Health Libraries Association (CHLA) / Association des bibliothèques de la santé du Canada (ABSC) 2017 41st Annual Conference, 2017, Edmonton, AB
Scope: National
Description: An annual May or June gathering of health science librarians to participate in continuing education courses & lectures, & to view products & services related to their work
Contact Information: Continuing Education, E-mail: ce@chla-absc.ca; Public Relations, E-mail: pr@chla-absc.ca
• Canadian Health Libraries Association (CHLA) / Association des bibliothèques de la santé du Canada (ABSC) 2018 42nd Annual Conference, 2018, St. John's, NL
Scope: National
Description: An annual May or June gathering of health science librarians to participate in continuing education courses & lectures, & to view products & services related to their work
Contact Information: Continuing Education, E-mail: ce@chla-absc.ca; Public Relations, E-mail: pr@chla-absc.ca
Publications:
• CHLA [Canadian Health Libraries Association] / ABSC Directory & Membership List
Type: Directory
Profile: For members only
• eNews [a publication of Canadian Health Libraries Association]
Type: Newsletter
• Journal of the Canadian Health Libraries Association / Journal de l'association des bibliothèques de la santé du Canada
Type: Journal; *Frequency:* Quarterly; *Accepts Advertising*; *Editor:* Vicky Duncan *ISSN:* 1708-6892
Profile: Feature articles, book reviews, & news
• Standards for Library & Information Services in Canadian Healthcare Facilities
Type: Monograph; *ISBN:* 0-9692171-4-5; *Price:* $30 Canadian Health Libraries Association; $35 Non-members
• Workload Measurement Systems: A Guide for Libraries
Type: Monograph; *ISBN:* 0-9692171-3-7; *Price:* $30 Canadian Health Libraries Association; $40 Non-members

Canadian Health Record Association *See* Canadian Health Information Management Association

Canadian Health Services Research Foundation *See* Canadian Foundation for Healthcare Improvement

Canadian Healthcare Engineering Society (CHES) / Société canadienne d'ingénierie des services de santé (SCISS)

#310, 4 Cataraqui St., Kingston ON K7K 1Z7
Tel: 613-531-2661; *Fax:* 613-531-0626
ches@eventsmgt.com
www.ches.org
Previous Name: Canadian Hospital Engineering Society

Canadian Associations

Overview: A medium-sized national organization founded in 1980
Mission: To be a forum for exchange of information & ideas related to excellence in communication & professional development in healthcare facilities management
Chief Officer(s):
Peter Whiteman, President
Membership: 700 individual; *Fees:* $126
Activities: *Awareness Events:* National Healthcare Facilities Engineering Week, October
Meetings/Conferences: • Canadian Healthcare Engineering Society 35th Annual Conference, September, 2015, Shaw Conference Centre, Edmonton, AB
Scope: National
Description: Theme: Healthcare Facilities & the Technology Highway

Canadian Hearing Impaired Hockey Association *See* Canadian Deaf Ice Hockey Federation

Canadian Hearing Instrument Practitioners Society (CHIPS)

#259, 185-9040 Blundell Rd., Richmond BC V6Y 1K3
www.chipscanada.com
Overview: A small national organization founded in 1998
Mission: The national professional organization for Hearing Instrument Practitioners who provide hearing healthcare services for hard of hearing people in Canada.
Member of: International Hearing Society
Chief Officer(s):
Allen Kirkham, Chair
Membership: *Fees:* $275 Board Certified Hearing Instrument Specialist, Graduate, Provisional, Corporate Members; $100 Industrial Members; $50 Associate Members

Canadian Hearing Society (CHS) / Société canadienne de l'ouïe

271 Spadina Rd., Toronto ON M5R 2V3
Tel: 416-928-2535; *Fax:* 416-928-2506
Toll-Free: 877-347-3427; *TTY:* 877-216-7310
info@chs.ca
www.chs.ca
www.facebook.com/pages/The-Canadian-Hearing-Society/164604840229034
twitter.com/wwwCHSca
Overview: A large national charitable organization founded in 1940
Mission: To provide services that enhance the independence of deaf, deafened, & hard of hearing people, & that encourage prevention of hearing loss
Chief Officer(s):
Chris Kenopic, President/CEO & Secretary
Stephanus Greeff, CFO & Vice-President, Finance
Katherine Hum-Antonopoulos, COO & Vice-President, Programs & Services
Susan Main, Vice-President, Fundraising & Strategic Communications
Deborah Pikula, Director, Human Resources
Finances: *Funding Sources:* Ontario government service contracts; Product sales; United Way
450 volunteer(s)
Membership: 7,000; *Fees:* $25
Activities: Providing counselling services, employment services, a hearing aid program;, Ontario Interpreter Service, general social services, & sign language classes; Engaging in advocacy activities; *Awareness Events:* Hearing Awareness Month, May; Deaf Awareness Week, third week of September; *Internships:* Yes; *Speaker Service:* Yes

Barrie Office
#1412, 64 Cedar Pointe Dr., Barrie ON L4N 5R7
Tel: 705-737-3190; *Fax:* 705-722-0381; *TTY:* 877-872-0585
Chief Officer(s):
Maggie Doherty-Gilbert, Regional Director

Belleville Office
Bayview Mall, #51, 470 Dundas St. East, Belleville ON K8N 1G1
Tel: 613-966-8995; *Fax:* 613-966-8365; *TTY:* 877-872-0586
Chief Officer(s):
Brian McKenzie, Regional Director

Brantford Office
#139, 225 Colborne St., Brantford ON N3T 2H2
Tel: 519-753-3162; *Fax:* 519-753-7447; *TTY:* 877-843-0370
Chief Officer(s):
Monte Hardy, Regional Director

Brockville Sub-Office
#205, 68 William St., Brockville ON K6V 4V5
Tel: 613-498-3933; *Fax:* 613-498-0363
Toll-Free: 877-817-8209
Chief Officer(s):
Brian McKenzie, Regional Director

Chatham-Kent Office
#201, 75 Thames St., Chatham ON N7L 1S4
Tel: 519-354-9347; *Fax:* 519-354-2083; *TTY:* 877-872-0589
Chief Officer(s):
David Kerr, Regional Director

Durham Regional Office
Braemor Center Plaza, #7, 575 Thornton Rd. North, Oshawa ON L1J 8L5
Tel: 905-404-8490; *Fax:* 905-404-2012
Toll-Free: 888-697-3617
Chief Officer(s):
Maggie Doherty-Gillbert, Regional Director

Elliot Lake Office
c/o Huron Lodge, 100 Manitoba Rd., Elliot Lake ON P5A 3T1
Tel: 705-848-5306; *Fax:* 705-848-1306
Toll-Free: 877-634-0179
Chief Officer(s):
Silvy Coutu, Regional Director

Guelph Office
#200, 2 Quebec St., Guelph ON N1H 2T3
Tel: 519-821-4242; *Fax:* 519-821-8846
Toll-Free: 888-697-3611
Chief Officer(s):
Victoria Baby, Regional Director

Hamilton Office
21 Hunter St. East, 2nd Fl., Hamilton ON L8N 1M2
Tel: 905-522-0755; *Fax:* 905-522-1336; *TTY:* 877-817-8208
info@chs.ca

Kenora Office
136 Main St. South, Kenora ON P9N 1S9
Tel: 807-468-7230; *Fax:* 807-468-8496
Toll-Free: 866-790-0011; *TTY:* 877-843-0373
Chief Officer(s):
Nancy Patterson, Regional Director

Kingston Regional Office
Frontenac Mall, 1300 Bath Rd., Unit D4, Kingston ON K7M 4X4
Tel: 613-544-1927; *Fax:* 613-544-1975
Toll-Free: 877-544-1927; *TTY:* 877-217-8209
Chief Officer(s):
Brian McKenzie, Regional Director

London Regional Office
181 Wellington St., London ON N6B 2K9
Tel: 519-667-3325; *Fax:* 519-667-9668; *TTY:* 888-697-3613
info@chs.ca

Mississauga
#300, 2227 South Millway, Mississauga ON L5L 3R6
Tel: 905-608-0271; *Fax:* 905-608-8241
Toll-Free: 866-603-7161; *TTY:* 877-634-0176
info@chs.ca
Chief Officer(s):
Victoria Baby, Regional Director

Muskoka Office
#103, 175 Manitoba Street, Bracebridge ON P1L 1S3
Tel: 705-645-8882
Toll-Free: 877-840-8882
Chief Officer(s):
Maggie Doherty-Gilbert, Regional Director

Niagara Office
Normandy Resource Centre, #501, 55 King St., St Catharines ON L2R 3H5
Tel: 905-984-4412; *Fax:* 905-984-8298; *TTY:* 877-634-0181
Chief Officer(s):
Monte Hardy, Regional Director

North Bay Office
#432, 101 Worthington St. East, North Bay ON P1B 1G5
Tel: 705-474-8090; *Fax:* 705-474-6075; *TTY:* 877-634-0174
Chief Officer(s):
Silvy Coutu, Regional Director

Ottawa Regional Office
#600, 2197 Riverside Dr., Ottawa ON K1N 7X3
Tel: 613-521-0509; *Fax:* 613-521-0838; *TTY:* 888-697-3650
info@chs.ca
Chief Officer(s):
Michel David, Regional Director
mdavid@chs.ca

Peterborough Office
315 Reid St., Peterborough ON K9J 3R2
Tel: 705-743-1573; *Fax:* 705-741-0708
Toll-Free: 800-213-3848; *TTY:* 888-697-3623
info@chs.ca
Chief Officer(s):
Maggie Doherty-Gilbert, Regional Director

Sarnia Office
420 East St. North, Sarnia ON N7T 6Y5
Tel: 519-337-8307; *Fax:* 519-337-6886; *TTY:* 877-634-0178
Chief Officer(s):
Marilyn Reid, Regional Director

Sault Ste. Marie Regional Office
130 Queen St. East, Sault Ste Marie ON P6A 1Y5
Tel: 705-946-4320; *Fax:* 705-256-7231
Toll-Free: 855-819-9169; *TTY:* 877-634-0179
Chief Officer(s):
Silvy Coutu, Regional Director

Simcoe York Regional Office
#105, 713 Davis Dr., Newmarket ON L3Y 2R3
Tel: 905-715-7511; *Fax:* 905-715-7109
Toll-Free: 877-715-7511
Chief Officer(s):
Maggie Doherty-Gilbert, Regional Director

Sudbury Regional Office
1233 Paris St., Sudbury ON P3E 3B6
Tel: 705-522-1020; *Fax:* 705-522-1060
Toll-Free: 800-479-4562; *TTY:* 877-817-8205
info@chs.ca
Chief Officer(s):
Silvy Coutu, Regional Director

Thunder Bay Regional Office
Victoriaville Centre, #35, 125 Syndicate Ave. South, Thunder Bay ON P7E 6H8
Tel: 807-623-1646; *Fax:* 807-623-4815
Toll-Free: 866-646-0514; *TTY:* 877-634-0183
info@chs.ca
Chief Officer(s):
Nancy Frost, Regional Director

Timmins Office
20 Wilcox St, Timmins ON P4N 3K6
Tel: 705-268-0771; *Fax:* 705-268-4598
Toll-Free: 877-872-0580; *TTY:* 705-268-0744
Chief Officer(s):
Silvy Coutu, Regional Director

Toronto (Central) Region
271 Spadina Rd., Toronto ON M5R 2V3
Tel: 416-928-2500; *Fax:* 416-928-2523
Toll-Free: 877-215-9530
Chief Officer(s):
Stephanie Ozorio, Regional Director

Waterloo Regional Office
#200, 120 Ottawa St. North, Kitchener ON N2H 3K5
Tel: 519-744-6811; *Fax:* 519-744-2390
Toll-Free: 800-668-5815; *TTY:* 888-697-3611
info@chs.ca

Windsor Regional Office
300 Giles Blvd. East, #3A, Windsor ON N9A 4C4
Tel: 519-253-7241; *Fax:* 519-253-6630; *TTY:* 877-216-7302
info@chs.ca

Canadian Hearing Society Foundation *See* Hearing Foundation of Canada

Canadian Heart Association *See* Canadian Cardiovascular Society

Canadian Heartland Training Railway

226 Christie Park View SW, Calgary AB T3H 2Z4
Tel: 403-601-8731; *Fax:* 403-601-8704
www.chtr.ca
Overview: A small national organization
Mission: To support the practical training needs of the railway industry in Canada & around the world
Member of: Railway Association of Canada; Railway Suppliers Association of Canada
Chief Officer(s):
Joe Bracken, President
joebracken@chtr.ca

Canadian Heavy Oil Association (CHOA)

#400, 500 - 5th Ave. SW, Calgary AB T2P 3L5
Tel: 403-269-1755; *Fax:* 403-453-0179
www.choa.ab.ca
www.linkedin.com/groups?gid=2795817
twitter.com/CDN_CHOA
Overview: A medium-sized national organization

Mission: To provide a technical, educational, & social forum for people employed in, or associated with, the oil sands & heavy oil industries
Chief Officer(s):
Kym Fawcett, President, 403-693-5054, Fax: 403-693-5050
Kerri Markle, Executive Director
Finances: *Funding Sources:* Membership fees; Sponsorships
Membership: 1,200+; *Fees:* $25 plus GST students; $100 plus GST regular members; *Member Profile:* Individuals employed in heavy oil exploration & production, service & supply, consulting, & government; Students
Activities: Providing continuing education; Offering networking opportunities with industry peers; *Library:* Canadian Heavy Oil Association Library; by appointment
Awards:
• CHOA Scholarships (Scholarship)
Amount: $2,000
• CHOA Bursary Program (Grant)
To support students with financial needs to pursue programs that mat lead to work in the heavy oil industry *Contact:* K.C. Yeung, Education Committee Chair, E-mail: office@choa.ab.ca
Meetings/Conferences: • Canadian Heavy Oil Association Conference 2015, 2015
Scope: National
Publications:
• CHOA [Canadian Heavy Oil Association] Handbook
Type: Handbook; *Price:* $60
Profile: Topics include markets & logistics, environment & regulatory best management practices, geology & geophysics, geostatistics, geomechanics, reservoir & wellbore simulation,drilling & completions, field testing, bitumen / heavy oil upgrading, & heavy oil research
• Journal of the Canadian Heavy Oil Association
Type: Journal; *Accepts Advertising*; *Editor:* Deborah Jaremko
Profile: Feature articles, technology information, news from the association, scholarship winners, volunteer recognition, & sponsor information

Canadian Hematology Society (CHS) / Société canadienne d'hématologie
#199, 435 St. Laurent Blvd., Ottawa ON K1K 2Z8
Tel: 613-748-9613; *Fax:* 613-748-6392
canadianhematology@uniserve.com
www.canadianhematologysociety.org
Overview: A small national organization founded in 1971
Mission: To represent members of the Society & provide information about hematology
Chief Officer(s):
Stephen Couban, President, 902-473-7006
stephen.couban@cdha.nshealth.ca
Membership: 296; *Fees:* $50; *Member Profile:* Canadian physicians & scientists with an interest in the discipline
Publications:
• Canadian Hematology Society Membership Directory
Type: Directory
• Canadian Hematology Society Newsletter
Type: Newsletter; *Frequency:* 3 pa

Canadian Hemerocallis Society
16 Douville Ct., Toronto ON M5A 4E7
Tel: 416-362-1682
www.distinctly.on.ca/chs
Also Known As: National Daylily Society of Canada
Overview: A small national organization
Mission: To promote, encourage & foster the development & improvement of the genus Hemerocallis
Chief Officer(s):
John P. Peat, President
jpeat@distinctly.on.ca
Membership: *Fees:* $25

Canadian Hemochromatosis Society (CHS) / Société canadienne de l'hémochromatose
#285, 7000 Minoru Blvd., Richmond BC V6Y 3Z5
Tel: 604-279-7135; *Fax:* 604-279-7138
Toll-Free: 877-223-4766
office@toomuchiron.ca
www.toomuchiron.ca
Overview: A medium-sized national charitable organization founded in 1982
Mission: To increase awareness among the public & medical community with regards to the importance of family screening, early diagnosis & treatment of Hemochromatosis
Member of: International Association of Haemochromatosis Societies
Affliation(s): Haemochromatosis Society of Great Britain; Haemochromatosis Society of Southern Africa; American Hemochromatosis Society Inc.; Association hémochromatose France; Haemochromatosis Society Australia; Iron Disorders Institute of America
Chief Officer(s):
Frank Erschen, President & Chair
Finances: *Annual Operating Budget:* $50,000-$100,000; *Funding Sources:* Donations; membership dues
Staff Member(s): 3; 5 volunteer(s)
Membership: 1,074; *Fees:* $20 senior; $30 adult; $45 family; *Committees:* Fundraising; Awareness Week; Memberships
Activities: Maintains a central registry of members & donors & their families; also provides support & information, speakers, & a Medical Advisory Board; *Awareness Events:* National Hemochromatosis Awareness Week, last week of May
Publications:
• Iron Filings: Newsletter of The Canadian Hemochromatosis Society
Type: Newsletter; *Frequency:* Semiannually; *Price:* Free for members
Profile: Current research, news about hemochromatosis, dietary information, stories, & CHS member information

Canadian Hemophilia Society (CHS) / Société canadienne de l'hémophilie
#400, 1255 rue University, Montréal QC H3B 3B6
Tel: 514-848-0503; *Fax:* 514-848-9661
Toll-Free: 800-668-2686
chs@hemophilia.ca
www.hemophilia.ca
Overview: A medium-sized national charitable organization founded in 1953
Mission: To find a cure & to provide services to people with hemophilia or other inherited bleeding disorders; to serve persons infected with HIV or hepatitis through blood & blood products
Affliation(s): World Federation of Hemophilia
Chief Officer(s):
David Page, National Executive Director
dpage@hemophilia.ca
Hélène Bourgaize, National Director, Volunteer Development & Human Resources
hbourgaize@hemophilia.ca
Deborah Franz Currie, National Director, Resource Development
dcurrie@hemophilia.ca
Finances: *Annual Operating Budget:* $1.5 Million-$3 Million; *Funding Sources:* Telemarketing; direct mail
Staff Member(s): 6; 45 volunteer(s)
Membership: 2,000 individual; *Committees:* Administration; Finance; Fundraising; Program; Research
Activities: *Awareness Events:* Hemophilia Day, Apr. 17; *Internships:* Yes; *Speaker Service:* Yes
Publications:
• All About Carriers
Number of Pages: 133
Profile: Comprehensive guide, for carriers of hemophilia A or B
• All About von Willebrand Disease
Number of Pages: 86
Profile: A comprehensive guide, for persons with the disease
• Canadian Hemophilia Society Annual Report & Financial Statement
Frequency: Annually
• Factor Deficiencies
Profile: A series of publications, with topics such as Factor XI Deficiency, An Inherited Bleeding Disorder, for patients, families, & healthcare providers
• Hemophilia Today
Type: Magazine; *Frequency:* 3 pa; *Editor:* François Laroche
Profile: Current news & relevant issues to inform the hemophilia & bleeding disorders community

Alberta Chapter
PO Box 44171, Edmonton AB T5V 1N6
Tel: 780-421-9851
Toll-Free: 866-425-9851
albertachapter@hemophilia.ca
www.hemophilia.ca/en/provincial-chapters/alberta
Chief Officer(s):
Jennifer Ruklic, Co-President
Sherik Spady, Co-President

British Columbia Chapter
PO Box 21161, Stn. Maple Ridge Sq., Maple Ridge BC V2X 1P7
Tel: 778-230-9661; *Fax:* 604-476-2432
chsbc@shaw.ca
www.hemophiliabc.ca
Mission: To help improve the lives of people with hemophilia
Chief Officer(s):
Curtis Brandell, President
Julia Martin, Administrator/Coordinator

Hemophilia Manitoba
944 Portage Ave., Winnipeg MB R3G 0R1
Tel: 204-775-8625; *Fax:* 204-774-9403
Toll-Free: 866-775-8625
info@hemophiliamb.ca
www.hemophiliamb.ca
www.facebook.com/186587534783298
twitter.com/HemophiliaMB
www.youtube.com/user/hemophiliamb
Chief Officer(s):
Christine Keilback, Executive Director

Hemophilia Ontario
#501, 65 Wellesley St. East, Toronto ON M4Y 1G7
Tel: 416-972-0641; *Fax:* 888-958-0307
Toll-Free: 888-838-8846
tcor@hemophilia.on.ca
www.hemophilia.ca/en/provincial-chapters/ontario
Chief Officer(s):
Terri-Lee Higgins, Executive Director
thiggins@hemophilia.on.ca

Hemophilia Saskatchewan
2366 Ave. C North, Saskatoon SK S7L 5X5
Tel: 306-653-4366
Toll-Free: 866-953-4366
hemosask@hemophilia.ca
www.hemophilia.ca/en/provincial-chapters/saskatchewan
Chief Officer(s):
Wendy Quinn, President

New Brunswick Chapter
37 Churchill Ave, Sackville NB E4L 3T3
Tel: 506-536-9007
www.hemophilia.ca/en/provincial-chapters/new-brunswick
Chief Officer(s):
Rachelle Kingsler, President
rkingsler@gmail.com

Newfoundland & Labrador Chapter
25 Main Rd., Canvendish NL A0B 1J0
e-mail: chsnlcc@nf.sympatico.ca
hemophilia.ca/en/provincial-chapters/newfoundland-and-labrador
Chief Officer(s):
Jeff Jerrett, President

Nova Scotia Chapter
988 J. Jordan Rd., Canning NS B0P 1H0
Tel: 902-403-2208
nshemophiliasociety@hotmail.com
www.hemophilia.ca/en/provincial-chapters/nova-scotia
Chief Officer(s):
Dianna Cunning, President

Prince Edward Island Chapter
PO Box 2951, Charlottetown PE C1A 8C5
www.hemophilia.ca/en/provincial-chapters/prince-edward-island
Chief Officer(s):
Shelley Mountain, President
msvv4@eastlink.ca

Section Québec
#1102, 2120, rue Sherbrooke est, Montréal QC H2K 1C3
Tél: 514-848-0666; *Téléc:* 514-904-2253
Ligne sans frais: 877-870-0666
info@schq.org
www.hemophilia.ca
www.facebook.com/27424888399?ref=ts
Affliation(s): Partenaire Santé Québec/COCQSida
Chief Officer(s):
François Laroche, Président

Canadian Hereford Association (CHA) / Association canadienne Hereford
5160 Skyline Way NE, Calgary AB T2E 6V1
Tel: 403-275-2662; *Fax:* 403-295-1333
Toll-Free: 888-836-7242
herefords@hereford.ca
www.hereford.ca
twitter.com/CAN_Hereford
Overview: A medium-sized national organization founded in 1890
Mission: To promote the consistent & economical production of beef; To strive to meet & exceed consumer expectations for tender, juicy, & flavourful beef products, through performance

measurement, genetic selection, appropriate handling, feeding, & processing
Member of: Canadian Beef Breeds Council
Affliation(s): Canadian Cattlemens Association
Chief Officer(s):
Gordon Stephenson, General Manager
gm@hereford.ca
Finances: *Funding Sources:* Membership fees; breeding records
Staff Member(s): 10
Membership: *Fees:* $150 standard; $50 young guns; $15 junior; *Member Profile:* Purebred breeders; farmers & ranchers; *Committees:* Marketing; Show; Pedigree; Hereford Breed Improvement
Activities: Organizing the Annual Hereford Convention, the National Hereford Youth Conference, & the National Hereford Show
Publications:
• Canadian Hereford Association Member Directory
Type: Directory
• Canadian Hereford Digest
Type: Magazine; *Accepts Advertising*
Profile: Information about the beef breed for purebred & commercial cattle producers

Canadian Heritage Information Network (CHIN) / Réseau canadien d'information sur le patrimoine (RCIP)

15 Eddy St., 7th Fl., Gatineau QC K1A 0M5
Tel: 819-994-1200; *Fax:* 819-994-9555
Toll-Free: 800-520-2446; *TTY:* 888-997-3123
service@chin.gc.ca
www.rcip-chin.gc.ca
Overview: A medium-sized national organization founded in 1972
Mission: To engage national & international audiences in Canadian heritage, through leadership & innovation in digital content, partnerships, & lifelong learning opportunities
Member of: Canadian Museums Association; International Committee for Documentation (CIDOC); Museum Computer Network.
Chief Officer(s):
Claudette Lévesque, Acting Director General, 819-934-5016
Paul Lima, Senior Policy Advisor, 819-934-5019
Julie Marion, Director, Program Development, 819-934-5024
Staff Member(s): 43
Membership: 1,500+; *Member Profile:* Canadian museums & heritage institutions
Activities: *Awareness Events:* Canadian Multiculturalism Day, June 27; *Internships:* Yes; *Speaker Service:* Yes

The Canadian Heritage of Québec *Voir* L'Héritage canadien du Québec

Canadian Highland Cattle Society (CHCS) / Société canadienne des éleveurs de bovins Highland

121 Rang 5 East, Saint-Donat-de-Rimouski QC G0K 1L0
Tel: 418-739-4477; *Fax:* 418-739-4477
highland@chcs.ca
www.chcs.ca
Overview: A small national organization founded in 1964
Mission: To regulate & promote breeding of Highland cattle in Canada.
Chief Officer(s):
Marise Labrie, Secretary-Manager
Finances: *Funding Sources:* Membership fees
Membership: *Fees:* $60 resident; $12 youth; $72 non-resident; $1200 life

Canadian Historical Association (CHA) / Société historique du Canada (SHC)

#501, 130 Albert St., Ottawa ON K1P 5G4
Tel: 613-233-7885; *Fax:* 613-565-5445
www.cha-shc.ca
www.facebook.com/215430858536628
twitter.com/CndHistAssoc
Overview: A large national charitable organization founded in 1922
Mission: To encourage historical research; To stimulate public interest in history; To promote the preservation of Canadian heritage
Member of: Humanities & Social Science Federation of Canada
Chief Officer(s):
Lyle Dick, President
Michel Duquet, Executive Director
mduquet@cha-shc.ca
Martin Laberge, Secretary, French Language
Jo-Anne McCutcheon, Secretary, English Language
Finances: *Funding Sources:* Social Sciences & Humanities Research Council of Canada
24 volunteer(s)
Membership: 1,900; *Fees:* $65 general; $100 professional; $25 student; $105 institutional; $40 retired; $50 affiliated organization; $120 sustaining; *Member Profile:* Interest in history; *Committees:* Advocacy; Communications; Outreach; Prizes; Publications; Census; Equity & Diversity; Nominating; Membership
Activities: Publishing historical works & documents; Lobbying archives, museums, governments, & granting agencies in the interest of historians, particularly on issues relating to the preservation of heritage materials & public access to historical documents
Awards:
• The Clio Prizes (Award)
• Albert B. Corey Prize (Award)
Established 1966 & jointly sponsored by the CHA & the American Historical Association; awarded every two years to the best book dealing with the history of Canadian-American relations or the history of both countries *Amount:* $1,000
• The Wallace K. Ferguson Prize (Award)
Established 1979; awarded annually for outstanding work in a field of history other than Canadian *Amount:* $1,000
• Hilda Neatby Prize (Award)
Awarded to best articles in English & French on women's history
• John Bullen Prize (Award)
Awarded to the outstanding PhD thesis on a historical topic in a Canadian university by a Canadian citizen or landed immigrant *Amount:* $500
• François-Xavier Garneau Medal (Award)
The Senior CHA Prize; awarded every five years to a book which represents an outstanding Canadian contribution to history *Amount:* $2,000
• Sir John A. Macdonald Prize (Award)
Established 1976; awarded annually for the nonfiction work of Canadian history "judged to have made the most significant contribution to an understanding of the Canadian past" *Amount:* $1,000
Meetings/Conferences: • Canadian Historical Association 2015 Annual Meeting (held in conjunction with the Congress of the Humanities & Social Sciences), June, 2015, University of Ottawa, Ottawa, ON
Scope: National
Description: An event for historians to showcase their research & to discuss issues related to the discipline
Contact Information: Program Chair: Heather MacDougall, E-mail: hmacdoug@uwaterloo.ca; Liaison with Program Committee: James Opp, E-mail: james_opp@carleton.ca
Publications:
• Becoming a Historian
Profile: Handbook with guidance & advice for graduate history students & junior history professors
• Canada's Ethnic Groups History Booklets
Profile: Series presents concise histories of aspects of immigration & ethnicity in Canada
• CHA [Canadian Historical Association] President's Report
Frequency: Annually
• CHA [Canadian Historical Association] Short Books
Number of Pages: 80
Profile: Series on international themes & issues, for undergraduate students & the educated public
• CHA [Canadian Historical Association] Bulletin
Frequency: 3 pa; *Editor:* Alexandra Mosquin & Jean Martin
Profile: News & comments of interest to professional historians in Canada
• Historical Booklets
Profile: Series presents concise accounts of historical problems in Canadian history
• Journal of the Canadian Historical Association / Revue de la Société historique du Canada
Type: Journal; *Frequency:* Annually; *Editor:* Wendy Mitchinson & D. Marshall *ISSN:* 0847-4478
Profile: Best papers presented at CHA's annual meeting
• Register of Post-Graduate Dissertations in Progress in History & Related Subjects

Canadian Historical Association, Archives Section *See* Association of Canadian Archivists

Canadian History of Education Association (CHEA) / L'Association canadienne d'histoire de l'éducation (ACHE)

University of Saskatchewan, College of Education, 28 Campus Dr., Saskatoon SK S7N 0X1
www.ache-chea.ca
www.facebook.com/achechea
twitter.com/CHEA_ACHE
Overview: A small national organization
Chief Officer(s):
Kristina Llewellyn, President
Meetings/Conferences: • Canadian History of Education Association 19th Biennial Conference, 2016, Waterloo, ON
Scope: National

Canadian HIV Trials Network (CTN) / Réseau canadien pour les essais VIH

#588, 1081 Burrard St., Vancouver BC V6Z 1Y6
Tel: 604-806-8327; *Fax:* 604-806-8210
Toll-Free: 800-661-4664
ctninfo@hivnet.ubc.ca
www.hivnet.ubc.ca
www.facebook.com/214053698628427
twitter.com/CIHR_CTN
www.youtube.com/user/CIHRCTN
Overview: A medium-sized national organization founded in 1990
Mission: To develop treatments, vaccines & a cure for HIV disease & AIDS through the conduct of scientifically sound & ethical clinical trials
Chief Officer(s):
Martin T. Schechter, National Director
Aslam Anis, National Co-Director
Finances: *Annual Operating Budget:* $3 Million-$5 Million; *Funding Sources:* Health Canada
Staff Member(s): 30

Atlantic Region
Victoria General Hospital, #ACC5014, 1278 Tower Rd., Halifax NS B3H 2Y9
Tel: 902-473-7742; *Fax:* 902-473-2023
Chief Officer(s):
David Haase, Regional Director

Ontario Region
University of Ottawa at Ottawa General Hospital, #12G, 501 Smyth Rd., Ottawa ON K1H 8L6
Tel: 613-737-8923; *Fax:* 613-737-8925
bcameron@ottawahospital.on.ca
Chief Officer(s):
William Cameron, Regional Director

Pacific Region
St. Paul's Hospital, #667, 1081 Burrard St., Vancouver BC V6Z 1Y6
Tel: 604-806-8640; *Fax:* 604-806-8527
Chief Officer(s):
Marianne Harris, Regional Director

Prairie Region
Southern Alberta HIV Clinic, #213, 906 - 8th Ave. SW, Calgary AB T2P 1H9
Tel: 403-234-2399; *Fax:* 403-262-4893
bryan.peffers@CRHA-health.ab.ca
Chief Officer(s):
John Gill, Regional Director

Québec Region
Institut thoracique de Montréal, #J8.03, 3650, rue St-Urbain, Montréal QC H2X 2P4
Tel: 514-849-5201; *Fax:* 514-843-2092
richard.lalonde@muhc.mcgill.ca
Chief Officer(s):
Richard Lalonde, Regional Director

Toronto & Area Office
Sunnybrook Health Science Centre, #226A, 2075 Bayview Ave., Toronto ON M4N 3M5
Tel: 416-480-5900; *Fax:* 416-480-5808
a.rachlis@utoronto.ca
Chief Officer(s):
Anita Rachlis, Associate Regional Director

Canadian HIV/AIDS Legal Network / Réseau juridique canadien VIH/sida

#600, 1240 Bay St., Toronto ON M5R 2A7
Tel: 416-595-1666; *Fax:* 416-595-0094
info@aidslaw.ca
www.aidslaw.ca
twitter.com/aidslaw
Overview: A medium-sized national charitable organization founded in 1992 overseen by Canadian AIDS Society
Mission: To promote the human rights of people living with & vulnerable to HIV/AIDS, in Canada & internationally; through research, legal & policy analysis, education, advocacy & community mobilization

Chief Officer(s):
Janet Butler-McPhee, Director of Communications, 416-595-1666 Ext. 228
jbutler@aidslaw.ca
Finances: *Annual Operating Budget:* $1.5 Million-$3 Million; *Funding Sources:* Federal government; donations; corporations; various international organizations
Staff Member(s): 11; 6 volunteer(s)
Membership: 250; *Fees:* $40 individual; *Member Profile:* Community AIDS organizations; harm reduction organizations
Activities: Projects on legal & ethical issues raised by HIV/AIDS; *Internships:* Yes; *Library:* Resource Centre; by appointment
Awards:
• Awards for Action on HIV/AIDS & Human Rights (Award)
To recognize individuals or organizations that have made an outstanding contribution to addressing HIV/AIDS & human rights issues
Publications:
• HIV / AIDS Policy & Law Review
Type: Journal; *Editor:* David Garmaise *ISSN:* 1712-624X; *Price:* $75 Canada; $125 international
Profile: Analysis & summaries of current developments in HIV/AIDS-related policy and law from an international perspective
• Legal Network News
ISSN: 1488-0997

Canadian Hockey League

#201, 305 Milner Ave., Toronto ON M1B 3V4
Tel: 416-332-9711; *Fax:* 416-332-1477
www.chl.ca
twitter.com/CHLHockey
Overview: A large national organization
Mission: To act as the umbrella organization for the three major junior hockey leagues in Canada: Ontario Hockey League, Western Hockey League & Quebec Major Junior Hockey League
Activities: Mastercard Memorial Cup; Home Hardward Top Prospects Game; Subway Super Series; CHL Import Draft; *Rents Mailing List:* Yes
Awards:
• Player of the Year (Award)
• Top Prospect Award (Award)
• Sportsman of the Year (Award)
• Rookie of the Year (Award)
• Top Scorer of the Year (Award)
• Humanitarian of the Year (Award)
• Scholastic Player of the Year (Award)
• Brian Kilrea CHL Coach of the Year (Award)
• Goaltender of the Year (Award)
• Defenceman of the Year (Award)

Canadian Hoisting & Rigging Safety Council

PO Box 282, Stn. B, Ottawa ON K1P 6C4
Tel: 604-336-4699; *Fax:* 604-336-4510
input@chrsc.ca
chrsc.ca
Overview: A large national organization
Mission: To create standardized regulations throughout the nation with regards to cranes, histing & rigging
Chief Officer(s):
Fraser Cocks, Chair, Board of Directors

Canadian Holistic Nurses Association (CHNA) / Association canadienne des infirmières en soins holistiques

e-mail: info@chna.ca
www.chna.ca
Overview: A small national organization founded in 1986
Mission: To further the development of holistic nursing practice; To promote CHNA standards of practice
Affliation(s): Canadian Nurses Association
Chief Officer(s):
Susan Morris, President
sbmorrisis@shaw.ca
Jane Aitken-Herring, Secretary
djherring@pei.sympatico.ca
Darlene Grabo, Membership
wellnow@eastlink.ca
Membership: *Fees:* $60 full members; $50 associate members; $30 students
Activities: Adhering to CNA Nursing Practice Standards & the CNA Code of Ethics for Nurses; Promoting holistic nursing practice, education, & research; Influencing the health care system; Supporting members; Providing networking opportunities
Publications:
• Canadian Holistic Nurses Association Member Directory
Type: Directory
• Canadian Holistic Nurses Association Newsletter
Type: Newsletter; *Editor:* Wendy Snefjella

Canadian Home & School & Parent-Teacher Federation *See* Canadian Home & School Federation

Canadian Home & School Federation (CHSF) / Fédération canadienne des associations foyer-école (FCAFE)

#110, 99-1500 Bank St., Ottawa ON K1H 1B8
www.canadianhomeandschoolfederation.org
Previous Name: Canadian Home & School & Parent-Teacher Federation
Overview: A large national charitable organization founded in 1927
Mission: To improve the quality of Canadian public education available to children & youth; To act as the national voice of parents with children in public schools
Affliation(s): Canadian Education Association; Breakfast for Learning; Canadian Teachers Federation; Canadian Association of Principals; Centre for Science in Public Interest; Media Awareness; Council of Ministers of Education Canada
Chief Officer(s):
Cynthia Richards, President
shore_bird@hotmail.com
Deb Giesbrecht, First Vice-President
dgiesbr@mymts.net
Charla Dorrington, Second Vice-President
cambeedorrington@bellaliant.net
Michelle Ercolini, Secretary-Treasurer
fullhouse0@rogers.com
Membership: *Member Profile:* Parents with children in public schools who belong to provincial affiliates
Activities: Advocating for children & youth; Promoting the health & social well-being of children & youth
Publications:
• Effective Beginnings: A Guide to New Partnerships in Schools
Author: J. Mansfield; *Editor:* M. Durkin & H. Kingdon; *ISBN:* 0-921077-27-0

Canadian Home Builders' Association (CHBA) / Association canadienne des constructeurs d'habitations

#500, 150 Laurier Ave. West, Ottawa ON K1P 5J4
Tel: 613-230-3060; *Fax:* 613-232-8214
chba@chba.ca
www.chba.ca
Previous Name: Housing & Urban Development Association of Canada
Overview: A large national organization founded in 1943
Mission: To assist its members in serving the needs & meeting the aspirations of Canadians for housing; To be the voice of the residential construction industry in Canada; To achieve an environment in which members can operate profitably; To promote affordability & choice in housing for all Canadians; To support the professionalism of members
Chief Officer(s):
Nichael Gough, National Coordinator, Association Services, 613-230-3060 Ext. 227
Jack Mantyla, National Coordinator, Education & Training, 613-230-3060 Ext. 226
John Kenward, Chief Operating Officer
Don Johnston, Senior Director, Technology & Policy, 613-230-3060 Ext. 225
Lynda Barrett, Director, Conferences & Special Events, 905-954-0730
John Bos, Director, Finance, 613-230-3060 Ext. 238
David Crenna, Director, Urban Issues, 613-230-3060 Ext. 236
David Foster, Director, Environmental Affairs, 613-230-3060 Ext. 232
Membership: *Member Profile:* New home builders; Renovators; Trade contractors; Leading manufacturers; Suppliers; Warranty program providers; Government housing agents; Service people; Professionals; *Committees:* Technical Research; National Education & Training; National Marketing; Governance
Activities: Promoting the interests of housing consumers; Liaising with all levels of government; Working to influence decision-makers on issues such as taxation & regulatory reform; Developing courses & workshops; Distributing industry news; *Awareness Events:* Renovation Month, October; New Homes Month
Awards:
• Beaver Award (Award)
• Maple Leaf Award (Award)
• Gordon S. Shipp Award (Award)
• William M. McCance Award (Award)
• Canadian Renovators' Council Award (Award)
• Riley Brethour Award (Award)
• R-2000 Builder of the Year Award (Award)
• CHBA Award of Honour Certificates (Award)
• Ken McKinlay Award (Award)
• Susan Chambers Award of Recognition (Award)
• Colonel Boss Award (Award)
• Community Service Award (Award)
• Dave Bell Memorial Award (Award)
Meetings/Conferences: • Canadian Home Builders' Association 2015 72nd National Conference, March, 2015, Marriott Halifax Harbourfront, Halifax, NS
Scope: National
Description: Featuring the Canadian Home Builders' Association Annual Meeting of Members, provincial caucus meetings, guest speakers, the association's annual economic session, presentation of the National SAM Awards, social events, & networking opportunities
Contact Information: Director, Conferences & Special Events: Lynda Barrett, Phone: 905-954-0730
Publications:
• Canadian Home Builders' Association Builders' Manual
Type: Book; *Number of Pages:* 400; *Price:* $65
Profile: A guide to building energy-efficient housing
• Connecting with Customers [a publication of the Canadian Home Builders' Association]
Type: Book; *Price:* $15
Profile: Practical information & strategies for new home builders to sell homes, including market research & marketing plans
• How to Manage Risk: A Canadian Home Builders' Association Guide for New Home Builders & Renovators
Type: Book; *Price:* $15
Profile: Featuring topics such as main insurance coverages & financial assurance instruments
• The Marketing Advantage: A Guide For Professional Home Renovators
Type: Book; *Price:* $15
Profile: Advice for home renovators, including information on advertising & presentations
• The National [a publication of the Canadian Home Builders' Association]
Type: Newspaper; *Frequency:* Quarterly; *Editor:* Kerry Gibbens
Profile: Current events in the housing industry

Canadian Home Builders' Association - Alberta

#328, 9707 - 110 St., Edmonton AB T5K 2L9
Tel: 780-424-5890; *Fax:* 780-426-0128
Toll-Free: 800-661-3348
info@chbaalberta.ca
www.chbaalberta.ca
Overview: A medium-sized provincial organization founded in 1962 overseen by Canadian Home Builders' Association
Mission: To work on building codes & standards, government relations, safety, education, energy efficient housing, & networking opportunities in an attempt to improve housing in Alberta
Chief Officer(s):
Sandra Young, President
SYoung@homesbyavi.com
Jim Rivait, Chief Executive Officer
jim.rivait@chbaalberta.ca
Pat Adams, Treasurer
patrick@parkgroup.ca
Membership: 1,200
Activities: *Speaker Service:* Yes
Awards:
• Awards in Excellence in Housing (Award)
Yearly award for homebuilders
Meetings/Conferences: • Canadian Home Builders' Association - Alberta Conference: BUILD 2015, September, 2015, Jasper, AB
Scope: Provincial
Description: BUILD is the acronym for Being a United Industry in Leadership & Development
Contact Information: conference@chbaalberta.ca

Canadian Home Builders' Association - British Columbia (CHBA BC)

c/o Bldg. NW5, British Columbia Institute of Technology Campus, 3700 Willingdon Ave., Burnaby BC V5G 3H2
Tel: 604-432-7112; *Fax:* 604-432-9038
Toll-Free: 800-933-6777
info@chbabc.org

www.chbabc.org
www.facebook.com/300300953336086
twitter.com/chbabc
Overview: A medium-sized provincial organization founded in 1967 overseen by Canadian Home Builders' Association
Mission: To act as the voice of British Columbia's residential construction industry; to foster an environment for effectiveness & professionalism in the industry; to maintain affordability & profitability in British Columbia's housing industry
Chief Officer(s):
Robert Capar, President
rob@maisondetre.ca
Neil Moody, CEO
neilmoody@chbabc.org
Staff Member(s): 6
Membership: 1,500; *Member Profile:* New home builders & renovators; Land developers; Trade contractors; Product & material manufacturers; Building product suppliers; Lending institutions; Insurance providers; Service professionals
Activities: Liaising with the provincial government on province-wide initiatives; offering courses for Master Builder credential; providing government information & reference materials; offering technical support services;; *Library:* CHBA BC Technical & Video Library
Awards:
• Georgie Awards (Award)
To celebrate excellence in home building
Publications:
• BC Homes Magazine
Type: Magazine; *Frequency:* Bimonthly; *Accepts Advertising*; *Editor:* Scott Whitemarsh
Profile: Issue in British Columbia's housing industry

Canadian Home Builders' Association - Calgary Region

#100, 7326 - 10th St. NE, Calgary AB T2E 8W1
Tel: 403-235-1911; *Fax:* 403-248-1272
info@chbacalgary.com
www.chbacalgary.com
Overview: A small local organization founded in 1946
Staff Member(s): 8; 220 volunteer(s)
Membership: 625; *Fees:* Schedule available

Canadian Home Builders' Association - New Brunswick / Association canadienne des constructeurs d'habitations - Nouveau-Brunswick

#207, 403 Regent St., Fredericton NB E3B 3X6
Tel: 506-459-7219; *Fax:* 506-450-4924
nbhome@nbnet.nb.ca
www.nbhome.nb.ca
www.facebook.com/137729068402
Overview: A small provincial organization founded in 1986 overseen by Canadian Home Builders' Association
Mission: To represent residential construction industry for New Brunswick consumers, members & government; To improve the performance of the housing industry
Chief Officer(s):
Claudia Simmonds-Lipka, CEO
Rick Turner, President
rt@hughessurveys.com
Staff Member(s): 2
Membership: *Member Profile:* Industry related; *Committees:* Technical Research; Government Liaison; Canadian Renovator's Council; Marketing; Urban Council; National Training & Education Advisory; Building Safety Advisory; Economic Research
Activities: *Speaker Service:* Yes; *Rents Mailing List:* Yes; *Library* by appointment

Fredericton Home Builders' Association
#207, 403 Regent St., Fredericton NB E3A 3X6
Tel: 506-459-7219; *Fax:* 506-450-4924
www.nbhome.nb.ca/Regions/FrederictonEn/Default.aspx

Greater Moncton Home Builders' Association
#2, 297 Collishaw St., Moncton NB E1C 9R2
Tel: 506-852-3377; *Fax:* 506-852-3871
gmhba@monctonhomebuilders.com
www.monctonhomebuilders.com
Chief Officer(s):
Denise Charron, Executive Director

Greater Saint John Home Builders' Association
PO Box 2581, Saint John NB E2L 4S8
Tel: 506-672-7487; *Fax:* 506-738-8145
sjhba@nb.aibn.com
www.nbhome.nb.ca/Regions/SaintJohnEn/Default.aspx
Chief Officer(s):
Linda D. Smith, Executive Officer

Sussex & District Home Builders' Association
PO Box 4733, Sussex NB E4E 5L9
Tel: 506-432-1534; *Fax:* 506-433-5906
www.nbhome.nb.ca/Regions/SussesEn/Default.aspx
Chief Officer(s):
Juanita Carhart, President & Executive Officer
juanita.carhart@gmail.com

Canadian Home Builders' Association - Newfoundland Labrador (CHBA-EN)

435 Blackmarsh Rd., St. John's NL A1E 1T7
Tel: 709-753-2000; *Fax:* 709-753-7469
admin@chbanl.ca
www.nfbuilders.com
Overview: A medium-sized provincial organization founded in 1956 overseen by Canadian Home Builders' Association
Membership: 29 local associations + 4,000 member companies; *Member Profile:* Builders; Developers; Renovators; Trade contractors; Manufacturers; Suppliers; Landscape & lawn care organizations; Financial & mortgage companies; Associations, boards, & housing corporations; Business services; Media
Activities: Facilitating networking opportunities; Delivering the R-2000 Initiative & EnerGuide for New Houses Program in Newfoundland and Labrador; Providing updates on standards, codes, & regulations; Offering consumer information & seminars; Presenting sales & marketing awards; Liaising with municipal planning departments & the provincial government; *Awareness Events:* New Homes Month; Renovation Month; *Library:* Consumer Resource Centre
Publications:
• Canadian Home Builders' Association - Eastern Newfoundland Member Directory
Type: Directory
Profile: Distributed to association members & consumers who visit the Consumer Resource Centre

Canadian Home Builders' Association - Northern British Columbia

#300, 1705 - 3rd Ave., Prince George BC V2L 3G7
Tel: 250-563-3306; *Fax:* 250-563-3815
info@chbanorthernbc.ca
www.chbanorthernbc.ca
Overview: A small local organization founded in 1974
Mission: To represent the interests of professionals & businesses in the home building sector of northern British Columbia
Member of: Canadian Home Builders' Association - British Columbia
Chief Officer(s):
Mark Peil, Executive Officer
Membership: 75; *Member Profile:* Developers, sub-contractors, builders, renovators, suppliers, financial organizations, & government agencies involved in the home building & renovating business in Prince George, British Columbia & the surrounding region
Activities: Engaging in advocacy activities for the home building industry; Hosting monthly Builder's Liason meetings with local building officials; Providing training; Offering networking opportunities; Promoting a Code of Ethics; *Awareness Events:* CHBA Northern BC Home Show
Publications:
• Canadian Home Builders' Association - Northern British Columbia Membership Directory
Type: Directory; *Frequency:* Annually; *Accepts Advertising*
Profile: Four thousand directories, featuring contact information for companies involved in the home building sector, are distributed eachyear

Canadian Home Builders' Association - Prince Edward Island (CHBA-PEI)

PO Box 24079, 13 Stratford Rd., Stratford PE C1B 1T4
Tel: 902-659-2256; *Fax:* 902-659-2279
chba.pei@bellaliant.com
nbhome.nb.ca/Regions/PeiEn/Default.aspx
Overview: A small provincial organization founded in 2009 overseen by Canadian Home Builders' Association
Mission: To be the voice of the residential construction industry in PEI; To achieve an environment in which membership can operate profitably; To promote affordability & choice in housing in PEI
Affiliation(s): Canadian Home Builders' Association - New Brunswick
Chief Officer(s):
Scott Costain, President, 902-436-8270
office@scotcor.com
Membership: *Member Profile:* New home builders, renovators, developers, trades, manufacturers, suppliers & professionals; Companies & individuals that do business in Prince Edward Island & beyond; Members commit to a Code of Ethics & act with integrity & professionalism
Activities: Monthly dinner meetings; Seminars; Annual Golf Tournament

Canadian Home Builders' Association - Saskatchewan

11-3012 Louise St., Saskatoon SK S7J 3L8
Tel: 306-955-5188; *Fax:* 306-373-3735
Toll-Free: 888-955-5188
info@chbasaskatchewan.com
www.chbasaskatchewan.com
www.facebook.com/CHBASaskatchewan
twitter.com/CHBASask
Previous Name: Saskatchewan Home Builders' Association
Overview: A medium-sized provincial organization founded in 1974 overseen by Canadian Home Builders' Association
Mission: To act as the voice of the residential construction industry in Saskatchewan; To promote professionalism in the industry
Chief Officer(s):
Alan H.J. Thomarat, Chief Executive Officer
Sarah Trefiak, Director, Marketing & Events, 306-955-5188 Ext. 226
Michelle Beckett, Coordinator, Research, 306-955-5188 Ext. 235
Gina White, Coordinator, Accountimg, 306-955-5188 Ext. 224
Activities: Stressing certification

Canadian Home Care Association (CHCA) / Association canadienne de soins et services à domicile

7111 Syntex Dr., 3rd Fl., Mississauga ON L5N 8C3
Tel: 289-290-4389; *Fax:* 289-290-4301
chca@cdnhomecare.ca
www.cdnhomecare.ca
twitter.com/CdnHomeCare
www.youtube.com/user/cdnhomecare
Overview: A medium-sized national organization founded in 1990
Mission: To promote the development, integration, delivery, public awareness & evaluation of quality home care services in Canada; to provide national leadership to strengthen & unify the home care sector; to collect & disseminate information about home care; to encourage or commission research; to influence policy & legislation; to establish a code of ethics
Chief Officer(s):
John Schram, President
Nadine Henningsen, Executive Director
Membership: 600; *Fees:* $200-$6,000; *Member Profile:* Organizations & individuals involved in coordination & delivery, research & policy making, funding & management of home care services
Activities: Current areas of focus: national standards; research; communication & liaison with other national organizations; education opportunities for members
Meetings/Conferences: • 2015 Home Care Summit, 2015
Scope: National

Canadian Home Furnishings Alliance (CHFA)

Toronto International Centre, PO Box 85, #239C, 6900 Airport Rd., Mississauga ON L4V 1E8
Tel: 905-677-6561; *Fax:* 905-677-5212
info@chfaweb.ca
www.chfaweb.ca
Overview: A medium-sized national organization
Mission: To represent manufacturers, importers, & distributors of furniture, furnishings, fixtures, & accessories
Chief Officer(s):
Laine Reynolds, Chair
Murray Vaughan, President
Dino Colalillo, Treasurer
Finances: *Funding Sources:* Membership fees
Membership: 100-499

Canadian Honey Council / Conseil canadien du miel

36 High Vale Cres., Calgary AB T3A 5K8
Tel: 403-475-3882
Toll-Free: 877-356-8935
chc-ccm@honeycouncil.ca
www.honeycouncil.ca
Overview: A medium-sized national organization founded in 1940

Mission: To promote, develop & maintain cooperation among all persons, organizations & government personnel involved with Canadian beekeeping industry
Affliation(s): Apimondia
Chief Officer(s):
Rod Scarlett, Executive Director
chc-ccm@honeycouncil.ca
Finances: *Annual Operating Budget:* $50,000-$100,000
Staff Member(s): 1
Membership: 375; *Fees:* Schedule available
Activities: *Speaker Service:* Yes; *Rents Mailing List:* Yes
Awards:
• Fred Rathje Memorial Award (Award)

Canadian Horse Breeders' Association (CHBA) / Société des Éleveurs de Chevaux Canadiens

#108, 59, rue Monfette, Victoriaville QC G6P 1J8
Tel: 819-367-2195; *Fax:* 819-367-2195
www.lechevalcanadien.ca
www.facebook.com/SECC.CHBA
Overview: A medium-sized international organization founded in 1895
Mission: To preserve & improve the Canadian horse; To promote & maintain breed standards; To provide services to breeders of the Canadian horse
Affliation(s): Canadian Livestock Records Corporation
Chief Officer(s):
Marie Josee Proulx, President, 819-367-2195
Pierre Lalonde, Vice-President, 819-278-4414, Fax: 819-278-3054
pierre.lalonde@xplornet.ca
David Campbell, Secretary-Treasurer
Dale Myggland, Director, Western Canada & Maritimes, & USA Representative, 780-842-4975, Fax: 780-842-6248
dmygg@telusplanet.net
Raymond Robichaud, Director, Ontario, 613-931-2060
fermerayann@yahoo.ca
Sandra Rowe, Director, Québec, 418-272-1264
lacadienne32@hotmail.com
Laura Lee Mills, Registrar, 613-731-7110 Ext. 314, Fax: 613-731-0704
lauralee.mills@clrc.ca
Membership: 1,100; *Fees:* $450 lifetime members; $45 / year active & junior members & supporters; $30 physical supporters over age 18; $10 physical supporters under age 18; *Member Profile:* Owners or co-owners of registered Canadian horses, from Canada, the United States, & Europe, who are at least 18 years of age; Junior members under 18 years of age; *Committees:* By-laws; Promotion; Annual General Meeting; Judgement & Classification; Futurity
Activities: Monitoring the registration, identification, & the keeping of the stud book for Canadian horses; Grading
Publications:
• Le cheval canadien
Type: Newsletter; *Frequency:* 3 pa; *Price:* Free with membership in the Canadian Horse Breeders' Association

Atlantic District
c/o Christie Riddell, 2626 South Rawdon Rd., RR#1, Mount Uniacke NS B0N 1Z0
www.canadianhorseatlantic.ca
Mission: To preserve, protect, & promote the Canadian horse breed
Chief Officer(s):
April Watson, President
watsonnhc@gmail.com
Nicole Sullivan, Secretary-Treasurer
hymagnum@gmail.com
• Canadian Horse Breeders' Association Atlantic District Club Newsletter
Type: Newsletter; *Editor:* Cathy Arsenault

Rocky Mountain District
c/o Heather Poff, 27131 Twp. Rd. 524, Spruce Grove AB T7X 3M9
Tel: 780-499-8458
dpoff@telus.net
www.canadianhorsebreeders.com
Mission: To preserve & promote the Canadian horse
Chief Officer(s):
Dale Myggland, President
dmygg@telusplanet.net
Patti Juutiand, Vice-President
spjuuti@mac.com
• Canadian Horse Breeders' Association Rocky Mountain District Newsletter
Type: Newsletter; *Price:* $20

Upper Canada District (Ontario)
PO Box 179, Hillsburgh ON N0B 1Z0
Tel: 519-855-6498; *Fax:* 519-855-6959
info@ucdcanadianhorse.ca
www.ucdcanadianhorse.ca
Mission: To preserve & promote the Canadian horse, Canada's National Horse
Chief Officer(s):
Ron Marino, President
marinoathome@hotmail.com
Virginia Pantling, Vice-President, 519-835-1620
virginia@canadianhorses.com
Brenda Pantling, Secretary-Treasurer, 519-885-6498
brenda@canadianhorses.com
• Canadian Horse Breeders' Association, Upper Canada District Newsletter
Type: Newsletter; *Frequency:* Bimonthly
Profile: News from the board of directors, show results, member profiles, articles, & forthcoming events

Canadian Horse Heritage & Preservation Society (CHHAPS)

c/o Judi Hayward, Five Winds Farm, 1697 Lockyer Rd., Roberts Creek BC V0N 2W1
e-mail: judihayward@dccnet.com
www.chhaps.org
Overview: A small international organization
Mission: To preserve the traditional type of Canadian horse; To ensure responsible care & stewardship of heritage animals; To recognize the heritage of the Canadian horse to the history of Canada
Chief Officer(s):
Betty Baxter, Chair
fivewindsfarm@dccnet.com
Lynda Flato, Treasurer
skyline@telusplanet.net
Judi Hayward, Secretary, Membership
judihayward@dccnet.com
Ken Morris, Liaison, USA Members
10nycav@usa.net
Elaine Ulrich, Editor, Newsletter
elaine.ullrich@yahoo.com
Membership: *Fees:* $30 / year all categories of membership; *Member Profile:* Owners & admirers of the Canadian horse breed, from any location, who are interested in the preservation of the Canadian horse; Junior members under 19 years of age
Activities: Promoting the Canadian horse breed; Educating members & the public about the Canadian horse breed, through clinics & educational events with guest speakers; Sponsoring shows & events for the Canadian horse; Encouraging the exchange of information with other horse organizations
Meetings/Conferences: • Canadian Horse Heritage & Preservation Society 2015 Annual General Meeting, 2015
Scope: National
Publications:
• Canadian Horse Heritage & Preservation Society Newsletter
Type: Newsletter; *Frequency:* Quarterly; *Editor:* Elaine Ulrich; *Price:* Free with membership in the Canadian Horse Heritage & Preservation Society

Canadian Horticultural Council (CHC) / Conseil canadien de l'horticulture

9 Corvus Ct., Ottawa ON K2E 7Z4
Tel: 613-226-4880; *Fax:* 613-226-4497
webmaster@hortcouncil.ca
www.hortcouncil.ca
Overview: A large national organization founded in 1922
Mission: To improve horticultural & allied industries including production, grading, packing, transportation, storage & marketing
Member of: CanAgPlus
Affliation(s): Canadian Potato Council; International Federation for Produce Standards; Potatoes Canada
Chief Officer(s):
Murray Porteous, President
Anne Fowlie, Executive Vice-President
afowlie@hortcouncil.ca
Finances: *Annual Operating Budget:* $500,000-$1.5 Million
Staff Member(s): 10
Membership: 120+ organizations; *Fees:* Amount based on national farm cash receipts; *Member Profile:* Organizations promoting development of horticultural industry; horticultural commodity organizations; federal & provincial government agriculture departments; *Committees:* Apple & Fruit; Crop, Plant Protection & Environment; Finance & Marketing; Food Safety; Greenhouse Production; Human Resources; Potato; Research & Technology; Science Advisory; Trade & Industry Standards; Vegetable
Activities: *Library*
Meetings/Conferences: • Canadian Horticultural Council 91st Annual General Meeting 2015, March, 2015, Fairmont Château Frontenac, Québec City, QC
Scope: National
Description: Members come together to deal with the challenges and opportunities facing Canada's horticultural industry.
Publications:
• Fresh Thinking [a publication of the Canadian Horticultural Council]
Type: Magazine; *Frequency:* s-a.
• Hort Shorts [a publication of the Canadian Horticultural Council]
Type: Newsletter

Canadian Horticultural Therapy Association

100 Westmount Rd., Guelph ON N1H 5H8
Tel: 519-822-9842
admin@chta.ca
www.chta.ca
www.facebook.com/119374542077?v=info
Overview: A small national organization
Mission: To promote the use & awareness of horticulture as a therapeutic modality; horticultural therapy is a process which uses plants, horticultural activities, & the natural world to promote awareness & well-being by improving the body, mind, & spirit
Chief Officer(s):
Judy-May Roberts, Chair
chair@chta.ca
Membership: *Fees:* $35 student; $55 individual; $95 corporate; *Member Profile:* Professionals such as occupational therapists, physiotherapists, recreation therapists, social workers, nurses, psychologists, landscape architects & designers, horticulturists, & people who have a passion for gardening

Canadian Hospice Palliative Care Association (CHPCA) / Association canadienne de soins palliatifs (ACSP)

Annex D, Saint-Vincent Hospital, 60 Cambridge St. North, Ottawa ON K1R 7A5
Tel: 613-241-3663; *Fax:* 613-241-3986
Toll-Free: 800-668-2785
Other Communication: Info Line: 1-877-203-4636
info@chpca.net
www.chpca.net
www.facebook.com/CanadianHospicePalliativeCare
twitter.com/CanadianHPCAssn
Overview: A large national charitable organization founded in 1991
Mission: CHPCA provides leadership in the pursuit of excellence in the care of people approaching death in Canada, in order to lessen suffering, loneliness, & grief. The national association works to develop national standards of practice for hospice palliative care.
Member of: Quality End of Life Care Coalition; HEAL; Canadian Care Giver Coalition; Health Charities Council of Canada
Chief Officer(s):
Sarah Walker, President
Ed McLaren, Secretary-Treasurer
Sharon Baxter, Executive Director
Finances: *Funding Sources:* Federal government; membership dues; corporate sponsors; sale of resources; donations
Staff Member(s): 10
Membership: 1,000-4,999; *Fees:* Schedule available, based on province or territory of residence; *Member Profile:* Members include Canadian & international health care organizations, providers, & volunteers.; *Committees:* Executive; Finance; Organizational Development; Awards; Physician Assisted Dying
Activities: Raising awareness of hospice palliative care; Increasing knowledge & skills of health care providers & volunteers; Supporting research; Advocating for improved hospice palliative care policy, resource allocation, & supports for caregivers; *Awareness Events:* National Hospice Palliative Care Week, May; Hike for Hospice Palliative Care, May
Awards:
• CHPCA Champion Award (Award)
• CHPCA Leadership Award (Award)
Publications:
• AVISO
Type: Newsletter; *Frequency:* Quarterly
• Canadian Hospice Palliative Care Association National Office Update
Type: Newsletter; *Frequency:* Monthly

Profile: Events, research news, awards, policy news, & resources
• Directory of Hospice Palliative Care Services
Type: Directory
Profile: Information on the availability of hospice palliative care services across Canada, featuring listings of programs & services, contact information, population served, & areaof care

Canadian Hospital Engineering Society ***See*** Canadian Healthcare Engineering Society

Canadian Hotel Marketing & Sales Executives (CHMSE)

26 Avonhurst Rd., Toronto ON M9A 2G8
Tel: 416-252-9800; *Fax:* 416-252-7071
info@chmse.com
www.chmse.com
www.linkedin.com/groups?home=&gid=3020813
twitter.com/CHMSE
Overview: A medium-sized provincial organization founded in 1980
Mission: To be the leading association in providing professional development opportunities to sales & marketing executives within the Canadian hospitality industry
Chief Officer(s):
Shelley Macdonald, Executive Director
Christopher White, President
christopher.white@eatonhotels.com
Finances: *Annual Operating Budget:* $50,000-$100,000; *Funding Sources:* Membership dues; strategic partnerships; sponsorships
Staff Member(s): 1; 12 volunteer(s)
Membership: 100; *Fees:* $299; $99 long distance; $25 application fee; *Member Profile:* Hotel members - employed in sales capacity in the hotel industry; Affiliate members - representatives of organizations which provide goods & services to the hotel industry; *Committees:* Membership; Programs; Communications; Students; Fundraising; Educational Development; Affiliates
Activities: Training programs for hospitality & sales professionals;
Publications:
• Canadian Hotel Marketing & Sales Executives Directory
Type: Directory
Profile: Listing of members
• Key Access
Type: Newsletter; *Frequency:* 3 pa; *Accepts Advertising*

Canadian Household Battery Association; Rechargeable Battery Recycling Corporation Canada ***See*** Call2Recycle Canada, Inc.

Canadian Housing & Renewal Association (CHRA) / Association canadienne d'habitation et de rénovation urbaine (ACHRU)

#902, 75 Albert St., Ottawa ON K1P 5E7
Tel: 613-594-3007; *Fax:* 613-594-9596
info@chra-achru.ca
www.chra-achru.ca
www.facebook.com/CHRA.ACHRU.ca
twitter.com/CHRAstaff
www.youtube.com/user/CanadianHousing/
Overview: A medium-sized national organization founded in 1968
Mission: To provide access to adequate & affordable housing.
Chief Officer(s):
Jody Ciufo, Executive Director
jciufo@chra-achru.ca
Finances: *Annual Operating Budget:* $250,000-$500,000; *Funding Sources:* Federal & provincial governments; private
Staff Member(s): 6
Membership: 250; *Fees:* Schedule available; *Member Profile:* Directors, managers, employees & tenants of territorial, provincial, municipal & private non-profit housing corporations, housing authorities & rehabilitation program agencies, elected representatives, academics, housing consultants, municipal planners, tenants associations & others interested in the field.; *Committees:* Executive; Finance; Nominations & Awards; Resolutions; Personnel; Membership Development; International; Policy Advisory
Activities: Heightens public awareness of housing issues & inequalities through advocacy, research, communications & promotes excellence in the management of social housing through education & training.; *Rents Mailing List:* Yes

Canadian Human Rights Foundation ***See*** Equitas - International Centre for Human Rights Education

Canadian Hunger Foundation (CHF)

323 Chapel St., Ottawa ON K1N 7Z2
Tel: 613-237-0180; *Fax:* 613-237-5969
Toll-Free: 866-242-4243
www.chf-partners.ca
Overview: A medium-sized national organization founded in 1961
Mission: To assist local NGOs in developing countries, with particular emphasis on food production, water supply security, & energy
Chief Officer(s):
Tony Breuer, Executive Director
Cynthia Farrell, Director, Technical Services
Mary Forbes, Director, Finance
Sandra Kiviaho, Director, Public Engagement
Neil Leslie, Director, Fundraising
Sue MacPherson, Director, Human Resources
Michael Jones, Officer, Communications

Canadian Hydrogen & Fuel Cell Association (CHFCA)

#900, 1188 West Georgia St., Vancouver BC V6E 4A2
Tel: 604-283-1040; *Fax:* 604-283-1043
info@chfca.ca
www.chfca.ca
www.linkedin.com/groups?mostPopular=&gid=3145006?mostPopular=&gid=3145
www.facebook.com/poweringnow
twitter.com/poweringnow
www.youtube.com/chfca
Merged from: Canadian Hydrogen Association (CHA) & Hydrogen & Fuel Cells Canada (H2FCC)
Overview: A small national organization founded in 2009
Mission: To act as the collective voice of the hydrogen & fuel cell technologies & products sector; To support Canadian corporations, educational institutions, & governments which develop & deploy hydrogen & fuel cell products & services in Canada
Chief Officer(s):
Eric Denhoff, President & Chief Executive Officer, 604-760-7176
edenhoff@chfca.ca
Membership: 70 organizations; *Fees:* Schedule available, based upon number of employees; *Member Profile:* Hydrogen & fuel cell technology & component firms; Fuelling system organizations; Fuel storage services; Engineering firms; Financial services
Activities: Increasing awareness of the economic, environmental, & social benefits of hydrogen & fuel cells; Supporting the development of regulations, codes, & standards; Facilitating demonstration projects, such as Hydrogen Village & the Hydrogen Highway; Supporting the safe & widespread application & commercialization of hydrogen & fuel cell products; Engaging in advocacy activities; Liasing with government stakeholders; Providing information to governments, media & the pubblic; Offering networking opportunities for members
Meetings/Conferences: • 8th Annual Hydrogen + Fuel Cells 2015 International Conference, April, 2015, Four Seasons Hotel, Vancouver, BC
Scope: International
Description: HFC2015 will feature prominent industry and government leaders as keynote speakers as well as plenary and parallel sessions focusing on key issues and new initiatives within the sector.
Contact Information: Michael Davis, Director, Client and Sponsor Services; Website: www.hfc2015.com; hfc2015@chfca.ca; Phone: 604-688-9655 Ext. 2
Publications:
• Canadian Capabilities Guide: Canada's Hydrogen & Fuel Cell Industry
Type: Guide
Profile: Profiles & critical information about companies & organizations in Canada's hydrogen & fuel cell sector
• Canadian Fuel Cell Commercialization Roadmap Update: Progress of Canada's Hydrogen & Fuel Cell Industry
Type: Guide
Profile: ISSN: 978-1-100-10468-360537E
• Canadian Hydrogen & Fuel Cell Association Newsletter
Type: Newsletter; *Frequency:* Quarterly
Profile: Association member news & successes
• Canadian Hydrogen & Fuel Cell Sector Profile
Type: Guide
Profile: Statistics about Canada's hydrogen & fuel cell sector

Canadian Hydrographic Association (CHA) / Association canadienne d'hydrographie

#1205, 4900 Yonge St., Toronto ON M2N 6A6
Tel: 416-512-5815
www.hydrography.ca
Overview: A small national organization founded in 1966
Mission: To advance the development of hydrography & associated activities in Canada; to further the knowledge & professional development of members; to enhance & demonstrate the public need for hydrography; & to help the development of hydrographic sciences in developing countries; & to embrace the desciplines of marine cartography, hydrographic surveying, offshore exploration, marine geodesy, & tidal studies.
Member of: International Federation of Hydrographic Societies
Affliation(s): Canadian Institute of Geomatics; The Hydrographic Society
Chief Officer(s):
Rob Hare, National President
wabbit@shaw.ca
Kirsten Greenfield, National Secretary
kirsten.greenfield@pwgsc-tpsgc.gc.ca
Christine Delbridge, National Treasurer, 905-336-4745
Christine.Delbridge@dfo-mpo.gc.ca
Finances: *Funding Sources:* Membership dues; Conferences & seminars; Sponsorships
Membership: *Fees:* Schedule available; *Member Profile:* Hydrographers; Workers in associated disciplines; persons interested in hydrography & marine cartography; *Committees:* Lighthouse; Student Award; Hydrographic; Website
Activities: Operating a Student Award Program; *Library:* Gerry Wade Memorial Library; by appointment
Awards:
• Canadian Hydrographic Association Award (Award)
Awarded to a student at any Canadian university or technological college who must be continuing into second year of a program in one of the following fields of study: hydrography, cartography, geomatics, survey sciences; award based on 70% or better GPA & financial need *Amount:* $2,000 scholarship
Publications:
• Lighthouse: The Journal of the Canadian Hydrographic Association
Type: Journal; *Frequency:* Semiannually; *Number of Pages:* 60; *Price:* $20 Canada; $25international
Profile: Timely scientific, technical, & non-technical articles about hydrography in Canada, news from the industry, & CHA activities & events

Atlantic Branch
PO Box 1006, Dartmouth NS B2Y 4A2
Tel: 902-426-0574
Chief Officer(s):
Bruce Anderson, Vice-President
Bruce.Anderson@dfo-mpo.gc.ca

Central Branch
867 Lakeshore Rd., Burlington ON L7R 4A6
e-mail: email@mcquestmarine.com
Chief Officer(s):
Ken McMillan, Vice-President

Ottawa Branch
615 Booth St., Ottawa ON K1A 0E6
Tel: 613-995-5249
Chief Officer(s):
Kian Fadaie, Vice-President
Kian.Fadaie@dfo-mpo.gc.ca

Pacific Branch
9860 West Saanich Rd., Sidney BC V8L 4B2
Tel: 250-363-6669; *Fax:* 250-363-6323
Chief Officer(s):
Craig Lessels, Vice-President
Craig.Lessels@dfo-mpo.gc.ca

Québec Branch
53, rue St-Germain Ouest, Rimouski QC G5L 4B4
Tel: 418-775-0812; *Fax:* 418-775-0654
Chief Officer(s):
Bernard Labrecque, Vice-President
Bernard.labrecque@dfo-mpo.gc.ca

Canadian Hydropower Association (CHA) / Association canadienne de l'hydroélectricité

#1402 - 150 Metcalfe St., Ottawa ON K2P 1P1
Tel: 613-751-6655; *Fax:* 613-751-4465
info@canadahydro.ca
canadahydro.ca
twitter.com/CanadaHydro
Overview: A small national organization founded in 1998
Mission: To provide leadership for the responsible growth & prosperity of the Canadian hydropower industry
Chief Officer(s):

Jacob Irving, President
jacob@canadahydro.ca
Membership: 16 generators; 21 industry; 8 associate; *Member Profile:* Hydroelectic generation; hydroelectric industry; Associated associations and organizations
Meetings/Conferences: • 14th Annual Forum on Hydropower 2015, May, 2015, Ottawa, ON
Scope: National
Contact Information: Yvonne Jack, yvonne@canadahydro.ca; URL: www.hydroforum.ca

Canadian Hypnotherapy Association (CHA)

121 Wallis St., Parksville BC V9P 1K7
Tel: 250-248-9297
Overview: A small national charitable organization founded in 1977
Mission: To determine standards for hypnotherapy in Canada & to promote the therapeutic value of hypnotherapy
Chief Officer(s):
Joe Friede, President
Finances: *Funding Sources:* Fees
Membership: *Fees:* $35 (student), $80 (full member); *Member Profile:* Training or practising hypnotherapists

Canadian Ice Carvers' Society / Société des sculpteurs de glace

ON
Tel: 613-836-1798
www.canadianicecarverssociety.com
Previous Name: Ottawa-Hull Ice Carvers' Society
Overview: A small international licensing organization founded in 1987
Mission: To promote mutual friendship & harmony amongst members & to pursue higher social recognition, artistic expression & technical perfection of ice carving through activities such as demonstrations, education & workshops
Chief Officer(s):
Ikuo Kanbayashi, President
ikanbayashi@rogers.com
Finances: *Funding Sources:* Contracts
Membership: *Member Profile:* Knowledge or interest in ice carving
Activities: Winterlude; Crystal Garden - ice carving competition

Canadian Icelandic Horse Federation (CIHF)

c/o Maria Badyk, PO Box 1, Stn. Site 1, RR#2, High River AB T1V 1N2
Tel: 403-603-7949
www.cihf.ca
Overview: A small national organization founded in 1979
Mission: To promote & maintain the purity of the Icelandic horse; to keep record of breeding and registration of Icelandic horse under the Canadian National Livestock Record System; to promote the awareness and secure the integrity of purebred Icelandic horses.
Member of: European Friends of the Icelandic Horse
Chief Officer(s):
Maria Badyk, President
Victoria Stoncius, Vice-President
vicky.stoncius@hotmail.com
Finances: *Funding Sources:* Equipment sales
Membership: 150; *Committees:* Breeding; Sport; Pleasure; Edcation/Youth; Multi Media; Sponsorship; World Championship; Membership/Promotion
Activities: *Speaker Service:* Yes

Canadian Image Processing & Pattern Recognition Society (CIPPRS) / Association canadienne de traitement d'images et de reconnaissance des formes (ACTIRF)

Dept. of Computer Sciences, Univ. of Western Ontario, Middlesex College 383, London ON N6A 5B7
Tel: 519-661-2111; *Fax:* 519-661-3515
www.cipprs.org
Overview: A medium-sized national organization
Mission: To promote research & development activities in image & signal processing for solving pattern recognition problems.
Affliation(s): Canadian Information Processing Society
Chief Officer(s):
John Barron, Treasurer
barron@csd.uwo.ca
Greg Dudek, President
dudek@cim.dot.mcgill.edu
Finances: *Funding Sources:* Conferences; membership fees
Membership: *Fees:* $30 regular; $20 student

Awards:
• Distinguished Service Award (Award)
• Young Investigator Award (Award)

Canadian Imaging Trade Association (CITA) / Association canadienne de l'industrie de l'imagerie

PO Box 71058, 570 Mulock Dr., Newmarket ON L3X 1Y8
Tel: 416-226-2750; *Fax:* 416-226-3347
cita2@sympatico.ca
www.citacanada.ca
Previous Name: Canadian Photo Video Trade Association
Overview: A medium-sized national organization founded in 1955
Mission: To promote traditional & emerging imaging technologies (manufacturers/importers & distributors of photographic & electronic imaging equipment & sensitized materials)
Chief Officer(s):
Dori Gospodaric, General Manager
Finances: *Annual Operating Budget:* $50,000-$100,000; *Funding Sources:* Membership fees
Staff Member(s): 1
Membership: 40 corporate + 5 associate + 7 senior/lifetime; *Fees:* Schedule available; *Member Profile:* Actively involved in manufacturing/distribution of photo imaging equipment supplies; *Committees:* Legislation; Industry Statistics; Promotion; Convention
Activities: CITA is part of a special committee that works in conjunction with the Canadian Standards Association to rationalize & simplify specifications of photo & imaging equipment, so that new products may reach the Canadian market more quickly; *Library*
Awards:
• Dealer of the Year Award (Award)
Publications:
• Image Line
Type: Newsletter
Profile: CITA activities

Canadian Importers Association Inc. *See* Canadian Association of Importers & Exporters

Canadian Independent Adjusters' Association (CIAA) / Association canadienne des experts indépendants (ACEI)

Centennial Centre, #100, 5401 Eglinton Ave. West, Toronto ON M9C 5K6
Tel: 416-621-6222; *Fax:* 416-621-7776
Toll-Free: 877-255-5589
info@ciaa-adjusters.ca
www.ciaa-adjusters.ca
Overview: A medium-sized national organization founded in 1953
Mission: To provide leadership for independent adjusters in Canada; To develop & maintain high standards of professionalism; To represent the interests of independent adjusters at the regional, provincial, & national levels
Chief Officer(s):
Patricia M. Battle, Executive Director, 416-621-6222, Fax: 416-621-7776
pbattle@ciaa-adjusters.ca
Marie C. Gallagher, President, 905-984-8282, Fax: 905-984-8290
marie.gallagher@graniteclaims.com
David Porter, 1st Vice-President, 604-699-6550, Fax: 604-659-6570
david.porter@graniteclaims.com
Albert Poon, 2nd Vice-President, 905-896-8181, Fax: 905-896-3485
apoon@cl-na.com
Dara Banga, Secretary, 416-400-8933, Fax: 416-915-4685
dara.banga@dsbclaims.com
Russell Fitzgerald, Treasurer, 780-488-2371, Fax: 780-488-0243
rfitzgerald@kernaghan.com
Membership: *Member Profile:* Canadian independent adjusters
Activities: Engaging in advocacy activities; Providing continuing education; Liaising with government, industry, & the public; Offering networking opportunities
Meetings/Conferences: • CIAA's 31st Annual General Meeting & Conference, 2015
Scope: National
Publications:
• CIAA [Canadian Independent Adjusters' Association] National Claims Manual
Type: Directory; *Frequency:* Annually; *Accepts Advertising*; *Number of Pages:* 150; *Price:* $45
Profile: Comprehensive resource publication for insurance claims management professionals throughout Canada, featuring sections such as provinciallegal limitation periods, insurance institutes, councils, & superintendents, provincial educational & licensing requirements, & Canadian ICPB offices
• Claims Canada
Type: Journal; *Frequency:* Bimonthly; *Accepts Advertising*; *Editor:* Laura Kupcis
Profile: Incorporating the previously titled magazine, The Canadian Independent Adjuster, the national property & casualty insurance claims & loss magazine interests stakeholders in the insurance claimsmanagement & adjustment process

Canadian Independent Film Caucus *See* Documentary Organization of Canada

Canadian Independent Music Association (CIMA)

30 St. Patrick St., 2nd Fl., Toronto ON M5T 3A3
Tel: 416-485-3152
members@cimamusic.ca
www.cimamusic.ca
twitter.com/StuartCIMA
Previous Name: Canadian Independent Record Production Association (CIRPA)
Overview: A medium-sized national organization founded in 1975
Mission: To lobby governments for support & copyright reform; to raise the profile of Canadian music abroad by promoting the industry at international events, particularly MIDEM, held annually in Cannes, France.
Affliation(s): Canadian Music Industry Database
Chief Officer(s):
Stuart Johnston, President, 416-485-3152 Ext. 232
stuart@cimamusic.ca
Donna Murphy, Vice-President, Operations, 416-485-3152 Ext. 225
donna@cimamusic.ca
Chris Martin, Coordinator, Research & Communications
chris@cimamusic.ca
Finances: *Funding Sources:* Membership dues; projects; government subsidies
Staff Member(s): 7
Membership: 375 organizations; *Fees:* Schedule available; *Member Profile:* Record labels; accountants; managers; record distributors; lawyers; producers; recording studios; publicists; promoters; *Committees:* Executive; Finance & Audit; Government Affairs; Ontario Advisory; Music Export Liaison; Talent Selection
Activities: Digital Media Distribution System; *Internships:* Yes

Canadian Independent Record Production Association (CIRPA) *See* Canadian Independent Music Association

Canadian Independent Recording Artists' Association (CIRAA)

118 Berkeley St., Toronto ON M5A 2W9
Toll-Free: 866-482-4722
memberservices@ciraa.ca
www.ciraa.ca
www.facebook.com/TheCIRAA
twitter.com/theciraa
Overview: A medium-sized national organization
Mission: To stimulate increased government funding for unsigned artists in Canada; to promote greater airplay for emerging artists
Chief Officer(s):
Gregg Terrence, President
Kathryn Rose, Secretary
James Porter, Treasurer
Membership: 8,000

Canadian Independent Telephone Association (CITA) / Association canadienne du téléphone indépendant

c/o Creative Events Management, #205, 1402 Queen St. West, Alton ON L7K 0C3
Tel: 519-940-0935; *Fax:* 519-940-1137
www.cita.ca
Overview: A medium-sized national organization founded in 1905
Mission: To promote the increase & improvement of telephone service in Canada; to promote & protect the common business interest of members; to produce & distribute literature; to represent the industry before regulatory bodies, either federal or provincial.
Chief Officer(s):

Margi Taylor, General Manager, 519-940-0935
mhtaylor@allstream.net
Finances: *Funding Sources:* Membership fees; showcase
Membership: 29 + 100 associate; *Fees:* Schedule available; *Member Profile:* Independant phone companies; Telephone equipment & service providers

Canadian Industrial Relations Association *Voir* Association canadienne des relations industrielles

Canadian Industrial Transportation Association *See* Freight Management Association of Canada

Canadian Infectious Disease Society *See* Association of Medical Microbiology & Infectious Disease Canada

Canadian Information Centre for International Credentials (CICIC) / Centre d'information canadien sur les diplômes internationaux

#1106, 95 St. Clair Ave. West, Toronto ON M4V 1N6
Tel: 416-962-9725; *Fax:* 416-962-2800
www.cicic.ca
www.linkedin.com/company/cicic---cicdi
www.facebook.com/CICIC.CICDI
twitter.com/CICIC_CICDI
Also Known As: CICDI
Overview: A medium-sized national organization founded in 1990 overseen by Council Of Ministers Of Education, Canada
Mission: To collect, organize, & distribute information; To act as a national clearinghouse & referral service; To support the recognition & portability of Canadian & international educational & occupational qualifications
Member of: Enic-Naric Networks; Imagine Education in Canada

Canadian Information Processing Society (CIPS) / L'Association canadienne de l'informatique (ACI)

National Office, #801, 5090 Explorer Dr., Mississauga ON L4W 4T9
Tel: 905-602-1370; *Fax:* 905-602-7884
Toll-Free: 877-275-2477
info@cips.ca
www.cips.ca
www.linkedin.com/groups?about=&gid=71785&trk=anet_ug_grppro
www.facebook.com/187610094599781
twitter.com/cips
Overview: A large national charitable organization founded in 1958
Mission: To define & foster the IT profession; To encourage & support the IT practitioner; To advance the theory & practice of IT, while safeguarding the public interest
Member of: International Federation for Information Processing; Institute for Certification of Computer Professionals; South Asian Regional Computer Confederation
Affliation(s): British Computer Society; Australian Computer Society; Association for Computing Machinery
Chief Officer(s):
Jon Nightingale, Chair, Governance Committee
Membership: 6,000; *Fees:* Schedule available; *Member Profile:* Open to business people, scientists, educators & others who make their careers in information technology (IT)
Activities: Awarding the Information Systems Professional of Canada (I.S.P.) designation
Awards:
- Gala Award (Award)
- Volunteeer of the Year (Award)
- CIPS Honorary Membership (Award)

The highest award available to CIPS members, awarded to those who have made an outstanding contribution to CIPS & to information processing in Canada
- C.C. Gotlieb CIPS Contribution (Award)

For members who are widely recognized for outstanding contribution to CIPS through years of substantial efforts for the society
- Gary Hadford Professional Achievement Award (Award)

For members who are recognized by their peers for their integrity & expertise, for their outstanding achievements in fields related to information processing, & who have a high degree of competence in their field

Alberta Chapter
PO Box 4091, Stn. C, #400, 1040 - 7th Ave. SW, Calgary AB T2T 5M9
Fax: 403-244-2340
Toll-Free: 877-247-7221
alberta@cips.ca
ab.cips.ca
Chief Officer(s):
Doug Brown, President
browndS@nucleus.com
Anthony B. Scott, Executive Director

British Columbia Chapter
#102, 211 Columbia St., Vancouver BC V6A 2R5
Tel: 604-681-2796; *Fax:* 604-681-4545
bc@cips.ca
bc.cips.ca
Chief Officer(s):
Jon Nightingale, President

Manitoba Chapter
PO Box 2610, Winnipeg MB R3C 4B3
e-mail: manitoba@cips.ca
mb.cips.ca
Chief Officer(s):
Linda Hunter, President

Newfoundland & Labrador Chapter
PO Box 21053, St. John's NL A1A 5B2
e-mail: nl@cips.ca
nl.cips.ca
Chief Officer(s):
Cheryl Lundrigan, President

Nova Scotia Chapter
PO Box 1612, Stn. Halifax Central, Halifax NS B3J 2Y3
e-mail: cipsns@cips.ca
ns.cips.ca
Chief Officer(s):
Chris Kendrick, Acting President & Treasurer
ckendrick@cips.ca

Ontario Chapter
cipsontario.ca

Réseau Action TI
Tour ouest, #355, 550, rue Sherbrooke ouest, Montréal QC H3A 1B9
Tél: 514-840-1240
info@actionti.com
www.actionti.com
www.linkedin.com/groups/Réseau-ACTION-TI-90428
www.facebook.com/ActionTI
twitter.com/ActionTI
www.youtube.com/reseauactionti
Chief Officer(s):
Lyne Bouchard, Présidente

Saskatchewan Chapter
PO Box 20073, Stn. Cornwall Center, Regina SK S4P 4J7
Tel: 306-352-1392
saskatchewan@cips.ca
sk.cips.ca
Chief Officer(s):
Derek Risling, President

Canadian Injured Workers Alliance (CIWA) / L'Alliance canadienne des victimes d'accidents et de maladies du travail (ACVAMT)

PO Box 10098, 1201 Jasper Dr., Thunder Bay ON P7B 6T6
Tel: 807-345-3429; *Fax:* 807-344-8683
Toll-Free: 877-787-7010
www.ciwa.ca
Overview: A medium-sized national organization founded in 1990
Mission: To support & strengthen the work of local & provincial groups by providing a forum for exchanging information & experiences; To provide training & educational resources in partnership with these groups to ensure that injured workers maintain control over their destinies & that the groups themselves be democratically controlled by the workers
Chief Officer(s):
Bill Cheodore, National Coordinator
Finances: *Annual Operating Budget:* $100,000-$250,000
Staff Member(s): 3; 20 volunteer(s)
Membership: 8; *Member Profile:* Provincial injured workers organizations
Activities: Offering conferences & workshops; Providing leadership training; Conducting a survey on the re-employment of injured workers; Engaging in research; *Speaker Service:* Yes; *Library:* Resource Centre
Publications:
- Highlights [a publication of the Canadian Injured Workers Alliance]

Type: Newsletter; *Frequency:* Quarterly; *Price:* $5 injured worker & unemployed;$10 individual; $15 organization
Profile: Information about provincial & national developments, government policies, & CIWA projects for injured workers' groups

Canadian Innovation Centre (CIC)

c/o Waterloo Research & Technology Park, #15, 295 Hagey Blvd., Waterloo ON N2L 6R5
Tel: 519-885-5870; *Fax:* 519-513-2421
Toll-Free: 800-265-4559
info@innovationcentre.ca
www.innovationcentre.ca
www.linkedin.com/company/canadian-innovation-centre
twitter.com/innovationctre
Overview: A medium-sized national organization founded in 1981
Mission: To advance innovation by helping our clients make better business decisions through information, education & commercialization.
Chief Officer(s):
Ted Cross, Chair
Josie Graham, CEO & Director, Projects and Studies
Staff Member(s): 10
Activities: *Library* by appointment
Awards:
- Market Research Services (Grant)

Assists individuals & established companies in commercializing their technologies & business ventures; will conduct preliminary & detailed market research, evaluate commercial potential, manage development & testing, assist in venture planning, provide training & education programs, & promote international technologies available for license*Eligibility:* Individual entrepreneurs, inventors/innovators & small businesses
- The Inventor's Assistance Program (Grant)

Provides an objective evaluation of a new idea which considers technical feasibility, available legal protection & market competition*Eligibility:* Individual entrepreneurs, inventors/innovators or small businesses

Canadian Insolvency Practitioners Association *See* Canadian Association of Insolvency & Restructuring Professionals

The Canadian Institute (CI) / L'Institut canadien

1329 Bay St., Toronto ON M5R 2C4
Tel: 416-927-7936; *Fax:* 416-927-1563
Toll-Free: 877-927-7936
customerservice@canadianinstitute.com
www.canadianinstitute.com
Overview: A small national organization
Mission: To monitor trends in public policy, the law, & major industry sectors; To provide business intelligence for Canadian decision-makers
Affliation(s): American Conference Institute (New York); C5 (London, UK)
Finances: *Funding Sources:* Sponsorships; Conference fees
Activities: Organizing conferences, executive briefings, & summits for senior delegates; Publishing materials for conferences

Canadian Institute for Advanced Research (CIFAR) / Institut canadien de recherches avancées (ICRA)

#1400, 180 Dundas St. West, Toronto ON M5G 1Z8
Tel: 416-971-4251; *Fax:* 416-971-6169
Toll-Free: 888-738-1113
info@cifar.ca
www.ciar.ca
www.linkedin.com/company/canadian-institute-for-advanced-research
www.facebook.com/CIFAR
twitter.com/cifar_news
Overview: A medium-sized national organization founded in 1982
Mission: To stimulate leading-edge research projects vital to Canada's future prosperity.
Chief Officer(s):
Alan Bernstein, President/CEO, 416-971-4255
abernstein@cifar.ca
Staff Member(s): 14
Membership: 400
Activities: Programs in cosmology, superconductivity, evolutionary biology, population health, human development, earth system evolution, the science of soft surfaces & interfaces, economic growth, nanoelectronics

Canadian Institute for Child & Adolescent Psychoanalytic Psychotherapy (CICAPP)

17 Saddletree Trail, Brampton ON L6X 4M5
Tel: 416-690-5464; *Fax:* 416-690-2746
info@cicapp.ca
www.cicapp.ca
Previous Name: Toronto Child Psychoanalytic Program

Overview: A small national organization founded in 1981
Mission: To provide training in psychodynamic child therapy; to foster the growth of the profession in Canada; to have input in shaping government policies; to promote ongoing research in child psychotherapy
Chief Officer(s):
Suzanne Pearen, Administrator
suzanne_pearen@rogers.com
Membership: 55; *Fees:* $215

Canadian Institute for Conflict Resolution (CICR) / Institut canadien pour la résolution des conflits

c/o St. Paul University, 223 Main St., Ottawa ON K1S 1C4
Tel: 613-235-5800; *Fax:* 613-235-5801
Toll-Free: 866-684-2427
info@cicr-icrc.ca
www.cicr-icrc.ca
Overview: A medium-sized national charitable organization founded in 1988
Mission: To foster, develop & communicate resolution processes for individuals, organizations & communities in Canada & internationally; to embody, within the conflict resolution process, the positive attributes of common sense, sensitivity, compassion & spirituality
Chief Officer(s):
Brian Strom, Executive Director
Activities: Works with a number of community organizations in areas such as community mediation training & conflict resolution processes, addressing such issues as multiculturalism, race relations & community relations; provides hands-on workshops

Canadian Institute for Energy Training (CIET) / Institut canadien de formation de l'énergie

#200, 160, rue Saint-Paul, Québec QC G1K 3W1
Tel: 418-692-2592; *Fax:* 418-692-4899
Toll-Free: 800-461-7618
info@cietcanada.com
www.cietcanada.com
Overview: A medium-sized national organization founded in 1994
Mission: To focus on the advancement of energy efficiency in industrial, commercial, & public sector organizations; To provide effective training solutions for the incorporation of energy management into organizational management priorities
Chief Officer(s):
Douglas Tripp, President
Finances: *Funding Sources:* Fees for service
Activities: Offers the following training courses: Certified Energy Manager (CEM); Certification à l'utilisation du logiciel de simulation RETScreenr; Certified Energy Auditor (CEA); Techniques d'amélioration de l'efficacité énergétique; Certified Measurement and Verification Professional (CMVP); Certified in the Use of RETScreenr (CRU); Mesurage et ciblage énergétique; & Certification CEM

Canadian Institute for Health Information (CIHI) / Institut canadien d'information sur la santé (ICIS)

#600, 495 Richmond Rd., Ottawa ON K2A 4H6
Tel: 613-241-7860; *Fax:* 613-241-8120
Other Communication: help@cihi.ca
communications@cihi.ca
www.cihi.ca
www.facebook.com/141785889231388
twitter.com/CIHI_ICIS
www.youtube.com/user/CIHICanada
Overview: A small national organization founded in 1994
Mission: To collect, analyze, & provide information about the health system in Canada & the health of Canadians; To support persons who use data for health & health-services research
Chief Officer(s):
David O'Toole, President & Chief Executive Officer, 613-694-6500
dotoole@cihi.ca
Brent Diverty, Vice-President, Programs, 613-694-6501
BDiverty@cihi.ca
Anne McFarlane, Vice-President, Western Canada & Developmental Initiatives, 250-220-2211
AMcFarlane@cihi.ca
Louise Ogilvie, Vice-President, Corporate Services, 613-694-6503
LOgilvie@cihi.caca
Jeremy Veillard, Vice-President, Research & Analysis, 416-549-5361
JVeillard@cihi.ca
Finances: *Funding Sources:* Federal, provincial, & territorial governments
Activities: Maintaining health databases, measurements, & standards; Developing reports; Raising awareness about services; *Speaker Service:* Yes
Publications:
• Canadian Institute for Health Information Annual Report
Type: Yearbook; *Frequency:* Annually
• CIHI [Canadian Institute for Health Information] Directions ICIS [Institut canadien d'information sur la santé]
Type: Newsletter *ISSN:* 1201-0383

CIHI Montréal
#300, 1010 Sherbrooke St. West, Montréal QC H3A 2R7
Tel: 514-842-2226; *Fax:* 514-842-3996
Chief Officer(s):
Caroline Heick, Executive Director, Ontario and Quebec, 416-549-5517
CHeick@cihi.ca

CIHI St. John's
#701, 140 Water St., St. John's NL A1C 6H6
Tel: 709-576-7006; *Fax:* 709-576-0952
Chief Officer(s):
Stephen O'Reilly, Executive Director, Atlantic Canada, 709-733-7064
SOReilly@cihi.ca

CIHI Toronto
#300, 4110 Yonge St., Toronto ON M2P 2B7
Tel: 416-481-2002; *Fax:* 416-481-2950
Chief Officer(s):
Caroline Heick, Executive Director, Ontario and Quebec, 416-549-5517
CHeick@cihi.ca

CIHI Victoria
#600, 880 Douglas St., Victoria BC V8W 2B7
Tel: 250-220-4100; *Fax:* 250-220-7090

Canadian Institute for Historical Microreproductions *See* Canadiana

Canadian Institute for Jewish Research (CIJR) / Institut canadien de recherche sur le Judaïsme

PO Box 175, Stn. H, Montréal QC H3G 2K7
Tel: 514-486-5544; *Fax:* 514-486-8284
cijr@isranet.org
www.isranet.org
www.facebook.com/162536567136089
twitter.com/cijr
Overview: A small national charitable organization founded in 1988
Mission: To increase public understanding of Jewish Israel & general Jewish world issues
Chief Officer(s):
Jack Kincler, National Chair
Nathan Elberg, International Chair
Baruch Cohen, Research Chair
Frederick Krantz, Director
Activities: Bringing up-to-date informtion about Jewish world-related issues to Jewish & non-Jewish communities, the media, & students; Maintaining the Middle East & Jewish World Databank, an archive of Jewish, Israel, & Middle East materials; Presenting regular Insider Briefing seminars & Community Colloquia
Publications:
• Canadian Institute for Jewish Research Daily Isranet Briefing
Type: Newsletter; *Frequency:* Daily; *Price:* Free with membership in the Canadian Institute for Jewish Research
Profile: Current issues affecting Jewish people, read by more than 60,00 people around the world
• Communiqué Isranet
Type: Newsletter; *Frequency:* Weekly; *Price:* Free with membership in the Canadian Institute for Jewish Research
Profile: Articles, documents, & opinion pieces about current issues impacting Jewish people
• Dateline: Middle East
Type: Magazine; *Price:* Free with membership in the Canadian Institute for Jewish Research
Profile: A magazine for students
• Israfax
Type: Magazine; *Frequency:* Quarterly; *Editor:* Frederick Krantz; *Price:* Free with membership in the Canadian Institute forJewish Research
Profile: Articles from international newspapers, journals, magazines, documents, & websites collected & distributed throughout Canada & around the globe

Canadian Institute for Mediterranean Studies (CIMS) / Institut canadien d'études méditerranéennes

c/o Carr Hall, Department of Italian Studies, University of Toronto, 100 St. Joseph St., Toronto ON M5S 1J4
www.utoronto.ca/cims
Merged from: Society for Mediterranean Studies; Canadian Mediterranean Institute
Overview: A medium-sized national charitable organization founded in 1996
Mission: To study all aspects of Mediterranean culture & civilization, past & present
Chief Officer(s):
Mario Crespi, Executive Director
mario.g.crespi@sympatico.ca
Finances: *Funding Sources:* Membership fees; Donations
Membership: *Fees:* Schedule available; *Member Profile:* Scholars interested in Mediterranean studies; Persons with an interest in the Mediterranean world
Activities: Facilitating research; Organizing public lectures; Sponsoring international interdisciplinary conferences
Publications:
• Canadian Institute for Mediterranean Studies Bulletin
Type: Newsletter; *Frequency:* Semiannually; *Price:* Free with Canadian Institute for Mediterranean Studies membership
Profile: Canadian Institute for Mediterranean Studies activities
• Scripta Mediterranea
Type: Journal; *Frequency:* Annually; *Editor:* Dr. Anthony Percival; *Price:* Free with Canadian Institute for Mediterranean Studiesmembership
Profile: Refereed scholarly journal, with articles & reviews on all aspects of Mediterranean culture & civilization, past & present

Ottawa
Desmarais Building, University of Ottawa, #1160, 55 Laurier Ave. East, Ottawa ON K1N 6N5
Tel: 819-684-8768
cimsottawa@gmail.com
Chief Officer(s):
Louise Terrillon-Mackay, President

Canadian Institute for NDE

135 Fennell Ave. West, Hamilton ON L8N 3T2
Tel: 905-387-1655; *Fax:* 905-574-6080
Toll-Free: 800-964-9488
info@cinde.ca
www.cinde.ca
www.facebook.com/297023083473
Also Known As: CINDE
Merged from: Canadian Society for Nondestructive Testing; NDE Institute of Canada
Overview: A medium-sized national organization founded in 1964
Mission: To advance scientific, engineering, technical knowledge in the field of nondestructive testing; to gather & disseminate information relating to nondestructive testing useful to individuals & beneficial to the general public; to promote nondestructive testing through courses of instruction, lectures, meetings, publications, conferences, etc.
Member of: NDE Institute of Canada
Chief Officer(s):
Larry Cote, President & CEO
l.cote@cinde.ca
Finances: *Annual Operating Budget:* $100,000-$250,000
Staff Member(s): 1
Membership: 50 corporate + 20 associate + 20 student + 20 senior/lifetime + 1,000 individual + 50 subscriptions; *Fees:* $60 individual; $160 sustaining; $475 corporate
Meetings/Conferences: • Canadian Institute for NDE NDT in Canada 2015 Conference, 2015
Scope: International
Contact Information: Phone: 905-387-1655 Ext. 238; events@cinde.ca
Publications:
• CINDE [Canadian Institute for NDE] Journal
Type: Journal; *Frequency:* Bimonthly; *Accepts Advertising*; *Price:* Free with Canadian Institute for NDE membership; $80 Canada; $110 USA; $135 overseas
Profile: Canadian Institute for NDE chapter reports, conferences, members, & board of directors, industry & international news, business directory, & new products supplies & services

Canadian Institute for Neutron Scattering (CINS)

Bldg. 459, Station 18, Canadian Neutron Beam Centre, Chalk River Labs, Chalk River ON K0J 1J0
Tel: 613-584-8297; *Fax:* 613-584-4040
www.cins.ca
Overview: A small international organization

Mission: To advance neutron scattering research; To promote the neutron scattering in science & technology
Chief Officer(s):
Dominic Ryan, President
dhryan@physics.mcgill.ca
Niki Schrie, Secretary-Treasurer
Niki.Schrie@nrc-cnrc.gc.ca
Membership: 400; *Member Profile:* Persons interested in neutron scattering research from government, academia, & industry; Graduate students
Activities: Providing educational activities

Canadian Institute for Photonics Innovations (CIPI)
Université Laval, Pavillion d'optique-photonique, #2111, 2375 rue de la Terrasse, Québec QC G1V 0A6
Tel: 418-656-3013; *Fax:* 418-656-2995
cipi@cipi.ulaval.ca
www.cipi.ulaval.ca
Overview: A medium-sized national organization
Mission: Photonics - science of generating, manipulating, transmitting & detecting light
Member of: Networks of Centres of Excellence
Chief Officer(s):
Robert Corriveau, President
robert.corriveau@cipi.ulaval.ca

Canadian Institute for Radiation Safety *See* Radiation Safety Institute of Canada

Canadian Institute for Research in Nondestructive Examination (CINDE)
135 Fennell Ave. West, Hamilton ON L8N 3T2
Tel: 905-387-1655; *Fax:* 905-574-6080
Toll-Free: 800-964-9488
www.cinde.ca
www.linkedin.com/groups/Canadian-Institute-NDE-4510204?trk=myg_ugrp_ov
www.facebook.com/pages/Canadian-Institute-for-NDE-CINDE/297023083473
Also Known As: Canadian Institute for NDE
Overview: A small national organization
Mission: To foster, coordinate & disseminate results of research, development & application of new or advanced NDE techniques in Canada; to promote technology transfer by encouraging collaboration between universities, research organizations & industrial or governmental users; to raise the profile of NDE research in Canada by publicizing the need for & economic benefits arising from advances in NDE
Chief Officer(s):
Larry Cote, President and CEO, 905-387-1655 Ext. 225
l.cote@cinde.ca
Membership: 100; *Member Profile:* Open to applied scientists & engineers who have a professional interest in conductor application of research in NDE
Activities: *Rents Mailing List:* Yes

Canadian Institute for the Administration of Justice (CIAJ) / Institut canadien d'administration de la justice (ICAJ)
Faculté de droit, Univ. de Montréal, PO Box 6128, Stn. Centre-Ville, #A3421, 3101, chemin de la Tour, Montréal QC H3C 3J7
Tel: 514-343-6157; *Fax:* 514-343-6296
ciaj@ciaj-icaj.ca
www.ciaj-icaj.ca
www.linkedin.com/groups?about=&gid=4113891
www.facebook.com/ciaj.icaj
twitter.com/ciaj_icaj
Overview: A medium-sized national charitable organization founded in 1974
Mission: To improve the quality of justice for all Canadians
Chief Officer(s):
Michèle Moreau, Executive Director
Donna Ventress, Coordinator, Publications & Communications
Finances: *Annual Operating Budget:* $100,000-$250,000; *Funding Sources:* Membership fees
Staff Member(s): 5
Membership: 1,678; *Fees:* $10 student; $75 retired; $150 individual; *Member Profile:* Anyone interested in the administration of justice; *Committees:* Administrative Tribunals; Communications; Court Administration; Criminal Law Reform Task Force; Education; Executive; Finance & Fundraising; International Initiatives; Membership; Nominations; Research
Meetings/Conferences: • Canadian Insititue for the Administration of Justice 2015 Annual Conference, 2015, Saskatoon, SK
Scope: National
Description: Theme: Aboriginal Peoples & the Law - "We're all in this together"
• Canadian Insititute for the Administration of Justice 2016 Annual Conference, 2016
Scope: National
Publications:
• CIAJ [Canadian Institute for the Administration of Justice] Newsletter
Type: Newsletter; *Frequency:* Irregular
Profile: CIIAJ information, conferences, events & awards, legislative information

Canadian Institute for the Relief of Pain & Disability (CIRPD)
National Office, #204, 916 West Broadway, Vancouver BC V5Z 1K7
Tel: 604-684-4148; *Fax:* 604-684-6247
Toll-Free: 800-872-3105
admin@cirpd.org
www.cirpd.org
www.linkedin.com/groups/Canadian-Institute-Relief-Pain-Disability-2262
www.facebook.com/CIRPD
twitter.com/cirpd
www.youtube.com/user/cirpdadmin
Previous Name: Physical Medicine Research Foundation
Overview: A small national charitable organization founded in 1985
Mission: To improve diagnosis & treatment for pain sufferers; To prevent & reduce pain & disability & improve the quality of life for people who suffer from muscle & joint pain
Affiliation(s): Canadian Cochrane Centre
Chief Officer(s):
Marc I. White, Executive Director
Adrienne Hook, President
William Dyer, Secretary
Janette Lyons, Treasurer
Finances: *Annual Operating Budget:* $250,000-$500,000; *Funding Sources:* Donations
Staff Member(s): 5
Membership: *Fees:* $12 people with chronic pain; $75 individual/organization; *Committees:* Nominations
Activities: Offering educational & research programs; Disseminating evidence-informed best practices; Establishing regional & international health care committees to bring together academics & clinicians from all health care disciplines to prevent & reduce disability; *Library:* Canadian Institute for the Relief of Pain & Disability Library;
Awards:
• Woodbridge Grants & Awards Program (Grant)
Categories include traffic & auto engineering related research; diagnosis & treatment related research; & disability prevention related research *Contact:* Dr. Jack Richman, Research Chair, Phone: 905-678-2924
Publications:
• Canadian Institute for the Relief of Pain & Disability Annual Report
Type: Yearbook; *Frequency:* Annually

Canadian Institute for Theatre Technology (CITT) / L'Institut Canadien des Technologies Scénographiques (ICTS)
PO Box 85041, 345 Laurier Blvd., Mont-Saint-Hilaire QC J3H 5W1
Tel: 613-482-1165; *Fax:* 613-482-1212
Toll-Free: 888-271-3383
info@citt.org
www.citt.org
www.facebook.com/group.php?gid=24629289772
Overview: A small national organization founded in 1990
Mission: To work for the betterment of the Canadian live performance community; To promote safe & ethical work practices
Affiliation(s): United States Institute for Theatre Technology (USITT); l'Organisation Internationale des Scénographes, Techniciens et Architectes de Théâtre / International Organization of Scenographers, Theatre Architects, & Technicians
Chief Officer(s):
Adam Mitchell, President
Gerry van Hezewyk, Vice-President
Mike Dickinson, Secretary
Eric Mongerson, Treasurer
Monique Corbeil, National Coordinator
Membership: *Member Profile:* Theatre consultants & architects; Managers; Designers; Manufacturers; Suppliers; Technicians; Educators; Students; *Committees:* Board development; Finance; Communications; Membership services; Annual conference programming
Activities: Encouraging industry standards; Engaging in advocacy activities; Promoting research; Organizing professional development activities for members; Offering networking opportunities; Recognizing excellent work
Awards:
• Dieter Penzhorn Memorial Award (for significant service to CITT / ICTS) (Award)
• CITT / ICTS Educational Achievement Award (Award)
• The Ron Epp Memorial Award for Professional Achievement (Award)
• CITT / ICTS Supplier (Corporate) Achievement Award (Award)
• CITT / ICTS Award of Technical Merit (Award)
• The Honorary Membership Award (Award)
Meetings/Conferences: • Canadian Institute for Theatre Technology Rendez-vous 2015: Annual Conference & Trade Show, August, 2015, Vancouver, BC
Scope: National
Contact Information: CITT / ICTS Phone: 613-482-1165, Toll-Free Phone: 1-888-271-3383, E-mail: info@citt.org
Publications:
• Canadian Institute for Theatre Technology Annual Report & Annual General Meeting Minutes
Type: Yearbook; *Frequency:* Annually
• Canadian Institute for Theatre Technology / L'Institut Canadien des Technologies Scénographiques Member Directory
Type: Directory
Profile: List of members by name, province, & caucus
• Stageworks
Type: Newsletter; *Accepts Advertising*
Profile: News from the national office & the International Organization of Scenographers, Theatre Architects, & Technicians, plus awards information

Alberta Section
AB
e-mail: alberta@citt.org
www.citt-alberta.org
Chief Officer(s):
Kevin Humphrey, Chair
Josh Gennings, Secretary
Mark Belkie, Treasurer
• Behind the Scene [a publication of the Canadian Institute for Theatre Technology, Alberta Section]
Type: Newsletter
Profile: Information & upcoming events from the Alberta Section of the Canadian Institute for Theatre Technology

Atlantic Region Section
e-mail: atlantic@citt.org
www.citt.org/atlantic.html
Jim Wilson, Section Committe Member, New Brunswick
Karl Simmons, Section Committe Member, Newfoundland & Labrador

British Columbia Section
BC
e-mail: bc@citt.org
www.citt.org/british_columbia.html
Chief Officer(s):
Jim Dobbs, Chair
Matt Frankish, Vice-Chair
Ace Martens, Secretary
Colin MacDuff, Treasurer

Ontario Section
PO Box 72051, 1630 Danforth Ave., Toronto ON M4C 1H0
e-mail: ontario@citt.org
www.citt.org/ontario.html
Chief Officer(s):
Sharon Secord, Chair
James McKernan, Secretary
Victor Svenningson, Treasurer

Québec Section
PO Box 85041, 345, boul Laurier, Mont-Saint-Hilaire QC J3H 5W1
e-mail: cqicts@citt.org
www.citt.org/quebec.html
www.facebook.com/CITTICTS
Mission: To contribute to the development of the theatre technology sector in Québec; To promote excellence in theatre technology
Member of: Quebec Council of Human Resources & Culture
Chief Officer(s):
Michel Desbiens, Chair
Martin Saintonge, Vice-Chair

Monique Corbeil, Secretary
Gilles Benoist, Treasurer

Canadian Institute in Greece (CIG)

Dionysiou Aiginitou 7, Athens GR-115 28 Greece
Tel: 30-210-722-3201; *Fax:* 30-210-725-7968
info@cig-icg.gr
www.cig-icg.gr
www.facebook.com/pages/The-Canadian-Institute-in-Greece/173666819462
twitter.com/CIGICG
www.youtube.com/channel/UCFJEoGzs3NPPdo-2qa1vNKA
Previous Name: Canadian Academic Institute in Athens
Overview: A small international organization founded in 1974
Mission: To promote academic & cultural exchanges between Canada & Greece; to serve the needs of Canadian scholars in Greece
Chief Officer(s):
David W. Rupp, Director
drupp@cig-icg.gr
Staff Member(s): 4
Membership: *Fees:* Schedule available; *Member Profile:* People interested in Greek history; *Committees:* Fellowship; Library; Permits; Publications; Bulletin

Canadian Institute of Actuaries (CIA) / Institut canadien des actuaires (ICA)

Secretariat, #1740, 360 Albert St., Ottawa ON K1R 7X7
Tel: 613-236-8196; *Fax:* 613-233-4552
head.office@cia-ica.ca
www.cia-ica.ca
twitter.com/CIA_Actuaries
Overview: A large national organization founded in 1965
Mission: To set & ensure educational & professional standards for members; To operate a review & disciplinary system; To maintain liaison with government authorities & other professions & organizations; To promote research
Chief Officer(s):
Michel C. Simard, Executive Director
executive.director@cia-ica.ca
Lynn Blackburn, Director, Professional Practice & Volunteer Services
Les Dandridge, Director, Communications & Public Affairs
Jacques Leduc, Director, Operations, Finance, & Administration
Alicia Rollo, Director, Membership, Education & Professional Development
Membership: *Fees:* #1,195 fellow; $1,015 associate (5 years or more); $350 associate (less than 5 years), affiliate & correspondent; *Member Profile:* Actuaries who meet policy on education & work experience requirements
Activities: Engaging in advocacy activities; Sponsoring programs for the education of members; *Library*
Meetings/Conferences: • Canadian Institute of Actuaries 2015 Annual Meeting, June, 2015, Ottawa, ON
Scope: National
Publications:
• (e)Bulletin: The Monthly Newsletter of the CIA [Canadian Institute of Actuaries]
Type: eNewsletter; *Frequency:* Monthly
Profile: Institute news & announcements

Canadian Institute of Biotechnology; Industrial Biotechnology Association of Canada *See* BIOTECanada

Canadian Institute of Bookkeeping (CIB)

PO Box 963, 31 Adelaide St. East, Toronto ON M5C 2K3
Tel: 416-925-9420; *Fax:* 416-929-8815
info@cibcb.com
www.cibcb.com
Overview: A small national organization
Mission: To promote the advancement of certified bookkeepers; To prepare persons for professional positions in a financial environment; To establish educational, ethical, & professional standards in the bookkeeping profession; To protect the public
Finances: *Funding Sources:* Membership fees
Membership: *Fees:* $50 enrolment fee; $240 certified bookkeeper; $192 associate; $156 student; *Member Profile:* Individuals working in the bookkeeping / accounting field, who have completed Level I & Level II of the academic program; Students, who are completing the academic & experience requirements to become certified
Activities: Enforcing the Code of Professional Conduct of CIB; Providing the CIB professional development program; Raising public awareness of certified bookkeepers
Publications:
• Canadian Institute of Bookkeeping Newsletter
Type: Newsletter; *Frequency:* Quarterly; *Price:* Free to members of the Canadian Institute of Bookkeeping
Profile: Information from the Institute

Canadian Institute of Chartered Business Planners (CICBP)

#210, 1117 First St. SW, Calgary AB T2R 0T9
Tel: 403-457-5144; *Fax:* 403-457-5133
Other Communication: Alternate E-mail: admin@cicbp.ca
info@cicbp.ca
www.cicbp.ca
Overview: A small national organization
Mission: To ensure high standards of practice & professionalism in business planning; To represent & protect the profession; To protect the public interest
Membership: *Member Profile:* Business planning professionals from across Canada; Members, who meet requirements, are entitled to use the designation, Chartered Business Planner (CBP); Students enrolled in the Institute's program or other programs accredited by the Institute
Activities: Training & certifying business planning professionals; Providing professional development opportunities; Promoting the specialized profession of business planning
Publications:
• Business Planning Review
Frequency: Semiannually
Profile: Articles & papers on business planning
• The Chartered Business Planner
Type: Newsletter; *Frequency:* Quarterly
Profile: Institute activities & members announcements

Canadian Institute of Chartered Business Valuators (CICBV) / L'Institut canadien des experts en évaluation d'entreprises

#710, 277 Wellington St. West, Toronto ON M5V 3H2
Tel: 416-977-1117; *Fax:* 416-977-7066
admin@cicbv.ca
cicbv.ca
Previous Name: Canadian Association of Business Valuators (CABV)
Overview: A medium-sized national licensing organization founded in 1971
Mission: To develop high professional standards for Canadian Chartered Business Valuators; To manage the Chartered Business Valuator (CBV) designation; To govern members of the Institute with a strict Code of Ethics & Practice Standards
Chief Officer(s):
Allister Byrne, FCA, President & CEO
byrnea@cicbv.ca
Bob Boulton, Director, Education & Standards
boultonb@cicbv.ca
Isabel Natale, Coordinator, Program
natalei@cicbv.ca
Lauren Kirshner, Coordinator, External Relations
kirshnerl@cicbv.ca
Megan Kennedy, Manager, Communications
kennedym@cicbv.ca
Deborah Pelle, Manager, Events
pelled@cicbv.ca
Judith Roth, Manager, Information Technology & Member Services
rothj@cicbv.ca
Staff Member(s): 7
Membership: 1,400+; *Member Profile:* Chartered Business Valuators in Canada, who work in the areas of corporate finance, securities valuation, disputes, & compliance; *Committees:* Accreditation/Membership; Audit; Awards; Communications/Branding; Conduct & Discipline; Continuing Education; Education; Executive; FCBV/LIFE Membership Selection; International; Nominating; Professional Practice & Standards; Publications; Research Institute; Strategic Planning; Publications; Liaison; Workshops
Activities: Offering professional development opportunities; Developing programs to test members; Encouraging research; Facilitating the exchange of ideas; Promoting the profession of business valuations; *Library:* Canadian Institute of Chartered Business Valuators Library
Publications:
• Bibliography
Profile: Listing of articles & conference papers published by the CICBV
• The Business Valuator
Type: Newsletter; *Frequency:* Quarterly
Profile: CICBV's activities, members, & students
• Canadian Institute of Chartered Business Valuators Annual Report
Type: Yearbook; *Frequency:* Annually
Profile: Summary of the Institute's yearly highlights
• Casebook
Profile: Summary of significant legal & tax cases related to valuation
• Handbook
Frequency: Annually
Profile: CICBV's by-laws, code of ethics, practice standards, policies, & member list
• The Journal of Business Valuation
Type: Journal; *Frequency:* Semiannually
Profile: Articles & papers related to the field of business valutation, plus the proceedings of the Canadian Institute of Chartered Business Valuators' biennial conferences
• The Valuation Law Review
Frequency: Annually
Profile: Publication consists of corporate securities law, family law, & taxation

Canadian Institute of Child Health (CICH) / Institut canadien de la santé infantile

#300, 384 Bank St., Ottawa ON K2P 1Y4
Tel: 613-230-8838; *Fax:* 613-230-6654
cich@cich.ca
www.cich.ca
Overview: A medium-sized national charitable organization founded in 1977
Mission: To promote the health & well-being of Canadian children through consultation, collaboration, research & advocacy by building alliances & coalitions & by creating resources on health promotion, disease & injury prevention relevant to child & family health in Canada; To identify issues of concern by monitoring the health & well-being of children in Canada; To promote & improve the health & well-being of mothers & infants in all settings; To promote the healthy physical development of children in a safe environment & reduce childhood injuries; To promote the healthy psycho-social development of children in supportive & nurturing environments; To facilitate empowerment of individuals & communities to achieve the above goals for Canadian children & their families; To facilitate collaborative work between consumers, professional, non-professional & government agencies that results in appropriate actions for identified needs
Member of: Canadian Coalition for the Prevention of Developmental Disabilities; Coalition of National Voluntary Organizations; Canadian Coalition on the Rights of the Child; Children's Alliance; Breastfeeding Committee for Canada; National Literacy & Health Program
Affiliation(s): Canadian Children's Environmental Health Network; Key Institution of Childwatch International; International Network for Child Health, Environment & Safety; WHO/European Environment Agency Working Group on the Environment & Children's Health
Chief Officer(s):
Robin Moore-Orr, D.Sc., R.D., Chair
Lynne Westlake, Secretary
Eleonore Benesch, Treasurer
Finances: *Funding Sources:* Government; Membership fees; Donations; Sale of publications; Sponsors; Foundations
185 volunteer(s)
Membership: 565; *Fees:* $15 youth; $35 individual; $65 hospital; $75 educational institution; $85 corporate
Publications:
• Child Health
Type: Newsletter; *Frequency:* Quarterly *ISSN:* 0838-9683; *Price:* Free with CICH membership
Profile: National news about child health & well-being issues

Canadian Institute of Credit & Financial Management *See* Credit Institute of Canada

Canadian Institute of Cultural Affairs / Institut canadien des affaires culturelles

655 Queen St. East, Toronto ON M4M 1G4
Tel: 416-691-2316; *Fax:* 416-691-2491
Toll-Free: 877-691-1422
ica@icacan.org
www.icacan.org
Also Known As: ICA Canada
Overview: A small national charitable organization founded in 1976
Mission: To empower people to develop leadership capacity; To contribute to positive social change
Chief Officer(s):
Nan Hudson, Executive Director
nhudson@icacan.org

Staci Kentish, Director, Community Facilitators' Initiative, 416-691-2316 Ext. 236
skentish@icacan.org
Finances: *Funding Sources:* Membership fees; Donations; Sponsorships
Staff Member(s): 3
Membership: *Committees:* Program Advisory
Activities: Presenting programs such as the Courage to Lead Program, the Youth as Facilitative Leaders Program (a skills development & mentorship program), & the Listen to the Drumming Program (to help communities in Kenya & Tanzania develop their own way to alleviate the HIV/AIDS crisis)

Canadian Institute of Energy (CIE)

#26, 181 Ravine Dr., Port Moody BC V3H 4T3
Tel: 604-949-1346; *Fax:* 604-469-3717
cienergybc@gmail.com
cienergybc.blogspot.ca
Overview: A medium-sized national organization founded in 1979
Mission: To provide a Canadian perspective on energy technology, business & policy, nationally & internationally, for those affected professionally or personally by energy issues; To encourage energy research, education & dissemination of topical information; To provide an unbiased forum for discussion & debate
Chief Officer(s):
Penny Cochrane, Chair
Melissa McArthur, Administrator
John Oliver, Treasurer
Finances: *Funding Sources:* Membership fees
6 volunteer(s)
Membership: 500; *Fees:* $60; *Member Profile:* Professionally involved in all aspects of energy, whether in exploring for sources, conducting energy research, converting or using energy, or in energy planning
Activities: *Speaker Service:* Yes; *Rents Mailing List:* Yes
Awards:
• Energy Scholarship Award (Award)
• Energy Research & Development Award (Award)
• Applied Energy Innovation Award (Award)

Canadian Institute of Entrepreneurship (CIE)

e-mail: coordinator@cienow.com
www.canadianinstituteofentrepreneurship.com
Overview: A small national organization
Mission: To promote education in entrepreneurship; To act as a registrar & facilitator
Membership: *Member Profile:* Students interested in obtaining the CIE designation, CE, Certified Entrepreneur; Persons with the designation, CE, Certified Entrepreneur
Activities: Granting the CIE Certification academic designation, in partnership with Canadian post-secondary institutions; Offering mentoring services
Publications:
• CIE Newsletter
Type: Newsletter
Profile: Information for student members & Certified Entrepreneurs

Canadian Institute of Financial Planning (CIFPs)

#600, 3660 Hurontario St., Mississauga ON L5B 3C4
Tel: 647-723-6450; *Fax:* 647-723-6457
Toll-Free: 866-933-0233
cifps@cifps.ca
www.cifps.ca
Overview: A medium-sized national organization founded in 1972
Mission: To train & qualify advisors to become Certified Financial Planners; To represent members on matters of common interest
Chief Officer(s):
Keith Costello, President & Chief Executive Officer
Anthony Williams, Vice-President, Academic Affairs
Andrew Cunningham, Director, Information Services
Robert Jeffrey, Director, Member Relations
Odele Burton, Corporate Secretary
Finances: *Funding Sources:* Sponsorships
Membership: 3,500+; *Member Profile:* Canadian financial planners; Financial planning students
Activities: Providing continuing education, mentorship, & support services; Advocating on issues that affect the financial planning profession in Canada; Promoting the financial planning profession to the public
Meetings/Conferences: • 2015 Canadian Institute of Financial Planning National Conference, June, 2015, The Westin Bayshore, Vancouver, BC
Scope: National
Publications:
• Canadian Institute of Financial Planning Magazine
Type: Magazine
Profile: Information about current trends & practices in the financial planning profession
• Canadian Institute of Financial Planning Newsletter
Type: Newsletter
Profile: Information about the Institute's activities & events for its members

Canadian Institute of Food Science & Technology (CIFST) / Institut canadien de science et technologie alimentaires (ICSTA)

#1311, 3-1750 The Queensway, Toronto ON M9C 5H5
Tel: 905-271-8338; *Fax:* 905-271-8344
cifst@cifst.ca
www.cifst.ca
Overview: A medium-sized national organization founded in 1951
Mission: To advance food science & technology; To act as a voice for scientific issues related to the Canadian food industry
Affliation(s): British Columbia Food Technolgists
Chief Officer(s):
Carol Ann Burrell, Executive Director, 905-271-8338, Fax: 905-271-8344
caburrell@cifst.ca
Belinda Elysée-Collen, President
belinda@internationalsugars.com
Finances: *Funding Sources:* Sponsorships
Membership: 1,200+; *Fees:* $43 student; $87.50 retired; $195 professional/associate; $550 sustaining; *Member Profile:* Food industry professionals from across Canada, such as scientists & technologists in industry, academia, & government; *Committees:* Awards; Executive; International Liaison; Membership Renewal; Nominating; Fellow Selection; Publication Editorial Advisory Council; Fellow Selection; Section Advisory Council; Atlantic; Quebec; Ontario; Manitoba; Alberta; British Columbia; Volunteer Implementation Task Force; Membership Marketing and Communications Task Force; Web Site Task Force; Publication Task Force; Scientific Expert Council Task Force
Activities: Exchanging scientific, educational, & business information; Engaging in advocacy activities; Liaising with related national & international organizations, such as Agriculture & Agri-Food Canada (AAFC) & the International Union of Food Science & Technology (IUFoST); Promoting professional development; Establishing Subject Interest Divisions, such as food process engineering, functional foods, government & regulatory affairs, microbiology, nutrition, packaging, & sensory evaluation
Meetings/Conferences: • 2016 World Congress of Food Science of Technology, August, 2016, Royal Dublin Society, Dublin
Scope: International
Description: IUFoST promotes the advancement of global food science and technology, fosters the worldwide exchange of scientific knowledge and ideas through the biennial World Congress and aims to strengthen food science and technology's role in helping secure the world's food supply and eliminate world hunger.
Contact Information: iufost2016@conferencepartners.ie; URL: www.iufost2016.com

Alberta Section
c/o Hisham Karami, Alberta Health Services, Queen Elizabeth II Hosp., Grand Prairie AB T8N 7E9
www.cifst.ca
Chief Officer(s):
Michael Gänzle, Chair, 780-492-0774, Fax: 780-492-4265
mgaenzle@ualberta.ca
Mirko Betti, Secretary-Treasurer, 780-248-1598
mirko.betti@ales.ualberta.ca
Hisham Karami, Director, Membership, 780-710-2071
hishamkarami@hotmail.com

Atlantic Section
c/o Joy Shinn, PEI Healthy Eating Alliance, #220, 40 Enman Cres., Charlottetown PE C1E 1E6
Tel: 902-940-9782
cifst.atlantic@gmail.com
www.cifst.ca
Chief Officer(s):
H.P. Vasantha Rupasinghe, Chair
vrupasinghe@dal.ca

Manitoba Section
c/o A. Tezcucano, Manitoba Agriculture, Food & Rural Initiatives, PO Box 100, 229 Main St. South, Morris MB R0G 1K0
e-mail: manitobasection@cifst.ca
www.cifst.ca
Chief Officer(s):
Aline Tezcucano, Chair, 204-795-7968, Fax: 204-746-2932
aline.tezcucano@gov.mb.ca
Prabal Ghosh, Secretary, 204-239-3164, Fax: 204-239-3180
Prabal.Ghosh@gov.mb.ca
David Adamik, Treasurer
adamik22@mts.net
Ketie Sandhu, Chair, Programs
ksandhu@gourmetbaker.com
• Canadian Institute of Food Science & Technology, Manitoba Section
Type: Yearbook; *Frequency:* Annually
Profile: Reports from executives & financial statements
• Food File
Type: Newsletter; *Editor:* D. Head (dagmarahead@gmail.com)
Profile: Section events & news, as well as industry interviews

Ontario Section
5 Fenwood Circle, Peterborough ON K9J 6M4
Tel: 866-437-6030; *Fax:* 866-719-5396
OntarioSection@cifst.ca
www.cifst.ca
Chief Officer(s):
Maureen Taylor, Chair, 905-567-2555 Ext. 29, Fax: 905-567-2556
maureen@theingredientcompany.com
• SciTech
Type: Newsletter; *Editor:* James Summers
Profile: Current activities of the Toronto section for members

Québec Section
c/o Manon Cloutier, 130, Place de Naples, Laval QC H7M 4A6
Tel: 450-663-6503; *Fax:* 450-663-6503
www.cifst.ca
Chief Officer(s):
Sam Choucha, Chair, 514-421-0303
sam.choucha@univarcanada.com
• Canadian Institute of Food Science & Technology, Québec Section Annual Report
Type: Yearbook; *Frequency:* Annually
Profile: A summary of the previous year's activities

Canadian Institute of Forestry / Institut forestier du Canada

c/o The Canadian Ecology Centre, PO Box 430, 6905 Hwy. 17 West, Mattawa ON P0H 1V0
Tel: 705-744-1715; *Fax:* 705-744-1716
Other Communication: questions@cif-ifc.org
admin@cif-ifc.org
www.cif-ifc.org
www.facebook.com/groups/53806339292
twitter.com/cif_ifc
www.youtube.com/user/CIFtube
Previous Name: Canadian Society of Forest Engineers
Overview: A large national organization founded in 1908
Mission: To act as the national voice of forest practitioners
Member of: International Union of Societies of Foresters
Chief Officer(s):
John Pineau, Chief Executive Officer
Matt Meade, Executive Director
Michel Vallée, President
Tattersall Smith, Vice-President
Finances: *Funding Sources:* Membership dues; Sponsorships
Membership: 2,200; *Fees:* $39.55 students; $67.80 retired members; $50 sustaining individuals; $111.87 active members & spousal; $192.10 current active members; *Member Profile:* Foresters; Forest technicians & technologists; Educators; Scientists, such as biologists & ecologists; Students; Others with a professional interest in forestry; *Committees:* National board of Directors; Executive; Awards; Silver Ring Accreditation
Activities: Providing national leadership in forestry; Promoting competence & knowledge of forestry for professionals; Presenting a national electronic lecture series; Providing workshops & seminars; Fostering public awareness & understanding of forestry issues; Presenting rings to graduates of Canadian forest technical & forestry baccalaureate programs; Offering field tours; Establishing demonstration forests; Providing networking opportunities; Liaising with the Canadian Council of Forest Ministers; *Speaker Service:* Yes

Awards:
• International Forestry Achievement Award (Award)
To recognize outstanding achievement in international forestry
• James M. Kitz Award (Award)
To honour contributions of forest practitioners who are new to the profession
• Canadian Forest Management Group Achievement Award (Award)
To honour outstanding achievement by teams & groups of natural resource managers, researchers, & NGO groups in the field of forest resource related activities in Canada
• Canadian Forestry Achievement Award (Award)
To recognize outstanding achievement in forestry in Canada
• Canadian Forestry Scientific Achievement Award (Award)
To honour unique achievement in forestry research in Canada
• Presidential Award (Award)
Presented to individuals who have made significant or consistent contributions to the practice & profession of forestry
• Section of the Year Award (Award)
Awarded to sections that exemplify the objects of the Canadian Institute of Forestry
• Tree of Life Award (Award)
To honour persons who have made superior contributions to forest renewal, sustainable forest resource management, or sustained yield integrated management of the forest & its intrinsic resources
• Gold Medal (Award)
For graduating students, selected by the head of each school, from each forestry baccalaureate school & each forestry diploma school in Canada
• Honourary Members (Award)
For a non-member who has made outstanding contributions to the advancement of forestry
• J. Michael Waldram Memorial Model Forest Fellowship (Scholarship)
For a Canadian Aboriginal youth enrolled in at least their second year in either a degree or diploma program in natural resource management at a Canadian university or college
• Fellows of the Institute (Award)
To recognize a member or ex-member who has made outstanding contributions to the advancement of forestry or to the Candian Institute of Forestry
Meetings/Conferences: • Canadian Institute of Forestry / Institut forestier du Canada 2015 107th Annual General Meeting & Conference, 2015
Scope: National
Description: Meetings, presentations, poster sessions, displays, & field trips
Publications:
• Canadian Institute of Forestry Annual Report
Type: Yearbook; *Frequency:* Annually
• Canadian Institute of Forestry E-news
Type: Newsletter; *Frequency:* Bimonthly
Profile: Information about the Institute, such as conferences, section updates, & member resources
• The Forestry Chronicle: The Official Journal of the Canadian Institute of Forestry
Type: Journal; *Frequency:* Bimonthly; *Accepts Advertising*; *Editor:* Brian Haddon; *Price:* $100 personal electronic & print; $300multi-users electronic & print
Profile: Practical & applied science & information for forest management planning & operations

Canadian Institute of Forestry, Newfoundland & Labrador (CIF-NL)

PO Box 793, Stn. Main, Corner Brook NL A2H 6G7
e-mail: newfoundland-labrador@cif-ifc.org
cif-ifc.org/site/newfoundland_labrador
Overview: A small provincial organization
Mission: To advance the stewardship of Canada's forest resources, provide national leadership in forestry, promote competence among forestry professionals, and foster public awareness of Canadian and international forestry issues.
Chief Officer(s):
Allan Masters, Director

Canadian Institute of Gemmology (CIG) / Institut canadien de gemmologie

c/o School of Jewellery Arts, PO Box 57010, Vancouver BC V5K 5G6
Tel: 604-530-8569
Other Communication: gemlab@cigem.ca
info@cigem.ca
www.cigem.ca
www.facebook.com/pages/Canadian-Institute-of-Gemmology/135719129830957
www.twitter.com/CIGemNews
Also Known As: Pacific Institute of Gemmology
Overview: A small national organization founded in 1990
Mission: To serve the jewellery industry & the general public
Chief Officer(s):
Wolf Kuehn, Executive Director
Activities: Offering C.I.G courses & training; Providing GemForum - The Information Exchange
Publications:
• CIGem News: The Newsletter of the Canadian Institute of Gemmology
Type: Newsletter; *Frequency:* Monthly
• Gemmology Canada
Type: Magazine; *Editor:* J. Wolf Kuehn *ISSN:* 0846-3611
Profile: Articles written by students of the Canadian Institute of Gemmology & other contributors

Canadian Institute of Geomatics (CIG) / Association canadienne des sciences géomatiques

#100D, 900 Dynes Rd., Ottawa ON K2C 3L6
Tel: 613-224-9851; *Fax:* 613-224-9577
admincig@magma.ca
www.cig-acsg.ca
Overview: A medium-sized national organization founded in 1882
Mission: Geomatics is commonly defined as a "discipline aimed at managing geographic data by means of the science & technology used to acquire, store, process, display & distribute them"; to advance the development of geomatics sciences in Canada; to enhance & demonstrate the public usefulness of geomatics; to further the professional development of its members; to foster cooperation between & promote unity of purpose among Canadian geomatics organizations; to represent & promote Canadian interests in geomatics internationally
Affliation(s): International Federation of Surveyors; International Society for Photogrammetry & Remote Sensing; International Cartographic Association; Commonwealth Association of Canada Lands Surveyors; Canadian Council of Land Surveyors; Canadian Hydrographic Association
Chief Officer(s):
David R. Stafford, Executive Director
exdircig@magma.ca
Lucie Lebrun-Ginn, Office Administrator
Finances: *Annual Operating Budget:* $100,000-$250,000; *Funding Sources:* Membership fees; events; contributions
Staff Member(s): 3; 30 volunteer(s)
Membership: 1,500; *Fees:* $95 member; $500 sustaining; $40 student; *Committees:* Cartography; Education; Engineering & Mining; Geodesy; Geospatial Data Infrastructures; Hydrography; GPS; Land Surveying; Land Information Management; Photogrammetry; Remote Sensing; Urban Regional Information; Annual Conferences
Activities: Geographical information systems (GIS); global positioning systems & remote sensing as tools & techniques in environmental monitoring & planning (ie. sustainable development); *Library* by appointment
Awards:
• Intermap Award (Award)
• Jim Jones Award (Award)
• John Carroll Geodesy Award (Award)
• Triathlon Award (Award)
• CIG Student Membership Award (Award)
• Hans Klinkenberg Memorial Scholarship Fund (Scholarship)
Publications:
• Geomatica
Type: Journal; *Frequency:* Quarterly; *Accepts Advertising*; *Price:* $275
Profile: Formerly the CISM Journal ACSGC, the surveying & mapping publication features both scientific & practical information, conferences, reviews, industry news, & new products

Canadian Institute of International Affairs / Institut canadien des affaires internationales *See* Canadian International Council

Canadian Institute of Iridology

233 Park Lawn Rd., Toronto ON M8Y 3J3
Tel: 416-231-6298; *Fax:* 905-824-0063
cdn_inst_of_irid@hotmail.com
www.cdninstiridology.com
Overview: A small national organization founded in 1989
Mission: To provide a professional teaching forum in the field of iridology
Affliation(s): The Iridologists' Association of Canada (Ir.A.C.)
Chief Officer(s):
Agota Csekey, President & Program Director
Activities: Offering training in the practice of iris analysis, including the Practitioner Diploma Program in Clinical Iridology

Canadian Institute of Management (CIM) / Institut canadien de gestion

National Office, 15 Collier St., Lower Level, Barrie ON L4M 1G5
Tel: 705-725-8926; *Fax:* 705-725-8196
Toll-Free: 800-387-5774
office@cim.ca
www.cim.ca
Overview: A medium-sized national licensing organization founded in 1942
Mission: To promote the senior management profession by offering a series of educational programs from single courses to professional certification
Chief Officer(s):
Matthew Jelavic, President
president@cim.ca
Betty Smith, Secretary
pastpresident@cim.ca
Deb Daigle, Treasurer
treasurer@cim.ca
Finances: *Funding Sources:* Corporate sponsorship
Membership: *Fees:* Schedule available; *Member Profile:* Canadian leaders in the management profession
Activities: Offering educational opportunities to enhance managerial skills; Certifying managers
Publications:
• Canadian Manager Magazine
Type: Magazine; *Frequency:* Quarterly; *Accepts Advertising*; *Editor:* Sheila Sproule; *Price:* Free to CIM members
Profile: Information about management developments
• Tips from the Top
Type: Newsletter; *Frequency:* Monthly; *Price:* Free for CIM members

Alberta - Northern & NWT Branch
PO Box 610, Stn. Main, Edmonton AB T5J 2K8
Tel: 780-455-7951
northernalberta@cim.ca
Affliation(s): Faculty of Extension, University of Alberta
Chief Officer(s):
Garry Kalawarny, Regional President, Western & Central
central@cim.ca

Alberta - Southern Branch
PO Box 53222, Stn. Marlborough, Calgary AB T2A 7L9
Tel: 705-725-8926; *Fax:* 705-725-8196
Toll-Free: 800-387-5774
cimsouthalberta@gmail.com
Affliation(s): University of Calgary; Southern Alberta Institute of Technology; Mount Royal College; Olds College; Red Deer College; DeVry Canada
Chief Officer(s):
Garry Kalawarny, Regional President, Western & Central
central@cim.ca

British Columbia & Yukon Branch
PO Box 346, 4974 Kingsway, Burnaby BC V5J 4M9
e-mail: bc@cim.ca
Chief Officer(s):
Garry Kalawarny, Regional President, Western & Central
central@cim.ca

Manitoba - Winnipeg Branch
1150 Waverley St., #B2, Winnipeg MB R3T 0P4
Tel: 204-474-8653
cim.winnipeg@mts.net
www.cim-winnipeg.ca
Affliation(s): University of Manitoba
Chief Officer(s):
Clayton McPherson, President
Garry Kalawarny, Regional President, Western/Central
central@cim.ca
• Manitoba Manager
Type: Newsletter; *Frequency:* Quarterly
Profile: Branch news, upcoming events, & articles

Maritime Branch
PO Box 463, Port Williams NS B0P 1T0
Tel: 902-670-0746
info@maritimecim.com
www.maritimecim.com
Chief Officer(s):
Katherine Hanks, President

Newfoundland & Labrador Branch
49 Anthony Ave., St. John's NL A1E 1X5

Tel: 709-437-7075; *Fax:* 709-437-7079
newfoundlandandlabrador@cim.ca
cimnl.ca
www.facebook.com/184069228310762
Affliation(s): Memorial University; Keyin College; Eastern College
Chief Officer(s):
Ken Noseworthy, Regional President, Eastern
eastern@cim.ca

Ontario - Grand Valley Branch
#167, 55 Northfield Dr. East, Waterloo ON N2K 3T6
Toll-Free: 800-387-5774
grandvalley@cim.ca
www.facebook.com/cimgrv
twitter.com/cimgrandvalley
Affliation(s): Conestoga College; Wilfrid Laurier University
Chief Officer(s):
Lorraine Gignac, Regional President, Ontario East
onteast@cim.ca

Ontario - Hamilton Branch
PO Box 57035, Stn. Jackson Square, Hamilton ON L8P 4W9
Tel: 905-561-9889; *Fax:* 866-774-2226
admin@cim-hamilton.com
cim-hamilton.com
Affliation(s): Mohawk College; McMaster University
Chief Officer(s):
Don Spaetzel, President, 905-690-1164
dspaetzel@cogeco.ca
• The Hamilton Scene
Type: Newsletter

Ontario - Lake Simcoe Branch
PO Box 1060, Barrie ON L4M 5E1
Tel: 705-326-6577
infolakesimcoe@cim.ca
Affliation(s): Georgian College of Applied Arts & Technology
Chief Officer(s):
Lorraine Gignac, Regional President, Ontario East
onteast@cim.ca
• Lake Simcoe Manager
Type: Newsletter

Ontario - London Branch
PO Box 611, Stn. B, London ON N6A 4Y4
Tel: 519-681-4168; *Fax:* 519-668-7866
cimlonbr@sympatico.ca
Affliation(s): University of Western Ontario
Chief Officer(s):
Beth Lahey, Regional President, Ontario West
ontwest@cim.ca
• London Manager
Type: Newsletter

Ontario - Niagara Branch
#264, 17 - 7000 McLeod Rd., Niagara Falls ON L2G 7K3
Toll-Free: 800-387-5774
niagara@cim.ca
Affliation(s): Niagara College of Applied Arts & Technology; Brock University
Chief Officer(s):
Beth Lahey, Regional President, Ontario West
ontwest@cim.ca

Ontario - Ottawa Valley Branch
#303, 320 Croyden Ave., Ottawa ON K2B 5P3
Tel: 613-831-0379
ottawa@cim.ca
Affliation(s): Carleton University; Algonquin College; St. Lawrence College; University of Ottawa
Chief Officer(s):
Lorraine Gignac, Regional President, Ontario East
onteast@cim.ca

Ontario - Sarnia Branch
258 Ross Ave., Sarnia ON N7T 1J9
Tel: 519-336-3544
sarnia@cim.ca
Affliation(s): Lambton College

Ontario - Toronto Branch
#210, 2800 - 14th St., Markham ON L3R 0E4
e-mail: toronto@cim.ca
Affliation(s): University of Toronto; Ryerson University; York University; Centennial College; Humber College; George Brown College; Seneca College

Québec - Montréal Branch
#200, 2140, boul Marie-Victorin, Longueuil QC J4G 1A9
Tél: 450-674-6775; *Téléc:* 450-646-9333
montreal@cim.ca
Affliation(s): Concordia University; McGill University; Université de Montréal; UNiversité du Québec; Sherbrooke Université
Chief Officer(s):
Pierre Jutras, Président
Caroline Coulombe, Secrétaire-Trésorière
Pierre Henri, Président régional, Québec
quebec@cim.ca

Saskatchewan - Saskatoon/Regina Branch
PO Box 8055, Saskatoon SK S7K 4R7
Fax: 866-812-0654
Toll-Free: 800-387-5774
saskatoon-regina@cim.ca
Affliation(s): University of Saskatchewan; CIM Distance Education
Chief Officer(s):
Garry Kalawarny, Regional President, Western & Central
central@cim.ca

Canadian Institute of Marketing / Institut canadien du marketing

205 Miller Dr., Georgetown ON L7G 6G4
Tel: 905-877-5369
www.professionalmarketer.ca
www.linkedin.com/groups?mostPopular=&gid=105823
www.facebook.com/groups/8099252591
twitter.com/regprofmarketer
www.youtube.com/user/canadianmarketer
Overview: A medium-sized international charitable organization founded in 1982
Mission: To improve the practice of marketing in Canada by encouraging the adoption of professional standards & qualifications by practitioners & employers, & by sponsoring activities related to marketing education & training; To be a means by which those engaged in all aspects of marketing as a professional activity can represent their views & interests to governments & agencies
Member of: Asia Pacific Marketing Federation
Affliation(s): Affiliated with 20 other Institutes of Marketing around the world
Chief Officer(s):
A. Grant Lee, Executive Director
grant.lee@professionalmarketer.ca
Faythe Pal, Chair
faythe@handsoftimeinc.com
John Jackson, Secretary-Treasurer
humanist.officiant@me.com
Shiv Seechurn, Registrar
shivseechurn@rogers.com
Membership: Over 50,000; *Fees:* Schedule available; *Member Profile:* No corporate memberships; each person has to apply for, & earn, the right of membership
Activities: Accredited marketing programs in the following colleges & universities: Algonquin College, Atkinson College, BC Institute of Technology, Seneca, Centennial, Concordia, Kingston College (Vancouver), Mount Allison, Ottawa, Ryerson, St. Lawrence College, University of Toronto, York University, Brock University; *Speaker Service:* Yes
Publications:
• Canadian Institute of Marketing Membership Directory
Type: Directory
Profile: Listing of members
• Canadian Institute of Marketing Services Directory
Type: Directory
Profile: Listing of accredited professionals who have the qualifications & experience to provide services in marketing
• Marketing Canada
Type: Journal; *Frequency:* Quarterly; *Accepts Advertising*; *Editor:* A. Grant Lee
Profile: Articles related to marketing theory, case studies, standards & ethics, & applications of principles

Canadian Institute of Mining & Metallurgy *See* Canadian Institute of Mining, Metallurgy & Petroleum

Canadian Institute of Mining, Metallurgy & Petroleum (CIM) / Institut canadien des mines, de la métallurgie et du pétrole

CIM National Office, #1250, 3500, boul de Maisonneuve ouest, Westmount QC H3Z 3C1
Tel: 514-939-2710; *Fax:* 514-939-2714
cim@cim.org
www.cim.org
Previous Name: Canadian Institute of Mining & Metallurgy
Overview: A large national organization founded in 1898
Mission: To act as a source of leadership for its members, by offering conferences & courses, liaising with government departments, commissioning special volumes & reports, & publishing technical papers
Chief Officer(s):
Jean Vavrek, Executive Director, 514-939-2710 Ext. 1301, Fax: 513-939-2714
jvavrek@cim.org
Chuck Edwards, President
chuck.edwards@amec.com
Jean-Marc Demers, Deputy Executive Director
jmdemers@cim.org
Lise Bujold, Director, Conferences & Exhibitions
lbujold@cim.org
Marjolaine Dugas, Director, Membership
mdugas@cim.org
Gérard Hamel, Director, Information Technology
ghamel@cim.org
Angela Hamlyn, Director, Media & Communications
ahamlyn@cim.org
Serge Major, Director, Finance & Admininstration
smajor@cim.org
Deborah Sauvé, Manager, Canadian Mining Metallurgical Foundation
dsauve@cim.org
Membership: 12,000+; *Member Profile:* Professionals in the Canadian minerals, metals, materials, & energy sectors, from industry, government, & academia; *Committees:* Central Publications; Audit; Bulletin; By-Laws; CIM Valuation of Mineral Properties; Education; Estimation Guidelines; Human Resources; International Advisory Liaison; Membership; President Elect Nominating; Public Affairs; Special Volumes
Activities: Providing technical forums & professional networking opportunities; Offering continuing education; Recognizing excellent programs; *Speaker Service:* Yes; *Library:* Canadian Institute of Mining, Metallurgy & Petroleum Library;
Awards:
• CIM Awards (Award)
The institute administers 27 awards recognizing achievement in mining, metallurgy & petroleum industries
• CIM Journalism Awards (Award)
Established 1985; presented to print, radio & television journalists in Canada for balanced & technically accurate news reporting, feature writing, radio & television broadcasting that best enhance public understanding of the minerals industry & its contribution to the economic & social well-being of Canada
Amount: $500 first prizes
• Medals for Bravery (Award)
Established 1933; medals are awarded in recognition of great valour displayed to save life in mines or plants of Canadian mining companies; an award is made only in a case where a person knowingly risks his/her life in attempting to rescue a fellow worker
• The Order of Santa Barbara (Award)
Established 1968; a silver medal is awarded to any woman who has made a significant contribution to the welfare of a mining community in Canada
Meetings/Conferences: • Canadian Institute of Mining, Metallurgy & Petroleum 2015 Annual Conference & Exhibition, May, 2015, Palais des Congrès, Montréal, QC
Scope: National
Description: A mining event, featuring a technical program, workshops, field trips, a student program, & a social program
Contact Information: Events Director: Lise Bujold; Phone: 514-939-2710, ext. 1308; E-mail: lbujold@cim.org
• 24th World Mining Congress & Expo, 2016, Centro Empresarial Sul América, Rio de Janeiro
Scope: International
Attendance: 1,500
• Canadian Institute of Mining, Metallurgy & Petroleum MassMin 2016: 7th Intl Conference & Exhibition on Mass Mining, 2016, Sydney
Scope: International
Description: Topics include mine design, rock flow modeling & prediction, mine automation, & mining methods
Publications:
• CIM [Canadian Institute of Mining, Metallurgy & Petroleum] Magazine
Type: Magazine; *Frequency:* 7 pa; *Accepts Advertising*; *ISSN:* 1718-4177; *Price:* Free for members; $160 non-members in Canada
Profile: Editorials, technical information, industry events, & industry information
• CIM [Canadian Institute of Mining, Metallurgy & Petroleum] Directory

Type: Directory; *Frequency:* Annually
Profile: Listing of individual & corporate CIM members
• CIM [Canadian Institute of Mining, Metallurgy & Petroleum] Reporter
Frequency: Annually
Profile: Official publication of the annual CIM Conference & Exhibition, for all registered delegates & visitors
• CIM [Canadian Institute of Mining, Metallurgy & Petroleum] Canadian Metallurgical Quarterly
Frequency: Quarterly *ISSN:* 0008-4433
Profile: Publishes original contributions on all aspects of metallurgy and materials science, including mineral processing,hydrometallurgy, pyrometallurgy, materials processing, physical metallurgy and the service behaviour of materials.

Canadian Institute of Mortgage Brokers & Lenders / Institut canadien des courtiers et des prêteurs hypothécaires *See* Canadian Association of Accredited Mortgage Professionals

Canadian Institute of Planners (CIP) / Institut canadien des urbanistes (ICU)

#1112, 141 Laurier Ave. West, Ottawa ON K1P 5J3
Tel: 613-237-7526; *Fax:* 613-237-7045
Toll-Free: 800-207-2138
general@cip-icu.ca
www.cip-icu.ca
Overview: A medium-sized national organization founded in 1919
Mission: To advance professional planning excellence, through the delivery of membership & public services in Canada & abroad
Affiliation(s): Alberta Professional Planners Institute; Saskatchewan Professional Planners Institute; Atlantic Planners Institute; Manitoba Professional Planners Institute; Ontario Professional Planners Institute; Ordre des urbanistes du Québec; Planning Institute of British Columbia
Chief Officer(s):
Steven Brasier, CAE, Executive Director
sbrasier@cip-icu.ca
Finances: *Funding Sources:* Membership fees
Membership: 7,500; *Member Profile:* Professional community & regional planners employed in the private sector in the consulting & land development industries & in the public sector at all levels of government.
Activities: *Awareness Events:* World Town Planning Day, November; *Internships:* Yes; *Rents Mailing List:* Yes
Meetings/Conferences: • Canadian Institute of Planners 2015 Conference: Thrive, June, 2015, Saskatoon, SK
Scope: National
Description: Educational sessions & workshops for professional planners from across Canada
Contact Information: Phone: 613-237-7526; Fax: 613-237-7045; E-mail: conference@cip-icu.ca; URL: www.thrive2015fleurir.ca

Canadian Institute of Plumbing & Heating (CIPH) / Institut canadien de plomberie et de chauffage

#504, 295 The West Mall, Toronto ON M9C 4Z4
Tel: 416-695-0447; *Fax:* 416-695-0450
Toll-Free: 800-639-2474
info@ciph.com
www.ciph.com
www.facebook.com/pages/CIPH/355926634482039
twitter.com/ciphnews
Overview: A large national organization founded in 1933
Mission: To act as a unified voice for plumbing, heating, hydronic, PVF, & waterworks across Canada
Chief Officer(s):
Ralph Suppa, President & General Manager
r.suppa@ciph.com
Elizabeth McCullough, General Manager, Trade Shows
e.mccullough@ciph.com
Kevin Wong, Coordinator, Member Services
k.wong@ciph.com
Stephen Apps, Contact, Education & Training
s.apps@ciph.com
Ken Tomihiro, Contact, Hydronics, Codes, & Standards
k.tomihiro@ciph.com
Membership: *Member Profile:* Companies throughout Canada that manufacture, sell, & distribute plumbing, heating, hydronic, PVF, & waterworks products & services; *Committees:* Executive / Finance; Nominating; Membership; Government Affairs; Region Hydronics; Charity Committee for Habitat for Humanity Canada; Manufacturers' Agents; Wholesalers' Division; Manufacturers' Division; Education & Training Council; Plumbing Industry Advisory Council; Canadian Hydronics Council; Industrial Pipe, Valve, & Fittings Council
Activities: Liaising with governments & organizations; Influencing the development of standards & codes; Raising awareness of safety; Providing education; Offering networking opportunities to share best practices
Meetings/Conferences: • Canadian Institute of Plumbing & Heating 2015 Annual Business Conference/Annual General Meeting, June, 2015, Fairmont Chateau Frontenac, Québec, QC
Scope: National
• Canadian Institute of Plumbing & Heating 2016 Annual Business Conference/Annual General Meeting, June, 2016, Fairmont Banff Springs, Banff, AB
Scope: National
Publications:
• Advocacy Link [a publication of the Canadian Institute of Plumbing & Heating]
Type: Newsletter
Profile: A summary of information about the Canadian Institute of Plumbing & Heating. the Industrial Pipes, Valves, & Fittings Council, & theCanadian Hydronics Council, involving code & standards, public safety, & education
• Canadian Institute of Plumbing & Heating Member Directory
Type: Directory
Profile: Listing of members by head office, plus further information such as sales offices & contacts
• CIPH [Canadian Institute of Plumbing & Heating] EconoLink
Profile: Results from surveys
• CIPH [Canadian Institute of Plumbing & Heating] Wholesalers Sales Statistics
Frequency: Monthly; *Price:* $325
Profile: A summary of sales survey results in six regions by product groups
• Pipeline
Type: Newsletter; *Frequency:* 3-4 pa
Profile: Information about the hydronics, plumbing, & PVF industries, educational products, trade shows, & association activities for Canadian Institute of Plumbing & Heating members, industry stakeholders, &government

Atlantic Region
c/o Mike Lovegrove, Wolseley Canada, 1270 St. George Blvd., Monton NB E1E 3S1
Tel: 506-853-8020; *Fax:* 506-858-7186
Chief Officer(s):
Mike Lovegrove, Region President
mike.lovegrove@wolseleyinc.ca
Kathy Saunders, Region Coordinator, 902-497-1084, Fax: 902-443-6888
kathysaunders@bellaliant.net

British Columbia Region
c/o Kathryn Fallis, 15316 Sequoia Dr., Surrey BC V3S 8N4
Tel: 778-867-5956; *Fax:* 604-594-5091
ciphbc@shaw.ca
Chief Officer(s):
Randy Kolstad, President, 604-444-2000
randyk@barobinson.ca
Ed Chubb, Treasurer
ed.chubb@mphsupply.com
Kathryn Fallis, Region Coordinator, 778-867-5956, Fax: 604-594-5091
ciphbc@shaw.ca
• British Columbia Plumbline Newsletter
Type: Newsletter; *Editor:* Kathryn Fallis
Profile: Industry events, profiles, & a British Columbia members' forum

Calgary, Alberta Region
PO Box 4520, Stn. C, Calgary AB T2T 5N3
Tel: 403-244-4487; *Fax:* 403-244-2340
Chief Officer(s):
Mike Stringer, President, 403-256-4900, Fax: 403-256-1208
sales@stringersales.com
Connie Pruden, Region Coordinator, 403-244-4487, Fax: 403-244-2340
conniep@associationsplus.ca
• CIPH [Canadian Institute of Plumbing & Heating] Updater - Calgary Region
Type: Newsletter
Profile: Local upcoming events, training opportunities, & member news

Edmonton, Alberta, Region
c/o Linda Wood Edwards, PO Box 11021, Stn. Main, Edmonton AB T5J 3K3
Tel: 780-466-9938; *Fax:* 780-468-4449
Chief Officer(s):
Linda Wood Edwards, Region Coordinator
lue42@shaw.ca
Jason Sjolie, Region President
jason@bartlegibson.com
• Backflow
Type: Newsletter
Profile: Upcoming events, course information, & regional activities

Manitoba Region
c/o Lisa Carbonneau, PO Box 2737, Winnipeg MB R3C 4B3
Tel: 204-832-1512; *Fax:* 204-897-8094
Chief Officer(s):
Ryan Bristow, Region President, 204-772-4341, Fax: 204-772-4402
rbristow@equipcoltd.com
Lise Carbonneau, Region Coordinator
whirlwind@shaw.ca
• Overflow
Type: Newsletter; *Editor:* Alan Thompson (alatho@ipexinc.com)
Profile: Upcoming events, company profiles, & region activities

Newfoundland Region
c/o Sheri Slaney, 16 Argus Pl., St. John's NL A1A 5N2
Tel: 709-753-4222; *Fax:* 709-753-6641
ciph.nl@gmail.com
Chief Officer(s):
John Ozon, Region President, 709-753-1670
jozon@kerrcontrols.ca
Sheri Slaney, Region Coordinator, 709-753-4222

Ontario Region
c/o Nancy Barden, 5827 - 6th Line, RR#1, Hillsburgh ON N0B 1Z0
Tel: 519-855-6474; *Fax:* 519-855-1747
Chief Officer(s):
Jon Leeson, Region President, 416-213-1585 Ext. 144
jleeson@desco.ca
Nancy Barden, Region Coordinator
barden@sympatico.ca
• The Flow
Type: Newsletter
Profile: Information about upcoming events & profiles

Québec Region
c/o Claude Robitaille, #106, 4460, ch des Cageux, Montréal QC H7W 2S7
Tél: 514-989-1002; *Téléc:* 514-681-1941
Chief Officer(s):
Claude Robitaille, Region Coordinator
claude.robitaille@mtaplus.com
Gilles Legault, Region President, 450-655-9588, Fax: 450-641-2737
glegault@ajpsylvain.com
• The Good Tip
Type: Newsletter
Profile: Information about forthcoming events & industry news

Saskatchewan Region
c/o Nicole Ursu, Uponor Ltd., PO Box 6030, Regina SK S4N 5T6
Chief Officer(s):
Nicole Ursu, Region President, 306-591-1883
nicole.ursu@uponor.com
Lovella Jones, Region Coordinator
lovella.jones@b-creative.ca
• Connection [a publication of Canadian Institute of Plumbing & Heating, Saskatchewan Region]
Type: Newsletter
Profile: Upcoming events, educational opportunities, & regional news

Canadian Institute of Professional Home Inspectors Inc.

#720, 999 West Broadway, Vancouver BC V5Z 1K5
Tel: 604-732-0617
info@edwitzke.com
www.edwitzke.com
Previous Name: Canadian Society of Home Inspectors Inc.
Overview: A medium-sized national organization founded in 1965
Mission: To inspect all components of building for structural soundness, damage assessment, dry rot, pest problems, energy efficiency, compliance with grading, zoning, legal requirements & safety laws; to inspect all manner of the buildings, including new or existing residential or commercial buildings to determine the condition of a building, for contractors in recommending procedures for compliance with legal requirements, or for insurance companies in assessing damages & general public
Chief Officer(s):

Ed R.R. Witzke, President, 604-309-3812
Activities: *Speaker Service:* Yes

Canadian Institute of Public & Private Real Estate Companies *See* Real Property Association of Canada

Canadian Institute of Public Health Inspectors (CIPHI) / Institut Canadien des inspecteurs en santé publique (ICISP)

#720, 999 West Broadway Ave., Vancouver BC V5Z 1K5
Tel: 604-739-8180; *Fax:* 604-738-4080
Toll-Free: 888-245-8180
Other Communication: office@ciphi.ca
questions@ciphi.ca
www.ciphi.ca
Previous Name: Canadian Institute of Sanitary Inspectors
Overview: A medium-sized national licensing organization founded in 1934
Mission: To protect the health of all Canadians; To advance the environmental & health sciences; To enhance the field of public health inspection through certification, information, & advocacy
Affliation(s): National Environmental Health Association (NEHA)
Chief Officer(s):
Adam Grant, National President
president@ciphi.ca
Membership: 1,000-4,999; *Fees:* Schedule available; *Member Profile:* Canadian public health inspectors; Environmental health officers
Activities: Providing professional development opportunities; *Awareness Events:* Environmental Public Health Week (EPHW), January; *Speaker Service:* Yes
Meetings/Conferences: • Canadian Institute of Public Health Inspectors 2015 81st Annual Educational Conference, 2015
Scope: National
Description: Featuring the presentation of Institute awards
Publications:
• Canadian Institute of Public Health Inspectors National Newsletter
Type: Newsletter
• Environmental Health Review
Frequency: Quarterly; *Editor:* Domenic Losito; *Price:* Free for Canadian Institute of Public Health Inspectors members

Canadian Institute of Quantity Surveyors (CIQS)

#19, 90 Nolan Ct., Markham ON L3R 4L9
Tel: 905-477-0008; *Fax:* 905-477-6774
admin@ciqs.org
www.ciqs.org
www.linkedin.com/groups/Canadian-Institute-Quantity-Surveyors-4837923
www.facebook.com/112909992224092
twitter.com/CIQS_Official
Overview: A medium-sized national organization
Mission: To represent the quantity surveying & construction estimating profession in Canada
Chief Officer(s):
Lois Metcalfe, Executive Director
execdir@ciqs.org
Mark Gardin, Chair
president@ciqs.org
Staff Member(s): 2
Membership: *Member Profile:* Professional Quantity Surveyors, Associate Quantity Surveyors, Construction Estimator Certified (CEC), Associate Construction Estimator, and fulland part-time students.

Canadian Institute of Quantity Surveyors - Ontario

#19, 90 Nolan Ct., Markham ON L3R 4L9
Tel: 905-477-3222; *Fax:* 905-477-6774
info@ciqs-ontario.org
www.ciqs-ontario.org
Also Known As: CIQS - Ontario
Overview: A small provincial organization
Mission: To maintain high standards for the industry & help its members gain employment
Member of: Canadian Institute of Quantity Surveyors
Chief Officer(s):
Lois Metcalfe, Administrator
lois.metcalfe@ciqs-ontario.org

Canadian Institute of Realtors *See* Real Estate Institute of Canada

Canadian Institute of Resources Law (CIRL) / Institut canadien du droit des ressources

Murray Fraser Hall, University of Calgary, #3353, 2500 University Dr. NW, Calgary AB T2N 1N4
Tel: 403-220-3200; *Fax:* 403-282-6182
cirl@ucalgary.ca
www.cirl.ca
Overview: A small national charitable organization founded in 1979
Mission: To undertake and promote research, education and publication on the law relating to Canada's renewable and non-renewable natural resources.
Chief Officer(s):
Allan Ingelson, Executive Director, 403-220-3200
Clifford D. Johnson, Chair
Finances: *Funding Sources:* Public and Private Sectors; Non-Governmental Organizations
Staff Member(s): 9
Activities: Sponsoring conferences, workshops & courses on aspects of resources law; *Library* Open to public by appointment
Publications:
• Canada Energy Law Service
Profile: Looseleaf guide to the regulatory regimes administered by the National Energy Board & the Alberta Energy & Utilities Board
• CIRL [Canadian Institute of Resources Law] Annual Report
Type: Yearbook; *Frequency:* Annually
• Resources [a publication of the Canadian Institute of Resources Law]
Type: Newsletter; *Frequency:* Quarterly *ISSN:* 0714-5918; *Price:* Free
Profile: Commentary on matters of concern in natural resources law & policy, developments in resources case & statute law, & CIRL new publications,courses, & conferences

Canadian Institute of Sanitary Inspectors *See* Canadian Institute of Public Health Inspectors

Canadian Institute of Steel Construction (CISC) / Institut canadien de la construction en acier (ICCA)

#200, 3760 - 14th Ave., Markham ON L3R 3T7
Tel: 905-946-0864; *Fax:* 905-946-8574
info@cisc-icca.ca
www.cisc-icca.ca
www.linkedin.com/company/986081
www.facebook.com/cisc.icca.ca
twitter.com/cisc_icca
Overview: A medium-sized national organization founded in 1942
Mission: To promote good design & safety, together with efficient & economical use of steel as a means of expanding the construction markets for structural steel, joists & platework
Member of: Standards Council of Canada; Canadian Standards Association; Canadian Welding Bureau; Welding Institute of Canada; Canadian Steel Trade & Employment Congress; Canadian Construction Association; Construction Specifications Canada; Transportation Association of Canada
Affliation(s): Canadian Steel Construction Council; Steel Structures Education Foundation
Chief Officer(s):
Jim McLagan, Chair
Ed Whalen, President
ewhalen@cisc-icca.ca
Staff Member(s): 14
Membership: 885; *Fees:* Schedule available; *Member Profile:* Organizations & individuals involved in the steel construction industry
Activities: *Speaker Service:* Yes; *Library* by appointment

Canadian Institute of Stress (CIS)

Toronto ON
Tel: 416-236-4218
info@stresscanada.org
www.stresscanada.org
www.facebook.com/TheCanadianInstituteOfStress
Overview: A small national organization founded in 1979
Mission: To provide programs & tools for individuals & workplaces to handle stress
Activities: Providing certification training; Offering web-based distance education for professionals; *Speaker Service:* Yes

Canadian Institute of Surveying *See* Association of Canada Lands Surveyors

Canadian Institute of the Arts for Young Audiences *See* Vancouver International Children's Festival

Canadian Institute of Traffic & Transportation (CITT) / Institut canadien du trafic et du transport

#400, 10 King St. East, Toronto ON M5C 1C3
Tel: 416-363-5696; *Fax:* 416-363-5698
info@citt.ca
www.citt.ca
Overview: A medium-sized national organization founded in 1958
Mission: To promote high standards of professionalism among transportation logisticians
Chief Officer(s):
Catherine Viglas, President
cviglas@citt.ca
Chrissy Aitchison, Senior Manager, Marketing & Strategic Initiatives
caitchison@citt.ca
Jennifer Traer, Manager, Events & Member Operations
jtraer@citt.ca
Maria Murjani, Program Administrator
mmurjani@citt.ca
Sue MacMillan, Program Manager
smacmillan@citt.ca
Staff Member(s): 6
Membership: 2,000+; *Member Profile:* Members must complete course of study to hold the designation, CITT
Activities: Offers the CITT Diploma Program

Canadian Institute of Transportation Engineers (CITE)

PO Box PO Box 81009, Harbour Square PO, 89 Queens Quay West, Toronto ON M5J 2V3
Tel: 202-785-0060; *Fax:* 202-785-0609
www.cite7.org
Overview: A large international organization overseen by Institute of Transportation Engineers
Mission: To facilitate the application of technology & scientific principles for modes of ground transportation
Chief Officer(s):
Peter Truch, President
president@cite7.org
Membership: 2,000+; *Member Profile:* Transportation engineers, planners, technologists and students across Canada.
Activities: Promoting professional development; Supporting education; Encouraging research; Increasing public awareness; Exchanging professional information
Meetings/Conferences: • Canadian Institute of Transportation Engineers / Ontario Traffic Council 2015 Conference, June, 2015, Regina, SK
Scope: National
Attendance: 150-350

Canadian Institute of Treated Wood *See* Wood Preservation Canada

Canadian Institute of Ukrainian Studies (CIUS) / Institut canadien d'études ukrainiennes

#4-30, Pembina Hall, University of Alberta, Edmonton AB T6G 2H8
Tel: 780-492-2972; *Fax:* 780-492-4967
cius@ualberta.ca
www.cius.ca
www.facebook.com/canadian.institute.of.ukrainian.studies
Overview: A small national organization founded in 1976
Mission: To develop Ukrainian scholarship in Canada; To organize research in Ukrainian & Ukrainian-Canadian studies
Chief Officer(s):
Volodymyr Kravchenko, Director
cius.director@ualberta.ca
Finances: *Funding Sources:* University of Alberta operating budget; Grants for projects; Income from endoment funds; Donations
Staff Member(s): 10
Activities: Directing the Kowalsky Program for the Study of Eastern Ukraine; Coordinating the Kule Ukrainian Canadian Studies Centre; Operating the Peter Jacyk Centre for Ukrainian Historical Research; Directing the Stasiuk Program for the Study of Contemporary Ukraine; Operating the Ukrainian Language Education Centre (E-mail: ulec@ualberta.ca); Managing the Ukrainian Knowledge Internet Portal Project Office (E-mail: ukip@ualberta.ca); Supporting Ukrainian studies internationally; Organizing lectures & a seminar series
Publications:
• CIUS [Canadian Institute of Ukrainian Studies] Newsletter
Type: Newsletter; *Editor:* B. Klid, M. Soroka, & M. Yurkevich
ISSN: 1485-7979
Profile: Information about the institute's endowment funds,

grants, awards, seminars & lectures, new publications, & researchprograms
• Journal of Ukrainian Studies
Type: Journal; *Frequency:* Semiannually
Profile: Scholarly journal about Ukrainian & Ukrainian-Canadian studies, featuring articles, reviews, literary translations, & guides to research

Toronto Office
University of Toronto, #308, 256 McCaul St., Toronto ON M5T 1W5
Tel: 416-978-6934; *Fax:* 416-978-2672
Chief Officer(s):
Frank E. Sysyn, Director
f.sysyn@utoronto.ca
Roman Senkus, Senior Editor, CIUS, 416-978-8669
r.senkus@utoronto.ca

• Internet Encyclopedia of Ukraine
Type: Encyclopedia; *Editor:* Roman Senkus (r.senkus@utoronto.ca)
Profile: A comprehensive work in English on Ukrainian history, geography, people, culture, & economy

Canadian Institute of Underwriters (CIU)

c/o Marian Kingsmill, DKCI Events (David Kingsmill Consultants Inc.), PO Box 91516, Stn. Roseland Plaza, 3023 New St., Burlington ON L7R 4L6
www.ciu.ca
Overview: A medium-sized national organization
Chief Officer(s):
Merv Gillson, Chair
merv.gillson@logiq3.com
Linda Wisleski, Treasurer
linda_wislesky@swissre.com
Russell Shaw, Incoming Treasurer
russell.shaw@rbc.com
Finances: *Funding Sources:* Sponsorships
Membership: *Fees:* $110; *Member Profile:* Members have attained their Fellow of the Academy of Life Underwriting & possess a minimum of five years experience in life & health underwriting; Associate members have attained their Associate of Academy of Life Underwriting & possess a minimum of two years experience of life & health underwriting
Activities: Facilitating the exchange of ideas on issues that affect the insurance industry; Providing educational opportunities
Meetings/Conferences: • Canadian Institute of Underwriters Annual General Meeting 2015, June, 2015, Marriott Toronto Downtown, Toronto, ON
Scope: National

Canadian Institutional Research & Planning Association (CIRPA) / Association canadienne de planification et de recherche institutionnelles (ACPRI)

c/o Concordia University, 1455 De Maisonneuve Blvd. West, Montréal QC H3G 1M8
Tel: 514-848-2424
www.cirpa-acpri.ca
www.linkedin.com/groups/CIRPA-ACPRI-Canadian-Institutional-Research-40
Previous Name: Canadian Institutional Researchers & Planners Association
Overview: A small national organization founded in 1994
Mission: To promote the professional interests of its members; to advance research on post-secondary education in general & to encourage studies of the operation of post-secondary institutions in particular; to promote good practice in institutional policy-making, management, planning & research; to encourage a closer cooperation between researchers on post-secondary education & institutional researchers, planners, managers & policy-makers; to encourage comparative studies of post-secondary systems
Affliation(s): Association of Institutional Research; European Air
Chief Officer(s):
Sharon Schultz, President
Membership: 230; *Fees:* $100; $50 student; *Committees:* Nominations

Canadian Institutional Researchers & Planners Association
See Canadian Institutional Research & Planning Association

Canadian Insurance Accountants Association (CIAA) / Association canadienne des comptables en assurance

c/o Taylor Enterprises Ltd., #310, 2175 Sheppard Ave. East, Toronto ON M2J 1W8
Tel: 416-971-7800; *Fax:* 416-491-1670
ciaa@ciaa.org
www.ciaa.org
Overview: A medium-sized national organization founded in 1934
Mission: To promote study, research, & development of management & insurance accounting
Chief Officer(s):
Catherine Fleming, Executive Assistant
Membership: 500-999; *Fees:* $100; *Member Profile:* Active members are employed by an insurance / reinsurance company, insurance / reinsurance broker, or an insurance agency; Associate members are involved in the supply of specialized knowledge or services to the insurance industry
Activities: Providing a professional development program, including courses, seminars, speakers, & conferences; Facilitating networking opportunities within the industry; *Speaker Service:* Yes
Meetings/Conferences: • Canadian Insurance Accountants Association 2015 51st Annual Conference, September, 2015, San Francisco, CA
Scope: National
Description: CIAA members, speakers, presenters, & exhibitors from across Canada
Publications:
• Canadian Insurance Accountants Association Membership Directory
Type: Directory; *Frequency:* Annually
Profile: Listings of CIAA members with their contact information

Canadian Insurance Claims Managers Association (CICMA)

c/o Insurance Bureau of Canada, PO Box 121, #2400, 777 Bay St., Toronto ON M5G 2C8
Tel: 416-362-2031; *Fax:* 416-361-5952
www.cicma.ca
Overview: A small national organization founded in 1952
Mission: To maintain a high standard of ethics among those who handle general insurance claims; To promote the general insurance industry in matters related to the settlement of claims; To advance administration to result in just settlement of claims
Chief Officer(s):
Lynn Prescott, President
lynn.prescott@assistplus.ca
Patrick O'Hara, Vice-President
pohara@millenniuminsurance.ca
Alex Lethbridge, Treasurer
alethbridge@insurancecorp.ca
Membership: *Member Profile:* Active members include officers of a general insurance company who are engaged in the administration of claims, & employees of general insurance companies whose responsibility involves the management of employees who administer claims; Life members have an established record of outstanding service in the association; Honorary members are senior officers of an association, government department, or administrative body; Associate members are persons who were previously active members in good standing; *Committees:* Arbitration; Communication; Constitution; Education; IBC Liaison; Membership/Association Enhancement; Treasurer; Website
Activities: Administering the Canadian Inter-Company Arbitration Agreement; Facilitating information exchange; Promoting mediation or arbitration to resolve claims
Publications:
• Insight
Type: Newsletter
Profile: Information on chapters & members; articles on topics relevant to members

Canadian Intergovernmental Conference Secretariat (CICS) / Secrétariat des conférences intergouvernementales canadiennes

PO Box 488, Stn. A, 222 Queen St., 10th Fl., Ottawa ON K1P 5V9
Tel: 613-995-2341; *Fax:* 613-996-6091
info@scics.gc.ca
www.scics.gc.ca
Mission: CICS was established in 1973 by the First Ministers as an agency of the federal & provincial governments. Governments recognized a need for a mechanism to serve on a continuing basis conferences of First Ministers & a growing number of intergovernmental meetings. CICS serves federal-provincial First Ministers' meetings, the Annual Premiers' Conference, the Eastern Canadian Premiers' & New England Governors' Conference & the Western Premiers' Conference. The core of the Secretariat's work is providing services to multilateral meetings of Ministers & Deputy Ministers in virtually every sector of government activity. The Secretariat's services are available to federal, provincial & territorial departments that are called upon to organize & chair such meetings. The agency's mandate & sole program are designed to relieve its clients of the numerous & various technical & administrative tasks associated with the planning & conduct of senior level intergovernmental conferences. The CICS maintains through its Information Services section, a document archives for the use of governments & the general public. Containing over 25,000 conference-related documents spanning every sector of conference activity, this collection is unique. The information contained in the archives is made available, as appropriate, to government institutions at the federal, provincial & territorial levels while unclassified material is also available to the public on request.
Chief Officer(s):
André McArdle, Secretary, 613-995-2345
Louise Seaward-Gagnon, Director, 613-995-4328
Louise.Seaward-Gagnon@scics.gc.ca

Canadian International Air Show (CIAS)

Press Bldg., Exhibition Place, 210 Princes' Blvd., 2nd Fl., Toronto ON M6K 3C3
Tel: 416-263-3650; *Fax:* 416-263-3654
info@cias.org
cias.org
www.facebook.com/torontoairshow
twitter.com/TorontoAirshow
Also Known As: Canadian Exhibition Airshows Inc.
Overview: A medium-sized local organization founded in 1949
Mission: To entertain the Toronto community with world-class air shows; to provide customized opportunities for our corporate partners; to support community groups through involvement in fund-raising & outreach programs
Member of: International Council of Air Shows; NorthEast Council of Airshows; Etobicoke Chamber of Commerce
Finances: *Funding Sources:* Metropolitan Toronto; independent sponsorship

Canadian International Council (CIC) / Conseil international du Canada

#210, 45 Willcocks St., Toronto ON M5S 1C7
Tel: 416-946-7209; *Fax:* 416-946-7319
Other Communication: technical@opencanada.org (technical issues)
info@opencanada.org
www.opencanada.org
www.facebook.com/CanadianInternationalCouncil
twitter.com/TheCIC
www.youtube.com/user/onlinecicvideos
Previous Name: Canadian Institute of International Affairs / Institut canadien des affaires internationales
Overview: A medium-sized international charitable organization founded in 1928
Mission: To strengthen Canada's role in international affairs; To advance research & dialogue on international affairs
Chief Officer(s):
Jennifer Jeffs, President, 416-946-7209
Laura Sunderland, Vice-President, Programs, 416-946-7071
lsunderland@opencanada.org
Deborah Shields, Director, Operations, 416-946-7273
dshields@opencanada.org
Kathryn McBride, Administrator, Office, 416-946-7209
kmcbride@opencanada.org
Finances: *Funding Sources:* Private supporters
Membership: *Fees:* $75 regular members; $35 students; *Member Profile:* Individuals & organizations interested in international affairs
Activities: Conducting policy research; Offering a fellowship program; Presenting seminars, discussions, & study groups
Awards:
• Globalist of the Year Award (Award)
Publications:
• Behind the Headlines [a publication of the Canadian International Council]
Editor: Robert Johnstone; *Price:* Free for CIC members
Profile: Articles on international issues, with an emphasis on their implications for Canada
• Foreign Policy for Canada's Tomorrow
Profile: Preliminary papers to outline critical issues which have not yet been peer reviewed
• International Insights
Profile: Canada's role in international security issues

• International Journal
Type: Journal; *Editor:* Rima Berns-McGown
Profile: Scholarly articles on international relations
• Strategic Datalink [a publication of the Canadian International Council]
Profile: Analytical paper on a timely, policy-relevant international security issue

Canadian International Dragon Boat Festival Society (CIDBFS)

Creekside Community Centre, 1 Athletes Way, Vancouver BC V5Y 0B1
Tel: 604-688-2382; *Fax:* 866-571-9004
info@dragonboatbc.ca
dragonboatbc.ca
www.facebook.com/thedragonboatbc
twitter.com/dragonboatbc
Also Known As: Rio Tinto Alcan Dragon Boat Festival
Previous Name: Dragon Boat Festival Society
Overview: A small national organization founded in 1989
Mission: To foster learning & exploration of Canada's diverse multicultural heritage through performing, visual & culinary arts, & dragon boat-racing
Member of: Vancouver Cultural Alliance
Chief Officer(s):
Ann Phelps, General Manager
Finances: *Funding Sources:* Government; corporate; donations; fund-raising
Staff Member(s): 12; 1000 volunteer(s)
Activities: Annual 3 day multicultural festival; year long education program on multiculturalism; *Speaker Service:* Yes

Canadian International DX Club (CIDX)

PO Box 67063, Stn. Lemoyne, St. Lambert QC J4R 2T8
e-mail: cidxclub@yahoo.com
www.anarc.org/cidx
Overview: A small international organization founded in 1962
Mission: To serve radio enthusiasts throughout the world
Member of: Association of North American Radio Clubs
Finances: *Funding Sources:* Membership fees
Membership: *Fees:* $10 members for outside Canada or the U.S.A.; $15 Canadian & U.S.A. members; *Member Profile:* Members of the radio monitoring community from around the world
Activities: Providing education about radio; Promoting the radio hobby
Publications:
• Messenger
Type: Newsletter; *Frequency:* Monthly; *Price:* Free with membership in the Canadian International DX Club
Profile: Information on all aspects of radio, such as AM, FM, shortwave, pirate broadcasting, & Internet & satellite radio

Canadian International Freight Forwarders Association, Inc. (CIFFA) / Association des transitaires internationaux canadiens, inc. (ATIC)

#480, 170 Attwell Dr., Toronto ON M9W 5Z5
Tel: 416-234-5100; *Fax:* 416-234-5152
Toll-Free: 866-282-4332
Other Communication: Policies & Procedures e-mail:
admin@ciffa.com
secretariat@ciffa.com
www.ciffa.com
Overview: A large international organization founded in 1948
Mission: To represent & support members of the Canadian international freight forwarding industry in providing the highest level of quality & professional services to their clients
Member of: Federation internationale des associations de transitaires et assimiles
Affliation(s): International Federation of Freight Forwarders Associations
Chief Officer(s):
Jeff Cullen, President
jeff.cullen@dhl.com
Gary Vince, First Vice-President
gary.vince@jas.com
Dwayne Hihn, Second Vice-President
dhihn@manitoulingroup.com
H. Ruth Snowden, Executive Director
ruths@ciffa.com
Bruce Rodgers, Treasurer
bruceprodgers@gmail.com
Paul Lobas, Secretary
paull@itn-logistics.com
Finances: *Annual Operating Budget:* $500,000-$1.5 Million; *Funding Sources:* Membership dues; education fees
Staff Member(s): 5; 20 volunteer(s)
Membership: 188 regular + 94 associate; *Fees:* Schedule available; *Committees:* Airfreight; By Laws; Customs; Education; Ethics & Standards; FIATA; Finance; Judicial; Membership; Seafreight; Security
Activities: CIFFA Professional Training Program; education courses; dangerous goods courses, topical workshops
Awards:
• CIFFA Scholarship (Scholarship)
To provide the children of CIFFA Regular Members with funds, so that they may pursue higher education at an accredited Canadian college or university *Amount:* $3,000
Publications:
• The Forwarder [a publication of Canadian International Freight Forwarders Association, Inc.]
Type: Magazine; *Accepts Advertising*

Central Division
PO Box 159, Stn. Toronto AMF, Mississauga ON L5P 1B1
Tel: 905-362-6000
Chief Officer(s):
Jodie Wilson, Chair
jodie.wilson@lcnav.com

Eastern Division
c/o Milgram International Shipping, #400, 645 Wellington St., Montréal QC H3C 0L1
Tel: 514-288-2358
Chief Officer(s):
Angelo Loffredi, Chair
aloffredi@milgram.com%20

Western Division
c/o Courtney Agencies Ltd., #802, 535 Thurlow St., Vancouver BC V6E 3L2
Tel: 604-684-7505
Chief Officer(s):
Paul Courtney, Chair
paul@courtney.ca

Canadian International Grains Institute

#1000, 303 Main St., Winnipeg MB R3C 3G7
Tel: 204-983-5344; *Fax:* 204-983-2642
cigi@cigi.ca
www.cigi.ca
www.facebook.com/278582516605
twitter.com/CigiWinnipeg
www.youtube.com/user/CIGIwinnipeg
Overview: A medium-sized international organization founded in 1972
Mission: To provide educational programs & technical activities in support of market development & promotion of world markets for Canada's grains, oilseeds & special crops
Chief Officer(s):
Earl Geddes, Chief Executive Officer
egeddes@cigi.ca
Heather Johnson, Director, Communications & Branding, 204-983-7678
hjohnson@cigi.ca
Finances: *Funding Sources:* Canadian Wheat Board; International Markets Bureau of Agriculture; Agri-Food Canada
Staff Member(s): 35
Activities: Provides an average of 35 programs annually

Canadian International Institute of Applied Negotiation (CIIAN) / L'Institut international canadien de la négociation pratique

68B Raddarz Rd., RR#2, Eganville ON K0J 1T0
Tel: 613-237-9050
ciian@ciian.org
www.ciian.org
www.facebook.com/145938635447384
twitter.com/CIIAN
Overview: A small international organization founded in 1992
Mission: To build sustainable peace at local, national, & international levels
Chief Officer(s):
Benjamin Hoffman, President
Evan Hoffman, Executive Director
ehoffman@ciian.org
Activities: Offering conflict prevention, dispute resolution, & peacebuilding programming, such as the Domestic Program, the International Program, the Violence Prevention Early Response Unit, & Special Programs; Providing courses & workshops, including a Certificate Program in Peacebuilding & Conflict Resolution; Conferring the professional designation of Registered Practitioner in Dispute Resolution (RPDR); Developing resources such as research papers, manuals, & videos; *Speaker Service:* Yes
Publications:
• CIIAN [Canadian International Institute of Applied Negotiation] News
Type: Newsletter; *Accepts Advertising*
Profile: Information about Canadian International Institute of Applied Negotiation projects, such as clinics & courses, scholarships, & forthcomingpublications
• The Mediator's Handbook for Durable Peace
Type: Handbook; *Author:* Evan Hoffman
Profile: The presentation of an original model of durable peace, plus practical tactics
• New Math for Human Relations
Type: Handbook; *Author:* Dr. Benjamin Hoffman; *Price:* $10
• The Peace Guerilla Handbook
Type: Handbook; *Author:* Dr. Benjamin Hoffman; *Price:* $11
Profile: Information for persons who must prevent violence or build peace

Canadian Internet Registration Authority (CIRA)

#306, 350 Sparks St., Ottawa ON K1R 7S8
Tel: 613-237-5335; *Fax:* 800-285-0517
www.cira.ca
www.linkedin.com/groups?gid=2456714
www.facebook.com/cira.ca
twitter.com/ciranews
www.youtube.com/ciranews
Overview: A small national organization founded in 1987
Mission: To operate the dot-ca internet country code.
Chief Officer(s):
Byron Holland, President & CEO
Staff Member(s): 6
Membership: *Member Profile:* Individuals who own a .ca domain name

Canadian Interoperability Technology Interest Group (CITIG)

c/o Canadian Association of Chiefs of Police, #100, 300 Terry Fox Dr., Kanata ON K2K 0E3
Tel: 613-595-1101
www.citig.ca
Overview: A medium-sized national organization founded in 2007
Mission: To improve communications interoperability in the field of Canadian public safety
Affliation(s): Canadian Association of Chiefs of Police (CACP); Canadian Association of Fire Chiefs (CAFC); Paramedic Chiefs of Canada (PCC)
Chief Officer(s):
Lance Valcour, O.O.M., Executive Director
Membership: 1,250; *Fees:* Free; *Member Profile:* First responders; members of government, non-governmental organizations, associations, academia & industry

Canadian Interuniversity Athletic Union *See* Canadian Interuniversity Sport

Canadian Interuniversity Sport (CIS) / Sport interuniversitaire canadien (SIC)

#N205, 801 King Edward, Ottawa ON K1N 6N5
Tel: 613-562-5670; *Fax:* 613-562-5669
feedback@universitysport.ca
www.cis-sic.ca
www.facebook.com/cissports
twitter.com/CIS_SIC
www.youtube.com/universitysport
Previous Name: Canadian Interuniversity Athletic Union
Overview: A medium-sized national organization overseen by Association of Universities & Colleges of Canada
Mission: To act as the national governing body for men's & women's university sport in Canada
Affliation(s): Atlantic University Sport; Québec Student Sport Federation; Ontario University Athletics; Canada West Universities Athletic Association
Chief Officer(s):
Pierre Lafontaine, CEO, 613-568-5670 Ext. 26
plafontaine@universitysport.ca
Staff Member(s): 9
Membership: 55 institutional (these are also members of four regional associations);

Canadian Intravenous Nurses Association *See* Canadian Vascular Access Association

Canadian Investor Protection Fund (CIPF) / Fonds canadien de protection des épargnants (FCPE)

First Canadian Place, PO Box 481, #2610, 100 King St. West, Toronto ON M5X 1E5
Tel: 416-866-8366; *Fax:* 416-360-8441
Toll-Free: 866-243-6981
info@cipf.ca
www.cipf.ca
Previous Name: National Contingency Fund
Overview: A medium-sized national organization founded in 1969
Mission: To foster a healthy & active capital market in Canada by contributing to the security & confidence of investors who have accounts with members of sponsoring self-regulatory organizations
Chief Officer(s):
Rozanne E. Reszel, President & Chief Executive Officer
Barbara Love, Senior Vice-President & Secretary
Linda Pendrill, Chief Financial Officer
Ilana Singer, Vice-President
Tammy Smith, Director, Risk Assessment
Donna Yiu, Director, Industry Policy & Risk
Membership: 100-499; *Member Profile:* Investment dealers who are members of our sponsoring self-regulatory organizations; *Committees:* Audit, Finance & Investment; Governance, Nominating & Human Resources; Coverage; Industry Risk

Canadian Investor Relations Institute (CIRI) / Institut canadien de relations avec les investisseurs

#601, 67 Yonge St., Toronto ON M5E 1J8
Tel: 416-364-8200; *Fax:* 416-364-2805
enquiries@ciri.org
www.ciri.org
Previous Name: National Investor Relations Institute Canada (NIRI Canada)
Overview: A medium-sized national organization founded in 1990
Mission: To advance the practice of investor relations; To raise the stature of the profession in Canada; To act as the voice of investor relations professionals throughout Canada
Chief Officer(s):
Yvette Lokker, President & Chief Executive Officer, 416-364-8200 Ext. 224
ylokker@ciri.org
Salisha Hosein, Director, Professional Development & Communications, 416-364-8200 Ext. 228
shosein@ciri.org
Kaitlin Beca, Coordinator, Programming, 416-364-8200 Ext. 221
kbeca@ciri.org
Karen Clutsam, Coordinator, Membership, 416-364-8200 Ext. 229
kclutsam@ciri.org
Jane Maciel, Executive Assistant & Specialist, Publications, 416-364-8200 Ext. 222
jmaciel@ciri.org
Finances: *Funding Sources:* Corporate donations
Membership: 600+; *Member Profile:* Executives who are responsible for communications between public corporations, the financial community, & investors, such as IR practitioners, IR consultants, & IR vendors; *Committees:* Audit; Certification Curriculum; Certification Governance; Corporate Donation Program; Editorial Board; Human Resources, Compensation & Corporate Governance; Issues; Membership; Resource & Education
Activities: Advancing the professional competency of members through professional development sessions; Engaging in advocacy activities; Encouraging research;
Meetings/Conferences: • Canadian Investor Relations Institute 28th Annual Conference, May, 2015, Fairmont Banff Springs, Banff, AB
Scope: National
Publications:
• CIRI [Canadian Investor Relations Institute] Newsline
Type: Newsletter; *Frequency:* Bimonthly; *Accepts Advertising*; *Price:* Free for Canadian Investor Relations Institute members
Profile: In-depth information about regulatory & accounting issues, capital markets, & IR practices, for members
• CIRI [Canadian Investor Relations Institute] wIRed
Type: Newsletter; *Frequency:* Weekly
Profile: Institute activities, job listings, & professional development events, for persons involved in the investor relations field
• CIRI [Canadian Investor Relations Institute] Membership Directory
Type: Directory
Profile: Listings of the Institute's members & their contact information
• A Guide to Developing an IR Program [a publication of the Canadian Investor Relations Institute]
• Investor Relations Compensation & Responsibilities Survey
• IR Focus [a publication of the Canadian Investor Relations Institute]
Frequency: Bimonthly; *Price:* Free for Canadian Investor Relations Institute members
Profile: Distributed with Newsline, the publication addresses a single professional challenge
• Issues Bulletin [a publication of the Canadian Investor Relations Institute]
Price: Free for Canadian Investor RelationsInstitute members
Profile: A production of the CIRI Issues Committee to update members on current developments affecting investor relations
• Standards & Guidance for Disclosure [a publication of the Canadian Investor Relations Institute]
Price: Free for Canadian Investor Relations Institute members
Profile: Featuring a Model Disclosure Policy template

Canadian Iris Society (CIS)

c/o Ed Jowett, 1960 Sideroad 15, RR#2, Tottenham ON L0G 1W0
Tel: 905-936-9941
cdniris@gmail.com
www.cdn-iris.ca
Overview: A small national organization founded in 1946
Mission: To encourage, improve & extend the cultivation of the Iris & to collaborate with other societies for this purpose, as well as to regulate the nomenclature & colour classification of this flower.
Chief Officer(s):
Ed Jowett, President
jowettfarm@copper.net
Nancy Kennedy, Secretary
xkennedy@sympatico.ca
Finances: *Funding Sources:* Membership dues; iris auctions
Membership: *Fees:* $20 1 year; $50 3 years; *Member Profile:* Amateur gardeners; gardening experts; horticulturists
Activities: June Iris Shows: Royal Botanical Gardens, Hamilton; Iris sales & auctions; *Awareness Events:* June Iris Shows

Canadian ISBN Agency (ISBN) / Agence canadienne de l'ISBN

Library & Archives Canada, 395 Wellington St., Ottawa ON K1A 0N4
Tel: 819-994-6872; *Fax:* 819-977-7517
Toll-Free: 866-578-7777
isbn@lac-bac.gc.ca
www.collectionscanada.gc.ca/isn/041011-1000-e.html
Also Known As: Canadian International Standard Book Number Agency
Overview: A small national organization founded in 1974
Member of: Library & Archives Canada
Affliation(s): International ISBN Agency
Activities: Assigns ISBNs for Canadian book publishers

Canadian IT Law Association / Association canadienne du droit des technologies de l'information

c/o Lisa Ptack, PO Box 918, 1 Promenade Circle, Thornhill ON L4J 8G7
www.it-can.ca
Also Known As: IT Can
Overview: A medium-sized national organization founded in 1997
Mission: To develop & encourage the use of technology law in Canada
Chief Officer(s):
Simon Hodgett, President, Executive Commitee
shodgett@osler.com
Lisa Ptack, Executive Director
lisa.ptack@rogers.com
Membership: *Fees:* Schedule available

Canadian Italian Business & Professional Association (CIBPA) / Association des gens d'affaires & professionnels italo-canadiens

#310, 8370, boul Lacordaire, Montréal QC H1R 3Y6
Tel: 514-254-4929; *Fax:* 514-254-4920
info@cibpamontreal.com
www.cibpamontreal.com
www.facebook.com/cibpa.montreal
twitter.com/CIBPAMONTREAL
Overview: A medium-sized international organization founded in 1949
Mission: To encourage high ethical standards & professional development; To voice concerns in order to protect the interests of members
Chief Officer(s):
Giovanni Chieffallo, President
Carole Gagliardi, Vice-President, Communications
Mike Goriani, Vice-President, Events
Roberto Rinaldi, Vice-President, Membership
Sam Spatari, Vice-President, Finance
Luisa Papa, Administrative Secretary
Membership: 400+; *Member Profile:* Business people & professionals of Italian origin or descent
Activities: Fostering trade & business dealings between members; Providing a bursary program

Canadian Italian Business & Professional Association of Ottawa (CIBPA)

1026 Baseline Rd., Ottawa ON K2C 0A6
e-mail: info@cibpaottawa.com
www.cibpa-ottawa.com
Overview: A small local organization founded in 1961
Mission: CIBPA promotes the recreational, cultural, social, artistic, charitable, business and professional activities of Italian Canadians in the National Capital Region and also encourages the participation of Italian Canadians in the economic and public affairs of this region and Canada.
Chief Officer(s):
Gino Milito, President
Membership: 1-99; *Fees:* $95 regular; $25 student
Awards:
• CIBPA Ottawa Scholarship Awards (Scholarship)

Canadian Italian Heritage Foundation (CIHF)

11 Director Ct., Woodbridge ON L4L 4S5
Tel: 905-850-4500; *Fax:* 905-850-4516
Overview: A medium-sized national charitable organization
Mission: To work with the Italian Canadian community to undertake projects in collaboration with other existing organizations that support & promote Italian heritage & culture through activities within Canada
Chief Officer(s):
Michael Tibollo, President
Awards:
• Canadian Italian Heritage Foundation Scholarship Award (Scholarship)
Eligibility: Must be between 16 and 28; must have one parent that is of Canadian-Italian descent
Meetings/Conferences: • Canadian Italian Heritage Foundation Renaissance Gala, 2015
Scope: National

Canadian Jesuits International (CJI)

70 Saint Mary St., Toronto ON M5S 1J3
Tel: 416-465-1824
Toll-Free: 800-448-2148
cji@jesuits.ca
www.canadianjesuitsinternational.ca
www.facebook.com/canadianjesuitsinternational
Also Known As: Canadian Jesuit Missions
Overview: A medium-sized national charitable organization founded in 1955
Mission: Committed to the service of faith & the promotion of justice for the poor of the world; especially dedicated to the educational needs of women, children, elderly & indigenous people at home & abroad
Chief Officer(s):
Jenny Cafiso, Director
Staff Member(s): 6
Activities: Support projects in Africa, India, Nepal, Jamaica, & Ukraine
Publications:
• Mission News
Type: Newsletter; *Frequency:* 3 pa
Profile: News & stories about people in developing countries

Canadian Jewellers Association (CJA)

#600, 27 Queen St. East, Toronto ON M5C 2M6
Tel: 416-368-7616; *Fax:* 416-368-1986
Toll-Free: 800-580-0942
www.canadianjewellers.com
Overview: A medium-sized national organization founded in 1923
Mission: To provide its members with information, services & techonology that allow them to flourish in their profession
Member of: The World Jewellery Confederation
Chief Officer(s):
David Ritter, President & CEO

Finances: *Funding Sources:* Trade show; membership dues
Membership: 1,090; *Fees:* Schedule available; *Member Profile:* Retailers; manufacturers; wholesalers; supply sector; *Committees:* Accredited Appraiser Program; Charity; Diamonds/Colored Stones; Ethics; Investment/Audit; Government Relations; Marketing/Public Relations; Membership Benefits; Membership Review; Insurance; Watch/Supply; Executive; Young Professional Networking
Activities: Benefits; series of industry-related courses of study; *Rents Mailing List:* Yes; *Library:* Tiffany/Gerstein Library;

Canadian Jewish Congress *See* The Centre for Israel & Jewish Affairs

Canadian Jiu-jitsu Council
PO Box 543, Madoc ON K0K 2K0
Tel: 613-473-4366
www.jiujitsucouncil.ca
Overview: A medium-sized national organization founded in 1968
Mission: A non-profit educational Martial Arts organization under the Canadian Province of Ontario Charter. The CJC is administered by a volunteer group of senior Black Belts whose objective is to guide and assist the growth of Jiujitsu in a friendly, healthy environment and to help more people get more benefits, knowledge and pleasure from the Martial Art and Science of Jiujitsu.
Chief Officer(s):
Robert Walthers, President
rwalther@kos.net
Membership: *Fees:* $40 club; $40 black belts; $25 senior students; $10 junior students

Canadian Journalism Foundation (CJF) / La Fondation pour le journalisme canadien
#500, 59 Adelaide St. East, Toronto ON M5C 1K6
Tel: 416-955-0394; *Fax:* 416-532-6879
www.cjf-fjc.ca
www.facebook.com/cjfprograms
twitter.com/cjffjc
Overview: A medium-sized national charitable organization founded in 1990
Mission: To honour outstanding achievements in the field of journalism in Canada through grants, awards & scholarships; to promote & support programs & seminars at or in conjunction with qualified educational institutions in journalism.
Chief Officer(s):
Natalie Turvey, Executive Director
nturvey@cjf-fjc.ca
Wendy Kan, Program Manager
wkan@cjf-fjc.ca
Finances: *Annual Operating Budget:* $250,000-$500,000; *Funding Sources:* Media and non-media corporations and foundations; membership dues.
Staff Member(s): 3
Activities: *Internships:* Yes

Canadian Journalists for Free Expression (CJFE) / Journalistes canadiens pour la liberté d'expression
PO Box 407, #1101, 555 Richmond St. West, Toronto ON M5V 3B1
Tel: 416-515-9622; *Fax:* 416-515-7879
cjfe@cjfe.org
www.cjfe.org
www.facebook.com/167459509971053
twitter.com/canadacjfe
Previous Name: The Canadian Committee to Protect Journalists
Overview: A medium-sized national charitable organization founded in 1982
Mission: To promote freedom of expression
Member of: International Freedom of Expression Exchange (IFEX)
Chief Officer(s):
Tom Henheffer, Executive Director
Arnold Amber, President
Finances: *Funding Sources:* Membership fees; donations; foundation grants
Staff Member(s): 12; 2 volunteer(s)
Membership: 300+; *Fees:* $25; *Member Profile:* Journalists; writers; producers; editors; publishers & others interested; *Committees:* Journalists in Exile
Activities: IFEX Clearing House operates an Action Alert Network & disseminates information on freedom of the press to organizations & individuals around the world; operates a Journalists in Distress Fund; training programs for journalists living in the developing world; *Awareness Events:* Word On The Street; World Press Freedom Day, May 3
Awards:
- Canadian International Press Freedom Awards (Award)

Canadian Junior Chamber *See* Junior Chamber International Canada

Canadian Junior Football League (CJFL)
www.cjfl.net
www.facebook.com/166507583399023
twitter.com/cjflnews
Overview: A large national organization founded in 1908
Mission: To foster community involvement & a positive environment; to teach discipline, perseverance & cooperation
Member of: Football Canada
Chief Officer(s):
Jim Pankovich, Commissioner
Frank Naso, Deputy Commissioner
Paul Shortt, Executive Director
Ryan Watters, Director, Communications & Digital Media
ryan@onairenterprises.com
Membership: 20 teams; *Member Profile:* Young men aged 17-22
Activities: Canadian Bowl (National championship)
Awards:
- Stewart MacDonald Executive of the Year (Award)
- Life Membership (Award)
- Ed Henick Meritorious Service (Award)
- Past Commissioners Community Service (Award)
- Gord Currie Coach of the Year (Award)
- Rookie of the Year (Award)
- Larry Wruck Defensive Player of the Year (Award)
- Peter Dalla Riva Offensive Player of the Year (Award)
- Intergold Cup Champions (Award)
- Jostens Cup Champions (Award)
- Leader Post Trophy Champions (Award)
- Armadale Cup Champions (Award)
- Paul Kirk Memorial Trophy (Award)
- John M Bannerman Memorial Trophy (Award)
- Canadian Bowl Champions (Award)

Canadian Junior Golf Association (CJGA)
#6, 170 West Beaver Creek Rd., Richmond Hill ON L4B 1L6
Tel: 905-731-6388; *Fax:* 905-731-6058
Toll-Free: 877-508-1069
info@cjga.com
www.cjga.com
www.facebook.com/cjga.ca
twitter.com/CJGA
Overview: A medium-sized national organization founded in 1993
Mission: To provide competition & instruction to junior golfers in Canada
Chief Officer(s):
Earl M. Fritz, Executive Director
earl.fritz@cjga.com
Staff Member(s): 28
Activities: Golf tours & competitions; kids programs

Canadian Katahdin Sheep Association Inc. (CKSA)
c/o Canadian Livestock Records Corporation, 2417 Holly Lane, Ottawa ON K1V 0M7
Tel: 613-731-7110; *Fax:* 613-731-0704
katahdin@clrc.ca
www.katahdinsheep.com
www.facebook.com/groups/CanadianKatahdins/
Overview: A small national organization founded in 1995
Mission: To provide a system for the development, identification, & registration of Katahdin sheep in Canada, through the Canadian Livestock Records Corporation Inc.; To address issues of concern to the Katahdin sheep industry; To expand the industry
Affliation(s): Canadian Livestock Records Corporation
Chief Officer(s):
Louis L'Arrivee, President, 306-769-8981, Fax: 306-769-8916
landjlarrivee@sasktel.net
Bonnie Ramsey, Vice-President, 204-662-4588, Fax: 204-662-4588
wickedsheep@hotmail.com
Ron Black, Secretary-Treasurer, 613-731-7110 Ext. 303, Fax: 613-731-0704
ron.black@clrc.ca
Lorna Woolsey, Registrar, 613-731-7110 Ext. 306, Fax: 613-731-0704
lorna.woolsey@clrc.ca
Laura Lee Mills, Registrar (French), 613-731-7110 Ext. 314, Fax: 613-731-0704
lauralee.mills@clrc.ca
Membership: 80; *Fees:* $10 junior members; $25 associate members; $50 renewed farm memberships, individual, or company; $60 new farm memberships; $1,000 life memberships; *Member Profile:* Persons, partnerships, or farms that own at least one Canadian-registered Katahdin sheep
Activities: Establishing & maintaining selective breeding standards; Promoting Katahdin sheep; Maintaining records of the transfer of ownership of Katahdin sheep; Compiling & publishing data relating to Katahdin sheep; Assisting in the implementation of research programs; Educating the public & members of the association
Meetings/Conferences: • Canadian Katahdin Sheep Association 2015 Annual General Meeting, 2015
Scope: National
Publications:
- Canadian Katahdin Sheep Association Breed Guidebook
Type: Guidebook
Profile: Characteristics, standards, procedures, identification, & registration
- Canadian Katahdin Sheep Association Newsletter
Type: Newsletter; *Frequency:* Quarterly; *Accepts Advertising*; *Editor:* Duane Rose; *Price:* Free with membership in the Canadian Katahdin Sheep Association
Profile: Association updates, articles, & photographs of Katahdin sheep

Canadian Kendo Federation (CKF) / Fédération canadienne de kendo
8013 Hunter St., Burnaby BC V5A 2B8
Tel: 604-420-0438; *Fax:* 604-420-1971
hokusa@kendo-canada.com
www.kendo-canada.com
www.facebook.com/KendoCanada
twitter.com/KendoCanada
Also Known As: Kendo Federation
Overview: A small national organization
Chief Officer(s):
Hiro Okusa, President
hiro_okusa@hotmail.com
Yoshiaki Taguchi, Vice-President
ytaguchi@kendo-canada.com
Christian d'Orangeville, 2nd Vice-President
cdorangeville@kendo-canada.com
Kim Taylor, Secretary
kataylor@kendo-canada.com
John Maisonneuve, Treasurer
maisonnj@canton.edu
Finances: *Funding Sources:* Membership fees; Donations; Sale of CKF souvenirs
Membership: *Fees:* $20 individuals; $75 clubs; *Committees:* Kendo Grading; Iaido Grading; Jodo Grading; Finance; Internal Review; Budget & Event; Team Canada; Secretary's; CKF History

Canadian Kennel Club (CKC) / Club canin canadien
#400, 200 Ronson Dr., Toronto ON M9W 5Z9
Tel: 416-675-5511; *Fax:* 416-675-6506
Toll-Free: 800-250-8040
Other Communication: orderdesk@ckc.ca
information@ckc.ca
www.ckc.ca
Overview: A large national organization founded in 1888
Mission: To provide registry services for all officially recognized breeds of purebred dogs; To provide governance for all CKC approved events; To encourage, guide, & advance the interests of purebred dogs & their responsible owners & breeders in Canada
Chief Officer(s):
Leslie Bahorie, Interim Executive Director
lbahorie@ckc.ca
Elio Furlan, Director, Events & Operations
efurlan@ckc.ca
Sonny Allinson, Manager, Marketing & Communications
sallinson@ckc.ca
Diane Draper, Manager, Regulatory Division
ddraper@ckc.ca
Finances: *Funding Sources:* Membership dues; Service fees
Membership: 25,000 individual + 700 clubs; *Fees:* $50 basic; $100 premier; *Committees:* Executive Performance and Compensation Review; Board Orientation & Education; Breed Standards; Club Relations; Event Officiating; Genetics & Medical; Legislation; Strategic Planning; Responsible Dog

Ownership; Appeal; Audit; Discipline; Registration; Show Modelling
Activities: *Library:* CKC Library; Open to public
Publications:
• Breeders' Showcase [a publication of the Canadian Kennel Club]
Accepts Advertising
• The Bulletin [a publication of the Canadian Kennel Club]
Type: Newsletter; *Frequency:* Monthly; *Price:* Free with CKC membership
• Directory of Breeders [a publication of the Canadian Kennel Club]
Type: Directory; *Accepts Advertising*
• Directory of Suppliers [a publication of the Canadian Kennel Club]
Type: Directory
• Dogs Annual
Type: Yearbook; *Frequency:* Annually; *Price:* Free with CKC membership
• Dogs in Canada
Type: Magazine; *Frequency:* Monthly; *Accepts Advertising*; *Editor:* Kelly Caldwell; *Price:* Free with CKC membership
Profile: Expert advice on topics such as dog behaviour, training, health, & nutrition
• Judges Directory [a publication of the Canadian Kennel Club]
Type: Directory
• Official Section [a publication of the Canadian Kennel Club]
Price: Free with Canadian Kennel Club membership

Canadian Kitchen Cabinet Association (CKCA) / Association canadienne de fabricants d'armoires de cuisine (ACAC)

1485 Laperriere Ave., Ottawa ON K1Z 7S8
Tel: 613-567-9171; *Fax:* 613-729-6206
info@ckca.ca
www.ckca.ca
Overview: A medium-sized national organization founded in 1968
Mission: To promote the interests & conserve the rights of those engaged in the manufacture of kitchen cabinets, bathroom vanities & related millwork as well as their suppliers & dealers.
Chief Officer(s):
Jake Wolter, President
Membership: 112; *Fees:* Schedule available; *Member Profile:* Manufacturers; Suppliers; Dealers; Associates

Canadian Knifemaker's Guild

PO Box 35022, Stn. Nelson Park, London ON N5W 5Z6
e-mail: info@canadianknifemakersguild.com
canadianknifemakersguild.com
Overview: A small national organization founded in 1994
Mission: To increase public awareness of knifemakers, not as makers of weapons, but as skilled & versatile craftspeople producing high quality knives
Chief Officer(s):
Wolfgang Loerchner, President
Wally Hayes, Vice-President
Membership: 40; *Fees:* $30-$150; *Member Profile:* Anyone involved in the craft of knifemaking

Canadian Laboratory Suppliers Association (CLSA) / Association canadienne de fournisseurs de laboratoire

#131, 525 Highland Rd. West, Kitchener ON N5P 4N3
Tel: 519-650-8028; *Fax:* 519-653-8749
www.clsassoc.com
Overview: A medium-sized national organization
Mission: The Canadian Labratory Suppliers Association is a group of scientific companies committed to promoting and serving the Canadian laboratory marketplace. It provides a non-competitive environment for executives of Canada's leading scientific suppliers to share ideas and concepts. The CLSA's objective is to provide market analysis on the scientific industry, and to understand and discuss issues that influence the Canadian laboratory scientific market.
Chief Officer(s):
Alan Koop, President & Chair
Finances: *Funding Sources:* Membership dues
Membership: 52 companies; *Fees:* Schedule available; *Member Profile:* Labratory supply Companies in Canada; *Committees:* New Members; Survey; Exhibits & Promotions; Resources; Social
Activities: Lab exhibits; market data & salary surveys

Canadian Labour Congress (CLC) / Congrès du travail du Canada (CTC)

National Headquarters, 2841 Riverside Dr., Ottawa ON K1V 8X7
Tel: 613-521-3400; *Fax:* 613-521-4655
www.canadianlabour.ca
www.facebook.com/clc.ctc
twitter.com/canadianlabour
www.youtube.com/canadianlabour
Overview: A large national licensing organization founded in 1956
Mission: To represent the interests of affiliated workers across Canada; To act as an umbrella organization for affiliated regional labour councils, provincial federations, Canadian unions, & international unions
Chief Officer(s):
Ken Georgetti, President
Barbara Byers, Executive Vice-President
Marie Clarke Walker, Executive Vice-President
Hassan Yussuff, Secretary-Treasurer
Karl Flecker, Director, Anti-Racism & Human Rights, 613-521-3400 Ext. 236
Andrew Jackson, Director, Social & Economic Policy, 613-521-3400 Ext. 262
Daniel Mallett, Director, Political Action, 613-521-3400 Ext. 322
Lucien Royer, Director, International, 613-521-3400 Ext. 270
Colleen Kilty, Manager, Human Resources, 613-521-3400 Ext. 325
Dennis Gruending, Contact, Communications, Media Calls, 613-526-7431
Membership: 3,000,000+; *Member Profile:* Affiliated workers in various occupations throughout Canada
Activities: Lobbying politicians; Organizing campaigns & rallies; Representing the Canadian labour movement when dealing with the media & business
Meetings/Conferences: • Canadian Labour Congress 2017 National Convention, 2017
Scope: National
Description: A convention for members of the labour movement to develop an Action Plan, based on committee reports, resolutions, & the discussion of policies

Atlantic Regional Office
2282 Mountain Rd., Moncton NB E1G 1B4
Tel: 506-858-9350; *Fax:* 506-858-9571
atlantic@clc-ctc.ca
www.canadianlabour.ca/atlantic-region
Mission: To serve labour councils & federations in New Brunswick, Nova Scotia, Prince Edward Island, & Newfoundland & Labrador
Chief Officer(s):
Paulette Sadoway, Director
psadoway@clc-ctc.ca
Serge Landry, Representative, Moncton, New Brunswick, 506-851-7088, Fax: 506-858-9571
slandry@clc-ctc.ca
Mary Shortall, Representative, St. John's, Newfoundland, 709-726-8745, Fax: 709-726-8661
mshortall@clc-ctc.ca
Tony Tracy, Representative, Halifax, Nov Scotia, 902-455-2965, Fax: 902-455-9130
ttracy@clc-ctc.ca

Ontario Regional Office
#401, 15 Gervais Dr., Toronto ON M3C 1Y8
Tel: 416-441-3710; *Fax:* 416-441-4073
ontario@clc-ctc.ca
www.canadianlabour.ca/ontario-region
Chief Officer(s):
Catherine Corcoran, Secretary
ccorcoran@clc-ctc.ca
Eddie Ste-Marie, Representative
estemarie@clc-ctc.ca
Gogi Bhandal, Representative
bbegin@clc-ctc.ca
Medhi Kouhestaninejad, Representative
mkouhestaninejad@clc-ctc.ca
Erin Harrison, Representative
eharrison@clc-ctc.ca
Federico Carvajal, Representative
fcarvajal@clc-ctc.ca

Pacific Regional Office
#201, 5118 Joyce St., Vancouver BC V5R 4H1
Tél: 604-430-6766; *Téléc:* 604-430-6762
pacific@clc-ctc.ca
www.canadianlabour.ca/pacific-region
Mission: To work with labour councils & federations of labour in British Columbia & the Yukon
Chief Officer(s):
Amber Hockin, Director
ahockin@clc-ctc.ca
Orion Irvine, Representative
oirvine@clc-ctc.ca
Ron Stipp, Representative
rstipp@clc-ctc.ca
Iris Taylor, Representative
itaylor@clc-ctc.ca
Chantel O'Neill, Representative
coneill@clc-ctc.ca

Prairie Regional Office
1888 Angus St., Regina SK S4T 1Z4
Tel: 306-525-6137; *Fax:* 306-525-9514
prairie@clc-ctc.ca
www.canadianlabour.ca/prairie-region
Mission: To work with labour councils & federations of labour in Alberta, Manitoba, Saskatchewan, the Northwest Territories, & Nunavut
Chief Officer(s):
Alex Furlong, Regional Director
afurlong@clc-ctc.ca
Cindy Murdoch, Representative, Manitoba
cmurdoch@clc-ctc.ca
Amanda Freistadt, Representative, Alberta
afreistadt@clc-ctc.ca
Darla Leard, Representative, Saskatchewan
dleard@clc-ctc.ca

Québec Regional Office
#12100, 565, boul Crémazie Est, Montréal QC H2M 2W3
Tél: 514-383-8000; *Téléc:* 514-383-8038
Ligne sans frais: 877-897-0057
ftq@ftq.qc.ca
www.ftq.qc.ca
Chief Officer(s):
Michel Arsenault, President, 514-383-8034, Fax: 514-383-8003
fvigeant@ftq.qc.ca (Francine Vigeant, President's Secretary)
René Roy, Secretary General, 514-383-8008, Fax: 514-383-8002
douellet@ftq.qc.ca

Canadian Labour International Film Festival (CLiFF)

Toronto ON
Tel: 416-579-0481
info@labourfilms.ca
labourfilms.ca
Overview: A medium-sized national organization founded in 2009
Mission: To produce a labour-oriented film festival in Canada, featuring films about workers & their conditions from Canada & around the world; To provide a venue where working people can tell their own stories in their own words & images; To encourage the production of films about working people
Chief Officer(s):
Frank Saptel, Festival Founder & Director
Activities: Partnering with other labour organizations; Assisting organizations & communities across Canada to host a film festival

Canadian Lacrosse Association (CLA) / Association canadienne de crosse (ACC)

Gladstone Sports & Health Centre, #310, 18 Louisa St., Ottawa ON K1R 6Y6
Tel: 613-260-2028; *Fax:* 613-260-2029
info1@lacrosse.ca
www.lacrosse.ca
www.facebook.com/CanadianLacrosseAssociation
twitter.com/LacrosseCanada
Overview: A medium-sized national licensing charitable organization founded in 1867
Mission: To promote, develop & preserve the sport of Lacrosse & its heritage as Canada's national summer sport.
Affliation(s): International Lacrosse Federation; International Federation of Women's Lacrosse Associations; Fédération internationale d'Inter-crosse; Canadian Lacrosse Foundation; Sport Canada; Coaching Association of Canada
Chief Officer(s):
Joey Harris, President
jjharris@mtsm.blackberry.com
Melissa McKenzie, Executive Director
melissa@lacrosse.ca
Jane Clapham, Senior Team Leader
jane@lacrosse.ca
Finances: *Annual Operating Budget:* $250,000-$500,000; *Funding Sources:* Sport Canada; membership fees; sponsors; donations; sales
Staff Member(s): 3

Membership: 11 provincial organizations; *Fees:* $350 - $1,050; *Member Profile:* Provincial associations/leagues; *Committees:* Equipment Review; Transfer Review; Appeals; Discipline; Aboriginal Development
Activities: *Awareness Events:* Lacrosse Week, 3rd week of May; *Internships:* Yes; *Speaker Service:* Yes; *Rents Mailing List:* Yes

Canadian Lacrosse Hall of Fame
PO Box 308, 65 - 6th Ave., New Westminster BC V3L 4Y6
Tel: 604-527-4640; *Fax:* 604-527-4641
info@canadianlacrossehalloffame.com
www.canadianlacrossehalloffame.org
Overview: A small national organization founded in 1967
Mission: To present the history of lacrosse in Canada & to induct worthy receipients into the Hall of Fame
Chief Officer(s):
Allan Blair, Curator
Activities: *Library:* Canadian Lacrosse Hall of Fame Archives; by appointment

Canadian Lactation Consultant Association (CLCA) / Association canadienne des consultantes en lactation
4 Innovation Dr., Dundas ON L9H 7S3
Tel: 905-689-3980; *Fax:* 905-689-1465
clca-accl@gmail.com
www.clca-accl.ca
www.linkedin.com/groups/Canadian-Lactation-Consultant-Association-CLCA
www.facebook.com/welcomeback/requests/#!/CLCA.ACCL
twitter.com/cdnlactation
Overview: A small national organization founded in 1986
Affliation(s): International Lactation Consultant Association
Chief Officer(s):
Lauretta Williams, Administrator
Activities: *Library:* CLCA/ACCL Lending Library; by appointment

Canadian Land Reclamation Association (CLRA) / Association canadienne de réhabilitation des sites dégradés (ACRSD)
PO Box 61047, Stn. Kensington, Calgary AB T2N 4S6
Tel: 403-289-9435
clra@telusplanet.net
www.clra.ca
Overview: A small national organization founded in 1975
Mission: To rehabilitate disturbed lands & waterways
Member of: International Affiliation of Land Reclamationists
Chief Officer(s):
Andrea Granger, President
agranger@shaw.ca
M. Anne Naeth, Vice-President
anne.naeth@ualberta.ca
Linda Jones, Secretary
clra@telusplanet.net
Finances: *Funding Sources:* Membership fees; Sponsorships
Membership: *Fees:* $15 full-time students & retirees; $50 regular members; $200 corporate members; *Member Profile:* Individuals & corporations interested in or engaged in reclamation activities; *Committees:* Nominations; Noranda; Watkin; Website
Activities: Facilitating the exchange of information & experience; Encouraging education in the field of land reclamation
Awards:
• William E. Coates Student Awards (Scholarship)
Amount: $500
• Dr. Edward M. Watkin Award (Award)
To recognize contributions that advance the progress of reclamation or the association
• Noranda Land Reclamation Award (Award)
To recognize outstanding achievement in land reclamation in Canada
Meetings/Conferences: • Canadian Land Reclamation Association / Association canadienne de réhabilitation des sites dégradés 2015 40th Annual General Meeting, June, 2015, Radisson Winnipeg Downtown, Winnipeg, MB
Scope: National
Description: Business affairs of the association
Contact Information: Lucie Labbe, Phone: 514-287-8500
Publications:
• Canadian Land Reclamation Association Annual Meeting Proceedings
Type: Yearbook; *Frequency:* Annually
• Canadian Reclamation
Type: Magazine; *Frequency:* Semiannually; *Accepts Advertising*; *Editor:* Tracy Patterson
Profile: Articles & illustrations
• Reclamation Newsletter
Type: Newsletter; *Frequency:* Semiannually
Profile: Articles & updates on all aspects of reclamation

Alberta Chapter
AB
www.clra.ca
Chief Officer(s):
Andrea Granger, Past President
granger.andrea@cleanharbors.com

Canadian Laser Aesthetic Surgery Society (CLASS)
2334 Heska Rd., Pickering ON L1V 2P9
Tel: 905-831-7248
Toll-Free: 877-578-0336
info@class.ca
www.class.ca
www.facebook.com/114244068599861
Overview: A small national organization founded in 1997
Mission: CLASS is active in the dissemination of information, education, preceptorship and promotion of quality in all forms of aesthetic laser surgery.
Chief Officer(s):
Pat Hewitt, Executive Secretary
Membership: *Member Profile:* Physicians who have achieved a specialty certification in either Dermatology, Plastic Surgery, Otolaryngology, or Ophthalmology.

Canadian Latvian Catholic Association
34 Edenvale Cres., Toronto ON M9A 4A4
Tel: 416-244-4576; *Fax:* 416-244-1513
Overview: A medium-sized national organization founded in 1949
Finances: *Annual Operating Budget:* Less than $50,000
10 volunteer(s)
Membership: 3,000 individual; *Fees:* $10 individual

Canadian Law & Economics Association
Faculty of Law, University of Toronto, 84 Queen's Park Cres., Toronto ON M5S 2C5
Tel: 416-978-0210; *Fax:* 416-978-7899
www.canlecon.org
Overview: A small national organization
Chief Officer(s):
Nadia Gulezko, Contact
n.gulezko@utoronto.ca

Canadian Law & Society Association (CLSA) / Association canadienne de droit et société (ACDS)
c/o Dept. of Law, Carleton University, 1125 Colonel Bay Dr., Ottawa ON K1S 5B6
e-mail: info@acds-clsa.org
www.acds-clsa.org
Overview: A small national organization founded in 1985
Mission: To encourage socio-legal inquiry both domestically & internationally
Member of: Canadian Federation for the Humanities & Social Sciences
Membership: *Fees:* Annually, $100 individual; $30 student; $50 Emeritus; *Member Profile:* Scholars from many disciplines, with an interest in the place of law in economic political, cultural, social life
Activities: Awaring prizes for scholarship
Meetings/Conferences: • Canadian Law & Society Association Annual Mid-Winter Meeting 2015, 2015
Scope: National
• Canadian Law & Society Association Annual Meeting 2015, June, 2015, Ottawa, ON
Scope: National
Publications:
• Canadian Journal of Law & Society / La Revue Canadienne Droit et Société (CJLS / RCDS)
Type: Journal; *Frequency:* Semiannually; *Accepts Advertising*; *Editor:* D. Moore; M. Valverde; M. Coutu *ISSN:* 0829-3201; *Price:* Free with CLSA / ACDSmembership; $90 Canada; $110 International
Profile: Original academic research in the field of law & society scholarship
• The CLSA / ACDS Bulletin
Type: Newsletter; *Frequency:* Semiannually; *Editor:* Kimberley White; *Price:* Free with CLSA / ACDS membership
Profile: Forum for for CLSA members to share information on developments & issues affecting Canadian law & society research

Canadian Lawyers Association for International Human Rights (CLAIHR)
www.claihr.ca
www.facebook.com/claihr
twitter.com/CLAIHR
Overview: A small national organization
Mission: To promote human rights globally through legal education, advocacy & law reform; to promote awareness of human rights issues within the legal community in Canada.
Membership: *Fees:* $50 general; $25 student

Canadian Lawyers Insurance Association (CLIA) / Association d'assurances des juristes canadiens (AAJC)
Office of the General Manager, #510, 36 Toronto St., Toronto ON M5C 2C5
Tel: 416-408-5293; *Fax:* 416-408-3721
info@clia.ca
www.clia.ca
Overview: A small national organization founded in 1988
Mission: To provide a reliable source of insurance on a non-profit basis; To ensure availability of reasonably priced insurance, & that premium rates reflect the loss experience of Canadian lawyers; To stabilize premiums in both mandatory & excess layers
Chief Officer(s):
Patrick Mahoney, General Manager
Norma Ibbetson, Assistant General Manager, 416-408-5294
Staff Member(s): 2
Membership: *Member Profile:* Participating law societies, which agree on standard limits & policy terms, in Alberta, Saskatchewan, Manitoba, New Brunswick, Nova Scotia, Prince Edward Island, Newfoundland & Labrador, Yukon, Northwest Territories, & Nunavut
Activities: Providing professional liability insurance for Canadian lawyers; Managing a Voluntary Excess Program in the provinces of British Columbia & Ontario, through the Canadian Bar Excess Liability Association
Publications:
• Canadian Lawyers Insurance Association Annual Report
Type: Yearbook; *Frequency:* Annually
Profile: A summary of the association's yearly activities
• Loss Prevention Bulletin
Type: Newsletter; *Editor:* Karen L. Dyck
Profile: Claim prevention techniques to help lawyers minimize the likelihood of being sued for malpractice
• Loss Prevention eBytes
Price: Loss prevention information for CLIA insured lawyers
• Safe & Effective Practice
Number of Pages: 106; *Author:* Jean Côté; *Editor:* Barry Vogel, Q.C.; *Price:* Free to members of the legal profession

Canadian League Against Epilepsy (CLAE)
c/o Secretariat Centreal, #6, 20 Crown Steel Dr., Markham ON L3R 9X9
Tel: 905-415-3917
clae@secretariatcentral.com
claegroup.org
Overview: A small national organization
Mission: To help Canadians affected by epilepsy; To develop therapeutic & preventative strategies to avoid the consequences of epilepsy
Affliation(s): Canadian Epilepsy Alliance; American Epilepsy Society; North American Commission for Epilepsy
Chief Officer(s):
S. Nizam Ahmed, President
snahmed@ualberta.ca
Elizabeth Donner, Secretary-Treasurer
elizabeth.donner@sickkids.ca
Finances: *Funding Sources:* Donations; Fundraising
Membership: *Fees:* $50 junior; $100 allied heatlh professionals; $150 active; *Member Profile:* Medical & basic sciences professionals, including physicians, neuropsychologists, & nurses; Students
Activities: Increasing awareness about epilepsy; Educating Canadians about epilepsy; Providing professional development opportunities; Supporting epilepsy research

Canadian League of Composers / La Ligue canadienne de compositeurs
Chalmers House, 20 St. Joseph St., Toronto ON M4Y 1J9
Tel: 416-964-1364; *Fax:* 416-961-7189
Toll-Free: 877-964-1364
clcomposers@gmail.com

composition.org
www.facebook.com/143305345702145
twitter.com/CLC_LCC
Overview: A small national organization
Mission: To represent the interests of composers & to monitor & influence the conditions that affect their livlihood and public image.
Chief Officer(s):
Jennifer Butler, President
Elisha Denbrug, General Manager
Membership: 400; *Fees:* $60; *Committees:* Executive; Advocacy; Awards; Communications; Professional; Membership

Canadian Lebanon Society of Halifax

c/o Community Centre, 255 Bedford Hwy., Halifax NS B3M 2K5
Tel: 902-444-4257
cls_halifax@hotmail.com
Overview: A small local organization founded in 1938
Mission: To act as the voice of Nova Scotia's Lebanese community; To service the Lebanese people of Nova Scotia; To promote the heritage & culture of the Lebanese community
Activities: Producing radio programs, a magazine, & festivals to promote the culture of the Lebanese community; Providing education about Lebanese culture & the Arabic language to youth; *Awareness Events:* Multicultural Festival, June; Annual Lebanese Summer Festival, July; Labanon's Independence Day, November

Canadian Lesbian & Gay Archives (CLGA)

PO Box 699, Stn. F, 34 Isabella St., Toronto ON M4Y 1N1
Tel: 416-777-2755
queeries@clga.ca
www.clga.ca
www.facebook.com/116735553447
twitter.com/clgarchives
Previous Name: Canadian Gay Archives
Overview: A medium-sized national charitable organization founded in 1973
Mission: To acquire, preserve & make available to the public information in any medium about lesbians & gays, with an emphasis on Canada.
Affliation(s): Association of Canadian Archivists; Ontario Association of Archives
Chief Officer(s):
Robert Windrum, President
Finances: *Annual Operating Budget:* Less than $50,000
Staff Member(s): 1; 25 volunteer(s)
Membership: 1,200
Activities: *Library:* James Fraser Library; Open to public by appointment

Canadian Library Association (CLA) / Association canadienne des bibliothèques (ACB)

#400, 1150 Morrison Dr., Ottawa ON K2H 8S9
Tel: 613-232-9625; *Fax:* 613-563-9895
Other Communication: membership@cla.ca
info@cla.ca
www.cla.ca
www.linkedin.com/groups?gid=4137241
www.facebook.com/group.php?gid=2229890224
twitter.com/cla_web
Overview: A large national charitable organization founded in 1946
Mission: To serve as the national public voice for Canada's library communities; To champion library values & the value of libraries; To influence public policy impacting libraries; To inspire & support learning; To collaborate to strengthen the library community
Member of: Book & Periodical Council; Cultural Human Resources Council (CHRC); International Federation of Library Associations & Institutions (IFLA)
Affliation(s): American Library Association
Chief Officer(s):
Pilar Martinez, President, 780-496-5522, Fax: 780-496-7097
pmartinez@epl.ca
DeYoung Marie, Vice President, 902-420-5532
marie.deyoung@smu.ca
Barbara H. Clubb, Interim Executive Director, 613-232-9625 Ext. 306
bclubb@cla.ca
Judy Green, Manager, Marketing & Communications, 613-232-9625 Ext. 322
jgreen@cla.ca
Geraldine Hyland, Manager, Member Services, 613-232-9625 Ext. 301
ghyland@cla.ca
Wendy Walton, Manager, Conference & Events, 613-232-9625 Ext. 302
wwalton@cla.ca
Penny Warne, Manager, Web & IT Infrastructure, 613-232-9625 Ext. 320
pwarne@cla.ca
Mary-Jo Romaniuk, Treasurer, 780-492-5958, Fax: 780-492-7925
mary-jo.romaniuk@ualberta.ca
Beverly Bard, Coordinator, Book Reviews, 613-232-9625 Ext. 324
bbard@cla.ca
Christopher Culhane, Coordinator, Young Canada Works, 613-232-9625 Ext. 321
ycw@cla.ca
Anita Fortier, Administrator, Orders, 613-232-9625 Ext. 310
orders@cla.ca
Finances: *Funding Sources:* Membership dues; Advertising; Sponsorships; Conference & Tradshow
Staff Member(s): 9
Membership: 3,987; *Fees:* $25 students; $50 retired, unemployed, LTD, parental leave; $100 individuals with salary under $40,000; $200 personal; $325-$1,000 institutional; *Member Profile:* Individuals, institutions, & groups interested in librarianship & in library & information services; *Committees:* Copright Advisory; Information Policy Advisory; Intellectual Freedom Advisory; Library Services for People with Print Disabilities Advisory; School Libraries Advisory; Conference Program Standing; Elections Standing; Finance Standing; Member Communications Standing; Nominations Standing; Participation Standing; Resolutions Standing
Activities: Engaging in national & international advocacy activities; Monitoring issues such as funding, copyright, & the Library Book Rate; Making representations to governments concerning issues affecting library & information services; Promoting public support for library & information services; Facilitating networking opportunities, such as CLA e-communities & CLA Listserv; Providing information & research services; *Awareness Events:* Canadian Library Month, October
Awards:
• W. Kaye Lamb Award for Service to Seniors (Award)
• Award for the Advancement of Intellectual Freedom in Canada (Award)
• CLA / ACB Information Today Award for Innovative Technology (Award)
• Amelia Frances Howard-Gibbon Illustrator's Award (Award)
• CLA / ACB Dafoe Scholarship (Scholarship)
• H.W. Wilson Scholarship (Scholarship)
• Young Adult Canadian Book Award (Award)
• Book of the Year for Children Award (Award)
• Outstanding Service to Librarianship Award (Award)
• CLA / ACB Ken Haycock Award for Promoting Librarianship (Award)
• CLA / ACB Student Article Contest (Award)
• Angela Thacker Memorial Award (Award)
• CLA / ACB Robert H. Blackburn Distinguished Paper Award (Award)
• CLA / Alan MacDonald Mentorship Award (Award)
• CLA / ACB Emerging Leader Award (Award)
• CLA / ACB Research & Development Grant (Grant)
• Chancellor Group Conference Grant (Grant)
• Best Poster Presentation Award (Grant)
Meetings/Conferences: • Canadian Library Association / Association canadienne des bibliothèques 70th National Conference & Trade Show 2015, June, 2015, Ottawa, ON
Scope: National
Attendance: 800+
Description: Featuring keynote speakers, workshops, social events, & a trade show
Contact Information: Manager, Conference & Events: Wendy Walton, Phone: 613-232-9625, ext. 302, E-mail: wwalton@cla.ca; Manager, Marketing & Communications (Trade show & sponsorship opportunities): Judy Green, Phone: 613-232-9625, ext. 322, E-mail: jgreen@cla.ca
• Canadian Library Association / Association canadienne des bibliothèques 71st National Conference & Trade Show 2016, June, 2016, Halifax Convention Centre, Halifax, NS
Scope: National
Attendance: 1,500
Description: Conference program includes educational workshops, keynote speakers, networking opportunities, & exhibitors at the trade show
Contact Information: Manager, Conference & Events: Wendy Walton, Phone: 613-232-9625, ext. 302, E-mail: wwalton@cla.ca; Manager, Marketing & Communications (Trade show & sponsorship opportunities): Judy Green, Phone: 613-232-9625, ext. 322, E-mail: jgreen@cla.ca
• Canadian Library Association / Association canadienne des bibliothèques 72nd National Conference & Trade Show 2017, 2017
Scope: National
Attendance: 800+
Description: Featuring keynote speakers, workshops, social events, & a trade show
Contact Information: E-mail: info@cla.ca
• Canadian Library Association / Association canadienne des bibliothèques 73rd National Conference & Trade Show 2018, 2018
Scope: National
Attendance: 800+
Description: Keynote speakers, an educational program, poster sessions, exhibits, & social events
Contact Information: E-mail: info@cla.ca
Publications:
• Canadian Library Association Annual Report
Type: Yearbook; *Frequency:* Annually
• CLA [Canadian Library Association] Digest
Type: Newsletter; *Frequency:* Biweekly
Profile: News, people highlights, career spotlights, "Shop CLA", & conference & award updates
• Feliciter
Type: Magazine; *Frequency:* 6 pa; *Accepts Advertising*; *Editor:* Judy Green *ISSN:* 0014-9802; *Price:* inc. in membership fee
Profile: Opinion pieces, columns, articles on professional concerns & developments, & news of the Canadian Library Association
• School Libraries in Canada
Type: Journal; *Frequency:* Quarterly *ISSN:* 1710-8535
Profile: Journal of the Canadian Association for School Libraries provides national support for the development & maintenance of school libraries, media centres & schoollibrary personnel; Free online publication for teacher-librarians & school librarians

Canadian Life & Health Insurance Association Inc. (CLHIA) / Association canadienne des compagnies d'assurances de personnes inc. (ACCAP)

#1700, 1 Queen St. East, Toronto ON M5C 2X9
Tel: 416-777-2221; *Fax:* 416-777-1895
info@clhia.ca
www.clhia.ca
twitter.com/clhia
Previous Name: Canadian Life Insurance Association
Overview: A large national organization founded in 1894
Mission: To represent the interests of member life & health insurance companies
Chief Officer(s):
Donald Guloien, Chair
Frank Swedlove, President
Wendy Hope, Vice-President, External Relations, 613-230-0031
whope@clhia.ca
Membership: 100-499; *Member Profile:* Life & health insurers licensed to do business in Canada; Insurance-related organizations
Activities: Facilitating the exchange of information about best practices & current developments; Compiling information & statistics
Publications:
• Canadian Life & Health Insurance Facts
Type: Yearbook; *Frequency:* Annually
Profile: Statistics on life & health insurance ownership & purchases, life & health insurance companies' income & expenses, pension plan coverages, assets & obligations, & operations inCanada
• Consumer Tips: RRSPs with Life Insurance Companies
Profile: CLHIA publication to assist Canadian consumers
• A Guide to Disability Insurance
Number of Pages: 20
Profile: A guide to understanding options for income replacement in the event of disability
• A Guide to Life Insurance
Type: Booklet; *Number of Pages:* 36
Profile: Consumer publication about types of policies, agent services, riders & dividends, & premiums
• A Guide to Supplementary Health Insurance
Number of Pages: 20
Profile: Resource to assist consumers
• A Guide to the Coordination of Benefits
Number of Pages: 12
Profile: Assistance in navigating the claims process

• A Guide to Travel Health Insurance
Number of Pages: 12
Profile: A review of the supplementary health insurance needed by Canadians when they travel ouside the province or country
• In The Loop
Type: Newsletter; *Frequency:* Monthly
Profile: Industry updates
• Key Facts About Segregated Fund Contracts
Number of Pages: 12
Profile: A guide for investors
• Provincial Facts & Figures
Frequency: Annually

Montréal Office
#630, 1001, boul de Maisonneuve ouest, Montréal QC H3A 3C8
Tel: 514-845-9004; *Fax:* 514-845-6182

Ottawa Office
#400, 46 Elgin St., Ottawa ON K1P 5K6
Tel: 613-230-0031; *Fax:* 613-230-0297

Canadian Life & Health Insurance OmbudService *See* OmbudService for Life & Health Insurance

Canadian Life Insurance Association *See* Canadian Life & Health Insurance Association Inc.

Canadian Life Insurance Medical Officers Association (CLIMOA) / Association Canadienne des Directeurs Médicaux en Assurance-Vie (ACDMAV)

#100, 32 Colonnade Rd., Ottawa ON K2E 7J6
Tel: 613-721-7061; *Fax:* 613-721-3581
climoa@unconventionalplanning.com
www.climoa.com
Overview: A small national organization
Mission: To help develop & coordinate doctors & others working in the health & life insurance industry
Chief Officer(s):
Bruce Boyd, President
Membership: *Fees:* $200 active; $100 associate; $35 emeritus; *Committees:* Medical Education; Professional Relations
Activities: Meetings; presentations

Canadian Limousin Association (CLA)

#13, 4101 - 19th St. NE, Calgary AB T2E 7C4
Tel: 403-253-7309; *Fax:* 403-253-1704
limousin@limousin.com
www.limousin.com
Overview: A large international organization founded in 1970
Mission: To provide collective service for Limousin breeders in Canada, record registration & produce Records of Performance on all registered animals; to promote & inform producers about Limousin cattle; to develop & implement educational agricultural programs
Member of: Canadian 4H; Canadian Beef Breeds Council
Chief Officer(s):
Bill Campbell, President
cam.limousin@xplornet.com
Anne Brunet-Burgess, General Manager
aburgess@limousin.com
Finances: *Annual Operating Budget:* $250,000-$500,000; *Funding Sources:* Registration of limousin cattle; membership dues
Staff Member(s): 6; 11 volunteer(s)
Membership: 750; *Fees:* Schedule available; *Member Profile:* Limousin cattle breeders; *Committees:* Advertising & Promotion; Breed Improvement; Export; Junior
Activities: *Library* by appointment
Publications:
• Bottom Line Newsletter
Type: Newsletter; *Frequency:* Semiannually
Profile: Information about breeders & breeding, sales, & beef industry trends
• Limousin Voice
Frequency: Quarterly; *Accepts Advertising*; *Editor:* Bryan Kostiuk; *Price:* $35
Profile: Includes a bull issue, a herd reference issue & a harvest of value issue

Canadian Linguistic Association (CLA) / Association canadienne de linguistique (ACL)

c/o University of Toronto Press, Journals Division, 5201 Dufferin Ave., Toronto ON M3H 5T8
www.chass.utoronto.ca/~cla-acl
Overview: A medium-sized national organization
Mission: To advance scientific study of linguistics & language in Canada
Member of: Humanities & Social Sciences Federation of Canada
Affliation(s): International Permanent Committee of Linguists
Chief Officer(s):
France Martineau, President
fmartin@uOttawa.ca
Ileana Paul, Secretary
ileana@uwo.ca
Carrie Dyck, Treasurer
cdyck@mun.ca
Finances: *Funding Sources:* Membership dues
6 volunteer(s)
Membership: 400 institutional + 360 individual; *Fees:* $45 individual; $50 institution
Meetings/Conferences: • Canadian Linguistic Association 2015 Conference (part of the Congress of the Humanities & Social Sciences), 2015
Scope: National
Description: Information from all areas of linguistics
Contact Information: Treasurer (travel grant information): Laura Colantoni E-mail: laura.colantoni@utoronto.ca
Publications:
• The Canadian Journal of Linguistics
Type: Journal; *Frequency:* Quarterly; *Accepts Advertising*; *Editor:* Sarah Cummins *ISSN:* 0008-4131; *Price:* Free with CLA membership; $65
Profile: Articles, as well as book reviews, about topics such as linguistic theory, phonology, phonetics, semantics, syntax, linguistic description ofnatural languages, historical linguistics, psycholinguistics, sociolinguistics, & first & second language acquisition

Canadian Literacy & Learning Network (CLLN) / Rassemblement canadien pour l'alphabétisation (RCA)

342A Elgin St., Ottawa ON K2P 1M6
Tel: 613-563-2464; *Fax:* 613-563-2504
clln@literacy.ca
www.literacy.ca
www.facebook.com/195237923820101
twitter.com/Cdn_Literacy
Overview: A medium-sized national charitable organization founded in 1978
Mission: To act as a national voice for literacy for Canadians
Member of: Prince Edward Island Literacy Alliance Inc.
Chief Officer(s):
Lindsay Kennedy, President & CEO, 613-563-2464 Ext. 222
lkennedy@literacy.ca
Finances: *Funding Sources:* Membership fees; Donations; employement & social development canada
Membership: *Member Profile:* Provincial & territorial literacy coalitions & organizations; Individual who support the mission & goals of MCL
Activities: Providing networking opportunities; Researching; Preparing special reports, such a briefs to the House of Commons; Liaising with government; Informing the general public about issues related to adult literacy; Developing & strengthening learners through the Learners Advisory Network; Communicating & collaborating to ensure Canadians have access to quality literacy education; Supporting people & organizations involved with adult literacy education;

Canadian Literary & Artistic Association / Association littéraire et artistique canadienne inc.

PO Box 20035, Stn. De Vinci, Repentigny QC J5Y 0K6
Tel: 514-993-1556
alaican@aei.ca
www.alai.ca
Also Known As: ALAI Canada
Overview: A small national organization founded in 1978
Mission: To promote & protect copyright as well as to study questions regarding the protection and the applicability of these rights.
Member of: International ALAI
Chief Officer(s):
Madeleine Lamothe-Samson, President
mlamothesamson@ogilvyrenault.com
Finances: *Funding Sources:* Membership fees
Membership: 145 individuals; *Fees:* $125 individuals; $160 institutions; $60 students; *Member Profile:* Any person interested in copyright who endorses the goals of ALAICanada may submit an application by completing an admission form or a copy thereof. Full standing members, corporate members, and students. Members of ALAI Canada originate from different circles: creators, performers, broadcasters, producters, jurists, teachers, members of the public administration.
Activities: Conferences, seminars, and congresses. Publishes documents dealing with copyright; and, on its own or in collaboration with other associations, it holds educational and training sessions on the topic.; *Speaker Service:* Yes

Canadian Liver Foundation (CLF) / Fondation canadienne du foie (FCF)

#801, 3100 Steeles Ave. East, Toronto ON L3R 8T3
Tel: 416-491-3353; *Fax:* 416-491-4952
Toll-Free: 800-563-5483
clf@liver.ca
www.liver.ca
www.facebook.com/6584473365
twitter.com/CdnLiverFdtn
www.youtube.com/user/clfwebmaster
Overview: A large national charitable organization founded in 1969
Mission: To reduce the incidence & impact of all liver disease by funding liver research & education; promote liver health through programs & publications
Chief Officer(s):
Morris Sherman, Chairman
Paul Derksen, Sec.-Treas.
Finances: *Annual Operating Budget:* Greater than $5 Million; *Funding Sources:* Donations; Fundraising; Government grants
Staff Member(s): 40; 300 volunteer(s)
Membership: 100-499
Activities: Programs for parents, youth; publications; *Awareness Events:* Help Fight Liver Disease Month, March; *Speaker Service:* Yes; *Rents Mailing List:* Yes; *Library* Open to public
Publications:
• Canadian Liver Foundation Annual Report
Type: Yearbook; *Frequency:* Annually

Atlantic Canada Regional Office/Halifax Chapter
#103-406, 287 Lacewood Dr., Halifax NS B3M 3Y7
Tel: 902-423-8538; *Fax:* 902-423-8811
Toll-Free: 866-423-8538
atlantic@liver.ca
Chief Officer(s):
Shayla Steeves, Regional Director

Bas St-Laurent Chapter
133 ch du Village, Saint-Onésime QC G0R 3W0
Tél: 418-856-4802; *Téléc:* 418-856-5033
Ligne sans frais: 866-333-4802
Chief Officer(s):
Nicole Laforest, Volunteer
nlaforest@liver.ca

British Columbia/Yukon Regional Office
#109, 828 West 8th Ave., Vancouver BC V5Z 1E2
Tel: 604-707-6430; *Fax:* 604-681-6067
Toll-Free: 800-856-7266
radmin@liver.ca
Chief Officer(s):
Elena Murgoci, Regional Director
emurgoci@liver.ca

Chatham/Kent Chapter
PO Box 23, Chatham ON N7M 5K1
Tel: 519-682-9805; *Fax:* 519-682-2184
clfchatham@liver.ca
Chief Officer(s):
Sheila Hughes, Development Manager

Cornwall Chapter
PO Box 1764, Cornwall ON K6H 5V7
Tel: 613-937-1781; *Fax:* 613-937-1781
slebano@liver.ca
Chief Officer(s):
Sue Lebano

Eastern Ontario Regional Office
PO Box 101, Kars (Ottawa) ON K0A 2E0
Tel: 613-489-5208; *Fax:* 613-489-5255
Chief Officer(s):
Annette Martin, Contact
amartin@liver.ca

Guysborough County & Area Chapter
PO Box 122, Guysborough NS B0H 1N0
Tel: 902-533-2959; *Fax:* 902-533-2106
guysboroughchapter@liver.ca
Chief Officer(s):
Dale O'Connor, Chapter President

London Chapter
Royal Bank Bldg., #1206, 383 Richmond St., London ON N6A 3C4

Tel: 519-659-0951; *Fax:* 519-659-4232
clflondon@liver.ca
Chief Officer(s):
Janeen Collins-Dera, Regional Coordinator
Manitoba Chapter
#210, 375 York Ave., Winnipeg MB R3C 3J3
Tel: 204-831-6231
Chief Officer(s):
Ruth Magnuson, Reginal Manager
rmagnuson@liver.ca
Moncton Chapter
#4-1010, 331 Elmwood Dr., Moncton NB E1A 7Y1
Tel: 506-855-0331
Chief Officer(s):
Nicole Underhill, Treasurer
Montréal Chapter
#1430, 1000, rue de la Gauchetière ouest, Montréal QC H3B 4W5
Tél: 514-876-4170; *Téléc:* 514-876-4172
montrealevents@liver.ca
Chief Officer(s):
Betty Esperanza, Regional Director
besperanza@liver.ca
Northern Alberta/Edmonton Regional Office
#209, 10240 - 124 St., Edmonton AB T5S 3W6
Tel: 780-444-1547; *Fax:* 780-481-7781
Toll-Free: 888-557-5516
rsandy@liver.ca
Chief Officer(s):
Vacant, President
Todd Hebert, Regional Director
thebert@liver.ca
Saint John Chapter
#222, 505 Rothesay Ave., Saint John NB E2J 2C6
Tel: 519-214-3511; *Fax:* 519-214-3715
saintjohnchapter@liver.ca
Chief Officer(s):
Kristen Wheaton, Chapter President
St. John's Chapter
PO Box 6382, 354 Water St., St. John's NL A1C 6J9
Tel: 709-753-1987; *Fax:* 709-753-1987
stjohnschapter@liver.ca
Chief Officer(s):
Leonard Stacey, Chapter President
Southern Alberta/Calgary Regional Office
#309, 1010 - 1st Ave. NE, Calgary AB T2E 7W7
Tel: 403-276-3390; *Fax:* 403-276-3423
Toll-Free: 888-557-5516
calgary@liver.ca
www.facebook.com/groups/78344543539
Todd Hebert, Chapter President
thebert@liver.ca
Toronto/GTA Chapter
#801, 3100 Steeles Ave. East, Markham ON L3R 8T3
Tel: 416-491-3353; *Fax:* 905-752-1540
Toll-Free: 800-563-5483
clf@liver.ca
Chief Officer(s):
Marsha Doucette, Regional Coordinator
mdoucette@liver.ca
Waterloo/Wellington Chapter
5 Clive Ave., Guelph ON N1E 3S2
Tel: 519-836-8309
clf@sentex.net
Chief Officer(s):
Theresa Stewart, Chapter President
Windsor/Essex Chapter
3147 Tecumseh Rd. East, Windsor ON N8W 1G9
Tel: 519-974-8008; *Fax:* 519-974-3348
clfwindsor@liver.ca
Chief Officer(s):
Anna Marie Letwin, Manager

Canadian Livestock Records Corporation (CLRC) / Société canadienne d'enregistrement des animaux

2417 Holly Lane, Ottawa ON K1V 0M7
Tel: 613-731-7110; *Fax:* 613-731-0704
Toll-Free: 877-833-7110
clrc@clrc.ca
www.clrc.ca
Previous Name: Canadian National Live Stock Records
Overview: A medium-sized national organization founded in 1905
Mission: To serve the Canadian seed stock industry; to be responsible to the member breed associations & Agriculture Canada for the maintenance of records, issuance of certificates, endorsement of changes of ownership, enrolment of members, registration of individuals, identification letters, collection of fees & the deposit of same into the appropriate breed association account
Chief Officer(s):
Ron Black, General Manager, 613-731-7110 Ext. 303
ron.black@clrc.ca
Finances: *Annual Operating Budget:* $500,000-$1.5 Million; *Funding Sources:* Fees for service
Staff Member(s): 11; 6 volunteer(s)
Membership: 52 livestock associations; *Fees:* Schedule available
Activities: *Library* Open to public

Canadian Llama & Alpaca Association (CLAA)

2320 - 41 Ave. NE, Calgary AB T2W 6W8
Tel: 403-250-2165; *Fax:* 403-291-9324
Toll-Free: 800-717-5262
info@claacanada.com
www.claacanada.com
Overview: A medium-sized national organization founded in 1987
Mission: To set up & maintain a reputable registry for Canadian llamas & alpacas
Chief Officer(s):
Susan Wipfli, President
skwipfli@sympatico.ca
Staff Member(s): 1
Membership: 718; *Fees:* $195 alpaca; $140 llama

Canadian Lowline Cattle Association (CLCA)

c/o Lee Monteith, PO Box 84, Edam SK S0M 0V0
Tel: 306-397-2584
www.canadianlowline.com
Overview: A small national organization founded in 1997
Mission: To support Lowline cattle breeders across Canada; To gain exposure & acceptance of the Lowline cattle breed in the agricultural world
Member of: Canadian Beef Breeds Council
Affiliation(s): Canadian Livestock Records Corporation
Chief Officer(s):
Lee Monteith, General Manager
cmonteith@littleloon.ca
Membership: 1-99; *Member Profile:* Breeders of Lowline cattle in Canada
Activities: Providing information about Lowline cattle
Publications:
• Sales Catalogue
Type: Catalogue

Canadian Luge Association / Association canadienne de luge

#323, 151 Canada Olympic Rd. SW, Calgary AB T3B 6B7
Tel: 403-202-6581
www.luge.ca
www.facebook.com/138340422883168
twitter.com/LugeCanada
Previous Name: Canadian Amateur Bobsleigh & Luge Association
Overview: A medium-sized national organization founded in 1990
Mission: To provide leadership & pursue success in promotion & development of all aspects of luge.
Chief Officer(s):
Tim Farstad, Executive Director
tfarstad@luge.ca
Finances: *Funding Sources:* donations; Fast Track Capital
Staff Member(s): 4
Membership: *Member Profile:* Provincial associations fully recognized by national association
Activities: *Internships:* Yes

Canadian Luing Cattle Association

c/o Blacketlees Farm, RR#4, Rimbey AB T0C 2J0
Tel: 403-843-0094; *Fax:* 403-843-0094
iaineaitken@gmail.com
www.luingcattle.com/luing.html
Overview: A small national organization founded in 1975
Mission: To develop & regulate the breeding of Luing cattle in Canada; To protect & assist breeders
Affiliation(s): Canadian Livestock Records Corporation
Chief Officer(s):
Jeff Longard, President, 780-682-3805
Paul Galbraith, Vice-President, 250-346-3100
Iain Aitken, Secretary-Treasurer, 403-843-0094, Fax: 403-843-0094
ieaitken@hotmail.com
Lisa Hutt, Registrar, 613-731-7110 Ext. 312, Fax: 613-731-0704
lisa.hutt@clrc.ca
Membership: 1-99; *Fees:* $35 / year; $10 junior membership (until member's 18th birthday); *Member Profile:* Breeders of Luing cattle in Canada
Activities: Encouraging the breeding of Luing cattle in Canada; Maintaining the Luing cattle breed in Canada; Compiling statistics about the industry; Publishing data & documents related to to breeding of Luing cattle; Supervising breeders of Luing cattle

Canadian Lumber Standards Accreditation Board (CLSAB)

#102, 28 Deakin St., Ottawa ON K2E 8B7
Tel: 613-482-2480; *Fax:* 613-482-6044
info@clsab.ca
www.clsab.ca
Overview: A medium-sized national organization founded in 1960
Chief Officer(s):
Alphonse Caouette, Chair
Chuck Dentelbeck, Secretary-Treasurer
Finances: *Funding Sources:* Membership dues; Assessment fees
Membership: 16; *Member Profile:* Lumber Regulatory Inspection Agency

Canadian Lung Association (CLA) / Association pulmonaire du Canada

National Office, #300, 1750 Courtwood Cres., Ottawa ON K2C 2B5
Tel: 613-569-6411; *Fax:* 613-569-8860
Toll-Free: 800-566-5864
info@lung.ca
www.lung.ca
www.facebook.com/canadianlungassociation
www.twitter.com/canlung
www.youtube.com/user/TheLungAssociation
Previous Name: The Canadian Association for the Prevention of Consumption & Other Forms of Tuberculosis; The Canadian Tuberculosis & Respiratory Disease Association
Overview: A large national charitable organization founded in 1900
Mission: To improve & promote lung health across Canada
Chief Officer(s):
Mary-Pat Shaw, Acting President & Chief Executive Officer
Connie Côté, Senior Director, National Lung Health Framework
Claudia Gongora, Director, Finance
Janis Hass, Director, Marketing & Communications
Janet Sutherland, Director, Canadian Thoracic Society/Canadian Respiratory Health Professiona
Anne Van Dam, Director, Research & Knowledge Translation
Christopher Wilson, Director, Public Affairs & Advocacy
Finances: *Funding Sources:* Donations; Fundraising; Sponsorships
Activities: Advocating for improvements to care for lung disease patients; Providing lung health information to governments & the public; Funding medical research; Coordinating the Christmas Seal campaign; *Awareness Events:* National Non-Smoking Week, January; Lung Cancer Month, November; COPD Awareness Week, November
Meetings/Conferences: • Canadian Respiratory Conference 2015, April, 2015, Ottawa, ON
Scope: National
Description: Jointly organized by the Canadian Lung Association, the Canadian Thoracic Society, the Canadian COPD Alliance, & the Canadian Respiratory Health Professionals
Contact Information: Web Site: www.lung.ca/crc; E-mail: crc@taylorandassociates.ca
• Canadian Respiratory Conference 2016, April, 2016, Halifax Convention Centre, Halifax, NS
Scope: National
Attendance: 650
Description: Jointly organized by the Canadian Lung Association, the Canadian Thoracic Society, the Canadian COPD Alliance, & the Canadian Respiratory Health Professionals
Contact Information: Web Site: www.lung.ca/crc; E-mail: crc@taylorandassociates.ca
Publications:
• Canadian Lung Association Annual Report
Type: Yearbook; *Frequency:* Annually

Canadian Lutheran World Relief (CLWR)

#600, 177 Lombard Ave., Winnipeg MB R3B 0W5
Tel: 204-694-5602; *Fax:* 204-694-5460
Toll-Free: 800-661-2597
clwr@clwr.mb.ca
www.clwr.org
www.facebook.com/CanadianLutheranWorldRelief
twitter.com/canlwr
www.youtube.com/user/CLWRvideo
Overview: A large national charitable organization founded in 1946
Mission: To provide development programming in Africa, Asia, Latin America, & the Middle East; To provide emergency relief in case of disaster; To enable sponsorships for refugee resettlement in Canada; To focus on development, peace building, alternative approaches to trade, education, & community building
Member of: Canadian Foodgrains Bank; The Lutheran World Federation; ACT Alliance; Canadian Churches in Action; Canadian Council for International Cooperation; Manitoba Council for International Cooperation; Saskatchewan Council for International Cooperation
Chief Officer(s):
Robert Granke, Executive Director, 204-631-0113
rgranke@clwr.mb.ca
Tom Brook, Director, Community Relations Team, 204-631-0115
tbrook@clwr.mb.ca
Elaine Peters, Director, Program Team, 204-631-0116
elainep@clwr.mb.ca
Lyn Stienstra, Director, Finance & Administration Team, 204-631-0507
lyn@clwr.mb.ca
Finances: *Funding Sources:* Evangelical Lutheran Church of Canada; Lutheran Church-Canada; Canadian Lutherans; Government
Staff Member(s): 21
Activities: *Speaker Service:* Yes
Publications:
• Canadian Lutheran World Relief Annual Report
Type: Yearbook; *Frequency:* Annually
Profile: Distributed to CLWR donors
• Canadian Lutheran World Relief Bulletin of Reports
Type: Yearbook; *Frequency:* Annually
Profile: CLWR activities & financial information
• CLWR [Canadian Lutheran World Relief] News Briefs
Type: Newsletter; *Frequency:* Weekly
Profile: Summary of significant CLWR-related news events in Canada or around the world
• CLWR [Canadian Lutheran World Relief] Monthly Briefs
Frequency: Monthly
Profile: Information for constituents about events in the developing world & the response of Canadians
• Four Corners [a publication of the Canadian Lutheran World Relief]
Type: Newsletter; *Frequency:* Semiannually
Profile: News about alternative trade to create opportunities for artists in the developing world
• Partnership Newsletter [a publication of the Canadian Lutheran World Relief]
Type: Newsletter; *Frequency:* Quarterly; *Editor:* Lorne Kletke
ISSN: 1916-2308
Profile: Inspirational stories about people in the developing world

Eastern Regional Office
#101, 470 Weber St. North, Waterloo ON N2L 6J2
Tel: 519-725-8777; *Fax:* 519-725-8776
Toll-Free: 888-255-0150
Chief Officer(s):
Jennifer Ardon, Contact
jardon@clwr.mb.ca

Western Regional Office
80 East 10 Ave., New Westminster BC V3L 4R5
Tel: 604-540-9760; *Fax:* 604-540-9795
Toll-Free: 888-588-6686
clwr@clwrbc.ca
Chief Officer(s):
Fikre M. Tsehai, Development Manager

Canadian Lyme Disease Foundation / Fondation canadienne de la maladie de lyme

2495 Reece Rd., Westbank BC V4T 1N1
Tel: 250-768-0978; *Fax:* 250-768-0946
www.canlyme.org
www.facebook.com/143033619666?ref=hl
www.twitter.com/canlyme
Also Known As: CanLyme
Overview: A small national charitable organization
Mission: To advance research about Lyme Disease in Canada
Affliation(s): International Lyme & Associated Diseases Society (ILADS)
Chief Officer(s):
Jim Wilson, President & Founder
jimwilson@telus.net
Finances: *Funding Sources:* Donations; Fundraising
Activities: Providing Canadian Lyme Disease news & research; *Library:* Canadian Lyme Disease Foundation Library

Canadian Lymphedema Foundation

414 Cliffe Ave. SW, Calgary AB T2S 0Z4
e-mail: info@lymphovenous-canada.ca
www.lymphovenous-canada.ca
Overview: A small national organization founded in 2002
Mission: To support lymphatic research & related programs in Canada that will lead to breakthroughs in understanding, treatment & prevention of lymphedema & related disorders
Affliation(s): Lymphovenous Canada
Finances: *Annual Operating Budget:* $50,000-$100,000
Membership: *Committees:* Fund raising; Scientific advisory
Activities: Scientific symposiums on the lymphatic systems; Quarterly meetings; Funding scientific research into lymphatic disorders

Canadian Machinery Vibration Association (CMVA) / Association canadienne en vibrations de machines (ACVM)

#1260, 225 The East Mall, Toronto ON M9B 0A9
Tel: 416-622-1170; *Fax:* 416-622-5376
val@cmva.com
www.cmva.com
Overview: A small national organization founded in 1993
Mission: A not-for-profit association dedicated to the advancement of machinery condition monitoring technologies.
Chief Officer(s):
Andy Woodcock, Executive Director
awoodcock@cmva.com
Finances: *Annual Operating Budget:* $100,000-$250,000
Membership: 550; *Fees:* $120 individual; $750 corporate
Meetings/Conferences: • Canadian Machinery Vibration Association 2015 Annual Seminar, 2015
Scope: National
Publications:
• Good Vibes
Type: Newsletter; *Frequency:* Quarterly; *Editor:* Val Zacharias

Canadian Magen David Adom for Israel (CMDA) / Magen David Adom canadien pour Israël

#3155, 6900, boul Decarie, Montréal QC H3X 2T8
Tel: 514-731-4400; *Fax:* 514-731-2490
Toll-Free: 800-731-2848
info@cmdai.org
www.cmdai.org
Overview: A small national charitable organization founded in 1976
Mission: To raise funds to purchase medical supplies to be sent to Israel
Member of: International Red Cross
Affliation(s): Magen David Adom, Israel
Chief Officer(s):
Arnold Rosner, National Executive Director
Finances: *Annual Operating Budget:* $250,000-$500,000
Staff Member(s): 1
Membership: 1,200; *Fees:* $18+; *Committees:* Executive; Finance; Marketing; Membership; Personnel
Activities: Fundraising events; concerts; guest speakers; games night; board meetings; *Awareness Events:* Israel Day, March; Israeli Street Festival, May or June; Mall Exhibitions

Calgary Chapter
PO Box 73112, RPO Woodbine, Calgary AB T2W 6E4
Tel: 403-251-6802
www.cmdai.org/calgary/
Chief Officer(s):
James Cohen, Co-Chair
s_s_wainer@shaw.ca

London Chapter
116 Maxwell Crt., London ON N5X 1Z3
Tel: 519-455-5411
www.cmdai.org/london/
Chief Officer(s):
Naomi Sheinbaum, Co-Chair
naomi8@sympatico.ca

Ottawa Chapter
95 Beaver Ridge, Ottawa ON K2E 6E5
Tel: 613-224-2500
www.cmdai.org/ottawa/
Chief Officer(s):
Seymour Eisenberg, President
seyeis@rogers.com

Toronto Chapter
#508, 4580 Dufferin St., Toronto ON M3H 5Y2
Tel: 416-780-0034; *Fax:* 416-780-0343
Toll-Free: 888-858-2632
toronto@cmdai.org
www.cmdai.org/toronto/
Chief Officer(s):
Iris Ehrent, Administrative Coordinator

Vancouver Chapter
#318, 101-1001 West Broadway, Vancouver BC V6H 4E4
Tel: 604-873-5244; *Fax:* 604-873-5246
vancouver@cmdai.org
www.cmdai.org/vancouver/

Canadian Maine-Anjou Association (CMAA)

5160 Skyline Way NE, Calgary AB T2E 6V1
Tel: 403-291-7077; *Fax:* 403-291-0274
cmaa@maine-anjou.ca
www.maine-anjou.ca
Overview: A small national organization founded in 1970
Mission: To encourage, develop, & regulate the breeding of Main-Anjou cattle in Canada
Member of: Canadian Beef Breeds Council
Chief Officer(s):
Stuart Byman, President
Murray Preece, Secretary
Brian Brown, Treasurer
Membership: *Member Profile:* Breeders engaged in propagation & breeding of Maine-Anjou cattle
Publications:
• The Maine Mail
Type: Magazine; *Frequency:* Bi-annually; *Editor:* Carolyn McCormack

Canadian Management Centre

150 York St., 5th Fl., Toronto ON M5H 3S5
Fax: 416-214-6047
Toll-Free: 877-262-2519
cmcinfo@cmcoutperform.com
www.cmctraining.org
www.linkedin.com/company/35861
twitter.com/canadianmgmt
www.youtube.com/user/CdnMgmtCtr
Overview: A large national organization
Mission: To play a key role in strengthening the ability of Canada's business leaders, managers & organizations to compete & succeed in today's challenging & changing business environment; To provide a full range of professional development & management education services to companies, government agencies, & individuals
Affliation(s): American Management Association International
Chief Officer(s):
John Wright, President & Managing Director
Jo Bouchard, Vice-President, Business Development
Andre Proulx, Vice-President, Marketing
Bernadette Smith, Vice-President, Learning Solutions
Activities: *Speaker Service:* Yes; *Rents Mailing List:* Yes
Awards:
• Canadian Management Centre Recognized Once Again for Innovation and Excellence in Leadership Training (Award)

Canadian Manufactured Housing Institute (CMHI)

#500, 150 Laurier Ave. West, Ottawa ON K1P 5J4
Tel: 613-563-3520; *Fax:* 613-232-8600
cmhi@cmhi.ca
www.cmhi.ca
www.linkedin.com/company/canadian-manufactured-housing-institute
twitter.com/CMHI_ICHU
plus.google.com/105246295798437075142
Overview: A medium-sized national organization founded in 1953
Mission: To be the voice of the manufactured housing industry in Canada; to seek, identify & solidify the development of new, profitable market opportunities for manufactured housing, both domestically & internationally; to promote housing affordability for all Canadians.
Chief Officer(s):
Dale Ball, President

Membership: *Fees:* $1000 national; $400 regional; *Member Profile:* Manufacturers; retailers; suppliers
Activities: *Library*

Canadian Manufacturers & Exporters (CME) / Manufacturiers et Exportateurs Canada

#1500, 1 Nicholas St., Ottawa ON K1N 7B7
Tel: 613-238-8888; *Fax:* 613-563-9218
www.cme-mec.ca
www.linkedin.com/companies/100367/Canadian+Manufacturers+%26+Exporters
twitter.com/cme_mec
www.youtube.com/manufacturingTV
Previous Name: Alliance of Manufacturers & Exporters Canada
Merged from: Canadian Manufacturers' Association (1871); Canadian Exporters' Association (1943)
Overview: A large national organization founded in 1996
Mission: To continuously improve the competitiveness of Canadian industry & to expand export business by: aggressive, effective advocacy to government at all levels; delivering timely, relevant information, programs & support of superior quality & value; providing opportunities for education, learning & professional growth; & promoting the development & implementation of advanced technology
Chief Officer(s):
Jayson Myers, President & Chief Executive Officer, 613-238-8888 Ext. 4231
jayson.myers@cme-mec.ca
Jeff Sholdice, Chief Financial Officer & Vice-President, Operations, 613-238-8888 Ext. 3245
jeff.sholdice@cme-mec.ca
Jeff Brownlee, Vice-President, Public Affairs & Partnerships, 613-238-8888 Ext. 4233
jeff.brownlee@cme-mec.ca
Joanne Heighway, Vice-President, Organizational Excellence, 613-238-8888 Ext. 3294
joanne.heighway@cme-mec.ca
John Knox, Vice-President, Sales & Marketing, 613-238-8888 Ext. 3258
john.knox@cme-mec.ca
Jean-Michel Laurin, Vice-President, Global Business Policy, 613-238-8888 Ext. 4238
jean-michel.laurin@cme-mec.ca
Craig Williams, Vice-President, National Programs, 604-713-7844
craig.williams@cme-mec.ca
Mathew Wilson, Vice-President, National Policy, 905-672-3466 Ext. 3242
mathew.wilson@cme-mec.ca
Finances: *Funding Sources:* Membership fees; Publication sales; Services
Membership: 5,000-14,999; *Fees:* Schedule available; *Member Profile:* Manufacturers, exporters, exporting companies, businesses & institutions servicing the manufacturing & exporting sectors; *Committees:* Environmental Quality; Export Financing; Insurance; Export Issues Roundtable; Export Promotion; Development Aid; Legislation; Market Access & Customs; Science & Technology; Service Exporters; Standards; Taxation & Financial Issues; Transportation
Activities: *Awareness Events:* Canadian Manufacturing Week, 2nd week of Oct.; *Speaker Service:* Yes
Meetings/Conferences: • Canadian Manufacturers & Exporters 2015 Dare to Compete Conference, March, 2015, RBC Convention Centre Winnipeg, Winnipeg, MB
Scope: National
Publications:
• 20/20: Canada's Industry Association Magazine
Type: Magazine; *Frequency:* Bimonthly; *Accepts Advertising*; *Editor:* Marie Morden
Profile: Information for Canadian industry to compete in the global economy, on subjects such as global competitiveness, workforce capability, energy, environment &efficiency, financial services, logistics, innovation, & CME strategy
• CME [Canadian Manufacturers & Exporters] Newsletter
Type: Newsletter

Alberta Division
#531, 10060 Jasper Ave., Edmonton AB T5J 3R8
Tel: 800-642-3871; *Fax:* 780-426-1509
www.cme-mec.ca
Chief Officer(s):
Neil Kaarsemaker, Director, Operations
neil.kaarsemaker@cme-mec.ca

Association des manufacturiers et des exportateurs du Québec
#210, 2000, rue Peel, Montréal QC H3A 2W5
Tél: 514-866-7774; *Téléc:* 514-866-9447
Ligne sans frais: 800-363-0226
info@meq.ca
qc.cme-mec.ca
Chief Officer(s):
Simon Prévost, Président
simon.prevost@meq.ca
José Jacome, Directeur général
jose.jacome@meq.ca

British Columbia Division
#540, 688 West Hastings St., Vancouver BC V6B 1P1
Tel: 604-713-7800; *Fax:* 604-713-7801
www.cme-mec.ca
Chief Officer(s):
Peter Jeffrey, Vice-President, 604-713-7804
peter.jeffrey@cme-mec.ca

Manitoba Division
110 Lowson Cres., Winnipeg MB R3P 2H8
Tel: 204-949-1454; *Fax:* 204-943-3476
www.cme-mec.ca
Chief Officer(s):
Ron Koslowsky, Vice-President
ron.koslowsky@cme-mec.ca

New Brunswick & Prince Edward Island Division
PO Box 7129, #12, 567 Coverdale Rd., Riverview NB E1B 4T8
Tel: 506-861-9071; *Fax:* 506-857-3049
www.cme-mec.ca
Chief Officer(s):
David Plante, Vice-President
david.plante@cme-mec.ca

Newfoundland & Labrador Division
Parsons Building, 90 O'Leary Ave., 1st Fl., St. John's NL A1B 2C7
Tel: 709-772-3682; *Fax:* 709-772-3213
www.cme-mec.ca
Chief Officer(s):
David Haire, Vice-President
david.haire@cme-mec.ca

Nova Scotia Division
Collins' Bank Building, #305, 1869 Upper Water St., Halifax NS B3J 1S9
Tel: 902-422-4477; *Fax:* 902-422-9563
Ann Janega, Vice President
ann.janega@cme-mec.ca

Ontario Division
#200, 6725 Airport Rd., Mississauga ON L4V 1V2
Tel: 800-268-9684; *Fax:* 905-672-1764
www.cme.mec.ca
Chief Officer(s):
Ian Howcroft, Vice-President
ian.howcroft@cme-mec.ca

Canadian Manufacturers of Chemical Specialties Association *See* Canadian Consumer Specialty Products Association

Canadian Marfan Association (CMA) / Association du syndrome de Marfan

PO Box 42257, Stn. Centre Plaza, 128 Queen St. South, Mississauga ON L5M 4Z0
Tel: 905-826-3223; *Fax:* 905-826-2125
Toll-Free: 866-722-1722
info@marfan.ca
www.marfan.ca
www.facebook.com/CanadianMarfanAssociation
twitter.com/CanadianMarfan
Overview: A medium-sized national charitable organization founded in 1986
Member of: International Federation of Marfan Syndrome Associations; Thoracic Aortic Disease (TAD) Coalition; Canadian Organization for Rare Disorders
Chief Officer(s):
Gandhi Sharmin, Executive Director
Finances: *Annual Operating Budget:* $100,000-$250,000; *Funding Sources:* Donations; Fundraising
Staff Member(s): 2; 150 volunteer(s)
Membership: 500; *Fees:* Donation
Activities: Increasing awareness of Marfan Syndrome through publications & information packages; Producing videos; Organizing presentations, seminars & conferences across Canada; Organizing Marfan regional support groups; Fostering & supporting research; *Awareness Events:* National Marfan Awareness Week, 3rd week of November; *Internships:* Yes; *Library:* Canadian Marfan Association Resource Centre; by appointment

Canadian Marine Manufacturers Association *See* National Marine Manufacturers Association Canada

Canadian Marine Officers' Union (AFL-CIO/CLC) / Syndicat canadien des officiers de la marine marchande (FAT-COI/CTC)

9670, Notre-Dame East, Montreal QC H1L 3P8
Tel: 514-354-8321; *Fax:* 514-354-8368
info@cmou.ca
www.cmou.ca
Overview: A medium-sized national organization
Chief Officer(s):
Richard Vezina, President
Membership: 1,225

Canadian Marine Pilots' Association (CMPA) / Association des pilotes maritimes du Canada (APMC)

#1302, 155 Queen St., Ottawa ON K1P 6L1
Tel: 613-232-7777; *Fax:* 613-232-7667
cmpa@tnpa.ca
www.marinepilots.ca
Overview: A small national organization founded in 1966
Mission: To represent Canadian marine pilots; To raise awareness of marine pilots' role to protect public safety; To ensure a healthy Canadian marine sector
Member of: International Maritime Pilots' Association; Canadian Merchant Service Guild
Chief Officer(s):
Simon Pelletier, President
Bernard Boissonneault, Vice-President
Laurentian Region
Mike Burgess, Vice-President
Great Lakes Region
Fred Denning, Vice-President
Pacific Region
Andrew Rae, Vice-President
Atlantic Region
Membership: 400; *Member Profile:* Marine pilots in Canada
Activities: Upholding a Code of Conduct for Canadian pilots; Contributing to matters of safety & regulatory issues; Collaborating with marine stakeholders to maintain a vibrant marine sector
Meetings/Conferences: • Canadian Marine Pilots' Association 5th Congress, 2017
Scope: National
Publications:
• The Canadian Pilot: The CMPA Newsletter
Type: Newsletter
Profile: Information, articles, & forthcoming events for pilots & other stakeholders in the industry

Canadian Maritime Industries Association *See* Shipbuilding Association of Canada

Canadian Maritime Law Association / Association canadienne de droit maritime

#900, 1000, rue de la Gauchetiére ouest, Montréal QC H3B 5H4
Tel: 514-849-4161; *Fax:* 514-849-4167
cmla@blg.com
www.cmla.org
Overview: A medium-sized national organization founded in 1951
Mission: To represent all Canadian commercial maritime interests for the uniform development of Canadian & international maritime law affecting marine transportation & related aspects
Member of: Comité maritime international
Chief Officer(s):
Robert C. Wilkins, Secretary-Treasurer
rwilkins@blg.com
Christopher J. Giaschi, President
giaschi@admiraltylaw.com
John G. O'Connor, National Vice-President
john.oconnor@lkd.ca
Finances: *Funding Sources:* Membership fees
Membership: 318 individual + 20 organizations; *Fees:* $105 individual; $500 organization; *Member Profile:* Individual, association, or corporate body resident in Canada; *Committees:* Executive; Liaison; Limitation of Liability; Marine Insurance; Special Liaison; Tanker Safety

Canadian Marketing Association (CMA) / Association canadienne du marketing (ACM)

#607, 1 Concorde Gate, Toronto ON M3C 3N6
Tel: 416-391-2362; *Fax:* 416-441-4062
info@the-cma.org
www.the-cma.org
www.linkedin.com/groups?mostPopular=&gid=47336
www.facebook.com/cdnmarketing
twitter.com/Cdnmarketing
Previous Name: Canadian Direct Marketing Association
Overview: A large national organization founded in 1967
Mission: To be the pre-eminent marketing association in Canada representing the integration & convergence of all marketing disciplines, channels & technologies
Affliation(s): European Direct Marketing Association; Direct Marketing Association - USA
Chief Officer(s):
John Gustavson, President & CEO
Peg Hunter, Chair
Finances: *Annual Operating Budget:* $1.5 Million-$3 Million; *Funding Sources:* Membership dues; events
Staff Member(s): 28; 400 volunteer(s)
Membership: 800 corporate; 1,200 total; *Member Profile:* Membership includes corporations & organizations which encompass Canada's major business sectors & which represent the integration & convergence of all marketing disciplines, channels & technologies; supports 480,000 jobs & generates more than $51 billion in overall annual sales; *Committees:* Special Interest Councils - Branding & Strategic Planning; Customer Relationship Management; Database & Marketing Technology; Integrated Marketing Communications; Not-for-Profit; Contact Centre; Direct Mail; E-Marketing
Activities: Responds to public policy issues; participates in a variety of government-led task forces & working groups on issues such as privacy, electronic commerce, consumer protection, the prevention of telemarketing fraud, & unsolicited bulk e-mail; forms internal task forces to develop self-regulatory policies on standards of business practice, ethics, privacy, & marketing to children & teenagers; enforces Code of Ethics & Standards of Practice & Privacy Code; *Rents Mailing List:* Yes
Awards:
• CMA Awards (Award)
20 categories; direct response campaigns from all media are considered
• CMA Student Awards (Award)
Meetings/Conferences: • 2015 Canadian Marketing Association Conference: CMAcreative, April, 2015
Scope: National
Description: A day with the leading creative minds in marketing and beyond, exploring the standout ideas and newest ways of thinking to help inspire and motivate you to make the next breakthrough in your life.
• 2015 Canadian Marketing Association Conference: CMAconnections, September, 2015
Scope: National
Description: CMAconnections focuses on all aspects of interaction between brands and their audience and consumer.
• 2015 Canadian Marketing Association Conference: CMAfuture, November, 2015
Scope: National
Description: A look at the newest methods, strategies and technology on the horizon; the best things you've never heard of.
• 2016 Canadian Marketing Association Conference: CMAideas, January, 2016
Scope: National
Description: Brings together a unique conference of creators, innovators and leaders with insights from unlikely places and undiscovered territories.
• 2016 Canadian Marketing Association Conference: CMAinsights, March, 2016
Scope: National
Description: CMAinsights will feature multiple content streams; focusing on both the marketer and the data practitioner.
Publications:
• Canadian Marketing Association Membership Directory & Buyers' Guide
Type: Directory; *Accepts Advertising*
Profile: Listing of companies & their services
• CMA [Canadian Marketing Association] Guide to E-mail Marketing
Type: Guide
Profile: Theory, best practices & practical advice, for marketers
• CMA [Canadian Marketing Association] Fundraiser's Handbook
Type: Handbook; *Number of Pages:* 35; *Price:* $15 members; $25 non-members
Profile: A guide to measurement & evaluation

British Columbia Association of Integrated Marketers
#102, 211 Columbia St., Vancouver BC V6A 2R5
Tel: 604-633-0033; *Fax:* 604-681-4545
info@bcaim.org
www.bcaim.org
www.facebook.com/group.php?gid=22340780165
twitter.com/BCAIM
Chief Officer(s):
Rob Dawson, President

Calgary Chapter
PO Box 5071, Stn. A, Calgary AB T2H 1X1
Tel: 403-860-8745; *Fax:* 403-974-2043
info@calgarycma.com
www.calgarycma.com
www.linkedin.com/companies/433702
twitter.com/calgarycma
www.flickr.com/calgarycma
Chief Officer(s):
Jim Carter, President
jim.carter@theclient.ca

Manitoba Chapter
PO Box 1973, Winnipeg MB R3C 3R3
Tel: 204-284-5642
www.cmamanitoba.com
www.facebook.com/marketingmanitoba
www.twitter.com/cma_manitoba
Chief Officer(s):
Kevin Gordon, Interim President
president@cmamanitoba.com

Ottawa Chapter
PO Box 8024, Stn. Alta Vista, Ottawa ON K1G 3H6
Fax: 613-248-4667
info@cmaottawa.com
www.cmaottawa.com
Chief Officer(s):
Sharon Daly, President
s.daly@calian.com

Association du marketing relationnel
#109, 1744, rue William, Montréal QC H3J 1R4
Tél: 514-904-1927
info@relationnel.ca
relationnel.ca
www.linkedin.com/groups?gid=1743317
www.facebook.com/AMRQuebec
twitter.com/AMRQuebec
www.youtube.com/user/AMRQuebec
Chief Officer(s):
Alex Langlois, Président

Canadian Masonry Contractors' Association (CMCA)

Canada Masonry Centre, 360 Superior Blvd., Mississauga ON L5T 2N7
Tel: 905-564-6622; *Fax:* 905-564-5744
www.canadamasonrycentre.com/cmca
Overview: A medium-sized national organization founded in 1967
Mission: To advance masonry technology, skills development & the use of masonry products in construction across Canada.
Member of: National Trade Contractors Coalition of Canada
Affliation(s): Ontario Masonry Contractors' Association; Metro Mason Contractors Association; Canada Masonry Centre
Finances: *Funding Sources:* Membership dues
Activities: *Speaker Service:* Yes; *Library* by appointment

Association des entrepreneurs en maçonnerie du Québec
#101, 4097, boul Saint-Jean Baptiste, Montréal QC H1B 5V3
Tél: 514-645-1113; *Téléc:* 514-645-1114
Ligne sans frais: 866-645-1113
aemq@aemq.com
www.aemq.com
www.linkedin.com/company/aemq—association-des-entrepreneurs-en-maçon
www.facebook.com/171902572902949
Chief Officer(s):
Marco Tommasel, Président

British Columbia & Yukon Chapter
3636 - 4th Ave. East, Vancouver BC V5M 1M3
Tel: 604-291-1458; *Fax:* 604-291-9482
info@masonrybc.org
www.masonrybc.org

Manitoba Masonry Contractors' Association
Manitoba Masonry Institute, 1447 Waverley St., Winnipeg MB R3T 0P7
Tel: 204-949-0688
mmi_mmca@mts.net
www.manitobamasonry.ca

Masonry Contractors' Association of Alberta, Northern Region
PO Box 44157, RPO Garside, Edmonton AB T5V 1N6
Tel: 780-851-7013; *Fax:* 780-851-7013
mcaanorth@mca-canada.com
www.mca-canada.com
Chief Officer(s):
Karen Schneider, Contact

Masonry Contractors' Association of Alberta, Southern Region
#169, 132-250 Shawville Blvd. SE, Calgary AB T2Y 2Z7
Tel: 587-998-4023
mcaasouth@mca-canada.com
www.mca-canada.com
Chief Officer(s):
Danine McDougall, Contact

Ontario Masonry Contractors' Association
360 Superior Blvd., Mississauga ON L5T 2N7
Tel: 905-564-6622
www.canadamasonrycentre.com/omca

Saskatchewan Masonry Institute
532 - 2nd Ave. North, Saskatoon SK S7K 2C5
Tel: 306-665-0622; *Fax:* 306-665-0621
info@saskmasonry.ca
www.saskmasonry.ca
Chief Officer(s):
Rob Walchuk, President

Canadian Massage Therapist Alliance (CMTA) *See* Massage Therapy Alliance of Canada

Canadian Masters Athletic Association (CMAA)

Tel: 416-380-2503
canadianmasters.ca
Previous Name: Canadian Masters Track & Field Association
Overview: A medium-sized national organization founded in 1972
Chief Officer(s):
Paul Osland, President
paul.osland@hotmail.com
Sherry Watts, Contact, Membership
pacertraining@yahoo.ca
Finances: *Funding Sources:* Membership fees
Membership: 1,527; *Member Profile:* Men & women 30 and up
Publications:
• The MASTERpiece
Type: Newsletter; *Frequency:* Irregular; *Price:* Free with CMAA membership
Profile: News, results, & upcoming events for Masters

Canadian Masters Cross-Country Ski Association (CMCSA) / Association canadienne des maîtres en ski de fond

c/o 2 MacNeil Cres., Stephenville NL A2N 3E3
Tel: 709-643-3259
www.canadian-masters-xc-ski.ca/en_index.htm
Overview: A medium-sized national organization founded in 1980
Mission: To promote Masters cross-country skiing across Canada, establish rules & regulations for activities, & representing members at meetings at the WMA.
Affliation(s): World Masters Cross-Country Ski Association; Cross-Country Canada
Chief Officer(s):
Bruce Legrow, National Director
bruce.legrow@nf.sympatico.ca
Finances: *Funding Sources:* Membership fees
Membership: *Fees:* $20; $35 in Québec; *Member Profile:* 30 years of age & over
Activities: Cross country ski races in Canada & abroad; Masters World Cup; Canadian Masters National Championships
Publications:
• Canadian Masters Cross-Country Ski Association Newsletter
Type: Newsletter; *Frequency:* Irregular; *Price:* Free with CMCSA membership
Profile: Information & upcoming events for Masters skiers

Alberta
c/o Dave Rees, 12 Spray Village, Canmore AB T1W 2T5
Tel: 403-707-5565
Chief Officer(s):

Dave Rees, Director
rees.ski@gmail.com
British Columbia
c/o Mike Bell, 4193B Gordon Dr., Kelowna BC V1W 1S4
Tel: 250-540-1273
Chief Officer(s):
Mike Bell, Director
mikebell10@gmail.com
Manitoba
c/o Danielle Papin, 126 Sherbrun St., Winnipeg MB R3G 2K4
Tel: 204-772-2535
Chief Officer(s):
Danielle Papin, Director
dpapin@mts.net
New Brunswick
c/o Roger Lévesque, 94 Pioneer Ave., Balmoral NB E8E 1E1
Tel: 506-826-2534
Chief Officer(s):
Roger Levesque, Director
Newfoundland/Labrador
c/o Bruce Legrow, 2 MacNeil Cres., Stephenville NL A2N 3E3
Tel: 709-643-3259
Chief Officer(s):
Bruce LeGrow, Director
bruce.legrow@nf.sympatico.ca
Ontario
c/o Russ Evans, 24 Cortina Cres., Hamilton ON L8K 4K4
Tel: 905-547-7162
Chief Officer(s):
Russ Evans, Director
revans@cogeco.ca
Québec
c/o Rock Ouimet, 546, rue de la Tourelle, Québec QC G1R 1E3
Chief Officer(s):
Rock Ouimet, Director
rock.ouimet@gmail.com
Saskatchewan
c/o Robin Butler, 531 Emmeline Key, Saskatoon SK S7J 5G8
Tel: 306-373-6658
Chief Officer(s):
Robin Butler, Director
skirobin@sasktel.net
Yukon
c/o Mary Whitley, 1 Chalet Cres., Whitehorse YT Y1A 3H1
Tel: 867-668-2903
Chief Officer(s):
Mary Whitley, Director
whitley@polarcom.com

Canadian Masters Track & Field Association *See* Canadian Masters Athletic Association

---

Canadian Mathematical Society (CMS) / Société mathématique du Canada

#209, 1785 St Laurent Blvd., Ottawa ON K1G 3Y4
Tel: 613-733-2662; *Fax:* 613-733-8994
office@cms.math.ca
www.cms.math.ca
www.facebook.com/canmathsoc
twitter.com/canadmathsoc
Overview: A medium-sized international charitable organization founded in 1945
Mission: To promote & advance the discovery, learning & application of mathematics
Member of: National Consortium for Scientific Societies
Chief Officer(s):
Johan Rudnick, Executive Director, 613-733-2662 Ext. 721
director@cms.math.ca
Finances: *Annual Operating Budget:* $500,000-$1.5 Million; *Funding Sources:* Membership; publications; donations
Staff Member(s): 9; 210 volunteer(s)
Membership: 1,068; *Fees:* $21-$249 individual; $98-$1092 institution; *Member Profile:* University professors; students; teachers & mathematicians; *Committees:* Education; Electronic Services; Finance; Advancement of Mathematics; Human Rights; International Affairs; Mathematical Competitions; Nominating; Publications; Research; Women in Mathematics
Activities: Meetings; publishing; competitions; mathematics awareness; electronic services; represents the Canadian mathematical community to federal & provincial governments; *Speaker Service:* Yes; *Rents Mailing List:* Yes
Awards:
• Canadian Mathematical Olympiad (Award)
Annual mathematics competition established to provide an opportunity for students to perform well on the Canadian Open Mathematics Challenge & to complete on a national basis. Fifteen cash prizes
Meetings/Conferences: • 2015 Canadian Mathematical Society Summer Meeting, June, 2015, University of Prince Edward Island, Charlottetown, PE
Scope: National
Publications:
• Canadian Journal of Mathematics (CJM)
Type: Journal
• Canadian Mathematical Bulletin (CMB)
Type: Journal
• Canadian Mathematical Society Notes
Type: Journal

Canadian Meat Council (CMC) / Conseil des viandes du Canada

#407, 1545 Carling Ave., Ottawa ON K1Z 8P9
Tel: 613-729-3911; *Fax:* 613-729-4997
info@cmc-cvc.com
www.cmc-cvc.com
Previous Name: Meat Packers Council of Canada
Overview: A medium-sized national organization founded in 1919
Mission: To express the views of the membership with government, all elements of the food industry, consumer organizations, the research & academic community, & the media; To foster high standards of industry integrity, & a vast range of wholesome, nutritional meat products
Chief Officer(s):
James M. Laws, Executive Director, 613-729-3911 Ext. 24
jiml@cmc-cvc.com
Ray Price, First Vice President-Treasurer
Finances: *Funding Sources:* Membership dues
Staff Member(s): 6
Membership: 66; *Member Profile:* Federally inspected packers & processors of meat; *Committees:* Beef, Veal & Lamb; Pork; Technical, Processed Meats, Environment; Foodservice; Special Events; Annual Conference; Administrative Committees
Activities: Responding to members' needs; Contributing to the competitiveness of the industry at both domestic & international levels; Providing a forum for members to discuss & consider matters relating to government regulations & activities, competitiveness, & dealings with other national trade associations; Working towards a free & expanding market environment; *Speaker Service:* Yes; *Library:* Council Library
Awards:
• Canadian Meat Council Associate Members Scholarship (Scholarship)
Meetings/Conferences: • Canadian Meat Council 2015 95th Annual Conference, 2015
Scope: National
Description: A meeting with a technical symposium & exhibits, a general session, as well as the announcement of scholarship recipients
Contact Information: Event Planner, Tanya Poirier, Phone: 613-729-3911 ext. 31
Publications:
• Food Service Meat Manual / Manuel des vaindes pour les services alimenaires
Type: Manual; *Number of Pages:* 40+; *Price:* $30 for 1-9 copies; $25 for 10+copies
Profile: The third revised edition that outines the cutting & trimming technniqes for 86 cuts of meat

---

Canadian Meat Goat Association (CMGA) / Canadienne de la Chèvre de Boucherie

c/o Karen Kolkman, PO Box 61, Annaheim SK S0K 0G0
Tel: 306-598-4322; *Fax:* 306-598-8901
info@canadianmeatgoat.com
www.canadianmeatgoat.com
Previous Name: Canadian Boer Goat Association
Overview: A small national organization founded in 1995
Mission: To support the development of a profitable meat goat breeding stock & meat industry in Canada; To provide animal registration; To establish breeding standards; To promote the industry & raise consumer demand for chevon
Affliation(s): Canadian Livestock Records Corporation
Chief Officer(s):
Karen Kolkman, General Manager, 306-598-4322, Fax: 306-598-8901
Kerry O'Donnell, President, 306-742-2050
kod@sasktel.net
Membership: *Fees:* $50 active members; $35 associate members; $20 junior members (persons under 18 years); *Member Profile:* Commercial meat goat & purebred seed stock producers across Canada; *Committees:* Executive; Advertising & Promotion; Breed Improvement; Membership; Show; Advisory; Nominating; Constitution; Hardship Case
Activities: Creating educational tools for commercial meat goat & purebred seed stock producers; Partnering in research; Introducing a youth program; Developing marketing tools in order to expand the market; Representing members at agricultural events throughout Canada
Publications:
• Canadian Meat Goat Association Membership Directory
Type: Directory; *Frequency:* Annually
• Canadian Meat Goat Journal
Type: Journal; *Frequency:* Quarterly; *Accepts Advertising*; *Price:* Free with Canadian Meat Goat Association membership
Profile: Management of goats; business practices; goat health issues, & marketing

---

Canadian Meat Science Association (CMSA) / Association scientifique canadienne de la viande (ASCB)

Dept. of Agricultural, Food & Nutritional Science, Univ. of Alberta, #4-10, Agriculture / Forestry Centre, Edmonton AB T6G 2P5
Tel: 780-492-3651; *Fax:* 780-492-5771
ruth.ball@ales.ualberta.ca
www.cmsa-ascv.ca
Overview: A medium-sized national organization
Mission: To promote the application of science & technology to the production, processing, packaging, distribution, preparation, evaluation, & utilization of all meat & meat products; To develop & promote useful, coordinated research, educational techniques, & service activities
Chief Officer(s):
Peter Purslow, President, 519-824-4120 Ext. 52099
ppurslow@uoguelph.ca
Sandra Gruber, President-Elect, 403-671-0781
gruber_sandra@lilly.com
Manuel Juárez, Sec.-Treas., 403-782-8118
manuel.juarez@agr.gc.ca
Sylvain Fournaise, Director at Large, 514-858-9000
sylvainfournaise@olymel.com
Membership: 13 corporate members; *Fees:* $60 professional; $200 corporate; $0 students; *Member Profile:* Individuals & corporations with an interest in the science of meat & meat products; *Committees:* Promotion & Membership; Education; Newsletter; Nominations & Elections; Symposium; Website & Electronic Communications; Audit
Activities: Providing forums & networking opportunities for discussion & dissemination of information; Promoting recognition of people engaged in meat science
Awards:
• Percy Gitelman Memorial Scholarship (Scholarship)
Sponsored jointly by the Canadian Meat Science Association and Newly Weds Foods, Inc. *Amount:* $3,000
• CMC Associate Members Scholarship (Scholarship)
To honour a promising graduate student who is studying Meat Science in Canada *Amount:* 3,000
Meetings/Conferences: • Canadian Meat Science Association 2015 Annual Meeting, 2015
Scope: National
• Canadian Meat Science Association 2015 Technical Symposium, 2015
Scope: National
Publications:
• Canadian Meat Science Association Membership Directory
Type: Directory; *Frequency:* Annually
Profile: A listing of persons & organizations throughout Canada with an interest in meat science
• CMSA [Canadian Meat Science Association] News
Type: Newsletter; *Frequency:* Quarterly
Profile: Activities of the meat sector & the association for CMSA members

---

Canadian Mechanical Contracting Education Foundation (CMCEF)

#601, 280 Albert St., Ottawa ON K1P 5G8
Tel: 613-232-5169; *Fax:* 613-235-2793
cmef@cmcef.org
www.cmcef.org
Overview: A medium-sized national organization founded in 1998 overseen by Mechanical Contractors Association of Canada
Mission: To ensure a stronger Mechanical Contracting Industry by initiating and conducting essential educational and research programs which enhance this industry's ability to operate

efficiently and economically for the benefit of those served by the industry.
Chief Officer(s):
Tania Johnston, Executive Director

Canadian Media Directors' Council (CMDC)

#1097, 1930 Yonge St., Toronto ON M4S 1Z4
Tel: 416-967-7282
bruce.claassen@genesismedia.com
www.cmdc.ca
Overview: A small national organization founded in 1966
Mission: To advance media advertising in Canada; To create more efficient processes to execute and administer media transactions by adopting industry-wide standards
Affliation(s): Institute of Communications and Advertising (ICA)
Chief Officer(s):
Penny Stevens, President, 416-597-0707 Ext. 32
pennys@mediaexperts.com
Janet Callaghan, Executive Director, 416-921-4049
js.callaghan@sympatico.ca
Membership: 38; *Member Profile:* Media professionals who represent advertising & media management companies in Canada
Activities: Liaising with government, media sellers, & advertising organizations; Providing continuing education program for media professionals

Canadian Media Guild (CMG) / La Guilde canadienne des médias

#810, 310 Front St. West, Toronto ON M5V 3B5
Tel: 416-591-5333; *Fax:* 416-591-7278
Toll-Free: 800-465-4149
info@cmg.ca
www.cmg.ca
www.facebook.com/pages/Canadian-Media-Guild/108304249197614
Previous Name: Canadian Wire Service Guild
Overview: A medium-sized national organization founded in 1950
Mission: To advance the interests of Guild members through collective bargaining
Affliation(s): CWA/SCA Canada
Chief Officer(s):
Carmel Smyth, National President
carmel@cmg.ca
Karen Wirsig, Coordinator, Communications
karen@cmg.ca
Membership: 6,000; *Member Profile:* Members work in the Canadian media & become part of a democratic trade union
Activities: Promoting good working environments; Providing training & education to assist members
Publications:
• G-Force
Type: Newsletter; *Frequency:* Quarterly; *Editor:* Karen Wirsig
Profile: Media issues & information for CMG members

Halifax Regional Office
#133, 1657 Barrington St., Halifax NS B3J 2A1
Tel: 902-471-6070
Chief Officer(s):
Gerald Whelan, Staff Representative, Atlantic Office
gerry@cmg.ca

Ottawa Regional Office
Ottawa ON
Toll-Free: 877-947-9477
Chief Officer(s):
Gabi Durocher, Staff Representative
gabi@cmg.ca

Vancouver Regional Office
Vancouver BC
Tel: 604-642-2554
Chief Officer(s):
Jean Broughton, Staff Representative, Western Office
jean@cmg.ca

Canadian Media Production Association

601 Bank St., 2nd Fl., Ottawa ON K1S 3T4
Tel: 613-233-1444; *Fax:* 613-233-0073
Toll-Free: 800-656-7440
ottawa@cmpa.ca
www.cmpa.ca
www.linkedin.com/company/canadian-media-production-association-cmpa-
www.facebook.com/theCMPA
twitter.com/CMPA_Updates
www.youtube.com/CMPAOnline
Previous Name: Canadian Film & Television Production Association
Overview: A medium-sized national organization founded in 1990
Mission: To represent the interests of media companies engaged in the production & distribution of English language television programs, feature films, & new media content throughout Canada
Chief Officer(s):
Norm Bolen, President & Chief Executive Officer, 613-688-0946 Ext. 328
norm.bolen@cmpa.ca
Jane Cheesman, Chief Financial Officer, 613-688-0947 Ext. 330
jane.cheesman@cmpa.ca
Marc Séguin, Senior Vice-President, Policy, 613-688-0948 Ext. 323
marc.seguin@cmpa.ca
Jay Thomson, Vice-President, Broadcasting Policy & Regulatory Affairs, 613-688-0949 Ext. 322
jay.thomson@cmpa.ca
Susanne Vaas, Vice-President, Business Affairs, 613-688-0950 Ext. 337
susanne.vaas@cmpa.ca
Anne Trueman, Director, Communications & Media, 613-688-0951 Ext. 327
anne.trueman@cmpa.ca
Sarolta Csete, Manager, National Mentorship Program & e-Services, 613-688-0952 Ext. 338
sarolta.csete@cmpa.ca
Lisa Moreau, Manager, Member Services & Special Events, 613-688-0900 Ext. 329
lisa.moreau@cmpa.ca
Membership: 100-499
Activities: *Library*
Meetings/Conferences: • Canadian Media Production Association 2015 Conference: Prime Time in Ottawa, March, 2015, Westin Ottawa, Ottawa, ON
Scope: National
Description: A learning & networking opportunity for business leaders from the feature film, television, interactive media, broadcasting, & telecommunications industries
Contact Information: Web Site: www.primetimeinottawa.ca; Manager, Member Services & Special Events: Lisa Moreau, E-mail: lisa.moreau@cmpa.ca
Publications:
• Canadian Media Production Association's Note to Members
Type: Newsletter; *Price:* Free with membership in the Canadian Media Production Association
Profile: Containing pertinent industry information

Canadian Medical & Biological Engineering Society (CMBES) / Société canadienne de génie biomédical inc. (SCGB)

1485 Laperrière Ave., Ottawa ON K1Z 7S8
Tel: 613-728-1759
secretariat@cmbes.ca
www.cmbes.ca
Overview: A medium-sized national organization founded in 1965
Mission: To advance the theory & practice of medical device technology; To advance individuals who are engaged in interdisciplinary work involving medicine, engineering, & the life sciences; To represent the interests of biomedical & clinical engineering to government agencies
Affliation(s): International Federation for Medical and Biological Engineering (IFMBE)
Chief Officer(s):
Murat Firat, President
murat.firat@uhn.on.ca
Mike Capuano, Chair, Professional Affairs
capuamik@hhsc.ca
Tim J. Zakutney, Chair, Awards
tzakutney@ottawaheart.ca
Martin Poulin, Treasurer
martin.poulin@viha.ca
Melanie Chayra, Secretariat, 613-728-1759
secretariat@cmbes.ca
Membership: 100-499; *Fees:* $35 students; $130 full members; $150 student institutional; Schedule for corporate members, based upon number of members per group
Activities: Offering continuing education; Providing networking opportunities; *Awareness Events:* Biomedical / Clinical Engineering Appreciation Week
Meetings/Conferences: • Canadian Medical & Biological Engineering Society 2015 38th Annual National Conference, June, 2015, Toronto, ON
Scope: National
Description: An annual gathering of Canadian biomedical engineering professionals for continuing education & networking opportunities. This year's conference is a collaboration with l'Association des physiciens et ingénieurs biomédicaux du Québec (APIBQ).
Contact Information: Chair, Long-Term Conference Planning: Sarah Kelso, E-mail: sarah.a.kelso@gmail.com
• The World Congress on Medical Physics & Biomedical Engineering: IUPESM 2015 (hosted by the Canadian Medical & Biological Engineering Society), June, 2015, Toronto, ON
Scope: National
Description: Co-hosted with the Canadian Organization of Medical Physicists (COMP)
Contact Information: E-mail: secretariat@cmbes.ca; Chair, Long-Term Conference Planning: Sarah Kelso, E-mail: sarah.a.kelso@gmail.com
• Canadian Medical & Biological Engineering Society 2016 39th Annual National Conference, 2016, Calgary, AB
Scope: National
Description: An annual gathering of Canadian biomedical engineering professionals for continuing education & networking opportunities. This year's conference is a collaboration with l'Association des physiciens et ingénieurs biomédicaux du Québec (APIBQ).
Contact Information: Chair, Long-Term Conference Planning: Sarah Kelso, E-mail: sarah.a.kelso@gmail.com
Publications:
• Canadian Medical & Biological Engineering Society Conference Proceedings & Abstracts
• Canadian Medical & Biological Engineering Society Career Booklet
Type: Booklet
Profile: Information for guidance counselors & employment centers
• Clinical Engineering Standards of Practice [a publication of the Canadian Medical & Biological Engineering Society]
Type: Guide; *Price:* Free with Cdn. Medical & Biological Engineering Society membership; $50 non-members
Profile: Criteria for health care institutions on the management of medical devices, the education & certificationrequirements for clinical engineers & biomedical engineering technologists & technicians & the promotion of professional development
• CMBES [Canadian Medical & Biological Engineering Society Inc.] Newsletter
Type: Newsletter; *Editor:* Dr. Gnahoua Zoabli; Pamela Wilson
ISSN: 1499-4089
Profile: Society activities, conferences, events, awards, chapters, & events

Canadian Medical Association (CMA) / Association médicale canadienne (AMC)

1867 Alta Vista Dr., Ottawa ON K1G 5W8
Tel: 613-731-8610; *Fax:* 613-236-8864
Toll-Free: 888-855-2555
Other Communication: cmatechsupport@cma.ca (Technical Support)
cmamsc@cma.ca
www.cma.ca
twitter.com/CMA_Docs
www.youtube.com/user/CanadianMedicalAssoc
Overview: A large national organization founded in 1867
Mission: To act as the national voice of physicians in Canada; To serve the Canadian medical community; To promote the highest standards of health & health care
Member of: World Medical Association
Affliation(s): Assn. of Cdn. Medical Colleges; Cdn. Anesthesiologists' Soc.; Cdn. Assn. of Medical Biochemists; Cdn. Assn. of Physicians with Disabilities; Cdn. Assn. of Physicians for the Environment; Cdn. Assn. of Radiation Oncologists; Cdn. Fedn. of Medical Students; Cdn. Infectious Disease Soc.; Cdn. Neurological/Neurosurgical/Clinical Neurophysiologists Societies; Cdn. Ophthalmological Soc.; Cdn. Orthopaedic Assn.; Cdn. Paediatric Soc.; Cdn. Psychiatric Assn; Cdn. Rheumatology Assn.; Cdn. Soc. of Addiction Medicine; Cdn. Soc. of Internal Medicine; Cdn. Soc. of Nuclear Medicine; Cdn. Soc. of Otolaryngoly
Chief Officer(s):
Anne Reid, President
Michael Golbey, Chair
Louis Francescutti, President Elect
Membership: Over 50,000; *Member Profile:* Practising physicians; Residents; Retired physicians; Students; *Committees:* Ethics; Political Action; Health Care & Promotion;

Health Policy & Economics; Education & Professional Development
Activities: Providing national & provincial advocacy; Offering practice management solutions; Providing courses through the CMA's Physician Management Institute, a leadership development program designed for physicians in the Canadian health care system
Awards:
• Medal of Honour (Award)
• Medal of Service (Award)
• May Cohen Award for Women Mentors (Award)
• Sir Charles Tupper Award for Political Action (Award)
• F.N.G. Starr Award (Award)
• Award for Excellence in Health Promotion (Award)
• Awards for Young Leaders (Award)
• Dr. William Marsden Award in Medical Ethics (Award)
• Physician Misericordia Award (Award)
Meetings/Conferences: • Canadian Medical Association 2015 148th Annual Meeting, August, 2015, Halifax, NS
Scope: National
Description: General Council is open to delegates & observers who must be Canadian Medical Association members or invited guests
Contact Information: Registration Officer, Phone: 1-800-663-7336, ext. 2383, E-mail: gcregistrations@cma.ca
• Canadian Medical Association 2016 149th Annual Meeting, August, 2016
Scope: National
Description: A meeting, featuring a business session to consider business & matters referred by the General Council
Contact Information: Registration Officer, Phone: 1-800-663-7336, ext. 2383, E-mail: gcregistrations@cma.ca
Publications:
• Canadian Health Magazine
Type: Magazine; *Frequency:* Quarterly; *Accepts Advertising*; *Editor:* Diana Swift; *Price:* $12 / year
Profile: A health & wellness resource for patients in a physician's waiting room
• Canadian Journal of Surgery (CJS)
Type: Journal; *Frequency:* Bimonthly; *Accepts Advertising*; *Editor:* E.J. Harvey, MD; G.L. Warnock, MD *ISSN:* 0008-428X; *Price:* $35 Canadian students & residents; $175 Canadian individuals; $270 institutions
Profile: Continuing medical education for Canadian surgical specialists
• Canadian Medical Association Complete Home Medical Guide
Type: Book *ISSN:* 1-55363-054-8; *Price:* $51.95 members
Profile: An 1104 page authoritative & user-friendly resource for physicians to recommend to patients
• Canadian Medical Association Conference Updates
Profile: The latest news from major clinical meetings
• Canadian Medical Association Journal (CMAJ)
Type: Journal; *Frequency:* Semimonthly; *Accepts Advertising*; *Editor:* Paul C. Hébert *ISSN:* 0820-3946; *Price:* $35 / issue Canadian; $40 / issue USA
Profile: Peer-reviewed original research, review articles, practice updates, drug alerts, health news, & commentaries for clinicians, available online& in print
• CMA [Canadian Medical Association] Bulletin
Type: Newsletter; *Frequency:* Semimonthly; *Editor:* Patrick Sullivan; Steve Wharry
Profile: A communication from the Canadian Medical Association, with news stories of interest to Canadian physicians, inserted in the Canadian MedicalAssociation Journal
• CMA [Canadian Medical Association] Driver's Guide: Determining Medical Fitness to Operate Motor Vehicles
Type: Guide; *Price:* Free for Canadian Medical Association members
Profile: Examples of sections include the following: Functional assessment - emerging emphasis; Reporting - when & why; Drivingcessation; Aging; Vision; Respiratory diseases; Psychiatric illness; Cardiovascular diseases; Seat belts & air bags; Motorcycles & off-road vehicles; Aviation; Railway; & Appendices
• CMA [Canadian Medical Association] Leadership Series: MD Pulse
Type: Magazine; *Price:* $8.95 / copy members; $14.95 nonmembers
Profile: Results of the National Physician Survey, prepared by the Canadian Medical Association in collaboration with the College of Family Physicians of Canada & theRoyal College of Physicians & Surgeons of Canada
• CMA [Canadian Medical Association] Leadership Series: Primary Care Reform
Type: Magazine; *Editor:* Dr. Albert Schumacher
Profile: An outline of primary care reform initiatives throughout Canada
• CMA [Canadian Medical Association] Leadership Series: Elder Care - Issues & Options
Type: Magazine; *Price:* $8.95 / copy members; $14.95 nonmemebers
Profile: An examination of the medical, social, & ethical dimensions of care for older patients
• CMA [Canadian Medical Association] Leadership Series: Women's Health - Research & Practice Issues for Canadian Physicians
Type: Magazine; *Price:* $8.95 / copy members; $14.95 nonmemebers
Profile: Published by the Canadian Medical Association in partnership with the Centre for Research inWomen's Health
• CMA [Canadian Medical Association] Complete Book of Mother & Baby Care
Type: Book; *Number of Pages:* 264; *Editor:* Anne Biringer MD, CCFP,FCFP; *ISBN:* 978-1-55363-154-5; *Price:* $24 members
Profile: Care for a mother & her baby, from conception to age three
• Future Practice
Type: Magazine; *Frequency:* Irregular; *Editor:* Pat Rich
Profile: Information for physicians about health information technology in Canada
• History of the Canadian Medical Association, 1954-94
Type: Book; *Number of Pages:* 388; *Author:* John Sutton Bennett, MD; *ISBN:* 0-920169-83-X; *Price:* $19.95 members
Profile: A comprehensive account of important events that continue to affect medicine in Canada
• Honour Due: the Story of Dr. Leonora Howard King
Type: Book; *Number of Pages:* 236; *Author:* Margaret I. Negodaeff-Tomsik; *ISBN:* 0-920169-33-3; *Price:* $19.95 members
Profile: The story of the first Canadian to work as a physician in China
• Lessons Learned: Reflections of Canadian Physician Leaders
Type: Book; *Number of Pages:* 123; *Editor:* Chris Carruthers, MD; *ISBN:* 978-1-897490-09-9; *Price:* $16.95 members
• MD Lounge
Type: Magazine; *Editor:* Dr. Francine Lemire et al.
Profile: Information & advice to strengthen relations between general practitioners, family physicians, & other specialists, published by the Canadian Medical Association in partnership withThe Royal College of Physicians & Surgeons of Canada & the College of Family Physicians of Canada
• PMI [Physician Management Institute] Newsletter: Leadership for Physicians
Type: Newsletter
Profile: Information about leadership theories & techniques

Canadian Medical Foundation (CMF) / La Fondation médicale canadienne

1870 Alta Vista Dr., Ottawa ON K1G 6R7
Tel: 613-520-7681; *Fax:* 613-520-7692
Toll-Free: 866-530-4979
info@cmf.ca
www.medicalfoundation.ca
twitter.com/CdnMedicalFound
www.youtube.com/CdnMedicalFoundation
Overview: A large national charitable organization founded in 1987
Mission: Physicians striving for excellence in health care through charitable action together & in partnership with others; organized, guided & funded by physicians CMF makes decisive, targeted funding decisions in areas physicians feel will provide the best impact
Chief Officer(s):
Ruth Collins-Nakai, Chair
Alison Forestell, Managing Director
Staff Member(s): 6; 9 volunteer(s)
Activities: Medical Education Program; Medical Outreach Program; Physician Health & Well-being Program; annual golf tournament; *Library*
Publications:
• Best Practice
Type: Newsletter; *Frequency:* Quarterly

The Canadian Medical Protective Association / Association canadienne de protection médicale

PO Box 8225, Stn. T, 875 Carling Ave., Ottawa ON K1G 3H7
Tel: 613-725-2000; *Fax:* 613-725-1300
Toll-Free: 800-267-6522
feedback@cmpa.org
www.cmpa-acpm.ca
www.linkedin.com/company/canadian-medical-protective-association
twitter.com/CMPAmembers
Overview: A large national organization founded in 1901
Mission: Founded by a group of Canadian doctors for their mutual protection against legal actions based on allegations of malpractice or negligence
Chief Officer(s):
Lawrence Groves, President, 204-728-4440
Lawrence Groves, 1st Vice-President, 204-728-4440
Edward Crosby, 2nd Vice-President, 613-737-8187
John E. Gray, Executive Director & CEO
Membership: 65,000; *Fees:* Schedule available; *Committees:* Audit; Executive; Case Review; Nominating; Communications Advisory; Investment; Extent of Assistance; Human Resources & Compensation; Legal Services; Research, Education & Risk Management
Publications:
• CMPA [The Canadian Medical Protective Association] Perspective
Type: Magazine; *Frequency:* q.

Canadian MedicAlert Foundation / Fondation canadienne MedicAlert

#800, 2005 Sheppard Ave. East, Toronto ON M2J 5B4
Tel: 416-696-0267; *Fax:* 800-392-8422
Toll-Free: 800-668-1507
www.medicalert.ca
www.facebook.com/medicalertcanada
twitter.com/medicalertCA
www.youtube.com/medicalertCA
Also Known As: MedicAlert
Overview: A large national charitable organization founded in 1961
Mission: To provide lifelong access to personal & medical information in order to protect & save the lives of its members; MedicAlert is a non-profit organization that provides all Canadians with medical protection in an emergency situation
Affiliation(s): MedicAlert Foundation International
Chief Officer(s):
Robert Ridge, President
Dorothy Scanion, Director, Finance & Corporate Affairs
Finances: *Funding Sources:* Membership fees; donations
Staff Member(s): 60
Membership: 1 million+ individuals + 12 board; *Fees:* Schedule available
Activities: Membership includes a stainless steel bracelet or necklet engraved with medical information, member ID number & a 24-hour emergency hotline number available in 140 languages worldwide; members also receive a wallet card that lists medications & the names & phone numbers of physicians & emergency contacts; *Awareness Events:* MedicAlert Month, May; *Internships:* Yes; *Speaker Service:* Yes

Canadian MedTech Manufacturers' Alliance (CMMA)

#900, 405 The West Mall, Toronto ON M9C 5J1
Tel: 416-620-1915; *Fax:* 416-620-1595
Toll-Free: 866-586-3332
cmma@medec.org
www.medec.org
Merged from: Trillium Medical Technology Association & MEDEC
Overview: A medium-sized provincial organization founded in 2011
Mission: To encourage the development of medical technology & to help this technology grow in international markets
Chief Officer(s):
Mary Palmer, Executive Director
mpalmer@medec.org
Membership: *Member Profile:* Medical technology companies

Canadian Melanoma Foundation (CMF)

c/o Div. of Dermatology, Univ. of British Columbia, 835 - 10th Ave. West, Vancouver BC V5Z 4E8
Tel: 604-875-4747; *Fax:* 604-873-9919
www.derm.ubc.ca/division/cmf/cmf1.htm
Overview: A small national organization
Mission: A non-profit organization dedicated to improving cancer prevention and cure.

Canadian Memorial Chiropractic College (CMCC)

6100 Leslie St., Toronto ON M2H 3J1
Tel: 416-482-2340; *Fax:* 416-482- 362
communications@cmcc.ca
www.cmcc.ca
Overview: A medium-sized national organization founded in 1945

Mission: To advance the art, science & philosophy of chiropractic; To educate chiropractors; To further the development of the chiropractic profession; To improve the health of society
Member of: Canadian Chiropractic Association
Chief Officer(s):
Mark Symchych, Chair
Jean A. Moss, DC, MBA, President
David Gryfe, Secretary-Treasurer
Finances: *Funding Sources:* Membership fees; Student tuition; Donations
Membership: 1,600; *Fees:* $715; *Member Profile:* Chiropractors across Canada & internationally
Activities: *Awareness Events:* Run/Walk for Chiropractic Education; *Speaker Service:* Yes; *Library:* CC Clemmer Health Sciences Library; by appointment
Meetings/Conferences: • Canadian Memorial Chiropractic College Event: Practice OpportUnity 2015, February, 2015, Toronto, ON
Scope: National
Description: An event for Canadian Memorial Chiropractic College students to meet industry professional, such as chiropractors & associated business vendors
Contact Information: General Information, Phone: 416-482-2340, ext. 200, E-mail: events@cmcc.ca; Sponsorship Information, E-mail: sponsorship@cmcc.ca
Publications:
• CMCC [Canadian Memorial Chiropractic College] Annual Report
Type: Yearbook; *Frequency:* Annually
• CMCC [Canadian Memorial Chiropractic College] Academic Calendar
Frequency: Annually
Profile: Academic programs & course descriptions
• CMCC [Canadian Memorial Chiropractic College] Research Report
Frequency: Irregular
Profile: A summary of research activities undertaken at CMCC
• Primary Contact: A Magazine for Canadian Chiropractors
Type: Magazine; *Frequency:* 3 pa; *Editor:* Janet Blanchard
Profile: Articles, continuing education, CMCC events, & members

Canadian Mental Health Association (CMHA) / Association canadienne pour la santé mentale (ACSM)

#1110, 151 Slater St., Ottawa ON K1P 5H3
Tel: 613-745-7750; *Fax:* 613-745-5522
www.cmha.ca
www.facebook.com/CANMentalHealth
twitter.com/CMHA_NTL
www.youtube.com/user/cmhanational
Overview: A large national charitable organization founded in 1918
Mission: To promote mental health as well as support the resilience & recovery of people experiencing mental illness, through advocacy, education, research & service
Affliation(s): Canadian Alliance on Mental Illness & Mental Health; Canadian Health Network
Chief Officer(s):
Peter Coleridge, National Chief Executive Officer, 613-745-7750 Ext. 221
pcoleridge@cmha.ca
Irene Merien, Chair
Sarah Smith, National Director, Fund Development
Mark Ferdinand, National Director, Public Policy
Finances: *Annual Operating Budget:* $3 Million-$5 Million; *Funding Sources:* Donations & bequests; corporate support; affiliated CMHA fees
Staff Member(s): 8; 10,0 volunteer(s)
Activities: *Awareness Events:* Mental Health Week, May; National Conference & AGM, TBC
Awards:
• Strengthening CMHA Award (Award)
• C.M. Hincks Award (Award)
• Consumer Involvement Award (Award)
Meetings/Conferences: • Canadian Mental Health Association 2015 Conference, 2015
Scope: National
Publications:
• CMHA [Canadian Mental Health Association] Annual Report
Type: Yearbook; *Frequency:* Annually
Profile: Details of CMHA initiatives & achievements

Alberta Division
Capital Place, #320, 9707 - 110 St. NW, Edmonton AB T5K 2L9
Tel: 780-482-6576; *Fax:* 780-482-6348
alberta@cmha.ab.ca
alberta.cmha.ca
Chief Officer(s):
Vacant, Executive Director
William (Bill) Bone, Chair

British Columbia Division
#1200, 1111 Melville St., Vancouver BC V6E 3V6
Tel: 604-688-3234; *Fax:* 604-688-3236
Toll-Free: 800-555-8222
info@cmha.bc.ca
www.cmha.bc.ca
www.facebook.com/CMHABCDIVISION
twitter.com/cmhabc
www.youtube.com/cmhabc
Chief Officer(s):
Beverly Gutray, Chief Executive Officer
bev.gutray@cmha.bc.ca

Division du Québec
#326, 911, rue Jean-Talon Est, Montréal QC H2R 1V5
Tél: 514-849-3291; *Téléc:* 514-849-8372
info@acsm.qc.ca
www.acsm.qc.ca
www.linkedin.com/company/association-canadienne-pour-la-sant-mentale—
www.facebook.com/189002251132456
twitter.com/ACSMDivisionQc
www.youtube.com/user/ACSMQC
Chief Officer(s):
Renée Ouimet, Directrice
reneeouimet@acsm.qc.ca

Manitoba Division
930 Portage Ave., Winnipeg MB R3G 0P8
Tel: 204-982-6100; *Fax:* 204-982-6128
office@cmhawpg.mb.ca
winnipeg.cmha.ca
www.facebook.com/cmha.manitoba
twitter.com/MbDivisionCMHA
www.youtube.com/user/CMHAWpg
Chief Officer(s):
Stephanie Skakun, Acting Executive Director

New Brunswick Division
#202, 403 Regent St., Fredericton NB E3B 3X6
Tel: 506-455-5231; *Fax:* 506-459-3878
nb.cmha.ca
www.facebook.com/CMHANB
Chief Officer(s):
Christa Baldwin, Executive Director
cbaldwin.cmhanb@rogers.com

Newfoundland & Labrador Division
70 The Boulevard, 1st Fl., St. John's NL A1A 1K2
Tel: 709-753-8550; *Fax:* 709-753-8537
Toll-Free: 877-753-8550
office@cmhanl.ca
www.cmhanl.ca
www.facebook.com/247087668665555
twitter.com/CMHANL
www.youtube.com/user/cmhanational
Chief Officer(s):
George Skinner, Executive Director

Nova Scotia Division
63 King St., Dartmouth NS B2Y 2R7
Tel: 902-466-6600; *Fax:* 902-466-3300
Toll-Free: 877-466-6606
cmhans@bellaliant.com
novascotia.cmha.ca
www.facebook.com/cmhansdivision
twitter.com/cmhansdivision
pinterest.com/cmhanovascotia
Chief Officer(s):
Gail Gardiner, Executive Director

Ontario Division
#2301, 180 Dundas St. West, Toronto ON M5G 1Z8
Tel: 416-977-5580; *Fax:* 416-977-2813
Toll-Free: 800-875-6213
info@ontario.cmha.ca
ontario.cmha.ca
www.facebook.com/cmha.ontario
twitter.com/CMHAOntario
www.youtube.com/cmhaontario
Chief Officer(s):
Camille Quenneville, CEO
cquenneville@ontario.cmha.ca

Prince Edward Island Division
PO Box 785, 178 Fitzroy St., Charlottetown PE C1A 7L9
Tel: 902-566-3034; *Fax:* 902-566-4643
division@cmha.pe.ca
pei.cmha.ca
www.facebook.com/CMHAPEIDivision
Chief Officer(s):
Reid Burke, Executive Director

Saskatchewan Division
2702 - 12th Ave., Regina SK S4T 1J2
Tel: 306-525-5601; *Fax:* 306-569-3788
Toll-Free: 800-461-5483
contactus@cmhask.com
www.cmhask.com
www.facebook.com/255440253328
Chief Officer(s):
Dave Nelson, Executive Director
daven@cmhask.com

Yukon Division
6 Bates Cres., Whitehorse YT Y1A 4T8
Tel: 867-668-7144
cmha.ca@gmail.com
twitter.com/CMHAYukon
Chief Officer(s):
Dudley Morgan, Executive Director

Canadian Merchant Navy Veterans Association Inc. (CMNVA) / L'Association des Anciens Combattants de la marine marchande canadienne Inc.

2108 Melrick Pl., Sooke BC V9Z 0M9
Tel: 250-642-2638
Overview: A medium-sized national organization founded in 1990
Mission: To renew old friendships & bring together ex-Canadian merchant seamen; to promote increased recognition of the role of the merchant navy during wartime; to liaise with government to obtain full benefits & pension as recognized veterans
Chief Officer(s):
Bruce Ferguson, President
Finances: *Annual Operating Budget:* Less than $50,000; *Funding Sources:* Membership dues; donations
200 volunteer(s)
Membership: 10 senior/lifetime + 900 individual + 20 honourary; *Fees:* $30 + $5 initiation fee; *Member Profile:* Canadian citizen who sailed on Canadian or allied deep-sea ships during WWI or II or Korean conflict; former allied merchant seamen who sailed during WWII or Korean conflict; family members of veterans; associate - peacetime Canadian seafarers; *Committees:* Government Liaison; Membership & Supply; Public Relations
Activities: Quarterly meetings within branches; *Awareness Events:* Merchant Navy Day, Sept. 3; Battle of Atlantic Day; *Speaker Service:* Yes

Canadian Merchant Service Guild (CMSG) / Guilde de la marine marchande du Canada (GMMC)

#234, 9 Antares Dr., Ottawa ON K2E 7V5
Tel: 613-727-6079; *Fax:* 613-727-6079
cmsgott@on.aibn.com
www.cmsg-gmmc.ca
Overview: A medium-sized national licensing organization founded in 1919
Mission: To promote the social, economic, cultural, educational & material interests of ships' masters, chief engineers, officers, pilots & of other persons whose employment is directly related to maritime operations
Affliation(s): International Transport Workers' Federation (ITF)
Chief Officer(s):
Mark Boucher, National President
Publications:
• Canadian Merchant Service Guild Bulletin
Type: Newsletter; *Frequency:* Irregular
Profile: Information for CMSG members
• Canadian Merchant Service Guild News
Type: Magazine; *Frequency:* Irregular; *Editor:* Mark Boucher
Profile: CMSG activities & branch news

Eastern Branch
c/o Quebec Office, #108, 3107 Hôtels Ave., Québec QC G1W 4W5
Tel: 418-650-6471; *Fax:* 418-650-1484
cmsg-gmmc.qc@bellnet.ca
www.cmsg-gmmc.ca
Mission: To act as a voice for the interests of Canadian Ships' Officiers and has been instrumental in successfully

lobbying for improvement to a host of regulations directly related to the safety of life at sea and the well-being of all seafarers.
Chief Officer(s):
Edward Day, President
Western Branch
#310, 218 Blue Mountain St., Coquitlam BC V3K 4H2
Tel: 602-939-8990; *Fax:* 602-939-8950
cmsgwb@cmsg.org
www.cmsg-gmmc.ca
Mission: To act as a voice for the interests of Canadian Ships' Officers and has been instrumental in successfully lobbying for improvement to a host ofregulations directly related to the safety of life at sea and the well-being of ll seafarers.
Chief Officer(s):
Mike Armstrong, President

Canadian Meteorological & Oceanographic Society (CMOS) / Société canadienne de météorologie et d'océanographie (SCMO)

PO Box 3211, Stn. D, Ottawa ON K1P 6H7
Tel: 613-990-0300; *Fax:* 613-990-1617
cmos@cmos.ca
www.cmos.ca
www.facebook.com/groups/338431655320
Previous Name: Canadian Meteorological Society
Overview: A large national charitable organization founded in 1967
Mission: To advance meteorology & oceanography in Canada
Member of: Canadian Consortium for Research; Partnership Group for Science & Engineering
Chief Officer(s):
Ian D. Rutherford, Executive Director
exec-dir@cmos.ca
Peter Bartello, President
president@cmos.ca
Bourque Sheila, Director, Education & Outreach
education@cmos.ca
Qing Liao, Office Manager, 613-991-4494
accounts@cmos.ca
Finances: *Annual Operating Budget:* $500,000-$1.5 Million; *Funding Sources:* Membership fees; Donations; Congress resignation fees
Staff Member(s): 3; 3 volunteer(s)
Membership: 800; *Fees:* $80; *Member Profile:* Meteorologists & oceanographers; Persons interested in meteorology & oceanography; Corporations & institutions; Government organizations; Students; *Committees:* Accreditation; Students; External Relations; Fellows; Awards: Scholarships; Scientific; Audit; Nominating
Activities: Participating in School Science Fairs; Accrediting consultants in meteorology & oceanography; Providing advice & suggestions to government & its departments on meteorological & oceanographic issues; Publications; Scholarships; Prizes & Awards; Public lectures; *Speaker Service:* Yes
Awards:
• Postgraduate Scholarship (Scholarship)
• Undergraduate Scholarship (Scholarship)
• Tertia M.C. Hughes Memorial Prize (Award)
• The J.P. Tully Medal in Oceanography (Award)
May be awarded each year to a person whose scientific contributions have had a significant impact on Canadian oceanography
• The President's Prize (Award)
May be awarded each year to a member or members of the Society for a recent paper or book of special merit in the fields of meteorology or oceanography. Eligibility: Paper must have been published in Atmosphere-Ocean, The CMOS bulletin, SCMO or another referred journal
• François J. Saucier Prize in Applied Oceanography (Award)
May be awarded each year to a member or members of the Society for an outstanding contribution to the application of oceanography in Canada
• The Rube Hornstein Medal in Operational Meteorology (Award)
May be awarded each year to an individual for outstanding operational meteorological service. The work for which the prize is granted may be cumulative over a period of years or may be a single notable achievement
• Dr. Andrew Thomson Prize in Applied Meteorology (Award)
May be awarded each year to a member or members of the Society for an outstanding contribution to the application of meteorology in Canada
• Neil J. Campbell Award for Exceptional Volunteer Service (Award)
The award may be made for an exceptional contribution in a single year or for contributions over an extended period.
Meetings/Conferences: • 49th Canadian Meteorological & Oceanographic Society Congress, May, 2015, Whistler Conference Centr, Whistler, BC
Scope: National
Publications:
• Atmosphere-Ocean
Type: Journal; *Frequency:* Quarterly *ISSN:* 0705-5900; *Price:* $50 individual; $125 institution
Profile: Scientific journal with original research, survey articles, & comments on published papers in the fields of atmospheric, oceanographic, & hydrological sciences
• Canadian Meteorological & Oceanographic Society Annual Review
Frequency: Annually; *Price:* Free with Canadian Meteorological & OceanographicSociety membership
Profile: Summaries of the Canadian Meteorological & Oceanographic Society yearly activities & the audited financial statement
• Canadian Meteorological & Oceanographic Society Annual Congress Program & Abstracts
Type: Yearbook; *Frequency:* Annually; *Price:* Free withCMOS membership; $50 non-members & institutions
Profile: Guide to the Canadian Meteorological & Oceanographic Society Annual Congress sessions & abstracts of papers to be presented
• CMOS [Canadian Meteorological & Oceanographic Society] Bulletin SCMO [Société canadienne de météorologie et d'océanographie]
Frequency: Bimonthly; *Accepts Advertising*; *Editor:* Paul-André Bolduc; *Price:* Free with CMOS / SCMO membership; $80 non-members & institutions
Profile: Technical articles, conferences, & events related to meteorology, oceanography,climatology, & meteorological & oceanographic history
• The Edmonton Tornado & Hailstorm: A Decade of Research
Author: R. Charlton, B. Kachman, L. Wojtiw; *Price:* $10
• Numerical Methods in Atmospheric & Oceanic Modelling: The André J. Robert Memorial Volume
Number of Pages: 634; *Editor:* C. Lin, R. Laprise, & H. Ritchie; *ISBN:* 0-9698414-4-2; *Price:* $39.95
Profile: Refereed papers by scientists on the art & science of numerical modelling, for students &researchers

Alberta Centre
Edmonton AB
Tel: 780-492-6706; *Fax:* 780-492-2030
Chief Officer(s):
Paul Myers, Vice Chair
pmyers@ualberta.ca
British Columbia Interior (Kelowna)
Prince George BC
Tel: 250-960-5785
Chief Officer(s):
Peter Jackson, Chair
peterj@unbc.ca
British Columbia Lower Mainland Centre
Vancouver BC
Tel: 604-822-2821
Chief Officer(s):
William Hsieh, Chair
whsieh@eos.ubc.ca
Centre de Québec
Québec QC
Tél: 418-654-3764; *Téléc:* 418-654-2600
yves_gratton@ete.inrs.ca
Chief Officer(s):
Yves Gratton, Chair
Centre de Rimouski
Rimouski QC
Chief Officer(s):
Yvonnick Le Clainche, Président
Halifax Centre
Dartmouth NS
Tel: 902-426-9963
Chief Officer(s):
Blair Greenan, Chair
Blair.Greenan@dfo-mpo.gc.ca
Montréal Centre
Montréal QC
Tel: 514-384-9990; *Fax:* 514-384-1598
Chief Officer(s):
Rabah Hammouche, Secretary-Treasurer
rabah@enviromet.qc.ca
New Brunswick Chapter
Fredericton NB
Tel: 506-477-3257; *Fax:* 506-453-4581
Chief Officer(s):
William Ward, President
Newfoundland Centre
St. John's NL
Tel: 709-772-8963; *Fax:* 709-772-4105
Chief Officer(s):
Fraser Davidson, Chair
Fraser.Davidson@dfo-mpo.gc.ca
Len Zedel, Secretary, 709-737-3106
zedel@mun.ca
Ottawa Centre
Ottawa ON
Tel: 613-831-5851
Chief Officer(s):
Ann McMillan, Chair
mcmillan@storm.ca
Saskatchewan Centre
Saskatoon SK
Tel: 306-933-8122
Chief Officer(s):
Virginia Wittrock, Chair
wittrock@src.sk.ca
Toronto Centre
Toronto ON
Tel: 416-736-2100; *Fax:* 416-739-5817
Chief Officer(s):
Tom McElroy, Chair
TMcElroy@yorku.ca
Oscar Koren, Secretary, 905-669-2365
okoren@sympatico.ca
Vancouver Island Centre
Victoria BC
Tel: 250-363-8233
Chief Officer(s):
Gregory Flato, Chair
greg.flato@ec.gc.ca
Winnipeg Centre
Winnipeg MB
Tel: 204-983-4513; *Fax:* 204-983-0109
Chief Officer(s):
Jim Slipec, Chair
jim.slipec@ec.gc.ca

Canadian Meteorological Society *See* Canadian Meteorological & Oceanographic Society

Canadian Meter Study Group

#903, 24 Marilyn Dr., Guelph ON N1H 8E9
www.postalhistorycanada.net/php/StudyGroups/Meter/
Overview: A small national organization
Mission: To study the history of Canadian metered mail in Canada
Affliation(s): Postal History Society of Canada
Chief Officer(s):
Ross W. Irwin, Contact
Membership: *Member Profile:* Individuals interested in the history of Canadian postage meters
Publications:
• Canada Meter Study Group Newsletter
Type: Newsletter

Canadian Micrographic Society; Canadian Information & Image Management Society *See* Association for Image & Information Management International - 1st Canadian Chapter

Canadian Micro-Mineral Association

660 Heathcliffe Place, Waterloo ON N2T 2P3
canadianmicrominerals.ca
Overview: A small national organization founded in 1964
Mission: To promote education & interest in micromineralogy & to encourage fellowship & goodwill among its members
Member of: Gem & Mineral Federation of Canada
Chief Officer(s):
Frank Ruehlicke, President, 519-880-2716
ruehlicke@rogers.com
Membership: 1-99; *Fees:* $15
Activities: Micro Symposium; Micro Workshop;

Canadian Midwifery Regulators Consortium (CMRC) / Consortium canadien des ordres des sages-femmes (CCOSF)

c/o College Of Midwives Of Manitoba, #235, 500 Portage Ave., Winnipeg MB R3C 3X1

Tel: 204-783-4520; *Fax:* 204-779-1490
www.cmrc-ccosf.ca
Overview: A small national organization founded in 2000
Mission: To facilitate inter-provincial mobility, to advocate for legislation, regulation, and standards of practice that support access to a high standard of midwifery care across the country, and to provide a forum for Canadian regulators to discuss and take action on issues of mutual concern.
Affliation(s): College of Midwives of British Columbia; Alberta Midwifery Health Disciplines Committee; College of Midwives Manitoba; College of Midwives of Ontario; Ordres des sages-femmes du Québec; Northwest Territories Health Professional Licensing (Midwifery)
Chief Officer(s):
Kris Robinson, Chairperson

Canadian Militaria Preservation Society (CMPS)
c/o MilArm Co. Ltd., 10769 - 99 St., 2nd Fl., Edmonton AB T5H 4H6
Tel: 780-424-5281; *Fax:* 800-894-7598
milarm@telus.net
www.milarm.com
www.facebook.com/milarmguns
www.youtube.com/user/TheMILARMchannel
Overview: A small local organization founded in 2000
Mission: To collect military items with an emphasis on Canadian militari
Affliation(s): Royal Alberta Museum; Heritage Community Foundation
Chief Officer(s):
Allan Kerr, Curator
R. Gordon McGowan, President
Activities: Producing a website & virtual museum on Alberta's homefront during World War II; Operating a museum containing Canadian militaria from 1812 to the present

Canadian Military Colleges Faculty Association (CMCFA) / Association des professeurs(es) des collèges militaires du Canada (APCMC)
Royal Military College of Canada, PO Box 17000, Stn. Forces, Kingston ON K7K 7B4
Tel: 613-541-6000
cmcfa-apcmc.ca
Overview: A small national organization
Chief Officer(s):
Jean-Marc Noel, President
Jean-Marc.Noel@rmc.ca
Membership: *Committees:* Grievance; Bargaining

Canadian Milking Shorthorn Society (CMSS)
203 Ferry Rd., Cornwall PE C0A 1H4
Tel: 902-439-9386; *Fax:* 902-436-0551
milking.shorthorn@gmail.com
www.cmss.on.ca
www.facebook.com/milkingshorthorn
Overview: A small national organization founded in 1920
Mission: To promote & encourage the development of milking shorthorn cattle.
Member of: Canadian Shorthorn Association
Chief Officer(s):
Ryan Barrett, Secretary-Manager
Dave Prinzen, President, 613-393-5087
daprinzen@sympatico.ca
Membership: *Fees:* $25 junior; $85 individual; $40 new member; *Member Profile:* Breeders; *Committees:* Show; Genetic Improvement; Promotion/Youth
Activities: American Milking Shorthorn Society Convention; National Milking Shorthorn Show.;

Canadian Mineral Analysts (CMA) / Analystes des minéraux canadiens
444 Harold Ave. West, Winnipeg MB R2C 2E2
Tel: 204-224-1443
www.canadianmineralanalysts.com
Overview: A small national organization founded in 1969
Mission: To promote communication among analysts in the mining industry & persons engaged in analytical procedures & the development of methods
Chief Officer(s):
John Gregorchuk, Managing Secretary, 204-224-1443
jgregorchuk@mts.net
Sean Murry, Treasurer, 604-270-2252
smurry@anachemia.com
Eric Arseneault, Executive Secretary, 506-522-7143
EArseneault@xstrata.com
Membership: *Fees:* $25 students & retired individuals; $40 new & renewing members; $1000 corporate members; *Member Profile:* Analysts employed in the mineral industry; Technical personnel connected with the provision of analyses
Activities: Providing educational opportunities; Assisting in the development of methods for element analysis; Compiling methods manuals for members; Liaising with laboratories of the Canadian mining industry; Supporting the Certified Assayers Foundation of British Columbia
Awards:
• Canadian Mineral Analysts Scholarships (Scholarship)
Awarded for courses in mineral sciences & chemical technology at Canadian colleges
Publications:
• Alchemist Digest: The CMA / SMA [Canadian Mineral Analysts / Analystes des minéraux canadiens] Newsletter
Type: Newsletter; *Editor:* Mark Lewis; *Price:* Free with CMA / SMA membership
• Proceedings of the Canadian Mineral Analysts / Analystes des minéraux canadiens Annual Meeting
Type: Yearbook; *Frequency:* Annually; *Price:* Free with CMA / SMA membership
• QC / QA Manual [a publication of the Canadian Mineral Analysts]
Type: Manual; *Price:* $30

Canadian Mineral Processors Society (CMP)
555 Booth St., Ottawa ON K1A 0G1
www.cmpsoc.ca
Overview: A medium-sized national organization overseen by Canadian Institute of Mining, Metallurgy & Petroleum
Mission: The Canadian Mineral Processors (CMP) is a Technical Society of the Canadian Institute of Mining, Metallurgy and Petroleum.
Chief Officer(s):
Janice Zinck, Secretary, 613-995-4221, Fax: 613-947-3325
jzinck@nrcan.gc.ca
Ray MacDonald, Treasurer, 613-829-4335, Fax: 613-947-3325
macdon@storm.ca
Meetings/Conferences: • 47th Canadian Mineral Processors Conference, January, 2015, Westin Hotel, Ottawa, ON
Scope: National

Canadian Mining Industry Research Organization (CAMIRO)
1545 Maley Dr., Sudbury ON P3A 4R7
Tel: 705-673-6595; *Fax:* 705-673-6588
info@camiro.org
www.camiro.org
Overview: A small national organization
Mission: To manage collaborative mining research in the divisions of exploration, mining, & metallurgical processing; To contribute to the safety, growth, & competitiveness of the Canadian mineral industry
Chief Officer(s):
Larry Urbanoski, Director, Research, Metallurgical Division
LUrbanoski@XstrataZinc.ca
Tom Lane, Director, Research Development, Exploration Division
tom.lane@sympatico.ca
Charles Graham, Contact, Mining Division
Membership: *Member Profile:* Corporations & organizations who wish to further the objects of the association
Activities: Initiating applied research

Canadian Modern Pentathlon Association *See* Pentathlon Canada

Canadian Modern Rhythmic Gymnastic Federation *See* Canadian Rhythmic Sportive Gymnastic Federation

Canadian Morgan Horse Association (CMHA) / Association des chevaux Morgan canadien inc.
PO Box 286, Port Perry ON L9L 1A3
Tel: 905-982-0060; *Fax:* 905-982-0097
info@morganhorse.ca
www.morganhorse.ca
Overview: A medium-sized national licensing organization founded in 1968
Member of: Equine Canada
Affliation(s): British Columbia Interior Morgan Horse Club; New Brunswick Morgan Horse Club; Nova Scotia Morgan Horse Club; Ontario Morgan Horse Club; Saskatchewan Morgan Horse Club
Chief Officer(s):
Bob Watson, President, 403-378-4323
Melissa MacKenzie, Eastern Vice-President, 506-832-5515
Laurie Ann Lyons, Western Vice-President, 250-571-4919
Mark Grootelaar, Treasurer, 204-444-2944
Membership: *Fees:* $25 youth; $40 associate; $50 regular membership; $1000 life membership; *Committees:* Awards; Equine Canada; Historical; Membership; Part Morgan; Promotion; Youth; Registry; Bylaws
Meetings/Conferences: • Canadian Morgan Horse Association Convection and Annual General Meeting, 2015, BC
Scope: National
Publications:
• British Columbia Interior Newsletter
Type: Newsletter
• The Canadian Morgan Magazine
Type: Magazine; *Frequency:* 5 pa; *Accepts Advertising*; *Editor:* C.L. Marriott; *Price:* Free with CMHA membership; $25 Canada; $35 international
• Journey: Nova Scotia Morgan Horse Newsletter
Type: Newsletter; *Editor:* Liz Devine
Profile: Provincial reports, Morgan show highlights, plus upcoming shows & meetings
• Registry Books
Profile: Volumes of Canadian registered Morgan Horses, for Morgan breeders & owners

Canadian Motion Picture Distributors Association *See* Motion Picture Association - Canada

Canadian Motorcycle Association (CMA) / Association motocycliste canadienne
605 James St. North, 4th Fl., Hamilton ON L8L 1J9
Tel: 905-522-5705; *Fax:* 905-522-5716
registration@canmocycle.ca
www.canmocycle.ca
Overview: A medium-sized national licensing organization founded in 1946
Mission: To encourage & develop motorcycling for the benefit & enjoyment of its members
Affliation(s): Fédération internationale motocycliste; Canadian Olympic Association; FIM North America Union
Chief Officer(s):
Marilyn Bastedo, Chief Executive Officer
mbastedo.cma@bellnet.ca
Joseph Godsall, President
Finances: *Annual Operating Budget:* $500,000-$1.5 Million; *Funding Sources:* Membership fees; event fees
Staff Member(s): 4; 150 volunteer(s)
Membership: 100 club + 150 lifetime + 9,000 individual; *Fees:* $30; $15 family (per individual); *Member Profile:* Interest in motorcycling; *Committees:* Technical; Road Safety; Environmental

Canadian Murray Grey Association (CMGA)
PO Box 157, Bragg Creek AB T0L OKO
Tel: 403-949-2199
cmgareg@telus.net
www.cdnmurraygrey.ca
Overview: A medium-sized national organization founded in 1970
Mission: To promote the genetics of Murray Grey Beef Cattle
Member of: Canadian Beef Breeds Council
Membership: *Fees:* $75 annual; $5 junior; $35 associate; $1000 lifetime; *Committees:* Financial; Promotion & Events; CBBC; Constitution; Herd Book; Nominating; Pedigree & Registration

Canadian Museums Association (CMA) / Association des musées canadiens
#400, 280 Metcalfe St., Ottawa ON K2P 1R7
Tel: 613-567-0099; *Fax:* 613-233-5438
Toll-Free: 888-822-2907
info@museums.ca
www.museums.ca
www.facebook.com/pages/Canadian-Museums-Association/107410072621904
twitter.com/musecdnCached
www.youtube.com/museumsdotca
Overview: A large national organization founded in 1947
Mission: To advance a strong, vital, & valued Canadian museum sector
Affliation(s): Alliance of Natural History Museums (ANHMC); Canadian Federation of Friends of Musesum (CFFM); Council of Museums Canada; Canadian Association of Zoos & Aquariums; Canadian Association of Science Centres; Canadian Art Museums Directors' Association (CAMDO); ICOM Canada; Organization of Military Museums of Canada (OMMC); Department of Canadian Heritage
Chief Officer(s):
Bill Greenlaw, President, 902-424-4986, Fax: 902-424-0560
greenlbe@gov.ns.ca

Nancy Noble, Vice-President, 604-730-5323, Fax: 604-736-5417
nnoble@museumofvancouver.ca
John G. McAvity, Executive Director & CEO, 613-567-0099 Ext. 226
jmcavity@museums.ca
Finances: *Annual Operating Budget:* Greater than $5 Million; *Funding Sources:* Membership fees; Donations; Government grants
Membership: 2,000; *Fees:* $85 voting individual; $100 - $2,750 institution, based on operating budget; $50 senior & student; $100 affiliate & foreign; $250 corporate; *Member Profile:* Members include museum professionals in Canada & abroad, non-profit museums, art galleries, science centres, aquaria, archives, sport halls of fame, artist-run centres, zoos, & historic sites throughout Canada.
Activities: Providing professional development & networking opportunities for members; Collaborating with other national & international organizations; Creating & delivering projects & programs; *Awareness Events:* Canadian Museums Day, November 23; *Internships:* Yes
Awards:
• The Awards of Outstanding Achievement (Award)
Deadline: November 15
• The Award of Distinguished Service (Award)
Deadline: November 15
• The Fellows of the CMA (Award)
Deadline: November 15
• The Barbara Tyler Award in Museum Leadership (Award)
Deadline: November 15
• ICOM Canada's International Achievement Award (Award)
Deadline: November 15
• The History Alive! Award of Excellence for History in Museums (Award)
Presented by the Canadian Museums Association (CMA) in partnership with Canada's History Society*Deadline:* July
• The Museums & Schools Partnership Award (Award)
Presented by the Canadian Museums Association (CMA) & the Canadian Teachers' Federation*Deadline:* November 15
• The Museum Volunteer Award (Award)
Presented by the Canadian Museums Association (CMA) & the Canadian Federation of Friends of Museums (CFFM)*Deadline:* November 15
Meetings/Conferences: • Canadian Museums Association 2015 Museum Enterprises Conference, January, 2015, Hilton Toronto Hotel, Toronto, ON
Scope: National
Description: Keynote sessions, educational presentations, workshops, & networking opportunities for museum professionals involved in operations, admissions, retail, & food services
Contact Information: Symposium Contact: Erin Caley, Phone: 613-567-0099, ext. 233; E-mail: ecaley@museums.ca
• Canadian Museums Association 2015 68th National Conference, April, 2015, Banff, AB
Scope: National
Description: A conference & tradeshow for Canadian museum professionals, such as directors, administrators, & curators
Contact Information: Conference contact: Megan Lafrenière, Phone: 613-567-0099, ext. 233, E-mail: mlafreniere@museums.ca
Publications:
• Muse [a publication of the Canadian Museums Association]
Type: Magazine; *Frequency:* Bimonthly; *Accepts Advertising*; *Price:* Free formembers; $35 non-members in Canada; $46 U.S.A.; $55 international
Profile: Current issues, solutions to challenges, current projects, industry best practices, book reviews, Canadian & international news, & opinion pieces

Canadian Mushroom Growers' Association *See* Mushrooms Canada

Canadian Music Centre (CMC) / Centre de musique canadienne

Chalmers House, 20 St. Joseph St., Toronto ON M4Y 1J9
Tel: 416-961-6601; *Fax:* 416-961-7198
info@musiccentre.ca
www.musiccentre.ca
www.facebook.com/CanadianMusic
twitter.com/cmcnational
www.youtube.com/user/CanadianMusicCentre
Overview: A medium-sized national charitable organization founded in 1959
Mission: To stimulate the awareness, appreciation & performance of Canadian music
Member of: Canadian Conference of the Arts; Orchestras Canada
Affliation(s): International Association of Music Information Centres; Canadian Music Libraries Association
Chief Officer(s):
Allan G. Bell, President
Elisabeth Bihl, Executive Director
ebihl@musiccentre.ca
Steve Wingfield, Acquisitions Coordinator, Music Publishing
swingfield@musiccentre.ca
Finances: *Annual Operating Budget:* $500,000-$1.5 Million; *Funding Sources:* 3 levels of government; universities & arts bodies; donations
Staff Member(s): 35; 5 volunteer(s)
Membership: 630 associate + 415 individual; *Fees:* Schedule available; *Member Profile:* Associate - composers selected by an adjudication committee; voting - individuals supporting or interested in work of the Centre; *Committees:* Admission Criteria; Education; Finance; Nominating
Activities: Extensive libraries; most music may be borrowed free of charge; substantial collection of recorded Canadian music is available for reference in each CMC office; the Imperial Oil McPeek Pops Collection of orchestral arrangements of Canadian popular music; CMC sells recordings of Canadian music, on CMC Centrediscs label & on other Canadian & international labels (CMC distributes a free catalogue listing the wide variety of tapes, records & CDs for sale at all CMC office; CMC also offers a mail order service); *Library:* Ettore Mazzolini Library; Open to public
Awards:
• Friends of Canadian Music Award (Award)
• Toronto Emerging Composer Award (Award)
• Prairie Region Emerging Composer Competition Award (Award)

British Columbia Region
837 Davie St., Vancouver BC V6Z 1B7
Tel: 604-734-4622; *Fax:* 604-734-4627
bcregion@musiccentre.ca
Chief Officer(s):
Bob Baker, Regional Director
bbaker@musiccentre.ca

Ontario Region
20 St. Joseph St., Toronto ON M4Y 1J9
Tel: 416-961-6601; *Fax:* 416-961-7198
ontario@musiccentre.ca
Chief Officer(s):
Matthew Fava, Regional Director
mfava@musiccentre.ca

Prairie Region
#911, 2500 University Dr. NW, Calgary AB T2N 1N4
Tel: 403-220-7403; *Fax:* 403-289-4877
prairie@musiccentre.ca
Mission: The CMC offers a wide collection of books, music periodicals, composer information, and CDs for sale or free listening. Many of these items are unavailable elsewhere. Services available at the centre include photocopying, audio dubbing and binding of scores. Whatever you are looking for in Canadian music, we will help you find it, hear it, borrow it or buy it.
Member of: Canadian Music Centre
Chief Officer(s):
John Reid, Regional Director

Région du Québec
#200, 1085, Côte du Beaver Hall, Montréal QC H2Z 1S5
Tél: 514-866-3477; *Téléc:* 514-866-0456
quebec@centremusique.ca
www.centremusique.ca
Chief Officer(s):
Sonia Pâquet, Regional Director
spaquet@musiccentre.ca

Canadian Music Competitions Inc. (CMC) / Concours de musique du Canada inc.

69, rue Sherbrooke ouest, Montréal QC H2X 1X2
Tel: 514-284-5398; *Fax:* 514-284-6828
Toll-Free: 877-879-1959
info@cmcnational.com
www.cmcnational.com
www.facebook.com/CMCnational
Overview: A medium-sized national organization
Mission: Faire participer a une véritable expérience nationale de musique, en étroite collaboration avec les institutions et les professeurs de musique du pays, les plus doués de nos jeunes musiciennes et musiciens canadiens.
Chief Officer(s):
Yolande Cardinal, Présidente
Julie Lebel, Directrice générale
jlebel@cmcnational.com
Staff Member(s): 3; 100 volunteer(s)
Membership: 1,000;

Canadian Music Educators' Association (CMEA) / Association canadienne des éducateurs de musique

#A-430A, Wilfrid Laurier University, Waterloo ON N2L 3C5
Tel: 778-896-7343
www.cmea.ca
twitter.com/CanadianMEA
Overview: A medium-sized national organization founded in 1959
Mission: To nurture a vital music learning community throughout Canada
Member of: International Society for Music Education
Affliation(s): International Society for Music Education
Chief Officer(s):
Mark Reid, President
markreid@cmea.ca
Kirsten MacLaine, Vice-President
kirstenmaclaine@cmea.ca
Finances: *Annual Operating Budget:* $50,000-$100,000; *Funding Sources:* Membership fees
22 volunteer(s)
Membership: 2,200; *Fees:* $25; *Committees:* Research Council; Awards/Honorary Membership; Retired Teachers; Student Chapters; Strategic Planning; Teacher Education; Evaluation; Advocacy
Activities: *Internships:* Yes; *Speaker Service:* Yes
Meetings/Conferences: • National Conference on Music Education 2015, July, 2015, Winnipeg, MB
Scope: National
Publications:
• Canadian Music Educator
Type: Newsletter

Canadian Music Festival Adjudicators' Association (CMFAA)

c/o School of Music, Queen's University, Kingston ON K7L 3N6
Tel: 613-533-6000; *Fax:* 613-533-6808
www.cmfaa.ca
Overview: A small national organization founded in 1960
Chief Officer(s):
John Hansen, President
john.hansen@acadiau.ca
Finances: *Funding Sources:* Membership fees
Membership: 250; *Fees:* $40; *Member Profile:* Three successful festival adjudications
Activities: *Rents Mailing List:* Yes

Canadian Music Library Association *See* Canadian Association of Music Libraries, Archives & Documentation Centres

Canadian Music Week Inc. (CMW)

5355 Vail Ct., Mississauga ON L5M 6G9
Tel: 905-858-4747; *Fax:* 905-858-4848
cmw.net
www.facebook.com/canadianmusicweek
twitter.com/CMW_Week
Overview: A medium-sized national organization
Mission: To organize the annual Canadian Music Week festival, convention & trade show
Chief Officer(s):
Neill Dixon, President
neill@cmw.net
Verle Mobbs, General Manager
verle@cmw.net
Cameron Wright, Director, Festival
concerts@cmw.net

Canadian Musical Reproduction Rights Agency (CMRRA) / Agence canadienne des droits de production musicaux limitée

#320, 56 Wellesley St. West, Toronto ON M5S 2S3
Tel: 416-926-1966; *Fax:* 416-926-7521
inquiries@cmrra.ca
www.cmrra.ca
Overview: A small national organization founded in 1976
Mission: Represents the majority of music publishers & copyright owners doing business in Canada; on their behalf, issues licences & collects royalties for the reproduction of copyrighted musical works on CDs, cassettes & other sound carriers, & in films, TV programs & advertising; owned by the Canadian Music Publishers Association
Chief Officer(s):

David A. Basskin, President
Fred Merritt, Vice-President, Finance & Administration
Staff Member(s): 50
Membership: *Member Profile:* Music publishers
Activities: *Speaker Service:* Yes

Canadian Mutual Fund Association ***See*** Investment Funds Institute of Canada

Canadian National Accelerated Christian Education Association ***See*** Accelerated Christian Education Canada

Canadian National Association of Real Estate Appraisers (CNAREA)

PO Box 157, #1, 175 2nd Ave. West, Qualicum Beach BC V9K 1S7
Fax: 866-836-6369
Toll-Free: 888-399-3366
cnarea@shaw.ca
www.cnarea.ca
Overview: A small national organization founded in 1992
Mission: To certify & regulate real property appraisers in Canada; To raise the standards of the real property appraising profession; To protect consumers
Member of: The Canadian Employee Relocation Council (CERC); Canadian Association of Acredited Mortgage Proffessionals (CAAMP)
Affiliation(s): Appraisal Foundation (Washington DC, USA); Appraisal Foundation Advisory Council (TAFAC); National Association of Independent Fee Appraisers (NAIFA)
Chief Officer(s):
Steven G. Coull, Chief Executive Officer
Robert B. Fraser, National President & Treasurer
rfraser16@cogeco.ca
James Carty, National Vice-President
jim@cartyappraisals.ca
Douglas Rishor, National Secretary, 705-741-2021
drishor@cnarea.ca
Finances: *Annual Operating Budget:* $1.5 Million-$3 Million
Staff Member(s): 10; 15 volunteer(s)
Membership: 1142; *Fees:* $700; *Member Profile:* Canadian professional real property appraisers, such as those with the following designations: DAR (Designated Appraiser Residential), DAC (Designated Appraiser Commercial), DAC (Designated Appraiser Commercial with a Specialty in Agricultural), DRP (Designated Reserve Planner), Certified Appraisal Reviewer & CMAR (Certified Mortgage Appraisal Reviewer); Associate members are those who have an an interest in the appraisal profession or who work with professional appraisers; Candidates are persons who want to further their education & experience to earn a designation
Activities: Offering continuing education opportunities; Maintaining the professionalism of members; Ensuring that members abide by a Code of Ethics; Providing designated members with professional liability insurance for error & omissions
Publications:
• CNAREA [Canadian National Association of Real Estate Appraisers] Newsletter
Type: Newsletter
Profile: Association activities & changes in insurance coverage

Canadian National Association of Trained Nurses ***See*** Canadian Nurses Association

Canadian National Autism Foundation (CNAF)

PO Box 66512, 38 King St. East, Stoney Creek ON L8G 5E5
Tel: 905-930-8682; *Fax:* 905-930-9744
info@cnaf.net
www.cnaf.net
Overview: A small national charitable organization founded in 2000
Mission: To increase autism awareness; To assist families; To raise funds to support Canadian-based autism research
Chief Officer(s):
Christine Fougere, President & Founder

Canadian National Baton Twirling Association (CNBTA)

c/o Lisa Ross, Treasurer, 7208 Concession 1, RR#2, Puslinch ON N0B 2J0
e-mail: info@cnbta.org
www.cnbta.org
Overview: A small national organization
Mission: To promote the sport of baton twirling in Canada; to offer twirling events & seminars
Affiliation(s): National Baton Twirling Association - USA; Global Alliance of National Baton Twirling & Majorette Associations
Chief Officer(s):
Kevan Latrace, President
cnbta.prez@gmail.com
Darlene King, National Technical Director/Co-Founder
darleneking@shaw.ca

Canadian National Committee for Irrigation & Drainage (CANCID)

9 Corvus Crt., Ottawa ON K2E 7Z4
Tel: 613-237-9363; *Fax:* 613-594-5190
executivedirector@cwra.org
www.cwra.org
twitter.com/cwraed
Previous Name: International Commission on Irrigation & Drainage - Canadian National Committee
Overview: A small international organization
Mission: To promote research, development, & application of technology among those interested in irrigation, drainage, & flood control
Affiliation(s): Canadian Water Resources Association (CWRA); International Commission on Irrigation & Drainage (ICID); Canadian Committee on Irrigation and Drainage; Canadian Society for Hydrologic Sciences; Student and Young Professionals
Chief Officer(s):
Brent Paterson, President, 403-381-5515, Fax: 403-381-5765
brent.paterson@gov.ab.ca
Laurie Tollefson, Secretary-Treasurer, 306-867-5404, Fax: 306-867-9656
tollefsonl@agr.gc.ca
Activities: Disseminating news about technical information & CANCID & ICID activities; Liaising with other ICID committees & related organizations
Awards:
• Ken Thompson Scholarship (Scholarship)
Eligibility: Graduate students whose programs of study focus on applied, natural, or social science aspects of water resources. *Amount:* $2,000
• Dillon Scholarship (Scholarship)
Eligibility: Graduate students whose programs of study focus on applied, natural, or social science aspects of water resources. *Amount:* $5,000
• General Canadian Water Resources Association Scholarship (Scholarship)
Eligibility: Graduate students whose programs of study focus on applied, natural, or social science aspects of water resources. *Amount:* $1,500 (3)

Canadian National Exhibition Association (CNEA) / Exposition nationale canadienne

Exhibition Place, Toronto ON M6K 3C3
Tel: 416-263-3800; *Fax:* 416-263-3838
info@theex.com
www.theex.com
Overview: A medium-sized national organization founded in 1879
Mission: The CNEA is responsible for the planning and presentation of the annual Canadian National Exhibition at Exhibition Place in Toronto, Ontario.
Chief Officer(s):
Brian Ashton, President
Sarah Fink, Corporate Secretary, 416-263-5201
sfink@theex.com
Membership: 125
Meetings/Conferences: • Canadian National Exhibition 2015, August, 2015, Canadian National Exhibition Place, Toronto, ON
Scope: National

Canadian National Federation of Independent Unions (CNFIU) / Fédération canadienne nationale des syndicats indépendants (FCNSI)

PO Box 416, 36 Main St. North, Campbellville ON L0P 1B0
Tel: 905-854-6868; *Fax:* 905-854-6869
Toll-Free: 800-638-9438
info@cnfiu.com
www.cnfiu.com
Overview: A medium-sized national organization founded in 1980
Mission: To encourage & promote the formation of independent unions
Affiliation(s): Division of Laborers' International Union of North America
Chief Officer(s):
Ann Waller, National President
ann.waller@cnfiu.com
Paul Dickson, Secretary-Treasurer
treasurer@cnfiu.com
Finances: *Annual Operating Budget:* $100,000-$250,000
Staff Member(s): 16
Membership: 3,500

Canadian National Institute for the Blind (CNIB) / INCA (INCA)

1929 Bayview Ave., Toronto ON M4G 3E8
Fax: 416-480-7700
Toll-Free: 800-563-2642
info@cnib.ca
www.cnib.ca
www.facebook.com/myCNIB
www.twitter.com/CNIB
www.youtube.com/cnibnatcomm
Also Known As: The Canadian National Institute for the Blind/Institut national canadien pour les aveugles
Overview: A large national charitable organization founded in 1918
Mission: To ameliorate the condition of persons with vision loss in Canada; To prevent blindness; To promote sight enhancement services; To direct services to more than 100,000 Canadians with vision loss, provided through a network of more than 57 service centres, within 13 provincial & territorial operating divisions; To provide library services, research, advocacy, public education, & accessible design consulting; To produce materials in alternative formats, including Braille & DAISY talking books; To supply assistive technologies for persons with vision loss
Affliation(s): World Blind Union; International Agency for the Prevention of Blindness
Chief Officer(s):
John M. Rafferty, President
Craig Lillico, CFO, Treasurer, & Vice-President
Sandra Levy, Chief People Officer Vice-President, Human Resource
Margaret McGrory, Executive Director & Vice-President, CNIB Library
Tim Alcock, Vice-President, Marketing & Communications
Keith Gordon, Vice-President, Research & Service Quality
Bill McKeown, Vice-President, Government Relations & Divisional Advancement
Finances: *Funding Sources:* United Way; Government; Corporate funding; Private fundraising
2000 volunteer(s)
Membership: 900; *Fees:* $15; $150 - life
Activities: Counselling & referral; Rehabilitation teaching; Orientation & mobility training; Providing library services; Researching blindness prevention; *Library:* CNIB Library
Awards:
• Arthur Napier Magill Distinguished Service Award (Award)
To recognize outstanding service in work for the blind & prevention of blindness services*Deadline:* February *Contact:* Shampa Bose, E-mail: shampa.bose@cnib.ca
• F.J.L. Woodcock / Sir Arthur Pearson Association of War Blinded Scholarship Program (Scholarship)
Eligibility: Outstanding students with low vision who will continue academic or vocational education at the post-secondary level*Deadline:* April
• Walter & Wayne Gretzky Scholarship Foundation Scholarships & Bursaries (Scholarship)
Eligibility: Blind & visually impaired students who plan to study at the post-secondary level *Amount:* $3,000-$5,000 *Contact:* Kim Kohler, Phone: 519-458-8665; E-mail: Kim.Kohler@cnib.ca
• E. (Ben) & Mary Hochhausen Access Technology Research Award (Award)
Eligibility: Applicants may be from any country*Deadline:* September *Amount:* up to $10,000 *Contact:* Trustees, The Hochhausen Fund, Phone: 416-486-2500, ext. 7622; E-mail: shampa.bose@cnib.ca
• Edie Mourre Transcriber's Scholarship (Scholarship)
Eligibility: A person enrolled in a braille transcriber's course, or registered to participate in a professional development activity relevant to braille transcription*Amount:* up to $1,000 *Contact:* Joy Charlton, Canadian Braille Authority, 1929 Bayview Ave, Toronto, ON M4G 3E8
• Canadian Braille Literacy Foundation Grant (Grant)
To provide funding for programs to promote braille literacy*Deadline:* June
• Dr. Dayton M. Forman Memorial Award (Award)
To honour leadership in the advancement of library & information services for Canadians living with vision loss or print disabilities

• Euclid Herie Leadership Award (Award)
Eligibility: Individuals of all ages in Alberta & the Northwest Territories *Amount:* $5,000 *Contact:* Herie Award Selection Committee, Phone: 780-488-4871; TTY: 780-482-2791; E-mail: alberta@cnib.ca
• Euclid Herie Assistive Technology Scholarship (Scholarship)
Eligibility: Students with vision loss in grades 10, 11, or 12 in a school in Alberta or the Northwest Territories*Deadline:* May *Contact:* Herie Award Selection Committee, Phone: 780-488-4871; TTY: 780-482-2791; E-mail: alberta@cnib.ca
• Scholarship for British Columbia Students with Visual Impairments (Scholarship)
Eligibility: A graduating student who exemplifies leadership activities & community service *Amount:* $2,000 *Contact:* Anne Wadsworth, Phone: 604-269-2205; E-mail: awadsworth@prcvi.org
• Scholarship Award of the Aliant Pioneer Volunteers (Scholarship)
A scholarship to assist with tuition costs while a student attends a post-secondary institution*Eligibility:* Students living with vision loss in Nova Scotia or Prince Edward Island *Amount:* $2,000
• Barney Danson Bursary (Grant)
Eligibility: Canadian students with vision loss who will attend a Canadian post-secondary institution *Amount:* $5,000 *Contact:* Shampa Bose, Phone: 416-486-2500, ext. 7622; E-mail: shampa.bose@cnib.ca
Meetings/Conferences: • CNIB 2015 National Braille Conference, 2015
Scope: National
Publications:
• The Canadian National Institute for the Blind Annual Review
Frequency: Annually
• CNIB [Canadian National Institute for the Blind] Vision
Type: Newsletter; *Frequency:* 3 pa
Profile: A nationally distributed newsletter presenting Canadian vision health issues, for consumers & professionals
• Insight [a publication of the Canadian National Institute for the Blind]
Type: Newsletter; *Frequency:* Monthly; *Price:* Free
Profile: Vision health information, consumer products & assistive technologies, & upcoming events

Alberta-Nortwest Territories
12010 Jasper Ave., Edmonton AB T5K 0P3
Tel: 780-488-4871; *Fax:* 780-482-0017
Toll-Free: 800-563-2642; *TTY:* 780-482-2791
alberta@cnib.ca
Chief Officer(s):
John McDonald, Regional Vice President, Alberta & Northwest Territories

British Columbia-Yukon Division
#100, 5055 Joyce St., Vancouver BC V5R 6B2
Tel: 604-431-2121; *Fax:* 604-431-2099
Toll-Free: 800-563-2642
Chief Officer(s):
John Mulka, Regional Vice President, British Columbia & Yukon

Division du Québec
3044, rue Delisle, Montréal QC H4C 1M9
Tél: 514-934-4622; *Téléc:* 514-934-2131
quebec@cnib.ca
Chief Officer(s):
Marie-Camille Blais, Directrice générale, Québec

E.A. Baker Foundation for the Prevention of Blindness
1929 Bayview Ave., Toronto ON M4G 3E8
Tel: 416-486-2500; *Fax:* 416-480-7700
www.cnib.ca
Mission: To provide research & fellowship grants to further education & research into eye disease & surgical expertise

Manitoba-Saskatchewan Division
1080 Portage Ave., Winnipeg MB R3G 3M3
Tel: 204-774-5421; *Fax:* 204-775-5090
manitoba@cnib.ca
Chief Officer(s):
Garry Nenson, Regional Vice President, Manitoba & Saskatchewan

New Brunswick Division
22 Church St., #T120-22, Moncton NB E1C 0P7
Tel: 506-857-4240; *Fax:* 506-857-3019
Toll-Free: 800-536-2642
Chief Officer(s):
Pam Gow-Boyd, Regional Vice President, Atlantic Canada

Newfoundland & Labrador Division
70 The Boulevard, St. John's NL A1A 1K2
Tel: 709-754-1180; *Fax:* 709-754-2018
Toll-Free: 800-563-2642
Chief Officer(s):
Pam Gow-Boyd, Regional Vice President, Atlantic Canada

Nova Scotia-PEI Division
6136 Almon St., Halifax NS B3K 1T8
Tel: 902-453-1480; *Fax:* 902-454-6570
Toll-Free: 800-563-2642
nspei@cnib.ca
Chief Officer(s):
Pam Gow-Boyd, Regional Vice President, Atlantic Canada

Ontario-Nunavut
1929 Bayview Ave., Toronto ON M4G 3E8
Tel: 416-486-2500; *Fax:* 416-480-7700
Toll-Free: 800-563-2642; *TTY:* 416-480-8645
Chief Officer(s):
Len Baker, Regional Vice President, Ontario & Nunavut

Canadian National Live Stock Records *See* Canadian Livestock Records Corporation

---

Canadian National Millers Association (CNMA)
#200, 265 Carling Ave., Ottawa ON K1S 2E1
Tel: 613-238-2293; *Fax:* 613-235-5866
www.canadianmillers.ca
Overview: A medium-sized national organization
Mission: To serve as a vehicle for consultation between the milling industry, government departments & agencies; to promote regulatory & public policy environment that enhances international competitiveness; to provide international trade development to the industry; to disseminate information about the industry & Canadian wheat flour quality; to work directly & in cooperation with the trade offices abroad
Chief Officer(s):
Gordon Harrison, President
gharrison@canadianmillers.ca
Donna Wiggins, Director, Administration
dwiggins@canadianmillers.ca
Finances: *Annual Operating Budget:* $250,000-$500,000
Staff Member(s): 2
Membership: 13 companies; *Member Profile:* Companies in the Canadian cereal grain milling industry

---

Canadian National Railways Police Association (Ind.) (CNRPA) / Association des policiers des chemins de fer nationaux du Canada (ind.)
c/o CN Headquarters, 935 de La Gauchetière St. West, Montréal QC H3B 2M9
Toll-Free: 800-465-9239
Also Known As: CNR Police Association
Overview: A small national organization founded in 1923
Chief Officer(s):
Gerry St. George, National President

Canadian Native Friendship Centre (CNFC)
15001 - 112 Ave., 2nd Fl., Edmonton AB T5G 2A4
Tel: 780-760-1900
www.cnfcedmonton.com
twitter.com/EdmontonCNFC
www.youtube.com/user/cnfcedmonton
Also Known As: CNFC Edmonton
Overview: A small local charitable organization founded in 1962 overseen by Alberta Native Friendship Centres Association
Mission: To improve the quality of life of Aboriginal Peoples in an urban environment by supporting self-determined activities encouraging equal access to & participation in Canadian society while respecting Aboriginal cultural distinctiveness
Member of: National Association of Friendship Centres; Alberta Native Friendship Centres Association
Chief Officer(s):
Adam North Peigan, Executive Director
Finances: *Funding Sources:* Federal & provincial government; United Way; donations
Staff Member(s): 5
Activities: Food & clothing banks; Aboriginal cultural awareness programs; recreation; fine art; crafts; dance classes; *Speaker Service:* Yes; *Library:* Resource Centre; Open to public
Publications:
• Aboriginal Voices of Survival, Resiliency & Community Wellness
Number of Pages: 49; *Editor:* Alana Ross et al.
Profile: Personal narratives from the Aboriginal community
• Welcome to our Home on Native Land: From The Voices of Urban Indigenous Peoples In Collaboration with The CNFC

Canadian Natural Health Association (CNHA)
#105, 5 Wakunda Pl., Toronto ON M4A 1A2
Tel: 416-686-7056
Toll-Free: 866-686-7056
Previous Name: Canadian Natural Hygiene Society
Overview: A medium-sized national charitable organization founded in 1960
Mission: To establish leadership in healthy, natural lifestyle education & support services; to assist by providing resources to help make people healthier
Chief Officer(s):
Mark Ansara, Executive Director
Finances: *Annual Operating Budget:* Less than $50,000; *Funding Sources:* Lectures; book sales; membership fees
Staff Member(s): 1; 25 volunteer(s)
Membership: 765; *Fees:* $40 individual; $20 seniors/students; $45 family
Activities: Publication & sales of literature on health; lectures & courses on health; Counselling; publication of newsletter; *Internships:* Yes; *Speaker Service:* Yes; *Library* Open to public by appointment

---

Canadian Natural Hygiene Society *See* Canadian Natural Health Association

---

Canadian Nature Federation *See* Nature Canada

Canadian Naturopathic Association *See* The Canadian Association of Naturopathic Doctors

---

Canadian Nautical Research Society (CNRS) / Société canadienne pour la recherche nautique
PO Box 34029, Ottawa ON K2J 4B0
www.cnrs-scrn.org
www.facebook.com/150946001632212
Overview: A medium-sized national charitable organization founded in 1982
Mission: To stimulate & promote nautical research in Canada; to enhance Canada's understanding of its maritime heritage; to foster communication in nautical affairs, to organize meetings, & to cooperate with other agencies promoting nautical research
Affliation(s): International Commission for Maritime History
Chief Officer(s):
Marice D. Smith, President
barque2@cogeco.ca
Finances: *Annual Operating Budget:* Less than $50,000; *Funding Sources:* Membership fees; donations
12 volunteer(s)
Membership: 45 institutional + 226 individual; *Fees:* $65 individual; $20 students; $90 institutional; +$10 for international; *Committees:* Editorial; Executive; Keith Matthews Award
Awards:
• Keith Matthews Prizes (Award)
Awarded annually to recognize outstanding books & journal articles on nautical research
• Gerald Panting New Scholars Award (Award)
Publications:
• Argonauta
Type: Newsletter; *Frequency:* Quarterly
Profile: Articles, research notes, & CNRS activities
• The Northern Mariner / Le Marin du nord
Type: Journal; *Frequency:* Quarterly; *Editor:* Roger Sarty
Profile: Refereed essays, documents, & book reviews on naval & maritime history in the North Atlantic & North Pacific, published in association with the North American Society forOceanic History

---

Canadian Navigation Society (CNS)
c/o Canadian Aeronautics & Space Institute, #104, 350 Terry Fox Dr., Kanata ON K2K 2W5
Tel: 613-591-8787; *Fax:* 613-591-7291
www.casi.ca/canadian-navigation-society
Overview: A small national charitable organization overseen by Canadian Aeronautics & Space Institute
Mission: To advance the science, technologies, & applications of navigation
Chief Officer(s):
Susan Skone, Society Chair
sskone@geomatics.ucalgary.ca
Activities: Promoting the publication of papers on topics related to navigation; Providing navigation & related technology information

---

Canadian Netherlands Business & Professional Association Inc. (CNBPA)
c/o Tom Vandeloo, KPMG Canada, Bay Adelaide Centre, Toronto ON M5H 2S5
Tel: 416-981-3424; *Fax:* 416-981-3424
info@cnbpa.ca

www.cnbpa.ca
www.linkedin.com/groups/Canadian-Netherlands-Business-Professional-Ass
twitter.com/cnbpa
Previous Name: Netherlands Business & Professional Association
Overview: A small local organization founded in 1979
Mission: To promote the economic & social interests of association members
Chief Officer(s):
Tom Vandeloo, President
Membership: *Fees:* $60 individuals; $300 corporate memberships; *Member Profile:* Professionals & business people with Dutch interests
Activities: Facilitating interaction with other European business organizations in Canada; Offering networking opportunities
Publications:
• Canadian Netherlands Business & Professional Association Member Directory
Type: Directory; *Price:* Free with CNBPA membership

Canadian Network for Asthma Care *See* Canadian Network for Respiratory Care

Canadian Network for Environmental Education & Communication (EECOM) / Réseau canadien d'éducation et de communication relatives à l'environnement

c/o 336 Rosedale Ave., Winnipeg MB R3L 1L8
e-mail: nswayze@eecom.org
www.eecom.org
www.facebook.com/112287385502920?ref=sgm
Overview: A small national charitable organization founded in 1993
Mission: To advance environmental learning in Canada; To promote environmental literacy & environmental stewardship; To contribute to a sustainable future
Chief Officer(s):
Natalie Swayzer, Executive Director, 204-221-2007
Grant Gardner, Chair, 709-737-8155
Rick Wishart, Treasurer, 204-467-3254
Finances: *Funding Sources:* Donations
Membership: *Fees:* $10 associates; $20 students; $40 individuals; $115 not-for-profit organizations; $280 corporations & government; *Member Profile:* Environmental educators, practitioners, researchers, scientists, administrators, & business representatives
Activities: Offering networking opportunities; Providing professional development resources & activities; Liaising with other organizations
Awards:
• EECom Awards for Excellence in Environmental Education (Award)
Publications:
• EECOM News
Type: Newsletter; *Frequency:* Bimonthly; *Editor:* Sue Wallace; *Price:* Free with Canadian Network for Environmental Education & Communication membership
Profile: Conferences, members, regional reports, awards, & announcements

Canadian Network for Improved Outcomes in Systemic Lupus Erythematosus (CaNIOS)

CaNIOS National Coordinating Ctr, Toronto Western Hospital, #10-306, 399 Bathurst St., Main Pavilion, Toronto ON M5T 2S8
Tel: 416-603-5800; *Fax:* 416-603-6288
cchau@uhnresearch.ca
www.canios.ca
Overview: A medium-sized national organization founded in 1995
Mission: To allow Canadian researchers to address questions important to patients with lupus & their families
Chief Officer(s):
Fortin Paul R., Chair
Cathy Chau, Administrator, Research Business
Finances: *Funding Sources:* Governmental agencies; Not-for-profit organizations & foundations
Activities: Maintaining a database of lupus patients through the National Lupus Registry
Publications:
• CaNIOSIn Touch: CaNIOS Research Participants Newsletter
Type: Newsletter; *Frequency:* Semiannually

Canadian Network for Innovation in Education (CNIE) / Réseau canadien pour l'innovation en éducation (RCIÉ)

#204, 260 Dalhousie St., Ottawa ON K1N 7E4
Tel: 613-241-0018; *Fax:* 613-241-0019
cnie-rcie@cnie-rcie.ca
www.cnie-rcie.ca
www.facebook.com/pages/CNIE-RCIÉ/178940428810638
twitter.com/CNIE_RCIE
Previous Name: Canadian Association for Distance Education (CADE); Association for Media & Technology in Education in Canada (AMTEC)
Merged from: Canadian Association for Distance Education; Association for Media & Technology in Education Canada
Overview: A medium-sized national charitable organization founded in 2007
Mission: To develop & promote the use of technologies, practices, & policies that foster access to learning for students
Chief Officer(s):
Lorraine Carter, Interim Co-President
lorrainec@nipissingu.ca
Diane Janes, Interim Co-President
diane_janes@cbu.ca
Sandy Hughes, Secretary-Treasurer
shughes@wlu.ca
Membership: *Fees:* $100 individual; $50 student & retired membership; $350 organizational (first 4 members + $85 each additional member; *Committees:* Awards; Website; Professional Development; International Relations; Sponsorship & External Relations

Canadian Network for Respiratory Care (CNRC) / Réseau Canadien pour les soins respiratoires (RCSR)

16851 Mount Wolfe Rd., Caledon ON L7E 3P6
Tel: 905-880-1092; *Fax:* 905-880-9733
Toll-Free: 855-355-4672
info@cnrchome.net
www.cnrchome.net
Previous Name: Canadian Network for Asthma Care
Overview: A small national charitable organization founded in 1994
Mission: To certify healthcare professionals as asthma & rspiratory educators (CAEs & CREs)
Chief Officer(s):
Cheryl Connors, Executive Director
Staff Member(s): 5
Membership: 21 organizations; *Member Profile:* Organizations & associations interested in respiratory health; Certified asthma & respiratory educators; *Committees:* Recertification; Certification Management; Exam; Item-writing; Medical Advisory; Strategic Planning; Finance/Fundraising; Conference Planning; Abstract
Meetings/Conferences: • Canadian Network for Respiratory Care Biennial National Respiratory Education Conference, November, 2015

Canadian Network of National Associations of Regulators (CNNAR) / Réseau canadien des associations nationales d'organismes de réglementation (RCANOR)

528 River Rd., Ottawa ON K1V 1E9
Tel: 613-739-4376
www.cnnar.ca
Overview: A medium-sized national organization founded in 2003
Mission: To support the self-regulation of professionals and occupations; to increase the understanding of the Canadian public, governments and others, of the value of self-regulation; facilitate collaboration at the national level amongst our members, federal government agencies and other national and international groups; monitor and respond to federal legislation and policy; serve as an information clearing house on common issues; and develop and share resources.
Membership: *Fees:* $750
Meetings/Conferences: • Canadian Network of National Associations of Regulators 2015 Conference, 2015
Scope: National

Canadian Network of Toxicology Centres (CNTC) / Réseau canadien des centres de toxicologie

Bovey Bldg., 2nd Fl., Gordon St., Guelph ON N1G 2W1
Tel: 519-824-4120; *Fax:* 519-837-3861
uoguelph.ca/ses/content/canadian-network-toxicology-centres
Overview: A medium-sized national organization founded in 1983
Mission: To be recognized & respected for excellence in research, training, analysis & communication of information focused on critical toxicology issues for ecosystem & human health; to achieve this through innovative, multi-disciplinary teamwork & partnerships between the public & private sector
Affliation(s): Metals in the Environment Research Network
Chief Officer(s):
Len Ritter, Executive Director
lritter@uoguelph.ca
Donna Warner, Program Coordinator
dwarner@uoguelph.ca
Finances: *Annual Operating Budget:* $1.5 Million-$3 Million; *Funding Sources:* Environment Canada; grants from government & industrial companies & associations
Staff Member(s): 4
Activities: 4 themes - Human Health & Environmental Risk Assessment; Metal Speciation at the Biological Interface; Endocrine Disrupters & Reproductive/Endocrines Toxicology; Immunotoxicology; also conducts research on a contract basis for government or industry, develops educational materials on toxicology for secondary school programs across Canada; risk assessments of complex mixtures;
Publications:
• CNTC [Canadian Network of Toxicology Centres] News
Type: Newsletter
Profile: Communication among CNTC member scientists & the public to increase education about toxicology
• CNTC [Canadian Network of Toxicology Centres] Science Briefs
Type: Newsletter
• CNTC [Canadian Network of Toxicology Centres] Annual Report
Type: Yearbook; *Frequency:* Annually
• CNTC [Canadian Network of Toxicology Centres] Annual Symposium Report
Type: Yearbook; *Frequency:* Annually

Canadian Network to Abolish Nuclear Weapons (CNANW)

30 Cleary Ave., Ottawa ON K2A 4A1
Tel: 613-233-1982; *Fax:* 613-233-9028
cnanw@web.ca
www.web.net/~cnanw/
Overview: A small national organization founded in 1996
Mission: CNANW and its members do work to educate the public, and conduct seminars, consultations and meetings with the public, officials and politicians in Canada and abroad. All this work is with the purpose of advancing the cause of nuclear disarmament and moving the world toward abolition of nuclear weapons
Affliation(s): Les Artistes pour la paix; Canadian Coalition for Nuclear Responsiblity; Canadian Federation of University Women; Canadian Peace Alliance; Canadian Voice of Women for Peace; Canadian Pugwash Group; Centre de Ressources sur la Non-Violence; Lawyers for Social Responsibility; Physicians for Global Survival; Project Ploughshares; Science for Peace; United Nations Association in Canada; Veterans Against Nuclear Arms; World Conference on Religion & Peace; World Federalist Movement - Canada

Canadian Neurological Sciences Federation (CCNS) / Fédération des sciences neurologiques du Canada

#709, 7015 Macleod Trail SW, Calgary AB T2H 2K6
Tel: 403-229-9544; *Fax:* 403-229-1661
info@cnsfederation.org
www.cnsfederation.org
Previous Name: Canadian Congress of Neurological Sciences
Overview: A medium-sized national organization
Mission: To enhance the care of patients with diseases of the nervous system; To act as the umbrella organization for the following societies: Canadian Neurological Society, Canadian Neurosurgical Society, Canadian Society of Clinical Neurophysiologists, & Canadian Association of Child Neurologists
Chief Officer(s):
Dan Morin, Chief Executive Officer
dan-morin@cnsfederation.org
Marika Fitzgerald, Manager, Finance & Administration
marika-fitzgerald@cnsfederation.org
Donna Irvin, Administrator, Membership Services
donna-irvin@cnsfederation.org
Lisa Bicek, Coordinator, Professional Development
lisa-bicek@cnsfederation.org
Cindy Leschyshyn, Editorial Coordinator, Journal, 403-229-9575
cindy-leschyshyn@cnsfederation.org
Membership: 1,000-4,999; *Fees:* Schedule available; *Member Profile:* Neurology & neurosurgery residents & fellows; *Committees:* Professional Development; Scientific Program; Planning

Activities: Providing a national forum for communication; Offering continuing medical education to members & the neurological medical profession; Encouraging fundamental & applied research; Increasing public awareness about neurological disorders; Advocating on behalf of the profession
Meetings/Conferences: • Canadian Neurological Sciences Federation 50th Annual Congress, June, 2015, Royal York Hotel, Toronto, ON
Scope: National
Description: Courses, lectures, oral & digital poster presentations, plus exhibits & social events
Contact Information: Canadian Neurological Sciences Federation, Phone: 403-229-9544
• Canadian Neurological Sciences Federation 51st Annual Congress, 2016
Scope: National
Description: Courses, lectures, oral & digital poster presentations, plus exhibits & social events
Contact Information: Canadian Neurological Sciences Federation, Phone: 403-229-9544
Publications:
• Canadian Journal of Neurological Sciences
Type: Journal; *Frequency:* 6 pa; *Editor:* Cindy Leschyshyn
Profile: Peer-reviewed clinical & basic neuroscience research articles, covering neurology, neurosurgery, clinical neurophysiology, & pediatric neurology
• Canadian Neurological Sciences Federation Membership Directory
Type: Directory; *Frequency:* Annually

Canadian Neurological Society (CNS) / Société canadienne de neurologie

#709, 7015 Macleod Trail SW, Calgary AB T2H 2K1
Tel: 403-229-9544; *Fax:* 403-229-1661
www.cnsfederation.org/
Overview: A medium-sized national organization overseen by Canadian Neurological Sciences Federation
Mission: To promote & encourage all aspects of neurology, including research, education, assessment & accreditation; provide for annual scientific sessions to promote the knowledge & practice of neurology
Chief Officer(s):
Dan Morin, CNSF CEO
dan-morin@cnsfederation.org
Lisa Bicek, Manager
lisa-bicek@cnsfederation.org
Marika Fitzgerald, Manager, Finance & Administration
marika-fitzgerald@cnsfederation.org
Staff Member(s): 7
Membership: 600; *Fees:* $325; $80 Junior; $170 associate; *Member Profile:* Neurologists, Neurology residents, those in other related medical fields
Awards:
• Francis McNaughton & André Barbeau Memorial Prizes (Award)
Best submitted papers based on work done during the neurology residency or in post-residency training; junior members or active members of the society within 2 years of obtaining certification are eligible *Amount:* $1,000, inscribed scroll; up to $1,000 to cover expenses to attend the annual meeting of the Canadia
Publications:
• The Canadian Journal of Neurological Sciences
Type: Journal; *Frequency:* Bimonthly; *Accepts Advertising*; *Editor:* G. Bryan Young; *Price:* Free with CNS membership
Profile: Peer-reviewed original articles

Canadian New Music Network (CNMN) / Réseau canadien pour les musiques nouvelles (RCMN)

#200, 1085, Côte du Beaver Hall, Montréal QC H2Z 1S5
e-mail: admin@reseaumusiquesnouvelles.ca
www.newmusicnetwork.ca
www.facebook.com/CNMN.RCMN
Overview: A medium-sized national organization founded in 2005
Mission: To improve communication, understanding & knowledge within the new music community; To represent the community in Canadian society, by working with the media, Canadian government & arts organizations
Affliation(s): Canadian Music Centre; Upstream Music Association
Chief Officer(s):
Emily Hall, Administrator
Kyle Brenders, President
Finances: *Funding Sources:* Government grants; Membership dues
Membership: 1841; *Fees:* Schedule available; *Member Profile:* Artists, ensembles, orchestras, production companies, record labels, music educators, music media, musicologists, music lovers & fans who believe in the importance & value of creative music making in Canadian society
Activities: Website & online directory of members; Biennial conference; Regional meetings; Tours;

Canadian Newspaper Association (CNA) / Association canadienne des journaux (ACJ)

c/o Newspapers Canada, #200, 890 Yonge St., Toronto ON M4W 3P4
Tel: 416-923-3567; *Fax:* 416-923-7206
Toll-Free: 877-305-2262
Other Communication: publisher@newspaperscanada.ca
info@newspaperscanada.ca
www.newspaperscanada.ca
Previous Name: Canadian Daily Newspaper Association
Merged from: Newspaper Marketing Bureau
Overview: A medium-sized national organization founded in 1996
Mission: To ensure the continuance of a free press to serve readers effectively, by combining the experience, expertise, & dedication of members; To increase the profile & effectiveness of Canada's newspaper industry
Affliation(s): Canadian Community Newspapers Association
Chief Officer(s):
Natalie Larivière, Chair
John Hinds, President & Chief Executive Officer, 877-305-2262 Ext. 244
jhinds@newspaperscanada.ca
Suzanne Raitt, Vice-President, Marketing & Innovation, 877-305-2262 Ext. 234
sraitt@newspaperscanada.ca
Eileen Barak, Director, Government Affairs, 877-474-6397, Fax: 613-270-8369
Susan Down, Managing Director, Dailies, 877-305-2262 Ext. 231
sdown@newspaperscanada.ca
Tina Ongkeko, Managing Director, Community Media, 877-305-2262 Ext. 325
tongkeko@newspaperscanada.ca
Finances: *Funding Sources:* Membership fees
Membership: *Member Profile:* English & French daily newspapers, with circulations which range from 3,500 to over 500,000 each day; Suppliers, vendors, & consultants to the newspaper industry
Activities: Monitoring & analyzing legislation which affects newspapers & the freedom of the press; Representing needs of members & the public in areas of public policy, marketing, & member services; Increasing awareness of the benefits of newspapers; Developing research projects; Providing educational activities; Offering business services, such as the Canadian Media Circulation Audit; Preparing marketing materials; *Library:* Canadian Newspaper Association Library; by appointment
Awards:
• Extra Awards (Award)
To recognize outstanding newspaper advertising in Canada
• Goff Penny Awards (Award)
A competition for young journalists from daily newspapers
• Great Ideas Awards (Award)
To honour the best ad campaigns, promotions, & special sections from community & daily newspapers
• Quill Awards (Award)
To recognize longstanding service in the newspaper industry
Meetings/Conferences: • Newspapers Canada 2015 Annual Conference & Trade Show, May, 2015, Sheraton Centre Toronto Hotel, Toronto, ON
Scope: National
Description: An annual spring event with speakers, presentations, & seminars covering a wide range of topics for both daily & weekly newspapers
Contact Information: Tina Ongkeko, E-mail: conference@newspaperscanada.ca
Publications:
• Advertising Linage Reports [publications of the Canadian Newspaper Association]
Frequency: Monthly
Profile: Total ROP linage, classified linage, & category linage
• Circulation Data Report [a publication of the Canadian Newspaper Association]
Type: Yearbook; *Frequency:* Annually
Profile: Circulation in Canada for CNA & CCMA members
• Circulation Rates Report [a publication of the Canadian Newspaper Association]
Type: Yearbook; *Frequency:* Annually
Profile: Information on circulation pricing, wholesale rates, weekly subscription rates, net profits to carriers, vending box pricing, & storepricing, for Canadian Newspaper Association & Canadian Community Newspapers Association members only
• News on News [a publication of the Canadian Newspaper Association]
Type: Newsletter; *Frequency:* Weekly; *Price:* Freewith membership in the Canadian Newspaper Association
Profile: Activities of the Canadian Newspaper Association & the Canadian Community Newspapers Association, industry news, annoucements, awards, & events
• Non-Publishing Days Report [a publication of the Canadian Newspaper Association]
Type: Yearbook; *Frequency:* Annually
• The Press & The Courts
Frequency: Bimonthly
Profile: A collection of court cases involving the media in Canada, particularly the written press
• The Publisher
Type: Journal; *Frequency:* Bimonthly; *Accepts Advertising*; *Price:* Free with membership in the Canadian Newspaper Association
Profile: Articles on newspaper industry trends & topics in Canada, including regulatory issues, new technology, production, & distribution
• Revenue Report [a publication of the Canadian Newspaper Association]
Frequency: Quarterly
• The Scoop [a publication of the Canadian Newspaper Association]
Type: Newsletter; *Frequency:* Monthly; *Price:* Free
Profile: A bulletin for media planners, advertisers, creative agencies, & buyers, featuring news stories, case studies, research reports, & innovations in thedaily & community newspaper industry

Canadian Northern Society (CNoS)

PO Box 1174, Camrose AB T4V 1X2
Tel: 780-672-3099
canadiannorthern@telus.net
www.canadiannorthern.ca
www.facebook.com/pages/Canadian-Northern-Society/211046248914713
Overview: A small local charitable organization founded in 1987
Mission: To preserve prairie heritage
Chief Officer(s):
Lorrie Tiegs, President
Norm Prestage, Vice-President
Shawn I. Smith, Treasurer
Dean Tiegs, Secretary
secretary@canadiannorthern.ca
Finances: *Funding Sources:* Donations; Fundraising; Grants
Membership: *Fees:* $20 full members; $10 associate; *Committees:* Camrose Railway Station Park & Morgan Railway Garden; Meeting Creek Grain Elevator & Railway Station Heritage Site; Big Valley Railway Station & Roundhouse Interpretive Park; Canora Chronicle; Audit
Activities: Preserving railway station sites at Camrose, Big Valley & Meeting Creek, Alberta, as well as the grain elevator at Meeting Creek
Publications:
• The Canora Chronicle
Type: Newsletter; *Frequency:* Quarterly; *Editor:* Dean Tiegs; Lorrie Tiegs; *Price:* Free with society membership
Profile: News about heritage tourism initiatives

Canadian Nuclear Association (CNA) / Association nucléaire canadienne

#1610, 130 Albert St., Ottawa ON K1P 5G4
Tel: 613-237-4262; *Fax:* 613-237-0989
www.cna.ca
www.facebook.com/TalkNuclear
twitter.com/talknuclear
www.youtube.com/talknuclear
Overview: A large national organization founded in 1960
Mission: To promote the orderly & sound development of nuclear energy for peaceful purposes in Canada & abroad; To promote & foster an environment favourable to the healthy growth of the uses of nuclear energy & radioisotopes; To encourage cooperation between various industries, utilities, educational institutions, government departments & agencies, which may have a common interest in the development of economic nuclear power & the uses of radioisotopes; To provide

a forum for the discussion & resolution of problems which are of concern to the members, the industry, or the Canadian public; To stimulate cooperation with other associations with similar objectives & purposes
Chief Officer(s):
Heather Kleb, Acting President & Chief Executive Officer, 613-237-4262 Ext. 111
klebh@cna.ca
Steve Coupland, Director, Environmental Affairs, 613-237-4262 Ext. 107
couplands@cna.ca
George Christidis, Director, Government Affairs, 613-237-4262 Ext. 108
georgec@cna.ca
Laura Allardyce, Officer, Communications & Digital Media, 613-237-4262 Ext. 110
allardycel@cna.ca
John Stewart, Director, Policy & Research, 613-237-4262 Ext. 103
stewartj@cna.ca
Marie-danielle Davis, Corporate Secretary/Director, Member Services, 613-237-4262 Ext. 102
davism@cna.ca
Finances: *Funding Sources:* Membership fees
Membership: 112; *Fees:* Based on company size & activity; *Member Profile:* Industries & enterprises interested in the development & application of nuclear energy for peaceful purposes including uranium producers, reactor manufacturers, electrical utilities, engineering companies, banks, employee unions, departments of federal & provincial governments, educational establishments; *Committees:* Communications; Regulatory Affairs; Climate Change
Activities: *Library*
Meetings/Conferences: • Canadian Nuclear Association Conference & Trade Show 2015, February, 2015, Westin Hotel, Ottawa, ON
Scope: National
Contact Information: conference@cna.ca
Publications:
• Nuclear Canada
Type: Newsletter; *Editor:* Colin G. Hunt
Profile: CNA activities & news about nuclear energy in Canada
• Nuclear Canada Yearbook
Type: Yearbook; *Frequency:* Annually
Profile: Information about the Canadian nuclear industry & a buyers' guide of nuclear products & services
• Nuclear Energy Handbook
Profile: Basic & factual information about nuclear energy

Canadian Nuclear Society (CNS) / Société nucléaire canadienne (SNC)
655 Bay St., 17th Fl., Toronto ON M5G 2K4
Tel: 416-977-7620; *Fax:* 416-977-8131
cns-snc@on.aibn.com
www.cns-snc.ca
Previous Name: The technical society of the Canadian Nuclear Association (CNA)
Overview: A medium-sized national organization founded in 1979
Mission: To promote the exchange of information about nuclear science & technology & its applications; To foster the beneficial utilization of nuclear science
Member of: Engineering Institute of Canada (EIC)
Chief Officer(s):
Adriaan Buijs, President
K.L. (Ken) Smith, Financial Administrator
Denise Rouben, Office Manager
cns-snc@on.aibn.com
Finances: *Funding Sources:* Sponsorships
Membership: *Fees:* $27.81 students; $48.41 retirees; $82.40 regular members; *Member Profile:* Individuals directly involved with nuclear technology; Students; Persons interested in nuclear topics; *Committees:* Program; CNA Interface; WIN Interface; COG Interface; OCI Interface; Branch Affairs; Education & Communication; Membership; Bulletin; Finance; Past Presidents'; Climate Change, The Nuclear Future, & Communication Advisory; Fusion; Honours & Awards; Universities / UNENE; Inter-society Relations; Young Generation; Representative to PAGSE
Activities: Providing education; Offering opportunities to network with colleagues in Canada & internationally
Awards:
• W.B. Lewis Medal (Award)
• Ian McRae Award of Merit (Award), Canadian Nuclear Society
• Outstanding Contribution Award (Award), Canadian Nuclear Society
• Innovative Achievement Award (Award), Canadian Nuclear Society
• Fellows of the Canadian Nuclear Society (Award), Canadian Nuclear Society
• John S. Hewitt Team Achievement Award (Award), Canadian Nuclear Society
• Education & Communication Award (Award), Canadian Nuclear Society
• R.E. Jervis Award (Award), Canadian Nuclear Society
• CNA International Award (Award), Canadian Nuclear Society
• CNS President's Award (Award), Canadian Nuclear Society
Meetings/Conferences: • Canadian Nuclear Society 2015 Annual Conference & CNS/CNA Student Conference, May, 2015, Saint John Trade & Convention Center, Saint John, NB
Scope: National
Description: A meeting open to all persons interested in nuclear science, nuclear engineering, & technology, featuring the presentation of Canadian Nuclear Society awards
Contact Information: Canadian Nuclear Society Office: Phone: 416-977-7620, E-mail: cns-snc@on.aibn.com; URL: www.cnsconference2015.org
• Canadian Nuclear Society 2015 17th International Conference on Environmental Degradation of Materials in Nuclear Power Systems - Water Reactors, August, 2015, Fairmont Château Laurier, Ottawa, ON
Scope: National
Contact Information: Canadian Nuclear Society Office: Phone: 416-977-7620, E-mail: cns-snc@on.aibn.com; URL: www.envdeg2015.org
• Canadian Nuclear Society 2015 7th International Conference on Modelling & Simulation in Nuclear Science & Engineering, October, 2015, Ottawa Marriott Hotel, Ottawa, ON
Scope: National
Contact Information: Canadian Nuclear Society Office: Phone: 416-977-7620, E-mail: cns-snc@on.aibn.com; URL: cns2015simulation.org
Publications:
• Canadian Nuclear Society Bulletin
Type: Journal; *Frequency:* Quarterly; *Editor:* Ric Fluke; *Price:* Free with Canadian Nuclear Society membership
Profile: Society news, conference reports, technical papers, articles, & letters
• Canadian Nuclear Society Proceedings
Profile: Information from Canadian Nuclear Society conferences or symposia

Canadian Numismatic Association ***See*** Royal Canadian Numismatic Association

Canadian Numismatic Research Society (CNRS)
PO Box 1351, Victoria BC V8W 2W7
www.nunetcan.net/cnrs/cnrs.htm
Overview: A small national organization founded in 1963
Mission: To promote reseach & study of numismatics
Chief Officer(s):
Ronald Greene, Secretary/Treasurer
ragreene@telus.net
Membership: *Member Profile:* Members are invited to join CNRS; Individuals must be engaged in numismatic research & have published the results of their research
Activities: Increasing public awareness & understanding of numismatics; Disseminating knowledge about numismatics related to Canada
Publications:
• Numismatica Canada
Frequency: Quarterly; *Price:* $15 non-members
Profile: Information about Canadian tokens, medals, modern municipal trade dollars, & other numismatic topics, published in conjunction with the Canadian Association of Token Collectors

Canadian Nurse Continence Advisors Association (CNCA)
c/o Jennifer Skelly, St. Joseph's Healthcare, King Campus, 2757 King St. East, Hamilton ON L8G 5E4
Tel: 905-573-4823
www.cnca.ca
Overview: A small national organization
Mission: To protect the quality standard associated with being an NCA
Chief Officer(s):
Jennifer Skelly, President
skelly@mcmaster.ca
Membership: *Fees:* $40 full; $30 affiliate; $20 student; *Member Profile:* Nurse Continence Advisors (NCA)

Canadian Nursery Landscape Association (CNLA)
Stn. Main, 7856 Fifth Line South, R.R.#4, Milton ON L9T 2X8
Tel: 905-875-1399; *Fax:* 905-875-1840
Toll-Free: 888-446-3499
info@canadanursery.com
www.canadanursery.com
twitter.com/cnlavictor
Previous Name: Canadian Nursery Trades Association; Landscape Canada
Overview: A medium-sized national organization founded in 1968
Mission: To coordinate provincial member groups in the Canadian horticultural industry; to set national standards; to work with government; to develop national priorities
Affliation(s): Flowers Canada; Canadian Ornamental Plant Foundation; Associated Landscape Contractors of America; International Garden Centres Association; North American Plant Protection Organization; American Nursery & Landscape Association; International Ornamental Growers Association; Canadian Plant Protection Advisory Committee; Canadian Horticultural Council
Chief Officer(s):
Victor Santacruz, Executive Director
victor@canadanursery.com
Finances: *Annual Operating Budget:* $500,000-$1.5 Million; *Funding Sources:* Membership dues; publications; management fees
Staff Member(s): 8; 21 volunteer(s)
Membership: 3,210; *Fees:* $115.23; *Member Profile:* Must be a supplier, active or associate member of one of the provincial organizations; *Committees:* Certification; Garden Centres; Growers; Human Resources; Insurance; Landscape
Awards:
• Award of Excellence for Landscape Construction/Installation (Award)
• Award of Excellence for Landscape Maintenance (Award)
Publications:
• Canadian Standards for Nursery Stock
Price: Free with CNLA membership
Profile: A set of minimum professional standards for for the nursery industry
• CNLA [Canadian Nursery Landscape Association] Newsbrief
Type: Newsletter; *Frequency:* Bimonthly; *Price:* Free with CNLA membership
Profile: National news about the industry & the association
• CNLA [Canadian Nursery Landscape Association] Membership Directory
Type: Directory; *Frequency:* Annually; *Price:* Free with CNLA membership

Canadian Nursery Trades Association; Landscape Canada ***See*** Canadian Nursery Landscape Association

Canadian Nurses Association (CNA) / Association des infirmières et infirmiers du Canada
50 Driveway, Ottawa ON K2P 1E2
Tel: 613-237-2133; *Fax:* 613-237-3520
Toll-Free: 800-361-8404
info@cna-aiic.ca
www.cna-aiic.ca
www.facebook.com/CNA.AIIC
twitter.com/canadanurses
www.youtube.com/user/CNAVideos
Previous Name: Canadian National Association of Trained Nurses
Overview: A large national organization founded in 1908
Mission: To advance the discipline of nursing; to advocate for public policy that incorporates the principles of primary health care & respects the principles, conditions & spirit of the Canada Health Act; To advance the regulation of Registered Nurses in the interest of the public; To advance international health policy & development in Canada
Member of: International Council of Nurses
Chief Officer(s):
Karima A. Velji, President
Barbara Shellian, President Elect
Anne Sutherland Boal, CEO
executiveoffice@cna-aiic.ca
Brenda Beauchamp, Director, Finance and Administration, 613-237-2159 Ext. 202
bbeauchamp@cna-aiic.ca
Finances: *Annual Operating Budget:* Greater than $5 Million; *Funding Sources:* Membership dues; Testing services; Sales & marketing
Membership: 11 provincial & territorial nursing associations, representing over 129,023 registered nurses; *Fees:* $27;

Member Profile: Provincial & territorial associations; Nursing students; National nursing groups, emerging groups & other groups
Activities: Collaborating with nurses, other health-care providers, health system stakeholders, & the public with the goal of sustaining quality practice & achieving positive client outcomes; Promoting awareness of the nursing profession; Setting standards for education, practice, research, & administration; *Awareness Events:* National Nursing Week, May; National Nursing Day, May 12; *Library:* Helen K. Mussallem Library
Awards:
• Jeanne Mance Award (Award)
To honour individuals who have made significant contributions to the health of Canadians & positively influenced nursing practice in Canada
• Employer Recognition Award (Award)
To recognize employers who demonstrate support for the certification process in nursing specialties
Meetings/Conferences: • Canadian Nurses Association 2015 Annual Meeting, 2015
Scope: National
Description: The highlights of the association's year
Contact Information: E-mail: info@cna-aiic.ca
• Canadian Nurses Association 2016 Annual Meeting & Biennial Convention, June, 2016, NB
Scope: National
Attendance: 1,000+
Description: One of Canada's largest nursing conferences, featuring presentations, speakers, workshops, & the opportunity to view new products in the health-care marketplace
Contact Information: E-mail: conferences@cna-aiic.ca
• Canadian Nurses Association 2017 Annual Meeting, 2017
Scope: National
Description: A business meeting attended by members of the provincial & territorial nursing associations & interested parties
Contact Information: E-mail: info@cna-aiic.ca
• Canadian Nurses Association 2018 Annual Meeting & Biennial Convention, June, 2018, AB
Scope: National
Attendance: 1,000+
Description: An opportunity for delegates from across Canada to discuss challenges in the nursing profession, share successes, participate in workshops, listen to speakers, & view new products from the health-care marketplace
Contact Information: E-mail: conferences@cna-aiic.ca
• Canadian Nurses Association 2019 Annual Meeting, 2019
Scope: National
Description: A review of the association's strategic initiatives during the past year
Contact Information: E-mail: info@cna-aiic.ca
• Canadian Nurses Association 2020 Annual Meeting & Biennial Convention, June, 2020, PE
Scope: National
Attendance: 1,000+
Description: A large Canadian nursing conference, featuring presentations, speakers, workshops, discussions, & the opportunity to see new products in the health-care marketplace
Contact Information: E-mail: conferences@cna-aiic.ca
• Canadian Nurses Association 2021 Annual Meeting, 2021
Scope: National
Description: A business meeting featuring a board report & a CEO update
Contact Information: E-mail: info@cna-aiic.ca
Publications:
• Access: The CNA [Canadian Nurses Association] Newsletter
Type: Newsletter; *Frequency:* Monthly
• Canadian Nurse
Type: Journal; *Frequency:* 9 pa; *Accepts Advertising*; *Editor:* Lisa Brazeau; *Price:* Free with membership in the Cannadian NursesAssociation
Profile: Peer-reviewed, evidence-based information about advances in the nursing profession & changes to the health system
• CNA [Canadian Nurses Association] Annual Report
Type: Yearbook; *Frequency:* Annually
Profile: Highlights of the association's activities & achievements throughout the year
• CNA [Canadian Nurses Association] Convention Communiqué
Profile: Periodic updates on the Canadian Nurses Association biennial convention
• CNA [Canadian Nuses Association] Now
Type: Newsletter
Profile: Reports, new products, CNA services & activities, nursing trivia, & nursing history
• CRNE [Canadian Registered Nurse Examination] Bulletin
Type: Newsletter
Profile: Information about the Canadian Registered Nurse Examination (CRNE)
• Nursing Now: Issues & Trends in Canadian Nursing
Type: Newsletter
Profile: Short papers

Canadian Nurses Foundation (CNF) / Fondation des infirmières et infirmiers du Canada

50 Driveway, Ottawa ON K2P 1E2
Tel: 613-237-2133; *Fax:* 613-237-3520
Toll-Free: 800-361-8404
info@cnf-fiic.ca
www.cnf-fiic.ca
www.facebook.com/CNA.AIIC
twitter.com/canadanurses
Overview: A medium-sized national charitable organization founded in 1962
Mission: To promote the health of Canadians by enhancing nursing education & research.
Chief Officer(s):
Christine Rieck Buckley, Executive Director
cbuckley@cnf-fiic.ca
Finances: *Funding Sources:* Special membership dues; corporate, foundation & individual donations
Awards:
• Study Awards (Scholarship)

Canadian Nurses Protective Society (CNPS) / Société de protection des infirmières et infirmiers du Canada (SPIIC)

#510, 1545 Carling Ave., Ottawa ON K1Z 8P9
Tel: 613-237-2092; *Fax:* 613-237-6300
Toll-Free: 800-267-3390
info@cnps.ca
www.cnps.ca
Overview: A small national organization founded in 1988
Mission: To offer legal liability protection related to nursing practice to eligible Registered Nurses
Affliation(s): College & Association of Registered Nurses of Alberta; Saskatchewan Registered Nurses' Association; College of Registered Nurses of Manitoba; Registered Nurses' Association of Ontario; Nurses Association of New Brunswick; College of Registered Nurses of Nova Scotia; Association of Registered Nurses of Prince Edward Island; Association of Registered Nurses of Newfoundland & Labrador; Registered Nurses Association of the Northwest Territories & Nunavut; Yukon Registered Nurses Association
Chief Officer(s):
Chantal Léonard, CEO
Activities: Providing legal & financial assistance for nurses in professional legal jeopardy; Offering information & educational opportunities about professional liability problems
Publications:
• infoLAW
Profile: Topics include operating room nursing, malpractice lawsuits, medication errors, & the nurse as a witness

Canadian Nursing Informatics Association (CNIA)

937 Cromwell Dr., Ottawa ON K1V 6K3
www.cnia.ca
www.facebook.com/group.php?gid=119735001344
Overview: A small national organization
Mission: To be the voice for Nursing Informatics in Canada; to catalyze the emergence of a new national association of nurse informaticians
Affiliation(s): Canadian Nurses Association
Chief Officer(s):
June Kaminski, President
Finances: *Annual Operating Budget:* Less than $50,000
Membership: 300; *Fees:* $52.50 general/associate; $157.50 institutional; $26.25 student

Canadian Nursing Students' Association (CNSA) / Association des étudiantes infirmières du Canada (AEIC)

Fifth Ave. Court, #15, 99 - 5th Ave., Ottawa ON K1S 5K4
Tel: 613-235-3150
communications@cnsa.ca
www.cnsa.ca
www.facebook.com/CNSA.AEIC
twitter.com/cnsa1
Previous Name: Canadian University Nursing Students' Association
Overview: A medium-sized national organization founded in 1971
Mission: To act as the official voice of nursing students in Canada; To strive to increase the legal, ethical, professional, & educational aspects of nursing
Affliation(s): Canadian Nurses Association; Canadian Association of Schools of Nursing
Chief Officer(s):
Evan Jolicoeur, President
president@cnsa.ca
Mary Strain, Vice-President & Director, Inter/IntraProfessional Education & Research
vp@cnsa.ca
Sarah Covino, Director, National Career & Leadership Development
leadership@cnsa.ca
Laura Gallant, Director, Communications
communications@cnsa.ca
Katherine Lamy, Director, Bilingualism & Translation
translation@cnsa.ca
Lise Schultz, Director, National Conference
conference@cnsa.ca
Katrina Vande Bunte, Director, International Health
international@cnsa.ca
Membership: *Member Profile:* Student bodies at a School of Nursing; Nursing students at a School of Nursing; Former individual members or distance members with a continuing interest in the association; Organizations or corporate bodies approved by the board of directors
Activities: Promoting the nursing profession; Providing a communication link among Canadian nursing students; Encouraging education; Liaising with other organizations concerned with nursing; Increasing awareness of the existence of & the need for nursing research
Meetings/Conferences: • Canadian Nursing Students' Association 2015 Annual Atlantic Regional Conference, 2015
Scope: Provincial
Description: A conference to promote professional & personal development & discussion in the field of nursing
Contact Information: E-mail: atlantic@cnsa.ca
• Canadian Nursing Students' Association 2015 Annual Québec Regional Conference, 2015, QC
Scope: Provincial
Description: A professional development opportunity for Québec's nursing students, featuring a business meeting for the region
Contact Information: E-mail: quebec-conference@cnsa.ca
• Canadian Nursing Students' Association 2015 Annual Ontario Regional Conference, 2015, ON
Scope: Provincial
Attendance: 400
Description: Registered nursing students & practical nursing students from across Ontario participate in the Ontario regional meeting, hospital tours, keynote speaker sessions, workshops, panel presentations, & social events
Contact Information: E-mail: ontario@cnsa.ca
• Canadian Nursing Students' Association 2015 Annual Western / Prairie Regional Conference, 2015
Scope: Provincial
Description: An event for nursing students showcasing keynote speakers, health panels, poster presentations, workshops, a career fair, regional executive meetings, & networking & social events
Contact Information: E-mail: prairie@cnsa.ca; west@cnsa.ca
• Canadian Nursing Students' Association 2015 National Conference, January, 2015, University of Saskatchewan - Regina Campus, Regina, SK
Scope: National
Attendance: 500+
Description: Keynote speakers, panels, debates, professional development sessions, & networking opportunities
Contact Information: National Conference Planning Committee, E-mail: conference@cnsa.ca
Publications:
• Canadian Nursing Students' Association Governing Bylaws
Profile: Some sections include rules, regulations, & policies of the association, the board of directors & officers, committees, membership, finances, amendments to bylaws, &meetings
• Canadian Nursing Students' Association Governing Rules & Regulations
Profile: Covering the power, duties, & meetings of the board of directors & officers, the duties & meetings of the regional executive, committees, & national & regionalconferences

Canadian Nutrition Society (CNS) / Société canadienne de nutrition (SCN)

#310, 2175 Sheppard Ave. East, Toronto ON M2J 1W8

Tel: 416-491-7188; *Fax:* 416-491-1670
Toll-Free: 888-414-7188
info@cns-scn.ca
www.cns-scn.ca
www.linkedin.com/groups?gid=4660487
www.facebook.com/canadiannutritionsociety
twitter.com/@CNS_SCN
Merged from: Canadian Society for Clinical Nutrition; Canadian Society for Nutritional Sciences
Overview: A medium-sized national organization founded in 2010
Mission: To promote nutrition science & education; To act as a voice for those engaged in furthering nutrition
Chief Officer(s):
Leah Gramlich, President, 780-735-6839, Fax: 780-735-5650
leah.gramlich@ualberta.ca
Robert Bertolo, Vice-President, Research
rbertolo@mun.ca
Maitreyi Raman, Vice-President, Health Professionals
maitreyi.raman@gmail.com
Lindsay Robinson, Secretary
Janis Randall Simpson, Treasurer
janis@uoguelph.ca
Melonie Hart, Manager, Operations, 416-491-7188, Fax: 416-491-1670
Finances: *Funding Sources:* Membership fees; Sponsorships
Membership: *Fees:* Schedule available; *Member Profile:* Graduates of post-secondary institutions with degrees or diplomas in nutrition-related disciplines; Members of provincially regulated health care professions; Students; *Committees:* Annual Scientific Meeting; Membership; Publications; Awards; Resources; Ethics; Communications; Canadian Malnutrition Task Force
Activities: Advocating for the promotion of health & the prevention & treatment of disease; Lobbying for research funding; Providing input into policy formulation; Promoting the application of best practices; Offering professional development; Providing networking opportunities
Awards:
• Khush Jeejeebhoy Award (Award)
To recognize the best application of clinical nutrition research findings to clinical practice
• Earle Willard McHenry Award (Award)
Awarded for distinguished service in the field of nutrition by a Canadian or Canadian-based individual *Contact:* Dr. Guylaine Ferland, CNS/SCN Awards Chair, E-mail: guylaine.ferland@umontreal.ca
• Nestlé Nutrition Student & Trainee Award (Award)
The Nestlé Nutrition Student & Trainee Competition is part of the Canadian Nutrition Society Annual Meeting
• PhD Dissertation Award (Award)
Presented for outstanding research contributing to the degree of PhD *Contact:* Dr. Guylaine Ferland, CNS/SCN Awards Chair, E-mail: guylaine.ferland@umontreal.ca
• Joanne Schweitzer Clinical Nutrition Research Abstract Award (Award)
• Centrum Foundation New Scientist Award for Outstanding Research (Award)
• IUNS Travel Subsidy Award (Award)
Meetings/Conferences: • Canadian Nutrition Society 2015 Protein Conference, January, 2015, Toronto Marriott Downtown Eaton Centre Hotel, Toronto, ON
Scope: National
Contact Information: Phone: 416-491-7188, Fax: 416-491-1670, E-mail: info@cns-scn.ca
• Canadian Nutrition Society 2015 5th Annual Meeting, May, 2015, RBC Convention Centre, Winnipeg, MB
Scope: National
Description: Conference sessions & the presentation of awards
Contact Information: Phone: 416-491-7188, Fax: 416-491-1670, E-mail: info@cns-scn.ca
Publications:
• CNS [Canadian Nutrition Society] Newsletter
Type: Newsletter

Canadian Obesity Network (CON) / Réseau Canadien en Obésité (RCO)

Li Ka Shing Centre for Health Research & Innovation, Univ. of Alberta, #1-116, 8602 - 112 St., Edmonton AB T6G 2E1
Tel: 780-492-8361; *Fax:* 780-492-9414
info@obesitynetwork.ca
www.obesitynetwork.ca
twitter.com/CanObesityNet
Overview: A small national organization founded in 2006
Mission: To foster knowledge translation, capacity building, & partnerships in the area of obesity in Canada; To find innovative & effective ways to treat & prevent obesity; To reduce the mental, physical, & economic burden of obesity
Chief Officer(s):
Anton Hart, Chair
Arya M. Sharma, Scientific Director
Staff Member(s): 8
Membership: 10,500; *Member Profile:* Obesity researchers; Health professionals; Stakeholders; Media members; *Committees:* Science
Activities: Facilitating networking among researchers, health professionals, policy makers, & stakeholders who are interested in obesity; Promoting research; Training researchers & practitioners; Building consensus on obesity policies; *Speaker Service:* Yes
Meetings/Conferences: • Canadian Obesity Summit 2015, April, 2015, Toronto, ON
Scope: National
Publications:
• Best Weight: A Practical Guide to Office-Based Obesity Management
Number of Pages: 100; *Author:* Dr. Y. Freedhoff; Dr. A.M. Sharma
Profile: A practical guide to managing obesity in a clinical setting
• Conduit
Type: Magazine; *Frequency:* Quarterly; *Accepts Advertising*; *Editor:* Brad Hussey
Profile: Articles about obesity research & networking activities throughout Canada
• Obesity + (Online Best Evidence Service In Tackling Obesity Plus)
Profile: Latest evidence for clinical practice on obesity

Canadian Occupational Health Nurses Association (COHNA) / Association canadienne des infirmières et infirmiers en santé du travail (ACIIST)

e-mail: karen.mazerolle@imperialgroup.ca
www.cohna-aciist.ca
Previous Name: National Association of Occupational Health Nurses
Overview: A medium-sized national organization founded in 1984
Mission: To promote national standards for occupational health nursing practice; to advance the profession by providing a national forum for the exchange of ideas & concerns; to enhance the profile of occupational health nurses; to improve the health & safety of workers; to contribute to the health of the community by providing quality health services to workers; to encourage continuing education
Affiliation(s): Canadian Nurses Association
Chief Officer(s):
Karen Mazerolle, President
karen.mazerolle@imperialgroup.ca
Marg Creen, Secretary/Treasurer
mcreen@tsh.to
Ellen Coe, Vice President
ellencoe@telus.net
Finances: *Annual Operating Budget:* Less than $50,000; *Funding Sources:* Membership dues
4 volunteer(s)
Membership: 2,400; *Fees:* $5; *Member Profile:* Member of provincial occupational health nurses group; *Committees:* Certification; Communication; Education; Finance
Activities: *Speaker Service:* Yes

Canadian Occupational Therapy Foundation (COTF) / La Fondation canadienne d'ergothérapie (FCE)

CTTC Bldg., #3401, 1125 Colonel By Dr., Ottawa ON K1S 5R1
Tel: 613-523-2268; *Fax:* 613-523-2552
Toll-Free: 800-434-2268
www.cotfcanada.org
www.facebook.com/239464269434993
Overview: A medium-sized national charitable organization founded in 1983
Mission: To fund & promote research & scholarship in occupational therapy in Canada
Chief Officer(s):
Sangita Kamblé, Executive Director, 613-523-2268 Ext. 241
skamble@cotfcanada.org
Anne McDonald, Executive Assistant, 613-523-2268 Ext. 226
amcdonald@cotfcanada.org
Finances: *Annual Operating Budget:* $50,000-$100,000; *Funding Sources:* Donations; Canadian Association of Occupational Therapists
Staff Member(s): 2; 20 volunteer(s)
Membership: 1,500; *Committees:* Research; Scholarship
Activities: Competitions for research; scholarship;
Awards:
• Masters & Docotral Scholarships (Scholarship)
Awarded annually to members of CAOT enrolled full-time or part-time in a masters or doctoral program in a discipline related to occupational therapy research*Eligibility:* Occupational Therapy students enrolled in Masters or Doctoral Research based programs. Must be current members of CAOT*Deadline:* October 1 *Amount:* $1,500; $3,000
• COTF Research Grants (Grant)
Amount: $2,000; $5,000
• Janice Hines Memorial Award (Award)
Awarded annually to a member of CAOT for an activity which supports the transfer of knowledge of best practices in pediatric occupational therapy *Amount:* $500
• Goldwin Howland Scholarship (Scholarship)
Awarded to a member of CAOT who has demonstrated leadership & vision within the profession *Amount:* $2,000
• Thelma Cardwell Scholarship (Scholarship)
Awarded annually to a member of CAOT enrolled full-time in a masters or doctoral level program who is able to demonstrate an outstanding contribution to occupational therapy *Amount:* $2,000

Canadian Office & Professional Employees Union (COPEU) / Le Syndicat canadien des employées et employés professionnels et de bureau (SEPB)

c/o Francine Doyon, #11100, boul 565 East Cremazie, Montreal QC H2M 2W2
copesepb.ca
Overview: A medium-sized national organization founded in 1933
Mission: A national labour union organization made up of 2 regional Councils and 39 Local unions comprising tens of thousands of members in several provinces across Canada.
Affiliation(s): Canadian Labour Congress (CLC)
Chief Officer(s):
Serge Cadieux, National President, 514-522-6511 Ext. 235, Fax: 514-522-9096
scadieux@copesepb.ca
Membership: 3,000,000; *Member Profile:* Office employees, technical and professional employees and sales representatives both in the private and public sectors.

Region 1 - Section locale 1012
#1.139, 8485 Christophe-Colomb, Montréal QC H2M 0A7

Region 1 - Section locale 434
#250, 1200 Papineau, Montreal QC H2K 4R5
Tél: 514-522-6511; *Téléc:* 514-528-7380
Ligne sans frais: 800-561-7372
sepb434@videotron.net
Chief Officer(s):
François Leduc, Président, 514-522-0434 Ext. 222

Region 1 - Section locale 463
1717 du Havre, Montreal QC H2K 2X3
Tél: 514-598-3259; *Téléc:* 514-598-3890
sepb463@gazmetro.com

Region 1 - Section locale 480
#250, 1200 Papineau, Montreal QC H2K 4R5
Tél: 514-522-6511
Ligne sans frais: 800-561-7372
lucsabou@magma.ca

Region 1 - Section locale 526
CP 1980, 4010 St-Andre Rd., Jonquiere QC G7S 5K5
Tél: 418-622-5170
Ligne sans frais: 800-295-7372
langis_lapointe@abitibiconsolidated.com

Region 1 - Section locale 571
303 Notre-Dame St. East, 4th Fl., Montreal QC H2Y 3Y8
Tél: 512-487-2419; *Téléc:* 514-872-3883
c_picotte@videotron.ca

Region 1 - Section locale 573
#250, 1200 Papineau, Montreal QC H2K 4R5
Tél: 514-522-6511; *Téléc:* 514-522-9000
Ligne sans frais: 800-561-7372
573@sepb.qc.ca

Region 1 - Section locale 574
#250, 1200 Papineau, Montreal QC H2K 4R5
Tél: 514-522-7574; *Téléc:* 514-522-0505
574@sepb.qc.ca
Chief Officer(s):
Loïc Breton, Président
lbreton@sepb.qc.ca

Region 1 - Section locale 575
#2200, 565, boul Crémazie est, Montreal QC H2M 2V7
Tél: 514-522-6511; *Téléc:* 514-522-5759
Ligne sans frais: 800-561-7372
sepb575.desjardins@videotron.net
www.sepb575.qc.ca

Region 1 - Section locale 576
444, Mountainview, Otterburn Park QC J3H 2K2
Tél: 450-672-4010; *Téléc:* 450-467-9347
rmace-burton@rsb.qc.ca

Region 1 - Section locale 577
#A105, 3200, boul Souvenir ouest, Laval QC H7V 1W9
Tél: 450-621-5600
jfitch@swlauriersb.qc.ca

Region 1 - Section locale 578
13, boul St-Laurent est, Longueuil QC J4H 4B7
Tél: 450-647-5884; *Téléc:* 450-647-5099
sepbmarie-victorin@qc.aira.com

Region 1 - Section locale 579
500, boul Dollard, Outremont QC H2V 3G2
Tél: 514-271-1194; *Téléc:* 514-271-1981
579@sepb.qc.ca

Region 1 - Section locale 610
CP 96565, 895, de la Gauchetière ouest, Montréal QC H3B 5J8
Tél: 514-280-7139
info@spstm.ca

Region 1 - Section locale 611
#250, 1200 Papineau, Montréal QC H2K 4R5
Tél: 514-522-6511; *Téléc:* 514-522-9000
Chief Officer(s):
Jacques Lamontagne, Président

Region 2 - Local 103
c/o Penny Wachter, President, 3145 Doran Rd., Pembroke ON K8A 6W8
Tel: 613-735-5496
cope103inthevalley@hotmail.com

Region 2 - Local 131
c/o Steve Reeves, President, 280 Willis Dr., Aurora ON L4G 7M3
Fax: 877-217-1437
Toll-Free: 800-746-5728

Region 2 - Local 151
c/o Assunta Young, President, PO Box 359, Marathon ON P0T 2E0
Tel: 807-229-2681; *Fax:* 807-229-3638

Region 2 - Local 225
c/o Daniel Mayville, President, PO Box 19, Stn. A, Ottawa ON K1N 8V1
Tel: 613-907-1626
correspondence@cope225sepb.ca
www.cope225sepb.ca
www.facebook.com/cope225sepb

Region 2 - Local 236
c/o Christine Bayko, President, 400 Westbury Cres., Thunder Bay ON P7C 4N4
Tel: 807-624-2255
chrisb@supercu.com

Region 2 - Local 24
c/o Frank Woit, President, 879 Callandar Bay Dr., Callender ON P0H 1H0
Tel: 705-752-1651
Frank.woit@sympatico.ca

Region 2 - Local 26
c/o Pauline Wallace, President, 433 Townline Rd., Sault Ste. Marie ON P6A 6K4
Tel: 705-949-6444
Chief Officer(s):
Jacques Morin, Président

Region 2 - Local 290
c/o Teena O'Keefe, President, 151 North Service Rd., Burlington ON L7R 4C2
Tel: 800-263-9120; *Fax:* 905-632-4733

Region 2 - Local 343
c/o Liz Fong, President, #701, 555 Richmond St. West, Toronto ON M5V 3B1
Tel: 416-703-4448; *Fax:* 416-703-8520
Toll-Free: 888-224-5553
cope343@on.aibn.com
www.cope343.com
www.facebook.com/pages/COPE-Ontario/201120949921790
twitter.com/PorterStrike

Region 2 - Local 429
c/o Judy McLeod, Kirkland Lake District Comp. School, PO Box 520, 60 Allen Ave., Kirkland Lake ON P2N 3J5
Tel: 705-567-4981; *Fax:* 705-568-8829

Region 2 - Local 454
c/o Maria Kullman, President, 1126 Roland St., Thunder Bay ON P7B 5M4
Tel: 807-345-6395; *Fax:* 807-344-8448

Region 2 - Local 468
c/o Valerie Francis-Roberts, President, PO Box 1202, #701, 555 Richmond St. West, Toronto ON M5V 3B1
Tel: 416-703-8515; *Fax:* 416-703-8520
jbest@copeontario.ca

Region 2 - Local 473
c/o Lynne Sims, President, 11 Golfview Cres., London ON N6C 5N1
Tel: 519-680-4013; *Fax:* 519-686-1392

Region 2 - Local 491
3731 Eastgate Dr. East, Regina SK S4Z 1A5
Tel: 306-525-5874; *Fax:* 306-781-8177
cope491.ca
Chief Officer(s):
Steve Smith, President
ssmith@cupe.ca

Region 2 - Local 521
c/o Bonnie Paterson, PO Box 7, Dryden ON P8N 2Y7
Tel: 807-223-8246; *Fax:* 807-223-8843

Region 2 - Local 523
c/o Shannon Lamontagne, President, 173 Lefebvre Peninsula Rd., Moonbeam ON P0L 2G0
Tel: 705-367-2799
shanron7@yahoo.ca
Chief Officer(s):
Ron Roberts, President
Susan Bellefeuille, Recording Secretary
Pauline Gauvin, Financial Secretary

Region 2 - Local 527
c/o Elaine Sinha, President, 580 Upper Wellington St., Hamilton ON L9A 3P9
Tel: 905-387-9843; *Fax:* 905-387-9919
Chief Officer(s):
Victor Lau, Secretary

Region 2 - Local 529
c/o Jody Etmanski, President, 372 Cartier St., North Bay ON P1B 8N5
Tel: 705-462-5030
raymondd@npsc.edu.on.ca

Region 2 - Local 550
PO Box 47108, Dundas SQ PO, 10 Dundas St. East, Toronto ON M5B 0A1
Tel: 416-671-3865
copelocal550@hotmail.com
www.copelocal550.ca

Region 2 - Local 81
C/o Dan Rogers, President, 1126 Roland St., Thunder Bay ON P7B 5H4
Tel: 807-473-3445

Region 2 - Local 96
c/o Cheryl Balacko, President, 319 River St., Thunder Bay ON P7A 3R3
Tel: 807-343-8335; *Fax:* 807-345-0428
cope96@tbaytel.net
Chief Officer(s):
Yves Ouellet, Président

Region 3 - Local 342
c/o Erin McGee, President, #403 D, 275 Broadway, Winnipeg MB R3C 4M6
Tel: 204-942-0899; *Fax:* 204-947-6513

Region 3 - Local 397
#109, 2709 - 12th Ave., Regina SK S4T 1J3
Tel: 306-352-4238; *Fax:* 306-347-2720
Toll-Free: 877-267-3397
cope397@sasktel.net
www.facebook.com/pages/COPE-Local-397/196363183824204
twitter.com/COPE397

Region 3 - Local 458
c/o Yvonne Bootsman, President, PO Box 11242, Edmonton AB T5J 3K5
Tel: 780-916-8997
cope458president@gmail.com

Region 4 - Local 378
4595 Canada Way, 2nd Fl., Burnaby BC V5G 1J9
Tel: 604-299-0378; *Fax:* 604-299-8211
Toll-Free: 800-665-6838
communications@cope378.ca
www.cope378.ca
www.facebook.com/COPE378
twitter.com/COPE378
www.youtube.com/378COPE
Mission: Part of the larger COPE National Union, Local 378, located in Burnaby, represents 12,000 employees of BC Hydro, Capilano University, TransLink, and other other workplaces throughout BC.
Affliation(s): B.C. Federation of Labour, Canadian Labour Congress
Chief Officer(s):
Andy Ross, President
aross@cope378.ca
Lori Mayhew, Secretary-Treasurer
lmayhew@cope378.ca
David Black, Vice President
davidblack@cope378.ca

Canadian Office Products Association (COPA)

#300, 2585 Skymark Ave., Mississauga ON L4W 5L6
Tel: 905-624-9462; *Fax:* 905-624-0830
info@copa.ca
www.copa.ca
www.linkedin.com/company/canadian-office-products-association
twitter.com/COPA_network
Previous Name: Stationery & Office Equipment Guild of Canada Inc.; Stationers' Guild of Canada Inc.
Overview: A small national organization founded in 1933
Mission: To help their memebers by providing them with business solutions that allow them to grow
Chief Officer(s):
Sam Moncada, President
smoncada@copa.ca
Membership: *Fees:* Schedule available dependant on type of business & annual sales; *Committees:* Awards; Finance; Business Network; Logistics; Golf; Data Factory

Canadian Oil Sands Network for Research & Development Inc. (CONRAD)

3608 - 33 St. NW, Calgary AB T2L 2A6
Tel: 403-210-5221; *Fax:* 403-210-5380
info@conrad.ab.ca
www.conrad.ab.ca
Overview: A large international organization founded in 1994
Mission: CONRAD is a network organized to faciliatate collaborative research in science & technology for Alberta oilsands.
Affiliation(s): WADE Canada
Chief Officer(s):
Carolyn Preston, CEO & Executive Director, Administration
preston@conrad.ab.ca
Stephanie Sutton, Executive Assistant, Administration
stephanie@conrad.ab.ca
Roger Melley, Treasurer, Administration
Finances: *Annual Operating Budget:* Greater than $5 Million; *Funding Sources:* Industry
Staff Member(s): 6; 50 volunteer(s)
Membership: 35 associations; *Fees:* $10,000-$50,000 general members; *Member Profile:* Regular members consist of universities, government agencies and companies involved in oilsands industry.
Activities: *Awareness Events:* CONRAD Clay Conference, bi-annual; CONRAD Water Conference & Workshops, bi-annual

Canadian Oilseed Processors Association (COPA)

#2150, 360 Main St., Winnipeg MB R3C 3Z3
Tel: 204-956-9500; *Fax:* 204-956-9506
copa@mymts.net
www.copaonline.net
Previous Name: Canola Crushers of Western Canada
Overview: A small national organization founded in 1992
Mission: To represent Canadian oilseed producers
Chief Officer(s):
Ken Stone, Chair
Staff Member(s): 3
Membership: 7; *Member Profile:* Major Oilseed Processors; *Committees:* Technical, Environmental & Safety; Oil Trading Rules; Meal Trading Rules; Food Feed Safety

Canadian Oldtimers' Hockey Association *See* Canadian Adult Recreational Hockey Association

Canadian Olympic Committee (COC) / Comité olympique canadien

Corporate Office, #900, 21 St. Clair Ave. East, Toronto ON M4T 1L9
Tel: 416-962-0262; *Fax:* 416-967-4902
digital@olympic.ca
www.olympic.ca
www.facebook.com/canadianolympicteam
twitter.com/cdnolympicteam
www.youtube.com/canadianolympicteam
Overview: A small national charitable organization founded in 1952
Mission: To be responsible for all aspects of Canada's involvement in the Olympic movement, including Canada's participation in the Olympic & Pan American Games & a wide variety of programs that promote the Olympic Movement in Canada through cultural & educational means.
Chief Officer(s):
Christopher Overholt, CEO & Secretary General
Finances: *Annual Operating Budget:* Greater than $5 Million; *Funding Sources:* National & international sponsors
Staff Member(s): 26; 400 volunteer(s)
Membership: 400
Activities: *Speaker Service:* Yes

Montréal
4141, av Pierre-de Coubertin, Montréal QC H1V 3N7
Tél: 514-861-3371

Ottawa
85 Albert St. 14th Fl., Ottawa ON K1P 6A4
Tel: 613-244-2020

Canadian Olympic Hall of Fame / Temple de la renommée olympique du Canada

c/o COC, #1400, 85 Albert St., Ottawa ON K1P 6A4
Tel: 613-244-2020; *Fax:* 613-244-0169
olympic.ca/canadian-olympic-hall-of-fame
Overview: A small national organization founded in 1948
Mission: To honor those who have served the cause of the Olympic Movement with distinction; those athletes, coaches, officials, administrators & volunteers whose dedication, sportsmanship & achievements have made an exemplary contribution to the Canadian Olympic Movement
Member of: Canadian Olympic Committee
Staff Member(s): 1; 6 volunteer(s)
Membership: 351

Canadian Oncology Societies

c/o Ottawa Hospital, 501 Smyth Rd., Ottawa ON K1H 8K6
Fax: 613-247-3511
Toll-Free: 877-990-9044
info@cos.ca
cos.ca
Overview: A small local organization
Mission: To increase & exchange knowledge in the field of oncology; to promote the application of such knowledge in the prevention and diagnosis of cancer and the care of cancer patients and their families; to promote interdisciplinary approaches to patient care and research in cancer; to provide a forum for the presentation and discussion of scientific knowledge and advances in oncology; to further continuing education for groups and indivduals involved in the care of patients who require special attention; support public cancer education programs; to support and assist the Canadian Cancer Society and the National Cancer Insitute; to advise government and other agencies on the provision of health services relevent to oncology.
Chief Officer(s):
Charles Pitts, Administrator

Canadian Opera Company (COC) / Compagnie d'opéra canadienne

145 Queen St. West, Toronto ON M5A 1E8
Tel: 416-363-6671; *Fax:* 416-363-5584
Toll-Free: 800-250-4653
tickets@coc.ca
www.coc.ca
www.facebook.com/canadianoperacompany
twitter.com/canadianopera
www.youtube.com/canadianopera
Overview: A large national charitable organization founded in 1950
Mission: To produce opera of the highest international standard while attracting growing public support & participation in opera through increased accessibility & education; To attract, develop & promote young Canadian singers, musicians, stage directors, conductors, designers, technical personnel & administrators; To encourage Canadian librettists & composers to compose new works
Member of: Opera America
Affliation(s): The Canadian Opera Foundation; Canadian Opera Volunteer Committee; Canadian Children's Opera Company
Chief Officer(s):
Alexander Neef, General Director
Robert Lamb, Managing Director
Finances: *Annual Operating Budget:* Greater than $5 Million; *Funding Sources:* Government; corporations; foundations; individuals; ticket sales
Staff Member(s): 60; 1200 volunteer(s)
Membership: 350 President's Council + 3,750 friends + 400 aged 19-29; *Fees:* $75+; *Member Profile:* Interest in opera; *Committees:* Finance; Fundraising; Planning
Activities: Produces six mainstage operas, one chamber opera, numerous concerts; summer camps; Annual Fine Wine Auction; golf tournament; *Awareness Events:* Opera Chats; Interactive Opera: Opera at Harbourfront; *Internships:* Yes; *Speaker Service:* Yes; *Library* Open to public

Canadian Operational Research Society (CORS) / Société canadienne de recherche opérationelle (SCRO)

PO Box 2225, Stn. D, Ottawa ON K1P 5W4
www.cors.ca
Overview: A small national organization founded in 1958
Mission: To advance the theory & practice of O.R. in Canada; to stimulate & promote contacts between people interested in the subject
Chief Officer(s):
Corinne MacDonald, President
corinne.macdonald@dal.ca
Dionne Aleman, Secretary
aleman@mie.utoronto.ca
Finances: *Funding Sources:* Membership fees
Membership: *Fees:* $110 individual; $55 retired; $45 student; *Committees:* Education; Membership; Program; Public Relations; Publications; Awards; Past President's Advisory Board; SIG
Activities: Operational research; educational activities; *Speaker Service:* Yes
Awards:
• Harold Larnder Prize (Award)
• Omond Solandt Award (Award)
• Practice Prize Competition (Award)
• Student Prize Competition (Award)
• Award of Merit (Award)
• Service Awards (Award)
Publications:
• Canadian Operational Research Society Membership Directory
Type: Directory; *Price:* Free with CORS membership
Profile: Listing of CORS members
• CORS [Canadian Operational Research Society] Bulletin / Bulletin de la SCRO [Société canadienne de recherche opérationelle]
Type: Newsletter; *Frequency:* Quarterly; *Editor:* Lise Arseneau
Profile: CORS activities, section news, awards, competitions, meetings & conferences
• INFOR: Information Systems & Operational Research
Type: Journal; *Accepts Advertising*; *Editor:* Bernard Gendron
ISSN: 0315-5986; *Price:* $65 individual; $95 institution; $70-$100international
Profile: Scientific papers on theory, methodology, & practice of operational research & information systems

Canadian Ophthalmological Society (COS) / Société canadienne d'opthalmologie (SCO)

#610, 1525 Carling Ave., Ottawa ON K1Z 8R9
Tel: 613-729-6779; *Fax:* 613-729-7209
cos@eyesite.ca
www.eyesite.ca
Overview: A medium-sized national organization founded in 1937
Mission: To assure the provision of optimal eye care to all Canadians by promoting excellence in ophthalmology & providing services to support its members in practice
Member of: Canadian Standards Association
Affliation(s): Canadian Medical Association; Concilium Ophthalmological Universale
Chief Officer(s):
Jennifer Brunet-Colvey, Chief Executive Officer
Finances: *Annual Operating Budget:* $500,000-$1.5 Million; *Funding Sources:* Membership dues; subscriptions; exhibits
2 volunteer(s)
Membership: 863 individual; *Fees:* Active: $500; Associate $200; Affiliate $200; Inter'l: $400; *Member Profile:* Physicians who have received certification of fellowship in opthamology from the Royal College of Family Physicians and Surgeons of Canada or has reveived a diploma of the American Board of Ophthalmology or their equivalent, or has received certification by the board of the province in which he or she practices, or holds other specialist qualifications in opthalmology as shall be acceptable to the Board
Activities: *Rents Mailing List:* Yes
Meetings/Conferences: • Canadian Ophthalmological Society 2015 Annual Meeting & Exhibition, June, 2015, Victoria Conference Centre, Victoria, BC
Scope: National
Contact Information: Registration Contact: Rita Afeltra, E-mail: rafeltra@cos-sco.ca; URL: www.cos-sco.ca/victoria2015
• Canadian Ophthalmological Society 2016 Annual Meeting & Exhibition, June, 2016, Shaw Centre, Ottawa, ON
Scope: National
Contact Information: cos@eyesite.ca

Canadian Oral History Association (COHA) / Société canadienne d'histoire orale (SCHO)

c/o University of Winnipeg, 515 Portage Ave., Winnipeg MB R3B 2E9
www.canoha.ca
Previous Name: Oral History Committee, Canadian Historical Association
Overview: A small national organization founded in 1974
Mission: To encourage & support the creation & preservation of sound recordings which document the history & culture of Canada; to develop standards of excellence & increase competence in the field of oral history through study, education & research.
Chief Officer(s):
Nolan Reilly, President
Janis Thiessen, Secretary-Treasurer
Finances: *Funding Sources:* Membership dues
Membership: *Fees:* $15 student; $20 individual; $30 institutional
Activities: *Rents Mailing List:* Yes; *Library* by appointment

Canadian Organic Growers Inc. (COG) / Cultivons Biologique Canada

#7519, 1145 Carling Ave., Ottawa ON K1Z 7K4
Tel: 613-216-0741; *Fax:* 613-236-0743
Toll-Free: 888-375-7383
office@cog.ca
www.cog.ca
www.facebook.com/CanadianOrganic
twitter.com/CanadianOrganic
Overview: A medium-sized national charitable organization founded in 1975
Mission: To conduct research into alternatives to traditional chemical & energy-intensive food growing practices; To provide a resource base & a forum open to all farmers & food growers interested in alternative agriculture; To foster the goals of a decentralized, bio-regionally-based food system; To endorse practices which promote & maintain long-term soil fertility, reduce fossil fuel uses, reduce pollution, recycle wastes & conserve non-renewable resources; To assist the farmer, grower, food processor & consumer, through education & demonstration, in understanding the value of organic foods
Member of: Canadian Environmental Network
Affliation(s): Atlantic Canadian Organic Regional Network; Certified Organic Associations of British Columbia; Ecological Farmers Association of Ontario; Saskatchewan Organic Directorate
Chief Officer(s):
Ashley St. Hilaire, Director, Operations
Finances: *Funding Sources:* Membership dues; Publications sale; Foundations; Governments
Membership: *Fees:* Donation based; *Member Profile:* Farmers; Gardeners; Consumers; Environmentalists; Writers; Wholesale marketers; *Committees:* Finance; Fundraising; Strategic Planning; Succession; By-laws & Policy & Procedures; Chapters; TCOG
Activities: *Awareness Events:* Organic Week, Sept.; *Library:* Mail-Lending Library
Awards:
• Mary Perlmutter Scholarship (Scholarship)
Awarded annually to a graduate student whose work within a recognized research institution is deemed beneficial to organic growers
Publications:
• The Canadian Organic Grower
Price: $18 + HST

Profile: Canada's voice for organics-reaching over 2,500 farmers, gardeners and consumers across Canada.
• Organic Statistics
Profile: Statistical overview of the Canadian organic sector for Canada & by province
• Practical Skills Handbooks
Profile: Resources for organic, transitioning, & conventional farmers on topics such as organic field crops & organic livestock

Durham
ON
Tel: 905-263-9907
info@durhamorganicgardeners.com
durhamorganicgardeners.com
www.facebook.com/DurhamOrganicGardeners
twitter.com/cogdurham
Chief Officer(s):
Vincent Powers, Contact

Hamilton
Hamilton ON
e-mail: greaterhamilton@cog.ca

Island Natural Growers (Gulf Islands)
106 Old Scott Rd., Salt Spring Island BC V8K 2L6
Tel: 250-537-5511
Chief Officer(s):
Rod Martens, Co-Chair, 250-931-1233
Anne Macey, Secretary

Organic Food Council of Manitoba
PO Box 68082, Stn. Osborne Village, Winnipeg MB R3L 2V9
Tel: 204-779-8546
organicfoodcouncil.org
www.facebook.com/OrganicFoodCouncilManitoba
Chief Officer(s):
Janine Gibson, Chapter Chair

Ottawa
Ottawa ON
Tel: 613-244-4000
cog.oso.chapter@cog.ca
cog.ca/ottawa
Chief Officer(s):
Adèle McKay, Project Manager

Perth/Waterloo/Wellington
ON
Toll-Free: 888-375-7383
office@cog.ca
www.cog.ca/pww
www.facebook.com/cogpww
twitter.com/cogpww

Toronto
Toronto ON
Tel: 647-367-7706
torontochapter@cog.ca
www.cogtoronto.org
www.facebook.com/COGTorontoChapter
Chief Officer(s):
Elizabeth Chrumka, Chapter Chair

Vancouver Island
BC
Tel: 250-642-3671
Chief Officer(s):
Mary Alice Johnson, Chapter Chair
mary@almfarms.org

Canadian Organization for Development through Education (CODE)

321 Chapel St., Ottawa ON K1N 7Z2
Tel: 613-232-3569; *Fax:* 613-232-7435
Toll-Free: 800-661-2633
codehq@codecan.org
www.codecan.org
www.facebook.com/group.php?gid=2380399600
www.youtube.com/user/TheCodecan
Previous Name: Overseas Book Centre
Overview: A large international charitable organization
Mission: To work with partners to bring tangible education results to the developing world for nearly 50 years; To enable people to learn by developing partnerships that provide resources for learning; To promote awareness & understanding; To encourage self-reliance
Member of: The Reading and Writing for Critical Thinking International Consortium; The Canadian Global Campaign for Education
Affliation(s): CODE Foundation; CODE Incorporated; International Book Bank
Chief Officer(s):
Lynn Beauregard, Chair
Scott Walter, Executive Director, 613-232-3569 Ext. 230
swalter@codecan.org
Finances: *Annual Operating Budget:* Greater than $5 Million; *Funding Sources:* Private sponsorship; Donations
Staff Member(s): 17
Activities: *Library*
Awards:
• The Burt Award (Award)
Recognizes excellence in young adult literature and provides young readers with engaging books that they want to read.
• The Burt Award for African Literature (Award)
• The Burt Award for First Nations, Métis and Inuit Literature (Award)
Publications:
• CODE Annual Report
Type: Yearbook; *Frequency:* Annually
Profile: A report published each autumn, with financial statements, program results, & articles from the field
• Ngoma [a publication of CODE]
Type: Newsletter; *Frequency:* Semiannually; *Price:* Donation of $20 or more
Profile: "Ngoma", meaning "talking drum" in Swahili, is published each spring & autumn, with information about programs, stories from the field, & forthcoming events
• Zikomo Kwambiri [a publication of CODE]
Type: Newsletter; *Frequency:* Quarterly
Profile: "Zikomo Kwambiri", meaning "thank you very much" in the Chichewa language of Malawi, is CODE's publication for donors, featuring articles & photographs from literacy projects

Canadian Organization for Rare Disorders (CORD)

#600, 151 Bloor St. West, Toronto ON M5S 1S4
Tel: 416-969-7464; *Fax:* 416-969-7420
Toll-Free: 877-302-7273
info@raredisorders.ca
raredisorders.ca
www.facebook.com/RareDisorders
twitter.com/Durhane
Overview: A small national charitable organization founded in 1995
Mission: To advocate for health policy that works for people with rare disorders; to promote research & services for all rare disorders in Canada; To increase access to genetic screening & genetic counselling for rare disorders
Chief Officer(s):
Durhane Wong-Rieger, President
durhane@sympatico.ca
John Adams, Vice-President
Stephen McElroy, Treasurer
Finances: *Funding Sources:* Alberta Gaming and Liquor Commission; BIOTECanada; Canadian Genetic Diseases Network; Health Canada; Donations
Membership: *Member Profile:* Organizations that represent all those with rare disorders
Activities: Liaising with governments, industry, clinicians, & researchers; Providing information; Connecting affected families; Supporting the Expensive Drugs for Rare Disorders program; *Awareness Events:* Annual International Rare Disease Day, Feb.
Publications:
• THE LINK Newsletter
Type: Newsletter; *Frequency:* Annually
Profile: Articles, conferences, & CORD activities

Edmonton - Alberta Chapter
15973 - 93rd A Ave. NW, Edmonton AB T5R 5J5
Toll-Free: 877-302-7273

Canadian Organization of Campus Activities (COCA)

#202, 509 Commissioners Rd. West, London ON N6J 1Y5
Tel: 519-690-0207; *Fax:* 519-681-4328
cocaoffice@coca.org
www.coca.org
Previous Name: Canadian Entertainment Conference
Overview: A medium-sized national organization founded in 1982
Mission: To strive to develop quality campus programming, through information sharing
Affliation(s): National Association for Campus Activities (USA)
Chief Officer(s):
Earle Taylor, Executive Director, 519-690-0207, Fax: 519-681-3284
Kenney Fitzpatrick, Chair, 902-457-6123, Fax: 902-457-0444
kenney@mountstudents.ca
Shea Dahl, Chair, National Conference Committee, 604-822-5336, Fax: 604-822-9019
programs@ams.ubc.ca
Finances: *Funding Sources:* Membership fees; Sponsorships
Staff Member(s): 1; 25 volunteer(s)
Membership: 65 colleges/universities; 100 companies/artists; *Fees:* $150 artists; $285 companies (associations, agencies, & suppliers); $300 institutions; *Member Profile:* Post-secondary institutions across Canada; Associate members, such as entertainers, booking agencies, artist management, & other suppliers to the campus entertainment & programming industry; *Committees:* Awards; National Conference; Education; Nominating; Communications; International Relations
Activities: Providing resources; Offering educational opportunities; Hosting national & regional conferences & meetings; Enabling blook booking with other schools; Providing networking opportunities with other members & campus buyers; Offering the COCA Job Network; Sponsoring regional events, such as Campus Idol & Campus Music Explosion; *Library:* Canadian Organization of Campus Activities Library
Meetings/Conferences: • Canadian Organization of Campus Activities 2015 National Conference, June, 2015, DoubleTree by Hilton West Edmonton, Edmonton, AB
Scope: National
Description: Educational sessions, plus showcases featuring music, films, & comedy, plus the Campus Activities Biz Hall trade show
• Canadian Organization of Campus Activities 2016 National Conference, June, 2016, Ottawa, ON
Scope: National
Description: Educational sessions, plus showcases featuring music, films, & comedy, plus the Campus Activities Biz Hall trade show
• Canadian Organization of Campus Activities 2015 National Conference, June, 2015, AB
Scope: National
Description: Educational sessions, plus showcases featuring music, films, & comedy, plus the Campus Activities Biz Hall trade show
Publications:
• Canadian Organization of Campus Activities Conference Manual
Type: Manual; *Frequency:* Annually
Profile: A manual from the Canadian Organization of Campus Activities National Conference
• COCA [Canadian Organization of Campus Activities] Membership Directory
Type: Directory
Profile: Available for Canadian Organization of Campus Activities members only
• COCA [Canadian Organization of Campus Activities] Notes
Type: Newsletter; *Frequency:* 3 - 4 pa; *Accepts Advertising*; *Editor:* Bill Mahon; *Price:* Free with Canadian Organization of Campus Activities membership
Profile: Reports from regions throughout Canada plus information about upcoming events

Canadian Organization of Medical Physicists (COMP) / L'Organisation canadienne des physiciens médicaux (OCPM)

PO Box 72024, Stn. Kanata North, Kanata ON K2K 2P4
Tel: 613-599-3491; *Fax:* 613-435-7257
admin@medphys.ca
www.medphys.ca
www.linkedin.com/groups?gid=4135236
www.facebook.com/CanadianMedphys
twitter.com/MedphysCA
Overview: A small national organization founded in 1989
Mission: To encourage the application of physics in medicine; To develop & protect professional standards; To encourage certification by the Canadian College of Physicists in Medicine
Member of: International Organization of Medical Physicists
Affliation(s): Canadian College of Physicists in Medicine; American Association of Physicists in Medicine; Institute of Physics and Engineering in Medicine
Chief Officer(s):
Nancy Barrett, Executive Director, 613-599-1948
nancy@medphys.ca
Gisele Kite, Administrator
admin@medphys.ca
Matthew G. Schmid, President
mschmid@bccancer.bc.ca
Glenn Wells, Secretary-Treasurer
gwells@ottawaheart.ca
Membership: *Member Profile:* Professional medical physicists who are practising in Canada; Scientists; Academics; Post-doctoral fellows; Graduate students in medical physics programs; National & international corporations; *Committees:*

Awards; Conference; Medal; Nominations; Professional Affairs; Radiation Safety & Technical Standards Advisory; Communications (Joint committee with CCPM); Finance (Joint committee with CCPM)
Activities: Promoting scientific knowledge & publication; Exchanging scientific or technical information; Promoting continuing education
Publications:
• InterACTIONS
Type: Newsletter; *Frequency:* Quarterly; *Accepts Advertising*; *Editor:* Dr. Parminder Basran
Profile: Newsletter of the Canadian Organization of Medical Physicists (COMP) & the Canadian College of Physicists in Medicine (CCPM) for their members
• Medical Physics
Type: Journal; *Price:* Free with COMP membership
• Physics in Medicine & Biology
Type: Journal; *Price:* $385

Canadian Organization of Professional Electrologists (COPE)
PO Box 402, Lundbreck AB T0K 1H0
Tel: 403-628-3522
Toll-Free: 800-665-2673
www.electrolysis.ca
Overview: A small national organization founded in 2000
Mission: To listen, learn and teach, to encourage open and objective dialogue; to foster peer support and camaraderie; to provide access to advanced, continuing education in electrolysis; to recognize quality electrolysis training centres; and to provide reliable information and referrals to the public.
Chief Officer(s):
Phyllis Tourond, National Chair
tourond@telusplanet.net
Membership: *Member Profile:* Electrologists who have had a minimum of 300 hours of instructional training

Canadian Organization of Small Business Inc. (COSBI)
5405, 129 Ave. NW, Edmonton AB T5A 0A3
Tel: 780-423-2672
Also Known As: The Voice of Business
Overview: A medium-sized national organization founded in 1979
Mission: To support & promote the interests of small business & independent professionals throughout Canada; to protect the free enterprise system & the interests of independent business; to function as a lobby & service organization dealing with all levels of government or large bureaucracy; to provide members with access to information vital to business success & to present the owner/manager's point of view to decision makers in both political & private sectors
Chief Officer(s):
Donald Richard Eastcott, Managing Director
Roy E. Shannon, Chair
Finances: *Annual Operating Budget:* $50,000-$100,000; *Funding Sources:* Membership fees; donations
Staff Member(s): 1; 200 volunteer(s)
Membership: 6,000; *Fees:* $150 or donation; *Member Profile:* Open to small independent business or service provider to small business; *Committees:* Taxation; Finance; Business Education; Trade & Economic Expansion; Government Relations; Ethics & Strategic Planning for Business; Home-Based Businesses; Business Action Teams
Activities: Voice of Business Network Program - representing similar organizations with regional or local focus on a national level; advocates & intermediaries for members; *Speaker Service:* Yes

Canadian Orienteering Federation (COF) / Fédération canadienne de course d'orientation
1239 Colgrove Ave. NE, Calgary AB T2C 5C3
Tel: 403-283-0807; *Fax:* 403-451-1681
info@orienteering.ca
www.orienteering.ca
www.facebook.com/orienteeringcanada
twitter.com/orienteeringcan
www.youtube.com/orienteeringcanada
Also Known As: Orienteering Canada
Overview: A large national organization founded in 1967
Mission: To provide leadership & resources to individuals involved in orienteering in Canada
Affiliation(s): International Orienteering Federation
Chief Officer(s):
Anne Teutsch, President
Bruce Rennie, Vice-President
Dave Graupner, Secretary
Tracy Bradley, Executive Director
Membership: *Member Profile:* Coaches, officials, volunteers, athletes, & youth leaders involved in orienteering; *Committees:* Coaching Program; High Performance; Officials Program; Sass Peepre Junior Development; Technical; Nominations; Finance & Audit; HR; Governance; Celebration, Awards & Recognition; Long Term Athlete Development; New Participant Recruitment; Mountain Bike Orienteering; Ski Orienteering
Activities: *Rents Mailing List:* Yes
Publications:
• Legends [a publication of the Canadian Orienteering Federation]
Type: Newsletter; *Frequency:* 3 pa *ISSN:* 0227-6658
Profile: COF newsletter with information on orienteering in certain regions, a section for juniors, & COF activities

Canadian Ornamental Plant Foundation (COPF) / Fondation canadienne des plantes ornementales
PO Box 26029, Guelph ON N1E 6W1
Tel: 519-341-6761; *Fax:* 519-341-6748
Toll-Free: 800-265-1629
info@copf.org
www.copf.org
Overview: A small national organization founded in 1964
Mission: To encourage new plant development by strengthening relations between growers & breeders for the benefit of the horticulture industry
Member of: aanadian Horticultural Council; International Plant Propagators Society
Chief Officer(s):
Victoria Turner Shoemaker, Executive Director
victoria@copf.org
Staff Member(s): 3
Membership: 660; *Fees:* Schedule available; *Member Profile:* Businesses involved in the horticulture industry
Activities: *Rents Mailing List:* Yes

Canadian Orthopaedic Association (COA) / Association canadienne d'orthopédie
#360, 4150, rue Ste-Catherine ouest, Montréal QC H3Z 2Y5
Tel: 514-874-9003; *Fax:* 514-874-0464
cynthia@canorth.org
www.coa-aco.org
twitter.com/CdnOrthoAssoc
Overview: A medium-sized national organization founded in 1948
Mission: To provide continuing medical education for orthopaedic surgeons
Chief Officer(s):
Douglas C. Thomson, CEO, 514-874-9003 Ext. 5
Finances: *Annual Operating Budget:* $500,000-$1.5 Million
Staff Member(s): 4
Membership: 950 individual; 50 associate; *Fees:* $475 individual; $25 associate
Meetings/Conferences: • Canadian Orthopaedic Association 2015 70th Annual Meeting & Canadian Orthopaedic Research Society 49th Annual Meeting, June, 2015, Fairmount Hotel Vancouver, Vancouver, BC
Scope: National
Contact Information: Meghan Corbeil, Contact; Phone: 514-874-9003 ext. 4; meghan@canorth.org; URL: www.coaannualmeeting.ca
• Canadian Orthopaedic Association 2016 71st Annual Meeting & Canadian Orthopaedic Research Society 50th Annual Meeting, June, 2015, Halifax Convention Centre, Halifax, NS
Scope: National
Attendance: 600
Publications:
• The Bulletin of the Canadian Orthopaedic Association
Type: Newsletter; *Frequency:* Quarterly; *Accepts Advertising*; *Editor:* Dr. Emil Schemitsch; *Price:* Free with COA membership
Profile: Current events & ideas in orthopaedics

Canadian Orthopaedic Foundation (COF) / Fondation orthopédique du Canada (FOC)
PO Box 7029, Innisfil ON L9S 1A8
Tel: 416-410-2341
Toll-Free: 800-461-3639
mailbox@canorth.org
www.canorth.org
Overview: A medium-sized national charitable organization founded in 1945
Mission: To foster excellence in the provision of health care to patients with musculoskeletal disease or injury, in a cost effective manner, based on significant outcome studies, by supporting research, educating its members & securing funding from government & other health care funding agencies
Affliation(s): World Orthopaedic Concern; Canadian Medical Association
Chief Officer(s):
James Waddell, Chair
Sandra Vlaar Ingram, Vice Chair
Finances: *Funding Sources:* Membership dues
Staff Member(s): 3
Membership: 1,084; *Fees:* $475; *Committees:* By-Laws; Membership; Exchange Fellowship; Programme; Annual Meetings; Nominating; Orthopaedic Practice & Economics; Finance; Planning & Development; Training, Education & Qualification; Ethics; Medical Devices; Public Relations: Orthopaedics Overseas; Safety & Accident Prevention
Activities: *Awareness Events:* Hip Hip Hooray Orthopaedic Walk, May; *Rents Mailing List:* Yes
Awards:
• I. Edouard Samson Award (Award)
Medal & $15,000 awarded for outstanding orthopaedic research by a young investigator; paper presented at the annual meeting of the Canadian Orthopaedic Research Society
Publications:
• OrthoLink
Type: Newsletter; *Frequency:* Quarterly
Profile: Information & practical tips for people interested in building & maintaining bone & joint health

Canadian Orthopaedic Nurses Association (CONA) / Association canadienne des infirmières et infirmiers en orthopédie
2035 Rosealle ln, West Kelowna BC V1Z 3Z5
Tel: 250-769-3640
www.cona-nurse.org
Overview: A medium-sized national organization founded in 1978
Mission: To foster professional growth of the membership in the assessment, treatment & rehabilitation of individuals with neuromuscular & skeletal alterations; to promote nursing research related to orthopaedics
Affliation(s): Canadian Nurses Association
Chief Officer(s):
Angela Dunklee-Clark, President
dunkleea@cdha.nshealth.ca
Finances: *Annual Operating Budget:* Less than $50,000; *Funding Sources:* Membership dues; conference fees
Staff Member(s): 1; 8 volunteer(s)
Membership: 535 individual; 10 associate; *Fees:* $50; *Member Profile:* Active - registered nurse, associate - all other health professionals
Activities: *Rents Mailing List:* Yes
Awards:
• CONA Continuing Education Award (Award)
• CONA Dr. Robert B. Salter Award (Award)
• CONA Excellence in Orthopaedic Nursing Practice Award (Award)
• COA Literary Award (Award)
• CONA Speakers Fund Award (Award)
• CONA Certification Scholarships (Scholarship)
• CONA Conference Grant (Grant)
Meetings/Conferences: • Canadian Orthopaedic Nurses Association 2015 Annual Conference, May, 2015, Fredericton Convention Center, Fredericton, NB
Scope: National
Contact Information: Nancy Schuttenbeld, Conference Chair; Nancy.schuttenbeld@horizonnb.ca
Publications:
• Orthoscope
Type: Newsletter; *Frequency:* Quarterly; *Editor:* Hélène Rainville; *Price:* Free with CONA membership
Profile: National newsletter with current events in orthopaedic nursing

Canadian Orthopaedic Residents Association (CORA) / L'Association Canadienne des Residents en Orthopédie (ACRO)
#450, 4150, rue Sainte-Catherine ouest, Montréal QC H3Z 2Y5
Tel: 514-874-9003; *Fax:* 514-874-0464
coraweb@canorth.org
www.coraweb.org
Overview: A small national organization
Mission: To foster & promote research & education in the field of Orthopaedic Surgery
Chief Officer(s):
Nadia Murphy, President
nlmurphy@dal.ca

Meetings/Conferences: • Canadian Orthopaedic Residents Association 2015 Annual Meeting, June, 2015, Vancouver, BC
Scope: National

Canadian Orthopractic Manual Therapy Association
#207, 1150 - 100 Ave., Edmonton AB T5K 0J7
Tel: 780-482-7428; *Fax:* 780-488-2463
info@orthopractic.org
www.orthopractic.org
Overview: A medium-sized national organization
Mission: To provide the public, fellow healthcare professionals, government & funding agencies with guidelines on the provision of safe & effective manual therapy including mobilization & manipulation
Membership: 115; *Fees:* $100

Canadian Orthoptic Council / Conseil canadien d'orthoptique
CHUL, 2705, boul Laurier, Ste. Foy QC G1V 4G2
Fax: 418-654-2188
info@orthopticscanada.org
www.orthopticscanada.org
Overview: A medium-sized national organization
Mission: To establish standards in the training of orthoptic students; to establish standards for orthoptic training centres; to provide examinations of orthoptic students in order to determine their proficiency in orthopotics & to award a certificate of competency to qualified students who pass the examinations; to require evidence of continuing education of certified orthoptists; to establish standards for the professional ethical conduct of certified orthoptists.
Affliation(s): Canadian Medical Association; Canadian Ophthalmological Society
Chief Officer(s):
Louis-Etienne Marcoux, Secretary-Treasurer
Cathie Day, Administrative Coordinator
Staff Member(s): 1

Canadian Outdoor Measurement Bureau *See* Canadian Out-of-Home Measurement Bureau

Canadian Out-of-Home Measurement Bureau (COMB)
#500, 111 Peter St., Toronto ON M5V 2B8
Tel: 416-968-3823; *Fax:* 416-968-9396
Toll-Free: 800-866-1189
www.comb.org
Previous Name: Canadian Outdoor Measurement Bureau
Overview: A medium-sized national organization
Chief Officer(s):
Karen Best, President
kbest@comb.org
Staff Member(s): 7
Membership: 21 plant operators + 8 advertisers + 39 advertising agencies + 6 associate + 3 limited members

Canadian Overseas Telecommunications Union
2170 Pierre Dupuy Ave., Montreal QC H3C 3R4
Tel: 514-866-9015
cotu.ca
Overview: A large national charitable organization
Mission: To maintain the benefits of the members of the union through collective bargaining
Chief Officer(s):
Daniel Séguin, President
president@cotu.ca

Canadian Owners & Pilots Association (COPA)
71 Bank St., 7th Fl., Ottawa ON K1P 5N2
Tel: 613-236-4901; *Fax:* 613-236-8646
copa@copanational.org
www.copanational.org
Overview: A medium-sized national charitable organization founded in 1954
Mission: The recognized voice of general aviation in Canada
Chief Officer(s):
Kevin Psutka, President
kpsutka@copanational.org
Finances: *Annual Operating Budget:* $500,000-$1.5 Million; *Funding Sources:* Membership dues; advertising
Staff Member(s): 9; 20 volunteer(s)
Membership: 17,000; *Fees:* $50 individual; $250 corporate; *Member Profile:* Pilots & aircraft owners; corporate members; *Committees:* Air Navigation Services National Advisory Group; Canadian Aviation Regulation Advisory Committee
Activities: COPA Flight Chapters located across Canada; *Library* Open to public
Publications:
• COPA [Canadian Owners & Pilots Association] Flight
Type: Newspaper; *Frequency:* Monthly; *Accepts Advertising*; *Editor:* Michel Hell; *Price:* Free with COPA membership
Profile: Aviation news for members, flying students, aviation medical examiners, air cadets, & government officials
• COPA [Canadian Owners & Pilots Association] Aviation Guides
Price: Free for members
Profile: Booklets on topics such as cross border operations, buying an aircraft, aircraft operating costs, & private aerodromes
• COPA [Canadian Owners & Pilots Association] e-NewsFlash
Type: Newsletter; *Frequency:* Monthly
Profile: COPA activities for members

Canadian Paediatric Society (CPS) / Société canadienne de pédiatrie
2305 St. Laurent Blvd., Ottawa ON K1G 4J8
Tel: 613-526-9397; *Fax:* 613-526-3332
info@cps.ca
www.cps.ca
www.linkedin.com/company/canadian-paediatric-society
www.facebook.com/CanadianPaediatricSociety
twitter.com/canpaedsociety
www.youtube.com/canpaedsociety
Overview: A medium-sized national organization founded in 1922
Mission: To advocate for the health needs of children & youth; to provide continuing education to paediatricians; to establish national guidelines for paediatric care & practice
Member of: International Paediatric Association
Chief Officer(s):
Andrew Lynk, President
Marie Adèle Davis, Executive Director
madavis@cps.ca
Elizabeth Moreau, Director, Communications & Public Education
elizabethm@cps.ca
Staff Member(s): 30
Membership: 3,000 individual; *Member Profile:* Certified paediatricians & associates; *Committees:* Action Committee for Children & Teens; Acute Care; Adolescent Health; Annual Conference; Awards; Bioethics; Community Paediatrics; Continuing Professional Development; Drug Therapy & Hazardous Substances; Fetus & Newborn; First Nations, Inuit & Métis Health; Healthy Active Living & Sports Medicine; Infectious Diseases & Immunization; Injury Prevention; Mental Health & Development Disabilities; Nutrition & Gastroenterology; Paediatric Human Resources Planning
Activities: Conducts Continuing Medical Education courses; *Rents Mailing List:* Yes; *Library* Open to public
Awards:
• Ross Award (Award)
• CPS Awards for Excellence (Award)
• CPS Research Award (Award)
Meetings/Conferences: • 92nd Canadian Paediatric Society Annual Conference 2015, June, 2015, Toronto, ON
Scope: National
Contact Information: Phone: 613-526-9397 ext. 2148, meetings@cps.ca, www.annualconference.cps.ca
• 93rd Canadian Paediatric Society Annual Conference 2016, June, 2016, Charlottetown, PE
Scope: National
Contact Information: Phone: 613-526-9397 ext. 2148, meetings@cps.ca, www.annualconference.cps.ca
• 94th Canadian Paediatric Society Annual Conference 2017, June, 2017, Vancouver, BC
Scope: National
Contact Information: Phone: 613-526-9397 ext. 2148, meetings@cps.ca, www.annualconference.cps.ca
Publications:
• CPS [Canadian Paediatric Society] News
Type: Newsletter; *Frequency:* 5 pa; *Accepts Advertising*; *Price:* Free with CPS membership
Profile: Current society activities for CPS members
• Paediatrics & Child Health
Type: Journal; *Accepts Advertising*; *Price:* Free with CPS membership
Profile: Educational information & research reports for clinicians, parents, & caregivers

Canadian Pain Society / Société canadienne pour le traitement de la douleur
#202, 1143 Wentworth St. West, Oshawa ON L1J 8P7
Tel: 905-404-9545; *Fax:* 905-404-3727
office@canadianpainsociety.ca
www.canadianpainsociety.ca
www.facebook.com/CanadianPain
twitter.com/canadianpain
Overview: A medium-sized national organization founded in 1982
Mission: To foster research on pain; To improve the management of patients with acute & chronic pain
Member of: International Association for the Study of Pain
Chief Officer(s):
M. Catherine Bushnell, President, 514-398-3493, Fax: 514-398-7464
catherine.bushnell@mcgill.ca
Diane LaChapelle, Secretary
Michael McGillion, Treasurer
Ellen Maracle-Benton, Office Manager
ellen@canadianpainsociety.ca
Judy Watt-Watson, President Elect
Membership: 850; *Fees:* $45 trainees; $150 regular members; *Member Profile:* Health professionals & basic scientists with an interest in pain research & management; Students, residents, & interns at the pre-doctoral, doctoral, or pre-professional level; *Committees:* Awards; Nomination; Scientific Program
Meetings/Conferences: • Canadian Pain Society 2015 36th Annual Scientific Meeting, May, 2015, Delta Hotel & Convention Centre, Charlottetown, PE
Scope: National
Description: The exchange of current information about pain assessment, pain mechanisms, & pain management for healthcare professionals, scientists, & trainees from clinical, research, industry, & policy settings
Contact Information: Office Manager, Canadian Pain Society Office: Ellen Maracle-Benton, E-mail: ellen@canadianpainsociety.ca
• Canadian Pain Society 2016 Annual Meeting, May, 2016, Winnipeg, MB
Scope: National
Description: The exchange of current information about pain assessment, pain mechanisms, & pain management for healthcare professionals, scientists, & trainees from clinical, research, industry, & policy settings
Contact Information: Office Manager, Canadian Pain Society Office: Ellen Maracle-Benton, E-mail: ellen@canadianpainsociety.ca
Publications:
• Canadian Pain Society Membership Directory
Type: Directory
Profile: Contact information for members
• CPS [Canadian Pain Society] Newsletter
Type: Newsletter; *Frequency:* Quarterly; *Editor:* E. Van Den Kerkhof (ev5@queensu.ca); *Price:* Free withmembership in th Canadian Pain Society
Profile: Updates from the Canadian Pain Society, including book reviews, a trainee corner, training opportunities, & forthcoming events
• Pain Research & Management
Type: Journal; *Frequency:* Quarterly; *Editor:* Ken Craig, PhD; *Price:* Free with membership in th Canadian Pain Society
Profile: The official journal of the Canadian Pain Society, featuring original articles & reviews

Canadian Paint & Coatings Association (CPCA) / Association canadienne de l'industrie de la peinture et du revêtement
#608, 170 Laurier Ave. West, Ottawa ON K1P 5V5
Tel: 613-231-3604; *Fax:* 613-231-4908
cpca@cdnpaint.org
www.cdnpaint.org
Overview: A medium-sized national organization founded in 1913
Mission: To represent the paint industry among the provincial, federal & municipal governments
Chief Officer(s):
Dale Constantinoff, Chair
Finances: *Annual Operating Budget:* $500,000-$1.5 Million
Staff Member(s): 5
Membership: 105 organizations
Activities: Seminars; annual convention; government relations;

Meetings/Conferences: • Canadian Paint and Coating Association 102nd Annual Conference, 2015
Scope: National
Description: Paint & coasting professionals gather to discuss the state of the Canadian paint & coasting industries.

Canadian Pallet Council (CPC) / Conseil des palettes du Canada
239 Division St., Cobourg ON K9A 3P9

Tel: 905-372-1871; *Fax:* 905-373-0230
info@cpcpallet.com
www.cpcpallet.com
Overview: A medium-sized national organization founded in 1977
Chief Officer(s):
Belinda Junkin, President/CEO, 905-372-1871 Ext. 105
bjunkin@cpcpallet.com
Finances: *Funding Sources:* Membership fees; royalties
Staff Member(s): 3
Membership: 1,300+; *Fees:* $485-$5,665
Publications:
• CPC [Canadian Pallet Council] Communiqué
Type: Newsletter; *Frequency:* Bimonthly; *Price:* Free with CPC membership
Profile: Pallet issues & topics of interest for members

Canadian Palomino Horse Association (CPHA)
c/o Lorraine Holdaway, 631 Hendershott Rd., RR#1, Hannon ON L0R 1P0
Tel: 905-692-4328
canadianpalomino@gmail.com
www.clrc.ca/palomino.shtml
Overview: A small national organization founded in 1952
Mission: To develop & promote the breeding of Palomino horses in Canada; To establish standards of breeding
Affliation(s): Canadian Livestock Records Corporation
Chief Officer(s):
Lorraine Holdaway, Secretary
Laura Lee Mills, Registrar, 613-731-7110 Ext. 314
lauralee.mills@clrc.ca
Membership: 15 regular; 9 lifetime; *Fees:* $20 regular annual membership; $75 life membership
Activities: Registering Palomino horses in Canada; Keeping a record of the breeding & origin of Palomino horses; Protecting & assisting breeders engaged in propagation & breeding; Compiling statistics on the industry

Canadian Paper Money Society (CPMS)
Attn: Dick Dunn, PO Box 562, Pickering ON L1V 2R7
Tel: 905-509-1146
info@cpmsonline.ca
www.nunetcan.net/cpms.htm
Overview: A small national organization founded in 1964
Mission: To encourage & support historical studies of banks & other paper money issuing authorities in Canada, to preserve their history & statistical records, & through research & publishing the results thereof, ensure that information, documents & other evidence of Canada's financial development will be preserved.
Chief Officer(s):
Dick Dunn, Secretary-Treasurer
Jared Stepleton, President
president@cpmsonline.ca
Finances: *Funding Sources:* Membership dues
Membership: *Fees:* $30 printed; $20 digital

Canadian Paralympic Committee (CPC) / Comité paralympique canadien
#310, 225 Metcalfe St., Ottawa ON K2P 1p9
Tel: 613-569-4333; *Fax:* 613-569-2777
www.paralympic.ca
www.facebook.com/CDNParalympics
twitter.com/CDNParalympics
www.youtube.com/user/CDNParalympics
Previous Name: Canadian Federation of Sport Organizations for the Disabled
Overview: A medium-sized national charitable organization founded in 1982
Mission: The CPC is responsible for creating an optimal environment for high-performance Canadian Paralympic Athletes to compete and win in the Paralympic and Parapan American Games, and by promoting their success, inspire all Canadians with a disability to get involved in sport.
Affliation(s): International Paralympic Committee
Chief Officer(s):
Karen O'Neill, CEO, 613-569-4333 Ext. 223
koneill@paralympic.ca
Gaétan Tardif, President
Finances: *Funding Sources:* Government; private & public sector
Staff Member(s): 22
Membership: 25 national organizations; *Member Profile:* Any National Sport Organization for Athletes with a Disability or National Sport Organization representing a sport on the Paralympic program, provided that such organization is properly constituted in Canada and is the recognized Canadian member of the appropriate international federation. Each active member shall be entitled to one (1) vote each at each meeting of members.; *Committees:* High Performance Committee; Paralympic Development Committee; Coach Council; Athlete School; Classification Taskforce
Activities: *Internships:* Yes; *Speaker Service:* Yes; *Library* by appointment

Canadian Paraplegic Association ***See*** Spinal Cord Injury Canada

Canadian Paraplegic Association ***See*** Spinal Cord Injury British Columbia

Canadian Paraplegic Association - Newfoundland & Labrador ***See*** Spinal Cord Injury Newfoundland & Labrador

Canadian Paraplegic Association (Alberta) ***See*** Spinal Cord Injury Alberta

Canadian Paraplegic Association (Manitoba)
#211, 825 Sherbrook St., Winnipeg MB R3A 1M5
Tel: 204-786-4753; *Fax:* 204-786-1140
Toll-Free: 800-720-4933
winnipeg@canparaplegic.org
www.cpamanitoba.ca
Overview: A medium-sized provincial organization overseen by Spinal Cord Injury Canada
Mission: To represent persons with spinal cord injuries in Manitoba
Chief Officer(s):
Ron Burky, Executive Director
rburky@canparaplegic.org
Darlene Cooper, Director, Rehabilitation Services
djcooper@canparaplegic.org
Membership: *Member Profile:* Persons living with disabilities, their families, & supporters
Activities: Offering information services, rehabilitation counselling, peer support, community advocacy, & employment services

Canadian Paraplegic Association (New Brunswick) Inc. ***See*** Ability New Brunswick

Canadian Paraplegic Association (Nova Scotia)
Halifax Shopping Centre, Tower 1, #317A, 7001 Mumford Rd., Halifax NS B3L 4N9
Tel: 902-423-1277; *Fax:* 902-492-1213
Toll-Free: 800-889-1889
halifax@canparaplegic.org
www.thespine.ca
Overview: A medium-sized provincial organization overseen by Spinal Cord Injury Canada
Chief Officer(s):
Kevin Lamarque, Chair
Angela Cook, Treasurer
Nancy Beaton, Executive Director
nbeaton@canparaplegic.org
Activities: *Awareness Events:* Wheel & Win, Feb.; Sail Able, July

Sydney - Cape Breton Regional Office
165 Townsend St., Sydney NS B1P 5E4
Tel: 902-562-3291; *Fax:* 902-562-2861
Toll-Free: 800-566-1887
sydney@canparaplegic.org
Chief Officer(s):
Lorna Griffin-Fillier, Rehabilitation Counsellor

Canadian Paraplegic Association (Prince Edward Island) (CPA-PEI)
14 Exhibition Dr., Charlottetown PE C1A 5Z5
Tel: 902-370-9523
cpapei.org
www.facebook.com/166802903349902
Overview: A small provincial organization overseen by Spinal Cord Injury Canada
Chief Officer(s):
Paul Cudmore, Executive Director
pcudmore@cpapei.org
Activities: *Awareness Events:* CPA Month, May

Canadian Paraplegic Association (Saskatchewan) (CPA-SK)
#311 - 38th St. East, Saskatoon SK S7K 0T1
Tel: 306-652-9644; *Fax:* 306-652-2957
saskatoon@canparaplegic.org
www.spinalcordinjurysask.com
Overview: A medium-sized provincial organization overseen by Spinal Cord Injury Canada
Mission: To provide services to persons with spinal cord injury & other mobility impairments in Saskatchewan
Chief Officer(s):
Darlene Stein, Executive Director
dstein@canparaplegic.org
Activities: Offering the Provincial Peer Support Program; Providing information, on topics such as home modification; Consulting about accessibility; Counselling; Engaging in advocacy activities; Offering employment services; *Awareness Events:* Annual Wheel Challenge for Everyone

Regina
3928 Gordon Rd., Regina SK S4S 6Y3
Tel: 306-584-0101; *Fax:* 306-584-0008
regina@canparaplegic.org

Canadian Paraplegic Association Ontario ***See*** Spinal Cord Injury Ontario

Canadian Parents for French (CPF)
#310, 176 Gloucester St., Ottawa ON K2P 0A6
Tel: 613-235-1481; *Fax:* 613-230-5940
cpf@cpf.ca
www.cpf.ca
www.facebook.com/CanadianParentsForFrench
twitter.com/CDNP4F
Overview: A large national charitable organization founded in 1977
Mission: To provide educational opportunities for young Canadians to learn & use the French language; To recognize & support English & French as Canada's two official languages; To create & promote opportunities for young Canadians to learn & use French as a second language
Chief Officer(s):
Lisa Marie Perkins, President
Robert Rothon, Executive Director, 613-235-1481 Ext. 24
rrothon@cpf.ca
Finances: *Funding Sources:* Membership fees; Donations from individuals, foundations & corporations; Grants & contributions
500 volunteer(s)
Membership: 10,000; *Fees:* $25 individual/family; $60 associate; *Member Profile:* Individuals, families & organizations interested in the promotion & creation of French second-language learning opportunities for young Canadians; *Committees:* Nominations; FSL Advisory
Activities: Organizing Concours d'Art Oratoire, a provincial/territorial public speaking competition for Core French, French immersion & French first language students; Training volunteers; *Speaker Service:* Yes; *Rents Mailing List:* Yes
Publications:
• CPF [Canadian Parents for French] National News
Type: Newsletter; *Accepts Advertising; ISSN:* 1202-7384
Profile: CFP activities, plus news & opinions to support learning French as a second language
• Helping Your Child Become Bilingual: A Tool Kit for Parents
Type: Booklet; *Number of Pages:* 30; *Price:* Free with CPF membership
• The State of French-Second-Language Education in Canada
Type: Yearbook; *Frequency:* Annually; *Price:* Free with CPF membership
Profile: Assessments of French-second language programs across Canada & examinations of the quality of national & provincial & territorial support for French-second languageprograms

Canadian Parking Association (CPA)
#350, 2255 St. Laurent Blvd., Ottawa ON K1G 4K3
Tel: 613-727-0700; *Fax:* 613-727-3183
info@canadianparking.ca
www.canadianparking.ca
www.linkedin.com/company/2241893?trk=tyah
www.facebook.com/173429676044219?sk=wall
twitter.com/canadianparking
Also Known As: Association canadienne du stationnement
Overview: A medium-sized national organization founded in 1983
Mission: The Association is the national organization that represents the parking industry & provides a dynamic forum for learning & sharing to enhance member's ability to serve the public & improve the economic vitality of communities.
Chief Officer(s):
Carole Whitehorne, Executive Director, 613-727-0700 Ext. 10
carole@canadianparking.ca
Membership: 320; *Fees:* $475 full

Meetings/Conferences: • Canadian Parking Association 2015 Conference & Trade Show, October, 2015, Vancouver, BC
Scope: National
• Canadian Parking Association 2016 Conference & Trade Show, October, 2016, Ottawa, ON
Scope: National

Canadian Parks & Recreation Association (CPRA) / Association canadienne des parcs et loisirs

PO Box 83069, 1180 Walkley Rd., Ottawa ON K1V 2M5
Tel: 613-523-5315
info@cpra.ca
www.cpra.ca
www.facebook.com/168910893249240?ref=hl
twitter.com/CPRA_ACPL
Overview: A large national charitable organization founded in 1945
Mission: To advocate on the benefits of parks & recreation services
Chief Officer(s):
Jennifer Reynolds, President
CJ Noble, Executive Director, 613-523-5315
cjnoble@cpra.ca
Sarah Wayne, Accountant, 613-523-5315
swayne@cpra.ca
Membership: 2,600+; *Member Profile:* Parks & recreation professionals; *Committees:* Finance; Strategic Development; Communications; Awards
Activities: Influencing policy direction; Promoting the benefits of parks & recreation; Providing information to members; Offering professional development opportunities; *Awareness Events:* Recreation & Parks Month, June
Awards:
• Claude Langelier Award for Young Professionals (Award)
• Award of Merit (Award)
• Citation of Outstanding Achievement (Award)
• Honourary Life Membership (Award)
• Boothman Bursary (Scholarship)
• Award of Excellence for Innovation (Award)
Publications:
• The Benefits Catalogue
Type: Catalogue; *Number of Pages:* 200
Profile: Research outlining why parks, recreation, fitness, arts, & culture are important to the development of healthy individuals & communities
• Canadian Parks & Recreation Association Annual Report
Type: Yearbook; *Frequency:* Annually
• Canadian Parks & Recreation Association Research Reports
Profile: Topics include A Workbook on Child Health & Poverty: A Shared Vision for Health Children; Recreation & Children & Youth Living in Poverty: Barriers, Benefits & SuccessStories; & Bridging the Recreation Divide: Listening to Youth & Parents from Low-income Families across Canada
• CPRA [Canadian Parks & Recreation Association] E-News
Type: Newsletter; *Frequency:* Quarterly; *Price:* Free with CPRA membership
Profile: CPRA activities, conferences, awards, news, resources, initiatives, & research
• CPRA [Canadian Parks & Recreation Association] Tool Kits
Type: Kit
Profile: Topics of tool kits include Making All Recreation Safe, Relevant Recreation, & Everybody Gets to Play

Canadian Parks & Wilderness Society (CPAWS) / Société pour la nature et les parcs du Canada (SNAP)

#506, 250 City Centre Ave., Ottawa ON K1R 6K7
Tel: 613-569-7226; *Fax:* 613-569-7098
Toll-Free: 800-333-9453
www.cpaws.org
www.facebook.com/cpaws
twitter.com/cpaws
www.youtube.com/cpawsnational
Previous Name: National & Provincial Parks Association (NPPAC)
Overview: A medium-sized national charitable organization founded in 1963
Mission: To act as the Canadian voice for public wilderness protection
Chief Officer(s):
Éric Hébert-Daly, National Executive Director
Ellen Adelberg, Director, Communications & Marketing
Finances: *Funding Sources:* Donations; Fundraising
Membership: 1,200; *Committees:* Conservation; Engagement; Governance
Activities: Increasing awareness & understanding of ecological principles; Providing educational programs; Liaising with government, First Nations, business, & other organizations;
Awards:
• J.B. Harkin Medal (Award)
To honour individuals who have made a significant contribution to the conservation of Canada's parks & wilderness
Publications:
• Canadian Wilderness
Type: Newsletter; *Frequency:* Semiannually; *Price:* Free with Canadian Parks & Wilderness Society membership
Profile: Wilderness conservation news & views from across Canada for Canadian Parks & Wilderness Society members
• Community Atlas Initiative [a publication of the Canadian Parks & Wilderness Society]
Profile: CPAWS works with communities near national parks to produce atlases about land use & the natural environment, such as the Gulf IslandsCommunity Atlas, the Riding Mountain Community Atlas, the St. Lawrence Islands Atlas, & the Bruce Penninsula Community Atlas
• CPAWS [Canadian Parks & Wilderness Society] Annual Report
Type: Yearbook; *Frequency:* Annually
Profile: CPAWS yearly highlights & financial information
• CPAWS [Canadian Parks & Wilderness Society] Research Reports
Frequency: Irregular
Profile: Conservation biology scientific report topics include Grizzly Challenge; Special Marine Areas in Newfoundland & Labrador; Ontario's Timber Harvesting Levels: Scienceor Wishful Thinking?; The State of the Alberta Parks & Protected Areas; & Uncertain Future: Woodland Caribou & Canada's Boreal Forest
• Gatineau Park: A Threatened Treasure
Type: Booklet; *Number of Pages:* 28
Profile: Information to ensure a sustainable future for Gatineau Park & its ecosystems
• More Than Trees: A Citizen's Guide to Making Conservation a Bigger Part of Forest Management
Type: Guide; *Number of Pages:* 91; *Editor:* Chris Henschel; Dave Pearce
Profile: A guide featuring advice fact sheets, compliance checklists, & the forest guardians reporting form
• Nahanni: Protected Forever
Type: Booklet; *Number of Pages:* 16
Profile: The expansion of the Nahanni National Park Reserve

Calgary - Southern Alberta Chapter
Kahanoff Centre, ?425 - 78th Ave. SW, Calgary AB T2V 5K5
Tel: 403-232-6686; *Fax:* 403-232-6988
infosab@cpaws.org
cpaws-southernalberta.org
facebook.com/cpawssab
twitter.com/cpawssab
www.youtube.com/cpawsnational
Chief Officer(s):
Grégoire Belland, Executive Director
gbelland@cpawscalgary.org
Gord James, Chair
• Green Notes
Type: Newsletter; *Frequency:* Semiannually; *Editor:* Shaun Fluker & Shelley Sopher
Profile: Articles & features about wilderness issues & campaigns

Edmonton - Northern Alberta Chapter
PO Box 52031, #202, 8540 - 109 St., Edmonton AB T6G 2T5
Tel: 780-424-5128; *Fax:* 780-424-5133
infonab@cpaws.org
www.cpawsnab.org
www.facebook.com/cpaws.northernalberta
twitter.com/cpawsnab
Mission: To maintain biodiversity & wilderness in northern Alberta
Chief Officer(s):
Catherine Shier, Executive Director
Jeannette Gysbers, Chair
Wally Friesen, Secretary
• Boreal Market News
Editor: Helene Walsh
Profile: Information for decision makers about developments in forest management
• News for the Wild
Type: Newsletter; *Frequency:* Semiannually; *Editor:* J. Gysbers; B. Ensslin; M. Avery; *Price:* Free for CPAWS members
Profile: Information about CPAWS campaigns in Alberta

Fredericton - New Brunswick Chapter
180 St John St., Fredericton NB E3B 4A9
Tel: 506-452-9902
cpawsnb@nb.sympatico.ca
www.cpawsnb.org
www.facebook.com/CPAWSNewBrunswick
twitter.com/RCnature
Mission: To work towards the permanent protection of wilderness areas in New Brunswick
Chief Officer(s):
Roberta Clowater, Executive Director
• Wild New Brunswick [a publication of the Canadian Parks & Wilderness Society, Fredericton Chapter]
Type: Newsletter; *Price:* Free for CPAWS NB members

Halifax - Nova Scotia Chapter
#101, 5435 Portland Pl., Halifax NS B3K 6R7
Tel: 902-446-4155; *Fax:* 902-446-4156
cpawsns.org
www.facebook.com/CPAWSNS
twitter.com/cpawsnovascotia
www.youtube.com/cpawsns;
www.flickr.com/photos/64626833@N02
Mission: To conserve Nova Scotia's wild places in parks & other protected areas as well as areas of ocean
Chief Officer(s):
Martin Willison, President & Chair
Chris Miller, Biologist, National Conservation
cmiller@cpaws.org
Rodrigo Menafra, Coordinator, Marine Conservation
marine@cpawsns.org
• Wild East: The Newsletter of CPAWS Nova Scotia
Type: Newsletter; *Frequency:* Semiannually; *Editor:* Jon Feldgajer & Chris Miller
Profile: Wilderness area updates, conservation profiles, & chapter reports

Montréal - Québec Chapter
#303, 727, St-Urbain, Montréal QC H2R 2Y5
Tél: 514-278-7627
www.snapqc.org
www.facebook.com/pages/SNAP-Québec/107424984239
twitter.com/snapqc
www.youtube.com/channel/UCrE5HMtv8GnNtZCxplQVlsw
Mission: To establish a network of protected areas across Québec; To provide effective management for existing protected areas; To protect the boreal forest
Chief Officer(s):
Brigitte Voss, Présidente
Patrick Nadeau, Directeur général, 514-278-7627 Ext. 226
Marie-Eve Allaire-Hébert, Coordonnatrice, Relations avec la communauté, 514-278-7627 Ext. 221
Jérôme Spaggiari, Coordonnateur, Conservation, 581-307-7627

Ottawa - Ottawa Valley Chapter
190 Bronson Ave., Ottawa ON K1R 6H4
Tel: 613-232-7297; *Fax:* 613-569-7098
www.cpaws-ov-vo.org
www.facebook.com/cpawsov
twitter.com/cpaws_ottawa
www.youtube.com/user/cpawsov
Chief Officer(s):
John McDonnell, Executive Director
jmcdonnell@cpaws.org

St. John's - Newfoundland & Labrador Chapter
The Environmental Gathering Place, PO Box 1027, Stn. C, 172 Military Rd., 3rd Fl., St. John's NL A1C 5M3
Tel: 709-726-5800; *Fax:* 709-726-2764
nlcoordinator@cpaws.org
www.cpawsnl.org
www.facebook.com/pages/CPAWS-NL/184526941575823
twitter.com/cpawsnl
www.youtube.com/user/cpawsnl;
www.flickr.com/photos/cpaws-nl
Mission: To foster management of protected areas in Newfoundland & Labrador; To promote the establishment of new marine & terrestrial protected areas in the province
Chief Officer(s):
Suzanne Dooley, Co-Executive Director
Tanya Edwards, Co-Executive Director
Leah Mahoney, Coordinator, Marine
• CPAWS - NL [Canadian Parks & Wilderness Society - Newfoundland & Labrador] Newsletter
Type: Newsletter; *Editor:* Emily White
Profile: Chapter reports

Saskatoon - Saskatchewan Chapter
PO Box 25106, Stn. River Hts., Saskatoon SK S7K 2B1

Tel: 306-469-7876
www.cpaws-sask.org
www.facebook.com/cpaws.sask
twitter.com/cpawsSK
Mission: To establish protected areas on Crown lands in Saskatchewan; To promote responsible land use
Affiliation(s): Saskatchewan Environmental Society; Nature Saskatchewan; Silva Forest Foundation
Chief Officer(s):
Sue Michalsky, Chair
Gord Vaadeland, Executive Director
gvaadeland@cpaws.org
Kjelti Anderson, Coordinator, Communications & Project
kanderson@cpaws.org
• Paws & Ponder: The Newsletter of the Canadian Parks & Wilderness Society, Saskatchewan Chapter
Type: Newsletter
Profile: Chapter activities & updates & book releases

Toronto - CPAWS Wildlands League Chapter
#380, 401 Richmond St. West, Toronto ON M5V 3A8
Tel: 416-971-9453; *Fax:* 416-979-3155
Toll-Free: 866-510-9453
info@wildlandsleague.org
www.wildlandsleague.org
www.facebook.com/259132727038
Mission: To save, protect, & enhance wilderness areas throughout Ontario
Kim Statham, B.Sc., M.E.S., President
Janet Summer, Executive Director
janet@wildlandsleague.org
• CPAWS [Canadian Parks & Wilderness Society] Wildlands League Chapter Annual Report
Type: Yearbook; *Frequency:* Annually
• Ontario's Timber Harvesting Levels
Type: Report
• Wild Notes [a publication of the Canadian Parks & Wilderness Society, Toronto Chapter]
Type: Newsletter; *Price:* Free with donations to the Wildlands League

Vancouver - British Columbia Chapter
#410, 698 Seymour St., Vancouver BC V6B 3K6
Tel: 604-685-7445; *Fax:* 604-685-6449
info@cpawsbc.org
www.cpawsbc.org
www.facebook.com/cpawsbc
twitter.com/CPAWSbc
www.youtube.com/user/CPAWSinBC/videos
Chief Officer(s):
Chloe O'Loughlin, Executive Director
Robert Penrose, President
Michaeln Barkusky, Treasurer
• CPAWS-BC [Canadian Parks & Wilderness Society - British Columbia] Chapter Newsletter
Type: Newsletter; *Frequency:* Quarterly; *Price:* Free for members
Profile: Information about conservation issues in British Columbia

Whitehorse - Yukon Chapter
PO Box 31095, 211 Main St., Whitehorse YT Y1A 5P7
Tel: 867-393-8080; *Fax:* 867-393-8081
info@cpawsyukon.org
cpawsyukon.org
www.facebook.com/CPAWS.Yukon
twitter.com/CPAWSYukon
www.youtube.com/cpawsyukon
Mission: To safeguard wilderness & wildlife in the Yukon
Jill Pangman, Chair
Mike Dehn, Executive Director

Winnipeg - Manitoba Chapter
#3, 303 Portage Ave., Winnipeg MB R3B 2B4
Tel: 204-949-0782
info@cpawsmb.org
cpawsmb.org
www.facebook.com/cpawsmb.org
twitter.com/cpawsmb
Chief Officer(s):
Amanda Karst, President
Ron Thiessen, Executive Director
• The Green Cottager Guide
Type: Manual; *Author:* Chanda Hunnie & Ron Thiessen; *Editor:* Donna Danyluk & Liz Dykman
Profile: Tips for cottagers, cottage associations, & non-governmental environmental organizations to ensure their environmental footprint is assmall as possible

• Parks & Wilderness
Type: Newsletter
Profile: Information, issues, & campaigns regarding the wilderness

Yellowknife - Northwest Territories Chapter
PO Box 1934, 5020 - 52nd St., Yellowknife NT X1A 2P5
Tel: 867-873-9893; *Fax:* 867-873-9593
nwtadmin@cpaws.org
cpawsnwt.org
Mission: To conserve the land, water, & wildlife of the Northwest Territories
Chief Officer(s):
Kris Brekke, Executive Director
Erica Janes, Coordinator, Conservation Outreach

Canadian Parks Partnership (CPP) / Partenaires des parcs canadiens
#360, 1414 - 8th St. SW, Calgary AB T2R 1J6
Tel: 613-567-0099
Overview: A medium-sized national organization founded in 1986
Mission: To support the overall enhancement of Canada's parks, historic sites & canals system & to foster public awareness, appreciation, understanding of & involvement in the system
Finances: *Annual Operating Budget:* Less than $50,000
Staff Member(s): 3
Membership: Over 60 associations across Canada which work on an individual level with their partner national & provincial park or historic site
Activities: Direct Volunteer Support Program - to help cooperating associations to be strong & effective partners to their local national/provincial parks & historic sites & other protected area sites across Canada; National Education Programs - reaching beyond the park gate to encourage public awareness, appreciation of & involvement in supporting our special places; Canadian Parks Partnership Fund - was established in 1992 to act as a community foundation; *Speaker Service:* Yes; *Rents Mailing List:* Yes

Canadian Partnership for Children's Health & Environment (CPCHE) / Le Partenariat canadien pour la santé des enfants et l'environnement (PCSEE)
#301, 130 Spadina Ave., Toronto ON M5V 2L4
Tel: 416-960-2284
info@healthyenvironmentforkids.ca
www.healthyenvironmentforkids.ca
Overview: A medium-sized national organization
Mission: The Canadian Partnership for Children's Health and Environment (CPCHE) is an affiliation of groups with overlapping missions to improve children's environmental health in Canada. Working across traditional boundaries, CPCHE provides common ground for organizations working to protect children's health from environmental contaminants.
Chief Officer(s):
Erica Phipps, Director
erica@healthyenvironmentforkids.ca

Canadian Partnership for Consumer Food Safety Education
R.R. #22, Cambridge ON N3C 2V4
Tel: 519-651-2466; *Fax:* 519-651-3253
brenda.watson@canfightbac.org
www.canfightbac.org
www.facebook.com/347282142037165?fref=ts
twitter.com/CanFightBac
Overview: A medium-sized national charitable organization founded in 1997
Mission: To educate consumers about their role in food safety; to reduce the incidence of foodborne illness in Canada
Chief Officer(s):
Brenda Watson, Executive Director
Finances: *Annual Operating Budget:* $100,000-$250,000
Membership: 35+

Canadian Pasta Manufacturers Association (CPMA)
#200, 265 Carling Ave., Ottawa ON K1S 2E1
Tel: 613-235-4010; *Fax:* 613-235-5866
www.pastacanada.com
Overview: A small national organization
Mission: To promote Canadian pasta as a healthy & affordable food choice
Finances: *Funding Sources:* Advancing Canadian Agriculture and Agri-Food (ACAAF) Program
Membership: *Member Profile:* Manufacturers of pasta made from durum wheat
Activities: Providing consumer education; Conducting surveys; Funding the health communications program called "Grains: They're Essential"; *Awareness Events:* World Pasta Day, Oct. 25

Canadian Pastry Chefs Guild Inc. (CPCG)
c/o Egon Keller, 36 Melrose Ave., Barrie ON L4M 2A7
Tel: 705-719-9654
www.canadianpastrychefsguild.ca
Overview: A small national organization founded in 2002
Mission: To promote trade education for pastry chefs throughout Canada; to improve trade standards
Chief Officer(s):
Al Criminisi, President
al@lentia.com
Daniel Gonzalez, Vice-President
pastryman@sympatico.ca
Nyree Allen, Secretary
nyree.allen@gmail.com
Egon Keller, CEO
freewind1@sympatico.ca
Membership: 200; *Fees:* $65; *Member Profile:* Members of the Guild, such as pastry chefs or executive pastry chefs in hotels, bakeries, restaurants, or wholesale & retail businesses, are approved by the Board of Directors & abide by a Code of Ethics; Members also include teachers & persons closely connected to the trade, such as equipment manufacturers & suppliers
Activities: Offering shows & competitions, recipes, & resources
Publications:
• The Guild Journal
Type: Newsletter; *Editor:* Richard Crossman; *Price:* Free with Guild membership
Profile: Guild activities

Canadian Patient Safety Institute (CPSI) / Institut canadien pour la sécurité des patients
#1414, 10235 - 101 St., Edmonton AB T5J 3G1
Tel: 780-409-8090; *Fax:* 780-409-8098
Toll-Free: 866-421-6933
info@cpsi-icsp.ca
www.patientsafetyinstitute.ca
www.linkedin.com/companies/canadian-patient-safety-institute
www.facebook.com/PatientSafety
www.twitter.com/Patient_Safety
www.youtube.com/patientsafetycanada
Overview: A small national organization founded in 2003
Mission: To work with patients, healthcare providers, organizations, regulatory bodies, & governments to provide safer healthcare for Canadians; To promote leading practices for patient safety within Canada's health system
Chief Officer(s):
Doug Cochrane, Chair
Hugh MacLeod, CEO
hmacleod@cpsi-icsp.ca
Cecilia Bloxom, Director, Communications
cbloxom@cpsi-icsp.ca
Finances: *Funding Sources:* Health Canada
Activities: Providing resources about patient safety; Identifying patient safety practices; Developing safety competencies; Promoting integration of patient safety practices into educational & training programs; *Awareness Events:* Canadian Patient Safety Week; *Library:* Canadian Patient Safety Institute Library
Publications:
• Patient Safety Matters: The CPSI Newsletter
Type: Newsletter
Profile: Institute updates, courses, appointments, profiles, funding, & upcoming events

Canadian Payday Loan Association (CPLA) / Association canadienne des prêteurs sur salaire (ACPS)
#1600, 25 Main St. West, Hamilton ON L8P 1H1
Tel: 905-522-2752; *Fax:* 905-522-2310
www.cpla-acps.ca
Previous Name: Canadian Association of Community Financial Service Providers
Overview: A small national organization founded in 2004
Mission: To represent the interests of the sector to governments & consumers, & to ensure that Association members adhere to national standards of best business practices for the industry
Chief Officer(s):
Stan Keyes, President
stan.keyes@cpla-acps.ca

Marian Ross, Executive Assistant
marian.ross@cpla-acps.ca
Membership: 764 retail outlets; *Fees:* $1,000 per store; *Member Profile:* Small-sum unsecured short-term credit (payday loan) providers who operate retail outlets across Canada

Canadian Payments Association (CPA) / Association canadienne des paiements (ACP)

180 Elgin St., 12th Fl., Ottawa ON K2P 2K3
Tel: 613-238-4173; *Fax:* 613-233-3385
info@cdnpay.ca
www.cdnpay.ca
Overview: A medium-sized national organization founded in 1980
Mission: To establish & operate safe & efficient national clearing & settlements systems; To facilitate the interaction of its systems with others involved in the exchange, clearing & settlement of payments; To facilitate the development of new payment methods & technologies
Chief Officer(s):
Janet Cosier, Chair
Eric Wolfe, Deputy Chair
Finances: *Funding Sources:* Membership dues
Staff Member(s): 80
Membership: 118; *Member Profile:* The Bank of Canada & all banks operating in Canada are required to be members. Other institutions eligible for membership are credit union centrals, federations of caisses populaires, trust companies, loan companies, other deposit-taking institutions, life insurance companies, securities dealers that are members of the Investment Dealers Association or the Bourse de Montréal, & money market mutual funds that meet certain requirements.; *Committees:* Executive; Finance; Stakeholder Advisory; Large-Value Transfer System (LVTS) Management; National Clearings; CPA Regulatory, Statutory and Policy Matters; Payments Risk; Cash Management Users
Activities: Monitoring payment system developments & related issues in Canada & abroad; *Library* by appointment
Publications:
• Canadian Payments Association Annual Review
Frequency: Annually
• Forum [a publication of the Canadian Payments Association]
Type: Newsletter; *Frequency:* Quarterly; *Editor:* Geoffroi Montpetit
Profile: Association activities & important payment developments

Canadian Payroll Association (CPA) / L'Association canadienne de la paie (ACP)

#1600, 250 Bloor St. East, Toronto ON M4W 1E6
Tel: 416-487-3380; *Fax:* 416-487-3384
Toll-Free: 800-387-4693
Other Communication: dialogue@payroll.ca
infoline@payroll.ca
www.payroll.ca
Overview: A large national organization founded in 1978
Mission: To provide payroll leadership, through advocacy & education
Chief Officer(s):
Patrick Culhane, President & Chief Executive Officer
Finances: *Funding Sources:* Membership fees; Education program; Training sessions
212 volunteer(s)
Membership: 13,500+; *Fees:* Schedule available; *Member Profile:* Corporate, Professional & Associate memberships available; *Committees:* Government Relations; Communications; Membership; Programs; Education; Volunteer Management
Activities: Providing the CPA Professional Development Series that covers all aspects of payroll training, including terminations, taxable benefits, year end reporting & new year requirements; *Awareness Events:* National Payroll Week, September; *Speaker Service:* Yes; *Library:* Infoline
Meetings/Conferences: • Canadian Payroll Association 2015 33rd Annual Conference & Trade Show: Payroll Champions, 2015, Sheraton Centre Toronto Hotel
Scope: National
Description: A payroll event, where compliance, employment standards, & strategic management leaders have the opportunity to advance their skills, to learn about the latest trends & issues, & to network with professionals from across Canada
Contact Information: Phone: 416-487-3380, ext. 111; E-mail: conference@payroll.ca
Publications:
• CPA [The Canadian Payroll Association] E-Source
Type: Newsletter; *Frequency:* Bimonthly
Profile: Legislation & compliance updates, payroll & human resources tips, & professional development opportunities
• Dialogue [a publication of The Canadian Payroll Association]
Type: Magazine; *Frequency:* Bimonthly
Profile: Articles, products, legislative updates, trends, case-studies, & industry related news about payroll administration
• Your Payroll Privacy Questions Answered
Author: Murray Long; *ISBN:* 0-9736167-2-5; *Price:* $39.95
Profile: For people responsible for payroll & related functions

Canadian Peace Alliance (CPA) / Alliance canadienne pour la paix

PO Box 13, 427 Bloor St. West, Toronto ON M5S 1X7
Tel: 416-588-5555; *Fax:* 416-588-5556
cpa@web.ca
www.acp-cpa.ca
www.facebook.com/268544019838244
twitter.com/CanadianPeace
Overview: A medium-sized national organization founded in 1985
Mission: To involve Canadians in the worldwide movement to stop the arms race, ensure the non-violent settlement of disputes & guarantee the security & well-being of all peoples.
Affiliation(s): Canadian Network to Abolish Nuclear Weapons; International Peace Bureau
Chief Officer(s):
Sid Lacombe, Coordinator, 416-588-5555
cpa@web.ca
Finances: *Funding Sources:* Membership dues; donations
Staff Member(s): 1
Membership: 156 groups; *Fees:* Schedule available; *Member Profile:* Acceptance of statement of unity; *Committees:* Steering
Activities: Facilitates member group campaigns for peace & disarmament; quarterly clearinghouse mailings; *Internships:* Yes; *Speaker Service:* Yes; *Rents Mailing List:* Yes; *Library:* Resource Centre; by appointment

Canadian Peacebuilding Coordinating Committee *See* Peacebuild: The Canadian Peacebuilding Network

Canadian Peacekeeping Veterans Association (CPVA)

PO Box 905, Kingston ON K7L 4X8
Tel: 506-627-6437
info@cpva.ca
www.cpva.ca
Overview: A small national organization founded in 1991
Mission: To assist Canadians who have served on peacekeeping missions
Member of: National Council of Veterans
Chief Officer(s):
Ray Kokkonen, President
kokkonen@nbnet.nb.ca
20 volunteer(s)
Membership: *Fees:* $20 regular; $25 associate; $100 group; *Member Profile:* Military, police & civilian veterans of peacekeeping missions; also open to those who served with Multinational Force & Observers, International Commission of Control & Supervision, International Commission for Supervision & Control
Activities: *Awareness Events:* Peacekeeping Memorial Day, Aug. 9; *Speaker Service:* Yes

Canadian Pediatric Endocrine Group (CPEG) / Groupe canadien d'endocrinologie pédiatrique (GCEP)

c/o Robert Barnes, M.D., Montreal Children's Hospital, #316E, 2300, rue Tupper, Montréal QC H3H 1P3
Tel: 514-412-4315; *Fax:* 514-412-4264
www.cpeg-gcep.net
Overview: A small national organization
Mission: To promote the study of pediatric endocrinology
Chief Officer(s):
Robert Barnes, Secretary-Treasurer
Membership: *Member Profile:* Paediatricians; Endocrinologists; Fellows in training; Nurses
Activities: Communicating information about pediatric endocrinology & diabetes;
Meetings/Conferences: • Canadian Pediatric Endocrine Group 2015 Scientific Meeting, February, 2015, Westin Nova Scotian, Halifax, NS
Scope: National

Canadian Pediatric Foundation (CPF) / La fondation canadienne de pédiatrie

2305 St. Laurent Blvd., Ottawa ON K1G 4J8
Tel: 613-526-9397; *Fax:* 613-526-3332
cpf@cps.ca
www.cps.ca
www.linkedin.com/company/canadian-paediatric-society/
www.facebook.com/CanadianPaediatricSociety
twitter.com/canpaedsociety
www.youtube.com/canpaedsociety
Overview: A medium-sized national organization founded in 1985
Mission: To promote improved health care & social well-being for the children of Canada, particularly for disadvantaged groups; to promote better standards of health care for children throughout the world, particularly where Canadian aid is active.
Chief Officer(s):
Marie Adèle Davis, Executive Director, 613-526-9397 Ext. 226
madavis@cps.ca
Membership: 150; *Committees:* Action Committee for Children and Teens; Acute Care; Adolescent Health; Annual Conference; Awards; Bioethics; Community Paediatrics; Continuing Professional Development; Drug Therapy and Hazardous Substances; Fetus and Newborn; First Nations, Inuit and Métis Health; Healthy Active Living and Sports Medicine; Infectious Diseases and Immunization; Injury Prevention; Mental Health and Development Disabilities; Nutrition and Gastroenterology; Paediatric Human Resources Planning
Meetings/Conferences: • Canadian Pediatric Foundation 92nd Annual Conference, June, 2015, Sheraton Centre Hotel, Toronto, ON
Scope: National
Contact Information: meetings@cps.ca; URL: www.annualconference.cps.ca

Canadian Pemphigus & Pemphigoid Foundation

#148, 6A-170 The Donway West, Toronto ON M3C 2E8
Tel: 647-382-9356
info@pemphigus.ca
www.pemphigus.ca
twitter.com/InfoCPPF
Overview: A medium-sized national charitable organization
Mission: To provide support to people who have pemphigus & pemphigoid & their families; To supply information to its member; To raise awareness about pemphigus & pemphigoid
Affiliation(s): International Pemphigus & Pemphigoid Foundation; Canadian Organization for Rare Disorders; Canadian Skin Patient Alliance
Chief Officer(s):
Victoria Carlan, Chair
Daria Parsons, Executive Director

Canadian Pension & Benefits Institute (CPBI) / Institut canadien de la retraite et des avantages sociaux (ICRA)

CPBI National Office, 1175, av Union, Montréal QC H3B 3C3
Tel: 514-288-1222; *Fax:* 514-288-1225
Other Communication: members@cpbi-icra.ca
info@cpbi-icra.ca
www.cpbi-icra.ca
www.linkedin.com/company/canadian-pension-&-benefits-institut
e
twitter.com/cpbi_icra
Overview: A medium-sized national organization founded in 1960
Finances: *Funding Sources:* Membership fees; Sponsorships; Event registration fees
Membership: 3,500+; *Member Profile:* Persons involved in pension, benefits, & investment issues in Canada & the United States
Activities: Analyzing best practices, related to to pensions, employee benefits, & investments; Offering continuing education; Facilitating the exchange of information; Providing member access to industry job postings
Meetings/Conferences: • Canadian Pension & Benefits Institute Forum 2015, May, 2015, New York Hilton Midtown, New York City, NY
Scope: International
Description: Theme: Definig Our Future
Publications:
• Canadian Pension & Benefits Institute Annual Report
Type: Yearbook; *Frequency:* Annually
• Canadian Pension & Benefits Institute Members' Directory
Type: Directory
Profile: Listing of Canadian Pension & Benefits Institute members & their contact information

Atlantic Region
1600 Bedford Hwy., Bedford NS B4A 1E8

Tel: 902-835-0391; *Fax:* 902-835-3628
atlantic@cpbi-icra.ca
www.cpbi-icra.ca
Mission: To provide members in Atlantic Canada with education & networking opportunities for the analysis of best practices & the exchange of information
Chief Officer(s):
Maria Hayes, Regional Administrator

Manitoba Region
80 Noble Ave., Winnipeg MB R2L 0J6
Tel: 204-667-5027; *Fax:* 204-477-5081
manitoba@cpbi-icra.ca
www.cpbi-icra.ca
Mission: To facilitate the exchange of best practices & information for pension, employee benefit, & investment professionals in Manitoba
Joan Turnbull, Regional Administrator
• Manitoba Momentum
Type: Newsletter
Profile: News from the CPBI Manitoba Regional Council, including upcoming local events, membership information, & credit updates

Northern Alberta Region
#3353, 11215 Jasper Ave., Edmonton AB T5K 0L5
Tel: 780-438-3398; *Fax:* 780-438-3399
albertanorth@cpbi-icra.ca
www.cpbi-icra.ca
Mission: To offer educational & networking opportunities to persons in northern Alberta involved in the pensions, employee benefits, & investments sectors
Shelly Petovar, Regional Administrator

Ontario Region
PO Box 64003, 200 Bay St., Toronto ON M5J 2T6
Fax: 905-643-2972
Toll-Free: 877-599-1414
ontario@cpbi-icra.ca
www.cpbi-icra.ca
Mission: To provide education & networking forums related to pensions, employee benefits, & investments in the Ontario region
Jackie Ablett, Regional Administrator

Pacific Region
PO Box 48542, Stn. Bentall, Vancouver BC V7X 1A3
Tel: 604-379-1946
pacific@cpbi-icra.ca
www.cpbi-icra.ca
Mission: To serve persons involved in the pensions, employee benefits, & investments sector in the Pacific region

Québec Region
1175, av Union, Montréal QC H3B 3C3
Tel: 514-288-7272; *Fax:* 514-288-1255
quebec@cpbi-icra.ca
www.cpbi-icra.ca
Mission: To facilitate the exchange of information & the analysis of best practices among persons employed in the fields of pensions, investments, & employee benefits in the Québec region
Chief Officer(s):
André Picard, Chair
Michèle Bernier, Treasurer
Myriam Beaudry, Regional Administrator

Saskatchewan Region
PO Box 353, White City SK S4L 5B1
Tel: 306-757-1013; *Fax:* 306-781-3316
saskatchewan@cpbi-icra.ca
www.cpbi-icra.ca
Mission: To support individuals involved in the pension, benefits, & investment sectors in Saskatchewan
Karen Lovelace, Regional Administrator
• CPBI [Canadian Pension & Benefits Institute] Saskatchewan News
Type: Newsletter; *Frequency:* 3 pa
Profile: Membership news, education updates, upcoming events, & sponsorship opportunities

Southern Alberta Region
PO Box 20065, 205 - 5th Ave. SW, Calgary AB T2P 4H3
Tel: 587-435-2724
albertasouth@cpbi-icra.ca
www.cpbi-icra.ca
Mission: To provide continuing education & networking opportunities for individuals involved in pensions, employee benefits, & investments in southern Alberta
Krista Esau, Regional Administrator

Canadian Pensioners Concerned Inc. (CPC) / Retraités canadiens en action (RCA)
6 Trinity Sq., Toronto ON M5G 1B1
Tel: 416-368-5222; *Fax:* 416-368-0443
Toll-Free: 888-822-6750
canpension@gmail.com
www.canpension.ca
Overview: A medium-sized national charitable organization founded in 1969
Mission: To provide joint action on seniors issues; To collect authoritative factual material & distribute it in usable form to relevant persons & authorities
Chief Officer(s):
Barbara Kilbourn, President
Sylvia Hall, Corporate Secretary
Jane Miller, Treasurer
Finances: *Funding Sources:* Donations; Membership fees
Membership: 1,200 in chapters & associated clubs + 50,000 with affiliated organizations; *Fees:* $25 individual; $45 institution; $50 affiliate/organization; *Member Profile:* Retired & semi-retired persons &/or their spouses over 55
Publications:
• Viewpoint
Type: Newsletter; *Frequency:* Quarterly; *Editor:* Dorothy Archer
Profile: Issues & CPC reports, meetings, awards, & news

Nova Scotia Division
#325, 7071 Bayers Rd., Halifax NS B3L 2C2
Tel: 902-455-7684; *Fax:* 905-455-1825
Chief Officer(s):
Joan Lay, President

Ontario Division
6 Trinity Sq., Toronto ON M5G 1B1
Tel: 416-368-5222
Toll-Free: 888-822-6750
canpension@gmail.com
www.canpension.ca
Chief Officer(s):
Barbara Kilbourn, President

Canadian Peony Society / Société canadienne de la pivoine
PO Box 28027, RPO Parkdale, 468 Albert St., Waterloo ON N2L 6J8
Other Communication: membership@peony.ca
info@peony.ca
www.peony.ca
Overview: A small national organization founded in 1998
Mission: To promote the growing, improving and use of peonies in the garden and for home decoration; to encourage peony breeding to produce distinctly Canadian peony hybrids; to locate and record locally bred peonies, and produce a national registry of collections and their location; and, to sponsor an annual peony show and encourage regional shows.
Membership: *Fees:* $15 individual; $275 lifetime

Canadian Percheron Association / Association canadienne du cheval Percheron
Rolla BC
Tel: 250-759-4981; *Fax:* 888-423-0049
canadapercheron@uniserve.com
www.canadianpercherons.com
Overview: A small national organization
Mission: To develop & encourage the breeding of purebred Percheron horses in Canada; To establish standards of breeding; To regulate the breeding of purebred Percheron horses
Chief Officer(s):
David Logies, President, 902-538-8505
Kathy Ackles, Contact
Membership: *Fees:* $50
Activities: Keeping a record of the breeding & origin of Percheron horses; Protecting & assisting breeders of purebred Percheron horses in compliance with the Animal Pedigree Act; Compiling statistics on the Percheron industry
Publications:
• Canadian Percheron Broadcaster
Type: Magazine; *Accepts Advertising*

Canadian Peregrine Foundation (CPF)
#20, 25 Crouse Rd., Toronto ON M1R 5P8
Tel: 416-481-1233
Toll-Free: 888-709-3944
info@peregrine-foundation.ca
www.peregrine-foundation.ca
Overview: A small national organization founded in 1998
Mission: The Canadian Peregrine Foundation is a registered charity dedicated to assisting the recovery of the peregrine falcon and other raptors at risk.
Membership: *Fees:* $30 single; $40 family

Canadian Periodical Publishers' Association; Canadian Magazine Publishers Association (CMPA) ***See*** Magazines Canada

Canadian Personal Trainers Network ***See*** Certified Professional Trainers Network

Canadian Pest Control Association ***See*** Canadian Pest Management Association

Canadian Pest Management Association (CPMA) / Association canadienne de la gestion parasitaire (ACGP)
PO Box 1748, Moncton NB E1C 9X5
Fax: 866-957-7378
Toll-Free: 866-630-2762
cpma@pestworld.org
www.pestworldcanada.org
Previous Name: Canadian Pest Control Association
Overview: A medium-sized national organization founded in 1943
Mission: To provide pest management information; To act as the voice of the pest management industry throughout Canada; Upholding the association's Code of Ethics
Affiliation(s): National Pest Management Association; Leadership Development Group; Minorities in Pest Management; Professional Women in Pest Management
Chief Officer(s):
Bill Melville, President
bmelville@orkincanada.com
Karen Furgiuele-Percy, Director, Business Development
kfurgiuele@gardexinc.com
Randy Hobbs, Director, Government Affairs
rhobbs@braemargroup.ca
Sean Rollo, Treasurer
srollo@pcocanada.com
Membership: *Member Profile:* Members of provincial & regional pest management associations; Suppliers
Activities: Offering training & networking opportunities; Conducting research; Offering assistance to consumers seeking a professional pest control company
Meetings/Conferences: • Pest Management Canada 2015, March, 2015, Westin Calgary, Calgary, AB
Scope: National
Description: Educational sessions, networking opportunities, & exhibits of products, services & techniques
Contact Information: E-mail: cpma@pestworld.org
Publications:
• Canada ePestWorld
Type: Newsletter; *Frequency:* Monthly; *Price:* Free with Canadian Pest Management Association membership
Profile: Timely national industry news & happenings, membership bulletins, & articles
• Pest Gazette
Type: Newsletter; *Frequency:* Quarterly; *Number of Pages:* 4
Profile: Educational information about seasonal pests for pest management consumers
• PestWorld
Type: Newsletter; *Frequency:* Bimonthly; *Price:* Free with Canadian Pest Management Association membership
Profile: Business techniques & tips, analysis of the pest management industry, field stories, technical updates, & legislative news

Canadian Petroleum Law Foundation ***See*** Canadian Energy Law Foundation

Canadian Petroleum Products Institute ***See*** Canadian Fuels Association

Canadian Pharmacists Association (CPhA) / Association des pharmaciens du Canada
1785 Alta Vista Dr., Ottawa ON K1G 3Y6
Tel: 613-523-7877; *Fax:* 613-523-0445
Toll-Free: 800-917-9489
Other Communication: members@pharmacists.ca
info@pharmacists.ca
www.pharmacists.ca
www.facebook.com/cpha
twitter.com/CPhAAPhC
Overview: A large national organization founded in 1907
Mission: To advance the profession of pharmacy to contribute to the health of Canadians; To represent & support pharmacists

across Canada
Member of: Canadian Council on Continuing Education in Pharmacy
Affiliation(s): Commonwealth Pharmaceutical Association; Fédération internationale pharmaceutique
Chief Officer(s):
Jeff Poston, Executive Director
jposton@pharmacists.ca
Paula MacNeil, President
Membership: 5,000-14,999; *Fees:* Free for new practitioners; $202 spouses; $336 active & supporting members; $2,200 corporate members; *Member Profile:* Individuals licensed to practice pharmacy in Canada, or holding a professional degree in pharmacy; Individuals or associations who support the mission of the association; Undergraduates, graduates, & those attending the IPG program; Corporate members; *Committees:* Standing Board; Ad Hoc; Coalitions; Advisory; Editorial Advisory
Activities: Advocating on behalf of the profession; Liaising with all levels of government & other health care stakeholders; Providing information & education; Promoting research, innovation, & health promotion; Participating in partnerships; *Library:* Canadian Pharmacists Association Library
Awards:
• Canadian Pharmacist of the Year Award (Award)
• CPhA Honourary Life Membership Award (Award)
• CPhA International Leadership Award (Award)
• CPhA Meritorious Service Award (Award)
• CPhA New Practitioner Award (Award)
• CPhA Patient Care Achievement Award for Health Promotion (Award)
• CPhA Patient Care Achievement Award for Innovation (Award)
• CPhA Patient Care Achievement Award for Specialty Practice (Award)
• CPhA Certificate of Recognition (Award)
Meetings/Conferences: • Canadian Pharmacists Association 2015 103rd Annual National Conference, May, 2015, The Westin Ottawa, Ottawa, ON
Scope: National
Description: An educational program, plus a trade show, & networking events for pharmacists from throughout Canada
Contact Information: E-mail: info@pharmacists.ca
• Canadian Pharmacists Association 2016 104th Annual National Conference, June, 2016, Vancouver, BC
Scope: National
Description: Educational oral & poster presentations, a trade show, an awards presentation, & networking events
Contact Information: E-mail: info@pharmacists.ca
• Canadian Pharmacists Association 2017 105th Annual National Conference, June, 2017, Québec, QC
Scope: National
Description: A continuing education program, a trade show, as well as social events of interest to pharmacists
Contact Information: E-mail: info@pharmacists.ca
• Canadian Pharmacists Association 2018 106th Annual National Conference, June, 2018, Winnipeg, MB
Scope: National
Description: A yearly event for Canadian pharmacists, featuring educational workshops, a trade show, awards, & social events
Contact Information: E-mail: info@pharmacists.ca
• Canadian Pharmacists Association 2019 107th Annual National Conference, 2019
Scope: National
Description: Professional development activities, workshops, & a trade show for pharmacists from across Canada
Publications:
• Canadian Pharmacists Association Annual Report
Type: Yearbook; *Frequency:* Annually
• Canadian Pharmacists Journal
Type: Journal; *Frequency:* Bimonthly; *Accepts Advertising*; *Editor:* Rosemary M. Killeen *ISSN:* 1715-1635; *Price:* Free with membership in the Canadian Pharmacists Association
Profile: Peer reviewed, clinical, & research articles plus reviews of interest for Canadian pharmacists
• Compendium of Pharmaceuticals & Specialties
Profile: Current Canadian drug information, including monographs for drugs, vaccines, & natural health products

Canadian Philatelic Society ***See*** The Royal Philatelic Society of Canada

Canadian Philosophical Association (CPA) / Association canadienne de philosophie (ACP)

c/o Louise Morel, Saint Paul University, 223 Main St., Ottawa ON K1S 1C4
Tel: 613-236-1393; *Fax:* 613-782-3005
administration@acpcpa.ca
www.acpcpa.ca
www.facebook.com/164300999481
twitter.com/acp_cpa
Overview: A large national charitable organization founded in 1958
Mission: To advance the discipline of philosophy in Canada
Member of: Canadian Federation for the Humanities
Affiliation(s): Fédération internationale des sociétés de philosophie
Chief Officer(s):
Louise Morel, Executive Director
Judy Pelham, Secretary, 416-736-2100 Ext. 44721
pelham@yorku.ca
Patrice Philie, Treasurer, 613-562-5800 Ext. 3684
pphilie@uottawa.ca
Eric Dayton, English Editor, Dialogue: Canadian Philosophical Review, 306-966-7844, Fax: 306-966-7845
dialogue@usask.ca
Mathieu Marion, Éditeur Francophone, Dialogue: Revue canadienne de philosophie, 514-987-3000 Ext. 4999, Fax: 514-987-6721
dialogue@er.uqam.ca
Staff Member(s): 1; 30 volunteer(s)
Membership: 800 individual; *Member Profile:* Philosophy professors & students; others interested in philosophy; *Committees:* Equity; Executive
Activities: *Awareness Events:* Congress
Meetings/Conferences: • 2015 Canadian Philosophical Association Congress, May, 2015, University of Ottawa, Ottawa, ON
Publications:
• Canadian Graduate Programs in Philosophy
• CPA [Canadian Philosophical Association] Bulletin
Type: Newsletter; *Frequency:* Semiannually; *Editor:* Christine Tappolet
Profile: CPA activities, announcements, book & student essay prize winners, resources, committee reports, & congress information
• Dialogue [a publication of the Canadian Philosophical Association]
Type: Journal; *Frequency:* Quarterly; *Editor:* Susan Dimock & Mathieu Marion; *Price:* Free with CPAmembership
Profile: Canadian philosophical review featuring peer reviewed articles & reviews in all aspects of philosophy

Canadian Philosophy of Education Society (CPES) / Société Canadienne de Philosophie de l'Education (SCPE)

c/o Ann Chinnery, Faculty of Education, Simon Fraser University, 8888 University Dr., Burnaby BC V5A 1S6
Tel: 778-782-8123; *Fax:* 778-782-8119
ann.chinnery@sfu.ca
www.philosophyofeducation.ca
Overview: A small national organization founded in 1972
Mission: Devoted to philosophical inquiry into educational issues and their relevance for developing educative, caring, and just teachers, schools, and communities.
Member of: Canadian Society for the Study of Education
Affiliation(s): Canadian Association of Foundations of Education
Chief Officer(s):
Douglas Simpson, Presdient
d.j.simpson@tcu.edu
Publications:
• Paideusis
Type: Journal

Canadian Photo Video Trade Association ***See*** Canadian Imaging Trade Association

Canadian Physical Education Association; Canadian Association for Health, Physical Education, Recreation, & Dance ***See*** Physical & Health Education Canada

Canadian Physicians for Aid & Relief (CPAR)

1425 Bloor St. West, Toronto ON M6P 3L6
Tel: 416-369-0865; *Fax:* 416-369-0294
Toll-Free: 800-263-2727
info@cpar.ca
www.cpar.ca
www.facebook.com/135666612320
twitter.com/cpar
Overview: A large international charitable organization founded in 1984
Mission: To help impoverished communities in developing nations become prosperous, while maintaining harmony with the environment; To tackle all aspects of poverty; To emphasize healthy community empowerment & integrated community based development
Chief Officer(s):
Kevin O'Brien, Executive Director
kobrien@cpar.ca
Todd Carmichael, Director, Programs
tcarmichael@cpar.ca
Andrew Williamson, Chair
Finances: *Funding Sources:* Government; Donations; Foundations
40 volunteer(s)
Activities: *Internships:* Yes

Canadian Physicians for Aid & Relief

1425 Bloor St. West, Toronto ON M6P 3L6
Overview: A medium-sized local organization founded in 1984
Chief Officer(s):
Jean Goerzen, Director of Programs
tcarmichael@cpar.ca

Canadian Physicians for Life

PO Box 1289, Ottawa ON K0A 2Z0
Tel: 613-728-5433; *Fax:* 613-728-5433
info@physiciansforlife.ca
www.physiciansforlife.ca
Overview: A small national charitable organization founded in 1975
Mission: To ensure reverence for every human life, regardless of age or infirmity; to protect & preserve human life, to relieve suffering, & to promote healing
Chief Officer(s):
Barbara McAdorey, Administrator
Williard Johnston, President
Robert Pankratz, Vice-President
Finances: *Funding Sources:* Donations
Membership: *Member Profile:* Canadian physicians
Publications:
• Vital Signs
Type: Newsletter; *Frequency:* Semiannually
Profile: Timely issues of interest to member physicians, Canadian Physicians for Life meetings, & activities

Canadian Physicians for the Prevention of Nuclear War ***See*** Physicians for Global Survival (Canada)

Canadian Physiological Society (CPS) / Société canadienne de physiologie

c/o Dr. Melanie Woodin, Dept. of Cell & Systems Biology, U. of Toronto, 25 Harbord St., Toronto ON M5S 3G5
www.cpsscp.ca
Overview: A medium-sized national charitable organization founded in 1935 overseen by Canadian Federation of Biological Societies
Mission: To disseminate & discuss scientific information of interest to researchers in physiology & biological sciences
Chief Officer(s):
Steven Barnes, President
Melanie Woodin, Secretary, 416-978-8646, Fax: 416-978-8532
m.woodin@utoronto.ca
Membership: *Fees:* $25 students; $65 associates; $100 regular; *Committees:* Nominating; Web Resources
Activities: Encouraging reseaerch in the physiological sciences; Fostering communication within the scientific community in Canada

Canadian Physiotherapy Association (CPA) / L'Association canadienne de physiothérapie

955 Green Valley Cres., Ottawa ON K2C 3V4
Tel: 613-564-5454; *Fax:* 613-564-1577
Toll-Free: 800-387-8679
information@physiotherapy.ca
www.physiotherapy.ca
www.linkedin.com/company/canadian-physiotherapy-association
www.facebook.com/CPA.ACP
twitter.com/physiocan
Overview: A large national organization founded in 1920
Mission: To provide leadership & direction to the profession; To foster excellence in practice, education & research; To promote high standards of health in Canada
Affiliation(s): World Confederation for Physical Therapy; Alliance of Physiotherapy Regulatory Boards of Canada; Canadian University Physiotherapy Academic Council; Health Action Lobby (HEAL); Physiotherapy Foundation of Canada; Accreditation Council for Canadian Physiotherapy Academic Programs
Chief Officer(s):
Robert Werstine, President

Finances: *Annual Operating Budget:* Greater than $5 Million; *Funding Sources:* Membership dues & programs; Products & services
Membership: 10,000; *Fees:* Schedule available; *Member Profile:* Graduates of accredited physiotherapy programs in Canada; Physiotherapists who hold or have held full registration or licensure anywhere in Canada; Graduates of physiotherapy programs who hold a full- or part-time academic faculty appointment in a physiotherapy program at a Canadian university; Students; Support workers; PTA students; Affiliates who are persons, corporations or associations who support CPA's mission; *Committees:* Awards; Finance; Manual Therapy; Membership & Affiliations; Nominations; Resolutions
Activities: *Awareness Events:* National Physiotherapy Month, April 20 - May 20; *Speaker Service:* Yes
Meetings/Conferences: • Canadian Physiotherapy Association 2015 Congress, June, 2015, Halifax, NS
Scope: National
Description: Educational courses, workshops, the presentation of scientific research, private practice leadership information, & networking opportunities for physiotherapists from across Canada
Contact Information: Registration Contact: Hope Caldwell, Phone: 1-800-387-8679, ext. 247, E-mail: hcaldwell@physiotherapy.ca
• Canadian Physiotherapy Association 2016 Congress, May, 2016, Victoria, BC
Scope: National
Description: Educational courses, workshops, the presentation of scientific research, private practice leadership information, & networking opportunities for physiotherapists from across Canada
Contact Information: Registration Contact: Hope Caldwell, Phone: 1-800-387-8679, ext. 247, E-mail: hcaldwell@physiotherapy.ca
Publications:
• Canadian Physiotherapy Association Annual Report
Type: Yearbook; *Frequency:* Annually
• Physiotherapy Canada
Type: Journal; *Frequency:* Quarterly; *Accepts Advertising*; *Editor:* Dina Brooks, BSc(PT), MSc, PhD; *Price:* Free to CPA members
Profile: The Canadian Physiotherapy Association's official peer-reviewed scientific & clinical studies journal
• Physiotherapy Practice
Type: Magazine; *Frequency:* 5 pa; *Accepts Advertising*; *Price:* Free to CPA members
Profile: Information for physiotherapy clinicians, including an annual Buyers Guide

Canadian Phytopathological Society (CPS) / Société Canadienne de Phytopathologie (SCP)

c/o Vikram Bisht, PO Box 1149, 65 - 3 Ave. NE, Carman MB R0G 0J0
Tel: 204-745-0260; *Fax:* 204-745-5690
www.cps-scp.ca
www.facebook.com/111761558875337
Overview: A medium-sized national organization founded in 1929
Mission: To encourage & support research, education, & dissemination of knowledge on the nature, cause, & control of plant diseases; To promote communication among plant pathologists; To broaden educational opportunities for members
Chief Officer(s):
Janice Elmhirst, President
Finances: *Funding Sources:* Membership fees
Membership: 365; *Committees:* International Cooperation; Website; Local Arrangements; Canadian liaison; Science Policy; Financial Advisory; Education; Nominations; Resolutions; Awards; Membership
Meetings/Conferences: • Canadian Phytopathological Society 2015 87th Annual Meeting, July, 2015
Scope: National
Description: The objectives of CPS are to encourage research, education, and the dissemination of knowledge on the nature, cause, and control of plant diseases.
Publications:
• Canadian Journal of Plant Pathology / Revue canadienne de phytopathologie
Type: Journal; *Frequency:* Quarterly; *Editor:* Zamir K. Punja
ISSN: 0706-0661; *Price:* $85 Canada individuals; $140 Canada institutions; $95-$105international individuals
Profile: Scientific research, reviews & information about plant pathology
• Canadian Plant Disease Survey / Inventaire des maladies des plantes au Canada
Editor: Dr. Robin Morrall, Coordinator
Profile: Records of plant diseases in Canada & assessments of losses from disease
• Diseases & Pests of Vegetable Crops in Canada
Number of Pages: 554; *Editor:* R. Howard, J. Garland, & W. Seaman
Profile: Joint publication of the Canadian Phytopathological Society & the Entomological Society of Canada
• Diseases of Field Crop Crops in Canada
Number of Pages: 304; *Editor:* Bailey, Gossen, Gugel & Morrall; *ISBN:* 0-9691627-6-6; *Price:* $35
Profile: Thorough, illustrated guide to identifying diseases of forage, pulse, oilseed, cereal, & specialty crops
• The Pest Management Research Report (PMRR)
Editor: Andrea Labaj
Profile: Information about integrated pest management (IPM) for researchers & advisors

Canadian Picture Pioneers (CPP)

#1762, 250 The East Mall, Toronto ON M9B 6L3
Tel: 416-368-1139; *Fax:* 416-368-1139
cdnpicturepioneers@rogers.com
www.canadianpicturepioneers.ca
Overview: A small national charitable organization founded in 1940
Mission: To provide assistance for the welfare of those in the motion picture industry in Canada
Chief Officer(s):
John Freeborn, Executive Director
Phil May, President
Paul Wroe, Secretary-Treasurer
Membership: 1,000+; *Member Profile:* Persons from all levels of the motion picture industry in Canada, whose period of service has been five years
Activities: Promoting good relations between those in the motion picture industry; to increase understanding between those in the motion picture industry & the public; Maintaining a trust fund;
Awards:
• Pioneer of the Year Award (Award)

Calgary - Alberta Branch
36 Silver Brook Dr. NW, Calgary AB T3B 3H3
Tel: 403-999-1134
www.members.shaw.ca/iron1
Chief Officer(s):
Louise Campbell, Contact

Halifax - Atlantic Branch
c/o Empire Theatres Ltd., 190 Chain Lake Dr., Halifax NS B2W 6A3
Tel: 902-876-4848
Chief Officer(s):
Ernie MacDonald, Contact

Montréal - Les Pionniers du cinéma du Québec
2396, rue Beaubien est, Montréal QC H2G 1N2
Tél: 514-722-6682; *Téléc:* 514-721-6684
info@pionniersducinema.qc.ca
www.pionniersducinema.qc.ca
Chief Officer(s):
Michael Mosca, President

Vancouver - British Columbia Branch
c/o #1, 1005 Jervis St., Vancouver BC V6E 3T1
Tel: 604-681-6487
Chief Officer(s):
John Pedersen, President

Canadian Piedmontese Association (CLRC)

2417 Holly Lane, Ottawa ON K1V 0M7
Tel: 613-731-7110; *Fax:* 613-731-0704
Toll-Free: 877-833-7110
clrc@clrc.ca
www.clrc.ca
Overview: A small national organization founded in 1983
Mission: To develop & regulate the breeding of Piedmontese cattle in Canada; To establish standards of breeding; To carry out a system of registration for Piedmontese cattle
Affliation(s): Canadian Livestock Records Corporation
Chief Officer(s):
Ron Black, General Manager
ron.black@clrc.ca
Glenn Clark, Systems Manager
glenn.clark@clrc.ca
Membership: *Fees:* $50 + $25 / year; $250 + $25 / year life membership; $100 associate life membership; $10 junior membership (under 18 years of age); *Member Profile:* Piedmontese breeders; *Committees:* Executive; Appraisal; Promotion; Breed Improvement; Membership; Junior Membership; Show & Sale; Advisory; Nomination
Activities: Keeping records of the breeding & origin of Piedmontese cattle; Compiling industry statistics; Publishing data & documents; Supervising breeders of Piedmontese cattle; Promoting the economic productivity of the breed;

Canadian Pinzgauer Association (CPA)

c/o Rob Smith, Box 8, Site 16, RR#2, Olds AB T4H 1P3
Tel: 403-507-2255; *Fax:* 403-507-8583
diamondt@airenet.com
www.pinzgauer.ca
Overview: A small national organization founded in 1972
Mission: To develop & regulate the breeding of Pinzgauer cattle in Canada; To protect & assist breeders
Member of: Canadian Beef Breeds Council
Affliation(s): Canadian Livestock Records Corporation
Chief Officer(s):
Rob Smith, CPA President
Lisa Hutt, Registrar, 613-731-7110 Ext. 312, Fax: 613-731-0704
Membership: 1-99; *Fees:* $75 / year active membership; $20 junior membership (under 18 years of age); $10 associate membeship; *Member Profile:* Canadian breeders of Pinzgauer cattle; *Committees:* Promotion; Breed Improvement; Membership; Junior Member; Advisory; Nominating; Finance
Activities: Promoting the breeding of Pinzgauer cattle in Canada; Keeping a record of the breeding & origin of Pinzgauer cattle; Compiling statistics; Publishing & preserving data; Maintaining breeding standards; Supervising breeders
Publications:
• Breeder Directory
Type: Directory
• Purely Pinzgauer
Type: Newsletter
Profile: Feature articles, meetings, & sale & show results

Canadian Plastics Industry Association (CPIA) / Association canadienne de l'industrie des plastiques

#125, 5955 Airport Rd., Mississauga ON L4V 1R9
Tel: 905-678-7748; *Fax:* 905-678-0774
www.plastics.ca
www.linkedin.com/company/1087578
www.facebook.com/IntelligentPlastics
twitter.com/CPIA_ACIP
Previous Name: Society of the Plastics Industry of Canada
Overview: A large national organization founded in 1997
Mission: To advance the prosperity & international competitiveness of the Canadian plastics industry in an environmentally & socially responsible manner
Chief Officer(s):
Paul Cohen, Chair
Carol Hochu, President & CEO, 905-678-7748 Ext. 229
Michael Hill, Director, Membership Development, 905-678-7748 Ext. 281
Finances: *Funding Sources:* Membership fees
Staff Member(s): 30
Membership: 500; *Fees:* $1,000-$16,000; *Member Profile:* Companies involved in Canadian plastics industry; *Committees:* Composites; Construction; EH&S; EPIC; Machinery; Mould Makers; Natural Composites; Vinyl
Activities: P3 Sustainability Management Program; Intelligent Plastics Campaign; *Speaker Service:* Yes; *Rents Mailing List:* Yes; *Library:* Technical Information Resource Centre; Open to public by appointment
Awards:
• Leader of the Year Award (Award), CPIA Plastics Awards
• Plastics Innovator of the Year Award (Award), CPIA Plastics Awards
• Plastics Newcomer of the Year Award (Award), CPIA Plastics Awards
• Plastics Stewardship Award (Award), CPIA Plastics Awards
• Recycled Plastics Product Award (Award), CPIA Plastics Awards
Publications:
• Canadian Plastics Industry Association Executive Summary
Type: Newsletter
Profile: Internal newsletter of the CPIA President & CEO for CPIA members only
• CPIA [Canadian Plastics Industry Association] Annual Report
Type: Yearbook; *Frequency:* Annually
• CPIA [Canadian Plastics Industry Association] Membership Directory
Type: Directory

• CPIA [Canadian Plastics Industry Association] Plastics Machinery & Moulds Export Directory
Type: Directory
• CPIA [Canadian Plastics Industry Association] NewsBrief
Type: Newsletter
• Green Building
Type: Newsletter
Profile: Publication of the Green Building Task Force of the Canadian Plastics Industry Association
• Member to Member [a publication of Canadian Plastics Industry Association]
Type: Newsletter
• News & Views [a publication of Canadian Plastics Industry Association]
Type: Newsletter
• Plastics in Class [a publication of Canadian Plastics Industry Association]
Type: Newsletter
• Plastics Perspectives [a publication of Canadian Plastics Industry Association]
Type: Newsletter

Western Region
#33020, 11198 - 84th Ave., Delta BC V4C 1L0
Tel: 604-581-1984; *Fax:* 604-581-1607

Canadian Plastics Sector Council (CPSC) / Conseil canadien sectoriel des plastiques

#1, 200 Colonnade Rd., Ottawa ON K2E 7M1
Tel: 613-231-4470; *Fax:* 613-231-3775
info@cpsc-ccsp.ca
www.cpsc-ccsp.ca
www.linkedin.com/groups?home=&gid=3122682&trk=anet_ug_hm
www.facebook.com/170596692956657
twitter.com/PlasticsHR
youtube.com/CanadianPlastics
Overview: A small national organization founded in 2000
Mission: To explore & address emerging human resources issues in the plastics processing industry
Chief Officer(s):
Amelia Siva, Executive Director
a.siva@cpsc-ccsp.ca
Finances: *Annual Operating Budget:* $500,000-$1.5 Million
Staff Member(s): 4
Publications:
• CPSC [Canadian Plastics Sector Council] Newsletter / Bulletin du CCSP [Conseil canadien sectoriel des plastiques]
Type: Newsletter; *Frequency:* 3 pa; *Editor:* Jérôme Bourgault
Profile: Feature articles & CPSC activities

Canadian Plowing Council *See* Canadian Plowing Organization

Canadian Plowing Organization

38 Parkin St., Salsbury NB E4J 2N4
Tel: 506-372-9427
info@canadianplowing.ca
www.canadianplowing.ca
Previous Name: Canadian Plowing Council
Overview: A small national charitable organization founded in 1955
Mission: To preserve the art of match plowing in Canada; to promote the efficient operation & use of farm machinery; to promote improved farm productivity & yield efficiency through proper seed bed preparation & soil management
Affiliation(s): World Ploughing Organization
Chief Officer(s):
Gary Keith, Secretary
Finances: *Annual Operating Budget:* Less than $50,000; *Funding Sources:* Donations
1 volunteer(s)
Membership: 30 affiliated countries
Activities: Organizes an annual Canadian Championship Plowing Contest at which a Canadian Senior Champion Plowman, a Reserve Champion Plowman & a Canadian Junior Champion Plowman are declared

Canadian Plumbing & Mechanical Contractors Association, BC Branch *See* Mechanical Contractors Association of British Columbia

Canadian Plywood Association

#100, 375 Lynn Ave., North Vancouver BC V7J 2C4
Tel: 604-981-4190; *Fax:* 604-985-0342
info@canply.org
www.canply.org
Also Known As: CANPLY
Overview: A medium-sized national organization
Mission: Canadian plywood organization.
Chief Officer(s):
Judy White, Office Manager
Nick Nagy, President
nagy@certiwood.com
Finances: *Annual Operating Budget:* $1.5 Million-$3 Million
Staff Member(s): 14
Membership: 1-99

Canadian Podiatric Medical Association (CPMA) / Association médicale podiatrique canadienne

#2063, 61 Broadway Blvd., Sherwood Park AB T8H 2C1
Toll-Free: 888-220-3338
askus@podiatrycanada.org
www.podiatrycanada.org
Overview: A small national organization founded in 1924
Mission: To effectively serve & provide guidance to its members & the podiatry profession in Canada; to serve the public; to provide the authoritative national voice for podiatrists in Canada; to recognize a particular responsibility to contribute to the development of national positions & standards related to the podiatric medical profession through education, research, materials & personnel
Member of: Federation of International Podiatrists
Affiliation(s): Canadian Podiatric Education Foundation (CPEF)
Chief Officer(s):
Jayne Jeneroux, Executive Director
Finances: *Annual Operating Budget:* $50,000-$100,000; *Funding Sources:* Membership dues; endorsement
Staff Member(s): 1
Membership: 250+; *Fees:* $300; *Member Profile:* Doctor of Podiatric Medicine; *Committees:* Insurance; Publications; Seal of Approval/Acceptance; By-Laws; Foot Health Awareness Month; Economic Development
Activities: Educational; political; *Awareness Events:* National Foot Health Awareness Month, May; *Internships:* Yes; *Rents Mailing List:* Yes
Publications:
• CPMA [Canadian Podiatric Medical Association] Newsletter
Type: Newsletter; *Frequency:* Semiannually; *Price:* Free with CPMA membership

Canadian Poetry Association (CPA) / Association canadienne de la poésie

c/o Pooka Press, PO Box 2648, Stn. Main, Vancouver BC V5B 3W8
e-mail: poemata@live.com
www.canadianpoetryassociation.webs.com
twitter.com/cpalit
Overview: A small national organization founded in 1985
Mission: To promote the reading, writing, publishing, purchasing & preservation of poetry in Canada through the individual efforts of its members
Finances: *Funding Sources:* Membership dues; Grants
Membership: *Fees:* $30 regular; $20 students/seniors; $40 international; $50 association; $150 library/bookstore; *Member Profile:* Poets & those interested in poetry
Activities: Operates a LISTSERV: cpa@sympatico.ca
Awards:
• Shaunt Basmajian Chapbook Award (Award)
Publications:
• Poemata
Type: Magazine; *Accepts Advertising*; *Editor:* Donna Allard
ISSN: 1203-6595
Profile: National forum for ideas, with markets, reviews, & CPA announcements, chapter reports & happenings

Atlantic Canada
#4-212, 331 Elmwood Dr., Moncton NB E1A 1X6

Canadian Police Association (CPA) / Association canadienne des policiers (ACP)

#100, 141 Catherine St., Ottawa ON K2P 1C3
Tel: 613-231-4168; *Fax:* 613-231-3254
cpa-acp@cpa-acp.ca
www.cpa-acp.ca
Overview: A large national organization founded in 1953
Chief Officer(s):
Tom Stamatakis, President
Denis Côté, Vice-President
Staff Member(s): 4
Membership: 52,000; *Member Profile:* Rank & file police officers
Activities: *Library:* Canadian Police Association Library
Meetings/Conferences: • 2016 Biennial Canadian Police Association Conference, 2016
Scope: National

Canadian Polish Congress (CPC) / Congrès canadien polonais

3055 Lake Shore Blvd. West, Toronto ON M8V 1K6
Tel: 416-532-2876; *Fax:* 416-532-5730
kongres@kpk.org
www.kpk.org
Overview: A large national charitable organization founded in 1944
Mission: To represent Polish-Canadians & to defend their interests; To coordinate & support the work of Polish-Canadian organizations in Canada; To foster Polish culture & assist Polish immigrants; To inform Canadians about Poland's contribution to culture & to maintain liaisons with Poland
Member of: Canadian Ethnocultural Council
Affiliation(s): Polonia of the Free World; Canadian Polish Research Institute; Adam Mickiewicz Foundation; Polish Combattants Association; Polish National Union
Chief Officer(s):
Teresa Berezowski, President
tberezowski@kpk.org
Jan Cytowski, First Vice-President, Polish Affairs
jcytowski@kpk.org
Ludwik Klimkowski, Vice-President, Canadian Affairs
lklimkowski@kpk.org
Teresa Szramek, Secretary-General
tszramek@kpk.org
Elizabeth Morgan, Treasurer
emorgan@kpk.org
Finances: *Funding Sources:* Membership fees
12 volunteer(s)
Membership: 25,000 individuals + 220 organizations; *Fees:* $6; *Committees:* Award; Audit; Litigation
Activities: *Library*

Alberta Branch
PO Box 1912, Stn. Main, Edmonton AB T5J 2P3
Tel: 780-425-2172; *Fax:* 780-432-6295
www.kpkalberta.com
Chief Officer(s):
Jaroslaw Nowinka, President
j.nowinka@shaw.ca

British Columbia Branch
1134 Kingsway, Vancouver BC V5V 3C8
Tel: 604-725-8712
kpkbritishcolumbia@gmail.com
www.kpkbritishcolumbia.com
www.facebook.com/KPKBritishColumbia
Chief Officer(s):
Beata Grodkowska, President

Hamilton Branch
374 Aurora Cres., Burlington ON L7N 2A9
Tel: 905-637-9333
Chief Officer(s):
Stanislaw Warda, President
Stanley.warda097@sympatico.ca

Kitchener Branch
601 Wellington St. North, Kitchener ON N2H 5J6
Tel: 519-623-3460
www.kpk-kitchener.org
Chief Officer(s):
Urszula Walkowska, President
uw@appaut.com

Manitoba Branch
768 Mountain Ave., Winnipeg MB R2W 1L7
Tel: 204-338-2888; *Fax:* 204-589-7878
kongres@shaw.ca
www.kpkmanitoba.ca
Chief Officer(s):
Grazyna Galezowska, President

Mississauga Branch
Mississauga ON
e-mail: mississauga.kpk@gmail.com
en.kpk-mississauga.org
www.youtube.com/user/kpkmississauga
Chief Officer(s):
Anna Mazurkiewicz, President, 905-206-0003
kpkmississauga@rogers.com

Niagara Branch
36 October Dr., St Catharines ON L2N 6J6
Tel: 905-934-3175
Chief Officer(s):
Jacek Kaminski, President

Oshawa Branch
418 Grange Ct., Oshawa ON L1G 7J1

Tel: 905-576-6726
kpkoshawa@gmail.com
Chief Officer(s):
Elizabeth Szczepanski, President
Ottawa Branch
Ottawa ON
www.kpk-ottawa.org
Chief Officer(s):
Piotr Nawrot, President
pnawrot@rogers.com
Québec Branch
63, rue Prince Arthur Est, Montréal QC H2X 1B4
Tel: 514-285-4880; *Fax:* 514-624-0416
Chief Officer(s):
Edward Sliz, President
esliz@rogers.com
Sudbury Branch
291 Albinson St., Sudbury ON P3C 3W2
Tel: 705-673-1931
ahmrozewski@sympatico.ca
Chief Officer(s):
Andrzej H. Mrozewski, President
ahmrozewski@sympatico.ca
Thunder Bay Branch
90 Banning St., Thunder Bay ON P7B 3H7
Tel: 807-344-5530
Chief Officer(s):
Henryk Bystrzycki, President
bbystrzycki@tbaytel.net
Toronto Branch
206 Beverley St., Toronto ON M5T 1Z3
Tel: 416-971-9848; *Fax:* 416-971-9848
president@kpk-toronto.org
www.kpk-toronto.org
Chief Officer(s):
Juliusz Kirejczyk, President
Windsor Branch
2050 Willistead Cres., Windsor ON N8Y 1K5
Tel: 519-256-4172
Chief Officer(s):
Jerzy Barycki, President

Canadian Polish Foundation / Fondation canadienne-polonaise
2453 Lake Shore Blvd. West, Toronto ON M8V 1C5
Tel: 647-762-3876
cdnpolishfdn@yahoo.ca
www.facebook.com/270776979652952
Overview: A small local organization founded in 1998

Canadian Polish Society
43 Facer St., St. Catharines ON L2M 5H4
Tel: 905-937-1413
office@canadianpolishsociety.com
www.canadianpolishsociety.com
www.facebook.com/102029093175788
Previous Name: Polish Society in Canada
Overview: A small local organization founded in 1928
Mission: To unite Canadians of Polish origin & Polish people in Canada; To represent Poles in all levels of government & political life; To create & to foster strong cultural, economic & social Polish community; To engage Polish business community in economic cooperation & exchange of information; To promote & preserve Polish cultural heritage & historical traditions; To organize cultural events & to assist & help Poles in need
Membership: 200+; *Member Profile:* Polish descent

Canadian Political Science Association (CPSA) / Association canadienne de science politique (ACSP)
#204, 260 Dalhousie St., Ottawa ON K1N 7E4
Tel: 613-562-1202; *Fax:* 613-241-0019
cpsa@csse.ca
www.cpsa-acsp.ca
Overview: A medium-sized national charitable organization founded in 1913
Mission: To encourage & develop political science & its relationship with other disciplines
Member of: Canadian Federation for the Humanities & Social Sciences; International Political Science Association; United Nations Educational, Scientific and Cultural Organization
Chief Officer(s):
Sally Rutherford, Executive Director
sally_rutherford@cpsa-acsp.ca
Reeta Tremblay, President
Michelle Hopkins, Administrator
Finances: *Annual Operating Budget:* $1.5 Million-$3 Million; *Funding Sources:* Membership fees; Institutional subsciptions to the Canadian Journal of Political Science; SSHRC grants; Provincial & federal funding
Staff Member(s): 2
Membership: 1,150 individuals; *Fees:* Students & those earning under $40K gross/yr.: $50 CPSA, $60 CPSA & SQSP; Regular: $150 CPSA; $170 CPSA & SQSP; *Member Profile:* Individuals interested in CPSA objectives, including representatives of political science departments, students, politicians, public servants, & persons from the private sector
Activities: Offering grants, scholarships, & fellowships; Sponsoring the Parliamentary Internship Program; *Internships:* Yes; *Rents Mailing List:* Yes
Meetings/Conferences: • Canadian Political Science Association 2015 Annual Conference (within the Congress of the Humanities & Social Sciences), June, 2015, University of Ottawa, Ottawa, ON
Scope: National
Description: A conference including the association's business & committee meetings, special presentations, workshops, & exhibits
Contact Information: Canadian Political Science Association Secretariat, E-mail: cpsa-acsp@cpsa-acsp.ca
Publications:
• Canadian Journal of Political Science (CJPS)
Type: Journal; *Frequency:* Quarterly; *Editor:* James Kelly; Daniel Salée; *Price:* Free for members of the CanadianPolitical Science Association
Profile: A journal of articles & book reviews sent to 3,000 subscribers
• Directory of Political Scientists in Canada
Type: Directory
Profile: Listings of political scientists & their research interests

Canadian Political Science Students' Association (CPSSA) / Association des Étudiants de Science Politique du Canada (AESPC)
University of Calgary, Dept. of Political Science, 2500 Universtiy Dr. NW, Calgary AB T2N 1N4
Tel: 613-562-1202; *Fax:* 613-241-0019
contact@cpssa.ca
www.cpssa.ca
ca.linkedin.com/company/canadian-political-science-students%27-associa
www.facebook.com/CPSSAAESPC
www.twitter.com/cpssa_aespc
instagram.com/cpssa_aespc
Overview: A medium-sized national organization founded in 1997
Mission: A national student organization representing students and student groups studying Political Science across the country.
Membership: *Committees:* Journal; Conference; Academic
Meetings/Conferences: • Canadian Political Science Students' Association 2015 Annual National Conference, 2015
Scope: National

Canadian Polo Association (CPA)
#100, 180 Renfrew Dr., Markham ON L3R 9Z2
Tel: 647-208-7656; *Fax:* 905-477-6897
info@polocanada.ca
www.polocanada.ca
www.facebook.com/polocanada
Also Known As: Polo Training Foundation Canada
Overview: A small national charitable organization founded in 1985
Mission: To develop & maintain standards of excellence for the sport of polo in Canada; To promote polo across the nation
Chief Officer(s):
Don Pennycook, President
Dave Offen, Vice-President
Cliff Sifton, Secretary
Gerald Levin, Treasurer
Finances: *Funding Sources:* Membership fees; Donations
Membership: *Fees:* $30 + GST juniors; $60 + GST adults; *Member Profile:* Individual junior & adult polo players, & clubs from across Canada
Activities: Supporting polo players & clubs across Canada; Providing resources; Raising awareness of polo & attracting new players to the game; Supporting training programs, educational workshops, & clinics for coaches, umpires, & players; Encouraging international competition; Offering junior polo programs; Facilitating communication between member clubs
Awards:
• Polo Canada Annual Scholarship (Scholarship)
Publications:
• Instructor's Manual
Type: Manual
Profile: Information for aspiring polo instructors who would like to become certified by Polo Canada

Canadian Pony Club (CPC)
PO Box 127, Baldur MB R0K 0B0
Fax: 204-535-2289
Toll-Free: 888-286-7669
ponyclub@escape.ca
www.canadianponyclub.org
Overview: A medium-sized national organization founded in 1934
Mission: To encourage & instruct young people to ride & care for their horses, while promoting loyalty, character & sportsmanship.
Member of: Equine Canada
Affliation(s): Ontario Equestrian Federation
Chief Officer(s):
Cathy Miller, National Chair
cmlmiller@sympatico.ca
Val Crowe, Administrator
pvcrowe@mts.net
Finances: *Funding Sources:* Fees
Membership: 3,500, in 150 branches; *Member Profile:* Young people between the ages of 6-21 who wish to learn all about horses; *Committees:* Management; Communications; Dressage; PPG; Rally; Testing; Tetrathlon; Finance; Human Resources; Education; Quiz; Show Jummping; Disciplines; Rally; Prince Philip Games
Activities: Instruction in dressage, show jumping, Tetrathlon
Awards:
• Three scholarships towards post-secondary education (Scholarship)
Alberta Central
PO Box 71, Tees AB T0C 2N0
Tel: 403-747-3013
www.canadianponyclub.org/albertacentral/index.htm
Chief Officer(s):
Mary Busch, Regional Chair
mbusch@xplornet.com
Alberta North
c/o 53315 Range Rd. 222, Ardrossan AB T8E 2M5
www.canadianponyclub.org/albertanorth/index.htm
Chief Officer(s):
Sandy Wallin, Regional Chair
swallin25@live.ca
Alberta South
Lethbridge AB
www.canadianponyclub.org/albertasouth
Chief Officer(s):
Colin Jorgensen, Regional Chair
jorgenc@telusplanet.net
British Columbia Interior North
www.canadianponyclub.org/bcin/index.htm
Chief Officer(s):
Sandy Agatiello, Regional Chair
sandyagatiello@yahoo.ca
British Columbia Islands
c/o 2040 Saddle Dr., Nanoose Bay BC V9L 5Z2
Tel: 250-468-7247
www.canadianponyclub.org/bcis/index.html
Chief Officer(s):
Susan Harrison, Regional Chair
toddsusan@shaw.ca
British Columbia Lower Mainland
www.canadianponyclub.org/bclm
Chief Officer(s):
Darcie Kerkhoven, Regional Chair
nicomen@xplornet.com
Central Ontario
Newmarket ON
www.canadianponyclub.org/centralontario/index.htm
Chief Officer(s):
Laurie Blake, Regional Chair, 905-830-0552
ljblake@rogers.com
Manitoba
www.canadianponyclub.org/manitoba/index.htm
Chief Officer(s):
Maria Berry, Regional Chair
meb@mts.net
New Brunswick/PEI
www.canadianponyclub.org/nbpei

Chief Officer(s):
Brad Woodward, Regional Chair
bradar@rogers.com

Nova Scotia
Kentville NS
www.canadianponyclub.org/ns/index.htm
Chief Officer(s):
Sheila Bower-Jacquard, Regional Chair, 902-678-6572
sheilabowerjacquard@bellaliant.net

St. Lawrence/Ottawa Valley
www.canadianponyclub.org/slov/index.htm
Chief Officer(s):
Liz Tucker, Regional Chair
tuck9@can.rogers.com

Saskatchewan
c/o Pelmac Stables, PO Box 66, RR7, Site 707, Saskatoon SK S7K 1N2
Tel: 306-933-4615; *Fax:* 306-933-3189
www.canadianponyclub.org/sask/index.html
Chief Officer(s):
Diana Pella, Regional Chair
pelmac@hughes.net

Western Ontario
c/o 3 Arkendo Dr., Oakville ON L6J 5T8
www.canadianponyclub.org/westernontario/index.htm
Chief Officer(s):
Del Zelmer, Regional Chair, 905-842-2458
delzel@cogeco.ca

Canadian Pony Society

746629 Township Rd. 4, #RR2, Princeton ON N0J 1V0
Tel: 519-458-8231
www.clrc.ca/pony.shtml
Overview: A small national organization founded in 1901
Mission: To encourage, develop & regulate the breeding of ponies in Canada by establishing standards of breeding & by carrying out a system of registration under the Canadian Livestock Records Corporation
Affliation(s): Canadian Livestock Records
Chief Officer(s):
Sandy Gunby, Secretary
Chris Bacher, Treasurer
Art Alderman, President
Finances: *Annual Operating Budget:* Less than $50,000
3 volunteer(s)
Membership: 100-499; *Fees:* $25
Activities: Members show at local fairs, Royal Winter Fair etc.

Canadian Poolplayers Association (CPA)

1000 Lake Saint Louis Blvd., Lake Saint Louis MO 63367 USA
Tel: 636-625-8611; *Fax:* 636-625-2975
playpool@wightman.ca
www.poolplayers.ca
www.facebook.com/34672444365
www.youtube.com/apaleagues
Also Known As: Canadian Pool League
Overview: A medium-sized national organization founded in 1989
Mission: Sanctions an international network of amateur pool leagues
Member of: Canadian Franchise Association
Affliation(s): American Pool Players Association
Chief Officer(s):
Larry Hubbart, Contact
Lindsay Dobson, Contact
Finances: *Funding Sources:* Membership dues
Staff Member(s): 4
Membership: 250,000; *Fees:* $25; *Member Profile:* Men & women over 19
Activities: Organized amateur pool league

Canadian Population Society

520-17 Aberdeen St., Ottawa ON K1S 3J3
e-mail: admin@canpopsoc.ca
www.canpopsoc.org
Overview: A small national organization
Mission: To work toward the improvement of knowledge and understanding about the quantitative and qualitative characteristics of human population
Chief Officer(s):
Eric Fong, President
fong@chass.utoronto.ca
Feng Hou, Sec.-Treas.
feng.hou@statcan.ca
Membership: *Fees:* $40 student; $75 regular; $350 lifetime; *Committees:* Awards; Canadian Federation of Humanities and Social Sciences; Federation of Canadian Demographers; International; Journal; National; Program; Student Paper Competition
Awards:
• Canadian Population Society Award (Award)
This award honors a Canadian scholar every two years who has shown outstanding commitment to the profession of demography and whose cumulative work has contributed in important ways to the advancement of the discipline in Canada, through publications, teaching and/or service.
Meetings/Conferences: • 2015 Canadian Population Society Annual Meeting, May, 2015, University of Ottawa, Ottawa, ON
Scope: National
Publications:
• Canadian Studies in Population
Type: Journal; *Editor:* Frank Trovato *ISSN:* 03801 489; *Price:* Free with CPS membership
Profile: Joint demographic publication of the Canadian Population Society & the University of Alberta
• CPS [Canadian Population Society] Newsletter
Type: Newsletter; *Frequency:* Semiannually; *Editor:* Laurie Goldmann
Profile: For CPS members

Canadian Pork Council (CPC) / Conseil canadien du porc (CCP)

#900, 200 Laurier Ave. West, Ottawa ON K1P 5Z9
Tel: 613-236-9239; *Fax:* 613-236-6658
info@cpc-ccp.com
www.cpc-ccp.com
Previous Name: Canadian Swine Council
Overview: A medium-sized national organization founded in 1966
Mission: To provide a leadership role in a concerted effort involving all levels of industry & government toward a common understanding & action plan for achieving a dynamic & prosperous pork industry in Canada.
Member of: Canadian Federation of Agriculture
Chief Officer(s):
Jean-Guy Vincent, Chair
Membership: 9 provincial; *Member Profile:* Hog producer marketing organizations
Activities: International trade food safety; quality assurance; environmental programs; *Library* Open to public by appointment

Canadian Porphyria Foundation Inc. (CPF) / La Fondation canadienne de la porphyrie

PO Box 1206, Neepawa MB R0J 1H0
Tel: 204-476-2800; *Fax:* 204-476-2800
Toll-Free: 866-476-2801
porphyria@cpf-inc.ca
www.cpf-inc.ca
Overview: A small national charitable organization founded in 1988
Mission: Dedicated to improving the quality of life for Canadians affected by the porphyrias through programs of awareness, education, service, advocacy & research; committed to promoting public & medical professional awareness; assembling, printing & distributing up-to-date educational information to physicians, health care personnel, diagnosed patients & others affected by porphyria; offering support programs to affected individuals & their families; promoting the family social welfare of affected individuals; educating & informing physicians & others in health care about the porphyrias so that early diagnosis & proper treatment will be realized; promoting & providing financial assistance for research; committed to encouraging, supporting & serving physicians & researchers in their efforts to find more effective treatments & to increasing physician, patient & community awareness & thereby cultivating support for research
Chief Officer(s):
Lois J. Aitken, President/Executive Director
Finances: *Annual Operating Budget:* $50,000-$100,000; *Funding Sources:* Fund-raising; Donations; Bequeaths; In memoriams; Philanthropic community
Staff Member(s): 3; 200 volunteer(s)
Membership: 2,500; *Member Profile:* People diagnosed with Porphyria & their families; medical personnel; interested persons, friends; *Committees:* Finance; Publicity; Newsletter; Member Services
Activities: Support groups, patient advocacy; confidential database; patient registry; educational information; list of safe/unsafe drugs; research fund development; fund-raising; *Awareness Events:* National Porphyria Day, June 1; *Speaker Service:* Yes
Publications:
• Canadian Porphyria Foundation National Newsletter
Type: Newsletter; *Frequency:* Semiannually
Profile: General information about porphyria

Canadian Port & Harbour Association ***See*** Association of Canadian Port Authorities

Canadian Portland Cement Association ***See*** Cement Association of Canada

Canadian Positive Psychology Association (CAPPA)

#703, 1 Eglinton Ave. East, Toronto ON M4P 3A1
Tel: 416-481-8930
info@positivepsychologycanada.com
www.positivepsychologycanada.com
Overview: A small national organization
Mission: A representive association for scholars and academics who are engaged in rigorous academic research in the field of positive psychology.
Chief Officer(s):
Louisa Jewell, President
Membership: *Fees:* $90 regualr; $30 student; *Member Profile:* Researchers, clinicians, educators, students, business owners, coaches, consultants, medical experts.
Meetings/Conferences: • 3rd Canadian Conference on Positive Psychology, 2015
Scope: National

Canadian Postmasters & Assistants Association (CPAA) / Association canadienne des maîtres de poste et adjoints (ACMPA)

281 Queen Mary St., Ottawa ON K1K 1X1
Tel: 613-745-2095; *Fax:* 613-745-5559
mail@cpaa-acmpa.ca
cpaa-acmpa.ca
Overview: A medium-sized national organization founded in 1902
Affliation(s): Canadian Labour Congress
Chief Officer(s):
Leslie A. Schous, National President
leslieschous@cpaa-acmpa.ca
Pierre Charbonneau, National Vice-President
pierrecharbonneau@cpaa-acmpa.ca
Shirley L. Dressler, National Vice President
shirleydressler@cpaa-acmpa.ca
Daniel L. Maheux, National Secretary-Treasurer
danielmaheux@cpaa-acmpa.ca
Staff Member(s): 9
Membership: 6,364
Publications:
• Communiqué
Type: Newsletter; *Frequency:* Semiannually; *Editor:* Karen E. MacDonald

Canadian Post-MD Education Registry (CAPER) / Système informatisé sur les stagiaires post-MD en formation clinique

#800, 265 Carling Ave., Ottawa ON K1S 2E1
Tel: 613-730-1204; *Fax:* 613-730-1196
caper@afmc.ca
www.caper.ca
twitter.com/CAPERCanada
Overview: A medium-sized national charitable organization founded in 1986
Mission: To provide accurate & timely data pertaining to Post-MD training & physician resources in Canada to assist medical schools, governments & other work longitudinal research pertaining to physicians training & supply
Affliation(s): Association of Faculties of Medicine of Canada
Chief Officer(s):
Steve Slade, Vice-President, Research & Analysis
sslade@caper.ca
Hélène LeBlanc, Executive Assistant
Finances: *Annual Operating Budget:* $250,000-$500,000; *Funding Sources:* Medical organizations; federal, provincial & territorial governments
Staff Member(s): 4
Membership: 1-99; *Committees:* Executive; Policy
Publications:
• CAPER [Canadian Post-MD Education Registry] Annual Census
Type: Report; *Frequency:* Annually *ISSN:* 1712-9184
Profile: Annual census of post-M.D. trainees
• CAPER [Canadian Post-MD Education Registry] Provincial Reports
Type: Report; *Frequency:* Annually

Canadian Poultry & Egg Processors Council (CPEPC)
#400, 1545 Carling Ave., Ottawa ON K1Z 8P9
Tel: 613-724-6605; *Fax:* 613-724-4577
www.cpepc.ca
Overview: A medium-sized national organization
Mission: To foster a climate of continuous improvement within the Canadian feather industry recognizing the need for increasing competitiveness
Chief Officer(s):
Robin Horel, President / CEO
robinhorel@cpepc.ca
Membership: *Member Profile:* Processors, packagers and distributors of chicken and turkey meat, graders and further processors of eggs and hatcheries in Canada
Meetings/Conferences: • Canadian Poultry and Egg Processors Council (CPEPC) Convention 2015, June, 2015, Winnipeg, MB
Scope: National

Canadian Power & Sail Squadrons (Canadian Headquarters) (CPS) / Escadrilles canadiennes de plaisance (ECP)
26 Golden Gate Ct., Toronto ON M1P 3A5
Tel: 416-293-2438; *Fax:* 416-293-2445
Toll-Free: 888-277-2628
hqg@cps-ecp.ca
www.cps-ecp.ca
www.facebook.com/groups/6654534451
twitter.com/cpsboat
www.youtube.com/CPSECP
Overview: A medium-sized national charitable organization founded in 1938
Mission: To increase awareness & knowledge of safe boating by educating & training members & the general public, by fostering fellowship among members, & establishing partnerships & alliances with organizations & agencies interested in boating
Member of: Canadian Safe Boating Council
Chief Officer(s):
Walter Kowalchuk, Executive Director, 416-293-2438 Ext. 0160
wkowalchuk@cps-ecp.ca
John Gullick, Manager, Government & Special Programs, 416-293-2438 Ext. 0155
jgullick@cps-ecp.ca
Finances: *Annual Operating Budget:* $1.5 Million-$3 Million
Staff Member(s): 13; 5000 volunteer(s)
Membership: 34,000; *Fees:* $30; *Member Profile:* Must pass specified examination & pay dues on annual basis; *Committees:* Public Relations; Training Department
Activities: *Library*
Meetings/Conferences: • Canadian Power and Sail Squadrons 2015 Annual General Meeting & Conference, October, 2015, Niagara Falls, ON
Scope: National

Canadian Powerlifting Federation *See* Canadian Powerlifting Union

Canadian Powerlifting Federation (CPF)
306 Castlefield Ave., Waterloo ON N2K 2N1
www.canadianpowerliftingfederation.com
www.facebook.com/117359724995464
Previous Name: Canadian Powerlifting Organization
Overview: A small national organization
Mission: Promoting powerlifting in Canada
Member of: World Powerlifting Congress; World Powerlifting Organization
Membership: *Member Profile:* Individuals & organizations, from across Canada, who are interested in powerlifting
Activities: Providing results from CPF meets & its affiliates
Publications:
• Maximum Power
Type: Newsletter

Canadian Powerlifting Organization *See* Canadian Powerlifting Federation

Canadian Powerlifting Union (CPU)
c/o Mike Armstrong, 4709 Fordham Cres. SE, Calgary AB T2A 2A5
Tel: 403-402-4142
www.powerlifting.ca
www.facebook.com/CDNpowerliftingunion
Previous Name: Canadian Powerlifting Federation
Overview: A medium-sized national organization founded in 1982
Mission: To oversee & regulate all IPF style powerlifting in Canada
Affliation(s): International Powerlifting Federation
Chief Officer(s):
Mark Giffin, President
mark@powerlifting.ca
Ryan Fowler, Chair, Coaching
rfowler@powerlifting.ca
Mike Armstrong, Secretary
mike@powerlifting.ca
Barry Antoniow, Treasurer
bantoniow@powerlifting.ca
Membership: *Committees:* Anti-Doping; Coaching; Team Selection; Funding; ParaPowerlifting

Canadian Prader-Willi Syndrome Association *See* Foundation for Prader-Willi Research in Canada

Canadian Precast / Prestressed Concrete Institute (CPCI) / Institut canadien du béton préfabriqué et précontraint
#100, 196 Bronson Ave., Ottawa ON K1R 6H4
Tel: 613-232-2619; *Fax:* 613-232-5139
Toll-Free: 877-937-2724
info@cpci.ca
www.cpci.ca
www.facebook.com/121188924614844
Overview: A medium-sized national organization founded in 1961
Mission: To stimulate & advance the common interests & general welfare of the structural precast/prestressed concrete industry, the architectural precast concrete industry & the post-tensioned concrete industry in Canada
Chief Officer(s):
Rob Burak, President
robert.burak@cpci.ca
Finances: *Annual Operating Budget:* $500,000-$1.5 Million
Staff Member(s): 3
Membership: 31 institutional
Activities: *Library* Open to public
Publications:
• CPCI [Canadian Precast / Prestressed Concrete Institute] Imagineering
Type: Magazine; *Accepts Advertising*; *Editor:* Jeanne Fronda
Profile: Feature articles, industry updates, member directory, "tech talk", marketing information, president's messages

The Canadian Press (CP) / La presse canadienne
36 King St. East, Toronto ON M5C 2L9
Tel: 416-364-0321; *Fax:* 416-364-0207
Other Communication: archives@cpimages.com
editorial@thecanadianpress.com
www.thecanadianpress.com
www.facebook.com/thecanadianpress
twitter.com/CdnPress
Overview: A large national organization founded in 1917
Mission: To operate as a national news cooperative, owned & financed by Canada's daily newspapers
Chief Officer(s):
Scott White, Editor-in-Chief
Philippe Mercure, Business Director, CPimages
Graeme Roy, Director, News Photography
James McCarten, Senior National Editor
Andrea Baillie, Editor, Entertainment
Neil Davidson, Editor, Sports
Paul Loong, Editor, World
John Valorzi, Editor, Business
Membership: 100 daily newspapers; *Committees:* Board of Directors; Executive
Activities: Providing news & information services to more than 600 radio & television stations, cable TV systems, internet sites, & commercial clients, delivered by satellite & web server; Offering a Picture Service that delivers nearly 1,000 photos a week; *Library*

Calgary Bureau
#700, 100 - 4th Ave. SW, Calgary AB T2P 3N2
Tel: 403-233-7004; *Fax:* 403-262-7520

Edmonton Bureau
#504, 10109 - 106 St. NW, Edmonton AB T5J 3L7
Tel: 780-428-6107; *Fax:* 780-428-0663
www.thecanadianpress.com

Fredericton Bureau
Press Gallery, PO Box 6000, 96 St. John St., Fredericton NB E3B 5H1
Tel: 506-458-5785; *Fax:* 506-457-9708

Halifax Bureau
#701, 1888 Brunswick St., Halifax NS B3J 2L4
Tel: 902-422-8496; *Fax:* 902-425-2675

Montréal Bureau
#100, 215, rue St-Jacques, Montréal QC H2Y 1M6
Tél: 514-849-3212; *Téléc:* 514-282-6915

Ottawa Bureau
PO Box 595, Stn. B, Ottawa ON K1P 5P7
Tel: 613-236-4122; *Fax:* 613-238-4452

Québec Bureau
#2.43, 1050, des Parlementaires, Québec QC G1R 5J1
Tel: 418-646-5377; *Fax:* 418-523-9686

Regina Bureau
#335, Press Gallery, Legislative Bldg., Regina SK S4S 0B3
Tel: 306-585-1011; *Fax:* 306-585-1027

St. John's Bureau
The Fortis Bldg., PO Box 5951, #901, 139 Water St., St. John's NL A1C 5X4
Tel: 709-576-0687; *Fax:* 709-576-0049

Vancouver Bureau
#250, 840 Howe St., Vancouver BC V6Z 2L2
Tel: 604-687-1662; *Fax:* 604-687-5040

Victoria Bureau
#350, Press Gallery, Legislative Building, Victoria BC V8V 1X4
Tel: 250-384-4912; *Fax:* 250-356-9597

Washington Bureau
National Press Bldg., 1100 - 13th St. NW, Washington DC 20005 USA
Tel: 202-641-9734

Winnipeg Bureau
#101, 386 Broadway Ave., Winnipeg MB R3C 3R6
Tel: 204-988-1780; *Fax:* 204-942-4788

Canadian Printable Electronics Industry Association (CPEIA)
170 Cheyenne Way, Ottawa ON K2J 5S6
Tel: 613-795-8181
cpeia-acei.ca
www.linkedin.com/company/canadian-printable-electronics-industry-assoc
twitter.com/CPEIA_ACEI
Overview: A medium-sized national organization founded in 2014
Mission: The Canadian Printable Electronics Industry Association (CPEIA) connects key Canadian and international players in industry, academia and government to build a strong Canadian PE sector.
Chief Officer(s):
Peter Kallai, Executive Director
pkallai@cpeia-acei.ca
Leo Valiquette, Director, Marketing and Communications
Membership: *Fees:* $50 students; $l00 indivuduals; $250 universities; $500 multinationals

Canadian Printing Industries Association (CPIA) / Association canadienne de l'imprimerie (ACI)
#1110, 151 Slater St., Ottawa ON K1P 5H3
Tel: 613-236-7208; *Fax:* 613-232-1334
Toll-Free: 800-267-7280
info@cpia-aci.ca
www.cpia-aci.ca
www.linkedin.com/company/canadian-printing-industries-association
Previous Name: Graphic Arts Industries Association; Canadian Printing & Imaging Association
Overview: A medium-sized national organization founded in 1939
Mission: To advance the quality of management in the printing & allied trades; to offer services through a network of local & related organizations including representations to various sectors; to enhance the image & profile of the industry
Affliation(s): Printing Industries of America
Chief Officer(s):
Anateresa Mendes-Collins, Executive Assistant
anateresa@cpia-aci.ca
Bob Elliott, President
belliott@cpia-aci.ca
Jamie Barbieri, Secretary-Treasurer
james.barbieri@groupepdi.com
Finances: *Annual Operating Budget:* $250,000-$500,000; *Funding Sources:* Membership dues
Staff Member(s): 2; 25 volunteer(s)

Membership: 300; *Member Profile:* Owners/senior executives of companies in pre-press, press, bindery & allied industries; *Committees:* Government Affairs; Membership
Activities: *Library*

Canadian Printing Ink Manufacturers' Association (CPIMA)
ON
Tel: 905-665-9310; *Fax:* 647-439-1572
www.cpima.org
Overview: A medium-sized national organization founded in 1932
Mission: To exchange information that will be of benefit to members, the ink industry, & the printing industry
Affliation(s): Society of British Ink Manufacturers; National Association of Printing Ink Manufacturers; Oil & Colour Chemists Organization of Ontario; International Paint & Printing Ink Council; Radtech International North America
Chief Officer(s):
Steve Marshall, President
Michelle Connolly, Executive Director
mconnolly@cpima.org
Finances: *Funding Sources:* Membership dues
Staff Member(s): 1
Membership: 6; *Member Profile:* Canadian ink manufacturers
Awards:
• The Jim Glynn Award (Award)
Publications:
• Canadian Printing Ink Manufacturers Association Technical Bulletins
Type: Newsletter; *Frequency:* Irregular
Profile: Topics include environmental issues, printing inks & food packaging, scrap ink, & UV inks health & saftey

Canadian Private Copying Collective (CPCC)
#403, 150 Eglinton Ave. East, Toronto ON M4P 1E8
Tel: 416-486-6832; *Fax:* 416-486-3064
Toll-Free: 800-892-7235
inquiries@cpcc.ca
www.cpcc.ca
Overview: A medium-sized national organization founded in 1999
Mission: To collect & distribute private copying royalties through a levy system on blank CDs, cassettes and minidiscs
Chief Officer(s):
Anna Bucci, Executive Director
abucci@cpcc.ca
Membership: *Member Profile:* Songwriters; recording artists; music publishers; record companies

Canadian Process Control Association (CPCA)
#25, 1250 Marlborough Ct., Oakville ON L6H 2W7
Tel: 905-844-6822; *Fax:* 905-901-9913
cpca@cpca-assoc.com
www.cpca-assoc.com
Previous Name: Industrial Instrument Manufacturers Association
Overview: A medium-sized national organization
Mission: To promote the industry & its members to customers, academia, & public bodies; To provide a forum to exchange technical, industry, & regulatory information; To develop industry statistics; To encourage professional & ethical behaviour & quality standards among members
Chief Officer(s):
Peter Dello, President, 905-670-2266
Membership: 51 corporate; *Fees:* Schedule available

Canadian Produce Marketing Association (CPMA) / Association canadienne de la distribution de fruits et légumes
162 Cleopatra Dr., Ottawa ON K2G 5X2
Tel: 613-226-4187; *Fax:* 613-226-2984
question@cpma.ca
www.cpma.ca
Previous Name: Canadian Fruit Wholesalers Association
Overview: A medium-sized national organization founded in 1924
Mission: To increase the market for fresh fruits & vegetables in Canada, by encouraging cooperation & information exchange in all segments, at the domestic & international level
Affliation(s): Canadian Horticultural Council
Chief Officer(s):
Jim DiMenna, Chair
Ron Lemaire, President
Finances: *Annual Operating Budget:* $1.5 Million-$3 Million; *Funding Sources:* Membership dues; Convention
Staff Member(s): 13; 40 volunteer(s)
Membership: 680; *Fees:* $1,139.25 active; $924 associate; $598.50 branch; *Member Profile:* Retailers, wholesalers, brokers, shippers, food service operators, carriers of fresh fruits & vegetables; *Committees:* Grower/Shipper; Marketing; Member services; NA Trade Task Force; Retail/Foodservice Marketing
Activities: *Library*
Meetings/Conferences: • Canadian Produce Marketing Association 2015 90th Annual Convention & Trade Show, April, 2015, Palais des congrès de Montréal, Montréal, QC
Scope: International
Attendance: 2,700
Description: Featuring business sessions, a trade show, a keynote speaker, & awards
Contact Information: Senior Manager, Convention & Trade Show: Carole Brault, CMP, Phone: 613-226-4187, ext. 219; E-mail: cbrault@cpma.ca; Manager, Trade Show & Events: Natalia Kaliberda, Phone: 613-226-4187, ext. 223; E-mail: nkaliberda@cpma.ca
• Canadian Produce Marketing Association 2016 91st Annual Convention & Trade Show, 2016
Scope: International
Description: Featuring business sessions, a trade show, a keynote speaker, & awards

Canadian Professional DJ Association Inc. (CPDJA)
PO Box 300, 3007 Kingston Rd., Toronto ON M1M 1P1
Tel: 416-234-2299; *Fax:* 866-964-2299
Toll-Free: 866-964-2299
www.cpdja.org
Previous Name: Canadian Association of Mobile Entertainers & Operators (CAMEO)
Overview: A small national organization
Mission: To provide benefits & programs to DJ Industry professionals at competitive rates & to provide a forum for these professionals to network & share information, mutual concerns & techniques
Chief Officer(s):
Dennis Hampson, Contact
dhampson@cpdja.ca
Membership: *Fees:* $64.95 general; $259 allied; $325 primary; $375 professional; *Member Profile:* DJs/KJs; Industry suppliers & retailers
Activities: Training; networking; promotion; service; information; dj directory;

Canadian Professional Golfers' Association *See* Professional Golfers' Association of Canada

Canadian Professional Sales Association (CPSA) / Association canadienne des professionnels de la vente
#400, 655 Bay St., Toronto ON M5G 2K4
Tel: 416-408-2685; *Fax:* 416-408-2684
Toll-Free: 888-267-2772
Other Communication: salessuccess@cpsa.com
customerservice@cpsa.com
www.cpsa.com
www.linkedin.com/groups?gid=1589497
www.facebook.com/CanadianProfessionalSalesAssociation
twitter.com/cpsa
Overview: A large national organization founded in 1874
Mission: To develop & serve sales professionals
Chief Officer(s):
Bob Medland, Chair
Harvey Copeman, CSP, President & CEO
Sylvain Tousignant, Vice-Chair
Ian Macdonald, Treasurer
Finances: *Funding Sources:* Membership fees
Membership: 30,000; *Fees:* $129 annual membership fee + $25 one-time administration fee; *Member Profile:* Sales & marketing professionals from throughout Canada; Students enrolled in a full-time sales or marketing program or in the continuing education division at a college or university recognized by the association
Activities: Providing sales training programs; Offering networking opportunities
Awards:
• CPSA Travel Awards (Award)
• C.H. Barnes Award (Award)
• Sales Excellence Award (Award)
Publications:
• Contact
Type: Magazine
• Sales Connexion
Type: Newsletter; *Frequency:* Biweekly; *Accepts Advertising*
Profile: Sales news, articles, tips, & job postings

Canadian Progress Charitable Foundation (CPCF)
c/o Canadian Progress Club, #143, 75 Lavinia St., New Glasgow NS B2H 1N5
Fax: 888-337-9826
Toll-Free: 877-944-4726
info@progressclub.ca
www.progressclub.ca
Overview: A small national charitable organization founded in 1968
Mission: To assist the Canadian Special Olympics
Member of: Canadian Progress Club
Chief Officer(s):
Michele Russell, President

Canadian Progress Club / Club progrès du Canada
#143, 75 Lavinia St., New Glasgow NS B2H 1N5
Fax: 888-337-9826
Toll-Free: 877-944-4726
info@progressclub.ca
www.progressclub.ca
twitter.com/ProgressClub
Overview: A medium-sized national charitable organization founded in 1922
Mission: To assist those in need as well as creating & preserving a spirit of friendship that is sincere; to advance the best interests of the community in which that club is located.
Chief Officer(s):
Juanita Soutar, National President
juanitasoutar@hotmail.com
Jana Cleary, National Business Administrator
jana.cleary@progressclub.ca
Membership: 600 individuals in 30 clubs; *Member Profile:* Open to both men & women wishing to assist within their community

Alberta North Zone
PO Box 183, St Albert AB T8N 1N3
Tel: 780-491-3501; *Fax:* 780-460-6697
www.progressclubab.ca
Chief Officer(s):
Carol Fergusson, Zone Director

Halifax Cornwallis
PO Box 31170, Halifax NS B3K 5Y1
Tel: 902-454-2971
club@cpchalifaxcornwallis.ca
www.cpchalifaxcornwallis.ca
www.linkedin.com/company/canadian-progress-club-halifax-cornwallis
www.facebook.com/CanadianProgressClubHalifaxCornwallis

Stampede City
125 Inglewood Grove SE, Calgary AB T2G 5R4
Tel: 403-282-1400; *Fax:* 403-338-1197
bullshooters@telus.net
www.stampedecityprogressclub.com

Canadian Propane Association (CPA) / Association canadienne du propane (ACP)
#616, 130 Albert St., Ottawa ON K1P 5G4
Tel: 613-683-2270; *Fax:* 613-683-2279
info@propane.ca
www.propane.ca
www.linkedin.com/groups/Canadian-Propane-Association-4355062
twitter.com/Propanedotca
Merged from: Propane Gas Association of Canada Inc.; Ontario Propane Association
Overview: A medium-sized national licensing organization founded in 2011
Mission: To act as the national voice of the Canadian propane industry; To supports its members in the development of a safe, environmentally responsible Canadian propane industry
Affliation(s): Propane Training Institute (PTI), a division of the CPA; Liquefied Petroleum Gas Emergency Response Corporation, a wholly owned subsidiary of the CPA
Chief Officer(s):
Andrea Labelle, General Manager & Director, Marketing
Steven Sparling, Chair
Allison Mallette, Director, Communications, 647-340-2208
allisonmallette@propane.ca
Peter Maddox, Regional Manager, Ontario, 416-903-8518
petermaddox@propane.ca
Finances: *Annual Operating Budget:* $1.5 Million-$3 Million; *Funding Sources:* Membership dues
Staff Member(s): 15
Membership: 380+; *Fees:* Schedule available; *Member Profile:* Producers; Wholesalers; Retailers; Transporters; Manufacturers

of appliances, cylinders, & equipment; Associates; *Committees:* Transportation; Environment; Marketing; Codes & Standards
Activities: Providing industry related training & emergency response; Promoting the interests of the industry; Engaging in regulatory relations; *Internships:* Yes
Meetings/Conferences: • Canadian Propane Association (CPC) 2015 Leadership Summit, 2015
Scope: National
Description: The summit provides the opportunity for leaders in the propane industy to share ideas & knowledge among each other
Publications:
• CPA Bulletin
Type: Newsletter; *Frequency:* Bimonthly
Profile: For members
• CPA Newsletter
Type: Newsletter; *Frequency:* Monthly
Profile: For members

Calgary Office
#800, 717 - 7th Ave. SW, Calgary AB T2P 0Z3
Tel: 403-543-6518; *Fax:* 403-543-6508
Toll-Free: 877-784-4636
training@propane.ca
www.propane.ca
Chief Officer(s):
Spencer Buckland, Vice-President & General Manager, 403-543-6090

Canadian Property Tax Association, Inc. (CPTA) / Association canadienne de taxe foncière, inc

#225, 6 Lansing Sq., Toronto ON M2J 1T5
Tel: 416-493-3276; *Fax:* 416-493-3905
www.cpta.org
Overview: A medium-sized national organization founded in 1967
Mission: To facilitate the exchange of information about industrial & commercial property tax issues throughout Canada
Chief Officer(s):
Brian K. Dell, President, 403-290-1601
bdell@wilcraft.com
Giselle Kakamousias, Executive Vice-President, 902-429-1811
gkakamousias@turnerdrake.com
Monica Keller, Vice-President, Administration, 403-237-1189
mkeller@talisman-energy.com
Louise Boutin, Vice-President, Communication, 514-282-7819
louise.boutin@lkd.ca
Viviane Marcotte, Managing Director, 416-493-3276
cpta@on.aibn.com
Membership: *Fees:* $415 first member; $205 second member; $100 retired member; *Member Profile:* Canadian corporate property companies, associations, tax officers, tax consultants, lawyers, & government officials
Activities: Studying legislation & making representations to government; Providing networking opportunities; *Library:* Canadian Property Tax Association Resource Library
Publications:
• Canadian Property Tax Association, Inc. Membership Directory
Type: Directory; *Frequency:* Annually; *Price:* Free with membership
Profile: Listing of Canadian Property Tax Association members, member companies, chapter executives, directors, & assessment offices
• Canadian Property Tax Association, Inc. Communications Update
Type: Newsletter; *Frequency:* Bimonthly; *Price:* Free withmembership
Profile: Chapter information, upcoming meetings, articles on current tax & assessment issues, new legislation & developments, & provincial case listings
• Tax Practices Across Canada & Appeals Procedures Manual
Type: Manual; *Frequency:* Annually; *Price:* Free with membership
Profile: Outline of procedures & tax practices in each province

Canadian Psychiatric Association (CPA) / Association des psychiatres du Canada

#701, 141 Laurier Ave. West, Ottawa ON K1P 5J3
Tel: 613-234-2815; *Fax:* 613-234-9857
Toll-Free: 800-267-1555
cpa@cpa-apc.org
www.cpa-apc.org
Overview: A medium-sized national organization founded in 1951
Mission: To forge a strong, collective voice for Canadian psychiatrists & to promote an environment that fosters excellence in the provision of clinical care, education & research
Affiliation(s): Canadian Medical Association; World Psychiatric Association
Chief Officer(s):
Ted Callanan, Sec.-Treas.
Alex Saunders, CEO
Finances: *Annual Operating Budget:* $1.5 Million-$3 Million; *Funding Sources:* Membership; government; industry; subscriptions
Staff Member(s): 22
Membership: 4,000; *Fees:* $469.50 active; $32.25 member-in-training; $156.50 associate/affiliate; $225.25 international; *Member Profile:* Members in following psychiatric practice interests: admin. psychiatry, adolescent/young adult psychiatry, affective disorders, alcohol & substance abuse disorder, psychoanalysis/psychodynamic therapy, anxiety disorder, attention deficit disorder, behaviorial & cognitive therapy, biological psychiatry, child abuse, conjoint therapy, community psychiatry, consultation-liaison, chronic care, chronic pain, development/learning disabilities, dissociative disorders, eating disorders, education, emergency & crisis intervention, epidemiology, family therapy, forensic psychiatry, gender disorders, general psychiatry, geriatric psychiatry, hospital psychiatry, infant/child psychiatry, inpatient/outpatient, marital & divorce therapy, mental retardation, mood disorders, occupational therapy, etc.; *Committees:* Education; Economics; Professional Standards & Practice; Provinces; Scientific & Research
Activities: Public Information Office responds to media & public information requests, & refers inquiries to member psychiatrists with interests &/or expertise in a specific area; Service Bureau provides a variety of administrative, financial, publishing & communication services to affiliated psychiatric organizations on a contract basis; CPA sponsors lectures & conference speakers; online access to electronic mail system, online conferencing, CPA bylaws, position & policy papers, calendar of events & publications; *Awareness Events:* Mental Illness Awareness Week, 2nd week of Oct.
Meetings/Conferences: • Canadian Psychiatric Association 65th Annual Conference / 65e Conférence annuelle de l'Association des psychiatres du Canada, October, 2015, The Fairmont Hotel Vancouver, Vancouver, BC
Scope: National
Attendance: 1200+
Contact Information: E-mail: conference@cpa-apc.org
• Canadian Psychiatric Association 66th Annual Conference / 66e Conférence annuelle de l'Association des psychiatres du Canada, September, 2016, The Westin Harbour Castle, Toronto, ON
Scope: National
Attendance: 1200+
Contact Information: E-mail: conference@cpa-apc.org
• Canadian Psychiatric Association 67th Annual Conference / 67e Conférence annuelle de l'Association des psychiatres du Canada, September, 2017, The Ottawa Convention Centre, Ottawa, ON
Scope: National
Attendance: 1200+
Contact Information: E-mail: conference@cpa-apc.org
• Canadian Psychiatric Association 68th Annual Conference / 68e Conférence annuelle de l'Association des psychiatres du Canada, September, 2018, The Westin Harbour Castle, Toronto, ON
Scope: National
Attendance: 1200+
Contact Information: E-mail: conference@cpa-apc.org

Canadian Psychiatric Research Foundation (CPRF) / Fondation canadienne de recherche en psychiatrie (FCRP)

#500, 2 Toronto St., Toronto ON M5C 2B6
Tel: 416-351-7757; *Fax:* 416-351-7765
Toll-Free: 800-915-2773
admin@healthymindscanada.ca
healthymindscanada.ca
www.facebook.com/healthymindscanada
twitter.com/Healthy_Minds
Also Known As: Healthy Minds Canada
Overview: A small national charitable organization founded in 1980
Mission: To discover better treatments & cures for mental illness & addiction, by funding mental health & addiction research to improve the health of Canadians
Chief Officer(s):
Katie W. Robinette, Executive Director, 416-351-7757 Ext. 24
Andrea Swinton, Director, Fund Development & Marketing
aswinton@cprf.ca
Finances: *Funding Sources:* Donations; Fundraising
Membership: 1,000-4,999
Activities: Funding research projects at universities & teaching hospitals throughout Canada; Advocating for mental health & addiction research investment;
Publications:
• Canadian Psychiatric Research Foundation Annual Report
Type: Yearbook; *Frequency:* Annually
• Today
Type: Newsletter; *Frequency:* Semiannually
Profile: News, articles, research, fundraising, & events
• When Something's Wrong: Ideas for Families
Type: Handbook
Profile: For parents & caregivers to help children
• When Something's Wrong: Strategies for the Workplace
Type: Handbook
Profile: For employers, human resource personnel, managers, disability management providers, occupational health & safety personnel, union representatives, & employees
• When Something's Wrong: Strategies for Teachers
Type: Handbook
Profile: For elementary & secondary school teachers & administrators

Canadian Psychoanalytic Society (CPS) / Société canadienne de psychanalyse (SCP)

7000 Côte-des-Neiges Chemin, Montréal QC H3S 2C1
Tel: 514-738-6105
www.psychoanalysis.ca
Overview: A small national licensing organization founded in 1967
Affiliation(s): International Psychoanalytic Association
Chief Officer(s):
Andrew Brook, President
Activities: Conferences; workshops & meetings; *Library:* CPS Library
Awards:
• Douglas Levin Essay Prize (Award)
Amount: Awarded biennially to candidates of the CPS branches
• Miguel Prados Essay Prize (Award)
Amount: Awarded biennially to members of the CPS
• Citation of Merit (Award)
Amount: Recognizes distinguished & enduring contributions by members to the profession of psychoanalysis

CPS Western Canadian Branch
c/o Nancy Briones, 7755 Yukon St., Vancouver BC V5X 2Y4
e-mail: info1@wbcps.org
www.wbcps.org
Chief Officer(s):
David Heilbrunn, President

Ottawa Psychoanalytic Society
c/o Somerset Psychologists, #201, 125 Somerset St. West, Ottawa ON K2P 0H7
Tel: 613-236-5608
contact@ottawaps.ca
ottawaps.ca
www.facebook.com/OttawaPsychoanalyticSociety
Chief Officer(s):
Arthur Leonoff, Director

Québec English Branch
7000, ch Côte des Neiges, Montréal QC H3S 2C1
Tel: 514-342-7444; *Fax:* 514-342-1062
cpsqeb@qc.aira.com
www.psychoanalysismontreal.com
Chief Officer(s):
Erica Robertson, President

Société psychanalytique de Montréal
7000, ch de la Côte-des-Neiges, Montréal QC H3S 2C1
Tél: 514-342-5208; *Téléc:* 514-342-9990
spsymtl@qc.aira.com
www.psychanalysemontreal.org
Chief Officer(s):
Louis Brunet, Président

Société psychanalytique de Québec
1180, rue Charles-Albanel, Sainte-Foy QC G1X 4T9
Tél: 418-877-8445; *Téléc:* 418-877-7056
info@spq-scp.ca
www.spq-scp.ca

South Western Ontario Psychoanalytic Society
London ON

Toronto Psychoanalytic Society
#203, 40 St. Clair Ave. East, Toronto ON M4T 1M9

Tel: 416-922-7770; Fax: 416-922-9988
torontopsychoanalysis.com
www.facebook.com/TorontoPsychoanalyticSociety
Chief Officer(s):
Rukhsana Bukhari, President

Canadian Psychological Association (CPA) / Société canadienne de psychologie (SCP)
#702, 141 Laurier Ave. West, Ottawa ON K1P 5J3
Tel: 613-237-2144; *Fax:* 613-237-1674
Toll-Free: 888-472-0657
cpa@cpa.ca
www.cpa.ca
www.linkedin.com/groups?about=&gid=3766289&trk=anet_ug_grppro
www.facebook.com/group.php?gid=146082642130174
twitter.com/CPA_SCP
www.youtube.com/user/CPAVideoChannel
Overview: A medium-sized national organization founded in 1939
Mission: To improve the health & welfare of Canadians by promoting psychological research, education, & practice
Affiliation(s): Canadian Register of Health Service Providers in Psychology; Council of Provincial Associations of Psychologists; International Union of Psychological Science; Canadian Federation for the Humanities & Social Sciences
Chief Officer(s):
Karen R. Cohen, Chief Executive Officer, 613-237-2144 Ext. 323
executiveoffice@cpa.ca
David Dozois, President
executiveoffice@cpa.ca
Phil Bolger, Chief Financial Officer, 613-237-2144 Ext. 329
pbolger@cpa.ca
John Service, Director, Practice Directorate, 613-237-2144 Ext. 336
Melissa Tiessen, Registrar & Director, Education Directorate, 613-237-2144 Ext. 333
Finances: *Annual Operating Budget:* Less than $50,000; *Funding Sources:* Membership dues; Government grants
Staff Member(s): 17
Membership: 5,000-14,999; *Member Profile:* Individuals with a masters or doctoral degree in psychology; Students enrolled in psychology or a related field; Foreign affiliates & special affiliates; retired members & fellows; *Committees:* Audit; By-laws, Rules & Procedures; Canadian National Committee for the International Union of Psychological Science; Convention; Education & Training; Elections; Ethics; Fellows & Awards; Finance; International Relations; Membership; Nominations; Past Presidents; Professional Affairs Committee; Public Policy; Publications; Scientific Affairs; Sections
Activities: Promoting the development & dissemination of psychological knowledge; Providing services to members; Advocating for psychology; Providing continuing education opportunities; *Awareness Events:* Mental Illness Awareness Week; *Rents Mailing List:* Yes
Meetings/Conferences: • Canadian Psychological Association 2015 76th Annual Convention, June, 2015, Westin Ottawa, Ottawa, ON
Scope: National
Description: An educational conference & exhibition
Contact Information: E-mail: convention@cpa.ca
• Canadian Psychological Association 2016 77th Annual Convention, June, 2016, Victoria Conference Centre & The Fairmont Empress Hotel, Victoria, BC
Scope: National
Description: An educational conference & exhibition
Contact Information: E-mail: convention@cpa.ca
Publications:
• Canadian Journal of Behavioural Science / La revue canadienne des sciences du comportement
Type: Journal; *Frequency:* Quarterly; *Accepts Advertising*; *Editor:* Todd Morrison; *Price:* $119 + GST/HST individuals in Canada; $289.00 + GST/HSTinstitutions in Canada
Profile: Original, empirical articles in the following areas of psychology:abnormal, behavioural, community, counselling, educational, environmental, developmental, health, industrial-organizational, clinical neuropsychological, personality, psychometrics, & social
• The Canadian Journal of Experimental Psychology
Type: Journal; *Frequency:* Quarterly; *Accepts Advertising*; *Editor:* Doug J. Mewhort *ISSN:* 0008-4255; *Price:* $119 + GST/HST individuals in Canada; $289.00 + GST/HST institutions in Canada
Profile: A journal of original research papers from the field of experimental psychology, published in partnershipwith the American Psychological Association
• Canadian Psychology
Type: Journal; *Frequency:* Quarterly; *Accepts Advertising*; *Editor:* Martin Drapeau, Ph.D.; *Price:* $119 + GST/HST individuals in Canada; $289.00 + GST/HST institutions inCanada
Profile: Generalist articles in areas of theory, research, & practice
• CPA [Canadian Psychological Association] News
Type: Newsletter; *Price:* Free with membership in the Canadian Psycological Association
Profile: Current information for members
• Psynopsis: Canada's Psychology Magazine
Type: Magazine; *Frequency:* Quarterly; *Accepts Advertising*; *Editor:* Karen R. Cohen *ISSN:* 1187-11809
Profile: Articles of interest to scientists, educators, & practitioners in psychology

Canadian Public Health Association (CPHA) / Association canadienne de santé publique (ACSP)
#300, 1565 Carling Ave., Ottawa ON K1Z 8R1
Tel: 613-725-3769; *Fax:* 613-725-9826
info@cpha.ca
www.cpha.ca
www.facebook.com/group.php?gid=159289860285?ref
twitter.com/CPHA_ACSP
Overview: A large national charitable organization founded in 1910
Mission: To represent public health in Canada; To support universal & equitable access to the necessary conditions to achieve health for all Canadians; To provide links to the international public health community
Affliation(s): World Health Organization; World Federation of Public Health Associations
Chief Officer(s):
Debra Lynkowski, Chief Executive Officer
Erica Di Ruggiero, Chair
James Chauvin, Director, Policy Development, 613-725-3769 Ext. 160
Ian Culbert, Director, Communications & Development, 613-725-3769 Ext. 142
Greg Penney, Director, Public Health Knowledge Centre, 613-725-3769 Ext. 150
Sarah Pettenuzzo, Manager, Conferences, 613-725-3769 Ext. 153
Finances: *Funding Sources:* Membership fees; Donations
Membership: 2,000; *Fees:* $88 students, retired persons, & low income individuals; $107 international students; $185 regular members; $200 regular international members; *Member Profile:* Individuals who support Canadian Public Health Association objectives, & who are engaged or interested in community or public health activities, such as professionals in public health practice, researchers, professors, & government workers
Activities: Advising decision-makers about public health system reform; Liaising with provincial & territorial public health associations & national & international agencies & organizations; Publishing & disseminating research results; *Speaker Service:* Yes
Awards:
• Aventis Pasteur International Award (Award)
• Ron Draper Health Promotion Award (Award)
• Certificate of Merit (Award)
• Student Award (Award)
• Honorary Life Membership (Award)
Awarded for exceptional excellence as an educator, researcher or practitioner in the field of public health, as demonstrated by achievements, valuable & outstanding research or distinguished service in the advancement of public health knowledge & practice
• R.D. Defries Award (Award)
The highest honour granted by the association; presented to the CPHA members who have made outstanding contributions in the broad field of public health; preference is given to Canadian contributions & individuals who have substantially supported the objectives of the association; the award carries with it an honorary life membership
• Janssen-Ortho Inc. Award (Award)
Presented to the candidate who has significantly advanced the cause, legitimized & stressed the responsibility & state of the art of public health
Meetings/Conferences: • Canadian Public Health Association 2015 Conference, May, 2015, Vancouver, BC
Scope: National
Description: A conference for policy-makers, researchers, environmental health professionals, academics, & students from across Canada
Contact Information: Conference Manager: Sarah Pettenuzzo, Phone: 613-725-3769, ext. 153; Conference Officer: Julie Paquette, Phone: 613-725-3769, ext. 126
• Canadian Public Health Association 2016 Conference, June, 2016, Toronto, ON
Scope: National
Description: A conference for policy-makers, researchers, environmental health professionals, academics, & students from across Canada
Contact Information: Conference Manager: Sarah Pettenuzzo, Phone: 613-725-3769, ext. 153; Conference Officer: Julie Paquette, Phone: 613-725-3769, ext. 126
• Canadian Public Health Association 2017 Conference, June, 2017, Ottawa, ON
Scope: National
Description: A conference for policy-makers, researchers, environmental health professionals, academics, & students from across Canada
Contact Information: Conference Manager: Sarah Pettenuzzo, Phone: 613-725-3769, ext. 153; Conference Officer: Julie Paquette, Phone: 613-725-3769, ext. 126
• Canadian Public Health Association 2018 Conference, June, 2018, Halifax, NS
Scope: National
Description: A conference for policy-makers, researchers, environmental health professionals, academics, & students from across Canada
Contact Information: Conference Manager: Sarah Pettenuzzo, Phone: 613-725-3769, ext. 153; Conference Officer: Julie Paquette, Phone: 613-725-3769, ext. 126
Publications:
• The Canadian Journal of Public Health
Type: Journal; *Frequency:* Bimonthly; *Accepts Advertising*; *Editor:* Debra Lynkowski; *Price:* Free with membership in the Canadian Public Health Association
Profile: Articles on public health, including epidemiology, nutrition, family health, environmental health, sexually transmitted diseases, gerontology, behavioural medicine,rural health, health promotion, & public health policy
• Canadian Public Health Association Annual Report
Type: Yearbook; *Frequency:* Annually
• CPHA [Canadian Public Health Association] Health Digest
Frequency: Quarterly; *Editor:* Debra Lynkowski; *ISBN:* 0703-5624; *Price:* Free with membership inthe Canadian Public Health Association
Profile: Incorporates the international newsletter, Partners Around the World, plus articles from across Canada & around the world

Canadian Public Health Association - NB/PEI Branch
NB
e-mail: nbpei.pha@gmail.com
Overview: A small provincial organization founded in 1952 overseen by Canadian Public Health Association
Mission: To maintain & improve the level of personal & community health
Chief Officer(s):
Kathleen Brennan, President
Anne Lebans, Secretary-Treasurer

Canadian Public Health Association - NWT/Nunavut Branch (NTNUPHA)
PO Box 1709, Yellowknife NT X1A 2P3
Overview: A small provincial organization overseen by Canadian Public Health Association
Chief Officer(s):
Faye Stark, President

Canadian Public Personnel Management Association ***See*** International Personnel Management Association - Canada

Canadian Public Relations Society Inc. (CPRS) / La Société canadienne des relations publiques
#346, 4195 Dundas St. West, Toronto ON M8X 1Y4
Tel: 416-239-7034; *Fax:* 416-239-1076
admin@cprs.ca
www.cprs.ca
twitter.com/CPRSNational
Overview: A medium-sized national organization founded in 1948
Mission: To oversee the practice of public relations practitioners in Canada, to ensure the protection of the public interest; To advance the professional stature of public relations practitioners; To promote the ethical practice of public relations & communications management
Chief Officer(s):

Karen Dalton, Executive Director
kdalton@cprs.ca
Jorge de Mendonca, Director, Finance & Information Systems
jd@cprs.ca
Monica Simmie, Director, Professional Development & Sponsorship
msimmie@cprs.ca
Elizabeth Tang, Manager, Membership, Communications, & Awards
etang@cprs.ca
Finances: *Funding Sources:* Membership fees; Sponsorships
Membership: 16 member societies; *Fees:* $220 plus GST/HST ($50 one time, new member initiation fee); *Member Profile:* Public relations practitioners in Canada; *Committees:* Audit & Investment; Awards; College of Fellows; Governance; Judicial & Ethics; Measurement; Membership Recruitment & Retention; Nominating; National Conference; Professional Development; Public Relations & Communications; Resource Library
Activities: Offering professional development activities; Communicating through social media (www.facebook.com/group.php?gid=2257458445); *Speaker Service:* Yes; *Library:* Canadian Public Relations Society Resource Library
Meetings/Conferences: • Canadian Public Relations Society / La Société canadienne des relations publiques 2015 National Summit, May, 2015, Montréal, QC
Scope: National
Description: An education conference, with networking opportunities with public relations professionals from across Canada
Contact Information: E-mail: admin@cprs.ca
• Canadian Public Relations Society / La Société canadienne des relations publiques 2016 National Summit, 2016
Scope: National
Description: An education conference, with networking opportunities with public relations professionals from across Canada
Contact Information: E-mail: admin@cprs.ca
Publications:
• Canadian Public Relations Society Annual Report
Type: Yearbook; *Frequency:* Annually
• Education Standard & Curriculum Guide
Type: Guide

CPRS Calgary
PO Box 2081, Stn. M, Calgary AB T2P 2M4
e-mail: communications@cprscalgary.com
www.cprscalgary.org
www.facebook.com/CPRSCalgary
twitter.com/CPRSCalgary
Mission: To represent communications professionals in Calgary, Alberta
Chief Officer(s):
Janice Robertson, President
president@cprscalgary.com
Del Simon, Secretary
secretary@cprscalgary.com
Jennifer Thomlinson, Treasurer
treasurer@cprscalgary.com
• CPRS [Canadian Public Relations Society Inc.] Calgary Annual Report
Type: Yearbook; *Frequency:* Annually
Profile: The society's year in review
• HOTwire [a publication of Canadian Public Relations Society Inc., Calgary]
Type: Newsletter
Profile: CPRS Calgary activities, articles, forthcoming events, award winners
• Independent Consultant Directory [a publication of Canadian Public Relations Society Inc., Calgary]
Type: Directory
Profile: A directory to assist organizations in sourcing public relations & communications expertise in Calgary

CPRS Edmonton
Edmonton AB
e-mail: communications@cprsedmonton.ca
www.cprsedmonton.ca
www.facebook.com/CPRSEdmonton
twitter.com/cprsedmonton
Mission: To advance the practice of ethical & effective public relations
Chief Officer(s):
Dan Vankeeken, President
president@cprsedmonton.ca
Tamara Vineberg, Secretary
secretary@cprsedmonton.ca
Jan Martin, Treasurer
treasurer@cprsedmonton.ca
Kelly Bowman, Co-Chair, Communications
communications@cprsedmonton.ca
Crystal Komanchuk, Co-Chair, Communications
communicationscochair@cprsedmonton.ca
• Consultants' Directory [a publication of the Canadian Public Relations Society Inc., Edmonton]
Type: Directory
Profile: A directory of public relations services
• PR Edmonton
Type: Newsletter; *Frequency:* Monthly
Profile: CPRS Edmonton board happenings, local news from the public relations field, resources, & case studies

CPRS Hamilton
PO Box 33517, Stn. Dundurn, Hamilton ON L8P 4X4
www.cprs-hamilton.ca
www.linkedin.com/groups?mostPopular&gid=768077
www.facebook.com/CPRSHamilton
twitter.com/CPRSHamilton
Mission: To serve public relations professionals from Hamilton, Halton, Niagara, & Southwestern Ontario; To promote ethical standards of professional practice
Chief Officer(s):
Bob Deans, Co-President
Alex Sévigny, Co-President

CPRS Manitoba
PO Box 441, Stn. Main, Winnipeg MB R3C 2H6
e-mail: info@cprs.mb.ca
www.cprs.mb.ca
www.facebook.com/CPRSManitoba
twitter.com/CPRSManitoba
Mission: To advance the profession of public relations in Manitoba
Chief Officer(s):
Tamara Bodi, President
Julie Kentner, Secretary
Lorne Kletke, Treasurer
• CPRS [Canadian Public Relations Society Inc.] Manitoba Annual Report
Type: Yearbook; *Frequency:* Annually
• Insight [a publication of Canadian Public Relations Society Inc., Manitoba]
Type: Newsletter
Profile: CPRS Manitoba awards, upcoming events, & activities

CPRS New Brunswick
c/o Chris Williams, Department of Energy, #M100, 1 Germain St., Saint John NB E2L 4V1
Tel: 506-738-8064
www.cprs.ca/societies/nb.aspx
Mission: To advance public relations & communications management throughout New Brunswick
Chief Officer(s):
Wayne Knorr, Vice-President, 506-460-2181
wayne.knorr@fredericton.ca
Chris Williams, Chair, Membership
willcomm@nb.sympatico.ca

CPRS Newfoundland & Labrador
St. John's NL
e-mail: cprsnlchapter@gmail.com
cprsnl.wordpress.com
www.facebook.com/CPRSNL
twitter.com/cprs_nl
Mission: To serve public relations & communications specialists in Newfoundland & Labrador
Chief Officer(s):
Sean Kelly, President

CPRS Nova Scotia
PO Box 1544, Halifax NS B3J 2Y3
www.cprs.ca
www.facebook.com/161426570557284
twitter.com/cprsns
Mission: To maintain high standards of practice for the public relations profession
Chief Officer(s):
Tom Peck, President

CPRS Ottawa / Gatineau
c/o Thornley Fallis, #730, 55 Metcalfe St., Ottawa ON K1P 6L5
Tel: 613-231-3355; *Fax:* 613-231-4515
info@cprsottawa.ca
www.cprsottawa.ca
www.linkedin.com/company/cprs-ottawa-gatineau
www.facebook.com/CPRSOttawaGatineau
twitter.com/CPRSOttawaGat
www.youtube.com/user/CPRSOttawaGatineau
Mission: To represent communications specialists from the National Capital Region; To maintain high professional standards
Chief Officer(s):
Léa Werthman, President, 613-286-0619
Natalie Bovair, Director, Accreditation
Stephanie Rochfort, Director, Membership
• VOX
Type: Newsletter; *Frequency:* Bimonthly
Profile: Information about the society's activities in the National Capital Region

CPRS Prince Edward Island
c/o Anna MacDonald, Media Relations Officer, University of PEI, PO Box 16, Mount Stewart PE C0A 1T0
www.cprs.ca/societies/pei.aspx
Mission: To advance the public relations profession in Prince Edward Island
Chief Officer(s):
Anna MacDonald, President
Kathy Maher, Vice-President
Doug Shackell, Secretary-Treasurer
Sheri Ostridge, Chair, Accreditation

CPRS Prince George
c/o Matt Wood, City of Quesnel, 410 Kinchant St., Quesnel BC V2J 7J5
cprsnorthernlights.com
Mission: To serve public relations professionals in the Prince George region of British Columbia
Chief Officer(s):
Alyson Gourley-Cramer, President
g.cramer@telus.net
Christine Finnerty, Vice-President & Co-Chair, Communications
christine.finnerty@redcross.ca
Reneé McCloskey, Secretary-Treasurer
rmccloskey@rdffg.bc.ca
Steve Raper, Co-Chair, Membership
steve.raper@northernhealth.ca
Matt Wood, Co-Chair, Membership, 250-991-7475, Fax: 250-992-2206
mwood@city.quesnel.bc.ca

CPRS Québec
#106, 7255, rue Alexandra, Montréal QC H2R 2Y9
Tél: 514-845-4441; *Téléc:* 514-842-4886
info@srq.qc.ca
www.sqprp.ca
Chief Officer(s):
David Barrett, Coprésident
Émilie Dutil-Bruneau, Coprésidente

CPRS Regina
PO Box 472, Regina SK S4P 3A2
www.cprsregina.sk.ca
www.linkedin.com/groups?gid=4076984
www.facebook.com/CPRSregina
Mission: To advance the professional stature of public relations in Regina, Saskatchewan
Chief Officer(s):
Natalie Tomczak, President
cprsreginapresident@gmail.com
Rose Brewster, Director, Events & Marketing
cprsreginarsvp@gmail.com
Ariane Whiting, Director, Membership
cprsreginamembership@gmail.com

CPRS Toronto
c/o Lois Marsh, CPRS Toronto Secretariat, #1801, 1 Yonge St., Toronto ON M5E 1W7
Tel: 416-360-1988; *Fax:* 416-369-0515
www.cprstoronto.com
Mission: To represent communications professionals in the Toronto area
Chief Officer(s):
Martin Waxman, President, 416-425-9143, Fax: 416-703-2495
Lindsay Peterson, First Vice-President & Contact, Membership, 416-425-9143
Vincent Power, Second Vice-President & Contact, Accreditation, 416-941-4422
Christine Edwardson, Secretary, 416-326-4956
Gerald Crowell, Treasurer
• CPRS [Canadian Public Relations Society Inc.] Toronto Member Directory

Type: Directory
Profile: For CPRS members only
• CPRS [Canadian Public Relations Society Inc.] Toronto Student Directory
Type: Directory
Profile: For CPRS members only
• New Perspective [a publication of the Canadian Public Relations Society Inc.]
Type: Newsletter; *Frequency:* Quarterly; *Accepts Advertising*; *Editor:* M. Martin (mjmartin@primus.ca)
Profile: CPRS Toronto activities, meeting highlights, book reviews, profiles, & articles related to publicrelations

CPRS Vancouver
#102, 211 Columbia St., Vancouver BC V6A 2R5
Tel: 604-633-1433; *Fax:* 604-681-4545
admin@cprsvancouver.com
www.cprsvancouver.com
www.facebook.com/CPRSVancouver
twitter.com/CPRSVancouver
Mission: To serve communications specialists & public relations practitioners in Vancouver; To encourage high professional standards for members
Chief Officer(s):
Regan Lal, President
reganlal@outlook.com
Kurt Heinrich, Vice-President
kheinrich@vsb.bc.ca
Ashley Curammeng, Treasurer
ashley_curammeng@vancity.com
Charlotte Sherry, Chair, Communications
charlotte@peakco.com
Ashley Castellan, Chair, Education
ashleycastellan@gmail.com

CPRS Vancouver Island
c/o Phil Saunders, Communications Officer, Royal Roads University, 2005 Sooke Rd., Victoria BC V9Y 5Y2
e-mail: info@cprs-vi.org
www.cprs-vi.org
www.facebook.com/group.php?gid=5917429578
Mission: To represent public relations professionals & students on Vancouver Island; To advance public relations & communications management
Chief Officer(s):
Dave Traynor, President
president@cprs-vi.org
Michelle May, Secretary
secretary@cprs-vi.org
Erin Kelly, Treasurer
treasurer@cprs-vi.org
Sarah Milner, Chair, Communications
communications@cprs-vi.org
Phil Saunders, Chair, Membership, 250-391-2526
membership@cprs-vi.org
• CPRS-VI [Canadian Public Relations Society Inc. - Vancouver Island] Newsletter
Type: Newsletter
Profile: Information for members, including local issues & coming events

Canadian Public Works Association (CPWA) / Association canadienne des travaux publics

797 Somerset St. West, Ottawa ON K1R 6R3
Tel: 202-408-9541; *Fax:* 202-408-9542
Toll-Free: 800-848-2792
cpwa@cpwa.net
www.cpwa.net
Overview: A medium-sized national organization founded in 1986
Mission: To improve the quality of public works services for Canadian citizens; To share information about public works issues that are unique to Canada
Chief Officer(s):
Darwin K. Durnie, President
Peter King, Executive Director
pking@apwa.net
Gail Clark, Manager, International Affairs
gclark@apwa.net
Brent Colbert, Consultant, Government Relations
bcolbert@tactix.ca
Laura Bynum, Contact, Media Relations
lbynum@apwa.net
Membership: *Member Profile:* Public works employees in Canada who are members of the American Public Works Association; Any person or organization in Canada with an interest in infrastructure & public works issues
Activities: Engaging in advocacy projects; Producing position statements; Facilitating the exchange of information for public works employees

Canadian Publishers' Council (CPC)

#203, 250 Merton St., Toronto ON M4S 1B1
Tel: 416-322-7011; *Fax:* 416-322-6999
www.pubcouncil.ca
Previous Name: Canadian Book Publishers' Council; Canadian Textbook Publishers Institute
Overview: A medium-sized national organization founded in 1910
Mission: To represent the interests of 18 companies who publish books & other media for elementary & secondary schools, colleges & universities, professional & reference, retail & library markets
Member of: Book & Periodical Council; CANARIE; Information Technology Association of Canada; Canadian Library Association; Canadian Booksellers Association; Ontario Library Association
Affliation(s): International Publishers Association
Chief Officer(s):
Jacqueline Hushion, Executive Director, External Relations, 416-322-7011 Ext. 222
jhushion@pubcouncil.ca
Colleen O'Neill, Executive Director, Trade (Consumer) & Higher Education Publishers' Groups, 416-322-7011 Ext. 226
coneill@pubcouncil.ca
Finances: *Funding Sources:* Membership fees; project grants
Staff Member(s): 3
Membership: 18 firms; *Fees:* Schedule available; *Member Profile:* Incorporated in Canada with primary role as book publishing; 5 titles in print & publishing minimum 1 book per year; affiliate - engaged in related activities; honorary - service to Council; associate
Activities: Professional Development Seminar Program; *Library*

Canadian Pulp & Paper Association ***See*** Forest Products Association of Canada

Canadian Pulp & Paper Association - Technical Section ***See*** Pulp & Paper Technical Association of Canada

Canadian Pulp & Paper Network for Innovation in Education & Research; Mechanical Wood-Pulps Network ***See*** Pulp & Paper Centre

Canadian Quarter Horse Association (CQHA)

c/o Sherry Clemens, Secretary, PO Box 2132, Moose Jaw SK S6H 7T2
Tel: 306-692-8393
admin@huntseathorses.com
www.cqha.ca
www.facebook.com/192652444096322
Overview: A small national organization
Mission: To address issues of concern to Canadian owners of American Quarter Horses; to be a communications vehicle for and with Canadian owners of American Quarter Horses; and to promote and market - both globally and within Canada - Canadian-bred and/or Canadian-owned American Quarter Horses.
Affliation(s): American Quarter Horse Association
Chief Officer(s):
Haidee Landry, President
hmqh@hotmail.com
Meetings/Conferences: • Canadian Quarter Horse Association 2015 Annual General Meeting, January, 2015, Holiday Inn, Cambridge, ON
Scope: National

Canadian Quaternary Association / Association canadienne pour l'étude du Quaternaire

c/o Kathryn Hargan, Department of Biology, Queen's University, 116 Barrie St., Kinsgton ON K7L 3N6
Tel: 613-533-6000
www.canqua.com
Also Known As: CANQUA
Overview: A small national organization founded in 1975
Mission: To study & advance knowledge of the quaternary period
Affliation(s): Geological Association of Canada
Chief Officer(s):
Sarah Finkelstein, President, 416-978-5613, Fax: 416-978-3938
finkelstein@es.utoronto.ca
Patrick Lajeunesse, Vice-President, 418-565-2131 Ext. 5879, Fax: 418-656-3960
patrick.lajeunesse@ggr.ulaval.ca
Kathryn Hargan, Secretary-Treasurer, 613-533-6000 Ext. 75143
kathrynhargan@gmail.com
Membership: 150; *Fees:* $0 students; $15 regular members; *Member Profile:* Persons interested in Canadian quaternary studies, such as geographers, geologists, biologists, botanists, archaeologists, & students
Activities: Disseminating information about the quaternary period; Cooperating with other quaternary associations
Awards:
• W.A. Johnston Medal (Award)
To recognize professional excellence in quaternary science
• Aleksis Dreimanis Doctoral Scholarship (Scholarship)
A student prize
• David Proudfoot Award (Award)
Awarded for the best student presentation at the Canadian Quaternary Association biennial meeting
• Guy Lortie Award (Award)
To recognize the best paper presented by a student at the Canadian Quaternary Association biennial meeting
Meetings/Conferences: • Canadian Quaternary Association (CANQUA) 2015 Biennial Meeting, 2015, St. John's, NL
Scope: National
Contact Information: Secretary-Treasurer: Kathryn Hargan, E-mail: kathrynhargan@gmail.com

Canadian Quilt Study Group (CQSG)

www.quilt.com/History/CanadianQuiltStudy.html
Overview: A small national organization founded in 1989
Mission: To encourage & to advance study & research about quiltmakers, quilts & quiltmaking; to promote contemporary quilts & to preserve historical quilts
Finances: *Annual Operating Budget:* Less than $50,000; *Funding Sources:* Membership dues; fundraising
5 volunteer(s)
Membership: 325 representing 10 countries; *Fees:* $15 individual; $20 overseas; $50 guilds; $50 supporting; $250 corporate sponsor; $500 corporate patron

Canadian Quilters' Association (CQA) / Association canadienne de la courtepointe (ACC)

6 Spruce St., Pasadena NL A0L 1K0
e-mail: administration@canadianquilter.com
www.canadianquilter.com
www.facebook.com/canadianquilterassociation
Overview: A medium-sized national organization founded in 1981
Mission: The promotion of a greater understanding, appreciation & knowledge of the art, techniques & heritage of patchwork, appliqué & quilting; the promotion of the highest standards of workmanship & design in both traditional & innovative work the fostering of a climate of cooperation amongst quiltmakers across the country.
Chief Officer(s):
Johanna Alford, President, 902-835-9780
Vivian Kapusta, Secretary/Publicist
Finances: *Annual Operating Budget:* Less than $50,000; *Funding Sources:* Membership dues; fundraising
9 volunteer(s)
Membership: 1,800 individuals; 12 regional contacts; *Fees:* $56.50, 1 yr.; $101.70, 2 yr.
Activities: *Library*
Awards:
• Dorothy McMurdie Award (Award)
• Teacher of the Year (Award)
• Agnes Boal Bursary (Scholarship)
Meetings/Conferences: • Quilt Canada 2015, June, 2015, University of Lethbridge, Lethbridge, AB
Scope: National
Description: National conference

Canadian Race Communications Association (CRCA)

PO Box 307, Shannonville ON K0K 3A0
e-mail: contact@crca1.com
www.crcamarshal.com
www.facebook.com/101660183249507
twitter.com/CRCA_Marshals
Overview: A medium-sized national licensing organization founded in 1959
Mission: To provide corner marshals for all forms of racing events
Chief Officer(s):

Wayne Walsh, President, 613-328-4945
iwwalsh@live.ca
Rick Helman, Treasurer & Director, Recruiting, 613-966-5922
rhelman@loyalistc.on.ca
Membership: *Fees:* $15
Publications:
• The Blue Flag [a publication of Canadian Race Communications Association]
Type: Newsletter; *Frequency:* Quarterly

Canadian Racing Pigeon Union Inc.
#C, 261 Tillson Ave., Tillsonburg ON N4G 5X2
Tel: 519-842-9771; *Fax:* 519-842-8809
Toll-Free: 866-652-5704
crpu@crpu.ca
www.crpu.ca
Overview: A medium-sized national organization founded in 1929
Mission: To promote the sport of pigeon racing in Canada
Affliation(s): Fédération colombophile internationale
Chief Officer(s):
Oscar DeVries, President
oscar@ol-devries.com
Shannon Beadow, Office Manager
shannon@crpu.ca
Staff Member(s): 1
Membership: 1,500; *Fees:* $40

Canadian Racquetball Association *See* Racquetball Canada

Canadian Radiation Protection Association (CRPA) / Association canadienne de radioprotection (ACRP)
PO Box 83, Carleton Place ON K7C 3P3
Tel: 613-253-3779; *Fax:* 888-551-0712
secretariat2007@crpa-acrp.ca
www.crpa-acrp.ca
Overview: A small national organization founded in 1982
Mission: To develop scientific knowledge for protection from the harmful effects of radiation; To encourage research; To assist in the development of professional standards in the discipline
Affliation(s): International Radiation Protection Association (IRPA).
Chief Officer(s):
Lois Sowden-Plunkett, President
lsowden@uottawa.ca
Christine Dehm, Treasurer
christine.dehm@uregina.ca
Membership: *Fees:* $565 corporate members; $140 full or associate members; $25 students; $70 retired; *Member Profile:* Individuals with training who are engaged in the science & practice of radiation protection
Activities: Promoting educational opportunities
Publications:
• CRPA [Canadian Radiation Protection Association] Bulletin
Type: Newsletter; *Frequency:* Quarterly
Profile: For Canadian Radiation Protection Association members only

Canadian Radio Technical Planning Board *See* Radio Advisory Board of Canada

Canadian Railroad Historical Association (CRHA) / Association canadienne d'histoire ferroviaire
110 St-Pierre St., Saint-Constant QC J5A 1G7
Tel: 450-632-2410; *Fax:* 450-638-1563
info@exporail.org
www.exporail.org
www.facebook.com/Exporail
twitter.com/Exporail
Overview: A medium-sized national charitable organization founded in 1932
Mission: To collect, preserve & disseminate information/items relating to the history of railways in Canada
Chief Officer(s):
C. Stephen Cheasley, President
Finances: *Annual Operating Budget:* $1.5 Million-$3 Million
Membership: *Fees:* $50 regular; $110 friend of the museum; *Committees:* Executive; Collection; Membership; Audit
Activities: *Library* by appointment

Calgary & South-Western Division
4515 Dalhart Rd. NW, Calgary AB T3A 1B9
Tel: 403-652-7279
www.exporail.org/en/crha/divisions
Chief Officer(s):
D. Walter Edgar, Vice-President
walter@dweco.com

Charny Division
#103, 5314, av des Belles-Amours, Charny QC G6X 1P2
Tel: 418-832-1502
info@groupe-traq.com
www.groupe-traq.com
Chief Officer(s):
Louis-François Garceau, President

Esquimalt & Nanaimo Division
2414 Dryfe St., Victoria BC V8R 5T2
Tel: 250-514-6497
info@encrha.com
www.encrha.com

Kingston Division
PO Box 1714, Kingston ON K7L 5V5
intercolonialrailway.com/CRHA/
Chief Officer(s):
Douglas Smith, President
DRGsmith@sympatico.ca

New Brunswick Division
2847 Main St., Hillsborough NB E4H 2X7
Tel: 506-734-3195
www.crhanb.ca
Mission: The Canadian Railroad Historical Association (NB Division), known as the CRHA (NB), is New Brunswick's most active railway heritage group with its focus to provide all members of the general public with information regarding all aspects of railway transportation in the Province of New Brunswick and thereby to provide the education, enjoyment and entertainment of the general public
Chief Officer(s):
J.A. Clowes, Contact
clowesja@sympatico.ca

Niagara Division
PO Box 20311, Stn. Grantham, St Catharines ON L2M 7W7
Chief Officer(s):
Andy Panko, Division Representative
apanko@niagara.com

Pacific Coast Division
PO Box 1006, Stn. A, Vancouver BC V6C 2P1
e-mail: railsmith@yahoo.ca

Prince George-Nechako-Fraser Division
PO Box 2408, Prince George BC V2N 2S6
Tel: 250-563-7351
trains@pgrfm.bc.ca

Rideau Valley Division
PO Box 962, 90 William St., Smiths Falls ON K7A 5A5
Tel: 613-283-5696

Selkirk Division
PO Box 2561, 719 Track St. W., Revelstoke BC V0E 2S0
Tel: 250-837-6060
railway@telus.net
www.railwaymuseum.com

Toronto & York Division
43 Marjory Ave., Toronto ON M4M 2Y2
Tel: 416-536-2894
Chief Officer(s):
Paul Bowles, Contact
pbtrainman@aol.com

Canadian Railway & Transit Manufacturers Association *See* Canadian Association of Railway Suppliers

Canadian Railway Club
PO Box 162, Stn. St-Charles, Kirkland QC H9H 0A3
Tel: 514-428-5903; *Fax:* 514-697-6238
cdnrailwayclub.mtl@hotmail.com
canadianrailwayclub.ca
Overview: A small national organization founded in 1902
Chief Officer(s):
Heather McGuire, Administrator
hemcguire@sympatico.ca
Membership: *Fees:* $30; *Member Profile:* Current or retired employees of railway companies; employees that produce railway accessories or services; those associated with railway companies; *Committees:* Executive; Arrangements; Membership & Attendance; Audit; Advertising

Canadian Ready Mixed Concrete Association (CRMCA) / Association canadienne du béton préparé
#3, 365 Brunel Rd., Mississauga ON L4Z 1Z5
Tel: 905-507-1122; *Fax:* 905-890-8122
www.crmca.ca
Previous Name: Canadian Concrete Paving Association
Overview: A medium-sized national organization founded in 1981
Finances: *Funding Sources:* Membership dues
Membership: 10; *Member Profile:* Provincial concrete organizations

The Canadian Real Estate Association (CREA) / Association canadienne de l'immeuble
200 Catherine St., 6th Fl., Ottawa ON K2P 2K9
Tel: 613-237-7111; *Fax:* 613-234-2567
Toll-Free: 800-842-2732
info@crea.ca
www.crea.ca
www.linkedin.com/company/1400987
www.facebook.com/CREA.ACI
www.twitter.com/CREA_ACI
Overview: A large national organization founded in 1943
Mission: To enhance member professionalism, competency & profitability; To advocate government policies which improve the industry's market environment & enhance individual rights with respect to the ownership of real property
Affliation(s): National Association of Realtors; International Real Estate Federation; International Consortium Real Estate Associations
Chief Officer(s):
Gary Simonsen, Chief Executive Officer
aohara@crea.ca
Laura Leyser, President
Beth Crosbie, Vice-President
Finances: *Funding Sources:* Membership dues; Publications
Membership: 90,000 licensed or registered brokers/agents & salespeople in 103 real estate boards, 10 provincial associations & 1 territorial association; *Fees:* $140; *Committees:* Federal Affairs; Audit; Provincial/Territorial Advisory

Canadian Recording Industry Association *See* Music Canada

Canadian Recreation Facilities Council
PO Box 534, Cochrane AB T0C 1C0
Tel: 403-851-7626; *Fax:* 403-851-9181
info@crfc.ca
www.crfc.ca
Overview: A medium-sized national organization
Mission: To encourage full representation from all provinces & territories; to promote facility programs at the provincial/territorial & national levels; to facilitate the exchange of information; to identify & encourage the development of projects & programs of a national interest; to develop & deliver an unified position on issues of a national interest; to strive for financial self-sufficiency
Chief Officer(s):
Larry Golby, Chair
944golby@telus.net
John Milton, Chief Executive Officer
Membership: 15; *Member Profile:* Provincial & Territorial Facility Associations

Canadian Recreational Canoeing Association *See* Paddle Canada

Canadian Recreational Vehicle Association (CRVA) / Association canadienne du véhicule récréatif
110 Freelton Rd., Freelton ON L0R 1K0
www.crva.ca
Overview: A medium-sized national organization founded in 1975
Mission: To promote recreational vehicle lifestyle
Membership: *Fees:* $282.50-$339; *Member Profile:* Manufacturers of RVs & their suppliers

Canadian Recruiters Guild *See* Association of Professional Recruiters of Canada

Canadian Red Angus Promotion Society
PO Box 39075, Lakewood Common SK S7V 0A9
Tel: 306-227-2992; *Fax:* 306-373-3515
office@redangus.ca
www.redangus.ca
Overview: A small national organization founded in 1972
Mission: To promote & advertise Canadian Red Angus cattle
Member of: Canadian Angus Association
Chief Officer(s):
Anson Lewis, President
Finances: *Funding Sources:* Membership dues; fund-raising
Membership: 135; *Committees:* Promotions & Show; Advertising; CCA Liaison; Red Roundup
Activities: Annual Farm Tour; Annual Red Roundup Sale; Red Angus Shows; advertising & promotion

Canadian Red Cross (CRC) / La Société la Croix-Rouge canadienne

170 Metcalfe St., Ottawa ON K2P 2P2
Tel: 613-740-1900; *Fax:* 613-740-1911
Toll-Free: 800-418-1111
Other Communication: shop@redcross.ca (online store inquiries); feedback@redcross.ca
WeCare@redcross.ca
www.redcross.ca
twitter.com/redcrossCanada
Overview: A large international charitable organization founded in 1896
Mission: To help people deal with situations that threaten: their survival & safety, their security & well-being, their human dignity, in Canada & around the world; To improve the lives of vulnerable people by mobilizing the power of humanity
Member of: International Red Cross & Red Crescent Societies
Affliation(s): International Committee of the Red Cross; International Federation of Red Cross & Red Crescent Societies (Geneva)
Chief Officer(s):
Conrad Sauvé, Secretary General & Chief Executive Officer
Claude Tremblay, Chief Financial & Operating Officer
Samuel Schwisberg, General Counsel & Corporate Secretary
Finances: *Funding Sources:* Public donations; United Way; Governments; Corporations
Staff Member(s): 6640; 22,0 volunteer(s)
Membership: 130,000
Activities: Providing international services & field operations, including emergency, water safety, & first aid services; Offering community services, such as veterans' services & home assistance; Violence, abuse & bullying prevention programs & services; International & Canadian disaster preparedness & response; Healthcare programs & services; *Awareness Events:* Red Cross Month, March; World Red Cross Day, May 8; *Library:* National Office Library; by appointment
Publications:
• Be Ready, Be Safe
Type: Booklet; *Number of Pages:* 60; *ISBN:* 978-1-55104-506-1
Profile: An activity booklet for 12 & 13 year old children
• Bug Out Activity Booklet: Get the Facts on Germs
Type: Booklet
Profile: Booklets for ages 6 to 8, 9 to 11, & 12 to 13, plus a family guide for ages 4 to 13
• Bug Out Facilitator Guide: Get the Facts on Germs
Type: Guide
Profile: Booklets for educators & caregivers of children from ages 6 to 8, 9 to 11, & 12 to 13
• Canadian Red Cross Society Annual Report
Type: Yearbook; *Frequency:* Annually
Profile: A review of Canadian & international disaster management, health & homecare services, humanitarian issues, donations, & financial information
• Canadian Red Cross Society: Working to Serve Humanity 2010-2015
Type: Report; *Number of Pages:* 20
Profile: A strategic plan for the future
• Drowning Research: Water Safety Poll
Type: Survey; *ISBN:* 0
Profile: Canadian parents concerned about safety in backyard pools
• Expect the Unexpected Facilitator's Guide
Type: Guide
Profile: Guides for educators using the Emergency Preparedness Program with students aged 7 to 8, 9 to 11, & 12 to 13
• Facing Fear: Helping Young People Deal with Terrorism & Tragic Events
Type: Guide; *ISBN:* 1-55104-277-0
Profile: Booklets with activities & lesson plans for students aged 5 to 7, 8 to 10, 11 to 13, & 14 to 16
• Facing the Unexpected, Be Prepared
Type: Booklet; *Number of Pages:* 44; *ISBN:* 978-1-55104-504-7
Profile: An activity booklet for children ages 10 & 11
• Integrating Emergency Management & High-Risk Populations: Survey Report & Action Recommendations
Type: Report; *Number of Pages:* 58
Profile: Prepared for Public Safety Canada by Canadian Red Cross
• It Can Happen, Be Ready
Type: Booklet; *Number of Pages:* 36; *ISBN:* 978-1-55104-502-3
Profile: An activity booklet for 7 & 8 year old children
• Let's Plan for The Unexpected
Type: Booklet; *Number of Pages:* 52; *ISBN:* 978-1-55104-508-5
Profile: An activity booklet for families
• Social Media During Emergencies
Type: Survey; *ISBN:* 0
Profile: Exploring how to use social media during an emergency
• Survive the Peace: Landmine Education & Community Involvement Guide
Type: Guide; *Number of Pages:* 54
Profile: Background information about the landmine crisis, learning activities, & ways to take action
• Your Emergency Preparedness Guide
Type: Guide; *Number of Pages:* 36
Profile: A publication from Public Safety Canada, in collaboration with the Canadian Red Cross, the Canadian Association of Chiefs of Police, the Canadian Association of Fire Chiefs, St. JohnAmbulance, & The Salvation Army, available in print, audio, Braille, large print, diskette, & CD

Atlantic Zone Office
Burnside Industrial Park, 133 Troop Ave., Dartmouth NS B3B 2A7
Tel: 902-423-3680; *Fax:* 902-422-6247

Division du Québec
6, place du Commerce, Verdun QC H3E 1P4
Tél: 514-362-2930; *Téléc:* 514-362-9991
Chief Officer(s):
Michel Léveillé, Directeur

Ontario Zone Office
5700 Cancross Ct., Mississauga ON L5R 3E9
Tel: 905-890-1000; *Fax:* 905-890-1008

Western Zone Office
#100, 1305 - 11 Ave. SW, Calgary AB T3C 3P6
Tel: 403-541-6100; *Fax:* 403-541-6129

Canadian Red Cross - Blood Services *See* Canadian Blood Services

Canadian Red Poll Cattle Association / Société Canadienne des Bovins Red Poll

2417 Holly Lane, Ottawa ON K1V 0M7
Tel: 613-731-7110; *Fax:* 613-731-0704
Toll-Free: 877-731-7110
redpoll@clrc.ca
www.clrc.ca/redpoll.shtml
Overview: A medium-sized national organization founded in 1906
Mission: To encourage development & regulation of breeding of purebred Red Poll cattle in Canada for improvement of Canadian beef cattle industry
Affliation(s): Canadian Livestock Records Corporation
Chief Officer(s):
Ron Black, Sec.-Treas.
Finances: *Annual Operating Budget:* Less than $50,000; *Funding Sources:* Membership dues; fees for service
Staff Member(s): 1; 13 volunteer(s)
Membership: 16; *Fees:* $60; *Committees:* Advertising; Performance Records

Canadian Regional Science Association *Voir* Association canadienne des sciences régionales

Canadian Register of Health Service Psychologists (CRHSP) / Répertoire canadien des psychologues offrant des services de santé (RCPOSS)

#300, 368 Dalhousie St., Ottawa ON K1N 7G3
Tel: 613-562-0900; *Fax:* 613-562-0902
info@crhspp.ca
www.crhspp.ca
Overview: A small national organization founded in 1985
Mission: To promote & protect public access to qualified health service providers in psychology
Chief Officer(s):
Pierre L.-J. Ritchie, Executive Director
L. Craig Turner, President
Myles Genest, Vice-President
Mark Lawrence, Secretary-Treasurer
Membership: 1,000-4,999; *Member Profile:* Psychologists providing health services
Activities: *Rents Mailing List:* Yes
Publications:
• Canadian Register of Health Service Providers in Psychology Annual Directory
Type: Directory; *Frequency:* Annually; *Price:* $26.75
Profile: Listing of all registrants

Canadian Registry of Tennessee Walking Horse (CRTWH)

c/o Leslie Hunchuk, Box 12, Site 12, RR#1, Millard AB T0L 1K0
Tel: 403-931-2105
secretary@crtwh.ca
www.crtwh.ca
www.facebook.com/crtwh
Overview: A small international organization
Mission: To register & record purebred Tennessee Walking Horses, both in Canada & internationally; To preserve the historical attributes of the Tennessee Walking Horse breed; To encourage improvement in the quality of the breed
Affliation(s): Equine Canada; Canadian Livestock Records Corporation
Chief Officer(s):
Fran Kerik, President
president@crtwh.ca
Bill Roy, Vice-President, 250-838-2066
vice-president@crtwh.ca
Leslie Hunchuk, Secretary, 403-931-2105
secretary@crtwh.ca
Dianne Little, Treasurer, 403-271-7391
treasurer@crtwh.ca
Membership: *Fees:* $10 youth members, under 18; $15 associate members; $25 full members; $35 non-Canadian residents; $200 individual life members; *Member Profile:* Canadian individuals, families, organizations, groups, corporations, & partnerships; International members
Activities: Promoting the Tennessee Walking Horse breed; Establishing standards of breeding; Cooperating with other breed associations & agricultural groups; Presenting awards
Publications:
• The Canadian Walker
Type: Newsletter
Profile: Association updates

Canadian Reiki Association (CRA)

#24, 2350 New St., Burlington ON L7R 4P8
Tel: 416-931-3465; *Fax:* 866-734-4540
Toll-Free: 800-835-7525
reiki@reiki.ca
www.reiki.ca
www.facebook.com/groups/6813158154/?ref=ts&fref=ts
Overview: A small national organization founded in 1997
Mission: Provides members with a national voice; encourages high educational standards; promotes ethical practices & teaching; assists the public with referrals to practitioners & teachers; committed to enlightening & educating communites about Reiki
Member of: Volunteer Canada
Chief Officer(s):
Bonnie Smith, President, 905-639-5980
bonnie@soulsjourney.ca
Staff Member(s): 1

Canadian Remote Sensing Society (CRSS) / Société canadienne de télédétection

c/o Canadian Aeronautics & Space Institute, #104, 350 Terry Fox Dr., Kanata ON K2K 2W5
Tel: 613-591-8787; *Fax:* 613-591-7291
casi@casi.ca
www.crss-sct.ca
Overview: A small national organization founded in 1978
Mission: To advance the art, science, engineering, & application of remote sensing in Canada; To uphold the Society's Code of Ethics
Member of: Canadian Aeronautics & Space Institute (CASI)
Chief Officer(s):
Monique Bernier, Chair
Anne Smith, Vice-Chair
Richard Fournier, Secretary-Treasurer
Activities: Disseminating technical remote sensing information; Developing a program for certification of remote sensing scientists & mapping scientists in GIS & photogrammetry
Meetings/Conferences: • Canadian Remote Sensing Society 2015 36th Canadian Symposium on Remote Sensing, June, 2015, Delta Hotel, St. John's, NL
Scope: National
• Canadian Remote Sensing Society 2016 37th Canadian Symposium on Remote Sensing, 2016, Winnipeg, MB
Scope: National
Publications:
• Canadian Journal of Remote Sensing (CJRS) / Journal canadien de télédétection (JCT)
Type: Journal; *Frequency:* Bimonthly; *Accepts Advertising*; *Editor:* Nicholas Coops; *Price:* $211.68 Canada; $206.30 USA; $217.20 International
Profile: Research articles & notes, technical notes, & review

papers on topics such asinformation processing methods, data acquisition, & applications

Canadian Renewable Energy Alliance (CanREA)

www.canrea.ca/site
Previous Name: Canadian Renewable Energy Association
Overview: A large national organization founded in 2006
Mission: To promote a global transition to energy conservation & efficiency, & the use of renewable energy. A founding member of the North American Alliance for Renewable Energy, CanREA & its members advocate to all levels of government & work with like-minded organizations worldwide to recommend new policy directions & practical strategies
Member of: North American Alliance for Renewable Energy
Affliation(s): BC Sustainable Energy Association; David Suzuki Foundation; Ecology Action Centre; Environmental Coalition of Prince Edward Island; The Falls Brook Centre; Green Communities Canada; Greenpeace Canada; Nova Scotia Cooperative Council; Ontario Sustainable Energy Association; Canadian Institute for Sustainable Living; Pembina Institute; Sierra Club Canada; Saskatchewan Environmental Society; Toronto Renewable Energy Coop; Windfall Ecology Centre
Chief Officer(s):
Jose Etcheverry, President
rejose@yorku.ca
Membership: 16; *Member Profile:* Registered & incorporated not-for-profit organizations which actively promote renewable energy policy & implementation & are in good standing under applicable laws
Activities: Conferences

Canadian Renewable Energy Association *See* Canadian Renewable Energy Alliance

Canadian Renewable Fuels Association (CRFA) / Association canadienne des carburants renouvelables

#605, 350 Sparks St., Ottawa ON K1R 7S8
Tel: 613-594-5528; *Fax:* 613-594-3076
l.ehman@greenfuels.org
www.greenfuels.org
Overview: A medium-sized national organization founded in 1984
Mission: To promote renewable fuel development & usage
Chief Officer(s):
Gordon Quaiattini, President
g.quaiattini@greenfuels.org
Deborah Elson, Director, Member Relations & Industry Promotions
D.Elson@greenfuels.org
Debby Marandola, Director, Operations
D.Marandola@greenfuels.org
Alison Ouellet, Director, Government Affairs
A.Ouellet@greenfuels.org
Finances: *Funding Sources:* Membership dues
Membership: 1-99; *Fees:* Schedule available based upon company's litres of production; $15,000 associate members; $5,000 supporting members; *Member Profile:* Representatives from all levels of the ethanol & biodiesel industries
Activities: Liaising with government; Promoting policy initiatives advantageous to ethanol & biodiesel fuel development; Increasing awareness of ethanol & biodiesel; Conducting research;
Meetings/Conferences: • Canadian Renewable Fuels 2015 12th Annual Summit, 2015
Scope: International
Description: A conference of interest to representatives from the ethanol & biodiesel industries, plus agricultural associations & petroleum companies
Contact Information: Director, Member Relations & Industry Promotions: Deborah Elson, E-mail: d.elson@greenfuels.org

Canadian Rental Association (CRA) / Association de location du Canada

112B Scurfield Blvd., Winnipeg MB R3Y 1G4
Tel: 204-452-1836; *Fax:* 204-453-3569
Toll-Free: 800-486-9899
www.crarental.org
www.facebook.com/canadianrental
twitter.com/canadianrental
www.youtube.com/canadianrental
Previous Name: Rental Association of Canada
Overview: A small national organization founded in 1964
Chief Officer(s):
Mandy Maeren, Executive Director
Finances: *Annual Operating Budget:* $100,000-$250,000
Staff Member(s): 2; 13 volunteer(s)
Membership: 500-999; *Committees:* Membership Benefit; Policy and Procedures; Social Media/Advertising; Trade Show; Website
Activities: *Library*

Canadian Reprography Collective *See* Access Copyright

Canadian Research Institute for the Advancement of Women (CRIAW) / Institut canadien de recherches sur les femmes (ICREF)

c/o Institute of Women's Studies, University of Ottawa, 143 Séraphin-Marion, Ottawa ON K1N 6N5
Tel: 613-562-5800
info@criaw-icref.ca
www.criaw-icref.ca
Overview: A medium-sized national organization founded in 1976
Mission: To advance the position of women in society through feminist & women-centred research; to encourage, coordinate & communicate research about the reality of women's lives & ensure an equal place for women & their experiences in the body of knowledge about Canada; to recognize & affirm the diversity of women's experiences; to demystify the research process & promote connections between research, social action & social change; to facilitate communication among feminist researchers & research organizations world-wide
Chief Officer(s):
Maria-Héléna Pacelli, Administrative Officer
Ann Denis, President
Finances: *Annual Operating Budget:* $250,000-$500,000; *Funding Sources:* Government; donations; membership fees; sales of publications; administration of projects
Staff Member(s): 4
Membership: 1,000 individual + 25 institutional; *Fees:* $15 student/low income; $30 regular; $55 supporting; $150 sustaining; $100 institutional; *Member Profile:* Independent researchers; students; academics; policy makers; journalists; community activists & women's centres
Activities: *Speaker Service:* Yes; *Library:* Resource Centre; Open to public
Publications:
• CRIAW [Canadian Research Institute for the Advancement of Women] Papers
Profile: Topics in the series include the following: Canada's Early Women Writers: Texts in English to 1859; Canadian Women's Autobiography in English: AnIntroductory Guide for Researchers & Teachers; & Feminist Engagement with the Law: The Legal Recognition of the Battered Woman Syndrome
• Feminist Perspectives
Profile: Topics in the series include the following: Gender-sensitive Theory & the Housing Needs of Mother-led Families: Some Concepts & Some Buildings; Reclaiming Body Territory; Role Muddles: The Stereotyping ofFeminists; & Towards Family Policies in Canada With Women in Mind
• Feminist Voices
Profile: Topics in this series include the following: Diaries in English by women in Canada, 1753-1995: an Annotated Bibliography; Invoking Community: Rethinking the Health of Lesbian & Bisexual Women; & Making NewFeminisms: A Conversation Between a Feminist Mother & Daughter

Canadian Research Management Association *See* Innovation Management Association of Canada

Canadian Resident Matching Service (CARMS)

#300, 171 Nepean St., Ottawa ON K2P 0B4
Tel: 613-237-0075
Toll-Free: 877-227-6742
help@carms.ca
www.carms.ca
www.linkedin.com/company/carms
www.facebook.com/carms.ca
twitter.com/carms_ca
www.youtube.com/user/CaRMSvideo
Overview: A small national organization founded in 1982
Mission: National organization that serves both eligible applicants & post graduate programs by offering fair & equitable access to medical residency training in Canada
Chief Officer(s):
Sandra Banner, Executive Director/CEO
Staff Member(s): 44
Membership: *Committees:* Executive; Finance & Audit; Nominating; Research & Data Policy; Awards; Scope of Services

Canadian Resort & Recreational Development Association (1992) *See* Canadian Resort Development Association

Canadian Resort Development Association (CRDA)

13061 - 15 Ave., South Surrey BC V4A 1K6
Tel: 604-538-7001; *Fax:* 604-538-7101
info@crda.com
www.crda.com
Previous Name: Canadian Resort & Recreational Development Association (1992)
Overview: A small national organization founded in 1980
Mission: To raise a better understanding of the value of the vacation ownership product; to ensure fair & ethical treatment by all industry participants, through legislation or industry self-management; to educate & inform within the membership & outwardly to the public.
Affliation(s): American Resort Development Association; All India Resort Development Association; Mexican Resort Development Association; Co-Operative Association of Resort Exchangers; Canadian Resort & Foodservices Association; Hotel Association of Canada; Resort Development Organisation
Chief Officer(s):
Jon Zwickel, President & CEO
Membership: 47; *Fees:* $0 - $3,000; *Member Profile:* Resort developers; marketers; suppliers

Canadian Respiratory Health Professionals (CRHP)

#300, 1750 Courtwood Cres., Ottawa ON K2C 2B5
Tel: 613-569-6411; *Fax:* 613-569-8860
crhpinfo@lung.ca
www.lung.ca/crhp
Merged from: Cdn Nurses Respiratory, Cdn Physiotherapy Cardio-Respiratory, & Respiratory Therapy Societies
Overview: A small national organization founded in 2004 overseen by Canadian Lung Association
Mission: To promote lung health & the prevention of lung disease
Affliation(s): Canadian Thoracic Society
Membership: *Fees:* $30 associate member; $45 full member; *Member Profile:* A multidisciplinary health professional section of The Canadian Lung Association, consisting of respiratory therapists, cardio-pulmonary physiotherapists, nurses, pharmacists, & other health professionals who work in the respiratory field
Activities: Advising the Canadian Lung Association on scientific matters, as well as professional & public education; Administering a research & fellowship program; Facilitating interprofessional collaboration
Meetings/Conferences: • Canadian Respiratory Conference 2015, April, 2015, Ottawa, ON
Scope: National
Description: Jointly organized by the Canadian Thoracic Society, the Canadian Respiratory Health Professionals, the Canadian COPD Alliance and the Canadian Lung Association
Publications:
• Airwaves - The Newsletter of the Canadian Respiratory Health Professionals
Type: Newsletter; *Price:* Free with CRHP membership
Profile: Information for Canadian Respiratory Health Professionals members

Canadian Restaurant & Foodservices Association *See* Restaurants Canada

Canadian Retransmission Collective (CRC) / Société collective de retransmission du Canada (SCR)

74 The Esplanade, Toronto ON M5E 1A9
Tel: 416-304-0290; *Fax:* 416-304-0496
info@crc-scrc.ca
www.crc-scrc.ca
Overview: A small national organization
Mission: To retransmit of royalties paid for the use of programs in broadcast signals that are classed as 'distant', or not transitted by the originating signal
Chief Officer(s):
Carol Cooper, President/CEO
Staff Member(s): 5

Canadian Rheumatology Association (CRA) / Société canadienne de rhumatologie

#244, 12 - 16715 Yonge St., Newmarket ON L3X 1X4
Tel: 905-952-0698; *Fax:* 905-952-0708
info@rheum.ca
rheum.ca
Overview: A small national organization
Mission: To represent Canadian rheumatologists & promote their pursuit of excellence in arthritis care & research in Canada through leadership, education & communication
Affliation(s): Canadian Medical Association, Royal College of Physicians & Surgeons of Canada

Chief Officer(s):
Carter Thorne, President
Jacob Karsh, Sec.-Treas.
Staff Member(s): 2
Membership: *Fees:* $400; *Member Profile:* Canadian & international rheumatologists; others with a focused area of interest in rheumatology; *Committees:* Access to Care; CRAJ; Human Resources; Education; Management; Liaison; Summer Studentship Program; Scientific; Therapeutics; Website; Media
Awards:
• Distinguished Rheumatologist Award (Award)
Eligibility: A CRA member *Amount:* $5,000
• Distinguished Investigator Award (Award)
Eligibility: A CRA member *Amount:* $2,500
• Teacher - Educator Award (Award)
Eligibility: A CRA member *Amount:* $2,500
• Young Investigator Award (Award)
Eligibility: A CRA member *Amount:* $2,500
• CRA/ARF Young Faculty Award for Excellence in Research (Award)
Eligibility: A CRA member *Amount:* $1,250
• Dr. Philip S. Rosen Endowment Fund (Award)
Amount: $1,000
• Ian Watson Memorial Award (Award)
Amount: $1,000
• Best Abstract by an Undergraduate Student (Award)
Amount: $1,000
Meetings/Conferences: • Canadian Rheumatology Association 2015 Annual Scientific Meeting, February, 2015, Fairmont Chateau Frontenac, Québec, QC
Scope: National
• Canadian Rheumatology Association 2016 Annual Scientific Meeting, February, 2016, Lake Louise, AB
Scope: National
Publications:
• Journal of the Canadian Rheumatology Association
Type: Journal; *Frequency:* Quarterly

Canadian Rhythmic Sportive Gymnastic Federation (CRSGF) / Fédération canadienne de gymnastique rythmique sportive
c/o 2288 Covington Pl., Victoria BC V8N 5N6
Tel: 250-472-3322; *Fax:* 250-472-2659
dfrattaroli@shaw.ca
Also Known As: Rhythmic Gymnastics Canada
Previous Name: Canadian Modern Rhythmic Gymnastic Federation
Overview: A medium-sized national organization founded in 1970
Mission: To promote Rhythmic Gymnastics for lifetime growth, fitness & the pursuit of excellence.
Chief Officer(s):
Danielle Frattaroli, GCG-RG Program Coordinator
Finances: *Annual Operating Budget:* $100,000-$250,000; *Funding Sources:* Government; donations; marketing; membership fees; sales
Staff Member(s): 1; 100 volunteer(s)
Membership: 10,000 registered; *Fees:* Schedule available
Activities: *Library*

Canadian Rock Mechanics Association (CARMA) / Association canadienne de méchanique des roches
c/o Civil Engineering Department, University of Toronto, 35 St. George St., Toronto ON M5S 1A4
www.carma-rocks.ca
Overview: A medium-sized national organization founded in 1980
Mission: To represent Canada to the international community of engineers working in the mining & civil engineering aspects of rock mechanics engineering
Member of: Canadian Geotechnical Society; Canadian Institute of Mining & Metallurgy
Affliation(s): International Society for Rock Mechanics
Chief Officer(s):
John Hadjigeorgiou, Chair
john.hadjigeorgiou@utoronto.ca
Luc Beauchamp, Secretary-Treasurer
lucbeauchamp@workplacesafetynorth.ca
6 volunteer(s)
Membership: 165
Awards:
• John Franklin Award (Award)
Recognizes an individual who has recently made an outstanding and published technical contribution in the fields of rock mechanics or rock engineering in Canada and/or internationally. Given biannually

Canadian Roofing Contractors' Association (CRCA) / Association canadienne des entrepreneurs en couverture (ACEC)
#100, 2430 Don Reid Dr., Ottawa ON K1H 1E1
Tel: 613-232-6724; *Fax:* 613-232-2893
crca@on.aibn.com
www.roofingcanada.com
Overview: A medium-sized national organization founded in 1960
Member of: Canadian Construction Association; National Trade Contractors Coalition of Canada; National Roofing Contactors Association
Affliation(s): Construction Specifications Canada
Staff Member(s): 4
Membership: 380; *Member Profile:* Companies actively engaged in the roofing & related sheet metal contracting business in Canada; *Committees:* Board of Directors; Executive; National Technical; Associate Members

Canadian Rope Skipping Federation (CRSF)
906 County Rd. 46, RR#3, Essex ON N8M 2X7
www.ropeskippingcanada.com
www.facebook.com/134193290003026
twitter.com/RopeSkippingCA
Also Known As: Rope Skipping Canada (RSC)
Previous Name: Canadian Skipping Association
Overview: A small national organization
Mission: To promote rope skipping as a fitness & recreational activity, as well as a competitive sport.
Chief Officer(s):
Bonnie Popov, General Manager

Canadian Rose Society (CRS)
116 Belsize Dr., Toronto ON M4S 1L7
Tel: 416-266-6303
Canrosesociety@aol.com
canadianrosesociety.org
www.facebook.com/canadianrosesociety
Previous Name: Rose Society of Ontario
Overview: A medium-sized national charitable organization founded in 1955
Mission: To provide information about rose growing, speakers, judges, nurseries & suppliers, & rose shows; To correspond with people with similar interests throughout Canada & around the world
Member of: World Federation of Rose Societies
Affliation(s): World Federation of Rose Societies
Chief Officer(s):
Barb Munton, Membership Sec.-Treas.
Finances: *Annual Operating Budget:* Less than $50,000; *Funding Sources:* Donations, membership fees, sales of goods & services
Membership: 500-999; *Fees:* $20 regular; $25 family; $30 affiliate society, nursery, institute;$35 U.S.A. members; $50 foreign; $15 all electronic subscriptions
Activities: *Speaker Service:* Yes; *Library:* Rose Book Library & Rose Slide Library
Publications:
• Canadian Rose Society Newsletter: Sharing your love of roses
Type: Newsletter
Profile: Business of the Canadian Rose Society & world rose news

Canadian Rugby Union *See* Football Canada

Canadian Rugby Union *See* Rugby Canada

Canadian Sablefish Association (CSA)
#24B, 12820 Trites Rd., Richmond BC V7E 3R8
Tel: 604-328-7835; *Fax:* 604-448-8582
info@canadiansablefish.com
www.canadiansablefish.com
Overview: A small national organization founded in 1987
Mission: To protect the interests & investments of sablefish fishermen & to explore & develop programs & policies for the protection & conservation of the Canadian sablefish resource & fishery

Canadian Safe Boating Council (CSBC) / Conseil canadien de la sécurité nautique
400 Consumers Rd., Toronto ON M2J 1P8
Tel: 905-820-4817
www.csbc.ca
Overview: A small national organization founded in 1991
Mission: To promote boating safety through the activities of our members & public awareness campaigns
Chief Officer(s):
Jean Murray, Chair
chair@csbc.ca
Finances: *Annual Operating Budget:* $100,000-$250,000
100 volunteer(s)
Membership: 135; *Fees:* $500 patron; $150 - organization; $75 - individual; *Committees:* Symposium; PFD Task Force; CASBA Awards; Communications
Activities: Boating safety education; *Awareness Events:* Safe Boating Awareness Week; *Speaker Service:* Yes

Canadian Safe School Network (CSSN)
229 Niagara St., Toronto ON M6J 2L5
Tel: 416-977-1050
info@canadiansafeschools.com
www.canadiansafeschools.com
www.facebook.com/CanadianSafeSchoolNetwork
twitter.com/CndnSafeSchools
Overview: A small national organization founded in 1997
Mission: To reduce youth violence & to make our schools & communities safer
Chief Officer(s):
Stuart Auty, President
Renee Goncalves, Coordinator, Communications & Event
Staff Member(s): 5

Canadian Sanitation Standards Association *See* Canadian Sanitation Supply Association

Canadian Sanitation Supply Association (CSSA) / Association canadienne des fournisseurs de produits sanitaires
PO Box 10009, 910 Dundas St. West, Whitby ON L1P 1P7
Tel: 905-665-8001; *Fax:* 905-430-6418
Toll-Free: 866-684-8273
www.cssa.com
www.facebook.com/group.php?gid=183837499478
twitter.com/CSSA_Canada
Previous Name: Canadian Sanitation Standards Association
Overview: A large national organization founded in 1957
Mission: To provide a high degree of professionalism, technical knowledge & business ethics within the membership; To promote greater public awareness, appreciation & understanding of the sanitation industry
Chief Officer(s):
Mike Nosko, Executive Director
mike@cssa.com
Catherine Fedak, Contact, Sales
cathie@cssa.com
Diane Mason, Contact, Accounting
dcm@cssa.com
10 volunteer(s)
Membership: 395 corporate + 10 associate + 15 senior/lifetime; *Fees:* Schedule available; *Member Profile:* Manufacturer or distributor of sanitation products & services; *Committees:* Long Range Planning; Government Liaison
Activities: *Library* by appointment
Awards:
• The Sam Tughan Achievement Award (Award)
Awarded every two years to any person, group or organization that represents a high degree of professionalism in business.
• Member of the Year Award (Award)
Recognizes a CSSA member who contributes significantly to the association in the previous year.
• The Builder Award (Award)
Given to the CSSA member who has donated time and effort to building the association over the years.
Meetings/Conferences: • Canadian Sanitation Supply Association's CanClean 2015, April, 2015, International Centre, Mississauga, ON
Scope: National
Publications:
• Canadian Sanitation Supply Association Update
Type: Newsletter; *Price:* Free with CSSA membership
Profile: CSSA activities, awards, chapter news, & events
• Canadian Sanitation Supply Association Bulletin
Type: Newsletter; *Price:* Free with CSSA membership
Profile: Information for CSSA members important to their business

Canadian Schizophrenia Foundation *See* International Schizophrenia Foundation

Canadian Scholarship Trust Foundation (CST) / Fondation fiduciaire canadienne de bourses d'études
#1600, 2235 Sheppard Ave. East, Toronto ON M2J 5B8

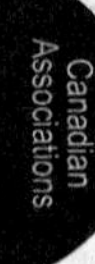

Tel: 416-445-7377; *Fax:* 416-445-1708
Toll-Free: 877-333-7377
cstplan@cst.org
www.cst.org
www.linkedin.com/company/cst-consultants-inc.
www.facebook.com/CSTConsultants
twitter.com/CSTConsultants
www.youtube.com/CSTConsultants
Also Known As: CST Foundation
Overview: A small national charitable organization founded in 1960
Mission: To assist parents & others to save for post-secondary education of children, by way of the Canadian Scholarship Trust Plan
Chief Officer(s):
Sherry MacDonald, President/CEO
Peter Bethlenfalvy, CFO

Canadian School Boards Association (CSBA) / Association canadienne des commissions/conseils scolaires

#515, 1410 rue Stanley, Montréal QC H3A 1P8
Tel: 514-289-2988; *Fax:* 514-849-8228
info@cdnsba.org
www.cdnsba.org
www.facebook.com/124194330966818
twitter.com/cdnsba
Previous Name: Canadian School Trustees' Association
Overview: A large national organization founded in 1923
Mission: To provide leadership for school boards throughout Canada by supporting the efforts of the provincial/territorial school board/trustee associations; To promote educational excellence at the elementary/secondary levels as a national imperative; To foster & promote the maintenance of the principles of local autonomy in education in Canada through elected representation; To provide for & maintain liaison with the Cabinet & all branches of the federal government & members of Parliament & to make representation on behalf of school boards in Canada; To maintain a national profile for school boards & to make representation on their behalf to other national organizations; To provide for interprovincial communication on issues & developments in public education that take place on a provincial/territorial, national or international level
Chief Officer(s):
Sandi Urban Hall, President
Finances: *Annual Operating Budget:* $250,000-$500,000; *Funding Sources:* Membership fees from school trustee/board associations
Staff Member(s): 3; 23 volunteer(s)
Membership: 250 school boards; *Member Profile:* Provincial/territorial associations of school trustees, school boards & boards of school trustees or of school commissioners; *Committees:* Executive
Activities: *Rents Mailing List:* Yes
Meetings/Conferences: • Canadian School Boards Association / Association canadienne des commissions/conseils scolaires 2015 Congress, 2015, Saskatoon, SK
Scope: National
• Canadian School Boards Association / Association canadienne des commissions/conseils scolaires 2016 Congress, 2016
Scope: National
Publications:
• Anaphylaxis: A Handbook for School Boards
Type: Handbook; *Number of Pages:* 74; *ISBN:* 0-920632-80-7
• CSBA [Canadian School Boards Association] InfoBackgrounder
Type: Newsletter; *Frequency:* Irregular
Profile: Topics include the following: Child Care; High School Completion Rates; & Copyright

Canadian School Trustees' Association *See* Canadian School Boards Association

Canadian Science & Technology Historical Association (CSTHA) / Association pour l'histoire de la science et de la technologie au Canada (AHSTC)

PO Box 8502, Stn. T, Ottawa ON K1G 3H9
cstha-ahstc.ca
Overview: A medium-sized national charitable organization founded in 1980
Mission: To foster the study of Canada's scientific & technological heritage through research, publication, teaching & preservation of artifacts & records
Chief Officer(s):
Suzanne Beauvais, Secretary
sbeauvais@technomuses.ca
Bertrum H. MacDonald, President
bertrum.macdonald@dal.ca
Finances: *Annual Operating Budget:* Less than $50,000; *Funding Sources:* Membership fees
Membership: 150; *Fees:* $27
Activities: *Rents Mailing List:* Yes

Canadian Science Writers' Association (CSWA) / Association canadienne des rédacteurs scientifiques

PO Box 75, Stn. A, Toronto ON M5W 1A2
Toll-Free: 800-796-8595
office@sciencewriters.ca
www.sciencewriters.ca
Overview: A small national organization founded in 1971
Mission: To foster excellence in science communication; To increase public awareness of Canadian science & technology
Chief Officer(s):
Kristina Bergen, Executive Director
Stephen Strauss, President
president@sciencewriters.ca
Membership: 450+; *Fees:* $75 regular members; $35 students; *Member Profile:* Professional science communicators in all media, who communicate science & technology to non-specialist audiences
Activities: Providing networking opportunities for communications officers in science & technology institutions, media professionals, educators, & technical writers; Offering workshops & public meetings; Encouraging awareness of the need for science coverage
Awards:
• Science in Society Book Awards (Award)
To honour outstanding contributions to science writing. *Amount:* Two $1000 annual awards
• Science in Society Journalism Awards (Award)
• Medal For Excellence In Health Research Journalism (Award)
• L'Oreal Excellence In Science Journalism Award (Award)
• Yves Fortier Earth Science Journalism Award (Award)
Meetings/Conferences: • Canadian Science Writers' Association 44th Annual Conference, May, 2015, Saskatoon, SK
Scope: National
Publications:
• Canadian Science Writers' Association Membership Directory
Type: Directory
Profile: For CSWA / ACRS members
• Science Link [a publication of the Canadian Science Writers' Association]
Type: Newsletter; *Editor:* Peter McMahon
Profile: Information for CSWA / ACRS members

Canadian Screen Institute *See* National Screen Institute - Canada

Canadian Seaplane Pilots Association (CSPA)

#1001, 75 Albert St., Ottawa ON K1P 5E7
Tel: 613-236-4901; *Fax:* 613-236-8646
Overview: A medium-sized national organization
Mission: To maintain communications among seaplane pilots; to represent them at all levels of government; to help develop regulations conducive to safe & pleasurable flying; to prepare & disseminate educational material; to advance among its members information & knowledge of seaplane flying.
Affiliation(s): Seaplane Pilots Association International
Chief Officer(s):
Chris Bullerdick, Director
Finances: *Annual Operating Budget:* $50,000-$100,000
Staff Member(s): 2; 10 volunteer(s)
Membership: 400; *Fees:* US$28
Activities: Fly-ins; safety seminars

Canadian Search Dog Association (CSDA)

PO Box 37103, Stn. Lynnwood Postal Outlet, Edmonton AB T5R 5Y2
e-mail: calgary.csda@outlook.com
canadiansearchdog.com
www.facebook.com/156258481071770
Previous Name: RCMP Civilian Search & Rescue Civilian Search Dog Program; RCMP Civilian Search Dog Association
Overview: A medium-sized provincial charitable organization founded in 1995
Mission: To generate a group of trained search workers & search dogs to aid the RCMP & other tasking agencies in the search for lost or missing persons
Finances: *Funding Sources:* Donations

Canadian Securities Administrators (CSA) / Autorités canadiennes en valeurs mobilières (ACVM)

CSA Secretariat, Tour de la Bourse, #2510, 800, Victoria Sq., Montréal QC H4Z 1J2
Tel: 514-864-9510; *Fax:* 514-864-9512
csa-acvm-secretariat@acvm-csa.ca
www.securities-administrators.ca
twitter.com/CSA_News
Overview: A small national organization
Mission: To coordinate & harmonize regulation of the Canadian capital markets; To foster fair & efficient capital markets; To reduce the risk of failure of market intermediaries
Chief Officer(s):
William S. Rice, Q.C., Chair
Kim Lachapelle, Secretary General
Membership: 13; *Member Profile:* Securities regulators of Canada's provinces & territories; *Committees:* Executive Directors; Enforcement; Market Oversight; Registrant Regulation; Investment Funds; Investor Education
Activities: Developing the Canadian Securities Regulatory System (CSRS) to harmonize securities regulation, policy, & practice; Educating investors; Providing educational resources about securities & investing; Protecting investors from improper or fraudulent practices; Authorizing individuals who provide investment services to the public; Supervising market intermediaries; Maintaining the databases, SEDAR & SEDI
Publications:
• Investor Education Annual Activity Report
Type: Report; *Frequency:* Annually
Profile: A summary of education initiatives
• Report on Enforcement Activities
Type: Report
Profile: Highlights of how Canadian securities regulators protect investors & the marketplace

Canadian Securities Institute (CSI) / L'Institut canadien des valeurs mobilières

200 Wellington St. West, 15th Fl., Toronto ON M5V 3C7
Tel: 416-364-9130; *Fax:* 416-359-0486
Toll-Free: 866-866-2601
customer_support@csi.ca
www.csi.ca
www.linkedin.com/groups?gid=3720042
www.facebook.com/csiglobal
twitter.com/CSIGlobalEd
csiblog.csi.ca
Previous Name: Institute of Canadian Bankers
Overview: A large national organization founded in 1970
Mission: To enhance the knowledge of securities & financial industry professionals & promote knowledge & understanding of investing among the public
Affliation(s): Investment Dealers Association of Canada; Montreal Exchange; Toronto Stock Exchange; Canadian Venture Exchange
Chief Officer(s):
Simon Parmar, Managing Director
Membership: *Committees:* Education
Activities: Granting CIM, PFP, MTI & CIWM professional designations as well as Fellow of the Canadian Securities Institute (FCSI) & Fellow, Institute of Canadian Bankers (FICB); Offering courses such as Investment Management, Financial Planning, Wealth Management, Derivatives, Compliance, Management & Leadership, Credit & Lending, Insurance, Licensing, Mutual Funds, Trading & Trust.; *Speaker Service:* Yes

Bureau de Montréal
#400, 625, boul René-Lévesque ouest, Montréal QC H3B 1R2
Ligne sans frais: 866-866-2601
Chief Officer(s):
Marc Flynn, Senior Vice-President, Regulatory Relations & Credentialing

Canadian Securities Institute Research Foundation / Fondation de recherche de l'Institut canadien des valeurs mobilières

200 Wellington St. West, 15th Fl., Toronto ON M5V 3G2
Tel: 416-681-2262; *Fax:* 416-364-8952
hirwin@csi.ca
www.csifoundation.com
Previous Name: Investor Learning Centre of Canada
Overview: A small national organization founded in 1993
Mission: Encourages, considers & supports realistic & creative ideas for research in issues pertaining to the Canadian capital markets to benefit investors & other participants with a national

&/or global perspective
Affliation(s): Canadian Securities Institute (CSI)
Staff Member(s): 10
Activities: Publications & seminars aimed at the novice investor; publications include: "How to Invest in Canadian Securities", "How to Read Financial Statements", "Investment Terms & Definitions", & "Career Oppoutunities in the Investment Industry"; Intelligent Investing seminar series provides a basic overview of investment principles, stocks, bonds, mutual funds & practical information on how to start investing & plan for retirement; *Library:* ILC Resource Centre

Canadian Security Association (CANASA) / L'Association canadienne de la sécurité

National Office, #201, 50 Acadia Ave., Markham ON L3R 0B3
Tel: 905-513-0622; *Fax:* 905-513-0624
Toll-Free: 800-538-9919
staff@canasa.org
www.canasa.org
www.linkedin.com/groups?mostPopular=&gid=3663787
www.facebook.com/169077016452968
twitter.com/CANASA_News
Previous Name: Canadian Alarm & Security Association
Overview: A large national organization founded in 1977
Mission: To act as the national voice of the security industry; To promote & protect the interests of members; To increase public awareness of the security industry's effectiveness in reducing risk; To develop & promote programs consistent with the needs of members; To develop & promote programs which will lead to the reduction of false dispatches & improved response; To influence regulations affecting the members
Chief Officer(s):
Donald Budden, President
JF Champagne, Executive Director, 905-513-0624 Ext. 222
jfchampagne@canasa.org
Steve Basnett, Director, Trade Shows & Events, 905-513-0624 Ext. 224
sbasnett@canasa.org
Mona Emond, Director, Marketing & Communications, 905-513-0624 Ext. 242
memond@canasa.org
Dave Kushner, Manager, Finance, 905-513-0624 Ext. 225
finance@canasa.org
Lynne Hewitson, Office Administrator, Membership Services, 905-513-0624 Ext. 221
membership@canasa.org
Finances: *Funding Sources:* Membership fees; Trade show
Membership: 1,300 companies in 10 chapters; *Fees:* Schedule available; *Member Profile:* Includes installing & monitoring companies, manufacturers, distributors, consultants & public safety organizations; Members install &/or monitor over 85% of all alarm systems in Canada; *Committees:* ASC; Audit; Exhibitor Advisory; Governance; Membership; Monitoring
Activities: Organizing professional development courses; Hosting members' meetings; *Library* by appointment
Publications:
• Canadian Security Association Annual Report
Type: Yearbook
• Canadian Security Association Directory of Members
Type: Directory
Profile: Listing of agents, consulting companies, consultants, installer & installer - monitoring businesses, distributors, monitors, manufacturers, security dirctors, privateguard services, & single installers
• Inside Security [a publication of the Canadian Security Association]
Type: Newsletter

Atlantic Chapter
Toll-Free: 800-538-9919
atmanager@canasa.org
www.facebook.com/218551091501584
Chief Officer(s):
Gordon Hebb, President
Natasha Morrisey, Chapter Manager
atmanager@canasa.org

British Columbia Chapter
BC
Chief Officer(s):
JF Champagne, Executive Director, Canadian Security Association
jfchampagne@canasa.org

Calgary Sub-Chapter
Fax: 905-513-0624
Toll-Free: 800-538-9919
www.facebook.com/192561264129079
Chief Officer(s):
Chris Strong, President
Karen Hamada, Chapter Manager
khamada@canasa.org

Edmonton Sub-Chapter
Toll-Free: 800-538-9919
www.facebook.com/156106294459786
Chief Officer(s):
Shawn Lazaruk, President
Karen Hamada, Chapter Manager
khamada@canasa.org

Golden Horseshoe Sub-Chapter
Toll-Free: 800-538-9919
www.facebook.com/117301578358860
Chief Officer(s):
Joseph Rossano, President
Lisa Padgett, Chapter Manager
lpadgett@canasa.org

Manitoba Chapter
Toll-Free: 800-538-9919
www.facebook.com/215516491821324
Chief Officer(s):
Ellery Demedash, President
Lisa Padgett, Chapter Manager
lpadgett@canasa.org

Ontario Chapter
Toll-Free: 800-538-9919
www.facebook.com/137690642972156
Chief Officer(s):
Jamie Couper, President
Lisa Padgett, Chapter Manager
lpadgett@canasa.org

Ottawa Sub-Chapter
Toll-Free: 800-538-9919
www.facebook.com/225959204098448
Chief Officer(s):
Richard McMullen, President
Lisa Padgett, Chapter Manager
lpadgett@canasa.org

Québec Chapter
Tél: 514-884-3343
Ligne sans frais: 800-538-9919
www.facebook.com/219357428095529
Chief Officer(s):
Michel Houde, President
Danielle Paquin, Regional Director
dpaquin@canasa.org

Southwestern Ontario Sub-Chapter
Toll-Free: 800-538-9919
www.facebook.com/122336791183288
Chief Officer(s):
Al Herrington, President
Lisa Padgett, Chapter Manager
lpadgett@canasa.org

Canadian Security Traders Association, Inc. (CSTA)

PO Box 3, 31 Adelaide St. East, Toronto ON M5C 2J6
e-mail: janice.cooper@canadiansta.org
www.canadiansta.org
Overview: A medium-sized national organization founded in 2000
Chief Officer(s):
Peggy Bowie, President, 416-926-5462
peggy_bowie@manulifeam.com
Membership: *Committees:* Audit; Conference; CSTA/STA Relationship; Nominating; Sponsorship; Speakers; Website
Meetings/Conferences: • Canadian Security Traders Association 22nd Annual Conference, August, 2015
Scope: National

Canadian Seed Growers' Association (CSGA) / Association canadienne des producteurs de semences

PO Box 8455, #202, 240 Catherine St., Ottawa ON K1G 3T1
Tel: 613-236-0497; *Fax:* 613-563-7855
seeds@seedgrowers.ca
www.seedgrowers.ca
Overview: A medium-sized national organization founded in 1904
Chief Officer(s):
Dale Apolphe, Executive Director, 613-236-0497 Ext. 224
adolphed@seedgrowers.ca
Staff Member(s): 8
Membership: 4,300
Meetings/Conferences: • Canadian Seed Growers' Association's 2015 Annual General Meeting, July, 2015, Marriott Chateau Champlain Hotel, Montréal, QC
Scope: National

Canadian Seed Trade Association (CSTA) / Association canadienne du commerce des semences (ACCS)

#505, 2039 Robertson Rd., Ottawa ON K2H 8R2
Tel: 613-829-9527; *Fax:* 613-829-3530
www.cdnseed.org
www.facebook.com/cdnseed
twitter.com/SeedInnovation
Overview: A medium-sized national organization founded in 1923
Mission: To foster an environment conducive to researching, developing, distributing & trading seed and associated technologies
Chief Officer(s):
Patty Townsend, Chief Executive Officer, 613-829-9527 Ext. 223
Peter Entz, President
Finances: *Funding Sources:* Membership fees
Staff Member(s): 3
Membership: 128; *Fees:* Schedule available; *Member Profile:* Plant breeders & those involved with the seed manufacturing industry; *Committees:* Biotechnology; Forage & Turf Committee; International Committee; Researchers East; Researchers West; Oilseeds, Pulses & Western Cereals; Intellectual Property; Corn, Soybeans & Eastern Cereals

Canadian Self Storage Association (CSSA)

PO Box 188, Coldwater ON L0K 1E0
Fax: 519-941-0877
Toll-Free: 888-898-8538
info@cssa.ca
www.cssa.ca
ca.linkedin.com/groups/Canadian-Self-Storage-Association-4106636
www.facebook.com/CanadianSelfStorageAssociation
twitter.com/cdnselfstorage/
Overview: A medium-sized national organization
Mission: The Canadian Self Storage Association brings together industry members through leadership, information, products, networking, services and government representation.
Affliation(s): American Self Storage Association
Chief Officer(s):
Troy McLellan, President
Membership: *Fees:* $499
Meetings/Conferences: • Canadian Self Storage Association 9th Annual Western Canadian Conference, Trade Show & Self Storage Facility Tours, April, 2015, Dalta Vancovuer Suites, Vancouver, BC
Scope: National

Canadian Service for Overseas Students & Trainees **See** Canadian Bureau for International Education

Canadian Sheep Breeders' Association (CSBA) / La société canadienne des éleveurs de moutons

PO Box 46, RR#2, Site 7, Bluffton AB T0C 0M0
Fax: 877-207-2541
Toll-Free: 866-956-1116
www.sheepbreeders.ca
Overview: A medium-sized national organization
Mission: To represent & promote sheep breeders
Chief Officer(s):
Trenholm Nelson, President, 819-826-3066
nelson@abacom.com
Kim MacDougall, Vice President, 306-545-6190, Fax: 306-543-3919
kmacdougall@supremebasics.com
Stacey White, General Manager
Membership: 1,100; *Fees:* $50; *Committees:* Executive & Finance; Spot Parentage; Health/Scrapie Canada/Eradication Working Group; Constitution; Promotion/Education/Information; Breed Standards/International Association Recognition; Genetics/GenOvis/Research; Classic & Model/Template

Canadian Sheep Federation / Fédération canadienne du mouton

130 Malcolm Rd., Guelph ON N1K 1B1
Tel: 613-652-1824; *Fax:* 866-909-5360
Toll-Free: 888-684-7739
info@cansheep.ca
www.cansheep.ca
Previous Name: Canada Sheep Council

Overview: A small national organization founded in 1990
Mission: To set national policy for the sheep industry; to endeavour to further the viability, expansion & prosperity of the Canadian sheep & wool industry.
Chief Officer(s):
Philip Kolodychuk, Chair
philk@abnorth.com
Carlena Patterson, Executive Director
corlena@cansheep.ca
Finances: *Funding Sources:* Provincial organizations; Federal funding
Staff Member(s): 2
Membership: 10 organizations; *Member Profile:* Canadian sheep producers

Canadian Sheet Steel Building Institute (CSSBI) / Institut canadien de la tôle d'acier pour le bâtiment (ICTAB)

#2A, 652 Bishop St. North, Cambridge ON N3H 4V6
Tel: 519-650-1285; *Fax:* 519-650-8081
info@cssbi.ca
www.cssbi.ca
www.linkedin.com/groups/Canadian-Sheet-Steel-Building-Institute-388674
www.facebook.com/197469816960835
twitter.com/cssbi
Overview: A medium-sized national organization founded in 1961
Mission: To make steel the material of choice for building construction in Canada.
Chief Officer(s):
Meredith Perez, Manager, Marketing
Membership: 29 corporate; *Member Profile:* Producers, fabricators & associates involved in the structural sheet steel industry

Canadian Shiatsu Society of British Columbia (CSSBC)

Lonsdale Quay Market, #101, 123 Carrie Cates Ct., North Vancouver BC V7M 3K7
Tel: 604-986-4964
info@shiatsupractor.org
www.shiatsupractor.org
Overview: A small provincial organization
Mission: To providing the highest educational & professional standards for Shiatsu Therapy in British Columbia; Providing the Shiatsupractor (SPR) certification
Membership: *Fees:* $100; *Member Profile:* Shiatsupractors in British Columbia

Canadian Shipowners Association (CSA) / Association des armateurs canadiens (AAC)

#705, 350 Sparks St., Ottawa ON K1R 7S8
Tel: 613-232-3539; *Fax:* 613-232-6211
shipowners.ca
twitter.com/canshipowners
Previous Name: Dominion Marine Association
Overview: A medium-sized national organization founded in 1903
Mission: To promote an economic & competitive Canadian marine transportation industry; to support a national policy conducive to the development & maintenance of the Canadian flag merchant fleet in the inland, coastal & Arctic waters of Canada & foster the growth of a Canadian flag deep sea merchant fleet.
Member of: International Chamber of Shipping; International Shipping Federation; Chamber of Maritime Commerce; Canada Maritime Law Association
Chief Officer(s):
Robert Lewis-Manning, President
Silvie Dagenais, Secretary-Treasurer
dagenais@shipowners.ca
Staff Member(s): 5
Membership: 6 corporate; *Committees:* Marine Environment; Marine Operations
Activities: Monitors Canadian & US government legislative/regulatory actions, initiatives by various international marine organizations, political trends, public policy relating to navigation, safety & the Canadian shipping environment; executes strategic communications & public relations campaigns to effectively represent the interests of member companies

Canadian Shire Horse Association (CSHA)

c/o Maggie Dube, PO Box 631, Wimborne AB T0M 2G0
e-mail: shires@telus.net
www.canadianshirehorse.com
Overview: A small national organization
Mission: To encourage, develop and regulate purebred Shire horses in Canada.
Chief Officer(s):
Lindsay LaRiviere, President
lelfarms@telus.net
Dale Campbell, Vice-President
campbell@pris.ca
Maxine Campbell, Secretary-Treasurer
cshasec@pris.ca
Fran Anderson, Registrar
Membership: *Fees:* $50 Canadian breeders; $30 associate members; $500 life memberships; *Member Profile:* Shire horse breeders & owners
Activities: Arranging procedures for registration of Shire horses; Setting standards for the breed; Providing information specific to Shire breeders & owners; Presenting show results for Shire horses
Publications:
• CSHA [Canadian Shire Horse Association] Newsletter
Type: Newsletter; *Editor:* Cindy Dopson; *Price:* Free with membership in the Canadian Shire Horse Association

Canadian Shooting Sports Association (CSSA)

116 Galaxy Blvd., Etobicoke ON M9W 4Y6
Tel: 416-679-9959; *Fax:* 416-679-9910
Toll-Free: 888-873-4339
info@cdnshootingsports.org
www.cdnshootingsports.org
Merged from: Ontario Handgun Association; Ontario Smallbore Federation
Overview: A medium-sized national organization
Mission: To provide the knowledge, guidance & services to ensure the continuation promotion of the shooting sports & related activities & to represent their interests to the government, the regulatory bodies, the media & the public
Affliation(s): Ontario Council of Shooters; Shooting Federation of Canada
Finances: *Funding Sources:* Membership fees
Membership: 15,000; *Fees:* $45; $80 family; $27 junior; $250 corporate; *Member Profile:* Member of a recognized shooting club
Activities: To provide liability insurance & training courses

Canadian Shorthorn Association

Canada Centre Bldg., Exhibition Park, PO Box 3771, Regina SK S4P 3N8
Tel: 306-757-2212; *Fax:* 306-525-5852
info@canadianshorthorn.com
www.canadianshorthorn.com
Overview: A medium-sized national organization founded in 1886
Member of: Canadian Beef Breeds Council
Chief Officer(s):
Belinda Wagner, Sec.-Treas.
Finances: *Annual Operating Budget:* $100,000-$250,000
Staff Member(s): 2
Membership: 600; *Fees:* $75

Canadian Simmental Association

#13, 4101 - 19 St. NE, Calgary AB T2E 7C4
Tel: 403-250-7979; *Fax:* 403-250-5121
Toll-Free: 866-860-6051
cansim@simmental.com
www.simmental.com
Overview: A small national organization founded in 1969
Mission: To encourage, develop, & regulate the breeding of Simmental cattle in Canada
Member of: Canadian Beef Breeds Council
Chief Officer(s):
Fraser Redpath, President, 204-529-2560, Fax: 204-529-2560
redsim2@gmail.com
Kelly Ashworth, First Vice-President
jashworth@sasktel.net
Randy Mader, Second Vice-President
rrmader@xplornet.com
Bruce Holmquist, General Manager
bholmquist@simmental.com
Staff Member(s): 9
Membership: *Fees:* $25 youth; $50 annual membership initiation; $50 annual administration; $25 annual membership; $200 life membership
Activities: Registering Simmental cattle in Canada; Keeping a record of the breeding and origin of all Simmental cattle; Protecting & assisting breeders engaged in the propagation & breeding of Simmental cattle; Compiling statistics on the industry; *Library:* CSA Library;
Publications:
• Canadian Simmental Association Annual Report
Type: Yearbook; *Frequency:* Annually
• Commercial Country [a publication of the Canadian Simmental Association]
Type: Magazine; *Frequency:* Semiannually; *Accepts Advertising*
Profile: Information for the commercial industry
• CSA [Canadian Simmental Association] Member Enewsletter
Type: Newsletter; *Frequency:* Monthly
Profile: Beef information, CSA activities, registry information, & events
• Simmental Country
Type: Magazine; *Frequency:* Bimonthly; *Accepts Advertising*; *ISSN:* 1709-5212; *Price:* $42 Canada; $65 USA; $130 International
Profile: Advertising & marketing needs for breeders

Canadian Sinfonietta Youth Orchestra (CSYO)

c/o Canadian Sinfonietta, 107 Glengrove Ave. West, Toronto ON M4R 1P1
Tel: 416-716-6997
cs.youthorchestra@gmail.com
csyo.wordpress.com
twitter.com/csyouthorch
Previous Name: Toronto Cultural Youth Orchestra
Overview: A small local organization founded in 1985 overseen by Orchestras Canada
Chief Officer(s):
Tak-Ng Lai, Music Director
Jennifer Mak, Manager
Membership: *Fees:* $180; *Committees:* Parent

Canadian Ski & Snowboard Association; Canadian Ski Association *See* Canadian Snowsports Association

Canadian Ski Coaches Federation *See* Canadian Ski Instructors' Alliance

Canadian Ski Council (CSC) / Conseil canadien du ski

21 - 4 St. East, Collingwood ON L9Y 1T2
Tel: 705-445-9140
info@skicanada.org
www.skicanada.org
www.facebook.com/152259956560
twitter.com/cdnskicouncil
www.pinterest.com/gosnow
Overview: A medium-sized national organization founded in 1977
Mission: To encourage participation in recreational skiing & snowboarding.
Member of: Canadian Society of Association Executives; Tourism Industry Association of Canada.
Affliation(s): Canadian Association for Disabled Skiing; Canadian Ski Instructors' Alliance; Canadian Ski Patrol; Canadian Association of Snowboard Instructors; Association des stations de ski du Québec; Atlantic Ski Area Association; Canadian Snowsports Association; Canada West Ski Areas Association; Ontario Snow Resorts Associations
Chief Officer(s):
Claude Péloquin, Chair
Patrick Arkeveld, President & CEO
Finances: *Funding Sources:* Sponsorship; associate membership; service fees; research
Membership: 11 organizations; *Committees:* Marketing & Research; Toronto Snow Show
Activities: Skier Development Programs; product development; research; *Speaker Service:* Yes; *Rents Mailing List:* Yes

Canadian Ski Instructors' Alliance (CSIA) / Alliance des moniteurs de ski du Canada

#220, 4900, rue Jean Talon ouest, Montréal QC H4P 1W9
Tel: 514-748-2648; *Fax:* 514-748-2476
Toll-Free: 800-811-6428
national@snowpro.com
www.snowpro.com
www.facebook.com/CSIAAMSC
www.youtube.com/user/CSIAAMSC
Overview: A large national organization founded in 1938
Mission: To promote professionalism & high standards for the profession of ski instruction; To certify ski instructors across Canada
Member of: Canadian Ski Council
Affliation(s): International Ski Instructors Association
Chief Officer(s):
Dan Ralph, Managing Director
dralph@snowpro.com

Lisa Cambise, Director, Shared Services
lisa@snowpro.com
Martin Jean, Director, Education & Membership Services
martinj@snowpro.com
Benoit Fournier, Coordinator, National Programs
benoit@snowpro.com
Finances: *Funding Sources:* Membership dues
Staff Member(s): 14
Activities: Providing education & leadership that contributes to a vibrant mountain experience for the skiing public; *Internships:* Yes
Publications:
• CSIA [Canadian Ski Instructors' Alliance] eBLAST
Type: Newsletter; *Frequency:* Monthly
Profile: CSIA activities
• Ski Pro
Type: Magazine; *Frequency:* Semiannually; *Accepts Advertising*; *Price:* Free with CSIA membership
Profile: CSIA news, teaching tips, techniques, industry updates, benefits, course schedules, job listings, & merchandise for ski instructors & coaches

Canadian Ski Instructors' Alliance (CSIA) / Fédération des entraîneurs de ski du Canada
#220, 4900 rue Jean Talon ouest, Montréal QC H4P 1W9
Tel: 514-748-2648; *Fax:* 514-748-2476
Toll-Free: 800-811-6428
national@snowpro.com
www.snowpro.com/en
www.youtube.com/user/CSIAAMSC
Previous Name: Canadian Ski Coaches Federation
Overview: A medium-sized national organization founded in 1938
Mission: To help produce the best skiers in the world for Canada
Chief Officer(s):
Dan Blankstein, Chair
dan@snowpro.com
Dan Ralph, Managing Director
dralph@snowpro.com
Staff Member(s): 13

Ontario
#209, 3 Concorde Gate, Toronto ON M3C 3N7
Tel: 416-426-7261; *Fax:* 416-426-7261
info@csiaontario.com
www.csiaontario.com
Chief Officer(s):
Miranda Sorensen, Chair

Canadian Ski Marathon (CSM) / Marathon canadien de ski (MCS)
60, rue Notre Dam, Montebello QC J0V 1L0
Tel: 819-483-0456; *Fax:* 819-483-0450
Toll-Free: 877-770-6556
ski@csm-mcs.com
www.csm-mcs.com
www.facebook.com/csmmcs
twitter.com/csmmcs
Overview: A medium-sized national charitable organization founded in 1967
Mission: The Canadian Ski Marathon is an historic cross-county ski tour for people of all ages in celebration of Canadian winter. Their mission is to organize an annual & fully supported weekend in the wilderness, the Canadian Ski Marathon provides a uniquely Canadian cross-country skiing event with a broad appeal.
Affliation(s): Tourisme Outaouais; Tourisme Laurentides
Chief Officer(s):
Paul "Boomer" Throop, President
paul.throop@forces.gc.ca
Danielle Blais, General Manager
Finances: *Annual Operating Budget:* $250,000-$500,000; *Funding Sources:* Sponsors; participants
Staff Member(s): 3; 500 volunteer(s)
Membership: 2,000; *Fees:* Schedule available
Activities: Cross-Country Ski Tour; *Internships:* Yes

Canadian Ski Patrol (CSP) / Patrouille canadienne de ski (PCS)
4531 Southclark Pl., Ottawa ON K1T 3V2
Tel: 613-822-2245; *Fax:* 613-822-1088
Toll-Free: 900-565-2777
info@skipatrol.ca
www.csps.ca
Overview: A medium-sized national charitable organization founded in 1940
Mission: To provide first aid & safety programs throughout Canada
Member of: Fédération Internationale des Patrouilles de Ski (FIPS) / International Federation of Ski Patrollers
Chief Officer(s):
Renée Scanlon, Office Manager
manager@skipatrol.ca
Al Knott, Chair
chairman@skipatrol.ca
Colin Saravanamuttoo, President & CEO, 613-822-2245 Ext. 224
csaravan@skipatrol.ca
Finances: *Funding Sources:* Sponsorships; Donations
Membership: 5,450; *Member Profile:* Volunteer patrollers, over the age of eighteen, who have undergone training sessions in first aid & rescue; *Committees:* Communications; Fund Development; Education; Finance & Administration; Operations
Activities: Patrolling over 200 resorts across Canada on alpine, Nordic, & tele-mark skis, as well as on snow boards; Providing year-round safety & rescue services by volunteering at non-skiing events during the summer; Presenting awards; Providing first aid training; *Awareness Events:* National First Aid Competition
Publications:
• SK-E Patrolling News
Type: Newsletter; *Frequency:* Monthly; *Editor:* Geoff Scotton
Profile: News about the organization & upcoming events for members
• Sweep
Type: Magazine; *Frequency:* Semiannually; *Editor:* A.P. Crawford

Coquitlam - Pacific South Division
c/o Greater Vancouver Zone, #4, 62 Fawcett Rd., Coquitlam BC V3K 6V5
e-mail: communications@skipatrolbc.com
www.skipatrolbc.com
Chief Officer(s):
Steve Gunderson, President, Greater Vancouver Zone
president@skipatrolvancouver.com
Justin Lane, President, Ogopogo Zone
president@cspsoz.com
Fred Haight, President, Inter-Mountain Zone
president@inter-mountain.ca
• The CRuD!: Newsletter of the Canadian Ski Patrol System, Canadian Ski Patrol System
Type: Newsletter; *Frequency:* Weekly
Profile: Area news & events

Dartmouth - Atlantic East Division
c/o Brian Smith, Queens Sq., #604, 45 Alderney Dr., Dartmouth NS B2Y 2N6
www.scotiazone.com
Chief Officer(s):
Bernie Robichau, President, Scotia Zone
b_robichau@bellaliant.net
• CSPS [Canadian Ski Patrol System] Scotia Zone Newsletter
Type: Newsletter; *Editor:* G. Leslie

Drayton Valley - Mountain Division
3513 - 49 Ave., Drayton Valley AB T7A 1E3
www.mountaindivision.ca
Chief Officer(s):
Dave Swindlehurst, President
dave.swindlehurst@weyerhaeuser.com
Carey Rowntree, Vice-President, Communications
rtree@shaw.ca
• Mountain Peaks: Newsletter of the Canadian Ski Patrol System, Mountain Division
Type: Newsletter
Profile: Upcoming events & division updates
• The Probe: The Voice of CSPS Calgary Zone
Type: Newsletter; *Frequency:* Monthly; *Editor:* Nicole Merz
Profile: Zone reports & forthcoming events

Labrador City - Atlantic West Division
e-mail: info@atlanticwest.ca
www.atlanticwest.ca
Mission: To promote safety & injury prevention; to provide high standards of education, certification, & delivery in first aid & rescue services
Chief Officer(s):
Craig Taggart, President
president@atlanticwest.ca
Doug Couture, Vice-President, Operations
operations@atlanticwest.ca

Manitoba Division
e-mail: info@cspsmanitoba.ca
www.cspsmanitoba.ca

Ontario Division
www.skipatrol.on.ca
www.facebook.com/Canadian.Ski.Patrol
Mission: To support the Canadian Ski Patrol System system through training & leadership
Chief Officer(s):
Guy Stewart, President
guystewart@rogers.com
William Wright, Vice-President, Communications
wjwright@execulink.com
• The Lift Lines: Newsletter of the Canadian Ski Patrol System, Ontario Division
Type: Newsletter
Profile: Division activities, reports, events, & awards

Pacific North Division

Saint-Jérome - Québec Division
CP 536, Saint-Jérome QC J7Z 5V3
Tél: 514-906-7099
Ligne sans frais: 866-747-8899
info@pcsq.qc.ca
www.pcsq.qc.ca
Eric Chastenais, President, Lanaudière Zone
zone-lanaudiere@pcsq.qc.ca
Jean-Charles Cote, President, Gatineau Zone
zone-gatineau@pcsq.qc.ca
Richard Patenaude, President, Laurentian Zone
zone-laurentienne@pcsq.qc.ca
Marco Romani, President, Eastern Townships Zone
zone-cantonsdelest@pcsq.qc.ca
• Le Câble: Newsletter of the Canadian Ski Patrol System, Eastern Townships Zone
Type: Newsletter
Profile: Information about education, ski swaps, meetings, & operations in the zone
• Snow Squall: Newsletter of the Canadian Ski Patrol System, Gatineau Zone
Type: Newsletter; *Frequency:* Biweekly; *Editor:* Mark Plante
Profile: Activities in the Gatineau Zone, including special events, instructor information, & awards

Saskatoon - Saskatchewan Division
c/o Saskatoon Patrol, 443 Franklin Cres., Saskatoon SK S7J 5G4
e-mail: csps@csps-saskatoon.ca
www.csps-saskatoon.ca

Canadian Skin Patient Alliance (CSPA)
#383, 136-2446 Bank St., Ottawa ON K1V 1A8
Tel: 613-440-4260; *Fax:* 877-294-1525
Toll-Free: 877-505-2772
info@skinpatientalliance.ca
www.skinpatientalliance.ca
www.facebook.com/CanadianSkin
twitter.com/canadianskin
Overview: A large national organization founded in 2007
Mission: To educate the public about skin health & to help patients experience skin health concerns
Affliation(s): AboutFace; Alberta Society of Melanoma; Alliance Québécoise du Psoriasis; BCCNS Life Support Network; British Columbia Lymphedema Association; Canadian Alopecia Areata Foundation; Canadian Burn Survivors Community; Canadian Pemphigus & Pemphigoid Foundation; Canadian Psoriasis Network; Canadian Skin Cancer Foundation; Cutaneous Lymphoma Foundation; DEBRA Canada, Epidermolysis Bullosa; Eczema Society of Canada; Neurofibromatosis Society of Ontario; Save Your Skin; Scieroderma Association of British Columbia; Scleroderma Society of Ontario; Canadian Association of Psoriasis Patients
Chief Officer(s):
Allan Stordy, President
Membership: *Committees:* Website; Advocacy; Affiliates; SKIN Conference Planning
Publications:
• Canadian Skin Magazine
Type: Magazine; *Frequency:* 4 times a year; *Editor:* Sheri Pilon
ISSN: 1923-0729
Profile: The magazine publishes articles regarding skin health

Canadian Skipping Association ***See*** Canadian Rope Skipping Federation

Canadian Sleep Society (CSS) / Société Canadienne du Sommeil (SCS)

c/o Reut Gruber, McGill University, Douglas Institute, 6875 LaSalle Blvd., Montréal QC H4H 1R3
Fax: 877-659-0760
Toll-Free: 866-239-2176
Other Communication: media@canadiansleepsociety.ca
info@canadiansleepsociety.ca
www.canadiansleepsociety.ca
Overview: A small national charitable organization founded in 1986
Mission: To further the advancement & understanding of sleep & its disorders through scientific study & public awareness
Chief Officer(s):
Shelly K. Weiss, President
president@canadiansleepsociety.ca
Membership: 100-499; *Fees:* $100; $40 technologist; $25 student; $1000 corporate

Canadian Slovak League

#6, 259 Traders Blvd. East, Mississauga ON L4Z 2E5
Tel: 905-507-8004
administrator@kanadskyslovak.ca
www.ksliga.com
Overview: A small national organization founded in 1932

Canadian Slovenian Chamber of Commerce (CSCC)

747 Browns Line, Toronto ON M8W 3V7
Tel: 416-251-8456; *Fax:* 416-252-2092
info@canslo.com
www.canslo.com
www.facebook.com/CanadianSlovenianChamberofCommerce
Overview: A small local organization founded in 1990
Mission: To promote Canadian Slovenian business and enterprise, communication between people in business & to create opportunities for business investment in Canada and abroad.
Membership: 80+
Activities: CSCC Business Directory (online)

Canadian Snack Food Association (CSFA) / Association canadienne des fabricants des grignotines

c/o Ileana Lima, PO Box 42252, 128 Queen St. South, Mississauga ON L5M 4Z0
Tel: 289-997-1379
ileanal@4reflections.com
canadiansnack.com
Overview: A medium-sized national organization founded in 1956
Mission: To provide the leadership required for sustained growth & competitiveness of the industry; to influence policy formulation, legislation & regulations at all levels of government in the best interests of the industry
Affliation(s): Canadian Horticultural Council
Chief Officer(s):
Calum MacLeod, President
Ileana Lima, Contact
Finances: *Annual Operating Budget:* Less than $50,000
Membership: 60 corporate; *Fees:* $2,000 business; $535 associate; US$400 international; *Member Profile:* Snack food manufacturers & suppliers

Canadian Snowbird Association (CSA) / Association canadienne des Snowbirds

180 Lesmill Rd., Toronto ON M3B 2T5
Tel: 416-391-9000; *Fax:* 416-441-7007
Toll-Free: 800-265-3200
csastaff@snowbirds.org
www.snowbirds.org
Overview: A small national organization founded in 1992
Mission: Dedicated to actively defending & improving the rights & privileges of travelling Canadians
Chief Officer(s):
Michael MacKenzien, Executive Director
Michael.MacKenzie@snowbirds.org
Robert Slack, President
Finances: *Annual Operating Budget:* $500,000-$1.5 Million; *Funding Sources:* Membership fees; special donations
Staff Member(s): 6; 9 volunteer(s)
Membership: 70,000; *Fees:* $25 one year; $325 lifetime; *Committees:* Membership; Promotion; Government Relations; Finance
Activities: Lifestyle presentations, Fall in Canada; Extravaganzas; Winter information meetings (Spring in the USA)
Publications:
• CSA [Canadian Snowbird Association] News / Nouvelles CSA
Type: Magazine; *Frequency:* Quarterly; *Accepts Advertising*; *Editor:* J. Ross Quigley *ISSN:* 1195-2393; *Price:* Free with CSA membership; $20 Canada non-members; $30 International non-members
Profile: Government information, articles, CSA activities, insurance updates, health information, advice, events, awards, book reviews &benefits
• CSA [Canadian Snowbird Association] Information Booklets
Profile: Topics include the following: The CSA Member Handbook; The CSA Travel Information Guide; & The CSA Travellers' Checklist

Canadian Snowboard Federation

#301, 333 Terminal Ave., Vancouver BC V6A 4C1
Tel: 604-568-1135; *Fax:* 604-568-1639
info@canadasnowboard.ca
www.canadasnowboard.ca
www.facebook.com/canadasnowboard
twitter.com/CanadaSnowboard
Also Known As: Canada~Snowboard
Overview: A medium-sized national organization
Mission: To be the national governing body of competitive snowboarding in Canada.
Chief Officer(s):
Steve Hills, Executive Director
steven@canadasnowboard.ca
Robert Joncas, Director, High Performance
lebob@canadasnowboard.ca
Nadia M'Seffar, Manager, Communications & Media Relations
nadia@canadasnowboard.ca
Activities: Freestyle; alpine; snowboardcross; para-snowboard

Canadian Snowsports Association (CSA) / L'Association canadienne des sports d'hiver (ACSH)

#202, 1451 West Broadway, Vancouver BC V6H 1H6
Tel: 604-734-6800; *Fax:* 604-669-7954
info@canadiansnowsports.com
www.canadiansnowsports.com
Previous Name: Canadian Ski & Snowboard Association; Canadian Ski Association
Overview: A large national organization founded in 1920
Mission: To develop elite amateur athletes; To pursue excellence at national & international level competition
Chief Officer(s):
Chris Robinson, President
David Pym, Managing Director
dpym@isrm.com
Lillian Alderton, Administrator
lillianalderton@hotmail.com
Membership: 700+ ski clubs + 97,000 members
Awards:
• John Semmelink Memorial Award (Award)
• Dee Road Memorial Award (Award)
• Patricia Ramage Volunteer of the Year Award (Award)

Canadian Soccer Association (CSA) / Association canadienne de soccer

Place Soccer Canada, 237 Metcalfe St., Ottawa ON K2P 1R2
Tel: 613-237-7678; *Fax:* 613-237-1516
info@soccercan.ca
www.canadasoccer.com
www.facebook.com/canadasoccer
twitter.com/CanadaSoccerEN
www.youtube.com/CanadaSoccerTV
Overview: A large national organization founded in 1912
Mission: To promote the growth & development of soccer for all Canadians at all levels; to provide leadership & good governance for the sport
Affliation(s): Féderation Internationale de Football Association, FIFA; Football Confederation; Canadian Olympic Association
Chief Officer(s):
Victor Montagliani, President
Peter Montopoli, General Secretary
Earl Cochrane, Deputy General Secretary
Sean Hefferman, CFO
Ray Clark, Director, Coaching & Player Development
rclark@canadasoccer.com
Cathy Breda, Manager, Administration
cbreda@soccercan.ca
Michèle Dion, Acting Director, Communications
mdion@soccercan.ca
Staff Member(s): 56
Membership: 850,000 registered players

Technical Office
BMO Field, 170 Princes' Blvd., Toronto ON M6K 3C3
Tel: 416-263-5890; *Fax:* 416-263-5891

Canadian Social Work Foundation (CSWF) / Fondation canadienne du service social

#402, 383 Parkdale Ave., Ottawa ON K1Y 4R4
Tel: 613-729-6668; *Fax:* 613-729-9608
Toll-Free: 855-729-2279
casw@casw-acts.ca
www.casw-acts.ca
www.facebook.com/Canadian.Association.of.Social.Workers
Overview: A small national charitable organization
Mission: To edit & publish books, papers, journals & other forms of literature respecting social work in order to disseminate information to the public; to encourage studies; to promote, develop & sponsor activities strengthening social work
Chief Officer(s):
Morel Caissie, President
Fred Phelps, Executive Director
Finances: *Funding Sources:* Donations
Staff Member(s): 4
Membership: *Fees:* $50 affiliate; $0 students

Canadian Society for Aesthetic (Cosmetic) Plastic Surgery (CSACPS) / Société canadienne de chirurgie plastique esthétique

2334 Heska Rd., Pickering ON L1V 2P9
Tel: 905-831-7750; *Fax:* 905-831-7248
info@csaps.ca
www.csaps.ca
www.facebook.com/csaps
Overview: A small national organization founded in 1972
Mission: To improve cosmetic surgery outcomes; To maintain high surgical standards of clinical practice
Chief Officer(s):
Gregory Waslen, M.D., President
Elizabeth Hall-Findlay, Vice-President
Felix-Andre Tetu, Secretary-Treasurer
Pat Hewitt, Secretariat
Membership: 160+; *Member Profile:* Certified specialists in plastic surgery, with a special focus on aesthetic surgery; *Committees:* Ethics; Judicial; Constitution / Bylaws; Public Relations; Nominating; Educational; CMPA Ad Hoc; Public Education Ad Hoc
Activities: Supporting research; Providing education
Meetings/Conferences: • 2015 Canadian Society for Aesthetic (Cosmetic) Plastic Surgery 42nd Annual Meeting, September, 2015, Montréal, QC
Scope: National

Canadian Society for Aesthetics (CSA) / Société canadienne d'esthétique (SCE)

c/o Dawson College, 4729, av de Maisonneuve, Westmount QC H3Z 1M3
www.csa-sce.ca
Overview: A small national organization founded in 1984
Mission: To keep aesthetic theorists in close touch with the creative & critical practices that are the basis of their discipline; to increase awareness of aesthetic issues among Canadian citizens & develop the intellectual & conceptual resources for dealing with them.
Member of: Humanities & Social Sciences Federation of Canada
Chief Officer(s):
Ira Newman, Anglophone President
inewman@mansfield.edu
Carl Simpson, Secretary, Membership
msimpson@wlu.ca
Finances: *Funding Sources:* Membership dues; HSSFC

Canadian Society for Analytical Sciences & Spectroscopy

PO Box 46122, 2339 Ogilvie Rd., Ottawa ON K1J 9M7
Tel: 613-933-3719; *Fax:* 613-954-5984
www.csass.org
Previous Name: Spectroscopy Society of Canada
Overview: A medium-sized national organization founded in 1957
Mission: To organize programs of scientific & general interest for the educational benefit of members & the public; to organize annual scientific conferences & workshops on various aspects of pure & applied spectroscopy in the chemical, biological, geochemical & metallurgical sciences
Affliation(s): Society for Applied Spectroscopy - USA; Colloquium Spectroscopicum Internationale; Chemical Institute of Canada; Canadian Society of Forensic Science
Chief Officer(s):
Graeme Spiers, President
gspiers@mirarco.org

Ana Delgado, Treasurer
ana.delgado@nrc.gc.ca
Membership: *Fees:* Schedule available

Canadian Society for Bioengineering (CSBE) / Société canadienne de génie agroalimentaire et de bioingénierie (SCGAB)

2028 Calico Crescent, Orleans ON K4A 4L7
Tel: 613-590-0975
bioeng@shaw.ca
www.bioeng.ca
Previous Name: Canadian Society for Engineering in Agricultural, Food & Biological Systems
Overview: A medium-sized national organization founded in 1958
Mission: To provide expertise in the areas of farm power & machinery, structures & environment, soil & water & electrical power & processing
Affiliation(s): American Society of Agricultural & Biological Engineers
Chief Officer(s):
James S. Townsend, Secretary
Ron MacDonald, President
rmacdonald@agviro.com
Finances: *Annual Operating Budget:* Less than $50,000; *Funding Sources:* Annual dues
Staff Member(s): 1; 17 volunteer(s)
Membership: 500 full + 200 students; *Fees:* Schedule available
Activities: Canadian Society for Bioengineering Foundation
Awards:
- John Turnbull Award (Award)
- John Clark Award (Award)
- Glenn Downing Award (Award)
- Jim Beamish Award (Award)
- Maple Leaf Award (Award)
- Industrial Award (Award)
- CSBE Fellow Award (Award)

Meetings/Conferences: • CSBE/SCGAB 2015 Annual General Meeting & Technical Conference, July, 2015, Delta Edmonton South Hotel & Conference Centre, Edmonton, AB
Scope: National
Description: The conference will include workshops, technical sessions, networking receptions, tours, a guest program, the CSBE Awards Banquet and the CSBE Annual General Meeting.
Contact Information: Local Organizing Committee Chair: Rick Atkins, rick.atkins@gov.ab.ca; URL: csbe-scgab.ca/edmonton2015
Publications:
- Canadian Biosystems Engineering Journal / Le Journal de la Société Canadienne de Génie Agroalimentaire et de Bioingénierie
Type: Journal; *Editor:* Ranjan Sri Ranjan; *Price:* $50 Canada non-members; $30 Canada CSBE / SCGAB members
Profile: Peer-reviewed papers
- Canadian Society for Bioengineering Annual Meeting Papers
Frequency: Annually
Profile: Presentations from conferences
- Perspectives: The Newsletter of CSBE [Canadian Society for Bioengineering] / Les Nouvelles de SCGAB
Type: Newsletter
Profile: Canadian Society for Bioengineering / Société canadienne de génie agroalimentaire et de bioingénierie activities,awards, chapter news, job opportunities, & events
- Resource [a publication of the Canadian Society for Bioengineering]
Type: Magazine; *Accepts Advertising*
Profile: Industry news & trends

Canadian Society for Brain, Behaviour & Cognitive Science (CSBBCS) / Société Canadienne des Sciences du Cerveau, du Comportement et de la Cognition

c/o Dept. of Psychology, University of British Columbia, Vancouver BC V6T 1Z4
e-mail: secretary@csbbcs.org
www.csbbcs.org
Overview: A small national organization
Mission: To advance Canadian research in experimental psychology & behavioral neuroscience
Member of: National Consortium of Scientific & Educational Societies
Chief Officer(s):
Penny Pexman, President
Peter Graf, Secretary-Treasurer
Membership: 400+; *Fees:* $70 regular; $40 associate/student; *Member Profile:* Students & people with PhDs in psychology & related fields
Meetings/Conferences: • Canadian Society for Brain, Behaviour & Cognitive Science Annual Meeting, June, 2015, Carleton University, Ottawa, ON

Canadian Society for Chemical Engineering (CSChE) / Société canadienne de génie chimique (SCGC)

c/o The Chemical Institute of Canada (CIC), #550, 130 Slater St., Ottawa ON K1P 6E2
Tel: 613-232-6252; *Fax:* 613-232-5862
Toll-Free: 888-542-2242
www.cheminst.ca
Overview: A medium-sized national organization overseen by Chemical Institute of Canada
Mission: To advance the principles & practice of chemical engineering throughout Canada; To ensure excellence in chemical engineering; To act as the national voice of chemical engineering professionals on issues related to chemical engineering, such as regulatory affairs & research funding
Chief Officer(s):
David Guss, President
david_guss@nexeninc.com
Roland Andersson, Executive Director
randersson@cheminst.ca
Amarjett Bassi, Vice-President
abassi@uwo.ca
Nicolas Abatzoglou, Director, Awards
Handan Tezel, Director, Conferences & Symposia
Madjid Mohseni, Director, Publications & Continuing Education
Francois Bertrand, Treasurer
Finances: *Funding Sources:* Membership fees
Membership: *Fees:* Schedule available; *Member Profile:* Chemical engineering professionals employed in academia, government, & industry
Activities: Promoting ethics & responsibility among members; Engaging in lobbying activities on behalf of members; Providing professional development activities; Organizing networking events; Increasing public awareness & understanding of chemical engineering;
Publications:
- The Canadian Journal of Chemical Engineering
Type: Journal; *Frequency:* Bimonthly

Canadian Society for Chemical Technology (CSCT) / Société canadienne de technologie chimique (SCTC)

#550, 130 Slater St., Ottawa ON K1P 6E2
Tel: 613-232-6252; *Fax:* 613-232-5862
Toll-Free: 888-542-2242
www.cheminst.ca
Overview: A small national organization overseen by Chemical Institute of Canada
Mission: To establish & maintain high standards in the profession of chemical technology throughout Canada
Chief Officer(s):
Donna McMahon, President
dmcmahon@suncor.com
Samantha Waytowich, Vice-President
swaytowich@leanscn.com
Roland Andersson, Executive Director
randersson@cheminst.ca
Kevin Ferris, Director, Certification
kferris@ferrischemicals.com
Finances: *Annual Operating Budget:* Less than $50,000; *Funding Sources:* Membership fees; Constituent fees; Certificates; Symposiums & courses
Membership: *Fees:* Schedule available; *Member Profile:* Chemical technology professionals, from academia, government, & industry; Students
Activities: Providing professional development opportunities; Certifying members Offering networking among technologists from industry, government, & academia; Increasing the public awareness of chemical technology

Canadian Society for Chemistry (CSC) / Société canadienne de chimie

#550, 130 Slater St., Ottawa ON K1P 6E2
Tel: 613-232-6252; *Fax:* 613-232-5862
Toll-Free: 888-542-2242
info@cheminst.ca
www.cheminst.ca
Overview: A small national organization overseen by Chemical Institute Of Canada
Mission: To represent the field of chemistry & the interests of chemists in industry, academia, & government; To advance the principles & practices of the chemical sciences for the betterment of society
Chief Officer(s):
Roland Andersson, Executive Director, 613-232-6252 Ext. 222
randersson@cheminst.ca
Joan Kingston, Director, 613-232-6252 Ext. 225
jkingston@cheminst.ca
Lucie Frigon, Manager, 613-232-6252 Ext. 240
lfrigon@cheminst.ca
Gale Thirlwall, Manager, Awards & Local Sections, 613-232-6252 Ext. 223
gthirlwall@cheminst.ca
Angie Moulton, Coordinator, Membership Services, 613-232-6252 Ext. 230
amoulton@cheminst.ca
Membership: *Member Profile:* Chemists
Activities: Holding four regional undergraduate student conferences annually in the Atlantic region, Québec, Southwestern Ontario, & Westen Canada; Advancing the public's understanding & appreciation of chemistry; Recommending standards of education in chemistry
Meetings/Conferences: • Canadian Society for Chemistry 2015 98th Canadian Chemistry Conference & Exhibition, June, 2015, Ottawa, ON
Scope: National
Contact Information: URL: www.csc2015.ca
• Canadian Society for Chemistry 2016 99th Canadian Chemistry Conference & Exhibition, June, 2016, Halifax Convention Centre, Halifax, NS
Scope: National
Attendance: 1,000
Publications:
- Canadian Chemical News / L'Actualité chimique canadienne
Type: Magazine; *Frequency:* 10 pa; *Accepts Advertising*; *Editor:* Terri Pavelic; *Price:* Free with membership in The Chemical Institute Of Canada
Profile: News about the Canadian & international chemical scene, for chemical professionals
- Canadian Journal of Chemistry
Type: Journal; *Frequency:* Monthly; *Editor:* Dr. Robert H. Lipson
ISSN: 1480-3291
Profile: Current research findings & articles, plus comprehensive reviews in all branches of chemistry

Canadian Society for Civil Engineering (CSCE) / Société canadienne de génie civil

4877, rue Sherbrooke ouest, Montréal QC H3Z 1G9
Tel: 514-933-2634; *Fax:* 514-933-3504
Other Communication: membership@csce.ca
info@csce.ca
www.csce.ca
Overview: A medium-sized national organization founded in 1887 overseen by The Engineering Institute of Canada
Mission: To develop & maintain high standard of civil engineering practice in Canada; To enhance the public image of the civil engineering profession
Chief Officer(s):
Doug Salloum, Executive Director
doug.salloum@csce.ca
Mahmoud Lardjane, Manager, Programs
mahmoud@csce.ca
Louise Newman, Manager, Communications
louise@csce.ca
Andrea Grimaud, Officer, Membership Liaison
membership@csce.ca
Membership: *Fees:* Schedule available; *Committees:* Infrastructure Renewal; Innovations & IT; International Affairs; Sustainable Development; Career Development; Honours & Fellowships; History
Activities: Offering continuing education & networking opportunities; Working with sister organizations; Promoting civil engineering
Meetings/Conferences: • Canadian Society for Civil Engineering 2015 Annual General Meeting & Conference, May, 2015, Regina, SK
Scope: National
Publications:
- Canadian Civil Engineer (CCE)
Type: Magazine; *Frequency:* 5 pa; *Accepts Advertising*; *Editor:* Louise Newman *ISSN:* 9825-7515; *Price:* $35 Canada & U.S.A.; $45 other countries
Profile: Technical activity reports, technical articles, corporate & personal achievement items, & networking news

• Canadian Journal of Civil Engineering (CJCE)
Type: Journal
Profile: Technical journal featuring scholarly papers devoted to civil engineering
• Canadian Society for Civil Engineering Annual Report
Type: Yearbook; *Frequency:* Annually
Profile: Reports from executives such as the president, the president-elect, the executive director, vice-president, committees, & the CSCE Foundation, in addition to theauditor's report & financial statements
• Canadian Society for Civil Engineering E-Bulletin
Type: Newsletter; *Frequency:* Monthly; *Accepts Advertising*
Profile: Featuring current industry & society news, trends, & forthcoming events of interest to over 7,000 subscribers
• Canadian Society for Civil Engineering President's E-Letter
Type: Newsletter; *Frequency:* Monthly
Profile: Information for members of the Canadian Society for Civil Engineering, including forthcoming programs & conferences
• Canadian Society for Civil Engineering Conference Proceedings
Type: Yearbook; *Frequency:* Annually
Profile: Proceedings usually include an abstract book & CD-ROM with details of the society's annual conference
• A Civil Society - A brief personal history of the CSCE [Canadian Society for Civil Engineering]

Canadian Society for Clinical Investigation (CSCI) / Société canadienne de recherches cliniques (SCRC)

114 Cheyenne Way, Ottawa ON K2J 0E9
Toll-Free: 877-968-9449
info@csci-scrc.ca
www.csci-scrc.ca
Overview: A medium-sized national organization founded in 1951
Mission: To promote research in the field of human health throughout Canada; to lobby for research funding; to support Canadian researchers in their endeavours & at all stages of their careers by supporting knowledge translation & fostering communities of health science researchers
Chief Officer(s):
Brent W. Winston, President
Finances: *Funding Sources:* Membership dues; grants
Membership: 440; *Fees:* $160; $50 Associate; $0 Emeritus; *Member Profile:* General - person with an active interest in research; associate - person who holds a doctoral level degree & is still in training
Awards:
• Distinguished Scientist Award (Award)
• CSCI/CAPM Core Medical Residents Research Award (Award)
• CSCI/CIHR Resident Research Prize (Award)
• CSCI/RCPSC/PAIRO Specialty Resident Research Awards (Award)
• Joe Doupe Young Investigator's Award (Award)
• Distinguished Service Award (Award)
• CSCI/RCPSC/CFBS G. Malcolm Brown Lecture (Award)
• CSCI/RCPSC Henry Friesen Award (Award)
Publications:
• Clinical & Investigative Medicine (CIM)
Type: Journal; *Frequency:* Bimonthly; *Editor:* David R. Bevan
Profile: Original research, policy changes that affect biological & medical science research, issues related to medical research funding, information for clinician-scientisttrainees

Canadian Society for Continental Philosophy (CSCP)

c/o Dept. of Philosophy, University of Calgary, 2500 University Dr. NW, Calgary AB T2N 1N4
www.c-scp.org
Previous Name: Canadian Society for Hermeneutics & Postmodern Thought
Overview: A small national organization
Mission: To be dedicated to the pursuit & exchange of philosophical ideas inspired by Continental European traditions; to provide a forum for scholarly interests in such fields as hermeneutics, existentialism, phenomenology, deconstruction, critical theory & poststructuralism
Chief Officer(s):
Shannon Hoff, President
Lorraine Markotic, Treasurer
Membership: *Fees:* $35 student/unwaged; $55 regular
Activities: Annual meetings

Canadian Society for Education through Art (CSEA) / Société canadienne d'éducation par l'art (SCEA)

PO Box 1700, Stn. CSC, University of Victoria, Victoria BC V8W 3N4
Tel: 250-721-7896; *Fax:* 250-721-7598
office.csea@gmail.com
www.csea-scea.ca
www.facebook.com/groups/187459137995296/?ref=ts&fref=ts
Overview: A medium-sized national organization founded in 1955
Mission: The Canadian Society for Education through Art, is a voluntary association and is the only Canadian national organization that brings together art educators, gallery educators, and others wtih simialr intersts and concerns.
Affliation(s): British Columbia Art Teachers' Association; Fine Arts Council, Alberta Teachers' Association; Saskatchewan Society for Education through Art; Manitoba Association of Art Educators; Ontario Society for Education through Art; Provincial Association of Art Teachers; Association québécoise des éducateurs spécialisés en arts plastiques; New Brunswick Arts Education Council; Nova Scotia Art Teachers' Association; PEI Art Teachers' Association; Art Council of the Newfoundland Teachers' Association; Canadian Art Gallery Educators
Chief Officer(s):
Miriam Cooley, President, 780-492-0902
miriam.cooley@ualberta.ca
Finances: *Annual Operating Budget:* Less than $50,000; *Funding Sources:* Membership fees
12 volunteer(s)
Membership: 350; *Fees:* $65; *Member Profile:* Represents all levels of education: elementary, secondary, college/university, ministries of education, art galleries/museums, and community education.
Activities: Canadian Children's Art Collection; archives; *Awareness Events:* Art Education Month, May
Awards:
• CSEA/Crayola Awards (Award)
Awarded to teachers of quality art programs in grades 3-6
• Student Scholarships (Scholarship)
Awarded to Canadian high school graduates planning to continue their art education

Canadian Society for Eighteenth-Century Studies (CSECS) / Société canadienne d'étude du dix-huitième siècle (SCEDS)

c/o Department of French, University of Manitoba, 427 Fletcher Argue Bldg., Winnipeg MB R3T 2N2
Tel: 204-474-9206
www.csecs.ca
Overview: A small national charitable organization founded in 1971
Mission: To sustain, in Canada, interest in eighteenth-century civilization in Europe & the New World; to encourage, from a wide interdisciplinary base, research on the eighteenth-century; to make known to eighteenth-century specialists the work done in this area in Canada.
Member of: Canadian Federation for the Humanities
Affliation(s): International Society for Eighteenth-Century Studies
Chief Officer(s):
Armelle St-Martin, President
armelle.stmartin@umanitoba.ca
Isabelle Tremblay, Secretary
Isabelle.Tremblay@rmc.ca
Julie Murray, Treasurer
julie_murray@carleton.ca
Finances: *Funding Sources:* Membership fees; Social Science & Humanities Federation of Canada
Awards:
• Mark Madoff Prize (Award)
For best graduate paper read at the conference
• D.W. Smith Eighteenth-Century Research Fellowship (Award)
Amount: $2,000 *Contact:* Betty A. Schellenberg, schellen@sfu.ca
Meetings/Conferences: • Canadian Society for Eighteenth-Century Studies 2015 Conference, October, 2015, Vancouer, BC
Contact Information: csecs@sfu.ca
Publications:
• The Canadian Society for Eighteenth-Century Studies Bulletin
Type: Journal; *Frequency:* Semiannually; *Editor:* Stéphanie Massé; K. James-Cavan
• Lumen
Type: Journal; *Frequency:* Annually; *Editor:* Barbara K. Seeber; Ugo Dionne *ISSN:* 0824-3298; *Price:* $29.95 Canada & U.S.A.; $50 international
Profile: Formerly known as Man and Nature / L'homme et la nature; Based on annual conference

Canadian Society for Engineering in Agricultural, Food & Biological Systems *See* Canadian Society for Bioengineering

Canadian Society for Engineering Management (CSEM) / Société canadienne de gestion en ingénierie

1295 Hwy. 2 East, Kingston ON K7L 4V1
Tel: 613-547-5989
louisem@cogeco.ca
www.csem-scgi.org
www.linkedin.com/groups/Canadian-Engineering-Management-4865922
Previous Name: EIC General Members Society
Overview: A medium-sized national organization founded in 1981 overseen by The Engineering Institute of Canada
Mission: To represent the interests & enhance the capabilities of engineers in management in order to promote & advance efficient management of commerce, industry & public affairs.
Chief Officer(s):
Aidan Gordon, President
Dominique Janssens, Sec.-Treas.
Finances: *Annual Operating Budget:* Less than $50,000; *Funding Sources:* Membership fees
Staff Member(s): 1; 8 volunteer(s)
Membership: 365; *Fees:* $85

Canadian Society for Epidemiology & Biostatistics (CESB) / Société canadienne d'épidémiologie et de biostatistique (SCEB)

c/o Pamela Wilson, The Willow Group, 1485 Laperriere Ave., Ottawa ON K1Z 7S8
Tel: 613-722-8796; *Fax:* 613-729-6206
secretariat@cseb.ca
www.cseb.ca
www.facebook.com/109122749151677
twitter.com/csebsceb
www.youtube.com/user/CSEBSCEB
Overview: A small national organization founded in 1990
Mission: To foster epidemiology & biostatistics research in Canada; To improve training in the disciplines of epidemiology & biostatistics in Canada
Chief Officer(s):
Susan Jaglal, President
Paul Arora, Secretary
Membership: *Fees:* $50 students; $100 full membership; *Member Profile:* Epidemiologists; Health care professionals; Researchers; Biostatisticians; Statisticians; Students
Activities: Facilitating communication among epidemiologists & biostatisticians
Meetings/Conferences: • Canadian Society for Epidemiology & Biostatistics 2015 Biennial Conference, 2015, Toronto, ON
Scope: National
Publications:
• Canadian Society for Epidemiology & Biostatistics Newsletter
Type: Newsletter
Profile: Information of interest to members of the Society

Canadian Society for Exercise Physiology (CSEP) / Société canadienne de physiologie de l'exercice (SCPE)

#370, 18 Louisa St., Ottawa ON K1R 6Y6
Tel: 613-234-3755; *Fax:* 613-234-3565
Toll-Free: 877-651-3755
info@csep.ca
www.csep.ca
www.facebook.com/group.php?gid=291577755198
twitter.com/CSEPdotCA
Previous Name: Canadian Association of Sport Sciences
Overview: A medium-sized national organization founded in 1967
Mission: To promote the generation, synthesis, transfer, & application of knowledge & research related to exercise physiology, encompassing physical activity, fitness, health, nutrition, epidemiology & human performance; To act as the voice for exercise physiology in Canada
Chief Officer(s):
Earl Noble, PhD, President
enoble@uwo.ca
Brian MacIntosh, PhD, Executive Director
brian@kin.ucalgary.ca
Peter Tiidus, PhD, Vice-President, Research
ptiidus@wlu.ca
Panagiota Klentrou, Treasurer
nota.klentrou@brocku.ca
Membership: 5,400; *Fees:* $20 first-time sponsored students; $50 students; $175 active & affiliate members; *Member Profile:*

Active members with the graduate degree, PhD, MD, or MSc; Affiliate members with a BSc, BA, BPE, BKin, or no degree; Organizations; Students currently enrolled full-time in university studies; Retired active members; *Committees:* Annual General Meeting Program; Applied Physiology, Nutrition, & Metabolism (APNM) Editorial; Finance; Graduate Student; CSEP Health & Fitness Program National Advisory; Knowledge Transfer; Physical Activity Measurement & Guidelines (PAMG) Steering; Expert Advisory (Scientific Advisors); CSEP Health & Fitness Program Executive; CSEP Certified Exercise Physiologist Technical; CSEP Certified Personal Trainer Technical; Strategic Health & Fitness Program Initiatives; CSEP Health & Fitness Program Marketing; Research Subcommittees (Existing & New Guidelines)
Activities: Offering the National Health & Fitness Program; Engaging in advocacy activities; Advertising job postings; Facilitating national communication through committees & networks; Providing networking opportunities
Awards:
- CSEP Young Investigator Award (Award)
- CSEP Honour Award (Award)
- Graduate Student Award (Award)
- CSEP / SCPE Undergraduate Student Award (Award)
- Health & Fitness Program Recognition Award (Award)

Meetings/Conferences: • Canadian Society for Exercise Physiology 2015 Annual General Meeting, 2015
Scope: National
Contact Information: E-mail: info@csep.ca
Publications:
- Active Living During Pregnancy: Physical Activitiy Guidelines for Mother & Baby
Type: Manual; *Number of Pages:* 40; *ISBN:* 978-1-896900-06-3; *Price:* $11.95
Profile: A resource for pregnant women who want to maintain activity during pregnancy
- Applied Physiology, Nutrition & Metabolism (APNM)
Type: Journal; *Editor:* Terry Graham, PhD; *Price:* Free with membership in the Canadian Society for Exercise Physiology
Profile: Original research articles, reviews, & commentaries on the application of physiology, nutrition, & metabolism to the study of humanhealth, physical activity, & fitness
- Canada's Physical Activity Guide to Healthy Active Living (Adults 20-55): PA Guide Handbook
Type: Handbook; *Number of Pages:* 32
Profile: Detailed advice & case studies about becoming more active, produced by the Public Health Agency of Canada (PHAC) & theCanadian Society for Exercise Physiology (CSEP)
- The Canadian Physical Activity, Fitness & Lifestyle Approach (CPAFLA)
Type: Manual; *Number of Pages:* 300; *ISBN:* 978-1-896900-16-2; *Price:* $70
Profile: CSEP Health & Fitness Program's health-related appraisal & counselling strategy
- Communiqué [a publication of the Canadian Society for Exercise Physiology]
Type: Newsletter; *Frequency:* Monthly; *Accepts Advertising*; *Price:* Free withmembership in the Canadian Society for Exercise Physiology
Profile: A member newsletter of the Canadian Society for Exercise Physiology, with job postings & information about forthcoming conferences
- CSEP [Canadian Society for Exercise Physiology] Member Directory
Type: Directory
Profile: A listing of the more 4,500 members of the Canadian Society for Exercise Physiology, to help users locate CSEP Certified Personal Trainers or CSEPCertified Exercise Physiologists
- The CSEP [Canadian Society for Exercise Physiology] Certified Exercise Physiologist Certification Guide
Type: Guide; *Number of Pages:* 144; *ISBN:* 978-1-896900-26-1; *Price:* $39.95
Profile: For candidates preparing for the theory & practical examination process to be recognized as CSEPCertified Exercise Physiologist
- CSEP [Canadian Society for Exercise Physiology] Certified Personal Trainer Study Guide
Type: Guide; *Number of Pages:* 52; *ISBN:* 978-1-896900-28-5; *Price:* $29.95
Profile: For candidates preparing to obtain the professional personal training certificate in Canada
- Inclusive Fitness & Lifestyle Services for all (dis)Abilities
Type: Manual; *Number of Pages:* 300; *ISBN:* 978-1-896900-10-0; *Price:* $55
Profile: Resources to provide fitness assessment & active living counselling services
- Physical Activity Guide for Children (6-9 Years of Age): Family Guide to Physical Activity for Children
Type: Guide; *Number of Pages:* 12
Profile: Advice about how children can be active, produced by the Public Health Agency of Canada (PHAC) & the CanadianSociety for Exercise Physiology (CSEP)
- Physical Activity Guide for Children (6-9 Years of Age): Teacher's Guide to Physical Activity for Children
Type: Guide; *Number of Pages:* 8
Profile: Advice for teachers about how children can be active, produced by the Public Health Agency of Canada (PHAC) & theCanadian Society for Exercise Physiology (CSEP)
- Physical Activity Guide for Older Adults (Over 55): PA Guide Handbook for Older Adults
Type: Handbook; *Number of Pages:* 32
Profile: Detailed advice with tips on increasing physical activity, produced by the Public Health Agency of Canada (PHAC) & the CanadianSociety for Exercise Physiology (CSEP)
- Physical Activity Guide for Youth (10-14 Years of Age): Family Guide to Physical Activity for Youth
Type: Guide; *Number of Pages:* 12
Profile: A support resource for families, produced by the Public Health Agency of Canada (PHAC) & the Canadian Society forExercise Physiology (CSEP)
- Physical Activity Guide for Youth (10-14 Years of Age): Teacher's Guide to Physical Activity for Youth
Type: Guide; *Number of Pages:* 8
Profile: A support resource for teachers, produced by the Public Health Agency of Canada (PHAC) & the Canadian Society forExercise Physiology (CSEP)
- Professional Fitness & Lifestyle Consultant (PFLC) Resource Manual
Type: Manual; *Number of Pages:* 250; *ISBN:* 978-1-896900-04-9; *Price:* $55
Profile: The practical requirements for certification as a CSEP Certified Exercise Physiologist

Canadian Society for Hermeneutics & Postmodern Thought
See *Canadian Society for Continental Philosophy*

Canadian Society for Horticultural Science (CSHS) / Société canadienne de science horticole (SCSH)

c/o Dept. of Plant & Animal Sciences, Nova Scotia Agricultural College, PO Box 550, Truro NS B2N 5E3
Tel: 902-893-6032; *Fax:* 902-897-9762
www.cshs.ca
Overview: A small national organization founded in 1956
Mission: To advance research, teaching, information, & technology related to all horticultural crops
Chief Officer(s):
Samir C. Debnath, President
samir.debnath@agr.gc.ca
Kris Pruski, Ph.D., Secretary-Treasurer
kpruski@nsac.ca
Membership: *Member Profile:* Scientists; Educators; Extension agents; Industry personnel; Students
Activities: Providing professional development opportunities; Organizing an annual conference & scientific meeting
Publications:
- Canadian Journal of Plant Science (CJPS)
Type: Journal; *Frequency:* Quarterly; *Editor:* Vaino Poysa
Profile: Shared with the Canadian Society of Agronomy (CSA)
- CSHS [Canadian Society for Horticultural Science] Newsletter
Type: Newsletter; *Frequency:* Quarterly
Profile: Society activities, issues, & events
- CSHS [Canadian Society for Horticultural Science] Membership Directory
Type: Directory; *Frequency:* Annually
Profile: Listings of Society members, plus information about governance, committees, & awards
- Program & Abstracts of the CSHS [Canadian Society for Horticultural Science] Annual Conference
Type: Yearbook; *Frequency:* Annually
Profile: The latest horticultural research

Canadian Society for Immunology (CSI)

c/o Dept. of Veterinary Microbiology, Univ. of Saskatchewan, 52 Campus Dr., Saskatoon SK S7N 5B4
Tel: 306-966-7214; *Fax:* 306-966-7244
Other Communication: membership@csi-sci.ca
info@csi-sci.ca
www.csi-sci.ca
Overview: A small national charitable organization founded in 1966
Mission: To foster & support immunology research & education across Canada
Member of: Research Canada
Chief Officer(s):
Hanne Ostergaard, President
hanne.ostergaard@ualberta.ca
Lori Coulthurst, Society Administrator
Membership: 250+; *Fees:* $30 students; $50 postdoctoral fellows, research associates, technicians of CSI members; $80 educational faculty & professionals; *Member Profile:* Members from hospitals, research institutes, & universities across Canada
Activities: Lobbying for immunology research funding; Liaising between membership & national funding agencies; Presenting awards
Meetings/Conferences: • Canadian Society for Immunology 28th Annual Conference, June, 2015, The Fairmount Winnipeg, Winnipeg, MB
Scope: National

Canadian Society for Industrial Security Inc. (CSIS) / Société canadienne de la sûreté industrielle (SCSI)

PO Box 57006, 2 King St. West, Hamilton ON L8P 4W9
Tel: 905-853-6523; *Fax:* 905-972-0404
Toll-Free: 800-461-7748
inquiries@csis-scsi.org
www.csis-scsi.org
Overview: A medium-sized national organization founded in 1954
Mission: To provide a forum for security issues; To develop high standards for security education; To promote professional security ethics
Chief Officer(s):
Fergus Keyes, President
president@csis-scsi.org
Robert A. Marentette, Executive Director
csisinc@sympatico.ca
Finances: *Funding Sources:* Membership dues; Profit from annual convention; Donations
Membership: *Member Profile:* Individuals engaged in security in Canada
Activities: Offering professional designations; Providing educational opportunites;
Publications:
- Canadian Security
Type: Magazine; *Frequency:* 9 pa; *Accepts Advertising*; *Editor:* Jennifer Brown
- Canadian Society for Industrial Security Inc. National Newsletter
Type: Newsletter; *Accepts Advertising*; *Editor:* Dennis Burton
Profile: Membership information, regional news, awards, conferences, CSIS services
- Canadian Society for Industrial Security Inc. Membership Directory
Type: Directory
- The Canadian Society for Industrial Security Inc. National Capital Region Newsletter
Type: Newsletter; *Frequency:* Quarterly; *Accepts Advertising*; *Editor:* Dennis Burton
Profile: Chapter information

Canadian Society for International Health (CSIH) / Société canadienne de la santé internationale

#1105, 1 Nicholas St., Ottawa ON K1N 7B7
Tel: 613-241-5785
csih@csih.org
www.csih.org
www.linkedin.com/groups/CSIH-Global-Health-Forum-3671985
www.facebook.com/CSIH.org
twitter.com/globalsante
Previous Name: Canadian Society for Tropical Medicine & International Health
Overview: A medium-sized international charitable organization founded in 1977
Mission: To promote international health & development through mobilization of Canadian resources; To advocate & facilitate research, education, & service activities in international health; To further Canadian strengths of progressive health policy & programming in all fields where global & domestic health concerns meet; To contribute to the evolving global understanding of health & development
Member of: Canadian Coalition for Global Health Research
Chief Officer(s):
Karam Ramotar, Co-Chair
Colleen Cash, Co-Chair
Janet Hatcher-Roberts, Executive Director, 613-241-5785 Ext. 302

Finances: *Annual Operating Budget:* $1.5 Million-$3 Million; *Funding Sources:* Membership fees; Contracts; CIDA; Competitive bids
Staff Member(s): 11; 30 volunteer(s)
Membership: 400; *Fees:* $50 regular; $25 student/retired/non-wage-earner; *Member Profile:* Persons with interest in health development, tropical medicine, health systems strengthening, & capacity building; *Committees:* Communication; Advocacy; Research
Activities: *Internships:* Yes
Meetings/Conferences: • Canadian Society for International Health's 22nd Canadian Conference on Global Health, November, 2015, Hilton Bonaventure, Montréal, QC
Scope: National
Description: The conference is the largest meeting of researchers, academics, decision makers, NGOs, policy makers, students & health care providers involved with global health in Canada.
Contact Information: Conference Manager: Sarah Brown, Phone: 613-241-5785 ext. 326, sbrown@csih.org
Publications:
• Synergy Online
Type: Newsletter; *Frequency:* Monthly
Profile: International health & development information, news bulletins, awards, conference information, & job listings

Canadian Society for Italian Studies (CSIS) / Société canadienne pour les études italiennes

c/o Sandra Parmegiani, School of Languages & Literatures, U of Guelph, 50 Stone Rd. East, Guelph ON N1G 2W1
Tel: 519-824-4120; *Fax:* 519-763-9572
sparmegi@uoguelph.ca
www.canadiansocietyforitalianstudies.camp7.org
Overview: A small national charitable organization
Mission: To foster & advance Italian studies in Canada & abroad
Chief Officer(s):
Roberto Perin, President, 416-736-2100 Ext. 88249, Fax: 416-487-6852
RPerin@glendon.yorku.ca
Paola Basile, Vice-President, 440-375-7542, Fax: 440-375-7005
pbasile@lec.edu
Sandra Parmegiani, Secretary-Treasurer, 519-824-4120 Ext. 54989, Fax: 519-763-9572
sparmegi@uoguelph.ca
Finances: *Funding Sources:* Donations; Social Sciences & Humanities Research Council of Canada
Membership: *Fees:* $35 students, retired persons, & PhDs without full-time employment; $60 institutions; $85 sustaining members; $100 couples; $120 patrons; *Member Profile:* Teachers of Italian Studies; Researchers who deal with Italian material
Activities: Facilitating the exchange of ideas; Disseminating information
Meetings/Conferences: • Canadian Society for Italian Studies 2015 Annual Conference, June, 2015, Sant'Anna Institute, Sorrento
Scope: International
Description: In conjunction with the 80th Congress of the Canadian Federation of the Humanities & Social Sciences
Publications:
• Biblioteca di Quaderni d'italianistica
Editor: Dr. Giuliana Katz
Profile: Translations & studies in linguistics, literary criticism, & pedagogy related to Italian culture
• Quaderni d'Italianistica
Type: Journal; *Frequency:* Semiannually; *Editor:* Konrad Eisenbichler; *Price:* $30 Canada individuals; $35 USA individuals; $40 international individuals
Profile: Peer-reviewed articles, published in English, French, & Italian

Canadian Society for Jewish Studies (CSJS) / Société Canadienne des études juives (SCEJ)

Dept. of Religion, Concordia Univ., 1455, boul de Maisonneuve ouest, Montréal QC H3G 1M8
e-mail: ira.robinson@sympatico.ca
www.csjs.ca
Overview: A small national organization founded in 2004
Mission: To provide a venue for the presentation of Jewish studies research & information, primarily for faculty members, graduate students, & independent scholars in Canada
Chief Officer(s):
Ira Robinson, President
ira.robinson@sympatico.ca
Daniel Maoz, Vice-President
Membership: 37; *Fees:* $30; *Member Profile:* All with an active scholarly interest in Canadian Jewish studies

Canadian Society for Mechanical Engineering (CSME) / Société canadienne de génie mécanique (SCGM)

1295 Hwy. 2 East, Kingston ON K7L 4V1
Tel: 613-547-5989; *Fax:* 613-547-0195
csme@cogeco.ca
www.csme-scgm.ca
Overview: A medium-sized national charitable organization founded in 1970 overseen by The Engineering Institute of Canada
Mission: To benefit Canada & the world by fostering excellence in the practice of mechanical engineering; To support members
Affliation(s): Engineering Institute of Canada
Chief Officer(s):
Rama B. Bhat, President
Membership: *Fees:* $15 students; $45 retired members; $85 first year membership; $115 professional affiliate; $125 full membership; *Member Profile:* Mechnical engineering personnel; Engineers in other disciplines who are interested in mechanical engineering; *Committees:* Executive; Regional Vice Presidents; Chairs Special; Chairs Standing; Chairs Technical
Activities: Providing continuing education; Arranging networking opportunities
Meetings/Conferences: • Canadian Society for Mechanical Engineering 2015 Congress, 2015
Scope: National
Description: A meeting of mechanical engineers, held every other year in a Canadian city, for discussion of research & issues important to the profession & related fields
Contact Information: Canadian Society for Mechanical Engineering, E-mail: csme@cogeco.ca
• Canadian Society for Mechanical Engineering 2015 25th Biennial Canadian Congress of Applied Mechanics (CANCAM), 2015
Scope: National
Description: Tech tracks at past conferences have included civil engineering, computational mechanics, dynamics & vibration, education in applied mechanics, fluid mechanics, manufacturing, mechatronics, micro-electro-mechanical systems, solid mechanics & materials, & thermodynamics & heat transfer
Contact Information: Canadian Society for Mechanical Engineering, E-mail: csme@cogeco.ca
Publications:
• CSME [Canadian Society for Mechanical Engineering] Bulletin
Type: Newsletter; *Frequency:* 3 pa; *Editor:* Kamran Siddiqui, PhD; *Price:* Free with membership in theCanadian Society for Mechanical Engineering
Profile: News & articles of a general technical nature, covering all aspects of the practice of mechanical engineering
• From Steam to Space. . . Contributions of Mechanical Engineering to Canadian Development
Number of Pages: 400; *Editor:* Andrew H. Wilson; *Price:* $25 softcover; $50 hardcover
Profile: Essays, memoirs, & photographs
• Transactions of the Canadian Society for Mechanical Engineering
Type: Journal; *Frequency:* Quarterly; *Editor:* Paul J. Zsombor-Murray *ISSN:* 0315-8977; *Price:* $40 / yearfor members of the Canadian Society for Mechanical Engineering
Profile: Scholarly papers of a reference or archival nature in the field of mechanical engineering or related disciplines

Canadian Society for Medical Laboratory Science (CSMLS) / Société canadienne de science de laboratoire médical (SCSLM)

33 Wellington Ave. North, Hamilton ON L8R 1M7
Tel: 905-528-8642; *Fax:* 905-528-4968
Toll-Free: 800-263-8277
www.csmls.org
www.facebook.com/csmls
twitter.com/csmls
www.youtube.com/user/csmls
Previous Name: Canadian Society of Laboratory Technologists
Overview: A large national licensing organization founded in 1937
Mission: To promote & maintain a nationally accepted standard of medical laboratory technology; To promote, maintain, & protect professional identity & interests of medical laboratory technologists
Member of: International Federation of Biomedical Laboratory Science
Affliation(s): International Association of Medical Laboratory Technologists; Intersociety Council of Laboratory Medicine; Conjoint Council on Accreditation of Allied Programs in Health Care
Chief Officer(s):
Tricia Vandenakker, President, 905-528-8642 Ext. 8009
Christine Nielsen, Executive Director, 905-667-8684
Finances: *Annual Operating Budget:* Greater than $5 Million; *Funding Sources:* Membership dues
Membership: 14,000+; *Fees:* $142 active & affiliate; $85 inactive; $62 certified retired; $112 laboratory assistant; $78-$102 student; *Member Profile:* Certified medical laboratory technologists; *Committees:* Marketing & Communications; Professional Development; Council on National Certification; National Advocacy Council; National Regulatory Council
Activities: Develops competency profiles; conducts examinations across Canada & issues certificates of qualification; offers certification in general medical laboratory technology, cytology & clinical genetics; *Awareness Events:* National Medical Laboratory Week, 3rd week of April
Awards:
• CSMLS Student Scholarship Program (Award)
Awarded to the best students who are enrolled in general medical laboratory technology, cytotechnology, or cytogenetics studies*Deadline:* November *Amount:* Five scholarships of $500 each
• E.V. Booth Scholarship Award (Award)
Awarded to certified medical laboratory technologists who are enrolled in studies leading to a degree in medical laboratory science *Amount:* Two awards of $500
• Honorary Awards & Fellowship Awards (Award)
• Distinguished Fellowship Award (Award)
• The A.R. Shearer Pride of the Profession Award (Award)
• The David Ball Community Service Award (Award)
• Siemens Healthcare Diagnostics Student Scholarship (Scholarship)
• Founders' Fund & International Founders' Fund Awards (Scholarship)
• Barbara Santalab-Rickey Memorial Award (Award)
• Leaders of Tomorrow National Congress Grant (Grant)
Meetings/Conferences: • Canadian Society for Medical Laboratory Science / Société canadienne de science de laboratoire médical LABCON2015, May, 2015, Fairmont Queen Elizabeth, Montreal, QC
Scope: National
Contact Information: Web Site: labcon.csmls.org; LABCON Hotline: 1-800-263-8277
• Canadian Society for Medical Laboratory Science / Société canadienne de science de laboratoire médical LABCON2016, May, 2016, Fairmont Queen Elizabeth, Montréal, QC
Scope: National
Contact Information: Staff Contact: Natalie Marino, Phone: 905-528-8642 ext. 8696
Publications:
• Canadian Journal of Medical Laboratory Science
Type: Journal; *Frequency:* Quarterly
Profile: Articles on trends in medical laboratory science & other professional issues, book reviews, & a regular column on laboratory safety

The Canadian Society for Mesopotamian Studies (CSMS) / La Société canadienne des études mésopotamiennes

c/o RIM Project, University of Toronto, 4 Bancroft Ave., 4th Fl., Toronto ON M5S 1C1
Tel: 416-978-4531; *Fax:* 416-978-3305
csms@chass.utoronto.ca
www.chass.utoronto.ca/csms
Previous Name: Society for Mesopotamian Studies
Overview: A small international charitable organization founded in 1980
Mission: To stimulate interest among the general public in the culture, history & archaeology of Mesopotamia, in particular the civilizations of Sumer, Babylon & Assyria, as well as neighbouring ancient civilizations
Affliation(s): Royal Inscriptions of Mesopotamia Project
Chief Officer(s):
Pail-Alain Beaulieu, President
Roy Thomas, Secretary-Treasurer
N.J. Johnson, Administrator
Finances: *Annual Operating Budget:* Less than $50,000; *Funding Sources:* Membership dues; donations; grant
3 volunteer(s)
Membership: 2 institutional + 35 student + 5 senior/lifetime + 96 individual + 17 family + 49 regular subscriber + 26 exchange subscriber; *Fees:* Schedule available

Activities: Public lectures; films & music; travel; exhibitions; research; archaeology; evening courses; *Library*
Publications:
• The Journal
Frequency: Annual; *Editor:* Dr. Douglas R. Frayne

Canadian Society for Molecular Biosciences (CSBM) / Société Canadienne pour Biosciences Moléculaires

c/o Rofail Conference & Management Services, 17 Dossetter Way, Ottawa ON K1G 4S3
Tel: 613-421-7229; *Fax:* 613-421-9811
contact@csmb-scbm.ca
www.csmb-scbm.ca
Previous Name: Canadian Biochemical Society
Merged from: Canadian Society for Biochemistry & Molecular & Cellular Biology; Genetics Society of Canada
Overview: A medium-sized national organization founded in 1958 overseen by Canadian Federation of Biological Societies
Chief Officer(s):
James Davie, President
Arthur Hilliker, Vice President
Finances: *Annual Operating Budget:* $100,000-$250,000; *Funding Sources:* Membership fees
12 volunteer(s)
Membership: 100 student + 50 senior/lifetime + 650 other; *Member Profile:* Demonstrated interest in biochemistry research
Activities: *Internships:* Yes; *Rents Mailing List:* Yes
Publications:
• CSBMCB [The Canadian Society of Biochemistry, Molecular & Cellular Biology] Bulletin
Type: Newsletter
Profile: CSBMCB activites, meeting minutes, lectures, awards, & news from member departments

Canadian Society for Mucopolysaccharide & Related Diseases Inc.

PO Box 30034, Stn. Parkgate, #202, 173 Forester St., North Vancouver BC V7H 2Y8
Tel: 604-924-5130; *Fax:* 604-924-5131
Toll-Free: 800-667-1846
info@mpssociety.ca
www.mpssociety.ca
ca.linkedin.com/pub/kirsten-harkins/0/920/0/
www.facebook.com/208787789156391
twitter.com/canmpssociety
Also Known As: The Canadian MPS Society
Overview: A small national charitable organization founded in 1984
Mission: To support families affected with MPS & related diseases
Member of: Canadian Organization for Rare Disorders
Chief Officer(s):
Bernie Geiss, Chair
Kirsten Harkins, Executive Director
kirsten@mpssociety.ca
Jill Ley, Executive Assistant
jill@mpssociety.ca
Finances: *Funding Sources:* Donations; Fundraising
Staff Member(s): 2; 20 volunteer(s)
Membership: 200; *Fees:* $30-$50; *Member Profile:* Affected families; Professionals; Individuals interested in supporting MPS
Activities: Offering education to medical professionals & the public about MPS & related diseases; Raising funds for research; Referring families; Offering financial aid to affected families; Engaging in advocacy activities; Offering bereavement support; *Awareness Events:* Canadian MPS Jeans Days; The MPS CUP
Publications:
• The Canadian MPS Society Annual Report
Type: Yearbook; *Frequency:* Annually; *Price:* Free with Canadian MPS Society membership
• The Canadian MPS Society Family Referral Directory
Type: Directory; *Frequency:* Annually; *Price:* Free with Canadian MPS Society membership
• The Connection
Type: Newsletter; *Frequency:* Quarterly; *Price:* Free with Canadian MPS Society membership
Profile: A resource for families affected with MPS & related diseases, featuring MPS news, care options, new treatment updates, clinical trials, medical updates, current research, events, fundraising, & familynews

Canadian Society for Pharmaceutical Sciences (CSPS) / Société canadienne des sciences pharmaceutiques (SCSP)

Katz Group Centre, University of Alberta, #2-020L, 11361 - 87 Ave., Edmonton AB T6G 2E1
Tel: 780-492-0950; *Fax:* 780-492-0951
www.cspscanada.org
Overview: A medium-sized national organization founded in 1997
Mission: To advance pharmaceutical R&D & education; to provide a forum for researchers, industry & government to advance pharmaceutical sciences & increase drug discovery & development in Canada
Chief Officer(s):
Barbara Scollick, Executive Director
scollick@cspscanada.org
Bev Berekoff, Administrator
bberekoff@cspscanada.org
Staff Member(s): 2
Membership: 400; *Fees:* $100 individual; $25 trainee; corporate varies
Meetings/Conferences: • Canadian Society for Pharmaceutical Sciences 2015 Annual Symposium, May, 2015, Eaton Chelsea Hotel, Toronto, ON
Scope: National
Description: Educational sessions, networking opportunities, & the presentation of awards
Contact Information: Phone: 780-492-0950
• Canadian Society for Pharmaceutical Sciences 2016 Annual Symposium, 2016
Scope: National
Description: Educational sessions, networking opportunities, & the presentation of awards
Contact Information: Phone: 780-492-0950
Publications:
• Canadian Society for Pharmaceutical Sciences Newsletter
Type: Newsletter
Profile: Information about pharmaceutical events & society happenings
• Journal of Pharmacy & Pharmaceutical Sciences
Type: Journal; *Editor:* Dr. Fakhreddin Jamali *ISSN:* 1482-1826
Profile: A peer-reviewed journal presenting review & original articles

Canadian Society for Psychomotor Learning & Sport Psychology (CSPLSP) / Société canadienne d'apprentissage psychomoteur et de psychologie du sport (SCAPPS)

c/o T. Welsh, Faculty of Kinesiology & Physical Education, U of T, #WS2022B, 55 Harbord St., Toronto ON M5S 2W6
www.scapps2013.org
twitter.com/scapps2013
Overview: A small national organization founded in 1977
Mission: To promote the study of motor development, motor learning, motor control, & sport psychology
Chief Officer(s):
Tim Welsh, President, 416-946-3303
t.welsh@utoronto.ca
Sean Horton, Secretary-Treasurer
Activities: Facilitating the exchange of scientific information related to psychomotor learning & sport psychology
Awards:
• Franklin Henry Young Scientist Award (Award)
Presented annually to an outstanding student scholar

Canadian Society for Quality (CSQ)

c/o Dr. Madhav Sinha, Winnipeg MB
Tel: 204-261-6606
csq@shaw.ca
canadianqualitycongress.com
www.linkedin.com/groups/CSQ-Canadian-Society-Quality-4357519
www.facebook.com/pages/Canadian-Society-for-Quality/118131451687238
www.twitter.com/csq9
Overview: A medium-sized national organization
Meetings/Conferences: • The 7th Canadian Quality Congress, September, 2015, Edmonton, AB
Scope: National

Canadian Society for Surgical Oncology (CSSO) / Société canadienne d'oncologie chirurgicale

c/o Jane Hanes, Princess Margaret Hospital, #3-130, 610 University Ave., Toronto ON M5G 2M9
Tel: 416-946-6583; *Fax:* 416-946-6590
www.cos.ca/csso
Overview: A small national organization founded in 1986
Mission: To encourage optimum cancer patient care through a multi-disciplinary treatment approach; To promote surgical oncology training programs in Canadian universities
Affliation(s): Royal College of Physicians & Surgeons of Canada (RCPSC); Canadian Oncology Societies
Chief Officer(s):
Rona Cheifetz, President
Jane Hanes
Finances: *Funding Sources:* Membership dues
Membership: *Fees:* $150; *Member Profile:* Oncologists of all disciplines
Activities: Facilitating communication between surgeons; Encouraging research in oncologic surgery

Canadian Society for the History & Philosophy of Science (CSHPS) / Société Canadienne d'Histoire et Philosophie des Sciences (SCHPS)

c/o Dr. Conor Burns, Department of History, Ryerson University, 350 Victoria St., Toronto ON M5C 2K3
www.yorku.ca/cshps1
Overview: A small national organization founded in 1959
Mission: To explore all aspects of science, past & present
Affliation(s): Canadian Society for the History & Philosophy of Mathematics (CSHPM)
Chief Officer(s):
Lesley Cormack, President
Conor Burns, Secretary-Treasurer
conor.burns@ryerson.ca
Membership: *Fees:* $25 students, retirees, & partially employed persons; $40 regular members; *Member Profile:* Interdisciplinary scholars, such as philosophers, historians, & sociologists; Persons interested in the history & philosophy of science; Students; Retirees; *Committees:* Programme; Nominating; Local Arrangements
Awards:
• Richard Hadden Award (Award)
Awarded for the best student paper presented at the annual meeting
Publications:
• Communiqué: Newsletter of the Canadian Society for the History & Philosophy of Science
Type: Newsletter; *Frequency:* 3 pa; *Editor:* S. Lachapelle (slachap@uoguelph.ca); *Price:* Free with Canadian Society for the History & Philosophy of Science membership
Profile: Information for members about the society's activities, such as membership news, congressevents, & announcements

Canadian Society for the History of Medicine (CSHM) / Société canadienne d'histoire de la médecine (SCHM)

c/o Brock University, Community Health Sciences, 500 Glendridge Ave., St. Catharines ON L2S 3A1
Tel: 905-688-5550; *Fax:* 905-688-8954
www.cshm-schm.ca
Overview: A small national organization founded in 1950
Mission: To promote the study & communication of the history of health & medicine
Chief Officer(s):
James Moran, President
jmoran@upei.ca
Sasha Mullaly, Vice-President
sasham@unb.ca
Dan Malleck, Secretary-Treasurer & Membership Coordinator
dmalleck@brocku.ca
Finances: *Funding Sources:* Social Sciences & Humanities Research Council (SSHRC); Associated Medical Services (AMS)
Membership: *Fees:* $30 student/retired/postdoctoral; $60 regular; $75 corporate; *Member Profile:* Individuals interested in a range of fields in the humanities & health sciences
Activities: Promoting research in all facets of the history of health and medicine
Meetings/Conferences: • Canadian Society for the History of Medicine 2015 Annual Conference (In conjunction with the 2015 Congress of the Humanities & Social Sciences), May, 2015, University of Ottawa, Ottawa, ON
Scope: National
Description: Events include the the annual AMS / Paterson Lecture by an historian of medicine, & the H.N. Segall Prize which honours the best student paper
Publications:
• Canadian Bulletin of Medical History / Bulletin canadien d'histoire de la médecine
Type: Journal; *Frequency:* Semiannually; *Editor:* Cheryl Krasnick Warsh *ISSN:* 0823-2105

Profile: Peer-reviewed original papers on all aspects of the history of medicine, health care, & relateddisciplines

Canadian Society for the Investigation of Child Abuse (CSICA)

PO Box 42066, Stn. Acadia, Calgary AB T2J 7A6
Tel: 403-289-8385
Other Communication: Alternate e-mail: csica@telus.net
csica@shaw.ca
www.csicainfo.com
www.facebook.com/takingaction
twitter.com/lynnbarrycsica
Previous Name: Calgary Society for the Investigation of Child Sexual Abuse
Overview: A small national charitable organization founded in 1985
Mission: To provide a coordinated professional approach to child abuse investigations; To support professionals, witnesses, & victims involved in the investigation of child abuse
Chief Officer(s):
Alice Gifford, Contact
Activities: Providing educational resources & services; Engaging in advocacy activities; Conducting research

Canadian Society for the Prevention of Cruelty to Children (CSPCC)

PO Box 700, 362 Midland Ave., Midland ON L4R 4P4
Tel: 705-526-5647; *Fax:* 705-526-0214
cspcc@bellnet.ca
www.empathicparenting.org
Overview: A medium-sized national charitable organization founded in 1975
Mission: To increase public awareness of the long-term consequences of child abuse & neglect; to encourage primary prevention initiatives for improved nurturing of children in their earliest years of life
Member of: Canadian Coalition for the Rights of Children
Affliation(s): EPOCH Worldwide; The Infant-Parent Institute, USA; Attachmente Parenting International; Center for Parent Education, USA
Chief Officer(s):
E.T. Barker, President
Finances: *Annual Operating Budget:* Less than $50,000; *Funding Sources:* Membership fees; donations
14 volunteer(s)
Activities: *Library*

Canadian Society for the Protection of Nature in Israel / La société canadienne pour la protection la nature en israél

#200, 25 Imperial St., Toronto ON M5P 1B9
Tel: 416-224-2318
cspnicanada@gmail.com
cspni.org
Overview: A small national charitable organization founded in 2011
Mission: A group of Canadian citizens with a desire to help protect Israel's treasured and threatened natural features.
Affliation(s): Society for the Protection of Nature in Israel; American Society for the Protection of Nature in Israel (ASPNI)

Canadian Society for the Study of Allergy; Canadian Academy of Allergy *See* Canadian Society of Allergy & Clinical Immunology

Canadian Society for the Study of Education (CSSE) / Société canadienne pour l'étude de l'éducation (SCÉÉ)

#204, 260 Dalhousie St., Ottawa ON K1N 7E4
Tel: 613-241-0018; *Fax:* 613-241-0019
csse-scee@csse.ca
www.csse-scee.ca
www.facebook.com/csse.scee
twitter.com/CSSESCEE
Overview: A medium-sized national charitable organization founded in 1972
Mission: To advance knowledge & inform practice in educational settings; to promote the advancement of Canadian research & scholarship in education; to provide for the discussion of studies, issues & trends in education, & for the dissemination of research findings; to promote exchange among members & other educational researchers in Canada & internationally; to foster partnerships &, through educational research, influence public policy & help determine the nature, structure & funding of the research agenda
Member of: Canadian Education Association; Canadian Federation of the Humanities & Social Sciences
Chief Officer(s):
Victor Glickman, President
Finances: *Annual Operating Budget:* $100,000-$250,000; *Funding Sources:* Membership fees; publications; conference
Staff Member(s): 1; 30 volunteer(s)
Membership: 28 institutional + 343 student + 19 senior/lifetime + 535 individual + 20 international associate; *Fees:* $100; $60 international; $50 student/retired; *Committees:* Government & External Relations; R&D; Professional Enhancement & Collaboration; Conference; Programme
Publications:
• The Canadian Journal of Education (CJE) / Revue canadienne de l'éducation
Type: Journal; *Frequency:* Quarterly; *Editor:* Dr. Julia Ellis; *Price:* Free with CSSE membership; $100 non-members
Profile: Educational scholarship in Canada
• Canadian Society for the Study of Education Membership Directory
Type: Directory
Profile: General contact information & descriptions of completed & ongoing researh
• CSSE [Canadian Society for the Study of Education] News
Type: Newsletter; *Frequency:* Monthly; *Price:* Free with CSSE membership
Profile: Educational issues, CSSE activities

Canadian Society for the Study of Fertility *See* Canadian Fertility & Andrology Society

Canadian Society for the Study of Higher Education (CSSHE) / La Société canadienne pour l'étude de l'enseignement supérieur (SCEES)

#204, 260 Dalhousie St., Ottawa ON K1N 7E4
Tel: 613-241-0018; *Fax:* 613-241-0019
csshe-scees@csse.ca
www.csshe-scees.ca
twitter.com/csshescees
Overview: A medium-sized national charitable organization founded in 1970
Mission: To advance the knowledge of post-secondary education through the promotion of research & its dissemination through publications & learned meetings
Chief Officer(s):
Kathleen Matheos, Treasurer
Walter Archer, President
walter.archer@ualberta.ca
Finances: *Funding Sources:* Membership fees; publication sales
Membership: *Fees:* $110; $50 students/retired; *Member Profile:* Faculty & students in universities, community colleges, administrators & trustees, professionals in government departments & agencies, others with an interest in Canadian post-secondary education; *Committees:* Awards; Nominating; Publications
Awards:
• Distinguished Member Award (Award)
For outstanding contribution to the CSSHE
• Research Award (Award)
For excellence in postsecondary education research
• Sheffield Award (Award)
For superior scholarly publication in the Journal
• George L. Geis Dissertation Award (Award)
For excellence in doctoral research on postsecondary education
• Masters Award (Award)
Publications:
• Canadian Journal of Higher Education (CJHE)
Type: Journal; *Editor:* Lesley Andres
Profile: Peer-reviewed articles about Canadian higher education for persons directly involved in higher education in Canada or very interested in the field
• Complete directory of CSSHE members / Bottin complet des membres de la SCÉES
Type: Directory
Profile: Listing of members by function or title

Canadian Society for the Study of Names (CSSN) / Société canadienne d'onomastique (SCO)

PO Box 2164, Stn. Hull, Gatineau QC J8X 3Z4
www.csj.ualberta.ca/sco
Overview: A small national charitable organization founded in 1967
Mission: CSSN promotes the study of all aspects of names & naming in Canada & elsewhere.
Member of: Canadian Federation for the Humanities & Social Sciences
Chief Officer(s):
Carol J. Léonard, Chair
carol.leonard@ualberta.ca
Léo La Brie, Secretary-Treasurer
Leo.Labrie@laposte.net
Finances: *Funding Sources:* Membership dues
Membership: *Fees:* $25 regular; $20 retired; $15 student; $37.50 family; $30 retired family; $400 life membership; *Member Profile:* Persons who share the objectives of the Society
Activities: Facilitating exchange of ideas among onomatologists, toponymists, & scholars in the related fields of literary onomastics & linguistic aspects of names
Meetings/Conferences: • Conference of the Canadian Society for the Study of Names, May, 2015, Ottawa, ON
Contact Information: Program Chair: Diane Dechief, diane.dechief@mail.utoronto.ca
Publications:
• The Name Gleaner
Type: Newsletter; *Frequency:* 3 pa; *Editor:* William Davey; *Price:* Free with membership dues
• Onomastica Canadiana
Type: Journal; *Frequency:* Semiannually; *Number of Pages:* 56; *Editor:* Benoît Leblanc; *Price:* $20 libraries

Canadian Society for the Study of Practical Ethics (CSSPE) / Société canadienne pour l'étude de l'éthique appliquée (SCEEA)

c/o Dept. of Philosophy, #618, Jorgenson Hall, Ryerson Univ., 350 Victoria St., Toronto ON M5B 2K3
Tel: 416-979-5000; *Fax:* 416-979-5362
www.csspe.ca
Overview: A small national organization founded in 1987
Mission: To study all areas of practical ethics, including environmental ethics, health care ethics, bioethics, & business ethics
Chief Officer(s):
Sandra Tomsons, President
stomsons@mts.net
Melany Banks, Secretary-Treasurer
mebanks@wlu.ca
Membership: *Fees:* $20 student; $35 Contract Faculty/Post doc/ Retired; $50 Full Time Faulty/Professional; $75 Contributing Membership; *Member Profile:* Persons interested in practical ethics, from a variety of fields, such as academia, business, & the civil service
Activities: Addressing ethical issues which arise in areas of learning & activitiy, such as the social sciences & professions
Meetings/Conferences: • 2015 Canadian Society for the Study of Practical Ethics Annual Meeting, 2015
Scope: National

Canadian Society for the Study of Religion (CSSR) / Société canadienne pour l'étude de la religion (SCER)

c/o Dr. Arlene Macdonald, #2.104, 301 University Blvd., Galveston TX 77555-1311 USA
www.cssrscer.ca
Overview: A small national organization founded in 1966
Mission: To promote research in the study of religion, with particular reference to Canada; To encourage a critical examination of the teaching of the discipline
Member of: International Association for the History of Religions (IAHR)
Affliation(s): Canadian Federation for the Humanities & Social Sciences (CFHSS)
Chief Officer(s):
Rubina Ramji, President
ruby_ramji@cbu.ca
Arlene Macdonald, Membership Secretary
almacdon@utmb.edu
Richard Mann, Treasurer
Richard_mann@carleton.ca
Membership: *Fees:* $50 students; $60 part-time & retired persons; $90 regular; *Member Profile:* Scholars engaged in various academic approaches to the study of religion
Meetings/Conferences: • Canadian Society for the Study of Religion Congress 2015, May, 2015, University of Ottawa, Ottawa, ON
Scope: Provincial
Description: Theme: "Capital Ideas"
Publications:
• Canadian Society for the Study of Religion Bulletin
Type: Newsletter; *Frequency:* Semiannually; *Editor:* Mark Chapman *ISSN:* 0708-952X; *Price:* Free with CSSR membership
Profile: CSSR activies, member news, departmental news, & conference information

• Studies in Religion / Sciences Religieuses
Type: Journal; *Price:* Free with CSSR membership

Canadian Society for the Study of the Aging Male (CSSAM) / Société canadienne pour l'Étude de l'Homme Vieillissant (SCEHV)

71 Dewlane Dr., Toronto ON M2R 2P9
Tel: 416-480-0010; *Fax:* 416-480-0010
secretariat@cssam.com
cssam.com
Previous Name: Canadian Andropause Society
Overview: A small national organization founded in 1998
Chief Officer(s):
David Greenberg, President
Membership: *Fees:* $65-$125

The Canadian Society for the Weizmann Institute of Science (CSWIS)

4700 Bathurst St., 2nd Fl., Toronto ON M2R 1W8
Tel: 416-733-9220; *Fax:* 416-733-9430
Toll-Free: 800-387-3894
info@weizmann.ca
www.weizmann.ca
www.linkedin.com/company/weizmann-canada
www.facebook.com/129788800406309
www.youtube.com/user/WeizmannCanada
Also Known As: Weizmann Canada
Overview: A medium-sized international charitable organization founded in 1964
Mission: To marshal Canadian support for the Weizmann Institute of Science in Rehovot, Israel; to help build & maintain scientific facilities; to acquire costly up-to-date research equipment & instrumentation; to set up endowments for research centres; to establish professional chairs & scholarships
Chief Officer(s):
Catherine Beck, Chair
Susan Stern, National Executive Vice-President
susan@weizmann.ca
Marni Brinder Byk, Manager, Development
marni@weizmann.ca
Finances: *Annual Operating Budget:* $500,000-$1.5 Million; *Funding Sources:* Donations
Staff Member(s): 4
Membership: 7,000; *Committees:* National Executive
Publications:
• Weizmann News [a publication of The Canadian Society for the Weizmann Institute of Science]
Type: Newsletter; *Frequency:* Quarterly
Profile: Information on news, events, awards, programs, & initiatives related to Weizmann Canada.

Calgary Office
2322 Carleton St. SW, Calgary ON T2T 3K7
Tel: 403-243-6549
Chief Officer(s):
Stanley Magidson, President

Montréal Office
#23, 2340, ch Lucerne, Montréal QC H3R 2J8
Tel: 514-342-0777; *Fax:* 514-342-0602
Chief Officer(s):
Susan Stern, National Executive Vice-President
susan@weizmann.ca

Canadian Society for Traditional Music (CSTM) / Société canadienne pour les traditions musicales (SCTM)

University of Alberta, 3-47 Arts Building, Edmonton AB T6G 2E6
e-mail: cstmsctm@ualberta.ca
www.yorku.ca/cstm
Also Known As: Canadian Folk Music Society
Overview: A medium-sized national charitable organization founded in 1956
Mission: Study & promotion of musical traditions of all cultures & communities in all their aspects
Member of: International Council for Traditional Music
Chief Officer(s):
Judith Klassen, President
judith@homeontheland.ca
Chris McDonald, Treasurer
chris_mcdonald@cbu.ca
Jessica Roda, Secretary
rodajessica@yahoo.com
Finances: *Annual Operating Budget:* Less than $50,000; *Funding Sources:* Membership dues; government & foundation grants
30 volunteer(s)
Membership: 200 individual + 100 institutional; *Fees:* $85 organization; $60 individual; $25 underemployed; *Member Profile:* Open
Activities: Mail order service of records, books, cassettes on Canadian folk music; acts in consultative/teaching capacity to teachers, performers, etc.; *Rents Mailing List:* Yes

Canadian Society for Training & Development (CSTD)

#315, 720 Spadina Ave., Toronto ON M5S 2T9
Tel: 416-367-5900; *Fax:* 416-367-1642
Toll-Free: 866-257-4275
info@cstd.ca
www.cstd.ca
www.linkedin.com/groups/CSTD-National-1944595?gid=1944595&trk=hb_side_
twitter.com/cstdnational
www.youtube.com/user/CSTDNational
Overview: A medium-sized national organization founded in 1946
Mission: To bring together individuals who share a common interest in training, personnel development & organizational development
Member of: Conference Board of Canada
Chief Officer(s):
Isabel Feher-Watters, Acting President
ifeher-watters@cstd.ca
Dale Wilcox, President
Finances: *Annual Operating Budget:* $500,000-$1.5 Million
Staff Member(s): 7; 100 volunteer(s)
Membership: 2,300; *Fees:* $295 new member; $225 renewal; *Member Profile:* Training & development professionals; *Committees:* Member Services; Professional Certification; Government Relations; Conference
Activities: Annual conference
Meetings/Conferences: • Canadian Society for Training & Development 2015 National Conference and Trade Show, November, 2015, Metro Toronto Convention Centre, North Building, Toronto, ON
Scope: National

Canadian Society for Transfusion Medicine (CSTM) / Société canadienne de médecine transfusionnelle

#6, 20 Crown Steel Dr., Markham ON L3R 9X9
Tel: 905-415-3917; *Fax:* 905-415-0071
Toll-Free: 855-415-3917
Other Communication: Toll-Free Fax: 866-882-7093
office@transfusion.ca
www.transfusion.ca
www.facebook.com/290163767690083
twitter.com/CanSocTransMed
Previous Name: Canadian Association of Immunohematologists
Overview: A medium-sized national organization founded in 1989
Mission: To promulgate throughout Canada a high level of ethics & professional standards; to create national & regional opportunities for the presentation & discussion of research & developments in this & allied fields; to initiate & maintain a program of continuing education; to promote good laboratory & good manufacturing practices; to establish mutually beneficial working relationships with relevant national & international societies & organizations & to be the primary voice for transfusion medicine in Canada
Chief Officer(s):
Gwen Clarke, President
president@transfusion.ca
Finances: *Annual Operating Budget:* Less than $50,000; *Funding Sources:* Membership fees
Membership: 450; *Committees:* Standards; Membership
Awards:
• Honorary Membership (Award)
• Ortho Award (Award)
• Blum Award (Award)
Meetings/Conferences: • Canadian Society for Transfusion Medicine Conference 2015, May, 2015, Fort Garry Hotel, Winnipeg, MB
Scope: National
Description: Theme: "Where Past and Future Meet"

Canadian Society for Tropical Medicine & International Health *See* Canadian Society for International Health

Canadian Society for Vascular Surgery (CSVS) / Société canadienne de chirurgie vasculaire

c/o Christiane Dowsing, Society Manager, 774 Echo Dr., Ottawa ON K1S 5N8
Tel: 613-730-6263; *Fax:* 613-730-1116
csvs@royalcollege.ca
canadianvascular.ca
Overview: A small national organization
Mission: To promote vascular health for Canadians
Chief Officer(s):
Jerry Chen, President
jec@interchange.ubc.ca
Gerrit Winkelaar, Secretary
gbwinkelaar@shaw.ca
Jacques Tittley, Treasurer
vascdisl@sympatico.ca
Thomas Forbes, Chair, Research Committee
tom.forbes@lhsc.on.ca
Ravi Sidhu, Chair, Education Committee
RSSidhu@providencehealth.bc.ca
Finances: *Funding Sources:* Membership fees; Sponsorships
Activities: Promoting research; Providing continuing medical education; Engaging in advocacy activities; Facilitating the exchange of ideas & information
Meetings/Conferences: • Canadian Society for Vascular Surgery 2015 37th Annual Meeting, September, 2015, Delta Victoria, Victoria, BC
Scope: National
Description: The annual general meeting of the society, plus continuing education sessions, lectures, exhibits, & social events
• Canadian Society for Vascular Surgery 2016 38th Annual Meeting, September, 2016, The Westin Nova Scotian, Halifax, NS
Scope: National
Description: The annual general meeting of the society, plus continuing education sessions, lectures, exhibits, & social events

Canadian Society for Yad Vashem

#218, 265 Rimrock Rd., Toronto ON M3J 3C6
Tel: 416-785-1333; *Fax:* 416-785-4536
Toll-Free: 888-494-7999
info@yadvashem.ca
www.yadvashem.ca
www.facebook.com/yadvashem
www.youtube.com/user/YadVashem
Overview: A medium-sized national charitable organization founded in 1986
Mission: To help support & finance the Canadian Pavilion for Holocaust Studies
Chief Officer(s):
Fran Sonshine, National Chair
Yaron Ashkenazi, Executive Director
Finances: *Funding Sources:* Donations
Activities: *Speaker Service:* Yes

Canadian Society of Addiction Medicine (CSAM) / La Société Medicale Canadienne sur l'Addiction (SMCA)

47 Tuscany Ridge Terrace NW, Calgary AB T3L 3A5
Tel: 403-813-7217
admin@csam-smca.org
www.csam-smca.org
Overview: A small national organization founded in 1989
Mission: To foster & promote medical sciences and clinical practice in the field of substance use disorders in Canada; To establish & promote standards of clinical practice
Affiliation(s): The International Society of Addiction Medicine
Chief Officer(s):
Ron Lim, President
Paul Sobey, President-Elect
Finances: *Funding Sources:* Corporate sponsorship
Membership: 370; *Fees:* $200 MD & PhD; $50 associate; $25 retired; $5 student/intern/resident; *Member Profile:* MD members; Associate members; PhD members; Honorary members; Medical students, interns, & residents; Retired members; *Committees:* Journal; Education; Membership; By-Laws; Standards; Website; Sponsorship; Nominations; Economics; Conference; Bilingual; Executive; Advocacy
Activities: Offering scientific & medical information about addiction; Providing networking opportunities; Promoting research & medical education; Increasing public awareness
Publications:
• CSAM [Canadian Society of Addiction Medicine] Bulletin
Type: Newsletter; *Frequency:* 3 pa; *Editor:* Dr. Michael Varenbut
Profile: CSAM conferences, reports, membership information, research updates, clinical experiences, & continuing education opportunities related toaddiction medicine

Canadian Associations

Canadian Society of Agronomy
S.C. Sheppard, PO Box 637, Pinawa MB R0E 1L0
Tel: 204-753-2747; *Fax:* 204-753-8478
www.agronomycanada.com
Overview: A medium-sized national organization
Mission: The mission of The Canadian Society of Agronomy is dedicated to enhancing cooperation and coorindation among agronomists, to recognizing significant achievements in agronomy and to providing the oppourtunity to report and evaluate information pertinent to agronomy in Canada. The goals and objects include networking; external relations and awareness; and internal communications and coordination.
Member of: Agricultural Institute of Canada
Chief Officer(s):
Steve Sheppard, PhD, Executive Director
sheppards@ecomatters.com
Membership: 300

Canadian Society of Air Safety Investigators (CSASI)
139 West 13th Ave., Vancouver BC V5Y 1V8
e-mail: avsafe@shaw.ca
www.beyondriskmgmt.com
Overview: A small international organization founded in 1975
Mission: To ensure air safety through investigation
Affliation(s): International Society of Air Safety Investigators
Chief Officer(s):
Barbara M. Dunn, President
Elaine M. Parker, Vice-President
Membership: *Fees:* $100 annual fee; $65 initiation fee; $25 student annual fee; $20 student initiation fee; *Member Profile:* Canadian aircraft accident investigators; Students
Publications:
• Canadian Society of Air Safety Investigators Proceedings
Price: Free with CSASA membership
Profile: Papers presented at each seminar
• Canadian Society of Air Safety Investigators Newsletter
Type: Newsletter; *Price:* Free with CSASA membership
• ISASI Forum
Frequency: Quarterly; *Price:* Free with CSASA membership

Canadian Society of Allergy & Clinical Immunology (CSACI) / Société canadienne d'allergie et d'immunologie clinique
PO Box 51045, Orleans ON K1E 3W4
Tel: 613-986-5869; *Fax:* 866-839-7501
info@csaci.ca
www.csaci.ca
Previous Name: Canadian Society for the Study of Allergy; Canadian Academy of Allergy
Overview: A small national organization founded in 1945
Mission: To ensure optimal patient care by advancing the knowledge & practice of allergy, clinical immunology, & asthma
Chief Officer(s):
Paul Keith, President
Sandy Kapur, Vice-President
David Fischer, Secretary-Treasurer
Finances: *Funding Sources:* Donations; Sponsorships
Membership: 475+; *Member Profile:* Clinical immunologists; Allergists; Asthma specialists; Allied health professionals; Medical students; Persons interested in the research & treatment of allergic diseases
Activities: Conducting research; Engaging in advocacy activities; Offering continuing professional development; Providing education to the public
Publications:
• Allergy, Asthma & Clinical Immunology: Official Journal of the Canadian Society of Allergy & Clinical Immunology
Type: Journal; *Frequency:* Quarterly; *Editor:* Richard Warrington
Profile: Articles to further the understanding & treatment of allergic &immunologic disease
• CSACI [Canadian Society of Allergy & Clinical Immunology] Newsletter / Bulletin CSAIC
Type: Newsletter; *Frequency:* Bimonthly
Profile: CSACI activities, events, & awards

Canadian Society of Animal Science (CSAS) / Société canadienne de science animale
c/o University of Alberta, Agriculture & Forestry Centre, #4-10, Edmonton AB T6G 2C8
Tel: 780-248-1700; *Fax:* 780-248-1900
www.csas.net
Overview: A medium-sized national organization founded in 1951
Mission: To provide opportunities to discuss the problems of the Canadian animal & poultry industries, with the objective of furthering advancements in these industries; To assist in the coordination of research, teaching & technology transfer related to the animal & poultry industries; To encourage publication of scientific information; To provide an annual forum for professionals in the agricultural industry to meet & discuss the most recent technological advancements in the field of animal & poultry science
Member of: Agricultural Institute of Canada
Chief Officer(s):
John Baah, President, 403-360-6310
john.baah@agr.gc.ca
Carolyn Fitzsimmons, Secretary-Treasurer
cfitzsim@ualberta.ca
Membership: *Member Profile:* Membership is open to persons currently or previously employed in research, teaching, administration, extension, production, marketing, or otherwise interested in any field pertaining to the animal industry. There are three categories for membership; regular, retired, or student members (undergraduate or graduate).; *Committees:* Awards; Membership
Awards:
• Honorary Life Memberships (Award)
• Young Scientist Award (Award)
• Fellowship Award (Award)
• Award for Excellence in Nutrition & Meat Sciences (Award)
• Animal Industries Award in Extension & Public Service (Award)
• Award for Technical Innovation in Enhancing Production of Safe Affordable Food (Award)
Meetings/Conferences: • 2015 Conference of the Canadian Society of Animal Science and the Canadian Meat Council, May, 2015, The Westin Hotel, Ottawa, ON
Scope: National

Canadian Society of Association Executives (CSAE) / Société canadienne d'association (SCDA)
#1100, 10 King St. East, Toronto ON M5C 1C3
Tel: 416-363-3555; *Fax:* 416-363-3630
Toll-Free: 800-461-3608
www.csae.com
Previous Name: Institute of Association Executives
Overview: A large national organization founded in 1951
Mission: To provide members with the environment, knowledge, & resources to develop excellence in not-for-profit leadership, through networking, education, advocacy, information, & research
Affliation(s): European Society of Association Executives; American Society of Association Executives; 7 Canadian Chapters of Society of Association Executives: British Columbia, Edmonton, Manitoba, Trillium, Ottawa-Gatineau, Quebec, Nova Scotia
Chief Officer(s):
Michael Anderson, President
Dave Cybak, Vice-President
Stewart Laszio, Director, Marketing, 416-363-3555 Ext. 235
stewart@csae.com
Josette Forde, Director, Chapter Relations & Education, 416-363-3555 Ext. 240
josette@csae.com
Gail McHardy, Director, Conferences & Events, 416-363-3555
gail@csae.com
Finances: *Annual Operating Budget:* 0; *Funding Sources:* 60% education & services; 40% member fees
Staff Member(s): 15
Membership: 600 corporate + 1,650 individual; *Fees:* All members pay fees to the national association; *Member Profile:* Association executives & businesses; *Committees:* Audit; Nominating; Honours & Awards; Government & Public Affairs; CAE Project Review Team; Policy Review
Activities: *Rents Mailing List:* Yes
Meetings/Conferences: • Canadian Society of Association Executives / Société canadienne d'association 2015 Conference & Showcase, October, 2015, Calgary, AB
Scope: National
Attendance: 500+
Contact Information: E-mail: events@csae.com
• Canadian Society of Association Executives / Société canadienne d'association 2016 Conference & Showcase, October, 2016, Toronto, ON
Scope: National
Attendance: 500+
Contact Information: E-mail: events@csae.com
• Canadian Society of Association Executives / Société canadienne d'association 2017 Conference & Showcase, October, 2017, St. John's, NL
Scope: National
Attendance: 500+
Contact Information: E-mail: events@csae.com
• Canadian Society of Association Executives / Société canadienne d'association 2018 Conference & Showcase, October, 2018, Ottawa, ON
Scope: National
Attendance: 500+
Contact Information: E-mail: events@csae.com
Publications:
• Association Magazine
Type: Magazine; *Accepts Advertising*
Profile: Practical advice regarding association management & governance membership recruitment, retention, lobbying & advocacy updates, revenue generation, data management, and necessary sector information

British Columbia Chapter
c/o British Columbia Bottle Depot Association, 9850 King George Hwy., Surrey BC V3T 4Y3
Tel: 604-930-0003; *Fax:* 604-930-0060
bcbd@telus.net
www.csae.com
www.linkedin.com/groups/British-Columbia-Chapter-Canadian-Society-4139
twitter.com/csaebc
Chief Officer(s):
Corinne Atwood, President
Kasey Nishimura, Vice-President, 604-941-5852, Fax: 604-941-5292
kasey.nishimura@deltahotels.com
Andy Fung, Treasurer, 604-687-2811 Ext. 123, Fax: 604-207-9535
andy@bcga.org

Edmonton Chapter
Edmonton AB
Tel: 780-466-9938
lue42@shaw.ca
www.csae.com/Chapters/Edmonton.aspx
Chief Officer(s):
Jim Humphries, Chapter President
humphriesj@shaw.ca
Meghan McConnan, Vice-President
Meghan.McConnan@ca.gt.com

Manitoba Chapter
c/o Certified General Accountants Association of Manitoba, 4 Donald St. South, Winnipeg MB R3L 2T7
www.csae.com/Chapters/Manitoba.aspx
Chief Officer(s):
Nadine Curtis, Chapter President
ncurtis@cga-manitoba.org

Nova Scotia Chapter
PO Box 22057, 7071 Bayers Rd., Halifax NS B3L 4T7
Tel: 902-292-3839; *Fax:* 902-457-1900
csae@ns.aliantzinc.ca
www.csae.com/Chapters/NovaScotia.aspx
Chief Officer(s):
Joanne Gorveatt, Chapter President
joanne.gorveatt@rbc.com
Dianne Swinemar, Vice-President
dswinemar@feednovascotia.ca

Ontario (Trillium) Chapter
39 River St., Toronto ON M5A 3P1
Tel: 416-646-1600; *Fax:* 416-646-9460
www.csae.com/trillium/
Mission: To act as the regional voice for association professionals; To facilitates the exchange of ideas, information, & experiences; To encourage personal & professional growth & prosperity for all members
Chief Officer(s):
Deborah Thompson, Vice President
Pauletten Vinette, Executive Director
Penny Marrett, President

Ottawa Gatineau Chapter
c/o Royal College of Physicians and Surgeons of Canada, 773 Echo Dr., Ottawa ON K1S 5N8
Tel: 613-730-6237
tcohen@rcpsc.edu
www.csae.com/ottawa
Mission: To provide the environment, knowledge, & resources its members need to develop excellence in not-for-profit leadership, through education, networking, advocacy, information, & research
Chief Officer(s):
Ted Cohen, Chapter President

Section du Québec
#1014, 3535, av Papineau, Montréal QC H2K 4J9
Tél: 514-984-0622
www.csae.com
twitter.com/scdaquebec
Chief Officer(s):
Chantal Demers, Présidente
chantal.demers@poelesfoyers.ca
Louis Moubarak, Directeur général
louism@managementcom.net

Canadian Society of Atherosclerosis, Thrombosis & Vascular Biology (CSATVB) / Société canadienne d'Athérosclérose, de Thrombose et de Biologie Vasculaire (SCATBV)

c/o Laurence Boudreault, Centre de recherche du CHU de Quebec, #TR-93, 2705, boul Laurier, Québec QC G1V 4G2
Tel: 418-656-4141; *Fax:* 418-654-2145
www.csatvb.ca
Previous Name: Canadian Atherosclerosis Society
Overview: A medium-sized national charitable organization founded in 1983
Mission: To provide means of communication between Canadian professionals interested in atherosclerosis; to promote research & education
Affiliation(s): International Atherosclerosis Society
Chief Officer(s):
Laurence Boudreault, Contact
laurence.boudreault@crchuq.ulaval.ca
Membership: 309; *Fees:* $100; *Member Profile:* Scientists, physicians, lipidologists, pathologists; *Committees:* Education; Finance; Long-Term Planning; Nominating
Awards:
• Young Investigator Awards (Award)
• Travel Awards (Award)
• Grant-in-aid (Grant)

Canadian Society of Biblical Studies (CSBS) / Société canadienne des études bibliques (SCEB)

c/o Prof. Robert A. Derrenbacker, Jr., Regent College, 5800 University Blvd., Vancouver BC V6T 2E4
www.ccsr.ca/csbs
Overview: A small national organization founded in 1933
Mission: To stimulate the critical investigation of the classical biblical literature & related literature
Chief Officer(s):
Terry Donaldson, President
terry.donaldson@utoronto.ca
Francis Landy, Vice-President
francis.landy@ualberta.ca
Robert A. Derrenbacker, Jr., Treasurer & Membership Secretary
rderrenbacker@regent-college.edu
Richard S. Ascough, Officer, Communications
rsa@queensu.ca
Membership: *Fees:* $35 students & retired & unemployed persons; $72 full membership; *Member Profile:* Individuals interested in all aspects of the academic study of the Bible
Meetings/Conferences: • Canadian Society of Biblical Studies 2015 Annual Meeting (in conjunction with the 2015 Congress of the Humanities & Social Sciences), May, 2015, University of Ottawa, Ottawa, ON
Scope: National
• Canadian Society of Biblical Studies 2016 Annual Meeting (in conjunction with the 2016 Congress of the Humanities & Social Sciences), 2016, Brock University, St Catharines, ON
Scope: National
• Canadian Society of Biblical Studies 2017 Annual Meeting (in conjunction with the 2017 Congress of the Humanities & Social Sciences), 2017
Scope: National
Publications:
• Canadian Society of Biblical Studies Membership Directory
Type: Directory
• The CSBS [Canadian Society of Biblical Studies] / SCÉB [Société canadienne des études bibliques] Bulletin
Type: Yearbook; *Frequency:* Annually; *Editor:* Richard S. Ascough; *Price:* Free withCSBS membership
Profile: CSBS membership news, events, annual general meeting minutes, & financial statements
• Studies in Religion / Sciences Religieuses
Type: Journal; *Price:* Free with CSBS membership
Profile: Refereed articles

Canadian Society of Cardiac Surgeons / Société des chirurgiens cardiaques

#1403, 222 Queen St., Ottawa ON K1P 5V9
Toll-Free: 877-569-3407
cscs@ccs.ca
www.ccs.ca/cscs
Previous Name: Canadian Society of Cardiovascular & Thoracic Surgeons
Overview: A small national organization
Mission: To promote cardiac surgery as a profession
Chief Officer(s):
David Ross, President
david.b.ross@albertahealthservices.ca
Roderick MacArthur, Secretary-Treasurer
roderick.macArthur@albertahealthservices.ca
Membership: *Fees:* $200; *Member Profile:* Canadian cardiovascular & thoracic surgeons

Canadian Society of Cardiology Technologists Inc. (CSCT) / Société canadienne des technologues en cardiologie inc.

PO Box 3121, Winnipeg MB R3C 4E6
Other Communication: education@csct.ca
info@csct.ca
www.csct.ca
Overview: A medium-sized national organization
Mission: To ensure a standard of excellence in the practice of cardiology technology in Canada
Affiliation(s): Canadian Cardiovascular Society (CCS)
Membership: 1,000+; *Member Profile:* Individuals employed in the field of cardiology
Activities: Providing continuing education;

Canadian Society of Cardiovascular & Thoracic Surgeons
See Canadian Society of Cardiac Surgeons

Canadian Society of Children's Authors, Illustrators & Performers (CANSCAIP) / La société canadienne des auteurs, illustrateurs et artistes pour enfants

#104, 40 Orchard View Blvd., Toronto ON M4R 1B9
Tel: 416-515-1559
office@canscaip.org
www.canscaip.org
www.facebook.com/groups/18960022544
twitter.com/CANSCAIP
Overview: A medium-sized national organization founded in 1977
Mission: To promote the growth of children's literature by establishing the rapport with teachers, librarians & children; to establish communication between publishers & society; to encourage the development of new writers, illustrators & performers
Member of: Canadian Children's Book Centre
Chief Officer(s):
Karen Krossing, President
Finances: *Funding Sources:* Membership fees; workshops; travelling art collection
16 volunteer(s)
Membership: 460 professional + 650 associates; *Fees:* $75 professional; $35 associate; *Member Profile:* Professional - must be published; Associate - any interested person
Activities: *Speaker Service:* Yes
Publications:
• CANSCAIP [Canadian Society of Children's Authors, Illustrators & Performers] News
Type: Newsletter; *Frequency:* Quarterly; *Price:* Free with CANSCAIP membership
Profile: Articles, interviews, new CANSCAIP members, awards, new books, publishers, & projects
• CANSCAIP [Canadian Society of Children's Authors, Illustrators & Performers] Monographs
Price: Free with CANSCAIP membership
Profile: Topics include How to Do a School Presentation & How to Negotiate an Illustrator Contract

Canadian Society of Chinese Medicine & Acupuncture (CSCMA)

#402, 245 Fairview Mall Dr., Toronto ON M2J 4T1
Tel: 416-597-6769; *Fax:* 416-597-9928
office@tcmcanada.org
www.tcmcanada.org
Overview: A small national organization founded in 1994
Mission: To unite traditional Chinese medicine (TCM) & acupuncture practitioners, & to advocate for legal recognition & regulation of TCM in Canada
Chief Officer(s):
Zhao Cheng, President
Gengmin Tang, Secretary General
Membership: 2,300; *Fees:* $100; $380 new member; *Committees:* Finance; Academic; Supervise; Public Relation; Promotion & Editing; General Affairs; Organizations Relation; Translator; Entertainment; Athletic Sports; Qigong, Taiji, Regimen; Insurance Affair; Continue Education
Publications:
• The Canadian Society of Chiense Medicine & Acupuncture Publication
Type: Journal

Canadian Society of Church History (CSCH) / Société canadienne d'histoire de l'Église

c/o Robynne R. Healey, Dept. of History, Trinity Western University, 7600 Glover Rd., Langley BC V2Y 1Y1
e-mail: robynne.healey@twu.ca
churchhistcan.wordpress.com
Overview: A small national organization founded in 1960
Mission: To encourage research in the history of Christianity, especially the history of Christianity in Canada
Member of: Canadian Corporation for Studies in Religion; Congress of Social Sciences & Humanities
Chief Officer(s):
Todd Webb, President
Marguerite Van Die, Vice-President & Program Chair
Robynne Rogers Healey, Administrative Secretary
John H. Young, Treasurer
Membership: *Fees:* $36 students; $53 retired academics; $60 individuals; *Member Profile:* Historians of Christianity in Canada & the United States
Meetings/Conferences: • Canadian Society of Church History 2015 Annual Meeting (in conjunction with the 2015 Congress of the Humanities & Social Sciences), May, 2015, University of Ottawa, Ottawa, ON
Scope: National
Publications:
• Historical Papers: Canadian Society of Church History
Type: Journal; *Frequency:* Annually; *Editor:* Robynne Rogers Healey; *Price:* Free with CSCH membership
Profile: A selection of papers delivered at the CSCH annual meeting

Canadian Society of Cinematographers (CSC)

#131, 3007 Kingston Rd., Toronto ON M1M 1P1
Tel: 416-266-0591; *Fax:* 416-266-3996
admin@csc.ca
www.csc.ca
www.facebook.com/groups/41958001658
Overview: A small national organization founded in 1957
Mission: To promote the art & craft of cinematography
Chief Officer(s):
Joan Hutton, President
joanhuttondesign@gmail.com
Susan Saranchuk, Executive Director
Finances: *Funding Sources:* Sponsorships
Membership: 600; *Member Profile:* Canadian film & video professionals involved in the production of feature films, documentaries, television series, specials, & commercials
Activities: Providing professional education for members; Disseminating technical & product information
Awards:
• The Roy Tash Award for Spot News Cinematography (Award)
• The Stan Clinton Award for News Essay Cinematography (Award)
• Student Cinematography (Award)
• Music Video Cinematography (Award)
• Docudrama Cinematography (Award)
• Robert Brooks Award for Documentary Cinematography (Award)
• Dramatic Short Cinematography (Award)
• Fritz Spiess Award for Commercial Cinematography (Award)
• TV Drama Cinematography (Award)
• Documentary (Award)
• TV Series Cinematography (Award)
• Theatrical Feature Cinematography (Award)
• Bill Hilson Award (Award)
• Fuji Film Award (Award)
• Kodak New Century Award (Award)
Publications:
• CSC [Canadian Society of Cinematographers] News
Type: Magazine; *Frequency:* 10 pa; *Accepts Advertising*; *Editor:* Wyndham Wise
Profile: Personal & corporate profiles, awards, illustrated production & technical features, industry news & informative columns
• CSC [Canadian Society of Cinematographers] Directory
Type: Directory; *Frequency:* Semiannually; *Accepts Advertising*
Profile: Register of members, & a list of sponsors

Canadian Society of Clinical Chemists (CSCC) / Société canadienne des clinico-chimistes

PO Box 1570, #310, 4 Cataraqui St., Kingston ON K7K 1Z7
Tel: 613-531-8899; *Fax:* 866-303-0626
office@cscc.ca
www.cscc.ca
Overview: A medium-sized national organization founded in 1965
Mission: To establish standards for diagnostic services in the practice of clinical biochemistry & clinical laboratory medicine
Chief Officer(s):
Edward Randell, President
Elizabeth Hooper, Executive Director
Ronald Booth, Treasurer
Membership: *Member Profile:* Clinical biochemists throughout Canada
Activities: Providing leadership, education, & research in the practice of clinical biochemistry & clinical laboratory medicine; Liaising with goverment, industry, & healthcare associations; Engaging in advocacy activities
Meetings/Conferences: • 2015 Canadian Society of Clinical Chemists Canadian Congress of Laboratory Medicine (CLMC), June, 2015, Hotel Le Westin, Montreal, QC
Scope: National
Description: Joint Conference of CSCC and the Canadian Association of Pathologists
Contact Information: www.clmc.ca/2015
• 2016 Canadian Society of Clinical Chemists Conference, 2016
Scope: National
Publications:
• Canadian Society of Clinical Chemists Member Handbook
Type: Yearbook; *Frequency:* Annually
• Clinical Biochemistry
Type: Journal; *Editor:* Edgard E. Delvin *ISSN:* 0009-9120
Profile: Analytical & clinical investigative articles related to molecular biology, chemistry, biochemistry, immunology, clinical investigation, diagnosis, therapy, & monitoring humandisease, for chemists, immunologists, biologists, & biochemists
• The CSCC [Canadian Society of Clinical Chemists] News
Type: Newsletter
Profile: Society activities & information for CSCC members

Canadian Society of Clinical Neurophysiologists (CSCN) / Société canadienne de neurophysiologistes cliniques

PO Box 5456, Stn. A, #709, 7015 Macleod Trail SW, Calgary AB T2H 2K6
Tel: 403-229-9544; *Fax:* 403-229-1661
www.cnsfederation.org
Overview: A small national organization founded in 1958 overseen by Canadian Neurological Sciences Federation
Mission: To promote & encourage all aspects of neurophysiology, including research & education, in addition to assessment & accreditation in the field
Member of: Canadian Neurological Sciences Federation
Affliation(s): Cdn. Brain Tumour Consortium; Cdn. Epilepsy Consortium; Cdn. Stroke Consortium; Cdn. League Against Epilepsy; Cdn. Headache Society; Cdn. Movement Disorders Group; Cdn. Network of MS Clinics; Cdn. Neurocritical Care Group; Amyotrophic Lateral Sclerosis Research Foundation; Consortium of Canadian Centres for Clinical Cognitive Research; Associate Societies: Assn. of Electromyography Technologists of Canada; Canadian Assn. of Electroneurophysiology Technologists; Canadian Assn. of Neuroscience; Canadian Assn. of Neuroscience Nurses; Canadian Assn. of Physical Medicine & Rehabilitation
Chief Officer(s):
Marika Fitzgerald, Contact
marika-fitzgerald@cnsfederation.org
Membership: 275; *Fees:* $380 clinical & research; $250 associate; *Member Profile:* Individuals who pass the EEG or EMG exam; Other persons require the names & signatures of two active CSCN members in support of their application for membership; Junior members need the signature of either an active member or their training program director; *Committees:* Executive; Membership; Nominating
Activities: Providing annual scientific sessions to promote the knowledge & practice of clinical neurophysiology; Providing physicians the opportunity to take exams in EEG &/or EMG
Awards:
• Herbert Jasper Prize (Award)
Awarded annually for the best submitted paper in clinical or basic neurophysiology by a resident or fellow in training; others also eligible *Amount:* honorarium, fees to attend the annual meeting of the CNS
Publications:
• Canadian Journal of Neurological Sciences
Type: Journal; *Frequency:* Bimonthly; *Accepts Advertising*; *Editor:* G. Bryan Young
Profile: Peer-reviewed original articles

Canadian Society of Clinical Perfusion (CSCP) / Société Canadienne de Perfusion Clinique (SCPC)

914 Adirondack Rd., London ON N6K 4W7
Fax: 866-648-2763
Toll-Free: 888-496-2727
cscp@cscp.ca
www.cscp.ca
www.facebook.com/group.php?gid=2361384057
Overview: A medium-sized national organization
Mission: To encourage & foster the development of the profession of clinical perfusion, through education & certification
Chief Officer(s):
Ray Van de Vorst, President
Marie-France Raymond, Vice-President
Filippo Berna, Treasurer
Membership: 257 + 10 corporate + 4 student + 2 honourary + 1 retired + 1 incorporated; *Fees:* $300 certified; $225 associate; $50 student; $240 institutional; $300 inactive (on approval of board of directors); $530-1200 corporate
Meetings/Conferences: • Canadian Society of Clinical Perfusion 2015 Annual General Meeting & Scientific Sessions, October, 2015, Toronto Convention Centre, Toronto, ON
Scope: National
Description: Continuing education sessions on product development involving the society's corporate members, a business meeting, Canadian Society of Clinical Perfusion cerification examinations held off site from the convention centre, the presentation of awards, & networking opportunities
Contact Information: Annual General Meeting Coordinator: Bill O'Reilly, E-mail: cscp@cscp.ca; Chair, Accreditation, Competency, & Examination: Manon Caouette, E-mail: cscp@cscp.ca; Contact, Professional Development: Philip Fernandes, E-mail: cscp@cscp.ca
Publications:
• The Perfusionist: The Official Publication of the Canadian Society of Clinical Perfusion]
Type: Journal; *Frequency:* 3 pa; *Accepts Advertising*; *Editor:* Andrew Beney, MSc, CPC, CCP
Profile: Approximately 350 issues are distributed to Canadian certified perfusionists,subscribing students, American perfusionists, & corporate members

Canadian Society of Club Managers (CSCM) / La Société canadienne des directeurs de club

2943B Bloor St. West, Toronto ON M8X 1B3
Tel: 416-979-0640; *Fax:* 416-979-1144
Toll-Free: 877-376-2726
national@cscm.org
www.cscm.org
Overview: A small national organization
Mission: To provide managers with the tools necessary to manage their clubs
Chief Officer(s):
Elizabeth Di Chiara, Executive Director
elizabeth@cscm.org
Finances: *Annual Operating Budget:* $250,000-$500,000
Staff Member(s): 5; 25 volunteer(s)
Membership: 560; *Fees:* Based on region; *Member Profile:* Managers of private or semi-private clubs in Canada; *Committees:* Executive; Editorial Advisory; Education; Technology; Certification

Canadian Society of Consultant Pharmacists (CSCP)

Winnipeg Regional Health Authority, 2109 Portage Ave., Winnipeg MB R3J 0L3
Tel: 204-831-2967; *Fax:* 204-831-2915
info@cscpharm.com
www.cscpharm.com
www.linkedin.com/groups/Canadian-Senior-Care-Pharmacists-4331158?gid=4
www.facebook.com/groups/256159589015
twitter.com/ASCPharm
Overview: A small national organization
Mission: To enhance the role of pharmacists working with clients in assisted living or long term care settings.
Affiliation(s): American Society of Consultant Pharmacists
Chief Officer(s):
Teresa Pitre, President
Finances: *Annual Operating Budget:* Less than $50,000
Membership: 150; *Fees:* Schedule available; *Member Profile:* Consultant pharmacists, long-term care providers
Activities: Support optimal pharmeceutical care of seniors & long term care residents

Canadian Society of Corporate Secretaries (CSCS)

#255, 55 St. Clair Ave. West, Toronto ON M4V 2Y7
Tel: 416-921-5449; *Fax:* 416-967-6320
Toll-Free: 800-774-2850
info@cscs.org
www.cscs.org
Overview: A medium-sized national organization founded in 1994
Mission: To provide members with the tools necessary to become expert in corporate secretarial practice & to strengthen the corporate secretary's profile in the company.
Chief Officer(s):
Pamela Smith, Administrative Director
pamela.smith@cscs.org
Lynn Beauregard, President
lynn.beauregard@cscs.org
Finances: *Annual Operating Budget:* $100,000-$250,000; *Funding Sources:* Membership dues; seminars & courses fees
Staff Member(s): 5; 30 volunteer(s)
Membership: 300; *Fees:* $124.69 individual; $708.75 corporate; *Member Profile:* Practicing corporate secretaries in Canada & other persons involved with corporate governance; *Committees:* Legal; Legislative
Activities: Training in corporate procedures;

Canadian Society of Customs Brokers (CSCB) / Société canadienne des courtiers en douane

#320, 55 Murray St., Ottawa ON K1N 5M3
Tel: 613-562-3543; *Fax:* 613-562-3548
Other Communication: students@cscb.ca
cscb@cscb.ca
www.cscb.ca
Previous Name: Canadian Association of Customs Brokers
Overview: A medium-sized international organization founded in 1921
Mission: To act as voice of the industry to all levels of government; To provide information to members on all matters affecting customs brokerage
Affliation(s): International Federation of Customs Brokers Associations
Chief Officer(s):
Bedard Melanie, Chair
Finances: *Funding Sources:* Membership dues
Membership: 160 corporate + 40 associate + 2,000 Certified Customs Specialists; *Fees:* Schedule available; *Member Profile:* Must be licensed customs broker or engaged in international trade or a certified customs specialist
Activities: Offering internet based & other distance education programs about customs & international trade; *Speaker Service:* Yes

Canadian Society of Cytology (CSC) / Société canadienne de cytologie

c/o Dr. Karim Khetani, #200, 10150 - 102 St. NW, Edmonton AB T5J 5E2
e-mail: karim1233@yahoo.com
cap-acp.org/cytology.cfm
Previous Name: Canadian Cytology Council
Overview: A small national charitable organization founded in 1961
Mission: To promote & support education in cytology; To maintain a high standard of practice within the discipline of cytopathology; To foster the development of cytopathology in Canada
Member of: Canadian Association of Pathologists / Association canadienne des pathologistes
Chief Officer(s):
Karim Khetani, Chair
Membership: *Fees:* $40 medical members; $10 cytotechnologists; *Member Profile:* Pathologists; Cytotechnologists with an interest in cytopathology
Activities: Conducting regular cytology surveys; Contributing to the development of the Guide for Training in General Pathology & cytotechnology training programs across Canada; Presenting awards; Facilitating the exchange of knowledge in cytopathology; Organizing educational programs; Developing guidelines for quality assurance programs in cytopathology
Publications:
• CSC [Canadian Society of Cytology] Bulletin
Type: Newsletter; *Frequency:* 3 pa

Canadian Society of Endocrinology & Metabolism (CSEM) / Société canadienne d'endocrinologie et métabolisme (SCEM)

#1403, 222 Queen St., Ottawa ON K1P 5V9
Tel: 613-594-0005; *Fax:* 613-569-6574
info@endo-metab.ca
www.endo-metab.ca
Overview: A small national organization founded in 1972
Mission: To advance the discipline of endocrinology & metabolism in Canada
Chief Officer(s):
Stephanie Kaiser, President
Jean-Patrice Baillargeon, Secretary-Treasurer
Membership: *Fees:* $100 active members; *Member Profile:* Clinical endocrinologists, educators, & researchers who provide health care, training, research in endocrinology; Graduate students, residents, & research fellows; emertius members; *Committees:* Awards; Continuing Professional Development; Program Planning; Residents Council/Review Course Planning; Clinical Practice Guidelines; eCHE
Activities: Advocating for excellence in endocrinology research, education, & patient care; Promoting research in endocrinology & metabolism; Providing continuing professional development opportunities
Meetings/Conferences: • Canadian Society of Endocrinology & Metabolism (CSEM) & Canadian Diabetes Association Professional Conference & Annual Meetings, November, 2015, Vancouver, BC
Scope: National
Description: Interactive workshops, oral abstract sessions, poster presentations. speakers addressing current diagnosis & treatment issues, a trade show, social activities, & networking opportunities
Contact Information: Chair, Program Planning Committee: Stephanie Kaiser, E-mail: CSEM@royalcollege.ca

Canadian Society of Environmental Biologists (CSEB) / Société canadienne des biologistes de l'environnement

PO Box 962, Stn. F, Toronto ON M4Y 2N9
www.cseb-scbe.org
Overview: A medium-sized national charitable organization founded in 1943
Mission: To further the conservation of natural resources of Canada & to promote the prudent management of these resources so as to minimize adverse environmental effects; to ensure high professional standards in education, research & management related to resources & environment; to advance the education of the public & to protect public interest on matters pertaining to the use of natural resources & the protection & management of the environment; to undertake environmental research & education programs; to assess & evaluate administrative & legislative policies having ecological significance in terms of conservation of resources & quality of the environment; to develop & promote policies that seek to achieve balance among resource management & utilization, protection of the environment & quality of life; to foster liaison among environmental biologists working within governmental, industrial & educational frameworks across Canada
Chief Officer(s):
Robert Stedwill, President, 306-585-1854
rstedwill@live.ca
Finances: *Annual Operating Budget:* Less than $50,000; *Funding Sources:* Membership dues
Staff Member(s): 2; 30 volunteer(s)
Membership: 500; *Fees:* $35; *Member Profile:* Regular - graduate from college or university in discipline of biological sciences, professionally engaged in teaching, management or research related to natural resources & the environment; Student - persons enrolled in accredited college or university in discipline of biological sciences & preparing themselves for professional work in teaching, management or research related to natural resources; Associate - supporters in general
Activities: *Speaker Service:* Yes; *Rents Mailing List:* Yes
Publications:
• CSEB [Canadian Society of Environmental Biologists] National Newsletter / Bulletin
Type: Newsletter; *Frequency:* Quarterly; *Accepts Advertising*; *Editor:* Gary Ash *ISSN:* 0318-5133; *Price:* Free with Canadian Society of Environmental Biologistsmembership
Profile: CSEB activities, & national & regional news, for members

Canadian Society of Exploration Geophysicists (CSEG)

#600, 640 - 8th Ave. SW, Calgary AB T2P 1G7
Tel: 403-262-0015
cseg.office@shaw.ca
www.cseg.ca
Overview: A medium-sized national organization founded in 1949
Mission: To promote the science of geophysics
Affiliation(s): Society of Exploration Geophysicists (USA); European Association of Geoscientists & Engineers
Chief Officer(s):
John Townsley, President
jtownsley@arcresources.com
Larry Herd, Vice-President
larryh@boydpetro.com
Jim Racette, Managing Director, 403-262-0015, Fax: 403-262-7383
jimra@shaw.ca
John Fernando, Director, Educational Services
john.fernando@sait.ca
Kelly Jamison, Director, Finance
kelly.jamison@divestco.com
Kristy Manchul, Director, Communications
kristy.manchul@cggveritas.com
Dave Nordin, Director, Member Service
denordin@telusplanet.net
Finances: *Funding Sources:* Membership fees
Membership: 1,800; *Member Profile:* Geophysicists involved in hydrocarbon exploration; Geologists; Field specialists; Technical specialists; Academics; Interested industry personnel; Corporate members
Activities: Offering a mentorship program; Exchanging technical information; Providing networking activities;
Meetings/Conferences: • Canadian Society of Exploration Geophysicists GeoConvention 2015 (Focus 2015), May, 2015, Calgary TELUS Convention Centre, Calgary, AB
Scope: National
Description: Technical information for persons involved in earth sciences, from geologists to reservior engineers, & managers
Contact Information: URL: www.geoconvention.com
Publications:
• Canadian Society of Exploration Geophysicists Annual Report
Type: Yearbook; *Frequency:* Annually
• The CSEG / CSPG Geophysical Atlas of Western Canadian Hydrocarbon Pools
Type: Atlas; *Editor:* Leonard V. Hills
• Recorder
Type: Magazine; *Frequency:* Monthly; *Accepts Advertising*
Profile: Canadian Society of Exploration Geophysicists membership news, & events, plus articles related to geophysics

Canadian Society of Forensic Science (CSFS)

PO Box 37040, 3332 McCarthy Rd., Ottawa ON K1V 0W0
e-mail: csfs@bellnet.ca
www.csfs.ca
Overview: A small national organization founded in 1953
Mission: To promote the study of forensic science; To maintain professional standards in the discipline of forensic science
Chief Officer(s):
G. Anderson, President
G. Verret, Secretary
D. Camellato, Treasurer
Membership: *Fees:* $30; *Member Profile:* Professionals with an interest in forensic science; *Committees:* Awards; Finance; Membership; Nominating; Publication; Informatics & Education; Drugs & Driving; Constitution; Alcohol Test; Accreditation
Activities: Addressing educational, scientific, & legal issues within forensic science
Publications:
• The Canadian Society of Forensic Science Journal
Type: Journal; *Frequency:* Quarterly; *Accepts Advertising*; *Price:* $115 Canada; $130 International
Profile: Original papers, & comments & reviews on the various aspects of forensic science, such as forensic chemistry, forensic odontology, forensic toxicology, forensic pathology,firearms examination, forensic biology, & forensic anthropology

Canadian Society of Forest Engineers *See* Canadian Institute of Forestry

Canadian Society of Gastroenterology Nurses & Associates (CSGNA)

#224, 1540 Cornwall Rd., Oakville ON L6J 7W5
Tel: 905-829-8794; *Fax:* 905-829-0242
Toll-Free: 866-544-8794
csgnaexecutiveassistant@csgna.com
www.csgna.com
Overview: A small national organization founded in 1984
Mission: To enhance the educational & professional growth of the membership within the resources available.
Member of: SIGNEA - the International Society of Gastroenterology Nurses & Associates
Affliation(s): Canadian Nurses Association
Chief Officer(s):
Lisa Westin, President
Jacqui Ho, Treasurer
treasurer@csgna.com
Finances: *Funding Sources:* Membership fees; donations; fundraising
Membership: 467 members + 19 local chapters; *Fees:* $100 active/affiliate; *Member Profile:* Work in field of gastroenterology

Calgary Chapter
South Health Campus Endoscopy Unit, 4448 Front St. SE, Calgary AB T3M 1M4
Chief Officer(s):
Bobbi Sheppy, President
sheppyfamily@shaw.ca

Edmonton Chapter
c/o Endoscopy Unit, Misericordia Community Hospital, 16940 - 87 Ave., Edmonton AB T5R 4H5
Chief Officer(s):
Yvonne Verklan, President
yvohver@gmail.com

Golden Horseshoe Chapter
ON
Chief Officer(s):
Jody Hannah, President
jhanah@stjosham.on.ca

Greater Toronto Chapter
c/o St. Joseph's Healthcentre, 30 The Queensway, Toronto ON M6R 1B5
Tel: 416-530-6000
Chief Officer(s):
Daysi Sandino, President
daysisandino@yahoo.ca

London & Area Chapter
London ON
Chief Officer(s):
Donna Pratt, President
Donna.Pratt@lhsc.on.ca

London Chapter
London ON
Chief Officer(s):
Donna Pratt, President
Donna.Pratt@lhsc.on.ca

Manitoba Chapter
MB
Chief Officer(s):
Carol Reidy, President
creidy@sbgh.mb.ca

New Brunswick/PEI Chapter
NB
Chief Officer(s):
Cathy Arnold Cormier, President
cathy.arnoldcormier@horizonnb.ca

Newfoundland Chapter
NL
Chief Officer(s):
June Peckham, President
j.peckham@nf.sympatico.ca

Nova Scotia Chapter
NS
Chief Officer(s):
Marleen Spencer, President
marleen.spencer@cdha.nshealth.ca

Okanagan Chapter
Kelowna General Hospital, Gastroenterology Unit, 2268 Pandosy St., Kelowna BC V1Y 1T2
Tel: 250-868-8465
Chief Officer(s):
Bethany Rode, President
behl@shaw.ca

Ottawa Chapter
Ottawa ON
Chief Officer(s):
Joanne Bertrand, President
joanne.l.bertrand@gmail.com

Regina Chapter
Regina SK
Chief Officer(s):

Jennifer McIntyre, President
Jennifer.Mcintyre@rqhealth.ca
Vancouver Regional Chapter
Vancouver BC

Canadian Society of Geriatric Medicine ***See*** Canadian Geriatrics Society

Canadian Society of Hand Therapists (CSHT) / Societe canadienne des therapeutes de la main (SCTM)

csht.org
www.facebook.com/324550384259629
twitter.com/handtherapists
Overview: A medium-sized national organization
Chief Officer(s):
Trevor Fraser, President
president@csht.org
Membership: *Fees:* $30; *Member Profile:* Occupational and physical therapists
Meetings/Conferences: • 2015 Annual Canadian Society of Hand Therapists Conference, May, 2015, Hyatt Regency Hotel, Montreal, QC
Scope: National

Canadian Society of Home Inspectors Inc. ***See*** Canadian Institute of Professional Home Inspectors Inc.

Canadian Society of Hospital Pharmacists (CSHP) / Société canadienne des pharmaciens d'hôpitaux

#3, 30 Concourse Gate, Ottawa ON K2E 7V7
Tel: 613-736-9733; *Fax:* 613-736-5660
info@cshp.ca
www.cshp.ca
Overview: A medium-sized national organization founded in 1947
Mission: To advance safe, effective medication use & patient care in hospitals & related health care settings throughout Canada; To act as an influential voice for hospital pharmacy; To encourge professional growth & practice excellence
Member of: Canadian Council on Continuing Education in Pharmacy
Chief Officer(s):
Myrella Roy, Executive Director
mroy@cshp.ca
Desarae Davidson, Administrator, Conferences
ddavidson@cshp.ca
Colleen Drake, Administrator, Publications
cdrake@cshp.ca
Anna Dudek, Administrator, Finance
adudek@cshp.ca
Robyn Rockwell, Administrator, Membership
rrockwell@cshp.ca
Finances: *Funding Sources:* Membership fees; Sponsorships
Membership: *Member Profile:* Hospital pharmacists across Canada; Residents & students; Hospital & industry corporate members; *Committees:* Advocacy; Bylaws: CSHP 2015 Steering; Educational Services; Finance & Audit; Government & Health Policy Planning; Membership; National Awards; Nominating; Pharmacy Specialty Networks Coordinating; Practice Standards Steering; Research
Activities: Developing standards; Facilitating research; Advocating for hospital pharmacy; Providing education, mentorship, & information; *Awareness Events:* Pharmacy Awareness Week
Meetings/Conferences: • Canadian Society of Hospital Pharmacists 2015 46th Annual Professional Practice Conference, January, 2015, Sheraton Centre Toronto Hotel, Toronto, ON
Scope: National
Attendance: 650
Description: Educational sessions for clinical practitioners & managers from across Canada
Contact Information: E-mail: info@cshp.ca
• Canadian Society of Hospital Pharmacists 2015 Annual Summer Educational Sessions, August, 2015, London, ON
Scope: National
Attendance: 250
Description: Workshops, plus the annual general meeting of the society
Contact Information: E-mail: info@cshp.ca
• Canadian Society of Hospital Pharmacists 2016 47th Annual Professional Practice Conference, January, 2016, Sheraton Centre Toronto Hotel, Toronto, ON
Scope: National
Attendance: 650
Description: Presentations about pharmacists' roles, pharmacy practice, & pharmacy programs
Contact Information: E-mail: info@cshp.ca
• Canadian Society of Hospital Pharmacists 2017 48th Annual Professional Practice Conference, 2017
Scope: National
Description: Informative sessions to educate & motivate participants
• Canadian Society of Hospital Pharmacists 2017 Annual Summer Educational Sessions, 2017
Scope: National
Description: The annual general meeting of the society & educational workshops held each year in partnership with one of the society's branches
Contact Information: E-mail: info@cshp.ca
Publications:
• Canadian Journal of Hospital Pharmacy
Type: Journal; *Frequency:* Bimonthly; *Accepts Advertising*; *Editor:* Mary H.H. Ensom *ISSN:* 0008-4123; *Price:* Free with Canadian Society of Hospital Pharmacistsmembership
Profile: A peer-reviewed scientific journal, featuring original research, case reports, & clinical reviews
• CSHP [Canadian Society of Hospital Pharmacists] eBulletin
Type: Newsletter; *Frequency:* Semimonthly; *Accepts Advertising*; *Price:* Free with Canadian Society of Hospital Pharmacists membership
Profile: Society news & career opportunities

Alberta
Edmonton AB
e-mail: deurich@ualberta.ca
www.cshp-ab.ca
Chief Officer(s):
Dean Eurich, President
Jeff Lanz, Treasurer
jeff.lanz@albertahealthservices.ca

British Columbia
#200, 1765 West 8th Ave., Vancouver BC V6J 1V8
e-mail: cshpbc@gmail.com
www.cshp-bc.com
www.facebook.com/pages/CSHP-BC/124009301064833
twitter.com/CSHPBCBranch
Chief Officer(s):
Michael Legal, President
Ivy Chow, Treasurer

Manitoba
200 Tache Ave., Winnipeg MB R3H 1A7
e-mail: info4@cshp-mb.ca
www.cshp-mb.ca
Chief Officer(s):
Patrick Fitch, President
Alyn Stavness, Treasurer

New Brunswick
NB
e-mail: webmaster@cshp-nb.ca
www.cshp-nb.ca
Chief Officer(s):
Leslie Manuel, President
Leslie.Manuel@horizonnb.ca
Rochelle Johnston, Director, Communication
Rochelle.Johnston@HorizonNB.ca

Newfoundland & Labrador
c/o PANL, 85 Thorburn Rd., St. John's NL A1E 1C1
e-mail: admin@cshp-nl.com
www.cshp-nl.com
Chief Officer(s):
Tiffany Lee, President
tiffany.lee@mun.ca
Angie Payne, Treasurer
Angie.Payne@easternhealth.ca
• Branch Out: The Newsletter of the Newfoundland & Labrador Branch Canadian Society of Hospital Pharmacists
Type: Newsletter
Profile: Membership, awards, advocacy, & professional development updates, as well as upcoming events

Nova Scotia
Halifax NS
www.cshp-ns.com
Chief Officer(s):
Lisa Nodwell, President
Lisa.Nodwell@cdha.nshealth.ca
Heather MacKeen, Treasurer
heather.mackeen@cdha.nshealth.ca

Ontario
#3, 30 Concourse Gate, Ottawa ON K2V 7V7
Tel: 613-736-9733; *Fax:* 613-736-5660
www.cshpontario.ca
Chief Officer(s):
Dawn Jennings, President
Helen Briggs, Treasurer

Prince Edward Island
Charlottetown PE
Chief Officer(s):
Wendy Cooke, President
wpcooke@gov.pe.ca
Kelly Herget, Treasurer
kcherget@ihis.org

Québec
Association des pharmaciens des établissements de santé, #320, 4050, rue Molson, Montréal QC H1Y 3N1
Tel: 514-286-0776; *Fax:* 514-286-1081
info@apesquebec.org
www.apesquebec.org
Chief Officer(s):
Linda Vaillant, Directrice générale
France Boucher, Directrice générale adjointe

Saskatchewan
c/o Saskatoon Health Region, Saskatoon SK
www.cshp-sk.org
Chief Officer(s):
Jaris Swidrovich, President
president@cshp-sk.org
Leslie Dagg, Treasurer
treasurer@cshp-sk.org
• The PostScript
Type: Newsletter; *Editor:* Z. Dumont (postscript@cshp-sk.org)
Profile: Canadian Society of Hospital Pharmacists, Saskatchewan Branch highlights, membership news, professional development information, & upcoming events

Canadian Society of Internal Medicine (CSIM) / Société canadienne de médecine interne (SCMI)

774 Echo Dr., Ottawa ON K1S 5N8
Tel: 613-730-6244; *Fax:* 613-730-1116
csim@royalcollege.ca
www.csimonline.com
Overview: A medium-sized national organization founded in 1984
Affliation(s): Canadian Medical Association
Chief Officer(s):
Maria Baccus, President
Finances: *Funding Sources:* Membership dues; grants
Membership: 700; *Fees:* $200 full; $30 residents in training; *Member Profile:* General internal medicine physicians/residents; *Committees:* Educational
Awards:
• Canadian Society of Internal Medicine's Education & Research Fund (Scholarship)
Support research and education for members of CSIM*Eligibility:* Resident & member of association*Deadline:* November
Publications:
• CJGIM (Canadian Journal of General Internal Medicine)
Type: Journal; *Frequency:* Quarterly
Profile: CSIM news, book reviews, articles, case reviews, history of medicine, & medical education

Canadian Society of Laboratory Technologists ***See*** Canadian Society for Medical Laboratory Science

Canadian Society of Landscape Architects (CSLA) / Association des architectes paysagistes du Canada (AAPC)

PO Box 13594, Ottawa ON K2K 1X6
Tel: 866-781-9799; *Fax:* 866-871-1419
info@csla.ca
www.csla.ca
Overview: A medium-sized national organization founded in 1934
Mission: To support the improvement &/or conservation of the natural, cultural, social & built environment; to promote visibility, recognition, acceptance & understanding of the profession by communicating its value in relation to that of the public good
Affliation(s): International Federation of Landscape Architects; Landscape Alliance
Chief Officer(s):
Elizabeth A. Sharpe, Executive Director
executive-director@csla.ca
Finances: *Annual Operating Budget:* $100,000-$250,000; *Funding Sources:* Membership dues
40 volunteer(s)

Membership: 1,250 individuals; *Fees:* $115; *Member Profile:* Qualified & experienced landscape architects who practise their profession by providing a variety of services ranging from advice, consultation & design to preparing working drawings, contract documents & supervising the implementation of various size construction projects
Meetings/Conferences: • 2015 Canadian Society of Landscape Architects Congress, May, 2015, Hilton Mexico City Reforma, Mexico City
Scope: National
• 2016 Canadian Society of Landscape Architects Congress, June, 2016, Fort Garry Hotel, Spa and Conference Centre, Winnipeg, MB
Scope: National
Publications:
• CSLA [Canadian Society of Landscape Architects] Bulletin
Type: Newsletter; *Frequency:* Monthly
Profile: News & events related to landscape architecture in Canada
• CSLA [Canadian Society of Landscape Architects] Membership Directory
Type: Directory
• CSLA [Canadian Society of Landscape Architects] Annual Report
Type: Yearbook; *Frequency:* Annually
• Landscapes / Paysages
Type: Journal; *Frequency:* Quarterly; *Accepts Advertising*
Profile: Articles about the professional practice of landscape architecture in Canada, related to culture, design, & the environment

Canadian Society of Mayflower Descendants
c/o Lynne Webb, 2927 Highfield Cres., Ottawa ON K2B 6G4
e-mail: administrator@csmd.org
csmd.org
www.facebook.com/canadiansocietyofmayflowerdescendants
twitter.com/CanMayflower
Overview: A small national organization founded in 1980
Mission: To promote the memory of the Mayflower pilgrims & to inform the public of this era of Canadian history
Affiliation(s): General Society of Mayflower Descendants - USA
Chief Officer(s):
Joyce Cutler, Governor
governor@csmd.org
Finances: *Funding Sources:* Membership dues; donations
Membership: 577; *Fees:* $45; *Member Profile:* Direct descendants of Mayflower passengers; *Committees:* Governance; Nominating; Publicity
Activities: *Internships:* Yes; *Speaker Service:* Yes; *Library:* Collection at North York Public Library; Open to public
Publications:
• Canadian Pilgrim
Type: Newsletter; *Frequency:* Semiannually; *Price:* Free with Canadian Society of Mayflower Descendants membership
Profile: Society news, & genealogical & historical information
• The Mayflower Quarterly
Type: Journal; *Frequency:* Quarterly; *Price:* Free with Society membership
Profile: Genealogical information

Canadian Society of Medical Evaluators (CSME)
#301, 250 Consumers Rd., Toronto ON M2J 4V6
Tel: 416-487-4040; *Fax:* 416-495-8723
Toll-Free: 888-672-9999
info@csme.org
www.csme.org
www.facebook.com/101574806684190
Overview: A small national organization
Mission: To serve Canadian physicians who perform medical & medicolegal evaluations for patients or as a professional service to the legal profession, employers, the workplace safety & insurance board & the insurance industry
Chief Officer(s):
Renee Levine, Executive Director
rlevine@csme.org
Membership: *Fees:* $295 associate; $450 general; *Committees:* Communications; Ethics; Education Programs; Guidelines; Membership

Canadian Society of Medievalists (CSM)
104 Mount Aubrun St., 5th Fl., Cambridge MA 02138 USA
Tel: 617-491-1622; *Fax:* 617-492-3303
csmtreasurer@gmail.com
www.canadianmedievalists.ca
www.facebook.com/pages/Canadian-Society-of-Medievalists
twitter.com/canMedievalists
Overview: A small national organization
Mission: The Canadian Society of Medievalists is an academic organization that promotes excellence in research for medieval studies.
Chief Officer(s):
John Osborne, President
Membership: *Fees:* $50 regular; $35 retired/unemployed/other; $30 student; $125 sustaining
Meetings/Conferences: • Canadian Society of Medievalists 2015 Conference, May, 2015, University of Ottawa, Ottawa, ON
Scope: National

Canadian Society of Microbiologists (CSM) / Société canadienne des microbiologistes
CSM-SCM Secretariat, 17 Dossetter Way, Ottawa ON K1G 4S3
Tel: 613-421-7229; *Fax:* 613-421-9811
info@csm-scm.org
www.csm-scm.org
Overview: A medium-sized national organization founded in 1958
Mission: To advance microbiology in all its aspects; to facilitate interchange of ideas between microbiologists
Affiliation(s): Youth Science Foundation; International Union of Microbiological Societies
Chief Officer(s):
Ivan Oresnik, President
Ayush Kumar, Secretary-Treasurer
Finances: *Annual Operating Budget:* $100,000-$250,000
Staff Member(s): 2
Membership: 450; *Fees:* $75; *Member Profile:* open; *Committees:* Education; Manpower Placement; Science Policy; Regulatory Issues
Meetings/Conferences: • The Canadian Society of Microbiologists 65th Annual Conference, June, 2015, University of Regina, Regina, SK
Scope: National
Description: In conjunction with the IUMS 2015 Congress
Contact Information: Congress Manager: Marie Lanouette, iums2014@nrc-cnrc.gc.ca
Publications:
• Canadian Society of Microbiologists Call for Abstracts
Type: Booklet; *Frequency:* Annually
Profile: Published in advance of the Annual General Meeting in November / December
• Canadian Society of Microbiologists Programme & Abstracts
Frequency: Annually
Profile: Published for the Annual General Meeting each May
• Canadian Society of Microbiologists Graduate Studies & Membership Directory
Type: Directory; *Frequency:* Biennially
• CSM [Canadian Society of Microbiologists] Newsletter
Type: Newsletter; *Frequency:* 3 pa

Canadian Society of Nephrology (CSN) / Société canadienne de néphrologie (SCN)
PO Box 25255, Stn. RDP, Montreal QC H1E 7P9
Tel: 514-643-4985
info@csnscn.ca
www.csnscn.ca
Overview: A small national organization founded in 1966
Mission: To advance the practice of Nephrology; To promote the highest quality of care for patients with renal diseases, by setting high standards for medical training & education; To encourage research in biomedical sciences related to the kidney, kidney disorders & renal replacement therapies
Member of: International Society of Nephrology
Affiliation(s): Royal College of Physicians & Surgeons of Canada
Chief Officer(s):
John Gill, President
jgill@providencehealth.bc.ca
Marcello Tonelli, Vice-President
mtonelli-admin@med.ualberta.ca
Sanjay Padeya, Secretary-Treasurer
spandeta@me.com
Braden Manns, President-Elect
braden.manns@albertahealthservices.ca
Filomena Picciano, Director, Operations
Finances: *Funding Sources:* Membership fees; Corporate sponsors
Membership: *Fees:* Schedule available; *Member Profile:* Any person with the degree of Doctor of Medicine or Doctor of Philosophy, or its equivalent, who has demonstrated a major, continued interest in nephrology; Corporations with links to Nephrology; *Committees:* Education; Scientific; Clinical Practice Guidelines; International Health; Nephrology Division Head; Website Advisory
Meetings/Conferences: • Canadian Society of Nephrology Annual General Meeting 2015, 2015
Scope: National
Publications:
• CSN [Canadian Society of Nephrology] Newsletter
Type: Newsletter; *Frequency:* Quarterly

Canadian Society of Nutrition Management / Société canadienne de gestion de la nutrition
#300, 1370 Don Mills Rd., Toronto ON M3B 3N7
Fax: 416-441-0591
Toll-Free: 866-355-2766
csnm@csnm.ca
www.csnm.ca
ca.linkedin.com/in/thecsnm
twitter.com/TheCSNM
Previous Name: Canadian Food Service Supervisors Association
Overview: A medium-sized national organization
Mission: To foster an environment in which members can achieve success in their chosen field.
Chief Officer(s):
Barbara Cockwell, President Elect
president-elect@csnm.ca
Jean Van Nus, President
president@csnm.ca
Membership: *Fees:* $40 student; $165 regular; $500 corporate; *Member Profile:* Graduates of a certified Nutrition Management program

Canadian Society of Ophthalmic Registered Nurses (CSORN) / Société canadienne des infirmières et infirmiers en opthalmologie
c/o Janet Powers, University of Ottawa Eye Institute, 501 Smyth Rd., Ottawa ON K1H 8L6
www.csorn.ca
Overview: A small national organization
Mission: To promote high standards of practice in ophthalmic nursing; To encourage good ocular care
Chief Officer(s):
Janet Powers, President, 613-737-8577
jpowers@ottawahospital.on.ca
Kathy Bruce, Vice-President
Marlene Griffin, Secretary
Wanda Mulrooney, Treasurer
Finances: *Funding Sources:* Membership fees; Sponsorships
Membership: 176; *Fees:* $25
Activities: Promoting research in the field of ophthalmic nursing; Liaising with government & related professional organizations; Providing continuing professional education for ophthalmic nurses; Encouraging & facilitating the sharing of knowledge among ophthalmic nurses; Educating the public about preventable & treatable ocular conditions
Publications:
• Canadian Society of Ophthalmic Registered Nurses Newsletter
Type: Newsletter
Profile: CSORN activities, including conference previews & reviews, executive news, updates from provincial representatives, & ophthalmology news

Canadian Society of Orthopaedic Technologists (CSOT) / Société canadienne des technologistes en orthopedie
#715A, 18 Wynford Dr., Toronto ON M3C 3S2
Tel: 416-445-4516; *Fax:* 416-489-7356
csot@look.ca
www.pappin.com/csot
Overview: A small national licensing organization founded in 1972
Mission: To promote & develop training programmes, professional standards; encourage uniform training programs & examinatios; promote & facilitate cooperation between Orthopaedic Technologists & the medical profession.
Chief Officer(s):
Patricia Ennis, President
ennis.60@hotmail.com
Pamela Smith, Registrar/Office Manager
Finances: *Annual Operating Budget:* $50,000-$100,000
Staff Member(s): 1
Membership: 400; *Fees:* $150 retired; $160 student; $170 associate; $225 registered/full
Publications:
• BodyCast
Type: Journal; *Frequency:* s-a.

• NewsCast
Type: Newsletter; *Frequency:* s-a.

Alberta Chapter
303 Chaparral Dr. SE, Calgary AB T2X 3L9
Tel: 403-201-2423
Chief Officer(s):
Pam Nadon, President

Graham Bell Chapter
26 Geneva Crt., Brantford ON L6S 1B8
Tel: 905-791-7970
Chief Officer(s):
Adam Bradley, President

Manitoba Chapter
c/o Pan Am Clinic, 75 Poseidon Bay, Winnipeg MB R3M 3E4
Tel: 204-925-1522
Chief Officer(s):
Mary Kate Turner, President

Niagara Chapter
22 Lyndon St. West, Thorold ON L2V 3J7
Tel: 906-321-6201
Chief Officer(s):
Stephanie Koch, President

Northtechs Chapter
6211-149 Ave., Edmonton AB T5A 1W1
Tel: 780-342-4056
Chief Officer(s):
Ellanore Gallagher, President

Wascana Chapter
200 Angus St., Regina SK S4R 3K4
Tel: 306-775-2100
Chief Officer(s):
Dustin Livingstone, President

Canadian Society of Otolaryngology - Head & Neck Surgery (CSO-HNS) / Société canadienne d'otolaryngologie et de chirurgie cervico-faciale

Administrative Office, 221 Millford Cres., Elora ON N0B 1S0
Tel: 519-846-0630; *Fax:* 519-846-9529
Toll-Free: 800-655-9533
cso.hns@sympatico.ca
www.entcanada.org
Overview: A medium-sized national charitable organization founded in 1947
Mission: To improve patient care in otolaryngology - head & neck surgery; To maintain high professional & ethical standards
Chief Officer(s):
Dale Brown, President
Sam Spafford, Secretary
Martin Corsten, Treasurer
Donna Humphrey, General Manager
Membership: *Member Profile:* Graduates in medicine, who also hold a certificate in otolaryngology - head & neck surgery of the Royal College of Physicians & Surgeons of Canada, or an equivalent qualification approved by the Board of Directors of the Society; Associates, who are training in an otolaryngology program approved by the Board of Directors of the Society; Affiliates, who are undertaking professional work in areas related to otolaryngology - head & neck surgery; Emeritus members; *Committees:* Awards; Budget; Bylaws; Convention; Economics; Electronic Communications; Ethics; Fellowship; Historian; Humanitarian; International Liaison; Long-Range Planning; Nominating; Physican Resources; Policy Action; Practice Guidelines; Public Relations; Publications; Residents; Safety; Undergraduate Education
Activities: Promoting research; Supporting education; Disseminating information
Meetings/Conferences: • Canadian Society of Otolaryngology - Head & Neck Surgery 2015 69th Annual Meeting: "Taking Care of Your Patients and Yourself - Work / Life Balance", June, 2015, RBC Convention Centre / Delta Hotel, Winnipeg, MB
Scope: National
Description: Scientific presentations for graduates in medicine who hold a certificate in otolaryngology & professionals who work in areas related to otolaryngology
Contact Information: Canadian Society of Otolaryngology Administrative Office: Phone: 519-846-0630, E-mail: cso.hns@sympatico.ca
• Canadian Society of Otolaryngology - Head & Neck Surgery 2016 70th Annual Conference, 2016, Québec, QC
Scope: National
Description: Scientific information for those who specialize in head & neck surgery
Contact Information: Canadian Society of Otolaryngology Administrative Office: Phone: 519-846-0630, E-mail: cso.hns@sympatico.ca
Publications:
• Journal of Otolaryngology - Head & Neck Surgery
Type: Journal; *Editor:* Dr. Erin Wright & Dr. Hadi Seikaly
Profile: Available for Society members

Canadian Society of Painters in Water Colour (CSPWC) / Société canadienne de peintres en aquarelle (SCPA)

80 Birmingham St., #B3, Toronto ON M8V 3W6
Tel: 416-533-5100
info@cspwc.com
www.cspwc.com
Overview: A medium-sized national organization founded in 1925
Mission: To promote the use of experimentation with water-based media; To encourage new artists
Member of: Visual Arts Ontario
Affliation(s): John B. Aird Gallery
Chief Officer(s):
William Rogers, President
Anita Cotter, Administrator
Finances: *Funding Sources:* Fundraising; grants
Membership: 265 + 210 associates; *Fees:* $125; $35 associate; *Member Profile:* Review of work by members
Activities: Annual open juried exhibitions; members exhibitions, workshops; scholarships for watercolour at various Canadian art colleges; *Awareness Events:* World Watercolour Day, Nov. 23; *Library* Open to public by appointment

Canadian Society of Palliative Care Physicians (CSPCP) / Société canadienne des médecins de soins palliatifs (SCMSP)

c/o Fraser Health Authority, #400, 13450 - 102 Ave., Surrey BC V3T 0H1
Tel: 604-341-3174; *Fax:* 604-587-4644
office@cspcp.ca
www.cspcp.ca
Overview: A medium-sized national organization
Mission: The CSPCP is a membership organization for patients and their families, though the advancement and improvement of palliative medicine and training.
Chief Officer(s):
Susan MacDonald, President
Kim Taylor, Executive Director
Membership: *Fees:* $10-$290; *Member Profile:* Clinicians, educators, academics, researchers and specialists dedicated to the improvement of palliative care; *Committees:* Undergrad Training; Postgrad Training; CPD; Sub-specialty/Liaison; Euthanasia/PAS; Human Resources; Communications/Membership
Awards:
• CSPCP Lifetime Achievement Award (Award)
• The Eduardo Bruera Award in Palliative Medicine (Award)
Meetings/Conferences: • 11th annual Advanced Palliative Medicine Conference "New Frontiers in Palliative Medicine", May, 2015, Westin Calgary, Calgary, AB
Scope: National

Canadian Society of Patristic Studies (CSPS) / Association canadienne des études patristiques

c/o Dr. S. Muir, Religious Studies, Concordia University College of AB, 7128 Ada Blvd., Edmonton AB T5B 4E4
www.ccsr.ca/csps
Overview: A small national organization founded in 1975
Mission: To encourage the academic study of the Church Fathers
Member of: Canadian Federation for the Humanities & Social Sciences / Fèderation canadienne des sciences humaines
Chief Officer(s):
Robert Kennedy, President
Lorraine Buck, Vice-President
George Bevan, Secretary
Steven Muir, Treasurer
Membership: *Fees:* $48 studemts & retired members (with subscription); $65 regular members (including subscription); *Committees:* Program; Nominating
Meetings/Conferences: • Canadian Society of Patristic Studies 2015 Annual Meeting, May, 2015, University of Ottawa, Ottawa, ON
Scope: National
Publications:
• Canadian Society of Patristic Studies Bulletin
Type: Newsletter; *Frequency:* Semiannually; *Editor:* Adriana Bara
Profile: Society activities, including information about recent & upcoming conferences, membership updates, research, & other scholarly activities in patristics

Canadian Society of Petroleum Geologists (CSPG)

#110, 333 - 5th Ave. SW, Calgary AB T2P 1G7
Tel: 403-264-5610; *Fax:* 403-264-5898
cspg@cspg.org
www.cspg.org
www.linkedin.com/groups/Canadian-Society-Petroleum-Geologists-4153517
www.facebook.com/CSPGOnline
Previous Name: Alberta Society of Petroleum Geologists
Overview: A medium-sized national organization founded in 1929
Mission: To advance the science of geology, especially as it relates to petroleum, natural gas & other fossil fuels; to promote the technology of exploration for finding & producing these resources; to foster the spirit of scientific research; to develop a sense of pride & community among Canadian Petroleum Geologists; to provide the means to ensure that the Canadian Petroleum Geologist is the best trained, best supported & most skillful practitioner in the world
Chief Officer(s):
Lis Bjeld, Executive Director, 403-513-1235
lis.bjeld@cspg.org
Finances: *Annual Operating Budget:* $250,000-$500,000; *Funding Sources:* Membership dues; publications; programs; trust fund
Staff Member(s): 3; 300 volunteer(s)
Membership: 3,500; *Fees:* $65; $20 students; $500 corporate
Activities: Education trust fund; member programs
Awards:
• CSPG Graduate Scholarships (Scholarship)
Three scholarships available (Atlantic, Ontario/Québec & Western) in petroleum geology, one in marine geoscience; awarded to a second year graduate student*Deadline:* May *Amount:* $1,500
Publications:
• The Bulletin of Canadian Petroleum Geology
Type: Journal; *Frequency:* Quarterly; *Accepts Advertising*; *Editor:* Denise Then *ISSN:* 0007-4802; *Price:* $120 Canada; $140USA; $170 International
Profile: Peer-reviewed scientific articles, technical papers, book reviews, & debates of interest to the Canadian petroleum geoscience community
• Canadian Society of Petroleum Geologists Calendar
Frequency: Annually
Profile: Photographs & CSPG, CSEG, APEGGA, & CWLS events
• Digital Atlas: Geological Atlas of the Western Canada Sedimentary Basin
Profile: Created by CSPG & the Alberta Geologic Survey (AGS)
• Reservoir [a publication of the Canadian Society of Petroleum Geologists]
Type: Magazine; *Frequency:* 11 pa; *Accepts Advertising*; *Editor:* Heather Tyminski; *Price:* $60 Canada; $70 USA; $80International
Profile: Industry articles & commentaries, conferences, upcoming events, & awards of interest to CSPG members

Canadian Society of Pharmacology & Therapeutics (CSPT) / Société de pharmacologie du Canada

c/o PATH Research Institute, #200, 25 Main St. West, Hamilton ON L8P 1H1
Tel: 905-523-7284
www.pharmacologycanada.org
Previous Name: Pharmacological Society of Canada; Canadian Society for Clinical Pharmacology
Overview: A medium-sized national organization founded in 1974 overseen by Canadian Federation of Biological Societies
Mission: To promote research & education in the disciplines of pharmacology & experimental therapeutics
Chief Officer(s):
Goebel Kathryn, Executive Administrator
kgaebel@pharmacologycanada.org
Richard Kim, President
richard.kim@lhsc.on.ca
Fiona Parkinson, Vice-President
parkins@cc.umanitoba.ca
Cindy Woodland, Secretary-Treasurer
cindy.woodland@utoronto.ca
Finances: *Funding Sources:* Sponsorships
Membership: *Fees:* $25 students; $50 associates; $75 regular members; $750 corporate members; *Member Profile:* Students; Postdoctoral fellows; Researchers & clinician scientists from academia, industry, & government; Corporations

Activities: Engaging in advocacy activities; Facilitating the exchange of expertise;
Awards:
• Pfizer Senior Scientist Award (Award)
• Piafsky Young Investigator Award (Award)
• Boehringer Ingelheim Postdoctoral Award (Award)
• CSPT Postdoctoral Award (Clinical) (Award)
• Peter Dresel Trainee Presentation Award (Award)
• William Mahon Trainee Presentation Award (Award)
• Piafsky Trainee Presentation Award (Award)
• Rhoderic Reiffenstein Trainee Presentation Award (Award)
• AstraZeneca Trainee Presentation Award (Award)
• Regular / Emeritus Travel Bursaries (Award)
• Trainee Travel Bursaries (Award)
• Service & Education Award (Award)
• Canadian Journal Publication Award (Award)
• Publication Award (Award)
Meetings/Conferences: • 2015 Canadian Society of Pharmacology & Therapeutics Meeting, June, 2015, Peter Gilgan Centre for Research and Learning Auditorium, Toronto, ON
Scope: National
Publications:
• The Canadian Journal of Clinical Pharmacology / Journal canadien de pharmacologie clinique
Type: Journal; *Editor:* Mitchell Levine *ISSN:* 1710-6222
Profile: Original research papers, case reports, & review articles about clinical pharmacology, drugs, &therapeutics
• Canadian Journal of Physiology & Pharmacology
Type: Journal; *Frequency:* Monthly; *Editor:* Dr. D.D. Smyth; Dr. Grant Pierce *ISSN:* 1205-7541
Profile: Current research in pharmacology, physiology, toxicology, & nutrition by scientists & experts, plus award lectures & symposiumreviews
• Canadian Society of Pharmacology & Therapeutics Newsletter
Type: Newsletter; *Frequency:* Semiannually; *Price:* Free with membership in the Canadian Society of Pharmacology & Therapeutics
Profile: Societal business plus significant events

Canadian Society of Physician Executives (CSPE) / Société canadienne des médecins gestionnaires

PO Box 59005, 1559 Alta Vista Dr., Ottawa ON K1G 5T7
Tel: 613-731-9331; *Fax:* 613-731-1779
www.cspexecs.com
twitter.com/CSPExecs
Overview: A small national organization founded in 1998
Mission: To develop physician leaders to be successful in health care leadership & management roles
Affiliation(s): Canadian Medical Association
Chief Officer(s):
Carol Rochefort, Executive Director
carol.rochefort@cma.ca
Membership: *Fees:* $150 regular members; $35 medical students & residents; *Member Profile:* Physician leaders & managers; Physicians interested in enhancing their effectiveness in management
Activities: Presenting awards; Providing networking opportunities; Offering educational programs
Publications:
• CSPE [Canadian Society of Physician Executives] Newsletter
Type: Newsletter; *Frequency:* Quarterly; *Price:* Free with CSPE membership
Profile: Information for Canadian physician managers & executives
• CSPE [Canadian Society of Physician Executives] Reports
Profile: Timely reports for CSPE members on topics such as Negotiating a Successful Contract & Physician Executive Compensation

Canadian Society of Plant Physiologists (CSPP) / Société canadienne de physiologie végétale (SCPV)

c/o Dr. Harold Weger, Department of Biology, University of Regina, 3737 Wascana Pkwy., Regina SK S4S 0A2
www.cspp-scpv.ca
twitter.com/cspbscbv
Overview: A small national organization founded in 1958
Mission: To promote the teaching & public awareness of plant physiology in Canada
Chief Officer(s):
Rob Guy, Senior Director
seniordirector@cspp-scpvca.ca
Bill Plaxton, President
president@cspp-scpvca.ca
Barry Micallef, Secretary
secretary@cspp-scpvca.ca
Harold G. Weger, Treasurer
treasurer@cspp-scpvca.ca
Membership: *Member Profile:* Plant scientists in Canada; Retired members; Students; Persons who live outside Canada are eligible for corresponding membership; *Committees:* Society (Gold) Medal Award; C.D. Nelson Award; David J. Gifford Tree Physiology Award; Gleb Krotkov Award; Ann Oaks Scholarship; Ragai Ibrahim Award; Communications; Education; Meeting Site; Nominating; Auditors
Activities: Facilitating the exchange of information; Promoting the importance of research in plant sciences; Liaising with other educational, non-profi, or governmental agencies or organizations to develop the science of plant physiology
Awards:
• C.D. Nelson Award (Award)
To honour outstanding research contributions to plant physiology
• Gleb Krotkov Award of the CSPP (Award)
To honour outstanding service to the Society
• The Gold Medal Award (The CSPP Medal) (Award)
To recognize either outstanding published contributions or distinguished service to plant physiology
• David J. Gifford Award in Tree Physiology (Award)
To recognize outstanding research contributions in tree physiology
• The President's Awards (Award)
To recognize the best student oral & poster presentations at the Annual General Meeting
• The Regional Directors' Awards (Award)
To recognize the best student oral & poster presentations at the Eastern and Western Regional Meetings
• Ragai Ibrahim Award (Award)
To recognize the best student paper
Publications:
• Canadian Society of Plant Physiologists Membership List
• CSPP [Canadian Society of Plant Physiologists] / SCPV [Société canadienne de physiologie végétale] Bulletin
Type: Newsletter; *Frequency:* Semiannually; *Editor:* Gordon Gray *ISSN:* 1183-9597
Profile: Issues related to plant biology, & CSPP / SCPV events, activites, awards, & financialinformation, of interest to society members

Canadian Society of Plastic Surgeons (CSPS) / Société canadienne des chirurgiens plasticiens

#4, 1469, boul St-Joseph est, Montréal QC H2J 1M6
Tel: 514-843-5415; *Fax:* 514-843-7005
csps_sccp@bellnet.ca
www.plasticsurgery.ca
Overview: A medium-sized national organization founded in 1947
Mission: To represent, promote & provide leadership for the descipline fo plastic surgery across Canada
Affiliation(s): Canadian Medical Association
Chief Officer(s):
Karyn Wagner, Executive Director
Patricia Bortoluzzi, President
Douglas Ross, Vice-President
Bryan Callaghan, Sec.-Treas.
Finances: *Annual Operating Budget:* $100,000-$250,000; *Funding Sources:* Membership dues
Staff Member(s): 1
Membership: 400; *Fees:* $500; *Member Profile:* Active members are specialists in plastic surgery who practise in Canada & are certified by the Royal College of Physicians & Surgeons of Canada, the American Board of Plastic Surgery &/or the Collège des médecins du Québec. Associate members are plastic surgeons who practise outside Canada, who in the past have attended one of the meetings of the Canadian Society of Plastic Surgeons, & who are known to the membership. Senior associate members are exempt from annual dues and must be 60+ yrs. of age. Junior members are registered in a plastic surgery training program, with membership proposed by their director. Honorary members are nominated by the Board to recognize their contribution of services; *Committees:* Ethics; RCPSC Plastic Surgery Specialty; Young Plastic Surgeons; Canadian Journal of Plastic Surgery; Annual Meeting Local Host
Meetings/Conferences: • Canadian Society of Plastic Surgeons 2015 69th Annual Meeting, June, 2015, Fairmont Empress Hotel, Victoria, BC
Scope: National
Description: An opportunity for participants to learn during the scientific program & to view exhibits
Contact Information: Phone: 514-843-5415; Fax: 514-843-7005, E-mail: csps_sccp@bellnet.ca
• Canadian Society of Plastic Surgeons 2016 70th Annual Meeting, June, 2016, Westin Hotel, Ottawa, ON
Scope: National
Description: An opportunity for participants to learn during the scientific program & to view exhibits
Contact Information: Phone: 514-843-5415; Fax: 514-843-7005, E-mail: csps_sccp@bellnet.ca
Publications:
• CSPS News: The Newsletter of the Canadian Society of Plastic Surgeons
Type: Newsletter; *Frequency:* Semiannually; *Editor:* Karyn Wagner
Profile: Message from the president, meeting highlights, upcoming workshops, member news
• Plastic Surgery
Type: Journal; *Editor:* Dr. E. Buchel

Canadian Society of Professional Event Planners (CanSPEP)

312 Oakwood Court, Newmarket ON L3Y 3C8
Tel: 905-868-8008; *Fax:* 905-895-1630
Toll-Free: 866-467-2299
infoc@cspep.ca
www.canspep.ca
Previous Name: Independent Meeting Planners Association of Canada, Inc.
Overview: A small national organization founded in 1996
Mission: To promote, support & provide education to independent meeting & event planners & create public awareness around the profession of meeting & event planning
Chief Officer(s):
Catherine Paull, President
catherine@cpmm.ca
Finances: *Annual Operating Budget:* $100,000-$250,000
Membership: 110; *Fees:* $225; *Member Profile:* Independent meeting/event planners
Activities: *Speaker Service:* Yes
Meetings/Conferences: • Canadian Society of Professional Event Planners 2015 Annual Conference, February, 2015, Saskatoon, SK
Scope: National

Canadian Society of Professionals in Disability Management (CSPDM)

c/o Pacific Coast University for Workplace Health Sciences, 4755 Cherry Creek Rd., Port Alberni BC V9Y 0A7
Tel: 778-421-0821; *Fax:* 778-421-0823
www.cspdm.ca
Overview: A small national organization founded in 2006
Mission: To minimize the socio-economic impact of disabling injuries & illnesses on employees & employers by establishing & supporting the practice of consensus based disability management through professional standards of quality innovation & leadership in the field
Member of: International Association of Professionals in Disability Management
Chief Officer(s):
Sheena Cook, Coordinator of Membership Services, 778-421-0821 Ext. 210
sheena.cook@cspdm.ca
Membership: 500
Activities: *Library*
Publications:
• CSPDM [Canadian Society of Professionals in Disability Management] Connections
Type: Newsletter; *Frequency:* Quarterly; *Editor:* Jim Chutka
Profile: Information and resources relevant to disability management

Canadian Society of Public Health Dentists *See* Canadian Association of Public Health Dentistry

Canadian Society of Questers

PO Box 1465, Salmon Arm BC V1E 4P6
e-mail: pinkrose4233@gmail.com
www.questers.ca
Overview: A small national organization founded in 1979
Mission: To promote the ancient art of divining in its many forms, including: dowsing for water, minerals, ley lines, & ancient ruins; questing/seeking for lost or stolen goods, missing persons, & answers to personal queries; radiesthesia to assist in good health by identifying allergies, determining supplements such as vitamins & minerals, & locating sources of disease; PSI to understand & develop the power of the mind
Chief Officer(s):
Carol Heywood, President, 541-846-6835
Membership: 25; *Fees:* $35 individual; $45 family

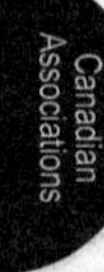

Meetings/Conferences: • Canadian Society of Questers Spring Conference 2015, 2015
Scope: National
• Canadian Society of Questers Fall Conference 2015, 2015
Scope: National

Canadian Society of Respiratory Therapists (CSRT) / La Société canadienne des thérapeutes respiratoires (SCTR)

#400, 301 Cooper St., Ottawa ON K1G 3Y6
Tel: 613-731-3164; *Fax:* 613-521-4314
Toll-Free: 800-267-3422
info@csrt.com
www.csrt.com
www.facebook.com/group.php?gid=37337032416
twitter.com/@CSRT_tweets
Overview: A medium-sized national organization founded in 1964
Mission: To provide leadership toward the advancement of cardiorespiratory care; To achieve excellence through the definition of roles, standards, & scope of clinical practice
Chief Officer(s):
Christiane Ménard, Executive Director, 613-731-3164 Ext. 222
James McCormick, President
Angela Coxe, President-Elect
Jeff Dmytrowich, Treasurer
Finances: *Annual Operating Budget:* $500,000-$1.5 Million
Staff Member(s): 5; 100 volunteer(s)
Membership: 3,000; *Fees:* $180
Activities: Providing education; Conducting research
Meetings/Conferences: • Canadian Society of Respiratory Therapists 2015 Annual Education Conference & Trade Show, May, 2015, Hyatt Regency Hotel, Calgary, AB
Scope: National
Attendance: 400+
Description: Featuring internationally renowned speakers, workshops, & presentations for respiratory therapists
Contact Information: Education Conference & Trade Show Contact: Lindsey Naddaf, Phone: 613-731-3164, ext. 231
• Canadian Society of Respiratory Therapists 2016 Annual Education Conference & Trade Show, 2016
Scope: National
Description: Featuring internationally renowned speakers, workshops, & presentations for respiratory therapists
Contact Information: Education Conference & Trade Show Contact: Lindsey Naddaf, Phone: 613-731-3164, ext. 231

Canadian Society of Safety Engineering, Inc. (CSSE) / Société canadienne de la santé et de la sécurité, inc.

39 River St., Toronto ON M5A 3P1
Tel: 416-646-1600; *Fax:* 416-646-9460
www.csse.org
www.linkedin.com/groups?gid=1558517
www.facebook.com/39373429711
twitter.com/csse
Previous Name: Ontario Society of Safety Engineering
Overview: A medium-sized national organization founded in 1949
Mission: To be the voice of safety in Canada
Affliation(s): American Society of Safety Engineers
Chief Officer(s):
Wayne Glover, Executive Director
wglover@csse.org
Peter Sturm, President
president@csse.org
Finances: *Annual Operating Budget:* $250,000-$500,000; *Funding Sources:* Membership dues; educational programs
Staff Member(s): 7; 50 volunteer(s)
Membership: 30 associate + 100 student + 45 senior/lifetime + 2,000 individual; *Fees:* $150; *Member Profile:* Open to those employed full-time in occupational health, safety & environment work
Activities: Certification program for Health & Safety Consultant; *Awareness Events:* Canadian Occupational Health & Safety Week, 1st week of June; *Speaker Service:* Yes; *Rents Mailing List:* Yes
Meetings/Conferences: • Canadian Society of Safety Engineering (CSSE) 2015 Professional Development Conference, September, 2015, Ottawa, ON
Scope: National
Publications:
• CSSE [Canadian Society of Safety Engineering, Inc.] Contact
Type: Newsletter; *Frequency:* Quarterly; *Price:* Free with CSSE membership; $100 non-members

Canadian Society of Soil Science (CSSS) / Société canadienne de la science du sol

Business Office, PO Box 637, Pinawa MB R0E 1L0
Tel: 204-753-2747; *Fax:* 204-753-8478
sheppards@ecomatters.com
www.csss.ca
Overview: A medium-sized national charitable organization
Mission: To be actively engaged in land use, soils research, & classification
Member of: Agricultural Institute of Canada
Affliation(s): International Union of Soil Science
Chief Officer(s):
Gordon Price, President
gprice@nsac.ca
Barbara Cade-Menun, Secretary
barbara.cade-menun@agr.gc.ca
Paul Bullock, Treasurer
bullockp@ms.umanitoba.ca
Finances: *Funding Sources:* Membership dues
Membership: 100-499; *Member Profile:* Open to those concerned with farming practices as they affect soil quality & the development of soil conserving cropping practices, or those concerned with non-agricultural uses of soils, including forestry, engineering, & reclamation
Activities: *Speaker Service:* Yes
Meetings/Conferences: • 2015 Canadian Society of Soil Science Annual Meeting, July, 2015, Montreal, QC
Description: Joint meeting with Association Québécoise de Spécialistes en Sciences du Sol (AQSSS)
Publications:
• Canadian Journal of Soil Science
Type: Journal; *Frequency:* Quarterly; *Editor:* Dr. F.J. Larney
Profile: International peer-reviewed original research related to the development, structure, use, & management of soils
• CSSS [Canadian Society of Soil Science] Newsletter
Type: Newsletter; *Frequency:* 3 pa; *Price:* Free with CSSS membership
Profile: CSSS activities, awards, events, & reports

Canadian Society of Sugar Artistry (CSSA)

35 - 19th St., Toronto ON M8V 3L4
Tel: 416-252-1294
www.cssainc.ca
www.facebook.com/101567256639834
Overview: A small national organization founded in 1983
Mission: Professional & non-professional society for those interested in sugar artistry
Member of: Arts Etobicoke
Chief Officer(s):
Ann Hetram, President
ann@cssainc.ca
Staff Member(s): 10
Membership: 200 individual; *Fees:* $25; *Committees:* Newsletter
Activities: Two workshops annually; one Cake Show & Fall Competition

Canadian Society of Teachers of the Alexander Technique (CANSTAT)

53 Bowden St., Toronto ON M4K 2X3
Toll-Free: 877-598-8879
info@CanSTAT.ca
www.canstat.ca
Overview: A small national organization
Mission: To establish & maintain standards for the certification of teachers and teacher training courses; to provide services to its members; to educate the public about the F. M. Alexander Technique.

Canadian Society of Technical Analysts (CSTA)

#436, 157 Adelaide St. West, Toronto ON M5H 4E7
Tel: 519-807-9178
Toronto@csta.org
www.csta.org
Overview: A large national organization
Mission: To provide a forum for those interested in & working in technical analysis; to promote technical analysis within the financial community
Chief Officer(s):
Reagan Yuke, Business Manager
bm@csta.org
William Chin, President
william@csta.org
Membership: *Fees:* $125; *Member Profile:* People working in the technical analysis field; people interested in technical analysis; *Committees:* Education; Finance

Canadian Society of Transplantation (CST) / Société canadienne de transplantation

774 Echo Dr., Ottawa ON K1S 5N8
Tel: 613-730-6274; *Fax:* 613-730-1116
cst@rcpsc.edu
www.cst-transplant.ca
Previous Name: Canadian Transplantation Society
Overview: A small national charitable organization
Mission: To provide leadership for the advancement of educational, scientific, & clinical aspects of transplantation in Canada
Chief Officer(s):
Marcelo Cantarovich, President
Shaf Keshavjee, Secretary-Treasurer
Finances: *Funding Sources:* Membership dues; Sponsorships
Membership: *Fees:* $25 associate member & trainee; $150 full member; $200 corporate; *Member Profile:* Medical doctor or scientist in the field of transplantation or an associated field; Person in a training program accredited by the Royal College of Physicians & Surgeons of Canada (or equivalent) in a field related to transplantation; Individual actively involved in transplantation clinical practice or research, such as a nurse practitioner or social worker; Person employed by an organization with corporate interests that are compatible with the interests & ethical standards of the Society
Activities: Implementing national strategies & policies; Promoting ethical practice in organ donation, clinical studies, & research; Encouraging research; Promoting high standards for education; Maintaining a national forum for scientists, surgeons, & physicians; Collaborating with related organizations
Meetings/Conferences: • Canadian Society of Transplantation 2015 Annual Scientific Conference, October, 2015, Vancouver, BC
Scope: National
Description: Co-hosted with the Banff Foundation of Allograft Pathology
• Canadian Society of Transplantation 2016 Annual Scientific Conference, 2016
Scope: National
Description: Annual meeting of the society, group meetings, symposia, poster presentations, award presentations, exhibits, & social events
Publications:
• CST [Canadian Society of Transplantation] News
Type: Newsletter; *Frequency:* 3 pa
Profile: Feature articles, plus information about the Canadian Society of Transplantation sent to all members

Canadian Society of Zoologists (CSZ) / Société canadienne de zoologie (SCZ)

c/o Biology Department, University of Western Ontario, London ON N6A 5B7
Tel: 519-661-3869
www.csz-scz.ca
Overview: A medium-sized national organization founded in 1961
Mission: To promote advancement & public awareness of zoology; To facilitate sharing of knowledge & ideas among all persons interested in science & practice of zoology; To organize discussions & debates of general interest
Affliation(s): Canadian Council on Animal Care; Canadian Federation of Biological Societies
Chief Officer(s):
Helga Guderley, Secretary, 418-656-2131 Ext. 3184, Fax: 418-656-2043
helga.guderley@bio.ulaval.ca
Louise Milligan, President
milligan@uwo.ca
Finances: *Funding Sources:* Membership fees
Membership: 373; *Fees:* $80 regular; $20 student, associate, & emeritus; *Member Profile:* Working in zoology; *Committees:* Membership; Recognition; Science Policy; Biodiversity; Animal Care Advisory; Collections Advisory; Outstanding Ph.D. Thesis; Communications; Nominating
Awards:
• CSZ Public Awarenss Award - Public Education Prize (Award)
Intended to recognize excellent in public education about zoology *Amount:* $300
• Helen Battle Award (Award)
Cash prize & scroll, given for the best student poster at the Annual Conference *Amount:* $200
• Leo Margolis Scholarship (Scholarship)
Presented to a Canadian who is registered in a graduate studies program at a Canadian university, whose research is in the field of fisheries biology *Amount:* $500

• CSZ Student Research Grant (Grant)
To assist students & post-doctoral fellows from Canadian Universities to conduct zoological research *Amount:* Up to $500
• CSZ Public Awareness Award; Best issue driven popular press article (Award)
Cash prize & scroll, intended to encourage & stimulate members to increase public awarenss of zoology through articles in the popular press *Amount:* $500
• Fry Award - Outstanding Biologist of the Year (Award)
Receives the Fry Medal, delivers the Fry Lecture at the AGM, full travel expenses are reimbursed
• Fry Award & Medal - Outstanding Zoologist of the Year (Award)
Recipient receives the Fry Medal, delivers the Fry Lecture at the Annual Meeting
• CSZ Distinguished Service Medal (Award)
Scroll & medal, presented at the AGM; recogizing members who have contributed to the well being of zoology in Canada, by working hard for the CSZ
• T.W.M. Cameron Outstanding Ph.D. Thesis Award (Award)
Recipient is invited to present a lecture of their dissertation to the AGM
• Hoar Award (Award)
Cash prize & scroll given for the best student paper presented orally at the Annual Conference *Amount:* $500
• CSZ New Investigator Award (Award)
Scroll & cash award to an individual, who since professional appointment, has made a significant contribution to zoology & may be considered a 'rising star' in their field *Amount:* Up to $500
Meetings/Conferences: • Canadian Society of Zoologists 2015 54th Annual Congress, May, 2015, University of Calgary, Calgary, AB
Scope: National
Description: A conference to advance the study of animals & their environment
Contact Information: Secretary: Helga Guderley, E-mail: helga.guderley@bio.ulaval.ca
Publications:
• Canadian Society of Zoologists / Société canadienne de zoologie Bulletin
Type: Newsletter; *Frequency:* 3 pa; *Editor:* Sally Leys *ISSN:* 0319-6674; *Price:* Free with CSZ / SCZ membership
Profile: CSZ / SCZ reports, events, articles, & interviews

Canadian Sociological Association (CSA)

PO Box 98014, 2126 Burnhamthorpe Rd. West, Mississauga ON L5L 5V4
Tel: 438-880-2182
office@csa-scs.ca
www.csa-scs.ca
www.linkedin.com/groups?mostPopular=&gid=3188569
www.facebook.com/134213209935255
Overview: A medium-sized national licensing organization founded in 1964
Mission: To promote research, publication & teaching in sociology in Canada
Member of: Humanities & Social Science Federation of Canada
Chief Officer(s):
J.S. Frideres, President
Finances: *Annual Operating Budget:* $100,000-$250,000; *Funding Sources:* Membership fees; grants
Staff Member(s): 3; 50 volunteer(s)
Membership: 1,550; *Fees:* Depends on status; *Member Profile:* Membership includes sociologists in education, government & business, students & individuals from other disciplines or affiliations who share a concern for sociology
Activities: *Rents Mailing List:* Yes; *Library* by appointment
Awards:
• Outstanding Services Awards (Award)
• Outstanding Contribution Awards (Award)
Given to recognize the work of eminent sociologists & anthropologists
• John Porter Award (Award)
Recognizes the best sociology book published in Canada in the past three years
Meetings/Conferences: • Canadian Sociological Association Congress 2015, June, 2015, University of Ottawa, Ottawa, ON
Scope: National
Description: In conjunction with the Canadian Federation of Humanities and Social Sciences.
Publications:
• Canadian Review of Sociology / Revue canadienne de sociologie
Type: Journal; *Frequency:* Quarterly; *Editor:* Harley Dickinson *ISSN:* 1755-6171; *Price:* Free with CSAmembership; $120 non-members
Profile: Formerly known as the Canadian Review of Sociology & Anthropology, the professional journal features articles & reviews
• Society / Société
Type: Newsletter; *Frequency:* 3 pa; *Editor:* Dr. Meir Amor *ISSN:* 0318-1794; *Price:* Free with CSA membership
Profile: Articles on matters of professional interest, such as teaching methods, research, public policy issues, & conditions of employment

Canadian Solar Industries Association

#605, 150 Isabella St., Ottawa ON K1S 1V7
Tel: 613-736-9077; *Fax:* 613-736-8938
Toll-Free: 866-522-6742
info@cansia.ca
www.cansia.ca
www.linkedin.com/groups/Canadian-Solar-Industries-Association-4208965
www.facebook.com/cansia
twitter.com/CanadianSIA
Also Known As: CanSIA
Overview: A medium-sized national organization founded in 1978
Mission: To develop a strong Canadian solar energy industry; To act as the voice for the solar energy industry in Canada
Chief Officer(s):
Michelle Chislett, Chair
John A. Gorman, President, 613-736-9077 Ext. 223
Wesley Johnston, Director, Policy & Research, 613-736-9077 Ext. 224
David Samuel, Director, Member Services & Operations, 613-736-9077 Ext. 225
Tiffany Shields, Administrator, Services & Communications, 613-736-9077 Ext. 228
Membership: 650 companies; *Member Profile:* Solar energy companies across Canada
Activities: Offering education & networking events for members; Liaising with federal & provincial governments
Meetings/Conferences: • Canadian Solar Industries Association 2015 Solar Ontario Conference & Showcase, 2015
Scope: National
Description: A one-day event for solar energy professionals, practitioners, stakeholders & advocates
• Canadian Solar Industries Association 2015 Solar Canada Conference & Exposition, 2015
Scope: National
Attendance: 4000+
Description: The presentation of timely topics for solar industry professionals from across Canada, featuring more than 60 speakers & 225 exhibitors
Contact Information: Web Site: www.solarcanadaconference.ca
Publications:
• Canadian Solar Industries Association Member Directory
Type: Directory; *Accepts Advertising*
Profile: A buyers' guide of companies & organizations across Canada involved in solar thermal & photovoltaics (PV) technologies
• Solar Beat Newsletter
Type: Newsletter; *Frequency:* Bimonthly
Profile: News from the solar industry
• SOLutions Magazine [a publication of the Canadian Solar Industries Association]
Type: Magazine; *Frequency:* Semiannually; *Accepts Advertising*
Profile: Information from the Canadian Solar Industries Association

Canadian South Devon Association (CSDA)

Calgary AB
Tel: 403-289-3836; *Fax:* 403-289-3886
www.southdevon.ca
Overview: A small national organization founded in 1975
Member of: Canadian Beef Breeds Council
Membership: *Member Profile:* Breeders of South Devon cattle in Canada

Canadian Soybean Council

#201, 100 Stone Rd. West, Guelph ON N1G 5L3
Tel: 519-767-4124
info@soybeancouncil.ca
www.soybeancouncil.ca
Previous Name: Soyfoods Canada
Overview: A small national organization founded in 2005
Mission: To encourage growth, integrity, & sustainability in the Canadian soyfoods industry by promoting soyfoods, including soy-based foods & ingredients, to consumers
Chief Officer(s):
John Johnston, Treasurer
Membership: *Member Profile:* Soybean growers & suppliers; soyfood processors & distributors; marketing firms

Canadian Space Society (CSS) / La société canadienne de l'espace

Bldg. E, PO Box 70009, Stn. Rimrock Plaza, 1115 Lodestar Rd., Toronto ON M3J 0H3
www.css.ca
Overview: A small national organization founded in 1983
Mission: To conduct technical & outreach projects; to promote the involvement of Canadians in space development
Chief Officer(s):
Kevin Shortt, President
president@css.ca
Marc Fricker, Vice-President
vp@css.ca
Gary McQueen, Treasurer
treasurer@css.ca
Membership: *Fees:* $75 professional; $40 students; *Member Profile:* Professionals & individuals interested in the exploration of the solar system, including engineers, teachers, environmentalists, & writers
Activities: Increasing knowledge of space & space-related technologies among members & the public; Providing feedback to the government on legislation that impacts Canadian space development;
Publications:
• Canadian Space Gazette
Frequency: Quarterly; *Accepts Advertising*
Profile: Current affairs in space development & exploration of interest to the Canadian space community

Canadian Special Crops Association (CSCA)

#1215, 220 Portage Ave., Winnipeg MB R3C 0A5
Tel: 204-925-3780; *Fax:* 204-925-4454
office@specialcrops.mb.ca
www.specialcrops.mb.ca
Overview: A medium-sized national organization founded in 1987
Mission: To encourage sustainable growth in the pulse industry by facilitating relations with growers
Membership: 110+; *Fees:* Schedule available; *Member Profile:* Companies involved in the merchandising of Canadian pulse & special crops

Canadian Special Olympics Inc. *See* Special Olympics Canada

Canadian Speckle Park Association (CSPA)

PO Box 773, Crossfield AB T0M 0S0
Tel: 403-946-4635; *Fax:* 403-946-4635
info@canadianspecklepark.ca
www.canadianspecklepark.ca
Overview: A small national organization founded in 1993
Mission: To register Speckle Park cattle; To issue certificates of registration & transfer ownership of Speckle Park cattle; To implement mandates for the improvement of the Speckle Park breed; To promote Speckle Park cattle
Member of: Canadian Beef Breeds Council
Affliation(s): Canadian Livestock Records Corporation
Chief Officer(s):
Rod Remin, Business Manager, 403-946-4635, Fax: 403-946-4635
Debbie Spencer, President, 306-957-2010, Fax: 306-957-2019
redneckfarrier@sasktel.net
Membership: 1-99; *Fees:* $25 / year active membership; $10 junior membership; $100 associate membership; *Member Profile:* Breeders of Speckle Park cattle in Canada
Activities: Developing markets for Speckle Park cattle

Canadian Sphagnum Peat Moss Association (CSPMA) / Association canadienne Tourbe de Sphaigne

#2208, 13 Mission Ave., St Albert AB T8N 1H6
Tel: 780-460-8280; *Fax:* 780-459-0939
cspma@peatmoss.com
www.peatmoss.com
www.facebook.com/peatmoss.canada
pinterest.com/peatmosscanada/
Overview: A medium-sized national organization founded in 1988
Mission: To promote the benefits of peat moss to horticulturists and home gardeners throughout North America.
Member of: Canadian Society of Association Executives
Chief Officer(s):

Paul Short, President
Finances: *Annual Operating Budget:* $250,000-$500,000; *Funding Sources:* Membership dues
Staff Member(s): 2
Membership: 34 producers; *Member Profile:* Producer/broker of Canadian peat moss; supplier to industry

Canadian Spice Association (CSA) / Association canadienne des épices

PO Box 88059, 7235 Bellshire Gate, Mississauga ON L5N 8A0
e-mail: contact@canadianspiceassociation.com
www.canadianspiceassociation.com
Overview: A medium-sized national organization founded in 1942
Mission: To foster & promote fellowship & goodwill among members; to advance the welfare of the Spice Trade & its commonly associated lines in Canada
Member of: American Spice Trade Association; Saskatchewan Herb & Seed Association
Affliation(s): American Spice Trade Association; The Saskatchewan Herb and Spice Association; European Spice Association
Chief Officer(s):
Tiina Henkusens, President
Finances: *Funding Sources:* Membership dues
Membership: 36 corporate; *Member Profile:* Organizations involved in the spice industry

Canadian Spinal Research Organization (CSRO)

#2, 120 Newkirk Rd., Richmond Hill ON L4C 9S7
Tel: 905-508-4000; *Fax:* 905-508-4002
Toll-Free: 800-361-4004
csro@globalserve.net
www.csro.com
www.facebook.com/196341387063476
www.youtube.com/user/CSROVideos
Overview: A medium-sized national organization founded in 1984
Mission: To improve the physical quality of life for people with spinal injuries; to reduce the incidence of spinal cord injuries through awareness programs for the public & prevention programs with targeted groups
Member of: Charities First
Chief Officer(s):
Michael Dorman, Executive Director, 800-361-4004 Ext. 221
mdorman@csro.com
Barry Munro, President
bmunro@csro.com
Finances: *Annual Operating Budget:* $1.5 Million-$3 Million; *Funding Sources:* Corporate; individual; donations
Staff Member(s): 7
Membership: 2,000+; *Fees:* $10; *Member Profile:* Anyone who is interested in supporting the search for a cure for spinal injuries & who submits the membership fee
Activities: Research work; prevention; awareness projects; *Internships:* Yes; *Speaker Service:* Yes
Publications:
• CSRO [Canadian Spinal Research Organization] Quarterly
Type: Magazine; *Frequency:* Quarterly

Canadian Sport Horse Association (CSHA)

PO Box 970, 7904 Franktown Rd., Richmond ON K0A 2Z0
Tel: 613-686-6161; *Fax:* 613-686-6170
csha@canadian-sport-horse.org
www.c-s-h-a.org
www.facebook.com/138540009572125
twitter.com/cdnsporthorse
Overview: A small national organization founded in 1933
Mission: To ensure the production & promotion of a sound, solid horse, with a good disposition, capable of competing successfully in the Olympic Disciplines at all levels of competition.
Member of: World Breeding Federation
Chief Officer(s):
Sue Ockendon, President
maplehurst@hotmail.ca
David Lancaster, Treasurer
dlancast@magma.ca
Staff Member(s): 1; 15 volunteer(s)
Membership: 718; *Fees:* $35 associate/youth; $80 individual; $800 life
Activities: Sport horse inspections; shows

Canadian Sport Massage Therapists Association (CSMTA) / Association canadienne des massothérapeutes du sport

1030 Burnside Rd. West, Victoria BC V8Z 1N3
Tel: 250-590-9861; *Fax:* 250-388-7835
natoffice@csmta.ca
www.csmta.ca
Overview: A medium-sized national licensing organization founded in 1987
Mission: To provide leadership in the field of sport massage therapy & education in Canada through the establishment of professional standards & qualifications of its members, as a certifying body
Affiliation(s): Canadian Olympic Committee; Expert Provider Group
Chief Officer(s):
Trish Schiedel, President
Roberta Graham, National Office Coordinator
Jessica Sears, Vice President
Monty Churchman, Secretary
Finances: *Annual Operating Budget:* Less than $50,000; *Funding Sources:* Membership fee; workshop
Staff Member(s): 1; 5 volunteer(s)
Membership: 70; *Member Profile:* 2,200-hr massage school or member of provincial association affiliated with CSMTA; *Committees:* Membership; Education; Certification; Examination
Activities: Enhances the health care needs of Canadian athletes through its National Sport Massage Certification Program (NSMCP) & the effective application of sport massage during all phases of their training, performance & competition; promotes a professional climate for the growth of sport massage therapy in Canada
Awards:
• Award of Excellence (Award)
Meetings/Conferences: • Canadian Sport Massage Therapists Association 2015 Annual General Meeting & Conference, 2015
Scope: National

Canadian Sport Parachuting Association (CSPA) / Association canadienne du parachutisme sportif (ACPS)

#204, 1468 Laurier St., Rockland ON K4K 1C7
Tel: 613-419-0908; *Fax:* 613-916-6008
office@cspa.ca
www.cspa.ca
Overview: A medium-sized national charitable organization founded in 1956
Member of: Aero Club of Canada
Chief Officer(s):
Debbie Flanagan, President
president@cspa.ca
Brian diCenzo, Vice-President
vp@cspa.ca
David Hodge, Executive Director
dave.hodge@cspa.ca
Membership: 2,000 + 48 member groups; *Fees:* $85; *Committees:* Coaching Working; Technical Safety; Competition & National Teams; Web / Information Technology
Activities: *Library*
Publications:
• Parachutist Information Manuals
Profile: Topics include skydiving skills, Canadian National Parachuting Championships Hosting, safety rules & recommendations, competitions, formation skydiving, & judge rating system

Canadian Sport Tourism Alliance (CSTA)

#600, 116 Lisgar St., Ottawa ON K2P 0C2
Tel: 613-688-5843; *Fax:* 613-238-3878
info@canadiansporttourism.com
www.canadiansporttourism.com
Overview: A small national organization founded in 2000
Mission: To market Canada internationally as a preferred sport tourism destination
Chief Officer(s):
Greg Stremlaw, Chair
gstremlaw@curling.ca
Rick Traer, CEO
rtraer@canadiansporttourism.com
Staff Member(s): 6
Membership: 200; *Committees:* Membership; Marketing & Communications; Research; Training & Education; Government Relations

Canadian Sporting Goods Association (CSGA) / Association canadienne d'articles de sport (ACAS)

#420, 300, rue du Saint-Sacrement, Montréal QC H2Y 1X4
e-mail: csga@csga.ca
www.csga.ca
Overview: A large national organization founded in 1945
Mission: To conduct quality trade shows; To provide forum responsive to the professional needs of its members; To initiate programs designed to stimulate sports activity participation as considered feasible
Affliation(s): World Federation of the Sporting Goods Industry
Chief Officer(s):
Andrew Prendergast, Chair
andrew.prendergast@newbalance.com
Michael Tadgell, Executive Director, 647-404-9799
mtadgell@rogers.com
Finances: *Funding Sources:* Membership dues; Trade shows
Membership: 2,000+ organizations; *Fees:* $400-1,000 supplier; $150-250 retailer; $50-150 sales rep; *Member Profile:* Bona fide members of the sporting goods industry
Activities: Conducting a market survey

Canadian Square & Round Dance Society (CSRDS)

c/o Lorraine Kozera, 24 Aspen Villa Dr., Oak Bank MB R0E 1J2
Toll-Free: 866-206-6696
info@squaredance.ca
www.csrds.ca
Overview: A medium-sized national organization
Mission: To link information about Canadian square & round dancing associations together in order to promote awareness, inspire activity, & to offer information
Chief Officer(s):
Lorraine Kozera, Secretary
lkozera@mymts.net
John Kozera, Director, Manitoba
Eric McCormack, President
ericmcc@nbnet.nb.ca

Canadian Squash Racquets Association *See* Squash Canada

The Canadian Stage Company

26 Berkeley St., Toronto ON M5A 2W3
Tel: 416-367-8243; *Fax:* 416-367-1768
www.canstage.com
www.facebook.com/cdnstage
twitter.com/canadianstage
www.youtube.com/user/canadianstage
Also Known As: CanStage
Overview: A medium-sized national charitable organization
Mission: To develop, produce & export the best in Canadian & international contemporary theatre
Member of: Professional Association of Canadian Theatres; Toronto Theatre Alliance
Chief Officer(s):
Matthew Jocelyn, Artistic & General Director
Staff Member(s): 48
Activities: Produces over 300 performances in four venues each year;

Canadian Stamp Dealers' Association (CSDA) / Association canadienne des négociants en timbres-poste (ACNTP)

PO Box 81, Stn. Lambeth, London ON N6P 1P9
e-mail: director@csdaonline.com
www.csdaonline.com
www.facebook.com/214870458990?ref=ts
Overview: A small national organization founded in 1942
Chief Officer(s):
John Sheffield, Executive Director
director@csdaonline.com
Rick Day, President
medallionstamps@cogeco.ca
Ian Kimmerly, Vice-President
ian@iankimmerly.com
Membership: *Member Profile:* Established full or part-time stamp dealers; Dealers from outside Canada must be a member of their country's trade association
Activities: Partnering with other major philatelic organizations
Publications:
• Beaver Tales [a publication of the Canadian Stamp Dealers' Association]
Type: Newsletter; *Price:* Free with CSDA membership
Profile: Industry news with current information
• Canadian Stamp Dealers' Association Membership Directory
Type: Directory; *Frequency:* Annually; *Price:* Free for collectors throughout the world

Canadian Standards Association (CSA)

#100, 5060 Spectrum Way, Mississauga ON L4W 5N6
Tel: 416-747-4000; *Fax:* 416-747-2473
Toll-Free: 800-463-6727
Other Communication: sales@csa.ca; seminars@csa.ca; elearning@csa.ca

member@csa.ca
www.csa.ca
Overview: A medium-sized national organization
Mission: To develop new standards & codes to meet needs, such as public health & safety & the facilitation of trade; To contribute to the global harmonization of standards; To serve government, industry, business, & consumers in Canada & the worldwide marketplace
Member of: CSA Group
Chief Officer(s):
Bonnie Rose, President
Finances: *Funding Sources:* Sponsorships
Activities: Presenting e-learning, seminars, & training opportunities, through the CSA Learning Centre, to assist people to understand standards; Reviewing & considering adopted & adapted standards from other organizations & countries
Meetings/Conferences: • Canadian Standards Association 2015 Annual Conference & Committee Week, June, 2015, Niagara Falls, ON
Scope: National
Attendance: 600+
Description: Educational presentations & committee meetings
Publications:
• Canadian Standards Association Annual Report
Type: Yearbook; *Frequency:* Annually
Profile: A review of the association's activities for the past year
• Perspectives [a publication of the Canadian Standards Association]
Type: Newsletter; *Editor:* James Harrison
Profile: Current information about standards development initiatives for members

Canadian Steel Construction Council (CSCC) / Conseil canadien de la construction en acier
#300, 201 Consumers Rd., Toronto ON M2J 4G8
Tel: 416-491-9898; *Fax:* 416-491-6461
Previous Name: Canadian Steel Industries Construction Council
Overview: A medium-sized national organization founded in 1960
Mission: To represent the manufacturers of steel products, including: open-web steel joists, steel platework, corrugated steel pipe, sheet steel, & steel fasteners; to promote the use of steel in construction through research & engineering
Affliation(s): Canadian Institute of Steel Construction; Steel Structures Education Foundation
Staff Member(s): 1
Membership: 9; *Committees:* Codes & Standards; Fire Protection
Activities: *Speaker Service:* Yes

Canadian Steel Door & Frame Manufacturers Association
See Canadian Steel Door Manufacturers Association

Canadian Steel Door Manufacturers Association (CSDMA)
#1801, 1 Yonge St., Toronto ON M5E 1W7
Tel: 416-363-7845; *Fax:* 416-369-0515
info@csdma.ca
www.csdma.org
Previous Name: Canadian Steel Door & Frame Manufacturers Association
Overview: A medium-sized national organization
Mission: To deliver standards and specifications regarding the manufacture and installation of steel doors, frames and related items, for the guidance of specifiers, end users, AEC professionals, and those interested in the construction trades at large.
Chief Officer(s):
Lois Marsh, Executive Director
Staff Member(s): 1
Membership: 13

Canadian Steel Industries Construction Council *See*
Canadian Steel Construction Council

Canadian Steel Producers Association (CSPA) / Association canadienne des producteurs d'acier (ACPA)
#906, 350 Sparks St., Ottawa ON K1R 7S8
Tel: 613-238-6049; *Fax:* 613-238-1832
info@canadiansteel.ca
www.canadiansteel.ca
www.facebook.com/220022834730294
twitter.com/CSPA_ACPA
Overview: A medium-sized national organization founded in 1986
Mission: To represent the steel producers that melt & pour steel in Canada
Chief Officer(s):
Ron Watkins, President
Finances: *Annual Operating Budget:* $500,000-$1.5 Million; *Funding Sources:* Membership dues
Staff Member(s): 4
Membership: 17; *Committees:* Communications; Environment; Climate Change; Statistics; Trade; Research & Development

Canadian Steel Trade & Employment Congress
#800, 234 Eglinton Ave. East, Toronto ON M4P 1K7
Tel: 416-480-1797; *Fax:* 416-480-2986
general@cstec.ca
www.cstec.ca
www.linkedin.com/company/canadian-steel-trade-and-employment-congress
twitter.com/SteelSkills
www.vimeo.com/user8234365
Overview: A medium-sized national organization
Mission: To provide a forum for communication among steel companies, steelworkers, & governments to work for the betterment of the industry & its workforce
Chief Officer(s):
Ken Delaney, Executive Director
kdelaney@cstec.ca
Staff Member(s): 5
Membership: *Committees:* Sector Study Steering

Canadian Stroke Network (CSN) / Réseau canadien contre les accidents cérébrovasculaires
#301, 600 Peter Morand Cres., Ottawa ON K1G 5Z3
Tel: 613-562-5696; *Fax:* 613-521-9215
info@canadianstrokenetwork.ca
www.canadianstrokenetwork.ca
www.linkedin.com/groups?gid=3012927&trk=myg_ugrp_ovr
www.facebook.com/canadianstrokenetwork
twitter.com/strokenetwork
www.youtube.com/user/strokenetwork
Overview: A small national organization founded in 1999
Mission: To reduce the physical, social, & economic consequences of stroke on individuals & society through leadership in research; To develop & implement national strategies in stroke research; To maximize health & economic benefits; To build a consensus across Canada on stroke policy
Member of: Canada's Network of Centres of Excellence
Chief Officer(s):
Pierre Boyle, Chair
Antoine Hakim, CEO & Scientific Director
Kevin Willis, Executive Director
Robin Millbank, Manager, Professional Development
Membership: 100+; *Member Profile:* Scientists; Clinicians; Rehabilitation specialists; Knowledge-translation experts from universities throughout Canada; *Committees:* Ethics; External Scientific Review; Planning & Priorities
Activities: Conducting a multi-disciplinary research program; Training Canadian scientists & clinicians; Promoting research excellence; Liaising with government, industry, & the non-profit sector; Supporting the Canadian Stroke Strategy
Meetings/Conferences: • Canadian Stroke Congress 2015, 2015
Scope: National
Publications:
• Canadian Stroke Network: Reducing the Impact of Stroke
Type: Newsletter
Profile: Information about stroke care

Canadian Student Leadership Association (CSLA)
2460 Tanner Rd., Victoria BC V8Z 5R1
studentleadership.ca
www.facebook.com/CanadianStudentLeadershipAssociation
twitter.com/CSLA_Leaders
Overview: A small national charitable organization founded in 1983
Chief Officer(s):
Don Homan, Chair
dhoman@studentleadership.ca
Bill Conconi, Executive Director
bconconi@studentleadership.ca
Membership: *Fees:* $90
Activities: Distributes leadership resources, materials; scholarships; organizes programs and events for its member schools
Meetings/Conferences: • Canadian Student Leadership Association 2015 Conference, September, 2015, Halifax, NS
Scope: National

Canadian Stuttering Association (CSA) / Association canadienne des bègues
PO Box 3027, Sherwood Park AB T8H 2T1
Tel: 416-840-5169
Toll-Free: 866-840-5169
csa@stutter.ca
www.stutter.ca
www.facebook.com/111972052148483
twitter.com/CSAStuttering
Previous Name: Canadian Association for People Who Stutter (CAPS)
Overview: A small national charitable organization founded in 1991
Mission: To support Canadians afflicted with the disorder of stuttering; To increase awareness of stuttering
Chief Officer(s):
Lisa Wilder, Coordinator, Editor, Webmaster
Membership: *Fees:* $20 full members; $10 associate members; *Member Profile:* Individuals who stutter; Families & friends of people who stutter; Professionals who work with people who stutter
Activities: Providing education & resources about stuttering; Offering self-help groups; Engaging in advocacy activities for people who stutter
Meetings/Conferences: • 2015 Canadian Stuttering Association Conference, 2015
Scope: National
Publications:
• CSA [Canadian Stuttering Association] Newsletter
Type: Newsletter; *Frequency:* Quarterly
Profile: Developments in research & therapy, personal stories, news from CSA members, & CSA events

Canadian Sugar Institute (CSI) / Institut canadien du sucre
Water Park Pl., #620, 10 Bay St., Toronto ON M5J 2R8
Tel: 416-368-8091; *Fax:* 416-368-6426
info@sugar.ca
www.sugar.ca
Overview: A medium-sized national organization founded in 1966
Member of: World Sugar Research Organization
Chief Officer(s):
Sandra Marsden, President
Tristin Brisbois, Manager, Nutrition & Scientific Affairs
tbrisbois@sugar.ca
Finances: *Annual Operating Budget:* $500,000-$1.5 Million; *Funding Sources:* Member companies
Staff Member(s): 5
Membership: 3 corporate; *Member Profile:* Sugar refining companies in Canada; *Committees:* Technical; Trade; Communications
Activities: *Library* by appointment
Publications:
• Carbohydrate News
Type: Newsletter; *Frequency:* Annually
Profile: Recent scientific information on carbohydrate for health & education professionals
• Consumer Materials
Profile: Topics include practical information about sugar, such as understanding the Glycemic Index, & from plant to food, The CSI Recipe Collection, & testing your sugar IQ
• Nature's Sweet Mystery
Profile: Teaching resource for grades four to six with background information, activity sheets, & resource suggestions

Canadian Supply Chain Food Safety Coalition / Coalition canadienne de la filière alimentaire pour la salubrité des aliments
19 Elm St., Ottawa ON K1R 6M9
Tel: 613-233-7175
cscfsc@monachus.com
foodsafetycoalition.ca
Overview: A medium-sized national organization founded in 2000
Mission: To initiate a national standard for food safety
Chief Officer(s):
Albert Chambers, Executive Director
Membership: 37; *Fees:* $750 national organization/allied member; $300 provincial/local organization

Canadian Swine Breeders' Association (CSBA) / L'Association canadienne des éleveurs de porcs
#2, 408 Dundas St., Woodstock ON N4S 1B9

Tel: 519-421-2354; *Fax:* 519-421-0887
info@canswine.ca
www.canswine.ca
Previous Name: Purebred Swine Breeders' Association of Canada
Overview: A medium-sized national organization founded in 1889
Mission: To improve & promote Canadian purebred swine; to lobby on behalf of purebred swine breeders in Canada; to direct & regulate purebred swine industry; to be involved in registration & transfer of following breeds: Berkshire, British Saddleback, Chester White, Duroc, Hampshire, Large Black, Pietrain, Poland China, Spotted, Tamworth, Welsh, Yorkshire, Landrace, Lacombe, Red Wattle (registration forms can be obtained from Canadian Livestock Records Corporation).
Chief Officer(s):
Rosemary Smart, General Manager
Finances: *Annual Operating Budget:* $100,000-$250,000
Staff Member(s): 3
Membership: 120; *Fees:* Schedule available; *Member Profile:* Four classes: honorary, life, annual, non-resident; *Committees:* Promotion

Canadian Swine Council *See* Canadian Pork Council

Canadian Swine Exporters Association (CSEA)

#2, 408 Dundas St., Woodstock ON N4S 1B9
Tel: 519-421-0997; *Fax:* 519-421-0887
csea@rogers.com
www.canadianswine.com
Overview: A small national organization
Mission: To assist the Canadian swine industry promote & market swine genetics worldwide
Chief Officer(s):
Nancy F. Weicker, Executive Director
Membership: 13; *Member Profile:* Represents the top exporters from Canada

Canadian Syringomyelia Network (CSN)

c/o The Forrestall Group, #4, 201 Whitehall Dr., Markham ON L3R 9Y3
Fax: 905-944-4844
www.csn.ca
Overview: A small national charitable organization founded in 1993
Mission: To provide information & support for persons with Syringomyelia & related conditions, plus their caregivers & families
Activities: Increasing public awareness of the effects of Syringomyelia; Organizing fundraising
Publications:
• The CSN News
Type: Newsletter; *Frequency:* Quarterly
Profile: Information & updates from the Canadian Syringomyelia Network

Canadian Table Soccer Association *See* Canadian Table Soccer Federation

Canadian Table Soccer Federation

Tel: 647-986-6719
terri@canadafoosball.ca
tablesoccerca.ning.com
Previous Name: Canadian Table Soccer Association
Overview: A small national organization
Mission: To oversee & monitor the growth of foosball in Canada.
Chief Officer(s):
Will Stanks, President
Eric Dunn, Vice-President

Canadian Table Tennis Association *See* Table Tennis Canada

Canadian Tarentaise Association (CTA)

c/p Rosalyn Harris, PO Box 1156, Shellbrook SK S0J 2E0
Toll-Free: 800-450-4181
canadiantarentaise@sasktel.net
www.canadiantarentaise.com
Overview: A small national organization founded in 1974
Mission: To develop, register & promote Tarentaise cattle in Canada.
Affliation(s): American Tarentaise Association; SOPEXA - Cambery, France
Chief Officer(s):
Wayne Collette, President, 303-452-1820
keyholekg@aol.com
Rosalyn Harris, Secretary
Finances: *Funding Sources:* Membership & registration fees
Staff Member(s): 1
Membership: 7; *Fees:* $25 junior; $60 active; $100 associate lifetime; $200 active lifetime; *Committees:* Advertising & Promotion; Nominationg; Breed Improvement & Memberships; Show & Sale; Advisory

Canadian Tax Foundation (CTF) / Foundation canadienne de fiscalité (FCF)

#1200, 595 Bay St., Toronto ON M5G 2N5
Tel: 416-599-0283; *Fax:* 416-599-9283
Toll-Free: 877-733-0283
www.ctf.ca
www.linkedin.com/groups?home=&gid=4000744
twitter.com/cdntaxfdn
Overview: A medium-sized national charitable organization founded in 1945
Mission: To create a greater understanding of the Canadian tax system; To improve the Canadian tax system
Chief Officer(s):
Penny Woolford, Chair
Gabrielle Richards, Vice-Chair
Debbie Selley, CGA, Treasurer
dselley@ctf.ca
Larry Chapman, FCPA, FCA, Executive Director & CEO
lchapman@ctf.ca
Judy Singh, Librarian
jisngh@ctf.ca
Membership: 11,000+; *Fees:* $29.75 student; $55 outside Canada; $115.50 retired; $175 academic & young practitioner; $350 individuals; *Member Profile:* Individuals & corporations from Canada & abroad
Activities: Providing tax information; Supporting members in their daily work in the taxation field; Conducting research projects; Contributing to tax & fiscal policy; *Library:* Douglas J. Sherbaniuk Research Centre
Awards:
• Douglas J. Sherbaniuk Distinguished Writing Award (Award)
• Student - Paper Award Competition (Award)
Meetings/Conferences: • Annual Tax Conference 2015, November, 2015, Palais des congrès de Montréal, Montréal, QC
Scope: National
Publications:
• Canadian Tax Foundation Conference Reports
Frequency: Annually; *Price:* Free with Canadian Tax Foundation membership
Profile: Proceedings & papers presented at conferences
• Canadian Tax Highlights / Faits saillants en fiscalité canadienne
Type: Newsletter; *Frequency:* Monthly; *Price:* Free with Canadian Tax Foundation membership
Profile: Analyses of current topics & developments in the taxation field
• Canadian Tax Journal
Type: Journal; *Frequency:* Quarterly; *Accepts Advertising*; *Editor:* Alan Macnaughton; Brian Carr; *Price:* Free with Canadian Tax Foundationmembership
Profile: Scholarly articles on tax topics, analyses of changes in tax law, summaries of provincial budget figures, & reviews of tax literature
• Tax for the Owner-Manager
Type: Newsletter; *Frequency:* Quarterly; *Price:* Free with Canadian Tax Foundation membership
Profile: Reports on tax developments, of interest to private corporations & their advisers

Québec Office
#2935, 1250, boul René-Lévesque ouest, Montréal QC H3B 4W8
Tel: 514-939-6323; *Fax:* 514-939-7353
Chief Officer(s):
Jane Meagher, Director, Québec Office
jmeagher@ctf.ca

Canadian Taxpayers Federation (CTF)

#265, 438 Victoria Ave. East, Regina SK S4N 0N7
Tel: 306-352-7199; *Fax:* 306-205-8339
Other Communication: vimeo.com/taxpayerdotcom
admin@taxpayer.com
taxpayer.com
www.facebook.com/TaxpayerDOTcom
twitter.com/taxpayerdotcom
www.youtube.com/taxpayerdotcom
Previous Name: Association of Saskatchewan Taxpayers; Resolution One Association of Alberta
Overview: A large national organization founded in 1990
Mission: To advocate for the common interest of taxpayers; To effect public policy change
Chief Officer(s):
Michael Binnion, Chair
Troy Lanigan, President & CEO
tlanigan@shaw.ca
Shannon Morrison, Vice-President, Operations
smorrison@taxpayer.com
Scott Hennig, Vice-President, Communications
shennig@taxpayer.com
Gregory Thomas, Director, Federal
federal.director@taxpayer.com
Melanie Harvie, Manager, Finance
mharvie@taxpayer.com
Finances: *Funding Sources:* Donations
Membership: 70,000; *Fees:* Free; *Member Profile:* Canadian citizens dedicated to lower taxes, less waste, & government accountability
Activities: Updating members about issues & actions; Conducting research; Issuing news releases & conducting media interviews; Making presentations to government; Organizing campaigns & petition drives; *Speaker Service:* Yes
Awards:
• The Federal Teddy (Award), The Ted Weatherill Awards (The Teddies)
• The Provincial/Municipal Teddy (Award), The Ted Weatherill Awards (The Teddies)
• The Lifetime Achievement Teddy (Award), The Ted Weatherill Awards (The Teddies)
• TaxFighter of the Year (Award)
Publications:
• Let's Talk Taxes [a publication of the Canadian Taxpayers Federation]
Frequency: Weekly
Profile: Commentaries for media outlets across Canada
• Municipal Ratepayers Guide [a publication of the Canadian Taxpayers Federation]
• TaxAction [a publication of the Canadian Taxpayers Federation]
Type: Newsletter; *Frequency:* Monthly
Profile: Canadian Taxpayers Federation news, government activities, & facts & figures
• TaxFacts [a publication of the Canadian Taxpayers Federation]
Profile: Issues of taxation & government spending at the provincial & federal levels
• The Taxpayer [a publication of the Canadian Taxpayers Federation]
Type: Magazine; *Frequency:* Quarterly; *Accepts Advertising*; *Number of Pages:* 48
Profile: Canadian Taxpayers Federation national happenings, campaign updates, articles by CTF researchers, & guest commentaries

Canadian Taxpayers Federation - Alberta (CTF)

PO Box 84171, Stn. Market Mall, 3625 Shaganappi Trail, Calgary AB T3A 5C4
Toll-Free: 800-661-0187
www.taxpayer.com
twitter.com/DFildebrandt
Overview: A medium-sized provincial organization overseen by Canadian Taxpayers Federation
Mission: To advocate on behalf of taxpayers across Alberta
Chief Officer(s):
Derek Fildebrandt, Director, Alberta, 403-690-4910
dfildebrandt@taxpayer.com
Finances: *Funding Sources:* Donations
Membership: *Member Profile:* Citizens of Alberta committed to lower taxes, reduced waste, & accountable government
Activities: Conducting research related to issues in Alberta; Organizing national initiatives at the regional level in Alberta; Holding press conferences & issuing news releases; *Speaker Service:* Yes

Canadian Taxpayers Federation - Altlantic Canada (CTF)

PO Box 34077, Stn. Scotia Square, 5201 Duke St., Halifax NS B3J 1N0
Tel: 902-407-5757
www.taxpayer.com
Overview: A medium-sized provincial organization overseen by Canadian Taxpayers Federation
Mission: To advocate on behalf of taxpayers across Atlantic Canada
Chief Officer(s):
Kevin Lacey, Director, 877-909-5757
atlantic.director@taxpayer.com

Finances: *Funding Sources:* Donations
Membership: *Member Profile:* Citizens of Atlantic Canada committed to lower taxes, reduced waste, & accountable government
Activities: Campaigning & organizing national initiatives at the regional level in Atlantic Canada; *Speaker Service:* Yes

Canadian Taxpayers Federation - British Columbia (CTF)
PO Box 20539, Stn. Howe St., Vancouver BC V6Z 2N8
Tel: 604-999-3319
www.taxpayer.com
twitter.com/jordanbateman
Overview: A medium-sized provincial organization founded in 1990 overseen by Canadian Taxpayers Federation
Mission: To advocate lower taxes, less waste & accountable government
Chief Officer(s):
Jordan Bateman, Director, British Columbia
jbateman@taxpayer.com
Finances: *Funding Sources:* Donations
Membership: *Member Profile:* British Columbia citizens who support lower taxes & government accountability
Activities: Conducting campaigns; Providing background information; *Speaker Service:* Yes

Canadian Taxpayers Federation - Ontario (CTF)
#283, 100 - 2 Toronto St., Toronto ON M5C 2B5
Toll-Free: 800-667-7933
www.taxpayer.com
twitter.com/CandiceMalcolm
Overview: A medium-sized provincial organization founded in 1990 overseen by Canadian Taxpayers Federation
Mission: To engage in advocacy activities specific to Ontario
Chief Officer(s):
Candice Malcolm, Director, Ontario
cmalcolm@taxpayer.com
Finances: *Funding Sources:* Donations
Membership: *Member Profile:* Ontario citizens dedicated to lower taxes, less waste, & accountable government
Activities: Organizing Canada-wide initiatives within Ontario; Conducting research; Preparing government presentations; Issuing news releases & dealing with media requests; *Speaker Service:* Yes

Canadian Taxpayers Federation - Saskatchewan & Manitoba (CTF)
PO Box 42123, 1881 Portage Ave., Winnipeg MB R3J 3X7
Tel: 204-982-2150; *Fax:* 204-982-2154
Toll-Free: 800-772-9955
www.taxpayer.com
twitter.com/colincraig1
Overview: A medium-sized provincial organization founded in 1989 overseen by Canadian Taxpayers Federation
Mission: To advocate on behalf of taxpayers in the prairie provinces
Chief Officer(s):
Colin Craig, Director, Prairies
ccraig@taxpayer.com
Finances: *Funding Sources:* Donations
Membership: *Member Profile:* Manitoba & Saskatchewan citizens who support lower taxes, reduced waste, & accountable government
Activities: Researching issues that affect the prairie provinces; Distributing background information; Organizing campaigns fo the prairies; Impacting public policy; *Speaker Service:* Yes

Canadian Teachers' Federation (CTF) / Fédération canadienne des enseignantes et des enseignants (FCE)
2490 Don Reid Dr., Ottawa ON K1H 1E1
Tel: 613-232-1505; *Fax:* 613-232-1886
Toll-Free: 866-283-1505
info@ctf-fce.ca
www.ctf-fce.ca
www.facebook.com/group.php?gid=147721021992584
twitter.com/CanTeachersFed
www.youtube.com/user/canadianteachers
Overview: A large national organization founded in 1920
Mission: To promotes a strong publicly funded education system for Canada, one that enhances the country's competitiveness in a knowledge based global economy & gives children the opportunity to become active, engaged citizens
Member of: Education International
Chief Officer(s):
Paul Taillefer, President
Calvin Fraser, Secretary General
Finances: *Annual Operating Budget:* $3 Million-$5 Million
Staff Member(s): 45
Membership: 17 provincial & territorial teacher organizations representing 240,000+ teachers; *Fees:* $21.80 per teacher/per year; *Committees:* Aboriginal Education; Diversity and Human Rights; French as a First Language; Status of Women; Nominations; Resolutions; Constitution and By-laws; Finance; Retirement
Activities: *Awareness Events:* National Media Education Week; *Library:* George A. Croskery Memorial Library
Awards:
• CTF Special Recognition Awards (Award)
• CTF Public Education Advocacy Award (Award)
• CTF Outstanding Aboriginal Educator Award (Award)
Meetings/Conferences: • Canadian Teachers' Federation 2015 Annual Francophone Symposium / Symposium de l'enseignement en français, February, 2015, Shaw Convetion Centre, Edmonton, AB
Scope: National
Description: Held jointly with The Manitoba Teachers' Society / Éducatrices et éducateurs francophones du Manitoba
Contact Information: Contact: Johanne Deschamps, Address: 2490, promenade Don Reid, Ottawa, ON K1H 1E1
• Canadian Teachers' Federation, Yukon Teachers' Association & the Government of Yukon 2015 Women's Issues Symposium, 2015, YT
Scope: National
• Canadian Teachers' Federation 2015 Annual General Meeting, 2015
Scope: National
Description: Approval of a budget for the upcoming year, a discussion & determination of policy priorities, & an election of directors
Contact Information: Director of Communications: Francine Filion, Phone: 613-688-4314
Publications:
• CTF [Canadian Teachers' Federation] Annual Report
Type: Yearbook; *Frequency:* Annually
Profile: The work of the federation as directed by policy & priorities under the leadership of the Board of Directors
• The CTF [Canadian Teachers' Federation] Handbook
Type: Handbook
Profile: A compilation of the constitution, by-laws, policy, & regulations
• Perspectives
Type: Newsletter; *Price:* Free
Profile: A forum for diverse perspectives on current education issues
• Vision
Type: Newsletter; *Price:* Free
Profile: Issues related to teaching & education across Canada

Canadian Team Handball Federation (CTHF) / Fédération canadienne de handball olympique (FCHO)
453, rue Jacob-Nicol, Sherbrooke QC J1J 4E5
Tel: 819-563-7937; *Fax:* 819-563-5352
handballcanada.ca
Overview: A medium-sized national charitable organization founded in 1966
Affliation(s): International Handball Federation; Pan American Team Handball Federation; Commonwealth Handball Federation
Chief Officer(s):
Rick Ryll, President
François LeBeau, Chief Operating Officer
f.leleau@videotron.ca
Finances: *Annual Operating Budget:* $500,000-$1.5 Million; *Funding Sources:* Sport Canada; COO; CAC
Staff Member(s): 1; 1 volunteer(s)
Membership: 15,000; *Fees:* $5; *Committees:* Management; Officials; Coaches; National Teams
Activities: Canadian Championship; Canada Cup; Pan-American Championships & Games; *Speaker Service:* Yes

Canadian Technical Asphalt Association (CTAA) / Association technique canadienne du bitume
#300, 895 Fort St., Victoria BC V8W 1H7
Tel: 250-361-9187; *Fax:* 250-361-9187
admin@ctaa.ca
www.ctaa.ca
Overview: A medium-sized national organization founded in 1955
Mission: To organize efforts of membership on a non-profit, public service basis; to assemble, correlate & disseminate technical information on characteristics & uses of bituminous materials; to conduct conferences at which characteristics & uses of asphaltic materials are discussed; to stimulate & encourage research on uses of asphaltic materials; to encourage colleges to teach students to study asphalt technology
Chief Officer(s):
Chuck McMillan, Secretary-Treasurer, 250-361-9187
admin@ctaa.ca
Finances: *Funding Sources:* Membership fees
Staff Member(s): 1
Membership: 700; *Fees:* $155; $400 sustaining; $0 student; *Member Profile:* Consultants; Contractors; Academia; Government
Meetings/Conferences: • Canadian Technical Asphalt Association 60th Annual Conference & Annual General Meeting, November, 2015, Ottawa, ON
Scope: National
Publications:
• CTAA Newsletter
Type: Newsletter
Profile: CTAA conferences, scholarships, financial information, awards, & membership information

Canadian Technion Society *See* Technion Canada

Canadian Technology Human Resources Board (CTHRB) / Bureau canadien des ressources humaines en technologie
#2, 285 McLeod St., Ottawa ON K2P 1A1
Tel: 613-233-1955
info@cthrb.ca
www.cthrb.ca
Overview: A small national organization founded in 1995
Mission: To promote the use & continuous revision of national technician & technologist standards across Canada; to lead Canadian industrial & occupational technology organizations in identifying & resolving human resource issues that are challenging the industry
Chief Officer(s):
Barry Gander, Director, Communications
Finances: *Annual Operating Budget:* $250,000-$500,000
Staff Member(s): 5; 15 volunteer(s)
Activities: *Internships:* Yes; *Speaker Service:* Yes; *Library:* Resource Centre; by appointment
Publications:
• TechNews
Type: Newsletter; *Frequency:* Monthly
Profile: Acivities affecting human resources & technology

Canadian Telecommunication Carriers Association *See* Frequency Co-ordination System Association

Canadian Telecommunications Consultants Association (CTCA)
PO Box 361, St. Davids ON L0S 1P0
Tel: 289-477-1465; *Fax:* 866-584-2822
Toll-Free: 866-584-2822
Other Communication: membership@ctca.ca
admin@ctca.ca
www.ctca.ca
Overview: A small national organization founded in 1985
Mission: CTCA advocates high standards of professionalism & expertise in the provision of telecommunications solutions. Towards this vision, the association encourages the dissemination & exchange of information among telecommunications consultants & organizations.
Chief Officer(s):
Kirk Glaze, President
Finances: *Funding Sources:* Membership dues; conference registrations
Membership: 1-99; *Fees:* $378.55 affiliate; $452 associate; $525.45 consultant; $728.85 supplier liaison group - primary representative; *Member Profile:* Independent telecommunications consultants
Activities: Providing networking, collaboration, & educational opportunities for members; Promoting integrity, competence, & professionalism among members according to its Code of Ethics & Professional Conduct; *Speaker Service:* Yes

Canadian Television Series Development Foundation *See* Independent Production Fund

Canadian Telework Association (CTA)
5749 Doyle Rd., Ottawa ON K4M 1B4
Tel: 613-692-0566
info@ivc.ca
www.ivc.ca/cta

Overview: A medium-sized national organization founded in 1997
Mission: To promote & develop telework in Canada
Chief Officer(s):
Bob Fortier, President
bobf@ivc.ca
Membership: 1,000; *Fees:* Free; *Member Profile:* Individuals; Corporate bodies; Academics; Governments
Activities: Providing information & recommendations to the government, private sector, & the media; Providing networking opportunities; *Awareness Events:* Canadian Telework Day
Publications:
• Telework News
Type: Newsletter; *Price:* Free
Profile: Information for CTA members

Canadian Tennis Association *See* Tennis Canada

Canadian Tenpin Federation, Inc. (CTF) / Fédération canadienne des dix-quilles, inc.

916 - 3 Ave. North, Lethbridge AB T1H 0H3
Tel: 403-381-2830; *Fax:* 403-381-6247
ctf@gotenpinbowling.ca
www.gotenpinbowling.ca
www.facebook.com/CanadianTenpinFederationInc
Overview: A large national organization founded in 1964
Mission: To promote & foster the sport of tenpin bowling in Canada by maintaining active membership in the world's appropriate affiliated tenpin organizations, providing competitive opportunities for all skill levels, culminating in the selection of a National Team; To encourage the development of skills through a national coaching certification program
Affliation(s): Fédération internationale des quilleurs
Chief Officer(s):
Cathy Innes, President
cathyinnes@hotmail.com
Stan May, Executive Director
stanmay@gotenpinbowling.ca
Gus Badali, Manager, Domestic Team
gusbadali@gotenpinbowling.ca
20 volunteer(s)
Membership: 80,000 + 74 clubs
Activities: *Awareness Events:* National Team Trials, every even year, May long weekend
Awards:
• Honour Score Award (Award)
• Special Achievement Awards (Award)
• Purchasable Awards (Award)
Youth & tournament awards may be purchased from the Federation
• Sport Bowling Awards (Award)
Meetings/Conferences: • Canadian Tenpin Federation, Inc. / Fédération canadienne des dix-quilles, inc. 2015 Annual General Meeting, 2015
Scope: National
Publications:
• CTF Connection
Type: Newsletter; *Frequency:* 5 pa; *Editor:* Hazel McLeary
Profile: CTF events, tournaments, member news, & provincial news

Canadian Test Centre Inc. (CTC) / Services d'évaluation pédagogique

#10, 80 Citizen Ct., Markham ON L6G 1A7
Tel: 905-513-6636; *Fax:* 905-513-6639
Toll-Free: 800-668-1006
info@canadiantestcentre.com
www.canadiantestcentre.com
www.youtube.com/user/CanadianTestCentre
Overview: A medium-sized national organization founded in 1980
Mission: To publish & distribute test products; to support teachers to make their testing programs work; to invest in research & development projects which aim to improve the measurement & evaluation of student ability & achievement.
Chief Officer(s):
Ernest W. Cheng, Managing Director
ernest.cheng@canadiantestcentre.com
Finances: *Annual Operating Budget:* $500,000-$1.5 Million
Staff Member(s): 14

Canadian Textile Association (CTA) / La Fédération canadienne du textile

13 Interlacken Dr., Brampton ON L6X 0Y1
Tel: 647-821-4649
www.cdntexassoc.com
Previous Name: Textile Federation of Canada
Merged from: Canadian Association of Textile Chemists & Colourists; Textile Society of Canada
Overview: A medium-sized national charitable organization founded in 2003
Mission: To advance & disseminate knowledge of textiles; to promote sound procedures of textile processing; to encourage & sponsor textile research & investigation; to assist in the establishment of standards in the textile industry; to promote & encourage schools, classes & libraries for the study of textile technology; to collaborate with international groups in advancing the foregoing objectives
Chief Officer(s):
John Secondi, President
Finances: *Funding Sources:* Social activities
Membership: *Fees:* $50-$800; *Member Profile:* Textile graduates; textile related workers, industry
Activities: The promotion of the textile industry & textile education

Canadian Theatre Critics Association (CTCA) / Association des critiques de théâtre du Canada

c/o Department of Theatre, York University, 4700 Keele St., Toronto ON M3J 1P3
e-mail: scenechanges@rogers.com
www.canadiantheatrecritics.ca
Overview: A small national organization founded in 1979
Mission: To promote excellence in theatre criticism; to encourage the dissemination of information on theatre on a national level; to encourage the awareness & development of Canadian theatre nationally & internationally through theatre criticism in all the media; to promote & encourage excellence in Canadian theatre through national awards; to improve the status & working conditions of theatre critics
Member of: International Association of Theatre Critics
Affliation(s): Capital Critics Association; Association québécoise des critiques de théâtre
Chief Officer(s):
Don Rubin, President
drubin@yorku.ca
Membership: 30; *Fees:* $45 individual; *Member Profile:* Full - minimum three years professional theatre reviewing, feature writing or broadcasting within the entertainment field; associate - minimum one year of professional regular theatre reviewing, feature writing or broadcasting within the entertainment field
Awards:
• The Herbet Whittaker/Drama Bench Award for Outstanding Contribution to Canadian Theatre (Award)
Presented annually to Canadian citizen or permanent resident working in any theatrical discipline who has demonstrated distinguished contribution in playwriting, performance, direction or design; named after Herbert Whittaker Founding Chairman of the Canadian Theatre Critics Assoc.

Canadian Theological Society (CTS) / Société théologique canadienne

c/o M. Beavis, St. Thomas More College, 1437 College Dr., Saskatoon SK S7N 0W6
e-mail: secretary@cts-stc.ca
cts-stc.ca
www.facebook.com/canadiantheologicalsociety
Overview: A small national organization founded in 1955
Mission: To promote theological reflection & writing in Canada
Member of: Canadian Corporation for the Study of Religion (CCSR)
Affliation(s): Canadian Congress of the Humanities & Social Sciences
Chief Officer(s):
Allen Jorgenson, President
ajorgenson@wlu.ca
Bob McKeon, Treasurer
rmckeon@shaw.ca
Membership: *Fees:* $86 full members; $61 associate members; $45 student, retired, & unwaged full members; $22 student, retired, & unwaged associate members; *Member Profile:* Theologians, clergy, scholars, & students from universities, seminaries, & churches; Lay people
Activities: *Awareness Events:* Annual Student Essay Contest
Meetings/Conferences: • Canadian Theological Society Conference (Congress), May, 2015
Scope: National

Canadian Theosophical Association

89 Promenade Riverside, St-Labtert QC J4R 1A3
Toll-Free: 866-277-0074
www.theosophical.ca
Previous Name: Canadian Federation of the Theosophical Society
Overview: A small national organization founded in 1924
Mission: To form a nucleus of the universal Brotherhood of Humanity without distinction of race, creed, sex, caste or colour; to encourage the study of comparative religion, philosophy & science; to investigate the unexplained laws of nature & the powers latent in man
Chief Officer(s):
Medardo Martinez Cruz, President
Finances: *Annual Operating Budget:* Less than $50,000
Membership: 150 institutional; *Fees:* $25

Canadian Therapeutic Riding Association / Association canadienne d'équitation thérapeutique

5420 Hwy. 6 North, RR#5, Guelph ON N1H 6J2
Tel: 519-767-0700
ctra@golden.net
www.cantra.ca
twitter.com/CanTRA_ACET
Also Known As: CanTRA
Overview: A large national charitable organization founded in 1980
Mission: To foster therapeutic riding for persons with disabilities by establishing riding standards in collaboration with the medical profession; To accredit programs, certify instructors & promote research; To promote equestian sport & competition for persons with disabilities
Member of: Riding for Disabled International; Canadian Paralympic Committee; Canadian Equestrian Federation
Finances: *Funding Sources:* Donations; Membership fees; Fund-raising
Membership: *Fees:* $40
Activities: Offering the Certification Program for Therapeutic Riding Instructors (CTRI); *Speaker Service:* Yes
Awards:
• Rhonda Davies Award for Outstanding Volunteer (Award)
• Andrea Gillies Award for Outstanding CanTRA Instructor (Award)
• Outstanding Therapy Horse (Award)
Publications:
• CanTRA [Canadian Therapeutic Riding Association] Caller / L'Appel ACET
Type: Newsletter; *Frequency:* Quarterly
Profile: CanTRA conferences, articles, events, bylaws changes, & clinics
• Communiqué [a publication of the Canadian Therapeutic Riding Association]
Type: Newsletter
Profile: Information for CanTRA members, published between CanTRA Caller newsletters

Canadian Thoracic Society (CTS) / Société canadienne de thoracologie (SCT)

c/o National Office, The Lung Association, #300, 1750 Courtwood Cres., Ottawa ON K2C 2B5
Tel: 613-569-6411; *Fax:* 613-569-8860
Toll-Free: 888-566-5864
ctsinfo@lung.ca
www.lung.ca/cts
Overview: A medium-sized international charitable organization founded in 1958 overseen by Canadian Lung Association
Mission: To enhance the prevention & treatment of respiratory diseases
Affliation(s): AllerGen; American College of Chest Physicians; American Thoracic Society; Canadian COPD Alliance; Canadian Respiratory Health Professionals; Canadian Society of Allergy & Clinical Immunology; European Respiratory Society; Guidelines International Network
Chief Officer(s):
George Fox, President
Janet Sutherland, Director
Jean Bourbeau, Secretary
Mark FitzGerald, Treasurer
Suzanne Desmarais, Manager, Communications & Membership
Suzanne McCoy, Manager, Continuing Professional Development
Finances: *Funding Sources:* Donations; Sponsorships
Membership: *Member Profile:* Canadian & international physicians & scientists
Activities: Developing & implementing clinical practice guidelines; Advising the Canadian Lung Association on medical matters & programs; Promoting lung health & the best respiratory practices; Providing educational & clinical practice resources; Organizing professional development opportunities, as an accredited continuing professional development (CPD)

provider, under the Royal College of Physicians & Surgeons of Canada's Maintenance of Certification program; Engaging in advocacy activities; Funding research
Meetings/Conferences: • Canadian Thoracic Society Better Breathing 2015: Global Threats, Local Responses, January, 2015, Toronto Marriott Downtown Eaton Centre, Toronto, ON
Scope: National
• Canadian Thoracic Society 2015 Annual General Meeting, April, 2015, Westin Ottawa, Ottawa, ON
Scope: National
Publications:
• Canadian Respiratory Journal (CRJ)
Type: Journal; *Price:* Free for North American members of the Canadian Thoracic Society
Profile: Original articles, controlled clinical trials, case reports, & reviews
• Canadian Thoracic Society Annual Report
Type: Yearbook; *Frequency:* Annually
• Canadian Thoracic Society E-Bulletin
Type: Newsletter
Profile: Updates for all members of the Society

Canadian Thoroughbred Horse Society (CTHS) / Société canadienne du cheval Thoroughbred

PO Box 172, Toronto ON M9W 5L1
Tel: 416-675-1370; *Fax:* 416-675-9525
info@cthsnational.com
www.cthsnational.com
www.facebook.com/CanadianThoroughbredHorseSocietyNationalDivision
Overview: A medium-sized national organization founded in 1906
Mission: To assist & afford a means for promotion of interests of those engaged in breeding of thoroughbreds; to protect members against unbusinesslike methods; to diffuse information among members & others; to secure uniformity in usage & business conditions; to determine requirements of horses as thoroughbreds by the Society; to promote, encourage & assist in livestock & agricultural exhibitions, fairs & racing; to sponsor, assist & conduct sales of thoroughbred stock; to compile statistics of the industry; to maintain efficient supervision of breeders of thoroughbred horses; to prevent, detect & punish fraud (ie. in registration of throughbreds).
Chief Officer(s):
Grant Watson, President
Fran Okihiro, Manager
fokihiro@cthsnational.com
Finances: *Annual Operating Budget:* $100,000-$250,000; *Funding Sources:* Membership dues; registration fees
Staff Member(s): 2
Membership: 1,421; *Fees:* Schedule available; *Member Profile:* Annual - owners of thoroughbreds for purpose of breeding in current year in Canada, registered in Stud Book recognized by the Society; associate annual - to be approved by National Board; *Committees:* Pedigree; Membership; Registration; Publications/Communications; Internal Committees (Constitution, Regional Sales)
Activities: *Library:* Documentation Centre; Open to public

Alberta Division
#218, 1935 - 32nd Ave. NE, Calgary AB T2E 7C8
Tel: 403-229-3609; *Fax:* 403-224-6909
cthsalta@telusplanet.net
www.cthsalta.com
www.facebook.com/cths.alberta
twitter.com/CTHSALTA
Mission: To promote the purchase of Alberta Thoroughbreds, keep records, organize sales, disseminate information, compile statistics and assist our membership with registration.
Chief Officer(s):
Jean Kruse, Manager

British Columbia Division
#201, 17687 - 56A Ave., Surrey BC V3S 1G4
Tel: 604-574-0145; *Fax:* 604-574-5868
cthsbc@cthsbc.org
www.cthsbc.org
Mission: To assist and afford a means for the promotion of the interest of those engaged in the breeding of Thoroughbreds, to protect it's members against unbusinesslike methods, to reform abuses, to diffuse information among its members and others and to secure uniformity in usage and business conditions.
Chief Officer(s):
Bette-Jean (B-J) Davidson, General Manager

Manitoba Division
PO Box 46152, Stn. Westdale, Winnipeg MB R3R 3S3
Tel: 204-832-1702; *Fax:* 204-831-6735
cthsmb@mts.net
www.cthsmb.ca
Mission: To assist breeders of Thoroughbred horses in Manitoba by aiding them with provincial bonus and incentive programs, the operation of auctions, and providing other services to members.
Chief Officer(s):
Jill Withers, Regional Secretary

Ontario Division
PO Box 172, Toronto ON M9W 5L1
Tel: 416-675-3602; *Fax:* 416-675-9405
cthsont@idirect.com
www.cthsont.com
Mission: To aim to ensure a viable future for its members by providing assistance and representation within the thoroughbred breeding industry
Chief Officer(s):
R. Glenn Sikura, President

Québec Division
c/o CTHS National Office, CP 172, Toronto ON M9W 5L1
Tél: 416-675-1370; *Téléc:* 416-675-9525
Mission: To assist breeders of Thoroughbred horses in Quebec, by aiding them with provincial bonus and incentive programs, the operation of auctions, and providing other services to members.

Saskatchewan Division
PO Box 1137, Saskatoon SK S7K 3N2
Mission: To assist breeders of Thoroughbred horses in Saskatchewan by aiding them with provincial bonus and incentive programs, the operation of auctions, and providing other services to members.

Canadian Tibetan Association of Ontario (CTAO)

40 Titan Rd., Toronto ON M8Z 2J8
Tel: 416-410-5606; *Fax:* 416-410-5606
www.ctao.org
Overview: A small provincial organization founded in 1980
Mission: To represent Tibetans in Ontario; To serve the needs of the Tibetan community in the province; To promote cross-cultural understanding
Chief Officer(s):
Tsering Tsomo, President
Ngawang Diki, Coordinator, Cultural
Activities: Assisting newcomers to Canada; Promoting the rights of all individuals; Encouraging Tibetan Canadians to participate in Candian society; Providing regular cultural programs to help community members keep their traditions alive; Fostering tolerance, through education & awareness activities

Canadian Tinnitus Foundation

#202, 15388 24th Ave., Surrey BC V4A 2I2
Tel: 604-317-2952
info@findthecurenow.org
www.findthecurenow.org
www.facebook.com/CanadianTinnitusFoundation
Overview: A medium-sized national organization
Mission: A not-for-profit organization working to expand awareness & generate funding for tinnitus research
Chief Officer(s):
Nathan Nowak, President
John Jabat, Vice-President
Brian Cassidy, Treasurer
Alexander Bridges, Executive Director
Finances: *Funding Sources:* Donations
Membership: *Fees:* $30

Canadian Tire Coupon Collectors Club (CTCCC) / Club de collectionneurs de coupons Canadian Tire

1120, place Charron, Blainville QC J7C 2T2
Tel: 450-419-7914; *Fax:* 450-430-7233
adamsdoug@rogers.com
www.ctccc.ca
Overview: A small national organization founded in 1990
Mission: To research, study & catalogue all merchant scrip issued by the Canadian Tire Corporation; to promote the collecting & trading of such scrip in numismatic circles; to archive a collection of the scrip with a major Canadian University
Member of: Canadian Numismatic Association
Affliation(s): Canadian Paper Money Society
Chief Officer(s):
Thayer Bouck, President
mgiammarco@sympatico.ca
Finances: *Annual Operating Budget:* Less than $50,000; *Funding Sources:* Membership fees; auction premiums
8 volunteer(s)
Membership: 450; *Fees:* $15; *Committees:* Audio-visual; Archive; Publishing
Activities: Displaying collections; *Library* by appointment
Publications:
• Bilodeau Guide
Price: $23.99 volume 1; $34 volume 2; $57.99 both volumes
Profile: Guide to Canadian Tire "money" in two volumes
• The Collector: The Canadian Tire Coupon Collectors Club Newsletter
Type: Newsletter; *Accepts Advertising*; *Price:* Free with CTCCC regular membership
Profile: Advertisement of wants of collectors, or items for sale to other collectors, & articles of interest to members

Canadian Tire Dealers Association

#5, 171 Ambassador Dr., Mississauga ON L5T 2J1
Tel: 905-795-3329; *Fax:* 905-795-3330
ctdaoffice@ctdealers.com
newsite.ctdealers.com
Overview: A small national organization founded in 1968
Mission: To provide an organization to promote the welfare of Canadian Tire (CT) Associate Dealers
Chief Officer(s):
Terry Connoy, Executive Director
Staff Member(s): 14

Canadian Titanic Society (CTS)

Site 25-73, Simcoe ON N3Y 5K7
Tel: 519-426-2330
canadiantitanicsociety@yahoo.ca
www.canadian-titanic-society.com
Also Known As: Titanic Historical Society of Canada
Overview: A small national organization founded in 1998
Mission: To preserve the history of the Titanic tragedy
Chief Officer(s):
Norm Lewis, President/ CEO & Founder
Finances: *Funding Sources:* Sponsors
Membership: *Member Profile:* National & international members

Canadian Tooling & Machining Association (CTMA)

#3, 140 McGovern Dr., Cambridge ON N3H 4R7
Tel: 519-653-7265; *Fax:* 519-653-6764
Toll-Free: 888-437-3661
info@ctma.com
www.ctma.com
Overview: A medium-sized national organization founded in 1963
Mission: To be an effective, broad-based, respected organization, representing the Canadian tooling & machining industry, nationally & internationally
Member of: International Special Tooling & Machining Association (ISTMA)
Affliation(s): Auto Parts; Canadian Foundry Association; Canadian Plastics Institute; GTMA England; PMPTB - Ohio, USA; SPI - Toronto; CAMM - Windsor
Chief Officer(s):
Les Payne, Executive Director
lpayne@ctma.com
Finances: *Annual Operating Budget:* $100,000-$250,000; *Funding Sources:* Membership dues
Staff Member(s): 3; 12 volunteer(s)
Membership: 160 corporate + 15 associate + 6 senior/lifetime; *Fees:* Schedule available; *Member Profile:* Corporate only; *Committees:* Pattern-Model Makers; Training
Activities: Annual Apprenticeship Competition
Publications:
• CTMA Buyers Guide

• CTMA Membership List
• CTMA View
Type: Newsletter; *Frequency:* Quarterly; *Accepts Advertising*

Canadian Tour Guide Association of British Columbia

PO Box 18515, 710 Granville St., Vancouver BC V6Z 0B3
e-mail: info@ctgaofbc.com
www.ctgaofbc.com
Previous Name: Canadian Tourist Guide Association of BC
Overview: A medium-sized provincial organization founded in 1989
Mission: To develop a professional standard of tour guiding for members; to encourage tourist guide certification; to be a voice for tourist guides; to provide a place to exchange information
Member of: World Federation of Tourist Guide Associations
Chief Officer(s):

Cheryl Lou Ornburn, President
president@ctgaofbc.com
Membership: *Fees:* $65 professional; $50 associate/alumni; $35 student/educator; *Member Profile:* Tour guides, directors & greeters

Canadian Tourist Guide Association of BC *See* Canadian Tour Guide Association of British Columbia

Canadian Tourism Human Resource Council (CTHRC) / Conseil canadien des ressources humaines en tourisme (CCHRT)

#608, 151 Slater St., Ottawa ON K1J 7W9
Tel: 613-231-6949; *Fax:* 613-231-6853
info@cthrc.ca
www.cthrc.ca
www.linkedin.com/company/canadian-tourism-human-resource-council
www.facebook.com/CTHRC
twitter.com/cthrc
www.youtube.com/user/TourismHRCouncil
Overview: A medium-sized national organization founded in 1993
Mission: An organization whose overall goal is to improve the quality of the Canadian labour force, and to assist businesses to be more flexible in meeting changing competitive demands.
Chief Officer(s):
Wendy Swedlove, President
Finances: *Annual Operating Budget:* $100,000-$250,000
Staff Member(s): 25
Membership: 86; *Member Profile:* Business; labour; education; national associations; prov./territorial associations; individuals

Canadian Tourism Research Institute

255 Smyth Rd., Ottawa ON K1H 8M7
Tel: 613-526-3280; *Fax:* 613-526-4857
Toll-Free: 866-711-2262
ctri@conferenceboard.ca
www.conferenceboard.ca/ctri/
Overview: A medium-sized national organization
Chief Officer(s):
Gregory Hermus, Associate Director
hermus@conferenceboard.ca

Canadian Toy Association / Canadian Toy & Hobby Fair (CTA) / L'Association canadienne du Jouet

#212, 7777 Keele St., Concord ON L4K 1Y7
Tel: 905-660-5690; *Fax:* 905-660-6103
info@cdntoyassn.com
www.cdntoyassn.com
Overview: A medium-sized national organization founded in 1932
Member of: International Council of Toy Industries
Chief Officer(s):
Carol McDonald, Contact, Media Relations
mail@mcmarketing.ca
Finances: *Annual Operating Budget:* $500,000-$1.5 Million
Staff Member(s): 2; 13 volunteer(s)
Membership: 155; *Member Profile:* Manufacturers, importers or distributors of toys, games, seasonal decorations & hobby products
Publications:
• Canadian Toy Association Newsletter
Type: Newsletter

Canadian Toy Collectors' Society Inc. (CTCS)

#245, 91 Rylander Blvd., Unit 7, Toronto ON M1B 5M5
e-mail: ctcsweb@hotmail.com
www.ctcs.org
Overview: A medium-sized national organization founded in 1970
Mission: To promote interest in the collection & display of all types of toys, childhood memorabilia & literature; to acquire, maintain & house a collection of toys & to restore & preserve Canadian toys of historic significance.
Affliation(s): Dufferin County Museum & Archives
Chief Officer(s):
Ron Blair, President
Finances: *Annual Operating Budget:* Less than $50,000; *Funding Sources:* Membership dues; model sales; toy show
12 volunteer(s)
Membership: 130; *Fees:* $50; *Committees:* Collections; Museum; Publicity; Toy Show
Activities: *Awareness Events:* Annual Canada's Greatest Collector's Toy Show

Canadian Toy Testing Council (CTTC) / Conseil canadien d'évaluation des jouets

1973 Baseline Rd., Ottawa ON K2C 0C7
Tel: 613-228-3155; *Fax:* 613-228-3242
cttc@toy-testing.org
www.toy-testing.org
www.facebook.com/CdnToyTesting
twitter.com/CdnToyTesting
Overview: A small national charitable organization founded in 1952
Mission: To encourage the design, manufacture & distribution of toys sensitive to children's needs through independent evaluation
Chief Officer(s):
Liliane Benoît, Executive Director
Finances: *Annual Operating Budget:* $100,000-$250,000
400 volunteer(s)
Membership: 400; *Fees:* $30; *Member Profile:* Educators, parents
Activities: National Media Conference on the "Best" toys, annual
Publications:
• Canadian Toy Testing Council Newsletter
Type: Newsletter; *Frequency:* Semiannually; *Editor:* Janet Hetherington; *Price:* Free with CTTC membership
Profile: Information about recent toys, & creative recommendations for children
• Toy Report
Type: Yearbook; *Frequency:* Annually; *Editor:* Judy Andrew Piel
Profile: Rating & a review of each toy tested

Canadian Track & Field Association *See* Athletics Canada

Canadian Trail & Mountain Running Association (CTMRA)

BC
www.mountainrunning.ca
Overview: A small national organization
Mission: To oversee the sport of mountain running in Canada.
Chief Officer(s):
Adrian Lambert, Contact
adrian.lambert@mountainrunning.ca
Activities: Championship series

Canadian Training Institute (CTI) / Institut canadien de formation

50 Euston Ave., Toronto ON M4J 3N3
Tel: 416-778-7056; *Fax:* 416-778-8103
Toll-Free: 877-889-6158
www.canadiantraininginstitute.com
Overview: A small national charitable organization founded in 1983
Mission: To contribute to the effectiveness of services delivered by criminal justice & related human service agencies in Canada
Affliation(s): Canadian Traumatic Stress Network; National Associations Active in Criminal Justice (NAACJ/ANIJC); American Probation & Parole Association (APPA); International Community & Corrections Association (ICCA)
Chief Officer(s):
John Sawdon, Executive Director
sawdon@cantraining.org
Finances: *Funding Sources:* Donations; Sponsorships
Activities: Liaising with government; Offering courses & workshops; Disseminating information; Training; Consulting; Conducting research; Breaking the Cycle program for youth involved in gangs
Publications:
• Canadian Training Institute Annual Report
Type: Yearbook; *Frequency:* Annually
• Community Corrections & Criminal Justice Work in Canada
• A Literature Review on Youth Violence: From Risk to Resiliency Utilizing a Developmental Perspective
Number of Pages: 128; *ISBN:* 0-921465-18-1; *Price:* $20
• Youth Justice in Canada: A Resource Manual
Type: Manual; *Number of Pages:* 310; *ISBN:* 0-921465-15-7; *Price:* $39 book; $45 binder

Canadian Trakehner Horse Society (CTHS)

PO Box 6009, New Hamburg ON N3A 2K6
Tel: 519-662-3209
cantrakhsivh@golden.net
www.cantrak.on.ca
www.facebook.com/pages/Canadian-Trakehner/203491652994222
Overview: A small national organization founded in 1974
Mission: To maintain a public registry of Trakehner horses, under the Canadian Livestock Records Corporation; to promote & preserve Trakehner horses in Canada
Chief Officer(s):
Judy Kirkby, President
judlenn@sasktel.net
Ingrid von Hausen, Registrar & Secretary
Laurel Glanfield, Treasurer
lglanfield@telus.net
Membership: *Fees:* $30 associate members; $45 single memberships; $80 families; $400 life memberships; *Member Profile:* Breeders, owners, & friends of Trakehner horses
Activities: Providing information & support to members
Publications:
• Canadian Trakehner
Type: Magazine; *Accepts Advertising*; *Price:* Free with CTHS membership
• Canadian Trakehner News
Type: Newsletter; *Frequency:* Quarterly; *Accepts Advertising*; *Price:* Free with CTHS membership

Canadian Translators & Interpreters Council *See* Canadian Translators, Terminologists & Interpreters Council

Canadian Translators, Terminologists & Interpreters Council (CTTIC) / Conseil des traducteurs, terminologues et interprètes du Canada (CTTIC)

#1202, One Nicholas St., Ottawa ON K1N 7B7
Tel: 613-562-0379; *Fax:* 613-241-4098
info@cttic.org
www.cttic.org
Previous Name: Canadian Translators & Interpreters Council
Overview: A medium-sized national charitable organization founded in 1956
Mission: To ensure uniform standards for the practice of the profession; to make available to the public a body of reliable professionals in translation, terminology & interpretation
Chief Officer(s):
Kristel Blais, Administrative Director
Faith Cormier, President
faith.cormier@cttic.org
Finances: *Annual Operating Budget:* $50,000-$100,000
Staff Member(s): 1; 4 volunteer(s)
Membership: 3,500 in 10 societies
Activities: Programs in translation, terminology, interpretation; certification examinations
Publications:
• CTTIC By-laws
• Symposium on Translation, Terminology & Interpretation in Cuba & Canada
Frequency: Biennially

Canadian Transplant Association (CTA) / Association canadienne des greffes

26 Morris St., Ottawa ON K1S 4A7
Toll-Free: 877-779-5991
cta@txworks.ca
www.organ-donation-works.org
www.facebook.com/CanadianTransplantAssociationandGames
twitter.com/CTACanada
Previous Name: Canadian Transplant Games Association
Overview: A medium-sized national charitable organization founded in 1989
Mission: To promote a healthy lifestyle for transplant recipients
Chief Officer(s):
Aubrey Goldstein, President
aubreygoldstein@txworks.ca
Neil Folkins, Director, Membership, 780-455-1655
neilfolkins@txworks.ca
Kathy Tachynski, Secretary
ktachynsk@txworks.ca
Michael J. Sullivan, Treasurer
msullivan@txworks.ca
Finances: *Funding Sources:* Membership fees; Donations; Fundraising
Membership: *Fees:* $30 individual members; $75 family membership; $300 lifetime individual membership; *Member Profile:* Transplant recipients; Persons committed to removing barriers to organ donation
Activities: Supporting organ & tissue donation awareness activities; Offering education about transplantation; Providing information about the National & World Transplant Games; Organizing social activities; *Speaker Service:* Yes
Awards:
• Gloria Santini Memorial Award (Award)

To honour dedication & perseverance in supporting the mission of the Canadian Transplant Association
Publications:
• The Living Proof
Type: Newsletter; *Frequency:* Quarterly; *Editor:* Jennifer Holman; *Price:* Free with membership in the Canadian Transplant Association
Profile: Canadian Transplant Association news, including event information, awards & inspiring stories

Alberta Region
AB
www.organ-donation-works.org

British Columbia Region
BC
www.organ-donation-works.org
Mission: To promote organ donation & transplantation throughout British Columbia
Chief Officer(s):
Margaret Benson, Regional Director, British Columbia
mmbenson@txworks.ca

New Brunswick (Eastern Provinces) Region
NB
www.organ-donation-works.org
Mission: Increasing awareness of organ & tissue donation in Newfoundland, Prince Edward Island, Nova Scotia, & New Brunswick
Chief Officer(s):
Mark Black, Regional Director, Eastern Provinces
markblack@txworks.ca

Ontario Region
ON
www.organ-donation-works.org
Mission: To encourage a healthy lifestyle for transplant recipients throughout Ontario
Chief Officer(s):
Sandra Holdsworth, Director, Ontario Region
sandraholdsworth@txworks.ca

Québec Region
c/o Gaston Martin, 101, rue Lavigne, Repentingny QC J6A 6B6
Tel: 450-654-3786
www.organ-donation-works.org
Chief Officer(s):
Gaston Martin, Director, Québec Region
gaston@txworks.ca

Saskatchewan Region
SK
www.organ-donation-works.org
Chief Officer(s):
Phil Gleim, Regional Director
philgleim@txworks.ca

Canadian Transplant Games Association ***See*** Canadian Transplant Association

Canadian Transplantation Society ***See*** Canadian Society of Transplantation

Canadian Transport Lawyers Association (CTLA)
24 Duncan St., 3rd Fl., Toronto ON M5V 2B8
Tel: 416-601-1340; *Fax:* 416-601-1190
marc@isaacsco.ca
www.ctla.ca
Overview: A small national organization
Mission: To provide a professional and social forum for lawyers engaged or otherwise interested in transportation law, regulatory policy, procedure and related legal interests.
Chief Officer(s):
Kim E. Stoll, President
Louis A. Amato-Gauci, Vice-President & Secretary
lamato-gauci@airdberlis.com
Douglas I. Evanchuk, Treasurer
devanchuk@mross.com
Roger Watts, Director, Communications
Membership: *Fees:* $100 - $195; *Member Profile:* Lawyers engaged in transportation law, regulatory policy, procedure, & related legal interests
Awards:
• C. Douglas MacLeod Memorial Scholarship (Scholarship)
Awarded annually to a student, or students, completing the second year of the LLB programme on the basis of outstanding academic performance generally, with an emphasis on achievements in constitutional and administrative law.
Publications:
• The Transportation Lawyer
Type: Journal; *Price:* Subscription included with Canadian Transport Lawyers Association membership fees

Canadian Transport Tariff Bureau Association ***See*** Freight Carriers Association of Canada

Canadian Transportation Equipment Association (CTEA) / Association d'équipement de transport du canada (AETC)
#3B, 16 Barrie Blvd., St. Thomas ON N5P 4B9
Tel: 519-631-0414; *Fax:* 519-631-1333
transportation@ctea.ca
www.ctea.ca
ca.linkedin.com/groups?gid=6508608
Overview: A medium-sized national organization founded in 1963
Mission: To promote excellence in commercial vehicle manufacturing; to develop standard practices
Chief Officer(s):
Don Moore, Executive Director
don.moore@atminc.on.ca
Kevin Last, President
Staff Member(s): 4
Membership: 544; *Fees:* $825; *Member Profile:* Commercial vehicle & component manufacturers; Dealers & distributors; Service providers
Activities: Lobbying; Providing access to technical & regulatory information; Offering networking opportunities; Encouraging research; *Speaker Service:* Yes
Meetings/Conferences: • CTEA 52nd Manufacturers Technical Conference, 2015
Publications:
• Buyer's Guide to Members' Products & Services
Profile: Equipment, products, & services offered by companies, for CTEA / AETC members & potential customers
• CTEA Membership Directory
Type: Directory; *Frequency:* Monthly
Profile: Contact information for CTEA's members
• CTEA Today
Type: Magazine; *Frequency:* Bimonthly; *Price:* Free with CTEA membership
Profile: CTEA activities & events, industry news, & articles on issues
• Xpress Newsletter
Type: Newsletter; *Price:* Free with CTEA / AETC membership
Profile: Membership information, industry news, employment referrals, technical papers, new products, & surveys

Canadian Transportation Research Forum (CTRF) / Groupe de recherches sur les transports au Canada
PO Box 23033, Woodstock ON N4T 1R9
Tel: 519-421-9701; *Fax:* 519-421-9319
www.ctrf.ca
twitter.com/ForCtrf
Overview: A medium-sized national charitable organization founded in 1967
Mission: To promote the development of research in transportation & related fields; to publish research papers through media & through national & regional forum meetings.
Chief Officer(s):
Marc-André Roy, President
mroy@cpcstrans.com
Carole Ann Woudsma, Secretary
cawoudsma@ctrf.ca
Jean Patenaude, Executive Vice-President
jean.patenaude@cn.ca
Mark Hemmes, Vice-President External
mhemmes@quorumcorp.net
Gerry Kolaitis, VP Finance/Treasurer
Gerry_Kolaitis@viarail.ca
Hanna Maoh, Vice-President Program/Publications
maohhf@uwindsor.ca
William Anderson, Vice-President Meetings
bander@uwindsor.ca
Garland Chow, VP Organization/Development
garland.chow@sauder.ubc.ca
Membership: *Fees:* $135 individual; $79 senior; $32 student; *Member Profile:* Open to anyone interested in any aspect of transportation; membership is individual rather than corporate; present membership is drawn from carriers, shippers, consultants & suppliers in the commercial sector, the policy, regulatory, planning & research environments at all levels of government, students & professors at universitites & community colleges
Awards:
• Scholarships for Graduate Study in Transportation (Scholarship)
In cooperation with several other organizations, offers up to five scholarships; field of study may be in business administration, civil engineering, economics, geography, law, planning, or other fields*Deadline:* February *Amount:* $4,000
• Student Research Paper Competition (Award)
Prizes awarded annually for student papers dealing with transportation; prizes are awarded for the best undergraduate papers, the best papers at the master's level, & the best papers at the doctorate level
Meetings/Conferences: • 50th Annual Canadian Transportation Research Forum Conference, May, 2015, Marriott Chateau Champlain, Montréal, QC
Scope: National

Canadian Transverse Myelitis Association (CTMA) / Association Canadienne de myélite transverse
263 Malcolm Circle, Dorval QC H9S 1T6
Tel: 514-636-9337
info@mytm.ca
mytm.ca
twitter.com/CTMAssociation
Overview: A medium-sized national organization
Mission: To help patients with transverse myelitis & their families build a network of support as well as to inform them of new research & treatment that has been discovered, and to raise awareness about the disorder
Chief Officer(s):
Kimberley Kotar, President & Founder
kimberley@mytm.ca

Canadian Trapshooting Association (CTA)
3118 - 7th Ave. East, Regina SK S4N 5V4
Overview: A medium-sized national organization founded in 1950
Mission: To promote clay target shooting as a recreational sport among shooters of every age, both sexes, & at every level of ability, the ultimate objective being to compete in the world championships held each year in Ohio
Member of: Amateur Trapshooting Association
Chief Officer(s):
Jim Wood, President
Finances: *Annual Operating Budget:* Less than $50,000; *Funding Sources:* Fees collected at the national championships
150 volunteer(s)
Membership: 1,800

Canadian Tribute to Human Rights (CTHR) / Monument canadien pour les droits de la personne (MCDP)
#170, 99 - 5th Ave., Ottawa ON K1P 5P5
e-mail: info@cthr-mcdp.com
www.cthr-mcdp.com
Also Known As: The Human Rights Monument
Overview: A small national charitable organization founded in 1984
Mission: To ensure public awareness of the presence in Ottawa of the Tribute monument as a symbol of Canadians' committment to preserving & fostering human rights; To promote use of the site as a focal point for all groups working for human rights in Canada & internationally; To spread the concept of public places dedicated to human rights in other capital cities of countries that have affirmed the UN Universal Declaration of Human Rights.
Finances: *Annual Operating Budget:* Less than $50,000; *Funding Sources:* Donations; grants
Activities: *Speaker Service:* Yes

Canadian Trucking Alliance (CTA) / L'Alliance canadienne du camionnage (ACC)
555 Dixon Rd., Toronto ON M9W 1H8
Tel: 613-236-9426; *Fax:* 866-823-4076
publicaffairs@cantruck.ca
www.cantruck.ca
Overview: A medium-sized national organization founded in 1937
Mission: To promote business excellence in trucking; to participate in the development of public policy which supports the economic growth, safety & prosperity of the industry; to provide services, including research, development, products & information to meet the needs of the industry.
Staff Member(s): 5
Membership: *Member Profile:* Motor carriers & associated trades
Activities: *Speaker Service:* Yes

Canadian Trucking Human Resources Council (CTHRC) / Conseil canadien des ressources humaines en camionnage
#203, 720 Belfast Rd., Ottawa ON K1G 0Z5
Tel: 613-244-4800; *Fax:* 613-244-4535
info@cthrc.com
www.cthrc.com
Overview: A medium-sized national organization
Mission: To respond to the human resource needs of the trucking industry
Affliation(s): CCA Truck Driver Training Ltd.; Capilano Truck Driver Training Institute; JVI Provincial Transportation & Safety Academy; Mountain Transport Institute Ltd.; Red Deer College; SK Driver Training Ltd.; Wheels On Ltd. / Training & Driver Training
Membership: *Committees:* Labour Market Information; Outreach; Foreign Credential Recognition; Gap; Professional Driver Recognition Program; Skills Upgrading
Activities: Conducting research; Training; Offering advice; Liaising with industry members
Publications:
• Industry in Motion: Canada's Trucking HR Newsletter
Type: Newsletter
Profile: Industry, government, & general information
• Sharing the Load: Activity Report

Canadian Turkey Marketing Agency *See* Turkey Farmers of Canada

Canadian Ukrainian Immigrant Aid Society (CUIAS)
2383 Bloor St. West, 2nd Fl., Toronto ON M6S 1P9
Tel: 416-767-4595; *Fax:* 416-767-2658
www.cuias.org
Overview: A small international organization founded in 1977
Mission: To sponsor & aid in settlement of Ukrainian refugees.
Member of: Ontario Council of Agencies Serving Immigrants
Affliation(s): Ukrainian Canadian Congress
Chief Officer(s):
Ludmila Kolesnichenko, Executive Director
lkolesnichenko@cuias.org
Finances: *Funding Sources:* Federal & provincial grants; donations; fees
Staff Member(s): 10

Canadian Ultimate Players Association *See* Ultimate Canada

Canadian Underwater Games Association (CUGA)
c/o Melanie Johnson, Secretary, #2002, 535 Nicola St., Vancouver BC V6G 3G3
e-mail: info@cuga.org
www.cuga.org
www.facebook.com/cuga.org
Overview: A small national organization founded in 1984
Mission: To oversee underwater sports in Canada.
Affliation(s): World Underwater Federation
Chief Officer(s):
Adam Jocksch, President
Activities: Underwater hockey & underwater rugby

Canadian Union of Brewery & General Workers, Local 325
1 Carlingview Dr., Toronto ON M9W 5E5
Tel: 416-675-2648; *Fax:* 416-675-6694
component325.ca
Overview: A small provincial organization founded in 1959
Member of: National Union of Public and General Employees
Chief Officer(s):
Glen Hamilton, President
Membership: *Member Profile:* Canadian Brewery Workers

Canadian Union of Communication Workers (Ind.) *Voir* Union canadienne des travailleurs en communication (ind.)

Canadian Union of Postal Workers (CUPW) / Syndicat des travailleurs et travailleuses des postes (STTP)
377 Bank St., Ottawa ON K2P 1Y3
Tel: 613-236-7238; *Fax:* 613-563-7861
feedback@cupw-sttp.org
www.cupw-sttp.org
Overview: A large national organization
Mission: CUPW is a democratic union. They are involved with various campaigns and activities which help support their members.
Member of: Canadian Labour Congress
Chief Officer(s):
Denis Lemelin, National President
George Kuehnbaum, National Sec.-Treas.
Membership: 54,000; *Member Profile:* Rural and suburban mail carriers, letter carriers, mail service couriers, postal clerks, mail handlers, mail despatchers, technicians, mechanics, electricians and electronic technicians.; *Committees:* Human Rights; Women's; Work Measurement
Meetings/Conferences: • Canadian Union of Postal Workers National Convention 2015, May, 2015
Scope: National

Canadian Union of Public Employees (CUPE) / Syndicat canadien de la fonction publique (SCFP)
1375 St. Laurent Blvd., Ottawa ON K1G 0Z7
Tel: 613-237-1590; *Fax:* 613-237-5508
cupemail@cupe.ca
www.cupe.ca
Overview: A large national organization founded in 1963
Mission: To advance the social, economic, & general welfare of both active & retired employees; To promote required legislation
Member of: Prince Edward Island Literacy Alliance Inc.
Affliation(s): Canadian Labour Congress; Public Services International; International Confederation of Free Trade Unions
Chief Officer(s):
Paul Moist, National President
Charles Fluery, National Secretary-Treasurer
Daniel Légère, General Vice-President
Lucie Levasseur, General Vice-President
Barry O'Neill, General Vice-President
Tom Graham, General Vice-President, Saskatchewan
Fred Hahn, General Vice-President, Ontario
Membership: 600,000+; *Member Profile:* Workers in the public service of Canada; *Committees:* National Advisory Committee on Pensions; National Global Justice; National Contracting Out & Privatization Coordinating; National Environment; National Health & Safety; National Health Care Issues; National Pink Triangle; National Women's; National Working Committee on Racism, Discrimination, & Employment Equity (National Rainbow Committee); National Child Care Working Group; Persons With Disabilities National Working Group; National Young Workers; National Literacy Working Group; National Political Action
Activities: Improving wages, working conditions, hours of work, & job security; Eliminating harassment & discrimination; Providing educational programs
Meetings/Conferences: • Canadian Union of Public Employees 2015 Human Rights Conference, February, 2015, RBC Convention Centre, Winnipeg, MB
Scope: National
Publications:
• Counterpoint
Type: Newsletter; *Frequency:* Quarterly; *Editor:* Catherine Louli
ISSN: 1920-2857
Profile: Available in print & online (1920-2865)
• CUPE Celebrates: Year in Review
Type: Yearbook; *Frequency:* Annually
Profile: Articles & facts about CUPE in Canada during the recent year
• CUPE International Solidarity Report
Type: Report; *Author:* Catherine Louli
• CUPE Literacy News
Type: Newsletter
Profile: Highlights of training programs & literacy workshops
• Economic Climate for Bargaining
Type: Newsletter; *Frequency:* Quarterly; *Editor:* Toby Sanger (tsanger@cupe.ca)
Profile: National & provincial economic outlooks
• FastFacts
Type: Newsletter
Profile: Current CUPE news & activities
• Global Justice
Type: Newsletter
Profile: Articles from around the world
• Privatization Watch
Type: Newsletter; *Frequency:* Monthly
Profile: News about contracting out & P3s, & profiles of public alternatives to privatization
• Tabletalk
Type: Newsletter; *Frequency:* Quarterly; *Editor:* Susan Attenborough
Profile: A bargaining resource, for CUPE local bargaining committees, elected officers, & servicing representatives

Alberta Division
#102, 10425 Princess Elizabeth Ave. NW, Edmonton AB T5G 0Y5
Tel: 780-484-7644; *Fax:* 780-489-2202
Toll-Free: 877-937-2873
larab@cupe.ca
www.cupealberta.ab.ca
twitter.com/cupeab
Mission: To work together for improved working conditions, better wages, & strong public services in Alberta
Marle Roberts, President
cupeabpresident@telus.blackberry.net
Jody Carey, Secretary
recording-secretary.cupe.ab@hotmail.com
Neil Ketler, Treasurer
cupe.abtreasurer@telus.blackberry.net
• The United Leader
Type: Newsletter

British Columbia Division
British Columbia Regional Office, #500, 4940 Canada Way, Burnaby BC V5G 4T3
Tel: 604-291-9119; *Fax:* 604-291-9043
Toll-Free: 800-664-2873
info@cupe.bc.ca
www.cupe.bc.ca
Chief Officer(s):
Robin Jones, Director
Anne Coupland, Assistant Director
Barry O'Neill, President
Mark Hancock, Secretary-Treasurer
• CUPE BC News
Type: Newsletter

Manitoba Division
Manitoba Regional Office, #703, 275 Broadway, Winnipeg MB R3C 4M6
Tel: 204-942-0343; *Fax:* 204-956-7071
Toll-Free: 800-552-2873
cupemb@mts.net
www.cupe.mb.ca
www.facebook.com/cupescfp
twitter.com/cupenat
www.youtube.com/user/cupescfp
Chief Officer(s):
Sandra Oakley, Regional Director
cupemb@mts.net
Kelly Moist, President
kmoist@cupe.mb.ca
Mike Davidson, Vice-President
mdavidson@cupe500.mb.ca

New Brunswick Division
Maritime Regional Office, 91 Woodside Lane, Fredericton NB E3C 0C5
Tel: 506-458-8059; *Fax:* 506-452-1702
nb.cupe.ca
Mission: To advance the efficiency of public employees in New Brunswick; To promote legislation in New Brunswick that furthers the interests of member unions
Daniel Légère, President, 506-869-0424, Fax: 506-758-9327
dlegere@cupe.ca
Sandy Harding, First Vice-President, 506-832-6022, Fax: 506-832-6022
sharding@cupe.ca
Minerva Porelle, Secretary-Treasurer, 506-466-6149
oporelle@nbnet.nb.ca
Gordon Black, Regional Director
gblack@cupe.ca
• The Signal [a publication of the Canadian Union of Public Employees, New Brunswick Division]
Type: Newspaper

Newfoundland & Labrador Division
St. John's Area Office, PO Box 8745, Stn. A, 36 Austin St., St. John's NL A1B 3T2
Tel: 709-753-0732; *Fax:* 709-753-2313
Toll-Free: 866-771-2873
www.nl.cupe.ca
Chief Officer(s):
Wayne Lucas, President
Dawn Lahey, Vice-President
Ed Whelan, Secretary-Treasurer

Nova Scotia Division
Atlantic Regional Office, #308, 7071 Bayers Rd., Sartlite Bldg., Halifax NS B3L 2C2
Tel: 902-455-4180; *Fax:* 902-455-5915
www.novascotia.cupe.ca
Mission: To work for equitable treatment for all members
Chief Officer(s):
Danny Cavanagh, President
dannycavanagh@eastlink.ca

Mike McNeil, Vice-President
michaelmcneil@ns.sympatico.ca
Dianne Frittenburg, Secretary-Treasurer
fritt@eastlink.ca
Jim Laverie, Recording Secretary
laverie@hotmail.com
Mary Jessome, Communication Editor
maryejess@hotmail.com
• Danny's Diary [a publication of Canadian Union of Public Employees, Nova Scotia Division]
Type: Newsletter

Ontario Division
Ontario Regional Office, #1, 80 Commerce Valley Dr. East, Markham ON L3T 0B2
Tel: 905-739-9739; *Fax:* 905-739-9740
info@cupe.on.ca
www.cupe.on.ca
Mission: To act as a political voice for affiliated locals throughout Ontario; To campaign for legislative, policy, & political change on issues affecting public services
Chief Officer(s):
Brian Atkinson, Regional Director
Randy Millage, Regional Director
André Lamoureux, Assistant Regional Director
Karen McNama, Assistant Regional Director
Linda Thurston-Neeley, Assistant Regional Director
Fred Hahn, President
Candace Rennick, Secretary-Treasurer
Michael Hurley, First Vice-President
Yolanda McClean, Second Vice-President
Andrea Madden, Third Vice-President
Henri Giroux, Fourth Vice-President
• Canadian Union of Public Employees Ontario Division Newsletter
Type: Newsletter; *Frequency:* Biweekly
Profile: Developments in CUPE Ontario sectors, campaign updates, & upcoming events

Prince Edward Island Division
Charlottetown Area Office, 100 Capital Dr., Charlottetown PE C1E 1E7
Tel: 902-566-4006
www.cupepei.ca
www.facebook.com/465650880124770
twitter.com/bmckinnonatcupe
Mission: To advance the efficiency of public employees & the labour movement in Prince Edward Island; To assist in the organization of unorganized workers
Chief Officer(s):
Lori Mackay, President
lmackay@cupe.ca
Leonard Crawford, Vice-President
leonardjcrawford@hotmail.com
Karyn Noble, Recording Secretary
noblehouse@pei.sympatico.ca
Linda Jones, Treasurer
bandljones@pei.sympatico.ca
• CUPE Prince Edward Island Newsletter
Type: Newsletter

Québec Division
Québec Regional Office, #7100, 565, boul Crémazie, Montréal QC H2M 2V9
Tél: 514-384-9681; *Téléc:* 514-384-9680
www.cupe.ca/quebec
www.facebook.com/pages/SCFP/177741812241442
twitter.com/SCFPQuebecInfos
Chief Officer(s):
Michel Bibeault, Regional Director
Linda Craig, Assistant Regional Director
Michel Parenteau, Assistant Regional Director
Serge Morin, Assistant Regional Director

Saskatchewan Division
Saskatchewan Regional Office, 3275 East Eastgate Dr., Regina SK S4Z 1A5
Tel: 306-757-1009; *Fax:* 306-757-0102
cupesask@sasktel.net
www.sk.cupe.ca
www.facebook.com/cupesask
www.twitter.com/CUPEsask
Mission: To present positions of the union to government & media
Chief Officer(s):
Aina Kagis, Regional Director
Tom Graham, President
cupesask@sasktel.net
Dolores Douglas, Vice-President
doldou@sasktel.net
Judy Henley, Secretary-Treasurer
rjhenner@sasktel.net
Debbie Hubick, Recording Secretary
debstan@sasktel.net
• CUPE Saskatchewan Bulletin
Type: Newsletter; *Frequency:* Weekly

Canadian Unitarian Council (CUC) / Conseil unitarien du Canada

#100, 344 Dupont St, Toronto ON M5R 1V9
Tel: 416-489-4121; *Fax:* 416-489-9010
Toll-Free: 888-568-5723
info@cuc.ca
www.cuc.ca
Also Known As: Unitarian Church
Overview: A medium-sized national charitable organization founded in 1961
Mission: To enhance, nurture & promote Unitarian & Universalist religion in Canada; to provide support for religious exploration, spiritual growth & social responsibility
Affliation(s): International Association for Religious Freedom; International Council of Unitarians & Universalists; Unitarian Universalist Minsters of Canada
Chief Officer(s):
Vidya Sudama, Financial Administrator, 416-489-4121
vidya@cuc.ca
Gary Groot, President
gary@cuc.ca
Finances: *Annual Operating Budget:* $250,000-$500,000; *Funding Sources:* Donations; membership dues
Staff Member(s): 6; 20 volunteer(s)
Membership: 50 institutional; *Fees:* congregations - assessment per member; *Committees:* Lay & Chaplaincy; Social Responsibility
Activities: *Library:* CUC Library; by appointment
Publications:
• The Canadian Unitarian
Frequency: Biannually; *Accepts Advertising; ISSN:* 0527-9860; *Price:* Free for members of CUC congregations; $9/yr. non-members
• Canadian Unitarian Council National Directory
Type: Directory; *Price:* Free for members of CUC congregations

Canadian Unitarians for Social Justice (CUJS)

Stn. 40011, Ottawa ON K1V 0W8
e-mail: membership@cusj.org
cusj.org
www.facebook.com/groups/cusjca
Overview: A medium-sized national organization founded in 1996
Mission: A national, liberal religious organization, founded to actively promote Unitarian values through social action.
Affliation(s): Canadian Unitarian Council
Chief Officer(s):
Frances Deverell, President
president@cusj.org
Finances: *Annual Operating Budget:* Less than $50,000
Membership: 350 individual
Publications:
• JUSTnews
Type: Newsletter; *Editor:* Philip Symons

Canadian University & College Conference Officers Association *See* Canadian University & College Conference Organizers Association

Canadian University & College Conference Organizers Association (CUCCOA) / Association des coordonnateurs de congrès des universités et des collèges du Canada (ACCUCC)

312 Oakwood Ct., Newmarket ON L3Y 3C8
Tel: 905-954-0102; *Fax:* 905-895-1630
inquiries@cuccoa.org
www.cuccoa.org
Previous Name: Canadian University & College Conference Officers Association
Overview: A small national organization founded in 1978
Mission: Exists for the purpose of information sharing, professional development & group marketing
Chief Officer(s):
Carol Ford, Manager
Finances: *Annual Operating Budget:* $50,000-$100,000
8 volunteer(s)
Membership: 75 institutions; *Fees:* $375; *Member Profile:* Normally restricted to universities & colleges in Canada

Canadian University & College Counselling Association (CUCCA) / Association canadienne de counseling universitaire et collégial

c/o Canadian Association of College & University Student Services, #310, 4 Cataraqui St., Kingston ON K7K 1Z7
Tel: 613-531-9210; *Fax:* 866-303-0626
contact@cacuss.ca
www.eventsmgt.com
Previous Name: University Counselling & Placement Association
Overview: A small national organization founded in 1963
Chief Officer(s):
Chris Mercer, President
Erin Bradford, Secretary/Treasurer
Membership: *Member Profile:* Individuals employed as counsellors & counselling psychologists, at Canadian post-secondary institutions, who counsel educators & graduate students in counselling-related programs
Activities: Providing professional development activities
Awards:
• CUCCA Student Award (Award)
To recognize student innovations in counselling or applied research
• CUCCA Professional Development Award (Award)
One award is available in counselling & another in applied research
• CUCCA Award of Service (Award)
Publications:
• Coast to Coast
Type: Newsletter

Canadian University Football Coaches Association (CUFCA)

c/o Dinos Football, University of Calgary, 2500 University Dr. NW, Calgary AB T2N 1N4
Tel: 403-210-8187
Overview: A small national organization founded in 1977
Mission: To improve the coaching of Canadian Interuniversity Athletic Union (CIAU) football teams; to improve the technical aspects of play in CIAU football
Affliation(s): Canadian Interuniversity Athletic Union
Chief Officer(s):
Blake Nill, President
bnill@ucalgary.ca
Membership: 60 individuals + 24 teams; *Fees:* $40

Canadian University Music Society (CUMS) / Société de musique des universités canadiennes (SMUC)

c/o Secretariat, #202, 10 Morrow Ave., Toronto ON M6R 2J1
Tel: 416-538-1650; *Fax:* 416-489-1713
Other Communication: membership@cums-smuc.ca
journals@interlog.com
www.cums-smuc.ca
Previous Name: Canadian Association of University Schools of Music
Overview: A medium-sized national charitable organization founded in 1979
Mission: To stimulate research, musical performance & composition; to improve instructional methods in university teaching; to provide a forum to exchange views on common problems, scholarly research in music & other matters of professional concern; to advise on new university programs & monitor existing programs
Member of: Humanities & Social Science Federation of Canada
Affliation(s): Social Sciences & Humanities Research Council of Canada
Chief Officer(s):
Mary Ingraham, President
Finances: *Annual Operating Budget:* Less than $50,000; *Funding Sources:* Social Sciences & Humanities Research Council of Canada; membership fees
Staff Member(s): 1
Membership: 45 institutional + 224 faculty & independent scholars + 48 students; *Fees:* $30-$70; *Member Profile:* Active interest in delivery & practice of music at post-secondary level in Canada; *Committees:* Standing Committee of Institutional Members
Awards:
• George Proctor Prize (Award)
Best paper presented by a graduate student at the CUMS annual conference
Meetings/Conferences: • 2015 Canadian University Music Society Annual Meeting, 2015
Scope: National

Canadian University Nursing Students' Association *See* Canadian Nursing Students' Association

Canadian University Press (CUP) / Presse universitaire canadienne

#5, 411 Richmond St. East, Toronto ON M5A 3S5
Tel: 416-962-2287; *Fax:* 416-966-3699
Toll-Free: 866-250-5595
president@cup.ca
www.cup.ca
www.facebook.com/canadianuniversitypress
twitter.com/canunipress
www.youtube.com/user/CUPonline
Overview: A medium-sized national organization founded in 1938
Mission: To elevate the standard of post-secondary student journalism; to foster communication among post-secondary student newspapers; to provide a national press service for post-secondary student newspapers; to provide facilities for the dissemination of news of importance to post-secondary students
Chief Officer(s):
Erin Hudson, President
president@cup.ca
Brendan Kergin, National Bureau Chief
national@cup.ca
Finances: *Annual Operating Budget:* $100,000-$250,000; *Funding Sources:* Membership fees; donations; grants
Staff Member(s): 20
Membership: 84 organizations; *Fees:* $300-$7,000; *Member Profile:* Democratically run post-secondary student newspapers; *Committees:* Caucuses: Women's; Racial Equality; LGBQ; Environment; Commissions: Priorities & Planning; Services & Finance; Membership
Activities: *Internships:* Yes; *Speaker Service:* Yes; *Rents Mailing List:* Yes; *Library:* CUP Resource Centre; by appointment

Canadian Urban Institute (CUI)

PO Box 612, #402, 555 Richmond St. West, Toronto ON M5V 3B1
Tel: 416-365-0816; *Fax:* 416-365-0650
cui@canurb.org
www.canurb.org
www.facebook.com/pages/Canadian-Urban-Institute/265253496954
twitter.com/canurb
Overview: A medium-sized national organization founded in 1990
Chief Officer(s):
Fred Eisenberger, President & Chief Executive Officer, 416-365-0816 Ext. 233
feisenberger@canurb.org
Andrew Farncombe, Vice-President, International Partnerships, 416-365-0816 Ext. 224
afarncombe@canurb.org
Glenn R. Miller, FCIP, RPP, Vice-President, Education & Research, 416-365-0816 Ext. 284
gmiller@canurb.org
Ed Mafa, CMA, Director, Finance, 416-365-0816 Ext. 226
emafa@canurb.org
Lisa Cavicchia, Program Manager, International Partnerships, 416-365-0816 Ext. 223
lcavicchia@canurb.org
Elena Dinu, Program Manager, International Partnerships, 416-365-0816 Ext. 251
edinu@canurb.org
Careesa Gee, Manager, Education & Events, 416-365-0816 Ext. 221
cgee@canurb.org
Simon Geraghty, Senior Engineering Researcher, Urban Solutions, 416-365-0816 Ext. 249
sgeraghty@canurb.org
Katelyn Margerm, Senior Engineering Researcher, 416-365-0816 Ext. 283
kmargerm@canurb.org
Membership: *Fees:* $135
Awards:
• Brownie Awards (Award)
• Urban Leadership Awards (Award)
Publications:
• The Urban Century
Type: Newsletter; *Frequency:* Annually; *Editor:* Philippa Campsi
ISSN: 1206-4599

Canadian Urban Libraries Council (CULC)

#4001, 1 King St. West, Toronto ON M5H 1A1
Tel: 416-699-1938; *Fax:* 866-211-2999
www.culc.ca
Previous Name: Council of Administrators of Large Urban Public Libraries
Overview: A medium-sized national organization founded in 1978
Mission: To identify the issues & choices available in developing urban public library services; to explore the philosophy & principles that govern public library service in urban areas; to comment on the state of public library service in Canada; to facilitate the exchange of ideas & information between member libraries; to influence legislation & financing of urban public libraries; to promote & work in conjunction with other library organizations in Canada to achieve an urban public library service which is comprehensive, economic & efficient; to provide the means for communication & information sharing between members of the public library community; to promote formal & informal cooperation with organizations & institutions in Canada & outside Canada whose goals & objectives are relevant to large urban public library service
Member of: Canadian Library Association; Canadian Association of Public Libraries; International Federation of Library Associations
Chief Officer(s):
Catherine Bliss, Chair
cbiss@markham.library.on.ca
Jefferson Gilbert, Executive Director
jgilbert@culc.ca
Finances: *Funding Sources:* Membership fees
Staff Member(s): 1
Membership: 46; *Fees:* $3500; *Member Profile:* Any single municipal urban public library system or urban library districts serving more than 100,000 population directly interested in aims & objectives of CULC
Activities: *Rents Mailing List:* Yes

Canadian Urban Transit Association (CUTA) / Association canadienne du transport urbain (ACTU)

#1401, 55 York St., Toronto ON M5J 1R7
Tel: 416-365-9800; *Fax:* 416-365-1295
www.cutaactu.ca
Overview: A large national organization founded in 1904
Mission: To represent the public transit community throughout Canada; To strengthen the industry
Chief Officer(s):
Michael W. Roschlau, President & Chief Executive Officer, 416-365-9800 Ext. 104
Becky Benaissa, Director, Finance & Administration, 416-365-9800 Ext. 108
Patrick Leclerc, Director, Marketing & Public Affairs, 613-788-7982
Paré Jean, Director, Research & Technical Services, 416-365-9800 Ext. 109
Nancy Ortenburg, Director, Training & Membership Development, 416-365-9800 Ext. 102
Maureen Shuell, Director, Events & Publications, 416-365-9800 Ext. 105
Membership: 503; *Member Profile:* Transit systems; Manufacturers & suppliers of transit equipment; Federal, provincial, & municipal government agencies; Consultants; Affiliated individuals & companies; *Committees:* Business Members; Communications & Public Affairs; Human Resources; Technical Services; Transit Board Members
Activities: Conducting research & preparing statistics; Providing technical & operational information; Liaising with government; Partnering with other transportation associations & community development stakeholders; Engaging in advocacy activities; Raising public awareness of transit's contributions to communities; *Library:* Canadian Urban Transit Association Library
Meetings/Conferences: • Canadian Urban Transit Association 2015 Annual Conference, May, 2015, Winnipeg, MB
Scope: National
Description: Professional development activities & networking opportunities, held in May or June each year
Contact Information: Phone: 416-365-9800
• Canadian Urban Transit Association 2015 Fall Conference & Trans-Expo, November, 2015, Montréal, QC
Scope: National
Description: An annual technical meeting which also features a display of products & services for sales opportunities & business to business marketing
Contact Information: Phone: 416-365-9800
• Canadian Urban Transit Association 2016 Annual Conference, May, 2016, Halifax, NS
Scope: National
Description: Professional development sessions & the presentation of Corporate Awards, held in May or June each year
• Canadian Urban Transit Association 2016 Fall Conference & Trans-Expo, November, 2016, Vancouver, BC
Scope: National
Description: A yearly technical conference, which also includes the presentation of Employee Awards based on accomplishments in areas such as attendance, safety, & acts of heroism
• Canadian Urban Transit Association 2017 Annual Conference, May, 2017, Montreal, QC
Scope: National
Description: Professional development sessions & the presentation of Corporate Awards, held in May or June each year
• Canadian Urban Transit Association 2017 Fall Conference & Trans-Expo, 2017
Scope: National
Description: A yearly technical conference, which also includes the presentation of Employee Awards based on accomplishments in areas such as attendance, safety, & acts of heroism
Publications:
• Canadian Transit Forum
Type: Magazine; *Frequency:* Y
Profile: Transit industry news in Canada, plus special conference issues in May/June & November/December
• Canadian Urban Transit Association's Buyer's Guide
Type: Guide
Profile: Products & services organized by categories
• CUTA Membership Directory
Type: Directory; *Frequency:* Annually; *Accepts Advertising*; *Price:* $50
Profile: Specific contact details for transit systems, suppliers, government agencies, consultants, & affiliate members
• EXPRESSions
Type: Newsletter; *Frequency:* Semimonthly
Profile: Association activities & forthcoming events
• Transit Vision 2040
Number of Pages: 74
Profile: An industry vision of the role of public transit in Canada

Ottawa Office
#200, 440 Laurier Ave. West, Ottawa ON K1R 7X6
Tel: 613-788-7982; *Fax:* 613-248-7965

Canadian Urethane Foam Contractors Association (CUFCA) / Association canadienne des entrepreneurs en mousse de polyuréthane

3200 Wharton Way, Mississauga ON L4X 2C1
Fax: 877-416-3626
Toll-Free: 866-467-7729
cufca@cufca.ca
www.cufca.ca
Overview: A small national licensing organization founded in 1985
Mission: To champion the polyurethane foam industry in Canada; To maintain high standards in the industry; to ensure the professionalism & profitability of the industry
Chief Officer(s):
Ryan Dalgleish, Executive Director
Andrew B. Cole, Chair
Jean Doucet, Secretary-Treasurer, 418-679-0497
Membership: *Fees:* $500 general membership & contractors; $3,500 manufacturers; *Member Profile:* Manufacturers; Contractors
Activities: Liaising with government agencies; Encouraging professional development; Providing a quality assurance program; Promoting use of ray polyurethane foam; Facilitating research; Publishing; Implementing standards for materials

Canadian Urethane Manufacturers Association (CUMA)

PO Box 5281, Penetanguishene ON L9M 2G4
Tel: 705-427-5383; *Fax:* 705-549-8197
www.cumahome.org
Overview: A medium-sized national organization founded in 1974
Chief Officer(s):
Scott Woodworth, President
Noel Campbell, Manager
manager@cumahome.org
Finances: *Annual Operating Budget:* Less than $50,000

Membership: 45 corporate; *Fees:* $375; *Member Profile:* Urethane processors & suppliers; *Committees:* Health; Safety; Environmental

Canadian Urologic Oncology Group (CUOG)

c/o Dr. Fred Saad, CUOG Chairman, 1560 Sherbrooke est, Montreal QC H2L 4M1
Tel: 514-890-8000
fred.saad.chum@ssss.gouv.qc.ca
www.cuog.org
Overview: A small national organization
Mission: Clinical research investigator network committed to furthering urology research in Canada
Affliation(s): Canadian Urological Association
Chief Officer(s):
Neil Fleshner, Chair
Finances: *Funding Sources:* Investigator agreements; review charges; consultancy fees

Canadian Urological Association (CUA) / Association des urologues du Canada

#1303, 1155, University St., Montréal QC H3B 3A7
Tel: 514-395-0376; *Fax:* 514-395-1664
cua@cua.org
www.cua.org
Overview: A medium-sized national organization founded in 1945
Affliation(s): Canadian Medical Association
Chief Officer(s):
Tiffany Pizioli, Executive Director
tiffany.pizioli@cua.org
Josephine Sciortino, Editorial Director CUAJ
josephine.sciortino@cua.org
Finances: *Annual Operating Budget:* $250,000-$500,000; *Funding Sources:* Annual dues; Annual Meeting; commercial donations
Staff Member(s): 5; 6 volunteer(s)
Membership: 600; *Fees:* $120; *Committees:* Interprovincial socioeconomic & manpower; Guidelines; Research
Activities: Supports CUA Scholarship Foundation to financially aid young researchers in urology
Meetings/Conferences: • Canadian Urological Association 2015 70th Annual Meeting, June, 2015, Westin Hotel, Ottawa, ON
Scope: National
• Canadian Urological Association 2016 71st Annual Meeting, June, 2016, Westin Hotel, Vancouver, BC
Scope: National
• Canadian Urological Association 2017 72nd Annual Meeting, June, 2017, Westin Harbour Castle Hotel, Toronto, ON
Scope: National
• Canadian Urological Association 2018 73rd Annual Meeting, June, 2018, Halifax Convention Centre, Halifax, NS
Scope: National
Attendance: 600
Publications:
• Canadian Urological Association Journal (CUAJ) / Journal de l'Association des urologues du Canada (JAUC)
Type: Journal; *Frequency:* Bimonthly; *Editor:* Dr. Laurence Klotz
Profile: Peer-reviewd original scientific research, reviews, resident studies, & case reports
• CUA News: Newsletter of the Canadian Urological Association
Type: Newsletter; *Frequency:* Semiannually
Profile: CUA activities, programs, events, awards, professional development, & committee reports

Canadian Utilities & Northland Utilities Employees' Association; Alberta Power Employees' Association *See* Canadian Energy Workers' Association

Canadian Vascular Access Association (CVAA) / Association canadienne d'Accès Vasculaire

PO Box 68030, 753 Main St. East, Hamilton ON L8M 3M7
Tel: 289-396-8824; *Fax:* 289-396-1624
cvaa@cvaa.info
www.cvaa.info
www.facebook.com/165776480198722
Previous Name: Canadian Intravenous Nurses Association
Overview: A medium-sized national organization founded in 1975
Mission: To establish & promote standards of intravenous therapy to enhance patient care & safety
Chief Officer(s):
Jocelyn Hill, President
Melissa McQueen, Executive Director
Membership: *Fees:* $110 regular/international; $80 retired; $15,000 platinum company; $10,000 gold company; $6,000 silver company; $3,000 bronze company; *Member Profile:* IV nurses & others involved with IV therapy; *Committees:* Professional Practice; Conference; Chapters & Membership; Constitution & Governance
Activities: *Library:* Documentation Centre
Awards:
• Maisie Townend Scholarship Award (Award)
Amount: Two $500 each
• Medex Canada Inc. Medical Products Editorial Award (Award)
Amount: $1,000
• Poster Presentations Award (Award)
Amount: $250 first prize; $150 second prize; $75 third prize
• Barbara Hill Award (Award)
• Certification Award (Award)
Amount: $100 & a plaque
• CINA Award (Award)
Publications:
• CVAA Journal
Type: Journal; *Price:* $42.80 Canada; $53.50 USA; $58.85 Other
Profile: Information regarding aspects of vascular access therapy
• Mainliner
Type: Newsletter; *Frequency:* Quarterly; *Price:* Free for CVAA members
Profile: Up-to-date information about happenings in the association, health care system, & industry

Winnipeg Chapter
Winnipeg MB
Chief Officer(s):
Belinda Waylett, President
bwaylett@exchange.hsc.mb.ca

Canadian Vehicle Manufacturers' Association (CVMA) / Association canadienne des constructeurs de véhicules

#400, 170 Attwell Dr., Toronto ON M9W 5Z5
Tel: 416-364-9333; *Fax:* 416-367-3221
Toll-Free: 800-758-7122
info@cvma.ca
www.cvma.ca
Previous Name: Canadian Automobile Chamber of Commerce
Overview: A medium-sized national organization founded in 1926
Mission: To create a framework within which member companies work together to achieve shared industry objectives on a range of important issues such as consumer protection, the environment, and vehicle safety
Member of: Canadian Society of Association Executives; Canadian Tax Foundation; Society of Automotive Engineers.
Chief Officer(s):
Mark A. Nantais, President
Finances: *Funding Sources:* Membership fees
Staff Member(s): 5
Membership: 4; *Member Profile:* Chrysler Canada Inc.; Ford Motor Company of Canada, Limited; General Motors of Canada Limited; Navistar Canada, Inc.
Activities: Canadian Motor Vehicle Arbitration Plan; *Speaker Service:* Yes; *Library* by appointment

Canadian Venture Capital Association *See* Canada's Venture Capital & Private Equity Association

Canadian Veterinary Medical Association (CVMA) / Association canadienne des médecins vétérinaires (ACMV)

339 Booth St., Ottawa ON K1R 7K1
Tel: 613-236-1162; *Fax:* 613-236-9681
admin@cvma-acmv.org
www.canadianveterinarians.net
twitter.com/CanVetMedAssoc
Overview: A medium-sized national organization founded in 1948
Mission: To represent the interests of the veterinary profession in Canada; commits to excellence within the profession & to the well-being of animals; promotes public awareness of the contribution of animals & veterinarians to society
Chief Officer(s):
Jost Am Rhyn, Executive Director, 613-236-1162 Ext. 114
Suzanne Lavictoire, Director, Membership Services & Communications, 613-236-1162 Ext. 118
slavictoire@cvma-acmv.org
Finances: *Annual Operating Budget:* $1.5 Million-$3 Million
Staff Member(s): 17
Membership: *Member Profile:* Graduates in veterinary medicine; *Committees:* National Issues; Animal Welfare; Business Management; Animal Health Technology/Veterinary Technician Accreditation Program; Professional Development; Environmental Advisory Group; National Examination Board; Editorial; Students of the CVMA; Student Liaison Advisory Group; CVMA Insurance Advisory Group
Activities: *Awareness Events:* Animal Health Week, Oct.
Awards:
• CVMA Industry Award (Award)
• Hill's Public Relations Award (Award)
• CVMA Award (Award)
Established 1966; awarded annually to a veterinary student in the third year at each of the four Canadian veterinary colleges; the recipient is selected by his/her classmates on the basis of achievement & leadership in student affairs
• R.V.L. Walker Award (Award)
Established 1986; awarded to an undergraduate student in one of the four veterinary colleges in Canada who has made the greatest contribution in promoting student interest in the Association; the recipient should have demonstrated active interest in student & college affairs & have a satisfactory student record
• The Schering Veterinary Award (Award)
Established 1985 to enhance progress in large animal medicine & surgery; award made to a veterinarian whose work in large animal practice, clinical research or basic sciences is judged to have contributed significantly to the advancement of large animal medicine, surgery & theriogenology, including herd health management; $1,000 & a plaque awarded
• CVMA Pet Food Certification & Nutrition Award (Award)
• The Small Animal Practitioner Award (Award)
Established 1987 to encourage progress in the field of small animal medicine & surgery; awarded to a veterinarian whose work in small animal practice, clinical research or basic sciences is judged to have contributed significantly to the advancement of small animal medicine, surgery, or the management of small animal practice, including the advancement of the public's knowledge of the responsibilities of pet ownership; $1,000 & a plaque awarded
• The CVMA Humane Award (Award)
Established 1986 to encourage care & well-being of animals; awarded to an individual (veterinarian or non-veterinarian) whose work is judged to have contributed significantly to the welfare & well-being of animals; $1,000 & a plaque awarded
Meetings/Conferences: • Canadian Veterinary Medical Association 2015 Convention and Annual General Meeting, July, 2015, Calgary, AB
Scope: National
Publications:
• Canadian Journal of Veterinary Research
Type: Journal; *Frequency:* Quarterly
• Canadian Veterinary Journal
Type: Journal; *Frequency:* Monthly

Canadian Vintage Motorcycle Group (CVMG)

33 Station Rd., Toronto ON M8V 2R1
e-mail: secretary@cvmg.ca
www.amcm.ca
Overview: A medium-sized national organization founded in 1968
Chief Officer(s):
Bill Hoar, President
president@cvmg.ca
Betty Anne Clark, Correspondence Secretary
Anthony Petti, Membership Secretary
membership@cvmg.ca
Membership: 1,700;

Canadian Vintners Association (CVA) / L'Association des vignerons du Canada

#200, 440 Laurier Ave. West, Ottawa ON K1R 7X6
Tel: 613-782-2283; *Fax:* 613-782-2239
info@canadianvintners.com
www.canadianvintners.com
www.facebook.com/CVAwine
twitter.com/cvawine
Previous Name: Canadian Wine Institute
Overview: A medium-sized national organization founded in 2001
Mission: To formulate & promote policies that will advance the interests & goals of the Canadian wine sector.
Member of: International Federation of Wine & Spirits; Alberta Liquor Industry RoundTable; World Wine Trade Group; Alcohol in Moderation
Affliation(s): Wine Council of Ontario; British Columbia Wine Institute, Winery Association of Nova Scotia
Chief Officer(s):
Dan Paszkowski, President & CEO

Staff Member(s): 4
Membership: 60 corporate; *Member Profile:* Licenced wineries & regional winery associations

Canadian Viola Society

c/o Ann Frederking, 2030 Woodglen Cres., Ottawa ON K1J 6G4
www.viola.ca
Overview: A small national organization
Mission: To improve communication among violists & enthusiasts both in Canada & worldwide
Affliation(s): International Viola Society
Chief Officer(s):
Jutta Puchhammer-Sédillot, President
president@viola.ca
Membership: *Fees:* $24 student/emeritus; $40 active; *Member Profile:* Musicians, amateurs & professionals

Canadian Vocational Association (CAV) / Association canadienne de la formation professionnelle (ACFP)

c/o Ms Jane Louks, PO Box 816, Ottawa ON K0A 2Z0
Tel: 613-838-3244; *Fax:* 613-838-5930
cva-acfp.org
www.linkedin.com/groups/Canadian-Vocational-Association-Association-ca
twitter.com/CVA_ACFP
Overview: A small national organization founded in 1960
Mission: A non-profit organization to promote and foster education and training which leads to occupational competence.
Chief Officer(s):
Pierre Morin, President, 450-812-7510
pmforminc@gmail.com
Membership: *Member Profile:* Post-secondary and secondary educational institutions, the business community and government officials from across Canada as well as internationally.
Publications:
• CVA Journal
Type: Journal; *Frequency:* Quarterly

Canadian Volkssport Federation (CVF) / Fédération canadienne volkssport (FCV)

PO Box 2668, Stn. D, Ottawa ON K1P 5W7
Tel: 613-234-7333
cvffcv@bellnet.ca
www.walks.ca
www.facebook.com/groups/VolkssportCanada
Overview: A medium-sized national organization founded in 1987
Mission: To promote non-competitive participation in walking & other recreational activities for fun, fitness & friendship
Member of: International Federation of Popular Sports
Chief Officer(s):
Ethel Hansen, President
ethelh@shaw.ca
Finances: *Annual Operating Budget:* Less than $50,000; *Funding Sources:* Sanctioning fees
Staff Member(s): 1; 150 volunteer(s)
Membership: 51 clubs; *Fees:* $50 club; *Member Profile:* Mostly ages 35-70; *Committees:* Board of Directors; Executive
Activities: Walking; swimming; skating; skiing - all non-competitively; *Speaker Service:* Yes
Awards:
• IVV's Individual Achievement Awards Program (Award)
Publications:
• Volkssport Canada
Type: Newsletter; *Frequency:* Quarterly; *Accepts Advertising*; *Price:* $15 Canada; $20 International
Profile: Canadian volkssporting events & recent developments

Canadian Warmblood Horse Breeders Association (CWHBA)

PO Box 21100, 2105 - 8th St. East, Saskatoon SK S7H 5N9
Tel: 306-373-6620; *Fax:* 306-374-0646
office@canadianwarmbloods.com
www.canadianwarmbloods.com
www.facebook.com/CanadianWarmblood
Overview: A small national organization founded in 1991
Mission: To further warmblood horse breeding in Canada through the provision of information to breeders & the maintenance of a uniform breeding program
Chief Officer(s):
Chris Gould, President
Chairman@canadianwarmbloods.com
Charmaine Bergman, Secretary-Treasurer
Secretary@canadianwarmbloods.com
Katryna, Office Manager
Membership: *Member Profile:* Breeders, owners, & friends of warmblood horses in Canada
Activities: Maintaining the Stud Book of Canadian Warmblood horses; Providing stallion & provincial mare inspections; Uniting warmblood horse breeders; Offering educational opportunities; Promoting breed shows & exhibitions; Increasing public understanding of Canadian warmblood horses
Awards:
• CWHBA Year-end High-point Awards (Award)
• CWHBA Ogilvy Equestrian Summer Circuit Awards (Award)
• CWHBA Achievement Award (Award)
• CWHBA Lifetime Performance Award (Award)
Publications:
• Breeder's Digest
Type: Newsletter; *Accepts Advertising*
• Stallion Directory
Type: Directory; *Frequency:* Annually

Canadian Warplane Heritage (CWH)

9280 Airport Rd., Mount Hope ON L0R 1W0
Tel: 905-679-4183; *Fax:* 905-679-4186
Toll-Free: 877-347-3359
museum@warplane.com
www.warplane.com
Also Known As: Canada's Flying Museum
Overview: A medium-sized national charitable organization founded in 1971
Mission: To acquire documents; perserve & maintain a complete collection of aircraft that were flown by Canadians & the Canadian military services from the beginning of World War II to the present, including other related aviation artifacts & memorabilia of significant historic importance to this period; to instruct, educate & entertain the general public through the maintenance & rotation of displays, flight demonstrations, special events & activities, & to encourage Canadians of all ages to become actively involved in the preservation of these aircraft & artifacts; to provide facilities for the restoration & protection, interpretation & exhibits of the collection; to maintain supportive exhibits in tribute to the thousands of men & women who built, serviced & flew these aircraft & in memory of those who did not return
Chief Officer(s):
Pamela Rickards, Vice President of Operations, 905-679-4183 Ext. 230
pam@warplane.com
Al Mickeloff, Manager, Marketing, 905-679-4183 Ext. 233
amickeloff@warplane.com
Finances: *Annual Operating Budget:* $3 Million-$5 Million; *Funding Sources:* Membership fees; grants; donations
Staff Member(s): 20; 300 volunteer(s)
Membership: 33,000; *Fees:* $100 adult; *Member Profile:* Interest in Canadian aviation/history
Activities: *Awareness Events:* Remembrance Day; *Internships:* Yes; *Speaker Service:* Yes; *Library* by appointment

Canadian Water & Wastewater Association (CWWA) / Association canadienne des eaux potables et usées (ACEPU)

#11, 1010 Polytek St., Ottawa ON K1J 9H9
Tel: 613-747-0524; *Fax:* 613-747-0523
admin@cwwa.ca
www.cwwa.ca
www.linkedin.com/company/canadian-water-and-wastewater-association
www.facebook.com/117350581695487
twitter.com/CWWACEPU
Overview: A medium-sized national organization founded in 1986
Mission: To represent the common interests of Canadian municipal water & wastewater systems to federal & interprovincial bodies
Member of: Canadian National Committee for the International Water Association
Chief Officer(s):
Dan Limacher, President
Staff Member(s): 8
Membership: *Member Profile:* Utility members are owners or operators of municipal infrastructure or services; Associate members are the private sector & academics; Subscription members are federal, provincial, or territorial government departments or agencies; *Committees:* Wastewater & Stormwater; National Water Efficiency; Drinking Water Quality; Water Protection Information; Biosolids; Energy
Activities: Monitoring policies, legislation, & standards; Liaising with federal & interprovincial organizations; Hosting workshops; Facilitating networking opportunities; Increasing & improving public awareness; Cooperating with regional water & wastewater associations
Awards:
• Steve Bonk Scholarship (Scholarship)
To provide educational assistance to persons embarking on careers associated with municipal water supply or wastewater *Amount:* $500
• Utility Excellence Awards (Award)
Awards for utility programs & initiatives in the areas of community outreach & risk taking
Meetings/Conferences: • Canadian Water & Wastewater Association 2015 National Water & Wastewater Conference, October, 2015, Whistler, BC
Scope: National
Description: An exchange of news & views from Canadian utility conservation specialists
Contact Information: Phone: 613-747-0524; Fax: 613-747-0523; E-mail: admin@cwwa.ca
Publications:
• Canadian Municipal Water News & Review / Journal et faits sur l'eau municipale canadienne
Type: Magazine; *Frequency:* Semiannually; *Accepts Advertising*
Profile: National & international news & events
• Canadian Water & Wastewater Association Conference Proceedings
• CWWA [Canadian Water & Wastewater Association] Membership Directory
Type: Directory; *Accepts Advertising*
Profile: Directory acts as association information as well as a buyers' guide
• CWWA [Canadian Water & Wastewater Association] Bulletin
Type: Newsletter; *Frequency:* 10 pa; *Accepts Advertising*
Profile: National information on water & wastewater developments, for CWWA members
• CWWA Members' Briefing Book: Current National Issues & Topics Concerning Water & Wastewater Management in Canada
Frequency: Quarterly
Profile: Briefing notes on current management topics that are national in nature, to assist managers & operators
• Directory of Sources of Contaminants Entering Municipal Sewer Systems
Type: Directory
Profile: Aid in identifying industrial, commercial, & institutional sources of contaminants entering municipal sewage treatment plants
• Guideline on Sampling, Handling, Transporting, & Analyzing Legal Wastewater Samples
• Meters Made Easy: A Guide to the Economic Appraisal of Alternative Metering Investment Strategies
Type: Guidebook
Profile: A tool to assist system owners & operators determine whether the introduction of meters will produce long-term savings inther community
• Municipal Water & Wastewater Rate Manual
Type: Manual
Profile: New & alternative approaches to traditional & current rate setting methods
• Municipal Water & Wastewater Rates Primer
Type: Monograph
Profile: An overview of topics on rate setting
• National Water Works Operator Training Manuals
Type: Manual
• Survey on Chloramine in Drinking Water Disinfection
• Water Safety Plans for Municipal Drinking Water Systems
Profile: Hazard Analysis & Critical Control Points (HACCP) plan for the source, treatment, & distribution of drinking water in Canada
• Water Treatment Principles & Applications

Canadian Water Network (CWN) / Réseau canadien de l'eau

University of Waterloo, 200 University Ave. West, Waterloo ON N2L 3G1
Tel: 519-888-4567; *Fax:* 519-883-7574
info@cwn-rce.ca
www.cwn-rce.ca
www.linkedin.com/company/canadian-water-network
www.facebook.com/CanadianWaterNetwork
twitter.com/CdnWaterNetwork
Overview: A medium-sized national organization founded in 2001
Mission: To create a national partnership in innovation that promotes environmentally responsible stewardship & opportunities with respect to Canada's water resources resulting

in sustained prosperity & improved quality of life for Canadians.
Member of: Networks of Centres of Excellence
Chief Officer(s):
Bernadette Conant, Executive Director, 519-888-4567
bconant@cwn-rce.ca
Mark Servos, Scientific Director, 519-888-4567 Ext. 36034
mservos@uwaterloo.ca
Finances: *Annual Operating Budget:* $3 Million-$5 Million
Staff Member(s): 8
Membership: 48 industrial, 65 government, 120 researchers, 200 students; *Fees:* None
Activities: Research funding, student development, national networking; *Internships:* Yes

Canadian Water Quality Association (CWQA)

#330, 295 The West Mall, Toronto ON M9C 4Z4
Tel: 416-695-3068; *Fax:* 416-695-2945
Toll-Free: 866-383-7617
k.wong@cwqa.com
www.cwqa.com
www.linkedin.com/groups/Canadian-Water-Quality-Association-3948494
Overview: A medium-sized national organization founded in 1967
Mission: To promote the individual right to quality water; To educate water quality professionals; To promote the growth of the water quality improvement industry; To serve as a unified voice in government & public relations; To provide a role in consumer education
Chief Officer(s):
Kevin Wong, Executive Director
Staff Member(s): 5
Membership: 106 dealers/distributors + 16 manufacturers/suppliers + 10 associates; *Fees:* $355 associate; Based on volume for dealer/distributor & manufacturer/supplier
Meetings/Conferences: • Canadian Water Quality Association 2015 Annual General Meeting, 2015
Scope: National
Publications:
• Canadian Water Quality Association Membership Directory
Type: Directory
Profile: A listing of members by their head office or main facility, for use by Canadian Water Quality Association members only
• Communiqué [a publication of the Canadian Water Quality Association]
Frequency: 11 pa

Canadian Water Resources Association (CWRA) / Association canadienne des ressources hydriques (ACRH)

c/o Membership Office, 9 Covus Crt., Ottawa ON K2E 7Z4
Tel: 613-237-9363; *Fax:* 613-594-5190
services@aic.ca
www.cwra.org
Overview: A large national charitable organization founded in 1948
Mission: To encourage recognition of the high priority & value of water
Affliation(s): Canadian Water & Wasterwater Association; International Water Resources Association; American Water Resources Association; British Hydological Society; American Institute of Hydrology
Chief Officer(s):
F.A. (Rick) Ross, Executive Director & Editor, Water News, 403-317-0017
executivedirector@cwra.org
André Saint-Hilaire, President, 418-654-3113
andre_st-hilaire@ete.inrs.ca
Paul H. Whitfield, Co-Editor, Canadian Water Resources Journal, 604-664-9238, Fax: 604-664-9004
paul.whitfield@ec.gc.ca
Brenda Toth, Secretary
Ed Dean, Treasurer
Membership: *Member Profile:* Individuals & organizations interested in the management of Canada's water resources, including private & public sector water resource managers, administrators, scientists, academics, students, & users
Activities: Increasing awareness & understanding of Canada's water resources; Providing a forum for the exchange of information; Participating with appropriate agencies in international water management activities
Awards:
• Ken Thompson Scholarship (Scholarship)
• Dillon Scholarship (Scholarship)
• The Hoskin Scientific Award (Award)
• Bill Stolte Student Paper Award (Award)
Meetings/Conferences: • 2015 Canadian Water Resource Association 68th National Confernece, June, 2015, Radisson Hotel, Winnipeg, MB
Scope: National
Publications:
• Canadian Perspectives on Integrated Water Resources Management
Type: Book; *Number of Pages:* 123; *Editor:* Dan Shrubsole; *Price:* $23
• Canadian Water Resources Association Conference Proceedings

• Canadian Water Resources Journal
Type: Journal; *Frequency:* Quarterly; *Editor:* Paul H. Whitfield
ISSN: 0701-1784
Profile: Research articles, technical notes, & review papers
• CWRA [Canadian Water Resources Association] Water News
Type: Newsletter; *Frequency:* Quarterly; *Editor:* F.A. (Rick) Ross
Profile: National & branch activities, international water resource information, a technical supplement, & a profile article
• Hydroscan: Airborne Laser Mapping of Hydrological Features & Resources
Type: Book; *Editor:* Chris Hopkinson et al.; *Price:* $15
• Predictions in Ungauged Basins
Type: Book; *Editor:* C. Spence et al.; *Price:* $15
• Reflections on Water: CWRA 1947 - 1997
Type: Book; *Author:* B. Mitchell; Robert de Loe; *Price:* $20

Canadian Water Ski Association *See* Water Ski & Wakeboard Canada

Canadian Water Well Association *See* Canadian Ground Water Association

Canadian Welding Bureau (CWB)

8260 Parkhill Dr., Milton ON L9T 5V7
Fax: 905-542-1318
Toll-Free: 800-844-6790
info@cwbgroup.org
www.cwbgroup.org
www.facebook.com/134949822909
twitter.com/cwbgroupandcwa
www.youtube.com/user/cwbgroup
Overview: A medium-sized national organization founded in 1947
Mission: To administrator certification programs for CSA Standards W47.1, W47.2, W186, W178.1 & W48 series; to provide support for welding-based programs in schools, education institutions, welding professionals & companies employing welding technology.
Chief Officer(s):
Douglas Luciano, President
Membership: 7,600 clients
Activities: *Speaker Service:* Yes; *Library:* Gooderham Centre for Industrial Learning

Alberta Region
#206, 2528 Ellwood Dr., Edmonton AB T6X 0A9
Toll-Free: 800-844-6790
info@cwbgroup.org
Chief Officer(s):
Bill Boyko, Regional Manager, Western Operations

Atlantic Region
#304, 73 Tacoma Dr., Dartmouth NS B2W 3Y6
Toll-Free: 800-844-6790
info@cwbgroup.org
Chief Officer(s):
Yvon Sénéchal, Regional Manager, Eastern Operations

Ontario Region
8260 Parkhill Dr., Milton ON L9T 5V7
Toll-Free: 800-844-6790
info@cwbgroup.org
Chief Officer(s):
Luis Romero, Regional Manager, Ontario

Québec Region
4321 Autoroute des Laurentides, Laval QC H7L 5W5
Toll-Free: 800-844-6790
info@cwbgroup.org
Chief Officer(s):
Yvon Sénéchal, Regional Manager, Eastern Operations

Western Region
#203, 1555 St. James St., Winnipeg MB R3H 1B5
Toll-Free: 800-844-6790
info@cwbgroup.org
Chief Officer(s):
Darcy Yantz, Regional Manager, Western Operations

Canadian Welfare Council *See* Canadian Council on Social Development

Canadian Well Logging Society (CWLS)

Scotia Centre, #2200, 700 - 2nd St. SW, Calgary AB T2P 2W1
Tel: 403-269-9366; *Fax:* 403-269-2787
www.cwls.org
Overview: A medium-sized national organization founded in 1957
Chief Officer(s):
Mike Seifert, Membership Chair, 403-269-3644
seifertm@telus.net
Harold S. Hovdebo, President, 403-750-5058
harold.hovdebo@huskyenergy.ca
Finances: *Annual Operating Budget:* Less than $50,000; *Funding Sources:* Membership fees; corporate sponsors
Membership: 500; *Fees:* $40; *Member Profile:* Oil industry petrophysical interests
Publications:
• CWLS [Canadian Well Logging Society] InSite
Type: Newsletter; *Frequency:* Quarterly; *Accepts Advertising*; *Editor:* Tyler Maksymchuk & Kelly Skuce; *Price:* Free with CWLS membership
Profile: Short articles, & upcoming events to inform CWLS members
• CWLS [Canadian Well Logging Society] Journal
Type: Journal; *Frequency:* Biennially; *Price:* Free with CWLS membership
Profile: Formal papers for people interested in formation evaluation
• CWLS [Canadian Well Logging Society] Annual Report
Type: Yearbook; *Frequency:* Annually; *Price:* Free with Canadian Well Logging Society membership

Canadian Welsh Black Cattle Society (CWBCS) / Société Canadienne des bovins Welsh Black

c/o Canadian Livestock Records Corporation, 2417 Holly Lane, Ottawa ON K1V 0M7
Tel: 613-731-7110; *Fax:* 613-731-0704
www.clrc.ca/welshblack.shtml
Overview: A small national organization founded in 1971
Chief Officer(s):
Randy Scott, President, 403-854-2135, Fax: 403-854-2135
Randy Kaiser, Vice-President
Arlin Strohschein, Secretary-Treasurer, 403-442-4372
Membership: *Fees:* $25; $150 lifetime; *Committees:* Bulletin; Website; Advertising & Promotions
Activities: Providing information about the Canadian Welsh black cattle breed
Publications:
• Breeders Directory
Type: Directory
Profile: Contact information for breeders of Canadian Welsh black cattle
• The Welsh Black Bulletin
Type: Newsletter; *Accepts Advertising*; *Editor:* Randy Scott

Canadian Western Agribition Association (CWA)

PO Box 3535, Regina SK S4P 3J8
Tel: 306-565-0565; *Fax:* 306-757-9963
info@agribition.com
www.agribition.com
Overview: A medium-sized local organization founded in 1971
Mission: To create an atmosphere to promote Canadian agricultural products & their development; to host the annual Canadian Western Agribition to increase interest in agriculture
Chief Officer(s):
Bryan Hadland, President
bhadland@sasktel.net
Matt Seymour, CEO & General Manager, 306-924-9600
mseymour@agribition.com
Sylvia Boyko, Manager, Finance & Office, 306-924-9583
sboyko@agribition.com
Finances: *Funding Sources:* Sponsorships
Activities: Providing educational information to the agricultural industry & the public; Encouraging competition; Promoting urban-rural relations; *Awareness Events:* Canadian Western Agribition, November
Publications:
• Ambassador
Type: Newsletter; *Frequency:* 5 pa
Profile: Agribition programs, shows, sponsors, awards, & livestock

Canadian Wheelchair Basketball Association (CWBA) / Association canadienne de basketball en fauteuil roulant (ACBFR)

#8, 6 Antares Dr., Phase 1, Ottawa ON K2E 8A9
Tel: 613-260-1296; *Fax:* 613-260-1456
Toll-Free: 877-843-2922
info@wheelchairbasketball.ca
www.wheelchairbasketball.ca
www.facebook.com/wheelchairbasketball
twitter.com/WCBballCanada
www.youtube.com/user/WheelchairBball
Also Known As: Wheelchair Basketball Canada
Overview: A medium-sized national charitable organization founded in 1994
Mission: To act as the governing body for wheelchair basketball in Canada
Member of: Canadian Paralympic Committee; International Wheelchair Basketball Federation
Affliation(s): Canada Basketball
Chief Officer(s):
Wendy Gittens, Executive Director
wgittens@wheelchairbasketball.ca
Paul Zachau, Director, High Performance
pzachau@wheelchairbasketball.ca
Jody Kingsbury, Manager, Communications
jkingsbury@wheelchairbasketball.ca
Catherine Ireland, Coordinator, Programs
Courtney Pollock, Coordinator, Communications
cpollock@wheelchairbasketball.ca
Ryan Lauzon, Coordinator, High Performance
rlauzon@wheelchairbasketball.ca
Staff Member(s): 11
Membership: 2,500
Publications:
• Around The Rim [a publication of the Canadian Wheelchair Basketball Association]
Type: Newsletter
• CWBA [Canadian Wheelchair Basketball Association] Annual Report
Type: Yearbook; *Frequency:* Annually

Canadian Wheelchair Sports Association (CWSA) / Association canadienne des sports en fauteuil roulant (ACSFR)

#108, 2255 St. Laurent Blvd., Ottawa ON K1G 4K3
Tel: 613-523-0004; *Fax:* 613-523-0149
info@cwsa.ca
www.cwsa.ca
www.facebook.com/wheelchairrugbycanada
twitter.com/wcrugbycanada
www.youtube.com/wheelsportscanada
Overview: A large national charitable organization founded in 1967
Mission: To promote excellence & develop opportunities for Canadians in wheelchair sport
Affliation(s): International Stoke Mandeville Wheelchair Sports Federation
Chief Officer(s):
Donald Royer, President
Cathy Cadieux, Executive Director
ccadieux@cwsa.ca
Duncan Campbell, Director, National Development, 604-333-3539, Fax: 604-333-3450
duncancampbell@cwsa.ca
Andy Van Neutegem, Director, High Performance, Fax: 250-220-2501
andyvan@cwsa.ca
Don Lane, Manager, Program, 613-523-0004, Fax: 613-523-0149
dlane@cwsa.ca
Arley McNeney, Coordinator, Communications, Fax: 604-333-3450
arley@cwsa.ca
Finances: *Funding Sources:* Federal government; Independent corporations; General public; Man in Motion Foundation
Staff Member(s): 7
Membership: *Member Profile:* Wheelchair athletes
Activities: Offering high performance sport programs for rugby; Engaging in advocacy activities

Canadian Wholesale Drug Association ***See*** Canadian Association for Pharmacy Distribution Management

Canadian Wildflower Society ***See*** North American Native Plant Society

Canadian Wildlife Federation (CWF) / Fédération canadienne de la faune

350 Michael Cowpland Dr., Kanata ON K2M 2W1
Tel: 613-599-9594; *Fax:* 613-599-4428
Toll-Free: 800-563-9453
info@cwf-fcf.org
www.cwf-fcf.org
www.facebook.com/pages/Canadian-Wildlife-Federation/778724 9430
twitter.com/CWF_FCF
www.youtube.com/user/CanadianWildlifeFed
Overview: A large national charitable organization founded in 1961
Mission: To promote the conservation of fish & wildlife, wildlife habitat & quality aquatic environments; To foster an understanding of natural processes; To ensure adequate stocks of wildlife for the use & enjoyment of all Canadians; To sponsor research; To cooperate with legislators, government & non-government agencies in achieving conservation objectives
Member of: World Conservation Union
Chief Officer(s):
Dave Powell, President
Lloyd Lintott, First Vice-President
Bob Morris, Second Vice-President
Guy Vezina, Secretary
John Ford, Treasurer
Finances: *Funding Sources:* Membership fees; Sales of merchandise; Donations
Membership: 300,000; *Fees:* $25; *Committees:* Affiliate; Associate Member; Audit; Awards; Constitution; Credentials; Energy; Environment; Fisheries; Forestry; Native Affairs; Nominating; Parks; Resolutions; Wildlife
Activities: Offering educational programs; Engaging in advocacy activities concering national & international conservation & environmental issues; *Awareness Events:* National Wildlife Week, April; Canadian Rivers Day, June; *Speaker Service:* Yes; *Rents Mailing List:* Yes; *Library* Open to public by appointment
Awards:
• Doug Clarke Memorial Award (Award), Canadian Conservation Achievement Awards Program
Presented annually to a Canadian Wildlife Federation affiliate for the most outstanding conservation project completed during the previous year by the affiliate or its clubs or members *Contact:* Sandy Baugartner
• Stan Hodgkiss Outdoorsman of the Year Award (Award), Canadian Conservation Achievement Awards Program
Presented annually to an outdoorsperson who has demonstrated an active commitment to conservation in Canada
• Roland Michener Conservation Award (Award), Canadian Conservation Achievement Awards Program
A trophy is given annually in recognition of an individual's outstanding achievement in the field of conservation in Canada
• Roderick Haig-Brown Memorial Award (Award), Canadian Conservation Achievement Awards Program
Awarded annually to an individual who has made a significant contribution to furthering the sport of angling &/or conservation & wise use of Canada's recreational fisheries resources
• Past Presidents' Canadian Legislator Award (Award), Canadian Conservation Achievement Awards Program
Presented annually to an elected provincial, territorial or federal legislator in recognition of a significant contribution toward the conservation of wildlife in Canada *Contact:* Sandy Baugartner
Publications:
• Biosphère [a publication of the Canadian Wildlife Federation]
Frequency: Bimonthly
Profile: French language edition of Canadian Wildlife, for young adults & adults
• Canadian Wildlife [a publication of the Canadian Wildlife Federation]
Type: Magazine; *Frequency:* Bimonthly
Profile: Stories about Canadian & international wildlife, plus CWF news & reports, for young adults & adults
• Wild [a publication of the Canadian Wildlife Federation]
Type: Magazine; *Frequency:* 8 pa
Profile: Educational information & games, for children between the ages of 6 & 12
• Your Big Backyard
Type: Magazine; *Frequency:* Monthly
Profile: Easy-to-read nature information, puzzles, & games, for children between the ages of 3 & 5

Canadian Wind Energy Association Inc. (CanWEA) / Association canadienne d'énergie éolienne

#710, 1600 Carling Ave., Ottawa ON K1Z 1G3
Tel: 613-234-8716; *Fax:* 613-234-5642
Toll-Free: 800-922-6932
info@canwea.ca
www.canwea.ca
www.facebook.com/163408037028327
twitter.com/canwindenergy
www.youtube.com/canwea
Overview: A small national organization founded in 1984
Mission: To promote the social, economic, & environmental benefits of wind energy in Canada; To encourage the appropriate development & application of wind energy; To create suitable environmental policy
Chief Officer(s):
Robert Hornung, President
Ariane Sabourin, Manager, Communications & Marketing
Jean-François Nolet, Vice-President, Policy & Government Affairs
Patrick Kirby, Bookkeeper, Finance
Sharon Fryer, Manager, Meetings and Events
Finances: *Funding Sources:* Membership fees; Conference & workshop fees
Membership: 420; *Member Profile:* Organizations & individuals who are involved in the development & application of wind energy technology, products, & services in Canada
Activities: Providing information about wind energy; Offering networking opportunities for all stakeholders; Facilitating research; Forming strategic alliances; *Library:* Canadian Wind Energy Association Library; by appointment
Awards:
• Individual Leadership Award (Award)
Awarded to an individual who has significantly advanced the wind energy industry in Canada.
• Group Leadership Award (Award)
Awarded to the government, corporation or non-profit organization that has contributed significantly to the advancement of wind energy in Canada.
• R.J. Templin Award (Award)
Awarded to any individual or organization who has undertaken scientific, technical, engineering or policy work that has significantly advanced the wind energy industry in Canada.
• Friend of Wind Award (Award)
Awarded in recognition of outstanding contributions made by individuals or groups in advancing awareness of the benefits of wind energy at the community level.
• The Matt Holder Community Connection Award (Award)
Awarded to an organization or individual who embodies the mandate of responsible development through a commitment to understand and build meaningful relationships with host communities.
Meetings/Conferences: • Canadian Wind Energy Association (CanWEA) 31st Annual Conference and Exhibition, October, 2015, Metro Toronto Convention Centre, Toronto, ON
Scope: National
Attendance: 2000
Description: To discuss the opportunities and latest developments in the wind energy industry.
Contact Information: events@canwea.ca
• Canadian Wind Energy Association (CanWEA) 32nd Annual Conference and Exhibition, 2016
Scope: National
Description: To discuss the opportunities and latest developments in the wind energy industry.
Contact Information: events@canwea.ca
Publications:
• CanWEA Members Directory
Type: Directory
Profile: Contact information & a profile of each CanWEA member
• WindLink
Type: Newsletter; *Frequency:* Semimonthly
Profile: Issues & events that affect the Canadian wind energy for CanWEA members, policymakers, & the public
• WindSight
Type: Magazine; *Frequency:* Quarterly
Profile: Detailed articles on Canadian wind energy projects & policy

Canadian Window & Door Manufacturers Association ***See*** Fenestration Canada

Canadian Wine Institute ***See*** Canadian Vintners Association

Canadian Wire Service Guild ***See*** Canadian Media Guild

Canadian Wireless Telecommunications Association (CWTA) / Association canadienne des télécommunications sans fil (ACTS)
#300, 80 Elgin St., Ottawa ON K1P 6R2
Tel: 613-233-4888; *Fax:* 613-233-2032
info@cwta.ca
www.cwta.ca
twitter.com/CWTAwireless
Previous Name: Radiocomm Association of Canada
Overview: A medium-sized national licensing charitable organization founded in 1970
Mission: The authority on wireless issues, trends & developments in Canada; represents cellular, PCS, messaging, mobile radio, fixed wireless & mobile satellite service providers as well as companies that develop & produce products & services for the industry.
Chief Officer(s):
Bernard Lord, President & Chief Executive Officer
blord@cwta.ca
Patrick Jim, Senior Vice-President
jpatrick@cwta.ca
Geiger J. Michael, Manager, IT
mgeiger@cwta.ca
Finances: *Funding Sources:* Membership fees; seminars; conferences; publications
Staff Member(s): 19
Membership: 182; *Fees:* Schedule available
Activities: *Rents Mailing List:* Yes

Canadian Women for Women in Afghanistan
PO Box 86016, Stn. Marda Loop, Calgary AB T2T 6B7
Tel: 403-244-5625
info@cw4wafghan.ca
www.cw4wafghan.ca
www.facebook.com/cw4wafghan
twitter.com/CW4WAfghan
Overview: A small national organization founded in 1996
Mission: CWWA is a volunteer, not-for-profit organization committed to supporting the empowerment of Afghan women and girls, with a network of chapters across Canada. It is registered charity, BN: 887718203RR0001.
Chief Officer(s):
Madeliene Tarasick, President
President@CW4WAfghan.ca
Janice Eisenhauer, Executive Director
ExecutiveDirector@CW4WAfghan.ca
Activities: Breaking Bread, a do-it-yourself potluck fundraiser, breakingbread@cw4wafghan.ca

Canadian Women in Communications (CWC) / Association canadienne des femmes en communication (AFC)
#300, 116 Lisgar St., Ottawa ON K2P 0C2
Tel: 613-706-0607; *Fax:* 613-706-0612
Toll-Free: 800-361-2978
cwcafc@cwc-afc.com
www.cwc-afc.com
Previous Name: Canadian Women in Radio & Television
Overview: A medium-sized national organization founded in 1991
Mission: To advance the role of women in the communications sector
Member of: The International Alliance for Women
Chief Officer(s):
Joanne Stanley, Executive Director, 613-706-0607 Ext. 102
jstanley@cwc-afc.com
Finances: *Annual Operating Budget:* $500,000-$1.5 Million; *Funding Sources:* Corporate
Staff Member(s): 5; 150 volunteer(s)
Membership: 1,500; *Fees:* $132.50 professional; $42.40 student; $99.38 Diamond; $112.63 Platinum; $119.25 Gold; *Committees:* Women on Boards; Strategic Review; Nominations & Governance; Communications & Membership; Chapter Liaison; Jeanne Sauvé; Annual Awards; Treasurer; Fundraising
Activities: Hosting an annual awards gala & chapter events;
Awards:
• CWC Annual Awards (Award)
• Jeanne Sauvé Professional Development Program (Scholarship)
• Career Accelerator Programs (Scholarship)
• CWC/CBC Transformer Award (Award)

Canadian Women in Radio & Television *See* Canadian Women in Communications

Canadian Women Voters Congress
19959 - 48 Ave., Langley BC V3A 3L2
e-mail: info@womenvoters.ca
womenvoters.ca
www.facebook.com/womenvoters
twitter.com/womenvotersca
Previous Name: Congress of Canadian Women-British Columbia
Overview: A small provincial charitable organization
Mission: To ensure women have equal opportunities in the elctoral process
Chief Officer(s):
Susan Lockhart, Contact
Activities: Operating the Women's Campaign School in Vancouver, British Columbia; holding workshops, talks & events

Canadian Women's Foundation / Fondation canadienne des femmes
#504, 133 Richmond St. West, Toronto ON M5H 2L3
Tel: 416-365-1444; *Fax:* 416-365-1745
Toll-Free: 866-293-4483; *TTY:* 416-365-1732
info@canadianwomen.org
www.cdnwomen.org
www.facebook.com/#!/CanadianWomensFoundation
Overview: A medium-sized national organization founded in 1989
Mission: To raise money to research, fund & share the best approaches to ending violence against women, moving low-income women out of poverty & building strong, resilient girls
Chief Officer(s):
Beverley Wybrow, President & CEO
Staff Member(s): 24; 500 volunteer(s)
Activities: Violence prevention grants; CWF Economic Development Fund; Girls Program
Publications:
• CWF [Canadian Women's Foundation] Annual Report
Type: Yearbook; *Frequency:* Annually
• Initiatives [a publicaton of the Canadian Women's Foundation]
Type: Newsletter
Profile: CWF information

Canadian Women's Health Network (CWHN) / Réseau canadien pour la santé des femmes (RCSF)
#203, 419 Graham Ave., Winnipeg MB R3C 0M3
Tel: 204-942-5500; *Fax:* 204-989-2355
Toll-Free: 888-818-9172
cwhn@cwhn.ca
www.cwhn.ca
www.facebook.com/CanadianWomensHealthNetwork
Overview: A medium-sized national organization founded in 1993
Mission: To recognize the importance of information sharing, education & advocacy for women's health & equality; To build & strengthen the women's health movement in Canada & thoroughout the world; To work to end the effects of discrimination based on gender, race, age, language, income, sexual orientation, ability, religion, & geographic region
Chief Officer(s):
Lydya Assayag, Executive Director
Finances: *Annual Operating Budget:* $250,000-$500,000
Staff Member(s): 9
Membership: 100-499; *Fees:* $15/1 year, $25/2 years individuals; $35 organizations
Activities: Provides easier access to health information, resources & research; produces user-friendly materials & resources; promotes & develops links to information & action networks; provides forums for debate; acts as "watchdog" on emerging issues & trends that may affect women's health; works to change inequitable health policies & practices; encourages community-based participatory research modes; promotes women's involvement in health research; Clearinghouse a collection of women-centred health-related resources; *Library:* Information Centre; Open to public

Canadian Women's Studies Association / L'association canadienne des études sur les femmes (CWSA / ACÉF) *See* Women's & Gender Studies et Recherches Féministes

Canadian Wood Council (CWC) / Conseil canadien du bois (CCB)
#400, 99 Bank St., Ottawa ON K1P 6B9
Tel: 613-747-5544; *Fax:* 613-747-6264
www.cwc.ca
Overview: A large national organization founded in 1959
Mission: To represent Canadian manufacturers of wood products; To insure market access for wood products; To communicate technical information; To organize educational programs for students & construction professionals
Chief Officer(s):
Michael Giroux, President
Helen Griffin, Vice-President, Codes & Engineering
Étienne Lalonde, Vice-President, Market Development
Ioana Lazea, Manager, Events
Natalie Tarini, Manager, Communications
Membership: 15 corporate; *Fees:* Schedule available; *Member Profile:* Manufacturers of Canadian wood products used in construction; *Committees:* Management: Audit, Finance & Risk Management; Membership; HR; Nominating. Operations: U.S. Affairs; Lumber Properties Steering Committee; Market Development; Fire & Structural Design; Canadian Wood Industries Forum on Market Access; Canadian Sustainable Building Partnership. Other: WoodWORKS!; Advisory Groups; Chairmen's Club
Activities: *Awareness Events:* Annual Wood WORKS! Awards Gala; Wood Solutions Fairs; *Library* by appointment
Awards:
• Honor Award (Award)
• Merit Award (Award)
• Citation Award (Award)
Publications:
• Canadian Wood Council Awards Book
Type: Yearbook; *Frequency:* Annually
Profile: Compilation of best projects submitted to the Wood Design Awards program
• Canadian Wood Council Technical Publications
Profile: Topics include the Wood Design Manual, Span Books, & Engineering Guides
• The CWC [Canadian Wood Council] Newsletter
Type: Newsletter; *Frequency:* Weekly
Profile: Trends & events that affect the wood products industry
• Wood Design & Building
Type: Magazine; *Frequency:* Quarterly; *Accepts Advertising*; *Editor:* Bernadette Johnson; *Price:* $24
Profile: Wood use in architecture & construction
• Wood WORKS!
Type: Newsletter; *Frequency:* Monthly
Profile: Resources for technical support, training opportunities, & educational events

Canadian Wood Pallet & Container Association (CWPCA) / Association canadienne des manufacturiers de palettes et contenants (ACMPC)
#11, 1884 Merivale Rd., Ottawa ON K2G 1E6
Tel: 613-521-6468; *Fax:* 613-521-1835
Toll-Free: 877-224-3555
info@canadianpallets.com
www.canadianpallets.com
twitter.com/canadianpallets
Overview: A small national organization founded in 1967
Mission: To promote the general welfare of the wooden pallet & container manufacturing industry; to improve services directly or otherwise; to cooperate with officers of government & business in any program considered essential to the national welfare or economy; to engage in any other lawful activities & enjoy powers, rights & privileges granted or conferred upon associations of a similar nature.
Member of: Partners in Protection
Affliation(s): National Wooden Pallet & Container Association; Western Pallet Association
Chief Officer(s):
Bill Eggertson, Executive Director
bill.eggertson@canadianpallets.com
Lori Devlin, Director, Member Services
lori.devlin@canadianpallets.com
Stephanie Poirier, CWPCP
Blair McEwen, President
bowmanvillewoodproducts@bellnet.ca
Finances: *Annual Operating Budget:* $500,000-$1.5 Million
Staff Member(s): 3
Membership: 550; *Fees:* $595 corporate; $525 associate; *Member Profile:* Active manufacturers & suppliers within wood pallet & container industry; *Committees:* Wood Waste Standards; Workers Compensation; Education
Activities: *Speaker Service:* Yes; *Library* Open to public

Canadian Wood Preservers Bureau *See* Canadian Wood Preservers Bureau

Canadian Wood Preservers Bureau (WPC) / Préservation du bois Canada
#202, 2141 Thurston Dr., Ottawa ON K1G 6C9
Tel: 613-737-4337; *Fax:* 613-247-0540
www.woodpreservation.ca
Previous Name: Canadian Wood Preservers Bureau
Overview: A small national organization founded in 1988

Mission: To provide a quality assurance program for the treated wood industry
Chief Officer(s):
Henry Walthert, Executive Director
henry@woodpreservation.ca
Finances: *Funding Sources:* Membership dues
Membership: *Member Profile:* Treated wood producers; consumer groups

Canadian Wood Truss Association (CWTA) / Association canadienne des fabricants de fermes de bois

Tel: 403-271-0520; *Fax:* 403-271-0520
cwta@telus.net
www.cwta.net
Overview: A small national organization
Mission: To act as the voice of the truss manufacturing industry; To develop & maintain uniform performance standards; To promote high standards of excellence for structural wood component manufacturers & distributors
Chief Officer(s):
Daniel Després, President
ddespres@leonchouinard.com
Jerry Cvach, Secretary
Russ Nicol, Treasurer
russn@allspan.com
Membership: 6 regional associations; *Member Profile:* Metal plate connected wood truss manufacturers; Structural wood component manufacturers
Activities: Providing educational activities
Publications:
• CWTA [Canadian Wood Truss Association] Training Manual
Type: Manual

The Canadian Woodlands Forum (CWF) / Forum canadien des opérations forestières

20 Coupar Terrace, Truro NS B2N 5L3
Tel: 902-897-6961; *Fax:* 902-897-6976
info@cwfcof.org
www.cwfcof.org
Overview: A medium-sized national organization founded in 1995
Mission: To support technology transfer & information sharing activities focusing on improving the competitiveness of forest operations
Chief Officer(s):
Peter Robichaud, Executive Director, 902-899-6420
probichaud@cwfcof.org
Finances: *Funding Sources:* Membership dues
Staff Member(s): 2
Membership: *Fees:* Schedule available

Sudbury
765 Brennan Rd., Sudbury ON P3C 1C4
Tel: 705-671-2444; *Fax:* 705-671-2446
Toll-Free: 877-671-2444
www.sciontario.org/sudbury

The Canadian Writers' Foundation Inc. (CWF) / La Fondation des écrivains canadiens inc.

PO Box 13281, Stn. Kanata, Ottawa ON K2K 1X4
Tel: 613-256-6937; *Fax:* 613-256-5457
info@canadianwritersfoundation.org
www.canadianwritersfoundation.org
Overview: A small national charitable organization founded in 1931
Mission: Strives to continue building the capital fund through donations
Chief Officer(s):
Marianne Scott, President, 613-733-4223, Fax: 613-733-8752
Suzanne Williams, Executive Secretary
Finances: *Annual Operating Budget:* $50,000-$100,000; *Funding Sources:* Donations; bequests; royalties; investment income
Staff Member(s): 1
Membership: 8; *Fees:* Annual donations; *Committees:* Executive; Advisory
Activities: Grants continued financial assistance to distinguished, senior Canadian writers in times of financial distress

Canadian Yachting Association *See* Sail Canada

Canadian Young Judaea

788 Marlee Ave., Toronto ON M6B 3K1
Tel: 416-781-5156; *Fax:* 416-787-3100
www.youngjudaea.ca
www.facebook.com/youngjudaea
twitter.com/CdnYoungJudaea
Overview: A medium-sized national organization
Mission: To empower its members through their Jewish indentity
Chief Officer(s):
Risa Epstein, National Executive Director
risa@youngjudaea.ca
Staff Member(s): 8
Membership: *Committees:* Educational; Fundraising; National Camp Board; Marketing & Communications
Activities: * Israel trips

Canadian Youth Business Foundation *See* Futurpreneur Canada

The Canadian Zionist Cultural Association (CZCA)

#201, 788 Marlee Ave., Toronto ON M6B 3K1
Tel: 416-783-3063; *Fax:* 416-787-7496
czcacanada@gmail.com
Overview: A small international charitable organization
Mission: To support humanitarian & educational programs in Israel
Chief Officer(s):
Talia Klein Leighton, Administrator
talia.klein@czca.org
Activities: Providing scholarships; Operating camps for soldiers' orphans

Canadian Zionist Federation (CZF) / La fédération sioniste canadienne

#206, 1, carré Cummings, Montréal QC H3W 1M6
Tel: 514-739-7300; *Fax:* 514-739-9412
czf@jazo.org.il
Overview: A large international organization founded in 1967
Mission: To promote the Zionist ideal among the Jewish population in Canada; To assist in strengthening the Jewish State of Israel; To enrich Canadian Jewish life through the provision of Jewish education & information on Israel & Zionism, through the promotion of Aliyah & activities among Jewish youth in Canada.
Member of: World Zionist Organization
Affliation(s): World Zionist Organization; Jewish Agency
Chief Officer(s):
Florence Simon, National Executive Director
Norman Stern, President
snstern@sympatico.ca
Finances: *Annual Operating Budget:* $50,000-$100,000
Staff Member(s): 5; 30 volunteer(s)
Membership: 1,000-4,999; *Fees:* Schedule available
Activities: *Speaker Service:* Yes

Central Region
4600 Bathurst St., 4th Fl., Toronto ON M2R 3V2
Tel: 416-633-3988; *Fax:* 416-635-2758
czf@jazo.org.il
Chief Officer(s):
Norman Stern, President
snstern@sympatico.ca

Eastern Region
5151, ch de la Cote-Saint-Luc, Montréal QC H3W 2H5
Tel: 514-739-7300; *Fax:* 514-739-9412

Midwest Region
#C300, 123 Doncaster St., Winnipeg MB R3N 2B2
Tel: 204-477-7400

Canadiana

#200, 440 Laurier Ave. West, Ottawa ON K1R 7X6
Tel: 613-235-2628; *Fax:* 613-235-9752
info@canadiana.org
www.canadiana.ca
www.facebook.com/pages/Canadiana/115437585187018
twitter.com/CanadianaCA
Previous Name: Canadian Institute for Historical Microreproductions
Overview: A medium-sized national charitable organization founded in 1978
Mission: To specialize in the digitization of, preservation of, & access to documentary heritage
Member of: Association for Canadian Studies; Canadian Library Association; Canadian History Association; Canadian Initiative on Digital Libraries
Chief Officer(s):
Lynn Copeland, President
Leslie Weir, Vice-President
Sylvie Belzile, Treasurer
Finances: *Funding Sources:* Subscriptions; Sales; National Library
Publications:
• Canadiana.org Annual Report
Type: Yearbook; *Frequency:* Annually
• Canadiana.org Bulletin
Type: Newsletter; *Frequency:* Bimonthly; *Editor:* Magdalene Albert
Profile: Updated information about the institute, its projects, & events
• Facsimile
Type: Newsletter; *Frequency:* Annually
Profile: Thematic issues, with essays, articles, queries, & news, for scholars & librarians who use the Canadiana.org Early Canadiana microfiche & online research collections

Canadian-Arab Business Council *See* Canada-Arab Business Council

Canadian-Croatian Chamber of Commerce

630 The East Mall, Toronto ON M9B 4B1
Tel: 416-641-2829; *Fax:* 416-641-2700
contactus@croat.ca
www.croat.ca
www.linkedin.com/groups/CanadianCroatianChamberofCommerce
www.facebook.com/CanadianCroatianChamberofCommerce
twitter.com/CroatChamber
Overview: A medium-sized national organization founded in 1995
Mission: The Canadian-Croatian Chamber of Commerce is a not-for-profit network of Croatian-Canadian businesses, professionals and organizations that has emerged as the voice of Croatian-Canadian business in Canada.
Chief Officer(s):
Wanita Kelava, Manager
Staff Member(s): 1
Activities: *Awareness Events:* Taste of Croatia Golf Tournament; Annual Business Excellence Awards

Canadian-Croatian Congress (CCC) / Kanadsko-Hrvatski Kongres

3550 Commercial St., Vancouver BC V5A 4E9
Tel: 604-871-7190; *Fax:* 604-879-2256
crocc@shaw.ca
www.crocc.org
Overview: A large national charitable organization founded in 1993
Mission: To represent the Croatian Canadian community before the people & Government of Canada
Member of: United Nations
Affliation(s): Croatian World Congress
Chief Officer(s):
Mijo Maric, President
mijo.maric@telekom.de
Finances: *Annual Operating Budget:* $250,000-$500,000; *Funding Sources:* Membership dues; donations
Staff Member(s): 20; 125 volunteer(s)
Membership: Over 50,000; *Member Profile:* Croatian community; *Committees:* Lobby; Humanitarian; Sports; Schools; Cultural; Investment; Emigration; Youth; Internet
Activities: *Library* by appointment

Canadian-Cuban Friendship Association Toronto (CCFA)

PO Box 99051, 1245 Dupont St., Toronto ON M6H 2A0
Tel: 416-410-8254; *Fax:* 905-951-7629
info@ccfatoronto.ca
www.ccfatoronto.ca
twitter.com/ccfatoronto
Also Known As: CCFA Toronto
Overview: A small international charitable organization founded in 1977
Mission: To promote cooperation & understanding between the people of Canada & Cuba; to fundraise to send material goods to Cuba, provide for Cubans passing through Toronto; to hold activities that help protect Canada's & Cuba's sovereignty
Member of: Canadian Network on Cuba
Chief Officer(s):
Elizabeth Hill, President
Finances: *Annual Operating Budget:* Less than $50,000
12 volunteer(s)
Membership: 100-499; *Fees:* $5-$25
Activities: Cultural & informational public meetings; *Speaker Service:* Yes
Publications:
• Amistad

Type: Newsletter; *Frequency:* Bimonthy
Profile: Articles pertaining to Cuban issues
• Amistad
Type: Newsletter; *Frequency:* Bimonthly
Profile: CCFA activities, events, & developments in Cuba

Canadian-Filipino Association of Yukon (CFAY)
Whitehorse YT
Tel: 867-336-4443
www.facebook.com/YukonFilipino
Overview: A small provincial organization
Mission: To assist Filipinos in Canada; to promote understanding between Filipinos and Canadians; to provide education & training opportunities to members of the Association; to organize recreational & cultural activities for members & others.
Chief Officer(s):
Mike Buensuceso, President

Canadian-Palestinian Education Exchange
612 Markham St., Toronto ON M6G 2L8
e-mail: info@cepal.ca
www.cepal.ca
Overview: A medium-sized national organization
Mission: To educate Palestinian refugees in Lebanon and raise awareness to Canadians about Palestinian refugees difficult conditions in Lebanon.
Chief Officer(s):
Alexandra Conliffe, President

Canadians Concerned About Violence in Entertainment (C-CAVE)
167 Glen Rd., Toronto ON M4W 2W8
e-mail: info@c-cave.com
www.c-cave.com
Overview: A small national organization founded in 1983
Mission: To provide public education on research findings related to media violence through popular culture, commodities marketed primarily to children, adolescents & adults.
Member of: Cultural Environment Movement
Affliation(s): Coalition for Responsible Television (CRTV)
Chief Officer(s):
Rose Anne Dyson, Media Contact
rose.dyson@c-cave.com
Finances: *Funding Sources:* Membership fees; private donations
Membership: *Fees:* $35 individual; $80 institution
Activities: *Speaker Service:* Yes; *Library:* Resource Centre; by appointment

Canadians for Ethical Treatment of Food Animals (CETFA)
PO Box 18024, 2225 - 41 Ave. West, Vancouver BC V6M 4L3
e-mail: care@cetfa.com
www.cetfa.com
www.facebook.com/cetfa.news
Overview: A medium-sized national organization founded in 1990
Mission: CETFA is an investigation-based, farm animal advocacy organization that promotes the humane treatment of animals raised for food. It works to educate the public about Canada's food industry by providing information on factory farming practices.
Chief Officer(s):
Patricia Oswald, President
Twyla Francois, Head, Investigation, 204-296-1375
twyla.1@mts.net
Membership: *Fees:* $10

Canadians for Health Research (CHR) / Les Canadiens pour la recherche médicale
PO Box 126, Westmount QC H3Z 2T1
Tel: 514-398-7478; *Fax:* 514-398-8361
info@chrcrm.org
www.chrcrm.org
www.facebook.com/300688209959308
Overview: A medium-sized national charitable organization founded in 1976
Mission: To further understanding & communication among the public, the scientific community & government; To promote stability & quality in Canadian health research; to meet goals through the direct provision of information on request, & development & circulation of literature & special programming; To sponsor periodic conferences, workshops, a journalism award, & a student essay competition
Chief Officer(s):
Tim Lougheed, Chair
Awards:
• Youth Health Awareness Award (Award)
• Aventis Pasteur Medal for Excellence in Health Research Journalist (Award)

Canadians of Bangladeshi Origin
84 Westhumber Blvd., Toronto ON M9W 3A4
Tel: 416-742-9818
Overview: A small national organization founded in 1972
Mission: To support persons of Banglasdeshi origin who live in Canada

Canadians' Choice Party (CCP)
#1, 927 Danforth Ave., Toronto ON M4J 1L8
Tel: 647-853-8858; *Fax:* 416-477-9386
canadianschoice@gmail.com
www.canadianschoice.com
www.facebook.com/people/Canadians-Choice/10000267577810 7
twitter.com/CanadiansChoice
www.youtube.com/CanadiansChoiceParty
Overview: A small provincial organization
Chief Officer(s):
Bahman Yazdanfar, Party Leader

Canadian-Scandinavian Foundation (CSF) / Fondation Canada-Scandinavie
1438, rue Fullum, Montréal QC H2K 3M1
www.thecsfoundation.com
Overview: A small international charitable organization founded in 1950
Mission: To raise funds to distribute to Canadian students who wish to travel to Denmark, Finland, Iceland, Norway or Sweden, to undertake studies at a Scandinavian institution; to promote study/research projects by offering travel busaries.
Chief Officer(s):
Noami Kramer, President
Membership: *Fees:* $25 friend; $50 donor; $75 benefactor; $100 patron/corporate
Activities: Research funding; dinners; *Speaker Service:* Yes
Awards:
• Brucebo Scholarships (Scholarship)
2 scholarships given each year to young Canadian artists and a grant to 1 Swedish artist
• Special Purpose Grants (Grant)
Travel grants in the range of $600 to $1,000, to help defray travel costs in connection with study visits

Canadienne de la Chèvre de Boucherie *See* Canadian Meat Goat Association

Les Canadiens pour la recherche médicale *See* Canadians for Health Research

Canaidan Association of Physician Assistants (CAPA)
#704, 265 Carling Ave., Ottawa ON K1S 2E1
Tel: 613-248-2272; *Fax:* 613-521-2226
Toll-Free: 877-744-2272
admin@capa-acam.ca
capa-acam.ca
www.facebook.com/CAPA.ACAM
twitter.com/CAPAACAM
Overview: A small national organization
Mission: Develops Canadian health care and advocates for the professions' model of cooperative, collaborative, patient centered quality health care.
Chief Officer(s):
Patrick Nelson, Executive Director
Membership: 500; *Member Profile:* Canadian physician assistants
Meetings/Conferences: • 2015 Canaidan Association of Physician Assistants Conference, October, 2015, Toronto, ON
Scope: National

CanAm Indian Friendship Centre of Windsor (CAIFC)
3837 Wyandotte St. East, Windsor ON N8Y 1G4
Tel: 519-253-3243; *Fax:* 519-253-7876
caifcwindsor@hotmail.com
ofifc.org/centres/CanAm_Indian_Friendship_Centre_of_Windsor.php
Overview: A small local charitable organization founded in 1981
Mission: To advocate on behalf of Aboriginal people in Windsor; To improve the quality of life of community members
Affliation(s): Ontario Federation of Indian Friendship Centres
Activities: Developing programs & services to meet community needs

Canards Illimités Canada *See* Ducks Unlimited Canada

Cancer Advocacy Coalition of Canada (CACC)
#1902, 2 Bloor St. West, Toronto ON M4W 3R1
Tel: 416-642-6472; *Fax:* 416-538-4874
Toll-Free: 877-472-3436
cacc@canceradvocacy.ca
www.canceradvocacy.ca
www.facebook.com/pages/Cancer-Advocacy-Coalition-of-Canada/57221457251
twitter.com/CancerAdvocacy1
canceradvocacy.tumblr.com
Overview: A medium-sized national organization
Mission: To ensure that Canadians receive the best cancer services; To benefit cancer survivors; To assist in shaping constructive change in the Canadian cancer system
Chief Officer(s):
Dauna Crooks, Chair
Larry Broadfield, Vice-Chair
Finances: *Funding Sources:* Donations; Fundraising; Sponsorships
Activities: Evaluating cancer system performance in Canada; Engaging in advocacy activities, related to patient, survivor, & family issues; Promoting positive cancer policies; Encouraging public funding for the control & prevention of cancer; Publishing assessments of the cancer system; Preparing positions papers, such as a position statement on isotopes
Publications:
• Report Card on Cancer in Canada
Frequency: Annually
Profile: Articles about the effectiveness of the cancer system in Canada

Cancer Care Ontario (CCO)
620 University Ave., Toronto ON M5G 2L7
Tel: 416-971-9800; *Fax:* 416-971-6888
www.cancercare.on.ca
www.linkedin.com/company/cancer-care-ontario
www.facebook.com/pages/Cancer-Care-Ontario/138101106232982
twitter.com/CancerCare_ON
Overview: A medium-sized provincial organization
Mission: To advise the Ontario government on all aspects of provincial cancer care; to provide information to health care providers & decision makers, & to motivate better cancer system performance
Chief Officer(s):
Ratan Ralliaram, Interim Chair
Michael Sherar, President & CEO
Finances: *Funding Sources:* Donations; provincial & federal funding
Membership: *Committees:* Audit & Finance; Corporate Governance/Nominating; Human Resources & Compensation; Strategic Planning, Performance & Risk Management

Cancer de l'ovaire Canada *See* Ovarian Cancer Canada

Cancer de la vessie Canada *See* Bladder Cancer Canada

Cancer du Colon Canada *See* Colon Cancer Canada

Cancer Patient Education Network Canada (CPEN - Canada)
e-mail: info@cancerpatienteducation.org
www.cancerpatienteducation.org
www.linkedin.com/groups?mostPopular=&gid=3300283
www.facebook.com/JoinCPEN
Overview: A small national organization
Mission: To support cancer care providers in Canada, in the provision of effective, accurate, & comprehensive patient education; To empower cancer patients & their families to participate effectively in their care; To improve health outcomes, through cancer patient, family, & community education; To develop national standards for best practice in cancer patient education programs at cancer centres, hospitals, & community organizations
Chief Officer(s):
Tamara Harth, Liaison, CPEN Canada
Membership: *Member Profile:* Health care professionals interested in cancer patient education at hospitals, cancer centers, & community organizations throughout Canada; Volunteers who participate in cancer patient education
Activities: Facilitating collaboration among leaders in cancer patient education; Promoting research in cancer patient education; Supporting the implementation & management of high quality patient education programs & resources; Providing educational information to cancer patients & families; Mentoring

health care professionals & care providers to educate others; Advocating for institutional allocation of funding for cancer patient education programs

Cancer Research Society / Société de recherche sur le cancer

#402, 625, av Président-Kennedy, Montréal QC H3A 3S5
Tel: 514-861-9227; *Fax:* 514-861-9220
Toll-Free: 866-343-2262
Other Communication: RechercheCancer.ca
info@src-crs.ca
CancerResearchSociety.ca
www.facebook.com/cancerresearchsociety
www.facebook.com/recherchecancer
Overview: A large national charitable organization founded in 1945
Mission: To support basic cancer research through funding & seed money. Grants & fellowships are allocated to universities & hospitals involved in research across Canada
Chief Officer(s):
Andy Chabot, Executive Director
achabot@src-crs.ca
Nathalie Giroux, Deputy Executive Director
ngiroux@src-crs.ca
Alain Laurendeau, Director, Administration & Finance
alaurendeau@src-crs.ca
Finances: *Annual Operating Budget:* Greater than $5 Million; *Funding Sources:* Donations
Staff Member(s): 24; 1000 volunteer(s)
Membership: 1,000; *Fees:* $500 life; $250 Governor; $200 executive; $100 benefactor; $50 patron; $25 general
Awards:
• Grants (Grant)
Institutional grants, fellowships, general research grants, award grants & special grants

Ottawa
#305, 200 Isabella St., Ottawa ON K1S 1V7
Fax: 613-233-1030
Toll-Free: 888-766-2262
ottawa@src-crs.ca

CancerCare Manitoba (CCMB)

MacCharles Unit, 675 McDermot Ave., Winnipeg MB R3E 0V9
Tel: 204-787-2197
Toll-Free: 866-561-1026
donate@cancercare.mb.ca
www.cancercare.mb.ca
twitter.com/cancercaremb
www.youtube.com/user/CancerCareMB
Also Known As: Action Cancer Manitoba
Overview: A small provincial organization founded in 1930
Mission: To provide exceptional care for patients & their families
Chief Officer(s):
Arnold Naimark, Chair
Dhali Dhaliwal, President & CEO
Valerie Wiebe, Chief Nursing Officer
Jeff Peitsch, Chief Operating Officer
Activities: Providing patient & family support services; Offering resources for health care professionals, patients & families; Providing education & training opportunities for health care professionals; Conducting research;

Candlelighters Childhood Cancer Support Programs, Inc.

#9, 21 Concourse Gate, Ottawa ON K2E 7S4
Tel: 613-715-9157
information@candlelighters.net
www.candlelighters.net
www.facebook.com/candlelightersottawa
twitter.com/Candlelighters1
www.flickr.com/photos/candlelighters
Overview: A small local organization
Mission: To help children cope with their cancer diagnosis; to raise awareness about childhood cancer & its effect on the patients
Chief Officer(s):
Jocelyn Lamont, Executive Director
jocelyn.lamont@candlelighters.net
Staff Member(s): 3
Membership: *Member Profile:* Families of children diagnosed with cancer

Candora Society of Edmonton

Abbottfield Mall, #248, 3210 - 118 Ave NW, Edmonton AB T5W 4W1
Tel: 780-474-5011; *Fax:* 780-474-5041
www.candora.ca
www.facebook.com/pages/Candora-Society/278741025491847
Overview: A small local charitable organization founded in 1989
Mission: To address the needs of low income residents of North East Edmonton, specifically the communities of Rundle and Abbottsfield which comprise about 1,400 low income multi family housing units.
Chief Officer(s):
Valerie Cudmore, Executive Director

CANDU Owners Group Inc. (COG)

655 Bay St, 17th Fl., Toronto ON M5G 2K4
Tel: 416-595-1888; *Fax:* 416-595-1022
cog@candu.org
www.candu.org
Overview: A small national organization founded in 1984
Mission: COG is a not-for-profit organization that provides programs for cooperation, mutual assistance & exchange of information for the support, development, operation, maintenance & economics of CANDU technology.
Affiliation(s): World Association of Nuclear Operators (WANO); Electric Power Research Institute (EPRI)
Membership: 11 (5 Cdn., 6 offshore); *Member Profile:* All CANDU reactor operators in the world

CANGRANDS Kinship Support

RR#1, McArthurs Mills ON K0L 2M0
Tel: 613-474-0035
grandma@cangrands.com
www.cangrands.com
Also Known As: Canadian Grandparents Support
Previous Name: Association to Reunite Grandparents & Families
Overview: A small national charitable organization founded in 1996
Chief Officer(s):
Betty Cornelius, President
Wendy Porter, Vice-President
Finances: *Annual Operating Budget:* Less than $50,000
3 volunteer(s)
Membership: 100; *Fees:* $25
Activities: Internet support; annual conference; *Awareness Events:* Grandparents Day, Sept. 10

Canine Federation of Canada (CFC)

265, rue des Peupliers, St-Bruno QC J3V 2M2
e-mail: info@caninecanada.ca
www.caninecanada.ca
www.facebook.com/120510128020298
Overview: A small national organization founded in 1989
Mission: To serve & protect the pure-bred dog in Canada; To register, keep pedigrees, & issue certificates concerning pure-bred dogs (Beauce Sheepdog, Auvergne Pointer, Dogue de Bordeaux, Coton de Tuléar, & Dogo Argentino)
Affiliation(s): Canadian Livestock Records Corporation
Chief Officer(s):
Suzanne Lavigne, President
Donna Deschambault, Vice-President
Karen Black, 2nd Vice-President
Johanne Parent, Secretary-Treasurer, 450-883-2113
ecselpro@gmail.com
Laura Lee Mills, Registrar, 613-731-7110 Ext. 314, Fax: 613-731-0704
lauralee.mills@clrc.ca
Membership: *Fees:* $40 Individual support membership; $45 Individual associate membership; $75 Kennel / breeders membership
Activities: Providing education about pure breeds of dogs; Establishing standards of breeding; Monitoring the breeders of pure-bred dogs; Implementing the rules & regulations governing dog shows & various trials for pure-bred dogs; Working with clubs; Promoting pure-bred dogs

Canine Vision Canada *See* Dog Guides Canada

CanLearn Society for Persons with Learning Difficulties

3930 - 20th St. SW, Calgary AB T2T 4Z9
Tel: 403-686-9300; *Fax:* 403-686-0627
Toll-Free: 877-686-9300
info@calgarylearningcentre.com
www.calgarylearningcentre.com
facebook.com/pages/canlearn-centre/197617023661313
twitter.com/canlearncentre
Also Known As: Calgary Learning Centre
Previous Name: Computer Learning & Information Centre Society of Calgary
Overview: A small local charitable organization founded in 1979
Mission: To provide programs & services for learning disabilities, attention deficit / hyperactivity disorder (AD / HD), & literacy issues
Chief Officer(s):
Krista Poole, CEO
Anne Price, Director
Robert Simpson, Chair
Finances: *Funding Sources:* Donations
Membership: *Fees:* Free
Activities: Offering professional development opportunities; Increasing awareness & knowledge through public education; Providing clinical services; Providing Power for Youth services to support young people in issues related to learning & literacy challenges; Assessing & consulting services; Initiating family literacy programs; *Library:* LearningLinks Resource Centre
Publications:
• CanLearn Society for Persons with Learning Difficulties Annual Report
Type: Yearbook; *Frequency:* Annually
• For the Love of Learning Newsletter
Type: Newsletter
Profile: Information for donors

Canmore Folk & Blues Club

PO Box 8098, Canmore AB T1W 2T8
Tel: 403-678-2524; *Fax:* 403-678-2524
info@canmorefolkfestival.com
www.canmorefolkfestival.com
www.facebook.com/320189857849
twitter.com/canmorefolk
www.youtube.com/user/CanmoreFolkFestival
Overview: A small local charitable organization founded in 1977
Mission: To educate & cultivate in the public an appreciation & enjoyment of the folk music of Canada & other countries; To provide opportunities for national & international folk performances to become known in the area; To stimulate international understanding through a common interest in folk music
Affiliation(s): Alberta Arts Festival Association
Chief Officer(s):
Sue Panning, Artistic Director
Finances: *Annual Operating Budget:* $100,000-$250,000
400 volunteer(s)
Membership: 14; *Committees:* Folk Festival

Cannington & Area Historical Society

PO Box 196, Cannington ON L0E 1E0
Tel: 705-432-3136
canningtonhistoricalsociety@hotmail.ca
www.canningtonhistoricalsociety.ca
Overview: A small local charitable organization founded in 1975
Mission: To promote the study & history of Cannington, Ontario; to operate the Cannington Historical Museum located in MacLeod Park, featuring a CNR caboose & five restored, heritage buildings.
Chief Officer(s):
Ted Foster, President
Allan Argue, Secretary
Finances: *Funding Sources:* Fund-raising; membership fees; quilt & craft sale
Activities: *Library:* Museum Archives; Open to public by appointment

Canoe Kayak New Brunswick

c/o Rob Neish, 1350 Regent St., Fredericton NB E3B 3Z4
Tel: 506-622-5050
communications@canoekayaknb.org
www.canoekayaknb.org
www.facebook.com/group.php?gid=11074266810
Also Known As: Canoe Kayak NB
Overview: A small provincial organization
Mission: Canoe-Kayak New Brunswick is a non-profit volunteer organization dedicated to the promotion of safe recreational paddling in the province of New Brunswick.
Member of: Paddle Canada
Chief Officer(s):
Rob Neish, President
president@canoekayaknb.org

Canoe Kayak Nova Scotia (CKNS)

5516 Spring Garden Rd., Halifax NS B3J 1G6
Tel: 902-425-5454; *Fax:* 902-425-5606
admin@ckns.ca

www.ckns.ca
www.facebook.com/canoekayakns
www.twitter.com/canoekayakns/
Previous Name: Canoe Nova Scotia
Overview: A medium-sized provincial organization founded in 1973
Member of: Paddle Canada
Chief Officer(s):
Karl Vollmer, President
president@ckns.ca

Canoe Kayak Ontario
c/o OCSRA, 2078 Lemay Cres., Ottawa ON K1G 2X4
Tel: 613-618-1715
canoeontario.org
Overview: A medium-sized provincial organization overseen by CanoeKayak Canada
Mission: Canoe Kayak Ontario is a collective voice for canoeing and kayaking in Ontario, which promotes the interests and supports the activities of its Affiliates.
Affiliation(s): Ontario Canoe Sprint Racing Affiliation; Ontario Marathon Canoe Racing Association; Whitewater Ontario
Activities: Collective voice for canoeing in Ontario

Canoe Kayak Saskatchewan (CKS)
1870 Lorne St., Regina SK S4P 2L7
Tel: 306-585-6366; *Fax:* 306-352-4153
cks@accesscomm.ca
www.saskcanoe.ca
Previous Name: Saskatchewan Canoe Association
Overview: A small provincial charitable organization founded in 1987 overseen by CanoeKayak Canada
Mission: To operate as the provincial sport governing body for canoe & kayak in Saskatchewan
Member of: CanoeKayak Canada
Chief Officer(s):
Janette Hamilton, President
Jan Hanson, Executive Director
cks@accesscomm.ca
Finances: *Funding Sources:* Saskatchewan Lotteries
Membership: *Fees:* $10 recreation, flatwater, & whitewater members; $15 marathon members; *Member Profile:* Competitive athletes; Novice athletes; Recreational paddlers; Coaches; Officials; Supporters
Activities: Encouraging participation; Developing excellence; Overseeing activities related to whitewater, recreation paddling, sprint racing (flatwater), & marathon
Publications:
• Stern Word
Type: Newsletter; *Frequency:* 3 or 4 pa; *Editor:* Fiona Vincent
Profile: Event information

Canoe Newfoundland & Labrador *See* Paddle Newfounfdland & Labrador

Canoe Nova Scotia *See* Canoe Kayak Nova Scotia

Canoe Ontario; Ontario Recreational Canoeing Association *See* Ontario Recreational Canoeing & Kayaking Association

CanoeKayak BC
#102A, 11410 Kingston St., Maple Ridge BC V2X 0Y5
Tel: 604-465-5268; *Fax:* 604-460-0587
info@canoekayakbc.ca
www.canoekayakbc.ca
www.facebook.com/canoekayakbc
twitter.com/CanoeKayakBC
Overview: A medium-sized provincial organization overseen by CanoeKayak Canada
Member of: CanoeKayak Canada
Chief Officer(s):
Mary Jane Abbot, Executive Director

CanoeKayak Canada (CKC)
#700, 2197 Riverside Dr., Ottawa ON K1H 7X3
Tel: 613-260-1818; *Fax:* 613-260-5137
www.canoekayak.ca
www.facebook.com/CanoeKayakCAN
twitter.com/CanoeKayakCAN
Previous Name: Canadian Canoe Association
Merged from: Whitewater Kayaking Association of British Columbia
Overview: A large national organization founded in 1900
Mission: To increase the number of Canadians participating in canoeing & kayaking; To enable participants to realize excellence by providing sound athlete development programs & membership support systems
Member of: International Canoe Federation; Pan American Canoe Federation
Chief Officer(s):
Casey Wade, Chief Executive Officer, 613-260-1818 Ext. 2203
cwade@canoekayak.ca
Sally Clare, Director, Finance, 613-721-0504
sally@sallyclare.com
John Edwards, Director, Domestic Development, 613-260-1818 Ext. 2201
jhedwards@canoekayak.ca
Peter Niedre, Director, Coach & Athlete Development, 613-260-1818 Ext. 2206
peterniedre@canoekayak.ca
Scott Logan, Director, Sprint High Performance, 902-499-9984
slogan@canoekayak.ca
Finances: *Funding Sources:* Sport Canada; Corporate Partners; Donations; Event Fees
3000 volunteer(s)
Membership: 25,000+; *Fees:* $35; *Member Profile:* Individuals, commercial or other groups; *Committees:* Board of Directors; Sprint; Whitewater; Marathon
Publications:
• Paddles Up [a publication of CanoeKayak Canada]
Type: Newsletter

CanoeKayak Canada - Atlantic Division *See* Atlantic Division, CanoeKayak Canada

CanoeKayak Canada Western Ontario Division (WOD)
c/o Alan Potts, 22 Bowes Garden Ct., Toronto ON M1C 4L8
www.westernontariodivision.com
www.facebook.com/436833409678565
twitter.com/CKC_WOD
Overview: A small provincial organization overseen by CanoeKayak Canada
Chief Officer(s):
Dean Jenkins, Registrar
dean.jenkins31@gmail.com
Alan Potts, Treasurer
avpotts@rogers.com

Canola Council of Canada
#400, 167 Lombard Ave., Winnipeg MB R3B 0T6
Tel: 204-982-2100; *Fax:* 204-942-1841
Toll-Free: 866-834-4378
admin@canolacouncil.org
www.canolacouncil.org
Overview: A medium-sized national organization founded in 1967
Mission: To enhance the Canadian canola industry's ability to profitably produce & supply seed, oil, & meal products that offer superior value to customers throughout the world.
Chief Officer(s):
Terry Youzwa, Chair, 306-862-5070
Patti Miller, President
millerp@canolacouncil.org
Finances: *Funding Sources:* Program grants; industry funding; sponsorships
Staff Member(s): 33
Membership: *Fees:* $500 regular; $250 affiliate; *Member Profile:* Involved/interested in Canada's canola industry
Activities: Crop production; research; market development; *Library*
Meetings/Conferences: • Canola Council of Canada 2015 Conference, March, 2015, Fairmont Banff Springs Hotel, Banff, AB
Scope: National
Contact Information: Communications Manager: Crystal Klippenstein, Phone: 204-982-7762, klippensteinc@canolacouncil.org; URL: convention.canolacouncil.org

Canola Crushers of Western Canada *See* Canadian Oilseed Processors Association

Canora Arts Council
PO Box 1083, Canora SK S0A 0L0
Tel: 306-563-5396
Other Communication: Alternate Phone: 306-563-5211
Overview: A small local organization
Member of: Organization of Saskatchewan Arts Councils

Canso Historical Society
PO Box 128, 1297 Union St., Canso NS B0H 1H0
Tel: 902-366-2516
Overview: A small local organization
Mission: To preserve, develop and identify the historic tradition and culture of the people of the Town of Canso and surrounding area.
Chief Officer(s):
Martha Kavanaugh, Contact
mkavanaugh@ns.sympatico.ca
Activities: Operates Whitman House Museum

Capacité Nouveau-Brunswick *See* Ability New Brunswick

Cape Breton Centre for Sexual Health
PO Box 1598, 150 Bentinck St., Sydney NS B1P 6R8
Tel: 902-539-5158; *Fax:* 902-539-0290
pp.cb@eastlink.ca
www.nssexualhealth.ca
Previous Name: Planned Parenthood Cape Breton
Overview: A small local organization founded in 1979
Member of: Nova Scotia Association for Sexual Health; Planned Parenthood Federation of Canada
Chief Officer(s):
Cathie Penny, Executive Director
Staff Member(s): 1; 10 volunteer(s)

Cape Breton Chamber of Voluntary Organizations (CBCVO)
150 Commercial St., Glace Bay NS B1A 3C1
cbhelp.ca/cbcvo
twitter.com/volCB
Overview: A small local organization
Mission: To provide opportunities of networking, support, collaboration & a voice for the voluntary sector in Cape Breton, similar to a chamber of commerce
Membership: *Fees:* $24; *Member Profile:* NGOs with a volunteer component; individuals connected to the volunteer sector
Activities: Lunch & Learn series; workshops

Cape Breton County Minor Hockey Association (CBCMHA)
PO Box 6003, 95 Keltic Dr., Coxheath NS B1S 3V9
Tel: 902-562-1767; *Fax:* 902-562-1833
cbcmha@ns.aliantzinc.ca
www.cbcmha.ca
Overview: A medium-sized local organization
Mission: The Cape Breton County Minor Hockey Association is dedicated to the advancement of minor hockey & promoting the development & personal growth of all participants through progressive leadership, by ensuring meaningful & equal opportunities, & providing enjoyable experiences in a safe & respectful environment.
Member of: Hockey Canada; Hockey Nova Scotia
Chief Officer(s):
Pam Reid, Executive Director
Membership: *Fees:* $162-$507

Cape Breton Injured Workers' Association (CBIWA)
714 Alexandra St., Sydney NS B1S 2H4
Tel: 902-539-4650; *Fax:* 902-539-4171
cbiwa@hotmail.ca
Overview: A small provincial organization
Mission: The Cape Breton Injured Workers Association is a volunteer group, located in Sydney, Nova Scotia working on behalf of injured workers by providing information, assisting with claims and appeals, and continuing a dialogue with the Workers' Compensation Board of Nova Scotia.
Finances: *Funding Sources:* Donations
Membership: *Fees:* $5

Cape Breton Island Building & Construction Trades Council
238 Vulcan Ave., Sydney NS B1P 5X2
Tel: 902-539-2661; *Fax:* 902-539-4462
Overview: A small local organization
Mission: To represent fifteen private enterprise unions
Member of: Nova Scotia Construction Sector Council - Industrial-Commercial-Institutional
Chief Officer(s):
Cliff Murphy, President
Membership: 4,000+
Awards:
• Cape Breton Island Building & Construction Trades Council & Unionized Cape Breton Contractors Entrance Scholarship (Scholarship)
To provide opportunities for students to access educational opportunities at the Nova Scotia Community College*Eligibility:* Students interested in the construction sector who are graduating from any high school in Cape Breton

Cape Breton Professional Musicians Association, AFM Local 355
PO Box 1812, 369 Prince St., Sydney NS B1P 6W4
Tel: 902-567-2909; *Fax:* 902-567-1042
cbpma2010@hotmail.com
www.capebretonmusicians.org
www.facebook.com/afm.org
twitter.com/MusiciansUnion
www.youtube.com/user/MusiciansUnion
Overview: A small local organization founded in 1966 overseen by American Federation of Musicians of the United States & Canada
Mission: To promote & protect the working conditions of Cape Breton Island professional musicians
Member of: American Federation of Musicians (AFM), Canadian Conference
Chief Officer(s):
Patricia Margaret Day, Acting President/Treasurer
Membership: *Fees:* $140

Cape Breton Regional Hospital Foundation
#209, 45 Weatherbee Rd., Sydney NS B1M 0A1
Tel: 902-567-7752
foundation@cbdha.nshealth.ca
www.becauseyoucare.ca
www.facebook.com/CapeBretonCares
twitter.com/BecauseUCare
www.youtube.com/channel/UC_GsK8t5w3UR8HTqjoxTJGQ
Overview: A small local charitable organization
Mission: To raise money on behalf of the Cape Breton Regional Hospital in order to improve the services provided to patients & to fund research
Chief Officer(s):
Brad Jacobs, CEO
jacobsb@cbdha.nshealth.ca
Staff Member(s): 6

Cape Breton Tourist Association *See* Tourism Cape Breton

Cape Breton University Centre for International Studies (CIS) / Centre d'études internationales
Cape Breton University, PO Box 5300, Sydney NS B1P 6L2
Tel: 902-563-1274
cbu-cis.ca
Overview: A small local organization founded in 1978
Mission: To develop greater general awareness of the relevance & importance of international affairs to Canadians; To carry out extensive public educational programs on development, multiculturalism, human rights, environmental issues & peace; To encourage research & publications, sponsor guest speakers, workshops & seminars; To seek linkages with other universities & institutions both in Canada & elsewhere; To negotiate international exchange agreements & coordinate technical assistance projects
Member of: Canadian Council for International Cooperation
Chief Officer(s):
Garry Leech, Director
garry_leech@cbu.ca
Finances: *Funding Sources:* University; government; projects
Activities: Lectures; seminars; youth conference; cultural events; *Speaker Service:* Yes; *Library* Open to public

Cape Breton University Faculty Association / Association des faculty du universitaire du Cap-Breton
Cape Breton University, PO Box 351, Stn. A, Sydney NS B1S 6H2
Tel: 902-563-1623; *Fax:* 902-563-1881
president@cbufa.ca
www.cbufa.ca
www.facebook.com/100307433386250?sk=wall
twitter.com/CBUFA
Previous Name: University College of Cape Breton Faculty Association of University Teachers
Overview: A small local organization founded in 1974
Affliation(s): Canadian Association of University Teachers
Chief Officer(s):
Chester Pyne, President
Finances: *Annual Operating Budget:* Less than $50,000; *Funding Sources:* Membership dues
Membership: 110

Cape Sable Historical Society
The Old Courthouse, PO Box 67, 2401 Hwy. 3, RR#1, Barrington NS B0W 1E0
Tel: 902-637-2185
barmusuemcomplex@eastlink.ca
www.capesablehistoricalsociety.com
www.facebook.com/209904499063299
Overview: A small local organization founded in 1932
Mission: To preserve the archives & genealogy of Cape Sable Island & the surrounding region, including Shelburne County & the Municipality of Barrington; To provide information about family history & the local history of the Cape Sable area; To act as the custodian of the Seal Island Light Museum, the Old Meeting House, the Western Counties Military Museum, & the Barrington Woolen Mill
Finances: *Funding Sources:* Membership fees; Research fees; Admission fees
Membership: *Fees:* $10
Activities: Offering research facilities, resources, & staff to assist visitors with genealogical research; *Library:* Genealogical Research Centre; Open to public

Capilano College Faculty Association *See* Capilano University Faculty Association

Capilano University Faculty Association (CFA)
#501E, 2055 Purcell Way, North Vancouver BC V7J 3H5
Tel: 604-984-4948
cfa@capilanou.ca
www.capilanofaculty.ca
Previous Name: Capilano College Faculty Association
Overview: A small local organization founded in 1969
Mission: To represent the faculty of Capilano University, by addressing issues of the faculty, such as professional development, workload, access to benefit plans, & appointments
Chief Officer(s):
Mark Battersby, President
mbatters@capilanou.ca
John Wilson, Vice-President; Chief Steward
jwilson@capilanou.ca
Jason Leslie, Secretary
jleslie@capilanou.ca
Janet Waters, Treasurer
jawaters@capilanou.ca
Colin Gilker, Officer, Professional Affairs
cgilker@capilanou.ca
Membership: 500+; *Member Profile:* Instructors from Capilano University, including the North Vancouver, Squamish, & Sunshine Coast campuses; *Committees:* Audit; Benefits Review; Cap College Naming Opportunities; Disability Rehabilitation; Dispute Resolution; Education Policy; Employee & Family Assistance; Equivalent Workload; Faculty Professional Development; Food Services; Harassment; Human Rights & International Solidarity; Joint Occupational Health & Safety; Mediation; Non Regular Faculty; Paid Ed Leave; Parking; Pension Liaison; Physical Environment; Placement Review; Social; Status of Women; Student Appeals; Trade Union Practices & Ethics; Transportation; Washroom Advertising
Publications:
• Capilano College Faculty Association Newsletter
Type: Newsletter
Profile: Union issues

The Capital Commission of Prince Edward Island Inc. / La Commission de la Capitale de l'Île-du-Prince-Édouard
#302, 52 Water St., Charlottetown PE C1A 7M4
Tel: 902-629-1864; *Fax:* 902-892-5486
Also Known As: Capital Commission
Overview: A medium-sized local organization founded in 1995
Mission: To promote & develop Charlottetown in its role as the Birthplace of Confederation in an authentic & accurate manner, resulting in diverse cultural & business opportunities for private enterprise
Member of: Tourism Industry Association of PEI; International Festivals & Events Association; PEI Convention Bureau; PEI Museum & Heritage Foundation, Greater Charlottetown Area Chamber of Commerce
Chief Officer(s):
Kim Green, Executive Director

Capital Region Beekeepers Association
c/o Alanya Smith, 2930 Prior St., Victoria BC V8T 3Y5
192.197.97.9/~vicbeekeepers/
Overview: A small local organization
Mission: To assist & educate member beekeepers
Membership: 100+; *Fees:* $25; *Member Profile:* Interested apiarists, as well as non-beekeepers, in the capital region area of British Columbia
Activities: Offering monthly meetings featuring a speaker, questions, & beekeeping information; Organizing a field day; Testing bees for nosema; Removing honey bees from yards; *Speaker Service:* Yes; *Library:* Capital Region Beekeepers Association Library
Publications:
• Beeline Newsletter
Type: Newsletter; *Frequency:* Monthly; *Price:* Free with Capital Region Beekeepers Association membership

Carberry & District Chamber of Commerce
PO Box 101, Carberry MB R0K 0H0
Tel: 204-834-6616
edo@townofcarberry.ca
www.townofcarberry.ca
Overview: A small local organization
Chief Officer(s):
Christinia Steen, President
Lori Scott, Secretary
Membership: *Fees:* $50

Carberry Plains Arts Council
PO Box 130, 122 Main St., Carberry MB R0K 0H0
Tel: 204-834-6617; *Fax:* 204-834-6619
crbyarts@westman.wave.ca
home.westman.wave.ca/~crbyarts
Overview: A small local organization
Mission: To promote & encourage use of the arts as an integral part of the community
Member of: Manitoba Association of Community Arts Councils Inc.
Chief Officer(s):
Sherry Howard, Administrative Director
Staff Member(s): 1

Carcinoid NeuroEndocrine Tumour Society Canada
#4103, 3219 Yonge St., Toronto ON M4N 3S1
Tel: 416-628-3189
Toll-Free: 844-628-6788
info@cnetscanada.ca
www.cnetscanada.org
www.facebook.com/cnetscanada
twitter.com/CNETSCanada
Also Known As: CNETS Canada
Overview: A large national charitable organization founded in 2007
Mission: To raise awareness about neuroendocrine tumours; to provide help & support to those suffering from this type of cancer; to fund research that treats neuroendocrine tumours
Chief Officer(s):
Jackie Herman, President
jackie.herman@cnetscanada.org
Activities: *Awareness Events:* NET Cancer Day, November

Cardiac Care Network of Ontario
#502, 4211 Yonge St., Toronto ON M2P 2A9
Tel: 416-512-7472; *Fax:* 416-512-6425
mail@ccn.on.ca
www.ccn.on.ca
Overview: A small provincial organization
Mission: To work as an advisory body to the Ministry of Health & Long-Term Care; To improve quality, efficiency, access, & equity in the delivery of the continuum of adult cardiac services in Ontario
Chief Officer(s):
Kori Kingsbury, Chief Executive Officer
Finances: *Funding Sources:* Ministry of Health & Long-Term Care
Staff Member(s): 16
Membership: 18; *Member Profile:* Cardiac centres in Ontario
Activities: Collecting & reporting information on surgery, catheterization, angioplasty, eps & ablations & ICDs

Cardiac Rehabilitation Network of Ontario (CRNO)
347 Rumsey Rd., Toronto ON M4G 1R7
Tel: 416-597-3422; *Fax:* 416-597-7027
www.crno.ca
Overview: A small provincial organization founded in 2002 overseen by Canadian Association of Cardiac Rehabilitation
Mission: Dedicated to the rehabilitation of individuals with cardiac disease, as well as the prevention of cardiac disease; advocacy on behalf of the patient through the advancement of health care services in Ontario
Chief Officer(s):
Terry Fair, Chair, 905-895-4521 Ext. 2805
TFair@southlakeregional.org
Andrew Lotto, Treasurer/Registrar, 905-895-4521 Ext. 6896
alotto@southlakeregional.org
Finances: *Funding Sources:* Membership dues

Membership: *Fees:* $25 regular; $100-$250 institutional dependant on number of members; *Member Profile:* Anyone involved in some capacity with an Ontario cardiac rehabilitation program

Cardiology Technologists' Association of British Columbia (CTABC)

PO Box 2575, 349 West Georgia St., Vancouver BC V6B 3W8
Toll-Free: 866-280-6535
www.ctabc.ca
Overview: A small provincial organization founded in 1975
Mission: To raise standards of practice & of patient care provided by cardiology technologists in British Columbia
Member of: Canadian Society of Cardiology Technologists (CSCT)
Affliation(s): Canadian Cardiovascular Society (CCS)
Chief Officer(s):
Shauna Ryall, CTABC President
president@ctabc.ca
Cheryl West, CTABC / CSCT Registrar
registrar@ctabc.ca
Jiannan Yu, Treasurer
treasurer@ctabc.ca
Membership: 400+; *Fees:* $145 registered cardiology technologists; $95 inactive; $75 students; $115 business, commercial, & industrial members; *Member Profile:* Registered cardiology technologists; Students
Activities: Increasing the level of competence of cardiology technologists; Maintaining professional standards; Providing education; *Library:* Lending Library
Awards:
• Marion Wright (Award)
Publications:
• Heart Copy: Cardiology Technologists' Association of BC Newsletter
Type: Newsletter
Profile: Association reports

Cardston & District Chamber of Commerce

PO Box 1212, 490 Main St., Cardston AB T0K 0K0
Tel: 403-795-1032; *Fax:* 403-653-2644
Info@CardstonChamber.com
www.cardstonchamber.com/
Overview: A small local organization
Mission: The Chamber of Commerce aims to promote and improve trade and commerce and to assit in providing economic growth, as well as civic and social being in our community and surrounding area.
Chief Officer(s):
Zenieth Gaynor, President
Jason Comin, Treasurer

Cardston & District Historical Society (CDHS)

PO Box 1830, Cardston AB T0K 0K0
Overview: A small local charitable organization founded in 1975
Mission: To collect & arrange for display historical items from Cardston & district; to collect & store local newspapers & make them available for research; to collect history books from Southern Alberta for interest & research
Chief Officer(s):
Shayne Tolman, Contact, 403-893-7722
neandertolman@gmail.com
Finances: *Funding Sources:* Municipality; government of Alberta
Activities: Operates both C.O. Card Home & Court House Museum, seasonal June 1 - Aug. 31; *Library* by appointment

CARE Canada

#100, 9 Gurdwara Rd., Ottawa ON K2E 7X6
Tel: 613-228-5600; *Fax:* 613-226-5777
Toll-Free: 800-267-5232
info@care.ca
www.care.ca
www.facebook.com/carecanada
twitter.com/CARE_CAN
www.youtube.com/carecanada
Overview: A large international charitable organization founded in 1946
Mission: To defend dignity and fight poverty by empowering the world's most vulnerable and greatest agent for change: women and girls
Chief Officer(s):
Kevin McCort, President/CEO
Gillian Barth, Executive Vice-President
Finances: *Annual Operating Budget:* Greater than $5 Million; *Funding Sources:* Federal government; multinationals; corporate & private donors
Staff Member(s): 102
Membership: 1-99
Activities: In over 80 countries, CARE works with the poorest communities to improve basic health and education, enhance rural livelihoods and food security, increase access to clean water and sanitation, expand economic opportunity, help vulnerable people adapt to climate change and provide lifesaving assistance during emergencies. CARE places special focus on working alongside women and girls living in poverty.; *Awareness Events:* Walk in Her Shoes, March; International Women's Day, March; Climb for CARE, January; *Internships:* Yes

Montréal Office
BP114 Succ St-Jacques, Montréal QC H3C 1C5
Tel: 514-458-0057
Chief Officer(s):
Marie-Eve Bertrand, Director
Marie-Eve.Bertrand@care.ca

Care Institute of Safety & Health Inc.

1770 East 18th Ave., Vancouver BC V5N 5P6
Tel: 604-873-6018; *Fax:* 604-873-4443
Toll-Free: 800-923-4566
sales@care-institute.com
www.care-institute.com
Overview: A small local organization
Mission: Safety training for individuals & organizations
Chief Officer(s):
Elaine Benes, President & CEO
elaine@care-institute.com
Activities: First aid training; transportation endorsement; WHMIS

Career Colleges Ontario (CCO)

#2, 155 Lynden Rd., Brantford ON N3R 8A7
Tel: 519-752-2124; *Fax:* 519-752-3649
info@careercolleges.ca
careercolleges.ca
www.linkedin.com/company/2653513?trk=tyah
www.facebook.com/careercollegesontario
twitter.com/yourcco
Previous Name: Private Career Educational Council; Ontario Association of Career Colleges
Overview: A medium-sized provincial organization founded in 1973
Mission: To act as the voice for the private career college sector in Ontario
Member of: National Association of Career Colleges
Chief Officer(s):
Paul Kitchin, Executive Director, 519-752-2124 Ext. 103
paulkitchen@careercollegesontario.ca
Lorna Mills, Manager, Office & Financial Aid, 519-752-2124 Ext. 104
lornamills@careercollegesontario.ca
Finances: *Funding Sources:* Membership dues; Sponsorships
Membership: 250+; *Member Profile:* Private career colleges in Ontario; *Committees:* Membership; International Students; OACC Services; Ministry Liaison; Public Relations, Marketing, & Communications; Conference; Student Success; Program Standards; Private Career Colleges Act Review; Performance Accountability Measures; General Accreditation / Apprenticeship / Online; TCAF; Employment Ontario; Career College Quality; Finance & Budget; Nomination; Deputy Minister PCC Advisory; Governance; Private Career College Tours; RICC Focus Group
Activities: Providing a central clearing house; Promoting the interests of members; Advocating on behalf of members; Participating in negotiating regulations & legislation that impact the sector; Offering development workshops;
Meetings/Conferences: • Career Colleges Ontario & National Association of Career Colleges (NACC) Annual Conference 2015 - All In With CCO, June, 2015, Niagara Falls, ON
Scope: Provincial
Description: A keynote address, professional development sessions, a business meeting, & networking opportunities
Contact Information: Career Colleges Ontario Administrative Assistant: Dena Stuart, Phone: 519-752-2124, ext. 200, Fax: 519-752-3649, E-mail: denastuart@careercollegesontario.ca
Publications:
• The 411
Type: Newsletter; *Frequency:* Quarterly
Profile: Information for high schools
• The OACC Voice
Type: Newsletter; *Frequency:* Monthly
Profile: Information for members

Career Management Association of BC; Labour Market & Career Information Association of British Columbia *See* British Columbia Career Development Association

Carefirst Seniors & Community Services Association

#501, 3601 Victoria Park Ave., Toronto ON M1W 3Y3
Tel: 416-502-2323; *Fax:* 416-502-2382
info@carefirstseniors.com
www.carefirstseniors.com
www.facebook.com/CarefirstSeniors
twitter.com/CarefirstSenior
Previous Name: Chinese Seniors Support Services Association
Overview: A small local charitable organization
Member of: United Way Greater Toronto, York Region, Peel Region
Finances: *Annual Operating Budget:* Greater than $5 Million; *Funding Sources:* Federal, provincial & municipal; membership dues; sales of goods & services
Staff Member(s): 350; 1200 volunteer(s)

Mississauga On-Site Drop-In Service
#81, 1177 Central Pkwy W., Mississauga ON L5C 4P3
Tel: 905-270-9988; *Fax:* 905-361-1082
mso@carefirstseniors.com
www.carefirstseniors.com
Chief Officer(s):
Percy Leung, Program Assistant
Helen Leung, Executive Director, 416-502-2323
helen.leung@carefirstseniors.com

South Toronto Office, Helen Lam Community Service Centre
479 Dundas St. West, Toronto ON M5T 1H1
Tel: 416-585-2013; *Fax:* 416-585-2892
sto@carefirstseniors.com
www.carefirstseniors.com/websites/content.php?id=18

Supportive Housing Services, Alexandra Park
#707, 91 Augusta Ave., Toronto ON M5T 2L2
Tel: 416-603-0909; *Fax:* 416-603-0436
shsa@carefirstseniors.com
www.carefirstseniors.com

Supportive Housing Services, Tam O'Shanter
#902, 3825 Sheppard Ave. East, Toronto ON M1T 3P6
Tel: 416-291-1800; *Fax:* 416-291-9586
shst@carefirstseniors.com
www.carefirstseniors.com

York Region Community Services Centre
#104A, 420 Hwy 7 East, Richmond Hill ON L4B 3K2
Tel: 905-771-3700; *Fax:* 905-763-3718
york@carefirstseniors.com
www.carefirstseniors.com/websites/content.php?id=18

Carefree Society

2832 Queensway St., Prince George BC V2L 4M5
Tel: 250-562-1394; *Fax:* 250-562-1393
carefree_society@telus.net
www.transitbc.com/regions/prg/accessible/handydart.cfm
Also Known As: handyDART
Overview: A small local charitable organization founded in 1971
Mission: To provide transportation services for the disabled
Affliation(s): BC Transit
Finances: *Annual Operating Budget:* $250,000-$500,000; *Funding Sources:* Provincial government; regional government
Staff Member(s): 12; 10 volunteer(s)
Membership: 15; *Fees:* $6; *Committees:* Accessible Transportation Awareness

Caregivers Nova Scotia

#2, 3433 Dutch Village Rd., Halifax NS B3N 2S7
Tel: 902-421-7390; *Fax:* 902-421-7338
Toll-Free: 877-488-7390
info@caregiversns.org
www.caregiversns.org
www.facebook.com/194077034023007?fref=ts
twitter.com/CaregiversNS
Previous Name: Family Caregivers Association of Nova Scotia
Overview: A small provincial organization
Mission: To support caregivers throughout Nova Scotia
Affliation(s): Canadian Caregiver Coalition
Chief Officer(s):
Mary Elizabeth MacLellan, President
Angus Campbell, Executive Director
director@caregiversns.org
Jennifer Briand, Coordinator, Capital District Caregiver Support
Western@CaregiversNS.org
Maggie Roach-Ganaway, Coordinator, Cape Breton Support
CapeBreton@CaregiversNS.org
Cindie Smith, Coordinator, Northern and Eastern Mainland Region Support
Northern@CaregiversNS.org

Finances: *Funding Sources:* Nova Scotia Department of Health - Continuing Care Services; Sponsorships
Membership: *Member Profile:* Individuals across Nova Scotia who care for & support family & friends who need assistance due to physical or mental disabilities
Activities: Providing education & information for caregivers across Nova Scotia; Offering assistance to caregivers by telephone & through peer support groups; Increasing public awareness of caregiver issues; Influencing public policy regarding caregivers, by participating in government task forces & working groups; Collaborating with other organizations to facilitate projects, such as the Working Together to Prevent Falling Among Seniors; *Awareness Events:* Caregivers' Awareness Week; *Library:* Caregivers Nova Scotia Library
Publications:
• Caregivers Nova Scotia News
Type: Newsletter; *Frequency:* Quarterly
Profile: Information about caregiving issues, forthcoming workshops, plus the experiences & concerns of caregivers

Carers ARK
103 Ferncliff Cres., Toronto ON L3S 4N6
Tel: 416-786-0347
carers.ark@gmail.com
www.carersark.org
www.facebook.com/carersark
Overview: A small national charitable organization
Mission: To inform caregivers of their rights, privilages, & obligations; to protect caregivers when necessary; to develop caregivers' leadership skills; to assist caregivers in their spiritual & professional growth; to create a link between caregivers & outside agencies
Affliation(s): Archdiocese of Toronto
Chief Officer(s):
Corazon Palomares, Contact, 905-294-3481
Finances: *Funding Sources:* Donations; membership fees; corporate sponsorship
Membership: *Member Profile:* Caregivers
Activities: Training courses; presentations; seminars; retreats; workshops; Prayer Link program (carersark.prayerlink@gmail.com)

Caribbean & African Chamber of Commerce of Ontario (CACCO)
PO Box 55328, Stn. Scarborough Town Centre, Toronto ON M1P 4Z7
Tel: 416-265-8603; *Fax:* 416-269-2081
www.cacco.ca
Overview: A medium-sized international organization founded in 1990
Mission: To promote, encourage & support the achievement of economic viability within the community it serves & enable advancement of the greater Canadian business community
Affliation(s): Ontario Chamber of Commerce; Board of Trade
Chief Officer(s):
Worrick Russel, Executive Chair, 416-265-8603
wrussell@web.net
Finances: *Annual Operating Budget:* Less than $50,000
20 volunteer(s)
Membership: 6 businesses; *Fees:* $100 institutional; $15 student; $50 individual; $75 non-profit

Caribbean Community Council of Calgary
#357, 1500 - 14 St. SW, Calgary AB T3C 1C9
Tel: 403-774-1300
admin@carifestcalgary.com
www.carifestcalgary.com
www.facebook.com/groups/48778073665
twitter.com/thecarifest
www.youtube.com/user/TheCarifest
Also Known As: Carifest
Previous Name: Calgary Caribbean Cultural Association
Overview: A small local organization founded in 1981
Mission: To contribute to the vibrancy of Calgary by staging an ethnic festival that portrays the Caribbean's rich history & diverse peoples
Finances: *Annual Operating Budget:* $50,000-$100,000
Staff Member(s): 1; 250 volunteer(s)
Activities: *Awareness Events:* Carifest Week, June; *Library* Open to public

Caribbean Students' Society of McGill University
#411, 3480 McTavish Rd., Montréal QC H3A 0E7
Tel: 514-398-1519
Overview: A small local organization
Mission: To foster unity among people from the Caribbean at McGill & in Montréal; to promote the Caribbean culture & student interests on the McGill campus
Member of: Students' Society of McGill University
Finances: *Funding Sources:* Students' Society of McGill University
Activities: Parties & dinners; annual culture show; community service; trips; Roots-AfroCaribbean Explosion 2000

Cariboo Action Training Society
#130, 1460 - 6th Ave., Prince George BC V2L 3N2
Tel: 250-563-9159; *Fax:* 250-563-9154
camptrapping.com
Overview: A medium-sized provincial organization founded in 1971
Mission: To conduct a wilderness behaviour modification program for male young offenders, who attend as a condition of probation programs

Cariboo Chilcotin Child Development Centre Association (CDC)
690 - 2nd Ave. North, Williams Lake BC V2G 4C4
Tel: 250-392-4481; *Fax:* 250-392-4432
www.cccdca.org
Overview: A medium-sized local organization founded in 1975
Mission: To work in partnership with families & the community; to provide a comprehensive continuum of quality developmental support services for children & their families
Member of: BC Association for Child Development & Rehabilitation
Chief Officer(s):
Jerry Tickner, President
Finances: *Annual Operating Budget:* $1.5 Million-$3 Million; *Funding Sources:* Government contracts; fees for service; donations
Staff Member(s): 35; 302 volunteer(s)
Membership: 12 institutional; 290 individual; *Fees:* $2
Activities: Child & Youth Care; Intensive Support & Supervision; FASD Key Worker & Parent Support Program; Infant Development; Occupational Therapy; Physiotherapy; Preschool; Speech & Language Therapy; Supported Child Development

Cariboo Chilcotin Coast Tourism Association
#204, 350 Barnard St., Williams Lake BC V2G 4T9
Tel: 250-392-2226; *Fax:* 250-392-2838
Toll-Free: 800-663-5885
info@landwithoutlimits.com
www.landwithoutlimits.com
www.facebook.com/CaribooChilcotinCoast
twitter.com/CarChiCoa
www.youtube.com/user/TheCCCTA
Previous Name: Cariboo Tourism Association
Overview: A small local organization founded in 1961 overseen by Council of Tourism Associations of British Columbia
Mission: To promote tourism products of the Cariboo Chilcotin Coast region of BC. Products & services include, access to an extensive image bank, travel guide & DVD, familiarization tour assistance, itinerary planning assistance, property inspection/recommendations, regional knowledge.
Affliation(s): Tourism BC; Council of Regional Tourist Associations; Cariboo Chilcotin Guide Outfitters Association; Guest Ranch Association of BC
Chief Officer(s):
Amy Thacker, CEO
amy@landwithoutlimits.com
Finances: *Funding Sources:* Membership fees; provincial/regional government
Staff Member(s): 4
Membership: *Member Profile:* Tourism product/service provider
Activities: *Speaker Service:* Yes; *Library:* CTA Library; by appointment

Cariboo Friendship Society
99 South 3rd Ave., Williams Lake BC V2G 1J1
Tel: 250-398-6831; *Fax:* 250-398-6115
admin@cfswl.ca
www.cariboofriendshipsociety.ca
Overview: A small local organization founded in 1969
Mission: To promote healthy lifestyles, & fostering fellowship & understanding between people by providing holistic programs & services to all.
Chief Officer(s):
Rosanna McGregor, Executive Director
rmcgregor@cfswl.ca
Finances: *Funding Sources:* Provincial/federal governments; private donations; fundraising events
Activities: Chiwid Transition House; Little Moccasins Learning Centre; Children Who Witness Abuse Program; Pregnancy Outreach/Family Outreach Program; Emergency Shelter Services; Mental Health Program; Low-Income Urban Aboriginal Housing; Tenant Relations Coordinator

Cariboo Tourism Association *See* Cariboo Chilcotin Coast Tourism Association

The Caritas Foundation
1880 Ormont Dr., Toronto ON M9L 2V4
Tel: 416-748-9988; *Fax:* 416-748-7341
info@caritasfoundation.ca
caritasfoundation.ca
Overview: A small local organization founded in 1980
Mission: To raise funds to support the programs provided by the Caritas Project
Affliation(s): Archdiocese of Toronto
Chief Officer(s):
Gianni Carparelli, Founder
Michael Tibollo, Chair
Anthony DiBattista, President
Walter Simone, Vice-President, Foundation
Finances: *Funding Sources:* Donations; fundraising
Activities: Community events; *Awareness Events:* Annual Golf Tournament; Annual Summerfest; Together Event

Caritas Project Community Against Drugs
1880 Ormont Dr., Toronto ON M9L 2V4
Tel: 416-748-9988; *Fax:* 416-748-7341
Toll-Free: 800-201-8138
help@caritas.ca
www.caritas.ca
Also Known As: Caritas
Overview: A small local organization founded in 1980
Mission: To prevent addiction through education & awareness; to provide a therapeutic community in order to rehabilitate those suffering from dependencies; to also aid people with mental health issues, behaviour problems, & family issues
Member of: Therapeutic Communities of America
Affliation(s): Archdiocese of Toronto
Chief Officer(s):
Gianni Carparelli, Founder
Michael Tibollo, Chair
Anthony DiBattista, President
Anthony Petonaci, Vice-President
Tullio Orlando, Executive Director
Finances: *Funding Sources:* Central Local Health Integration Network; donations; fundraising
Activities: Group sessions; day program; residential program; re-entry & transitional programs; aftercare; family support; public education; *Awareness Events:* Annual Golf Tournament; Annual Summerfest; Together Event

Carl Orff Canada Music for Children (COC)
c/o Joan Linklater, 88 Tunis Bay, Winnipeg MB R3T 2X1
Tel: 204-261-1893
www.orffcanada.ca
Overview: A medium-sized national organization founded in 1974
Mission: To encourage the development of a wholistic music education evolved from the pedagogical philosophy & approach of Carl Orff
Chief Officer(s):
Beryl Peters, President
petersb@cc.umanitoba.ca
Finances: *Annual Operating Budget:* $50,000-$100,000
17 volunteer(s)
Membership: 1,000; *Fees:* $75 institutional; $25 student; $50 individual
Meetings/Conferences: • Carl Orff Canada Music for Children 24th National Conference, April, 2016, Sheraton Cavalier Hotel, Saskatoon, SK
Scope: National

Carleton County Historical Society, Inc. (CCHS)
128 Connell St., Woodstock NB E7M 1L5
Tel: 506-328-9706; *Fax:* 506-328-2942
cchs@nb.aibn.com
www.cchs-nb.ca
Overview: A small local organization founded in 1960
Mission: To research and document local history; to acquire and preserve historical documents and artefacts relating to the area; and to refurbish historical buildings.
Chief Officer(s):
John Thompson, President
Membership: *Fees:* $20 student; $25 individual; $300 life

Carleton County Law Association (CCLA) / Association du barreau du comté de Carleton (ABCC)
Law Library, Ottawa Courthouse, #2004, 161 Elgin St., Ottawa ON K2P 2K1
Tel: 613-233-7386; *Fax:* 613-238-3788
Toll-Free: 866-637-3888
www.ccla-abcc.ca
www.linkedin.com/company/county-of-carleton-law-association
www.facebook.com/CCLA.ABCC
twitter.com/ccla_abcc
Overview: A small local organization founded in 1888
Mission: To advance the interests of it members; to promote the administration of justice
Chief Officer(s):
Jaye E. Hooper, President
hooper@williamsmcenery.com
Rick Haga, Executive Director
rhaga@ccla-abcc.ca
Wanda Walters, Administrator, Finance
wwalters@ccla-abcc.ca
Jennifer Walker, BAH, BEd, MLIS, Head Librarian
jwalker@ccla-abcc.ca
Membership: *Fees:* $52.50 - $309.75; *Member Profile:* Ottawa & Eastern Ontario lawyers
Activities: Offering continuing education programs; Providing networking opportunities; *Library:* County of Carleton Law Association Ottawa Courthouse Law Library
Publications:
• CCLA [Carleton County Law Association] Bulletin
Type: Newsletter; *Frequency:* Bimonthly
Profile: Updated policies & procedures for CCLA members
• Ottawa & Eastern Ontario Lawyers' Directory
Type: Directory; *Frequency:* Annually; *Accepts Advertising*; *Price:* $55 - $65

Carleton Literacy Council
100 Broadway St., Woodstock NB E7M 5C5
Tel: 506-328-4779
Overview: A small local organization founded in 1987
Mission: To provide free, private tutoring to illiterate & functionally illiterate adults in the area, thereby increasing the rate of literacy & ensuring a brighter future for these people
Affliation(s): Laubach Literacy of Canada
Chief Officer(s):
Angela Acott-Smith, Chair
angela.acottsmith@gnb.ca
Finances: *Annual Operating Budget:* Less than $50,000
40 volunteer(s)
Membership: 50 individual

Carleton Place & Beckwith Historical Society
267 Edmund St., Carleton Place ON K7C 3E8
Tel: 613-253-7013
www.cpbheritagemuseum.com
Overview: A small local charitable organization founded in 1984
Mission: To promote & educate on the subject of local history
Membership: *Fees:* $5 student; $7 senior; $10 individual; $15 family; $50 oraganization; $100 life
Activities: *Library* Open to public by appointment

Carleton Place & District Chamber of Commerce & Visitor Centre
132 Coleman St., Carleton Place ON K7C 4M7
Tel: 613-257-1976; *Fax:* 613-257-4148
manager@cpchamber.com
www.cpchamber.com
www.facebook.com/carletonplacechamber
Overview: A small local charitable organization founded in 1916
Mission: To encourage & foster free enterprise & economic development; to support good government & create & maintain a positive business climate in Carleton Place & surrounding district
Member of: Ontario Chamber of Commerce; Lanark County Tourism Association
Chief Officer(s):
Tracy Lamb, President, 613-257-1348
tlamb@mopani.ca
Finances: *Annual Operating Budget:* Less than $50,000; *Funding Sources:* Membership; fund-raising; town compensation
Staff Member(s): 1; 10 volunteer(s)
Membership: 205; *Fees:* $105 to $235 per annum, depending on number of employees; *Committees:* Expediting; Fund-raising; Membership; Planning; Tourism; Canada Day
Activities: Group Insurance; Networking Meetings; Certificates of Origin; Information Services; Complaint Service; public meetings; tourism information; *Awareness Events:* Industrial Awareness Week
Awards:
• Business Person of the Year (Award)

Carleton Road Industries Association (CRIA)
515 Carleton Rd., Lawrencetown NS B0S 1M0
Tel: 902-584-3332
admin@carleton515.ns.ca
www.carletonroadindustries.com
www.facebook.com/CarletonRoadIndustries
Overview: A small local charitable organization founded in 1977
Mission: To provide vocational & life skills training to adult residents of Annapolis & Kings Counties who have mental, intellectual, emotional &/or physical disabilities
Member of: DIRECTIONS Council for Vocational Services Society
Chief Officer(s):
Mackenzie Akin, Executive Director/Manager
Activities: Developmental services; employment programs; health & wellness program

Carleton University Academic Staff Association (CUASA) / Association du personnel enseignant de l'Université Carleton
Dunton Tower, Carleton University, #2004, 1125 Colonel By Dr., Ottawa ON K1S 5B6
Tel: 613-520-5607; *Fax:* 613-520-4426
cuasa@cuasa.ca
www.cuasa.ca
www.facebook.com/cuasaonline
twitter.com/cuasa
Overview: A medium-sized local organization founded in 1952
Mission: To serve as the collective bargaining agent for academic staff members at Ottawa's Carleton University; To promote the well-being of the academic community
Affliation(s): Canadian Association of University Teachers (CAUT); National Union of the Canadian Association of University Teachers (NUCAUT); CAUT Defence Fund; Ontario Confederation of University Faculty Associations (OCUFA); Ontario Federation of Labour; Ottawa District Labour Council; Canadian Labour Congress
Chief Officer(s):
Kimberly Benoit, Executive Director
kimberly.benoit@cuasa.ca
Chantal Dion, President
Staff Member(s): 4
Membership: 850+; *Member Profile:* Academic staff members at Carleton University in Ottawa; *Committees:* Collective Bargaining; Finance; Nominations & Elections; External Relations; Grievance Policy & Administration; Internal Affairs; Equity; Steering
Activities: *Library:* Carleton University Academic Staff Association Library
Publications:
• Academic Administrators' Handbook: A Guide to Responsibilities under the CUASA Collective Agreement
Type: Handbook; *Author:* Patricia Finn, LL.M
• CUASA Communiqué
Type: Newsletter; *Editor:* Janice Scammell

Carleton-Victoria Arts Council (CVAC)
c/o Pearl Black, 934 Route 590, Waterville, Carleton County NB E7P 1C4
Tel: 506-278-5154
carletonvictoriaarts@gmail.com
www.cvarts.ca
www.facebook.com/CVArtsC
twitter.com/CVArtsC
Overview: A small local organization founded in 1978
Mission: To provide Canadian entertainment & artists for a Canadian audience
Affliation(s): New Brunswick Arts Council
Chief Officer(s):
Peter McLaughlin, Contact
Activities: To promote/sponsor performances by Canadian/Eastern Canadian performing artists (music, theatre & dance); 4-6 shows annually;

Carleton-Victoria Forest Products Marketing Board & Wood Producers Association
151 Perkins Way, Florenceville NB E7L 3P6
Tel: 506-392-5584; *Fax:* 506-392-8290
info@cvwpa.ca
www.cvwpa.ca
Overview: A small local organization founded in 1975
Mission: To represent Private Woodlot Owners and Wood Producers from the counties of Carleton and Victoria (excluding the Parish of Drummond) in New Brunswick, Canada.
Member of: New Brunswick Federation of Woodlot Owners; Wood Products Group
Chief Officer(s):
Linda Bell, General Manager
linda.bell@cvwpa.ca
Staff Member(s): 9
Membership: *Member Profile:* Private woodlot owners

Carman & Community Chamber of Commerce
PO Box 249, Carman MB R0G 0J0
Tel: 204-750-3050
ccchamber@gmail.com
www.carmanchamberofcommerce.com
Overview: A small local organization founded in 1895
Affliation(s): Manitoba Chamber of Commerce
Chief Officer(s):
Paul Clark, President
Nikki Bartley, Executive Director
Finances: *Annual Operating Budget:* Less than $50,000; *Funding Sources:* Membership fees
Membership: 120+; *Fees:* $50-$100
Activities: Fun & Value Days; Fair Parade & Pancake Breakfest; Training Sessions; Area Promotion

Carnaval de Québec / Québec Winter Carnival
205, boul des Cèdres, Québec QC G1L 1N8
Tél: 418-626-3716; *Téléc:* 418-626-7252
Ligne sans frais: 866-422-7628
bonhomme@carnaval.qc.ca
www.carnaval.qc.ca
www.linkedin.com/BonhommeCarnaval
www.facebook.com/CarnavaldeQuebec
twitter.com/BHCarnaval
Aperçu: *Dimension:* grande; *Envergure:* provinciale; Organisme sans but lucratif; fondée en 1954
Mission: Depuis 50 ans, le Carnaval de Québec s'est donné la mission d'organiser annuellement une fête populaire hivernale dans le but de faire bénéficier à Québec une activité économique, touristique et sociale de première qualité dont les gens de la région seront fiers.
Membre(s) du bureau directeur:
Denis Simard, Président
Jean Pelletier, Directeur général
Stéphanie Paquet, Adjointe, Communications
Stephanie.Paquet@carnaval.qc.ca
Finances: *Budget de fonctionnement annuel:* Plus de $5 Million
Membre(s) du personnel: 70; 1400 bénévole(s)
Membre: 1-99
Activités: *Stagiaires:* Oui; *Service de conférenciers:* Oui

Caroline & District Chamber of Commerce
PO Box 90, Caroline AB T0M 0M0
Tel: 403-722-4066; *Fax:* 403-722-4002
ccoc@telus.net
www.carolinechamber.ca
Overview: A small local organization founded in 1980
Mission: To promote trade & commerce, support community & tourism development, encourage the growth of our businesses, & to voice local concerns to government.
Member of: Alberta Chamber of Commerce
Chief Officer(s):
Shannon Fagnan, Manager
Membership: *Fees:* $10 individual; $50 business
Activities: Big Horn Rodeo Parade; Christmas Light-Up; Campsite; *Library:* Caroline Municipal Library; Open to public

Carolinian Canada Coalition
Grosvenor Lodge, 1017 Western Rd., London ON N6G 1G5
Tel: 519-433-7077; *Fax:* 519-645-0981
info@carolinian.org
www.carolinian.org
www.facebook.com/caroliniancanada
twitter.com/caroliniancan
www.youtube.com/user/CarolinianCanada
Overview: A medium-sized local organization
Mission: To promote the protection and conservation of the Carolinian Life Zone of Southwestern Ontario.
Chief Officer(s):
Michelle Kanter, Executive Director
admin@carolinian.org
Staff Member(s): 12
Membership: *Committees:* Management; Fundraising; Finance; Audit; Nominations

Carousel Players
101 King St., 2nd Fl., St Catharines ON L2R 3H6
Tel: 905-682-8326; *Fax:* 905-682-9313
info@carouselplayers.com
www.carouselplayers.com
www.facebook.com/pages/Faces-of-Carousel/230586966952156
twitter.com/carouselplayers
Overview: A small local charitable organization founded in 1972
Mission: To use drama & theatre as a means of integrating & enlivening all aspects of the curriculum while developing the audience's awareness of & sensitivity to the experience of theatre
Member of: Professional Association of Canada Theatres; Theatre Ontario
Affliation(s): Theatre for Young Audiences Association
Chief Officer(s):
Pablo Felices-Luna, Artistic Director
pablo@carouselplayers.com
Jane Gardner, General Manager
jane@carouselplayers.com
Finances: *Funding Sources:* Canada Council; Ontario Arts Council
Staff Member(s): 4
Activities: *Speaker Service:* Yes

CARP
30 Jefferson Ave., Toronto M6K 1Y4
Tel: 416-363-8748; *Fax:* 416-363-8747
Toll-Free: 888-363-2279
Other Communication: Advocacy e-mail: advocacy@carp.ca
support@carp.ca
www.carp.ca
www.facebook.com/CARP
twitter.com/carpnews
www.zoomers.ca/group/CARP
Previous Name: Canadian Association of Retired Persons
Overview: A large national organization founded in 1984
Mission: The Association is a national, non-partisan organization that promotes the rights & quality of life of Canadians as they age through advocacy, education, information & CARP-recommended services & programs
Chief Officer(s):
Moses Znaimer, President
Eric Vengroff, General Manager & VP, Benefits
Susan Eng, Vice-President, Advocacy
Ross Mayot, Vice-President, Community
Finances: *Annual Operating Budget:* $1.5 Million-$3 Million; *Funding Sources:* Membership fees
Staff Member(s): 12; 500 volunteer(s)
Membership: 300,000 in 50 chapters; *Fees:* $14.95 - $34.95; *Member Profile:* No restrictions on membership
Activities: *Speaker Service:* Yes
Publications:
• CARP Health
Type: Newsletter
• CARP Lifestyle
Type: Newsletter
• CARP Savings
Type: Newsletter

Ajax-Pickering Chapter
e-mail: ajaxpickeringcarp@live.ca
www.apcarp20.ca

Barrie Chapter
Tel: 705-252-4756
barriecarp@gmail.com
www.barriecarp.org
Chief Officer(s):
Gwen Kavanagh, Chapter Chair

Brantford Chapter
e-mail: carpbrantford@gmail.com
www.carp.ca/category/community/regional/central/brantford
Chief Officer(s):
Andy Woodburn, Chapter Director, 519-759-2084

Brighton Belleville Quinte West Chapter
Tel: 613-475-9478
carpbbq@gmail.com
Chief Officer(s):
Mary Robertson, Chapter Chair

Brockville & Thousand Islands Chapter
56 King St. East, Brockville ON K6V 1B1
Tel: 613-802-0424
Chief Officer(s):
Dawn Edgley, Chapter Chair
edgley.carp@gmail.com

Calgary Chapter
Tel: 403-256-1181
carpcalgary@gmail.com
www.carp.ca/category/community/regional/western/calgary
Chief Officer(s):
Yasmin Kanji, Chapter Chair

Cambridge Chapter
www.carp.ca/category/community/regional/central/cambridge
Chief Officer(s):
Gail Goldman, Chapter Chair
g.goldman@carp.ca
Anthony Quinn, Chapter Liason, National Office, 888-363-2279 Ext. 274
a.quinn@carp.ca

Chatham-Kent Chapter
Tel: 519-354-8103
carpchathamkent@gmail.com
www.carp.ca/category/community/regional/central/chatham-kent
Chief Officer(s):
Carolynn Barko, Contact
Dena Ross, Contact

Edmonton Chapter
Tel: 780-450-4802
carp.edmonton@gmail.com
www.carp.ca/category/community/regional/western/edmonton
Chief Officer(s):
Bernice Rempel, Chapter Chair

Etobicoke Chapter
Tel: 416-399-2673
etobicokecarp@gmail.com
www.carp.ca/category/community/regional/central/etobicoke
Chief Officer(s):
Gary Hepworth, Chapter Chair

Fort McMurray Chapter
Tel: 587-645-5999
fortmcmurraycarp@gmail.com
www.carp.ca/category/community/regional/western/fort-mcmurray
Chief Officer(s):
Felix Berube, Chapter Chair

Fredericton Chapter
www.carp.ca/fredericton
www.facebook.com/171600369517582
Chief Officer(s):
Joanne Johnson, Chapter Chair

Georgian Bay Chapter
Tel: 705-888-9204
carpgeorgianbay14@gmail.com
www.carp.ca/category/community/regional/central/georgian-bay
Chief Officer(s):
Ian Kerr, Chapter Chair
iankerr@rogers.com

Haliburton Highlands Chapter
e-mail: carp.haliburton@gmail.com
carp.ca/category/community/regional/central/haliburton-highlands
Chief Officer(s):
Bob Stinson, Founding Chair

Halifax Chapter
Tel: 902-495-8284
anewvision@carpnovascotia.ca
www.carpnovascotia.ca
Chief Officer(s):
Bill VanGorder, Chapter President
president@carpnovascotia.ca

Halton Chapter
Tel: 905-319-7345
carphaltonchapter@gmail.com
www.carp.ca/category/community/regional/central/halton-region
Chief Officer(s):
Tom Carrothers, Chapter Director

Hamilton Chapter
e-mail: hamiltoncarp@gmail.com
www.carp.ca/category/community/regional/central/hamilton
Chief Officer(s):
Doug Stone, Chapter Chair
Lori Olyjnik, Chapter Co-Chair

Kingston Chapter
e-mail: carpkingston@gmail.com
www.carp.ca/category/community/regional/central/kingston
Chief Officer(s):
Victoria Pearson, Chapter Chair

Kitchener/Waterloo Chapter
PO Box 988, Kitchener ON N2G 4E3
Tel: 226-989-0001
info@carpkw.ca
www.carpkw.ca
Chief Officer(s):
Debby Fox, Chapter Chair
chapter25chair@carpkw.ca

London Chapter
Tel: 519-432-2789
carplondonchapter@gmail.com
www.carp.ca/category/community/regional/central/london
Chief Officer(s):
Dan Procop, Chapter Chair

Markham Chapter
e-mail: carp.markham@gmail.com
www.carp.ca/category/community/regional/central/markham
Chief Officer(s):
Terry D'Silva, Chapter Chair, 905-477-5727

Mississauga Chapter
www.carp.ca/category/community/regional/central/mississauga
Chief Officer(s):
Murray Etherington, Chapter Chair, 905-824-0919
murrayetherington@yahoo.com

Moncton Chapter
Tel: 506-389-9808
carpmonctonchapter@gmail.com
www.carp.ca/category/community/regional/eastern/moncton
Chief Officer(s):
Louise Gilbert, Interim Chapter Chair

Montréal - Metro West Chapter
#209, 3484, boul des Sources, Dollard des Ormeaux QC H9B 1Z9
Toll-Free: 888-286-8096
carp.ca/category/community/regional/central/montreal-metro-west
Chief Officer(s):
Marcus Tabachnick, Chapter Chair
chair.westislandcarp@gmail.com
Lee Royko, Vice-Chair, Communications/Community Relations
comm.westislandcarp@gmail.com
Al Shellard, Contact, Membership/Advocacy
member.westislandcarp@gmail.com

Newmarket Aurora Chapter
Tel: 416-805-6721
newmarket.aurora.carp@gmail.com
www.carp.ca/category/community/regional/central/newmarket-aurora
Chief Officer(s):
Kevin Dixon, Contact
kevin@kevindixon.ca
Winston Downer, Contact

Niagara Chapter
www.carp.ca/category/community/regional/central/Niagara
Chief Officer(s):
Jim Brown, Chapter Chair, 905-984-9225
jimbrown@remax-gc.com

North Bay Chapter
Tel: 705-478-0723
carpnorthbay@gmail.com
www.carp.ca/category/community/regional/central/north-bay
Chief Officer(s):
Betty Dean, Chapter Chair

North Fraser Chapter
e-mail: CARPnortfraserchapter@gmail.com
www.carp.ca/category/community/regional/western/north-fraser
Chief Officer(s):
Bruce Bird, Chapter Chair, 778-284-1189
brucebird@shaw.ca

North Vancouver Chapter
e-mail: carp.northshorevancouver@gmail.com
www.carp.ca/category/community/regional/western/north-vancouver
Chief Officer(s):
Lorna Goodwin, Chapter Chair

North York Chapter
Tel: 416-551-2678
carpnorthyork@gmail.com
www.carp.ca/category/community/regional/central/north-york
Chief Officer(s):

Max Wynter, Chapter Chair
Okanagan Valley Chapter
e-mail: carpokanagan@hotmail.com
www.carp.ca/category/community/regional/western/okanagan-valley
Alice Mah Wren, Chapter Co-Chair
Mary Ann Murphy, Chapter Co-Chair
Orillia Chapter
e-mail: orilliacarp@gmail.com
www.carp.ca/category/community/regional/central/orillia
Chief Officer(s):
Jim Gough, Vice-Chair
Ottawa Chapter
Tel: 613-755-0055
carpottawa@gmail.com
www.carp.ca/ottawa
Chief Officer(s):
Janet Gray, Chapter Director
Peterborough Chapter
www.carp.ca/category/community/regional/central/peterborough
Chief Officer(s):
Bob Geddes, Chapter Director, 705-745-3771
geddesbob@yahoo.ca
Prince Edward Island Chapter
e-mail: carp.pei@gmail.com
www.carp.ca/category/community/regional/eastern/pei
Chief Officer(s):
Barbara Sinden, Chapter Chair
Prince George Chapter
e-mail: pgcarpnews@gmail.com
www.carp.ca/category/community/regional/western/prince-george
Chief Officer(s):
Ken Biron, Chapter Chair
St. John's (Avalon) Chapter
Tel: 709-753-1187
carpavalon@gmail.com
www.carp.ca/category/community/regional/eastern/st-johns-avalon
Chief Officer(s):
Edgar Williams, Chapter Chair
Sault Ste. Marie Chapter
www.carp.ca/category/community/regional/central/sault-ste-marie
Chief Officer(s):
Marilyn Patterson, Chapter Director, 705-949-2299
marilyn.patterson@sympatico.ca
Scarborough Chapter
Tel: 416-491-2652
scarboroughcarp@gmail.com
www.carp.ca/category/community/regional/central/scarborough
Chief Officer(s):
Gary Butler, Chapter Chair
South Fraser Chapter
Tel: 204-837-4026
southfrasercarp@gmail.com
www.carp.ca/category/community/regional/western/south-fraser
www.facebook.com/SouthFraserCarp
twitter.com/SouthFraserCARP
Chief Officer(s):
Kim Richter, Chapter Chair
Sudbury Chapter
e-mail: carpsudbury09@gmail.com
www.carp.ca/category/community/regional/central/sudbury
Chief Officer(s):
Pat Douglas, Chapter Chair, 705-669-0045
Thunder Bay Chapter
www.carp.ca/category/community/regional/central/thunder-bay
Chief Officer(s):
Allen Richert, Chapter Chair, 807-768-4746
ahcr@shaw.ca
Toronto (Downtown) Chapter
e-mail: contactus@carpto2.ca
wwww.carpto2.ca
Chief Officer(s):
Adina Lebow, Chapter Chair
Toronto (Pink) Chapter
www.carp.ca/category/community/national/pink-carp
twitter.com/AgingWithPride
Vancouver Central Chapter
Toll-Free: 866-718-0274
carpvancouvercentral@gmail.com
www.carp.ca/category/community/regional/western/vancouver-central
Chief Officer(s):
Jeffrey Sefton, Chapter Chair
Vaughan Chapter
e-mail: carp.vaughan@gmail.com
www.carp.ca/category/community/regional/central/vaughan
Chief Officer(s):
George Mathew, Chapter Chair, 416-879-8470
Victoria Chapter
e-mail: CARPVictoriaChapter@gmail.com
www.carp.ca/category/community/regional/western/victoria
Chief Officer(s):
Ray Welch, Chapter Chair, 250-220-5870
Whitby Oshawa Clarington Chapter
e-mail: carpwoc@gmail.com
Chief Officer(s):
Irene Anderson, Chapter Chair, 416-521-5531
White Rock/Surrey Chapter
e-mail: carp.whiterock.surrey@gmail.com
www.carp.ca/whiterocksurrey
Chief Officer(s):
Ramona Kaptyn, Chapter Chair, 778-294-0787
April Lewis, Director, Communications, 604-536-8717
aprillewis.carp@gmail.com
Windsor-Essex Chapter
Tel: 519-890-2474
carp.windsor.essex@hotmail.ca
www.carp.ca/category/community/regional/central/windsor-essex
Chief Officer(s):
Sushil Jain, Chapter Chair
sjain42@yahoo.com
Winnipeg East Chapter
www.carp.ca/category/community/regional/western/winnipeg-east
Chief Officer(s):
Dallas Bagby, Contact, 204-661-6199
Darlene Demkey, Contact, 204-222-8120
John Plischke, Contact, 204-586-5501
Winnipeg West Chapter
Tel: 204-837-4026
carpwinnipegwest@gmail.com
www.carp.ca/category/community/regional/western/winnipeg-west
Chief Officer(s):
Gerry Otto, Chapter Chair

Carp Agricultural Society
PO Box 188, Carp ON K0A 1L0
Tel: 613-839-2172; *Fax:* 613-839-1961
info@carpfair.ca
www.carpfair.ca
Overview: A medium-sized local charitable organization founded in 1863
Mission: To improve agriculture & the quality of life in the community by educating members & the community; To provide a community forum for discussing agricultural issues; To foster community development & community spirit; To help provide markets for Ontario products; To encourage conservation of natural resources, including soil conservation, reforestation, rural & urban beautification
Member of: Carp BIA
Chief Officer(s):
Joyce Trafford, General Manager
Paul Caldwell, President, Agriculture
Heather Johnston, President, Homecraft
300 volunteer(s)
Membership: 500-999; *Committees:* Concessions; Light Horse; Heavy Horse; Gate; Parking; Dairy; Beef Cattle; Sheep; 4-H Club; Field Crops; Fruit & Vegetables; Grains & Seeds; Honey & Maple Syrup; Wine & Beer; Flowers; Domestic Science; Junior Department; Sewing, Needlework, & Crafts; Antiques; Story Book Farm

Le Carré des Lombes
#401, 2022, rue Sherbrooke Est, Montréal QC H2K 1B9
Tél: 514-287-9339
info@lecarredeslombes.com
www.lecarredeslombes.com
www.facebook.com/pages/Le-Carre-des-Lombes/161816823394
vimeo.com/danieledesnoyers
Aperçu: *Dimension:* petite; *Envergure:* locale; Organisme sans but lucratif; fondée en 1989
Mission: Diffuser des spectacles de danse; promouvoir la danse comme discipline artistique
Membre(s) du bureau directeur:
Danièle Desnoyers, Directrice artistique et chorégraphe
danieledesnoyers@lecarredeslombes.com
Membre(s) du personnel: 4

Carrefour canadien international *See* Canadian Crossroads International

Carrefour communautaire de Chibougamau
330, ch Merrill, Chibougamau QC G8P 2X4
Tél: 418-748-7266
carrefour_com@hotmail.com
Aperçu: *Dimension:* petite; *Envergure:* locale; fondée en 2001
Membre(s) du bureau directeur:
Brigitte Rosa, Responsable

Carrefour d'Actions Populaires
CP 426, Succ. Bureau-Chef, Saint-Jérôme QC J7Z 5V2
Tél: 450-432-8696; *Téléc:* 450-432-8696
www.carrefouractionspopulaire.com
Aperçu: *Dimension:* petite; *Envergure:* locale
Mission: À apporter aide et soutien aux personnes et aux familles moins fortunées
Membre(s) du bureau directeur:
Myriam Raymond, Coordonatrice
myriam@carrefouractionspopulaire.com

Carrefour d'entraide de Drummond (CEDI)
255, rue Brock, Drummondville QC J2C 1M5
Tél: 819-477-8105; *Téléc:* 819-477-7012
Aperçu: *Dimension:* petite; *Envergure:* locale; Organisme sans but lucratif; fondée en 1978
Mission: Organisme de dépannage vital, de consultation budgétaire pour personnes à faibles revenus; Cuisines collectives
Membre(s) du bureau directeur:
Lise Ledoux, Personne ressource
Finances: *Budget de fonctionnement annuel:* $100,000-$250,000
Membre(s) du personnel: 11; 10 bénévole(s)
Membre: 1-99

Carrefour de ressources en interculturel (CRIC)
#1, 1851, rue Defresne, Montréal QC H2K 2K2
Tél: 514-525-2778
info@criccentresud.org
www.criccentresud.org
Aperçu: *Dimension:* petite; *Envergure:* locale; fondée en 1999
Mission: Pour collecter des informations sur les cultures internationales afin de créer une meilleure compréhension entre les personnes d'origines culturelles différentes dans le centre-sud de Montréal
Membre(s) du bureau directeur:
Caroline Savard, Coordonnatrice
caroline@criccentresud.org
José Rebelo, Président, Conseil d'administration

Carrefour de solidarité internationale inc.
165, rue Moore, Sherbrooke QC J1H 1B8
Tél: 819-566-8595; *Téléc:* 819-566-8076
info@csisher.com
www.csisher.com
www.facebook.com/carrefour.solidarite.internationale
twitter.com/csisherbrooke
www.youtube.com/user/CSIsherbrooke
Également appelé: CSI - Sherbrooke
Aperçu: *Dimension:* petite; *Envergure:* internationale; Organisme sans but lucratif; fondée en 1976
Mission: Susciter la solidarité de la population de l'Estrie pour la justice sociale au plan international.
Membre(s) du bureau directeur:
Marco Labrie, Directeur général
marcolabrie@csisher.com
Membre(s) du personnel: 10
Membre: *Montant de la cotisation:* Barème
Activités: Quinzaine du commerce équitable, mai; Festival de Cinéma Images du Sud, avril; *Stagiaires:* Oui; *Service de conférenciers:* Oui; *Bibliothèque* Bibliothèque publique

Carrefour des Chrétiens du Québec pour la Santé *Voir* Carrefour Humanisation Santé

Carrefour des mouvements d'action catholique
435, rue du Roi, Québec QC G1K 2X1

Tél: 418-525-6187; *Téléc:* 418-525-6081
Nom précédent: Comité diosésain d'action catholique
Aperçu: *Dimension:* petite; *Envergure:* locale
Mission: Groupe de coordination des associations d'action catholique dans le diocèse de Québec
Membre(s) du bureau directeur:
Bernadette Dubuc, Contact
bernadette@mmtc-infor.com

Carrefour Humanisation Santé
CP 12, 1431, Fullum, Montréal QC H2K 3M3
Tél: 514-544-4154; *Téléc:* 514-259-0857
carrefour.humanisation@videotron.ca
Nom précédent: Carrefour des Chrétiens du Québec pour la Santé
Aperçu: *Dimension:* petite; *Envergure:* provinciale
Mission: Carrefour Humanisation-Santé est une association sans but lucratif qui vise l'humanisation des milieux de soins et de services de santé, en s'inspirant des valeurs judéo-chrétiennes. Elle met l'accent sur l'harmonisation entre la dimension humaine et spirituelle.
Membre(s) du bureau directeur:
Andrée Chapleau-Lorrain, Co-présidente
Pierre Côté, Co-président

Carrefour jeunesse emploi de l'Outaouais (CJEO)
350, boul de la Gappe, Gatineau QC J8T 7T9
Tél: 819-561-7712; *Téléc:* 819-561-1455
info@cjeo.qc.ca
www.cjeo.qc.ca
www.linkedin.com/company/carrefour-jeunesse-emploi-de-loutaouais
www.facebook.com/197339806961886
twitter.com/_cjeo
www.youtube.com/channel/UCTv0CrGXD-bjc03303Wj3MQ
Aperçu: *Dimension:* petite; *Envergure:* locale
Mission: Offrer des services qui visent à améliorer les conditions de vie des jeunes adultes de 16 à 35 ans en les accompagnant dans leur cheminement vers l'emploi, vers un retour aux études ou pour démarrer une entreprise.
Membre(s) du bureau directeur:
Martine Morissette, Directrice générale
direction@cjeo.qc.ca
Membre(s) du personnel: 36

Carrefour jeunesse emploi du Pontiac (CJEP)
CP 219, 80, rue Leslie, Campbell's Bay QC J0X 1K0
Tél: 819-648-5065
www.crep.qc.ca
Aperçu: *Dimension:* petite; *Envergure:* locale
Mission: Pour aider les jeunes à trouver des emplois et retournent à l'école
Membre(s) du bureau directeur:
Sylvie Landriault, Directrice générale
Membre(s) du personnel: 13
Membre: *Critères d'admissibilite:* Jeunes adultes

Carrefour Jeunesse Emploi Vallée-de-la-Gatineau (CJEVG)
217, rue Principale Sud, Maniwaki QC J9E 2A3
Tél: 819-441-1165; *Téléc:* 819-441-1195
info@cjevg.qc.ca
www.cjevg.qc.ca
www.facebook.com/carrefour.emploi
Aperçu: *Dimension:* petite; *Envergure:* locale
Mission: Pour aider les jeunes à trouver des emplois et retournent à l'école
Membre: *Critères d'admissibilite:* Jeunes adultes

Carrefour jeunesse-emploi Papineau (CJEP)
112, rue MacLaren Est, Gatineau QC J8L 1K1
Tél: 819-986-5248; *Téléc:* 819-986-9686
cjepapineau@cjepapineau.qc.ca
www.cjepapineau.qc.ca
Nom précédent: Action Emploi Papineau Inc.
Aperçu: *Dimension:* petite; *Envergure:* locale; fondée en 1986
Mission: Pour aider les jeunes à trouver des emplois et retournent à l'école
Membre(s) du bureau directeur:
Francine St-Jean, Directrice générale
Membre(s) du personnel: 13
Membre: *Critères d'admissibilite:* Jeunes adultes

Carrefour pour Elle
CP 21115, Succ. Jacques Cartier, Longueuil QC J4J 5J4
Tél: 450-651-5800
info@carrefourpourelle.org
www.carrefourpourelle.org
Aperçu: *Dimension:* petite; *Envergure:* locale
Mission: De fournir aux femmes et aux enfants qui sont victimes de violence un endroit sûr pour rester et pour leur offrir des compétences qui les aideront à surmonter les abus à l'avenir
Membre(s) du bureau directeur:
Sophie Boileau, Présidente, Conseil d'administration
Activités: Groupes de soutien; Recontres éclair; Groupes pour les énfants

Carrefour pour femmes inc. *See* Crossroads for Women Inc.

Carrefour Tiers-Monde (CTM)
365, boul Charest est, Québec QC G1K 3H3
Tél: 418-647-5853; *Téléc:* 418-647-5856
info@carrefour-tiers-monde.org
www.carrefour-tiers-monde.org
www.facebook.com/carrefourtiersmonde
Aperçu: *Dimension:* petite; *Envergure:* locale; fondée en 1969
Mission: Sensibiliser la population de la région de Québec aux problématiques de développement du Sud; offrir des occasions de formation pour ceux et celles qui veulent agir dans le domaine de la solidarité internationale; offrir un centre de ressources et de mobilisation aux individus et organismes de la région
Membre de: Association québécoise des organismes de coopérative internationale (AQOCI)
Membre(s) du bureau directeur:
Nicole Piché, Agente, Communication
npiche@carrefour-tiers-monde.org
Finances: *Budget de fonctionnement annuel:* $100,000-$250,000; *Fonds:* Par projet
Membre(s) du personnel: 4; 70 bénévole(s)
Membre: 15 institutionnels (13 000 membres); 60 individus; *Montant de la cotisation:* 75$ institutionnel; 10$ individu; *Comités:* Recherche de financement
Activités: Journées québécoises de solidarité internationale; journée de solidarité Nord-Sud; Au Sud comme au Nord... les enfants d'abord; *Evénements de sensibilisation:* Quinzaine du commerce équitable, mai; *Service de conférenciers:* Oui; *Bibliothèque:* Centre de documentation; Bibliothèque publique

Boutique ÉquiMonde
365, boul Charest Est, Québec QC G1K 3H3

Carrefour-Ressources
#50, 1e rue ouest, Sainte-Anne-des-Monts QC G4V 2G5
Tél: 418-763-7707; *Téléc:* 418-763-7767
carrefourressources@globetrotter.net
www.facebook.com/carrefourressources
Nom précédent: Action Budget Denis Riverin Inc.
Aperçu: *Dimension:* petite; *Envergure:* locale; Organisme sans but lucratif; fondée en 1986
Mission: Développer et offrir des services aux familles et personnes à faible revenu ou vivant avec des difficultés pour qu'elles acquièrent et accroissent leur autonomie et leurs compétences personnelles, familiales et sociales
Membre(s) du bureau directeur:
Charlotte Pouliot, Directrice
carrefourressources@globetrotter.net
Finances: *Budget de fonctionnement annuel:* $100,000-$250,000
Membre(s) du personnel: 10; 5 bénévole(s)
Membre: 33
Activités: Ateliers de cuisine; ateliers manuels; ateliers sur la consommation; service de répit; cuisine communautaire

Carrot River & District Board of Trade
PO Box 340, Carrot River SK S0E 0L0
Tel: 306-768-2533; *Fax:* 306-768-3491
Overview: A small local organization

Carstairs & District Historical Society
PO Box 1067, Carstairs AB T0M 0N0
Tel: 403-337-3710
info@roulstonmuseum.ca
carstairsroulstonmuseum.ca
Also Known As: Roulston Museum
Overview: A small local charitable organization founded in 1986
Mission: To preserve the heritage of Carstairs & District; to record the history of pioneer & contemporary life in the Carstairs area; to administer the Roulston Museum by collecting, preserving, exhibiting & interpreting artifacts relevant to the area; to assemble accurate archives
Finances: *Funding Sources:* Town of Carstairs; Mountain View County; Carstairs 20/20 Partnership; Alberta Museums Association
Activities: Garden party; pioneer supper; *Library:* Roulston Museum Archives; Open to public
Awards:
• Bessie Pointen Appreciation Award (Award)
Presented to a person/group who has made outstanding contributions to the preservation of our history

Carstairs Chamber of Commerce
PO Box 968, Carstairs AB T0M 0N0
Tel: 403-337-3710
carstairschamber@gmail.com
carstairs2020.ca/chamber/
www.facebook.com/carstairsonline
Overview: A small local organization
Mission: The Carstairs and Community Chamber of Commerce is an organization of local business people and community minded indivduals. The Chamber strives to promote the economic well-being of Carstairs and the surrounding community.
Chief Officer(s):
Dennis Schmick, President, 403-337-0009
Karen Kneeland, Vice-President, 403-337-3044
Membership: *Member Profile:* Membership included in a Town of Carstairs business license.

Casa Cultural Peruana
#404, 20 Bergamot Ave., Toronto ON M9W 1V9
Tel: 416-206-2337
www.casaculturalperuana.com
www.facebook.com/185320361494606
Overview: A small local organization founded in 2001
Mission: To promote and defend Peruvian Cultural Heritage
Activities: Folk dances; Cultural exchanges; Parties

Casa do Benfica / Benfica House of Toronto
1 Robina Ave., Toronto ON M6C 3Y4
Tel: 416-653-6370
Overview: A small local organization founded in 1969
Affliation(s): Sports Lisboa e Benfica (Lisbon, Portugal)
Chief Officer(s):
Joe Loureiro, Manager
Finances: *Funding Sources:* Provincial government
Activities: Cultural centre whose activities include dances, folk dancing, karate, soccer, special dinners, pageants & other social events

Casa do Ribatejo / Maison de Ribatejo
5979, rue Molson, Montréal QC H1Y 3C1
Tél: 514-729-7822
Également appelé: Ribatejo House
Aperçu: *Dimension:* petite; *Envergure:* locale

Casa dos Acores (Toronto) Inc / The Azorean House of Toronto
1136 College St., Toronto ON M6H 1B6
Tel: 416-603-2900; *Fax:* 416-603-0642
secretaria@cacores.ca
www.cacores.ca
www.facebook.com/pages/Casa-dos-Acores/12766509493
twitter.com/CasadosAcoresOn
Overview: A small local charitable organization founded in 1986
Affliation(s): Association of Portuguese Clubs
Chief Officer(s):
Fernando Faria, President
Finances: *Annual Operating Budget:* $100,000-$250,000
40 volunteer(s)
Membership: 400 individual; *Fees:* $60 individual
Activities: Portugese association hosting & organizing cultural events; *Library* Open to public

Casey House Hospice Inc.
9 Huntley St., Toronto ON M4Y 2K8
Tel: 416-962-7600; *Fax:* 416-962-5147
info@caseyhouse.on.ca
www.caseyhouse.com
www.linkedin.com/company/casey-house-foundation
www.facebook.com/CaseyHouseTO
twitter.com/caseyhouseTO
www.youtube.com/caseyhousetv
Overview: A small local organization founded in 1988 overseen by Canadian AIDS Society
Mission: To provide exemplary treatment, support and palliative care for people affected by HIV/AIDS, in collaboration with our communities.

Member of: Ontario Hospital Association; Canadian Palliative Care Association
Affliation(s): St. Michael's Hospital
Chief Officer(s):
Stephanie Karapita, CEO
Ann Stewart, Medical Director
Finances: *Funding Sources:* Ontario Ministry of Health; fundraising
200 volunteer(s)
Activities: Exceptional medical, palliative end-of-life care & support for people living with HIV/AIDS, their families & friends, provided in a 13-bed Hospice residence, & for up to 120 people at any one time through Home Hospice

Castle-Crown Wilderness Coalition (CCWC)
PO Box 2621, #202, 696 Kettles St., Pincher Creek AB T0K 1W0
Tel: 403-627-5059
office@ccwc.ab.ca
www.ccwc.ab.ca
www.facebook.com//269184503160443
Overview: A small local organization founded in 1989
Mission: To restore & maintain the Castle Wilderness within the Crown of the Continent Ecosystem
Chief Officer(s):
Gordon Petersen, President & Treasurer
Carolyn Aspeslet, Exective Director, 403-627-5059
James Tweedie, Director, Conservation
james@ccwc.ab.ca
Finances: *Funding Sources:* Membership fees; Donations; Conservation organizations; Fisheries & Oceans Canada
Membership: 500+; *Fees:* $10 individuals; $15 families; $25 groups; $110 supporting members; $250 life members
Activities: Sponsoring a stewardship program to monitor & restore the Castle Wilderness; Conducting hikes to raise awareness of the area; *Awareness Events:* Annual West Castle Wetland Ecological Reserve Weed Pull, July
Publications:
• Bringing it Back: A Restoration Framework for the Castle Wilderness
• The Castle Wilderness Environmental Inventory
• Castle Wilderness News
Type: Newsletter; *Frequency:* Quarterly; *Editor:* Judy Huntley
• The State of the Castle Wilderness: Annual Report
Type: Yearbook; *Frequency:* Annually

Castlegar & District Arts Council
PO Box 3501, Castlegar BC V1N 3W3
Tel: 250-365-8026
castlegararts@gmail.com
Overview: A small local organization
Mission: To promotes the arts in Castlegar and the surrounding area.
Member of: Assembly of BC Arts Councils
Chief Officer(s):
Jacquie Hamilton, Contact
jhamilton@direct.ca

Castlegar & District Chamber of Commerce (CDCoC)
1995 - 6th Ave., Castlegar BC V1N 4B7
Tel: 250-365-6313; *Fax:* 250-365-5778
info@castlegar.com
www.castlegar.com
Overview: A medium-sized local organization founded in 1946
Mission: To encourage a business climate which enables our membership & community to prosper
Member of: BC Chamber of Commerce; Canadian Chamber of Commerce
Chief Officer(s):
Kerry Hobbs, President
Finances: *Annual Operating Budget:* $100,000-$250,000; *Funding Sources:* Membership dues; City of Castlegar; provincial government
Staff Member(s): 2; 12 volunteer(s)
Membership: 225; *Fees:* Based on number of employees; *Committees:* Membership; Fund-raising; Education; Internet; Events
Activities: Golf tournament; member breakfasts & events; promotional materials; Christmas Light Up; 2010 Olympic Bid; Tourism Essentials; *Awareness Events:* Small Business Week; Chamber Week

Castlegar United Way
1995 - 6 Ave., Castlegar BC V1N 4B7
Tel: 250-365-7331; *Fax:* 250-365-5778
office@castlegar.unitedway.ca
www.castlegar.unitedway.ca
Overview: A medium-sized local charitable organization founded in 1947 overseen by United Way of Canada - Centraide Canada
Mission: To build & help sustain a quality of community life that is good for families & business.
Chief Officer(s):
Steve Martin, President
Finances: *Annual Operating Budget:* Less than $50,000
Staff Member(s): 1; 40 volunteer(s)
Membership: 9 agencies; *Committees:* Campaign Committee
Activities: *Awareness Events:* Kick Off Day, Sept.

Castor Fish & Game Association
c/o Alberta Fish & Game Association, 6924 - 104th St., Edmonton AB T6H 2L7
Tel: 780-437-2342; *Fax:* 780-438-6872
office@afga.org
www.afga.org/html/content/clubandzones
Overview: A small local organization
Member of: Alberta Fish & Game Association
Chief Officer(s):
Wes Wagar, Director, Zone 3, Alberta Fish & Game Association

Catalyst Theatre Society of Alberta
8529 Gateway Blvd., Edmonton AB T6E 6P3
Tel: 780-431-1750; *Fax:* 780-433-3060
info@catalysttheatre.ca
www.catalysttheatre.ca
Overview: A medium-sized provincial charitable organization founded in 1978
Mission: To create & present original Canadian work that explores new possibilities for theatre
Member of: Professional Association of Canadian Theatres (PACT); Canadian Conference for the Arts
Chief Officer(s):
Jonathan Christenson, Artistic Director
Staff Member(s): 7
Membership: *Committees:* Youth Advisory

Cataraqui Archaeological Research Foundation
611 Princess St., Kingston ON K7L 1E1
Tel: 613-542-3483
carf@carf.info
www.carf.info
www.facebook.com/Kingstonarchaeologicalcentre
twitter.com/carfkingston
Also Known As: Kingston Archaeological Centre
Overview: A small local charitable organization founded in 1983
Mission: To research & maintain archaeological resources in Ontario
Chief Officer(s):
Kip Parker, Executive Director
Finances: *Funding Sources:* Private & public donations; Corporate support
Staff Member(s): 4
Activities: Sponsoring archaeological research; Providing public education; Offering activities for all ages, such as a summer camp called, "Can You Dig It?"; *Awareness Events:* Public Archaeology Day, July; Archaeology Week, June; *Library:* Kingston Archaeological Centre Library; by appointment
Publications:
• Subsoil
Type: Newsletter; *Frequency:* s-a.; *Price:* Free for members of the Cataraqui Archaeological Research Foundation
Profile: Recent activities, upcoming events, articles, fiction

Cathedral Bluffs Symphony Orchestra (CBSO)
PO Box 51074, 18 Eglinton Sq., Toronto ON M1L 2K2
Tel: 416-879-5566
info@cathedralbluffs.com
www.cathedralbluffs.com
www.facebook.com/1376703615900205
twitter.com/cathedralbluff
www.youtube.com/channel/UCjQ5dDliajV95HIIIbQKMUQ
Previous Name: Cathedral Bluffs Symphony Orchestra of Scarborough
Overview: A small local charitable organization founded in 1985 overseen by Orchestras Canada
Mission: To provide residents of Scarborough with an opportunity to hear classical symphonic music performed by a live orchestra; to provide skilled amateur musicians & young soloists with an opportunity to perform
Member of: Scarborough Arts Council
Chief Officer(s):
Peggy Wong, Orchestra Director
Tim Hendrickson, President
Finances: *Funding Sources:* Box office; donations; government grants; fund-raising
Membership: *Member Profile:* Skilled musicians
Activities: A series of 5 concerts; 1 free concert at Scarborough Civic Centre during Arts Week; 1 Pops concert; *Library*

Cathedral Bluffs Symphony Orchestra of Scarborough *See* Cathedral Bluffs Symphony Orchestra

Catholic Association of Religious & Family Life Educators of Ontario (CARFLEO)
ON
e-mail: contact@carfleo.org
www.carfleo.org
www.facebook.com/Carfleo
www.twitter.com/TWEETcarfleo
www.youtube.com/VIDEOCARFLEO
Merged from: Catholic Religious Education Consultants of Ontario; Ontario Catholic Family Life Educators Network
Overview: A medium-sized local charitable organization founded in 2005
Chief Officer(s):
Paul Beaudette, Chair
BeaudetteP@hwcdsb.ca
Membership: *Member Profile:* Religious and Family Life Education in Ontario
Awards:
• Archbishop Pocock Award for Excellence in Religious Education (Award)
• Fr. Angus MacDougall S.J. Award (Award)
Meetings/Conferences: • CARFLEO Annual General Meeting & Conference, March, 2015, Queen of Apostles Retreat Centre, Mississauga, ON
Scope: Provincial

Catholic Bible Society *Voir* Société catholique de la Bible

Catholic Biblical Association of Canada (CBAC)
5650 Mavis Rd., Mississauga ON L5V 2N6
Tel: 905-568-4393
catholicbiblicalcanada@gmail.com
www.catholicbiblical.com
Previous Name: Canadian Catholic Biblical Association
Overview: A medium-sized national charitable organization founded in 1974
Mission: To foster knowledge & love of the Word of God as found in the Scriptures, through provision of a variety of sources, primarily to the Catholic community.
Affliation(s): Archdiocese of Toronto; World Catholic Biblical Federation
Chief Officer(s):
Jocelyn Monette, Executive Director
Finances: *Annual Operating Budget:* $100,000-$250,000
Membership: *Fees:* $30
Activities: Workshops; Bible in My Life program; children's summer program; pilgrimages; *Rents Mailing List:* Yes; *Library:* Resource Centre; Open to public

Catholic Charismatic Renewal Council (CCRC)
2671 Islington Ave. N., Toronto ON M9V 2X6
Tel: 416-466-0776; *Fax:* 905-454-0876
ccrctoronto@bellnet.ca
www.ccrctor.com
Also Known As: Catholic Charismatic Renewal
Overview: A small local organization
Mission: To offer service that facilitates, educates, & promotes, with activities & resources, the growth & development of the Catholic Charismatic Renewal, throughout the Catholic Communities of Metropolitan Toronto, the Regional Municipalities of York, Peel, a portion of Durham, the County of Simcoe, a portion of the County of Dufferin, & the Town of Orangeville; To promote Baptism of the Holy Spirit; To bring people of the church closer together by exercising the gifts of TheHoly Spirit; To be committed to daily prayer & scripture reading, the love & us of the sacraments, & attendance at mass
Affliation(s): Archdiocese of Toronto
Chief Officer(s):
Hilda Martin, Chair
Activities: Providing the Holy Eucharist with healing services, evangelization, Life in The Spirit seminars, devotional workshops, conferences & special rallies;Serving the local church & parish when called upon by bishops & priests; Providing faith instruction; Offering prayer groups

Catholic Charities of The Archdiocese of Toronto
#400, 1155 Yonge St., Toronto ON M4T 1W2

Tel: 416-934-3401; *Fax:* 416-934-3402
info@catholiccharitiestor.org
www.catholiccharitiestor.org
twitter.com/charitiescares
Previous Name: Council of Catholic Charities
Overview: A medium-sized local licensing charitable organization founded in 1913
Mission: Catholic Charities of the Archidiocese of Toronto is dedicated to ensuring the provision of health & social sciences & to provide leadership & advocacy on behalf of the member agencies & those in need. The people served live & work throughout the Greater Toronto Area, as well as in Simcoe, Durham, Peel, & York.
Affliation(s): Catholic Family Services of Toronto & 26 member agencies
Chief Officer(s):
Thomas Cardinal Collins, Chair
Kevin McGivney, President
Michael Fullan, Executive Director
Finances: *Annual Operating Budget:* $250,000-$500,000
Staff Member(s): 1; 10 volunteer(s)
Membership: *Committees:* Allocations; Audit; Catholic Agencies; Communications; Employee Pension & Benefit; Human Resources; Membership Review; Nominating; Social Justice/Advocacy
Activities: *Speaker Service:* Yes

Catholic Children's Aid Society of Hamilton (CCAS)
735 King St. East, Hamilton ON L8M 1A1
Tel: 905-525-2012; *Fax:* 905-525-5606
david.shea@hamiltonccas.on.ca
www.hamiltonccas.on.ca
Overview: A small local charitable organization founded in 1954
Mission: To provide child welfare services to the Roman Catholic population of the City of Hamilton
Member of: Ontario Association of Children's Aid Societies
Affliation(s): Council of Catholic Service Organziations
Chief Officer(s):
Ersilia DiNardo, Executive Director
Anne Niec, President
Finances: *Annual Operating Budget:* Greater than $5 Million; *Funding Sources:* Ontario Ministry of Community & Social Services
Staff Member(s): 180; 191 volunteer(s)
Membership: 100-499; *Fees:* $10
Activities: Annual general meeting; *Awareness Events:* Serendipity Auction, Nov.; *Internships:* Yes; *Speaker Service:* Yes

Catholic Children's Aid Society of Metropolitan Toronto *See* Catholic Children's Aid Society of Toronto

Catholic Children's Aid Society of Toronto (CCAS)
26 Maitland St., Toronto ON M4Y 1C6
Tel: 416-395-1500; *Fax:* 416-395-1581
pr@ccas.toronto.on.ca
www.ccas.toronto.on.ca
Previous Name: Catholic Children's Aid Society of Metropolitan Toronto
Overview: A medium-sized local charitable organization founded in 1894
Mission: CCAS investigates concerns that a child may be abused or neglected, then assesses the risk to the child & develops a plan to keep the child safe. It is mandated to provide protective services to Catholic children at any time. It is a registered charity, BN: 129863577RR0001.
Member of: Catholic Charities of the Archdiocese of Toronto
Chief Officer(s):
Stephen Taylor, President
Mary A. McConville, Executive Director
Finances: *Funding Sources:* Provincial government; private donations
Activities: Parental healthcare & child management training; foster care; Central Adoption Centre; *Awareness Events:* Child Abuse Prevention Campaign

North York Branch
30 Drewry Ave., Toronto ON M2M 4C4
Chief Officer(s):
Nyron Sookraj, Branch Manager

Scarborough Branch
1880 Birchmount Rd., Toronto ON M1P 2J7
Mission: On behalf of the Catholic community, this organization is committed to provide social services that protect children and strengthen family life.
Chief Officer(s):
Nancy DiNatale, Branch Manager

Scarborough Branch
843 Kennedy Rd., Toronto ON M1K 2E3
Chief Officer(s):
Domenic Gratta, Branch Manager

West Toronto Branch
Dufferin Mall, #219, 900 Dufferin St., Toronto ON M6H 4B1
Chief Officer(s):
Renée Walsh, Branch Manager

Catholic Church Extension Society of Canada *See* Catholic Missions in Canada

Catholic Civil Rights League (CCRL)
2305 Bloor Street West, Toronto ON M6S 1P1
Tel: 416-466-8244; *Fax:* 416-466-0091
Toll-Free: 844-722-2275
ccrl@ccrl.ca
www.ccrl.ca
www.youtube.com/user/CatholicCivilRights
Overview: A medium-sized national organization founded in 1985
Mission: To be witness for church teaching in public life; To combat anti-Catholic defamation in the media; To participate in debates on public policy
Affliation(s): Archdiocese of Toronto
Chief Officer(s):
Christian D. Elia, Executive Director
Finances: *Funding Sources:* Donations
Membership: *Fees:* $25 individuals; $15 students & seniors; $30 families; *Member Profile:* Catholics over the age of eighteen
Activities: Advocating with government & media
Awards:
• Archbishop Adam Exner Award for Catholic Excellence in Public Life (Award)
Publications:
• Civil Rights
Type: Newsletter; *Frequency:* Quarterly; *Editor:* Joanne McGarry; *Price:* Free with Catholic Civil Rights League membership
Profile: Regional roundup, current issues, & media watch

Catholic Community Services Inc. (CCS) / Services communautaires catholiques inc.
1857, boul de Maisonneuve ouest, Montréal QC H3H 1J9
Tel: 514-937-5351; *Fax:* 514-937-5548
info@ccs-montreal.org
www.ccs-montreal.org
facebook.com/pages/CCS-Montreal
twitter.com/CCSMontreal
www.youtube.com/channel/UCSlZdslLG8cmtCqm_Es2ATQ
Overview: A medium-sized local organization founded in 1974
Mission: To provide a broad spectrum of social services on behalf of the English-speaking Catholic community of the Diocese of Montréal
Chief Officer(s):
Fred James, Director General, 514-937-5351 Ext. 242
fredj@ccs-montreal.org
Finances: *Annual Operating Budget:* $1.5 Million-$3 Million
Staff Member(s): 33; 1104 volunteer(s)
Membership: 65; *Fees:* $10
Activities: Youth groups; home sharing; administrative & support services; community organization & development; family support programs; personal development & support groups; camping services; Almage Senior Centre; Teapot Senior Centre; Good Shepherd Community Centre; Home Support Program; volunteer coordination; Home Day Care Program; *Speaker Service:* Yes

Catholic Cross Cultural Services (CCS)
#401, 55 Town Centre Ct., Toronto ON M1P 4X4
Tel: 416-757-7010; *Fax:* 416-757-7399
www.cathcrosscultural.org
Previous Name: Catholic Immigration Bureau
Overview: A medium-sized international charitable organization overseen by Ontario Council of Agencies Serving Immigrants
Mission: To promote the settlement & integration of immigrants & refugees facing linguistic & cultural barriers through the provision of community based services
Affliation(s): Access for New Canadians
Chief Officer(s):
Carolyn Davis, Executive Director
Finances: *Annual Operating Budget:* $3 Million-$5 Million
Staff Member(s): 98; 20 volunteer(s)
Membership: 60; *Fees:* $20 individual; $35 organization

Brampton
#302, 8 Nelson St. West, Brampton ON L6X 4J2
Tel: 905-457-7740; *Fax:* 905-457-7769
Mission: To promote the settlement & integration of immigrants & refugees facing linguistic & cultural barriers through the provision of community based services.

Mississauga
3660 Hurontario St., 7th Fl., Mississauga ON L5B 3C4
Tel: 905-273-4140; *Fax:* 905-273-4176
Mission: To promote the settlement & integration of immigrants & refugees facing linguistic & cultural barriers through the provision of community based services.

Scarborough Region
#503, 1200 Markham Rd., Toronto ON M1H 3C3
Tel: 416-289-6766; *Fax:* 416-289-6198
Mission: To promote the settlement & integration of immigrants & refugees facing linguistic & cultural barriers through the provision of community based services.

Catholic Education Foundation of Ontario (CEFO)
80 Sheppard Ave. East, Toronto ON M2N 6E8
Tel: 416-229-5326; *Fax:* 416-229-5345
office@cefontario.ca
cefontario.ca
Overview: A small provincial charitable organization founded in 1976
Mission: To foster & promote the principles of Catholic education; to support parents in their role as primary educators; to assist the Church in its pastoral responsibilities to the schools; to encourage the establishment of Catholic schools; to promote equity of educational funding in Ontario
Chief Officer(s):
John J. Flynn, Executive Secretary

Catholic Family Counselling Centre; Catholic Social Services; Catholic Welfare Bureau *See* Mosaic Counselling & Family Services

Catholic Family Life Centre-Simcoe South; North Simcoe Catholic Family Life Centre *See* Catholic Family Services of Simcoe County

Catholic Family Service of Ottawa (CFS Ottawa) / Service familial catholique d'Ottawa
310 Olmstead St., Ottawa ON K1L 7K3
Tel: 613-233-8478; *Fax:* 613-233-9881
info@cfsottawa.ca
www.cfsottawa.ca
Previous Name: Catholic Family Service of Ottawa-Carleton
Overview: A small local charitable organization founded in 1940 overseen by Family Service Ontario
Mission: CFS Ottawa offers a range of social services in English & French to all residents of the Ottawa-Carleton area. Services include counselling, support to the victims or witnesses of family violence or sexual abuse, advocacy, community development. It is a registered charity, BN: 118841105RR0001.
Member of: Family Service Canada
Chief Officer(s):
Normand Levasseur, President
Franca DiDiomete, Executive Director
Finances: *Annual Operating Budget:* $1.5 Million-$3 Million; *Funding Sources:* Provincial/municipal government; United Way; private donations
Staff Member(s): 34; 15 volunteer(s)
Membership: 50
Activities: *Internships:* Yes

Catholic Family Service of Ottawa-Carleton *See* Catholic Family Service of Ottawa

Catholic Family Services of Hamilton (CFS)
#201, 447 Main St. East, Hamilton ON L8N 1K1
Tel: 905-527-3823; *Fax:* 905-546-5779
Toll-Free: 877-527-3823
intake@cfshw.com
www.cfshw.com
www.facebook.com/Catholic.Family.Services.Hamilton
Previous Name: Catholic Family Services of Hamilton-Wentworth
Overview: A small local organization founded in 1944 overseen by Ontario Association of Credit Counselling Services
Mission: To provide individual, marriage, family, & credit counselling services in the Hamilton & Burlington communities
Member of: Ontario Association of Credit Counselling Service
Affliation(s): Ontario Community Support Association; ONTCHILD; Family Services Ontario; Canadian Association for Community Care; Continuing Gerontological Education Cooperative; Older Persons' Mental Health & Addictions Network; Ontario Association on Developmental Diabilities;

Ontario Case Managers Association; Ontario Gerontology Association; Ontario Partnership on Aging Development Disabilities
Chief Officer(s):
Linda Dayler, Executive Director & Secretary
Teresa Hartnett, Chair
Kathleen Leach, Vice-Chair
Carol James, Treasurer
Paula Forbes, Associate Director
Mary Jefferson, Associate Director
Finances: *Funding Sources:* Government of Canada; Province of Ontario; City of Hamilton; United Way of Burlington & Greater Hamilton; Foundations such as ON Trillium Foundation
Activities: Offering programs, such as the Employee Assistance Program, Debt Management Program, K.I.D.S. (Kids in Divorced / Separated Situations), Men's Anti-Violence & Abuse Program, & the Senior's Intervention & Support Program; Providing mediation services, in areas such as the workplace, credit, estates, & commerce; Offering consumer credit education to the general public; Offering money management coaching

Catholic Family Services of Hamilton-Wentworth *See* Catholic Family Services of Hamilton

Catholic Family Services of Peel Dufferin (CFSPD)
Emerald Centre, #400, 10 Kingsbridge Garden Circle, Mississauga ON L5R 3K6
Tel: 905-897-1644; *Fax:* 905-897-2467
Toll-Free: 888-940-0584
info@cfspd.com
www.cfspd.com
Previous Name: Peel Dufferin Catholic Services
Overview: A small local charitable organization founded in 1981 overseen by Family Service Ontario
Mission: CFSPD is a multi-service counselling agency that supports families coping with difficulties, notably violence, trauma & abuse. Services are available in many languages to help people deal with such problems as depression, anxiety, grief, marital difficulties, parent-child conflict, developmental transitions & cutural adjustments. Offices in Mississauga & Brampton have walk-in clinics. The Society is a registered charity, BN: 119087823RR0001.
Member of: Catholic Charities; Archdiocese of Toronto; United Way of Peel Region
Chief Officer(s):
Andrea Broadley, President
Mark Creedon, Executive Director
Finances: *Annual Operating Budget:* $500,000-$1.5 Million
Staff Member(s): 30; 85 volunteer(s)
Activities: Individual, couple & family therapy; support groups; workshops; *Internships:* Yes; *Speaker Service:* Yes

Brampton Branch
#201, 60 West Dr., Brampton ON L6T 3T6
Tel: 905-450-1608; *Fax:* 905-450-8902
Toll-Free: 888-940-0584

Caledon Branch
#D8, 18 King St. East, Bolton ON L7E 1E8
Tel: 905-450-1608; *Fax:* 905-450-8902
Toll-Free: 888-940-0584
Chief Officer(s):
Dale Gillespie, Executive Director

Orangeville Branch
Dufferin Child & Family Services, 655 Riddell Rd., Orangeville ON L9W 4Z5
Toll-Free: 888-940-0584

Catholic Family Services of Saskatoon
#200, 506 - 25th St. East, Saskatoon SK S7K 4A7
Tel: 306-244-7773; *Fax:* 306-244-8537
staff@cfssaskatoon.sk.ca
www.cfssaskatoon.sk.ca
Overview: A small local charitable organization founded in 1940
Mission: To promote quality of life by developing & supporting the inherent strengths of individuals, families & the community
Member of: United Way of Saskatoon
Affliation(s): Family Service Canada; Family Service Saskatchewan
Chief Officer(s):
Trish St. Onge, Executive Director
Finances: *Annual Operating Budget:* $500,000-$1.5 Million; *Funding Sources:* Provincial & regional governments; United Way; Diocese of Saskatoon; community grants & donations
50 volunteer(s)
Membership: 1-99
Activities: Counselling; family & children's services; teen parent program; family to family ties program; families & schools together program; employee & family assistance prgrams, marriage preparation, work & family wellness presentations; event speakers; workshop presentations & consultations; *Library*

Catholic Family Services of Simcoe County (CFSSC)
#5, 20 Bell Farm Rd., Barrie ON L4M 6E4
Tel: 705-726-2503; *Fax:* 705-726-2570
info@cfssc.ca
www.cfssc.ca
www.facebook.com/CFSSC
twitter.com/CounselorSimcoe
Previous Name: Catholic Family Life Centre-Simcoe South; North Simcoe Catholic Family Life Centre
Overview: A small local charitable organization founded in 1979 overseen by Family Service Ontario
Mission: To offer professional social services to all residents of Simcoe South; services will be directed to the treatment of troubled families & individuals, as well as to strengthening & enriching family life & individual functioning in all their dimensions & contexts
Chief Officer(s):
Wanda Rae, Executive Director
wrae@cfssc.ca
Finances: *Annual Operating Budget:* $250,000-$500,000; *Funding Sources:* Charities; United Way
Staff Member(s): 20
Membership: 1-99
Activities: Family, individual & group counselling; family life education;

Catholic Family Services of Toronto (CFS Toronto) / Services familiaux catholiques de Toronto
Catholic Pastoral Centre, #200, 1155 Yonge St., Toronto ON M4T 1W2
Tel: 416-921-1163; *Fax:* 416-921-1579
info@cfsofto.org
www.cfsofto.org
Previous Name: Catholic Welfare Bureau
Overview: A medium-sized local charitable organization founded in 1922
Mission: CFS Toronto is a non-profit counselling agency for individuals, couples, & families. Within the context of Catholic beliefs, it offers a range of specialised programs, as well as a safe environment for women & families who are victims of abuse.
Member of: Catholic Charities of the Archdiocese of Toronto
Affliation(s): Family Service Canada; Family Service Ontario
Chief Officer(s):
Ken Yip-Chuck, President
Lucia Furgiuele, Secretary/Executive Director
Finances: *Annual Operating Budget:* $1.5 Million-$3 Million
Staff Member(s): 35; 18 volunteer(s)
Activities: *Library*

North Toronto Office
#300, 5799 Yonge St., Toronto ON M2M 3V3
Tel: 416-222-0048; *Fax:* 416-222-3321

The Catholic Foundation of Manitoba / Fondation catholique du Manitoba
622 Taché Ave., Winnipeg MB R2H 2B4
Tel: 204-233-4268; *Fax:* 204-233-1800
cfmb@mts.net
catholicfoundation.mb.ca
Overview: A medium-sized provincial organization founded in 1964
Mission: The vision of the Catholic Foundation is to provide for the needy, better the situation of the underprivileged, promote cultural advancement and scientific research, and promote the cultural life of the Catholic community of Manitoba by encouraging the funding of endowments and by providing prudent management of funds and responsible distribution of the derived revenue
Chief Officer(s):
Tom Lussier, President
Staff Member(s): 1; 18 volunteer(s)
Awards:
• Catholic Foundation of Manitoba Grants (Grant)
Eligibility: Religious, educational or social agency

Catholic Health Alliance of Canada / Alliance catholique canadienne de la santé
Annex C, Saint-Vincent Hospital, 60 Cambridge St. North, Ottawa ON K1R 7A5
Tel: 613-562-6262; *Fax:* 613-782-2857
www.chac.ca
Previous Name: Catholic Health Association of Canada; Catholic Hospital Association of Canada
Overview: A large national charitable organization founded in 1939
Mission: To strengthen & support the ministry of Catholic health care organizations & providers, through advocacy & governance
Chief Officer(s):
Mike Shea, Chair
James Roche, Executive Director
jroche@bruyere.org
Nuala Kenny, Ethics & Health Policy Advisor
nkenny@eastlink.ca
Finances: *Annual Operating Budget:* $1.5 Million-$3 Million; *Funding Sources:* Membership dues
Membership: 7 provincial associations + 23 sponsors & owners of health care organizations + 96 hospitals, long-term care organizations & health care professionals; *Fees:* Schedule available; *Member Profile:* Sponsor organizations of Catholic health care in Canada.
Awards:
• Midcareer Leadership Award (Award)
Eligibility: Nominees must be 45 years of age or younger & work in a Catholic health care organization
• Lifetime Achievement Award (Award)
Eligibility: Nominees must have sent the majority of their careers in Catholic health care
Meetings/Conferences: • Catholic Health Alliance of Canada 2015 Annual Conference: Standing Together at the Margins - Creating a Circle of Compassion, May, 2015, Sheraton Cavalier Hotel, Saskatoon, SK
Scope: National
Description: A conference featuring keynote speakers & the presentation of awards
Contact Information: Executive Director: James Roche, Phone: 613-562-6262, ext. 2164, E-mail: jroche@bruyere.org
Publications:
• Catholic Health Alliance of Canada Annual Report
Type: Yearbook; *Frequency:* Annually
Profile: Financial & executive reports
• Facing Death, Discovering Life
Number of Pages: 78; *Author:* James Roche; *ISBN:* 9780920705360; *Price:* $10.95
• Forming Health Care Leaders: A Guide
Number of Pages: 143; *ISBN:* 9780920705421; *Price:* $12.50
• Health Ethics Guide
Number of Pages: 122; *ISBN:* 9780920705018; *Price:* $12.50 members
• Lift Up Your Hearts to the Lord
Number of Pages: 104; *ISBN:* 9780920705056; *Price:* $4 members
• Living With Hope in Times of Illness
Number of Pages: 30; *Editor:* Barry McGrorry; Greg J. Humbert; *ISBN:* 9780920705407; *Price:* $2
• Spirituality & Health: What's Good for the Soul Can Be Good for the Body, Too
Number of Pages: 74; *Author:* James Roche; *ISBN:* 9780920705247; *Price:* $9.95

Catholic Health Association of British Columbia (CHABC)
9387 Holmes St., Burnaby BC V3N 4C3
Tel: 604-524-3427; *Fax:* 604-524-3428
smhouse@shawlink.ca
chabc.bc.ca
Overview: A medium-sized provincial organization founded in 1940 overseen by Catholic Health Association of Canada
Mission: To witness to the healing ministry and abiding presence of Jesus. Inspired by the Gospel, this Association strives to have a universal concern for health as a condition for full human development.
Member of: Catholic Health Association of Canada; Health Employers Association of British Columbia
Affliation(s): Euthanasia Prevention Coalition; Canadian Association of Parish Nurse Ministries
Chief Officer(s):
Dianne Doyle, President
Staff Member(s): 2
Membership: 114; *Committees:* Mission Intergration; Pastral Care; Ethics
Meetings/Conferences: • Catholic Health Association of BC 75th Annual General Meeting and Conference, 2054, BC
Scope: Provincial

Catholic Health Association of Canada; Catholic Hospital Association of Canada *See* Catholic Health Alliance of Canada

Canadian Associations

Catholic Health Association of Manitoba (CHAM) / Association catholique manitobaine de la santé (ACMS)

SBGH Education Bldg., #N5067, 409 Taché Ave., Winnipeg MB R2H 2A6
Tel: 204-235-3136; *Fax:* 204-235-3811
www.cham.mb.ca
Overview: A medium-sized provincial charitable organization founded in 1943
Mission: To carry out the healing ministry of the Catholic Church in the delivery of both health & social services in Manitoba; To treat the people of Manitoba with compassion & respect for all; to recognize the spiritual dimension integral to health & healing
Affliation(s): Bishops of Manitoba; Diocese of Churchill-Hudson Bay, Northwest Territories
Chief Officer(s):
Wilmar Chopyk, Executive Director
wchopyk@cham.mb.ca
Daniel Lussier, Chair
Membership: *Fees:* $20 personal members; $100 associate members; *Member Profile:* Organizations; Health care facilities; Individuals
Activities: Promoting collaboration in health care services; Providing education to health care professionals, parish workers, & volunteers; Engaging in advocacy activities for the needs of the vulnerable & disadvantaged; Promoting the dignity & sacredness of each person; *Awareness Events:* CHAC World Day of the Sick
Publications:
• CHAM [Catholic Health Association of Manitoba] Newsletter
Type: Newsletter
Profile: Educational information for members & CHAM activities

Catholic Health Association of New Brunswick (CHANB)

1773 Water St., Miramichi NB E1N 1B2
Tel: 506-778-5302; *Fax:* 506-778-5303
nbcha@nb.aibn.com
www.chanb.com
Overview: A small provincial organization founded in 1986 overseen by Catholic Health Association of Canada
Mission: The Catholic Health Association of New Brunswick is a provincial Christian organization promoting health care in the tradition of the Catholic Church. The Association fosters healing in all its aspects: Physical, psychological, social and spiritual
Chief Officer(s):
Robert Stewart, Executive Director
rstewart@health.nb.ca
Membership: 300

Catholic Health Association of Saskatchewan (CHAS)

1702 - 20 St. West, Saskatoon SK S7M 0Z9
Tel: 306-655-5330; *Fax:* 306-655-5333
cath.health@sasktel.net
www.chassk.ca
Overview: A medium-sized provincial charitable organization founded in 1943 overseen by Catholic Health Association of Canada
Mission: To provide leadership in mission, ethics, spiritual care, & social justice in Saskatchewan; To promote the sanctity of life & the dignity of all
Chief Officer(s):
Sandra Kary, Executive Director
sandra.chassk@sasktel.net
Brian Martin, President
Christopher Boychuk, Vice-President
Peter Martens, Secretary-Treasurer
Membership: *Fees:* $25 person members; $75 associations; *Member Profile:* Institutions, groups, & individuals who are interested in Catholic health care & support the work of the association
Activities: Providing education & resources to members; Offering programs, such as the Parish Home Ministry of Care Program & the Catholic Health Leadership Program; Engaging in advocacy activities with the government; Providing both provincial & national networking opportunities; *Awareness Events:* Mission Week; World Day of the Sick; *Library:* Catholic Health Association of Saskatchewan Resource Library;
Awards:
• Moola-Freer Scholarship & Award (Scholarship), Committee of the Board of Directors
Eligibility: Scholarship funds available to persons who have registered or are planning to register in a Palliative Care home study or certificate program.*Deadline:* June 30

Catholic Health Care Conference of Alberta *See* Christian Health Association of Alberta

Catholic Health Corporation of Ontario (CHCO)

PO Box 1879, 712 College Ave. West, Guelph ON N1H 7A1
Tel: 519-767-5600; *Fax:* 519-767-5602
chco@chco.ca
www.chco.ca
Overview: A medium-sized provincial organization overseen by Catholic Health Association of Canada
Mission: Sponsors member institutions & thereby continues and strengthens Catholic health care in Ontario
Chief Officer(s):
John P. Ruetz, President, 519-767-5600
Sarah Quackenbush, Consultant, Mission & Education, 705-522-1485
csjsarah@ontera.net

Catholic Health of Alberta *See* Covenant Health (Alberta)

Catholic Immigration Bureau *See* Catholic Cross Cultural Services

Catholic Immigration Centre + CIC Foundation (CIC)

219 Argyle Ave., Ottawa ON K2P 2H4
Tel: 613-232-9634; *Fax:* 613-232-3660
cic@cic.ca
www.cic.ca
Overview: A medium-sized national organization founded in 1984
Chief Officer(s):
Carl Nicolson, Executive Director
Membership: *Fees:* $10; *Member Profile:* All Canadian residents

Catholic Missions in Canada (CMIC) / Missions catholiques au Canada

#201, 1155 Yonge St., Toronto ON M4T 1W2
Tel: 416-934-3424; *Fax:* 416-934-3425
Toll-Free: 866-937-2642
info@cmic.info
www.cmic.info
www.facebook.com/catholicmissionsincanada
twitter.com/canadamissions
www.youtube.com/missioncanada
Previous Name: Catholic Church Extension Society of Canada
Overview: A large national charitable organization founded in 1908
Mission: To keep the Catholic faith in remote & poor communities throughout Canada
Member of: Association of Fundraising Professionals (Toronto); CAGGP
Chief Officer(s):
Thomas C. Collins, Apostolic Chancellor & Chair, Executive Committee
Philip J. Kennedy, President
president@cmic.info
John P. McGrath, Secretary
Finances: *Funding Sources:* Donations; Fundraising
Staff Member(s): 11; 1 volunteer(s)
Membership: 2; *Committees:* Executive; Allocations; Finance
Activities: Supporting over 600 missionaries who serve in home mission communities throughout Canada; *Speaker Service:* Yes
Awards:
• St. Joseph Award (Award)
Eligibility: Catholic missionary workers in Canada
Publications:
• Catholic Missions in Canada
Type: Magazine
Profile: Information about missionaries who serve in home mission communities across Canada
• Catholic Missions in Canada Annual Report
Type: Yearbook; *Frequency:* Annually
Profile: Featuring information on CMIC's expenses & distributions
• Catholic Missions in Canada E-Newsletter
Type: Newsletter
• John & Emily Visit Catholic Missions in Canada [a publication of Catholic Missions in Canada]
Type: Book
Profile: A soft-cover activity book for children 12 & under

Catholic Organization for Life & Family (COLF) (COLF) / Organisme catholique pour la vie et la famille (OCVF)

2500 Don Reid Dr., Ottawa ON K1H 2J2
Tel: 613-241-9461; *Fax:* 613-241-9048
ocvfcolf@cccb.ca
www.cccb.ca/site/eng/contact-us
Overview: A small national organization founded in 1996
Mission: To build a civilization of love; To promote respect for human life & the important role of the family
Affliation(s): Canadian Conference of Catholic Bishops (CCCB)
Chief Officer(s):
Michèle Boulva, Director, 613-241-9461 Ext. 141
Peter D. Murphy, Assistant Director, 613-241-9461 Ext. 162
Jocelyne Pagé, Administrative Assistant, 613-241-9461 Ext. 161
Finances: *Funding Sources:* Donations
Staff Member(s): 1
Activities: Promoting the teaching of the Catholic Church in circumstances from conception to natural death; Preparing & providing educational resources; Strengthening the role of the family; Participating in public debate about the family & respect for life; Collaborating with the Canadian Conference of Catholic Bishops & the Knights of Columbus
Publications:
• Catholic Organization for Life & Family Activity Report
Type: Yearbook; *Frequency:* Annually
Profile: Details about the organization's activities, projects, & initiatives
• Euthanasia & Assisted Suicide — Urgent Questions
• Life in the Balance: Workshop on Euthanasia & Assisted Suicide
Type: Guide
• Stem Cells: Astonishing Promises . . . But at What Cost?

The Catholic Principals' Council of Ontario (CPCO)

#3030, 2300 Yonge St., Toronto ON M4P 1E4
Tel: 416-483-1556; *Fax:* 416-483-2554
Toll-Free: 888-621-9190
info@cpco.on.ca
www.cpco.on.ca
twitter.com/CPCO2012
www.youtube.com/cpcotoronto
Overview: A small provincial organization
Mission: CPCO is a voluntary, professional association that serves more than 2,100 principals and vice-principals in twenty-nine Catholic school boards across Ontario
Chief Officer(s):
Paul Lacalamita, Executive Director
placalamita@cpco.on.ca
Paul Lacalamita, President
president@cpco.on.ca
Finances: *Annual Operating Budget:* $1.5 Million-$3 Million
Staff Member(s): 6; 6 volunteer(s)
Membership: 2,000 members who are principals & vice-principals in more than 1,300 elementary & secondary separate schools across Ontario; *Committees:* Communications; Member Security; Professional Development; Finance; Issues in Catholic Education
Activities: Advocacy, professional development; legal services; *Speaker Service:* Yes

Catholic Teachers Guild

80 Sackville St., Toronto ON M5A 3E5
Tel: 416-393-5204; *Fax:* 416-397-6586
catholicteachersguild.ca
Overview: A medium-sized national organization founded in 2000
Mission: To support & deepen the vocation of Catholic educators
Affliation(s): Archdiocese of Toronto
Chief Officer(s):
Barry White, President
barry.white@tcdsb.org
Finances: *Funding Sources:* Donations
Membership: *Fees:* $20 initial fee; $10 renewal fee; *Member Profile:* Active or retired Catholics involved in education at any level, including pre-school & post-secondary, who support the mission of the Guild; Catholic lay educators & volunteers who work in Catholic schools, public schools, private schools, & other educational institutions
Activities: Holding an Annual Education Mass & Lenten Retreat; Presenting lectures & workshops; Conducting book club meetings

Catholic Welfare Bureau *See* Catholic Family Services of Toronto

Catholic Women's League of Canada (CWL)

702C Scotland Ave., Winnipeg MB R3M 1X5

Fax: 888-831-9507
Toll-Free: 888-656-4040
info@cwl.ca
www.cwl.ca
Overview: A large national organization
Mission: To assist one another liver holier lives, while carrying out our daily occupations; To become an enlightened & dedicated member of the laity; to grow in relationship with Christ & the church; To carry out the work of Christ at home, in the community, & in the world; To serve the people of God; To ensure local leagues within Archdiocesan Parishes report to regional & provincial councils, & follow the constitution & bylaws of the CWL
Chief Officer(s):
Kim Scammell, Executive Director
executivedirector@cwl.ca
Martin W. Currie, Spiritual Advisor
Barbara Dowding, President
Judy Lewis, Secretary-Treasurer
Finances: *Funding Sources:* Donations
Membership: Over 50,000; *Member Profile:* Catholic women over sixteen years of age who wish to serve within their communities
Meetings/Conferences: • Catholic Women's League of Canada 2015 National Convention, August, 2015, Vancouver, BC
Scope: National
• Catholic Women's League of Canada 2016 National Convention, August, 2016, Halifax Convention Centre, Halifax, NS
Scope: National
Publications:
• The Canadian League [a publication of the Catholic Women's League of Canada]
Type: Newsletter; *Frequency:* 3 pa; *Price:* Free for Catholic Women's League of Canada members
Profile: Executive reports, meeting highlights, spiritual development, Christian family life, community, education, health, communications, laws,international relations, & provincial reports
• Catholic Women's League of Canada Annual Report
Type: Yearbook; *Frequency:* Annually
• Catholic Women's League of Canada Executive Handbook

Catholic Youth Studio - KSM Inc. (KSM)
183 Roncesvalles Ave., 2nd Fl., Toronto ON M6R 2L5
Tel: 416-588-0555; *Fax:* 416-588-9995
radio@catholicradio.ca
www.catholicradio.ca
www.facebook.com/KSMRADIO
twitter.com/KSMRADIO
Also Known As: Catholic Radio Toronto
Overview: A small local charitable organization founded in 1994
Mission: To reach those who have not yet experienced their "springtime of faith", by means of evangelization through modern forms of mass media; to broadcast a daily radio program, eleven hours per week in Polish, & to publish a magazine, in order to provide services to families
Affiliation(s): Archdiocese of Toronto
Chief Officer(s):
Marcin Serwin, Director
Finances: *Funding Sources:* Donations
Staff Member(s): 4; 50 volunteer(s)
Membership: *Member Profile:* Individuals who donate their talents & time at Catholic Youth Studio - KSM Inc., a media corporation for evangelization, in order to promote the Christian faith; Members are both youth & adults who share the Catholic Youth Studio's charism
Activities: Programming for youth, couples, & seniors; Providing faith instruction; *Awareness Events:* International Festival of Religious Song
Publications:
• Rodzina (Family)
Type: Magazine

Catholicland
21550 Bathurst St., Holland Landing ON L9N 1P6
Tel: 647-834-2046
Other Communication: 905-836-5928 (phone)
victor@catholicland.com
www.catholicland.com
Also Known As: Catholicland & Stella Maris Marina
Overview: A small local organization founded in 1989
Mission: To provide & promote a place (80 acres) for retreat, recreation, & reflection, in a Catholic environment, for families, parish groups, & youth; To assist other countries by volunteering services to those in need
Affiliation(s): Archdiocese of Toronto
Chief Officer(s):
Marilyn Carvalho, Contact
Victor Carvalho, Contact
Membership: *Fees:* $300 individual; $600 family for 5 on-site events with overnights & 10 without overnights; *Member Profile:* Roman Catholic individuals & families, faithful to the Magisterium, who wish to live their faith in fun & fellowship with others
Activities: Assisting those in need in Belize & Africa; Funding volunteers to pursue missions in countries where assistance is needed; Providing land & water based recreational programming for married couples, families, & youth; Offering retreat houses for reflection & retreats

CAUSE Canada
PO Box 8100, #207, 743 Railway Ave., Canmore AB T1W 2T8
Tel: 403-678-3332; *Fax:* 403-678-8869
Toll-Free: 888-552-2873
info@cause.ca
www.cause.ca
www.facebook.com/causecanada
twitter.com/causecanada
Also Known As: Christian Aid for Under-Assisted Societies Everywhere
Overview: A small international charitable organization founded in 1984
Mission: To support sustainable development projects in geographical regions where there is an under-representation of international aid organizations; it is the belief of CC that each individual is precious in the eyes of God & that to lack access to food, water & basic health care is to be deprived of the promise of a full & abundant life
Member of: Canadian Council for Christian Charities
Chief Officer(s):
Ron Remple, Chair
Beverley Carrick, Executive Director
bevcarrick@cause.ca
Finances: *Annual Operating Budget:* $500,000-$1.5 Million
Staff Member(s): 7; 55 volunteer(s)
Membership: 40
Activities: Primary health care; water & sanitation restoration; gender-specific develoment initiatives; microenterprine project; *Speaker Service:* Yes
Publications:
• CAUSE Canada Newsletter
Type: Newsletter

Cavalier Riding Club Ltd. (CRC)
705 Pine Glen Rd., Pine Glen NB E1J 1S1
Tel: 506-386-7652
cavalierridingclub.weebly.com
Also Known As: Greater Moncton Riding for the Disabled; CRC Therapeutic Horseback Riding for the Disabled
Overview: A small local organization
Mission: To use hippotherapy in order to treat certain physical and emotional conditions of the disabled.
Member of: Canadian Therapeutic Riding Association
Chief Officer(s):
Dianne LaRocque, President
diannelarocque@gmail.com

Cavelier de Lasalle Historical Society *Voir* Société historique Cavelier-de-LaSalle

Cayuga & District Chamber of Commerce
PO Box 118, 6 Cayuga St. North, Cayuga ON N0A 1E0
Tel: 905-772-5954; *Fax:* 905-772-2680
info@cayugachamber.ca
cayugachamber.ca
facebook.com/603613649649890
Overview: A small local organization founded in 1992
Mission: The mission of the Cayuga & District Chamber of Commerce is to effect and enhance total quality of life for area residents and to share their gifts with all visitors and tourists.
Chief Officer(s):
John Edelman, President
Membership: 72

CBC French Network Technicians' Union (Ind.) *Voir* Syndicat des technicien(ne)s et artisan(e)s du réseau français de Radio-Canada (ind.)

CCCC Relief & Development Group (R&D Group). *See* Canadian Christian Relief & Development Association

C.D. Howe Institute / Institut C.D. Howe
#300, 67 Yonge St., Toronto ON M5E 1J8
Tel: 416-865-1904; *Fax:* 416-865-1866
cdhowe@cdhowe.org
www.cdhowe.org
Overview: A medium-sized international organization founded in 1973
Mission: To identify current & emerging economic & social policy issues facing Canadians; to recommend particular policy options; to communicate conclusions of research to domestic & international audiences.
Chief Officer(s):
Finn Poschmann, Vice-President, Research
William B.P. Robson, President & CEO
Finances: *Funding Sources:* Membership dues
Staff Member(s): 24
Membership: *Fees:* Schedule available; *Member Profile:* Participation in & support of its activities from business, organized labor, associations, professions & interested individuals
Activities: *Speaker Service:* Yes; *Library* by appointment

CDC Centre-Sud
2187, rue Larivière, Montréal QC H2K 1P5
Tél: 514-521-0467; *Téléc:* 514-521-6923
info@cdccentresud.org
www.cdccentresud.org
www.facebook.com/222302597781803
Aperçu: *Dimension:* petite; *Envergure:* locale
Mission: Pour aider au développement socio-économique du centre-sud de Montréal
Membre(s) du bureau directeur:
François Bergeron, Directeur général
Membre: 60; *Critères d'admissibilite:* Les organismes communautaires; Les entreprises d'économie sociale
Activités: Assemblées communautaires

Cecebe Waterways Association (CWA)
c/o President, 332B Chapman Dr., Burks Falls ON P0A 1C0
Tel: 705-573-5090
www.cecebewaterways.ca
Overview: A medium-sized local organization
Mission: To represent families who are residents and/or landowners on Lake Cecebe.
Chief Officer(s):
Peggy Frederikse, President
pfrederikse@sympatico.ca
Membership: *Fees:* $30

Cedar Crest Society for Community Living
PO Box 1197, 410 Cedar Ave., 100 Mile House BC V0K 2E0
Tel: 250-395-4643; *Fax:* 250-395-4686
cedar_crest@bcinternet.net
www.cedarcrestsociety.com
Overview: A small local organization founded in 1973
Mission: To promote ongoing growth & development of any person with a mental handicap
Member of: British Columbia Association for Community Living
Finances: *Funding Sources:* Community donations, income from the Thrift Shop, contracts with the Ministry of Children & Family Services

The Celtic Way / La Route Celtique
324 Gosford South Rd., Inverness QC G0S 1K0
Tel: 418-453-3434; *Fax:* 418-453-3434
info@larouteceltique.org
www.larouteceltique.org
Overview: A small local organization founded in 2001
Mission: To promote the heritage of the Megantic region, Inverness in particular; to conduct historical & genealogical research, & communicate the results of that research to the public

Cement Association of Canada (CAC) / Association canadienne du ciment
#502, 350 Sparks St., Ottawa ON K1R 7S8
Tel: 613-236-9471; *Fax:* 613-563-4498
www.cement.ca
Previous Name: Canadian Portland Cement Association
Overview: A medium-sized national organization
Mission: Represents all of Canada's cement producers; aims to improve & extend the uses of cement & concrete through market development, engineering, research, education, & public affairs work
Chief Officer(s):
Michael McSweeney, President & CEO
mmcsweeney@cement.ca

Staff Member(s): 31
Membership: 10 companies; *Member Profile:* 100% of the manufacturers of Portland cement in Canada

Ontario Region
#704, 1500 Don Mills Rd., Toronto ON M3B 3K4
Tel: 416-449-3708; *Fax:* 416-449-9755
www.cement.ca
Mission: To engage the cement industry in a wide range of public policy issues - from sustainable infrastructure and climate change, to clean air and clean water.
Chief Officer(s):
Rico Fung, Director, Markets & Technical Affairs
rfung@cement.ca

Québec & Atlantic Region
#250-5, 1173 Charest Blvd. West, Québec QC G1N 2C9
Tel: 418-527-3973; *Fax:* 418-537-6876
Toll-Free: 888-591-3973
www.cement.ca
Mission: To engage the cement industry in a wide range of public policy issues - from sustainable infrastructure and climate change, to clean air and clean water.
Chief Officer(s):
Michel Binette, Vice-President, Legal, Public and Government Affairs, Québec & Atlantic Region
mbinette@cement.ca

Western Region (Calgary)
135 Silverado Range Hts SW, Calgary AB T2X 0B8
Tel: 403-250-3535; *Fax:* 403-261-3637
western@cement.ca
www.cement.ca
Mission: The Cement Association of Canada is the voice of Canada's cement industry representing 100% of cement producers in the country. Through the CAC, the cement industry is engaged in a wide range of public policy issues - from sustainable infrastructure and climate change, to clean air and clean water.
Chief Officer(s):
Todd Kruszewski, Director, Markets & Technical Affairs
tkruszewski@cement.ca

Western Region (Vancouver)
#820, 1200 West 73rd Ave., Vancouver BC V6P 6G5
Tel: 604-269-0582; *Fax:* 604-269-0585
www.cement.ca
Mission: To engage the cement industry in a wide range of public policy issues - from sustainable infrastructure and climate change, to clean air and clean water.
Chief Officer(s):
Andy Vizer, Director, Markets & Technical Affairs
avizer@cement.ca

Center for Research-Action on Race Relations (CRARR)
#610, 460 Saint-Catherine West, Montreal QC H3B 1A7
Tel: 514-939-3342; *Fax:* 514-939-9763
crarr@primus.ca
www.crarr.org
www.facebook.com/258996297500425?sk=wall
Overview: A medium-sized national organization founded in 1983
Mission: An independent, non-profit civil rights organization with the mandate to promote racial equality and combat racism in Canada.
Member of: Court Challenges Program of Canada
Chief Officer(s):
Fo Niemi, Executive Director
Finances: *Funding Sources:* Public and private institutions, unions, educational institutions and individual donors
Activities: Conferences, consultations and seminars on different race relations and civil rights issues; Awards; Training; Research-action projects; Charter research and litigation; *Rents Mailing List:* Yes

Centraide Abitibi Témiscamingue et Nord-du-Québec
1009, 6e rue, Val-d'Or QC J9P 3W4
Tél: 819-825-7139; *Téléc:* 819-825-7155
courrier@centraide-atnq.qc.ca
www.centraide-atnq.qc.ca
Aperçu: *Dimension:* moyenne; *Envergure:* provinciale; Organisme sans but lucratif; fondée en 1983 surveillé par United Way of Canada - Centraide Canada
Affliation(s): Chambre de Commerce; Comité prévention des crimes
Membre(s) du bureau directeur:
Huguette Boucher, Directrice générale
hboucher@centraide-atnq.qc.ca
Finances: *Budget de fonctionnement annuel:* $500,000-$1.5 Million
Membre(s) du personnel: 3; 1000 bénévole(s)
Membre: *Comités:* Administration; Campagne; Allocation des fonds; Priorités sociales; Candidature; Communications; Développement
Activités: *Service de conférenciers:* Oui

Centraide Bas St-Laurent
#303, 1555, boul. Jacques Cartier, Mont-Joli QC G5H 2W1
Tél: 418-775-5555; *Téléc:* 418-775-5525
direction@centraidebsl.org
www.centraidebsl.org
Aperçu: *Dimension:* petite; *Envergure:* locale; Organisme sans but lucratif; fondée en 1982 surveillé par United Way of Canada - Centraide Canada
Mission: Organisme sans but lucratif de lutte à la pauvreté et de soutien aux personnes démunies.
Membre(s) du bureau directeur:
Michel Daigle, Directeur général
Finances: *Budget de fonctionnement annuel:* $500,000-$1.5 Million
Membre(s) du personnel: 3; 100 bénévole(s)
Membre: 40; *Critères d'admissibilite:* Organismes communautaires; *Comités:* Comité des priorités; Comité d'allocations

Centraide Centre du Québec
154, rue Dunkin, Drummondville QC J2B 5V1
Tél: 819-477-0505; *Téléc:* 819-477-6719
Ligne sans frais: 888-477-0505
bureau@centraide-cdq.ca
www.centraide-cdq.ca
www.facebook.com/pages/Centraide_cdq/152071968150658
twitter.com/centraide_cdq
Nom précédent: Centraide Coeur du Québec
Aperçu: *Dimension:* petite; *Envergure:* locale; Organisme sans but lucratif; fondée en 1979 surveillé par United Way of Canada - Centraide Canada
Mission: Rassembler les personnes et les ressources du Centre-du-Québec afin de contribuer au développement social de la communauté et d'améliorer la qualité de vie de ses membres les plus vulnérables et ce, en lien avec les organismes communautaires.
Membre(s) du bureau directeur:
Isabelle Dionne, Directrice générale
idionne@centraide-cdq.ca
Membre(s) du personnel: 5
Membre: 1-99
Activités: Campagne annuelle de financement

Centraide Coeur du Québec *Voir* Centraide Centre du Québec

Centraide Côte-Nord/Secteur ouest *Voir* Centraide Haute-Côte-Nord/Manicouagan

Centraide de l'ouest québécois *Voir* Centraide Outaouais

Centraide de la région du Grand Moncton et du Sud-Est du NB Inc. *See* United Way of Greater Moncton & Southeastern New Brunswick

Centraide de Niagara Sud *See* United Way South Niagara

Centraide de Stormont, Dundas & Glengarry *See* United Way of Stormont, Dundas & Glengarry

Centraide du Grand Montréal / Centraide of Greater Montréal
493, rue Sherbrooke ouest, Montréal QC H3A 1B6
Tél: 514-288-1261; *Téléc:* 514-350-7282
info@centraide-mtl.org
centraide-mtl.org
www.facebook.com/centraide.du.grand.montreal
twitter.com/centraidemtl
www.youtube.com/user/CentraideMtl
Aperçu: *Dimension:* grande; *Envergure:* locale; fondée en 1974 surveillé par United Way of Canada - Centraide Canada
Mission: To maximize financial & volunteer resources in order to promote mutual aid, social commitment, & self-reliance as effective means of improving the quality of life of the community, & especially of its neediest members
Membre(s) du bureau directeur:
Michèle Thibodeau-DeGuire, Présidente et Directrice générale
Finances: *Budget de fonctionnement annuel:* $3 Million-$5 Million; *Fonds:* There is an annual campaign which begins on October 1st.
Membre(s) du personnel: 71
Membre: 200; *Montant de la cotisation:* 10 $
Activités: *Bibliothèque* rendez-vous

Centraide Duplessis
#101, 185, rue Napoléon, Sept-Iles QC G4R 4R7
Tel: 418-962-2011; *Fax:* 418-968-4694
administration@centraideduplessis.org
www.centraideduplessis.org
Overview: A small local organization overseen by United Way of Canada - Centraide Canada
Chief Officer(s):
Denis Miousse, Directeur général
direction@centraideduplessis.org

Centraide Estrie
1150, rue Belvédère sud, Sherbrooke QC J1H 4C7
Tél: 819-569-9281; *Téléc:* 819-569-5195
bureau@estrie.centraide.ca
www.estrie.centraide.ca
www.facebook.com/pages/Centraide-Estrie/177152949010458
www.youtube.com/user/centraideestrie
Aperçu: *Dimension:* petite; *Envergure:* locale; Organisme sans but lucratif; fondée en 1975 surveillé par United Way of Canada - Centraide Canada
Mission: Vise à soutenir les organismes bénévoles et communautaires engagés directement auprès des clientèles les plus démunies et vulnérables.
Membre(s) du bureau directeur:
Claude Forgues, Directeur général
Finances: *Budget de fonctionnement annuel:* $500,000-$1.5 Million
Membre(s) du personnel: 3; 1 bénévole(s)
Membre: 150

Centraide Gaspésie Iles-de-la-Madeleine
#216, 230, rte du Parc, Sainte-Anne-des-Monts QC G4V 2C4
Tél: 418-763-2171; *Téléc:* 418-763-7677
centraidegim@globetrotter.net
www.gim.centraide.ca
Aperçu: *Dimension:* petite; *Envergure:* locale; fondée en 1988 surveillé par United Way of Canada - Centraide Canada
Mission: Soulager la misère et la souffrance humaine.
Membre(s) du bureau directeur:
Yvon Lemieux, Directeur général
Finances: *Budget de fonctionnement annuel:* $250,000-$500,000
400 bénévole(s)
Membre: *Montant de la cotisation:* 20$

Centraide Gatineau-Labelle-Hautes-Laurentides
671, rue de la Madone, Mont-Laurier QC J9L 1T2
Tél: 819-623-4090; *Téléc:* 819-623-7646
bureau@centraideglhl.ca
www.gatineaulabellehlaurentides.centraide.ca
www.facebook.com/Centraide.Gatineau.Labelle.Hautes.Laurentides
Aperçu: *Dimension:* moyenne; *Envergure:* locale; fondée en 1985 surveillé par United Way of Canada - Centraide Canada
Membre(s) du bureau directeur:
Annie Lajoie, Directrice générale
Finances: *Budget de fonctionnement annuel:* $50,000-$100,000

Centraide Haute-Côte-Nord/Manicouagan
#301, 858, rue de Puyjalon, Baie-Comeau QC G5C 1N1
Tél: 418-589-5567; *Téléc:* 418-295-2567
centraidehcnman@globetrotter.net
www.centraidehcnmanicouagan.ca
Nom précédent: Centraide Côte-Nord/Secteur ouest
Aperçu: *Dimension:* moyenne; *Envergure:* locale; Organisme sans but lucratif surveillé par United Way of Canada - Centraide Canada
Membre(s) du bureau directeur:
Christine Brisson, Directrice générale

Centraide KRTB-Côte-du-Sud
100, 4e av, La Pocatière QC G0R 1Z0
Tél: 418-856-5105; *Téléc:* 418-856-4385
centraideportage@bellnet.ca
centraidekrtbcotedusud.org
Nom précédent: Centraide Portage-Taché
Aperçu: *Dimension:* petite; *Envergure:* locale surveillé par United Way of Canada - Centraide Canada

Mission: Notre mission est d'aider les gens, d'affecter les ressources en fonction des besoins, d'améliorer la qualité de vie de chacun et de renforcer le soutien communautaire. Donnez un coup de main au destin et participez aux efforts déployés par le Mouvement Centraide Portage-Taché.
Membre(s) du bureau directeur:
Sylvain Roy, Directeur général

Centraide Lanaudière

674, rue St-Louis, Joliette QC J6E 2Z6
Tél: 450-752-1999
www.centraide-lanaudiere.com
www.facebook.com/275362692481275
Aperçu: *Dimension:* moyenne; *Envergure:* locale; Organisme sans but lucratif; fondée en 1977 surveillé par United Way of Canada - Centraide Canada
Mission: Promouvoir l'entraide, le partage et l'engagement bénévole et communautaire
Membre de: Centraide Canada
Membre(s) du bureau directeur:
Sylvie Savoie, Directrice générale
Finances: *Budget de fonctionnement annuel:* $100,000-$250,000
Membre(s) du personnel: 3; 500 bénévole(s)
Membre: 148; *Critères d'admissibilite:* Etre résident de Lanaudière ou avoir sa place d'affaires ou son lieu de travail sur le territoire de Centraide Lanaudière; *Comités:* Cabinet de campagne; Conseil d'administration; Comité d'attribution de fonds
Activités: *Stagiaires:* Oui

Centraide Laurentides

#107, 880, Michèle-Bohec, Blainville QC J7C 5E2
Tél: 450-436-1584; *Téléc:* 450-951-2772
www.centraidelaurentides.org
www.facebook.com/centraidelaurentides
twitter.com/CentraideLauren
www.youtube.com/user/centraidelaurentides
Aperçu: *Dimension:* petite; *Envergure:* locale; Organisme sans but lucratif; fondée en 1962 surveillé par United Way of Canada - Centraide Canada
Mission: Contribuer, par la promotion du partage et de l'engagement bénévole et communautaire, à la construction d'une société d'entraide vouée à l'amélioration de la qualité de vie des personnes en difficulté
Membre(s) du bureau directeur:
Suzanne M. Piché, Directrice générale
spiche@laurentides.centraide.ca
Réjean Kingsbury, Présidente
Violette Gingras, Directrice de communications
vgingras@laurentides.centraide.ca
Finances: *Budget de fonctionnement annuel:* $1.5 Million-$3 Million
Membre(s) du personnel: 21; 1500 bénévole(s)
Activités: Mène une campagne de sollicitation à l'automne et soutient 75 organismes communautaires qui viennent en aide aux personnes dans le besoin, sur le territoire des Laurentides; opère trois comptoirs d'entraide; *Service de conférenciers:* Oui

Centraide Mauricie

90, Des Casernes, Trois-Rivières QC G9A 1X2
Tél: 819-374-6207; *Téléc:* 819-374-6857
centraide.mauricie@centraidemauricie.ca
www.centraidemauricie.ca
www.facebook.com/173989994047?ref=ts
Aperçu: *Dimension:* petite; *Envergure:* locale; Organisme sans but lucratif; fondée en 1956 surveillé par United Way of Canada - Centraide Canada
Mission: Travailler à un changement social pour une société plus juste, plus humaine et plus démocratique à travers la promotion de l'entraide, la solidarité et l'engagement bénévole afin de répondre aux besoins socio-économiques de notre communauté.
Membre de: Assemblée des Centraide du Québec
Membre(s) du bureau directeur:
Julie Colbert, Directrice générale
julie.colbert@centraidemauricie.ca
Finances: *Budget de fonctionnement annuel:* $500,000-$1.5 Million
Membre(s) du personnel: 3; 3200 bénévole(s)
Membre: 318; *Critères d'admissibilite:* Bénévole; donateur; organismes communautaires; *Comités:* Allocation de fonds; Communication; Finances; Orientation & Priorité
Activités: Campagne de financement annuelle; *Service de conférenciers:* Oui

Centraide of Greater Montréal *Voir* Centraide du Grand Montréal

Centraide Outaouais

74, boul. Montclair, Gatineau QC J8Y 2E7
Tél: 819-771-7751; *Téléc:* 819-771-0301
Ligne sans frais: 800-325-7751
information@centraideoutaouais.com
www.centraideoutaouais.com
www.facebook.com/pages/Centraide-Outaouais/346079120163
www.youtube.com/user/centraideoutaouais
Nom précédent: Centraide de l'ouest québécois
Aperçu: *Dimension:* moyenne; *Envergure:* locale; Organisme sans but lucratif; fondée en 1944 surveillé par United Way of Canada - Centraide Canada
Mission: Mobiliser le gens et rassembler les ressources pour améliorer la qualité de vie des personnes plus vulnérables et contribuer au développement de collectivités solidaires.
Membre(s) du bureau directeur:
Nathalie Lepage, Directrice générale
lepagen@centraideoutaouais.com
Finances: *Budget de fonctionnement annuel:* $1.5 Million-$3 Million
Membre(s) du personnel: 8; 5000 bénévole(s)
Activités: *Service de conférenciers:* Oui

Centraide PEI *See* United Way of Prince Edward Island

Centraide Portage-Taché *Voir* Centraide KRTB-Côte-du-Sud

Centraide Québec

#101, 3100, av Bourg-Royal, Québec QC G1C 5S7
Tél: 418-660-2100; *Téléc:* 418-660-2111
centraide@centraide-quebec.com
www.centraide-quebec.com
www.facebook.com/centraidequebec
www.youtube.com/user/CentraideQuebec
Aperçu: *Dimension:* moyenne; *Envergure:* locale; Organisme sans but lucratif; fondée en 1945 surveillé par United Way of Canada - Centraide Canada
Mission: Levées de fonds et attribution de subventions à 166 organismes communautaires pour aider les personnes les plus démunies
Membre(s) du bureau directeur:
Bruno Marchand, Président/Directeur général
Finances: *Budget de fonctionnement annuel:* Plus de $5 Million
Membre(s) du personnel: 30; 1200 bénévole(s)
Membre: 650; *Montant de la cotisation:* 5$

Centraide Richelieu-Yamaska

320, ave. de la Concorde nord, Saint-Hyacinthe QC J2S 4N7
Tél: 450-773-6679; *Téléc:* 450-773-4734
bureau@centraidery.org
www.richelieuyamaska.centraide.ca
www.facebook.com/pages/Centraide-Richelieu-Yamaska/199196286858982
Aperçu: *Dimension:* petite; *Envergure:* locale surveillé par United Way of Canada - Centraide Canada
Mission: Centraide Portage-Taché, c'est une organisation charitable, qui repose sur l'engagement bénévole et qui se donne comme mission d'améliorer les conditions de vie des plus démuni(e)s de son territoire.
Membre(s) du bureau directeur:
Daniel Laplante, Directrice générale
dan.laplante@centraidery.org

Centraide Saguenay-Lac St-Jean

#107, 475, boul. Talbot, Chicoutimi QC G7H 4A3
Tél: 418-543-3131; *Téléc:* 418-543-0665
info@centraideslsj.ca
www.centraidesaglac.ca
Aperçu: *Dimension:* moyenne; *Envergure:* locale; Organisme sans but lucratif; fondée en 1978 surveillé par United Way of Canada - Centraide Canada
Mission: Rassembler et développer des ressources financières et bénévoles afin d'aider les diverses communautés du Saguenay-Lac-St-Jean à organiser et à promouvoir l'entreaide, l'engagement social et la prise en charge afin d'améliorer la qualité de vie de sa collectivité et de ses membres les plus démunis et les plus vulnérables.
Membre(s) du bureau directeur:
Martin St-Pierre, Directeur général
martin.stpierre@centraideslsj.ca
Claude Fortin, Agente, Communication
claudie.fortin@centraideslsj.ca
Finances: *Budget de fonctionnement annuel:* $500,000-$1.5 Million
Membre(s) du personnel: 4; 3000 bénévole(s)
Membre: 95 organismes associés bénéficiaires de l'aide de Centraide; *Critères d'admissibilite:* Organismes communautaires
Activités: *Service de conférenciers:* Oui

Centraide sud-ouest du Québec

#200, 100, rue Ste-Cécile, Salaberry-de-Valleyfield QC J6T 1M1
Tél: 450-371-2061; *Téléc:* 450-377-2309
centraid@rocler.qc.ca
www.centraidesudouest.org
www.facebook.com/195796617125646
Aperçu: *Dimension:* moyenne; *Envergure:* locale; Organisme sans but lucratif; fondée en 1982 surveillé par United Way of Canada - Centraide Canada
Mission: Grâce à votre don, il y a du changement possible. En effet, la misère qu'elle soit physique, morale, psychologique ou matérielle peut toucher tout le monde, peu importe la classe sociale. Donner à Centraide Sud-Ouest, c'est susciter un changement positif dans notre communauté
Membre(s) du bureau directeur:
Steve Hickey, Directeur général
Finances: *Budget de fonctionnement annuel:* $50,000-$100,000
Membre(s) du personnel: 2; 1000 bénévole(s)
Membre: 12 conseils d'administration; *Critères d'admissibilite:* Etre un organisme à but non-lucratif; *Comités:* Allocation des fonds; Cabinet de campagne; Comité d'analyse des besoins et de Campagne
Activités: *Stagiaires:* Oui

Central 1 Credit Union

1441 Creekside Dr., Vancouver BC V6J 4S7
Tel: 604-734-2511; *Fax:* 855-772-6936
Toll-Free: 800-661-6813
communications@central1.com
www.central1.com
ca.linkedin.com/company/central-1-credit-union
www.facebook.com/Central1CreditUnion
twitter.com/Central1CU
www.youtube.com/user/central1creditunion
Previous Name: Credit Union Central of British Columbia
Merged from: Credit Union Central of British Columbia & Credit Union Central of Ontario
Overview: A medium-sized local organization founded in 1944 overseen by Credit Union Central of Canada
Mission: To act as the central financial facility, payments settlement centre, liquidity manager, & trade association for credit unions in British Columbia & Ontario; To provide financial stewardship, competitive advantage, & fair value for credit unions in British Columbia & Ontario
Member of: Credit Union Central of Canada
Affliation(s): Canadian Payments Association; INTERAC
Chief Officer(s):
Terry Enns, Chair
Don Wright, President & CEO
Helen Blackburn, CFO & Senior Vice-President, Strategy
Charles Milne, Chief Investment Officer
Jon Schubert, Interim Chief Risk Officer
Oscar van der Meer, Chief Technology & Payments Officer
Fred Wagner, Senior Vice-President, Trade Services
Membership: *Member Profile:* Credit unions in British Columbia & Ontario
Activities: Managing the liquidity reserves of member credit unions in both British Columbia & Ontario; Offering payments & Internet banking to member credit unions; Serving corporate customers with transaction & banking services; *Speaker Service:* Yes
Publications:
• The Coincident Economic Index (CEI)
Type: Newsletter; *Author:* David Hobden; Judy Wozencroft
Profile: A summary measure of the level & velocity of the economies of British Columbia & Metro Vancouver
• Co-operation, Conflict, & Consensus
Number of Pages: 290; *Author:* Dr. Ian MacPherson
Profile: The history of the British Columbia credit union movement
• Economic Analysis of British Columbia (The Analysis)
Type: Newsletter *ISSN:* 0824-3980
Profile: A non-politically biased, authoritative economic analyses of local, national, & international issues that affect British Columbia's economy
• Economics: B.C. Weekly Briefing
Type: Newsletter; *Frequency:* Weekly; *Editor:* David Hobden
ISSN: 1918-3535
Profile: Information on interest rates, employment trends, tax changes, the national debt, & other current economic issues

• Economics: Budget Analysis
Type: Report; *Frequency:* Irregular
Profile: Analysis of the British Columbia provincial economy
• Economics: Interest Rate Forecast
Type: Newsletter; *Frequency:* Monthly; *Editor:* Helmut Pastrick; David Hobden
Profile: Up-to-date interest, deposit, lending, & bank rate forecasts, with an assessment of factors that shape trends
• Economics: Lower Mainland Housing Updates
Type: Newsletter; *Editor:* Helmut Pastrick
Profile: Analysis of recent housing sales & price information for the real estate boards of Greater Vancouver & the Fraser Valley
• Economics: Vancouver Island Housing Updates
Type: Newsletter; *Editor:* Helmut Pastrick
Profile: Analysis of recent housing sales & price information for the real estate board of Victoria & Vancouver Island
• Enterprise: The Voice of Canadian Credit Unions
Type: Magazine; *Accepts Advertising*
Profile: Coverage of issues that impact Canada's credit union sector, such as restructuring, technology, & marketing

Mississauga - Ontario Region
2810 Matheson Blvd. East, Mississauga ON L4W 4X7
Tel: 905-238-9400
Toll-Free: 800-661-6813
communications@central1.com
www.central1.com
Mission: To enable the strength, stability, & growth of the credit union system
Affliation(s): Canadian Payments Association; INTERAC

Central Albera Soccer Association (CASA)
4108A - 60 St., Camrose AB T4V 3G7
Fax: 780-672-0035
casa9@telus.net
www.central-alta-soccer.ca
Overview: A small local organization overseen by Alberta Soccer Association
Member of: Alberta Soccer Association
Chief Officer(s):
Tammy Olson, Executive Director
Staff Member(s): 4

Central Alberta AIDS Network Society (CAANS)
Turning Point, 4611 - 50th Ave., Red Deer AB T4N 3Z9
Tel: 403-346-8858; *Fax:* 403-346-2352
Toll-Free: 877-346-8858
info@caans.org
www.caans.org
www.facebook.com/group.php?gid=7191549516
twitter.com@CAANSRedDeer
Overview: A small local charitable organization founded in 1988 overseen by Canadian AIDS Society
Mission: To carry out its charitable mission, which includes responsibility for HIV prevention & support, in the David Thompson Health Region, which extends from Drumheller to Drayton Valley & from Nordegg to the Saskatchewan border
Finances: *Funding Sources:* Donations; Fundraising; United Way Central Alberta; Alberta Community HIV Fund; Safe Communities Coalition of Central Alberta; Wild Rose Foundation
Staff Member(s): 10
Activities: Providing support, information, referrals, education, & research; Presenting harm reduction workshops; Providing a needle drop box program, a needle exchange program, syringe retrieval, & disposal training; Counselling; Engaging in advocacy activities for people affected by HIV; Offering a place to "drop-in"; Preparing informational displays & promotional materials for the public; Addressing stigma & discrimination issues; Liaising with other community organizations; *Awareness Events:* World AIDS Day, December 1

Central Alberta Gliding Club
Red Deer AB
Tel: 403-346-0543
www.cagcsoaring.ca
Overview: A small local organization founded in 1989
Mission: To train pilots for glider licences; To create opportunities for glider pilots to fly club-owned aircraft
Member of: Alberta Soaring Council; Innisfail Flying Club; Soaring Association of Canada
Chief Officer(s):
Shane Cockriell, Director
shane-o@telusplanet.net
Finances: *Funding Sources:* Membership dues

Central Alberta Realtors Association
4922 - 45 St., Red Deer AB T4N 1K6
Tel: 403-343-0881; *Fax:* 403-347-9080
office@CARAssociation.ca
www.rdreb.ca
www.facebook.com/243909398990726
twitter.com/CaraRedDeer
Overview: A small local organization overseen by Alberta Real Estate Association
Member of: Alberta Real Estate Association; The Canadian Real Estate Association
Chief Officer(s):
Judy Ferguson, Executive Officer
Ken Devoe, President
Membership: 650; *Member Profile:* Real estate brokers & agents

Central Alberta Women's Outreach Society (CAWOS)
4101 - 54 Ave, Red Deer AB T4N 7G3
Tel: 403-347-2480
Toll-Free: 866-347-2480
info@womensoutreach.ca
www.womensoutreach.ca
www.facebook.com/RDOutreachCentre
twitter.com/womensoutreach
Also Known As: Women's Outreach
Overview: A medium-sized local charitable organization founded in 1984
Mission: To help women who have chosen to pursue a safer, healthier and more secure life for themselves and their families.
Member of: Public Legal Education Network of Alberta
Chief Officer(s):
Barb Barber, Executive Director
Finances: *Funding Sources:* National, provincial & municipal government; foundations; donors
Activities: Working with women who are seeking change in lifestyles, relationships, parenting skills & financial stability; *Library* Open to public

Central Annapolis Valley Chamber of Commerce
PO Box 395, 831 Main St., Kingston NS B0P 1R0
Tel: 902-765-0344; *Fax:* 902-765-0141
Overview: A medium-sized local organization founded in 1945
Mission: To promote economic development in the Annapolis Valley, from West Hants to the District of Clare
Member of: Canadian Chamber of Commerce
Affliation(s): World Trade Centre
Chief Officer(s):
Kenneth L. Bower, President
Melissa Robinson, Secretary
Finances: *Annual Operating Budget:* $100,000-$250,000; *Funding Sources:* Memberships; grants
Staff Member(s): 1
Membership: 500; *Committees:* Business Development; Fisheries; Forestry; Transportation

Central Beekeepers' Alliance (CBA)
c/o Agricultural Research Centre, 850 Lincoln Rd., Fredericton NB E3B 9H8
Previous Name: Central New Brunswick Beekeepers Association
Overview: A small local organization founded in 1963
Mission: To promote & support beekeeping in central & southwestern New Brunswick; To provide assistance to new beekeepers; To offer information about honey bees & beekeeping to apiarists & the public
Chief Officer(s):
Michelle Flanagan, President
Natalie Duncan, Vice-President
Marlene Price, Secretary
Rick Atkinson, Treasurer
Membership: *Fees:* $5/year; *Member Profile:* Hobbyist & commercial beekeepers from central & southwestern New Brunswick
Activities: Organizing regular monthly meetings for members & anyone interested in beekeeping at the Agricultural Research Station in Fredericton; Providing field trips; Offering educational programs where persons can learn apiary skills; Arranging displays to inform the public;

Central British Columbia Railway & Forest Industry Museum Society
850 River Rd., Prince George BC V2L 5S8
Tel: 250-563-7351; *Fax:* 250-563-3697
trains@pgrfm.bc.ca
www.pgrfm.bc.ca
www.facebook.com/groups/47235038734
www.twitter.com/pgrailmuseum
Also Known As: Railway & Forestry Museum
Overview: A small local charitable organization founded in 1983
Mission: Administers Prince George Railway & Forest Industry Museum
Member of: Canadian Railway Historical Association; Canadian Museum Association; British Columbia Museum Association; American Railway Museum Association
Chief Officer(s):
Laura Williams, General Manager
Finances: *Annual Operating Budget:* $50,000-$100,000
Staff Member(s): 6; 15 volunteer(s)
Membership: 75; *Fees:* $15-$40
Activities: *Awareness Events:* Steam Day; Forester Day; Family Carnival; *Library:* Canfor Library; by appointment

Central Canada Broadcast Engineers (CCBE)
3 Jasmine Dr., Paris ON N3L 3P7
Fax: 519-442-1912
Toll-Free: 800-481-4649
information@ccbe.ca
www.ccbe.ca
Overview: A small provincial organization founded in 1951
Mission: To provide up-to-date technical information regarding the broadcast industry, including the following areas: television, radio, post production, towers & safety issues.
Chief Officer(s):
Peter Warth, President
peter@ccbe.ca

Central Canada Broadcasters Association *See* Ontario Association of Broadcasters

Central Canadian Federation of Mineralogical Societies (CCFMS)
c/o Natural History, Mineralogy, 100 Queen's Park, Toronto ON M5S 2C6
e-mail: info@ccfms.ca
www.ccfms.ca
Overview: A medium-sized national organization founded in 1969
Mission: To act as the voice for amateur rock, mineral, & lapidary clubs in central Canada
Chief Officer(s):
Russell Bruce, President, 416-284-9797
bruce12@bell.net
Ray Hainsworth, Secretary
eyciboy@yahoo.ca
Faye Meadows, Treasurer
fayemeadows@rogers.com
Membership: 25 clubs; *Member Profile:* Rock, mineral, & lapidary clubs for hobbyists in central Canada
Activities: Promoting the earth sciences; Encouraging exchange of information between societies, federations, & institutions; Educating rock & mineral collectors; Protecting collecting sites; *Speaker Service:* Yes

Central Carleton Chamber of Commerce
28 Palmer Rd., Waterville NB E7P 1B4
Tel: 506-375-4074
Overview: A small local organization
Mission: To promote economic development in the Waterville / Carleton area
Member of: New Brunswick Chamber of Commerce
Chief Officer(s):
Dale Albright, President
Membership: 150; *Member Profile:* Local businesses in the Waterville / Carleton region
Awards:
• Business of the Year (Award)
• Small Business of the Year (Award)

Central Coast Chamber of Commerce (CCCC)
PO Box 40, Denny Island BC V0T 1B0
Tel: 250-957-2656; *Fax:* 250-957-2422
www.dennyislandbc.ca/chamber-of-commerce.php
Overview: A small local organization
Finances: *Funding Sources:* Membership dues

Central Coast Communications Society (CCCS)
PO Box 278, Bella Coola BC V0T 1C0
Tel: 250-982-0094
info@belco.bc.ca
www.belco.bc.ca
www.facebook.com/141849752567359
Overview: A small local organization
Mission: To provide wireless high-speed Internet & dial-up access for the Bella Coola Valley

Chief Officer(s):
Mike Wigle, President
James Hindley, Technician
Lesley Harrison, Bookkeeper
cccsbookkeeper@belco.bc.ca

Central Interior Logging Association (CILA)
#201, 850 River Rd., Prince George BC V2L 5S8
Tel: 250-562-3368; *Fax:* 250-563-3697
Toll-Free: 877-562-5668
cila@pgonline.com
www.cila.bc.ca
www.facebook.com/280253495363132
Previous Name: Prince George & District Truck Loggers Association
Overview: A medium-sized local charitable organization founded in 1966
Mission: To present the views of members to all levels of government, its agencies, & the corporate sector
Chief Officer(s):
MaryAnne Arcand, Executive Director
maryanne@cila.ca
Membership: *Fees:* $413.40-$3174.70; *Member Profile:* Companies & individuals directly or indirectly engaged in logging or log hauling; manufacturers & suppliers of goods &/or services to the logging industry

Central Interior Regional Arts Council (CIRAC)
PO Box 4537, Williams Lake BC V2G 2V5
Tel: 604-629-9883
info@cirac.ca
www.cirac.ca
Overview: A small local charitable organization founded in 1976
Mission: To assist in development & promotion of the arts in the region
Member of: Assembly of BC Arts Councils; Canadian Conference of the Arts; Arts in Education Council
Chief Officer(s):
Sheri Ukrainetz, President
Finances: *Funding Sources:* Membership fees; donations; grants
Activities: *Library* by appointment

Central Neighbourhood House
349 Ontario St., Toronto ON M5A 2V8
Tel: 416-925-4363; *Fax:* 416-925-1545
central@cnh.on.ca
www.cnh.on.ca
www.facebook.com/pages/Central-Neighbourhood-House/147806825236720
Overview: A small local charitable organization founded in 1911 overseen by Canadian Association of Neighbourhood Services
Mission: To work with people to improve the quality of each stage of life, especially for those with few opportunities; to offer programs & services that enable us to listen, respond to & advocate for the needs, interests & aspirations of diverse & changing populations
Member of: United Way
Chief Officer(s):
Elizabeth Forestell, Executive Director
eforestell@cnh.on.ca
Finances: *Annual Operating Budget:* $3 Million-$5 Million
Membership: 100-499; *Fees:* $10
Activities: Children, youth & women's programs, day care, home support services, services for the homeless & under-housed, voice mail, stroke survivors program; *Speaker Service:* Yes

Central New Brunswick Beekeepers Association *See* Central Beekeepers' Alliance

Central Nova Tourist Association (CNTA)
65 Treaty Trail, Millbrook NS B6L 1W3
Tel: 902-893-8782; *Fax:* 902-893-2269
Toll-Free: 800-895-1177
info@centralnovascotia.com
www.centralnovascotia.com
www.facebook.com/pages/Central-Nova-Tourist-Association/62069285284
Overview: A small provincial organization founded in 1979 overseen by Tourism Industry Association of Nova Scotia
Mission: To contribute to the Central Nova area becoming the most important tourist destination in Nova Scotia, resulting in new tourism initiatives & strengthened businesses; we will accomplish this by working as a team dedicated to effective communication & production of our community
Member of: Tourism Industry Association of Canada
Chief Officer(s):
Joyce Mingo, Executive Director
joyce@centralnovascotia.com
Finances: *Funding Sources:* Federal & provincial governments; municipal grants; membership fees
Staff Member(s): 5
Membership: *Member Profile:* Tourism business
Activities: Trade shows; Visitors' Guide

Central Okanagan Child Development Association (COCDA)
1546 Bernard Ave., Kelowna BC V1Y 6R9
Tel: 250-763-5100; *Fax:* 250-862-8433
Toll-Free: 877-763-5100; *TTY:* 250-763-5103
info@cocda.com
www.cocda.com
Previous Name: Okanagan Neurological Association
Overview: A medium-sized local charitable organization founded in 1966
Mission: To support families in promoting the optimum development of children with challenges
Affliation(s): British Colombia Association of Child Development Centres
Chief Officer(s):
Wendy Falkowski, Executive Director
Staff Member(s): 45
Membership: 45; *Member Profile:* Individuals; family; corporate
Activities: Speech; physiotherapy; occupational therapy; infant development; autism program;

Central Okanagan Foundation (COF)
#217, 1889 Springfield Rd., Kelowna BC V1Y 5V5
Tel: 250-861-6160; *Fax:* 250-861-6156
info@CentralOkanaganFoundation.org
www.centralokanaganfoundation.org
www.facebook.com/centralokanaganfoundation
twitter.com/centralokanagan
Overview: A small national charitable organization founded in 1977
Mission: To provide an ongoing contribution to the quality of life in our community through the stewardship of entrusted funds, grant making & community leadership; To encourage all citizens to participate through the establishment of or contributions to endowment funds
Member of: Community Foundations of Canada
Affliation(s): Association of Canadian Foundations
Chief Officer(s):
Bruce Davies, Executive Director
bruce@centralokanaganfoundation.org
Louise Elliot, Chair
Finances: *Annual Operating Budget:* $100,000-$250,000
Staff Member(s): 3; 30 volunteer(s)
Membership: 140; *Committees:* Capital Development; Communication; Investment; Grants

Central Okanagan Indian Friendship Society *See* Ki-Low-Na Friendship Society

Central Okanagan Naturalists Club (CONC)
PO Box 21128, Stn. Orchard Park, Kelowna BC V1Y 9N8
www.okanagannature.org
Overview: A small local charitable organization founded in 1962
Mission: To promote the enjoyment of nature through environmental appreciation & conservation; To encourage wise use & conservation of natural resources & environmental protection.
Member of: Federation of BC Naturalists
Chief Officer(s):
Craig Lewis, President, 250-765-2511
begley1253@gmail.com
Membership: *Fees:* $14 student; $30 single; $42 family
Activities: Hiking; skiing; botany; ornithology; participating with City of Kelowna in environmental events; conservation; *Library:* CONC Library
Publications:
• Central Okanagan Naturalist Newsletter
Type: Newsletter; *Frequency:* 10 pa; *Editor:* Teresa Smith

Central Ontario Beekeepers' Association
c/o Brent Cole, Herb Guy's Honey House, 3807 County Rd. 36, Buckhorn ON K0L 1J0
Tel: 705-657-9971
registrar@centralontariobeekeepers.ca
www.centralontariobeekeepers.ca
Overview: A small local organization
Mission: To develop the beekeeping skills of local beekeepers; To promote beekeeping in central Ontario, including Peterborough, Peterborough County, Northumberland County, Haliburton County, & the City of Kawartha Lakes
Member of: Ontario Beekeepers' Association
Affliation(s): Canadian Association Insurance Program (CAP)
Chief Officer(s):
Glen McMullen, President
president@centralontariobeekeepers.ca
Membership: *Member Profile:* Commercial beekeepers & hobbyists from the central Ontario region
Activities: Conducting meetings for members; Organizing field days; Preparing informative displays about beekeeping; Providing information & networking oopportunities for beekeepers; Assisting members with problems encountered by beekeepers;

Central Ontario Developmental Riding Program (CODRP)
Pride Stables, 584 Pioneer Tower Rd., Kitchener ON N2P 2H9
Tel: 519-653-4686; *Fax:* 519-653-5565
info@pridestables.com
www.pridestables.com
www.facebook.com/PrideStables
Also Known As: Pride Stables
Overview: A small local charitable organization founded in 1973
Mission: To provide a safe, high-quality riding program for persons with disabilities; to foster personal growth & improvement through the use of horses as a medium for development & therapy with the assistance of volunteers
Member of: Ontario Equestrian Federation; Association of Riding Establishments of Ontario
Affliation(s): Ontario Therapeutic Riding Association (ONTRA)
Chief Officer(s):
Heather Mackneson, Executive Director
Finances: *Funding Sources:* Service clubs; company & individual donations; municipal grants; special events
Staff Member(s): 8; 250 volunteer(s)
Membership: 350+ riders; *Member Profile:* Physical, mental & behavioral challenges
Activities: Integrated summer camp; therapeutic horseback riding; *Speaker Service:* Yes; *Library* by appointment

Central Ontario Industrial Relations Institute (COIRI)
350 Bay St., 10th Fl., Toronto ON M5H 2S6
Tel: 905-373-1761; *Fax:* 905-373-0190
www.coiri.com
Overview: A medium-sized local organization founded in 1943
Mission: To represent organizations in labour relations, employment law, human rights, workers compensation, pay equity and other related employment issues.
Chief Officer(s):
Jane Stewart, Director, Publications
jane@coiri.com
Membership: *Fees:* $625

Central Ontario Musicians' Association (COMA)
100 Ahrens St. West, Kitchener ON N2H 4C3
Tel: 519-744-4891; *Fax:* 519-744-2279
info@centralontariomusicians.org
www.centralontariomusicians.org
Overview: A small local organization founded in 1906
Mission: To help develop musical skill
Member of: American Federation of Musicians (Local 226)
Chief Officer(s):
Paul Mitchell, President
mitchgroup@rogers.com
Membership: 400; *Fees:* $139
Activities: *Library* by appointment

Central Ontario Network for Black History
203 Rykert St., St Catharines ON L2R 7C2
Tel: 905-685-5222
Overview: A small local organization

Central Ontario Orchid Society (COOS)
PO Box 40074, 75 King St. South, Waterloo ON N2J 4V1
retirees.uwaterloo.ca/~jerry/coos
Overview: A small local organization founded in 1985
Mission: To promote & train people about growing orchids
Chief Officer(s):
Gerhard Kompter, Interim President, 519-745-3815
Christine Williams, Secretary, 519-747-1087
cwilliams3740@yahoo.caca
Finances: *Annual Operating Budget:* Less than $50,000
Membership: 100+; *Fees:* $15 individual; $20 family
Activities: Promote & train people about growing orchids; *Speaker Service:* Yes

Publications:
• The COOS [Central Ontario Orchid Society] Newsletter
Type: Newsletter; *Editor:* Cathy Ralston

Central Ontario Standardbred Association (COSA)
PO Box 297, 36 Main St. North, Campbellville ON L0P 1B0
Tel: 905-854-2672; *Fax:* 905-854-2644
cosaonline.com
Previous Name: Ontario Harness Horse Association
Overview: A small local organization founded in 2009 overseen by Standardbred Canada
Mission: To represent the interests of horsepeople racing at Woodbine & Mohawk Racetracks in central Ontario
Chief Officer(s):
Bill O'Donnell, President
bill.o'donnell@cosaonline.com
Membership: 1500; *Fees:* Free; *Member Profile:* Horse owners, breeders, caretakers, trainers, & drivers in central Ontario

Central St. Lawrence Real Estate Board *See* Rideau-St. Lawrence Real Estate Board

Central Service Association of Ontario (CSAO)
PO Box 225, Timmins ON P4N 7C9
Tel: 705-268-4763; *Fax:* 705-268-4421
csao@ntl.sympatico.ca
www.csao.net
www.linkedin.com/groups/Central-Services-Association-Ontario-CSAO-5036
www.facebook.com/pages/CSAO/237386583016742
twitter.com/CSAOCanada
Overview: A medium-sized provincial organization founded in 1963
Mission: Promotes & provides opportunities for all members within instrument/medical device reprocessing in a health-care setting
Chief Officer(s):
Denise Bosnjak, President
Louis Konstant, Vice-President
Finances: *Funding Sources:* Membership dues & services
Membership: *Fees:* $30 technician & associate; $40 management; *Member Profile:* Those involved in the instrument/device reprocessing in a health care setting.

Central Seven Association for Community Living *See* Community Living Durham North

Central Valley Naturalists *See* Abbotsford-Mission Nature Club

Central Vancouver Island Multicultural Society (CVIMS)
#101, 319 Selby St., Nanaimo BC V9R 2R4
Tel: 250-753-6911; *Fax:* 250-753-4250
www.cvims.org
www.facebook.com/pages/immigrant-welcome-centre/126098154087608
twitter.com/CVIMS
www.youtube.com/user/ImmigrantWelcomeCtr
Overview: A small local charitable organization
Mission: To offer immigrants such services as English language classes, employment & settlement assistance.
Member of: Affiliation of Multicultural Societies & Service Agencies of BC
Chief Officer(s):
Sharif Kishawi, President
Hilde Schlosar, Executive Director
hschlosar@cvims.org
Staff Member(s): 25
Membership: *Fees:* $10 individual; $20 group/family; $5 student; $50 corporate
Activities: Information Centre; interpreting & translation; assistance with governmental applications; cultural counselling

Central Vancouver Island Orchid Society
PO Box 1061, Nanaimo BC V9R 5Z2
www.cvios.com
Overview: A small local organization
Mission: To promote an interest in orchids & support research in the study of orchids
Chief Officer(s):
Shelley Rattink, President
Membership: *Fees:* $25
Activities: *Library*

Centrale de l'enseignement du Québec *Voir* Centrale des syndicats du Québec

La Centrale des caisses de crédit du Canada *See* Credit Union Central of Canada

Centrale des professionnelles et professionnels de la santé *Voir* Alliance du personnel professionnel et technique de la santé et des services sociaux

Centrale des syndicats démocratiques (CSD)
#300, 801, 4e rue, Québec QC G1J 2T7
Tél: 418-529-2956; *Téléc:* 418-529-6323
info@csd.qc.ca
www.csd.qc.ca
Aperçu: *Dimension:* grande; *Envergure:* provinciale; fondée en 1972
Mission: CSD est composée des associations de salariés constituées ou non en vertu de la Loi des syndicats professionnels qui y adhèrent et souscrivent aux objectifs de la CSD; CSD a comme première croyance la liberté de la personne humaine, tant dans son intelligence que dans la recherche de la satisfaction de ses besoins matériels; elle est donc libre de toute attache politique et se reconnaît comme un mouvement de fraternité et de solidarité dédié entièrement à la formation, à l'information, à la défense et à la promotion collective des travailleuses et des travailleurs.
Affiliation(s): Fédération démocratique de la métallurgie, des mines et des produits chimiques; Fédération des syndicats du textile et du vêtement inc.
Membre(s) du bureau directeur:
François Vaudreuil, Président
Membre(s) du personnel: 78
Membre: 61 000; *Critères d'admissibilite:* Un syndicat affilié qui croit à la CSD
Activités: *Bibliothèque* rendez-vous

Beauce
#11, 720, 1re av, Saint-Georges QC G5Y 2C8
Tél: 418-228-9577; *Téléc:* 418-228-9558

Centre du Québec
66, boul Labbé sud, Victoriaville QC G6S 1B5
Tél: 819-758-3174; *Téléc:* 819-758-7105

Estrie
1009, rue Galt ouest, Sherbrooke QC J1H 1Z9
Tél: 819-569-9377; *Téléc:* 819-569-9370

Mauricie
141, rue Beauchemin, Trois-Rivières QC G8T 7L4
Tél: 819-376-3339; *Téléc:* 819-376-3475

Montmagny - Bas St-Laurent
119, av Collin, Montmagny QC G5V 2S7
Tél: 418-248-5766; *Téléc:* 418-248-5799

Montréal
#2000, 9405, rue Sherbrooke Est, Montréal QC H1L 6P3
Tél: 514-899-1070; *Téléc:* 514-899-1216
www.csd.qc.ca

Richelieu - Yamaska
11, rue Chapleau, Granby QC J2G 6K1
Tél: 450-375-1122; *Téléc:* 450-375-1125

Saguenay - Lac St-Jean
3310, boul St-François, Jonquière QC G7X 2W9
Tél: 418-547-2622; *Téléc:* 418-547-2623

Centrale des syndicats du Québec (CSQ)
9405, rue Sherbrooke est, Montréal QC H1L 6P3
Tél: 514-356-8888; *Téléc:* 514-356-9999
Ligne sans frais: 800-465-0897
communications@csq.qc.net
www.csq.qc.net
www.facebook.com/lacsq
twitter.com/CSQ_centrale
www.youtube.com/user/csqvideos
Nom précédent: Centrale de l'enseignement du Québec
Aperçu: *Dimension:* grande; *Envergure:* provinciale; fondée en 1946
Mission: De regrouper dans un même mouvement des personnels salariés ayant des aspirations et des intérêts communs et de promouvoir leurs intérêts professionnels, sociaux, et économiques; dans cette perspective, elle travaille à établir un environnement syndical et professionnel exempt de harcèlement sexuel et favorise la vie syndicale par le partage des ressources; elle intervient au soutien direct de ses affiliés et assure différents services liés aux relations de travail et à la vie professionnelle (recherche dans le domaine de l'éducation, etc.)
Affiliation(s): Internationale de l'Éducation; Confédération des éducateurs d'Amérique
Membre(s) du bureau directeur:
Louise Rochefort, Directrice générale
rochefort.louise@csq.qc.net
Réjean Parent, Président
Finances: *Budget de fonctionnement annuel:* Plus de $5 Million
Membre(s) du personnel: 200
Membre: 180 000; *Critères d'admissibilite:* Personnel de l'éducation, de la santé et services sociaux de la petite enfance, des loisirs et des communications; *Comités:* Comité d'action sociopolitique; Comité en éducation pour un avenir viable; Comité de la condition des femmes; Comité des jeunes; Comité pour la diversité sexuelle
Activités: *Bibliothèque:* Centre de documentation; rendez-vous

Bureau de Québec
#100, 320, rue Saint-Joseph Est, Québec QC G1K 9E7
Tél: 418-649-8888; *Téléc:* 418-649-8800
Ligne sans frais: 877-850-0897
www.lacsq.org

Centre Afrika
1644, rue St-Hubert, Montréal QC H2L 3Z3
Tél: 514-843-4019; *Téléc:* 514-849-4323
centreafrika@centreafrika.com
www.centreafrika.com
www.facebook.com/centreafrika
www.youtube.com/channel/UCh07u7KOPIF43d_Qg-DPjQA
Aperçu: *Dimension:* petite; *Envergure:* locale; fondée en 1988
Mission: Activités sociales & culturelles et activités spirituelles/religieuses

Centre Afrique au Féminin
#106, 7000, av du Parc, Montréal QC H3N 1X1
Tél: 514-272-3274; *Téléc:* 514-272-8617
info@afriqueaufeminin.org
www.afriqueaufeminin.org
Aperçu: *Dimension:* petite; *Envergure:* locale
Mission: Offre un lieu de recontres pour toutes les femmes, ces familles & ce dans une ambiance conviviale; classes, activités, halte-garderie, dépannage alimentaire
Membre(s) du bureau directeur:
Magdalena Molineros, Coordonatrice Principale
magdalena@afriqueaufeminin.org
Membre(s) du personnel: 7

Centre Anti-Poison du Québec
1050, ch Sainte-Foy, #L, Québec QC G1S 4L8
Tél: 418-654-2731; *Téléc:* 418-654-2747
Ligne sans frais: 800-463-5060
Aperçu: *Dimension:* petite; *Envergure:* provinciale
Membre de: Canadian Association of Poison Control Centres

Centre canadien d'arbitrage commercial (CCAC) / Canadian Commercial Arbitration Centre (CCAC)
Place du Canada, #905, 1010, rue de la Gauchetière ouest, Montréal QC G1K 5V6
Tél: 514-448-5980; *Téléc:* 514-448-5948
Ligne sans frais: 877-909-3794
www.ccac-adr.org
Nom précédent: Centre d'arbitrage commercial national et international du Québec
Aperçu: *Dimension:* moyenne; *Envergure:* provinciale; Organisme sans but lucratif; fondée en 1986
Mission: Fournir des services de conciliation, de médiation et d'arbitrage pour les activités commerciales et de consommation; offrir des activités de formation aux arbitres et médiateurs; analyse de dossiers litigieux et études pour des organismes privés et publics
Membre de: International Federation of Commercial Arbitration Institutions
Membre(s) du bureau directeur:
Michel A. Jeanniot, Président
Julie Houle, Coordonnatrice
jhoule@ccac-adr.org
Finances: *Budget de fonctionnement annuel:* $250,000-$500,000
Membre(s) du personnel: 6
Membre: 100; *Montant de la cotisation:* 100$ à 500$; *Comités:* Conseil des Experts; Comité de gestion des dossiers
Activités: Colloques; séminaires; *Bibliothèque*

Centre Canadien d'Architecture *See* Canadian Centre for Architecture

Centre canadien d'étude et de coopération internationale (CECI) / Canadian Centre for International Studies & Cooperation
3000, rue Omer-Lavallée, Montréal QC H1Y 3R8
Tél: 514-875-9911; *Téléc:* 514-875-6469
Ligne sans frais: 877-875-2324
info@ceci.ca

www.ceci.ca
www.facebook.com/cecicooperation
twitter.com/CECI_Canada
www.youtube.com/commceci
Aperçu: *Dimension:* grande; *Envergure:* internationale; Organisme sans but lucratif; fondée en 1958
Mission: Le CECI combat la pauvreté et l'exclusion; renforce les capacités de développment des communautés défavorisées; appuie des initiatives de paix, de droits humains et d'équité; mobilise des ressources et favorise l'échange de savoir-faire.
Membre de: Conseil canadien pour la coopération internationale/Canadian Council for International Cooperation; Association québécoise des organismes de coopération internationale.
Membre(s) du bureau directeur:
Robert Perreault, Chair
Claudia Black, Executive Director
claudiab@ceci.ca
Finances: *Budget de fonctionnement annuel:* Plus de $5 Million
Membre(s) du personnel: 65; 150 bénévole(s)
Membre: 1-99
Activités: Cours de formation; initiation de jeunes adultes à la coopération internationale; publications thématiques; sensibilisation du public et collecte de fonds pour l'aide au développement; *Stagiaires:* Oui; *Service de conférenciers:* Oui; *Bibliothèque:* Centre de documentation; rendez-vous
Publications:
• CECI [Centre canadien d'étude et de coopération internationale] Infolettre
Type: Newsletter

Centre canadien d'hygiène et de sécurité au travail *See* Canadian Centre for Occupational Health & Safety

Centre canadien d'innovations des pêches *See* Canadian Centre for Fisheries Innovation

Centre canadien de leadership en éducation (CLÉ)

#B120, 2445 boul. St-Laurent, Ottawa ON K1G 6C3
Tél: 613-747-7021; *Téléc:* 613-747-7277
Ligne sans frais: 800-372-5508
info@leCLE.com
www.lecle.com
Aperçu: *Dimension:* petite; *Envergure:* nationale
Mission: Un organisme pancanadien sans but lucratif voué au développement et à l'épanouissement de la Francophonie canadienne.
Membre(s) du bureau directeur:
Louis Claude Tremblay, Directeur générale
lctremblay@lecle.com

Centre canadien de lutte contre l'alcoolisme et les toxicomanies *See* Canadian Centre on Substance Abuse

Centre canadien de politique alternative *See* Canadian Centre for Policy Alternatives

Centre canadien du film *See* Canadian Film Centre

Centre canadien pour l'éthique dans le sport *See* Canadian Centre for Ethics in Sport

Centre canadien-ukrainien de recherches et de documentation *See* Ukrainian Canadian Research & Documentation Centre

Le Centre commémoratif de l'Holocauste à Montréal *See* The Montréal Holocaust Memorial Centre

Centre Communautaire Bon Courage De Place Benoît / Place Benoît Bon Courage Community Centre

#2, 155 Place Benoît, Ville Saint-Laurent QC H4N 2H4
Tél: 514-744-0897; *Téléc:* 514-744-6205
info@centreboncourage.org
www.centreboncourage.org
twitter.com/CCBonCourage
Aperçu: *Dimension:* petite; *Envergure:* locale; fondée en 1991
Membre de: ROCAJQ, ROCQLD, ACCESSS, TCRI, ImagineCanada
Membre(s) du bureau directeur:
Mame Moussa Sy, Directeur
mm.sy@centreboncourage.org
Nafissatova Duquenoy, Adjointe Directeur
n.duquenoy@centreboncourage.org
Finances: *Budget de fonctionnement annuel:* $500,000-$1.5 Million
Membre(s) du personnel: 16; 107 bénévole(s)
Membre: 323 familles
Activités: Jeunesse, famille, petite enfance; *Bibliothèque:* Bibliothèque; Bibliothèque publique

Centre communautaire de counselling du Nipissing *See* Community Counselling Centre of Nipissing

Centre communautaire des gais et lesbiennes de Montréal (CCGLM)

CP 476, Succ. C, Montréal QC H2L 4K4
Tél: 514-528-8424; *Téléc:* 514-528-9708
info@ccglm.org
www.ccglm.org
www.facebook.com/ccglm
Aperçu: *Dimension:* petite; *Envergure:* locale; fondée en 1988
Mission: Organisme sans but lucratif qui agit pour améliorer la condition des membres de nos communautés - lesbiennes, gais, bisexuel(les), transexuel(les), transgenres, et allosexuel(les); bibliothèque
Membre(s) du bureau directeur:
Christian Tanguay, Director-General
Membre(s) du personnel: 3; 3 bénévole(s)
Membre: *Montant de la cotisation:* 10$ individu; 25$ groupe

Centre Communautaire Esprit Saint *Voir* Centro Comunitàrio Divino Espìrito Santo

Centre Communautaire Tyndale St-Georges *See* Tyndale St-Georges Community Centre

Centre culturel franco-manitobain (CCFM)

340, boul Provencher, Winnipeg MB R2H 0G7
Tél: 204-233-8972; *Téléc:* 204-233-3324
communication@ccfm.mb.ca
www.ccfm.mb.ca
www.facebook.com/people/Centre-Culturel-Franco-Manitobain/1549747456
Aperçu: *Dimension:* petite; *Envergure:* provinciale; Organisme sans but lucratif; fondée en 1972 surveillé par Fédération des communautés francophones et acadienne du Canada
Mission: De maintenir, d'encourager, de favoriser et de patronner, par tous les moyens possibles, toutes les formes d'activités culturelles de langue française, et de rendre la culture canadienne-française accesible à tous les résidents de la province.
Membre de: Federation Culturelle Canadienne Française; Association culturelle franco-manitobaine
Membre(s) du bureau directeur:
Sylviane Lanthier, Directrice générale
direction@ccfm.mb.ca

Le Centre culturel francophone de Vancouver (CCFV) / Vancouver Francophone Cultural Centre

1551 - 7 Ave. West, Vancouver BC V6J 1S1
Tél: 604-736-9806; *Téléc:* 604-736-4661
info@lecentreculturel.com
www.lecentreculturel.com
www.facebook.com//235198656529236
twitter.com/CCFV
Aperçu: *Dimension:* moyenne; *Envergure:* locale; Organisme sans but lucratif; fondée en 1975
Mission: Présenter des spectacles en langue française et expositions d'artistes francophones et francophiles, dans le but de rehausser l'appréciation artistique de l'ensemble de la population du Vancouver métropolitain; promouvoir l'éducation au moyen de services et de programmes éducatifs en langue française à l'ensemble de la population du Vancouver métropolitain
Membre de: Fédération des francophones de la Colombie-Britannique
Affliation(s): Conférence canadienne des arts; Réseau international pour la diversité culturelle; Réseau indépendant des diffuseurs d'événements artistiques unis (RIDEAU)
Membre(s) du bureau directeur:
Pierre Rivard, Directeur général
pierre.rivard@lecentreculturel.com
Finances: *Budget de fonctionnement annuel:* $500,000-$1.5 Million
Membre(s) du personnel: 4; 150 bénévole(s)
Membre: 1000; *Montant de la cotisation:* Barème
Activités: café-restaurant; des camps d'été pour les enfants; des ateliers récréatifs ou éducatifs; des expositions d'oeuvres d'art; vidéothèque; spectacles divers; bibliothèque; *Evénements de sensibilisation:* Festival d'Été; Coup de Coeur Francophone; *Bibliothèque* Bibliothèque publique
Prix, Bouses:
• Prix Mercure (Prix)
Remis à un individu qui a contribué à l'essor de la chanson d'expression française dans l'Ouest, que ce soit en tant qu'administrateur, musicien, promoteur, artiste de la scène ou autre artisan

Centre d'action bénévole de Montréal (CABM) / Volunteer Bureau of Montreal (VBM)

#300, 2015, rue Drummond, Montréal QC H3G 1W7
Tél: 514-842-3351; *Téléc:* 514-842-8977
info@cabm.net
cabm.net
www.facebook.com/benevolat
twitter.com/benevolat
Aperçu: *Dimension:* moyenne; *Envergure:* locale; fondée en 1937
Mission: Promotion de l'action bénévole
Membre de: Fédération des centres d'action bénévole du Québec; Bénévoles Canada
Affliation(s): International Association for Volunteer Effort
Membre(s) du bureau directeur:
André Guérard, Président
Kevin Cohalan, Directeur général
Finances: *Budget de fonctionnement annuel:* $250,000-$500,000; *Fonds:* Centraide du Grand Montréal; Agence de la santé et des services sociaux de Montréal
Membre(s) du personnel: 6
Membre: 100
Activités: *Evénements de sensibilisation:* Semaine de l'action bénévole/Volunteer Week, 3e semaine d'avril; *Service de conférenciers:* Oui; *Bibliothèque:* Centre de documentation; Bibliothèque publique

Centre d'action sida Montréal (Femmes) (CASMF) / Centre for AIDS Services of Montreal (Women)

1750, rue Saint-André, 3e étage, Montréal QC H2L 3T8
Tél: 514-495-0990; *Téléc:* 514-495-8087
casm@netrover.net
www.netrover.com/~casm
Aperçu: *Dimension:* petite; *Envergure:* locale
Mission: Offrir des services aux femmes affectées et infectées par le VIH/SIDA ainsi qu'aux membres de leur famille; ces actions, priorisant les besoins particuliers des femmes, ont pour but d'augmenter leur pouvoir à déterminer la qualité de leur propre vie
Membre de: Canadian AIDS Society; Fédération des femmes du Québec; Conseil des femmes de Montréal; Coalition des organismes communautaires québécois de lutte contre le sida
Membre: *Critères d'admissibilite:* Groupes des femmes séropositives, bénévoles, proches
Activités: Sessions d'informations sur le VIH/SIDA; ateliers sur la sexualité, l'estime de soi, les VIH/SIDA et les MTS; kiosques; projets ponctuels; ligne d'information, d'écoute et de références; intervention individuelle; accompagnement; fonds de dépannage; service de gardiennage; café-rencontre; diverses activités sociales; lobbying; levée de fonds

Centre d'adaptation de la main-d'oeuvre aérospatiale du Québec (CAMAQ)

5300, rue Chauveau, Montréal QC H1N 3V7
Tél: 514-596-3311; *Téléc:* 514-596-3388
info@camaq.org
www.camaq.org
twitter.com/CAMAQ_aero
Également appelé: Comité sectoriel de main-d'ouvre en aérospatiale
Aperçu: *Dimension:* petite; *Envergure:* provinciale; Organisme sans but lucratif; fondée en 1983
Mission: Susciter et d'appuyer la concertation des partenaires de l'industrie aérospatiale dans leurs efforts d'adaptation et de développement de la main-d'oeuvre.
Membre(s) du bureau directeur:
Nathalie Paré, Directrice générale
Finances: *Fonds:* Emploi Québec

Centre d'aide et de lutte contre les agressions à caractère sexuel de Châteauguay / Châteauguay Sexual Assault Center

CP 47030, Châteauguay QC J6K 5B7
Tél: 450-699-8258; *Téléc:* 450-699-7295
info@calacs-chateauguay.ca
Également appelé: CALACS Châteauguay
Nom précédent: Centre d'aide et de prévention d'assauts sexuels de Châteauguay
Aperçu: *Dimension:* petite; *Envergure:* locale; Organisme sans but lucratif; fondée en 1979
Mission: Cet organisme offre les services suivants: aide aux femmes âgées de 14 ans et plus ayant vécu une agression à caractère sexuel, sans discrimination en raison de

l'appartenance ethnique, culturelle, religieuse ou de l'orientation sexuelle; informe la population et la sensibilise à la problématique des agressions à caractère sexuel; suscite des réflexions afin de favoriser des changements sociaux et politiques
Membre de: Regroupement québecois des centres d'Aide et de Lutte contre les agressions à caractère sexuel
Membre(s) du bureau directeur:
Carole Cayer, Contact
Finances: *Budget de fonctionnement annuel:* $250,000-$500,000; *Fonds:* Gouvernement provincial
Membre(s) du personnel: 6
Membre: 1-99
Activités: *Stagiaires:* Oui; *Bibliothèque* rendez-vous

Centre d'aide et de lutte contre les agressions à caractère sexuel de Granby

CP 63, Granby QC J2G 8E2
Tél: 450-375-3338; *Téléc:* 450-375-0802
info@calacs-granby.qc.ca
www.calacs-granby.qc.ca
www.facebook.com/#!/calacs.degranby?fref=ts
Également appelé: CALACS-Granby
Aperçu: *Dimension:* petite; *Envergure:* locale; Organisme sans but lucratif; fondée en 1986
Mission: Le CALACS de Granby est un organisme féministe à but non lucratif qui lutte contre les agressions sexuelles et toute autre forme de violence sexuelle.
Membre de: Centre d,aide et de lutte contre les agressions à caractère sexuel (CALACS) de Granby
Affliation(s): Regroupement québécois des CALACS
Membre(s) du bureau directeur:
Carole Thériault, Contact
caroletheriault@calacs-granby.qc.ca
Finances: *Budget de fonctionnement annuel:* $100,000-$250,000; *Fonds:* Programme de soutien aux organismes communautaires (PSOC)
Membre(s) du personnel: 4; 15 bénévole(s)
Membre: 60; *Montant de la cotisation:* Don volontaire; *Critères d'admissibilite:* Femmes 18 ans et plus; *Comités:* Journal; Action vigilance; membership
Activités: Récréactives; formation en autodéfense pour femmes et adolescentes; mobilisation ponctuelle; *Evénements de sensibilisation:* Journée d'action contre la violence sexuelle faite aux femmes, sep..; *Stagiaires:* Oui; *Service de conférenciers:* Oui

Centre d'aide et de prévention d'assauts sexuels de Châteauguay ***Voir*** Centre d'aide et de lutte contre les agressions à caractère sexuel de Châteauguay

Centre d'aide personnes traumatisées crâniennes et handicapées physiques Laurentides (CAPTCHPL)

CP 11, Saint-Jérôme QC J7Z 5T7
Tél: 450-431-2860; *Téléc:* 450-431-7955
Ligne sans frais: 888-431-3437
lecaptchpl@sympatico.ca
www.captchpl.org
twitter.com/Captchpl
Aperçu: *Dimension:* petite; *Envergure:* locale
Mission: Pour aider les personnes souffrant de lésions cérébrales et physiquement handicapées dans la région des Laurentides du Québec; Pour favoriser l'intégration sociale des personnes handicapées physiques et de lésions cérébrales
Membre de: Regroupement des associations de personnes traumatisées craniocérébrales du Québec / Coalition of Associations of Craniocerebral Trauma in Quebec
Membre(s) du bureau directeur:
Michel Lajeunesse, Directeur général
Membre(s) du personnel: 9
Membre: *Critères d'admissibilite:* Les personnes atteintes de lésions cérébrales ou de handicaps physiques, et leurs familles, dans la région des Laurentides du Québec; *Comités:* Journal; Maison Matte Laurentides; Négociations SAAQ
Activités: Promouvoir les intérêts de cerveau blessés et handicapés physiques; Accroître la sensibilisation de lésion cérébrale et handicaps physiques dans la région des Laurentides; Promotion de la prévention; Fournir des services de soutien et d'information aux familles et amis de personnes qui sont victimes de traumatismes crâniens ou handicapés physiques; Offrir une éducation; Se référant personnes vers les ressources appropriées

Centre d'amitié autochtone de Montréal Inc. ***See*** Native Friendship Centre of Montréal Inc.

Centre d'amitié autochtone de Val-d'Or / Val-d'Or Native Friendship Centre

1272, 7e rue, Val-d'Or QC J9P 6W6
Tél: 819-825-6857; *Téléc:* 819-825-7515
info@caavd.ca
www.caavd.ca
www.facebook.com/caavd
www.youtube.com/user/caavd1
Aperçu: *Dimension:* petite; *Envergure:* locale; fondée en 1974
Mission: Offrir des services de qualité en milieu urbain, adaptés aux besoins des Autochtones; améliorer la qualité de vie et le mieux-être des Autochtones; respecter et diffuser la culture autochtone; faciliter les relations harmonieuses avec la communauté non-autochtone; contribuer à l'augmentation de la richesse collective.
Membre(s) du bureau directeur:
Oscar Kistabish, Président
Édith Cloutier, Directrice générale
Membre(s) du personnel: 44

Centre d'amitié autochtone du Québec (CAAQ) / Friendship Centre of Québec

234, rue St-Louis IX, Loretteville QC G2B 1L4
Tél: 418-843-5818; *Téléc:* 418-843-8960
caaqadm@bellnet.ca
www.rcaaq.info
Aperçu: *Dimension:* petite; *Envergure:* locale; Organisme sans but lucratif; fondée en 1979
Mission: Maintenir à Québec un lieu de rencontre afin de satisfaire les besoins culturels, matériels et sociaux des autochtones; fournir des installations centrales, convenables et appropriées; sensibiliser le public en général, aux besoins spécifiques des autochtones qui migrent en milieu urbain et faciliter leur acceptation; offrir des facilités d'hébergement à court et moyen terme aux autochtones de passage à Québec, venant y chercher différents services; améliorer la qualité de vie des autochtones en milieu urbain en leur prêtant assistance
Membre de: Association d'affaires des Premiers Peuples - Régie régionale de la Santé & Services sociaux; Regroupement des centres d'amitié autochtone du Québec
Affliation(s): Association nationale des centres d'amitié
Membre(s) du bureau directeur:
Jocelyne Gros-Louis, Directrice générale
Finances: *Budget de fonctionnement annuel:* $500,000-$1.5 Million
Membre(s) du personnel: 1; 75 bénévole(s)
Membre: 250; *Montant de la cotisation:* 3$
Activités: Activités socioculturelles; communautaires; formation; services sociaux; service d'hébergement; garderie, service de garde à contribution réduite, de 7$/jour; centre de jour; Café Roreke; souper traditionnel pour les autochtones; *Evénements de sensibilisation:* Journée nationale des Autochtones; Journée mondiale du diable; *Bibliothèque* Bibliothèque publique

Centre d'animation de développement et de recherche en éducation (CADRÉ)

1940, boul Henri-Bourassa est, Montréal QC H2B 1S2
Tél: 514-381-8891; *Téléc:* 514-381-4086
www.cadre.qc.ca
Aperçu: *Dimension:* moyenne; *Envergure:* provinciale; Organisme sans but lucratif; fondée en 1968
Membre(s) du bureau directeur:
Paul Boisvenu, Directeur général
Finances: *Budget de fonctionnement annuel:* $500,000-$1.5 Million
Activités: *Bibliothèque* Bibliothèque publique

Centre d'arbitrage commercial national et international du Québec ***Voir*** Centre canadien d'arbitrage commercial

Centre d'éducation et d'action des femmes de Montréal (CÉAF)

2422, boul de Maisonneuve Est, Montréal QC H2K 2E9
Tél: 514-524-3901; *Téléc:* 514-524-2183
www.ceaf-montreal.qc.ca
www.facebook.com/329404080465297
Aperçu: *Dimension:* petite; *Envergure:* locale; fondée en 1972
Mission: D'offrir des consultations à court terme, des références et informations; De proposer un programme d'activités sur 3 sessions: cafés-rencontres, autodéfense, groupe de soutien, comité journal et d'action, une chorale, etc.
Activités: *Service de conférenciers:* Oui; *Bibliothèque*

Centre d'entraide et de ralliement familial (CERF)

#101, 105, rue Ontario Est, Montréal QC H2X 1G9
Tél: 514-288-8314; *Téléc:* 514-288-4176
info@cerf-montreal.org
www.cerf-montreal.org
twitter.com/C_E_R_F
Aperçu: *Dimension:* petite; *Envergure:* locale; fondée en 1995
Mission: Améliorer la qualité de vie des familles

Centre d'entrepreneuriat et PME (CEPME) / Centre for Entrepreneurship & Small Business

Faculté des sciences de l'administration, Pavillon Palasis-Prince, 2325, rue De La Terrasse, Québec QC G1K 7P4
Tél: 418-656-2490; *Téléc:* 418-656-2624
centre.pme@fsa.ulaval.ca
www.fsa.ulaval.ca/cepme/
Aperçu: *Dimension:* petite; *Envergure:* internationale; Organisme sans but lucratif; fondée en 1993
Mission: Initier et coordonner des études sur l'entrepreneuriat et la PME; promouvoir l'apprentissage; développer des activités de formation et de perfectionnement; élaborer du matériel pédagogique et didactique; favoriser le partenariat et la participation des entrepreneurs; susciter les échanges d'expertise aux niveaux régional, national et international
Affliation(s): Fondation de l'entrepreneurship du Québec; Canadian Council for Small Business & Entrepreneurship; Canadian Foundation for Economic Education; International Council for Small Business; International Small Business Congress; Centre SAHEL
Finances: *Budget de fonctionnement annuel:* $50,000-$100,000; *Fonds:* Projets; contrats
Membre(s) du personnel: 2; 2 bénévole(s)
Membre: 5; *Critères d'admissibilite:* Universitaires; *Comités:* Orientation; Consultation
Activités: Recherches; conférences; séminaires; *Service de conférenciers:* Oui; *Bibliothèque* rendez-vous

Centre d'entreprise des femmes du Manitoba ***See*** Women's Enterprise Centre of Manitoba

Centre d'étude de la pratique d'assurance ***See*** Centre for Study of Insurance Operations

Centre d'étude des niveaux de vie ***See*** Centre for the Study of Living Standards

Centre d'études internationales ***See*** Cape Breton University Centre for International Studies

Centre d'études sur l'apprentissage et la performance ***See*** Centre for the Study of Learning & Performance

Centre d'Histoire de Saint-Hyacinthe

650, rue Girouard Est, Saint-Hyacinthe QC J2S 2Y2
Tél: 450-774-0203; *Téléc:* 450-250-8127
infos@chsth.com
www.chsth.com
www.facebook.com/histoiremaskoutaine
twitter.com/histoiredemaska
Aperçu: *Dimension:* petite; *Envergure:* locale
Mission: Promouvoir et encourager l'étude de l'histoire. Le Centre d'histoire de Saint-Hyacinthe est né de la fusion du Centre d'archives du Séminaire de Saint-Hyacinthe et de la Société d'histoire régionale de Saint-Hyacinthe
Membre(s) du bureau directeur:
Luc Cordeau, Directeur général
Marie-Marthe Bélisle, Responsable de la généalogie
Membre(s) du personnel: 4
Activités: Service de recherches en généalogie; consultation d'archives; vente de matériel généalogique; cours de généalogie; conférences

Centre d'information canadien sur les diplômes internationaux ***See*** Canadian Information Centre for International Credentials

Centre d'information communautaire d'Ottawa ***See*** Community Information Centre of Ottawa

Centre d'information communautaure et de dépannage Ste-Marie (CICD)

2766, rue de Rouen, Montréal QC H2K 1N3
Tél: 514-526-4908; *Téléc:* 514-526-9050
cicdsm@cam.org
www.cam.org/~cicdsm
Aperçu: *Dimension:* petite; *Envergure:* locale; fondée en 1972
Mission: Pour aider les moins fortunés sur Saint Marie et Saint Jacques région en offrant des services sociaux gratuits et abordable
Membre(s) du bureau directeur:
Pierrette Malépart, Présidente, Conseil d'administration

www.cija.ca
www.facebook.com/cijainfo
twitter.com/cijainfo
Previous Name: Canadian Jewish Congress
Overview: A medium-sized national charitable organization founded in 1919
Mission: To act as decision-making body of the Jewish community in Canada; to act on behalf of Canadian Jewish community on issues & concerns affecting Jews in Canada & around the world; to foster interaction between interests & needs of Jewish community in Canada & Canadian society at large on a broad range of political, charitable & social justice issues
Affliation(s): World Jewish Congress; Conference on Jewish Material Claims Against Germany, Inc.; Memorial Foundation for Jewish Culture
Chief Officer(s):
Paul Michaels, Director, Research & Senior Media Relations
pmichaels@cija.ca
Staff Member(s): 25; 125 volunteer(s)
Membership: 1,000-4,999; *Committees:* Archives; Community Relations; Holocaust Remembrance; Legal Advisory; Religious & Interreligious Affairs; Social Action
Activities: *Library:* National Jewish Archives; Open to public by appointment
Awards:
• Samuel Bronfman Medal (Award)
• Saul Hayes Human Rights Award (Award)
• Brian A. Finestone Memorial Award (Award)
• Monroe Abbey Award (Award)

Calgary Jewish Federation
1607 - 90 Ave. SW, Calgary AB T2V 4V7
Tel: 403-253-8600; *Fax:* 403-253-7915
www.jewishcalgary.org
Mission: Canadian Jewish Congree works to foster a Canada where Jews, as part of the multicultural fabric of this country, live in and contribute to an environment of oppourtunity and mutual respect. CJC fulfulls this mission through its mandate of proactive defense of the security, status and rights of the community; seeking the support of governments on a range of policy issues identified by Jewish Federations in Canada; and promotion of the values of the Charter of Rights and Freedoms in Canada and human rights at home and abroad.
Member of: Canadian Jewish Congress
Chief Officer(s):
Drew Staffenberg, Executive Director
dstaffenberg@jewishcalgary.org

Jewish Federation of Edmonton
7200 - 156 St., Edmonton AB T5R 1X3
Tel: 780-487-0585; *Fax:* 780-481-1854
www.jewishedmonton.org
Mission: Canadian Jewish Congress works to foster a Canada where Jews, as part ofthe multicultural fabric of this country, live in and contribute to an environment of opportunity and mutual respect. CJC fulfills this mission through its mandate of proactive defense of the security, status and rights of the community; seeking the support of governments on a range of policy issues identified by Jewish Federations in Canada; and promotion of the values of the Charter of Rights and Freedoms in Canada and human rights at home and abroad.
Member of: Canadian Jewish Congress

Jewish Federation of Winnipeg
#300C, 123 Doncaster St., Winnipeg MB R3N 2B2
Tel: 204-477-7400; *Fax:* 204-477-7405
www.jewishwinnipeg.org
twitter.com/fedtweet
Mission: Canadian Jewish Congress works to foster a Canada where Jews, as part ofthe multicultural fabric of this country, live in and contribute to an environment of opportunity and mutual respect. CJC fulfills this mission through its mandate of proactive defense of the security, status and rights of the community; seeking the support of governments on a range of policy issues identified by Jewish Federations in Canada; and promotion of the values of the Charter of Rights and Freedoms in Canada and human rights at home and abroad.
Chief Officer(s):
Robert Freedman, Chief Executive Officer
bfreedman@jewishwinnipeg.org

Québec Region
1, carré Cummings, Montréal QC H3W 1M6
Tel: 514-345-6411; *Fax:* 514-345-6412
Chief Officer(s):
Sara Saber-Freedman, Executive Vice President, 514-343-8703
sfreedman@cija.ca

Centre for Jewish Education (CJE)
UJA Federation of Greater Toronto, Sherman Campus, 4600 Bathurst St., 4th Fl., Toronto ON M2R 3V2
Tel: 416-635-2883; *Fax:* 416-633-7535
cjetoronto.com
Previous Name: Ontario Association of Jewish Dayschools; Ontario Jewish Association for Equity in Education
Overview: A medium-sized provincial organization founded in 1984
Affliation(s): UJA Federation of Greater Toronto
Chief Officer(s):
Joel Kurtz, Executive Director
Membership: 1-99

Centre for Legislative Exchange *See* Parliamentary Centre

Centre for Medicine, Ethics & Law
McGill University, #201, 3690, rue Peel, Montréal QC H3A 1W9
Tel: 514-398-7400; *Fax:* 514-398-4668
Overview: A small national organization founded in 1986
Mission: To undertake & promote research across the fields of health law & bioethics

The Centre for Peace in the Balkans
PO Box 1500-1292, Toronto ON M9C 4V5
Tel: 416-201-9729; *Fax:* 416-201-7397
scontact@balkanpeace.org
www.balkanpeace.org
Overview: A small international organization
Mission: To advocate a balanced & accurate presentation of the current socio-political situation on the Balkan Peninsula through peaceful means & the presentation of pertinent materials

Centre for Research & Education in Human Services
#300, 73 King St. West, Kitchener ON N2G 1A7
Tel: 519-741-1318; *Fax:* 519-741-8262
general@communitybasedresearch.ca
www.communitybasedresearch.ca
Also Known As: Centre for Community Based Research
Overview: A small national organization founded in 1982
Mission: Focused on strengthening communities through social research.
Chief Officer(s):
Joanna Ochocka, Executive Director
Kokila Khanna, President
Activities: Community research projects in Ontario & across Canada
Publications:
• Evaluation Handbook
Number of Pages: 215; *Author:* Andrew Taylor & Janos Botschner; *Price:* $69
• Pathways to Inclusion
Number of Pages: 276; *Author:* John Lord & Peggy Hutchison; *Price:* $29.50
• Shifting the Paradigm in Community Mental Health
Number of Pages: 295; *Author:* Geoff Nelson, John Lord et al.; *Price:* $25

Centre for Research on Latin America & The Caribbean (CERLAC)
8th Fl., York Research Tower, York University, 4700 Keele St., Toronto ON M3J 1P3
Tel: 416-736-5237; *Fax:* 416-736-5688
cerlac@yorku.ca
www.yorku.ca/cerlac
Overview: A medium-sized international organization founded in 1978
Mission: To offer an interdisciplinary research unit concerned with economic development, political & social organization & cultural contributions of Latin America & the Caribbean; to build academic & cultural links between these regions & Canada; informs researchers, policy advisors & public on matters concerning the regions; to assist in development of research & teaching institutions that directly benefit people of the regions
Affliation(s): Canadian Association for Latin American & Caribbean Studies; Development Education Centre; OXFAM-Canada; Centre for Spanish Speaking People; CCIC; AFG: KAIROS
Chief Officer(s):
Eduardo Canel, Director
ecanel@yorku.ca
Staff Member(s): 6
Activities: Research & conferences on the Americas; Migration & Refugee Flows/Population & Development Projects; Rural Development Project; Religions Project; Human Rights Project; *Speaker Service:* Yes; *Rents Mailing List:* Yes; *Library:* CERLAC Documentation Centre; by appointment

Centre for Research on Violence Against Women & Children
Faculty of Educ. Bldg., Univ. of Western Ontario, #1118, 1137 Western Rd., London ON N6G 1G7
Tel: 519-661-4040; *Fax:* 519-850-2464
www.crvawc.ca
Overview: A small provincial organization
Mission: To promote the development of community-centred, action research on violence against women & children; To facilitate the cooperation of individuals, groups, & institutions representing the diversity of the community to pursue research questions & training opportunities to understand & prevent abuse
Chief Officer(s):
Anna-Lee Straatman, Centre Manager
astraat2@uwo.ca

Centre for Spanish Speaking Peoples
2141 Jane St., 2nd Fl., Toronto ON M3M 1A2
Tel: 416-533-8545; *Fax:* 416-533-5731
info@spanishservices.org
www.spanishservices.org
www.facebook.com/CPGHH
twitter.com/CSSPToronto
www.youtube.com/user/CSSPtoronto
Overview: A small local organization founded in 1973 overseen by Ontario Council of Agencies Serving Immigrants
Mission: To assist the Spanish speaking community in Metro Toronto
Chief Officer(s):
Raul Burbano, President
Finances: *Annual Operating Budget:* $1.5 Million-$3 Million
120 volunteer(s)
Activities: *Library:* Spanish Language Library; Open to public by appointment

Centre for Study of Insurance Operations (CSIO) / Centre d'étude de la pratique d'assurance
#500, 110 Yonge St., Toronto ON M5C 1T4
Tel: 416-360-1773; *Fax:* 416-364-1482
Toll-Free: 800-463-2746
helpdesk@csio.com
www.csio.com
www.linkedin.com/company/csio
twitter.com/csio
Overview: A medium-sized national organization
Mission: To act as the national standards association for property & casualty insurance by representing property & casualty industry initiatives; to provide a competitive advantage for the independent broker distribution channel
Chief Officer(s):
Steve Whitelaw, Chair
Catherine Smola, President & CEO
Membership: 100-499; *Member Profile:* Broker associations; Insurance companies; Insurance vendors
Activities: Developing & maintaining XML Standards, Electronic Data Interchange (EDI) Standards, Terminology Standards, Form Standards, Web Screen Standards, Industry owned & managed CSIOnet, & Forums for Implementations of Standards; Participating in ACORD Standards Plenary & Working Groups & the Insurance Global Standards Working Group; Developing & designing property & casualty industry application forms; Providing members with access to forms & standards; Offering educational sessions & networking opportunities

Montréal Office
#1305, 1155, rue University, Montréal QC H3B 3A7
Tel: 514-393-8200; *Fax:* 514-393-3625
Toll-Free: 877-393-2372

Centre for Suicide Prevention (CSP)
#320, 105 - 12 Ave. SE, Calgary AB T2G 1A1
Tel: 403-245-3900; *Fax:* 403-245-0299; *Crisis Hot-Line:* 406-266-4357
csp@suicideinfo.ca
www.suicideinfo.ca
www.linkedin.com/company/centre-for-suicide-prevention
twitter.com/cspyyc
suicideinfo.tumblr.com
Previous Name: Suicide Information & Education Centre
Overview: A medium-sized provincial charitable organization founded in 1982

Mission: CSP educates people with the information, knowledge and skills necessary to respond to the risk of suicide.
Member of: Canadian Association for Suicide Prevention
Affliation(s): Canadian Mental Health Association - Alberta Division
Chief Officer(s):
Diane Yackel, Executive Director
Finances: *Funding Sources:* User fees, government contracts, community grants, special events, memorial and individual donations
Staff Member(s): 11
Activities: Training workshops, online courses, webinars, literature scans and reviews, library database access, lending library and knowledge translation publications.; *Library:* Resource Centre; Open to public

Centre for the Study of Classroom Processes *See* Centre for the Study of Learning & Performance

Centre for the Study of Learning & Performance (CSLP) / Centre d'études sur l'apprentissage et la performance (CEAP)
Université Concordia, #LB581, 1450, boul de Maisonneuve ouest, Montréal QC H3G 2V8
Tel: 514-848-2424; *Fax:* 514-848-4520
cslp@education.concordia.ca
doe.concordia.ca/cslp
Previous Name: Centre for the Study of Classroom Processes
Overview: A small national organization founded in 1988
Mission: The objectives of the CSLP are fourfold: to increase the theoretical and practical understanding of the factors that promote and hinder the learning and performance of complex skills; to provide training and support to educators and administrators; to provide the educational community with material and intellectual resources regarding new ideas in education; and to train students who have an interest in learning and performance and who are enrolled in graduate studies within the departments with which the centre and its members are affiliated.
Chief Officer(s):
Philip C. Abrami, Director
abrami@education.concordia.ca
Anne Wade, Manager & Information Specialist
wada@education.concordia.ca
Finances: *Funding Sources:* National government; provincial government; foundations; internal grants
Membership: 70
Activities: Research & training, Bi-annual Research Fair; *Internships:* Yes; *Speaker Service:* Yes; *Library:* CSLP Information Resource Centre; Open to public

Centre for the Study of Living Standards (CSLS) / Centre d'étude des niveaux de vie
#710, 151 Slater St., Ottawa ON K1P 5H3
Tel: 613-233-8891; *Fax:* 613-233-8250
info@csls.ca
www.csls.ca
Overview: A medium-sized national charitable organization founded in 1995
Chief Officer(s):
Andrew Sharpe, Executive Director
Finances: *Funding Sources:* Federation & provincial governments; Foundations
Staff Member(s): 2
Activities: Conducting research on living standards, productivity, & economical well-being issues
Publications:
• The International Productivity Monitor
Editor: Andrew Sharpe
Profile: Journal, published twice annually

Centre for Transportation Engineering & Planning (C-TEP)
c/o Stantec, Transportation, #200, 325 - 25 St. SE, Calgary AB T2A 7H8
Tel: 403-607-4482; *Fax:* 403-716-8129
Overview: A medium-sized national organization
Mission: To provide professional development & research related to Canadian transportation engineering & planning; to provide a forum for collaboration between institutions & various levels of government; to act as a resource centre for the transportation engineers & planners
Chief Officer(s):
Jason Meliefste, President
Neil Little, Executive Director
nlittle@c-tep.com
Membership: 42; *Fees:* Schedule available

Centre for Women in Business (CWB)
c/o Mount Saint Vincent University, The Meadows, 166 Bedford Hwy., 2nd Fl., Halifax NS B3M 2J6
Tel: 902-457-6449; *Fax:* 902-443-4687
Toll-Free: 888-776-9022
cwb@msvu.ca
www.centreforwomeninbusiness.ca
www.linkedin.com/company/1539340
www.facebook.com/centreforwomeninbusiness
twitter.com/cwb_ns
www.youtube.com/user/CentreWomenBusiness
Overview: A medium-sized local organization
Mission: To help women entrepreneurs start, grow & advance their businesses
Affliation(s): Centre for Entrepreneurship Education & Development Inc.
Chief Officer(s):
Sandi Findlay-Thompson, Chair
Tanya Priske, Executive Director
Membership: *Fees:* $57.50-$1,150
Activities: Conferences; networking events
Publications:
• BizBeat [a publication of the Centre for Women in Business]
Type: Newsletter

Centre franco-ontarien de folklore (CFOF)
935, ch du Lac Ramsey, Sudbury ON P3E 2C6
Tél: 705-675-8986; *Téléc:* 705-675-5809
cfof@cfof.on.ca
www.cfof.on.ca
fr-fr.facebook.com/126335660730527
Aperçu: *Dimension:* petite; *Envergure:* provinciale; Organisme sans but lucratif; fondée en 1972
Mission: Cueillette, conservation et diffusion du partimoine franco-ontarien, en particulier, le patrimoine oral
Membre de: Association études canadiennes
Membre(s) du bureau directeur:
Janik Aubin-Robert, Présidente
Activités: *Bibliothèque:* Bibliothèque du CFOF et Bibliothèque de généalogie; rendez-vous

Centre franco-ontarien de ressources pédagogiques (CFORP)
435, rue Donald, Ottawa ON K1K 4X5
Tél: 613-747-8000; *Téléc:* 613-747-2808
Ligne sans frais: 877-742-3677
cforp@cforp.ca
www.cforp.ca
twitter.com/CFORP
Aperçu: *Dimension:* moyenne; *Envergure:* provinciale; Organisme sans but lucratif; fondée en 1974
Mission: Le Centre franco-ontarien de ressources pédagogiques (CFORP) est un centre multiservices en éducation qui produit et diffuse des ressources pédagogiques et qui offre des services destinés à soutenir l'éducation en langue française.
Cet organisme à but non lucratif appuie le développement et l'épanouissement de l'éducation en langue française à l'aide de services, comme la formation professionnelle du personnel scolaire et l'impression de documents, et de projets novateurs, tels des ressources numériques et des cours multimédias en ligne. La Librairie du Centre, propriété du CFORP, offre depuis 1992 des services non seulement au milieu scolaire, mais aussi à toute la communauté francophone et francophile. Tous les profits des ventes à la librairie sont réinvestis dans la production de nouvelles ressources pédagogiques.
Membre de: Association canadienne d'éducation de langue française (ACELF); Association nationale des éditeurs de livres (ANEL)
Affliation(s): Librairie du Centre
Membre(s) du bureau directeur:
Gilles Leroux, Directeur général Ext. 253
gilles.leroux@cforp.ca
Michel Goulet, Directeur, Développement et Édition Ext. 243
michel.goulet@cforp.ca
Guy Dubois, Directeur, Formation professionnelle Ext. 294
guy.dubois@cforp.ca
Hubert Lalande, Directeur, Production multimédia Ext. 260
hubert.lalande@cforp.ca
Michel Levesque, Directeur, Librairie du Centre Ext. 226
michel.levesque@cforp.ca
Daniel Forget, Directeur, Imprimerie Ext. 233
daniel.forget@cforp.ca
Lise Gélinas, Directrice, Communications/Marketing Ext. 244
lise.gelinas@cforp.ca
Penny Bell, Directrice, Finances et Ressources humaines Ext. 234
penny.bell@cforp.ca
Finances: *Budget de fonctionnement annuel:* $3 Million-$5 Million
Membre(s) du personnel: 140
Membre: 1-99
Activités: Production et distribution de ressources pédagogiques de langue française; *Stagiaires:* Oui; *Bibliothèque:* Librairie du Centre; Bibliothèque publique
Publications:
• Mon mag à moi
Type: Magazine; *Frequency:* 8-12 ans

Centre francophone d'informatisation des organisations (CEFRIO)
#575, 888, rue Saint-Jean, Québec QC G1R 5H6
Tél: 418-523-3746; *Téléc:* 418-523-2329
www.cefrio.qc.ca
www.linkedin.com/groups?gid=3697317
www.facebook.com/CEFRIOTIC
twitter.com/cefrio
Nom précédent: Centre francophone de recherche en informatisation des organisations
Aperçu: *Dimension:* petite; *Envergure:* provinciale; Organisme sans but lucratif; fondée en 1987
Mission: Aider les organisations québécoises à utiliser les techniques de l'information de manière à être plus performantes, plus productives et plus innovatrices
Membre(s) du bureau directeur:
Jacqueline Dubé, Présidente-directrice générale
Membre(s) du personnel: 24
Membre: 150; *Montant de la cotisation:* Variable, selon le nombre d'employés
Activités: *Bibliothèque:* Centre de documentation

Bureau à Montréal
#471, 550, rue Sherbrooke ouest, Montréal QC H3A 1B9
Tél: 514-840-1245; *Téléc:* 514-840-1275

Centre francophone de recherche en informatisation des organisations *Voir* Centre francophone d'informatisation des organisations

Centre francophone de Toronto (CFT)
20 Lower Spadina Ave., Toronto ON M5V 2Z1
Tél: 416-203-1220; *Téléc:* 416-203-1165
www.centrefranco.org
Nom précédent: Conseil des organismes francophones du Toronto Métropolitain; Centre francophones du Toronto Métropolitain
Aperçu: *Dimension:* moyenne; *Envergure:* locale; Organisme sans but lucratif; fondée en 1977
Mission: Permettre à la population francophone du grand Toronto d'avoir accès à des services d'information, d'orientation et d'encadrement susceptibles de promouvoir la dimension humaine, culturelle et communautaire des multiples visages de la francophonie
Affliation(s): Assemblée des centres culturels de l'Ontario; Centraide
Membre(s) du bureau directeur:
Lise Marie Baudry, Directrice générale
Finances: *Budget de fonctionnement annuel:* $500,000-$1.5 Million
Membre(s) du personnel: 12; 50 bénévole(s)
Membre: 20 individu; 5 institutionnel; *Montant de la cotisation:* 30$ institutionnel; 10$ individu
Activités: Consultation personnalisée dans les domaines de l'établissement; service de conseils d'emploi; accès à des offres d'emploi; *Bibliothèque*

Centre historique de St-Armand
166, rue Quinn, St-Armand QC J0J 1N0
Tel: 450-248-3393
Overview: A small local organization founded in 2002

Centre indien cri de Chibougamau
95, rue Jaculet, Chibougamau QC G8P 2G1
Tél: 418-748-7667
cicc@lino.com
Aperçu: *Dimension:* petite; *Envergure:* locale; fondée en 1969
Mission: Centre social pour les Autochtones de la région; centre d'exposition pour les artisans cri
Membre(s) du bureau directeur:
Jo-Ann Toulouse, Directice générale

Centre info-énergie *See* Canadian Centre for Energy Information

Centre intégré d'employabilité locale des Collines-de-l'Outaouais (CIEL)
1694, Montée de la Source, Cantley QC J8V 3H6
Tél: 819-457-4480; *Téléc:* 819-457-1024
Ligne sans frais: 877-770-2435
info@cielcollines.org
www.cielcollines.org
www.facebook.com/160819140628575
Aperçu: *Dimension:* petite; *Envergure:* locale
Mission: Pour aider les jeunes à trouver des emplois et retournent à l'école
Membre(s) du bureau directeur:
Josiane Groulx, Directrice éxécutive
jgroulx@cielcollines.org
Membre: *Critères d'admissibilite:* Jeunes adultes

Centre interdisciplinaire de recherches sur les activités langagières (CIRAL)
Pavillon Charles-de-Koninck, Université Laval, #2260-A, Faculté des lettres, Québec QC G1V 0A6
Tél: 418-656-2131
www.ciral.ulaval.ca
Nom précédent: Centre international de recherche en aménagement linguistique
Aperçu: *Dimension:* petite; *Envergure:* internationale; fondée en 1967
Mission: Le Centre interdisciplinaire de recherches sur la activités langagières (CIRAL) regroupe cinq équipes régulières, une vingtaine de chercheurs et quelque soixante-dix étudiants de deuxième et troisième cycles. Tous partagent la même conception des questions linguistiques ; la langue est indissociable de l'histoire et de la culture des groupes qui la parlent, et elle évolue en fonction des contacts interethniques et des pressions socioculturelles qui s'exercent sur elle.
Membre(s) du bureau directeur:
Aline Francoeur, Directrice
aline.francoeur@lli.ulaval.ca
Finances: *Fonds:* Subventions; Université Laval
Membre(s) du personnel: 3
Membre: 28 + 80 étudiants gradués; *Critères d'admissibilite:* Chercheur
Activités: Recherches en aménagement du corpus de la langue; recherches en aménagement du statut des langues; diffusion des travaux de recherches; formation des chercheur-e-s; collaboration avec d'autres centres ou universités et service au milieu; *Bibliothèque* Bibliothèque publique

Centre international de criminologie comparée (CICC) / International Centre for Comparative Criminology
CP 6128, Succ. Centre-Ville, Montréal QC H3C 3J7
Tél: 514-343-7065; *Téléc:* 514-343-2269
cicc@umontreal.ca
www.cicc.umontreal.ca
www.facebook.com/246261298771123
twitter.com/ciccTweet
www.youtube.com/cicctv
Aperçu: *Dimension:* petite; *Envergure:* internationale; fondée en 1969
Mission: Travaux de recherche en criminologie sur le comportement criminel ou déviant de la personne qui le pose ou le subit, et la réaction sociale au crime
Affiliation(s): Université de Montréal et Université du Québec à Trois-Rivières
Finances: *Budget de fonctionnement annuel:* $3 Million-$5 Million; *Fonds:* FQRSC, Université de Montréal
Membre(s) du personnel: 5
Membre: 38; *Critères d'admissibilite:* Chercheur; professeur
Activités: Colloques; séminaires; débats; conférences; *Evénements de sensibilisation:* Bourses de rédaction, de cueillette de données, de colloque, recherche et société, entente de collaboration chercheur du milieu de pratique
Publications:
• Bulletin CICC-Hebdo
Frequency: hebdomadaire
Profile: Un plateforme d'échange sur l'actualité criminologique
• CICC INFO
Frequency: semi-annuel
Profile: Le bulletin d'information du CICC

Centre international de documentation et d'échanges de la francophonie (CIDEF)
Pavillon Louis-Jacques Casault, Université Laval, #6411, 1055 av du Séminaire, Québec QC G1V 0A6
Tél: 418-656-2131
afi@com.ulaval.ca
www.afi.com.ulaval.ca
Aperçu: *Dimension:* moyenne; *Envergure:* internationale; fondée en 1984
Mission: Constituer et diffuser une documentation internationale de la francophonie.
Membre(s) du bureau directeur:
Charles Moumouni, Directeur de publication
Charles.Moumouni@com.ulaval.ca
Membre(s) du personnel: 2
Activités: Francophonie internationale; *Stagiaires:* Oui

Centre international de recherche en aménagement linguistique *Voir* Centre interdisciplinaire de recherches sur les activités langagières

Centre international de solidarité ouvrière (CISO)
#3500, 565, Crémazie est, Montréal QC H2M 2V6
Tél: 514-383-2266; *Téléc:* 514-383-1143
ciso@ciso.qc.ca
www.ciso.qc.ca
www.facebook.com/profile.php?id=100002425138083
twitter.com/CQCAM
Aperçu: *Dimension:* petite; *Envergure:* internationale; Organisme sans but lucratif; fondée en 1975
Membre de: Association québécoise des organismes coopération internationale
Membre(s) du bureau directeur:
Michèle Asselin, Coordonnateur, 514-383-2266 Ext. 225
Finances: *Budget de fonctionnement annuel:* $500,000-$1.5 Million
Membre(s) du personnel: 3; 30 bénévole(s)
Membre: *Montant de la cotisation:* 5-35 individuel; 50-400 organisationnel

Centre international Match *See* MATCH International Centre

Centre international pour la prévention de la criminalité (CIPC) / International Centre for the Prevention of Crime (ICPC)
#803, 465, rue St-Jean, Montréal QC H2Y 2R6
Tél: 514-288-6731; *Téléc:* 514-288-8763
cipc@crime-prevention-intl.org
www.crime-prevention-intl.org
www.linkedin.com/company/570491?trk=companies_home_ycp_logo_internatio
www.facebook.com/PreventionofCrime
twitter.com/ICPC_CIPC
Également appelé: ICPC
Aperçu: *Dimension:* moyenne; *Envergure:* internationale; Organisme sans but lucratif; fondée en 1994
Mission: Pour aider les pays et les villes à améliorer la sécurité des collectivités et à réduire la criminalité et la violence grâce à une prévention efficace
Membre(s) du bureau directeur:
Daniel Cauchy, Directeur général
Finances: *Fonds:* Gouvernemental
Membre(s) du personnel: 11
Membre: 99; *Montant de la cotisation:* Barème; *Comités:* Comité consultatif et d'orientation; Comité scientifique
Activités: *Stagiaires:* Oui; *Service de conférenciers:* Oui; *Bibliothèque:* Centre de documentation; Bibliothèque publique rendez-vous

Centre international pour le développement de l'inforoute en français (CIDIF)
167, boul Hébert, Edmundston NB E3V 4H2
Tél: 506-737-5280; *Téléc:* 506-737-5281
info@cidif.org
www.cidif.org
www.linkedin.com/company/cidif
twitter.com/cidif
Aperçu: *Dimension:* petite; *Envergure:* internationale
Mission: Fournir des outils et des services spécialisés afin de contribuer à rendre l'utilisation de logiciels et l'internet transparente aux usagers de différentes cultures et de différentes langues
Membre(s) du bureau directeur:
Réal Gervais, Propriétaire et président
Éric Bélanger, Directeur

Centre interuniversitaire de recherche en économie quantitative (CIREQ)
Pavillon Lionel-Groulx, Université de Montréal, CP 6128, Succ. Centre-Ville, 3150, rue Jean-Brillant, local C-6088, Montréal QC H3C 3J7
Tél: 514-343-6557; *Téléc:* 514-343-5831
www.cireqmontreal.com
Nom précédent: Centre de recherche et développement en économique
Aperçu: *Dimension:* moyenne; *Envergure:* internationale; fondée en 2002
Mission: Recherches dans les domaines de l'économétrie théorique et appliquée, de l'économie financière et de la théorie économique
Membre(s) du bureau directeur:
Emanuela Cardia, Dirctrice, 514-343-6111 Ext. 2449
emanuela.cardia@umontreal.ca
Finances: *Fonds:* FQRSC; Université de Montréal; Université McGill et Université Concordia
Membre(s) du personnel: 4
Membre: 50; *Critères d'admissibilite:* Chercheurs
Activités: Colloques; ateliers; conférences spéciales; séminaires; *Stagiaires:* Oui; *Service de conférenciers:* Oui; *Bibliothèque:* Centre de documentation; Bibliothèque publique

Centre Jean-Claude Malépart
2633, rue Ontario Est, Montréal QC H2K 1W8
Tél: 514-521-6884; *Téléc:* 514-521-6760
info@cjcm.ca
cjcm.ca
www.facebook.com/centrejcm
www.youtube.com/centrejcm
Aperçu: *Dimension:* petite; *Envergure:* locale
Mission: Pour améliorer la qualité de vie des résidents de la région en offrant des activités de loisirs abordables
Membre(s) du bureau directeur:
Adrien Michaud, Directeur
amichaud@cjcm.ca
Activités: Sport, Arts; Artisanat; Activités informatiques

Le Centre jeunesse de la Montérégie
575 rue Adoncour, Longueuil QC J4G 2M6
Tél: 450-679-0140; *Téléc:* 450-679-3731
www.centrejeunessemonteregie.qc.ca/
Aperçu: *Dimension:* moyenne; *Envergure:* locale; fondée en 1995
Mission: Offrir aux enfants et aux adolescents en difficulté de même qu'à leurs parents, des services d'aide spécialisée qui visent leur sécurité, leur protection, leur responsabilisation et leur autonomie
Membre(s) du bureau directeur:
Marc Rodier, Président
Camil Picard, Secrétaire
Membre(s) du personnel: 1000
Membre: 1,000-4,999
Activités: La protection de l'enfance et de la jeunesse et l'aide aux parents de ces enfants et adolescents; l'aide et la responsabilisation des jeunes contrevenants et le support aux parents; l'adaptation, la réadaptation et l'intégration sociale des enfants et des adolescents en difficulté; l'aide aux jeunes mères (pères) en difficulté d'adaptation; le placement d'enfants et d'adolescents en milieu substitut; l'urgence D.P.J. (24 heurs/7 jours par semaine); *Stagiaires:* Oui; *Bibliothèque:* Centre de documentation

Centre jeunesse de Montréal - Institut universitaire (CJMIU)
4675, rue Bélanger, Montréal QC H1T 1C2
Tél: 514-593-3979
courrier@cjm-iu.qc.ca
www.centrejeunessedemontreal.qc.ca
www.facebook.com/cjmiu.fanpage
www.youtube.com/user/centrejeunessemtl
Nom précédent: Le Centre jeunesse de Montréal; Les Centres jeunesse de Montréal; Centre Marie-Vincent
Aperçu: *Dimension:* petite; *Envergure:* locale; fondée en 1993
Membre(s) du bureau directeur:
Jean-Marc Potvin, Directeur général
Membre(s) du personnel: 3
Activités: *Bibliothèque:* Bibliothèque du Centre jeunesse de Montréal - Institut universita; rendez-vous
Publications:
• Défe jeunesse
Profile: Journal

Le Centre jeunesse de Montréal; Les Centres jeunesse de Montréal; Centre Marie-Vincent *Voir* Centre jeunesse de Montréal - Institut universitaire

Le centre jeunesse de Québec (CJQ)
2915, av du Bourg-Royal, Beauport QC G1C 3S2

Tél: 418-661-6951; *Téléc:* 418-661-2845
communication.cj03@ssss.gouv.qc.ca
www.centrejeunessedequebec.qc.ca
Aperçu: *Dimension:* moyenne; *Envergure:* locale
Mission: Dispense des services psychosociaux, des services d'adaptation, des services de réadaptation et des services d'intégration sociale aux jeunes et aux mères en difficulté de la région de Québec ainsi qu'à leur famille
Membre(s) du bureau directeur:
Jacques Laforest, Directeur général

Centre local de développement Rouyn-Noranda (CLD R-N)

161, av Murdoch, Rouyn-Noranda QC J9X 1E3
Tél: 819-792-0142; *Téléc:* 819-762-7139
info@cldrn.ca
www.cldrn.ca
www.facebook.com/pages/CLD-Rouyn-Noranda/359012320874266
twitter.com/cldrouynnoranda
Aperçu: *Dimension:* petite; *Envergure:* locale; Organisme sans but lucratif; fondée en 1998
Mission: De soutenir et de promouvoir les entreprises locales afin de les aider à prospérer
Membre(s) du bureau directeur:
André Rouleau, Directeur général
Membre(s) du personnel: 17
Activités: Développement économique

Centre Montérégien de réadaptation (CMR)

5300, ch. de Chambly, St-Hubert QC J3Y 3N7
Tél: 450-676-7447; *Téléc:* 450-676-0047
Ligne sans frais: 800-667-4369; *TTY:* 450-676-9841
Autres numéros: ATME sans frais: 1-866-676-1411
16cmr@ssss.gouv.qc.ca
cmrmonteregie.ca
Aperçu: *Dimension:* petite; *Envergure:* locale; fondée en 1991
Mission: Pour aider à la réhabilitation des personnes handicapées physiques et les troubles du langage
Membre(s) du bureau directeur:
Martin Girard, Président, Conseil d'administration
Hélène Duval, Directrice générale, 450-676-7447 Ext. 2400, Fax: 450-676-0047
Membre: *Critères d'admissibilité:* Les personnes handicapées physiques et les troubles du langage

Centre multiethnique de Québec (CMQ)

369, de la Couronne, 3e étage, Québec QC G1K 6E9
Tél: 418-687-9771; *Téléc:* 418-687-9063
cmq1@webnet.qc.ca
www.centremultiethnique.org
Également appelé: Fraternité multiculturelle
Aperçu: *Dimension:* moyenne; *Envergure:* locale; Organisme sans but lucratif; fondée en 1960
Mission: Accueillir les nouveaux arrivants et les soutenir dans leur intégration dans la société d'accueil
Membre de: Table de concertation pour les réfugiés et immigrants
Membre(s) du bureau directeur:
Karine Verreault, Directrice
Finances: *Budget de fonctionnement annuel:* $250,000-$500,000; *Fonds:* gouvernement provincial et fédéral
Membre(s) du personnel: 11; 50 bénévole(s)
Membre: 10 institutionnel; 300 individus; *Critères d'admissibilité:* Intérêt pour la cause des immigrants
Activités: *Stagiaires:* Oui

Le Centre parlementaire *See* Parliamentary Centre

Centre patronal de santé et sécurité du travail du Québec (CPSSTQ) / Employers Center for Occupational Health & Safety of Quebec

#1000, 500, rue Sherbrooke ouest, Montréal QC H3A 3C6
Tél: 514-842-8401; *Téléc:* 514-842-9375
www.centrepatronalsst.qc.ca
Aperçu: *Dimension:* grande; *Envergure:* provinciale; Organisme sans but lucratif; fondée en 1983
Mission: Fournir de l'information et de la formation en SST aux entreprises regroupées par les associations patronales membres du Centre patronal
Membre de: Société canadienne des directeurs d'associations
Membre(s) du bureau directeur:
Claude Gosselin, Président
Denise Turenne, Direction générale
d.turenne@centrepatronalsst.qc.ca
Diane Rochone, Directrice, Communications
d.rochon@centrepatronalsst.qc.ca
Finances: *Budget de fonctionnement annuel:* $3 Million-$5 Million
Membre(s) du personnel: 24; 7 bénévole(s)
Membre: 90+; *Montant de la cotisation:* 25$; *Critères d'admissibilite:* Associations d'employeurs
Activités: Cours; colloques; *Stagiaires:* Oui; *Service de conférenciers:* Oui; *Bibliothèque:* Centre de documentation
Publications:
• Convergence [a publication of the Centre patronal de santé et sécurité du travail du Québec]
Type: Journal
• SST Bonjour ! [a publication of the Centre patronal de santé et sécurité du travail du Québec]
Type: Newsletter

Centre pour la défense de l'intérêt public *See* The Public Interest Advocacy Centre

Centre pour les droits à l'égalité au logement *See* Centre for Equality Rights in Accommodation

Centre pour les victimes d'agression sexuelle de Fredericton *See* Fredericton Sexual Assault Crisis Centre

Centre Psycho-Pédagogique de Québec Inc.

École Saint-François, 1000, rue du Joli-Bois, Québec QC G1V 3Z6
Tél: 418-650-1171; *Téléc:* 418-650-1145
www.cppq.qc.ca
Aperçu: *Dimension:* petite; *Envergure:* provinciale
Membre(s) du bureau directeur:
Donald Gilbert, Président
Membre: *Critères d'admissibilite:* L'école Saint-François aide les enfants, les parents et les écoles en fournissant une ressource appropriée à l'intérieur d'un enseignement personnalisé, dispensé de la troisième année du primaire à la troisième année du secondaire dans le but de favoriser l'intégration sociale de filles et garçons présentant des difficultés d'adaptation scolaire.
Activités: Classe nature; sortie thématiques et culturelles en groupe; atelierss; service d'orientation; clinique juridique; *Stagiaires:* Oui

Centre québécois de la déficience auditive (CQDA) / Québec Centre of Hearing Impaired

#202, 2494, boul Henri-Bourassa est, Montréal QC H2B 1T9
Tél: 514-278-8704; *Téléc:* 514-278-8238
info@cqda.org
www.cqda.org
Aperçu: *Dimension:* petite; *Envergure:* provinciale; Organisme sans but lucratif; fondée en 1975
Mission: Regrouper les organismes dans le domaine de la surdité au Québec; aider les personnes déficientes auditives; identifier leurs besoins; sensibiliser le public à leur problématique; surveiller et défendre leurs droits et leurs intérêts; créer plus de services répondant à leurs besoins
Membre de: Confédération des organismes de personnes handicapées du Québec
Affliation(s): Confédération des organismes de personnes handicapées du Québec; Conseil des canadiens avec déficiences; KEROUL; Association des sourds du Canada; Association des Malentendants canadiens
Membre(s) du bureau directeur:
Martin Bergevin, Directeur
Finances: *Budget de fonctionnement annuel:* $100,000-$250,000
Membre(s) du personnel: 3; 20 bénévole(s)
Membre: 70; *Montant de la cotisation:* 75$ membre actif; 100$ membre associé; *Critères d'admissibilité:* Association de sourds et malentendants ou liée à la surdité
Activités: Information; formation; soutien aux membres; concertation; défense des droits et des intérêts; *Service de conférenciers:* Oui; *Listes de destinataires:* Oui

Centre québécois du droit de l'environnement (CQDE) / Québec Environmental Law Centre

454, av Laurier Est, Montréal QC H2J 1E7
Tél: 514-272-2666; *Téléc:* 514-447-9455
info@cqde.org
www.cqde.org
www.facebook.com/DroitEnvironnementQC
Aperçu: *Dimension:* petite; *Envergure:* provinciale; Organisme sans but lucratif; fondée en 1989
Mission: Promouvoir le droit de l'environnement comme outil de protection de la santé publique et du patrimoine collectif
Membre(s) du bureau directeur:
Cédric Gagnon-Ducharme, Président
Marie-Josée Caya, Trésorière
Karine Péloffy, Secrétaire
Finances: *Budget de fonctionnement annuel:* $100,000-$250,000
Membre: 120; *Montant de la cotisation:* 10$ étudiant; 20$ membre individuel; 50$ entreprise
Activités: *Service de conférenciers:* Oui; *Bibliothèque* Bibliothèque publique rendez-vous

Centre sida amitié (CSA)

527, rue St-Georges, Saint-Jérôme QC J7Z 5B6
Tél: 450-431-7432; *Téléc:* 450-431-6536
csa1@qc.aira.com
www.facebook.com/pages/centre-sida-amiti%C3%A9/124552904252226
twitter.com/Sidaamitie
Aperçu: *Dimension:* petite; *Envergure:* locale; Organisme sans but lucratif; fondée en 1989 surveillé par Canadian AIDS Society
Membre(s) du bureau directeur:
Hugo Bissonnet, Directeur général
Membre(s) du personnel: 25; 15 bénévole(s)
Activités: soutien; éducation/prévention; ligne info-sida; *Stagiaires:* Oui; *Service de conférenciers:* Oui

Centre Sportif de la Petite Bourgogne / Little Burgundy Sports Centre

1825, rue Notre-Dame ouest, Montréal QC H3J 1M5
Tel: 514-932-0800
centresportifdelapetitebourgogne.com
Overview: A small local organization founded in 1997
Chief Officer(s):
Dickens Mathurin, Director General, 514-932-0800 Ext. 24
serviceclient@centresportif-cspb.com

Centre St-Pierre

1212, rue Panet, Montréal QC H2L 2Y7
Tél: 514-524-3561; *Téléc:* 514-524-5663
csp@centrestpierre.org
www.centrestpierre.org
Aperçu: *Dimension:* petite; *Envergure:* locale
Mission: Pour offrir une organisation communautaire avec les valeurs chrétiennes incorporés dans ses services
Membre(s) du bureau directeur:
Lise Roy, Directrice générale
Activités: Animation; pstchothérapie; service d'accompagnement psycho-spirituel; dynamique du couple et mariage chrétien

Centre Wellington Chamber of Commerce

400 Tower St. South, Fergus ON N1M 2P7
Tel: 519-843-5140; *Fax:* 519-787-0983
Toll-Free: 877-242-6353
chamber@cwchamber.ca
www.cwchamber.ca
Overview: A small local organization founded in 1999
Mission: To promote the social, civic & economic development of our community & serve as the voice of business
Member of: Canadian Chamber of Commerce; Ontario Chamber of Commerce
Chief Officer(s):
Deb Dalziel, General Manager
Finances: *Annual Operating Budget:* $250,000-$500,000
Staff Member(s): 2
Membership: 370; *Fees:* $165 minimum; *Committees:* Ways & Means; Business; Government Affairs; Member Services; Communications; Golf; Awards of Excellence
Activities: Golf Tournament; AGM; education sessions
Awards:
• Citizen of the Year Award (Award)

Les Centres jeunesse de l'Outaouais (CJO)

105, boul Sacré-Coeur, Gatineau QC J8X 1C5
Tél: 819-771-6631; *Téléc:* 819-771-8221
Ligne sans frais: 800-567-6810
www.cjoutaouais.qc.ca
Merged from: Centre de services sociaux de l'Outaouais; Centre de réadaptation les jeunes de l'Outaouais
Aperçu: *Dimension:* petite; *Envergure:* locale; Organisme sans but lucratif; fondée en 1942
Mission: Nous assurons la protection des jeunes; nous amenons les jeunes à assumer leurs responsabilités et à se réadapter à la société en les aidant à retrouver un équilibre personnel et social; nous aidons enfants et adultes à se préparer à une adoption; nous aidons les enfants adoptés et parents naturels à reprendre contact; nous offrons notre expertise dans certaines causes de divorce; nous assurons aux jeunes un éventail de ressources d'hébergement
Membre de: Association des Centres jeunesse du Québec

Membre(s) du bureau directeur:
Luc Cadieux, Directeur général, 819-771-2990 Ext. 2145
Finances: *Budget de fonctionnement annuel:* Plus de $5 Million
Membre(s) du personnel: 450
Membre: 17; *Critères d'admissibilité:* Membre du CA Collèges électoraux
Activités: Services psychosociaux; services de réadaptation; urgence sociale 24 heures par jour, 7 jours par semaine; *Stagiaires:* Oui; *Bibliothèque*

Les Centres jeunesse de la Mauricie et du Centre de Québec

1455, boul du Carmel, Trois-Rivières QC G8Z 3R7
Tél: 819-378-5481
Ligne sans frais: 800-567-8520
www.cjmcq.qc.ca
Nom précédent: Les Centres jeunesse Mauricie-Bois-Francs
Aperçu: *Dimension:* petite; *Envergure:* locale; fondée en 1996
Mission: Assurer la sécurité et le développement; assurer la responsabilisation des jeunes; aider les enfants, les jeunes, leurs parents et les jeunes mSres vivant des difficultés majeures au plan de leur fonctionnement; intervenir dans leur démarche de changement de leur situation personnelle, familiale et sociale

Membre(s) du bureau directeur:
Renée St-Amand, Directrice générale

Les Centres jeunesse Mauricie-Bois-Francs ***Voir*** Les Centres jeunesse de la Mauricie et du Centre de Québec

Centreville Chamber of Commerce

PO Box 628, Centreville NB E7K 3H5
Tel: 506-276-3674; *Fax:* 506-276-9891
centreville.chamber@aernet.ca
Overview: A small local organization founded in 1985
Chief Officer(s):
Kathy Simonson, Staff
Robert Taylor, President
Membership: 45 individual; *Committees:* Tourism; Membership; Streets & Roads; Special Events; Agriculture; Business & Commercial; Sports & Recreation

Centro Comunitàrio Divino Espìrito Santo / Centre Communautaire Esprit Saint

86872 rue de Forbin-Janson, Montréal QC H1K 2J9
Tél: 514-353-1550
Également appelé: Saint Esprit Community Centre
Aperçu: *Dimension:* petite; *Envergure:* locale

Cercle canadien de Toronto ***Voir*** Club canadien de Toronto

Cercle d'expression artistique Nyata Nyata

4374, boul St-Laurent, 2e étage, Montréal QC H2W 1Z5
Tél: 514-849-9781
Ligne sans frais: 877-692-8208
info@nyata-nyata.org
www.nyata-nyata.org
www.facebook.com/153132964772900
www.youtube.com/user/nyatanyata
Également appelé: Nyata Nyata
Aperçu: *Dimension:* petite; *Envergure:* locale; Organisme sans but lucratif
Mission: Pour créer musical et l'art chorégraphique dans le but de développer l'art de la danse et les compétences des artistes.
Membre(s) du bureau directeur:
Zab Maboungou, Directrice artistique
Membre(s) du personnel: 5; 3 bénévole(s)

Cercle de la finance internationale de Montréal / International Finance Club of Montréal

CP 63123, 40, Place du Commerce, Montréal QC H3E 1V6
Tél: 514-933-1451; *Téléc:* 514-933-1508
cfim@cercledelafinance.qc.ca
www.cercledelafinance.qc.ca
Nom précédent: Cercle des banquiers internationaux de Montréal
Aperçu: *Dimension:* petite; *Envergure:* internationale; fondée en 1984
Mission: Promouvoir au sein de la communauté financière les activités et les services de ses membres
Membre(s) du bureau directeur:
Luc St-Arnault, Président
Gérard Mournier, Trésorier
gerard.mounier@ccd.desjardins.com
1 bénévole(s)
Membre: 150; *Montant de la cotisation:* 500$ corporatifs; 125$ individuels; 50$ étudiants; *Critères d'admissibilité:* Dirigeants d'institutions et d'organismes financiers à orientation internationale
Activités: *Stagiaires:* Oui; *Listes de destinataires:* Oui

Cercle des banquiers internationaux de Montréal ***Voir*** Cercle de la finance internationale de Montréal

Cercle des bénévoles du Musée des beaux-arts du Canada ***See*** Volunteer Circle of the National Gallery of Canada

Cercle des Fermières - Chibougamau

CP 417, Chibougamau QC G8P 2X7
Tél: 418-672-4877
www.cfq.qc.ca
Aperçu: *Dimension:* petite; *Envergure:* locale surveillé par Cercles de Fermières du Québec
Membre(s) du bureau directeur:
Colombe Bergeron, Responsable
colombeberge@hotmail.com

Le Cercle Molière

340, boul Provencher, Winnipeg MB R2H 0G7
Tél: 204-233-8053; *Téléc:* 204-233-2373
info@cerclemoliere.com
www.cerclemoliere.com
www.facebook.com/cercle.moliere
twitter.com/CercleMoliere
Aperçu: *Dimension:* moyenne; *Envergure:* provinciale; Organisme sans but lucratif; fondée en 1925
Mission: Présenter des spectacles de théâtre en français au Manitoba
Membre de: Association des compagnies de théâtre de l'Ouest; Association des théâtres francophones du Canada; Conférence canadienne des arts
Membre(s) du bureau directeur:
Geneviève Pelletier, Directrice artistique et générale
genevieve@cerclemoliere.com
Finances: *Fonds:* Conseil des arts du Manitoba; Conseil des arts du Canada; Patrimoine Canadien
Membre(s) du personnel: 7
Activités: Spectacles (grand public et jeunes publics), lectures, école de théâtre, festival de théâtre adolescent, grande soirée de levée de fonds; *Stagiaires:* Oui; *Service de conférenciers:* Oui

Cercle national des jounalistes du Canada ***See*** National Press Club of Canada Foundation

Le Cercle Saint-François ***See*** The Kindness Club

Cercles de fermières du Québec (CFQ)

1043, rue Tiffin, Longueuil QC J4P 3G7
Tél: 450-442-3983; *Téléc:* 450-442-4363
cerfer@videotron.ca
www.cfq.qc.ca
www.facebook.com/283417910957
Aperçu: *Dimension:* moyenne; *Envergure:* provinciale; Organisme sans but lucratif; fondée en 1915
Mission: Association apolitique de femmes vouées à l'amélioration des conditions de vie de la femme et de la famille et à la transmission du patrimoine artisanal et culturel
Membre(s) du bureau directeur:
Louise Lagarde, Présidente
cerfer@videotron.ca
Finances: *Budget de fonctionnement annuel:* $100,000-$250,000
Membre(s) du personnel: 3
Membre: 38 000; *Montant de la cotisation:* 20$; *Critères d'admissibilite:* Femme 14+; *Comités:* Dossiers; Communications; Arts Textiles; Recrutement
Publications:
• L'Actuelle
Profile: Magazine

Cercles des jeunes naturalistes (CJN)

Jardin botanique de Montréal, #262, 4101, rue Sherbrooke est, Montréal QC H1X 2B2
Tél: 514-252-3023; *Téléc:* 514-254-8744
info@jeunesnaturalistes.org
www.jeunesnaturalistes.org
www.facebook.com/161347170575251
twitter.com/AdrienRivard
www.youtube.com/watch?v=LiGi1B0bYtc
Aperçu: *Dimension:* grande; *Envergure:* nationale; Organisme sans but lucratif; fondée en 1931
Mission: Nous initions les jeunes à l'étude des sciences de la nature et à la protection de l'environnement
Membre de: Regroupement Loisir Québec
Membre(s) du bureau directeur:
André St-Arnaud, Président
Vicky Lesieur, Coodonnatrice générale
Finances: *Budget de fonctionnement annuel:* $50,000-$100,000; *Fonds:* Gouvernement provincial pour la gestion du Siège social; OSBL
Membre(s) du personnel: 3; 15 bénévole(s)
Membre: 2 000; *Montant de la cotisation:* 35$ individuel; 50$ famille; *Comités:* Voir notre site internet
Activités: Camps nature; animations dans les cercles avec les Jeunes Naturalistes sur les sciences de la nature; activités parascolaires et dans les écoles; formation pour animateurs; trousses d'animations; festival provincial annuel; *Bibliothèque*
Publications:
• Les Naturalistes [a publication of Cercles des jeunes naturalistes]
Type: Revue

Cereal & District Board of Trade

PO Box 85, Cereal AB T0J 0N0
Tel: 403-326-3818; *Fax:* 403-326-3800
Overview: A small local organization
Membership: 15; *Fees:* $2

Cerebral Palsy Association in Alberta (CPAA)

12001 - 44 St. SE, Calgary AB T2Z 4G9
Tel: 403-543-1161; *Fax:* 403-543-1168
Toll-Free: 800-363-2807
admin@cpalberta.com
www.cpalberta.com
www.facebook.com/groups/2323799542
twitter.com/CPAlberta
www.youtube.com/user/CerebralPalsyAlberta
Overview: A medium-sized provincial organization founded in 1976
Mission: To improve the quality of life of persons with cerebral palsy through a broad range of programs, education, support of research, & the delivery of needed services to people with cerebral palsy & their families; To encourage persons with cerebral palsy to develop & pursue meaningful goals & achievements in life; To raise awareness in society of the abilities of individuals with cerebral palsy
Chief Officer(s):
Janice Bushfield, Executive Director
janice@cpalberta.com
Mezaun Lakha-Evin, Associate Executive Director
Mezaun@cpalberta.com
Joanne Dorn, Director, Development
jdorn@cpalberta.com
Mariana Nimara, Director, Administration
mariana@cpalberta.com
Shyam Poudyal, Manager, Finance
shyam@cpalberta.com
Finances: *Annual Operating Budget:* $250,000-$500,000; *Funding Sources:* Fundraising; United Way; Donations; Grants; Sales of used clothing; Bottle recycling
Staff Member(s): 40; 300 volunteer(s)
Membership: 2,800; *Fees:* Free
Activities: Increasing public awareness; Engaging in advocacy activities; Researching; Recreation & sports; Youth transitions program; Support services; *Speaker Service:* Yes; *Library:* Resource Centre; Open to public

Cerebral Palsy Association of British Columbia (CPABC)

#330, 409 Granville St., Vancouver BC V6C 1T2
Tel: 604-408-9484; *Fax:* 604-408-9489
Toll-Free: 800-663-0004
www.bccerebralpalsy.com
www.facebook.com/cerebral.palsy.39
Also Known As: CP Association of BC
Overview: A medium-sized provincial organization founded in 1954
Mission: To raise awareness of cerebral palsy in the community; To assist those living with cerebral palsy to reach to maximum; To work to see those living with cerebral palsy realize their place as equals within a diverse society; To provide support & services that facilitate these needs; To make a Life Without Limits for people with disabilities
Member of: Better Business Bureau
Chief Officer(s):
Andy Yu, President
Feri Dehdar, Executive Director
Finances: *Annual Operating Budget:* $100,000-$250,000
Staff Member(s): 8; 30 volunteer(s)

Membership: 1,500; *Fees:* Free; *Committees:* Charitable Funders Network
Activities: Dance, yoga, resource & community outreach; *Awareness Events:* Cerebral Palsy Week, June; *Library:* Resource Library; Open to public
Awards:
• Tanabe Bursary (Scholarship)

Cerebral Palsy Association of Manitoba Inc. (CPAM)
#105, 500 Portage Ave., Winnipeg MB R3C 3X1
Tel: 204-982-4842; *Fax:* 204-982-4844
Toll-Free: 800-416-6166
office@cerebralpalsy.mb.ca
www.cerebralpalsy.mb.ca
Overview: A medium-sized provincial charitable organization founded in 1974
Mission: To enrich the lives of individuals affected by cerebral palsy through services, advocacy, education & peer support
Chief Officer(s):
Laura Schnellert, Director, Membership & Programs
lauras@cerebralpalsy.mb.ca
Finances: *Annual Operating Budget:* $50,000-$100,000
Staff Member(s): 1; 50 volunteer(s)
Membership: 400; *Fees:* $10 family & individual; $25 institution
Activities: *Speaker Service:* Yes; *Library:* Cerebral Palsy Library; Open to public

Cerebral Palsy Association of Newfoundland & Labrador (CPNL)
PO Box 23059, Stn. Churchill Square, St. John's NL A1B 4R9
Tel: 709-753-9922
Previous Name: Newfoundland Cerebral Palsy Association Inc.
Overview: A small provincial charitable organization founded in 1961
Mission: To improve the quality of life of persons with cerebral palsy through a broad range of programs, education, support of research & the delivery of needed services to people with cerebral palsy & their families
Member of: Atlantic Cerebral Palsy Association
Finances: *Funding Sources:* Donations; grants
Activities: Social events; meetings; Disability Awareness Project; *Library* by appointment

Cerebral Palsy Foundation (St. John) Inc.
PO Box 2152, Saint John NB E2L 3V1
Tel: 506-648-0322
mail@cpfsj.ca
www.cpfsj.ca
Overview: A small local organization
Membership: *Fees:* $5 individual; $10 family
Awards:
• Gertrude Aarela Memorial Scholarship
Eligibility: New Brunswick high school student with cerebral palsy planning on attending a post-secondary institution*Deadline:* May 15 *Amount:* $1000

Cerebral Palsy Sports Association of British Columbia (CPSABC)
6235C - 136th St., Surrey BC V3X 1H3
Tel: 604-599-5240; *Fax:* 604-599-5241
sportinfo@sportabilitybc.ca
sportabilitybc.ca
www.facebook.com/pages/SportAbility/48152344944
twitter.com/SportAbilityBC
www.youtube.com/SportAbilityBC
Also Known As: SportAbility BC
Overview: A medium-sized provincial charitable organization founded in 1976 overseen by Canadian Cerebral Palsy Sports Association
Mission: To provide sports & recreational opportunities for people with cerebral palsy, head injury, stroke & similar disabilities at the local, regional, provincial & national level; To provide access to appropriate programming for members including segregated & integrated opportunities
Member of: Canadian Cerebral Palsy Sports Association
Affliation(s): Sport BC
Chief Officer(s):
Chris Duehrsen, President
Terrie Moore, Executive Director
tmoore@sportabilitybc.ca
Finances: *Annual Operating Budget:* $250,000-$500,000; *Funding Sources:* Fundraising; Sport BC; Gaming
Staff Member(s): 5
Membership: *Fees:* $25 senior/individual/family; *Member Profile:* Physically disabled or interested in volunteering; *Committees:* Risk Management
Activities: *Library* by appointment
Publications:
• Sportability [a publication of the Cerebral Palsy Sports Association of British Columbia]
Type: Newsletter

Certification Council of Early Childhood Educators of Nova Scotia (CCECENS)
#100, 1200 Tower Rd., Halifax NS B3H 4K6
Tel: 902-423-8199
Toll-Free: 800-565-8199
ccecens@cccns.org
www.cccns.org/cert/home.html
Overview: A small provincial organization
Mission: Committed to the development of a high quality, professional, certified body of Early Childhood Educators
Affliation(s): Canadian Child Care Federation
Chief Officer(s):
Pat Hogan, President
Janice MacKinnon, Registrar
Finances: *Annual Operating Budget:* Less than $50,000
Membership: 52; *Fees:* $35; *Member Profile:* Early childhood educators & administrators

Certified Dental Assistants of BC (CDABC)
#504, 602 West Hastings St., Vancouver BC V6B 1P2
Tel: 604-714-1766; *Fax:* 604-714-1767
Toll-Free: 800-579-4440
info@cdabc.org
www.cdabc.org
Overview: A small provincial organization overseen by Canadian Dental Assistants Association
Chief Officer(s):
Marlene Robinson, Executive Director
Arlene Cearns, President
Finances: *Funding Sources:* Grant
Staff Member(s): 5; 50 volunteer(s)
Membership: 5,700; *Fees:* $25 student; $125 active/associate
Activities: *Awareness Events:* Dental Assistants Recognition Week, March

Certified General Accountants Association - Yukon Territory
PO Box 31536, Main St., Whitehorse YT Y1A 6K8
Tel: 867-668-4461; *Fax:* 867-668-8635
www.cga.org/canada/yukon
Also Known As: CGA - Yukon
Overview: A medium-sized provincial licensing organization founded in 1983 overseen by Chartered Professional Accountants of the Yukon
Chief Officer(s):
Robert Fendrick, FCGA, President
Membership: *Member Profile:* Certified General Accountants of Yukon, who are also associate members, in good standing, with the Certified General Accountants Association of British Columbia; Certified General Accountant students from Yukon
Activities: Ensuring members' adherence to CGA - BC's Code of Ethical Principles & Rules of Conduct; Providing professionl development opportunities (note that CGA Yukon will integrate under the CPA banner)

Certified General Accountants Association of Alberta
#100, 325 Manning Rd. NE, Calgary AB T2E 2P5
Tel: 403-299-1300; *Fax:* 403-299-1339
Toll-Free: 800-661-1078
manningreception@albertaaccountants.org
www.cga-alberta.org
www.facebook.com/cgaalberta
twitter.com/cgaalberta
www.youtube.com/user/CGAAlberta
Also Known As: CGA - Alberta
Overview: A medium-sized provincial licensing organization overseen by Alberta Accountants Unification Agency
Mission: To represent the provincial interests of Certified General Accountants & students; To establish & enforce professional competency & ethical standards
Chief Officer(s):
Larry Presiloski, MBA, FCGA, Chief Operating Officer
lpresiloski@cga-alberta.org
Membership: 9,000; *Member Profile:* Certified General Accountants who meet the educational requirements of the association, plus students from Alberta
Activities: Providing advisory services for public practitioners; Creating networking opportunities; Promoting the Certified General Accountant identity; Offering job search assistance; Offering professional development opportunities (note that CGA Alberta will integrate under the CPA banner)

Certified General Accountants Association of British Columbia
#300, 1867 West Broadway, Vancouver BC V6J 5L4
Tel: 604-732-1211; *Fax:* 604-732-1252
Toll-Free: 800-565-1211
info@cga-bc.org
www.cga-bc.org
twitter.com/cgabc
Also Known As: CGA - BC
Overview: A medium-sized provincial licensing organization founded in 1951 overseen by Chartered Professional Accountants of British Columbia
Mission: To act as the governing & regulatory body responsible for Certified General Accountants in British Columbia; To train & certify British Columbia's Certified General Accountants
Chief Officer(s):
John Pankratz, President
Bruce Hurst, 1st Vice-President
Bill Caulfield, Executive Director & Secretary
Stephen Spector, Treasurer
Membership: 14,000+ Certified General Accountants & Certified General Accountant students; *Member Profile:* British Columbia's Certified General Accountants & Certified General Accountant students
Activities: Presenting a mentorship program for newcomers to Canada; Providing professional development activities (note that CGA BC will integrate under the CPA banner)
Meetings/Conferences: • Certified General Accountants Association of British Columbia 2015 65th Annual General Meeting, Conference, & Trade Show, 2015
Scope: Provincial
Description: A provincial conference about recent developments in the profession for Certified General Accountants & other professional accountants

Certified General Accountants Association of Canada *See* Chartered Professional Accountants Canada

Certified General Accountants Association of Manitoba
4 Donald St. South, Winnipeg MB R3L 2T7
Tel: 204-477-1256; *Fax:* 204-453-7176
Toll-Free: 800-282-8001
info@cga-manitoba.org
www.cga-manitoba.org
Also Known As: CGA - Manitoba
Overview: A medium-sized provincial licensing organization founded in 1973 overseen by Chartered Professional Accountants of Manitoba
Mission: To provide professional support services for the accounting profession in Manitoba; To ensure commitment to the Code of Ethical Principles & Rules of Conduct; To empower members to excel
Chief Officer(s):
Grant B. Christensen, B.A., B.Comm.(H, Chief Executive Officer
Zachary R. Minuk, Manager, Business Development, 204-924-4416
zminuk@cpamb.ca
Nadine Morrill, Director, Finance & Administration
Bruce Granke, Director, Professional Regulation & Communications
Membership: *Member Profile:* Certified General Accountants & students from Manitoba
Activities: Organizing awareness campaigns, such as the annual Tax Tips series; Offering professional training events; Professional development opportunities (note that CGA Manitoba will integrate under the CPA banner)
Awards:
• The John Leslie Award (Award)
• The Fellowship Award (Award)
• Life Membership Award (Award)
• Honorary Membership (Award)

Certified General Accountants Association of New Brunswick / Association des comptables généraux accrédités du Nouveau-Brunswick
PO Box 5100, #403, 236 St. George St., Moncton NB E1C 8R2
Tel: 506-857-0939; *Fax:* 506-855-0887
Toll-Free: 877-462-4262
cganb@cga-nb.org
www.cga-nb.org
www.facebook.com/306759089364264
twitter.com/CGANewBrunswick
Also Known As: CGA - New Brunswick

Overview: A medium-sized provincial organization founded in 1962 overseen by Chartered Professional Accountants of New Brunswick
Mission: To advance the interests of Certified General Accountants & to inform the public in New Brunswick; To provide education & professional services to members; To uphold the Code of Ethical Principles & Rules of Conduct to protect the public
Chief Officer(s):
Trudy Dryden, FCGA, Executive Director
tdryden@cga-nb.org
Finances: *Funding Sources:* Sponsorships
Membership: *Member Profile:* Certified General Accountants & students from New Brunswick
Activities: Conducting research; Engaging in advocacy activities; Recruiting new students; Delivering the Program of Professional Studies in New Brunswick; Offering an annual conference; Providing advisory services for public practitioners; Offering an employment referral service; Offering continuing professional development opportunities (note that CGA New Brunswick will integrate under the CPA banner);

Certified General Accountants Association of Newfoundland & Labrador (CGA-NL)
#500, 95 Bonaventure Ave., St. John's NL A1B 2X5
Tel: 709-579-1863; *Fax:* 709-579-0838
Toll-Free: 800-563-2426
office@cganl.org
www.cganl.org
www.facebook.com/CGANL
twitter.com/cganl
Also Known As: CGA - Newfoundland & Labrador
Overview: A medium-sized provincial licensing organization founded in 1962 overseen by Chartered Professional Accountants of Newfoundland & Labrador
Mission: To protect the public through commitment to The CGA Newfoundland & Labrador Code of Ethical Principles & Rules of Conduct & The CGA Newfoundland & Labrador Independence Standard; To advocate on issues to advance the interests of Certified General Accountants in Newfoundland & Labrador
Chief Officer(s):
Michael Kennedy, B. Comm., CGA, Chair
Membership: *Member Profile:* Certified General Accountants & students from Newfoundland & Labrador
Activities: Delivering the Program of Professional Studies in Newfoundland & Labrador; Informing the public of important issues; Conducting research; Publishing reports & policy positions; Offering job search assistance; Providing continuing professional development (note that CGA-NL will integrate under the CPA banner)

Certified General Accountants Association of Nova Scotia
#230, 1801 Hollis St., Halifax NS B3J 3N4
Tel: 902-425-4923; *Fax:* 902-425-4983
office@cga-ns.org
www.cga-ns.org
www.facebook.com/195665448488
twitter.com/cga_nova_scotia
Also Known As: CGA - Nova Scotia
Overview: A medium-sized provincial organization founded in 1982 overseen by Chartered Professional Accountants Canada
Mission: To control the professional standards, conduct, & discipline of Certified General Accountants from Nova Scotia; To grant the exclusive right to the CGA designation
Chief Officer(s):
Stana Colovic, CGA (Hon.), Chief Executive Officer
Membership: *Member Profile:* Certified General Accountants & students from Nova Scotia
Activities: Upholding the Code of Ethical Practice & Rules of Conduct (CEPROC); Assisting members in job searches; Providing professional development activities (note that CGA Nova Scotia will integrate under the CPA banner once legislation is approved)

Certified General Accountants Association of Ontario
240 Eglinton Ave. East, Toronto ON M4P 1K8
Tel: 416-322-6520; *Fax:* 416-322-6481
Toll-Free: 800-668-1454
info@cga-ontario.org
www.cga-ontario.org
www.linkedin.com/company/cga-ontario
twitter.com/CGA_Ontario
Also Known As: CGA - Ontario
Overview: A large provincial licensing organization founded in 1913 overseen by Chartered Professional Accountants of Ontario
Mission: To regulate qualification, performance, & discipline standards for Certified General Accountants throughout Ontario; To grant exclusive rights to the CGA designation
Chief Officer(s):
Doug Brooks, FCGA, Chief Executive Officer
Membership: 21,000 Certified General Accountants + 8,000 students; *Member Profile:* Certified General Accountants & students from the province of Ontario
Activities: Engaging in advocacy activities; Informing Certified General Accountants & the public; Conducting surveys; Offering continuing professional development opportunities (note that CGA Ontario will integrate under the CPA banner)
Awards:
• Chapter Distinguished Service Award (Award)
Eligibility: Member of CGA-Ontario who has performed outstanding service
• Ivy Thomas Award (Award)
Eligibility: Member of CGA-Ontario who has received recognition for artistic or business practice, service or charitable involvement
• Donna MacGregor Outstanding Volunteer Award (Award)
Eligibility: Member of CGA-Ontario who has performed volunteer service to the community
• Ontario Distinguished Service Award (Award)
Eligibility: Member of CGA-Ontario who has performed distinguished service to the association
• Lorna Henderson Outstanding Mentor Award (Award)
Eligibility: Member of CGA-Ontario who has made a contribution to the study & developmente of students

Certified General Accountants Association of Prince Edward Island
PO Box 3, #105, 18 Queen St., Charlottetown PE C1A 4A1
Tel: 902-368-7237; *Fax:* 902-368-3627
contact@cga-pei.org
www.cga-pei.org
Also Known As: CGA - Prince Edward Island
Overview: A medium-sized provincial organization founded in 1968 overseen by Chartered Professional Accountants of Prince Edward Island
Mission: To provide professional support services to the accounting profession in Prince Edward Island
Chief Officer(s):
Sherry Ross, BBA, CGA, President
Membership: 175+; *Member Profile:* Certified General Accountants & students from Prince Edward Island
Activities: Providing continuing education opportunities (note that CGA-PEI will integrate under the CPA banner)

Certified General Accountants Association of Saskatchewan
#101, 4581 Parliament Ave., Regina SK SW4 0G3
Tel: 306-359-0272; *Fax:* 306-347-8580
general@cga-saskatchewan.org
www.cga-saskatchewan.org
twitter.com/cgaSaskatchewan
Also Known As: CGA - Saskatchewan
Overview: A medium-sized provincial licensing organization founded in 1978 overseen by Chartered Professional Accountants of Saskatchewan
Mission: To ensure members' commitment to the Certified General Accountants Association of Saskatchewan Code of Ethics; To promote excellence in accounting standards & practices; To advance the interests of Saskatchewan's Certified General Accountants
Chief Officer(s):
Prabha Vaidyanathan, Executive Director
pvaidyanathan@cga-saskatchewan.org
Finances: *Funding Sources:* Sponsorships; Membership dues
Membership: *Member Profile:* Certified General Accountants & students from Saskatchewan
Activities: Delivering the Program of Professional Studies in Saskatchewan; Offering advisory services for public practitioners; Providing an employment referral service; Conducting research; Informing the public about important issues; Hosting information nights & development events; Providing continuing professional development (note that CGA - Saskatchewan will integrate under the CPA banner)

Certified General Accountants Association of the Northwest Territories & Nunavut
PO Box 128, 5016 - 50th Ave., Yellowknife NT X1A 2N1
Tel: 867-873-5620; *Fax:* 867-873-4469
admin@cga-nwt-nu.org
www.cga-nwt-nu.org
Also Known As: CGA NWT/Nunavut
Overview: A medium-sized provincial charitable organization founded in 1977 overseen by Chartered Professional Accountants Canada
Mission: To provide training & professional support services to accountants in the Northwest Territories & Nunavut; To grant the exclusive rights to the CGA designation; To advance the interests of members; To protect the public; To advocate for the public interest
Chief Officer(s):
Biswanath Chakrabarty, CGA, President
Membership: *Member Profile:* Certified General Accountants in the Northwest Territories & Nunavut, who have completed the CGA Program of Professional Studies, the CGA national exams, an approved degree, & the practical experience requirement; Certified General Accountants students
Activities: Enforcing professional standards & discipline members; Promoting the profession of accountancy in the north; Liaising with governments, regulatory authorities, & the community; Offering professional development opportunities (note that CGA NWT/Nunavut will integrate under the CPA banner once legislation is approved);

Certified Management Accountants of Newfoundland & Labrador (CMA-NL)
#500, 95 Bonaventure Ave., St. John's NL A1B 2X5
Tel: 709-726-3652; *Fax:* 709-753-3609
www.cma-nl.com
Also Known As: CMA Canada - Newfoundland & Labrador
Overview: A medium-sized provincial licensing organization founded in 1951 overseen by Chartered Professional Accountants of Newfoundland & Labrador
Chief Officer(s):
Mark A. Bradbury, FCMA, Chief Executive Officer, 709-726-3652
mbradbury@cma-nl.com
Finances: *Annual Operating Budget:* $100,000-$250,000
Membership: 100-499
Activities: Offering continuing professional development (note that CMA-NL will integrate under the CPA banner)

Certified Management Accountants of Nova Scotia
#300, 1559 Brunswick St., Halifax NS B3J 2G1
Tel: 902-422-5836; *Fax:* 902-423-1605
Toll-Free: 800-565-7198
admin@cma-ns.com
www.cma-ns.com
Also Known As: CMA Nova Scotia
Previous Name: Society of Management Accountants of Nova Scotia
Overview: A medium-sized provincial organization overseen by Chartered Professional Accountants Canada
Mission: To promote standards of excellence in management accounting
Chief Officer(s):
Nancy Foran, CMA, FCMA, C.Di, Chief Executive Officer
nforan@cma-ns.com
Finances: *Funding Sources:* Membership fees
Activities: Offering professional development activities (note that CMA Nova Scotia will integrate under the CPA banner once legislation is approved)

Certified Management Accountants of Prince Edward Island (CMA-PEI)
Dominion Building, PO Box 301, #600, 97 Queen St., Charlottetown PE C1A 7K7
Tel: 902-894-4290; *Fax:* 902-894-4791
info@cpapei.ca
www.cma-pei.com
Also Known As: CMA Prince Edward Island
Overview: A large provincial licensing organization overseen by Chartered Professional Accountants Canada
Chief Officer(s):
Tanya O'Brien, CPA, CA, Chief Executive Officer
Activities: Offering professional development opportunities (note that CMA-PEI will integrate under the CPA banner)

Certified Organic Associations of British Columbia (COABC)
#202, 3002 - 32nd Ave., Vernon BC V1T 2L7
Tel: 250-260-4429; *Fax:* 250-260-4436
office@certifiedorganic.bc.ca
www.certifiedorganic.bc.ca
Overview: A medium-sized provincial organization founded in 1994

Mission: To maintain a credible set of organic production & processing standards
Chief Officer(s):
Jen Gamble, Administrator
admin@certifiedorganic.bc.ca
Staff Member(s): 3
Activities: Cyber-Help; Canadian Organic Initiative; Organic Environmental Farm Program; Organic Harvest Awards; Organic Sector Development Program; Standards
Meetings/Conferences: • 2015 Certified Organic Associations of British Columbia Conference, February, 2015, Chilliwack, BC
Scope: Provincial
Publications:
• BC Organic Grower
Frequency: Quarterly

Certified Professional Trainers Network (CPTN)
122 D'Arcy St., Toronto ON M5T 1K3
Tel: 416-979-1654
info@cptn.com
www.cptn.com
www.facebook.com/600340323384521
Previous Name: Canadian Personal Trainers Network
Overview: A small national organization founded in 1991
Mission: The organization integrates current research and practical applications for education, communication, professional development and marketing opportunities for Personal Trainers to maintain a leading edge on professional training developments.
Chief Officer(s):
Susan Lee, President
Membership: *Fees:* $64.41
Activities: Offers certification for professional trainers

Certified Technicians & Technologists Association of Manitoba (CTTAM)
#602, 1661 Portage Ave., Winnipeg MB R3J 3T7
Tel: 204-784-1088; *Fax:* 204-784-1084
admin@cttam.com
www.cttam.com
Previous Name: Manitoba Society of Certified Engineering Technicians & Technologists Inc.
Overview: A medium-sized provincial organization founded in 1965 overseen by Canadian Council of Technicians & Technologists
Mission: To advance the professional recognition & development of certified applied science technicians & technologists in a manner that serves the public interest
Member of: Science & Technology Awareness Network
Chief Officer(s):
Tracey Kucheravy, CET, President
president@cttam.com
Terry Gifford, CAE, Executive Director, 204-784-1080
Robert B. Chochinov, CET, Registrar, 204-784-1081
Finances: *Funding Sources:* Membership fees
Membership: 2,600; *Fees:* $155; *Member Profile:* Open to those employed in all aspects of engineering technology (civil, mechanical, electrical, electronic, computer, instrumentation, surveying, design & drafting, structural, construction) provided they meet the academic requirements
Activities: *Internships:* Yes
Awards:
• Scholarships (Scholarship)
Amount: Three $600 scholarships

Ceta-Research Inc.
PO Box 10, Trinity NL A0C 2S0
Tel: 709-464-3269; *Fax:* 709-464-3700
beamish@oceancontact.com
www.oceancontact.com/research/research.html
Overview: A medium-sized local organization founded in 1990
Mission: To undertake the rescue of entrapped whales & dolphins; to conduct research on whales; To organize a discovery in animal communication using Rhythm Bases Communication
Chief Officer(s):
Peter Beamish, Co-Director
Christine Beamish, Co-Director
Finances: *Annual Operating Budget:* $100,000-$250,000
Staff Member(s): 30
Membership: 5,000 individual;

CFA Society Calgary (CFASC)
PO Box 118, #100, 111 - 5th Ave. SW, Calgary AB T2P 3Y6
Tel: 403-249-2009; *Fax:* 403-206-0650
admin@cfacalgary.com
www.cfacalgary.com
www.linkedin.com/in/calgarycfasociety
www.facebook.com/CalgaryCFA
twitter.com/CFACalgary
Also Known As: CFA Calgary
Overview: A small local organization founded in 1976
Mission: To establish & maintain a standard level of ethics to benefit the organization & the community
Member of: CFA Institute
Chief Officer(s):
Chris Hooper, CFA, President
Jade Piraux, Coordinator, Communications/Events, 403-454-0773
events@cfacalgary.com
Finances: *Annual Operating Budget:* $500,000-$1.5 Million; *Funding Sources:* Events registration; Sponsorship; Member dues
Staff Member(s): 2; 30 volunteer(s)
Membership: 1330; *Fees:* $65 USD; *Member Profile:* Investment professionals; *Committees:* Executive; Audit; Programs; Conference; Social
Activities: Professional development; Candidate support; Networking events; Career development
Awards:
• Access Scholarship (Scholarship)
Eligibility: Interest in CFA Program with plans for enrollment*Deadline:* September 15
Meetings/Conferences: • Calgary CFA Society - 38th Annual Forecast Dinner, January, 2015, Telus Convention Centre, Calgary, AB
Scope: Local

CFA Society Toronto
#701, 120 Adelaide St. West, Toronto ON M5H 1T1
Tel: 416-366-5755; *Fax:* 416-366-6716
www.cfatoronto.ca
Also Known As: Toronto Chartered Financial Analyst Society
Previous Name: Toronto CFA Society; Toronto Society of Financial Analysts
Overview: A small local organization
Mission: To lead the investment profession in our local community by setting the highest standards of education, integrity & professional excellence
Affliation(s): CFA Institute
Chief Officer(s):
Sue Lemon, Chief Executive Officer & Director
Staff Member(s): 3
Membership: 7,000; *Committees:* Programming; Continuing Education; Corporate Finance; Equity; Fixed Income; Portfolio Management; Private Client; Risk Management & Alternative Investments; Career Management; External Relations & Advocacy; Kitchener-Waterloo; Awards & University Relations; Finance; Member Communications; Membership; Mentorship

CFA Society Vancouver
PO Box 54080, Vancouver BC V7M 3L5
Tel: 604-435-9889; *Fax:* 888-635-0265
info@cfavancouver.com
www.cfasociety.org/vancouver
twitter.com/cfavancouver
Previous Name: Vancouver Society of Financial Analysts
Overview: A small local organization
Member of: Association for Investment Management & Research
Chief Officer(s):
Daren Atkinson, President
Virginia Coles, Executive Administrator
Membership: 1054; *Fees:* US$225

CFA Society Winnipeg
PO Box 2684, Winnipeg MB R3C 4B3
Tel: 204-471-3640
info@cfawinnipeg.ca
www.cfasociety.org/winnipeg/
Previous Name: Winnipeg Society of Financial Analysts
Overview: A small local organization
Member of: Association for Investment Management & Research
Chief Officer(s):
Graeme Hay, President
Meetings/Conferences: • CFA Society Winnipeg 50th Annual Forecast Dinner, January, 2015, RBC Convention Centre, Winnipeg, MB
Scope: Provincial

C.G. Jung Foundation of Ontario
223 St. Clair Ave. West, 3rd Fl., Toronto ON M4V 1R3
Tel: 416-961-9767; *Fax:* 416-961-6659
info@cgjungontario.com
www.cgjungontario.com
Also Known As: Ontario Association of Jungian Analysts
Overview: A small local charitable organization founded in 1971
Mission: To disseminate information about the psychological teachings of Carl Gustav Jung through lectures, seminars, workshops, a library & a bookstore; a list of Jungian analysts is available for referral
Member of: International Association of Jungian Analysts
Chief Officer(s):
Roger Larade, President, 416-937-9459
rlarade@rogers.com
John Affleck, Vice-President
j_affleck@primus.ca
Jean Connon Unda, Treasurer
jcunda@sympatico.ca
Beverly Clarkson, Secretary
Jackson Graham, Programme Coordinator
grahamjackson13@rogers.com
Staff Member(s): 3; 20 volunteer(s)
Membership: 200; *Committees:* ON Regulation; Graduation
Activities: Word & Image Bookshop; training institute since 2000; *Speaker Service:* Yes; *Library:* Fraser Boa Library
Publications:
• Chiron [a publication of the C.G. Jung Foundation of Ontario]
Type: Newsletter; *Editor:* Robert Black *ISSN:* 1918-6142

Chabad Lubavitch Youth Organization
4691 Van Horne, Montréal QC H3W 1H3
Tel: 514-738-4654; *Fax:* 514-738-3341
www.chabad.org/centers
Overview: A medium-sized local organization
Affliation(s): Chabad Project PRIDE; Jewish Business Network
Chief Officer(s):
Shalom Chriqui
Staff Member(s): 15; 300 volunteer(s)
Membership: 500 student; 3,000 individual

Chaeo Chow Association of Eastern Canada
568 Dundas St. West, Toronto ON M5T 1H5
Tel: 416-340-0839; *Fax:* 416-340-6386
Also Known As: CCA Youth Group
Previous Name: Chao Chow Association Of Ontario
Overview: A small local organization
Mission: CCA promotes Chinese Chaeo Chow culture & provides programs for seniors & activities for young people.

Chamber of Commerce Niagara Falls, Canada
4056 Dorchester Rd., Niagara Falls ON L2E 6M9
Tel: 905-374-3666
www.niagarafallschamber.com
www.facebook.com/368306856223
twitter.com/NFChamber
www.youtube.com/user/NFChamber
Previous Name: Niagara Falls Chamber of Commerce
Overview: A small local organization founded in 1889
Mission: To maintain & improve trade & commerce; To promote the economic, civic & social welfare of the Municipality
Member of: Canadian Chamber of Commerce
Chief Officer(s):
Tim Parker, Chair
Carolyn Bones, President
Finances: *Funding Sources:* Membership fees
Staff Member(s): 4
Membership: 780; *Fees:* Schedule available; *Committees:* Government Affairs; Education; Industrial; Marketing

Chamber of Commerce of Brantford & Brant (BRCC)
77 Charlotte St., Brantford ON N3T 2W8
Tel: 519-753-2617; *Fax:* 519-753-0921
www.brantfordbrantchamber.com
www.facebook.com/197455726976322
twitter.com/BtfdBrantChambr
Previous Name: Brantford Regional Chamber of Commerce
Overview: A small local organization founded in 1866
Mission: To promote the free enterprise system through improved trade & commerce; to advance the economic, civic & social welfare of the City of Brantford & its surrounding region; to assist & or cooperate with those organizations embodying similar objectives.
Chief Officer(s):
Cathy Oden, President
Charlene Nicholson, CEO
charlene@brcc.ca
Finances: *Annual Operating Budget:* $250,000-$500,000; *Funding Sources:* Membership dues; programs

Staff Member(s): 5; 200 volunteer(s)
Membership: 820; *Fees:* Based on number of employees; *Committees:* Aesthetic Awards; Ambassador; Building & Grounds; Business Excellence; Corporate Challenge; Education; Finance; Golf Tournament; Highway #403; Marketing; Membership; Outlook Panel; Planning & Administration; Policy & Procedure; Political Awareness; President's Event; Program; Trade Show; Women's Networking
Activities: *Speaker Service:* Yes; *Library* Open to public
Awards:
• Business Excellence Awards (Award)

Chamber of Commerce of the City of Grand Forks, Grand Forks Board of Trade ***See*** Boundary Country Regional Chamber of Commerce

Chamber of Commerce Serving Coquitlam, Port Coquitlam, Port Moody ***See*** Tri-Cities Chamber of Commerce Serving Coquitlam, Port Coquitlam & Port Moody

Chamber of Marine Commerce (CMC) / Chambre du commerce maritime (CCM)
#700, 350 Sparks St., Ottawa ON K1R 7S8
Tel: 613-233-8779; *Fax:* 613-233-3743
email@cmc-ccm.com
www.cmc-ccm.com
Previous Name: Great Lakes Waterways Development Association
Overview: A large national organization founded in 1959
Mission: To bring together all sectors of the economy that rely on a cost efficient & safe marine transportation system
Chief Officer(s):
Ray Johnston, President
rjohnston@cmc-ccm.com
Stephen J. Brooks, Vice-President
sbrooks@cmc-ccm.com
Julia Fields, Manager, Communications
jfields@cmc-ccm.com
Finances: *Funding Sources:* Membership dues
Membership: 180+ institutional; *Member Profile:* Major Canadian & American shippers, ports & marine service providers, domestic & international shipowners
Activities: *Speaker Service:* Yes

Chamber of Mines of Eastern British Columbia
215 Hall St., Nelson BC V1L 5X4
Tel: 250-352-5242
chamberofmines@netidea.com
cmebc.com
www.facebook.com/ChamberOfMinesEasternBC
Overview: A medium-sized provincial organization founded in 1921
Mission: To act as advocate for the mining industry in British Columbia; to provide a collective voice on behalf of prospectors & miners; to provide information on exploration & mining; to educate the public through accessibility to mineral museum & library.
Member of: BC Mining Association; BC/Yukon Chamber of Mines
Membership: *Fees:* $40 individual; $100 2-10 employees; $200 11-30 employees; $300 31-50 employees; $500 51+ employees
Activities: *Library*

Chambre d'immeuble d'Ottawa ***See*** Ottawa Real Estate Board

Chambre d'immeubles de Québec ***Voir*** Chambre immobilière de Québec

Chambre de commerce acadienne et francophone de l'Ile-du-Prince-Édouard
CP 67, Wellington PE C0B 2E0
Tél: 902-854-3439; *Téléc:* 902-854-3099
Aperçu: *Dimension:* petite; *Envergure:* locale
Membre(s) du bureau directeur:
Jeannette Arsenault, Contact
Membre: 40; *Montant de la cotisation:* 25 $

Chambre de commerce au Coeur de la Montérégie (CCCM)
#101, 2055, rue Du Pont, Marieville QC J3M 1J8
Tél: 450-460-4019; *Téléc:* 450-460-2362
info@coeurmonteregie.com
www.coeurmonteregie.com
Nom précédent: Chambre de Commerce de Marieville
Aperçu: *Dimension:* petite; *Envergure:* locale; fondée en 1930
Mission: Regroupement volontaire de personnes du milieu dans un but de développement économique, civique et social des membres
Membre de: Chambre de Commerce de Québec; Chambre de Commerce du Canada
Membre(s) du bureau directeur:
Yanick Marchand, Président
ymarchand@coeurmonteregie.com
Finances: *Budget de fonctionnement annuel:* Moins de $50,000; *Fonds:* Dons; Profit des activités
Membre(s) du personnel: 2
Membre: 100-150; *Montant de la cotisation:* Dépend du nombre d'employés de la compagnie
Activités: Tournois de golf; déjeuners; causeries; rencontres de réseautage

Chambre de commerce Baie-des-Chaleurs
119, av Grand-Pré, Bonaventure QC G0C 1E0
Tél: 418-392-9832
www.ccmrcbonaventure.com
Nom précédent: Chambre de commerce de Bonaventure/St-Siméon/St-Élzear
Aperçu: *Dimension:* petite; *Envergure:* locale
Membre(s) du bureau directeur:
Maurice Quesnel, Directeur Général, 418-534-0050
maurice@ccmrcbonaventure.com
Membre: *Montant de la cotisation:* Varie de 100$ à 1000$

Chambre de commerce Bellechasse-Etchemins
129-B, boul Bégin, Sainte-Clare QC G0R 2V0
Tél: 418-563-1131; *Téléc:* 418-907-9797
ccb-e.ca
www.facebook.com/381810975165087
Aperçu: *Dimension:* petite; *Envergure:* locale
Membre(s) du bureau directeur:
Yvon Laflamme, Président
MVLAFLA@globetrotter.net

Chambre de Commerce Bois-des-Filion - Lorraine
CP 72012, Bois-des-Filion QC J6Z 4N9
Tél: 450-818-3481
info@ccbdfl.com
www.ccbdfl.com
www.facebook.com/155697847806886
Aperçu: *Dimension:* petite; *Envergure:* locale
Membre(s) du bureau directeur:
Danielle Dauphin, Trésorier
Membre: *Montant de la cotisation:* 64$ Membre corporatif; 75$ Membre individuel

Chambre de commerce Canada-Pologne
5570 Waverly Rue, Montréal QC H2T 2Y1
Overview: A medium-sized international organization

Chambre de commerce Canado-Suisse (Montréal) Inc. ***See*** Swiss Canadian Chamber of Commerce (Montréal) Inc.

Chambre de commerce Canado-Tunisienne (CCCT) / Tunisian Canadian Chamber of Commerce
#710, 276, rue Saint-Jacques, Montréal QC H2Y 1N3
Tél: 514-847-1281
info@cccantun.com
www.cccantun.ca
Aperçu: *Dimension:* petite; *Envergure:* internationale; fondée en 1996
Mission: Le fer de lance du partenariat canado-tunisien; fournir des informations privilégiées sur les spécificités du marché tunisien; soutenir dans votre recherche de partenaires d'affaires tunisiens; appuyer dans la démarche de mise en marché de vos produits et services en Tunisie
Membre de: Chambre de commerce du Québec
Membre: *Critères d'admissibilite:* Tous les secteurs orientés à l'export/Tunisie
Activités: Événements, conférences, réception délégation tunisienne; mission Maghreb (Tunisie, Algerie, Maroc, Lybie)

Chambre de commerce d'Amos-région (CCAR)
644, 1e av ouest, Amos QC J9T 1V3
Tél: 819-732-8100; *Téléc:* 819-732-8101
www.ccar.qc.ca
www.facebook.com/ChambredecommerceAmos
twitter.com/ccamosregion
Aperçu: *Dimension:* petite; *Envergure:* locale
Mission: La Chambre de commerce d'Amos-région (CCAR) est le plus important rassemblement des gens d'affaires de la MRC Abitibi. En effet, la CCAR est un organisme regroupant 300 membres actifs en provenance de tous les milieux d'affaires: commerces, industries, professionnels, travailleurs autonomes et plus.
Membre(s) du bureau directeur:
Anne Turcotte, Directrice général, 819-732-8100 Ext. 203
anne.turcotte@ccar.qc.ca

Chambre de Commerce d'industrie Les Moulins
#204, 760, montée Masson, Lachenaie QC J7K 3B6
Tél: 450-966-1536; *Téléc:* 450-966-1531
info@ccimoulins.com
www.ccimoulins.com
www.facebook.com/LaChambreDeCommerceEtDindustrieLesMoulins
Aperçu: *Dimension:* petite; *Envergure:* locale; fondée en 1935
Mission: La Chambre de commerce de Terrebonne se veut un regroupement volontaire de commerçants, professionnels et gens d'affaires qui ont pour but le développement économique, touristique, civique et social du territoire de Terrebonne. La solidarité qu'elle favorise entre les gens d'affaires de tous les secteurs, et les services qu'elle leur offre constituent une des forces de ce regroupement.
Affliation(s): Chambre de commerce du Canada; Chambre de commerce du Québec; Chambre de commerce régionale de Lanaudière; Réseau canadien de centres de services aux entreprises; Centre local de développement économique des Moulins (CLDEM); Centre local d'emploi de Terrebonne; Société de développement touristique des Moulins; Conseil de développement bioalimentaire de Lanaudière.
Membre(s) du bureau directeur:
Vicky Marchand, Directrice générale
vicky@ccimoulins.com
Membre(s) du personnel: 4
Membre: 800; *Montant de la cotisation:* 100$ OBNL; 150$ régulier

Chambre de commerce d'Orléans ***See*** Orléans Chamber of Commerce

Chambre de Commerce de Baie-Comeau ***Voir*** Chambre de commerce de Manicouagan

Chambre de commerce de Beauceville
CP 5142, Beauceville QC G5X 2P5
Tél: 418-774-1020
info@chambredecommercedebeauceville.com
www.chambredecommercedebeauceville.com
Aperçu: *Dimension:* petite; *Envergure:* locale; Organisme sans but lucratif; fondée en 1925
Mission: Participer au développement économique de la ville de Beauceville
Affliation(s): Chambre de commerce du Québec; Chambre du commerce du Canada
Membre(s) du bureau directeur:
Jacques Gagné, Président
Finances: *Budget de fonctionnement annuel:* Moins de $50,000
10 bénévole(s)
Membre: 125; *Montant de la cotisation:* Barème
Activités: *Service de conférenciers:* Oui

Chambre de commerce de Bonaventure/St-Siméon/St-Élzear ***Voir*** Chambre de commerce Baie-des-Chaleurs

Chambre de commerce de Bouctouche ***See*** Bouctouche Chamber of Commerce

Chambre de commerce de Brandon
151, rue Saint-Gabriel, Saint-Gabriel-de-Brandon QC J0K 2N0
Tél: 450-835-2105; *Téléc:* 450-835-2991
france.brisebois@qc.aira.com
Aperçu: *Dimension:* petite; *Envergure:* locale; fondée en 1926
Mission: Développement commercial, industriel et touristique de la région
Affliation(s): Chambre de commerce du Québec
Membre(s) du bureau directeur:
France Brisebois, Directrice générale
Finances: *Budget de fonctionnement annuel:* Moins de $50,000
14 bénévole(s)
Membre: 120; *Montant de la cotisation:* 100 $

Chambre de Commerce de Cap-des-Rosiers
1127, boul de Cap-des-Rosiers, Cap-des-Rosiers QC G4X 6G3
Aperçu: *Dimension:* petite; *Envergure:* locale
Membre(s) du bureau directeur:
Gérard O'Connor, Secrétaire

Chambre de commerce de Carleton
629, boul Perron, Carleton QC G0C 1J0
Tél: 418-364-1004
Aperçu: *Dimension:* petite; *Envergure:* locale

Chambre de commerce de Causapscal
5, rue St-Jacques sud, Causapscal QC G0J 1J0

Tél: 418-756-6048
Aperçu: *Dimension:* petite; *Envergure:* locale

Chambre de commerce de Charlevoix
#209, 11, rue Saint-Jean-Baptiste, Baie-Saint-Paul QC G3Z 1M1
Tél: 418-760-8648
info@creezdesliens.com
www.creezdesliens.com
www.facebook.com/chambrecommercecharlevoix
Nom précédent: Chambre de Commerce de Charlevoix-Ouest
Aperçu: *Dimension:* petite; *Envergure:* locale; Organisme sans but lucratif; fondée en 1940
Mission: De promouvoir les intérêts de ses membres afin de les aider à prospérer
Membre de: Chambre de Commerce de Québec
Membre(s) du bureau directeur:
Johanne Côté, Coordonnatrice
johanne.cote@creezdesliens.com
Membre(s) du personnel: 2
Membre: *Montant de la cotisation:* Barème
Activités: *Service de conférenciers:* Oui

Chambre de Commerce de Charlevoix-Ouest *Voir* Chambre de commerce de Charlevoix

Chambre de commerce de Chibougamau
#4, 600, 3e rue, Chibougamau QC G8P 1P1
Tél: 418-748-4827; *Téléc:* 418-748-6179
info@ccchibougamau.com
www.ccchibougamau.ca
Aperçu: *Dimension:* petite; *Envergure:* locale; Organisme sans but lucratif; fondée en 1954
Affiliation(s): Chambre de Commerce du Québec et du Canada
Membre(s) du bureau directeur:
Alain Bradette, Président
Finances: *Budget de fonctionnement annuel:* Moins de $50,000
Membre(s) du personnel: 1; 8 bénévole(s)
Membre: 400; *Montant de la cotisation:* 50$, 100$, 150$, 200$, 250$; *Critères d'admissibilite:* Commerçants et particuliers; *Comités:* Membres, interne, économique et politique
Activités: Gala des lauréats; dégustations vins et fromages; grandes virées; *Stagiaires:* Oui; *Service de conférenciers:* Oui; *Bibliothèque:* Bibliothèque de Chibougamau; Bibliothèque publique

Chambre de commerce de Chicoutimi *Voir* Chambre de commerce du Saguenay

Chambre de commerce de Clair
CP 1025, Clair NB E7B 2J5
Tél: 506-992-6030; *Téléc:* 506-992-6041
info@chambrecommerceclair.com
www.chambrecommerceclair.com
Aperçu: *Dimension:* petite; *Envergure:* locale; fondée en 1973
Mission: Pour promouvoir les entreprises locales et les aider à grandir
Membre(s) du bureau directeur:
Marie-Josée Michaud, Responsable
marie-josee.michaud@gnb.ca
Membre: 55

Chambre de commerce de Clare / Clare Chamber of Commerce
CP 35, Pointe-de-l'Église NS B0W 1M0
Tél: 902-769-5312; *Téléc:* 902-769-5500
contact@commercedeclare.ca
www.commercedeclare.ca
Aperçu: *Dimension:* petite; *Envergure:* locale; fondée en 1949
Mission: La Chambre de commerce de Clare représente les intérêts de la région au travers des défis économiques et sociaux; première Chambre française de la Nouvelle-Écosse
Membre(s) du bureau directeur:
Paul Emile LeBlanc, Président
Membre: 100; *Montant de la cotisation:* 50$
Activités: *Listes de destinataires:* Oui

Chambre de commerce de Cocagne, Notre-Dame et Grande-Digue
CP 166, 190 Cormier Cross Roads, Cocagne NB E4R 2J5
Tél: 506-576-6005; *Téléc:* 506-576-6073
cormier@carcajou.com
Aperçu: *Dimension:* petite; *Envergure:* locale

Chambre de commerce de Collette
11731, rte 126, Collette NB E4Y 1G4
Tél: 506-622-0752; *Téléc:* 506-622-0477
Aperçu: *Dimension:* petite; *Envergure:* locale
Membre(s) du bureau directeur:
Maurice Desroches, Président, 506-775-2898

Chambre de commerce de Cowansville et région
#150, 104, rue du Sud, Cowansville QC J2K 2X2
Tél: 450-266-1665; *Téléc:* 450-266-4117
cccr@chambre-cowansville.com
www.chambre-cowansville.com
www.facebook.com/cowansville
Aperçu: *Dimension:* petite; *Envergure:* locale; fondée en 1968
Mission: Participe activement au développement économique de la ville tout en lui assurant une fenêtre ouverte sur le monde
Membre(s) du bureau directeur:
Marc Blanchette, Président
Michel Fleury, Directeur général
Membre: 175

Chambre de commerce de Danville-Shipton
CP 599, Danville QC J0A 1A0
Tél: 819-839-2742; *Téléc:* 819-839-2347
info@ccdanville.com
www.ccdanville.com
Également appelé: Chambre de commerce de Danville
Aperçu: *Dimension:* petite; *Envergure:* locale; fondée en 1957
Membre(s) du bureau directeur:
Isabelle Lodge, Présidente
Martine Satre, Vice-Présidente
Pierre Picard, Trésorier
Sylvie Beauchemin, Secrétaire
11 bénévole(s)
Membre: 75

Chambre de commerce de Disraéli
CP 5008, 846, av Champlain, Disraéli QC G0N 1E0
Tél: 418-449-2955; *Téléc:* 418-449-1669
chambcommdisraeli@tlb.sympatico.ca
chambrecommercedisraeli.com
www.facebook.com/ChambreCommerceDisraeli
Aperçu: *Dimension:* petite; *Envergure:* locale; fondée en 1952
Membre de: Québec Chamber of Commerce
Membre(s) du bureau directeur:
Guylaine Dubuc, Présidente
Finances: *Budget de fonctionnement annuel:* Moins de $50,000
Membre: 70; *Montant de la cotisation:* 50$

Chambre de commerce de Dolbeau-Mistassini
#300, 1341, boul Wallberg, Dolbeau-Mistassini QC G8L 1H3
Tél: 418-276-6638; *Téléc:* 418-276-9518
info@cdcdm.com
Aperçu: *Dimension:* petite; *Envergure:* locale; Organisme sans but lucratif; fondée en 1946
Mission: La Chambre de commerce de Dolbeau-Mistassini fait partie intégrante du développement des ses municipalités ainsi que de sa grande région
Membre(s) du bureau directeur:
Mélanie Robert, Directrice générale
Finances: *Budget de fonctionnement annuel:* Moins de $50,000
Membre: 155; *Montant de la cotisation:* 100$
Activités: *Service de conférenciers:* Oui

Chambre de commerce de East Angus et Région *Voir* Chambre de commerce du Haut-Saint-François

Chambre de commerce de Ferme-Neuve
125, 12e rue, Ferme-Neuve QC J0W 1C0
Tél: 819-587-3882
ch.comm.fn@tlb.sympatico.ca
www.municipalite.ferme-neuve.qc.ca/Chambre_de_commerce.asp
Aperçu: *Dimension:* petite; *Envergure:* locale; Organisme sans but lucratif; fondée en 1959
Membre de: Chambre de commerce du Québec
Membre(s) du bureau directeur:
Alexandre Sarrazin, Président
Finances: *Budget de fonctionnement annuel:* Moins de $50,000
Membre: 93; *Montant de la cotisation:* 100$; *Critères d'admissibilite:* Commerce vente au détail

Chambre de Commerce de Fermont
CP 419, #6C, 299, Le Carrefour, Fermont QC G0G 1J0
Tél: 418-287-3000; *Téléc:* 418-287-3001
Aperçu: *Dimension:* petite; *Envergure:* locale; Organisme sans but lucratif; fondée en 1998
Mission: Regrouper les gens d'affaires; soutenir l'intérêt des membres; favoriser les liens régionaux; promouvoir l'achat local; intervenir dans différents dossiers soci-économiques
Membre de: Chambre de commerce du Québec
Membre(s) du bureau directeur:
Johanne Nolin, Directrice générale
Finances: *Budget de fonctionnement annuel:* Moins de $50,000
Membre: 78; *Montant de la cotisation:* Barème

Chambre de commerce de Fleurimont
924, rue King Est, Sherbrooke QC J1G 1L2
Tél: 819-565-7991; *Téléc:* 819-565-3160
info@ccfleurimont.com
icifleurimont.com/ccfleurimont
Aperçu: *Dimension:* petite; *Envergure:* locale; Organisme sans but lucratif; fondée en 1998
Mission: Agit à titre d'organisme rassemblant les gens d'affaires et comme regroupement de gens d'affaires pour le développement économique; par le biais d'activités d'information de formation ou sociales, assumer le leadership permettant le rapprochement des gens d'affaires afin de créer une synergie essentielle à un milieu dynamique.
Membre(s) du bureau directeur:
François Lemieux, Directeur général
dg@ccfleurimont.com
Membre(s) du personnel: 2
Membre: 628; *Montant de la cotisation:* 140$ individuel; 190$ entreprise 2-5 employés; 230$ entreprise 6-20 employés; 280$ entreprise 21 employés; *Critères d'admissibilite:* Gens d'affaires; *Comités:* Affaires publiques; Gala d'Excellence Desjardins Entreprises; affaires Entr'ELLES
Activités: Gala souper; déjeuner conférence

Chambre de commerce de Forestville
40, route 138 Ouest, Forestville QC G0T 1E0
Tél: 418-587-1585
www.repertoire-chambres.fccq.ca
Aperçu: *Dimension:* petite; *Envergure:* locale

La Chambre de Commerce de Fredericton *See* Fredericton Chamber of Commerce

Chambre de commerce de Gatineau
#100, 45, rue de Villebois, Gatineau QC J8T 8J7
Tél: 819-243-2246; *Téléc:* 819-243-3346
ccgatineau@ccgatineau.ca
www.ccgatineau.ca
www.facebook.com/ccgatineau
Aperçu: *Dimension:* petite; *Envergure:* locale
Membre(s) du bureau directeur:
Karl Lavoie, Directeur général
karl.lavoie@ccgatineau.ca
Membre: *Montant de la cotisation:* Entreprise 900 $, regulier 275 $, jeune personne (x) 137.50 $

Chambre de Commerce de Hawkesbury et région *See* Hawkesbury & Region Chamber of Commerce

La Chambre de commerce de l'Atlantique *See* Atlantic Chamber of Commerce

Chambre de commerce de l'Est de la Beauce
CP 719, Saint-Prosper QC G0M 1Y0
Tél: 418-594-1219
info@ccestbeauce.com
www.ccestbeauce.com
Nom précédent: Chambre de Commerce de St-Prosper
Aperçu: *Dimension:* petite; *Envergure:* locale; Organisme sans but lucratif; fondée en 1960
Mission: Rassembler et représenter les gens d'affaires du territoire afin de contribuer efficacement au développement socio-économique
Membre de: Fédération des chambres de commerce du Québec
Membre(s) du bureau directeur:
Suzanne Lantagne, Présidente
Finances: *Budget de fonctionnement annuel:* Moins de $50,000
Membre(s) du personnel: 1; 16 bénévole(s)
Membre: 110; *Montant de la cotisation:* Selon le nombre d'employés; *Critères d'admissibilite:* Travailleur autonome, entreprises, etc.
Activités: *Service de conférenciers:* Oui

Chambre de commerce de l'Est de Montréal
#100, 5600, rue Hochelaga, Montréal QC H1N 3L7
Tél: 514-354-5378; *Téléc:* 514-354-5340
info@ccemontreal.ca
www.ccemontreal.ca
www.linkedin.com/company/chambre-de-commerce-de-l%27est-de-montr-al
www.facebook.com/ChambrecommEst
twitter.com/ChambrecommEst
Aperçu: *Dimension:* petite; *Envergure:* locale

Mission: La Chambre de commerce de l'Est de Montréal a pour mission de défendre et de promouvoir les intérêts économiques et sociaux des 30 000 entreprises qui composent son territoire.
Membre(s) du bureau directeur:
Isabelle Foisy, Directrice générale
ifoisy@ccemontreal.ca
Membre(s) du personnel: 10
Membre: *Montant de la cotisation:* Barème; *Comités:* Communications; Développment des Affairs; Développment durable; Enjeux socioéconomiques; Exportation; Audit; Gouvernance et planification stratégique; Conours des prix estim; Classique de golf; Anjou; Quartier Latin - les Faubourgs

Chambre de commerce de l'Est de Portneuf
CP 4031, Pont-Rouge QC G3H 3R4
Tél: 418-873-4085; *Téléc:* 418-873-4599
ccep@globetrotter.net
www.portneufest.com
Aperçu: *Dimension:* petite; *Envergure:* locale
Mission: Pour promouvoir ses membres et de contribuer à leur succès commericial
Membre(s) du bureau directeur:
Karine Lacroix, Directrice
Membre: *Montant de la cotisation:* Barème

Chambre de commerce de l'Ile d'Orléans (CCIO)
490, côte du Pont, Saint-Pierre-Ile-d'Orléans QC G0A 4E0
Tél: 418-828-0880; *Téléc:* 418-828-2335
Ligne sans frais: 866-941-9411
ccio@videotron.ca
cciledorleans.com
Aperçu: *Dimension:* petite; *Envergure:* locale
Mission: Organisme à but non lucratif et apolitique, la CCIO dessert plus de 220 membres répartis sur l'île d'Orléans, Beauport, Côte-de-Beaupré et Québec
Affliation(s): Chambre de commerce de Québec
Membre(s) du bureau directeur:
Sylvie Ann Tremblay, Directrice générale
Finances: *Budget de fonctionnement annuel:* $100,000-$250,000
Membre(s) du personnel: 2; 13 bénévole(s)
Membre: 220; *Montant de la cotisation:* Barème; *Critères d'admissibilite:* Affaire-tourisme-conjoint

Chambre de commerce de l'Ouest-de-l'Ile de Montréal / West Island Chamber of Commerce
#602, 1000, boul Saint-Jean, Pointe-Claire QC H9R 5P1
Tél: 514-697-4228; *Téléc:* 514-697-2562
info@wimcc.ca
www.ccoim.ca
www.facebook.com/CCOIM.WIMCC
Aperçu: *Dimension:* petite; *Envergure:* locale; fondée en 1979
Mission: D'assurer le bien-être économique de ses membres et de sa communauté d'affaires.
Membre de: Chambre de commerce du Québec; Chambre de commerce du Canada
Membre(s) du bureau directeur:
Joseph Huza, Directeur exécutif
jhuza@ccoim.ca
Membre(s) du personnel: 2
Membre: 484; *Montant de la cotisation:* Barème; *Comités:* Accueil-recrutement; Communication; Conseil des gouverneurs; Avantages commerciaux

Chambre de Commerce de la Baie Georgienne Sud *See* Southern Georgian Bay Chamber of Commerce

Chambre de commerce de la Haute-Gaspésie
96, boulevard Sainte-Anne ouest, Sainte-Anne-des-Monts QC G4V 1R3
Tél: 418-763-2200; *Téléc:* 418-763-3473
cchg@globetrotter.net
www.cchg.qc.ca
Aperçu: *Dimension:* petite; *Envergure:* locale
Mission: La Chambre de commerce de la Haute-Gaspésie se veut un organisme apolitique voué à la défense des intérêts économiques généraux de ses membres et au développement économique de la Haute-Gaspésie
Membre(s) du bureau directeur:
Hugo Caissy, LL.B, Président

Chambre de commerce de la Haute-Matawinie
521, rue Brassard, Saint-Michel-des-Saints QC J0K 3B0
Tél: 450-833-1334; *Téléc:* 450-833-1334
infocchm@satelcom.qc.ca
www.haute-matawinie.com
Aperçu: *Dimension:* petite; *Envergure:* locale
Mission: Regrouper les leaders de tout son territoire intéressés à travailler au bien-être économique, civique et social du milieu et au développement de ses ressources
Membre(s) du bureau directeur:
France Chapdelaine, Directrice générale
chamhm@satelcom.qc.ca
Membre: *Critères d'admissibilite:* Entreprises locales

Chambre de Commerce de la Jacques-Cartier
4517, rte de Fossambault, RR#3, Ste-Catherine-de-la-J-Cartier QC G0A 3M0
Tél: 418-875-4103
Aperçu: *Dimension:* petite; *Envergure:* locale

Chambre de commerce de la MRC de L'Assomption
#100, 522, rue Notre-Dame, Repentigny QC J6A 2T8
Tél: 450-581-3010; *Téléc:* 450-581-5069
info@ccmrclassomption.ca
www.ccmrclassomption.ca
Nom précédent: Chambre de commerce Pierre-Le Gardeur De Repentigny
Aperçu: *Dimension:* petite; *Envergure:* locale; fondée en 2012
Mission: La Chambre de commerce est un réseau de gens d'affaires qui a pour mission de favoriser le développement économique et social de la région, dans un esprit de concertation
Membre de: Chambre de Commerce du Québec
Membre(s) du bureau directeur:
Peter Fogarty, Président
Linda Mallette, Directrice générale
Finances: *Budget de fonctionnement annuel:* $100,000-$250,000
Membre(s) du personnel: 2; 15 bénévole(s)
Membre: 536; *Montant de la cotisation:* 55$ OSBL; 80$ membre délégué; 110$ membre jeune entrepreneur; 150$ membre principal; *Critères d'admissibilite:* Commercial; institutionnel; industriel; service
Activités: Dîners; conférences; golf; petits-déjeuner formation; *Service de conférenciers:* Oui

Chambre de commerce de la MRC de la Matapédia
#403, 123, rue Desbiens, Amqui QC G5J 3S5
Tél: 418-629-5765; *Téléc:* 418-629-5530
information@ccmrcmatapedia.qc.ca
www.ccmrcmatapedia.qc.ca
www.facebook.com/CCMRCM
plus.google.com/107383797735234822116
Aperçu: *Dimension:* petite; *Envergure:* locale; Organisme sans but lucratif; fondée en 2006
Mission: Travaille au bien-être économique, civique et social de la région et au développement de ses ressources; a pour but de traduire en actes les aspirations collectives de sa circonscription territoriale.
Affliation(s): Fédération des Chambres de commerce du Québec
Membre(s) du bureau directeur:
Chantal St-Pierre, Directrice générale
Membre(s) du personnel: 1
Membre: 200+; *Montant de la cotisation:* Barème; *Comités:* Achat matapédien; Organisateur du Gala; Projets spéciaux
Activités: *Stagiaires:* Oui

Chambre de commerce de la MRC de Rivière-du-Loup
298, boul. Armand-Thériault, Rivière-du-Loup QC G5R 4C2
Tél: 418-862-5243; *Téléc:* 418-862-5136
info@monreseaurdl.com
www.ccmrcrdl.com
www.facebook.com/pages/Chambre-de-commerce-MRC-RDL/172373320738
twitter.com/monreseaurdl
Nom précédent: Chambre de Commerce de Rivière-du-Loup
Aperçu: *Dimension:* petite; *Envergure:* locale; Organisme sans but lucratif; fondée en 1889
Mission: Favoriser le développement socio-économique de la région de Rivière-du-Loup; défendre les intérêts de ses membres auprès des différentes instances politiques; favoriser le réseautage entre ses membres
Membre de: Fédération des chambres de commerce du Québec
Membre(s) du bureau directeur:
Julie Lamontagne, Directeur général
direction@monreseaurdl.com
Finances: *Budget de fonctionnement annuel:* $100,000-$250,000
Membre(s) du personnel: 2; 21 bénévole(s)
Membre: 700+; *Montant de la cotisation:* Selon le nombre d'employés; *Critères d'admissibilite:* Entrepreneur
Activités: *Listes de destinataires:* Oui

Chambre de commerce de la région d'Acton
Édifice de la Gare, 980, rue Boulay, Acton Vale QC J0H 1A0
Tél: 450-546-0123; *Téléc:* 450-546-2709
ccracton@cooptel.qc.ca
www.chambredecommerce.info
Aperçu: *Dimension:* petite; *Envergure:* locale
Mission: Promouvoir l'action commerciale, sociale, communautaire.
Membre de: Chambre de commerce du Québec
Membre(s) du bureau directeur:
Joanne Joannette, Directrice générale
Membre: 115; *Montant de la cotisation:* Barème

Chambre de commerce de la région d'Asbestos
CP 34, Asbestos QC J1T 3M9
Tél: 819-300-1484
ccidessources@lives.ca
www.lccra.com
Aperçu: *Dimension:* petite; *Envergure:* locale
Mission: A pour objectif de regrouper en association les gens d'affaires et les personnes qui s'occupent de promotion, d'entraide et de planification économique, commerciale et industrielle sur le territoire immédiat de la MRC de la région d'Asbestos
Membre(s) du bureau directeur:
Denis Beaubien, Président
Membre: 275
Activités: tournoi de golf annuel; repas-conférences

Chambre de commerce de la région d'Edmundston
1, ch Canada, Edmundston NB E3V 1T6
Tél: 506-737-1866; *Téléc:* 506-737-1862
info@ccedmundston.com
www.ccedmundston.com
www.facebook.com/ChambredecommerceEdmundston
twitter.com/CCEdmundston
www.flickr.com/photos/ccedmundston
Aperçu: *Dimension:* petite; *Envergure:* locale; fondée en 1907
Affliation(s): Chambre de commerce du Nouveau-Brunswick; Chambre de commerce des Provinces Atlantiques; Chambre de commerce du Canada; Chambre de commerce Internationale
Membre(s) du bureau directeur:
Gilles Daigle, Présidente
gdaigle@qualityinnnb.com
Marc Long, Directeur général
marclong@ccedmundston.com
Membre: *Montant de la cotisation:* Barème

Chambre de commerce de la région de Berthier / D'Autray
960, av Gilles-Villeneuve, Berthierville QC J0K 1A0
Tél: 450-836-4689
www.ccberthier-dautray.com
Aperçu: *Dimension:* petite; *Envergure:* locale
Mission: L'organisme travaille au développement économique de ses membres et de sa communauté et intervient, au besoin, dans divers dossiers
Membre(s) du bureau directeur:
Louis-Simon Lamontagne, Président, 450-889-8742
Finances: *Budget de fonctionnement annuel:* $50,000-$100,000
Membre: 150; *Montant de la cotisation:* Barème

Chambre de commerce de la region de Cap-Pelé
CP 1219, Cap-Pelé NB E4N 3B1
Tél: 506-332-0118
chambredecommerce@yahoo.ca
www.cap-pele.com/chamber.cfm
Aperçu: *Dimension:* petite; *Envergure:* locale; fondée en 1994
Membre(s) du bureau directeur:
Albert E. LeBlanc, Président
Gilles Haché, Secrétaire

Chambre de commerce de la région de Weedon
280, 9e av, Weedon QC J0B 3J0
Tél: 819-560-8555
admin@ccweedon.com
www.ccweedon.com
Aperçu: *Dimension:* petite; *Envergure:* locale; Organisme sans but lucratif; fondée en 1957
Mission: Favoriser le développement économique par le réseautage et la concertation
Affliation(s): Chambre de Commerce du Québec
Membre: 55

Chambre de Commerce de la Rive-Sud de Québec *Voir* Chambre de commerce de Lévis

Chambre de Commerce de la Vallée de St-Sauveur *Voir* Chambre de commerce et de tourisme de la Vallée de Saint-Sauveur/Piedmont

Chambre de commerce de Lac-Brome
CP 3654, #316, 1, rue Knowlton, Lac-Brome QC J0E 1V0
Tél: 450-242-2870
info@cclacbrome.com
www.cclacbrome.com
Aperçu: *Dimension:* petite; *Envergure:* locale
Mission: Pour promouvoir le commerce dans la ville et d'offrir à ses membres des services pour aider à développer leur entreprise
Membre(s) du bureau directeur:
Suzanne Gregory, Directrice générale
Membre(s) du personnel: 1
Membre: 44;

Chambre de commerce de Lévis
#225, 5700, rue JB Michaud, Lévis QC G6V 0B1
Tél: 418-837-3411; *Téléc:* 418-837-8497
cclevis@cclevis.ca
www.cclevis.com
www.linkedin.com/groups?home=&gid=2918725
www.facebook.com/cclevis?sk=wall
twitter.com/cclevis
Nom précédent: Chambre de Commerce de la Rive-Sud de Québec
Aperçu: *Dimension:* petite; *Envergure:* locale; fondée en 1872
Mission: La Chambre de commerce de Lévis est le leader et le rassembleur de la communauté des affaires. Elle contribue activement au développement de sa région dans un esprit de concertation
Membre de: Chambre de commerce du Québec
Membre(s) du bureau directeur:
Jérôme Gaudreault, Directeur générale
Finances: *Budget de fonctionnement annuel:* Moins de $50,000
Membre(s) du personnel: 3
Membre: 900; *Montant de la cotisation:* Barème; *Comités:* Recrutement; Gestion des Ressources Humaines; Aile jeunesse; 5 à 7; Foire de l'emploi; Cocktail Dînatoire; Tournoi de hockey des entreprises de la CCL; organisateur des Pléiades; concours du Gala les Pléiades; Tournoi de golf; Colloque en affaires; conférences; économie; Programme Prêt à entreprendre; financement; Lunch au féminin; gouvernance

Chambre de commerce de Malartic
CP 368, 550, 4e av, Malartic QC J0Y 1Z0
Tél: 819-757-2332
Aperçu: *Dimension:* petite; *Envergure:* locale
Membre(s) du bureau directeur:
Dalila Dupuis, Secrétaire

Chambre de commerce de Manicouagan
22, place la Salle, 2ème étage, Baie-Comeau QC G4Z 1K3
Tél: 418-296-2010; *Téléc:* 418-296-5397
info@ccmanic.qc.ca
www.ccmanic.qc.ca
www.facebook.com/ChambrecommerceManicouagan
Nom précédent: Chambre de Commerce de Baie-Comeau
Aperçu: *Dimension:* petite; *Envergure:* locale
Mission: Favoriser le progrès de l'entreprise privée en encourageant l'entrepreneuriat et en jouant un rôle de catalyseur dans le développement économique, social et régional
Membre(s) du bureau directeur:
Michel Truchon, Président
Membre: *Montant de la cotisation:* Barème

Chambre de Commerce de Maniwaki *Voir* Chambre de commerce et d'industrie de Maniwaki

Chambre de Commerce de Marieville *Voir* Chambre de commerce au Coeur de la Montérégie

Chambre de commerce de Mascouche
#204, 760, Montée Masson, Mascouche QC J7K 3B6
Tél: 450-966-1536; *Téléc:* 450-966-1531
info@ccmascouche.com
www.ccmascouche.com
www.facebook.com/chambre.de.commerce.de.mascouche
Aperçu: *Dimension:* petite; *Envergure:* locale; fondée en 1976
Membre de: Chambre de commerce du Québec
Membre(s) du bureau directeur:
Vicky Marchand, Directrice générale
Finances: *Budget de fonctionnement annuel:* $50,000-$100,000
Membre: 151; *Montant de la cotisation:* 150$

Chambre de commerce de Mont-Laurier
360, du Pont, Mont-Laurier QC J9L 2R4
Tél: 855-623-3642; *Téléc:* 819-623-5220
info@ccmont-laurier.com
www.ccmont-laurier.com
Aperçu: *Dimension:* petite; *Envergure:* locale; fondée en 1931
Mission: Développement des affaires
Membre de: Fédération des chambre de commerce du Québec; Chambre de commerce du Canada
Membre(s) du bureau directeur:
Éric Tourangeau, Président
Jocelyn Girouard, Vice-Présidente
Audrey Lebel, Directrice générale
Finances: *Budget de fonctionnement annuel:* $100,000-$250,000
Membre(s) du personnel: 2; 12 bénévole(s)
Membre: 260; *Montant de la cotisation:* Barème
Activités: *Stagiaires:* Oui; *Service de conférenciers:* Oui

Chambre de commerce de Montmagny
63, av de la Gare, Montmagny QC G5V 2T1
Tél: 418-248-3111; *Téléc:* 418-241-5779
adjointe@ccmontmagny.com
www.ccmontmagny.com
www.facebook.com/group.php?gid=145029165537435
twitter.com/ccmontmagny
Aperçu: *Dimension:* petite; *Envergure:* locale; fondée en 1912
Membre(s) du bureau directeur:
Myriam Bossé, Directeur général
Finances: *Budget de fonctionnement annuel:* Moins de $50,000
Membre: 150

Chambre de commerce de Mont-Tremblant
990, rue Lauzon, Mont-Tremblant QC J8E 3J5
Tél: 819-425-8441; *Téléc:* 819-425-7949
info@ccdemonttremblant.com
www.ccm-t.ca
www.facebook.com/ccmtremblant
Aperçu: *Dimension:* petite; *Envergure:* locale; fondée en 1983
Mission: La Chambre assure le maintien de conditions socio-économiques propices à la croissance des affaires et la promotion des intérêts de ses membres
Membre(s) du bureau directeur:
Dominique Laverdure, Présidente
dlaverdure.adm@ccm-t.ca
Françoise Tardif, Directrice générale
francoise.tardif@ccm-t.ca
Finances: *Budget de fonctionnement annuel:* Moins de $50,000
Membre: 610; *Montant de la cotisation:* Barème

Chambre de commerce de Nipissing Ouest *See* West Nipissing Chamber of Commerce

Chambre de commerce de Notre Dame
PO Box 107, Notre Dame de Lourdes MB R0G 1M0
Tel: 204-248-2073; *Fax:* 204-248-2847
Overview: A small local organization
Chief Officer(s):
Lise Deleurme, President
deleurme@mymts.net
Joey Dupasquler, Secretary

Chambre de commerce de Port-Cartier
CP 82, Port-Cartier QC G5B 2G7
Tél: 418-766-8047; *Téléc:* 418-766-6367
popco@globetrotter.net
Aperçu: *Dimension:* petite; *Envergure:* locale; fondée en 1979
Membre de: Chambre de Commerce du Québec; Chambre de Commerce du Canada
Membre(s) du bureau directeur:
Jean-Marie Potvin, Président
Membre: 140; *Comités:* Municipal; Industriel; Commercial; Touristique; Recrutement

Chambre de commerce de Rawdon
3874, rue Queen, Rawdon QC J0K 1S0
Tél: 450-834-2282; *Téléc:* 450-834-3084
ccdr@bellnet.ca
www.chambrecommercerawdon.ca
www.linkedin.com/in/chambrecommercerawdon
www.facebook.com/chambrecommercerawdon
Aperçu: *Dimension:* petite; *Envergure:* locale; fondée en 1934
Mission: Contribuer à l'essor de la municipalité en assurant l'avancement du commerce, de l'industrie et du tourisme
Membre(s) du bureau directeur:
Pénélope Lefebvre, Président
Membre: 120

Chambre de Commerce de Rivière-du-Loup *Voir* Chambre de commerce de la MRC de Rivière-du-Loup

Chambre de commerce de Rogersville / Rogersville Chamber of Commerce
#5, 11101, rue Principale, Rogersville NB E4Y 2N2
www.rogersvillenb.com/la-fierte-acadienne/chambre-de-commerces
Aperçu: *Dimension:* petite; *Envergure:* locale
Membre de: Chambre de commerce des provinces atlantiques
50 bénévole(s)
Membre: 75; *Montant de la cotisation:* 20$ institutionnel, 10$ individu

Chambre de Commerce de Saint Louis de Kent
83A rue Beauséjour, Saint-Louis-de-Kent NB E4X 1A6
Tel: 506-876-3475; *Fax:* 506-876-3477
Overview: A small local organization
Chief Officer(s):
René Côté, Présidente

Chambre de commerce de Saint-Bruno *Voir* Chambre de commerce Mont-Saint-Bruno

Chambre de commerce de Saint-Côme
1661A, rue Principale, Saint-Côme QC J0K 2B0
Tél: 450-883-2730
info@stcomelanaudiere.ca
www.stcomelanaudiere.com
www.facebook.com/chambredecommercesaintcome
Aperçu: *Dimension:* petite; *Envergure:* locale; Organisme sans but lucratif; fondée en 1976
Membre(s) du bureau directeur:
Carole Lachance, Présidente
Membre: *Critères d'admissibilite:* Entreprises locales
Activités: Tournoi de golf en juillet

Chambre de commerce de Sainte-Adèle
Promenades Sainte-Adèle, #134, 555, boul de St-Adèle, Sainte-Adèle QC J8B 1A7
Tél: 450-229-2644; *Téléc:* 450-229-1436
chambredecommerce@sainte-adele.net
www.sainte-adele.net
Aperçu: *Dimension:* petite; *Envergure:* locale
Mission: Pour promouvoir le commerce et à aider leurs membres à prospérer
Membre(s) du bureau directeur:
Guy Goyer, Directeur général
guy.goyer@sainte-adele.net
Membre(s) du personnel: 2
Membre: 472

Chambre de commerce de Saint-Ephrem
CP 2015, Saint-Éphrem QC G0M 1R0
Tél: 418-484-2681
info@ccstephrem.com
www.ccstephrem.com
www.facebook.com/chambre.stephrem
Nom précédent: Chambre de commerce St-Éphrem-de-Beauce
Aperçu: *Dimension:* petite; *Envergure:* locale; fondée en 1948
Mission: La mission de la chambre de commerce de Saint-Éphrem est d'appuyer ses membres aux développements de leurs entreprises, tout en veillant à l'épanouissement économique de la municipalité
Membre de: Chambre de Commerce du Québec
Membre(s) du bureau directeur:
France St-Pierre, Présidente
Finances: *Budget de fonctionnement annuel:* Moins de $50,000
Membre: 70; *Montant de la cotisation:* 112,88$ entreprises; 56,44$ individuel

Chambre de commerce de Ste-Julienne
1799, rte 125, Sainte-Julienne QC J0K 2T0
Tél: 819-831-3551; *Téléc:* 819-831-3551
Aperçu: *Dimension:* petite; *Envergure:* locale; Organisme sans but lucratif; fondée en 1979
Membre(s) du bureau directeur:
Nicole Bourgie, Secrétaire

Chambre de commerce de Ste-Justine
167, rte 204, Sainte-Justine QC G0R 1Y0
Tél: 418-383-3207; *Téléc:* 418-383-3223
chambredecommercestejustine@sogetel.net
stejustine.net/chambre
Aperçu: *Dimension:* petite; *Envergure:* locale
Mission: Pour maintenir une économie saine à Saint-Justine

Membre(s) du bureau directeur:
Bruno Turcotte, Président
Membre: 100+; *Montant de la cotisation:* Barème

La chambre de commerce de Saint-Malo & District
CP 328, Saint-Malo MB R0A 1T0
Aperçu: *Dimension:* petite; *Envergure:* locale
Membre(s) du bureau directeur:
Joël Fouasse, Co-président, 204-347-5455
jfouasse@rrvsd.ca
Gilles Maynard, Co-président, 204-347-5079
gam@mts.net

Chambre de commerce de Saint-Quentin Inc.
144D, rue Canada, Saint-Quentin NB E8A 1G7
Tél: 506-235-3666; *Téléc:* 506-235-1804
www.facebook.com/ChambreDeCommerceDeStQuentin
Aperçu: *Dimension:* petite; *Envergure:* locale; fondée en 1946
Mission: Réunir ceux et celles qui veulent promouvoir et protéger les intérêts de la ville de Saint-Quentin et de sa région immédiate; encourager tous les citoyens à participer à la prospérité et croissance de la communauté; favoriser et améliorer l'industrie, le commerce et le bien-être économique, civique et social de la communauté
Membre(s) du bureau directeur:
Marc Beaulieu, Président
Pascale Bellavance, Secrétaire
Activités: Expositions commerciales et industrielles; journal pour membres; conférences lors de la semaine de la P.M.E.; projets d'été pour étudiants; réunions des membres tous les 3 mois; réunion annuelle en janvier; *Service de conférenciers:* Oui

Chambre de commerce de Sept-Iles
#237, 700, boul Laure, Sept-Iles QC G4R 1Y1
Tél: 418-968-3488; *Téléc:* 418-968-3432
ccsi@globetrotter.net
www.ccseptiles.com
Aperçu: *Dimension:* moyenne; *Envergure:* locale; Organisme sans but lucratif; fondée en 1952
Membre(s) du bureau directeur:
Ginette Lehoux, Directrice générale
Finances: *Budget de fonctionnement annuel:* $100,000-$250,000
Membre(s) du personnel: 2; 15 bénévole(s)
Membre: 502; *Montant de la cotisation:* 100$

Chambre de commerce de Sherbrooke
#202, 9, rue Wellington Sud, Sherbrooke QC J1H 5C8
Tél: 819-822-6151; *Téléc:* 819-822-6156
info@ccsherbrooke.ca
www.ccsherbrooke.ca
Aperçu: *Dimension:* petite; *Envergure:* locale
Mission: De favoriser et promouvoir le développement socio-économique de l'entreprise privée, défendre les intérêts de ses membres grâce à l'exercice de son leadership et assurer le maintien de conditions propices à la croissance des affaires de sa communauté
Affiliation(s): La jeune chambre de commerce de Sherbrooke
Membre(s) du bureau directeur:
Louise Bourgault, Directrice générale
lbourgault@ccsherbrooke.ca
Membre(s) du personnel: 5
Membre: 1,413; *Montant de la cotisation:* 175$ association; 70$ enterprise; *Comités:* Finance; Activités, Marketing, Recrutement et Service aux Membres; Gold; Opinion; Gala Reconnaissance Estrie; Grand Estrien; Achat Local; Économie Interculturelle

Chambre de commerce de Shippagan inc.
227, boul J.D. Gauthier, Shippagan NB E8S 1N2
Tél: 506-336-3993
chambredecommercedeshippagan@nb.aibn.com
www.facebook.com/512672818829033
Aperçu: *Dimension:* petite; *Envergure:* locale
Membre(s) du bureau directeur:
Shelley Robichaud, Présidente

Chambre de commerce de St-Côme-Linière (CCSCL)
1614, 6e rue, Saint-Côme-Linière QC G0M 1J0
Tél: 418-685-2630; *Téléc:* 418-685-2630
chambredecommerce@stcomeliniere.com
www.stcomeliniere.com/c_ccommerce.php
www.facebook.com/CCSCL
Aperçu: *Dimension:* petite; *Envergure:* locale; fondée en 1993
Mission: Sa mission est de défendre d'abord et avant tout, les membres qui la composent et de faire valoir leurs points de vue, leurs objectifs et leurs attentes
Membre(s) du bureau directeur:
Sylvain Bourque, Président
Membre: 63; *Montant de la cotisation:* Barème

Chambre de commerce de St-Donat
536A, rue Principale, Saint-Donat-de-Montcalm QC J0T 2C0
Tél: 819-424-2833
Aperçu: *Dimension:* petite; *Envergure:* locale; Organisme sans but lucratif; fondée en 1949
Mission: La Chambre de commerce de Saint-Donat est un regroupement de gens d'affaires provenant de tous les secteurs d'activités, partageant leurs efforts afin de promouvoir le mieux-être économique, civique et social de Saint-Donat. Pour ce faire, la Chambre valorise la participation, l'entraide et l'esprit d'entrepreneurship de ses membres
Membre(s) du bureau directeur:
Diane Champagne, Agente de liaison
Finances: *Budget de fonctionnement annuel:* $50,000-$100,000
Membre: 147; *Montant de la cotisation:* 100$

Chambre de commerce de St-Eugène-de-Guigues
CP 1013, 9, 1ere Avenue Ouest, Saint-Eugène-de-Guigues QC J0Z 3L0
Tél: 819-785-2057
Aperçu: *Dimension:* petite; *Envergure:* locale
Membre(s) du bureau directeur:
Lillian Matteau, Secrétaire

Chambre de commerce de St-Frédéric
850, rue de l'Hôtel-de-Ville, Saint-Frédéric QC G0N 1P0
Tél: 418-426-3104; *Téléc:* 418-426-3357
www.saint-frederic.com
Aperçu: *Dimension:* petite; *Envergure:* locale; Organisme sans but lucratif; fondée en 1971
Mission: Promouvoir le développement commercial, industriel et résidentiel de la Municipalité de St-Frédéric; remplir le parc industriel existant; attirer de nouveaux investisseurs et de nouveaux résidents
Membre(s) du bureau directeur:
Monique Morin-Cyr, Secrétaire
Andre Lessard, Président
Finances: *Budget de fonctionnement annuel:* Moins de $50,000
Membre: 1-99
Activités: *Evénements de sensibilisation:* Souper-bénéfice; *Bibliothèque:* Rayon de Soleil

Chambre de commerce de St-Georges
#310, 8585, boul Lacroix, Ville de Saint-Georges Beauce QC G5Y 5L6
Tél: 418-228-7879; *Téléc:* 418-228-8074
administration@ccstgeorges.com
www.ccstgeorges.com
www.facebook.com/ccstgeorges
Aperçu: *Dimension:* petite; *Envergure:* locale; fondée en 1931
Mission: Rassembler et représenter les gens d'affaires de Saint-Georges et la région, afin de contribuer efficacement au développement socio-économique de notre communauté
Membre de: Conseil Économique de Beauce; Office de Tourisme de Beauce
Affliation(s): Chambre de commerce du Québec; Chambre de commerce du Canada
Membre(s) du bureau directeur:
André Boily, Directrice générale
boily.andre@ccstgeorges.com
Finances: *Budget de fonctionnement annuel:* $50,000-$100,000
Membre(s) du personnel: 2
Membre: 310; *Montant de la cotisation:* Barème

Chambre de commerce de St-Jean-de-Dieu
CP 392, 32 Principale sud, Saint-Jean-de-Dieu QC G0L 3M0
Tél: 418-963-3402
Aperçu: *Dimension:* petite; *Envergure:* locale
Membre(s) du bureau directeur:
Chantale Rioux, Secrétaire

Chambre de commerce de St-Jules-de-Beauce
CP 81, 169, Rang 3, Saint-Jules QC G0N 1R0
Tél: 418-397-1870
Aperçu: *Dimension:* petite; *Envergure:* locale
Membre(s) du bureau directeur:
Sylvain Cloutier, Président

Chambre de commerce de St-Léonard
8370, boul. Lacordaire, Saint-Léonard QC H1R 3Y6
Tél: 514-325-4232; *Téléc:* 514-955-8544
info@saintleonardenaffaires.com
saintleonardenaffaires.com
fr-ca.facebook.com/207992709237477
twitter.com/chambrestleo
Aperçu: *Dimension:* petite; *Envergure:* locale; fondée en 1979
Mission: Défendre des interêts de ses membres et de la communauté d'affaires de son territoire
Membre(s) du bureau directeur:
Nick Fiasche, Président
Membre: *Montant de la cotisation:* 175$

Chambre de Commerce de St-Prosper *Voir* Chambre de commerce de l'Est de la Beauce

Chambre de Commerce de St-Raymond *Voir* Chambre de commerce régionale de St-Raymond

Chambre de commerce de Timmins *See* Timmins Chamber of Commerce

Chambre de commerce de Tring-Jonction
CP 1012, Tring-Jonction QC G0N 1X0
Tél: 418-426-1230
c_de_commerce_tring@hotmail.com
Aperçu: *Dimension:* petite; *Envergure:* locale
Membre(s) du bureau directeur:
Marc Paré, Président

Chambre de commerce de Valcourt et Région
980, rue St-Joseph, Valcourt QC J0E 2L0
Tél: 450-532-3263; *Téléc:* 450-532-5855
info@valcourtregion.com
www.valcourtregion.com
ca.linkedin.com/pub/valcourt-région/80/52/1ab
twitter.com/valcourtregion
Aperçu: *Dimension:* petite; *Envergure:* locale; fondée en 1987
Mission: D'améliorer les activités économiques, sociales et civiques de la région de vacourt
Membre de: Chambre de commerce du Québec
Affiliation(s): Chambre de commerce régionale de l'Estrie
Membre(s) du bureau directeur:
Sonia Gauthier, Présidente
Membre: 55; *Montant de la cotisation:* 100$
Activités: *Listes de destinataires:* Oui

Chambre de commerce de Val-d'Or (CCVD)
#200, 921, 3e av, Val-d'Or QC J9P 1T4
Tél: 819-825-3703; *Téléc:* 819-825-8599
ccvd@cablevision.qc.ca
www.ccvd.qc.ca
www.linkedin.com/company/chambre-de-commerce-de-val-d'or
www.facebook.com/232034766863790
twitter.com/CCVDcom
www.youtube.com/user/CCVDCom
Aperçu: *Dimension:* petite; *Envergure:* locale
Mission: Etre partenaire du développement économique et social de la communauté valdorienne et à cette fin, mobiliser, appuyer et représenter ses membres, défendre leurs intérêts.
Membre(s) du bureau directeur:
Marcel H. Jolicoeur, Président
Hélène Paradis, Directrice générale
hparadis@ccvd.qc.ca
Membre: *Montant de la cotisation:* 91,98$

Chambre de commerce de Ville-Marie (CCVM)
1, rue Industrielle, Ville-Marie QC J9V 1S3
Tél: 819-629-2918; *Téléc:* 819-622-1801
ccvm@mrctemiscamingue.qc.ca
www.facebook.com/105241086218211
Aperçu: *Dimension:* petite; *Envergure:* locale; Organisme sans but lucratif; fondée en 1908
Mission: Est un groupe de personnes qui ont l'habilité de planifier, l'intelligence d'initier, le courage de dénoncer et d'exécuter tout ce qui est susceptible d'améliorer la santé, le bien-être, la culture et le développement économique des citoyens et des gens d'affaires du Témiscamingue
Membre(s) du bureau directeur:
Anne-Marie Demers, Secrétaire
Finances: *Budget de fonctionnement annuel:* $100,000-$250,000
Membre(s) du personnel: 1; 10 bénévole(s)
Membre: 100-499

La Chambre de commerce de Welland/Pelham *See* The Welland/Pelham Chamber of Commerce

Chambre de commerce de Winnipeg *See* Winnipeg Chamber of Commerce

Chambre de commerce des Bois-Francs *Voir* Chambre de commerce et d'industrie des Bois-Francs et de l'Érable

Chambre de commerce des Iles Lamèque et Miscou inc.
CP 2075, Lamèque NB E8T 3N5
Tél: 506-344-3222; *Téléc:* 506-344-3266
cc.lamequemiscou@lameque.ca
www.lameque.ca
Aperçu: *Dimension:* petite; *Envergure:* locale
Mission: De promouvoir les intérêts si ses membres afin de les aider à prospérer
Membre(s) du bureau directeur:
Jules Haché, Président
Membre: 88; *Montant de la cotisation:* Barème

Chambre de commerce des Iles-de-la-Madeleine (CCIM)
Édifice Fernand Cyr, #103, 735, ch Principal, Cap-aux-Meules QC G4T 1G8
Tél: 418-986-4111; *Téléc:* 418-986-4112
info@ccim.qc.ca
www.ccim.qc.ca
Aperçu: *Dimension:* petite; *Envergure:* locale; Organisme sans but lucratif; fondée en 1962
Mission: La Chambre de commerce des Iles rend des services directs et collectifs de toute nature aux membres qui en font partie. Comme corps public, défendre et promouvoir les intérêts de ses membres et de sa communauté auprès des différents paliers de gouvernements
Membre de: Chambre du commerce du Québec; Chambre du commerce du Canada
Membre(s) du bureau directeur:
Gino Thorne, Président
Finances: *Budget de fonctionnement annuel:* $100,000-$250,000
Membre(s) du personnel: 3; 15 bénévole(s)
Membre: 250; *Montant de la cotisation:* 100-320; *Critères d'admissibilite:* PHE
Activités: Gala des Eloizes; *Evénements de sensibilisation:* Forum économique; *Service de conférenciers:* Oui; *Listes de destinataires:* Oui; *Bibliothèque* rendez-vous

La Chambre de commerce du Canada *See* The Canadian Chamber of Commerce

Chambre de commerce du Centre-de-la-Mauricie *Voir* Chambre de commerce et d'industrie de Shawinigan

Chambre de commerce du district de Granby-Bromont *Voir* Chambre de commerce Haute-Yamaska et Région

Chambre de Commerce du district de Trois-Rivières *Voir* Chambre de commerce et d'industries de Trois-Rivières

Chambre de commerce du Grand Bathurst *See* Greater Bathurst Chamber of Commerce

Chambre de commerce du Grand Caraquet Inc
39-1, boul St-Pierre ouest, Caraquet NB E1W 1B7
Tél: 506-727-2931; *Téléc:* 506-727-3191
chambre@nb.aira.com
www.chambregrandcaraquet.com
Aperçu: *Dimension:* petite; *Envergure:* locale; fondée en 1937
Mission: La Chambre de commerce du Grand Caraquet a comme mission de participer au développement économique de toute la région et donc de favoriser la prospérité de gens d'affaires et l'essor de leurs entreprises
Membre(s) du bureau directeur:
Normand Mourant, Présidente
Aline Landry, Directrice générale
Membre(s) du personnel: 1
Membre: *Montant de la cotisation:* Barème

Chambre de commerce du grand de Châteauguay
#100, 15, boul Maple, Châteauguay QC J6J 3P7
Tél: 450-698-0027; *Téléc:* 450-698-0088
info@ccgchateauguay.ca
www.ccgchateauguay.ca
www.facebook.com/ChambreDeCommerceChateauguay
Aperçu: *Dimension:* petite; *Envergure:* locale
Mission: La Chambre de commerce et d'industrie de Châteauguay a un conseil d'administration dynamique et responsable, engagé et motivant par leurs expériences et leurs connaissances. Des plus présentes dans le milieu la CCIC par des actions et des présences dans des comités et autres.
Membre(s) du bureau directeur:
Isabelle Poirier, Directrice générale par intérim
Membre: *Montant de la cotisation:* 180$; *Critères d'admissibilite:* Entreprises de Grand Châteauguay

Chambre de commerce du Grand Joliette
500, rue Dollard, Joliette QC J6E 4M4
Tél: 450-759-6363; *Téléc:* 450-759-5012
info@ccgj.qc.ca
www.ccgj.qc.ca
Aperçu: *Dimension:* petite; *Envergure:* locale
Membre(s) du bureau directeur:
Mélanie Dufresne, Présidente
André Hénault, Directeur général
ahenault@ccgj.qc.ca
Membre: *Montant de la cotisation:* 50$ membre junior/sénior; 125$ membre individuel; 150$ membre corporatif

Chambre de commerce du Grand Moncton *See* Greater Moncton Chamber of Commerce

Chambre de commerce du Grand Shediac *See* Greater Shediac Chamber of Commerce

Chambre de commerce du Grand Sudbury *See* Greater Sudbury Chamber of Commerce

Chambre de commerce du Grand Tracadie-Sheila
#399, 124, rue de Couvent, Tracadie NB E1X 1E1
Tel: 506-394-4028; *Fax:* 506-394-4899
ccgtracadie-sheila@nb.aibn.com
ca.linkedin.com/pub/chambre-de-commerce-du-grand-tracadie-sheila-inc/4
www.facebook.com/111012852315372
Overview: A small local organization founded in 2009
Mission: De promouvoir et de développer le commerce dans la région
Member of: Canadian Chamber of Commerce
Chief Officer(s):
Rebecca Preston, Directrice générale

Chambre de commerce du Haut St-Maurice *Voir* Chambre de commerce et d'industrie du Haut St-Maurice

Chambre de commerce du Haut-Richelieu
Centre Ernest-Thuot, 75, 5e av, Saint-Jean-sur-Richelieu QC J2X 1T1
Tél: 450-346-2544; *Téléc:* 450-346-3812
info@cchautrichelieu.qc.ca
www.cchautrichelieu.qc.ca
www.linkedin.com/company/chambre-de-commerce-du-haut-richelieu
www.facebook.com/94909227051
Aperçu: *Dimension:* petite; *Envergure:* locale; fondée en 1894
Mission: Pour aider à développer l'économie de la région et aider à développer le commerce
Membre(s) du bureau directeur:
Claude Demers, Directeur général
Membre: 575; *Montant de la cotisation:* 70$ individuel; 100$ jeunesse; 135$ 1 à 25 employés; 200$ 25 à 99 employés; 300$ 100+ employés; *Comités:* Exécutif; Recrutement; Gala de L'excellence; Agroalimentaire; Programmation; Jeunesse

Chambre de commerce du Haut-Saint-François
221, St-Jean Ouest, East Angus QC J0B 1R0
Tél: 819-832-4950; *Téléc:* 819-832-4950
info@chambredecommercehsf.com
www.chambredecommercehsf.com
Nom précédent: Chambre de commerce de East Angus et Région
Aperçu: *Dimension:* petite; *Envergure:* locale; Organisme sans but lucratif; fondée en 2010
Mission: Promouvoir le commerce et les industries dans la région
Membre de: Chambre de Commerce du Québec; Chambre de Commerce Régionale de l'Estrie
Membre(s) du bureau directeur:
Guy Boulanger, Président
kamiko@acncanada.net
Nancy Grenier, Directrice générale
Finances: *Budget de fonctionnement annuel:* $50,000-$100,000
Membre(s) du personnel: 1; 17 bénévole(s)
Membre: 1-99; *Montant de la cotisation:* 113,95$

Chambre de commerce du Montréal métropolitain / Board of Trade of Metropolitan Montréal
#6000, 380, rue Saint-Antoine ouest, Montréal QC H2Y 3X7
Tél: 514-871-4000; *Téléc:* 514-871-1255
info@ccmm.qc.ca
www.ccmm.qc.ca
Merged from: Montréal Board of Trade; Chambre de commerce de Montréal
Aperçu: *Dimension:* moyenne; *Envergure:* locale; Organisme sans but lucratif
Mission: Est le porte-parole du milieu des affaires et de la communauté en matière de croissance et de réussite économique; agit comme rassembleur et catalyseur des forces vives de l'économie métropolitaine; s'engage dans des secteurs clés du développement économique; favorise le développement d'un membership représentatif, fort, fier et engagé; offre des services adaptés aux besoins; prône une philosophie d'action axée sur la crédibilité, la pro-activité et l'impact.
Membre(s) du bureau directeur:
Michel Leblanc, Président et chef de la direction
Guy Jobin, Vice-Président, Services aux entreprises
Finances: *Budget de fonctionnement annuel:* $3 Million-$5 Million
Membre(s) du personnel: 85
Membre: 5,000-14,999
Activités: *Bibliothèque:* Info Entrepreneurs; Bibliothèque publique

Chambre de Commerce du Rouyn-Noranda régional *Voir* Chambre de commerce et d'industrie de Rouyn-Noranda

Chambre de commerce du Saguenay
194, rue Price ouest, Chicoutimi QC G7J 1H1
Tél: 418-543-5941; *Téléc:* 418-543-5576
info@ccsaguenay.ca
www.ccsaguenay.ca
Nom précédent: Chambre de commerce de Chicoutimi
Aperçu: *Dimension:* petite; *Envergure:* locale
Membre(s) du bureau directeur:
Éric Dufour, Président
dufour.eric@rcgt.com
Marie-Josee Morency, Directrice générale
mjmorency@ccsaguenay.ca

Chambre de commerce du Témiscouata
CP 147, 871 Commerciale, Notre-Dame-du-Lac QC G0L 1X0
Tél: 418-714-2735
info@temiscouata.cc
www.cctemiscouata.com
Aperçu: *Dimension:* petite; *Envergure:* locale
Membre(s) du bureau directeur:
Michaël Lang, Président

Chambre de commerce du Transcontinental
CP 2004, Rivière-Bleue QC G0L 2B0
Tél: 418-893-5504; *Téléc:* 418-893-2889
cctrans@sympatico.ca
pages.globetrotter.net/cctrans
Aperçu: *Dimension:* petite; *Envergure:* locale; fondée en 1950
Mission: La mission première de la Chambre de commerce est de stimuler le développement socio-économique des gens d'affaires et des citoyens du Transcontinental
Membre(s) du bureau directeur:
Sylvain Lafrance, Président
Finances: *Budget de fonctionnement annuel:* Moins de $50,000

Chambre de commerce Duparquet
CP 369, Duparquet QC J0Z 1W0
Tél: 819-948-2030
Aperçu: *Dimension:* petite; *Envergure:* locale
Membre de: Chambre de Commerce du Québec
Membre(s) du bureau directeur:
Jasmine Therrien, Secrétaire
Finances: *Budget de fonctionnement annuel:* Moins de $50,000
Membre: 15

Chambre de commerce East Broughton
CP 916, East Broughton QC G0N 1G0
Tél: 418-351-0143
cceastbroughton@hotmail.com
cceastbroughton.com
Aperçu: *Dimension:* petite; *Envergure:* locale
Membre(s) du bureau directeur:
Annie Roy, Secrétaire
Membre: 65; *Montant de la cotisation:* 60$ Commerce, 20$ particulier

Chambre de commerce et d'industrie Beauharnois-Valleyfield
#400, 100, rue Sainte-Cécile, Salaberry-de-Valleyfield QC J6T 1M1
Tél: 450-373-8789; *Téléc:* 450-373-8642
ccibv@rocler.com
www.ccibv.ca
www.facebook.com/ccibv
Aperçu: *Dimension:* petite; *Envergure:* locale

Mission: De miser sur pied d'activités et de services propres à aider les gens d'affaires; de promouvoir des intérêts économiques régionaux face aux décideurs politiques et cela sous forme d'études, de consultations, d'expertises, de propositions et de représentations et enfin promotion du commerce local et régional
Membre(s) du bureau directeur:
Sylvie Villemure, Directrice générale
Membre: 550; *Montant de la cotisation:* 201,21$ régulier; 432,16$ corporatif; *Comités:* Tourisme; Relations municipales/intermunicipales et intergouvernementales; Dossiers économiques; Événements; Marketing et communication; Recrutement, renouvellement et intégration dans le milieu

Chambre de commerce et d'industrie d'Abitibi-Ouest (CCAO)
#203, 99, 5e Av est, La Sarre QC J9Z 3A8
Tél: 819-333-9836; *Téléc:* 819-333-5737
ccao@ccao.qc.ca
www.ccao.qc.ca
Aperçu: *Dimension:* petite; *Envergure:* locale; fondée en 1953
Mission: La Chambre de commerce d'Abitibi-Ouest est une organisation sans but lucratif composée d'entreprises oeuvrant dans tous les secteurs d'activités, qui contribuent au développement économique en défendant la liberté d'entreprendre par l'exercice de son leadership, de son pouvoir de représentation et d'action.
Membre(s) du bureau directeur:
Stéphanie Bédard, Directrice générale
Membre: 350;

Chambre de commerce et d'industrie d'Argenteuil
#225, 580, rue Principale, Lachute QC J8H 1Y7
Tél: 450-562-1947; *Téléc:* 450-562-1896
info@cciargenteuil.com
cciargenteuil.com/francais/Accueil.php
Aperçu: *Dimension:* petite; *Envergure:* locale
Mission: Regroupement de gens d'affaires d'Argenteuil
Membre(s) du bureau directeur:
Mélanie Guérard, Directrice générale

Chambre de commerce et d'industrie de Bécancour; Chambre de commerce de Bécancour *Voir* Chambre de commerce et d'industrie du Coeur-du-Québec

Chambre de commerce et d'industrie de Drummond (CCID)
CP 188, 234, rue Saint-Marcel, Drummondville QC J2B 6V7
Tél: 819-477-7822; *Téléc:* 819-477-2823
info@ccid.qc.ca
www.ccid.qc.ca
Aperçu: *Dimension:* petite; *Envergure:* locale; fondée en 1902
Mission: La Chambre de commerce et d'industrie de Drummond est vouée au développement d'une économie solide et viable. Elle constitue une voix privilégiée de la communauté d'affaires drummondvilloise
Membre(s) du bureau directeur:
Alain Côté, Directeur général
acote@ccid.qc.ca
Membre: 1 100; *Montant de la cotisation:* Barème; *Comités:* Affaires commerciales; Affaires industrielles; Affaires publiques; Affaires au féminin; Commandites; Finances; Golf; Recrutement et services aux membres; Réseautage; Gala des Napoléon

Chambre de commerce et d'industrie de la MRC de Maskinongé
396, Ste-Élisabeth, Louiseville QC J5V 1M8
Tél: 819-228-8582; *Téléc:* 819-228-8989
Ligne sans frais: 866-900-8582
servicemembres@cci-maskinonge.ca
www.ccimm.qc.ca
Aperçu: *Dimension:* petite; *Envergure:* locale
Mission: Promouvoir le développement économique, social et culturel de la MRC de Maskinongé
Membre(s) du bureau directeur:
Fannie Trudel, Coordonnatrice, service aux membres
Membre: 400

Chambre de commerce et d'Industrie de la région de Coaticook (CCIRC)
150, rue Child, Coaticook QC J1A 2B3
Tél: 819-849-4733; *Téléc:* 819-849-6828
info@ccircoaticook.ca
www.ccircoaticook.ca
Aperçu: *Dimension:* petite; *Envergure:* locale; Organisme sans but lucratif; fondée en 1899
Mission: Promouvoir et défendre le bien-être économique, civique et social des municipalités faisant partie de son territoire; stimuler le développement des ressources
Membre(s) du bureau directeur:
Dominic Arsenault, Présidente
Finances: *Budget de fonctionnement annuel:* Moins de $50,000
Membre: 250; *Montant de la cotisation:* Barème

Chambre de commerce et d'industrie de la région de Richmond
CP 3119, Richmond QC J0B 2H0
Tél: 819-826-5854
info@ccrichmond.com
www.ccrichmond.com
Aperçu: *Dimension:* petite; *Envergure:* locale; Organisme sans but lucratif; fondée en 1894
Mission: De travailler au bien être économique, civique, et social de la région de Richmond, et au développement de ses ressources en stimulant le commerce, l'industrie et le tourisme
Membre de: Féderation des chambres de commerce du Québec; Chambre de commerce du Canada
Membre(s) du bureau directeur:
Hélène Tousignant, Présidente
Christian Bazinet, Vice-président
Rémi-Mario Mayette, Secrétaire
Ginette Coutu-Poirier, Trésorière
Membre: 53
Activités: Soupers, conférences mensuelles

Chambre de commerce et d'industrie de la Rive-Sud
#101, 85, rue Saint-Charles ouest, Longueuil QC J4H 1C5
Tél: 450-463-2121; *Téléc:* 450-463-1858
info@ccirs.qc.ca
www.ccirs.qc.ca
www.linkedin.com/groups?mostPopular=&gid=1621977
www.facebook.com/184970904850383
twitter.com/CCIRS2010
Aperçu: *Dimension:* petite; *Envergure:* locale; fondée en 1974
Mission: De représenter les entreprises agissant sur son territoire; De prendre position sur les grands enjeux; D'offrir des services en lien avec leurs objectifs de réussite; en développant des partenariats et des occasions de maillage.
Membre(s) du bureau directeur:
Hélène Bergeron, Directrice générale
hbergeron@ccirs.qc.ca
Membre(s) du personnel: 10
Membre: 1,900; *Montant de la cotisation:* Barème; *Comités:* Accueil industriel; Développment durable; Femmes; Golf; Main-d'oeuvre; Aile jeunesse nouvelle génération d'affaires; Prix excellence; Relève; Rendez-vous; Transport

Chambre de commerce et d'industrie de la Rivière-Du-Nord *Voir* Chambre de commerce et d'industrie St-Jérôme

Chambre de commerce et d'industrie de la Vallée-du-Richelieu
#102, 230, rue Brébeuf, Beloeil QC J3G 5P3
Tél: 450-464-3733; *Téléc:* 450-446-4163
www.ccivr.com
www.linkedin.com/groups/CCIVR-Chambre-commerce-dindustrie-ValléeduRich
www.facebook.com/CCIVR
twitter.com/CCIVR
Nom précédent: Chambre de Commerce Vallée du Richelieu
Aperçu: *Dimension:* petite; *Envergure:* locale
Mission: De développer continuellement de nouveaux services pour ses membres, des services et des activités qui peuvent contribuer à faire connaître leur entreprise.
Membre(s) du bureau directeur:
Anne Durocher, Directrice générale
anne.durocher@ccivr.com
Membre(s) du personnel: 3
Membre: 777; *Montant de la cotisation:* Barème

Chambre de commerce et d'industrie de Laval (CCIL)
#200, 1555, boul Chomedey, Laval QC H7V 3Z1
Tél: 450-682-5255; *Téléc:* 450-682-5735
info@ccilaval.qc.ca
www.ccilaval.qc.ca
www.linkedin.com/company/ccilaval---chambre-de-commerce-et-d%27industr
www.facebook.com/CCILaval
twitter.com/CCILaval
Aperçu: *Dimension:* petite; *Envergure:* locale; Organisme sans but lucratif; fondée en 1967
Mission: Assumer un leadership au sein des affaires à Laval par l'organisation d'activités de sensibilisation, d'information et de formation; défendre et promouvoir les intérêts des entreprises membres auprès de toute instance décisionnelle sur le plan des règles, des lois et du climat des affaires
Membre de: Chambre de Commerce du Québec; Chambre de Commerce du Canada
Membre(s) du bureau directeur:
Stéphane Corbeil, Président
Chantal Provost, Directrice générale
cprovost@ccilaval.qc.ca
Finances: *Budget de fonctionnement annuel:* $1.5 Million-$3 Million
Membre(s) du personnel: 15; 150 bénévole(s)
Membre: 2 000; *Montant de la cotisation:* Barème; *Critères d'admissibilite:* Propriétaires, cadres supérieurs et professionnels d'entreprises diverses; *Comités:* Jeunes; Science et technologie; Ressources humaines; Transports
Activités: *Stagiaires:* Oui; *Service de conférenciers:* Oui; *Listes de destinataires:* Oui; *Bibliothèque:* Centre de documentation CCIL; rendez-vous

Chambre de commerce et d'industrie de Maniwaki (CCIM)
186, rue King, Maniwaki QC J9E 3N6
Tél: 819-449-6627; *Téléc:* 819-449-7667
Ligne sans frais: 866-449-6728
info@ccimaniwaki.com
www.ccimaniwaki.com
Nom précédent: Chambre de Commerce de Maniwaki
Aperçu: *Dimension:* petite; *Envergure:* locale; Organisme sans but lucratif; fondée en 1983
Mission: Rassembler les gens d'affaires et intervenants du milieu des affaires pour contribuer au développement du mieux-être économique des entreprises et promouvoir le développement socio-économique de l'entreprise privée, défendre les intérêts de ses membres grâce à l'exercice de son leadership et assurer le maintien de conditions propices à la croissance des affaires de sa communauté
Membre de: Chambre de Commerce du Québec; Association touristique de l'Outouais
Membre(s) du bureau directeur:
Denis Bonhomme, Président
Sophie Beaudoin, Directrice générale
sophie.beaudoin@cjevg.qc
Finances: *Budget de fonctionnement annuel:* $100,000-$250,000
Membre(s) du personnel: 2; 25 bénévole(s)
Membre: 200; *Montant de la cotisation:* Barème; *Critères d'admissibilite:* Entrepreneur
Activités: Salon du Commerce; Gala PME; Tournoi de golf de la CCIM

Chambre de commerce et d'industrie de Mirabel
#208, 13665, boul du Curé Labelle, Mirabel QC J7J 1L2
Tél: 450-433-1944
info@ccimirabel.com
www.ccimirabel.com
www.linkedin.com/company/2279237
www.facebook.com/153917731347845
twitter.com/CCIMirabel
Aperçu: *Dimension:* petite; *Envergure:* locale
Membre(s) du bureau directeur:
Thierry Lefebvre, Président
tlefebvre@lltnotaires.com

Chambre de commerce et d'industrie de Montréal-Nord (CRIMN)
#207, 5835, boul Léger, Montréal-Nord QC H1G 6E1
Tél: 514-329-4453; *Téléc:* 514-329-5318
www.ccimn.qc.ca
www.facebook.com/231433036889071
Aperçu: *Dimension:* petite; *Envergure:* locale; Organisme sans but lucratif; fondée en 1947
Mission: La Chambre de commerce et d'industrie de Montréal-Nord est un regroupement volontaire d'entreprises et de cadres, hommes et femmes, qui se sont réunis dans le but de promouvoir le progrès civique, commercial et industriel de leur communauté
Membre de: Chambre de Commerce du Québec
Membre(s) du bureau directeur:
Palmina Panichella, Directrice générale
palmina.panichella@ccimn.qc.ca
Finances: *Budget de fonctionnement annuel:* $50,000-$100,000
Membre: 200; *Montant de la cotisation:* Barème

Chambre de commerce et d'industrie de Québec
17, rue St-Louis, Québec QC G1R 3Y8
Tél: 418-692-3853; *Téléc:* 418-694-2286
info@ccquebec.ca
www.ccquebec.ca
www.linkedin.com/groups?mostPopular=&gid=1833061
www.facebook.com/154731684555439
fr.twitter.com/ccquebecca
Nom précédent: Chambre de Commerce et d'industrie du Québec métropolitain
Aperçu: *Dimension:* moyenne; *Envergure:* locale; fondée en 1809
Mission: Pour représenter les entreprises au Québec
Affiliation(s): Chambre de commerce du Canada
Membre(s) du bureau directeur:
Eric Lavoie, Président, Conseil d'administration
Alain Kirouac, Président et chef de la direction
Membre(s) du personnel: 16
Membre: 4,600; *Montant de la cotisation:* 190$+
Activités: *Service de conférenciers:* Oui; *Listes de destinataires:* Oui

Chambre de commerce et d'industrie de Roberval
CP 115, Roberval QC G8H 2N4
Tél: 418-275-3504; *Téléc:* 418-275-6895
info@ccroberval.ca
www.ccroberval.ca
www.facebook.com/ChambreCommerceRoberval
Nom précédent: Chambre de commerce et d'industrie du secteur Roberval
Aperçu: *Dimension:* petite; *Envergure:* locale; Organisme sans but lucratif; fondée en 1921
Mission: Assurer le développement économique de son milieu en représentant les intérêts de ses membres auprès des intervenants socio-économiques et politiques
Affiliation(s): Chambre de Commerce du Québec; Chambre de Commerce du Canada
Membre(s) du bureau directeur:
Mélanie Paul, Coprésidente
Denis Taillon, Coprésident
Pascal Gagnon, Directeur général
Finances: *Budget de fonctionnement annuel:* Moins de $50,000
Membre(s) du personnel: 1; 16 bénévole(s)
Membre: 180; *Montant de la cotisation:* 175-200; *Critères d'admissibilité:* Commerçant, professionnel, fonctionnaire
Activités: Tournois de golf sur glace du Lac St-Jean; dégustation de vin/fromage, mois de novembre; gala méritas; *Stagiaires:* Oui; *Service de conférenciers:* Oui

Chambre de commerce et d'industrie de Rouyn-Noranda (CCIRN)
70, av du Lac, Rouyn-Noranda QC J9X 4N4
Tél: 819-797-2000; *Téléc:* 819-762-3091
reseau@ccirn.qc.ca
www.ccirn.qc.ca
www.facebook.com/10150100860385648
twitter.com/CCIRN
Nom précédent: Chambre de Commerce du Rouyn-Noranda régional
Aperçu: *Dimension:* moyenne; *Envergure:* locale; fondée en 1927
Membre de: Chambre de commerce du Canada; Corporation des Cadres des Chambres de commerce du Québec; Fédération des chambres de commerce du Québec
Membre(s) du bureau directeur:
Guy Veillet, Présidente
veillet.guy@hydro.qc.ca
Finances: *Budget de fonctionnement annuel:* $100,000-$250,000
Membre(s) du personnel: 7; 15 bénévole(s)
Membre: 1,100; *Montant de la cotisation:* 100$+; *Critères d'admissibilité:* Gens d'affaires et professionnels; *Comités:* ComaXAT
Activités: Gala; causeries; formation; promotion des membres; *Service de conférenciers:* Oui

Chambre de commerce et d'industrie de Shawinigan
1635, 5e av, Shawinigan-Sud QC G9P 1M8
Tél: 819-536-0777; *Téléc:* 819-536-0039
info@ccishawinigan.ca
www.ccishawinigan.ca
twitter.com/CCIShawinigan
Nom précédent: Chambre de commerce du Centre-de-la-Mauricie
Aperçu: *Dimension:* petite; *Envergure:* locale
Mission: Promouvoir et développer la région économique du Centre-de-la-Mauricie
Membre(s) du bureau directeur:
Nancy Déziel, Présidente
ndeziel@cnete.qc.ca
Geneviève Bédard, Directrice générale
genevieve@ccishawinigan.ca
Finances: *Budget de fonctionnement annuel:* Moins de $50,000
Membre: 100-499; *Montant de la cotisation:* 125-815
Activités: *Stagiaires:* Oui

Chambre de commerce et d'industrie de St-Félicien *Voir* Chambre de commerce et d'industrie secteur Saint-Félicien inc.

Chambre de commerce et d'industrie de St-Joseph-de-Beauce
CP 5042, Saint-Joseph-de-Beauce QC G0S 2V0
Tél: 418-397-5980; *Téléc:* 418-397-5982
Aperçu: *Dimension:* petite; *Envergure:* locale
Membre(s) du bureau directeur:
Marielle Bertrand, Adjointe administrative

Chambre de commerce et d'industrie de St-Laurent
#204, 935, Décarie, Saint-Laurent QC H4L 3M3
Tél: 514-333-5222; *Téléc:* 514-333-0937
info@ccstl.qc.ca
www.ccstl.qc.ca
Aperçu: *Dimension:* petite; *Envergure:* locale; Organisme sans but lucratif; fondée en 1981
Mission: De rassembler, informer et défendre les intérêts de ses membres.
Membre de: Fédération des Chambres de Commerce du Québec
Membre(s) du bureau directeur:
Sylvie Séguin, Directrice générale
seguins@ccsl-mr.com
Membre(s) du personnel: 4
Membre: 385; *Montant de la cotisation:* Barème

Chambre de commerce et d'industrie de Thetford Mines (CCITM)
81, rue Notre-Dame ouest, Thetford Mines QC G6G 1J4
Tél: 418-338-4551; *Téléc:* 418-335-2066
www.ccitm.com
Également appelé: Chambre de commerce et d'industrie de l'Amiante
Aperçu: *Dimension:* petite; *Envergure:* locale
Mission: Promotion des intérêts des membres; offre et analyse de services collectifs; susciter des initiatives bénéfiques à l'ensemble par la communication, l'information et la formation.
Membre(s) du bureau directeur:
Louis Thivierge, Directeur général
dg.ccamiante@bellnet.ca
Finances: *Budget de fonctionnement annuel:* $100,000-$250,000

Chambre de commerce et d'industrie de Varennes (CCIV)
2368, boul Marie-Victorin, Varennes QC J3X 1R7
Tél: 450-652-4209; *Téléc:* 450-652-4244
info@cciv.ca
www.cciv.ca
Aperçu: *Dimension:* petite; *Envergure:* locale; fondée en 1952
Mission: De défendre les intérêts de ses membres afin de faire prospérer leur entreprise
Membre(s) du bureau directeur:
Marie-Claude Lévesque, Coordonnatrice
Membre(s) du personnel: 1
Membre: 191; *Montant de la cotisation:* Barème

Chambre de commerce et d'industrie des Bois-Francs et de l'Érable
122, rue de l'Acqueduc, Victoriaville QC G6P 1M3
Tél: 819-758-6371; *Téléc:* 819-758-4604
ccibf@ccibf.com
www.ccibf.qc.ca
Nom précédent: Chambre de commerce des Bois-Francs
Aperçu: *Dimension:* petite; *Envergure:* locale; fondée en 1903
Mission: La Chambre de commerce et d'industrie des Bois-Francs et de l'Érable est, depuis 1903, un rassemblement volontaire et dynamique de dirigeant(e)s d'entreprise provenant de tous secteurs d'activité économique et de toute personne qui partage sa mission et sa vision. ®Ses membres ont pour mission commune d'initier, sous l'entité ®Chambre de commerce et d'industrie¯, des actions concertées favorisant le développement économique et social du groupe et de travailler ensemble à l'avancement des 35 municipalités des MRC d'Arthabaska et de l'Érable.
Membre(s) du bureau directeur:
Marie-France Béliveau, Directrice générale
mfbeliveau@ccibfe.com

Chambre de commerce et d'industrie du bassin de Chambly (CCIB)
929, boul. de Périgny, Chambly QC J3L 5H5
Tél: 450-658-7598; *Téléc:* 450-658-3569
info@ccibc.qc.ca
www.ccibc.qc.ca
Aperçu: *Dimension:* petite; *Envergure:* locale
Mission: Développer, promouvoir et stimuler l'esprit commercial entre les membres, les villes et la collectivité
Membre(s) du bureau directeur:
Pierre Cardinal, Président
Finances: *Budget de fonctionnement annuel:* Moins de $50,000
Membre(s) du personnel: 1
Membre: 300;

Chambre de commerce et d'industrie du Coeur-du-Québec
1045, av Nicolas Perrot, Bécancour QC G9H 3B7
Tél: 819-294-6010; *Téléc:* 819-294-6020
Ligne sans frais: 877-994-6010
info@ccicq.ca
www.ccicq.ca
www.facebook.com/pageccicq
Nom précédent: Chambre de commerce et d'industrie de Bécancour; Chambre de commerce de Bécancour
Aperçu: *Dimension:* petite; *Envergure:* locale; fondée en 1973
Mission: La Chambre de commerce favorise le développement d'un réseau d'affaires représentatif, visionnaire, influent et engagé. Elle est la voix du milieu des affaires et de la communauté en matière de croissance et de réussite économiques et agit comme rassembleur et catalyseur des forces vives de l'économie locale
Membre(s) du bureau directeur:
Jean-Denis Girard, Président

Chambre de commerce et d'industrie du Haut St-Laurent
CP 1914, 8, rue King, Huntingdon QC J0S 1H0
Tél: 450-264-5252; *Téléc:* 450-264-5111
cdechsl@suroit.com
www.cdechsl.com
Aperçu: *Dimension:* petite; *Envergure:* locale; fondée en 1984
Membre(s) du bureau directeur:
Daniel Légaré, Président
Membre: 100

Chambre de commerce et d'industrie du Haut St-Maurice
547-C, rue Commerciale, La Tuque QC G9X 3A7
Tél: 819-523-9933; *Téléc:* 819-523-9939
cchsm@lino.com
www.ccihsm.ca
Nom précédent: Chambre de commerce du Haut St-Maurice
Aperçu: *Dimension:* petite; *Envergure:* locale
Membre(s) du bureau directeur:
Michael Scarpino, Président
Manon Côté, Directrice générale

Chambre de Commerce et d'industrie du Québec métropolitain *Voir* Chambre de commerce et d'industrie de Québec

Chambre de commerce et d'industrie du secteur Normandin
1048, rue St-Cyrille, Normandin QC G8M 4R9
Tél: 418-274-2004; *Téléc:* 418-274-7171
ccinormandin@hotmail.com
www.facebook.com/chambredecommercesecteurnormandin
Aperçu: *Dimension:* petite; *Envergure:* locale
Membre(s) du bureau directeur:
Doris Ratte, Vice-présidente
Roger Bussiere, Trésorier
Hélène Cadieux, Directrice
Paulo Duchesne, Directeur
Nancy Gaudreault, Directrice
Gilles Morin, Directeur
Dany Tremblay, Directrice
Julie Trottier, Directrice
Nicole Bilodeau, Relationniste
Membre: 70; *Critères d'admissibilité:* Commerçants; Entrepreneurs; Professionnels

Activités: *Événements de sensibilisation:* Foire commerciale, aux années impaires

Chambre de commerce et d'industrie du secteur Roberval
Voir Chambre de commerce et d'industrie de Roberval

Chambre de commerce et d'industrie du Sud-Ouest de Montréal

#32, 410, av Lafleur, Montréal QC H8R 3H6
Tél: 514-365-4575; *Téléc:* 514-365-0487
info@ccisom.ca
www.ccisom.ca
Aperçu: *Dimension:* petite; *Envergure:* locale; fondée en 1952
Mission: Territoire desservi: Lachine, Lasalle, Verdun et Sud-Ouest.
Affliation(s): Chambre de commerce du Canada; Fédération des Chambres de commerce du Québec
Membre(s) du personnel: 2
Membre: 397

Chambre de commerce et d'industrie Lac-Saint-Jean-Est

640, rue Côté-Ouest, Alma QC G8B 7S8
Tél: 418-662-2734; *Téléc:* 418-669-2220
cci@ccilacsaintjeanest.com
www.ccilacsaintjeanest.com
Aperçu: *Dimension:* petite; *Envergure:* locale; fondée en 1933
Membre(s) du bureau directeur:
Kathleen Voyer, Directrice générale
kvoyer@ccilacsaintjeanest.com

Chambre de commerce et d'industrie Les Maskoutains

780, av de L'Hôtel-de-ville, Saint-Hyacinthe QC J2S 5B2
Tél: 450-773-3474; *Téléc:* 450-773-9339
chambre@chambrecommerce.ca
www.chambrecommerce.ca
www.facebook.com/cclesmaskoutains
twitter.com/CCILM_1892
Aperçu: *Dimension:* petite; *Envergure:* locale; Organisme sans but lucratif; fondée en 1983
Mission: Vise, par le regroupement représentatif des forces de son milieu, à élaborer, développer et/ou parrainer toutes actions favorisant l'épanouissement du développement économique et social de la région tout en assurant la promotion et la défense des intérêts de ses membres.
Membre de: Chambre de Commerce du Québec; Chambre de Commerce du Canada
Membre(s) du bureau directeur:
Claire Sarrasin, Directrice générale
csarrasin@chambrecommerce.ca
Membre(s) du personnel: 2
Membre: 511; *Montant de la cotisation:* 75$ étudiant; 100$ particulier/travailleur autonome/communautaire; 125$ additionnel; 180$ entreprise; 250$ soutien; *Comités:* Agriculture et agroalimentaire; Formation Passion détail; Vision stratégique; Train de banlieue; Réseau RH

Chambre de commerce et d'industrie Magog-Orford

355, rue Principale ouest, Magog QC J1X 2B1
Tél: 819-843-3494; *Téléc:* 819-769-0292
info@ccimo.qc.ca
www.ccimo.qc.ca
Aperçu: *Dimension:* petite; *Envergure:* locale
Membre(s) du bureau directeur:
Robert Théorêt, Président
Jérémy Parent, Directeur général
Membre: *Montant de la cotisation:* Barème

Chambre de commerce et d'industrie MRC de Deux-Montagne (CCI2M)

67A, boul Industriel, Saint-Eustache QC J7R 5B9
Tél: 450-491-1991; *Téléc:* 450-491-1648
info@chambrecommerce.com
www.chambrecommerce.com
www.facebook.com/CCI2M
twitter.com/CCISE
Aperçu: *Dimension:* petite; *Envergure:* locale; Organisme sans but lucratif; fondée en 2014
Membre de: Association touristique des Basses Laurentides
Affliation(s): Chambre de Commerce du Québec
Membre(s) du bureau directeur:
Michel Goyer, Directeur
Membre(s) du personnel: 6
Membre: 650; *Montant de la cotisation:* Barème; *Comités:* Évaluation de rendement des administrateurs et du directeur général; Financement; Mise en nomination des administrateurs; Offre de services; Recrutement de nouveaux membres; Relève; Vérification des politiques; Veille des intérêts d'affaires; Du verre à la fourchette 3e édition; La Classique des Gouverneurs 55e édition; Saveurs d'Oktobre; Soirée Encan; Projet IMPACC

Chambre de commerce et d'industrie Nouvelle-Beauce (CCINB)

CP 684, #C, 700, rue Notre-Dame nord, Sainte-Marie QC G6E 2K9
Tél: 418-387-2006; *Téléc:* 418-387-8223
Ligne sans frais: 866-387-2005
info@ccinb.ca
www.ccinb.ca
Aperçu: *Dimension:* petite; *Envergure:* locale; Organisme sans but lucratif; fondée en 1930
Mission: Réseautage d'entreprises, organisation d'activités pour les contacts commerciaux
Membre de: Fédération des Chambres de Commerce
Membre(s) du bureau directeur:
Mario Cantin, Président
Johanne Côté, Directrice générale
johanne.cote@ccinb.ca
Finances: *Budget de fonctionnement annuel:* $50,000-$100,000
Membre(s) du personnel: 3
Membre: 225; *Montant de la cotisation:* Barème; *Critères d'admissibilite:* Industriel et commerce
Activités: Business café; dîner conférence; activités de formation en entreprises; gala de reconnaissance

Chambre de commerce et d'industrie régionale de Saint-Léonard-d'Aston

#1, 370, rue Principale, Saint-Léonard-d'Aston QC J0C 1M0
Tél: 819-399-2020
Aperçu: *Dimension:* petite; *Envergure:* locale
Membre: *Montant de la cotisation:* Barème

Chambre de commerce et d'industrie Rimouski-Neigette

CP 1296, #101, 125, rue de l'Évêché, Rimouski QC G5L 8M2
Tél: 418-722-4494; *Téléc:* 418-722-4494
info@ccrimouski.com
www.ccrimouski.com
www.facebook.com/233406713347742
Aperçu: *Dimension:* petite; *Envergure:* locale; Organisme sans but lucratif; fondée en 1908
Mission: Représenter les gens d'affaires rimouskois auprès des décideurs locaux, régionaux, provinciaux et nationaux; favoriser l'élaboration de nouvelles orientations de développement pour la région; favoriser les échanges fructueux entre nos membres
Membre(s) du bureau directeur:
Jérome Dufour-Gallant, Président
Finances: *Budget de fonctionnement annuel:* $100,000-$250,000
Membre: 700; *Montant de la cotisation:* Selon le nombre d'employés; *Critères d'admissibilite:* Commerces, entreprises, travailleurs automnes, institutions

Chambre de commerce et d'industrie secteur Saint-Félicien inc.

CP 34, 1209, boul Sacré-Coeur, Saint-Félicien QC G8K 2P8
Tél: 418-679-2097; *Téléc:* 418-679-8183
sarah.michaud@chambre-sf.com
www.chambre-sf.com
Nom précédent: Chambre de commerce et d'industrie de St-Félicien
Aperçu: *Dimension:* petite; *Envergure:* locale; Organisme sans but lucratif; fondée en 1950
Mission: Travailler au bien-être économique, civique et social de la ville de Saint-Félicien et au développement de ses ressources
Membre de: Fédération des chambres de commerce du Québec
Membre(s) du bureau directeur:
Marie-Noël Gagnon, Présidente, 418-679-1331
marie.noel.gagnon@clcw.ca
Jean Tremblay, Directeur général
Finances: *Budget de fonctionnement annuel:* $50,000-$100,000
Membre(s) du personnel: 2; 12 bénévole(s)
Membre: 125; *Montant de la cotisation:* Barème; *Critères d'admissibilite:* Commerces, industries, professionnels; *Comités:* Marketing, communication, développement, finance
Activités: Colloque, formation, conférence, dîner; *Stagiaires:* Oui; *Service de conférenciers:* Oui; *Listes de destinataires:* Oui

Chambre de commerce et d'industrie Sorel-Tracy métropolitain

#112, 67, rue George, Sorel-Tracy QC J3P 1C2
Tél: 450-742-0018; *Téléc:* 450-742-7442
info@ccstm.qc.ca
www.ccstm.qc.ca
Aperçu: *Dimension:* petite; *Envergure:* locale
Mission: La loi fédérale des chambres de commerce au Canada donne leur mandat aux chambres de commerce dans les termes suivant : ".. Aux fins de favoriser et d'améliorer le commerce et le bien-être économique, civique et social de son district."
Membre(s) du bureau directeur:
Marcel Robert, Directeur général
marcel.robert@ccstm.qc.ca

Chambre de commerce et d'industrie St-Jérôme (CCISJ)

#20, 236, rue de Parent, Saint-Jérôme QC J7Z 1Z7
Tél: 450-431-4339; *Téléc:* 450-431-1677
www.ccisj.qc.ca
www.facebook.com/CCISJ
twitter.com/ccisj
Nom précédent: Chambre de commerce et d'industrie de la Rivière-Du-Nord
Aperçu: *Dimension:* petite; *Envergure:* locale; fondée en 1898
Mission: La CCISJ est un organisme voué à la promotion et à la prospérité du milieu des affaires. En effet, par ses activités de formation, de promotion et de réseautage, la CCISJ favorise la réussite des entreprises, petites et grandes. Par ses interventions publiques au nom de la communauté des affaires, elle se fait aussi le porte-parole des intervenants économiques régionaux, dont elle défend les intérêts
Membre(s) du bureau directeur:
Raphaelle Prévost, Directrice, Développement des affaires et relations publiques
Membre: *Montant de la cotisation:* Barème

Chambre de commerce et d'industrie Thérèse-De Blainville (CCITB)

#202, 141, rue St-Charles, Ste-Thérèse QC J7E 2A9
Tél: 450-435-8228; *Téléc:* 450-435-0820
info@ccitb.ca
www.ccitb.ca
www.linkedin.com/company/chambre-de-commerce-et-d'industrie-th-r-se-de
www.facebook.com/CCITB
twitter.com/laccitb
www.youtube.com/user/CCITB85
Aperçu: *Dimension:* petite; *Envergure:* locale
Membre de: Canadian Chamber of Commerce; Ontario Chamber of Commerce
Membre(s) du bureau directeur:
Samuel Bergeron, Président
Membre: 605; *Montant de la cotisation:* Barème; *Comités:* Midis d'affaires; Forum sur les enjeux économiques; Golf

Chambre de commerce et d'industrie Vaudreuil-Dorion

450, rue Aimé-Vincent, 2e étage, Vaudreuil-Dorion QC J7V 5V5
Tél: 450-424-6886
www.ccivs.ca
Aperçu: *Dimension:* petite; *Envergure:* locale
Mission: Un regroupement de personnes qui ont l'habilité de planifier, l'intelligence d'initier, le courage d'énoncer et l'énergie d'exécuter tout ce qui est susceptible d'améliorer la santé, le bien-être, la culture et le développement économique des gens d'affaires et des citoyens.
Membre(s) du bureau directeur:
Nadine Lachance, Directrice générale
Membre(s) du personnel: 1
Membre: 370+; *Montant de la cotisation:* Barème; *Comités:* Aménagement du territoire; Commandite; Budget-Comptabilité; Service aux membres/Développement des affaires/Industriel/Logement abordable; Gala; Golf; Jeunesse; Rayonnement régional/Grands dossiers régionaux; S.A.A.Q.; Hôpital; Vaudreuil-Dorion; Informatique; Tourisme, Culture et Art

Chambre de commerce et d'industries de Trois-Rivières

CP 1045, #200, 225, rue des Forges, Trois-Rivières QC G9A 5K4
Tél: 819-375-9628; *Téléc:* 819-375-9083
info@ccitr.net
www.ccitr.net
Nom précédent: Chambre de Commerce du district de Trois-Rivières
Aperçu: *Dimension:* petite; *Envergure:* locale; fondée en 1881

Mission: Défendre les entreprises privées et d'améliorer la communauté
Membre de: Chambre de Commerce du Québec
Membre(s) du bureau directeur:
Caroline Beaudry, Directrice générale
caroline.beaudry@ccitr.net
Membre(s) du personnel: 6
Membre: 900; *Montant de la cotisation:* Barème; *Critères d'admissibilite:* Gens d'affaires; *Comités:* Stratégie Vigie; Soirée de dégustation Les vins du monde; Gala Radisson; Cocktail du Nouvel An; Séduction; Entrepreneuriat; Tournoi de golf
Activités: Déjeuner P.M.E.; Midi Causerie; formation; colloque; *Service de conférenciers:* Oui; *Bibliothèque* Bibliothèque publique

Chambre de commerce et de tourisme de Gaspé
8, rue de la Marina, Gaspé QC G4X 3B1
Tél: 418-368-8525; *Téléc:* 418-368-8549
info@cctgaspe.org
cctgaspe.org
www.facebook.com/chambredecommerceetdetourismedegaspe
Aperçu: *Dimension:* petite; *Envergure:* locale; Organisme sans but lucratif
Mission: Défendre les intérêts des membres et promouvoir l'activité économique
Membre de: Fédération des chambres de commerce du Québec
Membre(s) du bureau directeur:
Olivier Nolleau, Directeur général
direction@cctgaspe.org
Finances: *Budget de fonctionnement annuel:* Moins de $50,000
Membre(s) du personnel: 4
Membre: 600; *Montant de la cotisation:* Barème; *Critères d'admissibilite:* Gens d'affaires

Chambre de commerce et de tourisme de la Vallée de Saint-Sauveur/Piedmont
30, rue Filion, Saint-Sauveur QC J0R 1R0
Tél: 450-227-2564; *Téléc:* 450-227-6480
Ligne sans frais: 877-528-2553
info@valleesaintsauveur.com
www.valleesaintsauveur.com
Nom précédent: Chambre de Commerce de la Vallée de St-Sauveur
Aperçu: *Dimension:* petite; *Envergure:* locale
Membre(s) du bureau directeur:
Pierre Urquhart, Directeur général

Chambre de commerce et de tourisme de St-Adolphe-d'Howard
CP 326, Saint-Adolphe-d'Howard QC J0T 2B0
info@st-adolphe.com
www.st-adolphe.com
Aperçu: *Dimension:* petite; *Envergure:* locale
Mission: Promouvoir l'intérêt socio-économique de nos commerçants et travailleurs autonomes
Membre(s) du bureau directeur:
Michel Couture, Président, 819-327-2359
mcouture@mcformcoach.com

Chambre de commerce et industrie Mont-Joli-Mitis
CP 183, #304, 1553, boul Jacques-Cartier, Mont-Joli QC G5H 2V9
Tél: 418-775-4366; *Téléc:* 418-775-4366
info@ccimontjolimitis.com
www.ccimontjolimitis.com
Aperçu: *Dimension:* petite; *Envergure:* locale; fondée en 1930
Membre(s) du bureau directeur:
Libellia St-Arnaud, Président
presidence@ccimontjolimitis.com

Chambre de commerce française au canada (CCFC) / French Chamber of Commerce
#202, 1819, boul René-Lévesque Ouest, Montréal QC H3H 2P5
Tél: 514-281-1246; *Téléc:* 514-289-9594
info@ccfcmtl.ca
www.ccfcmtl.ca
ca.linkedin.com/pub/chambre-de-commerce-française-au-canada/26/148/374
www.facebook.com/147358495336342
twitter.com/CCFCcanada
Aperçu: *Dimension:* moyenne; *Envergure:* internationale; Organisme sans but lucratif; fondée en 1886
Mission: Favoriser les échanges entre la France et le Canada; aider à trouver des partenaires
Membre de: Chambre de commerce du Québec
Membre(s) du bureau directeur:
Véronique Loiseau, Directrice générale
direction@ccfcmtl.ca
Membre(s) du personnel: 7
Membre: *Montant de la cotisation:* 1600$ honneur; 825$ corporatif; 300$ individuel; 150$ jeune de la CCFC; 100 euros ami de la chambre; *Critères d'admissibilite:* Corporation; *Comités:* Membership; Ressources Humaines; Service d'Appui aux Entreprises; Convention d'affaires Canada-France; Publications; Déjeuners-Conférences; Tournoi de Golf; Grand Bal; Jeunes de la CCFC

Chambre de commerce francophone de Saint-Boniface (CCFSB) / St-Boniface chamber of Commerce
CP 204, #212, 383, boul. Provencher, Saint-Boniface MB R2H 3B4
Tél: 204-235-1406; *Téléc:* 204-233-1017
info@ccfsb.mb.ca
www.ccfsb.mb.ca
www.facebook.com/312566845445683?ref=tn_tnmn
twitter.com/ccfsbstboniface
Aperçu: *Dimension:* petite; *Envergure:* locale; Organisme sans but lucratif
Mission: La Chambre de commerce francophone de Saint-Boniface a pour mission de favoriser, d'améliorer et de promouvoir l'industrie, le développement, le commerce et le bien-être civique, social et économique régional. La Chambre désire servir tout commerce/entreprise du Manitoba désirant oeuvrer/communiquer en français. De plus la Chambre encourage l'usage du français dans le milieu de travail
Membre(s) du bureau directeur:
Paul Prenovault, Président
Membre(s) du personnel: 1; 11 bénévole(s)
Membre: 150; *Montant de la cotisation:* Barème

Chambre de commerce francophone de Vancouver (CCFC)
1555, 7e av ouest, Vancouver BC V6J 1S1
Tél: 604-601-2124
info@ccfvancouver.com
ccfvancouver.com
www.linkedin.com/company/chambre-de-commerce-francophone-de-vancouver
www.facebook.com/ccfvancouver
twitter.com/ccfvancouver
Aperçu: *Dimension:* petite; *Envergure:* locale; fondée en 1983
Mission: Organisme à but non-lucratif dont le mandat est de développer et d'améliorer les rapports commerciaux entre gens d'affaires d'expression française en Colombie-Britannique
Membre(s) du bureau directeur:
Térence Doucet, Président
terence@ledoucetdesigngroup.ca

Chambre de commerce gaie du Québec (CCGQ) / The Québec Gay Chamber of Commerce
#100, 1307 rue Ste-Catherine Est, Montréal QC H2L 2H4
Tél: 514-522-1885
Ligne sans frais: 888-647-2247
info@ccgq.ca
www.ccgq.ca
www.linkedin.com/groups?home=&gid=946577
www.facebook.com/ccgq.ca
Aperçu: *Dimension:* petite; *Envergure:* locale
Mission: Défendre et promouvoir les intérêts de la communauté lesbienne et gaie d'affaires du Québec et favoriser le rayonnement de ses membres
Membre de: Fédération chambres de commerce du Québec
Membre(s) du bureau directeur:
Marc-Antoine Saumier, Président
Finances: *Fonds:* Variées
Membre(s) du personnel: 2
Membre: 600+; *Montant de la cotisation:* 11,49$ étudiant; 91,97$ OBNL; 172,45$ professionel; 287,42$ enterprise; 574,85$ governeur; *Critères d'admissibilite:* Professionnel, commerçant
Activités: Tous les derniers mercredis de chaque mois activités de réseautage (6 à 8) chez un membre corporatif différent chaque mois; AGA fin septembre; conférence déjeuner ou lunch cinq fois par an; *Service de conférenciers:* Oui
Prix, Bouses:
• Prix Phenicia (Prix)

Chambre de commerce Haute-Yamaska et Région (CCHYR)
650, rue Principale, Granby QC J2G 8L4
Tél: 450-372-6100; *Téléc:* 450-696-1119
info@cchyr.com
cchyr.ca
Nom précédent: Chambre de commerce du district de Granby-Bromont
Aperçu: *Dimension:* petite; *Envergure:* locale; fondée en 1900
Membre de: FCCQ
Membre(s) du bureau directeur:
Michel Rouillard, Président et Chef-Mentor
Céline Gagnon, Directrice générale
celine.gagnon@cchyr.com
Membre: 700; *Montant de la cotisation:* Barème
Activités: *Service de conférenciers:* Oui; *Bibliothèque*

Chambre de commerce Hemmingford—Napierville—Saint-Rémi
1009, rue Notre-Dame, Saint-Rémi QC J0L 2L0
Tél: 450-615-0512; *Téléc:* 450-615-0612
chambredecommercejardinsdenapierville.com
Aperçu: *Dimension:* petite; *Envergure:* locale; Organisme sans but lucratif
Membre(s) du bureau directeur:
Karine Demers, Présidente
Membre: 107

Chambre de commerce Indo-Canada *See* Indo-Canada Chamber of Commerce

Chambre de commerce juive *See* Jewish Chamber of Commerce

Chambre de commerce Kamouraska-L'Islet (CCKL)
#208, 1000, 6e av, La Pocatière QC G0R 1Z0
Tél: 418-856-6227; *Téléc:* 418-856-6462
Ligne sans frais: 877-856-6227
cckl@qc.aira.com
www.cckl.org
Nom précédent: Chambre de Commerce la Pocatière
Aperçu: *Dimension:* petite; *Envergure:* locale; fondée en 1959
Mission: Regrouper des gens d'affaires ou des gens concernés par des activités commerciales sur son territoire; les représenter, leur assurer des services de liaison et faire le suivi des dossiers que lui confie l'assemblée de ses membres et/ou le conseil d'administration; faire des représentations nécessaires auprès de toutes instances afin de défendre et promouvoir les points de vue de la Chambre, tout en respectant les priorités d'intervention que lui dicte l'assemblée des membres.
Membre de: Fédération des Chambres de commerce du Québec
Membre(s) du bureau directeur:
Gabriel Hudon, Président
Finances: *Budget de fonctionnement annuel:* $100,000-$250,000
Membre(s) du personnel: 2
Membre: 384; *Montant de la cotisation:* 25-400; *Critères d'admissibilite:* Gens d'affaires
Activités: Déjeuners, dîners et soupers conférence; vins et fromages; tournois de golf; galas; colloques

Chambre de Commerce la Pocatière *Voir* Chambre de commerce Kamouraska-L'Islet

Chambre de commerce Latino-américaine du Québec (CCLAQ)
CP 33, 1111, rue du Phare, Laval QC H7R 6H5
Tél: 604-730-0790
marketing@cclaq.ca
cclaq.itout.ca
ca.linkedin.com/in/cclaq
www.facebook.com/CCLAQ.CA
twitter.com/CCLAQ
plus.google.com/113923936639158701998/posts
Aperçu: *Dimension:* petite; *Envergure:* provinciale
Mission: La Chambre offre à ses membres des occasions variées leur permettant de développer des relations pour échanger sur les opportunités d'affaires au Québec, dans les Amériques et dans le Monde.
Membre: *Critères d'admissibilite:* Des personnes issus de la communauté latino-américaine et québécoises qui oeuvrent au sein d'entreprises établies au Québec.

Chambre de commerce Mont-Saint-Bruno (CCMSB)
CP 123, Saint-Bruno QC J3V 4P8
Tél: 450-653-0585; *Téléc:* 450-653-6967
info@ccstbruno.ca
www.ccstbruno.ca
Nom précédent: Chambre de commerce de Saint-Bruno
Aperçu: *Dimension:* petite; *Envergure:* locale; fondée en 1956

Mission: Promouvoir et développer l'économie locale; représenter les membres devant les instances gouvernementales, municipales et commerciales; participer au bien-être économique, civique et social
Affliation(s): Chambre de commerce du Québec; Chambre de commerce du Canada
Membre(s) du bureau directeur:
Daniel Tousignant, CGA, Président
dan.tousignant@videotron.ca
Jacques Laliberté, Directeur général
Finances: *Budget de fonctionnement annuel:* Moins de $50,000
Membre: 200; *Montant de la cotisation:* 145$; *Critères d'admissibilité:* Autonomes; industries; commerces; professionnels
Activités: Conférences; tournoi de golf; gala du mérite économique, critérium cycliste

Chambre de commerce MRC du Rocher-Percé
#121-2, 129, boul René-Levesque Ouest, Chandler QC G0C 1K0
Tél: 418-689-6998
info@ccrocherperce.org
www.ccrocherperce.org
www.facebook.com/174787679389490
Aperçu: *Dimension:* petite; *Envergure:* locale; fondée en 1960
Membre(s) du bureau directeur:
Roger Clavet, Directeur général
Membre(s) du personnel: 1
Membre: 1-99; *Montant de la cotisation:* Barème

Chambre de commerce Notre-Dame-du-Nord
3, rue Principale sud, Notre-Dame-du-Nord QC J0Z 3B0
Tél: 819-723-2586
www.municipalite.notre-dame-du-nord.qc.ca
Aperçu: *Dimension:* petite; *Envergure:* locale; fondée en 1949
Membre(s) du bureau directeur:
Ken Armitage, Président, 819-723-2814

Chambre de commerce Pierre-Le Gardeur De Repentigny *Voir* Chambre de commerce de la MRC de L'Assomption

Chambre de commerce région de Matane
CP 518, Matane QC G4W 3P5
Tél: 418-562-9344; *Téléc:* 418-562-7734
info@ccmatane.com
www.ccmatane.com
Aperçu: *Dimension:* petite; *Envergure:* locale
Mission: La Chambre de commerce - région de Matane est un groupe de personnes qui ont l'habilité de planifier, l'intelligence d'initier, le courage d'énoncer et l'énergie d'exécuter tout ce qui est susceptible d'améliorer la santé, le bien-être, la culture et le développement économique des gens d'affaires et des citoyens de la MRC
Membre(s) du bureau directeur:
Richard Godbout, Président
Membre: 300; *Montant de la cotisation:* Barème

Chambre de commerce région de Mégantic
4336, rue Laval, Lac-Mégantic QC G6B 1B8
Tél: 819-583-5392
www.ccrmeg.com
Aperçu: *Dimension:* petite; *Envergure:* locale; fondée en 1909
Mission: Contribuer au développement de la région du Granit en faisant la promotion de l'entrepreneuriat en en supportant son essor et son dynamisme
Membre de: Chambre de Commerce du Canada; Fédération des Chambres de Commerce du Québec; Chambre de Commerce Régional de l'Estrie
Membre(s) du bureau directeur:
Pascal Hallé, Président
Isabelle Hallé, Directrice générale
Membre: 249; *Critères d'admissibilite:* Entreprises locales

Chambre de commerce régional de Campbellton *See* Campbellton Regional Chamber of Commerce

Chambre de commerce régionale de St-Raymond (CCRSR)
#100, 1, av St-Jacques, Saint-Raymond QC G3L 3Y1
Tél: 418-337-4049; *Téléc:* 418-337-8017
ccrsr@cite.net
www.ccrsr.qc.ca
Nom précédent: Chambre de Commerce de St-Raymond
Aperçu: *Dimension:* petite; *Envergure:* locale; fondée en 1967
Mission: De soutenir et appuyer ses membres commerçants, entrepreneurs, gens d'affaires et individus évoluant dans le milieu des affaires de Saint-Raymond, Saint-Léonard et de Rivière-à-Pierre

Membre(s) du bureau directeur:
Hughes Genois, Président
hugues@primeverts.com
Membre: 171

Chambre de commerce régionale de Windsor
CP 115, Windsor QC J1S 2L7
Tél: 819-434-5936
www.ccrwindsor.com
Aperçu: *Dimension:* petite; *Envergure:* locale
Mission: Pour aider à développer le commerce dans la région de Windsor afin que leurs membres sont en mesure de prospérer
Membre(s) du bureau directeur:
Guillaumme Lussier, Président
Membre: 100; *Montant de la cotisation:* 103,48$

Chambre de commerce Ste-Émélie-de-l'Énergie
400, rue St-Michel, Sainte-Émélie-de-l'Énergie QC J0K 2K0
Tél: 450-886-1658
Aperçu: *Dimension:* petite; *Envergure:* locale

Chambre de commerce Saint-Lin-Laurentides
#101, 704, rue St-Isidore, Saint-Lin-Laurentides QC J5M 2V2
Tél: 450-439-3704; *Téléc:* 450-439-2066
Aperçu: *Dimension:* petite; *Envergure:* locale
Membre(s) du bureau directeur:
André Corbeil, Président

Chambre de commerce secteur ouest de Portneuf
#2, 295, rue Gauthier, Saint-Marc-des-Carrières QC G0A 4B0
Tél: 418-268-5447
ccsop@portneufouest.com
www.portneufouest.com
Aperçu: *Dimension:* petite; *Envergure:* locale
Mission: De promouvoir et de soutenir ses membres
Membre(s) du bureau directeur:
Guillaume Béliveau Côté, Chargé de projets
g.beliveau.cote@portneufouest.com
Membre(s) du personnel: 3
Membre: 132; *Montant de la cotisation:* Barème

Chambre de commerce St-Éphrem-de-Beauce *Voir* Chambre de commerce de Saint-Ephrem

Chambre de commerce St-Félix de Valois
15, ch Joliette, Saint-Félix-de-Valois QC J0K 2M0
Tél: 450-889-8161; *Téléc:* 450-889-1590
ccst-flx@stfelixdevalois.qc.ca
www.stfelixdevalois.qc.ca
Aperçu: *Dimension:* petite; *Envergure:* locale; Organisme sans but lucratif; fondée en 1969
Mission: La mission de la Chambre de Commerce de Saint-Félix-de-Valois est de travailler au bien-être économique, civique et social de Saint-Félix-de-Valois et au développement de ses ressources en regroupant les leaders de tout son territoire intéressés à oeuvrer en ce sens
Membre(s) du bureau directeur:
Johanne Dufresne, Directrice générale
Membre(s) du personnel: 2
Membre: 167; *Critères d'admissibilite:* Entrepreneurs; industrie; aviculteurs; agriculteurs
Activités: Souper des fêtes et membres honorifiques; conférences-causeries; amicale de golf; *Stagiaires:* Oui; *Service de conférenciers:* Oui; *Bibliothèque*

Chambre de commerce St-Jean-de-Matha
204L, rue Principale, Saint-Jean-de-Matha QC J0K 2S0
Tél: 450-886-0599; *Téléc:* 450-886-3123
info@chambrematha.com
www.chambrematha.com
Aperçu: *Dimension:* petite; *Envergure:* locale; fondée en 1973
Mission: Travailler à la promotion de ses membres, ainsi qu'au développement commercial, culturel et social de son village
Membre de: Fédération des Chambres de Commerce du Québec
Membre(s) du bureau directeur:
Sylvain Binette, Président
Sophie Moreau, Coordinatrice
Membre: 108

Chambre de commerce St-Martin de Beauce
CP 2022, 131, 1e av Est, Saint-Martin QC G0M 1B0
Tél: 418-382-5549
chambre@st-martin.qc.ca
www.st-martin.qc.ca
Aperçu: *Dimension:* petite; *Envergure:* locale; Organisme sans but lucratif; fondée en 1985
Mission: Travailler au développement économique civique et social de la localité de St-Martin-De-Beauce
Affliation(s): Chambre de commerce du Québec; Chambre de commerce du Canada
Membre(s) du bureau directeur:
Pascal Bergeron, Président
Activités: *Listes de destinataires:* Oui

Chambre de commerce Témiscaming-Kipawa (CCTK)
CP 442, 760, chemin Kipawa, Témiscaming QC J0Z 3R0
Tél: 819-627-6160; *Téléc:* 819-627-3390
cctk@temiscaming.net
www.temiscaming.net/chambre-commerce
Aperçu: *Dimension:* petite; *Envergure:* locale
Membre de: Chambre de commerce du Québec
Membre(s) du bureau directeur:
Guylaine Létourneau, Présidente

Chambre de commerce Vallée de la Missisquoi
858, rte Missisquoi, Bolton Centre QC J0E 1G0
Tél: 450-292-4217; *Téléc:* 450-292-4224
Aperçu: *Dimension:* petite; *Envergure:* locale; fondée en 1989
Mission: Promouvoir la région et ses commerces; encourager la venue de nouveaux commerces; encourager et accueillir les jeunes entrepreneurs
Membre de: Chambre de commerce du Québec
Finances: *Budget de fonctionnement annuel:* $50,000-$100,000

Chambre de commerce Vallée de la Petite-Nation
185, rue Henri-Bourassa, Papineauville QC J0V 1R0
Tél: 819-427-8450
ccvpn@videotron.ca
www.ccvpn.org
www.facebook.com/ccvpn
Aperçu: *Dimension:* petite; *Envergure:* locale
Mission: Pour stimuler l'économie et la croissance des entreprises locales à travers des projets d'intérêt commun
Membre(s) du bureau directeur:
Jean Careau, Directeur général
direction.ccvpn@videotron.ca
Membre(s) du personnel: 2
Membre: 150; *Montant de la cotisation:* 100$ travailleur autonome/entreprise de moins de 3 ans d'existenc; 180$ entreprise de plus de 3 ans d'existence

Chambre de Commerce Vallée du Richelieu *Voir* Chambre de commerce et d'industrie de la Vallée-du-Richelieu

Chambre de l'assurance de dommages (CHAD)
#1200, 999, boul de Maisonneuve ouest, Montréal QC H3A 3L4
Tél: 514-842-2591; *Téléc:* 514-842-3138
Ligne sans frais: 800-361-7288
info@chad.qc.ca
www.chad.ca
www.linkedin.com/company/2579212
Nom précédent: Association des courtiers d'assurances de la Province de Québec
Aperçu: *Dimension:* grande; *Envergure:* provinciale; Organisme de réglementation; fondée en 1999
Mission: Assurer la protection du public en matière d'assurance de dommages et d'expertise en règlement de sinistres; encadrer de façon préventive et disciplinaire la pratique professionnelle des individus et des organisations oeuvrant dans ces domaines
Membre(s) du bureau directeur:
Diane Beaudry, Chair
Maya Raic, Présidente-directrice générale
Finances: *Budget de fonctionnement annuel:* $1.5 Million-$3 Million
Membre(s) du personnel: 34
Membre: 14 500+; *Critères d'admissibilite:* Agents; courtiers; experts en sinistre; *Comités:* Déontologie et de règles de pratique; Discipline; Gouvernance et d'éthique; Nomination; Vérification; Développement professionnel; Affaires de régulation
Activités: *Service de conférenciers:* Oui
Prix, Bouses:
• Le prix Marcel-Tassé (Prix)

Chambre de la sécurité financière (CSF)
300, rue Léo-Pariseau, 26e étage, Montréal QC H2X 4B8
Tél: 514-282-5777; *Téléc:* 514-282-2225
Ligne sans frais: 800-361-9989
renseignements@chambresf.com
www.chambresf.com
www.linkedin.com/company/1004475
www.facebook.com/ChambreSF

www.twitter.com/ChambreSF
www.youtube.com/chambresf
Nom précédent: Association des intermédiaires en assurance de personnes du Québec
Aperçu: *Dimension:* moyenne; *Envergure:* provinciale; Organisme sans but lucratif; fondée en 1999
Mission: Assurer la protection du public en maintenant la discipline et en veillant à la formation et à la déontologie de ses membres
Membre(s) du bureau directeur:
Luc Labelle, Président et chef de la direction
Finances: *Budget de fonctionnement annuel:* Plus de $5 Million
Membre(s) du personnel: 50; 320 bénévole(s)
Membre: 32 000; *Montant de la cotisation:* 275$; *Critères d'admissibilité:* Exerçant dans les disciplines suivantes: l'assurance de personnes; l'assurance collective de personnes; la planification financière; le courtage en épargne collective; le courtage en plans de bourses d'études; *Comités:* Discipline; Réglementation; Gouvernance; Sections; Vérification et finances; Formation et développement professionnel; Relève
Activités: Assemblée générale annuelle; camp de formation

Chambre des huissiers de justice du Québec (CHJQ)

#970, 507, Place-d'Armes, Montréal QC H2Y 2W8
Tél: 514-721-1100; *Téléc:* 514-721-7878
Ligne sans frais: 800-500-7022
chjq@chjq.ca
www.huissiersquebec.qc.ca
Aperçu: *Dimension:* petite; *Envergure:* provinciale
Mission: La Chambre a pour principale fonction d'assurer la protection du public. A cette fin, elle doit notamment contrôler l'exercice de la profession par ses membres
Membre(s) du bureau directeur:
André Bizier, Président/Directeur général par intérim
president@chjq.ca
Finances: *Budget de fonctionnement annuel:* $500,000-$1.5 Million
Membre(s) du personnel: 9
Membre: *Comités:* La formation professionnelle et la formation continue obligatoire; Les normes d'équivalence pour la délivrance d'un permis; Conciliation et arbitrage des comptes d'honoraires; Conseil de discipline; Inspection professionnelle; Révision; La réforme du tarif

Chambre des notaires du Québec

#600, 1801, av McGill College, Montréal QC H3A 0A7
Tél: 514-879-1793; *Téléc:* 514-879-1923
Ligne sans frais: 800-263-1793
www.cnq.org
www.youtube.com/user/ChambreDesNotaires
Également appelé: Ordre des notaires du Québec
Aperçu: *Dimension:* moyenne; *Envergure:* provinciale; Organisme de réglementation; fondée en 1847
Mission: D'assurer principalement la protection du public utilisateur des services professionnels de notaire.
Membre de: Union internationale du notariat latin
Affiliation(s): Fédération des professions juridiques
Membre(s) du bureau directeur:
Christian Tremblay, Directeur général
Membre: *Critères d'admissibilité:* Stage de la CNQ; *Comités:* Consultatif du Centre d'expertise en droit immobilier; Consultatif en droit des personnes, de la famille et des successions; D'arbitrage des comptes d'honoraires des notaires; Gouvernance et d'éthique de la Chambre des notaires du Québec; Formation continue; Formation des notaires; Législation; Placements; Réglementation; Révision; Sélection pour le programme de bourses d'études supérieures; Vérification et prospectives financières; Communications; Inspection professionnelle; Fonds d'études notariales; Fonds d'indemnisation; Régime de retraite; Exercice illégal de la profession de notaire
Activités: *Stagiaires:* Oui; *Service de conférenciers:* Oui; *Bibliothèque*

Chambre du commerce maritime *See* Chamber of Marine Commerce

Chambre immobilière Centre du Québec Inc.

139C, rue Hériot, Drummondville QC J2C 2B1
Tél: 819-477-1033; *Téléc:* 819-474-7913
Ligne sans frais: 877-546-8320
chambre@cgocable.ca
www.immobiliercentreduquebec.com
Aperçu: *Dimension:* moyenne; *Envergure:* locale surveillé par Fédération des Chambres immobilières du Québec
Membre de: The Canadian Real Estate Association
Membre(s) du bureau directeur:
Marie-Paule Landry, Adjointe exécutive
Denis A. Jackson, Présidente
denisa.jackson@sympatico.ca

Chambre immobilière de l'Abitibi-Témiscamingue Inc. (CIAT)

#203, 33, av Horne, Rouyn-Noranda QC J9X 4S1
Tél: 819-762-1777; *Téléc:* 819-762-4030
ciat@cablevision.qc.ca
www.ciat.qc.ca
Aperçu: *Dimension:* petite; *Envergure:* locale; Organisme sans but lucratif; fondée en 1985 surveillé par Fédération des Chambres immobilières du Québec
Membre de: The Canadian Real Estate Association
Membre(s) du bureau directeur:
Robert Brière, Président
robertbbriere@royallepage.ca
Gilles Langlais, Directeur général
Membre: 58 courtiers

Chambre immobilière de l'Estrie inc.

19, rue King ouest, Sherbrooke QC J1H 1N4
Tél: 819-566-7616; *Téléc:* 819-566-7688
info@mon-toit.net
www.mon-toit.net
Aperçu: *Dimension:* moyenne; *Envergure:* locale surveillé par Fédération des Chambres immobilières du Québec
Mission: Promouvoir et protéger les intérêts de l'industrie immobilière du Québec afin que les Chambres et les membres accomplissent avec succès leurs objectifs d'affaires.
Membre de: The Canadian Real Estate Association
Membre(s) du bureau directeur:
Lucien Choquette, Président

Chambre immobilière de l'Outaouais

106, boul Sacré-Coeur, Gatineau QC J8X 1E1
Tél: 819-771-5221; *Téléc:* 819-771-8715
info@avecunagent.com
www.avecunagent.com
www.facebook.com/104740336281495
twitter.com/avecuncourtier
Aperçu: *Dimension:* petite; *Envergure:* locale surveillé par Fédération des Chambres immobilières du Québec
Mission: De fournir à ses membres les outils nécessaires pour réussir
Membre de: The Canadian Real Estate Association
Membre(s) du bureau directeur:
Chantal Legault, Directrice générale
Membre: 500; *Comités:* Activités récréatives; Formation; Révision des Règlements et Politiques; Action politique; Communication et visibilité

Chambre immobilière de la Haute Yamaska Inc. (CIHY) / Haute Yamaska Real Estate Board

#3, 45, rue Centre, Granby QC J2G 5B4
Tél: 450-378-6702; *Téléc:* 450-375-5268
administration.cihy@videotron.ca
Aperçu: *Dimension:* petite; *Envergure:* locale; fondée en 1984 surveillé par Fédération des Chambres immobilières du Québec
Mission: Offrir des services de formation et d'information pour les agents immobiliers.
Membre de: The Canadian Real Estate Association
Membre(s) du bureau directeur:
Lise Desrochers, Directrice générale

Chambre immobilière de la Mauricie Inc. / Trois-Rivières Real Estate Board

1275, boul des Forges, Trois-Rivières QC G8Z 1T7
Tél: 819-379-9081; *Téléc:* 819-379-9262
info@cimauricie.com
www.cimauricie.com
Aperçu: *Dimension:* moyenne; *Envergure:* locale; Organisme sans but lucratif; fondée en 1962 surveillé par Fédération des Chambres immobilières du Québec
Membre de: The Canadian Real Estate Association
Membre(s) du bureau directeur:
Lise Girardeau, Directrice générale
cimauricie@cgocable.ca
Membre(s) du personnel: 2
Membre: 1,200; *Critères d'admissibilité:* Détenir un certificat d'agent ou de courtier immobilier
Activités: *Service de conférenciers:* Oui

Chambre immobilière de Lanaudière Inc.

765, boul Manseau, Joliette QC J6E 3E8
Tél: 450-759-8511; *Téléc:* 450-759-6557
cil@immobilierlanaudiere.com
www.immobilierlanaudiere.com
Aperçu: *Dimension:* moyenne; *Envergure:* locale; fondée en 1982 surveillé par Fédération des Chambres immobilières du Québec
Membre de: The Canadian Real Estate Association
Membre(s) du bureau directeur:
Louise Renaud, Directrice générale
Membre(s) du personnel: 1
Membre: 160

Chambre immobilière de Québec

600, ch du Golf, Ile-des-soeurs QC H3E 1A8
Tél: 514-762-0212; *Téléc:* 514-762-0365
Ligne sans frais: 866-882-0212
info@fciq.ca
www.fciq.ca
twitter.com/fciq_eco
Nom précédent: Chambre d'immeubles de Québec
Aperçu: *Dimension:* moyenne; *Envergure:* locale surveillé par Fédération des Chambres immobilières du Québec
Mission: Promouvoir et protéger les intérêts de l'industrie immobilière du Québec afin que les Chambres et les membres accomplissent avec succès leurs objectifs d'affaires.
Membre de: The Canadian Real Estate Association
Membre(s) du bureau directeur:
Gina Gaudreault, Président
Membre: 12 chambres immobilières; *Critères d'admissibilite:* Chambres immobilières

Chambre immobilière de Saint-Hyacinthe Inc.

CP 667, Saint-Hyacinthe QC J2S 7P5
Tél: 450-799-2210; *Téléc:* 450-799-2230
chimmob@cgocable.ca
www.chambreimmobilieresthyacinthe.com
Aperçu: *Dimension:* petite; *Envergure:* locale; fondée en 1984 surveillé par Fédération des Chambres immobilières du Québec
Mission: Promouvoir et protéger les intérêts de l'industrie immobilière du Québec afin que les Chambres et les membres accomplissent avec succès leurs objectifs d'affaires.
Membre de: The Canadian Real Estate Association
Membre(s) du bureau directeur:
Pierre Tanguay, Président
Membre: 100

Chambre immobilière des Laurentides (CIL)

570, boul. des Laurentides, Piedmont QC J0R 1K0
Tél: 450-240-0006
Ligne sans frais: 800-263-3511
info@cilaurentides.ca
www.cilaurentides.ca
www.facebook.com/OptionLaurentides
Également appelé: Un PRO du Nord
Aperçu: *Dimension:* petite; *Envergure:* locale; Organisme sans but lucratif; fondée en 1982 surveillé par Fédération des Chambres immobilières du Québec
Mission: De promouvoir et à développer des intérêts professionnels, économiques et sociaux de ses membres
Membre de: The Canadian Real Estate Association
Membre(s) du bureau directeur:
Francine Soucy, Présidente
fsoucy@immobilierlaurentien.com
Daniel Vandal, Directrice générale
Membre: 600 courtiers et agents immobiliers; *Critères d'admissibilité:* Courtiers et agents immobiliers de la région

Chambre immobilière du Grand Montréal / Greater Montréal Real Estate Board

600, ch du Golf, Ile-des-Soeurs QC H3E 1A8
Tél: 514-762-2440; *Téléc:* 514-762-1854
Ligne sans frais: 888-762-2440
cigm@cigm.qc.ca
www.cigm.qc.ca
Aperçu: *Dimension:* moyenne; *Envergure:* locale surveillé par Fédération des Chambres immobilières du Québec
Mission: De protéger les intérêts commerciaux de ses membres afin de développer leur succès
Membre de: The Canadian Real Estate Association
Membre(s) du bureau directeur:
Éric Charbonneau, Directeur général
Membre: 10,000+

Chambre immobilière du Saguenay-Lac St-Jean Inc. (CISL)

#140, 2655, boul du Royaume, Jonquière QC G7S 4S9

Tél: 418-548-8808; *Téléc:* 418-548-2588
chambre@immobiliersaguenay.com
www.immobiliersaguenay.com
www.facebook.com/immobilier.saguenay
Aperçu: *Dimension:* moyenne; *Envergure:* locale; Organisme sans but lucratif; fondée en 1954 surveillé par Fédération des Chambres immobilières du Québec
Mission: Regrouper les membres afin de leur fournir des services, assurer la qualité de leur travail, défendre et promouvoir leurs intérêts; protéger et promouvoir le commerce de l'immobilier et encourager l'accès à la propriété; offrir de la formation et du perfectionnement dans le domaine immobilier afin d'assurer et de garantir le professionnalisme de l'industrie; faciliter au public en général l'accès à l'information dans le domaine immobilier
Membre de: The Canadian Real Estate Association
Membre(s) du bureau directeur:
Ginette Gaudreault, Directrice générale
ginetteg@immobiliersaguenay.com
Finances: *Budget de fonctionnement annuel:* $100,000-$250,000
Membre(s) du personnel: 2; 7 bénévole(s)
Membre: 150; *Montant de la cotisation:* 225$; *Critères d'admissibilite:* Courtiers, agents et professionnels de l'immobilier
Activités: Cours de perfectionnement;

Chambres de commerce des provinces de l'Atlantique *See* Atlantic Provinces Chambers of Commerce

Champlain Coin Club
Orillia ON
Tel: 705-327-1789
ChamplainCoinClub@gmail.com
Overview: A small local organization
Chief Officer(s):
Doug McGarvey, Secretary

The Champlain Society
University of Toronto Press, 5201 Dufferin St., Toronto ON M3H 5T8
Tel: 416-538-1650; *Fax:* 416-667-7881
info@champlainsociety.ca
www.champlainsociety.ca
Overview: A medium-sized national charitable organization founded in 1905
Chief Officer(s):
Christina Becker, Administrator
Finances: *Annual Operating Budget:* $50,000-$100,000; *Funding Sources:* Membership fees; donations
6 volunteer(s)
Membership: 750; *Fees:* $75 individual; $85 institutions; *Member Profile:* Readers of Canadian history; libraries; *Committees:* Executive; Publications; Special Events; Membership; Funding; Nominations
Activities: Administers Chalmers Award for best book in Ontario history; publish an annual volume of edited documentary history
Awards:
• The Floyd S. Chambers Award in Ontario History
Awarded annually to the best book on Ontario history *Amount:* $2000
Publications:
• General Series
Type: Book
Profile: Documents on the Canadian experience, described by an expert in the field

Change for Children Association (CFCA)
10808 - 124 St., 2nd Fl., Edmonton AB T5M 0H3
Tel: 780-448-1505; *Fax:* 780-448-1507
cfca@changeforchildren.org
www.changeforchildren.org
www.facebook.com/change4children
twitter.com/change4justice
www.youtube.com/user/cfca100/videos
Also Known As: Change for Children
Overview: A small international charitable organization founded in 1976
Mission: To support local projects in various parts of the Global South; To identify the root causes of poverty & provide assistance to find solutions; To ensure that all donor dollars go directly to the people; To educate Canadians about the Global South through literature, lectures & discussions; To bring about an awareness of our global interdependence & solicit support for greater justice & equality
Member of: Alberta Council for Global cooperation
Chief Officer(s):
Lorraine Swift, Projects Coordinator
Shelaine Sparrow, Development Coordinator
Fiona Cavanagh, Education Coordinator
Sharon Strong, President
Finances: *Annual Operating Budget:* $500,000-$1.5 Million
Staff Member(s): 3; 72 volunteer(s)
Membership: 3,000; *Fees:* Donations of $10 & over; *Committees:* Executive; Finance; Development
Activities: International development; global education; development cafe; development dinner; *Internships:* Yes; *Speaker Service:* Yes; *Library* Open to public

The Change Foundation
PO Box 42, #2501, 200 Front St. West, Toronto ON M5V 3M1
Tel: 416-205-1353; *Fax:* 416-205-1440
asunnak@changefoundation.com
www.changefoundation.ca
www.twitter.com/TheChangeFdn
Overview: A large local organization founded in 1996
Mission: To promote, support & improve health & health care delivery through four activity areas: applied research, grants for Change Initiatives, & knowledge transfer through development & education programs
Chief Officer(s):
Cathy Fooks, President & CEO
cfooks@changefoundation.com
Sine MacKinnon, Director of Communications
smackinnon@changefoundation.com

Channel Port Aux Basques & Area Chamber of Commerce
PO Box 1389, Channel-Port-aux-Basques NL A0M 1C0
Tel: 709-695-3688; *Fax:* 709-695-7925
Overview: A small local organization
Chief Officer(s):
Gary O'Brien, Secretary
Terry Anderson, President

Chantiers jeunesse
4545, av Pierre-de Coubertin, Montréal QC H1V 3R2
Tél: 514-252-3015; *Téléc:* 514-251-8719
Ligne sans frais: 800-361-2055
cj@cj.qc.ca
www.cj.qc.ca
www.facebook.com/Chantiersjeunesse
Nom précédent: Mouvement québécois des chantiers jeunesse
Aperçu: *Dimension:* moyenne; *Envergure:* provinciale; Organisme sans but lucratif; fondée en 1980
Mission: Favoriser le développement de jeunes citoyens actifs et engagés, à appuyer le développement d'une communauté et du plein potentiel des personnes en offrant des lieux d'apprentissages et de formation en collaboration avec des partenaires d'ici et d'ailleurs et ce dans un esprit de solidarité et de respect des différences
Membre de: Regroupement loisir Québec; Conseil Québécois du Loisir; Alliance européenne des organismes des organisations de service volontaire
Affliation(s): Secrétariat au loisir et au sport; Ministère de santé et services sociaux
Membre(s) du bureau directeur:
Stéphanie Fey, Président
Finances: *Fonds:* Provincial Government
Membre(s) du personnel: 5
Membre: *Montant de la cotisation:* 10$ indiviuel; 25$ organisme; *Critères d'admissibilite:* Jeunes de 16 - 30 ans
Activités: Projects de travail volontaire au Québec et à l'étranger; *Stagiaires:* Oui

Chants Libres, compagnie lyrique de création
#303, 1908, rue Panet, Montréal QC H2L 3A2
Tél: 514-841-2642
creation@chantslibres.org
www.chantslibres.org
www.facebook.com/ChantsLibres
twitter.com/ChantsLibres
www.youtube.com/user/chantslibres
Aperçu: *Dimension:* petite; *Envergure:* locale; fondée en 1990
Mission: Réunir des créateurs de toutes les disciplines (musique, théâtre, arts plastiques, arts électroniques, vidéo etc.) autour d'un point commun: la voix
Membre(s) du bureau directeur:
Pauline Vaillancourt, Directrice générale
Membre(s) du personnel: 4

Chao Chow Association Of Ontario *See* Chaeo Chow Association of Eastern Canada

Chapel Hill Historical Society
PO Box 46, Shag Harbour NS B0W 3B0
Tel: 902-723-2949
chapelhills@gmail.com
www.chapelhillmuseumns.com
Overview: A small local charitable organization founded in 1980
Mission: To promote heritage & history of the area
Member of: Federation of the Nova Scotian Heritage; Nova Scotia Lighthouse Preservation Society
Activities: Operates Chapel Hill Museum June 1 - Sept. 15; *Library:* Chapel Hill Museum; Open to public

Chapitre de Québec *Voir* Sign Association of Canada

CHARGE Syndrome Canada
PO Box 61509, Stn. Fennell, Hamilton ON L8T 5A1
Tel: 519-752-4685; *Fax:* 519-758-9919
admin@chargesyndrome.ca
www.chargesyndrome.ca
Overview: A small national charitable organization founded in 2003
Mission: To raise money for the sufferers of CHARGE Syndrome, as well as CHARGE Syndrome research

Charlotte Seafood Employees Association / Association des employés de Charlotte Seafood
c/o 669 Main St., Blacks Harbour NB E5H 1K1
Tel: 506-456-3391; *Fax:* 506-456-1569
Overview: A medium-sized local organization
Chief Officer(s):
William Beney, President
Membership: 744

Charlottetown Area Baseball Association
c/o Baseball PEI, PO Box 302, 40 Enman Cres., Charlottetown PE C1A 7K7
Tel: 902-569-0583; *Fax:* 902-368-4548
Toll-Free: 800-247-6712
baseball@sportpei.pe.ca
www.baseballpei.ca/caba/index.php
Overview: A medium-sized local organization
Member of: Baseball PEI
Chief Officer(s):
Bob Quilliam, Contact, Peewee Try-outs
rquilliam@gmail.com
J.D. Geldert, Website Administrator
fifa_jade5@hotmail.com

Charlottetown Board of Trade *See* Greater Charlottetown & Area Chamber of Commerce

Charlottetown Downtown Residents Association (CDRA)
e-mail: cdrainpei@gmail.com
www.facebook.com/185367578171566?sk=notes
Overview: A medium-sized local organization
Mission: To create a vibrant and safe downtown community and to offer a forum for discussion, deliberation and consensus on matters affecting the downtown City Area and the Waterfront.
Membership: *Fees:* $10; *Member Profile:* Open to any person residing in the downtown Charlottetown City Area bounded by Euston Street and inclusively between West Street and Esher Street.

CharterAbility
PO Box 60024, Oakville ON L6J 6G4
Tel: 905-466-2016
info@charterability.com
www.charterability.com
Overview: A small local organization
Mission: To promote accessible boating & provide a barrier-free, fully accessible, charter boat service on Lake Ontario for groups of people of all ages with disabilities or mobility impairments
Chief Officer(s):
Stephen Cull, Founder & President, 905-844-7208
sjc@charterability.com

Chartered Accountants' Education Foundation of Alberta (CAEF)
c/o Manulife Place, Institute of Chartered Accountants of Alberta, #580, 10180 - 101st St., Edmonton AB T5J 4R2
Toll-Free: 800-232-9406
www.albertacas.ca/CAEducationFoundation.aspx
Previous Name: Alberta CA Profession's Non-Profit Foundation
Overview: A small provincial organization founded in 1982
Mission: To support accounting & business education in Alberta; To promote the excellence of the CA profession

Chief Officer(s):
Alex Tutschek, Chair
Finances: *Funding Sources:* Member's annual $60 contribution; Donations
Activities: Supporting post-secondary institutions, accounting educators, & students, through university operational funding, a Teaching Prize, student conferences & career information events, plus scholarships, awards, & bursaries
Publications:
• Chartered Accountants' Education Foundation Report to the Community
Type: Report
• Chartered Accountants' Education Foundation Annual Report
Type: Yearbook; *Frequency:* Annually

The Chartered Institute of Logistics & Transport in North America (CILT) / Institut agréé de la logistique et des transports Amérique du Nord

#205, 1435 Sandford Fleming Ave., Ottawa ON K1G 3H3
Tel: 613-738-3003; *Fax:* 613-738-3033
requestinfo@ciltna.com
www.ciltna.com
Also Known As: CILT in North America
Previous Name: Chartered Institute of Transport Canadian Division
Overview: A medium-sized international organization founded in 1919
Mission: To promote, encourage, coordinate study & advancement of science & art of transportation.
Member of: Chartered Institute of Transport
Chief Officer(s):
Bob Armstrong, President, 416-418-3990
armstrong@ciltna.com
David Collenette, Chair
david.collenette@hillandknowlton.ca
Finances: *Funding Sources:* Membership fees, conferences, workshop revenue
Staff Member(s): 1; 15 volunteer(s)
Membership: 250; *Fees:* Schedule available; *Member Profile:* Individuals with experience, interest & education in the transportation field.; *Committees:* Regional

Manitoba Region
73 Nassena Cres., Winnipeg MB R2P 0K8
Tel: 204-633-4956
Chief Officer(s):
David Bibby, Regional Chair

Pacific Region
c/o CILTNA, #900, 275 Slater St., Ottawa ON K1P 5H9
Tel: 613-688-1438; *Fax:* 613-688-0966
www.linkedin.com/groups/CILTNA-Pacific-Chapter-4942351
Chief Officer(s):
Marian Robson, Regional Chair

Chartered Institute of Secretaries *See* Institute of Chartered Secretaries & Administrators - Canadian Division

Chartered Institute of Transport Canadian Division *See* The Chartered Institute of Logistics & Transport in North America

Chartered Professional Accountants Canada (CPA) / Comptables professionnels agréés du Canada

277 Wellington St. West, Toronto ON M5V 3H2
Tel: 416-977-3222; *Fax:* 416-977-8585
Toll-Free: 800-268-3793
Other Communication: CGA-Canada Legacy Content: www.cga-canada.org
member.services@cpacanada.ca
www.cpacanada.ca
www.linkedin.com/company/cpa-canada
twitter.com/CPAcanada
Also Known As: CPA Canada
Merged from: Canadian Institute of Chartered Accountants; Certified Management Accountants of Canada; CGA-Canada
Overview: A large national licensing organization founded in 1902
Mission: To foster public confidence in the chartered accountant profession; To assist members to excel; To oversee a single, unified professional accounting designation known as CPA, including all 40 of the accounting bodies in Canada (note that some provinces/regions will be represented by a merged CPA body, while others will be represented by the legacy bodies until integration is complete)
Chief Officer(s):
Kevin Dancey, FCPA, FCA, President & CEO
Stephen Anisman, CPA, CMA, Chief Financial Officer
Joy Thomas, MBA, FCPA, FCMA, Executive Vice-Presidnet
Tashia Batstone, MBA, FCPA, FCA, Vice-President, Education Services
Gord Beal, CPA, CA, M.Ed., Vice-President, Research, Guidance & Support
Nicholas Cheung, CPA, CA, Vice-President, Member Services
Gale Evans, CPA, CMA, C.Dir, Vice-President, Administration
Nancy Foran, CMA, FCMA, C.Di, Vice-President, International - The Americas
Lyle Handfield, CPA, FCGA, Vice-President, Asia & Pacific
Gabe Hayos, FCPA, FCA, Vice-President, Taxation
Heather Whyte, MBA, APR, Vice-President, Strategic Communications, Branding & Public Affairs
Cairine Wilson, MBA, CAE, Vice-President, Corporate Citizenship
Membership: 190,000+
Activities: Providing continuing education opportunities;
Awards:
• Corporate Reporting Awards (Award)
National awards for corporate reporting, recognizing the best in the country.
Meetings/Conferences: • Chartered Professional Accountants Canada 1st National SR&ED Symposium, February, 2015, Toronto, ON
Scope: National
Publications:
• CPA Magazine [a publication of the Chartered Professional Accountants]
Type: Magazine; *Frequency:* 10 pa; *Accepts Advertising*; *Editor:* Okey Chigbo *ISSN:* 0317-6878; *Price:* $32 members, $55non-members; $45 students; $5.50 single issue
Profile: An information resource for Canadian chartered accountants & financial executives

Burnaby Office
#100, 4200 North Fraser Way, Burnaby BC V5J 5K7
Tel: 604-669-3555; *Fax:* 604-689-5845
Toll-Free: 800-663-1529

Montréal Office
680, rue Sherbrooke Ouest, 17e étage, Montréal QC H3A 2M7

Ottawa Office
#1201, 350 Sparks St., Ottawa ON K1R 7S8
Tel: 613-789-7771; *Fax:* 613-789-7772

Chartered Professional Accountants of British Columbia (CPABC)

BC
e-mail: info@bccpa.ca
www.bccpa.ca
www.linkedin.com/groups?home=&gid=8136632
www.facebook.com/cpabc
twitter.com/cpa_bc
www.youtube.com/user/cpabritishcolumbia
Also Known As: CPA British Columbia
Overview: A large provincial licensing organization overseen by Chartered Professional Accountants Canada
Mission: To oversee the integration of the Institute of Chartered Accountants of British Columbia (ICABC), the Certified General Accountants of British Columbia (CGA-BC), & Chartered Management Accountants of BC (CMA-BC) under the Chartered Professional Accountants (CPA) banner; to administer the CPA designation in BC
Chief Officer(s):
Richard Rees, CPA, FCA, ICABC, Chief Executive Officer
Meetings/Conferences: • Chartered Professional Accountants of British Columbia Spring Leadership Conference 2015, 2015, BC
Scope: Provincial
• Chartered Professional Accountants of British Columbia Fall Leadership Conference 2015, 2015, BC
Scope: Provincial

Chartered Professional Accountants of Manitoba (CPAMB)

#1675, 1 Lombard Place, Winnipeg MB R3B 0X3
Tel: 204-942-8248; *Fax:* 204-943-7119
cpamb@cpamb.ca
www.cpamb.ca
www.linkedin.com/groups/CPA-Manitoba-6573960
www.facebook.com/CPAmanitoba
twitter.com/CPAManitoba
Also Known As: CPA Manitoba Joint Venture
Overview: A large provincial licensing organization founded in 2014 overseen by Chartered Professional Accountants Canada
Mission: To oversee the integration of the Institute of Chartered Accountants of Manitoba (CA Manitoba), the Certified General Accountants Association of Manitoba (CGA Manitoba), & the Certified Management Accountants of Manitoba (CGA Manitoba) under the Chartered Professional Accountants (CPA) banner; to administer the CPA designation in BC
Chief Officer(s):
Gary Hannaford, FCA, Chief Executive Officer, 204-924-4410
ghannaford@cpamb.ca

Chartered Professional Accountants of New Brunswick (CPANB) / Comptables professionnels agréés Nouveau-Brunswick

#602, 860 Main St., Moncton NB E1C 1G2
Tel: 506-830-3300; *Fax:* 506-830-3310
Other Communication: CPA Atlantic School of Business, URL: cpaatlantic.ca
info@cpanewbrunswick.ca
www.cpanewbrunswick.ca
Also Known As: CPA New Brunswick
Overview: A large provincial licensing organization founded in 2014 overseen by Chartered Professional Accountants Canada
Mission: To oversee the integration of the New Brunswick Institute of Chartered Accountants (NBICA), the Certified General Accountant of New Brunswick (CGA-NB), & the Certified Management Accountants of NB (CMA-NB) under the Chartered Professional Accountants (CPA) banner; to administer the CPA designation in New Brunswick
Chief Officer(s):
Nancy Whipp, CPA, CA, Chief Executive Officer
Membership: 2,200+

Chartered Professional Accountants of Newfoundland & Labrador (CPA NL)

NL
Other Communication: CPA Atlantic School of Business, URL: cpaatlantic.ca
cpanl.ca
Overview: A large provincial licensing organization founded in 2014 overseen by Chartered Professional Accountants Canada
Mission: To oversee the integration of the Institute of Chartered Accountants of Newfoundland & Labrador (ICANL), the Certified Management Accountants of Newfoundland & Labrador (CMA-NL), & the Certified General Accountants Association of Newfoundland (CGA-NL) under the Chartered Professional Accountants (CPA) banner; to administer the CPA designation in Newfoundland & Labrador
Chief Officer(s):
Arnold Adey, CMA, Co-chair, CPANL Transitional Steering Committee
Michael Kennedy, CGA, Co-chair, CPANL Transitional Steering Committee
John O'Brien, CA, Co-chair, CPANL Transitional Steering Committee

Chartered Professional Accountants of Ontario

69 Bloor St. East, Toronto ON M4W 1B3
Tel: 416-962-1841; *Fax:* 416-962-8900
Toll-Free: 800-387-0735
customerservice@cpaontario.ca
www.cpaontario.ca
Also Known As: CPA Ontario; The Institute of Chartered Accountants of Ontario
Merged from: Institute of Chartered Accountants of Ontario; CGA Ontario; CMA Ontario
Overview: A medium-sized provincial licensing organization founded in 1879 overseen by Chartered Professional Accountants Canada
Mission: Mission is to foster public confidence in the Chartered Professional Accountant profession, by acting in the public interest & helping members excel. CPA Ontario sets & enforces high standards of practice, qualification & education; promotes professional excellence & ethical conduct; encourages continuous improvement of capabilities among members; promotes the profession while serving as it's primary voice in Ontario
Member of: Ontario Chamber of Commerce; Metro Toronto Board of Trade
Chief Officer(s):
Carol Wilding, President/CEO
Nora Murrant, Executive Vice-President/COO
Tom Warner, Vice-President/Registrar
Finances: *Annual Operating Budget:* Greater than $5 Million; *Funding Sources:* Membership fees; CA education & professional development programs

Membership: 80,000 chartered accountants + 20,000 CA students
Activities: Conferences, meetings, awards, continuing education, speakers, tax clinics, children's charities & other community initiatives;
Awards:
• Award of Outstanding Merit (Award)
Eligibility: Member of the institute

Chartered Professional Accountants of Prince Edward Island (CPAPEI)

PE
Other Communication: CPA Atlantic School of Business, URL: cpaatlantic.ca
www.cpapei.ca
Overview: A large provincial licensing organization founded in 2014 overseen by Chartered Professional Accountants Canada
Mission: To oversee the integration of the Certified General Accountants, the Certified Management Accountants, & the Institute of Chartered Accountants of PEI under the Chartered Professional Accountants (CPA) banner; to administer the CPA designation in PEI
Chief Officer(s):
Cleve Myers, CPA, FCA, Chair, Oversight Committee
Sherry Ross, CPA, CGA, Vice-Chair, Oversight Committee
Jean Kimpton, CPA, FCMA, Secretary, Oversight Committee
Chris Gallant, CPA, CA, Treasurer, Oversight Committee
Tanya O'Brien, CPA, CA, Chief Executive Officer, 902-894-4290
tobrien@cpapei.ca

Chartered Professional Accountants of Saskatchewan

#101, 4581 Parliament Ave., Regina SK S4W 0G3
Tel: 306-359-0272; *Fax:* 306-347-8580
Overview: A large provincial licensing organization founded in 2014 overseen by Chartered Professional Accountants Canada
Mission: To oversee the integration of the Institute of Chartered Accountants of Saskatchewan, Certified Management Accountants of Saskatchewan, & Certified General Accountants Association of Saskatchewan under the Chartered Professional Accountants (CPA) banner; to administer the CPA designation in Saskatchewan
Chief Officer(s):
Shelley Thiel, FCA, Chief Executive Officer

Chartered Professional Accountants of the Yukon (CPAYT)

YT
Overview: A large provincial licensing organization founded in 2014 overseen by Chartered Professional Accountants Canada
Mission: To oversee the integration of the Certified Management Accountants Society of the Yukon (CMAYT), the Certified General Accountants Association of the Yukon (CGA-YT), & the Institute of Chartered Accountants of the Yukon (ICAYT) under the Chartered Professional Accountants (CPA) banner; to administer the CPA designation in the Yukon
Chief Officer(s):
Bilsky Jason, CA, President, ICAYT
Fendrick Robert, FCGA, President, CGA-YT
Kelly Steele, CMA, Chair, CMAYT

Chartered Shorthand Reporters' Association of Ontario (CSRAO)

#425, 157 Adelaide St. West, Toronto ON M5H 4E7
Tel: 613-435-0794
membership@csrao.net
www.csrao.net
Overview: A small provincial licensing organization founded in 1891
Mission: To qualify & maintain qualifications of verbatim court reporters; To offer training & education to prospective reporters; To liaise with governments to ensure use of new technology
Affliation(s): National Court Reporters Association
Chief Officer(s):
Tracey Davis, President
president@csrao.net
9 volunteer(s)
Membership: 100 associate + 50 student + 200 senior/lifetime + 50 other; *Fees:* $30 student/affiliate/retired fellow/retired associate; $100 fellows; *Member Profile:* Fellow - by examination; associate - by occupation; student - by attendance at recognized school; *Committees:* Training & Education; Official Reporters; Technology

Chase & District Chamber of Commerce

PO Box 592, 400 Shuswap Ave., Chase BC V0E 1M0
Tel: 250-679-8432; *Fax:* 250-679-3120
admin@chasechamber.com
www.chasechamber.com
Also Known As: Chase Info Centre
Overview: A small local organization founded in 1954
Mission: To promote & improve trade, commerce, economic, civic & social welfare of the district
Member of: BC Chamber of Commerce; Canadian Chamber of Commerce
Chief Officer(s):
Andy Phillips, President
Finances: *Annual Operating Budget:* $50,000-$100,000; *Funding Sources:* Membership dues; government grants
Staff Member(s): 1; 12 volunteer(s)
Membership: 101; *Fees:* $100-$200

Châteauguay Sexual Assault Center ***Voir*** Centre d'aide et de lutte contre les agressions à caractère sexuel de Châteauguay

Chateauguay Valley English-Speaking Peoples' Association (CVESPA)

1493, rte 138, CP 1357, Huntingdon QC J0S 1H0
Tel: 450-264-5386; *Fax:* 450-264-5387
Overview: A medium-sized local organization founded in 1983
Mission: To assure preservation, maintenance & on-going development of English-speaking population in Southwest Québec; to encourage continuous development of their institutions & cultural heritage; to assure full participation & representation of English-speaking community in all aspects of Québec society; to promote positive attitudes in English-speaking community to participate fully & harmoniously with French-speaking population; to foster activities which would bring the two communities together to improve their mutual understanding
Member of: Québec Community Group Network
Finances: *Annual Operating Budget:* $100,000-$250,000; *Funding Sources:* Membership dues; donations; fundraising; government
Staff Member(s): 2; 40 volunteer(s)
Membership: 6,000
Activities: Public information meetings; seminars; workshops; *Speaker Service:* Yes

Chatham & District Association for Community Living ***See*** Community Living Chatham-Kent

Chatham & District Chamber of Commerce ***See*** Chatham-Kent Chamber of Commerce

Chatham & District Labour Council ***See*** Chatham-Kent Labour Council

Chatham Outreach for Hunger

PO Box 953, Chatham ON N7M 5L3
Tel: 519-351-8381
bjl@ciaccess.com
www.outreachforhunger.com
Also Known As: Food Bank
Overview: A small local charitable organization founded in 1988
Mission: To provide food to low income families on an emergency basis
Member of: Ontario Association of Food Banks; Food Banks Canada
Finances: *Funding Sources:* Community supported
Activities: *Speaker Service:* Yes

Chatham Railroad Museum Society

PO Box 434, 2 McLean St., Chatham ON N7M 5K5
Tel: 519-352-3097
crms@mnsi.net
www.chathamrailroadmuseum.ca
www.facebook.com/pages/Chatham-Railroad-Museum-CRMS/195849387130379
Overview: A small local charitable organization founded in 1989
Mission: To present history from a retired CN baggage car
Staff Member(s): 3; 10 volunteer(s)
Membership: 1-99

Chatham-Kent Big Sisters Association Inc. ***See*** Big Brothers Big Sisters of Chatham-Kent

Chatham-Kent Chamber of Commerce

54 Fourth St., Chatham ON N7M 2G2
Tel: 519-352-7540; *Fax:* 519-352-8741
info@chatham-kentchamber.ca
www.chatham-kentchamber.ca
Previous Name: Chatham & District Chamber of Commerce
Overview: A medium-sized local organization
Chief Officer(s):
G.A. (Gail) Antaya, President & CEO, 519-352-7540 Ext. 22
gail@chatham-kentchamber.ca
Membership: 400

Chatham-Kent Labour Council

280 Merritt Ave., Chatham ON N7M 3G1
Tel: 519-351-6621; *Fax:* 519-351-9403
cklc@kent.net
www.kent.net/cklc/index.htm
Previous Name: Chatham & District Labour Council
Overview: A small local organization founded in 1958 overseen by Ontario Federation of Labour
Mission: To group together local labour councils and unions
Member of: Ontario Federation of Labour; Canadian Labour Congress
Chief Officer(s):
Jeff McFadden, President
jeff_mcfadden@hotmail.com
Elizabeth Cannon, Secretary
ecannon@cogeco.ca

Chatham-Kent Multiple Birth Association

Chatham ON
Tel: 519-825-9075
chatham@multiplebirthscanada.org
www.multiplebirthscanada.org/~chatham
Overview: A small local organization founded in 1987 overseen by Multiple Births Canada
Membership: *Fees:* $30

Chatham-Kent Real Estate Board

PO Box 384, 252 Wellington St. W., Chatham ON N7M 5K5
Tel: 519-352-4351; *Fax:* 519-351-1498
ckreb@mnsi.net
boards.mls.ca/chatham
Overview: A small local organization overseen by Ontario Real Estate Association
Member of: The Canadian Real Estate Association
Chief Officer(s):
Randy Korpan, President
Finances: *Funding Sources:* Membership fees
Activities: *Library*

Chebucto Community Net (CCN) / Réseau communautaire Chebucto (RCC)

#006, Chase Bldg., Dalhousie University, Halifax NS B3H 4R2
Tel: 902-494-2449; *Fax:* 902-494-1242
office@chebucto.ns.ca
www.chebucto.ns.ca
www.facebook.com/pages/Chebucto-Community-Net/191676037573945
twitter.com/ChebuctoCommNet
plus.google.com/109471644185457910515
Overview: A small local charitable organization founded in 1994
Mission: To provide the technology, infrastructure & training to enable all people in the Greater Halifax Region to participate in an electronic public space
Membership: *Fees:* Schedule available

Chebucto Symphony Orchestra

PO Box 27024, 5595 Fenwick St., Halifax NS B3H 4M8
Tel: 902-431-7654
info@chebuctosymphony.ca
www.chebucto.ns.ca/Culture/ChebuctoSymphony
www.facebook.com/ChebuctoSymphony
Also Known As: Chebucto Orchestral Society of Nova Scotia
Overview: A small local charitable organization founded in 1976 overseen by Orchestras Canada
Mission: To provide an opportunity for amateur musicians to perform the great symphonic works & to bring classical music to local audiences
Member of: Orchestras Canada
Affliation(s): SOCAN
Chief Officer(s):
Gina McFetridge, Chair
Volker Metz, Treasurer
Membership: 1-99; *Fees:* $150 regular; $50 students; *Member Profile:* Talented amateur musicians from the Halifax Regional Municipality
Activities: Performance of a minimum of four public concerts per annum, in a repertoire focused on classical works; has performed four world premiers of modern works over the past eight years; *Library:* Music Library; Open to public

Chedoke Numismatic Society
c/o Bruce Brace, 654 Hiawatha Blvd., Ancaster ON L9G 3A5
Overview: A small local organization
Member of: Royal Canadian Numismatic Association
Chief Officer(s):
Bruce Brace, Contact
brace@cogeco.ca

Cheer Canada
c/o Alberta Cheerleading Association, 52 Meadowood Cres., Sherwood Park AB T8A 0L7
Tel: 780-417-0050; *Fax:* 780-417-0093
Toll-Free: 888-756-9220
Other Communication: Funding, E-mail: funding@cheercanada.net
info@cheercanada.net
cms.cheercanada.net
www.facebook.com/171764516220976
twitter.com/cheercanada
Overview: A medium-sized national organization founded in 2011
Mission: To provide the following to provincial cheerleading organizations: ease of travel between provinces & territories; national coaches' & judges' training & certification programs; insurance for athletes & coaches; & funding for teams.
Affliation(s): International All Star Federation Worlds; US All Star Federation
Membership: 9 associations; *Member Profile:* Provincial cheerleading associations

Cheer Nova Scotia
NS
www.cheerns.com
Aperçu: *Dimension:* petite; *Envergure:* provinciale surveillé par Cheer Canada
Mission: To promote cheerleading in Nova Scotia.
Membre de: Cheer Canada
Membre(s) du bureau directeur:
Megan Spencer, President
president@cheerns.com
Alicia Grant, Treasurer & Administrative Registrar
alicia@halifaxcheerelite.ca
Monique Johnson, Contact, Communications
communicator@cheerns.com

Chemainus & District Chamber of Commerce
PO Box 575, 9796 Willow St., Chemainus BC V0R 1K0
Tel: 250-246-3944; *Fax:* 250-246-3251
chamber@chemainus.bc.ca
www.chemainus.bc.ca
www.facebook.com/ChemainusVisitorCentreAndChamberOfCommerce
twitter.com/ChemainusCOC
Overview: A small local organization founded in 1949
Member of: BC Chamber of Commerce; Canadian Chamber of Commerce; Tourism BC; Tourism Association of Vancouver Island; Tourism Victoria
Chief Officer(s):
Jeanne Ross, Chamber Coordinator
Marlie Kelsey, Coordinator, Visitor Centre
visitorcentre@chemainus.bc.ca
Finances: *Funding Sources:* Municipality of North Cowichan; BC Tourism; Service Canada
Staff Member(s): 2; 20 volunteer(s)
Membership: 120; *Member Profile:* Businesses
Activities: Participating in the Chemainus Giant Street Market & the Cheamainus Wednesday Market; *Awareness Events:* Golden Brush Awards & Silent Auction

Chemainus Food Bank
PO Box 188, 9814 Willow St., Chemainus BC V0R 1K0
Tel: 250-246-4816; *Fax:* 250-246-9060
Also Known As: Harvest House
Overview: A small local charitable organization overseen by Food Banks British Columbia
Member of: Food Banks British Columbia; Food Banks Canada
Chief Officer(s):
Sylvia Massey, Contact
sylviamassey@shaw.ca
Finances: *Annual Operating Budget:* $50,000-$100,000
25 volunteer(s)
Membership: 25; *Fees:* $5

Chemical Institute of Canada (CIC) / Institut de chimie du Canada
#550, 130 Slater St., Ottawa ON K1P 6E2
Tel: 613-232-6252; *Fax:* 613-232-5862
Toll-Free: 888-542-2242
info@cheminst.ca
www.cheminst.ca
www.linkedin.com/company/chemical-institute-of-canada
www.facebook.com/ChemicalInstituteOfCanada
fr.twitter.com/CIC_ChemInst
www.flickr.com/photos/61234653@N08
Overview: A large national organization founded in 1945
Mission: To maintain all branches of the professions of chemical sciences & chemical engineering in their proper status among other learned & scientific professions; To encourage original research & develop & maintain high standards in profession; To enhance usefulness of profession to the public
Affliation(s): Canadian Society for Chemical Engineering; Canadian Society for Chemical Technology; Canadian Society for Chemistry
Chief Officer(s):
Roland Andersson, Executive Director, 613-232-6252 Ext. 222
randersson@cheminst.ca
Joan Kingston, Director, Finance & Administration, 613-232-6252 Ext. 225
jkingston@cheminst.ca
Gale Thirlwall, Manager, Awards & Local Sections, 613-232-6252 Ext. 223
gthirlwall@cheminst.ca
Luke Andersson, Coordinator, Marketing, 613-232-6252 Ext. 227
landersson@cheminst.ca
Angie Moulton, Coordinator, Membership Services, 613-232-6252 Ext. 230
amoulton@cheminst.ca
Anne Campbell, Officer, Conference Programs, 613-232-6252 Ext. 235
acampbell@cheminst.ca
Finances: *Funding Sources:* Membership fees
Membership: 6,000; *Fees:* Schedule available; *Member Profile:* Open to those interested in chemistry & chemical technology & engineering with appropriate background; *Committees:* Finance; Fellowship
Activities: *Awareness Events:* National Chemistry Week; *Speaker Service:* Yes; *Rents Mailing List:* Yes
Awards:
• The Chemical Institute of Canada Award for Environmental Improvement (Award)
A plaque & certificate & up to $500 travel assistance awarded to a company, individual, team or organization in Canada for a significant achievement in pollution prevention, treatment or remediation in Canada *Contact:* Awards Manager, E-mail: awards@cheminst.ca
• The Catalysis Award (Award)
Awarded biennially to an individual who has made a distinguished contribution to the field of catalysis; sponsored by the Canadian Catalysis Foundation *Amount:* A rhodium-plated silver medal & travel expense to present the award lecture
• Chemical Institute of Canada Awards (Award)
The institute administers several awards & scholarships in chemistry, chemical engineering, & macromolecular science or engineering
• The Macromolecular Science & Engineering Lecture Award (Award)
Established 1989; awarded annually to an individual who has made a distinguished contribution to macromolecular science & engineering *Amount:* $1,500 & a framed scroll provided by Novacor Chemicals Ltd.
• Pestcon Graduate Scholarship (Scholarship)
For M.Sc. or Ph.D. students for research into alternate pest control strategies*Deadline:* March *Amount:* $3,000
• Union Carbide Award for Chemical Education (Award)
Established 1961; awarded annually to recognize an individual who has made outstanding contributions in Canada to education at any level in the field of chemistry or chemical engineering *Amount:* $1,000, a scroll & up to $400 in travel expenses if required
• Polysar Awards of the CIC for High School Chemistry Teachers (Award)
Two awards a year recognizing excellence in the teaching of chemistry at the secondary level in Canada *Amount:* $500, a scroll & membership in the CIC
• Sarnia Chemical Engineering Community Scholarship (Scholarship)
Awarded to an undergraduate student about to enter the final year of studies at a Canadian university in chemical engineering; based on academic excellence & demonstrated contributions to the Canadian Society for Chemical Engineering *Amount:* $1,000
• The Chemical Institute of Canada Medal (Award)
Established 1951; a palladium medal is awarded as a mark of distinction & recognition to a person who has made an outstanding contribution to the science of chemistry or chemical engineering in Canada
• The Montreal Medal (Award)
Established 1956; awarded annually as a mark of distinction & honour to a resident of Canada who has shown significant leadership in or has made an outstanding contribution to the profession of chemistry or chemical engineering in Canada
Amount: A medal & up to $300 travel expenses if required
Meetings/Conferences: • 98th Canadian Chemistry Conference & Exhibition, June, 2015, Ottawa Convention Centre, Ottawa, ON
Scope: National
Contact Information: Website: www.csc2015.ca; info@csc2015.ca; Phone: 613-232-6252; Fax: 613-232-5862; Toll-free: 888-542-2242
• 65th Canadian Chemical Engineering Conference, October, 2015, Calgary, AB
Scope: National
Contact Information: URL: csche2015.ca
• 66th Canadian Chemical Engineering Conference, 2016, Québec City, QC
Scope: National
Publications:
• Canadian Chemical News
Type: Magazine; *Frequency:* Bimonthly
• The Canadian Journal of Chemical Engineering
Type: Journal

Chemins du soleil
1155, rue Alexandre de Sève, Montréal QC H2L 2T7
Tél: 514-528-9991
admin@cheminsdusoleil.org
cheminsdusoleil.org
www.facebook.com/leschemins
Aperçu: *Dimension:* petite; *Envergure:* locale
Mission: Pour offrir des activités récréatives, culturelles, sportives et éducatives pour les jeunes vivant dans le centre-sud de Montréal
Membre(s) du bureau directeur:
Daniel Lauzon, Directeur
daniel.lauzon@cheminsdusoleil.org
Membre(s) du personnel: 5
Activités: *Evénements de sensibilisation:* Magasin-Partage de la Rentrée Scolaire (août); Magasin-Partage de Noël (décembre)

Chemistry Industry Association of Canada (CIAC)
#805, 350 Sparks St., Ottawa ON K1R 7S8
Tel: 613-237-6215; *Fax:* 613-237-4061
info@canadianchemistry.ca
www.canadianchemistry.ca
www.linkedin.com/company/chemistry-industry-association-of-canada/
www.facebook.com/ChemistryCanada
twitter.com/ChemistryCanada
Previous Name: Canadian Chemical Producers' Association
Overview: A medium-sized national organization founded in 1962
Mission: To represent the interests of chemical manufacturers; To promote the ethic, "Responsible Care"; To act responsibly, with accountability & openness
Chief Officer(s):
Richard Paton, President & CEO, 613-237-6215 Ext. 231
Pierre Gauthier, Vice-President, Public Affairs, 613-237-6215 Ext. 225
David Podruzny, Vice-President, Business & Economics, 613-237-6215 Ext. 229
Gordon Lloyd, Vice-President, Technical Affairs, 613-237-6215 Ext. 243
Bob Masterson, Vice-President, Responsible Care, 613-237-6215 Ext. 234
Membership: 60+; *Member Profile:* Companies that manufacture or formulate chemicals, with a commitment to ethics & codes; Companies that directly manage chemicals; Companies that supply goods or services to the chemical industry; Responsible care partnership associations & responsible care supporting associations
Activities: Communicating values & concerns of the chemcial producing industry to member companies, governments, & the public; Supporting & sharing successful practices; Promoting improved safety & environmental performance;
Publications:
• Catalyst

Frequency: Quarterly; *Accepts Advertising*; *Editor:* Michael Bourque
Profile: Feature articles & departments about the management of chemicals throughout their life cycle

Alberta Regional Office
#223, 97 - 53017 Range Rd., Androssan AB T8E 2M3
Tel: 780-922-5902
Chief Officer(s):
Al Schulz, Regional Director
alschulz@telusplanet.net

British Columbia Regional Office
#13, 1238 Cardero St., Vancouver BC V6G 2H6
Tel: 778-888-6461
Chief Officer(s):
Lorna Young, Regional Director
lyoung@canadianchemistry.ca

Ontario Regional Office
41 Cornerbrook Dr., Toronto ON M3A 1H5
Tel: 416-445-9353
Chief Officer(s):
Norm Huebel, Regional Director
nhuebel@sympatico.ca

Québec Regional Office
8910, rue Deschambault, Saint-Léonard QC H1R 2C4
Tel: 514-324-1308
Chief Officer(s):
Jules Lauzon, Regional Director
jlauzon@videotron.ca

Chesley & District Chamber of Commerce
PO Box 406, 106 - 1st Ave. South, Chesley ON N0G 1L0
Tel: 519-363-9837
townofchesley.com
Overview: A small local organization
Chief Officer(s):
Stacy Charlton, Treasurer
Membership: 60; *Fees:* $85; *Member Profile:* Business owners

Chess & Math Association (CMA) / Association échecs et maths (AEM)
3423 St. Denis St., Montréal QC H2X 3L2
Tel: 514-845-8352; *Fax:* 514-845-8810
www.chess-math.org
Overview: A medium-sized national organization founded in 1985
Chief Officer(s):
Larry Bevand, Executive Director
Finances: *Annual Operating Budget:* $1.5 Million-$3 Million
Staff Member(s): 20; 25 volunteer(s)
Membership: 10,000; *Fees:* $15 institutional; $15 student; $15 individual

Ottawa Branch
250 Bank St., Ottawa ON K2P 1X4
Tel: 613-565-3662; *Fax:* 613-565-5190
Chief Officer(s):
Paul Maisonneuve, Manager

Toronto Branch
701 Mount Pleasant Rd., Toronto ON M4S 2N4
Tel: 416-488-5506; *Fax:* 416-486-4637
www.chess-math.org

Chess Federation of Canada / Fédération canadienne des échecs
#356, 17A-218 Silvercreek Pkwy. North, Guelph ON N1H 8E8
Tel: 519-265-1789
info@chess.ca
www.chess.ca
www.linkedin.com/groups?home=&gid=3949499
www.facebook.com/163031117086480
twitter.com/ChessCanada
www.youtube.com/ChessCanada
Overview: A medium-sized national charitable organization founded in 1872
Mission: To coordinate chess play across Canada
Affliation(s): Fédération internationale des échecs
Chief Officer(s):
Vlad Drkulec, President
president@chess.ca
Michael von Keitz, Executive Director
Staff Member(s): 2
Membership: 1,866; *Fees:* Schedule available; *Committees:* Kalev Pugi Fund; National Appeals; Tournament Director & Organizer; Olympic; Olympic Fundraising; Youth

Chester Municipal Chamber of Commerce
PO Box 831, #13, 4171 Hwy. 3, Chester NS B0J 1J0
Tel: 902-275-4709; *Fax:* 902-275-4629
info@chesterns.com
www.chesterns.com
www.facebook.com/138252302853117
Overview: A small local organization founded in 1935
Chief Officer(s):
Jo-Ann Grant, President
Finances: *Annual Operating Budget:* Less than $50,000; *Funding Sources:* Membership dues; fundrasing
Membership: 200+; *Fees:* $45 retired/non-profit; $90-$360 business

Chester Municipal Heritage Society (CMHS)
PO Box 628, 133 Central St., Chester NS B0J 1J0
Tel: 902-275-3826
lordlyhouse@ns.aliantzinc.ca
chester-municipal-heritage-society.ca
www.facebook.com/180126828677505
www.youtube.com/user/lordlymuseum
Overview: A small local charitable organization founded in 1981
Mission: To encourage & promote interest in & preservation of local heritage & our built heritage
Member of: Federation of the Nova Scotian Heritage
Affliation(s): South Shore Tourism Association; Chester Chamber of Commerce
Chief Officer(s):
Carol Nauss, Chair
Finances: *Funding Sources:* Fundraising; donations
Membership: *Fees:* $15 individual; $25 family; $100 supporter; $250 contributer; $500 patron; $1000 benefactor; *Committees:* Fundraising; Newsletter/Parkbookings; Art Show/Christmas Show; Membership; Auction; Nominating; Acquisitions/Research/Program; Building
Activities: Ooperates Lordly House Museum; House & Harbour Tour

Cheticamp Association for Community Living (CACL)
PO Box 550, Cheticamp NS B0E 1H0
www.cheticampcacl.ca
Overview: A small local organization overseen by Nova Scotia Association for Community Living
Mission: To help each client to reach his or her potential; to encourage & facilitate the growth of each client; to integrate clients into the community
Member of: DIRECTIONS Council for Vocational Services Society; Nova Scotia Association for Community Living
Chief Officer(s):
Bill Barnet, President
Jeanne Chiasson, Executive Director/Manager
Activities: Green Door workshop; woodworking studio; residential services; L'Attique second hand clothing store

Chetwynd & District Chamber of Commerce
PO Box 870, 5217 North Access Rd., Chetwynd BC V0C 1J0
Tel: 250-788-3345; *Fax:* 250-788-3655
manager@chetwyndchamber.ca
www.chetwyndchamber.ca
Overview: A small local organization
Member of: BC Chamber of Commerce
Chief Officer(s):
Tonia Richter, Executive Director
Sheree Smith, President
Finances: *Annual Operating Budget:* Less than $50,000; *Funding Sources:* Fees for service; fundraising
2 volunteer(s)
Membership: 82

Les Chevaliers de Colomb du Québec / Knights of Columbus of Québec
670, av Chambly, Saint-Hyacinthe QC J2S 6V4
Tél: 450-768-0616; *Téléc:* 450-768-1660
Ligne sans frais: 866-893-3681
conact@chevaliersdecolomb.com
www.chevaliersdecolomb.com
Aperçu: *Dimension:* moyenne; *Envergure:* provinciale
Mission: Un groupe d'entraide et une société fraternelle, qui unit des hommes de foi; l'ordre n'est pas rattaché à la structure juridique de l'Église catholique mais c'est un ordre de laïcs catholiques et exclusivement masculin
Membre: 104 000 individus

Les Chevaliers de Colomb du Québec, District No 37, Conseil 5198
124, rue des Forces Armées, Chibougamau QC G8P 2K5
Tél: 418-748-2411
dd37cc@hotmail.com
www.chevaliersdecolomb.com
Aperçu: *Dimension:* petite; *Envergure:* locale
Membre(s) du bureau directeur:
Danny Bouchard, Député de district, 418-748-6482
Gaston Deroy, Grand Chevalier

Chez les français de L'Anse-à-Canards inc.
CP 337, RR#1, l'Anse-à-Canards NL A0N 1R0
Tél: 709-642-5498; *Téléc:* 709-642-5294
cfac_bdb@hotmail.com
www.francotnl.ca/CFAC
Aperçu: *Dimension:* petite; *Envergure:* locale; fondée en 1972
Mission: S'engage à préserver et à promouvoir la langue et la culture française des communautés de L'Anse-à-Canards et de Maison d'Hiver.
Affliation(s): La Fédération des francophones de Terre-Neuve et du Labrador; L'Association francophone du Labrador.
Membre(s) du bureau directeur:
Bernard Félix, Président
Robert Félix, Agent culturel
Activités: Le Jour de l'Armistice; La Chandeleur; festival folklorique

Chezzetcook Historical Society
PO Box 7, Head Chezzetcook NS B0J 1N0
Tel: 902-827-4177
www.rootsweb.ancestry.com/~nschezhs
Overview: A small local organization founded in 1974
Mission: To preserve articles or information of historical value from East Chezzetcook, Porter's Lake, West Chezzetcook & Seaforth areas
Member of: Federation of the Nova Scotian Heritage

Chicken Farmers of Canada (CFC) / Les Producteurs de poulet du Canada
#1007, 350 Sparks St., Ottawa ON K1R 7S8
Tel: 613-241-2800; *Fax:* 613-241-5999
cfc@chicken.ca
chicken.ca
www.facebook.com/chickenfarmers
twitter.com/chickenfarmers
www.youtube.com/user/chickenfarmers1
Previous Name: Canadian Chicken Marketing Agency
Overview: A large national organization founded in 1978
Mission: To build an evidence-based, consumer driven Canadian chicken industry that provides opportunities for profitable growth for all stakeholders
Member of: Canadian Federation of Agriculture
Chief Officer(s):
Dave Janzen, Chair
Mike Dungate, Executive Director
mdungate@chicken.ca
Lisa Bishop-Spencer, Manager, Communications
lbishop@chicken.ca
Finances: *Annual Operating Budget:* $500,000-$1.5 Million
Staff Member(s): 22
Membership: 2,700 Canadian chicken producers; *Committees:* Executive; Finance; Policy; Production; Consumer Relations; Representatives
Publications:
• Allocation Calendar [a publication of Chicken Farmers of Canada]
Type: Calendar; *Frequency:* Annually
Profile: Information on the chicken industry
• Chicken Farmer Newsletter [a publication of Chicken Farmers of Canada]
Type: Newsletter; *Frequency:* Monthly
• Chicken Farmers of Canada 5-year Strategic Plan
Type: Report
• Chicken Farmers of Canada Annual Report
Type: Yearbook; *Frequency:* Annually
• Chicken Fax/Repères [a publication of Chicken Farmers of Canada]
Type: Newsletter; *Frequency:* Monthly
Profile: Canadian chicken market trends
• Data Booklet [a publication of Chicken Farmers of Canada]
Type: Booklet; *Frequency:* Annually
Profile: Yearly overview of the Canadian chicken industry
• Geneva Watch [a publication of Chicken Farmers of Canada]
Type: Newsletter; *Frequency:* Weekly; *Editor:* Charles Akande
Profile: Information on World Trade Organization negoiations involving agriculture; published by Dairy Farmers of Canada, Chicken Farmers of Canada, EggFarmers of Canada, Turkey Farmers of Canada and Canadian Hatching Egg Producers

• Good Business, Great Chicken [a publication of Chicken Farmers of Canada]
Type: Guide
Profile: Information on the chicken industry
• Storage Stocks [a publication of Chicken Farmers of Canada]
Type: Report; *Frequency:* Monthly
Profile: Information on Canadian chicken storage stocks

Chicken Farmers of New Brunswick / Les Éleveurs de poulets du Nouveau-Brunswick
#103, 277 Main St., Fredericton NB E3A 1E1
Tel: 506-452-8085; *Fax:* 506-451-2121
nbchicken@nb.aibn.com
Overview: A medium-sized provincial organization overseen by Chicken Farmers of Canada
Mission: To control the marketing of chickens in the area within its jurisdiction; To cooperate with similar boards in other areas; To stimulate & increase the demand for chickens produced in New Brunswick; To improve the process of marketing
Chief Officer(s):
Marc Cormier, Chair
Louis Martin, Secretary-Manager
5 volunteer(s)

Chicken Farmers of Newfoundland & Labrador
PO Box 8098, St. John's NL A1B 3M9
Tel: 709-747-1493; *Fax:* 709-747-0544
www.nlchicken.com
Previous Name: Newfoundland Chicken Marketing Board
Overview: A medium-sized provincial organization overseen by Chicken Farmers of Canada
Member of: Chicken Farmers of Canada
Chief Officer(s):
Ron Walsh, Executive Director
rwalsh@nlchicken.com
Finances: *Annual Operating Budget:* $250,000-$500,000

Chicken Farmers of Nova Scotia
531 Main St., Kentville NS B4N 1L4
Tel: 902-681-7400; *Fax:* 902-681-7401
chicken@nschicken.com
www.nschicken.com
Overview: A medium-sized provincial organization founded in 1966 overseen by Chicken Farmers of Canada
Finances: *Funding Sources:* Levy system for chicken farmers
Membership: 84; *Member Profile:* Chicken farmers in Nova Scotia

Chicken Farmers of Saskatchewan (CFS)
Rumley Building, #201, 224 Pacific Ave., Saskatoon SK S7K 1N9
Tel: 306-242-3611; *Fax:* 306-242-3286
www.saskatchewanchicken.ca
Overview: A medium-sized provincial organization founded in 1966 overseen by Chicken Farmers of Canada
Affliation(s): Chicken Farmers of Canada
Chief Officer(s):
Gale Kellington, Office Manager
Gale@saskatchewanchicken.ca
Finances: *Funding Sources:* Levy system for chicken producers
Staff Member(s): 5
Membership: 70; *Committees:* Saskatchewan Chicken Industry Development Fund (SCIDF)

Chief Dan George Foundation
315 Dollarton Hwy., North Vancouver BC V7H 1B1
Tel: 604-924-2338; *Fax:* 604-924-2339
Overview: A small local organization

Chiefs of Ontario
#804, 111 Peter St., Toronto ON M5V 2H1
Tel: 416-597-1266; *Fax:* 416-597-8365
Toll-Free: 877-517-6527
www.chiefs-of-ontario.org
twitter.com/chiefsofontario
vimeo.com/chiefsofontario;
www.flickr.com/photos/chiefsofontario
Overview: A medium-sized provincial organization
Mission: To enable the political leadership to discuss regional, provincial & national priorities affecting First Nation people in Ontario & to provide a unified voice on these issues.
Affliation(s): Assembly of First Nations
Chief Officer(s):
Pam Montour, Executive Director
executive.director@coo.org
Staff Member(s): 33

Child & Family Services of Timmins & District *See* North Eastern Ontario Family & Children's Services

Child & Family Services of Western Manitoba (C&FS Western)
800 McTavish Ave., Brandon MB R7A 7L4
Tel: 204-726-6030; *Fax:* 204-726-6775
Toll-Free: 800-483-8980
info@cfswestern.mb.ca
www.cfswestern.mb.ca
Previous Name: Children's Aid Society of Western Manitoba
Overview: A medium-sized local charitable organization founded in 1899
Mission: To ensure children are safe in strong loving families within caring communities
Member of: Child Welfare League of Canada
Chief Officer(s):
Patrick Hogan, President
Candace Kowalchuk, Speicalist, Human Resources, 204-726-6030
hr@cfswestern.mb.ca
Finances: *Annual Operating Budget:* Less than $50,000; *Funding Sources:* Government; United Way; private donations; rural campaigns; service clubs; foundations
Staff Member(s): 160; 46 volunteer(s)
Membership: 120; *Fees:* $10/1 yr.; $25/3 yrs.
Activities: Child protection services; family counselling; family support worker program; Family Resource Centre; family aid program; shared service programs; summer programs; parent-child home program; preschool enrichment; Victoria Day Care; unmarried parent service; sexual abuse treatment; adoption; post-adoption; foster care; *Library*

Child & Parent Resource Institute (CPRI)
600 Sanatorium Rd., London ON N6H 3W7
Tel: 519-858-2774; *Fax:* 519-858-3913
Gillian.Kriter@ontario.ca
www.cpri.ca
Previous Name: Children's Psychiatric Research Institute
Overview: A medium-sized local organization founded in 1960
Mission: To enhance the quality of life of children & youth with complex mental health or developmental challenges; to assist their families so these children & youth can reach their full potential
Member of: Ontario Association of Children's Mental Health Centres
Chief Officer(s):
Anne Stark, Administrator
Finances: *Annual Operating Budget:* Greater than $5 Million
Staff Member(s): 400; 80 volunteer(s)
Activities: *Speaker Service:* Yes; *Library:* Dr. Joseph Pozsonyi Memorial Library; Open to public

Child & Youth Care Association of Alberta (CYCAA)
#204, 12013 - 76 St., Edmonton AB T5B 2C9
Tel: 780-448-7254; *Fax:* 780-448-9159
cycaa@telus.net
www.cycaa.com
www.facebook.com/ChildAndYouthCareAssociationOfAlberta
twitter.com/CYCAA1
Overview: A small provincial organization founded in 1972
Mission: To promote, improve & maintain progressive standards of child/youth care services; To encourage an active public interest in child/youth care services
Member of: Alberta Association of Services for Children & Families
Affliation(s): Council of Canadian Child & Youth Care Associations
Chief Officer(s):
Pat Foran, President
Finances: *Annual Operating Budget:* Less than $50,000
Staff Member(s): 3; 20 volunteer(s)
Membership: 750; *Fees:* $55 full member; $45 associate; $115 certified member; $100 agency member; *Member Profile:* Child & youth care workers, not daycare workers
Activities: Certification program for child & youth care workers; *Library*
Awards:
• Scholarships for CYC students at designated colleges (Scholarship)
• Child & Youth Care Worker of the Year (Award)

Child & Youth Care Association of Newfoundland & Labrador (CYCANAL)
PO Box 632, St. John's NL A1C 5K8
Tel: 709-368-6125; *Fax:* 709-739-1857
cycanl@nl.rogers.com
www.cycanl.ca
Overview: A small provincial organization
Mission: To advocate for child & youth in general &, specifically, those in care; to provide members with up-to-date information on developments in the field of Child & Youth Care through newsletters & journals; To promote the field of Child & Youth Care as a profession through the development of standards & ethics for those working in the field; To provide members with a forum to network with others in the field
Chief Officer(s):
Charles Thomases, President
Membership: *Fees:* $30 full membership; $15 student membership; *Committees:* Public Relations; Standards; Finance/Fundraising; Newsletter

The Child Abuse Survivor Monument Project (CASMP)
274 Rhodes Ave., Toronto ON M4L 3A3
Tel: 416-469-4764; *Fax:* 416-963-8892
mci@irvingstudios.com
www.irvingstudios.com/child_abuse_survivor_monument
www.facebook.com/ChildAbuseMonument
twitter.com/ChildAbuseMnumt
www.youtube.com/user/ChildAbuseMonument
Also Known As: Survivor Monument Project
Overview: A small local charitable organization founded in 1995
Mission: To build a memorial monument for & by survivors of child abuse to assist with the personal & social healing of the ravages of child abuse
Affliation(s): Children's Aid Foundation
Chief Officer(s):
Michael C. Irving, Artistic Director
Finances: *Funding Sources:* Private donations; government grants
Activities: *Speaker Service:* Yes; *Library:* CASMP Library; by appointment

Child Care Advocacy Association of Canada (CCAAC) / Association canadienne pour la promotion des services de garde à l'enfance (ACPSGE)
#704, 151 Slater St., Ottawa ON K1P 5H3
Toll-Free: 866-878-3096
info@ccaac.ca
www.ccaac.ca
Previous Name: Canadian Day Care Advocacy Association
Overview: A medium-sized national licensing organization founded in 1982
Mission: To work toward expanding the child care system & improving its quality; To advocate for the development of an affordable, comprehensive, high-quality, not-for-profit child care system that is supported by public funds & accessible to every Canadian family who wishes to use it
Member of: National Action Committee on the Status of Women
Affliation(s): Canadian Labour Congress; Public Service Alliance; Canadian Union of Public Employees
Chief Officer(s):
Ann McCrorie, Chair, 306-531-4833
Sue Delanoy, Coordinator, 306-956-1796
suedelanoy@kaphouse.ca
Membership: 1,000; *Fees:* $15 individual/family; $50 organization/group; $5 full-time student
Activities: *Speaker Service:* Yes

Child Care Connection Nova Scotia (CCCNS)
#100, 1200 Tower Rd., Halifax NS B3H 4K6
Tel: 902-423-8199; *Fax:* 902-492-8106
Toll-Free: 800-565-8199
Other Communication: resource@cccns.org
info@cccns.org
www.cccns.org
Overview: A small provincial organization founded in 1989
Mission: To provide resources & support to early childhood practitioners throughout Nova Scotia
Chief Officer(s):
Barb Bigelow, Co-Chair
Donna Stapleton, Co-Chair
Elaine Ferguson, Executive Director
Pat McCormack, Coordinator, Office & Resources
Finances: *Funding Sources:* Nova Scotia Department of Community Services; Advertising, publication, & product sales; Income from events
Staff Member(s): 2

Membership: *Member Profile:* Early childhood practitioners in Nova Scotia
Activities: Providing professional development activities; Raising the public image of early childhood practice; Engaging in advocacy activities; Producing fact sheets; *Library:* Child Care Connection Resource Library
Publications:
• A Best Practices Approach to Regulated Child Care within a Framework that Supports Good Outcomes for Children
Author: E. Ferguson; K. Flanagan Rochon
• Child Care Administrator Credentialing In Canada, A Work In Progress Appendix A; Appendix B; & Appendix C
Author: T. McCormick Ferguson; E. Ferguson
• Child Care Centre Directory
Type: Directory
Profile: Listings of licensed centres in Nova Scotia, including information such as address, capacity, children's age range, number of staff, & type of program
• Child Care Connection Nova Scotia Report to Stakeholders
Type: Yearbook; *Frequency:* Annually
• ConnectioNS [a publication of Child Care Connection Nova Scotia]
Type: Journal; *Frequency:* 2-3 pa; *Accepts Advertising*; *Editor:* E. Elaine Ferguson *ISSN:* 0843-6304
Profile: Distributed to Nova Scotia's child care centres & other organizations & individuals
• Maximizing Child Care Services: The Role of Owners & Boards
Author: T. McCormick Ferguson; E. Ferguson
• Retention & Recruitment Challenges in Canadian Child Care
Author: Elaine Ferguson; Connie Miller
• Toward a Best Practices Framework for Licensing Child Care Facilities in Canada
Author: E. Ferguson; K. Flanagan Rochon

Child Care Providers Resource Network of Ottawa-Carleton

#275, 30 Colonnade Rd., Ottawa ON K2E 7J6
Tel: 613-749-5211; *Fax:* 613-749-6650
info@ccprn.com
www.ccprn.com
www.facebook.com/234504449898448?ref=ts
www.youtube.com/childcareproviders/
Overview: A small provincial organization
Mission: The Child Care Providers Resource Network of Ottawa-Carleton, is a non-profit, charitable organization committed to providing support, information, training and resources to individuals who offer child care in a home setting.
Chief Officer(s):
Doreen Cowin, Executive Director
doreen@ccprn.com
Activities: Workshops; Children's events; Bi-monthly newsletter; *Library:* Resource Library

Child Development Centre Society of Fort St. John & District

10417 - 106th Ave., Fort St John BC V1J 2M8
Tel: 250-785-3200; *Fax:* 250-785-3202
info@cdcfsj.ca
www.cdcfsj.ca
Overview: A small local charitable organization founded in 1973
Mission: To promote the treatment & education of children with special needs, to ensure that they & their families are effectively & locally served with dignity & respect.
Member of: BC Association for Child Development & Intervention
Affiliation(s): Cerebral Palsy Association of British Columbia
Chief Officer(s):
Andy Ackerman, President
Penny Gagnon, Executive Director
Finances: *Funding Sources:* Regional government; private & corporate donors
Activities: Operation of the Child Development Centre (CDC) with programs including physiotherapy, speech therapy, occupational therapy, Early Learning Program

Child Evangelism Fellowship of Canada

PO Box 165, Stn. Main, 337 Henderson Hwy., Winnipeg MB R3C 2G9
Tel: 204-943-2774; *Fax:* 204-943-9967
Toll-Free: 866-943-2774
info@cefcanada.org
www.cefcanada.org
Also Known As: CEF Canada
Overview: A medium-sized national charitable organization founded in 1937
Mission: CEF Canada is a bible-centred organization of born-again believers whose purpose is to evangelize & disciple children with the gospel of Jesus Christ.
Member of: Canadian Council of Christian Charities
Affiliation(s): Child Evangelism Fellowship Inc.; CEF of Nations
Chief Officer(s):
Jerry Hanson, National Director
jhanson@cefcanada.org
Finances: *Annual Operating Budget:* $500,000-$1.5 Million; *Funding Sources:* Individual, corporate & church donations
Staff Member(s): 45; 200 volunteer(s)
Membership: 8
Activities: Children's Ministries Institute; offers courses/programs, materials & training for Christian education among children

Child Evangelism Fellowship - Atlantic
PO Box 134, Moncton NB E1C 8R9
Tel: 506-378-4775
Chief Officer(s):
Ron Wiebe, Provincial Director
rwiebe@cefcanada.org

Child Evangelism Fellowship of Alberta
2115 - 5 Ave. NW, Calgary AB T2N 0S6
Fax: 800-561-0686
Toll-Free: 800-561-5315
info@cefalberta.org
www.cefalberta.org
www.facebook.com/cefalberta
Chief Officer(s):
Jerry Durston, Provincial Director
jerry.durston@cefministries.org

Child Evangelism Fellowship of British Columbia
#204, 18515 - 53 Ave., Surrey BC V3S 7A4
Tel: 604-576-7796; *Fax:* 604-582-0491
Toll-Free: 855-576-7796
info@cefbc.com
www.cefbc.com
Chief Officer(s):
Dennis Quin, Provincial Director
dennisq@cefbc.com

Child Evangelism Fellowship of Manitoba
179 Henderson Hwy., Winnipeg MB R2L 1L5
Tel: 204-663-3300; *Fax:* 204-667-1026
cefmb@mts.net
cefmanitoba.org
Chief Officer(s):
Matthew Maniate, Provincial Director

Child Evangelism Fellowship of Ontario
335 Robinson Rd., RR #4, Brantford ON N3T 5L7
Tel: 519-751-1233; *Fax:* 519-751-2233
info@cefontario.org
www.cefontario.org
www.facebook.com/139808322733114
Chief Officer(s):
Rob Lukings, Provincial Director
rlukings@cefontario.org

Child Evangelism Fellowship of Saskatchewan
74 Marquis Cres., Regina SK S4S 6J9
Tel: 306-584-9622; *Fax:* 306-584-1308
info@cefsask.org
www.cefsask.org
www.facebook.com/cefsask
twitter.com/cefsask
Chief Officer(s):
Jerry Durston, Provincial Director
jdurston@cefsask.org

Québec
2225, rue Mistral, Brossard QC J4Y 2T3
Tél: 450-926-3357
info@aeecefquebec.org
aeecefquebec.org
Chief Officer(s):
Mary Porter, Directrice
Jenne Phillips, Directrice

Child Find British Columbia

#208, 2722 Fifth St., Victoria BC V8T 4B2
Tel: 250-382-7311; *Fax:* 250-382-0227
Toll-Free: 888-689-3463
childvicbc@shaw.ca
childfindbc.com
Overview: A small provincial charitable organization founded in 1984 overseen by Child Find Canada Inc.
Mission: To assist in the search & location of missing children, providing support to law enforcement & families; To educate & prevent the abduction & exploitation of children & provide awareness
Member of: Association of Missing & Exploited Children's Organizations; Chamber of Commerce
Chief Officer(s):
Steve Orcherton, Executive Director
Finances: *Annual Operating Budget:* $100,000-$250,000; *Funding Sources:* Fundraising; sponsorships; grants & foundations
Staff Member(s): 3; 500 volunteer(s)
Activities: *Awareness Events:* Annual Michael Dunahee Dance, April; Fun Run, April; Green Ribbon Day, May 25; *Speaker Service:* Yes

Child Find Canada Inc. (CFC)

PO Box 237, Oakville MB R0H 0Y0
Tel: 204-870-1298
childcan@aol.com
Overview: A small national charitable organization founded in 1988
Mission: Supports provincial Child Find organizations in the location of & education in the prevention of missing children; increases national awareness of issues relating to missing children; advocates for the protection & rights of children.
Member of: Canadian Coalition for the Rights of Children; Association of Missing & Exploited Children (AMEC)
Finances: *Funding Sources:* Corporate & individual donations
Membership: 9 provincial offices; *Member Profile:* Over 18 years of age; police security clearance; references; application; personal suitability
Activities: Prevention & education material; child & baby identification kits

Child Find Manitoba *See* Canadian Centre for Child Protection

Child Find Newfoundland/Labrador

#217, 31 Peet St., St. John's NL A1B 3W8
Tel: 709-738-4400
Toll-Free: 800-387-7962
childnfld@aol.com
www.childfind.ca
Overview: A medium-sized provincial organization overseen by Child Find Canada Inc.
Mission: To prevent missing children; To support the search for missing children

Child Find Nova Scotia

PO Box 523, #110, 1568 Hollis Street, Halifax NS B3J 2R7
Tel: 902-454-2030; *Fax:* 902-429-6749
Toll-Free: 800-682-9006
childns@aol.com
www.childfind.ns.ca/
Overview: A medium-sized provincial organization
Chief Officer(s):
Lynn McMillan, President
Dianna Cann, Executive Director

Child Find Ontario

#303B, 75 Front St. East, Toronto ON M5E 1V9
Tel: 416-987-9684
Toll-Free: 866-543-8477
mail@childfindontario.ca
www.childfindontario.ca
Overview: A small provincial charitable organization founded in 1983 overseen by Child Find Canada Inc.
Mission: To assist in the search & recovery process of missing children
Affiliation(s): Ontario Community Links (1-800-447-6047); local police stns, including LaSalle Police Service & Hamilton Police Service Community Policing Centres
Finances: *Funding Sources:* Donations
Activities: Fingerprinting events; information booths; abduction education; assistance in search for missing children; *Speaker Service:* Yes

Northern Ontario Office
303 York St., Sudbury ON P3E 2A5
Tel: 705-671-9888

Child Find PEI Inc.

8 Belvedere Ave., Charlottetown PE C1A 6A1
Tel: 902-566-5935; *Fax:* 902-368-1389
Toll-Free: 800-387-7962
childfind@pei.aibn.com
www.childfindpei.com
www.facebook.com/459667334088816
Overview: A small provincial charitable organization founded in 1988 overseen by Child Find Canada Inc.

Mission: To assist in the location of missing children; to increase awareness of the problem of missing children; to teach ways to prevent abduction; to provide assistance & support to families of a missing child.
Member of: Association of Missing & Exploited Children's Organizations
Affliation(s): PEI Amber Alert
Chief Officer(s):
Megan DeCoste, President
Staff Member(s): 1; 50 volunteer(s)
Activities: "All About Me ID" (fingerprinting clinics), educational videos, distribution of brochures & pamphlets, public displays at community events, & distribution of missing children posters; *Awareness Events:* Green Ribbon of Hope Campaign, May; *Speaker Service:* Yes; *Library* Open to public

Child Find Saskatchewan Inc.

#202, 3502 Taylor St. East, Saskatoon SK S7H 5H9
Tel: 306-955-0070; *Fax:* 306-373-1311
Toll-Free: 800-513-3463
childfind@childfind.sk.ca
www.childfind.sk.ca
www.facebook.com/pages/Child-Find-Saskatchewan/121799723998
Overview: A small provincial charitable organization founded in 1984 overseen by Child Find Canada Inc.
Mission: To locate missing & abducted children & reunite them with their lawful parent or guardian; To increase public awareness of the need to protect children; To educate both parents & child on street proofing technology & to support families of missing children
Affliation(s): Chamber of Commerce
Chief Officer(s):
Phyllis Hallatt, President
Finances: *Annual Operating Budget:* $100,000-$250,000; *Funding Sources:* Private & corporate donations
Staff Member(s): 3; 50 volunteer(s)
Membership: 1-99
Activities: All About Me ID; I'm OK; education programs on child personal safety, streetproofing, runaways & prevention of abductions; national picture distribution; poster distribution; *Awareness Events:* Missing Children's Month, May; *Speaker Service:* Yes; *Library* Open to public by appointment

CHILD Foundation (CHILD)

U.B.C. Campus, #201, 2150 Western Parkway, Vancouver BC V6T 1V6
Tel: 604-736-0645; *Fax:* 604-228-0066
Toll-Free: 877-672-4453
ch_i_l_d@telus.net
www.child.ca
Also Known As: Children with Intestinal & Liver Disorders
Overview: A small provincial charitable organization founded in 1995
Mission: To help an almost forgotten group of youngsters who suffer from incurable digestive disorders such as Crohn's Disease, Ulcerative Colitis & related IBD (intestinal & bowel disorders) & liver disorders; To find a cure through research for these diseases
Member of: Vancouver Board of Trade
Affliation(s): CHILD Foundation USA
Chief Officer(s):
Grace M. McCarthy, Chair
Mary Parsons, President & CEO
J. Lindsay Gordon, Governor
Finances: *Annual Operating Budget:* $100,000-$250,000
Staff Member(s): 2; 75 volunteer(s)
Membership: 75; *Member Profile:* Business leaders & members of families of Crohn's or Colitis patients
Activities: *Awareness Events:* Fashion for CHILD; Snowbirds Fly for CHILD; Doormen's Dinner for CHILD; Golf for CHILD; *Speaker Service:* Yes

Child Haven International / Accueil international pour l'enfance

19014 - 7th Conc., RR#1, Maxville ON K0C 1T0
Tel: 613-527-2829; *Fax:* 613-527-1118
fred@childhaven.ca
www.childhaven.ca
Overview: A small international charitable organization founded in 1985
Mission: To assist any child of any nationality who needs in-country care or a private family home; To provide institutions & cottage or village industries for giving training in handcrafts, music, agricultural methods; To promote the integrity of the family by providing help for adolescents or adults who have special needs & by community development & medical aid projects
Affliation(s): Child Haven International - USA, India, Nepal
Finances: *Annual Operating Budget:* $250,000-$500,000; *Funding Sources:* Individual & foundation donations
Staff Member(s): 4; 100 volunteer(s)
Membership: *Member Profile:* Gandhian organization: vegetarian, no regard for caste, race, gender
Activities: Operates three homes in India & one in Nepal for destitute women & children; support groups in Ottawa, Glengarry County, Cornwall, Toronto, Vancouver, Montréal, Calgary, Hamilton, Victoria & Waterloo; *Internships:* Yes; *Speaker Service:* Yes

Child Welfare League of Canada (CWLC) / Ligue pour le bien-être de l'enfance du Canada (LBEC)

226 Argyle Ave., Ottawa ON K2P 1B9
Tel: 613-235-4412; *Fax:* 613-235-7616
info@cwlc.ca
www.cwlc.ca
www.facebook.com/CWLC.LBEC
Overview: A large national charitable organization founded in 1994
Mission: To provide public education on the needs of all children, youth & their families through research, information & other services directed toward enhancing & improving public awareness; to facilitate the development of standards in services to children, youth & their families; to encourage excellence in the delivery of these services
Member of: Canadian Coalition for the Rights of Children
Affliation(s): Child Welfare League of America
Chief Officer(s):
Mike DeGagné, Chair
Gordon Phaneuf, MSW, RSW, Chief Executive Officer
gord@cwlc.ca
Finances: *Annual Operating Budget:* $250,000-$500,000; *Funding Sources:* Membership dues; consultation fees; projects; conference income; sustaining grant
Staff Member(s): 8
Membership: 135 organizations; *Fees:* Schedule available; *Member Profile:* Professionals who support the welfare & protection of children
Activities: Training programs for professional staff, caregivers, volunteers; information resource for public & organizations; program reviews; looking after children program; Centre of Excellence for Child Welfare; *Awareness Events:* Atlantic Canada Child Welfare Forum; *Internships:* Yes; *Speaker Service:* Yes; *Rents Mailing List:* Yes; *Library:* Canadian Resource Centre on Children & Youth; Open to public
Awards:
• Youth Achievement Award (Award)
Honours a young person (under 21) who is either in care or has left care, & has demonstrated commitment to self-improvement & contributed to the positive image of youth
• Advocacy Award (Award)
Awarded to an individual or organization that has made a positive impact on public opinion regarding child welfare in Canada
• Research & Program Excellence Award (Award)
Honours excellence in child welfare research
• Children's Services Award (Award)
Awarded to a staff member or team that has shown commitment, creativity & dedication in their work in the child welfare sector
• Foster Parent Award (Award)
Awarded to a foster parent or foster family that has provided outstanding care to the children &/or youth placed in his or her care
Publications:
• The Child Welfare League of Canada Newsletter
Type: Newsletter

Childcare Resource & Research Unit

225 Brunswick Ave., Toronto ON M5S 2M6
Tel: 416-926-9264; *Fax:* 416-964-8239
contactus@childcarecanada.org
www.childcarecanada.org
www.facebook.com/112088688872463?sk=wall
twitter.com/childcarepolicy
Overview: A small national organization
Chief Officer(s):
Martha Friendly, Coordinator
mfriendly@childcarecanada.org

Childhood Cancer Canada Foundation

#801, 21 St. Clair Ave. East, Toronto ON M4T 1L9
Tel: 416-489-6440; *Fax:* 416-489-9812
Toll-Free: 800-363-1062
info@childhoodcancer.ca
www.childhoodcancer.ca
www.facebook.com/ChildhoodCancerCanada
twitter.com/chldhdcancercan
Overview: A large national organization founded in 1987
Mission: To help improve the lives of children suffering from cancer through family support programs; to fund cancer research
Chief Officer(s):
Megan Davidson, President & CEO
Finances: *Annual Operating Budget:* $1.5 Million-$3 Million

British Columbia Childhood Cancer Parent's Association
British Columbia Children's Hospital, #A127A, 4480 Oak St., Vancouver BC V6H 3B8
Tel: 604-875-2345

Candlelighters Newfoundland & Labrador
PO Box 5846, St. John's NL A1C 5X3
Tel: 709-745-4448
Toll-Free: 866-745-4448
info@Candlelightersnl.ca
www.candlelightersnl.ca
www.facebook.com/CandlelightersNL
twitter.com/CandlelighterNL
Chief Officer(s):
Amanada Kinsman, Coordinator, Provincial Family Program
coordinator@candlelightersnl.ca

Manitoba - Candlelighters Childhood Cancer Support Group
PO Box 350, RR#1, Winkler MB R6W 4A1
e-mail: support@manitobacandlelighters.ca
www.manitobacandlelighters.ca
Chief Officer(s):
Denis Foidart, Chair, 204-737-2684
denlis@wiband.ca

ON - Candlelighters Simcoe
6 Emily Ct., Barrie ON L4N 6B4
Tel: 705-737-4296; *Fax:* 705-737-4836
Chief Officer(s):
Barbara Johnson, Coordinator
albarbjohnson@sympatico.ca

SK - Candlelighters - Prince Albert
350 - 30th St. East, Prince Albert SK S6V 1Z4
Tel: 306-922-5101
Chief Officer(s):
Leslie Blacklock, Contact
leslie.blacklock@aodbt.com

SK - Regina Candlelighters
100 cardinal Cres., Regina SK S4S 4Y7
Tel: 306-529-3292
sask.candlelighters@sasktel.net
Chief Officer(s):
David Achter, Contact
Tangy Achter, Contact

Children & Family Services for York Region *See* York Region Children's Aid Society

Children of the World Adoption Society Inc. / Société d'adoption enfants du monde inc.

815 Lippmann Rd., 2nd. Fl., Laval QC H7S 1G3
Tel: 514-332-6332; *Fax:* 514-688-9339
Toll-Free: 800-381-3588
info@enfantsdumonde.org
www.enfantsdumonde.org
Overview: A small international organization founded in 1989
Mission: To help parents adopt children from foreign countries in compliance with the laws & traditions of those countries, in a spirit of humanitarian co-operation.
Affliation(s): Secrétariat à l'Adoption Internationale (SAI); Quebec Association of Youth Centres
Chief Officer(s):
Hélène Duval, President
Activities: International adoption

Lower St. Lawrence - Gaspé Office
PO Box 417, 7 Bossé St., Saint-Antonin QC G0L 2J0
Tel: 418-868-1889; *Fax:* 418-868-1889
Chief Officer(s):
Martin Desrosiers, Regional Coordinator
mdesros@videotron.ca

Saguenay - Lac-St-Jean Office
238, rue Olier, Chicoutimi QC G7G 4J3
Tel: 418-545-8536; *Fax:* 418-543-8211
Chief Officer(s):

Sylvie Tremblay, Regional Coordinator
boivinsylvieguy@videotron.ca

The Children's Aid Foundation of York Region
#19, 201 Millway Ave., Vaughan ON L4K 5K8
Tel: 905-738-8675
support@cafry.org
www.cafyr.org
Overview: A small local organization
Chief Officer(s):
Larry Garber, President

Children's Aid Society of Algoma / Société de l'aide à l'enfance d'Algoma
191 Northern Ave. East, Sault Ste Marie ON P6B 4H8
Tel: 705-949-0162; *Fax:* 705-949-4747
Toll-Free: 888-414-3571
www.algomacas.org
Overview: A small local organization founded in 1902
Mission: To protect the children of Algoma; to promote their well-being in a manner that reflects community standards & the spirit or legislation, while making efficient use of community & society resources
Member of: Ontario Association of Children's Aid Societies
Chief Officer(s):
Wes Moore, President
Kim Streich-Poser, Executive Director
Finances: *Annual Operating Budget:* Greater than $5 Million; *Funding Sources:* Ministry of Children and Youth Services
Membership: *Member Profile:* Resident of Algoma, 18 yrs. & over, who believe in the CAS mission statement

Blind River Officer
9 Lawton St., Blind River ON P0R 1B0
Tel: 705-356-1464; *Fax:* 705-356-0773

Elliot Lake Office
29 Manitoba Rd., Elliot Lake ON P5A 2A7
Tel: 705-848-8000; *Fax:* 705-848-5145

Hornepayne Office
#7, 8 - 2nd St., Hornepayne ON P0M 1Z0
Tel: 807-868-2624

Wawa Office
31 Algoma St., Wawa ON P0S 1K0
Tel: 705-856-2960; *Fax:* 705-856-7379

Children's Aid Society of Brant
PO Box 774, 70 Chatham St., Brantford ON N3T 5R7
Tel: 519-753-8681; *Fax:* 519-753-6090
Toll-Free: 888-753-8681; *TTY:* 519-753-8323
www.casbrant.ca
Also Known As: Brant Children's Aid Society
Overview: A small local organization founded in 1894
Mission: To work with families & the community to safeguard a permanent, nurturing family for all children at risk of abuse, neglect or abandonment.
Member of: Ontario Association of Children's Aid Societies
Affliation(s): Contact Brant; Lansdowne Children's Centre; St. Leonard's Community Services; Brant County Health Unit; Nova Vita Domestic Violence Prevention Services
Chief Officer(s):
Harry Emmott, President
Andrew Koster, Executive Director
Finances: *Annual Operating Budget:* Greater than $5 Million
Membership: *Fees:* $5; *Committees:* Finance/Governance; Strategic Services Directions

Children's Aid Society of Metropolitan Toronto *See* Children's Aid Society of Toronto

Children's Aid Society of Ottawa (CASO) / La Société de l'aide à l'enfance d'Ottawa
1602 Telesat Ct., Gloucester ON K1B 1B1
Tel: 613-747-7800; *Fax:* 613-747-4456; *TTY:* 613-742-1617
yourcasquestion@casott.on.ca
www.casott.on.ca
www.facebook.com/ottawacas
twitter.com/OttawaCas
www.youtube.com/user/casott123
Previous Name: Ottawa-Carleton Children's Aid Society
Overview: A small local charitable organization founded in 1893
Mission: To protect the children & youth of the Ottawa area from abuse & neglect, as regulated by Ontario's Ministry of Children & Youth Services & as governed by the Child & Family Services Act
Chief Officer(s):
Deborah Shortt, President
Finances: *Funding Sources:* Government of Ontario
Activities: Offering information sessions about foster care & adoption; *Awareness Events:* Child Abuse Prevention Month, October; Foster Family Week, October
Publications:
• Children's Aid Society of Ottawa Annual Report
Type: Yearbook; *Frequency:* Annually
• Community-Based Aboriginal-Inuit Agencies of Ottawa
• Positive Parenting
Profile: Resource also available in Arabic, Farsi, Chinese, Farsi, Somali, & Spanish
• What is Child Abuse

Children's Aid Society of Oxford County
92 Light St., Woodstock ON N4S 6H1
Tel: 519-539-6176; *Fax:* 519-537-6664
Toll-Free: 800-250-7010
info@casoxford.on.ca
www.casoxford.on.ca
Also Known As: CAS Oxford
Previous Name: Oxford Family & Child Services
Overview: A small local organization founded in 1895
Mission: The Society is committed to serving & promoting the best interests, protection & well-being of children, while supporting the autonomy, integrity & cultural diversity of families and communities
Member of: Ontario Association of Children's Aid Societies
Chief Officer(s):
Don Woolcott, President
Bruce Burbank, Executive Director
Finances: *Annual Operating Budget:* $1.5 Million-$3 Million; *Funding Sources:* Provincial government
Staff Member(s): 100; 75 volunteer(s)
Activities: Screening/training/counseling foster & adoptive parents; offering guidance to families for protecting children; investigates reports of possible abuse or neglect of children.; *Internships:* Yes; *Speaker Service:* Yes

Children's Aid Society of Simcoe County
#7, 60 Bell Farm Rd., Barrie ON L4M 5G6
Tel: 705-726-6587; *Fax:* 705-726-9788
Toll-Free: 800-461-4236
www.simcoecas.com
Overview: A medium-sized local organization
Mission: To provide guidance & counseling to families & protection for children
Chief Officer(s):
Susan Carmichael, Executive Director
Finances: *Annual Operating Budget:* Greater than $5 Million
140 volunteer(s)

Children's Aid Society of the City of Kingston & County of Frontenac
817 Division St., Kingston ON K7K 4C2
Tel: 613-545-3227; *Fax:* 613-542-4428
Toll-Free: 855-445-3227
info@facsfla.ca
www.casfrontenac.ca
www.facebook.com/502994029764357
twitter.com/FACSFLA
www.youtube.com/user/FACSFLA
Previous Name: Frontenac Children's Aid Society
Overview: A small local charitable organization founded in 1994
Mission: To provide professional child protection services which safeguard children, support nurturing environments & strengthen families.
Member of: Ontario Association of Children's Aid Societies
Affliation(s): Community Living Kingston; Kingston Interval House; Northern Frontenac Community Services; Frontenac Community Mental Health Services; Pathways for Children & Youth; Youth Diversion Program
Membership: *Member Profile:* Residents of Frontenac County
Activities: Coordination of foster care & adoption; investigation of possible child abuse or neglect; counseling; *Speaker Service:* Yes

Children's Aid Society of the District of Nipissing & Parry Sound / La Société d'aide à l'enfance Nipissing & Parry Sound
433 McIntyre St. West, North Bay ON P1B 2Z3
Tel: 705-472-0910
Toll-Free: 877-303-0910
www.parnipcas.org
Previous Name: Nipissing Children's Aid Society for the District of Nipissing & Parry Sound
Overview: A small local licensing charitable organization founded in 1907
Mission: To promote the well-being & protection of children & youth, and advocates for their fundamental entitlements.
Member of: Ontario Association of Children's Aid Societies
Chief Officer(s):
Rick Sapinski, President
boardpresident@parnipcas.org
Finances: *Funding Sources:* Ontario Ministry of Children & Youth Services; donations
Activities: Screening/training of foster parents; adoption services; assisting young mothers; counseling; Near North Youth Centre; providing services that maintain & enhance the natural environments of home & community, that will insure the safety of children, youth & the public; establishing partnerships with other community services

Children's Aid Society of the Districts of Sudbury & Manitoulin (CAS) / La Société d'aide à l'enfance des districts de Sudbury et de Manitoulin
#3, 319 Lasalle Blvd., Sudbury ON P3A 1W7
Tel: 705-566-3113; *Fax:* 705-521-7372
Toll-Free: 800-272-4334
www.casdsm.on.ca
Merged from: Sudbury Children's Aid Society; Manitoulin Children's Aid Society
Overview: A medium-sized local charitable organization founded in 1971
Mission: To build positive futures for our children
Member of: Ontario Association of Children's Aid Societies
Finances: *Funding Sources:* Provincial government
Activities: Publishes information pamphlets; volunteer recognition event; *Speaker Service:* Yes
Awards:
• Youth In Care Bursary (Award)
• Foster Parent Recognition Event (Award)

Chapleau Office
34 Birch St. East, Chapleau ON P0M 1K0
Tel: 705-864-0329; *Fax:* 705-864-2133

Manitoulin Office
9050 Hwy. 6, #E, Little Current ON P0P 1K0
Tel: 705-368-2810; *Fax:* 705-368-3200
Toll-Free: 800-461-3583

Children's Aid Society of the Region of Peel
West Tower, 6860 Century Ave., Mississauga ON L5N 2W5
Tel: 905-363-6131; *Fax:* 905-363-6133
Toll-Free: 888-700-0996
mail@peelcas.org
www.peelcas.org
Also Known As: Peel Children's Aid
Overview: A medium-sized local charitable organization founded in 1944
Mission: To protect children & strengthen families & communities through partnership
Chief Officer(s):
Paul Zarnke, Executive Director
Finances: *Annual Operating Budget:* $1.5 Million-$3 Million
Staff Member(s): 371; 250 volunteer(s)
Membership: 94; *Fees:* $5; *Member Profile:* Must work or live in the region of Peel
Activities: *Awareness Events:* Use Your Voice Campaign, Oct.; *Speaker Service:* Yes

Children's Aid Society of Toronto (CASMT)
30 Isabella St., Toronto ON M4Y 1N1
Tel: 416-924-4646
Other Communication: Foster Care Inquiries: fostering@TorontoCAS.ca
inquiries@torontocas.ca
www.casmt.on.ca
Previous Name: Children's Aid Society of Metropolitan Toronto
Overview: A large local organization founded in 1891
Mission: To protect children from emotional, sexual & physical harm by working with individual children & their families; to provide a high standard & continuity of substitute parental care for those children who cannot remain at home; to develop prevention programs
Member of: Ontario Association of Children's Aid Societies; Child Welfare League of Canada; Child Welfare League of America
Chief Officer(s):
Jessica Hill, Chair
David Rivard, CEO
Finances: *Annual Operating Budget:* Greater than $5 Million; *Funding Sources:* 100% provincial government
Staff Member(s): 624; 703 volunteer(s)

Membership: 1,318; *Fees:* $10; *Committees:* Audit & Risk; Diversity
Activities: *Internships:* Yes; *Speaker Service:* Yes
Publications:
• Communicate [a publication of the Children's Aid Society of Toronto]
Type: Newspaper

Children's Aid Society of Western Manitoba ***See*** Child & Family Services of Western Manitoba

Children's Arts Umbrella Association
1286 Cartwright St., Vancouver BC V6H 3R8
Tel: 604-681-5268; *Fax:* 604-681-5272
info@artsumbrella.com
www.artsumbrella.com
www.facebook.com/artsumbrella
twitter.com/artsumbrella
www.youtube.com/user/artsumbrellabc
Also Known As: Arts Umbrella
Overview: A small local charitable organization founded in 1979
Mission: Canada's visual & performing arts institute for young people of ages 2 to 19
Chief Officer(s):
Jamie Pitblado, Chair
Lucille Pacey, President & CEO
Finances: *Annual Operating Budget:* $3 Million-$5 Million; *Funding Sources:* Government; fundraising; private sector corporations
300 volunteer(s)

The Children's Broadcast Institute ***See*** Youth Media Alliance

Children's Cottage Society
845 McDougall Rd. NE, Calgary AB T2E 5A5
Tel: 403-283-4200; *Fax:* 403-283-4393; *Crisis Hot-Line:* 403-233-2273
www.childrenscottage.ab.ca
www.facebook.com/childrenscottagecalgary
twitter.com/childrnscottage
www.youtube.com/user/ChildrensCottage
Overview: A small local charitable organization
Mission: To prevent violence towards children & ensure a safe environment for them
Chief Officer(s):
Patty Kilgallon, Executive Director, pkilgallon@childrenscottage.ab.ca
Finances: *Annual Operating Budget:* $100,000-$250,000; *Funding Sources:* Provincial & municipal governments; foundation grants; donations; fundraising
Staff Member(s): 16; 1670 volunteer(s)

Children's Education Funds Inc. (CEFI)
3221 North Service Rd., Burlington ON L7N 3G2
Tel: 905-331-8377; *Fax:* 905-331-9977
Toll-Free: 800-246-1203
www.cefi.ca
Overview: A medium-sized national organization founded in 1990
Mission: To help build a better society through the education of children.

Children's Health Foundation of Vancouver Island
2390 Arbutus Rd., Victoria BC V8N 1V7
Tel: 250-519-6977; *Fax:* 250-519-6715
childrenshealthvi.org
www.linkedin.com/company/2291213
www.facebook.com/queenalexandrafoundation
twitter.com/childrensvi
www.youtube.com/user/QAFoundation
Overview: A small local organization founded in 1922
Mission: To support children in need by raising funds towards improving their health and well being
Chief Officer(s):
Linda Hughes, Chief Executive Officer, 250-519-3721
Linda.M.Hughes@viha.ca
Margot McLaren Moore, Chair, Board of Directors
Staff Member(s): 10
Activities: Fundraising

Children's Health Foundations
345 Westminster Ave., London ON N6C 4V3
Tel: 519-432-8564; *Fax:* 519-432-5907
Toll-Free: 888-834-2696
chf@childhealth.ca
childhealth.ca
www.facebook.com/CHFHope
twitter.com/CHFHope
www.youtube.com/user/ChildrensRaisingHope
Overview: A small local charitable organization founded in 1922
Mission: To help raise funds for children's hospitals in order to provide patients with improved health care services & to fund research
Chief Officer(s):
Susan Crowley, President & CEO
scrowley@childhealth.ca
Staff Member(s): 20
Activities: Fundraising

Children's Heart Association for Support & Education (CHASE)
Tel: 416-410-2427
kidheart@angelfire.com
www.angelfire.com/on/chase
Overview: A small national organization founded in 1984
Mission: Organization committed to promoting awarness about congenital heart disease; to provide encouragement to families affected by CHD; driven to become the leading provider of resoures to education & support those who seek an understanding of the disease.
Finances: *Annual Operating Budget:* Less than $50,000
Membership: 527; *Member Profile:* Families & professionals dealing with congenital heart disease.; *Committees:* Awarenes; Fundraising; Social
Activities: *Awareness Events:* Feb. 14 CHD Day; *Library:* CHIP; Open to public

Children's Heart Society
PO Box 52088, Stn. Gardeau, Edmonton AB T6G 2T5
Tel: 780-454-7665
childrensheart@shaw.ca
www.childrensheart.org
www.facebook.com/childrenshearts
twitter.com/childrenshearts
Overview: A small local organization
Mission: To support children with heart disease & their families
Chief Officer(s):
Shannon Moroz, President
Membership: *Fees:* $30

Children's Hospital Foundation of Manitoba
#CE501, 840 Sherbrook St., Winnipeg MB R3A 1S1
Tel: 204-787-4000; *Fax:* 204-787-4114
Toll-Free: 866-953-5437
goodbear.mb.ca
www.facebook.com/childrenshospitalfoundation
twitter.com/chfmanitoba
www.youtube.com/user/DRGoodbear1
Overview: A large provincial charitable organization founded in 1971
Mission: To help raise funds for the Winnipeg Children's Hospital & the Manitoba Institute of Child Health in order to provide patients with improved health care services & to fund research
Chief Officer(s):
Lawrence Prout, President & CEO
lprout@hsc.mb.ca
Finances: *Annual Operating Budget:* Greater than $5 Million
Staff Member(s): 20
Membership: *Committees:* Advisory Council; Child Health Advisory Council; Development; Finance; Human Resources; Investment; Marketing & Communications; Nominating/Governance
Activities: Fundraising

Children's Hospital Foundation of Saskatchewan
#1, 345 - 3 Ave. South, Saskatoon SK S7K 1M6
Tel: 306-931-4887
Toll-Free: 888-808-5437
info@chfsask.ca
www.childrenshospitalsask.ca
www.facebook.com/CHFSask
twitter.com/childhospitalsk
www.youtube.com/user/ChildHospitalSK
Overview: A small provincial charitable organization
Mission: To help raise funds for the Children's Hospital of Saskatchewan in order to provide patients with improved health care services & to fund research
Chief Officer(s):
Robert Hawkins, Chair
Activities: Fundraising

Children's Hospital of Eastern Ontario Foundation
415 Smyth Rd., Ottawa ON K1H 8M8
Tel: 613-737-2780; *Fax:* 613-738-4818
Toll-Free: 800-561-5638
www.cheofoundation.com
www.facebook.com/CHEOkids
twitter.com/cheohospital
www.youtube.com/user/CHEOvideos
Also Known As: Children's Hospital Foundation
Overview: A medium-sized local charitable organization founded in 1974
Mission: To advance the physical, mental, & social well-being of children & their families in Eastern Ontario & Western Quebec by raising, managing, & disbursing funds; To support the Children's Hospital of Eastern Ontario
Member of: Children's Miracle Network Telethon
Chief Officer(s):
Len Hanes, Director, Communications
lhanes@cheofoundation.com
Finances: *Funding Sources:* Fundraising
Activities: *Speaker Service:* Yes

Children's International Summer Villages (Canada) Inc. (CISV) / Villages internationaux d'enfants
233 Chaplin Cres., Toronto ON M5P 1B1
e-mail: canada@cisv.org
www.ca.cisv.org
Overview: A medium-sized national organization founded in 1957
Mission: To promote cross-cultural friendship, through educational programs for youth & adults in 60 countries; To prepare indivduals to become active & contributing members of a peaceful society; To stimulate the life-long development of amicable relationships & effective & appropriate leadership towards a fair & just world
Member of: Canadian Council for International Cooperation

Children's Mental Health Ontario (CMHO) / Santé Mentale pour Enfants Ontario (SMEO)
#309, 40 St. Clair Ave. East, Toronto ON M4T 1M9
Tel: 416-921-2109; *Fax:* 416-921-7600
Toll-Free: 888-234-7054
info@cmho.org
www.kidsmentalhealth.ca
www.facebook.com/kidsmentalhealth
twitter.com/kidsmentalhlth
www.youtube.com/2013changetheview
Also Known As: Ontario Association of Children's Mental Health Centres
Overview: A medium-sized provincial charitable organization founded in 1972
Mission: To promote, support & strengthen a sustainable system of mental health services for children, youth & their families
Member of: Child Welfare League of Canada
Chief Officer(s):
Gordon Floyd, President & CEO
Finances: *Annual Operating Budget:* $1.5 Million-$3 Million; *Funding Sources:* Membership dues
Staff Member(s): 15
Membership: 85; *Fees:* 0.3% of annual operating budget for cmh services + $585; *Member Profile:* Children's mental health centres
Activities: Annual conference; Webinars; *Awareness Events:* Children's Mental Health Week, May
Meetings/Conferences: • Children's Mental Health Ontario Annual Conference 2015, 2015, ON
Scope: National

Children's Miracle Network
#C10, 4220 Steeles Ave. West, Woodbridge ON L4L 3S8
Tel: 905-265-9750; *Fax:* 905-265-9749
childrensmiraclenetwork.ca
www.facebook.com/cmnhospitals
twitter.com/cmncanada
www.youtube.com/cmnhospitals
Overview: A large national charitable organization
Mission: To raise funds for children's hospitals
Chief Officer(s):
John Lauck, President & CEO
Jenni Debartolo, Chief People Officer
John Hartman, Chief Operating Officer
Craig Sorensen, Chief Concept Officer
Clark Sweat, Chief Corporate Partnership Officer
Finances: *Funding Sources:* Fundraising

Children's Oncology Care of Ontario Inc. ***See*** Ronald McDonald House Toronto

Children's Psychiatric Research Institute *See* Child & Parent Resource Institute

Children's Rehabilitation & Cerebral Palsy Association; Children's Centre for Ability *See* British Columbia Centre for Ability Association

Children's Resource & Consultation Centre of Ontario

100 St. Clair Ave. West, Toronto ON M4V 1N3
Tel: 416-923-7771
www.ontarioadoptions.com
Overview: A small provincial organization
Mission: The Centre is an adoption agency licensed both domestically and internationally in Bangladesh, Hong Kong, India, Jamaica, Lebanon, Pakistan, Philippines, Thailand, Trinidad & U.S.
Chief Officer(s):
Michael Blugerman, Executive Director
Activities: Consultation on adoptive planning

Children's Safety Association of Canada

PO Box 551, 2110 Kipling Ave. North, Toronto ON M9W 4K0
Toll-Free: 888-499-4444
info@safekid.org
www.safekid.org
www.facebook.com/388063844595114
twitter.com/CHASAorg
Overview: A small national organization founded in 1992
Mission: The Association provides information on child safety.
Chief Officer(s):
Andre Brisebois, President
Membership: *Member Profile:* Parents of children 0-5
Activities: Free window blind repair kits; free identification & print kits; free 32 page safety info kit; free scalding prevention stickers
Publications:
• Child Safety
Type: magazine

Children's Wish Foundation of Canada / Fondation canadienne rêves d'enfants

#350, 1101 Kingston Rd., Pickering ON L1V 1B5
Tel: 905-839-8882; *Fax:* 905-839-3745
Toll-Free: 800-700-4437
nat@childrenswish.ca
www.childrenswish.ca
www.linkedin.com/company/children's-wish-foundation-of-canada
www.facebook.com/ChildrensWish
twitter.com/Childrens_wish
Overview: A large national charitable organization founded in 1984
Mission: The Foundation grants wishes to children suffering from a high risk, life-threatening illnesses
Chief Officer(s):
Chris Kotsopoulos, CEO
chris.kotsopoulos@childrenswish.ca
Linda Marco, Vice-President, Development
janet.turner@childrenswish.ca
Paul St-Germain, Director, Communications
paul.stgermain@childrenswish.ca
Finances: *Annual Operating Budget:* Greater than $5 Million; *Funding Sources:* Donations
Staff Member(s): 90
Activities: *Awareness Events:* Wishmaker Parade, Oct. 14

Alberta & N.W.T. Chapter - Calgary
#271, 339 - 50 Ave. SE, Calgary AB T2G 2B3
Tel: 403-265-9039; *Fax:* 403-265-1704
Toll-Free: 800-267-9474
ab@childrenswish.ca
www.facebook.com/ChildrensWishAB
twitter.com/ChildrensWishAB
Chief Officer(s):
Kyla Martin, Chapter Director
kyla.martin@childrenswish.ca

Alberta & N.W.T. Chapter - Edmonton
#4, 10016 - 29A Ave, NW, Edmonton AB T6N 1A8
Tel: 780-340-9039; *Fax:* 587-881-0064
Toll-Free: 800-267-9474
ab@childrenswish.ca
www.facebook.com/ChildrensWishAB
twitter.com/ChildrensWishAB
Chief Officer(s):
Elizabeth LoPresti, Chapter Director
elizabeth.lopresti@childrenswish.ca

British Columbia & Yukon Chapter
#450, 319 West Pender St., Vancouver BC V6B 1T3
Tel: 604-299-2241; *Fax:* 604-299-1228
Toll-Free: 800-267-9474
bc@childrenswish.ca
www.facebook.com/ChildrensWishBC
twitter.com/cwfbc
Chief Officer(s):
Jennifer Petersen, Chapter Director
jennifer.petersen@childrenswish.ca

Division Québec Est
Halles Fleur de Lys, #206, 245, rue Soumande, Québec QC G1M 3H6
Tél: 418-650-2111; *Téléc:* 418-650-3466
Ligne sans frais: 800-267-9474
qe@revesdenfants.ca
www.facebook.com/revesenfants
twitter.com/Reves_denfants
Chief Officer(s):
Pierre-Luc Berthiaume, Directrice du chapitre
pierre-luc.berthiaume@childrenswish.ca

Division Québec Ouest
#418, 4200, rue St. Laurent, Montréal QC H2W 2R2
Tél: 514-289-1777; *Téléc:* 514-298-8504
Ligne sans frais: 800-267-9474
qw@revesdenfants.ca
www.facebook.com/revesenfants
twitter.com/Reves_denfants
Chief Officer(s):
Juli Meilleur, Directeur du chapitre
Juli.Meilleur@childrenswish.ca

Manitoba & Nunavut Chapter
350 St. Mary Ave., Winnipeg MB R3C 3J2
Tel: 204-945-9474; *Fax:* 204-945-9479
Toll-Free: 800-267-9474
mb@childrenswish.ca
www.facebook.com/ChildrensWishMB
twitter.com/ChildrensWishMB
Chief Officer(s):
Maria Toscano, Chapter Director
maria.toscano@childrenswish.ca

National Capital Region
#103, 1390 Prince of Wales Dr., Ottawa ON K2C 3N6
Tel: 613-221-9474; *Fax:* 613-221-9441
Toll-Free: 800-267-9474
ncr@childrenswish.ca
www.facebook.com/ChildrensWishNatCap
twitter.com/ChildrensWishNC
Chief Officer(s):
Sue Walker, Chapter Director
Sue.Walker@childrenswish.ca

New Brunswick Chapter
#C202, 600 Main St., Saint John NB E2K 1J5
Tel: 506-632-0099; *Fax:* 506-635-6924
Toll-Free: 800-267-9474
nb@childrenswish.ca
www.facebook.com/ChildrensWishFoundationNB
twitter.com/NBChildrensWish
Chief Officer(s):
Gerry Beresford, Chapter Director
gerry.beresford@childrenswish.ca

Newfoundland & Labrador Chapter
#211 - 31 Peet St., St. John's NL A1B 3W8
Tel: 709-739-9553; *Fax:* 709-726-9474
Toll-Free: 800-267-9474
nl@childrenswish.ca
www.facebook.com/ChildrensWishNL
twitter.com/cwfnl
Chief Officer(s):
Edie Newton, Chapter Director
edie.newton@childrenswish.ca

Nova Scotia Chapter
#105, 238 Brownlow Ave., Dartmouth NS B3B 2B4
Tel: 902-492-1984; *Fax:* 902-492-1908
Toll-Free: 800-267-9474
ns@childrenswish.ca
www.facebook.com/ChildrensWishNS
twitter.com/ChildrensWishNS
Chief Officer(s):
Cheryl Matthews, Chapter Director
cheryl.matthews@childrenswish.ca

Ontario Chapter
#360, 1101 Kingston Rd., Pickering ON L1V 1B5
Tel: 905-427-5353; *Fax:* 905-427-0536
Toll-Free: 800-267-9474
on@childrenswish.ca
www.facebook.com/ChildrensWishON
twitter.com/ChildrensWishON
Chief Officer(s):
Sandra Harris, Director, Ontario Region
sandra.harris@childrenswish.ca

Prince Edward Island Chapter
Midtown Plaza, #7, 375 University Ave., Charlottetown PE C1A 4N4
Tel: 902-566-5526; *Fax:* 902-894-8412
Toll-Free: 800-267-9474
pei@childrenswish.ca
www.facebook.com/ChildrensWishPE
twitter.com/ChildrensWishPE
Chief Officer(s):
Beth Corney Gauthier, Chapter Director
beth.corneygauthier@childrenswish.ca

Saskatchewan Chapter
PO Box 309, 3602 Millar Ave., Saskatoon SK S7K 3L3
Tel: 306-955-0511; *Fax:* 306-653-9474
Toll-Free: 800-267-9474
sk@childrenswish.ca
Chief Officer(s):
Gay Oldhaver, Chapter Director
gay.oldhaver@childrenswish.ca

Children's Writers & Illustrators of British Columbia Society (CWILL BC)

c/o Mary Jane Muir, #406, 2938 Laurel St., Vancouver BC V5Z 3T3
e-mail: membership@cwill.bc.ca
www.cwill.bc.ca
www.facebook.com/CWILLBC
cwillbc.wordpress.com
Overview: A small provincial organization founded in 1994
Mission: To publicize & promote members' books; to provide support & allows for information exchange about creating books for young people; to communicate with other arts groups in BC & Canada.
Member of: Vancouver Cultural Alliance
Chief Officer(s):
Lori Sherritt-Fleming, President
Finances: *Funding Sources:* Membership fees
Membership: 150; *Fees:* $55; *Member Profile:* Published writers & illustrators
Activities: *Speaker Service:* Yes; *Library:* Collection of books at UBC Education Library

Chilliwack & District Real Estate Board

#1, 8433 Harvard Pl., Chilliwack BC V2P 7Z5
Tel: 604-792-0912; *Fax:* 604-792-6795
cadreb@telus.net
cadreb.com
twitter.com/ChilliwackREB
Overview: A medium-sized local organization overseen by British Columbia Real Estate Association
Mission: To serve the real estate needs of Chilliwack, Agassiz, Hope, Boston Bar and Harrison.
Member of: The Canadian Real Estate Association
Chief Officer(s):
Steve Lerigny, Executive Officer
Staff Member(s): 4

Chilliwack Chamber of Commerce

#16, 45966 Yale Rd., Chilliwack BC V2P 2M3
Tel: 604-793-4323; *Fax:* 604-793-4303
info@chilliwackchamber.com
www.chilliwackchamber.com
www.linkedin.com/company/chilliwack-chamber-of-commerce
www.facebook.com/pages/Chilliwack-Chamber-of-Commerce/140662687837
twitter.com/chwkchamber
www.youtube.com/user/ChilliwackChamber?ob=0
Overview: A small local organization founded in 1903
Mission: To promote economic growth & development for the benefit of the commercial, agricultural, industrial, civic & social well-being of the district
Member of: Canadian Chamber of Commerce; Better Business Bureau; BC Chamber of Commerce; Vancouver Coast & Mountains Tourism Region
Chief Officer(s):
Kevin Gemmell, President
Patti MacAhonic, Executive Director
Patti.MacAhonic@chilliwackchamber.com

Finances: *Funding Sources:* Provincial & municipal government; fundraising
Staff Member(s): 2
Membership: 555; *Fees:* $116 non-profit/retired; $168-$578 business; *Committees:* Agriculture; Business Education & Development; Membership; Public Relations; Retail; Special Events; Tourism
Activities: Forestry Task Force; Shop Local Program; *Speaker Service:* Yes; *Library:* Business Information Centre; Open to public

Chilliwack Community Arts Council
Chilliwack Cultural Centre, 9201 Corbould St., Chilliwack BC V2P 2A4
Tel: 604-392-8888; *Fax:* 604-392-8008
info@chilliwackartscouncil.com
chilliwackartscouncil.com
www.facebook.com/ChilliwackArts
www.youtube.com/user/ChwkArtsCouncil?feature=mhum
Overview: A small local organization founded in 1960
Mission: To enrich the quality of life for the residents of Chilliwack by the effective use of resources & volunteers to encourage education & participation in the arts
Member of: Assembly of BC Arts Councils; BC Touring Council; BC Bluegrass Association
Finances: *Annual Operating Budget:* $500,000-$1.5 Million
Staff Member(s): 12; 100 volunteer(s)
Membership: 350; *Fees:* $15 individual; $25 family/group; $100 corporation
Activities: Concerts, Bluegrass Festival, craft market, film screenings
Awards:
• Community Arts Council Fine Arts Awards
Eligibility: A full-time, post-secondary student in the Fine Arts field, past or present resident of Chilliwack*Deadline:* April 1 *Amount:* $500
• Mary Elizabeth Allan Memorial Award
Eligibility: A full-time, post-secondary student in the Theatre field, past or present resident of Chilliwack*Deadline:* April 1 *Amount:* $500
• Jenny Child Memorial Award
Eligibility: A full-time, post-secondary student in a Fine Arts field, past or present resident of Chilliwack*Deadline:* April 1 *Amount:* $500
• Robert (Bob) Forsythe Memorial Award
Eligibility: A full-time, post-secondary student in the Theatre field, past or present resident of Chilliwack*Deadline:* April 1 *Amount:* $500

Chilliwack Field Naturalists
#216, 45598 McIntosh Dr., Chilliwack BC V2P 1J3
Tel: 604-796-9182
postmaster@chilliwackfieldnaturalists.freeservers.com
www.chilliwackfieldnaturalists.com
Overview: A small local organization founded in 1970
Mission: To promote the enjoyment of nature through environmental appreciation & conservation; To encourage wise use & conservation of natural resources & environmental protection
Member of: Federation of BC Naturalists
Chief Officer(s):
Janne Perrin, President
djperrin@uniserve.com
Membership: 60 individual; *Fees:* $25 individual; $35 family; *Committees:* Conservation; Education
Activities: Field trips; meetings & speakers; education; *Awareness Events:* Christmas Bird Count, December

Chilliwack Society for Community Living (CSCL)
9353 Mary St., Chilliwack BC V2P 4G9
Tel: 604-792-7726; *Fax:* 604-792-7962
administration@cscl.org
www.cscl.org
www.facebook.com/cscl.org
twitter.com/CSCLtweets
Overview: A small local charitable organization founded in 1954
Mission: CSCL is an accredited, non-profit, charitable organization that seeks to promote & enhance the quality of life for people with developmental disabilities.
Chief Officer(s):
Helen Tolmie, President
Brenda Gillette, Executive Director
brenda.gillette@cscl.org
Membership: 100
Activities: Adult day services; adult community services; community housing coordination; children's services; short-term respite care services

Chilliwack Symphony Orchestra & Chorus (CSO)
PO Box 521, Stn. Main, Chilliwack BC V2P 6H7
Tel: 604-795-0521
chilliwacksymphony@gmail.com
chilliwacksymphony.com
www.facebook.com/Chilliwack.Symphony.Orchestra.and.Chorus
Overview: A small local organization founded in 1999 overseen by Orchestras Canada
Chief Officer(s):
Paula Dewit, Music Director
Membership: 147

China Canada Investment Association (CCIA)
#503, 3601 Hwy #7 East, Markham ON L3R 0M3
Tel: 905-305-6865
ccia2002@gmail.com
cciacanada.com
Also Known As: Canadian Chinese Investment Association
Overview: A small national organization founded in 2010
Mission: To advocate for cultural & economic exchanges between China & Canada
Chief Officer(s):
Sophia Ming Sun, President
Membership: *Member Profile:* Representitives from sectors such as financial services, real estate, legal services, manufacturing, construction, transportation, mining & energy, information & communication technology, high-tech & education

China Council for the Promotion of International Trade - Canadian Office (CCPIT)
#908, 150 York St., Toronto ON M5H 3S5
Tel: 416-363-8561; *Fax:* 416-363-0152
ccpitcanada@gmail.com
overseas.ccpit.org/ca
Overview: A medium-sized international organization founded in 1952
Chief Officer(s):
Yun Chang, Contact
changyun@ccpit.org
Staff Member(s): 3

China Inland Mission *See* OMF International - Canada

Chinese Benevolent Association of Vancouver (CBA)
108 East Pender St., Vancouver BC V6A 1T3
Tel: 604-681-1923; *Fax:* 604-682-0073
info@cbavancouver.ca
www.cbavancouver.ca
Also Known As: Shanghai Alley & Canton Alley
Overview: A small local organization founded in 1906
Mission: To provide support and leadership within the Chinese Canadian community.
Member of: Chinese Canadian National Council
Activities: Establishment of an affliated society to provide low cost housing; fund-raising campaigns to aid victims of natual disasters; Spring Festival Parade

Chinese Canadian Association of Prince Edward Island (CCAPEI)
36 Massey Dr., Charlottetown PE C1E 1R6
Overview: A small provincial organization

Chinese Canadian Chiropractic Society (CCCS)
#102, 7381 Kennedy Rd., Markham ON L3R 5B5
Tel: 905-513-9559; *Fax:* 905-513-0187
Overview: A small national organization founded in 2001
Mission: Created in order to educate the Chinese community about the benefits of chiropractic care
Chief Officer(s):
Sabrina Chen-See, President
Membership: 30

Chinese Canadian National Council (CCNC) / Conseil national des canadiens chinois
#507, 302 Spadina Ave., Toronto ON M5T 2E7
Tel: 416-977-9871; *Fax:* 416-977-1630
national@ccnc.ca
www.ccnc.ca
Overview: A medium-sized national organization founded in 1980
Mission: To promote the rights of all individuals, in particular, those of Chinese Canadians & to encourage their full & equal participation in Canadian society; to create an environment in Canada in which the rights of all individuals are fully recognized & protected; to promote understanding & cooperation between Chinese Canadians & all other ethnic, cultural, & racial groups in Canada; to encourage & develop in persons of Chinese descent, a desire to know & respect their historical & cultural heritage, & to educate them in adopting a creative & positive attitude towards the Chinese Canadian contribution to society & the Chinese Canadian heritage
Member of: Canadian Ethnocultural Council; National Organization of Immigrants of Visible Minority Women; National Action Committee of Status of Women
Affliation(s): Canadian Council for Refugees; Coalition for a Just Immigration Refugee Policy
Chief Officer(s):
Victor Wong, Executive Director
Activities: *Speaker Service:* Yes; *Library* by appointment

AB - Calgary Chinese Community Service Association
#108, 197 - 1 St. SW, Calgary AB T2P 4M4
Tel: 403-265-8446; *Fax:* 403-233-0070
cccsa@cadvision.com
Chief Officer(s):
Lloyd Wong, Co-Chair
Edith Chan, Co-Chair

British Columbia - United Chinese Community Enrichment Service Society
28 West Pender St., Vancouver BC V6B 1R6
Tel: 604-684-1628; *Fax:* 604-408-7234
www.successbc.ca
Mission: Provides services in settlement, English as a second language training, employment, family and youth counselling, business and economic development, health care, housing, and community and volunteer development.
Queenie Choo, CEO

Nfld. - Chinese Association of Newfoundland & Labrador
PO Box 7311, St. John's NL A1E 3Y5
Tel: 709-754-1470
Chief Officer(s):
Betty Wong, President
bwong@mun.ca

NS - Chinese Society of Nova Scotia
PO Box 29055, Stn. Halifax Shopping Centre, Halifax NS B3L 4T8
e-mail: csnsca@gmail.com
www.cs-ns.com
Chief Officer(s):
Yonggan Zhao, President

ON - CCNC London
1701 Trafalgar St., London ON N5W 1X2
Tel: 519-451-0760
info@londonccnc.ca
www.londonccnc.ca
Chief Officer(s):
Joan Lee, President

ON - CCNC Ottawa
391 Bank St., 2nd Fl., Ottawa ON K2P 1Y3
Tel: 613-996-8139
Chief Officer(s):
Jonas Ma, President

ON - CCNC Toronto
#123, 215 Spadina Ave., Toronto ON M5T 2C7
Tel: 416-596-0833
info@ccnctoronto.ca
www.facebook.com/CCNCTO
Chief Officer(s):
Kristyn Wong-Tam, President

ON - Central Ontario Chinese Cultural Centre
#9, 100 Campbell Ave., Kitchener ON N2H 4X8
Tel: 519-576-6168
info@coccc.net
www.coccc.net
www.facebook.com/COCCC
Chief Officer(s):
Shu Hing Man, President
president@coccc.net

ON - Chinese Canadians for Equity in York Region
PO Box 51, #97C2, 4350 Steeles Ave., Markham ON L3R 9V4
Chief Officer(s):
Amy Lam, President

ON - Lambton Chinese Canadian Association
PO Box 301, Sarnia ON N7T 7J2
Chief Officer(s):
Song Choo, President
ksyinc@ebtech.net

Chinese Cultural Association of Saint John (CCASJ)
PO Box 2661, Saint John NB E2L 4Z1
Tel: 506-645-1910
info@ccasj.org
www.ccasj.org
www.facebook.com/534026059992706
Overview: A small local organization founded in 1984
Mission: CCASJ provides public education of Chinese culture & heritage; promotes understanding & goodwill among all Canadians
Member of: Chinese Canadian National Council
Finances: *Funding Sources:* Saint John Community Arts Funding Program
Membership: 150; *Fees:* $10 individual; $15 family
Activities: Dragonboat racing; fund-raising for local charities; Chinese language classes; Asian Heritage Gala; Canada Day People's Parade

Chinese Cultural Centre (CCC)
50 East Pender St., Vancouver BC V6A 3V6
Tel: 604-658-8850; *Fax:* 604-687-6260
www.cccvan.com
www.facebook.com/cccvan
Also Known As: Chinese Cultural Centre of Greater Vancouver
Overview: A small local charitable organization founded in 1973
Mission: To preserve & promote Chinese cultural heritage; to foster better understanding among cultural groups; to facilitate cultural exchange.
Member of: Vancouver Cultural Alliance
Affliation(s): Chinese Benevolent Association of Vancouver; Vancouver Multicultural Society; Cultural Human Resources Council
Chief Officer(s):
Daisey Yau, Executive Director
Mike Jang, Chair
Finances: *Funding Sources:* Provincial government; facility rental; telethons, radiothons & raffles
Membership: 1,200; *Fees:* $15 individual; $30 family; $10 seniors/students; $2,000 life membership
Activities: Chinatown Arts & Cultural Festival; Chinese Language School & educational classes for adults & childeren; exhibition of visual arts; museum programs; concerts; film festivals & other community events; summer camp; museum & archives; *Internships:* Yes; *Speaker Service:* Yes

Richmond Office
#860, 4400 Hazelbridge Way, Richmond BC V6X 3R8
Tel: 604-658-8875; *Fax:* 604-658-8854

Chinese Cultural Centre of Greater Toronto (CCC)
5183 Sheppard Ave. East, Toronto ON M1B 5Z5
Tel: 416-292-9293; *Fax:* 416-292-9215
info@cccgt.org
www.cccgt.org
www.facebook.com/171784883266
Overview: A medium-sized local charitable organization founded in 1989
Mission: To promote Chinese culture within the multicultural context of Canadian society; to facilitate communication & understanding between Canada & Southeast Asian countries in culture, education & trade
Chief Officer(s):
Ming-Tat Cheung, President & Chair
Membership: *Fees:* $22 individual; $11 student/senior; $33 family; *Committees:* Operations; Programs; Special Events; Building & Facilities; Finance; Culture & Education; Marketing & Sponsorship; IT; Legal Consultant; Outreach
Activities: *Library:* Richard Charles Lee Resource Centre

Chinese Family Life Services Project *See* Chinese Family Services of Ontario

Chinese Family Service of Greater Montréal *Voir* Service à la famille chinoise du Grand Montréal

Chinese Family Services of Ontario
#229, 3330 Midland Ave., Toronto ON M1V 5E7
Tel: 416-979-8299; *Fax:* 416-979-2743
Toll-Free: 866-979-8298; *TTY:* 416-979-5898
info@chinesefamilyso.com
www.chinesefamilyso.com
Previous Name: Chinese Family Life Services Project
Overview: A small local charitable organization founded in 1988 overseen by Ontario Council of Agencies Serving Immigrants
Mission: To offer service that help Chinese immigrants settle in Canada
Chief Officer(s):
Patrick Au, Executive Director
Finances: *Annual Operating Budget:* $1.5 Million-$3 Million; *Funding Sources:* Government levels; United Way Toronto & York; donations
Staff Member(s): 25
Activities: Family life education programs; group counseling; domestic violence intervention program; addiction therapy; youth services; sexual orientation counseling; employment assistance program; internships; *Speaker Service:* Yes

Chinese Interpreter & Information Services; Chinese Information & Community Services of Greater Toronto; Centre for Information & Community Servi *See* Centre for Immigrant & Community Services

Chinese Medicine & Acupuncture Association of Canada (CMAAC)
154 Wellingston St., London ON N6B 2K8
Tel: 519-642-1970; *Fax:* 519-642-2932
cmaac@execulink.com
www.cmaac.ca
Overview: A medium-sized national organization founded in 1983
Mission: To unite practitioners of Eastern & Western Medicine; Establishment of high standards of education & training for practitioners; Promotion & attendance at international conferences; Assisting in the exchange of scientific research; acting as an educational vehicle for the public.
Member of: World Federation of Acupuncture
Affliation(s): World Wildlife Fund Canada; Canadian Health Care Anti-Fraud Association
Chief Officer(s):
Wei Ling Qiu, President
Membership: 756; *Fees:* $100; *Member Profile:* Practitioners of acupuncture & Chinese medicine

Alberta Chapter
414 Lee Ridge Rd., Edmonton AB T6K 0N7
Tel: 780-497-5168; *Fax:* 403-274-5077
Chief Officer(s):
King Sang Wong, President

British Columbia Chapter
#P401, 2212 Oxford St., Vancouver BC V5L 1G1
Tel: 604-434-1646; *Fax:* 604-434-1646
Chief Officer(s):
Dana Mah, President
danajmah@gmail.com

Manitoba Chapter
1036 Portage Ave., Winnipeg MB R3G 0S2
Tel: 204-284-4047; *Fax:* 204-284-5755
Chief Officer(s):
Lin Liu, President
liulin1036@hotmail.com

New Brunswick Chapter
91 Roseberry St., Campbellton NB E3N 2G6
Tel: 506-753-4421
Chief Officer(s):
Steve Lambert, President
slambert@nbnet.nb.ca

Newfoundland Chapter
#3, 54 Conception Bay Hwy., Conception Bay South NL A1W 3A1
Chief Officer(s):
Michelle Collett, President
collettmichele@hotmail.com

Nova Scotia Chapter
6066 Quinpool Rd., Halifax NS B3L 1A1
Tel: 902-832-0688; *Fax:* 902-835-3298
ccanm@ns.sympatico.ca
Chief Officer(s):
Diana Tong Li, President
acup@eastlink.ca

Ontario Office
117 King St. East, Oshawa ON L1H 1B9
Tel: 905-721-4917; *Fax:* 905-721-4336
Chief Officer(s):
Jane Cheung, Vice-President, External Relations
jane.cheung@cmaac.ca

Québec Chapter
#307, 340 McLeod St., Ottawa ON K2P 1A4
Tel: 613-569-8947; *Fax:* 613-569-8947
Chief Officer(s):
Gasan Askerow, President
askerow@bell.net

Saskatchewan Chapter
3829B Albert St. South, Regina SK S4S 3R4
Tel: 306-584-9888; *Fax:* 306-584-9888
allnatural@sasktel.net
Chief Officer(s):
Diana Dong Yue Zhang, President
allnatural@sasktel.net

Chinese Neighbourhood Society of Montréal / Amitié Chinoise de Montréal
15 Viger Rd. West, 3rd Fl., Montréal QC H2Z 1E6
Tel: 514-866-7133; *Fax:* 514-866-8636
Overview: A small local organization
Member of: Chinese Canadian National Council
Chief Officer(s):
Kenneth Cheung, President

Chinese Professionals Association of Canada (CPAC)
4150 Finch Ave. East, Toronto ON M1S 3T9
Tel: 416-298-7885; *Fax:* 416-298-0068
office@chineseprofessionals.ca
www.chineseprofessionals.ca
Overview: A large national organization founded in 1992
Mission: To advocate for the interests of association members & the Chinese Canadian community
Chief Officer(s):
Hugh Zhao, President
Banggu Jiang, Vice-President
Longhuan Kim, Executive Advisor & Treasurer
Yolanda Yao, General Manager
Finances: *Funding Sources:* Corporate sponsorships
Membership: 20,000+; *Fees:* $100 individual & student; Schedule for group & corporate; *Member Profile:* Chinese Canadian professionals; *Committees:* Executive; International Exchange; Finance; Membership; Program; Recreation, Culture & Entrepreneurship; Resources Development
Activities: Facilitating professional development; Providing networking opportunities; Assisting association members with settlement & integration in Canadian society; Offering training & education to internationally trained professionals & families
Publications:
• New Horizon
Type: Newspaper; *Frequency:* Monthly
Profile: Association activies, past & forthcoming events, & professional development oppotunities

Chinese Seniors Support Services Association *See* Carefirst Seniors & Community Services Association

Chinook Applied Research Association (CARA)
PO Box 690, Oyen AB T0J 2J0
Tel: 403-664-3777; *Fax:* 403-664-3007
cara-1@telus.net
www.areca.ab.ca/carahome.html
Overview: A small local organization overseen by Agricultural Research & Extension Council of Alberta
Mission: To expand agricultural research
Member of: Agricultural Research & Extension Council of Alberta
Chief Officer(s):
Dianne Westerlund, Manager
cara-dw@telus.net
Audrey Bamber, Agrologist, Crops
cara-ab@telus.net
Lacey Ryan, Agrologist, Forage
cara-ca@telus.net
Membership: *Fees:* $20 (annual); $80 (5 years)
Publications:
• Grain, Grass & Growth [a publication of Chinook Applied Research Association]
Type: Newsletter

Chinook Musical Society
159 Lake Adams Cres. SE, Calgary AB T2J 3N2
Tel: 403-271-3719
general@saturdaynightspecial.ca
www.saturdaynightspecial.ca
Overview: A small local organization founded in 1976
Chief Officer(s):
David McIntyre, President
Activities: Presents between 9 and 10 Saturday evening concerts per year

Chinook Regional Hospital Foundation (CRHF)
960 - 19th St. South, Lethbridge AB T1J 1W5
Tel: 403-388-6001; *Fax:* 403-388-6604
info@crhfoundation.com
www.crhfoundation.ca

www.facebook.com/crhfoundation.ca
twitter.com/crh_foundation
Overview: A small local charitable organization
Mission: To raise, receive & distribute funds for equipment & programs in order to enhance patient services at Chinook Regional Hospital; Primarily fund the purchase & maintenance of equipment that will enhance care & attract medical specialists
Chief Officer(s):
Everett Duerksen, Chair
Jason Vanden Hoek, Executive Director
Finances: *Funding Sources:* Donations; Fundraising
Activities: *Awareness Events:* Care from the Heart Radiothon, Feb.; Golf Tournament, Aug.; Christmas Tree Festival & Lights of Hope, Dec.

Chipman Community Care Inc.

PO Box 435, 93 Bridge St., Chipman NB E4A 3N4
Tel: 506-339-5565; *Fax:* 506-339-6823
Overview: A small local charitable organization founded in 1987
Mission: To promote total community wellness among youth to seniors
Member of: Association of Food Banks & C.V.A.'s for New Brunswick; Atlantic Alliance of Food Banks & C.V.A.'s
Chief Officer(s):
Mary West, President
Finances: *Annual Operating Budget:* $100,000-$250,000; *Funding Sources:* Federal & Provincial grants; NB Protestant Orphanage; Village of Chipman; Fundraising
Staff Member(s): 2; 19 volunteer(s)
Membership: 15; *Committees:* Social; Building; Telethon; Housing; Youth
Activities: Food, Clothing bank; low-income housing; youth centre

Chiropractic Awareness Council (CAC)

#126, 17A - 218 Silvercreek Pkwy. North, Guelph ON N1H 9E9
Tel: 519-822-1879; *Fax:* 519-822-1239
Toll-Free: 877-997-9927
totalhealth@chiropracticawarenesscouncil.org
www.chiropracticawarenesscouncil.org
Overview: A small national organization founded in 1998
Mission: To promote public awareness of chiropractic life principles by promoting an awareness of the devastating effects of vertebral subluxation complex on the expression of human health potential; To educate the public with the conviction that chiropractic care is a integral aspect of health for people of all ages & to society in general
Member of: Chiropractic Coalition
Chief Officer(s):
Steven Silk, Chair
Finances: *Annual Operating Budget:* $100,000-$250,000; *Funding Sources:* Membership fees
Staff Member(s): 1; 8 volunteer(s)
Membership: 350; *Fees:* $295; *Member Profile:* Chiropractors, staff, students, corporations; *Committees:* CCO; Convention; Public Awareness; Student Affairs
Activities: *Speaker Service:* Yes

Chiropractic Foundation for Spinal Research *See* Canadian Chiropractic Research Foundation

Chiropractors' Association of Saskatchewan (CAS)

3420A Hill Ave., Regina SK S4S 0W9
Tel: 306-585-1411; *Fax:* 306-585-0685
cas@saskchiropractic.ca
www.saskchiropractic.ca
www.youtube.com/user/SaskChiro
Overview: A medium-sized provincial organization founded in 1943 overseen by Canadian Chiropractic Association
Mission: To standardize & elevate chiropractic methods
Chief Officer(s):
Shane Taylor, President
Lori Foster, Executive Director
Finances: *Annual Operating Budget:* $500,000-$1.5 Million; *Funding Sources:* Membership dies
Staff Member(s): 3; 50 volunteer(s)
Membership: 200; *Committees:* Investigation; Discipline
Activities: Regulating chiropractic care in Saskatchewan; Promoting chiropractic profession; *Internships:* Yes

Chisholm Services for Children

5724 South St., Halifax NS B3H 1S4
Tel: 902-423-9871; *Fax:* 902-422-3725
info@chisholm4children.ca
www.chisholm4children.ca
Overview: A medium-sized provincial charitable organization founded in 2004
Mission: A non-profit organization offering a long-term care program, specializes in early intervention.
Chief Officer(s):
Wade Johnston, Executive Director

Choiceland & District Chamber of Commerce

c/o Town of Choiceland, PO Box 279, 115 - 1st St. East, Choiceland SK S0J 0M0
Tel: 306-428-2070; *Fax:* 306-428-2071
Overview: A small local organization
Mission: Supporting business and community in the town of Choiceland.
Chief Officer(s):
Frank H. Bond, President, 306-428-2300
growplan@sasktel.net
Colleen F Digness, Secretary
choiceland.town@sasktel.net

Choirs Ontario

1442 Bayview Ave., #A, Toronto ON M4G 3A7
Tel: 416-923-1144; *Fax:* 416-929-0415
Toll-Free: 866-935-1144
www.choirsontario.org
Also Known As: Ontario Choral Federation
Overview: A medium-sized provincial organization
Mission: To promote choral singing in communities, schools & universities, places of worship, etc. throughout Ontario.
Chief Officer(s):
Rachel Rensink-Hoff, President
Elizabeth Shannon, Executive Director
eshannon@choirsontario.org
Staff Member(s): 2
Membership: *Fees:* Schedule available
Awards:
• The Ruth Watson Henderson Choral Composition Prize (Award)
• The Leslie Bell Prize for Choral Conducting (Award)
Offered every two years and administered by the Ontario Arts Council

Chorale Les Voix de la Vallée du Cuivre de Chibougamau inc.

CP 129, Chibougamau QC G8P 2K6
Tél: 418-748-6892
Aperçu: *Dimension:* petite; *Envergure:* locale
Membre(s) du bureau directeur:
Bruno Marceau, Président

Chosen People Ministries (Canada) (CPM)

PO Box 58103, Stn. Dufferin-Lawrence, Toronto ON M6A 3C8
Tel: 416-250-0177; *Fax:* 416-250-9235
Toll-Free: 888-442-5535
info@chosenpeople.ca
www.chosenpeople.ca
Also Known As: Beth Sar Shalom Mission
Overview: A medium-sized national charitable organization founded in 1894
Mission: To share the Good News of Jesus the Messiah and help others do the same
Chief Officer(s):
Jorge Sedaca, National Director
Finances: *Annual Operating Budget:* $500,000-$1.5 Million; *Funding Sources:* Donations
Staff Member(s): 14
Activities: *Speaker Service:* Yes

Chown Adult Day Care Centre

Taoist Building, 94 East 15th Ave., Vancouver BC V5T 2R5
Tel: 604-879-0947; *Fax:* 604-879-0121
chownadc@shaw.ca
chownadc.com
www.facebook.com/pages/Chown-Adult-Day-Centre/236969846432675
Overview: A small local charitable organization
Mission: The Centre serves frail elders, disabled older & younger adults who need support to maintain health, & live in their community as independently as possible.
Member of: British Columbia Association of Community Care; Health Employers Association of British Columbia
Finances: *Funding Sources:* Provincial Government; Donations
Staff Member(s): 9
Activities: fitness & creative arts programs; chat groups; health services;

Chris Spencer Foundation

Bentall Centre, PO Box 48284, Vancouver BC V7X 1A1
Tel: 604-608-2560
Overview: A small local charitable organization founded in 1949
Mission: To provide grants to charitable organizations supporting boys & girls in Canada in the Greater Vancouver & Lower Fraser Valley area of B.C.

The Christian & Missionary Alliance in Canada (C&MA) / L'Alliance chrétienne et missionnaire au Canada

#100, 30 Carrier Dr., Toronto ON M9W 5T7
Tel: 416-674-7878; *Fax:* 416-674-0808
Other Communication: vimeo.com/cmaincanada
info@cmacan.org
www.cmacan.org/home
www.facebook.com/CMAllianceinCanada
twitter.com/CMAinCanada
www.youtube.com/user/cmacan
Also Known As: The Alliance Church
Overview: A large national charitable organization founded in 1981
Mission: To proclaim the truth of God's Word & to disciple people of all nations, particularly where Christ has not been named, emphasizing the Lordship of Jesus Christ & the person & work of the Holy Spirit, & looking for the coming of the Lord; to establish & nurture churches related in fellowship with C&MA around the world, dedicated to evangelism & missions; to establish local churches throughout Canada; to teach & train believers for the work of the ministry of Christ; to provide fellowship for individual believers of kindred spirit with one another without affecting their denominational relations; to encourage the cooperation of such evangelical groups of churches or Christians as may be disposed to send their missionaries through C&MA & contribute their missionary offerings through the general treasury
Member of: Canadian Council of Christian Charities; Alliance World Fellowship
Affliation(s): Alliance Life Magazine; Al Hayat Ministries; Evangelical Fellowship of Canada
Chief Officer(s):
David Hearn, President
Finances: *Annual Operating Budget:* Greater than $5 Million; *Funding Sources:* Donations
Staff Member(s): 1642
Membership: 430 churches + 48,922 baptized + 132,323 inclusive members + 205 Canadian International Workers

Canadian Midwest District (CMD) Office
2950 Arens Rd., Regina SK S4V 1N8
Tel: 306-586-3549
office@cma-cmd.ca
www.cma-cmd.ca
www.facebook.com/260082770709468
Chief Officer(s):
Al Fedorak, District Superintendent, 306-586-3549

Canadian Pacific District (CPD) Office
#101 - 17660 65A Ave., Surrey BC V3S 5N4
Tel: 604-372-1922; *Fax:* 604-372-1923
cpdoffice@pacificdistrict.ca
pacificdistrict.ca
www.facebook.com/123480364431374
twitter.com/PacificDistrict
www.youtube.com/user/PacificDistrict
Chief Officer(s):
Errol Rempel, District Superintendent, 604-372-1922

Central Canadian District (CCD) Office
155 Panin Rd., Burlington ON L7P 5A6
Tel: 905-639-9615; *Fax:* 905-634-7044
www.cmaccd.com
Chief Officer(s):
Brian Thom, District Superintendent, 902-639-9615 Ext. 215
thom@cmaccd.com

Eastern Canadian District (ECD) Office
#12, 11 Stanley Ct., Whitby ON L1N 8P9
Tel: 905-430-0955
www.sea2sea.ca
Chief Officer(s):
John Healey, District Superintendent

St. Lawrence District (SLD) Office
#215, 5473, av Royalmount, Mont-Royal QC H4P 1J3
Tel: 514-733-0343; *Fax:* 514-733-0683
acmpq@bellnet.ca
www.acmqc.org/en/
Chief Officer(s):
Yvan Fournier, District Superintendent

Western Canadian District (WCD) Office
#333, 30 Springborough Blvd. SW, Calgary AB T3H 0N9

Tel: 403-265-7900; *Fax:* 403-265-4599
office@transformcma.ca
www.cmawdo.org
www.facebook.com/groups/transformcma
www.youtube.com/user/WesternCanDistrict
Chief Officer(s):
Brent Trask, District Superintendent

Christian Aid Mission *See* Intercede International

Christian Blind Mission International (CBMI)
PO Box 800, 3844 Stoufville Rd., Stouffville ON L4A 7Z9
Tel: 905-640-6464; *Fax:* 905-640-4332
Toll-Free: 800-567-2264
cbm@cbmcanada.org
www.cbmcanada.org
www.facebook.com/pages/cbm-Canada/101857609865125
twitter.com/cbmCanada
www.youtube.com/user/cbmcanada
Overview: A medium-sized international charitable organization founded in 1978
Mission: With core values based on Christian faith, CBMI serves the blind & disabled in the developing world, irrespective of nationality, race, sex, or religion; prevents & treats blindness & other disabilities through medical care, rehabilitation training & integration programs; helps people to help themselves.
Member of: Canadian Council of Christian Charities
Chief Officer(s):
Ted Dueck, Chair
Ed Epp, Executive Director
Finances: *Annual Operating Budget:* Greater than $5 Million
Staff Member(s): 28; 45 volunteer(s)
Activities: Talking Book Library; Craft Store; works with nearly 600 mission agencies, local churches, Christian relief organizations & self-help groups overseas; *Rents Mailing List:* Yes; *Library:* Talking Book Library; Open to public

Christian Brethren Churches of Québec (CBCQ) / Églises de frères chrétiens du Québec (EFCQ)
PO Box 1054, #101, 1520, rue King ouest, Sherbrooke QC J1H 5L3
Tel: 819-820-1693
Also Known As: Plymouth Brethren
Overview: A medium-sized provincial charitable organization founded in 1942
Mission: To handle affairs for local affiliated churches regarding government & affairs of civil status
Chief Officer(s):
Pierre Munger, General Director
Finances: *Annual Operating Budget:* Less than $50,000; *Funding Sources:* Dues from local churches
2 volunteer(s)

Christian Catholic Church Canada (CCRCC) / Église catholique-chrétien Canada
PO Box 2043, Stn. Hull, Gatineau QC J8X 3Z2
Tel: 613-738-2942; *Fax:* 613-738-7835
info@ccrcc.ca
www.ccrcc.ca
Previous Name: Canadian Chapter of the International Council of Community Churches
Overview: A large international charitable organization founded in 1858
Mission: Advancing the kingdom of God through worship, pastoral work, & fellowship. Parishes in Ottawa-Gatineau, North Bay, Montreal
Affliation(s): International Council of Community Churches (ICCC), ICCC Canada, World Council of Churches
Chief Officer(s):
Serge A. Thériault, Évêque et président
sergeatheriault@hotmail.com
Finances: *Annual Operating Budget:* Less than $50,000; *Funding Sources:* Clergy; churches; benefactors
Staff Member(s): 15; 25 volunteer(s)
Membership: 1,000-4,999; *Fees:* $200 church; $50 clergy; *Committees:* Order of the Crown of Thorns
Activities: Church ministry; Seminary program; Counselling & mediation services; *Library:* Archives; Open to public by appointment

Christian Children's Fund of Canada (CCFC)
1200 Denison St., Markham ON L3R 8G6
Tel: 905-754-1001; *Fax:* 905-754-1002
Toll-Free: 800-263-5437
Other Communication: media@ccfcanada.ca
donor-relations@ccfcanada.ca
www.ccfcanada.ca
www.facebook.com/CCFC
www.twitter.com/ccfc
www.youtube.com/YCCCC
Overview: A large international organization founded in 1960
Mission: To focus upon community development ministry, starting with basic assistance & leading to programs stressing self-help & eventual independence; To work with colleagues & partners in developing countries; To reach out to children & families of all faiths
Member of: Canadian Council of Christian Charities; Better Business Bureau; ChildFund Alliance; Imagine Canada
Affliation(s): Canadian Marketing Association; Association of Fundraising Professionals
Chief Officer(s):
Mark Lukowski, Chief Executive Officer
Felicitas Adrian, Vice-President, Fund Development & Communications
Jim Carrie, Vice-President, Global Operations
Jeff Hogan, Vice-President, Finance & Corporate Services
Finances: *Funding Sources:* Donations
200 volunteer(s)
Membership: 30,000+; *Fees:* $39/month suggested donation
Activities: Working to help those affected by HIV/AIDS; Providng water & sanitation; Offering education; *Internships:* Yes; *Speaker Service:* Yes
Publications:
• Child Essentials Newsletter
Type: Newsletter
• ChildVoice
Type: Magazine; *Editor:* Vicki Quigley
Profile: Magazine for donors featuring stories of sponsored children

Christian Church (Disciples of Christ) in Canada (DISCAN) / Église chrétienne (Disciples du Christ) au Canada
PO Box 1, Springfield ON N0L 2J0
Tel: 519-269-9800
ccinca@eastlink.ca
www.disciplesofchrist.ca
Previous Name: All-Canada Committee of the Christian Church (Disciples of Christ)
Overview: A small national charitable organization founded in 1922
Member of: The Canadian Council of Churches
Affliation(s): The Christian Church (Disciples of Christ) in USA
Chief Officer(s):
Janet Fountain, Moderator, 902-354-5988
pjfountain@eastlink.ca
Richard E. (Rick) Hamilton, Interim Regional Minister
Finances: *Annual Operating Budget:* $100,000-$250,000; *Funding Sources:* Donations
Staff Member(s): 2
Membership: 4,000 + 30 churches; *Committees:* Archives; Biennial Convention; Christian Nurture, Service, Witness; Church Development; College; Ministry
Activities: *Internships:* Yes; *Speaker Service:* Yes; *Library:* Resource Centre

The Christian Episcopal Church of Canada (CECC)
9280 #2 Rd., Richmond BC V7E 2C8
Tel: 604-275-7422
xnec1662@gmail.com
www.xnec.ca
Also Known As: Traditional Anglican Church in Canada
Overview: A small national charitable organization founded in 1991
Member of: Anglican Communion
Affliation(s): Christian Episcopal Church in the USA
Chief Officer(s):
Robert D. Redmile
Finances: *Annual Operating Budget:* $100,000-$250,000; *Funding Sources:* Donations
Staff Member(s): 12; 40 volunteer(s)
Membership: 450; *Fees:* Free-will offerings; *Member Profile:* Baptised & confirmed Anglican Christians; *Committees:* Parochial Church Council, Assembly & Consistory; Diocesan Synod & Diocesan Council
Activities: Traditional Anglican faith & worship according to the Book of Common Prayer

Christian Farmers Federation of Ontario (CFFO)
7660 Mill Rd., RR#4, Guelph ON N1H 6J1
Tel: 519-837-1620; *Fax:* 519-824-1835
cffomail@christianfarmers.org
www.christianfarmers.org
twitter.com/CFFOnt
www.youtube.com/user/ChristianFarmers
Overview: A large provincial organization founded in 1954
Mission: A professional organization for Christian family farm entrepreneurs; a general farm organization with an interest in a broad range of agricultural, rural & social issues that impact upon the quality of the family life & family businesses of members; as a professional organization, committed to enabling members as producers, as marketers & as citizens, developing both the entrepreneurial & community leadership of members; through involvement in public policy, promotes a family farm & stewardship perspective; as a confessional organization, committed to being upfront about the Christian value system that motivates members, in order to make the wisdom of the Christian faith available to farm practice & farm policy
Affliation(s): AG Care; Christian Farmers Federation of Alberta; Christian Environmental Council; Rural Development Advisory Committee
Chief Officer(s):
Lorne Small, President
Nathan Stevens, Interim Manager & Director, Policy Development
stevens@christianfarmers.org
Finances: *Annual Operating Budget:* $500,000-$1.5 Million; *Funding Sources:* Membership fees
Staff Member(s): 5
Membership: 4,172; *Fees:* $157.50; *Member Profile:* Full-time commercial family farm entrepreneurs; part-time, hobby & lifestyle farmers; all those who have directed their farm organization fee to CFFO when they register with the Ontario Ministry of Agriculture, Food & Rural Affairs as part of the farm business registration process; *Committees:* Supply Management; Pork Producers; Sheep Producers; Stewardship & Policy East; Stewardship & Policy West
Activities: Our Farm Environmental Agenda (drafted by a coalition of Christian Farmers Federation of Ontario, AGCare, Ontario Federation of Agriculture, & the Ontario Farm Animal Council) outlines the strong commitment of farmers, through farm plans, to document present environmental conditions on their farms, develop a strategy for making appropriate changes, document actual farm practices & use that data for the development of new farm environmental initiatives; *Speaker Service:* Yes

Christian Health Association of Alberta (CHAA)
132 Warwick Rd., Edmonton AB T5X 4P8
Tel: 780-488-8074; *Fax:* 780-475-7968
chaaa@compusmart.ab.ca
www.chaaa.ab.ca
Previous Name: Catholic Health Care Conference of Alberta
Overview: A medium-sized provincial charitable organization founded in 1943 overseen by Catholic Health Association of Canada
Mission: Represents the shared vision & values of those seeking to make visible Jesus the Healer; provides support & leadership to members & the community through education, advocacy & collaboration
Chief Officer(s):
Glyn J. Smith, Administrator
Finances: *Annual Operating Budget:* $50,000-$100,000
Staff Member(s): 1; 13 volunteer(s)
Membership: 22 health facilities + 29 associate + 48 personal + 10 life; *Fees:* $25 individual; $75 associate

Christian Heritage Party of British Columbia
PO Box 275, Smithers BC V0J 2N2
Tel: 250-847-3777
info@BCHeritageParty.ca
www.bcheritageparty.ca
Also Known As: CHP British Columbia
Previous Name: British Columbia Heritage Party
Overview: A small provincial organization founded in 2010
Mission: The party advocates in favour of establishing a constitution to govern the province of British Columbia
Chief Officer(s):
Wilf Hanni, Party Leader

Christian Heritage Party of Canada (CHP) / Parti de l'héritage du Canada
PO Box 4958, Stn. E, Ottawa ON K1S 5J1
Tel: 819-281-6686; *Fax:* 819-281-7174
Toll-Free: 888-868-3247
nationaloffice@chp.ca
www.chp.ca
www.facebook.com/groups/CHPCanada

twitter.com/CHPCanada
www.youtube.com/user/christianheritage
Also Known As: Canada's Responsible Alternative
Overview: A large national organization founded in 1986
Mission: To provide true Christian leadership & uphold biblical principles in federal legislation; To attain the leadership of the federal government of Canada through the existing democratic process
Affliation(s): CHP New Zealand; Christian Heritage International Political Society
Chief Officer(s):
Jim Hnatiuk, National Leader
leader@chp.ca
Rod Taylor, Deputy Leader
deputyleader@chp.ca
Louis (Luke) Kwantes, President
nationalpres@chp.ca
Finances: *Annual Operating Budget:* $250,000-$500,000; *Funding Sources:* Membership fees & donations
Staff Member(s): 3
Membership: 6,000+; *Fees:* $25 individual; $40 family; $200 individual lifetime; $300 husband & wife
Activities: *Speaker Service:* Yes

Christian Labour Association of Canada (CLAC) / Association chrétienne du travail du Canada

2335 Argentia Rd., Mississauga ON L5N 5N3
Tel: 905-812-2855; *Fax:* 905-812-5556
Toll-Free: 800-268-5281
headoffice@clac.ca
www.clac.ca
www.facebook.com/clacunion
twitter.com/clacunion
www.youtube.com/user/CLACunion
Overview: A medium-sized national organization founded in 1952
Mission: To promote labour relations based on the social principles of justice, respect & dignity; To stand up for fair wages, reasonable work hours, good benefits, a dependable retirement savings plan, job security, professional development & opportunities for advancement
Member of: World Organization of Workers
Chief Officer(s):
Dick Heinen, Executive Director, 780-454-6181
dheinen@clac.ca
Hank Beekhuis, Ontario Provincial Director, 905-812-2855
hbeekhuis@clac.ca
Dennis Perrin, Prairies Director, 780-792-5292
David Prentice, BC Director, 604-888-7220
dprentice@clac.ca
Wayne Prins, Alberta Director
Staff Member(s): 250
Membership: 55,000
Activities: Training programs; *Speaker Service:* Yes; *Library* by appointment

Calgary Regional Office
#232, 2333 - 18 Ave. NE, Calgary AB T2E 8T6
Tel: 403-686-0288; *Fax:* 403-686-0357
Toll-Free: 866-686-0288
calgary@clac.ca
Chief Officer(s):
Randy Klassen, Regional Director
rklassen@clac.ca

Edmonton Regional Office
14920 - 188 Ave., Edmonton AB T5V 1B8
Tel: 780-454-6181; *Fax:* 780-451-3976
Toll-Free: 877-863-5154
edmonton@clac.ca
Chief Officer(s):
Ryan Timmermans, Regional Director
rtimmermans@clac.ca

Fort McMurray Regional Office
8129 Fraser Ave., Unit A, Fort McMurray AB T9H 0A2
Tel: 780-792-5292
fortmcmurray@clac.ca
Chief Officer(s):
Jayson Bueckert, Regional Director

Fort St. John/Northeastern BC Regional Office
PO Box 2, #210, 10504 - 100th Ave., Fort St. John BC V1J 1Z2
Tel: 250-785-5005
fortstjohn@clac.ca
Chief Officer(s):
David Prentice, BC Director

GTA/Central/Northern Ontario Regional Office
2335 Argentia Rd., Mississauga ON L5N 5N3
Tel: 905-812-2855
Toll-Free: 800-268-5281
mississauga@clac.ca
Chief Officer(s):
J.D. Alkema, Regional Director

Kelowna/Southern Interior, BC Regional Office
#105, 2040 Springfield Rd., Kelowna BC V1Y 9N7
Tel: 250-868-9111
Toll-Free: 866-757-2522
kelowna@clac.ca
Chief Officer(s):
Jim Oostenbrink, Regional Director

Kitchener/Cambridge/Waterloo Regional Office
64 Saltsman Dr., Cambridge ON N3H 4R7
Tel: 519-653-3002
Toll-Free: 877-701-2522
cambridge@clac.ca
Chief Officer(s):
Ian DeWaard, Representative

Niagara/Hamilton/Brant Regional Office
PO Box 219, 89 South Service Rd., Grimsby ON L3M 4G3
Tel: 905-945-1500; *Fax:* 905-945-7200
Toll-Free: 800-463-2522
grimsby@clac.ca
Chief Officer(s):
Isobel Farrell, Regional Director
ifarrell@clac.ca

Ottawa/Eastern Ontario Regional Office
#100, 38 Antares Dr., Ottawa ON K2E 7V2
Tel: 613-238-2522; *Fax:* 613-238-9255
Toll-Free: 888-279-2522
ottawa@clac.ca
Chief Officer(s):
Brendan Kooy, Regional Director

Saskatoon Regional Office
PO Box 38089, #8, 2345 Ave. CN, Saskatoon SK S7L 5Z5
Tel: 306-649-2522; *Fax:* 306-649-2526
Toll-Free: 877-649-2522
saskatoon@clac.ca
Chief Officer(s):
Dennis Perrin, Regional Director

Southwestern Ontario Regional Office
455 Keil Dr. South, Chatham ON N7M 6M4
Tel: 519-354-4831; *Fax:* 519-354-3723
Toll-Free: 800-561-2522
chatham@clac.ca
Chief Officer(s):
Trish Douma, Regional Director
tdouma@clac.ca

Vancouver/Lower Mainland Regional Office
#100, 19955 - 81A Ave., Langley BC V2Y 0C7
Tel: 604-888-7220; *Fax:* 604-455-1565
Toll-Free: 800-331-2522
langley@clac.ca
Chief Officer(s):
David Prentice, BC Director

Winnipeg Regional Office
#100, 185 Provencher Blvd., Winnipeg MB R2H 0G4
Tel: 204-989-0198; *Fax:* 204-942-6967
Toll-Free: 877-989-2522
winnipeg@clac.ca
Chief Officer(s):
Geoff Dueck Thiessen, Regional Director
gduecktthiessen@clac.ca

Christian Medical & Dental Society of Canada (CMDS)

#1 - 197D Main St., Steinbach MB R5G 1Y5
Tel: 204-326-2523; *Fax:* 204-326-3098
Toll-Free: 888-256-8653
office@cmdscanada.org
www.cmdscanada.org
Overview: A medium-sized provincial organization founded in 1971
Mission: To uphold a Christian view of medicine & dentistry; to understand & minister to the spiritual needs of colleagues; to create educational materials about public policy & health; to develop programs that promote a Christian view of medical ethics; & to support local group activities, plan conferences, & locate mentorship & other opportunities.
Member of: International Christian Medical & Dental Association
Chief Officer(s):
Larry Worthen, Executive Director
lworthen@cmdscanada.org
Abraham Ninan, President
Shalea Piteau, Treasurer
Sue McLoughlin, Secretary
Finances: *Funding Sources:* Dues; Donations
Membership: *Fees:* $365 Full-time Medical & Dental Practitioners; $180 Part-time Practitioners; $55 Residents; $25 Medical or Dental Students or Missionaries; *Member Profile:* Christian physicians, dentists, & students who wish to integrate faith with professional practice
Activities: Offers workshops & conferences; supports a toll-free helpline for medical & dental trainees; publishes a Members Directory & other literature; offers mission opportunities

Christian Record Braille Foundation Inc. *See* Christian Record Services Canada

Christian Record Services Canada

PO Box 31119, #119, 1300 King St. East, Oshawa ON L1H 8N9
Tel: 905-436-6938; *Fax:* 905-436-7102
Toll-Free: 888-899-0006
page@christianrecordservices.ca
www.crsblindservices.ca
twitter.comCRSBfriends
www.youtube.com/user/chrecord
Also Known As: National Camps for the Blind
Previous Name: Christian Record Braille Foundation Inc.
Overview: A medium-sized national charitable organization founded in 1899
Mission: To enrich the lives of blind, deaf, visually, physically & hearing impaired persons regardless of race, creed, economic status or sex.
Member of: Christian Camping International; Canadian Camping Association
Chief Officer(s):
Patricia L. Page, Executive Director
p.page@christianrecordservices.ca
Finances: *Annual Operating Budget:* $500,000-$1.5 Million; *Funding Sources:* Public contribution
Staff Member(s): 14
Activities: Magazines in braille, large print & on audio cassette; full-vision books (a combination of print & braille for blind parents with sighted children); Bible Correspondence School (Bible study guides available in braille, in large print, on audio cassettes & in easy English for the deaf); National Camps for the Blind; personal visitation; glaucoma screenings; deaf services.; *Library:* Lending Library for the Blind

Christian Reformed Church in North America (CRCNA)

PO Box 5070, Stn. LCD 1, 3475 Mainway, Burlington ON L7R 3Y8
Tel: 905-336-2920; *Fax:* 905-336-8344
Toll-Free: 800-730-3490
crcna@crcna.ca
www.crcna.org
www.facebook.com/crcna
www.twitter.com/crcna
Overview: A large international organization founded in 1857
Mission: The denominational office in Canada coordinates the work of the Church in Canada, overseeing the Committee for Contact with the Government (social justice issues), urban Aboriginal Ministry Centres (Edmonton, Regina, Winnipeg), & ecumenical involvement in KAIROS task forces (KAIROS: Canadian Ecumenical Justice Initiatives)
Affliation(s): National Association of Evangelicals; Reformed Ecumenical Council; World Alliance of Reformed Churches; Canadian Council of Churches; Evangelical Fellowship of Canada
Chief Officer(s):
Ben Vandezande, Interim Director
executive-director@crcna.org
Finances: *Annual Operating Budget:* Greater than $5 Million; *Funding Sources:* Gifts & donations
Staff Member(s): 225
Membership: In US & Canada: 245,217 members in more than 1,000 congregations; *Committees:* Abuse Prevention; Back to God Hour; Calvin College; Calvin Theological Seminary; CRC Publications; Home Missions; World Missions; World Relief; Chaplaincy Ministries; CRC Loan Fund; Disability Concerns; Fund for Smaller Churches; Pastor-Church Relations; Pensions & Insurance; Race Relations; Historical; Interchurch Relations; Sermons for Reading Services
Activities: *Awareness Events:* Sea to Sea Celebration Rally; *Speaker Service:* Yes

Publications:
• The Banner
Type: Magazine; *Frequency:* Monthly; *Editor:* Rev Bob De Moor

Christian Reformed World Relief Committee *See* World Renew

Christian Stewardship Services (CSS)
#214A, 500 Alden Rd., Markham ON L3R 5H5
Tel: 905-947-9262; *Fax:* 905-947-9263
Toll-Free: 800-267-8890
admin@csservices.ca
www.csservices.ca
Overview: A medium-sized national charitable organization founded in 1976
Mission: To connect families, faith, & finances for efficient estate & gift planning; To promote Biblical stewardship
Member of: Canadian Council of Christian Charities
Affliation(s): Diaconal Ministries of the Christian Reformed Church
Chief Officer(s):
Maynard Wiersma, Executive Director
maynardw@csservices.ca
Mary Benn, Administrator, Finance & Systems
finance@csservices.ca
Henry Eygenraam, Coordinator, Special Projects and Succession Plans
eygenraam@csservices.ca
Finances: *Funding Sources:* Christian charities, including churches & schools; Social service organizations
Activities: Providing advice about will & estate planning; Offering the Growing & Giving program, featuring presentations & workshops
Publications:
• Advancing Stewardship
Type: Newsletter; *Frequency:* Semiannually
Profile: Information about the organization & its work
• Christian Stewardship Services Annual Report
Type: Yearbook; *Frequency:* Annually

Christie-Ossington Neighbourhood Centre (CONC)
854 Bloor St. West, Toronto ON M6G 1M2
Tel: 416-534-8941; *Fax:* 416-534-8704
www.conccommunity.org
Overview: A medium-sized local charitable organization founded in 1994
Mission: To improve the quality of life in the Christie Ossington community by working in collaboration with residents, community institutions, agencies, local businesses and stakeholders to create a safe and healthy community.
Chief Officer(s):
Lynn Daly, Executive Director
lynn@conc.ca
Finances: *Funding Sources:* Government, United Way, Donations
Staff Member(s): 43

Christina Lake Chamber of Commerce
1675 Hwy. 3, Christina Lake BC V0H 1E2
Tel: 250-447-6161; *Fax:* 250-447-6161
info@christinalake.com
www.christinalake.com
Overview: A small local organization
Member of: BC Chamber of Commerce
Finances: *Funding Sources:* Membership dues
7 volunteer(s)
Membership: 52; *Fees:* $100
Activities: Fishing derby; winter fest; trail & park development

Christmas Exchange / Partage de Noël
PO Box 5167, Ottawa ON K2C 3H4
Tel: 613-226-6434; *Fax:* 613-226-7522
info@christmas-exchange.com
www.christmas-exchange.com
www.linkedin.com/company/the-caring-and-sharing-exchange-l%27-change-c
www.facebook.com/pages/Christmas-Exchange/17514594027
twitter.com/CS_Exchange
www.youtube.com/user/CaringandSharingX
Overview: A small local organization founded in 1915
Mission: To provide seasonal food assistance, as food hamper or redeemable store vouchers to families in need.
Affiliation(s): Salvation Army Toy Centre; Child & Youth Friendly Ottawa
Chief Officer(s):
Wayne Crutchlow, President
Cindy Smith, Executive Director
Staff Member(s): 5; 331 volunteer(s)
Activities: Maintenance of database coordinated with other community groups to avoid duplication of giving

Christmas Tree Farmers of Ontario (CFTO)
9251 County Rd. 1, Palgrave ON L0N 1P0
Fax: 905-729-0548
Toll-Free: 800-661-3530
www.christmastrees.on.ca
Overview: A small provincial organization founded in 1950
Member of: Canadian Christmas Tree Growers Association
Chief Officer(s):
Shirley Brennan, Executive Director
Membership: *Fees:* Member $195; Senior member $250; Plus member $360; Associate member $130; Subscriber $80;
Member Profile: Christmas tree farmers

Christos Metropolitan Community Church
Trinity St. Paul's Centre, 427 Bloor St. West, Toronto ON M5S 1X7
Tel: 416-925-7924; *Fax:* 416-922-8587
Also Known As: Christos MCC
Overview: A small local charitable organization founded in 1984
Mission: Ministry by and for the LGBT community of Toronto.
Member of: Universal Fellowship of Metropolitan Community Churches
Chief Officer(s):
Deana Dudley, Pastor
Judi Bonner, Secretary
Finances: *Annual Operating Budget:* Less than $50,000
Staff Member(s): 1; 8 volunteer(s)
Membership: 30
Activities: Weekly worship services; spirituality-based study groups; social events;

Chronic Pain Association of Canada (CPAC)
PO Box 66017, Stn. Heritage, #130, 2323 - 111 St., Edmonton AB T6J 6T4
Tel: 780-482-6727; *Fax:* 780-433-3128
cpac@chronicpaincanada.com
www.chronicpaincanada.com
Previous Name: North American Chronic Pain Association of Canada
Overview: A medium-sized national charitable organization founded in 1986
Mission: To advance the treatment & management of chronic intractable pain; to develop research projects to promote the discovery of a cure for this disease; to educate both the health care community & the public
Chief Officer(s):
Terry Bremner, President
Barry Ulmer, Executive Director
Finances: *Annual Operating Budget:* Less than $50,000; *Funding Sources:* Donations
Staff Member(s): 1; 2 volunteer(s)
Membership: 1,200; *Fees:* $15; *Member Profile:* Individuals interested in chronic pain; 26 self-help groups
Activities: Self-help groups; education & research; networking with organizations of contiguous purpose; *Awareness Events:* Chronic Pain Awareness Week, 2nd week of Nov.; *Speaker Service:* Yes; *Library* by appointment

Chrysotile Institute / Instit du Chrysotile
#1640, 1200, av McGill College, Montréal QC H3B 4G7
Tel: 514-877-9797; *Fax:* 514-877-9717
info@chrysotile.com
www.chrysotile.com
Overview: A medium-sized national organization founded in 1984
Mission: To promote the implementation & enforcement of effective regulations, standards, work practices & techniques for the safe use of asbestos.
Chief Officer(s):
Denis Hamel, Director General
Activities: Participates in international missions by providing information, consultation, or training of a technical, medical & scientific nature for processors & users in other countries; gathers & disseminates medical, scientific & technical data about asbestos & substitute fibres; *Library* by appointment

CHUM Charitable Foundation; CHUM's Kid's Crusade Foundation *See* CP24 CHUM Christmas Wish

Church Council on Justice & Corrections (CCJC) / Conseil des églises pour la justice et la criminologie (CÉJC)
#303, 200 Isabella St., Ottawa ON K1S 1V7
Tel: 613-563-1688; *Fax:* 613-237-6129
info@ccjc.ca
www.ccjc.ca
www.linkedin.com/company/the-church-council-on-justice-and-corrections
www.facebook.com/180318678672186?v=wall
twitter.com/CCJCCanada
www.youtube.com/channel/UCbL3WH8MfWbUp-31s9gPjoQ?feature=mhee
Overview: A medium-sized national charitable organization founded in 1972
Mission: To strengthen churches' ministry in fields of crime prevention, justice & corrections; to initiate, encourage & support programs which sensitize congregations & educate volunteer groups to participate in development of community responses to crime, justice & corrections; to promote a healing justice; to examine & respond to policy concerns with assistance of churches; to call on churches to address issues; to provide resources to churches & other related organizations.
Member of: National Associations Active in Criminal Justice
Affliation(s): The Network - Interaction for Conflict Resolution
Chief Officer(s):
Janet Handy, Executive Director
jhandy@ccjc.ca
Lorraine Berzins, Communication Chair of Justice, 613-563-1688 Ext. 2
lberzins@ccjc.ca
Finances: *Annual Operating Budget:* $250,000-$500,000
Staff Member(s): 3
Membership: 46 directors + 292 supporting; *Fees:* $40 individuals; $200 organizations; *Committees:* Steering
Activities: *Internships:* Yes; *Speaker Service:* Yes
Awards:
• Ron Wiebe Restorative Justice Award (Award)

CEJC Québec
#322, 2715, ch côte Ste-Catherine, Montréal QC H3T 1B6
Tél: 514-738-5075; *Téléc:* 514-735-2935
cejcq-provincial@sympatico.ca
Chief Officer(s):
Laurent Champagne, Coordinateur

The Church Lads' Brigade (CLB)
PO Box 28126, 82 Harvey Rd., St. John's NL A1B 4J8
Tel: 709-722-1737; *Fax:* 709-722-1734
info@theclb.ca
www.theclb.ca
twitter.com/TheCLB_NL
Overview: A medium-sized national organization founded in 1892
Mission: The advancement of Christ's kingdom among youth, the promotion of Christian charity, reverence, discipline, self-respect, respect for others & all that lends towards true Christian character
Affliation(s): The Church Lads' & Church Girls' Brigade (UK)
Chief Officer(s):
Bernard Davis, Executive Director
Finances: *Annual Operating Budget:* $50,000-$100,000; *Funding Sources:* Donations; building rentals; fundraising
Staff Member(s): 1; 200 volunteer(s)
Membership: 800; *Fees:* $20; *Member Profile:* Boys & girls of all religious affiliations
Activities: Youth activities; recreational, educational & social; *Internships:* Yes; *Library:* CLB Archives; Open to public by appointment

Church Library Association of British Columbia
615 Banks Ave. West, Parksville BC V9P 2S1
Tel: 604-264-5821
clabc.ca@gmail.com
www.clabc.ca
www.facebook.com/ca.clabc
Overview: A small provincial organization founded in 1971
Mission: To help church libraries in British Columbia make the most of their resources
Chief Officer(s):
June Wynne, President
Membership: *Member Profile:* Churches & church librarians in British Columbia
Activities: Helping churches create pro-active, engaging libraries
Publications:
• The Rare Bird
Type: Newsletter; *Frequency:* 4 times a year *ISSN:* 0380-2566
Profile: A forum for exchange of news & ideas among members; Newsletter also includes book reviews & news articles

Church Library Association of Ontario (CLAO)

c/o Margaret Godefroy, CLAO Membership Secretary, #603, 155 Navy St., Oakville ON L6J 2Z7
Tel: 905-845-0222
agodefroy@cogeco.ca
www.churchlibraries.ca
www.facebook.com/churchlibraryassociationofontario
Overview: A small provincial organization founded in 1969
Mission: To help church libraries in Ontario make the most of their resources
Chief Officer(s):
Arthur McClelland, President & Archivist, 519-679-5830
arthur.mcclelland@lpl.london.on.ca
Marcella Haanstra, Coordinator, Outreach, 905-309-5284
mknibbe13@hotmail.com
Margaret Godefroy, Membership Secretary, 905-845-0222
agodefroy@cogeco.ca
Jane Rocoski, Coordinator, Resources, 905-725-0910
grocoski1204@rogers.com
Mary Ryan, Coordinator, Conferences
ryanms39@gmail.com
Jo-Anne Vandermey, Treasurer, 905-563-7616
jovdmey@cogeco.ca
Margaret Godefroy, Secretary, Membership, 905-845-0222
agodefroy@cogeco.ca
Michelle Rickard, Editor, Newsletter
mkrickard@sympatico.ca
Membership: *Fees:* $15; *Member Profile:* Churches & church librarians in Ontario
Activities: Helping churches create pro-active, engaging libraries
Meetings/Conferences: • Church Library Association of Ontario 2015 Annual Spring Conference, 2015, ON
Scope: Provincial
Description: A Saturday conference, usually held in a southern Ontario location, featuring workshops, speakers, networking opportunities, exhibitors, & a book swap
Contact Information: conference@clao.ca
• Church Library Association of Ontario 2015 Annual Fall Conference, 2015, ON
Scope: Provincial
Description: A Saturday event in a southern Ontario location, featuring technical, administrative, & promotional workshops
Contact Information: conference@clao.ca
• Church Library Association of Ontario 2016 Annual Spring Conference, 2016, ON
Scope: Provincial
Description: A Saturday conference, usually held in a southern Ontario location, featuring workshops, speakers, networking opportunities, exhibitors, & a book swap
Contact Information: conference@clao.ca
• Church Library Association of Ontario 2016 Annual Fall Conference, 2016, ON
Scope: Provincial
Description: A Saturday event in a southern Ontario location, featuring technical, administrative, & promotional workshops
Contact Information: conference@clao.ca
Publications:
• Library Lines
Type: Newsletter; *Frequency:* Quarterly; *Editor:* June Wilson
Profile: Articles, book reviews, & practical information for church libraries

Church of England in Canada *See* The Anglican Church of Canada

Church of God of Prophecy in Canada

Eastern Canada Head Office, 5145 Tomken Rd., Mississauga ON L4W 1P1
Tel: 905-625-1278; *Fax:* 905-625-1316
info@cogop.ca
www.cogop.ca
Overview: A medium-sized national charitable organization
Mission: The Church of God of Prophecy has its roots in the Holiness/Pentecostal tradition and has felt a special burden to call attention to the principle of unity in the body of Christ, while faithfully proclaiming the gospel of Jesus Christ before a watching world.
Finances: *Annual Operating Budget:* $100,000-$250,000
Staff Member(s): 3
Membership: 31 churches
Activities: *Internships:* Yes; *Speaker Service:* Yes

Church of Jesus Christ of Latter-day Saints

c/o Toronto Ontario Temple, 10060 Bramalea Rd., Brampton ON L6R 1A1
Tel: 905-799-1122; *Fax:* 905-799-1140
www.lds.org
www.facebook.com/LDS
twitter.com/ldschurch
www.pinterest.com/ldschurch/
Overview: A medium-sized national organization founded in 1830
Membership: 190,265 members + 479 congregations in Canada
Activities: *Speaker Service:* Yes; *Library:* Family History Library; by appointment

Church of Scientology of Toronto

77 Peter St., Toronto ON M5V 2G4
Tel: 416-925-2145
toronto@scientology.net
www.scientology.ca
Overview: A medium-sized local organization
Member of: Church of Scientology

Church of the Good Shepherd

116 Queen St. North, Kitchener ON N2H 2H7
Tel: 519-743-3845; *Fax:* 519-743-3375
office@shepherdsway.ca
www.shepherdsway.ca
Also Known As: Swedenborgian Church
Overview: A small local organization
Chief Officer(s):
John Maine, Minister
Staff Member(s): 2
Membership: 140 individual

The Churches' Council on Theological Education in Canada: an Ecumenical Foundation (CCTE) / Le Conseil des Églises pour l'éducation théologique au Canada: une fondation oecuménique

47 Queen's Park Cres., Toronto ON M5S 2C3
Tel: 416-928-3223; *Fax:* 416-928-3563
director@ccte.ca
www.ccte.ca
Overview: A small national organization founded in 1962
Mission: To provide for the coordination of consultation, research, & administration of grants awarded by the Council, in order to promote the development of theological education for ministry
Affiliation(s): Association of Theological Schools
Chief Officer(s):
Rafael Vallejo, Executive Director
Robert Smith, President
Finances: *Annual Operating Budget:* $100,000-$250,000
Staff Member(s): 2; 24 volunteer(s)
Membership: 24 individual

Churchill Chamber of Commerce

PO Box 176, Churchill MB R0B 0E0
Tel: 204-675-2022; *Fax:* 204-675-2021
Toll-Free: 888-389-2327
churchillchamber@mts.net
churchillchamberofcommerce.ca
Overview: A small local organization
Chief Officer(s):
Louise Lawrie, President
lawriemb@mymts.net
Patricia Penwarden, Secretary
arcticmusher@hotmail.com

Churchill Park Family Care Society

3311 Centre St. NW, Calgary AB T2E 2X7
Tel: 403-266-4656; *Fax:* 403-264-5657
cpfirst@churchillpark.ca
www.churchillpark.ca
Overview: A small local organization founded in 1970
Mission: To offer quality child care; To help families & caregivers access support & emergency assistance
Chief Officer(s):
Sharon Reib, Executive Director
Dionne Harlos, Senior Director, Human Resources & Administration
Dharlos@churchillpark.ca
Don Ballance, Director, Finance
Montana Desjardins, Director, Operations
Tristan Katz, Director, Operations
Dina Ottoni-Barristessa, Director, Operations
Christie Scarlett, Director, Operations
Shefali Geoffroy Chateau, Manager, Business
Activities: Sharing resources to help with child rearing; Accommodating children with special needs

La Cinémathèque québécoise

335, boul de Maisonneuve est, Montréal QC H2X 1K1
Tél: 514-842-9763; *Téléc:* 514-842-1816
info@cinematheque.qc.ca
www.cinematheque.qc.ca
Également appelé: Musée de l'image en mouvement
Aperçu: *Dimension:* moyenne; *Envergure:* provinciale; Organisme sans but lucratif; fondée en 1963
Mission: Conservation et mise en valeur du patrimoine cinématographique et télévisuel; promouvoir la culture cinématographique; créer des archives de cinéma; acquérir et conserver des films ainsi que toute la documentation qui s'y rattache; projeter ces films et exposer ces documents de facon non commerciale à des fins historique, pédagogique et artistique.
Membre de: Fédération internationale des archives du film
Membre(s) du bureau directeur:
Iolande Cadrin-Rossignol, Directrice générale
Fabrice Montal, Directeur, Programmation
Jean Gagnon, Directeur, Collections
Claude Bouffard, Directrice, Administration et finances
Jeanine Basile, Directrice, Communications et marketing
Finances: *Budget de fonctionnement annuel:* $1.5 Million-$3 Million; *Fonds:* Ministère de la Culture et des communications du Québec; Patrimoine canadien, Conseil des arts du Canada
Membre(s) du personnel: 54; 2 bénévole(s)
Membre: 500; *Montant de la cotisation:* 120$; *Critères d'admissibilite:* Tous ceux qui s'intéressent à l'histoire, l'actualité et l'avenir du cinéma, de la télévision et des nouveaux médias
Activités: *Bibliothèque:* Médiathèque Guy-L.-Coté; Bibliothèque publique

CIO Association of Canada (CIOCAN)

National Office, #204, 7270 Woodbine Ave., Markham ON L3R 4B9
Tel: 905-752-1899; *Fax:* 905-513-1248
Toll-Free: 877-865-9009
national@ciocan.ca
www.ciocan.ca
Overview: A large national organization founded in 2004
Mission: To facilitate networking, sharing of best practices & executive development, & to drive advocacy on issues facing IT Executives/CIOs. Chapters: Calgary, Edmonton, Toronto, Vancouver & Victoria
Chief Officer(s):
Gary Davenport, President, National Board of Directors
Membership: 300 nation-wide; *Fees:* $375 academic; $600 associate; $750 full; *Member Profile:* IT executives; Chief Information Officers
Activities: Networking events; seminars; outreach; advocacy; research; scholarships; leadership development
Meetings/Conferences: • CIO Peer Forum 2015, April, 2015, Vancouver Convention Centre, Vancouver, BC
Scope: National
Description: The theme is "Action is Eloquence: Creating Value from Innovation." Hosted by the CIO Association's Toronto & Ottawa Chapters.
Contact Information: Alex Buhler, CIO Peer Forum Co-Chair; national@ciocan.ca

Calgary Chapter
www.ciocan.ca/Chapters/Calgary
Chief Officer(s):
Paul Parzen, President

Edmonton Chapter
www.ciocan.ca/Chapters/Edmonton
Chief Officer(s):
Dean Doige, President

Toronto Chapter
www.ciocan.ca/Chapters/Toronto
Chief Officer(s):
Mary Anne Ballantyne, President

Vancouver Chapter
#610, 142 - 757 West Hastings St., Vancouver BC V6C 1A1
Tel: 604-461-0246
admin@ciocan-vancouver.ca
www.ciocan.ca/Chapters/Vancouver
Chief Officer(s):
Alex Buhler, President
Lisa Bateman, Contact

Victoria Chapter
www.ciocan.ca/Chapters/Victoria
Chief Officer(s):
Ian McLeod, President

CIRANO
2020, rue University, 25e étage, Montréal QC H3A 2A5
Tel: 514-985-4000; *Fax:* 514-985-4039
webmaster@cirano.qc.ca
www.cirano.qc.ca
Also Known As: Center for Interuniversity Research & Analysis of Organizations
Overview: A medium-sized provincial organization founded in 1998
Mission: To bolster firms' efficiency & competitive edge through the rapid transfer of new knowledge generated by its research; to encourage the integration of organizations' knowledge & preoccupations & practitioners' experience into teaching & research programs; to develop & keep in Québec world-class research teams who perform scientific analyses of organizations & strategic behaviour; to contribute to training a new generation of top-tier scientists & professionals in Québec

Circle of Eagles Lodge
1470 East Broadway, Vancouver BC V5N 1V6
Tel: 604-874-9610; *Fax:* 604-874-3858
Toll-Free: 888-332-6357
www.circleofeagles.com
Overview: A medium-sized local organization founded in 1970
Mission: To provide services to incarcerated Native men; to assist Native ex-offenders in becoming productive, contributing members of society
Chief Officer(s):
Ken Clement, President
Finances: *Annual Operating Budget:* $250,000-$500,000
Activities: Post-release residential house; hands-on job development & lifeskills program; individual counselling; temporary financial assistance; social orientation; shelter & food services; liaison between inmates, corrections & the community; assisting Native clubs within the institutions

Circulation Management Association of Canada (CMC) / Association canadienne des chefs de tirage
c/o Target Audience Management Inc., #6, 50 Main St. East, Beeton ON L0G 1A0
Tel: 905-729-1046; *Fax:* 905-729-4432
admin@thecmc.ca
thecmc.ca
www.facebook.com/180627152014026
twitter.com/CircCanada
Previous Name: Canadian Circulation Management Association
Overview: A small national organization founded in 1981
Mission: To provide professional development, promotes fellowship within the circulation profession & raises the profile of circulation professionals by rewarding outstanding achievement.
Affliation(s): Newspaper Association of America
Chief Officer(s):
Tony Danas, President
tony.danas@gmail.com
Ron Sellwood, Director, Communications, 416-754-3900 Ext. 285
rons@ctcmagazines.com
Brian Gillet, Administrator
Membership: *Fees:* $139; *Member Profile:* Circulation professionals of the Canadian magazine industry
Activities: *Rents Mailing List:* Yes
Awards:
• ACE Awards (Award)
Eligibility: Demonstration of excellent circulation work in Cdn. publishing industry
• Magazine Marketer of the Year Award (Award)
Eligibility: Having produced a body of work or notable achievement/contribution in the Cdn. magazine marketing field

Publications:
• The Circulator

Cities of New Brunswick Association
PO Box 1421, Stn. A, Fredericton NB E3B 5E3
Tel: 506-452-9292; *Fax:* 506-452-9898
cnba_acnb@bellaliant.com
Overview: A medium-sized provincial organization
Chief Officer(s):
Denis Roussel, Executive Director
Finances: *Funding Sources:* Membership dues

Citizen Advocacy Montreal *Voir* Parrainage civique Montréal

Citizen Advocacy Society of Medicine Hat & District
#209, 1865 Dunmore Rd. SE, Medicine Hat AB T1A 1Z8
Tel: 403-527-9787; *Fax:* 403-527-9780
www.medicinehatcitizenadvocacy.webs.com
www.facebook.com/134258909947679
Also Known As: Medicine Hat & District Citizen Advocacy Society
Overview: A small local charitable organization founded in 1981
Mission: To help build & support relationships between people who are socially isolated & people who are considered well adjusted members of our community; To ensure that people with different abilities achieve equal rights & opportunities; To support one-on-one friendships with volunteers; To offer support, guidance, spokesmanship & social inclusion

Citizen Scientists
1749 Meadowvale Rd., Toronto ON M1B 5W8
e-mail: info@citizenscientists.ca
www.citizenscientists.ca
Overview: A medium-sized local organization founded in 2001
Mission: To monitor local watersheds, foster local environmental stewardship, and educate volunteers and the public.

Citizens Concerned About Free Trade (CCAFT)
PO Box 8052, Saskatoon SK S7K 4R7
Tel: 306-244-5757; *Fax:* 306-244-3790
ccaftnat@sk.sympatico.ca
www.davidorchard.com/ccaft
Overview: A small national organization
Mission: To provide information & mobilize those opposed to the Free Trade Agreements & the loss of Canadian sovereignty; to have Canada exercise the termination clauses of both the FTA & NAFTA so that the country can protect its resources & play an independent role in world affairs
Membership: 5,000

Toronto Office
#202, 9 Bloor St. East, Toronto ON M4W 1A9
Tel: 416-922-7867; *Fax:* 416-922-7883
ccafttor@sympatico.ca
www.davidorchard.com/ccaft

Vancouver Office
PO Box 4185, Vancouver BC V6B 3Z6
Tel: 604-683-3733; *Fax:* 604-683-3749
ccaftvan@telus.net

Citizens for a Safe Environment (CSE)
Tel: 416-461-1092
info@csetoronto.org
www.csetoronto.org
Overview: A medium-sized local organization founded in 1983
Mission: To promomote waste management practices that protect the health of Toronto citizens, their communities and the environment.
Member of: Ontario Environmental Network
Activities: *Awareness Events:* Green Tea Parties; *Speaker Service:* Yes

Citizens for an Oak Ridges Trail *See* Oak Ridges Trail Association

Citizens for Public Justice (CPJ)
#501, 309 Cooper St., Ottawa ON K2P 0G5
Fax: 613-232-1275
Toll-Free: 800-667-8046
cpj@cpj.ca
www.cpj.ca
www.facebook.com/citizensforpublicjustice
twitter.com/publicjustice
Overview: A medium-sized national organization
Mission: To promote public justice in Canada by shaping key public policy debates through research and analysis, publishing and public dialogue. CPJ encourages citizens, leaders in society and governments to support policies and practices which reflect God's call for love, justice and stewardship.
Chief Officer(s):
Joe Gunn, Executive Director
Sarah Shepherd, Coordinator, Communications
sarah@cpj.ca
Staff Member(s): 9
Membership: 1500; *Fees:* $50 individual; $25 low income; $10 student
Activities: *Internships:* Yes

Citizens for Public Justice *See* CPJ Corp.

Citizens for Safe Cycling (CfSC)
PO Box 248, Stn. B, Ottawa ON K1P 6C4
Tel: 613-722-4454; *Fax:* 613-722-4454
Other Communication: membership@safecycling.ca
info@safecycling.ca
www.safecycling.ca
www.facebook.com/safecycling
twitter.com/CfSC_Ott
Overview: A medium-sized local organization founded in 1984
Mission: To promote cycling as fun, healthy, safe, economical, and environmentally-friendly transportation and recreation.
Chief Officer(s):
Hans Moor, President
president@safecycling.ca

Citizens' Environment Alliance of Southwestern Ontario *See* Citizens' Environment Alliance of Southwestern Ontario

Citizens' Environment Alliance of Southwestern Ontario (CEA)
1950 Ottawa St., Windsor ON N8Y 1R7
Tel: 519-973-1116; *Fax:* 519-973-8360
ceaadmin@cogeco.net
www.citizensenvironmentalliance.org
www.facebook.com/group.php?gid=4417742199
Previous Name: Citizens' Environment Alliance of Southwestern Ontario
Overview: A small local charitable organization founded in 1985
Mission: CEA is a non-profit, grass-roots, international, education & research organization that aims to protect, restore & enhance the quality of the local environment in the Detroit-St. Clair Rivers corridor & in the Essex-Kent regions of the Great Lakes Basin; educate the public about environmental problems & solutions as they relate to the Great Lakes ecosystems & in particular to Southwestern Ontario. It is a registered charity, BN: 899837850RR0001.
Member of: Canadian Environmental Network; Ontario Environment Network; Environmental Action Ontario
Affliation(s): Canadian Environmental Network (RCEN); Ontario Environmental Network (OEN); Lake Erie Millennium Network (LEMN); Ontario Water Conservation Alliance
Finances: *Annual Operating Budget:* $50,000-$100,000
20 volunteer(s)
Membership: 100-499; *Fees:* Donations; *Committees:* Endangered Species; Toxic Trackers; Air Quality; Area Clean-up Team
Activities: "State of the Detroit River" boat tour; annual "Weenie Award" night; endangered natural spaces; toxic trackers; air quality; Detroit River clean-up; waste management; *Speaker Service:* Yes; *Rents Mailing List:* Yes; *Library:* Environmental & Resource Library; Open to public

Citizens' Environment Watch (CEW)
#380, 401 Richmond St. West, Toronto ON M5V 3A8
Tel: 647-258-3280; *Fax:* 416-979-3155
info@citizensenvironmentwatch.org
www.citizensenvironmentwatch.org
Overview: A medium-sized national organization founded in 1996
Mission: To provide communities the tools for education, monitoring and influencing positive change and to encourage people to take an active role in restoring and sustaining nature.
Chief Officer(s):
Meredith Cochrane, Executive Director
Finances: *Annual Operating Budget:* $250,000-$500,000; *Funding Sources:* Government, Foundations
Staff Member(s): 4

Citizens' Opposed to Paving the Escarpment (COPE)
PO Box 20014, 2211 Brant St., Burlington ON L7P 0A4
e-mail: mail@cope-nomph.org
www.cope-nomph.org
www.facebook.com/pages/Highway-No-Way/146644585393483?v=wall
twitter.com/StopHwy
Overview: A large local organization
Mission: To preserve the Niagara Escarpment, by ensuring that no new highway corridors are paved across the Niagara Escarpment & that all viable alternatives to the proposed Mid-Peninsula Highway are fully considered
Affliation(s): Coalition on the Niagara Escarpment; Sierra Club
Membership: 1000+; *Fees:* Donations of $10 or more

Citizenship Council of Manitoba Inc. *See* Immigrant Centre Manitoba Inc.

Citroën Autoclub Canada
49 Alabaster Dr., Brampton ON L6V 4G9

citroenvie.com
Overview: A medium-sized national organization
Mission: To promote preservation, restoration & recognition of all Citroëns
Chief Officer(s):
George Dyke, President, 647-896-3202
gdyke@sympatico.ca
Membership: *Fees:* US$20 basic; US$30 full; US$40 overseas
Activities: Meetings; rallies & tours; special tool-lending service

City Clerks & Election Officers Association ***See*** Alberta Municipal Clerks Association

City Farmer - Canada's Office of Urban Agriculture
PO Box 74567, Stn. Kitsilano, Vancouver BC V6K 4P4
Tel: 604-685-5832
cityfarmer@gmail.com
www.cityfarmer.org
Overview: A small national organization founded in 1978
Mission: To encourage gardening in an urban environment
Chief Officer(s):
Michael Levenston, Executive Director
Activities: Research Garden functions as the City of Vancouver's Compost Demonstration Garden & site of the Compost Hotline: 604-736-2250;

City Index Referral Association ***See*** Community Food Sharing Association

The City of Greater Sudbury Developmental Services
245 Mountain St., Sudbury ON P3B 2T8
Tel: 705-674-1451
www.cgsds.ca
Previous Name: Sudbury & District Association for Community Living
Overview: A small local organization
Member of: Ontario Agencies Supporting Individuals with Special Needs (OASIS)
Chief Officer(s):
Pascal Joseph, President
Mila Wong, Executive Director
mwong@vianet.ca

City of Waterloo Staff Association
Waterloo City Hall, PO Box 337, 100 Regina St. South, Waterloo ON N2J 4A8
Tel: 519-886-1550; *Fax:* 519-747-8760
www.city.waterloo.on.ca
Overview: A small local organization
Mission: The Association is a labour group that represents inside workers who provide administrative, program management & supervisory support for the City's operations.
Membership: 220

Civic Institute of Professional Personnel (CIPP) / L'Institut professionnel du personnel municipal (IPPM)
#270, 117 Centrepointe Dr., Ottawa ON K2G 5X3
Tel: 613-241-3730; *Fax:* 613-241-4461
admin@cipp.on.ca
www.cipp.on.ca
www.facebook.com/CIPPOttawa
twitter.com/CIPPOttawa
Overview: A small local organization
Mission: CIPP represents members in the negotiation and administration of their rights under their respective collective agreements.
Chief Officer(s):
Doug Laviolette, President
Sheila Stansislawski, Executive Director
sheilas@cipp.on.ca
Staff Member(s): 5
Membership: *Member Profile:* Professional public sector employees; *Committees:* City Negotiating; OCHC Negotiating; Grievance Arbitration Approval; Policy & Education

Civil Air Search & Rescue Association (CASARA)
c/o John Kelly, National Administrator, 3025 Ness Ave., #C, Winnipeg MB R2Y 2J2
Tel: 204-953-2290
Nationaladministrator@casaranational.ca
casara.biz
Overview: A large national organization founded in 1984
Mission: To promote aviation safety; To support Canada's Search & Rescue (SAR) program
Chief Officer(s):
John Davidson, President
John Kelly, National Administrator
Brian Bishop, Vice-President, Training & Operations
Mike Daniels, Vice-President, Finance & Administration
Doug MacDonald, Vice-President, Plans & Equipment
Membership: 2,000+ pilots, navigators, & spotters
Awards:
• Volunteer Award (Award)
Recognizes the exceptional service of a volunteer.
• Continuation Pilot Training Award (Award)
Presented annually to one of the top graduates of the power pilot training program.
• CASARA Scholarships (Scholarship)
Amount: $300-$5,000

Civil Constables Association of Nova Scotia (CCANS)
8 Evergreen Dr., Truro NS B2N 5J1
www.nsbailiff.ca
Overview: A small provincial organization founded in 2002
Mission: To represent bailiffs & process servers from Nova Scotia
Chief Officer(s):
Michael Lutes, President
Membership: *Fees:* $60 civil constables; $45 associate/corporate members; *Member Profile:* Appointed civil constable individuals in Nova Scotia; Corporations or individuals who have a direct involvement in the civil enforcement industry in Nova Scotia may be associate members

Civil Service Association of Ontario ***See*** Ontario Public Service Employees Union

Clan Donald Canada
PO Box 417, Trenton NS B0K 1X0
Tel: 902-752-6616
ebmac@ns.sympatico.ca
www.clandonaldcanada.ca
www.facebook.com/group.php?gid=171824577402
Overview: A medium-sized national organization founded in 1996
Mission: To maintain contact with members of Clan Donald around Canada
Chief Officer(s):
Priscilla Sharkey, Secretary
thesharkeys@eastlink.ca
Glenda McDonell, High Commissioner
glendamgm@sympatico.ca

Clan Farquharson Association of Canada
PO Box 23045, Stn. Dartmouth, Dartmouth NS B3A 4S9
www.clanfarquharsoncanada.ca
www.facebook.com/ClanFarquharsonOfCanada
Overview: A small national organization founded in 1984
Mission: To promote & preserve the heritage & interests of the Scottish clan of Farquharson through history, genealogy, social events, literature & language (Gaelic).
Member of: Nova Scotia Scottish Clans Association
Chief Officer(s):
David E. Coutts, President, 519-900-3771
dcouttsca2012@hotmail.ca
Finances: *Funding Sources:* Membership fees
Membership: *Fees:* $20 Individual; $25 Family; $20 Associate Member; *Member Profile:* Persons of Scottish descent related to Clan Farquharson

Clan Fraser Society of Canada (CFSC)
c/o W. Neil Fraser, #1101, 71 Charles St. East, Toronto ON M4Y 2T3
Tel: 416-920-6851
enquiry@clanfraser.ca
www.clanfraser.ca
Previous Name: Clan Fraser Society of North America, Canadian Region
Overview: A small national organization founded in 1868
Mission: To collect & disseminate information on history & the exploits of Frasers in Canada & Scotland; To act as liaison with clan chiefs
Affliation(s): Clan Fraser Society of Australia; Clan Fraser Society of New Zealand; Clan Fraser Society of Scotland & the UK
Chief Officer(s):
W. Neil Fraser, Chair
Finances: *Annual Operating Budget:* Less than $50,000
5 volunteer(s)
Membership: 650 individual; *Fees:* $25; *Member Profile:* People with the surname of Fraser or septs of Clan Fraser
Activities: Fraser history & genealogy in Canada & Scotland
Publications:
• Clan Fraser: A History
Author: Flora Marjory Fraser; *Price:* $28 hardcover; $22 paperback

Clan Fraser Society of North America, Canadian Region ***See*** Clan Fraser Society of Canada

Clan Gunn Society of North America - Eastern Canada Branch
c/o Edward Gunn, 10485 Vanier Rd., Québec QC G2B 3N4
Tel: 418-842-6563
www.clangunn.com
Overview: A small provincial organization founded in 2001
Mission: To unite all family members; to renew pride in family & clan by fostering kinship & increasing knowledge & understanding of Scottish history through cultural activities.
Chief Officer(s):
Ted Gunn, Co-Commissioner
gunn@upc.qc.ca
Louise Gunn, Co-Commissioner
Finances: *Annual Operating Budget:* Less than $50,000; *Funding Sources:* Membership fees; donations
Publications:
• Gunnsmoke
Type: newsletter

Clan Lamont Society of Canada
#317, 9049 Commercial St., New Minas NS B4N 5A4
e-mail: info@clanlamont.ca
www.clanlamont.ca
Also Known As: Clan MacEaracher
Overview: A small international charitable organization founded in 1986
Mission: To promote the Gaelic language in Nova Scotia; to help with cost of restoration of Kilfinnan Church in Scotland; To promote Celtic music & customs
Member of: Federation of Scottish Clans in Nova Scotia; Canadian Association of Scottish Societies of Canada
Affliation(s): Clan Lamont Scotland, Australia, USA
Chief Officer(s):
David Wimsett, President
Ian Patrick, Chief's Commissioner in Canada
Elsie Turner, Treasurer
Finances: *Annual Operating Budget:* Less than $50,000; *Funding Sources:* Membership dues; fundraising
6 volunteer(s)
Membership: 100; *Fees:* $15 individual; $20 family; *Member Profile:* All persons interested in Scottish culture; *Committees:* History Research
Activities: Meetings; outings; Highland games; Tartan Day; Lamont Memorial Day; Robbie Burns Day; *Awareness Events:* Tartan Day in Canada, April 6; Lamont Memorial Days, June 1-3

Clan MacKenzie Society in the Americas, Canadian Chapter ***See*** Clan Mackenzie Society of Canada

Clan Mackenzie Society of Canada
580 Rebecca St., Oakville ON L6K 3N9
clanmackenzie.ca
Previous Name: Clan MacKenzie Society in the Americas, Canadian Chapter
Overview: A small national charitable organization founded in 1986
Mission: To support history, culture & education of MacKenzies & Clan in Canada, Scotland & worldwide
Affliation(s): Clan MacKenzie Societies in Scotland, USA, Australia, New Zealand
Chief Officer(s):
Norman S. MacKenzie, President
dmjrmac@sympatico.ca
Alan McKenzie, Treasurer
alan@mkz.com
Mary-Lou Oyler, Secretary & Commissioner, Toronto
secmloyl@sympatico.ca
Finances: *Annual Operating Budget:* Less than $50,000; *Funding Sources:* Membership dues; sales; lotteries; donations
12 volunteer(s)
Membership: 400+; *Fees:* $20
Activities: Tent at Highland Games across Canada; annual dinner & picnic; *Awareness Events:* Highland Games; *Library:* Private Collection

Clan MacLeod Societies of Canada (CMSC)
Ottawa ON

Tel: 613-733-2887
www.clanmacleod-canada.com
Overview: A medium-sized national organization founded in 1935
Mission: The Societies aim to strengthen bonds of clan fellowship across Canada; to advance knowledge about the history in Canada of the MacLeods & septs; to maintain & procure documents & genealogical records for the National Archives; to encourage appreciation & performance of Celtic Arts (music, piping & dancing); to assist in the restoration & repair of places & objects of historical interest.
Member of: World Associate Clan MacLeod Societies
Chief Officer(s):
Jim MacLeod, President
glenelg.macleod@gmail.com

Alberta Branch
AB
Tel: 403-284-0175; *Fax:* 403-851-5231
info@clanmacleod.ca
clanmacleod.ca
Chief Officer(s):
Randy MacLeod, President
brenda33@telus.net

British Columbia Interior Branch
BC
Chief Officer(s):
Neil McLeod, President
nrinmerritt@telus.net

Central Ontario Branch
ON
Tel: 647-692-7407
clanmacleod.centralontario@gmail.com
Chief Officer(s):
Karen Macleod McCrimmon, President
mccrimmon.karen@gmail.com

Glengarry Ontario Branch
PO Box 92, 5 Maxwell St., Ingleside ON K0C 1M0
Tel: 613-537-2541
www.clanmacleod-canada.com
Chief Officer(s):
Joan McEwan, President
trd15@glen-net.ca

Manitoba Branch
MB
Tel: 204-453-5933
Chief Officer(s):
Bruce McLeod, President
bfmacleod@mymts.net

Ottawa Branch
Ottawa ON
Tel: 613-623-9492
Chief Officer(s):
Ann McCrimmon, President
ann.mccrimmon@ocdsb.ca

Vancouver Branch
Vancouver BC
Tel: 604-589-2299
clanmacleodsocietygv.blogspot.ca
www.facebook.com/pages/MacLeod/385314628266032
Chief Officer(s):
Mark MacLeod, President
mr.mmacleod@gmail.com

Vancouver Island Branch
BC
Tel: 250-746-3997
Chief Officer(s):
Malcolm E. MacLeod, President
macleod-m-k@shaw.ca

Clan Matheson Society of Nova Scotia
88 Beaumont Dr., Lower Sackville NS B4C 1V6
Tel: 902-865-5735
Overview: A small provincial organization founded in 1985
Chief Officer(s):
Albert Matheson, President
albert.matheson@clanmatheson.org
Finances: *Funding Sources:* Fundraising events

Clans & Scottish Societies of Canada (CASSOC)
c/o Secretary, #78, 24 Fundy Bay Blvd., Toronto ON M1W 3A4
Tel: 416-492-1623
editor@cassoc.ca
www.cassoc.ca
Overview: A medium-sized national charitable organization founded in 1976
Mission: To foster the organization of & cooperation between Scottish associations, federations, clans, societies & groups through initiation & coordination of projects & undertakings; to advance Scottish cultural heritage in Canada
Chief Officer(s):
Ian A. Munro, Chair
chair@cassoc.ca
Jo Ann M. Tuskin, Secretary
secretary@cassoc.ca
Finances: *Annual Operating Budget:* Less than $50,000; *Funding Sources:* Membership fees
75 volunteer(s)
Membership: 64 organizations; *Fees:* $50
Activities: Booth at Scottish events (Highland Games, etc.); newsletter; telephone service; *Speaker Service:* Yes

Clare Chamber of Commerce *Voir* Chambre de commerce de Clare

Clarenville Area Chamber of Commerce
292A Memorial Dr., Clarenville NL A5A 1P1
Tel: 709-466-5800; *Fax:* 709-466-5803
Toll-Free: 866-466-5800
info@clarenvilleareachamber.net
www.clarenvilleareachamber.net
www.facebook.com/clarenvillearea.chamberofcommerce
Overview: A small local organization
Mission: To promote Clarenville as a tourist destination & to improve economic development
Chief Officer(s):
Brian Smith, President
Ina Marsh, Office Manager
Finances: *Annual Operating Budget:* $50,000-$100,000
Staff Member(s): 2; 16 volunteer(s)
Membership: 110; *Fees:* $59 - $299; *Committees:* Public Relations; Events; Profit; Economic Development Advisory; Finance; Physician Recruitment

Claresholm & District Chamber of Commerce
PO Box 1092, Claresholm AB T0L 0T0
Tel: 403-625-4229
info@claresholmchamber.com
www.claresholmchamber.com
Overview: A small local organization
Mission: The Claresholm Chamber of Commerce was resurrected in 1994 and has maintained a continuous membership of approximately 100 members. Their organization is made up of volunteers representing a huge cross-section of the many types of businesses in Claresholm. Their main goals are to promote Claresholm as a strong, united community encouraging new business as well as finding ways to help their existing business grow and prosper.
Chief Officer(s):
Linda Petryshen, President, 403-625-4646
m65710bomotel6.com
Membership: 105

Classical & Medieval Numismatic Society (CMNS)
3329 Queen St. East, Toronto ON M4E 1E8
e-mail: cmns.info@gmail.com
www.cmns.ca
Overview: A small international organization founded in 1991
Mission: To promote & encourage study & research in the field of numismatics & history as they relate to ancient & medieval coinage & related subjects; to publish the writings that are the result of such activity.
Member of: Royal Canadian Numismatic Association; Numismatic Network Canada; American Numismatic Society; American Numismatic Association
Finances: *Funding Sources:* Membership dues; donations; grants
Membership: *Member Profile:* Collectors, historians, students; those interested in ancient & medieval coinage & history
Activities: Publish quarterly journal; hold educations meeting & programs; *Speaker Service:* Yes; *Library* by appointment

Classical Accordion Society of Canada
3296 Cindy Cr., Mississauga ON L4Y 3J6
Tel: 905-625-0422
Overview: A small national organization founded in 1979
Chief Officer(s):
Joseph Macerollo, President
Finances: *Annual Operating Budget:* $50,000-$100,000
6 volunteer(s)
Membership: 26 individual; 15 associate
Activities: *Rents Mailing List:* Yes

Classical Association of Canada (CAC) / Société canadienne des études classiques (SCEC)
Guy Chamberland, Classical Studies, Thorneloe College, Laurentian University, Sudbury ON P3E 2C6
Tel: 416-736-2100
www.cac-scec.ca
Overview: A small national charitable organization founded in 1947
Mission: To advance the study of the civilizations of the Roman & Greek worlds; To promote teaching of classical civilizations & languages in Canadian schools; To encourage research in classical studies
Affliation(s): Canadian Federation for the Humanities & Social Sciences; Fédération Internationale des Études Classiques; Canadian Institute in Greece
Chief Officer(s):
Patrick Baker, President
president@cac-scec.ca; patrick.baker@hst.ulaval.ca
Bonnie MacLachlan, Vice-President
vice-president@cac-scec.ca
Guy Chamberland, Secretary
secretary@cac-scec.ca; gchamberland@laurentian.ca
Ingrid Holmberg, Treasurer
treasurer@cac-scec.ca
Finances: *Funding Sources:* Donations
Activities: Increasing public awareness of the importance of classical studies; Promoting the study of women, gender, & sexuality in the ancient world, through the Women's Network; Liaising with other Canadian & international scholarly associations; *Speaker Service:* Yes
Awards:
• Desmond Conacher Scholarship (Scholarship)
Eligibility: Students entering graduate studies in classics or a related discipline *Amount:* $2,500
• Undergraduate Essay Contest (Award)
Eligibility: Undergraduate students taking Classics courses at Canadian universities
• National Greek & Latin Sight Translation Competitions (Award)
Eligibility: Canadian students at the high school & university level*Deadline:* January
• Grace Irwin Award for Classics (Award)
Eligibility: Secondary school teachers of Latin, Ancient Greek, or Classical Civilization who is seeking to upgrade abilities *Amount:* $500
• Graduate Student Presentation Prize (Award)
To honour a graduate student who delivers the best paper at the annual meeting of The Classical Association of Canada
Meetings/Conferences: • Classical Association of Canada Annual Conference 2015, May, 2015, University of Toronto, Toronto, ON
Scope: National
Publications:
• The Canadian Classical Electronic Bulletin
Type: Newsletter; *Editor:* Guy Chamberland
• Directory of Classical Scholars & Programmes in Canadian universities
Type: Directory
• Mouseion
Type: Journal; *Frequency:* 3 pa; *Editor:* Brad Levett
Profile: A scholarly publication published by the University of Calgary Press for the Classical Association of Canada
• Phoenix
Type: Journal; *Editor:* Michele George
Profile: An international scholarly publication published by the University of Toronto Press for the Classical Association of Canada

Clay Tree Society for People with Developmental Disabilities
838 Old Victoria Rd., Nanaimo BC V9R 6A1
Tel: 250-753-5322; *Fax:* 250-753-2749
claytree@shaw.ca
www.claytree.org
www.facebook.com/ClayTreeSociety
Overview: A small local organization founded in 1957
Mission: The Society is a non-profit, registered organization that provides support to individuals with developmental disabilities with programs focusing on community inclusion & recreation, life skills, volunteer opportunities, artistic exploration, personal empowerment & independence.
Chief Officer(s):
Veronica (Roni) Harrison, President
Glenys Patmore, Executive Director
glenys.claytree@shaw.ca

La Clé d'la Baie en Huronie - Association culturelle francophone

#5, 2, promenade Marsellus, Barrie ON L4N 0Y4
Tél: 705-725-9755; *Téléc:* 705-725-1955
Autres numéros: Penetanguishene Tél: 705-549-3116; Télé: 705-549-6463
lacle@lacle.ca
www.lacle.ca
Également appelé: La Clé d'la Baie
Aperçu: *Dimension:* petite; *Envergure:* locale; Organisme sans but lucratif; fondée en 1996
Mission: La Clé d'la Baie est un organisme catalyseur au service de la communauté francophone du comté de Simcoe; promouvoir la participation active des membres de la communauté; rechercher l'épanouissement et le développement harmonieux de la communauté francophone, tout en lui permettant de vivre sa langue, sa culture, son identité et son héritage
Membre(s) du bureau directeur:
Pierre Casault, Directeur général
pcasault@lacle.ca
Finances: *Budget de fonctionnement annuel:* $500,000-$1.5 Million; *Fonds:* Gouvernement féderal et provincial; autofinancement
Membre(s) du personnel: 40; 150 bénévole(s)
Membre: 100-499; *Critères d'admissibilite:* francophones; *Comités:* Exécutif; Socioculturel; Radio; Actions politiques
Activités: Spectacles, camps d'été, radio communautaire, développement communautaire; *Service de conférenciers:* Oui

Clean Air Foundation *See* Summerhill Impact

Clean Air Strategic Alliance (CASA)

10035 - 108 St., 10th Fl., Edmonton AB T5J 3E1
Tel: 780-427-9793; *Fax:* 780-422-3127
casa@casahome.org
www.casahome.org
www.facebook.com/419768864745652
twitter.com/CleanAirSA
www.flickr.com/photos/81460374@N02
Overview: A medium-sized provincial organization founded in 1994
Mission: To manage strategic issues of air quality in Alberta; To represent three levels of government, as well as industry & NGOs; To plan for, organize, & commit resources related to air quality in Alberta
Chief Officer(s):
Norman MacLeod, Executive Director
Finances: *Funding Sources:* Industry; Government; Donations
Staff Member(s): 5

Clean Annapolis River Project (CARP)

PO Box 395, Annapolis Royal NS B0S 1A0
Tel: 902-532-7533; *Fax:* 902-532-3038
Toll-Free: 888-547-4344
carp@annapolisriver.ca
www.annapolisriver.ca
www.facebook.com/183264721694056
twitter.com/CARPAnnapolis
Overview: A medium-sized local charitable organization founded in 1990
Mission: To promote, encourage & assist with the wise use of the resources of the Annapolis Watershed; Water quality monitoring program
Chief Officer(s):
Monik Richard, Executive Director
monikrichard@annapolisriver.ca
Finances: *Annual Operating Budget:* $250,000-$500,000; *Funding Sources:* Private & public
Staff Member(s): 12; 60 volunteer(s)
Membership: 100; *Fees:* $5 student; $7 individual; $10 family; $25 NGO; $100 lifetime
Activities: Environment monitoring; habitat restoration; climate change issues; water quality issues; public awareness; *Internships:* Yes; *Speaker Service:* Yes; *Library* by appointment

Clean Calgary Association *See* Green Calgary

Clean Energy BC

#354, 409 Granville St., Vancouver BC V6C 1T2
Tel: 604-568-4778; *Fax:* 604-568-4724
Toll-Free: 855-568-4778
www.cleanenergybc.org
www.linkedin.com/groups/Clean-Energy-Association-BC-4767428
www.facebook.com/781621211850050?xprOpenPopup=1
twitter.com/CleanEnergyBC
Previous Name: Independent Power Association of BC
Overview: A small provincial organization founded in 1992
Mission: To ensure that British Columbia's independent power producer industry is a contributor to the electricity market in the province
Chief Officer(s):
Paul Kariya, Executive Director
paul.kariya@cleanenergybc.org
Donald MacLachlan, Contact, Media & Communications
claritymediapr@gmail.com
Lisa Bateman, Coordinator, Events
lisa.bateman@cleanenergybc.org
Kristen McIntyre, Contact, Membership Services, Registration, & Administration
kristen.mcintyre@cleanenergybc.org
Membership: *Committees:* Conference; First Nations; Hydro; Market Development; Public Affairs; Regulatory; Thermal; Transmission; Wind
Activities: Engaging in policy implementation
Meetings/Conferences: • Clean Energy BC 2015 13th Annual Conference, 2015, BC
Scope: Provincial
Description: An event featuring guest speakers, short courses, exhibits, & field trips,
Contact Information: Coordinator, Events: Lisa Bateman, E-mail: lisa.bateman@cleanenergybc.org

Clean North

736A Queen St. East, Sault Ste Marie ON P6A 2A9
Tel: 705-945-1573
info@cleannorth.org
www.cleannorth.org
Also Known As: The Sault & District Recycling Association
Overview: A small provincial organization founded in 1989
Mission: This citizens' group promotes environmental protection through reduction, reuse & recycling of residential & industrial waste in Sault Ste. Marie & the Algoma District.
Member of: Northwatch; Ontario Environmental Network
Affliation(s): Ontario Environment Network; Northwatch
Chief Officer(s):
David Trowbridge, Chair
Finances: *Annual Operating Budget:* $50,000-$100,000; *Funding Sources:* Membership dues; fundraising; foundations; grants
210 volunteer(s)
Membership: 350; *Fees:* $10 & $15
Activities: Recycling phone books; dry cells; Christmas trees; *Internships:* Yes; *Speaker Service:* Yes; *Library:* Environmental Resource Room; Open to public

Clean Nova Scotia (CNS)

126 Portland St., Dartmouth NS B2Y 1H8
Tel: 902-420-3474; *Fax:* 902-424-5334
Toll-Free: 888-380-5008
cns@clean.ns.ca
www.clean.ns.ca
www.facebook.com/pages/Clean-Nova-Scotia/117505381665669
twitter.com/CleanNovaScotia
www.youtube.com/user/CleanNovaScotia1
Previous Name: The Clean Nova Scotia Foundation
Overview: A medium-sized provincial charitable organization founded in 1988
Mission: To inspire positive environmental change in Nova Scotia
Chief Officer(s):
Judy McMullen, Executive Director, 902-420-3476
judym@clean.ns.ca
Jill Murphy, Director, Finance, 902-420-7939
jmurphy@clean.ns.ca
Marlene Parsons, Director, Human Resources, 902-420-7945
mparsons@clean.ns.ca
Gina Patterson, Director, Programs, 902-420-7937
patterson@clean.ns.ca
Katie Abriel, Manager, Climate Change Education Programs, 902-420-7936
kabriel@clean.ns.ca
Joe Moar, Manager, Home Energy Evaluations, 902-420-7928
jmoar@clean.ns.ca
David Ashley, Coordinator, Ship to Shore Program, 902-420-7940
adavid@clean.ns.ca
Neil Bailey, Coordinator, Waste Programs, 902-420-7943
nbailey@clean.ns.ca
Steve Fairbairn, Coordinator, Green Schools Nova Scotia, 902-420-7948
sfairbairn@clean.ns.ca
Spencer Fowlie, Coordinator, Farms-to-School, 902-420-7933
sfowlie@clean.ns.ca
Valerie Francella, Coordinator, Adopt-a-Watershed, 902-420-3473
vfrancella@clean.ns.ca
Derek Gillis, Coordinator, Drive Wiser / Fleet Wiser Program, 902-420-7944
Wiserdgillis@clean.ns.ca
Leann Grosvold, Coordinator, Communications, 902-420-8803
lgrosvold@clean.ns.ca
Lisa Privett, Coordinator, Environmental Home Assessment Program, 902-420-6593
Kari Riddell, Coordinator, Litterless Road Tour, 902-420-7924
riddell@clean.ns.ca
Finances: *Funding Sources:* Donations; Sponsorships
Membership: *Member Profile:* Persons & businesses committed to the creation of a sustainable & healthy environment in Nova Scotia
Activities: Providing environmental education & information; *Awareness Events:* Commuter Challenge; Clean Across Nova Scotia
Meetings/Conferences: • Clean Nova Scotia 2015 Annual General Meeting, June, 2015, NS
Scope: Provincial
Description: Reports from executives, a review of finances, & information about envrionmental programming
Contact Information: Coordinator, Communications: Leanna Grosvold, E-mail: lgrosvold@clean.ns.ca
Publications:
• A Carbon Offsetting Primer
Author: Gina Patterson
• Clean & Green Newsletter
Type: Newsletter *ISSN:* 1715-7897; *Price:* Free with Clean Nova Scotia membership
Profile: Environmental articles & tips, plus a list of interesting websites
• Clean Nova Scotia Annual Report
Type: Yearbook; *Frequency:* Annually
• Clean Nova Scotia Strategic Plan
Profile: A direction for the organization's activities during the next three to five years
• A Guide to Energy Efficiency for Religious Buildings in Nova Scotia
Type: Guide; *Number of Pages:* 50
Profile: Sections of the guide include getting started, the walk-through audit, how to do a greenhouse gas inventory, youth group engagement, energy efficiencyimprovements, a case study, a master checklist, resources for churches, & references

The Clean Nova Scotia Foundation *See* Clean Nova Scotia

Clearwater & District Chamber of Commerce

#201, 416 Eden Rd., Clearwater BC V0E 1N1
Tel: 250-674-2646; *Fax:* 250-674-3693
info@clearwaterbcchamber.com
www.clearwaterbcchamber.com
Overview: A small local organization founded in 1956
Chief Officer(s):
Sheena vanDyk
Finances: *Annual Operating Budget:* Less than $50,000; *Funding Sources:* Membership dues
Staff Member(s): 2
Membership: 100; *Fees:* $94.50-$220.50 business; $31.50 individual; $57.75 organization; *Member Profile:* Business
Activities: *Library:* Business Information Centre;
Awards:
• Annual Awards
Annual award, given to Citizen, Youth, Employee, Retail/Service and Tourism Business of the Year

Clearwater & District Food Bank *See* Clearwater & District Food Bank Society

Clearwater & District Food Bank Society

741 Clearwater Village Rd., Clearwater BC V0E 1N0
Tel: 250-674-3697; *Fax:* 250-674-3402
Previous Name: Clearwater & District Food Bank
Overview: A small local organization overseen by Food Banks British Columbia
Member of: Food Banks British Columbia
Chief Officer(s):
Heather Stanley, Contact
pandhlc@telus.net

Les Clefs d'Or Canada
c/o Sofitel Luxury Hotels, 1155 Sherbrooke Ouest, Montréal QC H3A 2N3
Tel: 514-788-3046
president@lesclefsdorcanada.org
www.lesclefsdorcanada.org
Overview: A small national organization founded in 1976
Mission: To grow & promote Les Clefs d'Or & the concierge profession
Chief Officer(s):
Heather Crosby, National Secretary
Hugo Legrand, President
Finances: *Funding Sources:* corporate sponsorship
Membership: 55 individual; 19 professional affiliate; *Fees:* $300 and up; *Member Profile:* Hotel concierge

Clements Centre Society
5856 Clements St., Duncan BC V9L 3W3
Tel: 250-746-4135; *Fax:* 250-746-1636
administration@clementscentre.org
clementscentre.org
www.facebook.com/214754818591076
Previous Name: Cowichan Valley Association for Community Living
Overview: A small local charitable organization founded in 1957
Mission: To provide support & services to individuals with developmental disabilities & their families in the Cowichan Valley, promoting the acceptance & inclusion of all people
Member of: British Columbia Association for Community Living; Canadian Association for Community Living
Affliation(s): Commission on Accreditation of Rehabilitation Facilities (CARF); Thrifty Foods
Chief Officer(s):
Leslie Welin, President
Dominic Rockall, Executive Director
drockall@clementscentre.org
Finances: *Funding Sources:* Ministry for Children & Families; United Way; Duncan Volunteer Fire Department; BC Gaming Commission
Activities: Child development services; residential services; adult day programs; *Speaker Service:* Yes; *Library:* Toy Resource Lending Library; by appointment

Climate Action Network - Canada
#412, 1 Nicholas St., Ottawa ON K1N 7B7
Tel: 613-241-4413
Toll-Free: 866-373-2990
info@climateactionnetwork.ca
www.climateactionnetwork.ca
www.facebook.com/climate.action.network.canada
twitter.com/CANRACCanada
www.youtube.com/user/CANRACCanada
Overview: A small national organization
Mission: To support & empower Canada's governments, private sector, labour & civil society by designing, developing & implementing effective strategies to reduce greenhouse gas emissions at international, national & local levels; To prevent dangerous levels of human interference with the global climate system
Chief Officer(s):
Christian Holz, Executive Director
cholz@climateactionnetwork.ca
Membership: *Fees:* $40

Climb Yukon Association
YT
e-mail: info@climbyukon.net
www.climbyukon.net
Overview: A small provincial organization
Mission: To develop to the climbing community in the Yukon as a recreational opportunity for adults & youth, to raise awareness of & address access & safety concerns.

Clinical Nurse Specialist Association of Ontario (CNS)
c/o Registered Nurses' Association of Ontario, 158 Pearl St., Toronto ON M5H 1L3
Tel: 416-599-1925
cns-ontario.mao.ca
www.facebook.com/113210988761198?fref=ts
twitter.com/cnsig
youtube.com/cnsig
Overview: A small provincial organization founded in 1977
Mission: To support the role of advanced nursing practice in Ontario; To address issues that affect clinical nursing practice
Member of: Registered Nurses' Association of Ontario
Chief Officer(s):
Paul-André Gauthier, Co-President & Director of Finance
Membership: *Fees:* $40 / year (including membership in the Canadian Association of Advanced Practice Nurses); *Member Profile:* Registered Nurses' Association of Ontario members or affiliates who are committed to advanced nursing practice
Activities: Promoting & clarifying the role of advanced nursing practice throughout Ontario; Presenting educational events, such as workshops; Supporting research in nursing; Providing professional networking opportunities; Engaging in lobbying activities
Awards:
• Clinical Nurse Specialist of the Year Award (Award)
To recognize outstanding professional achievement as a clinical nurse specialist in the domains of advanced nursing practice *Contact:* Mitzi G. Mitchell, E-mail: mitzi.mitchell@rogers.com or mitzim@yorku.ca
• CNSIG Education Award (Award)
Amount: $1,000 *Contact:* Mitzi G. Mitchell, E-mail: mitzim@yorku.ca or Mitzi.mitchell@rogers.com
Publications:
• Clinical Nurse Specialist Newsletter
Type: Newsletter; *Frequency:* Quarterly; *Editor:* Dania Versailles
Profile: Group activities, articles, plus event reviews & announcements

Cloverdale & District Chamber of Commerce
#5748, 176 St., Cloverdale BC V3S 4C8
Tel: 604-574-9802; *Fax:* 604-574-9122
clovcham@axion.net
www.cloverdale.bc.ca
www.facebook.com/CloverdaleChamber
twitter.com/CloverdaleCOC
Overview: A small local organization founded in 1949
Mission: To promote & improve trade, commerce, economic, civic & social welfare in the district of Cloverdale Surrey
Member of: Surrey Regional Chamber of Commerce
Chief Officer(s):
Brian Young, President
brian@surreygolf.com
Bill Reid, Executive Director
Staff Member(s): 2; 11 volunteer(s)
Membership: 130; *Fees:* $100

Club 'Les Pongistes d'Ungava'
109, rue Obalski, Chibougamau QC G8P 2E9
Tél: 418-748-4903
Aperçu: *Dimension:* petite; *Envergure:* locale
Membre(s) du bureau directeur:
Lynn Labbé, Contact
labbelynn@hotmail.com

Club alpin du Canada *See* Alpine Club of Canada

Le Club BMW du Canada *See* BMW Clubs Canada

Club canadien de Toronto
#66030, 1116 ave Wilson, Toronto ON M3M 3G1
Tél: 416-243-0662; *Téléc:* 416-243-9655
info@clubcanadien.ca
www.clubcanadien.ca
www.facebook.com/pages/Club-canadien-de-Toronto/372838496115999
twitter.com/clubcanadienTO
Nom précédent: Cercle canadien de Toronto
Aperçu: *Dimension:* petite; *Envergure:* locale; Organisme sans but lucratif; fondée en 1986
Mission: Donner l'occasion aux francophones et francophiles à Toronto d'échanger, de s'enrichir et d'établir des contacts. Le Club agit comme un élément catalyseur et rassembleur de la grande communauté francophone des milieux d'affaires, académiques, culturels et gouvernementaux
Membre(s) du bureau directeur:
Yannick Rose, Président
Jean-C. Martin, Directeur général
Finances: *Budget de fonctionnement annuel:* $100,000-$250,000; *Fonds:* Privé
Membre(s) du personnel: 1; 30 bénévole(s)
Membre: 350; *Montant de la cotisation:* 30$ étudiant; 70$ individuelle; 120$ couple; 215$ (pour 4 délégué(s) d'une même entreprise); *Critères d'admissibilite:* Gens d'affaires de Bay St.
Activités: Déjeuners d'affaires mensuels; *Service de conférenciers:* Oui

Club canin canadien *See* Canadian Kennel Club

Club cycliste de la Montérégie
#201, 1204, rue Sentier, Longueuil QC J4N 1S4
Tél: 450-647-2012
admin@clubcyclistemonteregie.qc.ca
clubcyclistemonteregie.qc.ca
Aperçu: *Dimension:* petite; *Envergure:* locale
Mission: De donner à ses membres la possibilité de rester en forme grâce à vélo
Membre(s) du bureau directeur:
André Desjardins, Président, Conseil d'administration

Club d'astronomie Quasar de Chibougamau
783, 6e rue, Chibougamau QC G8P 2W4
Tél: 418-748-4642
www.faaq.org/clubs/quasar/
Aperçu: *Dimension:* petite; *Envergure:* locale
Membre(s) du bureau directeur:
Pierre Bureau, Président
pbureau@hotmail.com
Membre: *Montant de la cotisation:* 7,50$ étudiant; 10$ personnes âgées; 15$ adulte; 20$ famille

Club d'auto-neige Chibougamau inc.
CP 43, Chibougamau QC G8P 2K5
Tél: 418-748-3065
rene.martel@motoneigechibougamau.ca
www.motoneigechibougamau.ca
Aperçu: *Dimension:* petite; *Envergure:* locale
Membre(s) du bureau directeur:
Mario Simard, Président

Club d'électricité du Québec inc. *Voir* Association de l'industrie électrique du Québec

Club d'observateurs d'oiseaux de Laval (COOL)
Pavillon du Bois Papineau, #214, 3235, boul St Martin Est, Laval QC H7E 5G8
Tél: 450-664-4718
lavalcool2@hotmail.com
www.lavalcool.com
Aperçu: *Dimension:* petite; *Envergure:* locale; Organisme sans but lucratif; fondée en 1989
Mission: Étude et observation des oiseaux sauvages et la protection de leurs habitats.
Affliation(s): Association québécoise des groupes d'ornithologues
Membre: *Montant de la cotisation:* 35$ familial; 25$ individu; 40$ corporatif

Club d'Ornithologie de Longueuil
CP 21099, Succ. Jacques Cartier, Longueuil QC J4J 5J4
Tél: 514-724-8383
ornitho_longueuil@hotmail.com
col.quebecoiseaux.org
www.facebook.com/315821868435402
Aperçu: *Dimension:* petite; *Envergure:* locale; fondée en 1988
Mission: De promouvoir l'observation des oiseaux et pour aider à garder les oiseaux sécurité
Membre(s) du bureau directeur:
Daniel Ouellette, Président, Conseil d'administration
Membre: 300+; *Montant de la cotisation:* 25$ Individuelle; 30$ Famille
Activités: Voyages d'observation d'oiseaux; Conférences
Publications:
• Le Chardonneret
Type: Bulletin; *Frequency:* 3 fois par ans; *Editor:* Josette Laplante
Profile: Les articles qui contiennent nouvelles sur le club, écrits par ses membres

Club d'ornithologie de Mirabel (COMIR)
CP 3418, 9009, Rte Arthur-Sauvé, Mirabel QC J7N 2T8
Tél: 450-258-4924
admin@comirabel.org
comirabel.org
Aperçu: *Dimension:* petite; *Envergure:* locale; fondée en 1999
Mission: Le territoire couvert part le COMIR s'étend de la rivière des Mille-Iles au Sud, Prévost au Nord, la rivière des Outaouais (Rivière Rouge) à l'Ouest et la route 117 à l'Est.
Affliation(s): Regroupement QuébecOiseaux
Membre(s) du bureau directeur:
Normande Lapensée, Présidente
Denis Lauzon, Vice-président
Membre: 165 familles
Activités: Rencontre d'initiation à l'ornithologie; présentations; conférences; sorites & observations d'oiseaux; observations nocturnes; recontres sociales & pique-niques

Club de boxe Chibougamau *Voir* La Zone Boxe 49

Club de collectionneurs de coupons Canadian Tire ***See*** Canadian Tire Coupon Collectors Club

Club de curling Mont-Bruno

1390, rue Goyer, St-Bruno QC J3V 3Z3
Tél: 450-653-6913
Info2@CurlingMontBruno.com
www.curlingmontbruno.com
Aperçu: *Dimension:* moyenne; *Envergure:* locale; fondée en 1960
Affliation(s): Association Canadienne de curling; Curling Québec; Association régionale curling Montréal
Membre(s) du bureau directeur:
Alain Beaumier, Président, Conseil d'adminitration
Membre: *Montant de la cotisation:* 80$ - 1,015$
Activités: Tournoi de curling

Club de garçons et filles de Moncton Inc. ***See*** Boys & Girls Clubs of New Brunswick

Le Club de gemmologie et de minérlogie de Montréal ***Voir*** Montréal Gem & Mineral Club

Club de généalogie de Sainte-Julie ***Voir*** Société de généalogie de la Jemmerais

Club de golf Chibougamau-Chapais inc.

CP 81, 130, rue des Forces-Armées, Chibougamau QC G8P 3A1
Tél: 418-748-4709; *Téléc:* 418-748-2471
golfchibougamau@hotmail.com
Nom précédent: Club de golf de Chibougamau inc.
Aperçu: *Dimension:* petite; *Envergure:* locale
Membre(s) du bureau directeur:
Michael Lallemand, Directeur général
Membre(s) du personnel: 12; 10 bénévole(s)

Club de golf de Chibougamau inc. ***Voir*** Club de golf Chibougamau-Chapais inc.

Club de karaté Shotokan Chibougamau

576, Bordeleau, Chibougamau QC G8P 1A6
Tél: 418-748-4048
www.karatechibougamau.com
Aperçu: *Dimension:* petite; *Envergure:* locale; fondée en 1972
Membre(s) du bureau directeur:
France Bélanger, Présidente
Claude Bédard, Instructeur chef, 418-770-6933
cbedard@karatechibougamau.com

Club de l'âge d'or Les intrépides de Chibougamau

126, rue des Forces-Armées, Chibougamau QC G8P 3A1
Tél: 418-748-6703
Aperçu: *Dimension:* petite; *Envergure:* locale
Membre(s) du bureau directeur:
Darquise St-Georges, Présidente, 418-748-2400

Club de marche de Québec

15, rue Jean de Brébeuf, Québec QC G2A 2V7
www.clubdemarche.net
Aperçu: *Dimension:* petite; *Envergure:* locale
Mission: Pour engager la communauté dans les activités de l'ordre
Membre(s) du bureau directeur:
Nicole Thivierge, Présidente, Conseil d'administration, 418-842-7950
Membre: *Montant de la cotisation:* 20$
Activités: Marches en ville; Randonnées pédestres; Activitées sociales

Club de marche de Rimouski

CP 444, Succ. A, Rimouski QC G5L 7C3
Tél: 514-725-3696
CMR1994@hotmail.com
www.rimouskiweb.com
Aperçu: *Dimension:* petite; *Envergure:* locale
Mission: Pour organiser des randonnées de groupe et l'exploration scénique du Québec
Membre: *Montant de la cotisation:* 15$

Club de marche moi mes souliers

3155, rue Fortin, Trois-Rivières QC G8Z 2C3
Tél: 819-373-1109
www.moimessouliers.com
Aperçu: *Dimension:* petite; *Envergure:* locale; fondée en 1993
Mission: Pour pouvoir promenades au Canada et aux États-Unis pour ses membres
Membre(s) du bureau directeur:
Louis Giroux, Président, Conseil d'administration
louis.giroux13@cgocable.com
Membre: 100; *Montant de la cotisation:* 20$ individuelle; 30$ Famille

Club de natation Natchib inc.

CP 213, Chibougamau QC G8P 2K7
Tél: 418-748-8038
Aperçu: *Dimension:* petite; *Envergure:* locale
Membre(s) du bureau directeur:
Marie-Josée Audet, Président

Club de naturalistes de Prince George ***See*** Prince George Naturalists Club

Club de Numismates du Bas St-Laurent (CNBSL)

CP 1475, Rimouski QC G5L 8M3
Tél: 418-723-8586
www.cnbsl.org
Aperçu: *Dimension:* petite; *Envergure:* locale; fondée en 1979
Mission: De fournir un lieu de rencontre pour ceux qui s'intéressent à la collecte de pièces de monnaie
Membre(s) du bureau directeur:
Gaétan Aubin, Président
gaubin@globetrotter.net
Membre: *Montant de la cotisation:* Barème

Club de patinage artistique Les lames givrées inc.

CP 453, Chibougamau QC G8P 2X9
Tél: 418-748-2671
leslamesgivrees@hiotmail.com
Aperçu: *Dimension:* petite; *Envergure:* locale
Membre(s) du bureau directeur:
Joline Bélanger, Présidente, 418-748-2339

Club de photo de Boucherville

Centre Mgr Poissant, Café Belle-Lurette, 566, boul. Marie-Victorian, Boucherville QC J4B 1X1
Tél: 450-449-1649
clubphotoboucherville.org
Aperçu: *Dimension:* petite; *Envergure:* locale
Mission: De créer un réseau de photographes qui sont capables d'encourager et d'aider les uns les autres
Membre(s) du bureau directeur:
Nicole Boucher, Présidente, Conseil d'administration

Club de photographie L'Oeil qui voit de Saint-Hubert

#A2 - A3, 2060, rue Holmes, Saint-Hubert QC J4T 1R8
Tél: 514-686-3633
info@oeilquivoit.com
oeilquivoit.com
www.facebook.com/oeilquivoit
Aperçu: *Dimension:* petite; *Envergure:* locale; fondée en 1986
Mission: Pour partager une passion pour la photographie parmi ses membres
Membre(s) du bureau directeur:
Nathalie Madore, Présidente, Conseil d'administration
Activités: Ateliers techniques; conférences

Club de plein air Les Aventuriers

4545, av Pierre-de-Coubertin, Montréal QC H1V 0B2
Tél: 514-374-6078
info@aventuriers.qc.ca
www.aventuriers.qc.ca
Aperçu: *Dimension:* petite; *Envergure:* locale; fondée en 1976
Mission: Pour rassembler les gens afin de réaliser des activités de plein air
Membre: *Montant de la cotisation:* 30$ individuel; 30$ monoparental; 50$ familial
Activités: Canot; Vélo; Randonnée pédestre et raquette; Kayak de mer; Ski de randonnée
Publications:
• L'Écope
Type: Journal
Profile: Articles et photos des membres du club

Club de trafic de Québec

CP 2501, Succ. Normandie, Saint-Nicholas QC G7A 4X5
info@clubtraficqc.com
www.clubtraficqc.org
Aperçu: *Dimension:* moyenne; *Envergure:* provinciale; Organisme sans but lucratif; fondée en 1960
Mission: Regrouper les représentants oeuvrant dans le domaine du transport de la grande région de Québec
Membre(s) du bureau directeur:
Benoit Latour, Président
b.latour@pmtroy.com
Finances: *Budget de fonctionnement annuel:* $100,000-$250,000
Membre: 137; *Montant de la cotisation:* 85$

Club de vol à voile de Québec

CP 9276, Sainte-Foy QC G1V 4B1
Tél: 418-337-4905
www.cvvq.net
www.facebook.com/CVVQPlaneur
twitter.com/Planeur_Quebec
Aperçu: *Dimension:* petite; *Envergure:* locale; fondée en 1954
Mission: Les principaux objectifs de notre association sont de fournir une plate-forme d'opération sécuritaire pour la pratique de notre sport et d'offrir une formation de qualité à de nouveaux adeptes qui se joignent à nous.
Membre(s) du bureau directeur:
Pierre Beaulieu, Président
Membre: *Montant de la cotisation:* Barème; *Comités:* Aménagement; Planification de la flotte; Recrutement

Club de Vol à Voile MSC ***See*** Montréal Soaring Council

Club des collectionneurs d'épinglettes Inc. (CCE) / Pin Collectors' Club

clubepinglettes@hotmail.com
pincollectors.unblog.fr
Aperçu: *Dimension:* petite; *Envergure:* nationale; Organisme sans but lucratif; fondée en 1984
Mission: Regrouper les collectionneurs d'épinglettes intéressés
Membre(s) du bureau directeur:
Gilles Labine, Président
Finances: *Budget de fonctionnement annuel:* Moins de $50,000
12 bénévole(s)
Membre: 200; *Montant de la cotisation:* Selon la formule d'adhésion, renouvellement: 24$
Activités: Rencontres mensuelles des membres par région; expositions régionales; Festival d'épinglettes;

Club des débrouillards

4475 rue Frontenac, Montréal QC H2H 2S2
scientifix@lesdebrouillards.com
www.lesdebrouillards.qc.ca
Aperçu: *Dimension:* grande; *Envergure:* provinciale
Mission: Pour faire découvrir aux jeunes le bonheur de la lecture et développer leur goût de la découverte et de la science
Membre: 24,000; *Critères d'admissibilite:* Jeunes intéressées à la science
Publications:
• Les Débrouillards [a pubication of the Club des débrouillards]
Type: Magazine

Club des Garçons et Filles d'Ottawa ***See*** Boys & Girls Clubs of Ontario

Club des ornithologues de Québec inc. (COQ)

Domaine de Maizerets, 2000, boul Montmorency, Québec QC G1J 5E7
Tél: 418-661-3544
coq@coq.qc.ca
www.coq.qc.ca
Aperçu: *Dimension:* petite; *Envergure:* provinciale; fondée en 1955
Mission: Faire connaître les oiseaux, loisir, protection de l'avifaune et des habitats, participation à des activités scientifiques.
Membre de: Regroupement QuébecOiseaux
Membre(s) du bureau directeur:
Norbert Lacroix, Président
norbert.lacroix@mat.ulaval.ca
Marguerite Larouche, Vice-président
marlarou@sympatico.ca
Louis Messely, Secrétaire
lmessely@mediom.qc.ca
Finances: *Budget de fonctionnement annuel:* Moins de $50,000; *Fonds:* Cotisations des membres, support de la Ville de Québec pour les espaces de rangement et les locaux
75 bénévole(s)
Membre: 700; *Montant de la cotisation:* 25 $ / année; *Comités:* Conseil d'administration; Plusieurs autres comités
Activités: Publication du Bulletin ornithologique; Excursions, conférences, cours, compilation de données d'observation; *Service de conférenciers:* Oui
Meetings/Conferences: • Virée ornithologique Québec 2015, May, 2015, Four Points by Sheraton Québec, Québec, QC
Scope: Provincial

Publications:
• Bulletin ornithologique
Editor: Pierre Otis

Club des sports moteur d'Ottawa ***See*** Motorsport Club of Ottawa

Club export agro-alimentaire du Québec ***Voir*** Groupe export agroalimentaire Québec - Canada

Club garcons et filles de Lachine ***See*** Boys & Girls Clubs of Québec

Club garçons et filles de LaSalle ***See*** Boys & Girls Clubs of Québec

Club informatique de Brossard (RIB)

Centre Georges-Henri Brossard, #111, 3205, boul. Rome, Brossard QC J4Y 1R2
Tél: 450-656-3348; *Téléc:* 450-678-4801
ribnathaliecroteau@videotron.ca
clubrib.org
Aperçu: *Dimension:* petite; *Envergure:* locale; fondée en 2005
Mission: de partager les connaissances et aider les membres à apprendre à utiliser les ordinateurs, les téléphones cellulaires intelligents et les tablettes
Membre: *Montant de la cotisation:* 35$

Club informatique de Longueuil (CIL)

930, rue Saint-Jacques, Longueuil QC J4H 3E2
Tél: 450-670-5268
admin@clubinfolongueuil.qc.ca
clubinfolongueuil.qc.ca
twitter.com/clubCIL
Aperçu: *Dimension:* petite; *Envergure:* locale
Mission: Pour partager des informations utiles sur la façon d'utiliser un ordinateur
Membre(s) du bureau directeur:
Fernand Laurin, Président, Conseil d'administration
Membre(s) du personnel: 7
Membre: *Montant de la cotisation:* 25$; *Critères d'admissibilite:* Gens de la Rive-Sud de Montréal

Club informatique Mont-Bruno

1585, rue Montarville, Saint-Bruno-sur-Richelieu QC J3V 3T8
Tél: 450-653-3755
cimbcc@cimbcc.org
cimbcc.org
Aperçu: *Dimension:* petite; *Envergure:* locale
Mission: De partager les connaissances et aider les membres à apprendre à utiliser un ordinateur
Membre(s) du bureau directeur:
Réjean Côté, Président, Conseil d'administration
60+ bénévole(s)

Club Kiwanis Chibougamau

CP 61, Chibougamau QC G8P 2K5
Tél: 418-770-8303
Aperçu: *Dimension:* petite; *Envergure:* locale
Membre(s) du bureau directeur:
Yves Lachaine, Président

Club Lions de Chibougamau

CP 11, Chibougamau QC G8P 2K5
Tél: 418-770-9366
lionschibougamau@hotmail.com
lionschibougamau.icr.qc.ca
Aperçu: *Dimension:* petite; *Envergure:* locale
Membre(s) du bureau directeur:
Mario Asselin, Président

Club nautique de Chibougamau inc.

CP 395, Chibougamau QC G8P 2X8
Tél: 418-748-6180
Aperçu: *Dimension:* petite; *Envergure:* locale
Membre(s) du bureau directeur:
Mario Paradis, Président

Club Optimiste de Rivière-du-Loup inc.

CP 1344, Rivière-du-Loup QC G5R 4L9
Tél: 418-862-8454; *Téléc:* 418-862-3366
service@optimiste.org
www.optimiste.org
Aperçu: *Dimension:* petite; *Envergure:* locale
Mission: Les clubs Optimistes inspirent le meilleur chez les jeunes depuis 1919 en rencontrant les besoins des jeunes de toutes les collectivités du monde. Ils organisent des projets de service communautaire positifs qui visent à tendre la main à la jeunesse.

Membre(s) du bureau directeur:
Jean-Louis Dorval, Trésorier

Club photo Évasion

1540, rue Montarville, Saint-Bruno QC J3V 3T7
Tél: 438-274-9424
clubphotoevasion@gmail.com
clubphotoevasion.com
Aperçu: *Dimension:* petite; *Envergure:* locale; fondée en 1985
Mission: D'aider ses membres partagent leurs connaissances et leur amour de la photographie et de développer leurs compétences
Membre(s) du bureau directeur:
Suzanne Tremblay, Présidente, Conseil d'administration
Membre: *Montant de la cotisation:* 75$

Club portugais de Montréal ***Voir*** Clube Portugal de Montreal

Club progrès du Canada ***See*** Canadian Progress Club

Club Richelieu Boréal de Chibougamau

CP 522, Chibougamau QC G8P 2X9
Tél: 418-748-2398
Aperçu: *Dimension:* petite; *Envergure:* locale
Membre(s) du bureau directeur:
Julie Poirier, Responsable

Club Shorthorn du Québec ***See*** Québec Shorthorn Association

Club timbres et monnaies de Sorel inc.

CP 542, Succ. Bureau-Chef, Sorel-Tracy QC J3P 5N9
Tél: 450-855-1648
Aperçu: *Dimension:* petite; *Envergure:* locale
Membre de: Fédération québécoise de philatélie - Montréal
Membre(s) du bureau directeur:
Éric Forest, Président
ricky.itg@gmail.com

Club Vélogamik

CP 594, Chibougamau QC G8P 2Y8
Tél: 418-748-6406
info@velogamik.com
www.velogamik.com
www.facebook.com/groups/342270345795228
Également appelé: Vélogamik Chibougamau
Aperçu: *Dimension:* petite; *Envergure:* locale
Membre(s) du bureau directeur:
Fabien Laprise, Président

Club violettes Longueuil

CP 5000, 1 boul. Curé Poirier Est, Longueuil QC J4K 4Y7
Tél: 450-628-4791
club_violettes_longueuil@hotmail.com
club-violettes-longueuil.org
Aperçu: *Dimension:* petite; *Envergure:* locale; fondée en 1991
Mission: Encourager la culture de la violette africaine pour les personnes vivant à Longueuil
Membre(s) du bureau directeur:
Pierre Laforest, Président, Conseil d'administration
Membre: *Montant de la cotisation:* 20$ individu; 25$ couple

Clube Oriental Português de Montreal / Est club portugais de Montréal

4000, rue Courtai, Montréal QC H3S 1C2
Tél: 514-342-4373
Également appelé: Montreal Portuguese Oriental Club
Aperçu: *Dimension:* petite; *Envergure:* locale

Clube Portugal de Montreal / Club portugais de Montréal

4397 boul St-Laurent, Montréal QC H7H 1G7
Tél: 514-844-1406
Également appelé: Montreal Portuguese Club
Aperçu: *Dimension:* petite; *Envergure:* locale

Clubs 4-H du Québec

#202, 6500 boul. Arthur-Sauvé, Laval QC H7R 3X7
Tél: 450-314-1942; *Téléc:* 450-314-1952
info@clubs4h.qc.ca
www.clubs4h.qc.ca
Aperçu: *Dimension:* moyenne; *Envergure:* provinciale; fondée en 1942
Mission: Susciter et développer, chez le jeune, une préoccupation active pour la conservation de l'arbre, du milieu forestier et de l'environnement; développer le sens des autres, le sens des responsabilités, l'esprit d'initiative, la créativité, le sens de l'émerveillement et le respect pour tout ce qui vit; contribuer à répandre dans le public une mentalité de conservation envers l'environnement, en posant des gestes concrets pour l'amélioration de la qualité de la vie
Membre de: Regroupement Loisir Québec; Conseil québecois du loisir
Membre(s) du bureau directeur:
Andrée Gignac, Directrice
agignac@clubs4h.qc.ca
Finances: *Budget de fonctionnement annuel:* $100,000-$250,000; *Fonds:* Financement municipal, provincial, et fédéral; les frais d'adhésion; collecte de fonds
Membre(s) du personnel: 4; 300 bénévole(s)
Membre: 30 institutionnel; 1 000 individu; *Montant de la cotisation:* $100/club
Activités: *Evénements de sensibilisation:* Mois de l'arbre et des forêts, mai

Clubs garçons & filles du Canada ***See*** Boys & Girls Clubs of Canada

Clydesdale Horse Association of Canada

c/o Marlene Langille, 395 Foxbrook Rd., RR#2, Hopewell NS B0K 1C0
Tel: 902-923-2600
mlangille@auracom.com
www.canadianclydesdales.ca
Overview: A small national organization founded in 1886
Mission: To establish standards of breeding; To develop & regulate the breeding of Clydesdale horses in Canada; To enhance the image, usability, & marketability of the Clydesdale horse
Affliation(s): Canadian Livestock Records Corporation
Chief Officer(s):
Marlene Langille, Secretary
Membership: *Fees:* $37.66 NB, ON, NL; $38 PEI; $38.33 NS; $35 all other provinces; *Member Profile:* Any person who is interested in the well-being & advancement of purebred Clydesdale horses
Activities: Collecting & preserving the breeding & orign of Clydesdale horses; Compiling statistics of the industry; Educating the public about Clydesdale horses; Protecting & assisting breeders; Supervising breeders
Publications:
• Canadian Clydesdale Contact
Type: Magazine; *Frequency:* Annually; *Price:* Free with membership in the Clydesdale Horse Association of Canada
Profile: News & results of Clydesdale shows from throughout Canada

CMA Canada - Alberta

#300, 1210 - 8th St. SW, Calgary AB T2R 1L3
Tel: 403-269-5341; *Fax:* 403-262-5477
Toll-Free: 877-262-2000
reception@cma-alberta.com
www.cma-alberta.com
www.linkedin.com/company/cma-alberta
www.facebook.com/127048308618
twitter.com/CMAAlberta
www.flickr.com/photos/cmaalberta
Previous Name: Society of Management Accountants of Alberta
Overview: A medium-sized provincial licensing organization founded in 1944 overseen by Alberta Accountants Unification Agency
Mission: To develop & advance the competencies & market relevance of CMAs through accreditation, education, & high standards
Chief Officer(s):
John Carpenter, BA, MBA, FICB, President & CEO
Finances: *Annual Operating Budget:* $1.5 Million-$3 Million; *Funding Sources:* Membership dues
Membership: 7,400+; *Fees:* $677.59 + GST; *Member Profile:* University or college graduate; entrance exam & two-year professional program & 24 months practical experience
Activities: Careers-on-Line; CMA Professional Program; Continuing Professional Education (note that CMA Alberta will integrate under the CPA banner); *Library*
Awards:
• Certified Management Accountants Awards (Scholarship)
Amount: Maximum of $1,500; up to 5 awards

CMA Canada - British Columbia (CMABC)

#1000, 900 West Hastings St., Vancouver BC V6C 0C4
Tel: 604-687-5891; *Fax:* 604-687-6688
Toll-Free: 800-663-9646
cmabc@cmabc.com
www.cmabc.com
Also Known As: Certified Management Accountants of British Columbia

Previous Name: Society of Management Accountants of British Columbia
Overview: A medium-sized provincial licensing organization founded in 1945 overseen by Chartered Professional Accountants of British Columbia
Mission: To be pre-eminent in management accounting by ensuring that the body of knowledge is available, by setting & enforcing the standards of competence, ensuring availability of CMAs in the defined territory, & supporting research; to optimize the performance of enterprises by driving the continuous development of financial & strategic management professionals & shaping the strategic leadership competencies of CMAs
Chief Officer(s):
Vinetta Peek, CMA (Hon), CMA, President & CEO, 604-484-7002
vinetta@cmabc.com
Finances: *Annual Operating Budget:* $3 Million-$5 Million; *Funding Sources:* Membership dues
Membership: 5,000; *Fees:* $855.75
Activities: Professional education; professional development (note that CMABC will integrate under the CPA banner)

CMA Canada - Manitoba
#1675, 1 Lombard Pl., Winnipeg MB R3C 0X3
Tel: 204-943-1538; *Fax:* 204-943-7119
Toll-Free: 800-841-7148
cpamb@cpamb.ca
www.cma-manitoba.com
Overview: A medium-sized provincial organization founded in 1947 overseen by Chartered Professional Accountants of Manitoba
Mission: To support members in leading organizations in the application of advanced management practices
Chief Officer(s):
Ron Stoesz, CMA, FCMA, Chief Executive Officer, 204-987-4564
rstoesz@cpamb.ca
Finances: *Funding Sources:* Membership
Membership: *Member Profile:* Accreditation process including examinations
Activities: Professional development opportunities (note that CMA Manitoba will integrate under the CPA banner)

CMA Canada - Northwest Territories & Nunavut (CMA NWT&NU)
PO Box 512, Yellowknife NT X1A 2N4
Tel: 867-876-1290; *Fax:* 867-920-2503
www.cma-nwt.com
Overview: A small provincial organization overseen by Chartered Professional Accountants Canada
Chief Officer(s):
George Blandford, CMA, Contact
george@blandford.ca
Activities: Providing professional development opportunities (note that CMA NWT&NU will integrate under the CPA banner once legislation is approved)

CMA Canada - Ontario
#1100, 25 York St., Toronto ON M5J 2V5
Tel: 416-977-7741; *Fax:* 416-977-6079
Toll-Free: 800-387-2991
info@gocpaontario.ca
www.cmaontario.org
Also Known As: Certified Management Accountants of Ontario
Previous Name: The Society of Management Accountants of Ontario
Overview: A large provincial licensing organization founded in 1941 overseen by Chartered Professional Accountants of Ontario
Mission: To optimize the performance of enterprises by driving the continuous development of management accounting & shaping the strategic competences of CMA's
Chief Officer(s):
Carol Wilding, FCPA, FCA, President & CEO
Beth Deazeley, Corporate Secretary & Registrar
Andrew Gall, Vice-President & Treasurer, Corporate Services
Janet Treasure, Vice-President, Professional Development
Finances: *Annual Operating Budget:* Greater than $5 Million; *Funding Sources:* Membership dues; program fees
Membership: 25,000; *Fees:* Schedule available; *Member Profile:* University degree & practical experience
Activities: Offers management development program; offers professional development opportunities (note that CMA Ontario will integrate under the CPA banner); *Library:* Member Services Centre; Open to public

CMA Canada - Saskatchewan
#101, 4581 Parliament Ave., Regina SK S4W 0G3
Tel: 306-359-6461; *Fax:* 306-347-8580
Toll-Free: 800-667-3535
info@cma-sask.org
www.cma-saskatchewan.com
Overview: A medium-sized provincial licensing organization founded in 1929 overseen by Chartered Professional Accountants of Saskatchewan
Chief Officer(s):
Betty Hoffart, CMA, FCMA, Chief Executive Officer
bhoffart@cma-sask.org
Activities: Providing continuing professional development (note that CMA - Saskatchewan will integrate under the CPA banner)

CMA Canada - Yukon
c/o Certified Management Accountants of British Columbia, #1000, 900 West Hastings St., British Columbia BC V6C 0C4
Tel: 604-687-5891; *Fax:* 604-687-6688
cmabc@cmabc.com
www.cmabc.com
Overview: A small provincial organization founded in 1975 overseen by Chartered Professional Accountants of the Yukon
Mission: To promote standards of excellence in management accounting
Chief Officer(s):
Kelly Steele, Chair
Kelly.Steele@wgh.yk.ca
Activities: Providing professionl development opportunities (note that CMA Yukon will integrate under the CPA banner)

CNEC - Partners International
#56, 8500 Torbram Rd., Brampton ON L6T 5C6
Tel: 905-458-1202; *Fax:* 905-458-4339
Toll-Free: 800-883-7697
info@partnersinternational.ca
www.partnersinternational.ca
twitter.com/Partnersintlcan
www.youtube.com/user/partnerscanada
Also Known As: Partners International
Overview: A small local organization
Mission: Partners Canadians with indigenous Christian ministries to spread the Word of God.
Chief Officer(s):
Harry Doxsee, Chair

CNTU Federation - Construction (CNTU) *Voir* Fédération CSN - Construction (CSN)

COACH - Canada's Health Informatics Association (COACH)
#301, 250 Consumers Rd., Toronto ON M2J 4V6
Tel: 416-494-9324; *Fax:* 416-495-8723
Toll-Free: 888-253-8554
info@coachorg.com
www.coachorg.com
www.linkedin.com/company/coach-canada's-health-informatics-association
www.facebook.com/group.php?gid=196625113752686
twitter.com/COACH_HI
Overview: A large national organization founded in 1975
Mission: To improve the health of Canadians & enhance the management of Canada's health system by advancing the practice of health information management & effective utilization of associated technologies
Member of: International Medical Informatics Association
Chief Officer(s):
Don Newsham, Chief Executive Officer
dnewsham@coachorg.com
Shannon Bott, Executive Director, Operations
sbott@coachorg.com
Linda Miller, Executive Director, CHIEF: Canada's Health Informatics Executive Forum
lmiller@coachorg.com
John Schinbein, Executive Director, CTF Telehealth Forum
jschinbein@coachorg.com
Neil Gardner, President
Mike Barron, Sec.-Tres., 709-752-6009
mike.barron@nlchi.nl.ca
Finances: *Annual Operating Budget:* $500,000-$1.5 Million; *Funding Sources:* Membership fees; workshops; conferences
Staff Member(s): 8; 45 volunteer(s)
Membership: 400 institutional + 20 student + 30 lifetime + 400 individual; *Fees:* Schedule available; *Member Profile:* Interest in health informatics; *Committees:* HIP@work Task Force; CTF Advisory Commitee; HIP Resources Task Force; HIP Steering Committee; HIP@school Task Force; Exam Committee; Dr. Pat Ceresia Leads P&S Steering Committee; EP Advisory Committee
Awards:
• Canadian Health Informatics Award (Award)
• Chairman's Award of Excellence (Award)
• Corporate Citizenship - Multi-National Company (Award)
• Corporate Citizenship - Small to Medium Enterprise (Award)
• merging Leader in Health Informatics (Award)
• Leadership in the Field of Health Informatics Award (Award)
• Steven Huesing Scholarship (Scholarship)
Meetings/Conferences: • Canada's Health Informatics Association 2015 Annual Geenral Meeting, 2015
Scope: National
• ANHIX (Alberta Network for Heath Information eXchange) and COACH (Canada's Health Informatics Association) Conference 2015, February, 2015, Delta Calgary South, Calgary, AB
Scope: National
Contact Information: COACH Program Coordinatior: Cheryl Cornelio, ccornelio@coachorg.com

Coaches Association of British Columbia *See* ViaSport

Coaches Association of Ontario (CAO)
#108, 3 Concorde Gate, Toronto ON M3C 3N7
Fax: 416-426-7331
Toll-Free: 888-622-7668
www.ontariobobsleighskeleton.ca
www.linkedin.com/company/coaches-association-of-ontario
www.facebook.com/coachesontario
twitter.com/coaches_ont
www.youtube.com/user/CoachesOntario
Overview: A medium-sized provincial organization founded in 2002
Mission: To represent coaches in Ontario
Chief Officer(s):
Susan Kitchen, Executive Director
susan@coachesontario.ca
Finances: *Funding Sources:* Federal & provincial government; Ontario Trillium Foundation
Staff Member(s): 7
Activities: Sport workshops; Webinars
Meetings/Conferences: • 2015 Ontario Coaches Conference, February, 2015, Sheraton Parkway North, Richmond Hill, ON
Scope: Provincial

Coaches Association of PEI (CAPEI)
40 Enman Cres., Charlottetown PE C1E 1E6
Tel: 902-368-4110; *Fax:* 902-368-4548
Toll-Free: 800-247-6712
Other Communication: Toll free fax: 800-235-5687
sports@sportpei.pe.ca
www.sportpei.pe.ca
www.facebook.com/pages/Sport-PEI/176050449103403
twitter.com/SportPEI
Overview: A small provincial organization founded in 1992 overseen by Sport PEI Inc.
Mission: To educate, develop & promote coaching & coaches for the benefit of athletes, sport & the community in general; To encourage fair play, integrity & the pursuit of excellence
Member of: Coaching Association of Canada
Chief Officer(s):
Gemma Koughan, Executive Director
gkoughan@sportpei.pe.ca
Finances: *Funding Sources:* Membership fees; fundraising
Staff Member(s): 8
Membership: 50 organizations

Coaching Association of Canada (CAC) / Association canadienne des entraîneurs
#300, 141 Laurier Ave. West, Ottawa ON K1P 5J3
Tel: 613-235-5000; *Fax:* 613-235-9500
www.coach.ca
www.facebook.com/coach.ca
Overview: A large national charitable organization founded in 1971
Mission: To improvo implementation & delivery of National Coaching Certification Program; To establish coaching as viable career within the Canadian sports system; To increase the number of qualified full-time & part-time remunerated coaches at various levels within the sport system
Affliation(s): Professional Arm: Canadian Professional Coaches Association
Chief Officer(s):
Gabor Csepregi, Chair
John Bales, CEO, 613-235-5000 Ext. 2363
Cyndie Flett, Vice-President, Research & Development, 613-235-5000 Ext. 2379

Nancy Spotton, Vice-President, Sales & Marketing, 613-235-5000 Ext. 0
Marc Schryburt, Director, Finance & Administration, International Programs, 613-235-5000 Ext. 2365
Julie Parkins-Forget, Manager, Marketing & Communications, 613-235-5000 Ext. 2382
Finances: *Funding Sources:* Sport Canada; Corporations; Foundations
Membership: *Committees:* Coaching Research
Activities: Offering the following programs: National Coaching Certification Program (NCCP); Sport Nutrition; Petro-Canada Sport Leadership sportif; Investors Group Community Coaching Conferences; *Speaker Service:* Yes
Awards:
• Petro-Canada Coaching Excellence Awards (Award)
• Geoff Gowan Award (Award)
• Investors Group Volunteer Sport Administrator Award (Award)
• Queen Elizabeth II Diamond Jubilee Medal (Award)
Meetings/Conferences: • Coaching Association of Canada Petro-Canada Sport Leadership Sportif Conference 2015, November, 2015, RBC Convention Centre and the Delta Winnipeg, Winnipeg, MB
Scope: National
Description: An inpiring event for coaches, featuring guest speakers & the presentation of sport leadership awards
Contact Information: Phone: 613-235-5000

Coaching Manitoba
145 Pacific Ave., Winnipeg MB R2B 2Z6
Tel: 204-925-5692; *Fax:* 204-925-5624
Toll-Free: 888-887-7307
www.coachingmanitoba.ca
Overview: A small provincial organization
Mission: To train coaches in Manitoba
Member of: Sport Manitoba
Chief Officer(s):
Greg Guenther, Director, 204-925-5669
greg.guenther@sportmanitoba.ca
Staff Member(s): 4

Coady International Institute (CII)
St. Francis Xavier University, PO Box 5000, Antigonish NS B2G 2W5
Tel: 902-867-3960; *Fax:* 902-867-3907
Toll-Free: 866-820-7835
coady@stfx.ca
www.coady.stfx.ca
www.facebook.com/coady.international.institute
twitter.com/coadystfx
www.youtube.com/user/CoadyInstitute
Overview: A large international charitable organization founded in 1959
Mission: Promotes learning in individuals & organizations engaged in community-driven action to achieve wellbeing, global justice, peace & participating democracy
Member of: Canadian Council for International Cooperation
Chief Officer(s):
John Gaventa, Director
Finances: *Annual Operating Budget:* $1.5 Million-$3 Million
Staff Member(s): 28
Membership: *Committees:* University Advisory
Activities: Conferences & presentations; publishes occasional papers; *Awareness Events:* Coady Celebrates, Nov 1; *Internships:* Yes; *Library:* Marie Michael Library; Open to public

Coal Association of Canada (CAC)
#150, 205 - 9th Ave. SE, Calgary AB T2G 0R3
Tel: 403-262-1544; *Fax:* 403-265-7604
Toll-Free: 800-910-2625
info@coal.ca
www.coal.ca
www.twitter.com/coalcanada
Overview: A medium-sized national organization
Mission: To promote coal as a vital energy source that is abundant, safe, reliable, environmentally and economically acceptable.
Chief Officer(s):
Ann Marie Hann, President
hann@coal.ca
Michelle Mondeville, Director, Communications and Stakeholder Relations
mondeville@coal.ca
Membership: 78 corporate
Meetings/Conferences: • Coal Association of Canada 2015 Association Conference & Trade Show, September, 2015, Westin Bayshore Hotel, Vancouver, BC
Scope: National
Contact Information: Linda Kool; kool@coal.ca

Coaldale & District Chamber of Commerce
PO Box 1117, 1401 - 20 Ave., Coaldale AB T1M 1M9
Tel: 403-345-2358; *Fax:* 403-345-2339
info@coaldalechamber.com
www.coaldalechamber.com
Overview: A small local organization
Mission: The Chamber of Commerce is a community based volunteer business organization that brings elements of the business commuity together in a single influential and respected voice by speaking on behalf of the business community. Chambers provide leadership on issues of the community, provincial and federal concerns. Chambers provide an effective lobby to ensure a positive climate.
Member of: Alberta Chamber of Commerce; Canadian Chamber of Commerce
Chief Officer(s):
John Pollemans, President
Finances: *Annual Operating Budget:* Less than $50,000; *Funding Sources:* Membership fees; grant
20 volunteer(s)
Membership: 150; *Fees:* Schedule available

Coalition After Property Tax Reform (CAPTR)
c/o WRAFT, PO Box 263, #200, 131 Bloor St. West, Toronto ON M5S 1R8
Tel: 416-929-9885
bobtopp1@gmail.com
Overview: A medium-sized provincial organization
Mission: To fight for a five per cent cap on annual property assessment increase & reforms to the property tax system in Ontario
Chief Officer(s):
Bob Topp, Executive Director
Membership: 700 ratepayer groups

Coalition Avenir Québec
#499, 4020, rue Saint-Ambroise, Montréal QC H4C 2C7
Tél: 514-800-6000; *Téléc:* 514-800-0081
Ligne sans frais: 866-416-2960
info@coalitionavenirquebec.org
coalitionavenirquebec.org
www.facebook.com/coalitionavenir
twitter.com/coalitionavenir
www.youtube.com/user/AvenirCoalition
Aperçu: *Dimension:* petite; *Envergure:* provinciale; fondée en 2011
Membre(s) du bureau directeur:
François Legault, Chef
Stéphane Le Bouyonnec, Président

Coalition canadien contre la peine de mort *See* Canadian Coalition Against the Death Penalty

Coalition canadienne de l'énergie géothermique *See* Canadian GeoExchange Coalition

Coalition canadienne de la filière alimentaire pour la salubrité des aliments *See* Canadian Supply Chain Food Safety Coalition

Coalition canadienne de la santé *See* Canadian Health Coalition

Coalition canadienne des aidants et aidantes naturels *See* Canadian Caregiver Coalition

Coalition canadienne des organismes bénévoles en santé *See* Health Charities Coalition of Canada

Coalition canadienne pour un accès équitable à la technologie digitale *See* Canadian Coalition for Fair Digital Access

Coalition d'une vie active pour les aîné(e)s *See* Active Living Coalition for Older Adults

Coalition des centres anti-viol de l'Ontario *See* Ontario Coalition of Rape Crisis Centres

Coalition des communautés en santé de l'Ontario *See* Ontario Healthy Communities Coalition

Coalition des familles homoparentales *Voir* Coalition des familles LGBT

Coalition des familles LGBT / LGBT Family Coalition
Montréal QC
Tél: 514-846-7600
info@familleslgbt.org
www.familleslgbt.org
Nom précédent: Coalition des familles homoparentales
Aperçu: *Dimension:* petite; *Envergure:* locale; fondée en 1998
Mission: Milite pour la reconnaissance légale et sociale des familles homoparentales; groupe bilingue de parents lesbiens, gais, bisexuels et transgenres. Québec: 418-523-5572
Membre(s) du bureau directeur:
Mona Greenbaum, Directrice générale
mona@familleslgbt.org
Membre: *Montant de la cotisation:* 40$ par famille

Coalition des femmes de l'Alberta
Bldg. 2, #300, 8627, rue Marie-Anne-Gaboury, Edmonton AB T6C 3N1
Tél: 780-468-2288; *Téléc:* 780-468-2210
femmes@coalitionfemmes.ab.ca
www.coalitionfemmes.ab.ca
Nom précédent: Coalition des femmes francophones de l'Alberta; Association des groupes de femmes francophones de l'Alberta
Aperçu: *Dimension:* petite; *Envergure:* provinciale; Organisme sans but lucratif; fondée en 2002
Mission: Développer et favoriser des activités variées de sensibilisation, d'animation, de revendication et de formation qui répondent aux besoins des femmes francophones de l'Alberta
Affiliation(s): Alliance des femmes de la francophonie canadienne; Conseil de développement économique de l'Alberta; Institut Guy-Lacombe de la famille; Réseau canadien de santé des femmes
Membre(s) du bureau directeur:
Gioia Sallustio-Jarvis, Présidente
Vicky Choquette, Vice-présidente
Geneviève Labrie, Trésorière
Fabienne Bühl, Agente de développement
Membre(s) du personnel: 1
Membre: *Critères d'admissibilite:* Femme francophone de l'Alberta
Activités: Ateliers; conférences; sensibilisation aux dossiers socio-politiques touchant les femmes, développement personnel, leadership, estime de soi, confiance en soi, gestion du temps, l'art de parler en public; consultations provinciales; *Service de conférenciers:* Oui
Publications:
• Bulletin de la Coalition [a publication of Coalition des femmes de l'Alberta]
Type: Bulletin

Coalition des femmes francophones de l'Alberta; Association des groupes de femmes francophones de l'Alberta *Voir* Coalition des femmes de l'Alberta

Coalition des organismes communautaires québécois de lutte contre le sida (COCQ-SIDA)
1, rue Sherbrooke est, Montréal QC H2X 3V8
Tél: 514-844-2477; *Téléc:* 514-844-2498
Ligne sans frais: 866-535-0481
info@cocqsida.com
www.cocqsida.com
www.facebook.com/COCQSIDA
twitter.com/COCQSIDA
Aperçu: *Dimension:* moyenne; *Envergure:* provinciale; Organisme sans but lucratif; fondée en 1990
Mission: Représenter les membres afin de favoriser l'émergence et le soutien d'une action concertée dans les dossiers d'intérêt commun; faire reconnaître l'expertise et l'apport des organismes communautaires et non-gouvernementaux dans la lutte contre le sida.
Membre(s) du bureau directeur:
Hélène Légaré, Présidente
Ken Monteith, Directeur général
d.g@cocqsida.com
Finances: *Budget de fonctionnement annuel:* $100,000-$250,000
Membre(s) du personnel: 5; 15 bénévole(s)
Membre: 25 organismes; *Montant de la cotisation:* 100-400; *Critères d'admissibilite:* Groupes communautaires
Activités: *Service de conférenciers:* Oui; *Bibliothèque* rendez-vous

Coalition des organismes d'aînés et d'aînées de l'Ontario *See* Ontario Coalition of Senior Citizens' Organizations

Coalition for a Smoke-Free Nova Scotia
PO Box 822, Lower Sackville NS B4V 3V3

Tel: 902-864-9633; *Fax:* 902-484-6946
Toll-Free: 866-777-7374
carivanlingen@smokefreens.ca
www.smokefreens.ca
Also Known As: Smoke-Free Nova Scotia
Previous Name: Nova Scotia Council on Smoking & Health
Overview: A small provincial organization
Mission: Committed to the achievement of a tobacco-free Nova Scotia
Member of: Canadian Council on Smoking & Health
Finances: *Funding Sources:* Provincial government grants; Membership fees
Membership: 31; *Fees:* $20-200; *Member Profile:* Health professionals; Health agencies; Individuals
Activities: Media strategies; Public presentaions; Educational material; Consultations with government; *Awareness Events:* National Non-Smoking Week

Coalition for Active Living (CAL)
#301, 2197 Riverside Dr., Ottawa ON K1H 7X3
Tel: 613-277-9979
info@activeliving.ca
www.activeliving.ca
Overview: A small national organization
Mission: To ensure that environments in which people live support regular physical activity.
Chief Officer(s):
Christa Costas-Bradstreet, Co-Chair
Nancy Dubois, Co-Chair
Finances: *Funding Sources:* Physical Activity Contribution Program of Health Canada
Staff Member(s): 1
Membership: 100+ organiations

Coalition for Competitive Telecommunications
#880, 45 O'Connor St., Ottawa ON K1P 1A4
Tel: 613-566-7053; *Fax:* 613-566-2026
Overview: A small national organization founded in 2003
Mission: To be the authoritative voice for Canadian business & institutional users of telecom equipment & services on critical legislative, regulatory & policy issues affecting business operations
Chief Officer(s):
Ian C. Russell, Chair

Coalition for Gay Rights in Ontario ***See*** Coalition for Lesbian & Gay Rights in Ontario

Coalition for Gun Control / Coalition pour le contrôle des armes
PO Box 90062, 1488 Queen St. West, Toronto ON M6K 3K3
Tel: 416-604-0209
coalitionforguncontrol@gmail.com
www.guncontrol.ca
twitter.com/CGCguncontrol
Overview: A small local organization founded in 1990
Mission: To reduce gun crimes; to promote strict laws on gun control

Bureau de Montréal
1301, rue Sherbrooke, Montréal QC H2L 1M3
Tél: 514-528-2360
cgc.montreal@gmail.com
twitter.com/CGCmontreal

Coalition for Lesbian & Gay Rights in Ontario (CLGRO) / Coalition pour les droits des lesbiennes et personnes gaies en Ontario
PO Box 822, Stn. A, Toronto ON M5W 1G3
Tel: 416-392-6878
www.clgro.org
Previous Name: Coalition for Gay Rights in Ontario
Overview: A medium-sized provincial organization founded in 1975
Mission: To work towards feminism, lesbian, gay & bisexual liberation by engaging in public struggle for full human rights, by promoting access & diversity within our communities, & by strengthening cooperative networks for lesbian, gay & bisexual activism
Affiliation(s): International Lesbian & Gay Association
40 volunteer(s)
Membership: 24 groups + 450 individuals; *Fees:* $40; $20 students or unwaged
Activities: *Speaker Service:* Yes

Coalition for Music Education in British Columbia (CME)
#839, 1641 Lonsdale Ave., Langley BC V7M 2J5
Tel: 604-888-7385; *Fax:* 604-888-7853
www.cmebc.org
Overview: A small provincial organization
Mission: To protect & promote public school music education in British Columbia
Affliation(s): Coalition for Music Education in Canada
Membership: *Fees:* $20 individual; $40 group; $100 patron; $250 corporate; $500 benefactor

Coalition for Music Education in Canada (CMEC)
PO Box 556, Agincourt ON M1S 3C5
Tel: 416-298-2871; *Fax:* 416-298-5730
cmec.convio.net
www.facebook.com/pages/Music-Makes-Us/166549336704277
twitter.com/musicmakesus_ca
youtube.com/musicmondaycanada
Overview: A small national organization
Mission: To raise the awareness & understanding of the role that music plays in Canadian culture; To advocate for the contribution that music education makes in the lives of all Canadians
Chief Officer(s):
Holly Nimmons, Executive Director
Staff Member(s): 2
Publications:
- Coalition for Music Education in Canada Newsletter
Type: Newsletter; *Frequency:* Irregular; *Editor:* Norman Mould

Coalition for the Protection of Human Life ***See*** Campaign Life Coalition

Coalition Jeunesse Sierra ***See*** Sierra Youth Coalition

Coalition nationale des citoyens inc. ***See*** The National Citizens Coalition

Coalition of Associations of Craniocerebral Trauma in Quebec ***Voir*** Regroupement des associations de personnes traumatisées craniocérébrales du Québec

Coalition of BC Businesses (COBCB)
PO Box 12125, #2410, 555 West Hastings St., Vancouver BC V6B 4N6
Tel: 604-682-8366
info@coalitionbcbusiness.ca
www.coalitionbcbusiness.ca
twitter.com/CoalitionBC
Overview: A small provincial organization founded in 1992
Mission: To represent the interests of businesses, with an aim to help foster a positive relationship between employers & employees in labour & employment policy.
Membership: *Member Profile:* Associations who represent small- & medium-sized businesses in various sectors in BC

Coalition of Rail Shippers (CRS)
c/o Canadian Industrial Transportation Association, #405, 580 Terry Fox Dr., Ottawa ON K2L 4C2
Tel: 613-599-3283; *Fax:* 613-599-1295
Overview: A medium-sized national organization founded in 2005
Mission: To provide input to government on matters affecting Canadian, rail freight transportation.
Chief Officer(s):
Robert H. Ballantyne, Chair, 613-599-8993 Ext. 223, Fax: 613-294-4569
ballantyne@bellnet.ca
Membership: *Member Profile:* Shipping industry associations

Coalition on the Niagara Escarpment (CONE)
193 James St. South, Hamilton ON L8P 3A8
Tel: 905-529-4955; *Fax:* 905-529-9503
cone@niagaraescarpment.org
www.niagaraescarpment.org
Overview: A small local organization founded in 1978
Mission: CONE is a non-profit alliance of environmental groups, conservation organizations, and concerned citizens and businesses dedicated to the protection of Ontario's Niagara Escarpment.
Affiliation(s): The Greenbelt Foundation, Niagara Escarpment Foundation
Chief Officer(s):
Robert Patrick, President
Membership: 26 organizations; *Fees:* $35 individual; $60-$120 corporate

La coalition ontarienne pour la justice sociale ***See*** Ontario Coalition for Social Justice

Coalition pour l'alphabétisme du Nouveau-Brunswick ***See*** Literacy Coalition of New Brunswick

Coalition pour le contrôle des armes ***See*** Coalition for Gun Control

Coalition pour les droits des lesbiennes et personnes gaies en Ontario ***See*** Coalition for Lesbian & Gay Rights in Ontario

Coalition québécoise pour le contrôle du tabac (CQCT)
#200, 4126, rue St-Denis, Montréal QC H2W 2M5
Tél: 514-598-5533; *Téléc:* 514-598-5283
coalition@cqct.qc.ca
www.cqct.qc.ca
Aperçu: *Dimension:* petite; *Envergure:* provinciale
Membre(s) du bureau directeur:
Flory Doucas, Codirectrice
Louis Gauvin, Cofondateur & Codirecteur
Heidi Rathjen, Cofondatrice & Codirectrice
Membre(s) du personnel: 5

Coalition sida des sourds du Québec (CSSQ)
Edifice Plessis, #320, 2075, rue Plessis, Montréal QC H2L 2Y4
Ligne sans frais: 877-535-5556; *TTY:* 800-855-0511
info@cssq.org
www.cssq.org
Aperçu: *Dimension:* petite; *Envergure:* provinciale; Organisme sans but lucratif; fondée en 1992 surveillé par Canadian AIDS Society
Mission: Informer et mettre en garde la communauté sourde du Québec contre les risques de contracter le Sida et les ITSS (Infections transmissibles sexuellement par le sang); dispenser des services et activités aux personnes sourdes et malentendantes atteintes du VIH/Sida et de l'ITSS
Affliation(s): Coalition des organismes communautaires québécois de lutte contre le sida
Membre(s) du bureau directeur:
Donald Pilling, Président
Michel Turgeon, Directeur général
direction@cssq.org
Finances: *Budget de fonctionnement annuel:* $50,000-$100,000
Membre(s) du personnel: 4; 30 bénévole(s)
Membre: 36 individus; 6 étudiants; 14 membres associés; *Montant de la cotisation:* 15$ réguliers; 10$ étudiants; 100$ associés; *Critères d'admissibilite:* Clientèle - population sourde et malentendante du Québec; personnes sourdes vivant avec le VIH/SIDA; personnes sourdes proches; aucune limite d'âge
Activités: Activités d'éducation/prévention; groupe de support pour personnes atteintes et leurs proches; accompagnement et soutien des pairs; ligne d'écoute (TTY); rencontres individuelles; counselling; services psychosociaux (en collaboration avec l'institut Raymond Dewar); information; orientation; références; vidéo: le Sida frappe aussi les Sourds; un manuel illustré pour l'éducation et la prévention du VIH/Sida; un répertoire de signes LSQ pertinents au VIH/Sida; *Stagiaires:* Oui; *Service de conférenciers:* Oui

Coalition to Oppose the Arms Trade (COAT)
541 McLeod St., Ottawa ON K1R 5R2
Tel: 613-231-3076
overcoat@rogers.com
coat.ncf.ca
www.facebook.com/group.php?gid=2337208773
Overview: A medium-sized national organization
Mission: To actively oppose the arms trade and support the anti-war movement.
Chief Officer(s):
Richard Sanders, Coordinator
Publications:
- Press for Conversion
Frequency: 3 pa; *Price:* $8 per issue; $25 annual subscription

Coalition to Save the Elms ***See*** Trees Winnipeg

Coast Forest & Lumber Association ***See*** Coast Forest Products Association

Coast Forest Products Association (CFPA)
#1200, 1090 West Pender St., Vancouver BC V6E 2N7
Tel: 604-891-1237; *Fax:* 604-682-8641
info@coastforest.org
www.coastforest.org
twitter.com/CoastForest
www.youtube.com/user/CoastForest
Also Known As: Coast Forest
Previous Name: Coast Forest & Lumber Association

Overview: A medium-sized international organization founded in 1994
Mission: To promote the interests & protect the rights of those engaged in the coast forest industry in BC
Member of: Canadian Wood Council; Business Council of BC; Vancouver Board of Trade
Chief Officer(s):
Rick Jeffrey, President/CEO
Finances: *Funding Sources:* Coast Forest Industry; Partnership funding for lumber promotion in Japan & China
Staff Member(s): 6
Membership: 19; *Member Profile:* Logging companies &/or lumber manufacturing companies
Activities: User-pay menu programs; log security; Japan & China lumber promotion

Coast Foundation Society (CFS)
293 East 11 Ave., Vancouver BC V5T 2C4
Tel: 604-872-3502; *Fax:* 604-879-2363
info@coastmentalhealth.com
www.coastmentalhealth.com
Overview: A medium-sized provincial charitable organization founded in 1974
Mission: To promote recovery of persons with mental illness
Member of: Canadian Council of Health Services Association
Chief Officer(s):
Jeniffer Clarke, Chair
Darrell Burnham, Executive Directro
darrellb@coastmentalhealth.com
Finances: *Funding Sources:* Donations; government grants; membership fees; BC Housing
Membership: *Fees:* $10
Activities: AGM; Courage to Come Back; Endeavour; Christmas crafts fair; picnic; *Awareness Events:* Mental Health Week, May; *Library:* Resource Centre; Open to public

Coast Waste Management Association (CWMA)
1185 Rolmar Cres., Cobble Hill BC V0R 1L4
Tel: 250-733-2213; *Fax:* 250-733-2214
Toll-Free: 886-386-2962
info@cwma.bc.ca
www.cwma.bc.ca
Overview: A small local organization
Mission: To facilitate communication between members; to provide networking & educational opportunities
Chief Officer(s):
Malcolm Harvey, Chair, 604-831-7203
malcolm_harvey@telus.net
Will Burrows, Executive Director
info@cwma.bc.ca
Membership: 136; *Member Profile:* Members of the solid waste industry on Vancouver Island, the Gulf Islands & the Sunshine Coast
Publications:
• CWMA [Coast Waste Management Association] News
Type: Newsletter; *Frequency:* q.
• CWMA [Coast Waste Management Association] E-bulletins
Type: Bulletin

Coastal Ecosystems Research Foundation
General Delivery, Dawson's Landing BC V0N 1M0
Tel: 44-0-7745-730873; *Fax:* 815-327-0173
info@cerf.bc.ca
www.cerf.bc.ca
Overview: A small local organization founded in 1995
Mission: To fund ecological research through eco-tourism
Chief Officer(s):
William Megill, Ph.D., Research Director
Finances: *Annual Operating Budget:* $50,000-$100,000; *Funding Sources:* Provincial & national government
Staff Member(s): 4
Membership: 120
Activities: Week-long "research adventure" in which people can participate in all aspects of our research while living a wilderness adventure along the southern Central Coast of British Columbia; this program almost completely funds our research focused on grey & humpback whales studies of the subtidal intertidal & coastal forest zones

Coastal Jazz & Blues Society (CJBS)
295 - 7th Ave. West, 2nd Fl., Vancouver BC V5Y 1L9
Tel: 604-872-5200; *Fax:* 604-872-5250
Toll-Free: 888-438-5200
cjbs@coastaljazz.ca
www.coastaljazz.ca
www.facebook.com/profile.php?id=100000842108783
twitter.com/vanjazzfest
Also Known As: TD Vancouver International Jazz Festival
Overview: A small local charitable organization founded in 1986
Mission: To produce concerts, festivals & events featuring a comprehensive & diverse range of artists representing jazz, blues & improvised music
Member of: Vancouver Cultural Alliance
Affliation(s): Westcan Jazz Association; Jazz Festivals Canada
Chief Officer(s):
Fatima Amarshi, Executive Director
Ken Pickering, Artistic Director
John Orysik, Media Director
Finances: *Annual Operating Budget:* $3 Million-$5 Million; *Funding Sources:* Earned income; sponsorship; grant; donations; memberships
Staff Member(s): 10; 750 volunteer(s)
Membership: 170; *Fees:* $50; *Member Profile:* Producer & presenter of concerts, festivals & workshops
Activities: TD Vancouver International Jazz Festival; *Internships:* Yes

Coastal Zone Canada Association (CZCA)
c/o Jennifer Barr, Dalhousie University, PO Box 15000, 6414 Coburg Rd., Halifax NS B3H 4R2
Tel: 902-494-4650; *Fax:* 902-494-1334
czcadmin@dal.ca
www.czca-azcc.org
Overview: A small local organization founded in 1993
Mission: A society of coastal zone management professionals and others interested in and supportive of Integrated Coastal Zone Management goals in Canada and abroad.
Membership: *Fees:* $20-$40
Meetings/Conferences: • Coastal Zone Canada 2016, June, 2016, Toronto, ON
Scope: National
Contact Information: Peter Zuzek; pzuzek@baird.com

The Coaster Enthusiasts of Canada
e-mail: cec@chebucto.org
www.cec.chebucto.org
Overview: A small national organization
Chief Officer(s):
Richard Bonner, Contact
Membership: *Member Profile:* Group of persons whose primary interest is robots, amusement parks, rides, fairs & exhibitions

Cobequid Arts Council
605 Prince St., Truro NS B2N 1G2
Tel: 902-897-4004
marigold@downtowntruro.ca
www.marigoldcentre.ca
www.facebook.com/marigoldcentre
twitter.com/MarigoldCentre
marigoldcentre.tumblr.com
Also Known As: Marigold Culture Centre
Overview: A small local organization founded in 1978
Mission: To direct, coordinate & advise on arts & cultural activities in Colchester area, Nova Scotia; To act as liaison between arts organizations in the region
Member of: Performing Arts Sponsors Organization of Nova Scotia
Chief Officer(s):
Al Rosen, Executive director, 902-893-2718, Fax: 902-895-9712
al.rosen@marigoldcentre.ca
Finances: *Funding Sources:* Government; fundraising
Staff Member(s): 4
Membership: *Fees:* $25 deck hand; $75 captain; $150 admiral; *Member Profile:* Interest in arts & culture
Activities: Fundraising; Performance

Cobourg & District Chamber of Commerce *See* Northumberland Central Chamber of Commerce

Cobourg & District Chamber of Commerce
Northumberland Mall, 1111 Elgin St. West, Cobourg ON K9A 5H7
Tel: 905-372-5831; *Fax:* 905-372-2411
info@threecubed.ca
Overview: A medium-sized local organization founded in 1907
Member of: Ontario Chamber of Commerce; Canadian Chamber of Commerce
Chief Officer(s):
Kevin Ward, Manager
kward@cobourgchamber.com
Finances: *Annual Operating Budget:* $100,000-$250,000
Staff Member(s): 2
Membership: 350; *Committees:* Finance & Long Range Planning; Government Relations; Membership; Marketing & Tourism; Promotion & Special Events; Business Relations

Cobourg & District Historical Society (CDHS)
200 Ontario St., Cobourg ON K9A 5P4
Tel: 905-377-0413
archivist@cdhsarchives.org
Overview: A small local charitable organization founded in 1980
Mission: To preserve & understand the history of Cobourg & surrounding area of Hamilton & Haldimand Townships, with a primary focus being the conservation of the Archives, a collection of historical documents & photographs.
Member of: Ontario Historical Society; Archives Associations
Finances: *Funding Sources:* Membership dues; government grants
Activities: Exhibits; open houses; tours; monthly meetings with guest speakers; *Library:* The Cobourg & District Historical Society Archives; Open to public
Publications:
• Historical Review
Type: Journal; *Frequency:* Annually
• Historically Speaking
Type: Newsletter; *Frequency:* Monthly

Cobourg Community Information Centre Inc. *See* Info Northumberland

Cobourg-Port Hope District Real Estate Board *See* Northumberland Hills Association of Realtors

Cocaine Anonymous (CA)
#148, 33 Hazelton Ave., Toronto ON M5R 2E3
Tel: 416-927-7858
Toll-Free: 866-622-4636
questions@ca-on.org
www.ca-on.org
Overview: A small local organization founded in 1987
Mission: Cocaine Anonymous is a fellowship of men and women who share their experience, strength and hope with each other so that they may solve their common problem and help others to recover from their addiction.
Membership: *Member Profile:* A desire to be free of all mood/mind altering substances
Activities: 12-step meetings

Cochrane & District Chamber of Commerce
PO Box 996, Cochrane AB T4C 1B1
Tel: 403-932-0320; *Fax:* 403-541-0915
c.business@cochranechamber.ca
www.cochranechamber.ca
Overview: A small local organization founded in 1978
Finances: *Annual Operating Budget:* $50,000-$100,000
Staff Member(s): 1; 12 volunteer(s)
Membership: 268; *Fees:* $140-$350 based on number of employees; $140 associate

CODE
321 Chapel St., Ottawa ON K1N 7Z2
Tel: 613-232-3569; *Fax:* 613-232-7435
Toll-Free: 800-661-2633
Other Communication: donor.donateur@codecan.org
codehq@codecan.org
www.codecan.org
www.facebook.com/code.org
www.youtube.com/user/TheCodecan
Also Known As: Canadian Organization for Development through Education
Overview: A large international charitable organization founded in 1959
Mission: To enable people to learn by developing partnerships that provide resources for learning, to promote awareness & understanding & to encourage self-reliance; To support training for teachers & librarians; To coordinate book donations from North American publishers to schools & libraries in the developing world
Member of: Canadian Council for International Cooperation
Affliation(s): International Book Bank; CODE Europe; CODE Inc.; CODE Foundation
Chief Officer(s):
Scott Walter, Executive Director, 613-232-3569 Ext. 230
Brian Coburn, Director, Finance & Administration, 613-232-3569 Ext. 224
Ann Collins, Director, Marketing & Public Engagment, 613-232-3569 Ext. 232
Sean Maddox, Director, Development, 613-232-3569 Ext. 236

Canadian Associations

Dominique Naud, Manager, Communications, 613-232-3569 Ext. 252
Finances: *Funding Sources:* Individual; Corporate donations; CIDA
4500 volunteer(s)
Membership: 30; *Fees:* $20; *Committees:* Governance; Audit; Human Resources
Activities: Organizing Adopt a Library to support a community library in Tanzania, Ethiopia or Malawi

Co-Dependents Recovery Society
PO Box 306, Stn. Main, Surrey BC V3T 5B6
Tel: 604-239-1042; *Fax:* 888-675-8325
board@cdrs.ca
www.cdrs.ca
Overview: A small local organization
Mission: To translate & distribute material to Co-dependents Annoymous groups at a reduced cost, and to help promote Co-dependents Annoymous across Canada
Membership: *Member Profile:* Adults seeking healthy relationships

CoDevelopment Canada (CODEV)
#260, 2747 East Hastings St., Vancouver BC V5K 1Z8
Tel: 604-708-1495; *Fax:* 604-708-1497
codev@codev.org
www.codev.org
www.facebook.com/CoDevCanada
twitter.com/CoDevCanada
Overview: A small international charitable organization founded in 1985
Mission: To initiate social change in Latin American, facilitating relationships between Northern & Southern organizations that share a commitment to workers' rights, community development & women's rights.
Member of: BC Council for International Cooperation
Affliation(s): CUPE Global Justice; Hospital Employees' Union (HEU); World Community Development Education Society (WCDES)
Chief Officer(s):
Joey Hartman, President
Barbara Wood, Executive Director
bwood@codev.org
Finances: *Funding Sources:* Canadian International Development Agency; Global Development Fund; private donors
Staff Member(s): 7
Membership: *Fees:* $10 student/retired/low income; $25 individual; $40 family; $50-$500+ organization
Activities: Solidarity work in Latin America; workshops; film festivals; concerts; *Internships:* Yes

A Coeur d'Homme
#135, 947, av Royale, Québec QC G1E 1Z9
Tél: 418-660-7799; *Téléc:* 418-660-8053
Ligne sans frais: 877-660-7799
acoeurdhomme@videotron.ca
www.acoeurdhomme.com
Également appelé: Réseau d'aide aux hommes pour une société sans violence
Nom précédent: Association des ressources intervenant auprès des hommes ayant des comportement violent
Aperçu: *Dimension:* moyenne; *Envergure:* provinciale
Mission: Association qui a pour mission d'agir comme ambassadeur de ses membres afin de promouvoir, au niveau socio-politique, un réseau oeuvrant en transformation sociale visant des rapports égalitaires et sans violence
Membre(s) du bureau directeur:
Rémi Bilodeau, Directeur général
dgacdh@videotron.ca
Membre(s) du personnel: 2
Membre: 29 organismes communautaires répartis dans 15 régions du Québec

A coeur joie Nouveau-Brunswick Inc. (ACJ)
1, rue des Arts, Saint-Antoine-de-Kent NB E0A 2X0
Tél: 506-525-2707
Aperçu: *Dimension:* petite; *Envergure:* provinciale; fondée en 1971
Mission: Promotion du chant chorale par des stages de formation, des rencontres, des semaines chantantes; permettre l'accès à tous à de la documentation chorale, (des milliers de titres et des nouveautés annuelles)
Membre de: Conseil international à coeur joie
Finances: *Budget de fonctionnement annuel:* Moins de $50,000; *Fonds:* Gouvernement régional
12 bénévole(s)
Membre: 16; *Montant de la cotisation:* 50$ par chorale, plus 2$ par choriste; *Critères d'admissibilite:* Présidents et directeurs généraux d'associations et chefs de choeur
Activités: Les Arcadiades; *Stagiaires:* Oui; *Service de conférenciers:* Oui; *Bibliothèque:* Centre de Documentation; Bibliothèque publique

Coffee Association of Canada (CAC) / Association du café du Canada
#1100, 120 Eglinton Ave. East, Toronto ON M4P 1E2
Tel: 416-510-8032; *Fax:* 416-320-5075
info@coffeeassoc.com
www.coffeeassoc.com
ca.linkedin.com/groups?gid=5060649
Overview: A medium-sized national organization founded in 1991
Mission: To address industry-wide issues on behalf of members, keeping them fully informed, & allowing them to focus on the proprietary concerns of building their businesses
Chief Officer(s):
Sandy McAlpine, President
sandym@coffeeassoc.com
Staff Member(s): 2
Membership: 23; *Fees:* Schedule available; *Member Profile:* Company or corporation involved in the coffee industry in Canada: importers, roasters, wholesalers, retailers

Colchester Community Workshops Foundation
PO Box 314, 168 Arthur Street, Truro NS B2N 5C5
Tel: 902-893-4799; *Fax:* 902-896-6533
ccw@ns.sympatico.ca
www.colchestercommunityworkshops.com
www.facebook.com/226607440782048
Overview: A small local organization founded in 1999
Mission: To create & manage funds for the exclusive benefit of the Colchester Community Workshops by providing a facility & resources to support its clients who seek to earn an independent lifestyle
Chief Officer(s):
Don Hoadley, Executive Director/Manager
Activities: Golf tournament

Colchester Historical Society
PO Box 412, Truro NS B2N 5C5
Tel: 902-895-6284; *Fax:* 902-895-9530
colchesterhistoreum.ca
Also Known As: Colchester Historical Museum
Overview: A small local charitable organization founded in 1954
Mission: To gather, compile & preserve artifacts & printed documents of historic value & interest; To gather & record stories until now unwritten, which exist only in the memory of older people; To promote the marking of historic sites within the county by suitable plaques, etc.; To cooperate with civic officials in civic celebrations of a historic nature
Member of: Heritage Canada; Federation of the Nova Scotian Heritage; Canadian Museums Association; Council of Canadian Archives; Council of Nova Scotia Archives
Chief Officer(s):
Joe Ballard, President
Finances: *Funding Sources:* Provincial government; membership fees; municipal government; corporate; private donors
Membership: *Fees:* $20 individual; $25 family; $30 institution; $200 life; *Committees:* Archives; Core Exhibit; Marketing; Fundraising; Heritage; Human Resources
Activities: Maintains a museum & Archives/Research Library; exhibits 6 times a year; *Library:* Colchester Historical Society Archives; Open to public
Awards:
• Heritage Awards Program (Award)

Colchester-East Hants Regional Library Foundation
754 Prince St., Truro NS B2N 1G9
Tel: 902-895-0235; *Fax:* 902-895-7149
libfound@cehpubliclibrary.ca
lovemylibrary.ca/library-foundation
Overview: A small local charitable organization
Mission: Aims to maintain and enhance the library system
Chief Officer(s):
Edith M. Patterson, Chair
Janet D. Pelley, Regional Library Director
Activities: Books by Mail; Home Reader Service; Satellite Library Service; Annual Library Giving Campaign

Cold Lake Native Friendship Centre
PO Box 1978, 5015 - 55 St., Cold Lake AB T9M 1P4
Tel: 780-594-7526; *Fax:* 780-594-1599
cold1@telus.net
anfca.com/friendship-centres/cold-lake
Previous Name: Grand Centre Canadian Native Friendship Centre
Overview: A small local charitable organization overseen by Alberta Native Friendship Centres Association
Mission: The Centre aims to facilitate the advancement of cultural, social, recreation between Natives & non-Native people of Cold Lake area.
Member of: Alberta Native Friendship Centres Association (ANFCA)
Chief Officer(s):
Agnes Gendron, Executive Director
Finances: *Annual Operating Budget:* $50,000-$100,000
Staff Member(s): 14; 50 volunteer(s)
Membership: 213; *Fees:* $1
Activities: Youth Centre Drop-in; Friday Hot Lunch; AES Workers; Probation; Youth Justice; Referrals

Cold Lake Regional Chamber of Commerce
PO Box 454, Cold Lake AB T9M 1P1
Tel: 780-594-4747; *Fax:* 780-594-3711
Toll-Free: 800-840-6140
info@coldlakechamber.ca
www.coldlakechamber.ca
www.facebook.com/120651524644643
twitter.com/ColdLakeChamber
Overview: A small local organization
Mission: To act as the unified business organization of choice; To promote progression & professionalism; To provide support to members
Member of: Alberta Chamber of Commerce
Chief Officer(s):
Trevor Benoit, President
Sherri Bohme, Executive Director
Finances: *Funding Sources:* Membership dues; Projects
Staff Member(s): 3
Membership: 320; *Fees:* Schedule available based on number of employees; *Member Profile:* Local businesses
Activities: Organizing a Sports Show, a Community Fish Fry, & the Business of the Year Awards; Producing a community guide; *Internships:* Yes

Cole Harbour Ringette Association (CHRA)
c/o CHRA Registrar, 6 Braeloch Court, Lake Loon NS B2W 6C8
coleharbourringette.ca
Overview: A small local organization overseen by Ringette Nova Scotia
Member of: Ringette Nova Scotia
Chief Officer(s):
Sarah Ronahan, President
presidentchra@gmail.com
Membership: 16 teams; *Fees:* schedule

Cole Harbour Rural Heritage Society (CHRHS)
471 Poplar Dr., Cole Harbour NS B2W 4L2
Tel: 902-434-0222
farm.museum@ns.aliantzinc.ca
www.coleharbourfarmmuseum.ca/chrhs.html
Overview: A small local charitable organization founded in 1973
Mission: To protect & increase awareness of the natural history & cultural resources of Cole Harbour & the surrounding area; To foster appreciation & respect for the resources of the Cole Harbour region
Finances: *Funding Sources:* Community support
Membership: *Fees:* $20 individuals; $30 families
Activities: Administering the Cole Harbour Rural Heritage Farm Museum, a community museum that preserves & interprets the agricultural history of Cole Harbour; Preserving the former Methodist Chapel, now known as the Cole Harbour Meeting House; Advocating for the protection of natural history in the Cole Harbour area; Providing education about the ecosystem of the region; Promoting careful use of sensitive lands around Cole Harbour

Collaboration Santé Internationale (CSI)
1001, ch de la Canardière, Québec QC G1J 5G5
Tél: 418-522-6065; *Téléc:* 418-522-5530
csi@csiquebec.org
www.csiquebec.org
Aperçu: *Dimension:* grande; *Envergure:* internationale; Organisme sans but lucratif; fondée en 1968
Mission: Soutenir nos Canadiens impliqués dans les dispensaires et les hôpitaux des pays en voie de développement en leur fournissant le matériel de travail; recueillir, sélectionner, et expédier dans les pays du tiers-monde, par l'intermédiaire de

Canadiens qui oeuvrent dans le domaine de la santé, des médicaments et de l'équipement médical et hospitalier; parrainer des projets de construction et d'aménagement de dispensaires et d'hôpitaux et soutenir des équipes de médecins et de techniciens spécialisés dans le domaine de la santé publique
Membre de: Association Québecoise des Organismes de Coopération Internationale; Conseil Canadien pour la Coopération Internationale; Canadian International Development Agency
Membre(s) du bureau directeur:
Nicole Blouin, Président
Finances: *Budget de fonctionnement annuel:* $500,000-$1.5 Million
Membre(s) du personnel: 23; 210 bénévole(s)
Membre: 14 000
Activités: *Evénements de sensibilisation:* Soupers bénéfices; Rencontres en écoles et universités; *Service de conférenciers:* Oui
Publications:
• Bulletin de Collaboration Santé Internationale
Type: Bulletin

Collaborative Centre for Justice & Safety
3737 Wascana Pkwy., Regina SK S4S 0A2
Tel: 306-337-2570
www.justiceandsafety.ca
Overview: A small provincial organization
Chief Officer(s):
Steve Palmer, Executive Director
steve.palmer@uregina.ca
Staff Member(s): 2

Collectif action alternative en obésité *Voir* ÉquiLibre - Groupe d'action sur le poids

Collectif des femmes immigrantes du Québec (CFIQ)
7124, rue Boyer, Montréal QC H2S 2J8
Tél: 514-279-4246; *Téléc:* 514-279-8536
info@cfiq.ca
www.cfiq.ca
Aperçu: *Dimension:* moyenne; *Envergure:* provinciale; Organisme sans but lucratif; fondée en 1983
Mission: Préparation à l'emploi des immigrants, formation, placement à Montréal et en région
Affiliation(s): Relais femmes
Membre(s) du bureau directeur:
Aoura Bizzarri, Directrice générale
aoura@cfiq.ca
Marie-Josée Duplessis, Adjointe à la direction
marie-josee@cfiq.ca
Finances: *Budget de fonctionnement annuel:* $500,000-$1.5 Million; *Fonds:* Subventions
Membre(s) du personnel: 10; 7 bénévole(s)
Membre: 45; *Montant de la cotisation:* 5 $; *Critères d'admissibilite:* Individus ou groupes de femmes immigrantes
Activités: Ateliers en employabilité, café rencontre, coaching, atelier de français, atelier d'anglais et atelier pour les mères immigrantes; *Stagiaires:* Oui; *Service de conférenciers:* Oui; *Bibliothèque:* Cyber Emploi

Collectif féministe Rouyn-Noranda/Centre de femmes "Entre-Femmes"
CP 1051, 60, rue du Terminus ouest, Rouyn-Noranda QC J9X 5C8
Tél: 819-764-4714; *Téléc:* 819-764-4715
entrefemmes@sympatico.ca
centreentrefemmes.abitemis.info
www.facebook.com/centreentrefemmes.rouynnoranda
Aperçu: *Dimension:* moyenne; *Envergure:* locale; fondée en 1973
Mission: Alternative à l'isolement psycho-social des femmes; réseau d'entraide et d'action; permettre à des femmes isolées, souvent démunies, d'entreprendre avec d'autres femmes, un processus d'autonomie sur des plans économiques, affectifs, sociaux
Membre de: L'R des centres de femmes du Québec
Affliation(s): Fédération du Québec pour le planning des naissances; Regroupement des centres des femmes du Québec
Finances: *Budget de fonctionnement annuel:* $50,000-$100,000; *Fonds:* Gouvernement provincial
Membre(s) du personnel: 3; 15 bénévole(s)
Activités: *Stagiaires:* Oui

Collectif pour un Québec sans pauvreté
#309, 165, rue Carillon, Québec QC G1K 9E9
Tél: 418-525-0040; *Téléc:* 418-525-0740
collectif@pauvrete.qc.ca
www.pauvrete.qc.ca
Aperçu: *Dimension:* petite; *Envergure:* provinciale
Mission: Est à la fois un mouvement et un espace citoyen qui vise à générer de façon pluraliste et non partisane, avec les personnes en situation de pauvreté et toute personne ou organisation qui veut y contribuer, les conditions nécessaires pour établir les bases permanentes d'un Québec sans pauvreté
Membre(s) du bureau directeur:
Claude Goulet, Adjoint administratif

The College & Association of Registered Nurses of Alberta (CARNA)
11620 - 168 St., Edmonton AB T5M 4A6
Tel: 780-451-0043; *Fax:* 780-452-3276
Toll-Free: 800-252-9392
carna@nurses.ab.ca
www.nurses.ab.ca
www.facebook.com/albertarns
www.twitter.com/albertarns
www.youtube.com/carnavideo
Previous Name: Alberta Association of Registered Nurses
Overview: A large provincial licensing organization founded in 1916 overseen by Canadian Nurses Association
Mission: To set nursing practice standards & to ensure Albertans receive safe, competent, & ethical nursing services
Chief Officer(s):
Dianne Dyer, President
Finances: *Annual Operating Budget:* Greater than $5 Million; *Funding Sources:* Membership fees
Staff Member(s): 85; 300 volunteer(s)
Membership: 33,000; *Fees:* Schedule available; *Committees:* Competence; Appeals; Registration Review; Complaint Review; Audit; Elections & Resolutions; Provincial Executive; Leadership Review; Appointments; Awards Selection
Activities: Registers, disciplines & provides professional development activities; *Awareness Events:* National Nursing Week, May; *Library:* Museum & Archives; Open to public by appointment
Publications:
• Alberta RN
Type: Magazine; *Frequency:* Quarterly

College & Association of Respiratory Therapists of Alberta (CARTA)
#370, 6715 - 8 St. NE, Calgary AB T2E 7H7
Tel: 403-274-1828; *Fax:* 403-274-9703
Toll-Free: 800-205-2778
Denise.Holmberg@carta.ca
www.carta.ca
Previous Name: Alberta College & Association of Respiratory Therapy
Overview: A medium-sized provincial licensing organization founded in 1971
Mission: To serve & protect the public interest by guiding & regulating the profession of respiratory therapy; to provide professional services to our members
Member of: Federation of Regulated Health Professions of Alberta
Affliation(s): Respiratory Therapy Labour Mobility Consortium
Chief Officer(s):
Greg Hind, President
Bryan Buell, Executive Director
Bryan.Buell@carta.ca
Staff Member(s): 2; 20 volunteer(s)
Membership: 867; *Fees:* $333
Activities: Education forum & tradeshow; annual meetings

College & University Retiree Associations of Canada (CURAC) / Associations de retraités des universités et collèges du Canada
#997, 7B Pleasant Blvd., Toronto ON M4T 1K2
e-mail: curac@curac.ca
www.curac.ca
Overview: A medium-sized national organization
Mission: To facilitate communication among college & university retirees in all parts of Canada; To collect & disseminate information about retirement policies, pensions, & benefits; To continue relationships of retirees with their colleges & universities; To address other matters of mutual interest
Chief Officer(s):
George Brandie, President
François Gallays, Secretary
Membership: *Fees:* $10 associate; $50-$300 associations; $500-$1000 affiliate

Collège canadien de généticiens médicaux *See* Canadian College of Medical Geneticists

Collège canadien des leaders en santé *See* Canadian College of Health Leaders

Collège canadien des physiciens en médecine *See* Canadian College of Physicists in Medicine

Collège des médecins de famille du Canada *See* College of Family Physicians of Canada

Collège des médecins du Québec (CMQ)
2170, boul René-Lévesque ouest, Montréal QC H3H 2T8
Tél: 514-933-4441; *Téléc:* 514-933-3112
Ligne sans frais: 888-633-3246
info@cmq.org
www.cmq.org
www.facebook.com/257741694238490
twitter.com/CMQ_org
Aperçu: *Dimension:* moyenne; *Envergure:* provinciale; Organisme sans but lucratif; fondée en 1847
Mission: Promouvoir une médecine de qualité pour protéger le public et contribuer à l'amélioration de la santé des Québécois
Membre de: Conseil interprofessionnel du Québec
Affliation(s): Federation of Medical Licensing Authorities of Canada
Membre(s) du bureau directeur:
Charles Bernard, Président-directeur général
pdg@cmq.org
Yves Robert, Secrétaire
yrobert@cmq.org
Finances: *Budget de fonctionnement annuel:* Plus de $5 Million
Membre(s) du personnel: 115
Membre: 20 568; *Critères d'admissibilite:* Médecine
Activités: Direction générale, direction de l'amélioration de l'exercice; direction des études médicales; direction des enquêtes; *Listes de destinataires:* Oui; *Bibliothèque:* Centre du documentation
Prix, Bouses:
• Grand prix du Collège (Prix)
annuel depuis 1997
Meetings/Conferences: • Collège des médecins du Québec Colloque et assemblée génerale annuelle 2015, May, 2015, Paliais des congrés de Montréal, Montréal, QC
Scope: Provincial

Collège des médecins et chirurgiens du Nouveau-Brunswick *See* College of Physicians & Surgeons of New Brunswick

Collège des psychologues du Nouveau-Brunswick *See* College of Psychologists of New Brunswick

College of Alberta Denturists (CAD)
Sun Life Place, #270, 10123 - 99th St., Edmonton AB T5J 3H1
Tel: 780-429-2330; *Fax:* 780-429-2336
Toll-Free: 800-260-2742
reception.cofabdent@telus.net
www.collegeofabdenturists.ca
Overview: A medium-sized provincial organization founded in 2002
Mission: Governing the profession of denturism in the province of Alberta, the College of Alberta Denturists strives to ensure that Albertans will receive ethical, professional and safe denturist services.
Chief Officer(s):
Jennifer Auld, President
Cara-Lee Voss-Seiler, Vice-President
Peter Portlock, Registrar
registrar@collegeofabdenturists.ca
Membership: *Member Profile:* Regulated Members have approval to provide independent denturist services as indicated in the Denturists Profession Regulation. Provisional Regulated Members have graduated from a three-year denturist training program & are in the process of completing the College's registration examinations. Some Provsisional Regulated Members are authorized to provide denturist services while under direct supervision of a College approved Regulated Member. Intern members have graduated from a denturist training program & are in the process of completing their required internship & challenging licensure examinations. Honorary members are appointed by the Council of the College of Alberta Denturists. These individuals are not provided with a practice permit & cannot legally provide any denturist services.; *Committees:* Examination; Conference Planning; Registration; Standards

Publications:
• Wild Rose Denturist
Type: Newsletter; *Frequency:* 3 pa; *Editor:* Charles Gulley; Lorrie Rees

College of Alberta Professional Foresters
#200, 10544 - 106 St., Edmonton AB T5H 2X6
Tel: 780-432-1177; *Fax:* 780-432-7046
office@capf.ca
www.capf.ca
Previous Name: Alberta Registered Professional Foresters Association
Overview: A medium-sized provincial licensing organization founded in 1988
Mission: To maintain an accurate register of registered professional foresters in Alberta; To set standards of professional conduct & competence for members; To administer the title, Registered Professional Forester (RPF)
Member of: Canadian Federation of Professional Foresters Associations
Affliation(s): Alberta Forest Technologists Association; Canadian Institute of Forestry
Chief Officer(s):
Noel St. Jean, President
ngjstjean@shaw.ca
Doug Krystofiak, Executive Director & Registrar
registrar@capf.ca
Finances: *Funding Sources:* Membership fees
Staff Member(s): 2
Membership: *Member Profile:* B.Sc. in Forestry + professional examination + 2 yr. Forester-in-Training period; *Committees:* Executive; Competence; Registration; Policy, Act, Regulation & Bylaws; Finance; Nominating; Program; Transformation Steering
Awards:
• Frank Appleby Professional Award (Award)

College of Alberta Psychologists
Sun Life Place, #2100, 10123 - 99th St., Edmonton AB T5J 3H1
Tel: 780-424-5070
Toll-Free: 800-659-0857
www.cap.ab.ca
Overview: A small provincial organization
Mission: To serve the interests of the public & guide the profession of psychology
Chief Officer(s):
Roger Gervais, President
Membership: *Committees:* Oral Examinations; Hearing Tribunals / Complaint Review; Registration Advisory; Practice Advisory

College of Applied Biology British Columbia
#205, 733 Johnson St., Victoria BC V8W 3C7
Tel: 250-383-3306; *Fax:* 250-383-2400
cab@cab-bc.org
www.cab-bc.org
Overview: A small provincial licensing organization
Mission: To uphold & protect the public interest by: preserving & protecting the scientific methods & principles that are the foundation of the applied bilogical sciences; To uphold the principles of stewardship of aquatic & terrestrial ecosystems & biological resources; To ensure the integrity, objectivity & expertise of its members
Chief Officer(s):
Brian Churchill, President
Pierre Lachetti, Executive Director
Finances: *Annual Operating Budget:* $250,000-$500,000
Staff Member(s): 4; 30 volunteer(s)
Membership: 1,500

College of Audiologists & Speech-Language Pathologists of Ontario (CASLPO) / Ordre des audiologistes et des orthophonistes de l'Ontario (OAOO)
PO Box 71, #5060, 3080 Yonge St., Toronto ON M4N 3N1
Tel: 416-975-5347; *Fax:* 416-975-8394
Toll-Free: 800-993-9459
www.caslpo.com
Overview: A medium-sized provincial licensing organization
Mission: To regulate the practice of the professions & govern the members; To develop, establish & maintain standards of qualification; To assure the quality of the practice of the professions; Develop & maintain a code of ethics & standards
Chief Officer(s):
Vicky Papaioannou, President
Brian O'Riordan, Registrar, 416-975-5347 Ext. 215
boriordan@caslpo.com
Finances: *Annual Operating Budget:* $3 Million-$5 Million; *Funding Sources:* Membership dues & services; investment income
Staff Member(s): 9
Membership: 3,000; *Fees:* $200 students, graduates & those with 2+ yrs. expc.; $100 application fee; annual fee ($300 students & recent graduates; $600 regular) is prorated; *Member Profile:* Speech-Language Pathologists & Audiologists; *Committees:* Executive; ICRC; Discipline; Fitness to Practice; Patient Relations; Quality Asssurance; Registration; Finance; Audiology Practice; SLP Practice

College of Chiropodists of Ontario (COCOO)
#2102, 180 Dundas St. West, Toronto ON M5G 1Z8
Tel: 416-542-1333; *Fax:* 416-542-1666
Toll-Free: 877-232-7653
info@cocoo.on.ca
www.cocoo.on.ca
Overview: A small provincial licensing organization
Mission: To protect public interest by ensuring competent care is given by chiropodists & podiatrists in Ontario
Chief Officer(s):
Sheila Lefkowitz, Contact
slefkowitz@cocoo.on.ca
Membership: 500; *Fees:* $950; *Member Profile:* Practicing Chiropodists & Podiatrists in Ontario

College of Chiropractors of Alberta; Alberta Chiropractic Association ***See*** Alberta College & Association of Chiropractors

College of Chiropractors of British Columbia (CCBC)
#125, 3751 Shell Rd., Richmond BC V6X 2W2
Tel: 604-270-1332; *Fax:* 604-278-0093
Toll-Free: 866-256-1474
info@bcchiro.com
www.bcchiro.com
Previous Name: British Columbia College of Chiropractors
Overview: A medium-sized provincial organization
Mission: To deal with concerns from the public or practitioners regarding BC doctors of chiropractic
Affliation(s): British Columbia Chiropractic Association
Chief Officer(s):
David Olson, Chair
Shannon Patterson, Vice Chair
Membership: *Committees:* Registration; Inquiry (Bylaw 16); Discipline (Bylaw 17); Quality Assurance (Bylaw 18); Patient Relations (Bylaw 19)
Awards:
• College of Chiropractors of British Columbia Research Awards (Award)
To honour College of Chiropractors of British Columbia members for their research papers
Meetings/Conferences: • College of Chiropractors of British Columbia 2015 Annual General Meeting, 2015, BC
Scope: Provincial
Description: A meeting of College of Chriopractors of British Columbia registrants that is open to the public
Contact Information: Phone (attendance information): 604-270-1332, E-mail: info@bcchiro.com
Publications:
• College of Chriopractors of British Columbia Annual Report
Type: Yearbook; *Frequency:* Annually
Profile: Reports from the chair, the registrar, & committee chairs
• College of Chriopractors of British Columbia Professional Conduct Handbook
Type: Handbook; *Number of Pages:* 36
Profile: Contents include the code of ethics plus the standards, limits, & conditions of practice

College of Chiropractors of Ontario
#902, 130 Bloor St. West, Toronto ON M4S 1N5
Tel: 416-922-6355; *Fax:* 416-925-9610
Toll-Free: 877-577-4772
cco.info@cco.on.ca
www.cco.on.ca
Overview: A small provincial organization
Chief Officer(s):
Jo-Ann Willson, Registrar
jpwillson@cco.on.ca
Membership: *Committees:* Executive; Inquiries, Complaints & Reports; Disipline; Fitness to Practise; Patient Relations; Quality Assurance; Registration; Advertising

College of Dental Hygienists of British Columbia (CDHBC)
#600, 3795 Carey Rd., Victoria BC V8Z 6T8
Tel: 250-383-4101; *Fax:* 250-383-4144
Toll-Free: 800-778-8277
cdhbc@cdhbc.com
www.cdhbc.com
Overview: A small provincial licensing organization founded in 1995
Mission: Responsible for establishing, monitoring & enforcing standards that assures the public of safe, ethical & competent dental hygiene care
Chief Officer(s):
Jennifer Lawrence, Registrar
Finances: *Funding Sources:* Membership dues
Staff Member(s): 6
Membership: 2500; *Fees:* $400 practicing; $200 non-practicing; *Committees:* Registration; Quality Assurance; Inquiry; Discipline

College of Dental Hygienists of Nova Scotia (CDHNS)
Armdale Professional Centre, #11, 2625 Joseph Howe Dr., Halifax NS B3L 4G4
Tel: 902-444-7241; *Fax:* 902-444-7242
info@cdhns.ca
cdhns.ca
Overview: A small provincial organization founded in 2009 overseen by Canadian Dental Hygienists Association
Mission: To advance the profession & contribute to the health of the public
Chief Officer(s):
Wendy Stewart, Chair
Joyce Lind, Vice-President
Finances: *Annual Operating Budget:* Less than $50,000
Staff Member(s): 2; 40 volunteer(s)
Membership: 400+
Activities: Public health education; *Awareness Events:* National Dental Hygienists' Week, April; *Speaker Service:* Yes; *Library:* CDHNS Resource Centre
Publications:
• The Unison
Type: Newsletter; *Frequency:* Quarterly; *Editor:* Rosemary Bourque
Profile: Available to members of the CDHNS and to other provincial Dental Hygiene Associations across Canada

College of Dental Surgeons of British Columbia (CDSBC)
#500, 1765 West 8th Ave., Vancouver BC V6J 5C6
Tel: 604-736-3621; *Fax:* 604-734-9448
Toll-Free: 800-663-9169
info@cdsbc.org
www.cdsbc.org
Overview: A large provincial licensing organization founded in 1908
Mission: Registers, licenses & regulates dentists & certified dental assistants. Assures British Columbians of professional standards of health care, ethics, & competence by regulating dentistry in a fair & reasonable manner; administers the Dentists Act
Chief Officer(s):
Jerome Marburg, Registrar & CEO
Finances: *Annual Operating Budget:* $500,000-$1.5 Million; *Funding Sources:* Membership fees
Staff Member(s): 22; 200 volunteer(s)
Membership: 3,170 dentists + 6,500 certified dental assistants; *Fees:* $2,478 licence fee for new dentists; $325 for new dental assistants; *Member Profile:* Dentist or certified dental assistant; *Committees:* Accreditation; Audit; CDA Advisory; CDA Examiniation; Exam Qualification Review Sub Committee; Election & Awards; Ethics; Finance; Inquiry; Practice Standards; Professional Conduct; Quality Assurance; Registration
Activities: *Awareness Events:* College Awards Ceremony; *Internships:* Yes; *Rents Mailing List:* Yes
Awards:
• Honoured Member Award (Award)
• Distinguished Service Award (Award)
• Award of Merit (Award)
Meetings/Conferences: • 2015 Annual General Meeting of the College of Dental Surgeons of British Columbia, June, 2015, Vancouver Marriott Pinnacle Downtown Hotel, Vancouver, BC
Scope: Provincial

College of Dental Surgeons of Saskatchewan
Tower at Midtown, #1202, 201 - 1 Ave. South, Saskatoon SK S7K 1J5
Tel: 306-244-5072; *Fax:* 306-244-2476
cdss@saskdentists.com
www.saskdentists.com

Overview: A medium-sized provincial licensing organization founded in 1906 overseen by Canadian Dental Association
Mission: To operate as a provincial licensing body
Member of: Canadian Dental Association
Chief Officer(s):
Bernie White, Registrar
bernie@saskdentists.com
Frank Hohn, President
Brent Dergousoff, Vice-President

College of Dental Technicians of British Columbia (CDT)
#N208, 5811 Cooney Rd., Richmond BC V6X 3M1
Tel: 604-278-8324; *Fax:* 604-278-8325
Toll-Free: 877-666-8324
info@cdt.bc.ca
www.cdt.bc.ca
Overview: A small provincial organization founded in 1995
Mission: To serve and protect the public by regulating the profession of dental technology.

College of Dental Technologists of Alberta (CDTA)
#7, 9340 - 50 St. NW, Edmonton AB T6B 2L5
Tel: 780-469-0615; *Fax:* 780-469-1340
membersinfo@cdta.ca
www.cdta.ca
Overview: A medium-sized provincial organization founded in 1990
Mission: Regulates the profession of Dental Technology in the province of Alberta.
Chief Officer(s):
Gary Wakelam, President
Jason Lohr, Vice-President
Clarence Spring, Treasurer
Staff Member(s): 6

College of Dental Technologists of Ontario
#300, 2100 Ellesmere Rd., Toronto ON M1H 3B7
Tel: 416-438-5003; *Fax:* 416-438-5004
info@cdto.ca
www.cdto.ca
Previous Name: Governing Board of Dental Technicians of Ontario
Overview: A small provincial licensing organization
Mission: To serve & protect the public interest by regulating & guiding the dental technology profession
Chief Officer(s):
J. David McDonald, Registrar
jdmcdonald@cdto.ca
Finances: *Annual Operating Budget:* $250,000-$500,000; *Funding Sources:* Membership registration
Staff Member(s): 3
Membership: 482 individual; *Fees:* Application fee $150; General Certificate: $994.36; Inactive Certificate: $300; *Member Profile:* Must pass registration examination; *Committees:* Council; Executive; Registration; Complaints; Discipline; Quality Assurance; Patient Relations; Fitness to Practice
Activities: *Speaker Service:* Yes

College of Denturists of British Columbia (CDBC)
#101, 309 - Sixth St., New Westminster BC V3L 3A7
Tel: 604-515-0533; *Fax:* 604-515-0534
registrar@cd.bc.ca
www.cd.bc.ca
Overview: A small provincial organization
Mission: To serve & protect the public; To exercise its powers & discharge its responsibilities under all enactments in the public interest
Chief Officer(s):
Jim Connolly, Chair
Publications:
• College of Denturists of British Columbia Newsletter
Type: Newsletter; *Frequency:* Irregular

College of Denturists of Ontario (CDO)
#903, 180 Bloor St. West, Toronto ON M5S 2V6
Tel: 416-925-6331; *Fax:* 416-925-6332
Toll-Free: 888-236-4326
info@denturists-cdo.com
www.denturists-cdo.com
www.linkedin.com/company/college-of-denturists-of-ontario
Overview: A small provincial licensing organization founded in 1973
Mission: To regulate, govern & develop the profession while serving the public interest
Affliation(s): Benard & Associates; Robin Bigglestone (Robin's Ready Inc.); Shannon Hawkshaw, John Seychuck, & Ivy Tse (Adams & Miles LLP)
Chief Officer(s):
Abena Buahene, Registrar
abuahene@denturists-cdo.com
Finances: *Funding Sources:* License, examination, incorporation, & membership fees
Staff Member(s): 7
Membership: *Fees:* $2,147; *Committees:* Executive; Inquiries, Complaints & Reports; Registration; Discipline; Fitness; Patient Relations; Quality Assurance; Qualifying Examination; Professional Practice; Qualifying Examinations Appeals; Nominating

College of Dietitians of Alberta
#740, 10707 - 100 Ave., Edmonton AB T5J 3M1
Tel: 780-448-0059; *Fax:* 780-489-7759
Toll-Free: 866-493-4348
office@collegeofdietitians.ab.ca
www.collegeofdietitians.ab.ca
Overview: A small provincial licensing organization overseen by Dietitians of Canada
Mission: The College is the regulatory body of registered dieticians/nutritionists in Alberta, setting entry requirements, standards of practice. It is accountable to both the government & the public.
Chief Officer(s):
Doug Cook, Executive Director & Registrar
Membership: 900

College of Dietitians of British Columbia (CDBC)
#409, 1367 West Broadway, Vancouver BC V6H 4A7
Tel: 604-736-2016; *Fax:* 604-736-2018
Toll-Free: 877-736-2016
info@collegeofdietitiansbc.org
www.collegeofdietitiansbc.org
Overview: A medium-sized provincial licensing organization founded in 2004 overseen by Dietitians of Canada
Mission: To serve & protect the nutritional health of the public through quality dietetic practice
Chief Officer(s):
Fred Hubbard, Registrar
Finances: *Annual Operating Budget:* $500,000-$1.5 Million
Staff Member(s): 4; 21 volunteer(s)
Membership: 1,189; *Fees:* $525 registration fee; *Committees:* Inquiry; Quality Assurance; Registration; Discipline

College of Dietitians of Manitoba
#36, 1313 Border St., Winnipeg MB R3H 0X4
Tel: 204-694-0532; *Fax:* 204-889-1755
Toll-Free: 866-283-2823
office.cdm@mts.net
www.manitobadietitians.ca
Overview: A small provincial organization overseen by Dietitians of Canada
Mission: To act as the regulating body within the province for dietitians & the profession of dietetics, setting education standards, ensuring competency of members.
Member of: Alliance of Dietetic Regulatory Bodies
Chief Officer(s):
Michelle Hagglund, Registrar
Finances: *Funding Sources:* Membership fees
Membership: *Fees:* $525; *Member Profile:* B.Sc. & accredited dietetic internship; *Committees:* Complaints; Executive; Board of Assessors; Screening; Audit; Finance

College of Dietitians of Ontario (CDO) / L'Ordre des diététistes de l'Ontario
PO Box 30, #1810, 5775 Yonge St., Toronto ON M2M 4J1
Tel: 416-598-1725; *Fax:* 416-598-0274
Toll-Free: 800-668-4990
information@cdo.on.ca
www.cdo.on.ca
Also Known As: CDO
Overview: A medium-sized provincial licensing charitable organization founded in 1993 overseen by Dietitians of Canada
Mission: To promote awareness of & access to competent, high quality nutritional care for Ontarians.
Member of: The Federation of Health Regulatory Bodies of Ontario; Alliance of Canadian Dietetic Regulatory Bodies; Council of Licensure, Enforcement and Regulation
Chief Officer(s):
Mary Lou Gignac, Registrar & Executive Director
gignacm@cdo.on.ca
Finances: *Funding Sources:* Membership fees
Staff Member(s): 12
Membership: *Committees:* Registration; Quality Assurance; Inquiries, Complaints and Reports; Patient Relations; Discipline; Fitness to Practice; Legislative Issues; Executive; Elections
Activities: *Speaker Service:* Yes

College of Family Physicians of Canada (CFPC) / Collège des médecins de famille du Canada
2630 Skymark Ave., Mississauga ON L4W 5A4
Tel: 905-629-0900; *Fax:* 905-629-0893
Toll-Free: 800-387-6197
info@cfpc.ca
www.cfpc.ca
twitter.com/FamPhysCan
www.youtube.com/user/CFPCMedia
Overview: A large national organization founded in 1954
Mission: To improve the health of Canadians by promoting high standards of medical education & care in family practice, by contributing to public understanding of healthful living, by supporting ready access to family physician services, & by encouraging research & disseminating knowledge about family medicine
Chief Officer(s):
Marie-Dominique Beaulieu, MD, CCFP, FCFP, President
Kathy Lawrence, MD, CCFP, FCFP, President-Elect & Chair
Calvin Gutkin, MD, CCFP (EM), Executive Director/CEO
executive@cfpc.ca
Finances: *Annual Operating Budget:* Greater than $5 Million; *Funding Sources:* Membership & examination fees
Staff Member(s): 84
Membership: 28,623 physicians; *Fees:* Schedule available; *Member Profile:* Licensed physicians in good standing & engaged in the practice of family medicine; residents & medical students; specialists; *Committees:* Accreditiation; Advisory Committee on Family Practice; ALSO; Board of Examiners; Bylaws; CACI; Collaborative Committee on Rural Education; Environmental Health Steering; Equity & Diversity; Ethics; Examinations in Emergency medicine; Examinations in Family Medicine; Family Medicine Forum Advisory; Finance & Audit; Governance Advisory; History & Narrative in Family Medicine; Honours & Awards; Janus Project Steering; Membership Advisory; National Committee on Continuing Professional Development; Nominating; Patient Education; Self Learning; Undergraduate Education; and others...
Activities: Administers a Research & Education Foundation; *Library:* Canadian Library of Family Medicine
Awards:
• Leadership Awards for Residents & Medical Students (Award)
• W. Victor Johnston Award (Award)
• Ian McWhinney Award (Award)
• Irwin Bean Award (Award)
• Family Physician Research Grants (Grant)
• Family Physician Study Grants (Grant)
• Janus Scholarships (Scholarship)
• Hollister King Study Grant (Grant)
• Nadine St-Pierre Award (Award)
• Bob Robertson Award (Award)
• Research Awards for Residents (Award)
• D.I. Rice Merit Award (Award)
Awarded annually to a renowned leader in family medicine to allow travel for a period of approximately one month in order to engage in educational activities *Amount:* $10,000 plus travel expenses
• D.M. Robb Research Award (Award)
Awarded annually to a community-based family physician to conduct research in family medicine *Amount:* $2,500
• CFP Research Award (Award)
Sponsored by Canadian Family Physician; awarded to the author of the best article of original research published in the Canadian Family Physician during the previous year *Amount:* $1,000
• Ortho French & English Literary Award (Award)
Sponsored by Ortho Pharmaceutical (Canada) Ltd.; awarded to the best article written in French & published in Canadian Family Physician during the current year *Amount:* $1,000 & certificate

• Family Physician of the Year Award (Award)
Sponsored by Janseen Ortho; awarded to physicians who have been in family practice for a minimum of 15 years & members of the college for at least 10 years, & who have made outstanding contributions to family medicine, to their communities & to the college
Meetings/Conferences: • College of Family Physicians of Canada / Collège des médecins de famille du Canada 2015 Annual General Meeting, 2015, ON
Scope: Provincial

Publications:
• Canadian Family Physician [a publication of the College of Family Physicians of Canada]
Type: Journal
Profile: Current issues & developments in family medicine
• eNews [a publication of the College of Family Physicians of Canada]
Type: Newsletter; *Frequency:* Monthly
• Kaléidoscope [a publication of the College of Family Physicians of Canada]
Type: Newsletter
Profile: Developments in family medicine research
• Section of Residents Newsletter [a publication of the College of Family Physicians of Canada]
Type: Newsletter
Profile: Information for family medicine residents

Alberta Chapter
Centre 170, #370, 10403 - 172 St., Edmonton AB T5S 1K9
Tel: 780-488-2395; *Fax:* 780-488-2396
info@acfp.ca
www.acfp.ca
Mission: To act as a respected voice for family practice in Alberta; To advance excellence in family practice
Chief Officer(s):
Cathy Scrimshaw, President
Terri Potter, Executive Director

British Columbia College of Family Physicians
#350, 1665 West Broadway, Vancouver BC V6J 1X1
Tel: 604-736-1877; *Fax:* 604-736-4675
office@bccfp.bc.ca
www.bccfp.bc.ca
Mission: The British Columbia College of Family Physicians (BCCFP) is a national voluntary organization of family physicians that represents family physicians/general practitioners in the discipline of Family Medicine.
Chief Officer(s):
Shari Claremont, President
Ian Tang, Manager, Project Development

Manitoba College of Family Physicians
#240, 1695 Henderson Hwy., Winnipeg MB R2G 1P1
Tel: 204-668-3667; *Fax:* 204-668-3663
info@mcfp.mb.ca
www.mcfp.mb.ca
Mission: The College strives to improve the health of Canadians by promoting high standards of medical education and care in family practice, by contributing to public understanding of healthy living, by supporting ready access to family physician services and by encouraging research and disseminating knowledge about family medicine.
Chief Officer(s):
Paul Sawchuk, President
Amanda Wellnitz, Administrator

New Brunswick College of Family Physicians
950 Picot Ave., Bathurst NB E2A 4Z9
Tel: 506-548-4707; *Fax:* 506-548-4761
nbcfp@bellaliant.com
www.nbcfp.ca
www.facebook.com/Nbcfp
Mission: The College of Family Physicians of Canada is a national voluntary organization of family physicians that makes continuing medical education of its members mandatory.
Chief Officer(s):
Anick Pelletier, President
Karine DeGrâce, Administrator

Newfoundland & Labrador Chapter
c/o Discipline of Family Medicine, Health Sciences Centre, #2422, 300 Prince Philip Dr., St. John's NL A1B 3V6
Tel: 709-744-3434; *Fax:* 709-777-7913
cfpcdebbie@hotmail.com
nl.cfpc.ca
Mission: The College of Family Physicians of Canada is a national voluntary organization of family physicans that makes continuing medical education of its members mandatory.
Member of: The College of Family Physicians of Cananda
Chief Officer(s):
Charlene Fitzgerald, President
Debbie Rideout, Administrator

Nova Scotia College of Family Physicians
Mill Cove Plaza, #207, 967 Bedford Hwy., Bedford NS B4A 1A9
Tel: 902-499-0303; *Fax:* 902-457-2584
admin@nsfamdocs.com
www.nsfamdocs.com
Mission: The College of Family Physicians of Canada is a national voluntary organization of family physicians that makes continuing medical education of its members mandatory.
Chief Officer(s):
Michelle Ciach, President
Cathie W. Carroll, Executive Director

Ontario College of Family Physicians
340 Richmond St. West, Toronto ON M5V 1X2
Tel: 905-867-9646; *Fax:* 905-867-9990
Toll-Free: 800-670-6237
ocfp@cfpc.ca
www.ocfp.on.ca
Mission: The Ontario College of Family Physicians (OCFP) is the Ontario Chapter of the College of Famiy Physicians of Canada and is a provincial, voluntary, not-for-profit organization whose mandate includes undergraduate education, the contiuing professional development of family physicians and the maintenance of high standards of medical care and education in family practice.
Chief Officer(s):
Jessica Hill, Chief Executive Officer
Jonathan Kerr, President

Prince Edward Island Chapter
14 Royalty Rd., Charlottetown PE C1E 1T8
Tel: 902-894-2605; *Fax:* 902-894-3975
pei.cfp@pei.aibn.com
pei.cfpc.ca
Chief Officer(s):
Lana Beth Barkhouse, President
Rosemary Burke-Perry, Administrator

Saskatchewan Chapter
PO Box 7111, Saskatoon SK S7K 4J1
Tel: 306-665-7714; *Fax:* 306-665-7714
scfp@shaw.ca
www.skcfp.ca
Chief Officer(s):
Paula Schwann, President
Lois Hislop, Executive Administrator

Section du Québec
#202, 3210, av Jacques-Bureau, Laval QC H7P 0A9
Tél: 450-973-2228; *Téléc:* 450-973-4329
Ligne sans frais: 800-481-5962
cqmf@bellnet.ca
www.cqmf.qc.ca
Mission: The Quebec chapter of the College of Family Physicians of Canada operate independently and is governed by its own rules. Its activities depend on committed family physicians who volunteer to serve on our Executive Committee and in special working groups working to establish relations with government, other provincial organizations, and local media.
Chief Officer(s):
Nicole Cloutier, Executive Director
Dominique Deschênes, President

College of Hearing Aid Practioners of Alberta (CHAPA)
4017 - 63 St., Camrose AB T4V 2X2
Fax: 780-678-3282
Toll-Free: 866-990-4327
www.chapa.ca
Overview: A medium-sized provincial organization founded in 2002
Mission: To regulate the hearing aid practitioner profession; to ensure clients are receiving the best possible treatment & equipment so that they are able to hear to the best of their ability.
Membership: *Fees:* $625 hearing aid practitioner & registered hearing aid practitioner; $50 student; $250 associate or out-of-province/inactive; $150 interim

College of Licensed Practical Nurses of Alberta (CLPNA)
13163 - 146 St., Edmonton AB T5L 4S8
Tel: 780-484-8886; *Fax:* 780-484-9069
Toll-Free: 800-661-5877
info@clpna.com
www.clpna.com
www.linkedin.com/company/college-of-licensed-practical-nurses-of-alber
www.facebook.com/CLPNA
twitter.com/clpna
www.youtube.com/clpna
Previous Name: Professional Council of Licensed Practical Nurses
Overview: A medium-sized provincial licensing organization founded in 1985 overseen by Canadian Council of Practical Nurse Regulators
Mission: To regulate & lead the profession in a manner that protects & serves the public through excellence in Practical Nursing.
Chief Officer(s):
Linda L. Stanger, Executive Director/Registrar
lstanger@clpna.com
Finances: *Funding Sources:* Membership dues
Staff Member(s): 21
Membership: 10,623; *Fees:* $350; $50 associate; *Member Profile:* Licensed Practical Nurses; *Committees:* Registration & Competence; Hearing Tribunal; Complaint Review; Education Standards
Activities: *Library*

College of Licensed Practical Nurses of BC (CLPNBC)
#260, 3480 Gilmore Way, Burnaby BC V5G 4Y1
Tel: 778-373-3100; *Fax:* 778-373-3102
Toll-Free: 877-373-2201
info@clpnbc.org
www.clpnbc.org
Overview: A medium-sized provincial licensing organization founded in 1965 overseen by Canadian Council of Practical Nurse Regulators
Mission: To regulate practical nursing in the public interest
Finances: *Annual Operating Budget:* $500,000-$1.5 Million; *Funding Sources:* Membership dues 88%; other 12%
Staff Member(s): 12; 12 volunteer(s)
Membership: 6,000; *Fees:* $225; *Member Profile:* Licensed practical nurses; *Committees:* Registration; Inquiry/Discipline Hearing; Education & Accreditation; Quality Assurance; Policy; Finance
Activities: *Speaker Service:* Yes
Awards:
• John MacKay Financial Bursary for Student PN in Need (Award)

College of Licensed Practical Nurses of Manitoba (CLPNM)
463 St. Anne's Rd., Winnipeg MB R2M 3C9
Tel: 204-663-1212; *Fax:* 204-663-1207
Toll-Free: 877-663-1212
info@clpnm.ca
www.clpnm.ca
Overview: A small provincial organization overseen by Canadian Council of Practical Nurse Regulators
Mission: The governing body for the Licensed Practical Nurses in Manitoba. The College's duty is to carry out its activities and govern its members in a manner that serves and protects the public interest. The College establishes requirements to enter the profession and assures the quality of the practice of LPNs through the development and enforcement of standards and practice and continuing competence programs.
Chief Officer(s):
Jennifer Breton, LPN, RN, BN, Executive Director
jbreton@clpnm.ca
Barb Palz, Business Manager
bpalz@clpnm.ca
Membership: *Fees:* Schedule available

College of Licensed Practical Nurses of Newfoundland & Labrador (CLPNNL)
9 Paton St., St. John's NL A1B 4S8
Tel: 709-579-3843; *Fax:* 709-579-8268
Toll-Free: 888-579-2576
info@clpnnl.ca
www.clpnnl.ca
Previous Name: Newfoundland Council for Nursing Assistants
Overview: A small provincial licensing organization overseen by Canadian Council of Practical Nurse Regulators
Mission: To regulate the practice of Licensed Practical Nurses in Nnewfound & Labrador; to promote safety and protection of the general public through the provision of safe, competent and ethical nursing care.
Chief Officer(s):
Paul D. Fisher, Executive Director/Registrar
pfisher@clpnnl.ca
Finances: *Annual Operating Budget:* $500,000-$1.5 Million
Staff Member(s): 4
Membership: *Committees:* Complaints Authorization; Discipline Panel; Education; Finance

College of Licensed Practical Nurses of Nova Scotia (CLPNNS)
Starlite Gallery, #302, 7071 Bayers Rd., Halifax NS B3L 2C2
Tel: 902-423-8517; *Fax:* 902-425-6811
Toll-Free: 800-718-8517
www.clpnns.ca
Previous Name: Licensed Practical Nurses Association of Nova Scotia; Nova Scotia Certified Nursing Assistants Association
Overview: A medium-sized provincial organization founded in 1956 overseen by Canadian Council of Practical Nurse Regulators
Mission: To represent licensed practical nurses within the health care system; to protect the public by providing safe, competent nursing care.
Chief Officer(s):
Ann Mann, Executive Director/Registrar
ann@clpnns.ca
Finances: *Funding Sources:* Membership fees
Staff Member(s): 8
Membership: *Fees:* $280; *Committees:* Complaints; Professional Conduct
Activities: *Internships:* Yes; *Speaker Service:* Yes; *Library:* Video Library
Awards:
• Best Bedside Nurse Award (Award)

College of Massage Therapists of British Columbia (CMTBC)
#304, 1212 West Broadway, Vancouver BC V6H 3V1
Tel: 604-736-3404; *Fax:* 604-736-6500
Toll-Free: 877-321-3404
info@cmtbc.ca
www.cmtbc.ca
Overview: A medium-sized provincial organization founded in 1994
Mission: To regulate the message therapy profession in order to protect the public
Chief Officer(s):
Susan Addario, Registrar & CEO
registrar@cmtbc.ca
Finances: *Funding Sources:* Membership dues
Staff Member(s): 7
Membership: *Member Profile:* Massage therapists; *Committees:* Discipline; Finance & Audit; Governance & Human Resources; Inquiry; Patient Relations; Quality Assurance; Registration

College of Massage Therapists of Ontario (CMTO) / L'Ordre des massothérapeutes de l'Ontario
#810, 1867 Yonge St., Toronto ON M4S 1Y5
Tel: 416-489-2626; *Fax:* 416-489-2625
Toll-Free: 800-465-1933
cmto@cmto.com
www.cmto.com
Overview: A medium-sized provincial licensing organization founded in 1919
Mission: To promote the highest possible quality of massage therapy practice; To protect the public by providing massage therapy in a safe & ethical manner; To serve its members
Member of: Federation of Health Regulatory Colleges of Ontario
Chief Officer(s):
Corinne Flitton, Registrar & CEO
Finances: *Annual Operating Budget:* Greater than $5 Million; *Funding Sources:* Membership dues; examination fees; investment income
Staff Member(s): 24
Membership: 11,200; *Fees:* $571 regular; $173 inactive; *Member Profile:* Massage therapist - MT or Registered Massage Therapist - RMT designation; *Committees:* Appeals; Client Relations; Discipline; Executive; Fitness to Practise; Inquiries, Complaints & Reports; Quality Assurance; Registration

College of Medical Radiation Technologists of Ontario / Ordre des technologues en radiation médicale de l'Ontario
#200, 375 University Ave., Toronto ON M5G 2J5
Tel: 416-975-4353; *Fax:* 416-975-4355
Toll-Free: 800-563-5847
info@cmrto.org
www.cmrto.org
Overview: A medium-sized provincial organization
Mission: To serve & protect the people of Ontario through self-regulation of the profession
Chief Officer(s):
Linda Gough, Registrar
lgough@cmrto.org

College of Midwives of British Columbia (CMBC)
#207, 1682 West 7th Ave., Vancouver BC V6J 4S6
Tel: 604-742-2230; *Fax:* 604-730-8908
information@cmbc.bc.ca
www.cmbc.bc.ca
Overview: A small provincial licensing organization founded in 1995
Mission: To serve & protect the public interest by registering competent midwives who will practise safely & ethically in British Columbia
Chief Officer(s):
Jane Kilthei, Registrar & Executive Director, 604-742-2234
registr@cmbc.bc.ca
Finances: *Annual Operating Budget:* $500,000-$1.5 Million; *Funding Sources:* Membership fees
Staff Member(s): 5; 9 volunteer(s)
Membership: 110; *Fees:* $1,800; *Member Profile:* Registered midwives; *Committees:* Executive; Registration; Quality Assurance; Inquiry; Client Relations; Discipline; Aboriginal
Activities: Regulation of the profession; set education & registration requirements & standards of practice;

College of Midwives of Manitoba
#230, 500 Portage Ave., Winnipeg MB R3C 3X1
Tel: 204-783-4520; *Fax:* 204-779-1490
admin@midwives.mb.ca
www.midwives.mb.ca
Overview: A medium-sized provincial organization founded in 1997
Mission: To justify public trust and confidence, to uphold and enhance the good standing and reputation of the profession, to serve the interests of society and, above all, to safeguard the interests of individual clients.
Chief Officer(s):
Patty Eadie, Executive Director
director@midwives.mb.ca
Finances: *Funding Sources:* Provincial funding; membership dues; sales of goods & services; pension plan
Staff Member(s): 3
Membership: *Fees:* $1600

College of Midwives of Ontario / Ordre des Sages-Femmes de l'Ontario
#303, 21 St. Clair Ave. East, Toronto ON M4T 1L9
Tel: 416-640-2252; *Fax:* 416-640-2257
admin@cmo.on.ca
www.cmo.on.ca
Overview: A medium-sized provincial licensing organization founded in 1993
Mission: Ensures that its members provide competent & ethical care to the clients they serve; Establishes standards that ensure its members are responsive to individual & community needs; Promotes a model of care for the profession that encourages informed choice for the client and participation of women by providing standards
Chief Officer(s):
Kelly Dobbin, Registrar-CEO, 416-640-2252 Ext. 226
registrar@cmo.on.ca
Barbara Borland, President
Wendy Murko, Vice-President
Finances: *Funding Sources:* Membership fees
Staff Member(s): 11
Publications:
• College of Midwives of Ontario Member Communiqué
Type: Newsletter; *Frequency:* Quarterly
Profile: Practice notes, news, & updates

College of Naturopathic Doctors of Alberta (CNDA)
PO Box 21142, 813 - 14th St. NW, Calgary AB T2N 2A4
Tel: 403-266-2446
aanpsecretary@gmail.com
www.naturopathic-alberta.com
twitter.com/CollegeNDAB
Previous Name: Alberta Association of Naturopathic Practitioners
Overview: A small provincial organization overseen by The Canadian Association of Naturopathic Doctors
Chief Officer(s):
Alissa Gaul, President
Finances: *Annual Operating Budget:* Less than $50,000; *Funding Sources:* Membership dues
6 volunteer(s)
Membership: 73; *Member Profile:* Naturopathic professionals

College of Naturopathic Physicians of British Columbia (CNPBC)
#840, 605 Robson St., Vancouver BC V6B 5J3
Tel: 604-688-8236; *Fax:* 604-688-8476
Toll-Free: 877-611-8236
office@cnpbc.bc.ca
www.cnpbc.bc.ca
Previous Name: Association of Naturopathic Physicians of British Columbia
Overview: A small provincial licensing organization founded in 1936
Mission: To set standards of professional practice amongst naturopathic physicians in BC.
Chief Officer(s):
Karen Parmar, President
Howard Greenstein, CEO & Registrar
registrar@cnpbc.bc.ca
Staff Member(s): 3
Membership: *Fees:* $1,650 active; $200 associate; *Member Profile:* All licensed & registered naturopathic physicians; *Committees:* Advertising; Discipline; Examination; Finance & Administration; Inquiry; Patient Relations; Pharmacopoeia & Diagnostics Referral; Registration; Quality Assurance

College of Nurses of Ontario (CNO) / Ordre des infirmières et infirmiers de l'Ontario
101 Davenport Rd., Toronto ON M5R 3P1
Tel: 416-928-0900; *Fax:* 416-928-6507
Toll-Free: 800-387-5526
cno@cnomail.org
www.cno.org
Overview: A large provincial licensing organization founded in 1963 overseen by Canadian Council of Practical Nurse Regulators
Mission: To protect the public's right to quality nursing services by providing leadership to the nursing profession in self-regulation
Chief Officer(s):
Anne Coghlan, Executive Director
Finances: *Funding Sources:* Membership fees
Staff Member(s): 130
Membership: 145,000 registered nurses + registered practical nurses; *Fees:* $125; *Committees:* Disipline; Executive; Finance; Fitness to Practice; Inquiries, Complaints & Reports; Quality Assurance; Registration
Activities: *Library*

College of Occupational Therapists of British Columbia (COTBC)
Yarrow Bldg., #219, 645 Fort St., Victoria BC V8W 1G2
Tel: 250-386-6822; *Fax:* 250-383-4144
Toll-Free: 866-386-6822
info@cotbc.org
www.cotbc.org
Overview: A small provincial licensing organization
Mission: To establish standards of practice & conduct; To enhance quality assurance; To monitor quality of practice & continuing competence; To improve competence of occupational therapists; To investigate complaints; To enforce standards
Chief Officer(s):
Kathy Corbett, Registrar-CEO
Cindy McLean, Deputy Registrar
Finances: *Annual Operating Budget:* $500,000-$1.5 Million; *Funding Sources:* Application fees; Registration fees
Staff Member(s): 4
Membership: 1600; *Fees:* $350 practicing; $75 non-practicing

College of Occupational Therapists of Manitoba (COTM) / L'Ordre des ergothérapeutes du Manitoba
#7, 120 Maryland St., Winnipeg MB R3G 1L1
Tel: 204-957-1214; *Fax:* 204-775-2340
Toll-Free: 866-957-1214
otinfo@cotm.ca
www.cotm.ca
Previous Name: Association of Occupational Therapists of Manitoba
Overview: A small provincial licensing organization founded in 1971
Mission: To register occupational therapists in Manitoba; to investigate complaints; to administer The Occupational Therapists Act
Affliation(s): Association of Canadian Occupational Therapy Regulatory Organizations
Chief Officer(s):
Sharon Kathleen Eadie, Executive Director
sharon.eadie@cotm.ca
Finances: *Funding Sources:* Membership fees
Staff Member(s): 3

Membership: *Fees:* Schedule available; *Committees:* Executive; Practice Issues; Investigation; Inquiry; Communications; Continuing Competence; Legislation

College of Occupational Therapists of Nova Scotia (COTNS)

Mumford Professional Centre, #2132B, 6960 Mumford Rd., Halifax NS B3L 4P1
Tel: 902-455-0556; *Fax:* 902-455-0621
admin@cotns.ca
www.cotns.ca
Overview: A medium-sized provincial organization
Mission: Regulates the practice of occupational therapists by ensuring safe and ethical services that will protect the public it serves.
Chief Officer(s):
Pauline Cousins, Chair
Allanna Jost, Treasurer
Gayle Salsman, Registrar
Membership: 483; *Fees:* $375 annual fee; *Committees:* Continuing competency; Nominations; Advisory Committee for the College Complains Process; Practice; Credentials

College of Occupational Therapists of Ontario (COTO) / Ordre des ergothérapeutes de l'Ontario

PO Box 78, #900, 20 Bay St., Toronto ON M5J 2N8
Tel: 416-214-1177; *Fax:* 416-214-1173
Toll-Free: 800-890-6570
info@coto.org
www.coto.org
www.linkedin.com/company/college-of-occupational-therapists-of-ontario
Overview: A medium-sized provincial licensing organization
Mission: Self-governing body that protects the public interest & improves their health & well-being by registering, regulating & supporting the ongoing competency of Occupational Therapists
Chief Officer(s):
Jane Cox, President
Elinor Larney, Registrar
elarney@coto.org
Finances: *Annual Operating Budget:* $3 Million-$5 Million; *Funding Sources:* Registration & application fees
Staff Member(s): 17
Membership: *Fees:* $657.55 + HST: annual renewal; $200 + HST: new application fee; $40 + HST: re-instatement fee; *Committees:* Inquiries, Complaints & Reports; Discipline; Fitness to Practice; Patient Relations; Quality Assurance; Registration

College of Opticians of Alberta (COA)

201, 2528 Ellwood Dr. SW, Edmonton AB T6X 0A9
Tel: 780-429-2694; *Fax:* 780-426-5576
Toll-Free: 800-263-6026
www.opticians.ab.ca
www.facebook.com/pages/Opticians-of-Alberta/301105265172
Previous Name: Alberta Opticians Association; Alberta Guild of Opthalmic Dispensers
Overview: A medium-sized provincial organization founded in 1965
Mission: To promote the advancement of knowledge, skills & competence of members & encourage education & training programs while representing members on all issues affecting the profession; to act as a regulatory body; to provide opportunities for opticians to improve their skills while advancing competency through education & cooperation with other eye care professions
Member of: Opticians Association of Canada
Affliation(s): National Accreditation Committee of Opticians
Chief Officer(s):
Maureen Hussey, Executive Director & Registrar
mhussey@opticians.ab.ca
Finances: *Annual Operating Budget:* $250,000-$500,000; *Funding Sources:* Membership dues
Staff Member(s): 6
Membership: 760; *Fees:* $620 opticians; $770 contact lens practitioners
Activities: *Internships:* Yes

College of Opticians of British Columbia (COBC)

#403, 1505 West 2nd Ave., Vancouver BC V6H 3Y4
Tel: 604-278-7510; *Fax:* 604-278-7594
Toll-Free: 888-771-6755
reception@cobc.ca
www.cobc.ca
www.facebook.com/CollegeofOpticiansBC
twitter.com/CO_BritishC
www.youtube.com/user/LicensedOptician
Overview: A small provincial licensing organization founded in 1994
Mission: To govern the practice of opticianry in BC.
Chief Officer(s):
Raheem Savja, Chair
Connie Chong, Registrar & Executive Director
cchong@cobc.ca
Finances: *Funding Sources:* Licensing fees
Staff Member(s): 4
Membership: 1,118; *Fees:* Schedule available; *Committees:* Discipline; Executive; Inquiry; Quality Assurance; Registration; Patient Relations
Activities: Assessment, registration & licensing of all opticians & contact lens fitters; handle complaints & inquiries

College of Opticians of Ontario (COO)

#902, 85 Richmond St. West, Toronto ON M5H 2C9
Tel: 416-368-3616; *Fax:* 416-368-2713
Toll-Free: 800-990-9793
mail@coptont.org
www.coptont.org
Overview: A medium-sized provincial organization
Mission: Regulates and improves the practice of Opticians in the public interest, and values professionalism, fairness, efficiency, accountability and accessiblity.
Affliation(s): Federation of Health Regulatory Colleges of Ontario
Chief Officer(s):
Fazal Khan, Registrar
fkhan@coptont.org
Staff Member(s): 8
Membership: *Fees:* $120 student; $835 individual; *Committees:* Executive; Inquiries, Complaints & Reports; Patient Relations; Quality Assurance; Registration; Fitness to Practise; Discipline; Governance

College of Optometrists of BC

#1204, 700 West Pender St., Vancouver BC V6C 1G8
Tel: 604-623-3464; *Fax:* 604-623-3465
optometry_board@telus.net
www.optometrybc.com
Previous Name: Board of Examiners in Optometry in B.C.
Overview: A medium-sized provincial organization
Mission: To serve & protect the public interest by guiding the profession of optometry in British Columbia
Chief Officer(s):
Dale Dergousoff, Chair
Robin Simpson, Registrar
Stanka Jovicevic, Chief Administrative Officer
Meetings/Conferences: • College of Optometrists of BC 2015 Annual General Meeting, 2015, BC
Scope: Provincial
Description: The presentation of financial statements, as well as reports from the chair, the registrar, the deputy registrar, & college board members
Contact Information: Chief Administrative Officer & Assistant to the Registrar: Stanka Jovicevic, E-mail (general information): college@optometrybc.ca
Publications:
• College of Optometrists of BC Annual Report
Type: Yearbook; *Frequency:* Annually
Profile: A year end summary
• College of Optometrists of BC Registrant Directory
Type: Directory
Profile: Public information in the Register includes a registrant's name, class, registration number, business address, & business telephone number
• The Examiner: The Official Newsletter of The College of Optometrists of BC
Type: Newsletter
Profile: Messages from the Chair & the Registrar, plus information about fees, bylaws, & new registrants

College of Optometrists of Ontario / Ordre des optométristes de l'Ontario

#901, 1867 Yonge St., Toronto ON M4S 1Y5
Tel: 416-962-4071; *Fax:* 416-962-4073
Toll-Free: 888-825-2554
www.collegeoptom.on.ca
Overview: A medium-sized provincial licensing organization founded in 1919
Mission: To serve the public interest by guiding the profession
Chief Officer(s):
Richard Kniaziew, President
Paula Garshowitz, Registrar
Louise Kassabian, Manager, Membership & Office Administration
lkassabian@collegeoptom.on.ca
Finances: *Annual Operating Budget:* $500,000-$1.5 Million
Staff Member(s): 9
Membership: 2,371; *Fees:* $750; *Member Profile:* Professional optometrists; *Committees:* Executive; Registration; Inquiries, Complaints & Reports; Quality Assurance; Discipline; Patient Relations; Fitness to Practise; Optometry Review; Clinical Practice Panel
Activities: *Rents Mailing List:* Yes; *Library:* Irving Baker Library

College of Pharmacists of British Columbia

#200, 1765 - 8 Ave. West, Vancouver BC V6J 5C6
Tel: 604-733-2440; *Fax:* 604-733-2493
Toll-Free: 800-663-1940
info@bcpharmacists.org
www.bcpharmacists.org
Overview: A medium-sized provincial licensing organization founded in 1891 overseen by National Association of Pharmacy Regulatory Authorities
Mission: Safe & effective pharmacy practice outcomes for the people of British Columbia.
Member of: Canadian Council on Continuing Education in Pharmacy
Chief Officer(s):
Doug Kipp, Chair, 250-342-6612
dougkipp@gmail.com
Bob Nakagawa, Registrar, 604-676-4201
bob.nakagawa@bcpharmacists.org
Ashifa Keshavji, Director, Practice Reviews & Competency, 604-676-4246
ashifa.keshavji@bcpharmacists.org
Finances: *Annual Operating Budget:* $3 Million-$5 Million; *Funding Sources:* License & registration fees
Staff Member(s): 22; 300 volunteer(s)
Membership: 4,379; *Fees:* $585; *Member Profile:* Pharmacists licensed to practice in BC; *Committees:* Audit; Board of Examiners; Community Practice Advisory Committee; Discipline; Drug Advisory; Ethics Advisory; Executive; Hospital Pharmacy; Inquiry; Long-term Care; PharmaNet; Resolutions
Activities: *Internships:* Yes
Awards:
• Past President's Award (Award)
• Certificate of Merit (Award)
• Certificate of Honour (Award)
• Certificate of Recognition (Award)
• Bowl of Hygeia (Award)

College of Pharmacists of Manitoba

200 Tache Ave., Winnipeg MB R2H 1A7
Tel: 204-233-1411; *Fax:* 204-237-3468
info@cphm.ca
mpha.in1touch.org
Previous Name: Manitoba Pharmaceutical Association
Overview: A small provincial organization founded in 1878 overseen by National Association of Pharmacy Regulatory Authorities
Mission: To administer the Manitoba Pharmaceutical Act; to give license to & monitors pharmacists in the province, setingt standards of practice & investigating complaints.
Member of: Canadian Council on Continuing Education in Pharmacy; National Assn. of Pharmacy Regulatory Authorities (NAPRA); District 5, National Assn. of Boards of Pharmacy
Chief Officer(s):
Glenda Marsh, President
Ronald Guse, Registrar
Membership: *Committees:* Awards & Nominating; Executive; Finance & Risk Management; Governance; Professional Development; Standards of Practice

College of Physical Therapists of Alberta *See* Physiotherapy Alberta - College + Association

College of Physical Therapists of British Columbia (CPTBC)

#1420, 1200 West 73rd Ave., Vancouver BC V6P 6G5
Tel: 604-730-9193; *Fax:* 604-730-9273
info@cptbc.org
www.cptbc.org
Overview: A medium-sized provincial organization founded in 1994 overseen by Canadian Alliance of Physiotherapy Regulators
Mission: To serve and protect the public by ensuring that Physical Therapists provide high quality, competent and ethical services.
Member of: Canadian Alliance of Physiotherapy Regulators
Chief Officer(s):
Brenda Hudson, Registrar
brenda_hudson@cptbc.org

Finances: *Annual Operating Budget:* $500,000-$1.5 Million
Staff Member(s): 5
Membership: 2,661; *Fees:* Varies

College of Physicians & Surgeons of Alberta (CPSA)
#2700, 10020 - 100 St. NW, Edmonton AB T5J 0N3
Tel: 780-423-4764; *Fax:* 780-420-0651
Toll-Free: 800-561-3899
info@cpsa.ab.ca
www.cpsa.ab.ca
Overview: A medium-sized provincial licensing organization founded in 1905 overseen by Federation of Regulatory Authorities of Canada
Mission: To serve the public & guide the medical profession; to identify factors affecting competent medical practice; to promote quality improvement in medical practice; to ensure practitioners meet our registration standards; to resolve complaints involving practitioners fairly & effectively.
Chief Officer(s):
Trevor Theman, Registrar
Trevor.Theman@cpsa.ab.ca
Finances: *Funding Sources:* Membership fees
Staff Member(s): 48
Membership: 9,014 individual; *Fees:* $800 physcian; $500 professional corporation; *Member Profile:* Physicians practicing medicine in Alberta; *Committees:* Competence; Medical Informatics; Finance & Audit; Infection Prevention and Control; Physician Health Monitoring; Physician Prescribing Practices; Medical Facility Accreditation; Physician Performance; Executive; Complaint Review; Nominating; TPP Steering
Activities: Licensing & disciplinary body for the physicians & surgeons of Alberta

College of Physicians & Surgeons of British Columbia (CPSBC)
#300, 699 Howe St., Vancouver BC V6C 0B4
Tel: 604-733-7758; *Fax:* 604-733-3503
Toll-Free: 800-461-3008
www.cpsbc.ca
Overview: A medium-sized provincial licensing organization founded in 1886 overseen by Federation of Regulatory Authorities of Canada
Chief Officer(s):
M.A. Docherty, President
Finances: *Annual Operating Budget:* Greater than $5 Million; *Funding Sources:* Licensure fees
Staff Member(s): 60
Membership: 10,500
Activities: *Library:* Medical Library Service

College of Physicians & Surgeons of Manitoba (CPSM)
#1000, 1661 Portage Ave., Winnipeg MB R3J 3T7
Tel: 204-774-4344; *Fax:* 204-774-0750
Toll-Free: 877-774-4344
cpsm@cpsm.mb.ca
cpsm.mb.ca
Also Known As: CPS Manitoba
Overview: A medium-sized provincial licensing organization founded in 1871 overseen by Federation of Regulatory Authorities of Canada
Chief Officer(s):
Margaret Burnett, President
William Pope, Registrar & CEO
theregistrar@cpsm.mb.ca
Finances: *Annual Operating Budget:* $1.5 Million-$3 Million
Staff Member(s): 25
Membership: 2,200; *Fees:* $950; *Committees:* Executive; Audit; Nominating; Central Standards; Complaints; Investigation; Inquiry; Appeals; Program Review

College of Physicians & Surgeons of New Brunswick / Collège des médecins et chirurgiens du Nouveau-Brunswick
#300, One Hampton Rd., Rothesay NB E2E 5K8
Tel: 506-849-5050; *Fax:* 506-849-5069
Toll-Free: 800-667-4641
info@cpsnb.org
www.cpsnb.org
Overview: A medium-sized provincial licensing organization founded in 1981 overseen by Federation of Regulatory Authorities of Canada
Chief Officer(s):
Ed Schollenberg, Registrar
Staff Member(s): 2
Membership: 1,313
Activities: *Rents Mailing List:* Yes

College of Physicians & Surgeons of Newfoundland & Labrador
#603, 139 Water St., St. John's NL A1C 1B2
Tel: 709-726-8546; *Fax:* 709-726-4725
cpsnl@cpsnl.ca
www.cpsnl.ca
Previous Name: Newfoundland Medical Board
Overview: A medium-sized provincial licensing organization founded in 1893 overseen by Federation of Regulatory Authorities of Canada
Mission: To protect the public; to regulate the practice of medicine & medical practitioners
Chief Officer(s):
Robert W. Young, Registrar
William Moulton, Chair
Membership: 13
Publications:
• College of Physicians & Surgeons of Newfoundland & Labrador Annual Report
Type: Yearbook; *Frequency:* Annually
• Practice Dialogue [a publication of the College of Physicians & Surgeons of Newfoundland & Labrador]
Type: Newsletter
Profile: Published under authority of the Registrar

College of Physicians & Surgeons of Nova Scotia (CPSNS)
#5005, 7071 Bayers Rd., Halifax NS B3L 2C2
Tel: 902-422-5823; *Fax:* 902-422-7476
Toll-Free: 877-282-7767
info@cpsns.ns.ca
www.cpsns.ns.ca
www.linkedin.com/company/2497006
www.facebook.com/291670920671
Previous Name: Provincial Medical Board of Nova Scotia
Overview: A medium-sized provincial licensing organization founded in 1872 overseen by Federation of Regulatory Authorities of Canada
Mission: To govern the practice of medicine in the public interest
Chief Officer(s):
Ethel Cooper-Rosen, President
Finances: *Annual Operating Budget:* $1.5 Million-$3 Million; *Funding Sources:* Licensing fees
Staff Member(s): 10
Membership: 2,026; *Fees:* $850; *Member Profile:* Physicians; *Committees:* Executive; Investigation (A, B & C); Finance; Policy & Standards; Credentials; Nominating; Practice Improvement

College of Physicians & Surgeons of Ontario (CPSO)
80 College St., Toronto ON M5G 2E2
Tel: 416-967-2603; *Fax:* 416-961-3330
Toll-Free: 800-268-7096
Other Communication: inquiries@cpso.on.ca
feedback@cpso.on.ca
www.cpso.on.ca
Overview: A large provincial licensing organization founded in 1866 overseen by Federation of Regulatory Authorities of Canada
Mission: To ensure the best quality care for the people of Ontario by the doctors of Ontario
Chief Officer(s):
Robert Byrick, President
Rocco Gerace, Registrar
Finances: *Annual Operating Budget:* Greater than $5 Million; *Funding Sources:* Membership dues
Staff Member(s): 235
Membership: 30,000; *Fees:* $1,530; *Member Profile:* Physicians; *Committees:* Executive; Inquiries, Complaints & Reports; Discipline; Registration; Education; Finance; Medical Review; Quality Assurance; Methadone; Outreach; Patient Relations; Premises Inspection
Awards:
• The Council Award (Award)
Eligibility: Ontario physicians
Publications:
• Dialogue
Type: Magazine
• Methadone News: Patient Forum
Type: Newsletter

College of Physicians & Surgeons of Prince Edward Island
14 Paramount Dr., Charlottetown PE C1E 0C7
Tel: 902-566-3861; *Fax:* 902-566-3986
cpspei.ca
Previous Name: Medical Council of Prince Edward Island
Overview: A small provincial licensing organization founded in 1988 overseen by Federation of Regulatory Authorities of Canada
Mission: To act as the regulatory body for physicians in the province, responsible for licensing all medical doctors, maintaining medical standards, handling complaints from the public, & delivering disciplinary action.
Chief Officer(s):
Cyril Moyse, Registrar
cmoyse@collegeofphysicians.pe.ca
Staff Member(s): 4
Membership: *Member Profile:* Licensed physician in PEI
Activities: *Rents Mailing List:* Yes

College of Physicians & Surgeons of Saskatchewan (CPSS)
#500, 321A - 21st St. East, Saskatoon SK S7K 0C1
Tel: 306-244-7355; *Fax:* 306-244-0090
Toll-Free: 800-667-1668
cpss@quadrant.net
www.quadrant.net/cpss/
Overview: A medium-sized provincial organization founded in 1905 overseen by Federation of Regulatory Authorities of Canada
Mission: To be responsible for licencing properly qualified medical practitioners, developing and ensuring the standards of practice in all fields of medicine, investigating and disciplining of all doctors whose standards of medical care, ethical or professional conduct are questioned.
Chief Officer(s):
Bryan Salte, Associate Registrar
David Pulin, Deputy Registrar
Karen Shaw, Registrar
Finances: *Funding Sources:* Membership fees
Membership: *Committees:* Medical Imaging; Alternate Dispute Resolution/Mediation; Complaints and The Complaints Resolution Advisory; Competency Assessment and Maintenance; Discipline and The Discipline; ECG; Health Care Facilities Credentialling; Laboratory Quality Assurance Program; Practice Enhancement Program; Prescription Review Program
Activities: *Rents Mailing List:* Yes

College of Physiotherapists of Manitoba (CPM)
#211, 675 Pembina Hwy., Winnipeg MB R3M 2L6
Tel: 204-287-8502; *Fax:* 204-474-2506
info@manitobaphysio.com
www.manitobaphysio.com
Overview: A small provincial licensing organization founded in 1957 overseen by Canadian Alliance of Physiotherapy Regulators
Mission: To protect the public by ensuring quality physiotherapy is provided to the public
Member of: Canadian Alliance of Physiotherapy Regulators
Chief Officer(s):
Lori Stobart, Chair
cpmchair@manitobaphysio.com
Brenda McKechnie, Registrar/Executive Director
Staff Member(s): 3
Membership: 700; *Fees:* $300; *Committees:* Complaints; Continuing Competency; Continuing Competency Evaluations; Ethics; Inquiry; Legislative; Governance & Nominating; Physiotherpay Standards
Publications:
• In Touch Newsletter [a publication of the College of Physiotherapists of Manitoba]
Type: Newsletter

College of Physiotherapists of Ontario (CPO) / Ordre des physiothérapeutes de l'Ontario
#901, 375 University Ave., Toronto ON M5G 2J5
Tel: 416-591-3828; *Fax:* 416-591-3834
Toll-Free: 800-583-5885
info@collegept.org
www.collegept.org
Overview: A medium-sized provincial organization founded in 1994 overseen by Canadian Alliance of Physiotherapy Regulators
Mission: To protect & serve the public interest by ensuring that physiotherapists provide high quality, competent & ethical services
Member of: Canadian Alliance of Physiotherapy Regulators
Affliation(s): Federation of Health Regulatory Colleges of Ontario; Canadian Physiotherapy Association; Ontario

Physiotherapy Association; Federation of State Boards of Physical Therapy; World Confederation of Physical Therapy
Chief Officer(s):
Rod Hamilton, Associate Registrar, Policy Ext. 232
rhamilton@collegept.org
Jan Robinson, Registrar & CEO
Karin Micheelsen, Communications Director
Finances: *Annual Operating Budget:* $1.5 Million-$3 Million; *Funding Sources:* Membership fees
Staff Member(s): 19
Membership: 6,300; *Fees:* $600; *Member Profile:* Physiotherapists registered to practice in Ontario; *Committees:* Executive; Fitness to Practise; Complaints; Discipline; Patient Relations; Registration; Quality Management; Nominations
Activities: Registering physiotherapists for practice in Ontario; dealing with concerns about members' practices from the public; annual meeting, June; *Speaker Service:* Yes
Awards:
• Award of Distinction (Award)

College of Podiatrists of Manitoba (COPOM)

#512, 428 Portage Ave., Winnipeg MB R3C 0E2
Tel: 204-942-3256
www.copom.org
Overview: A small provincial licensing organization
Mission: The College is a provincial regulatory body that protects the public by ensuring podiatrists in Mantioba follow the standards of practice defined in The Podiatry Act, 2001.
Chief Officer(s):
Iain Palmer, Chair
Martin Colledge, Registrar
Registrar@copom.org
Membership: *Member Profile:* Provincially registered podiatrists

College of Psychologists of British Columbia (CPBC)

#404, 1755 West Broadway, Vancouver BC V6J 4S5
Tel: 604-736-6164; *Fax:* 604-736-6133
Toll-Free: 800-665-0979
www.collegeofpsychologists.bc.ca
Overview: A medium-sized provincial organization
Mission: To regulate the profession of psychology in the public interest in accordance with the Health Professions Act of British Columbia by setting the standards for competant and ethical practice, promoting excellence and taking action when standards are not met.
Chief Officer(s):
Andrea Kowaz, Registrar
Susan D. Turnbull, Director, Practice Support
Staff Member(s): 3
Membership: *Fees:* $1200 active register; $600 limited register (non-practicing or out-of-province); $150 limited register (retired); *Committees:* Registration; Quality Assurance; Inquiry; Discipline; Patient Relations
Publications:
• The Chronicle
Type: Newsletter

College of Psychologists of New Brunswick (CPNB) / Collège des psychologues du Nouveau-Brunswick

PO Box 201, Stn. A, Frederiction NB E3B 4Y9
Tel: 506-382-1994; *Fax:* 506-857-9813
cpnb@nbnet.nb.ca
www.cpnb.ca
Overview: A small provincial licensing organization founded in 1965
Mission: To regulate the practice of psychology; to represent the interests of its members
Chief Officer(s):
Louise Morin, President
Carole Cormier-Rioux, Registrar
carole.c.rioux@nb.aibn.com
Staff Member(s): 3

The College of Psychologists of Ontario (CPO)

#500, 110 Eglinton Ave. West, Toronto ON M4R 1A3
Tel: 416-961-8817; *Fax:* 416-961-2635
Toll-Free: 800-489-8388
cpo@cpo.on.ca
www.cpo.on.ca
www.facebook.com/group.php?gid=110923675626180
Overview: A large provincial licensing organization
Mission: To monitor & regulate the practice of psychology in Ontario
Chief Officer(s):
Milan Pomichalek, College Council President
Catherine Yarrow, Registrar & Executive Director
Finances: *Annual Operating Budget:* Greater than $5 Million; *Funding Sources:* Registration & application fees
Staff Member(s): 16
Membership: 3,000+; *Member Profile:* Psychologists & Psychological Associates; *Committees:* Executive; Registration; Quality Assurance; Fitness to Practice; Client Relations; Inquiries, Complaints & Reports; Discipline; Jurisprudence & Ethics Examination Committee
Publications:
• The College of Psychologists of Ontario Standards of Professional Conduct
Type: Manual; *Number of Pages:* 22
Profile: Members of the College of Psychologists must adhere to the standards while practicing the profession
• e-Bulletin [a publication of the College of Psychologists of Ontario
Type: Newsletter
Profile: Articles, discipline proceedings, by-law amendments, & committee & council news

College of Registered Dental Hygienists of Alberta (CRDHA)

#302, 8657 - 51 Ave., Edmonton AB T6E 6A8
Tel: 780-465-1756; *Fax:* 780-440-0544
Toll-Free: 877-465-1756
info@crdha.ca
www.crdha.ca
Overview: A small provincial licensing organization
Mission: To regulate the practice of dental hygeine for the public; To advance the profession of dental hygiene
Chief Officer(s):
Brenda Walker, CEO & Registrar
Finances: *Annual Operating Budget:* $3 Million-$5 Million
Membership: *Member Profile:* Registered dental hygienists in Alberta; *Committees:* Registration; Competence

College of Registered Nurses of British Columbia (CRNBC)

2855 Arbutus St., Vancouver BC V6J 3Y8
Tel: 604-736-7331; *Fax:* 604-738-2272
Toll-Free: 800-565-6505
info@crnbc.ca
www.crnbc.ca
twitter.com/CRNBC
Previous Name: Registered Nurses Association of British Columbia
Overview: A large provincial licensing organization founded in 1912 overseen by Canadian Nurses Association
Mission: To provide safe & appropriate nursing practice regulated by nurses in the public interest; To promote good practice, prevent poor practice & intervene when practice is unacceptable
Chief Officer(s):
Cynthia Johansen, CEO/Registrar
ceo@crnbc.ca
Barb Crook, Chair
Finances: *Annual Operating Budget:* Greater than $5 Million; *Funding Sources:* Membership fees; grants; sales
Staff Member(s): 80; 500 volunteer(s)
Membership: 35,000; *Member Profile:* Registered nurses; *Committees:* Certified Practices Approval; Disipline; Education Program Review; Finance and Audit; Inquiry; Nominations; Nurse Practitioner Examination; Nurse Practitioner Standards; Quality Assurance; Registration
Activities: *Speaker Service:* Yes; *Library* by appointment
Awards:
• Award of Distinction in Nursing (Award)
• Award of Excellence in Nursing Administration (Award)
• Award of Excellence in Nursing Education (Award)
• Award of Excellence in Nursing Practice (Award)
• Award of Excellence in Nursing Research (Award)
• Award of Advocacy (Award)
• Rising Star (Award)
• Award of Merit (Award)
• Award of Honour (Award)
Meetings/Conferences: • College of Registered Nurses of British Columbia 2015 Annual General Meeting, 2015, BC
Scope: Provincial
Publications:
• Nursing Matters
Type: Newsletter; *Frequency:* 10-11 times pa

College of Registered Nurses of Manitoba (CRNM)

890 Pembina Hwy., Winnipeg MB R3M 2M8
Tel: 204-774-3477; *Fax:* 204-775-6052
Toll-Free: 800-665-2027
info@crnm.mb.ca
www.crnm.mb.ca
www.facebook.com/collegeofrnsmb
Previous Name: Manitoba Association of Registered Nurses
Overview: A medium-sized provincial licensing organization founded in 1913 overseen by Canadian Nurses Association
Mission: To regulate the practice of registered nurses & to advance the quality of nursing to protect the public interest
Chief Officer(s):
Cathy Rippin-Sisler, President
president@crnm.mb.ca
Diane Wilson Máté, Executive Director
dwmate@crnm.mb.ca
Lisa Fraser, Manager, Communications
lfraser@crnm.mb.ca
Staff Member(s): 30

College of Registered Nurses of Nova Scotia (CRNNS)

#4005, 7071 Bayers Rd., Halifax NS B3L 2C2
Tel: 902-491-9744; *Fax:* 902-491-9510
Toll-Free: 800-565-9744
info@crnns.ca
www.crnns.ca
Previous Name: Registered Nurses Association of Nova Scotia
Overview: A medium-sized provincial licensing organization founded in 1910 overseen by Canadian Nurses Association
Mission: Registered nurses regulating their profession to promote excellence in nursing practice.
Chief Officer(s):
Donna Denney, Executive Director, 902-491-9744 Ext. 223
dd@crnns.ca
Finances: *Annual Operating Budget:* $1.5 Million-$3 Million; *Funding Sources:* Membership fees
Staff Member(s): 22
Membership: 9,300; *Fees:* $442.96; *Member Profile:* Registered nurses
Meetings/Conferences: • College of Registered Nurses of Nova Scotia 2015 Education Forum, May, 2015, NS
Scope: Provincial

College of Registered Psychiatric Nurses of Alberta

#201, 9711 - 45 Ave., Edmonton AB T6E 5V8
Tel: 780-434-7666; *Fax:* 780-436-4165
Toll-Free: 877-234-7666
crpna@crpna.ab.ca
www.crpna.ab.ca
Previous Name: Registered Psychiatric Nurses Association of Alberta
Overview: A medium-sized provincial organization
Mission: To protect & servce the public interest by ensuring members provide safe, competent and ethical practice; to address the needs of members and the public through education, regulation, advocacy.
Chief Officer(s):
Chris Watkins, President
Barbara Lowe, Executive Director
Membership: *Committees:* Finance; Education; Continuing Competence; Personnel; Recognition & Awards; Education Fund Selection

College of Registered Psychiatric Nurses of B.C. (CRPNBC)

#307, 2502 St. John's St., Port Moody BC V3H 2B4
Tel: 604-931-5200; *Fax:* 604-931-5277
Toll-Free: 800-565-2505
www.crpnbc.ca
Overview: A small provincial organization
Mission: to serve and protect the public through self-regulation, assuring a safe, accountable, and ethical level of psychiatric nursing practice.
Chief Officer(s):
Donna Higenbottam, Executive Director & Registrar
Staff Member(s): 4
Membership: *Fees:* $357 Pracicing Members; $63 Non-Practicing Members
Publications:
• The Communicator
Type: Magazine; *Frequency:* 4 pa; *Editor:* Jacqollyne Keath

College of Registered Psychiatric Nurses of British Columbia

#307, 2502 St. Johns St., Port Moody BC V3H 2B4

Tel: 604-931-5200; *Fax:* 604-931-5277
Toll-Free: 800-565-2505
www.crpnbc.ca
Previous Name: Registered Psychiatric Nurses Association of British Columbia
Overview: A medium-sized provincial organization founded in 1974
Mission: To serve & protect the public; to assure a safe, accountable & ethical level of psychiatric nursing practice
Chief Officer(s):
Dorothy Jennings, Chair
Kyong-ae Kim, Executive Director & Registrar
Staff Member(s): 8
Publications:
• The Communicator
Type: Magazine; *Frequency:* Quarterly; *Accepts Advertising*; *Editor:* Dr. Jacqollyne Keath

College of Registered Psychiatric Nurses of Manitoba (CRPNM)

1854 Portage Ave., Winnipeg MB R3J 0G9
Tel: 204-888-4841; *Fax:* 204-888-8638
www.crpnm.mb.ca
Previous Name: Registered Psychiatric Nurses Association of Manitoba
Overview: A medium-sized provincial licensing organization founded in 1960
Mission: To ensure that members of the profession provide safe & effective psychiatric nursing services to the public of Manitoba, in accordance with the Registered Psychiatric Nurses Act
Chief Officer(s):
Laura Panteluk, Executive Director
Activities: *Library*
Publications:
• Annual Report of The College of Registered Psychiatric Nurses of Manitoba
Type: Yearbook; *Frequency:* Annually
• CRPNM [College of Registered Psychiatric Nurses of Manitoba] Advisor

College of Registered Psychotherapists of Ontario (CRPO)

163 Queen St. East, 4th Fl., Toronto ON M5A 1S21
Tel: 416-862-4801; *Fax:* 416-974-4079
Toll-Free: 888-661-4801
info@crpo.ca
www.crpo.ca
Overview: A small provincial licensing organization
Mission: To regulate the profession of psychotherapy & to maintain professional, ethical standards.
Chief Officer(s):
Joyce Rowlands, Registrar
Membership: *Committees:* Client Relations; Discipline; Examination; Executive; Fitness to Practise; Inquiries, Complaints & Reports; Nominations & Elections; Quality Assurance; Registration

College of Respiratory Therapists of Ontario (CRTO)

#2103, 180 Dundas St. West, Toronto ON M5G 1Z8
Tel: 416-591-7800; *Fax:* 416-591-7890
Toll-Free: 800-261-0528
questions@crto.on.ca
www.crto.on.ca
twitter.com/theCRTO
www.youtube.com/user/TheCRTO
Overview: A medium-sized provincial licensing organization
Mission: To regulate the profession of respiratory care in the public interest
Chief Officer(s):
Carrie-Lynn Meyer, President
Staff Member(s): 8
Membership: *Fees:* $500; *Committees:* Fitness to Practice; Quality Assurance; Registration; ICRC; Discipline; Patient Relations; Professional Practice; Executive

College of the Rockies Faculty Association (CORFA)

PO Box 8500, 2700 College Way, Cranbrook BC V1C 5L7
Tel: 250-489-8251
www.corfa.org
Previous Name: East Kootenay Community College Faculty Association
Overview: A small local organization
Member of: College & Institutes Educators Association (CIEA)
Affliation(s): Cranbrook Labour Council; Federation of Post-Secondary Educators of BC; Canadian Association of University Teachers
Chief Officer(s):
Leslie Molnar, President
Finances: *Annual Operating Budget:* $50,000-$100,000
Staff Member(s): 1
Membership: 150; *Committees:* Disability Management; Education Policy; Human Rights & International Solidarity; Non-Regular Faculty; Occupational Health & Safety; Pension Advisory; Professional Development; Status of women

College of Traditional Chinese Medicine Practitioners & Acupuncturists of British Columbia (CTCMABC)

1664 - West 8th Ave., Vancouver BC V6J 1V4
Tel: 604-738-7100; *Fax:* 604-738-7171
info@ctcma.bc.ca
www.ctcma.bc.ca
Overview: A small provincial organization founded in 1996
Mission: To protect the public by establishing a system of mandatory registration in which practitioners have to meet and maintain standards in TCM and acupuncture care established by the College.
Chief Officer(s):
Mary S. Watterson, Registrar
registrar@ctcma.bc.ca
Publications:
• Balance
Type: Newsletter; *Frequency:* 4 pa

College of Veterinarians of British Columbia (CVBC)

#107, 828 Harbourside Dr., North Vancouver BC V7P 3R9
Tel: 604-929-7090; *Fax:* 604-929-7095
Toll-Free: 800-463-5399
reception@cvbc.ca
www.cvbc.ca
Previous Name: British Columbia Veterinary Medical Association
Overview: A medium-sized provincial licensing organization founded in 1907 overseen by Canadian Veterinary Medical Association
Mission: To serve members by promoting their professional image, providing a forum for addressing issues of importance to the profession, offering continuing education & protecting their interests & rights; to protect & serve animals & animal custodians through evaluation of veterinary competence & facility quality & by enforcing the Veterinarians Act & Bylaws
Chief Officer(s):
Larry W. Odegard, Registrar & CEO
John Brocklebank, Deputy Registrar
Finances: *Funding Sources:* Membership dues
Staff Member(s): 8
Membership: 2,445; *Fees:* Schedule available; *Member Profile:* Veterinarians

College of Veterinarians of Ontario (CVO)

2106 Gordon St., Guelph ON N1L 1G6
Tel: 519-824-5600; *Fax:* 519-824-6497
Toll-Free: 800-424-2856
inquiries@cvo.org
www.cvo.org
Overview: A medium-sized provincial licensing organization founded in 1872
Mission: To protect the public by regulating & enhancing the veterinary profession in Ontario
Chief Officer(s):
Ken Bridge, President
Christine Simpson, Acting Registrar
csimpson@cvo.org
Membership: *Committees:* Executive; Accreditation; Discipline; Registration; Complaints
Activities: *Rents Mailing List:* Yes
Publications:
• College of Veterinarians of Ontario Update
Editor: Susan J. Carlyle *ISSN:* 0821-6320
Profile: Comprehensive, accurate & defensible information about regulatory issues for members

Collège royal canadien des organistes *See* Royal Canadian College of Organists

Collège Royal des Chirurgiens Dentistes du Canada *See* Royal College of Dentists of Canada

Le Collège royal des médecins et chirurgiens du Canada *See* The Royal College of Physicians & Surgeons of Canada

Colleges and Institutes Canada (CICan) / Collèges et instituts Canada

#701, 1 Rideau St., Ottawa ON K1N 8S7
Tel: 613-746-2222; *Fax:* 613-746-6721
info@collegesinstitutes.ca
www.collegesinstitutes.ca
www.facebook.com/collegesinstitutes
twitter.com/CollegeCan
instagram.com/College_can
Previous Name: Association des collèges communautaires du Canada
Overview: A large national organization
Mission: Colleges and Institutes Canada (CICan) is the national, voluntary membership organization representing publicly supported colleges, institutes, cégeps and polytechnics in Canada and internationally.
Chief Officer(s):
Denise Amyot, President & CEO, 613-746-6492
damyot@accc.ca
Finances: *Annual Operating Budget:* Greater than $5 Million; *Funding Sources:* Canadian International Development Agency (CIDA); membership fees
Staff Member(s): 55
Membership: 150 colleges, institutes & groups; *Fees:* Based on overall operating revenue of each institution; *Member Profile:* Regular (publicly-funded institutions); Associates (privately-funded institutions & educational organizations); *Committees:* Canadian Program Advisory & International Program Advisory Committies; Program Review
Activities: Awards Program; Canadian College Partnership Program; Student Mobility Program
Awards:
• Indigenous Education Excellence (Award)
• Innovation in Applied Research Excellence (Award)
• Internationalization Excellence (Award)
• Leadership Excellence (Award)
• Program Excellence (Award)
• Staff Excellence (Award)
• Student Leadership Excellence (Award)
• Teaching Excellence (Award)
Meetings/Conferences: • Colleges and Institutes Canada 2015 Conference, May, 2015, RBC Convention Centre, Winnipeg, MB
Scope: National
Attendance: 800
Description: Provides an opportunity for colleges, institutes, cégeps, university colleges and polytechnics to share their success stories and help shape a new direction for the future.

Collèges et instituts Canada *See* Colleges and Institutes Canada

Colleges Ontario

PO Box 88, #1600, 20 Bay St., Toronto ON M5J 2N8
Tel: 647-258-7670; *Fax:* 647-258-7699
www.collegesontario.org
www.facebook.com/CollegesOntario
twitter.com/CollegesOntario
www.youtube.com/user/CollegesOntario1?feature=mhee
Previous Name: Association of Colleges of Applied Arts & Technology of Ontario
Overview: A medium-sized provincial organization
Mission: To advance a strong college system for Ontario
Chief Officer(s):
Linda Franklin, President & CEO, 647-258-7676
franklin@collegesontario.org
Membership: Ontario's 24 colleges of applied arts & technology; *Fees:* Pro-rated
Activities: *Speaker Service:* Yes
Awards:
• Premier's Awards (Award)
The Premier's Awards recognize outstanding college graduates from Ontario's 24 public colleges. Presented annually in six categories: Business, Community Services, Creative Arts and Design, Health Sciences, Recent Graduate and Technology.
Contact: Keiko Kataoka, kataoka@collegesontario.org
• Minister's Lifetime Achievement Award (Award)
Recognizes success in advancing Ontario college education.
Contact: Keiko Kataoka, kataoka@collegesontario.org

Heads, Libraries and Learning Resources (HLLR)
ON
Tel: 905-845-9430; *Fax:* 905-845-4123
www.hllr.org
Mission: HLLR's mandate is to advocate on behalf of students for the best possible college library services and resources, to provide a forum for the discussion of issues, trends, and concerns related to the field of learning resources in Ontario Colleges.
Chief Officer(s):

Jason Bird, Chair, 705-759-2554 Ext. 2402, Fax: 705-235-7299
Jason.Bird@saultcollege.ca

Collingwood & District Historical Society

PO Box 181, Collingwood ON L9Y 3Z5
Tel: 705-446-1820
www.historicallyspeakingcdhs.ca
www.facebook.com/collingwoodhistoricalsociety
www.youtube.com/channel/UC9SzLj34EcxEVN8LsAIUJGQ
Overview: A small local organization founded in 1976
Mission: To research, record, preserve & promotoe public interest in the history of the Collingwood district; to identify structures of historical & architectural merit in the district & promotes their preservation.
Member of: Heritage Canada, Ontario Historical Society; Simcoe County Historical Association
Chief Officer(s):
Bruce Mackison, President
Joan Miller, Secretary
Finances: *Funding Sources:* Membership fees
Membership: *Fees:* $20 individual; $30 couple/corporate
Activities: Tours of historic homes; regular meetings with speakers
Publications:
• Historically Speaking
Type: newsletter

Collingwood & District United Way *See* United Way of South Georgian Bay

Collingwood Chamber of Commerce

25 Second St., Collingwood ON L9Y 1E4
Tel: 705-445-0221; *Fax:* 705-445-6858
info@collingwoodchamber.com
www.collingwoodchamber.com
Overview: A small local organization founded in 1880
Mission: To act as the recognized voice of business committed to the enhancement of economic prosperity in the Collingwood area
Affliation(s): Canadian Chamber of Commerce; Ontario Chamber of Commerce
Chief Officer(s):
John Alsop, President
Trish Irwin, General Manager & CEO
tirwin@collingwoodchamber.com
Finances: *Annual Operating Budget:* $100,000-$250,000
Staff Member(s): 2; 16 volunteer(s)
Membership: 525; *Fees:* $107-$516; *Member Profile:* Business; non-profit organizations; individuals; *Committees:* Government; Marketing
Activities: Training seminars; social; networking events

Collingwood Community Living *See* E3 Community Services

Colon Cancer Canada / Cancer du Colon Canada

#204A, 5915 Leslie St., Toronto ON M2H 1J8
Tel: 416-785-0449; *Fax:* 416-785-0450
Toll-Free: 888-571-8547
info@coloncancercanada.ca
www.coloncancercanada.ca
www.facebook.com/coloncancercda
twitter.com/ColonCancerCda
Previous Name: National Colorectal Cancer Campaign
Overview: A small national organization founded in 1996
Mission: To raise public awareness for the disease of colorectal cancer & to raise money for vital research
Chief Officer(s):
Bunnie Schwartz, President/Co-Founder
hmschwartz@rogers.com
Amy Lerman-Elmaleh, Executive Director/Co-Founder
amy@coloncancercanada.ca
Staff Member(s): 5
Activities: Charity golf tournament; fundraisers; *Awareness Events:* Colon Cancer Awareness Month, March

Colorectal Cancer Association of Canada (CCAC)

#204, 60 St. Clair Ave. East, Toronto ON M4T 1N5
Tel: 416-920-4333; *Fax:* 416-920-3004
information@colorectal-cancer.ca
www.colorectal-cancer.ca
www.facebook.com/group.php?gid=28102673065
www.twitter.com/coloncanada
www.youtube.com/user/ccac1230
Overview: A small national organization
Mission: To support people with colorectal cancer, their families & caregivers; to improve the quality of life of patients & increase awareness of the disease
Chief Officer(s):
Barry D. Stein, President
barrys@colorectal-cancer.ca
Activities: *Awareness Events:* Colorectal Cancer Awareness Month, March

Columbia Valley Chamber of Commerce (CVCC)

PO Box 1019, Invermere BC V0A 1K0
Tel: 250-342-2844; *Fax:* 250-342-3261
info@cvchamber.ca
www.cvchamber.ca
www.facebook.com/167124979984316
twitter.com/cv_chamber
Overview: A small local organization founded in 1991
Mission: To promote the economic prosperity of the area & its residents
Affliation(s): British Columbia Chamber of Commerce
Chief Officer(s):
Rose-Marie Regitnig, President
Susan E. Clovechok, Executive Director
Finances: *Annual Operating Budget:* $100,000-$250,000; *Funding Sources:* British Columbia Ministry of Small Business, Tourism, & Culture; District of Invermere; Membership dues; Fundraising
Staff Member(s): 1
Membership: 320; *Fees:* $100 - $650; *Member Profile:* Business; professionals & individuals
Activities: *Awareness Events:* Chamber Week, Feb.; Small Business Week, Oct.; *Library* Open to public

Columbia Valley Chamber of Commerce; Invermere Business Committee; Fairmont Business Association; Windermere Board of Trade *See* Radium Hot Springs Chamber of Commerce

Comité canadien d'action sur le statut de la femme *See* National Action Committee on the Status of Women

Comité canadien de catalogage *See* Canadian Committee on Cataloguing

Comité canadien du MARC *See* Canadian Committee on MARC

Comité canadien sur l'histoire du travail *See* Canadian Committee on Labour History

Comité condition féminine Baie-James

#203, 552, 3e Rue, Chibougamau QC G8P 1N9
Tél: 418-748-4408; *Téléc:* 418-748-2486
ccfbj@tlb.sympatico.ca
ccfbj.com
Aperçu: *Dimension:* moyenne; *Envergure:* locale; fondée en 2001
Mission: A pour mission l'amélioration des conditions de vie des Jamésiennes
Membre(s) du bureau directeur:
Gérald Lemoine, Présidente
Membre: 5 membres individuelles; 13 associations

Comité culturel "La Chaussée"

CP 165, Cap-Pelé NB E0A 1J0
Tél: 506-577-6683; *Téléc:* 506-577-2035
Aperçu: *Dimension:* petite; *Envergure:* locale; Organisme sans but lucratif; fondée en 1979
Mission: Le Comité culturel La Chaussée oeuvre en collaboration avec la municipalité, les écoles et autres organismes communautaires, pour promouvoir la fierté communautaire à travers la création et l'expression dans divers domaines culturels: théâtre, musique populaire et traditionnelle, spectacles, littérature et beaux-arts.
Membre de: Conseil de promotion et de diffusion de la culture
Membre(s) du bureau directeur:
Réginald Vautour, Contact, 506-577-4787
Finances: *Budget de fonctionnement annuel:* Moins de $50,000
6 bénévole(s)
Membre: 1-99; *Critères d'admissibilite:* Oeuvre en collaboration avec la municipalité, les écoles et autres organismes communautaires, pour promouvoir la fierté communautaire à travers la création et l'expression dans divers domaines culturels: théâtre, musique populaire et traditionnelle, spectacles, littérature et beaux-arts

Comité d'action des citoyennes et citoyens de Verdun

3972, rue de Verdun, Verdun QC H4G 1K9
Tél: 514-769-2228; *Téléc:* 514-769-0825
www.cacv-verdun.org
Aperçu: *Dimension:* petite; *Envergure:* locale; fondée en 1975
Mission: Le CACV soutien les personnes les plus démunies afin qu'elles améliorent leurs conditions de vie dans une optique de prise en charge
Membre(s) du bureau directeur:
Chantal Lamarre, Directrice
Membre(s) du personnel: 4

Comité d'action Parc Extension (CAPE)

#03, 419, St-Roch, Montréal QC H3N 1K2
Tél: 514-278-6028; *Téléc:* 514-278-0900
Aperçu: *Dimension:* petite; *Envergure:* locale; fondée en 1986
Mission: A pour mission d'améliorer les conditions de vie de tous les citoyens/citoyennes du quartier Parc Extension
Membre(s) du bureau directeur:
Denis Giraldeau, Coordonnateur

Comité de bénévolat de Rogersville

#12, 11133, rue Principale, Rogersville NB E4Y 2N4
Tél: 506-775-2783
Aperçu: *Dimension:* petite; *Envergure:* locale
Mission: Aider les familles démunies en leur fournissant une boîte de nourriture
Membre de: Association of Food Banks & C.V.A. for New Brunswick; Atlantic Alliance of Food Banks & C.V.A.
Finances: *Budget de fonctionnement annuel:* Moins de $50,000
Membre: 1-99; *Montant de la cotisation:* 25$

Comité de parents du Nouveau-Brunswick *Voir* Association francophone des parents du Nouveau-Brunswick

Comité de solidarité tiers-monde/Trois-Rivières *Voir* Comité de solidarité/Trois-Rivières

Comité de solidarité/Trois-Rivières

942, rue Ste-Geneviève, Trois-Rivières QC G9A 3X6
Tél: 819-373-2598; *Téléc:* 819-373-7892
comitedesolidarite@cs3r.org
www.cs3r.org
Nom précédent: Comité de solidarité tiers-monde/Trois-Rivières
Aperçu: *Dimension:* petite; *Envergure:* internationale; Organisme sans but lucratif; fondée en 1973
Mission: De contribuer à l'édification d'un monde plus juste et plus harmonieux où l'ensemble des peuples et des citoyens et citoyennes qui en font partie se partageraient équitablement les ressources et les richesses de la planète; promouvoir la solidarité avec les peuples de l'Afrique, de l'Amérique latine, du Moyen-Orient; se concrétise par des activités d'information, d'éducation, et des campagnes publiques que le Comité organise dans les écoles, les médias, les organisations populaires et syndicales et dans le grand public
Membre de: Solidarité Canada Sahel; Solidarité Populaire Québec; Corporation développement communautaire
Affliation(s): Association québécoise des organismes de coopération internationale
Finances: *Budget de fonctionnement annuel:* $500,000-$1.5 Million
Membre(s) du personnel: 8; 50 bénévole(s)
Membre: 2 500; *Comités:* Action solidaire; Jeunesse; Femme et développement; Réseau d'urgence; Communication
Activités: Rendez-vous ethnique; animation Tiers Monde; stages à l'étranger; campagnes de solidarité; *Stagiaires:* Oui; *Bibliothèque* Bibliothèque publique

Comité des citoyens et citoyennes du quartier Saint-Sauveur

301, rue Carillon, Québec QC G1K 5B3
Tél: 418-529-6158; *Téléc:* 418-529-9455
cccqss@bellnet.ca
www.cccqss.org
www.facebook.com/CCCQSS
Aperçu: *Dimension:* petite; *Envergure:* locale
Membre: *Montant de la cotisation:* 3$ les personnes sans emploi; 5$ ceux qui travaillent

Comité des orphelins victimes d'abus (COVA)

1710, rue Beaudry, MontréAl QC H2L E37
Tél: 514-523-3843
Aperçu: *Dimension:* petite; *Envergure:* locale
Mission: De faire respecter les droits des orphelins qui ont été abusés physiquement et sexuellement

Comité des personnes atteintes du VIH du Québec (CPAVIH)
#310, 2075, rue Plessis, Montréal QC H2L 2Y4
Tél: 514-521-8720; *Téléc:* 514-521-9633
Ligne sans frais: 800-927-2844
Aperçu: *Dimension:* moyenne; *Envergure:* provinciale; Organisme sans but lucratif; fondée en 1987
Mission: Informer les personnes vivant avec le VIH/SIDA; promouvoir leurs droits afin d'améliorer leur qualité de vie
Membre de: Canadian AIDS Society
Finances: *Budget de fonctionnement annuel:* $250,000-$500,000; *Fonds:* Gouvernemental; corporatif; privé
Membre(s) du personnel: 5; 30 bénévole(s)
Membre: 350; *Montant de la cotisation:* 1$; *Critères d'admissibilité:* Personnes attientes du VIH/SIDA
Activités: Info-traitements; info juridique; activités socio-culturelles; centre de documentation; *Bibliothèque:* Centre de documentation; rendez-vous

Comité diosésain d'action catholique *Voir* Carrefour des mouvements d'action catholique

Comité du patrimoine paysager estrien (CPPE)
#300, 230, rue King Ouest, Sherbrooke QC J1H 1P9
Tél: 819-563-1911
info@paysagesestriens.qc.ca
www.paysagesestriens.qc.ca
Aperçu: *Dimension:* petite; *Envergure:* locale; fondée en 2001
Mission: Sensibiliser, informer et promouvoir la préservation et la valorisation du patrimoine paysager estrien auprès de la collectivité régionale.
Activités: Campagne de sensibilisation et d'information; causerie-conférence; affiche promotionnelle; rédaction d'une Charte du patrimoine paysager estrien

Comité du SIDA d'Ottawa *See* AIDS Committee of Ottawa

Comité du sida de North Bay et de la région *See* AIDS Committee of North Bay & Area

Comité intergouvernemental de recherches urbaines et régionales *See* Intergovernmental Committee on Urban & Regional Research

Comité logement de Lacine-Lasalle
426, rue St-Jacques Ouest, Lachine QC H8R 1E8
Tél: 514-544-4294; *Téléc:* 514-366-0505
logement.lachine-lasalle@videotron.ca
Aperçu: *Dimension:* petite; *Envergure:* locale
Membre(s) du bureau directeur:
Daniel Chainey, Responsable

Comité logement du Plateau Mont-Royal
#328, 4450, rue St-Hubert, Montréal QC H2J 2W9
Tél: 514-527-3495; *Téléc:* 514-527-6653
clplateau@yahoo.ca
sites.google.com/site/comitelogementplateau
Aperçu: *Dimension:* petite; *Envergure:* locale; fondée en 1975

Comité logement Rosemont
#R-145, 5350, rue Lafond, Montréal QC H1X 2X2
Tél: 514-597-2581; *Téléc:* 514-524-9813
info@comitelogement.org
www.comitelogement.org
www.facebook.com/comitelogement
Aperçu: *Dimension:* petite; *Envergure:* locale; fondée en 1977
Mission: Défendre et promouvoir les droits des locataires du quartier Rosemont
Membre(s) du bureau directeur:
Martine Poitras, Coordonnatrice
Membre(s) du personnel: 4
Membre: 500-600; *Montant de la cotisation:* 3$

Comité olympique canadien *See* Canadian Olympic Committee

Comité paralympique canadien *See* Canadian Paralympic Committee

Comité pour la justice sociale *See* Social Justice Committee

Comité québécois femmes et développement (CQFD)
#540, 1001, rue Sherbrooke Est, Montréal QC H2L 1L3
Tél: 514-871-1086; *Téléc:* 514-871-9866
Aperçu: *Dimension:* petite; *Envergure:* provinciale; fondée en 1984 surveillé par Association Québécoise des organismes de coopération internationale
Mission: Le CQFD est un regroupement de femmes du milieu des organismes de coopération internationale, du milieu universitaire, syndical et groupes de femmes du Québec. Ses objectifs sont de favoriser la concertation, la réflexion et le partenariat entre groupes de femmes du Nord et du Sud

Comité régional d'éducation pour le développement international de Lanaudière (CRÉDIL)
200, rue de Salaberry, Joliette QC J6E 4G1
Tél: 450-756-0011; *Téléc:* 450-759-8749
info@credil.qc.ca
www.credil.qc.ca
www.facebook.com/credil.joliette
Aperçu: *Dimension:* petite; *Envergure:* locale; Organisme sans but lucratif; fondée en 1976
Mission: Promouvoir l'éducation au développement international dans la région de Lanaudière, la solidarité avec des organisations populaires d'ici et celles d'autres pays pour appuyer les initiatives de partenariat, l'initiation et support d'engagements concrets en appui aux efforts de justice dans le monde; accueil de nouveaux arrivants dans la région de Lanaudière.
Affliation(s): Association québécoise d'organismes de coopération internationale; Emploi Québec
Membre(s) du bureau directeur:
Daniel Tessier, Coordonnateur par intérim
coordination@credil.qc.ca
Finances: *Fonds:* Ministère de l'Immigration et des Communautés culturelles; Ministère des Relations internationales
Membre(s) du personnel: 6
Membre: *Montant de la cotisation:* 10$ individuel; 50$ organisationnel; *Critères d'admissibilité:* Individuel et corporatif
Activités: Journées québécoises de la solidarité internationale; stages de coopération internationale; kiosque de produits équitables; aide aux devoirs; jumelage; logement; *Événements de sensibilisation:* Journées québécoises de la solidarité internationale, nov.; *Stagiaires:* Oui

Comité régional des associations pour la déficience intellectuelle (CRADI)
#100, 5095 - 9e avenue, Montréal QC H1Y 2J3
Tél: 514-255-8111; *Téléc:* 514-255-3444
cradi@cradi.com
www.cradi.com
Aperçu: *Dimension:* petite; *Envergure:* locale
Membre(s) du bureau directeur:
Djamila Benabdelkader, Présidente
Membre: 31

Comité Social Centre-Sud (CSCS)
1710, rue Beaudry, MontréAl QC H2L 3E7
Tél: 514-596-7092; *Téléc:* 514-596-7093
webmestre@comitesocialcentresud.org
www.comitesocialcentresud.org
Aperçu: *Dimension:* petite; *Envergure:* locale; fondée en 1971
Mission: Pour aider les membres de la communauté à faire face aux injustices sociales qu'ils peuvent faire face et leur offrir une éducation dans divers domaines
Membre(s) du bureau directeur:
Loriane Séguin, Directrice générale
cscs.direction@comitesocialcentresud.org
Membre: *Montant de la cotisation:* 5$
Activités: Événements; sorties; cours; atelier de couture

Comité UNICEF Canada *See* UNICEF Canada

Commercial & Press Photographers Association of Canada (CAPPAC) *See* Professional Photographers of Canada 1970 Incorporated

Commercial Seed Analysts Association of Canada Inc. (CSAAC)
#208, 301 Rothesay St., Douglas MB R0K 0K0
Tel: 204-763-4610
csaacexecutivedirector@gmail.com
www.seedanalysts.ca
Overview: A medium-sized national licensing organization founded in 1944
Mission: To help determine the future of the seed industry; to enhance professionalism through ongoing education; to provide customers with seed analysis services & information
Chief Officer(s):
Christine DeRooy, President
cderooy@hylandseeds.com
Betty Girard, Executive Director
csaacexecutivedirector@gmail.com
Membership: 100+; *Fees:* $60-$350; *Committees:* Membership; Research & Review; Historical; Special; Technical; Ethics; Exam; CSI Reps; CSGA Standard & Stock Seed; Nomination; CSAAC By-law Review
Activities: Exams & accreditation
Awards:
• The Marie Greeniaus Award (Award)
Publications:
• Breaking Dormancy [a publication of the Commercial Seed Analysts Association of Canada Inc.]
Type: Newsletter; *Frequency:* Monthly

Commission canadienne d'histoire militaire (CCHM) / Canadian Commission of Military History (CCMH)
Quartier général de la Défense nationale, 101 Colonel By Dr., Ottawa ON K1A 0K2
Téléc: 613-990-8579
Aperçu: *Dimension:* petite; *Envergure:* nationale; fondée en 1973
Mission: La CCHM est une organisation bénévole, ne comptant qu'un Conseil de direction, sans membres, collaborant à la Commission internationale d'histoire militaire (CIHM) du Comité international des Sciences historiques (CISH) de Genève, Suisse; La Commission canadienne cherche à servir de lien entre les historiens militaires canadiens et la communauté internationale des chercheurs et écrivains en histoire militaire; La Commission canadienne travaille aussi à mieux faire connaître l'histoire militaire canadienne au Canada et à l'étranger
Membre de: Comité international des sciences historiques
Affiliation(s): Commission internationale d'histoire militaire
Membre(s) du bureau directeur:
Serge Bernier, Directeur
Finances: *Budget de fonctionnement annuel:* Moins de $50,000
3 bénévole(s)
Membre: 3 organisations regroupant des historiens
Activités: Représentations canadiennes auprès de la Commission internationale pour l'histoire militaire (CIHM); participation à l'organisation du congrès international annuel de la CIHM; liaisons diverses avec les autres commissions nationales participantes de la CIHM; participation à la préparation de la bibliographie international annuelle du Comité de bibliographie de la CIHM; financement d'activités canadiennes dans le domaine de l'histoire militaire

Commission canadienne du lait *See* Canadian Dairy Commission

Commission canadienne pour l'UNESCO *See* Canadian Commission for UNESCO

Commission canadienne pour la théorie des machines et des mécanismes (CCToMM) / Canadian Committee for the Theory of Machines & Mechanisms
Faculté de génie mécanique, Université du Nouveau Brunswick, CP 4400, Fredericton NB E3B 5A3
Tél: 506-458-7454; *Téléc:* 506-453-5025
www.cctomm.mae.carleton.ca
Aperçu: *Dimension:* petite; *Envergure:* nationale; fondée en 1993
Mission: Promouvoir le développement dans le domaine des machines et des mécanismes par la recherche théorique et expérimentale et leurs applications pratiques.
Membre de: International Federation for the Theory of Machines & Mechanisms (IFToMM)
Membre(s) du bureau directeur:
Marc Arsenault, Secrétaire général
marc.arsenault@laurentian.ca
Scott Nokleby, Responsable des communications
scott.nokleby@uoit.ca
Membre: *Montant de la cotisation:* 50$

Commission Coopération Environnementale *See* Commission for Environmental Cooperation

La Commission Crie-Naskapie *See* Cree-Naskapi Commission

Commission culturelle fransaskoise *Voir* Conseil culturel fransaskois

Commission d'enseignement spécial des provinces de l'Atlantique *See* Atlantic Provinces Special Education Authority

Commission de coopération environnementale *See* Commission for Environmental Cooperation

La Commission de la Capitale de l'Ile-du-Prince-Édouard *See* The Capital Commission of Prince Edward Island Inc.

Commission de la Médiathèque Père-Louis-Lamontagne
300 Beaverbrook Rd., Miramichi NB E1V 1A1
Tél: 506-627-4084; *Téléc:* 506-627-4592
mediathequep@gnb.ca
www.mpll.nb.ca
Aperçu: *Dimension:* petite; *Envergure:* locale; Organisme sans but lucratif; fondée en 1986
Mission: Travailler à l'amélioration constante des services offerts par la Médiathèque Père-Louis-Lamontagne
Membre(s) du bureau directeur:
Jeannine Morris, Présidente
Laura Richard, Trésorière
Véronique Deniger, Secrétaire
Finances: *Budget de fonctionnement annuel:* Moins de $50,000
Membre: 7
Activités: *Service de conférenciers:* Oui; *Bibliothèque:* Médiathèque Père-Louis-Lamontagne; Bibliothèque publique

Commission de Ski pour Personnes Handicapées du Québec (CSPHQ)
165 Place Lilas, Pincourt QC J7V 5B6
Tél: 514-425-8894; *Téléc:* 514-425-8894
disabledskiing.ca/?page_id=139
Aperçu: *Dimension:* petite; *Envergure:* provinciale surveillé par Canadian Association for Disabled Skiing
Mission: Promouvoir et pratiquer le ski alpin
Membre de: Ski Québec; Canadian Association for Disabled Skiing
Membre(s) du bureau directeur:
Henry Wohler, President
henry@disabledskiing.ca
Membre: *Critères d'admissibilite:* Adolescent et adulte ayant une déficience physique
Activités: Cours de ski alpin adapté (luge, bi-ski)

Commission des sépultures de guerre du Commonwealth - Agence canadienne *See* Commonwealth War Graves Commission - Canadian Agency

Commission des services financiers de l'Ontario *See* Financial Services Commission of Ontario

Commission des services financiers et des services aux consommateurs *See* Financial & Consumer Services Commission

Commission Électrotechnique Internationale - Comité National du Canada *See* International Electrotechnical Commission - Canadian National Committee

Commission for Environmental Cooperation (CEC) / Commission Coopération Environnementale
Secretariat, #200, 393, rue St-Jacques ouest, Montréal QC H2Y 1N9
Tel: 514-350-4300; *Fax:* 514-350-4314
info@cec.org
www.cec.org
Mission: The Commission for Environmental Cooperation (CEC) is an international organization created by Canada, Mexico & the United States under the North American Agreement on Environmental Cooperation (NAAEC). The CEC was established to address regional environmental concerns, help prevent potential trade & environmental conflicts & to promote the effective enforcement of environmental law. The Agreement complements the environmental provisions of the North American Free Trade Agreement (NAFTA).
Chief Officer(s):
Irasema Coronado, Executive Director
Marco Antonio Heredia Fragoso, Program Manager, Environmental Law, 514-350-4302
maheredia@cec.org
Orlando Cabrera-Rivera, Program Manager, Air Quality & PRTR, 514-350-4323
ocabrera@cec.org
Heidy G. Rivasplata, Project Coordinator, Chemicals Management, 514-350-4378
hrivasplata@cec.org

Commission for Environmental Cooperation (CEC) / Commission de coopération environnementale (CCE)
#200, 393, St-Jacques St. West, Montréal QC H2Y 1N9
Tel: 514-350-4300; *Fax:* 514-350-4314
info@cec.org
www.cec.org
Overview: A medium-sized international organization founded in 1995
Mission: Created by Canada, Mexico & the United States to address regional environmental concerns; to help prevent potential trade & environmental conflicts, & to promote the effective enforcement of environmental law
Chief Officer(s):
Evan Lloyd, Executive Director
Nathalie Daoust, Secretary, 514-350-4310
Finances: *Annual Operating Budget:* Greater than $5 Million; *Funding Sources:* Three NAFTA governments, Canada, Mexico, United States
Staff Member(s): 55
Membership: 1-99
Activities: *Internships:* Yes

Mexico Office
Progreso #3, Viveros de Coyoacán, Mexico DF 04110 Mexico
Tel: 52-555 659 5021; *Fax:* 52-555-659 5023
Chief Officer(s):
Juan Rafael Elvira Quesada

La Commission internationale de juristes (section canadienne) *See* International Commission of Jurists (Canadian Section)

Commission nationale des parents francophones (CNPF)
2445, boul St-Laurent, #B182, Ottawa ON K1G 6C3
Tél: 613-288-0958; *Téléc:* 613-688-1367
Ligne sans frais: 800-665-5148
cnpf@cnpf.ca
cnpf.ca
www.facebook.com/219249894852875
twitter.com/parentsfranco
www.vimeo.com/cnpf
Aperçu: *Dimension:* moyenne; *Envergure:* provinciale; fondée en 1979 surveillé par Fédération des communautés francophones et acadienne du Canada
Mission: Pour soutenir les branches provinciales de l'organisation et les aider à fournir de l'aide aux parents
Affliation(s): Association canadienne d'éducation de langue française; Fédération nationale des conseils scolaires francophones; Ministère du Patrimoine canadien; Ministère de l'Emploi et du Développement social Canada; Commissariat aux langues officielles; Secrétariat aux affaires intergouvernementales canadiennes
Membre(s) du bureau directeur:
Adèle David, Directrice générale
Véronique Legault, Présidente
Membre(s) du personnel: 3
Membre: 12 organisations

Committee of Presidents of Universities of Ontario *See* Council of Ontario Universities

Committee on Canadian Labour History *See* Canadian Committee on Labour History

Committee on Learning Resources (CLR) *See* Colleges Ontario

Commonwealth Association for Public Administration & Management (CAPAM)
#202, 291 Dalhousie St., Ottawa ON K1N 7E5
Tel: 819-956-7961; *Fax:* 613-701-4236
capam@capam.org
www.capam.org
www.linkedin.com/company/commonwealth-association-for-public-administr
www.facebook.com/CAPAMorg
twitter.com/CAPAM_
Overview: A small international organization founded in 1994
Mission: To provide a forum to exchange information, innovations & experiences of public service management; to enhance Commonwealth cooperation, to improve managerial competence & organizational excellence in governance.
Affliation(s): African Association for Public Administration and Management (AAPAM); Arab Urban Development Institute; Association of Management Development Institutions in South Asia (AMDISA); Caribbean Centre for Development Administration (CARICAD); Institute of Public Administration Australia (IPAA); Public Management and Policy Association - United Kingdom (PMPA)
Chief Officer(s):
Ali Hamsa, President
Gay Hamilton, Executive Director & CEO
ghamilton@capam.org
Finances: *Funding Sources:* Membership dues; government agencies internationally
Staff Member(s): 4
Membership: 1,100; *Fees:* US$180 individual; US$3900 institutional; *Member Profile:* Individuals, institutions & professional organizations, representatives of all levels of government, both elected & appointed officials, the academic community & the private sector
Activities: *Library:* Practice Knowledge Centre; by appointment

Commonwealth Association of Museums (CAM)
c/o Catherine C. Cole, 10023 - 93rd St., Edmonton AB T5H 1W6
Tel: 780-424-2229; *Fax:* 780-424-2229
www.maltwood.uvic.ca/cam
Overview: A small international organization founded in 1974
Mission: To improve museums & their societies in the Commonwealth & around the world; To high standards of museum activity throughout the Commonwealth; To create & strengthen links between museums & persons in the museum profession; To involve children & youth in museum development & activities
Chief Officer(s):
Rooksana Omar, President
rooksano@gmail.com
Michael Gondwe, Vice-President
michaelgondwe9@gmail.com
Amareswar Galla, Ph.D, Vice-President
Timothy Mason, International Treasurer
tim.mason@bigfoot.com
Catherine C. Cole, Secretary General
CatherineC.Cole@telus.net
Finances: *Funding Sources:* Membership fees; Commonwealth Foundation
Membership: *Member Profile:* Individuals, associations, & institutions from Commonwealth nations; Associate members from outside the Commonwealth
Activities: Collaborating with Commonwealth governments, non-governmental organizations, & other museum organizations; Offering professional development activities, such as a distance learning program, seminars, & workshops; Disseminating information, such as occasional papers & conference, workshop, & symposia proceedings & reports; Facilitating networking opportunities
Publications:
• Bulletin of the Commonwealth Association of Museums
Frequency: Irregular *ISSN:* 1026-5155; *Price:* Free with membership in the Commonwealth Association of Museums; $20 for 3 issues
Profile: Updates for association members; including recent & forthcoming meetings
• The Commonwealth Association of Museums On-Line International Journal
Type: Journal; *Editor:* L. Irvine; M. Segger; B. Winters
Profile: A compilation of papers presented at conferences & meetings

Commonwealth Forestry Association - Canadian Chapter (CFA)
c/o Prof. Shashi Kant, Faculty of Forestry, University of Toronto, 33 Willcocks St., Toronto ON M5S 3B3
www.cfa-international.org
www.facebook.com/groups/152010068195576/#!/groups/152010068195576
twitter.com/CFAforestry
Overview: A small international organization founded in 1921
Mission: To promote the conservation and sustainable management of the world's forests and the contribution they make to peoples' livelihoods
Member of: Commonwealth Forestry Association, UK
Chief Officer(s):
Shashi Kant, Regional Director, The Americas
shashi.kant@utoronto.ca
Finances: *Annual Operating Budget:* Less than $50,000
1 volunteer(s)
Membership: 60; *Fees:* $108; *Member Profile:* Professional foresters

The Commonwealth Games Association of Canada Inc. *See* Commonwealth Games Canada

Commonwealth Games Canada (CGC) / Jeux du Commonwealth Canada
#120, 2255 St. Laurent Blvd., Ottawa ON K1G 4K3
Tel: 613-244-6868; *Fax:* 613-244-6826
info@commonwealthgames.ca
www.commonwealthgames.ca
www.facebook.com/265526150138420

twitter.com/cgc_jcc
www.youtube.com/user/cgcTVjcc
Previous Name: The Commonwealth Games Association of Canada Inc.
Overview: A small international organization founded in 1977
Affliation(s): Commonwealth Games Federation - London, England
Chief Officer(s):
Brian MacPherson, Chief Executive Officer
brian@commonwealthgames.ca
Kelly Laframboise, Administrative Manager
kelly@commonwealthgames.ca
Finances: *Annual Operating Budget:* $100,000-$250,000
Staff Member(s): 2; 60 volunteer(s)
Membership: 60 individual
Activities: *Internships:* Yes; *Library* Open to public

The Commonwealth of Learning (COL)
#1200, 1055 Hastings St. West, Vancouver BC V6E 2E9
Tel: 604-775-8200; *Fax:* 604-775-8210
info@col.org
www.col.org
www.facebook.com/COL4D
twitter.com/colkm
Overview: A large international organization founded in 1988
Mission: To create & widen access to education & to improve its quality, utilising distance education techniques & associated communications technologies to meet the particular requirements of member countries
Affliation(s): Commonwealth Educational Media Centre for Asia (CEMCA); Commonwealth Secretariat; Commonwealth Foundation; Commonwealth Connects
Chief Officer(s):
John Daniel, President & CEO
Vis Naidoo, Vice-President
Finances: *Annual Operating Budget:* Greater than $5 Million; *Funding Sources:* Voluntary pledges; strategic partnerships
Staff Member(s): 40
Membership: 54 commonwealth governments; *Fees:* Voluntary contributions; *Member Profile:* Commonwealth Member Governments
Activities: Strengthens member countries' capacities to develop the human resources required for their economic & social advancement; activities are carried out in collaboration with governments, relevant agencies, universities & colleges; operations are currently consolidated under four key functions - communications & information technologies; materials, training for distance educators, & information & advisory services; *Awareness Events:* Commonwealth Day, second Monday of March; *Internships:* Yes; *Library:* Information Resource Centre; by appointment

Commonwealth War Graves Commission - Canadian Agency (CWGC) / Commission des sépultures de guerre du Commonwealth - Agence canadienne (CSGC)
#1707, 66 Slater St., Ottawa ON K1A 0P4
Tel: 613-992-3224; *Fax:* 613-995-0431
cwgc-canada@vac-acc.gc.ca
www.cwgc-canadianagency.ca
Overview: A medium-sized international organization founded in 1917
Mission: To ensure Commonwealth War Burials in the Americas (including the Caribbean) are marked & maintained; To ensure maintenance of memorials to the missing; To keep records & registers; To discharge Commission duties for Commonwealth war graves in the Americas (comprising some 3,350 cemeteries & over 20,000 commemorations)
Affliation(s): Commonwealth War Graves Commission
Chief Officer(s):
David Kettle, Canandian Agency Director
Finances: *Funding Sources:* Governments of Canada, Australia, India, New Zealand, South Africa, & United Kingdom
Staff Member(s): 9
Activities: *Speaker Service:* Yes

La communauté bahá'íe du Canada *See* The Bahá'í Community of Canada

La communauté coréenne du grand Montréal *See* Korean Community of Greater Montréal

Communauté de l'Emmanuel *See* Emmanuel Community

Communauté Laotienne du Québec (CLQ) / Lao Community of Québec
#400, 6555, ch de la Côte-des-Neiges, Montréal QC H3S 2A6
Tél: 514-341-1057; *Téléc:* 514-341-8404
information@romel-montreal.ca
www.romel-montreal.ca
Aperçu: *Dimension:* petite; *Envergure:* provinciale; fondée en 1982
Mission: La Communauté Laotienne du Québec est un des organismes fondateurs du Regroupement des organismes du Montréal ethnique pour le logement (ROMEL); ROMEL centralise toute l'information sur l'habitation et informe les membres des communautés culturelles sur les programmes et services en matière d'habitation.
Membre de: Regroupement des organismes du Montréal ethnique pour le logement
Affliation(s): Federation des Associations Lao du Canada
Membre(s) du bureau directeur:
Mazen Houdeib, Directeur général
Membre(s) du personnel: 13
Activités: Donne des services d'interprète et d'accompagnement; information sur l'habitation

La Communauté lithuanienne du Canada *See* The Lithuanian Canadian Community

Communauté musulmane du Québec *See* Muslim Community of Québec

Communauté sépharade unifiée du Québec (CSUQ)
#216, 1, carré Cummings, Montréal QC H3W 1M6
Tél: 514-733-4998; *Téléc:* 514-733-3158
info@csuq.org
www.csuq.org
Également appelé: La Voix sépharade
Nom précédent: Association Sépharade Francophone
Aperçu: *Dimension:* moyenne; *Envergure:* provinciale; Organisme sans but lucratif; fondée en 1966
Mission: Préserver la culture et le patrimoine sépharade; défendre les intérêts de la population sépharade et la représenter auprès des divers paliers gouvernementaux ainsi que d'autres associations communautaires
Membre de: Fédération - CJA
Finances: *Budget de fonctionnement annuel:* $500,000-$1.5 Million
Membre(s) du personnel: 10; 200 bénévole(s)
Membre: 25 000; *Comités:* Administration; Affaires religieuses; Affaires sociales; Éducation et Culture; Financement; Information; Planification communautaire; Relations publiques; Ressources humaines
Activités: La Commission de l'Information, un comité permanent, informe toute la population sépharade des réalisations et projets de la communauté ainsi qu' une information culturelle, religieuse et générale; *Bibliothèque* rendez-vous

Communauté vietnamienne au Canada, région de Montréal
#495, 6655, ch Côte-des-Neiges, Montréal QC H3S 2B4
Tél: 514-340-9630; *Téléc:* 514-340-1926
communaute.viet.montreal@gmail.com
vietnam.ca
Aperçu: *Dimension:* petite; *Envergure:* locale; fondée en 1954
Membre de: Vietnamese Canadian Federation
Membre(s) du bureau directeur:
Lê Minh Thinh, Directeur exécutif
Activités: Immigration et Intégration; Cours et formation;

Communicative Disorders Assistant Association of Canada (CDAAC)
PO Box 55009, 1800 Sheppard Ave. East, Toronto ON M2J 3Z6
Tel: 647-974-6147
info@cdaac.ca
www.cdaac.ca
www.facebook.com/106123889530114
twitter.com/CDAAC
Overview: A small national organization
Mission: To unite members of the profession & protect the character & status of the profession; To maintain & improve the qualifications & standards of the profession; to represent the members in their relationships with other associations, government, colleges, & other national & international organizations; To promote & achieve statutory regulations for members; To provide the public with information regarding our profession & membership; To provide support & share information for the mutual benefit of members
Chief Officer(s):
Brenda Nur
Membership: *Fees:* $60; $25 student; *Member Profile:* Communicative Disorders Assistants
Activities: *Library:* Resource Library

Communion & Liberation Canada
#314, 1857 boul de Maisonneuve ouest, Montréal QC H3H 1J9
Tel: 514-667-5709
clonline.ca
Also Known As: CL Canada
Previous Name: Gioventù Studentesca (Student Youth)
Overview: A small national organization founded in 1954
Mission: To educate to Christian maturity; to collaborate in the mission of the Church in all facets of contemporary life
Chief Officer(s):
Julian Carron, President, Fraternity of CL
Filomena Vecchio-Scandinavo, Contact, 416-746-2015
mena_vecchio@yahoo.ca
Finances: *Funding Sources:* Donations
Membership: *Member Profile:* Male & female adults & children who wish to participate in the ecclesial movement
Activities: Providing a weekly catechesis, known as a School of Community, for adults to meet in order to read, meditate, & discuss; Offering "Little School" meetings for children
Publications:
• Traces
Type: Magazine; *Frequency:* Monthly; *Editor:* Davide Perillo; *Price:* $45
Profile: International magazine of the Movement of Communion & Liberation, with testimonies from around the world, articles on the life of the Church, & cultural, social, & politicaltopics

Communist Party of BC (CPCBC)
706 Clark Dr., Vancouver BC V5L 3J1
Tel: 604-254-9836; *Fax:* 604-254-9803
cpinfo.bc@gmail.com
Overview: A small provincial organization overseen by Communist Party Of Canada
Chief Officer(s):
Samuel Hammond, Party Leader

Communist Party of Canada (CPC) / Parti Communiste du Canada
Central Committee, 290A Danforth Ave., Toronto ON M4K 1N6
Tel: 416-469-2446
info@cpc-pcc.ca
www.communist-party.ca
www.facebook.com/CommunistPartyOfCanada
twitter.com/compartycanada
flickr.com/photos/communist-party-of-canada
Overview: A small national organization founded in 1921
Mission: To establish a socialist society in Canada, in which the principal means of producing & distributing wealth will be the common property of society as a whole.
Chief Officer(s):
Miguel Figueroa, Party Leader
Finances: *Funding Sources:* Membership dues
Membership: *Committees:* Alberta; British Columbia; Saskatchewan; Manitoba; Ontario; Atlantic
Activities: *Library:* CPC Resource Centre
Publications:
• People's Voice
Type: Newspaper; *Frequency:* Monthly

Communist Party of Canada (Alberta) (CPC-A)
PO Box 68112, 70 Bonnie Doon, Edmonton AB T6C 4N6
Tel: 780-465-7893; *Fax:* 780-463-0209
naomirankin@shaw.ca
www.communistparty-alberta.ca
Overview: A small provincial organization overseen by Communist Party Of Canada
Chief Officer(s):
Naomi Rankin, Party Leader

Communist Party of Canada (Manitoba) (CPC-M)
387 Selkirk Ave., Winnipeg MB R2W 2M3
Tel: 204-586-7824
cpc-mb@mts.net
Overview: A small provincial organization overseen by Communist Party Of Canada
Chief Officer(s):
Darrell Rankin, Party Leader

Communist Party of Canada (Marxist-Leninist) (CPC(ML)) / Parti communiste du Canada (marxiste-léniniste)
National Headquarters, 1876, rue Amherst, Montréal QC H2L 3L7
Tel: 514-522-1373; *Fax:* 514-522-1373
Toll-Free: 800-263-4203

office@cpcml.ca
www.cpcml.ca
Also Known As: The Marxist-Leninist Party of Canada
Overview: A small national organization founded in 1970
Mission: The Party holds that the attainment of communism will bring the complete emancipation of the working class. It holds that all people have claims on the society by virtue of being human and that this is the overriding principle of society, along with gender equality and freedom of conscience & lifestyle.
Chief Officer(s):
Anna Di Carlo, Party Leader
Hélène Héroux, Chief Agent

Communist Party of Canada (Ontario) (CPCO)
290A Danforth Ave., Toronto ON M4K 1N6
Tel: 416-469-2446
info@communistpartyontario.ca
www.communistpartyontario.ca
www.facebook.com/RowleyCPCO
Overview: A small provincial organization overseen by Communist Part Of Canada
Chief Officer(s):
Elizabeth Rowley, Party Leader

Communitas Supportive Care Society
#103, 2776 Bourquin Cres. West, Abbotsford BC V2S 6A4
Tel: 604-850-6608; *Fax:* 604-850-2634
Toll-Free: 800-622-5455
office@communitascare.com
www.communitascare.com
www.linkedin.com/company/communitas-supportive-care-society
www.facebook.com/group.php?gid=121270768851
Previous Name: Mennonite Central Committee Supportive Care Services Society
Overview: A small local organization
Mission: Provide various resources to persons living & dealing with mental, physical &/or emotional disabilities.
Member of: Association for Community Living; Community Social Services Employers Association; Psychosocial Rehabilitation Canada; BC Association for Child Development & Intervention; Denominational Health Association; Fraser Valley Brain Injury Association
Affliation(s): Jean Vanier; Henri Nouwen; Copeland Centre for Wellness & Recovery; International Initiative for Mental Health; Living Room; Mental Health Commission of Canada; STEP Enterprises; Mennonite Central Committee (British Columbia & Canada); Mennonite Disaster Service; Ten Thousand Villages
Chief Officer(s):
Steve Thiessen, CEO
Marlyce Friesen, Co-Chair
Henry Wiens, Co-Chair
Finances: *Annual Operating Budget:* Greater than $5 Million
Activities: *Awareness Events:* Curl for Care, Jan.

Communitech
#100, 151 Charles St. West, Kitchener ON N2G 1H6
Tel: 519-888-9944; *Fax:* 519-804-2225
www.communitech.ca
www.linkedin.com/groups/Communitech-2071521
www.facebook.com/communitechpage
twitter.com/communitech
Previous Name: Communitech Technology Association
Overview: A small local organization founded in 1997
Mission: to support technology companies in the Kitchener-Waterloo Region; to promote networking among professionals & a sharing of ideas; to foster the creation of new companies & coaches them through early stages.
Chief Officer(s):
Iain Klugman, President & CEO
iain.klugman@communitech.ca
Staff Member(s): 24
Membership: *Fees:* Schedule available based on number of employees; *Member Profile:* Technology companies; service providers; educational institutions; municipal entities
Activities: Canadian Digital Media Network (CDMN); monthly lunch & breakfast; Annual Spring Conference

Communitech Technology Association *See* Communitech

Community & Family Services of Chatham *See* Family Service Kent

Community & Hospital Infection Control Association Canada / Association pour la prévention des infections à l'hôpital et dans la communauté - Canada
PO Box 46125, Stn. Westdale, Winnipeg MB R3R 3S3
Tel: 204-897-5990; *Fax:* 204-895-9595
Toll-Free: 866-999-7111
Other Communication: Membership e-mail: chicamembership@mts.net
chicacanada@mts.net
www.chica.org
www.facebook.com/179334712101680
twitter.com/CHICACanada
Also Known As: CHICA-Canada
Overview: A medium-sized national charitable organization founded in 1976
Mission: To promote excellence in the practice of infection prevention & control; to employ evidence based practice & application of epidemiological principles to improve the health of Canadians
Member of: International Federation of Infection Control (IFIC)
Chief Officer(s):
Jim Gauthier, President, 613-548-5567 Ext. 5754
gauthij2@providencecare.ca
Staff Member(s): 2; 50 volunteer(s)
Membership: 1,700; *Fees:* $195
Activities: Education; Communication; Standards; Research; Consumer awareness; *Library*
Meetings/Conferences: • CHICA 2015 National Education Conference, June, 2015, Victoria, BC
Scope: National
Publications:
• Canadian Journal of Infection Control
Type: Journal; *Frequency:* Quarterly; *Editor:* Pat Piaskowski, RN, HBScN, CIC; *Price:* Free with CHICA-Canada membership
Profile: Information relevant to the practice of infection control in hospitals & communities
• Community & Hospital Infection Control Association Canada Annual Member & Source Guide
Type: Yearbook; *Frequency:* Annually; *Price:* Free with CHICA-Canada membership

Community Action Resource Centre (CARC)
1652 Keele St., Toronto ON M6M 3W3
Tel: 416-652-2273; *Fax:* 416-652-8992
www.communityarc.ca
www.facebook.com/CommunityActionResourceCentre
twitter.com/communityarc
Merged from: Connect Information Post; Community Information Centre For The City Of York
Overview: A medium-sized local charitable organization founded in 2004
Mission: To build the capacity of communities by mobilizing resources & providing supportive social services, for the empowerment of individuals & groups with a focus on serving the most vulnerable and disadvantaged.
Finances: *Funding Sources:* Government, United Way, Donations
Membership: *Fees:* Free

Community Action Resource Centre (CARC)
1652 Keele St., Toronto ON M6M 3W3
Tel: 416-652-2273; *Fax:* 416-652-8992
www.communityarc.ca
www.facebook.com/CommunityActionResourceCentre
twitter.com/communityarc
Merged from: Community Information Centre for the City of York & Connect Information Post
Overview: A small local charitable organization founded in 2004 overseen by InformOntario
Mission: Mobilizing resources and providing supportive social services for the empowerment of individuals and groups.
Finances: *Funding Sources:* Provincial governemt; United Way Toronto; Industry Canada
Activities: Clothing bank; individual & family support; voicemail; income tax clinics; access to computers

Community AIDS Treatment Information Exchange *See* Canadian AIDS Treatment Information Exchange

Community Arts Council of Fort St. James
PO Box 846, Fort St James BC V0J 1P0
Tel: 250-996-8233
www.facebook.com/FortArts
Overview: A small local organization
Mission: To bring amateur theatre & film to the Fort St. James community
Member of: Assembly of BC Arts Councils
Finances: *Funding Sources:* Municipal & provincial government

Community Arts Council of Greater Victoria (CACGV)
3220 Cedar Hil Rd., Victoria BC V8P 3Y3
Tel: 250-475-7123
info@cacgv.ca
www.cacgv.ca
www.facebook.com/145619592158880
twitter.com/CACGV
Overview: A small local charitable organization founded in 1965
Mission: To promote public awareness of & opportunities in arts & culture activities; to ensure that the arts remain a priority in government budget planning.
Member of: BC Assembly of Arts Councils
Chief Officer(s):
Judy Moore, President
Finances: *Annual Operating Budget:* $100,000-$250,000; *Funding Sources:* Provincial & CRD government; donations; BCAC
150 volunteer(s)
Membership: *Fees:* $10 student; $30 individual; $150 patron; *Member Profile:* Individuals & groups; artists of all disciplines; instructors; *Committees:* Nomination; Performance; Visual Arts; Literary
Activities: Resource & Information Centre; Members Art Gallery; arts in education; community development; group grants; *Internships:* Yes; *Library:* CACGV Resource Centre; Open to public
Awards:
• Michael Blake Watercolour Award (Award)
• Erika Kurth Scholarship/Bursary Award (Scholarship)

Community Arts Council of Prince George & District
2820 - 15 Ave., Prince George BC V2M 1T1
Tel: 250-562-6935; *Fax:* 250-562-0436
info@studio2880.com
www.studio2880.com
Also Known As: Studio 2880 Arts Center
Overview: A small local organization founded in 1969
Mission: To support, encourage & promote all arts in Prince George and District, providing a creative climate to nurture artistic talent.
Member of: Assembly of BC Arts Councils; Prince George Chamber of Commerce; CIRAC; Canadian Conference of the Arts
Chief Officer(s):
Wendy Young, Executive Director
executive@studio2880.com
Staff Member(s): 9
Membership: 180 individual + 57 member groups; *Fees:* $20 individual; $50 guild or club; *Member Profile:* Arts groups & artistic individuals
Activities: Studio Fair; Arts Gallery of Honour; Spring Arts Bazaar; Try Us Out Festival; Summer Day Camp of the Arts
Awards:
• Scholarship Fund (Scholarship)
Eligibility: Local high school students interested in visual, performing or literary arts *Amount:* $500

Community Arts Council of Richmond (CACR)
PO Box 36546, Stn. Seafair, Richmond BC V7C 5M4
e-mail: richmondartscouncil@gmail.com
www.richmondartscouncil.org
www.facebook.com/227503713954030
twitter.com/RichmondBCArts
Overview: A medium-sized local charitable organization founded in 1970
Mission: To promote the arts & artisans in Richmond, British Columbia; To advocate for the arts & artists; To support emerging & disabled artists
Affliation(s): Arts BC; Alliance for Arts; BC Arts Council; Richmond Chamber of COmmerce; Heritage Canada
Chief Officer(s):
Natasha Lozovsky-Burns, President
Klaas Focker, Vice-President
Lee Beaudry, Secretary
Margaret Stephens, Treasurer & Administrator
Finances: *Funding Sources:* Donations; Fundraising
Membership: 29; *Fees:* $10 associate; $15 student; $20 supprting; $35 participating artists; $100 group; $100 individual lifetime; $500 group lifetime; *Member Profile:* Artists from the Richmond, British Columbia area, such as painters, jewellers, sculptors, musicians, potters, wood turners, weavers; Supporting members, such as non-artists who support the work of the council
Activities: Operating the Artisans' Galleria & gift shop in Steveston, British Columbia; Presenting art exhibitions, such as

the annual Indian Summer Art Show; Offering grants; Providing publicity for members; Assisting members with the sale of their work; Working with other non-profit community groups
Publications:
• Community Arts Council of Richmond Newsletter
Type: Newsletter
Profile: Information about forthcoming exhibitions & events
• Community Arts Council of Richmond Member Directory
Type: Directory
Profile: Listings of artists & their artistic medium

Community Arts Council of T'Lagunna ***See*** Maple Ridge Pitt Meadows Arts Council

Community Arts Council of the Alberni Valley
3061 - 8 Ave., Port Alberni BC V9Y 2K5
Tel: 250-724-3412
communityarts@shawcable.com
www.portalberniarts.com
www.facebook.com/CommunityArtsCouncilOfTheAlberniValley
Also Known As: Rollin Art Centre
Overview: A small local charitable organization
Mission: To enrich life in the community through the promotion of arts, with a focus on collecting, protecting, conserving & presenting work by local artists.
Member of: Assembly of BC Arts Councils
Finances: *Funding Sources:* Civic; provincial grants; gallery & gift shop sales; box office; fundraising
Activities: Public gardens; visual arts gallery & programs; performing arts series; special events; art programs & classes

Community Association for Riding for the Disabled (CARD)
4777 Dufferin St., Toronto ON M3H 5T3
Tel: 416-667-8600; *Fax:* 416-739-7520
info@card.ca
www.card.ca
Overview: A medium-sized local charitable organization founded in 1969
Mission: To improve the lives of children & adults with disabilities through quality therapeutic riding programs
Member of: Canadian Therapeutic Riding Association
Affliation(s): Ontario Therapeutic Riding Association
Chief Officer(s):
Penny Smith, Executive Director
Penny@card.ca
Finances: *Funding Sources:* Government; fundraising; special events; corporate donations; private donations
Staff Member(s): 9; 350 volunteer(s)
Membership: 600; *Fees:* $25
Activities: Summer program; Ride-a-thon; dinner; auction

Community Care Belleville ***See*** Community Care for South Hastings

Community Care for South Hastings
55 South Pinnacle St., Belleville ON K8N 3A1
Tel: 613-969-0130; *Fax:* 613-969-1719
ccsh@ccsh.ca
www.ccsh.ca
Previous Name: Community Care Belleville
Overview: A small local charitable organization founded in 1980
Mission: To provide programs & services that assist clients to remain in their own homes for as long as possible.
Member of: Ontario Community Support Association; SEO Community Support Services Network
Affliation(s): Pensioners Concerned
Finances: *Funding Sources:* United Way Quinte; Donations; Local Health Integration Network, Parrot Foundation
Membership: *Fees:* $5
Activities: Meals On Wheels (hot and frozen); Escorted Transportation; House Care; Crisis Intervention & Support; Reassurance and Safety, Congregate Dining, Therapeutic Activity, Service Arrangement and Coordination, 55 Alive Drive Refresher, Footcare; *Speaker Service:* Yes

Deseronto Office
331 Edmon St., Deseronto ON
Tel: 613-396-6591; *Fax:* 613-396-6592

Community Care Peterborough
#2, 180 Barnardo Ave., Peterborough ON K9H 5V3
Tel: 705-742-7067; *Fax:* 705-745-6011; *TTY:* 705-742-2075
centofc@commcareptbo.org
www.commcareptbo.org
Overview: A small local charitable organization founded in 1984 overseen by InformOntario
Mission: The association is a network of community offices that provides essential services to seniors & disabled, so they may remain living at home. It is a non-profit, registered charity, BN: 136680865RR0001.
Member of: United Way
Chief Officer(s):
Jim Patterson, President
Danielle Belair, Executive Director
Finances: *Funding Sources:* Provincial; foundations; private donations
Activities: Caremobile; Meals on Wheels; Diner's Club; reassurance phone calls; arranging brokered workers for home maintenance; *Awareness Events:* Kilometres for Care, Apr.; Half-Marathon, Nov.; *Rents Mailing List:* Yes
Publications:
• The Thread
Type: Newsletter

Apsley Office
PO Box 303, 168 Burleigh St., Apsley ON K0L 1A0
Tel: 705-656-4589; *Fax:* 705-656-2542
apsley@commcareptbo.org
Chief Officer(s):
Peggy Downey, Coordinator

Chemung Office
549 Ennis Rd., Ennismore ON K0L 1T0
Tel: 705-292-8708; *Fax:* 705-292-8750
chemung@commcareptbo.org
Chief Officer(s):
Denise Gould, Coordinator

Harvey Office
PO Box 12, 1937 Lakehurst Rd., Buckhorn ON K0L 1J0
Tel: 705-657-2171; *Fax:* 705-657-3457
harvofc@commcareptbo.org
Chief Officer(s):
Lynda McKerr, Coordinator

Havelock Office
107 Concessiojn St. North, Havelock ON K0L 1Z0
Tel: 705-778-7831; *Fax:* 705-778-7924
havelock@commcareptbo.org
Chief Officer(s):
Tammy Ross, Coordinator

Lakefield Office
PO Box 001, 40 Rabbit St., Lakefield ON K0L 2H0
Tel: 705-652-8655; *Fax:* 705-652-7332
lakfield@commcareptbo.org
Chief Officer(s):
Lorri Rork, Coordinator

Millbrook Office
PO Box 257, 22 King St. East, Millbrook ON L0A 1G0
Tel: 705-932-2011; *Fax:* 705-932-4058
millofc@commcareptbo.org
Chief Officer(s):
Karen Morton, Coordinator

Norwood Office
PO Box 436, 2368 King St. East, Norwood ON K0L 2V0
Tel: 705-639-5631; *Fax:* 705-639-2511
norwood@commcareptbo.org
Chief Officer(s):
Kelly Small, Coordinator

Community Connection (CDIC)
PO Box 683, 275 First St., Collingwood ON L9Y 4E8
Tel: 705-444-0040; *Fax:* 705-445-1516
info@communityconnection.ca
www.communityconnection.ca
twitter.com/211CentralEast
Also Known As: Collingwood & District Information Centre
Overview: A medium-sized local charitable organization founded in 1969 overseen by InformOntario
Mission: To offer free & confidential information & referral services to anyone needing help
Member of: InformCanada; Alliance of Information & Referral Systems
Affliation(s): United Way
Chief Officer(s):
Donald Wright, Chair
Pamela Hillier, Executive Director
Finances: *Annual Operating Budget:* $500,000-$1.5 Million; *Funding Sources:* Municipal government; United Way; fundraising
Staff Member(s): 8; 3 volunteer(s)
Membership: 22; *Fees:* $25
Activities: Free legal advice clinic; *Rents Mailing List:* Yes
Awards:
• ACICO Accreditation (Award)

Community Counselling & Resource Centre (CCRC)
540 George St. North, Peterborough ON K9H 3S2
Tel: 705-743-2272; *Fax:* 705-742-3015
ccrc@ccrc-ptbo.com
www.ccrc-ptbo.com
www.facebook.com/CCRC.Peterborough
twitter.com/CCRC_Ptbo
Overview: A small local charitable organization overseen by Ontario Association of Credit Counselling Services
Mission: To provide professional & confidential counselling, support, & resources related to financial management in Peterborough, Haliburton, Kawartha Lakes, & Northumberland Counties in Ontario
Member of: Ontario Association of Credit Counselling Services; United Way of Peterborough & District
Affliation(s): Family Services Canada
Chief Officer(s):
Mike Burger, President
Finances: *Funding Sources:* Donations
Activities: Offering money management, budgeting, debt, & bankruptcy counselling; Establishing community partnerships; Providing preventative education; Offering debt repayment programs

Community Counselling Centre of Nipissing / Centre communautaire de counselling du Nipissing
361 McIntyre St. East, North Bay ON P1B 1C9
Tel: 705-472-6515; *Fax:* 705-472-4582
www.cccnip.com
Previous Name: Family Life Centre
Overview: A small local charitable organization founded in 1972 overseen by Ontario Association of Credit Counselling Services
Mission: To provide professional community & credit counselling services, plus developmental, addiction, & sexual assault services, to individuals, couples, & families in North Bay & the surrounding community
Member of: Ontario Association of Credit Counselling Services
Chief Officer(s):
Alan McQuarrie, Executive Director
amcquarrie@cccnip.com
Finances: *Funding Sources:* Donations
Activities: Arranging groups such as The Overcoming Abuse Group, The Women's Assertiveness Group, & the Dawn Youth Group for youth experiencing problems related to the use of substances; Offering employee & family assistance programs; Providing education to the public; Offering consulting services to community organizations & industries;

Community Development Council Durham (CDCD)
#4, 458 Fairall St., Ajax ON L1S 1R6
Tel: 905-686-2661; *Fax:* 905-686-4157
info@cdcd.org
www.cdcd.org
Previous Name: Social Development Council Ajax-Pickering; Ajax/Pickering Social Development Council
Overview: A small local charitable organization founded in 1970
Mission: To create, to advocate & to support policies, attitudes & actions which enhance individual, family & community growth
Member of: Social Planning Network of Ontario; Canadian Council of Social Development
Chief Officer(s):
Pinder Da Silva, President
Finances: *Annual Operating Budget:* $250,000-$500,000; *Funding Sources:* United Way; Region of Durham; Federal government
Staff Member(s): 11; 100 volunteer(s)
Membership: 100+; *Fees:* $15 student/senior; $25 individual; $50 non-profit; $75 corporate
Activities: Social research; community planning; information centre; rent bank; housing; immigration & settlement services; breakfast program; annual meeting, April

Community Development Council of Belleville & District ***See*** Community Development Council of Quinte

Community Development Council of Quinte
65 Station St., Belleville ON K8N 2S6
Tel: 613-968-2466; *Fax:* 613-968-2251
www.cdcquinte.co
www.facebook.com/214450471935888
twitter.com/cdcquinte
Also Known As: CDC Quinte
Previous Name: Community Development Council of Belleville & District
Overview: A small local charitable organization founded in 1989
Mission: To promote the planning & provision of health & social services to ensure area residents are provided with the

necessities of life & an opportunity to improve their quality of living.
Member of: Social Planning Network of Ontario
Chief Officer(s):
Ruth Ingersoll, Executive Director
Activities: Task Force on Hunger; Hungry for Action; Anti-Poverty Research Projects; Good Food Box Program; Good Lunch Box Program; Collective Kitchens; Planting Seeds for Change; Second Helping; NEXUS; Non-Dinner Dinner; Quality of Life Index Project; Healthy Community Week; How to Start Your Own Food Co-op; *Speaker Service:* Yes; *Library* Open to public

Community Development Halton (CDH)
860 Harrington Ct., Burlington ON L7N 3N4
Tel: 905-632-1975; *Fax:* 905-632-0778
Toll-Free: 855-395-8807
office@cdhalton.ca
www.cdhalton.ca
www.facebook.com/ComDevHalton
twitter.com/ComDevHalton
www.youtube.com/user/cdhweb
Previous Name: Halton Social Planning Council & Volunteer Centre
Overview: A small local charitable organization founded in 1970
Mission: To improve the quality of life for community residents, focusing on research, community planning & promotion of volunteerism.
Member of: Community Information Online Consortium (CIOC); Ontario Volunteer Centre Network
Chief Officer(s):
John Searles, President
Joey Edwardh, Executive Director
Finances: *Annual Operating Budget:* $500,000-$1.5 Million; *Funding Sources:* United Ways of Burlington, Greater Hamilton & Oakville; Ontario Trillium Foundation; Municipal government
Staff Member(s): 10
Membership: *Fees:* $5 unemployed; $25 adult; $50 small organization; $100 medium organization; $150 large organization
Activities: Workshops, seminars;

Community Economic Development Institute
Cape Breton University, PO Box 5300, Sydney NS B1P 6L2
Tel: 902-539-5300; *Fax:* 902-562-0119
Toll-Free: 888-959-9995
ced@capebretonu.ca
Overview: A small local organization founded in 1995
Mission: To promote general economic improvement on Cape Breton Island; to enhance capacity of community organizations, which can serve as models for other communities throughout Canada
Member of: National Congress for Community Economic Development
Chief Officer(s):
George Karaphillis, Contact
george_karaphillis@cbu.ca
Activities: *Speaker Service:* Yes; *Library* Open to public

Community Energy Association (CEA)
#1400, 333 Seymour St., Vancouver BC V6B 5A6
Tel: 604-628-7076; *Fax:* 778-786-1613
info@communityenergy.bc.ca
www.communityenergy.bc.ca
Overview: A medium-sized provincial charitable organization founded in 1993
Mission: To support local governments in British Columbia in energy conservation & climate change activities
Chief Officer(s):
Dale Littlejohn, Executive Director, 604-628-7076
dlittlejohn@communityenergy.bc.ca
Patricia Bell, Senior Community Energy Planner, 604-936-0470
pbell@communityenergy.bc.ca
Megan Lohmann, Senior Energy Planner, 250-423-7212
Finances: *Funding Sources:* Membership revenues; Fundraising
Activities: Communicating with elected officials, municipal & regional district staff, & First Nations in British Columbia; Offering advisory services to local governments regarding energy innovations; Promoting energy efficiency & renewable energy for infrastructure; Encouraging local governments to consider energy in land planning & development; Conducting research on energy related topics; *Speaker Service:* Yes
Publications:
• Community Energy Association Directory
Type: Directory
Profile: Listings of association members
• Energy Brief for Elected Officials
Type: Guide
Profile: Information for local government leaders
• Heating Our Communities
Type: Guide
Profile: A renewable energy guide produced for local government leaders

Community Enhancement & Economic Development Society (CEEDS)
6810 Horse Lake Rd., Lone Butte BC V0K 1X3
Tel: 250-395-3580
ceeds@bcinternet.net
www.horselakefarmcoop.ca/ceeds
Overview: A small local organization founded in 1971
Mission: To promote small scale organic farming & to provide food, fuel & shelter to the memebers of the group
Member of: International WWOOF Association
Activities: Organic farming; animal husbandry; bee-keeping; *Speaker Service:* Yes

Community Enhancement Association
105B Walker St., Truro NS B2N 4B1
Tel: 902-893-1911; *Fax:* 902-893-4474
Overview: A small local organization
Mission: The Association acts as a vehicle for continuing cultivation & development of the African Nova Scotian community of Colchester County.
Finances: *Funding Sources:* federal government
Activities: Training youth for employment

Community Financial Counselling Services (CFCS)
#516, 238 Portage Ave., Winnipeg MB R3C 0B9
Tel: 204-989-1900; *Fax:* 204-989-1908
Toll-Free: 888-573-2383
www.debthelpmanitoba.com
www.facebook.com/204965096269852
twitter.com/debthelpmb
Previous Name: Credit Counselling Canada - Manitoba
Overview: A small provincial charitable organization founded in 1974
Mission: To offer respectful & effective debt management services to vulnerable & high risk populations, in Manitoba, for no cost or minimal cost
Member of: Credit Counselling Canada; United Way of Winnipeg
Chief Officer(s):
John Silver, Executive Director
Finances: *Funding Sources:* United Way; Department of Finance, Province of Manitoba; Manitoba Lotteries Commission; Private donations
Activities: Providing financial counselling; Assisting persons to develop decision-making skills & self-management abilities; Offering community education & information to increase knowledge of financial counselling; Collaborating with other helpful organizations, such as The Workers Compensation Board, to offer an itegrated service; Offering the Gambling Project, funded by the Manitoba Lotteries Corporation, in partnership with the Addictions Foundation of Manitoba; Providing income tax preparation for social assistance recipients

Community Folk Art Council of Metro Toronto (CFAC)
173B Front St. East, Toronto ON M5A 3Z4
Tel: 416-368-8743; *Fax:* 416-368-4345
cfac.toronto@sympatico.ca
www.cfactoronto.com
Overview: A medium-sized local organization founded in 1968
Mission: To promote the preservation, development & advancement of the cultural & artistic heritage of the peoples of Canada, especially within Metro Toronto
Member of: Folklore Canada International
Chief Officer(s):
Wendy Limbertie, Executive Director
Finances: *Annual Operating Budget:* $50,000-$100,000
Staff Member(s): 1
Membership: 300 groups; *Fees:* $50 individual; $100 group; *Member Profile:* Arts groups & individuals preserving & promoting heritage & traditions

Community Food Sharing Association
PO Box 6291, 21 Mews Pl., St. John's NL A1C 6J9
Tel: 709-722-0130
cfsa.nf.net
Previous Name: City Index Referral Association
Overview: A small local organization
Mission: To act as a central collection & distribution point for member agencies throughout the province, with a goal to eliminate chronic hunger & alleviate poverty.
Member of: Newfoundland & Labrador Association of Food Distribution & Voluntary Action; Atlantic Alliance of Food Banks & C.V.A.'s; Food Banks Canada
Chief Officer(s):
Wanda Drodge, Chair

Community Foundation for Greater Toronto *See* Toronto Community Foundation

Community Foundation for Kingston & Area (CFGK)
165 Ontario St., Kingston ON K7L 2Y6
Tel: 613-546-9696; *Fax:* 613-531-9238
www.cfka.org
www.linkedin.com/company/community-foundation-for-kingston-&-area
twitter.com/CFKingstonArea
www.youtube.com/user/cfkaed
Previous Name: The Martello Tower Society
Overview: A small local organization founded in 1995
Mission: To raise funds for enhancing the quality of life of the community
Member of: Community Foundations of Canada
Chief Officer(s):
Greg Fisher, President
Vikram Varma, Executive Director
vikram@cfka.org
Finances: *Annual Operating Budget:* $100,000-$250,000; *Funding Sources:* Donations; corporations; grants
Staff Member(s): 3; 60 volunteer(s)
Membership: *Committees:* Strategic Planning; Marketing & Communications; Investment; Finance; Grants; Nominating; Fund Development; Special Celebrations; Ripples Editorial Board; Youth Advisory
Activities: Grant making
Awards:
• The Community Foundation for Kingston & Area Grant (Grant)

The Community Foundation of Durham Region
PO Box 322, 701 Rossland Rd. East, Whitby ON L1N 9K3
Tel: 905-430-6507
info@durhamcommunityfoundation.ca
www.durhamcommunityfoundation.ca
ca.linkedin.com/in/durhamcf
www.facebook.com/Durhamcf
Overview: A small local charitable organization founded in 1995
Mission: To provide & administer charitable capital endowment funds & donations for the benefit of the citizens of the region
Member of: Community Foundations of Canada
Chief Officer(s):
Vivian Curl, Executive Director
vivian@durhamcommunityfoundation.ca
Finances: *Annual Operating Budget:* $250,000-$500,000; *Funding Sources:* Donations
Staff Member(s): 1
Membership: *Committees:* Asset Development; Odyssey Ball; Grants; Hole in Won Golf; Investment; Marketing

Community Foundation of Greater Québec *Voir* Fondation communautaire du Grand-Québec

Community Foundation of Lethbridge & Southwestern Alberta
404 - 8 St. South, Lethbridge AB T1J 2J7
Tel: 403-328-5297; *Fax:* 403-328-6061
office@cflsa.ca
cflsa.ca
www.facebook.com/cflsa
twitter.com/LethFoundation
Overview: A small local charitable organization founded in 1966
Mission: To receive & administer donations in trust for charitable, educational & cultural purposes
Member of: Community Foundations of Canada
Chief Officer(s):
George Hall, Executive Director
ghall@cflsa.ca
Staff Member(s): 2
Membership: *Committees:* Executive; Development; Audit; Governance; Grants; Investment; Nomination; Vital Signs

Community Foundation of Ottawa (CFO) / Fondation communautaire d'Ottawa
#301, 75 Albert St., Ottawa ON K1P 5E7

Tel: 613-236-1616; *Fax:* 613-236-1621
info@cfo-fco.ca
communityfoundationottawa.ca
www.facebook.com/229469483746057
twitter.com/Ottawa_Gives
www.youtube.com/user/cfottawagives
Previous Name: Community Foundation of Ottawa-Carleton
Overview: A small national charitable organization founded in 1987
Mission: To accumulate funds from bequests, endowments, memorials & other charitable gifts to be held in trust in order to generate income, which in turn is used for a range of charitable interests & needs; to give grants to not-for-profit organizations in all sectors that are recognized as registered charities.
Affliation(s): Community Foundations of Canada; Council on Foundations - USA
Chief Officer(s):
Brian Toller, Chair
Marco Pagani, President & CEO
Finances: *Annual Operating Budget:* $250,000-$500,000; *Funding Sources:* United Way; donors
Staff Member(s): 13
Membership: *Committees:* Grants; Nominating; Inventestment; Governance; Finance & Audit; Impact Investing
Activities: Annual celebration; *Internships:* Yes; *Speaker Service:* Yes

Community Foundation of Ottawa-Carleton *See* Community Foundation of Ottawa

Community Futures Development Association of British Columbia

#C230, 7871 Stave Lake St., Mission BC V2V 0C5
Tel: 604-289-4222
www.communityfutures.ca
www.linkedin.com/company/community-futures-british-columbia
www.facebook.com/CommunityFuturesBC
twitter.com/Comm_FuturesBC
plus.google.com/+communityfutures
Also Known As: Community Futures British Columbia
Overview: A medium-sized provincial organization founded in 1992
Mission: To coordinate community economic development initiatives in British Columbia; To encourage economic diversification in rural communities; To improve economic conditions in British Columbia; To promote long-term community economic sustainability; To enhance regional competitiveness
Chief Officer(s):
Wendy Smitka, Chair
Marie Gallant, Executive Director
mgallant@communityfutures.ca
Garry Angus, Provincial Coordinator, Entrepreneurs with Disabilities Program (EDP)
gangus@communityfutures.ca
Vanessa Tveitane, Administrator, Communications & Office
vtveitane@communityfutures.ca
Membership: 34 organizations; *Fees:* $1,000 active members; *Member Profile:* Community Futures offices throughout British Columbia, such as Community Futures Central Kootenay, Community Futures North Okanagan, & Community Futures Sunshine Coast
Activities: Supporting community economic development strategies; Engaging in advocacy activities; Providing resources on topics such as starting a business, financing a business, & accessing government programs & services; Funding projects submitted by affiliated Community Futures locations, as part of the Rural Economic Diversification Initiative of British Columbia project, which is a joint initiative between Community Futures British Columbia & the Western Economic Diversification Canada

Community Futures Manitoba Inc. (CFM)

#559, 167 Lombard Ave., Winnipeg MB R3B 0V3
Tel: 204-943-2905; *Fax:* 204-956-9363
info@cfmanitoba.ca
www.cfmanitoba.ca
www.facebook.com/pages/Community-Futures-Manitoba/127795190636750
Overview: A medium-sized provincial organization
Mission: To strengthen rural economies in Manitoba; To promote the rural & northern region of Manitoba & its economic opportunities
Affliation(s): Western Economic Diversification Canada
Chief Officer(s):
Jason Denbow, Executive Director
jdenbow@cfmanitoba.ca
Susan Bater, Coordinator, Entrepreneurs with Disabilities Program, Rural & Northern Manitob
edpinfo@mts.net
Janet Charron, Coordinator, Aboriginal Business Service Network
jcharron@cfmanitoba.ca
Christine Landry, Coordinator, Projects
Finances: *Funding Sources:* Government of Canada, through Western Economic Diversification Canada
Membership: 16 Community Future organizations; *Member Profile:* Community Future organizations throughout rural & northern Manitoba
Activities: Assisting in community economic development, through the development of long-term plans; Enabling entrepreneurship across rural & northern Manitoba; Providing business counselling, training, & resources; Offering access to business loans;
Meetings/Conferences: • 19th Annual Vision Quest Conference & Trade Show 2015, May, 2015, RBC Covention Centre, Winnipeg, MB
Scope: Provincial
Attendance: 1,000+
Description: An annual event for business leaders, innovators, & entrepreneurs, from Manitoba, Saskatchewan, Alberta, northern Ontario, Nunavut, Northwest Territories, & the United States, to discuss & promote Aboriginal business & community development, featuring interactive workshops, motivational keynote presentations from business leaders, a trade show with more than 80 booths, & social & networking events
Contact Information: Vision Quest Conferences Inc., Phone: 204-942-5049, Toll-Free Phone: 1-800-557-8242; URL: www.vqconference.com
• Community Futures Manitoba Inc. 2015 Annual Provincial Conference, 2015, MB
Scope: Provincial
Attendance: 150
Description: A yearly event to explore economic development issues in Manitoba, featuring keynote addresses
Contact Information: E-mail: info@cfmanitoba.ca
Publications:
• Community Futures Manitoba Inc. Annual Report
Type: Yearbook; *Frequency:* Annually
Profile: An overview of the organization's activities, plus goals & strategies
• Futurescape [a publication of Community Futures Manitoba]
Type: Newsletter
Profile: Updates on ways the Community Futures Program assists rural Manitobans to diversify & grow their communities

Community Futures Network Society of Alberta (CFNA)

Bldg. B, PO Box 184, #3209, 101 Sunset Dr., Cochrane AB T4C 0B4
Tel: 403-851-9995; *Fax:* 403-851-9905
Toll-Free: 877-482-3672
cfna.albertacf.com
Overview: A medium-sized provincial organization
Mission: To work towards an economically strong & diversified rural Alberta; To support Community Futures organizations throughout rural Alberta; To facilitate the sustainability of the Community Futures program
Chief Officer(s):
Shane Stewart, Chair
Jon Close, Executive Director, 403-851-9995 Ext. 2
Judy McMillan-Evans, Manager, Projects & Capacity Building
Finances: *Funding Sources:* Western Economic Diversification Canada
Membership: 27 organizations; *Member Profile:* Alberta Community Futures organizations
Activities: Supporting the delivery of Community Futures initiatives; Developing & implementing community-based economic development & diversification strategies; Offering small business loans; Delivering the Self Employment Program; Providing the Entrepreneurs with Disabilities Program

Community Futures Saskatchewan

c/o Vickie Newmeyer, PO Box 2167, 125 - 1st Ave. East, Kindersley SK S0L 1S0
Tel: 306-463-1850; *Fax:* 306-463-1855
Toll-Free: 888-919-3800
cfsask.ca
www.facebook.com/cfsask
twitter.com/cfsaskatoon
Overview: A small provincial organization founded in 1985
Mission: To work as a grassroots economic renewal initiative, through local entrepreneur development & community & social economic development in rural & northern Saskatchewan; To support & guide persons who are interested in setting up a small business
Chief Officer(s):
Lori Ries, Chair
Jason Denbow, Executive Director
Finances: *Funding Sources:* Western Economic Diversification Canada
Membership: *Member Profile:* Local Community Futures Development Corporations in Saskatchewan
Activities: Assisting persons in Saskatchewan who wish to establish or expand a small business; Providing business skills training; Offering business loans; Delivering the Entrepreneurs with Disabilities program;
Publications:
• I Am an Entrepreneur
Type: Workbook; *Number of Pages:* 98
Profile: A self assessment guide about starting a business

Community Futures West Yellowhead

221 Pembina Ave., Hinton AB T7E 2B3
Tel: 780-865-1224
Toll-Free: 800-263-1716
www.cfwestyellowhead.com
Overview: A small local organization
Mission: To diversify the economy of the West Yellowhead region through entrepreneurship & community development
Chief Officer(s):
Johannes Zwart, Chair
Nancy Robbins, General Manager
Finances: *Funding Sources:* Federal government
Activities: Business training & development; business loans

Community Futures Wild Rose

PO Box 2159, #101, 331 - 3 Ave., Strathmore AB T1P 1K2
Tel: 403-934-8888; *Fax:* 403-934-6492
Toll-Free: 888-881-9675
wildrose.albertacf.com
Previous Name: Wild Rose Economic Development Corporation
Overview: A small local organization founded in 1929
Mission: To maintain, improve & expand existing businesses & to attract new ones to Three Hills
Affliation(s): Economic Development Association of Alberta
Chief Officer(s):
Alice Booth, Chair
Ron Cox, General Manager
Finances: *Funding Sources:* Regional Government
8 volunteer(s)
Membership: 1-99

Community Health Nurses of Canada (CHNC) / Infirmières et infirmiers en santé communautaire au Canada

182 Clendenan Ave., Toronto ON M6P 2X2
Tel: 647-239-9554; *Fax:* 416-426-7280
info@chnc.ca
www.chnc.ca
Overview: A medium-sized national organization founded in 1987
Mission: To act as the voice of community health nurses across Canada; To respond to issues which affect community health nurses
Member of: Canadian Nurses Association (CNA)
Affliation(s): Registered Nurses Association Community Health Nurses Initiatives Group
Chief Officer(s):
Kate Thompson, President
kate_chnc@rogers.com
Evelyn Butler, Administrative Manager
evelyn.cbutler@gmail.com
Ruth Schofield, Secretary
schofir@mcmaster.ca
Anne Clarotto, Treasurer
anne.clarotto@interiorhealth.ca
Yvette Laforet-Fliesser, Officer, Communications
yvette.laforetfliesser@mlhu.on.ca
Membership: *Member Profile:* Community health nurses throughout Canada; Provincial & territorial community health nursing interest groups; *Committees:* Bylaws, Constitution, & Annual General Meeting; Certification, Standards, & Competencies; Communication / Membership; Education / Professional Development; Political Action / Advocacy
Activities: Facilitating communication among community health nurses throughout Canada; Developing standards of practice & a community health nursing certification process

Meetings/Conferences: • Community Health Nurses of Canada 2015 10th National Community Health Nurses Conference, June, 2015, Winnipeg, MB
Scope: National
Description: A meeting of persons interested in community health nursing for educational sessions, workshops, posters, & exhibits
Contact Information: E-mail: info@chnc.ca
Publications:
• Community Health Nurses of Canada Newsletter
Type: Newsletter; *Price:* Free with Community Health Nurses of Canada membership
Profile: Association communications to members
• Community Health Nursing Standards of Practice
• Community Health Nursing Standards Toolkit
Profile: A resource to facilitate use of standards
• Community Health Nursing Vision 2020: Shaping the Future
• Public Health Nursing Competencies
• Public Health Nursing Practice in Canada: A Review of the Literature

Community Heritage Federation ***See*** Community Museums Association of Prince Edward Island

Community Heritage Ontario (CHO)
24 Conlins Rd., Toronto ON M1C 1C3
Tel: 416-282-2710
communityheritageontario.ca
www.facebook.com/215682445171022
twitter.com/CHOntario
Overview: A medium-sized provincial charitable organization founded in 1991
Mission: Umbrella organization to the volunteer, municipally-appointed heritage advisory committees (LACACs); encourages the development of same & furthers the identification, preservation, interpretation & wise use of community heritage
Member of: Heritage Canada
Chief Officer(s):
Roscoe Petkovic, President, 905-877-4586
roscoepetkovic@communityheritageontario.ca
Richard Schofield, Secretary/Treasurer
rickschofield@communityheritageontario.ca
Finances: *Funding Sources:* Membership fees; grants
Membership: 140 MHC; 23 individuals; *Fees:* $60 group; $25 individual; $15 student; $100 corporate; *Member Profile:* Heritage associations in Ontario
Activities: *Speaker Service:* Yes

Community Information - Essex ***See*** Essex Community Services

Community Information & Referral Centre Thunder Bay (CIRC)
Victoria Mall, 125 Syndicate Ave., Thunder Bay ON P7E 6H8
Tel: 807-626-1720; *Fax:* 807-625-9427
Toll-Free: 866-624-1729; *TTY:* 888-622-4651
info@lspc.ca
www.lspc-circ.on.ca
Overview: A small local organization founded in 1983 overseen by InformOntario
Mission: To provide accurate, up-to-date information on community services, organizations, clubs, events & activities; To assist organizations & the general public in accessing information & the resources they require & identify gaps in services; To work with individuals & groups to meet their needs & improve community well-being
Affliation(s): A program of the Lakehead Social Planning Council
Chief Officer(s):
Kristen Tomcko, Supervisor
Finances: *Annual Operating Budget:* $50,000-$100,000; *Funding Sources:* Grants; donations; fundraising events; sale of services
Staff Member(s): 1; 4 volunteer(s)

Community Information & Referral Society
Community Village, 4728 Ross St., Ded Deer AB T4N 1X2
Tel: 403-346-4636; *Fax:* 403-340-8193
info@volunteerreddeer.ca
volunteerreddeer.ca
Also Known As: Volunteer Red Deer
Overview: A small local charitable organization
Mission: To deliver volunteer services to non-profit & community service organizations
Chief Officer(s):
Bill Farr, Chair
Finances: *Funding Sources:* Provincial government; corporate sponsors
Awards:
• Great Kids Awards (Award)

Community Information Centre Belle River ***See*** Lakeshore Community Services

Community Information Centre of Ottawa (CIC) / Centre d'information communautaire d'Ottawa
PO Box 41146, #1910 St-laurent Blvd, Ottawa ON K1G 1A4
Tel: 613-241-4636; *Fax:* 613-761-9077
Toll-Free: 877-761-9076; *TTY:* 866-540-0565
info@cominfo-ottawa.org
www.cominfo-ottawa.org
Overview: A medium-sized local charitable organization founded in 1974
Mission: To provide a link between individuals & organizations in Ottawa & the community resources or services they need through information & referral services in both official languages
Member of: InformOntario; InformCanada
Chief Officer(s):
Marie-Andrée Carrière, Executive Director
Finances: *Annual Operating Budget:* $100,000-$250,000; *Funding Sources:* City of Ottawa; United Way of Ottawa; directory sales
Staff Member(s): 5; 6 volunteer(s)
Activities: Information & referral: gathers & maintains a database; publishes a directory; refers clients to appropriate service/agencies; *Rents Mailing List:* Yes; *Library* Open to public

Community Information Fairview (CIF)
Fairview Mall, PO Box U219A, 1800 Sheppard Ave. East, Toronto ON M2J 5A7
Tel: 416-493-0752; *Fax:* 416-493-0823
communityinfo@on.aibn.com
www.communityinfofairview.org
Overview: A small local organization founded in 1971
Mission: To provide accessible space within Fairview Mall to better serve the community; To assure equality of access to CIF services to the best of our abilities; To provide full access to people with physical & mental impairments; to improve & build partnerships with other community organizations & the private sector; To assist community development activities; To assist other community organizations to attain their goals; To promote the development of a Community Resource Centre
Member of: Federation of Community Information Centres of Toronto; Inform Canada
Chief Officer(s):
Susan Knisch, Executive Director
susan@communityinfofairview.org
Finances: *Annual Operating Budget:* $50,000-$100,000
Staff Member(s): 1; 2 volunteer(s)
Membership: 30; *Member Profile:* Volunteers with 50 hrs of community service
Activities: Information; legal clinic

Community Information Hamilton (CIH)
Hamilton Public Library, PO Box 2700, 55 York Blvd., 5th Fl., Hamilton ON L8N 4E4
Tel: 905-528-0104; *Fax:* 905-528-7764
informationhamilton.ca
www.facebook.com/Inform.Hamilton
twitter.com/informhamilton
Also Known As: Inform Hamilton
Previous Name: Community Information Service Hamilton-Wentworth
Overview: A small local charitable organization founded in 1971
Mission: To connect people with community & government services; To provide individuals, organizations, business & governments with information on resources available in Hamilton-Wentworth
Member of: Inform Ontario; ACICO/Inform Canada
Finances: *Annual Operating Budget:* $100,000-$250,000; *Funding Sources:* City of Hamilton; United Way; publication sales
Staff Member(s): 6; 14 volunteer(s)
Membership: 30; *Fees:* $5
Activities: *Library* Open to public

Community Information Service Hamilton-Wentworth ***See*** Community Information Hamilton

Community Integration Services Society (CISS)
2175 Mary Hill Rd., Port Coquitlam BC V3C 3A2
Tel: 604-461-2131; *Fax:* 778-285-5520
www.gociss.org
Overview: A small local organization
Chief Officer(s):
Shari Mahar, Executive Director
smahar@gociss.org

Community Involvement of the Disabled (CID)
#5, 28 Hillview Ave., Sydney NS B1P 2H4
Tel: 902-564-9817; *Fax:* 902-564-5758
Overview: A small local charitable organization founded in 1977
Mission: Advocacy for persons with disabilities
Member of: Nova Scotia League for Equal Opportunities
Activities: *Library* Open to public

Community Kitchen Program of Calgary
3751 - 21 St. NE, Calgary AB T2E 6T5
Tel: 403-275-0258; *Fax:* 403-274-2967
www.ckpcalgary.ca
twitter.com/ckpcalgary
Overview: A small local charitable organization overseen by Alberta Food Bank Network Association
Mission: Working with individuals, families and communities to facilitate and/or enable initiatives that reduce hunger.
Chief Officer(s):
Marilyn Gunn, Executive Director
mgunn@ckpcalgary.ca

Community Legal Assistance Society
#300, 1140 West Pender St., Vancouver BC V6E 4G1
Tel: 604-685-3425; *Fax:* 604-685-7611
Toll-Free: 888-685-6222
www.clasbc.net
www.facebook.com/204399496259131
twitter.com/clasbc
Overview: A large local organization founded in 1971
Mission: To provide legal assistance to persons who are physically, mentally, socially, economically or otherwise disadvantaged, through litigation, test cases, public education & law reform endeavours
Affliation(s): Legal Services Society; Law Foundation of British Columbia
Chief Officer(s):
Aleem Bharmal, Executive Director
Finances: *Annual Operating Budget:* $1.5 Million-$3 Million; *Funding Sources:* Provincial government
Staff Member(s): 35; 17 volunteer(s)
Membership: 27 individual; *Fees:* $10 institutional; $1 individual

Community Legal Education Association (Manitoba) Inc. (CLEA) / Association d'éducation juridique communautaire (Manitoba) inc.
#205, 414 Graham Ave., Winnipeg MB R3C 0L8
Tel: 204-943-2382; *Fax:* 204-943-3600
mctroszko@communitylegal.mb.ca
Overview: A medium-sized provincial charitable organization founded in 1984
Mission: To provide legal education & information programs to Manitobans
Chief Officer(s):
Mary Troszko, Executive Director
Heather Dixon, President
Finances: *Funding Sources:* Law Society of Manitoba; The Manitoba Law Foundation; Justice Canada; Youth Justice Policy; The Winnipeg Foundation; Investors Group; Legal Aid MB
Activities: Provision of school programs plus workshops & classes in the community; Law Phone-In & Lawyer Referral Program; Publication of pamphlets, booklets & education kits; *Speaker Service:* Yes; *Library* Open to public
Publications:
• CLEA [Community Legal Education Association (Manitoba) Inc.] Newsletter
Type: Newsletter; *Frequency:* Semiannually
• Manitoba Legal Services Directory
Type: Directory; *Price:* $20

Community Legal Education Ontario (CLEO)
#600, 119 Spadina Ave., Toronto ON M5V 2L1
Tel: 416-408-4420; *Fax:* 416-408-4424
cleo@cleo.on.ca
www.cleo.on.ca
Overview: A medium-sized provincial charitable organization founded in 1974
Mission: To provide public legal education services & programs that benefit the low income community, disadvantaged persons,

such as immigrants & refugees, seniors, women, & injured workers in Ontario
Finances: *Funding Sources:* Legal Aid Ontario; Department of Justice Canada
Activities: Provision of CLEONet, a web site for community workers & advocates; Publication of information on various legal topics; Six Languages Text & Audio Project to improve access to legal information by low-income people in the Chinese, Arabic, Tamil, Urdu, Spanish, & Somali linguistic communities; Research

Community Legal Information Association of Prince Edward Island (CLIA PEI)
Sullivan Bldg., 1st Fl., PO Box 1207, Fitzroy St., Charlottetown PE C1A 7M8
Tel: 902-892-0853
Toll-Free: 800-240-9798
www.cliapei.ca
www.facebook.com/CLIAPEI
twitter.com/cliapei
www.youtube.com/CLIAPEI
Overview: A medium-sized provincial charitable organization founded in 1985
Mission: To provide Islanders with understandable, useful information about the Canadian laws & the justice system
Member of: Prince Edward Island Literacy Alliance Inc.; Public Legal Education Association of Canada
Chief Officer(s):
Barry Arsenault, President
David Daughton, Executive Director
Finances: *Annual Operating Budget:* $100,000-$250,000; *Funding Sources:* Justice Canada; provincial government; Law Foundation of PEI
Staff Member(s): 3; 100 volunteer(s)
Membership: 50; *Fees:* $2
Activities: *Speaker Service:* Yes; *Library* Open to public

Community Living Ajax-Pickering & Whitby
36 Emperor St., Ajax ON L1S 1M7
Tel: 905-427-3300; *Fax:* 905-427-3310
info@apwcommunityliving.org
www.cl-apw.org
Previous Name: Ajax, Pickering & Whitby Association for Community Living
Overview: A small local organization founded in 1957 overseen by Community Living Ontario
Member of: Community Living Ontario
Chief Officer(s):
Barbara Andrews, Executive Director
Chris Cook, President
Staff Member(s): 140
Membership: 300; *Fees:* $10

Community Living Algoma
99 Northern Ave. East, Sault Ste Marie ON P6B 4H3
Tel: 705-253-1700; *Fax:* 705-253-1777
Toll-Free: 800-448-8097
www.communitylivingalgoma.org
Overview: A large local charitable organization founded in 1954 overseen by Community Living Ontario
Mission: That all people live in a state of dignity in their community, where they can access the supports needed to ensure full inclusion
Member of: Community Living Ontario
Chief Officer(s):
Lila Cyr, Chair
John Policicchio, Executive Director, 705-253-1700 Ext. 3001
john_policicchio@cla-algoma.org
Finances: *Annual Operating Budget:* Greater than $5 Million
Staff Member(s): 122
Membership: 154; *Fees:* $15 individual & affiliate; $50 corporate; *Committees:* Planning Development & Advocacy; Education; Finance; Human Resources & French Language Services; Quality Enhancement
Activities: Residential, support & vocation services; day programs; *Awareness Events:* Awareness Week, May; *Library* by appointment
Publications:
• News & Views [a publication of Community Living Algoma]
Type: Newsletter

Community Living Alternatives Society (CLAS)
46B Chipman Dr., Kentville NS B4N 3V7
Tel: 902-681-8920; *Fax:* 902-681-2850
clas@ns.sympatico.ca
www.clasnovascotia.com
Overview: A small local charitable organization founded in 1976
Mission: Provides quality community living opportunities for individuals with intellectual challenges; promotes & facilitates the exercise of individual rights, the fulfillment of responsibilities & the participation of individuals within their community
Chief Officer(s):
Brian Wolfe, Executive Director
Staff Member(s): 130

Community Living Association (Lanark County) (CLA (LC))
178 Townline Rd., Carleton Place ON K7C 2C2
Tel: 613-257-8040; *Fax:* 613-257-5679
www.clalanark.ca
Overview: A small local charitable organization founded in 1965 overseen by Community Living Ontario
Mission: To help all persons live in a state of dignity, share all elements of living in the community & have the opportunity to participate effectively
Member of: Community Living Ontario
Chief Officer(s):
Elizabeth Snyder, President
Tony Pacheco, Executive Director
tony@clalanark.ca
Finances: *Annual Operating Budget:* $1.5 Million-$3 Million
Staff Member(s): 87; 20 volunteer(s)
Membership: 50; *Fees:* $10; *Committees:* Fundraising, Association Well-Being; Health & Safety
Activities: Individual day & residential support throughout Larnark County, focused in Almonte, Carleton Place, Smiths Falls & Perth; *Speaker Service:* Yes; *Library* Open to public

Community Living Association for South Simcoe (CLASS)
125 Dufferin St. South, Alliston ON L9R 1E9
Tel: 705-435-4792; *Fax:* 705-435-2766
www.class.on.ca
www.facebook.com/400120446712712?ref=hl
Overview: A small local organization founded in 1962 overseen by Community Living Ontario
Mission: To advocate that persons with developmental disabilities live in a state of dignity, have equal opportunity to maximize individual potential for personal growth & participate in all elements of life in the community
Member of: Ontario Agencies Supporting Individuals with Special Needs
Chief Officer(s):
Tom Eagan, President
Carolyn Garton, Director, Financial Services
carolyn@class.on.ca
Staff Member(s): 109
Membership: 70; *Fees:* $15
Activities: *Internships:* Yes

Community Living Association for the Little Divide; Lac La Biche & District Association for the Handicapped *See* Lac La Biche Disability Services

Community Living Association for York South; York South Association for Community Living *See* Community Living York South

Community Living Atikokan (CLA)
PO Box 2054, 114 Gorrie St., Atikokan ON P0T 1C0
Tel: 807-597-2259; *Fax:* 807-597-1495
www.cl-atikokan.ca
Previous Name: Atikokan & District Association for the Developmental Services
Overview: A small local charitable organization founded in 1969
Member of: Community Living Ontario
Chief Officer(s):
Dennis Brown, President
Jim Turner, Executive Director, 807-597-2020
jim.turner@cl-atikokan.ca
Finances: *Annual Operating Budget:* $500,000-$1.5 Million; *Funding Sources:* Ministry of Community & Social Services; fundraising
Staff Member(s): 17
Activities: Group living; supported independent living; training & leisure centre; & transition program. Services include: yard maintenance; auto detailing; catering services; laundry services; janitorial services; Chips R' Us; wedding decoration; mail pick-up & delivery; collating; paper shredding; & promotional buttons.

Community Living Brantford
366 Dalhousie St., Brantford ON N3S 3W2
Tel: 519-756-2662; *Fax:* 519-756-7668
communitylivingbrant@clbrant.com
www.clbrant.com
Previous Name: Brantford & District Association for Community Living
Overview: A small local charitable organization founded in 1952 overseen by Community Living Ontario
Mission: To promote full citizenship & respect for all people, through education, support, & services designed to meet the diverse developmental needs of children, adults, & their families
Member of: Ontario Agencies Supporting Individuals with Special Needs (OASIS); Community Living Ontario
Chief Officer(s):
Janet Reansbury, Executive Director
janetreansbury@clbrant.com
Ryan Kirk, President
Finances: *Annual Operating Budget:* Greater than $5 Million; *Funding Sources:* Ontario Ministry of Community & Social Services; contract revenue; membership fees; fundraising
Staff Member(s): 250; 20 volunteer(s)
Membership: 300; *Fees:* $10 individual; $15 family; $5 associate; *Member Profile:* Parents, interested citizens; *Committees:* Public Education; Resource Management; Quality Enhancement
Activities: Operates 12 group homes, a Day Program for 100 adults & a Day Program for 45 adults with multiple challenges; provides support for over 70 individuals who live on their own; provides peer support groups for teens; adult literacy program; provides advocacy & support to parents & family members; *Speaker Service:* Yes
Awards:
• Leo Mahon Memorial Scholarship (Award)
Awarded to a student entering post-secondary education who would benefit the field of Developmental Handicaps *Amount:* $1,000

Community Living Cambridge
160 Hespeler Rd., Cambridge ON N1R 6V7
Tel: 519-623-7490; *Fax:* 519-740-8073
info@communitylivingcambridge.ca
www.communitylivingcambridge.ca
Previous Name: Cambridge Association for the Mentally Handicapped
Overview: A small local charitable organization founded in 1954
Mission: To ensure that all people who have a mental handicap live in a state of dignity & are provided with the opportunity to become self-sufficient & to realize their individual potential
Member of: Community Living Ontario
Affliation(s): Ontario Association For Community Living
Chief Officer(s):
Terry Lake, President
Michael J. Mullen, Executive Director, 519-623-7490 Ext. 2240
mmullen@clcambridge.ca
Finances: *Annual Operating Budget:* Greater than $5 Million; *Funding Sources:* Provincial government; legacies & bequests; private donations; memberships; fees for services; fundraising
100 volunteer(s)
Membership: 100; *Fees:* $10 family; *Committees:* Executive; Personnel; Health & Safety
Activities: Preschool resources; recreation; family services; residential services; vocational & adult day services; supported employment services & community options;

Community Living Campbellford/Brighton (CLCB)
PO Box 1360, 65 Bridge St. East, Campbellford ON K0L 1L0
Tel: 705-653-1821; *Fax:* 705-653-5738
Toll-Free: 866-528-0825
admin@communitylivingcampbellford.com
www.communitylivingcampbellford.com
www.linkedin.com/company/community-living-campbellford-brighton
www.facebook.com/CLCfordBrighton
twitter.com/clcfordbrighton
Previous Name: Campbellford & District Association for Community Living
Overview: A small local organization founded in 1960 overseen by Community Living Ontario
Mission: To provide support & services to people, and promote opportunities for personal growth within their community
Member of: Community Living Ontario
Chief Officer(s):
Nancy Brown, Executive Director
nbrown@communitylivingcampbellford.com
Finances: *Annual Operating Budget:* Greater than $5 Million; *Funding Sources:* Government grants
Staff Member(s): 122; 25 volunteer(s)

Membership: 75; *Fees:* $15

Community Living Chatham-Kent
PO Box 967, Chatham ON N7M 5L3
Tel: 519-352-1174; *Fax:* 519-352-5459
www.clc-k.ca
Previous Name: Chatham & District Association for Community Living
Overview: A small local organization founded in 1955 overseen by Community Living Ontario
Mission: To support individuals with intellectual disabilities & their families so that they are able to participate fully in their community.
Member of: Community Living Ontario
Chief Officer(s):
Stephen Andari, President
Lu-Ann Cowell, Executive Director
lcowell@clc-k.ca
Staff Member(s): 260
Membership: *Fees:* $10 single/family

Community Living Dryden (CLD)
280 Arthur St., Dryden ON P8N 1K8
Tel: 807-223-3364; *Fax:* 807-223-5784
cldsl.ca
www.facebook.com/96367942643
Previous Name: Dryden & District Association for Community Living
Overview: A small local organization founded in 1968
Mission: To provide support programs to individuals with developmental & intellectual disabilities in the Dryden, Sioux Lookout & Hudson area, offering programs directly & encouraging active involvement in the community.
Member of: Community Living Ontario
Chief Officer(s):
Dean Osmond, President
Heather Fukushima, Acting Executive Director
Membership: 27; *Fees:* $15 single; $20 family; $100 coporate; $200 corporate gold

Community Living Dufferin
065371 County Rd. 3, East Garafraxa ON L9W 7J8
Tel: 519-941-8971; *Fax:* 519-941-9121
info@communitylivingdufferin.ca
www.communitylivingdufferin.ca
www.facebook.com/communitylivingdufferin
twitter.com/cldufferin
www.youtube.com/user/CLDufferin
Previous Name: Dufferin Association for Community Living
Overview: A small local charitable organization founded in 1954 overseen by Community Living Ontario
Mission: To encourage people with developmental disabilities & their families to pursue enriched connections within their community.
Member of: Community Living Ontario; Canadian Association for Community Living
Chief Officer(s):
Pat Dunwoody, President
Sheryl Chandler, Executive Director
sheryl@communitylivingdufferin.ca
Finances: *Funding Sources:* Ministry of Community & Social Services; Dufferin County; foundations; fundraising
Membership: 1-99; *Fees:* $10
Activities: Residential Alternatives; Options Program; community outreach; employment services; Rolling Hills Children's Place; Summer Inclusion Program; Preschool Resource Program

Community Living Dundas County (CLDC)
PO Box 678, 55 Allison Ave., Morrisburg ON K0C 1X0
Tel: 613-543-3737; *Fax:* 613-543-4432
cldc@cldc.ca
www.cldc.ca
Previous Name: Dundas County Community Living Inc.
Overview: A small local organization
Mission: To advocate for the inclusion of people with an intellectual disability in their communities, promoting opportunities for their personal growth, providing training & resources for them & their families.
Member of: Community Living Ontario
Chief Officer(s):
Marja Smellink, President
Deborah Boardman, Executive Director
dboardman@cldc.ca
Finances: *Funding Sources:* Provincial government, donations
Activities: Social, leisure-based day support; transitional support from school to community; support for securing employment

Community Living Durham North
#2, 60 VanEdward Dr., Port Perry ON L9L 1G3
Tel: 905-985-8511; *Fax:* 905-985-0799
cldn.ca
twitter.com/CLDurhamNorth
Previous Name: Central Seven Association for Community Living
Overview: A small local charitable organization founded in 1967 overseen by Community Living Ontario
Mission: To provide services to people with developmental disabilities in the northern portion of Durham Region - Brock, Scugog & Uxbridge townships; to promote the idea that all people live in a state of dignity, share in all elements of living in the community & have the opportunity to participate effectively
Affliation(s): Canadian Association for Community Living; Ontario Association for Community Living
Chief Officer(s):
Jamie Ross, President
Terry Coyne, Vice-President
Finances: *Annual Operating Budget:* $3 Million-$5 Million; *Funding Sources:* Donations
Staff Member(s): 135; 35 volunteer(s)
Membership: 70; *Fees:* $10

Community Living Elgin (CLE)
400 Talbot St., St Thomas ON N5P 1B8
Tel: 519-631-9222; *Fax:* 519-633-4392
info@communitylivingelgin.com
www.eacl.on.ca
Previous Name: Elgin Association for Community Living
Overview: A small local charitable organization founded in 1958
Mission: To provide support & services, primarily to people with developmental disabilities & their families to enable them to participate at full potential within the community
Member of: Community Living Ontario
Chief Officer(s):
Bob Ashcroft, President
Tom McCallum, Executive Director
t.mccallum@communitylivingelgin.com
Finances: *Funding Sources:* Provincial government; United Way; fundraising
Activities: Adult Development Centre; Friendco, a workshop providing contract work to manufacturing companies; Family Enrichment Centre; Parent-Child Place; toy lending library; *Speaker Service:* Yes

Community Living Espanola
345 Centre St., Espanola ON P5E 1E4
Tel: 705-869-0442; *Fax:* 705-869-0446
clespanola.ca
www.facebook.com/506858389367383
twitter.com/clespanola
Previous Name: Espanola & District Association for Community Living
Overview: A small local charitable organization
Mission: To provide services to individuals with intellectual challenges, fostering meaningful living for those with developmental disabilities.
Member of: Community Living Ontario
Chief Officer(s):
Louise Laplante, Executive Director
louise.laplante@clespanola.ca
Kathy Lewis, President
Membership: 36; *Fees:* $3

Community Living Essex County
Essex Centre, 372 Talbot St. North, Essex ON N8M 2W4
Tel: 519-776-6483; *Fax:* 519-776-6972
communitylivingessex.org
Overview: A large local charitable organization founded in 1961 overseen by Community Living Ontario
Mission: To provide programs & supports for people with a developmental disability & their families; that all people have the right to live in a state of dignity & share in all elements of living in the community with the opportunity to participate effectively
Member of: Community Living Ontario
Chief Officer(s):
Marg Prince, President
Nancy Wallace-Gero, Executive Director
Finances: *Annual Operating Budget:* Greater than $5 Million; *Funding Sources:* Ontario Ministry of Community & Social Services; donations; fundraising
Staff Member(s): 600
Membership: 650+; *Fees:* $10 individual & affiliate; $150 corporate
Activities: *Awareness Events:* Ruthven Apple Festival, Sept.; Jingle Bell Run/Walk & Wheel, Nov.; *Speaker Service:* Yes; *Library* Open to public
Publications:
• The Profile [a publication of Community Living Essex County]
Type: Newsletter; *Frequency:* q.

Amherstburg - Channel Office
260 Bathurst St., Amherstburg ON N9V 1Y9
Tel: 519-736-4446; *Fax:* 519-736-9982
Chief Officer(s):
Anne Garrod, Director, Supports & Services, West Area, 519-776-6483 Ext. 262
annegarrod@communitylivingessex.org

Leamington - Southshore Office
245 Talbot St. West, Leamington ON N8H 1N8
Tel: 519-326-1816; *Fax:* 519-326-7794
Chief Officer(s):
Lee-Anne Dupuis, Director, Supports & Services, South Area, 519-776-6483 Ext. 263
leeannedupuis@communitylivingessex.org

Tecumseh - Northshore Office
13158 Tecumseh Rd. East, Tecumseh ON N8N 3T6
Tel: 519-979-0057; *Fax:* 519-979-2881
Chief Officer(s):
Sue Grando, Director, Supports & Services, North Area, 519-776-6483 Ext. 236
suegrando@communitylivingessex.org

Community Living Fort Erie (CLFE)
PO Box 520, 615 Industrial Dr., Fort Erie ON L2A 5Y1
Tel: 905-871-6770; *Fax:* 905-871-3339
pcopeland@clfe.ca
www.clfe.ca
Overview: A small local charitable organization founded in 1954 overseen by Community Living Ontario
Mission: That all people with developmental disability live in a state of dignity, share in all elements of living in the community & have the opportunity to participate effectively
Member of: Community Living Ontario
Chief Officer(s):
Maureen Brown, Executive Director, 905-871-6770 Ext. 224
mbrown@clfe.ca
Linda Thwaifes, President
Finances: *Annual Operating Budget:* $3 Million-$5 Million; *Funding Sources:* Ministry of Community & Social Services; fundraising
Staff Member(s): 130; 60 volunteer(s)
Membership: 150; *Fees:* $10; *Committees:* Nominating; Executive
Activities: Accommodation services; employment services; supported independent living; parent resource centre; friendship camp; inclusion community camps for children; volunteer services; *Awareness Events:* Community Living Month, May; *Library* by appointment

Community Living Fort Frances & District (CLFFD)
PO Box 147, 340 Scott St., Fort Frances ON P9A 3M5
Tel: 807-274-5556; *Fax:* 807-274-5009
clffd@vianet.ca
www.communitylivingfortfrances.com
Overview: A small local charitable organization founded in 1975
Mission: To ensure that all people live in a state of dignity, sharing & participating in all elements of living in the community
Member of: Community Living Ontario
Chief Officer(s):
Alanna J. Barr, Executive Director
ajbarr@clfortfrances.com
Denise Bliss, President
Finances: *Annual Operating Budget:* $3 Million-$5 Million
Staff Member(s): 80; 20 volunteer(s)
Membership: 20; *Committees:* Planning & Development; Public Relations; Services

Community Living Glengarry (CLG)
332 MacDonald Blvd., Alexandria ON K0C 1A0
Tel: 613-525-4357; *Fax:* 613-525-4360
info@clglen.on.ca
clglen.on.ca
www.facebook.com/114656748615866
Previous Name: Glengarry Association for Community Living
Overview: A small local organization
Mission: To support individuals who are intellectually challenged by creating an inclusive community where everyone can live to

Activities: *Awareness Events:* The Chair Affair, May; Chuckles for Charity, Oct.
Publications:
• Community Living Oakville Newsletter
Type: Newsletter

Community Living Ontario (CLO) / Intégration communautaire Ontario

#403, 240 Duncan Mill Rd., Toronto ON M3B 3S6
Tel: 416-447-4348; *Fax:* 416-447-8974
Toll-Free: 800-278-8025
info@communitylivingontario.ca
www.communitylivingontario.ca
www.facebook.com/communitylivingontario
twitter.com/CLOntario
www.youtube.com/user/comlivon
Also Known As: The Ontario Association for Community Living
Overview: A large provincial charitable organization founded in 1953 overseen by Canadian Association for Community Living
Mission: To lobby on behalf of people with intellectual disabilities in Ontario; To ensure that every person in Ontario has access to supports to live with dignity & to participate in the community of his/her choice
Member of: Canadian Association for Community Living
Chief Officer(s):
Chris Beesley, CEO, 416-447-4348 Ext. 227
cbeesley@communitylivngontario.ca
Keith Dee, Director, Membership Services, 416-447-4348 Ext. 242
kdee@communitylivingontario.ca
Kimberley Gavan, Director, Community Development, 416-447-4348 Ext. 234
kgavan@communitylivingontario.ca
Gordon Kyle, Director, Social Policy & Government Relations, 416-447-4348 Ext. 230
gkyle@communitylivingontario.ca
Finances: *Funding Sources:* Local associations; Fundraising
25 volunteer(s)
Membership: 12,000+ individuals + 117 local associations; *Member Profile:* Individuals; Local Community Living associations; *Committees:* Awards; By-Laws/Resolutions; Communications Strategies; Community Living Inclusion Project Committee; Conference; Council of Community Living Ontario; Executive; Federation Well Being Committee; Finance; Government Relations; Nominations; Social Policy
Meetings/Conferences: • 2015 Community Living Ontario 62nd Annual Conference, 2015, ON
Scope: Provincial

Community Living Oshawa / Clarington

39 Wellington St. East, Oshawa ON L1H 3Y1
Tel: 905-576-3011; *Fax:* 905-576-9754
www.communitylivingoc.ca
www.facebook.com/CommunityLivingOshawaClarington
twitter.com/community_cloc
Previous Name: Oshawa / Clarington Association for Community Living
Overview: A large local charitable organization founded in 1954 overseen by Community Living Ontario
Mission: To enable the community to welcome & support citizens with developmental handicaps as valued, participating & contributing members
Member of: Community Living Ontario
Affliation(s): Developmental Services Ontario
Chief Officer(s):
Garry Cooke, President
Terri Gray, Executive Director, 905-576-3011 Ext. 323
tgray@communitylivingoc.ca
Finances: *Annual Operating Budget:* $3 Million-$5 Million; *Funding Sources:* Donations; Membership dues; Government funding
Staff Member(s): 200; 40 volunteer(s)
Meetings/Conferences: • Community Living Oshawa / Clarington 2015 Annual General Meeting, 2015, ON
Scope: Local
Publications:
• News & Views [a publication of Community Living Oshawa / Clarington]
Type: Newsletter; *Frequency:* Quarterly; *Price:* Free with membership in Community Living Oshawa / Clarington
Profile: Information for Community Living members

Community Living Owen Sound & District

769 - 4 Ave. East, Owen Sound ON N4K 2N5
Tel: 519-371-9251; *Fax:* 519-371-5168
Previous Name: Owen Sound & District Association for the Mentally Retarded
Overview: A medium-sized local organization founded in 1954 overseen by Community Living Ontario
Mission: To assist people with developmental needs to live, work, & participate in the community as equal & valued partners
Member of: Community Living Ontario
Chief Officer(s):
Rick Hill, Executive Director
rhill@comlivos.on.ca
Debbie Earnes, President
Finances: *Annual Operating Budget:* $1.5 Million-$3 Million; *Funding Sources:* Ministry of Community & Social Services; donations
Staff Member(s): 150; 117 volunteer(s)
Membership: *Committees:* Nominating
Activities: *Library*

Community Living Parry Sound (CLPS)

38 Joseph St., Parry Sound ON P2A 2G5
Tel: 705-746-9330; *Fax:* 705-746-6151
mail@clps.ca
www.clps.ca
www.facebook.com/communitylivingparrysound
Overview: A small local charitable organization founded in 1962 overseen by Community Living Ontario
Mission: To provide services & opportunities that enable individuals with developmental disabilities to effectively participate in their community according to their interests & abilities.
Member of: Community Living Ontario; Ontario Agencies Supporting Individuals with Special Needs
Chief Officer(s):
Jo Ann Poglitshose, President
Jo-Anne Demick, Executive Director
jdemick@clps.ca
Finances: *Funding Sources:* Provincial government; fundraising
Membership: *Fees:* $10; $100 lifetime
Activities: *Library* Open to public by appointment
Awards:
• Community Living Parry Sound Bursary (Scholarship)

Addie St. Residence
15 Addie St., Parry Sound ON P2A 2K2
Tel: 705-746-7300
Chief Officer(s):
Jill Reevie, Director, Accommodation Services
jreevie@clps.ca

Community Living Peterborough (CLP)

223 Aylmer St., Peterborough ON K9J 3K3
Tel: 705-743-2411
contact@communitylivingpeterborough.ca
www.communitylivingpeterborough.ca
www.facebook.com/CommunityLivingPtbo?v=wall&ref=sgm
twitter.com/CLPeterborough
www.youtube.com/user/CommunityLivingPtbo
Overview: A small local charitable organization founded in 1953 overseen by Community Living Ontario
Mission: To inspire respect & equality for people living with an intellectual disability in Peterborough, Ontario
Member of: Community Living Ontario
Chief Officer(s):
Jack Gillan, Chief Executive Officer, 705-743-2412 Ext. 516
jgillan@communitylivingpeterborough.ca
Joanne Duquette, Director, Business & Administration, 705-743-2412 Ext. 513
jduquette@communitylivingpeterborough.ca
Barb Hiland, Director, Operations, 705-743-2412 Ext. 544
bhiland@communitylivingpeterborough.ca
Cindy Hobbins, Manager, Community Development, Communications, & Quality Enhancement, 705-743-2412 Ext. 525
chobbins@communitylivingpeterborough.ca
Pat McNamara, Manager, Transitional Aged Youth, Supported Housing, 705-743-2412 Ext. 522
pmcnamara@communitylivingpeterborough.ca
A.J. McNaught, Coordinator, Volunteers, 705-743-2412 Ext. 551
ajmcnaught@communitylivingpeterborough.ca
Lisa Clarke, Officer, Community & Fund Development, 705-743-2412 Ext. 539
lclarke@communitylivingpeterborough.ca
Heather Grosney, Officer, Communications, 705-743-2412 Ext. 549
hgrosney@communitylivingpeterborough.ca
Finances: *Funding Sources:* Donations; Fundraising
Activities: Offering job training; Providing a workforce to Peterborough companies, through the Small Business Resource Centre; Facilitating suitable living options for adults over the age of 21; Supporting families; Increasing community knowledge; Coordinating educational workshops for parents; Providing school & employment advocacy
Publications:
• Opening Doors . . . to Building Inclusive Communities
Type: Newsletter
Profile: Community Living Peterborough activities & campaign updates

Community Living Port Colborne-Wainfleet

100 MacRae Ave., Port Colborne ON L3K 2A8
Tel: 905-835-8941; *Fax:* 905-835-5515
www.portcolbornecommunityliving.com
Previous Name: Port Colborne District Association for Community Living, Inc.
Overview: A medium-sized local organization founded in 1962 overseen by Community Living Ontario
Mission: To promote the idea that all people should live in a state of dignity, share in all elements of living in the community & have equal opportunity to participate effectively
Member of: Community Living Ontario
Chief Officer(s):
Vickie Moreland, Executive Director
vmoreland@cogeco.ca
Membership: *Fees:* $5

Community Living Prince Edward (County)

#1, 67 King St., Picton ON K0K 2T0
Tel: 613-476-6038; *Fax:* 613-476-2868
info@clpe.on.ca
www.clpe.on.ca
Previous Name: Prince Edward Association for Community Living
Overview: A small local charitable organization founded in 1965 overseen by Community Living Ontario
Mission: To provide services to facilitate the participation of people with developmental disabilities into community life.
Member of: Community Living Ontario
Chief Officer(s):
Brian Smith, Executive Director
brian.smith@clpe.on.ca
Finances: *Funding Sources:* Ontario government; client fees; donations
Membership: *Fees:* $5
Activities: Advocacy & services

Community Living Quinte West (CLQW)

11 Canal St., Trenton ON K8V 4K3
Tel: 613-394-2222; *Fax:* 613-394-0381
communitylivingquintewest@clqw.ca
clqw.ca
Previous Name: Trenton & District Association for Community Living
Overview: A small local charitable organization founded in 1959 overseen by Community Living Ontario
Mission: To provide services to persons with developmental handicaps & their families so they may participate full in their community.
Member of: Community Living Ontario
Chief Officer(s):
Michelle Earle, President
Starr Olsen, Executive Director
starr@clqw.ca
Finances: *Funding Sources:* Fundraising

Community Living Renfrew County South

PO Box 683, 326 Raglan St. South, Renfrew ON K7V 4E7
Tel: 613-432-6763; *Fax:* 613-432-9465
commliving@clrcs.com
www.clrcs.com
Previous Name: Renfrew & District Association for the Mentally Retarded
Overview: A small local organization founded in 1965 overseen by Community Living Ontario
Mission: To achieve state of existence in which all persons live in dignity, share in all elements of living in the community & have the opportunity to participate effectively
Member of: Community Living Ontario; Canadian Association for Community Living
Chief Officer(s):
Jennifer Creeden, Executive Director
jcreeden@clrcs.com
Esther Roberts, President
Finances: *Annual Operating Budget:* $1.5 Million-$3 Million

Staff Member(s): 38; 20 volunteer(s)
Membership: 100; *Fees:* $5; *Committees:* Finance; Personnel; planning & Priorities
Activities: Vocational supports; residential supports; respite supports;

Community Living St. Marys & Area Association
PO Box 1618, 300 Elgin St. East, St Marys ON N4X 1B9
Tel: 519-284-1400; *Fax:* 519-284-3120
www.communitylivingstmarys.ca
Overview: A small local organization founded in 1962
Mission: To develop an ability & willingness in our community to welcome & support all people as valued, participating & contributing members by continuing to promote a fully integrated community
Member of: Community Living Ontario
Chief Officer(s):
Marg McLean, Executive Director
margm@communitylivingstmarys.ca
Finances: *Annual Operating Budget:* $500,000-$1.5 Million; *Funding Sources:* Fundraising
Staff Member(s): 50
Membership: 75; *Fees:* $5
Activities: *Library* Open to public

Community Living Sarnia & District *See* Community Living Sarnia-Lambton

Community Living Sarnia-Lambton (CLSL)
#202, 551 Exmouth St., Sarnia ON N7T 7J4
Tel: 519-332-0560; *Fax:* 519-332-3446
clsd@communitylivingsarnia.org
www.communitylivingsarnia.org
Previous Name: Community Living Sarnia & District
Overview: A small local charitable organization founded in 1955 overseen by Community Living Ontario
Mission: To ensure persons with developmental disabilities & their families live & share in all aspects of the community & that they have opportunites to participate fully.
Member of: Community Living Ontario; Ontario Agencies Supporting Individuals with Special Needs (OASIS)
Chief Officer(s):
Earle Kilner, President
John Hagens, Executive Director
Finances: *Annual Operating Budget:* Greater than $5 Million; *Funding Sources:* Federal & provincial governments; United Way; corporate & private donations
Staff Member(s): 210; 100 volunteer(s)
Membership: *Fees:* Donations; *Committees:* Executive; Resource; Resource Development; Fund Raising

Community Living Sioux Lookout (CLSL)
PO Box 1258, Sioux Lookout ON P8T 1B8
Tel: 807-737-1447; *Fax:* 807-737-3833
www.clsiouxlookout.com/index2-SL.htm
Previous Name: Sioux Lookout & Hudson Association for Community Living
Overview: A small local charitable organization founded in 1965
Mission: To ensure that all persons who are developmentally disabled have the opportunity to live a meaningful & satisfying life as equals in the community by providing opportunities for personal growth through education, training, employment, accommodation, support, advocacy, & an informed public
Member of: Community Living Ontario
Chief Officer(s):
Vince Kastrukoff, President
Michael Hull, B.A., M.A., Executive Director
Finances: *Annual Operating Budget:* $1.5 Million-$3 Million; *Funding Sources:* Membership fees; fundraising
Staff Member(s): 58
Membership: 1-99; *Fees:* $25 corporate; $5 general; *Committees:* Strategic Directions; Executive Finance; Fund Raising
Activities: Programs include: Residential Services; Vocational Services; Supported Independent Living; Transitions Program; Community Connections Program; & Video Conferencing Program;

Community Living Society (CLS)
#490, 6400 Roberts St., Burnaby BC V5G 4C9
Tel: 604-451-8699; *Fax:* 604-451-5708
contactus@communitylivingsociety.ca
www.communitylivingsociety.ca
Overview: A medium-sized local charitable organization founded in 1978
Mission: To support each individual to live with dignity & to thrive as a fully participating citizen within their community
Member of: British Columbia Association for Community Living
Chief Officer(s):
Ross Chilton, Executive Director
rchilton@cls-bc.org
Finances: *Funding Sources:* Government
Staff Member(s): 25
Membership: *Fees:* $5 single; $10 family; $100 life; *Committees:* Finance; Branding; Executive; Fund Development; Aging with Dignity; Orientation; Governance

Community Living South Huron
146 Main St., Dashwood ON N0M 1N0
Tel: 519-237-3637; *Fax:* 519-237-3190
clsh@hay.net
www.clsh.ca
Overview: A small local charitable organization founded in 1968 overseen by Community Living Ontario
Mission: To provide support to individuals with developmental challenges to participate in & contribute to all aspects of family & community life
Member of: Community Living Ontario
Chief Officer(s):
Bruce Shaw, Executive Director
Donna Greb, President
Finances: *Annual Operating Budget:* $1.5 Million-$3 Million; *Funding Sources:* Community & social services
Staff Member(s): 85; 20 volunteer(s)
Membership: 50; *Fees:* $20 family
Activities: *Rents Mailing List:* Yes

Community Living South Muskoka
15 Depot Dr., Bracebridge ON P1L 0A1
Tel: 705-645-5494; *Fax:* 705-645-4621
info@clsm.on.ca
www.clsm.on.ca
Overview: A medium-sized local organization founded in 1967 overseen by Community Living Ontario
Mission: To promote that all persons should live in a state of dignity, share in all elements of living in the community, & have the opportunity to participate effectively
Chief Officer(s):
David Morrison, Chair
Ann Kenney, Chief Executive Officer
Finances: *Annual Operating Budget:* $3 Million-$5 Million
Staff Member(s): 145; 60 volunteer(s)
Membership: 1-99

Community Living Stormont County (CLSC) / Intégration communautaire comté de Stormont
280 - 9 St. West, Cornwall ON K6J 3A6
Tel: 613-938-9550; *Fax:* 613-938-2033
www.communitylivingstormontcounty.ca
www.facebook.com/201683936572529
Overview: A medium-sized local charitable organization founded in 1958 overseen by Community Living Ontario
Mission: To help all people live in a state of dignity, share in all elements of living in the community & have the opportunity to participate effectively
Member of: Community Living Ontario
Chief Officer(s):
Dick D'Alessio, Executive Director
d.dalessio@clstormont.ca
Stephane Perrault, President
president@clstormont.ca
Finances: *Funding Sources:* Ministry of Community & Social Services; Ministry of Housing; fundraising; donations
Activities: Early Childhood Integration Support Service supports pre-school children in community based nursery schools & day care centres; adults 18 years of age & up may be supported in residential, recreational & work settings in the community; referrals; networking & advocacy; *Library:* Resource Room; by appointment

Community Living Stratford & Area
112 Frederick St., Stratford ON N5A 3V7
Tel: 519-273-1000; *Fax:* 519-273-6277
info@clsa.ca
www.clsa.ca
Previous Name: Stratford Area Association for Community Living
Overview: A small local charitable organization founded in 1957 overseen by Community Living Ontario
Member of: Community Living Ontario
Chief Officer(s):
Muriel Boyd, Executive Director
John Buechler, President
Finances: *Annual Operating Budget:* $3 Million-$5 Million; *Funding Sources:* Provincial government; fundraising
Staff Member(s): 160; 30 volunteer(s)
Membership: 80; *Fees:* $5 single; $10 family; *Member Profile:* Parents; community members; agencies; *Committees:* Finance
Activities: *Awareness Events:* Swing into Spring, May

Community Living Temiskaming South
PO Box 1149, 513 Amwell St., Haileybury ON P0J 1K0
Tel: 705-672-2000; *Fax:* 705-672-2722
www.clts.ca
Overview: A small local organization
Member of: Community Living Ontario
Chief Officer(s):
Sherwin Knight, Executive Director
sknight@clts.ca

Community Living Thunder Bay (CLTB)
1501 Dease St., Thunder Bay ON P7C 5H3
Tel: 807-622-1099; *Fax:* 807-622-8528
info@cltb.ca
www.cltb.ca
Previous Name: Lakehead Association for Community Living
Overview: A small local charitable organization founded in 1954 overseen by Community Living Ontario
Mission: To advocate for the rights & quality of life of people served; To educate & support the community to share the vision of the association; To provide services & supports to people served & to their families; To be accountable to people servee, their families, the membership of CLTB, & the community
Member of: Community Living Ontario
Chief Officer(s):
Rick Piccinin, President
Sandra Buosi, Interim Executive Director
sbuosi@cltb.ca
Finances: *Annual Operating Budget:* Greater than $5 Million; *Funding Sources:* The Ministry of Community and Social Services; United Way; fundraising; donations
Staff Member(s): 420; 175 volunteer(s)
Membership: 150; *Fees:* $5 individual; $10 family; $40 agency; *Member Profile:* Family & friends of people with a developmental disability; *Committees:* Rights; Education; Parents Group; Public Awareness
Activities: Support & advocacy services for people with a developmental disability & their families; *Speaker Service:* Yes

Publications:
• The Advocate
Type: Newsletter; *Frequency:* Bi-annually

Community Living Timmins Intégration Communautaire
166 Brousseau Ave., Timmins ON P4N 5Y4
Tel: 705-268-8811; *Fax:* 705-267-2011
admin@cltic.ca
www.communitylivingtimmins.com
Overview: A medium-sized local organization founded in 1955 overseen by Community Living Ontario
Mission: To help all persons to live in a state of dignity, share in all elements of living in the community & have the opportunity to participate effectively
Member of: Community Living Ontario
Chief Officer(s):
Johanne Rondeau-Bernier, Executive Director
jrondeau@cltic.ca
Finances: *Funding Sources:* Government; United Way; fundraising
Membership: *Committees:* Management-Finance; Parents Advisory; Support Services; Public Education; Housing; Nominations; Health & Safety; Employer/Employee Relations
Activities: *Awareness Events:* Community Living Month, May; *Internships:* Yes; *Library:* Resource Centre
Awards:
• Harold Beattie Award (Award)
• Northern College Bursary (Scholarship)

Community Living Toronto
20 Spadina Rd., Toronto ON M5R 2S7
Tel: 416-968-0650
cltoronto.ca
www.facebook.com/CLToronto
twitter.com/cltoronto
Previous Name: Toronto Association for Community Living
Overview: A medium-sized local charitable organization founded in 1951 overseen by Community Living Ontario

Mission: To ensure that persons with an intellectual disability live in a state of dignity, share in all elements of living in their community & have equal opportunity to participate effectively
Member of: Community Living Ontario; United Way of Greater Toronto
Affliation(s): Canadian Association for Community Living
Chief Officer(s):
Garry Pruden, Chief Executive Officer
gpruden@cltoronto.ca
Chris Stringer, President
Membership: *Member Profile:* Families & supporters of people with an intellectual disability
Activities: Support of people with an intellectual disability & their families; *Speaker Service:* Yes

Community Living Upper Ottawa Valley
PO Box 1030, 894 Pembroke St., Pembroke ON K8A 5P8
Tel: 613-735-0659; *Fax:* 613-735-1373
info@communitylivingupperottawavalley.ca
www.communitylivingupperottawavalley.ca
Previous Name: Pembroke & District Association for Community Living
Overview: A medium-sized local charitable organization founded in 1958 overseen by Community Living Ontario
Mission: To assist developmentally handicapped individuals to live in a state of dignity, share in all elements of the community & have the opportunity to participate effectively
Member of: Community Living Ontario
Chief Officer(s):
Paul Melcher, Executive Director
paulmelcher@communitylivingupperottawavalley.ca
Finances: *Annual Operating Budget:* $1.5 Million-$3 Million
Staff Member(s): 65; 25 volunteer(s)
Membership: 185; *Fees:* $5 individual/associate; $15 household; $50 corporate; $100 lifetime
Activities: Support to families; parent relief; supported living; family home program; community employment; outreach; *Awareness Events:* Community Living Month, May

Community Living Victoria
3861 Cedar Hill Cross Rd., Victoria BC V8P 2M7
Tel: 250-477-7231; *Fax:* 250-477-6944
communitylivingvictoria.ca
Previous Name: Victoria Association for Community Living
Overview: A small local charitable organization founded in 1955
Mission: To support people with developmental disabilities by nurturing their ability to choose, promoting inclusion in the community & creating a sense of belonging
Member of: British Columbia Association for Community Living
Affliation(s): Canadian Association for Community Living
Chief Officer(s):
Ellen Tarshis, Executive Director
etarshis@clvic.ca
Finances: *Funding Sources:* United Way; government; private donations
Membership: *Fees:* $20 single; $35 family/organization; *Member Profile:* General public
Activities: *Awareness Events:* Community Living Day; *Library* by appointment

Community Living Walkerton & District (CLWD)
PO Box 999, 19 Durham St. East, Walkerton ON N0G 2V0
Tel: 519-881-3713; *Fax:* 519-881-0531
www.clwalkerton.org
Previous Name: Walkerton & District Community Support Services
Overview: A small local charitable organization founded in 1956 overseen by Community Living Ontario
Mission: To ensure that persons with developmental disabilities & their families have the opportunity to live & effectively participate in their community.
Member of: Community Living Ontario
Chief Officer(s):
Rick Hill, Executive Director
rhill@clwalkerton.org

Community Living Wallaceburg (CLW)
1100 Dufferin Ave., Wallaceburg ON N8A 2W1
Tel: 519-627-0777; *Fax:* 519-627-8905
Toll-Free: 800-620-4425
www.getintocommunityliving.com
www.facebook.com/CLWallaceburg
twitter.com/clwallaceburg
www.youtube.com/CLWallaceburg
Previous Name: Wallaceburg & Sydenham District Association for Community Living
Overview: A small local charitable organization founded in 1956 overseen by Community Living Ontario
Mission: To provide a range of accommodation, community & employment services to enable people with developmental disabilities to realize their potential within inclusive communities.
Member of: Community Living Ontario; Ontario Agencies Supporting Individuals with Special Needs; Ontario Association on Developmental Disabilities; Integration Action for Inclusion in Education & Community; National Conference of Executives of the Arc
Chief Officer(s):
Derek McGivern, President
David Katzman, Executive Director
david@getintocommunityliving.com
Membership: *Fees:* $5 single; $10 family

Community Living Welland Pelham
535 Sutherland Ave., Welland ON L3B 5A4
Tel: 905-735-0081; *Fax:* 905-735-9431
communityliving@cl-wellandpelham.ca
www.cl-wellandpelham.ca
www.facebook.com/CLWellandPelham
twitter.com/CLWellandPelham
www.youtube.com/CLWellandPelham
Previous Name: Welland District Association for Community Living
Overview: A small local organization
Mission: To promote the inclusion of mentally disabled people
Member of: Community Living Ontario
Chief Officer(s):
Heather Schneider, President
Barbara Vyrostko, Executive Director
barbvyrostko@cl-wellandpelham.ca

Community Living West Nipissing (CLWN) / Intégration communautaire de Nipissing ouest
75 Railway St., Sturgeon Falls ON P2B 3A1
Tel: 705-753-1665; *Fax:* 705-753-2482
clwn@vianet.ca
communitylivingwestnipissing.com
Previous Name: West Nipissing Association for Community Living
Overview: A small local charitable organization founded in 1970 overseen by Community Living Ontario
Mission: To build a community where everyone belongs, one person at a time; To bea welcoming community that respects all its members in their diversity, their contributions, & their aspirations
Member of: Community Living Ontario
Chief Officer(s):
Sylvie Bélanger, Executive Director
sylviebelanger@vianet.ca
Louise Gauthier, President
Finances: *Annual Operating Budget:* $3 Million-$5 Million; *Funding Sources:* Government; Fundraising; Sale of goods & services
Staff Member(s): 95; 50 volunteer(s)
Membership: 41; *Fees:* $5
Activities: *Library*

Community Living West Northumberland
275 Cottesmore Ave., Cobourg ON K9A 4E3
Tel: 905-372-4455; *Fax:* 905-372-2783
info@communitylivingwestnorthumberland.ca
www.communitylivingwestnorthumberland.ca
Previous Name: Port Hope/Cobourg & District Association for Community Living
Overview: A small local charitable organization founded in 1959 overseen by Community Living Ontario
Mission: To provide support to individuals with an intellectual disability, helping them to particpate fully in the community.
Member of: United Way; Ontario Association for Community Living
Chief Officer(s):
Patrick Houlihan, Chair
Cathy Timlin, Executive Director
Finances: *Funding Sources:* Ministry of Community & Social Services
Staff Member(s): 8
Activities: Skills training; vocational employment; social recreational support for people with developmental challeges; EARN-ODSP Employment Support Provider

Community Living Wiarton & District *See* Bruce Peninsula Association for Community Living

Community Living Windsor (CLW)
7025 Enterprise Way, Windsor ON N8T 3N6
Tel: 519-974-4221; *Fax:* 519-974-4157
general@clwindsor.org
Previous Name: Windsor Community Living Support Services
Overview: A medium-sized local organization founded in 1953 overseen by Community Living Ontario
Member of: Community Living Ontario; Canadian Association for Community Living; OASIS
Chief Officer(s):
John Fairley, President
Xavier Noordermeer, Executive Director
Finances: *Annual Operating Budget:* Greater than $5 Million; *Funding Sources:* Government; foundation; donations; fees
Staff Member(s): 300; 75 volunteer(s)
Membership: 250; *Fees:* $11 individuals; $14 families
Activities: *Speaker Service:* Yes; *Library* Open to public

Community Living York South (CLYS)
101 Edward Ave., Richmond Hill ON L4C 5E5
Tel: 905-884-9110; *Fax:* 905-737-3284
Toll-Free: 877-737-3475
info@communitylivingyorksouth.ca
www.communitylivingyorksouth.ca
www.facebook.com/167103456661415
twitter.com/CLYorkSouth
Previous Name: Community Living Association for York South; York South Association for Community Living
Overview: A large local charitable organization founded in 1954 overseen by Community Living Ontario
Mission: To assist all individuals with a developmental disability to choose & access those aspects of daily living which enhance their quality of life in this community
Member of: Community Living Association for Ontario
Affliation(s): United Way
Finances: *Annual Operating Budget:* Greater than $5 Million; *Funding Sources:* United Way; donations; provincial government
Staff Member(s): 230; 200 volunteer(s)
Membership: 1,000+ families; *Committees:* Executive; External Rights Review; Task Forces: Housing; Aging; Financial; Investment
Publications:
• Access [a publication of Community Living York South]
Type: Newsletter

Markham Office
#5 & 6, 144 Main St. Markham North, Markham ON L3P 5T3
Tel: 905-294-4971; *Fax:* 905-472-5409

Vaughan Office
#6, 136 Winges Rd., Woodbridge ON L4L 6C3
Tel: 905-264-7262; *Fax:* 905-264-7850

Community Microskills Development Centre
1 Vulcan St., Toronto ON M9W 1L3
Tel: 416-247-7181; *Fax:* 416-247-1877
Toll-Free: 877-979-3999
admin@microskills.ca
www.microskills.ca
www.linkedin.com/company/93300
www.facebook.com/MicroSkillsBetterFuture
twitter.com/MicroSkills
www.youtube.com/user/MicroSkillsCentre
Previous Name: Rexdale Community Microskills Development Centre
Overview: A small local charitable organization founded in 1984 overseen by Ontario Council of Agencies Serving Immigrants
Mission: To assist the unemployed, with a focus on immigrants, racial minorities, youth & women, to acquire skills needed for economic, social & political equality in society.
Member of: Onestep, CED Learning Network
Affliation(s): Teachers of English as a Second Language Ontario
Chief Officer(s):
Karen Webb, Chair
Kay Blair, Executive Director
kblair@microskills.ca
Finances: *Annual Operating Budget:* Greater than $5 Million; *Funding Sources:* All levels of government; foundations; corporate donors
Staff Member(s): 103; 200 volunteer(s)
Membership: *Fees:* $10 Microskills graduate/unemployed; $25 employed; $50 non-profit organization; $150 coporation
Activities: Settlement & after-school programs; employment counselling; *Speaker Service:* Yes; *Library:* MicroSkills Employment Resource Centre

Community Museums Association of Prince Edward Island
PO Box 22002, Charlottetown PE C1A 9J2
Tel: 902-892-8837; *Fax:* 902-892-1459
info@museumspei.ca
www.museumspei.ca
www.facebook.com/116764358400112
Previous Name: Community Heritage Federation
Overview: A medium-sized provincial organization founded in 1983
Mission: To foster & support museums, historical societies & other non-profit organizations concerned with heritage of PEI.
Member of: Heritage Canada; Canadian Museums Association
Chief Officer(s):
David Panton, President
Barry King, Executive Director
Finances: *Funding Sources:* Membership fees; federal & provincial grants
Staff Member(s): 1
Membership: 37 museums; *Fees:* $15 individual; $30 organization/associate; $100 patron; *Member Profile:* Community museums; educational institutions; individuals

Community of Christ - Canada East Mission
390 Speedvale Ave. East, Guelph ON N1E 1N5
Tel: 519-822-4150; *Fax:* 519-822-1236
Toll-Free: 888-411-7537
cheryl@communityofchrist.ca
www.communityofchrist.ca/index.php/cem
Also Known As: Saints' Church
Previous Name: Reorganized Church of Jesus Christ of Latter Day Saints (Canada)
Overview: A medium-sized local charitable organization founded in 1830
Mission: To promote communities of joy, hope, love, & peace
Chief Officer(s):
Tim Stanlick, Canada East Mission President
tim@communityofchrist.ca
Jim Poirier, Canadian Bishop & Financial Officer
jim@communityofchrist.ca

Community of Christ - Canada West Mission (CWM)
Stn. 88, Edgerton AB T0B 1K0
Tel: 877-411-2632; *Fax:* 403-239-3542
Toll-Free: 877-411-2632
www.communityofchrist.ca/west/west.htm
Overview: A medium-sized local organization
Mission: To promote communities of joy, hope, love, & peace
Chief Officer(s):
Greg Goheen, President & CFO, 403-537-2565
greg@communityofchrist.ca
Membership: 15 congregations and missions
Publications:
• Family Camps, Youth Camps, Retreats
Type: Directory
Profile: Dates, directors & registrars of upcoming camps & retreats
• The Mission Messenger
Type: Newsletter
Profile: Articles & events to inform members & friends of the church

Community One Foundation
PO Box 760, Stn. F, Toronto ON M4Y 2N6
Tel: 416-920-5422
info@communityone.ca
www.communityone.ca
Previous Name: Lesbian & Gay Community Appeal Foundation
Overview: A medium-sized local charitable organization founded in 1980
Mission: To raise & disburse funds for the advancement of lesbian, gay, bisexual & transgender projects, artists & organizations; to fund projects in the areas of health & social services, arts & culture, research & education, political & legal
Member of: Canadian Centre for Philanthropy
Chief Officer(s):
Craig Daniel, Board Co-Chair
Andrea Love, Board Co-Chair
Calvin Chiu, Treasurer
Finances: *Annual Operating Budget:* $50,000-$100,000
20 volunteer(s)
Membership: 1,000 individual
Activities: *Speaker Service:* Yes

Community Planning Association of Alberta (CPAA)
#205, 10940 - 166A St., Edmonton AB T5P 3V5
Tel: 780-432-6387; *Fax:* 780-452-7718
cpaa@cpaa.biz
www.cpaa.biz
Overview: A small provincial organization
Mission: The Community Planning Association of Alberta is an organization dedicated to the promotion of community planning in the Province of Alberta.
Chief Officer(s):
Gloria Wilkinson, Chair
Finances: *Annual Operating Budget:* $100,000-$250,000
Staff Member(s): 3; 100 volunteer(s)
Membership: *Fees:* $25 student; $100 individual; $250 group
Awards:
• Community Planning of Association Scholarship (Scholarship)
Amount: $1000
Meetings/Conferences: • Community Planning Association of Alberta Planning Conference 2015, April, 2015, Black Knight Inn, Red Deer, AB
Scope: Provincial

Community Resource Centre (Killaloe) Inc. (CRC)
PO Box 59, 15 Lake St., Killaloe ON K0J 2A0
Tel: 613-757-3108; *Fax:* 613-757-0208
Toll-Free: 888-757-3108
info@crc-renfrewcounty.com
www.crc-renfrewcounty.com
Also Known As: The Resource Centre
Overview: A small local charitable organization founded in 1987 overseen by InformOntario
Mission: To improve the quality of life in the community by supporting and encouraging improved family life, cooperation, right livelihood and social development.
Member of: Ontario Association of Family Resource Programs; FRP Canada
Affliation(s): Ontario Community Action Program for Children; Canada Prenatal Nutrition Coation
Chief Officer(s):
Joanne King, Executive Director
Finances: *Annual Operating Budget:* $250,000-$500,000
Staff Member(s): 12; 40 volunteer(s)
Membership: 35; *Fees:* Free; *Member Profile:* Citizens of rural Renfrew County
Activities: Information & referral; prenatal nutrition; second hand clothing store; mobile toy & book lending library; mobile information centre for rural communities in southwest Renfrew County; programs for pre-school children accompanied by an adult; *Awareness Events:* Toy Bus Day in the Park; *Library:* Toy & Book Library

Community Resource Connections of Toronto (CRCT)
210 Dundas St. West, 4th Fl., Toronto ON M5G 2E8
Tel: 416-482-4103; *Fax:* 416-482-5237
crct@crct.org
www.crct.org
Previous Name: Community Resources Consultants of Toronto
Overview: A medium-sized local charitable organization founded in 1974
Mission: To provide counselling & consultation on mental health issues, programs, services; To promote development, research & education in area of mental health
Finances: *Funding Sources:* Ministry of Health and Long-Term Care; Ontario Trillium Foundation; Heritage Canada; City of Toronto - Access and Equity Grant; EJLB Foundation
Activities: Hostel outreach program; rehabilitation services; court diversion program; health promotion; *Library* by appointment

Community Resources Consultants of Toronto *See* Community Resource Connections of Toronto

Community Sector Council, Newfoundland & Labrador (CSC)
25 Anderson Ave., St. John's NL A1B 3E4
Tel: 709-753-9860; *Fax:* 709-753-6112
Toll-Free: 866-753-9860
csc@cscnl.ca
communitysector.nl.ca
Previous Name: Community Services Council, Newfoundland & Labrador
Overview: A small local charitable organization founded in 1975
Mission: The Council aims to enhance the volunteer sector of society, bringing together community organizations, governments & individuals, so they may identify common needs & concerns. It helps to formulate policy objectives & develop strategies & services to bring about an inclusive society that ideally supports all. It is a registered charity, BN: #133028027RR0001.
Chief Officer(s):
Penelope Rowe, CEO
pennyrowe@cscnl.ca
Finances: *Annual Operating Budget:* $500,000-$1.5 Million
Staff Member(s): 20; 20 volunteer(s)
Membership: 1-99
Activities: *Awareness Events:* Volunteer Week; National Child Day; *Internships:* Yes; *Speaker Service:* Yes; *Library* Open to public by appointment

Community Services Council, Newfoundland & Labrador
See Community Sector Council, Newfoundland & Labrador

Community Social Services Employers' Association (CSSEA)
Two Bentall Centre, PO Box 232, #800, 555 Burrard St., Vancouver BC V7X 1M8
Tel: 604-687-7220; *Fax:* 604-687-7266
Toll-Free: 800-377-3340
cssea@cssea.bc.ca
www.cssea.bc.ca
Overview: A medium-sized provincial organization founded in 1994
Mission: To strive for excellence & innovation in human resources & labour relations
Chief Officer(s):
Gentil Mateus, Chief Executive Officer
gmateus@cssea.bc.ca
Thomas Marshall, Director, Communications
tmarshall@cssea.bc.ca
Finances: *Annual Operating Budget:* $3 Million-$5 Million
Staff Member(s): 21
Membership: 202

Community Support Centre Haldimand-Norfolk (CSCHN)
103 Inverness St., Caledonia ON N3W 1B1
Tel: 905-765-4408; *Fax:* 289-284-0571
info@haldnor-communitysupport.ca
haldnor-communitysupport.ca
Previous Name: Haldimand Community Support Centre
Overview: A small local charitable organization founded in 1986
Mission: To provide comprehensive client-driven community support/services to individuals and families within Haldimand-Norfolk.
Member of: United Way of Haldimand-Norfolk
Chief Officer(s):
Andrea Gee, Office Manager
Finances: *Annual Operating Budget:* $50,000-$100,000
Staff Member(s): 2; 15 volunteer(s)
Membership: 1-99; *Fees:* $5-100 individual; $25-150 organizations/businesses
Activities: *Library* Open to public

Community Torchlight Guelph/Wellington/Dufferin
PO Box 1027, Guelph ON N1H 6N1
Tel: 519-821-3760; *Fax:* 519-821-8190
Toll-Free: 888-821-3760; *Crisis Hot-Line:* 877-822-0140
info@communitytorchlight.com
www.communitytorchlight.com
www.linkedin.com/pub/community-torchlight/23/2a2/236
twitter.com/CommunityTorch
Previous Name: Distress Centre Wellington/Dufferin; Guelph Distress Centre
Overview: A small local charitable organization founded in 1969 overseen by Distress Centres Ontario
Mission: To provide a free, 24-hour listening, referral & crisis assistance telephone service to Guelph & rural Wellington & Dufferin counties
Chief Officer(s):
John Jones, Executive Director
jjones@communitytorchlight.com
Finances: *Funding Sources:* United Way of Guelph & Wellington; Ontario Ministry of Health & Long-Term Care
Staff Member(s): 5
Activities: Operates Crisis line 519-821-0140/1-877-0140; Distress line 519-821-3760/1-888-821-3760; TeleCheck 519-941-6991; Youth support line 519-821-5469/1-888-821-3760; Emergency shelter line 519-767-6594/1-888-821-3760

Comox Valley Chamber of Commerce (CVCC)
2040 Cliffe Ave., Courtenay BC V9N 2L3
Tel: 250-334-3234; *Fax:* 250-334-4908
Toll-Free: 888-357-4471

admin@comoxvalleychamber.com
www.comoxvalleychamber.com
www.facebook.com/ComoxValleyChamber
twitter.com/cxValleyChamber
Overview: A medium-sized local organization founded in 1919
Mission: To support, promote & represent the best interests of our members in municipal, provincial & national issues.
Member of: BC Chamber of Commerce
Chief Officer(s):
Tracey McGinnis, Chair
Dianne Hawkins, President & CEO
dhawkins@comoxvalleychamber.com
Finances: *Funding Sources:* Membership dues
Staff Member(s): 5
Membership: *Fees:* Schedule available

Comox Valley Child Development Association
237 - 3rd St., Courtenay BC V9N 1E1
Tel: 250-338-4288; *Fax:* 250-338-9326
info@cvcda.ca
www.cvcda.ca
www.facebook.com/157683204244728
www.youtube.com/watch?v=asJV-7FleJo
Overview: A small local organization
Mission: Serves children in the Comox Valley region who need extra support
Chief Officer(s):
Heather McFetridge, Executive Director
Activities: Annual Telethon; *Library:* Lending Library
Publications:
• Oasis
Type: Newsletter; *Frequency:* Quarterly

Comox Valley Community Arts Council (CVCAC)
c/o Comox Valley Centre for the Arts, #202, 580 Duncan St., Courtenay BC V9N 2M7
Tel: 250-338-4417
info@comoxvalleyarts.org
www.comoxvalleyarts.org
www.facebook.com/ComoxValleyArts
twitter.com/CVCartscouncil
Overview: A small local charitable organization founded in 1965
Mission: To promote & foster cultural, educational & artistic activities in the Comox Valley
Affliation(s): Canadian Conference of the Arts; Assembly of BC Arts Councils; Pacific Regional Arts Council; Courtenay Recreational Association; Tourism Comox Valley; Comox Valley Chamber of Commerce
Chief Officer(s):
Dallas Stevenson, Executive Director
Finances: *Funding Sources:* Provincial & municipal governments; private & individual donations; fundraising
Staff Member(s): 2
Membership: *Fees:* $20 individual; $35 group
Activities: Trumpeter Swan Festival juried art show; Annual Community Juried Show; community art project; Art in the Park children's art program; banner project; Endowment Fund; concert series; exhibitions; *Library:* Resource Room; Open to public

Comox Valley Food Bank Society
PO Box 3028, 1491 McPhee St., Courtenay BC V9N 5N3
Tel: 250-338-0615
comoxvfbsociety@shaw.ca
Overview: A small local charitable organization overseen by Food Banks British Columbia
Mission: To provide food to the needy in Comox Valley.
Member of: Food Banks British Columbia
Chief Officer(s):
Jeff Hampton, President
jeffandsusan@shaw.ca

Comox Valley Therapeutic Riding Society (CVTRS)
PO Box 3666, Courtenay BC V9N 7P1
Tel: 250-338-1968; *Fax:* 250-338-4137
cvtrs@telus.net
www.cvtrs.com
Also Known As: Therapeutic Riding
Overview: A small local charitable organization founded in 1986
Mission: To provide a therapeutic riding program for physically, mentally & emotionally disabled, hearing & visually impaired children & adults
Member of: Canadian Therapeutic Riding Association
Affliation(s): North American Handicapped Riding Association
Chief Officer(s):
Margaret Hind, Program Director
Finances: *Funding Sources:* United Way; donations; fundraising
Staff Member(s): 13; 175 volunteer(s)
Membership: 130; *Fees:* $20 individual; $30 group/family
Activities: Therapy with the use of a horse

Comox Valley United Way
PO Box 3097, Courtenay BC V9N 5N3
Tel: 250-338-1151
www.uwcnvi.ca
Overview: A small local organization overseen by United Way of Canada - Centraide Canada

Compagnie d'opéra canadienne *See* Canadian Opera Company

Compagnie de Danse ethnique Migrations *Voir* Compagnie de danse Migrations

Compagnie de danse Migrations
880, av Pére-Marquette, Québec QC G1S 24A
Tél: 418-684-3132
migrationsdanse@gmail.com
www.migrationsdanse.com
Nom précédent: Compagnie de Danse ethnique Migrations
Aperçu: *Dimension:* petite; *Envergure:* locale; Organisme sans but lucratif; fondée en 1981
Mission: Création, formation, production et diffusion de la danse et musique traditionnelle québécoise et des cultures du monde
Membre de: Office du Tourisme et des Congrès de la Communauté Urbaine de Québec
Affliation(s): Folklore Canada International
Finances: *Fonds:* Conseil des Arts et Lettres du Québec; Ville de Québec
Activités: Spectacles - Galas Danse et Musique du Monde; *Stagiaires:* Oui; *Service de conférenciers:* Oui

La Compagnie des philosophes
100, rue St-Laurent Ouest, Montréal QC J4H 1M1
Tél: 450-670-8775
philosophes@me.com
cdesphilosophes.org
Aperçu: *Dimension:* petite; *Envergure:* locale
Mission: Promouvoir la pensée et les théories philosophique des choses qui peuvent être utilisés dans la vie quotidienne
Membre(s) du bureau directeur:
Jacques Perron, Directeur général
jacquesjperron@me.com
Membre: *Montant de la cotisation:* 25$
Activités: Les dimanches philo; journées thématiques et fins de semaines philosophiques; ciné-clubs philosophiques; cafés-philo

Compagnie Marie Chouinard
4499, av de l'esplanade, Montréal QC H2W 1T2
Tél: 514-843-9036; *Téléc:* 514-843-7616
info@mariechouinard.com
www.mariechouinard.com
www.facebook.com/pages/Compagnie-Marie-Chouinard/90299878696
twitter.com/mariechouinard
www.youtube.com/user/MarieChouinard
Aperçu: *Dimension:* petite; *Envergure:* locale
Mission: Pour être dédié à des interprétations modernes et uniques de la danse, nouvelle chorégraphie artistique, et l'expression à travers les mouvements du corps humain.
Membre(s) du bureau directeur:
Marie Chouinard, Directrice générale et artistique
Bernard Dubreuil, Directeur général délégué

Compagnie vox théâtre
#202, 112, rue Nelson, Ottawa ON K1N 5R7
Tél: 613-241-1090; *Téléc:* 613-241-0250
info@voxtheatre.ca
www.voxtheatre.ca
www.facebook.com/pages/Vox-Théâtre/220424964644192
Également appelé: Vox Théâtre
Aperçu: *Dimension:* petite; *Envergure:* locale; Organisme sans but lucratif; fondée en 1979
Mission: Avec son travail de création, ses productions de théâtre chanté, ses accueils de spectacle pluridisciplinaires et ses tournées, la compagnie Vox Théâtre présente une programmation complète pour les enfants et leur propose aussi des activités de formation
Membre de: Association des théâtres francophones du Canada; Théâtre Action
Membre(s) du bureau directeur:
Pier Rodier, Direction artistique et générale
prodier@voxtheatre.ca
Finances: *Fonds:* Conseil des Arts du Canada; Patrimoine canadien; Conseil des arts de l'Ontario, Ville d'Ottawa
Membre(s) du personnel: 2
Activités: Théâtre de création francophone pour les enfants; services d'ateliers en théâtre et d'autres formes des arts de la scène

Les companies de recherche pharmaceutique du Canada *See* Canada's Research-Based Pharmaceutical Companies (Rx&D)

Company of Master Mariners of Canada
c/o Captain G.O. Baugh Memorial Fund, 13375 - 14A Ave., Surrey BC V4A 7P9
www.mastermariners.ca
Overview: A medium-sized national organization founded in 1967
Mission: To maintain the standard of ability & professional conduct of the officers, & also develop education, training & qualifications for young cadets
Affliation(s): Master Mariner organizations in the UK, USA, South Africa, Australia & NZ
Chief Officer(s):
John McCann, National Master
jmccann@sjport.com
Ivan Lantz, Secretary
lantzivan@gmail.com
Yezdee Kooka, Membership Chair
ykooka@sympatico.ca
Finances: *Funding Sources:* Membership dues
Membership: *Fees:* $80 senior/associate/companion; $50 full; *Member Profile:* Master Mariners
Activities: *Speaker Service:* Yes
Publications:
• From The Bridge
Type: Newsletter; *Frequency:* Quarterly; *Editor:* David Whitaker (whitknit@shaw.ca)

Capital Division
PO Box 56104, 407 Laurier Ave. West, Ottawa ON K1R 7Z1
Chief Officer(s):
Michael Hubbard, Divison Master

Fundy Division
c/o 33 Cove Cres., Rothesay NB E2E 5C6
Chief Officer(s):
John McCann, Division Master

Great Lakes Division
8 Unwin Ave., Toronto ON M5A 1A1
Chief Officer(s):
Frank Hough, Division Master

Maritimes Division
PO Box 315, Stn. Main, Dartmouth NS B2Y 3Y5
Chief Officer(s):
Rick Gates, Division Master
patrickgates@bellaliant.net

Montréal Division
#326, 300, rue St-Sacrement, Montréal QC H2Y 1X4
Chief Officer(s):
Don Coelho, Division Master

Newfoundland & Labrador Division
PO Box 4920, St. John's NL A1C 5R3
Chief Officer(s):
Christopher Hearn, Division Master
christopher.hearn@mi.mun.ca

Vancouver Division
c/o D. Rose, 6050 Cartier St., Vancouver BC V6M 3A9
Chief Officer(s):
Don Rose, Division Master

Vancouver Island Division
#6, 912 Brulette Pl., Mill Bay BC V0R 2P2
Chief Officer(s):
Geoffrey Vale, Division Master, 250-743-9656
gvale33@hotmail.com

Company of Women
1353 Cleaver Dr., Oakville ON L6J 1W5
Tel: 905-338-1771; *Fax:* 905-338-3018
www.companyofwomen.ca
www.linkedin.com/groups?homeNewMember=&gid=1795964&trk=
www.facebook.com/pages/Company-of-Women/106951892707614
twitter.com/companyofwomen
Overview: A small local organization
Chief Officer(s):
Anne Day, Founder
anne@companyofwomen.ca

Membership: *Fees:* $195 full; $115 social; $285 corporate; $95 youth
Publications:
• Company
Profile: Quarterly magazine

The Comparative & International Education Society of Canada (CIESC) / La Société canadienne d'éducation comparée et internationale (SCECI)
University of Western Ontario, #2, 1151 Richmond St., London ON N6A 5B8
www.edu.uwo.ca/ciesc/
Overview: A small international charitable organization founded in 1967
Mission: To promote international knowledge & understanding in education; To examine educational systems in international & comparative framework
Member of: Canadian Society for the Study of Education
Affliation(s): World Congress of Comparative Education Societies
Chief Officer(s):
Marianne Larsen, President
mlarsen@uwo.ca
Finances: *Annual Operating Budget:* Less than $50,000
Membership: 150 Canada & abroad; *Fees:* $30
Awards:
• Michel LaFerrière Award (Award)
• Douglas Ray Award
Publications:
• Canadian & International Education / Education canadienne et international
Type: Journal; *Editor:* Suzanne Majhanovich

Compassion Canada
PO Box 5591, London ON N6A 5G8
Tel: 519-668-0224; *Fax:* 866-685-1107
Toll-Free: 800-563-5437
info@compassion.ca
www.compassion.ca
Overview: A medium-sized international charitable organization founded in 1963
Mission: To provide sponsors for children in Third World countries; to aid community development projects in cooperation with Canadian International Development Agency; to be an advocate for children, to release them from their spiritual, economic, social & physical poverty & to enable them to become responsible & fulfilled Christian adults
Member of: Better Business Bureau; Canadian Council of Christian Charities; Association of Evangelical Relief & Development Organizations; Evangelical Fellowship of Canada
Chief Officer(s):
Barry Slauenwhite, President & CEO
Finances: *Funding Sources:* Donations; government grants
Activities: *Speaker Service:* Yes

Compensation Employees' Union (Ind.) (CEU) / Syndicat des employés d'indemnisation (ind.)
#120, 13775 Commerce Pkwy., Richmond BC V6V 2V4
Tel: 604-278-4050; *Fax:* 604-278-5002
www.ceu.bc.ca
www.facebook.com/313873122023339
twitter.com/CEUOurUnion
Overview: A medium-sized provincial organization founded in 1974
Mission: The Compensation Employees' Union was certified in 1974. The CEU is an all inclusive bargaining unit representing all workers at the Workers' Compensation Board that are not excluded by law. The membership ranges from cleaners, support positions, technicial positions, officer level positions, physiologists, and lawyers.
Member of: National Union of Public and General Employees
Chief Officer(s):
Sandra Wright, President
Candace Philpitt, Secretary
Finances: *Annual Operating Budget:* $500,000-$1.5 Million
Staff Member(s): 5
Membership: 2,100
Activities: *Library*

Compétences Canada *See* Skills Canada

Compost Council of Canada / Conseil canadien du compost
16 Northumberland St., Toronto ON M6H 1P7
Tel: 416-535-0240; *Fax:* 416-536-9892
Toll-Free: 877-571-4769
info@compost.org
www.compost.org
www.facebook.com/people/Compost-Council/100001137258465
Overview: A medium-sized national organization founded in 1991
Mission: To advance organics residuals recycling & compost use; To contribute to environmental sustainability
Chief Officer(s):
Susan Antler, Executive Director
Activities: Providing resources for the Canadian compost industry; *Awareness Events:* Compost Week, May
Meetings/Conferences: • Compost Council of Canada 2015 25th Annual National Compost Conference, 2015
Scope: National
Description: Current developments in the composting industry, such as research, processing improvements, & community developments
Contact Information: E-mail: info@compost.org
Publications:
• Compost Matters
Type: Newsletter
Profile: Information for members of the Compost Council of Canada, such as regulations, members, grants, workshops, conferences, & awareness events

Comptables professionnels agréés du Canada *See* Chartered Professional Accountants Canada

Comptables professionnels agréés Nouveau-Brunswick *See* Chartered Professional Accountants of New Brunswick

Compton County Historical Museum Society (CCHMS) / Société du Musée historique du Comté de Compton
Eaton COrner Museum, 374 Rte 253, Cookshire-Eaton QC J0B 1M0
Tel: 819-875-5256
info@eatoncorner.ca
www.eatoncorner.ca
Overview: A small local charitable organization founded in 1959 overseen by Fédération des sociétés d'histoire du Québec
Mission: To operate the county museum; to promote the study & appreciation of the history of Eaton Corner & Compton County; to erect monuments, memorials & plaques; to maintain archives
Member of: Quebec Anglophone Heritage Network
Chief Officer(s):
Marc Nault, President
Finances: *Funding Sources:* Fundraising; membership fees
Membership: *Fees:* $10 individual; $15 family; $75 lifetime; *Committees:* Activities; Collections & Archives; Exhibition Development; Museum Administration; Buildings & Grounds; Heritage Gardens & Landscaping; Fundraising
Activities: Irish Variety Evening; Heritage Costume Dance; Hymn Sings at the Museum (music by a treadle-powered harmonium); Foliage & Heritge Tour; *Library:* Compton County Historical Museum Society Resource Centre; Open to public

Compton Historical Society / Société d'histoire de Compton
6280, rte Louis St. Laurent, Compton QC J0B 1L0
Tel: 819-835-9117
Overview: A small local organization founded in 1993
Chief Officer(s):
Russell Nichols, President
Finances: *Annual Operating Budget:* Less than $50,000
4 volunteer(s)
Membership: *Fees:* $5 individual; $10 family
Activities: Publishing books on local history; restoration of abandoned cemeteries

Computer Learning & Information Centre Society of Calgary *See* CanLearn Society for Persons with Learning Difficulties

Computer Modelling Group (CMG)
#200, 1824 Crowchild Trail NW, Calgary AB T2M 3Y7
Tel: 403-531-1300; *Fax:* 403-289-8502
cmgl@cmgl.ca
www.cmgroup.com
Overview: A small international organization founded in 1978
Mission: To develop technology transfer of oil & gas reservoir simulation software; To provide practical solutions for reservoir modelling & simulation, advanced software, advanced oil recovery (EOR/IOR) processes, reservoir engineering, consulting, training & technical support
Chief Officer(s):
Ken M. Dedeluk, President & CEO
ken.dedeluk@cmgl.ca
David Hicks, Vice-President, Eastern Hemisphere
James C. Erdle, Vice-President, USA & Latin America
jim.erdle@cmgl.ca

Europe Office
Howbery Park, #4, Isis Building, Wallingford OX10 8ba
United Kingdom
Tel: 44-1491-832447
CMG-sales-Europe@cmgl.ca
Chief Officer(s):
Steve Webb, General Manager

Middle East Office
Building 12, PO Box 500 446, #320, Dubai Internet City, Dubai United Arab Emirates
Tel: 971-4-434-5190; *Fax:* 971-4-423-0740
CMG-sales-ME@cmgl.ca
Chief Officer(s):
David Hicks, Vice President, Eastern Hemisphere

South America Office
Centro Empresarial Eurobuilding, Calle La Guarita, #2-A, Caracas Venezuela
Tel: 58-212-993-0463; *Fax:* 58-212-993-0315
CMG-sales-LA@cmgl.ca
Chief Officer(s):
Carlos Granado, Manager, Venezuela & Trinidad

USA office
#860, 450 Gears Rd., Houston TX 77067 USA
Tel: 281-872-8500; *Fax:* 281-872-8577
CMG-sales-USA@cmgl.ca
Chief Officer(s):
Jim Erdle, Vice-President, USA & Latin America

Computer-Using Educators of BC
c/o BC Teachers Federation, #100, 550 West 6 Ave., Vancouver BC V5Z 4P2
Tel: 604-871-1848
Toll-Free: 800-663-9163
cuebc.ca
twitter.com/cuebc
Overview: A small provincial organization
Mission: To promote the educational uses of computer technology in British Columbia schools
Member of: BC Teachers' Federation
Chief Officer(s):
Mike Silverton, President
msilverton@cuebc.ca
Activities: Conferences; newsletter

Conayt Friendship Society
PO Box 1989, Merritt BC V1K 1B8
Tel: 250-378-5107; *Fax:* 250-378-6676
conayt.com
Overview: A small local organization founded in 1968
Mission: To improve holistically the quality of life, cultural distinctiveness, & the strengthening of friendship & cooperation between the Aboriginal & Non-Aboriginal people in the Nicola Valley.
Chief Officer(s):
George Girouard, Executive Director
george@conayt.com
Staff Member(s): 20
Membership: *Fees:* $2 individual; $5 family
Activities: Housing services; counselling; out-patient services; anger management workshop; family preservation program; day camps; prenatal/nutrition program; selders network

Conception Bay Area Chamber of Commerce
#3, 702 Conception Bay Hwy., Conception Bay South NL A1X 3A5
Tel: 709-834-5670
info@cbachamber.com
www.conceptionbaysouth.ca/business/chamber-of-commerce
Overview: A small local organization
Member of: Newfoundland & Labrador Chamber of Commerce
Awards:
• Business Recognition Awards
Awards to Entrepreneur of the Year, Best New Business of the Year, and Best Established Business of the Year

Concerned Children's Advertisers
#200, 10 Alcorn Ave., Toronto ON M4V 3A9
Tel: 416-484-0871; *Fax:* 416-484-6564
info@cca-arpe.ca
cca-arpe.ca
Overview: A medium-sized national organization founded in 1990

Mission: To produce campaigns such as public service announcements, curricula & advice for families, in order to responsibly handle issues such as drug abuse, child abuse, child safety, self-esteem, bullying, media literacy & healthy lifestyles.
Affliation(s): Canadian Association of Principals; Canadian Teachers' Federation; The Canadian Home & School Federation; Dietitians of Canada; Active Living Alliance
Chief Officer(s):
Craig Hutchison, Chair
Sherry MacLauchlan, Vice-Chair
Russ Ward, Treasurer
Membership: *Member Profile:* Canadian companies who produce responsible marketing & advertising campaigns aimed at children & their families

Concerned Friends of Ontario Citizens in Care Facilities (CFOCCF)
140 Merton St., 2nd Fl., Toronto ON M4S 1A1
Tel: 416-489-0146
Toll-Free: 855-489-0146
info@concernedfriends.ca
www.concernedfriends.ca
Overview: A small provincial charitable organization founded in 1980
Mission: To address the issue of quality physical & emotional care & the general conditions facing residents of long-term care facilities; to bring concerns to the attention of the provincial government to work for constructive changes in statutes & regulations; to provide information to residents & their relatives about their rights & responsibilities under government legislation.
Affliation(s): Self Help Resource Centre of Greater Toronto
Chief Officer(s):
Lois Dent, Contact
Finances: *Funding Sources:* Ontario Trillium Foundation; membership dues; donations; sale of publications
Membership: *Fees:* $20 regular; $15 senior; *Member Profile:* Associate or employee of a long-term care facility; *Committees:* Advocacy; Volunteer

Concordia Caribbean Students' Union (CCSU)
Concordia University, Hall Building, #H-733-3, 1455 boul. de Maisonneuve Ouest, Montréal QC H3G 1M8
Tel: 514-848-2424
concordia.caribbean@gmail.com
ccsu.concordia.ca
Overview: A small local organization
Mission: The mission of CCSU is to educate and promote Caribbean culture to the entire student body, including those of non-caribbean descent. We also help facilitate the transition of the new Carribean students to Concordia and Montreal's social scene.

Concordia University Faculty Association (CUFA) / Association des professeurs de l'Université Concordia
7141 Sherbrooke St. West, #HB-109, Montréal QC H4B 1R6
Tel: 514-848-2424; *Fax:* 514-848-3997
cufa@alcor.concordia.ca
www.cufa.net
Overview: A medium-sized local organization
Mission: To represent its members at Concordia University, which includes full-time faculty, including those on limited and extended term and professional librarians
Chief Officer(s):
Lucie Lequin, President
Lucie.Lequin@concordia.ca
Staff Member(s): 2

Concordia University Part-time Faculty Association (CUPFA) / Association des professeures et professeurs à temps partiel de l'Université Concordia (APTPUC)
Sir George Williams Campus, #K-340, 1455 de Maisonneuve Blvd. West, Montréal QC H3G 1M8
Tel: 514-848-3691; *Fax:* 514-848-3648
cupfa@alcor.concordia.ca
www.cupfa.org
Overview: A small local organization
Mission: CUPFA is a certified, non-affliated labour organization aiming to improve the working conditions of the part-time faculty & maintain harmonious relations between them & Concordia University.
Chief Officer(s):
Dave Douglas, President
Staff Member(s): 2
Membership: *Committees:* Finance; Grievance; Professional Development; Negotiating

Concours de musique du Canada inc. ***See*** Canadian Music Competitions Inc.

Concrete Forming Association of Ontario (CFAO)
70 Leek Cres., Richmond Hill ON L4B 1H1
Tel: 416-499-4000; *Fax:* 416-499-8752
Overview: A small provincial organization founded in 1971
Mission: Contractors are engaged in highrise formwork within the ICI (industrial, commercial, institutional) sectors of the construction industry in Ontario
Member of: Toronto Construction Association
Chief Officer(s):
Rocco Lotito, Director
Finances: *Annual Operating Budget:* Less than $50,000; *Funding Sources:* Membership dues; industry funds
10 volunteer(s)
Membership: 10; *Fees:* $200
Awards:
• Civil Engineering Award (Award)
The Scholarship Committee of the Department of Civil Engineering takes into consideration the following factors: work experience, interest, career aspirations in the construction industry; family affiliations in any respect of the industry; financial need; academic proficiency; priority consideration to first-time applicants, however, a previous award winner may be considered given extenuating circumstances (i.e. financial need)*Eligibility:* Ryerson Polytechnic University students who have completed their first or second year of the Civil Engineering program & who are continuing on into the second or third year on a full-time basis in the immediate year following *Amount:* $500

Concrete Precasters Association of Ontario (CPA)
5001 Dufferin Ave., Wallaceburg ON N8A 4M9
Tel: 866-853-0310; *Fax:* 866-853-0311
info@cpaontario.com
www.cpaontario.com
Overview: A small provincial organization founded in 1991
Mission: To unite, improve & represent the interests of the precast concrete manufacturers in Ontario
Chief Officer(s):
Jason Schoenfeld, President
Brian Hoffman, Administrator
Staff Member(s): 2
Membership: 80; *Committees:* Membership; Technical; Marketing; Convention; Safety

Conditionnement physique Noueau-Brunswick ***See*** Fitness New Brunswick

Condominium Home Owners' Association of British Columbia (CHOA)
#200, 65 Richmond St., New Westminster BC V3L 5P5
Tel: 604-584-2462; *Fax:* 604-515-9643
Toll-Free: 877-353-2462
info@choa.bc.ca
www.choa.bc.ca
Overview: A medium-sized provincial organization founded in 1976
Mission: To promote the understanding of strata property living & the interests of strata property owners by providing advisory services, education, advocacy, resources, & support for its members
Chief Officer(s):
Tony Gioventu, Executive Director
tony@choa.bc.ca

Confectionery Manufacturers Association of Canada (CMAC) / Association canadienne des fabricants de confiseries
#301, 885 Don Mills Rd., Toronto ON M3C 1V9
Tel: 416-510-8034; *Fax:* 416-510-8043
info@cmaconline.ca
www.confectioncanada.com
Overview: A medium-sized national organization founded in 1919
Mission: To increase confectionery consumption & production; to achieve global competitiveness; to grow confectionery consumption in a responsible manner as an enjoyable food that is part of a healthy, active lifestyle.
Chief Officer(s):
Leslie Ewing, Executive Director
lesliewing@sympatico.ca
Finances: *Funding Sources:* Membership dues
Membership: 8 active + 24 associate; *Member Profile:* Active - chocolate, sugar confection & chewing gum manufacturers; Associate - suppliers to the industry; *Committees:* Communications; Category Development; Government Relations

Confederacy of Mainland Mi'kmaq (CMM)
PO Box 1590, 57 Martin Cresc., Truro NS B2N 6N7
Tel: 902-895-6385; *Fax:* 902-893-1520
Toll-Free: 877-892-2424
www.cmmns.com
Overview: A medium-sized provincial organization founded in 1986
Mission: To proactively promote and assist Mi'kmaw communities' initiatives toward self determination and enhancement of community.
Chief Officer(s):
Donald M. Julien, Executive Director
Membership: 6 communities

Confederation College Aboriginal Student Association ***See*** Oshki Anishnawbeg Student Association

Confédération des associations d'étudiants et étudiantes de l'Université Laval (CADÉUL)
Pavillon Maurice-Pollack, Université Laval, #2265, 2305 rue de l'Université, Québec QC G1V 1A6
Tél: 418-656-7931; *Téléc:* 418-656-3328
cadeul@cadeul.ulaval.ca
www.cadeul.com
www.facebook.com/CADEUL
twitter.com/cadeul
www.youtube.com/user/CADEUL
Aperçu: *Dimension:* moyenne; *Envergure:* locale
Mission: La Confédération des associations d'étudiants et étudiantes de l'Université Laval est l'association étudiante qui représente tous les ëtudiants inscrits au premier cycle à l'Université Laval.
Membre(s) du bureau directeur:
Caroline Aubry-Abel, Présidente
presidence@cadeul.ulaval.ca
Thierry Bouchard-Vincent, Vice-président, L'enseignement et à la recherche
enseignement@cadeul.ulaval.ca
Dominique Caron Bélanger, Vice-présidente, Affaires internes
interne@cadeul.ulaval.ca
Florence Côté, Vice-présidente, Affaires externes
externes@cadeul.ulaval.ca
Thomas Pouliot, Directeur, Services
directeur@cadeul.ulaval.ca
Membre(s) du personnel: 19

Confédération des Éducateurs physiques du Québec ***Voir*** Fédération des éducateurs et éducatrices physiques enseignants du Québec

Confédération des Organismes de Personnes Handicapées du Québec (COPHAN)
#300, 2030 boulevard Pie-IX, Montréal QC H1V 2C8
Tél: 514-284-0155; *Téléc:* 514-284-0775
info@cophan.org
www.cophan.org
Nom précédent: Confédération des organismes provinciaux de personnes handicapées du Québec
Aperçu: *Dimension:* moyenne; *Envergure:* provinciale; Organisme sans but lucratif; fondée en 1985
Mission: Milite pour la défense des droits et la promotion des intérêts des personnes ayant des limitations fonctionnelles, de tous âges
Membre de: Conseil de canadiens avec déficiences
Membre(s) du bureau directeur:
Richard Lavigne, Directeur général
direction@cophan.org
Léon Bossé, Président
Membre(s) du personnel: 3; 63 bénévole(s)
Membre: 40 associations; *Montant de la cotisation:* 75 $; *Critères d'admissibilite:* Association qui promeut les intérets et défend les droits des personnes handicapées

Confédération des organismes familiaux du Québec (COFAQ)
#205, 4360 rue D'Iberville, Montréal QC H2H 2L8
Tél: 514-521-4777; *Téléc:* 514-521-6272
famille@cofaq.qc.ca
www.cofaq.qc.ca
Aperçu: *Dimension:* grande; *Envergure:* nationale; Organisme sans but lucratif; fondée en 1972
Mission: Représenter les familles et revendiquer leurs droits auprès des diverses instances publiques et privées; promouvoir des projets innovateurs et le développement d'expertises

satisfaisant aux besoins des familles et leurs organisations; réaliser des activités de soutien auprès des membres
Membre de: Institut Vanier de la famille; Réseau pour un Québec famille; Carrefour action municipal et famille
Membre(s) du bureau directeur:
Paule Blain Clotteau, Vice-présidente
Franciene Mucci, Trésorière
Membre(s) du personnel: 10
Membre: 40 organismes; *Montant de la cotisation:* 40-75; *Critères d'admissibilité:* Organismes familiaux ou regroupement d'organismes

Confédération des organismes provinciaux de personnes handicapées du Québec *Voir* Confédération des Organismes de Personnes Handicapées du Québec

Confederation des peuples autochtones du Québec (CPAQ) / Confederation of Aboriginal People of Québec (CAPQ)
121, Montée de la Mer-Bleue, L'Ascension QC J0T 1W0
Tél: 819-663-4044; *Téléc:* 819-663-6466
info@cpaq.ca
www.cpaq.ca
Aperçu: *Dimension:* moyenne; *Envergure:* provinciale
Mission: Organisation provinciale qui représente les intérêts des Autochtones du Québec qui sont membres d'une de leurs communautés affiliées
Membre(s) du bureau directeur:
Guillaume Carle, Grand-Chef
Membre: *Montant de la cotisation:* $30

Confédération des syndicats nationaux (CSN) / Confederation of National Trade Unions
1601, av De Lorimier, Montréal QC H2K 4M5
Tél: 514-598-2155; *Téléc:* 514-598-2089
csncommunications@csn.qc.ca
www.csn.qc.ca
www.facebook.com/LaCSN
twitter.com/laCSN
Aperçu: *Dimension:* grande; *Envergure:* nationale; Organisme sans but lucratif; fondée en 1921
Mission: La Confédération limite ses activités principalement au Québec, quoique certains locaux soient établis hors de la province; comprend 9 fédérations, 13 conseils centraux et 2 800 syndicats
Affliation(s): Confédération internationale des syndicats libres
Membre(s) du bureau directeur:
Pierre Patry, Trésorier
Jacques Létourneau, Présidente
Jean Lortie, Secrétaire générale
Finances: *Budget de fonctionnement annuel:* Plus de $5 Million
Membre(s) du personnel: 450
Membre: 280 000; *Comités:* Le comité confédéral de santé et sécurité; Le comité national de la condition féminine; Le comité confédéral sur les relations interculturelles; Le comité national des jeunes; Le comité confédéral des LGBT
Activités: Réunion du conseil confédéral, 4 fois par an, à Montréal et Québec; *Stagiaires:* Oui; *Bibliothèque:* Service de documentation
Publications:
• Perspectives CSN
Type: Magazine

Confédération nationale des cadres du Québec (CNCQ)
2430, ch Ste-Foy, Québec QC G1V 1TZ
Tél: 418-877-1500; *Téléc:* 418-877-4469
www.cncq.qc.ca
Aperçu: *Dimension:* grande; *Envergure:* provinciale; Organisme sans but lucratif; fondée en 1992
Mission: Venir en aide et supporter les associations affiliées de cadres.
Affliation(s): Confédération internationale des cadres
Membre(s) du bureau directeur:
Michel Mathieu, Président
m.mathieu@saq.qc.ca
Finances: *Budget de fonctionnement annuel:* $100,000-$250,000
Membre(s) du personnel: 1
Membre: 15 associations représentant 20 000 cadres; *Montant de la cotisation:* 4,00$/membre d'une association affiliée

Confederation of Aboriginal People of Québec *Voir* Confederation des peuples autochtones du Québec

Confederation of Alberta Faculty Associations (CAFA)
Univ. of Alberta, 11043 - 90 Ave., Edmonton AB T6G 2E1
Tel: 780-492-5630; *Fax:* 780-436-0516
www.ualberta.ca/~cafa/
twitter.com/cafaab
Overview: A medium-sized provincial organization overseen by Canadian Association of University Teachers
Mission: CAFA is a professional organization of faculty and faculty association in Alberta Universities. The objects of the Conferdation are to promote the quality of education in the province and to promote the well-being of Alberta Universities and their academic staff. Comprised of four associations: The Association of Academic Staff University of Alberta, Athabasca University Faculty Association, The Faculty Association of the University of Calgary and The University of Lethbridge Faculty Association.
Chief Officer(s):
John Nicholls, Executive Director, 780-492-5630
john.nicholls@ualberta.ca
Lori Morinville, Administrative Officer, 780-492-5630
lori.morinville@ualberta.ca
Membership: 3,511 individuals + 6 organizations
Awards:
• CAFA Distinguished Academic Awards (Award)
Recognizes members, who through their research and/or other scholarly, creative or professional activities, have made outstanding contributions to the community beyond the university. Eligibility: Current member of one of the academic staff associations within CAFA

Confederation of Canadian Wushu Organizations *See* WushuCanada

Confederation of National Trade Unions *Voir* Confédération des syndicats nationaux

Confederation of Ontario University Staff Associations (COUSA)
ON
www.cousa.on.ca
Overview: A medium-sized local organization founded in 1974
Mission: To provide support and advocacy for the non-academic staff of Ontario's universities.
Chief Officer(s):
Barry Diacon, President, 905-252-9140 Ext. 24986
bdiacon@sympatico.ca
Membership: 5 unions

Confederation of Resident & Ratepayer Associations (CORRA)
63 The South Kingsway, Toronto ON M6S 3T4
e-mail: corratoronto@gmail.com
Overview: A small local organization
Mission: The association coordinates the activities of & lobbies for member associations to promote better urban life & beneficial legislation. It acts as watchdog to protect city neighbourhoods, parks & waterfront.
Chief Officer(s):
William Roberts, Chair, 416-769-3162
willadvocate@aol.com
Finances: *Annual Operating Budget:* Less than $50,000; *Funding Sources:* Membership dues
8 volunteer(s)
Membership: *Fees:* $50; *Member Profile:* Resident & ratepayer associations

Confederation of University Faculty Associations of British Columbia (CUFA BC)
#315, 207 West Hastings St., Vancouver BC V6B 1H7
Tel: 604-646-4677; *Fax:* 604-646-4676
www.cufa.bc.ca
Overview: A medium-sized provincial organization overseen by Canadian Association of University Teachers
Chief Officer(s):
Robert Clift, Executive Director
David Mirhady, President, 778-782-3906
Awards:
• CUFA/BC Distinguished Academics Awards (Award)

Confédération québécoise des coopératives d'habitation (CQCH)
#202, 840, rue Raoul-Jobin, Québec QC G1N 1S7
Tél: 418-648-6758; *Téléc:* 418-648-8580
Ligne sans frais: 800-667-9386
info@cqch.qc.ca
www.cooperativehabitation.coop
Aperçu: *Dimension:* moyenne; *Envergure:* provinciale; Organisme sans but lucratif; fondée en 1987
Membre(s) du bureau directeur:
Guillaume Brien, Directrice générale
guillaume.brien@reseaucoop.com
Michèle La Haye, Présidente, Conseil d'administration
Finances: *Budget de fonctionnement annuel:* $500,000-$1.5 Million
Membre(s) du personnel: 10
Membre: 7; *Critères d'admissibilite:* Fédérations des coopératives d'habitation

Confédération québécoise des coopératives d'habitation en Outaouais
#106, 178, boul Greber, Gatineau QC J8T 6Z6
Tél: 819-243-3717; *Téléc:* 819-243-5356
cooperativehabitation.coop
Aperçu: *Dimension:* petite; *Envergure:* locale; fondée en 1985
Mission: Pour promouvoir le logement coopératif au Québec
Membre de: Confédération québécoise des coopératives d'habitation
Membre(s) du bureau directeur:
Nathalie Mercier, Coordonnatrice
nmercier@logeaction.com
Finances: *Budget de fonctionnement annuel:* $250,000-$500,000
Membre: 1-99
Activités: Services aux membres; développement de nouvelles coopératives; gestion de coopératives d'habitation et d'organismes sans but lucratif

Le Conference Board du Canada *See* The Conference Board of Canada

The Conference Board of Canada / Le Conference Board du Canada
255 Smyth Rd., Ottawa ON K1H 8M7
Tel: 613-526-3280; *Fax:* 613-526-4857
Toll-Free: 866-711-2262
www.conferenceboard.ca
Overview: A medium-sized national organization founded in 1954
Mission: To be dedicated to applied research, notably in public policy, economic trends, & organizational performance
Chief Officer(s):
Anne Golden, President & CEO
Glen Hodgson, Sr. VP & Chief Economist
Perry Eisenschmid, Vice-President, Marketing, Sales & IT
Finances: *Funding Sources:* Fees for service to the public & private sectors
Activities: The Business & Environment Research Program provides research & networking facilities for business & government in the economics, business management & public policy aspects of environmental issues. Other activities include conferences, publishing & disseminating research, & facilitating networking & training for leadership; *Library:* Information Centre; by appointment
Awards:
• National Awards in Governance (Award)
Awarded to boards of directors that have demonstrated excellence in governance & have implemented successful innovations in their governance practices; overall award for innovation & sector specific awards for public, private & not for profit sectors
• National Awards for Excellence in Business-Education Partnership (Award)
Awarded to partnerships that have a demonstrated record of success in promoting the importance of science, technology &/or mathematics; linking education & the world of work, promoting teacher development, encouraging students to stay in school, expanding vocational &/or apprenticeship training *Contact:* Mary Ann McLaughlin

Conférence canadienne des arts *See* Canadian Conference of the Arts

Conférence des associations de la défense *See* Conference of Defence Associations

Conférence des coopératives forestières du Québec *Voir* Fédération québécoise des coopératives forestières

Conférence des évêques catholiques du Canada *See* Canadian Conference of Catholic Bishops

Conférence des recteurs et des principaux des universités du Québec (CREPUQ) / Conference of Rectors & Principals of Quebec Universities
c/o Conférence des recteurs et des principaux, #200, 500, rue Sherbrooke ouest, Montréal QC H3A 3C6
Tél: 514-288-8524; *Téléc:* 514-288-0554
info@crepuq.qc.ca
www.crepuq.qc.ca
Aperçu: *Dimension:* moyenne; *Envergure:* provinciale; fondée en 1963
Mission: Est un organisme privé qui regroupe, sur une base volontaire, tous les établissements universitaires québécois; sert de forum permanent d'échanges et de concertation qui permet aux gestionnaires de partager leurs expériences en vue d'améliorer l'efficacité générale du système universitaire québécois.
Membre(s) du bureau directeur:
Daniel Zizian, Directeur général, 514-288-8524 Ext. 201
daniel.zizian@crepuq.qc.ca
Finances: *Fonds:* Les cotisations annuelles des membres
Membre(s) du personnel: 33
Membre: 7 établissements universitaires québécois
Activités: *Bibliothèque*

Conference ferroviaire de Teamsters Canada *See* Teamsters Canada Rail Conference

Conférence générale des assemblées de dieu canadiennes *See* General Conference of the Canadian Assemblies of God

Conference of Defence Associations (CDA) / Conférence des associations de la défense
#412A, 151 Slater St., Ottawa ON K1P 5H3
Tel: 613-236-1252; *Fax:* 613-236-8191
cda@cda-cdai.ca
www.cdacanada.ca
twitter.com/CDAInstitute
Overview: A medium-sized national charitable organization founded in 1932
Mission: To place before people of Canada problems of defence & the well-being of Canada's Armed Forces
Affliation(s): Conference of Defence Associations Institute
Chief Officer(s):
Alain Pellerin, Executive Director
director@cda-cdai.ca
Peter Forsberg, Officer, Public Affairs
pao@cda-cdai.ca
Finances: *Funding Sources:* Individual subscriptions; Vimy Award dinner
Staff Member(s): 4
Membership: 52 associations; *Member Profile:* Associate - The Air Cadet League of Canada; Army, Navy, Air Force Veterans in Canada; Atlantic Chief & P.O.'s Association; The Army Cadet League of Canada; Canadian NATO Defence College Association; The Canadian Airborne Forces Association; The Canadian Defence Industries Association; The Canadian Institute of Strategic Studies; The Canadian War Museum; The Dominion of Canada Rifle Association; The Federation of Military & United Services Institutes of Canada; Military Engineering Institute of Canada; The Military Public Affairs Association of Canada; The Navy League of Canada; Organization of Military Museums of Canada; Reserves 2000; Royal Military Colleges Club of Canada; *Committees:* Executive
Activities: Seminars & symposiums; *Internships:* Yes; *Speaker Service:* Yes
Awards:
• The Vimy Award (Award)
To recognize one Canadian who has made a significant contribution to the defence & security of our nation & the preservation of our democratic values

Conference of Independent Schools (Ontario) (CIS)
PO Box 27, Whitby ON L1N 5R7
Tel: 905-665-8622; *Fax:* 905-665-8635
admin@cisontario.ca
www.cisontario.ca
twitter.com/CISOntario
Overview: A small provincial organization founded in 1983 overseen by Federation of Independent Schools in Canada
Mission: To provide a collegial forum to promote excellence in education among its member schools
Member of: Canadian Accredited Independent Schools
Affliation(s): National Association of Independent Schools
Chief Officer(s):
Ian Campbell, Executive Director
director@cisontario.ca
Finances: *Annual Operating Budget:* $100,000-$250,000; *Funding Sources:* Membership dues
Staff Member(s): 2
Membership: 45 Member schools; *Member Profile:* Not-for-profit independent schools

Conference of New England Governors & Eastern Canadian Premiers
Council Secretariat, PO Box 2044, #1006, 5161 George St., Halifax NS B3J 2Z1
Tel: 902-424-7590; *Fax:* 902-424-8976
info@cap-cpma.ca
www.cap-cpma.ca
Mission: To expand economic ties among the Atlantic provinces, Québec, & six New England states; To foster energy exchanges; To coordinate numerous policies & programs, in areas such as transportation, forest management, tourism, small-scale agriculture & fisheries; To enact policy resolutions that call on actions by the state & provincial governments, as well as by the two national governments; To promote natural gas, resource & infrastructure development
Membership: *Member Profile:* Premiers of the Atlantic provinces & Québec; Governors of six New England States
Activities: Hosting conferences of the Premiers & Governors to discuss issues of common interest; Convening meetings of state & provincial officials; Organizing workshops & roundtables; Preparing reports & studies; Monitoring & acting on common issues in the northeast region, such as electric restructuring

Conference of Rectors & Principals of Quebec Universities *Voir* Conférence des recteurs et des principaux des universités du Québec

Conference of Representatives of the Governing Bodies of the Legal Profession in the Provinces of Canada *See* Federation of Law Societies of Canada

Conference pour l'harmonisation des lois au Canada *See* Uniform Law Conference of Canada

Conference Society of Alberta *See* Alberta Congress Board

Conflict Resolution Network Canada / Réseau pour la résolution de conflits Canada
Conrad Grebel University College, 84 Waterloo University Campus, Waterloo ON N2L 3G6
Tel: 519-885-0880; *Fax:* 519-885-0806
www.crnetwork.ca
Previous Name: The Network: Interaction for Conflict Resolution
Overview: A medium-sized national charitable organization founded in 1988
Mission: To promote collaborative conflict resolution in Canada; To encourage people to develop more effective approaches to conflict resolution in their communities; To provide services to mediators, lawyers, teachers, community organizers, researchers, managers, & justice system personnel
Member of: Canadian Centre for Philanthropy
Chief Officer(s):
Kathleen Cleland Moyer, Co-Executive Director
Finances: *Annual Operating Budget:* $250,000-$500,000
Staff Member(s): 8
Membership: 800; *Fees:* $100; *Committees:* Private Foundations; Public Sector; Sales & Services
Activities: Producing publications & resources for schools & youth; *Rents Mailing List:* Yes; *Library* by appointment

Conflict Resolution Saskatchewan Inc.
PO Box 3765, Regina SK S4P 3N8
Tel: 306-565-3939; *Fax:* 306-586-6711
Toll-Free: 866-565-3938
admin@conflictresolutionsk.ca
www.conflictresolutionsk.ca
Previous Name: Mediation Saskatchewan
Overview: A small provincial organization
Affliation(s): Family Mediation Canada
Chief Officer(s):
Dreena Horner, President
building.blocks@shaw.ca
Membership: *Fees:* $25 introductory; $250 organizational/sponsor

Confrérie de la librairie ancienne du Québec (CLAQ)
CP 1056, Succ. C, Montréal QC H2L 4V3
Tél: 514-273-4963
Autres numéros: cote@bibliopolis.net
claqsec@bibliopolis.net
www.bibliopolis.net/claq
Aperçu: *Dimension:* petite; *Envergure:* provinciale; fondée en 1987
Mission: Promouvoir l'intérêt pour le livre ancien

Congregation Beth Israel - British Columbia
#305, 950 West 41st Ave., Vancouver BC V5X 2N7
Tel: 604-731-4161; *Fax:* 604-731-4989
info@bethisrael.ca
www.bethisrael.ca
www.youtube.com/watch?v=KtToCfl0Hjw&feature=youtu.be
Overview: A small local organization founded in 1932
Mission: The congregation is dedicated to the strengthening of all aspects of Jewish life, including worship & Torah study, religious, educational & social activities for all ages, & the observance of life cycle events.
Member of: United Synagogue of Conservative Judaism
Chief Officer(s):
Catherine Epstein, President
Jonathan Infeld, Klei Kodesh
rabbiinfeld@bethisrael.ca
Shannon Etkin, Executive Director
shannon@bethisrael.ca
Activities: Youth programs; Hebrew school; facility rental; Rabbi Wilfred & Phyllis Solomon Museum; *Library:* Moe Cohen Library

Congrégation de Sainte-Croix - Les Frères de Sainte-Croix / Congregation of Holy Cross
4901, rue du Piedmont, Montréal QC H3V 1E3
Tél: 514-731-7828; *Téléc:* 514-731-7820
saintecroixcsc@yahoo.ca
www.ste-croix.qc.ca
Aperçu: *Dimension:* petite; *Envergure:* locale
Mission: Congrégation religieuse catholique qui oeuvre en éducation, en milieu paroissial et dans divers autres secteurs de la société
Membre(s) du bureau directeur:
Réjean Charette, Supérieur provincial

Congregation of Holy Cross *Voir* Congrégation de Sainte-Croix - Les Frères de Sainte-Croix

Congregation of Missionaries of the Precious Blood, Atlantic Province
310 Central Ave., Fort Erie ON L2A 3T3
Tel: 905-871-0692
preciousbloodatlantic.org
Overview: A small local charitable organization founded in 1987
Mission: To be rooted in the word of God & reach out to the marginalized
Chief Officer(s):
Jeffrey Finley, Provincial Director
frjf@aol.com

Congregation of St-Basil (Basilian Fathers) (CSB)
95 St. Joseph St., Toronto ON M5S 3C2
Tel: 416-921-6674; *Fax:* 416-920-3413
contact@basilian.org
www.basilian.org
www.youtube.com/user/cavalka124
Also Known As: Basilian Fathers
Overview: A small international organization founded in 1822
Mission: Roman Catholic congregation of priests whose primary apostolate is education, parishes, & Hispanic ministry in Canada, USA, Mexico, Colombia, & France
Member of: RC Church
Chief Officer(s):
Michael P. Cerretto, Secretary General
Ronald P. Fabbro, Superior General
Finances: *Annual Operating Budget:* Less than $50,000
3 volunteer(s)
Membership: 325; *Member Profile:* Priests; Students for the priesthood
Activities: *Library* by appointment

Congregational Christian Churches in Canada (CCCC)
442 Grey St., #H, Brantford ON N3S 7N3
Tel: 519-751-0606; *Fax:* 519-751-0852
Toll-Free: 866-868-8702
cccnationaloffice@bellnet.ca
www.cccc.ca
Overview: A small national charitable organization founded in 1821
Mission: To celebrate & serve Jesus Christ in the 21st century through shared concern for others.
Chief Officer(s):

David Schrader, National Pastor
nationalpastor@bellnet.ca
Bill MacDougall, Chair
b-pmacdougall@ns.sympatico.ca
Kim Adeniran, Administrative Assistant
ccccnationaloffice@bellnet.ca
Finances: *Annual Operating Budget:* $100,000-$250,000
Staff Member(s): 2
Membership: 8,000 + 100 churches across Canada; *Fees:* $50; *Member Profile:* Churches or individuals in accord with CCCC's Statement of Faith and Founding Principles as set out in their By-Law and Supplementary Letters Patent.
Activities: *Internships:* Yes

Congrès canadien polonais ***See*** Canadian Polish Congress

Congrès des Peuples Autochtones ***See*** Congress of Aboriginal Peoples

Congrès des ukrainiens canadiens ***See*** Ukrainian Canadian Congress

Congrès du travail du Canada ***See*** Canadian Labour Congress

Congrès germano-canadien ***See*** German-Canadian Congress

Congrès mondial des ukrainiens ***See*** Ukrainian World Congress

Congrès national canadien-portugais ***See*** Portuguese Canadian National Congress

Congrès national des italo-canadiens ***See*** National Congress of Italian Canadians

Congress of Aboriginal Peoples (CAP) / Congrès des Peuples Autochtones

867 St. Laurent Blvd., Ottawa ON K1K 3B1
Tel: 613-747-6022; *Fax:* 613-747-8834
info@abo-peoples.org
www.abo-peoples.org
www.facebook.com/pages/Congress-of-Aboriginal-Peoples/178584242154616
twitter.com/CAPChief
www.youtube.com/user/TheCAPOttawa
Previous Name: Native Council of Canada
Overview: A large national organization
Mission: To represent approximately 3/4 million Aboriginal people living off-reserve in Canada
Chief Officer(s):
Betty Ann Lavellee, National Chief
Jim Devoe, Chief Operating Officer
jim@abo-peoples.org
Finances: *Annual Operating Budget:* $3 Million-$5 Million; *Funding Sources:* Heritage Canada; Health Canada; Privy Council Office
Membership: Over 50,000
Activities: *Internships:* Yes

Congress of Black Lawyers & Jurists of Québec

#500, 445, boul St-Laurent, Côte-Des-Neiges N QC H3S 2B8
Tel: 514-954-3471; *Fax:* 514-954-3451
Overview: A medium-sized provincial organization
Mission: Please call prior to visit

Congress of Canadian Women-British Columbia ***See*** Canadian Women Voters Congress

Congress of Union Retirees Canada (CURC) / Association des syndicalistes retraités du Canada (ASRC)

2841 Riverside Dr., Ottawa ON K1V 8X7
Tel: 613-526-7422; *Fax:* 613-521-4655
curc.clc-ctc.ca
www.facebook.com/315702295180775
twitter.com/UnionRetirees
Overview: A large national organization founded in 1993
Mission: To ensure that the concerns of senior citizens & union retirees are heard across Canada
Affliation(s): Canadian Labour Congress
Chief Officer(s):
Pat Kerwin, President
Len Hope, First Vice-President
Doug MacPherson, Second Vice-President
Bob McGarry, Secretary
Betty Ann Bushell, Treasurer
Membership: *Fees:* Schedule available; *Member Profile:* Individual union retirees; Spouses of union retiree; Current unionmembers, over 50 years of age

Connect Society - D.E.A.F. Services

6240 - 113 St., Edmonton AB T6H 3L2
Tel: 780-454-9581; *Fax:* 780-447-5820; *TTY:* 780-454-9581
info@connectsociety.org
www.connectsociety.org
Previous Name: Association for the Hearing Handicapped
Overview: A small local charitable organization founded in 1963
Mission: To bring about the full participation in society of deaf & hard of hearing individuals & their families
Chief Officer(s):
Caterina Snyder, Manager, Resource & Communications
csnyder@connectsociety.org
Finances: *Annual Operating Budget:* $500,000-$1.5 Million
Membership: 1-99
Activities: Early Intervention Program; Early Childhood Services; Family Support Program; Stay & Study; Community Living Support Services; *Speaker Service:* Yes

Connexions Information Sharing Services

#201, 812A Bloor St. West, Toronto ON M6G 1L9
Tel: 416-964-7799
mailroom@connexions.org
www.connexions.org
www.facebook.com/ConnexionsOnline
twitter.com/connexi0ns
Overview: A small national organization founded in 1975
Mission: To connect people working for social justice with information, ideas, groups & the history of social change movements.
Chief Officer(s):
Ulli Diemer, Coordinator
Finances: *Annual Operating Budget:* Less than $50,000
Staff Member(s): 3; 20 volunteer(s)
Activities: *Rents Mailing List:* Yes; *Library* Open to public by appointment

Conseil albertain de la coopération

#104, 402 - 30 Ave. NE, Calgary AB T2E 2E3
Tél: 403-276-8250
www.coopzone.coop
Aperçu: *Dimension:* moyenne; *Envergure:* provinciale; fondée en 1956
Membre(s) du bureau directeur:
Hazel Corcoran, Coordinatrice

Conseil atlantique des ministres de l'Éducation et de la Formation ***See*** Council of Atlantic Ministers of Education & Training

Conseil atlantique du Canada ***See*** Atlantic Council of Canada

Conseil canadien d'évaluation des jouets ***See*** Canadian Toy Testing Council

Conseil canadien d'orthoptique ***See*** Canadian Orthoptic Council

Conseil canadien de certification en architecture ***See*** Canadian Architectural Certification Board

Conseil canadien de développement social ***See*** Canadian Council on Social Development

Conseil canadien de droit international ***See*** Canadian Council on International Law

Le Conseil canadien de l'agrément des programmes de pharmacie ***See*** The Canadian Council for Accreditation of Pharmacy Programs

Conseil canadien de l'aviation et de l'aérospatiale ***See*** Canadian Council for Aviation & Aerospace

Le conseil canadien de l'éducation permanente en pharmacie ***See*** The Canadian Council on Continuing Education in Pharmacy

Conseil canadien de l'énergie ***See*** Energy Council of Canada

Conseil canadien de l'horticulture ***See*** Canadian Horticultural Council

Conseil canadien de la construction en acier ***See*** Canadian Steel Construction Council

Conseil Canadien de la Coopération ***Voir*** Conseil canadien de la coopération et de la mutualité

Conseil canadien de la coopération et de la mutualité (CCCM)

#400, 275, rue Bank, Ottawa ON K2P 2L6
Tél: 613-238-6712; *Téléc:* 613-567-0658
info@coopscanada.coop
canada.coop
www.facebook.com/792260167456516
twitter.com/CoopFrancoCan
Nom précédent: Conseil Canadien de la Coopération
Aperçu: *Dimension:* petite; *Envergure:* nationale; Organisme sans but lucratif; fondée en 1946
Mission: Le Conseil vise à promouvoir la coopération en vue du développement socio-économique des communautés francophones du Canada.
Affiliation(s): Alliance coopérative internationale
Membre(s) du bureau directeur:
Denyse Guy, Directrice générale
dguy@canada.coop
Finances: *Fonds:* Gouvernement fédéral
Membre(s) du personnel: 8
Membre: 61; *Critères d'admissibilite:* Conseils provinciaux de la coopération
Activités: Initiative de développement coopératif; adaptation agricole: une approche coopérative; séminaire de perfectionnement en leadership coopératif; chroniques "Culture action"; conférence de santé; programme "Jeune dirigeant stagiaire"; *Evénements de sensibilisation:* Semaine de la coopération; *Bibliothèque:* C.C.C.; rendez-vous
Prix, Bouses:
• Ordre du Mérite Coopératif Canadien (Prix)

Conseil canadien de la fourrure ***See*** The Fur Council of Canada

Conseil canadien de la lutte antiparasitaire en milieu urbain ***See*** Urban Pest Management Council of Canada

Le Conseil canadien de la réadaptation et du travail ***See*** Canadian Council on Rehabilitation & Work

Conseil canadien de la sécurité ***See*** Canada Safety Council

Conseil canadien de la sécurité nautique ***See*** Canadian Safe Boating Council

Conseil canadien de protection des animaux ***See*** Canadian Council on Animal Care

Conseil canadien des administrateurs en transport motorisé ***See*** Canadian Council of Motor Transport Administrators

Conseil canadien des administrateurs universitaires en éducation physique et kinésiologie ***See*** Canadian Council of University Physical Education & Kinesiology Administrators

Conseil canadien des archives ***See*** Canadian Council of Archives

Conseil canadien des associations en ressources humaines ***See*** Canadian Council of Human Resources Associations

Le Conseil canadien des aveugles ***See*** The Canadian Council of the Blind

Conseil canadien des bureaux d'éthique commerciale ***See*** Canadian Council of Better Business Bureaus

Conseil canadien des chefs d'entreprise ***See*** Canadian Council of Chief Executives

Conseil canadien des directeurs provinciaux et des commissaires des incendies ***See*** Council of Canadian Fire Marshals & Fire Commissioners

Le Conseil canadien des Églises ***See*** The Canadian Council of Churches

Conseil canadien des examens chiropratiques ***See*** Canadian Chiropractic Examining Board

Le Conseil canadien des Examinateurs pour les Arpenteurs-géomètres ***See*** Canadian Board of Examiners for Professional Surveyors

Conseil canadien des femmes musulmanes ***See*** Canadian Council of Muslim Women

Conseil Canadien des Géoscientifiques Professionnels ***See*** Canadian Council of Professional Geoscientists

Conseil canadien des infirmières et infirmiers en nursing cardiovasculaire ***See*** Canadian Council of Cardiovascular Nurses

Conseil canadien des laboratoires indépendants *See* Canadian Council of Independent Laboratories

Conseil canadien des ministres de l'environnement *See* Canadian Council of Ministers of the Environment

Conseil canadien des ministres des forêts *See* Canadian Council of Forest Ministers

Conseil canadien des normes de la radiotélévision *See* Canadian Broadcast Standards Council

Conseil canadien des organismes de motoneige *See* Canadian Council of Snowmobile Organizations

Conseil canadien des pêcheurs professionnels *See* Canadian Council of Professional Fish Harvesters

Conseil canadien des piscines et spas *See* Pool & Hot Tub Council of Canada

Conseil canadien des PME et de l'entrepreneuriat *See* Canadian Council for Small Business & Entrepreneurship

Conseil canadien des professionnels en securité agréés *See* Board of Canadian Registered Safety Professionals

Conseil canadien des responsables de la réglementation d'assurance *See* Canadian Council of Insurance Regulators

Conseil canadien des ressources humaines en camionnage *See* Canadian Trucking Human Resources Council

Conseil canadien des ressources humaines en tourisme *See* Canadian Tourism Human Resource Council

Conseil canadien des RH du secteur de l'alimentation *See* Canadian Grocery HR Council

Le Conseil canadien des soins respiratoires inc. *See* Canadian Board for Respiratory Care Inc.

Conseil canadien des techniciens et technologues *See* Canadian Council of Technicians & Technologists

Conseil canadien du bois *See* Canadian Wood Council

Conseil canadien du commerce de détail *See* Retail Council of Canada

Conseil canadien du compost *See* Compost Council of Canada

Conseil canadien du miel *See* Canadian Honey Council

Conseil canadien du porc *See* Canadian Pork Council

Conseil canadien du ski *See* Canadian Ski Council

Conseil canadien du transport de passages *See* Motor Carrier Passenger Council of Canada

Le Conseil canadien pour l'avancement de l'éducation *See* Canadian Council for the Advancement of Education

Conseil canadien pour la coopération internationale *See* Canadian Council for International Co-operation

Conseil canadien pour le commerce autochtone *See* Canadian Council for Aboriginal Business

Conseil canadien pour le contrôle du tabac *See* Canadian Council for Tobacco Control

Conseil Canadien pour les Amériques *See* Canadian Council for the Americas

Le Conseil canadien pour les partenariats public-privé *See* The Canadian Council for Public-Private Partnerships

Conseil canadien pour les réfugiés *See* Canadian Council for Refugees

Conseil canadien sectoriel des plastiques *See* Canadian Plastics Sector Council

Conseil central de l'Estrie (CSN) (CCSNE)

180, rue de l'Acadie, Sherbrooke QC J1H 2T3
Tél: 819-563-6515; *Téléc:* 819-563-4242
Également appelé: Conseil central des syndicats nationaux de l'Estrie (CSN)
Aperçu: *Dimension:* petite; *Envergure:* locale; Organisme sans but lucratif; fondée en 1925
Mission: Promouvoir et défendre les intérêts professionels, économiques, sociaux, culturels et moraux des travailleuses et travailleurs et de leur syndicats affiliés; parmi ses objectifs immediats, le conseil général s'interesse à l'expansion du syndicalisme et au plein exercise du droit d'association dans la région
Membre de: Confédération des syndicats nationaux

Conseil central du Montréal métropolitain (CCMM-CSN)

1601, av De Lorimier, Montréal QC H2K 4M5
Tél: 514-598-2021; *Téléc:* 514-598-2020
receptionccmm@csn.qc.ca
www.ccmm-csn.qc.ca
www.facebook.com/Conseil.Central.Montreal.Metropolitain.CSN
Aperçu: *Dimension:* petite; *Envergure:* locale
Membre(s) du bureau directeur:
Mireille Bénard, Coordonnatrice
mireille.benard@csn.qc.ca
Membre(s) du personnel: 15

Conseil Commercial Canada - Albanie *See* Canada - Albania Business Council

Conseil commercial Canada Chine *See* Canada China Business Council

Conseil commercial canadien-arménien inc. *See* Canadian Armenian Business Council Inc.

Conseil communautaire Beausoleil

300, ch Beaverbrook, Miramichi NB E1V 1A1
Tél: 506-627-4135; *Téléc:* 506-627-4592
contact@carrefourbeausoleil.ca
www.ccbmiramichi.com
www.facebook.com/carrefourbeausoleil
twitter.com/CCBInc
www.youtube.com/carrefourbeausoleil
Aperçu: *Dimension:* petite; *Envergure:* locale
Mission: Assurer l'épanouissement de la communauté francophone de la Miramichi par la promotion de la langue et de la culture françaises en offrant des programmes et des services qui répondent aux besoins de cette communauté
Membre de: Conseil de promotion et de diffusion de la culture
Membre(s) du bureau directeur:
Sylvain Melançon, Directeur général
sylvain.melancon@carrefourbeausoleil.ca

Conseil communautaire Notre-Dame-de-Grâce / Notre-Dame-de-Grâce Community Council

#204, 5964, av Notre-Dame-de-Grâce, Montréal QC H4A 1N1
Tél: 514-484-1471
ndgcc@ndg.ca
www.ndg.ca
Aperçu: *Dimension:* petite; *Envergure:* locale
Membre(s) du bureau directeur:
Halah Al-Ubaidi, Directrice générale
admin@ndg.ca
Membre(s) du personnel: 14; 3 bénévole(s)

Conseil communautaire Samuel-de-Champlain *Voir* Association régionale de la communauté francophone de Saint-Jean inc.

Conseil communauté en santé du Manitoba (CCS)

#400, 400, av Taché, Saint-Boniface MB R2H 3C3
Tél: 204-235-2393; *Téléc:* 204-237-0984
ccs@ccsmanitoba.ca
ccsmanitoba.ca
Aperçu: *Dimension:* petite; *Envergure:* provinciale; fondée en 2004 surveillé par Société santé en français
Membre(s) du bureau directeur:
Annie Bédard, Directrice générale
Membre(s) du personnel: 5

Conseil consultatif canadien de la radio *See* Radio Advisory Board of Canada

Conseil consultatif mixte de l'industrie des animaux de compagnie *See* PIJAC Canada

Conseil consultatif sur la condition féminine de la Nouvelle-Écosse *See* Nova Scotia Advisory Council on the Status of Women

Conseil coopératif acadien de la Nouvelle-Écosse (CCANE)

CP 667, Chéticamp NS B0E 1H0
Tél: 902-224-2205
coopacadien@ns.sympatico.ca
www.conseilcoopne.ca
www.facebook.com/162273307127445
Aperçu: *Dimension:* petite; *Envergure:* locale; Organisme sans but lucratif; fondée en 1980
Mission: Le Conseil coopératif acadien de la Nouvelle-Écosse a pour mission de promouvoir le développement coopératif acadien de la Nouvelle-Écosse.
Membre de: Le Conseil canadien de la coopération
Affiliation(s): Le magasin coopératif de Chéticamp; La Caisse Populaire Acadienne; La Coopérative Radio Chéticamp Ltée; The Co-operators; La coopérative La Résidence Acadienne; St. Joseph's Credit Union; La Caisse populaire de Clare Ltée
Membre(s) du bureau directeur:
Angus Lefort, Président
Membre: 7

Conseil culturel de la Montérégie inc *Voir* Conseil montérégien de la culture et des communications

Conseil culturel fransaskois (CCF) / Fransaskois Cultural Council

#216, 1440 - 9e av Nord, Regina SK S4R 8B1
Tél: 306-565-8916; *Téléc:* 306-565-2922
Ligne sans frais: 877-463-6223
ccf@culturel.sk.ca
www.culturel.sk.ca
www.facebook.com/Fransaskois
Nom précédent: Commission culturelle fransaskoise
Aperçu: *Dimension:* petite; *Envergure:* provinciale; Organisme sans but lucratif; fondée en 1974
Mission: Faire une plus grande place à la culture francophone et fransaskoise dans les écoles fransaskoises et d'immersion; renforcer les "systèmes" de diffusion en mettant en place différents moyens d'appuyer le travail des diffuseurs (ex: appui organisationnel, tournées d'artistes, outils de promotion); favoriser le cheminement professionnel des artistes en leur donnant les outils nécessaires dans les cinq domaines suivants: formation, création, production, diffusion, promotion; faire reconnaître l'importance du secteur culturel et artistique francophone par la communauté de la Saskatchewan et par les organismes fransaskois
Membre de: Fédération culturelle canadienne-française; SaskCulture
Membre(s) du bureau directeur:
Suzanne Compagne, Directrice générale
direction@culturel.ca
Finances: *Fonds:* Patrimoine canadien; Sasklotteries; BMLO (Bureau de la minorité de langue officielle)
Membre(s) du personnel: 6
Membre: *Critères d'admissibilité:* Association porte-parole des arts et de la culture des francophones en Saskatchewan
Activités: Ateliers InPA; programmation annuelle culturelle, scolaire, artistique; Gala fransaskois de la chanson
Prix, Bouses:
- Le lys d'art (Prix)

Conseil d'Adoption du Canada *See* Adoption Council of Canada

Conseil d'alphabétisation de l'ouest du Québec *See* Western Québec Literacy Council

Conseil d'alphabétisation de Yamaska *Voir* Yamaska Literacy Council

Conseil d'artisanat du Nouveau-Brunswick *See* New Brunswick Crafts Council

Conseil d'information et éducation sexuelles du Canada *See* Sex Information & Education Council of Canada

Conseil d'initiatives des ressources de construction *See* Construction Resource Initiatives Council

Conseil d'intervention pour l'accès des femmes au travail (CIAFT)

#403, 110, rue Ste-Thérèse, Montréal QC H2Y 1E6
Tél: 514-954-0220; *Téléc:* 514-954-1230
info@ciaft.qc.ca
www.femmesautravail.qc.ca
www.facebook.com/CIAFT
Aperçu: *Dimension:* petite; *Envergure:* provinciale; Organisme sans but lucratif; fondée en 1982
Mission: Oeuvrer à la défense, la promotion et le développement de services, de politiques et de mesures favorisant la réponse aux besoins spécifiques des femmes en matière de travail; faire reconnaître les droits des femmes au travail et obtenir l'égalité professionnelle des femmes
Affiliation(s): Fédération des femmes du Québec
Membre(s) du bureau directeur:
Nathalie Goulet, Présidente
ngoulet@ciaft.qc.ca

Membre(s) du personnel: 2
Membre: 41 groupes; *Montant de la cotisation:* 40$ individuelle; 100$ organisme

Conseil de commerce Canada-Inde *See* Canada-India Business Council

Conseil de commerce canado-arabe *See* Canada-Arab Business Council

Conseil de conservation de l'Ontario *See* Conservation Council of Ontario

Conseil de coopération de l'Ontario (CCO)

#201, 435, boul St-Laurent, Ottawa ON K1K 2Z8
Tél: 613-745-8619; *Téléc:* 613-745-4649
Ligne sans frais: 866-290-1168
info@cco.coop
www.cco.coop
www.linkedin.com/company/conseil-de-la-coop-ration-de-l'ontario
www.facebook.com/LeConseildelacooperationdelOntario
twitter.com/ccocoop
www.youtube.com/user/conseilcoopontario
Aperçu: *Dimension:* moyenne; *Envergure:* provinciale; fondée en 1964
Mission: Favoriser la prise en charge socio-économique de la communauté francophone de l'Ontario par le biais de la coopération
Membre de: Conseil canadien de la coopération
Affliation(s): Association canadienne française de l'Ontario
Membre(s) du bureau directeur:
Luc Morin, Directeur général
luc.morin@cco.coop
Finances: *Fonds:* Office des affaires francophones; Patrimoine canadien; Secrétariat aux affaires intergouvernementale
Membre(s) du personnel: 5
Membre: *Montant de la cotisation:* 25$ + 1$ par membre pour les coopératives; 10$ individuel; *Critères d'admissibilite:* Etre une coopérative francophone de l'Ontario ou un projet de coopérative en développement
Activités: Consultation; formation; information; développement; ateliers; appui technique (étude de faisabilité, incorporation, plan d'affaire); *Stagiaires:* Oui; *Service de conférenciers:* Oui

Conseil de développement du loisir scientifique (CDLS)

CP 1000, Succ. M, 4545, av Pierre-de Coubertin, Montréal QC H1V 3R2
Tél: 514-252-3027; *Téléc:* 514-252-3152
info@cdls.qc.ca
www.cdls.qc.ca
Aperçu: *Dimension:* moyenne; *Envergure:* provinciale; Organisme sans but lucratif; fondée en 1968
Mission: La promotion d'activités scientifiques, particulièrement chez les jeunes
Membre de: Regroupement Loisir Québec; Fondation Science Jeunesse Canada
Membre(s) du bureau directeur:
Nathalie Beaudry, President
Finances: *Budget de fonctionnement annuel:* $500,000-$1.5 Million
Membre(s) du personnel: 9; 20 bénévole(s)
Membre: 1-99

Conseil de développement économique des municipalités bilingues du Manitoba (CDEM)

#200, 614, rue Des Meurons, Winnipeg MB R2H 2P9
Tél: 204-925-2320; *Téléc:* 204-237-4618
Ligne sans frais: 800-990-2332
www.cdem.com
Nom précédent: Association des municipalités bilingues du Manitoba
Aperçu: *Dimension:* petite; *Envergure:* provinciale; fondée en 1996
Mission: Encourager, stimuler et organiser le développement économique dans les municipalités bilingues
Membre(s) du bureau directeur:
Louis Allain, Directeur général, 204-925-2322
lallain@cdem.com

Conseil de formation pharmaceutique continue *See* Council for Continuing Pharmaceutical Education

Conseil de l'artisanat de la Colombie-Britannique *See* Crafts Association of British Columbia

Conseil de l'enveloppe du bâtiment du Québec (CEBQ) / Québec Building Envelope Council (QBEC)

12465 - 94E av, Montréal QC H1C 1H6
Tél: 514-943-0251; *Téléc:* 514-943-0300
www.cebq.org
Aperçu: *Dimension:* moyenne; *Envergure:* provinciale; fondée en 1989
Mission: Organiser des forums afin de faciliter la discussion et le transfert de technologies auprès de l'industrie de la construction
Membre de: National Building Envelope Council
Membre(s) du bureau directeur:
Mario D. Gonçalves, Président
m.goncalves@cebq.org
Nathalie Martin, CPA, CGA, Directrice
n.martin@cebq.org
Finances: *Budget de fonctionnement annuel:* Moins de $50,000
2 bénévole(s)
Membre: 500; *Montant de la cotisation:* 120$ individuel; 360$ corporatif; *Critères d'admissibilite:* Professionnel de la construction
Activités: Conférences mensuelles; cours sur l'enveloppe du bâtiment; Envol: banque de données d'articles et publications sur l'enveloppe du bâtiment; *Service de conférenciers:* Oui; *Bibliothèque*
Meetings/Conferences: • 6ième Colloque Annuel sur l'Enveloppe du bâtiment du Québec, April, 2015, Palais des congrès de Montréal, Montréal, QC
Scope: Provincial

Le Conseil de l'industrie de la motocyclette et du cyclomoteur *See* Motorcycle & Moped Industry Council

Conseil de l'industrie forestière du Québec (CIFQ) / Québec Forestry Industry Council (QFIC)

#200, 1175, av Lavigerie, Sainte-Foy QC G1V 4P1
Tél: 418-657-7916; *Téléc:* 418-657-7971
info@cifq.qc.ca
www.cifq.qc.ca
Nom précédent: Association des manufacturiers de bois de sciage du Québec
Aperçu: *Dimension:* grande; *Envergure:* provinciale
Mission: Représente la très grande majorité des entreprises de sciage résineux, de pâtes, papiers, cartons et panneaux oeuvrant au Québec; se consacre à la défense des intérêts de ces entreprsies, à la promotion de leur contribution au développement socio-économique, à la gestion intégrée et à l'aménagement durable des forêts, de même qu'à l'utilisation optimale des ressources naturelles; oeuvre auprès des instances gouvernementales, des organismes publics et parapublics, des organisations et de la population; encourage un comportement responsable de ses membres en regard des dimensions environnementales, économiques et sociales de leurs activités.
Membre(s) du bureau directeur:
André Tremblay, Président-CEO
Membre(s) du personnel: 40
Membre: 200 compagnies; *Critères d'admissibilite:* Membres réguliers - compagnies possédant une ou des usines de sciage ou de rabotage ou papetière; membres remanufacturiers - compagnies dont la fonction consiste à transformer le bois en provenance d'une scierie; membres associés - grossistes, manufacturiers d'équipements, consultants, sociétés financières dont les activités sont reliées à celles des membres réguliers
Activités: *Listes de destinataires:* Oui
Prix, Bouses:
• Bourses académiques de l'Université Laval (Bourse d'études)
Publications:
• Fibrexpression
Type: Bulletin

Conseil de l'industrie laitière du Québec inc. *Voir* Conseil des industriels laitiers du Québec inc.

Conseil de l'Ontario pour la coopération internationale *See* Ontario Council for International Cooperation

Conseil de la conservation du Nouveau-Brunswick *See* Conservation Council of New Brunswick

Conseil de la coopération de L'Ile-du-Prince-Édouard

CP 124, RR#1, Wellington Station PE C0B 2E0
Tél: 902-854-2667; *Téléc:* 902-854-2981
Aperçu: *Dimension:* moyenne; *Envergure:* provinciale

Conseil de la Coopération de la Saskatchewan (CCS)

#205, 1440, 9e av, Regina SK S4R 8B1
Tél: 306-566-6000
Ligne sans frais: 800-670-0879
info@ccs-sk.ca
www.ccs-sk.ca
www.facebook.com/conseilcoopsk
twitter.com/ccs_sk_ca
www.youtube.com/user/conseilcoopsk
Aperçu: *Dimension:* petite; *Envergure:* provinciale; Organisme sans but lucratif; fondée en 1947
Mission: Le CCS s'engage à trouver les moyens et les ressources nécessaires afin d'offire des programmes et des services qui: permettent la mise en oeuvre d'une stratégie de développement diversifiée à l'intérieur de la communauté fransaskoise; assurent un support aux projets de développement économique communautaire; appuient la création et l'épanouissement d'entreprises fransaskoises
Affliation(s): Conseil Canadien de la Coopération; Réseau de développement économique et d'employabilité
Membre(s) du bureau directeur:
Robert Therrien, Directeur général
robert.therrien@ccs-sk.ca
Membre(s) du personnel: 14
Membre: *Montant de la cotisation:* 5$; *Critères d'admissibilite:* Entreprise; caisse populaire; association économique; individu; coopérative

Conseil de la coopération du Québec *Voir* Conseil québécois de la coopération et de la mutualité

Conseil de la culture de L'Abitibi-Témiscamingue (CRCAT)

150, av du Lac, Rouyn-Noranda QC J9X 4N5
Tél: 819-764-9511; *Téléc:* 819-764-6375
Ligne sans frais: 877-764-9511
info@ccat.qc.ca
www.ccat.qc.ca
www.facebook.com/290070211341
twitter.com/CultureAT
Aperçu: *Dimension:* petite; *Envergure:* locale; Organisme sans but lucratif; fondée en 1977
Mission: Unir tous les agences, corporations, corps publics et municipaux, associations et organismes, entreprises et personnes oeuvrant dans le domaine culturel de la région; contribuer à la définition des orientations et au développement de l'activité culturelle dans le meilleur intérêt régional; faire connaître la réalité et les particularités de la culture en Abitibi-Témiscamingue à l'extérieur de la région
Membre(s) du bureau directeur:
Madeleine Perron, Directrice générale
madeleine.perron@ccat.qc.ca
Finances: *Fonds:* Ministère de la Culture et des Communications du Québec
Membre(s) du personnel: 5
Membre: 780; *Montant de la cotisation:* 25$ individu; 60$ organisme; *Critères d'admissibilite:* S'intéresser à la vie culturelle; demeurer en Abitibi-Témiscamingue
Activités: Cours de formation et perfectionnement; *Listes de destinataires:* Oui; *Bibliothèque* Bibliothèque publique

Conseil de la culture de la Gaspésie (CCG)

169, av Grand Pré, Bonaventure QC G0C 1E0
Tél: 418-534-4139; *Téléc:* 418-534-4113
Ligne sans frais: 800-820-0883
info@culturegaspesie.org
www.zonegaspesie.qc.ca
www.facebook.com/culturegaspesie
www.youtube.com/user/joelgauthier
Aperçu: *Dimension:* petite; *Envergure:* locale; Organisme sans but lucratif; fondée en 1992
Mission: Promouvoir et défendre les interêts du milieu culturel tout en travaillant à favoriser une meilleure visibilité des produits culturels gaspésiens
Membre de: Les arts et la ville; ATR Gaspésie
Membre(s) du bureau directeur:
Anick Loisel, Directrice générale
aloisel@culturegaspesie.org
Membre(s) du personnel: 5
Membre: 200+; *Montant de la cotisation:* 25$ individu; 60$ organisme; 75$ entreprise; *Critères d'admissibilite:* Artistes; organismes culturels; municipalités

Conseil de la culture de la région de Québec/Chaudière-Appalaches *Voir* Conseil de la culture des régions de Québec et de Chaudière-Appalaches

Conseil de la culture de la région Saguenay/Lac-St-Jean/Chibougamau/Chapais *Voir* Conseil régional de la culture Saguenay-Lac-Saint-Jean

Conseil de la culture de Lanaudière
165, rue Lajoie Sud, Joliette QC J6E 5K9
Tél: 450-753-7444; *Téléc:* 450-753-9047
Ligne sans frais: 866-334-7444
info@culturelanaudiere.qc.ca
www.culturelanaudiere.qc.ca
Aperçu: *Dimension:* petite; *Envergure:* locale; Organisme sans but lucratif; fondée en 1978
Mission: Voir au développement culturel régional
Membre(s) du bureau directeur:
Andrée Saint-Georges, Directrice générale
andree.saint-georges@culturelanaudiere.qc.ca
Membre(s) du personnel: 3
Membre: 392; *Montant de la cotisation:* 40-200
Activités: *Listes de destinataires:* Oui

Conseil de la culture des Laurentides (CCL)
#400, 223, rue St-Georges, Saint-Jérôme QC J7Z 5A1
Tél: 450-432-2425; *Téléc:* 450-432-8434
Ligne sans frais: 866-432-2680
ccl@culturelaurentides.com
www.culturelaurentides.com
Nom précédent: Conseil de la culture et des communications des Laurentides
Aperçu: *Dimension:* moyenne; *Envergure:* locale; Organisme sans but lucratif; fondée en 1978
Mission: Appuyer le développement des arts et de la culture sur son territoire; regrouper, représenter et offrir des services aux intervenants de l'ensemble des domaines artistiques et culturels des Laurentides; mener des actions de sensibilisation, de représentation, de promotion et de développement auprès des principaux acteurs du milieu culturel régional; jouer un rôle conseil auprès des différents partenaires
Affliation(s): Conférence régionale des élus (CRÉ)
Membre(s) du bureau directeur:
Mélanie Gosselin, Directrice générale
direction@culturelaurentides.com
Finances: *Budget de fonctionnement annuel:* $250,000-$500,000
Membre(s) du personnel: 6; 15 bénévole(s)
Membre: 400; *Montant de la cotisation:* 25-250; *Critères d'admissibilite:* Membre individuel (artiste, artisan et intervenant); membre associé (hors région); organisme sans but lucratif, organisme public ou parapublic; entreprise privée; milieu municipal et MRC (Municipalité régionale de comté); *Comités:* Communications et nouvelles technologies de communications; Grands Prix; Métiers d'art
Activités: Contribuer au développement culturel régional; inventorier les ressources et organismes culturels de la région; agir comme agent de décentralisation des services culturels; être représentatif du milieu culturel régional; faire des recommandations auprès du ministère de la Culture et des Communications et du Conseil des arts et des lettres du Québec dans les secteurs d'activité professionnelle suivant les arts et les lettres, l'histoire, la conservation et la mise en valeur de notre patrimoine, et le design; *Bibliothèque:* Centre de documentation; Bibliothèque publique
Prix, Bouses:
• Colloque sur la culture (Prix)
• Grands prix de la culture des Laurentides (Prix)

Conseil de la culture des régions de Québec et de Chaudière-Appalaches
#120, 310, boul Langelier, Québec QC G1K 5N3
Tél: 418-523-1333; *Téléc:* 418-523-9944
ccr@culture-quebec.qc.ca
www.culture-quebec.qc.ca
www.facebook.com/conseilculture
twitter.com/conseilquebec
www.youtube.com/user/conseilculturegc
Nom précédent: Conseil de la culture de la région de Québec/Chaudière-Appalaches
Aperçu: *Dimension:* petite; *Envergure:* locale
Mission: Favoriser le développement des arts et de la culture sur son territoire
Membre(s) du bureau directeur:
Philippe Sauvageau, Président
Manon Laliberté, Directrice générale
Finances: *Fonds:* Ministère de la Culture et des Communications; Emploi-Québec; Conseil des arts et des lettres du Québec
Activités: Programmes de formation; services-conseils et accompagnement; gestion de projets; recherche
Prix, Bouses:
• Prix d'excellence des arts et de la culture (Prix)
Eligibility: Décernés à ceux et celles qui contribuent à l'excellence de l'activité artistique et culturelle de la grande région de la Capitale Nationale
• Prix du patrimoine (Prix)
Eligibility: Reconnaître les réalisation et actions en conservation et mise en valeur du patrimoine

Conseil de la culture du Bas-Saint-Laurent (CRCBSL)
CP 873, 88, Saint-Germain Ouest, Rimouski QC G5L 7C9
Tél: 418-722-6246; *Téléc:* 418-724-2216
info@crcbsl.org
crcbsl.org
www.facebook.com/113141962078442
twitter.com/CultureBSL
www.youtube.com/user/ConseildelacultureBS
Aperçu: *Dimension:* moyenne; *Envergure:* locale; Organisme sans but lucratif; fondée en 1976
Mission: Contribuer au développement culturel de la région; être un agent de décentralisation des services culturels; identifier, analyser les besoins et les points de vue de la région et promouvoir la défense des intérêts culturels des membres; assurer une planification au niveau de la région en collaboration avec ses membres
Membre de: Conférence canadienne des arts
Membre(s) du bureau directeur:
Ginette Lepage, Directrice générale
ginette.lepage@crcbsl.org
Membre(s) du personnel: 6
Membre: *Montant de la cotisation:* 60$ institutionnel; 25$ individu; *Critères d'admissibilite:* Etre un artiste ou un organisme culturel
Activités: *Listes de destinataires:* Oui; *Bibliothèque* rendez-vous

Conseil de la culture du Coeur-du-Québec; Conseil de la culture et des communications de la Mauricie *Voir* Culture Mauricie

Conseil de la culture et des communications des Laurentides *Voir* Conseil de la culture des Laurentides

Conseil de la Saskatchewan pour la co-opération internationale *See* Saskatchewan Council for International Co-operation

Conseil de la sécurité en fertilisation *See* Fertilizer Safety & Security Council

Conseil de la souveraineté du Québec (CSQ)
49, rue Archambault, Repentigny QC J6A 1A2
Tél: 514-303-6561
unis@souverainete.info
www.souverainete.info
www.facebook.com/Conseildelasouverainete
twitter.com/ConseilSouvQc
www.youtube.com/channel/UCuGyZrxvZFB2F0miMYm6EaA
Aperçu: *Dimension:* petite; *Envergure:* provinciale
Mission: A toute latitude pour stimuler dans la population québécoise l'idéal de souveraineté, faire valoir la nécessité de celle-ci pour l'avenir de la nation québécoise, être à l'origine d'initiatives originales pour garder la souveraineté à l'ordre du jour et appuyer toute initiative en ce sens
Membre(s) du bureau directeur:
Gilbert Paquette, Président

Conseil de la transformation agroalimentaire et des produits de consommation (CTAC) / Council of Food Processing & Consumer Products
#102, 200, rue MacDonald, Saint-Jean-sur-Richelieu QC J3B 8J6
Tél: 450-349-1521; *Téléc:* 450-349-6923
info@conseiltac.com
www.conseiltac.com
www.linkedin.com/company/1237456
Nom précédent: Association des manufacturiers de produits alimentaires du Québec
Merged from: Conseil de la boulangerie du Québec; Association des abattoirs avicoles du Québec
Aperçu: *Dimension:* moyenne; *Envergure:* provinciale; Organisme sans but lucratif; fondée en 1954
Mission: Le porte-parole officiel des manufacturiers de produits alimentaires du Québec qui s'y regroupent à titre de membres fabricants; canalise les représentations des manufacturiers, en particulier auprès des gouvernements; coordonne l'action des membres en vue de promouvoir leurs intérêts économiques, sociaux et professionnels; suscite l'éducation des consommateurs sur les valeurs d'une bonne alimentation; favorise la promotion des produits fabriqués par les membres; établit des liaisons entre les manufacturiers, les producteurs, les fournisseurs, les distributeurs, les consommateurs et les autres maillons de la chaîne alimentaire; encourage la recherche dans les domaines de l'agriculture, de l'alimentation et du marketing
Membre(s) du bureau directeur:
Sylvie Cloutier, Présidente-directrice générale
Finances: *Budget de fonctionnement annuel:* $500,000-$1.5 Million
Membre(s) du personnel: 5
Membre: 400; *Critères d'admissibilite:* Fabricants; fournisseurs; distributeurs; *Comités:* Activités sociales; Agriculture; Environnement; Mise en marché; Négociations; Nomination; Recrutement; Santé et securité du travail; Travail

Conseil de planification sociale d'Ottawa-Carleton *See* Social Planning Council of Ottawa-Carleton

Conseil de planification sociale Region de Sudbury *See* Social Planning Council of Sudbury Region

Conseil de presse de l'Ontario *See* Ontario Press Council

Conseil de presse du Québec (CPQ) / Québec Press Council
#A208, 1000, rue Fullum, Montréal QC H2K 3L7
Tél: 514-529-2818; *Téléc:* 514-873-4434
Ligne sans frais: 877-250-3060
info@conseildepresse.qc.ca
conseildepresse.qc.ca
twitter.com/MagazineCPQ
Aperçu: *Dimension:* petite; *Envergure:* provinciale; Organisme sans but lucratif; fondée en 1973
Mission: Le Conseil de presse du Québec est un organisme privé, à but non lucratif, qui ouvre depuis près de quarante ans à la protection de la liberté de la presse et à la défense du droit du public à une information de qualité. Son action s'étend à tous les médias d'information distribués ou diffusés au Québec, qu'ils soient membres ou non du Conseil, qu'ils appartiennent à la presse écrite ou électronique.
Membre(s) du bureau directeur:
Guy Amyot, Secrétaire général
guy.amyot@conseildepresse.qc.ca
Julien Acosta, Directeur des communications
julien.acosta@conseildepresse.qc.ca
Finances: *Budget de fonctionnement annuel:* $500,000-$1.5 Million
Membre(s) du personnel: 5; 22 bénévole(s)
Membre: 22; *Montant de la cotisation:* barème; *Critères d'admissibilite:* Médias; Journalistes; Public; *Comités:* Comité des plaintes; Comité d'appel
Activités: Ombudsman de la presse au Québec; *Stagiaires:* Oui; *Service de conférenciers:* Oui; *Bibliothèque:* Centre de documentation

Conseil de recherche en réassurance *See* Reinsurance Research Council

Conseil de recherches en sciences naturelles et en génie du Canada *See* Natural Sciences & Engineering Research Council of Canada

Conseil de sécurité d'Ottawa *See* Ottawa Safety Council

Conseil des 4-H du Canada *See* Canadian 4-H Council

Conseil des académies canadiennes *See* Council of Canadian Academies

Conseil des aéroports du Canada *See* Canadian Airports Council

Conseil des archives du Nouveau-Brunswick *See* Council of Archives New Brunswick

Conseil des arts de Hearst (CAH)
75, 9e rue, Hearst ON P0L 1N0
Tél: 705-362-4900; *Téléc:* 705-362-4600
www.conseildesartsdehearst.ca
Aperçu: *Dimension:* petite; *Envergure:* locale; fondée en 1978
Mission: Le Conseil des Arts de Hearst développe auprès de sa communauté un intérêt pour les arts et la culture francophone. Il offre des expériences artistiques et culturelles de qualité qui sont mémorables et signifiantes. Il encourage le rayonnement d'artistes de langue française par le biais d'une programmation variée

Membre(s) du bureau directeur:
Shana Vernier, Président
Valérie Picard, Directrice générale
dg@conseildesartsdehearst.ca
Finances: *Budget de fonctionnement annuel:* $250,000-$500,000
Membre(s) du personnel: 3; 60 bénévole(s)
Membre: 400; *Montant de la cotisation:* 20 $ individuelle; 35 $ familiale; 40 $ entreprise ou organisme
Activités: Le Festival de musique (mars); bingo (mars & novembre); Soirée Dégustation (juin); Le Festival National de L'Humour (septembre)

Conseil des arts de l'Ontario *See* Ontario Arts Council

Conseil des arts de la communauté urbaine de Montréal *Voir* Conseil des arts de Montréal

Conseil des arts de Montréal (CAM)

Édifice Gaston Miron, 1210, rue Sherbrooke est, Montréal QC H2L 1L9
Tél: 514-280-3580; *Téléc:* 514-280-3784
artsmontreal@ville.montreal.qc.ca
www.artsmontreal.org
www.facebook.com/ArtsMontreal
twitter.com/ConseilArtsMtl
Nom précédent: Conseil des arts de la communauté urbaine de Montréal
Aperçu: *Dimension:* moyenne; *Envergure:* locale; fondée en 1956
Mission: Soutenir, encourager et harmoniser les initiatives d'ordre artistique et culturel sur le territoire de la ville de Montréal.
Membre de: Chambre de commerce du Montréal métropolitain; Conférence canadienne des arts; Conseil régional de développement de l'Ile de Montréal; Les arts et la ville; Corporation du Faubourg St-Laurent
Membre(s) du bureau directeur:
Nathalie Maillé, Directrice générale et sec. conseil
nmaille.p@ville.montreal.qc.ca
France Laroche, Directrice de l'administration
france.laroche@ville.montreal.qc.ca
Finances: *Budget de fonctionnement annuel:* Plus de $5 Million
Membre(s) du personnel: 15
Membre: 21; *Critères d'admissibilite:* Organismes professionnels oeuvrant dans les disciplines des arts visuels, du cinéma et des arts médiatiques, de la danse, de la littérature, des nouvelles pratiques artistiques, de la musique et du théâtre; *Comités:* Arts visuels et littérature; Danse, cinéma et arts multidisciplinaires; Musique; Théâtre; Jeunes publics; Arts et arrondissements
Activités: Programme général d'aide financière; Jouer dans l'île; Art et communauté; Jeunes publics - public de demain; Grand Prix du Conseil des art; Programme d'échanges culturels; Services et expertise; Maison du Conseil des arts
Prix, Bouses:
• Grand Prix annuel du Conseil des arts (Prix)
Reconnaît annuellement l'excellence d'une production ou d'un événement réalisé sur le territoire de la Ville de Montréal dans l'une des disciplines suivantes : arts visuels, arts médiatiques, cinéma et vidéo, danse, littérature, musique et théâtre *Amount:* Bourse de 25 000$ + prix de reconnaissance

Conseil des arts de Sudbury *See* Sudbury Arts Council

Conseil des arts des TNO *See* Northwest Territories Arts Council

Conseil des arts du Manitoba *See* Manitoba Arts Council

Conseil des arts et des lettres du Québec

79, boul René Lévesque est, 3e étage, Québec QC G1R 5N5
Tél: 418-643-1707; *Téléc:* 418-643-4558
Ligne sans frais: 800-897-1707
info@calq.gouv.qc.ca
www.calq.gouv.qc.ca
www.facebook.com/group.php?gid=12468994038
twitter.com/LeCALQ
Également appelé: CALQ
Aperçu: *Dimension:* moyenne; *Envergure:* provinciale; fondée en 1993
Mission: Soutenir dans toutes les régions du Québec la création, l'expérimentation, la production et la diffusion dans les domaines des arts de la scène (théâtre, danse, musique, chanson, arts du cirque), des arts médiatiques (arts numériques, cinéma et vidéo), des arts multidisciplinaires, des arts visuels, de la littérature et du conte, des métiers d'art et de la recherche architecturale et d'en favoriser la reconnaissance et le rayonnement au Québec, au Canada et à l'étranger.
Membre(s) du bureau directeur:
Marie DuPont, Président du conseil d'administration, 514-864-3350
marie.dupont@calq.gouv.qc.ca
Stéphan La Roche, Président & Directeur général, 514-864-4333
micheline.bahl-levasseur@calq.gouv.qc.ca
Membre(s) du personnel: 72
Activités: *Bibliothèque:* Centre de documentation

Conseil des bio-industries du Québec; Association québécoise des bio-industries *Voir* BIOQuébec

Le Conseil des Canadiens *See* The Council of Canadians

Conseil des Canadiens avec déficiences *See* Council of Canadians with Disabilities

Conseil des directeurs médias du Québec (CDMQ)

#925, 2015, rue Peel, Montréal QC H3A 1T8
Tél: 514-990-1899
www.cdmq.ca
www.facebook.com/170319683021723
Aperçu: *Dimension:* petite; *Envergure:* provinciale; Organisme sans but lucratif
Mission: Etre un point de convergence d'opinions et d'information, un instrument de défense des intérêts des clients/agences et un outil de promotion et de stimulation de la fonction média
Affiliation(s): Association canadienne des annonceurs; Association des agences de publicitéu Québec; Canadian Media Directors' Council; Publicité Club de Montréal
Membre(s) du bureau directeur:
Michèle Savard, Présidente
michele.savard@carat.com

Conseil des doyens et des doyennes des facultés de droit du Canada *See* Council of Canadian Law Deans

Le Conseil des Églises pour l'éducation théologique au Canada: une fondation oecuménique *See* The Churches' Council on Theological Education in Canada: an Ecumenical Foundation

Conseil des églises pour la justice et la criminologie *See* Church Council on Justice & Corrections

Conseil des experts-comptables de la province de l'Ontario *See* Public Accountants Council for the Province of Ontario

Conseil des fabricants de bois *See* Wood Manufacturing Council

Le Conseil des femmes de Montréal *See* Montréal Council of Women

Conseil des industriels laitiers du Québec inc. (CILQ) / Québec Dairy Council Inc.

#200, 8585, boul St-Laurent, Montréal QC H2P 2M9
Tél: 514-381-5331; *Téléc:* 514-381-6677
info@cilq.ca
cilq.ca
Nom précédent: Conseil de l'industrie laitière du Québec inc.
Aperçu: *Dimension:* grande; *Envergure:* provinciale; fondée en 1963
Mission: Regrouper les entreprises laitières industrielles du Québec qui s'occupent des différentes phases de la transformation, distribution et commercialisation du lait et des produits laitiers; promotion, protection et développement de leurs intérêts économiques, sociaux et professionnels
Membre(s) du bureau directeur:
Normand Pomerleau, Président du CA
Pierre M. Nadeau, Président-directeur général
pierre.nadeau@cilq.ca
Charles Langlois, Vice-président, Affaires économiques & Approvisionnement
charles.langlois@cilq.ca
Yolaine Villeneuve, Directrice, Affaires publiques & corporatives
yolaine.villeneuve@cilq.ca
Finances: *Budget de fonctionnement annuel:* $250,000-$500,000
Membre(s) du personnel: 4
Membre: 90 réguliers
Prix, Bouses:
• Prix Donat-Roy (Prix)

Conseil des jeux du Canada *See* Canada Games Council

Conseil des métiers d'art du Québec (ind.) (CMA) / Québec Crafts Council (Ind.)

Marché Bonsecours, #400, 390, rue St-Paul Est, Montréal QC H2Y 1H2
Tél: 514-861-2787; *Téléc:* 514-861-9191
Ligne sans frais: 855-515-2787
info@metiersdart.ca
www.metiers-d-art.qc.ca
Nom précédent: Société de mise en marché des métiers d'art inc.
Aperçu: *Dimension:* moyenne; *Envergure:* provinciale; fondée en 1985
Mission: Pour distribuer les créations métiers d'art auprès des grossistes canadiens et étrangers.
Membre(s) du bureau directeur:
Patrice Bolduc, Adjoint du directeur général
patrice.bolduc@metiersdart.ca
Membre(s) du personnel: 19
Membre: 900; *Montant de la cotisation:* Barème

Conseil des ministres de l'éducation (Canada) *See* Council of Ministers of Education, Canada

Conseil des normes de la publicité *Voir* Les normes canadiennes de la publicité

Conseil des organismes francophones de la région de Durham (COFRD)

Suite D, 57 rue Simcoe sud, Oshawa ON L1H 4G4
Tél: 905-434-7676; *Téléc:* 905-434-7260
www.cofrd.org
www.facebook.com/librairieducentre.aucofrd
Aperçu: *Dimension:* petite; *Envergure:* locale; Organisme sans but lucratif; fondée en 1984
Mission: Oeuvrer au développement, à l'épanouissement et à la vitalité de la population francophone de la région de Durham; offrir grammation et des services accessibles qui répondent aux besoins de l'ensemble de la communauté d'expression française
Membre de: Réseau Ontario; AFO; Théâtre Action
Membre(s) du bureau directeur:
Didier Luchmun, Président
Elaine Legault, Directrice générale
elegault@cofrd.org
Finances: *Budget de fonctionnement annuel:* $100,000-$250,000; *Fonds:* Patrimoine canadien
Membre(s) du personnel: 9; 60 bénévole(s)
Membre: 23 organismes francophones de la région de Durham; *Comités:* Finances; prélèvements de fonds
Activités: Culturelles, socio-économiques, sociales; *Bibliothèque:* Librarie du centre; Bibliothèque publique

Conseil des organismes francophones du Toronto Métropolitain; Centre francophones du Toronto Métropolitain *Voir* Centre francophone de Toronto

Conseil des palettes du Canada *See* Canadian Pallet Council

Conseil des premiers ministres des Maritimes/Conseil des premiers ministres de l'Atlantique *See* Council of Maritime Premiers/Council of Atlantic Premiers

Conseil des relations internationales de Montréal (CORIM)

#1424, 1550, rue Metcalfe, Montréal QC H3A 1X6
Tél: 514-340-9622; *Téléc:* 514-340-9904
courrier@corim.qc.ca
www.corim.qc.ca/home
Aperçu: *Dimension:* petite; *Envergure:* locale; fondée en 1985
Mission: Le CORIM a pour mission de favoriser une plus grande connaissance des affaires internationales et susciter par ses événements et ses partenariats une collaboration plus étroite entre les divers milieux montréalais intéressés aux questions internationales
Membre(s) du bureau directeur:
Pierre Lemonde, Président-directeur général
plemonde@corim.qc.ca
Membre: *Montant de la cotisation:* $25 étudiant; 100$ individuel; 395$ organisme sans but lucratif; 850$ corporatif; 1 850$ membre gouverneur; 5 000$+ membre gouverneur émérite

Conseil des ressources humaines de l'industrie du vêtement *See* Apparel Human Resources Council

Conseil des ressources humaines de l'industrie minière *See* Mining Industry Human Resources Council

Conseil des Soins Palliatifs *See* Council on Palliative Care

Le Conseil des sports des handicapées de la capitale nationale inc. *See* National Capital Sports Council of the Disabled Inc.

Conseil des technologies de l'information et des communications du Canada *See* Information & Communications Technology Council of Canada

Conseil des traducteurs, terminologues et interprètes du Canada *See* Canadian Translators, Terminologists & Interpreters Council

Conseil des travailleurs de Sept-îles et du Golfe *Voir* Conseil régional FTQ Sept-Iles et Côte-Nord - Bureau régional FTQ Côte Nord

Conseil des universités de l'Ontario *See* Council of Ontario Universities

Conseil des viandes du Canada *See* Canadian Meat Council

Conseil du bâtiment durable du Canada *See* Canada Green Building Council

Conseil du loisir scientifique de l'Estrie (CLSE)

195, rue Marquette, Sherbrooke QC J1H 1L6
Tél: 819-565-5062; *Téléc:* 819-565-4534
clse@csrs.qc.ca
www.clse.qc.ca
Aperçu: *Dimension:* moyenne; *Envergure:* locale; Organisme sans but lucratif; fondée en 1981
Mission: Développer le loisir scientifique dans la région; encourager les carrières scientifiques chez les jeunes
Membre de: Conseil de développement du loisir scientifique
Membre(s) du bureau directeur:
Jeannine Provencher
Finances: *Fonds:* Gouvernement régional
Membre(s) du personnel: 4; 60 bénévole(s)
Membre: 26 institutionnel; 1 800 étudiant; 20 individu

Conseil du loisir scientifique de Québec *Voir* Boîte à science - Conseil du loisir scientifique du Québec

Conseil du Manitoba pour la coopération internationale *See* Manitoba Council for International Cooperation

Conseil du patronat du Québec (CPQ) / Québec Employers Council

#510, 1010, rue Sherbrooke ouest, Montréal QC H3A 2R7
Tél: 514-288-5161; *Téléc:* 514-288-5165
Ligne sans frais: 877-288-5161
www.cpq.qc.ca
www.linkedin.com/groups/Conseil-patronat-Québec-2908454
www.facebook.com/conseilpatronat
twitter.com/conseilpatronat
www.youtube.com/user/CPQ2010
Aperçu: *Dimension:* moyenne; *Envergure:* provinciale; fondée en 1969
Mission: Le Conseil du patronat du Québec a pour mission de s'assurer que les entreprises puissent disposer au Québec des meilleures conditions possibles- notamment en metiére de capital humain- afin de prospereer de fason durable dans un contexte de concurrence mondiale.
Membre(s) du bureau directeur:
Yves-Thomas Dorval, Président
president@cpq.qc.ca
Patrick Lemieux, Conseiller, Communications
plemieux@cpq.qc.ca
Finances: *Budget de fonctionnement annuel:* $500,000-$1.5 Million
Membre(s) du personnel: 14
Membre: 53 associations + 200 entreprises
Activités: *Service de conférenciers:* Oui; *Bibliothèque* rendez-vous

Conseil du peuplier du Canada *See* Poplar Council of Canada

Conseil du recyclage de l'Ontario *See* Recycling Council of Ontario

Conseil du travail d'Ottawa et du district *See* Ottawa & District Labour Council

Conseil du travail de Montréal *Voir* Conseil régional FTQ Montréal Métropolitain

Conseil du travail de Saguenay-Lac-St-Jean *Voir* Conseil régional FTQ Saguenay-Lac-St-Jean-Chibougamau-Chapais

Conseil du troisuème âge de Saint-Lambert / St. Lambert Council for Seniors

Maison Desaulniers, 574, av Notre-Dame, St-Lambert QC J4P 2K9
Tél: 450-671-1757; *Téléc:* 450-923-6608
stlambertseniors@sympatico.ca
stlambertseniors.ca
Aperçu: *Dimension:* petite; *Envergure:* locale; fondée en 1973
Mission: Pour aider les aînés à participer à des activités de groupe
Membre(s) du bureau directeur:
Elwyn Llewelyn, Président, Conseil d'administration
Membre: *Montant de la cotisation:* 30$; *Critères d'admissibilite:* Toute gens qui habite sur la Ville de St-Lambert, ou toute gens qui va à l'église à St-Lambert qui a 55 ans et plus.
Activités: Album souvenir; Artisanat; Bridge; Club de courtepointes; Club de moélisme de chemin de fer; Club d'informatique; Scrabble; Billard; Voyages

Conseil économique des provinces de l'Atlantique *See* Atlantic Provinces Economic Council

Conseil économique du Nouveau-Brunswick inc. (CÉNB)

#314, 236, rue St-Georges, Moncton NB E1C 1W1
Tél: 506-857-3143; *Téléc:* 506-857-9906
Ligne sans frais: 800-561-4446
cenb@cenb.com
www.cenb.com
www.facebook.com/cenbinc
Aperçu: *Dimension:* petite; *Envergure:* provinciale; Organisme sans but lucratif; fondée en 1979
Mission: Être le porte-parole de la communauté d'affaires francophone du NB
Membre(s) du bureau directeur:
Robert Moreau, Président
president@cenb.com
Anne Hébert, Directrice générale
anne@cenb.com
Membre(s) du personnel: 10
Membre: 1 000; *Montant de la cotisation:* Barème; *Critères d'admissibilite:* Entreprises et francophones du monde des affaires

Conseil en crédit du Canada *See* Credit Counselling Canada

Conseil ethnoculturel du Canada *See* Canadian Ethnocultural Council

Conseil francophone de la chanson (CFC)

2190, ch Hamel, Sherbrooke QC J1R 0P8
Tél: 819-820-0589
sg@conseilfrancophone.org
www.chanson.ca
Aperçu: *Dimension:* petite; *Envergure:* internationale; fondée en 1986
Mission: Promouvoir la chanson et les musiques de l'espace francophone
Membre(s) du bureau directeur:
Jacques Labrecque, Vice-président, Amérique du nord
jacques.labrecque@usherbrooke.ca
Finances: *Fonds:* Ministère de la Culture et des Communications (Québec)

Conseil FTQ Drummondville

175, rue Saint-Marcel, Drummondville QC J2B 2E1
Tél: 819-475-1320
syndicat_metallos_7885@hotmail.com
Aperçu: *Dimension:* petite; *Envergure:* locale surveillé par Fédération des travailleurs et travailleuses du Québec

Conseil international d'études canadiennes *See* International Council for Canadian Studies

Conseil international des associations de design graphique *See* International Council of Graphic Design Associations

Le Conseil international des organisations de lutte contre le SIDA *See* International Council of AIDS Service Organizations

Conseil international du Canada *See* Canadian International Council

Conseil interprofessionnel du Québec (CIQ) / Québec Interprofessional Council

Tour ouest, #890, 550, rue Sherbrooke ouest, Montréal QC H3A 1B9
Tél: 514-288-3574; *Téléc:* 514-288-3580
courrier@professions-quebec.org
www.professions-quebec.org
Aperçu: *Dimension:* grande; *Envergure:* provinciale; fondée en 1965
Mission: Forum d'échange et de concertation de même que la voix collective des ordres professionnels; mandat d'organisme conseil auprès de l'autorité publique
Membre(s) du bureau directeur:
Jean-François Thuot, Directeur général
jfthuot@professions-quebec.org
François Renauld, Président
presidence@professions-quebec.org
Finances: *Budget de fonctionnement annuel:* $500,000-$1.5 Million
Membre(s) du personnel: 5; 200 bénévole(s)
Membre: 45 ordres professionnels; *Comités:* Communications; Directions générales; Formation; Inspection professionnelle; Secrétaires de comité de discipline; Syndics

Conseil jeunesse francophone de la Colombie-Britannique (CJFCB) / British Columbian Francophone Youth Council

#229B, 1555, 7e av Ouest, Vancouver BC V6J 1S1
Tél: 604-736-6970; *Téléc:* 604-732-3236
information@cjfcb.com
www.cjfcb.com
www.facebook.com/CJFCB
twitter.com/cjfcb
instagram.com/conseiljeunessecb
Aperçu: *Dimension:* petite; *Envergure:* provinciale; Organisme sans but lucratif; fondée en 1989
Mission: Promouvoir, encourager et offrir des opportunités de formation aux jeunes francophones de la Colombie-Britannique afin de développer leur plein potentiel; encourager le développement de regroupements de la jeunesse francophone, au niveau local et régional; faire vivre les avantages de garder et de développer la langue et la culture francophone aux jeunes francophones de la C-B; assurer le développement et l'accroissement de partenariats avec la communauté globale; offrir des opportunités de regroupement aux jeunes francophones de la C-B, et ce au niveau provincial, interprovincial et national; offrir aux jeunes francophones de la C-B des renseignements sur les activités, services et programmes disponibles à la jeunesse francophone
Membre de: Fédération de la jeunesse canadienne-française inc.; Fédération des francophones de la Colombie-Britannique
Affiliation(s): Conseil scolaire-francophone de la C-B
Membre(s) du bureau directeur:
Shadie Bourget, Présidente
Rémi Marien, Directeur général
direction@cjfcb.com
Finances: *Fonds:* Patrimoine Canadien; Ministère de l'Éducation en CB; Développement des ressources humaines Canada
Membre(s) du personnel: 4
Membre: *Critères d'admissibilite:* Jeunes francophones et francophiles 12 à 25 ans
Activités: Parlement jeunesse francophone de la C-B; parlement franco-canadien du Nord et de l'Ouest; jeux francophone de la C-B, du Nord et de l'Ouest; jeux de la francophonie canadienne; camp de leadership, animation culturelle; formation diverses

Conseil jeunesse provincial (Manitoba) (CJP) / Provincial Youth Council

340, boul Provencher, Saint-Boniface MB R2H 0G7
Tél: 204-237-8947; *Téléc:* 204-237-5076
direction@conseil-jeunesse.mb.ca
www.conseil-jeunesse.mb.ca
www.facebook.com/conseil.jeunesse.provincial
twitter.com/CjpManitoba
www.youtube.com/CjpManitoba
Aperçu: *Dimension:* petite; *Envergure:* provinciale; Organisme sans but lucratif; fondée en 1974
Mission: Sensibiliser les jeunes à leur identité franco-manitobaine et de promouvoir le regroupement et le développement des jeunes au point de vue politique, éducatif, culturel et économique
Membre de: Fédération de la jeunesse canadienne-française inc.
Membre(s) du bureau directeur:
Roxane Dupuis, Directrice générale
direction@conseil-jeunesse.mb.ca
Membre(s) du personnel: 6

Membre: *Critères d'admissibilite:* Jeunes francophones du Manitoba de 14 à 25 ans
Activités: Pleine lune; Stage de leadership; Projet étudiants animateurs; Rassemblement Intense des Francophones Rigolos Adolescents et l'Fun; programme d'animation culturelle

Le Conseil médical du Canada *See* Medical Council of Canada

Conseil mixte du syndicat des employés de gros, de détail et de magasins à rayons de la Saskatchewan (CTC) *See* Saskatchewan Joint Board, Retail, Wholesale & Department Store Union (CLC)

Conseil montérégien de la culture et des communications (CMCC)

#130, 80, rue Saint-Laurent Ouest, Longueuil QC J4H 1L8
Tél: 450-651-0694; *Téléc:* 450-651-6020
Ligne sans frais: 877-651-0694
info@culturemonteregie.qc.ca
www.culturemonteregie.qc.ca
fr.facebook.com/179952732502
twitter.com/conseilculture
Nom précédent: Conseil culturel de la Montérégie inc
Aperçu: *Dimension:* petite; *Envergure:* provinciale; Organisme sans but lucratif; fondée en 1978
Mission: Assurer le rassemblement et la concertation des intervenants culturels de la Montérégie; contribuer à établir les priorités de développement culturel de ce territoire; conseiller la Ministre de la culture et des communications
Membre de: Table de concertation des conseils régionaux de la culture
Affliation(s): Conseil régional de développement de la Montérégie
Membre(s) du bureau directeur:
Dominic Trudel, Directeur général
dtrudel@culturemonteregie.qc.ca
Membre(s) du personnel: 7
Membre: 310; *Montant de la cotisation:* Barème; *Critères d'admissibilite:* Regroupe toute personne majeure ayant sa résidence ou sa place d'affaires sur le territoire et tout organisme (corporation ou groupement volontaire) qui a son siège social ou son principal établissement sur le territoire de la Montérégie
Activités: *Bibliothèque* Bibliothèque publique rendez-vous

Conseil multiculturel du Nouveau-Brunswick *See* New Brunswick Multicultural Council

Conseil national d'éthique en recherche chez l'humain *See* National Council on Ethics in Human Research

Conseil National de l'Enveloppe du Bâtiment *See* National Building Envelope Council

Conseil national des associations barbadiennes au Canada *See* National Council of Barbadian Associations in Canada

Conseil national des associations canadiennes des Philippines *See* National Council of Canadian Filipino Associations

Conseil national des associations d'anciens combattants au Canada *See* National Council of Veteran Associations

Conseil national des canadiens chinois *See* Chinese Canadian National Council

Le Conseil national des femmes du Canada *See* The National Council of Women of Canada

Conseil national des femmes métisses, inc. *See* Métis National Council of Women

Conseil National des Relations Canado-Arabes *See* National Council on Canada-Arab Relations

Conseil national du meuble

4360, rue Tanguay, Laval QC H7R 5Z5
Tél: 450-962-5757
Nom précédent: Corporation des marchands de meubles du Québec
Aperçu: *Dimension:* moyenne; *Envergure:* nationale
Membre(s) du bureau directeur:
Denis Bourgault, Directeur général

Le conseil national du secteur des produits de la mer *See* National Seafood Sector Council

Conseil national Société de Saint-Vincent de Paul (SSVP) / Society of Saint Vincent de Paul

2463, rue Innes, Ottawa ON K1B 3K3
Tél: 613-837-4363; *Téléc:* 613-837-7375
Ligne sans frais: 866-997-7787
national@ssvp.ca
www.ssvp.ca
Aperçu: *Dimension:* grande; *Envergure:* nationale; Organisme sans but lucratif; fondée en 1846
Mission: To live the Gospel message through personal contact with those in need & helping in all possible ways
Membre(s) du bureau directeur:
Penny Craig, President
president@ssvp.ca
Marianne Angus, Secretary
Germain Souligny, Treasurer
Finances: *Budget de fonctionnement annuel:* $100,000-$250,000; *Fonds:* Donations
Membre: 5,000-14,999
Publications:
• National President's Newsletter [a publication of the Society of Saint Vincent de Paul]
Type: Newsletter
• VincentPaul Canada: The Magazine of The Society of St. Vincent de Paul
Type: Magazine; *Frequency:* Quarterly; *Editor:* Jean-Noël Cormier *ISSN:* 0703 6477

British Columbia & Yukon Regional Council
1738 East Hastings, Vancouver BC V5L 1S5
e-mail: pres.bc@ssvp.ca
www.ssvp.bc.ca

Edmonton
PO Box 11532, Stn. Main, Edmonton AB T5J 3K7
Tel: 780-757-5225
ssvpedmonton@gmail.com
www.ssvpedmonton.ca

Halifax Particular Council
2170 Barrington St., Halifax NS B3K 2W4
Tel: 902-422-2049

Ottawa Central Council
#303, 207 Bank St., Ottawa ON K2P 2N2
Tel: 613-241-1225
bernie-on-ca-ssvp@rogers.com

Toronto Central Council
240 Church St., Toronto ON M5B 1Z2
Tel: 416-364-5577; *Fax:* 416-364-2055
info@ssvptoronto.cam
www.ssvptoronto.ca

Vancouver Island
4349 West Saanich Rd., Victoria BC V8Z 3E8
Tel: 250-727-0007; *Fax:* 250-727-0771
info@svdpvictoria.com
www.svdpvictoria.com
Membre(s) du bureau directeur:
Angela Hudson, Executive Director
Megan Misovic, President

Western Regional Council - Lethbridge
c/o St. Basil's Church, 604 - 13th St. North, Lethbridge AB T1H 2S7
Tel: 403-328-5493
www.ssvpwr.ca
Membre(s) du bureau directeur:
Lucille Boisvert, Contact
boksteynjsr@memlane.com

Conseil oecuménique des chrétiennes du Canada *See* Women's Inter-Church Council of Canada

Le Conseil ontarien d'évaluation des qualifications *See* Qualifications Evaluation Council of Ontario

Conseil ontarien de commerce des véhicules automobiles *See* Ontario Motor Vehicle Industry Council

Conseil Ontarien de Recherche en Loisir *See* Ontario Research Council on Leisure

Conseil ontarien des études supérieures *See* Ontario Council on Graduate Studies

Le Conseil ontarien pour le jeu responsable *See* Responsible Gambling Council (Ontario)

Conseil patronal de l'environnement du Québec (CPEQ)

#504, 640, rue Saint-Paul ouest, Montréal QC H3C 1L9
Tél: 514-393-1122; *Téléc:* 514-393-1146
info@cpeq.qc.ca
www.cpeq.qc.ca
Aperçu: *Dimension:* moyenne; *Envergure:* provinciale
Mission: De promouvoir les intérêts de l'industrie et l'entreprise en matière d'environnement
Membre(s) du bureau directeur:
Hélène Lauzon, Présidente
Membre(s) du personnel: 8
Membre: 212 enterprises + 32 associations; *Montant de la cotisation:* Barème

Conseil pédagogique interdisciplinaire du Québec (CPIQ)

#202, 1319, ch de Chambly, Longueuil QC J4J 3X1
Tél: 450-928-8770; *Téléc:* 450-928-8771
secretariat@conseil-cpiq.qc.ca
www.conseil-cpiq.qc.ca
Aperçu: *Dimension:* moyenne; *Envergure:* provinciale; fondée en 1968
Mission: Regroupement des associations professionnelles d'enseignants pour la promotion de la pédagogie et la qualité de l'enseignement au Québec
Membre(s) du bureau directeur:
Louise Trudel, Directrice générale
Membre: 21 associations; *Montant de la cotisation:* 2,30$ par membres d'associations pour membres actifs; 150$ membres associés; *Critères d'admissibilite:* Associations professionnelles d'enseignants; *Comités:* Vérification et finances; Gouvernance; Promotion du CPIQ et de ses associations et de recrutement; Publications; Linsertion professionnelle du personnel enseignant
Activités: Liste des publications sur le site web

Conseil pour l'enseignement de la lecture aux analphabètes de Montréal *See* Reading Council for Literacy Advance in Montréal

Conseil pour le développement de l'alphabétisme et des compétences des adultes du Nouveau-Brunswick (CODACNB)

#314, 236, rue Saint-Georges, Moncton NB E1C 1W1
Ligne sans frais: 866-473-4404
codacnb@codacnb.ca
www.codacnb.ca
www.facebook.com/alphabetisationNB
Aperçu: *Dimension:* petite; *Envergure:* provinciale; Organisme sans but lucratif; fondée en 1989
Mission: Promouvoir l'alphabétisation en français au Nouveau-Brunswick; assurer une concertation des intervenants en alphabétisation en français au Nouveau-Brunswick
Membre de: Fédération canadienne pour l'alphabétisation en français
Membre(s) du bureau directeur:
Patrick Jeune, Directeur général
patrick.jeune@codacnb.ca
Claudia Dubé, Sec.-trés.
Chantal Imbeault-Jean, Présidente
presidence@codacnb.ca
Membre(s) du personnel: 6
Membre: 13; *Critères d'admissibilite:* Conseils d'alphabétisation
Activités: *Bibliothèque:* Centre de ressources; rendez-vous
Prix, Bouses:
• Bourse Denise Poirier (Prix)
Pour rendre hommage à une personne qui a réussi le programme d'alphabétisation et qui a pour but de continuer ses études et qui a contribué à l'avancement de l'alphabétisation dans sa communauté

Conseil provincial du soutien scolaire

#7100, 565 boul Crémazie est, Montréal QC H2M 2V9
Tél: 514-384-9681; *Téléc:* 514-384-9680
www.cpss.qc.ca
Aperçu: *Dimension:* moyenne; *Envergure:* provinciale
Mission: Négocier la convention collective; de voir à son application et de promouvoir la qualité de vie de ses membres
Membre(s) du bureau directeur:
Pierre Degray, Président
Membre: 7,500; *Comités:* Sous-Traitance; Santé/Sécurité; Équité salariale; Mobilisation; Négociation

Conseil québécois de la coopération et de la mutualité (CCQ)

#204, 5955, rue Saint-Laurent, Lévis QC G6V 3P5
Tél: 418-835-3710; *Téléc:* 418-835-6322
info@coopquebec.coop
www.coopquebec.qc.ca

www.facebook.com/quebec.coop
twitter.com/CQCMCOOP
Nom précédent: Conseil de la coopération du Québec
Aperçu: *Dimension:* moyenne; *Envergure:* provinciale; fondée en 1939
Mission: Pour unir des organisations coopératives du Québec pour favoriser l'action concertée de ses membres, promouvoir l'authenticité coopérative, défendre les intérêts de ses membres
Affliation(s): Conseil canadien de la coopération; Alliance coopérative internationale
Membre(s) du bureau directeur:
Gaston Bédard, Directeur général intérimaire
gastonbedard@coopquebec.coop
Membre(s) du personnel: 21
Membre: 43; *Critères d'admissibilite:* Toute organisation appliquant les règles d'action coopérative énoncées par l'Alliance coopérative internationale peut être représentée
Activités: *Bibliothèque*

Conseil québécois de la franchise (CQF)

2115, boul des Laurentides, Laval QC H7M 4M2
Tél: 514-340-6018; *Téléc:* 450-967-2749
info@cqf.ca
www.cqf.ca
www.linkedin.com/groups/Franchise-Entrepreneurship-3934413
www.facebook.com/ConseilQuebecoisDeLaFranchise
twitter.com/info_cqf
www.youtube.com/user/lecqf
Aperçu: *Dimension:* petite; *Envergure:* provinciale; fondée en 1984
Mission: • promouvoir la franchise entre les entreprises au Québec
Membre(s) du bureau directeur:
Pieere Garceau, Président-directeur général
pierregarceau@cqf.ca
Membre: 325; *Montant de la cotisation:* Barème; *Critères d'admissibilite:* Franchiseurs et fournisseurs; *Comités:* Exécutif; Affaires légales; Communications; Formation; Gala et Temple de la renommée; Tournoi de golf; Jury Prix Maillon d'or; Mises en candidature Prix Maillon d'or; Prix Hommage; Relations publiques et Collège des experts; Semaine de l'entrepreneurship en franchise

Conseil québécois de la musique (CQM)

#302, 1908, rue Panet, Montréal QC H2L 3A2
Tél: 514-524-1310; *Téléc:* 514-524-2219
Ligne sans frais: 866-999-1310
info@cqm.qc.ca
www.cqm.qc.ca
Aperçu: *Dimension:* moyenne; *Envergure:* provinciale; Organisme sans but lucratif; fondée en 1987
Mission: Rassembler les professionels du secteur de la musique de concert (musiques ancienne médiévale, baroque, de la Renaissance, classique, romantique, moderne, contemporaine, Jazz, électronacqoustique, du monde); promouvoir la discipline et soutenir son rayonnement
Membre de: Conseil international de la musique; Les Arts et la Ville
Affliation(s): Conseil international de la musique
Membre(s) du bureau directeur:
Sylvie Gamache, Directrice générale
Finances: *Budget de fonctionnement annuel:* $250,000-$500,000
Membre(s) du personnel: 4
Membre: 300; *Montant de la cotisation:* Barème; *Critères d'admissibilite:* Organismes et individus oeuvrant professionnellement en musique de concert
Activités: Divers colloques; conférences; ateliers de formation; *Evénements de sensibilisation:* Journée internationale de la musique
Prix, Bouses:
• Prix Opus (Prix)
Eligibility: Souligne l'excellence de la musique de concert au Québec dans différents répertoires musicaux

Conseil québécois des arts médiatiques (CQAM)

3995, rue Berri, Montréal QC H2L 4H2
Tél: 514-527-5116
Ligne sans frais: 888-527-5116
www.cqam.org
Aperçu: *Dimension:* moyenne; *Envergure:* provinciale
Membre(s) du bureau directeur:
Robin Dupuis, Président
Isabelle L'Italien, Directrice générale
dg@cqam.org

Conseil québécois des gais et lesbiennes du Québec (CQGL)

CP 182, Succ. C, Montréal QC H2L 4K1
Tél: 514-759-6844
info@conseil-lgbt.ca
www.cqgl.ca
www.facebook.com/CQLGBT
twitter.com/cqlgbt
Aperçu: *Dimension:* petite; *Envergure:* provinciale
Mission: A pour mission concrétiser notre leitmotive 'S'engager pour l'égalité sociale'. Adresse civique: #100, 1307, rue Sainte-Catherine Est, Montréal, QC.
Membre(s) du bureau directeur:
Steve Foster, Directeur général
dg@conseil-lgbt.ca
Membre: *Montant de la cotisation:* 20$ étudiants; 40$ individus; 50$ organismes à but non lucratif

Le Conseil Québécois du Chardon Inc. ***See*** Québec Thistle Council Inc.

Conseil québécois du commerce de détail (CQCD) / Retail Council of Québec

#910, 630, rue Sherbrooke ouest, Montréal QC H3A 1E4
Tél: 514-842-6681; *Téléc:* 514-842-7627
Ligne sans frais: 800-364-6766
cqcd@cqcd.org
www.cqcd.org
Aperçu: *Dimension:* moyenne; *Envergure:* provinciale; Organisme sans but lucratif; fondée en 1978
Mission: Promouvoir, représenter et valoriser le secteur du commerce de détail au Québec et les détaillants qui en font partie afin d'assurer le sain développement et la prospérité du secteur
Membre(s) du bureau directeur:
Léopold Turgeon, Président
Chantale Bélanger, Directrice, Comptabilité et administration
cbelanger@cqcd.org
Finances: *Budget de fonctionnement annuel:* $500,000-$1.5 Million
Membre(s) du personnel: 12; 75 bénévole(s)
Membre: 5,000 établissements commerciaux; *Montant de la cotisation:* Barème

Conseil québécois du théâtre (CQT)

#808, 460, rue Ste-Catherine Ouest, Montréal QC H3B 1A7
Tél: 514-954-0270; *Téléc:* 514-954-0165
Ligne sans frais: 866-954-0270
cqt@cqt.qc.ca
www.cqt.ca
www.facebook.com/ConseilQuebecoisDuTheatre
twitter.com/cqt_theatre
www.youtube.com/user/ChaineCQT
Aperçu: *Dimension:* moyenne; *Envergure:* provinciale; fondée en 1983
Mission: Promouvoir et défendre les intérêts du milieu théâtral et le représenter auprès des diverses instances; concerter, animer et informer la communauté théâtrale sur toutes les questions qui touchent la pratique théâtrale; promouvoir et développer le théâtre
Membre de: L'institut internationale du théâtre
Membre(s) du bureau directeur:
Hélène Nadeau, Directrice générale
direction@cqt.qc.ca
Pier DuFour, Adjointe à la direction
Membre(s) du personnel: 7
Membre: 216; *Comités:* Actions politiques; Animation du milieu; Avenir du théâtre; Balises de succession; Conditions socioéconomiques; Formation continue; Formation professionnelle; Nouveaux modèles de gestion; Promotion collective du théâtre; Théâtre jeune public
Activités: *Evénements de sensibilisation:* Journée mondiale du théâtre; *Bibliothèque*

Conseil québécois sur le tabac et la santé / Québec Council on Tobacco & Health

#302, 4126, rue St-Denis, Montréal QC H2W 2M5
Tél: 514-948-5317; *Téléc:* 514-948-4582
info@cqts.qc.ca
www.cqts.qc.ca
www.facebook.com/317301810228
twitter.com/cqts
Aperçu: *Dimension:* moyenne; *Envergure:* provinciale; Organisme sans but lucratif; fondée en 1976
Mission: Promouvoir la santé du fumeur et du non-fumeur; faire le lien entre les associations, groupes bénévoles et autres intéressés à la santé publique; trouver des approches et des moyens pour améliorer l'éducation face à l'usage du tabac
Membre de: Conseil canadien pour le contrôle du tabac
Membre(s) du bureau directeur:
Mario Bujold, Directeur général
Marie-Soleil Boivin, Agente, Communication et relations médias
Finances: *Budget de fonctionnement annuel:* $250,000-$500,000
Membre: 600
Activités: *Evénements de sensibilisation:* Semaine québécoise sans tabac

Conseil régional de Baie Comeau (Manicouagan) - Bureau régional FTQ Côte Nord

#309, 1041, rue de Mingan, Baie-Comeau QC G5C 3W1
Tél: 418-295-3551; *Téléc:* 418-589-7620
crhcnmanicouagan@cgocable.ca
www.cotenord.ftq.qc.ca
Aperçu: *Dimension:* petite; *Envergure:* locale surveillé par Fédération des travailleurs et travailleuses du Québec

Conseil régional de l'Age d'Or de l'Est du Québec ***Voir*** Fédération des Clubs de l'Age d'Or de l'Est du Québec

Conseil régional de l'environnement de la Gaspésie et des Iles-de-la-Madeleine (CREGIM)

#103, 106-A, Port Royal, Bonaventure QC G0C 1E0
Tél: 418-534-4498
Ligne sans frais: 877-534-4498
cregim@globetrotter.net
www.cregim.org
www.facebook.com/269353189800151?ref=hl
twitter.com/CREGIM1
Aperçu: *Dimension:* petite; *Envergure:* locale; fondée en 1995
Mission: Regrouper et représenter des organismes proenvironnementaux et des individus voués à la protection et la mise en valeur de l'environnement, auprès de toutes les instances concernées; favoriser la concertation et assurer l'établissement de priorités et de suivi en matière d'environnement; favoriser et promouvoir des stratégies d'actions concertées; agir à titre d'organisme ressource aux services des intervenants régionaux
Affliation(s): Regroupement national des Conseils régionaux en environnement
Membre(s) du bureau directeur:
Caroline Duchesne, Directrice
caroline.cregim@globetrotter.net
Steve Pronovost, Présidente
Monette Bujold, Secrétaire adjointe-administrative
monette.cregim@globetrotter.net
Finances: *Budget de fonctionnement annuel:* $50,000-$100,000; *Fonds:* Gouvernement provincial; gouvernement régional; gouvernement municipal
Membre(s) du personnel: 4; 9 bénévole(s)
Membre: 119; *Montant de la cotisation:* 100$ institutionnel; 10$ individu; 30$ associé

Conseil régional de la culture de l'Outaouais

432, boul Alexandre-Taché, Gatineau QC J9A 1M7
Tél: 819-595-2601; *Téléc:* 819-595-9088
Ligne sans frais: 855-595-2601
info@crco.org
www.crco.org
www.linkedin.com/in/communicationcrco
www.facebook.com/275021145886146
twitter.com/Culture07
Aperçu: *Dimension:* petite; *Envergure:* locale; fondée en 1976
Mission: Conseiller, concerter, consulter et représenter le milieu culturel et artistique de la région de l'Outaouais, en ayant comme objectif principal le développement du secteur.
Membre(s) du bureau directeur:
Julie Martineau, Directrice Générale
direction@crco.org
Membre(s) du personnel: 4
Membre: *Montant de la cotisation:* 15$ étudiant; 20$ ami; 30$ titulaire; 50-75 organisme sans but lucratif; 85$ entreprise; 100$ insitutionnel; 125-1000 municipal; 250$ MRC

Conseil régional de la culture et des communications de la Côte-Nord (CRCCCN)

22, Place La Salle, 1er étage, Baie-Comeau QC G4Z 1K3
Tél: 418-296-1450; *Téléc:* 418-296-1457
Ligne sans frais: 866-295-6744
secretariat@culturecotenord.com
www.culturecotenord.com
www.facebook.com/crcccn
Aperçu: *Dimension:* petite; *Envergure:* locale; Organisme sans but lucratif; fondée en 1973

Mission: Développer les arts et lettres, la culture et les communications dans la région; offrir des services de qualité à ses membres
Membre(s) du bureau directeur:
Marie-France Lévesque, Directrice générale
dg@culturecotenord.com
Membre(s) du personnel: 3
Membre: 257; *Montant de la cotisation:* 20$ individu; 35$ organisme; 50-100 municipalité; *Critères d'admissibilité:* Organismes culturels et artistes
Activités: Forums; formation; remise de prix; promotion du tourisme; développement des médias communautaires et autochtones; services de secrétariat; *Listes de destinataires:* Oui; *Bibliothèque*
Prix, Bouses:
• Prix d'Excellence Culture et Communications Côte-Nord (Prix)

Conseil régional de la culture Saguenay-Lac-Saint-Jean (CRC)
1640 av Hamilton est, Alma QC G8B 4Z1
Tél: 418-662-6623; *Téléc:* 418-662-1071
secretariat@crc02.qc.ca
www.ccr-sl.qc.ca
Nom précédent: Conseil de la culture de la région Saguenay/Lac-St-Jean/Chibougamau/Chapais
Aperçu: *Dimension:* petite; *Envergure:* locale; Organisme sans but lucratif; fondée en 1977
Mission: Développer les arts, la culture et la communication au Saguenay-Lac-Saint-Jean en exerçant les rôles de concertation, représentation, information, consultation de promotion de services aux membres et au milieu culturel
Membre(s) du bureau directeur:
Lucien Frenette, Directeur général
direction@crc02.qc.ca
Lyne L'Italien, Présidente
lyne@theatrelarubrique.com
Finances: *Budget de fonctionnement annuel:* $100,000-$250,000
Membre(s) du personnel: 5
Membre: 200; *Montant de la cotisation:* Barème; *Critères d'admissibilité:* Organismes culturels et scolaires; individus; municipalités; *Comités:* Conseil d'administration; Comité exécutif
Activités: *Bibliothèque* rendez-vous

Conseil régional des personnes âgées italo-canadiennes de Montréal
671, rue Ogilvy, Montréal QC H3N 1N4
Tél: 514-273-6588; *Téléc:* 514-273-6636
craic@securenet.net
www.craic.ca
Aperçu: *Dimension:* moyenne; *Envergure:* locale; Organisme sans but lucratif; fondée en 1974
Mission: Favoriser le maintien à domicile des personnes âgées et leur autonomie physique et intellectuelle; améliorer la qualité de vie des personnes âgées dans leur environnement naturel le plus longtemps possible
Membre(s) du bureau directeur:
Franco Rocchi, Contact
Membre: 13,000
Activités: Popote roulante; traduction; accompagnement; repas communautaires; cours et activités éducatives, récréatives, culturelles; assistance aux immigrants;

Conseil régional FTQ Abitibi-Témiscamingue - Nord-du-Québec
#3100, 201, rue du Terminus ouest, Rouyn-Noranda QC J9X 2P7
Tél: 819-762-1354; *Téléc:* 819-762-1411
crftq-atndq@ftq.qc.ca
www.abitibi-nordqc.ftq.qc.ca
Aperçu: *Dimension:* petite; *Envergure:* locale surveillé par Fédération des travailleurs et travailleuses du Québec

Conseil régional FTQ Bas St-Laurent - Gaspésie-Iles-de-la-Madeleine
#608, 2, rue Saint-Germain est, Rimouski QC G5L 8T7
Tél: 418-722-8232; *Téléc:* 418-722-8380
crftq-bslgi@ftq.qc.ca
www.bsl-gaspesie.ftq.qc.ca
Aperçu: *Dimension:* petite; *Envergure:* locale surveillé par Fédération des travailleurs et travailleuses du Québec

Conseil régional FTQ de l'Ouatouais
#311, 259, boul Saint-Joseph, Gatineau QC J8V 2R1
Tél: 819-777-4473; *Téléc:* 819-777-1973
ftq07@bellnet.ca
www.outaouais.ftq.qc.ca

Aperçu: *Dimension:* petite; *Envergure:* locale surveillé par Fédération des travailleurs et travailleuses du Québec

Conseil régional FTQ de la Haute-Yamaska - Bureau régional FTQ - Montérégie
CP 244, 370, rue Principale, Granby QC J2G 8E5
Tél: 450-378-3557; *Téléc:* 450-378-4172
conseilregionalf.t.q.h.y@qc.aira.com
www.monteregie.ftq.qc.ca
Aperçu: *Dimension:* petite; *Envergure:* locale surveillé par Fédération des travailleurs et travailleuses du Québec

Conseil régional FTQ de la Mauricie et du Centre-du-Québec - Bureau régional FTQ - Maurice et Centre du Québec
7080, boul Marion, Trois-Rivières-Ouest QC G9A 6G4
Tél: 819-378-4049; *Téléc:* 819-378-4362
CRFTQMCQ@ftq.qc.ca
www.mauriciecentreqc.ftq.qc.ca
Aperçu: *Dimension:* petite; *Envergure:* locale surveillé par Fédération des travailleurs et travailleuses du Québec

Conseil régional FTQ du Richelieu - Bureau régional FTQ - Montérégie
#6200, 4805, boul Lapinière, Brossard QC J4Z 0G2
Tél: 450-926-6200; *Téléc:* 450-926-6204
sgirard@ftq.qc.ca
www.monteregie.ftq.qc.ca
Aperçu: *Dimension:* petite; *Envergure:* locale surveillé par Fédération des travailleurs et travailleuses du Québec

Conseil régional FTQ du Suroît - Bureau régional FTQ - Montérégie
3 rue Bay, Salaberry-de-Valleyfield QC J6S 1X3
Tél: 450-567-0170
daniełmallette@cgocable.ca
www.monteregie.ftq.qc.ca
Aperçu: *Dimension:* petite; *Envergure:* locale surveillé par Fédération des travailleurs et travailleuses du Québec

Conseil régional FTQ Estrie
790, rue de la Rand, Sherbrooke QC J1H 1W7
Tél: 819-562-3922; *Téléc:* 819-563-6916
ftq-estrie@qc.aira.com
www.estrie.ftq.qc.ca
Aperçu: *Dimension:* petite; *Envergure:* locale; Organisme sans but lucratif surveillé par Fédération des travailleurs et travailleuses du Québec
Affiliation(s): Fédération des travailleurs et travailleuses du Québec
Membre(s) du bureau directeur:
Harold Arseneault, Président

Conseil régional FTQ Montréal Métropolitain
#2500, 565, boul Crémazie est, Montréal QC H2M 2V6
Tél: 514-387-3666; *Téléc:* 514-387-4393
crftqmm@ftq.qc.ca
www.montrealmetro.ftq.qc.ca
Nom précédent: Conseil du travail de Montréal
Aperçu: *Dimension:* moyenne; *Envergure:* locale; fondée en 1886 surveillé par Fédération des travailleurs et travailleuses du Québec
Affiliation(s): Fédération des travailleurs et travailleuses du Québec
Membre(s) du bureau directeur:
Danielle Casara, Présidente
dcasara@ftq.qc.ca
Activités: *Stagiaires:* Oui

Conseil régional FTQ Québec et Chaudière-Appalaches (CRQCA)
#120, 5000, boul des Gradins, Québec QC G2J 1N3
Tél: 418-622-4941; *Téléc:* 418-623-9932
crqca@videotron.ca
www.quebec-chaudiereappalaches.ftq.qc.ca
Aperçu: *Dimension:* petite; *Envergure:* locale surveillé par Fédération des travailleurs et travailleuses du Québec
Affiliation(s): Fédération des travailleurs et travailleuses du Québec
Membre(s) du bureau directeur:
Sébastien Boies, Président, 416-622-4941, Fax: 416-623-9932
crqca@videotron.ca
Yves Marcoux, Vice-Président
Louise Lemieux, Secrétaire archiviste
Roch Lessard, Trésorier

Conseil régional FTQ Saguenay-Lac-St-Jean-Chibougamau-Chapais (CRFTQSLSJ)
#100, 2679, boul du Royaume, Jonquière QC G7S 5T1
Tél: 418-699-0199; *Téléc:* 418-699-7179
ftqsaglac@ftq.qc.ca
www.saglac-chibougamauchapais.ftq.qc.ca
Nom précédent: Conseil du travail de Saguenay-Lac-St-Jean
Aperçu: *Dimension:* petite; *Envergure:* locale; Organisme sans but lucratif; fondée en 1965 surveillé par Fédération des travailleurs et travailleuses du Québec
Membre de: Fédération des travailleurs et travailleuses du Québec; Congrès du travail du Canada
Affliation(s): Fédération des travailleurs et travailleuses du Québec
Membre(s) du bureau directeur:
Michel Routhier, Président
Finances: *Budget de fonctionnement annuel:* $50,000-$100,000
Membre(s) du personnel: 2; 50 bénévole(s)
Membre: 16,000;

Conseil régional FTQ Sept-Iles et Côte-Nord - Bureau régional FTQ Côte Nord
#203, 737, boul Laure, Sept-Iles QC G4R 1Y2
Tél: 418-962-3551
bmethot@ftq.qc.ca
www.cotenord.ftq.qc.ca
Nom précédent: Conseil des travailleurs de Sept-Îles et du Golfe
Aperçu: *Dimension:* petite; *Envergure:* locale surveillé par Fédération des travailleurs et travailleuses du Québec
Affiliation(s): Fédération des travailleurs et travailleuses du Québec

Conseil sectoriel de la construction *See* Construction Sector Council

Conseil sectoriel de la police *See* Police Sector Council

Le Conseil sur le vieillissement d'Ottawa *See* The Council on Aging of Ottawa

Conseil unitarien du Canada *See* Canadian Unitarian Council

Conservation Council of New Brunswick (CCNB) / Conseil de la conservation du Nouveau-Brunswick
180 St. John St., Fredericton NB E3B 4A9
Tel: 506-458-8747; *Fax:* 506-458-1047
info@conservationcouncil.ca
www.conservationcouncil.ca
www.facebook.com/ccnbaction
twitter.com/cc_nb
www.youtube.com/user/ccnbactiontv
Overview: A medium-sized provincial charitable organization founded in 1969
Mission: To generate awareness of the ecological foundations of our quality of life; To promote public policies with respect to the integrity of natural systems & to contribute to a sustainable society; To advocate appropriate remedies to pressing environmental problems such as ground water contamination & hazardous wastes
Member of: New Brunswick Environmental Network; Canadian Environmental Networks
Affiliation(s): Friends of the Earth Canada
Chief Officer(s):
Céline Delacroix, Executive Director
Stephanie Coburn, President
Finances: *Funding Sources:* Enterprise activities; Special events; Contracts for special projects
Staff Member(s): 6
Activities: *Rents Mailing List:* Yes

Conservation Council of Ontario (CCO) / Conseil de conservation de l'Ontario
#132, 215 Spadina Ave., Toronto ON M5T 2C7
Tel: 416-533-1635; *Fax:* 416-979-3936
cco@web.ca
www.weconserve.ca/cco
Overview: A medium-sized provincial charitable organization founded in 1951
Mission: To build a strong conservation movement across Ontario
Chief Officer(s):
Ben Marans, President
Chris Winter, Executive Director
cco@web.ca
Karen Sun, Secretary

Membership: *Member Profile:* Municipalities, businesses, organizations, & individuals dedicated to conservation & a healthy environment
Activities: Increasing public awareness of conservation; Developing a provincial fund to support conservation efforts throughout Ontario
Meetings/Conferences: • Conservation Council of Ontario 2015 Annual Meeting, 2015, ON
Scope: Provincial
Description: An overview of strategic direction & the election of new members
Contact Information: E-mail: info@weconserve.ca

Conservation de la faune au Canada *See* Wildlife Preservation Canada

Conservation Foundation of Greater Toronto

5 Shoreham Dr., Toronto ON M3N 1S4
Tel: 416-667-6279; *Fax:* 416-667-6275
Other Communication: thelivingcity.org
fdn@trca.on.ca
www.trca.on.ca
Also Known As: The Living City Foundation
Previous Name: The Metropolitan Toronto & Region Conservation Foundation; The Conservation Foundation of Greater Toronto
Overview: A small local charitable organization founded in 1961
Mission: To acquire & manage regional greenspace & watershed conservation lands; To support watershed management, reforestation, wildlife habitats, public access & recreation, historic sites, & environmental rehabilitation of natural spaces
Affliation(s): The Toronto & Region Conservation Authority
Chief Officer(s):
Linda Craib, Admin Coordinator & Sr. Researcher
lcraib@trca.on.ca
David Love, Executive Director
dlove@trca.on.ca
Finances: *Annual Operating Budget:* $250,000-$500,000; *Funding Sources:* Donors include businesses, industries, other foundations, estates, conservation organizations & individuals
20 volunteer(s)
Membership: 20; *Committees:* Board; Campaign; Executive; Members
Activities: Tree For Life Program; Kortright Centre for Conservation; Conservation Education Field Centres (conservation education schools at Albion Hills, Cold Creek & Claremont Conservation Areas); conservation libraries & scholarships; Don River; Greenspace Strategy (the authority's conservation vision for the 21st century - urges greater cooperation between the authority, the province & the municipalities in managing the regional watershed; also advocates protection of the Oak Ridges Moraine complex
Awards:
• The Conservation Foundation of Greater Toronto Scholarship (Scholarship)
Eligibility: Students enrolled in conservation-related studies
Amount: $1,500

Conservation Halton Foundation

2596 Britannia Rd. West, Burlington ON L7P 0G3
Tel: 905-336-1158; *Fax:* 905-336-7014
web@hrca.on.ca
www.conservationhalton.on.ca
www.facebook.com/ConservationHalton
twitter.com/CH_Comm
Previous Name: Halton Foundation
Overview: A small local charitable organization
Mission: To raise funds for Conservation Halton projects & programs that protect & enhance the natural environment
Chief Officer(s):
Jim A. Sweetlove, Chair, Conservation Halton Foundation
John Vice, Chair, Conservation Halton
Brian Hobbs, Director, Development, Conservation Halton Foundation
Finances: *Annual Operating Budget:* $100,000-$250,000
Publications:
• Focus on Conservation [a publication of Conservation Halton Foundation]
Type: Newsletter

Conservation Ontario

PO Box 11, 120 Bayview Pkwy., Newmarket ON L3R 4W3
Tel: 905-895-0716; *Fax:* 905-895-0751
info@conservationontario.ca
www.conservation-ontario.on.ca
www.facebook.com/126861190733330
twitter.com/conont
Also Known As: Association of Conservation Authorities of Ontario
Overview: A medium-sized provincial organization founded in 1946
Mission: To represent & support a network of community-based environmental organizations; To ensure conservation, restoration, & responsible management of Ontario's wetlands, woodlands, & natural habitat
Chief Officer(s):
Dick Hibma, Chair
chair@conservationontario.ca
Kim Gavine, General Manager
kgavine@conservationontario.ca
Bonnie Fox, Manager, Policy & Planning
bfox@conservationontario.ca
Mike Walters, Manager, Source Water Protection
mwalters@conservationontario.ca
Jo-Anne Rzadki, Coordinator, Watershed Stewardship
jrzadki@conservationontario.ca
Rick Wilson, Coordinator, Water Resources Information Program (WRIP)
rwilson@conservationontario.ca
Jane Lewington, Specialist, Marketing & Communications
jlewington@conservationontario.ca
Finances: *Funding Sources:* Levies provided by the conservation authorities
Staff Member(s): 13
Membership: 36 organizations; *Member Profile:* Ontario's conservation authorities; Community-based watershed management agencies
Activities: Developing programs to protect life & property from natural hazards, such as erosion & flooding; Encouraging watershed stewardship practices; Promoting teh expertise of conservation authorities in managing Ontario's environment
Publications:
• Adaptive Management of Stream Corridors in Ontario
Type: Report
Profile: A planning & design guide
• An Evaluation of Water Resource Monitoring Efforts in Support of Agricultural Stewardship in Watersheds of the Great Lakes
Type: Report
Profile: Produced by Conservation Ontario in partnership with the Ontario Ministry of Agriculture, Food &Rural Affairs
• Conservation Ontario Annual Report
Type: Yearbook; *Frequency:* Annually
• Conservation Ontario E-Bulletin
Type: Newsletter
Profile: Information & updates on issues about conservation authorities
• Cost Benefit Analysis of Agricultural Source Water Protection Beneficial Management Practices
Type: Report
Profile: Agricultural beneficial management practices such as plant buffers, soile testing, crop covers, & crop rotation to protect thequality & supply of water
• Guide to Conservation Areas
Type: Guide; *Number of Pages:* 64
Profile: A guide to 261 conservation areas among 36 conservation authorities in Ontario
• Innovations in Water Management
Type: Report
Profile: Place-based environmental management approaches
• Navigating Ontario's Future: A Water Budget Overview for Ontario
Type: Report; *Number of Pages:* 36
• Navigating Ontario's Future: Overview of Integrated Watershed Management in Ontario
Type: Report; *Number of Pages:* 122
• Navigating Ontario's Future: Water Management Framework
Type: Report; *Number of Pages:* 32
Profile: Contents include the need for a framework, developing the water management framework, the use of the framework in Ontario, & next steps
• Ontario Drinking Water Stewardship Program Outreach & Education Toolkit
Type: Kit
Profile: A communication toolkit for each Source Protection Region & Source Protection Area in Ontario
• Protecting People & Property: A Business Case for Investing in Flood Prevention & Control
Type: Report; *Number of Pages:* 56; *Author:* M. Fortin
Profile: Subjects addressed include the evolution of flood management, accomplishments, flood frequency & severity, responding tofuture risks, & costs & benefits of improvements
• Sensitivity Mapping & Local Watershed Assessments for Climate Change Detection & Adaptation Monitoring
Type: Report; *Number of Pages:* 77
Profile: Topics include Ontario sensitivity assessment using GIS mapping, climate change detection monitoring, & climatechange adaptation monitoring
• Walkerton Inquiry
Type: Report
Profile: A summary of Conservation Ontario's participation in part II of the Walkerton Inquiry, including a position paper entitled "The Importance of Watershed Management in Protecting Ontario's Drinking WaterSupplies"
• Water Resources Information Project
Type: Report
Profile: The current state of water information in Ontario

Conservative Party of Canada / Parti conservateur du Canada

#1204, 130 Albert St., Ottawa ON K1P 5G4
Tel: 613-755-2000; *Fax:* 613-755-2001
Toll-Free: 866-808-8407
www.conservative.ca
www.facebook.com/cpcpcc
twitter.com/CPC_HQ
www.youtube.com/cpcpcc;
www.flickr.com/photos/30107029@N04
Previous Name: Progressive Conservative Party of Canada, Canadian Alliance Party; Canadian Conservative Reform Alliance
Overview: A large national organization founded in 2003
Mission: The Conservative Party provided Canadians with an alternative to the Liberal government. It developed innovative and practical new policy ideas such as the Federal Accountability Act, the Public Transit Tax Credit and the Apprenticeship Incentive Grant- ideas Conservatives would later implement in government.
Chief Officer(s):
Stephen Harper, Leader

Conservatory Canada

#61, 45 King St., London ON N6A 1B8
Tel: 519-433-3147; *Fax:* 519-433-7404
Toll-Free: 800-461-5367
officeadmin@conservatorycanada.ca
www.conservatorycanada.ca
www.facebook.com/ConservatoryCanada
twitter.com/conservatorycan
www.youtube.com/user/ConservatoryCanada
Previous Name: Western Board of Music
Overview: A medium-sized local licensing charitable organization founded in 1934
Mission: To promote achievement in music through a comprehensive program of study, evaluation & recognition for teachers & students; to foster the development of musical talent & potential
Chief Officer(s):
Warwick Victoria, National Executive Director
victoria@conservatorycanada.ca
Staff Member(s): 3
Activities: Provides a standardized system of music examinations & education to students in Canada; annual conference; workshops

Conserver Society of Hamilton & District Inc.

c/o EcoHouse, 22 Veevers Dr., Hamilton ON L8K 5P5
e-mail: contact@conserversociety.ca
www.conserversociety.ca
Overview: A small local charitable organization founded in 1969
Mission: To promote a healthy, sustainable environment in Hamilton, Ontario & the surrounding area; To provide public education about environmental issues
Chief Officer(s):
Pete Wobschall, Chair, 905-540-8787 Ext. 117
Finances: *Funding Sources:* Donations; Membership fees; Sponsorships
Membership: *Fees:* $10 individuals; $20 families; $40 organizations
Activities: Partnering with like-minded organizations
Publications:
• Environmental Advocate
Type: Newsletter; *Price:* Free with membership in the Conserver Society of Hamilton & District Inc.
Profile: Information related to envrionmental issues

Consolidated Credit Counseling Services of Canada, Inc.

#400, 505 Consumers Rd., Toronto ON M2J 4V8
Tel: 416-915-5200; *Fax:* 800-656-4187
Toll-Free: 888-287-8506
counsellor@consolidatedcredit.ca
www.consolidatedcredit.ca
www.linkedin.com/company/consolidated-credit-counseling-services-of-ca
www.facebook.com/consolidatedcreditcanada
twitter.com/debt_free_2day
plus.google.com/107802209722404534513
Overview: A medium-sized national charitable organization overseen by Ontario Association of Credit Counselling Services
Mission: To provide professional, unbiased counselling & educational services to people distressed about debts; To encorage personal fi nancial literacy
Member of: Ontario Association of Credit Counselling Services
Chief Officer(s):
Jeffrey Schwartz, Executive Director
jschwartz@consolidatedcredit.ca
Activities: Providing education to consumers on topics such as budgeting, managing credit, cutting costs, & surviving layoffs; Offering consumer debt strategies
Publications:
• All About Credit
Type: Booklet; *Number of Pages:* 20; *Price:* Free
• Avoiding Foreclosure
Type: Booklet; *Number of Pages:* 14; *Price:* Free
• Budgeting 101: Your Money Guide for Getting Through School
Type: Booklet; *Number of Pages:* 24; *Price:* Free
Profile: Practical information for students
• Budgeting Made Easy
Type: Booklet; *Number of Pages:* 20; *Price:* Free
• Coping with Financial Stress
Type: Booklet; *Number of Pages:* 16; *Price:* Free
• Credit in a New Country: A Guide to Credit in Canada
Type: Booklet; *Number of Pages:* 16; *Price:* Free
• Cutting Car Costs
Type: Booklet; *Number of Pages:* 16; *Price:* Free
• Divorce & Your Credit
Type: Booklet; *Number of Pages:* 16; *Price:* Free
• Holiday Survival Guide
Type: Booklet; *Number of Pages:* 18; *Price:* Free
• Identity Theft
Type: Booklet; *Number of Pages:* 16; *Price:* Free
• Make the Most of Your Credit Score
Type: Booklet; *Number of Pages:* 12; *Price:* Free
• Managing Your Money: Why It is Important to Start Young
Type: Booklet; *Number of Pages:* 7; *Price:* Free
• Money Savers for New Parents: Tips for Raising Baby Without Breaking the Bank
Type: Booklet; *Number of Pages:* 14; *Price:* Free
• Planning your Golden Years: A Retirement Guide
Type: Booklet; *Number of Pages:* 16; *Price:* Free
• Repair Your Credit
Type: Booklet; *Number of Pages:* 16; *Price:* Free
• Save Energy, Save Money
Type: Booklet; *Number of Pages:* 6; *Price:* Free
• Savings & Chequing
Type: Booklet; *Number of Pages:* 14; *Price:* Free
• Shop Smart & Save
Type: Booklet; *Number of Pages:* 16; *Price:* Free
• Surviving a Layoff: Keeping it Together when Losing a Job
Type: Booklet; *Number of Pages:* 16; *Price:* Free
• Talking Money with Your Kids
Type: Booklet; *Number of Pages:* 16; *Price:* Free
• Taxes: Save Money, Solve Problems
Type: Booklet; *Number of Pages:* 6; *Price:* Free
• Vacation Budgeting
Type: Booklet; *Number of Pages:* 16; *Price:* Free
• The Wedding Planner
Type: Booklet; *Number of Pages:* 16; *Price:* Free
• When Love, Marriage, & Money Come Together
Type: Booklet; *Number of Pages:* 6; *Price:* Free
• Women & Money
Type: Booklet; *Number of Pages:* 6; *Price:* Free

Consort Chamber of Commerce

PO Box 490, 4901 - 50 Ave., Consort AB T0C 1B0
Tel: 403-577-3623; *Fax:* 403-577-2024
Overview: A small local organization
Mission: Promoting business and tourism in the area.
Chief Officer(s):
Peter G. Ringrose, Executive Director
peter.ringrose@lawsociety.nf.ca

Consortium canadien des ordres des sages-femmes *See* Canadian Midwifery Regulators Consortium

Consortium de bibliothèques du Manitoba *See* Manitoba Library Consortium Inc.

Constance Lethbridge Rehabilitation Centre *Voir* Centre de réadaptation Constance-Lethbridge

Construction Association of New Brunswick Inc. (CANB)

59 Avonlea Ct., Fredericton NB E3C 1N8
Tel: 506-459-5770; *Fax:* 506-457-1913
canb4@nbnet.nb.ca
www.constructnb.ca
Overview: A small provincial organization founded in 1971 overseen by Canadian Construction Association
Mission: To co-ordinate a consensus to effectively present the Industry's collective views to various client groups, partic-ularly to relevant departments and agencies of the provincial government.
Chief Officer(s):
John Landry, Executive Director
Membership: 1192; *Member Profile:* Construction related associations

Construction Association of Nova Scotia

#3, 260 Brownlow Ave., Dartmouth NS B3B 1V9
Tel: 902-468-2267; *Fax:* 902-468-2470
cans@cans.ns.ca
www.cans.ns.ca
Overview: A medium-sized provincial organization overseen by Canadian Construction Association
Mission: To represent the interests of its members
Chief Officer(s):
Duncan Williams, President
dwilliams@cans.ns.ca
Staff Member(s): 13
Membership: 760+; *Fees:* $1,507 full; $660 associate; *Member Profile:* Companies involved in construction work

Construction Association of Prince Edward Island (CAPEI)

PO Box 728, Charlottetown PE C1A 7L3
Tel: 902-368-3303; *Fax:* 902-894-9757
admin@capei.ca
www.capei.ca
Overview: A medium-sized provincial organization overseen by Canadian Construction Association
Mission: To foster, promote & advance the interests & efficiency of Prince Edward Island's construction industry
Chief Officer(s):
Ross D. Barnes, General Manager
ross@capei.ca
Grant MacPherson, President
gmacpherson@macleanconstruction.com
Staff Member(s): 3
Membership: 148; *Fees:* schedule; *Member Profile:* Construction related enterprises
Publications:
• CAPEI [Construction Association of Prince Edward Island] Project Newsletter
Type: Newsletter; *Frequency:* Weekly
• Construction Association of Prince Edward Island Membership Directory
Type: Directory
Profile: Guide for public of CAPEI members' company information
• Working for You [a publication of the Construction Association of Prince Edward Island]
Type: Newsletter

Construction Association of Québec *Voir* Association de la construction du Québec

Construction Association of Rural Manitoba Inc.

950B - 10th St., Brandon MB R7A 6B5
Tel: 204-727-4567; *Fax:* 204-727-1048
Toll-Free: 800-798-7483
carm@wcgwave.ca
www.carm.ca
Overview: A small provincial charitable organization founded in 1913
Mission: To provide services & representation to members; To act as a liaison between members & consumers of construction services & other interested groups for the betterment of the industry
Chief Officer(s):
Heather Dodds, General Manager
carmgm@wcgwave.ca
Finances: *Annual Operating Budget:* $100,000-$250,000
Staff Member(s): 3
Membership: 190; *Fees:* $250+
Activities: *Library*

Construction Association of Thunder Bay (CATB)

857 North May St., Thunder Bay ON P7C 3S2
Tel: 807-622-9645; *Fax:* 807-623-2296
information@catb.on.ca
www.catb.on.ca
Overview: A small local organization founded in 1949 overseen by Canadian Construction Association
Mission: To improve conditions and inform people about the construction industry and shine a light on industry relationships and practices, standards for business ethics, education and labour matters.
Member of: COCA; Canadian Construction Association; Link 2 Build
Membership: 214; *Fees:* $992 general contractor/trade contractor/manufacturer/supplier; $496 allied professional; $525 architect/enginner/designer; *Member Profile:* Professional Builders; Specialty Trade Contractors; Manufacturers; Suppliers; Design Consultants; Infrastructure Builders

Construction Employers Coordinating Council of Ontario (CECCO)

#708, 6299 Airport Rd., Mississauga ON L4V 1N3
Tel: 905-677-6200; *Fax:* 905-677-7634
cecco@bellnet.ca
www.cecco.org
Overview: A small provincial organization founded in 1979
Mission: Coordinates collective bargaining on behalf of designated Employer Bargaining Agencies responsible for the negotiation of province-wide, single-trade agreements applicable to the ICI sectors of the construction industry.
Chief Officer(s):
David Brisbin, Executive Director
david.brisbin@hotmail.com
Staff Member(s): 2; 6 volunteer(s)
Membership: 24; *Member Profile:* Construction employer bargaining agencies

Construction Labour Relations - An Alberta Association (CLRA)

Calgary Office, #207, 2725 - 12 St. NE, Calgary AB T2E 7J2
Tel: 403-250-7390; *Fax:* 403-250-5516
Toll-Free: 800-450-7204
www.clra.org
Previous Name: Alberta Construction Labour Relations Association
Overview: A medium-sized provincial organization founded in 1971
Mission: To represent construction employers in collective bargaining, collective agreement administration, administrative labour law, lobbying.
Member of: Canadian Construction Association
Finances: *Funding Sources:* Membership fees
Membership: *Member Profile:* General construction union contractor
Activities: *Library:* Catalogue; Open to public

Edmonton Office
#904, 10050 - 112 St., Edmonton AB T5K 2J1
Tel: 780-451-5444; *Fax:* 780-451-5447
Toll-Free: 800-450-7204
www.clra.org
Mission: To provide industrial, commercial and institutional construction employers assistance in bargaining, developing public policy, training, dealing with unions, administration and collective bargaining.

Construction Labour Relations Association of British Columbia

PO Box 820, 97 - 6 St., New Westminster BC V3L 4Z8
Tel: 604-524-4911; *Fax:* 604-524-3925
wendym@clra-bc.com
www.clra-bc.com
Overview: A small provincial organization founded in 1969
Chief Officer(s):
Clyde Scollan, President
clydes@clra-bc.com
Wendy Mazur, Office Manager

Construction Labour Relations Association of Newfoundland & Labrador Inc. (CLRA)
Ultramar Bldg., Main Floor, PO Box 8144, Stn. A, 39 Pippy Pl., St. John's NL A1B 3M9
Tel: 709-753-5770; *Fax:* 709-753-5771
clranl@clranl.com
www.clranl.com
Overview: A small provincial organization
Chief Officer(s):
Neil Chaplin, President

Construction Maintenance & Allied Workers (CMAW)
1450 Kootenay St., Vancouver BC V5K 4R1
Tel: 604-437-0471; *Fax:* 604-437-1110
reception@cmaw.ca
www.cmaw.ca
twitter.com/CMAWunion
Previous Name: British Columbia Carpenters Union
Overview: A medium-sized provincial organization founded in 2004
Mission: The objects of the Council are to organize workers; encourage an apprenticeship system & higher standard of skill; to develop, improve & enforce the program & standards of occupational safety & health; to cultivate friendship; to develop good public relations with the community; to assist each other to secure employment & to reduce the hours of daily labour
Chief Officer(s):
Jan Noster, President
jan.noster@cmaw.ca
Paul Nedelec, Secretary-Treasurer
pnedelec@cmaw.ca
Kim Ballantyne, Office Administrator
kim@cmaw.ca
Finances: *Annual Operating Budget:* $500,000-$1.5 Million
Membership: 7,000+; *Member Profile:* Carpenters; carpenter apprentices; lathers; millwrights; floorlayers; industrial workers; other construction trades & school board employees

Construction Management Bureau Limited *See* Nova Scotia Construction Labour Relations Association Limited

Construction Owners Association of Alberta (COAA)
Sun Life Place, #800, 10123 - 99 St. NW, Edmonton AB T5J 3H1
Tel: 780-420-1145; *Fax:* 780-425-4623
coaa-mail@coaa.ab.ca
www.coaa.ab.ca
Overview: A medium-sized provincial organization
Mission: COAA provides leadership to enable the Alberta heavy industrial construction and industrial maintenance industries to be successful in a drive for safe, effective, timely and productive project execution.
Chief Officer(s):
Ernie Tromposch, President
Membership: *Member Profile:* Principal Members who are users of construction services in their day-to-day operations.; *Committees:* Safety; Productivity; Workforce Development; Contracts
Meetings/Conferences: • Construction Owners Association of Alberta Best Practices Conferences 2015, 2015, AB
Scope: Provincial

Construction Resource Initiatives Council (CRI) / Conseil d'initiatives des ressources de construction
#609 Donald B. Munro Dr., Carp ON K0A 1L0
Tel: 613-795-4632; *Fax:* 613-839-0704
info@cricouncil.com
www.cricouncil.com
www.linkedin.com/groups/Construction-Resource-Initiatives-Council-3819
www.facebook.com/330962370266752
twitter.com/CRICouncil
Overview: A small national organization
Mission: To develop strategies that help the building industry achieve the goal of zero waste production.
Chief Officer(s):
Renée L. Gratton, President & CEO
renee.gratton@cricouncil.com
Membership: 137; *Fees:* Schedule available; *Member Profile:* Those who sipport the council & its goals

Construction Safety Association of Manitoba (CSAM)
1447 Waverly St., Winnipeg MB R3T 0P7
Tel: 204-775-3171; *Fax:* 204-779-3505
safety@constructionsafety.ca
www.constructionsafety.ca
Overview: A small provincial organization founded in 1989
Mission: To promote safe work practices & procedures throughout Manitoba's construction industry; To provide news about changes to health & safety regulations; To offer information about accident prevention methods
Member of: Canadian Federation of Construction Safety Associations
Chief Officer(s):
Sean Scott, Executive Director
sean@constructionsafety.ca
Derek Pott, Manager, Client Services
derek@constructionsafety.ca
Tara Zukewich, Program Manager
tara@constructionsafety.ca
Mitch Calvert, Coordinator, Marketing & Innovations
mitch@constructionsafety.ca
Marla Fillion, Coordinator, Training & Program
marla@constructionsafety.ca
Finances: *Funding Sources:* Manitoba contractors, through a surchrge on a percentage of their assessment premiums collected by the Workers Compensation Baord
Activities: Developing training programs; Working with the Workers Compensation Board of Manitoba & the Workplace Saftey & Health Branch
Meetings/Conferences: • Construction Safety Association of Manitoba 2015 The Safety Conference, February, 2015, RBC Convention Centre, Winnipeg, MB
Scope: Provincial
Attendance: 2,000+
Description: A safety & health conference for construction owners, supervisors, foremen, safety committees, workers, & students, featuring workshops & a trade show with more than 100 exhibitors
Contact Information: Executive Director, Construction Safety Association of Manitoba: Sean Scott, Phone: 204-775-3171, Fax: 204-779-3505, E-mail: sean@constructionsafety.ca
• Construction Safety Association of Manitoba 2015 21st Annual Westman Safety Conference, 2015, MB
Scope: Provincial
Description: An event that caters to industries in the Westman region, by offering specialized training in areas such as emergency preparedness & response, safety administration, as well as information about changes to workplace safety & health regulations
Contact Information: Westman Office, Phone: 204-728-3456, Fax: 204-571-0678
Publications:
• Construction Safety Association of Manitoba Newsletter
Type: Newsletter; *Price:* Free, as part of themandate to assist construction employers in safety matters
Profile: Information & education about safety regulatory matters & accident prevention methods for building construction employers throughout Manitoba

Construction Safety Association of Ontario *See* Infrastructure Health & Safety Association

Construction Safety Network *See* BC Construction Safety Alliance

Construction Sector Council (CSC) / Conseil sectoriel de la construction (CSC)
#1150, 220 Laurier Ave. West, Ottawa ON K1P 5Z9
Tel: 613-569-5552; *Fax:* 613-569-1220
info@csc-ca.org
www.csc-ca.org
Overview: A medium-sized national organization
Mission: To identify critical human resources challenges in the construction industry; To find common solutions & approaches
Chief Officer(s):
Rosemary Sparks, Executive Director

Construction Specifications Canada (CSC) / Devis de construction Canada
#312, 120 Carlton St., Toronto ON M5A 4K2
Tel: 416-777-2198; *Fax:* 416-777-2197
info@csc-dcc.ca
www.csc-dcc.ca
www.linkedin.com/groups?mostRecent=&gid=1911916&trk=eml-anet_dig-h_gn-
www.facebook.com/120516191352386?ref=ts
Previous Name: Specification Writers Association of Canada
Overview: A large national organization founded in 1954
Mission: To improve communication, contract documentation, & technical information in the construction industry
Affliation(s): Construction Specification Foundation; Construction Specifications Canada/Alberta Section Training Trust Fund; Construction Specifications Institute; Canadian Standards Assoc.; Mechanical Contractors Assoc. of Canada; Ontario Bid Depository Council; Alberta Building Envelope Council; Alberta Roofing Contractor's Assoc.; Canadian Institute of Plumbing & Heating; Assoc. of Professional Engineers of Canada; Royal Architectural Institute of Canada; Canadian Construction Assoc.; Toronto Construction Assoc.; Society of the Plastics Industry of Canada; Thermal Insulation Assoc. of Canada
Chief Officer(s):
Claude Giguère, President
cgiguere@pageaumorel.com
Finances: *Annual Operating Budget:* $500,000-$1.5 Million; *Funding Sources:* Sale of technical documents; membership fees
Staff Member(s): 4
Membership: 650 specifier architects & engineers + 750 industrial manufacturers, suppliers & contractors; *Fees:* $235; $50 student; *Member Profile:* Interested & involved in the dissemination of construction specifications & related documentation; incorporates specifiers, architects, engineers, construction product manufacturers & distributors, general & trade contractors; chapter-based association with chapters in Halifax, Quebéc, Montréal, Ottawa, Toronto, Hamilton/ Niagara, Grand Valley, London, Winnipeg, Regina, Saskatoon, Edmonton, Calgary & Vancouver; *Committees:* Awards; Conferences; Executive; Finance; French Language Publications; Legislative; Professional Development & Education; Technical Studies
Activities: National education programs consists of Technical Documents Programs including Home Study Course for Architectural Specifiers, & courses leading to the Registered Specification Writer (RSW) designation; *Speaker Service:* Yes; *Rents Mailing List:* Yes
Awards:
• CSC Awards
Awards of merit, National and Chapter
Meetings/Conferences: • Construction Specifications Canada Conference 2015, May, 2015, Winnipeg, MB
Scope: National
Publications:
• Construction Canada
Type: Magazine

Construction Technology Centre Atlantic (CTCA)
#229, 15 Dineen Dr., Fredericton NB E3B 5A3
Tel: 506-453-4789; *Fax:* 506-453-4819
CTCA@unb.ca
Overview: A small local organization founded in 1988
Mission: To assist industry in increasing awareness & access to the latest technological advances in construction management, for both the office and the job site.
Member of: Canadian Construction Research Board (CCRB); Canadian Technology Network (CTN)
Affliation(s): National Research Council (NRC); Industrial Research Assistance Program (IRAP)
Finances: *Funding Sources:* Consulting & training
Activities: Distribution of new technologies & information to the architectural, engineering & construction industries

Consulting Engineers of Alberta (CEA)
Phipps-McKinnon Building, #870, 10020 - 101A Ave., Edmonton AB T5J 3G2
Tel: 780-421-1852; *Fax:* 780-424-5225
info@cea.ca
www.cea.ca
Overview: A medium-sized provincial organization founded in 1978 overseen by Association of Consulting Engineering Companies - Canada
Mission: To provide leadership to foster a positive business environment for the consulting engineering firms in Alberta; To promote the engineering industry; To enhance interests & opportunities of CEA members; To provide society with high standards of engineering design & safety
Chief Officer(s):
Wendy Cooper, Executive Director
Gord Johnston, President
gord.johnston@stantec.com
Ken Pilip, Registrar
Sharon Moroskat, Manager, Finance & Administration
smoroskat@cea.ca
Hiju Song, Manager, Events & Communications
hsong@cea.ca
Finances: *Funding Sources:* Membership fees; Sponsorships
Membership: *Committees:* Board of Directors; Buildings; City of Calgary Liaison; City of Edmonton Liaison; Environmental;

Industrial; Municipal Liaison; Small Firm; Transportation; Transportation Conference; Young Professionals' Group
Activities: Protecting legislative & regulatory interests; Offering a forum to exchange ideas; Providing training programs & information; *Speaker Service:* Yes
Meetings/Conferences: • Consulting Engineers of Alberta 2015 18th Annual Tri-Party Transportation Conference & Trade Show Exhibition, 2015, AB
Scope: Provincial
Attendance: 700+
Description: Keynote speakers, forums, & workshops about transportation infrastructure in Alberta
Contact Information: Manager, Business Services/Events: Kary Kremer, E-mail: kkremer@cea.ca
• Consulting Engineers of Alberta 2015 37th Annual General Meeting, 2015, AB
Scope: Provincial
Description: Presentations by guest speakers plus the business meeting for consulting engineers in Alberta
Contact Information: Manager, Business Services/Events: Kary Kremer, E-mail: kkremer@cea.ca
Publications:
• Bullet [a publication of the Consulting Engineers of Alberta]
Type: Newsletter
Profile: Information for Consulting Engineers of Alberta, such as forthcoming meetings, sponsorship opportunities, & social events
• CEA [Consulting Engineers of Alberta] Progress Report on Salaries
Frequency: Annually
Profile: Salary recommendations
• CEA [Consulting Engineers of Alberta] Annual Report
Type: Yearbook; *Frequency:* Annually
• Consulting Engineers of Alberta Directory of Members
Type: Directory
Profile: Listing of members, including location & size of firms
• Consulting Engineers Rate Guidelines
Profile: Standard hourly rates for engineers, technicians, & technologists in Alberta

Consulting Engineers of British Columbia (CEBC)

#1258, 409 Granville St., Vancouver BC V6C 1T2
Tel: 604-687-2811; *Fax:* 604-688-7110
info@acec-bc.ca
www.acec-bc.ca
Overview: A medium-sized provincial organization founded in 1976 overseen by Association of Consulting Engineering Companies - Canada
Mission: To improve the commercial environment for consulting engineering firms
Chief Officer(s):
Glenn Martin, Executive Director
glenn@cebc.org
Jack Lee, President
Glen Martin, Executive Director
Alla Samusevich, Coordinator, Accounting & Events
alla@cebc.org
Membership: *Member Profile:* Consulting engineering firms across British Columbia that provide services to the built & natural environment; *Committees:* Building Engineering; Municipal Engineering; Resource & Energy; Transportation; Business Practice; Membership Affairs; Young Professsionals' Group; Okanagan/Thompson Liaison; Vancouver Island Liaison
Activities: Lobbying to policymakers in districts, provincial & municipal governments, & private sector clients; Coordinating a common industry approach to issues; Promoting CEBC members' consulting services; Providing networking, educational, & professional development opportunities
Awards:
• Awards for Engineering Excellence (Award)
To honour outstanding achievements in engineering
Meetings/Conferences: • Consulting Engineers of British Columbia 2015 Annual Transportation Conference, January, 2015, Hilton Metrotown, Burnaby, BC
Scope: Provincial
Description: An event presenting educational & networking opportunities to enhance business development. Theme: Future Trends and Topics in the BC Transportation Industry
Contact Information: Coordinator, Accounting & Events: Alla Samusevich
• Consulting Engineers of British Columbia 2015 Awards Gala, April, 2015, Vancover Convention Centre, Vancouver, BC
Scope: Provincial
Description: The presentation of the Awards for Engineering Excellence in categories such as buildings, municipal, transportation, natural resources, energy & industry, & soft engineering
Contact Information: Coordinator, Accounting & Events: Alla Samusevich
Publications:
• Consulting Engineers of British Columbia Annual Report
Type: Yearbook; *Frequency:* Annually
Profile: The association's profile, reports from the president, executive director, treasurer, & the committees, the minutes from the annual general meeting, awards, &events
• Directory of CEBC [Consulting Engineers of British Columbia] Member Firms
Type: Directory
Profile: Listings of Consulting Engineers of British Columbia members, available for the public

Consulting Engineers of Manitoba Inc. (CEM)

PO Box 1547, Stn. Main, Winnipeg MB R3C 2Z4
Tel: 204-774-5258; *Fax:* 204-779-0788
acec-mb.ca
twitter.com/acec_manitoba
Overview: A medium-sized provincial organization founded in 1978 overseen by Association of Consulting Engineering Companies - Canada
Mission: To promote & enhance the business interests of the consulting engineers of Manitoba; to lead in the application of technology for the benefit of society
Affiliation(s): Association of Professional Engineers of Manitoba; International Federation of Consulting Engineers; Manitoba Association of Architects
Chief Officer(s):
Shirley E. Tillett, Executive Director
cemca@shaw.ca
Steve Reaburn, President
Finances: *Annual Operating Budget:* $50,000-$100,000;
Funding Sources: Membership dues
Membership: 31 firms; *Member Profile:* Offer primarily consulting engineering services to public; *Committees:* Contract; First Nations; Golf Tournament; MWSB/PFRA; Private Industry Liasion; Public Relations; Transportation; Water & Environment; Professional Development; Young Professionals
Activities: *Speaker Service:* Yes

Consulting Engineers of Nova Scotia (CENS)

PO Box 613, Stn. M, Halifax NS B3J 2R7
Tel: 902-461-1325; *Fax:* 902-461-1321
cens@eastlink.ca
www.cens.org
Previous Name: Nova Scotia Consulting Engineers Association
Overview: A medium-sized provincial organization founded in 1973 overseen by Association of Consulting Engineering Companies - Canada
Mission: To enable the consulting engineering industry in Nova Scotia to capitalize on opportunities to grow; To promote employment of member firms
Chief Officer(s):
Skit Ferguson, Executive Director
Membership: 61 companies; *Member Profile:* Nova Scotia based companies in the business of engineering & related services
Activities: Maintaining high professional standards in the industry; Increasing awareness about the work & employment of consulting engineers
Meetings/Conferences: • Consulting Engineers of Nova Scotia (CENS) 2015 Annual General Meeting, 2015
Scope: Provincial

Consulting Engineers of Ontario (CEO)

#405, 10 Four Seasons Pl., Toronto ON M9B 6H7
Tel: 416-620-1400; *Fax:* 416-620-5803
www.ceo.on.ca
Overview: A medium-sized provincial organization founded in 1975 overseen by Association of Consulting Engineering Companies - Canada
Mission: To further the maintenance of high professional standards in consulting engineering profession; to promote cordial relations among various consulting firms in Ontario; to foster interchange of professional management & business experience & information among consulting engineers; to develop regional representation & participation in affairs of the association
Chief Officer(s):
Barry Steinburg, Chief Executive Officer
rmartin@ceo.on.ca
Saskia Martini-Wong, Manager, Operations & Corporate Services
smartini@ceo.on.ca
Holly Romero, Coordinator, Communication
hromero@ceo.on.ca
Finances: *Annual Operating Budget:* $250,000-$500,000
Staff Member(s): 6
Membership: 250 firms
Activities: *Speaker Service:* Yes
Meetings/Conferences: • Consulting Engineers of Ontario 2015 Annual General Meeting, 2015, ON
Scope: Provincial

Consulting Engineers of Québec *Voir* Association des ingénieurs-conseils du Québec

Consulting Engineers of Saskatchewan (CES)

#12, 2010 - 7 Ave., Regina SK S4R 1C2
Tel: 306-359-3338; *Fax:* 306-522-5325
ces@sasktel.net
www.ces.sk.ca
Previous Name: Association of Consulting Engineers of Saskatchewan
Overview: A small provincial organization founded in 1977 overseen by Association of Consulting Engineering Companies - Canada
Mission: To further the maintenance of high professional standards in consulting engineering profession; To promote cordial relations among various consulting firms in Saskatchewan; To foster interchange of professional management & business experience & information among consulting engineers; To develop regional representation & participation in affairs of the association
Chief Officer(s):
Mel Leu, P.Eng, Chair
Beverly MacLeod, Executive Director
Finances: *Annual Operating Budget:* $50,000-$100,000
Staff Member(s): 2; 100+ volunteer(s)
Membership: 49 firms + 9 associates; *Committees:* Building; Communications; Environment/Water Resources; Human Resources; Industry Resources; Transportation; Young Professionals Group (YPG); CEG Task Groups
Awards:
• CES Brian Eckel Award (Award)
To promote the consulting engineering industry. Eligibility: CES member firms
• CES Young Professional Award (Award)
Eligibility: Young professionals who demonstrates excellence in; his/her field of expertise; the business of consulting engineering/geoscience; dedication to his/her consulting engineering/geoscience association and community; as well as increasing awareness of the value of young professionals in the Saskatchewan consulting engineering/geoscience industry.

Consulting Engineers of Yukon (CEY)

c/o EBA Engineering Consultants Ltd., #6, 151 Industrial Rd., Whitehorse YT Y1A 2V3
Tel: 867-668-3068; *Fax:* 867-668-4349
cey@eba.ca
www.cey.ca
Overview: A small provincial organization founded in 1983 overseen by Association of Consulting Engineering Companies - Canada
Mission: To maintain high professional standards in the consulting engineering profession; To promote cordial relations among various consulting firms in the Yukon; to foster interchange of professional management & business experience & information among consulting engineers; To develop regional representation & participation in affairs of the association
Chief Officer(s):
Richard Trimble, Executive Director
Membership: 21 firms

Consulting Foresters of British Columbia

PO Box 98, Pender Island BC V0N 2M0
Tel: 250-656-8818
info@cfbc.bc.ca
www.cfbc.bc.ca
Overview: A small provincial organization founded in 1968
Mission: To maintain high professional standards in forestry consulting; To advance contact between its members, client groups, & the public at large
Chief Officer(s):
Bruce Blackwell, President
Mike Trepanier, Secretary
Membership: 80; *Fees:* $200-$1000

Consumer Electronics Marketers of Canada: A Division of Electro-Federation Canada (CEMC)
#300, 180 Attwell Dr., Mississauga ON M9W 6A9
Tel: 905-602-8877; *Fax:* 416-679-9234
info@electrofed.com
www.cemc-efc.ca
Overview: A medium-sized national organization
Mission: To represent the consumer electronic marketing industry; To provide information for CEMC members to help them make good business decisions; To report on the status of the consumer electronics market
Chief Officer(s):
Robert Gumiela, Chair
Susan Winter, Vice-President
swinter@electrofed.com
Membership: *Member Profile:* Manufacturers, importers, & distributors of consumer electronic products in Canada
Activities: Harmonizing standards; Addressing regulatory issues; Collecting statistical information

Consumer Health Organization of Canada (CHOC)
#1901, 355 St. Clair Ave. West, Toronto ON M5P 1N5
Tel: 416-924-9800; *Fax:* 416-924-6404
info@consumerhealth.org
www.consumerhealth.org
Overview: A medium-sized national organization founded in 1975
Mission: To encourage the prevention of all kinds of illness through knowledge; to help the individual, the family & the community to enjoy the benefits of a more wholesome lifestyle; to promote harmony & cooperation between like-minded groups.
Affliation(s): National Health Federation in US
Chief Officer(s):
Libby Gardon, President
Membership: *Fees:* $45
Activities: *Speaker Service:* Yes
Meetings/Conferences: • North America's Premier Natural Health Show 38th Annual Convention and Exhibition (Total Health 2015), April, 2015, Metro Toronto Convention Centre, Toronto, ON
Scope: International
Description: Speakers will focus on creating good health and preventing disease using natural methods: energy medicine, organic gardening, traditional farming, agricultural biodiversity, healthy homes, ecologically based communities, renewable energy source and preserving a healthy environment for our children. We as consumers must choose foods and medicines which do no harm to people, animals or our planet.
Contact Information: Phone: 416-924-9800 or 1-877-389-0996; Fax: 416-924-6404; Website: www.totalhealthshow.com

Consumer Health Products Canada
#406, 1111 Prince of Wales Dr., Ottawa ON K2C 3T2
Tel: 613-723-0777; *Fax:* 613-723-0779
info@chpcanada.ca
www.chpcanada.ca
www.linkedin.com/company/consumer-health-products-canada
www.facebook.com/chpcanada
twitter.com/chp_can
www.youtube.com/CHPCanada0
Also Known As: CHP Canada
Previous Name: Nonprescription Drug Manufacturers Association of Canada; NDMAC, Advancing Canadian Self-Care
Overview: A medium-sized national organization founded in 1896
Mission: To contribute to quality of life & cost-effective health care for Canadians by creating & maintaining an environment for the growth of responsible self-medication.
Member of: World Self-Medication Industry
Chief Officer(s):
Adam Kingsley, Acting President
adam.kingsley@chpcanada.ca
Gerry Harrington, Director, Public Affairs
gerry.harrington@chpcanada.ca
Finances: *Annual Operating Budget:* $500,000-$1.5 Million
Staff Member(s): 9; 70 volunteer(s)
Membership: 45; *Fees:* $1,000 - $2,000; *Member Profile:* Manufacturers of over-the-counter medicines; associate - suppliers of goods & services to manufacturers; *Committees:* Digital communications; Associates; Over the counter; Natural health product; Provinvial & Professional; Conference

Consumer Policy Institute (CPI)
225 Brunswick Ave., Toronto ON M5S 2M6
Tel: 416-964-9223; *Fax:* 416-964-8239
cpi@eprf.ca
www.c-p-i.org/cpi
Overview: A small local organization founded in 1980
Mission: A project of the Energy Probe Research Foundation (EPRF), CPI focuses on the force of the individual consumer, the empowerment of the general public brought about by the communications revolution & trade liberalization, circumstances that are eroding the power of traditional authorities in society. CPI understands this individual empowerment must be rooted in a sense of responsibility to other people & to the environment. The Institute is activly involved in a number of campaigns, covering a wide range of such fields as health care, tranportation, economic policy, automobile insurance & airports.
Chief Officer(s):
Lawrence Solomon, Executive Director
lawrence.solomon@nextcity.com

Consumer Protection BC
PO Box 9244, Victoria BC V8W 9J2
Tel: 604-320-1667; *Fax:* 250-920-7181
Toll-Free: 888-564-9963
www.consumerprotectionbc.ca
www.facebook.com/ConsumerProtectionBC
twitter.com/consumerprobc
www.youtube.com/user/ConsumerProBC
Previous Name: Business Practices & Consumer Protection Authority of British Columbia
Overview: A small provincial organization founded in 2004
Mission: To deliver consumer protection services throughout British Columbia; promote fairness and understanding in the marketplace; and enforce consumer protection laws in BC.
Chief Officer(s):
Robert Gialloreto, President & CEO

Consumers Council of Canada (CCC)
Commercial Bldg., #201, 1920 Yonge St., Toronto ON M4S 3E2
Tel: 416-483-2696
www.consumerscouncil.com
Overview: A small national organization
Chief Officer(s):
Aubrey LeBlanc, President
Ken Whitehurst, Executive Director
Membership: *Fees:* $50 individual

Consumers' Association of Canada (CAC) / Association des consommateurs du Canada
436 Gilmour St., 3rd Fl., Ottawa ON K2P 0R8
Tel: 613-238-2533; *Fax:* 613-238-2538
info@consumer.ca
www.consumer.ca
Overview: A large national organization founded in 1947
Mission: To represent & articulate the best interests of Canadian consumers to all levels of government & to all sectors of society by continually earning recognition as the trusted voice of the consumer on a national basis; to inform & educate consumers on marketplace issues; To work with government & industry to solve marketplace problems; To focus its work in the areas of food, health, trade, standards, financial services, communications industries & other marketplace issues as they emerge
Chief Officer(s):
Bruce Cran, President
Mel Fruitman, Vice-President
Finances: *Funding Sources:* Membership fees; project grants; donations
Membership: *Member Profile:* Open; *Committees:* Health; Economics & Finance
Activities: Consumer literacy program; consumer referral, information, education; consumer representation - standards development & implementation, multi-stakeholder working groups & advisory committees, special purpose task forces; *Speaker Service:* Yes

Contact Centre Canada
Toronto ON
canadacontact.ca
www.linkedin.com/groups/Canada-Contact-Centre-Association-5119908
www.facebook.com/CanadaContact
twitter.com/canadacontact
Overview: A medium-sized national organization
Mission: To contribute to the health & prosperity of the customer contact centre industry & of its workforce
Chief Officer(s):
Robert Campbell, Contact
Membership: *Member Profile:* Contact centre organizations; labour representatives; provincial industry associations; educational institutions; vendors & consultants that provide services to the Canadian contact centre industry

Contact Point
#200, 18 Spadina Rd., Toronto ON M5R 2S7
Tel: 416-929-2510; *Fax:* 416-923-2536
contactpoint@ceric.ca
www.contactpoint.ca
Overview: A small national organization
Mission: A practitioner-driven, Canadian website dedicated to providing multi-sectoral career development practitioners and career counsellors with career resources, learning and networking.
Affliation(s): The Counselling Foundation of Canada
Chief Officer(s):
Jennifer Browne, President
Publications:
• Canadian Journal of Career Development
Type: Journal; *Editor:* Rob Shea
• Contact Point Bulletin
Type: Newsletter; *Frequency:* Quarterly

Contagious Mountain Bike Club (CMBC)
4061 - 4th Ave., Whitehorse YT Y1A 1H1
Tel: 867-668-4990
Other Communication: CMBC URL: cmbcyukon.ca
info@cmbcyukon.ca
sportyukon.com/member/cycling-association-of-yukon
www.facebook.com/groups/141110515614
Also Known As: Cycling Association of Yukon
Overview: A small provincial organization
Mission: To promote off-road cycling in the Yukon.
Chief Officer(s):
Sierra Van Der Meer, President

Contemporary Dancers Canada ***See*** Winnipeg's Contemporary Dancers

Conteurs du Canada ***See*** Storytellers of Canada

Continental Automated Buildings Association (CABA) / Association continentale pour l'automatisation des bâtiments
#210, 1173 Cyrville Rd., Ottawa ON K1J 7S6
Tel: 613-686-1814; *Fax:* 613-744-7833
Toll-Free: 888-798-2222
caba@caba.org
www.caba.org
www.facebook.com/group.php?gid=108759039149175
twitter.com/caba_news
www.youtube.com/cabaconf
Also Known As: North America's Home & Building Automation Association
Previous Name: Canadian Automated Buildings Association
Overview: A medium-sized national organization founded in 1988
Mission: To promote advanced technologies for the automation of homes & buildings in North America; To create opportunities for members
Chief Officer(s):
Ronald J. Zimmer, President & Chief Executive Officer, 613-686-1814 Ext. 230
zimmer@caba.org
Ken Gallinger, Director, Marketing, 613-686-1814 Ext. 229
gallinger@caba.org
George Grimes, Director, Business Development, 613-686-1814 Ext. 226
grimes@caba.org
John L. Hall, Director, Research, 613-686-1814 Ext. 227
hall@caba.orga.org
Rawlson O'Neil King, Director, Communications, 613-686-1814 Ext. 225
king@caba.org
Activities: Providing information, education, & networking opportunities related to home & building automation; Encouraging research & development in the use of technology & integrated systems; *Library:* Research Library
Publications:
• CABA [Continental Automated Buildings Association] eBulletin
Type: Newsletter; *Accepts Advertising*
Profile: Industry & membership developments
• CABA [Continental Automated Buildings Association] Information Series
Profile: Industry intelligence for the home & large building automation & integrated systems sector

• CABA [Continental Automated Buildings Association] Event Reports
Profile: Information about industry-related conferences & events
• iHomes & Buildings
Type: Magazine; *Accepts Advertising*
Profile: Up-to-date information on trends & products in the industry

Continuing Care Association of Nova Scotia (CCANS)

c/o Sunshine Personal Home Care, 38A Withrod Dr., Halifax NS B3N 1B1
Tel: 902-446-3140
ccans@eastlink.ca
www.nsnet.org/ccans
Previous Name: Association of Licensed Nursing Homes (ALNH); Associated Homes for Special Care (AHSC)
Overview: A small provincial organization founded in 1964
Mission: To represent continuing care facilities throughout Nova Scotia
Chief Officer(s):
Marty Wexler, President, 902-492-0681
Finances: *Funding Sources:* Membership fees
Membership: 51 organizations; *Fees:* $365; *Member Profile:* Organizations across Nova Scotia, such as nursing homes, adult residential centres, regional rehabilitation centres, residential care facilities, licensed group homes, small option homes for persons with disabilities or seniors, & supported apartments
Activities: Engaging in advocacy activities; Liaising with Nova Scotia's Department of Community Services & Department of Health; Supporting caregivers; Offering educational opportunities; Providing a supportive network
Meetings/Conferences: • Continuing Care Association of Nova Scotia 2015 AGM, June, 2015, Liscomb Lodge, Marie Joseph, NS
Scope: Provincial

Continuing Legal Education Society of BC

#500, 1155 West Pender St., Vancouver BC V6E 2P4
Tel: 604-669-3544; *Fax:* 604-669-9260
Toll-Free: 800-663-0437
custserv@cle.bc.ca
www.cle.bc.ca
Overview: A medium-sized provincial organization founded in 1965
Mission: To meet the present & future educational needs of the legal profession in British Columbia
Chief Officer(s):
Ronald G. Lamperson, Chair
Finances: *Funding Sources:* Course registrations; Publication sales
Membership: *Member Profile:* British Columbia lawyers & their support staff
Activities: Provision of courses on a great range of topics; Publication of practice-oriented books
Publications:
• Case Digest Connection
Profile: Timely digest of cases decided by the British Columbia superior courts, selected Provincial Court decisions, & Supreme Court of Canada cases which originated in British Columbia

Convention & Visitors Bureau of Sarnia/Lambton *See* Tourism Sarnia Lambton

Convention & Visitors Bureau of Windsor, Essex County & Pelee Island *See* Tourism Windsor Essex Pelee Island

Convention canadienne des baptistes du Sud *See* Canadian Convention of Southern Baptists

Convention des Églises Baptistes de l'Atlantique *See* Convention of Atlantic Baptist Churches

Convention of Atlantic Baptist Churches (CABC) / Convention des Églises Baptistes de l'Atlantique

1655 Manawagonish Rd., Saint John NB E2M 3Y2
Tel: 506-635-1922; *Fax:* 506-635-0366
cabc@baptist-atlantic.ca
www.baptist-atlantic.ca
www.linkedin.com/company/2498898
www.facebook.com/atlanticbaptist
twitter.com/atlanticbaptist
plus.google.com/101053298635931681383
Also Known As: Atlantic Baptist Convention
Previous Name: United Baptist Convention of the Maritime Provinces
Overview: A medium-sized local charitable organization founded in 1905 overseen by Canadian Baptist Ministries
Mission: To resource pastors, churches, & people; To facilitate a shared mission on behalf of churches; To establish & maintain professional standards & ethics for clergy
Chief Officer(s):
Peter Reid, Executive Minister
peter.reid@baptist-atlantic.ca
Greg Jones, Associate Executive Minister
greg.jones@baptist-atlantic.ca
Finances: *Annual Operating Budget:* $1.5 Million-$3 Million
Staff Member(s): 20
Membership: *Committees:* Acadia Divinity College; Acadia University; Atlantic Baptist Mission Board; Atlantic Baptist Senior Citizen's Homes Inc.; Atlantic Baptist University; Atlantic Baptist Foundation; Baptist Bookroom; Nominating; Historical; Pension & Insurance Board; Board of Ministerial Standards & Education
Activities: Providing seminars, conferences, stewardship education, & retreats; *Speaker Service:* Yes
Meetings/Conferences: • Oasis: Refreshment for the Journey, August, 2015, Acadia University, Wolfville, NS
Scope: Provincial
Contact Information: URL: oasis.baptist-atlantic.ca
Publications:
• Convention Update
Type: Newsletter; *Frequency:* Monthly
• Youth & Family Update
Type: Newsletter; *Frequency:* Monthly

Conway Workshop Association

PO Box 568, 63 Shreve St., Digby NS B0V 1A0
Tel: 902-245-5391; *Fax:* 902-245-5539
conwayworkshop@ns.sympatico.ca
www.conwayworkshop.com
Overview: A small local organization
Mission: To help people with disabilities develop life skills so that they may live as independently as possible
Member of: DIRECTIONS Council for Vocational Services Society
Chief Officer(s):
Jill Baxter, Executvie Director

Coop des Producteurs d'arbres de Noël du N.-B. *See* New Brunswick Christmas Tree Growers Co-op Ltd.

La Coop Fédérée

#200, 9001, boul de l'Acadie, Montréal QC H4N 3H7
Tél: 514-384-6450; *Téléc:* 514-384-7176
information@lacoop.coop
www.lacoop.coop
www.linkedin.com/company/55527
twitter.com/LaCoop_federee
www.youtube.com/user/LaCoopfederee
Nom précédent: Coopérative fédérée du Québec
Aperçu: *Dimension:* grande; *Envergure:* provinciale; fondée en 1922 surveillé par Canadian Federation of Agriculture
Mission: La CFQ fournit aux agriculteurs, directement ou par l'entremise de ses coopératives sociétaires, une vaste gamme de biens et de services nécessaires à l'exploitation de leur entreprise, y compris des produits pétroliers; de plus, elle transforme et commercialise sur les marchés locaux et internationaux divers produits agricoles: viande porcine, volaille, etc.
Membre(s) du bureau directeur:
Denis Richard, Président
Finances: *Budget de fonctionnement annuel:* Plus de $5 Million
Membre(s) du personnel: 7
Membre: 95 coopératives
Activités: *Stagiaires:* Oui

Coop kayak des îles

60, av du Parc, Trois-Pistoles QC G0L 4K0
Tél: 418-851-4637
info@kayaksdesiles.com
www.kayaksdesiles.com
www.facebook.com/124709937578452
Aperçu: *Dimension:* petite; *Envergure:* locale; fondée en 1999
Mission: Pour faire du kayak de mer plus accessible
Membre(s) du bureau directeur:
Mikaël Rioux, Chef-guide
Membre(s) du personnel: 6
Membre: *Montant de la cotisation:* 350$ par deux places; 150$ par une place

Cooper Institute / L'Institut Cooper

81 Prince St., Charlottetown PE C1A 4R3
Tel: 902-894-4573; *Fax:* 902-368-7180
www.cooperinstitute.ca
www.facebook.com/pages/Cooper-Institute/156027014448502
Overview: A small provincial organization founded in 1984
Mission: To promote programs that are focussed on livable income for all, food sovereignty & cultural diversity & inclusion; to conduct research & popular education projects on provincial, national & international level.
Chief Officer(s):
Joe Byrne, President
Staff Member(s): 3
Membership: 14
Awards:
• The Reverend Vincent Murnghan Memorial Scholarship
Offered to a qualified refugee or foreign student displaying commitment to working for social justice and to improving the living conditions in the community and on the planet, and academic achievement or evidence of academic potential. It is hoped that this scholarship will further Father Murnaghan's vision of justice and capacity-building by enabling a qualified refugee or foreign student to proceed with his/her studies.
Amount: $1000

La coopérative de Solidarité de Répit et d'Etraide (COOP SORE)

170, rue des Épinettes, Morin-Heights QC J0R 1H0
Tél: 450-226-2466; *Téléc:* 450-226-2211
sore@cgocable.ca
coopsore.org
Aperçu: *Dimension:* petite; *Envergure:* locale; Organisme sans but lucratif
Mission: De créer une communauté de soignants où les idées et les informations sont fournies afin d'apporter de nouveaux éléments à leur emploi en aidant les personnes âgées
Membre(s) du bureau directeur:
Claire Lefebvre, Coordinatrice, 450-226-2466
Cecile Belanger, Présidente, Conseil d'administration
Membre(s) du personnel: 5
Membre: *Montant de la cotisation:* 10$ pour les membres; *Critères d'admissibilite:* Personnes qui sonts des proches aidant, ou personne qui désire soutenir l'organisation

Coopérative fédérée du Québec *Voir* La Coop Fédérée

Cooperative Housing Association of Newfoundland & Labrador (CHANAL)

PO Box 453, #204, 75 Barbour Dr., Mount Pearl NL A1N 2C4
Tel: 709-747-5615; *Fax:* 709-747-5606
chanal@nl.rogers.com
www.chfcanada.coop/eng/pages2007/feds_1_1.asp
Overview: A small provincial organization founded in 1990
Member of: Cooperative Housing Federation of Canada
Staff Member(s): 1
Membership: 25

Cooperative Housing Federation of British Columbia (CHF BC)

#200, 5550 Fraser St., Vancouver BC V5W 2Z4
Tel: 604-879-5111; *Fax:* 604-879-4611
Toll-Free: 866-879-5111
info@chf.bc.ca
www.chf.bc.ca
www.facebook.com/pages/CHF-BC/123651397671685
twitter.com/chfbc
www.youtube.com/user/coopsbc;
www.flickr.com/photos/bchousingcoops
Overview: A medium-sized provincial organization founded in 1982
Mission: To expand non-profit co-operative housing; to promote better housing conditions in BC; to share skills & information with the co-operative housing community; represent housing co-ops to governments & the general public
Chief Officer(s):
Thom Armstrong, Executive Director, 604-879-5111 Ext. 143
tarmstrong@chf.bc.ca
Finances: *Annual Operating Budget:* $500,000-$1.5 Million; *Funding Sources:* Membership dues; fees for service; grants
Staff Member(s): 10; 12 volunteer(s)
Membership: 210; *Fees:* $300 B + C members; $2.80/unit/month class A members; *Committees:* Diversity; Board of Directors; Finance; Education; Communication
Activities: Co-operative Housing Investment Pool; Education Program; Legal Services; Bulk Purchasing; Member Card; *Speaker Service:* Yes; *Library:* Resource Centre
Awards:
• Mary Flynn Award of Cooperation (Award)

Cooperative Housing Federation of Canada (CHF Canada) / Fédération de l'habitation coopérative du Canada (FHCC)
#311, 225 Metcalfe St., Ottawa ON K2P 1P9
Tel: 613-230-2201; *Fax:* 613-230-2231
Toll-Free: 800-465-2752
info@chfcanada.coop
www.chfc.ca
www.facebook.com/105594649486310
twitter.com/CHFCanada
www.youtube.com/user/coophousing
Overview: A medium-sized national organization founded in 1968
Mission: To unite, represent, & serve the co-op housing community across Canada
Chief Officer(s):
Nicholas Gazzard, Executive Director
ngazzard@chfcanada.coop
David Granovsky, Coordinator, Government Relations
dgranovsky@chfcanada.coop
Membership: *Committees:* Federations; Diversity; Finance & Audit; Risk Underwriting Fund Administration
Meetings/Conferences: • Cooperative Housing Federation of Canada 2015 Annual General Meeting, June, 2015, Charlottetown, PE
Scope: National
Attendance: 850
Description: Training for co-op volunteers & staff; Business meeting; Youth forum; Elections for the Board of Directors; Group caucuses
• Cooperative Housing Federation of Canada 2020 Annual General Meeting, May, 2020, Halifax Convention Centre, Halifax, NS
Scope: National
Description: Training for co-op volunteers & staff; Business meeting; Youth forum; Elections for the Board of Directors; Group caucuses
Publications:
• CHF [Cooperative Housing Federation of Canada] Annual Report
Type: Yearbook; *Frequency:* Annually
• Newsbriefs [a publication of the Cooperative Housing Federation of Canada]
Type: Newsletter; *Frequency:* Quarterly; *Editor:* Merrilee Robson
Profile: News, issues, & events that affect Canadian housing co-operatives

Manitoba Office
#192, 162-2025 Corydon Ave., Winnipeg MB R3P 0N5
Tel: 204-947-5411; *Fax:* 204-947-5412
Toll-Free: 888-591-3301
www.chfcanada.coop/eng/pages2007/chfc_6.asp
Chief Officer(s):
Tammy Robinson, Program Manager, Manitoba
trobinson@chfcanada.coop
• Newsbriefs, Manitoba Edition [a publication of the Cooperative Housing Federation of Canada]
Type: Newsletter; *Frequency:* Quarterly; *Editor:* Tammy Robinson
Profile: News, issues & events that affect Manitoba housing co-operatives

Nova Scotia Office
Tower 1, #300, 202 Brownlow Ave., Halifax NS B3B 1T5
Tel: 902-423-7119; *Fax:* 902-423-7058
Toll-Free: 866-213-2667
Chief Officer(s):
Karen Brodeur, Program Manager, Cooperative Services
kbrodeur@chfcanada.coop
Debbie Hamilton, Member Services Coordinator
dhamilton@chfcanada.coop

Ontario Region
#313, 720 Spadina Ave., Toronto ON M5S 2T9
Tel: 416-366-1711; *Fax:* 416-366-3876
Toll-Free: 800-268-2537
info@chfcanada.coop
www.chfcanada.coop/eng/pages2007/onthome.asp
Chief Officer(s):
Patrick Newman, Regional Director, Ontario
pnewman@chfcanada.coop
• Bulletin for Ontario-program Co-ops
Profile: Information about work at provincial & municipal levels for co-ops
• Newsbriefs, Ontario Edition [a publication of the Cooperative Housing Federation of Canada]
Type: Newsletter; *Editor:* Keith Moyer
Profile: News, issues, & events that affect Ontario housing co-operatives
• SHRA [Social Housing Reform Act] Details
Profile: Educational series about the Social Housing Reform Act for Ontario-program co-ops

Vancouver Office
#200, 5550 Fraser St., Vancouver BC V5W 2Z4
Tel: 604-879-4116; *Fax:* 604-879-4186
Toll-Free: 877-533-2667
info@chf.bc.ca
www.chf.bc.ca
www.facebook.com/pages/CHF-BC/123651397671685
twitter.com/chfbc
www.youtube.com/user/coopsbc;
www.flickr.com/photos/bchousingcoops
Chief Officer(s):
Scott Jackson, Program Manager, National Communications
sjackson@chfcanada.coop

Cooperative Housing Federation of Toronto (CHFT)
#306, 658 Danforth Ave., Toronto ON M4J 5B9
Tel: 416-465-8688; *Fax:* 416-465-8337
info@coophousing.com
chft.coop
Overview: A small local organization founded in 1974
Chief Officer(s):
Tom Clement, Executive Director
tom@coophousing.com
Staff Member(s): 8
Membership: 160 housing co-operatives

Co-operatives & Mutuals Canada (CMC) / Coopératives et mutuelles Canada
#400, 275 Bank St., Ottawa ON K2P 2L6
Tel: 613-238-6712; *Fax:* 613-567-0658
info@coopscanada.coop
canada.coop
www.facebook.com/792260167456516
twitter.com/CoopsCanada
Overview: A large national organization founded in 2014
Mission: To unite co-operatives & mutuals from various industry sectors & regions of Canada
Affliation(s): International Co-operative Alliance
Chief Officer(s):
Leo Leblanc, President
Denyse Guy, Executive Director
dguy@canada.coop
Madeleine Brillant, Director, Corporate Affairs
mbrillant@canada.coop
Membership: 60 Co-operatives & Mutuals; *Member Profile:* Co-operatives & mutuals in Canada
Activities: Assisting developing organizations; providing relevant news & data to members; educational programs; lobbying; providing a forum for members; *Awareness Events:* Co-op Week, Oct.

Coopératives et mutuelles Canada *See* Co-operatives & Mutuals Canada

Copian
Sterling House, 767 Brunswick St., Fredericton NB E3B 1H8
Tel: 506-457-6900; *Fax:* 506-457-6910
Toll-Free: 800-720-6253
contact@copian.ca
www.copian.ca
twitter.com/Copian_E
Previous Name: National Adult Literacy Database
Overview: A small national charitable organization founded in 1989
Mission: To provide an information network, in both official languages; to support the Canadian literacy community: adult learners, practitioners, organizations & governments
Chief Officer(s):
Bill Stirling, CEO
bill.stirling@copian.ca
Finances: *Annual Operating Budget:* $500,000-$1.5 Million
Staff Member(s): 15; 1 volunteer(s)
Activities: *Awareness Events:* Family Literacy Day, January 27

The Coptic Orthodox Church (Canada)
St. Mark's Coptic Orthodox Church, 41 Glendinning Ave., Toronto ON M1W 3E2
Tel: 416-494-4449
mail@coptorthodox.ca
www.stmark.toronto.on.coptorthodox.ca
Overview: A small national organization
Member of: The Canadian Council of Churches; Coptic Orthodox Patriarchate
Chief Officer(s):
M.A. Marcos, Protopriest

Coquitlam Area Fine Arts Council; ARC Arts Council *See* Arts Connect TriCities Arts Council

Corbrook Awakening Abilities
581 Trethewey Dr., Toronto ON M6M 4B8
Tel: 416-245-5565
info@corbrook.com
www.corbrook.com
www.facebook.com/pages/Corbrook/201701949899274
Overview: A small local organization
Mission: To provide personal development & meaningful work opportunities for people with varying ability levels
Chief Officer(s):
Judy Cooper, President
Deepak Soni, Executive Director
Membership: *Member Profile:* Persons 18 years of age or older with a development disability; *Committees:* Finance; Human Resources; Governance; Business Resources
Activities: Employment services; personalized services; REVEL program; Youth Centred Day Respite Services; Learning & Literacy programs

Corner Brook & District Labour Council
PO Box 203, Corner Brook NL A2H 6C7
Overview: A small local organization
Member of: Newfoundland & Labrador Federation of Labour

Corner Brook Chamber of Commerce *See* Greater Corner Brook Board of Trade

Cornerstone Counselling Society of Edmonton
#302, 10140 - 117 St., Edmonton AB T5K 1X3
Tel: 780-482-6215; *Fax:* 780-482-7199
office@cornerstonecounselling.com
www.cornerstonecounselling.com
Overview: A small local charitable organization founded in 1977
Mission: To provide professional psychological services aimed at promoting wholeness of life through counselling education, assessment & training; services provided to individuals, families & couples in need regardless of income & sensitivity to individual physical, emotional, cultural & spiritual dimensions
Chief Officer(s):
Sheila Stauffer, Executive Director
Staff Member(s): 29
Activities: Individual, marital & family therapy; psycho/educational programs; Ryan Smyth Golf Tournament; annual banquet; *Speaker Service:* Yes

Cornwall & Area Chamber of Commerce
#100, 113 Second St. East, Cornwall ON K6J 1Y5
Tel: 613-933-4004
info@cornwallchamber.com
www.cornwallchamber.com
www.facebook.com/ChamberCornwall
twitter.com/chambercornwall
Previous Name: Cornwall Chamber of Commerce
Overview: A small local organization founded in 1890
Mission: To promote the commercial, agricultural, industrial & communal interests of the city of Cornwall & area; To maintain just & equitable principles in business & professional usage
Member of: Canadian Chamber of Commerce; Ontario Chamber of Commerce
Chief Officer(s):
Rick Shaver, President
Lezlie Strasser, Executive Manager
Finances: *Annual Operating Budget:* $250,000-$500,000
Staff Member(s): 7; 14 volunteer(s)
Membership: 700; *Fees:* $75 associate; $110-$400 business; $400 institutional; $110 non-profit
Activities: *Speaker Service:* Yes

Cornwall & District Labour Council
21 Water St. West, Cornwall ON K6J 1A1
Tel: 613-933-8670
info@cornwalllabour.ca
www.cornwalllabour.ca
Overview: A small local organization overseen by Ontario Federation of Labour
Member of: Ontario Federation of Labour
Membership: 10,000

Cornwall & District Real Estate Board
407B Pitt St., Cornwall ON K6J 3R3

Tel: 613-932-6457; *Fax:* 613-932-1687
www.mls-cornwall.com
Overview: A small local organization overseen by Ontario Real Estate Association
Member of: The Canadian Real Estate Association
Chief Officer(s):
Johanna Murray, Executive Officer, 613-932-6457
Membership: 176

Cornwall & Seaway Valley Tourism
11 Water St. West, Cornwall ON K6J 1A1
Tel: 613-938-4748; *Fax:* 613-938-4751
Toll-Free: 800-937-4748
info@cornwalltourism.com
www.cornwalltourism.com
Overview: A small local organization founded in 1993
Mission: To promote Cornwall & Seaway Valley as a viable visitor & convention destination
Member of: Tourism Industry Association of Canada
Chief Officer(s):
Michael Lalonde, Executive Manager
Finances: *Annual Operating Budget:* $100,000-$250,000; *Funding Sources:* Membership dues; City of Cornwall; united counties of Stormont, Dundas, Glengarry
Staff Member(s): 3
Membership: 175; *Fees:* $70-$250; *Member Profile:* Tourism businesses in Cornwall & Seaway Valley
Activities: *Library*

Cornwall Chamber of Commerce ***See*** Cornwall & Area Chamber of Commerce

Cornwall Police Association (CPA) / Association de la police de Cornwall
340 Pitt St., Cornwall ON K6J 3P9
e-mail: cpa@cornwallpoliceassociation.ca
www.cornwallpoliceassociation.ca
Overview: A small local organization founded in 1954
Chief Officer(s):
Dave MacLean, President
maclean.d@cornwallpoliceassociation.ca
Membership: 128

Cornwall Township Historical Society
17109 Valade Rd., St Andrews ON K0C 2A0
Tel: 613-932-4390
info@cornwalltwphistorical.ca
www.cornwalltwphistorical.ca
Overview: A small local charitable organization founded in 1977
Mission: To preserve & promote local history
Chief Officer(s):
Maureen McAlear, Contact
Finances: *Annual Operating Budget:* Less than $50,000; *Funding Sources:* Heritage grant; raffles; fundraisers
Membership: 108; *Fees:* $5 single; $8 family; $35 life
Activities: Operates local museum

Coronach Community Chamber of Commerce
PO Box 577, Coronach SK S0H 0Z0
Tel: 306-267-2077; *Fax:* 306-267-2047
Overview: A small local organization
Affiliation(s): Saskatchewan Chamber of Commerce
Chief Officer(s):
J. Marshall, President
S. Nelson, Secretary
Finances: *Annual Operating Budget:* Less than $50,000
Staff Member(s): 4
Membership: 1-99; *Fees:* $50
Activities: Agricultural Fair

Coronation Chamber of Commerce
PO Box 960, Coronation AB T0C 1C0
Tel: 403-578-4111
Overview: A small local organization
Mission: Thier mission is to promote and facilitate economic and community development in Coronation and District. Their vision revolves around acting as a catalyst in promoting economic development and encouraging activities that help to achieve a vibrant community where people wnat to live, work, and play.
Member of: Alberta Chamber of Commerce
Chief Officer(s):
Jody Shipman, President, 403-578-4580
Finances: *Annual Operating Budget:* Less than $50,000
Membership: 1-99; *Fees:* $50
Activities: Trade show

Corporate Art Collectors Association ***Voir*** Association des collections d'entreprises

Corporation culturelle Latino-Américaine de l'Amitié (COCLA)
1357, rue Saint-Louis, Montréal QC H4L 2P4
Tél: 514-748-0796; *Téléc:* 514-748-7210
cocla.mtl@gmail.com
www.coclamontreal.org
Aperçu: *Dimension:* petite; *Envergure:* internationale; fondée en 1984
Mission: Accueillir les nouveaux-arrivants d'origine latino-américaine et d'autres ethnies culturelles; soutenir les besoins vitaux de ceux-ci tels la nourriture, le logement, le vêtement, le transport et la communication; réaliser les programmes d'éducation permettant à ces nouveaux-arrivants leur adaptation à la société québécoise et canadienne
Membre de: L'Église Unie du Canada/The United Church of Canada
Affiliation(s): Moisson Montréal; Renaissance Montréal
Membre(s) du bureau directeur:
Julio Rivera-Gamarra, Directeur général
direction@coclamontreal.org
Membre(s) du personnel: 3
Activités: Groupe de femmes; service d'interprètes; conférences; cours de langue; camp d'été; ateliers

Corporation de développement économique communautaire Centre-Sud/Plateau Mont-Royal (CDEC-CSPMR)
#11, 425, rue Sherbrooke Est, Montréal QC H2L 1J9
Tél: 514-845-2332; *Téléc:* 514-845-7244
infor@cdec-cspmr.org
www.cdec-cspmr.org
www.facebook.com/CDECCSPMR
twitter.com/CDECCSPMR
Aperçu: *Dimension:* petite; *Envergure:* locale; fondée en 1986
Mission: Pour améliorer la situation économique et sociale des personnes vivant dans Centre-Sud, Plateau Mont-Royal, Saint-Louis et Mile-End
Membre: 90; *Montant de la cotisation:* 10$ individuelle; 25$ organisme

Corporation des agronomes du Québec ***Voir*** Ordre des agronomes du Québec

Corporation des approvisionneurs du Québec (CAQ)
Complexe Tassé, #302, 895, boul Séminaire nord, Saint-Jean-sur-Richelieu QC J3A 1J2
Tél: 450-357-0033; *Téléc:* 450-357-0044
Ligne sans frais: 800-977-1877
info@caq.qc.ca
www.caq.qc.ca
www.facebook.com/CorpoAppQc
Nom précédent: Purchasing Management Association of Canada - Québec Institute
Aperçu: *Dimension:* petite; *Envergure:* provinciale; Organisme sans but lucratif; Organisme de réglementation surveillé par Supply Chain Management Association
Mission: La Corporation des approvisionneurs du Québec assure le développement professionnel de ses membres et veille à promouvoir et favoriser l'implantation des meilleures pratiques en matière de gestion de la chaîne d'approvisionnement au sein des entreprises québécoises afin que la valeur stratégique de l'approvisionnement puisse contribuer pleinement à l'essor des entreprises et à la société québécoise.
Membre(s) du bureau directeur:
Pierre St-Jean, Président
Membre: 1,100+

Corporation des associations de détaillants d'automobiles ***See*** Canadian Automobile Dealers' Association

Corporation des bibliothécaires professionnels du Québec (CBPQ) / Corporation of Professional Librarians of Québec
#215, 1453 Beaubien est, Montréal QC H2G 3C6
Tél: 514-845-3327; *Téléc:* 514-845-1618
info@cbpq.qc.ca
www.cbpq.qc.ca
www.facebook.com/bibliothecairesprofessionels
twitter.com/CBPQ_QC
Aperçu: *Dimension:* moyenne; *Envergure:* provinciale; fondée en 1969
Mission: Développer les services de bibliothèques; établir des normes de compétence; encourager et stimuler la recherche en bibliothéconomie; promouvoir et développer les intérêts professionnels de ses membres
Membre(s) du bureau directeur:
Régine Horinstein, Directrice générale
dg@cbpq.qc.ca
Saint-Marseille Josée, Présidente
joseesaintmarseille@hotmail.com
Guylaine Beaudry, Vice-President
Mohammed Harti, Trésorier
harti.mohammed@uqam.ca
Finances: *Budget de fonctionnement annuel:* $100,000-$250,000; *Fonds:* Frais de cotisation; Revenus de formation
Membre(s) du personnel: 3; 40 bénévole(s)
Membre: 700; *Montant de la cotisation:* 60$ étudiant; 260$ titulaire; 130$ associé; *Critères d'admissibilite:* Maîtrise de bibliothéconomie/sciences de l'information; *Comités:* Perfectionnement; Argus; Bulletin Corpo-Clip; Formation; Admission; Élections; Règlements, résolutions et discipline; Mise en candidature; Congrès annuel; Site de la CBPQ; Mentorat
Activités: Congrès; Mentorat; Formation; Activités rencontre; Campagne de communication; *Stagiaires:* Oui; *Service de conférenciers:* Oui
Prix, Bouses:
• Prix bibliothécaire de l'année (Prix)
Stimuler et reconnaître l'excellence parmi les membres; attirer l'attention des médias sur les récipiendaires de cette distinction honorifique et sur la nature des réalisations primées; orienter des perceptions; le prix comporte les volets suivants: distinction honorifique, remise d'une épinglette en or, publicité entourant l'événement*Eligibility:* Être bibliothécaire exercant au Québec, présenter un projet innovant réalisé durant les 24 mois précédents*Deadline:* 30 juin *Amount:* 500$ et cotisation gratuite
Meetings/Conferences: • Congrès des milieux documentaires du Québec 2015, 2015
Scope: Provincial
Publications:
• Argus
Type: Revue; *Frequency:* 3 fois par ans; *Accepts Advertising*; *Editor:* Maude Laplante & Joachim Luppens
Profile: Un revue contenant des articles et des nouvelles se rapportant aux bibliothécaires et de l'industrie de la bibliothèque
• Argus
Type: Revue *ISSN:* 0315-9930
Profile: La revue propose des articles sur l'industrie de la bibliothèque, de la culture numérique et leur impact.
• Corpoclip
Type: Bulletin; *Frequency:* 4 fois par ans *ISSN:* 0843-140X
Profile: Un bulletin de nouvelles de la corporation à l'intérêt des membres

Corporation des bijoutiers du Québec (CBQ) / Québec Jewellers' Corporation
868, rue Brissette, Sainte-Julie QC J3E 2B1
Tél: 514-485-3333; *Téléc:* 450-649-8984
info@cbq.qc.ca
www.cbq.qc.ca
Aperçu: *Dimension:* moyenne; *Envergure:* provinciale; Organisme sans but lucratif; fondée en 1952
Mission: La promotion des membres, la défence de leurs intérêts économiques et sociaux et le développement du professionnalisme chez les membres; garantir au public un meilleur service et l'intégrité des bijoutiers membres; accroître la compétence des gens du métier; favoriser l'exercise du métier selon l'art et la science
Membre de: Association des professionels en exposition du Québec (APEQ)
Membre(s) du bureau directeur:
André Marchand, Président
Lise Petitpas, Directrice générale
lisepetitpas@cbq.qc.ca
Finances: *Budget de fonctionnement annuel:* $250,000-$500,000
Membre(s) du personnel: 2; 20 bénévole(s)
Membre: 550; *Montant de la cotisation:* 190$ - 350$
Activités: *Bibliothèque*

Corporation des Chemins Craig et Gosford
2600, boul Frontenac Ouest, Thetford Mines QC G6H 2C6
Tél: 418-423-3333; *Téléc:* 418-423-3331
Ligne sans frais: 877-335-7141
www.craig-gosford.ca
Aperçu: *Dimension:* petite; *Envergure:* locale; fondée en 2000
Mission: Mettre en valeur l'histoire et le patrimoine religieux des vieux axes routiers Craig et Gosford.
Membre(s) du bureau directeur:

Cindy White, Vice-présidente

Corporation des concessionnaires d'automobiles du Québec inc. (CCAQ)

#750, 140, Grande-Allée est, Québec QC G1R 5M8
Tél: 418-523-2991; *Téléc:* 418-523-3725
Ligne sans frais: 800-463-5189
info@ccaq.com
www.ccaq.com
Aperçu: *Dimension:* grande; *Envergure:* nationale; Organisme sans but lucratif; fondée en 1945
Mission: Offre une multitude de services aux membres; représenter ses membres
Membre de: Canadian Automobile Dealers Association
Affliation(s): CarrXpert; Occasion en On; ULTRA
Membre(s) du bureau directeur:
Lise Roy, Vice-présidente, Administration
lroy@ccaq.com
Membre(s) du personnel: 40
Membre: 825; *Montant de la cotisation:* Selon le nombre de véhicles vendus; *Critères d'admissibilite:* Détenir une franchise d'un constructeur; *Comités:* Comité de gestion; conseil d'administration
Activités: *Service de conférenciers:* Oui

Corporation des entrepreneurs généraux du Québec (CEGQ)

6800, boul Pie IX, Saint-Léonard QC H1X 2C8
Tél: 514-325-8454; *Téléc:* 514-325-0612
Ligne sans frais: 877-425-8454
lmartin@cegq.com
www.cegq.com
www.linkedin.com/groups/Corporation-entrepreneurs-g%C3%A9n%C3%A9raux-Q
www.facebook.com/freudibili
www.twitter.com/la_cegq
Aperçu: *Dimension:* petite; *Envergure:* provinciale; fondée en 1996
Mission: Voué exclusivement à la défense des intérêts collectifs et des droits des entrepreneurs généraux, oeuvrant principalement dans le secteur ICI (industriel, commercial et institutionnel)
Membre(s) du bureau directeur:
Luc Martin, Vice président exécutif
lmartin@cegq.com

Corporation des entrepreneurs spécialisés du Grand Montréal inc. (CESGM)

#500, 5181, rue d'Amiens, Montréal-Nord QC H1G 6N9
Tél: 514-955-3548; *Téléc:* 514-955-6623
Ligne sans frais: 800-772-3746
www.cesgm.com
Aperçu: *Dimension:* moyenne; *Envergure:* locale; Organisme sans but lucratif; fondée en 1988
Mission: Aider les entreprises en construction à réussir leurs examens de compétence à la régie du bâtiment; à faire démarrer leur entreprise et à rester en affaires
Membre de: Fédération des Associations et Corporations en Construction du Québec inc.
Membre(s) du bureau directeur:
Jean-Yves Paris, Directeur général
jyparis@cesgm.com
Ronald Marin, Président
rmarin@cesgm.com
Membre: *Critères d'admissibilite:* Tous les domaines en construction
Activités: Offrir des cours de perfectionnement; cours en administration; lecture de plan; estimation; gestion de travaux; sécurité, etc.; *Stagiaires:* Oui; *Bibliothèque:* Biblio CESGM;

Corporation des entreprises de traitement de l'air et du froid (CETAF) / Corporation of Air Treatment & Cold Processing Enterprises

#203, 6555, boul Métropolitain Est, Montréal QC H1P 3H3
Tél: 514-735-1131; *Téléc:* 514-735-3509
Ligne sans frais: 866-402-3823
cetaf@cetaf.qc.ca
www.cetaf.qc.ca
Aperçu: *Dimension:* moyenne; *Envergure:* provinciale; Organisme sans but lucratif; fondée en 1964
Mission: Représenter et défendre les intérêts de ses membres; règlementer leur discipline et leur conduite professionnelle; favoriser et encourager la formation permanente
Membre(s) du bureau directeur:
Claudette Carrier, Directrice générale
claudette.carrier@cetaf.qc.ca
Membre(s) du personnel: 4
Membre: 320 entreprises; *Critères d'admissibilite:* Détenir une licence de la RBQ #4230.1, 4230.2, 4230.3, 4234, 4250.4 ou 4509; *Comités:* Arénas; Bureau de l'efficacité et de l'innovation énergétiques; Discipline; Formation et perfectionnement; Événements spéciaux; Gaz métro; HRAI; Hydro-Québec/Énercible; MCEE; Recrutement et services aux membres; Rédaction du climapresse et revenus publicitaires
Activités: Mecanex-Climatex: Exposition commerciale - le carrefour annuel des professionnels de l'installation, de la vente et du service, dans l'industrie du traitement de l'air et du froid; séminaires; programme de formation et de perfectionnement; tournoi de golf annuel; *Bibliothèque* rendez-vous
Publications:
• ClimaPresse
Profile: Une revue technique et professionnelle d'expression française, publiée 6 fois l'an

Corporation des infirmières et infirmiers de salle d'opération du Québec (CIISOQ)

CP 63, 10, Place du Commerce, Brossard QC J4W 3L7
info@ciisoq.ca
www.ciisoq.ca
facebook.com/ciisoq
Aperçu: *Dimension:* moyenne; *Envergure:* provinciale surveillé par Operating Room Nurses Association of Canada
Membre(s) du bureau directeur:
Philippe Willame, Président
presidence@ciisoq.ca

Corporation des maîtres électriciens du Québec (CMEQ) / Corporation of Master Electricians of Québec

5925, boul Décarie, Montréal QC H3W 3C9
Tél: 514-738-2184; *Téléc:* 514-738-2192
Ligne sans frais: 800-361-9061
www.cmeq.org
Aperçu: *Dimension:* moyenne; *Envergure:* provinciale; Organisme de réglementation; fondée en 1950 surveillé par Canadian Electrical Contractors Association
Mission: Augmenter la compétence des membres; règlementer la conduite des membres et de la profession; faciliter et encourager les membres à se familiariser avec des nouvelles techniques; chercher des solutions pratiques aux problèmes communs de l'industrie électrique
Membre: *Critères d'admissibilite:* Titulaire d'une licence d'entrepreneur en électricité
Activités: *Service de conférenciers:* Oui; *Listes de destinataires:* Oui

Corporation des maîtres mécaniciens en tuyauterie du Québec (CMMTQ) / Corporation of Master Pipe Mechanics of Québec

8175, boul St-Laurent, Montréal QC H2P 2M1
Tél: 514-382-2668; *Téléc:* 514-382-1566
Ligne sans frais: 800-465-2668
www.cmmtq.org
Aperçu: *Dimension:* moyenne; *Envergure:* provinciale; Organisme sans but lucratif; fondée en 1949
Mission: Augmenter la compétence et l'habilité de ses membres en vue d'assurer au public une plus grande sécurité et protection au point de vue de l'hygiène et de la santé
Membre de: Heating, Refrigeration & Air Conditioning Institute of Canada
Membre(s) du bureau directeur:
André Bergeron, Directeur général
Alain Daigle, Président
Finances: *Budget de fonctionnement annuel:* $500,000-$1.5 Million
Membre(s) du personnel: 21
Membre: 2 200; *Montant de la cotisation:* 660$; *Critères d'admissibilite:* Entrepreneur en mécanique du bâtiment
Activités: Mécanex
Publications:
• L'Entre-Presse
Type: Newsletter; *Frequency:* Biweekly

Corporation des marchands de meubles du Québec *Voir* Conseil national du meuble

Corporation des officiers municipaux agréés du Québec (COMAQ) / Corporation of Chartered Municipal Officers of Québec

Édifice Lomer-Gouin, #R02, 575, rue Saint-Amable, Québec QC G1R 2G4
Tél: 418-527-1231; *Téléc:* 418-527-4462
Ligne sans frais: 800-305-1031
info@comaq.qc.ca
www.comaq.qc.ca
Aperçu: *Dimension:* moyenne; *Envergure:* provinciale; fondée en 1968
Mission: Regrouper les cadres municipaux des cités et villes du Québec; promouvoir la formation professionnelle par l'organisation de cours; protéger les intérêts sociaux-économiques des membres.
Membre(s) du bureau directeur:
Julie Faucher, Diretrice générale
julie.faucher@comaq.qc.ca
Membre: 650 officiers municipaux; *Critères d'admissibilite:* Gestionnaires municipaux; *Comités:* Formation professionnelle; Technologies de l'information; Législation; Finances et fiscalité municipales; Carrefour; Congrès; Recrutement; Scrutins; TPS-TVQ
Activités: Cours aménagement et urbanisme; scrutins municipaux; rédaction d'articles - information; étude des lois municipales des cités et villes; *Listes de destinataires:* Oui

Corporation des praticiens en médecine douce du Canada (CPMDQ)

CP 51071, 101, boul Cardinal-Léger, Pincourt QC J7V 9T3
Téléc: 514-221-3740
Ligne sans frais: 800-624-6627
info@cpmdq.com
www.cpmdq.com
Aperçu: *Dimension:* petite; *Envergure:* provinciale; fondée en 1991
Mission: De contribuer à l'essor d'une société où les individus, leurs familles et leurs communautés seraient responsables et capables d'assurer le développement et l'amélioration de leur santé physique, psychologique, spirituelle et sociale, grâce à des solutions globales, novatrices et durables.
Membre(s) du bureau directeur:
Brigitte Girard, Contact
brigitte@cpmdq.com
Membre: *Montant de la cotisation:* 350$; *Critères d'admissibilite:* Thérapeute en médecine paramédical

Corporation des propriétaires immobiliers du Québec (CORPIQ)

Centre Laennec, #500, 1750, av de Vitre, Québec QC G1J 1Z6
Tél: 418-529-4985; *Téléc:* 418-529-0806
Ligne sans frais: 800-529-4985
corpiq@corpiq.com
www.corpiq.com
Aperçu: *Dimension:* moyenne; *Envergure:* provinciale; fondée en 1980
Membre de: Canadian Federation of Appartment Association
Finances: *Budget de fonctionnement annuel:* $1.5 Million-$3 Million
Membre(s) du personnel: 15; 12 bénévole(s)
Membre: 9 500; *Montant de la cotisation:* 135-475
Activités: Information; représentation; regroupement et achats

Corporation des services d'ambulance du Québec

#205, 455, rue Marais, Vanier QC G1M 3A2
Tél: 418-681-4448; *Téléc:* 418-681-4667
Ligne sans frais: 800-463-6773
info@csaq.org
www.csaq.org
Aperçu: *Dimension:* petite; *Envergure:* provinciale; fondée en 1972
Mission: Pour offrir une gamme de services et d'avantages à ses membres et à défendre les intérêts de ces derniers auprès des différentes instances gouvernementales, auprès de ses membres au Québec.
Affliation(s): Association des hôpitaux du Québec
Membre(s) du bureau directeur:
Denis Perrault, Directeur général
denis.perrault@csaq.org

Corporation des thanatologues du Québec (CTQ)

#115, 4600, boul Henri-Bourassa, Québec QC G1H 3A5
Tél: 418-622-1717; *Téléc:* 418-622-5557
Ligne sans frais: 800-463-4935
info@corpothanato.com
www.domainefuneraire.com
www.facebook.com/corporation.thanatologues.quebec?fref=ts
twitter.com/corpothanato
Aperçu: *Dimension:* moyenne; *Envergure:* provinciale; fondée en 1956
Mission: Représenter le domaine funéraire, supporter son évolution promouvoir l'excellence et contribuer au développement d'affaire de ses membres pour le mieux être de la population

Membre(s) du bureau directeur:
René Goyer, Président
Finances: *Budget de fonctionnement annuel:* $500,000-$1.5 Million
Membre(s) du personnel: 2; 20 bénévole(s)
Membre: 400
Activités: *Listes de destinataires:* Oui

Corporation des thérapeutes du sport du Québec (CTSQ)

#SP165, 7141, rue Sherbrooke ouest, Montréal QC H4B 1R6
Tél: 514-848-2424
admin@ctsq.qc.ca
www.ctsq.qc.ca
Aperçu: *Dimension:* petite; *Envergure:* provinciale; Organisme sans but lucratif; Organisme de réglementation
Membre de: Canadian Athletic Therapists Association
Membre(s) du bureau directeur:
Jaime Sochasky-Livingston, President
president@ctsq.qc.ca
Sabrina Hanna, Executive Director
Finances: *Budget de fonctionnement annuel:* Moins de $50,000
Membre: 100-499
Activités: Développement professionnel ainsi que réglementation et attribution de licences professionnelles

Corporation des traducteurs, traductrices, terminologues et interprètes du Nouveau-Brunswick (CTINB) / Corporation of Translators, Terminologists & Interpreters of New Brunswick

CP 427, Fredericton NB E3B 4Z9
Tél: 506-458-1519
ctinb@nbnet.nb.ca
www.ctinb.nb.ca
Aperçu: *Dimension:* moyenne; *Envergure:* provinciale; Organisme sans but lucratif; fondée en 1970 surveillé par Canadian Translators, Terminologists & Interpreters Council
Mission: Donner à ses membres une voix collective; promouvoir le perfectionnement professionnel de ses membres; veiller à ce que ses membres respectent son Code de déontologie; faire connaître le rôle professionnel de ses membres dans la société; protéger l'intérêt public en faisant subir des examens d'admission à la CTINB et d'agrément des membres ainsi qu'en examinant les plaintes reçues à l'égard des membres; entretenir des liens avec les organismes semblables et avec les établissements de formation universitaire dans les domaines de la traduction, de la terminologie et de l'interprétation
Affliation(s): Fédération internationale des traducteurs
Finances: *Budget de fonctionnement annuel:* Moins de $50,000
Membre(s) du personnel: 1; 5 bénévole(s)
Membre: 150 agrées + 60 associés; *Montant de la cotisation:* 135$ agrées; 70$ associés; *Comités:* Agrément; adhésion; discipline
Activités: Ateliers de perfectionnement professionnel; *Evénements de sensibilisation:* Journée nationale et internationale de la traduction

Corporation du patrimoine et du tourisme religieux de Québec

20, rue de Buade, Québec QC G1R 4A1
Tél: 418-694-0665; *Téléc:* 418-692-5860
info@patrimoine-religieux.com
www.patrimoine-religieux.com
Aperçu: *Dimension:* moyenne; *Envergure:* provinciale
Mission: La Corporation veille à l'animation, à l'interpretation et à la mise en valeur du patrimoine religieux de Québec.
Activités: Visites thématiques et pèlerinages, programmation, activités éducatives, service d'animation, service de documentation et d'information

Corporation l'Espoir

#511, 55, rue Dupras, LaSalle QC H8R 4A8
Tél: 514-367-3757; *Téléc:* 514-367-0444
www.corporationespoir.org
www.facebook.com/296348483713938
Aperçu: *Dimension:* petite; *Envergure:* locale; Organisme sans but lucratif; fondée en 1976
Mission: Regroupe des parents de personnes qui présentent une déficience intellectuelle; maintien dans le milieu familial, l'intégration et la participation sociale de toutes les personnes handicapées
Affliation(s): Association du Québec pour l'intégration sociale
Membre(s) du bureau directeur:
Réjean Turbide, Président
Caroline Langevin, Directrice générale
caroline@corporationespoir.org
Membre: 350; *Montant de la cotisation:* $15
Publications:
• Défi [a publication of Corporation l'Espoir]
Type: Journal

Corporation of Air Treatment & Cold Processing Enterprises *Voir* Corporation des entreprises de traitement de l'air et du froid

Corporation of BC Land Surveyors *See* Association of British Columbia Land Surveyors

Corporation of Chartered Municipal Officers of Québec *Voir* Corporation des officiers municipaux agréés du Québec

Corporation of Master Electricians of Québec *Voir* Corporation des maîtres électriciens du Québec

Corporation of Master Pipe Mechanics of Québec *Voir* Corporation des maîtres mécaniciens en tuyauterie du Québec

Corporation of Professional Librarians of Québec *Voir* Corporation des bibliothécaires professionnels du Québec

Corporation of Translators, Terminologists & Interpreters of New Brunswick *Voir* Corporation des traducteurs, traductrices, terminologues et interprètes du Nouveau-Brunswick

Corporation pour la formation et le développement ERS *See* ERS Training & Development Corporation

Corporation professionnelle des audioprothésistes du Québec *Voir* Ordre des audioprothésistes du Québec

Corporation professionnelle des conseillers et conseillères d'orientation du Québec *Voir* Ordre des conseillers et conseillères d'orientation du Québec

Corporation professionnelle des infirmières et infirmiers auxiliaires du Québec *Voir* Ordre des infirmières et infirmiers auxiliaires du Québec

Corporation professionnelle des technologistes médicaux du Québec *Voir* Ordre professionnel des technologistes médicaux du Québec

Corporation professionnelle des technologues professionnelles du Québec *Voir* Ordre des technologues professionnels du Québec

Corporations des assureurs directs de dommage (CADD)

c/o La Capitale assurances générales inc., 625, rue St-Amable, Québec QC G1R 2G5
Tél: 418-266-9762
secretariat@cadd.ca
www.cadd.ca
Aperçu: *Dimension:* petite; *Envergure:* provinciale
Membre(s) du bureau directeur:
Henry Blumenthal, Président
Jean Mathieu Potvin, Secrétaire Trésorier

Le Corps Canadien des Commissionnaires *See* The Canadian Corps of Commissionaires

Corridor Community Options for Adults (CCOA)

21 Convent Rd., Enfield NS B2T 1C9
Tel: 902-883-9404; *Fax:* 902-883-1251
Overview: A small local organization
Member of: DIRECTIONS Council for Vocational Services Society
Chief Officer(s):
Ross Young, Executive Director/Manager
ccoa.manager@gmail.com

Corrugated Steel Pipe Institute (CSPI) / Institut pour tuyaux de tôle ondulée

#2A, 652 Bishop St. North, Cambridge ON N3H 4V6
Tel: 519-650-8080; *Fax:* 519-650-8081
info@cspi.ca
www.cspi.ca
Overview: A medium-sized national organization
Mission: To promote & encourage general & wider use of corrugated steel pipe for drainage & other uses across Canada; to initiate & support research, marketing, promotion, public relations & advertising programs designed to broaden the markets for CSP products; to cooperate with public & private agencies engaged in the formulation of specifications & designs for drainage & other underground structures; to provide the industry & the public with documented experience & up-to-date technical information on CSP products & their proper use & application; to enhance, through responsible public relations practices, the reputation & image of the Canadian CSP industry; to cooperate with allied industry & government authorities; to encourage & participate in educational endeavours in colleges & universities.
Chief Officer(s):
David J. Penny, Marketing Manager
djpenny@cspi.ca
Activities: *Library* Open to public

Corsa Ontario

401 Beechwood Cr., Burlington ON L7L 3P7
Tel: 905-833-6858
www.corsaontario.com
Overview: A small provincial organization founded in 1969
Mission: To preserve Corvairs
Member of: Corvair Society of America
Chief Officer(s):
Jim Diell, Interim President
njdl@sympatico.ca
Finances: *Annual Operating Budget:* Less than $50,000
10 volunteer(s)
Membership: 65; *Fees:* $25

Cosmetologists' Association of British Columbia; Cosmetology Industry Association of British Columbia *See* BeautyCouncil

Cosmetology Association of Nova Scotia (CANS)

126 Chain Link Dr., Halifax NS B3S 1A2
Tel: 902-468-6477; *Fax:* 902-468-7147
Toll-Free: 800-765-8757
www.nscosmetology.ca
Overview: A medium-sized provincial licensing organization founded in 1962
Mission: To apply standards ensuring the safety of the public & practitioners
Chief Officer(s):
Lloyd Petrie, Chair
Finances: *Annual Operating Budget:* $250,000-$500,000; *Funding Sources:* Membership fees
Staff Member(s): 3; 11 volunteer(s)
Membership: 5,000; *Fees:* $35 - $45

Cosmopolitan Music Society

8426 Gateway Blvd. NW, Edmonton AB T6E 4B4
Tel: 780-432-9333; *Fax:* 780-439-2595
generalmanager@cosmopolitanmusic.org
cosmopolitanmusic.org
www.facebook.com/group.php?gid=128862577139033
Overview: A small local charitable organization founded in 1963
Chief Officer(s):
Cheryl Balay, General Manager
generalmanager@cosmopolitanmusic.org
Staff Member(s): 2; 50+ volunteer(s)
Membership: 250

COSTI Immigrant Services

Education Centre, 1710 Dufferin St., Toronto ON M6E 3P2
Tel: 416-658-1600; *Fax:* 416-658-8537
info@costi.org
www.costi.org
Overview: A small local organization founded in 1981
Mission: To provide educational, social & employment support to help immigrants in the greater Toronto area attain self-sufficiency in Canadian society. Services are provided in over 60 languages.
Chief Officer(s):
Bruno M. Suppa, President
Mario J. Calla, Executive Director
Finances: *Funding Sources:* Federal, provincial, municipal governments; United Way; private charitable foundations
Membership: *Fees:* $10 voting/individual associate; $25 orngantizational associate; *Committees:* Finance; Human Resources; Women's Services; Public Relations; Development Council
Activities: Referrals; work placement; language training; translation/interpretation; settlement services; family counselling; service for seniors

Brampton - Language, Employment & Settlement Services
Centennial Mall, #3, 227 Vodden St. East, Brampton ON L6V 1N2
Tel: 905-459-6700; *Fax:* 905-459-3626

Brampton & Caledon Employment Centre
#300, 10 Gillingham Dr., Brampton ON L6X 5A5
Tel: 905-459-8855; *Fax:* 905-459-9015
bramptonemployment@costi.org

Caledonia Centre
700 Caledonia Rd., Toronto ON M6B 3X7
Tel: 416-789-7925; *Fax:* 416-789-3499
employ@costi.org

Corvetti Education Centre
760 College St., Toronto ON M6G 1C4
Tel: 416-534-7400; *Fax:* 416-534-2482
edu@costi.org

Jane St. Hub
1541 Jane St., Toronto ON M9N 2R3
Tel: 416-645-7575; *Fax:* 416-645-7580

Markham - Enhanced Language Training Services
7220 Kennedy Fields Plaza, Markham ON L3P 7P2
Tel: 905-479-7926; *Fax:* 905-479-7425

Markham North - Language, Settlement & Skills Training Services
#102-103, 8400 Woodbine Ave., Markham ON L3R 4N7
Tel: 289-846-3645; *Fax:* 905-477-6478
esltmarkham@costi.org

Mississauga Centre
6750 Winston Churchill Blvd., #8A, Mississauga ON L5N 4C4
Tel: 905-567-0482; *Fax:* 905-567-0144
mississaugaemployment@costi.org

North York Centre
Sheridan Mall, #114, 1700 Wilson Ave., Toronto ON M3L 1B2
Tel: 416-244-0480; *Fax:* 416-244-0379
nyork@costi.org

Reception Centre
100 Lippincott St., Toronto ON M5S 2P1
Tel: 416-922-6688; *Fax:* 416-922-6668
reception@costi.org

Richmond Hill - Language, Settlement & Skills Training Services
9325 Yonge St., Richmond Hill ON L4C 0A8
Tel: 289-842-3124; *Fax:* 905-884-3163

Toronto - Employment Services
Weston Square, 35 King St., Toronto ON M9N 3R8
Tel: 416-588-2240; *Fax:* 416-244-2583
westonemployment@costi.org
Chief Officer(s):
Joe MacDonald, President

Vaughan - Language, Settlement & Skills Training Services
9100 Jane St., Bldg. H, Vaughan ON L4K 0A4
Tel: 905-761-1155; *Fax:* 905-761-2080

Vaughan Centre
#1, 7800 Jane St., Concord ON L4K 4R6
Tel: 905-669-5627; *Fax:* 905-669-1127
vaughanemployment@costi.org
Chief Officer(s):
Julie Darboh, General Manager
darboh@costi.org
Samantha Timbers, Manager
timbers@costi.org

Costume Society of Ontario (CSO)
PO Box 981, Stn. F, Toronto ON M4Y 2N9
e-mail: costumesocietyontario@gmail.com
www.costumesociety.ca
www.facebook.com/CostumeSocietyofOntario
Overview: A small provincial organization founded in 1970
Mission: To promote education in dress throughout the ages to individuals who share an interest in costume or textile history, theatrical costuming, or fashion design; to encourage the preservation of historic costume & related source material
Activities: Regular program of lectures, seminars, workshops, & field trips

Côte-des-Neiges Black Community Association Inc. ***Voir*** Association de le communauté noire de Côte-des-Neiges inc.

Couchiching Institute on Public Affairs (CIPA)
#301, 250 Consumers Rd., Toronto ON M2J 4V6
Tel: 416-642-6374; *Fax:* 416-495-8723
Toll-Free: 866-647-6374
couch@couchichinginstitute.ca
www.couchichinginstitute.ca
www.facebook.com/couchichinginstitute
twitter.com/couchiching
couchichinginstitute.tumblr.com
Overview: A small international charitable organization founded in 1932
Mission: To bring together interested Canadians to discuss important public policy issues with experts & other members of the general public
Chief Officer(s):
Amanuel Melles, President
Shannon Bott, Executive Director, 416-494-1440 Ext. 229
sbott@couchichinginstitute.ca
Finances: *Annual Operating Budget:* $100,000-$250,000; *Funding Sources:* Charitable, corporate, personal & government donations; membership & conference fees
Staff Member(s): 6
Membership: *Fees:* $2500 Coporate; $75 individual; $25 student; *Member Profile:* Individuals interested in public affairs; *Committees:* Program; Marketing & Communications; Conversations & Roundtables; Fundraising; Big Picture; Partnerships; Youth & Young Professionals
Awards:
• Couchiching Award for Public Policy Leadership (Award)
• The Aczel Fund (Scholarship)
• The Fresh Minds Fund (Scholarship)
• Kurt Swinton Fund (Scholarship)
Meetings/Conferences: • 2015 Couchiching Summer Conference, August, 2015
Description: The conference's theme is the politics & potential of sport. Issues will be discussed involving sports as entertainment, the violence of sports, sports & gender as well as sports & drugs
Contact Information: Phone: 416-642-6374; couch@couchichinginstitute.ca

Council Fire Native Cultural Centre ***See*** Toronto Council Fire Native Cultural Centre

Council for a Tobacco-Free Manitoba ***See*** Manitoba Tobacco Reduction Alliance

Council for Advancement of Native Development Officers (CANDO)
9635 - 45 Ave., Edmonton AB T6E 5Z8
Tel: 780-990-0303; *Fax:* 780-429-7487
Toll-Free: 800-463-9300
cando@edo.ca
www.edo.ca
Overview: A medium-sized national organization
Mission: To build capacity to strengthen Aboriginal economies
Chief Officer(s):
Paul Donald, President
Ray Wanuch, Executive Director

Council for Automotive Human Resources (CAHR)
#801, 10 Four Seasons Pl., Toronto ON M9B 6H7
Tel: 416-621-2614; *Fax:* 416-621-5926
Toll-Free: 866-242-2078
info@cahr-crha.ca
www.linkedin.com/company/council-for-automotive-human-resources
Overview: A medium-sized national organization
Mission: To develop leadership in building skills & driving innovation, fundamental skills required for the industry today & in the future, & the continual drive to improve through innovation

Council for Black Aging
3021 Delisle, Montréal QC H4C 1M8
Tel: 514-935-4951; *Fax:* 514-935-8466
Overview: A medium-sized local organization
Mission: The Council for Black Aging works as an advocate for the needs of Black seniors, undertaking activities designed to advance the interests of Black elders, keeping Black seniors better informed of issues relating to the availability of health and social services, and developing a unique day centre and a nursing home for Black elders.
Chief Officer(s):
Elisee Faure, Contact

Council for Continuing Pharmaceutical Education (CCPE) / Conseil de formation pharmaceutique continue (CFPC)
#350, 3333 boul de la Côte-Vertu, Saint-Laurent QC H4R 2N1
Tel: 514-333-8362; *Fax:* 514-333-1119
Toll-Free: 888-333-8362
info@ccpe-cfpc.com
www.ccpe-cfpc.com
Previous Name: Council for the Accreditation of Pharmaceutical Manufacturers Representatives of Canada
Overview: A small national organization founded in 1969
Mission: To provide educational programs to establish improved professional standards within the Canadian pharmaceutical industry; To better meet the needs & expectations of our internal & external stakeholders in the healthcare industry
Chief Officer(s):
Michelle Austin, Coordinator, Corporate Customers
Finances: *Annual Operating Budget:* $500,000-$1.5 Million
Staff Member(s): 6; 15 volunteer(s)
Membership: 60; *Member Profile:* Representatives associated with member companies who by their functions interface with other partners in the Canadian Health Care system

Council for the Accreditation of Pharmaceutical Manufacturers Representatives of Canada ***See*** Council for Continuing Pharmaceutical Education

Council for the Arts in Ottawa (CAOO)
Arts Ct., 2 Daly Ave., Ottawa ON K1N 6E2
Tel: 613-569-1387
council@arts-ottawa.on.ca
www.arts-ottawa.on.ca
www.facebook.com/groups/7734715604
twitter.com/CAOOttawa
Overview: A small local organization founded in 1982
Mission: To encourage & develop an appreciation for the arts in the Ottawa region
Chief Officer(s):
Peter Honeywell, Executive Director
peter@arts-ottawa.on.ca
Zoë Ashby, Creative Director
zoe@arts-ottawa.on.ca
Finances: *Annual Operating Budget:* $50,000-$100,000
Membership: *Fees:* $10 student; $20 individual; $50 patron; $50-$150 arts group; $250 corporate; $1000 sponsorship patron
Awards:
• The CAO Corel Endowment Fund Arts Award (Award)
• Victor Tolgesy Arts Award (Award)
• RBC Emerging Artist Award (Award)
• Business Recognition Award (Award)

Council of Administrators of Large Urban Public Libraries ***See*** Canadian Urban Libraries Council

Council of Administrators of Large Urban Public Libraries (CALUPL)
c/o Library Services Branch, Ministry of Municipal Affairs and Housing, PO Box 9490, Victoria BC V8W 9N7
Tel: 250-356-1791; *Fax:* 250-953-3225
Overview: A medium-sized national organization
Mission: To identify the issues & choices available in developing urban libraryservices; to explore the philosophy & principles which govern public library service in urban areas; to comment on the state of public library service in contemporary Canada in an endeavour to encourage the development of urban public library service; to facilitate the exchange of ideas & information between member libraries; to influence the legislation & financing of urban public libraries wherever possible.

Council of Agencies Serving South Asians (CASSA)
#212, 2401 Eglinton Ave. East, Toronto ON M1K 2N8
Tel: 416-932-1359; *Fax:* 416-932-9305
cassa@cassa.on.ca
www.cassaonline.com
www.facebook.com/314846981872986
twitter.com/CASSACanada
www.youtube.com/user/CASSAvid?feature=mhee
Overview: A small local organization
Mission: To advocate for & support existing as well as emerging agencies; to ensure that the social service needs of the community are met; To play an active role in eliminating all forms of discrimination in society
Chief Officer(s):
Neethan Shan, Executive Director
Maya Bhullar, President
Membership: *Fees:* $10 individual; $20 organization

Council of Archives New Brunswick (CANB) / Conseil des archives du Nouveau-Brunswick
PO Box 1204, Stn. A, Fredericton NB E3B 5C8
Tel: 506-453-4327; *Fax:* 506-453-3288
archives.advisor@gnb.ca
www.canbarchives.ca/canb
Overview: A small provincial organization founded in 1985 overseen by Canadian Council of Archives
Mission: To address the needs of the archival institutions in New Brunswick; To provide training & information on developments in the profession; To encourage information sharing & cooperation in educational opportunities with Maritime sister provinces & national associations
Chief Officer(s):
Fred Farrell, Manager, Private Sector Records
fred.farrell@gnb.ca

Amanda Tomé, President
amanda.tome@unb.ca
Finances: *Funding Sources:* Subventions; government grants
Staff Member(s): 1
Membership: 49; *Fees:* $35; *Member Profile:* Institutions; communities; museums
Awards:
• CANB-NB Provincial Grant (Grant)
Deadline: September 14
Meetings/Conferences: • Council of Archives New Brunswick AGM 2015, 2015, NB
Scope: Provincial
• Council of Archives New Brunswick AGM 2016, 2016, NB
Scope: Provincial

Council of Atlantic Ministers of Education & Training (CAMET) / Conseil atlantique des ministres de l'Éducation et de la Formation (CAMEF)

PO Box 2044, Halifax NS B3J 2Z1
Tel: 902-424-5352; *Fax:* 902-424-8976
camet-camef@cap-cpma.ca
www.camet-camef.ca
Previous Name: Atlantic Provinces Education Foundation
Overview: A medium-sized local organization founded in 1982
Mission: To allow the ministers responsible for education & training in New Brunswick, Nova Scotia, Newfoundland & Labrador, & Prince Edward Island to collaborate & respond to needs identified in public & post-secondary education; To enhance cooperation in public & post-secondary education to improve learning for Atlantic Canadians
Chief Officer(s):
Rhéal Poirier, Secretary, 902-424-3295
rpoirier@cap-cpma.ca
Sylvie Martin, Regional Coordinator, 902-424-8906
smartin@cap-cpma.ca

Council of Atlantic Premiers (CAP)

Council Secretariat, PO Box 2044, #1006, 5161 George St., Halifax NS B3J 2Z1
Tel: 902-424-7590; *Fax:* 902-424-8976
info@cap-cpma.ca
www.cap-cpma.ca
Mission: The mandate of the Council is to promote Atlantic Canadian interests on national issues. To accomplish this, the Council seeks to establish common views & positions to ensure that Atlantic Canadians & their interests are well represented in national debates. The work of the Council of Atlantic Premiers builds on the ongoing work of the Council of Maritime Premiers & the Conference of Atlantic Premiers. The premiers are committed to work together on behalf of Atlantic Canadians to strengthen the economic competitiveness of the region, improve the quality of public services to Atlantic Canadians and/or improve the cost-effectiveness of delivering public services to Atlantic Canadians.
Chief Officer(s):
Tim Porter, Secretary to Council, 902-424-7600
tporter@cap-cpma.ca
Membership: *Member Profile:* Premiers of New Brunswick, Newfoundland & Labrador, Nova Scotia & Prince Edward Island

Council of Canadian Academies / Conseil des académies canadiennes

#1401, 180 Elgin St., Ottawa ON K2P 2K3
Tel: 613-567-5000; *Fax:* 613-567-5060
info@scienceadvice.ca
www.scienceadvice.ca
twitter.com/Scienceadvice
Previous Name: Canadian Academies of Science
Overview: A small national organization founded in 2005
Mission: To support independent, expert assessment of the science underlying issues of public concern.
Chief Officer(s):
Margaret Bloodworth, Chair
Janet Bax, Interim President, 613-567-5000 Ext. 267
janet.bax@scienceadvice.ca
Tom Bursey, Vice-President, Corporate Services & CFO, 613-567-5000 Ext. 224
tom.bursey@scienceadvice.ca
Finances: *Funding Sources:* Federal government
Staff Member(s): 28
Membership: 3; *Member Profile:* Royal Society of Canada; Canadian Academy of Engineering; Canadian Academy of Health Sciences; *Committees:* Scientific Advisor; Executive; Audit & Finance; Investment; Nominations, Selection & Governance; Human Resources & Compensation

Council of Canadian Fire Marshals & Fire Commissioners (CCFMFC) / Conseil canadien des directeurs provinciaux et des commissaires des incendies

c/o 491 McLeod Hill Rd., Fredericton NB E3A 6H6
Tel: 506-453-1208; *Fax:* 506-457-0793
CCFMFC@rogers.com
www.ccfmfc.ca
Overview: A medium-sized national organization founded in 1921
Mission: To contribute to a reduction in the number of fire deaths
Chief Officer(s):
Duane McKay, President
Harold Pothier, Vice-President
Philippa Gourley, Secretary-Treasurer
Activities: Advising on & promoting legislation, policies, & procedures; Participating in the development of standards & codes; Arranging national fire loss statistics; Supporting professional development of the Canadian fire service; Identifying trends related to the causes of fire; Providing a forum for the exchange of information on fire safety matters; Offering advice to accredited agencies involved in the testing & certification of fire protection equipment

Council of Canadian Law Deans (CCLD) / Conseil des doyens et des doyennes des facultés de droit du Canada (CDFDC)

c/o Bridgitte Pilon, Executive Director, 57 Louis Pasteur, Ottawa ON K1N 6N5
Tel: 613-824-9233; *Fax:* 613-824-9233
brigitteccld@rogers.com
www.ccld-cdfdc.ca
Overview: A small national organization overseen by Association of Universities & Colleges of Canada
Chief Officer(s):
Brigitte Pilon, Executive Director
Finances: *Annual Operating Budget:* Less than $50,000
Staff Member(s): 1
Membership: 22; *Member Profile:* Heads of various law schools & departments across Canada
Activities: Two meetings per year; sponsorship of law teaching forum

The Council of Canadians (COC) / Le Conseil des Canadiens

#700, 170 Laurier Ave. West, Ottawa ON K1P 5V5
Tel: 613-233-2773; *Fax:* 613-233-6776
Toll-Free: 800-387-7177
inquiries@canadians.org; www.canadians.org
www.facebook.com/groups/2228697837
twitter.com/councilofcdns
www.youtube.com/councilofcanadians
Overview: A medium-sized national organization founded in 1985
Mission: With chapters across the country, The Council of Canadians is Canada's largest citizens' organization, working to protect Canadian independence in areas such as energy & environment, health care & fair trade. The Council provides a critical voice on key national issues: safeguarding our social programs, promoting economic justice, renewing Canada's democracy, asserting Canadian sovereignty, promoting alternatives to corporate-style free trade & preserving the environment
Chief Officer(s):
Maude Barlow, National Chairperson
Finances: *Annual Operating Budget:* $500,000-$1.5 Million; *Funding Sources:* Membership dues; donations
Staff Member(s): 15
Membership: 100,000; *Fees:* $45
Activities: Campaigns: Deep Integration (the increasing harmonisation of Canadian policies in key areas with those of the U.S.); Health Care; Trade; Water; Energy; Food; Peace; Blue Planet Project; *Rents Mailing List:* Yes; *Library* Open to public by appointment

Atlantic
#211, 2099 Gottigen St., Halifax NS B3K 3B2
Tel: 902-422-7811
Toll-Free: 877-772-7811
atlantic@canadians.org
www.facebook.com/groups/307287381978/
Chief Officer(s):
Angela Giles, Regional Organizer

British Columbia & Yukon
#700, 207 West Hastings St., Vancouver BC V6B 1H7
Tel: 604-688-8846
Toll-Free: 888-566-3888
bc-yukon@canadians.org
Chief Officer(s):
Harjap Grewal, Regional Organizer

Ontario, Québec, Nunavut
#210, 116 Spadina Ave., Toronto ON M5V 2K6
Tel: 416-979-5554
Toll-Free: 800-208-7156
ontario-quebec@canadians.org
Chief Officer(s):
Stuart Trew, Regional Organizer

Prairies
#34, 9912 - 106 St., Edmonton AB T5K 1C5
Tel: 780-429-4500
Toll-Free: 877-729-4500
prairies@canadians.org
Chief Officer(s):
Sheila Muxlow, Regional Organizer

Council of Canadians with Disabilities (CCD) / Conseil des Canadiens avec déficiences

#926, 294 Portage Ave., Winnipeg MB R3C 0B9
Tel: 204-947-0303; *TTY:* 204-947-4757
ccd@ccdonline.ca
www.ccdonline.ca
www.facebook.com/ccdonline
twitter.com/ccdonline
www.youtube.com/ccdonline
Overview: A medium-sized national organization founded in 1976
Mission: To improve the status of disabled citizens in Canadian society; to promote self-help for persons with disabilities; to provide a democratic structure for disabled citizens to voice concerns; to monitor federal legislation; to share information & cooperate with disabled persons' organizations in Canada & in other countries; to establish a positive image of disabled Canadians
Member of: Disabled Peoples International
Affliation(s): Consumer Organization of Disabled People of Newfoundland & Labrador; PEI Council of the Disabled; Nova Scotia League for Equal Opportunities; PUSH-Ontario; Manitoba League of the Physically Handicapped; Saskatchewan Voice of the Handicapped; Alberta Committee of Disabled Citizens; British Columbia Coalition of the Disabled; Association canadienne des sourds; DAWN Canada; National Network on Mental Health; Thalidomide Victims of Canada; National Education Association of Disabled Students; People First of Canada
Chief Officer(s):
Laurie Beachell, National Coordinator
Tony Dolan, Chair
Finances: *Funding Sources:* Human Resources Development
Membership: 17 organizations; *Member Profile:* Consumer controlled advocacy associations; *Committees:* Access to Technology; Human Rights; International Development; Social Policy; Transportation
Activities: *Speaker Service:* Yes; *Library* by appointment

Council of Catholic Charities *See* Catholic Charities of The Archdiocese of Toronto

Council of Catholic School Superintendents of Alberta (CCSSA)

c/o Betty Turpin, Holy Family Catholic Regional Division No. 37, 10307- 99 St., Peace River AB T8S 1R5
Toll-Free: 800-285-8712
superintendents@ccssa.ab.ca
www.ccssa.ab.ca. twitter.com/CCSSAB
Overview: A small provincial organization
Mission: Provides a forum for discussion regarding the direction & development of Catholic Education in Alberta
Chief Officer(s):
George Zeigner, Executive Director, 403-863-1079
Membership: 35

Council of Federal Libraries / Conseil des bibliothèques du gouvernement fédéral *See* Federal Libraries Coordination Secretariat

Council of Food Processing & Consumer Products *Voir* Conseil de la transformation agroalimentaire et des produits de consommation

Council of Forest Industries (COFI)

Pender Place I Business Building, #1501, 700 Pender St. West, Vancouver BC V6C 1G8

Tel: 604-684-0211; *Fax:* 604-687-4930
info@cofi.org; www.cofi.org
Also Known As: Canadian Forest Industries Council
Overview: A medium-sized provincial organization
Mission: To be the voice of the British Columbia interior forest industry; To offer member companies services in areas such as international market & trade development, community relations, public affairs, quality control, & forest policy
Chief Officer(s):
Ken Higginbotham, Chair
John Allan, President & Chief Executive Officer
Paul J. Newman, Executive Director, Market Access & Trade
newman@cofi.org
Doug Routledge, Vice-President, Forestry & Northern Operations
routledge@cofi.org
Anne Mauch, Director, Regulatory Issues
mauch@cofi.org
Membership: *Member Profile:* Companies that operate production facilities in forest dependent communities in the interior of British Columbia
Activities: Advocating for British Columbia's forest industry; Liaising with government about the development & implementation of policies related to British Columbia's forest sector; Increasing public awareness about the importance of the forest sector
Meetings/Conferences: • Council of Forest Industries 2015 Annual Convention, April, 2015, Prince George, BC
Scope: National
Description: A meeting about issues affecting the forestry industries of British Columbia.
Contact Information: Phone: 604-684-0211; Fax: 604-687-4930
• Council of Forest Industries 2016 Annual Convention, April, 2016, Kelowna, BC
Scope: National
Description: A meeting about issues affecting the forestry industries of British Columbia.
Contact Information: Phone: 604-684-0211; Fax: 604-687-4930
• Council of Forest Industries 2017 Annual Convention, April, 2017, Prince George, BC
Scope: National
Description: A meeting about issues affecting the forestry industries of British Columbia.
Contact Information: Phone: 604-684-0211; Fax: 604-687-4930
• Council of Forest Industries 2015 Annual Convention, April, 2018, Kelowna, BC
Scope: National
Description: A meeting about issues affecting the forestry industries of British Columbia.
Contact Information: Phone: 604-684-0211; Fax: 604-687-4930
Publications:
• British Columbia Forest Industry Fact Book
Type: Book
Profile: Sections include the world's forests & forest industry; Canada's forests & forest industry; competitiveness; land use, forest management, & the environment; & British Columbiaforest industry statistical tables
• COFI [Council of Forest Industries] News: Month in Review
Type: Newsletter
Profile: Council of Forest Industries events & British Columbia forest industry news
• Council of Forest Industries Annual Report
Type: Yearbook; *Frequency:* Annually
Profile: A review of operations & the financial report
• Quarterly Stumpage Update [a publication of the Council of Forest Industries]
Profile: Including British Columbia stumpage parameters & average stumpage prices

Council of Marine Carriers
#215, 3989 Henning Dr., Burnaby BC V5C 6P8
Tel: 604-687-9677; *Fax:* 604-687-1788
cmc@comc.cc, www.comc.cc
Overview: A small national organization founded in 1972
Chief Officer(s):
Leo Stradiotti, President
ole@dccnet.com
Staff Member(s): 3

Council of Maritime Premiers/Council of Atlantic Premiers (CMP/CAP) /Conseil des premiers ministres des Maritimes/Conseil des premiers ministres de l'Atlantique
PO Box 2044, #1006, 5161 George St., Halifax NS B3J 2Z1
Tel: 902-424-7590; *Fax:* 902-424-8976
info@cap-cpma.ca
www.cap-cpma.ca
Overview: A small local organization founded in 1971
Chief Officer(s):
Tim Porter, Secretary
tporter@cap-cpma.ca
Finances: *Annual Operating Budget:* $500,000-$1.5 Million; *Funding Sources:* Regional government
Staff Member(s): 15

Council of Ministers of Education, Canada (CMEC) / Conseil des ministres de l'éducation (Canada)
#1106, 95 St. Clair Ave. West, Toronto ON M4V 1N6
Tel: 416-962-8100; *Fax:* 416-962-2800
information@cmec.ca
www.cmec.ca
Overview: A medium-sized national organization founded in 1967
Chief Officer(s):
Andrew Parkin, Director General
a.parkin@cmec.ca
Colin Bailey, Director, Communications
c.bailey@cmec.ca
Jean-Gilles Pelletier, Director, Administration
jg.pelletier@cmec.ca
Christy Bressette, Coordinator, Aboriginal Education
c.bressette@cmec.ca
Pierre Brochu, Coordinator, Assessment
p.brochu@cmec.ca
Ruby Chow, Coordinator, Operations & CMEC Affairs
r.chow@cmec.ca
Nicole Cloutier, Coordinator, Financial Services
ncloutier@cmec.ca
Amanda Hodgkinson, Coordinator, Education Data & Research
a.hodgkinson@cmec.ca
Katerina Sukovski, Coordinator, Education & Literacy
k.sukovski@cmec.ca
Finances: *Funding Sources:* Membership dues
Membership: 13 institutional; *Member Profile:* Provincial & territorial departments responsible for education

Council of Nova Scotia Archives (CNSA)
6016 University Ave., Halifax NS B3H 1W4
Tel: 902-424-7093
advisor@councilofnsarchives.ca
www.councilofnsarchives.ca
www.facebook.com/536190566445902
Overview: A medium-sized provincial charitable organization founded in 1983 overseen by Canadian Council of Archives
Mission: To foster education of archival standards & practices to preserve Nova Scotia's documentary heritage; To promote archival standards, procedures, & practices
Chief Officer(s):
Jamie Serran, Advisor, Archives
advisor@councilofnsarchives.ca
Staff Member(s): 2
Membership: 100+; *Fees:* $55 General; $50 Individual; $25 Student; Schedule for institutions; *Member Profile:* Archivists & archives in Nova Scotia, such as university archives, religious archives, community archives, museums, provincial archives, corporations, & heritage associations; *Committees:* Executive; Education; Awards; Preservation; Arch Way; Renewal & Sustainability
Activities: Advocating for the importance of archives, preservation, & public access; Liaising with the Canadian Council of Archives; Providing training & advisory services; Establishing the CNSA Acquisition Strategy for cooperative acquisitition practices in Nova Scotian archives; *Library:* CNSA Lending Library; by appointment
Awards:
• Carman V. Carroll Award for Outstanding Achievement in Archival Preservation (Award)
• Anna Hamilton Award for Outstanding Voluntary Service to the Nova Scotian Archival Community (Award)
• Dr. Phyllis R. Blakeley Award for Archival Excellence (Award)
Meetings/Conferences: • Council of Nova Scotia Archives Annual Conference 2015, 2015, NS
Scope: Provincial
• Council of Nova Scotia Archives Annual Conference 2016, 2016
Scope: Provincial

Council of Ontario Construction Associations (COCA)
#2001, 180 Dundas St. West, Toronto ON M5G 1Z8
Tel: 416-968-7200; *Fax:* 416-968-0362
info@coca.on.ca
www.coca.on.ca
www.linkedin.com/company/2397076?trk=tyah
www.facebook.com/172643879452017
www.twitter.com/ICIconstruction
Overview: A large provincial organization founded in 1974
Mission: To contribute to the long-term growth & profitability of the construction industry in Ontario; To speak with a unified voice to government, the industry & the public.
Chief Officer(s):
Ian Cunningham, President, 416-968-7200 Ext. 224
icunningham@coca.on.ca
Staff Member(s): 4
Membership: 32 organizations; *Committees:* Labour Legislation; Environment; WSIB; Taxation; Occupational Health & Safety; Employment Practices; Human Resources
Activities: *Speaker Service:* Yes
Meetings/Conferences: • Council of Ontario Construction Associations Annual General Meeting 2015, 2015, ON
Scope: Provincial

Council of Ontario Universities (COU) / Conseil des universités de l'Ontario
#1100, 180 Dundas St. West, Toronto ON M5G 1Z8
Tel: 416-979-2165; *Fax:* 416-979-8635
cou@cou.on.ca
www.cou.on.ca
www.facebook.com/CouncilofOntarioUniversities
twitter.com/OntUniv
Previous Name: Committee of Presidents of Universities of Ontario
Overview: A medium-sized provincial charitable organization founded in 1962
Mission: To work with & on behalf of members to meet public policy expectations related to accountability, diversity of educational opportunity, financial self-reliance, & responsiveness to educational & marketplace needs
Chief Officer(s):
Alastair Summerlee, Chair
Bonnie M. Patterson, President & CEO
bpatterson@cou.on.ca
Nancy Sullivan, Interim Executive Director, Corporate Services
Barbara Hauser, Secretary to Council & Sr. Advisor
bhauser@cou.on.ca
Membership: *Committees:* Executive; Government & Community Relations; Nominations; Relationships with Other Post-Secondary Institutions; Human Rights
Activities: Advocating; Researching; Communicating to public; Processing university applications

Council of Outdoor Educators of Ontario (COEO)
c/o Sport Alliance Ontario, 3 Concorde Gate, Toronto ON M3C 3N7
e-mail: info@coeo.org
www.coeo.org
www.facebook.com/group.php?gid=5715637275
Overview: A medium-sized provincial charitable organization founded in 1969
Mission: To promote outdoor education in a safe manner; to develop environmental awareness of the outdoors; to act as a professional body for outdoor educators in Ontario
Member of: North American Association of Environmental Educators
Finances: *Annual Operating Budget:* Less than $50,000
20 volunteer(s)
Membership: 30 student + 10 senior/lifetime + 200 individual; *Fees:* $35 student; $50 individual; $60 family
Activities: *Speaker Service:* Yes
Meetings/Conferences: • Council of Outdoor Educators of Ontario (COEO) 2015 Conference, January, 2015, Mono Cliffs Outdoor Education Centre, Orangeville, ON
Scope: National
Description: Theme: "Make Peace with Winter"
Publications:
• Pathways: The Ontario Journal of Outdoor Education
Type: Journal; *Frequency:* Quarterly

Council of Parent Participation Preschools in British Columbia (CPPP)
#4, 4340 Carson St., Burnaby BC V5J 2X9
Tel: 604-435-4430; *Fax:* 604-434-0443
Toll-Free: 800-488-0660
Other Communication: cppadmin@telus.net
cnclbc@telus.net
www.cpppreschools.bc.ca

Overview: A medium-sized provincial organization founded in 1945
Mission: To provide a high standard of education for pre-schoolers (3 & 4 year-olds) & also a planned adult education program, through the co-operative efforts of parents & supervisors
Affliation(s): Parent Cooperative Preschools International
Chief Officer(s):
Jean Beale, Executive Director
Staff Member(s): 3; 1500 volunteer(s)
Membership: 39 institutional + 1,500 individual; *Fees:* $60 family metro; $45 family provincial

Council of Post Secondary Library Directors, British Columbia (CPSLD)

c/o G. Makarewicz, Director, Library & Bookstore Svs., Langara College, 100 West 49th Ave., Vancouver BC V5Y 2Z6
e-mail: admin@cpsld.ca
www.cpsld.ca
Overview: A small provincial organization
Mission: To represent library directors from British Columbia's post secondary education institutions; To strengthen the post secondary library system in British Columbia to benefit both students & stakeholders
Chief Officer(s):
Todd Mundle, President
tmundle@sfu.ca
Grace Makarewicz, Secretary, 604-323-5460
gmakarewicz@langara.bc.ca
Janet Beavers, Treasurer, 250-782-5251
jbeavers@nlc.bc.ca
Membership: *Member Profile:* Library directors or chief librarians from not-for-profit post secondary education institutions in British Columbia
Activities: Engaging in advocacy activities; Facilitating communication on issues of common concern
Meetings/Conferences: • Council of Post Secondary Library Directors, British Columbia, Spring 2015 Meeting, May, 2015, BC
Scope: Provincial
Description: A meeting of British Columbia's library directors of not-for-profit post secondary education institutions, with the goal to strengthen the post secondary library system in the province
• Council of Post Secondary Library Directors, British Columbia, Fall 2015 Meeting, 2015, BC
Scope: Provincial
Description: A meeting held each autumn with a program of interest to library directors & chief librarians from not-for-profit post secondary education institutions in British Columbia
Publications:
• CPSLD [Council of Post Secondary Library Directors, British Columbia] Newsletter
Type: Newsletter; *Frequency:* Semiannually; *Editor:* Katherine Plett
Profile: Reports from British Columbia's post secondary institutions

Council of Prairie & Pacific University Libraries (COPPUL)

Bennett Library, 8888 University Dr., Burnaby BC V5A 1S6
Tel: 778-782-9404; *Fax:* 778-782-3023
www.coppul.ca
twitter.com/coppul
Previous Name: Council of Prairie University Libraries
Overview: A small provincial organization founded in 1968
Mission: To coordinate the activities of the Prairie & Pacific university libraries in promoting enhanced information services by means of cooperative collection development, resource sharing, rapid document delivery, & other such methods of transmitting or sharing resources; to act as an information sharing body
Member of: Canadian Library Association
Chief Officer(s):
Gwen Bird, Executive Director
execdir@coppul.ca
Finances: *Annual Operating Budget:* $50,000-$100,000; *Funding Sources:* Membership fees
Staff Member(s): 3
Membership: 20; *Fees:* Pro-rated on basis of university operating budget; *Member Profile:* Western university libraries & other university libraries (affiliate member) which support the goals of the Council; *Committees:* Digitization; Distance Education; Public Services; Resource Sharing; Systems; Data Librarians; Collections
Meetings/Conferences: • Council of Prairie & Pacific University Libraries Fall Meeting 2015, 2015
Scope: National

Council of Prairie University Libraries *See* Council of Prairie & Pacific University Libraries

Council of Private Investigators - Ontario (CPIO)

#204, 43 Keefer Crt., Hamilton ON L8E 4V4
Tel: 416-955-9450
www.cpi-ontario.com
Previous Name: Association of Investigators & Guard Agencies of Ontario Inc.
Overview: A small provincial organization
Mission: To represent the interests of private investigators in Ontario
Chief Officer(s):
Debbra MacDonald, President
president@cpi-ontario.com
Charlie Robb, Administration Manager, 519-471-4681
Finances: *Annual Operating Budget:* $50,000-$100,000; *Funding Sources:* Membership dues
Staff Member(s): 1; 1 volunteer(s)
Membership: 350-400; *Fees:* $25-$350 + GST
Activities: Educational meetings & seminars; *Speaker Service:* Yes

Council of the Haida Nation - Haida Fisheries Program (HFP)

PO Box 589, Stn. Masset, Old Masset BC V0T 1M0
Tel: 250-626-5252; *Fax:* 250-626-3403
Toll-Free: 888-638-7778
www.haidanation.ca/Pages/programs/fisheries.html
Overview: A small local organization
Mission: The Program provides advice to the Council of the Haida Nation about actions, political or otherwise, on the marine habitat & environment. It assesses all commerical/recreational fisheries & any plans affecting marine resources. Its priority is the protection of Aboriginal rights & title of the Haida people.
Chief Officer(s):
Robert Davis, Treasurer
Activities: Pallant Creek hatchery; Integrated Marine Use Plan; abalone stewardship

Council of Tourism Associations of British Columbia (COTA)

PO Box 3636, 349 West Georgia St., Vancouver BC V6B 3Y8
Tel: 604-685-5956
www.cotabc.com
Previous Name: Tourism Industry Association of BC
Overview: A medium-sized provincial organization founded in 1991
Mission: To advocate the interests of members to provincial & federal governments, businesses & media, in order to inform them of the opportunities & concerns of the tourism industry; To promote tourism in British Columbia
Chief Officer(s):
Stephen Regan, President & CEO, 604-685-5910
sregan@tiabc.ca
Kitka Neyedli, Coordinator, Membership & Industry Relations Coordinator, 604-685-5956
kneyedli@tiabc.ca
Peter Larose, Director, Policy & Planning, 604-685-5996
Staff Member(s): 4
Membership: *Member Profile:* Associations whose members are engaged in tourism-related services
Activities: Organizing a tourism industry conference; Preparing reports & strategies; Advising governments on tourism policy development; Chairing the the Air Issues Monitoring Consortium

Council of Yukon First Nations (CYFN)

2166 - 2nd Ave., Whitehorse YT Y1A 4P1
Tel: 867-393-9200; *Fax:* 867-668-6577
reception@cyfn.net
www.cyfn.ca
Overview: A small provincial organization
Mission: The Council of Yukon First Nations is the central political organization for the First Nation people of the Yukon. It's mission is to serve the needs of First Nations within the Yukon and the MacKenzie delta.
Chief Officer(s):
Ruth Massie, Grand Chief
ruth.massie@cyfn.net
Michelle Kolla, Executive Director
michelle.kolla@cyfn.net
Membership: 11 Yukon First Nations; *Committees:* Education; Finance & Administration; Circumpolar Relations; Natural Resources & Environment; Self-Government Secretariat; Justice Program; Health & Social; Yukon Native Language Centre; Training Policy; Yukon Aboriginal Sports Circle

The Council on Aging of Ottawa (COA) / Le Conseil sur le vieillissement d'Ottawa (CSV)

#101, 1247 Kilborn Pl., Ottawa ON K1H 6K9
Tel: 613-789-3577; *Fax:* 613-789-4406
coa@coaottawa.ca
www.coaottawa.ca
Previous Name: Ottawa-Carleton Council on Aging
Overview: A small local charitable organization founded in 1975
Mission: To enhance the qualilty of life of all seniors in Ottawa; To work with & for seniors in the community to voice issues & concerns to all levels of government & the general public
Chief Officer(s):
Kathy Yach, President
Finances: *Annual Operating Budget:* $100,000-$250,000; *Funding Sources:* City of Ottawa; United Way/Centraide Ottawa; Ministry of Health & LTC
Staff Member(s): 5
Membership: 380; *Fees:* $15 individual; $50 organization/agency; $8 student; *Member Profile:* Seniors; individuals; community organizations & professionals; *Committees:* Seven standing committees, working groups & projects
Activities: Senior Accessible Health Care Forum; COA Spring Luncheon; AGM; projects & various forums; *Library:* COA Library; Open to public

Council on Aging, Windsor - Essex County (COA)

c/o Centres for Seniors Windsor, 635 McEwan Ave., Windsor ON N9B 2E9
Tel: 519-254-9342; *Fax:* 519-254-1869
information@councilonaging.ca
www.councilonaging.ca
Overview: A small local charitable organization founded in 1988
Mission: To enhance the quality of life of seniors in Windsor - Essex County in Ontario; To assist in the development & coordination of services for local seniors
Member of: Provincial Network of Councils
Chief Officer(s):
Elaine O'Neill, President
Bruce Draper, Vice-President
Deana Johnson, Executive Director
deana@councilonaging.ca
Finances: *Funding Sources:* Ontario Trillum Foundation; Sponsorships; Fundraising
Activities: Advocating on behalf of seniors; Increasing public awareness about issues related to aging; Conducting research & needs assessments; Providing education; Offering information & referral services; *Speaker Service:* Yes

Council on American-Islamic Relations Canada *See* National Council of Canadian Muslims

Council on Drug Abuse (CODA)

#120, 215 Spadina Ave., Toronto ON M5T 2C7
Tel: 416-763-1491; *Fax:* 416-979-3936
info@drugabuse.ca
drugabuse.ca
www.facebook.com/186232391465114
Overview: A small national charitable organization founded in 1969
Mission: To prevent & reduce substance abuse, primarily among youth, by sponsoring education programs in schools
Chief Officer(s):
Lorraine Patterson, Chair
Finances: *Funding Sources:* Federal government; foundations; corporations; individual donors
Activities: *Speaker Service:* Yes; *Library* by appointment

Council on Palliative Care / Conseil des Soins Palliatifs

3605, rue de la Montagne, Montréal QC H3G 2M1
Tel: 514-845-0795; *Fax:* 514-845-1732
fmpa202@aol.com
www.council-on-palliative-care.org
www.facebook.com/CouncilOnPalliativeCare
twitter.com/PalliativeCares
Overview: A small national organization founded in 1994
Mission: To work in association with McGill University to raise public awareness & support of palliative care; To increase the availability of palliative care
Chief Officer(s):
Kappy Flanders, Chair

Activities: Liaising with healthcare planners, educators, practitioners, & the community; Providing information about palliative care
Publications:
• Council on Palliative Care Newsletter
Type: Newsletter
Profile: Council news, articles about palliative care, meeting highlights, & upcoming events

Counselling & Support Services of S.D. & G. / Centre de counselling familial de Cornwall et Comtés unis

26 Montreal Rd., Cornwall ON K6H 1B1
Tel: 613-932-4610; *Fax:* 613-932-5765
admin@css-sdg.ca
www.css-sdg.ca
Previous Name: Family Counselling Centre of Cornwall & United Counties
Overview: A small local organization founded in 1938 overseen by Ontario Association of Credit Counselling Services
Mission: To offer professional credit & family counselling as well as support services to persons in Cornwall & the United Counties; To support adults with a developmental disability to live within the community & to achieve their potential
Member of: United Way; Family Service Ontario
Chief Officer(s):
Raymond Houde, Executive Director
Finances: *Funding Sources:* Sponsorships; Ministry of Community & Social Services
Activities: Providing educational services; Offering community integration services; Engaging in advocacy activities; Offering counselling in areas such as personal, couple, & family issues; Providing programs, such as the Employee Assistance Program, Creative Coping for Kids & Changing Directions;

The Counselling Foundation of Canada

#200, 18 Spadina Rd., Toronto ON M5R 2S7
Tel: 416-923-8953; *Fax:* 416-923-2536
info@counselling.net
www.counselling.net
Overview: A small national organization founded in 1959
Mission: To engage in charitable and educational activities for the benefit of people; thus enabling them to improve their lifestyles and make a more effective contribution to their communities.
Affliation(s): Contact Point
Chief Officer(s):
Donald G. Lawson, Chairman

Counselling Services of Belleville & District (CSBD)

12 Moira St. East, Belleville ON K8P 2R9
Tel: 613-966-7413; *Fax:* 613-966-2357
csbd@csbd.on.ca
www.csbd.on.ca
Overview: A small local charitable organization founded in 1978 overseen by Family Service Ontario
Mission: To offer behavioural assessment & counselling, advocacy & support to families & individuals.
Affliation(s): YMCA, for summer camps
Finances: *Funding Sources:* Government; county; United Way of Quinte; fees, donations
Activities: Adult Protective Services; Autism Intervention Program; Family Court Clinic; Infant & Child Development Program

Counterpoint Community Orchestra

PO Box 41, 552 Church St., Toronto ON M4Y 2E3
Tel: 416-654-9806
info@ccorchestra.org
www.ccorchestra.org
www.facebook.com/CounterpointCommunityOrchestra
twitter.com/CounterpointCCO
Overview: A small local organization founded in 1984 overseen by Orchestras Canada
Mission: To foster pride as a LGBT positive orchestra; to perform for the community & promote equality within Toronto
Chief Officer(s):
Terry Kowalczuk, Music Director
Membership: *Committees:* Bylaws/Board Development; Concert; Fundraising; Program; Marketing & Promotion; Publishing

The County & District Law Presidents' Association (CDLPA)

731 - 9th St. West, Owen Sound ON N4K 3P5
Tel: 519-371-9247; *Fax:* 519-371-2664
cdlpa@bellnet.ca
www.cdlpa.org
twitter.com/CDLPA
Overview: A small local organization
Mission: To advance & represent the interests of member associations throughout the province of Ontario; to serve the legal profession & the people of Ontario in pursuit of the continued delivery of excellent legal services in each county, district or region in Ontario; to preserve the independence of the Bar
Chief Officer(s):
Cheryl Siran, Chair, 807-468-9831
csiran@HSLlaw.ca
Michael Ras, Director of Public Affairs, 647-228-2339
mike.ras@cdlpa.org
Finances: *Annual Operating Budget:* $100,000-$250,000
Staff Member(s): 1; 11 volunteer(s)
Membership: 46; *Member Profile:* Presidents of County & District Law Associations in Ontario; *Committees:* The County Law Library; Professional Governance; Court Resources; Judiciary and Government; Legal Services; Real Estate Law; Rules & Practice Issues; Legal Aid

County of Perth Law Association

Perth Courthouse, 1 Huron St., Stratford ON N5A 5S4
Tel: 519-271-1871; *Fax:* 519-271-3522
Toll-Free: 866-365-0218
perthlaw@on.aibn.com
www.libraryco.ca/library/county-of-perth-law-association
Overview: A small local organization founded in 1883
Chief Officer(s):
Wendy Hearder-Moan, Library Manager
Membership: 50; *Member Profile:* Lawyers
Activities: *Library:* Law Library

Couples for Christ Canada (CFC)

3553 Southwick St., Toronto ON L5M 7C4
Tel: 416-816-3931; *Fax:* 416-321-8498
couplesforchristcanada.ca
Overview: A small national organization
Mission: To renew & strengthen Christian family life
Affliation(s): Archdiocese of Toronto
Chief Officer(s):
Eduardo Clarito, Contact
junclarito@gmail.com
Activities: Conferences; summits; concerts; CFC Youth program; *Awareness Events:* Live Loud, Dec.

Couples for Christ Edmonton
couplesforchristcanada.ca/edmonton

Couples for Christ Montréal
couplesforchristcanada.ca/montreal

Couples for Christ Vancouver
#250, 2981 Simpson Rd., Richmond BC V6X 2R2
Tel: 604-270-9463; *Fax:* 604-270-6855
couplesforchristcanada.ca/vancouver

Couples for Christ Winnipeg
404 Notre Dame Ave., Winnipeg MB R3B 1R1
Tel: 204-775-7503
couplesforchristcanada.ca/winnipeg

Couples For Christ Foundation for Family & Life (CFCFFL)

#7, 2250 Midland Ave., Scarborough ON M1P 4R9
Tel: 416-335-3358; *Fax:* 416-335-0051
cfcffl@cfcfflcanada.org
www.cfcfflcanada.org
Overview: A small national charitable organization founded in 2007
Mission: To engage in activities & services which focus on evangelization, family life renewal, & defense of the culture of life; To provide ministries, such as Missions & Evangelization, Social Ministries (work for justice & the poor), Pastoral Support (formation & work for life), & Communities Support (financial, legal, music, & commuications support)
Affliation(s): Archdiocese of Toronto
Chief Officer(s):
Eden Ben, Country Coordinator
Vuoleen Ben, Country Coordinator
Finances: *Funding Sources:* Donations
Membership: *Member Profile:* Couples, & single people must attend & complete the Christian Life Seminar (CLS) given by CFCFFL; Youth must attend & complete a Christian Youth Camp given by the Family Ministry of CFCFFL
Activities: Offering prayer groups for youth, singles, & couples; Presenting retreats, seminars, & conferences;

Couples For Christ (CFC)

156 Shorting Rd., Toronto ON M1S 3S6
Tel: 416-321-1937; *Fax:* 416-321-8498
cfctoronto@cfc-canada.org
couplesforchristcanada.ca
Overview: A small national charitable organization founded in 1981
Mission: To provide services, such as evangelization for adults & youth, & family renewal; to offer CFC family ministries, such as CFC Kids For Christ, CFC Youth For Christ, CFC Singles For Christ, CFC Handmaids of the Lord (a community of Christian women helping other women renew & live their Christian faith), & CFC Servants of the Lord (community of men who are either bachelors, married, separated, divorced or widowers); to work with the poor; to ensure governance by the CFC Council in Manila in each country where CFC exists
Affliation(s): Archdiocese of Toronto
Chief Officer(s):
Fulgencio (Sonny) Bautista, Contact
Finances: *Funding Sources:* Donations
Membership: *Member Profile:* Couples & single people who desire to join the CFC ministries must attend a Christian Life Program, which focuses on lay & family viewpoints; Graduates of the Christian Life Program apply for membership & must be approved by the area council; For teens & young children, weekend camps are held; CFC members are part of an association recognized by the Council of the Pontifical Laity as an International Association of the Lay Faithful
Activities: Counselling; Providing faith instruction & prayer groups; Offering marriage preparation & family planning services; Assisting immigrants & refugees through Immigrant & Refugee Centres; Offering religious goods & books; Helping the separated, divorced, & widowed; Providing study centres; Hosting monthly assemblies; Assisting the parish in any capacity given by the parish priest; Conducting RCIA & prolife activities; Presenting Christian Life Programs & pastoral formation teachings

Courtenay & District Historical Society

207 - 4th St., Courtenay BC V9N 1G7
Tel: 250-334-0686; *Fax:* 250-338-0619
museum@island.net
www.courtenaymuseum.ca
www.facebook.com/courtenaymuseum
twitter.com/courtenaymuseum
www.youtube.com/user/courtenaymuseum
Also Known As: Courtenay & District Museum & Archives
Overview: A small local charitable organization founded in 1953
Mission: To maintain the museum of local historic & palaentological artifacts.
Member of: Canadian Museums Association; BC Museums Association
Affliation(s): British Columbia Paleontological Alliance; Comox Valley Naturalists Society; Royal Tyrrell Museum; Comox Valley Family History Group; Comox Valley Tourism; Downtown Courtenay
Membership: *Fees:* $21 single; $31.50 family; $52.50 corporate; $210 life
Activities: Capes Escape, the museum's 1930s style home; *Library:* Research Centre; Open to public by appointment

Courtenay Gem & Mineral Club

2616 Mabley Rd., Courtenay BC V9N 9K2
Tel: 250-703-3444
Overview: A small local organization
Member of: British Columbia Lapidary Society
Chief Officer(s):
Russell Ball, Contact
dj_fossil@hotmail.com
Activities: Meetings 3rd Tues. of every month

Courtiers indépendants en sécurité financière du Canada
See Independent Financial Brokers of Canada

Covenant Health (Alberta) (ACHC)

3033 66 St. NW, Edmonton AB T6K 4B2
Tel: 780-735-9000
www.covenanthealth.ca
Previous Name: Catholic Health of Alberta
Overview: A small provincial organization
Chief Officer(s):
Patrick Dumelie, CEO
Membership: 14 Catholic health care facilities;

Covenant House Toronto

20 Gerrard St. East, Toronto ON M5B 2P3

Tel: 416-598-4898; *Fax:* 416-204-7030
Toll-Free: 800-435-7308
cino@covenanthouse.on.ca
www.covenanthouse.on.ca
www.facebook.com/covenanthousetoronto
twitter.com/covenanthouseto
Overview: A large local charitable organization founded in 1982
Mission: To provide a crisis shelter for homeless & runaway youth, who are 16 to 21 years of age; to offer assessment, counselling, & referral services
Affliation(s): Covenant House International
Chief Officer(s):
Stephen Corbett, Past Chair
Bruce Rivers, Executive Director
Rose Cino, Contact, Communications
cino@covenanthouse.on.ca
Finances: *Annual Operating Budget:* $3 Million-$5 Million; *Funding Sources:* Donations; Municipal funding; ShareLife
Staff Member(s): 112; 100 volunteer(s)
Membership: 1 corporate + 17 individual
Activities: *Awareness Events:* Sleep Out for Street Kids; GMP Capital Inc. Wine & Dine Gala, June; Covenant House Golf Classic; *Speaker Service:* Yes
Publications:
• Good Samaritan News [a publication of Covenant House Toronto]
Type: Newsletter

Coverdale Centre for Women Inc.
10 Culloden Court, Saint John NB E2L 3B9
Tel: 506-634-1649; *Fax:* 506-634-1647
coverdaleprograms@gmail.ca
www.coverdalecenterforwomen.com
Overview: A small local organization
Mission: Coverdale Center for Women Inc. provides programs and services for women including self-development programs in groups and individual counseling. It is a drop-in center where women can find support, referrals to community services, general counseling, addiction counselling, positive recreation, and self-improvement courses.
Chief Officer(s):
Mary Saulnier-Taylor, Executive Director, 506-634-0840
mary@coverdalecenterforwomen.ca
Activities: *Awareness Events:* International Women's Month; Purple Ribbon Campaign

Cowichan Consort Orchestra & Choir
PO Box 10, Cowichan Bay BC V0R 1N0
Tel: 604-748-8982
info@cowichanconsort.com
www.cowichanconsort.com
Overview: A small local organization overseen by Orchestras Canada
Chief Officer(s):
Rob Fox, President

Cowichan Intercultural Society
#205, 394 Duncan St., Duncan BC V9L 3W4
Tel: 250-748-3112
office@cis-iwc.org
www.cisduncan.ca
www.facebook.com/177342358949472
twitter.com/CISiwc
www.youtube.com/user/interculturalsociety
Previous Name: Cowichan Valley Intercultural & Immigrant Aid Society
Overview: A small local organization founded in 1981
Mission: To provide services & support to new Canadians to help them integrate into the Cowichan Valley communities.
Member of: Affiliation of Multicultural Societies & Service Agencies of BC
Chief Officer(s):
Lynn Weaver, Executive Director
lynn@cis-iwc.org
Finances: *Annual Operating Budget:* $500,000-$1.5 Million; *Funding Sources:* Federal, provincial governments; donations; special events; affinitive progams
Staff Member(s): 18; 167 volunteer(s)
Membership: *Fees:* $10 individual; $15 family; $30 corporate
Activities: ESL classes; employment assistance; children's summer programs

Cowichan Lake District Chamber of Commerce
PO Box 824, 125C South Shore Rd., Lake Cowichan BC V0R 2G0
Tel: 250-749-3244; *Fax:* 250-749-0187
info@cowichanlake.ca
www.cowichanlake.ca
Overview: A small local organization founded in 1946
Affliation(s): Canadian Chamber of Commerce
Chief Officer(s):
Rita Dustow, President
rita@cowichanlake.ca
Finances: *Annual Operating Budget:* Less than $50,000; *Funding Sources:* Donations; membership dues
Staff Member(s): 1
Membership: 62; *Fees:* $80-$130 business; $50 non-profit; *Committees:* Breakfast on the Town; Heritage Days; Shop Talk; Sunshine; Tourist Information
Activities: Daffy Daze, Apr.; Heritage Dayz, May; Lake Days, June; December Madness & Santa Parade

Cowichan Therapeutic Riding Association (CRTA)
c/o Providence Farm, 1843 Tzouhalem Rd., Duncan BC V9L 5L6
Tel: 250-746-1028; *Fax:* 250-746-1033
info@ctra.ca
www.ctra.ca
Overview: A small local charitable organization founded in 1985
Mission: To use horses to help persons with various disabilities in the Cowichan area of British Columbia achieve physical & mental health, behavioral, communication, cognitive, & social goals; To provide therapeutic or sporting activities in a safe environment with qualified instruction in order to improve the quality of life for persons with disabilities
Chief Officer(s):
Jennifer Barnes van Elk, Executive Director
Colleen Hunt, Manager, Operations
Staff Member(s): 16; 85 volunteer(s)
Activities: Receiving referrals from doctors, psychologists, physiotherapists, schools, & other health care organizations; Offering individualized riding programs; Providing a training program & workplace for persons with barriers to employment; Educating the public to see the contributions of persons with disabilities
Publications:
• The Leading Rein
Type: Newsletter; *Accepts Advertising*
Profile: Updates from the association, including a calendar of events, & information on upcoming riding programs

Cowichan United Way
1 Kenneth Place, Duncan BC V9L 5G3
Tel: 250-748-1312; *Fax:* 250-748-7652
office@cowichan.unitedway.ca
www.cowichan.unitedway.ca
twitter.com/uwcowichan
Overview: A small local charitable organization founded in 1976 overseen by United Way of Canada - Centraide Canada
Mission: To fundraise for charities; To provide guidance & counsel to charitable organization; To take leadership role in raising awareness of community needs
Chief Officer(s):
Mike Murphy, President
Carol Stenberg, Executive Director
Finances: *Annual Operating Budget:* $250,000-$500,000
Staff Member(s): 3; 140 volunteer(s)
Membership: 1,000-4,999
Activities: Fundraises for 21 local community organizations; *Speaker Service:* Yes

Cowichan Valley Arts Council
2687 James St., 2nd Fl., Duncan BC V9L 2X5
Tel: 250-746-1633
cvartscouncil@shaw.ca
www.cowichanvalleyartscouncil.ca
Overview: A small local organization founded in 1971
Mission: The Council is a non-profit organization that promotes the understanding & appreciation of art among local residents, & encourages the community to participate in artistic activities. It is a registered charity, BN: 867654022RR0001.
Member of: Assembly of BC Arts Councils
Chief Officer(s):
Judy Brayden, President
Finances: *Funding Sources:* British Columbia Arts Council
Staff Member(s): 2; 130 volunteer(s)
Membership: 250; *Fees:* $20 individual; $10 student; $35 family; $40 group; $50 business
Activities: Cowichan Valley Arts Centre

Cowichan Valley Association for Community Living *See* Clements Centre Society

Cowichan Valley Basket Society
5810 Garden St., Duncan BC V9L 3V9
Tel: 250-746-1566
cvbs@shaw.ca
www.cvbs.ca
www.facebook.com/285894211554071
Overview: A small local charitable organization founded in 1988 overseen by Food Banks British Columbia
Mission: To provide food to the needy in the Cowichan Valley.
Member of: Food Banks British Columbia
Affliation(s): Food Banks Canada
Chief Officer(s):
Colleen Fuller, Manager
Finances: *Funding Sources:* Donations

Cowichan Valley Intercultural & Immigrant Aid Society *See* Cowichan Intercultural Society

Cowichan Valley Naturalists' Society (CVNS)
PO Box 361, Duncan BC V9L 3X5
Tel: 250-746-6141
cvns@naturecowichan.net
www.naturecowichan.net/CVNS
Overview: A small local organization founded in 1962
Affliation(s): BC Nature: The Federation of British Columbia Naturalists
Chief Officer(s):
John Scull, Vice-President
Membership: *Fees:* $25 families of Young Naturalists Club members; $30 individuals; $35 families; *Member Profile:* Naturalists in the Cowichan Valley of British Columbia
Activities: Providing educational programs; Organizing nature hikes
Publications:
• Valley Naturalist [a publication of the Cowichan Valley Naturalists' Society]
Type: Newsletter; *Price:* Free with memberships in the Cowichan Valley Naturalists' Society
Profile: Information & events for naturalists in the Cowichan Valley

CP24 CHUM Christmas Wish
Bell Media, 299 Queen St. West, Toronto ON M5V 2Z5
Tel: 416-384-4199
thewish@bellmedia.ca
www.ctv.ca/TheWish
Previous Name: CHUM Charitable Foundation; CHUM's Kid's Crusade Foundation
Overview: A small local charitable organization founded in 1966
Mission: To provide financial assistance to charitable organizations and social service agencies
Activities: CP24/CHUM Christmas Wish

CPE du Carrefour
2355, rue Provençale, Montréal QC H2K 4P9
Tél: 514-526-8444
www.cpeducarrefour.qc.ca
Nom précédent: Garderie du Carrefour
Aperçu: *Dimension:* petite; *Envergure:* locale; fondée en 1979
Mission: De fournir des soins de qualité et une éducation aux enfants
Membre(s) du bureau directeur:
André Rémillard, Directeur général

CPJ Corp. (CPJ)
#501, 309 Cooper St., Ottawa ON K2P 0G5
Tel: 613-232-0275; *Fax:* 613-232-1275
Toll-Free: 800-667-8046
cpj@cpj.ca
www.cpj.ca
www.facebook.com/citizensforpublicjustice
twitter.com/publicjustice
www.youtube.com/user/c4pj
Previous Name: Citizens for Public Justice
Overview: A medium-sized national charitable organization founded in 1963
Mission: To promote public justice in Canada byshaping key public policy debates through research & analysis, publishing & public dialogue; CPJ encourages citizens, leaders in society & governments to support policies & practices which reflect God's call for love, justice & stewardship
Chief Officer(s):
Joe Gunn, Executive Director
joe@cpj.ca
Finances: *Funding Sources:* Membership dues; donations; grants
Staff Member(s): 10

Chief Officer(s):
Karen Milley, Contact
kmilley@ccsnl.ca

Credit Counselling Services of Southwestern Ontario *See* Financial Fitness Centre

Credit Counselling Society

#440, 88 Sixth St., New Westminster BC V3L 5B3
Tel: 604-527-8999; *Fax:* 604-527-8008
Toll-Free: 888-527-8999
info@nomoredebts.org
www.nomoredebts.org
www.facebook.com/nomoredebts
twitter.com/nomoredebts_org
Overview: A small provincial organization overseen by Credit Counselling Canada
Mission: To help consumers resolve debt & money problems & gain control over their finances
Member of: Credit Counselling Canada
Activities: For services in Nanaimo: 201 Selby St.; and in Victoria: 547 Michigan St. For both locations call 1-888-527-8999

Abbotsford
#209, 2316 McCallum Rd., Abbotsford BC V2S 3P4
Tel: 604-859-5757; *Fax:* 604-527-8008
Toll-Free: 888-527-8999

Burnaby
Central Park Business Centre, #300, 3665 Kingsway, Vancouver BC V5R 5W2
Tel: 604-527-8999; *Fax:* 604-527-8008
Toll-Free: 888-527-8999

Calgary
#210, 1935 32 Ave. NE, Calgary AB T2E 7C8
Tel: 403-263-9905
Toll-Free: 888-527-8999
Chief Officer(s):
Jim Thorne, Executive Director

Delta - Surrey
#228, 7164 - 120th St., Surrey BC V3W 3M8
Tel: 604-527-8999; *Fax:* 604-527-8008
Toll-Free: 888-527-8999

Edmonton
#201, 10612 - 124 St. NW, Edmonton AB T5N 1S4
Tel: 780-701-0083
Toll-Free: 888-527-8999

Hamilton
1 Hunter Street East, Hamilton ON L8N 3W1
Tel: 905-538-5035
Toll-Free: 888-527-8999

Kelowna
Stewart Centre Building, #230, 1855 Kirschner Rd., Kelowna BC V1Y 4N7
Tel: 250-860-3000; *Fax:* 604-527-8008
Toll-Free: 888-527-8999

London
City Centre Building, Tower B, 6th Floor, #651, 380 Wellington St., London ON N6A 5B5
Tel: 519-286-0801
Toll-Free: 888-527-8999

Nanaimo
Oceanview Executive Centre, #203, 335 Wesley St., Nanaimo BC V9R 2T5
Tel: 250-741-8558
Toll-Free: 888-527-8999

Ottawa
#514, 130 Albert St., Ottawa ON K1P 5G4
Tel: 613-234-0505
Toll-Free: 888-527-8999

Port Coquitlam
Tri-City Business Centre, #2300, 2850 Shaughnessy St., Port Coquitlam BC V3C 6K5
Tel: 604-527-8999; *Fax:* 604-527-8008
Toll-Free: 888-527-8999

Regina
Broad Street Business Centre, #322, 845 Broad St., Regina SK S4R 8G9
Tel: 306-525-6999
Toll-Free: 888-527-8999

Surrey - Guildford
#201, 15399 - 102A Ave., Surrey BC V3R 7K1
Tel: 604-527-8999; *Fax:* 604-527-8008
Toll-Free: 888-527-8999

Toronto
#700, 2 Bloor St. West, Toronto ON M4W 3R1
Tel: 647-776-0485
Toll-Free: 888-527-8999

Vancouver
#495, 1140 West Pender St., Vancouver BC V6E 4G1
Tel: 604-527-8999; *Fax:* 604-527-8008
Toll-Free: 888-527-8999

Victoria
Cook Medical Building, #214, 1175 Cook St., Victoria BC V8V 4A1
Tel: 250-382-9559
Toll-Free: 888-527-8999

Winnipeg
Power Building, #611, 428 Portage Ave., Winnipeg MB R3C 0E2
Tel: 204-942-8789
Toll-Free: 888-527-8999

Credit Counselling Thames Valley; Family Service London *See* Family Service Thames Valley

Credit Institute of Canada (CIC) / L'Institut canadien du crédit

219 Dufferin St., #216C, Toronto ON M6K 3J1
Tel: 416-572-2615; *Fax:* 416-572-2619
Toll-Free: 888-447-3324
geninfo@creditedu.org
www.creditedu.org
www.linkedin.com/groups/Credit-Collections-Management-Professionals-23
www.facebook.com/creditedu
twitter.com/creditinstitute
www.youtube.com/user/creditinstitute
Previous Name: Canadian Institute of Credit & Financial Management
Overview: A medium-sized national charitable organization founded in 1928
Mission: To provide credit education for credit & financial professionals in Canada
Chief Officer(s):
Mike MacPhee, Chair, President, & Dean
Reggie Delovitch, General Manager
rdelovitch@creditedu.org
Nawshad Khadaroo, Senior Manager, Operations & Certification
mgredu@creditedu.org
George Brown, Treasurer
Hélène Dorciné, Coordinator, Membership
hdorcine@creditedu.org
Finances: *Funding Sources:* Membership fees; CIC Store
Staff Member(s): 8
Membership: *Fees:* $150; *Member Profile:* Credit & financial professionals; *Committees:* Audit
Activities: Offering credit & financial management training; Providing credit management resources; Granting designations in credit management, such as CCP (formerly FCI) & ACI; Awarding academic achievements through a national awards program; Offering networking opportunities; Providing the Credit Institute Employment Referral Program; Monitoring & reacting to legislative issues relevant to the industry; *Library:* Credit Reference Library; by appointment
Publications:
• Bankruptcy & Insolvency Act - A Creditor's Perspective
Price: $45 + GST members; $55 + GSTnon-members
Profile: Topics include an overview of the Bankruptcy & Insolvency Act, effects of bankruptcy on creditors, & effects of bankruptcy on debtors
• Credit Institute of Canada Handbook, Volume 1
Type: Handbook; *Price:* $149 + GST members; $169+ GST non-members
Profile: Topics include credit investigations, financial statement analysis, securities, bankruptcy & insolvency, & credit department organization & reporting
• Credit Institute of Canada Handbook, Volume 2
Type: Handbook; *Price:* $149 + GST members; $169 + GST non-members
Profile: Topics include international credit management, credit fraud, & an introduction to e-commerce
• Credit Institute of Canada Membership Directory
Type: Directory
Profile: A listing of current members by individual & company name
• Credit Institute of Canada Student Handbook
Type: Yearbook; *Frequency:* Annually
• To Your Credit
Type: Newsletter; *Frequency:* Quarterly
Profile: Available to members

Atlantic Chapter
e-mail: atlantic@creditedu.org
atlantic.creditedu.org
Chief Officer(s):
Roger McCaie, President
mccaie.roger@midlandtransport.com

British Columbia Chapter
#79, 16995 - 64th Ave., Cloverdale BC V3S 0V9
Tel: 604-576-7611; *Fax:* 604-576-7612
info@cicbcchapter.org
cicbcchapter.org
Chief Officer(s):
Laureen Carroll, President

Calgary Chapter
PO Box 4651, Calgary AB T2T 5P1
e-mail: calgary@creditedu.org
calgary.creditedu.org
Chief Officer(s):
Ken Spurr, President, 403-291-1013 Ext. 231
kspurr@shoemakerdrywall.com

Conestoga Chapter
Conestoga ON
e-mail: conestoga@creditedu.org
conestoga.creditedu.org
Chief Officer(s):
Wilma Potter, President, 905-595-3234
wpotter@colortech.com

Edmonton Chapter
Edmonton AB
e-mail: edmonton@creditedu.org
edmonton.creditedu.org
Chief Officer(s):
David Hopkyns, President, 888-797-7727 Ext. 2380, Fax: 877-425-1522
dhopkyns@metcredit.com

Hamilton & District Chapter
1239 Baldwin Dr., Oakville ON L6J 2W4
e-mail: cichamilton@gmail.com
hamilton.creditedu.org
Chief Officer(s):
Frank Morson, President, 905-816-5156, Fax: 905-819-7358
fmorson@russelmetals.com

Manitoba Chapter
PO Box 476, Winnipeg MB R3C 2J3
e-mail: manitoba@creditedu.org
manitoba.creditedu.org
Chief Officer(s):
Debbie Baines, President
debbie.baines@standardaero.com

Montréal/Québec City Chapter
CP 285, Kirkland QC H9H 0A4
Téléc: 450-373-3309
Ligne sans frais: 866-990-8533
icc.mtl@sympathico.ca
www.creditedu.org/chapters/chapters/montreal_quebec/index.html
Chief Officer(s):
Carole Boutin, Président, 514-281-5392, Fax: 514-381-3775
c.boutin@corwik.com

Ottawa Chapter
Ottawa ON
e-mail: ottawa@creditedu.org
ottawa.creditedu.org

Saskatchewan Chapter
PO Box 7884, Saskatoon SK S7K 4R6
Tel: 306-931-9682
cicsaskchapter@sasktel.net
creditedu.org
Chief Officer(s):
Geri Meyer, President
geri@chfsask.ca

South Western Ontario Chapter
ON
e-mail: swo@creditedu.org
swo.creditedu.org
Chief Officer(s):
Christine Chase, President, 519-681-3264 Ext. 111, Fax: 519-658-1204
christine_chase@ryder.com

Toronto Chapter
13 Mullord Ave., Ajax ON L1Z 1K7
Tel: 905-426-7929; *Fax:* 905-426-2344
toronto@creditedu.org
www.cictoronto.org

Chief Officer(s):
Gail Maguire, President
gail.maguire@kellogg.com
Erin Marcelino, Executive Administrator

Credit Union Central of Alberta ***See*** Alberta Central

Credit Union Central of British Columbia ***See*** Central 1 Credit Union

Credit Union Central of Canada (CUCC) / La Centrale des caisses de crédit du Canada

Corporate Office, #1000, 151 Yonge St., Toronto ON M5C 2W7
Tel: 416-232-1262; *Fax:* 416-232-9196
Toll-Free: 800-649-0222
Other Communication: conferences@cucentral.com
inquiries@cucentral.com
www.cucentral.ca
www.linkedin.com/company/credit-union-central-of-canada
www.facebook.com/CanadianCentral
twitter.com/CanadianCentral
Also Known As: Canadian Central
Previous Name: Canadian Cooperative Credit Society
Overview: A large national organization founded in 1953
Mission: To act as the national voice for the Canadian credit union system; To facilitate the national cooperative movement; To provide services to ensure best practices are met at all credit unions; To develop opportunities for cooperative growth
Affliation(s): Concentra Financial Services Association
Chief Officer(s):
Daniel Burns, Chair
David Phillips, President & CEO
Cheryl Byrne, Vice-President, Knowledge Services
Stephen Fitzpatrick, Vice-President & CFO, Corporate Services
Brigitte Goulard, Vice-President, Policy
Brenda O'Connor, Vice-President, General Counsel & Corporate Secretary
Gary Rogers, Vice-President, Financial Policy
Staff Member(s): 46
Membership: 8 provincial credit union centrals + 1 federation of caisses populaires; *Member Profile:* Provincial credit union centrals; Federation of caisses populaires; *Committees:* Canadian central Board of Directors; Business Issues; Credit Union Social Responsibility; National Lenders; Legislative Affairs; Finance Policy; National Young Leaders; Risk Management Policy; CUSOURCE Board of Directors; Cooperative EFT Development Association; Cooperative Network Services; Research Advisory Council
Activities: Providing liquidity for the Canadian system; Establishing the National Mentorship Program, to match employees in senior positions with high potential employees
Awards:
• Community Economic Development Award (Award)
Meetings/Conferences: • Credit Union Central of Canada 2015 National Lending Conference, 2015
Scope: National
Contact Information: Credit Union Central of Canada Communications Department Contact: Edith Wilkinson, Phone: 416-232-3421, Fax: 416-232-3734, E-mail: wilkinsone@cucentral.com
• Credit Union Central of Canada 2015 Annual General Meeting & Canadian Conference for Credit Union Leaders, May, 2015, Banff, AB
Scope: National
Contact Information: Credit Union Central of Canada Communications Department Contact: Edith Wilkinson, Phone: 416-232-3421, Fax: 416-232-3734, E-mail: wilkinsone@cucentral.com
Publications:
• Atlantic Focus [a publication of the Credit Union Central of Canada]
Type: Newsletter
• Canadian Central Annual Report
Type: Yearbook; *Frequency:* Annually
• National System Results [a publication of the Credit Union Central of Canada]
Type: Report; *Frequency:* Quarterly
Profile: Financial information from the Canadian credit union system

Credit Union Central of Manitoba (CUCM)

#400, 317 Donald St., Winnipeg MB R3B 2H6
Tel: 204-985-4700; *Fax:* 204-949-0217
cuinfo@cucm.org
www.creditunion.mb.ca
Overview: A small provincial organization overseen by Credit Union Central of Canada
Mission: To act as the trade association for credit unions in Manitoba; To represent Manitoba's fifty-five credit unions
Member of: Credit Union Central of Canada
Chief Officer(s):
Garth Manness, Chief Executive Officer
John Hamilton, Manager, Knowledge Services & Communications
Activities: Engaging in advocacy activities; Providing services, such as product & service research & development, consulting, banking services, & financial & capital management
Meetings/Conferences: • Credit Union Central of Manitoba - Conference and AGM 2015, March, 2015, Brandon, MB
Scope: Provincial
Publications:
• Credit Union Central of Manitoba Annual Report
Type: Yearbook; *Frequency:* Annually

Credit Union Central of Newfoundland & Labrador ***See*** Newfoundland & Labrador Credit Union

Credit Union Central of Nova Scotia; Credit Union Central of New Brunswick; Credit Union Central of Prince Edward Island ***See*** Credit Unions Atlantic Canada

Credit Union Central of Ontario; Ontario Credit Union League Ltd. ***See*** Central 1 Credit Union

Credit Unions Atlantic Canada

PO Box 9200, 6074 Lady Hammond Rd., Halifax NS B3K 5N3
Tel: 902-453-0680; *Fax:* 902-455-2437
Toll-Free: 800-668-2879
atlanticcreditunions.ca
twitter.com/AtlCreditUnions
Also Known As: Atlantic Credit Unions; Atlantic Central
Previous Name: Credit Union Central of Nova Scotia; Credit Union Central of New Brunswick; Credit Union Central of Prince Edward Island
Overview: A small provincial organization founded in 1934 overseen by Credit Union Central of Canada
Mission: To represent & support the credit unions of Nova Scotia, New Brunswick, Newfoundland & Labrador, & Prince Edward Island; To manage the system's liquidity reserve requirements
Member of: Credit Union Central of Canada
Chief Officer(s):
Michael Leonard, President & CEO
Sharon Arnold, CCO & Senior Vice-President, Finance
Victoria Mainprize, Corporate Secretary & Vice-President, Corporate Service
Activities: Providing financial services, such as investment banking services; offering trade association & support services, such as human resources, legal advice, consulting, & provincial marketing & communication; raising awareness of the work of credit unions; *Awareness Events:* Credit Union Day, October
Publications:
• Credit Union Central of Nova Scotia Yearbook
Type: Yearbook; *Frequency:* Annually

Charlottetown Office
281 University Ave., Charlottetown PE C1A 7M4
Tel: 902-566-3350; *Fax:* 902-368-3534
Toll-Free: 800-668-2879

Riverview Office
663 Pinewood Rd., Riverview NB E1B 5R6
Tel: 506-857-8184; *Fax:* 506-857-9431
Toll-Free: 800-332-3320

Credit Valley Conservation Foundation

1255 Old Derry Rd. West, Mississauga ON L5N 6R4
Tel: 905-670-1615; *Fax:* 905-670-2210
Toll-Free: 800-668-5557
cvc@creditvalleyca.ca
www.creditvalleyca.ca
www.facebook.com/creditvalleyconservation
twitter.com/cvc_ca
www.youtube.com/user/CreditValleyCA;
www.flickr.com/photos/cvca
Overview: A small local organization founded in 1954
Mission: To raise funds & awareness in support of Credit Valley Conservation's goal of an environmentally healthy river for economically & socially healthy communities
Chief Officer(s):
Pat Mullin, Chair, 905-896-5200
Lou Maieron, Vice-Chair
Finances: *Funding Sources:* 67% from member municipalities; 20% generated by Credit Valley Conservation Foundation
Activities: Publishing a coffee table book; raising funds for the development of the Elora Cataract Trailway & Glassford Arboretum Trail; provides an annual bursary to a student at the University of Guelph & University of Toronto (Erindale); *Library:* Resource Library
Publications:
• Credit Cascades [a publication of the Credit Valley Conservation Foundation]
Frequency: Quarterly
Profile: Updates on work being done by the CVC.
• Currents [a publication of the Credit Valley Conservation Foundation]
Frequency: s-a.
Profile: A means of connecting the public to the Credit River Watershed.
• The Source [a publication of the Credit Valley Conservation Foundation]
Frequency: Monthly
Profile: Credit River Watershed news, profiles, tips, & opportunities.

Creelman Agricultural Society

PO Box 46, Creelman SK S0G 0X0
Tel: 306-722-3735; *Fax:* 306-722-3740
CreelmanKid@gmail.com
www.creelmanagsociety.ca
www.facebook.com/CreelmanAgSociety
Overview: A small local organization
Mission: To improve agriculture & the quality of life in the community by educating members & the community; To provide a community forum for discussion of agricultural issues; To encourage conservation of natural resources
Member of: Saskatchewan Association of Agricultural Societies & Exhibitions
Chief Officer(s):
Christine Procyk, Secretary
cmprocyk@yahoo.ca
Activities: *Awareness Events:* Creelman Fair, July

Cree-Naskapi Commission / La Commission Crie-Naskapie

#305, 222 Queen St., Ottawa ON K1P 5V9
Tel: 613-234-4288; *Fax:* 613-234-8102
Toll-Free: 888-236-6603
www.creenaskapicommission.net
Overview: A small local organization founded in 1984
Mission: To monitor the implementation of the Cree-Naskapi (of Quebec) Act.
Chief Officer(s):
Richard Saunders, Chair
saunders1943@sympatico.ca
Brian Shawana, Director General
brian@creenaskapicommission.net
Staff Member(s): 5
Activities: *Library* by appointment

Cremona Water Valley & District Chamber of Commerce

PO Box 356, Cremona AB T0M 0R0
Tel: 403-637-2030
info@cremonawatervalley.com
www.cremonawatervalley.com
www.facebook.com/CremonaWaterValley
Overview: A small local organization
Member of: Alberta chambers Commerce
Chief Officer(s):
Linda Newsome, President
Membership: 9

Crescent Beach ***See*** Association of Neighbourhood Houses BC

Cresteramics Society for the Handicapped

PO Box 927, 921 Railway Blvd., Creston BC V0B 1G0
Tel: 250-428-7412; *Fax:* 250-428-7489
cceramic@telus.net
crestonvalley.com/cresteramics
Overview: A small provincial charitable organization founded in 1974
Mission: To provide opportunities for developmentally challenged youths & adults to produce ceramics as a viable business
Member of: Kootenay Society for Community Living; BC Association for Community Living
Chief Officer(s):
Beth Kastelan, President
Donna McCready, Executive Director
Finances: *Annual Operating Budget:* $250,000-$500,000
Membership: 60

Activities: Summer program; supported work program

Creston & District Historical & Museum Society (CDHMS)
219 Devon St., Creston BC V0B 1G3
Tel: 250-428-9262; *Fax:* 250-428-9262
mail@creston.museum.bc.ca
www.creston.museum.bc.ca
www.facebook.com/CrestonMuseum
twitter.com/CrestonMuseum
Also Known As: Creston Museum
Overview: A small local charitable organization founded in 1971
Mission: To collect, preserve & exhibit the human & natural history of the Creston Valley for the education & entertainment of the local & visiting public
Member of: British Columbia Museums Association; Archives Association of BC; Creston Chamber of Commerce; Community of Creston Arts Council
Chief Officer(s):
Ian Currie, President
Finances: *Funding Sources:* Rental fees; tax money; admission revenues
Membership: *Fees:* $10 individual; $25 family; $100 patron
Activities: Guided tours; special exhibits; school programs; public outreach programs; research facilities; special events; *Library:* Creston Archives; Open to public

Creston Valley Chamber of Commerce
PO Box 268, 121 Northwest Blvd. (Hwy. 3), Creston BC V0B 1G0
Tel: 250-428-4342; *Fax:* 250-428-9411
Toll-Free: 866-528-4342
info@crestonvalleychamber.com
www.crestonvalleychamber.com
Overview: A small provincial organization founded in 1910
Mission: To be a catalyst for sustainable economic growth by providing education, networking & advocacy to government
Member of: BC Chamber of Commerce; Canadian Chamber of Commerce; International Selkirk Loop
Chief Officer(s):
Rob Schepers, President, 250-428-9388
Finances: *Annual Operating Budget:* $50,000-$100,000; *Funding Sources:* Town of Creston; Regional District; fundraising; membership fees
Staff Member(s): 1; 5 volunteer(s)
Membership: 200; *Fees:* $115-$400; *Committees:* Membership; Promotional Services; Tourism; Natural Resources
Activities: *Library:* Business Information Resource Desk

Creston Valley Prospectors & Lapidary Club
c/o 1114 Adler St., RR#4, Creston BC V0B 1G4
Tel: 250-428-5061
Overview: A small local organization
Affliation(s): British Columbia Lapidary Society; Gem & Mineral Federation of Canada
Chief Officer(s):
Gerry Rehwald, Contact, 250-428-0236
rehwaldg@telus.net
Membership: *Member Profile:* Persons in the Creston Vally area of British Columbia who are interested in collecting & polishing rocks & stones to make jewelry
Activities: Hosting monthly meetings; Offering summer camps; Teaching lapidary

La Crete & Area Chamber of Commerce
PO Box 1088, 10406 - 100 St., La Crete AB T0H 2H0
Tel: 780-928-2278; *Fax:* 780-928-2234
admin@lacretechamber.com
lacretechamber.com
www.facebook.com/190321804359596
twitter.com/LaCreteChamber
Overview: A small local charitable organization
Mission: The Chamber will be the organization of choice committed to the growth of business & enhancement of social, cultural & educational standards which contribute to the economic prosperity & quality of life to La Crete & area
Chief Officer(s):
Larry Neufeld, Manager
Finances: *Annual Operating Budget:* $50,000-$100,000; *Funding Sources:* Membership fees; Fund raising; Municipality
Staff Member(s): 3
Membership: 119; *Fees:* $35 individual; *Member Profile:* Business
Activities: Spring Trade Show; Monthly membership meeting 1st Monday of each month; *Library* Open to public

Cricket Alberta (ACA)
#203, 1528 - 16 Ave. SW, Calgary AB T3C 0Z8
Tel: 403-775-7206
acacricket@gmail.com
www.cricketalberta.com
www.facebook.com/155440747942009
twitter.com/CricketAlberta
Previous Name: Alberta Cricket Association
Overview: A small provincial organization founded in 1975 overseen by Cricket Canada
Member of: Cricket Canada
Chief Officer(s):
Chris James, President
csnjames@gmail.com
Finances: *Annual Operating Budget:* $50,000-$100,000; *Funding Sources:* Government; casino; membership fees
30 volunteer(s)
Membership: 500; *Fees:* $500 team; *Member Profile:* 10 to 55 years of age; *Committees:* Executive; By-Laws; Juniors
Activities: Competitions; school cricket; coaching; training camps

Cricket Canada
#301, 3 Concorde Gate, Toronto ON M3C 3N7
Tel: 416-426-7209
cricketcanada@gmail.com
www.gocricketgocanada.com
www.facebook.com/GoCricketCanada
twitter.com/canadiancricket
Also Known As: Canadian Cricket Association
Overview: A large national organization founded in 1892
Mission: To foster growth & development of cricket in Canada
Affliation(s): International Cricket Council; Kanga Ball Canada
Chief Officer(s):
Ravin Moorthy, President
Finances: *Funding Sources:* Ministry of Heritage; International Cricket Council Volunteer Donations
130 volunteer(s)
Membership: 30 senior/lifetime + 400 teams + 15,500 players; *Fees:* $85 per team
Activities: *Internships:* Yes; *Speaker Service:* Yes

Cricket Council of Ontario (CCO)
PO Box 55227, Stn. PM, 1800 Sheppard Ave. East, Toronto ON M2J 5B9
Tel: 416-602-8163
www.cricketcouncilofontario.ca
www.facebook.com/CricketOntario
Previous Name: Ontario Cricket Association Inc.
Overview: A medium-sized provincial organization founded in 2009 overseen by Cricket Canada
Mission: To be the provincial governing body of the sport of cricket in Ontario.
Member of: Cricket Canada
Chief Officer(s):
Leslie Soobrian, President
Nasser Khan, General Secretary
Rudy Lochan, Assistant Secretary-Treasurer
anava@rogers.com
Membership: 9 associations/leagues
Activities: *Rents Mailing List:* Yes

Cricket New Brunswick (CNB)
NB
cricketnb.org
www.facebook.com/CNB.Fredericton
Also Known As: Cricket NB
Previous Name: New Brunswick Cricket Association
Overview: A small provincial organization overseen by Cricket Canada
Mission: To facilitate the development & growth of the sport of cricket; To establish cricket as a competitive sport in New Brunswick; To promote participation in schools
Member of: Cricket Canada
Chief Officer(s):
Dunu Eliaba, President
dunu@cricketnb.org
Krista Steeves, General Secretary
6 volunteer(s)
Membership: 1-99; *Fees:* $75 full
Activities: Awareness lessons; Cricket camps

The Crime Writers of Canada (CWC)
#4C, 240 Westwood Rd., Geulph ON N1H 7W9
e-mail: info@crimewriterscanada.com
www.crimewriterscanada.com
Overview: A small national organization founded in 1982
Mission: To promote Canadian crime writing
Chief Officer(s):
Vicki Delany, Chair
Finances: *Funding Sources:* Membership fees; grant from Canadian Heritage; sponsorships by Canadian publishers
Membership: *Fees:* $85 associate; $125 professional; *Member Profile:* Authors of crime fiction, true crime & genre/reference criticism & promoters thereof: agents, editors, publishers, specialty booksellers & teachers of post-secondary courses on the genre
Activities: *Speaker Service:* Yes
Awards:
• The Arthur Ellis Awards (Award)
Established 1984; awarded annually in the following categories: best crime novel (by a previously published novelist), best crime non-fiction, best first crime novel (by a previously unpublished novelist), best crime short story, best juvenile crime book, & best crime writing in French

Criminal Lawyers' Association (CLA)
#1, 189 Queen St. East, Toronto ON M5A 1S2
Tel: 416-214-9875; *Fax:* 416-968-6818
www.criminallawyers.ca
Overview: A medium-sized national organization founded in 1971
Mission: To be the voice for criminal justice & civil liberties in Canada
Affliation(s): US National Association of Criminal Defence Lawyers; The Canadian Counsel of Criminal Defence Lawyers (CCCDL); The County & District Law President's Association (CDLPA)
Chief Officer(s):
Anthony Laycock, Executive Director
anthony@criminallawyers.ca
Norm Boxall, President
Membership: 1,000+; *Member Profile:* Criminal law practitioners
Activities: Advising all levels of government & the judiciary on issues relating to legislation & the administration of criminal justice; Assisting members in practice of criminal litigation; Developing continuing education programs for criminal law practitioners; Hosting an annual criminal defence law conference
Awards:
• G. Arthur Martin Criminal Justice Medal (Award)
For an outstanding contribution to criminal justice

Crisis Centre North Bay
PO Box 1407, North Bay ON P1B 8K6
Tel: 705-472-6204; *Fax:* 705-472-6236
info@crisiscentre-nb.on.ca
www.crisiscentre-nb.on.ca
Overview: A small local charitable organization founded in 1972 overseen by Distress Centres Ontario
Mission: To help people in crises by providing temporary room & board as well as rehabilitation services
Staff Member(s): 70

Crohn's & Colitis Canada / Crohn's et Colitis Canada
#600, 60 St. Clair Ave. East, Toronto ON M4T 1N5
Tel: 416-920-5035; *Fax:* 416-929-0364
Toll-Free: 800-387-1479
support@crohnsandcolitis.ca
www.crohnsandcolitis.ca
www.facebook.com/crohnsandcolitis.ca
twitter.com/getgutsyCanada
www.youtube.com/user/getgutsy
Previous Name: Crohn's & Colitis Foundation of Canada; Canadian Foundation for Ileitis & Colitis
Overview: A medium-sized national charitable organization founded in 1974
Mission: To find a cure for Crohn's disease & ulcerative colitis; To raise funds for medical research; To educate individuals with inflammatory bowel disease, their families, health professionals, & the public
Chief Officer(s):
Lindee David, CEO
Har Grover, Chair
Mark Ram, Secretary
Byron Sonberg, Treasurer
Activities: *Awareness Events:* M&M Meat Shops Charity BBQ Day, May; Gutsy Walk, June; All That Glitters Gala, November

Alberta/NWT Region
#3100, 246 Stewart Green SW, Calgary AB T3H 3C8
Tel: 403-569-8477; *Fax:* 403-569-1552
Toll-Free: 888-884-2232
canderson@ccfc.ca
Chief Officer(s):

Paul Evered, Executive Director, WeEstern ReEgion
Atlantic Canada Region
PO Box 173, Lower Sackville NS B4C 2S9
Tel: 902-422-8137; *Fax:* 902-422-6552
Toll-Free: 800-265-1101
atlanticcanada@ccfc.ca
Chief Officer(s):
Tracy Durkee-Jones, Regional Director
British Columbia/Yukon Region
Nordel Mall, PO Box 33060, 33398 - 84 Ave., Delta BC V4C 8E6
Tel: 604-230-6650; *Fax:* 604-596-3187
britishcolumbia@ccfc.ca
Chief Officer(s):
Paul Evered, Executive Director, Western Canada
pevered@ccfc.ca
Bureau du Québec
#420, 1980, rue Sherbrooke Ouest, Montréal QC H3H 1E8
Tél: 514-342-0666; *Téléc:* 514-342-1011
Ligne sans frais: 800-461-4683
quebec@ccfc.ca
Chief Officer(s):
Edna Mendelson, Directrice régionale
emendelson@ccfc.ca
Manitoba/Saskatchewan Region
600-60 St. Clair Ave. East, Toronto ON M4T 1N5
Tel: 416-920-5035; *Fax:* 416-929-0364
Toll-Free: 800-387-1479
ccfc@ccfc.ca
www.ccfc.ca
twitter.com/isupportibd
Chief Officer(s):
Rea Ganesh, Regional Director
rganesh@ccfc.ca
Ontario Region
#600, 60 St. Clair Ave. East, Toronto ON M4T 1N5
Tel: 416-920-5035; *Fax:* 416-929-0364
Toll-Free: 800-387-1479
admin_ontario@ccfc.ca
Chief Officer(s):
Rea Ganesh, Executive Director
rganesh@ccfc.ca

Crohn's & Colitis Foundation of Canada; Canadian Foundation for Ileitis & Colitis *See* Crohn's & Colitis Canada

Crohn's et Colitis Canada *See* Crohn's & Colitis Canada

Crop Protection Institute of Canada *See* CropLife Canada

CropLife Canada
#612, 350 Sparks St., Ottawa ON K1R 7S8
Tel: 613-230-9881
www.croplife.ca
twitter.com/croplifecanada
www.youtube.com/croplifecanada
Previous Name: Crop Protection Institute of Canada
Overview: A medium-sized national organization founded in 1952
Mission: To represent Canada's plant science industry; To foster the developmment of the industry; To build Canadians' trust & appreciation for plant science innovations
Member of: CropLife International
Chief Officer(s):
Lorne Hepworth, President, 613-230-9881 Ext. 3225
hepworth@croplife.ca
Maria Trainer, Managing Director, Regulatory Affairs
trainer@croplife.ca
Nadine Sisk, Vice President, Communications & Member Services
siskn@croplife.ca
Russel Hurst, Executive Director, Stewardship & Sustainability
hurstr@croplife.ca
Annie Hau, Vice-President, Finance & Administration
hsua@croplife.ca
Pierre Petelle, Vice-President, Chemistry
petellep@croplife.ca
Dennis Prouse, Vice-President, Government Affairs
proused@croplife.ca
Janice Tranberg, Vice-President, Western Canada, 306-373-4052
tranbergj@croplife.ca
Finances: *Funding Sources:* Sponsorships
Staff Member(s): 16
Membership: 36; *Member Profile:* Developers, manufacturers, & distributors of plant science innovations
Activities: Conducting research; Promoting the code of conduct
Meetings/Conferences: • GrowCanada Conference 2015, 2015
Scope: National
Description: Provides a platform to connect with industry leaders from across the country, explore cutting edge insight and build a stronger and more vibrant Canadian agricultural sector that ultimately contributes to a better world.
Contact Information: URL: www.growcanadaconference.ca

Croquet Canada
24 Deloraine Ave., Toronto ON M5M 2A7
e-mail: croquet@sympatico.ca
www.croquet.ca
Overview: A large national organization
Mission: To promote & develop croquet in Canada
Chief Officer(s):
Paul Emmett, President, 416-225-7535
pemmett@sympatico.ca
Membership: *Fees:* $20; *Committees:* Handicap; Selection; CroqCan

Cross Country Alberta (CCA)
Percy Page Centre, 11759 Groat Rd., Edmonton AB T5M 3K6
Tel: 780-415-1738; *Fax:* 780-427-0524
manager@xcountryab.net
www.xcountryab.net
www.facebook.com/CrossCountryAlberta
twitter.com/xcountryab
Overview: A medium-sized provincial organization overseen by Cross Country Canada
Mission: To lead, develop, & promote the sport of cross-country skiing througout Alberta
Member of: Cross Country Canada
Chief Officer(s):
Les Parsons, Chair
chairperson@xcountryab.net
Michael Neary, Manager, Sport
Staff Member(s): 2
Membership: 3,890; *Fees:* $55 club; $10 adult; $5 teen; $3 child
Activities: Quality service; leadership & skier development; management & education

Cross Country British Columbia (CCBC)
#106, 3003 - 30th St., Vernon BC V1T 9J5
Tel: 250-545-9600; *Fax:* 250-545-9614
office@crosscountrybc.ca
www.crosscountrybc.ca
Also Known As: Cross Country BC
Overview: A small provincial organization overseen by Cross Country Canada
Mission: The association is the governing body for the sport of cross country skiing in BC.
Member of: Cross Country Canada
Membership: 14,000

Cross Country Canada (CCC) / Ski de fond Canada (SFC)
c/o Bill Warren Training Centre, #100, 1995 Olympic Way, Canmore AB T1W 2T6
Tel: 403-678-6791; *Fax:* 403-678-3885
Toll-Free: 877-609-3215
info@cccski.com
www.cccski.com
www.facebook.com/138553616175807
twitter.com/cccski
www.flickr.com/photos/cccski
Overview: A medium-sized national charitable organization
Mission: To develop & deliver programs designed to achieve international excellence in cross-country skiing; to provide national programs for continuous development of cross-country skiing from introductory experience to international excellence, for participants of all ages & abilities, fostering the principles of ethical conduct & fair play
Member of: True Sport
Affliation(s): Canadian Ski & Snowboard Association
Chief Officer(s):
Richard Lemoine, President, 416-464-5875
rlemoine@lhgroup.com
Davin MacIntosh, Executive Director
dmacintosh@cccski.com
Cathy Sturgeon, Director, Administration & Communication
csturgeon@cccski.com
Kyle Seeley, Contact, Nunavut
kseeley@gov.nu.ca
Finances: *Annual Operating Budget:* $500,000-$1.5 Million
Staff Member(s): 25
Membership: 55,000; *Committees:* Marketing; Women's; Events; High Performance; Coach & Athlete Development; Fundraising; Para-Nordic
Activities: *Internships:* Yes
Awards:
• Dave Rees Award (Award)
• The Firth Award (Award)
• Volunteer of the Year (Award)
• Sponsor of the Year (Award)
• Media Award (Award)
• Sofie Manarin Award (Award)
• Ski to School Scholarship (Scholarship)

Cross Country New Brunswick / Ski de fond Nouveau-Brunswick
1450 Maria St., Bathurst NB E2A 3G2
Tel: 506-542-2617; *Fax:* 506-542-2638
skis@nbnet.nb.ca
www.xcski-nb.ca
Overview: A medium-sized provincial organization overseen by Cross Country Canada
Mission: To promote cross country skiing among the general population of New Brunswick; To provide a sense of leadership; To offer a variety of programs & services
Member of: Cross Country Canada
Chief Officer(s):
Dave Moore, Chair
moored@bellaliant.net
Linda LeClair, Treasurer, 506-826-1939
marline@nb.sympatico.ca
Marie-Eve Cyr, Liaison, 506-548-5707

Cross Country Newfoundland & Labrador
c/o Gerry Rideout, 301 Curtis Cres., Labrador City NL A2V 2B8
Tel: 709-944-5842
www.crosscountrynl.com
Overview: A medium-sized provincial organization overseen by Cross Country Canada
Chief Officer(s):
Gerry Rideout, President
rideoutg@crrstv.net

Cross Country Northwest Territories *See* Northwest Territories Ski Division

Cross Country Nova Scotia; Nordic Ski Nova Scotia *See* Cross Country Ski Nova Scotia

Cross Country Ontario (CCO)
738 River St., Thunder Bay ON P7A 3S8
Tel: 807-768-4617
admin@xco.org
www.xco.org
Overview: A medium-sized provincial organization overseen by Cross Country Canada
Mission: To govern the sport of cross country skiing in Ontario.
Member of: Cross Country Canada
Chief Officer(s):
Don Nixon, Chair
chair@xco.org
Liz Inkila, Director, Administration
admin@xco.org
Al White, Director, Technical
Alanwhite2001@rogers.com
Pavlina Sudrich, Ontario Coach, High Performance Committee
coachpav@xco.org
Meetings/Conferences: • Cross Country Ontario 2015 Annual General Meeting, 2015, ON
Scope: Provincial
Description: Board meetings are held each month by telephone, & the annual general meeting takes place each May
Contact Information: Administrative Director: Liz Inkila, E-mail: admin@xco.org

Cross Country PEI
PO Box 532, Souris PE C0A 2B0
Overview: A small provincial organization overseen by Cross Country Canada
Mission: The association is the governing body for the sport of cross country skiing in PEI.
Member of: Cross Country Canada
Chief Officer(s):
Steve O'Brien, Contact
srobrien@eastlink.ca

Cross Country Saskatchewan (CCS)
1860 Lorne St., Regina SK S4P 2L7

Curling Québec
4545, av Pierre-de Coubertin, Montréal QC H1V 0B2
Tél: 514-252-3088; *Téléc:* 514-252-3342
Ligne sans frais: 888-292-2875
info@curling-quebec.qc.ca
www.curling-quebec.qc.ca
www.facebook.com/pages/Curling-Québec/122740094410707
twitter.com/curlingquebec
Également appelé: Fédération québécoise de curling
Aperçu: *Dimension:* moyenne; *Envergure:* provinciale; Organisme sans but lucratif; fondée en 1976 surveillé par Canadian Curling Association
Mission: Offrir aux amateurs de curling, et à tous ceux désirant le devenir, la possibilité de jouer au curling à l'intérieur d'une structure organisée appuyée par divers services
Membre de: Fédération mondiale de curling
Membre(s) du bureau directeur:
Marco Berthelot, Directeur général
mferraro@curling-quebec.qc.ca
Membre: 10 000; *Comités:* Excellence; Championnats; Junior

CurlManitoba Inc.
#309, 145 Pacific Ave., Winnipeg MB R3B 2Z6
Tel: 204-925-5723; *Fax:* 204-925-5720
mca@curlmanitoba.org
www.curlmanitoba.org
www.facebook.com/323935420031
twitter.com/curlmanitoba
Merged from: Manitoba Ladies Curling Association
Overview: A medium-sized provincial organization founded in 2000 overseen by Canadian Curling Association
Mission: To promote the sport of curling in Manitoba.
Affliation(s): Canadian Curling Association
Chief Officer(s):
Craig Baker, Executive Director
cbaker@curlmanitoba.org
Rob Van Kommer, President
president@curlmanitoba.org
Staff Member(s): 7
Membership: *Fees:* Schedule available; *Committees:* Finance; Board Development; Executive
Activities: Learn to curl clinics; coaching courses; ice technician courses; business of curling courses; club ice & rock consultation; game promotion; competition organization; establishment & governance of competition rules & regulations
Awards:
• Outstanding Achievements (Award)
• Scholarships (Scholarship)
• Honourary Life Memberships (Award)

Curriculum Services Canada (CSC) / Service des programmes d'études Canada
#1450, 439 University Ave., Toronto ON M5G 1Y8
Tel: 416-591-1576; *Fax:* 416-591-1578
Toll-Free: 800-837-3048
csc@curriculum.org
www.curriculum.org
www.facebook.com/pages/Curriculum-Services-Canada/141397422559967
twitter.com/CSCorganization
Overview: A medium-sized national organization
Mission: The Pan-Canadian standards agency for quality assurance in learning products and programs. It is a not-for-profit and provides services including development, implementation, evaluation, and accreditation of teaching and/or learning resources, and the delivery of web-based professional learning opportunities across Canada and internationally.
Affliation(s): The Curriculum Foundation
Chief Officer(s):
Amy Coupal, Executive Director
Ardeth Staz, Chair

The Cursillo Movement of the Archdiocese of Toronto
PO Box 70038, 10661 Chinguacousy Rd., Brampton ON L7A 0N5
Tel: 416-776-4358
cursillotoronto.com
Also Known As: Cursillo
Overview: A small local organization
Affliation(s): Archdiocese of Toronto
Chief Officer(s):
Terrance McKenna, Spiritual Director
pearsonchaplaincy@yahoo.com
Gabriel Ferdinand, Lay Director
gabriel.ferdinand@gmail.com
Activities: Three-day weekends; group reunions
Publications:
• The Fourth Day [a publication of The Cursillo Movement of the Archdiocese of Toronto]
Type: Newsletter

Cursillos in Christianity Movement of the Archdiocese of Toronto
PO Box 70038, 10661 Chinguacousy Rd., Brampton ON L7A 0N5
Tel: 416-776-4358
pearsonchaplaincy@yahoo.com
www.cursillotoronto.com
Overview: A large local charitable organization founded in 1944
Mission: To discover & understand, in a profound & intense way, God's deep love; To share this belief in the everyday environment, particularly with those who are distant from the Christian faith & the Church
Affliation(s): Archdiocese of Toronto
Chief Officer(s):
Gabriel Ferdinand, Lay Director
gabriel.ferdinand@gmail.com
Membership: 15,000; *Member Profile:* Men & women who desire to encounter themselves, Christ, & others, & to transform this encounter into friendship with Christ & others; Individuals who have first experienced a Cursillo weekend may attend any Cursillo gathering in the world
Activities: Spreading faith in all environments; Offering Linguistic Cursillo Groups (Chinese, French, Hungarian, Korean, Spanish, & Vietnamese) in the Archdiocese of Toronto; Providing faith instruction & renewal programs; Sharing prayer life & apostolic activities
Publications:
• The Fourth Day
Type: Newsletter

CUSO International
#200, 44 Eccles St., Ottawa ON K1R 6S4
Tel: 613-829-7445; *Fax:* 613-829-7996
Toll-Free: 888-434-2876
questions@cusointernational.org
www.cusointernational.org
www.facebook.com/cusovso
twitter.com/CusoIntl
www.youtube.com/cusointernational
Previous Name: CUSO-VSO; Canadian University Service Overseas
Overview: A large international charitable organization founded in 1961
Mission: To work through skilled volunteers to aid global social justice; to address poverty, human rights violations, HIV/AIDS, inequity & environmental degradation; to give Canadians information, the experiences & the tools they need to become active global citizens.
Member of: VSO International; Canadian Council for International Cooperation; Global Campaign for Education (GCE); Global Citizens for Change Coalition; Canadian Make Poverty History Campaign
Affliation(s): CJEO Youth Avenue Internationale; El Salvador Cultural Partnership; International Model Forest Partnership; Canadian Community Economic Development Network (CCEDNet); Marbek Resource Consultants
Chief Officer(s):
Derek Evans, Executive Director
derek.evans@cusointernational.org
Finances: *Annual Operating Budget:* Greater than $5 Million; *Funding Sources:* Grants; Donations; CIDA
Staff Member(s): 58; 576 volunteer(s)
Activities: Works in over 40 countries, Canada's largest volunteer-sending agency; *Internships:* Yes; *Speaker Service:* Yes

Atlantic Regional Office
#500, 1001 Sherbrooke Rd. East, Montreal QC H2L 1L3
Tel: 514-276-8528
atlanticconnect@cusointernational.org
Mission: To promote policies for developing global sustainability.

Toronto Office
#166, 215 Spadina Ave., Toronto ON M5T 2C7
Tel: 647-478-4089
outreach@cusointernational.org
Mission: To support alliances for global social justice; to work with people striving for freedom, gender & racial equality, self-determination & cultural survival; to share information, human & material resources; to promote policies for developing global sustainability.
Chief Officer(s):
Jessica Dubelaar, Public Engagement Officer

Québec Regional Office
#500, 1001 Sherbrooke St. East, Montréal QC H2L 1L3
Tel: 514-276-8528
quebecconnect@cusointernational.org
Chief Officer(s):
Christine Messier, Public Engagement Officer
christine.messier@cusointernational.org

CUSO-VSO; Canadian University Service Overseas *See* CUSO International

Customs & Immigration Union (CIU) / Syndicat des douanes et de l'immigration (SDI)
1741 Woodward Dr., Ottawa ON K2C 0P9
Tel: 613-723-8008; *Fax:* 613-723-7895
web@ciu-sdi.ca
www.ciu-sdi.ca
www.facebook.com/ciu-sdi
twitter.com/ciusdi_en
Previous Name: Customs Excise Union Douanes Accise (CEUDA)
Overview: A medium-sized national organization founded in 1968 overseen by Public Service Alliance of Canada (CLC)
Mission: To address CIU-SDI members' concerns on a timely basis
Affliation(s): Canadian Professional Police Association (CPPA); Child Find Canada; Mother Against Drunk Driving (MADD Canada); Canadian Federation of Students (CFS); Canadian American Border Trade Alliance (CABTA); Canadian Labour Congress (CLC); Canadian Manufacturers and Exporters (CME); Fédération des travailleurs et travailleuses du Québec; Federation of Canadian Municipalities (FCM); Labour College of Canada; National Treasury Employees Union (NTEU), U.S.; Public Service Alliance of Canada (PSAC)
Chief Officer(s):
Jean-Pierre Fortin, National President
Jason McMichael, First National Vice-President
Michelle Tranche-Montagne, Contact, Communications
michelle.tranchemontagne@ciu-sdi.ca
Staff Member(s): 11
Membership: *Committees:* CIU-SDI Standing Finance; By-Laws; Union/Management Relations; Component Collective Bargaining; National Occupational Safety & Health; Honours & Awards; Human Resources Working; Border Security; Joint Union/Management Employment Equity; CIU-SDI Standing Equal Opportunities; Immigration Transition Advisory
Activities: Hosting a national convention; Appearing as a witness before Parliamentary Committees, House of Commons and Senate; Conducting national lobbying campaigns

Customs Excise Union Douanes Accise (CEUDA) *See* Customs & Immigration Union

Cut Knife Chamber of Commerce
PO Box 504, Cut Knife SK S0M 0N0
Tel: 306-398-2060; *Fax:* 306-398-2062
Overview: A small local organization

Cycling Association of the Yukon
4061, 4th Ave., Whitehorse YT Y1A 1H1
Tel: 867-668-4990
Overview: A small provincial organization overseen by Cycling Canada Cyclisme
Member of: Cycling Canada Cyclisme; Sport Yukon
Chief Officer(s):
Sue Richards, President
susanlearichards@gmail.com

Cycling British Columbia (CBC)
#201, 210 West Broadway, Vancouver BC V5Y 3W2
Tel: 604-737-3034; *Fax:* 604-737-3141
membership@cyclingbc.net
cyclingbc.net
www.facebook.com/122018951154516
twitter.com/raceinbc
www.youtube.com/user/cyclingbc
Also Known As: Cycling BC
Previous Name: Bicycling Association of BC
Overview: A medium-sized provincial organization founded in 1974 overseen by Cycling Canada Cyclisme
Mission: To enable, enhance, & encourage cycling in British Columbia
Member of: Cycling Canada Cyclisme
Chief Officer(s):

Richard Wooles, Executive Director
richard@cyclingbc.net
Diana Hardie, Director, Finance & Administration
diana@cyclingbc.net
Tara Mowat, Coordinator, High Performance
tara@cyclingbc.net
Staff Member(s): 7
Membership: *Fees:* Schedule available; *Committees:* Governance Review; Female Program Development
Activities: *Rents Mailing List:* Yes
Awards:
• BC Cup Champions (Award)
• Club, Coach, Organizer, Commissaire of the Year Awards (Award)

Cycling Canada Cyclisme

#203, 2197 Riverside Dr., Ottawa ON K1H 7X3
Tel: 613-248-1353; *Fax:* 613-248-9311
general@cyclingcanada.ca
www.cyclingcanada.ca
www.facebook.com/CyclingCanada
twitter.com/CyclingCanada
www.youtube.com/user/CanadianCycling
Previous Name: Canadian Cycling Association
Overview: A medium-sized national organization founded in 1882
Mission: To organize & promote cycling in Canada, including BMX, road racing, track, & mountain biking, for sport & fitness.
Chief Officer(s):
Greg Mathieu, CEO & Secretary General
greg.mathieu@cyclingcanada.ca
Jacques Landry, Director, High Performance
jacques.landry@cyclingcanada.ca
Mathieu Boucher, Director, Performance Development
mathieu.boucher@cyclingcanada.ca
Brett Stewart, Director, Finance & Administration
brett.stewart@cyclingcanada.ca
Publications:
• Athlete Bios [a publication of the Canadian Cycling Association]
• Canadian Cycling Association / Association cycliste canadienne Directory
Type: Directory
• CCA [Canadian Cycling Association] Annual Report
Frequency: Annually
• Cycling Long Term Athlete Development Model

Cycling PEI (CPEI)

Sport PEI, PO Box 302, 40 Enman Cresent, Charlottetown PE C1A 7K7
Tel: 902-368-4985; *Fax:* 902-368-4548
www.cpei.ca
twitter.com/cyclingpei
Overview: A small provincial organization overseen by Cycling Canada Cyclisme
Mission: To develop cycling in PEI
Member of: Cycling Canada Cyclisme
Chief Officer(s):
David Sims, President
sims@cpei.ca
Mike Connolly, Executive Director
mconnolly@sportpei.pe.ca
Membership: *Fees:* $20 youth general; $30 senior general; $30 youth citizen; $40 senior citizen; $50 youth UCI racing license; $90 senior UCI racing license
Activities: *Awareness Events:* Red Mud Mountain Mayhem, Aug.

Cyclo-Nature

4693, rue de Lanaudière, Montréal QC H2L 3P6
info@cyclonature.org
www.cyclonature.org
Aperçu: *Dimension:* petite; *Envergure:* locale; fondée en 1974
Mission: Pour réunir des gens qui sont enthousiastes au sujet des activités de plein air et de vélo

Cypress Hills Ability Centres, Inc. (CHACI)

PO Box 579, 395 7th St. West, Shaunavon SK S0N 2M0
Tel: 306-297-2776; *Fax:* 306-297-2574
information@chaci.com
www.chaci.com
Previous Name: Shaunawan Ability Centre
Merged from: Cypress Hills Developmental Association & Shaunawan Ability Centre
Overview: A small local organization founded in 1974
Mission: To provie holistic support services for individuals with disabilties to develop as participatory citizens
Affliation(s): Saskatchewan Association of Rehabilitation Centres
Chief Officer(s):
Phyllis Edgington, Chief Executive Officer
chaciceo@sasktel.net
Finances: *Annual Operating Budget:* $500,000-$1.5 Million; *Funding Sources:* Provincial government
Staff Member(s): 40; 2 volunteer(s)
Membership: 7 individual; *Fees:* $1 individual
Activities: Accreditation through Saskatchewan Association of Rehabilitation Centres; *Awareness Events:* Bowlathon, Feb.

Cypress Hills Registered Horse Breeders' Association

c/o William & Donna Beierbach, PO Box 416, Maple Creek SK S0N 1N0
Tel: 306-299-2073
1yquarterhorses@gmail.com
www.cypresshorsebreeders.com
Overview: A small local organization
Membership: 23; *Member Profile:* Registered horse breeders in the Cypress Hills region of southwestern Saskatchewan & southeastern Alberta
Activities: Hosting The Annual Cypress Hills Registered Horse Breeders Production Sale each September; Providing information about members' ranch histories, breedings programs, & sales

Cypress River Chamber of Commerce

PO Box 261, Cypress River MB R0K 0P0
Tel: 204-743-2119; *Fax:* 204-743-2339
www.cypressriver.ca
Overview: A small local organization
Chief Officer(s):
Jim Cassels, President
cypressmotorinnone@hotmail.com

Cypriot Federation of Canada / Fédération chypriote du Canada

6 Thorncliff Park Dr., Toronto ON M4H 1H1
Tel: 416-696-7400; *Fax:* 416-696-9465
cypriotfederation@rogers.com
cypriotfederation.ca
Overview: A small national organization
Member of: Canadian Ethnocultural Council

Cystic Fibrosis Canada / Fibrose Kystique Canada

National Office, #601, 2221 Yonge St., Toronto ON M4S 2B4
Tel: 416-485-9149; *Fax:* 416-485-0960
Toll-Free: 800-378-2233
info@cysticfibrosis.ca
www.cysticfibrosis.ca
www.facebook.com/CysticFibrosisCanada
twitter.com/CFCanada
www.youtube.com/CysticFibrosisCanada
Previous Name: Canadian Cystic Fibrosis Foundation
Overview: A large national charitable organization founded in 1960
Mission: To help people with Cystic Fibrosis through funding research towards a cure or control; To support high quality care; To promote public awareness; To raise & allocate funds
Member of: Canadian Centre for Philanthropy
Affliation(s): Cystic Fibrosis Worldwide
Chief Officer(s):
Maureen Adamson, President & CEO, 416-485-9149 Ext. 225
Ken Chan, Vice-President, Advocacy, Research & Healthcare, 416-485-9149 Ext. 234
David Gilmer, CFRE, Vice-President, Funds Development & Marketing
Aida Fernandes, Director, Medical / Scientific & Community Programs, 416-485-9149 Ext. 229
Barb Gull, Director, Finance & Accounting, 416-485-9149 Ext. 239
Cheryl Woods, Director, Community Development, 416-485-9149 Ext. 243
Alice Awweh, National Events & Partner Relations Officer, 416-485-9149 Ext. 293
Christine Beyaert, Social Media & Communications Officer, 416-485-9149 Ext. 291
Finances: *Funding Sources:* Donations; Fundraising
Membership: 50 chapters; *Committees:* Executive; Adult CF; Advisory
Activities: Many scientific grants & awards; research programs; *Awareness Events:* Cystic Fibrosis Month, May; *Speaker Service:* Yes
Publications:
• Breathe - Final Report [a publication of Cystic Fibrosis Canada]
Type: Report
• Canadian Patient Data Registry Report [a publication of Cystic Fibrosis Canada]
Type: Report
• Candid Facts [a publication of Cystic Fibrosis Canada]
Type: Newsletter; *Frequency:* Quarterly *ISSN:* 0226-2347
Profile: News about events, research, & treatments for CFC members, donors, partners, & friends
• CFC [Cystic Fibrosis Canada] Annual Report
Type: Yearbook; *Frequency:* Annually
• Circle of Friends [a publication of Cystic Fibrosis Canada]
Frequency: Semiannually; *Editor:* Carole Varin; *Price:* Free for adults with CF & other interested persons
Profile: National newsletter for Canadian adults with cystic fibrosis
• Cystic Fibrosis Canada Grants & Awards Guide [a publication of Cystic Fibrosis Canada]
Type: Guide
• The Guide: Resources for the CF Community [a publication of Cystic Fibrosis Canada]
Type: Guide
• Insights [a publication of Cystic Fibrosis Canada]
Type: Newsletter
Profile: For the CF community, support groups, & other interested persons

Cystic Fibrosis Québec *Voir* Fibrose kystique Québec

Czech & Slovak Association of Canada

PO Box 564, 3044 Bloor St. West, Toronto ON M8X 2Y8
Tel: 416-925-2241; *Fax:* 416-925-1940
ustredi@cssk.ca
www.cssk.ca
Previous Name: Czechoslovak Association of Canada
Overview: A medium-sized national organization founded in 1939
Mission: To develop the highest standards of citizenship in Canadians of Czech or Slovak origin by encouraging, carrying on & participating in activities of national, patriotic, cultural & humanitarian nature; to act in matters affecting status rights & welfare of Canadians of Czech or Slovak origin; to cultivate in members appreciation of their mother tongue, cultural heritage & historical traditions; to promote growth of spirit in toleration, understanding & goodwill between all ethnic elements in Canada; to conduct research & encourage studies.
Member of: Canadian Ethnocultural Council; OCASI
Chief Officer(s):
Marie Fuchsová, President
Activities: *Library* by appointment

Czech Cultural Club *See* Edmonton Czech Language Society

Czechoslovak Association of Canada *See* Czech & Slovak Association of Canada

Dads Can

c/o St. Joseph's Health Care, PO Box 34, 268 Grosvenor St., London ON N6A 4V2
Tel: 519-646-6095
Toll-Free: 888-323-7226
www.dadscan.ca
Overview: A small national charitable organization
Mission: To "re-enculture" a fatherhood ideal by promoting responsible & involved fathering through the support of men's personal development into fatherhood & healthy fathering patterns
Chief Officer(s):
Neil R. Campbell, President/Executive Director
Finances: *Annual Operating Budget:* Less than $50,000
Membership: 1-99
Activities: *Speaker Service:* Yes

Daily Bread Food Bank

191 New Toronto St., Toronto ON M8V 2E7
Tel: 416-203-0050; *Fax:* 416-203-0049
info@dailybread.ca
www.dailybread.ca
www.facebook.com/DailyBreadFoodBank
twitter.com/@DailyBreadTO
Overview: A small local organization
Mission: To feed hungry people; to eliminate the need for food banks
Member of: Canadian Association of Food Banks
Chief Officer(s):

Gail Nyberg, Executive Director Ext. 230
gail@dailybread.ca
Finances: *Annual Operating Budget:* $3 Million-$5 Million
Staff Member(s): 40; 160 volunteer(s)
Membership: 160; *Fees:* $25; *Member Profile:* Food agencies in the Greater Toronto Area who distribute food to people in need
Activities: Annual Spring, Fall & Winter food drives; *Awareness Events:* Holiday Drive, December; *Library:* Learning Centre;

Dairy Farmers of Canada (DFC) / Les Producteurs laitiers du Canada (PLC)

21 Florence St., Ottawa ON K2P 0W6
Tel: 613-236-9997; *Fax:* 613-236-0905
info.policy@dfc-plc.ca
www.dairyfarmers.ca
twitter.com/dfc_plc
Overview: A medium-sized national organization founded in 1934 overseen by Canadian Federation of Agriculture
Mission: To coordinate action of dairy producer organizations on all issues of national scope; to collaborate with relevant agencies in elaboration of national policies of interest to Canadian dairy industry.
Member of: International Dairy Federation
Chief Officer(s):
Wally Smith, President
Richard Doyle, Executive Director
Finances: *Funding Sources:* In partnership with Agriculture & Agri-Food Canada & the National Science & Engineering Research Council
Membership: *Member Profile:* Dairy producers; organizations; breed-related organizations; milk recording; *Committees:* Promotion
Activities: Promotion & marketing of dairy products such as cheese & butter as well as nutrition communications directed to health officials & consumers; *Library*
Awards:
- Canadian Cheese Grand Prix (Award)
- Graduate Student Award in Dairy Research (Award)
- Pure Determination Fund (Scholarship)

Montréal Office
#700, 1801, av McGill College, Montréal QC H3A 2N4
Tel: 514-284-1092; *Fax:* 514-284-0449
Toll-Free: 800-361-4632
info@dfc-plc.ca

Dairy Farmers of Manitoba (DFM) / Producteurs Laitiers du Manitoba

PO Box 724, 36 Scurfield Blvd., Winnipeg MB R3C 2K3
Tel: 204-488-6455; *Fax:* 204-488-4772
Toll-Free: 800-567-1671
general@milk.mb.ca
www.milk.mb.ca
Previous Name: Manitoba Milk Producers
Overview: A small provincial organization founded in 1974
Mission: To represent the interests of dairy farmers of Manitoba at the provincial & national levels; To produce milk according to the highest standards; To sell milk from Manitoba's dairy farmers to processors
Chief Officer(s):
David Wiens, Chair
Finances: *Funding Sources:* Manitoba's dairy farmers
Membership: *Member Profile:* Dairy farmers in Manitoba
Activities: Developing advertising programs

Dairy Farmers of New Brunswick (DFNB) / Producteurs laitiers du Nouveau-Brunswick

PO Box 5034, Sussex NB E4E 5L2
Tel: 506-432-4330; *Fax:* 506-432-4333
nbmilk@nbmilk.org
www.nbmilk.org
Overview: A small provincial organization
Mission: To represent the interests of dairy farmers in New Brunswick; To produce high quality milk
Chief Officer(s):
Steve Michaud, General Manager
stevem@nbmilk.org
Danielle Kennedy, Contact, Producer Services
danielle@nbmilk.org
Veronica McEwen, Contact, Transportation
veronica@nbmilk.org
Cassandra Murray, Contact, Producer Services
cassandra@nbmilk.org
Finances: *Funding Sources:* Dairy farmers of New Brunswick
Membership: *Member Profile:* New Brunswick's dairy farmers
Activities: Marketing raw milk

Dairy Farmers of Newfoundland & Labrador (DFNL)

27 Sagona Ave., Mount Pearl NL A1N 4P8
Tel: 709-364-6634; *Fax:* 709-364-8364
milk@dfnl.nf.net
www.dfnl.ca
Overview: A small provincial organization founded in 1983
Mission: To regulate milk production in Newfoundland & Labrador
Member of: Dairy Farmers of Canada
Chief Officer(s):
Harry Burden, Executive Director
harryburden@dfnl.nf.net
Staff Member(s): 4
Membership: 34

Dairy Farmers of Nova Scotia (DFNS)

#100, 4060 Hwy. 236, Lower Truro NS B6L 1J9
Tel: 902-893-6455; *Fax:* 902-897-9768
hboyd@dfns.ca
www.dfns.ca
Overview: A medium-sized provincial organization founded in 2001
Mission: To provide a regulatory and administrative service to Nova Scotia's dairy producers.
Chief Officer(s):
Brian Cameron, General Manager, 902-893-6455 Ext. 1
bcameron@dfns.ca
Barron Blois, Chair
Membership: 250
Meetings/Conferences: • Dairy Farmers of Nova Scotia Annual General Meetin 2015, January, 2015, Best Western Glengarry, Truro, NS
Scope: Provincial

Dairy Farmers of Ontario (DFO)

6780 Campobello Rd., Mississauga ON L5N 2L8
Tel: 905-821-8970; *Fax:* 905-821-3160
questions@milk.org
www.milk.org
Overview: A small provincial organization founded in 1995
Mission: To provide leadership and excellence in the production and marketing of Canadian milk.
Staff Member(s): 74
Membership: *Member Profile:* Dairy farmers in Ontario
Activities: Developing advertising programs
Meetings/Conferences: • Dairy Farmers of Ontario Annual Meeting 2015, January, 2015, Fairmont Royal York Hotel, Toronto, ON
Scope: Provincial

Dairy Nutrition Council of Alberta *See* Alberta Milk

Dalhousie Faculty Association / Association des professeurs de Dalhousie

PO Box 15000, 6280 South St., Halifax NS B3H 4R2
Tel: 902-494-3722; *Fax:* 902-494-6740
dfa@dal.ca
dfa.ns.ca
twitter.com/dalfacultyassoc
Overview: A medium-sized local organization
Mission: To represent the interests of all Dalhousie University staff & faculty members in employment relations matters
Chief Officer(s):
Kevin Grundy, President
Kevin.Grundy@dal.ca
Lynn Purves, Administrative Officer
Staff Member(s): 4
Membership: 870; *Committees:* Executive; Grievance

Dalhousie Medical Research Foundation

PO Box 15000, Halifax NS B3H 4R2
Tel: 902-494-3502; *Fax:* 902-494-1372
Toll-Free: 888-866-6559
dmrf@dal.ca
www.dmrf.ca
Overview: A small local charitable organization
Mission: To provide funds to the research department of the Dalhousie Medical school & other affiliated health care facilities
Affliation(s): Dalhousie Medical School
Chief Officer(s):
Jyl MacKinnon, Executive Director
Jyl.MacKinnon@Dal.ca
Staff Member(s): 5
Membership: *Committees:* Scientific Advisory

Dalhousie University School of Information Management Associated Alumni

Kenneth C. Rowe Management Bldg., #4010, 6100 University Ave., Halifax NS B3H 4R2
Tel: 902-494-3656; *Fax:* 902-494-2451
sim@dal.ca
sim.management.dal.ca
www.facebook.com/groups/228106125569
twitter.com/sim_aluni
blogs.dal.ca/sim
Overview: A small local organization founded in 1974
Mission: To advance the interests of information professionals, particularly their education; to promote the objectives & best interests of the Dalhousie School of Information Management & the professional objectives & interests of the individual members of the Associated Alumni.
Chief Officer(s):
Jessica Babineau, Chair
jlbabineau@gmail.com

Dance Centre

Scotiabank Dance Centre, 677 Davie St., Level 6, Vancouver BC V6B 2G6
Tel: 604-606-6400; *Fax:* 604-606-6401
info@thedancecentre.ca
www.thedancecentre.ca
www.facebook.com/thedancecentre
twitter.com/dancecentre
Overview: A small local charitable organization founded in 1986
Mission: To raise the profile of dance in BC; to serve as a focal point & advocate for issues & concerns affecting the entire dance community; to coordinate the resources & activities of this wide ranging community
Member of: Alliance for Arts and Culture; CanDance Network; Canadian Dance Assembly; World Dance Alliance Americas
Chief Officer(s):
Heather Bray, Marketing Manager
Mirna Zagar, Executive Director
executivedirector@thedancecentre.ca
Finances: *Annual Operating Budget:* $250,000-$500,000; *Funding Sources:* Government; private; earned
Staff Member(s): 7; 30 volunteer(s)
Membership: 220; *Fees:* $50-75 individual; $90-315 corporate; *Member Profile:* Dance companies; independent artists; educators; dance enthusiasts & supporters; *Committees:* Artistic Advisory; Fundraising
Activities: Administration; video production; consultation; presentation; advocacy; operation of Scotiabank Dance Centre facility; *Awareness Events:* International Dance Day, April 29; *Internships:* Yes; *Library:* Dr. Yosef Wosk Video Library
Awards:
- The Isadora Award (Award)

Awarded for excellence in dance & significant contribution to the dance community & to the art form
Publications:
- Dance Central

Type: Online Publication; *Frequency:* Bimonthly; *Accepts Advertising*; *Editor:* Andreas Kahre
Profile: The publication features interviews with people in the dance community

The Dance Centre (TDC)

Scotiabank Dance Centre, 677 Davie St., 6th Fl., Vancouver BC V6B 2G6
Tel: 604-606-6400; *Fax:* 604-606-6401
info@thedancecentre.ca
www.thedancecentre.ca
www.facebook.com/thedancecentre
twitter.com/dancecentre
www.youtube.com/thedancecentrebc
Overview: A small local charitable organization founded in 1986
Mission: To increase the exposure of performing arts through the presentation of interdisciplinary performances & workshops; to present contemporary dance work & interdisciplinary dance/theatre/music performances of the highest quality; to act as a catalyst & animator for dance & associated arts in the community & to offer infrastructure & presentation support of that activity
Chief Officer(s):
Mima Zagar, Executive Director
executivedirector@thedancecentre.ca
Staff Member(s): 27
Membership: *Fees:* $25 student; $50 associate; $75 full; $90 emerging company; schedule for companies dependant on annual budget; *Member Profile:* Dancers, choreographers, teachers & companies

Dance Collective *See* Ruth Cansfield Dance

Dance Manitoba Inc.

Pantages Playhouse Theatre, #204, 180 Market Ave. East, Winnipeg MB R3B 0P7
Tel: 204-989-5260; *Fax:* 204-989-5268
info@dancemanitoba.org
www.dancemanitoba.org
www.facebook.com/210968142294814
Overview: A small provincial organization
Mission: To promote the development of dance through festivals, workshops, & showcases
Chief Officer(s):
Nicole Owens, Executive Director
Membership: 146; *Fees:* $25 adult; $15 youth/student; $35 organization

Dance Nova Scotia

1113 Marginal Rd., Halifax NS B3H 4P7
Tel: 902-422-1749; *Fax:* 902-422-0881
office@dancens.ca
www.dancens.ca
www.facebook.com/dance.scotia
twitter.com/dancenovascotia
pinterest.com/dancens1
Also Known As: DANS
Overview: A medium-sized provincial charitable organization founded in 1974
Mission: To promote, stimulate & encourage the development of dance as a cultural, educational & social activity
Member of: Cultural Federations of Nova Scotia
Chief Officer(s):
Megan Matheson Hamilton, Executive Director
Finances: *Annual Operating Budget:* $100,000-$250,000; *Funding Sources:* Government; program revenue
Staff Member(s): 2; 40 volunteer(s)
Membership: 125; *Fees:* $25 individual; $50 organization; *Member Profile:* Dance teachers; dance organizations; *Committees:* Education; Professional Dance Artists
Activities: Studio performance series; studio rental; curriculum for public schools; summer programs; *Awareness Events:* International Day of Dance; *Library* Open to public by appointment

Dance Ontario Association / Association Ontario Danse

The Distillery District, #304, 15 Case Goods Lane, Toronto ON M5A 3C4
Tel: 416-204-1083; *Fax:* 416-204-1085
contact@danceontario.ca
www.danceontario.ca
Overview: A small provincial organization founded in 1976
Mission: To support the advancement of all forms of dance; To offer a unified voice on dance issues
Chief Officer(s):
Peter Ryan, Chair
Jennifer Watkins, Vice-Chair
Rosslyn Jacob Edwards, Executive Director
Jade Jager Clark, Secretary
Debbie Kapp, Treasurer
Finances: *Funding Sources:* Donations; Fundraising
Membership: 600+; *Fees:* $10 students; $25 affiliates & associates; $30 individuals; $60 groups; *Member Profile:* Persons who make their careers in dance professions; Persons who are interested in dance; Persons affiliated with a member group of Dance Ontario; Students; Groups, such as schools, studios, & associations, in the field of dance
Activities: Promoting all forms of dance & the development of performance facilities; Producing dance programs; Giving advice & industry information; Facilitating communication amongst the dance community; Offering referrals to dance services; Providing networking opportunities; Training management; Organizing workshops in areas such as kinetics & choreography
Publications:
• Dance Ontario Directory
Type: Directory
Profile: Listings of members, their professions, & services
• Dance Ontario Newsletter
Type: Newsletter
Profile: Information about member performance & events

Dance Oremus Danse (DOD)

240 Dovercourt Rd., Toronto ON M6J 3E1
Tel: 416-536-9002; *Fax:* 416-536-9002
www.danceoremusdanse.org
Overview: A small local charitable organization founded in 1983
Mission: To increase the public's appreciation of the aesthetic arts by promoting & encouraging the philosophy, movement practices & dance forms of Isadora Duncan (1877-1927) & European neo-classical dance, via seminars, workshops, courses on dance, performance, publishing & other media
Chief Officer(s):
Paul James Dwyer, Founder/Artistic Director
pauljamesdwyer@yahoo.ca
Finances: *Funding Sources:* Private; corporate
Activities: *Library* Open to public by appointment

Dance Saskatchewan Inc.

205A Pacific Ave., Saskatoon SK S7K 1N9
Tel: 306-931-8480; *Fax:* 306-244-1520
Toll-Free: 800-667-8480
dancesask@sasktel.net
www.dancesask.com
Overview: A medium-sized provincial charitable organization founded in 1979
Mission: To support & enhance the development of all dance forms; to preserve & promote dance in Saskatchewan; to represent & educate about dance; to encourage a passion for dance; to create a viable, unified organization which represents & advocates dance interests; to foster a respect & acceptance of dance which encourages free expression of cultural identity; to establish an active, vibrant environment which focuses on job creation, performance & cultural diversity within a central dance facility
Member of: World Dance Alliance; Dance & Child International; SaskCulture Inc.
Affiliation(s): Canadian Association of Professional Dance Organizations
Chief Officer(s):
Linda Coe-Kirkham, Executive Director
Finances: *Funding Sources:* Saskatchewan Lotteries; charitable donations
Staff Member(s): 9
Membership: *Fees:* Schedule available; *Member Profile:* Culturally diverse group of people
Activities: Dance flooring; workshops; community assistance in the development of social/ethnic dance forms; scholarships & grants; Dare to Dance & Summer Steps; *Speaker Service:* Yes; *Library* Open to public

Dance Umbrella of Ontario (DUO)

476 Parliament St., Toronto ON M4X 1P2
Tel: 416-504-6429; *Fax:* 416-504-8702
duo@danceumbrella.net
www.danceumbrella.net
www.facebook.com/DanceUmbrellaofOntario
twitter.com/danceumbrella
Overview: A small provincial organization founded in 1988
Mission: To assist & support professional dance creators in Ontario dance centres
Member of: Canadian Conference for the Arts
Affiliation(s): Arts Vote; Dance Ontario
Chief Officer(s):
Jennifer Bennett, Managing Director
Finances: *Funding Sources:* Canada Council of the Arts; Ontario Arts Council; Toronto Arts Council; Ontario government
Staff Member(s): 5
Membership: *Member Profile:* Dance professionals
Activities: *Library:* The Dance Plant; by appointment

Dancemakers

#301, 15 Case Goods Ln., Toronto ON M5A 3C4
Tel: 416-367-1800
info@dancemakers.org
dancemakers.org
www.facebook.com/dancemakersTO
twitter.com/DancemakersTO
www.youtube.com/user/dancemakerstoronto
Overview: A small local charitable organization founded in 1974
Mission: To bring dance of challenging physicality & emotional impact to audiences by drawing on the diverse talents & individual strengths of its artists; to develop & support works which both provoke & entertain
Member of: Canadian Dance Assembly; Dance Ontario
Chief Officer(s):
Michael Trent, Artistic Director
michael@dancemakers.org
Robert Sauvey, Executive Director
robert@dancemakers.org
Finances: *Funding Sources:* Government & private sector
Staff Member(s): 15

Dancer Transition Resource Centre (DTRC) / Centre de ressources et transition pour danseurs (CRTD)

The Lynda Hamilton Centre, #500, 250 The Esplanade, Toronto ON M5A 1J2
Tel: 416-595-5655; *Fax:* 416-595-0009
Toll-Free: 800-667-0851
nationaloffice@dtrc.ca
www.dtrc.ca
www.facebook.com/dtrcnews
twitter.com/dancetransition
www.youtube.com/user/DancerTransition
Overview: A medium-sized national charitable organization founded in 1985
Mission: TO hels dancers make necessary transitions into, within & from professional performing, as well as operating a resource centre for the dance community & the public, offering seminars, education materials & information.
Member of: Dance Ontario; Association of Dance in Universities & Colleges in Canada; International Organization for the Transition of Professional Dancers; Ontario Coalition of Arts Service Organizations; Canadian Conference of the Arts
Affliation(s): Alberta Canada; Ballet BC; Danse Montréal; Ballet Kelowna; Compagnoe Marie Chouinard; Les Grands Ballets; National Ballet of Canada; O Vertigo; Toronto Dance Theatre; Winnipeg Contemporary Dancers; Dancemakers & the Centre for Creation; Danny Grossman Dance; Decidedly Jazz Danceworks; Canada's Royal Winnipeg Ballet
Chief Officer(s):
Amanda Hancox, Executive Director
ahancox@dtrc.ca
Garry Neil, Chair
Finances: *Funding Sources:* Government; private; corporations; foundations; donations; special events; membership dues
Staff Member(s): 13
Membership: *Fees:* $75-$250; *Member Profile:* Open to dancers who agree to contribute 1% of their salary equally matched by their companies; dancers may also join on individual basis; *Committees:* Advisory; Artistic Resource
Activities: Counselling Referral Program to assist dancers find employment within & outside dance profession; Dancer Awareness Program; Public Awareness Program; Dancer Award Fund; annual conference "on the MOVE"; *Library* Open to public

Awards:
• Anne M. Delicaet Bursary (Award)
To help fund tuition, books &/or supplies for applicant in their third year of full-time retraining/grants received from the DTRC *Amount:* Award amount is discretionary
• Sara Symons Bursary (Award)
Open to all recipients of at least one year of funding under type C grant who are continuing their studies *Amount:* Amount is discretionary
• Lynda Hamilton Award (Award)
Awarded annually to a dancer in transition who has completed two years of study & requires a third to complete or continue the proposed course of study *Amount:* $18,000 subsistence & $4,000 for tuition & supplies
• Peter F. Bronfman Memorial Award (Award)
It is earmarked for a second or third year of retraining & subsistence & may be only awarded for the full amount *Amount:* $18,000 subsistence & $4,000 for tuition & supplies
• Karen Kain Award (Award)
Given to a dancer entering a second or subsequent year of full-time retraining *Amount:* Award is discretionary
• Grants for Retraining & Subsistence (Grant)
• Erik Bruhn Memorial Award (Award)
Awarded yearly to a dancer who has completed stream 1 & requires a second year to complete or continue proposed course of study *Amount:* $18,000 for subsistence & $4,000 for tuition & supplies
• Zella Wolofsky/Doug Wright Bursary (Award)
Awarded to a dancer with a degree from a recognized university & who is in second or subsequent year of professional program or doing graduate studies or second degree *Amount:* $2,000 for any purpose

British Columbia
#712, 402 West Pender St., Vancouver BC V6B 1T6
Tel: 604-899-0755; *Fax:* 604-899-0752
bcoffice@dtrc.ca
Chief Officer(s):
Zaena Campbell, Program Officer

Québec
#313, 3680, rue Jeanne-Mance, Montréal QC H2X 2K5
Tel: 514-284-1515
bureauqc@crtd.ca

Chief Officer(s):
Parise Mongrain, Program Officer

DanceSport Alberta (DSAB)
AB
e-mail: president@dancesportalberta.org
www.dancesportalberta.org
Overview: A medium-sized provincial organization founded in 1989 overseen by Canada DanceSport
Chief Officer(s):
Theresa Jenkins, President

DanceSport Atlantic (DAA)
3273 Beaver Bank Rd., Lower Sackville NS B4C 2S6
Tel: 902-865-9914
dancesport.chebucto.org
Overview: A medium-sized provincial organization overseen by Canada DanceSport
Chief Officer(s):
John McDermott, Contact

DanceSport Québec (DSQ)
4545 ave Pierre-De Coubertin, Montréal QC H1V 0B2
Tél: 514-418-8264
Ligne sans frais: 800-474-5746
info@dansesportquebec.com
dansesportquebec.com
Aperçu: *Dimension:* moyenne; *Envergure:* provinciale surveillé par Canada DanceSport

Dania Home Society
4279 Norland Ave., Burnaby BC V5G 3Z6
Tel: 604-299-2414; *Fax:* 604-299-7775
info@dania.bc.ca
www.dania.bc.ca
Overview: A small local charitable organization founded in 1941
Mission: To operate housing & care facilities for the elderly, maintaining a distinctly Danish style in keeping with the heritage & wishes of the founders
Member of: Federation of Danish Associations in Canada
Affiliation(s): Fraser Health Authority
Chief Officer(s):
Kjeld Christensen, President
Margaret Douglas-Matthews, Executive Director
Membership: *Fees:* $15 annual; $150 life
Activities: Dania Home; Dania Manor; Carl Mortensen Manor

Danish Canadian Chamber of Commerce (DCCC)
Tel: 416-923-1811; *Fax:* 416-962-3668
info@dccc.ca
www.dccc.ca
Overview: A small international organization founded in 1992
Mission: To help promote business relations between Denmark & Canada; to be a forum for discussions concerning Danish-Canadian trade; to be an advisory & consultative body available to Canadian & Danish governmental representatives
Member of: The European Union Chamber of Commerce
Chief Officer(s):
Anders Fisker, Chair
Finances: *Annual Operating Budget:* Less than $50,000; *Funding Sources:* Membership fees
Membership: 100; *Fees:* $95 individual; $400 corporate; $750 sponsor
Activities: Luncheon meetings; corporate presentations; conferences & seminars; social events

Danish Canadian Club of Calgary
727 - 11 Ave. SW, Calgary AB T2R 0E3
Tel: 403-261-9774; *Fax:* 403-261-6631
dcc@danishclubcalgary.com
www.danishclubcalgary.com
www.facebook.com/TheDanishCanadianClub
Overview: A small local licensing organization founded in 1933
Member of: Federation of Danish Associations in Canada
Chief Officer(s):
Ben Kromand, President
Peter Christensen, General Manager
peter.christensen@danishclubcalgary.com
Finances: *Funding Sources:* Membership dues; fundraising; banquets
Membership: *Fees:* $30

Danish Canadian National Museum Society (DCNMS)
PO Box 92, Spruce View AB T0M 1V0
Tel: 403-728-0019; *Fax:* 403-728-0020
Toll-Free: 888-443-4114
manager@danishcanadians.com
danishcanadians.com
twitter.com/danishcanadians
Also Known As: Danish Canadian National Museum & Gardens
Overview: A small national charitable organization founded in 1992
Mission: To enrich Canada through the Danish Canadian National Museum, located in Dickson, Alberta; To preserve & promote the culture & history of the Danes in Canada for a greater understanding & celebration of all humanity
Affiliation(s): Federation of Danish Associations in Canada
Chief Officer(s):
Steve Morck, President
Faye Kjearsgaard, Manager
Finances: *Annual Operating Budget:* $100,000-$250,000
Staff Member(s): 1; 100 volunteer(s)
Membership: 700+; *Fees:* $25 individual; $30 family; $100 organization; *Committees:* Development & Maintenance; Programs, Events & Volunteer; Museum
Activities: *Awareness Events:* St. Hans Fest, June

Danish Canadian Society of Saint John
112 Birch Cres. East, Rothesay NB E2H 1S6
Tel: 506-847-1021
Overview: A small local organization founded in 1987
Member of: Federation of Danish Associations in Canada
Affiliation(s): Multicultural Association of Saint John
Finances: *Funding Sources:* Membership fees
Membership: *Member Profile:* Danish descent or interest

The Danish Club of Ottawa
PO Box 55032, 240 Sparks St., Ottawa ON K1P 1A1
e-mail: info@danishclubottawa.com
www.danishclubottawa.com
www.facebook.com/DanishClubofOttawa
Overview: A small local organization founded in 1975
Mission: To promote customs, traditions & other matters peculiar to Danish culture; to foster good relations between Canada & Denmark
Member of: Federation of Danish Associations in Canada
Chief Officer(s):
Ted Hansen, President
Finances: *Funding Sources:* Membership fees; activities; bazaar
10 volunteer(s)
Membership: 270 individual; *Fees:* $25 family; $15 single; $17 senior couple; $10 senior single; *Committees:* Bazaar; Church
Activities: *Speaker Service:* Yes

Danish Heritage Society of Dickson *See* Dickson Store Museum Society

Danse-Cite inc
#426, 3680, rue Jeanne-Mance, Montréal QC H2X 2K5
Tél: 514-525-3595
info@danse-cite.org
www.danse-cite.org
www.facebook.com/dansecite
twitter.com/dansecite
www.youtube.com/user/DANSECITE
Aperçu: *Dimension:* petite; *Envergure:* locale; fondée en 1982
Mission: Création et production de spectacles de danse contemporain
Membre de: Regroupement québécois de la danse
Membre(s) du bureau directeur:
Daniel Soulières, Directeur artistique
Membre(s) du personnel: 8

Dartmouth Adult Services Centre (DASC)
#24, 10 Akerley Blvd., Dartmouth NS B3B 1J4
Tel: 902-468-6606; *Fax:* 902-468-5359
www.dasc-ns.ca
www.facebook.com/DASCIndustries
Overview: A small local organization
Mission: To provide a vocational day program for adults with intellectual disabilities
Member of: DIRECTIONS Council for Vocational Services Society
Chief Officer(s):
Susan Ehler, Chair
Cathy Deagle-Gammon, Executive Director
director@dasc-ns.ca
Activities: Services include: The Button People; Mailing Services; The Alter Bread Company; & Packaging & Assembly
Publications:
• DASC [Dartmouth Adult Services Centre] Newsletter
Type: Newsletter; *Frequency:* q.

Dartmouth Historical Association
Tel: 902-469-2018
www.dartmouthheritagemuseum.ns.ca/dhmDartmouthHistAssoc.html
Overview: A small local charitable organization founded in 1993
Mission: To administer the Leighton Dillman Scholarship Fund; To encourage research & to discuss policies affecting Dartmouth's heritage; To study future plans of Dartmouth; To publish books on local history; To place plaques in public buildings that have been named for people
Affiliation(s): Federation of Nova Scotian Heritage
Chief Officer(s):
Harry Chapman, President
hechapman@eastlink.ca
Finances: *Annual Operating Budget:* Less than $50,000; *Funding Sources:* Membership fees; Book sale
10 volunteer(s)
Membership: 200 individual; *Fees:* $8 individual
Activities: *Awareness Events:* Halifax Explosion Remembrance, Dec. 6; *Speaker Service:* Yes

Dartmouth N.S. Family History Centre
44 Cumberland Dr., Dartmouth NS B2V 2C7
Tel: 902-462-0628
nsgna.ednet.ns.ca/fhc/index.html
Overview: A small local organization
Mission: To do genealogical research
Member of: The Church of Jesus Christ Latter-Day Saints
Finances: *Annual Operating Budget:* Less than $50,000
Staff Member(s): 13; 12 volunteer(s)
Activities: *Library* Open to public

Dartmouth Ringette Association
NS
dartmouthringette.com
Overview: A small local organization overseen by Ringette Nova Scotia
Member of: Ringette Nova Scotia
Chief Officer(s):
Andrea Temple, President
ea.mom4@gmail.com
Membership: 11 teams

Darts Alberta
PO Box 163, #14, 9977 - 178 St. NW, Edmonton AB T5T 6J6
Tel: 780-908-0475
www.dartsalberta.com
Overview: A small provincial organization overseen by National Darts Federation of Canada
Mission: To provide recreational & competitive opportunities for darts players of all levels in Alberta.
Member of: National Darts Federation of Canada
Chief Officer(s):
Bill Hatter, President, 403-548-2939, Fax: 403-504-4029
president@dartsalberta.com
Sandi Orr, Administrator
administrator@dartsalberta.com
Activities: Sport programs; educational opportunities for coaches & officials; recognition programs

Darts BC Association (DBCA)
BC
e-mail: executive@dartsbc.ca
www.dartsbc.ca
www.facebook.com/BcDarts
Overview: A small provincial organization overseen by National Darts Federation of Canada
Mission: To be the provincial governing body for the sport of darts in British Columbia.
Member of: National Darts Federation of Canada
Chief Officer(s):
Ray Bode, President
president@dartsbc.ca
Suzie Letude, Provincial Director
provincialdirector@dartsbc.ca
Membership: 8 leagues/associations

Darts Ontario
ON
Tel: 905-426-7493; *Fax:* 905-426-8270
provincialdirector@dartsontario.com
www.dartsontario.com
Overview: A small provincial organization overseen by National Darts Federation of Canada
Mission: To promote the sport of darts on the provincial, national & world levels.
Member of: National Darts Federation of Canada

Chief Officer(s):
Susan Hine, President & Provincial Director
president@dartsontario.com
Katie Murphy, Secretary, 905-534-1426, Fax: 905-534-1464
secretary@dartsontario.com
Membership: *Fees:* $18 affiliate; $20 youth; $23 adult

Daughters of Isabella
40 Bashford Rd., Ajax ON L1S 3Y2
e-mail: info@daughtersofisabella.org
www.daughtersofisabella.org
Overview: A small local charitable organization
Mission: To unite Catholic women; To uphold the teachings of the Catholic Church & high ideals of life & morals; To extend the circle of friends for Catholic women & to establish bonds among Catholic women throughout the world; To pursue good in society; To foster growth of Catholic women in every aspect of life, including spiritual, social, & charitable; To ensure governance by The International Circle of the Daughters of Isabella; To implement programs & projects consistent with the laws & rules of the organization's constitution
Chief Officer(s):
Monique Kelly, Contact
moniquehkelly@gmail.com
Membership: *Member Profile:* Catholic women over the age of sixteen
Activities: Conducting monthly business & social meetings; Acting upon the sponsorship of charitable, spiritual, civic, & social programs; Holding ceremonies for the installation of officers & the conferral of degrees for new members

Dauphin & District Allied Arts Council Inc. (DDAAC)
104 - 1st Ave. NW, Dauphin MB R7N 1G9
Tel: 204-638-6231
info@watsonartcentre.com
www.watsonartcentre.com
Overview: A small local charitable organization founded in 1972
Mission: To promote the arts in Dauphin & district through ongoing programs in visual & performing arts, workshops & arts-related activities.
Member of: Manitoba Arts Network
Chief Officer(s):
Michelle Nyquist, President
Susan Kowalski, Administrator
Finances: *Funding Sources:* Provincial government; City of Dauphin; rentals
Membership: *Fees:* $12 Senior; $15 Single; $20 Family; $30 Affiliate; $50 Corporate; $100 Associate
Activities: Arts programming; gallery; art in library; *Speaker Service:* Yes

Dauphin & District Chamber of Commerce
100 Main St. South, Dauphin MB R7N 1K3
Tel: 204-622-3140; *Fax:* 204-622-3141
info@dauphinchamber.ca
www.dauphinchamber.ca
Overview: A small local organization founded in 1903
Member of: Manitoba Chamber of Commerce
Chief Officer(s):
Alyson Sametz, President
a.sametz@dauphincoop.com
Finances: *Annual Operating Budget:* Less than $50,000; *Funding Sources:* Membership dues; group insurance administration fees; grants
Staff Member(s): 1
Membership: 180; *Fees:* $40-$400; *Committees:* Membership; Tourism; Newsletter; Finance; Annual Dinner; Marketing; Events; Youth
Awards:
• Community Appreciation Award (Award)
• Don Persson Memorial Award (Award)

Dauphin Friendship Centre (DFC)
210 - 1st Ave. NE, Dauphin MB R7N 1A7
Tel: 204-638-5707; *Fax:* 204-638-4799
dfcexec@mts.net
www.dauphinfriendshipcentre.com
www.facebook.com/DauphinFriendshipCenter
Overview: A small local charitable organization founded in 1974
Mission: To enhance the quality of life for Aboriginal & Non-Aboriginal people in the community by working together to provide services & programs to meet the needs of its membership & community.
Affliation(s): Manitoba Association of Friendship Centres; National Association of Friendship Centres
Membership: *Fees:* $1
Activities: Children's Christmas Party; Adult Christmas Dinner & Dance; Halloween Howl; Annual Aboriginal Festival; Youth program; Craft/Sewing club; volunteer appreciation luncheon; quarterly networking luncheon; annual youth Christmas dance; Annual National Aboriginal Solidarity Day activities; bingos; *Library*
Awards:
• DFC Scholarships/Bursaries (Award)

Davenport-Perth Neighbourhood & Community Health Centre (DPNCHC)
1900 Davenport Rd., Toronto ON M6N 1B7
Tel: 416-656-8025; *Fax:* 416-656-1264
info@dpnchc.ca
dpnchc.com
Overview: A medium-sized local charitable organization founded in 1984
Mission: The Davenport-Perth Neighbourhood Centre (DPNC) is a multi-service agency located in the west end of Toronto dedicated to encouraging people to work together and take action to improve the political, social, economic, spiritual and cultural life of the whole community.
Chief Officer(s):
Wade Hilier, President
Finances: *Annual Operating Budget:* Greater than $5 Million; *Funding Sources:* Federal, provincial & municipal governments; foundations; donations; United Way; fundraising

David Foster Foundation
212 Henry St., Victoria BC V9A 3H9
Tel: 250-475-1223; *Fax:* 250-475-1193
Toll-Free: 877-777-7675
info@davidfosterfoundation.com
www.davidfosterfoundation.org
www.facebook.com/pages/David-Foster-Foundation/109610495747154?ref=mf
Overview: A small local charitable organization founded in 1986
Mission: To provide financial assistance to families of children undergoing transplant surgery; to raise public awareness regarding organ donation
Chief Officer(s):
Michael Ravenhill, CEO
mravenhill@davidfosterfoundation.com

David Suzuki Foundation (DSF)
#219, 2211 West 4 Ave., Vancouver BC V6K 4S2
Tel: 604-732-4228
Toll-Free: 800-453-1533
contact@davidsuzuki.org
www.davidsuzuki.org
www.facebook.com/DavidSuzuki
twitter.com/DavidSuzukiFDN
www.youtube.com/user/DavidSuzukiFDN
Overview: A small national charitable organization founded in 1991
Mission: To seek out & commission the best, most up-to-date research to help reveal ways we can live in balance with nature; to support the implementation of ecologically sustainable models - from local projects, such as habitat restoration, to international initiatives, such as better frameworks for economic decisions; to ensure the solutions developed through research & application to reach the widest possible audience, & help mobilize broadly supported change; to urge decision makers to adopt policies which encourage & guide individuals & businesses, so their daily decisions reflect the need to act within nature's constraints
Member of: Canadian Renewable Energy Alliance
Chief Officer(s):
Tara Cullis, President
James Hoggan, Chair
Peter Robinson, CEO
Staff Member(s): 69
Membership: *Committees:* Governance; Quebec Orientation; Finance & Audit; Investment; Program; Development

Dawson City Chamber of Commerce
PO Box 1006, Dawson YT Y0B 1G0
Tel: 867-993-5274; *Fax:* 867-993-6817
office@dawsoncitychamberofcommerce.ca
www.dawsoncitychamberofcommerce.ca
Overview: A small local organization
Chief Officer(s):
Dina Grenon, President

Dawson Creek & District Chamber of Commerce
10201 - 10th St., Dawson Creek BC V1G 3T5
Tel: 250-782-4868; *Fax:* 250-782-2371
info@dawsoncreekchamber.ca
www.dawsoncreekchamber.ca
Overview: A small local organization founded in 1944
Mission: To lead, promote & protect the economic & social prosperity of Dawson Creek & District
Affliation(s): BC Chamber of Commerce
Chief Officer(s):
Denis Labelle, President
Denis@greensmartmanufacturing.com
Kathleen Connolly, Executive Director
Kathleen@dawsoncreekchamber.ca
Finances: *Annual Operating Budget:* $100,000-$250,000; *Funding Sources:* Membership dues; service fees
Staff Member(s): 5; 20 volunteer(s)
Membership: 268; *Fees:* $85-$500; *Committees:* Agriculture; Economic Development; Education; Transportation
Activities: *Rents Mailing List:* Yes

Dawson Creek Construction Association
1000 - 102 Ave., Dawson Creek BC V1G 2C1
Tel: 250-782-4704; *Fax:* 250-782-2524
Overview: A small local organization
Chief Officer(s):
Tom van Spronsen, President

Dawson Creek Society for Community Living
1334 - 102 Ave., Dawson Creek BC V1G 2C6
Tel: 250-782-2611; *Fax:* 250-782-2662
info@dcscl.org
www.dcscl.org
Overview: A small local organization founded in 1958
Mission: To assist people with disabilities to become full community participants through training, education, support & advocacy
Member of: British Columbia Association for Community Living
Chief Officer(s):
Marla Reed, Executive Director
mreed@dcscl.org
Finances: *Funding Sources:* BC Housing Management Commission; Central Mortgage & Housing Corp.; Community Living BC; Northern Health Authority
Activities: Semi-Independent Living program; Opportunity Centre; Aurora Housing; Southview Housing Project, a seniors apartment complex;

Daybreak *See* L'Arche Ontario

Deaf Children's Society of B.C. (DCS)
#200, 7355 Canada Way, Burnaby BC V3N 4Z6
Tel: 604-525-6056; *Fax:* 604-525-7307; *TTY:* 604-525-9390
www.deafchildren.bc.ca
www.facebook.com/pages/Deaf-Childrens-Society-of-BC/146576198745766
Previous Name: Deaf Children's Society of British Columbia
Overview: A small provincial charitable organization founded in 1975
Mission: To help deaf children and their families in the province
Chief Officer(s):
Janice Springfield, Executive Director
Finances: *Funding Sources:* Provincial government; fundraisers
Staff Member(s): 11
Membership: *Fees:* $30
Activities: Early Literacy, preschool, speech-language & sign-language programs; summer playgroup; *Library:* DCS Library; Open to public

Deaf Children's Society of British Columbia *See* Deaf Children's Society of B.C.

Deafness Advocacy Association Nova Scotia (DAANS)
Halifax NS
Tel: 902-425-0240; *TTY:* 902-425-0119
daans@ns.sympatico.ca
www.facebook.com/109727935783155
Overview: A small provincial charitable organization founded in 1979
Mission: The Association promotes the rights & needs of the deaf, hard-of-hearing, late-deafened & deafblind in the province.
Member of: Canadian Association of the Deaf
Activities: Support; advocacy; special projects; education; human rights; *Speaker Service:* Yes; *Library* Open to public

Dease Lake & District Chamber of Commerce
PO Box 338, Dease Lake BC V0C 1L0
Tel: 250-771-3900; *Fax:* 250-771-3900
Overview: A small local organization

Member of: BC Chamber of Commerce
5 volunteer(s)

Debden & District Chamber of Commerce
PO Box 91, Debden SK S0J 0S0
Tel: 306-724-2020; *Fax:* 306-724-2220
Overview: A small local organization
Mission: To promote business development & tourism in the area.
Chief Officer(s):
Rhonda Peterson, President
Amelie Patrick, Secretary
Activities: Historical research; tourism development; business promos; new business setups; highway safety;

DeBolt & District Pioneer Museum Society
PO Box 447, Debolt AB T0H 1B0
Tel: 780-957-3957; *Fax:* 780-957-2934
deboltmuseum@gmail.com
Overview: A small local charitable organization founded in 1975
Mission: To preserve the history of the rural pioneer in DeBolt & district; To research & publish books on history of the area
Member of: Alberta Museum Association
Affliation(s): Spirit of the Peace
Chief Officer(s):
Fran Moore, Curator & President
Finances: *Annual Operating Budget:* Less than $50,000; *Funding Sources:* Donations; book sales; municipal & provincial grants; lottery funds; quilt raffles; hall rental
25 volunteer(s)
Membership: 50; *Fees:* $1; *Member Profile:* Retired & homemakers; *Committees:* Exhibits; Legion Hall
Activities: Thursday morning workshops; published four local history books; *Awareness Events:* Heritage Day, mid-August; *Library* by appointment

DEBRA Canada
#3, 1500 Upper Middle Rd., Oakville ON L6M 3H5
Toll-Free: 800-313-3012
Other Communication: French Phone: 866-433-0676
debra@debracanada.org
debracanada.org
twitter.com/DEBRACanada
Overview: A medium-sized national organization
Mission: To support patients of Epidermolysis Bullosa & their families & provide funding for the medical needs of patients
Chief Officer(s):
Gena Brumitt, President
gena@debracanada.org
Activities: *Awareness Events:* Epidermolysis Bullosa Awareness Week, Oct.

Decidedly Jazz Danceworks
1514 - 4th St. SW, Calgary AB T2R 0Y4
Tel: 403-245-3533; *Fax:* 403-245-3584
djd@decidedlyjazz.com
www.decidedlyjazz.com
www.facebook.com/pages/Decidedly-Jazz-Danceworks/162890170398000
twitter.com/DecidedlyJazz
www.youtube.com/user/decidedlyjazz
Overview: A small local organization
Mission: To create concert jazz dance that sustains the spirit and traditions of jazz; to mix groove, African roots, rhythm, improvisation, interplay with musicians, and deeply human soul, has distinguished DJD on the international jazz dance stage; to offer a season of performances, touring, and jazz classes.
Chief Officer(s):
Kimberley Cooper, Artistic Director
Kathi Sundstrom, Executive Director
Staff Member(s): 12

Deep River Symphony Orchestra (DRSO)
PO Box 398, Deep River ON K0J 1P0
Tel: 613-584-4264
drsoemail@gmail.com
www.drso.ca
Overview: A small local organization founded in 1952 overseen by Orchestras Canada
Mission: To promote the development & enjoyment of music in the Upper Ottawa Valley
Member of: Ontario Federation of Symphony Orchestras; Deep River Community Association; Valley Arts Council
Chief Officer(s):
Peter Morris, Music Director
Jane Craig, President
drsoemail@gmail.com
Finances: *Funding Sources:* Subscriptions; donations; fund-raising; Ontario Arts Council; Town of Deep River
Activities: 10 public concerts each season; *Library* Open to public

Deep Roots Music Cooperative
PO Box 2360, Wolfville NS B4P 2G9
Tel: 902-542-7668
info@deeprootsmusic.ca
www.deeprootsmusic.ca/cooperative
www.facebook.com/DeepRoots
Overview: A small national organization
Mission: To develop year-round musical programs culminating in an annual festival, and to encourage meaningful connections between cultures, community groups, artists and audiences.
Chief Officer(s):
Peter Mowat, Chair
100 volunteer(s)
Membership: *Fees:* $10 or 15 hours volunteer time
Activities: Canadian Deep Roots Music Festival

Deer Lake Chamber of Commerce
9A Church St., Deer Lake NL A8A 1C9
Tel: 709-635-3260; *Fax:* 709-635-5857
info@deerlakechamber.com
www.deerlakechamber.com
Overview: A small local organization founded in 1960
Member of: Atlantic Provinces Chamber of Commerce
Affliation(s): Newfoundland Chambers of Commerce
Chief Officer(s):
Todd Lee, Treasurer
Susan Goulding, Executive Director
Jim Goudie, President
Finances: *Annual Operating Budget:* Less than $50,000
Staff Member(s): 1
Membership: 167; *Fees:* Individual $50; 1-5 $60; 6-11 $70; 12+ $80; *Committees:* Executive; Fundraising; Small Business; Tourism
Activities: *Awareness Events:* Small Business Week, October

Defense environmentale *See* Environmental Defence

Dejinta Beesha Multi-Service Centre
8 Taber Rd., Toronto ON M9W 3A4
Tel: 416-743-1286; *Fax:* 416-743-1233
info@dejinta.org
dejinta.org
Overview: A medium-sized local charitable organization founded in 1994
Mission: To provide settlement, integration, recreation, health, employment, education, & social services to the community; Offering services in English, French, Italian, Arabic, Somali, & Kiswahili
Chief Officer(s):
Mohamed Gilao, Executive Director
mgilao@dejinta.org
Finances: *Funding Sources:* Government; Donations
Staff Member(s): 9

Delburne & District Chamber of Commerce
PO Box 341, Delburne AB T0M 0V0
Tel: 403-749-3606; *Fax:* 403-749-2800
www.delburne.ca
Overview: A small local organization
Mission: Promoting and supporting business in the area.
Chief Officer(s):
Brenda Smith, President, 403-749-3023

Deloraine & District Chamber of Commerce
PO Box 748, Deloraine MB R0M 0M0
Tel: 204-747-2655; *Fax:* 204-747-2927
deloraine.org/business/coc.html
Overview: A small local organization
Mission: To support and promote business in the area.
Member of: Manitoba Chamber of Commerce
Chief Officer(s):
Deb Calverley, President
debcalv@mts.net
Grant Cassils, Contact
Finances: *Annual Operating Budget:* Less than $50,000; *Funding Sources:* Municipal governments; membership fees
20 volunteer(s)
Membership: 75; *Fees:* $50

Delta Arts Council (DAC)
11489 - 84 Ave., Delta BC V4C 2L9
Tel: 604-596-1025
deltaartscouncil@gmail.com
www.deltaartscouncil.ca
www.facebook.com/197425190124
twitter.com/DeltaArtCouncil
Overview: A small local charitable organization founded in 1969
Mission: To foster cultural & artistic activities within the community, by encouraging amateur, emergent and professional artists
Member of: Assembly of BC Arts Councils
Chief Officer(s):
Janet Law, President
Finances: *Funding Sources:* Municipal, provincial & federal government; fundraising
Membership: *Fees:* $10 student; $25 individual; $40 family/non-profit; $50 artists group; $100 corporate
Activities: Tsawwassen Arts Centre; Firehall Centre for the Arts; Gallery North; Arts Alive; juried exhibitions; monthly TV shows; Maddfest; Xmas Craft Fair; ongoing art classes; summer art camp; garden party; monthly performances; 4 Arts resource centres: Arts & Coffee Corner; *Library:* Resource Centre; Open to public
Awards:
- Scholarships (Scholarship)

Delta Chamber of Commerce
6201 - 60 Ave., Delta BC V4K 4E2
Tel: 604-946-4232; *Fax:* 604-946-5285
admin@deltachamber.ca
www.deltachamber.ca
www.linkedin.com/pub/delta-chamber-of-commerce/22/541/89
www.facebook.com/169103131415
twitter.com/deltachamber
www.youtube.com/user/DeltaChamber
Overview: A small local charitable organization founded in 1910
Mission: To create & maintain a prosperous environment for business, industry, tourism & commerce in our community
Member of: BC Chamber of Commerce
Chief Officer(s):
Paul Roaf, Executive Director
execdirector@deltachamber.ca
Kelly Guichon, Chair
Finances: *Annual Operating Budget:* $250,000-$500,000; *Funding Sources:* Membership dues; municipal
Staff Member(s): 3; 25 volunteer(s)
Membership: 400; *Fees:* Schedule available; *Committees:* Marketing & Communications; Sustainable Economy; Tourism; Transportation; Membership; Agriculture; Education
Activities: Monthly networking lunches; business trade show; Tour de Delta; *Speaker Service:* Yes; *Library:* Business Centre; Open to public
Awards:
- Citizen & Business of the Year Awards (Award)

Delta Community Career & Living Society *See* Delta Community Living Society

Delta Community Living Society (DCLS)
#1, 3800 - 72 St., Delta BC V4K 3N2
Tel: 604-946-9508; *Fax:* 604-940-9683
dcls@dcls.ca
dcls.ca
Previous Name: Delta Community Career & Living Society
Overview: A small local charitable organization founded in 1963
Mission: To support adults who have a developmental disability & their families; To seek to improve their quality of life by assisting in personal goals & developing life skills to become valued citizens
Member of: British Columbia Association for Community Living
Chief Officer(s):
Anita Sihota, Executive Director
Membership: *Fees:* $10 individual; $15 family; $75 corporate/club
Activities: *Library* by appointment

Delta Family Resource Centre
#5, 2972 Islington Ave., Toronto ON M9L 2K6
Tel: 416-747-1172; *Fax:* 416-747-7415
contactus@dfrc.ca
www.dfrc.ca
www.facebook.com/pages/Delta-Family-Resource-Centre/337007286321251
twitter.com/DeltaFamilyRC
Overview: A medium-sized local charitable organization
Mission: To support the needs of families & children within the community; Offering services in English, Spanish, Italian, Hindi, Punjabi, Laotian, Gujarati, Somali, Cantonese, Tamil, Mandarin, Thi, Ewe, Twi, Urdu, Dari, & Ga
Chief Officer(s):

Rosalyn Miller, Executive Director
Finances: *Funding Sources:* Government; Foundations; Donations; United Way
Membership: *Fees:* $2 regular member; $20 associate member/organization/group

Delta Rockhound Gem & Mineral Club
5457 - 4A Ave., Delta BC V4M 1H6
Tel: 604-943-5518
Overview: A small local organization founded in 1968
Member of: British Columbia Lapidary Society
Chief Officer(s):
Mary Cool, Contact
coolgirl@dccnet.com
Finances: *Funding Sources:* Membership fees
Activities: Field trips; meetings 3rd Mon. every month;

Delta Symphony Society ***See*** Richmond Delta Youth Orchestra

Democracy Watch
PO Box 821, Stn. B, #412, 1 Nicholas St., Ottawa ON K1P 5P9
Tel: 613-241-5179; *Fax:* 613-241-4758
info@democracywatch.ca
democracywatch.ca
www.facebook.com/DemocracyWatch
twitter.com/democracywatchr
www.youtube.com/dwatchcda
Overview: A medium-sized national organization
Mission: To advocate for democratic reform, government accountability, and corporate responsibility.
Chief Officer(s):
Duff Conacher, Coordinator
Finances: *Funding Sources:* Donations

Denesoline Corporation Ltd.
PO Box 72, Lutsel K'e NT X0E 1A0
Tel: 867-370-3095; *Fax:* 867-370-3976
Previous Name: Lutsel K'E Development Corporation
Overview: A small local organization founded in 1990
Mission: Owned by the Lutsel K'e Dene Band, the corporation is a business development company which administers contracts for firefighting, ice road maintenance, survey stake production, hunting & outfitting, residential constuction & general contracting. It also has formed joint ventures with & has investment equity in other industry corporations.
Affliation(s): Ta'egera Corporation; Great Slave Helicopters Ltd.
Chief Officer(s):
Roy Shields, CEO

Dental Association of Prince Edward Island (DAPEI)
184 Belvedere Ave., Charlottetown PE C1A 2Z1
Tel: 902-892-4470
dapei@pei.sympatico.ca
www.dapei.ca
Overview: A small provincial licensing organization founded in 1931 overseen by Canadian Dental Association
Mission: DAPEI sees itself as a partner, a policy advisor, and decision maker with the public, government and its members, regarding the availability, accessibility, and affordibility of appropriate and high quality dental services for islanders.
Member of: Canadian Dental Association
Chief Officer(s):
Travis McLean, President
Brian Barrett, Executive Director
Staff Member(s): 2
Membership: 76; *Member Profile:* Dentists; dental specialists
Activities: *Awareness Events:* Dental Health Month, April; *Speaker Service:* Yes; *Rents Mailing List:* Yes

Dental Council of Prince Edward Island
184 Belvedere Ave., Charlottetown PE C1A 2Z1
Tel: 902-892-4470; *Fax:* 902-892-4470
Overview: A small provincial licensing organization

Dental Technicians Association of Saskatchewan
PO Box 8035, Saskatchewan SK S7K 4R7
Tel: 306-764-5525
sask.dtas@hotmail.com
Overview: A small provincial organization
Mission: To represent & regulate the dental technicians of Saskatchewan.

Denturist Association of British Columbia
#312C, 9801 King George Hwy., Surrey BC V3T 5H5
Tel: 604-582-6823; *Fax:* 604-582-0317
info@denturist.bc.ca
www.denturist.bc.ca
Overview: A small provincial organization overseen by Denturist Association of Canada
Chief Officer(s):
Maria Green, President

Denturist Association of Canada (DAC) / Association des denturologistes du Canada (ADC)
66 Dundas St. East, Belleville ON K8N 1C1
Tel: 613-968-9467
Toll-Free: 877-538-3123
dacdenturist@bellnet.ca
www.denturist.org
Previous Name: Interprovincial Denturist Societies
Overview: A medium-sized national organization founded in 1971
Mission: To promote oral health in Canada through the profession of denturism.
Member of: International Federation of Denturists
Membership: 12 associations; *Member Profile:* Provincial denturist associations
Activities: *Speaker Service:* Yes; *Rents Mailing List:* Yes
Awards:
- Robert Perreault Memorial Award (Award)
- George Connolly Denturist of the Year Award (Award)

Denturist Association of Manitoba
PO Box 70006, #1, 1660 Kenaston Blvd., Winnipeg MB R3P 0X6
Tel: 204-897-1087; *Fax:* 204-488-2872
Toll-Free: 866-897-1087
administrator@denturistmb.org
www.denturistmb.org
Overview: A small provincial licensing organization founded in 1970 overseen by Denturist Association of Canada
Mission: To represent Manitoba denturists & ensure high quality, low cost delivery of dentures direct to the public
Member of: International Federation of Denturists
Chief Officer(s):
Paul Hrynchuk, President
Jennifer Peters, Administrator
Finances: *Annual Operating Budget:* $50,000-$100,000; *Funding Sources:* Membership fees
Staff Member(s): 1
Membership: 61; *Fees:* $1,300; *Member Profile:* Licensed denturist
Activities: *Internships:* Yes

Denturist Association of Newfoundland & Labrador
9 Bay Bulls Rd., Kilbride NL A1G 1A2
Tel: 709-364-4813
info@denturistassociationnl.ca
www.denturistassociationnl.ca
Overview: A small provincial organization overseen by Denturist Association of Canada
Mission: To promote denturist as a profession & provide services for its members
Member of: The Denturist Associationg of Canada; International Federation of Denturists
Chief Officer(s):
Steve Browne, President
Membership: 23

Denturist Association of Northwest Territories
PO Box 1506, Yellowknife NT X1A 2P2
Tel: 867-766-3666; *Fax:* 867-669-0103
Overview: A small provincial organization overseen by Denturist Association of Canada

Denturist Association of Ontario (DAO)
#106, 5780 Timberlea Blvd., Mississauga ON L4W 4W8
Tel: 905-238-6090; *Fax:* 905-238-7090
Toll-Free: 800-284-7311
info@denturistassociation.ca
denturistassociation.ca
Overview: A small provincial organization overseen by Denturist Association of Canada
Mission: To develop services that address current needs & future concerns & are the primary providers of dental prosthetics & related services.
Member of: The Denturist Association of Canada
Chief Officer(s):
Nancy Tomkins, President
Susan Tobin, Chief Administrative Officer
Membership: 500+
Activities: Fabrication & repair of dentures; visitation services; *Library*

Denturist Society of Nova Scotia
c/o Della Sangster, 134 Arthur St., Truro NS B2N 1Y1
Tel: 902-893-8010; *Fax:* 902-893-1094
info@nsdenturistsociety.ca
www.nsdenturistsociety.ca
Overview: A small provincial licensing organization overseen by Denturist Association of Canada
Member of: Denturist Association of Canada
Chief Officer(s):
Della Sangster, Vice President

Denturist Society of Prince Edward Island
Summerside Denture Clinic, 191 Pope Rd., A, Summerside PE C1N 5C6
Tel: 902-892-3253
ssidedentclinic@eastlink.ca
Overview: A small provincial organization overseen by Denturist Association of Canada

Design Exchange (DX)
Toronto Dominion Centre, PO Box 18, 234 Bay St., Toronto ON M5K 1B2
Tel: 416-363-6121; *Fax:* 416-368-0684
Other Communication: membership@dx.org
info@dx.org
www.dx.org
Also Known As: The Group for the Creation of a Design Centre in Toronto
Overview: A medium-sized national organization founded in 1987
Mission: To provide a design museum & centre for design research & education; To raise awareness & understanding of design
Chief Officer(s):
Tim Gilbert, Interim President, 416-216-2145
tim@gilbertslaw.ca
Finances: *Funding Sources:* Donations; Sponsorships
Membership: *Member Profile:* Designers, students, & business professionals
Activities: Offering programs to promote the value of Canadian design; Showcasing good Canadian design; Organizing competitions; Presenting awards; Fundraising

Designers d'intérieur du Canada ***See*** Interior Designers of Canada

Desta Black Youth Network
Padua Centre, 1950, rue St-Antoine ouest, Montréal QC H3J 1A5
Tel: 514-932-7597; *Fax:* 514-932-9468
friendsofdesta@gmail.com
www.destanetwork.ca
www.facebook.com/pages/DESTA-Black-Youth-Network/75367875687
Overview: A small local organization
Mission: To provide an outreach initiative to young adults, from ages 18 to 25, within the Black community; To mentor marginalized youth in the areas of education, employment, & personal growth; To empower vision, strengthen authentic identity, & promote excellence
Chief Officer(s):
Frances Waithe, Executive Director
Staff Member(s): 4

Destination Halifax
#802, 1800 Argyle St., Halifax NS B3J 3N8
Tel: 902-422-9334; *Fax:* 902-492-3175
Toll-Free: 877-422-9334
info@destinationhalifax.com
www.destinationhalifax.com
www.facebook.com/DestinationHalifax
twitter.com/HfxNovaScotia
www.youtube.com/user/destinationhalifax;
pinterest.com/halifaxns
Also Known As: Meet Halifax
Previous Name: Greater Halifax Conventions & Meetings Bureau
Overview: A small local organization founded in 2002
Mission: To increase Greater Halifax's market share of the meetings & conventions market by promoting the region as a destination for meetings, conventions, exhibitions & special events; To provide meeting planners with a full range of services which will promote & build attendance at their Halifax meetings; To create business opportunities for bureau members & to develop pre- & post- conference travel opportunities
Chief Officer(s):

Stuart Jolliffe, Chair
stuart.jolliffe@deltahotels.com
Patricia Lyall, President & CEO, 902-429-4574
plyall@destinationhalifax.com
Catherine Porter, Director of Group Sales, 902-422-2161
cporter@destinationhalifax.com
Finances: *Annual Operating Budget:* $500,000-$1.5 Million
Staff Member(s): 12
Membership: 150; *Fees:* Varies; *Member Profile:* An organization company that books & services meetings & conventions
Activities: *Speaker Service:* Yes

Destination Sherbrooke
785, rue King Ouest, Sherbrooke QC J1H 1R8
Tél: 819-821-1919
Ligne sans frais: 800-561-8331
info@destinationsherbrooke.com
www.destinationsherbrooke.com
www.facebook.com/destinationsherbrooke
twitter.com/DSherbrooke
www.youtube.com/user/destinationsherb
Nom précédent: Tourisme Sherbrooke; Société de développement économique de la région sherbrookoise - Tourisme
Aperçu: *Dimension:* petite; *Envergure:* locale
Mission: Créer, animer, obtenir et administrer les activités touristiques pour la ville de Sherbrook; favoriser la recherche et le développement des dossiers touristiques; assurer la promotion du secteur touristique; agir comme expert conseil dans le domaine touristique auprès de la Société de développement économique de Sherbrooke
Membre(s) du bureau directeur:
Denis Bernier, Directeur général
denis.bernier@destinationsherbrooke.com
Membre(s) du personnel: 6

Destination Southwest Nova Association (DSWNA)
PO Box 1390, Lunenburg NS B0J 2C0
Tel: 902-634-8844
Toll-Free: 877-552-4040
info@destinationsouthwestnova.com
www.destinationsouthwestnova.com
Previous Name: South Shore Tourism Association
Overview: A small local organization founded in 1961
Mission: To represent the tourism industry on behalf of the private sector; to promote the business of tourism, culture & heritage in that area of Nova Scotia known as the South Shore region
Chief Officer(s):
Jeanette Joudrey, General Manager, 902-521-4658
Finances: *Annual Operating Budget:* $50,000-$100,000
Staff Member(s): 6
Membership: 100-499; *Fees:* $50 individual

Deutsch-Kanadische Industrie- und Handelskammer *See* Canadian German Chamber of Industry & Commerce Inc.

A deux mains *See* Head & Hands

Deux/Dix *See* Two/Ten Charity Trust of Canada Inc.

Developing Countries Farm Radio Network *See* Farm Radio International

Development & Peace / Développement et paix
1425, boul René-Lévesque ouest, 3e étage, Montréal QC H3G 1T7
Tel: 514-257-8711; *Fax:* 514-257-8497
info@devp.org
www.devp.org
www.facebook.com/devpeace
twitter.com/DevPeace
www.youtube.com/devpeacetv;
www.flickr.com/photos/devpedu/sets
Also Known As: Canadian Catholic Organization for Development & Peace
Overview: A large international charitable organization founded in 1967
Member of: Caritas Internationalis; Conseil canadien pour la coopération internationale / Canadian Council for International Cooperation
Affiliation(s): Coopération internationale pour le développement et la solidarité
Chief Officer(s):
G. Gagnon, Contact
Finances: *Funding Sources:* Donations; Canadian International Development Agency (provision of grants for projects & programs)
Staff Member(s): 61; 5,00 volunteer(s)
Membership: 10,000; *Fees:* 5$
Activities: Providing financial support for projects in the developing world; Contributing to emergency relief; Engaging in advocacy activities related to crises & issues in developing countries
Publications:
• Development & Peace Annual Report
Frequency: Annually
• Global Village Voice [a publication of Development & Peace]
Type: Newsletter; *Frequency:* 3 pa *ISSN:* 0383-6703

Alberta/Mackenzie
8421 - 101st Ave., Edmonton AB T6A 0L1
Tel: 587-224-9017
Chief Officer(s):
Sara Farid, Contact
sfarid@devp.org

British Columbia/Yukon
2690 Stockton Cres., Abbotsford BC V2S 4K2
Tel: 604-864-6383
john.gabor@devp.org
Chief Officer(s):
John Gabor, Contact

Manitoba
622 Tache Ave., Saint-Boniface MB R2H 2B4
Tel: 204-231-2848; *Fax:* 204-231-7471
ccodpmb@gmail.com
Chief Officer(s):
Janelle Delorme, Contact

Nouveau-Brunswick
CP 212, Edmundston NB E3V 3K8
Tél: 506-258-6376; *Téléc:* 506-263-8513
estelle.dumont-paillard@devp.org
Chief Officer(s):
Estelle Dumont-Paillard, Contact

Nova Scotia/New Brunswick/PEI/Newfoundland & Labrador
#205, 59 Inglis Pl., Antigonish NS B2N 4B5
Tel: 902-897-0469; *Fax:* 902-897-2852
Chief Officer(s):
Tara Hurford, Contact
thurford@devp.org

Ontario - Central
#400, 80 Hayden St., Toronto ON M4Y 3G2
Tel: 416-922-1592; *Fax:* 416-922-0957
Chief Officer(s):
Luke Stocking, Contact
lstocking@devp.org

Ontario - Eastern
1247 Kilborn Pl., Ottawa ON K1H 6K9
Tel: 613-738-9644; *Fax:* 613-738-0130
Chief Officer(s):
Genevieve Gallant, Contact
ggallant@devp.org

Ontario - Southwestern
698 King St. West, Hamilton ON L8P 1C7
Tel: 905-521-5632
Chief Officer(s):
Nana Kojo Damptey, Contact
nkdamptey@devp.org

Québec - Gatineau/Ottawa (French)
180, boul Mont-Bleu, Gatineau QC J8Z 3J5
Tél: 819-771-8391; *Téléc:* 819-778-8969
Chief Officer(s):
Jean-François Langlais, Contact
jflanglais@devp.org

Québec - Montréal
1425, boul René-Lévesque Ouest, 3e étage, Montréal QC H3G 1T7
Tél: 514-257-8711; *Téléc:* 514-257-8497
Chief Officer(s):
Jean-Paul St-Germain, Contact
jpstgermain@devp.org
Marie-Sophie Villeneuve, Contact
msvilleneuve@devp.org

Québec - Québec
1073, boul René-Lévesque Ouest, Québec QC G1S 4R5
Tél: 418-683-9901; *Téléc:* 418-683-9331
Chief Officer(s):
Elisabeth Desgranges, Contact
edesgranges@devp.org
Pascal André Charlebois, Contact
pcharlebois@devp.org

Saskatchewan
PO Box 1838, Battleford SK S0M 0E0
Tel: 306-937-7675
Chief Officer(s):
Armella Sonntag, Contact
asonntag@devp.org

Developmental Disabilities Resource Centre of Calgary (DDRC)
4631 Richardson Way SW, Calgary AB T3E 7B7
Tel: 403-240-3111; *Fax:* 403-240-3230
info@ddrc.com
www.ddrc.ca
www.linkedin.com/company/ddrc_2
www.facebook.com/DDRCCalgary
twitter.com/DDRC_Calgary
www.youtube.com/DDRCCalgary
Overview: A medium-sized local charitable organization founded in 1952
Mission: To facilitate personal choice & build the community's capacity to include person's with developmental disabilities
Member of: Alberta Association for Community Living
Chief Officer(s):
Helen Cowie, Chief Executive Officer
Finances: *Funding Sources:* Government contracts; fees for service; private fundraising; commercial ventures
Membership: *Fees:* $15 individual; $20 family
Activities: Awards of Distinction; *Speaker Service:* Yes

Développement et paix *See* Development & Peace

Devis de construction Canada *See* Construction Specifications Canada

Devon & District Chamber of Commerce
#104, 32 Athabasca Ave., Devon AB T9G 1G2
Tel: 780-987-5177; *Fax:* 780-987-5135
devoncc@telus.net
www.devon.ca/Business/ChamberofCommerce.aspx
Overview: A small local organization
Member of: Alberta Chamber of Commerce
Chief Officer(s):
Jeff Millar, President
Barry Breau, Manager
Finances: *Annual Operating Budget:* Less than $50,000
Membership: 65; *Fees:* $60; *Member Profile:* Businesses in & near Devon, Alberta

Dewdney-Alouette Railway Society (DARS)
22520 - 116 Ave., Maple Ridge BC V2X 0S4
Tel: 604-463-5311; *Fax:* 604-463-5317
mrmuseum@telus.net
www.mapleridgemuseum.org
Overview: A small local organization
Mission: The Society preserves the railway history of Maple Ridge, promotes the craft of model railroading, & offers advice to the public who are engaged in the building & operating of model railroads.
Affiliation(s): National Model Railway Association; Pacific Northwest Region 7th Division Society; BC Heritage Society; Maple Ridge Historical Society; Maple Ridge Museum
Chief Officer(s):
Dick Sutcliff, Contact
ras1@uniserve.com
Activities: Port Haney diorama

Diabète Québec (ADQ) / Diabetes Quebec
#300, 8550, boul Pie-IX, Montréal QC H1Z 4G2
Tél: 514-259-3422; *Téléc:* 514-259-9286
Ligne sans frais: 800-361-3504
info@diabete.qc.ca
www.diabete.qc.ca
www.facebook.com/179747505687
twitter.com/DiabeteQuebec
Également appelé: Association Diabète Québec
Nom précédent: Association du Diabète du Québec
Aperçu: *Dimension:* moyenne; *Envergure:* provinciale; fondée en 1954
Mission: Regrouper les diabétiques et favoriser l'entraide; les renseigner sur les façons de faire face à la maladie; informer le grand public et le sensibiliser à la condition de personnes souffrant du diabète; ouvrir de nouvelles voies dans le domaine de la recherche pour en venir à triompher du diabète
Membre de: Fédération Internationale du Diabète
Membre(s) du bureau directeur:

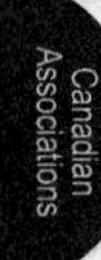

Serge Langlois, Président-directeur général Ext. 229
direction@diabete.qc.ca
Sylvie Lauzon, Chef des opération, Directrice, Développement
lauzon@diabete.qc.ca
Finances: *Budget de fonctionnement annuel:* $1.5 Million-$3 Million
Membre(s) du personnel: 16; 2 bénévole(s)
Membre: 25,000; *Montant de la cotisation:* 20$ membre régulier; *Comités:* Conseil d'administration; Conseil d'administration; Conseil professionnel de Diabète Québec
Activités: Congrès scientifique; service téléphonique InfoDiabète; formation; concours; publications; *Événements de sensibilisation:* Mois du diabète nov.; *Service de conférenciers:* Oui
Prix, Bouses:
• Bourses d'été et Subvention de démarrage (Brouse)
Eligibility: Étudiants niveaux Bac, M.Sc. et Ph.D.; Médecins chercheurs*Deadline:* Mars *Amount:* 3000$ à 25,000$
Publications:
• Plein Soleil
Type: Magazine; *Editor:* Louise Bouchard
Profile: Traite des sujets en relation avec le diabète : alimentation, traitement, activité physique, recherche, vivre avec le diabète, etc.

Diabetes Quebec ***Voir*** Diabète Québec

Diabetes Research Foundation ***See*** Juvenile Diabetes Research Foundation Canada

Dial-a-Tutor
#4-5074, 5845 Yonge St., Toronto ON M2M 4K3
Tel: 416-607-6401
dialatutor.ca
twitter.com/tutorsforless
Also Known As: Tutors For Less
Overview: A small local organization founded in 1996
Mission: To provide individualized, in-home tutoring sessions.
Finances: *Funding Sources:* Hourly service fees

Diamond Valley Chamber of Commerce
PO Box 61, Turner Valley AB T0L 2A0
Tel: 403-819-4994
info@diamondvalleychamber.ca
diamondvalleychamber.ca
Overview: A small local organization
Mission: To work with local municipal councils, business associations and local organizations to promote the area working on a regional development plan for business and events.
Member of: Alberta Chamber of Commerce
Chief Officer(s):
Bev Geier, President
Finances: *Annual Operating Budget:* Less than $50,000
5 volunteer(s)
Membership: 28; *Fees:* $95

Dickson Store Museum Society
PO Box 146, Spruce View AB T0M 1V0
Tel: 403-728-3355; *Fax:* 403-728-3351
dicksonstoremuseum@gmail.com
www.dicksonstoremuseum.com
Previous Name: Danish Heritage Society of Dickson
Overview: A small local charitable organization founded in 1985
Mission: TO manage the Dickson Store Museum; To preserve the history of Dickson & area pioneers
Member of: Federation of Danish Associations in Canada; Museums Alberta; Central Alberta Regional Museums Network
Finances: *Funding Sources:* Grants; donations; sales; membership dues; fundraising events
Membership: *Fees:* $10 single or family; $100 life
Activities: Home On the Range project; maintaining Dickson Store Museum, open to the public, tour & school groups; the museum contains hardware, dry goods & groceries which were available in the 1930s; the second floor is furnished as a typical 1930s home; the original post-office serves as a gift-shop; officially opened by Queen Margrethe II; *Awareness Events:* Dickson Harvest Festival, Oct.; Scandinavian Julestue, Nov.; *Library:* Archives; by appointment

Didsbury & District Historical Society
PO Box 1175, 2110 - 21 Ave., Didsbury AB T0M 0W0
Tel: 403-335-9295
ddhs@telusplanet.net
www.didsburymuseum.com
Overview: A small local charitable organization founded in 1978
Mission: To preserve, research, display, & interpret items about the founding, settlement, & development of the Town of Didsbury, Alberta
Chief Officer(s):
Jim Curran, Contact, 403-335-0003
Finances: *Funding Sources:* Donations; Fundraising; Grants
Membership: *Fees:* $5 single; $10 family
Activities: Providing education about local history;

Didsbury Chamber of Commerce
PO Box 981, 1811 - 20 St., Didsbury AB T0M 0W0
Tel: 403-335-3265; *Fax:* 403-335-3267
info@didsburychamber.ca
www.didsburychamber.ca
www.facebook.com/218454541526303
Overview: A small local organization founded in 1962
Mission: To increase communication within the business community and beyond; To keep their members informed on Chamber activities
Chief Officer(s):
Shelley Fakir, President
Membership: 75; *Committees:* Member Services; Marketing; Didsbury Art, Travel & Trade Expo; Special Event; Small Business Week; Policy/Issues; Strategic Plan

Les diététistes du Canada ***See*** Dietitians of Canada

Dietitians of Canada (DC) / Les diététistes du Canada
#604, 480 University Ave., Toronto ON M5G 1V2
Tel: 416-596-0857; *Fax:* 416-596-0603
centralinfo@dietitians.ca
www.dietitians.ca
Previous Name: Canadian Dietetic Association
Overview: A medium-sized national organization founded in 1935
Mission: To advance health, through food & nutrition; To act as the voice of the profession in Canada
Chief Officer(s):
Marsha Sharp, Chief Executive Officer
Corinne Eisenbraun, Director, Professional Practice Development
Janice Macdonald, Director, Communications
Marlene Wyatt, Director, Professional Affairs
Patricia Sierra, Manager, Finance & Administration
Finances: *Funding Sources:* Membership fees; Sponsorships
Membership: *Member Profile:* Registered & registration eligible dietitians; Internationally educated dietitians; Retired dietitians; Academics; Students in accredited undergraduate dietetics & internship programs
Activities: Engaging in advocacy activities; Developing standards; Offering workshops, webinars, & podcasts; Providing nutrition information; Facilitating access to counselling, consultations, & media interviews; Organizing networking opportunities; *Awareness Events:* Nutrition Month, March; National Dietitians' Day, March
Meetings/Conferences: • Dietitians of Canada 2015 Annual National Conference, June, 2015, Québec City, QC
Scope: National
Description: A learning & networking event for dietitians
Contact Information: General information events@dietitians.ca
Publications:
• Canadian Journal of Dietetic Research & Practice
Type: Journal; *Frequency:* Quarterly; *Editor:* Dawna Royall; Marie-Claude Paquette *ISSN:* 1486-3847
Profile: A peer-reviewed publication, featuring manuscripts of original research, professional practice, & reviews
• Dietitians of Canada Annual Report
Type: Yearbook; *Frequency:* Annually

Digby & Area Board of Trade
PO Box 641, Digby NS B0V 1A0
Tel: 902-245-2553
Overview: A small local organization
Chief Officer(s):
Kristy Herron, President
Membership: *Fees:* $24 individual; $60 business

Digital Imaging Association (DIA)
Tel: 416-482-2223
www.digitalimagingassoc.ca
Previous Name: Ontario Prepress Association
Overview: A small provincial organization founded in 1989
Chief Officer(s):
Marg Macleod, Manager
marg@digitalimagingassoc.ca
Finances: *Annual Operating Budget:* $50,000-$100,000
20 volunteer(s)
Membership: 80 companies; *Fees:* $100 individual; $200-$850 corporate; *Member Profile:* Suppliers & manufacturers of equipment & consumables used in the pre-press, printing & finishing industries

Digital Nova Scotia (ITANS)
Technology Innovation Centre, 1 Research Dr., Dartmouth NS B2Y 4M9
Tel: 902-423-5332; *Fax:* 877-282-9506
info@digitalnovascotia.com
www.digitalnovascotia.com
www.facebook.com/groups/2384141607
twitter.com/digitalns
www.youtube.com/user/digitalnovascotia
Previous Name: Information Technology Industry Alliance of Nova Scotia; Software Industry Association of Nova Scotia
Overview: A medium-sized provincial organization founded in 1989
Mission: To be dedicated to the development & growth of the digital technologies industry in Nova Scotia
Member of: CATAAtlantic
Chief Officer(s):
Michael McConnell, Chief Executive Officer
michael@digitalnovascotia.com
Jason K. Powell, President
jason.powell@digitalnovascotia.com
John Leahy, Vice-President
Ken Lee, Director, Events
David T. Fraser, Secretary
Steven Carr, Treasurer

Dignity Canada Dignité
PO Box 2102, Stn. D, Ottawa ON K1P 5W3
Tel: 613-746-7281
info@dignitycanada.org
www.dignitycanada.org
Overview: A medium-sized national organization
Mission: To voice the concerns of Roman Catholic sexual minorities; To promote the development of sexual theology, justice, & acceptance of the lesbian & gay community; To reinforce a sense of dignity & to encourage gay men & lesbian women to become more active members in the Church & society
Chief Officer(s):
Frank Testin, President
president@dignitycanada.org
Norman Prince, Secretary
Finances: *Funding Sources:* Donations
Activities: Encouraging spiritual development, education, & social involvement

Dignity Toronto Dignité
175 Windermere Ave., Toronto ON M6S 3J8
Tel: 416-925-9872
toronto@dignitycanada.org
dignitycanada.org/toronto.html
www.facebook.com/dignitytoronto
Overview: A small local organization founded in 1974 overseen by Dignity Canada Dignité
Mission: To support & affirm gay & lesbian Roman Catholics through spiritual development, education, social involvement, equity issues, & social events
Member of: Dignity Canada Dignité
Chief Officer(s):
Frank Testin, President
president@dignitycanada.org
Finances: *Annual Operating Budget:* Less than $50,000
Membership: 20; *Fees:* $30
Activities: Monthly liturgical meeting to support gay & lesbian Roman Catholics; social gatherings

Dignity Vancouver Dignité
PO Box 3016, Stn. Terminal, Vancouver BC V6B 3X5
e-mail: vancouver@dignitycanada.org
Overview: A small local organization founded in 1977 overseen by Dignity Canada Dignité
Mission: The organization works within the Catholic Church & with other Catholic groups to reform the church's theological stance pertaining to sexual minorities. It supports gay & lesbian Catholics & their friends, encouraging participation in educational, spiritual, & social activities.
Member of: Dignity Canada Dignité
Chief Officer(s):
Dennis Benoit, President, 604-669-3677
president@dignitycanada.org
Finances: *Annual Operating Budget:* Less than $50,000

Membership: 12; *Fees:* $35 individual; *Member Profile:* Roman Catholic gays, lesbians, friends

Dignity Winnipeg Dignité

PO Box 1912, Winnipeg MB R3C 3R2
Tel: 204-779-6446
winnipeg@dignitycanada.org
www.dignitycanada.org
Overview: A small provincial organization founded in 1970 overseen by Dignity Canada Dignité
Mission: To bring together gay & lesbian Catholics & their friends; To encourage a process of self-understanding & personal integration with respect to issues, including spirituality & sexuality
Member of: Dignity Canada Dignité
Chief Officer(s):
Thomas Novak, National Chaplain, 204-287-8583
Finances: *Annual Operating Budget:* Less than $50,000
3 volunteer(s)
Membership: 20; *Fees:* $25 (optional); *Member Profile:* LGBT community; non-gay men & women, encompassing a broad spectrum of professions, political beliefs, ethnic & linguistic backgrounds & economic levels
Activities: Regular liturgies/discussion groups; annual retreat; social events; brochures; *Speaker Service:* Yes

Diman Association Canada (Lebanese) (DAC)

c/o Diman Lebanese Centre, 345 Kearney Lake Rd., Bedford NS B4B 1H6
Tel: 902-457-3221
dimanassociation@gmail.com
Overview: A small national organization founded in 1973
Member of: Multicultural Association of Nova Scotia
Affliation(s): Diman Association Australia; Diman Association Lebanon (NADEE)
Chief Officer(s):
Samir Metlej, President
Finances: *Funding Sources:* Private donations
Membership: *Member Profile:* Over 15 years of age & from Diman

Diocèse militaire du Canada

USFC (O), Site Uplands, Édifice 469, Ottawa ON K1A 0K2
Tél: 613-990-7824; *Téléc:* 613-991-1056
carlone.l@forces.gc.ca
www.eveques.qc.ca/dioceses/Militaire.html
Aperçu: *Dimension:* petite; *Envergure:* nationale; Organisme sans but lucratif; fondée en 1987 surveillé par Canadian Conference of Catholic Bishops
Mission: Fournir une dimension spirituelle et morale à toutes les activités affectant le moral et le bien-être des membres catholiques des Forces canadiennes, leurs familles et les employés civils du Ministère de la Défense nationale
Membre de: La Conférence des évêques catholiques du Canada
Membre(s) du bureau directeur:
Donald Thériault, Évêque
Membre(s) du personnel: 3
Activités: *Bibliothèque:* Centre d'entraînement des aumôniers de Borden

Direct Sellers Association of Canada (DSA) / Association de ventes directes du Canada

#250, 180 Attwell Dr., Toronto ON M9W 6A9
Tel: 416-679-8555; *Fax:* 416-679-1568
info@dsa.ca
www.dsa.ca
www.facebook.com/322698510777
twitter.com/dsacanada
Overview: A small national organization founded in 1954
Mission: To represent companies that manufacture & distribute goods & services through independent sales contractors, away from a fixed retail location; To encourage strong consumer protection, through Codes of Ethics & Business Practices; To engage in discussion with government & industry; To act as the voice of the direct selling industry to government in pursuit of better business opportunities for Canadian entrepreneurs.
Chief Officer(s):
Angela Abdallah, Chair
Ross Creber, President & Secretary
Membership: 48

Direction Chrétienne Inc.

#520, 1450, rue City Councillors, Montréal QC H3A 2E6
Tel: 514-878-3035; *Fax:* 514-878-8048
info@direction.ca
www.direction.ca
Also Known As: Christian Direction
Overview: A small provincial charitable organization founded in 1964
Mission: Rendre visite aux communautés chrétiennes locales et particulièrement celles des grands centres urbains afin de se faire connaître et partager son mandat
Chief Officer(s):
Glenn Smith, Executive Director
Finances: *Annual Operating Budget:* $500,000-$1.5 Million
Staff Member(s): 13; 3 volunteer(s)
Membership: 1-99

DIRECTIONS Council for Vocational Services Society

#920, 99 Wyse Rd., Dartmouth NS B3A 4S5
Tel: 902-466-2220; *Fax:* 902-461-2220
www.directionscouncil.org
Previous Name: Workshop Council of Nova Scotia
Overview: A medium-sized provincial organization
Mission: To promote the abilities & inclusion of persons with disabilities by supporting member agencies
Chief Officer(s):
Bob Bennett, President
Membership: 28 agencies

Directors Guild of Canada (DGC) / La Guilde canadienne des réalisateurs

#600, 111 Peter St., Toronto ON M5V 2H1
Tel: 416-925-8200; *Fax:* 416-925-8400
Toll-Free: 888-972-0098
mail@dgc.ca
www.dgc.ca
twitter.com/DGCnational
vimeo.com/dgcnational; www.flickr.com/photos/dgcnational
Overview: A medium-sized national organization founded in 1962
Mission: To represent key creative & logistical personnel in the film & television industry; to promote & advance the quality & vitality of Canadian feature film
Chief Officer(s):
Sturla Gunnarsson, President
Brian Baker, National Executive Director
Staff Member(s): 18
Membership: 3,800+; *Member Profile:* Directors; Assistant Directors; Unit Directors; Art Directors; Assistant Art Directors; Set Designers; Production Designers; Assistant Production Managers; Location Managers; Assistant Location Managers; Unit Managers; Supervising Picture Editors; Picture Editors; Post Production Supervisors; Supervising Sound Editors; Sound Editors; Music Editors; Documentary Editors; Commercial Editors; Assistant Picture Editors; Assistant Sound Editors; Production Secretaries; Production Coordinators; Technical Coordinators; Post Production Coordinators; Production Assistants; Production Accountants; Art Department Trainees; Trainee Assistant Editors & any trainee, apprentice or other assistant of each category above
Activities: *Internships:* Yes; *Speaker Service:* Yes

Directors Guild of Canada (DGC)

#600, 111 Peter St., Toronto ON M5V 2H1
Tel: 416-925-8200; *Fax:* 416-925-8400
Toll-Free: 888-972-0098
mail@dgc.ca
www.dgc.ca
Overview: A small national organization founded in 1998
Mission: To collect, administer & distribute, on a collective basis, royalties & levies to which film & television directors are entitled under the national copyright legislation of certain countries in Europe
Member of: Director's Guild of Canada
Chief Officer(s):
Gerry Barr, National Executive Director & CEO
mchu@dgc.ca
Membership: *Fees:* $50

Alberta District Council
#133, 2526 Battleford Ave. SW, Calgary AB T3Z 7J4
Tel: 403-217-8672; *Fax:* 403-217-8678
dgc@dgcalberta.ca
www.dgc.ca/alberta
Chief Officer(s):
Hudson Cooley, Chair
Carol Romanow, Business Agent

Atlantic Regional District Council
#501B, 1496 Lower Water St., Halifax NS B3J 1R9
Tel: 902-492-3424; *Fax:* 902-492-2678
info@dgcatlantic.ca
www.dgc.ca/atlanticregion
www.facebook.com/groups/membersofthedgcatlanticregion
Chief Officer(s):
Shauna Hatt, Chair
James B. Nicholson, Business Agent
jamesbn@dgcatlantic.ca

British Columbia District Council
#430, 1152 Mainland St., Vancouver BC V6B 2X4
Tel: 604-688-2976; *Fax:* 604-688-2610
info@dgcbc.com
www.dgc.ca/bc
www.facebook.com/257912354261860
twitter.com/DGCBC
Chief Officer(s):
Nicholas Kendall, Chair
Crawford Hawkins, Executive Director
chawkins@dgcbc.com

Conseil du Québec
#708, 4200, boul Saint-Laurent, Montréal QC H2W 2R2
Tél: 514-844-4084; *Téléc:* 514-844-1067
action@dgc.ca
www.dgc.ca/quebec
Chief Officer(s):
Anne Sirois, Présidente
Geneviève Courcy, Coordinnatrice administrative
gcourcy@dgc.ca

Manitoba District Council
The Union Centre, #202B, 275 Broadway, Winnipeg MB R3C 4M6
Tel: 204-940-4301; *Fax:* 204-942-2610
www.dgcmanitoba.ca
Chief Officer(s):
Cathie Edgar, President
Scott McLaren, Business Agent
smclaren@dgc.ca

Ontario District Council
#500, 111 Peter St., Toronto ON M5V 2H1
Tel: 416-925-8200; *Fax:* 416-925-8400
Toll-Free: 888-972-0098; *Crisis Hot-Line:* 416-557-6223
odc@dgcontario.ca
www.dgc.ca/ontario
Chief Officer(s):
Alan Goluboff, Chair
alan@goluboff.ca
Bill Skolnik, Executive Director & CEO
bskolnik@dgcontario.ca

Saskatchewan District Council
c/o DGC National Office, #600, 111 Peter St., Toronto ON M5V 2H1
Toll-Free: 888-972-0098
sdc@dgc.ca
www.dgcsask.com
Chief Officer(s):
Bob King, Chair
Catherine Middleton, Business Agent
cmiddleton@dgc.ca

Disability Awareness Consultants

146 Haslam St., Toronto ON M1N 3N7
Tel: 416-267-5939; *Fax:* 416-267-8183
disabilityawarenessconsultants.com
Previous Name: Handidactis
Overview: A small local organization
Mission: The firm offers training & awareness programs to company employees so they can work comfortably with clients & coworkers who have disabilities. It helps companies to be in compliance with the Accessibility for Ontarians with Disabilities Act.
Chief Officer(s):
Lauri Sue Robertson, President
laurisue@bell.net
Finances: *Funding Sources:* Fee-based services
Staff Member(s): 5

Disabled Consumers Society of Colchester (DCSC)

PO Box 1794, Truro NS B2N 5Z5
Tel: 902-895-2110
Overview: A small local organization
Mission: The Disabled Consumers Society of Colchester (DCSC) is an advocacy organization working to enhance the lives of individuals with disabilities.
Member of: Nova Scotia League for Equal Opportunities
Chief Officer(s):
William King, President
Membership: *Fees:* $5

Activities: Drug assistance plan; technical aids and equipment for disabled persons; bus service for disabled persons

Disabled Individuals Alliance (DIAL)

Bethune Bldg., #262, 1278 Tower Rd., Halifax NS B3H 2Y9
Tel: 902-422-6888; *Fax:* 902-425-0766
MAJ@ns.sympatico.ca
www.nsnet.org/dial
Overview: A small local organization founded in 1978
Mission: DIAL (Disabled Individuals Alliance) is a cross-disability consumer group formed to bring together persons with varying disabilities and interested non-disabled individuals, enabling the disabled as a whole to speak out with a unified voice as to their common needs and goals.
Member of: Nova Scotia League for Equal Opportunities
Membership: *Member Profile:* People with disabilities; families of people with disabilities; supporters of people with disabilities

Disabled Peoples' International (DPI) / Organisation mondiale des personnes handicapées

#402, 214 Montreal Rd., Ottawa ON K1L 8L8
Tel: 613-563-2091; *Fax:* 613-563-3861
secretariat.dpi@gmail.com
www.dpi.org
Overview: A small international charitable organization founded in 1981
Mission: To promote the human rights of disabled people through full participation, equalization of opportunity & development
Affliation(s): United Nations; International Labour Organization
Chief Officer(s):
Javed Abidi, Chair
chairperson.dpi@gmail.com
Finances: *Annual Operating Budget:* $500,000-$1.5 Million
Staff Member(s): 5; 3 volunteer(s)
Membership: 135 National Assemblies; 1,300 e-news members; *Fees:* $50 developing country; $500 developed country; *Committees:* Human Rights; Francophone; Peace; Women's Independent Living; Education; Constitutional
Activities: *Internships:* Yes

Disabled Persons Community Resources *See* The In Community

Disabled Sailing Association of BC (DSA)

#318, 425 Carrall St., Vancouver BC V6B 6E3
Tel: 604-688-6464; *Fax:* 604-688-6463
info@disabilityfoundation.org
www.disabilityfoundation.org
www.facebook.com/DisabilityFoundation
twitter.com/disabilityfdn
Overview: A small provincial charitable organization founded in 1985
Mission: To help people with disabilities live independent lives
Affliation(s): BC Sport & Fitness Council for the Disabled
Chief Officer(s):
Matthew Wild, Communications Coordinator
matthew@disabilityfoundation.org
Membership: 6 non profit societies
Activities: Adopt-a-boat program; sailing experiences

Disabled Skiers Association of BC *See* BC Adaptive Snowsports

DisAbled Women's Network of Canada / Réseau d'Action des Femmes Handicapées du Canada

#505, 110, rue Ste. Thérèse, Montréal QC H2Y 1E6
Tel: 514-396-0009; *Fax:* 514-396-6585
Toll-Free: 866-396-0074
admin@dawncanada.net
www.dawncanada.net
www.facebook.com/dawnrafhcanada
Also Known As: DAWN-RAFH Canada
Overview: A small national organization founded in 1985
Mission: DAWN Canada's mission is to end the poverty, isolation, discrimination & violence experienced by women with disabilities; to ensure that they get the services & support needed, as well as the access to opportunities granted non-disabled people; to engage all levels of government & the wider disability & women's sectors & other stakeholders in addressing key issues.
Member of: National Action Committee on the Status of Women
Affliation(s): Council of Canadians with Disabilities
Chief Officer(s):
Carmela Sebastiana Hutchison, President
hutch@efirehose.net
Bonnie L. Brayton, National Executive Director
Finances: *Annual Operating Budget:* $100,000-$250,000
Staff Member(s): 5; 200 volunteer(s)
Membership: 300-400; *Fees:* Free; *Member Profile:* Women with disAbilities; *Committees:* Women's Partnership; Equality Rights; Health; Technology

Disaster Recovery Institute Canada (DRIC)

PO Box 552, #201, 200 Sanders Street, Kemptville ON K0G 1J0
Tel: 613-258-2271; *Fax:* 613-258-1447
Toll-Free: 888-728-3742
info@dri.ca
www.dri.ca
Also Known As: DRI CANADA
Overview: A small national organization founded in 1996
Mission: To provide the leadership & best practices that serve as a base of common knowledge for all business continuity/disaster recovery planners & organizations throughout our industry
Affliation(s): DRI International; Canadian Centre for Emergency Preparedness
Chief Officer(s):
Grant Whittaker, Executive Director
Dieter Raths, Certification & Membership Administ
Malcolm Smeaton, President
Finances: *Annual Operating Budget:* $250,000-$500,000; *Funding Sources:* Training courses; application fees; membership fees
Staff Member(s): 5; 20 volunteer(s)
Membership: 750; *Member Profile:* Passing of exam, review by committee; *Committees:* Certification; Education
Activities: Education & training; professional certification; promotion of the business continuity/disaster recovery field; major business continuity/emergency preparedness conferences throughout North America
Awards:
• Award of Excellence (Award)

Disc BC

BC
discbc.com
Also Known As: BC Disc Sports
Previous Name: BC Disc Sports Society
Overview: A small provincial organization
Mission: To be the provincial governing body of disc sports in British Columbia.
Affliation(s): BC Ultimate
Chief Officer(s):
Craig Sheather, President
Membership: 187; *Fees:* $5 through a recognized club; $10 individual
Activities: Disc golf; double disc court; freestyle; goaltimate; guts; ultimate

Discalced Carmelite Secular Order - Canada (OCDS)

11 Tangle Briarway, Toronto ON M2J 2M5
Tel: 416-223-2830; *Fax:* 416-223-9418
ocds.secretariat.ca@sympatico.ca
www.ocds.ca
Overview: A small national organization
Mission: To live in allegiance to Jesus Christ; To meditate on the law of the Lord; To engage in spiritual reading; To live an intense life of faith, hope, & charity
Affliation(s): Order of Our Lady of Mount Carmel; St. Teresa of Jesus; Archdiocese of Toronto
Finances: *Funding Sources:* Fundraising
Membership: *Member Profile:* Men & women, over the age of eighteen, who are constant in professing the Catholic faith; Members may not be professed members of another Order
Activities: Engaging in Daily Mass, morning & evening prayer from the Liturgy of the Hours, night, & mental prayer, & monthly formation meetings
Publications:
• Carmel-Lights
Type: Newsletter

Discovery Islands Chamber of Commerce

PO Box 790, Quathiaski Cove BC V0P 1N0
Tel: 250-285-2724
Toll-Free: 866-285-2724
chamber@discoveryislands.ca
www.discoveryislands.ca/chamber
Overview: A small local organization
Chief Officer(s):
Lynden McMartin, President
Membership: *Fees:* $15 individual; $25 small business; $50 business

Distance Riders of Manitoba Association (DRMA)

PO Box 36, Gr 36, RR#2, Dugald MB R0E 0K0
Tel: 204-444-2314
www.distanceridersofmanitoba.ca
Overview: A small provincial organization founded in 1993 overseen by Canadian Long Distance Riding Association
Mission: DRMA promotes endurance riding in the province of Manitoba & brings together equestrians interested in the sport.
Member of: Manitoba Horse Council; Canadian Long Distance Riding Association
Affliation(s): American Endurance Ride Conference
Chief Officer(s):
Myna Cryderman, President, 204-534-2390
myna@goinet.ca
Maura Leahy, Treasurer & Membership Contact
Maura.Leahy@live.ca
Membership: 30; *Fees:* $20 single; $25 family; $15 junior; *Member Profile:* Manitoba equestrians
Activities: Supervised rides; competitions

Distress Centre Niagara Inc.

195 East Main St., Welland ON L3B 3W7
Fax: 905-732-5966; *Crisis Hot-Line:* 905-688-3711
dcniagara@distresscentreniagara.com
distresscentreniagara.com
Overview: A small local organization founded in 1970 overseen by Distress Centres Ontario
Mission: To provide a no-cost confidential telephone support service by trained volunteers to assist anyone in need in the Niagara area
Finances: *Funding Sources:* United Way; Donations
Activities: *Speaker Service:* Yes

Distress Centre North Halton

PO Box 85, Georgetown ON L7G 4T1
Tel: 905-877-0655; *Fax:* 905-877-0655; *Crisis Hot-Line:* 905-877-1211
dcnhalton@bellnet.ca
www.distresscentrenorthhalton.ca
Overview: A small local organization founded in 1973 overseen by Distress Centres Ontario
Mission: To provide confidential listening, emotional support, referrals & information, & crisis intervention
Finances: *Funding Sources:* United Way; donations
Activities: Bereavement Support Program

Distress Centre of Durham Region (DCD)

306 Brock St. Nprth, Whitby ON L1N 4H7
Tel: 905-430-3511; *Fax:* 905-430-1381; *TTY:* 800-452-0688
dcd@distresscentredurham.com
www.distresscentredurham.com
Overview: A small local charitable organization founded in 1970
Mission: To help people in distress to cope, by providing emotional support, crisis/suicide management & community education
Member of: Distress Centres Ontario; Canadian Association of Suicide Prevention
Chief Officer(s):
Victoria Kehoe, Executive Director
victoria@distresscentredurham.com
Finances: *Annual Operating Budget:* $100,000-$250,000; *Funding Sources:* United Way; public donors; fundraising events
Staff Member(s): 3; 100 volunteer(s)
Membership: 100
Activities: Free, confidential 24-hr telephone helpline; crisis intervention; community education; suicide & homicide survivor support groups; adolescent suicide awareness program; *Awareness Events:* 5K Walk for Suicide Awareness, Sept.; *Speaker Service:* Yes

Distress Centre of Ottawa & Region (DCOR) / Centre de détresse d'Ottawa et la région

PO Box 3457, Stn. C, Ottawa ON K1Y 4J6
Tel: 613-238-1089; *Fax:* 613-722-5217; *Crisis Hot-Line:* 613-238-3311
www.dcottawa.on.ca
Also Known As: Distress Centre Ottawa
Previous Name: Distress Centre Ottawa/Carleton
Overview: A small local charitable organization founded in 1969 overseen by Distress Centres Ontario
Mission: The Distress Centre is a non-profit organization that provides 24/7 confidential telephone services for emotional support, suicide prevention/intervention, postvention, crisis intervention, information referral & education services. It is a registered charity, BN: 108079815RR0001
Affliation(s): American Association of Suicidology; Canadian

Association for Suicide Prevention; International Association for Suicide Prevention
Chief Officer(s):
Cathy McLeod, President
Finances: *Annual Operating Budget:* $500,000-$1.5 Million
Staff Member(s): 7; 150 volunteer(s)
Membership: 200+; *Committees:* Human Resources; Nominating; Executive; Promotion; Auction Planning
Activities: *Awareness Events:* Festival of Chocolate, Feb.; Leadercast Leadership Event, May; *Internships:* Yes; *Speaker Service:* Yes

Distress Centre Ottawa/Carleton *See* Distress Centre of Ottawa & Region

Distress Centre Peel
PO Box 48021, Stn. Dundas Sheppard, Mississauga ON L5A 4G8
Tel: 905-278-7055
Toll-Free: 800-363-0971; *TTY:* 905-278-4890; *Crisis Hot-Line:* 905-278-7208
mail@distresscentrepeel.com
www.distresscentrepeel.com
Overview: A small local charitable organization founded in 1973 overseen by Distress Centres Ontario
Mission: To improve callers' lives by providing confidential, 24-7 telephone support through trained, non-judgmental, caring volunteers
Affliation(s): United Way of Peel Region
Chief Officer(s):
Linda Gerger, Executive Director
Finances: *Funding Sources:* United Way; Trillium Foundation; Fundraising
Activities: Peel elder abuse support line 905-278-3141; *Internships:* Yes; *Speaker Service:* Yes

Distress Centre Wellington/Dufferin; Guelph Distress Centre *See* Community Torchlight Guelph/Wellington/Dufferin

Distress Centres of Toronto
PO Box 243, Stn. Adelaide, Toronto ON M5C 2J4
Tel: 416-598-0166; *TTY:* 416-408-0007; *Crisis Hot-Line:* 416-408-4357
info@torontodistresscentre.com
www.torontodistresscentre.com
twitter.com/DC_TO
www.youtube.com/user/DistressCentres
Overview: A small local organization founded in 1967
Mission: To assist emotionally distressed individuals deal with those issues they are currently unable to manage.
Affliation(s): Ontario Association of Distress Centres
Chief Officer(s):
Karen Letofsky, Executive Director, 416-598-0168
Karen@torontodistresscentre.com
Staff Member(s): 11
Activities: *Speaker Service:* Yes; *Rents Mailing List:* Yes

Distress Centres Ontario (DCO)
#1016, 30 Duke St. West, Kitchener ON N2H 3W5
Tel: 416-486-2242; *Fax:* 519-342-0970
info@dcontario.org
www.dcontario.org
Previous Name: Ontario Association of Distress Centres
Overview: A medium-sized provincial charitable organization founded in 1971
Mission: To transfer best practices between member centres; To promote, support & sustain member agencies
Chief Officer(s):
Karen Letofsky, Chair
Elizabeth Fisk, Executive Director
Membership: 15; *Member Profile:* Distress centres in Ontario
Activities: Hosting an annual meeting; Offering networking opportunities for member centres; Providing educational forums & training; Forming partnerships to assist in offering support, referral, & mental health services; Increasing public awareness; Liaising with funding bodies, government, & the public; *Awareness Events:* World Suicide Prevention Day, September

Distress Line Sarnia
Bldg. 1030, 1086 Modeland Rd., 2nd Fl., Sarnia ON N7S 6L2
Tel: 519-336-3000; *Fax:* 519-336-8517; *Crisis Hot-Line:* 888-347-8737
info@familycounsellingctr.com
www.familycounsellingctr.com
Also Known As: Family Counselling Centre
Overview: A small local charitable organization founded in 1973 overseen by Distress Centres Ontario
Mission: To help strengthen people & their relationships with others
Member of: Distress Centres Ontario
Chief Officer(s):
Tim Butler, Executive Director
Donna Martin, Program Coordinator
donna@familycounsellingctr.com
Finances: *Annual Operating Budget:* $50,000-$100,000; *Funding Sources:* United Way
Staff Member(s): 1; 55 volunteer(s)
Membership: 16; *Committees:* Suicide Prevention; Volunteer Co-Ordinators' Association; Senior Information Network
Activities: Conferences; resources; meetings; *Awareness Events:* Suicide Awareness Week; *Internships:* Yes; *Speaker Service:* Yes

District 69 Association for the Disabled *See* Parksville & District Association for Community Living

District 69 Community Arts Council *See* Oceanside Community Arts Council

District Indian Youth Club *See* Red Lake Indian Friendship Centre

District of Mission Arts Council
33529 - 1st Ave., Mission BC V2V 1H1
Tel: 604-826-0029; *Fax:* 604-826-0090
info@missionartscouncil.ca
www.missionartscouncil.ca
www.facebook.com/MissionArtsCentre
twitter.com/missionartscncl
Also Known As: Mission Arts Council
Overview: A small local charitable organization founded in 1972
Mission: To foster the development & appreciation of the arts by providing cultural & educational activities for the community of the District of Mission
Member of: Assembly of BC Arts Councils; South West Regional Arts Council
Chief Officer(s):
Nancy Arcand, Executive Director
nancy@missionartscouncil.ca
Finances: *Annual Operating Budget:* $50,000-$100,000; *Funding Sources:* Membership dues; grants; donations
Staff Member(s): 1; 60 volunteer(s)
Membership: *Fees:* $30 individual; $45 family; $75 group; $20 seniors; $5 MYAC student; $10 non-voting; *Member Profile:* Interest in the arts; *Committees:* Volunteer; Gallery; ArteScapes; Children's Festival; Christmas Craft Fair; Envision Twilight Concers; Events; Fundraising; Gift Shop; Halloween Haunted Mansion; Home Routes; Art Shows; Website
Activities: Art related workshops & festivals; Studio Tour; Children's Art Fest; Banner Festival; Gallery; *Awareness Events:* Children's Festival, June; Christmas Market, Nov.

Dive B.C. *See* British Columbia Diving

Dive Ontario
216 Gilwood Park Dr., Penetang ON L9M 1Z6
Tel: 705-355-3483; *Fax:* 705-355-4663
contactus@diveontario.com
www.diveontario.com
www.facebook.com/DiveOntario
Overview: A small provincial organization
Mission: To provide programs & services to its members
Affliation(s): Community & recreation centres around the province; Dive Plongeon Canada
Chief Officer(s):
Bernie Olanski, President
bernie@lexcor.ca
Membership: 11 clubs; *Member Profile:* Diving clubs in Ontario; *Committees:* HP Implementation; Sport Development; Media & Marketing

Diving Plongeon Canada (DPC) / Association canadienne du plongeon amateur Inc.
#312, 700 Industrial Ave., Ottawa ON K1G 0Y9
Tel: 613-736-5238; *Fax:* 613-736-0409
cada@diving.ca
www.diving.ca
www.facebook.com/DivingPCanada
twitter.com/DivingPlongeon
Also Known As: Canadian Amateur Diving Association Inc.
Overview: A medium-sized national charitable organization founded in 1967
Mission: To promote the growth & awareness of diving in Canada; To contribute to the development of globally accepted standards of diving; To support the rules & regulations of international competition
Member of: FINA
Affliation(s): Aquatics Federation of Canada; Swimming Natation Canada; Synchronized Swimming; Water Polo Canada
Chief Officer(s):
Penny Joyce, Chief Operating Officer
penny@diving.ca
Mitch Geller, Chief Technical Officer
mitch@diving.ca
Scott Cranham, Director, Talent Management
scott@diving.ca
Jeff Feeney, Manager, Events & Communications
jeff@diving.ca
Finances: *Funding Sources:* Government; Self Funding; Donations; Sponsorships
Staff Member(s): 10
Membership: 67 local diving clubs + 4,000 high performance athletes; *Member Profile:* Diving associations; Local diving clubs; High performance athletes; *Committees:* Athlete; Technical; Officials; Rules & Regulations
Activities: Providing programs & services for participants to achieve excellence & self-fulfillment; Obtaining media coverage & increasing spectators at events; Developing elite athletes; Communicating with members; Hosting an annual general meeting; Presenting DPC awards

Division de l'Atlantique de l'association Canadienne des Géographes *See* Canadian Association of Geographers

Dixon Hall
58 Sumach St., Toronto ON M5A 3J7
Tel: 416-863-0499; *Fax:* 416-863-9981
info@dixonhall.org
www.dixonhall.org
www.facebook.com/DixonHallToronto
twitter.com/dixon_hall
Overview: A medium-sized local charitable organization founded in 1929
Mission: To create opportunities for people of all ages to dream, to achieve and to live full and rewarding lives.
Chief Officer(s):
Kate Stark, Executive Director
Finances: *Funding Sources:* Government, Foundations, Donations, United Way
Membership: *Committees:* Strategic Planning; Finance & Audit; Fundraising, Development & Communications; Governance; Programs

Doctors Manitoba
20 Desjardins Dr., Winnipeg MB R3X 0E8
Tel: 204-985-5888; *Fax:* 204-985-5844
Toll-Free: 888-322-4242
general@docsmb.org
www.docsmb.org
Previous Name: Manitoba Medical Association
Overview: A medium-sized provincial organization founded in 1908 overseen by Canadian Medical Association
Mission: To advocate for Manitoba physicians, representing their professional & economic interests.
Chief Officer(s):
Debbie Bride, Communications Coordinator
dbride@docsmb.org
Robert Cram, CEO
rcram@docsmb.org
Finances: *Funding Sources:* Membership dues
Staff Member(s): 17
Membership: 2,272; *Member Profile:* Manitoba physicians, medical students & residents

Doctors Nova Scotia
25 Spectacle Lake Dr., Dartmouth NS B3B 1X7
Tel: 902-468-1866; *Fax:* 902-468-6578
info@doctorsns.com
www.doctorsns.com
Previous Name: Medical Society of Nova Scotia
Overview: A medium-sized provincial organization founded in 1862 overseen by Canadian Medical Association
Mission: To maintain the integrity of the medical profession; To represent members; To promote high quality health care & disease prevention in Nova Scotia
Member of: Canadian Medical Association
Chief Officer(s):
Nancy MacCready-Williams, CEO
John Chiasson, President
Membership: 2,200 physicians + 700 medical students & residents; *Member Profile:* Doctors, medical students, & residents in Nova Scotia

Activities: Educating the public on healthy lifestyle choices; Partnering with organizations; Offering the Youth Running for Fun Program; Voicing physician concerns with the health-care system; Advising on health-related policies & legislation
Meetings/Conferences: • Doctors Nova Scotia 2015 Annual Conference, June, 2015, Membertou Trade & Convention Centre, Cape Breton, NS
Scope: Provincial

Doctors of BC
#115, 1665 West Broadway, Vancouver BC V6J 5A4
Tel: 604-736-5551; *Fax:* 604-638-2917
Toll-Free: 800-665-2262
communications@doctorsofbc.ca
www.doctorsofbc.ca
twitter.com/doctorsofbc
Previous Name: British Columbia Medical Association
Overview: A medium-sized provincial organization founded in 1900 overseen by Canadian Medical Association
Mission: To promote a social, economic & political climate in which members can provide the citizens of British Columbia with the highest standard of health care while achieving maximum professional satisfaction & fair economic reward.
Chief Officer(s):
William Cunningham, President
president@doctorsofbc.ca
Activities: Programs to explore & articulate concerns regarding environmental health issues in a fashion which will best enable an informed public to participate in an open, valid, scientifically based analysis of issues involved; to assist society in development of policies dealing with environmental health issues; to enhance public health & harmony between humans & nature; Waste Management; Water Quality; Air Quality; *Internships:* Yes; *Speaker Service:* Yes; *Rents Mailing List:* Yes
Awards:
• Dr David M. Bachop Gold Medal for Distinguished Medical Service (Award)
• Dr. Cam Coady Medal of Excellence (Award)
• Dr Don Rix Award for Physician Leadership (D.B. Rix Award) (Award)
• Doctors of BC Silver Medal of Service Award (Award)
Publications:
• BC Medical Journal
Type: Journal; *Editor:* Jay Draper

Doctors without Borders Canada (MSF) / Médecins sans frontières Canada (MSF-C)
#402, 720 Spadina Ave., Toronto ON M5S 2T9
Tel: 416-964-0619; *Fax:* 416-963-8707
Toll-Free: 800-982-7903
msfcan@msf.ca
www.msf.ca
www.linkedin.com/company/6952
www.facebook.com/msf.english
twitter.com/MSF_Canada
www.youtube.com/user/MSFCanada
Also Known As: MSF Canada
Overview: A small national charitable organization founded in 1991
Mission: To offer assistance to populations in distress, to victims of natural or man-made disasters & to victims of armed conflict, without discrimination & irrespective of race, religion, creed or political affiliation.
Affliation(s): Association MSF - Canada
Chief Officer(s):
Heather Culbert, President
Stephen Cornish, Executive Director
Finances: *Annual Operating Budget:* Greater than $5 Million
Staff Member(s): 57
Activities: Sending medical & non-medical volunteers overseas to provide humanitarian relief during conflicts, epidemics & natural disasters; *Internships:* Yes; *Speaker Service:* Yes; *Rents Mailing List:* Yes; *Library* by appointment

Québec Office
#220, 1470, rue Peel, Montréal QC H3A 1T1
Tél: 514-845-5621; *Téléc:* 514-845-3707
Ligne sans frais: 866-878-5621
msfqc@msf.ca

Documentaristes du Canada ***See*** Documentary Organization of Canada

Documentary Organization of Canada (DOC) / Documentaristes du Canada
Centre for Social Innovation, #126, 215 Spadina Ave., Toronto ON M5T 2C7
Tel: 416-599-3844; *Fax:* 416-979-3936
Toll-Free: 877-467-4485
info@docorg.ca
www.docorg.ca
Previous Name: Canadian Independent Film Caucus
Overview: A small national organization founded in 1983
Mission: To support the art of independent documentary filmmaking & filmmakers in Canada
Member of: Observatoire du Documentaire; Canadian Conference of the Arts
Chief Officer(s):
Pepita Ferrari, Chair
Staff Member(s): 2
Membership: 650; *Fees:* $157.50 individual; $52.50 student; $525 associate; *Member Profile:* Directors; producers; craftspeople
Activities: Toronto, Ottawa-Gatineau, British Columbia, Atlantic, Québec, Newfoundland Chapters;
Publications:
• POV Magazine
Frequency: Quarterly

Dog Guides Canada
PO Box 907, 152 Wilson St., Oakville ON L6K 0G6
Tel: 905-842-2891; *Fax:* 905-842-3373
Toll-Free: 800-768-3030; *TTY:* 905-842-1585
info@dogguides.com
www.dogguides.com
www.facebook.com/LFCDogGuides
twitter.com/LFCDogGuides
Also Known As: Lions Foundation of Canada Dog Guides and Sibtech Creations
Previous Name: Canine Vision Canada
Overview: A medium-sized national organization founded in 1985
Mission: Provides Dog Guides to Canadians through three programs: Canine Vision Canada; Hearing Ear Dogs of Canada; Special Skills Dogs of Canada
Member of: Lions Foundation of Canada
Chief Officer(s):
Sandy Turney, Executive Director
sandyturney@dogguides.com
Finances: *Annual Operating Budget:* $3 Million-$5 Million
Staff Member(s): 35; 2000 volunteer(s)
Activities: *Speaker Service:* Yes

Doggone Safe
2295 Mohawk Trail, Campbellville ON L0P 1B0
Tel: 905-854-3232; *Fax:* 905-854-3271
Toll-Free: 877-350-3232
www.doggonesafe.com
www.facebook.com/DoggoneSafe
www.youtube.com/clickerpuppytrainer
Overview: A small national organization
Mission: To prevent dog bites; To help children & families learn how to be safe around familiar & unfamiliar dogs; To support victims of dog bites
Chief Officer(s):
Joan Orr, President
joanorr@doggonesafe.com
Membership: *Fees:* $20
Activities: Offering Be a Tree, Be Doggone Smart, & Be Doggone Smart at Home seminars for children, workers, & parents

Dominion Automobile Association Limited
PO Box 5817, London ON N6A 4T3
Toll-Free: 877-322-1033; *Crisis Hot-Line:* 519-434-2185
www.daa.ca
Overview: A small national organization
Mission: To provide road assistance to members.
Affliation(s): MADD Canada
Chief Officer(s):
Jackie McTaggart, Chief Operating Officer
Membership: *Member Profile:* Automobile owners
Activities: Battery boost; locked car service; tire change; fuel delivery, towing

Dominion Marine Association ***See*** Canadian Shipowners Association

Dominion of Canada Rifle Association (DCRA) / L'Association de tir dominion du canada
45 Shirley Blvd., Ottawa ON K2K 2W6
Tel: 613-829-8281; *Fax:* 613-829-0099
office@dcra.ca
www.dcra.ca
Overview: A small national charitable organization founded in 1868
Chief Officer(s):
Jim Thompson, Executive Director
Stan E. Frost, Executive Vice-President
T.F. deFaye, President
Finances: *Annual Operating Budget:* $100,000-$250,000
Staff Member(s): 3; 60 volunteer(s)
Membership: 1,000; *Member Profile:* 10 provincial rifle associations; Yukon Rifle Association; National Capital Region Rifle Association
Activities: Annual Canadian Fullbore Rifle Championships

Dominion Rabbit & Cavy Breeders Association (DR&CBA)
c/o Maureen Dyke, 243099 - 5th Side Rd., RR#1, Grand Valley ON L0N 1G0
www.drcba.ca
Overview: A small national organization founded in 1909
Mission: To promote & encourage the hobby of raising purebred rabbits & cavies for market, for show & for pleasure
Chief Officer(s):
Neil Taylor, President
nstaylor@sympatico.ca
Maureen Dyke, Secretary-Treasurer
maureendyke@sympatico.ca
Membership: 100+; *Fees:* $16 family; $12 adult; $8 youth; *Member Profile:* Rabbit & cavy enthusiasts
Activities: Shows; sweepstakes awards program; workshops; youth member program; licensing of judges; publishes standards
Awards:
• Sweepstakes Awards (Award)

The Donkey Sanctuary of Canada (DSC)
PO Box 27063, Stn. Clair, Guelph ON N1L 0C1
Tel: 519-836-1697; *Fax:* 519-821-0698
info@thedonkeysanctuary.ca
www.thedonkeysanctuary.ca
www.facebook.com/TheDonkeySanctuary
twitter.com/DonkeySancCa
www.youtube.com/user/DonkeySanctuary001
Overview: A small national charitable organization founded in 1992
Mission: To provide a lifelong home to unwanted, neglected or abused donkeys & mules; To offer animal welfare education; To offer a life skills & companion animal program to people with unique needs
Chief Officer(s):
Katharine Harkins, Executive Director
Finances: *Annual Operating Budget:* $500,000-$1.5 Million; *Funding Sources:* Private donations & foundation grants
Staff Member(s): 9; 35 volunteer(s)
Activities: *Awareness Events:* Donkey Day, 2nd Sunday in June; *Internships:* Yes; *Speaker Service:* Yes

Donner Canadian Foundation / Fondation canadienne Donner
8 Prince Arthur Ave., 3rd Fl., Toronto ON M5R 1A9
Tel: 416-920-6400; *Fax:* 416-920-5577
www.donnerfoundation.org
Overview: A small national organization founded in 1950
Mission: In addition to ongoing funding of public policy research, the Foundation supports environmental, international development, and social service projects.
Chief Officer(s):
Helen McLean, Executive Director
mclean@donner.ca
Amy Buskirk, Senior Program Officer
buskirk@donner.ca
Awards:
• The Donner Prize (Award)
Award of $35,000 for the best book on Canadian public policy; five runners-up prizes of $5,000 each

Donneurs d'organes du Canada ***See*** Organ Donors Canada

Door & Hardware Institute in Canada
#310, 2175 Sheppard Ave. East, Toronto ON M2J 1W8
Tel: 416-492-6502; *Fax:* 416-491-1670
www.dhicanada.ca
twitter.com/dhicanada
Overview: A small international organization founded in 1977
Mission: To serve Canadian members as the professional development, information, advocate & certification resource for the total distribution process in the architectural openings industry.
Chief Officer(s):

Lawrence Beatty, President
lawrence.beatty@shanahans.com
Carolyne Vigon, Executive Director, 416-492-6502 Ext. 251
carolyne@taylorenterprises.com
Staff Member(s): 6
Membership: 700 Canadian + 5,000 international; *Fees:* Schedule available; *Committees:* Strategic Planning; Finance; Education; Membership; Marketing & Communications; Codes; Program

Doorsteps Neighbourhood Services

#106, 200 Chalkfarm Dr., Toronto ON M3L 2H7
Tel: 416-243-5480; *Fax:* 416-243-7406
www.doorsteps.ca
Overview: A medium-sized local charitable organization
Mission: To focus on community education, prevention, & the enhancement of resiliency of individuals & communities
Chief Officer(s):
Carol Thames, Executive Director
cthames@doorsteps.ca
Finances: *Annual Operating Budget:* $500,000-$1.5 Million; *Funding Sources:* Government; United Way
Staff Member(s): 12

Dorchester & Westmorland Literacy Council

c/o 132 Lockhart Ave., Moncton NB E1C 6R7
Tel: 506-379-4064; *Fax:* 506-379-4204
Overview: A small local charitable organization
Mission: The Council provides educational opportunities to inmates at Dorchester & Westmorland institutions.
Affliation(s): Laubach Literacy New Brunswick
Chief Officer(s):
Bill Cairns, Contact
William.Cairns@CSC-SCC.gc.ca

Dorval Historical Society *Voir* Société historique de Dorval

Douglas College Faculty Association (DCFA) / Association des professeurs du Collège Douglas

PO Box 2503, New Westminster BC V3L 5B2
Tel: 604-527-5166; *Fax:* 604-520-1496
www.dcfa.ca
Overview: A small local organization
Mission: To act as the bargaining agent for faculty at Douglas College in New Westminster & Coquitlam, BC; to negotiate wages, benefits and working conditions for its members; to ensure the representation of faculty interests; to represent faculty facing complaints; to liaise with other labour groups.
Chief Officer(s):
Erin Rozman, President
rozmane@douglascollege.ca
Lil Mairs, Administrative Assistant
mairsl@douglas.bc.ca
Membership: *Committees:* Contract; Occupational Health & Safety; Rehabilitation

Down Syndrome Association of Ontario (DSAO)

#304, 300 Earl Grey Dr., Ottawa ON K2T 1C1
Tel: 905-439-6644
info@dsao.ca
www.dsao.ca
www.facebook.com/DSAOntario
twitter.com/DSAOntario
Overview: A small provincial charitable organization
Mission: To ensure equality for people with down syndrome
Meetings/Conferences: • 2015 Down Syndrome Association of Ontario Conference, 2015, ON
Scope: Provincial

Down Syndrome Association of Toronto (DSAT)

#303, 40 Wynford Dr., Toronto ON M3C 1J5
Tel: 416-966-0990
info@dsat.ca
www.dsat.ca
www.facebook.com/dsatoronto
twitter.com/DSAToronto
www.youtube.com/user/DSAToronto
Overview: A small local charitable organization founded in 1987
Mission: To pursue civil & human rights, equality of opportunity & the full integration of persons with Down syndrome; To ensure that all students with Down syndrome are welcomed in regular classes in neighbourhood schools with appropriate support services
Chief Officer(s):
Bhaskar Thiagarajan, President
Membership: *Fees:* $40
Activities: Social & information network; educational seminars & family-centered social events; *Awareness Events:* Down Syndrome Awareness Week, Nov.; *Rents Mailing List:* Yes; *Library* Open to public by appointment

Down Syndrome Research Foundation & Resource Centre (DSRF)

1409 Sperling Ave., Burnaby BC V5B 4J8
Tel: 604-444-3773; *Fax:* 604-431-9248
Toll-Free: 888-464-3773
info@dsrf.org
www.dsrf.org
www.facebook.com/109779455702001
twitter.com/DSRFcanada
www.youtube.com/user/DSRFCANADA
Overview: A small national charitable organization founded in 1995
Mission: To maximize the ability of people with Down Syndrome to lead independent lives & to participate in the community in which they live
Member of: Down Syndrome International
Chief Officer(s):
John N. Flintoft, Chair
Dawn McKenna, Executive Director
dawn@dsrf.org
Finances: *Annual Operating Budget:* $500,000-$1.5 Million
Staff Member(s): 8; 15 volunteer(s)
Membership: 200; *Fees:* $30; *Member Profile:* Parents, educators, general public
Activities: Video conference; summer school; fall conference; speech-language programs; health clinics; *Library* Open to public

Downtown Business Association of Edmonton (DBA)

10121 Jasper Ave., Edmonton AB T5J 4X6
Tel: 780-424-4085
info@edmontondowntown.com
www.edmontondowntown.com
www.facebook.com/190749960939389
twitter.com/DBAyeg
Overview: A medium-sized local organization founded in 1985
Mission: To promote downtown as the preferred place to work, shop, live & enjoy
Chief Officer(s):
Penny Omell, Chair
Jim Taylor, Executive Director
Finances: *Funding Sources:* Municipal levy & sponsorships
Membership: 1,831; *Member Profile:* Downtown businesses; *Committees:* Business Recruitment; Operations; Marketing; Executive
Activities: Family Day; Light-Up Downtown; Indoor Santa Parade; Chili Cook-Off

The Downtown Churchworkers' Association *See* Moorelands Community Services

Downtown Legal Services (DLS)

Fasken Martineau DuMoulin Centre for Legal Services, 655 Spadina Ave., Toronto ON M5S 2H9
Tel: 416-934-4535; *Fax:* 416-934-4536
law.dls@utoronto.ca
downtownlegalservices.ca
Also Known As: University of Toronto Community Legal Clinic
Overview: A small local organization founded in 1972
Mission: To provide legal assistance to those who cannot afford other legal services.
Member of: Association of Student Legal Aid Societies of Ontario
Affliation(s): University of Toronto Faculty of Law; Out of the Cold, for homeless clients; MealTrans, for transgendered clients; Red Door, a shelter for abused women and their children
Chief Officer(s):
Lisa Cirillo, Executive Director
Martha Turner, Office Manager
Finances: *Funding Sources:* Legal Aid Ontario
Staff Member(s): 6
Membership: *Member Profile:* Students at faculty of law
Activities: Legal assistance in summary conviction, criminal, academic, landlord/tenant, employment & immigration; Public Interest Advocacy clinical education programs; *Internships:* Yes; *Speaker Service:* Yes; *Library:* DLS Library

Downtown Truro Partnership (DTP)

PO Box 912, 605 Prince St., Truro NS B2N 5G7
Tel: 902-895-9258; *Fax:* 902-895-9712
contactus@downtowntruro.ca
www.downtowntruro.ca
www.facebook.com/pages/Downtown-Truro-Partnership/170541396310251
Overview: A small local organization founded in 1979
Chief Officer(s):
Debbie Elliott, Executive Director

Downtown Vancouver Association (DVA)

PO Box 21013, #11, 200 Burrard St., Vancouver BC V6C 3L6
Tel: 604-468-7382
info@thedva.com
www.thedva.com
Overview: A medium-sized local organization founded in 1946
Mission: To promote downtown Vancouver as the focus of urban activities in the Lower Mainland & the Province of British Columbia; to enhance the economic, commercial & social welfare of Downtown Vancouver; To study & advance any project, plan or improvement designed to benefit the City as a whole, & Downtown Vancouver in particular; To provide cooperation & aid to individuals or groups in projects designed to benefit the City & Downtown Vancouver; To regularly communicate to the public concerning the health & welfare of the whole City & the downtown; To commit to action on all matters that benefit the City & Downtown Vancouver
Member of: International Downtown Association
Affliation(s): Downtown Vancouver Business Improvement Association
Chief Officer(s):
Melissa Picher Kelly, Executive Director
melissa@thedva.com
Finances: *Annual Operating Budget:* $50,000-$100,000; *Funding Sources:* Membership fees
Staff Member(s): 1
Membership: 200 corporate + 10 institutional + 10 associate + 100 individual; *Fees:* $120-$1,400; *Committees:* Planning & Development; Retail; Taxation & Assessment; Tourism; Transportation & Communications; Arts & Culture
Activities: Networking monthly speaker series;

Dr. H. Bliss Murphy Cancer Care Foundation

Dr. H. Bliss Murphy Cancer Centre, 300 Prince Philip Dr., St. John's NL A1B 3V6
Tel: 709-777-2133; *Fax:* 709-777-2372
cancercarefoundation.nl.ca
www.facebook.com/cancercarefoundation
twitter.com/Cancercarefdn
www.youtube.com/user/Cstarz76
Overview: A small local charitable organization
Mission: To raise money on behalf of the Dr. H. Bliss Murphy Cancer Centre in order to improve the services offered to patients & to fund research
Chief Officer(s):
Lynette Hillier, Executive Director
lynette.hillier@easternhealth.ca
Staff Member(s): 7
Membership: *Committees:* Executive; Finance

Dr. James Naismith Basketball Foundation / La fondation de basketball Dr James Naismith

2729 Draper Ave., Ottawa ON K2H 7A1
Tel: 613-256-3610
www.naismithbasketball.ca
Also Known As: Naismith Foundation; Naismith Museum & Hall of Fame
Overview: A medium-sized national charitable organization founded in 1989
Mission: To establish & operate the Naismith International Basketball Centre which will reflect the remarkable heritage & development of Naismith's game in Canada & around the world.
Affliation(s): Basketball Canada
Finances: *Funding Sources:* Fundraising; merchandise sales; special events
Activities: To preserve, conserve & promote the life & times of Dr. James Naismith & his gift to mankind - basketball, through the museum & related programs; *Library:* Naismith Basketball Resource Collection; by appointment

Dragon Boat Canada (DBC) / Bateau-Dragon Canada (BDC)

PO Box 51517, Toronto M4E 3V7
Tel: 613-482-1377
dragonboat.ca
www.facebook.com/DBC.BDC
twitter.com/DragonBoatCda
Overview: A medium-sized national organization

Mission: To be the official governing of dragon boat racing in Canada.
Member of: International Dragon Boat Federation
Chief Officer(s):
Chloe Greenhalgh, Executive Director
director@dragonboat.ca
Membership: *Fees:* Schedule available

Dragon Boat Festival Society *See* Canadian International Dragon Boat Festival Society

Drainage Superintendents Association of Ontario (DSAO)

PO Box 100, Bradford ON L3Z 2A7
Tel: 905-778-4321
dsao@dsao.net
www.dsao.net
Overview: A medium-sized provincial organization founded in 1984
Mission: To improve the knowledge of drainage through the exchange of ideas & information; to consider & deal with construction, maintenance of, & improvement to drainage works; to unite the drainage superintendents & commissioners for the promotion of better maintenance, repair & improvement of drainage works in Ontario.
Chief Officer(s):
Eric Westerberg, President
ericw@chatham-kent.ca
Sarah Murray, Executive Secretary
smurray@townofbwg.com
Finances: *Funding Sources:* Membership fees
Membership: *Fees:* $175

Bluewater
Woolwich ON
Tel: 519-880-2708; *Fax:* 519-880-2709
Chief Officer(s):
Greg Nancekivell, Board Director
greg@dietricheng.com

Central Region
Bradford West Gwillimbury ON
Tel: 905-778-4321; *Fax:* 905-775-0153
dsao@dsao.net
Chief Officer(s):
Frank Jonkman, Past President, DSAO
fjonkman@townofbwg.com

Eastern Region
Ottawa ON
Tel: 613-580-2424; *Fax:* 613-489-2880
dsao@dsao.net
Chief Officer(s):
Eric Cryderman, Board Director
eric.cryderman@ottawa.ca

Elgin/Lambton/Middlesex
Sarnia ON
Tel: 519-332-0330; *Fax:* 519-332-0776
dsao@dsao.net
Chief Officer(s):
David Moores, Board Director
david.moores@sarnia.ca

Essex/Chatham/Kent
Chatham-Kent ON
Tel: 519-360-1998; *Fax:* 519-436-3240
dsao@dsao.net
Chief Officer(s):
Eric Westerberg, President, DSAO
ericw@chatham-kent.ca

Niagara Region
Norfolk County ON
Tel: 519-582-2100; *Fax:* 519-582-4571
dsao@dsao.net
Chief Officer(s):
Bill Mayes, Vice-President, DSAO
bill.mayes@norfolkcounty.ca

Drayton Valley & District Chamber of Commerce (DVDCC)

PO Box 5318, Drayton Valley AB T7A 1R5
Tel: 780-542-7578; *Fax:* 780-542-2688
www.dvchamber.com
Overview: A small local organization founded in 1961
Mission: To promote & enhance free enterprise & the economy of Drayton Valley & district.
Member of: Alberta Chamber Executives; Alberta Chamber of Commerce; Canadian Chamber of Commerce
Chief Officer(s):
Tom Campbell, President
dvchamberpresident@gmail.com
Finances: *Annual Operating Budget:* $100,000-$250,000
Staff Member(s): 2; 12 volunteer(s)
Membership: 130+; *Fees:* $65-$295; *Committees:* Agriculture; Advisory; Business Development; Natural Resources; Policy Development & Review; Retail Merchants; Tourism; Trade Show; AGM; Membership
Activities: Spring Trade Show & Sale; Fall Trade Show; Parade Entries; host seminars & speakers; Junior Achievement; *Library:* Tourism Information Centre; Open to public
Awards:
• Best Business Award (Award)
• Chamber Spirit Award (Award)

Drayton Valley Association for Community Living *See* Beehive Support Services Association

Dreams Take Flight

PO Box 7000, Stn. Airport, Dorval QC H4Y 1J2
Tel: 204-479-5267
www.dreamstakeflight.ca
www.facebook.com/DreamsTakeFlightCanada
twitter.com/DreamsTakeFlght
Overview: A small national charitable organization founded in 1989
Mission: To provide Disney vacations to children with mental & physical disabilities
Chief Officer(s):
Bev Watson, President
beverly.watson@aircanada.ca

Drinks Ontario

41 Hatherton Cres., Toronto ON M3A 1P6
Tel: 416-699-9535; *Fax:* 416-699-3907
www.drinksontario.com
Previous Name: The Ontario Imported Wine-Spirit-Beer Association (OIWSBA)
Overview: A medium-sized provincial organization founded in 1958
Mission: To represent the interests of manufacturers, agents, importers, marketing groups, trade offices and distributors of beverage alcohol products in Ontario.
Chief Officer(s):
Ian Campbell, Executive Director
ian.campbell@drinksontario.com
Membership: 99; *Fees:* Schedule available; *Member Profile:* Provincial trade association representing manufacturers, agents, importers, marketing groups, international trade offices & distributors of imported alcohol products in Ontario

Drive Canada

#100, 208 Legget Dr., Ottawa ON K2K 1Y6
Tel: 613-287-1515; *Fax:* 613-248-3484
Toll-Free: 866-282-8395
info.drivecanada@shaw.ca
drivecanada.ca
Previous Name: Canadian Driving Society
Overview: A small national organization founded in 1983
Mission: To represent competitive & non-competitive drivers
Member of: Equine Canada
Affliation(s): American Driving Society
Chief Officer(s):
Simon Rosenman, Chair, Canadian Driving Committee
cdc.drivecanada@shaw.ca
Kathleen Winfield, Chair, Regional Council
regionalcouncil.drivecanada@shaw.ca
Wendy Gayfer, Program Coordinator, FEI Non-Olympic Disciplines
wgayfer@equinecanada.ca
Membership: *Member Profile:* Recreational & competitive drivers, coaches & officials; *Committees:* Athlete Development; Coaching Development; Combined Driving; Communications; Competitions; Draft Driving; Finance; High Performance; Licensed Officials; Pleasure Driving; Recreational Driving; Rules
Activities: Promotes sport of carriage driving; trains & evaluates coaches & officials; *Library*
Awards:
• Top Driver (Award)
Publications:
• Drive Canada E-Bulletin
Type: Newsletter

Driving School Association of Ontario (DSAO)

#111, 557 Dixon Rd., Toronto ON M9W 6K1
Tel: 416-247-2278; *Fax:* 416-247-4883
info@dsao.com
www.dsao.com
Overview: A small provincial organization founded in 1975
Mission: To maintain & improve the professional standards of driver education.
Membership: *Member Profile:* Driving Schools in Ontario

DRS Earthwise Society; Delta Recycling Society *See* Earthwise Society

Drumheller & District Chamber of Commerce (DDCC)

PO Box 999, 60 First Ave. West, Drumheller AB T0J 0Y0
Tel: 403-823-8100; *Fax:* 403-823-4469
info@drumhellerchamber.com
www.drumhellerchamber.com
www.facebook.com/drumchamber
twitter.com/DrumChamber
Overview: A small local organization founded in 1921
Member of: Canadian Chamber of Commerce; Alberta Chamber of Commerce
Chief Officer(s):
Ed Mah, President
Heather Bitz, General Manager
Staff Member(s): 4; 13 volunteer(s)
Membership: 240; *Fees:* $100-$250 business; $70 owner/farmer/non-profit; $130 government agency; $999 corporate; *Committees:* Tourism; Downtown Merchants; Golf Tournament

Drumheller Museum Society *See* Badlands Historical Centre

Dryden & District Association for Community Living *See* Community Living Dryden

Dryden District Chamber of Commerce (DDCC)

284 Government St., Hwy. 17, Dryden ON P8N 2P3
Tel: 807-223-2622; *Fax:* 807-223-2626
Toll-Free: 800-667-0935
Other Communication: Alternate e-mail: chamber@mail.drytel.net
chamber@drytel.net
www.drydenchamber.ca
Overview: A small local organization founded in 1931
Mission: To represent & strengthen the business community & membership through promoting & lobbying business concerns on the municipal, provincial & federal levels of government
Member of: Ontario Chamber of Commerce; Canadian Chamber of Commerce; Northwestern Ontario Associated Chambers of Commerce
Affliation(s): Sunset County Travel Association; Patricia Regional Tourist Council; Kenora District Camp Owners Association
Chief Officer(s):
Stafanie Armstrong, Chair
Alana Lobreau, Executive Coordinator
Finances: *Annual Operating Budget:* $100,000-$250,000; *Funding Sources:* Membership dues; fees for service; fundraising
Staff Member(s): 2; 14 volunteer(s)
Membership: 207; *Fees:* Schedule available
Activities: Home & Trade Show; Canada Day; Business Education; Retail Promotion; Santa Claus Parade; *Awareness Events:* Annual Business Excellence Awards
Awards:
• Business Excellence Awards (Award)

Dryden Native Friendship Centre

74 Queen St., Dryden ON P8N 1A4
Tel: 807-223-4180; *Fax:* 807-223-6275
dnfc@drytel.net
Overview: A small local organization founded in 1984
Member of: Ontario Federation of Indian Friendship Centres
Chief Officer(s):
Sally Ledger, Executive Director
Activities: Referrals for students; School Lunch Program; workshops; assistance to transients; helping social assistance clients; children's summer programs; Native language & cultural training; legal clinic.

Ducks Unlimited Canada (DUC) / Canards Illimités Canada

PO Box 1160, Mallard Bay at Hwy. 220, Stonewall MB R0C 2Z0
Tel: 204-467-3000; *Fax:* 204-467-9028
Toll-Free: 800-665-3825
Other Communication: member@ducks.ca
webfoot@ducks.ca

www.ducks.ca
www.facebook.com/ducksunlimitedcanada
twitter.com/ducanada
www.youtube.com/user/DucksUnlimitedCanada
Also Known As: DU Canada
Overview: A large national charitable organization founded in 1938
Mission: To conserve, restore & manage wetlands & associated habitats for waterfowl, as well as for the benefit of other wildlife & people
Affiliation(s): North American Waterfowl Management Plan (NAWMP)
Chief Officer(s):
Gregory E. Siekaniec, Chief Executive Officer
Tom Worden, President
James A. Fortune, Chief Operating Officer
Sandy Gousseau, National Director, Communications & Marketing
Grant Monck, National Director, Development
Henry Murkin, National Director, Conservation
Loraine Nyokong, National Director, Fundraising & Membership
Gary Goodwin, Executive Corporate Secretary & Counsel
Finances: *Annual Operating Budget:* Greater than $5 Million; *Funding Sources:* Donations; Fundraising; Corporate partners; Government agencies
Staff Member(s): 368; 6,20 volunteer(s)
Membership: 139,000; *Fees:* $35; *Committees:* Executive; Governance; Risk & Finance; Conservation Planning; Membership & Revenue; Personnel Policy; Nominating
Activities: Conducting on-the-ground habitat conservation projects, research, education programs & public policy work to stop wetland loss; *Library:* Ducks Unlimited Film & Video Library
Publications:
• Conservator
Type: Magazine; *Frequency:* 5 pa; *Accepts Advertising*
Profile: Feature articles from the world of wetland & waterfowl conservation
• Ducks Unlimited Canada Annual Report
Type: Yearbook; *Frequency:* Annually
Profile: A yearly tracking of Ducks Unlimited Canada's scientific research, conservation programs, partnerships, volunteers, & supporters

Alberta Provincial Office
17915 - 118th Ave., Edmonton AB T5S 1L6
Tel: 780-489-2002; *Fax:* 780-489-1856
Toll-Free: 866-479-3825
du_edmonton@ducks.ca

British Columbia Provincial Office
#511, 13370 - 78th Ave., Surrey BC V3W 0H6
Tel: 604-592-0987; *Fax:* 604-592-0930
Toll-Free: 800-665-3825
du_surrey@ducks.ca

Manitoba Provincial Office
#2, 545 Conservation Dr., Brandon MB R7A 7L8
Tel: 204-729-3500; *Fax:* 204-727-6044
du_brandon@ducks.ca

New Brunswick Provincial Office
752 Union St., Fredericton NB E3A 3P2
Tel: 506-458-8848; *Fax:* 506-458-9921
Toll-Free: 888-920-3330
du_fredericton@ducks.ca

Newfoundland & Labrador Provincial Office
19 Conway St., Grand Falls-Windsor NL A2A 2P4
Tel: 709-486-7674; *Fax:* 709-489-1554
Toll-Free: 877-516-1554
du_newfoundland@ducks.ca
Chief Officer(s):
Ian Barnett, Director, Regional Operations

Northwest Territories Office
PO Box 1438, #4A, 4921 - 49th St., Yellowknife NT X1A 2P1
Tel: 867-873-6744

Nova Scotia Provincial Office
PO Box 430, #64, Hwy. 6, Amherst NS B4H 3Z5
Tel: 902-667-8726; *Fax:* 902-667-0910
Toll-Free: 866-903-8257
du_amherst@ducks.ca
Chief Officer(s):
Mark Gloutney, Provincial Manager

Ontario Provincial Office
#1, 740 Hurontario Rd., Barrie ON L4N 6C6
Tel: 705-721-4444; *Fax:* 705-721-4999
Toll-Free: 888-402-4444
du_barrie@ducks.ca

Prince Edward Island Provincial Office
Farm Centre, #113, 420 University Ave., Charlottetown ON C1A 7Z5
Tel: 902-569-4544; *Fax:* 902-569-4674
du_charlottetown@ducks.ca
Chief Officer(s):
Jamie Fortune, Director, Regional Operations

Québec Provincial Office
#260, 710, rue Bouvier, Québec QC G2J 1C2
Tél: 418-623-1650; *Téléc:* 418-623-0420
du_quebec@ducks.ca
Chief Officer(s):
Bernard Filion, Directeur provincial

Saskatchewan Provincial Office
PO Box 4465, 1030 Winnipeg St., Regina SK S4R 8P8
Tel: 306-569-0424; *Fax:* 306-565-3699
Toll-Free: 866-252-3825
du_regina@ducks.ca

Yukon Territory Office
PO Box 31775, 308 Hanson St., Whitehorse YT Y1A 6L3
Tel: 867-668-3824

Dufferin Arts Council (DAC)
PO Box 21052, 150 - 1 St., Orangeville ON L9W 4S7
dufferinartscouncil.com
Previous Name: Shelburne Arts Council
Overview: A small local organization founded in 1992
Mission: Fundraising for scholarship awards; Other support activities; Social events to raise quality of community involvement in & appreciation of the arts (drama, music, painting, sculpture, etc.)
Chief Officer(s):
Pina Di Leo, President, 647-389-2568
Membership: *Fees:* $25 individual; $35 family; *Committees:* Nomination; Grants

Dufferin Association for Community Living *See* Community Living Dufferin

Dufferin Child & Family Services
655 Riddell Rd., Orangeville ON L9W 3H7
Tel: 519-941-1530
dcafs.on.ca
Overview: A small local organization
Mission: To advocate for & provide coordinated, quality services for children, families & individuals
Chief Officer(s):
Bonnie Jones, President
Activities: Child protection services; child mental health program; developmental support services; autism services

Dufferin County Beekeepers' Association
Erin ON
Tel: 519-833-0714
Overview: A small local organization
Mission: To provide education for the beekeepers of Dufferin County
Member of: Ontario Beekeepers' Association
Chief Officer(s):
Tom Fox, President
tomjfox1957@gmail.com
Membership: *Member Profile:* Beekeepers in Dufferin County, Ontario
Activities: Organizing monthly meetings at Holmes Agro Ltd, in Orangeville; Offering a forum for networking

Dufferin Peel Educational Resource Workers' Association (DPERWA)
#106, 5805 Whittle Rd., Mississauga ON L4Z 2J1
Tel: 905-501-1622; *Fax:* 905-501-1623
www.dperwa.com
Overview: A small local organization founded in 1986
Mission: DPERWA is the official, certified bargaining body for all Educational Assistants, Designated Early Childhood Educators & Supply ERWs employed with the Dufferin Peel Catholic District School Board.
Chief Officer(s):
Diane Kossel, President
president@dperwa.com
Membership: *Member Profile:* Educational Resource Workers with certificates or degrees from recognized colleges or universities
Activities: *Library*

The Duke Ellington Society - Toronto Chapter #40 (TDES)
Toronto ON
e-mail: tdes40@live.com
www.torontodukeellingtonsociety.com
www.facebook.com/tdes40
Overview: A small international organization founded in 1959
Mission: To promote the music of Duke Ellington & to have discussions about his influence
Chief Officer(s):
Martin Loomer, President
Membership: *Fees:* $35 individual; $50 family; *Member Profile:* Jazz fans, active musicians, & students
Activities: Bursaries given to students in jazz performance programs; *Speaker Service:* Yes
Awards:
• TDES Scholarships (Scholarship)

Dunbar Lapidary Club
c/o Dunbar Community Centre, 4747 Dunbar St., Vancouver BC V6S 2H2
Overview: A small local organization
Member of: Lapidary Rock & Mineral Society of British Columbia

Duncan Board of Trade *See* Duncan-Cowichan Chamber of Commerce

Duncan-Cowichan Chamber of Commerce (DCCC)
381 Trans-Canada Hwy., Duncan BC V9L 3R5
Tel: 250-748-1111; *Fax:* 250-746-8222
Toll-Free: 888-303-3337
manager@duncancc.bc.ca
www.duncancc.bc.ca
Previous Name: Duncan Board of Trade
Overview: A medium-sized local organization founded in 1908
Mission: To advocacy, service, education, support, & opportunity to engage the business community
Chief Officer(s):
Cathy Mailhot, Manager
Finances: *Funding Sources:* Sponsorships
Membership: 350
Activities: Providing networking, educational, & marketing opportunities to members; Promoting tourism throughout the region; Operating a Visitor Centre; Assisting new businesses & entrepreneurs; Providing regional & community information; Helping people relocate to the area; Liaising with organizations to promote growth; *Awareness Events:* Culinary Gala; Cowichan Wine & Culinary Festival; *Library:* Lending Library
Awards:
• Black Tie Service Awards (Award)

Dundalk Historical Society
c/o Dorothy Hames, RR 1, Procton Station ON N0C 1L0
Overview: A small local organization
Chief Officer(s):
Dorothy Hames, Contact
Finances: *Annual Operating Budget:* Less than $50,000; *Funding Sources:* Membership fees
Membership: 20; *Fees:* $4

Dundas County Community Living Inc. *See* Community Living Dundas County

Dundas Valley Orchestra
#2, 1603 Main St. West, Hamilton ON L8S 1E6
Tel: 905-528-9620
www.dundasvalleyorchestra.ca
www.facebook.com/DundasValleyOrchestra
Overview: A small local charitable organization overseen by Orchestras Canada
Mission: To organize two community concerts per year & occasional concerts at local nursing homes by amateur musicians of all ages
Chief Officer(s):
Laura M. Thomas, Music Director
Activities: *Library:* Sheet Music Library

Dundas West Residents Association *See* The West Bend Community Association

Dunnville Chamber of Commerce
PO Box 124, 231 Chestnut St., Dunnville ON N1A 2X1
Tel: 905-774-3183; *Fax:* 905-774-9281
dunnvillecoc@shaw.ca
www.dunnvillechamberofcommerce.ca
Overview: A small local organization founded in 1988
Mission: To promote both present & new business enterprises; To promote tourism & the development of appropriate facilities; to coordinate recreational & cultural events
Member of: Ontario Chamber of Commerce

Chief Officer(s):
Sandy Passmore, Office Manager, 905-774-6526
Finances: *Annual Operating Budget:* Less than $50,000; *Funding Sources:* Membership dues
Staff Member(s): 4; 4 volunteer(s)
Membership: 130; *Fees:* Sliding scale; *Committees:* Agriculture; Newsletter; Program; Tourism
Activities: *Awareness Events:* Mudcat Festival, 2nd weekend in June; *Speaker Service:* Yes

Durham & District Chamber of Commerce *See* West Grey Chamber of Commerce

Durham Avicultural Society of Ontario (DAS)

ON
www.birdclub.ca
Overview: A small local organization founded in 1977
Mission: To serve breeders in Durham & surrounding area; To improve fellowship among breeders & between clubs; To exchange ideas & educate members for betterment of the fancy through breeding & exhibiting; To encourage members to deal fairly with fellow breeders; To keep birds in good physical condition & not overextend breeding
Member of: Avicultural Advancement Council of Canada
Chief Officer(s):
Jacquie Blackburn, Secretary
jacquies.parrots@sympatico.ca
Membership: 150; *Fees:* $15 junior; $35 individual/family; $25 senior
Activities: *Library*
Awards:
• Canadian Parrot Conference Aviculturist Service Award (Award)
• DAS Patron Award (Award)

Durham Chamber Orchestra

Whitby ON
e-mail: info@durhamchamberorchestra.com
www.durhamchamberorchestra.com
www.facebook.com/DurhamChamberOrchestra
Previous Name: Ajax-Pickering Chamber Orchestra
Overview: A small local organization overseen by Orchestras Canada
Chief Officer(s):
Andrew Uranowski, Music Director
Membership: 30

Durham Deaf Services (DDS)

750 King St. East, Oshawa ON L1H 1G9
Tel: 905-579-3328; *Fax:* 905-728-1183; *TTY:* 905-579-6495
info@durhamdeaf.org
www.durhamdeaf.org
www.facebook.com/durhamdeafservices
www.youtube.com/user/DurhamDeafServices
Overview: A small local charitable organization founded in 1982
Mission: To offer services & educational programs to promote self-reliance within the deaf, deafened & hard-of-hearing community; to increase awareness of deaf culture.
Affliation(s): Ontario Association of the Deaf, Canadian Association of the Deaf
Chief Officer(s):
Yvonne Brown, Executive Director
Finances: *Funding Sources:* Federal & provincial government; United Way; William F. Hayball Foundation
Staff Member(s): 9
Membership: *Fees:* $15 senior/student; $20 senior couple; $25 individual; $35 family; $60 organization
Activities: Durham Deaf Club; *Speaker Service:* Yes; *Library:* Resource Centre; Open to public

Durham Parents of Multiples (DPOM)

PO Box 70607, Whitby ON L1N 2K0
Toll-Free: 888-358-5145
Other Communication: durham@multiplebirthscanada.org
durhamparentsofmultiples@yahoo.ca
www.multiplebirthscanada.org/~durham
Overview: A small local organization overseen by Multiple Births Canada
Mission: Providing support services for parents of multiple birth children in Durham Region.
Membership: *Fees:* $35 single parent; $40 family

Durham Personal Computer Users' Club (DPCUC)

PMB #110, #27, 300 King St. East, Oshawa ON L1H 8J4
Tel: 905-623-2787
www.durhampc-usersclub.on.ca
Overview: A small local organization founded in 1986
Chief Officer(s):
John Sylvestervich, President, 905-723-6797
jsylvest@rogers.com
Anne Delong, Vice-President, 905-623-6975
annedelong@timetraces.com
Bob Bell, Director, Publicity, 905-571-6748
bob@rgbell.ca
Linda Netten, Director, Membership
linnetten@idirect.com
Mark Stanisz, Director, Program, 905-436-6482
mark@markstanisz.com
Membership: *Fees:* $40; *Member Profile:* Computer enthusiasts from Ontario's Durham Region
Activities: Hosting general monthly meetings; Establishing Special Interst Groups
Publications:
• PC Monitor
Type: Newsletter; *Frequency:* Monthly; *Price:* Free with membership in the Durham Personal Coputer Users' Club
Profile: News & tips from the club

Durham Region Association of REALTORS (DRAR)

#14, 50 Richmond St. East, Oshawa ON L1G 7C7
Tel: 905-723-8184; *Fax:* 905-723-7531
drar@durhamrealestate.org
www.durhamrealestate.org
www.facebook.com/DurhamRegionalAssociationofREALTORS
Previous Name: Oshawa & District Real Estate Board
Overview: A small local organization founded in 1954 overseen by Ontario Real Estate Association
Mission: To pursue excellence & professionalism in real estate through commitment & service
Member of: The Canadian Real Estate Association
Chief Officer(s):
Christine Marquis, President, 905-432-7200, Fax: 905-432-1260
chmarquis@trebnet.com
Smith Ian, President-Elect, 905-432-7200, Fax: 905-432-1260
B. Cail Maclean, Executive Officer
Cail@DurhamRealEstate.org
Finances: *Annual Operating Budget:* $500,000-$1.5 Million; *Funding Sources:* Membership dues
Staff Member(s): 8
Membership: 900+; *Fees:* $1,356; *Committees:* Professional Standards; Political Action
Activities: Charity campaigns; annual golf tournament

Durham Region Beekeepers' Association

Sunderland ON
Tel: 905-852-0733
Overview: A small local organization
Mission: To share beekeeping techniques in Durham Region
Member of: Ontario Beekeepers' Association
Chief Officer(s):
Toni Beckmann, President
tbeckmann@andrewswireless.net
Membership: *Member Profile:* Beekeepers in Durham Region, Ontario
Activities: Providing a forum for networking; Organizing meetings at the Scugog Christian School in Prince Albert; Offering support services to the region's beekeepers

Durham Region Law Association (DRLA)

601 Rossland Rd. East, Whitby ON L1N 9G7
Tel: 905-668-2177; *Fax:* 905-668-0692
durhamregionlawassociation.com
Overview: A small local organization founded in 1879
Chief Officer(s):
Deborah Hastings, President
Staff Member(s): 1
Activities: Golf Tournament; *Library:* Durham District Courthouse Library;

Durham Regional Labour Council (DRLC)

115 Albert St., Oshawa ON L1H 4R3
Tel: 905-579-5188
durhamlc@durhamlabour.ca
www.durhamlabour.com
www.facebook.com/groups/265277607614
Previous Name: Oshawa & District Labour Council
Overview: A large local organization founded in 1942 overseen by Ontario Federation of Labour
Mission: To advocate workers' rights & to better the quality of life for workers, their families, & their communities
Member of: Ontario Federation of Labour
Affliation(s): Canadian Labour Congress
Chief Officer(s):
Jim Freeman, President
Bill Stratton, Sec.-Treas.
Finances: *Annual Operating Budget:* $50,000-$100,000
Staff Member(s): 1
Membership: 50,000+; *Fees:* $.20 per member per month; *Committees:* Women's; Education; Human Rights; Union Label & Labour Day; Community Outreach; Membership; Strike Support
Activities: *Awareness Events:* Labour Day, Sept.; *Speaker Service:* Yes

Durham Regional Police Association

725 Conlin Rd., Whitby ON L1R 2W8
Tel: 905-655-5566; *Fax:* 905-655-5066
info@drpa.ca
www.drpa.ca
Overview: A small local organization
Mission: The Association is the negotiating body for employees, both uniform & civilian, of the Durham Regional Police Services.
Affliation(s): Police Association of Ontario; Canadian Police Association
Chief Officer(s):
Randy Henning, President
Staff Member(s): 5
Membership: 800 uniform members + 300 civilian members; *Member Profile:* Employees of the Durham Regional Police Services
Activities: Child Safety Handbook

Durham Youth Orchestra (DYO)

c/o John Beaton, 168 Gladstone Ave., Oshawa ON L1J 4E7
Tel: 905-579-2401
www.dyomusic.com
Overview: A small local organization founded in 1993 overseen by Orchestras Canada
Chief Officer(s):
John Beaton, Music Director
jbeaton@dyomusic.com
Membership: *Fees:* $350

Dutch Canadian Association of Greater Toronto Inc.

207 Newton Dr., Toronto ON M2M 2P2
Tel: 416-229-1753
Overview: A small local organization founded in 1960

Dutch Canadian Business Club of Calgary (DCBC)

Calgary AB
www.dcbc.ca
www.linkedin.com/pub/gijs-van-rooijen/5/36a/51
Overview: A small local organization
Mission: To bring together entrepreneurs of Dutch heritage for the purpose of networking, business seminars, business promotion & celebrating Dutch tradition
Chief Officer(s):
Gijs van Rooijen, President
Membership: 160
Activities: Spring business market; Stampede Barbeque; an Indonesian evening; Christmas dinner; Business Excursion; Computer Clinic; Dutch Movie Night; Business Exchange; Experience Exchange

Dutch-Canadian Association Ottawa Valley/Outaouais

PO Box 78061, Stn. Meriline, Ottawa ON K2E 1B1
e-mail: info@dutchinottawa.ca
www.dutchinottawa.ca
Overview: A small local organization founded in 1990
Mission: To provide Dutch Canadians with a home feeling of gezelligheid by organizing events
Chief Officer(s):
Anouk Hoedeman, President
Finances: *Annual Operating Budget:* Less than $50,000
40 volunteer(s)
Membership: 220; *Fees:* $15 single; $25 couple
Activities: Sinterklaas, Koninginnedag, Koek en Zepie, Tulip festival

Dying with Dignity (DWD) / Mourir dans la dignité

#802, 55 Eglinton Ave. East, Toronto ON M4P 1G8
Tel: 416-486-3998; *Fax:* 416-486-5562
Toll-Free: 800-495-6156
info@dyingwithdignity.ca
www.dyingwithdignity.ca
www.facebook.com/DWDCanada
twitter.com/DWDCanada
www.youtube.com/user/DWDCanada
Overview: A medium-sized national charitable organization founded in 1980

Mission: To improve the quality of dying for all Canadians in accordance with their own wishes, values & beliefs
Affliation(s): World Federation of Right to Die Societies
Chief Officer(s):
Wanda Morris, Executive Director
wanda@dyingwithdignity.ca
Finances: *Annual Operating Budget:* $50,000-$100,000; *Funding Sources:* Membership fees; donations; fundraising
Staff Member(s): 4; 20 volunteer(s)
Membership: 7,000; *Fees:* $40-$75; *Committees:* Membership; Social Action; Counselling
Activities: Counselling & advocacy; *Speaker Service:* Yes; *Library* Open to public by appointment

Dystonia Medical Research Foundation Canada / Fondation de recherches médicales sur la dystonie
#305, 121 Richmond St. West, Toronto ON M5H 2K1
Tel: 416-488-6974; *Fax:* 416-488-5878
Toll-Free: 800-361-8061
www.dystoniacanada.org
www.facebook.com/DMRFC
Also Known As: DMRF Canada
Overview: A small international charitable organization founded in 1976
Mission: To advance & support research relating to dystonia; to build awareness about the illness in order to educate both medical & lay communities; to sponsor patient & family support groups & programs.
Member of: Dystonia Medical Research Foundation
Chief Officer(s):
Diane S. Gillespie, Executive Director
dianegillespie@dystoniacanada.org
Finances: *Funding Sources:* Contributions
Staff Member(s): 2
Activities: Support group meetings; grass roots & national awareness; advocacy; education through regional symposiums; fund research; *Library*

Alberta - Calgary Support Group
c/o Developmental Disabilities Resource Centre, 4631 Richardson Way SW, Calgary AB T3E 7B7
Toll-Free: 800-361-8061
Chief Officer(s):
Margaret Roy, Contact, 403-271-4438
roymg@telusplanet.net

British Columbia - Kelowna Area Support Group
Kelowna BC
Tel: 250-763-7739
Chief Officer(s):
Anne Skomedal, Contact
rskomedal@shaw.ca

Manitoba - Winnipeg Support Group
Winnipeg MB

New Brunswick - Moncton Support Group
Moncton NB
Chief Officer(s):
Shirley Sharkey, Contact, 506-204-2722
j.s.sharkey@rogers.com

Nova Scotia - Port Hawesbury Area Contact
Port Hawkesbury NS
Chief Officer(s):
Marcellin Chiasson, Contact, 902-625-1811
marcellin.chiasson@ns.sympatico.ca

Nunavut - Iqaluit Area Contact
Iqaluit NU
Tel: 867-979-3791
info@dystoniacanada.org
Chief Officer(s):
Sharon Gee, Contact
sharon_gee@hotmail.com

Ontario - Golden Triangle Support Group
c/o Judy Harsch, #808, 7 Christopher Ct., Guelph ON N1G 4V6
Mission: Servicing the Waterloo-Kitchener, Cambridge & Guelph area
Chief Officer(s):
Judy Harsch, Contact, 519-767-9721
jjmarie@rogers.com

Ontario - Hamilton Support Group
Hamilton ON
Chief Officer(s):
Laurie Bell, Contact, 905-774-4111
landbell@rogers.com

Ontario - London Support Group
London ON
Chief Officer(s):
Michelle & Bruce Goodhue, Contacts, 519-455-7457
bgood137@sympatico.ca

Ontario - Ottawa Support Group
Ottawa ON
Tel: 613-224-6888
Toll-Free: 800-361-8061
Chief Officer(s):
John Heney, Contact
jjheney@netrover.com

Ontario - Sudbury Support Group
Sudbury ON
Chief Officer(s):
Mary Guy, Contact, 705-524-0606
maryguy@personainternet.com

Ontario - Toronto Support Group
Toronto ON
Chief Officer(s):
Wendy Paul, Contact, Membership co-ordinator & support, 416-789-0154
dmrft@rogers.com

Québec - Montréal Support Group
Montréal QC
Chief Officer(s):
Chloe Belisle, Contact, 514-696-0949
chloe.belise@videotron.ca

Saskatchewan - Saskatoon Support Group
SK
Chief Officer(s):
Diane Haugen, Contact, 306-477-0577
dystonia@sasktel.net

Dystrophie musculaire Canada *See* Muscular Dystrophy Canada

Dze L K'ant Indian Friendship Centre Society
PO Box 2920, Smithers BC V0J 2N0
Tel: 250-847-5211; *Fax:* 250-847-5144
www.dzelkant.com
Overview: A small local charitable organization founded in 1974 overseen by British Columbia Association of Aboriginal Friendship Centres
Mission: The Centre is a community-based organization providing programs & services to enhance self-reliance, self-efficiency & self-awareness among Aboriginal people.
Member of: BC Association of Aboriginal Friendship Centres
Chief Officer(s):
Annette Morgan, Executive Director
Genevieve Poirier, Program Director
Staff Member(s): 16
Activities: A variety of programs, including: family support; legal support; mental health/HIV/AIDS workshops; addiction counselling; hospital liaison; community action for children; pregnancy outreach; youth after-school activities

E3 Community Services (E3)
100 Pretty River Pkwy. North, Collingwood ON L9Y 4X2
Tel: 705-445-6351
e3@e3.ca
www.e3.ca
Previous Name: Collingwood Community Living
Overview: A medium-sized local charitable organization founded in 1962
Mission: To educate, enable & enrich clients, staff & community
Member of: Ontario Agencies Supporting Individuals with Special Needs (OASIS)
Chief Officer(s):
Gordon Anton, CEO
Farel Anderson, President
Membership: *Member Profile:* Parents & other interested community members
Activities: *Library* Open to public

Eagle Valley Arts Council (EVAC)
Red Barn Arts Centre, PO Box 606, 1226 Riverside Rd., Sicamous BC V0E 2V0
Tel: 250-836-2220
www.eaglevalleyartscouncil.com
Overview: A small local organization founded in 1980
Mission: To encourage & coordinate arts & culture in the community by developing programs & services, primarily at the Red Barn Arts Centre, which it owns & operates.
Member of: Assembly of BC Arts Councils; Thompson Okanagan Network of Arts Councils
Affliation(s): Heritage Canada
Chief Officer(s):
Carla Krens, President
Finances: *Funding Sources:* Grants; functions; rentals; programs
Membership: 9; *Member Profile:* Arts groups
Activities: Art exhibitions, concerts & plays

Eaglesland Albanian Society of BC
#220, 102 - 15910 Fraser Hwy., Surrey BC V4N 0X9
Tel: 604-507-8334
info@eaglesland.org
www.eaglesland.org
Overview: A small local organization
Mission: To promote & provide education as well as recreational events for the Albanian community living in Vancouver
Chief Officer(s):
Estref Resuli, President, Board of Directors
Activities: Parties; National Celebrations; Picnics; Sporting events; Youth & student meeting

Early Childhood Care & Education New Brunswick (ECCENB) / Soins et éducation à la petite enfance Nouveau-Brunswick
#300, 56 Avonlea Ct., Fredericton NB E3C 1N8
Tel: 506-454-4765; *Fax:* 506-854-8333
Toll-Free: 888-834-7070
eccenb.sepenb@nb.aibn.com
Overview: A medium-sized provincial organization founded in 1999
Mission: To support early childhood educators in New Brunswick
Affliation(s): Canadian Child Care Federation
Chief Officer(s):
Marjolaine St-Pierre, Executive Director, 506-454-4765 Ext. 4
marjolaine.stpierre@nb.aibn.com
Finances: *Funding Sources:* Membership fees
Membership: *Fees:* $40 students, parents, & seniors; $60 early childhood educators; $300 corporations; *Member Profile:* Individuals employed in a child care facility; Seniors; Parents; Students; Corporations
Publications:
• Early Childhood Care & Education New Brunswick Newsletter
Type: Newsletter; *Price:* Free with Early Childhood Care & Education New Brunswick membership

Early Childhood Development Association of Prince Edward Island (ECDA)
#115B, 3 Brighton Rd., Charlottetown PE C1A 8T6
Tel: 902-369-1866; *Fax:* 902-569-7900
Toll-Free: 866-368-1866
www.earlychildhooddevelopment.ca
twitter.com/ECDAofPEI
Overview: A small provincial organization founded in 1974
Mission: To promote & support early childhood development programs & services throughout Prince Edward Island
Member of: Prince Edward Island Literacy Alliance Inc.
Affliation(s): Canadian Child Care Federation
Chief Officer(s):
Alice Taylor, Provincial President
tayloram@eastlink.ca
Sonya Hooper, Executive Director
s.hooper@earlychildhooddevelopment.ca
Membership: *Fees:* $30 students; $60-$100 licensed child care facilities; $80 associate members; $90 early childhood assistants; $100 professional members; *Member Profile:* Persons certified as an early childhood educators; Early childhood assistants; Licensed child care facilities; Corporate members that provide services to child care facilities; Associate members who support the association's mission; Students
Activities: Encouraging research; Providing resources about early childhood development; Offering professional development opportunities for early childhood educators; Liaising with government; Providing networking activities; *Awareness Events:* Early Childhood Education Week; *Library:* Early Childhood Development Association of PEI Resource Library
Publications:
• Early Childhood Development Association of Prince Edward Island Newsletter
Type: Newsletter; *Frequency:* Quarterly; *Price:* Free with membership in the Early Childhood Development Association of PEI

Early Childhood Educators of British Columbia (ECEBC)
2774 East Broadway, Vancouver BC V5M 1Y8
Tel: 604-709-6063; *Fax:* 604-709-6077
Toll-Free: 800-797-5602

membership@ecebc.ca
www.ecebc.ca
www.facebook.com/groups/ecebc
twitter.com/ECEBC1
Overview: A small provincial organization founded in 1969
Mission: To provide a network of support & services for members through a regional branch network; To promote professional development & high standards of practice; advocates for child care practitioners, young children & families; To participate in the development of child care training & professional development opportunities; To liaise with other early childhood provincial & national organizations.
Member of: Canadian Child Care Federation
Affliation(s): Westcoast Child Care Resource Centre; Child Care Advocacy Forum
Chief Officer(s):
Taya Whitehouse, President
tayawhitehead@hotmail.com
Emily Mlieczko, Executive Director
executive.director@ecebc.ca
Finances: *Funding Sources:* Membership dues
Staff Member(s): 3
Membership: *Fees:* $50; *Member Profile:* ECE qualified or ECE student; associate membership available for those in a related field

Early Childhood Intervention Program (ECIP) Sask. Inc.

c/o Early Childhood Development & Integrated Services, 2220 College Ave., Regina SK S4P 4V9
Tel: 306-787-6532; *Fax:* 306-787-0277
www.education.gov.sk.ca/ecip
Overview: A small local charitable organization founded in 1981
Mission: To provide a link between families & other professionals, working collaboratively with child care providers, speech & language pathologists, phyiotherapists, occupational therapists, nurses, physicians, teachers & school administrators to build trust & achieve mutually identified goals for the children & families.
Finances: *Funding Sources:* United Way
Activities: Consultation; liaising with the Government of Saskatchewan & other organizations; developing training programs for staff; *Awareness Events:* Early Childhood Intervention Program (ECIP) Week, April

Kindersley - West Central ECIP Inc.
PO Box 775, 125 - 1st Ave. East, Kindersley SK S0L 1S0
Tel: 306-463-6822; *Fax:* 306-463-6898
westcentralecip@sasktel.net

La Ronge - Children North ECIP Inc.
#106, 708 La Ronge Ave., La Ronge SK S0J 1L0
Tel: 306-425-6600; *Fax:* 306-425-6667
ChildrenNorthECIP@mcrrha.sk.ca
Chief Officer(s):
Daina Lapworth, Contact
daina.lapworth@mcrrha.sk.ca

Lloydminster - Midwest Family Connections
Co-op Plaza, #103, 4910 - 50th St., Lower Level, Lloydminster SK S9V 0Y5
Tel: 306-825-5911; *Fax:* 306-825-5912
Toll-Free: 866-651-5911
info@midwestfamilyconnections.ca
www.midwestfamilyconnections.ca
Chief Officer(s):
Sherri Husch Foote, Executive Director
sherri@midwestfamilyconnections.ca

Meadow Lake - Meadow Lake & Area Early Childhood Services Inc.
PO Box 2368, 201 - 4th Ave. East, Meadow Lake SK S0M 1V0
Tel: 306-236-4247; *Fax:* 306-236-1479
meadowlake.ecip@sasktel.net

Moose Jaw - South Central ECIP Inc.
#37, 1322 - 11th Ave. NW, Moose Jaw SK S9H 4L9
Tel: 306-692-2616; *Fax:* 306-692-2377
southcentral.ecip@sasktel.net

North Battleford - Battlefords ECIP Inc.
PO Box 1297, North Battleford SK S9A 3L8
Tel: 306-446-4545; *Fax:* 306-446-0575
becip@sasktel.net
www.becip.org
www.facebook.com/saskatchewan.ecip
Chief Officer(s):
Colleen Sabraw, Executive Director

Prince Albert - Prince Albert ECIP Inc.
3041 Sheman Dr., Prince Albert SK S6V 7B7
Tel: 306-922-3247; *Fax:* 306-763-5244
paecip@sasktel.net
Member of: Saskatchewan Early Childhood Intervention Program

Regina - Regina Region ECIP
#305, 1102 - 8th Ave., Regina SK S4R 1C9
Tel: 306-374-5021
ecip.rr@sasktel.net

Saskatoon - Prairie Hills ECIP Inc.
Kinsmen Children's Centre, 1319 Colony St., Saskatoon SK S7N 2Z1
Tel: 306-655-1083; *Fax:* 306-655-1449
Chief Officer(s):
Arlene Trask, Contact
arlene.trask@saskatoonhealthregion.ca

Swift Current - Swift Current ECIP Inc.
El Wood Bldg., PO Box 486, 350 Cheadle St. West, 3rd Fl., Swift Current SK S9H 3W3
Tel: 306-773-3600; *Fax:* 306-778-6633
swiftcurrentecip@sasktel.net
Chief Officer(s):
Wayne Cormier, Executive Director

Tisdale - North East ECIP Inc.
PO Box 1675, 610 - 100A St., Tisdale SK S0E 1T0
Tel: 306-873-3411; *Fax:* 306-873-3452
neecip@sasktel.net

Weyburn - Holy Family RCSSD 140
110 Souris Ave., Weyburn SK S4H 2Z8
Tel: 306-842-7025; *Fax:* 306-842-7033
wec.ecip@sasktel.net
Chief Officer(s):
Lynn Colquhoun, Contact
lynn.colquhoun@holyfamilyrcssd.ca

Weyburn - Weyburn & Area ECIP Inc.
405 Coteau Ave., Weyburn SK S4H 1H2
Tel: 306-842-2686; *Fax:* 306-842-0723
wecip@sasktel.net

Yorkton - Parkland ECIP Inc.
83 North St., Yorkton SK S3N 0G9
Tel: 306-786-6988; *Fax:* 306-786-7116
parklandecip@sasktel.net
Chief Officer(s):
Michelle Yaschuk, Executive Director

Early Music Vancouver (EMV)

1254 - 7 Ave. West, Vancouver BC V6H 1B6
Tel: 604-732-1610; *Fax:* 604-732-1602
staff@earlymusic.bc.ca
www.earlymusic.bc.ca
www.facebook.com/earlymusicvancouver
twitter.com/earlymusicvan
Also Known As: Vancouver Society for Early Music
Overview: A small local charitable organization founded in 1970
Mission: To foster increased understanding & appreciation of early music by providing educational programs, high quality concerts at reasonable prices featuring both local & internationally acclaimed musicians & by providing informative publications
Member of: Early Music America; Vancouver Alliance for Arts & Culture; American Recorder Society
Chief Officer(s):
José Verstappen, Executive Director
Finances: *Annual Operating Budget:* $500,000-$1.5 Million; *Funding Sources:* Public & private sectors
Staff Member(s): 8; 100 volunteer(s)
Membership: 100-499; *Fees:* $35
Activities: Winter concert series; winter workshops & master classes; the Vancouver Early Music Program & Festival; workshops for musicians of all levels; summer concert series;

Earth Day Canada (EDC) / Jour de la terre Canada

#503, 111 Peter St., Toronto ON M5V 2H1
Tel: 416-599-1991; *Fax:* 416-599-3100
Toll-Free: 888-283-2784
info@earthday.ca
www.earthday.ca
www.facebook.com/EarthDayCanada
twitter.com/earthdaycanada
www.youtube.com/user/EarthDayCanada
Overview: A medium-sized national charitable organization founded in 1991
Mission: To improve the state of the environment by motivating & helping Canadians to achieve local solutions
Affliation(s): Earth Day Network; 3,500 community-based organizations
Chief Officer(s):
Jed Goldberg, President
jgoldberg@earthday.ca
Keith Treffry, Director, Communications
keith@earthday.ca
Paul Bubelis, Chair
Finances: *Funding Sources:* Sponsorships; Donations
Membership: 5,000 organizations
Activities: Coordinating & promoting Earth Day; Circulating educational materials; Initiating & coordinating environmental projects; Offering programs, such as EcoKids; *Awareness Events:* Earth Day, April; Earth Month

Earth Energy Society of Canada (EESC) / Société canadienne de l'énergie du sol (SCES)

7885 Jock Trail, Richmond ON K0A 2Z0
Tel: 613-822-4987; *Fax:* 613-822-4987
info@earthenergy.ca
www.earthenergy.ca
Also Known As: GeoCanada
Previous Name: Canadian Earth Energy Association
Overview: A medium-sized national organization founded in 1985
Mission: To represent the ground-source/geothermal heat pump industry by promoting quality installations & earth energy technology
Chief Officer(s):
Bill Eggertson, Consultant, 613-222-6920
Eggertson@EarthEnergy.ca

Earthroots

#410, 401 Richmond St. West, Toronto ON M5V 3A8
Tel: 416-599-0152; *Fax:* 416-340-2429
Other Communication: www.wolvesontario.org
info@earthroots.org
www.earthroots.org
www.facebook.com/groups/16937496801
www.myspace.com/156509574
Previous Name: Earthroots Coalition; Temagami Wilderness Society
Overview: A medium-sized local organization founded in 1986
Mission: To preserve Ontario's ancient forests & other threatened ecosystems
Affliation(s): Temagami Wilderness Society
Chief Officer(s):
Amber Ellis, Executive Director
amber@earthroots.org
Josh Garfinkel, Senior Campaigner
joshg@earthroots.org
Finances: *Annual Operating Budget:* $250,000-$500,000; *Funding Sources:* Individual donors
Staff Member(s): 5; 40 volunteer(s)
Membership: 12,000; *Fees:* $40 donation
Activities: Works to protect wilderness, wildlife & watersheds through research, education & action; *Library* by appointment

Earthroots Coalition; Temagami Wilderness Society *See* Earthroots

Earthsave Canada (ESC) / SauveTerre

PO Box 2213, Stn. Terminal, #106 - 1850 Lorne St., Vancouver BC V6B 3W2
Tel: 604-731-5885; *Fax:* 604-731-5805
office@earthsave.ca
earthsavecanada.wildapricot.org
www.youtube.com/earthsavecanada
www.facebook.com/EarthsaveCanada
twitter.com/earthsavecanada
Overview: A small national charitable organization founded in 1990
Mission: To promote awareness of the health, ethical & environmental consequences of our food choices; To advocate transition to a plant-based diet for better health, a cleaner environment & a more compassionate world
Affliation(s): EarthSave International
Chief Officer(s):
David Steele, President
Carolyn Mill, Office Manager
Finances: *Annual Operating Budget:* $100,000-$250,000; *Funding Sources:* BC Gaming; Individual donations; Memberships; Retail sales
Staff Member(s): 2; 250 volunteer(s)
Membership: 500; *Fees:* $24 senior; $36 individual; $48 family; $96 corporate; $12 youth/student
Activities: Wellness Show; Healthy Living Expo; monthly potlucks; monthly dine-outs; Healthy School Lunch Program; Taste of Health; Vegeterian Food Festival; *Awareness Events:*

Taste of Health, Vegetarian Food Festival, Oct.; World Veg Week Fundraiser, Nov.; Vegstock; *Library* Open to public
Publications:
• Canada Earthsaver [a publication of Earthsave Canada]
Type: Newsletter; *Frequency:* Quarterly

Earthsave Whistler
e-mail: whistler@earthsave.ca
earthsavewhistler.com
www.facebook.com/EarthsaveWhistler
twitter.com/earthsavewhstlr
pinterest.com/earthsavewhstlr

Earthwise Society
6400 - 3rd Ave., Delta BC V4L 1B1
Tel: 604-946-9828
info@earthwisesociety.bc.ca
www.earthwisesociety.bc.ca
www.facebook.com/earthwisebc
twitter.com/EarthwiseBC
Previous Name: DRS Earthwise Society; Delta Recycling Society
Overview: A small local organization
Chief Officer(s):
Kathy Martin, President
Activities: Market Day; Root to Rise: Yoga Event; Music in the Garden; Family Harvest Box; workshops; Ecotours; education resources

East Coast Aquarium Society (ECAS)
c/o 91 Deerbrooke Dr., Dartmouth NS B2V 1X2
ECAS.ca
www.facebook.com/eastcoastaquariumsociety
Overview: A medium-sized local organization founded in 2004
Mission: To further the aquarium hobby and promote the practice of keeping tropical fish.
Member of: Canadian Association of Aquarium Clubs; Federation of American Aquarium Societies
Chief Officer(s):
Kathryn Purdy, President
kat@eastcoastaquariumsociety.ca
Kelly Lively Jones, Director, Membership
klivelyjones@eastlink.ca

East Coast Music Association (ECMA) / Association de la musique de la côte est
PO Box 31237, Halifax NS B3K 5Y1
Tel: 902-423-3411; *Fax:* 888-519-0346
Toll-Free: 800-513-4953
www.ecma.ca
Also Known As: East Coast Music Awards
Overview: A medium-sized local organization founded in 1989
Mission: To develop, foster, promote & celebrate East Coast music locally & globally
Affiliation(s): Music Industry Associations; Canadian Academy of Recording Arts & Science; FACTOR
Chief Officer(s):
Andria Wilson, Interim Executive Director
andria@ecma.com
Staff Member(s): 6
Membership: *Fees:* $60 individual; $500 lifetime; $25 student; *Member Profile:* Music industry professionals, musicians, fans
Awards:
• East Coast Music Awards (Award)
General Categories: Male Artist of the Year, Female Artist of the Year, Group of the Year, Songwriter of the Year, Single of the Year, Video of the Year, Album of the Year, New Artist(s) of the Year, Entertainer of the Year; Genre Specific Categories: Country Recording of the Year, Pop Recording of the Year, Rock Recording of the Year, Instrumental Recording of the Year, Alternative Recording of the Year, Jazz Recording of the Year, Blues Recording of the Year, Gospel Recording of the Year, Children's Recording of the Year, Bluegrass Recording of the Year, Urban Recording of the Year, Classical Recording of the Year, Roots/Traditional Recording of the Year, Folk Recording of the Year; Cultural Categories: Francophone Recording of the Year

East Durham Historical Society ***See*** Municipality of Port Hope Historical Society

East End Literacy ***See*** Centre for Community Learning & Development

East End Literacy ***See*** Toronto Centre for Community Learning & Development

East European Genealogical Society, Inc. (EEGS)
PO Box 2536, Winnipeg MB R3C 4A7
Tel: 204-989-3292
info@eegsociety.org
www.eegsociety.org
www.facebook.com/155052604506503
Overview: A small national charitable organization founded in 1996
Chief Officer(s):
Mavis Menzies, President
Chris Bukoski, Vice-President
Finances: *Annual Operating Budget:* Less than $50,000
12 volunteer(s)
Membership: 450; *Fees:* $38
Activities: Monthly meetings; workshops; lectures; *Library*

East Georgian Bay Historical Foundation
8 Queen St. East, Elmvale ON L0L 1P0
Tel: 705-322-3000; *Fax:* 705-322-0771
Overview: A small local charitable organization founded in 1981
Mission: The Society aims to preserve the heritage of the Districts of Muskoka, Parry Sound, & the County of Simcoe & has published several titles on the history of the region.
Chief Officer(s):
Gary E. French, President
french@bellnet.ca
Finances: *Annual Operating Budget:* Less than $50,000
4 volunteer(s)
Membership: 1-99
Activities: Local history publishing; heritage conservation advocacy; *Library*

East Gwillimbury Chamber of Commerce (EGCOC)
PO Box 199, 1590 Queensville Side Rd., Queensville ON L0G 1R0
Tel: 905-478-8447; *Fax:* 905-478-8786
Other Communication: egcoc@egcoc.org
www.egcoc.org
Overview: A small local organization
Chief Officer(s):
Kathy Scammell, Office Manager
Membership: 50; *Fees:* $226; *Committees:* Administration; Policy & By-Law; Strategic Development; Member Services; Networking & Special Events; Advocacy & Community Outreach; Tow E.G. Business Development
Activities: Networking events

East Hants & District Chamber of Commerce (EHDCC)
Parker Place Mall, Upper Level, 8 Old Enfield Rd., Enfield NS B2T 1C9
Tel: 902-883-1010; *Fax:* 902-883-7862
info@ehcc.ca
www.ehcc.ca
www.linkedin.com/groups?gid=4076625&trk=hb_side_g
www.facebook.com/171077252957659
Overview: A small local organization founded in 1986
Mission: To influence any major issues which are deemed to have an impact on the economic strength, prosperity & interests of communities; To provide members with services designed to improve their business opportunities
Member of: Atlantic Provinces Chamber of Commerce; Nova Scotia Chamber of Commerce
Chief Officer(s):
Heather Kerr, Manager
Richard Ramsay, President
Finances: *Annual Operating Budget:* Less than $50,000; *Funding Sources:* Membership dues
Staff Member(s): 1
Membership: 100; *Fees:* $50.29 individual/non-profit; $171.76 government; $85.88-$300.58 business
Activities: Trade shows; travel bureau; maps; *Awareness Events:* Showcase of East Hants, May
Awards:
• Student Entrepreneurship (Award)
• Business Entrepreneurship (Award)

East Hants Historical Society
PO Box 121, Maitland NS B0N1T03
e-mail: hantshistorical@gmail.com
www.ehhs.weebly.com
www.facebook.com/pages/East-Hants-Historical-Society/241534932553607
Overview: A small local charitable organization founded in 1967
Mission: To preserve & promote the history of East Hants, Nova Scotia; To provide genealogical resources
Chief Officer(s):
Nancy Doane, Co-Chair, Museum Committee, 902-632-2504
f.wallace@ns.sympatico.ca
Doug Lynch, Co-Chair, Museum Committee, 902-261-2293
dglynch8@gmail.com
Finances: *Funding Sources:* Donations
Membership: *Fees:* $5 / year
Activities: Maintaining & operating a museum in the former Lower Selma United Church; *Library:* East Hants Historical Society Research Library; Open to public

East Kootenay Chamber of Mines
#201, 12 - 11th Ave. South, Cranbrook BC V1C 2P1
Tel: 250-489-2255; *Fax:* 250-426-8755
www.ekcm.org/chamber2
Overview: A small local organization
Chief Officer(s):
Ross Stanfield, President

East Kootenay Community College Faculty Association ***See*** College of the Rockies Faculty Association

East Kootenay District Labour Council
#104, 105 - 9th Ave. South, Cranbrook BC V1C 2M1
Tel: 250-426-2670
ekdlc@telus.net
Overview: A small local organization overseen by British Columbia Federation of Labour
Mission: To advance the economic & social welfare of workers in the East Kootenay region of British Columbia
Affiliation(s): Canadian Labour Congress (CLC)
Chief Officer(s):
Jackie Spain, President
jspain@uniserve.com
Kevin Staneland, First Vice-President
kevstaneland@telus.net
Matt Rose, Treasurer
mrose@telus.net
Activities: Promoting interests of affiliates; Raising awareness of workers' rights; Sponsoring community events, such as the East Kootenay Labour Day Picnic; Hosting events to mark the Day of Mourning

East Prince Youth Development Centre (EPYDC)
98 Water St., Summerside PE C1N 4N6
Tel: 902-436-2815
epydc@epydc.org
www.epydc.org
www.facebook.com/262790347085606
Overview: A small local organization
Mission: Dedicated to helping youth with health, education, & employment problems to achieve their goals
Chief Officer(s):
Melissa Gallant, Manager
melissagallant@epydc.org
Staff Member(s): 6

East Toronto Community Legal Services
1320 Gerrard St. East, Toronto ON M4L 3X1
Tel: 416-461-8102; *Fax:* 416-461-7497
www.etcls.ca
Overview: A small local organization
Mission: To provide legal advice & representation in the areas of: Landlord/Tenant; Immigration; Employment Insurance & Employment Law; Canada Pension; Criminal Injuries Compensation; Consumer Law; Small Claims Court matters; Ontario Works/Ontario Disability Support Program (ODSP).
Finances: *Funding Sources:* Legal Aid Ontario
Staff Member(s): 7
Activities: Chinese-speaking lawyer on Tues. afternoons; *Speaker Service:* Yes

East Wellington Advisory Group for Family Services ***See*** East Wellington Community Services

East Wellington Community Services (EWCS)
PO Box 786, 45 Main St., Erin ON N0B 1T0
Tel: 519-833-9696; *Fax:* 519-833-7563
info@ew-cs.com
www.eastwellingtoncommunityservices.com
www.facebook.com/east.wellington
Previous Name: East Wellington Advisory Group for Family Services
Overview: A small local charitable organization founded in 1984
Mission: To provide essential services to the community in order to strengthen it
Member of: Inform Ontario; Community Support Association
Chief Officer(s):
Allan Alls, President
Kari Simpson, Executive Director

Finances: *Funding Sources:* Guelph/Wellington United Way; public donations; fundraising events & activities; Ministry of Health
Staff Member(s): 15
Activities: Employment services; Human Resources Job Bank; Foodshare; volunteer transportation program; income tax clinics; public access terminal to the internet; information & referrals; child care resource centre; seniors centre; seniors day program

East York - Scarborough Reading Association

#309, 1315 Lawrence Ave. East, Toronto ON M3A 3R3
Tel: 416-444-7473; *Fax:* 416-444-9282
eys@readingfortheloveofit.com
www.readingfortheloveofit.com
www.facebook.com/groups/141629316964/
twitter.com/eysreading
www.youtube.com/user/EYSReadingAssn
Overview: A small local organization
Mission: Committed to improving the quality of literacy instruction and encouraging the development of a lifelong interest in reading.
Chief Officer(s):
Kathy Lazarovits, Président
Meetings/Conferences: • East York-Scarborough Reading Association Reading for the Love of It Confernece 2015, February, 2015, Sheraton Centre Hotel, Toronto, ON
Scope: Local

East York Historical Society (EYHS)

10 McKayfield Rd., Toronto ON M4J 4P7
e-mail: eyhs@eastyork.org
www.eastyork.org/eyhs.html
Overview: A small local organization founded in 1980
Mission: To disseminate historical information; To arouse an interest in the past; To encourage the preservation of the historical, archaeological & architectural heritage of East York by publishing or printing material, by marking buildings, sites or other features of the historical landscapes, by holding public meetings, lectures & exhibitions, & by undertaking a variety of information sharing, publicity & public education programs
Member of: Ontario Historical Society; Toronto Historical Association
Chief Officer(s):
Jane Pitfield, President
Finances: *Annual Operating Budget:* Less than $50,000; *Funding Sources:* Membership fees; sale of desktop flags; provincial government; Toronto Public Library
10 volunteer(s)
Membership: 120; *Fees:* $15 individual; $20 family; $7 student
Activities: Lectures; trips to historical sites; erecting historical plaques in East York community; discussion group meetings
Publications:
• East York Inklings [a publication of the East York Historical Society]
Type: Newsletter; *Frequency:* 5 pa

East York Learning Experience (EYLE)

266 Donlands Ave., Toronto ON M4J 5B1
Tel: 416-425-2666; *Fax:* 416-425-0682
eyle@idirect.com
eyle.toronto.on.ca
Overview: A small local organization founded in 1986
Mission: A literacy program serving East York, parts of East Toronto and west Scarborough.
Affliation(s): Metro Toronto Movement for Literacy; Ontario Literacy Coalition; Community Literacy of Ontario; Community Social Planning Council
Chief Officer(s):
Gail McCullough, Director
Finances: *Annual Operating Budget:* $100,000-$250,000
Staff Member(s): 3; 90 volunteer(s)
Membership: 100; *Member Profile:* Adults 18+; *Committees:* Fundraising; Program; Newsletter; Learners
Activities: Computer-based learning services; tutoring; *Awareness Events:* Word on the Street

Eastend & District Chamber of Commerce

PO Box 534, Eastend SK S0N 0T0
Tel: 306-295-4070; *Fax:* 306-295-3571
Overview: A small local organization
Member of: Saskatoon Chamber of Commerce
Chief Officer(s):
Bonnie Gleim, President
Stephanie Morris, Secretary
Finances: *Annual Operating Budget:* Less than $50,000
Membership: 45

Eastend Arts Council

PO Box 415, Eastend SK S0N 0T0
Tel: 306-295-3281
admin@stegnerhouse.ca
www.stegnerhouse.ca
Overview: A small local charitable organization founded in 1978
Mission: The Council is a non-profit organization that operates the Wallace Stegner House as an artists' retreat.
Chief Officer(s):
Anne Davis, President
Finances: *Funding Sources:* Federal & provinicial governments; foundations; trusts; private donors
Activities: Missoula Children's Theatre; biannual art show & local events that involve the arts; Stegner House Dinner
Awards:
• Wallace Stegner Grant for the Arts (Grant)
Eligibility: Graduating student at Eastend High School whose submitted composition is chosen by the committee *Amount:* $500, plus 1-yr. free residence at retreat

The Easter Seal Society (Ontario) (TESS) / Société du timbre de Pâques de l'Ontario

#700, One Concorde Gate, Toronto ON M3C 3C6
Tel: 416-421-8377; *Fax:* 416-696-1035
Toll-Free: 800-668-6252
info@easterseals.org
www.easterseals.org
www.facebook.com/MoneyMart24HourRelay
twitter.com/easterssealsont
www.youtube.com/user/Eastersealsont
Overview: A large provincial charitable organization founded in 1922 overseen by Easter Seals Canada
Mission: To help children with physical disabilities achieve their full individual potential & future independence
Member of: National Society of Fundraising Executives; Canadian Centre for Philanthropy; Ontario Association for Children's Treatment Centres
Affliation(s): BC Lions Society for Children with Disabilities; Newfoundland Society for the Physically Disabled; Québec Easter Seal Society; Easter Seal Ability Council - Alberta; Saskatchewan Abilities Council; Society for Manitobans with Disabilities; Rotary Club of Charlottetown; Abilities Foundation of Nova Scotia; CRCD New Brunswick branch; National Easter Seal Society, USA
Chief Officer(s):
Duncan Hawthorne, Chair
Carol Lloyd, President & CEO
Finances: *Annual Operating Budget:* Greater than $5 Million; *Funding Sources:* 94% public + 1% investment income + 1% government grants + 3% fees for services + 1% other
Staff Member(s): 140; 1500 volunteer(s)
Membership: 500+; *Member Profile:* Board members; past employees; past ambassadors; key supporters & volunteers; parents; *Committees:* Executive; Board Affairs; Services; Provincial Council; Finance; Audit; Fundraising; Professional Advisory; Human Resources
Activities: Directing services to physically disabled children, usually up to age 19 & their families; Providing programs, research, advocacy & public education; *Speaker Service:* Yes; *Library:* Easter Seal Resource Centre & Archives; Open to public
Awards:
• Leaders of Tomorrow Scholarship Fund (Scholarship)
Eligibility: Youth & young adults who have participated in a Leaders of Tomorrow workshop*Deadline:* May
• Beatrice Drinnan Spence Scholarship Fund (Scholarship)
Eligibility: Youth & young adults with physical disabilities*Deadline:* May
• Rose Brodie Provincial Ambassador Scholarship Fund (Scholarship)
Eligibility: Former Provincial Ambassadors (Timmy / Tammy)*Deadline:* May
• Frank Henry Ralph Pounsett Scholarship Fund (Scholarship)
Eligibility: Youth & young adults with physical disabilities*Deadline:* May
• Truelove Dell Scholarship Fund (Scholarship)
Eligibility: Easter Seals youth who demonstrate outstanding community service in the Greater Toronto Area*Deadline:* May
• Sal Iacono Family Bursary Endowment Fund (Scholarship)
Eligibility: Youth & young adults pursuing post secondary education at Algonquin College*Deadline:* May

Eastern Region - Kingston
#304, 863 Princess St., Kingston ON K7L 5N4
Tel: 613-547-4126
Toll-Free: 888-667-0043

Eastern Region - Ottawa
#350, 1101 Prince of Wales Dr., Ottawa ON K2C 3W7
Tel: 613-226-3051
Toll-Free: 800-561-4313

Northern Region - Sault Ste. Marie
364 Queen St. East, Sault Ste. Marie ON P6A 1Z1
Tel: 705-945-1279
coconnor@easterseals.org

Northern Region - Sudbury
#F, 887 Notre Dame Ave., Sudbury ON P3A 2T2
Tel: 705-566-8858; *Fax:* 705-566-3122
Toll-Free: 800-316-5730
Chief Officer(s):
Judy Hyde, Regional Manager

Northern Region - Thunder Bay
#201, 91 Cumberland St. South, Thunder Bay ON P7B 6A7
Tel: 807-345-7622
Toll-Free: 800-267-3778

Western Region - Burlington / Mississauga / Oakville
PO Box 209, 4035 Fairview St., Burlington ON L7L 6E8
Tel: 289-208-1040
Chief Officer(s):
Susan Smith, Regional Manager
ssmith@easterseals.org

Western Region - London / Sarnia
Bruce Power Recreation Centre, #1, 2265 Oxford St. West, London ON N6K 4P1

Western Region - Windsor
PO Box 7097, Stn. Sandwich West, Windsor ON N9C 3Z1
Tel: 519-944-0044
Toll-Free: 888-535-5623

Easter Seals Canada / Timbres de Pâques Canada

#401, 40 Holly St., Toronto ON M4S 3C3
Tel: 416-932-8382; *Fax:* 416-932-9844
Toll-Free: 877-376-6362
info@easterseals.ca
www.easterseals.ca
www.facebook.com/pages/Easter-Seals-Canada/16770287059?ref=ts
twitter.com/easterseals
Also Known As: Canadian Rehabilitation Council for the Disabled
Previous Name: Easter Seals/March of Dimes National Council
Overview: A medium-sized national charitable organization founded in 1962
Mission: To enhance the quality of life, self-esteem, & self-determination of Canadians with physical disabilities; To support the social & economic integration of people with disabilities
Member of: Imagine Canada's Ethical Code Program
Chief Officer(s):
Max Beck, Chief Executive Officer
mbeck@easterseals.ca
Greg Sarney, National Director, Development
gsarney@easterseals.ca
Jason Eano, Manager, Business Development
jason@easterseals.ca
Brian Chan, Outreach Coordinator, National Programs
bchan@easterseals.ca
Lydia Chan, Coordinator, National Programs
lchan@easterseals.ca
Finances: *Funding Sources:* Sponsorships; Donations
Membership: *Committees:* Executive & Investment; Nominations; Audit; Licensee Relations & Intellectual Property; CEOs
Activities: Delivering programs & services; Raising awareness of disability issues; *Awareness Events:* Easter Seals; Easter Seals Telethon
Awards:
• The CRCD Award (Award)
Established 1969 by the Board of Directors of the Canadian Rehabilitation Council for the Disabled to recognize & celebrate exceptional leadership & personal achievement by a person with a disability
• The Easter Seals Canada Leadership Award (Award)
Established in 1959 as the Timmy Award, is intended to celebrate & recognize outstanding leadership & dedication by a volunteer to children with disabilities, through involvement with Easter Seals
Meetings/Conferences: • Easter Seals 2015 64th Annual Rogers Conn Smythe Sports Celebrities Dinner & Auction in Support of Easter Seals Kids, February, 2015, Royal York Hotel, Toronto, ON
Scope: National

Description: An event to raise money for youth & young adults with physical disabilities
Contact Information: Development Officer, Special Events (Marketing): Catherine Harwood, Phone: 416-421-8377, ext. 309, E-mail: charwood@easterseals.org; Development Officer, Special Events (Volunteers): Lauren Squizzato, Phone: 416-421-8377, ext. 316; URL: connsmythedinner.com
Publications:
• Easter Seals Canada Annual Report
Type: Yearbook; *Frequency:* Annually
Profile: Messages from the Chair of the Board & the Chief Executive Officer, information about the organization's programs & fundraising efforts, & the treasurer's report
• Easter Seals' Our Stories
Type: Newsletter; *Frequency:* Quartely; *Editor:* Cheryl McNamara

Easter Seals New Brunswick (ESNB) / Les Timbres de Pâques N.-B.

65 Brunswick St., Fredericton NB E3B 1G5
Tel: 506-458-8739; *Fax:* 506-457-2863
www.easterseals.nb.ca
www.facebook.com/246795441998452
twitter.com/EasterSealsNB
Also Known As: Canadian Rehabilitation Council for the Disabled (New Brunswick)
Overview: A medium-sized provincial charitable organization founded in 1966 overseen by Easter Seals Canada
Mission: To provide rehabilitation services & programs to persons with disabilities in New Brunswick; To improve public attitudes towards disabled persons; To provide disabled persons with new opportunities; to provide orthopedic appliances, rehabilitative equipment, technical aids & computers; To advocate on behalf of disabled persons; To serve as information resource centre for disabled persons, students, the public & health professionals; To hold the franchise for the Easter Seals campaign; To provide interprovincial transportation assistance to treatment & diagnostic centres
Chief Officer(s):
Julia Latham, Executive Director
Doug Bridgman, President
Finances: *Annual Operating Budget:* $500,000-$1.5 Million; *Funding Sources:* Public donations; fee for service
Staff Member(s): 11; 25 volunteer(s)
Membership: 500; *Fees:* $10
Activities: *Speaker Service:* Yes

Easter Seals Newfoundland & Labrador

206 Mount Scio Rd., St. John's NL A1B 4L5
Tel: 709-754-1399; *Fax:* 709-754-1398
Toll-Free: 888-601-6767
info@easterseals.nf.ca
www.easterseals.nf.ca
www.facebook.com/EasterSealsNL
Previous Name: Newfoundland Society for the Physically Disabled Inc.
Overview: A medium-sized provincial organization founded in 1950 overseen by Easter Seals Canada
Mission: To maximize the abilities & enhancing the lives of children & youth with physical disabilities through recreational, social & other therapeutic programs, direct assistance, education & advocacy.
Chief Officer(s):
Mark Lane, Executive Director/CEO
mark@eastersealsnl.ca
Staff Member(s): 7
Activities: Fundraising

Easter Seals Nova Scotia (AFNS)

3670 Kempt Rd., Halifax NS B3K 4X8
Tel: 902-453-6000; *Fax:* 902-454-6121
easterseals@easterseals.ns.ca
www.easterseals.ns.ca
www.facebook.com/ESnovascotia
twitter.com/Eastersealsns
Previous Name: Abilities Foundation of Nova Scotia
Overview: A medium-sized provincial charitable organization founded in 1931 overseen by Easter Seals Canada
Mission: To enable Nova Scotians with physical disabilities to enhance their quality of life by realizing their individual potential
Chief Officer(s):
Thomas G. Merriam, President & CEO
t.merriam@easterseals.ns.ca
Faye Joudrey, Co-ordinator, Client & Equipment Services
f.joudrey@easterseals.ns.ca
Finances: *Annual Operating Budget:* $500,000-$1.5 Million; *Funding Sources:* Mail campaign; special events
Staff Member(s): 15; 800 volunteer(s)
Membership: 110; *Fees:* $10; *Committees:* Program; Development
Activities: Financial assistance; accessible camping; job skills; training centre; recreation; *Awareness Events:* Easter Seals 24-Hour Relay, July; *Library* Open to public

Easter Seals/March of Dimes National Council ***See*** Easter Seals Canada

Eastern Canada Orchid Society (ECOS)

12, rue Dephoure, Dollard des Ormeaux QC H9B 1C2
Tel: 514-684-3904
info@ecosorchids.ca
www.ecosorchids.ca
www.facebook.com/ECOSorchids
Overview: A small national organization founded in 1953
Mission: ECOS is a non-profit group of orchid hobbyists dedicated to promoting the art, science & culture of raising orchids in the Montréal area.
Affiliation(s): Canadian Orchid Congress; American Orchid Society
Chief Officer(s):
Brian Dunbar, President
Membership: *Fees:* $30 individual; $35 couple
Activities: Orchidfête; *Library*

Eastern Canadian Galloway Association

1001 Hwy. 97, RR#3, Puslinch ON N0B 2J0
Tel: 905-659-2311; *Fax:* 905-659-2670
www.galloway.ca/ecga
Overview: A small local licensing organization founded in 1967
Mission: To promote the breeding of Galloway cattle in Ontario, Québec & Atlantic Provinces.
Member of: Canadian Galloway Association
Chief Officer(s):
Marie Blake, President, 519-291-2797
Ciaran McIlwraith, Secretary
msciaran@aol.com
Membership: 21

Eastern Charlotte Chamber of Commerce (ECCC)

www.ecchamber.ca
Overview: A small local organization
Member of: Atlantic Provinces Chamber of Commerce; Canadian Chamber of Commerce
Chief Officer(s):
Dorothy Gaudet, President
Irene Wright, Secretary
iwright.eccc@nb.aibn.com
Finances: *Annual Operating Budget:* Less than $50,000; *Funding Sources:* Membership fees; insurance
Membership: 58; *Fees:* Schedule available

Eastern Fishermen's Federation

PO Box 907, Grand Manan NB E5G 4M1
Tel: 506-662-8416; *Fax:* 506-662-8336
eff@nb.aibn.com
www.easternfishermensfederation.ca
Overview: A small local organization founded in 1979
Mission: To unite & inform member fishing organizations on issues of common interest.
Chief Officer(s):
Eugene O'Leary, President
eugeneol@yahoo.ca
Membership: 22 organizations; *Member Profile:* Fishermen's associations in Eastern Canada

Eastern Ontario Archivists Association ***See*** Archives Association of Ontario

Eastern Ontario Beekeepers' Association (EOBA)

c/o David Gray, PO Box 375, 1222 Bankfield Rd., Manotick ON K4M 1A4
Tel: 613-692-3363
info@all-things.com
www.all-things.com/eoba
Overview: A small local organization
Mission: To assist persons interested in bees & beekeeping in eastern Ontario; To promote improvement in eastern Ontario's beekeeping industry
Member of: Ontario Beekeepers' Association
Chief Officer(s):
Noel Peter, Director
ve3dpn@rac.ca
Juliet Bancroft, Director
jetpets@hotmail.com
Martin Damus, Director
Damusm@inspection.gc.ca
David Gray, Director, 613-692-3363
Joanne Levac, Director
mark.lauterbach@sympatico.ca
Craig McCaffrey, Director, 613-692-4020
Membership: 87; *Member Profile:* Any individual residing in eastern Ontario who is interested in beekeeping
Activities: Helping members with problems associated with beekeeping; Disseminating timely information about beekeeping; Liaising with the Ontario Ministry of Agriculture & Food; Educating the public; Exchanging ideas about beekeeping amongst members
Publications:
• Eastern Ontario Beekeepers Association Newsletter
Type: Newsletter
Profile: Information about association business, plus forthcoming meetings & events

Eastern Ontario Concert Orchestra ***See*** Quinte Symphony

Eastern Ontario Model Forest

PO Box 2111, 10 Campus Dr., Kemptville ON K0G 1J0
Tel: 613-258-8241; *Fax:* 613-258-8363
modelforest@eomf.on.ca
www.eomf.on.ca
Overview: A small local organization
Mission: To demonstrate how partners, representing a diversity of forest values, can work together to achieve sustainable forest management using innovative, region-specific approaches
Member of: Canadian Model Forest Network
Chief Officer(s):
Jim McCready, President
Elizabeth Holmes, General Manager
eholmes@eomf.on.ca

Eastern Ontario Travel Association ***See*** Ontario East Tourism Association

Eastern Ottawa Chamber of Commerce

5470 Canotek Rd., Gloucester ON K1J 9H4
Tel: 613-745-3578; *Fax:* 613-745-8575
Previous Name: Gloucester Chamber of Commerce
Overview: A small local organization founded in 1986
Mission: To serve the community & represent the interests of business in a politically & financially independent manner
Member of: National Capital Business Alliance; Ontario Chamber of Commerce; Canadian Chamber of Commerce
Chief Officer(s):
David Brault, President
Finances: *Annual Operating Budget:* Less than $50,000; *Funding Sources:* Membership fees
Staff Member(s): 1; 12 volunteer(s)
Membership: 175; *Fees:* $185-$776.50; *Member Profile:* Small & medium sized businesses in Ottawa east & south
Activities: *Internships:* Yes

Eastern Prince Edward Island Chamber of Commerce

PO Box 1593, 540 Main St., Montague PE C0A 1R0
Tel: 902-838-4030; *Fax:* 902-838-4031
www.epeicc.ca
Previous Name: Southern Kings & Queens Chamber of Commerce
Overview: A small local organization founded in 2002
Mission: To provide an economic advantage to business members by providing them with priority customer referrals; to represent them in community endeavours; to provide them with networking capabilities unavailable to non-members
Chief Officer(s):
Chris Nicholson, President, 902-313-0529
Stella Jamieson, Executive Director
Membership: *Fees:* Schedule available

Eastern Shore Fisherman's Protection Association

PO Box 55, Musquodoboit Harbour NS B0J 2L0
Tel: 902-845-2408; *Fax:* 902-845-2629
nellie@esfpa.ca
Overview: A small local organization founded in 1957
Mission: To develop opportunities to protect & maintain the interests of fishermen along the Eastern shore
Member of: Eastern Fisherman's Federation
Chief Officer(s):
Norma Richardson, President, 902-885-3563
Wayne D. Eddy, Vice-President, 902-465-6169

Sheldon Keating, Sec.-Treas., 902-845-2865
Chris Snow, Secretary, 902-654-2066
Finances: *Funding Sources:* Membership dues
Staff Member(s): 3; 150 volunteer(s)
Membership: 200; *Fees:* $100

Eastern Shore Ringette Association (ESRA)

NS
easternshoreringette.ca
Overview: A small local organization overseen by Ringette Nova Scotia
Member of: Ringette Nova Scotia
Chief Officer(s):
Mary Stienburg, President
presidentESRA@gmail.com
Membership: 3 teams; *Member Profile:* Teams with players 4-10; Teams with players 18+

Eastern Shore Volunteer Food Bank

Lakehill Dr., Musquodoboit Harbour NS B3E 1L6
Tel: 902-889-9243
Overview: A small local organization
Member of: Nova Scotia Food Bank Association; Atlantic Alliance of Food Banks & C.V.A.'s; Food Banks Canada

Eastern Shores Independent Association for Support Personnel (ESIASP)

c/o Eastern Shores School Board, 40, rue Mountsorrel, New Carlisle QC G0C 1Z0
Tel: 418-752-2247; *Fax:* 418-752-6447
esiasp@navigue.com
Overview: A small local organization
Chief Officer(s):
Louise C. Jones, President

Eastern Townships Association of Teachers *See* Appalachian Teachers' Association

Eastern Townships Resource Centre (ETRC) / Centre de recherche des cantons de l'est

Bishop's University, 2600 College St., Sherbrooke QC J1M 1Z7
Tel: 819-822-9600
etrc@ubishops.ca
www.etrc.ca
www.facebook.com/easterntownshipresourcecentre
Overview: A small local organization founded in 1982
Mission: To promote the study of the history, culture & society of the Eastern Townships of Québec, with a special focus on the English-speaking communities; to preserve the region's living & archival heritage.
Chief Officer(s):
Fabian Will, Executive Director, 819-822-9600 Ext. 2647
Staff Member(s): 3
Activities: Funding regional & community-based research projects; holding conferences & forums; exhibitions; preserving archival collections; *Internships:* Yes; *Library:* Old Library, Bishop's University; Open to public
Publications:
• Journal of the Eastern Townships Studies/Revue d'études des Cantons-de-l'Est
Type: journal
Profile: JETS is a bilingual, interdisciplinary dissemination of research, articles, notes, criticism, personal accounts & descriptions of archival fondsrelevant to the Eastern Townships.

Eastern Veterinary Technician Association (EVTA)

146 East St., Port Hood NS B0E 2W0
Tel: 902-787-2437
www.evta.ca
Overview: A small local organization founded in 1988
Member of: Canadian Association of Animal Health Technologists & Technicians
Affliation(s): Canadian Veterinary Medical Association
Chief Officer(s):
Joye Sears, President
Beverly MacDonald, Executive Director
bev@evta.ca
Finances: *Funding Sources:* Donations; membership fees
Membership: *Fees:* $20 student; $150 regular; *Member Profile:* Registered Veterinary Technicians; those who have passed the Veterinary Technician National Examination
Activities: *Awareness Events:* Veterinary Technician Week, Oct.
Awards:
• Veterinary Technician of the Year Award (Award)
• EVTA Bursary (Grant)
For students *Amount:* $100

EastGen

5653 Hwy. 6 North, RR#5, Guelph ON N1H 6J2
Tel: 519-821-2150; *Fax:* 519-763-6582
Toll-Free: 888-821-2150
info@eastgen.ca
www.eastgen.ca
Merged from: Eastern Breeders Inc. & Gencor
Overview: A large local organization founded in 2011
Mission: EastGen is a farmer- directed AI cooperative located in South-western Ontario
Chief Officer(s):
Charles Bennett, President
Finances: *Annual Operating Budget:* $3 Million-$5 Million
Staff Member(s): 305
Membership: 8,583; *Fees:* $10

Eastview Neighbourhood Community Centre

86 Blake St., Toronto ON M4J 3C9
Tel: 416-392-1750; *Fax:* 416-392-1175
contact@eastviewcentre.com
www.eastviewcentre.com
www.facebook.com/EastviewNeighbourhoodCommunityCentre
twitter.com/eastviewcentre
Overview: A small local charitable organization
Mission: To provide programs for children, adults, seniors & immigrants.
Member of: Boys & Girls Clubs of Canada
Affliation(s): Toronto-Danforth Early Years Centre; Toronto District School Board; Daily Bread Food Bank
Chief Officer(s):
Bev Wolfus, Chair & President
Kerry Bowser, Executive Director
Finances: *Funding Sources:* All 3 levels of government; corporations; foundations; private donations
Staff Member(s): 16
Membership: *Fees:* $5 child/youth; $10 adult/senior; $20 family
Activities: A variety of recreational programs for each age group; ESL & Mandarin classes; immigrant support group; food bank;

Eating Disorder Association of Canada (EDAC) / Association des Troubles Alimentaires du Canada (ATAC)

ON
e-mail: edacatac@gmail.com
www.edac-atac.ca
www.twitter.com/EDACATAC
Overview: A small national organization
Mission: EDAC-ATAC aims to serve the needs of those whose lives are impacted by eating disorders.
Chief Officer(s):
Jadine Cairns, President
Meetings/Conferences: • Eating Disorder Association of Canada 5th Biennial Conference, 2016, Winnipeg, MB
Scope: National

Eatonia & District Chamber of Commerce

PO Box 370, Eatonia SK S0L 0Y0
Tel: 306-967-2506; *Fax:* 306-967-2267
Overview: A small local organization
Member of: Saskatchewan Chamber of Commerce
Membership: 40; *Fees:* $25

Eatonia Arts Council

PO Box 39, Eatonia SK S0L 0Y0
Tel: 204-967-2550
Overview: A small local organization founded in 1988
Mission: To encourage people in the community, especially the youth, to become involved in the arts, drawing, painting, taking photos or doing crafts.
Member of: Organization of Saskatchewan Arts Councils
Activities: Annual Adjudicated Art Show

Eau Vive *See* WaterCan

Echo-Edson Cultural Heritage Organization

4818 - 7 Ave., Edson AB T7E 1K8
Tel: 780-723-3582
echored@telus.net
Also Known As: Red Brick Arts Centre & Museum
Overview: A small local organization founded in 1985
Mission: To restore & maintain the Red Brick School built in 1913 & to operate it as an arts centre & museum
Member of: Alberta Museums Association
Chief Officer(s):
Betty Stiltzenberger, President

Finances: *Annual Operating Budget:* $50,000-$100,000; *Funding Sources:* Provincial, federal & municipal government; donations; rentals
Staff Member(s): 2; 15 volunteer(s)
Membership: 1-99
Activities: Art classes & shows; tours; theatre & dance

Échographie Canada *See* Sonography Canada

The Eckhardt-Gramatté Foundation

54 Harrow St., Winnipeg MB R3M 2Y7
Tel: 204-452-9750; *Fax:* 204-477-6511
egf@egre.mb.ca
www.egre.mb.ca
Overview: A small national organization founded in 1982
Mission: Established in honour of Sonia & Walter Gramatté; to advance public appreciation, understanding & knowledge of the music & artistic works of these two individuals
Chief Officer(s):
Lynda Hiebert, Executive Director
Finances: *Annual Operating Budget:* $50,000-$100,000
Staff Member(s): 3
Activities: *Library* by appointment

Eckville & District Chamber of Commerce

PO Box 609, Eckville AB T0M 0X0
www.eckvillechamber.com
Overview: A small local organization

L'Écluse des Laurentides

22a, rue Goyer, Saint-Sauveur QC J0R 1R0
Tel: 450-744-1393; *Fax:* 450-744-1335
ecluse@cgocable.ca
ecluse.org
Overview: A small local organization
Chief Officer(s):
Vickie Laframboise, Contact, 450-569-7197

Éco Entreprises Québec (EEQ)

#600, 1600, boul René-Lévesque ouest, Montréal QC H3H 1P9
Tél: 514-987-1491; *Téléc:* 514-987-1598
service@ecoentreprises.qc.ca
www.ecoentreprises.qc.ca
Aperçu: *Dimension:* petite; *Envergure:* provinciale; fondée en 2003
Mission: Organisme privé sans but lucratif; représenter les entreprises assujetties à la Loi sur la qualité de l'environnement qui mettent sur le marché québécois des contenants et emballages et des imprimés.
Membre(s) du bureau directeur:
Maryse Vermette, Présidente-directrice générale
mvermette@ecoentreprises.qc.ca
Marie-Andrée Prénoveau, Directrice, Affaires corporatives, relations externes et communications
mprenoveau@ecoentreprises.qc.ca
Membre: 3 000
Prix, Bouses:
• Prix Phénix (Prix)

Ecoforestry Institute Society (EIS)

PO Box 5070, Stn. B, Victoria BC V8R 6N3
Tel: 604-595-0655
www.ecoforestry.ca
Overview: A small national charitable organization founded in 1992
Mission: To provide ecologically sound alternatives to current ruinous industrial forestry practices; To support preservation of ancient & natural forests; to encourage restoration of plantation tree farms to natural forest status
Member of: BC Environmental Network; Forest Stewardship Council
Chief Officer(s):
Sharon Chow, Treasurer
martchow@islandnet.com
Finances: *Annual Operating Budget:* $50,000-$100,000; *Funding Sources:* Foundations; donations; subscriptions
Staff Member(s): 1; 12 volunteer(s)
Membership: 250; *Fees:* $10
Activities: Provides community outreach through conferences, videos & publications; helps community watershed & land trusts set up ecoforestry programs; *Speaker Service:* Yes
Publications:
• Ecoforestry
Editor: Irv Penner
Profile: No longer published, but back-copies are available.

Ecojustice Canada Society

#214, 131 Water St., Vancouver BC V6B 4M3

Tel: 604-685-5618; *Fax:* 604-685-7813
Toll-Free: 800-926-7744
www.ecojustice.ca
www.facebook.com/ecojustice
twitter.com/ecojustice_ca
Also Known As: Ecojustice
Previous Name: Sierra Legal Defence Fund
Overview: A medium-sized national charitable organization founded in 1990
Mission: To provide legal representation to environmental groups that cannot afford to go to court against large institutions when important wilderness values are at stake; to bring selected cases with the ultimate goal of establishing an aggregate of strong legal precedents that recognize environmental values; to provide professional advice on the development of environmental legislation
Chief Officer(s):
Cathy Wilkinson, President & Chair
Deborah Curran, Vice-Chair
Mike Cormack, Treasurer
Ronald H. Pearson, Secretary
Devon Page, Executive Director
Finances: *Annual Operating Budget:* $1.5 Million-$3 Million; *Funding Sources:* Individual donors; private foundations
Staff Member(s): 49; 10 volunteer(s)
Membership: 5,000-14,999
Activities: Free legal services; litigation; *Internships:* Yes

Alberta Office
#900, 1000 - 5th Ave. SW, Calgary AB T2P 4V1
Tel: 403-705-0202; *Fax:* 403-264-8399

Ecojustice Clinic at the University of Ottawa
c/o University of Ottawa, Faculty of Law, #107, 35 Copernicus St., Ottawa ON K1N 6N5
Tel: 613-562-5800; *Fax:* 613-562-5319

Toronto Office
Centre for Green Cities, #401, 550 Bayview Ave., Toronto ON M4W 3X8
Tel: 416-368-7533; *Fax:* 416-363-2746

École internationale de français (EIF)
CP 500, Trois-Rivières QC G9A 5H7
Tél: 819-376-5124; *Téléc:* 819-376-5166
Ligne sans frais: 888-343-8645
eif@uqtr.ca
www.uqtr.ca/eif
www.facebook.com/EIF.UQTR
twitter.com/eifuqtr
Aperçu: *Dimension:* petite; *Envergure:* internationale; fondée en 1974
Mission: Offre des programmes intensifs d'immersion en français
Affliation(s): Conseil des Ministres de l'Éducation du Canada
Membre(s) du bureau directeur:
Hélène Marcotte, Directrice
Daniel Lavoie, Coordonnateur
Finances: *Budget de fonctionnement annuel:* $50,000-$100,000
Membre(s) du personnel: 50
Membre: 11 institutionnel; *Critères d'admissibilite:* Apprenants de 18 ans et plus
Activités: Excursions, soirées; *Stagiaires:* Oui; *Service de conférenciers:* Oui

Ecological Agriculture Projects (EAP) / Projets pour une agriculture écologique (PAE)
Macdonald Campus of McGill University, Sainte-Anne-de-Bellevue QC H9X 3V9
Tel: 514-398-7771; *Fax:* 514-398-7621
ecological.agriculture@mcgill.ca
eap.mcgill.ca
Overview: A small national organization founded in 1974
Mission: To facilitate the establishment of nutritional, just, & sustainable food systems worldwide
Affliation(s): International Federation of Organic Agriculture Movements
Finances: *Annual Operating Budget:* $100,000-$250,000
Staff Member(s): 1
Membership: *Fees:* $40 individual; $60 organization; $500 sustaining; $1,250 organization
Activities: *Speaker Service:* Yes; *Library* Open to public by appointment
Meetings/Conferences: • 34th Annual Guelph Organic Conference & Expo 2015, January, 2015, Guelph University Centre, Guelph, ON
Scope: Local
Attendance: 830
Contact Information: Website: www.guelphorganicconf.ca; Twitter: twitter.com/GuelphOrganic; Phone: 519-824-4120 Ext. 56311

Ecological Farmers of Ontario (EFO)
5420 Hwy. 6 North, RR#5, Guelph ON N1H 6J2
Tel: 519-822-8606; *Fax:* 519-822-5681
Toll-Free: 877-822-8606
info@efao.ca
www.efao.ca
Overview: A medium-sized provincial charitable organization founded in 1979
Mission: To provide information about ecological farming practices in Ontario
Chief Officer(s):
Chris Litster, President
Shauna Bloom, Manager, Programs
programs@efao.ca
Caitlin Hill, Coordinator, Communications & Outreach
outreach@efao.ca
Karen Maitland, Coordinator, Membership Services
Smith Dave, Treasurer
Finances: *Funding Sources:* George Cedric Metcalf Foundation; Ontario Trillium Foundation; Friends of Greenbelt Foundation
Membership: *Member Profile:* Ontario farmers; *Committees:* Energy & farming; Peak oil; Soil & carbon
Activities: Providing access to advice; Organizing farm tours;
Publications:
• Ecological Farmers of Ontario Newsletter
Type: Newsletter; *Editor:* Fiona Wagner

Ecology Action Centre (EAC)
2705 Fern Lane, Halifax NS B3K 4L3
Tel: 902-429-2202; *Fax:* 902-405-3716
info@ecologyaction.ca
www.ecologyaction.ca
www.facebook.com/EcologyActionCentre
twitter.com/ecologyaction
Overview: A medium-sized provincial organization founded in 1971
Mission: To act as a voice for Nova Scotia's environment; To build a healthier, more sustainable Nova Scotia
Member of: Canadian Renewable Energy Alliance
Chief Officer(s):
Maggy Burns, Managing Director, 902-429-5287
centre@ecologyaction.ca
Rochelle Owen, Co-Chair
Finances: *Funding Sources:* Membership dues; Donations
Membership: 2,400; *Fees:* $20 student/senior; $40 organizational/regular; $60 family; $120 supporting; *Committees:* Coastal & Water; Marine; Wilderness Issues; Transportation; Energy Issues; Food Action; Built Environment
Activities: Communication; Education and Programming; Research; Advocacy; *Internships:* Yes; *Speaker Service:* Yes; *Library* Open to public

Ecology North
5013 - 51 St. St., Yellowknife NT X1A 2N4
Tel: 867-873-6019
admin@ecologynorth.ca
www.ecologynorth.ca
Overview: A small local organization founded in 1971
Mission: To promote appreciation & protection of the natural environment of the Northwest Territories; To foster public awareness through seminars & outdoor activities; To provide a forum for communication of ideas on environmental issues between the scientific community, government & the peoples of the Northwest Territories
Member of: Canadian Environmental Network
Chief Officer(s):
John Carr, Board Member
Dawn Tremblay, Program Coordinator
Christine Wenman, Coordinator, Northern Waters Program
Finances: *Annual Operating Budget:* $50,000-$100,000
Staff Member(s): 2
Membership: 200; *Fees:* $25 individual; $40 family; *Committees:* Recycling; Botanical Gardens/Volunteer Development; Endangered Species
Activities: Participates in environmental hearings; reviews legislation & policy; sponsors a wide range of activities such as bird walks & nature hikes; public education seminars on various aspects of the northern environment; community recycling programs such as Rent-a-Plate; *Awareness Events:* Earth Week, April; Folk on the Rocks; *Library:* Recycling Resource Centre

Economic Developers Alberta (EDA)
Suite 127, #406, 917 - 85 St. Southwest, Calgary AB T3H 5Z9
Tel: 403-214-0224; *Fax:* 403-214-0224
Toll-Free: 866-671-8182
www.edaalberta.ca
www.linkedin.com/groups/Economic-Developers-Alberta-1448077
www.facebook.com/518610924817696
twitter.com/edaalberta
Previous Name: Economic Developers Association of Alberta
Overview: A small provincial organization founded in 1974
Mission: To enhance the economic development profession in Alberta, providing a network of communication, information & education
Affliation(s): Economic Developers Association of Canada; Canadian Association of Petroleum Producers
Chief Officer(s):
Jeff Penney, President
Leann Hackman-Carty, Chief Executive Officer
leann@edaalberta.ca
Finances: *Annual Operating Budget:* $100,000-$250,000; *Funding Sources:* Membership fees
Staff Member(s): 4
Membership: 100-499; *Fees:* $68 student; $137 associate/corporate individual & elected official; $205 regular
Activities: *Speaker Service:* Yes
Awards:
• Economic Developer of the Year Award (Award)
• Alex Metcalf Awards (Award)
• Marketing Awards (Award)
• President's Award (Award)
Meetings/Conferences: • Economic Developers Alberta 2015 Annual Conference, April, 2015, Delta Kananaskis, Kananaskis, AB
Scope: Provincial

Economic Developers Association of Alberta *See* Economic Developers Alberta

Economic Developers Association of Canada (EDAC) / Association canadienne de développement économique (ACDE)
7 Innovation Dr., Flamborough ON L9H 7H9
Tel: 905-689-8771; *Fax:* 905-689-5925
info@edac.ca
www.edac.ca
twitter.com/E_D_A_C
Previous Name: Industrial Developers Association of Canada
Overview: A medium-sized national organization founded in 1968
Mission: To contribute to Canada's economic, social, & environmental well-being by advancing economic development; To enhance professional competence & ethical service
Affliation(s): Provincial partners: APDEQ, EDA, EDABC, IEDC, EDCO, SEDA, Economic Developers Association of MB; Federal Economic Development Initiative in Northern ON; NS Association of Regional Development Authorities; Enterprise Network. Federal partners: Agriculture & Agri-Food Canada; Atlantic Canada Opportunities Agency; Canadian Commercial Corporation, Dept. of Environment, Dept. of Finance, Export Development Corp., Industry Canada, Invest in Canada, National Research Council, Public Works & Government Services, Revenue Can., Smart Communities 'Empowering Canadians', Statistics Can., CIDA, ICCI, HRSDC
Chief Officer(s):
Penny A. Gardiner, Chief Executive Officer
gardiner@edac.ca
Serge Cote, President
serge.cote@admtl.com
John Watson, 1st Vice-President
john@investcomoxvalley.com
G.J. Borduas, 2nd Vice-President
gborduas@thamescentre.on.ca
David Emerson, Treasurer
emerson@unbsj.ca
Membership: 1,000+; *Fees:* Schedule available; *Member Profile:* Economic development practitioners; Students
Activities: Liaising internationally, federally, provincially, & municipally; Providing professional development opportunities; Ensuring members follow the association's "Code of Ethics"; *Rents Mailing List:* Yes
Awards:
• Marketing Canada Awards (Award)
• EDAC / RBC Financial Group Economic Development Achievement of The Year Award (Award)

Meetings/Conferences: • Economic Developers Association of Canada 47th Annual Conference, September, 2015, Whitehorse, YT
Scope: National
Publications:
• Commuique
Type: Newsletter; *Editor:* Susan Touchette

Economic Developers Association of Manitoba (EDAM)
#700, 177 Lombard Ave., Winnipeg MB R3B 0W5
Tel: 204-795-2000; *Fax:* 204-925-8000
info@edamonline.ca
www.edamonline.ca
www.linkedin.com/groups/Economic-Developers-Association-Manitoba-32020
www.facebook.com/160988724423
Overview: A small provincial organization founded in 1993
Mission: EDAM is an independent, non-profit, incorporated association aiming to improve communication within the economic development profession.
Affliation(s): Economic Development Association of Canada; similar provincial associations
Chief Officer(s):
Colleen Engel, Chair
Shelley Morris, Manager
Membership: *Fees:* $150 individual; $325 organization; $400 associate/corporate; $50 student; *Member Profile:* Anyone engaged in economic development in Manitoba; *Committees:* Executive; Communications; Forum

Economic Developers Council of Ontario Inc. (EDCO)
6506 Marlene Ave., Cornwall ON K6H 7H9
Tel: 613-931-9827; *Fax:* 613-931-9828
edco@edco.on.ca
www.edco.on.ca
www.linkedin.com/company/economic-developers-council-of-ontario
twitter.com/edco1edco
Previous Name: Ontario Industrial Development Council Inc.
Overview: A medium-sized provincial organization founded in 1957
Mission: To provide a forum for economic development related educational activities; to increase the profile of EDCO & the profession; to encourage & create an awareness of economic development issues with relevant government agencies; to promote & develop Ontario as a premier location for economic activity by increasing employment & prosperity, & enhancing the quality of life within the Ontario municipalities.
Member of: Economic Developers Association of Canada; International Economic Development Council; Ontario East Economic Development Commission; Northwestern Ontario Development Network
Chief Officer(s):
Jennifer Patterson, President
Heather Lalonde, Executive Director
Finances: *Funding Sources:* Membership dues; corporate sponsors
Membership: *Fees:* Schedule available; *Member Profile:* Persons directly or indirectly engaged in business & economic development for benefit of Ontario
Activities: *Speaker Service:* Yes
Awards:
• Ontario Economic Development Awards (Award)
• Economic Development Achievement Award (Award)
Meetings/Conferences: • Economic Developers Council of Ontario 2015 Conference, February, 2015, Hamilton Convention Center, Hamilton, ON
Scope: Provincial

Economic Development Association of British Columbia *See* British Columbia Economic Development Association

Economic Development Brandon (EDB)
City of Brandon, 410 - 9th St., Brandon MB R7A 6A2
Tel: 204-729-2132; *Fax:* 204-729-8244
Toll-Free: 866-729-2132
econdev@brandon.ca
www.economicdevelopmentbrandon.com
www.facebook.com/144423528948225
Previous Name: Brandon Economic Development Board
Overview: A small local organization founded in 2001
Member of: Brandon Chamber of Commerce; Economic Developers Association of Canada (EDAC); International Economic Development Council (IEDC)
Chief Officer(s):
Sandy Trudel, Director, Economic Development, 204-729-2131
s.trudel@brandon.ca
Finances: *Annual Operating Budget:* $100,000-$250,000; *Funding Sources:* City of Brandon
Staff Member(s): 3
Activities: Providing relocation & business assistance; *Speaker Service:* Yes; *Library:* Economic Development Brandon Photo Library; Open to public

Economic Development Professionals Association of Québec *Voir* Association des professionnels en développement économique du Québec

Economic Development Winnipeg Inc. (EDW)
#300, 259 Portage Ave., Winnipeg MB R3B 2A9
Tel: 204-954-1997
www.economicdevelopmentwinnipeg.com
www.linkedin.com/company/economic-development-winnipeg-inc.
twitter.com/EDWinnipeg
www.youtube.com/user/EDWinnipeg
Overview: A medium-sized local organization founded in 2002
Mission: To act as Winnipeg's economic development & tourism services agency, by marketing the city & providing related economic development & tourism services
Chief Officer(s):
Marina R. James, President & CEO
Greg Dandewich, Senior Vice-President, 204-954-1982
greg@economicdevelopmentwinnipeg.com
Chantal Sturk-Nadeau, Senior Vice-President, Tourism, 204-954-1987
chantal@tourismwinnipeg.com
Activities: Providing information, statistics, & resources about Winnipeg; Assisting in meeting & event plans; Promoting travel to Winnipeg; Developing partnerships; Supporting the attraction, expansion, & retention of business in Winnipeg; Leveraging investment in targeted projects & sectors

Economics Society of Northern Alberta (ESNA)
PO Box 1434, Edmonton AB T5J 2N6
www.esna.ca
www.linkedin.com/groups/Economics-Society-Northern-Alberta-6612956
Overview: A small local organization founded in 1965
Mission: To bring together individuals interested in the field of economics & provides regular meetings for discussion & exchange of ideas relating to applied economics; to promote public awareness & understanding of current economic problems, issues & achievements.
Chief Officer(s):
Mark Parsons, President
Finances: *Funding Sources:* Membership dues; event fees; individual donations
Activities: Annual conferences; luncheons with speakers; *Speaker Service:* Yes

Economists', Sociologists' & Statisticians' Association *See* Canadian Association of Professional Employees

EcoPerth
2196 Old Brooke Rd., RR#2, Maberry ON K0H 2B0
Tel: 613-267-6463; *Fax:* 613-268-2907
info@ecoperth.on.ca
www.ecoperth.on.ca
Overview: A small local organization
Mission: To promote local projects that are environmentally sustainable and economically efficient in the Perth, Ontario area.
Chief Officer(s):
Bob Argue, Executive Director
bob@ecoperth.on.ca

Éco-Quartier Sainte-Marie
2151, rue Parthenais, MontréAl QC H2K 3T3
Tél: 514-523-9220; *Téléc:* 514-523-2653
eqsm@qc.aira.com
www.eco-quartiersm.ca
Aperçu: *Dimension:* petite; *Envergure:* locale
Mission: Pour aider financièrement les organismes communautaires qui travaillent dans le domaine de l'environnement et de créer une ville plus écologique
Membre(s) du bureau directeur:
Marie-Noëlle Foschini, Directrice générale
André Gagnon, Président, Conseil d'administration

EcoSource Mississauga
Meadowvale South Recreation Centre, 6600 Falconer Dr., 2nd Fl., Mississauga ON L5N 1M2
Tel: 905-274-6222; *Fax:* 905-858-8927
info@ecosource.ca
www.ecosource.ca
www.facebook.com/EcosourceGreen
twitter.com/EcoSourceGreen
Overview: A small local charitable organization founded in 1979
Mission: To offer education & programs related to the environment
Chief Officer(s):
Stephanie Crocker, Executive Director
scrocker@ecosource.ca
Carolyn Bailey, Associate Director
cbailey@ecosource.ca
Sierra Frank, Manager, School Programs
sfrank@ecosource.ca
Angie Sanchez, Coordinator, School Campaign
asanchez@ecosource.ca
Tooba Shakeel, Coordinator, School Waste Action
tshakeel@ecosource.ca
Finances: *Funding Sources:* Donations; Foundations; Municipal government agencies; Corporations
Publications:
• Gardens & Agriculture
Type: Newsletter; *Editor:* Carolyn Bailey
Profile: Updates about community projects through the EcoSource Urban Agriculture & Community Gardens initiatives
• Peel Environmental Youth Alliance (PEYA)
Type: Newsletter; *Frequency:* Semimonthly; *Editor:* Rahul Mehta
Profile: Environmental events & opportunities for students in the Region of Peel
• Trailblazers
Type: Newsletter
Profile: Information for Region of Peel educators about environmental teaching resources & events

Ecotrust Canada
#90, 425 Carrall St., Vancouver BC V6B 6E3
Tel: 604-682-4141; *Fax:* 604-862-1944
info@ecotrust.ca
ecotrust.ca
www.facebook.com/ecotrust.ca
twitter.com/ecotrustcanada
www.youtube.com/user/EcotrustCanada
Overview: A small provincial charitable organization
Mission: To improve environmental sustainability in British Columbia
Affliation(s): Ecotrust; Ecotrust Australia; Forest Stewardship Council; Heiltsuk Nation; Na' Na' kila Institute; Qqs Projects Society; Raincoast Conservation Society; West Coast Aquatic Management Board; Shorebank Enterprise Group; ShoreBank Pacific; Tsleil-Waututh Nation; Vancity
Chief Officer(s):
Brenda Reid-Kuecks, President
Staff Member(s): 31

EcoWatch Canada (EWC)
e-mail: seeds@telusplanet.net
www.ecowatchcanada.org
www.linkedin.com/company/ecowatch-canada
www.facebook.com/ecowatchcanada
twitter.com/ecowatchcanada
ecowatchcanada.wordpress.com
Overview: A medium-sized national charitable organization founded in 2008
Mission: To improve the environmental quality, to educate our future generations, and to raise awareness among our community by partnering with local businesses, community leaders, government officials, schools and neighbors.
Chief Officer(s):
Carmen Ng, Executive Director

L'Écrit Tôt
4050, rue Grande Allée, Montréal QC J4T 2W2
Tél: 450-443-1411; *Téléc:* 450-443-3772
ecritot@bellnet.ca
ecritot.ca
Aperçu: *Dimension:* petite; *Envergure:* locale
Mission: Aider les gens qui sont analphabètes développent la lecture et de l'écriture et de sensibiliser de l'analphabétisme
Membre(s) du bureau directeur:
Annie Beaudin, Directrice générale
Membre: *Montant de la cotisation:* 5$

Écrivains Francophones d'Amérique
1995, rue Sherbrooke Ouest, Montréal QC H3A 1H9
Tél: 514-318-2590
lesecrivainsfrancophones@yahoo.ca

ecrivainsfrancophones.com
www.facebook.com/111361458891464
Nom précédent: Société des écrivains canadiens
Aperçu: *Dimension:* petite; *Envergure:* nationale; fondée en 1936
Mission: Grouper en association les écrivains de langue française, de nationalité canadienne, domiciliés ou non au Canada, auteurs d'un ou de plusieurs livres publiés au Canada ou ailleurs par des éditeurs homologués; servir et défendre les intérêts de la littérature canadienne; prendre toutes les mesures nécessaires ou opportunes pour assurer le respect de la propriété littéraire de ses membres.
Membre(s) du bureau directeur:
Gino Levesque, Responsable
Membre: *Critères d'admissibilite:* Écrivains
Activités: Participation aux Salons du livre; conférences; lectures publiques; dîners-causeries; rencontres auteur-lecteurs, etc.; *Service de conférenciers:* Oui
Prix, Bouses:
• Prix de la SEC (Prix)
Attribué chaque année à un roman, à un essai ou à un recueil de poèmes, chacun de ces trois genres littéraires revenant une année sur trois. Le Prix n'est attribué qu'à des ouvrages publiés en français au Canada

Les écrivains indépendants d'Ottawa *See* Ottawa Independent Writers

Ecumenical Coalition for Economic Justice; GATT-Fly *See* KAIROS: Canadian Ecumenical Justice Initiatives

Ecumenical Committee of Manitoba *See* Association of Christian Churches in Manitoba

Ecumenical Forum of Canada *See* The Canadian Churches' Forum for Global Ministries

Eczema Society of Canada / Société d'Eczéma du Canada
PO Box 25009, 417 The Queensway South, Keswick ON L4P 2C7
Tel: 905-535-0776
director@eczemahelp.ca
www.eczemahelp.ca
Previous Name: Canadian Eczema Society for Education & Research
Overview: A small national charitable organization founded in 1997
Mission: To disseminate information about eczema & its treatment to both patients, families & their doctors; To encourage & fund basic research on eczema; To increase public awareness of eczema in society in general
Chief Officer(s):
Amanda Cresswell-Melville, President/Executive Director
Membership: *Member Profile:* Patients; parents of patients; doctors

Edam & District Board of Trade
PO Box 430, Edam SK S0M 0V0
Tel: 306-397-2242; *Fax:* 306-397-2555
Overview: A small local organization founded in 1940
Chief Officer(s):
Arnold Poole, President
Evelyn M Cooper, Secretary
Membership: 60
Activities: *Rents Mailing List:* Yes

EDAM Performing Arts Society (EDAM)
303 East 8th Ave., Vancouver BC V5T 1S1
Tel: 604-876-9559
info@edamdance.org
www.edamdance.org
www.facebook.com/pages/Edam-Dance/159929590739220
twitter.com/edamdance
Overview: A small local charitable organization founded in 1982
Mission: To explore new directions in dance & the performing arts
Member of: The Dance Centre; Alliance for Arts & Culture
Chief Officer(s):
Peter Bingham, Artistic Director
Mona Hamill, General Manager
Finances: *Funding Sources:* Canada Council; BC Arts Council; City of Vancouver; Vancouver Foundation; BC Gaming Branch

Eden Community Food Bank (ECFB)
#2, 3185 Unity Dr., Mississauga ON L5L 4L5
Tel: 905-785-3651
info@edenfoodbank.org
edenfoodbank.org
www.facebook.com/edencommunityfoodbank
twitter.com/edenfoodbank
Overview: A small local organization founded in 1990
Mission: To provide food to the less fortunate & promote healthy eating
Chief Officer(s):
Bill Crawford, Executive Director
bill.crawford@edenfoodbank.org
Staff Member(s): 7
Membership: *Committees:* Finance; Fundraising; HR; Marketing; Events

Edgerton & District Chamber of Commerce
PO Box 303, Edgerton AB T0B 1K0
Tel: 780-755-3933
Overview: A small local organization

Edgerton & District Historical Society
PO Box 174, Edgerton AB T0B 1K0
Tel: 780-755-2189; *Fax:* 780-755-2181
Overview: A small local charitable organization
Mission: To present artifacts that depict the history of Edgerton, Alberta & the surrounding region at the six buildings that make up the Edgerton Museum
Chief Officer(s):
Carl Bergerud, Contact
Finances: *Funding Sources:* Donations; Fundraising
Activities: Maintaining the original Grand Trunk Pacific Station, the Battle Valley School, & the Egerton Methodist Church

Edith Lando Charitable Foundation
1499 Angus Dr., Vancouver BC V6H 1V2
Fax: 604-731-1041
r_beiser@telus.net
www.edithlando.com
Overview: A small local charitable organization founded in 1973
Mission: To support programs that nurture self-esteem of young children
Chief Officer(s):
Roberta Beiser, Director
Finances: *Annual Operating Budget:* $50,000-$100,000
2 volunteer(s)
Activities: Grants note made for operating, capital projects, conferences, deficit financing, endowments; grants are made for special projects, seed money, matching funds, programs, research

Editors' Association of Canada (EAC) / Association canadienne des réviseurs (ACR)
#505, 27 Carlton St., Toronto ON M5B 1L2
Tel: 416-975-1379; *Fax:* 416-975-1637
Toll-Free: 866-226-3348
info@editors.ca
www.editors.ca
twitter.com/eac_acr
Previous Name: Freelance Editors' Association of Canada
Overview: A medium-sized national organization founded in 1979
Mission: To promote & maintain standards of professional editing & publishing; to set guidelines to help editors secure fair pay & good working conditions, fosters networking among editors & cooperates with other publishing associations in areas of common concern.
Member of: Book & Periodical Council; Canadian Conference of the Arts; Cultural Human Resources Council
Affiliation(s): Canadian Conference of the Arts
Chief Officer(s):
Vacant, President
president@editors.ca
Carolyn L. Burke, Executive Director
executivedirector@editors.ca
Finances: *Funding Sources:* Membership dues; conference fees
Membership: 1,500; *Fees:* $260 voting & qualifying members; $130 student & emeritus; *Member Profile:* Membership categories include students, qualifying members, voting members, emeritus members, & honorary life members. Voting members have completed at least 500 hours of editorial work over the 12 months preceding application for membership. Qualifying membership is open to anyone with an interest in editing.; *Committees:* Certification Steering; Conference; Newsletter; Francophone Affairs; Marketing & Public Affairs; Member Communications; Member Services; Professional Standards; Publications; Training & Development; Volunteer Management; External Liaison; Human Resources; Nominating
Activities: Sponsoring professional development seminars; establishing guidelines to help editors secure fair working conditions; facilitating networking
Awards:
• Tom Fairley Award for Editorial Excellence (Award)
Eligibility: Open to all editors, both freelance & in-house, for any editorial work published in Canada in English or French *Amount:* $2,000
• Claudette Upton Scholarship (Scholarship)
Eligibility: Current member of EAC *Amount:* $1,000 to attend national conference, association workshops or purchase EAC publications
Meetings/Conferences: • Editors' Association of Canada Conference 2015-Editing Goes Global, June, 2015, Metro Toronto Convention Centre, Toronto, ON
Scope: National
• Editors' Association of Canada Conference 2016, 2016, Vancouver, BC
Scope: National
Publications:
• Active Voice / La Voix active
Type: Newsletter; *Frequency:* Quarterly; *Editor:* Wilf Popoff; Michelle Boulton
• Editing Canadian English
Number of Pages: 258; *ISBN:* 1-55199-045-8
• Editors' Association of Canada Certification: Study Guide and Exemplars
Profile: Guides for editors through the certification process
• Meeting Editorial Standards
ISBN: 1-55322-003-X
• Professional Editorial Standards
Profile: Skills & knowledge needed for editing in English-language media in Canada

British Columbia
PO Box 1688, Stn. Bentall Centre, Vancouver BC V6C 2P7
e-mail: bc@editors.ca
www.facebook.com/EAC.BC
twitter.com/EditorsBC
Chief Officer(s):
Micheline Brodeur, Chair
bcchair@editors.ca

National Capital Region
PO Box 62035, Stn. E, Ottawa ON K1C 7H8
e-mail: ncr@editors.ca
www.linkedin.com/groups?gid=1858228
twitter.com/EditorsNCR
Chief Officer(s):
Maureen Moyes, Executive Director

Prairie Provinces
Edmonton AB
Chief Officer(s):
Emily Staniland, Branch Contact
Volunteer-with-PPB@editors.ca

Québec/Région de l'Atlantique
CP 46042, Pointe-Claire QC H9R 5R4
rqa-qac@editors.ca
www.facebook.com/326039037428133
twitter.com/RQA_QAC
Chief Officer(s):
Karen Schell, Administratrice

Toronto
PO Box 5833, Stn. A, Toronto ON M5W 1P2
Tel: 416-975-5528; *Fax:* 416-492-1719
toronto@editors.ca
www.facebook.com/EACToronto
twitter.com/EACToronto
Chief Officer(s):
Lisa Jemison, Chair
toronto_br_chair@editors.ca

Edmonton & District Council of Churches (EDCC)
c/o Garneau United Church, #123, 11148 - 84 Ave., Edmonton AB T6G 0V8
Tel: 780-439-2501; *Fax:* 780-439-3067
admin@EDCCunity.org
www.edccunity.org
Overview: A small local organization founded in 1942
Mission: To express through fellowship, consultation, cooperation, & service, the essential unity of the Christian church; To maintain open relationships & foster dialogue with other faith groups & inter-faith organizations; To provide support & monitoring for chaplaincy programs
Affiliation(s): Canadian Council of Churches
Chief Officer(s):

Julien Hammond, President, 780-469-1010 Ext. 2271, Fax: 780-465-3003
jhammond@caedm.ca
Finances: *Annual Operating Budget:* Less than $50,000
Staff Member(s): 1; 7 volunteer(s)
Membership: 22; *Fees:* $60 denominational member; $30 individual member; *Member Profile:* Christian denominations; *Committees:* Ecumenical Coordinators; Week of Prayer for Christian Unity Service Planning Committee; Way of the Cross Planning Committee; No Room in the Inn Planning Committee
Activities: Organization of events; distribution of information; participation in interdenominational projects; *Awareness Events:* Week of Prayer for Christian Unity, Jan.; Good Friday Way of the Cross; No Room in the Inn Fundraising for Low Income Housing, Dec.
Awards:
• Rev. Marilyn McClung Memorial Award for Ecumenism (Award)
Eligibility: Individuals who have made outstanding or specific contributions to the Edmonton & District Council of Churches' ecumenical efforts *Contact:* Julien Hammond

Edmonton & District Labour Council

#201, 10425 Princess Elizabeth Ave., Edmonton AB T5G 0Y5
Tel: 780-474-4747; *Fax:* 780-477-1064
edlc@telusplanet.net
www.edlc.ca
Overview: A medium-sized local organization founded in 1906 overseen by Alberta Federation of Labour
Mission: To advocate rights of workers through City Hall & school boards; to provide monthly forum for exchanging information on developments in unions; to facilitate unity in labour; to support & organize rallies; to offer strike support; to maintain involvement in civic boards & committees
Member of: Canadian Labour Congress; Alberta Federation of Labour
Affliation(s): Parkland Institute; Aspen Foundation; Edmonton Community Foundation
Chief Officer(s):
Brian Henderson, President
Finances: *Annual Operating Budget:* $100,000-$250,000
Staff Member(s): 1; 140 volunteer(s)
Membership: 40,000 local union; *Fees:* $5; *Member Profile:* Any organization already affiliated to the Canadian Labour Congress; *Committees:* Education; Political Action; Community Services; Strike Support; Peace; Finance
Activities: Labour Day BBQ for the Unemployed; Labour Appreciation Night; *Speaker Service:* Yes; *Library* by appointment

Edmonton (Alberta) Nerve Pain Association (EANPA)

14016 - 91 A Ave., Edmonton AB T5R 5A7
Tel: 780-217-9306
Neuropathy_nervepain@hotmail.com
www.edmontonnervepain.ca
Overview: A medium-sized provincial charitable organization
Mission: To support people suffering from neuropathic pain.
Chief Officer(s):
Claude M. Roberto, President

Edmonton Aboriginal Senior Centre (NSC)

Cottage E, 10107 - 134 Ave., Edmonton AB T5E 1J2
Tel: 780-476-6595
manager@easc.ca
www.easc.ca
Previous Name: Métis Women's Council of Edmonton
Overview: A small local charitable organization founded in 1986
Mission: To promote welfare, education & interests of Aboriginal seniors within the Edmonton area
Finances: *Funding Sources:* City of Edmonton community services; Alberta Municipal Affairs
Staff Member(s): 4
Activities: Native Seniors Drop-in Centre; Outreach Program; Urban Native Housing Registry; *Speaker Service:* Yes

Edmonton Arts Council (EAC)

Prince of Wales Armouries, 10440 - 108 Ave., 2nd Fl., Edmonton AB T5H 3Z9
Tel: 780-424-2787; *Fax:* 780-425-7620
www.edmontonarts.ab.ca
www.facebook.com/pages/Edmonton-Arts-Council/14999897487 9
twitter.com/artsedmonton
Overview: A small local organization
Mission: To support & promote the arts community in Edmonton; to provide support to festivals, arts organizations & individual artists
Affliation(s): Arts Habitat Association of Edmonton
Chief Officer(s):
Brian Webb, Chair
Paul Moulton, Executive Director
pmoulton@edmontonarts.ca
Staff Member(s): 18
Membership: 298; *Fees:* $25 individual full/associate; $50 organization full/associate; free - students; *Member Profile:* Artists, arts & festival organizations; individuals, businesses, government members, corporations & media supporting the arts in Edmonton; *Committees:* Equity
Activities: Public Art Conservation project; Graffiti Zones program; transitory public art; community public art; Percent for Art acquisition program
Awards:
• Lee Fund for the Arts Grant (Grant)
Eligibility: 18 years of age or older; resident of greater Edmonton region; Canadian citizen or landed immigrant *Amount:* $10,000 max.
• Project Grant for Individual Artists (Grant)
Eligibility: Emerging or established professional artist; resides in City of Edmonton; has peer recognition; has received public exposure*Deadline:* July 1 *Amount:* $25,000 maximum
• Cultural Diversity in the Arts Awards (Grant)
Eligibility: From ethnically diverse cultural background; Edmonton resident; 18 yrs. or older; working in any artistic medium, including but not limited to, dance, theatre, music, literary arts, storytelling & other oral traditions, fine craft, media arts or visual arts*Deadline:* October *Amount:* 12 awards, $7.500 each

Edmonton Association of the Deaf (EAD)

#203, 11404 - 142 St., Edmonton AB T5M 1V1
Fax: 780-436-4639
eadoffice@shawcable.com
Overview: A small local charitable organization
Affliation(s): Alberta Association of the Deaf; Alberta Cultural Society Deaf; Alberta Deaf Sports Association
Chief Officer(s):
Calvin Novak, President
tenten@shaw.ca
Finances: *Annual Operating Budget:* Less than $50,000
20 volunteer(s)
Membership: 100-499; *Fees:* $15 senior; $25 adults
Activities: Deaf social night; deaf summer camp; senior citizens

Edmonton Bicycle & Touring Club (EBTC)

PO Box 52017, Stn. Garneau, Edmonton AB T6G 2T5
Tel: 780-424-2453
info@bikeclub.ca
www.bikeclub.ca
www.facebook.com/groups/21002145481
Overview: A small local organization founded in 1978
Affliation(s): Alberta Bicycle Association
Chief Officer(s):
Ron Chapman, President
rwchipper@shaw.ca
Finances: *Annual Operating Budget:* $50,000-$100,000
7 volunteer(s)
Membership: 301; *Fees:* $30 single, add $15 for additional family member over 17 yrs.; *Member Profile:* Single, married, families, all ages & walks of life
Activities: Day & overnight cycling trips; cross-country skiing; social events; *Awareness Events:* Tour de l'Alberta

Edmonton Boxing & Wrestling Commission ***See*** Edmonton Combative Sports Commission

Edmonton Centre for Equal Justice ***See*** Edmonton Community Legal Centre

Edmonton CFA Society

Standard Life Centre, PO Box 479, #21, 10405 Jasper Ave., Edmonton AB T5J 3N4
Toll-Free: 866-494-3732
info@edmontoncfa.ca
www.edmontoncfa.ca
Also Known As: Edmonton Society of Financial Analysts
Overview: A small local charitable organization founded in 1976
Mission: To promote professional & ethical standards in Edmonton, Alberta's investment industry; To advance the interests of members
Member of: CFA Institute
Chief Officer(s):
Chris Turchansky, President
cturchansky@atb.com
Brett Kimak, Vice-President
brett.kimak@aimco.alberta.ca
Rodney Lance Babineau, Secretary
rod.babineau@gov.ab.ca
Theresa Walton, Treasurer
theresa.walton@telus.com
Finances: *Funding Sources:* Sponsoships
Membership: *Member Profile:* Individuals in the investment community in Edmonton, such as pension fund managers, security analysts, stockbrokers, & investment counsellors; *Committees:* CFA Prep Courses; Membership; Programs
Activities: Encouraging professional development through the CFA Program in Edmonton; Presenting programs, with speakers on topics related to the investment industry; Facilitating the exchange of information between members, Edmonton's financial community, the international investment community, & the general public; Raising awareness of the investment industry & the CFA designation;
Publications:
• Edmonton CFA Society Annual Report
Type: Yearbook; *Frequency:* Annually
• News & Views [a publication of the Edmonton CFA Society]
Type: Newsletter
Profile: Society activities & forthcoming events

Edmonton Chamber Music Society

PO Box 60354, Stn. U of Alberta, Edmonton AB T6G 2S6
Tel: 780-433-4532
ecms@edmontonchambermusic.org
www.edmontonchambermusic.org
www.facebook.com/edmonton.chambermusicsociety
twitter.com/ECMS4
www.youtube.com/user/ViolaChambers
Overview: A small local organization founded in 1954
Mission: To present a series of six to eight chamber music concerts each season
Chief Officer(s):
Verna Quon, Contact
vquon@telusplanet.net
Finances: *Funding Sources:* Municipal government, provincial government; donations; ticket sales

Edmonton Chamber of Commerce

World Trade Centre, Sun Life Place, #700, 9990 Jasper Ave., Edmonton AB T5J 1P7
Tel: 780-426-4620; *Fax:* 780-424-7946
info@edmontonchamber.com
www.edmontonchamber.com
ca.linkedin.com/in/edmontonchamber
www.facebook.com/EdmontonChamber
twitter.com/edmontonchamber
www.youtube.com/edmontonchamber
Overview: A medium-sized local organization founded in 1889
Mission: To facilitate economic growth by providing information, business opportunities, educational programs & services in the area of international trade; to positively influence Edmonton's business environment
Member of: World Trade Centre Association
Chief Officer(s):
James Cumming, President/CEO
Robin Bobocel, Vice President, Public Affairs
Finances: *Funding Sources:* Membership fees
Membership: *Fees:* Schedule available; *Committees:* Policy; Executive
Activities: Seminars & luncheons; trade missions; information & research; import/export guide; *Internships:* Yes; *Speaker Service:* Yes; *Library:* World Trade Centre Library
Awards:
• Centennial Scholarship (Scholarship)

Edmonton Chamber of Voluntary Organizations

Bonnie Doon Shopping Centre, #255, 82 Ave. & 83 St., Edmonton AB T6C 4E3
Tel: 780-428-5487; *Fax:* 780-428-1930
director@ecvo.ca
www.ecvo.ca
www.facebook.com/173734905672
twitter.com/Edmcvo
Overview: A small local organization
Mission: To provide leadership & mobilize the collective resources of the voluntary sector; To enhance programs, services, operations & governance of not-for-profit organizations in the Edmonton region
Chief Officer(s):
Russ Dahms, Executive Director
director@ecvo.ca

Edmonton Classical Guitar Society
14104 Vallerview Dr., Edmonton AB T5R 5T8
Tel: 587-708-2044; *Fax:* 780-489-9583
www.edmontonclassicalguitarsociety.org
Overview: A small local organization founded in 1995
Mission: To foster an appreciation for the classical guitar by providing a forum for listening, learning, performing & teaching.
Chief Officer(s):
David Grainger Brown, President
Membership: *Fees:* $30 regular; $60 partner; $100 sustaining
Activities: Regular concerts

Edmonton Combative Sports Commission (ECSC)
10250 - 101 St. NW, 13th Fl., Edmonton AB T6J 3P4
Tel: 780-495-0382; *Fax:* 780-429-6976
ecsc.ca
Previous Name: Edmonton Boxing & Wrestling Commission
Overview: A small local licensing organization founded in 1938 overseen by Canadian Professional Boxing Federation
Mission: The ECSC regulates, governs & controls boxing, wrestling & full-contact karate bouts & contests within Edmonton; enforces the CPBF safety code.
Member of: Canadian Professional Boxing Federation
Affliation(s): Association of Boxing Commissions
Chief Officer(s):
Pat Reid, Executive Director
pat.reid@edmonton.ca
Finances: *Annual Operating Budget:* $50,000-$100,000; *Funding Sources:* Permit fees
24 volunteer(s)
Membership: 8; *Member Profile:* By City Council appointment
Awards:
• Barney O'Connor Boxer of the Year Award (Award)

Edmonton Community Legal Centre (ECLC)
10056 - 101A Ave., Edmonton AB T5J 0C8
Tel: 780-702-1725; *Fax:* 780-702-1726
intake@eclc.ca
www.eclc.ca
Previous Name: Edmonton Centre for Equal Justice
Overview: A small local organization
Mission: To provide free legal advice, representation, referral & legal education to low-income Edmontonians
Chief Officer(s):
Lori Shortreed, Executive Director
Staff Member(s): 7; 62 volunteer(s)

Edmonton Community Networks (ECN)
c/o Tera-Byte Dot Com Inc., Terminal Level, 10004 - 104 Ave., Edmonton AB T5J 0K1
Tel: 780-413-1868; *Fax:* 780-413-1869
Toll-Free: 877-837-2298
support@ecn.ab.ca
www.ecn.ab.ca
Also Known As: Edmonton FreeNet
Overview: A small local charitable organization founded in 1994
Mission: To promote internet literacy by providing low cost internet access & training classes. It has installed access terminals in libraries & other public locations for free internet usage by the Edmonton community.
Member of: Edmonton Chamber of Commerce
Activities: Internet access; training & education; community building;

Edmonton Composers' Concert Society (ECCS) / L'association des compositeurs d'Edmonton
#302, 11124 - 68th Ave., Edmonton AB T6H 2C2
Tel: 780-432-1618
Overview: A small local charitable organization founded in 1985
Mission: To sponsor concerts which feature Canadian composers
Member of: Alberta Motion Picture Industries Association
Chief Officer(s):
Piotr Grella-Mozejko, Artistic Director & General Manager
Finances: *Annual Operating Budget:* Less than $50,000; *Funding Sources:* The Canada Council for the Arts; Winspear Fund; SOCAN Foundation; Alberta Foundation for the Arts
Membership: 90; *Fees:* $25 full; $10 associate; *Member Profile:* Interest in contemporary music: composer, performer, auditor
Activities: Annual New Music Festival; "New Music Alberta" concert series; CD releases; *Library*

Edmonton Construction Association (ECA)
10215 - 176 St., Edmonton AB T5S 1M1
Tel: 780-483-1130; *Fax:* 780-484-0299
contact@edmca.com
www.edmca.com
Overview: A medium-sized provincial organization founded in 1931 overseen by Canadian Construction Association
Mission: To provide up-to-date information relating to activities in the commercial, institutional & industrial construction industry; to provide access for the membership to tender documents necessary to the bidding process; to provide effective representation to government & industry-related organizations
Member of: International Builders Exchange Executives
Affliation(s): Alberta Construction Association; COOLNET Edmonton
Chief Officer(s):
Barry Pfau, President
Finances: *Funding Sources:* Membership fees; contract document sales; affinity program residuals
Membership: 1,000+; *Fees:* $1,824 regular; $400 associate; *Member Profile:* Engaged in commercial, institutional, industrial, roads, highways & bridge construction; *Committees:* Executive; Education; Membership; Trade Definitions; Social; Nominating
Activities: Municipal government liaison; Plan Room (plans open to tender available for viewing); COOLNET Edmonton Electronic Plan Room; Plans Deposit Guarantee Program; *Library*

Edmonton Czech Language Society
8623 - 33 Ave., Edmonton AB T6K 2X9
Tel: 780-462-5817
Previous Name: Czech Cultural Club
Overview: A small local organization
Mission: To provide cultural & support services for the Czech community
Chief Officer(s):
Milos Hajek, President
Stanya Kresta, Secretary/Alternative
Activities: Sports, cultural & social activities

Edmonton Dental Assistants Association (EDAA)
4 Elbow Dr., Devon AB T9G 1M5
Tel: 780-987-2022; *Fax:* 780-987-2022
edaa@interbaun.com
edaa.ab.ca
www.facebook.com/431730580181670
Overview: A small local organization
Chief Officer(s):
Debbie Hartt, President
Membership: *Member Profile:* Dental assistants in Edmonton
Activities: *Awareness Events:* National Dental Assistants Week, March

Edmonton District Soccer Association (EDSA)
17415 - 106A Ave., Edmonton AB T5S 1M7
Tel: 780-413-0140; *Fax:* 780-481-4619
www.edsa.org
www.facebook.com/99060275311
twitter.com/EdmontonSoccer
Overview: A small local organization overseen by Alberta Soccer Association
Member of: Alberta Soccer Association
Chief Officer(s):
Mike Thome, Executive Director
mthome@edsa.org
Staff Member(s): 8

Edmonton Economic Development Corporation (EEDC)
World Trade Centre Edmonton, 9990 Jasper Ave. 3rd Fl., Edmonton AB T5J 1P7
Tel: 780-424-9191
Toll-Free: 800-661-6965
www.eedc.ca
www.linkedin.com/company/edmonton-economic-development-corp.
www.facebook.com/EdmontonEconomicDevelopmentCorp
twitter.com/eedc
www.youtube.com/eedcedmonton
Overview: A small local organization
Mission: To foster entrepreneurship & economic growth in Edmonton
Chief Officer(s):
Brad Ferguson, President & CEO
BFerguson@edmonton.com
Derek Hudson, Chief Operating Officer, 780-401-7681
dhudson@edmonton.com
Kevin Weidlich, Vice-President, Marketing & Communications, 780-917-7890
kweidlich@edmonton.com
Activities: Overseeing the following divisions: Edmonton Tourism, Enterprise Edmonton, the Shaw Conference Centre & the Edmonton Research Park

Edmonton Tourism
c/o Edmonton Economic Development Corporation, World Trade Centre, 9990 Jasper Ave. 3rd Fl., Edmonton AB T5J 1P7
Tel: 780-424-9191
Toll-Free: 800-463-4667
info@exploreedmonton.com
exploreedmonton.com
www.facebook.com/EdmontonTourism
twitter.com/edmontontourism
instagram.com/exploreedmonton
Mission: Edmonton Tourism creates, implements, & evaluates tourism marketing initiatives for Greater Edmonton, working with both public & private tourism industry partners. It is a division of the Edmonton Economic Development Corporation (EEDC), an independent corporate entity established by the City to promote economic growth & development.
Chief Officer(s):
Maggie Davison, Vice-President, Edmonton Tourism, EEDC, 780-917-7623
mdavison@edmonton.com

Edmonton Epilepsy Association (EEA)
11007 - 124 St. NW, Edmonton AB T5M 0J5
Tel: 780-488-9600; *Fax:* 780-447-5486
Toll-Free: 866-374-5377
info@edmontonepilepsy.org
www.edmontonepilepsy.org
Overview: A small local charitable organization founded in 1961
Mission: To ensure the well-being of persons with epilepsy through increased public awareness & education to further to address specific concerns both personal & social that these individuals experience
Member of: United Way
Affliation(s): Canadian Epilepsy Alliance; Epilepsy Canada
Chief Officer(s):
Gary Sampley, Executive Director/COO
gary@edmontonepilepsy.org
Staff Member(s): 5
Membership: *Fees:* $15; *Member Profile:* Persons with epilepsy; caregivers; health/educational professionals
Activities: Awareness; education; support; *Awareness Events:* Epilepsy Month, Mar.; *Speaker Service:* Yes; *Library* Open to public

Edmonton Executives Association
PO Box 4044, Edmonton AB T6E 4S8
Tel: 780-413-1979; *Fax:* 780-413-1975
director@eea.org
www.eea.org
Overview: A small local organization
Mission: To help business leaders in Edmonton by providing direct business, referrals & information.
Member of: International Executives Association
Membership: 179; *Fees:* $375 + GST initiation; $1366 + GST annual dues; *Member Profile:* Business owners, executives; membership is limited to one firm per business or professional sector

Edmonton Federation of Community Leagues (EFCL)
7103 - 105 St., Edmonton AB T6E 4G8
Tel: 780-437-2913; *Fax:* 780-437-4710
info@efcl.org
www.efcl.org
Overview: A medium-sized local organization founded in 1921
Chief Officer(s):
Allan Bolstad, Executive Director
allan.bolstad@efcl.org
Finances: *Annual Operating Budget:* $100,000-$250,000; *Funding Sources:* Regional government
Staff Member(s): 6; 40 volunteer(s)
Membership: 148 institutional; 50,000+ individual; *Fees:* $425 institutional; *Member Profile:* Community leagues; *Committees:* Performing Arts; Planning & Development
Activities: Parent body for 148 community leagues & approximately 10-12 affiliated groups including, but not limited to, sports, neighbourhood watch, youth camps

Edmonton Fire Fighters Union
#200, 7024 - 101 Ave., Edmonton AB T6A 0H7

Tel: 780-429-9020; *Fax:* 780-420-1667
effu@edmontonfirefighters.com
www.edmontonfirefighters.com
Overview: A small local organization founded in 1917
Mission: EFFU is the offical lobbying & negotiating body for its members. Its designation is IAFF Local 209.
Member of: Canadian Association of Fire Fighters
Affliation(s): International Association of Fire Fighters; Muscular Dystrophy Canada
Chief Officer(s):
Greg Holubowich, President
gregholubowich@edmontonfirefighters.com
Bud McCarthy, Treasurer
budmccarthy@edmontonfirefighters.com
Membership: 1000; *Member Profile:* Uniformed dispatchers, fire fighters, inspectors, investigators, mechanics, & support personnel in Edmonton
Activities: Firefighters Burn Treatment Society, Edmonton Chapter; fundraising events for various charities

Edmonton Folk Music Festival

PO Box 4130, 10115 - 97A Ave., Edmonton AB T6E 4T2
Tel: 780-429-1899; *Fax:* 780-424-1132
admin@efmf.ab.ca
www.edmontonfolkfest.org
www.facebook.com/EdmontonFolkMusicFestival
twitter.com/edmfolkfest
www.youtube.com/EdmontonFolkFest
Overview: A small international charitable organization founded in 1980
Mission: The festival in a not-for-profit society dedicated to bringing in the best of folk music from around the world.
Finances: *Annual Operating Budget:* $1.5 Million-$3 Million
Staff Member(s): 14; 2000 volunteer(s)
Membership: *Member Profile:* Must be a volunteer in good standing
Activities: Edmonton Folk Music Festival, August;

Edmonton Health Care Citizenship Society *See* Action for Healthy Communities

Edmonton Heritage Festival Association (EHFA)

10125 - 157 St., Edmonton AB T5P 2T9
Tel: 780-488-3378; *Fax:* 780-455-9097
info@heritage-festival.com
www.heritage-festival.com
www.facebook.com/EdmontonHeritageFestivalAssociation
Overview: A small local charitable organization founded in 1976
Mission: To present an annual family oriented Multicultural Festival to raise public awareness, understanding & appreciation for the cultural diversity which characterizes our unique international community
Member of: Northwest Festivals Association; National Tour Association
Chief Officer(s):
Jack Little, Executive Director
jacklittle@heritage-festival.com
Wendy Carter, Volunteer Coordinator
wendy@heritage-festival.com
Finances: *Annual Operating Budget:* $250,000-$500,000
Staff Member(s): 2; 1200 volunteer(s)
Activities: *Internships:* Yes; *Speaker Service:* Yes; *Library* by appointment

Edmonton Humane Society for the Prevention of Cruelty to Animals (EHSPCA)

13620 - 163 St. NW, Edmonton AB T5V 0B2
Tel: 780-471-1774; *Fax:* 780-479-8946
ehs@edmontonhumanesociety.com
www.edmontonhumanesociety.com
www.facebook.com/EdmontonHumaneSociety
twitter.com/edmontonhumane
www.youtube.com/user/EdmontonHumane
Also Known As: Edmonton Humane SPCA
Previous Name: Edmonton Society for the Prevention of Cruelty to Animals
Overview: A small local charitable organization founded in 1910
Mission: To protect animals from suffering; To promote life long committment to animal welfare & dignity
Member of: Canadian Federation of Humane Societies; Canadian Association of Animal Welfare Administrators
Affliation(s): World Society for the Protection of Animals
Chief Officer(s):
Stephanie McDonald, Chief Executive Officer
Finances: *Funding Sources:* Fee for service contracts with the municipality of Edmonton & outlying municipalities
Membership: *Fees:* $5 senior; $20 individual; $25 family; $100 corporate; $5 junior
Activities: Adopts animals out to new homes; Lost & Found animal registry; Rural registry; investigates animal abuse; *Awareness Events:* Pets in the Park, July; *Speaker Service:* Yes; *Rents Mailing List:* Yes; *Library* Open to public

Edmonton Immigrant Services Association (EISA)

#201, 10720 - 113 St., Edmonton AB T5H 3H8
Tel: 780-474-8445; *Fax:* 780-477-0883
www.eisa-edmonton.org
www.facebook.com/edmontonEISA
twitter.com/EISA_Edmonton
Overview: A small local charitable organization founded in 1976
Mission: To help immigrants & refugees adapt & fully integrate in Canadian society; to promote cross-cultural understanding; to initiate programs & services to bridge cultural gaps.
Member of: Alberta Association of Immigrant Serving Agencies
Affliation(s): Northern Alberta Alliance on Race Relations
Chief Officer(s):
Rajiv Sinha, Chair
Janette De Cordova, Treasurer
Finances: *Funding Sources:* Federal, provincial, municipal, individual donors
Activities: Interpretation/translation services; ESL classes; human rights education classes; school settlement support; summer camp; mentorship & host services;

Edmonton Inner City Housing Society (EICHS)

9430 - 111 Ave., Edmonton AB T5G 0A4
Tel: 780-423-1339; *Fax:* 780-423-1166
offmngr@telusplanet.net
www.eichs.org
Also Known As: The Intermet Housing Society of Edmonton
Overview: A small local charitable organization founded in 1983
Mission: To provide affordable housing to low-income & disadvantaged people of Edmonton's inner city & to facilitate tenant involvement in the management of their housing & society
Chief Officer(s):
Cecilia Blasetti, President
Cameron McDonald, Executive Director
Finances: *Annual Operating Budget:* $500,000-$1.5 Million; *Funding Sources:* Provincial government; city grants; donations; rental income
Staff Member(s): 14; 60 volunteer(s)
Membership: 100-499

Edmonton Insurance Association (EIA)

c/o Portage Mutual Insurance Co., #1340 First Edmonton Place, 10665 Jasper Ave., Edmonton AB T5J 3S9
www.edmontoninsuranceassociation.com
www.linkedin.com/groups?gid=4330904&trk=hb_side_g
www.facebook.com/groups/EdmontonInsurance/
Previous Name: Insurance Women of Edmonton
Overview: A small local organization founded in 1981
Mission: Non-profit, voluntary association dedicated to promoting education, fellowship and loyalty
Member of: Canadian Association of Insurance Women
Chief Officer(s):
Dawn Mercier, President
dawn.mercier@economical.com
Finances: *Annual Operating Budget:* Less than $50,000
8 volunteer(s)
Membership: 50; *Fees:* $50

Edmonton Interdistrict Youth Soccer Association (EIYSA)

Sprucewoods Business Park, #307, 8925 - 51 Ave., Edmonton AB T5E 5J3
Tel: 780-462-3537; *Fax:* 780-444-4321
admin@eiysa.com
www.eiysa.com
Overview: A small local organization overseen by Alberta Soccer Association
Member of: Alberta Soccer Association
Chief Officer(s):
Barrie White, President & COO
exdir@eiysa.com
Staff Member(s): 6
Membership: 11 teams

Edmonton International Baseball Foundation (EIBF)

PO Box 33006, Stn. Glenwood, Edmonton AB T5P 4V8
Tel: 780-756-1183
postmaster@baseballeibf.ca
baseballeibf.ca
Overview: A small international organization founded in 1979
Mission: To help develop amateur baseball through financial assistance; to host international amateur baseball events
Affliation(s): Baseball Canada; International Baseball Federation
Chief Officer(s):
Ron Hayter, Chair
ron.hayter@baseballeibf.ca
Activities: Championships & world cups; four scholarships awarded annually

Edmonton International Film Festival Society (EIFFS)

#201, 10816A - 82nd Ave., Edmonton AB T6E 2B3
Tel: 780-423-0844
info@edmontonfilmfest.com
www.edmontonfilmfest.com
www.facebook.com/edmontonfilmfest
twitter.com/edmfilmfest
www.youtube.com/user/Edmontonfilmfest
Overview: A small international charitable organization founded in 2004
Mission: To produce a film festival for 9 days each autumn showing international, independent films in categories that include contemporary, world cinema, Canadian, documentary, alternative, shorts.
Chief Officer(s):
Kerrie Long, Festival Producer
Staff Member(s): 15

Edmonton Japanese Community Association

6750 - 88 St., Edmonton AB T6E 5H6
Tel: 780-466-8166; *Fax:* 780-465-0376
office@ejca.org
www.ejca.org
Overview: A small local organization
Mission: To help incorporate people of Japanese origin into Canadian society & ro preserve Japanese culture in Canada
Member of: National Association of Japanese Canadians
Chief Officer(s):
Stephanie Bozzer, President
Membership: *Fees:* $20 single; $35 family
Activities: Cultural programs; Japanese language classes; clubs & groups; *Awareness Events:* Fall Bazaar, Nov.; *Library:* Gordon Hirabashi Library
Publications:
• Moshi Moshi [a publication of the Edmonton Japanese Community Association]
Type: Newsletter; *Frequency:* bi-m.

Edmonton Jazz Society (EJS)

11 Tommy Banks Way, Edmonton AB T6E 2M2
Tel: 780-432-0428; *Fax:* 780-433-3773
programming@yardbirdsuite.com
www.yardbirdsuite.com
www.facebook.com/YardbirdSuite
twitter.com/yardbirdsuite
Also Known As: Yardbird Suite
Overview: A small local organization founded in 1973
Mission: To present, promote & develop the performance of live Jazz music in the City of Edmonton
Member of: Western Jazz Association
Chief Officer(s):
Adrian Albert, President
Membership: *Fees:* $30 student/senior; $50 regular; $300 silver; $500 gold
Activities: Concert Program; Littlebirds Educational Band Project; Jazzworks Festival

Edmonton Law Librarians Association *See* Edmonton Law Libraries Association

Edmonton Law Libraries Association (ELLA)

PO Box 47093, 62 Edmonton City Centre, Edmonton AB T5J 4N1
edmontonlawlibraries.ca
Previous Name: Edmonton Law Librarians Association
Overview: A small local organization
Mission: To provide professional services & to create networks between professionals in the law library field.
Chief Officer(s):
Shaunna Mireau, Chair
chair@edmontonlawlibraries.ca
Christine Watson, Secretary-Treasurer
secretary@edmontonlawlibraries.ca
Membership: *Fees:* $25; *Committees:* Head Start; Last Copy

Edmonton Library Association *See* Greater Edmonton Library Association

Edmonton Minor Soccer Association (EMSA)

Edmonton South Soccer Centre, 6520 Roper Rd., Edmonton AB T6B 3K8
Tel: 780-413-3672; *Fax:* 780-490-1652
edmontonsoccer.com
www.facebook.com/254791561239153
twitter.com/YEGMinorSoccer
Overview: A small local organization overseen by Alberta Soccer Association
Member of: Alberta Soccer Association
Chief Officer(s):
Juan Ortiz, Executive Director
juano@edmontonsoccer.com
Staff Member(s): 6
Membership: 89 teams

Edmonton Motor Dealers' Association (EMDA)

www.emdacars.com
Overview: A small local organization founded in 1953
Mission: To promote cooperation, discussion & the exchange of ideas & business methods between members of the association; To encourage the participation of members in industry & PR events, such as the Edmonton Motor Show, that enhance the image of industry in Edmonton; To represent the industry to government; To collect & disseminate information relative to the industry; To regulate the industry; to support educative initiatives
Member of: Motor Dealers Association of Alberta
Finances: *Annual Operating Budget:* $50,000-$100,000; *Funding Sources:* Auto show
Membership: 63; *Fees:* $120

Edmonton Musicians' Association (EMA)

#302, 10765 - 98 St., Edmonton AB T5H 2P2
Tel: 780-422-2449; *Fax:* 780-423-4212
info@afmedmonton.ca
www.afmedmonton.ca
Also Known As: Local 390, American Federation of Musicians
Overview: A small local organization founded in 1907
Mission: To provide services which protect their members, facilitate networking & allow them access to a pension plan & other resources, such as instrument/gear insurance
Member of: American Federation of Musicians
Chief Officer(s):
E. Eddy Bayens, President
Edith Stacey, Office Manager
Membership: *Fees:* $150
Activities: Assistance in applying for P2 visa to work in the U.S.

Edmonton Numismatic Society

PO Box 78057, Stn. Collingwood, Edmonton AB T5T 6A1
Tel: 780-270-6312
www.edmontoncoinclub.com
www.facebook.com/131811960187905
twitter.com/ENSCoinClub
Overview: A small local organization founded in 1954
Chief Officer(s):
David Peter, President
president_ens@yahoo.ca
Mitch Goudreau, Secretary
secretary_ens@yahoo.ca
Membership: *Fees:* $15-$40 regular; $5-$20 junior; $15-$40 family
Publications:
• The Planchet [a publication of the Edmonton Numismatic Society]
Type: Newsletter; *Frequency:* 10 pa; *Editor:* Roger Grove

Edmonton Opera Association

15230 - 128 Ave., Edmonton AB T5V 1A8
Tel: 780-424-4040; *Fax:* 780-429-0600
edmopera@edmontonopera.com
www.edmontonopera.com
www.facebook.com/EdmontonOpera
twitter.com/edmontonopera
Overview: A small local charitable organization founded in 1963
Mission: To develop & promote opera as a dynamic & progressive art form; to attract & challenge audiences & artists through a creative program of opera production & education
Member of: Opera Canada; Opera America; Canadian Actors' Equity Association
Chief Officer(s):
Tim Yakimec, General Manager
tim.yakimec@edmontonopera.com
Finances: *Funding Sources:* Grants; fundraising; sponsorship; box office; individual & corporate donations
Staff Member(s): 15
Activities: Four operas produced per season; lecture prior to each performance educating the audience about opera; four opera brunches per season at local hotel with brief performances by each opera's principals; four opera overtures per season which include a chance for the public to meet each opera's creative team; *Library*

Edmonton Persons Living with HIV Society *See* Living Positive

Edmonton Police Association (EPA) / Association de la police d'Edmonton

10158 - 97 Ave., Edmonton AB T5K 2T5
Tel: 780-496-8600; *Fax:* 780-428-0374
www.edmontonpoliceassociation.ca
Overview: A small local organization founded in 1972
Member of: Canadian Police Association
Affliation(s): Alberta Federation of Police Associations
Chief Officer(s):
Tony Simioni, President
Bill Clark, Treasurer
Finances: *Annual Operating Budget:* $500,000-$1.5 Million
Staff Member(s): 5
Membership: 1,100; *Member Profile:* Serving officers up to rank of staff sergeant
Activities: Labour relations; disciplinary representations; charity & welfare obligations

Edmonton Radial Railway Society (ERRS)

PO Box 76057, Stn. Southgate, Edmonton AB T6H 5Y7
Tel: 780-437-7721; *Fax:* 780-437-3095
info@edmonton-radial-railway.ab.ca
www.edmonton-radial-railway.ab.ca
www.facebook.com/edmontonstreetcar
twitter.com/yegstreetcar
Overview: A small national charitable organization founded in 1980
Mission: The Society collects, preserves & restores vintage streetcars, primarily those from 1908-1951.
Member of: Canadian Museum Association
Affliation(s): Association of Tourist Railroads and Railway Museums; Alberta Museums Association; Virtual Museum of Canada
Chief Officer(s):
Hans Ryffel, President
Finances: *Annual Operating Budget:* $100,000-$250,000; *Funding Sources:* Municipal, provincial & federal governments; donations
60 volunteer(s)
Membership: 130; *Fees:* $20
Activities: Operating 2 historic street railway lines within Edmonton from May to Oct.; streetcar museum; streetcar chartering service; restoration, maintenance and operation of historic streetcars; *Library*
Publications:
• The Trip Sheet
Type: Newsletter; *Frequency:* Quarterly

Edmonton Reptile & Amphibian Society (ERAS)

PO Box 52128, 8210 - 109 St., Edmonton AB T6G 2T5
Tel: 780-429-0934
www.edmontonreptiles.com
www.facebook.com/EdmontonREPTILES
twitter.com/EdmontonREPTILE
Overview: A small local organization
Chief Officer(s):
Ian Kanda, President
president@edmontonreptiles.com
Membership: *Fees:* $36
Awards:
• Annual ERAS Legacy Award (Award)
Recognizes outstanding efforts of a society member each year.
Publications:
• The Herp Digest
Type: Newsletter; *Frequency:* Quarterly
Profile: Available to all ERAS Members

Edmonton Soaring Club (ESC)

PO Box 472, Edmonton AB T5J 2K1
Tel: 780-363-3860
info@edmontonsoaringclub.com
www.edmontonsoaringclub.com
Overview: A small local organization founded in 1957
Mission: To promote soaring & provide enthusiasts with the means to practice soaring
Member of: Soaring Association of Canada
Affliation(s): Alberta Soaring Council; other soaring clubs
Membership: *Fees:* $600 adult; $405 spouse; $440 student 21-24; $380 student Û; $300 air cadet; $50 non-flying
Activities: Flying gliders; teaching how to fly; expeditions; social events

Edmonton Social Planning Council (ESPC)

#37, 9912 - 106 St., Edmonton AB T5K 1C5
Tel: 780-423-2031; *Fax:* 780-425-6244
edmontonspc@gmail.com
www.edmontonsocialplanning.ca
www.facebook.com/pages/Edmonton-Social-Planning-Council/37296571206
twitter.com/edmontonspc
Overview: A medium-sized provincial charitable organization founded in 1940
Mission: To provide leadership within the community by addressing & researching social issues, informing public discussion & influencing social policy
Chief Officer(s):
Susan Morrissey, Executive Director, 780-423-2031 Ext. 353
Vasant Chotai, President
Finances: *Annual Operating Budget:* $250,000-$500,000; *Funding Sources:* United Way of the Alberta Capital Region; Edmonton Community Foundation; Edmonton Community Investment Operating Grant; AB Gaming & Liquor Commission
Staff Member(s): 5; 54 volunteer(s)
Membership: *Fees:* Limited Income/Student $5; Associate $15; Individual $25; Corporate (Small) $50; Corporate (Large) $75; *Committees:* Finance; Policy; Advocacy; Board Development; Casino
Activities: Monitoring social issues & trends; Producing publications on a variety of social issues; Conducting surveys & presenting reports; Researching & analyzing policies; Partnering with other organizations to meet community needs; Providing public education; Advocating; *Awareness Events:* Lunch & Learn; *Internships:* Yes; *Speaker Service:* Yes; *Library:* ESPC Resource Library;

Edmonton Society for the Prevention of Cruelty to Animals *See* Edmonton Humane Society for the Prevention of Cruelty to Animals

Edmonton Space & Science Foundation (ESSF)

11211 - 142 St., Edmonton AB T5M 4A1
Tel: 780-452-9100; *Fax:* 780-455-5882
info@telusworldofscienceedmonton.com
www.telusworldofscienceedmonton.com
www.facebook.com/EdmontonScience
twitter.com/twosedm
Also Known As: Telus World of Science - Edmonton
Overview: A small local organization founded in 1978
Mission: To inspire & motivate people to learn about & contribute to science & technology advances that strengthen themselves, their family & community
Chief Officer(s):
George Smith, President & CEO
Finances: *Annual Operating Budget:* $3 Million-$5 Million; *Funding Sources:* Revenue; donations; grants
Staff Member(s): 82; 265 volunteer(s)
Membership: 5,000-14,999; *Fees:* Schedule available
Activities: Community courses; Mobile Astronomy program; Challenger Missions; Summer camps; IMAX films; full-dome shows; observatory; *Library* by appointment

Edmonton Stamp Club (ESC)

PO Box 399, Edmonton AB T5J 2J6
Tel: 780-437-1787
www.edmontonstampclub.com
Overview: A small local organization founded in 1912
Mission: To promote & encourage all aspects of philately for the benefit of all members
Member of: Royal Philatelic Society of Canada; American Philatelic Society
Chief Officer(s):
Rob Schutte, Secretary, Membership, 780-989-1260
Finances: *Annual Operating Budget:* Less than $50,000; *Funding Sources:* Membership dues; shows
Staff Member(s): 12; 10 volunteer(s)
Membership: 300; *Fees:* $25 individual; $35 family; *Member Profile:* Interest in stamp collecting
Activities: Meetings held twice a month; Junior Club; auctions; seminars; *Awareness Events:* National Show, 3rd weekend in March

Publications:
• ESC [Edmonton Stamp Club] Bulletin
Type: Newsletter; *Frequency:* Monthly
Profile: Online newsletter.

Edmonton Symphony Orchestra (ESO)
9720 - 102 Ave., Edmonton AB T5J 4B2
Tel: 780-428-1108; *Fax:* 780-425-0167
info@winspearcentre.com
www.edmontonsymphony.com
www.facebook.com/edmontonsymphony
twitter.com/edmsymphony
www.youtube.com/edmontonsymphony
Overview: A small local charitable organization founded in 1952 overseen by Orchestras Canada
Mission: To foster appreciation & enjoyment of live, professional orchestral music through presenting concert performances, educational & community programs
Member of: Edmonton Arts Council
Affliation(s): International Alliance of Theatrical Stage Employees, Moving Picture Technicians, Artists & Allied Crafts of the US & Canada
Chief Officer(s):
Rob McAlear, Artistic Administrator
rob.mcalear@winspearcentre.com
Annemarie Petrov, Executive Director
annemarie.petrov@winspearcentre.com
Finances: *Funding Sources:* Government; private sector; earned revenues
Staff Member(s): 43
Activities: Enbridge Symphony Under the Sky; Deloitte & Touche Beat Beethoven Road Race; *Library*

Edmonton Telephone Historical Information Centre Foundation *See* Telephone Historical Centre

Edmonton Trout Fishing Club
Edmonton AB
e-mail: info@edmontontrout.ca
www.edmontontrout.ca
www.facebook.com/EdmontonTroutFishingClub
Overview: A small local charitable organization founded in 1953
Mission: To foster, instruct & promote the art of fly tying, fly casting, & the betterment of trout fishing among its members
Member of: Alberta Fish & Game Association
Chief Officer(s):
Ron Sohnle, Membership Coordinator
Finances: *Funding Sources:* Membership fees; auction
Membership: *Fees:* $35
Activities: Shares stream enhancement projects with Trout Unlimited

Edmonton Tumblewood Lapidary Club (ETLC)
11B St. Anne St., St Albert AB T8N 1E8
e-mail: edmontonlapidary@gmail.com
www.edmontonlapidary.ca
www.facebook.com/EdmontonTumblewoodLapidaryClub
Overview: A small local charitable organization
Mission: To promote the lapidary hobby in Edmonton & surrounding areas.
Member of: Alberta Federation of Rock Clubs
Affliation(s): Gem & Mineral Federation of Canada
Membership: *Fees:* $25 single; $35 family
Activities: Collecting, cutting, polishing & displaying rocks, gems & minerals; *Speaker Service:* Yes

Edmonton Twin & Triplet Club (ETTC)
PO Box 809, Edmonton AB T5J 2L8
Tel: 780-455-5520
edmonton@multiplebirthscanada.org
www.ettc.ca
www.facebook.com/pages/Edmonton-Twin-and-Triplet-Club/103081349749564
twitter.com/EdmTwin_Triplet
Overview: A small local organization overseen by Multiple Births Canada
Mission: To provide moral support and guidance for parents, to promote an interest in, and supply information about multiple births.
Activities: *Library*
Awards:
• The Edmonton Twin and Triplet Club Scholarship (Scholarship)
Eligibility: Edmonton or area resident; full-time postsecondary student*Deadline:* December 31 *Amount:* $1,000 (8) or $500 (16)
Publications:
• The Twindow
Type: Newsletter; *Frequency:* 9 pa

Edmonton Weavers' Guild (EWG)
PO Box 37009, Stn. Lynwood Post Office, 10139 - 87 Ave., Edmonton AB T5R 5Y2
Tel: 780-425-9280
info@edmontonweavers.org
edmontonweavers.org
Overview: A small local organization founded in 1953
Mission: To provide an opportunity for local weavers, spinners & dyers to meet, exchange ideas & learn; To foster inspiration & growth; To enhance public awareness of fibre arts through regular study groups, public classes, sales & demonstrations
Affliation(s): Handweavers, Spinners & Dyers of Alberta; Guild of Canadian Weavers; Handweavers Guild of America
Finances: *Annual Operating Budget:* Less than $50,000; *Funding Sources:* Annual sale; provincial & city grants
Membership: 130; *Fees:* $50; *Member Profile:* Anyone with knowledge of or interest in spinning, weaving, dyeing
Activities: Classes; workshops; demonstrations; displays; *Awareness Events:* Annual Sale, 1st Sat. in Nov.; *Library:* Guild Library
Publications:
• Webs & Wheels [a publication of the Edmonton Weavers' Guild]
Type: Newsletter; *Frequency:* 5 pa.

Edmonton Youth Orchestra Association (EYO)
PO Box 66041, Stn. Heritage, Edmonton AB T6J 6T4
Tel: 780-436-7932; *Fax:* 780-436-7932
eyo@shaw.ca
www.eyso.com
Overview: A small local charitable organization founded in 1952 overseen by Orchestras Canada
Mission: To provide young musicians with the opportunity to develop their orchestral skills & increase their knowledge & appreciation of music, while enriching the cultural life of the community through concerts & benefit performances
Chief Officer(s):
Michael Massey, Music Director
Finances: *Funding Sources:* Government grants; corporate sponsorship; individual donors; foundations

Edmonton Zone Medical Staff Association (EZMSA)
Edmonton AB
Tel: 780-735-2924; *Fax:* 780-735-9091
Overview: A small local organization
Mission: Represents physicians working in the Capital Region of Alberta (Edmonton) in a number of forums including the Regional Medical Advisory Committee, Physician's Liason Committee & the Minister of Health for Alberta
Chief Officer(s):
Robert Broad, President, 780-735-2924
Laurie Wear, Administrator
laurie.wear@covenanthealth.ca
Finances: *Funding Sources:* Membership dues
Membership: *Member Profile:* Physicians; Oral Surgeons; Clinical doctoral laboratory scientists
Activities: Continuing education; Edmonton Zone Medical Staff Association Golf Tournament; Edmonton Doctor's Curling League; Annual banquet

Edmonton's Food Bank
PO Box 62061, 11508 - 120 St. NW, Edmonton AB T5M 4B5
Tel: 780-425-2133; *Fax:* 780-426-1590
www.edmontonsfoodbank.com
www.facebook.com/pages/Edmontons-Food-Bank/154812271277151
twitter.com/yegfoodbank
Overview: A medium-sized local charitable organization overseen by Alberta Food Bank Network Association
Mission: Collects surplus and donated food for the effective distribution, free of charge, to people in need in the community while seeking solutions to the causes of hunger.
Member of: Food Banks Canada
Chief Officer(s):
Marjorie Bencz, Executive Director

Edson & District Chamber of Commerce
221-55 St, Edson AB T7E 1L5
Tel: 780-723-4918; *Fax:* 780-723-5545
manger@edsonchamber.com
www.edsonchamber.com
Overview: A small local organization founded in 1912
Mission: To be the voice of the business community, dedicated to the enhancement of trade & commerce in Edson.
Member of: Alberta Chamber of Commerce; Canadian Chamber of Commerce; Yellowhead Highway Association
Chief Officer(s):
Heather Kelly, Executive Director
Finances: *Annual Operating Budget:* $50,000-$100,000; *Funding Sources:* Membership fees; special events; annual campaign; government employment grants
Staff Member(s): 2; 30 volunteer(s)
Membership: 240; *Fees:* $52.50-$420; *Member Profile:* Financial; industry; retail; manufacturing; educational; service; hospitality; fitness, etc.; *Committees:* Finance; Bylaws/Policy; Government Relations; Member Relations/Nominations; Retail; Small Business Week; Golf Tournament; Secretaries Day; Trade Show; Sidewalk Jamboree; Women's Fair; Christmas Party/Parade
Activities: *Library* Open to public
Awards:
• Small Business of the Year Award (Award)
• Volunteer of the Year Award (Award)
• Employee of the Year Award (Award)
• Best Service Award (Award)
• Corporate Citizen Award (Award)
• Parade Awards (Award)
• Trade Show Awards (Award)

Edson Association for the Developmentally Handicapped
See Supporting Choices of People Edson

Edson Friendship Centre
#13, 5023 - 3rd Ave., Edson AB T7E 1X7
Tel: 780-723-5494; *Fax:* 780-723-4359
efc99@telus.net
edsonfriendshipcentre.com
Overview: A small local charitable organization founded in 1986 overseen by Alberta Native Friendship Centres Association
Member of: National Association of Friendship Centre; Alberta Native Friendship Centres Association
Chief Officer(s):
Valerie Findlay, Executive Director
Finances: *Annual Operating Budget:* $250,000-$500,000
Staff Member(s): 15; 30 volunteer(s)
Membership: 110; *Fees:* $3
Activities: *Library:* Resource Library; Open to public

Éduc'alcool
#1000, 606, rue Cathcart, Montréal QC H3B 1K9
Tél: 514-875-7454; *Téléc:* 514-875-5990
Ligne sans frais: 888-252-6651
info@educalcool.qc.ca
www.educalcool.qc.ca
www.facebook.com/279669212081870
Aperçu: *Dimension:* moyenne; *Envergure:* provinciale; Organisme sans but lucratif; fondée en 1989
Mission: Promouvoir la consommation équilibrée et responsable de l'alcool par des activités d'éducation, de sensibilisation et de communication; coordonner les actions de différents organismes nationaux oeuvrant dans le même but
Affliation(s): Conseil international sur les problemes de l'alcoolisme et des toxicomanies
Membre(s) du bureau directeur:
Hubert Sacy, Directeur général
Finances: *Budget de fonctionnement annuel:* $1.5 Million-$3 Million
Membre(s) du personnel: 2
Membre: 125; *Critères d'admissibilite:* Associations professionnelles, organismes parapublics, individus interessés aux objectifs de l'organisme
Activités: Campagnes d'éducation, de prévention et d'information sur l'alcool
Prix, Bouses:
• Bourse Marie-Soleil Tougas (Prix)

Educating for Peace
ON
www.global-ed.org/e4p/
Also Known As: E4P
Overview: A small national organization founded in 1985
Mission: To promote & strengthen peace education in the public & secondary school system in Ottawa-Carleton & Canada
Member of: Global Education Network
Chief Officer(s):
Blodwen Piercy, Contact, 613-749-8929
jepiercy@cyberus.ca
Penny Sanger, Contact, 613-233-7133
pennysanger@sympatico.ca
Finances: *Annual Operating Budget:* Less than $50,000
3 volunteer(s)
Membership: 1-99; *Member Profile:* Teachers; parents
Activities: *Library:* Peace Education Resources; by appointment

Education Assistants Association of the Waterloo Region District School Board (EAA)
465 Philip St., Waterloo ON N2L 6C7
Tel: 519-745-4221
Overview: A small local organization
Chief Officer(s):
Kiki Bamberger, President

Éducation physique et santé Canada *See* Physical & Health Education Canada

Education Safety Association of Ontario; Municipal Health & Safety Assn; Ontario Safety Assn. for Community & Healthcare *See* Public Services Health & Safety Association

Education Support Staff of the Ontario Secondary School Teachers' Federation - District 24 - Waterloo (ESS/OSSTF)
225 Centennial Ct., Kitchener ON N2B 3X2
Tel: 519-571-0331; *Fax:* 519-571-9288
www.d24.osstf.ca
Previous Name: Educational Support Staff Association
Overview: A small provincial organization
Mission: To represent education workers in the Waterloo region
Chief Officer(s):
Sherry Freund, President
sfreund@bellnet.ca
Membership: 2,700+; *Member Profile:* Office, clerical & technical support staff for Waterloo Region District School Board; *Committees:* Political Action; Education Services; Status of Women; Human Rights
Activities: *Speaker Service:* Yes

Education Wife Assault *See* Springtide Resources

Educational Computing Organization of Ontario (ECOO) / Organisation ontarienne pour la cybernétique en éducation
ON
e-mail: communications@ecoo.org
www.ecoo.org
twitter.com/ecooWeb
Overview: A small provincial organization founded in 1979
Mission: To disseminate information to computer using teachers across the curriculum, from kindergarten to post-secondary education
Chief Officer(s):
Mark Carbone, President
ecoopresident@ecoo.org
Membership: 1,000-4,999; *Fees:* Schedule available

Educational Support Staff Association *See* Education Support Staff of the Ontario Secondary School Teachers' Federation - District 24 - Waterloo

Educators for Distributed Learning PSA (British Columbia) (EDLPSA)
c/o BC Teachers' Federation, #100, 550 West 6 Ave., Vancouver BC V5Z 4P2
Tel: 604-592-4263
bcedlpsa@gmail.com
bcedl.ca
Previous Name: British Columbia Educators for Distributed Learning Provincial Specialist Association
Overview: A small provincial organization
Mission: To promote distributed learning, as well as hospital-homebound instruction, to the public
Member of: BC Teachers' Federation
Chief Officer(s):
David Comrie, President
dcomrie@sd73.bc.ca

EduNova
#200, 1533 Barrington St., Halifax NS B3J 1Z4
Tel: 902-424-8274; *Fax:* 902-424-8134
info@edunova.ca
www.edunova.ca
www.facebook.com/pages/EduNova/212866282085259
twitter.com/edunova_news
www.youtube.com/edun0va
Overview: A small provincial organization
Mission: To work with members in order to raise the profile of education & training expertise in Nova Scotia. EduNova is the only provincial education & training cooperative in Canada
Chief Officer(s):
Wendy Luther, President & CEO, 902-424-4058
wendy@edunova.ca

Membership: 30+; *Member Profile:* Universities; community college campuses; English-language school boards; private language schools; independent schools; consultants & training partners

effect:hope
#200, 90 Allstate Pkwy., Markham ON L3R 6H3
Tel: 905-886-2885; *Fax:* 905-886-2885
Toll-Free: 888-537-7679
info@effecthope.org
info@effecthope.org
www.linkedin.com/company/3068053
www.facebook.com/effecthope
twitter.com/effecthope
www.youtube.com/user/effecthope
Also Known As: Leprosy Mission Canada
Previous Name: The Mission to Lepers
Overview: A medium-sized national organization founded in 1892
Mission: To provide care & support to leprosy patients in many parts of the world including India, Bangladesh, and Nigeria.
Member of: Canadian Council of Christian Charities
Affliation(s): The Leprosy Mission International
Chief Officer(s):
Peter Derrick, Executive Director
Finances: *Annual Operating Budget:* Greater than $5 Million; *Funding Sources:* Federal & provincial funding agencies; individual contributions
Membership: *Committees:* Audit
Activities: *Speaker Service:* Yes; *Library* Open to public by appointment

Efile Agents & Tax Preparers Association of Canada *See* EFILE Association of Canada

EFILE Association of Canada (EAC) / Association de TED du Canada (ATC)
PO Box 20040, Kelowna BC V1Y 9H2
Fax: 866-511-6879
Toll-Free: 866-384-4066
swatson@efile.ca
www.efile.ca
Previous Name: Efile Agents & Tax Preparers Association of Canada
Overview: A medium-sized national organization founded in 1993
Mission: To facilitate the operation of tax practices; To communicate the concerns of members to the Canada Revenue Agency, federal & provincial ministries of revenue, & tax software providers; To request remediation; To promote the electronic filing of personal & corporate tax returns
Chief Officer(s):
Steve Watson, Executive Director
swatson@efile.ca
Membership: *Fees:* $140 plus GST / HST; *Member Profile:* Tax practitioners, throughout Canada, from sole proprietors to large national firms
Activities: Meeting with senior managers of Canada Revenue Agency to discuss tax policies & administrative issues that affect tax practitioners; Lobbying for changes to facilitate the operation of tax practitioners; Encouraging member proficiency; Offering resources to members
Publications:
• CRA (Canada Revenue Agency) Tax Centre Directory
Type: Directory
• EAC / ATC Annual Submission to the CRA
Frequency: Annually; *Price:* Free to EFILE Association of Canada members
Profile: Results of a survey of EFILE Association of Canada members to learn the issues that hinder their work
• Impact
Type: Newsletter; *Frequency:* 3 pa; *Price:* Free to EFILE Association of Canada members
Profile: Association information updates plus issues in the tax & EFILE service industry

Egale Canada
185 Carlton St., Toronto ON M5A 2K7
Tel: 416-964-7887; *Fax:* 416-963-5665
Toll-Free: 888-204-7777
egale.canada@egale.ca
www.egale.ca
www.facebook.com/EgaleCanada
twitter.com/egalecanada
Overview: A medium-sized national organization founded in 1986
Mission: To advance equality & justice for lesbian, gay, bisexual & transgendered persons, & their families in Canada
Chief Officer(s):
Hilary Cook, Director
Finances: *Funding Sources:* Donations
Membership: *Committees:* Executive; Legal Issues; Political Action; Fundraising; Equal Marriage; Intersections; Trans Caucus; Two-Spirited & People-of-Colour Caucus; International Affairs; Adopt-an-MP; Planned Giving; Finance; Bylaws & Policies; Nominations; Elections
Activities: Implementing the Safe Schools Campaign; Intervening before the Supreme Court of Canada; Appearing before federal Parliamentary Committees; Providing public education; Hosting an annual general meeting; Conducting surveys

Egg Farmers of Canada (EFC) / Producteurs d'oufs du Canada
21 Florence St., Ottawa ON K2P 0W6
Tel: 613-238-2514; *Fax:* 613-238-1967
Other Communication: Market Information e-mail: econo@eggs.ca
info@eggs.ca
www.eggs.ca
www.facebook.com/eggs
www.youtube.com/getcracking
Previous Name: Canadian Egg Marketing Agency
Overview: A large national organization founded in 1972 overseen by Canadian Federation of Agriculture
Mission: To forcast demand for eggs; to promote eggs nationally; to develop national standards for egg farming
Member of: Canadian Federation of Agriculture
Affliation(s): World Trade Organization (WTO)
Chief Officer(s):
Peter Clarke, Chair
Tim Lambert, CEO
Membership: 1,000 farm families
Publications:
• Dedicated to Quality [a publication of the Egg Farmers of Canada]

Église adventiste du septième jour au Canada *See* Seventh-day Adventist Church in Canada

L'Église anglicane du Canada *See* The Anglican Church of Canada

Église apostolique de Pentecôte du Canada inc. *See* Apostolic Church of Pentecost of Canada Inc.

Église catholique-chrétien Canada *See* Christian Catholic Church Canada

Église chrétienne (Disciples du Christ) au Canada *See* Christian Church (Disciples of Christ) in Canada

Église Luthérienne du Canada *See* Lutheran Church - Canada

Église méthodiste libre du Canada *See* Free Methodist Church in Canada

Église presbytérienne au Canada *See* Presbyterian Church in Canada

Église Réformée St-Jean
3407A, av du Musee, Montréal QC H4E 4L7
Tél: 514-767-3165
jzoellner@erq.qc.ca
www.stjean.erq.qc.ca
Aperçu: *Dimension:* moyenne; *Envergure:* provinciale
Mission: The majority of our members are French-speaking Québecers practising various occupations in society, blue and white collared workers. People coming from a wide range of cultural, regional and national backgrounds also contribute to a rich diversity. People of all ages can be found amongst us: young children, adolescents, students, the middle-aged and the retired. The dynamic nature of our church can be seen in the presence of many young families. We recognise that the Lord Jesus Christ, head of the Church, has assembled us, with our children in a community which holds one vision, one love, one faith and one hope: to live for His Glory and to serve Him where He has placed us.
Affiliation(s): Christian Reformed Church; Presbyterian Church of North America
Membre(s) du bureau directeur:
Jean Zoellner, Pastor

L'Église Unie du Canada *See* United Church of Canada

Église Unie du Canada ***See*** United Church of Canada Foundation

Églises de frères chrétiens du Québec ***See*** Christian Brethren Churches of Québec

EIC General Members Society ***See*** Canadian Society for Engineering Management

The EJLB Foundation
#1050, 1350, rue Sherbrooke ouest, Montréal QC H3G 1J1
Tel: 514-843-5112; *Fax:* 514-843-4080
general@ejlb.qc.ca
www.ejlb.qc.ca
Overview: A small local organization founded in 1983
Mission: Provides grants to organizations with areas of interest in mental health and the environment
Chief Officer(s):
Kevin Leonard, Executive Director
Awards:
• The EJLB Foundation Grant (Grant)

Eldee Foundation
#1720, 1080, Côte du Beaver Hill, Montréal QC H2Z 1S8
Tel: 514-397-0816; *Fax:* 514-397-0816
www.eldeefoundation.ca
Overview: A small local charitable organization founded in 1961
Mission: To provides grants mostly for education & medical research to organizations primarily for the benefit of persons of the Jewish faith
Chief Officer(s):
Harry J.F. Bloomfield, Vice-President
David A. Johnson, Sec.-Treas.
Neri J. Bloomfield, President
Membership: *Fees:* $10; *Member Profile:* Yukoners 55 years of age and over

Elder Active Recreation Association (ERA)
Sport Yukon Bldg., 4061, 4th Ave., Whitehorse YT Y1A 1H1
Tel: 867-633-5010
elderactive@sportyukon.com
www.yukon-seniors-and-elders.org/era.home.htm
Overview: A medium-sized provincial organization
Mission: To enhance the quality of life of Yukon seniors & elders by supporting them in living healthy lives with independence & dignity; to support seniors & elders in helping other seniors & elders to live full, active & healthy lives, & to develop active communities throughout the Yukon where seniors & elders can make positive lifestyle choices, exchange wisdom & connect with others in friendship, recreation & creativity
Chief Officer(s):
Tom Parlee, President
hillparlee@northwestel.net
Hank Leenders, Vice-President
hleenders@northwestel.net

Elder Mediation Canada (EMC)
e-mail: admin@eldermediation.ca
www.eldermediation.ca
Overview: A medium-sized national organization
Mission: To advance the practice of elder mediation in Canada; to improve the qualifications & effectiveness of mediators
Affliation(s): Elder Mediation International Network; Family Mediation Canada

Elderhostel Canada ***See*** Routes to Learning Canada

Electric Mobility Canada (EMC) / Mobilité Électrique Canada
#309, 9-6975 Meadowvale Town Centre Circle, Mississauga ON L5N 2V7
Tel: 905-301-5950; *Fax:* 905-826-0157
www.emc-mec.ca
www.linkedin.com/pub/al-cormier/15/985/559
www.facebook.com/240477292643669?ref=ts
twitter.com/EMC_MEC
www.youtube.com/user/ElectricMobilityCA
Overview: A small national organization
Mission: Electric Mobility Canada is a national membership-based not-for-profit organization dedicated exclusively to the promotion of electric mobility as a readily available and important solution to Canada's emerging energy and environmental issues.
Chief Officer(s):
Chris Hill, President & CEO
chris.hill@emc-mec.ca
Membership: 125; *Committees:* Government Relations; Working Group on PEV Readiness; Electric Bus
Meetings/Conferences: • 7th Annual Electric Vehicles Conference & Trade Show 2015, May, 2015, Westin Nova Scotian, Halifax, NS
Scope: National
Contact Information: Twitter: twitter.com/EVVEconf; Website: www.emc-mec.ca/evve2015

Electric Vehicle Council of Ottawa (EVCO)
PO Box 4044, Stn. E, Ottawa ON K1S 5B1
e-mail: info@evco.ca
www.evco.ca
www.youtube.com/EVCOdotCA
Overview: A small local organization founded in 1980
Mission: To promote the use of electric vehicles as a viable transportation alternative
Chief Officer(s):
Darryl McMahon, President
president@evco.ca
Barry Hoover, Vice-President
bhoover@evco.ca
David French, Treasurer
dfrench@evco.ca
Activities: Offering technical literature; Organizing displays, demonstrations, talks, & competitions; Hosting monthly meetings; Participating in advocacy projects; *Library:* Electric Vehicle Council of Ottawa Print & Video Library
Publications:
• EV Circuit
Type: Newsletter
Profile: Information for members of the Electric Vehicle Council of Ottawa

Electric Vehicle Society of Canada (EVS)
c/o #40, 55 Kelfield St., Toronto ON M9W 5A3
Tel: 416-788-7438
info@evsociety.ca
www.evsociety.ca
www.linkedin.com/company/electric-vehicle-society-of-canada
www.facebook.com/EVSociety
Overview: A medium-sized national organization founded in 1991
Mission: To investigate & promote clean transportation technologies
Chief Officer(s):
Emile Stevens, President
president@evsociety.ca
Membership: *Fees:* $20 students, spouses, & seniors; $30 adults; $50 families; $100 corporations; *Member Profile:* Engineers; Environmentalists; Enthusiasts for electric energy for propulsion
Activities: Providing a forum for member discussions; Examining modes of electric transportation
Publications:
• Electric Vehicle Conversion Manual: A Workshop Guide for High Schools
Type: Manual; *Number of Pages:* 85; *Author:* Neil Gover et al.
Profile: Contents include the move to sustainable transportation, getting started, basics of electrical energy & electricity, starting theconversion, & EV performance & evaluation
• EVSurge [a publication of the Electric Vehicle Society of Canada]
Type: Newsletter; *Frequency:* Bimonthly; *Editor:* Robert Weekley; *Price:* Free with Electric VehicleSociety of Canada membership
Profile: Electric Vehicle Society of Canada events, membership information, & articles about activities in the EV world

Electrical & Mechanical Engineering Association (EMEA) / Association du génie électronique et mécanique
PO Box 1000, Stn. Main, Borden ON L0M 1C0
Tel: 705-423-2598
EMEBranchGEM@forces.gc.ca
Www.emebranchgem.ca
www.facebook.com/eme.branchgem
twitter.com/emebranchgem
Overview: A small national organization founded in 1945
Mission: To uphold the EME Branch of the Canadian Forces; to represent the interests of the Branch to defense associations & the federal government
Member of: Conference of Defence Associations
Membership: *Member Profile:* Retired or active members of the EME Branch of the Canadian Armed Forces
Activities: Annual general meeting; seminars; regular meetings with guest speakers;

Electrical Construction Association of Hamilton (ECA Hamilton)
#102, 370 York Blvd., Hamilton ON L8R 3L1
Tel: 905-522-1070; *Fax:* 905-522-2199
ecah@on.aibn.com
www.ecahamilton.ca
Overview: A small local organization founded in 1946
Affliation(s): Electrical Contractors Association of Ontario; International Brotherhood of Electrical Workers, Local 105
Chief Officer(s):
Mark Lloyd, President
Finances: *Funding Sources:* Membership fees
Membership: 56; *Member Profile:* Electrical contractors
Activities: Apprenticeship training; negotiating collective agreements

Electrical Contractors Association of Alberta (ECAA)
17725 - 103 Ave., Edmonton AB T5S 1N8
Tel: 780-451-2412; *Fax:* 780-455-9815
Toll-Free: 800-252-9375
ecaa@ecaa.ab.ca
www.ecaa.ab.ca
www.facebook.com/179555132080555
Also Known As: ECA Alberta
Overview: A medium-sized provincial organization overseen by Canadian Electrical Contractors Association
Mission: To work towards increased contractors knowledge & efficiency; improved communication between industry sections; government liaison for training qualifications & regulations; overall improvement of the electrical industry
Chief Officer(s):
Sheri McLean, Executive Director
smclean@ecaa.ab.ca
Membership: 500; *Fees:* Schedule available; *Member Profile:* Electrical contractors; *Committees:* Apprenticeship; Associate Liaison; Convention; ECAA Industry Appointment; Finance; Fire Technical Council; Labour Relations; Labour Relations Non-Union; Labour Relations Union; Membership; Nominations; PEC Discipline; PEC Education; PEC Marketing; PEC Practice Review; PEC Registration; Ways & Means

Electrical Contractors Association of BC (ECA-BC)
#201, 3989 Henning Dr., Burnaby BC V5C 6N5
Tel: 604-294-4123; *Fax:* 604-294-4120
www.eca.bc.ca
www.youtube.com/ecabctv
Overview: A medium-sized provincial organization founded in 1952 overseen by Canadian Electrical Contractors Association
Mission: To promote use of electricity; to strengthen, encourage & promote electrical contracting industry; to promote functions assisting businessmen to become more efficient & profitable.
Affliation(s): National Electrical Contractors Association
Chief Officer(s):
Deborah Cahill, President
Finances: *Funding Sources:* Membership dues
Staff Member(s): 3
Membership: 225; *Fees:* Schedule available; *Member Profile:* Electrical contractors engaged in electrical work; *Committees:* Communications; Education & Training; Electrical Heritage Society of BC; Electrical Joint Training; Governance; Lobby Task Force; Negotiating; New Membership; Subcontract Program
Activities: *Internships:* Yes; *Speaker Service:* Yes; *Rents Mailing List:* Yes

Electrical Contractors Association of London (ECAL)
4140 Gore Rd., RR#1, Dorchester ON N0L 1G4
Tel: 519-268-1060; *Fax:* 519-268-1061
Overview: A small local organization founded in 1961
Member of: Electrical Contractors of Ontario
Chief Officer(s):
Wayne Crockett, Manager
w.crockett@bell.net

Electrical Contractors Association of New Brunswick Inc. (ECANB)
PO Box 322, Fredericton NB E3B 4Y9
Tel: 506-452-7627; *Fax:* 506-452-1786
dwe@eca.nb.ca
www.eca.nb.ca
Overview: A small provincial organization founded in 1964 overseen by Canadian Electrical Contractors Association
Affliation(s): Construction Association of New Brunswick Inc.; Canadian Construction Association
Chief Officer(s):
David Ellis, Executive Director
Finances: *Annual Operating Budget:* $50,000-$100,000

Staff Member(s): 2
Membership: 21 corporate; *Fees:* Schedule available

Electrical Contractors Association of Ontario (ECAO)
#460, 170 Attwell Dr., Toronto ON M9W 5Z5
Tel: 416-675-3226; *Fax:* 416-675-7736
Toll-Free: 800-387-3226
ecao@ecao.org
www.ecao.org
Also Known As: ECA Ontario
Overview: A medium-sized provincial organization founded in 1948 overseen by Canadian Electrical Contractors Association
Mission: To serve & represent the interests of the electrical contracting industry
Member of: Canadian Electrical Contractors Association; Ontario Joint Standard Practices Committee; Construction Bid Depository of Ontario
Affiliation(s): 13 Area Electrical Contractors Associations (ECAs); Council of Ontario Construction Associations; Provincial Advisory Committee for the Construction & Maintenance Electrician; Electrical Contractor Registration Agency (ECRA) for Master Electrician & Electrical Contractor Licensing
Chief Officer(s):
Eryl Roberts, Executive Vice President, 416-675-3226 Ext. 311
eroberts@ecao.org
Bill McKee, Treasurer
Lucy Roberts, Contact, Public Relations & Member Services
lroberts@ecao.org
Membership: *Member Profile:* Bona fide electrical contractors with a contractual relationship with the International Brotherhood of Electrical Workers (IBEW); *Committees:* Board Of Directors; Contractor & Industry Standards; Electrical Trade Bargaining Agency; Human Resources; Member Services; Power & Utility Sector; Public Relations & Communications
Activities: Making representations on behalf of the industry to government; Developing standard practices

Electrical Contractors Association of Quinte-St. Lawrence
#2, 1575 John Counter Blvd., Kingston ON K7M 3L5
Tel: 613-541-0633; *Fax:* 613-541-0863
Overview: A small local organization
Affiliation(s): Electrical Contractors Association of Ontario
Chief Officer(s):
Jeff Green, Manager
greenj@bellnet.ca

Electrical Contractors Association of Saskatchewan
c/o Michael Fougere, 320 Gardiner Park Ct., Regina SK S4V 1R9
Tel: 306-525-0171
Overview: A medium-sized provincial organization overseen by Canadian Electrical Contractors Association
Mission: To voice the concerns of electrical contractors in Saskatchewan; To improvethe electrical industry
Affiliation(s): Canadian Electrical Contractors Association; National Electrical Contractors Association; Saskatoon Electrical Contractors Association; Saskatchewan Construction Association, Electrical Contractors Association of BC; Saskatchewan Construction Safety Association; Electrical Contractors Association of Alberta; Electrical Contractors Association of Ontario
Chief Officer(s):
Michael Fougere, Executive Director
Membership: *Committees:* Apprenticeship & Training; Membership; Code Revisions; Standard Contract Practices; Public Relations; Annual Meeting & Convention
Activities: Communicating with members; Increasing contractors' knowledge & efficiency; Promoting exchange of ideas between all electrical contracting industry sections; Liaising with government for qualifications, training, & regulations; Hosting annual general meetings

Electrical Contractors Association of Thunder Bay (ECATB)
910 Cobalt Cres., Thunder Bay ON P7B 5W3
Tel: 807-623-4174; *Fax:* 807-623-4572
ecatb@tbaytel.net
Overview: A small local organization
Member of: Electrical Contractors Association of Ontario
Chief Officer(s):
Karyn Sundell, Executive Vice-President

Electricity Distributors Association (EDA)
#1100, 3700 Steeles Ave. West, Vaughan ON L4L 8K8
Tel: 905-265-5300; *Fax:* 905-265-5301
Toll-Free: 800-668-9979
email@eda-on.ca
www.eda-on.ca
www.facebook.com/EDAMembersAssistSandy
twitter.com/EDA_ONT
Previous Name: Municipal Electric Association
Overview: A large provincial organization founded in 1986
Mission: To be the voice of Ontario's electricity distributors, the publicly & privately owned companies that deliver electricity to Ontario homes, businesses & public institutions. Focus is on advocacy & representation to government, analysis of legislation & market regulations, communication & networking among members & industry colleagues
Chief Officer(s):
Charlie Macaluso, President & CEO, 905-265-5363
John Loucks, Vice President, Association & Member Affairs, 905-265-5317
Teresa Sarkesian, Vice President, Policy & Government Affairs, 905-265-5313
Finances: *Annual Operating Budget:* Greater than $5 Million; *Funding Sources:* Membership dues
Staff Member(s): 18; 100 volunteer(s)
Membership: 256; *Fees:* $750 commercial member; *Member Profile:* Public & privately owned electricity distributors
Meetings/Conferences: • Electricity Distributors Association Executive Symposium 2015, 2015
Scope: Provincial

Electricity Human Resources Canada (EHRC)
#405, 2197 Riverside Dr., Ottawa ON K1H 7X3
Tel: 613-235-5540; *Fax:* 613-235-6922
info@electricityhr.ca
electricityhr.ca
www.facebook.com/278647015504485?sk=wall
twitter.com/electricityHR
Previous Name: Electricity Sector Council
Overview: A medium-sized national organization
Mission: Collective national partnership of business, labour & education working to develop a highly skilled workforce for the industry now & in the future
Chief Officer(s):
Michelle Branigan, Chief Executive Officer
Staff Member(s): 6
Membership: *Fees:* $1,000-$6,000

Electricity Sector Council *See* Electricity Human Resources Canada

Electro-Federation Canada Inc. (EFC)
#300, 180 Attwell Dr., Toronto ON M9W 6A9
Tel: 905-602-8877; *Fax:* 905-602-5686
Toll-Free: 866-602-8877
www.electrofed.com
www.linkedin.com/groups?gid=3236862&trk=hb_side_g
twitter.com/EFC_Tweets
Overview: A medium-sized national organization founded in 1995
Mission: To represent members provincially, federally, & internationally on issues affecting the electro-technical business
Chief Officer(s):
Jim Taggart, President/CEO, 647-260-3093
jtaggart@electrofed.com
Ken Frankum, Chair
Philip Lefrancq, Vice-President, Finance & Administration, 647-260-3086
plefrancq@electrofed.com
Wayne Edwards, Vice-President, Sustainability & Electrical Safety, 647-258-7483
wedwards@electrofed.com
Membership: 300 companies; *Member Profile:* Companies that manufacture, distribute, & service electrical, electronics, & telecommunications products; *Committees:* Canadian Appliance Manufacturers Association; Consumer Electronics Marketers of Canada; Electrical Equipment Manufacturers Association of Canada; Supply & Manufacturers' Reps Councils; Installation Maintenance & Repair Sector Council & Trade Association; Electro-Federation Canada Alumni Association
Activities: Collecting & disseminating market data; Providing networking opportunities; Hosting annual conferences; Researching; Offering educational programs; Communicating with members; Promoting the industry; Conducting surveys
Awards:
• Industry Recognition Award (IRA) (Award)
Presented annually to an individual who has influenced the Canadian electrical and/or electronics industries, either as a current or retired industry delegate, or as an industry supporter.
• Annual Marketing Awards Program (Award)
This awards program is designed to recognize organizations demonstrating marketing excellence and innovation within the Canadian electrical manufacturing, distribution and electronics industry. Eligibility: Current EFC member
Meetings/Conferences: • Electro-Federation Canada Annual Conference 2015, May, 2015
Scope: National
Contact Information: Nathalie Lajoie; Phone: 647-258-7484
• Electro-Federation Canada Annual Conference 2016, May, 2016
Scope: National
Contact Information: Nathalie Lajoie; Phone: 647-258-7484

Electronic Commerce Council of Canada *See* GS1 Canada

Electronic Frontier Canada Inc. (EFC) / Frontière électronique du Canada
20 Richmond Ave., Kitchener ON N2G 1Y9
Tel: 905-525-9140; *Fax:* 905-546-9995
www.efc.ca
Overview: A small national organization founded in 1994
Mission: To ensure that the principals embodied in the Canadian Charter of Rights & Freedoms are protected as new computing, communications & information technologies emerge.
Affiliation(s): Electronic Frontier Foundation, San Francisco
Chief Officer(s):
David Jones, President
djones@efc.ca
Jeffrey Shallit, Vice-President/Treasurer, 519-888-4804
shallit@efc.ca
Richard Rosenberg, Vice-President, 604-822-4142
rosen@efc.ca
Finances: *Funding Sources:* Membership fees & donations
Membership: *Fees:* $20 student; $40 regular
Activities: Research & education on issues such as the impact of information, computing & communication technologies on Canadian society; email discussion list; *Speaker Service:* Yes

Electronics Import Committee (EIC)
PO Box 189, Stn. Don Mills, Toronto ON M3C 2S2
Tel: 416-595-5333
info@iecanada.com
www.iecanada.com
Overview: A small national organization overseen by The Canadian Association of Importers & Exporters
Mission: To represent members' interests before government & regulatory bodies.
Chief Officer(s):
Joy Nott, President
Staff Member(s): 6
Membership: *Fees:* $1,175 regular corporate; $1,995 leadership circle corporate; *Member Profile:* Canadian Importers Association membership; *Committees:* Food
Activities: *Speaker Service:* Yes

Electronics Product Stewardship Canada (EPSC)
#403, 550 Bayview Ave., Toronto ON M4W 3X8
Tel: 647-351-7415
info@epsc.ca
www.epsc.ca
twitter.com/EPSC_Canada
Overview: A medium-sized national organization founded in 2003
Mission: To design, promote & implement sustainable solutions for electronics waste
Chief Officer(s):
Shelagh Kerr, President/CEO
shelagh@epsc.ca
Nathan B. MacDonald, Director, Environmental Programs
nathan@epsc.ca
Staff Member(s): 2
Membership: 16 leading electronics manufacturers

Elementary Teachers' Federation of Ontario (ETFO) / Fédération des enseignantes et des enseignants de l'élémentaire de l'Ontario (FEEO)
136 Isabella St., Toronto ON M4Y 1P6
Tel: 416-962-3836; *Fax:* 416-642-2424
Toll-Free: 888-838-3836
www.etfo.ca
www.facebook.com/ETFOprovincialoffice
twitter.com/etfonews
www.youtube.com/user/ETFOprovincial

Merged from: Federation of Women Teachers' Associations of Ontario; Ontario Public School Teachers' Federation
Overview: A large provincial organization founded in 1998
Mission: To regulate relations between employees & employer, including but not limited to securing & maintaining, through collective bargaining, the best possible terms & conditions of employment; To advance the cause of education & the status of teachers & educational workers; To promote a high standard of professional ethics & a high standard of professional competence; To foster a climate of social justice in Ontario & continue a leadership role in such areas as anti-poverty, non-violence & equity; To promote & protect the interests of all members of the Federation & the students in their care; To cooperate with other organizations in Ontario, Canada & elsewhere, having the same or like objects
Member of: Ontario Teachers' Federation; Ontario Federation of Labour; Canadian Labour Congress
Chief Officer(s):
Sam Hammond, President
shammond@etfo.org
Susan Swackhammer, First Vice-President
sswackhammer@etfo.org
Finances: *Annual Operating Budget:* Greater than $5 Million
Staff Member(s): 100
Membership: 73,000; *Fees:* Statutory members 1.6% earnings; Associate membership $100; Retired members as an associate $15; *Member Profile:* Teachers; occasional teachers; educational workers; *Committees:* Aboriginal Education; Annual Meeting; Anti-Racist Education; Arts; Awards; Collective Bargaining; Disability Issues; Early Years; Education Support Personnel; Environmental; French as a Second Language; Gender Issues; Human Rights; Intermediate Division; International Assistance; Lesbian, Gay, Bi-sexual & Transgender Members; Men's Focus; New Members; Occasional Teacher; Occupational Health & Safety; Pension; Political Action; Professional Development/Curriculum; Professional Relations; Special Education; Status of Women; Teacher Education/Faculty Liaison
Awards:
• Doctoral Scholarship (Scholarship)
• Honorary Life Membership (Award)
• Rainbow Visions Award (Award)
Honorary life membership award
• Bursaries for Sons & Daughters of ETFO Members Entering a Faculty of Education (Grant)
• Master's Scholarship - Women's Program (Scholarship)
• Outstanding Role Model for Women Award - Women's Program (Award)
• Women Working in Social Activism on behalf of Women & Children - Women's Program (Award)
• Women Who Develop Special Projects in Science & Technology - Women's Program (Award)
• Aboriginal Women in Education Bursaries - Women's Program (Grant)
• Doctoral Scholarship - Women's Program (Scholarship)
• Master's Scholarship (Scholarship)
• Women's Studies Scholarship (Scholarship)
• Children's Literature Award (Scholarship)
• Humanitarian Award for an ETFO Member (Award)
• Humanitarian Award for Non-ETFO Member (Award)
• Health & Safety Activist Award (Scholarship)
• Member Service & Engagement Award (Scholarship)
• New Member Award (Scholarship)
• Native as a Second Language Qualification Bursary (Scholarship)
• Writer's Award (Award)
• Writer's Award - Women's Program (Award)
• Anti-Bias Curriculum Development Award (Award)
• ETFO Bursaries (Designated Groups) (Grant)
• ETFO Bursaries - Women's Program (Designated Persons) (Grant)
• Arts & Culture Award (Award)
• Curriculum Development Award - Women's Program (Award)
• Curriculum Development Award (Award)
• Bev Saskoley Anti-Racism Scholarship (Scholarship)
• Bev Saskoley Anti-Racism Scholarship - Women's Program (Scholarship)
Meetings/Conferences: • Elementary Teachers' Federation of Ontario 2015 Women's Conference, 2015, ON
Scope: Provincial
Contact Information: Program Contact: Evelyn Doucett, Phone: 416-962-3836, ext. 2214, E-mail: edoucett@etfo.org
• Elementary Teachers' Federation of Ontario 2015 ICT Conference: Technology for Teachers, January, 2015, ETFO Provincial Office and OISE, Toronto, ON
Scope: Provincial
Description: A workshop designed to help members expand their presentation skills
Contact Information: Workshop Contacts: Ruth Dawson, Phone: 416-962-3836, ext. 2278, E-mail: rdawson@etfo.org; Jane Bennett, 416-962-3836, ext. 2277, E-mail: jbennett@etfo.org; Joanne Myers, Phone: 416-962-3836, ext. 2279, E-mail: jmyers@etfo.org
• Elementary Teachers' Federation of Ontario 2015 .. and still we rise, February, 2015, Fairmont Royal York Hotel, Toronto, ON
Scope: Provincial
Description: Annual leadership conference for women
Contact Information: Conference Contact: Kalpana Makan, E-mail: kmakan@etfo.org
• Elementary Teachers' Federation of Ontario 2015 Annual Meeting, 2015, ON
Scope: Provincial
Publications:
• @ETFO [Elementary Teachers' Federation of Ontario] eNewsletter
Type: Newsletter
• ETFO [Elementary Teachers' Federation of Ontario] Voice
Type: Magazine; *Accepts Advertising*; *Editor:* Izida Zorde
• ETFO [Elementary Teachers' Federation of Ontario] Stewards' Mailing
Type: Newsletter

Élèves ontariens contre l'ivresse au volant *See* Ontario Students Against Impaired Driving

Les éleveurs de dindon du Canada *See* Turkey Farmers of Canada

Les Éleveurs de dindons du Nouveau-Brunswick *See* Turkey Farmers of New Brunswick

Éleveurs de porcs du Québec
#120, 555, boul Roland-Therrien, Longueuil QC J4H 4E9
Tél: 450-679-0540; *Téléc:* 450-679-0102
leseleveursdeporcs@upa.qc.ca
www.leseleveursdeporcsduquebec.com
www.facebook.com/Porcduquebec
twitter.com/PorcQc
www.youtube.com/user/leporcduquebec
Nom précédent: Fédération des producteurs de porcs du Québec
Aperçu: *Dimension:* moyenne; *Envergure:* provinciale; fondée en 1966
Mission: A l'ordre du jour du Plan agroenvironnemental de la production porcine on trouve; l'application de plans de fertilisation sur toutes les fermes; la diminution des rejets de phosphore et d'azote pour éviter la surfertilisation; la réduction des odeurs; l'utilisation du lisier comme matière fertilisante; mise en place d'actions collectives.
Membre de: Canadian Pork Council
Affliation(s): Union des producteurs agricoles du Québec
Membre(s) du bureau directeur:
David Boissonneault, Président
Membre: 3,560; *Comités:* Naisseurs; Finisseurs

Les Éleveurs de poulets du Nouveau-Brunswick *See* Chicken Farmers of New Brunswick

Éleveurs de volailles du Québec
#250, 555, boul Roland-Therrien, Longueuil QC J4H 4G1
Tél: 450-679-0530; *Téléc:* 450-679-5375
evq@upa.qc.ca
volaillesduquebec.qc.ca
Nom précédent: Fédération des producteurs de volailles du Québec
Aperçu: *Dimension:* moyenne; *Envergure:* provinciale; Organisme sans but lucratif; fondée en 1970
Mission: A pour mission l'étude, la défense et le développement des intérêts économiques, sociaux et moraux de ses membres; favorise et stimule la mobilisation et la participation de ses membres tout en les consultant et en les informant; développe et renforce la mise en marché collective des poulets et des dindons produits au Québec, en mettant en place des services garantissant le fonctionnement optimal du plan conjoint et des autres outils de mise en marché
Membre de: Union des producteurs agricoles; Producteurs de poulet du Canada; Office canadien de commercialisation du dindon
Membre(s) du bureau directeur:
Jean-Paul Bouchard, Président
Finances: *Budget de fonctionnement annuel:* Plus de $5 Million
Membre(s) du personnel: 26
Membre: 800; *Critères d'admissibilite:* Producteurs de poulets ou de dindons

Elgin Association for Community Living *See* Community Living Elgin

Elgin Baptist Association
ON
elginbaptist.wordpress.com
Overview: A small local organization founded in 1874 overseen by Canadian Baptists of Ontario and Quebec
Mission: To bring together Baptist churches & to promote the interests of the members
Member of: Canadian Baptists of Ontario & Quebec; Canadian Baptist Ministries; Baptist World Alliance
Chief Officer(s):
Margaret Bell, Moderator
plainschurch@rogers.com
Membership: 8 churches; *Member Profile:* Baptist churches in Elgin County

Elgin-St.Thomas United Way Services *See* United Way Elgin-St. Thomas

Eli Bay Relaxation Response Institute
#201, 1352 Bathurst St., Toronto ON M5R 3H7
Tel: 416-932-2784; *Fax:* 416-932-2971
Toll-Free: 877-435-4229
Other Communication: Presentation & Workshop e-mail: info@kmprod.com
www.elibay.com
Also Known As: The Relaxation Response Ltd.
Overview: A small local organization founded in 1978
Mission: To empower individuals & organizations with mind-body skills proven to effectively release stress anywhere & anytime
Chief Officer(s):
Eli Bay, Founder
Finances: *Annual Operating Budget:* $250,000-$500,000
Staff Member(s): 3
Activities: Training, keynotes & A/V resources for stress control & change management; *Speaker Service:* Yes

Elie Chamber of Commerce
PO Box 175, Elie MB R0H 0H0
Tel: 204-353-2892; *Fax:* 204-353-2286
Overview: A small local organization
Chief Officer(s):
Bob Whitechurch, Chair, LUD of Elie, 204-353-2360

Elizabeth Fry Society of BC *See* Canadian Association of Elizabeth Fry Societies

Elizabeth Fry Society of Québec *Voir* Canadian Association of Elizabeth Fry Societies

Elizabeth Greenshields Foundation / Fondation Elizabeth Greenshields
#1, 1814, rue Sherbrooke ouest, Montréal QC H3H 1E4
Tel: 514-937-9225; *Fax:* 514-937-0141
egreen@total.net
www.elizabethgreenshieldsfoundation.org
Overview: A small international charitable organization founded in 1955
Mission: To assist artists in the early stages of their careers or in formative years (painting, drawing, printmaking, sculpture) who have demonstrated technical competence in representational or figurative art (abstract art cannot be accepted)
Chief Officer(s):
Micheline Leduc, Secretary
Staff Member(s): 2
Membership: 10
Awards:
• Artist Grant (Grant)
Amount: $10,000

Elizabeth House / Maison Elizabeth
2131 Marlowe, Montréal QC H4A 3L4
Tel: 514-482-2488; *Fax:* 514-482-9467
questions@maisonelizabethhouse.com
www.maisonelizabethhouse.com
Overview: A small provincial charitable organization founded in 1968
Mission: To provide a continuum of specialized services to pregnant adolescents & women, mothers & babies, fathers, & families experiencing significant difficulty in adjusting to pregnancy & to their new roles as parents & caregivers; To

support clients as they make choices & are directed to appropriate resources either in-house or in the community; To serve the anglophone community throughout the province of Quebec
Chief Officer(s):
Linda Schachtler, Executive Director
linda.schachtler.elizabeth@ssss.gouv.qc.ca
Activities: Rehabilitation Services; Pre-Natal and Mother-Baby Programs; Semi-Supervised and Transitional Apartment ProgramsSupported independent Living; Family Assistance Program; Education Programs; Child Stimulation Program; Summer Day Camp

Elk Point Chamber of Commerce
PO Box 639, Elk Point AB T0A 1A0
Tel: 780-724-3810; *Fax:* 780-724-4087
www.elkpoint.ca/chamber-commerce.html
Overview: A small local organization
Chief Officer(s):
Lesia Porcina, Vice-President
Vicki Brooker, Secretary
Membership: 41

Elk Valley Society for Community Living (EVSCL)
PO Box 1464, Fernie BC V0B 1M0
Tel: 250-423-7635
ymcp@telus.net
Previous Name: Elk Valley Society for the Handicapped
Overview: A small local charitable organization
Member of: Kootenay Regional Society for Community Living
Affliation(s): B.C. Association for Community Living
Membership: 17; *Member Profile:* People with special needs, their families & advocates; *Committees:* Housing; Education; Fundraising; Summer Program
Activities: Summer program for children with special needs; advocate for integration of special needs into schools, community activities

Elk Valley Society for the Handicapped *See* Elk Valley Society for Community Living

Elkford Chamber of Commerce
PO Box 220, 4A Front St., Elkford BC V0B 1H0
Tel: 250-865-4614; *Fax:* 250-865-2442
Toll-Free: 877-355-9453
info@elkfordchamberofcommerce.com
www.elkfordchamberofcommerce.com
Overview: A small local charitable organization founded in 1981
Member of: Canadian Chamber of Commerce; BC Chamber of Commerce; Tourism Rockies
Chief Officer(s):
Susan Robitaille, Manager
Ian Benson, President
Finances: *Annual Operating Budget:* $50,000-$100,000; *Funding Sources:* Membership dues; grants
Staff Member(s): 1; 15 volunteer(s)
Membership: 80; *Fees:* Schedule available; *Member Profile:* Interest in the promotion & development of the community of Elkford
Activities: Two annual festivals; Wilderness Classic Sled Dog Derby; Visitor Info Centre; Business Info Centre; Summer Job Bank; *Awareness Events:* Chamber Week; Small Business Week; Mining Week; *Library:* Business Library; Open to public

Elkhorn Chamber of Commerce
PO Box 418, Elkhorn MB R0M 0N0
www.elkhornchamberofcommerce.ca
Overview: A small local organization founded in 1899
Chief Officer(s):
Bob Nesbitt, Chamber Secretary
rnesbitt@mts.net
Tricia Forsythe, President
triden@mts.net
Membership: 39

Elliot Lake & District Chamber of Commerce
PO Box 81, #102, 1 Horne Walk, Elliot Lake ON P5A 2J6
Tel: 705-848-3974; *Fax:* 705-461-8039
elchamber@onlink.net
www.elliotlakechamber.com
Overview: A small local organization founded in 1958
Mission: To promote & improve trade & the economic, civic & social welfare of the Elliot Lake District
Member of: Ontario Chamber of Commerce; Algoma Kinniwabi Travel Association
Chief Officer(s):
Todd Stencill, President
Finances: *Annual Operating Budget:* Less than $50,000; *Funding Sources:* Membership fees
Staff Member(s): 1
Membership: 133; *Fees:* $75-$270; *Committees:* Municipal Liaison; Awards Banquet; Golf Tournament
Activities: Business development; Small Business Awards; Fall Extravaganza; Spring Trade Show

Elora Arts Council (EAC)
PO Box 3084, Elora ON N0B 1S0
Tel: 519-846-9638
eloraartscouncil@gmail.com
www.artscouncil.elora.on.ca
Overview: A small local organization founded in 1985
Mission: To support the arts in all displines, including visual art, music, writing, theatre & film, giving particular encouragement to emerging artists in the community.
Affliation(s): Puppets Elora; Elora Poetry Centre; Elora Community Theatre; Gallery Music Group; Elora Centre for the Arts; Guelph Arts Council; Wellington County; Township of Centre Wellington; Ontario Trillium Foundation
Chief Officer(s):
Barbara Lee, Chair
Melanie Morel, Treasurer
Finances: *Funding Sources:* Ontario Trillium Foundation
Membership: *Fees:* $15 individual; $25 family/group; *Committees:* Art In Public Places
Activities: Juried art shows; Elora Writers' Festival; concerts

Elora Centre for Environmental Excellence *See* Elora Environment Centre

Elora Environment Centre
PO Box 1100, 75 Melville St., 2nd Fl., Elora ON N0B 1S0
Tel: 519-846-8464; *Fax:* 519-846-8464
Toll-Free: 866-865-7337
info@eloraenvironmentcentre.ca
www.ecee.on.ca
Previous Name: Elora Centre for Environmental Excellence
Overview: A small local charitable organization founded in 1993
Mission: The Centre a not-for-profit organization focused on providing leadership in community-based environmental initiatives for both urban & rural communities. Areas of experience include: energy efficiency, greenhouse gas reduction, water efficiency, sustainable transportation, environmental education. It is a registered charity, BN: 138373196RR0001.
Member of: Green Communities Canada
Affliation(s): Ontario Environmental Network; Centre for Applied Renewable Energy; GreenPathways; several municipal governments & hydro-electric companies
Chief Officer(s):
Jennifer McLellan, Chair
Matt Vermeulen, Acting General Manager
manager@eloraenvironmentcentre.ca
Finances: *Annual Operating Budget:* $50,000-$100,000; *Funding Sources:* Fees from clients; Natural Resources Canada
Staff Member(s): 7
Activities: Home energy evaluations; NeighbourWoods tree steward program; *Speaker Service:* Yes

Elrose & District United Appeal *See* United Way of Elrose & District Corp.

Elsa Wild Animal Appeal of Canada
PO Box 45051, 2482 Yonge St., Toronto ON M4P 3E3
Tel: 416-489-8862
info@elsacanada.com
www.elsacanada.com
Also Known As: Elsa Canada
Overview: A small national charitable organization founded in 1972
Mission: To help save endangered wildlife species in Canada
Chief Officer(s):
Betty Henderson, President
Finances: *Funding Sources:* Donations; membership fees; fundraising

Embalmers' Association *See* Ontario Funeral Service Association

Embroiderers' Association of Canada, Inc. (EAC)
c/o Membership Director, 168 Kroeker Ave., Steinbach MB R5G 0L8
www.eac.ca
Overview: A medium-sized national charitable organization founded in 1973
Mission: To preserve traditional techniques & promote new challenges in embroidery through education & networking; to offer courses in embroidery & certifies teachers.
Member of: International Council of Needlework Associations
Chief Officer(s):
Beryl Burnett, President
president@eac.ca
Dianna Thorne, Treasurer
treasurer@eac.ca
Finances: *Funding Sources:* Membership dues; seminars fees
Membership: 1,500; *Fees:* Schedule available
Activities: Correspondence courses; exhibitions; competitions; awards; online store; *Speaker Service:* Yes; *Library:* Leonida Leatherdale Needle Arts Library; by appointment

Alberta - Calgary Guild of Needle & Fibre Arts
739 - 20 Ave. NW, Calgary AB T2M 1E1
www.cgnfa.ca
Chief Officer(s):
Anne Joy, President

Alberta - Edmonton Needlecraft Guild
PO Box 76027, Stn. Southgate, Edmonton AB T6H 5Y7
e-mail: contacts@edmneedlecraftguild.org
www.edmneedlecraftguild.org
www.facebook.com/pages/Edmonton-Needlecraft-Guild/107443652618019

Alberta - Lakeland Needle Art Guild
Cold Lake AB
Tel: 780-594-5608

British Columbia - Arrowsmith Needle Arts
c/o Qualicum Beach Civic Centre, 747 Jones St., Qualicum Beach BC V9K 1S4
e-mail: 1waddell@telus.net

British Columbia - Campbell River Needlearts Guild
Campbell River BC

British Columbia - Comox Valley Needlearts Guild
c/o Berwick House, 1700 Comox Ave., Comox BC V9M 4H4
e-mail: cvnaginfo@shaw.ca

British Columbia - Embroiderers' Guild of Victoria
Victoria BC
Tel: 250-386-7933
www.embroiderersguildvictoria.ca
www.facebook.com/pages/Embroiderers-Guild-of-Victoria/137878173039610

British Columbia - Island Stitchery Guild
Nanaimo BC
islandstitcheryguild.org

British Columbia - North Peace Needle Arts Guild
Fort St John BC

British Columbia - Okanagan Guild of Needlearts
PO Box 266, #101, 1865 Dilworth Dr., Kelowna BC V1V 9T1
www.ogna.org
Chief Officer(s):
Heather Fedick, President

British Columbia - Semiahmoo Guild of Needlearts
White Rock BC

British Columbia - Shuswap NeedleArts Guild
Tappen BC
Tel: 250-832-0972
shuswapneedlearts@gmail.com

British Columbia - Vancouver Guild of Embroiderers
Vancouver BC
e-mail: vge.information@gmail.com
www.vgeweb.ca

Manitoba - Winnipeg Embroiderers' Guild
c/o 371 Risbey Cres., Winnipeg MB R2Y 2C5
www.winnipegembroiderersguild.ca
Chief Officer(s):
Linda Lassman, President
wegpres@gmail.com

N.B. - Chickadee Chapter of Needle Arts
Dieppe NB

N.B. - Embroiderers' Guild of Fredericton
c/o Stepping Stone Senior Centre, 15 Saunders St., Fredericton NB E3B 1M9

N.B. - Kingston Peninsula Stitchers' Guild
Kingston NB
Tel: 506-763-2470
Chief Officer(s):
Anne Titus, Contact

N.B. - Pleasant Valley Stitchers
c/o Belleisle Community Centre, 1648 Rte. 124, Springsfield NB E5T 2J8
Tel: 506-839-2474

Chief Officer(s):
Mary McConchie, Contact
kmmcco@nb.aibn.com
NL - St. John's Guild of Embroiderers
St. John's NL
N.S. - Alderney Needlearts Guild
Dartmouth NS
N.S. - Marigold Guild of Needle Arts
c/o Cheryl Kienzle, 168 Teviot Pl., Valley NS B6L 4K8
marigoldguildofneedlearts.ca
Chief Officer(s):
Kim Fielding, President
N.S. - Stitchery Guild of Bedford
Bedford NS
N.S. - Town Clock Stitchers
Halifax NS
www.townclockstitchers.ca
Member of: Embroiderers' Association of Canada
Ontario - Cataraqui Guild of Needle Arts
#802, 829 Norwest Rd., Kingston ON K7P 2N3
e-mail: cgna@quiltskingston.org
quiltskingston.org/cgna
Chief Officer(s):
Diane Dukoff, President
Ontario - Embroiderers' Guild of Peterborough
Peterborough ON
Tel: 705-742-2201
Ontario - Norfolk's Own Needle Arts Guild
c/o Jane Hunter, 374 - 13 St., RR#4, Simcoe ON N3Y 4K3
Chief Officer(s):
Jane Hunter, Contact, 519-426-6238
Ontario - Ottawa Valley Guild of Stitchery
c/o 6 Epworth Dr., Ottawa ON K2G 2L5
e-mail: ovgs@hotmail.com
www.ovgs.ca
Ontario - Quinte Needlearts Guild
Belleville ON
Tel: 613-967-7917
Chief Officer(s):
Marg Whittleton, President, 613-476-7723
Ontario - Simcoe County Embroidery Guild
c/o Midhurst Community Centre, 24 Doran Rd., Midhurst ON L0L 1X0
Ontario - Toronto Guild of Stitchery
#1087, 7B Pleasant Blvd., Toronto ON M4T 1K2
e-mail: tgsinfo@tgsweb.ca
tgsweb.ca
www.facebook.com/374104039360534
Member of: Embroiderers' Association of Canada, Inc.
Ontario - Tulip Tree Needlearts
Chatham-Kent ON
P.E.I. - Island Treasures Needleart Guild
55 Hillside Dr., Summerside PE C1N 6C2
Tel: 902-436-1525
Chief Officer(s):
Judy Bowser, President
judybowser@hotmail.com
P.E.I. - Lady's Slipper Needle Arts Guild
PO Box 1259, Montague PE C0A 1R0
Tel: 902-838-2795
Chief Officer(s):
Carol Nicholson, Contact
jcnichol@pei.sympatico.ca
Québec - Lakeshore Creative Stitchery Guild/La Guilde des Travaux à l'Aiguille du Lakeshore
c/o Stewart Hall, 176, ch du Bord-du-Lac, Pointe-Claire QC H9S 4J7
e-mail: info@lcsg-gtal.ca
lcsg-gtal.ca
Chief Officer(s):
Rosemary Sookman, President
Saskatchewan - Bridge City Needlearts Guild
Saskatoon SK
e-mail: info@bcng.ca
bcng.ca
www.facebook.com/pages/Bridge-City-NeedleArts-Guild/158192510870267
Chief Officer(s):
Maggie Sim, President
president@bcng.ca
Saskatchewan - Pine Needle Arts Guild
Nipawin SK
Saskatchewan - Regina Stitchery Guild
PO Box 785, Regina SK S4P 3A8
e-mail: mail@reginastitcheryguild.ca
www.reginastitcheryguild.ca
www.facebook.com/pages/Regina-Stitchery-Guild/223276807685622
Yukon Guild of Needlearts
Whitehorse YT

Emil Skarin Fund

c/o The Senate, 150 Assiniboia Hall, University of Alberta, Edmonton AB T6G 2E8
Tel: 780-492-2268; *Fax:* 780-492-2448
senate.office@ualberta.ca
www.senate.ualberta.ca/en/EmilSkarinFund.aspx
Overview: A small provincial charitable organization founded in 1976
Mission: To support humanities & arts projects of value to public as well as to the University of Alberta (proposals originating outside Alberta will not be considered)
Chief Officer(s):
Sandra Kereliuk, Executive Officer
Finances: *Funding Sources:* Endowment

Emily Carr University of Art & Design Faculty Association (ECUADFA)

c/o Emily Carr University of Art + Design, 1399 Johnston St., Vancouver BC V6H 3R9
Tel: 604-844-3866; *Fax:* 604-844-3801
www.ecuadfa.org
www.facebook.com/pages/Emily-Carr-Faculty-Association/230132540366781
Overview: A small local organization
Mission: TO act as the bargaining agent for the faculty members of Emily Carr University of Art & Design (including sessional instructors, lecturers, adjunct faculty, regular faculty, & non-teaching faculty, such as counselors, librarians).
Member of: Federation of Post-Secondary Educators of British Columbia (FPSE)
Affliation(s): Canadian Association of University Teachers (CAUT)
Chief Officer(s):
Rita Wong, President

Emmanuel Community / Communauté de l'Emmanuel

QC
e-mail: info@emmanuelcommunity.com
www.emmanuelca.info
www.facebook.com/172877582427
Overview: A small local organization founded in 1992
Mission: To commit to a contemplative & apostolic life at the heart of the Catholic Church; To participate in the fulfillment of the mission of the Church in the modern world; To advance in the life of holiness
Chief Officer(s):
Laurent Albisetti, Canada, 418-977-1977
Activities: Helping one another materially, fraternally, & spiritually
Publications:
• He is Alive / Il est vivant
Type: Magazine; *Frequency:* Monthly

Emmanuel Relief & Rehabilitation International (Canada) (EIC)

PO Box 4050, 3967 Stouffville Rd., Stouffville ON L4A 8B6
Tel: 905-640-2111; *Fax:* 905-640-2186
Toll-Free: 866-269-6312
info@eicanada.org
www.eicanada.org
www.linkedin.com/company/emmanuel-international-canada
www.facebook.com/239293974881
Also Known As: Emmanuel International
Overview: A large national charitable organization founded in 1983
Mission: To encourage, strengthen, & assist churches worldwide to meet the spiritual & physical needs of the poor in accordance with the Holy Scriptures through programs of relief, rehabilitation, community development, evangelism, & church planting
Member of: Canadian Council of Christian Charities
Chief Officer(s):
Richard McGowan, Executive Director, Canada
Finances: *Annual Operating Budget:* $1.5 Million-$3 Million; *Funding Sources:* Government; donations
Staff Member(s): 14; 3 volunteer(s)
Membership: 1-99; *Member Profile:* Seven National Affiliates: Australia, Brazil, Canada, Malawi, The Philippines, The United Kingdom & The United States
Activities: Development, relief, rehabilitation & spiritual outreach programs; *Internships:* Yes
Publications:
• Emmanuel Relief & Rehabilitation International Annual Report
Type: Yearbook

Emmanus Canada

e-mail: emmauscanada@sympatico.ca
www3.sympatico.ca/pcmax
Overview: A small national organization
Mission: To deepend & nurture members' faith
Affliation(s): Archdiocese of Toronto
Chief Officer(s):
Claude Sam-Foh, Chair
Loretta Liu, Treasurer
Paul McAuley, Spiritual Director

Emo Chamber of Commerce

c/o Township of Emo, PO Box 520, 39 Roy St., Emo ON P0W 1E0
Tel: 807-482-2378; *Fax:* 807-482-2741
www.twspemo.on.ca/chamberofcommerce.html
Overview: A small local organization
Member of: Northwestern Ontario Associated Chambers of Commerce
Chief Officer(s):
Dave Goodman, Vice-President
Mary Goodman, Treasurer
Membership: 30
Activities: *Awareness Events:* Spring Fever Days; Holly Daze

Empire Club of Canada

Fairmont Royal York Hotel, 100 Front St. West, Level H, Toronto ON M5J 1E3
Tel: 416-364-2878; *Fax:* 416-364-7271
info@empireclub.org
www.empireclub.org
www.linkedin.com/groups/Empire-Club-Canada-2488065
www.facebook.com/169851787973
twitter.com/Empire_Club
www.flickr.com/photos/empire_club
Overview: A small national organization founded in 1903
Mission: To present prominent speakers from professions such as businesses, labour, education, government & cultural organizations.
Chief Officer(s):
Noble Chummar, President
Membership: *Fees:* $75 adult; $40 senior student; $200 corporate

EmployAbilities

10909 Jasper Ave., 4th Fl., Edmonton AB T5J 3L9
Tel: 780-423-4106
employ@employabilities.ab.ca
www.employabilities.ab.ca
www.facebook.com/EmployAbilities
twitter.com/employabilities
Overview: A medium-sized provincial charitable organization
Mission: To promote & enhance employment & learning opportunities for persons with disabilities
Chief Officer(s):
John Ough, President
Finances: *Funding Sources:* All levels of government; fundraising; donations

Employees Association of Milltronics - CNFIU Local 3005 / Association des employés de Milltronics (FCNSI)

PO Box 4225, Peterborough ON K9J 7B1
Tel: 705-745-2431; *Fax:* 705-741-0466
Overview: A small local organization founded in 1977
Chief Officer(s):
Baswick Al, President

Employees' Association Hammond Manufacturing Company Ltd.

c/o Hammond Manufacturing Co. Ltd., 394 Edinburgh Rd. North, Guelph ON N1H 1E5
Tel: 519-822-2962; *Fax:* 519-822-0715
Overview: A small local organization
Chief Officer(s):
Bill Robinson, President
Membership: 270; *Member Profile:* Employees of Hammond Manufacturing

Employees' Union of St. Mary's of the Lake Hospital - CNFIU Local 3001 / Association des employés, l'Hôpital Saint Mary's of the Lake (FCNSI)
340 Union St., Kingston ON K7L 5A2
Tel: 613-544-5220; *Fax:* 613-544-8527
Overview: A small local organization

Employers Center for Occupational Health & Safety of Quebec ***Voir*** Centre patronal de santé et sécurité du travail du Québec

Employers' Council of BC ***See*** Business Council of British Columbia

Employment & Education Centre (EEC)
PO Box 191, 105 Strowger Blvd., Brockville ON K6V 5V2
Tel: 613-498-2111; *Fax:* 613-498-2116
Toll-Free: 800-926-0777; *TTY:* 613-498-1610
info@eecentre.com
eecentre.com/ticcs.php
Also Known As: 1000 Islands Credit Counselling Services
Overview: A small local organization founded in 1996 overseen by Ontario Association of Credit Counselling Services
Mission: To offer employment, debt, credit, & student loan counselling services to persons in Brockville & the 1,000 Islands region of Ontario; To provide resources about life skills, job searches, & financial management
Member of: Ontario Association of Credit Counselling Services
Chief Officer(s):
Sherri Simzer, Executive Director
Deborah Alarie, Manager, Employment Services
deborah@eecentre.com
Blake McKim, Officer, Communications & Public Relations
blake@eecentre.com
Finances: *Funding Sources:* Government of Canada
Activities: Helping persons find solutions to their money management issues, through debt repayment programs; Presenting workshops, such as budget planning courses; Offering cash flow analysis; *Library:* Employment & Education Centre Resource Centre; Open to public

Employment Assistance Services (Skills for Change) ***See*** JVS of Greater Toronto

Emunah Women of Canada
#18, 7005 Kildare Rd., Côte Saint-Luc QC H4W 1C1
Tel: 514-485-2397; *Fax:* 514-483-3624
Toll-Free: 877-485-2397
emunahcanada@emunahcanada.org
www.emunahcanada.org
Also Known As: Mizrachi Hapoel Hamizrachi Women's Organization of Canada
Overview: A small local charitable organization founded in 1943
Mission: To provide social welfare services to cildren
Member of: World Emunah; Canadian Jewish Congress; Canadian Zionist Organization
Chief Officer(s):
Aryella Weisz, President
aryella@emunahcanada.org
Membership: *Fees:* $36
Activities: *Speaker Service:* Yes

Toronto Chapter
#300, 333 Wilson Ave., Toronto ON M3H 1T2
Tel: 416-636-0036; *Fax:* 416-636-0039
toronto@emunahcanada.org
Mission: To strengthen religious consciousness, provide social care & religious & secular education for children & youth, with selective vocational & academic training; provides care for approximately 8,000 children in over 127 day care centres & nurseries across Israel; educates more than 2,000 girls in 6 high schools & supports 5 children's homes & youth villages for more than 600 children
Chief Officer(s):
Roberta Newman, Co-President
Alina Mayer, Co-President

En ligne directe ***See*** Ability Online Support Network

Enactus Canada
#800, 920 Yonge St., Toronto ON M4W 3C7
Tel: 416-304-1566; *Fax:* 416-864-0514
Toll-Free: 800-766-8169
info@acecanada.ca
www.acecanada.ca
www.linkedin.com/groups/ACE-Advancing-Canadian-Entrepreneurship-118030
www.facebook.com/EnactusCanada
twitter.com/Enactus_Canada
www.youtube.com/user/EnactusCanada
Previous Name: Advancing Canadian Entrepreneurship Inc.; Canada's Future Entrepreneurial Leaders
Overview: A small national organization
Mission: Enactus is a national charitable organization that is teaching and igniting young Canadians to create brighter futures for themselves and their communities.
Chief Officer(s):
Ian Aitken, Chair
Nicole Almond, President
Staff Member(s): 10

Enasco - Institute of Social Service for Workers of Italian Origin ***See*** 50 & Piu Enasco

End Legislated Poverty (ELP)
PO Box 2359, Stn. Main, 349 West Georgia St., Vancouver BC V6B 3W5
Tel: 604-879-1209
elp@vcn.bc.ca
www.vcn.bc.ca/~elp
www.facebook.com/127936363907270
Overview: A small local organization founded in 1985
Mission: To organize low income people; to educate on the need to end poverty; to encourage unity & cooperation between unpaid & paid working people; to include low income people from marginalized communities
Chief Officer(s):
Dan Blake, Chair
Staff Member(s): 3; 250 volunteer(s)
Membership: 34; *Fees:* $1
Activities: *Library:* Resource Centre; by appointment

Enderby & District Arts Council (EDAC)
PO Box 757, Enderby BC V0E 1V0
e-mail: contact@enderbyartscouncil.com
www.enderbyartscouncil.com
www.facebook.com/1455855661326469
Overview: A small local charitable organization founded in 1991
Mission: To organize & provide grants for such cultural activities as workshops, public art (such as murals and sculpture), lectures & entertainment in the Enderby area.
Member of: Okanagan Mainline Arts Council
Finances: *Funding Sources:* municpal support; BC Arts Council; donations
Membership: *Fees:* $10 adult; $3 youth; $18 community organization; $20 corporate

Enderby & District Chamber of Commerce
PO Box 1000, 700 Railway St., Enderby BC V0E 1V0
Tel: 250-838-6727; *Fax:* 250-838-0123
Toll-Free: 877-213-6509
info@enderbychamber.com
www.enderbychamber.com
www.facebook.com/EnderbyChamber
twitter.com/EnderbyChamber
Overview: A small local organization
Mission: To encourage, promote & develop the interest of business for the prosperity of the whole community
Member of: BC Chamber of Commerce
Chief Officer(s):
Darren Robinson, Executive Director
darren@enderbychamber.com
Cora Prevost, Interim President
Finances: *Annual Operating Budget:* $100,000-$250,000; *Funding Sources:* Government; membership fees
Staff Member(s): 1; 25 volunteer(s)
Membership: 130; *Fees:* $30-$300

Enderby & District Museum Society
PO Box 367, 901 George St, Highway 97A, Enderby BC V0E 1V0
Tel: 250-838-7170
edms@jetstream.net
www.enderbymuseum.ca
www.facebook.com/enderbymuseum
twitter.com/enderbymuseum
Overview: A small local charitable organization founded in 1973
Mission: To collect, preserve, research, exhibit & interpret a collection of representative objects & supporting archival material relevant to the human & natural history of Enderby & district
Affiliation(s): BC Museums Association; Archives Association of BC
Chief Officer(s):
Naomi Fournier, Curator/Administrator
Finances: *Annual Operating Budget:* Less than $50,000; *Funding Sources:* City & regional district; donations
Staff Member(s): 1; 14 volunteer(s)
Membership: 105; *Fees:* $10 individual; $15 family
Activities: Guest speakers; Teas; Displays for special events; Research facility; *Library* Open to public

Ending Relationship Abuse Society of British Columbia (ERA)
8451 Harvard Pl., Chilliwack BC V2P 7Z5
Tel: 604-792-8090; *Fax:* 604-792-8090
www.erabc.ca
Previous Name: BC Association of Counsellors of Abusive Men
Overview: A small provincial organization founded in 1993
Mission: To establish a network of BC counsellors of men who are abusive in relationships
Chief Officer(s):
Jane Katz, Co-Chair
Ron Schwartz, Co-Chair, 250-661-1878
Carol Seychuk, Secretary, 250-847-9000
Finances: *Annual Operating Budget:* Less than $50,000; *Funding Sources:* Membership fees; conference fees
Membership: 74; *Fees:* $40; *Member Profile:* Counsellors of abusive men; program administrators; board members; funders; parole & probation officers; alcohol & drug counsellors
Activities: Annual fall conference; advocacy; maintenance of Guiding Principles; *Speaker Service:* Yes
Awards:
• Tony McNaughton Award (Award)
Awarded for bravery in opposing violence
• Alayne Hamilton Award (Award)
Awarded for bravery in opposing violence
• Community Service Award (Award)
Awarded for bravery in opposing violence

Ending Violence Association of British Columbia (EVA BC)
#1404, 510 West Hastings St., Vancouver BC V6B 1L8
Tel: 604-633-2506; *Fax:* 604-633-2507
evabc@endingviolence.org
www.endingviolence.org
www.facebook.com/EndingViolence.org
twitter.com/EndViolenceBC
Previous Name: British Columbia Association of Specialized Victim Assistance & Counselling Programs
Overview: A medium-sized provincial organization
Mission: To work as a provincial coordinating & networking organization for sexual assault centres, specialized victim assistance, & stopping the violence counselling programs; To assist those providing front line service
Chief Officer(s):
Tracy Porteous, Executive Director
porteous@endingviolence.org
Jennifer Woods, Co-chair
Bally Bassi, Co-chair
Finances: *Funding Sources:* Provincial Government
Staff Member(s): 13
Membership: 193 member programs; *Fees:* Schedule available

The Endometriosis Network
790 Bay St., 8th Fl., Toronto ON M5G 1N8
Tel: 416-591-3963
info@endometriosisnetwork.ca
www.endometriosisnetwork.ca
Previous Name: Toronto Endometriosis Network
Overview: A small national organization founded in 1987
Mission: To increase public & professional awareness of endometriosis; To encourage professional medical research toward early diagnosis & cure of endometriosis; To provide support & education to sufferers & their families
Affliation(s): Endometriosis Sisterhood
Chief Officer(s):
Katie McLeod, Director, Local Outreach & Community Development
katie@endometriosisnetwork.ca
Finances: *Annual Operating Budget:* Less than $50,000; *Funding Sources:* Membership dues; donations
Membership: *Fees:* $30; *Committees:* Education; Finance; Fundraising
Activities: Support groups; information packages; referrals; public meetings

Endurance Riders Association of British Columbia (ERABC)
5068 - 47A Ave., Delta BC V4K 1T8

Tel: 604-940-6958
tobytrot@telus.net
www.erabc.com
Overview: A small provincial organization founded in 1989
Mission: ERABC fosters interest in the equestrian sport of endurance riding & promotes training & competition opportunities for beginning & advanced riders. It also assists in the development & preservation of courses or terrain suitable for endurance competitions.
Affliation(s): Endurance Canada
Chief Officer(s):
June Melhuish, President
junemelhuish@gmail.com
Terre O'Brennan, Ride Manager
Finances: *Annual Operating Budget:* Less than $50,000
Membership: 1-99; *Fees:* $20 seniors; $12.50 junior; $40 family
Activities: *Awareness Events:* Ride Over the Rainbow

Endurance Riders of Alberta (ERA)

AB
Tel: 780-797-5404
enduranceridersofalberta.com
www.facebook.com/269711222453
Overview: A small provincial organization founded in 1981
Mission: To promote education & good horsemanship through endurance riding
Member of: Alberta Equestrian Federation; Canadian Long Distance Riding Association
Affliation(s): Canadian Long Distance Riding Association
Chief Officer(s):
Owen Fulcher, President
erapresident@live.ca
Membership: *Fees:* $30 individual; $60 family; $25 junior
Activities: Host clinics; sanctions endurance events in Alberta
Awards:
• High Points & Mileage Awards (Award)
• Darlene Keys Family Award (Award)
• Elaine Delbeke Memorial Partners Award (Award)
• Ron Janzen Memorial Sportsmanship Award (Award)

Énergie Solaire Québec

CP 540, Succ. St-Laurent, Ville St-Laurent QC H4L 4V7
Tél: 514-392-0095
www.esq.qc.ca
Aperçu: *Dimension:* petite; *Envergure:* provinciale
Mission: Promouvoir l'utilisation de l'énergie solaire au Québec
Membre: *Montant de la cotisation:* 40$ individuel
Activités: Souper solaire; clinique solaire; concours Cocktail Transport

Energy Action Council of Toronto (EnerACT)

51 Wolseley St., 5th Fl., Toronto ON M5T 1A4
Tel: 416-488-3966; *Fax:* 416-203-3121
Overview: A small local organization
Mission: To accelerate the change in society's usage of energy away from environmentally inappropriate forms towards conservation & renewable energy; To encourage the further application of technologies which contribute to energy conservation & the wider use of renewable energy; To broaden society's understanding of the relationship between energy & the environment & the potential for meeting society's energy needs through conservation & renewable energy technologies; To assist in the development of public policies which encourage energy conservation & the use of renewable energy
Chief Officer(s):
Mark Fernandez, Project Coordinator
Fraser Stewart, Executive Director
Membership: *Fees:* Schedule available

Energy Council of Canada / Conseil canadien de l'énergie

#608, 350 Sparks St., Ottawa ON K1R 7S8
Tel: 613-232-8239; *Fax:* 613-232-1079
krystal.piamonte@energy.ca
www.energy.ca
Previous Name: World Energy Council - Canadian Member Committee
Overview: A medium-sized national organization founded in 1924
Mission: To foster a greater understanding of energy issues; To enhance the effectiveness of the Canadian energy strategy
Member of: World Energy Council
Chief Officer(s):
Greg Schmidt, President
greg.schmidt@energy.ca
Brigitte Svarich, Director, Operations
brigitte.svarich@energy.ca
Staff Member(s): 3
Membership: 75+; *Member Profile:* Representatives from all facets of Canada's energy sector
Activities: Providing networking opportunities; Sponsoring forums & conferences; Disseminating current energy reports & information; Contributing to the development of the Canadian energy policy
Meetings/Conferences: • Energy Council of Canada Annual General Meeting 2015, 2015
Scope: National

Energy Probe Research Foundation (EPRF)

225 Brunswick Ave., Toronto ON M5S 2M6
Tel: 416-964-9223; *Fax:* 416-964-8239
webadmin@eprf.ca
epresearchfoundation.wordpress.com
www.facebook.com/277852842290873
Overview: A large national charitable organization founded in 1980
Mission: To educate Canadians about the benefits of conservation & renewable energy; to help Canada secure long-term energy self-sufficiency in the shortest possible time with the fewest disruptive effects & with the greatest societal, environmental & economic benefits; to provide business, government & the public with information on energy & energy-related issues; to help Canada contribute to global harmony & prosperity; recipient of the 1990 Lieutenant Governor's Conservation Award, the first time that an environmental organization has been so honoured; divisions include Energy Probe, Probe International, Environment Probe, Margaret Laurence Fund, Consumer Policy Institute, Environmental Bureau of Investigations, Urban Renaissance Institute
Affliation(s): Energy Probe; Probe International; Environment Probe; Consumer Policy Institute; Urban Renaissance Institute; Environmental Bureau of Investigation; Three Gorges Probe; Canadian Environmental News Network
Chief Officer(s):
Patricia Adams, President
Elizabeth Brubaker, Executive Director, Environment Probe
Finances: *Annual Operating Budget:* $1.5 Million-$3 Million; *Funding Sources:* Donations
Staff Member(s): 15; 10 volunteer(s)
Membership: 50,000 supporters
Activities: Policy research & education; *Internships:* Yes; *Speaker Service:* Yes; *Library* Open to public
Awards:
• The Margaret Laurence Fund (Grant)
Grants & scholarships are made to foster an understanding of peace & the environment upon which the fate of the planet rests*Eligibility:* Recipients of the grants & scholarships are limited to students, authors, researchers, & publishers, working with the foundation in collaborative projects approved by the directors

Enfant-Retour Québec / Missing Children Quebec

#420, 6830, av du Parc, Montréal QC H3N 1W7
Tél: 514-843-4333; *Téléc:* 514-843-8211
Ligne sans frais: 888-692-4673
info@enfant-retourquebec.ca
www.enfant-retourquebec.ca
www.facebook.com/182144014082
twitter.com/enfantretourqc
Nom précédent: Réseau Enfants Retour Canada
Aperçu: *Dimension:* moyenne; *Envergure:* provinciale; Organisme sans but lucratif; fondée en 1985
Mission: Assister les parents à la recherche de leurs enfants portés disparus; aider également les professionnels, avocats, policiers, travailleurs sociaux impliqués dans une situation de disparition d'enfant ou de prévention contre une disparition; réseau international de communication et d'aide qui oeuvre également à sensibiliser la population au problème des enfants disparus et exploités par des affiches, émissions, documents
Membre de: Association of Missing & Exploited Children's Organizations (AMECO)
Membre(s) du bureau directeur:
Yves J. Beauchesne, Président
Pina Arcamone, Directrice générale
Nancy Duncan, Directrice, Programmes d'assistance aux familles
Finances: *Budget de fonctionnement annuel:* $250,000-$500,000
Membre(s) du personnel: 7; 230 bénévole(s)
Membre: *Montant de la cotisation:* Dor voluntaire
Activités: Défi annuel Bateaux-Dragons; Classique de golf; *Evénements de sensibilisation:* Journée nationale des enfants disparus, 25 mai; Journée provinciale d'identification d'enfants; *Stagiaires:* Oui; *Service de conférenciers:* Oui; *Bibliothèque* Bibliothèque publique rendez-vous

Enform: The Safety Association for the Upstream Oil & Gas Industry

Head Office, 5055 - 11th St. NE, Calgary AB T2E 8N4
Tel: 403-516-8000; *Fax:* 403-516-8166
Toll-Free: 800-667-5557
customerservice@enform.ca
www.enform.ca
Previous Name: Petroleum Industry Training Service
Overview: A large national licensing charitable organization founded in 2005
Mission: To improve the Canadian upstream oil & gas industry's safety performance; To prevent work-related injuries in the upstream oil & gas industry in Canada
Affliation(s): Canadian Association of Geophysical Contractors (CAGC); Canadian Association of Oilwell Drilling Contractors (CAODC); Canadian Association of Petroleum Producers (CAPP); Canadian Energy Pipeline Association (CEPA); Petroleum Services Association of Canada (PSAC); Small Explorers & Producers Association of Canada (SEPAC); Petroleum Human Resources Council of Canada; Western Canadian Spill Services
Chief Officer(s):
Duane Mather, Chair
Cameron MacGillivray, President & CEO
L. Harman, Vice President, Operations
R. Ogilvie, Vice President, Corporate Services
Activities: Providing training courses; Offering saftey information; Promoting shared safety practices in the Canadian oil & gas industry; Providing the Small Employers Certificate of Recognition (SECOR), the Certificate of Recognition (COR), & the Petroleum Competency Program
Meetings/Conferences: • Petroleum Safety Conference 2015, May, 2015, Banff, AB
Scope: National
Contact Information: URL: www.psc.ca
Publications:
• Enform Insider
Type: Newsletter

British Columbia Office
#1240, 9600 - 93rd Ave., Fort St. John BC V1J 5Z2
Tel: 250-785-6009; *Fax:* 250-785-6013
Toll-Free: 855-436-3676

Genesee - Enform Ignition Training Facility
Genesee AB
Tel: 780-955-7770

Nisku Training Facility
1020 - 20th Ave., Nisku AB T9E 7Z6
Tel: 780-955-7770; *Fax:* 780-955-2454
Toll-Free: 800-667-5557

Saskatchewan Office
1912 Prince of Wales Dr., Regina BC S4Z 1A4
Tel: 306-337-9600; *Fax:* 306-337-9610
Toll-Free: 877-336-3676

The Engineering Institute of Canada (EIC) / L'Institut canadien des ingénieurs (ICI)

1295 Hwy. 2 East, RR#1, Kingston ON K7L 4V1
Tel: 613-547-5989; *Fax:* 613-547-0195
jplant1@cogeco.ca
www.eic-ici.ca
Overview: A large national charitable organization founded in 1887
Mission: To further the development of engineering in Canada; to stimulate the advancement of the quality & scope of Canadian engineering; to meet regularly with other engineering organizations & industries to promote understanding & improvement of the profession, the diffusion of engineering information & to provide Canadian representation in specialized engineering fields; to interact with government agencies & departments for the purpose of influencing decision making on matters relating to engineering & technology; to cooperate with the provincial engineering licensing bodies, The Canadian Council of Professional Engineering, The Association of Consulting Engineers of Canada, The Canadian Academy of Engineering & other engineering organizations in matters of common interest; to promote interaction with specific interest groups; to collaborate with universities & educational institutions
Affliation(s): Engineers Canada; Association of Canadian Engineering Companies; Canadian Academy of Engineering; International Association for Continuing Education & Training

(IACET); Internation Association for Continuing Engineering Education (IACEE)
Chief Officer(s):
Tony Bennett, P.Eng, President
John Plant, PhD, FCAE, FIEE, Executive Director
Xiaohua Wu, PhD, Treasurer
Jean Zu, PhD, PEng, Vice-President
Louise McNamara, Office Manager, 613-547-5989
louisem@cogeco.ca
Finances: *Annual Operating Budget:* $100,000-$250,000; *Funding Sources:* Membership fees; Con Ed quality, Assurance program, Career Site
Staff Member(s): 1; 20 volunteer(s)
Membership: 11 member societies; *Fees:* $2.50 per regular member of the member society; *Member Profile:* Join one of the member societies: Canadian Society for Civil Engineering; Canadian Society for Mechanical Engineering; Canadian Geotechnical Society; Canadian Society for Engineering in Management; IEEE - Canada; Canadian Society for Chemical Engineering; *Committees:* Executives, Council, Honours & Awards; History & Archives; Life Members Organization
Activities: Promotes the creation, exchange & dissemination of technical information; organizes conferences & symposia & promotes continuing education for engineers; supports engineering student advancement; maintains an official Registry of Continuing Education Units & Professional Development Activities; *Library:* Archives at University of Ontario Inst.; Open to public
Awards:
• EIC Fellows & Medals (Kennedy, Smith, Lo, Stirling & CPR) (Award)
• The Julian C. Smith Medal (Award)
• The John B. Stirling Medal (Award)
Established in 1987 in honour of Dr. John B. Stirling, a past president of the EIC & an outstanding engineer; medal is awarded in recognition of leadership & distinguished service at the national level within the institute &/or its member societies
• Canadian Pacific Rail Engineering Medal (Award)
Established 1987 in appreciation of CP Rail's contribution to the development of Canada; awarded in recognition of leadership & distinguished service at the local level within the institute &/or its member societies
• The Sir John Kennedy Medal (Award)
Established in 1927 in commemoration of the great services rendered in the field of engineering by Sir John Kennedy, a past president of the EIC; medal is awarded every two years by the council in recognition of outstanding merit in the profession or of noteworthy contributions to the science of engineering or to the benefit of the institute
Meetings/Conferences: • 4th Climate Change Technology Conference (CCTC 2015), May, 2015, Hotel Omni Mont-Royal, Montreal, QC
Scope: National

Engineers Canada / Ingénieurs Canada
#1100, 180 Elgin St., Ottawa ON K2P 2K3
Tel: 613-232-2474; *Fax:* 613-230-5759
Toll-Free: 877-408-9273
Other Communication: Executive e-mail: executive.office@engineerscanada.ca
info@engineerscanada.ca
www.engineerscanada.ca
www.facebook.com/EngineersCanada
twitter.com/engineerscanada
www.youtube.com/user/EngineersCanada
Previous Name: Canadian Council of Professional Engineers
Overview: A large national organization founded in 1936
Mission: To establish & maintain a common bond between constituent associations; To assist constituent associations to meet their common needs & those of their members by coordinating standards, procedures, & programs across Canada; To represent the engineering profession with respect to national & international affairs; To increase the profile & prestige of the engineering profession
Affliation(s): World Federation of Engineering Organizations
Chief Officer(s):
Kim Allen, FEC, P.Eng., CEO
kim.allen@engineerscanada.ca
Marie Carter, FEC, P.Eng., COO
marie.carter@engineerscanada.ca
Marc Bourgeois, FIC (Hon.), Director, Communications & Public Affairs
marc.bourgeois@engineerscanada.ca
Gordon Griffith, FEC, P.Eng, ing, Director, Education
gordon.griffith@engineerscanada.ca
Ken McMartin, FEC, P.Eng., Director, Professional & International Affairs
ken.mcmartin@engineerscanada.ca
Finances: *Funding Sources:* Membership dues
Membership: 10 provincial + 2 territorial associations representing 250,000 professional engineers; *Committees:* Canadian Engineering Accreditation Board (CEAB); Canadian Engineering Qualifications Board (CEQB); International; Awards
Activities: *Awareness Events:* National Engineering Month, March
Awards:
• Meritorious Service Award for Professional Service (Award)
For outstanding contribution to a professional, consulting or technical engineering association or society in Canada
• Gold Medal Award (Award)
• Meritorious Service Award for Community Service (Award)
Awarded for exemplary voluntary contribution to a community organization or humanitarian endeavour
• Young Engineer Achievement Award (Award)
Awarded for outstanding contribution in a field of engineering by an engineer 35 years of age or younger
• Medal for Distinction in Engineering Education (Scholarship)
Awarded for exemplary contribution to engineering teaching at a Canadian University
• Gold Medal Award (Award)
Awarded for exceptional individual achievement & distinction in a field of engineering
• Gold Medal Student Award (Award)
• National Award for an Engineering Project or Achievement (Award)
• Engineers Canada Fellowship (Award)
Meetings/Conferences: • Engineers Canada Board, Annual & Executive Committee Meetings 2015, May, 2015, Calgary, AB
Scope: National
Publications:
• Engineers Canada Newsletter
Type: Newsletter

Engineers Canada (EC) / Ingénieurs Canada (IC)
#1100, 180 Elgin St., Ottawa ON K2P 2K3
Tel: 613-232-2474; *Fax:* 613-230-5759
Other Communication: communications@engineerscanada.ca
info@engineerscanada.ca
www.engineerscanada.ca
www.linkedin.com/company/engineers-canada
www.facebook.com/EngineersCanada
twitter.com/engineerscanada
www.youtube.com/user/EngineersCanada
Overview: A small national organization founded in 1936
Mission: Regulates the practice of engineering in Canada and license the country's more than 160,000 professional engineers.
Member of: Canadian Network of National Associations of Regulators
Chief Officer(s):
Kim Allen, Chief Executive Officer
Kim.allen@engineerscanada.ca
Marc Bourgeois, Director, Communications & Public Affairs
marc.bourgeois@engineerscanada.ca
Activities: *Awareness Events:* National Engineering Month, March
Publications:
• Engineering on the Hill
Type: Newlsetter; *Frequency:* Semiannually
Profile: Reports on issues on Parliament Hill of interest to the engineering profession.

Engineers Nova Scotia
1355 Barrington St., Halifax NS B3J 1Y9
Tel: 902-429-2250; *Fax:* 902-423-9769
Toll-Free: 888-802-7367
info@engineersnovascotia.ca
www.engineersnovascotia.ca
Overview: A medium-sized provincial licensing organization founded in 1920 overseen by Engineers Canada
Mission: To establish, maintain & develop standards of knowledge & skill, standards of qualification & practice, & standards of professional ethics; To promote public awareness of the role of the association
Member of: Engineers Canada
Chief Officer(s):
Len White, P.Eng., Chief Executive Officer & Registrar
Perry Mitchelmore, P.Eng., President
Finances: *Funding Sources:* Membership dues
230 volunteer(s)
Membership: 5,000+; *Committees:* Public Relations; Student Affairs; Awards; Building; Professional Development; Professional Practice; Construction; Consulting Practice; Zones; Engineering Week; Finance; Publications; Information Highway; Salary; Employee Engineers
Activities: *Awareness Events:* National Engineering Week, March; *Internships:* Yes; *Speaker Service:* Yes
Meetings/Conferences: • Engineers Nova Scotia 2015 Annual General Meeting, 2015, NS
Scope: Provincial
Description: A business meeting with guest speakers for professional engineers & engineers-in-training in Nova Scotia
Contact Information: E-mail: info@engineersnovascotia.ca

Engineers Without Borders (EWB) / Ingénieurs sans Frontières (ISF)
#601, 366 Adelaide St. West, Toronto ON M5V 1R9
Tel: 416-481-3696; *Fax:* 416-352-5360
Toll-Free: 866-481-3696
info@ewb.ca
www.ewb.ca
www.facebook.com/ewbcanada
www.twitter.com/ewb
www.youtube.com/user/ewbcanada
Overview: A small international organization
Mission: To promote human development through access to technology
Chief Officer(s):
George Roter, CEO & Co-Founder
george@ewb.ca
Alex Conliffe, VP of Operations
Staff Member(s): 13
Meetings/Conferences: • Engineers Without Borders 2015 National Conference, January, 2015, Montréal, QC
Scope: National

Englehart & District Chamber of Commerce
PO Box 171, Englehart ON P0J 1H0
englehartchamber.weebly.com
Overview: A small local organization
Chief Officer(s):
Stacey Borgford, President
Membership: 50

English Additional Language Learners Provincial Specialist Association
c/o BC Teachers Federation, #100, 550 West 6 Ave., Vancouver BC V5Z 4P2
Tel: 604-871-2283; *Fax:* 205-871-2286
Toll-Free: 800-663-9163
ellpsa.ca
twitter.com/ESLPSA
Overview: A small provincial organization founded in 1989
Mission: To improve & promote English as a second language learning
Member of: BC Teachers' Federation
Chief Officer(s):
Marc Tremblay, President
mtremblay@sd45.bc.ca

English-Language Arts Network (ELAN)
#610, 460 Ste-Catherine West, Montréal QC H3B 1A7
Tel: 514-935-3312
Toll-Free: 866-935-3312
admin@quebec-elan.org
www.quebec-elan.org
Overview: A medium-sized provincial organization founded in 2005
Mission: Québec-wide network of English-speaking artists from all disciplines to promote the sharing of expertise, ideas & resources
Affliation(s): Québec Drama Federation; Québec Writers' Federation; Association of English Language Publishers of Québec
Chief Officer(s):
Guy Rodgers, Executive Director
Staff Member(s): 4; 1 volunteer(s)
Membership: 800; *Fees:* $10-$50; *Member Profile:* Anglophone artists who work in Québec, including writers, visual artists, actors, musicians, filmmakers, playwrights, dancers, etc.; *Committees:* Professional Development Group; Outreach Group; Social Events Group
Activities: Resource sharing; collective promotion; professional development; arts advocacy; *Internships:* Yes

Enokhok Development Corporation Ltd.
#200, 9405 - 45 Ave. NW, Edmonton AB T6E 6B9
Tel: 780-452-5784; *Fax:* 780-482-2267
Toll-Free: 866-452-5623

info@enokhok.com
www.enokhok.com
Overview: A small local organization founded in 1984
Mission: The company is a general contractor that also owns & manages rental property in Cambridge Bay, Kugluktuk and Gjoa Haven.

Enokhok Inn & Suits - Campbridge Bay
PO Box 103, Cambridge Bay NU X0B 0C0
Tel: 867-983-2532; *Fax:* 867-983-2271
info@enokhok.com

Les Enseignants et enseignantes retraités de l'Ontario ***See*** The Retired Teachers of Ontario

Ensemble contemporain de Montréal (ECM+)

3890, rue Clark, Montréal QC H2W 1W6
Tél: 514-524-0173; *Téléc:* 514-524-0179
info@ecm.qc.ca
www.ecm.qc.ca
www.facebook.com/135587246763
Aperçu: *Dimension:* petite; *Envergure:* locale; Organisme sans but lucratif surveillé par Orchestras Canada
Membre(s) du bureau directeur:
Natalie Watanabe, Directrice générale
Membre(s) du personnel: 6
Activités: *Listes de destinataires:* Oui

Ensemble vocal Ganymède

CP 476, Succ. C, Montréal QC H2L 4K4
Tél: 514-528-6302
contacter@evganymede.com
www.evganymede.com
Aperçu: *Dimension:* petite; *Envergure:* locale; fondée en 1991
Mission: Choeur d'hommes
Membre(s) du bureau directeur:
Yvan Sabourin, Directeur

Entertainment Software Association of Canada (ESAC)

#408, 130 Spadina Ave., Toronto ON M5V 2L4
Tel: 416-620-7171; *Fax:* 416-620-7085
theesa.ca
www.facebook.com/EntertainmentSoftwareAssociationofCanada
twitter.com/ESACanada
www.youtube.com/TheESACanada
Overview: A small national organization
Mission: To advocate on behalf of its members before government committees; to provide research services to its members
Chief Officer(s):
Jayson Hilchie, President & CEO
Staff Member(s): 4
Membership: 21 companies

Entomological Society of Alberta (ESA)

Dept. of Agricultural, Food & Nutritional Science, U of Alberta, 410 Ag/For Bldg., Edmonton AB T6G 2P5
Tel: 780-492-6893; *Fax:* 780-492-4265
www.entsocalberta.ca/esa.htm
Overview: A small provincial organization founded in 1952
Mission: To foster the advancement, exchange & dissemination of the knowledge of insects in relation to their importance in agriculture, forestry, public health & industry
Member of: Entomological Society of Canada
Chief Officer(s):
Lloyd Dosdall, President
lloyd.dosdall@ualberta.ca
Caroline Whitehouse, Treasurer, 780-492-3929, Fax: 780-492-9234
cmw7@ualberta.ca
Finances: *Annual Operating Budget:* Less than $50,000
Membership: 108; *Fees:* $10

Entomological Society of British Columbia (ESBC)

e-mail: info@entsocbc.ca
blogs.sfu.ca/groups/esbc
www.linkedin.com/groups/Entomological-Society-British-Columbia-4760901
www.facebook.com/groups/135038946598013
twitter.com/EntSocBC
Overview: A small provincial organization founded in 1902
Member of: Entomological Society of Canada
Chief Officer(s):
Ward Strong, President
Leo Rankin, Secretary
scholarships@entsocbc.ca
Max Salomon, Treasurer
membership@entsocbc.ca
15 volunteer(s)
Membership: 230; *Fees:* $20; *Member Profile:* Professional; amateur; student entomologists
Activities: *Library:* Pacific Forestry Centre
Awards:
• Student Research Presentation Awards (Award)
• Graduate Student Travel Grants (Grant)

Entomological Society of Canada (ESC)

393 Winston Ave., Ottawa ON K2A 1Y8
Tel: 613-725-2619
entsoc.can@bellnet.ca
www.esc-sec.ca
twitter.com/CanEntomologist
Overview: A small national organization founded in 1863
Mission: The Society promotes research, disseminating knowledge of insects, and encourages the continued participation of all "students and lovers of Entomology".
Chief Officer(s):
Rebecca Hallett, President, 519-824-4120 Ext. 54488, Fax: 519-837-0442
rhallett@uoguelph.ca
Membership: *Member Profile:* Amateurs & professionals; *Committees:* Youth and Amateur Encouragement; Awards; Microscope; Newsletter Editor; Regional Director to ESC
Meetings/Conferences: • Entomological Society of Canada 2015 Annual Meeting, 2015
Scope: National
• 2016 Entomological Society of Canada Annual Meeting and International Congress of Entomology, September, 2016, Orlando, FL
Scope: National
Publications:
• The Canadian Entomologist
Type: Journal; *Frequency:* 6 pa; *Editor:* Dr. Christopher Buddle
Profile: Publishes original research papers and scientific notes dealing with all facets of entomology.

Entomological Society of Manitoba Inc. (ESM)

Agriculture Canada, Research Station, 195 Dafoe Rd., Winnipeg MB R3T 2M9
Tel: 204-983-1450; *Fax:* 204-983-4604
iwise@agr.gc.ca
home.cc.umanitoba.ca/~fieldspg
Overview: A small provincial charitable organization founded in 1945
Mission: To encourage & promote the field of entomology; To provide a forum to enable individuals with an interest in entomology to acquire & share information
Affliation(s): Entomological Society of Canada
Chief Officer(s):
David Wade, Secretary
Bob Lamb, President
Finances: *Annual Operating Budget:* Less than $50,000; *Funding Sources:* Donations; membership fees; interest income; fundraising
25 volunteer(s)
Membership: 106; *Fees:* $25; *Member Profile:* Professional & amateur entomologists; *Committees:* Endowment Fund; Finance; Scientific Program; Newsletter; Youth Encouragement & Public Education; Social; Scholarships & Awards; Fundraising; Nomination; Membership; Scrtineers; Archivist; Common Names of Insects; Web Page
Activities: Scientific paper symposia; public education presentations on entomology; *Library:* Agriculture & Agrifood Canada Resource Centre
Awards:
• ESM Scholarship (Scholarship)
• ESM Student Award (Award)
• SWAT Award (Award)

Entomological Society of Ontario (ESO)

c/o Vista Centre, PO Box 83025, 1030 Bank St., Ottawa ON K1V 1A3
Tel: 603-736-3393
www.entsocont.ca
Overview: A small provincial organization founded in 1863
Mission: To foster interest in entomology
Chief Officer(s):
Bruce Gill, President, 613-759-1842, Fax: 613-759-6938
bruce.gill@inspection.gc.ca
Nicole McKenzie, Secretary
nicole_mckenzie@hc-sc.gc.ca
Finances: *Annual Operating Budget:* Less than $50,000
Membership: 100-499; *Member Profile:* Amateurs & professionals
Activities: *Library*
Meetings/Conferences: • Entomological Society of Ontario 2015 152nd Annual General Meeting, 2015
Scope: Provincial
Description: A gathering of entomologists of all disciplines
Publications:
• Journal of the Entomological Society of Ontario
Type: Journal; *Frequency:* Annually

Entomological Society of Saskatchewan (ESS)

c/o Agriculture & Agri-Food Canada, 107 Science Pl., Saskatoon SK S7N OX2
Tel: 306-956-7287; *Fax:* 306-956-7247
www.entsocsask.ca
Overview: A small provincial organization founded in 1952
Mission: The Society promotes the significance of entomology to the general public & provides a forum for those interested in the field to communicate. It also works in conjunction with other similar societies.
Member of: Entomological Society of Canada
Chief Officer(s):
Margaret Gruber, President
margaret.gruber@agr.gc.ca
Finances: *Annual Operating Budget:* Less than $50,000
Membership: *Fees:* $20; $5 student; *Member Profile:* Amateurs & professionals; *Committees:* Youth and Amateur Encouragement; Awards; Microscope; Newsletter Editor; Regional Director to ESC
Activities: North American butterfly count; insect inventory of endangered/protected ecosystems; talks & presentations, displays at schools; *Speaker Service:* Yes; *Rents Mailing List:* Yes

Entraide - femmes de Gatineau inc. ***Voir*** Entraide familiale de l'Outaouais inc.

Entraide familiale de l'Outaouais inc.

310-B, rue Notre-Dame, Gatineau QC J8P 1L1
Tél: 819-669-0686
entraidefamiliale.wordpress.com
www.facebook.com/EntraideFamilialeOutaouais
twitter.com/EFOutaouais
www.youtube.com/user/EntraideFamiliale
Nom précédent: Entraide - femmes de Gatineau inc.
Aperçu: *Dimension:* petite; *Envergure:* locale; Organisme sans but lucratif; fondée en 1990
Mission: Pour fournir des services essentiels à ceux qui en ont besoin mais ne peut pas se le permettre
Membre(s) du bureau directeur:
Diane Tremblay, Directrice générale
dtremblay@entraidefamiliale.com
Membre(s) du personnel: 5
Membre: 1 873; *Critères d'admissibilite:* Être prestataire d'aide sociale, ou avoir un revenu de moins de 20 000 par année pour 1 famille de 4 personnes
Activités: *Bibliothèque* Bibliothèque publique

Entraide Léo-Théorêt

2000B, rue Alaxandre-de-Sève, Montéal QC H2L 2W4
Tél: 514-521-0095
entraideleotheoret@hotmail.com
Aperçu: *Dimension:* petite; *Envergure:* locale
Mission: Pour aider les moins fortunés en leur offrant des services sociaux abordables
Affiliation(s): Corporateion de développment communautaire centre-sud; Table de concertation et d'intervention po9ur une garantie alimentaire

Entraide universitaire mondiale du Canada ***See*** World University Service of Canada

Entre Nous Femmes Housing Society

#21, 3550 SE Marine Dr., Vancouver BC V5S 4R3
Tel: 604-451-4412; *Fax:* 604-451-4415
enf@telus.net
www.enfhs.org
Also Known As: ENF Housing
Overview: A small local charitable organization founded in 1985
Mission: To provide & manage safe, affordable community homes & townhouses for female-led, single parent families in the Greater Vancouver Area; to operate 345 housing units.
Member of: British Columbia Non-Profit Housing Association
Chief Officer(s):
Tracy McCullough, Executive Director
Membership: *Fees:* $2

Publications:
• ENF Newsletter
Type: Newsletter; *Frequency:* Semiannually

Entre-amis Lavallois inc
4490, 10e rue, Laval QC H7R 6A9
Tél: 450-962-4058
Aperçu: *Dimension:* petite; *Envergure:* provinciale
Mission: Offrir une activité culturelle et de rencontre aux personnes atteintes de déficience intellectuelle
Membre: *Critères d'admissibilité:* Personnes vivant avec une déficience intellectuelle
Activités: Soirées de danse

Entrepreneurs with Disabilities Network (EDN)
1575 Brunswick St., Halifax NS B3J 2G1
ednns.ca
www.facebook.com/EntrepreneurswithDisabilitiesNetwork
twitter.com/EDNns
Overview: A small provincial organization founded in 2004
Mission: To encourage entrepreneurship to people with disabilities; to understand the needs of entrepreneurs with disabilities & to represent them; to work on behalf of entrepreneurs with disabilities to advise government, business service providers & others on how best to serve them
Affliation(s): Centre for Entrepreneurship Education & Development Inc.
Chief Officer(s):
Brian Aird, Executive Director
Awards:
• Entrepreneur of the Year Awards (Award)
Publications:
• EDN [Entrepreneurs with Disabilities Network] Newsletter
Type: Newsletter; *Frequency:* q.

Entrepreneurship Institute of Canada
PO Box 40043, 75 King St. South, Waterloo ON N2J 4V1
Tel: 519-885-1559*Tel:* 1-877-993-9921; *Fax:* 519-885-0990
Toll-Free: 800-665-4497
entinst@sympatico.ca
www.entinst.ca
Also Known As: The Entrepreneurial Community Corporation of Canada
Overview: A medium-sized national organization founded in 1986
Mission: To distribute support & educational resources of interest to entrepreneurs to corporations, institutions, human resources departments, post-secondary educational institutions, training departments, business resource centres, libraries, & business owners across Canada & the United States

Enviro-Accès Inc.
#150, 85, rue Belvédère nord, Sherbrooke QC J1H 4A7
Tél: 819-823-2230; *Téléc:* 819-823-6632
enviro@enviroaccess.ca
www.enviroaccess.ca
Également appelé: Centre pour l'avancement des technologies environnementales
Aperçu: *Dimension:* moyenne; *Envergure:* provinciale; fondée en 1993
Mission: Supporter les petites et moyennes entreprises qui oeuvrent dans le domaine de l'environnement en leur offrant les services professionnels nécessaires au développement de leurs projets et de leurs affaires.
Membre(s) du bureau directeur:
Manon Laporte, Présidente-directrice générale
mlaporte@enviroaccess.ca
Membre(s) du personnel: 9
Membre: 1-99

Montréal
#440, 50, rue Sainte-Catherine Ouest, Montréal QC H2X 3V4
Tél: 514-284-5794; *Téléc:* 514-284-6034
Membre(s) du bureau directeur:
Maude Lauzon-Gosselin, Directrice de projets
mlauzongosselin@enviroaccess.ca

Environment Resources Management Association
PO Box 857, Grand Falls-Windsor NL A2A 2P7
Tel: 709-489-7350
info@exploitsriver.ca
www.exploitsriver.ca/association.php
Overview: A medium-sized national organization founded in 1984
Mission: To promote the development of the Exploits River as a major Atlantic Salmon producing river.
Staff Member(s): 50

Environmental & Outdoor Education Council of Alberta *See* Global, Environmental & Outdoor Education Council

Environmental Abatement Council of Ontario (EACO)
70 Leek Cres., Richmond Hill ON L4B 1H1
Tel: 416-499-4000; *Fax:* 416-499-8752
mthorburn@tcanetworks.com
www.eacoontario.com
Previous Name: Ontario Asbestos Removal Contractors Association
Overview: A medium-sized provincial organization founded in 1992
Mission: To collect, generate & disseminate information concerning environmental abatement & other hazardous environmental health issues
Chief Officer(s):
Mary Thorburn, Secretary/Manager Ext. 114
mthorburn@tcaconnect.com
Finances: *Annual Operating Budget:* Less than $50,000; *Funding Sources:* Membership dues
Staff Member(s): 10; 30 volunteer(s)
Membership: 25 corporate; *Fees:* $625 general/contractor; $75 associate

Environmental Action Barrie - Living Green
Barrie ON
www.livinggreenbarrie.com
twitter.com/livinggreenbarr
Overview: A small local charitable organization founded in 1990
Mission: To provide education & awareness about environmental issues for the people of Barrie, Ontario & neighbouring communities; To promote environmentally friendly practices
Chief Officer(s):
Mike Fox, Executive Director
Erich Jacoby-Hawkins, Board Member
erich@livinggreenbarrie.com; erich@livinggreen.info
Finances: *Funding Sources:* Donations
Activities: Carrying out eco-projects; Providing articles related to environmental issues; Offering environmental information & activities through a web site, as a web site based organization; *Speaker Service:* Yes

Environmental Careers Organization of Canada / L'Organisation pour les carrières en environnement du Canada
#200, 308 - 11th Ave. SE, Calgary AB T2G 0Y2
Tel: 403-233-0748; *Fax:* 403-269-9544
info@eco.ca
www.eco.ca
www.facebook.com/ecocanada
twitter.com/ecocanada
Also Known As: ECO Canada
Previous Name: Canadian Council for Human Resources in the Environment Industry
Overview: A medium-sized national organization founded in 1992
Mission: To provide services to all participants in the environmental sector, including educators, students, practitioners, & employers
Chief Officer(s):
Hubert Bourque, Chair
Jon Ogryzlo, Sec.-Treas.
Grant S. Trump, President/CEO
Michael Kerford, Vice-President
Janelle Thomlinson, Director, Marketing & Communications
Finances: *Funding Sources:* Government of Canada's Sector Council Program
Activities: Providing career information & a job board; Recruiting; Offering ECO Canada internships; Providing professional development opportunities to practitioners; Offering employee retention strategies to employers; Providing tools for career change & career development; Disseminating human resource statistics & trends; Increasing Aboriginal employment in the environment sector through career awareness, training, & employment resources

Environmental Coalition of Prince Edward Island (ECO-PEI)
c/o Voluntary Resource Centre, 81 Prince St., Charlottetown PE C1A 4R3
Tel: 902-651-2575
mail@ecopei.ca
www.ecopei.ca
Overview: A small provincial organization founded in 1988
Mission: To work in partnership in order to understand & improve the Island's environment
Member of: Canadian Renewable Energy Alliance
Chief Officer(s):
Gary Schneider, Co-Chair
Membership: *Fees:* $10 basic; $25 supporting; $100 corporate
Publications:
• ECO-NEWS [a publication of the Environmental Coalition of Prince Edward Island]
Type: Newsletter

Environmental Defence / Defense environmentale
#300, 116 Spadina Ave., Toronto ON M5V 2K6
Tel: 416-323-9521; *Fax:* 416-323-9301
Toll-Free: 877-399-2333
info@environmentaldefence.ca
www.environmentaldefence.ca
www.facebook.com/EnvironmentalDefenceCanada
twitter.com/envirodefence
Previous Name: Canadian Environmental Defence Fund
Overview: A medium-sized national charitable organization founded in 1984
Mission: To protect the environment & human health; To research, educate, & initiate action in the courts when necessary
Member of: Canadian Environmental Network
Chief Officer(s):
Tim Gray, Executive Director, 416-323-9521 Ext. 288
Finances: *Annual Operating Budget:* $500,000-$1.5 Million
25 volunteer(s)

Environmental Education Association of the Yukon (EEAY)
Whitehorse YT
e-mail: eeyukon@gmail.com
taiga.net/YukonEE
Overview: A small provincial organization
Mission: To promote environmental education in the Yukon and foster communication between individuals and groups with and interest in environmental education.
Member of: EENorth; Canada's Arctic Environmental Education Network

Environmental Education Ontario (EEON)
32 Springdale Dr., Kitchener ON N2K 1P9
Tel: 519-579-3097
admin@eeon.org
www.eeon.org
twitter.com/GREENINGONTARIO
Overview: A small local charitable organization founded in 2000
Mission: To promote the facilitation, development & implementation of education on sustainable environments in Ontario
Member of: Education Alliance for a Sustainable Ontario
Finances: *Funding Sources:* Federal & provincial governments; foundations
Membership: *Member Profile:* Environmental & ecological educators, concerned citizens, parents, & representatives from non-governmental organizations & government agencies
Activities: Listserv; meetings; representations; *Speaker Service:* Yes
Meetings/Conferences: • Environmental Education Ontario Spring Event and Annual General Meeting 2015, 2015, ON
Scope: Provincial
Contact Information: admin@eeon.org

Environmental Educators' Provincial Specialist Association (EEPSA)
c/o British Columbia Teachers' Federation, #100, 550 - 6th Ave. West, Vancouver BC V5Z 4P2
Tel: 604-871-2283
eepsa.org
www.facebook.com/eepsa.bc
twitter.com/EEPSA
Overview: A medium-sized provincial organization founded in 1972
Mission: To promote, through public education, greater awareness, understanding & appreciation of the environment & to encourage global citizenship through the development of active decision making
Member of: BC Teachers' Federation
Chief Officer(s):
Selina Metcalfe, President
selmet@shaw.ca
Finances: *Funding Sources:* Membership dues
Membership: 200; *Fees:* $15 student; $25 BCTF members; $45.68 associate

Environmental Health Association of British Columbia (EHABC)
PO Box 30033, RPO Reyolds, Victoria BC V8X 5E1
Tel: 250-658-2027
Other Communication: ehabc.wordpress.com
info@ehabc.org
www.ehabc.org
www.facebook.com/353025931439290
Overview: A medium-sized provincial charitable organization founded in 1993
Mission: To raise awareness within the medical community, educational institutions, and the general public to prevent further cases of environmental sensitivity from occurring.
Affliation(s): EHA Nova Scotia; EHA Québec; EHA Ontario; EHA Alberta
Membership: *Fees:* $25

Environmental Health Association of Nova Scotia (EHANS)
PO Box 31323, Halifax NS B3K 5Y5
Toll-Free: 800-449-1995
ehans@environmentalhealth.ca
www.environmentalhealth.ca
www.facebook.com/165405756830794
Previous Name: Nova Scotia Allergy & Environmental Health Association
Overview: A small provincial organization founded in 1985
Chief Officer(s):
Eric Slone, President
Membership: *Fees:* $25 individual; $35 family; $75 supporting

Environmental Health Association of Ontario (EHA Ontario)
PO Box 33023, Ottawa ON K2C 3Y9
Tel: 613-860-2342
helpline@ehaontario.ca
www.ehaontario.ca
Previous Name: Allergy & Environmental Health Association
Overview: A small provincial charitable organization founded in 1975
Mission: To promote awareness of environmental conditions that may be harmful to human health, & advocates less-contaminated sources of food, water, clothing, personal & home care products, home furnishings & building materials
Member of: Human Ecology Foundation of Canada
Affliation(s): EHA Nova Scotia; EHA Québec; EHA Alberta; EHA BC
Finances: *Funding Sources:* Donations; Membership fees
Membership: *Fees:* $28; *Member Profile:* Individuals with environmental sensitivities & their families
Activities: *Library:* AEHA-Ottawa Library

Environmental Health Association of Québec *Voir* Association pour la santé environnementale du Québec

Environmental Health Foundation of Canada (EHFC)
c/o Tim Roark, 3301 - 164A St., Surrey BC V3S 0G5
Tel: 778-574-1188
www.ehfc.ca
Overview: A small national charitable organization founded in 1989 overseen by Canadian Institute of Public Health Inspectors
Mission: To advance environmental health in Canada through the development & implementation of education & research initiatives
Chief Officer(s):
Tim Roark, Treasurer
trustees@ehfc.ca
Membership: *Member Profile:* Members of the environmental public health profession; industry representatives; educational institutions; government

The Environmental Law Centre (Alberta) Society (ELC)
#800, 10025 - 106 St., Edmonton AB T5J 1G4
Tel: 780-424-5099; *Fax:* 780-424-5133
Toll-Free: 800-661-4238
elc@elc.ab.ca
www.elc.ab.ca
www.facebook.com/environmentallawcentre
twitter.com/ELC_Alberta
www.youtube.com/ELCAlberta
Also Known As: Environmental Law Centre
Overview: A small provincial charitable organization founded in 1982
Mission: To conduct research in environmental & natural resources law, policy & procedure; to educate the public on environmental law; to operate an environmental law information & referral service for the benefit of the public; to monitor relevant municipal, provincial & federal environmental laws, policies & procedures, & make recommendations for reform
Member of: Alberta Environmental Network
Chief Officer(s):
Cindy Chiasson, Executive Director
cchiasson@elc.ab.ca
Finances: *Annual Operating Budget:* $500,000-$1.5 Million; *Funding Sources:* Funded in part by the Alberta Law Foundation & through public support
Staff Member(s): 11
Membership: 13
Activities: *Speaker Service:* Yes; *Rents Mailing List:* Yes
Awards:
• Sir John A. Mactaggart Essay Prize (Scholarship)
Open to undergraduate & graduate students attending a recognized law school in Canada; prizes will be awarded for essays of high quality which address an issue in environmental law which is orginal, significant & relevant to Canada *Amount:* First prize is $500 plus a bound volume of the author's choice from Carswell; winning essay will als

Environmental Managers Association of British Columbia (EMABC)
PO Box 3741, Vancouver BC V6B 3Z8
Tel: 604-998-2226; *Fax:* 604-998-2226
info@emaofbc.com
www.emaofbc.com
www.linkedin.com/groups/Environmental-Managers-Association-BC-1856767
twitter.com/emaofbc
Overview: A medium-sized provincial organization
Mission: To encourage education, share knowledge among members and create a forum for environmental management issues in the industrial, commercial and institutional sectors, serve as a key resource of environmental information for members and explore existing and emerging environmental issues.
Chief Officer(s):
Patrick Johnstone, President
pjohnstone@richmond.ca
Don Bryant, Executive Director
don@consultdlb.com
Membership: 67 corporate; *Fees:* $450
Meetings/Conferences: • 2015 Environmental Managers Association of British Columbia Workshop, February, 2015, Simon Fraser University, Segal Building, Vancouver, BC
Scope: Provincial
Description: Theme: Supporting BC's Resource Sectors Toward Successful Development

Environmental Services Association of Alberta (ESAA)
#102, 2528 Ellwood Dr. SW, Edmonton AB T6X 0A9
Tel: 780-429-6363; *Fax:* 780-429-4249
Toll-Free: 800-661-9278
info@esaa.org
www.esaa.org
Previous Name: Alberta Special Waste Services Association
Overview: A medium-sized provincial organization founded in 1987
Mission: To act as the voice of Alberta's environment industry
Chief Officer(s):
Craig Robertson, President
Randy Neumann, Secretary
Skip Kerr, Treasurer
Joe Barraclough, Director, Industry & Government Relations, 780-429-6363 Ext. 224
Joe Chowaniec, Director, Program & Event Development, 780-429-6363 Ext. 223
chowaniec@esaa.org
Membership: 200+ organizations; *Fees:* $475
Activities: Communicating with all levels of government; Providing networking opportunities; Offering market & industry information
Meetings/Conferences: • Environmental Services Association of Alberta Environment Business 2015, February, 2015, Edmonton, AB
Scope: Provincial
Contact Information: URL: www.environmentbusiness.ca, Phone: 780-429-6363 x 223
• Environmental Services Association of Alberta 2015 Water Technology (WaterTech) Symposium, April, 2015, Delta Lodge Kananaskis, Kananaskis, AB
Scope: Provincial
Attendance: 300+
Description: A water technology transfer event for environmental professionals.
Contact Information: URL: www.esaa-events.com/watertech; Director, Program & Event Development: Joe Chowaniec, Phone: 780-429-6363, ext. 223, E-mail: chowaniec@esaa.org; Exhibit Information, E-mail: exhibits@esaa-events.com; Sponsorship Information, E-mail: sponsors@esaa-events.com

• Environmental Services Association of Alberta 2015 Remediation Technologies (RemTech) Symposium, October, 2015, Fairmont Banff Springs Hotel, Banff, AB
Scope: Provincial
Description: Remediation technology information for environmental professionals, such as engineering firms, pipeline companies, drill companies, energy marketers, natural gas producers, oil & gase services companies, environmental consulting firms, & mining companies
Contact Information: URL: www.esaa-events.com/remtech; Director, Program & Event Development: Joe Chowaniec, Phone: 780-429-6363, ext. 223, E-mail: chowaniec@esaa.org; Exhibit Information, E-mail: exhibits@esaa-events.com; Sponsorship Information, E-mail: sponsors@esaa-events.com
Publications:
• B.I.D.S. (Business Initiative Development Service)
Type: Newsletter; *Frequency:* Weekly
Profile: Environmental business opportunities, news, & marketing information for the buyers & sellers of environmental goods & services
• Environmental Association of Alberta Annual Report
Type: Yearbook; *Frequency:* Annually
• The ESAA [Environmental Services Association of Alberta] Weekly News
Type: Newsletter; *Frequency:* Weekly; *Accepts Advertising*
Profile: Association happenings, such as conferences & job opportunities, for Environmental Services Association of Alberta members
• The Regulatory Review [a publication of the Environmental Services Association of Alberta]
Frequency: Monthly
Profile: Current information on environmental policies & law, produced by the Environmental Services Association of Alberta & the EnvironmentalLaw Center

Environmental Services Association of Nova Scotia (ESANS)
Woodside Industrial Park, #211-2, 1 Research Dr., Dartmouth NS B2Y 4M9
Tel: 902-463-3538; *Fax:* 902-466-6889
contact@esans.ca
www.esans.ca
Also Known As: Nova Scotia Environmental Business Network
Overview: A medium-sized provincial organization founded in 1994
Mission: ESANS is a province-wide business organization dedicated to the promotion of environmental products, services & organizations within the environmental industry.
Chief Officer(s):
Norval Collins, President
ncollins@cefconsultants.ns.ca
Sandra Lynch, Operations Manager
sandra@esans.ca
Finances: *Annual Operating Budget:* $100,000-$250,000; *Funding Sources:* Membership; projects; government
Staff Member(s): 1
Membership: 100-499; *Fees:* Schedule available; *Member Profile:* Individuals & companies/organizations involved in the environmental industry; *Committees:* Communications; Membership; Finance
Activities: *Awareness Events:* Membership Appreciation Social; *Internships:* Yes; *Rents Mailing List:* Yes

Environmental Studies Association of Canada (ESAC) / Association canadienne d'études environnementales
c/o Dean's Office, Faculty of Environmental Studies, Univ. of Waterloo, Waterloo ON N2L 3G1
Tel: 519-888-4442; *Fax:* 519-746-0292
Toll-Free: 866-437-2587
www.esac.ca
www.facebook.com/218543575398
twitter.com/esaccanada
Overview: A small national organization founded in 1993
Mission: To to advance research & teaching activities in areas related to environmental studies in Canada
Chief Officer(s):

Chris Ling, Co-President
chris.ling@royalroads.ca
Shirley Thompson, Co-President
s.thompson@ad.umanitoba.ca
Membership: *Fees:* $45 student & unwaged & small NGO; $95 faculty & professional; $125 institutional; *Member Profile:* Members include individuals, who are interested in social science & humanities approaches to environmental issues, from educational institutions, government agencies, & private sector & non-profit organizations.
Meetings/Conferences: • The Environmental Studies Association of Canada (ESAC) 2015 Conference, 2015
Scope: National
Publications:
• Directory of ESAC [Environmental Studies Association of Canada] Members
Type: Directory; *Frequency:* Annually
Profile: Listing of ESAC members, with their areas of interest & research
• Rhizome [a publication of the Environmental Studies Association of Canada]
Type: Newsletter; *Editor:* Angela Waldie
Profile: Information about conferences, research projects, events, new publications, & teaching materials

Environmental Youth Alliance (EYA)
#517, 119 Pender St. West, Vancouver BC V6B 1S5
Tel: 604-689-4446
info@eya.ca
www.eya.ca
www.facebook.com/EnvironmentalYouthAlliance
twitter.com/EnviroYA
www.youtube.com/user/EnviroYouthAlliance
Overview: A small local organization founded in 1989
Mission: To save the earth through non-violent means; To promote change by educating people on our interconnectedness with Nature & involving youth in action projects; To create a youth movement that is activist-oriented & works towards environmental respect & protection.
Chief Officer(s):
Hartley Rosen, Managing Director
hartley@eya.ca
Finances: *Annual Operating Budget:* $100,000-$250,000; *Funding Sources:* Federal, provincial & municipal government; foundations
Staff Member(s): 2; 25 volunteer(s)
Membership: 10,000
Activities: Stewardship of urban sites; *Speaker Service:* Yes; *Library* by appointment

Environnement jeunesse
Maison du développement durable, #400, 50, rue Sainte-Catherine Ouest, Montréal QC H2X 3V4
Tél: 514-252-3016; *Téléc:* 514-254-5873
Ligne sans frais: 866-377-3016
infoenjeu@enjeu.qc.ca
enjeu.qc.ca
www.facebook.com/environnement.jeunesse
twitter.com/ENJEUquebec
vimeo.com/channels/enjeu
Également appelé: ENJEU
Aperçu: *Dimension:* moyenne; *Envergure:* provinciale; fondée en 1979
Mission: Promouvoir la conservation et l'amélioration de la qualité de l'environnement; développer chez les jeunes les qualités favorisant leur implication sociale.
Affiliation(s): Réseau québécois des groupes écologistes; Association québécoise pour la promotion de l'éducation relative à l'environnement
Membre(s) du bureau directeur:
Jérôme Normand, Directeur général
jnormand@enjeu.qc.ca
Membre(s) du personnel: 12
Membre: 1027 individuel + 167 collectif; *Montant de la cotisation:* 10$ étudiant; 20$ individuel; 50$ collectif; 35$ famille; 100$ souien; 1000$ donateur
Activités: Tient une assemblée générale annuelle; organise un colloque annuel, La Bise D'Automne; tient des comités inter-groupes; réalise L'Écologie en Action, un vaste projet d'éducation et d'action relatifs à l'environnement; offre un Service d'Activités en Formation et en Éducation Relatives à l'Environnement; produit une panoplie d'outils de qualité visant à soutenir l'action des groupes membres; participe à des processus de consultation publique; *Service de conférenciers:* Oui

Envol SRT
#302, 92, boul St-Raymond, Gatineau QC J8Y 1S7
Tél: 819-770-1622; *Téléc:* 819-771-5566
envoladmin@videotron.ca
www.envolsrt.org
Aperçu: *Dimension:* petite; *Envergure:* locale
Mission: Pour aider les jeunes qui ont un problème persistant de santé mentale à trouver un emploi
Membre: *Critères d'admissibilite:* Jeunes adultes qui ont un problème persistant de santé mentale

Ephemera Society of Canada
36 Macauley Dr., Thornhill ON L3T 5S5
e-mail: ephemera@tht.net
Overview: A small national organization founded in 1987
Mission: The Society preserves, studies & exhibits Canada's cultural heritage in the medium of printing.
Chief Officer(s):
E. Richard McKinstry, President
Membership: *Member Profile:* Researchers, dealers, collectors, historians
Activities: Regular membership meetings; lectures

Épilepsie Canada *See* Epilepsy Canada

Épilepsie Ontario *See* Epilepsy Ontario

Epilepsy & Seizure Association of Manitoba
#4, 1805 Main St., Winnipeg MB R2V 2A2
Tel: 204-783-0466; *Fax:* 204-784-9689
Toll-Free: 866-374-5377
epilepsy.seizures.mb@mts.net
www.manitobaepilepsy.org
Also Known As: Manitoba Epilepsy Association
Overview: A small provincial charitable organization founded in 1975
Mission: To improve the quality of life of persons with epilepsy through a broad range of programs, education, support of research & services.
Member of: Canadian Epilepsy Alliance
Chief Officer(s):
Jim Cook, President
Chris Vander Aa, Vice-President
Diane Wall, Secretary
Ruby Fife, Treasurer
Finances: *Funding Sources:* Donations & fundraisers
Activities: Library Loan; Information & Referral; Support Group; Community Education; Support group in Brandon 204/725-3599; *Speaker Service:* Yes; *Library:* Resource Centre; Open to public

Epilepsy Association of Calgary / Association d'épilepsie de Calgary
4112 - 4th St. NW, Calgary AB T2K 1A2
Tel: 403-230-2764; *Fax:* 403-230-5766
Toll-Free: 866-374-5377
info@epilepsycalgary.com
www.epilepsycalgary.com
www.facebook.com/EpilepgyCalgary
twitter.com/epilepsycalgary
Overview: A small local organization founded in 1955
Mission: To address community needs related to epilepsy; to improve the quality of life of persons with epilepsy through a broad range of programs, education, advocacy, support
Affiliation(s): Canadian Epilepsy Alliance/Alliance Canadienne d'Epilepsié
Chief Officer(s):
Kathy Fyfe, Executive Director
kathyf@epilepsycalgary.com
Finances: *Funding Sources:* Memberships; donations; fundraising activities; United Way; Rotary Club
Staff Member(s): 5
Activities: *Awareness Events:* Epilepsy Education Month, Nov.; Purple Day for Epilepsy Awareness, March 26; *Speaker Service:* Yes; *Library* Open to public by appointment

Central Alberta Office
4811 - 48th St., Red Deer AB T4N 1S6
Tel: 403-358-3358; *Fax:* 403-358-3595
Chief Officer(s):
Norma Jaskela, Program Coordinator
centralabinfo@epilepsycalgary.com

Epilepsy Association of Nova Scotia (EANS)
#306, 5880 Spring Garden Rd., Halifax NS B3H 1Y1
Tel: 902-429-2633; *Fax:* 902-425-0821
Toll-Free: 866-374-5377
info@epilepsyns.com
www.epilepsyns.com
Overview: A small provincial charitable organization founded in 1980
Mission: To provide support for people with epilepsy; to promote awareness, public understanding, & encourages research into the causes, treatment & prevention of epilepsy.
Member of: Epilepsy Foundation of America; Canadian Epilepsy Alliance
Chief Officer(s):
Suzanne Robichaud, President
Iris Elliott, Executive Director
iris@epilepsyns.com
Finances: *Funding Sources:* Donations; fundraising activities; grants
Membership: *Fees:* $15; *Committees:* Fundraising; Human Resources & Finance; Education; Nominations
Activities: Workshops; seminars; support groups; counselling & referral; education programs to schools, employers, institutions, mall displays; interviews with the media; newspaper ads; door-to-door campaign; *Speaker Service:* Yes; *Library:* Resource Library; Open to public by appointment
Publications:
• Epicure
Type: Newsletter; *Frequency:* 3 pa

Epilepsy Canada (EC) / Épilepsie Canada
#336, 2255B Queen St. East, Toronto ON M4E 1G3
Fax: 905-764-1231
Toll-Free: 877-734-0873
epilepsy@epilepsy.ca
www.epilepsy.ca
Overview: A medium-sized national charitable organization founded in 1966
Mission: To enhance the quality of life for persons affected by epilepsy; To promote & support research into all aspects of epilepsy; To facilitate educational initiatives; To increase public & professional awareness of epilepsy; To fund research; To encourage governments to address the needs of people with epilepsy
Member of: International Bureau for Epilepsy (IBE); Canadian League Against Epilepsy
Chief Officer(s):
W. McIntyre Burnham, National President
mac.burnham@utoronto.ca
Finances: *Funding Sources:* Donations; Corporate support
Activities: *Awareness Events:* National Epilepsy Awareness Month, March
Awards:
• Epilepsy Scholarship Awards (Scholarship)

Epilepsy Ontario / Épilepsie Ontario
#803, 3100 Steeles Ave. East, Markham ON L3R 8T3
Tel: 905-474-9696; *Fax:* 905-474-3663
Toll-Free: 800-463-1119
info@epilepsyontario.org
epilepsyontario.org
www.facebook.com/epilepsyontario1
twitter.com/EpilepsyOntario
Overview: A medium-sized provincial charitable organization founded in 1956
Mission: To promote optimal quality of life for people living with seizure disorders; to advocate for awareness, support services & research into these disorders and maintains a network of local agencies, contacts & associates to provide services, counselling & referrals.
Affiliation(s): Canadian Epilepsy Alliance; Epilepsy Canada
Chief Officer(s):
Rozalyn Werner-Arcé, Executive Director
rozalyn@epilepsyontario.org
Finances: *Funding Sources:* Gaming; public donations; special events
Membership: 17 chapters; *Fees:* Schedule available; *Member Profile:* Provincial/local chapters; *Committees:* Executive
Activities: Conferences; children's camp; chapter development; education; youth camps; *Speaker Service:* Yes; *Library:* Resource Centre; Open to public by appointment

Durham Region
#3, 310 Byron St. South, Whitby ON L1N 4P8
Tel: 905-430-3090; *Fax:* 905-430-3080
support@epilepsydurham.com
www.epilepsydurham.com
www.facebook.com/304187106330134
www.youtube.com/user/DurhamEpilepsy
Chief Officer(s):
Dianne McKenzie, Executive Director
dianne.mckenzie@epilepsydurham.com

Halton Peel Hamilton Region
#4, 2160 Dunwin Dr., Mississauga ON L5L 5M8
Tel: 905-450-1900
Toll-Free: 855-734-2111
info@epilepsypeel.org
epilepsyhaltonpeel.org
www.facebook.com/epilepsy.haltonpeelhamilton
twitter.com/EpilepsyHPH
www.youtube.com/channel/UCMs-90lDVPBUXoUi4tUv0Zw
Chief Officer(s):
Cynthia Milburn, Executive Director
executive.director@ehph.org

Huron-Perth
PO Box 1111, 19 Main St. South, Seaforth ON N0K 1W0
Tel: 519-527-0033; *Fax:* 519-527-2533
Toll-Free: 877-427-0033
ed.epilepsy@tcc.on.ca
www.epilepsyhpb.ca
www.facebook.com/EpilepsyHuronPerthBruceGrey
Chief Officer(s):
Andrea Longstaff, Executive Director

London & Area
690 Hale St., London ON N5W 1H4
Tel: 519-433-4073; *Fax:* 519-433-4079
support@epilepsysupport.ca
www.epilepsysupportcentre.com
www.facebook.com/epilepsysupport
twitter.com/EpilepsySC
www.youtube.com/user/EpilepsyLondon
Chief Officer(s):
Donna Pammer, Executive Director

Ottawa-Carleton
#207, 211 Bronson Ave., Ottawa ON K1R 6H5
Tel: 613-594-9255
Toll-Free: 866-374-5377
info@epilepsyottawa.ca
www.epilepsyottawa.ca
www.facebook.com/256201539316
twitter.com/Epilepsy_Ottawa
Chief Officer(s):
Peter Andrews, President

Peterborough & Area
Charlotte Mews, PO Box 2453, #4, 203 Simcoe St., Peterborough ON K9J 7Y8
Tel: 705-876-0311; *Fax:* 705-876-0109
Toll-Free: 800-463-1119
epilepsyptbo@yahoo.ca
Chief Officer(s):
Tom Appleby, Executive Director

Simcoe County
Victoria Village, #10, 72 Ross St., Barrie ON L4N 1G3
Tel: 705-737-3132; *Fax:* 705-737-5045
Toll-Free: 866-374-5377
epilepsysimcoecounty@rogers.com
www.facebook.com/epilepsysimcoecountybarrie

Southeastern Ontario
100 Stuart St., Kingston ON K7L 2V6
Tel: 613-542-6222; *Fax:* 613-548-4162
Toll-Free: 866-374-5377
admin@epilepsyresource.org
www.epilepsyresource.org
www.facebook.com/218186528201770
twitter.com/EpilepsyResourc
Chief Officer(s):
Susan Harrison, Executive Director
susanharrison@epilepsyresource.org

Timmins
733 Ross Ave. East, Timmins ON P4N 8S8
Tel: 705-264-2933; *Fax:* 705-264-0350
Toll-Free: 866-374-5377
info@seizurebraininjurycentre.com
www.seizurebraininjurycentre.com
www.facebook.com/seizurebraininjurycentre
twitter.com/letstalkbrain
Chief Officer(s):
Rhonda Latendresse, Executive Director
rhondal@seizurebraininjurycentre.com
Jacques Arbic, President

Toronto
#210, 468 Queen St. East, Toronto ON M5A 1T7
Tel: 416-964-9095; *Fax:* 416-964-2492
info@epilepsytoronto.org
www.epilepsytoronto.org
www.facebook.com/epilepsytoronto
twitter.com/epilepsytoronto
Chief Officer(s):
Geoff Bobb, Executive Director
gbobb@epilepsytoronto.org

Waterloo/Wellington
#5, 165 Hollinger Cres., Kitchener ON N2K 2Z2
Tel: 519-745-2112; *Fax:* 519-745-2435
epilepsy@epilww.com
www.epilww.com
www.linkedin.com/company/2661873
www.facebook.com/epilww
twitter.com/epilepsy_ww
Chief Officer(s):
Jennifer Lyon, Service Co-ordinator

Windsor/Essex County
Epilepsy Support Centre, 690 Hale St., London ON N5W 1H4
Tel: 519-433-4073; *Fax:* 519-433-4079
support@epilepsysupport.ca
epilepsysupport.ca
www.facebook.com/epilepsysupport
twitter.com/EpilepsySC
www.youtube.com/user/EpilepsyLondon
Chief Officer(s):
Mary Secco, Director, Strategic Initiatives

York Region
11181 Yonge St., Richmond Hill ON L4S 1L2
Tel: 905-508-5404; *Fax:* 905-508-0920
info@epilepsyyork.org
www.epilepsyyork.org
www.facebook.com/epilepsyyorkregion
Chief Officer(s):
Paul Raymond, Executive Director

Epilepsy Saskatoon
#203, 320 - 21 St. West, Saskatoon SK S7M 4E6
Tel: 306-665-1939; *Fax:* 306-665-0300
epilepsysaskatoon@sasktel.net
www.epilepsysask.com
www.facebook.com/EpilepsySaskatoon
www.pinterest.com/epilepsysask
Overview: A small local charitable organization founded in 1978
Mission: To improve the quality of life of persons with epilepsy through a broad range of programs, education, support of research & the delivery of needed services to people with epilepsy & their families
Member of: Canadian Epilepsy Alliance
Finances: *Funding Sources:* Membership fees; United Way
Activities: *Awareness Events:* Epilepsy Month, Mar.; *Speaker Service:* Yes; *Rents Mailing List:* Yes; *Library:* ES Resource Centre

Equestrian Association for the Disabled
8360 Leeming Rd., RR#3, Mount Hope ON L0R 1W0
Tel: 905-679-8323
admin@tead.on.ca
www.tead.on.ca
www.facebook.com/groups/10456337610/?fref=ts
Also Known As: TEAD
Overview: A small local charitable organization founded in 1978
Mission: To enhance the life of children & adults with physical, mental, & emotional handicaps, through equestrian therapy
Chief Officer(s):
Bill Evoy, Executive Director, 905-679-8323 Ext. 225
bill@tead.on.ca
Allison Woodall, Coordinator, Volunteers
Pat Bullock, Instructor, Riding
pat@tead.on.ca
Finances: *Funding Sources:* Donations; Grants; Fundraising
Membership: *Fees:* $10 individuals; $15 families; $25 groups; $100 companies; $1,000 corporate or lifetime memberships
Activities: Offering riding therapy, rehabilitation, & recreation to children & adults with disabilities
Publications:
• The Rocking Horse Review
Type: Newsletter; *Frequency:* Quarterly; *Price:* Free with membership in the Equestrian Association for the Disabled
Profile: Volunteer & rider news, plus upcoming events

ÉquiLibre - Groupe d'action sur le poids
#304, 7200, rue Hutchison, Montréal QC H3N 1Z2
Tél: 514-270-3779; *Téléc:* 514-270-1974
Ligne sans frais: 877-270-3779
info@equilibre.ca
www.equilibre.ca
Nom précédent: Collectif action alternative en obésité
Aperçu: *Dimension:* petite; *Envergure:* locale; Organisme sans but lucratif
Mission: Favoriser la prévention et la diminution des problèmes reliés au poids et à l'image corporelle par l'élaboration d'actions de sensibilisation, et la conception de programmes et d'outils éducatifs à l'intention de la population et des professionnels de la santé
Membre(s) du bureau directeur:
Fannie Dagenais, Directrice
fannie.dagenais@equilibre.ca
Finances: *Budget de fonctionnement annuel:* $100,000-$250,000
Membre(s) du personnel: 10
Membre: 100-499

Equine Association of Yukon (EAY)
PO Box 30011, Whitehorse YT Y1A 5M2
e-mail: equineyukon@gmail.com
equineyukon.weebly.com
www.facebook.com/EquineYukon
Overview: A small provincial organization
Mission: To be the governing body for equine sports in the Yukon.
Membership: *Fees:* $20 junior; $30 senior; $70 family

Equine Canada (EC) / Canada Hippique
#100, 2685 Queensview Dr., Ottawa ON K2B 8K2
Tel: 613-248-3433; *Fax:* 613-248-3484
Toll-Free: 866-282-8395
inquiries@equinecanada.ca
www.equinecanada.ca
www.facebook.com/385910086067
twitter.com/Equine_Canada
Previous Name: Canadian Equestrian Federation
Overview: A large national licensing charitable organization founded in 1977
Mission: To promote & develop a unified Canadian Equine Community, an economically viable horse industry, & access to the use of horses for leisure, sport & commerce
Affiliation(s): Provincial Partners: Horse Council of B.C., Alberta Equestrian Federation, Saskatchewan Horse Federation, Manitoba Horse Council, Ontario Equestrian Federation, Fédération Équestre du Quebec, New Brunswick Equestrian Association, PEI Horse Council, Nova Scotia Equestrian Federation, Newfoundland Equestrian Association, Canadian Pony Club
Chief Officer(s):
Mike Gallagher, President
mike4755@nb.sympatico.ca
Michael Arbour, CMA, Interim CEO/CFO, 613-248-3433 Ext. 108
marbour@equinecanada.ca
Craig Andreas, COO, 613-248-3433 Ext. 145
candreas@equinecanada.ca
Finances: *Funding Sources:* Government of Canada; Donations; Memberships
Membership: 56 corporate + 1,165 associate + 4,897 senior + 183 lifetime + 1,736 junior + 436 junior associate; *Fees:* $250 corporate-syndicate; $35 associate; $78 senior; $700 lifetime; $58 junior; $25 junior associate; *Member Profile:* License Profile: Senior Competitive License Holder - owner, lessee, agent, trainer, or EC certified coach; Junior Competitive License Holder - under 18 with the same qualifications; Lifetime - senior license holder level with the same qualifications; Corporate-syndicate - corporations, business enterprises & syndicates which own a horse or horses; Associate - wishes to compete in EC Provincial Circuit shows, or a member of a breed association competing at EC member shows in that breed's classes only; *Committees:* Audit; Bylaws & Governance; Equine ID; ERRR; Ethics; Finance; Health & Welfare; Nomination; Joint Steering; Recognition & Awards; Technology; Sport Council Committees: Athletes; Coaching; Competitions; Equine Medications; Finance; High Performance; Human Medications; National Rules; Officials; Stewards
Activities: Coaching program; Rider preparation program; *Awareness Events:* Horse Week; *Rents Mailing List:* Yes
Awards:
• Canadian Bred Horse of the Year (Award)
• Canadian Breeder of the Year (Award)
• Equestrian of the Year - The Doctor George Jacobsen Trophy (Award)
• Junior Equestrian of the Year - The Gillian Wilson Trophy (Award)
• Volunteer of the Year (Award)
Presented by BFL Canada

• Media Award - The Susan Jane Anstey Trophy (Award)
Presented by BFL Canada
• Just Add Horses Environmental Award (Award)
Presented by BFL Canada
• Lifetime Achievement Award (Award)
Presented by BFL Canada
Meetings/Conferences: • Equine Canada 2015 Annual Convention & Awards Gala, March, 2015, Crowne Plaza Gatineau-Ottawa, Ottawa, ON
Scope: National
Description: Meetings & clinics, plus the Equine Canada Awards Gala, for persons involved in equestrian sport, recreations, & industry from across Canada
Contact Information: Manager, Events: Fleur Tipton, Phone: 613-287-1515, ext. 111, E-mail: ftipton@equinecanada.ca
Publications:
• Horse Life
Type: Magazine
Profile: Updates for dressage, driving, endurance, eventing, hunter/jumper, paraequestian, reining, vaulting, breeds, industry news

Equitas - Centre international d'éducation aux droits humains *See* Equitas - International Centre for Human Rights Education

Equitas - International Centre for Human Rights Education / Equitas - Centre international d'éducation aux droits humains
#1100, 666 Sherbrooke St. West, Montréal QC H3A 1E7
Tel: 514-954-0382; *Fax:* 514-954-0659
info@equitas.org
www.equitas.org
www.linkedin.com/groups/Equitas-International-Centre-Human-Rights-1828
twitter.com/equitasintl
www.youtube.com/user/EquitasHRE
Previous Name: Canadian Human Rights Foundation
Overview: A medium-sized national charitable organization founded in 1967
Mission: To provide human rights education in Canada & abroad, based on the principles elaborated in the Universal Declaration of Human Rights
Chief Officer(s):
Rob Yalden, President
Ian Hamilton, Executive Director
ihamilton@equitas.org
Staff Member(s): 23
Activities: *Internships:* Yes; *Speaker Service:* Yes

Eriksdale & District Chamber of Commerce
PO Box 434, Eriksdale MB R0C 0W0
Tel: 204-739-2606
www.eriksdale.com
Overview: A small local organization
Chief Officer(s):
Keith Lundale, President
klundale@mts.net

Erin Soaring Society
ON
Tel: 905-838-5000
Overview: A small local organization overseen by Soaring Association of Canada
Chief Officer(s):
Peter Rawes, Contact
peter_rawes@rogers.com

Eritrean Canadian Community Centre of Metropolitan Toronto (ECCC)
579 St. Clair Ave. West, Toronto ON M6C 1A3
Tel: 416-658-8580; *Fax:* 416-658-7442
info@eccctoronto.ca
www.eccctoronto.ca
Overview: A small local organization founded in 1985
Mission: To provide immigrant & refugee settlement services & create an environment for building capacity in the Eritrean community of Toronto.

Ernest C. Manning Awards Foundation / Fondation des Prix Ernest C. Manning
#267, 3553 - 31 St. NW, Calgary AB T2L 2K7
Tel: 403-930-4332; *Fax:* 403-930-4329
info@manningawards.ca
www.manningawards.ca
www.linkedin.com/company/ernest-c-manning-awards-foundation
www.facebook.com/ManningAwards
twitter.com/manningawardsca
www.youtube.com/user/TheManningAwards
Overview: A small national organization
Mission: To recognize & encourage innovation in Canada. An independent committee of expert evaluators chooses the award winners from a selection of nominees & their decision is final.
Chief Officer(s):
John K. Read, Chair
Membership: *Committees:* Selection
Awards:
• The Manning Awards (Award)
Given annually to Canadian innovators who have conceived & developed new concepts, procedures, processes or products of benefit to Canada; awards may be in any area of activity*Deadline:* February *Amount:* One $100,000 Principal Award; one $25,000 Award of Distinction; two $10,000 Innovation prizes
• Young Canadian Innovation Awards (Award)
Amount: $4,000 ea./8 recipients

Errington Therapeutic Riding Association (ETRA)
Pyramid Stables, PO Box 462, 7581 Harby Rd., Lantzville, Parksville BC V9P 2G6
e-mail: etrainfo@shaw.ca
www.etra.ca
Overview: A small local organization founded in 1989
Mission: ETRA is an independent, non-profit association that gives people with disabilities the chance to ride a horse, to improve their physical and/or mental well-being, & enhance their sense of achievement & self-worth.
Member of: CanTRA; B.C. Therapeutic Riding Association
Affliation(s): BC Therapeutic Riding Association; Canadian Therapeutic Riding Association
Chief Officer(s):
Barry Galenzoski, President
barry.galenzoski@etra.ca
Finances: *Annual Operating Budget:* Less than $50,000; *Funding Sources:* Provincial government; rider fees; donations; community organizations
40 volunteer(s)
Membership: 112; *Fees:* $5; *Committees:* Volunteer Coordinator; Program Coordinator; Pledge Ride; Horse & Stable Care; Newsletter; Publicity
Activities: *Speaker Service:* Yes

ERS Training & Development Corporation (ERS) / Corporation pour la formation et le développement ERS
#810, 5250, rue Ferrier, Montréal QC H4P 1L4
Tel: 514-731-3419; *Fax:* 514-731-4999
ers@erstraining.ca
www.erstraining.ca
Overview: A medium-sized national charitable organization founded in 1986
Mission: To promote development & training; to identify the needs of youth; to develop & promote training skills & employment readiness; to seek out & put in place programs for the improvement of youth circumstances; to implement programs so that all may achieve full potential
Chief Officer(s):
Peter L. Clément, Président et directeur général
peterclement@erstraining.ca
Finances: *Annual Operating Budget:* $250,000-$500,000
Staff Member(s): 8; 7 volunteer(s)
Membership: 15; *Fees:* $25 annually
Activities: *Internships:* Yes

Est club portugais de Montréal *Voir* Clube Oriental Português de Montreal

Escadrilles canadiennes de plaisance *See* Canadian Power & Sail Squadrons (Canadian Headquarters)

Eskasoni Fish & Wildlife Commission (EFWC)
4115 Shore Rd., Eskasoni NS B1W 1C2
Tel: 902-379-2024; *Fax:* 902-379-2159
info@efwc.ca
www.efwc.ca
Overview: A small local organization founded in 1991
Mission: To facilitate the Aboriginal Fisheries Strategy agreement; to create partnerships with other agencies & organizations dealing with fish & wildlife

The ESOP (Employee Share Ownership Plan) Association *See* ESOP Association Canada

ESOP Association Canada (ESOP)
www.esop-canada.com
Previous Name: The ESOP (Employee Share Ownership Plan) Association
Overview: A small national organization founded in 1990
Mission: To promote & assist the implementation of employee share ownership through education, networking & lobbying
Member of: Canadian Advanced Technology Alliance
Affliation(s): National Centre for Employee Ownership
Staff Member(s): 1; 12 volunteer(s)
Membership: *Fees:* $240

Espanola & District Association for Community Living *See* Community Living Espanola

Espanola & District Chamber of Commerce *See* LaCloche Foothills Chamber of Commerce

Esperanto Association of Canada (KEA) / Association canadienne d'esperanto
6358-A, rue de Bordeaux, Montréal QC H2G 2R8
www.esperanto.ca/en/kea
Also Known As: Kanada Esperanto-Asocio
Overview: A small national charitable organization founded in 1958
Mission: To promote & teach the neutral international language of Esperanto
Affliation(s): Universal Esperanto Association - Rotterdam
Chief Officer(s):
Normand Fleury, President
Finances: *Annual Operating Budget:* Less than $50,000; *Funding Sources:* Membership fees; donations
Staff Member(s): 1; 9 volunteer(s)
Membership: 40 lifetime + 150 individual; *Fees:* $10 limited income; $30 individual; $45 family; $750 life; *Member Profile:* Interest in international language; *Committees:* Esperanto Book Service; Publications; Nominations
Activities: Correspondence courses; examination service; mail-order book service, 514/272-0151; publishing of books & periodicals in & on the language Esperanto; *Awareness Events:* Week of International Friendship, last full week of Feb.; Zamenhof Day, Dec. 15; *Internships:* Yes; *Speaker Service:* Yes; *Rents Mailing List:* Yes; *Library:* Libraro Ludovika; by appointment

Esperanto-Rondo de Toronto (ERT) / Toronto Esperanto Circle
4 Craig Alan Ct., Toronto ON M9P 1K4
Tel: 416-536-1300; *Fax:* 416-536-5110
esperanto.toronto@gmail.com
esperanto.ca/toronto
Previous Name: Toronto Esperanto-Klubo
Overview: A small local organization founded in 1950
Mission: To provide a social home base for individuals wishing to learn & practise the international language, Esperanto; To provide the necessary information & courses about Esperanto
Affliation(s): Canadian Esperanto Association
Chief Officer(s):
Scott Dawson, President
Kathy Toy, Vice-President
Alice Kazmierowski, Secretary
Finances: *Annual Operating Budget:* Less than $50,000
Membership: 20; *Fees:* $15 individual
Activities: Weekly meetings; *Speaker Service:* Yes; *Library* by appointment

Esprit Orchestra
#511, 174 Spadina Ave., Toronto ON M5T 2C2
Tel: 416-815-7887; *Fax:* 416-815-7337
info@espritorchestra.com
www.espritorchestra.com
www.facebook.com/pages/Esprit-Orchestra/162784130429573
twitter.com/espritorchestra
www.youtube.com/EspritOrchestra
Overview: A small local charitable organization founded in 1983 overseen by Orchestras Canada
Mission: To present "new music" programs & collaborative arts events; to act as an example for new music groups to develop similar programs which strengthen the new music community as a whole
Chief Officer(s):
Gloria Baldwin, Director, Development & Operations
Alex Pauk, Music Director
Finances: *Funding Sources:* Government; private foundations; individual donations
Staff Member(s): 5

Activities: Concerts; education series; outreach programs; recording for film

Esquimalt Chamber of Commerce

PO Box 36019, 1153 Esquimalt Rd., Victoria BC V9A 7J5
Tel: 250-704-2525; *Fax:* 250-380-6932
admin@esquimaltchamber.ca
esquimaltchamber.ca
www.facebook.com/EsquimaltChamber
twitter.com/esqchamber
Overview: A small local organization founded in 1947
Chief Officer(s):
Chuck Palmer, President, 250-727-9191
chuck.palmer@investorsgroup.com
Finances: *Annual Operating Budget:* Less than $50,000; *Funding Sources:* Membership dues
30 volunteer(s)
Membership: 139; *Fees:* $150 regular; $120 home-based; $95 retired; *Member Profile:* Business licence to operate within municipality of Esquimalt
Activities: *Speaker Service:* Yes

Essa Historical Society

c/o Olive Lee, 20 Henry St., Thornton ON L0L 2N0
Tel: 705-458-9971
Overview: A small local organization founded in 1979
Mission: To update the history of Essa Township; to promote the preservation of historical buildings & landmarks.
Member of: Ontario Historical Society
Affliation(s): Simcoe County Historical Society
Chief Officer(s):
Arnold Banting, President, 705-719-6535
Olive Lee, Secretary
teddylee1@rogers.com
Membership: *Fees:* $10 single; $20 couple
Activities: Undertakes historical research & identifies historical landmarks in Essa Township
Publications:
• Early History of Ivy
Type: book
Profile: A collection of photos & information on the hamlet of Ivy

Les EssentiElles

Centre de la francophonie, 302, rue Strickland, Whitehorse YT Y1A 2K1
Tél: 867-668-2636; *Téléc:* 867-668-3511
elles@essentielles.ca
www.lesessentielles.ca
Aperçu: *Dimension:* moyenne; *Envergure:* locale
Mission: De représenter les intérêts des femmes francophones du Yukon.
Membre de: Fédération nationale des femmes canadiennes françaises; Réseau canadien pour la santé des femmes; Nouveau Départ; Assemblée des aînées et aînés francophones du Canada; Association franco-yukonnaise; Partenariat communauté en santé; Partenariat communauté en éducation
Membre(s) du bureau directeur:
Ketsia Houde, Directrice
Membre(s) du personnel: 3
Activités: Projet: Le Partenariat communauté en santé

Essex Community Services (ECS)

#7, 35 Victoria Ave., Essex ON N8M 1M4
Tel: 519-776-4231; *Fax:* 519-776-4966
ecs@essexcs.on.ca
www.essexcs.on.ca
Previous Name: Community Information - Essex
Overview: A small local charitable organization founded in 1975 overseen by InformOntario
Mission: The organization provides a number of services to members of the community, including door-to-door transporation assistance for seniors, coat collection for children, income tax clinic, job bank, community resource library.
Affliation(s): Inform Canada
Chief Officer(s):
Kelly Stack, Executive Director
director@essexcs.on.ca
Staff Member(s): 5; 40 volunteer(s)
Activities: "Share the Warmth"; job kiosk; fundraising; community crisis centre; children's crisis centre; Hiatus House; counselling; housing info services; Care-A-Van; Foot Care Clinic; Income Tax Clinic; Coats for Kids; Letter Carrier's Alert; Security Reassurance; *Library:* Resource

Essex County Cattlemen's Association

#310, 5568 Lakeshore Rd., RR#2, Essex ON N0P 1J0
Tel: 519-687-2530; *Fax:* 519-687-3792
Overview: A small local organization
Affliation(s): Ontario Cattlemen's Association
Chief Officer(s):
Shawn Morris, President
shawn@jackmorrisauctions.com

Essex County Orchid Society

280 Howards Ave., Windsor ON N0R 1L0
essexcountyorchidsociety.webs.com
www.facebook.com/EssexCountyOrchidSociety
Overview: A small local organization founded in 2009
Mission: To provide knowledge & information to its members
Member of: Canadian Orchid Congress; American Orchid Society; Mid-America Orchid Congress
Chief Officer(s):
Barb Morden, President
barbmorden@cogeco.ca
Membership: *Fees:* $20 single; $25 family

Essex County Stamp Club (Windsor)

Tel: 519-966-2276
www.essexcountystampclub.com
Overview: A small local organization founded in 1978
Mission: To promote stamp collecting to all ages; To learn by collecting & taking care of a collection
Affliation(s): American Philatelic Society; Royal Philatelic Society of Canada
Chief Officer(s):
Brian Cutler, President
cutler@mnsi.net
Finances: *Annual Operating Budget:* Less than $50,000; *Funding Sources:* Membership fees; annual show
Staff Member(s): 5
Membership: 62; *Fees:* $15; *Member Profile:* All ages 18+; *Committees:* Executive
Activities: Slide shows; guest speakers; auction; youth program; *Awareness Events:* WINPEX Annual Show, 1st Sat. in March

Essex Law Association

245 Windsor Ave., Windsor ON N9A 1J2
Tel: 519-252-8418; *Fax:* 519-252-9686
info@essexlaw.ca
www.essexlaw.ca
Overview: A small local organization founded in 1884
Chief Officer(s):
Ronald Reaume, President
Staff Member(s): 2
Membership: 500+; *Fees:* $105 regular/affiliated; $50 faculty
Activities: *Library:* County Courthouse Library
Awards:
• Essex Law Association Centennial Scholarship (Scholarship)
Eligibility: Students in the law program at the University of Windsor
Publications:
• Caveat
Type: Newsletter

Essex-Kent Cage Bird Society

1647 Jefferson Blvd., Windsor ON N8T 2V6
Tel: 519-948-6398
www.essexkentcbs.com
Overview: A small local organization founded in 1976
Mission: To promote the caring, breeding & keeping of all cage birds in captivity; To establish interest & to educate the members & the general public in the proper care of cage birds; To collect & make available any scientific knowledge on the breeding, care & improvement of any species of cage birds
Member of: Avicultural Advancement Council of Canada
Affliation(s): Avian Preservation Foundation; National Finch & Softbill Society; National Cockatiel Society; African Lovebird Society; North American Parrot Society
Chief Officer(s):
Alfred Mion, President, 519-948-6398
julianne@mnsi.net
Finances: *Annual Operating Budget:* Less than $50,000; *Funding Sources:* Donations; exhibitions
Membership: 165; *Fees:* $30 family or single; $20 junior; *Member Profile:* Bird keepers & breeders, exhibitors & pets
Activities: 2 shows per year - Young Feather Show (Summer); Annual Show (Fall); monthly meetings with occasional guest speakers

Esterhazy & District Chamber of Commerce

PO Box 778, Esterhazy SK S0A 0X0
Tel: 306-745-5405; *Fax:* 306-745-6797
esterhazy.ed@sasktel.net
www.facebook.com/group.php?gid=195692180461817
Overview: A small local organization
Mission: To contribute to the development & growth of the business environment in Esterhazy Saskatchewan & the surrounding area
Member of: Saskatchewan Chamber of Commerce
Finances: *Annual Operating Budget:* Less than $50,000
Membership: 60; *Fees:* $85

Estevan & District Labour Committee

270 Duncan Rd., Estevan SK S4A 4A6
Overview: A small local organization overseen by Saskatchewan Federation of Labour
Mission: To promote the interests of affiliates in Estevan, Saskatchewan & the surrounding region; To advance the economic & social welfare of workers
Affliation(s): Canadian Labour Congress (CLC)
Chief Officer(s):
Sammy Dryden, Acting President, 306-634-3292
s.g.dryden@sasktel.net
Activities: Presenting educational opportunities; Raising awareness of occupational health & safety; Organizing a ceremony to mark the annual Day of Mourning for Workers Killed & Injured on the Job

Estevan Arts Council

Souris Valley Aquatic & Leisure Centre, 701 Souris Ave., Estevan SK S4A 2T1
Tel: 306-634-3942
estevanartscouncil@sasktel.net
www.estevanartscouncil.com
Overview: A small local charitable organization founded in 1967
Mission: To promote the arts & culture in Estevan & area
Member of: Organization of Saskatchewan Arts Councils
Finances: *Annual Operating Budget:* $50,000-$100,000; *Funding Sources:* Grants; donations; workshop fees; ticket sales
Staff Member(s): 1; 15 volunteer(s)
Membership: 15; *Committees:* Stars for Saskatchewan; Koncerts for Kids; Visual Arts
Activities: Art, painting, drawing, ceramics & pottery classes; "koncerts for kids"; Stars for Saskatchewan Concert Series

Estevan Chamber of Commerce

#2, 322 - 4th St., Estevan SK S4A 0T8
Tel: 306-634-2828; *Fax:* 306-634-6729
admin@estevanchamber.ca
www.estevanchamber.ca
www.linkedin.com/company/estevan-chamber-of-commerce
www.facebook.com/347557745256291
twitter.com/EstevanChamber
Also Known As: Estevan Chamber
Overview: A small local organization founded in 1904
Mission: To improve the business climate and community well being
Member of: Saskatchewan Chamber of Commerce; Canadian Chamber of Commerce; Canada North America Trade Corridor; SKEconomic Developers Association, Economic Developers Association of Canada, Tourism Saskatchewan
Chief Officer(s):
Ken Rowan, President
Michel Cyrenne, Executive Director, 306-637-2151
michel@estevanchamber.ca
Rebecca Howie, Marketing & Events Coordinator, 306-637-2150
rebecca@estevanchamber.ca
Manpreet Sangha, Economic Development Officer, 306-637-2191
manpreet@estevanchamber.ca
Finances: *Funding Sources:* Membership fundraising; business directory sales, events, contracted services
Staff Member(s): 4
Membership: 343; *Fees:* Schedule available; *Member Profile:* Any reputable person, directly or indirectly engaged or interested in trade, commerce or the economic & social welfare of the district; *Committees:* Economic Development & Tourism
Activities: All candidates political forums; community-wide customer service evaluation; trade show; Farmers' Appreciation; educational seminars; leadership seminars; advocacy for business community, economic developmeny, tourism development; *Awareness Events:* Farmers Appreciation, Feb.; Leadership Seminar, Estevan Business Excellence Awards, Showcase; Pure Energy Weekend, Kickoff to Christmas
Awards:
• Estevan Comprehensive High School Bursary (Scholarship)
• South East Regional College Bursary (Scholarship)

Estevan Exhibition Association
PO Box 100, 811 Souris Ave., Estevan SK S4A 2A2
Tel: 306-634-5595; *Fax:* 306-634-8833
eea@sasktel.net
Overview: A small local organization founded in 1905
Mission: To promotes agriculture, recreation & the development of community spirit.
Member of: Western Canada Fairs; CAFE; Saskatchewan Southeast Tourism Association; Estevan Chamber of Commerce; Saskatchewan Association of Agricultural Societies & Exhibitions (SAASE)
Chief Officer(s):
Dallas Spencer, President
Activities: Annual Estevan Fair; Annual Rodeo; Rumble in the Dirt Cabaret

Eston Arts Council
PO Box 327, Eston SK S0L 1A0
Overview: A small local charitable organization
Member of: Organization of Saskatchewan Arts Councils
Finances: *Annual Operating Budget:* Less than $50,000; *Funding Sources:* Fundraising; grants
25 volunteer(s)
Membership: 1-99
Activities: Art shows; drama presentations

Eston United Way
PO Box 23, Eston SK S0L 1A0
Tel: 306-962-3962
cassjacqui@sasktel.net
Overview: A small local organization overseen by United Way of Canada - Centraide Canada
Mission: Raising money in order to create positive and lasting changes in communities.

Estonian Evangelical Lutheran Church Consistory (EELC)
383 Jarvis St., Toronto ON M5B 2C7
Tel: 416-925-5465; *Fax:* 416-925-5688
e.e.l.k@eelk.ee
www.eelk.ee
Overview: A small national organization founded in 1950
Mission: EELC is an independent, self-governing church which functions on democratic grounds, calls together congregations, ordains pastors, holds services & carries out religious ceremonies according to the Service Book, the Statutes & the established order. The Consistory is the government of the EELC.
Affliation(s): Lutheran World Federation; World Council of Churches
Chief Officer(s):
Udo Petersoo, Archbishop & Dean of Canada
udo.petersoo@eelk.ee
Staff Member(s): 4; 10 volunteer(s)
Membership: 7,200 + 13 churches

ETC Group
ETC Headquarters, #206, 180 Metcalfe St., Ottawa ON K2P 1P5
Tel: 613-241-2267; *Fax:* 613-241-2506
etc@etcgroup.org
www.etcgroup.org
www.linkedin.com/company/2587794
www.facebook.com/theetcgroup
plus.google.com/115793847250050059887#115793847250050059887/posts
Also Known As: Action Group on Erosion, Technology & Concentration
Previous Name: Rural Advancement Foundation International
Overview: A small international organization founded in 1985
Chief Officer(s):
Mooney Pat Roy, Executive Director
Staff Member(s): 8; 2 volunteer(s)
Activities: *Library:* ETC Group Resource Library; by appointment

Ethics Practitioners' Association of Canada (EPAC) / Association des praticiens en éthique du Canada (APEC)
51 Dalgleish Ave., Kingston ON K7L 5H6
Tel: 613-547-2615; *Fax:* 613-822-8133
service@epac-apec.ca
www.epac-apec.ca
Overview: A small national organization
Mission: To enable individuals to work successfully in the field of ethics in organizations by enhancing the quality & availability of ethics advice & services across Canada
Chief Officer(s):
Allan Pedden, Chair
Membership: *Fees:* $75 individual; $150 organization; $25 student; *Committees:* Membership; Revenue Generation; Communications; Education; Governance & Planning; Audit & Risk Management; Workshop Task Force; Privacy
Activities: *Internships:* Yes
Publications:
• PAC/APEC Magazine
Type: Magazine

EthicsCentre.ca
#1801, 1 Yonge St., Toronto ON M5E 1W7
Tel: 416-368-7525; *Fax:* 416-369-0515
info@ethicscentre.ca
www.ethicscentre.ca
www.linkedin.com/company/2455638
twitter.com/ethicscentre
Also Known As: Canadian Centre for Ethics & Corporate Policy
Overview: A small national charitable organization founded in 1988
Mission: To champion the application of ethical values in the decision making processes of businesses & other organizations
Chief Officer(s):
Hélène Yaremko-Jarvis, Executive Director
hmyj@ethicscentre.ca
Lois Marsh, Contact, Administration
lmarsh@ethicscentre.ca
Finances: *Annual Operating Budget:* $50,000-$100,000
Staff Member(s): 2; 30 volunteer(s)
Membership: 100; *Fees:* $50-$100 individual; $250-$999 business; $1000-$2499 contributing; $2500-$4999 supporting; $5000-$9999 sustaining; *Committees:* Program; Communications; Development; Nominating & Governance
Activities: Luncheon series; *Speaker Service:* Yes

Ethiopiaid
#900, 275 Slater St., Ottawa ON K1P 5H9
Tel: 613-697-4843
info@ethiopiaid.ca
www.ethiopiaid.ca
twitter.com/EthiopiaidCAN
Overview: A medium-sized international organization founded in 1989
Mission: Ethiopiaid aims to create lasting and positive change in Ethiopia by tackling the problems of poverty, ill health and poor education.
As a fundraising organisation, it donates directly to local community projects in Ethiopia.

Ethiopian Association in Toronto (EAT)
1950 Danforth Ave., Toronto ON M4C 1J4
Tel: 416-694-1522; *Fax:* 416-694-8736
office@ethiocommun.org
www.ethiocommun.org
Overview: A small local organization founded in 1981 overseen by Ontario Council of Agencies Serving Immigrants
Chief Officer(s):
Busha Taa, President
Staff Member(s): 18
Membership: 1,500; *Fees:* $15
Activities: new-comers settlement services; crisis counselling; seniors programs; *Awareness Events:* Ethiopian-Canadian Day, September

Etobicoke Historical Society
c/o Montgomery's Inn, 4709 Dundas St. West, Toronto ON M9A 1A8
www.etobicokehistorical.com
www.facebook.com/pages/Etobicoke-Historical-Society/427420737349716
twitter.com/EtobHistory
Overview: A small local charitable organization founded in 1958
Mission: To engage in the collection, preservation & publication of material relevant to the history & heritage of Etobicoke; to support the preservation & restoration of historically significant properties in the community; to collect & catalogue a panorama of photographs of Etobicoke
Member of: Ontario Historical Society
Chief Officer(s):
James Geneau, President
james@united-thinking.com
Finances: *Funding Sources:* Provincial government; membership fees
Membership: *Fees:* $20 institution; $25 individual; $35 couple; $200 individual life; $250 couple life

Etobicoke Humane Society (EHS)
1500 Royal York Rd., Suite B, 2nd Fl., Toronto ON M9P 3B6
Tel: 416-249-6100; *Fax:* 416-249-6100
www.etobicokehumanesociety.com
www.facebook.com/etobicokehumanesociety
Overview: A medium-sized local charitable organization founded in 1987
Mission: To protect, care for, & advance the welfare of animals
Member of: Canadian Federation of Humane Societies
Affliation(s): Ontario Society for the Prevention of Cruelty to Animals (OSPCA)
Chief Officer(s):
Daniel Kushnir, Treasurer
Audrey Verge, Vice-President
William Blain, President
Michelle Anselmi, Vice-President
Finances: *Annual Operating Budget:* $50,000-$100,000; *Funding Sources:* Public donations; bequests; special events
40 volunteer(s)
Membership: 2,500; *Fees:* $25 regular; $50 special; *Committees:* Cat Adoption; Dog Adoption; Executive; Finance; Administration; Education; Fundraising; Animal Protection Services; PR; Membership/Volunteers; Shelter
Activities: Annual Dog Walk-a-Thon; Tag Day; Paws & Claws; Petsmart Santa Photos; *Library:* Pet Care Library; Open to public

Etobicoke North Community Information Centre *See* Albion Neighbourhood Services

Etobicoke Philharmonic Orchestra (EPO)
PO Box 60002, Stn. Thorncrest, 1500 Islington Ave, Toronto ON M9A 5G2
Tel: 416-239-5665
info@eporchestra.ca
www.eporchestra.ca
www.facebook.com/eporchestra
twitter.com/eporchestra
Overview: A small local charitable organization founded in 1960 overseen by Orchestras Canada
Mission: To provide an opportunity for trained amateur musicians to perform together & become acquainted with an orchestral repertoire; to provide the community with symphonic music, competently performed in a local setting; to assist serious music students in their studies through performance experience & a scholarship program
Member of: Arts Etobicoke; Ontario Federation of Symphony Orchestras
Chief Officer(s):
Judy Gargaro, General Manager
Domenic Meffe, President
Finances: *Funding Sources:* Government grants; fundraising projects; box office; corporate donations
Staff Member(s): 8; 36 volunteer(s)
Membership: 68 individual
Activities: *Library*

Eucahristic Apostles of the Divine Mercy (EADM)
c/o Rolando & Susan Dela Rosa, 49 Parsons Pl., Thornhill ON L4J 7Y4
Tel: 647-239-9350
smartinezd@hotmail.com
www.divinemercytoronto.com
www.youtube.com/user/DivineMercyWorks
Also Known As: EADM Cenacle Prayer Group of Toronto
Overview: A small local organization
Mission: To encourage members to care for the rejected, the lonely, the disabled, the elderly, & the dying
Affliation(s): Archdiocese of Toronto
Chief Officer(s):
Mario Salvadori, Spiritual Director
Activities: Meetings; youth retreat

European Evangelistic Crusade, Inc. *See* Global Outreach Mission Inc.

European Union Chamber of Commerce in Toronto (EUCOCIT)
#1500, 480 University Ave., Toronto ON M5G 1V2
Tel: 416-598-7087; *Fax:* 416-598-1840
info@eucocit.com
www.eucocit.com
www.linkedin.com/groups/European-Union-Chamber-Commerce-in-2924006
www.facebook.com/111523778875074
Overview: A large international organization founded in 1995

Mission: To strengthen economic ties between Canada & Europe; to act as the business voice of and the one point of contact for European business interests in Canada
Chief Officer(s):
Thomas Beck, President
Finances: *Funding Sources:* Membership fees; event revenue; sponsorships
Membership: 26; *Fees:* $250

Eva's Initiatives
#370, 215 Spadina Ave., Toronto ON M5T 2C7
Tel: 416-977-4497; *Fax:* 416-977-6210
info@evas.ca
www.evasinitiatives.com
twitter.com/evasinitiatives
Overview: A small local organization founded in 1992
Mission: To create opportunities for homeless youth
Chief Officer(s):
Maria Crawford, Executive Director
Staff Member(s): 110; 75 volunteer(s)
Awards:
• Eva's Initiatives - Award for Innovation
Three awards given to organizations working with the homeless or at-risk youth *Amount:* $5000

Evangel Hall Mission (EHM)
552 Adelaide St. West, Toronto ON M5V 3W8
Tel: 416-504-3563
information@evangelhall.ca
www.evangelhall.ca
www.facebook.com/104062456304727?fref=ts
twitter.com/ehm_1913
Overview: A small local charitable organization founded in 1913
Mission: A community agency delivering programs that deal with poverty and homelessness, offering a continuum of care from emergency food, clothing and shelter to transitional and long-term housing.
Affliation(s): Presbyterian Church in Canada
Activities: Health clinic; drop-in centre; laundry facilities; clothing drive; Out of the Cold program; youth programs
Publications:
• Faith, Hope, Love
Type: Book; *Price:* $50
Profile: A special commemorative book to celebrate 100 years of service to the community.

Evangel Hall Mission
552 Adelaide St. West, Toronto ON M5V 3W8
Tel: 416-504-3563; *Fax:* 416-504-8056
information@evangelhall.ca
www.evangelhall.ca
www.facebook.com/pages/ehm-Evangel-Hall-Mission/104062456304727
twitter.com/ehm_1913
www.youtube.com/user/TheEhm1913
Overview: A medium-sized local charitable organization
Mission: To provide food, shelter & social programs to homeless people in Toronto
Chief Officer(s):
Joseph Taylor, Executive Director
joseph.taylor@evangelhall.ca
Staff Member(s): 22

Evangelical Covenant Church of Canada (ECCC)
PO Box 23117, RPO McGillvray, Winnipeg MB R3R 5S3
Tel: 204-269-3437; *Fax:* 204-269-3584
office@covchurch.ca
www.canadacovenantchurch.org
Overview: A medium-sized national charitable organization founded in 1904
Member of: World Relief Canada; The Evangelical Fellowship of Canada; The Canadian Council of Christian Charities
Chief Officer(s):
Jeff Anderson, ECCC Conference Superintendent
ccc1@mts.net
Finances: *Funding Sources:* Donations
Membership: *Member Profile:* Evangelical Covenant Churches in Canada

Evangelical Fellowship of Canada (EFC) / Alliance évangélique du Canada
PO Box 5885, Stn. Beaver Creek, #103, 9821 Leslie St., Richmond Hill ON L4B 0B8
Tel: 905-479-5885; *Fax:* 905-479-4742
Toll-Free: 866-302-3362
efc@evangelicalfellowship.ca
www.evangelicalfellowship.ca
www.facebook.com/theefc
twitter.com/theefc
www.youtube.com/user/theEFCca
Overview: A medium-sized national charitable organization founded in 1964
Mission: EFC is the national association of evangelical Christians in Canada. Its aims are to be a public advocate of the gospel of Jesus Christ; to provide an evangelical identity which unites Canadian Christians of diverse backgrounds; to express biblical views on current issues; to assist individuals & groups in proclaiming the gospel & advancing Christian values.
Member of: World Evangelical Fellowship
Chief Officer(s):
Bill Fietje, Chair
Bruce J. Clemenger, President
Finances: *Annual Operating Budget:* $1.5 Million-$3 Million; *Funding Sources:* General & corporate donations; member & subscriber fees
Staff Member(s): 20; 90 volunteer(s)
Membership: 32 evangelical denominations + 110 organizations + 1,200 churches
Activities: Task forces: Evangelism; Women in Ministry; Aboriginal; Global Mission; Commissions: Education; Religious Liberty; Social Action; *Internships:* Yes; *Speaker Service:* Yes
Awards:
• Brian Stiller Leadership Award (Award)

Centre for Faith & Public Life
#1410, 130 Albert St., Ottawa ON K1P 5G4
Tel: 613-233-9868; *Fax:* 613-233-0301
ottawa@evangelicalfellowship.ca

Evangelical Lutheran Church in Canada (ELCIC)
#600, 177 Lombard Ave., Winnipeg MB R3B 0W5
Tel: 204-984-9173; *Fax:* 204-984-9185
Toll-Free: 888-786-6707
www.elcic.ca
www.facebook.com/CanadianLutherans
twitter.com/elcicinfo
Overview: A medium-sized national charitable organization founded in 1986
Mission: The Church shares the gospel of Jesus Christ with people in Canada & around the world through the proclamation of the Word, celebration of the sacraments, & through service in Christ's name. It functions through three major entities; nationally as the ELCIC, regionally as synods, & locally as congregations.
Member of: Canadian Council of Churches; Lutheran Council in Canada; Lutheran World Federation; World Council of Churches
Affliation(s): Anglican Church of Canada
Chief Officer(s):
Susan Johnson, Bishop, 204-984-9157
sjohnson@elcic.ca
Trina Gallop, Director, Communications & Stewardship, 204-984-9172
tgallop@elcic.ca
Gloria McNabb, Director, Finance & Administration, 204-984-9178
gmcnabb@elcic.ca
Finances: *Annual Operating Budget:* $1.5 Million-$3 Million; *Funding Sources:* Donations
Staff Member(s): 20
Membership: 153,000 individuals; 607 congregations; *Member Profile:* Current members in a congregation
Publications:
• Canada Lutheran
Type: Magazine; *Frequency:* Monthly; *Editor:* Kenn Ward
Profile: To engage the Evangelical Lutheran Church in Canada in a dynamic dialogue in which information, inspiration and ideas are shared in a thoughtful and stimulating way.

British Columbia Synod
80 - 10th Ave. East, New Westminster BC V3L 4R5
Tel: 604-524-1318; *Fax:* 604-524-9255
bcsynod@elcic.ca
www.bcsynod.org
Chief Officer(s):
Gregory Mohr, Bishop
gmohr@elcic.ca

Eastern Synod
74 Weber St. West, Kitchener ON N2H 3Z3
Tel: 519-743-1461; *Fax:* 519-743-4291
wegr@easternsynod.org
www.easternsynod.org
www.facebook.com/ESynodELCIC
twitter.com/ESynodELCIC
Chief Officer(s):
Michael J. Pryse, Bishop

Manitoba/Northwestern Ontario Synod
935 Nesbitt Bay, Winnipeg MB R3T 1X5
Tel: 204-889-3760; *Fax:* 204-896-0272
mnosynod@elcic.ca
www.mnosynod.org
www.facebook.com/123283781082392
Chief Officer(s):
Elaine Sauer, Bishop
esauer@elcic.ca

Saskatchewan Synod
714 Preston Ave., Saskatoon SK S7H 2V2
Tel: 306-244-2474; *Fax:* 306-664-8677
smckeown-closs@elcic.ca
www.sasksynod.elcic.ca
Chief Officer(s):
Cindy Halmarson, Bishop
chalmarson@elcic.ca

Synod of Alberta & the Territories
10014 - 81 Ave. NW, Edmonton AB T6E 1W8
Tel: 780-439-2636; *Fax:* 780-433-6623
Toll-Free: 866-430-2636
abtsynod@elcic.ca
www.albertasynod.ca
Chief Officer(s):
Larry Kochendorfer, Bishop

Evangelical Medical Aid Society Canada (EMAS)
#1, 20 Freel Lane, Stouffville ON L4A 5B9
Tel: 905-642-4661; *Fax:* 905-642-1616
Toll-Free: 866-648-0664
www.emascanada.org
Overview: A medium-sized international charitable organization founded in 1948
Mission: To heal, teach & serve in a Christlike manner
Chief Officer(s):
Peter Agwa, Executive Director
Ellen Watson, Director, Administration
ellen@emascanada.org
Finances: *Annual Operating Budget:* $500,000-$1.5 Million; *Funding Sources:* Private donations
Staff Member(s): 2; 200 volunteer(s)
Membership: 30
Activities: Healthcare-related programs with a spiritual component
Publications:
• EMASsary
Type: Newsletter; *Editor:* Ellen Watson

Evangelical Mennonite Conference (EMC)
440 Main St., Steinbach MB R5G 1Z5
Tel: 204-326-6401; *Fax:* 204-326-1613
www.emconf.ca
www.facebook.com/emconference
Overview: A medium-sized national charitable organization founded in 1812
Mission: To encourage local churches to work together on missions in Canada & around the world
Chief Officer(s):
Tim Dyck, General Secretary
Finances: *Annual Operating Budget:* $1.5 Million-$3 Million; *Funding Sources:* Donations
Membership: 7,300
Activities: *Library:* Evangelical Mennonite Conference Archives
Publications:
• The Messenger
Type: Magazine; *Frequency:* Monthly; *Editor:* Terry Smith *ISSN:* 0701-3299
Profile: The Messenger's purpose is to inform the general public about activities and events in the denomination and provide instruction on godliness and victorious living.

The Evangelical Order of Certified Pastoral Counsellors of America (EOCPCA)
3350 Fairview St., Burlington ON L7N 3L5
Tel: 905-639-0137; *Fax:* 905-333-8901
eocpc@cogeco.ca
www.eocpc.com
Previous Name: Order of Certified Pastoral Counsellors of America
Overview: A medium-sized national organization founded in 1982
Mission: To promote a Christian-oriented order; to certify & accredit pastoral counsellors by federal charter
Member of: Canadian Christian Counsellors Association;

Canadian Christian Clinical Counsellors College
Affiliation(s): California State Christian University
Chief Officer(s):
Stephen Hambly, Contact
Finances: *Annual Operating Budget:* $500,000-$1.5 Million
Staff Member(s): 3
Membership: 1,200 individual; *Fees:* $100-400

Evangelical Tract Distributors (EDT)
PO Box 146, Stn. Main, 12151 - 67 St. NW, Edmonton AB T5J 2G9
Tel: 780-477-1538; *Fax:* 780-477-3795
etdsupport@evangelicaltract.com
www.evangelicaltract.com
Overview: A small national organization founded in 1935
Mission: EDT is a non-profit organization that prints & distributes Christian gospel tracts free of charge. It is a registered charity, BN: 130522659RR0001.
Chief Officer(s):
John Harder, President/Managing Director
Publications:
• The Evangelist
Type: Newsletter; *Frequency:* Monthly

Evansburg & Entwistle Chamber of Commerce
PO Box 598, Evansburg AB T0E 0T0
Tel: 780-727-3526
info@partnersonthepembina.com
www.partnersonthepembina.com
Overview: A small local charitable organization
Mission: The Evansburg and Entwitle Chamber of Commerce are commiteed to community and economic development within the hamlets and surrounding areas. Many dedicated business people assit in moving the Chambers benefits and goals forward for the betterment of their communities.
Member of: Alberta Chambers of Commerce
Chief Officer(s):
Eric Karlzen, President
Al Hagman, Vice-President
20 volunteer(s)
Membership: 53; *Fees:* $60 business; $30 individual

Eventing Canada [!]
59 Hillside Dr., Toronto ON M4K 2M1
Tel: 416-429-1415
www.eventingcanada.com
Overview: A small national organization founded in 1996
Mission: To independently promote the sport of eventing
Chief Officer(s):
Sue Grocott, Contact
sgrocott@eventingcanada.com

Evergreen
#300, 550 Bayview Ave, Toronto ON M4W 3X8
Tel: 416-596-1495; *Fax:* 416-596-1443
Toll-Free: 888-426-3138
Other Communication: donate@evergreen.ca
info@evergreen.ca
www.evergreen.ca
Previous Name: The Evergreen Foundation
Overview: A medium-sized national charitable organization founded in 1991
Mission: To bring communities & nature together for the benefit of both; To create sustaining, healthy, dynamic outdoor spaces by engaging people & encouraging local stewardship
Chief Officer(s):
Geoff Cape, Executive Director
gcape@evergreen.ca
Seana Irvine, Chief Operating officer
seana@evergreen.ca
Finances: *Funding Sources:* Donations; Sponsorships
Activities: Creating innovative resources; Transforming school grounds & home landscapes; Conserving publicly accessible land; Hosting conferences; *Library*

Québec Office
5764, av Monkland, CP 107, Montréal QC H4A 1E9
Tel: 888-426-3138; *Fax:* 416-596-1443
infoqc@evergreen.ca
Chief Officer(s):
Kathleen Usher, Contact, Evergreen Québec

Vancouver Office
#107, 555 Great Northern Way, Vancouver BC V5T 1E2
Tel: 604-689-0766; *Fax:* 604-669-6222
infobc@evergreen.ca
Chief Officer(s):
Bill Sinclair, Regional Director, Western Canada

The Evergreen Foundation *See* Evergreen

Evergreen Theatre Society
2633 Hochwald Ave. SW, Calgary AB T3E 7K2
Tel: 403-228-1384; *Fax:* 403-229-1385
Toll-Free: 877-840-9746
info@evergreentheatre.com
www.evergreentheatre.com
www.facebook.com/pages/Evergreen-Theatre/229733167114546
twitter.com/evergreen_th
Overview: A small local charitable organization founded in 1991
Mission: To create innovative, entertaining, accessible education-tangible choices for a healthy & sustainable future
Chief Officer(s):
Valmai Goggin, Artistic Producer
valmai@evergreentheatre.com
Sean Fraser, Executive Director
sean@evergreentheatre.com
Staff Member(s): 6
Activities: *Internships:* Yes

Ex Libris Association
c/o Faculty of Information Studies, University of Toronto, 140 St. George St., Toronto ON M5S 3G6
e-mail: ExLibris@fis.utoronto.ca
exlibris.fis.utoronto.ca
Overview: A small national charitable organization founded in 1986
Mission: To encourage the publication of the history of Canadian libraries & librarianship & the identification & preservation of materials relating to library history in Canada which are not at present collected, organized or preserved by any other organization; To serve as a voice for retired librarians on important library-related issues
Chief Officer(s):
Carrol Lunau, President
Jean Weihs, Recording & Correspondence Secretary
Finances: *Annual Operating Budget:* Less than $50,000; *Funding Sources:* Membership dues; Donations
15 volunteer(s)
Membership: 215; *Fees:* $25 regular; *Member Profile:* Retired librarians & others interested in association's objectives
Awards:
• W. Kaye Lamb Award for Service to Seniors (Award)
Meetings/Conferences: • Ex Libris Association 2015 Annual General Meeting & Conference, 2015, Toronto, ON
Scope: National
Description: A one-day program with speakers on issues of current interest & trends in the library & archives community
Contact Information: Chair, Annual Conference: Richard Ficek, E-mail: exLibris@fis.utoronto.ca

Examinateurs canadiens en optométrie *See* Canadian Examiners in Optometry

Exempt Market Dealers Association of Canada; Limited Markets Dealers Association of Canada *See* Private Capital Markets Association of Canada

Exhibitions Association of Nova Scotia (EANS)
40 Gateway Rd., Halifax NS B3M 1M9
Tel: 902-443-2039
www.eans.ca
Overview: A small provincial organization
Mission: To promote such events as fairs & exhibitions across the province.
Chief Officer(s):
Glen E. Jefferson, Executive Director
glen.jefferson@ns.sympatico.ca

Experimental Aircraft Association of Canada *See* Recreational Aircraft Association

Exploits Regional Chamber of Commerce
PO Box 272, 2B Mill Rd., Grand Falls-Windsor NL A2A 2T5
Tel: 709-489-7512; *Fax:* 709-489-7532
info@exploitschamber.com
www.exploitschamber.com
Previous Name: Grand Falls-Windsor Chamber of Commerce
Overview: A small local organization
Member of: Newfoundland & Labrador Chamber of Commerce; Atlantic Provinces Chamber of Commerce; Canadian Chamber of Commerce
Chief Officer(s):
Scott Kenny, President
Ron Aucoin, Executive Director
Staff Member(s): 1
Membership: 200; *Fees:* $110-$184; *Member Profile:* Businesses

Exploits Valley Society for the Prevention of Cruelty to Animals
13A Duggan St., Grand Falls-Windsor NL A2A 2P7
Tel: 709-489-3604
evspca@yahoo.com
www.envision.ca/webs/exploitsvalleyspca
www.facebook.com/EVSPCA
Also Known As: Exploits Valley SPCA
Overview: A small local organization founded in 1971
Mission: To care for animals humanely through sheltering & public education.
Member of: Canadian Federation of Humane Societies
Chief Officer(s):
Sheila Baird, Manager

Explorer's Club (Canadian Chapter)
171 Brentwood Rd. North, Toronto ON M8X 2C8
Tel: 416-239-8840
Other Communication: www.explorers.org
explorersclubcanada@hotmail.com
www.explorersclub.ca
Overview: A medium-sized national organization founded in 1979
Mission: To promote field sciences & exploration of land, sea, air & space
Affiliation(s): Explorer's Club (New York)
Chief Officer(s):
Jason Schoonover, Communications Director
Simon Donato, Chair
simon@adventurescience.ca
Finances: *Annual Operating Budget:* Less than $50,000
Staff Member(s): 11
Membership: 110; 3,000 worldwide; *Fees:* US$120-450; *Member Profile:* Field scientists; *Committees:* Exploration; Student Recruitment; Events; Membership; Communications; Executive; Regional
Activities: *Speaker Service:* Yes

Explorers & Producers Association of Canada (EPAC)
#1060, 717 - 7th Ave. SW, Calgary AB T2P 0Z3
Tel: 403-269-3454; *Fax:* 403-269-3636
info@explorersandproducers.ca
www.explorersandproducers.ca
Previous Name: Small Explorers & Producers Association of Canada
Overview: A small national organization founded in 1986
Mission: To represent & promote the interests of small producers & explorers, not only to government & regulatory bodies, but to other sectors of the conventional oil & gas industry; To educate the public at large about the importance of emerging companies in resource development in Western Canada, & investment opportunities available in the growing segment of the oilpatch; To propose long-term, effective fiscal & operating strategies for the ongoing health & vitality of this important sector of the Canadian economy
Chief Officer(s):
Jim Screaton, Chair
Gary Leach, Executive Director
Staff Member(s): 3; 24 volunteer(s)
Membership: 387 corporate; *Fees:* $500-$3,335
Awards:
• EPAC Awards (Award)
The EPAC Awards will promote and celebrate Canadian oil and gas achievement, business success and entrepreneurship. The awards aim to recognize, motivate and inspire Canadians to continue innovating and advancing our nation's energy industry. Eligibility: Award categories this year include Top Emerging, Top Junior, Top Intermediate/Senior and Top International.
• CAPP-EPAC Scholarship Fund for Alberta Post- Secondary Students (Scholarship)
Eligibility: Alberta post-secondary institutions in qualifying fields of study.

Expo agricole de Chicoutimi
CP 8222, Succ. Racine, 350, boul Université est, Chicoutimi QC G7H 5B7
Tél: 418-545-8597; *Téléc:* 418-545-9243
info@expoagricoledechicoutimi.com
www.expoagricoledechicoutimi.com
Nom précédent: Société d'agriculture de Chicoutimi
Aperçu: *Dimension:* petite; *Envergure:* locale
Affiliation(s): Association des expositions agricoles du Québec
Membre(s) du bureau directeur:

Louis-Joseph Jean, Directeur général
expoagricole@qc.aira.com
Finances: *Fonds:* Gouvernement régional
Membre(s) du personnel: 1; 6 bénévole(s)
Membre: 70 individu; 5 associé; *Montant de la cotisation:* 10$ individu; 100$ associé
Activités: Exposition agricole;

Exposition nationale canadienne ***See*** Canadian National Exhibition Association

Eye Bank of BC (EBBC)

Jim Pattison Pavilion North - B205, 855 West 12th Ave, Vancouver BC V5Z 1M9
Tel: 604-875-4567; *Fax:* 604-875-5316
Toll-Free: 800-667-2060
eyebankofbc@vch.ca
www.eyebankofbc.ca
www.facebook.com/EyeBankBC
Overview: A medium-sized provincial charitable organization founded in 1983
Mission: To acquire human donor eye tissue for the purposes of corneal transplant, scelra grafts & medical research.
Member of: Eye Bank Association of America
Affliation(s): Canadian National Institute for the Blind; Eye Bank Association of America; Canadian Ophthalmological Society
Chief Officer(s):
Linda Wong, Manager
J. Martin McCarthy, Medical Director
Finances: *Annual Operating Budget:* $100,000-$250,000; *Funding Sources:* BC government, Health Care Division
Staff Member(s): 10
Activities: *Awareness Events:* Organ Donor Awareness, last week in Apr.; *Speaker Service:* Yes; *Library* by appointment

Eye Bank of Canada - Ontario Division

Dept. of Ophthalmology & Vision Sciences, University of Toronto, 1929 Bayview Ave., Toronto ON
Tel: 416-978-7355; *Fax:* 416-978-1522
eye.bank@utoronto.ca
www.eyebank.utoronto.ca
Also Known As: Ontario Eye Bank
Overview: A small provincial charitable organization founded in 1955
Mission: To provide donated eye tissue for surgical use in those whose vision can be restored or improved through corneal transplantation or other eye surgery
Affliation(s): Canadian National Institute for the Blind; University of Toronto
Chief Officer(s):
Fides Coloma, Manager
Finances: *Annual Operating Budget:* $500,000-$1.5 Million; *Funding Sources:* Ontario Ministry of Health
Staff Member(s): 8
Activities: *Speaker Service:* Yes
Awards:
• Certificates of Merit to Top Donor Hospitals, individuals & organizations who volunteer time & service (Award)

F. David Malloch Memorial Foundation ***See*** Malloch Foundation

Fabricants de produits alimentaires du Canada ***See*** Food Processors of Canada

Facility Association

PO Box 121, #2400, 777 Bay St., Toronto ON M5G 2C8
Tel: 416-863-1750; *Fax:* 416-868-0894
Toll-Free: 800-268-9572
mail@facilityassociation.com
www.facilityassociation.com
Overview: A medium-sized national organization founded in 1979
Mission: To ensure the availability of automobile insurance for owners & licensed drivers of motor vehicles who may otherwise have difficulty obtaining such insurance.
Chief Officer(s):
David J. Simpson, President & CEO
Membership: *Member Profile:* All property & casualty companies writing automobile business in all provinces & territories except BC, Manitoba, Québec & Saskatchewan.

The Factory: Hamilton Media Arts Centre

228 James St. North, Hamilton ON L8R 2L3
Tel: 905-577-9191
info@hamiltonmediaarts.org
www.hamiltonmediaarts.com
www.facebook.com/factorymedia
twitter.com/FactoryMediaArt
www.youtube.com/user/tfhmac
Also Known As: The Factory
Overview: A small local organization
Mission: To support an artist-driven resource center dedicated to the production and promotion of creatively diverse forms of independent film, video, and time-based multimedia arts in Hamilton and the surrounding region.
Chief Officer(s):
Ernest Gibson, Chair
Finances: *Funding Sources:* Canada Council for the Arts; Ontario Arts Council; City of Hamilton
Membership: *Fees:* $25 associate/student/senior; $45 full; $175 organizational

Facultés d'agriculture et de médecine vétérinaire du Canada ***See*** Canadian Faculties of Agriculture & Veterinary Medicine

Faculty Association of Medicine Hat College / Association des professeurs du Collège de Medicine Hat

c/o Medicine Hat College, 299 College Dr. SE, Medicine Hat AB T1A 3Y6
Tel: 403-504-3616; *Fax:* 403-504-3666
facultyassoc@mhc.ab.ca
www.mhc.ab.ca/Employees/FacultyAssociation.aspx
Overview: A small local organization
Mission: To represent the interests of its members in all contractual matters
Member of: Alberta Colleges & Institutes Faculties Association (ACIFA)
Chief Officer(s):
Elizabeth Pennefather-O'Brien, President
eobrien@mhc.ab.ca
Monika Farmer, Contact
Membership: *Committees:* Health & Safety; Bylaws; Worload Review; Social; Short Term Leave Review; Negotiations; Negotiations Advisory; Faculty Evluation; Professional Development

Faculty Association of Red Deer College (FARDC) / Association des professeurs du Collège Red Deer

c/o Red Deer College, PO Box 5005, 100 College Blvd., Red Deer AB T4N 5H5
Tel: 403-343-4092
extension.rdc.ab.ca/portal/fardc
Overview: A small local organization founded in 1968
Mission: To encourage its members to pursue professional & personal growth through teaching
Affliation(s): Alberta College & Institute Faculties Association
Chief Officer(s):
Ken Heather, President
ken.heather@rdc.ab.ca
Finances: *Funding Sources:* Membership dues
Membership: 400 individual; *Member Profile:* Academic staff members are designated by the Board of Governors at Red Deer College; *Committees:* Academic Council; Faculty Performance; Negotiations; Professional Development; Academic Policy; Awards Advisory; Benefits Advisory; CAT Fund; Curriculum; Dispute Resolution; Employee Award & Recognition; Faculty Scholarship Recognition; Faculty Workload; Occupational Health & Safety; Research & Scholarship; Students Awards Selection; Student Dispute, Appeal & Misconduct

Faculty Association of the College of New Caledonia (FACNC) / Association des professeurs du Collège de New Caledonia

3477 - 15th Ave., Prince George BC V2N 3Z3
Tel: 250-564-7880; *Fax:* 250-563-2776
facnc_local3@telus.net
www.facultyassoc-cnc.com
Overview: A small local organization overseen by College Institute Educators' Association of British Columbia
Chief Officer(s):
George Davison, President
Finances: *Annual Operating Budget:* $100,000-$250,000
Membership: 360; *Committees:* Professional Development; Political Action; Disability Management; CNC Occupational Health & Safety; Education Leave; Social; Human Rights; Education Policy; Status of Non-Regular Faculty; North Central Labour; Status of Women; Pension Liaison; Contract

Faculty Association of the Open Learning Agency ***See*** Thompson Rivers University Open Learning Faculty Association

Faculty Association of University of Saint Thomas (FAUST) / Association des professeurs de l'Université Saint-Thomas

St. Thomas University, Edmund Casey, #211, 51 Dineen Dr., Fredericton NB E3B 5G3
Tel: 506-452-9667
faust@stu.ca
www.faustnb.ca
Overview: A small local organization
Mission: To promote the welfare & interests of the association & its members
Member of: Federation of New Brunswick Faculty Associations; Canadian Association of University Teachers
Chief Officer(s):
Mary Lou Babineau, President
maryloub@stu.ca
Bonnie Huskins, Professional Officer, 506-452-9667
Membership: *Committees:* Communications; Benefits; Equity; Health & Safety; Part-time Issues; SoOcial; Grievance; Joint; Harassment Policy; Bargaining

FADOQ - Mouvement des Ainés du Quebec ***Voir*** FADOQ

The Fair Rental Policy Organization of Ontario (FRPO)

#105, 20 Upjohn Rd., Toronto ON M3B 2V9
Tel: 416-385-1100; *Fax:* 416-385-7112
Toll-Free: 877-688-1960
info@frpo.org
www.frpo.org
www.facebook.com/117940918260439
www.youtube.com/user/FRPO2011
Overview: A small provincial organization
Chief Officer(s):
Vince Brescia, President & CEO
vbrescia@frpo.org

Fair Vote Canada (FVC)

#408, 283 Danforth Ave., Toronto ON M4K 1N2
Tel: 416-410-4034
office@fairvote.ca
www.fairvotecanada.org
www.facebook.com/fairvotecanada
twitter.com/FairVoteCanada
www.youtube.com/user/FairVoteCanada
Overview: A small national organization
Mission: FVC is a national, multi-partisan citizens' campaign to promote voting system reform, specifically for proportional elections. It advocates for a national process that enables Canadian voters to choose which voting system shall be used to elect their representatives.
Chief Officer(s):
Kelly Carmichael, Executive Director
Staff Member(s): 2

Fairview & District Chamber of Commerce

PO Box 1034, 10912 - 103 Ave., Fairview AB T0H 1L0
Tel: 780-835-5999; *Fax:* 780-835-5991
www.fairviewchamber.com
Overview: A small local licensing organization
Mission: To provide leadership to ensure a stable business base & networking system.
Member of: Alberta Chamber of Commerce; Canadian Chamber of Commerce; Mighty Peace Tourism
Chief Officer(s):
Sharon Noullett, President
Debie Knudsen, Executive Director
Finances: *Annual Operating Budget:* $50,000-$100,000; *Funding Sources:* Membership dues; events
10 volunteer(s)
Membership: 106; *Fees:* $80.25-$214

Fairview Applied Research Association ***See*** Peace Agricultural Research & Demonstration Association

Fais-Un-Voeu Canada ***See*** Make-A-Wish Canada

Falcon, West Hawk & Caddy Lakes Chamber of Commerce (FWHLCC)

PO Box 187, Falcon Beach MB R0E 0N0
Tel: 204-349-3134; *Fax:* 204-349-3134
falconwesthawkchamber.com
Overview: A small local organization
Mission: To promote the communities of Falcon Lake, West Hawk Lake & surrounding areas
Member of: Manitoba Chamber of Commerce
Affliation(s): Canadian Chamber of Commerce
Chief Officer(s):

Bob Harbottle, President
rharbott@mts.net
Finances: *Annual Operating Budget:* Less than $50,000; *Funding Sources:* Membership fees
Membership: 55; *Fees:* $125; $75 associate; *Committees:* Architectural; Tourism

Falher Chamber of Commerce

PO Box 814, 11 Central Ave. SW, Falher AB T0H 1M0
Tel: 780-837-2364
Overview: A small local organization founded in 1940
Mission: To promote the area's economy & encourage business & industrial development, broaden the tax base & provide employment opportunities in Falher & area.
Affliation(s): Falher & Area Economic Development & Tourism
Staff Member(s): 1
Membership: 45; *Fees:* Based on number of employees

Falher Friendship Corner Association (FFCA)

PO Box 453, Falher AB T0H 1M0
Tel: 780-837-2153; *Fax:* 780-837-2254
Overview: A small local organization
Mission: To promote the welfare of people with handicaps & their families
Member of: Alberta Association for Community Living

Falkland Chamber of Commerce

PO Box 92, Hwy. 97, Falkland BC V0B 1M5
Tel: 250-379-2252
www.falklandbc.ca
Overview: A small local organization
Finances: *Funding Sources:* Membership dues
Membership: 8;

Falls Brook Centre

476 West Glassville Rd., Glassville NB E7L 1W4
Tel: 506-246-1114; *Fax:* 506-246-1116
admin@fallsbrookcentre.ca
www.fallsbrookcentre.ca
Overview: A small local organization
Mission: Situated on 400 acres of rural forest and farmland, the Centre is a sustainable community demonstration and training centre. On-site activities and features include solar and wind energy systems, organic gardening, forest trails, herbariums and tree nurseries, and a conference centre. The Centre promotes sustainability and collaborates with the community to provide alternatives.
Member of: Canadian Renewable Energy Alliance
Affliation(s): Canadian Coalition for Biodiversity
Chief Officer(s):
Marc Gionet, Executive Director
Staff Member(s): 6
Activities: Education and Outreach; Community Development; International Work; workshops and workbees

Falun Dafa Canada

Toronto ON
Tel: 416-731-6000
Toll-Free: 866-325-8622
toronto-1@falundafa.ca
falundafa.ca
Also Known As: Falun Gong
Overview: A medium-sized national organization
Mission: To improve body, mind & spirit; The ancient practice was introduced to the public by Mr. Li Hongzhi in 1992 in China; There are now more than 100 million practitioners around the world; The ultimate objective is to assimilate to the supreme principle: Truthfulness, Compassion, & Tolerance (Zhen, Shan, Ren)

Familial GI Cancer Registry *See* Zane Cohen Centre for Digestive Diseases Familial Gastrointestinal Cancer Registry

Family & Children's Services Niagara (FACS)

PO Box 24028, 82 Hannover Dr., St. Catharines ON L2R 7P7
Tel: 905-937-7731; *Fax:* 905-646-7085
Toll-Free: 888-937-7731
info@facsniagara.on.ca
www.facsniagara.on.ca
Also Known As: FACS Niagara
Overview: A large local charitable organization founded in 1898
Mission: The Society focuses on the protection of children, supporting those in need of safe homes. It provides guidance & counselling services to families, & investigates all reports of possible child abuse or neglect.
Member of: Ontario Association of Children's Aid Societies
Chief Officer(s):
Chris Steven, Executive Director
Finances: *Annual Operating Budget:* Greater than $5 Million; *Funding Sources:* 100% Province of Ontario (core services); donations
Staff Member(s): 360; 240 volunteer(s)
Membership: 50; *Fees:* $25; *Member Profile:* Reside or work in Niagara, 18 years old; *Committees:* Standing Board
Activities: Child protection & family services; adoption services; nursery school-parent enrichment program; family counselling centre; regional adolescent centre; mobile toy lending library; Ontario Early Years Program (Niagara South); *Awareness Events:* Child Abuse & Neglect Prevention Month, Oct.; *Internships:* Yes; *Speaker Service:* Yes

Niagara Falls Branch
7900 Canadian Dr., Niagara Falls ON L2E 6S5

Welland Branch
654 South Pelham St., Welland ON L3C 3C8

Family & Children's Services of Guelph & Wellington County (F&CS)

PO Box 1088, 275 Eramosa Rd., Guelph ON N1H 6N3
Tel: 519-824-2410; *Fax:* 519-763-9628
Toll-Free: 800-265-8300
info@fcsgw.org
www.fcsgw.org
www.facebook.com/371460589598793
twitter.com/fcsgw
Also Known As: Children's Aid Society of Guelph & Wellington County
Overview: A small local charitable organization founded in 1934
Mission: To provide help & support services for families to ensure that children are protected from physical & emotional abuse or neglect.
Member of: Ontario Association of Children's Aid Societies
Chief Officer(s):
Daniel Moore, Executive Director
Finances: *Annual Operating Budget:* Greater than $5 Million
Staff Member(s): 140; 160 volunteer(s)
Membership: *Fees:* $5

County Office
PO Box 29, 6484 Wellington Rd. 7, Elora ON N0B 1S0
Fax: 519-846-1005
Toll-Free: 800-265-8300
Mission: To advocate & provide for the protection of children, to support & strengthen families, & promote the well-being of children in our communities.

Shelldale Centre Branch
PO Box 1088, 20 Shelldale Cres., Guelph ON N1H 6N3
Fax: 519-766-4537
Toll-Free: 800-265-8300

Family & Children's Services of Lanark, Leeds & Grenville

438 Laurier Blvd., Brockville ON K6V 6C5
Tel: 613-498-2100; *Fax:* 613-498-2108
Toll-Free: 800-481-7834
www.casbrock.com
Merged from: Children's Aid Society of Lanark & Smiths Falls; Family & Children's Services of Leeds & Grenville
Overview: A small local organization overseen by Family Service Ontario
Mission: To protect children & ensure the safety of those in need; to provide care for those children under concern, as well as guidance & counselling to families to prevent circumstances requiring the protection of children.

Gananoque Office
#300, 375 William St., Gananoque ON K7G 1T2
Tel: 613-382-8220; *Fax:* 613-382-3579

Kemptville Office
PO Box 1299, 5 Clothier St. East, Kemptville ON K0G 1J0
Tel: 613-258-1460; *Fax:* 613-258-4459

Family & Children's Services of Renfrew County

#100, 77 Mary St., Pembroke ON K8A 5V4
Tel: 613-735-6866; *Fax:* 613-735-6641
Toll-Free: 800-267-5878
inquiries@fcsrenfrew.on.ca
www.fcsrenfrew.on.ca
Previous Name: Renfrew Family & Child Services
Overview: A medium-sized local charitable organization founded in 1935
Mission: To support & enhance the lives of children, youth, & families in Ontario's County of Renfrew by providing essential, mandated, & volutary services; To improve the quality of life for children, youth, & adults with developmental disabilities
Member of: Ontario Association of Children's Aid Societies
Chief Officer(s):
Arijana Tomicic, Executive Director
Staff Member(s): 142; 110 volunteer(s)
Membership: 18; *Fees:* $10; *Member Profile:* Board members; Volunteers; Community; *Committees:* Executive; Finance; Personnel; Services
Activities: Providing crisis intervention services; Investigating cases of neglect; Providing child protection services; Arranging financial assistance & safe shelter; Counselling individuals & families; Organizing foster care & adoption services; Providing developmental services, such as infant development, behaviour, & speech programs, as well as service coordination; Offering educational programs; Arranging family visitations & exchanges; Providing after school tutorial services, such as The Kumon Method; *Awareness Events:* Purple Ribbon - Child Abuse Prevention Month, October
Awards:
• Service Awards to Foster Parents (Award)
• Staff Recognition (Award)

Renfrew Office
331 Martin St., Renfrew ON K7V 1A1
Tel: 613-432-4821; *Fax:* 613-432-9278
Toll-Free: 800-267-5878

Family & Children's Services of the District of Rainy River (FACS)

820 Lakeview Dr., Kenora ON P9N 3P7
Tel: 807-467-5437; *Fax:* 807-467-5539; *Crisis Hot-Line:* 800-465-1100
www.krrcfs.ca
Also Known As: Kenora-Patricia Child & Family Services
Overview: A small local charitable organization founded in 1935
Mission: To ensure the safety of children & youth; to provide a variety of services to protect them; to investigate any concerns of their abuse or neglect.
Member of: Ontario Association of Children's Aid Societies; Children's Mental Health Associations of Ontario
Chief Officer(s):
Bill Leonard, Executive Director
Finances: *Funding Sources:* Provincial
Activities: Child welfare; children's mental health; child development; supervised access; family relief; *Speaker Service:* Yes; *Library:* FACS Library; Open to public
Publications:
• Developmental Services Newsletter [a publication of the Family & Children's Services of the District of Rainy River]
Type: Newsletter; *Frequency:* Bimonthly
• Family & Children's Services of the District of Rainy River Newsletter
Type: Newsletter; *Frequency:* 7 pa

Atikokan Office
211 Main St. West, Atikokan ON P0T 1C0
Tel: 807-597-2700; *Fax:* 807-597-6920

Dryden Office
175 West River Rd., Dryden ON P8N 2Z4
Tel: 807-223-5325; *Fax:* 807-223-5324

Fort Frances Office
240 - 1st St. East, Fort Frances ON P9A 1K5
Tel: 807-274-7787; *Fax:* 807-274-6646

Red Lake Office
201 Howey St., Red Lake ON P0V 2M0
Tel: 807-727-2165; *Fax:* 807-727-2645

Sioux Lookout Office
41 King St., Sioux Lookout ON P8T 1B7
Tel: 807-737-3250; *Fax:* 807-737-2611

Family & Community Support Services Association of Alberta (FCSSAA)

Belmead Professional Bldg., #106, 8944 - 182 St., Edmonton AB T5T 2E3
Tel: 780-415-4790; *Fax:* 780-415-4793
fcssaa@telus.net
www.fcssaa.ab.ca
Previous Name: Preventative Social Services Association
Overview: A medium-sized provincial organization founded in 1981
Mission: To advocate on behalf of local communities & programs to the general public, municipal governments, regional services, provincial & national agencies, & authorities; To educate individuals, communities, boards, & staff
Chief Officer(s):
Sharlyn White, Executive Director, 780-422-0133
Jeff Carlson, President
Judy Macknee, Executive Assistant
fcssaa-admin@telus.net

Membership: 100-499; *Fees:* Schedule available; *Member Profile:* FCSS programs in Alberta representing municipalities & Métis settlements
Activities: Hosting conferences; Sharing information about FCSS programs; Developing resources; *Library:* FCSSAA Resource Bank

Family Caregivers Association of Nova Scotia *See* Caregivers Nova Scotia

Family Caregivers' Network Society (FCNS)
526 Michigan St., Victoria BC V8V 1S2
Tel: 250-384-0408; *Fax:* 250-361-2660
fcns@telus.net
www.fcns-caregiving.org
Overview: A small local charitable organization founded in 1989
Mission: To provide support & education on family caregiving issues in Victoria, British Columbia & the surrounding region
Chief Officer(s):
Barb MacLean, Executive Director
Rick Hoogendoorn, President
Carolyn Thoms, Vice-President
Irene Laing, Secretary
Yolande DeMont, Treasurer
Finances: *Funding Sources:* Membership fees; Donations; Fundraising
Membership: *Fees:* $20 individuals; $30 non-profit organizations; $50 corporate members
Activities: Hosting workshops for family caregivers; Organizing regular family caregiver support groups; Offering telephone or in-person support; Providing information & referrals; *Library:* Family Caregivers' Network Society Resource Lending Library; Open to public
Meetings/Conferences: • Family Caregivers' Network Society 2015 Annual General Meeting, 2015, BC
Scope: Provincial
Publications:
• Facilitator's Manual: Educational Activities to Support Family Caregivers
Price: $75
Profile: Featuring facilitation techniques, outlines for workshops, & learning activities for healthcare provider training programs
• Medical Information Package
Price: Free with membership in theFamily Caregivers' Network Society; $3 non-members
Profile: Including a medical information record, information about incapacity planning, plus information from the British Columbia Transplant Society & the Heart & Stroke Foundation
• Network News [a publication of the Family Caregivers' Network Society]
Type: Newsletter; *Frequency:* Bimonthly; *Price:* Free with membership in the Family Caregivers' Network Society
Profile: Informative articles about caregiving issues & notices of upcoming events
• Resource Guide for Family Caregivers
Type: Handbook; *Number of Pages:* 160; *Price:* $15 FCNS members; $20 non-members
Profile: Practical information to help caregivers make decisions
• Resource Guide for Family Caregivers
Type: Handbook; *Number of Pages:* 160; *Price:* $15 FCNS members; $20 non-members
Profile: Practical information to help caregivers make decisions

Family Coalition Party of Ontario (FCP)
PO Box 85023, 210 Mohawk Rd. East, Hamilton ON L9A 2H0
Tel: 905-538-5327; *Fax:* 905-538-1739
Toll-Free: 888-327-2386
office@familycoalitionparty.com
www.familycoalitionparty.com
www.linkedin.com/profile/view?id=231081844&trk=tab_pro
www.facebook.com/fcp.ontario
twitter.com/FCP_Ontario
www.youtube.com/user/thefcpchannel
Overview: A small provincial organization
Chief Officer(s):
Eric Ames, Interim Party Leader
Lynne Scime, President
Finances: *Annual Operating Budget:* $50,000-$100,000
100 volunteer(s)
Membership: *Fees:* $10 individual; $20 family

Family Counselling & Support Services for Guelph-Wellington (FCSS)
109 Surrey St. East, Guelph ON N1H 3P7
Tel: 519-824-2431
Toll-Free: 800-307-7078
info@familyserviceguelph.on.ca
www.familyserviceguelph.on.ca
Previous Name: Guelph-Wellington Counselling Centre
Overview: A small local charitable organization founded in 1987 overseen by Ontario Association of Credit Counselling Services
Mission: To provide professional counselling, support, educational, & advocacy services for the citizens of the Guelph-Wellington region
Member of: Credit Counselling Canada; Ontario Association of Credit Counselling Services
Affliation(s): Family Service Ontario; Family Service Canada
Finances: *Funding Sources:* Donations; Local institutions
Activities: Providing counselling in areas such as relationships, family violence, credit & debt, & addictions & gambling; Engaging in advocacy activities; Offering groups, such as the separation & divorce recovery group, building peaceful families, anger management for men, & healing the trauma of early childhood incest & sexual abuse issues; Providing programs, such as the Employee Assistance Program, Debt Management Program, & the Case Management Services Program for individuals with developmental disabilities
Publications:
• Family Counselling & Support Services for Guelph-Wellington Annual Report
Type: Yearbook; *Frequency:* Annually

Family Counselling Centre of Brant, Inc.
54 Brant Ave., Brantford ON N3T 3G8
Tel: 519-753-4173; *Fax:* 519-753-9287
office@fccb.ca
www.fccb.ca
Previous Name: Family Service Bureau of Brantford & Brant County, Inc.
Overview: A small local organization founded in 1914 overseen by Ontario Association of Credit Counselling Services
Mission: To offer professional & ethical counselling services to persons in need in Brantford & the Brant County Region of Ontario
Member of: Ontario Association of Credit Counselling Services
Activities: Providing individual, couple, family, group, & credit counselling; Engaging in advocacy activities; Providing creditor mediation services; Offering an employee assistance program; Providing family relief services; Assisting with community integration; Offering behaviour therapy consultation to nurseries, preschools, schools, community agencies, caregivers, individuals, & families; Operating early learning & parenting centres; Increasing community awareness of individual & family issues; Providing informative resources
Publications:
• Family Matters
Type: Newsletter
Profile: Issue topics include aging parents, fostering self, & working through depression
• Solutions
Type: Newsletter
Profile: A newsletter from the Family Services Employee Assistance Program

Family Counselling Centre of Cornwall & United Counties *See* Counselling & Support Services of S.D. & G.

Family Counselling of Cambridge & North Dumfries
18 Walnut St., Cambridge ON N1R 2E7
Tel: 519-621-5090; *Fax:* 519-622-9394
fcccnd@golden.net
www.fcccnd.com
www.facebook.com/265770970176327
Also Known As: Family Counselling Centre of Cambridge & North Dumfries
Previous Name: Family Services Cambridge & North Dumfries
Overview: A small local organization founded in 1940
Member of: Family Services Canada; Family Services Ontario
Chief Officer(s):
Bobbye Goldenberg, Executive Director
Staff Member(s): 12

Family Day Care Services (Toronto)
#400, 155 Gordon Baker Rd., Toronto ON M2H 3N5
Tel: 416-922-9556; *Fax:* 416-922-5335
childcareservices@familydaycare.com
www.familydaycare.com
Previous Name: Protestant Children's Home
Overview: A large local charitable organization founded in 1851 overseen by Family Service Ontario
Mission: To meet the needs of children & families; To aid in optimum development of the child, be it physical care, social, emotional or cognitive development; To assist & support the family unit to function more effectively economically, socially & emotionally
Member of: Home Child Care Association of Ontario
Chief Officer(s):
S. Gopikrishna, President
Joan Arruda, CEO
Finances: *Annual Operating Budget:* Greater than $5 Million; *Funding Sources:* United Way; provincial government; fundraising
Staff Member(s): 263
Activities: *Speaker Service:* Yes

Family History Society of Newfoundland & Labrador
#101A, 66 Kenmount Rd., St. John's NL A1B 3V7
Tel: 709-754-9525; *Fax:* 709-754-6430
fhs@fhsnl.ca
www.fhsnl.ca
www.facebook.com/144749998869923
twitter.com/fhsnl
Previous Name: Newfoundland & Labrador Genealogical Society Inc.
Overview: A medium-sized provincial organization founded in 1984
Mission: To encourage & promote the study of family history in Newfoundland & Labrador; To collect & preserve local genealogical & historical records & materials; to foster education in genealogical research
Chief Officer(s):
Don Tarrant, President
John Fitzgerald, Secretary
Finances: *Funding Sources:* Membership fees
Membership: *Fees:* $42/yr; $700/life; *Member Profile:* All individuals, groups, & institutions
Activities: *Library:* The Family History Resource Centre; Open to public

Family Life Centre *See* Community Counselling Centre of Nipissing

Family Mediation Canada (FMC) / Médiation Familiale Canada
#180, 55 Northfield Dr. East, Waterloo ON N2K 3T6
Tel: 519-585-3118; *Fax:* 416-849-0643
Toll-Free: 877-362-2005
fmc@fmc.ca
www.fmc.ca
Overview: A medium-sized national charitable organization founded in 1985
Mission: To improve the provision for cooperative conflict resolution in areas such as separation & divorce, child welfare, adoption, parent & teen counselling, age-related issues, & wills & estates
Affliation(s): Mediate BC Society; Alberta Family Mediation Society; Conflict Resolution Saskatchewan Inc.; Family Mediation Manitoba Inc.; Ontario Association for Family Mediation; Association de médiation familiale du Québec; Family Mediation Nova Scotia; Mediation PEI Inc.; Mediation Yukon Society
Chief Officer(s):
Mary Damianakis, President
mediate@gmail.com
Linda Bonnell, Secretary
lindabonnell@shaw.ca
Carrie Cekerevac, Manager, Operations
carrie@fmc.ca
Membership: *Member Profile:* Lawyers; Human services professionals; Social workers; Health care professionals; *Committees:* Executive; Finance; Certification; PLAR; Governance; Public Outreach; Diversity; Education & Professional Development; Membership; Awards; Nominations; Government Relations; Practice & Ethics
Activities: Providing information; Referring families to family mediators throughout Canada; Promoting mediation & other forms of conflict resolution; Hosting an annual general meeting; Posting jobs; *Library*

New Brunswick
c/o Donihee Consulting, 417 Pelton Rd., Saint John NB E2K 5H6
Tel: 506-634-2883; *Fax:* 506-634-0877
pat@doniheeconsulting.com

Newfoundland & Labrador
Mission: Mediation & dispute resolution in Newfoundland & Labrador is provided by the Family Justice Services Division of the Department of Justice, through 11 offices across the province.
Chief Officer(s):

Judy McCann-Beranger, Provincial Representative
judy@peopleconcepts.ca
Eric Skoglund, Provincial Representative
ericskoglund@gov.nl.ca
Northwest Territories
Mission: Mediation services in the Northwest Territories are provided by the Department of Justice
Chief Officer(s):
Joe Pintarics, Provincial Representative
paasco@mts.net

Family Mediation Manitoba Inc. (FMM)
PO Box 2369, Winnipeg MB R3C 4A6
Tel: 204-989-5330; *Fax:* 204-694-7555
info@familymediationmanitoba.ca
www.familymediationmanitoba.ca
Overview: A small provincial organization founded in 1986
Mission: To promote family mediation in Manitoba
Affliation(s): Family Mediation Canada
Chief Officer(s):
Karen Burwash, President
president@familymediationmanitoba.ca
Finances: *Funding Sources:* Membership fees
Membership: *Fees:* $25 student; $50 regular; *Member Profile:* Individuals working in the field of mediation in Manitoba
Activities: Seminars; educational material; networking;
Publications:
• Directory of Mediators [a publication of Family Mediation Manitoba Inc.]
Type: Directory

Family Mediation Nova Scotia (FMNS)
c/o Keith Wallis, #306, 35 Commercial St., Truro NS B2N 3H9
e-mail: mirkwoodmediation@ns.aliantzinc.ca
Overview: A small provincial organization
Mission: The purpose of Family Mediation Nova Scotia is to promote accessible, quality mediation services for families. FMNS provides information about family mediation to the public, promotes professional development & establishes standards of practice for family mediators.
Affliation(s): Family Mediation Canada
Chief Officer(s):
Charlene Moore, Past President
charlene.moore@nslegalaid.ca
Keith Wallis, Vice-President

Family of the Immaculate Heart of Mary
368 Melville Ave., Maple ON L6A 2N8
Tel: 905-832-1893; *Fax:* 905-832-3954
Overview: A small local organization founded in 2007
Mission: To serve God & promote the Roman Catholic Faith
Affliation(s): Archdiocese of Toronto
Chief Officer(s):
Solidea Didonato, Contact
mario.didonato@rogers.com
Activities: Parish missions; spiritual exercises; worship

Family Prayer Mission (Ontario) (FPM)
2478 Callum Ave., Mississauga ON L5B 2H9
Tel: 905-896-2854; *Fax:* 905-896-3553
familyprayer@sympatico.ca
www.familyprayermission.org
Overview: A small local charitable organization founded in 1989
Mission: To strengthen family bonds through prayer & worship
Affliation(s): Archdiocese of Toronto
Chief Officer(s):
Rappai Nedumpara, President
Thomas Kalarathil, Spiritual Director
Membership: *Fees:* $15
Activities: Retreats

Family Service Association of Halifax
West End Mall, #S14, 6960 Mumford Rd., Halifax NS B3L 4P1
Tel: 902-420-1980; *Fax:* 902-423-9830
Toll-Free: 888-886-5552
admin@fshalifax.com
www.fshalifax.com
Overview: A medium-sized local organization
Mission: To offer professional, confidential counselling and education services to enable people to function more effectively at home, in the community and in their work environment.
Chief Officer(s):
Mary Clancy, Chair
Valerie Bobyk, Executive Director

Family Service Association of Toronto *See* Family Service Toronto

Family Service Bureau of Brantford & Brant County, Inc. *See* Family Counselling Centre of Brant, Inc.

Family Service Canada (FSC) / Services à la famille - Canada
c/o 312 Parkdale Ave., Ottawa ON K1Y 4X45
Toll-Free: 877-451-1055
www.familyservicecanada.org
Overview: A medium-sized national organization founded in 1982
Mission: To promote families as the primary source of nurturing & development of individuals, their relationship in families & communities, through promoting & ensuring the best policies & services for families in Canada.
Member of: Coalition of National Voluntary Organizations
Chief Officer(s):
Heather Underhill, Manager, Operations
heatherp@familyservicecanada.org
Finances: *Funding Sources:* Membership fees; grants
Membership: 33 agencies; *Fees:* Schedule available; *Member Profile:* Family service agencies, corporations, national & provincial organizations, government agencies & interested individuals
Awards:
• Leadership Award (Award)

Family Service Centre of Ottawa-Carleton / Centre de service familial d'Ottawa-Carleton
312 Parkdale Ave., Ottawa ON K1Y 4X5
Tel: 613-725-3601; *Fax:* 613-725-5651; *TTY:* 613-725-6175
fsfo@familyservicesottawa.org
familyservicesottawa.org
www.facebook.com/familyservicesottawa
Overview: A medium-sized local organization founded in 1914 overseen by Family Service Ontario
Mission: To strengthen all aspects of family & community living through the provision of family focused, professional social services in the areas of counselling, family life education, social planning & advocacy
Affliation(s): Family Service Canada
Chief Officer(s):
Kathryn Ann Hill, Executive Director
Finances: *Annual Operating Budget:* $3 Million-$5 Million; *Funding Sources:* United Way; Government; Fees; Donations; Fundraising; Grants; Interest
Staff Member(s): 90; 130 volunteer(s)
Activities: *Speaker Service:* Yes

Family Service Kent / Services à la Famille - Kent
50 Adelaide St., Chatham ON N7M 6K7
Tel: 519-354-6221; *Fax:* 519-354-5152
Toll-Free: 855-437-5368
familyservicekent.com
Previous Name: Community & Family Services of Chatham
Overview: A small local charitable organization founded in 1969 overseen by Ontario Association of Credit Counselling Services
Mission: To provide confidential counselling services by extensively trained & experienced persons to individuals & groups in Chatham-Kent communities
Member of: Ontario Association of Credit Counselling Services
Affliation(s): Canadian Family Services Accreditation Program; Association of Credit Counselling Services
Chief Officer(s):
Brad Davis, Executive Director
Finances: *Funding Sources:* United Way; Ministry of Community & Social Services; Ministry of Children & Youth Services; Ministry of Health & Long Term Care; Employee Assistance
Activities: Providing counselling services, in areas such as credit & sexual assault; Offering programs, such as the Credit Counselling Program, Employee Assistance Program, CHAP (Community Home Support Assisting People), APSW (Advocacy & Protective Service Worker), & the KIDS Team (Kent Inter-Disciplinary Support);

Family Service Moncton Inc. / Services à la famille - Moncton, Inc
#T410, 22 Church St., Moncton NB E1C 0P7
Tel: 506-857-3258; *Fax:* 506-858-8315
Toll-Free: 800-390-3258
fsmoncton@rogers.com
www.fsmoncton.com
Overview: A small local organization founded in 1986
Affliation(s): Family Service Canada
Chief Officer(s):
Brenda Robinson, Chair
Maurice D. LeBlanc, RSW, MPA, CEO
Finances: *Annual Operating Budget:* $500,000-$1.5 Million
Staff Member(s): 15; 10 volunteer(s)

Family Service Ontario / Services à la famille - Ontario
#630, 190 Attwell Dr., Toronto ON M9W 6H8
Tel: 416-231-6003; *Fax:* 416-231-2405
www.familyserviceontario.org
Overview: A medium-sized provincial charitable organization founded in 1974
Mission: To support & assist member family service agencies
Affliation(s): Ontario Association of Credit Counselling Services; Family Services Canada; Catholic Charities; United Way; Canadian Council of Social Development
Chief Officer(s):
John Ellis, Executive Director
Membership: 48 agencies

Family Service Thames Valley (FSTV)
125 Woodward Ave., London ON N6J 2H1
Tel: 519-433-0159
fstv@familyservicethamesvalley.com
www.familyservicethamesvalley.com
Previous Name: Credit Counselling Thames Valley; Family Service London
Overview: A small local organization founded in 1967 overseen by Ontario Association of Credit Counselling Services
Mission: To provide counselling & support services for individuals, families, & organizations in London & its surrounding communities; To promote wise money management by consumers
Chief Officer(s):
Louise Pitre, Executive Director
Activities: Offering a credit & bankruptcy counselling program to provide solutions to debt problems; Intervening with creditors; Providing educational seminars for groups; Offering organization & employee care programs; *Speaker Service:* Yes

Family Service Toronto (FST)
355 Church St., Toronto ON M5B 1Z8
Tel: 416-595-9230; *Fax:* 416-595-0242
sau@familyservicetoronto.org
www.fsatoronto.com
Previous Name: Family Service Association of Toronto
Overview: A small local charitable organization founded in 1914
Mission: To help low-income individuals & families in need.
Member of: Family Service Ontario; United Way
Affliation(s): Family Service Canada
Chief Officer(s):
Lan Nguyen, President
Margaret Hancock, Executive Director
Membership: *Fees:* Free; *Committees:* Financial Affairs; Governance
Activities: Counselling for individuals, couples & families; support for lesbians & gay men; support for people affected by HIV/AIDS; community development; counselling for battered women & abusive men; counselling, family life education & mediation for families undergoing separation, divorce & remarriage; promoting physical & emotional well-being for seniors & their caregivers; support for children & adults with developmental disabilities & their families; Bolton Camp; advocating for social policy; *Internships:* Yes; *Speaker Service:* Yes; *Library* Open to public

Family Services Cambridge & North Dumfries *See* Family Counselling of Cambridge & North Dumfries

Family Services of Greater Vancouver (FSGV)
1616 - 7th Ave. West, Vancouver BC V6J 1S5
Tel: 604-731-4951; *Fax:* 604-733-7009
contactus@fsgv.ca
www.fsgv.ca
Overview: A medium-sized local charitable organization founded in 1928
Mission: To strengthen people, families, & communities; To provide a diverse range of professional support & counselling services to those who are experiencing challenges in their lives
Member of: Family Service Canada; Alliance for Children & Families; Child Welfare League of Canada
Affliation(s): Commission of Accreditation & Rehabilitation Facilities
Chief Officer(s):
Caroline Bonesky, Chief Executive Officer
Renata Aebi, Vice-President, Youth & Employment Services
Roberta Haas, Chief Executive Officer, Human Resources & Corporate Services
Cheryl Mixon, Vice-President, Adoption, Family, & Child Services

Beth Rees, Vice-President, Employee Assistance Services
Lisa Whittaker, Vice-President, Counselling, Community Education, Trauma, & Victim Services
Kam Rai, Director, Finance
151 volunteer(s)
Membership: 35
Activities: Offering professional counselling, consultation, education, & other supportive programs for people of all ages & income levels; *Library*
Publications:
• Family Services of Greater Vancouver Newsletter
Type: Newsletter
Profile: Association happenings & supporter stories

Family Services Perth-Huron (FSPH)

142 Waterloo St., Stratford ON N5A 4B4
Tel: 519-273-1020; *Fax:* 519-273-6993
Toll-Free: 800-268-0903
office@debtontario.com
www.debtontario.com
Also Known As: Grey Bruce Credit Counselling
Overview: A small local charitable organization founded in 1975 overseen by Ontario Association of Credit Counselling Services
Mission: To provide professional, confidential counselling & family support services to individuals & families in Bruce, Grey, Huron, & Perth Counties
Member of: Credit Counselling Canada; Ontario Association of Credit Counselling Services; United Way
Chief Officer(s):
Susan Melkert, Executive Director
Activities: Coordinating respite care; Teaching literacy & numeracy skills; Providing programs, such as the Debt Management Program, Employee Assistance Program; Family Home Program, & the Familiy Violence Program for Men; Offering mediation services; Promoting consumer credit education;

Family Services Thunder Bay *See* Thunder Bay Counselling Centre

Family Services Windsor-Essex Counselling & Advocacy Centre

#105A, 235 Eugenie St. West, Windsor ON N8X 2X7
Tel: 519-966-5010; *Fax:* 519-256-5258
Toll-Free: 888-933-1831
info@fswe.ca
www.familyserviceswe.ca
Previous Name: Windsor Catholic Family Service Bureau
Overview: A small local charitable organization
Mission: To strengthen the ability of individuals, families & communities to reach their potential within the context of Catholic beliefs, values & teachings, while affirming the cultural, racial & specific differences of people
Chief Officer(s):
Mary Reaume, Executive Assistant
Tim Ellard, Executive Director
Finances: *Funding Sources:* United Way; government; fees
Activities: *Speaker Service:* Yes

Family Supports Institute Ontario

#206, 489 College St., Toronto ON M6G 1A5
Tel: 416-538-0628
program.manager@fsio.ca
www.fsio.ca
Overview: A small provincial organization
Mission: The Family Supports Institute Ontario exists to advance the well-being of families.
Member of: Canadian Association of Family Resource Programs (FRP Canada)
Chief Officer(s):
Karen Vallée, Contact

Fanshawe Community Orchestra *See* London Community Orchestra

The Farha Foundation / La Fondation Farha

#100, 576, rue Sainte-Catherine est, Montréal QC H2L 2E1
Tel: 514-270-4900; *Fax:* 514-270-5363
farha@farha.qc.ca
www.farha.qc.ca
www.facebook.com/FondationFARHAFoundation
twitter.com/FarhaFoundation
Overview: A medium-sized provincial charitable organization founded in 1992
Mission: To raise funds to improve the quality of life for persons living with HIV & AIDS throughout Québec
Chief Officer(s):
Nancy Farha, Executive Director (interim) Ext. 223
n.farha@farha.qc.ca
Finances: *Annual Operating Budget:* $500,000-$1.5 Million; *Funding Sources:* Private donations
Staff Member(s): 7; 800 volunteer(s)
Membership: 1-99; *Committees:* Events; Grant; Executive
Activities: *Awareness Events:* Ça Marche - AIDS Fundraising Walk; *Speaker Service:* Yes

Farm & Food Care Foundation

#106, 100 Stone Rd. West, Guelph ON N1G 5L3
e-mail: info@ farmcarefoundation.ca
www.farmcarefoundation.ca
Overview: A small national charitable organization founded in 2011
Mission: Develops and supports programs to communicate with Canadians helping to build confidence and trust in Canadian food and farming.

Farm & Food Care Ontario

#106, 100 Stone Rd. West, Guelph ON N1G 5L3
Tel: 519-837-1326; *Fax:* 519-837-3209
www.farmfoodcare.org
www.facebook.com/FarmFoodCare
twitter.com/farmfoodcare
www.youtube.com/user/FarmandFoodCare
Merged from: Ontario Farm Animal Council; Agricultural Groups Concerned about Resources and the Environment
Overview: A medium-sized provincial organization founded in 2012
Mission: To support & promote the responsible production & marketing of livestock & poultry by Ontario farmers & through a variety of initiatives, to better inform the public of the excellence of animal agriculture
Finances: *Funding Sources:* Memberships; corporate sponsorships; grants
Staff Member(s): 3
Membership: *Fees:* $250-$30,000
Activities: Consumer & producer displays; public speaking; agri-food spokespeople training; media relations; industry representation & services; referral & research

Farm & Ranch Safety & Health Association (FARSHA)

#311, 9440 - 202 St., Langley BC V1M 4A6
Tel: 604-881-6078; *Fax:* 604-881-6079
Toll-Free: 877-533-1789
farmsafe@farsha.bc.ca
www.farsha.bc.ca
www.facebook.com/FARSHABC
www.twitter.com/FARSHA_OHS
www.youtube.com/farshavideos
Overview: A medium-sized provincial organization founded in 1993
Mission: To reduce the number of accidents on farms & ranches in British Columbia through an active program of education & training in all regions of the province
Chief Officer(s):
Ralph McGinn, Chair
Bruce Johnson, Executive Director
bruce@farsha.bc.ca
Staff Member(s): 4
Activities: *Library* Open to public

Farm Management Canada

#300, 250 City Centre Ave., Ottawa ON K1R 6K7
Tel: 613-237-9060; *Fax:* 613-237-9330
Toll-Free: 888-232-3262
info@fmc-gac.com
www.fmc-gac.com
www.facebook.com/fmc.gac
twitter.com/FMC_GAC
www.youtube.com/user/fmcgac
Previous Name: Canadian Farm Business Management Council
Overview: A medium-sized national organization founded in 1992
Mission: To advance farm business management so that managers have access to the skills & tools for success
Chief Officer(s):
Heather Watson, Executive Director, 613-237-9060 Ext. 31
heather.watson@fmc-gac.com.
Finances: *Annual Operating Budget:* $1.5 Million-$3 Million
Staff Member(s): 8
Membership: 57 organizations; *Member Profile:* Associations; producers; governments; individuals; corporations
Activities: *Speaker Service:* Yes

Farm Radio International / Radios Rurales Internationales

1404 Scott St., Ottawa ON K1Y 4M8
Tel: 613-761-3650; *Fax:* 613-798-0990
Toll-Free: 888-773-7717
info@farmradio.org
www.farmradio.org
www.linkedin.com/company/farm-radio-international
www.facebook.com/farmradio
twitter.com/farmradio
www.youtube.com/farmradioint
Previous Name: Developing Countries Farm Radio Network
Overview: A medium-sized international charitable organization founded in 1979
Mission: To increase food supplies & to improve the nutrition, health & quality of life of small-scale farmers in developing countries through a coordinating network of broadcasters & others who exchange information about simple, practical sustainable farming techniques & health practices; To support broadcasters to strengthen small scale farmers & rural life
Member of: Canadian Centre for Philanthropy; Ontario Council for International Cooperation; Canadian Council for International Cooperation
Chief Officer(s):
Kevin Perkins, Executive Director
kperkins@farmradio.org
Finances: *Annual Operating Budget:* $250,000-$500,000; *Funding Sources:* Private donations; government grants; CIDA
Staff Member(s): 6; 10 volunteer(s)
Membership: 500; *Fees:* Free to radio stations in developing countries; *Member Profile:* Rural radio broadcasters in developing countries
Activities: *Library*
Publications:
• Network News
Type: Newsletter
Profile: Provides information about the program and the people involved in the organization, as well as updates on Canada's international development program.

Farmers of North America (FNA)

#318, 111 Research Dr., Saskatoon SK S7N 3R2
Tel: 306-665-2294; *Fax:* 306-651-0444
Toll-Free: 877-362-3276
info@fna.ca
www.fna.ca
Overview: A large national organization founded in 1998
Mission: To improve farm profitability across Canada
Membership: 10,000

Farmers of North America Strategic Agriculture Institute (FNA-SAG)

Head Office, #318, 111 Research Dr., Saskatoon SK S7N 3R2
Tel: 306-665-5032; *Fax:* 306-665-4513
www.fnastrategicag.ca
Overview: A large national organization founded in 2008 overseen by Canadian Federation of Agriculture
Mission: To identify new methods for farm profitability; to identify policy & regulatory issues affecting profitability, & to help advocate for change; to identify areas of needed research
Member of: Canadian Federation of Agriculture
Chief Officer(s):
Bob Friesen, CEO
bfriesen@fna.ca
Jonathan Warnock, Director, Research
jwarnock@fna.ca

Farmers' Markets Canada (FMC) / Les Marchés agricoles Canada (MAC)

c/o Robert T. Chorney, 54 Bayshore Rd., R.R.#4, Brighton ON K0K 1H0
Tel: 613-475-2913
Toll-Free: 800-387-3276
fmo@farmersmarketsontario.com
www.farmersmarketscanada.ca
Overview: A large national organization
Mission: The mission of FMC is to promote farmers' markets and develop national initiatives and partnerships to further the viability, growth and prosperity of the Canadian farmers' market industry.
Chief Officer(s):
Robert T. Chorney, President
fmo@farmersmarketsontario.com

Farmers' Markets of Nova Scotia Cooperative Ltd. (FMNS)

PO Box 33008, Halifax NS B3L 4T6

Tel: 902-425-9776
FMNS@farmersmarketsnovascotia.ca
farmersmarketsnovascotia.ca
www.facebook.com/FarmersMarketsNovaScotia
Overview: A small provincial organization founded in 2004 overseen by Farmers' Markets Canada
Mission: Maintaining and developing a network of farmers' markets throughout Nova Scotia.
Chief Officer(s):
Rowena Hopkins, Executive Director
Publications:
• The Vine
Type: Newsletter

Farmers' Markets Ontario (FMO)
54 Bayshore Rd., Brighton ON K0K 1H0
Tel: 613-475-4769; *Fax:* 613-475-2913
Toll-Free: 800-387-3276
fmo@farmersmarketsontario.com
www.farmersmarketsontario.com
www.facebook.com/pages/Farmers-Markets-Ontario/111525108903511?ref=hl
twitter.com/FarmersMktsOnt
Overview: A large provincial organization founded in 1991 overseen by Farmers' Markets Canada
Mission: Promotes and encourages farmers' markets in Ontario, develops information to help farmers who may be new at farmers' markets, researches what consumers are looking for when they buy Ontario food via direct marketing channels, and undertake consumer awareness and marketing activities to promote these efforts.
Chief Officer(s):
Robert T. Chorney, Executive Director
Membership: *Fees:* $141-$395 vendors; $141-$339 associate
Publications:
• Market Matters
Type: Newsletter

FarmFolk CityFolk
#203, 1661 Duranleau St., Vancouver BC V6H 3S3
Tel: 604-730-0450
Toll-Free: 877-730-0452
info@farmfolkcityfolk.ca
www.farmfolkcityfolk.ca
www.facebook.com/FarmFolkCityFolk
twitter.com/ffcf
Previous Name: FarmFolk/CityFolk Society
Overview: A small local charitable organization founded in 1993
Mission: To work with others for a local, sustainable food system; to make connection between farm & city, producer & consumer, grower & eater that creates sustainable communities; To protect foodlands, support farmers & food producers, & connect communities
Chief Officer(s):
Heather Johnstone, Chair
Nicholas Scapillati, Execxutive Director
Finances: *Annual Operating Budget:* $100,000-$250,000; *Funding Sources:* Foundations; memberships; donations
Staff Member(s): 4; 80 volunteer(s)
Membership: 15 institutional; 200 student; 200 individual; 20 associate; *Fees:* $500+ corporate; $100 farm; $50 family; $30 individual; *Member Profile:* Not-for-profit, charitable organization
Activities: Events, projects, education; *Awareness Events:* "Feast of Fields" Fundraiser, Sept.; *Library:* FarmFolk/CityFolk Resource Library; Open to public

FarmFolk/CityFolk Society *See* FarmFolk CityFolk

Farming Smarter (SARA)
#100, 5401 - 1st Ave. South, Lethbridge AB T1J 4V6
Tel: 403-381-5118; *Fax:* 403-382-4526
Other Communication: Blog:
www.farmingsmarterblog.blogspot.ca
sara.research@connectcomm.ca
www.farmingsmarter.com
www.facebook.com/farmingsmarter
twitter.com/farmingsmarter
www.youtube.com/farmingsmarter
Overview: A small local organization founded in 1994 overseen by Agricultural Research & Extension Council of Alberta
Mission: To improve sustainability & efficiency of farming methods throughout Southern Alberta
Member of: Agricultural Research & Extension Council of Alberta
Chief Officer(s):
Ron Lamb, Chair
Ken Coles, General Manager, 403-317-0757
ken@farmingsmarter.com
Publications:
• Farming Smarter Newsletter
Type: Newsletter

Faro Humane Society
PO Box 315, Faro YT Y0B 1K0
Tel: 867-994-2713; *Fax:* 867-994-3154
Overview: A small local organization
Mission: To protect dogs, cats, horses, birds, livestock, lab animals, wildlife & the environment.
Member of: Canadian Federation of Humane Societies

FAST (Fighting Antisemitism Together)
c/o CIJA, Manulife Centre, PO Box 19514, 55 Bloor St. West, Toronto ON M4W 3T9
Tel: 416-925-7499; *Fax:* 416-925-3531
www.fightingantisemitism.com
Overview: A small local organization founded in 2005
Chief Officer(s):
Nancy Greco, Senior Manager, Administration
nancy.greco@bmo.com
Elizabeth Comper, Founder
Tony Comper, Founder
Membership: *Member Profile:* Non-Jewish Canadian business & community leaders
Activities: "Choose Your Voice: Antisemitism in Canada" - educational program for students in grades 6-8

F.A.S.T.
#7B, 2441 Lakeshore Rd. West, Oakville ON L6L 5V5
Tel: 905-469-6338
Toll-Free: 888-651-5186
www.familytalk.ca
Also Known As: Family Adolescent Straight Talk Inc.
Overview: A small local charitable organization
Mission: F.A.S.T. helps people to recover from substance abuse/addicitons, by providing a safe environment in to receive crisis counselling, reconcile with family, friends and employers, and participate in ongoing individual and group therapy.
Chief Officer(s):
Jim Harkins, Executive Director/Senior Counselor
Staff Member(s): 5

FaunENord
CP 422, 512, rte 167 sud, Chibougamau QC G8P 2X8
Tél: 418-748-4441; *Téléc:* 418-748-1110
faunenord@lino.com
www.faunenord.org
www.facebook.com/pages/FaunENord/220907094605740
Aperçu: *Dimension:* petite; *Envergure:* locale
Mission: Une entreprise vouée à la promotion & à l'aménagement durable des ressources fauniques & des écosystèmes
Membre(s) du bureau directeur:
Isabelle Milord, Présidente

Federal Association of Security Officials (FASO) / Association fédérale des représentants de la sécurité
PO Box 2384, Stn. D, Ottawa ON K1P 5W5
Fax: 613-773-5787
Toll-Free: 888-330-3276
info@faso-afrs.ca
faso-afrs.ca
Overview: A medium-sized national organization founded in 1992
Mission: To enhance the performance & career development of federal security officers through enhancing the security function in government & improving the professionalism of security officers.
Chief Officer(s):
Claude J.G. Levesque, President
Membership: *Member Profile:* Federal government employees & employees of agencies who are subject to the Policy on Government Security

Federal Liberal Association of Nunavut
c/o Liberal Party of Canada, #600, 81 Metcalf St., Ottawa ON K1P 6M8
Toll-Free: 888-542-3725
assistance@liberal.ca
Overview: A small provincial organization
Mission: Representing the Liberal Party in Nunavut
Chief Officer(s):
Michel Potvin, President

Federal Libraries Coordination Secretariat
Place de la Cité, 550 de la Cité Blvd., Gatineau QC K1A 0N4
Tel: 613-410-9752; *Fax:* 819-934-7534
FLCS-SCBGF@lac-bac.gc.ca
Previous Name: Council of Federal Libraries / Conseil des bibliothèques du gouvernement fédéral
Overview: A medium-sized national organization founded in 1976
Mission: To coordinate federal libraries service reports to the Recordkeeping & Library Coordination Office of the Government Records Branch
Chief Officer(s):
Anne Chartrand, Resources Officer, Federal Libraries Consortium
Membership: *Member Profile:* All library and library-like entities within the federal government

Federal Superannuates National Association *See* National Association of Federal Retirees

Federated Women's Institutes of Canada (FWIC) / Fédération des instituts féminins du Canada
PO Box 209, 359 Blue Lake Rd., St George ON N0E 1N0
Tel: 519-448-3873; *Fax:* 519-448-3506
fwican@gmail.com
www.fwic.ca
Overview: A large national charitable organization founded in 1919
Mission: To act as a united voice for Women's Institutes of Canada; To promote Canadian agriculture & community living
Chief Officer(s):
Marie Kenny, President, 902-368-8285
mkfwic@gmail.com
Finances: *Funding Sources:* Membership fees
Staff Member(s): 2
Membership: 18,000; *Member Profile:* Any member in good standing of any provincial unit, institute, or body of women; *Committees:* Agriculture; Canadian Industries; Citizenship & Legislation; Education & Cultural Activities; Home Economics & Health; International Affairs; Constitution & By-laws; Finance; Resolutions; Publicity; Recruitment & Extension; Hoodless Homestead; Unity; Environment
Activities: Providing resources; Intitiating programs; Providing inter-communication opportunities; Hosting conferences, workshops & meetings
Awards:
• Erland Lee Award of Appreciation (Award)
Publications:
• Federated News [a publication of the Federated Women's Institutes of Canada]
Type: Newsletter; *Frequency:* s-a.

Federated Women's Institutes of Ontario (FWIO)
7382 Wellington Rd. 30, RR#5, Guelph ON N1H 6J2
Tel: 519-836-3078; *Fax:* 519-836-9456
fwio@fwio.on.ca
www.fwio.on.ca
www.facebook.com/home.php?sk=group_7156866227
Overview: A medium-sized provincial charitable organization founded in 1897 overseen by Federated Women's Institutes of Canada
Mission: To assist & encourage women to become more knowledgeable & responsible citizens; To promote & develop good family life skills; To help discover, stimulate & develop leadership; To help identify & resolve need in the community
Member of: Associated Country Women of the World
Chief Officer(s):
Lynn Ruigrok, Executive Director
lynnr@fwio.on.ca
Finances: *Annual Operating Budget:* $250,000-$500,000; *Funding Sources:* Membership dues; fundraising; gala events
Staff Member(s): 5; 1000 volunteer(s)
Membership: 10,500; *Fees:* $38 branch; $40 associate; *Member Profile:* Persons 16 years of age & over; *Committees:* Membership; Convention; Education; Erland Lee Museum; Budget; Home & Country Editorial; Personnel; Resolutions; Scholarship
Activities: Rose Health Programs

Fédération acadienne de la Nouvelle-Écosse (FANE)
La Maison acadienne, 54, rue Queen, Dartmouth NS B2Y 1G3
Tél: 902-433-0065; *Téléc:* 902-433-0066
fane@federationacadienne.ca
www.federationacadienne.ca
Aperçu: *Dimension:* moyenne; *Envergure:* provinciale; fondée en 1968 surveillé par Fédération des communautés francophones et acadienne du Canada

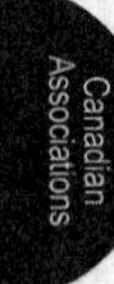

Mission: Un regroupement d'organismes régionaux, provinciaux et institutionnels d'expression française qui s'engage à promouvoir l'épanouissement et le développement global de la communauté acadienne et francophone de la Nouvelle-Écosse.
Membre de: Fédération canadienne pour l'alphabétisation en français; Société nationale des Acadiens
Membre(s) du bureau directeur:
Marie-Claude Rioux, Directrice générale, 902-433-0064
dg@federationacadienne.ca
Membre(s) du personnel: 9
Membre: 29 associations
Activités: *Bibliothèque* Bibliothèque publique

Centre communautaire La Picasse
CP 70, 3435 Rte 206, Petit de Grat NS B0E 2L0
Tél: 902-226-0149; *Téléc:* 902-226-0549
lapicasse@lapicasse.ca
www.lapicasse.ca
twitter.com/LaPicasse
Membre(s) du bureau directeur:
Yvon Samson, Directrice générale
direction@lapicasse.ca

Community education center Étoile de l'Acadie
15 Inglis St., Sydney NS B1P 7C6
Tél: 902-564-0432
etoile@eastlink.ca
www.etoiledelacadie.com
Membre(s) du bureau directeur:
Patrick DeLamirande, Président
president@etoiledelacadie.com

Conseil acadien de Par-en-Bas
CP 63, 4258, Rte 308, Tusket NS B0W 3M0
Tél: 902-648-2253; *Téléc:* 902-648-2340
www.capeb.ca
www.facebook.com/350741674069
Membre(s) du bureau directeur:
Clyde deViller, Directrice générale
cdeviller@capeb.ca

Conseil communautaire du Grand-Havre
201C du Portage Ave., Dartmouth NS B2X 3T4
Tél: 902-435-3244; *Téléc:* 902-435-1255
info@ccgh.ca
ccgh.ca
www.linkedin.com/in/conseilcommunautaire
www.facebook.com/126180694133823
twitter.com/ccghavre
www.youtube.com/user/conseilcommunautaire
Membre(s) du bureau directeur:
Claude Renaud, President

Société acadienne de Clare
CP 167, 795 Comeauville, Saulnierville NS B0W 2Z0
Tél: 902-769-0955; *Téléc:* 902-769-0979
sa.clare@ns.aliantzinc.ca
www.saclare.ca
Membre(s) du bureau directeur:
Diane Besner, Présidente

Société Acadienne Sainte-Croix
1154, chemin Pomquet Monks Head, Antigonish NS B2G 2L4
Tél: 902-386-2679; *Téléc:* 902-735-3069
societesaintecroix.ca
www.facebook.com/176029749128363
Membre(s) du bureau directeur:
Rollande Dubé, Directrice générale
dg@societesaintecroix.ca

Société Saint-Pierre
CP 430, 15584 Cabot Trail Hwy, Cheticamp NS B0E 1H0
Tél: 902-224-2642; *Téléc:* 902-224-1579
lestroispignons@ns.sympatico.ca
lestroispignons.com/ssp/en/index.php
www.facebook.com/pages/Les-Trois-Pignons/249801311699866
twitter.com/LesTroisPignons
Membre(s) du bureau directeur:
Lisette Aucoin-Bourgeois, Directrice générale
lisettebourgeois@ns.sympatico.ca

Fédération aquatique du Canada ***See*** Aquatic Federation of Canada

Fédération autonome du collégial (ind.) (FAC) / Autonomous Federation of Collegial Staff (Ind.)

#400, 1259, rue Berri, Montréal QC H2L 4C7
Tél: 514-848-9977; *Téléc:* 514-848-0166
Ligne sans frais: 800-701-1369
Aperçu: *Dimension:* moyenne; *Envergure:* provinciale; fondée en 1988
Mission: Défendre et développer les intérêts économiques, sociaux, pédagogiques et professionnels du personnel enseignant des cégeps; défendre le droit d'association, la libre négociation et la liberté d'action syndicale; négocier et s'assurer de l'application des conventions collectives; de représenter ses syndicats affiliés partout où leurs intérêts sont débattus.
Membre(s) du bureau directeur:
Alain Dion, Président
Membre: 4 000 individus; 18 sections locales; *Critères d'admissibilité:* Syndicat d'enseignant-es de cégep; faire parvenir votre demande à la FAC; *Comités:* Négociation; Information; Affaires pédagogiques; Condition féminine; Pratiques syndicales; Application convention collective; Solidarité internationale

Fédération Auto-Québec ***Voir*** Auto Sport Québec

Fédération baton canadienne ***See*** Canadian Baton Twirling Federation

Fédération Canada-France

c/o Ghislaine P. Turcotte, 3328, prom Riverside, Ottawa ON K1V 8P1
www.canadafrance.org
Nom précédent: Fédération canadienne France-Canada
Aperçu: *Dimension:* petite; *Envergure:* internationale
Membre(s) du bureau directeur:
Jean Paul Turcotte, Président
Ghislaine P. Turcotte, Trésoriere
Membre: *Montant de la cotisation:* 10$ étudiant; 20$ adulte; 35$ couple

Fédération canadienne d'agrément des conseillers en toxicomanie ***See*** Canadian Addiction Counsellors Certification Federation

La fédération canadienne d'aromathérapistes ***See*** Canadian Federation of Aromatherapists

Fédération canadienne d'escrime ***See*** Canadian Fencing Federation

Fédération canadienne de baseball amateur ***See*** Baseball Canada

Fédération canadienne de course d'orientation ***See*** Canadian Orienteering Federation

Fédération canadienne de culturisme ***See*** Canadian Bodybuilding Federation

Fédération canadienne de gymnastique rythmique sportive ***See*** Canadian Rhythmic Sportive Gymnastic Federation

Fédération canadienne de handball olympique ***See*** Canadian Team Handball Federation

Fédération canadienne de kendo ***See*** Canadian Kendo Federation

Fédération canadienne de l'agriculture ***See*** Canadian Federation of Agriculture

Fédération canadienne de l'entreprise indépendante ***See*** Canadian Federation of Independent Business

Fédération canadienne de la faune ***See*** Canadian Wildlife Federation

Fédération canadienne de robotique ***See*** Canadian Federation for Robotics

Fédération canadienne des amis de musées ***See*** Canadian Federation of Friends of Museums

Fédération canadienne des Associations de propriétaires immobiliers ***See*** Canadian Federation of Apartment Associations

Fédération canadienne des associations des professeurs de musique ***See*** Canadian Federation of Music Teachers' Associations

Fédération canadienne des associations foyer-école ***See*** Canadian Home & School Federation

Fédération canadienne des clubs des femmes de carrières commerciales et professionnelles ***See*** The Canadian Federation of Business & Professional Women's Clubs

Fédération canadienne des dix-quilles, inc. ***See*** Canadian Tenpin Federation, Inc.

Fédération canadienne des doyens des écoles d'administration ***See*** Canadian Federation of Business School Deans

Fédération canadienne des échecs ***See*** Chess Federation of Canada

Fédération canadienne des enseignantes et des enseignants ***See*** Canadian Teachers' Federation

Fédération canadienne des épiciers indépendants ***See*** Canadian Federation of Independent Grocers

Fédération canadienne des étudiantes et étudiants ***See*** Canadian Federation of Students

Fédération canadienne des étudiants et étudiantes en génie ***See*** Canadian Federation of Engineering Students

Fédération canadienne des femmes diplômées des universités ***See*** Canadian Federation of University Women

La Fédération canadienne des festivals de musique ***See*** Federation of Canadian Music Festivals

Fédération canadienne des gemmes et des minéraux ***See*** Gem & Mineral Federation of Canada

Fédération canadienne des infirmières et infirmiers en santé mentale ***See*** Canadian Federation of Mental Health Nurses

Fédération canadienne des jeunes ligues ***See*** Canadian Federation of Junior Leagues

Fédération canadienne des métiers d'art ***See*** Canadian Crafts Federation

Fédération canadienne des municipalités ***See*** Federation of Canadian Municipalities

Fédération Canadienne des Orthothérapeutes ***See*** Canadian Federation of Orthotherapists

Fédération Canadienne des Retraités ***See*** Canadian Federation of Pensioners

Fédération canadienne des sciences de la Terre ***See*** Canadian Federation of Earth Sciences

Fédération Canadienne des Sciences Humaines ***See*** Canadian Federation for the Humanities & Social Sciences

Fédération canadienne des services de garde à l'enfance ***See*** Canadian Child Care Federation

La Fédération canadienne des syndicats d'infirmières/infirmiers ***See*** Canadian Federation of Nurses Unions

Fédération canadienne du mouton ***See*** Canadian Sheep Federation

La Fédération canadienne du textile ***See*** Canadian Textile Association

Fédération canadienne du vêtement ***See*** Canadian Apparel Federation

Fédération canadienne France-Canada ***Voir*** Fédération Canada-France

La Fédération canadienne incorporée de bridge ***See*** Canadian Bridge Federation

Fédération canadienne nationale des syndicats indépendants ***See*** Canadian National Federation of Independent Unions

Fédération canadienne volkssport ***See*** Canadian Volkssport Federation

La Fédération Canado-Arabe ***See*** Canadian Arab Federation

Fédération chypriote du Canada ***See*** Cypriot Federation of Canada

Fédération CSN - Construction (CSN) / CNTU Federation - Construction (CNTU)

2100, boul de Maisonneuve Est, 4e étage, Montréal QC H2K 4S1
Tél: 514-598-2044; *Téléc:* 514-598-2040
www.csnconstruction.qc.ca
www.facebook.com/csnconstruction
Aperçu: *Dimension:* moyenne; *Envergure:* provinciale
Mission: Pour défendre les droits de leurs membres et de leur assurer de bonnes conditions de travail

Membre(s) du bureau directeur:
Pierre Brassard, Président
pierre.brassard@csnconstruction.qc.ca
Karyne Prégent, Secrétaire général
karyne.pregent@csn.qc.ca
Membre(s) du personnel: 4
Membre: 18,000

Fédération Culinaire Canadienne *See* Canadian Culinary Federation

Fédération culturelle acadienne de la Nouvelle-Écosse (FECANE)

54, rue Queen, Dartmouth NÉ B2Y 1G3
Tél: 902-466-1610; *Téléc:* 902-466-7970
www.fecane.com
www.facebook.com/infofecane
twitter.com/InfoFecane
Nom précédent: Fédération des festivals acadiens de la Nouvelle-Écosse
Aperçu: *Dimension:* petite; *Envergure:* provinciale; Organisme sans but lucratif; fondée en 1990
Mission: Développer et de promouvoir les différents produits artistiques acadiens de la N.E. Nos activités se concentrent sur les différentes communautés acadiennes de la N.E. mais peuvent également se dérouler à l'extérieur de la province
Membre(s) du bureau directeur:
Martin Théberge, Directeur général
Membre(s) du personnel: 3
Membre: *Montant de la cotisation:* Barème
Activités: Promotion et développement de la culture acadienne en Nouvelle Écosse

Fédération culturelle canadienne-française (FCCF)

Place de la Francophonie, #405, 450 Rideau St., Ottawa ON K1N 5Z4
Tél: 613-241-8770; *Téléc:* 613-241-6064
Ligne sans frais: 800-267-2005
info@fccf.ca
www.fccf.ca
www.facebook.com/infofccf
twitter.com/infofccf
Aperçu: *Dimension:* moyenne; *Envergure:* nationale; fondée en 1977
Mission: Défendre et promouvoir les arts et la culture de la francophonie canadienne hors-Québec.
Membre de: Conseil canadiens des arts; Conseil francophone de la chanson; Conseil des ressources humaines du secteur culturel
Membre(s) du bureau directeur:
Éric Dubeau, Directeur général, 613-241-8770 Ext. 24
edubeau@fccf.ca
Finances: *Budget de fonctionnement annuel:* $500,000-$1.5 Million
Membre(s) du personnel: 3; 32 bénévole(s)
Membre: 14 associations culturelles provinciales; *Montant de la cotisation:* 800$

Fédération culturelle de L'Ile-du-Prince-Édouard inc. (FCIPE)

5, promenade Acadienne, Charlottetown PE C1C 1M2
Tél: 902-368-1895; *Téléc:* 902-370-7334
fcipe@ssta.org
www.fcipe.ca
www.facebook.com/federation.culturelle
Aperçu: *Dimension:* petite; *Envergure:* provinciale; fondée en 1990
Mission: Développement culturel de la communauté acadienne et francophone
Affiliation(s): Commission culturelle de l'Atlantique; Fédération culturelle canadienne-française
Membre(s) du bureau directeur:
Michelle Blanchard, Présidente
Membre: 13; *Montant de la cotisation:* 10$ individuel; 50$ organisme; *Critères d'admissibilite:* Comité culture; musée; centre d'art
Activités: *Stagiaires:* Oui; *Bibliothèque* Bibliothèque publique

Fédération culturelle finno-canadienne *See* Finnish Canadian Cultural Federation

Fédération cycliste du Québec *Voir* Fédération québécoise des sports cyclistes

Fédération d'agriculture biologique du Québec (FABQ)

#100, 555, boul Roland-Therrien, Longueuil QC J4H 3Y9
Tél: 450-679-0530; *Téléc:* 450-670-4867
fabq@upa.qc.ca
www.fabqbio.ca
Aperçu: *Dimension:* petite; *Envergure:* provinciale; fondée en 1989
Mission: Promouvoir l'étude, la défense et le développement des intérêts économiques, sociaux et moraux de ses membres; administrer tout le programme de la mise en marché; étudier des problèmes relatifs à la production; coopérer à la vulgarisation des techniques de production biologique; renseigner le producteur sur la production et la vente de produits biologiques certifiés
Membre(s) du bureau directeur:
Gérard Bouchard, Président
Finances: *Budget de fonctionnement annuel:* $50,000-$100,000
Membre(s) du personnel: 1; 7 bénévole(s)
Membre: 200; *Montant de la cotisation:* 125$; *Critères d'admissibilite:* Producteurs agricoles biologiques
Activités: Promotion générique; développement de marchés; information

Fédération d'athlétisme du Québec *Voir* Fédération québécoise d'athlétisme

Fédération d'escrime du Québec

CP 1000, Succ. M, 4545, av Pierre-de Coubertin, Montréal QC H1V 0B2
Tél: 514-252-3045; *Téléc:* 514-254-3451
info@escrimequebec.qc.ca
www.escrimequebec.qc.ca
www.facebook.com/280110325350969
Aperçu: *Dimension:* moyenne; *Envergure:* provinciale surveillé par Canadian Fencing Federation
Membre de: Fédération canadienne d'escrime
Membre(s) du bureau directeur:
Maître Dominique Teisseire, Directeur, Technique et administratif
dominiqueteisseire@hotmail.com

Fédération de balle au mur du Canada *See* Canadian Handball Association

Fédération de basketball du Québec (FBBQ) / Québec Basketball Federation

4545, av Pierre-de Coubertin, Montréal QC H1V 0B2
Tél: 514-252-3057; *Téléc:* 514-252-3357
Ligne sans frais: 866-557-3057
www.basketball.qc.ca
www.facebook.com/BasketballQc
twitter.com/BasketballQc
www.youtube.com/user/BasketballQc
Également appelé: Basketball Québec
Aperçu: *Dimension:* grande; *Envergure:* provinciale; Organisme sans but lucratif; fondée en 1970 surveillé par Canada Basketball
Mission: Développement et promotion de la discipline; Formation de joueurs, entraîneurs et arbitres; organisation de compétitions provinciales; Programme Poursuite de l'Excellence (Équipes et Espoirs du Québec)
Membre(s) du bureau directeur:
Olga Hrycak, Présidente
Daniel Grimard, Directeur général
dgrimard@basketball.qc.ca
Mélissa Dion, Coordonnatrice, Communications et marketing
mdion@basketball.qc.ca
Membre(s) du personnel: 7
Membre: 35,000 personnes
Activités: *Stagiaires:* Oui; *Service de conférenciers:* Oui

Fédération de Boulingrin du Québec *See* Québec Lawn Bowling Federation

Fédération de cheerleading du Québec (FCQ)

4545, av Pierre-de Coubertin, Montréal QC H1V 0B2
Tél: 514-252-3145; *Téléc:* 514-252-3146
Ligne sans frais: 866-694-3145
info@cheerleadingquebec.com
www.cheerleadingquebec.com
www.facebook.com/252273871484094
Aperçu: *Dimension:* petite; *Envergure:* provinciale surveillé par Cheer Canada
Membre de: Cheer Canada
Membre(s) du bureau directeur:
Jocelyn Deslaurier, Président
Catherine Marois Blanchet, Directrice générale
cmblanchet@cheerleadingquebec.com

Fédération de crosse du Québec (FCQ)

CP 1000, Succ. M, 4545, av Pierre-de Coubertin, Montréal QC H1V 3R2
Tél: 450-464-6606; *Téléc:* 514-251-8038
crosse@crosse.qc.ca
www.crosse.qc.ca
Aperçu: *Dimension:* moyenne; *Envergure:* provinciale; fondée en 1971 surveillé par Canadian Lacrosse Association
Mission: Offrir des services et des programmes axés vers le développement du sport de la crosse sur un plan régional et international
Membre de: Fédération Internationale d'Inter-Crosse; Canadian Lacrosse Association
Affiliation(s): Sports Québec; Regroupement Loisir Québec
Membre(s) du bureau directeur:
Guy Blondeau, Président
guyblondeau43@gmail.com
Pierre Filion, Directeur
pierrefilion@videotron.ca
Finances: *Budget de fonctionnement annuel:* $100,000-$250,000
Membre(s) du personnel: 2; 45 bénévole(s)
Membre: 39 000; *Montant de la cotisation:* 15-100; *Comités:* Commission tecchnique; Commission de développement; Interventions stratégiques
Activités: Stages de formation, conférences, ligues d'inter-crosse, compétitions; *Stagiaires:* Oui; *Service de conférenciers:* Oui

Fédération de football amateur de Québec *Voir* Football Québec

Fédération de golf du Québec / Québec Golf Federation

4545, av Pierre-de Coubertin, Montréal QC H1V 0B2
Tél: 514-252-3345; *Téléc:* 514-252-3346
golfquebec@golfquebec.org
www.golfquebec.org
www.facebook.com/golfquebec
twitter.com/golf_quebec
www.youtube.com/user/GolfQuebecMedias
Également appelé: Golf Québec
Nom précédent: Association de golf du Québec
Aperçu: *Dimension:* moyenne; *Envergure:* provinciale; Organisme sans but lucratif; fondée en 1920 surveillé par Royal Canadian Golf Association
Mission: Assurer le leadership; Favoriser la croissance et le développement du golf amateur dans toute la province tout en préservant l'intégrité et les traditions du jeu
Membre(s) du bureau directeur:
Jean-Pierre Beaulieu, Directeur général, 514-252-3345 Ext. 3732
jpbeaulieu@golfquebec.org
François Roy, Directeur général adjoint, 514-252-3345 Ext. 3476
froy@golfquebec.org
Éric Couture, Directeur, Tournois, 514-252-3345 Ext. 3594
ecouture@golfquebec.org
Serge Rocheleau, Coordonnateur, Services aux membres, 514-252-3345 Ext. 3755
srocheleau@golfquebec.org
Membre(s) du personnel: 9; 250 bénévole(s)
Membre: 61 000; *Montant de la cotisation:* 29$

Fédération de gymnastique du Québec (FGQ) / Québec Gymnastics Federation

4545, av Pierre-de Coubertin, Montréal QC H1V 0B2
Tél: 514-252-3043; *Téléc:* 514-252-3169
info@gymnastique.qc.ca
www.gymnastique.qc.ca
www.facebook.com/fedgymnastique.duqc
twitter.com/FGQ01
Aperçu: *Dimension:* grande; *Envergure:* provinciale; fondée en 1971
Mission: Promouvoir et assurer le développement do la gymnastique à travers tout le Québec; favoriser l'éclosion des talents en vue d'une participation aux plans national et international; unir et coordonner les efforts de toutes les personnes intéressées dans le sport de la gym
Membre de: Canadian Gymnastics Federation
Membre(s) du bureau directeur:
Serge Sabourin, Président
Helen Brossard, Vice-présidente
Membre(s) du personnel: 11
Membre: *Critères d'admissibilite:* Athléthes, entraîneurs, membres

Activités: *Événements de sensibilisation:* Semaine de la prévention; *Stagiaires:* Oui; *Bibliothèque* Bibliothèque publique

Fédération de l'âge d'or du Québec *Voir* Réseau FADOQ

Fédération de l'habitation coopérative du Canada *See* Cooperative Housing Federation of Canada

Fédération de l'industrie manufacturière (FIM-CSN)

#204, 2100, boul de Maisonneuve est, Montréal QC H2K 4S1
Tél: 514-529-4937; *Téléc:* 514-529-4935
fim@csn.qc.ca
www.fim.csn.qc.ca
www.facebook.com/FIMCSN
www.youtube.com/FIMcsn
Nom précédent: Fédération de la métallurgie
Aperçu: *Dimension:* grande; *Envergure:* provinciale; fondée en 2011
Membre de: Confédération des syndicats nationaux
Membre(s) du bureau directeur:
Alain Lampron, Président
Vacant, Secrétaire-Trésorier
Finances: *Budget de fonctionnement annuel:* $100,000-$250,000
Membre(s) du personnel: 10
Membre: 30 000 + 320 sections locales; *Critères d'admissibilite:* Ajusteurs, assembleurs, bobineurs, camionneurs, chimistes, commis, comptables, carrossiers, dessinateurs, électriciens, employé-es de soutien, fondeurs, journaliers, machinistes, magasiniers, mécaniciens, métallurgistes, mineurs, opérateurs, peintres, plombiers, secrétaires, soudeurs, techniciens, tuyauteurs; *Comités:* Surveillance; Santé sécurité et environnement; Formation; Jeunes; Condition féminine
Activités: *Bibliothèque*

Baie-Comeau
999, rue Comtois, Baie-Comeau QC G5C 2A5
Tél: 418-589-6353; *Téléc:* 418-589-6873
fim.baie-comeau@csn.qc.ca
Membre(s) du bureau directeur:
Marie-Ellen Tremblay, Secrétaire

Joliette
190, rue Montcalm, 1er étage, Joliette QC J6E 5G4
Tél: 450-759-4142; *Téléc:* 450-759-3234
fim.joliette@csn.qc.ca
Membre(s) du bureau directeur:
Michèle Côté, Secrétaire

Québec
#350, 155, boul Charest est, Québec QC G1K 3G6
Tél: 418-647-5845; *Téléc:* 418-647-5884
fim.quebec@csn.qc.ca
Membre(s) du bureau directeur:
Dany Vallée, Secrétaire

Rimouski
124, rue Sainte-Marie, Rimouski QC G5L 4E3
Tél: 418-723-7797
fim.rimouski@csn.qc.ca
Membre(s) du bureau directeur:
Isabelle Albert, Secrétaire

Rouyn-Noranda
243, rue Murdoch, Rouyn-Noranda QC J9X 1E8
Tél: 819-764-9541; *Téléc:* 819-764-4405
fim.abitibi@csn.qc.ca
Membre(s) du bureau directeur:
Sylvie Gaudet, Secrétaire

Saguenay
73, rue Arthur-Hamel, Saguenay QC G7H 3M9
fim.saguenay@csn.qc.ca

Shawinigan
#101, 550, av Broadway, Shawinigan QC G9N 1M3
Tél: 819-536-4434; *Téléc:* 819-536-7030
fim.shawinigan@csn.qc.ca
Membre(s) du bureau directeur:
Lise Lessard, Secrétaire

Sherbrooke
#220, 180, Côte de l'Acadie, Sherbrooke QC J1H 2T3
Tél: 819-563-5006; *Téléc:* 819-563-4242
fim.sherbrooke@csn.qc.ca
Membre(s) du bureau directeur:
Micheline Asselin, Secrétaire

Sorel-Tracy
815, rte Marie-Victorin, Sorel-Tracy QC J3R 1L1
Tél: 450-743-5502; *Téléc:* 450-743-6127
fim.sorel@csn.qc.ca
Membre(s) du bureau directeur:
Anne Aussant, Secrétaire

Val-d'Or
609, av Centrale, Val-d'Or QC J9P 1P9
Tél: 819-825-4458; *Téléc:* 819-825-4383
fim.abitibi@csn.qc.ca
Membre(s) du bureau directeur:
Sylvie Gaudet, Secrétaire

Fédération de l'informatique du Québec *Voir* Réseau ACTION TI

Fédération de l'Union des producteurs agricoles de la Beauce *Voir* Fédération de l'UPA de la Beauce

Fédération de l'UPA - Abitibi-Témiscamingue

970, av Larivière, Rouyn-Noranda QC J9X 4K5
Tél: 819-762-0833; *Téléc:* 819-762-0575
abitibi-temiscamingue@upa.qc.ca
Aperçu: *Dimension:* moyenne; *Envergure:* locale; fondée en 1976
Mission: L'étude, la défense et le développement des intérêts économiques, sociaux et moraux de ses membres, en l'occurence les producteurs et productrices agricoles
Affliation(s): Confédération de l'UPA
Membre(s) du bureau directeur:
Linda Lavoie, Coordonnatrice, Centre d'emploi agricole
Finances: *Budget de fonctionnement annuel:* $500,000-$1.5 Million; *Fonds:* Gouvernement provincial
Membre(s) du personnel: 16
Membre: 720; *Critères d'admissibilite:* Producteurs et productrices agricoles

Fédération de l'UPA - Bas-Saint-Laurent

284, rue Potvin, Rimouski QC G5L 7P5
Tél: 418-723-2424; *Téléc:* 418-723-6045
bas-saint-laurent@upa.qc.ca
www.bas-saint-laurent.upa.qc.ca
Aperçu: *Dimension:* moyenne; *Envergure:* locale
Membre(s) du bureau directeur:
Gilbert Marquis, Président
Membre: 2 500

Fédération de l'UPA - Mauricie

230, rue Vachon, Ttrois-Rivières QC G8T 8Y2
Tél: 819-378-4033; *Téléc:* 819-371-2712
mauricie@upa.qc.ca
www.mauricie.upa.qc.ca
Aperçu: *Dimension:* moyenne; *Envergure:* locale
Membre(s) du bureau directeur:
Jean-Marie Giguère, Président
Membre: 1 587;

Fédération de l'UPA de la Beauce

2550, 127e rue est, Saint-Georges QC G5Y 5L1
Tél: 418-228-5588; *Téléc:* 418-228-3943
Nom précédent: Fédération de l'Union des producteurs agricoles de la Beauce
Aperçu: *Dimension:* petite; *Envergure:* locale
Mission: Oeuvrer à l'amélioration des conditions de vie des producteurs et productrices agricoles de la région, tant du point de vue économique, social que moral
Membre(s) du bureau directeur:
Paul Doyon, Président
Membre(s) du personnel: 33
Membre: 3 000
Activités: *Listes de destinataires:* Oui

Fédération de l'UPA de Saint-Hyacinthe

3800, boul Casavant ouest, Saint-Hyacinthe QC J2S 8E3
Tél: 450-774-9154; *Téléc:* 450-778-3797
st-hyacinthe@upa.qc.ca
www.st-hyacinthe.upa.qc.ca
www.facebook.com/157943824245129
Aperçu: *Dimension:* moyenne; *Envergure:* locale; Organisme sans but lucratif; fondée en 1931
Mission: Défendre les droits des agriculteurs et leur fournir différents services
Affiliation(s): Confédération de l'UPA
Membre(s) du bureau directeur:
Carole Meunier, Directrice régionale
cmeunier@upa.qc.ca
Réjean Bessette, Président
Finances: *Budget de fonctionnement annuel:* $100,000-$250,000
Membre(s) du personnel: 42
Membre: 6 300; *Montant de la cotisation:* 490$ institutionnel; 245$ individu; *Critères d'admissibilite:* Agriculteurs; agricultrices; *Comités:* Agriculture durable; aménagement; comptabilité fiscale; développement bioalimentaire régional; environnement; finances; fiscalité municipale; main-d'oeuvre; services - conseils; vie syndicale
Activités: Syndicalisme agricole et formation; comptabilité et fiscalité; centre agricole

Fédération de l'UPA de Saint-Jean-Valleyfield

6, rue du Moulin, Saint-Rémi-de-Napierville QC J0L 2L0
Tél: 450-454-5115
st-jean-valleyfield@upa.qc.ca
www.upasjv.qc.ca
Aperçu: *Dimension:* moyenne; *Envergure:* provinciale; Organisme sans but lucratif; fondée en 1931
Mission: Défendre les intérêts des producteurs agricoles
Membre de: Union des producteurs agricoles
Membre(s) du bureau directeur:
Bernard Vincent, Président
Finances: *Budget de fonctionnement annuel:* $500,000-$1.5 Million
Membre: 4 300; *Critères d'admissibilite:* Producteurs agricoles

Fédération de la faune du Nouveau-Brunswick *See* New Brunswick Wildlife Federation

Fédération de la jeunesse canadienne-française inc. (FJCF)

#403, 450 Rideau St., Ottawa ON K1N 5Z4
Tél: 613-562-4624; *Téléc:* 613-562-3995
Ligne sans frais: 800-267-5173
fjcf@fjcf.ca
www.fjcf.ca
www.facebook.com/fjcf.ca
twitter.com/FJCF_Canada
www.flickr.com/photos/fjcf_canada
Aperçu: *Dimension:* moyenne; *Envergure:* nationale; Organisme sans but lucratif; fondée en 1974 surveillé par Fédération des communautés francophones et acadienne du Canada
Mission: Etre le porte-parole national de la jeunesse canadienne-française et acadienne; assurer l'épanouissement de la jeunesse dans les secteurs de l'éducation, des arts et communications, des loisirs et de l'économie; augmenter la visibilité de la FJCF et de ses membres auprès de leurs différentes clientèles; augmenter les occasions pour les jeunes d'utiliser la langue française; renforcer le sentiment d'appartenance des jeunes, pour qu'ils soient des agents de changement dans leur communauté.
Membre(s) du bureau directeur:
Sylvian Groulx, Directeur Général
Membre(s) du personnel: 8
Membre: 11
Activités: Jeux de la francophonie canadienne; Parlement jeunesse pancanadien; Réseau international de la jeunesse; *Stagiaires:* Oui; *Service de conférenciers:* Oui

Fédération de la jeunesse franco-ontarienne (FESFO)

#202, 135, rue Alice, Ottawa ON K1L 7X5
Tél: 613-260-8055; *Téléc:* 613-260-5346
Ligne sans frais: 877-260-8055
info@fesfo.ca
www.fesfo.ca
www.facebook.com/fesfo
twitter.com/laFESFO
www.youtube.com/user/LaFESFO
Nom précédent: Fédération des Élèves du secondaire franco-ontarien
Aperçu: *Dimension:* moyenne; *Envergure:* provinciale; Organisme sans but lucratif; fondée en 1975
Mission: S'assure que la jeunesse franco-ontarienne participe pleinement au développement de sa communauté
Affiliation(s): Fédération de la jeunesse canadienne-française
Membre(s) du bureau directeur:
Andrée Newell, Directrice générale
anewell@fesfo.ca
Membre(s) du personnel: 12
Membre: 25 000; *Critères d'admissibilite:* Agé entre 14 et 18 ans
Activités: Ateliers de formation; consultations auprès des membres; formation en leadership et estime de soi; activisme et lobbying politique; *Événements de sensibilisation:* Jeux Franco-Ontariens; Forums "Organizzaction"; Parlement jeunesse francophone de l'Ontario; *Service de conférenciers:* Oui

Fédération de la métallurgie *Voir* Fédération de l'industrie manufacturière (FIM-CSN)

Fédération de la relève agricole du Québec (FRAQ)

#105, 555, boul Roland-Therrien, Longueuil QC J4H 4E7

Tél: 450-679-0530; *Téléc:* 450-679-2375
fraq@upa.qc.ca
www.fraq.qc.ca
www.facebook.com/fraqreleve
twitter.com/LaFraq
www.youtube.com/user/lesbobtrotteurs
Aperçu: *Dimension:* moyenne; *Envergure:* provinciale; fondée en 1982
Mission: Améliorer les conditions d'établissement en agriculture et travailler à une meilleure préparation des jeunes qui se destinent à une carrière en production agricole
Membre de: Union des producteurs agricoles
Membre(s) du bureau directeur:
Yourianne Plante, Directrice générale par intérim
yplante@upa.qc.ca
Membre(s) du personnel: 3
Membre: 2,000; *Montant de la cotisation:* Barème; *Critères d'admissibilite:* Jeunes âgés entre 16 et 35 ans intéressés à l'agriculture

Fédération de la santé et des services sociaux (FSSS)

1601, av de Lorimier, Montréal QC H2K 4M5
Tél: 514-598-2210; *Téléc:* 514-598-2223
fsss@fsss.qc.ca
www.fsss.qc.ca
Aperçu: *Dimension:* grande; *Envergure:* nationale
Mission: De promouvoir et sauvegarder la santé, la sécurité et les intérêts des personnes employées des établissements affiliés ou en voie d'affiliation; de représenter ses membres auprès de la Confédération des syndicats nationaux en lui soumettant toutes questions d'intérêt général; de représenter ses membres, de concert avec le CSN, partout où les intérêts généraux des travailleuses et travailleurs le justifient; d'aider à conclure, en faveur des syndicats affiliés, des conventions collectives de travail et en favoriser l'application; de collaborer à l'éducation des travailleuses et travailleurs et à la formation de responsables et militantes et militants syndicaux; d'assurer les services à ses syndicats affiliés; de favoriser et d'établir des liens inter-syndicaux avec les autres travailleuses et travailleurs dans le secteur public et para-public et dans le secteur privé du Québec et du Canada
Membre de: Confédération des syndicats nationaux
Membre(s) du bureau directeur:
Jeff Begley, Président par intérim et Vice-président, Responsable du secteur privé
vp.prive@fsss.qc.ca
Denyse Paradis, Secrétaire-trésorière
sec.tres@fsss.qc.ca
Membre(s) du personnel: 110
Membre: 125 000 membres; 897 sections locales; *Critères d'admissibilite:* Etre un sydicat affilié à la Confédération des syndicats nationaux et à la Fédération des affaires sociales
Activités: *Bibliothèque*

Fédération de lutte olympique du Québec / Québec Wrestling Association

4545, av Pierre de Couberlin, Montréal QC H1V 3R2
Tél: 514-252-3044
www.quebecolympicwrestling.ca
Aperçu: *Dimension:* moyenne; *Envergure:* provinciale surveillé par Canadian Amateur Wrestling Association

Fédération de nage synchronisée *Voir* Synchro-Québec

Fédération de natation du Québec (FNQ)

CP 1000, Succ. M, 4545, av Pierre-de Coubertin, Montréal QC H1V 3R2
Tél: 514-252-3200; *Téléc:* 514-252-3232
fnq@fnq.qc.ca
www.fnq.qc.ca
www.facebook.com/163831313666941
twitter.com/fednatationqc
Aperçu: *Dimension:* moyenne; *Envergure:* provinciale surveillé par Swimming Canada
Membre de: Swimming Canada
Affliation(s): Éducation, Loisir et Sport Québec; AQUAM Équipes; Groupe Hospitalité Westmont (Quality et Comfort Inn); Location Sauvageau; Trophies Dubois; Westjet; Financière Manuvie; McAuslan
Membre(s) du bureau directeur:
Bernard Charron, Directeur général
bcharron@fnq.qc.ca

Fédération de Netball du Québec / Québec Amateur Netball Federation (QANF)

CP 1000, Succ. M, 4545, av Pierre-de Coubertin, Montréal QC H1V 3R2
Tél: 514-486-2769
www.netballquebec.ca
www.facebook.com/197372537001817
Également appelé: Netball Québec
Aperçu: *Dimension:* moyenne; *Envergure:* provinciale; fondée en 1974 surveillé par Netball Canada
Mission: Promouvoir et développer le netball féminin au Québec
Membre de: Netball Canada
Affliation(s): International Federation of Netball Associations
Membre(s) du bureau directeur:
Avice Roberts-Joseph, Présidente
Donna Baker, Secrétaire
Lecita Audain, Trésoriere
Membre: 750; *Montant de la cotisation:* 35$; *Comités:* Technique
Activités: Tournois; Ligues; Cliniques pour entraîneurs et arbitres

Fédération de patinage artistique du Québec (FPAQ)

4545, av Pierre-de Coubertin, Montréal QC H1V 0B2
Tél: 514-252-3073; *Téléc:* 514-252-3170
patinage@patinage.qc.ca
www.patinage.qc.ca
www.facebook.com/patinageqc
Aperçu: *Dimension:* grande; *Envergure:* provinciale; fondée en 1969
Mission: Rendre accessible à tous, les programmes de Patinage Canada, que ce soit par amour, par plaisir ou pour atteindre l'excellence; a l'unisson, nous contribuons ainsi à l'avancement de notre sport.
Membre(s) du bureau directeur:
Sylvie Simard, Présidente
ssimard@patinage.qc.ca
Any-Claude Dion, Directrice générale, 514-252-3073 Ext. 3550

Membre(s) du personnel: 10
Membre: 40 000; 18 associations régionales; 242 organismes locaux
Prix, Bouses:
- Bénévole par excellence (Prix)
- Médaillés québécois (Prix)
- Temple de la renommée (Prix)
- Trophée Josée-Chouinard (Prix)

Fédération de Patinage de Vitesse du Québec

930, av Roland Beaudin, Sainte-Foy QC G1V 4H8
Tél: 418-651-1973; *Téléc:* 418-651-1977
Ligne sans frais: 877-651-1973
fpvq@fpvq.org
www.fpvq.org
Aperçu: *Dimension:* petite; *Envergure:* provinciale surveillé par Speed Skating Canada
Mission: Depuis un peu plus d'un mois déjà, les athlètes du Centre national courte piste sont en entraînement hors glace sous la surveillance des entraîneurs et avec la grande collaboration du groupe Actiforme.
Membre de: Speed Skating Canada
Membre(s) du bureau directeur:
Robert Dubreuil, Directeur général
Membre(s) du personnel: 6

Fédération de pétanque du Québec

4545, av Pierre-de Coubertin, Montréal QC H1V 0B2
Tél: 514-252-3077
petanque@petanque.qc.ca
www.petanque.qc.ca
www.facebook.com/189251017803912
Aperçu: *Dimension:* moyenne; *Envergure:* provinciale
Mission: Développement du sport de pétanque
Membre(s) du bureau directeur:
Janick Provencher, Présidente
Membre: 4 000; 14 organismes régionaux

Fédération de ressources d'hébergement pour femmes violentées et en difficulté du Québec (FRHFVDQ)

CP 55036, Succ. Maisonneuve, Montréal QC H1W 0A1
Tél: 514-878-9757; *Téléc:* 514-878-9755
info@fede.qc.ca
www.fede.qc.ca
Aperçu: *Dimension:* moyenne; *Envergure:* provinciale; Organisme sans but lucratif; fondée en 1987
Mission: La Fédération promouvoit et défend les intérêts des maisons d'hébergement pour femmes violentées et en difficulté membres en tenant compte de leur autonomie, de leurs particularités, de leurs similitudes et de leurs différences et ce, dans un esprit de partenariat et de concertation
Membre de: Relais Femmes; Féderation des Femmes du Québec; Table des Regroupements provinciaux des organismes communautaires et bénévoles
Finances: *Budget de fonctionnement annuel:* $100,000-$250,000
Membre: 40; *Montant de la cotisation:* 1% subvention de base; *Critères d'admissibilite:* Maisons d'hébergement
Activités: Formation; representation; sensibilisation;

Fédération de rugby du Québec (FRQ) / Quebec Rugby Union

CP 1000, Succ. M, 4545, av Pierre-de Coubertin, Montréal QC H1V 3R2
Tél: 514-252-3189; *Téléc:* 514-252-3159
info@rugbyquebec.qc.ca
www.rugbyquebec.qc.ca
www.facebook.com/98779487768
twitter.com/RugbyQuebec
Aperçu: *Dimension:* moyenne; *Envergure:* provinciale surveillé par Rugby Canada
Mission: Promouvoir le sport et la santé physique en général, et sans limiter ce qui précède le sport du rugby; organiser des tournois de Rugby dans la province de Québec; regrouper les associations régionales et les clubs de Rugby du Québec
Membre de: Rugby Canada
Membre(s) du bureau directeur:
Martin Cormier, Directeur général
Membre(s) du personnel: 3
Membre: 2 610

Fédération de soccer du Québec (FDSDQ)

#210, 955, av Bois-de-Boulogne, Laval QC H7N 4G1
Tél: 450-975-3355; *Téléc:* 450-975-1001
courriel@federation-soccer.qc.ca
www.federation-soccer.qc.ca
www.facebook.com/195926650532157
twitter.com/FDSDQ
www.youtube.com/user/FederationSoccerQC
Également appelé: Soccer Québec
Nom précédent: Fédération québécoise de soccer football
Aperçu: *Dimension:* grande; *Envergure:* provinciale; fondée en 1911 surveillé par Canadian Soccer Association
Membre de: Canadian Soccer Association
Membre(s) du bureau directeur:
Brigitte Frot, Directrice générale
b.frot@federation-soccer.qc.ca
Éric Leroy, Directeur, Technique
eleroy@federation-soccer.qc.ca
Kambiz Ebadi, Directeur, Compétitions
k.ebadi@federation-soccer.qc.ca
Finances: *Fonds:* Société de Promotion du Soccer
Membre: 82 000; *Comités:* Exécutif; Compétitions; Provincial Arbitrage; Technique
Publications:
- Cyber Nouvelles de la Fédé [a publication of the Fédération de soccer du Québec]
Type: Infolettre

Fédération de sociétés mutuelles d'assurance générale (Groupe promutuel)

#400, 2000 boul. Lebourgneuf, Québec QC G2K 0B6
Ligne sans frais: 866-999-2433
federation@promutuel.ca
www.promutuel.ca
Aperçu: *Dimension:* petite; *Envergure:* provinciale; fondée en 1852
Mission: Promouvoir et offrir des produits d'assurance et des services financiers qui répondent aux attentes des membres-assurés et des clients et souvent les précèdent
Affliation(s): Association canadienne des compagnies d'assurance mutuelles; Société de coopération pour le développement international
Membre(s) du bureau directeur:
Sylvain Fauchon, Chef de la direction
Membre(s) du personnel: 1800
Membre: 24 sociétés mutuelles d'assurance; *Critères d'admissibilite:* Client en assurance dommages
Activités: Assurance; services financiers;

Fédération de tennis de table du Québec (FTTQ)

4545, av Pierre-de Coubertin, Montréal QC H1V 0B2

Tél: 514-252-3064; *Téléc:* 514-251-8038
www.tennisdetable.ca
www.facebook.com/tennisdetableQC
Aperçu: *Dimension:* moyenne; *Envergure:* provinciale surveillé par Table Tennis Canada
Membre de: Table Tennis Canada
Membre(s) du bureau directeur:
Rémi Tremblay, Directeur général
Membre(s) du personnel: 3

Fédération de tir à l'arc du Québec (FTAQ)

CP 1000, Succ. M, 4545, av Pierre-de Coubertin, Montréal QC H1V 3R2
Tél: 514-252-3054; *Téléc:* 514-252-3165
ftaq@ftaq.qc.ca
www.ftaq.qc.ca
Aperçu: *Dimension:* petite; *Envergure:* provinciale surveillé par Archery Canada Tir à l'Arc
Membre de: Archery Canada Tir à l'Arc
Membre(s) du bureau directeur:
Glenn Gudgeon, Président
president@ftaq.qc.ca
Membre(s) du personnel: 3
Membre: 3 000

Fédération de tir du Canada *See* Shooting Federation of Canada

Fédération de voile du Québec

4545, av Pierre-de-Coubertin, Montréal QC H1V 0B2
Tél: 514-252-3097; *Téléc:* 514-252-3044
Ligne sans frais: 866-864-5372
fvq@voile.qc.ca
www.voile.qc.ca
www.facebook.com/voilequebec
Aperçu: *Dimension:* petite; *Envergure:* provinciale; fondée en 1970 surveillé par Sail Canada
Mission: Encourager et promouvoir la pratique de la voile, sous toutes ses formes au Québec
Membre(s) du bureau directeur:
Marc-André Littée, Président
Membre: *Comités:* Voile adaptée; Élite; Circuit du Québec; Régie de course; Croisière et plaisance; Formation dériveur; Formation croisière

Fédération de volleyball du Québec (FVBQ)

4545, av Pierre-de Coubertin, Montréal QC H1V 3R2
Tél: 514-252-3065; *Téléc:* 514-252-3176
info-fvbq@volleyball.qc.ca
www.volleyball.qc.ca
www.facebook.com/VolleyballQC
twitter.com/volleyballqc
www.youtube.com/volleyballquebec
Également appelé: Volleyball Québec
Aperçu: *Dimension:* moyenne; *Envergure:* provinciale; Organisme sans but lucratif; fondée en 1968 surveillé par Volleyball Canada
Mission: Régir le volleyball à l'intérieur et à l'extérieur du Québec; promouvoir le volleyball; former les intervenants impliqués dans l'encadrement du participant; offrir des services aux membres
Affliation(s): Sports Québec; Regroupement loisirs Québec
Membre(s) du bureau directeur:
Martin Gérin-Lajoie, Directeur général
mgl@volleyball.qc.ca
Finances: *Budget de fonctionnement annuel:* $500,000-$1.5 Million; *Fonds:* Gouvernement provincial
Membre(s) du personnel: 5; 100 bénévole(s)
Membre: 20,000; *Critères d'admissibilité:* Entraîneurs, athlètes, arbitres, adeptes, bénévoles; *Comités:* Entraîneurs; Arbitres; Élite; Techniques
Activités: Volleybal compétitif et récréatif; édition, publication et vente de documents techniques et pédagogiques; programme de formation des entraîneurs; vente de vidéos; *Stagiaires:* Oui; *Service de conférenciers:* Oui; *Bibliothèque* rendez-vous

Fédération de Water-Polo du Québec (FWPQ) / Water Polo Québec

4545, av Pierre-de Coubertin, Montréal QC H1V 0B2
Tél: 514-252-3098; *Téléc:* 514-252-5658
www.waterpolo-quebec.qc.ca
www.facebook.com/federationwaterpoloquebec
Aperçu: *Dimension:* petite; *Envergure:* provinciale; Organisme sans but lucratif surveillé par Water Polo Canada
Mission: Regrouper en association représentative, toute personne qui s'adonne à l'activité du water-polo; sensibiliser la population du Québec à cette activité de loisirs; favoriser le développement sous toutes ses formes
Membre de: Sports Québec; Regroupement Loisirs Québec; Water Polo Canada
Membre(s) du bureau directeur:
Guy Lapointe, Président
Ariane Clavet-Gaumont, Directrice générale
Finances: *Fonds:* Ministère de l'Éducation.
Activités: Coordonne les programmes des équipes féminines et masculines du Québec; sanctionne les différents tournois provinciaux; organise des stages, cliniques et autres événements

Fédération des Agricotours du Québec *Voir* Association de l'Agricotourism et du Tourisme Gourmand

Fédération des agriculteurs et agricultrices francophones du Nouveau-Brunswick (FAAFNB)

18, rue de l'École, Edmundston NB E3V 1X6
Tél: 506-735-4886; *Téléc:* 506-737-4070
faafnb@nbnet.nb.ca
Aperçu: *Dimension:* petite; *Envergure:* provinciale; Organisme sans but lucratif; fondée en 1985
Mission: Promouvoir et défendre les intérêts des agriculteurs et agricultrices francophones du Nouveau-Brunswick, sur le plan provincial et national; participer au développement de l'agriculture et l'épanouissement des producteurs et productrices agricoles francophones du Nouveau-Brunswick
Membre de: Conseil économique du Nouveau-Brunswick; Construction Association of New Brunswick
Membre(s) du bureau directeur:
Paul-Emile Soucy, Président
Diane Côté, Directrice executive
Finances: *Budget de fonctionnement annuel:* $50,000-$100,000
Membre(s) du personnel: 5
Membre: 200; *Critères d'admissibilité:* Producteur agricole

Fédération des agricultrices du Québec (FAQ)

555, boul Roland-Therrien, Longueuil QC J4H 4E7
Tél: 450-679-0540; *Téléc:* 450-463-5228
fed.agricultrices@upa.qc.ca
www.agricultrices.com
Aperçu: *Dimension:* moyenne; *Envergure:* provinciale; Organisme sans but lucratif; fondée en 1987
Mission: Valoriser la profession; créer un réseau entre les femmes; avoir une force politique capable de défendre les intérêts des agricultrices; prodiguer de la formation
Membre de: L'Union des producteurs agricoles
Membre: 1,000-4,999; *Critères d'admissibilité:* Agricultrice, membre de soutien

Fédération des aînées et aînés francophones du Canada (FAAFC)

#300, 450 rue Rideau, Ottawa ON K1N 5Z4
Tél: 613-564-0212; *Téléc:* 613-564-0212
info@faafc.ca
www.faafc.ca/fr
Nom précédent: L'Assemblée des aînées et aînés francophones du Canada
Aperçu: *Dimension:* moyenne; *Envergure:* nationale; fondée en 1992
Mission: Défendre les droits des personnes à la retraite; défendre les droits des préretraités; programmes intergénérationnels; protection de la langue et la culture française
Membre(s) du bureau directeur:
Roger Doiron, Président
Jean-Luc Racine, Directeur général
Michel Vézina, Premier vice-président, Saskatchewan
André Faubert, Deuxième vice-présidente, Québec
Richard Martin, Trésorier, Terre-Neuve & Labrador
Mélina Gallant, Secrétaire, Ile-du-Prince-Édouard
Marie-Christine Aubrey, Administratrice, Territoire du Nord-Ouest
Louis Bernardin, Administrateur, Manitoba
Roland Gallant, Administrateur, Nouveau-Brunswick
Charles Gaudet, Administrateur, Nouvelle-Écosse
Claire Grisé, Administratrice, Colombie-Britannique
Germaine Lehodey, Administratrice, Alberta
Francine Poirier, Administratrice, Ontario
Roxanne Thibaudeau, Administratrice, Yukon
Finances: *Budget de fonctionnement annuel:* $100,000-$250,000
Membre: *Montant de la cotisation:* Barème

Fédération des aînés et des retraités francophones de l'Ontario (FAFO)

#001, 1173, ch Cyrville, Ottawa ON K1J 7S6
Tél: 613-747-0469; *Téléc:* 613-747-8378
Ligne sans frais: 800-530-5870
info@fafo.on.ca
www.fafo.on.ca
Nom précédent: Fédération des aînés francophones de l'Ontario
Aperçu: *Dimension:* moyenne; *Envergure:* provinciale; Organisme sans but lucratif; fondée en 1978
Mission: Promouvoir les retraités et aînés francophones et francophiles de l'Ontario et être leur porte-parole officiel; améliorer la qualité de vie des retraités et aînés francophones de l'Ontario
Affliation(s): Assemblée des retraités et des aînées francophones du Canada
Membre(s) du bureau directeur:
Erina Termine, Directrice générale
dg@fafo.on.ca
Finances: *Budget de fonctionnement annuel:* $250,000-$500,000; *Fonds:* Patrimoine Canada; Ressources humaines Canada; Procureur général du Canada; Nouveaux horizons
Membre(s) du personnel: 2; 30 bénévole(s)
Membre: 10 500; *Montant de la cotisation:* 20$; *Comités:* Finances; congrès; logement
Activités: Journées santé; foires d'information;

Fédération des aînés Franco-Albertains (FAFA)

#136, 8627, rue Marie-Anne-Gaboury, Edmonton AB T6C 3N1
Tél: 780-465-8965; *Téléc:* 780-468-6535
bureau@fafalta.ca
www.fafalta.ca
Aperçu: *Dimension:* petite; *Envergure:* provinciale; fondée en 1991
Mission: Protéger les droits des aînés francophones en Alberta et favoriser leur plein épanouissement
Membre de: La Société généalogique; Alberta Council on Aging
Membre(s) du bureau directeur:
Yannick Freychet, Directeur général
yannick.freychet@fafalta.ca
Membre(s) du personnel: 1
Membre: *Critères d'admissibilité:* Gens qui a 50+ ans et qui parle français
Activités: Conférences; ateliers; congrès; assemblée annuelle

Fédération des aînés franco-manitobains inc. (FAFM)

#107, 400, rue des Meurons, Saint-Boniface MB R2H 3H3
Tél: 204-235-0670; *Téléc:* 204-231-7071
Ligne sans frais: 855-235-0670
info@fafm.mb.ca
www.fafm.mb.ca
Aperçu: *Dimension:* moyenne; *Envergure:* provinciale; Organisme sans but lucratif; fondée en 1977
Mission: Revendique et représente les intérêts des francophones de 55 ans et plus
Membre(s) du bureau directeur:
Gérard Curé, Directeur général
Membre: *Montant de la cotisation:* 15$
Activités: Activités en groupe; sessions d'information; tournois de golf; pièces de théâtre; service d'écoute

Fédération des aînés francophones de l'Ontario *Voir* Fédération des aînés et des retraités francophones de l'Ontario

Fédération des aînés fransaskois (FAF)

#213, 308 - 4e av nord, Saskatoon SK S7K 2L7
Tél: 306-653-7442
aines@sasktel.net
www.fransaskois.info/federation-des-aines-fransaskois-n583.htm l
Aperçu: *Dimension:* petite; *Envergure:* provinciale; Organisme sans but lucratif; fondée en 1983
Mission: La FAF a pour but de favoriser le développement et l'épanouissement des personnes âgées et retraitées de 50 ans et plus francophones en Saskatchewan
Membre de: Assemblée des aînées et aînés francophones du Canada; Saskatchewan Seniors Mechanism; Provincial Advisory Comittee of Older Persons
Membre: *Critères d'admissibilité:* Personnes âgées et retraitées de 50 ans et plus
Activités: Épluchette de blé d'Inde; Fête de Noël; cours Internet; conférences; fête fransaskoise; ateliers divers (santé, formation); jeux des aînés

Fédération des apiculteurs du Québec

Maison de l'UPA, #225, 555, boul Roland-Therrien, Longueuil QC J4H 4E7

Tél: 450-679-0540; *Téléc:* 450-463-5226
apiculteur@upa.qc.ca
www.apiculteursduquebec.com
Nom précédent: Fédération des producteurs de miel du Québec
Aperçu: *Dimension:* petite; *Envergure:* provinciale; fondée en 1979
Mission: Défendre les intérêts des apiculteurs de Québec
Membre de: Conseil canadien du miel
Affiliation(s): Union des producteurs agricoles (UPA); Conseil canadien du miel
Membre(s) du bureau directeur:
Léo Buteau, Président
Finances: *Budget de fonctionnement annuel:* $100,000-$250,000
Membre(s) du personnel: 1
Membre: 150; *Montant de la cotisation:* Barème; *Critères d'admissibilite:* Apiculteur

Fédération des associations danoises du Canada *See* Federation of Danish Associations in Canada

Fédération des associations de familles monoparentales et recomposées du Québec (FAFMRQ) / Federation of Single-Parent Family Associations of Québec

584, rue Guizot est, Montréal QC H2P 1N3
Tél: 514-729-6666; *Téléc:* 514-729-6746
fafmrq.info@videotron.ca
www.fafmrq.org
twitter.com/FAFMRQ
Aperçu: *Dimension:* moyenne; *Envergure:* provinciale; Organisme sans but lucratif; fondée en 1974
Mission: Travailler à améliorer les conditions socio-économiques des familles monoparentales et recomposées du Québec.
Membre(s) du bureau directeur:
Sylvie Lévesque, Directrice générale
fafmrq.sylvie@videotron.ca
Membre(s) du personnel: 3
Membre: 35 associations; *Montant de la cotisation:* Barème
Activités: Rencontres; colloques; *Stagiaires:* Oui

Fédération des associations de juristes d'expression française de common law (FAJEF)

117B, rue Egénie, Winnipeg MB R2H 0X9
Tél: 204-415-7551; *Téléc:* 204-415-4482
reception@fajef.com
www.accesjustice.ca
Aperçu: *Dimension:* moyenne; *Envergure:* provinciale; fondée en 1992 surveillé par Fédération des communautés francophones et acadienne du Canada
Mission: Pour fournir un soutien et de représenter ses membres
Membre(s) du bureau directeur:
Rénald Rémillard, Directeur général
Allan Darner, Président
Membre: *Critères d'admissibilite:* Associations de juristes francophones qui défendent les droits des francophones

Fédération des Associations de Musiciens-Éducateurs du Québec (FAMÉQ)

55, rue Greenfield, Longueil QC J4V 2J6
Tél: 450-466-6799
info@fameq.org
www.fameq.org
www.facebook.com/204489629683586
Aperçu: *Dimension:* moyenne; *Envergure:* provinciale; fondée en 1967
Mission: Représentater les musiciens éducateurs; participer à la concertation et mobilisation des musiciens éducateurs; promouvoir l'éducation musicale
Membre(s) du bureau directeur:
Maryse Forand, Directrice générale
dg@fameq.org
Membre: *Montant de la cotisation:* 90$ personnes en exercice; 60$ retraités; 30$ étudiants
Activités: Journée de la musique; concours; chorales; formation

Fédération des associations de parents francophones de l'Ontario *Voir* Parents partenaires en éducation

Fédération des associations de professeures et professeurs d'université du Nouveau-Brunswick *See* Federation of New Brunswick Faculty Associations

Fédération des associations du sport scolaire de l'Ontario *See* Ontario Federation of School Athletic Associations

Fédération des Associations et Corporations en Construction du Québec

#500, 5181, rue d'Amiens, Montréal QC H1G 6N9
Tél: 514-955-8508; *Téléc:* 514-955-6623
info@faccq.org
www.faccq.org
Aperçu: *Dimension:* moyenne; *Envergure:* provinciale; fondée en 1993
Mission: Promouvoir les droits des entrepreneurs; défendre leurs intérêts; vulgariser les Lois et règlements régissant l'industrie de la construction
Membre(s) du bureau directeur:
Ronald Marin, Président
rmarin@faccq.org

Fédération des associations étudiantes du campus de l'université de Montréal (FAÉCUM)

#B1265, 3200, rue Jean-Brillant, Montréal QC H3T 1N8
Tél: 514-343-5947
info@faecum.qc.ca
www.faecum.qc.ca
www.facebook.com/FAECUM
twitter.com/FAECUM
Aperçu: *Dimension:* grande; *Envergure:* locale; fondée en 1976
Mission: Représenter, les étudiants de l'Université par l'intermédiaire de leurs Associations; défendre leurs droits et intérêts dans le domaine académique et au niveau social, économique, culturel et politique
Membre de: Fédération étudiante universitaire du Québec
Membre(s) du bureau directeur:
Mireille Mercier Roy, Secrétaire général
sg@faecum.qc.ca
Richard Kabaka, Directeur général
dg@faecum.qc.ca
Membre: 82 associations qui représentent 37 000 membres; *Montant de la cotisation:* Barème; *Critères d'admissibilite:* associations étudiantes
Activités: Programme de radio A la bonne heure

Fédération des associations foyer-école du Québec Inc. *See* Québec Federation of Home & School Associations Inc.

Fédération des associations roumaines du Canada *Voir* Fondation roumaine de Montréal

Fédération des astronomes amateurs du Québec

4545, av Pierre-de Coubertin, Montréal QC H1V 3R2
Tél: 514-252-3038
info@faaq.org
www.faaq.org
Aperçu: *Dimension:* petite; *Envergure:* provinciale; Organisme sans but lucratif; fondée en 1976
Mission: Représenter et regrouper les individus, groupes (clubs) et institutions reliés à l'astronomie amateur au Québec
Affiliation(s): Conseil Québécois du Loisir; Regroupement Loisir Québec; Association Française d'Astronomie; International Dark-sky Association
Membre(s) du bureau directeur:
Rémi Laccasse, Président
Membre: *Montant de la cotisation:* 15$ individu; 75$ corporatifs éducationnels; 125$ corporatifs institutionnels; *Critères d'admissibilite:* Astronome amateur
Activités: Bibliothèque virtuelle

Fédération des aveugles du Québec inc. *See* Québec Federation of the Blind Inc.

Fédération des caisses Desjardins du Québec

100, av des Commandeurs, Lévis QC G6V 7N5
Tél: 418-835-8444
Ligne sans frais: 866-835-8444
www.desjardins.com
www.linkedin.com/company/desjardins
www.facebook.com/Desjardinsgroup
twitter.com/desjardinsgroup
www.youtube.com/user/desjardinsgroup
Aperçu: *Dimension:* grande; *Envergure:* provinciale
Mission: To support the Desjardins caisses in Québec.
Membre(s) du bureau directeur:
Monique F. Leroux, Chair, President & CEO, Desjardins Group
L.-Daniel Gauvin, Senior Vice-President & General Manager, Caisse centrale Desjardins & Capital Desjardins Inc.
Membre: 255 individuals in 17 councils

Abitibi-Témiscamingue - Nord du Québec
602, 3e av, Val-d'Or QC J9P 1S5
Tél: 819-825-2843; *Téléc:* 819-825-7083
Ligne sans frais: 866-588-2843

Bas St-Laurent
CP 880, 100, rue Julien-Rehel, Rimouski QC G5L 7C9
Tél: 418-723-3368; *Téléc:* 418-722-9527
Ligne sans frais: 888-880-9824

Centre-du-Quebec
460, boul Saint-Joseph, Drummondville QC J2C 2A8
Tél: 819-474-2524; *Téléc:* 819-417-4212
Ligne sans frais: 855-474-2524

Chaudière-Appalaches
#300, 1017, boul Vachon Nord, Sainte-Marie QC G6E 1M3
Tél: 418-386-1333; *Téléc:* 418-386-1330
Ligne sans frais: 877-707-1333

Estrie
#300, 1815, rue King ouest, Sherbrooke QC J1J 2E3
Tél: 819-821-3220; *Téléc:* 819-821-9229
Ligne sans frais: 800-481-3220

Gaspésie/Iles-de-la-Madeleine
CP 190, 473, boul Perron, Maria QC G0C 1Y0
Tél: 418-759-3456; *Téléc:* 418-759-3801
Ligne sans frais: 866-381-3456

Lanaudière
820, montée Masson, Mascouche QC J7K 3B6
Tél: 450-474-2474; *Téléc:* 450-474-5774

Laval-Laurentides
#210, 2550, boul Daniel-Johnson, Laval QC H7T 2L1
Tél: 450-978-2212; *Téléc:* 450-978-1123

Mauricie
1200, rue Royale, Trois-Rivières QC G9A 4J2
Tél: 819-376-1200; *Téléc:* 819-379-1438
Ligne sans frais: 877-375-4987

Montérégie
850, boul Casavant ouest, Saint-Hyacinthe QC J2S 7S3
Tél: 450-261-8888; *Téléc:* 450-261-8886
Ligne sans frais: 866-465-8888

Montréal
Niveau Promenade, CP 244, Succ. Desjardins, #100, 52 complexe Desjardins, Montréal QC H5B 1B4
Tél: 514-281-7101; *Téléc:* 514-281-6232

Outaouais
655, boul Saint-René ouest, Gatineau QC J8T 8M4
Tél: 819-568-5368; *Téléc:* 819-568-9063
Ligne sans frais: 877-568-5368

Québec-Rive-Sud
#600, 1610, boul Alphonse-Desjardins, Lévis QC G6V 0H1
Tél: 418-834-4343; *Téléc:* 418-833-2098
Ligne sans frais: 866-771-4343

Rive-Sud de Montréal
#100, 1850, av Panama, Brossard QC J4W 3C6
Tél: 450-671-3720; *Téléc:* 450-671-2431

Saguenay-Lac-Saint-Jean-Charlevoix
#700, 1685, boul Talbot, Saguenay QC G7H 7Y4
Tél: 418-543-1700; *Téléc:* 418-549-7244

Fédération des caisses populaires acadiennes

Édifice Martin-J.-Légère, CP 5554, 295, boul St-Pierre ouest, Caraquet NB E1W 1B7
Tél: 506-726-4000; *Téléc:* 506-726-4001
www.acadie.com
www.facebook.com/caissespopulairesacadiennes
twitter.com/CPAcadiennes
Aperçu: *Dimension:* moyenne; *Envergure:* provinciale; fondée en 1945
Mission: Améliorer la qualité de vie de ceux et celles qui y adhèrent tout en contribuant à l'autosuffisance socio-économique de la collectivité acadienne du Nouveau-Brunswick, dans le respect de son identité linguistique et ses valeurs coopératives
Membre(s) du bureau directeur:
Camille H. Thériault, Président/Directeur général
Membre(s) du personnel: 1000
Membre: 155,000

Fédération des cégeps

500, boul Crémazie est, Montréal QC H2P 1E7
Tél: 514-381-8631; *Téléc:* 514-381-2263
comm@fedecegeps.qc.ca
www.fedecegeps.qc.ca
www.facebook.com/monretouraucegep
Aperçu: *Dimension:* moyenne; *Envergure:* provinciale; fondée en 1969
Mission: De promouvoir le développement de l'enseignement collégial; au nom de ses membres, la Fédération établit des contacts et étudie des dossiers communs avec différents partenaires gouvernementaux et privés, notamment en ce qui

concerne les affaires pédagogiques, étudiantes, matérielles et financières, et les ressources humaines du réseau
Membre(s) du bureau directeur:
François Dornier, Président
Jean Beauchesne, Président-directeur général
jean.beauchesne@fedecegeps.qc.ca
Membre: 46
Activités: *Bibliothèque* rendez-vous

Fédération des centres d'action bénévole du Québec (FCABQ)
1557, av Papineau, Montréal QC H2K 4H7
Tél: 514-843-6312; *Téléc:* 514-843-6485
Ligne sans frais: 800-715-7515
info@fcabq.org
www.fcabq.org
www.facebook.com/fcabq
Aperçu: *Dimension:* moyenne; *Envergure:* provinciale; Organisme sans but lucratif; fondée en 1972
Mission: Promouvoir l'action bénévole au Québec; former un centre d'action bénévole; organiser la semaine de l'action bénévole.
Membre de: Bénévoles Canada
Affliation(s): International Association for Volunteer Effort
Membre(s) du bureau directeur:
Fimba Tankoano, Directeur général
direction@fcabq.org
Membre(s) du personnel: 4
Membre: 111
Activités: *Stagiaires:* Oui; *Service de conférenciers:* Oui; *Bibliothèque*

Fédération des centres de ressourcement Chrétien
CP 87127, Succ. Charlesbourg, 870, Carré de Tracy Est, Québec QC G1G 5E1
Tél: 418-623-5597
fcrc@ressourcementchretien.qc.ca
www.ressourcementchretien.qc.ca
Aperçu: *Dimension:* moyenne; *Envergure:* provinciale; fondée en 1960
Mission: Pour aider les centres chrétiens avec leurs buts
Membre(s) du bureau directeur:
Michel Paquet, Président, Conseil d'administration
4 bénévole(s)

Fédération des chambres de commerce du Québec (FCCQ)
#1100, 555, boul René-Lévesque ouest, Montréal QC H2Z 1B1
Tél: 514-844-9571; *Téléc:* 514-844-0226
Ligne sans frais: 800-361-5019
info@fccq.ca
www.fccq.ca
www.linkedin.com/groups/Fédération-chambres-commerce-Québec-4659438
www.facebook.com/FCCQ.Reseau
twitter.com/FCCQ
Aperçu: *Dimension:* petite; *Envergure:* provinciale; fondée en 1909
Mission: Promouvoir la liberté d'entreprendre qui s'inspire de l'initiative et dela créativité afin de contribuer à la richesse collective en coordonnant l'apport du travail de tous. Vision: Positionner la FCCQ comme le regroupement incontournable des intérêts d'affaires sur l'échiquier socio-économique et politique du Québec.
Membre(s) du bureau directeur:
Françoise Bertand, Présidente-directrice générale
francoise.bertrand@fccq.ca
Finances: *Budget de fonctionnement annuel:* $1.5 Million-$3 Million
Membre: 40 000 entreprises

Fédération des Chambres immobilières du Québec (FCIQ)
600, ch du Golf, Ile-Des-soeurs QC H3E 1A8
Tél: 514-762-0212; *Téléc:* 514-762-0365
Ligne sans frais: 866-882-0212
info@fciq.ca
www.fciq.ca
twitter.com/fciq_eco
Aperçu: *Dimension:* grande; *Envergure:* provinciale; Organisme sans but lucratif; fondée en 1991
Mission: Promouvoir et protéger les intérêts de l'industrie immobilière du Québec afin que les Chambres et les membres accomplissent avec succès leurs objectifs d'affaires
Membre de: The Canadian Real Estate Association
Membre(s) du bureau directeur:
Normand Racine, Président du conseil d'administration
Chantal de Repentigny, Directrice adjointe, Communication et relations avec l'industrie, 514-762-0212 Ext. 130
chantal.derepentigny@fciq.ca
Membre: 8 500

Fédération des chorales de la Nouvelle-Écosse *See* Nova Scotia Choral Federation

Fédération des chorales du Nouveau-Brunswick *See* New Brunswick Choral Federation

Fédération des citoyens aînés du Nouveau-Brunswick inc. *See* New Brunswick Senior Citizens Federation Inc.

Fédération des clubs de croquet du Québec (FCCQ)
CP 1000, Succ. M, 4545, av Pierre-de Coubertin, Montréal QC H1V 3R2
Tél: 514-252-3032
croquet@fqjr.qc.ca
croquet.quebecjeux.org
Aperçu: *Dimension:* petite; *Envergure:* provinciale; fondée en 1973
Membre(s) du bureau directeur:
Jacques Noël, Président, 819-379-8035
Membre: 635; *Montant de la cotisation:* 10$ individu

Fédération des clubs de fers du Québec
4545, av Pierre-de Coubertin, Montréal QC H1V 0B2
Tél: 514-252-3032
fers@fqjr.qc.ca
fers.quebecjeux.org
www.youtube.com/channel/UCeSkkidR7WTe1nZ3uw3T5UA
Aperçu: *Dimension:* moyenne; *Envergure:* provinciale; fondée en 1961 surveillé par Horseshoe Canada
Mission: La FCFQ veut promouvoir la pratique du lancer de fers. Elle favorise les rencontres et les tournois qui contribuent au développement de la discipline. Elle distribue de l'information, donne des cours et des démonstrations
Membre de: Horseshoe Canada
Membre(s) du bureau directeur:
Michel Favreau, Président, 450-535-6580
Membre: *Montant de la cotisation:* 10$ individuel; 30$ club/ligue/ville

Fédération des Clubs de l'Age d'Or de l'Est du Québec (FCADEQ)
#207, 148, av Belzile, Rimouski QC G5L 3E4
Tél: 418-722-6066; *Téléc:* 418-722-6077
www.fcadeq.org
Nom précédent: Conseil régional de l'Age d'Or de l'Est du Québec
Aperçu: *Dimension:* moyenne; *Envergure:* locale; Organisme sans but lucratif; fondée en 1972
Mission: Favoriser le bien-être collectif des membres; représenter et défendre les droits des aînés et des 50 ans et plus auprès des organismes locaux, régionaux et des instances provinciales et fédérales
Membre(s) du bureau directeur:
René Paquette, Directeur général
Finances: *Budget de fonctionnement annuel:* $250,000-$500,000
Membre(s) du personnel: 4; 100 bénévole(s)
Membre: 34 000; *Montant de la cotisation:* 20$; *Critères d'admissibilité:* 50 ans et plus

Fédération des clubs de motoneigistes du Québec (FCMQ)
CP 1000, Succ. M, 4545, av Pierre-de Coubertin, Montréal QC H1V 3R2
Tél: 514-252-3076; *Téléc:* 514-254-2066
Ligne sans frais: 844-253-4343
info@fcmq.qc.ca
www.fcmq.qc.ca
www.facebook.com/FCMQ40
twitter.com/Fed_MotoneigeQc
Aperçu: *Dimension:* moyenne; *Envergure:* provinciale; Organisme sans but lucratif; fondée en 1974
Mission: La Fédération des clubs de motoneigistes du Québec est un organisme à but non lucratif, voué au développement et à la promotion de la pratique de la motoneige dans tout le Québec
Membre(s) du bureau directeur:
Serge Ritcher, Président
Finances: *Budget de fonctionnement annuel:* $3 Million-$5 Million
Membre(s) du personnel: 10; 3000 bénévole(s)
Membre: 228; *Montant de la cotisation:* 250$/club

Fédération des comités de parents de la Province de Québec inc *Voir* Fédération des comités de parents du Québec inc.

Fédération des comités de parents du Québec inc. (FCPQ)
2263, boul Louis-XIV, Québec QC G1C 1A4
Tél: 418-667-2432; *Téléc:* 418-667-6713
Ligne sans frais: 800-463-7268
courrier@fcpq.qc.ca
www.fcpq.qc.ca
www.facebook.com/fcpq.parents
twitter.com/fcpq
Nom précédent: Fédération des comités de parents de la Province de Québec inc
Aperçu: *Dimension:* petite; *Envergure:* provinciale
Mission: De défendre et de promouvoir les droits et les intérêts des parents des élèves des écoles publiques primaires et secondaires de façon à assurer la qualité de l'éducation offerte aux enfants
Membre(s) du bureau directeur:
Gaston Rioux, Président
president@fcpq.qc.ca
Marc Charland, Directeur général
Jonatan Bérubé, Conseiller aux communications
communications@fcpq.qc.ca
Membre: *Comités:* Exécutif; Éthique

La Fédération des commissions scolaires du Québec (FCSQ)
CP 10490, Succ. Sainte-Foy, 1001, av Bégon, Québec QC G1V 4C7
Tél: 418-651-3220; *Téléc:* 418-651-2574
Autres numéros: www.flickr.com/photos/79682608@N03
info@fcsq.qc.ca
www.fcsq.qc.ca
twitter.com/fcsq
www.youtube.com/user/fcsq2011/videos
Aperçu: *Dimension:* grande; *Envergure:* provinciale; fondée en 1947
Mission: Tout en conservant ses tâches premières de coordination et d'unification, la mission de la Fédération s'est élargie, au fil des ans, pour rencontrer deux objectifs principaux : contribuer à promouvoir l'éducation ainsi que représenter et défendre avec détermination les intérêts des commissions scolaires.
Membre de: Association canadienne d'éducation de langue française
Membre(s) du bureau directeur:
Josée Bouchard, Présidente
Pâquerette Gagnon, Directrice générale
Finances: *Budget de fonctionnement annuel:* $3 Million-$5 Million
Membre(s) du personnel: 50
Membre: 61 commissions scolaires
Activités: *Evénements de sensibilisation:* Assemblée générale; *Bibliothèque*
Meetings/Conferences: • Congrès d'orientation de la FCSQ 2015, 2015
Scope: National
Publications:
• Commissaires [a publication of La Fédération des commissions scolaires du Québec]
Type: Bulletin
• Savoir [a publication of La Fédération des commissions scolaires du Québec]
Type: Magazine

Fédération des communautés francophones et acadienne du Canada (FCFAC)
#300, 450 rue Rideau, Ottawa ON K1N 5Z4
Tél: 613-241-7600; *Téléc:* 613-241-6046
info@fcfa.ca
www.fcfa.ca
www.facebook.com/FCFACanada
twitter.com/fcfacanada
Nom précédent: Fédération des francophones hors Québec
Aperçu: *Dimension:* grande; *Envergure:* nationale; Organisme sans but lucratif; fondée en 1975
Mission: Défendre et promouvoir les droits et les intérêts des communautés francophones et acadiennes qu'elle représente.
Membre(s) du bureau directeur:
Suzanne Bossé, Directrice générale
s.bosse@fcfa.ca
Marie-France Kenny, Présidente
presidence@fcfa.ca

Membre: 22 corporations à but non-lucratif; *Montant de la cotisation:* 500$
Activités: *Stagiaires:* Oui; *Listes de destinataires:* Oui; *Bibliothèque* Bibliothèque publique rendez-vous

Fédération des coopératives d'habitation de l'Estrie (FCHE)
548, rue Dufferin, Sherbrooke QC J1H 4N1
Tél: 819-566-6303; *Téléc:* 819-829-1593
fche@reseaucoop.com
Aperçu: *Dimension:* petite; *Envergure:* locale
Membre de: Confédération québécoise des coopératives d'habitation

Fédération des coopératives d'habitation de la Mauricie et du Centre-du-Québec (FECHMACQ)
#230, 235 rue Hénòt, Drummondville QC J2C 6X5
Tél: 819-477-6986; *Téléc:* 819-477-3827
Ligne sans frais: 888-477-6986
info@fechmacq.ca
www.cooperativehabitation.coop
Aperçu: *Dimension:* petite; *Envergure:* locale
Membre de: Confédération québécoise des coopératives d'habitation
Membre(s) du bureau directeur:
Mireille Pepin, Directrice générale
mpepin@fechmacq.ca
Michel Legault, Président
Membre(s) du personnel: 3

Fédération des coopératives d'habitation du Royaume Saguenay Lac-Saint-Jean
#110, 30, rue Racine est, Chicoutimi QC G7H 1P5
Tél: 418-543-6858; *Téléc:* 418-543-4698
fechas@qc.aira.com
www.cooperativehabitation.coop
Également appelé: FECHAS
Aperçu: *Dimension:* petite; *Envergure:* locale; Organisme sans but lucratif; fondée en 1990
Mission: Développer de nouvelles coopératives d'habitation; regrouper les coopératives d'habitation; offrir des services à ses membres COOP et OSBL en logement social
Membre de: Confédération québécoise des coopératives d'habitation (CQCH)
Membre(s) du bureau directeur:
Dennis Bolduc, Coordonnateur au dév. et affaires
Régine Lalancette, Coordonnatrice administrative
Marie-Andrée Turcotte, Présidente
Finances: *Budget de fonctionnement annuel:* $100,000-$250,000; *Fonds:* Gouvernement provincial
Membre(s) du personnel: 3; 5 bénévole(s)
Membre: 33 coopératives; 12 OBNL; *Montant de la cotisation:* 40$

Fédération des coopératives d'habitation intermunicipale du Montréal métropolitain (FECHIMM) / Montréal Federation of Housing Cooperatives
#202, 3155, rue Hochelaga, Montréal QC H1W 1G4
Tél: 514-843-6929; *Téléc:* 514-843-5241
info@fechimm.coop
www.fechimm.coop
www.facebook.com/146339935412999
twitter.com/FECHIMM
Aperçu: *Dimension:* petite; *Envergure:* locale
Mission: D'unir les coopératives de logement en leur fournissant des formations et des ateliers
Membre de: Confédération québécoise des coopératives d'habitation
Membre(s) du bureau directeur:
Francine Néméh, Directrice générale
fnemeh@fechimm.coop
Membre(s) du personnel: 32
Membre: 440 coopératives membres

Fédération des coopératives d'habitation Montérégiennes (FÉCHAM)
#310, 150, rue Grant, Longueuil QC J4H 3H6
Tél: 450-651-5520; *Téléc:* 450-651-5522
Ligne sans frais: 888-651-5520
Autres numéros: Télécopieur sans frais: 1-888-651-5522
info@fecham.coop
www.cooperativehabitation.coop
Aperçu: *Dimension:* petite; *Envergure:* locale; fondée en 1983
Mission: L'Association vise à regrouper les coops d'habitation en Montérégie; représenter et défendre les membres et leur offrir des services; promouvoir la formule coop sans but lucratif en habitation
Membre de: Confédération québécoise des coopératives d'habitation
Affiliation(s): Confédération québécoise des coopératives d'habitation; Fédération de l'habitation coopérative du Canada
Membre(s) du bureau directeur:
Sophie Rousseau-Loiselle, Directrice générale
sophierousseauloiselle@fecham.coop
Finances: *Budget de fonctionnement annuel:* $250,000-$500,000; *Fonds:* Gouvernement provincial et revenus autonomes
Membre(s) du personnel: 7; 7 bénévole(s)
Membre: 1-99; *Critères d'admissibilite:* Cooperatives d'habitation situées sur le territoire de la Montérègie
Activités: *Stagiaires:* Oui

Fédération des coopératives de Québec, Chaudière-Appalaches (FECHAQC)
#205A, 275, rue du Parvis, Québec QC G1K 6G7
Tél: 418-648-1354; *Téléc:* 418-648-9991
Ligne sans frais: 866-313-2667
info@fechaqc.qc.ca
Aperçu: *Dimension:* petite; *Envergure:* locale; fondée en 1981
Membre de: Confédération québécoise des coopératives d'habitation

Fédération des courtiers en fonds mutuels *See* Federation of Mutual Fund Dealers

Fédération des dames d'Acadie *Voir* Fédération des femmes acadiennes et francophones du Nouveau-Brunswick

Fédération des dentistes spécialistes du Québec (FDSQ) / Federation of dental specialists of Quebec
#302, 14, ch Bates, Outremont QC H2V 1A8
Tél: 514-737-4901
info@fdsq.qc.ca
www.fdsq.qc.ca
www.facebook.com/543154982403967
Aperçu: *Dimension:* petite; *Envergure:* provinciale; fondée en 1972
Mission: De promouvoir des intérêts professionnels de ses membres; de développer scientifique des spécialistes de la médecine dentaire.
Membre(s) du bureau directeur:
Victor Legault, Président

Fédération des Écrivaines et Écrivains du Québec *See* Québec Writers' Federation

Fédération des éducateurs et éducatrices physiques enseignants du Québec (FEEPEQ)
2500, boul de l'Université, Sherbrooke QC J1K 2R1
Tél: 819-821-8000; *Téléc:* 819-821-7970
info@feepeq.com
www.feepeq.com
www.facebook.com/180360724546
twitter.com/feepeq
Nom précédent: Confédération des Éducateurs physiques du Québec
Aperçu: *Dimension:* moyenne; *Envergure:* provinciale; Organisme sans but lucratif; fondée en 1960
Mission: Répresenter plus du tiers des éducateurs/trices physiques oeuvrant activement partout au Québec
Affiliation(s): Sports Québec; Fédération québécoise du sport étudiant
Membre(s) du bureau directeur:
Patrick Parent, Président
Nathalie Morneau, Directrice, Opérations
Finances: *Budget de fonctionnement annuel:* $100,000-$250,000
Membre(s) du personnel: 4; 40 bénévole(s)
Membre: 1 700; *Montant de la cotisation:* Barème; *Critères d'admissibilite:* Éducateur physique enseignant selon les régions d'appartenance; *Comités:* Exécutif; finances; partenariats; publications; pédagogie; professionnalisation; congrès, dossiers Internet
Activités: Formation; information; sensibilisation; congrès; Mouvement Pupilles de l'Enseignement Public; *Service de conférenciers:* Oui; *Listes de destinataires:* Oui; *Bibliothèque* rendez-vous

Fédération des Élèves du secondaire franco-ontarien *Voir* Fédération de la jeunesse franco-ontarienne

Fédération des employées et employés de services publics inc. (CSN) (FEESP) / Federation of Public Service Employees Inc. (CNTU)
1601, av de Lorimier, Montréal QC H2K 4M5
Tél: 514-598-2231; *Téléc:* 514-598-2398
feesp.courrier@csn.qc.ca
www.feesp.csn.qc.ca
www.facebook.com/feespcsn
Aperçu: *Dimension:* moyenne; *Envergure:* nationale; Organisme sans but lucratif
Mission: Il est composé de quatre personnes élues, du coordonnateur ou coordonnatrice des services et de la personne déléguée syndicale.
Affiliation(s): Conféderation des syndicats nationaux
Membre(s) du bureau directeur:
Nathalie Arguin, Secéraire-générale
Membre: 55 000 + 400 sections locales; *Comités:* Formation; Condition féminine; Santé-sécurité-environnement

Fédération des enseignantes et des enseignants de l'élémentaire de l'Ontario *See* Elementary Teachers' Federation of Ontario

Fédération des enseignantes et des enseignants de l'Ontario *See* Ontario Teachers' Federation

Fédération des enseignants de cégeps
9405, rue Sherbrooke Est, Montréal QC H1L 6P3
Tél: 514-356-8888; *Téléc:* 514-354-8535
Ligne sans frais: 800-465-0897
fec@csq.qc.net
www.fec.csq.qc.net
www.facebook.com/feccsq
twitter.com/feccsq
Aperçu: *Dimension:* moyenne; *Envergure:* provinciale surveillé par Centrale des syndicats du Québec
Mission: De protéger les intérêts de ses membres
Affiliation(s): Centrale des syndicats du Québec
Membre(s) du bureau directeur:
Mario Beauchemin, President
fec.beauchemin.mario@csq.qc.net
Membre: 13 sections locales; *Comités:* Négociation; D'information, de formation et d'application de la convention collective; Condition des femmes; Relève syndicale; Formation continue; Vigilance

Fédération des enseignants de l'Ile-du-Prince-Édouard *See* Prince Edward Island Teachers' Federation

Fédération des enseignants de la Colombie-Britannique *See* British Columbia Teachers' Federation

Fédération des enseignants des écoles juives *See* Federation of Teachers of Jewish Schools

Fédération des enseignants des écoles secondaires de l'Ontario *See* Ontario Secondary School Teachers' Federation

Fédération des enseignants du Nouveau-Brunswick *See* New Brunswick Teachers' Association

Fédération des enseignants et des enseignantes de la Saskatchewan *See* Saskatchewan Teachers' Federation

Fédération des entraîneurs de ski du Canada *See* Canadian Ski Instructors' Alliance

Fédération des établissements d'enseignement privés (FEEP)
1940, boul Henri-Bourassa est, Montréal QC H2B 1S2
Tél: 514-381-8891; *Téléc:* 514-381-4086
Ligne sans frais: 888-381-8891
info@feep.qc.ca
www.cadre.qc.ca
Nom précédent: Association des institutions d'enseignement secondaire; Association québécoise des Écoles secondaires privées
Aperçu: *Dimension:* moyenne; *Envergure:* provinciale; Organisme sans but lucratif; fondée en 1968
Mission: Soutien des établissements membres sur les plans administratifs, pédagogiques et de la vie scolaire; représentation auprès du gouvernement
Membre(s) du bureau directeur:
Paul Boisvenu, Directeur général
boisvenup@feep.qc.ca
Membre: 181; *Critères d'admissibilite:* Établissements d'enseignement privés
Activités: *Bibliothèque:* Centre de documentation; Bibliothèque publique rendez-vous

Fédération des étudiants en médecine du Canada *See* Canadian Federation of Medical Students

Fédération des familles et amis de la personne atteinte de maladie mentale (FFAPAMM) / Federation of Families & Friends of Persons with a Mental Illness

#203, 1990, rue Jean-Talon nord, Sainte-Foy QC G1N 4K8
Tél: 418-687-0474; *Téléc:* 418-687-0123
Ligne sans frais: 800-323-0474
info@ffapamm.com
www.ffapamm.qc.ca
Aperçu: *Dimension:* moyenne; *Envergure:* provinciale; Organisme sans but lucratif; fondée en 1986
Mission: La FFAPAMM se veut le porte-parole provincial des associations de familles et amis de la personne atteinte de maladie mentale. Tout en ayant à coeur de défendre et promouvoir les intérêts de ses membres, elle a également le mandat de les soutenir dans leur développement, de sensibiliser l'opinion publique aux problèmes reliés à la maladie mentale et de créer des programmes de communication et d'éducation.
Membre(s) du bureau directeur:
Hélène Fradet, Directrice générale
Membre(s) du personnel: 3
Membre: *Critères d'admissibilite:* Associations d'entraide pour familles et amis de la personne atteinte de maladie mentale

Fédération des familles-souches du Québec (FFSQ)

CP 10090, Succ. Sainte-Foy, Québec QC G1V 4C6
Tél: 418-653-2137; *Téléc:* 418-653-6387
ffsq@qc.aira.com
www.ffsq.qc.ca
Aperçu: *Dimension:* moyenne; *Envergure:* provinciale; Organisme sans but lucratif; fondée en 1983
Mission: Favoriser les regroupements en associations de familles; fournir différents services techniques et de l'aide-conseil
Membre de: Conseil Québecois de Loisir et Regroupement Loisir Québec
Membre(s) du bureau directeur:
Lucie Moisan, Présidente
lucmoi@globetrotter.net
Yves Boisvert, Directeur
yboisvert@ffsq.qc.ca
Membre(s) du personnel: 4
Membre: 218
Activités: Congrès annuel; journées d'information à l'automne; ateliers de formation; *Service de conférenciers:* Oui

La Fédération des femmes acadiennes de la Nouvelle-Écosse (FFANE)

54, rue Queen, Dartmouth NS B2Y 1G3
Tél: 902-433-2088; *Téléc:* 902-433-0066
Ligne sans frais: 877-433-2088
info@femmesacadiennes.ca
www.ffane.ca
Nom précédent: Association des femmes acadiennes en marche de la région de Richmond
Aperçu: *Dimension:* petite; *Envergure:* locale; Organisme sans but lucratif
Mission: Promouvoir le développement du plein potential de la femme acadienne du comté de Richmond
Membre de: Fédération des Acadiennes de la Nouvelle-Écosse
Affliation(s): Association des acadiennes de la Nouvelle-Ecosse
Membre(s) du bureau directeur:
Micheline Gélinas, Directrice générale
dg@femmesacadiennes.ca
Finances: *Fonds:* Gouvernement régional

Fédération des femmes acadiennes et francophones du Nouveau-Brunswick (FFAFNB)

1309, Sunset, Bathurst NB E2A 3N8
Tél: 506-546-3033; *Téléc:* 506-546-6688
ffafnb@nb.aibn.com
www.ffafnb.org
Nom précédent: Fédération des dames d'Acadie
Aperçu: *Dimension:* petite; *Envergure:* locale; fondée en 1968
Mission: FDA regroupe les femmes francophones du N.-B. dans le but de promouvoir les intérêts et de défendre les droits des femmes et des francophones du N.-B; favorise toute action visant l'épanouissement des femmes et des francophones et leur plein accès à l'égalité et à la justice sociale
Membre de: La Fédération nationale des femmes canadiennes-françaises
Membre(s) du bureau directeur:
Lisette Surette, Présidente
Della Collette Lacenaire, Vice-présidente
Membre: *Montant de la cotisation:* Membre d'un cercle : 20 $; Membre individuelle : 25 $; Groupe membre : 50 $

Fédération des femmes du Québec (FFQ)

#309, 110, rue St-Thérèse, Montréal QC H2Y 1E6
Tél: 514-876-0166; *Téléc:* 514-876-0162
info@ffq.qc.ca
www.ffq.qc.ca
www.facebook.com/FFQMMF
twitter.com/LaFFQ
www.flickr.com/photos/laffq
Aperçu: *Dimension:* moyenne; *Envergure:* provinciale; fondée en 1966
Mission: Pour défendre les droits et intérêts des femmes
Membre(s) du bureau directeur:
Alexa Conradi, Présidente
Eve-Marie Lacasse, Coordonnatrice, 514-876-0166 Ext. 1505
emlacasse@ffq.qc.ca
Membre(s) du personnel: 6
Membre: 197; *Critères d'admissibilite:* Toute association exclusivement ou majoritairement composée de femmes; *Comités:* Travail

Fédération des femmes médecins du Canada *See* Federation of Medical Women of Canada

Fédération des festivals acadiens de la Nouvelle-Écosse *Voir* Fédération culturelle acadienne de la Nouvelle-Écosse

La Fédération des festivals de musique du Nouveau-Brunswick inc. *See* New Brunswick Federation of Music Festivals Inc.

La Fédération des francophones de la Colombie-Britannique (FFCB)

1575 - 7e av ouest, Vancouver BC V6J 1S1
Tél: 604-732-1420; *Téléc:* 604-732-3236
ffcb@ffcb.ca
www.ffcb.ca
www.facebook.com/FederationFrancophoneCB
Aperçu: *Dimension:* moyenne; *Envergure:* provinciale; Organisme sans but lucratif; fondée en 1945
Mission: Promouvoir, représenter et défendre les droits et intérêts des francophones de la Colombie-Britannique et protéger leur patrimoine linguistique et culturel
Membre de: La Fédération des communaute@s francophones et acadienne au Canada
Membre(s) du bureau directeur:
Yves Trudel, Directeur général
ytrudel@ffcb.ca
Finances: *Fonds:* Heritage Canada/Patrimoine canadien
Membre: 37 associations; *Montant de la cotisation:* 200$
Activités: *Bibliothèque:* Centre de ressources francophones; Bibliothèque publique
Prix, Bouses:
• Prix Napoléon Gareau (Prix)
Prix de reconnaissance du dénouement des bénévoles de la Colombie-Britannique; décerné annuellement
• Prix Cornouiller d'or (Prix)
En guise de reconnaissance au fonctionnaire d'un ministère ou d'une institution fédéral(e) ou provincial(e), qui s'est distinguée en matière de francophonie; décerné annuellement

La Fédération des francophones de Terre-Neuve et du Labrador (FFTNL)

#233, 65, ch Ridge, St. John's NL A1B 4P5
Tél: 709-722-0627; *Téléc:* 709-722-9904
info@fftnl.ca
www.fftnl.ca
www.facebook.com/FrancoTnl
twitter.com/FrancoTnl
Nom précédent: Les Terre-Neuviens français
Aperçu: *Dimension:* petite; *Envergure:* provinciale; fondée en 1971
Mission: Organisme sans but lucratif qui travaille à la défense et à la promotion des droits et intérêts de la communauté francophone et acadienne de Terre-Neuve-et-Labrador
Activités: Carnaval d'hiver; bingos; marche de la St-Jean-Baptiste

Fédération des francophones hors Québec *Voir* Fédération des communautés francophones et acadienne du Canada

Fédération des harmonies du Québec *Voir* Fédération des harmonies et des orchestres symphonies du Québec

Fédération des harmonies et des orchestres symphonies du Québec (FHOSQ)

4545, av Pierre-de Coubertin, Montréal QC H1V 0B2
Tél: 514-252-3026; *Téléc:* 514-252-3115
info@fhosq.org
www.fhosq.org
www.facebook.com/162997715993
twitter.com/FHOSQ
Nom précédent: Fédération des harmonies du Québec
Aperçu: *Dimension:* moyenne; *Envergure:* provinciale; fondée en 1927 surveillé par Canadian Band Association
Mission: Contribuer au développement et à l'amélioration des harmonies en tant que loisir éducatif et culturel
Affliation(s): Fédération des associations de musiciens éducateurs du Québec
Membre(s) du bureau directeur:
Chantal Isabelle, Directrice générale
Membre: 350 harmonies, orchestres et stage bands; *Montant de la cotisation:* 130$ ordinaires; 80$ affins
Activités: *Service de conférenciers:* Oui; *Bibliothèque*

Fédération des infirmières et infirmiers du Québec *Voir* Fédération interprofessionnelle de la santé du Québec

Fédération des instituts féminins du Canada *See* Federated Women's Institutes of Canada

Fédération des intervenantes en petite enfance du Québec (FIPEQ)

9405, rue Sherbrooke Est, Montréal QC H1L 6P3
Tél: 514-356-8888; *Téléc:* 514-356-9999
Ligne sans frais: 800-465-0897
fipeq@csq.qc.net
Aperçu: *Dimension:* petite; *Envergure:* provinciale; fondée en 1985
Mission: La Fédération des intervenantes en petite enfance du Québec (FIPEQ) est vouée à la promotion de la profession, à la défense des droits et des intérêts ainsi qu'à l'amélioration des conditions de vie de toutes les intervenantes, tant travailleuses autonomes que salariées, oeuvrant au service des centres de la petite enfance.
Membre(s) du bureau directeur:
Kathleen Courville, Présidente

Fédération des jeunes francophones du Nouveau-Brunswick Inc. (FJFNB)

#101, 51, rue Highfield, Moncton NB E1L 5N2
Tél: 506-857-0926; *Téléc:* 506-388-1368
Ligne sans frais: 877-353-6200
fjfnb@fjfnb.nb.ca
www.fjfnb.nb.ca
www.facebook.com/299405679140
twitter.com/fjfnb
www.youtube.com/lafjfnb
Aperçu: *Dimension:* moyenne; *Envergure:* provinciale; Organisme sans but lucratif; fondée en 1987
Mission: Réunir les jeunes francophones, acadiens et acadiennes du N.-B. âgés de 14 à 21 ans afin d'assurer le développement et l'épanouissement de cette jeunesse
Membre de: Fédération de la jeunesse canadienne-française inc.
Membre(s) du bureau directeur:
Rémi Goupil, Directeur général
directeur@fjfnb.nb.ca
Membre(s) du personnel: 11
Membre: 10,000 étudiants; *Critères d'admissibilite:* Conseil des étudiants des écoles francophones du N.-B.
Activités: Conseil des présidents; colloque sur le leadership; programmes d'échanges internationaux; programmes d'échanges de jeunes travailleurs; programmes d'échanges en agriculture; camps musicaux; Échanges Jeuness Canada; Forums Jeunesses Canada; *Stagiaires:* Oui

Fédération des loisirs-danse du Québec (FLDQ)

4545, av Pierre-de-Coubertin, Montréal QC H1V 3N7
Tél: 514-252-3029
Également appelé: Danse Québec
Aperçu: *Dimension:* petite; *Envergure:* provinciale
Membre(s) du bureau directeur:
France Dagenais, Présidente

Fédération des médecins omnipraticiens du Québec (FMOQ) / Québec Federation of General Practitioners

2, Place Alexis Nihon, #2000, 3500, boul. de Maisonneuve ouest, Montréal QC H3G 1R8

Tél: 514-878-1911; *Téléc:* 514-878-4455
Ligne sans frais: 800-361-8499
info@fmoq.org
www.fmoq.org
Aperçu: *Dimension:* moyenne; *Envergure:* provinciale; fondée en 1963
Mission: Étude et défense des intérêts économiques, sociaux, moraux et scientifiques des associations et de leurs membres; promouvoir et développer le rôle de l'omnipraticien dans les sphères de la vie économique, sociale, scientifique et culturelle en définissant d'une façon objective le statut propre à l'omnipraticien
Membre de: World Organization of National Colleges; Academies & Academic Associations of General Practitioners/Family Physicians
Membre(s) du bureau directeur:
Louis Godin, Président-directeur général
lgodin@fmoq.org
Finances: *Budget de fonctionnement annuel:* Plus de $5 Million
Membre: 7 841; *Montant de la cotisation:* 1030$
Activités: *Service de conférenciers:* Oui; *Bibliothèque:* Centre de documentation; rendez-vous

Fédération des médecins résidents du Québec inc. (ind.) (FMRQ) / Québec Federation of Residents (Ind.)

#510, 630, rue Sherbrooke ouest, Montréal QC H3A 1E4
Tél: 514-282-0256; *Téléc:* 514-282-0471
Ligne sans frais: 800-465-0215
fmrq@fmrq.qc.ca
www.fmrq.qc.ca
www.facebook.com/fmrqc
Aperçu: *Dimension:* moyenne; *Envergure:* provinciale; fondée en 1966
Mission: D'étudier, de défendre et de développer les intérêts économiques, sociaux, moraux et scientifiques des syndicats et des leurs membres.
Membre(s) du bureau directeur:
Jean Gouin, Executive Director
Patrick Labelle, Administrative Director
Membre(s) du personnel: 16
Membre: 3,500

Fédération des médecins spécialistes du Québec (FMSQ)

CP 216, Succ. Desjardins, #3000, 2, Complexe Desjardins, Montréal QC H5B 1G8
Tél: 514-350-5000; *Téléc:* 514-350-5100
Ligne sans frais: 800-561-0703
communications@fmsq.org
www.fmsq.org
www.facebook.com/laFMSQ
twitter.com/FMSQ
Aperçu: *Dimension:* moyenne; *Envergure:* provinciale; fondée en 1965
Mission: Défendre et promouvoir les intérêts économiques, professionnels et scientifiques des médecins spécialistes
Membre(s) du bureau directeur:
Gaétan Barrette, Président
Membre(s) du personnel: 50
Membre: 9 500
Activités: *Bibliothèque:* Centre de documentation

Fédération des Métis du Manitoba *See* Manitoba Métis Federation

Fédération des Moissons du Québec inc. *Voir* Association québécoise des banques alimentaires et des Moissons

Fédération des ordres des médecins du Canada *See* Federation of Regulatory Authorities of Canada

Fédération des ordres des médecins du Canada *See* Federation of Medical Regulatory Authorities of Canada

Fédération des ordres professionnels de juristes du Canada *See* Federation of Law Societies of Canada

Fédération des OSBL d'habitation de Montréal

#105, 1650 rue St-Timothée, Montréal QC H2X 3P1
Tél: 514-527-6668; *Téléc:* 514-527-7388
fohm@videotron.ca
fohm.rqoh.com
Aperçu: *Dimension:* petite; *Envergure:* locale
Mission: Soutenir le développement de logements à but non lucratif et de fournir des logements abordables pour les locataires à faible revenu à Montréal
Affliation(s): Réseau québécois des OSBL d'habitation

Membre(s) du bureau directeur:
Claudine Laurin, Directrice générale
Membre: 216
Activités: Activités de formation; Des forums pour tennants et les personnes âgées; Réunions

Fédération des ouvriers des chantiers navals de la Colombie-Britannique (CTC) *See* Shipyard General Workers' Federation of British Columbia (CLC)

Fédération des parents acadiens de la Nouvelle-Écosse (FPANE)

54, rue Queen, Dartmouth NS B2Y 1G3
Tél: 902-435-2060; *Téléc:* 902-433-0066
Ligne sans frais: 877-326-4553
fpane@fpane.ca
www.fpane.ca
Aperçu: *Dimension:* petite; *Envergure:* provinciale; Organisme sans but lucratif
Affliation(s): Commission nationale des parents francophones
Membre(s) du bureau directeur:
Louise d'Entremont, Directrice générale par intérim
Finances: *Budget de fonctionnement annuel:* $50,000-$100,000
Membre(s) du personnel: 1; 15 bénévole(s)
Membre: 1-99;

Fédération des parents de l'Ile-du-Prince-Édouard (FPIPE)

5 Maris Stella Ave., Summerside PE C1N 6M9
Tél: 902-436-4881; *Téléc:* 902-436-6936
coord3@ssta.org
fpipe.org
www.facebook.com/parentsipe
twitter.com/fpipeorg
Aperçu: *Dimension:* petite; *Envergure:* provinciale
Mission: Promouvoir l'éducation et la culture acadienne et française, en travaillant pour la mise sur pied et le développement d'institutions préscolaires et scolaires de français langue première à l'Ile-du-Prince-Édouard
Affliation(s): Commission nationale des parents francophones
Membre(s) du bureau directeur:
Nicole Drouin, Directrice générale
Anastasia Des Roches, Coordonnatrice
Membre(s) du personnel: 1
Membre: 10 comités DE PARENTS

Fédération des parents francophones de Colombie-Britannique (FPFCB)

#223, 1555 - 7e av Ouest, Vancouver BC V6J 1S1
Tél: 604-736-5056; *Téléc:* 604-736-1259
Ligne sans frais: 800-905-5056
info@fpfcb.bc.ca
www.fpfcb.bc.ca
Nom précédent: Association des parents francophones de la Colombie-Britannique
Aperçu: *Dimension:* moyenne; *Envergure:* provinciale; Organisme sans but lucratif; fondée en 1980
Mission: Appuyer les parents de la Colombie Britanique dans leur rôle de premier éducateur de leurs enfants et de promouvoir leur participation à l'établissement d'un milieu éducatif et communautaire qui favorise le plein épanouissement français des enfants et des familles
Affliation(s): Commission nationale des parents francophones
Membre(s) du bureau directeur:
Marie-Andrée Asselin, Directrice administrative
Finances: *Budget de fonctionnement annuel:* $250,000-$500,000
Membre(s) du personnel: 4
Membre: 1-99; *Montant de la cotisation:* 20$; *Critères d'admissibilite:* Association locale de parents
Activités: Semaine nationale de la francophonie; congrès annuel; *Stagiaires:* Oui; *Service de conférenciers:* Oui; *Bibliothèque:* Centre de ressources Tire-Lire

Fédération des parents francophones de l'Alberta (FPFA)

#114, 8627 rue Marie-Anne-Gaboury nord-ouest, Edmonton AB T6C 3N1
Tél: 780-468-6934; *Téléc:* 780-469-4799
Autres numéros: direction@fpfa.ab.ca
info@fpfa.ab.ca
www.fpfa.ab.ca
Nom précédent: Association albertaine des parents francophones
Aperçu: *Dimension:* moyenne; *Envergure:* provinciale; Organisme sans but lucratif; fondée en 1986
Mission: Favoriser la participation dynamique des parents à l'éducation francophone de leurs enfants, au foyer, à l'école et dans la communauté de l'Alberta
Membre de: La Commission nationale des parents francophones (CNPF)
Membre(s) du bureau directeur:
Mireille Péloquin, Directrice générale, 780-468-6934
Marie-Chantal Daval-Bérillon, Adjointe-administrative, 780-468-6934
Corinne Collins, Responsable, la petite enfance, 780-468-6934
corinnecollins@fpfa.ab.ca
Membre: 1-99;

Fédération des parents francophones de Terre-Neuve et du Labrador (FPFTNL)

65, ch Ridge, St. John's NL A1B 4P5
Tél: 709-722-7669; *Téléc:* 709-722-7696
Ligne sans frais: 888-749-7669
www.fpftnl.ca
Aperçu: *Dimension:* petite; *Envergure:* provinciale; fondée en 1989
Membre de: Association canadienne d'éducation de langue française; La Commission nationale des parents francophones; Association of Early Childhood Educators, Newfoundland and Labrador; Fédération des francophones de Terre-Neuve et du Labrador
Affliation(s): Commission nationale des parents francophones
Membre: 6 comités parents
Activités: Concours littéraire provincial; visites d'écoles

Fédération des policiers du Québec (ind.) *Voir* Fédération des policiers et policières municipaux du Québec (ind.)

Fédération des policiers et policières municipaux du Québec (ind.) (FPMQ) / Québec Federation of Policemen (Ind.)

7955, boul Louis-Hippolyte-La Fontaine, Anjou QC H1K 4E4
Tél: 514-356-3321; *Téléc:* 514-356-1158
Ligne sans frais: 800-361-0321
info@fpmq.org
www.fpmq.org
Nom précédent: Fédération des policiers du Québec (ind.)
Aperçu: *Dimension:* moyenne; *Envergure:* provinciale; fondée en 1965
Mission: L'étude et la défense des intérêts économiques, professionnels, sociaux et moraux de ses associations-membres et de tous les policiers que celles-ci regroupent.
Membre(s) du bureau directeur:
Denis Côté, Président
dcote@fpmq.org
Christine Beaulieu, Directrice, Communications
cbeaulieu@fpmq.org
Josée Poisson, Secrétaire, Finances
jpoisson@fpmq.org
Membre(s) du personnel: 5
Membre: 3 685 + 30 sections locales; *Critères d'admissibilite:* Associations syndicales de policiers municipaux
Activités: Congrès, Tournois de golf, Gala du Ménite policier

Fédération des producteurs acéricoles du Québec (FPAQ) / Québec Maple Syrup Producers Federation

#525, 555, boul Roland-Therrien, Longueuil QC J4H 4G5
Tél: 450-679-7021; *Téléc:* 450-679-0139
info@siropderable.ca
www.siropderable.ca
Aperçu: *Dimension:* petite; *Envergure:* provinciale; fondée en 1966

Fédération des producteurs d'agneaux et moutons du Québec (FPAMQ)

CP 8484, #545, 555, boul Roland-Therrien, Longueuil QC J4H 4E7
Tél: 450-679-0540; *Téléc:* 450-674-4415
info@agneauduquebec.com
www.agneauduquebec.com
www.facebook.com/127544713953964
Aperçu: *Dimension:* moyenne; *Envergure:* provinciale; fondée en 1981
Mission: Défendre les droits économiques, sociaux et moraux des producteurs d'agneaux du Québec; organiser la mise en marché des produits
Affliation(s): Union des producteurs agricoles
Membre(s) du bureau directeur:
Amina Baba-Khelil, Directrice générale
Finances: *Budget de fonctionnement annuel:* $250,000-$500,000
Membre(s) du personnel: 7

Membre: 12 syndicats; 960 adhérents; *Critères d'admissibilité:* Producteurs d'agneaux et de moutons

Fédération des producteurs d'oeufs de consommation du Québec (FPOCQ)

#320, 555, boul Roland-Therrien, Longueuil QC J4H 4E7
Tél: 450-679-0530; *Téléc:* 450-679-0855
www.oeuf.ca
www.facebook.com/lesoeufs?v=wall
Aperçu: *Dimension:* moyenne; *Envergure:* provinciale; Organisme de réglementation; fondée en 1964
Mission: Favoriser le développement durable de l'industrie québécoise des oeufs et ce par: le respect de l'environnement et le bien-être des animaux; en procurant un revenu équitable aux intervenants du secteur; en répondant aux attentes des consommateurs avec des oeufs et produits de haute qualité
Membre de: L'Union des producteurs agricoles; L'Office canadien de commercialisation des oeufs
Membre(s) du bureau directeur:
Serge Lefebvre, Président
Finances: *Budget de fonctionnement annuel:* Plus de $5 Million
Membre(s) du personnel: 13
Membre: 103; *Critères d'admissibilité:* Détenir un quota de production et de mise en marché

La Fédération des producteurs de bois du Québec (FPBQ)

#565, 555, boul Roland-Therrien, Longueuil QC J4H 4E7
Tél: 450-679-0530; *Téléc:* 450-679-4300
bois@upa.qc.ca
www.fpbq.qc.ca
Aperçu: *Dimension:* moyenne; *Envergure:* provinciale; fondée en 1970
Mission: Défendre les intérêts de l'ensemble des propriétaires de boisés du Québec ainsi que l'élaboration et la promotion des politiques souhaitables et nécessaires pour atteindre cet objectif; représenter les propriétaires de boisés privés auprès des pouvoirs publics et des autres groupes de la société au niveau provincial et national; coordonner l'ensemble des activités des Syndicats et Offices de producteurs de bois ainsi que l'établissement, le maintien et le développement entre eux d'une étroite collaboration
Affliation(s): Union des producteurs agricoles
Membre(s) du bureau directeur:
Marc-André Côté, Directeur
macote@upa.qc.ca
Finances: *Budget de fonctionnement annuel:* $500,000-$1.5 Million
Membre(s) du personnel: 9

Fédération des producteurs de bovins du Québec (FPBQ) / Federation of Québec Beef Producers

#305, 555, boul Roland-Therrien, Longueuil QC J4H 4G2
Tél: 450-679-0530; *Téléc:* 450-442-9348
www.bovin.qc.ca
Aperçu: *Dimension:* moyenne; *Envergure:* provinciale; Organisme sans but lucratif; fondée en 1974
Mission: Regrouper et défendre les intérêts professionnels et économiques des producteurs de bovins du Québec; administrer et appliquer le plan conjoint des producteurs de bovins du Québec
Affliation(s): Union des producteurs agricoles
Membre(s) du bureau directeur:
Claude Viel, Président
Guy Gallant, Vice-président
Finances: *Budget de fonctionnement annuel:* $1.5 Million-$3 Million; *Fonds:* Publicité et promotion du veau; fonds de recherche et développement
Membre(s) du personnel: 37
Membre: 12 000 entreprises agricoles; *Critères d'admissibilité:* Producteurs agricoles
Activités: *Listes de destinataires:* Oui

Fédération des producteurs de cultures commerciales du Québec (FPCCQ)

#505, 555, boul Roland-Therrien, Longueuil QC J4H 3Y9
Tél: 450-679-0540; *Téléc:* 450-679-6372
fpccq@fpccq.qc.ca
www.fpccq.qc.ca
www.facebook.com/SIMFPCCQ
Aperçu: *Dimension:* petite; *Envergure:* provinciale; fondée en 1975
Affliation(s): Union des producteurs agricoles (UPA)
Membre(s) du bureau directeur:
Christian Overbeek, Président
Membre: 11 syndicats

Fédération des producteurs de lait du Québec (FPLQ)

555, boul Roland-Therrien, Longueuil QC J4H 3Y9
Tél: 450-679-0530; *Téléc:* 450-679-5899
fplq@upa.qc.ca
www.lait.org
Aperçu: *Dimension:* grande; *Envergure:* provinciale; fondée en 1983
Mission: Défense et promotion des intérêts professionnels et sociaux des producteurs de lait et mise en marché du lait de la ferme.
Membre de: Producteurs laitiers du Canada
Affliation(s): Union des producteurs agricoles
Finances: *Budget de fonctionnement annuel:* Plus de $5 Million*Fonds:* Fonds de recherche
Membre(s) du personnel: 40
Membre: 14 syndicats; 6 300 fermes laitières; 13 000 producteurs et productrices de lait; *Critères d'admissibilité:* Producteurs de lait
Activités: *Service de conférenciers:* Oui
Publications:
• Le producteur de lait québécois [a publication of Fédération des producteurs de lait du Québec]
Type: Revue; *Frequency:* 10 fois par an

Fédération des producteurs de miel du Québec ***Voir*** Fédération des apiculteurs du Québec

Fédération des producteurs de pommes de terre du Québec (FPPTQ)

#375, 555, boul Roland-Therrien, Longueuil QC J4H 4E7
Tél: 450-679-0530; *Téléc:* 450-679-5595
fpptq@upa.qc.ca
www.fpptq.qc.ca
Aperçu: *Dimension:* moyenne; *Envergure:* provinciale; fondée en 1966
Mission: Organisation de la mise en marché
Affliation(s): L'union des producteurs agricoles
Membre(s) du bureau directeur:
Clément Lalancette, Directeur général
clementlalancette@upa.qc.ca
Membre(s) du personnel: 6

Fédération des producteurs de porcs du Québec ***Voir*** Éleveurs de porcs du Québec

Fédération des producteurs de volailles du Québec ***Voir*** Éleveurs de volailles du Québec

Fédération des professionnèles (FPCSN) / Quebec Federation of Managers & Professional Salaried Workers (CNTU)

1601, av de Lorimier, Montréal QC H2K 4M5
Tél: 514-598-2143; *Téléc:* 514-598-2491
Ligne sans frais: 888-633-2143
www.fpcsn.qc.ca
Nom précédent: Fédération des professionnelles et professionnels salarié(e)s et des cadres du Québec
Aperçu: *Dimension:* moyenne; *Envergure:* provinciale; Organisme sans but lucratif; fondée en 1964
Mission: Regroupe plus de 7000 professionnèles oeuvrant dans différents secteurs d'activités: santé et services sociaux, organismes gouvernementaux, éducation, secteur municipal, médecines alternatives, secteur juridique, intégration à l'emploi, professionnèles autonomes, organismes communautaires, etc
Membre de: Confédération des syndicats nationaux
Membre(s) du bureau directeur:
Michel Tremblay, Président
michel.tremblay@csn.qc.ca
Lucie Dufour, Secrétaire générale
lucie.dufour@csn.qc.ca
Membre(s) du personnel: 10
Membre: 7 142 + 28 sections locales; *Critères d'admissibilité:* Professionnel de travail social ou secteur communautaire, universitaire, aide juridique
Activités: Congrès au printemps; *Stagiaires:* Oui

Fédération des professionnelles et professionnels de l'éducation du Québec (FPPE) / Québec Federation of Professional Employees in Education

9405, rue Sherbrooke est, Montréal QC H1L 6P3
Tél: 514-356-0505; *Téléc:* 514-356-1324
infos@fppe.qc.ca
www.fppe.qc.ca
twitter.com/FPPECSQ
www.youtube.com/user/FPPECSQ
Nom précédent: Fédération des syndicats de professionnelles et professionnels de commissions scolaires du Québec
Aperçu: *Dimension:* grande; *Envergure:* provinciale; Organisme sans but lucratif; fondée en 1985 surveillé par Centrale des syndicats du Québec
Mission: De promouvoir et de développer les intérêts professionnels, sociaux et économiques des professionnelles et professionnels de l'éducation du Québec ainsi que de défendre les droits fondamentaux compris à l'intérieur des chartes, le droit d'association, le droit à la libre négociation et le droit à la liberté d'action syndicale; de représenter ses syndicats affiliés à un niveau national; d'orienter et de coordonner la représentation de ses syndicats affiliés auprès des instances de la Centrale; de diriger et de coordonner la négociation des conventions collectives; de concilier les conflits qui peuvent naître entre les syndicats affiliés; de mettre à la disposition des syndicats affiliés et de leurs membres des services de qualité en matière de négociation et d'application des conditions de travail et des droits sociaux, d'information et de formation syndicale.
Membre(s) du bureau directeur:
Johanne Pomerleau, Président
fppe.pomerleau.johanne@csq.qc.net
Jean-Marie Comeau, Vice-présidente
fppe.comeau.jean-marie@csq.qc.net
Sylvie Simoneau, 2e Vice-président
Pierre Jobin, 3e Vice-président
Finances: *Budget de fonctionnement annuel:* $3 Million-$5 Million
Membre(s) du personnel: 10
Membre: 6 500 + 20 syndicats; *Montant de la cotisation:* 0,74% du traitement; *Critères d'admissibilité:* Professionnels de l'éducation; *Comités:* Santé-Sécurité; Affaires Financières; Condition de Femmes; Jeunes; Statuts; Élections

Syndicat des professionnelles et professionnels scolaires de la Gaspésie et des Iles-de-la-Madeleine (SPPGIM)

237, 9e rue, Paspébiac QC G0C 2K0
Tél: 418-534-3003; *Téléc:* 418-752-6447
a01.gaspesie@csq.qc.net
www.fppe.qc.ca/sppgim/accueil.html
Membre(s) du bureau directeur:
Steeve Loisel, Président

Syndicat des professionnelles et professionnels de l'éducation du Bas St-Laurent (SPPEBSL)

150, rue Émile-Labbé, Amqui QC G5J 1J4
Tél: 418-629-6200; *Téléc:* 418-629-5674
a02.bas.st.laurent@csq.qc.net
www.fppe.qc.ca/sppebsl/accueil.html
Membre(s) du bureau directeur:
Diane Bélanger, Présidente

Syndicat des professionnelles et professionnels des commissions scolaires du Grand-Portage (SPGP)

41, rue Caron, Notre-Dame-du-Lac QC G0L 1X0
Tél: 418-853-3420; *Téléc:* 418-899-0809
a03.grand.portage@csq.qc.net
www.fppe.qc.ca/spgp/accueil.html
Membre(s) du bureau directeur:
Jonanne Gingras, Présidente
johannedulac@hotmail.com

Syndicat des professionnelles et professionnels des commissions scolaires de la Rive-Sud de Québec (SPCSRSQ)

4568, rue des Bosquets, St-Augustin de Desmaurres QC G3A 1C4
Tél: 418-871-2656
a04.rive.sud.quebec@csq.qc.net
www.fppe.qc.ca/spcsrsq/accueil.html
Membre(s) du bureau directeur:
Marc Bernier, Président

Syndicat des professionnelles et professionnels de commissions scolaires de Beauce-Appalache (SPPBA)

CP 11, 178, ch du Lac Algonquin, Ste-Rose-de-Watford QC G0R 4G0
Tél: 418-228-5541; *Téléc:* 418-267-4599
a05.beauce.appalaches@csq.qc.net
www.fppe.qc.ca/sppba/accueil.html
Membre(s) du bureau directeur:
Élaine Robitaille, Présidente

Syndicat des professionnelles et professionnels des commissions scolaires de l'Estrie (SPPCSE)

2985, ch Norbel, RR#4, Canton Magog QC J1X 5R9
Tél: 450-263-3772; *Téléc:* 450-263-1205
a07.estrie@csq.qc.net
www.sppcse.qc.ca

Membre(s) du bureau directeur:
Constance Peacock, Présidente

Syndicat des professionnelles et professionnels de Richelieu Yamaska (SPPRY)
726, rue Chaput, Granby QC J2H 2X7
Tél: 450-263-6660
www.fppe.qc.ca/sppry/accueil.html
Membre(s) du bureau directeur:
Robert Huard, Président
huardr@csvdc.qc.ca

Syndicat des professionnelles et professionnels de commissions scolaires du Sud de la Montérégie (SPPSM)
CP 415, LaPrairie QC J5R 3Y3
Tél: 450-659-4272
a09.sud.moneregie@csq.qc.net
www.sppsm.ca
Membre(s) du bureau directeur:
Martin Lévesque, Président

Syndicat des professionnelles et professionnels de commissions scolaires de la Montérégie (SPPCSM)
7500, ch Chambly, Saint-Hubert QC J3Y 3S6
Tél: 450-670-3130; *Téléc:* 450-461-3750
a10.monteregie@csq.qc.net
www.sppcsm.ca
Membre(s) du bureau directeur:
Roger Tremblay, Président

Syndicat des professionnelles et professionnels du milieu de l'éducation de Montréal (SPPMÉM)
#200, 5927, rue Boyer, Montréal QC H2S 2H8
Tél: 514-254-6993; *Téléc:* 514-254-4744
info@sppmem.ca
www.sppmem.ca
Membre(s) du bureau directeur:
Paul Cousineau, Présidente
presidence@sppmem.ca

Syndicat des professionnelles et professionnels de l'Ouest de Montréal (SPPOM)
#440, 100, boul Alexis-Nihon, Saint-Laurent QC H4M 2N7
Tél: 514-748-5983; *Téléc:* 514-748-5822
sppom@sppom.qc.ca
www.fppe.qc.ca/sppom/accueil.html
Membre(s) du bureau directeur:
Diane Jacques, Présidente

Syndicat des professionnelles et professionnels des services éducatifs de la Région de Montréal (SPPSERM)
2323, boul Daniel Johnson, Laval QC H7T 1H8
Tél: 450-686-6333
a13.region.de.montreal@csq.qc.net
www.smaesp.org
Membre(s) du bureau directeur:
Dominic Di Stefano, Président

Syndicat des professionnelles et professionnels en milieu scolaire du Nord-Ouest (SPPMSNO)
194, 1e rue ouest, La Sarre QC J9Z 1V3
Tél: 819-333-5591; *Téléc:* 819-339-2347
a16.nord.ouest@csq.qc.net
www.fppe.qc.ca/sppmsno/accueil.html
Membre(s) du bureau directeur:
Rose Marquis, Présidente

Syndicat des professionnelles et professionnels de l'éducation des Laurentides-Lanaudière (SPPÉLL)
#109, 995, rue Labelle, Saint-Jérôme QC J7Y 5N7
Tél: 450-758-3570; *Téléc:* 450-438-1694
www.sppell.qc.ca
Membre(s) du bureau directeur:
Daniel Simon, Président
daniel.simon@xplornet.ca

Syndicat des professionnelles et professionnels de commissions scolaires du Lac St-Jean, Pays-des-Bleuets et Baie-James (SPPLPB)
148, av Pednault, Roberval QC G8H 3G4
Tél: 418-275-4136
a22.lac.st.jean@csq.qc.net
www.fppc.qc.ca/spplpb/accueil.html
Membre(s) du bureau directeur:
Maxime Goulet, Président

Syndicat des professionnelles et professionnels de l'éducation du Saguenay (SPPÉS)
210, ch des Vacanciers, RR#2, Labrecque QC G0W 2W0
Tél: 418-548-3113
a23.saguenay@csq.qc.net
www.fppe.qc.ca/sppes
Membre(s) du bureau directeur:
Richard Brisson, Président
richard.brisson@csjonquiere.qc.ca

Syndicat des professionnelles et professionnels de la Haute Côte Nord (SPPHCN)
40, av Michel-Hémon, Baie-Comeau QC G4Z 2K4
Tél: 418-232-6231
www.fppe.qc.ca/spphcn/accueil.html
Membre(s) du bureau directeur:
Chantale Paré, Présidente
chantale.pare@csestuaire.qc.ca

Syndicat des professionnelles et professionnels du Nord-Est du Québec (SPPNEQ)
34, rue Vallée, Port-Cartier QC G5B 2K4
Tél: 418-766-7171; *Téléc:* 418-766-5246
a25.nord.est@csq.qc.net
www.fppe.qc.ca/sppneq/accueil.html
Membre(s) du bureau directeur:
Guy Buteau, Président

Syndicat du personnel professionnel de l'éducation du Coeur et du Centre du Québec (SPPECCQ)
CP 1414, Trois-Rivières QC G9A 5L2
Tél: 819-693-1442; *Téléc:* 819-375-9659
sppeccq.csq@cgocable.ca
www.fppe.qc.ca/sppecq/accueil.html
Membre(s) du bureau directeur:
Denis Bastarache, Président

Syndicat du personnel professionnel des commissions scolaires de la Région de Québec (SPPRÉQ)
#100, 320, rue St-Joseph est, Québec QC G1K 9E7
Tél: 418-649-7726; *Téléc:* 418-525-0772
a26.region.quebec@csq.qc.net
www.sppreq.ca
Membre(s) du bureau directeur:
Lise Therrien, Présidente

Fédération des professionnelles et professionnels salarié(e)s et des cadres du Québec ***Voir*** Fédération des professionnèles

Fédération des professionnels chinois canadiens (Québec) ***See*** Federation of Chinese Canadian Professionals (Québec)

Fédération des propriétaires de lots boisés du Nouveau-Brunswick inc. ***See*** New Brunswick Federation of Woodlot Owners Inc.

Fédération des quilles du Canada ***See*** Bowling Federation of Canada

Fédération des sciences neurologiques du Canada ***See*** Canadian Neurological Sciences Federation

Fédération des scouts de l'Atlantique
126, ch Gerard, Haut-Saint-Antoine NB E4V 3B1
Tél: 506-525-2093; *Téléc:* 506-525-9548
scoutatl@nb.sympatico.ca
Aperçu: *Dimension:* moyenne; *Envergure:* locale; Organisme sans but lucratif; fondée en 1975
Mission: Promotion et développement du scoutisme francophone dans les provinces de l'Atlantique; formation des adultes à l'animation scoute; faire vivre aux jeunes de 7 à 21 ans l'aventure et la philosophie du scoutisme en leur permettant de prendre une part active dans leur formation
Membre de: Association des Scouts du Canada
Membre: *Critères d'admissibilite:* Jeunes âgés de 7 à 21 ans
Activités: *Stagiaires:* Oui

District Boishébert
Fredericton NB

District d'Edmundston
Edmundston NB

District de Chéticamp
Chéticamp NS

District de Gloucester
Paquetville NB

Fédération des scouts de l'ouest
67, Berwick Cres. NO, Calgary AB T3K 1P7
Tél: 403-274-0463; *Téléc:* 403-275-3749
scouts.ouest@home.com
members.shaw.ca/scouts.ouest/
Aperçu: *Dimension:* petite; *Envergure:* locale
Membre de: Scouts du Canada
Membre(s) du bureau directeur:
Roseline Cyr, Secrétariat

Fédération des secrétaires professionnelles du Québec (FSPQ)
#390-1, 1173, boul Charest ouest, Québec QC G1N 2C9
Tél: 418-527-5041; *Téléc:* 418-527-2160
Ligne sans frais: 866-527-5041
info@fspq.qc.ca
www.fspq.qc.ca
www.linkedin.com/groups?gid=2340718
twitter.com/FSPQ
Aperçu: *Dimension:* moyenne; *Envergure:* provinciale
Mission: Travail à la valorisation de la profession.
Membre(s) du bureau directeur:
Anick Blouin, Présidente
Membre: *Montant de la cotisation:* 95$ agréée; 45$ étudiante; 387,35$ corporatif

Fédération des sociétés canadiennes d'assistance aux animaux ***See*** Canadian Federation of Humane Societies

Fédération des sociétés d'histoire du Québec
4545, av Pierre-de Coubertin, Montréal QC H1V 0B2
Tél: 514-252-3031; *Téléc:* 514-251-8038
Ligne sans frais: 866-691-7207
fshq@histoirequebec.qc.ca
www.histoirequebec.qc.ca
twitter.com/FederationHQ
Aperçu: *Dimension:* moyenne; *Envergure:* nationale; Organisme sans but lucratif; fondée en 1965
Mission: Regrouper les organisations historiques de Québec.
Membre de: Heritage Canada
Membre(s) du bureau directeur:
Richard M. Bégin, Président
beginrm@ca.intern.net
Membre(s) du personnel: 2
Membre: *Montant de la cotisation:* 30$ indiviuel; 138$ institutionnel; *Critères d'admissibilite:* Société d'histoire, de généalogie, du patrimoine ou affinitaire; *Comités:* Patrimoine
Activités: *Bibliothèque:* Centre de documentation; rendez-vous
Prix, Bouses:
• Prix Léonidas-Bélanger (Prix)
Eligibility: Reconnaît le travail de diffusion réalisé par un organisme
• Prix Rodolphe-Fournier (Prix)
Eligibility: Prix décerné pour la promotion de la recherche en histoire du notariat
• Prix Honorius-Provost (Prix)
Eligibility: Reconnaît le travail bénévole

Fédération des sociétés d'horticulture et d'écologie du Québec (FSHÉQ)
CP 1000, Succ. M, 4545, av Pierre-de Coubertin, Montréal QC H1V 3R2
Tél: 514-252-3010; *Téléc:* 514-251-8038
fsheq@fsheq.com
www.fsheq.com
www.facebook.com/305119346270307?fref=ts
Aperçu: *Dimension:* moyenne; *Envergure:* provinciale; Organisme sans but lucratif; fondée en 1978
Mission: Regrouper tous les organismes voués à l'horticulture; faire la promotion de l'horticulture.
Membre(s) du bureau directeur:
Thérèse Tourigny, Directrice générale
ttourigny@fsheq.com
Finances: *Budget de fonctionnement annuel:* $50,000-$100,000
3 bénévole(s)
Membre: 280; *Montant de la cotisation:* 90$; *Critères d'admissibilite:* Sociétés d'horticulture
Activités: *Service de conférenciers:* Oui

Fédération des Syndicats de l'Enseignement (FSE)
CP 100, 320, rue Saint-Joseph est, Québec QC G1K 9E7
Tél: 418-649-8888; *Téléc:* 418-649-1914
fse@csq.qc.net
www.fse.qc.net
www.facebook.com/FSECSQ
twitter.com/FSECSQ
Aperçu: *Dimension:* grande; *Envergure:* provinciale; Organisme sans but lucratif; fondée en 1988 surveillé par Centrale des syndicats du Québec
Mission: Promouvoir les intérêts professionnels, sociaux et économiques du personnel enseignant des commissions scolaires; orienter et coordonner la représentation des syndicats affiliés auprès des instances de la Centrale et de représenter les syndicats affiliés là où leurs intérêts et leurs droits sont débattus; assumer prioritairement la responsabilité des négociations, les aspects sectoriels des relations du travail et de l'action juridique ainsi que les questions professionnelles à caractère sectoriel;

favoriser la concertation entre les syndicats affiliés et concilier les divergences qui pourraient naître entre eux.
Membre(s) du bureau directeur:
Laurier Caron, Directeur général
caron.laurier@csq.qc.net
Finances: *Budget de fonctionnement annuel:* $3 Million-$5 Million
Membre: 75 000; un regroupement de 35 syndicats; *Comités:* Élection; finances et de péréquation; statuts et règlements; formation générale des jeunes; formation professionnelle; éducation des adultes; interprétation et d'application de la convention collective

Fédération des syndicats de la santé et des services sociaux (F4S-CSQ)

9405, rue Sherbrooke est, Montréal QC H1L 6P3
Tél: 514-356-8888; *Téléc:* 514-356-2845
info@f4s.gs
www.f4s.gs
Aperçu: *Dimension:* petite; *Envergure:* provinciale
Mission: S'assurer que ses membres travaillent dans des conditions de sécurité; de représenter les intérêts de ses membres au cours des conventions collectives
Membre(s) du bureau directeur:
Claude Demontigny, Président
demontigny.claude@csq.qc.net

Fédération des syndicats de professionnelles et professionnels de commissions scolaires du Québec *Voir* Fédération des professionnelles et professionnels de l'éducation du Québec

Fédération des trappeurs gestionnaires du Québec (FTGQ)

1737, rue de Champigny Est, Québec QC G2G 1A6
Tél: 418-872-7644; *Téléc:* 418-872-6131
Ligne sans frais: 866-260-7644
ftgq@ftgq.qc.ca
www.ftgq.qc.ca
Aperçu: *Dimension:* moyenne; *Envergure:* provinciale; fondée en 1976
Affiliation(s): Association provinciale des trappeurs de l'Abitibi-Témiscamingue; Association des trappeurs du Bas Saint-Laurent; Association régionale des trappeurs de Chaudière-Appalaches; Regroupement des trappeurs de la Côte-Nord; Association provinciale des trappeurs indépendants, Conseil Estrie; Association provinciale des trappeurs indépendants, Conseil de la Gaspésie; Association des trappeurs du Haut-Saint-Maurice; Association régionale des trappeurs Laurentides/Labelle; Association régionale des trappeurs Laurentiens; Association des trappeurs Mauricie/Bois-Francs
Membre(s) du bureau directeur:
Érick Tremblay, Président
tremblay-erick@hotmail.com

Fédération des travailleurs et travailleises du Québec (FTQ) / Québec Federation of Labour

#12100, 565, boul Crémazie Est, Montréal QC H2M 2W3
Tél: 514-383-8000; *Téléc:* 514-383-8038
Ligne sans frais: 877-897-0057
ftq@ftq.qc.ca
www.ftq.qc.ca
www.facebook.com/laFTQ
twitter.com/FTQnouvelles
Aperçu: *Dimension:* moyenne; *Envergure:* provinciale surveillé par Canadian Labour Congress
Membre(s) du bureau directeur:
Michel Arsenault, Président
fvigeant@ftq.qc.ca
Membre: 600 000+

Fédération des travailleurs et travailleuses du Nouveau-Brunswick *See* New Brunswick Federation of Labour

Fédération des travailleurs et travailleuses du Québec - Construction

#2900, 565, boul Crémazie est, Montréal QC H2M 2V6
Tél: 514-381-7300; *Téléc:* 514-381-5173
Ligne sans frais: 877-666-4060
www.ftqconstruction.org
www.facebook.com/Construction
twitter.com/FTQConstruction
www.youtube.com/user/FTQconstruction
Également appelé: FTQ-Construction
Aperçu: *Dimension:* grande; *Envergure:* provinciale surveillé par Fédération des travailleurs et travailleuses du Québec
Mission: On peut facilement affirmer que la mission d'une association syndicale est quasi sans limite. La FTQ-Construction a, bien entendu, de manière très précise le mandat de négocier les conventions collectives applicables dans les sous secteurs d'activités (industriel, commercial et institutionnel, génie civil et voirie, résidentiel) et de voir à leur application. Mais bien au-delà de ce mandat traditionnel, la FTQ-Construction veut s'assurer d'être présent dans l'ensemble des débats représentant un intérêt pour les travailleurs et les travailleuses qu'il représente.
Affiliation(s): Fraternité inter-provinciale des ouvriers en électricité; Fraternité provinciale des ouvriers en électricité; Fraternité nationale des charpentiers-menuisiers; Union des opérateurs de machinerie lourde; Assn. des manoeuvres interprovinciaux; Assn. nationale des travailleurs en réfrigération, climatisation & protection-incendie; Assn. canadienne des métiers de la truelle; Union nationale des poseurs de systèmes intérieurs & revêtements souples; Assn. nationale des ferblantiers & couvreurs; Assn. nationale des peintres & métiers connexes; Fraternité internationale des peintres & métiers connexes
Membre(s) du bureau directeur:
Yves Ouellette, Directeur général
Membre: 73,000

Fédération des unions de familles inc. *Voir* La Fédération québécoise des organismes communautaires Famille

Fédération dramatique du Québec *See* The Québec Drama Federation

Fédération du baseball amateur du Québec

CP 1000, Succ. M, 4545, av Pierre-de Coubertin, Montréal QC H1V 3R2
Tél: 514-252-3075; *Téléc:* 514-252-3134
Ligne sans frais: 800-361-2054
info@baseballquebec.qc.ca
www.baseballquebec.com
www.facebook.com/baseballquebec
twitter.com/baseballquebec
Également appelé: Baseball Québec
Aperçu: *Dimension:* moyenne; *Envergure:* provinciale surveillé par Baseball Canada
Mission: La mission de la Fédération du baseball amateur du Québec inc. est de : Donner un cadre général d'ordre et de discipline à tous les intervenants du baseball québécois; Reconnaître le droit pour tous les joueurs d'évoluer au baseball selon des normes et critères précis; Donner un cadre pour l'application d'une réglementation uniforme dans tout le Québec; Fournir les moyens à chacun de s'amuser, de participer et de se perfectionner afin de donner un idéal à ceux qui aspirent à une carrière.
Membre(s) du bureau directeur:
Gilles Taillon, Directeur général
gtaillon@baseballquebec.qc.ca

Fédération du commerce (CSN)

1601, av De Lorimier, Montréal QC H2K 4M5
Tél: 514-598-2421; *Téléc:* 514-598-2304
infofc@csn.qc.ca
www.fc-csn.ca
Aperçu: *Dimension:* moyenne; *Envergure:* provinciale
Membre(s) du bureau directeur:
Serge Fournier, Président
serge.fournier@csn.qc.ca
Membre: 28,500 + 360 sections locales; *Comités:* Santé sécurité environnement; Avantages sociaux; Femmes

Fédération du personnel de l'enseignement privé (FPEP)

9405, rue Sherbrooke est, Montréal QC H1L 6P3
Tél: 514-356-8888; *Téléc:* 514-356-1866
fpep@csq.qc.net
www.fpep.csq.qc.net
Aperçu: *Dimension:* moyenne; *Envergure:* provinciale; Organisme sans but lucratif; fondée en 1986
Membre de: Centrale des syndicats du Québec
Membre(s) du bureau directeur:
Francine Lamoureux, Présidente, 514-356-8888 Ext. 2810
lamoureux.francine@csq.qc.net
Martine Dion, Première Vice-Présidente, 514-356-8888 Ext. 2813
dion.martine@csq.qc.net
Denis Benoit, Deuxième Vice-Président
fpep@csq.qc.net
Stéphane Lévis, Secrétaire
fpep@csq.qc.net
Marie-Josée Noël, Trésorerie
fpep@csq.qc.net
Finances: *Fonds:* Grille tarifaire
Membre(s) du personnel: 11
Membre: 2 800 individu; 43 unités; *Montant de la cotisation:* 0.576% du salaire; *Critères d'admissibilite:* Organisation syndicale; *Comités:* Élections; Élèves handicapés ou en difficulté d'adaptation ou d'apprentissage (HDAA); Comité du personnel professionnel et de soutien (CPPS); Environnement; Action professionnel
Activités: Relations du travail et d'action professionnelle

Fédération du personnel de soutien scolaire (CSQ) (FPSS) / Federation of Support Staff

9405, rue Sherbrooke est, 4e étage, Montréal QC H1L 6P3
Tél: 514-356-8888; *Téléc:* 514-493-3697
webfpss@csq.qc.net
www.fpss.csq.qc.net
www.facebook.com/fpss.csq
twitter.com/FPSSCSQ
Également appelé: FPSS-CSQ
Aperçu: *Dimension:* moyenne; *Envergure:* provinciale; Organisme sans but lucratif; fondée en 1998 surveillé par Centrale des syndicats du Québec
Mission: Le seul regroupement au Québec représentant exclusivement du personnel de soutien scolaire des écoles et des centres. Elle est affiliée à la Centrale des syndicats du Québec (CSQ)
Membre(s) du bureau directeur:
Diane Cinq-Mars, Présidente
Membre: 22 000, 17 syndicats, 22 commissions scolaires; *Comités:* Comités de vie professionnelle
Activités: *Evénements de sensibilisation:* Journée nationale du personnel de soutien scolaire CSQ, sept.

Fédération du personnel du loisir, de la culture et du communautaire (CEQ) (FPLCC)

9405, rue Sherbrooke est, Montréal QC H1L 6P3
Tél: 514-356-8888; *Téléc:* 418-649-8888
Ligne sans frais: 877-850-0897
fplcc@csq.qc.net
www.csq.qc.net
Aperçu: *Dimension:* moyenne; *Envergure:* provinciale; fondée en 1979 surveillé par Centrale des syndicats du Québec
Mission: Regroupe les syndicats qui représentent le personnel oeuvrant dans les secteurs du loisir, du sport, de la culture du tourisme et du communautaire
Membre(s) du bureau directeur:
Réjean Parent, Président
Finances: *Budget de fonctionnement annuel:* $50,000-$100,000
Membre: 320; *Critères d'admissibilite:* Salariés syndiqués

Fédération du personnel professionnel des collèges (FPPC)

9405, rue Sherbrooke est, Montréal QC H1L 6P3
Tél: 514-356-8888; *Téléc:* 514-356-3377
fppc@csq.qc.net
www.fppc.csq.qc.net
www.facebook.com/166365983458347
twitter.com/fppc_csq
Aperçu: *Dimension:* moyenne; *Envergure:* provinciale; fondée en 1975 surveillé par Centrale des syndicats du Québec
Mission: Défendre et promouvoir la fonction professionnelle dans les collèges
Membre(s) du bureau directeur:
Bernard Bérubé, Président
berube.bernard@csq.qc.net
Finances: *Budget de fonctionnement annuel:* $250,000-$500,000
Membre(s) du personnel: 2
Membre: 900
Activités: *Service de conférenciers:* Oui

Fédération du personnel professionnel des universités et de la recherche (FPPU)

873, rue du Haut-Boc, Trois-Rivières QC G9A 4W7
Tél: 819-840-4544; *Téléc:* 819-840-4294
info@fppu.ca
www.fppu.ca
www.facebook.com/518734318146156
Aperçu: *Dimension:* moyenne; *Envergure:* provinciale; fondée en 1978 surveillé par Centrale des syndicats du Québec
Mission: La FPPU est la seule organisation syndicale regroupant exclusivement le personnel professionnel des universités et de la recherche

Finances: *Budget de fonctionnement annuel:* $250,000-$500,000
Membre: 1,600 + 10 sections locales

Fédération du plongeon amateur du Québec (FPAQ)

4545, av Pierre-de Coubertin, Montréal QC H1V 0b2
Tél: 514-252-3096; *Téléc:* 514-252-3094
info@plongeon.qc.ca
www.plongeon.qc.ca
www.facebook.com/plongeonquebec
twitter.com/PlongeonQuebec
www.youtube.com/user/PlongeonQuebec
Également appelé: Plongeon Québec
Aperçu: *Dimension:* moyenne; *Envergure:* provinciale; fondée en 1971
Mission: Régir le plongeon sur l'ensemble du territoire québécois; promouvoir le plongeon et sa pratique; tenir et organiser des stages de formation et des compétitions de plongeon; regrouper les associations de plongeon
Membre de: Diving Plongeon Canada; Sports-Québec; AQUM; Club de la médaille d'or; Institut national du sport-Montréal
Membre(s) du bureau directeur:
Isabelle Cloutier, Directrice exécutive
icloutier@plongeon.qc.ca
Finances: *Budget de fonctionnement annuel:* $250,000-$500,000
Membre(s) du personnel: 3; 100+ bénévole(s)
Membre: 3,000; *Montant de la cotisation:* 15$ - 50$; *Comités:* Entraîneurs; Officiels; L'élite
Activités: *Stagiaires:* Oui; *Service de conférenciers:* Oui

Fédération du Québec pour le planning des naissances (FQPN)

#405, 110, rue Ste-Thérèse, Montréal QC H2Y 1E6
Tél: 514-866-3721; *Téléc:* 514-866-1100
info@fqpn.qc.ca
www.fqpn.qc.ca
Aperçu: *Dimension:* moyenne; *Envergure:* provinciale; fondée en 1972
Mission: Promouvoir les droits des femmes dans le domaine de la santé, particulièrement la reproduction et la sexualité; promouvoir l'accès à une information critique et fiable, la liberté de choix et le consentement des femmes face à leur propre corps.
Membre de: La Table des fédérations et des organismes nationaux pour l'éducation populaire autonome; Comité québécois femmes et développement; Women Global Network for Reproductive Rights; Réseau canadien pour la santé des femmes; Health Action International
Membre(s) du bureau directeur:
Sophie de Cordes, Coordonnatrice générale
Membre: 41; *Montant de la cotisation:* 5$ personnes à faible revenu; 30$ individuel; 75$ organismes et groupes communautaires; 150$ associations professionnelles
Activités: Information; éducation populaire; actions collectives; lobbying; *Service de conférenciers:* Oui; *Bibliothèque* rendez-vous

Fédération du saumon atlantique ***See*** Atlantic Salmon Federation

Fédération du travail de l'Alberta ***See*** Alberta Federation of Labour

Fédération du travail de l'Ile-du-Prince-Édouard ***See*** Prince Edward Island Federation of Labour

Fédération du travail de l'Ontario ***See*** Ontario Federation of Labour

Fédération du travail de la Colombie-Britannique ***See*** British Columbia Federation of Labour

Fédération du travail de la Nouvelle-Écosse ***See*** Nova Scotia Federation of Labour

Fédération du travail de la Saskatchewan ***See*** Saskatchewan Federation of Labour

Fédération du travail de Terre-Neuve et du Labrador ***See*** Newfoundland & Labrador Federation of Labour

Fédération du travail des Territoires du Nord ***See*** Northern Territories Federation of Labour

Fédération du travail du Manitoba ***See*** Manitoba Federation of Labour

Fédération du travail du Yukon ***See*** Yukon Federation of Labour

Fédération équestre du Québec inc. (FEQ)

4545, av Pierre-de Coubertin, Montréal QC H1V 0B2
Tél: 514-252-3053; *Téléc:* 514-252-3068
Ligne sans frais: 866-575-0515
infocheval@feq.qc.ca
www.feq.qc.ca
www.facebook.com/386728291214
www.youtube.com/EquestreQuebec
Aperçu: *Dimension:* moyenne; *Envergure:* provinciale; Organisme sans but lucratif; fondée en 1970
Mission: Promotion et développement de l'activité équestre au Québec
Membre de: Canadian Equestrian Federation
Membre(s) du bureau directeur:
Richard Mongeau, Directeur général
rmongeau@feq.qc.ca
Membre: 12,000; *Montant de la cotisation:* 46$ junior; 56$ senior

Fédération étudiante universitaire du Québec (FEUQ) / Québec University Students' Federation

15, Marie-Anne Ouest, 2e étage, Montréal QC H2W 1B6
Tél: 514-396-3380; *Téléc:* 514-396-7140
Ligne sans frais: 877-396-3380
Autres numéros: www.flickr.com/photos/feuq
feuq@feuq.qc.ca
www.feuq.qc.ca
www.facebook.com/page.FEUQ
twitter.com/feuq
Aperçu: *Dimension:* grande; *Envergure:* provinciale; fondée en 1989
Mission: Défendre et promouvoir les droits des étudiantes et étudiants universitaires du Québec
Membre de: Union internationale étudiante
Membre(s) du bureau directeur:
Martine Desjardins, Président
president@feuq.qc.ca
Yanick Grégoire, Vice-président exécutive
vpe@feuq.qc.ca
Francis Lafortune, Directeur administratif
da@feuq.qc.ca
Finances: *Budget de fonctionnement annuel:* $500,000-$1.5 Million
Membre(s) du personnel: 8
Membre: 120 000 (15 associations étudiantes); *Montant de la cotisation:* 2,50$

Federation for Scottish Culture in Nova Scotia (FSCNS)

PO Box 811, Lower Sackville NS B4C 3V3
e-mail: info@scotsns.ca
www.scotsns.ca
Overview: A medium-sized provincial organization founded in 1982
Mission: To act as the voice for Nova Scotia's clans, Scottish-cultural communities, & cultural associations; To create appreciation for the Scottish culture, traditions, & heritage
Chief Officer(s):
Thomas (Tom) E.S. Wallace, President
Daniel G. Campbell, 1st Vice-President
Audrey Manzer, Secretary
Al Matheson, Treasurer
Finances: *Funding Sources:* Fundraising
Membership: *Fees:* $15 individuals; $30 clan societies, Scottish cultural organizations, family associations; *Member Profile:* Any individual interested in learning more about Scottish culture; Clan societies; Scottish-cultural organizations; *Committees:* Audit; By-laws; Media Relations; Membership; Newsletter; Nominating; President's Advisory Council; Scholarship; Finance & Fundraising
Activities: Building partnerships with the Scottish community & sister organizations; Preserving & promoting Scottish culture & heritage
Awards:
- Federation of Scottish Clans in Nova Scotia Scholarship (Scholarship)

Fédération franco-ténoise (FFT)

CP 1325, Yellowknife NT X1A 2N9
Tél: 867-920-2919; *Téléc:* 867-873-2458
info@franco-nord.com
www.federation-franco-tenoise.com
Aperçu: *Dimension:* moyenne; *Envergure:* provinciale; fondée en 1978 surveillé par Fédération des communautés francophones et acadienne du Canada
Mission: Afin de promouvoir et de préserver la communauté francophone des Territoires du Nord-Ouest
Affliation(s): Association des francophones du delta du Mackenzie; Association des francophones de Fort Smith; Association des parents ayants droit de Yellowknife; Association franco-culturelle de Hay River; Association franco-culturelle de Yellowknife; Azimut Communications
Membre(s) du bureau directeur:
Richard Létourneau, Président
president@franco-nord.com
Membre(s) du personnel: 5

Fédération indépendante des syndicats affiliés (ind.) ***Voir*** Fédération indépendante des syndicats autonomes

Fédération indépendante des syndicats autonomes (FISA) / Independent Federation of Autonomous Unions

#201, 1778, boul Wilfrid-Hamel, Québec QC G1N 3Y8
Tél: 418-529-4571; *Téléc:* 418-529-4695
Ligne sans frais: 800-407-3472
info@fisa.ca
www.fisa.ca
Nom précédent: Fédération indépendante des syndicats affiliés (ind.)
Aperçu: *Dimension:* moyenne; *Envergure:* provinciale; Organisme sans but lucratif; fondée en 1947
Mission: Fournir des services d'organisation, de conseils, de représentation et d'aide financière aux associations membres.
Membre(s) du bureau directeur:
Jean Gagnon, Président
Activités: *Stagiaires:* Oui; *Service de conférenciers:* Oui

Montréal
#220, 2220, boul Lapinière, Montréal QC J4W 1M2
Tél: 514-736-2787; *Téléc:* 450-766-3473
Ligne sans frais: 800-353-3472
info.montreal@fisa.ca
fisa.ca/contact/montreal

Saguenay
3798, rue du Roi-Georges, Jonquière QC G7X 1T3
Tél: 418-547-9389; *Téléc:* 418-547-7143
Ligne sans frais: 877-547-9389
info.saguenay@fisa.ca
fisa.ca/contact/saguenay

Fédération interdisciplinaire de l'horticulture ornementale du Québec (FIHOQ)

#300E, 3230, rue Sicotte ouest, Saint-Hyacinthe QC J2S 7B3
Tél: 450-774-2228; *Téléc:* 450-774-3556
fihoq@fihoq.qc.ca
www.fihoq.qc.ca
www.facebook.com/fihoq
Aperçu: *Dimension:* moyenne; *Envergure:* provinciale; fondée en 1977
Mission: Grouper en fédération les associations professionnelles qui s'occupent d'horticulture ornementale au Québec; étudier, promouvoir, protéger et développer de toutes manières les intérêts économiques, sociaux et professionnels de ses membres; imprimer, éditer des revues, journaux, périodiques et plus généralement, toutes publications du domaine de l'horticulture ornementale aux fins d'information, de culture professionnelle et de propagande; organiser et tenir des cours, conférences, congrès, assemblées, expositions et autres réunions pour la promotion, le développement et la vulgarisation de l'horticulture ornementale; promouvoir la protection du consommateur dans le domaine de l'horticulture ornementale; assurer une représentation tant sur le plan local et national, que sur le plan international des personnes oeuvrant dans le domaine de l'horticulture ornementale au Québec.
Affliation(s): Association internationale des producteurs en horticulture; Conseil canadien de l'horticulture; Conseil québécois de l'horticulture
Membre(s) du bureau directeur:
Luce Daigneault, Directrice générale
luce.daigneault@fihoq.qc.ca
Lise Gauthier, Président
Membre(s) du personnel: 11
Membre: 10 associations
Activités: *Stagiaires:* Oui

Fédération Internationale des Culturistes ***See*** International Federation of Bodybuilders

Fédération internationale du vieillissement ***See*** International Federation on Aging

Fédération interprofessionnelle de la santé du Québec (FIQ)

1234, av Papineau, Montréal QC H2K 0A4
Tél: 514-987-1141; *Téléc:* 514-987-7273
Ligne sans frais: 800-363-6541
info@fiqsante.qc.ca
www.fiqsante.qc.ca
www.facebook.com/FIQSante
WWW.twitter.com/FIQSante
www.youtube.com/FIQSante
Nom précédent: Fédération des infirmières et infirmiers du Québec
Aperçu: *Dimension:* grande; *Envergure:* provinciale; fondée en 1987
Mission: Améliorer les conditions de travail des infirmières, infirmiers & cardiorespiratoires; s'associer aux luttes des femmes et être présente dans les débats concernant les orientations du système de santé
Membre(s) du bureau directeur:
Régine Laurent, Présidente
Finances: *Budget de fonctionnement annuel:* Plus de $5 Million
Membre(s) du personnel: 150
Membre: 57 000 + 61 syndicats; *Comités:* Condition féminine; éducation-animation; élection; fonds de défense syndicale; jeunes; évaluation des publications; santé & sécurité du travail; vérification interne; ad hoc Solidarité
Activités: *Bibliothèque*

FIQ - Abitibi-Témiscamingue
#106, 170, av Principale, Rouyn-Noranda QC J9X 4P7
Tél: 819-797-1748; *Téléc:* 819-797-1937
Ligne sans frais: 800-567-6564

FIQ - Estrie
#110, 2630, rue King ouest, Sherbrooke QC J1J 2H1
Tél: 819-346-4914; *Téléc:* 819-563-9825
Ligne sans frais: 800-567-2776

FIQ - Gaspésie Bas St-Laurent
#219, 84, rue St-Germain est, Rimouski QC G5L 7K1
Tél: 418-723-2251; *Téléc:* 418-723-7928
Ligne sans frais: 800-463-0628

FIQ - Mauricie Bois-Francs
#305, 465, 5e Rue, Shawinigan QC G9N 1E5
Tél: 819-346-4914; *Téléc:* 819-563-9825
Ligne sans frais: 800-567-2776

FIQ - Outaouais
#230, 370, boul Gréber, Gatineau QC J8T 5R6
Tél: 819-568-4243; *Téléc:* 819-568-0493
Ligne sans frais: 800-567-9651

FIQ - Québec
1260, rue du Blizzard, Québec QC G2K 0J1
Tél: 418-626-2226; *Téléc:* 418-626-2111
Ligne sans frais: 800-463-6770
www.fiqsante.qc.ca/fr/contents/pages/accueil.html
www.facebook.com/FIQSante
twitter.com/FIQSante
www.youtube.com/user/FIQSante

FIQ - Saguenay/Lac St-Jean
451, rue Racine est, Chicoutimi QC G7H 1T5
Tél: 418-690-2252; *Téléc:* 418-690-3216
Ligne sans frais: 800-567-8105

Fédération maritime du Canada ***See*** Shipping Federation of Canada

La Fédération mondiale de chiropratique ***See*** World Federation of Chiropractic

Fédération mondiale de l'hémophilie ***See*** World Federation of Hemophilia

Fédération motocycliste du Québec (FMQ) / Quebec Motorcyclist Federation

#460, 9675, av Papineau, Montréal QC H1R 3J2
Tél: 514-252-8121
fmq@fmq.qc.ca
www.fmq.qc.ca
www.facebook.com/FmqFederationMotocyclisteDuQuebec
Aperçu: *Dimension:* moyenne; *Envergure:* provinciale; fondée en 1974
Mission: La promotion du motocyclisme, de ses intérêts et la défense de ses droits; enseignement de la sécurité à motocyclette
Membre de: Motorcycle Alliance of Canada (MAC)
Membre(s) du bureau directeur:
Gilles Dubois, Président
gillesdubois@fmq.qc.ca
Membre: 5 000; *Montant de la cotisation:* 50$ individu; *Critères d'admissibilite:* Motocyclistes de tous les âges
Activités: Congrès annuel; Salon de la Moto à Montréal et Québec; table de concertation; cours Moto Pro FMQ; *Stagiaires:* Oui

Fédération nationale de dards du Canada ***See*** National Darts Federation of Canada

Fédération nationale des communications (CSN) (FNC) / National Federation of Communication Workers (CNTU)

1601, av de Lorimier, Montréal QC H2K 4M5
Tél: 514-598-2132; *Téléc:* 514-598-2431
fnc@fncom.org
www.fncom.org
Aperçu: *Dimension:* moyenne; *Envergure:* nationale; fondée en 1972
Mission: La défense des intérêts économiques, sociaux, politiques et professionnels des membres.
Membre de: Confédération des syndicats nationaux
Membre(s) du bureau directeur:
Pierre Roger, Président
pierre.roger@fncom.org
Finances: *Budget de fonctionnement annuel:* $500,000-$1.5 Million
Membre: 90 sections locales;

Fédération nationale des enseignants et des enseignantes du Québec (FNEEQ) / National Federation of Québec Teachers

1601, av de Lorimier, Montréal QC H2K 4M5
Tél: 514-598-2241; *Téléc:* 514-598-2190
fneeq.reception@csn.qc.ca
www.fneeq.qc.ca
www.facebook.com/FneeqCSN
twitter.com/FneeqCSN
Aperçu: *Dimension:* moyenne; *Envergure:* provinciale; fondée en 1969
Mission: La Fédération nationale des enseignantes et des enseignants du Québec (FNEEQ) est une fédération de la CSN qui regroupe les syndicats de l'enseignement. La mission première de la FNEEQ est l'amélioration des conditions de travail par l'entremise de la négociation et de l'application d'une convention collective entre un employeur et le personnel enseignant et salarié
Membre(s) du bureau directeur:
Jean Trudelle, Président
Finances: *Budget de fonctionnement annuel:* $1.5 Million-$3 Million
Membre(s) du personnel: 12
Membre: 25000; 80 syndicats répartis en 3 groupes: 37 syndicats de CÉGEPs; 8 syndicats de chargés de cours d'universités; 31 syndicats d'établissements privés; *Comités:* École et Société; Femmes; Santé-Sécurité; Assurances et Retraite; Action Internationale

Fédération nationale des femmes canadiennes-françaises; Fédération des femmes canadiennes-françaises ***Voir*** Alliance des femmes de la francophonie canadienne

Fédération nationale des retraités ***See*** National Pensioners Federation

Fédération nationale des services de préparation au mariage (FNSPM)

CP 1480, Trois-Rivières QC G9A 5L6
Tél: 819-379-1432; *Téléc:* 819-379-2496
www.fnspm.ca
Également appelé: Fédération Nationale SFM
Aperçu: *Dimension:* moyenne; *Envergure:* nationale; Organisme sans but lucratif
Mission: Offrir en collaboration avec les diocèses un service d'accompagnement aux couples ayant choisi le mariage catholique; accompagner sur le plan humain et chrétien, les personnes ayant choisi de s'engager dans un projet de vie à deux
Membre(s) du bureau directeur:
Simon Bournival, Directeur général
directiongenerale@fnspm.ca
Membre(s) du personnel: 2
Activités: Formation; production d'outils pédagogiques; soutien technique aux équipes; *Stagiaires:* Oui

Fédération nationale du MFC - Mouvement des Femmes Chrétiennes ***Voir*** Secrétariat nationale du MFC - Mouvement des femmes Chrétiennes

Fédération nationale lettone au Canada ***See*** Latvian National Federation in Canada

Fédération nautique du Canada ***See*** Canadian Boating Federation

Federation of Aboriginal Foster Parents (FAFP)

3455 Kaslo St., Vancouver BC V3M 3H4
Tel: 604-291-7091; *Fax:* 604-291-7098
Toll-Free: 866-291-7091
info@fafp.ca
www.fafp.ca
Overview: A medium-sized provincial organization
Mission: The Federation of Aboriginal Foster Parents represents Foster Parents providing quality care for Aboriginal children in a nurturning, culturally appropriate environment
Chief Officer(s):
Stephen W. Kozey, Executive Director
skozey@fafp.ca
Faye Poirier, President
Rick Poitras, Vice-President
Finances: *Funding Sources:* provincial & federal funding
Membership: *Fees:* $10 5 yr. single; $20 5 yr. couple; $5.5 yr associate; $50 1 yr. corporate

Federation of Asian Students (FAS) ***See*** University of Alberta South East Asian Students' Association

Federation of Automobile Dealer Associations of Canada ***See*** Canadian Automobile Dealers' Association

Federation of British Columbia Writers (FBCW)

PO Box 3887, Stn. Terminal, Vancouver BC V6B 2Z3
Tel: 604-683-2057
info@bcwriters.ca
www.bcwriters.ca
Overview: A medium-sized provincial organization founded in 1976
Mission: To develop, support, inform, & promote writers in British Columbia; To foster a community for writing in British Columbia
Chief Officer(s):
Ben Nuttall-Smith, President
president@bcwriters.ca
Finances: *Funding Sources:* Membership dues; Fundraising; Corporate & private sponsorships; Province of British Columbia's BC Arts Council & Direct Access Program
Membership: 650+; *Fees:* $65; *Member Profile:* Emerging & established writers; Persons interested in federation authors' works
Activities: Providing programs & resources; Organizing an annual writing contest; Arranging author visits to schools; Providing reading opportunities; Offering promotional services; Conducting workshops; Networking opportunities;

Federation of Broomball Associations of Ontario

515 Gascon St., Russell ON K4R 1C6
Tel: 613-445-0904; *Fax:* 613-445-9844
www.ontariobroomball.ca
Previous Name: Broomball Federation of Ontario
Overview: A medium-sized provincial organization overseen by Ballon sur glace Broomball Canada
Mission: To serve broomball players, coaches, & leagues in Ontario
Member of: Ballon sur glace Broomball Canada
Chief Officer(s):
Gerry Wever, President
gerry.wever@ontariobroomball.ca
Finances: *Annual Operating Budget:* $50,000-$100,000
20 volunteer(s)
Membership: 4,000; *Fees:* $175-$335 team; *Committees:* Officials; Coaching; Executive
Activities: Hosting high school tournaments, qualifier tournaments, junior provincials, & senior provincials; Conducting coaching clinics

Federation of Calgary Communities (FCC)

#301, 1609 - 14 St. SW, Calgary AB T3C 1E4
Tel: 403-244-4111; *Fax:* 403-244-4129
fcc@calgarycommunities.com
www.calgarycommunities.com
www.facebook.com/FederationofCalgaryCommunities
twitter.com/FedYYC
www.youtube.com/user/FederationCalgary
Overview: A small local licensing organization founded in 1961
Mission: To enhance Calgary communities
Chief Officer(s):

Leslie Evans, Executive Director
leslie.evans@calgarycommunities.com
Melanie McDonald, President
Finances: *Annual Operating Budget:* $100,000-$250,000
Staff Member(s): 1; 25 volunteer(s)
Membership: 114
Activities: *Library* Open to public

Federation of Canada-China Friendship Associations

159 Oakmount Rd. SW, Calgary AB T2V 4X3
Tel: 819-777-8434
www.fccfa.ca
Overview: A small international organization
Mission: To work with students from the Peoples' Republic of China studying in Canada; To take groups to China; To welcome delegations coming from China; To promote cultural exchanges
Chief Officer(s):
Sheila Foster, President
fosterst@shaw.ca
Membership: 1,800

Federation of Canadian Archers Inc. *See* Archery Canada Tir à l'Arc

Federation of Canadian Artists (FCA)

1241 Cartwright St., Vancouver BC V6H 4B7
Tel: 604-681-2744; *Fax:* 604-681-2740
fcaoffice@artists.ca
artists.ca
www.facebook.com/111266735581892
Overview: A medium-sized national charitable organization founded in 1941
Mission: To share & promote the visual arts
Chief Officer(s):
Andrew McDermott, President, 604-603-8945
mcdermottart@hotmail.com
Alfonso Tejada, 1st Vice-President, 604-988-4801
atejada@shaw.ca
Kathy Hildebrandt, 2nd Vice-President, 403-239-6127
khilde@shaw.ca
Patrick Meyer, Office Administrator, 604-681-2744
Mila Kostic, Director, Gallery, 604-681-8534
fcagallery@artists.ca
Peter Kiidumae, Secretary, 604-684-7542
peterkiidumae@shaw.ca
Susie Cipolla, Treasurer, 604-932-1880
susiecipollaart@gmail.com
Finances: *Funding Sources:* Membership fees; Government & foundation grants; Donations; Sponsorships; Fundraising; Revenue from education programs; Painting & other retail sales
Staff Member(s): 3
Membership: 2,000+; *Fees:* $10 regular; $50 supporting; $75 associate/senior; *Member Profile:* Artists & art lovers from across Canada; *Committees:* Fundraising; Communications; Education; Standards; Membership
Activities: Offering visual art exhibitions & education
Publications:
• Art Avenue
Type: Magazine; *Frequency:* Bimonthly; *Editor:* Kelli Kadokawa; *Price:* Free with membership in the Federation of Canadian Artists
Profile: Articles, images of recently exhibited works, member news, forthcoming events, & painting tips

Federation of Canadian Electrolysis Associations (FCEA)

PO Box 1777, Pictou NS B0K 1H0
Tel: 902-485-4557
Toll-Free: 888-333-2783
fcea@fcea.org
www.fcea.org
Overview: A small national organization
Mission: Dedicated to promoting professionalism and education in permanent hair removal.
Affliation(s): The Association of Professional Electrologists of BC, Electrolysis Society of Alberta; Saskatchewan Electrologists Association Incorporated; Manitoba Electrologists Association Inc.; Atlantic Association of Professional Electrologists; Federation of Canadian Electrolysis Associations Ontario Chapter
Chief Officer(s):
Gail MacDonald, President

Federation of Canadian Independent Deposit Brokers *See* Registered Deposit Brokers Association

Federation of Canadian Municipalities (FCM) / Fédération canadienne des municipalités

24 Clarence St., Ottawa ON K1N 5P3
Tel: 613-241-5221; *Fax:* 613-241-7440
federation@fcm.ca
www.fcm.ca
www.linkedin.com/company/federation-of-canadian-municipalities
www.facebook.com/pages/FCM/201746766534992
twitter.com/FCM_online
Previous Name: Canadian Federation of Mayors & Municipalities
Overview: A large national organization founded in 1901
Mission: FCM is the national voice of municipal government that represents the interests of municipalities on policy & program matters that fall within federal jurisdiction. Its goal in serving elected municipal officials is the improvement of the quality of life in all communities.
Chief Officer(s):
Berry Vrbanovic, President
ceo@fcm.ca
Basil L. Stewart, President
Finances: *Funding Sources:* Membership fees; advertising; trade show; market research
Membership: 1,600+; *Fees:* Schedule available based on population; *Member Profile:* Members include Canada's cities, small urban & rural communities, & provincial & territorial municipal associations.; *Committees:* Standing Committees: Increasing Women's Participation in Municipal Government; Community Safety & Crime Prevention; Environmental Issues & Sustainable Development; International Relations; Municipal Finance & Intergovernmental Arrangements; Municipal Infrastructure & Transportation Policy; Northern Forum; Rural Forum; Social Economic Development
Activities: Promoting strong, effective, & accountable municipal government; *Rents Mailing List:* Yes
Awards:
• Race Relations Awards (Award)
• FCM/CH2M Hill Canada Awards (Award)
• The Roll of Honour (Award)
• Outstanding International Volunteer Contribution Awards (Award)
• Ann MacLean Award for Outstanding Service by a Woman in Municipal Politics (Award)
Recognizes retired women municipal politicians who have shown exemplary service to their community and constituents and to mentoring women who want to run for elected office.
• Canadian Women in Municipal Government Scholarship (Scholarship)
Eligibility: The scholarship is open to female students enrolled in any year of study in secondary school and who are contributing to their school's leadership team or student council. *Amount:* $500 (5)
• Mayor Andrée Boucher Memorial Scholarship (Scholarship)
Eligibility: Female college or university student deemed to have submitted the best research paper on a topic related to women in politics. *Amount:* $2,000
Meetings/Conferences: • Federation of Canadian Municipalities 2015 Sustainable Communities Conference and Trade Show, February, 2015, London Convention Centre, London, ON
Scope: National
Description: This year's theme is "Building Momentum for Sustainability."
• Federation of Canadian Municipalities 2015 Annual Conference & Trade Show, June, 2015, Shaw Conference Centre, Edmonton, AB
Scope: National
• Federation of Canadian Municipalities 2018 Annual Conference & Trade Show, June, 2018, Halifax Convention Centre, Halifax, NS
Scope: National
Publications:
• Federation of Canadian Municipalities Annual Report
Type: Yearbook; *Frequency:* Annually
• Forum: Canada's National Municipal Magazine
Type: Magazine; *Frequency:* Bimonthly; *Accepts Advertising*; *Editor:* Robert Ross
Profile: Recent municipal-sector developments

Federation of Canadian Music Festivals (FCMF) / La Fédération canadienne des festivals de musique

C/O Executive Director, 14004 - 75th Ave. NW, Edmonton AB T5R 2Y5
Fax: 780-758-1227
Toll-Free: 877-323-3263
info@fcmf.org
www.fcmf.org
Overview: A large national organization founded in 1949
Mission: Umbrella organization for 230+ local & provincial festivals; to develop & encourage Canadian talent in the performance & knowledge of classical music; to encourage the study & practice of the art of music alone or in conjunction with related arts; to organize the National Music Festival in which winners from each province participate
Affliation(s): Canadian Conference of the Arts; provincial music festival organizations
Chief Officer(s):
Marilyn Wiwcharuk, President
Marilyn_wiwcharuk@shaw.ca
Rhéal Fournier, Vice-President
fournierrh@xplornet.ca
Heather Bedford Clooney, Executive Director
Finances: *Annual Operating Budget:* Less than $50,000; *Funding Sources:* Affiliation & membership fees; donations
Membership: 230+ local festivals; *Fees:* $50 regular; $100 sustaining; $200 patron; $500 life; *Member Profile:* Competitors, volunteers, adjudicators, music lovers; *Committees:* Syllabus; History; Finance; Planning; Adjudicator Selection; Marketing & Communications; Musical Theatre
Activities: *Awareness Events:* National Music Festival; *Speaker Service:* Yes; *Rents Mailing List:* Yes
Publications:
• Più Mosso [a publication of the Federation of Canadian Music Festivals]
Type: Newsletter

Federation of Canadian Naturists (FCN)

PO Box 186, Stn. D, Toronto ON M9A 4X2
Tel: 416-410-6833; *Fax:* 416-410-6833
Toll-Free: 888-512-6833
information@fcn.ca
www.fcn.ca
Overview: A small national organization founded in 1985
Mission: To promote naturism (social nudism) as a healthy, wholesome & completely natural lifestyle
Member of: Canadian Magazine Publishers' Association
Affliation(s): International Naturist Federation
Chief Officer(s):
Karen Grant, President
kgrant@fcn.ca
Finances: *Annual Operating Budget:* $50,000-$100,000; *Funding Sources:* Membership dues; subscribers fees
20 volunteer(s)
Membership: 2,400; *Fees:* $50 Canada; $55 USA; $60 elsewhere
Activities: *Speaker Service:* Yes
Publications:
• Going Natural
Price: $40 CAD subscription; $45 USD; $50 international
Profile: Quarterly magazine

Federation of Canadian Turkish Associations (FCTA)

#15, 1170 Sheppard Ave. West, Toronto ON M3K 2A3
Tel: 647-955-1923; *Fax:* 647-776-3111
info@turkishfederation.ca
www.turkishfederation.ca/en/home_en.html
Overview: A large national organization founded in 1985
Mission: To support & encourage activities of member associations aimed at making Turkish culture & Turks better known; To promote closer relations with Canadians & other ethnic communities
Member of: Canadian Ethnocultural Council
Finances: *Funding Sources:* Membership fees; grants; sponsorships
Membership: 17 associations which include 50,000 members; *Committees:* General Assembly; External Relations; Community Relations; Executive; Audit; Honour
Activities: *Speaker Service:* Yes; *Rents Mailing List:* Yes

Federation of Chinese Canadian Professionals (Ontario) (FCCP)

Coral Place, 55 Glenn Hawthorne Blvd., Mississauga ON L5R 3S6
Tel: 905-890-3235; *Fax:* 905-568-5293
www.fccpontario.com
Overview: A small provincial charitable organization founded in 1975
Mission: Fosters the promotion, cooperation, & growth among Chinese Canadian Professionals from various disciplines, including: accounting, architecture, biomedical, chiropractic,

dental, education, engineering, information technology, legal, medical, pharmacy, & physiotherapy
Chief Officer(s):
Josephine Kiang, President
Membership: 1,200 individual + 12 professional subsections

Federation of Chinese Canadian Professionals (Québec) (FCCP Québec) / Fédération des professionnels chinois canadiens (Québec)

PO Box 1004, Stn. B, Montréal QC H3B 3K5
Tel: 514-747-2488
htan222@yahoo.ca
www.fccp.ca
Overview: A medium-sized provincial organization founded in 1993
Mission: To promote the well-being of Chinese Canadian professionals in Québec; To liaise & cooperate with Chinese Canadian professionals in other parts of Canada & throughout the world; To provide a strong voice for the group
Chief Officer(s):
Howard Tan, President
htan222@yahoo.ca
John Chen, Vice-President
Renee Chin, Treasurer
Finances: *Funding Sources:* Sponsorships
Membership: *Committees:* Audit; Constitution; Corporate Sponsorship; Membership & Directory; Mentorship; Newsletter; Nomination / Election; Promotion / Recruitment; Scholarship; Youth; Awards; Strategic Task Force; Website
Activities: Exchanging professional knowledge; Developing Chinese professional businesse; Offering advice to professionals & students; Liaising with government agencies; Organizing seminars; Providing scholarships; Offering networking opportunities

Federation of Dance Clubs of New Brunswick (FDCNB)

c/o President, 35 Berwick St., Fredericton NB E3A 4Y2
Tel: 506-472-1444
www.squaredancenb.ca
Previous Name: New Brunswick Federation of Dance Clubs
Overview: A medium-sized provincial organization overseen by Canadian Square & Round Dance Society
Mission: Strives to be New Brunswick's family of dancers, expounding the virtues of dance-related recreational activity in each and every region of the province, actively involved with training, teaching, instructing, informing & assisting others to learn more about new & not so new dance-related ideas.
Member of: Canadian Square & Round Dance Society
Chief Officer(s):
Terry Hebert, President
sdcaller@nbnet.nb.ca

Federation of Danish Associations in Canada / Fédération des associations danoises du Canada

679 Eastvale Ct., Gloucester ON K1J 6Z7
home.ca.inter.net/~robuch/dan-fed.htm
Also Known As: The Danish Federation
Overview: A medium-sized national organization founded in 1981
Mission: To promote cooperation among Danish Canadian organizations; To promote preservation & understanding of Danish tradition & heritage
Chief Officer(s):
Rolf Buschardt Christensen, National President
Ole D. Larsen, National Vice-President
Ella Wolder, National Secretary
Sue Anne Nielsen, National Treasurer
Membership: 41 organizations
Activities: Exchanging ideas & experiences; Coordinating joint projects; Organizing heritage seminars & conferences; Building a national museum; Providing support & assistance to members

Alberta-Northwest Territories Region
231 - 40th Ave. NE, Calgary AB T2E 2M8
Tel: 403-276-6700; *Fax:* 403-230-9499
Chief Officer(s):
Karsten Dalberg, President

Manitoba-Saskatchewan Region
961 - 111 St., North Battleford SK S9A 2K2
Tel: 306-446-2334
Chief Officer(s):
Betty Wilson, Regional President
bettywilson@sk.sympatico.ca

Ontario Region
54 Lesgay Cres., Toronto ON M2J 2J1
Tel: 416-493-1594; *Fax:* 416-495-9289
Chief Officer(s):
Eva Terp, Regional President
terpeva@passport.ca

Pacific Region
8594 Sunbury Place, Delta BC V4C 3Y7
Tel: 604-951-4842
Chief Officer(s):
Solvejg Nielsen, President

Québec Region
#702, 6900, rue Cote St Luc, Westmount QC H3Z 2V5
Tel: 514-484-1665
intergit@hotmail.com
Chief Officer(s):
Ole D. Larsen, Regional President

Federation of dental specialists of Quebec *Voir* Fédération des dentistes spécialistes du Québec

Federation of Families & Friends of Persons with a Mental Illness *Voir* Fédération des familles et amis de la personne atteinte de maladie mentale

Federation of Foster Families of Nova Scotia (FFFNS)

#350, 99 Wyse Rd., Dartmouth NS B3A 4S5
Tel: 902-424-3071; *Fax:* 902-424-5199
Toll-Free: 800-565-1884
colecf@gov.ns.ca
www.fosterfamilies.ns.ca
Previous Name: Federation of Foster Family Associations of Nova Scotia
Overview: A medium-sized provincial charitable organization founded in 1976
Mission: To act as the voice for all foster parents in Nova Scotia; to ensure assistance & support for foster families & Foster Family Associations
Member of: Canadian Foster Family Association
Affliation(s): NS Council for the Family; Child Welfare League of Canada; International Foster Care Organization
Chief Officer(s):
Gary Landry, Executive Director
landrygp@gov.ns.ca
Wendell Fraser, Chair, 902-862-8916
ds.fraser@ns.sympatico.ca
Patricia Norman, Vice-Chair, 902-863-8351
pat-norman@hotmail.com
Joanne Mutton, Treasurer, 902-742-9497
jeam@bellaliant.net
Finances: *Funding Sources:* Provincial funding
Staff Member(s): 6
Membership: *Member Profile:* Foster parents; *Committees:* Provincial Foster Care Policy; P.R.I.D.E Provincial Education; Provincial Awareness & Recruitement
Activities: *Awareness Events:* Foster Family Week, Oct.; *Library:* Federation of Foster Families of Nova Scotia Library
Awards:
- The Thelma Goodall Memorial Bursary (Scholarship)
- The Jenny Cajolais Memorial Bursary (Scholarship)

Federation of Foster Family Associations of Nova Scotia *See* Federation of Foster Families of Nova Scotia

Federation of Health Regulatory Colleges of Ontario (FHRCO) / Ordres de réglementation des professionnels de la santé de l'Ontario (ORPSO)

PO Box 244, #301, 396 Osborne St., Beaverton ON L0K 1A0
Tel: 416-493-4076; *Fax:* 866-814-6456
www.regulatedhealthprofessions.on.ca
Overview: A medium-sized provincial organization
Mission: Federation of the colleges that regulate health professionals in Ontario; Established in order to protect the public's right to safe, effective, ethical health care
Chief Officer(s):
Linda Gough, President
Membership: 26; *Member Profile:* Health regulatory colleges in Ontario

Federation of Independent School Associations of BC (FISA)

150 Robson St., Vancouver BC V6B 2A7
Tel: 604-684-6023; *Fax:* 604-684-3163
info@fisabc.ca
www.fisabc.ca
Overview: A medium-sized provincial organization founded in 1966 overseen by Federation of Independent Schools in Canada
Mission: To assist independent schools in maintaining their independence while seeking fair treatment for them in legislative & financial terms.
Chief Officer(s):
Peter Froese, Executive Director
Doug Lauson, President
Finances: *Annual Operating Budget:* $100,000-$250,000; *Funding Sources:* Membership fees
Staff Member(s): 2
Membership: 200 schools + 4 associations
Activities: *Speaker Service:* Yes

Federation of Junior Leagues of Canada *See* Canadian Federation of Junior Leagues

Federation of Korean Canadian Associations

Tel: 514-481-4008; *Fax:* 514-481-6860
federationkca@gmail.com
www.koreancanadian.org
Overview: A small local organization
Member of: Canadian Ethnocultural Council

Federation of Law Reform Agencies of Canada (FOLRAC)

c/o Manitoba Law Reform Commission, 405 Broadway, 12th Fl., Winnipeg MB R3C 3L6
Tel: 604-822-0142; *Fax:* 604-822-0144
folracanada@gmail.com
www.folrac.com
Overview: A medium-sized national organization founded in 1990
Mission: Collection of 8 law reform agencies, from various provinces, who meet yearly to exchange information.
Chief Officer(s):
Greg Steele, President

Federation of Law Societies of Canada (FLSC) / Fédération des ordres professionnels de juristes du Canada

World Exchange Plaza, #1810, 45 O'Connor St., Ottawa ON K1P 1A4
Tel: 613-236-7272; *Fax:* 613-236-7233
info@flsc.ca
www.flsc.ca
Previous Name: Conference of Representatives of the Governing Bodies of the Legal Profession in the Provinces of Canada
Overview: A medium-sized national organization founded in 1926
Mission: To coordinate the law societies of Canada; To act as a voice for Canadian law societies
Affliation(s): International Bar Association; Union Internationale des Avocats
Chief Officer(s):
Marie-Claude Bélanger-Richard, President, 506-853-1970
mcbelanger@smss.com
Jonathan G. Herman, Chief Executive Officer
jherman@flsc.ca
Bob Linney, Director, Communications
blinney@flsc.ca
Membership: 14 law societies; *Member Profile:* Law societies in Canada, which regulate notaries in Québec & lawyers in the remainder of Canada in the public interest
Activities: Assessing & certifying the qualifications of persons with international legal credentials, through the National Committee on Accreditation; Offering the National Criminal Law Program & the National Family Law Program; Sponsoring continuing legal education programs; Studying matters of concern to the legal profession in Canada; Offering a forum for the exchange of views & information; Operating CanLII, a publicly accessible & free online search engine; Improving public understanding of the legal profession in Canada;

Federation of Medical Regulatory Authorities of Canada (FMRAC) / Fédération des ordres des médecins du Canada (FOMC)

#103, 2283 St. Laurent Blvd., Ottawa ON K1G 5A2
Tel: 613-738-0372; *Fax:* 613-738-9169
info@fmrac.ca
www.fmrac.ca
Overview: A medium-sized national organization
Mission: To provide a national structure for the provincial and territorial medical regulatory authorities to present and pursue issues of common concerns and interest, and to share, consider and develop positions on such matters; and to develop services and benefits for its Members.
Chief Officer(s):

Fleur-Ange Lefebvre, Executive Director/CEO
falefebvre@fmrac.ca
Staff Member(s): 3
Membership: 13
Meetings/Conferences: • Federation of Medical Regulatory Authorities of Canada 2015 AGM & Conference, June, 2015, Fredericton, NB
Scope: National
• Federation of Medical Regulatory Authorities of Canada 2016 AGM & Conference, 2016
Scope: National

Federation of Medical Women of Canada (FMWC) / Fédération des femmes médecins du Canada

780 Echo Dr., Ottawa ON K1S 5R7
Tel: 613-569-5881; *Fax:* 613-569-4432
Toll-Free: 877-771-3777
fmwcmain@fmwc.ca
www.fmwc.ca
Overview: A large national organization founded in 1924
Mission: Committed to the professional, social, & personal advancement of women physicians & to the promotion of the well-being of women in the medical profession & in society at large
Affliation(s): Canadian Medical Association; Medical Women's International Association
Chief Officer(s):
Crystal Cannon, President
Finances: *Annual Operating Budget:* $50,000-$100,000; *Funding Sources:* Membership fees; sponsors; corporate
Membership: 600 members, 21 branches; *Fees:* Schedule available; *Member Profile:* Women medical students; women physicians; associate member - men or non-physician women commited to the advancement of women's health; *Committees:* Maude Abbott Fund; Finance; Awards; Nominating
Activities: 21 branches across Canada; *Awareness Events:* Women's Health Day; National Cervical Cancer Awareness Week, October; *Speaker Service:* Yes
Awards:
• Maude Abbot Loan (Award)
• May Cohen Award (Award)
• Margaret Owens-Waite Memorial Fund (Award)
• Enid Johnson MacLeod Award (Award)
• The Reproductive Health Award (Award)
• Student Leadership Award (Award)
• Jessie McGeachy Award (Award)
• Dr. Shelagh Lindsay Medical Award (Award)

Federation of Metro Toronto Tenants' Associations (FMTA)

#500, 27 Carlton St., Toronto ON M5B 1L2
Tel: 416-646-1772; *Crisis Hot-Line:* 416-921-9494
hotline@torontotenants.org
www.torontotenants.org
Overview: A medium-sized local organization founded in 1974
Mission: To inform & educate tenants; To encourage the organization of tenants; To lobby for tenant protection laws; To promote affordable housing
Membership: *Fees:* $15 individuals; $5 seniors, students & unemployed; $25 organizations; $10 tenants' associations
Activities: Offering the tenant hotline for referrals & information about tenant rights; Helping tenants to challenge rent increases & to promote better maintenance in buildings, through the outreach & organizing team; Providing workshops on tenants' rights; Assisting tenants through the Tenant Defence Fund; Offering Landlord and Tenant Board preparation

Federation of Mountain Clubs of British Columbia (FMCBC)

Mountain Equipment Co-op Store, PO Box 18673, 130 West Broadway, 2nd Fl., Vancouver BC V5T 4E7
Tel: 604-873-6096; *Fax:* 604-873-6086
fmcbc@mountainclubs.org
www.mountainclubs.org
www.facebook.com/129423370477517
twitter.com/mountainclubs
Overview: A small provincial charitable organization founded in 1980
Mission: To promote hiking & mountaineering
Member of: Donations; Membership dues
Chief Officer(s):
Scott Webster, President
Jodi Appleton, Manager, Program and Administration
admin.manager@mountainclubs.org
Membership: 3500; *Fees:* Individual $25
Publications:
• Cloudburst
Type: Newsletter
• Training Manuals
Type: Manual
Profile: Training manuals to support courses in mountaineering, climbing, avalanche safety and other outdoor skills

Federation of Music Festivals of Nova Scotia

PO Box 31, Lunenberg NS B0J 2C0
Tel: 902-640-2448
www.musicfestivalsnovascotia.ca
Overview: A medium-sized provincial organization overseen by Federation of Canadian Music Festivals
Chief Officer(s):
Pamela Rogers, Secretary
pamelasrogers@gmail.com

Federation of Mutual Fund Dealers (FMFD) / Fédération des courtiers en fonds mutuels

c/o S. Kegie, Executive Director, 44 Faversham Cres., Etobicoke ON M9C 3X6
Tel: 416-621-8857
www.fmfd.ca
Overview: A medium-sized national organization founded in 1996
Mission: To be the representative voice of mutual fund distribution in Canada; to provide a forum for stakeholders; to advocate for members
Chief Officer(s):
Sandra Kegie, Executive Director, 647-409-8369
skegie@rogers.com
Membership: 27 dealers + 25 affiliates; *Fees:* $550-$5,500 dealer; $175-$5,500 affiliate
Activities: Networking; education opportunities; meetings with trade associations, lobby groups, regulators & individuals in order to further the federation's mandate;

Federation of New Brunswick Faculty Associations (FNBFA) / Fédération des associations de professeures et professeurs d'université du Nouveau-Brunswick (FAPPUNB)

#204, 361 Victoria St., Fredericton NB E3B 1W5
Tel: 506-458-8977; *Fax:* 506-458-5620
www.fnbfa.ca
Overview: A small provincial organization founded in 1973 overseen by Canadian Association of University Teachers
Mission: To promote interests of teachers, librarians & researchers in universities & colleges of New Brunswick; to advance standards of professions & to seek to improve quality of higher education in the Province.
Chief Officer(s):
Jean Sauvageau, President
jsauvageau@stu.ca
Elisabeth Hans, Executive Director
elisabeth.hans@fnbfa.ca
Staff Member(s): 2
Membership: 6 organizations representing 1,800 members; *Member Profile:* University professor & librarian associations; *Committees:* Communications; Prix Nicole Raymond Award; Legal Defense Fund; Collective Bargaining; George P. Semeluk Scholarship
Activities: *Speaker Service:* Yes
Awards:
• George P. Semezuk Scholarship (Scholarship)
• Prix Nicole Raymond Award (Award)
• Daniel Bélanger Medal of Achievement (Award)

Federation of Newfoundland & Labrador Square Dance

c/o Avalon Stompers Square Dance Club, 16 Edmonton Place, St. John's NL A1A 2N7
Tel: 709-579-0980
Overview: A small provincial organization
Member of: Canadian Square & Round Dance Society
Chief Officer(s):
Jim Critch, President

Federation of North American Explorers (FNE)

c/o Paul Ritchi, 43 Bluesky Cres., Richmond Hill ON L4C 8J2
Tel: 416-435-6593
info@fneexplorers.com
www.fneexplorers.com
www.facebook.com/128721180527013
twitter.com/PaulRitchi
Also Known As: FN Explorers
Overview: A small local charitable organization founded in 1956
Mission: To deliver traditional values to youth, from a Catholic faith perspective; To provide youth a same gender, education for life program experience
Member of: International Union of European FSE Guides & Scouts (Union Internationale des Guides et Scouts d'Europe)
Affliation(s): Archdiocese of Toronto
Chief Officer(s):
Paul Ritchi, General Commissioner & Founder
paul.ritchi@gmail.com
Finances: *Funding Sources:* Donations
Membership: *Member Profile:* Youth must be baptized Christians, or being prepared for baptism. Adults must also be baptized Christians, or being prepared for baptism, & volunteers must clear a police background check
Activities: Participating in camping weekends, outdoor survival skills, & community service; Earning badges by successfully completing certain activities;

Federation of Northern Ontario Municipalities (FONOM)

88 Riverside Dr., Kapuskasing ON P5N 1B3
Tel: 705-337-4454; *Fax:* 705-337-1741
fonom.info@gmail.com
www.fonom.org
Overview: A medium-sized local organization founded in 1960
Mission: To act as the voice for the people of northeastern Ontario communities; To work for the betterment of municipal government by striving for improved legislation respecting local government in northern Ontario
Member of: Association of Municipalities of Ontario
Chief Officer(s):
Alan Spacek, President
Finances: *Funding Sources:* Membership fees; Provincial grants; Sponsorships
Membership: 111; *Member Profile:* Municipal governments from the following districts: Cochrane, Algoma, Manitoulin, Nipissing, Parry Sound, Sudbury, & Timiskaming
Meetings/Conferences: • Federation of Northern Ontario Municipalities 2015 55th Annual Conference, May, 2015, Holiday Inn, Sudbury, ON
Scope: Local
Description: A meeting for northern Ontario's municipal decision makers, featuring exhibits by suppliers, vendors, & professionals who provide services to municipalities
Contact Information: E-mail: fonom.info@gmail.com

Federation of Nova Scotia Naturalists *See* Nature Nova Scotia (Federation of Nova Scotia Naturalists)

Federation of Nova Scotian Heritage *See* Association of Nova Scotia Museums

Federation of Nunavut Teachers *See* Nunavut Teachers Association

Federation of Ontario Bed & Breakfast Accommodation (FOBBA)

PO Box 998, Guelph ON N1H 6N1
e-mail: talk2us@fobba.com
www.fobba.com
Overview: A small provincial organization founded in 1986
Mission: To represent the interest of independent bed & breakfast operators, country inns, bed & breakfast associations & registries, to the public & various governmenta agencies
Chief Officer(s):
Troy Gee, President
president@fobba.com
Diane Tolstoy, Membership Director
membership@fobba.com
Finances: *Annual Operating Budget:* $50,000-$100,000
Membership: 100-499; *Member Profile:* Bed & breakfast owner/operators

Federation of Ontario Cottagers' Associations (FOCA)

#201, 159 King St., Peterborough ON K9J 2R8
Tel: 705-749-3622; *Fax:* 705-749-6522
info@foca.on.ca
www.foca.on.ca
Overview: A medium-sized provincial organization founded in 1963
Mission: To ensure a healthy future for waterfront Ontario; To support the interests of Ontario's cottagers
Chief Officer(s):
Terry Rees, Executive Director, 705-749-3622 Ext. 4
trees@foca.on.ca

Tracy Logan, Contact, Programs, 705-749-3622 Ext. 3
programs@foca.on.ca
Finances: *Funding Sources:* Membership fees; Sponsorships; Donations
Membership: 550+; *Fees:* $37.50 individuals; $75 associations; *Member Profile:* Ontario cottagers' associations; Individuals, such as waterfront property owners; *Committees:* Property Tax
Activities: Providing information about issues that affect cottage properties; Offering networking opportunities;
Meetings/Conferences: • Federation of Ontario Cottagers' Associations 2015 Spring Annual General Meeting, 2015, ON
Scope: Provincial
Contact Information: Phone: 705-749-3622, ext. 5; E-mail: communications@foca.on.ca
Publications:
• Federation of Ontario Cottagers' Associations Report to Members
Type: Newsletter; *Price:* Free with Federation of Ontario Cottagers' Associations membership
Profile: Federation activities
• Lake Stewards Newsletter
Type: Newsletter; *Frequency:* Annually; *Price:* Free with Federation of Ontario Cottagers' Associations membership

Federation of Ontario Memorial Societies - Funeral Consumers Alliance (FOOMS-FCA)

c/o Funeral Advisory & Memorial Society of Toronto, 55 St. Philips Rd., Toronto ON M9P 2N8
Tel: 416-241-6274
info@fams.ca
www.myfuneralplan.org
Overview: A small provincial charitable organization
Mission: To coordinate all memorial societies in Ontario
Chief Officer(s):
Al Gruno, Vice-President
Art Read, Treasurer
Pearl Davie, President
Finances: *Annual Operating Budget:* Less than $50,000
20 volunteer(s)
Membership: 10 societies; 51,000 members; *Fees:* Percentage of membership fees from 11 societies; *Committees:* Publicity; Legislation
Activities: Annual meeting; *Speaker Service:* Yes

Federation of Ontario Naturalists *See* Ontario Nature

Federation of Ontario Public Libraries (FOPL)

c/o North York Central Library, 5720 Yonge St., Toronto ON M2N 5N9
Tel: 416-395-5638; *Fax:* 416-395-0743
admin@fopl.ca
www.fopl.ca
www.facebook.com/160173540675944
twitter.com/FOPLnews
Overview: A medium-sized provincial organization
Mission: The Federation's strategic focus includes advocacy, research and development, marketing, and consortia purchasing.
Member of: Knowledge Ontario
Chief Officer(s):
Larry Stewart, Chair
Ian Ross, Vice-Chair
ianross@whitbylibrary.on.ca
Stephen Abram, Executive Director
sabram@fopl.ca
Membership: 195; *Member Profile:* Libraries in Ontario

Federation of Painting & Decorating Contractors of Toronto

#305, 211 Consumers Rd., Toronto ON M2J 4G8
Tel: 416-498-1897; *Fax:* 416-498-6757
Toll-Free: 800-461-3630
info@ontpca.org
www.ontpca.org
Overview: A small local organization founded in 1078
Mission: To foster, develop & maintain unity & stability among its members; To act as the bargaining agent in all matters involving organized labour; To provide services & educational opportunities; To act as a communication liaison between industry groups; To uphold & improve the standards of the painting & decorating trade; To keep members informed on questions of public importance & of any proposed legislation affecting the industry
Member of: Ontario Painting Contractors Association
Chief Officer(s):
Andrew Sefton, Executive Director
Finances: *Annual Operating Budget:* $50,000-$100,000
Staff Member(s): 2; 30 volunteer(s)
Membership: 60; *Fees:* Through provincial collective agreement; *Member Profile:* Unionized commercial, industrial & institutional painting contractors

Federation of Portuguese Canadian Business & Professionals Inc. (FPCBP)

1136 College St., Toronto ON M6H 1B6
Tel: 416-537-8874; *Fax:* 416-537-9706
info@fpcbp.com
www.fpcbp.com
www.facebook.com/143576472378864
Overview: A small national organization founded in 1981
Mission: To promote Portuguese culture & heritage; To foster business & community development in the Greater Toronto area
Chief Officer(s):
Isabel Christina Bento Martins, President
Francine Antonio, Vice-President
Josie Caldas, Secretary
Sergio Ruivo, Treasurer
Finances: *Funding Sources:* Sponsorships; Grants
Activities: Advocating on behalf of members; Enhancing political visibility; Partnering with other community groups; Organizing events, such as monthly business forums & social activities; Promoting business interaction & developing networking opportunities; Encouraging & improving academic excellence amongst Portuguese-Canadians; Fostering professionalism; Engaging Portuguese youth & the community to recognize & celebrate Portuguese history & heritage
Awards:
• FPCBP Scholarship (Scholarship)
To recognize the outstanding academic achievements of our Luso Canadian youth
• FPCBP Business Excellence Awards (Scholarship)
To recognize individuals in the business & professional community who demonstrate excellence in their field of work
Publications:
• FPCBP Directory
Type: Directory

Federation of Prince Edward Island Municipalities Inc. (FPEIM)

1 Kirkdale Rd., Charlottetown PE C1E 1R3
Tel: 902-566-1493; *Fax:* 902-566-2880
info@fpeim.ca
www.fpeim.ca
Overview: A large provincial organization founded in 1957
Mission: To represent the interests of the cities, towns & communities within PEI; To secure united action for the protection of individual municipalities & municipal interests as a whole; To act as a clearing house for the collection, exchange & dissemination of information of concern & interest to member municipalities; To provide training, education & development opportunities for elected & appointed municipal officials
Member of: Federation of Canadian Municipalities
Affliation(s): Association of Municipal Administrators, PEI
Chief Officer(s):
John Dewey, Executive Director
jdewey@fpeim.ca
Bruce MacDougall, President
president@fpeim.ca
Finances: *Annual Operating Budget:* $100,000-$250,000; *Funding Sources:* Small government grant; membership fees
Staff Member(s): 2; 13 volunteer(s)
Membership: 43 municipalities; *Fees:* Per capita fee; *Member Profile:* Incorporated municipality; *Committees:* Finance; Resolutions; Constitution; Annual Meeting; Semi-Annual Meeting; Transportation; Membership; Nominating; Resolutions; Policy
Activities: Monthly board meetings; 2 full membership meetings per year; bi-monthly information updates to membership; liaising with provincial municipal associations across Canada as well as provincial & federal government departments; *Awareness Events:* Municipal Government Week; *Library* by appointment
Awards:
• The Gilbert C. Bell Memorial Award (Scholarship)
Presented annually to a full-time undergraduate student who exemplifies an interest in a career in Public Administration by obtaining the highest mark in Public Administration Course #311 - Public Policy & Administration 1, in that academic year
• Municipal Achievement Award (Award)
Awarded annually to a municipality that has demonstrated a commitment to improving the quality of life of its residents through innovative local projects & activities; two awards presented each year: one award to a municipality with a population of 1,500 & under; one award to a municipality with a population over 1,500; open to FPEI Municipalities members
• Bruce H. Yeo Award (Award)

Federation of Public Service Employees Inc. (CNTU) *Voir* Fédération des employées et employés de services publics inc. (CSN)

Federation of Québec Alzheimer Societies *Voir* Fédération québécoise des sociétés Alzheimer

Federation of Québec Beef Producers *Voir* Fédération des producteurs de bovins du Québec

Federation of Regulatory Authorities of Canada (FMRAC) / Fédération des ordres des médecins du Canada

#103, 2283 St. Laurent Blvd., Ottawa ON K1G 5A2
Tel: 613-738-0372; *Fax:* 613-738-9169
info@fmrac.ca
www.fmrac.ca
Overview: A medium-sized national licensing organization founded in 1968
Mission: To provide a national structure for the provincial & territorial medical regulatory authorities; To present & pursue issues of common concern & interest; To share, consider, & develop positions on such matters
Chief Officer(s):
Rocco Gerace, President
Fleur-Ange Lefebvre, Executive Director & CEO
falefebvre@fmrac.ca
Finances: *Funding Sources:* Membership fees
Staff Member(s): 4
Membership: 13; *Member Profile:* Provincial & territorial regulatory authorities; *Committees:* Accreditation & Education Advisory; Executive; Nominating; Risk Management

Federation of Saskatchewan Indian Nations

Asimakaniseekan Askiy Reserve, #100, 103A Packham Ave., Saskatoon SK S7N 4K4
Tel: 306-665-1215; *Fax:* 306-244-4413
www.fsin.com
Previous Name: Federation of Saskatchewan Indians
Overview: A small provincial organization overseen by Congress of Aboriginal Peoples
Mission: To honour the spirit & intent of the First Nations Treaties & their rights; to foster the economic, educational & social endeavours of the First Nation people & adherence to democratic procedure & civil law.
Chief Officer(s):
Kim Jonathan, Interim Chief
Membership: 74 First Nations
Activities: Education & Training Secretariat;

Office of Treaty Governance Processes
#100, 130A Packham Ave., Saskatoon SK S7N 4K4
Tel: 306-665-1215; *Fax:* 306-244-4413

Federation of Saskatchewan Indians *See* Federation of Saskatchewan Indian Nations

Federation of Saskatchewan Surface Rights Association (FSSRA)

PO Box 53, Lone Rock SK S0M 1K0
Tel: 306-387-6650; *Fax:* 306-387-6650
Overview: A small provincial organization founded in 1982
Mission: To aid in reclamation concerns in land, gas lines, rail lines, compensation, environmental issues & legislation
Affliation(s): Alberta Surface Rights Federation
Chief Officer(s):
Terry Crush, Contact
Membership: 1-99; *Member Profile:* Farmers
Activities: *Speaker Service:* Yes

Federation of Senior Citizens & Pensioners of Nova Scotia (FSCPNS)

c/o Bernie LaRusic, 21 Grandview St., Sydney NS B1P 3N4
Tel: 902-562-1901
Previous Name: Nova Scotia Federation of Senior Citizens & Pensioners
Overview: A medium-sized provincial organization founded in 1973
Mission: To help seniors maintain the health services & pension incomes that they now have
Member of: National Federation of Senior Citizens & Pensioners
Chief Officer(s):
Bernie LaRusic, President
bernielarusic_392@hotmail.com

Membership: *Member Profile:* A member of a senior citizens club

Federation of Single-Parent Family Associations of Québec *Voir* Fédération des associations de familles monoparentales et recomposées du Québec

Federation of Support Staff *Voir* Fédération du personnel de soutien scolaire (CSQ)

Federation of Teachers of Jewish Schools (FTJS) / Fédération des enseignants des écoles juives

#3265, 6900 Decarie Blvd., Montréal QC H3X 2T8
Tel: 514-738-6852; *Fax:* 514-738-9660
info@ftjs.org
www.ftjs.org
Overview: A medium-sized local organization founded in 1947
Mission: To promote the advancement of professional economic & social welfare of its members by securing collective agreements; to engage in activities conducive to the well-being & furthering of Jewish, Hebrew & secular education
Chief Officer(s):
Mordechai Antal, President
Membership: *Fees:* Schedule available; *Member Profile:* Those teaching in Jewish schools in Montréal
Activities: Annual general meeting

Federation of Temporary Help Services *See* Association of Canadian Search, Employment & Staffing Services

Fédération professionnelle des journalistes du Québec (FPJQ)

#105, 1012, av Mont Royal est, Montréal QC H2J 1X6
Tél: 514-522-6142; *Téléc:* 514-522-6071
info@fpjq.org
www.fpjq.org
www.facebook.com/pages/FPJQ/256594304445143
twitter.com/fpjq
www.youtube.com/channel/UCCxQxREz2d3ff-55-8sFqHg
Aperçu: *Dimension:* moyenne; *Envergure:* provinciale; fondée en 1969
Mission: Pour défendre la liberté d'expression pour la presse et le droit du public à la connaissance
Membre(s) du bureau directeur:
Caroline Locher, Directrice générale
caroline.locher@fpjq.org
Membre(s) du personnel: 3
Membre: *Montant de la cotisation:* 46$ étudiant; 82$ associé/membre professionnel gagnant moins de 25 000 $/an; 174$ professional
Activités: Congrès annuel des journalistes; Sessions de prfectionnement Defense de la liberté de la presse; Droit du public à l'information; Prix et bourses journalistiques; Emmission de la carte de presse

Fédération provinciale des comités de parents du Manitoba (FPCP)

81, chemin Quail Ridge, Winnipeg MB R2Y 2A9
Tél: 204-237-9666; *Téléc:* 204-231-1436
Ligne sans frais: 866-666-8108
fpcp@fpcp.mb.ca
www.entreparents.mb.ca
Aperçu: *Dimension:* moyenne; *Envergure:* provinciale; Organisme sans but lucratif; fondée en 1976
Mission: Appuyer les membres dans le développement des milieux, familial, éducatif (préscolaire et scolaire) et communautaire, propices à l'épanouissement des familles francophones
Membre de: Commission nationale des parents francophones
Membre(s) du bureau directeur:
Geneviève Boudreau, Directrice générale
genevieve@fpcp.mb.ca
Finances: *Budget de fonctionnement annuel:* $250,000-$500,000
Membre(s) du personnel: 8
Membre: 80 regroupements membres; *Comités:* Parents du niveau scolaire; Parents du niveau préscolaire; Parents des mini-centres du CRÉE; Réseau provincial de garderies familiales francophones
Activités: Formation; animation; ressources; représentation; soutien; *Bibliothèque:* Centre de ressources éducatives à l'enfance (CRÉE); Bibliothèque publique

Fédération Québécoise Boxe Olympique (FQBO)

4545, av Pierre-de Coubertin, Montréal QC H1V 0B2
Tél: 514-252-3047; *Téléc:* 514-254-2144
Ligne sans frais: 866-241-3779
info@fqbo.qc.ca
www.fqbo.qc.ca
www.facebook.com/groups/5136898117
Également appelé: Boxe Québec
Aperçu: *Dimension:* moyenne; *Envergure:* provinciale surveillé par Canadian Amateur Boxing Association
Membre de: Canadian Amateur Boxing Association
Membre(s) du bureau directeur:
Kenneth Piché, Directeur général
kenpiche@fqbo.qc.ca
Membre: 2 000

Fédération québécoise d'athlétisme (FQA)

4545, av Pierre-de Coubertin, Montréal QC H1V 0B2
Tél: 514-252-3041; *Téléc:* 514-252-3042
fqa@athletisme.qc.ca
www.athletisme.qc.ca
www.facebook.com/athletismequebec
twitter.com/Athl_FQA
www.youtube.com/athletismequebec
Nom précédent: Fédération d'athlétisme du Québec
Aperçu: *Dimension:* moyenne; *Envergure:* provinciale; Organisme sans but lucratif; fondée en 1968 surveillé par Athletics Canada
Mission: Promouvoir l'athlétisme au Québec
Membre de: Athletics Canada
Membre(s) du bureau directeur:
Sylvain Proulx, Président
Laurent Godbout, Directeur général
lgodbout@athletisme.qc.ca
Membre(s) du personnel: 6
Membre: *Montant de la cotisation:* Barème; *Critères d'admissibilite:* Coureurs sur route; athlètes; entraîneurs; officiels; membres associés; *Comités:* Technique provinciale; Officiels, règlements et organisations; Jeunes
Activités: *Service de conférenciers:* Oui

Fédération québécoise de ballon sur glace

4545, av Pierre-de Coubertin, Montréal QC H1V 3R2
Tél: 514-252-3078
fqbg.comm@gmail.com
www.fqbg.net
www.facebook.com/157977357723290
Aperçu: *Dimension:* moyenne; *Envergure:* provinciale
Mission: La Fédération Québecoise de Ballon sur Glace a pour but de promouvoir le sport du ballon sur glace dans la province de Québec
Membre de: Fédération canadienne de ballon sur glace
Membre(s) du bureau directeur:
Normand Perreault, Président
normandperreault8@gmail.com

Fédération québécoise de camping et de caravaning inc. (FQCC)

CP 100, 1560, rue Eiffel, Boucherville QC J4B 5Y1
Tél: 450-650-3722; *Téléc:* 450-650-3721
Ligne sans frais: 877-650-3722
info@fqcc.ca
www.fqcc.ca
www.facebook.com/LaFQCC
Aperçu: *Dimension:* grande; *Envergure:* provinciale; fondée en 1967
Mission: Unir les adepts du camping et du caravaning; entreprendre et coordonner des actions relatives au camping et au caravaning.
Membre de: Fédération internationale de camping et de caravaning
Membre(s) du bureau directeur:
Martin Healey, Président
Michel Quintal, Trésorier
Finances: *Budget de fonctionnement annuel:* $500,000-$1.5 Million
Membre(s) du personnel: 10
Membre: 45 000 familles membres; *Montant de la cotisation:* 45$
Activités: *Service de conférenciers:* Oui

Fédération québécoise de canoë-kayak d'eau vives

4545, av Pierre-de Coubertin, Montréal QC H1V 3R2
Tél: 438-333-1913
fqckev@kayak.qc.ca
www.federationkayak.qc.ca
www.facebook.com/fqckev
pinterest.com/fqckev
Aperçu: *Dimension:* petite; *Envergure:* provinciale; fondée en 1971 surveillé par CanoeKayak Canada
Mission: Promouvoir le sport et la pratique d'activités en eau vive au Québec
Membre de: CanoeKayak Canada
Membre(s) du bureau directeur:
Patrick Lévesque, Coordonnateur

Fédération québécoise de course d'orientation *See* Orienteering Québec

Fédération Québécoise de Dynamophilie (FQD)

679, av du Parc, Sherbrooke QC J1N 3N5
Tél: 819-864-4810
www.fqd-quebec.com
www.facebook.com/dynamophilie
Aperçu: *Dimension:* petite; *Envergure:* provinciale surveillé par Canadian Powerlifting Union
Mission: Promouvoir, contrôler et développer la dynamophilie auprès de la population du Québec.
Affliation(s): Canadian Powerlifting Union; International Powerlifting Federation
Membre(s) du bureau directeur:
Louis Lévesque, Président
louis.lvesque2@sympatico.ca
Membre: *Montant de la cotisation:* 55$; 45$ les moins de 18 ans

Fédération québécoise de handball olympique (FQHO)

CP 1000, Succ. M, 4545, av Pierre-de Coubertin, Montréal QC H1V 3R2
Tél: 514-252-3067; *Téléc:* 514-252-3176
handball@handball.qc.ca
www.handball.qc.ca
Aperçu: *Dimension:* petite; *Envergure:* locale
Mission: Handball Québec est le seul organisme reconnu par le Secrétariat au Loisir et au Sport du Gouvernement du Québec pour régir le handball au Québec.
Membre de: Canadian Team Handball Federation
Membre(s) du bureau directeur:
Michelle Lortie, Directrice
mlortie@handball.qc.ca
Membre: *Comités:* Comité Technique d'Arbitrage; Comité de discipline

Fédération québécoise de hockey sur glace *Voir* Hockey Québec

Fédération québécoise de l'autisme et des autres troubles envahissants du développement (FQATED) / Québec Federation for Autism & Other Pervasive Developmental Disorders

#200, 7675, boul Saint-Laurent, Montréal QC H2R 1W9
Tél: 514-270-7386; *Téléc:* 514-270-9261
Ligne sans frais: 888-830-2833
info@autisme.qc.ca
www.autisme.qc.ca
www.facebook.com/198123333548170
Nom précédent: Société québécoise de l'autisme
Aperçu: *Dimension:* moyenne; *Envergure:* provinciale; Organisme sans but lucratif; fondée en 1976 surveillé par Autism Society Canada
Mission: Promouvoir et défendre les droits et les intérêts de la personne autiste ou ayant un trouble envahissant du développement afin qu'elle accède à une vie digne et à une meilleure autonomie sociale possible.
Membre(s) du bureau directeur:
Jo-Ann Lauzon, Directrice générale
direction@autisme.qc.ca
Finances: *Fonds:* Gouvernement
Membre(s) du personnel: 3
Membre: 16 organismes; *Montant de la cotisation:* 50$ organismes communautaires; 100$ autres organismes; *Critères d'admissibilite:* Organismes offrant des services aux personnes autistes ou ayant un trouble envahissant du développement
Activités: Défense des droits; information-formation; promotion; vie associative; *Stagiaires:* Oui; *Bibliothèque:* Centre de documentation

Fédération québécoise de la faune *Voir* Fédération québécoise des chasseurs et pêcheurs

Fédération québécoise de la marche

4545, av Pierre-de Coubertin, Montréal QC H1V 0B2
Tél: 514-252-3157; *Téléc:* 514-252-5137
Ligne sans frais: 866-252-2065
infomarche@fqmarche.qc.ca
www.fqmarche.qc.ca
www.facebook.com/138582999548977

twitter.com/QuebecMarche
www.youtube.com/user/fqmarche
Aperçu: *Dimension:* moyenne; *Envergure:* provinciale; Organisme sans but lucratif; fondée en 1978
Mission: Promotion de la marche et de la randonnée pedestre; support au développement de lieux de marche
Membre de: Conseil québécois du loisir
Membre(s) du bureau directeur:
Daniel Pouplot, Directeur général
dpouplot@fqmarche.qc.ca
Finances: *Budget de fonctionnement annuel:* $250,000-$500,000
Membre(s) du personnel: 5; 26 bénévole(s)
Membre: 3 000 individu; 100 clubs; *Montant de la cotisation:* 29,50$ individu; 35,50$ famille; *Comités:* Marches populaires; Raquette; Sentiers-Québec
Activités: *Evénements de sensibilisation:* Festival de la marche, oct.; Festival de la raquette, fév.; *Bibliothèque* Bibliothèque publique
Prix, Bouses:
• Prix sentiers Québec (Prix)
• Certificat du Randonneur émérite québecois (Prix)
• Padelima (Brouse)

Fédération québécoise de la montagne et de l'escalade (FQME)

4545, av Pierre-de Coubertin, Montréal QC H1V 0B2
Tél: 514-252-3004; *Téléc:* 514-252-3201
Ligne sans frais: 866-204-3763
fqme@fqme.qc.ca
www.fqme.qc.ca
www.facebook.com/63976115917
twitter.com/Escalade_FQME
Aperçu: *Dimension:* petite; *Envergure:* provinciale; Organisme sans but lucratif; fondée en 1969
Mission: Regrouper les adeptes de l'escalade et de l'alpinisme au Québec; promouvoir l'escalade (rocher et glace) et le ski de l'alpinisme et de randonnée en montagne; promouvoir une pratique sécuritaire de ces activités; protéger et rendre accessibles les différents sites d'escalade et de grande randonnée à skis au Québec
Membre de: Canadian Avalanche Association; Outdoor Recreation Coalition of America (ORCA)
Affliation(s): Union internationale des associations d'alpinisme
Membre(s) du bureau directeur:
André St-Jacques, Directeur des opérations
operations@fqme.qc.ca
Finances: *Budget de fonctionnement annuel:* $100,000-$250,000
Membre: 2 000; *Montant de la cotisation:* 30$ adulte; 10$ jeune; *Comités:* Formation; Site; Expédition
Activités: Amateur d'activités montagnes; *Stagiaires:* Oui; *Bibliothèque:* Centre de documentation; rendez-vous

Fédération québécoise de naturisme (FQN)

CP 1000, Succ. M, 4545, av Pierre-de Coubertin, Montréal QC H1V 3R2
Tél: 514-252-3014
fqn@fqn.qc.ca
www.fqn.qc.ca
www.facebook.com/fedquenat
Aperçu: *Dimension:* moyenne; *Envergure:* provinciale; fondée en 1977
Mission: Regrouper les naturistes; promouvoir et favoriser le développement de la pratique du naturisme au Québec
Affliation(s): Regroupement Loisir Québec; Fédération naturiste internationale
Finances: *Budget de fonctionnement annuel:* Moins de $50,000; *Fonds:* Provincial government
9 bénévole(s)
Membre: 400 individus; 4 institutionels; *Montant de la cotisation:* $22 jeune; $42 régulier
Activités: Sports et loisirs naturistes organisés durant l'année

Fédération québécoise de philatélie (FQP)

CP 1000, Succ. M, 4545, av Pierre-de Coubertin, Montréal QC H1V 3R2
Tél: 514-252-3035
fqp@philatelie.qc.ca
www.philatelie.qc.ca
Également appelé: Philatélie Québec
Aperçu: *Dimension:* moyenne; *Envergure:* provinciale; Organisme sans but lucratif; fondée en 1971
Mission: Promouvoir la pratique de la philatélie
Affliation(s): Regroupement Loisir-Québec
Membre(s) du bureau directeur:
Yves Rochefort, Président
Finances: *Budget de fonctionnement annuel:* Moins de $50,000
50 bénévole(s)
Membre: 300 institutionnel; 5 000 individu; 100 associé; *Montant de la cotisation:* 20$ institutionnel; 8$ individu
Activités: Expositions; Salon Philatélique; Quoffilex; *Stagiaires:* Oui; *Bibliothèque* rendez-vous

Fédération québécoise de soccer football *Voir* Fédération de soccer du Québec

Fédération québécoise de tennis *Voir* Tennis Québec

Fédération québécoise de tir (FQT) / Québec Shooting Federation

CP 1000, Succ. M, 4545, av Pierre-de Coubertin, Montréal QC H1V 3R2
Tél: 514-252-3056; *Téléc:* 514-252-3060
Ligne sans frais: 888-514-7847
fqt@fqtir.qc.ca
www.fqtir.qc.ca
Aperçu: *Dimension:* petite; *Envergure:* provinciale; Organisme sans but lucratif; fondée en 1978
Mission: La FQT est un organisme à but non lucratif voué à la promotion du tir sportif sur tout le territoire de la province du Québec et qui est reconnue et subventionnée par l'intermédiaire du Secrétariat au loisir et au sport (Gouvernement du Québec)
Membre de: Fédération de tir du Canada; Shooting Federation of Canada
Affliation(s): Regroupment Loisir Québec; Sports Québec
Membre(s) du bureau directeur:
Gilles Bédard, Directeur exécutif
gbedard@fqtir.qc.ca
Gérald Tousignant, Président
Finances: *Budget de fonctionnement annuel:* $250,000-$500,000; *Fonds:* Gouvernement du Québec
Membre(s) du personnel: 3; 400 bénévole(s)
Membre: 6,000; *Montant de la cotisation:* 55$ régulier; 20$ sportif; 10$ junior (21 ans et -); *Comités:* Carabine; pistolet; plateaux; chasse; moderne; poudre noire; pratique pour policiers et civils
Activités: Assemblée général annuelle; *Stagiaires:* Oui

Fédération québécoise des activités subaquatiques (FQAS)

4545, av Pierre-de Coubertin, Montréal QC H1V 0B2
Tél: 514-252-3009; *Téléc:* 514-254-1363
Ligne sans frais: 866-391-8835
info@fqas.qc.ca
www.fqas.qc.ca
www.facebook.com/FederationQuebecoisedesActivitesSubaquatiques
Aperçu: *Dimension:* moyenne; *Envergure:* provinciale; Organisme sans but lucratif; fondée en 1970
Mission: Regrouper les adeptes de la plongée et des activités subaquatiques; promouvoir la sécurite dans la pratique des activités subaquatiques; informer et renseigner ses membres et la population sur les bienfaits de la pratique; promouvoir ces activités comme moyen de formation et comme loisir
Affliation(s): Confédération mondiale des activités subaquatiques
Membre(s) du bureau directeur:
Jean-Sébastien Naud, Directeur général
jsnaud@fqas.qc.ca
Finances: *Budget de fonctionnement annuel:* $250,000-$500,000; *Fonds:* Gouvernement provincial
Membre(s) du personnel: 2; 150 bénévole(s)
Membre: 100 institutionnel + 2 200 individu; *Montant de la cotisation:* 180$ institutionnel; 25$ individu
Activités: *Stagiaires:* Oui; *Service de conférenciers:* Oui; *Bibliothèque:* Librairie FQAS; rendez-vous

Fédération québécoise des centres communautaires de loisir inc. (FQCCL)

2301, 1re av, Québec QC G1L 3M9
Tél: 418-686-0012; *Téléc:* 418-686-0021
Ligne sans frais: 888-686-8356
fqccl@fqccl.org
www.fqccl.org
Aperçu: *Dimension:* petite; *Envergure:* locale; Organisme sans but lucratif; fondée en 1976
Mission: Regroupe les centres pour qu'ils s'entraident dans leur cheminement; veille à la formation des intervenants et des bénévoles; aide à améliorer le bien-être et le développement de leur communauté locale; promeut les initiatives nouvelles des centres, spécialement dans la prise en charge des milieux les plus démunis; aide les centres dans leur financement
Membre de: Conseil québécois du loisir
Membre(s) du bureau directeur:
Sylvain Turcotte, Président
Finances: *Budget de fonctionnement annuel:* $250,000-$500,000; *Fonds:* Gouvernement provincial
Membre(s) du personnel: 12; 100 bénévole(s)
Membre: 58 institutionnel; *Critères d'admissibilite:* Centre communautaire de loisir
Activités: *Stagiaires:* Oui; *Service de conférenciers:* Oui

Fédération québécoise des chasseurs et pêcheurs

162, rue du Brome, Saint-Augustin-de-Desmaures QC G3A 2P5
Tél: 418-878-8901; *Téléc:* 418-878-8980
Ligne sans frais: 888-523-2863
info@fedecp.qc.ca
www.fedecp.qc.ca
www.facebook.com/116805682100
twitter.com/FederationCP
Nom précédent: Fédération québécoise de la faune
Aperçu: *Dimension:* moyenne; *Envergure:* provinciale; fondée en 1946 surveillé par Canadian Wildlife Federation
Mission: Contribuer, dans le respect de la faune et de ses habitats, à la gestion du développement et à la perpétuation de la chasse et de la pêche comme activités traditionnelles et sportives
Membre(s) du bureau directeur:
Pierre Latraverse, Président
Marjorie Alain, Responsable des relations publiques
marjoriealain@fedecp.qc.ca
Membre: 200 associations; *Montant de la cotisation:* 39,95$ membre individuel; *Critères d'admissibilite:* Chasseurs, pêcheurs

Fédération québécoise des coopératives en milieu scolaire (FQCMS)

#200, 3188, ch Sainte-Foy, Québec QC G1X 1R4
Tél: 418-650-3333; *Téléc:* 418-651-3860
www.fqcms.com
Aperçu: *Dimension:* grande; *Envergure:* provinciale; fondée en 1983
Mission: Regroupe 60 coopératives en milieu scolaire
Membre(s) du bureau directeur:
Francis Viens, Président du conseil
Jean-Emmanuel Bouchard, Président de la Fédération
André Gagnon, Directeur général
andre.gagnon@coopsco.com
Membre: 400 000 membres

Bureau d'Anjou
#501, 7333, place Des Roseraies, Anjou QC H1M 2X6
Tél: 514-352-1121; *Téléc:* 514-352-1764

Fédération québécoise des coopératives forestières (FQCF)

#200, 3188, ch Sainte-Foy, Québec QC G1X 1R4
Tél: 418-651-0388; *Téléc:* 418-651-3860
www.fqcf.coop
Nom précédent: Conférence des coopératives forestières du Québec
Aperçu: *Dimension:* moyenne; *Envergure:* provinciale; fondée en 1985
Mission: La Fédération québécoise des coopératives forestières (FQCF) regroupe et représente dans des domaines d'intérêts communs l'ensemble des coopératives forestières de travailleurs, les coopératives de travailleurs actionnaires et les coopératives de solidarité actives dans le milieu forestier, et ce dans toutes les régions du Québec
Membre(s) du bureau directeur:
Jocelyn Lessard, Directeur général
j.lessard@fqcf.coop
Cathy Gagnon, Adjointe administrative
cathyg@fqcf.coop
Finances: *Budget de fonctionnement annuel:* $500,000-$1.5 Million
Membre(s) du personnel: 4
Membre: 44;

Fédération québécoise des directeurs et directrices d'établissements d'enseignement (FQDE)

#100, 7855, boul Louis-H-Lafontaine, Anjou QC H1K 4E4
Tél: 514-353-7511; *Téléc:* 514-353-2064
Ligne sans frais: 800-361-4258
info@fqde.qc.ca
www.fqde.qc.ca
twitter.com/fqde/

Aperçu: *Dimension:* moyenne; *Envergure:* provinciale; Organisme sans but lucratif; fondée en 1961
Mission: Défendre les droits des directeurs, directrices, directeurs adjoints, directrices adjointes d'établissements d'enseignement, sans oublier de promouvoir l'excellence dans la direction des établissements d'enseignement au Québec: en supportant des associations de directions d'établissement d'enseignement; en faisant en sorte que les directions d'établissement d'enseignement aient un environnement de travail favorisant la réalisation du projet éducatif; en s'assurant que les directions d'établissement d'enseignement maintiennent une compétence de gestionnaire de haute qualité.
Membre(s) du bureau directeur:
Marc Brunelle, Secrétaire
Chantal Longpré, Présidente
Finances: *Budget de fonctionnement annuel:* $500,000-$1.5 Million
Membre(s) du personnel: 10
Membre: 23 associations (2300 membres) + 1 association de 2430 retraités; *Montant de la cotisation:* 1% du traitement
Activités: *Service de conférenciers:* Oui

Fédération québécoise des échecs (FQE) / Québec Chess Federation

CP 1000, Succ. M, Montréal QC H1V 3R2
Tél: 514-252-3034; *Téléc:* 514-251-8038
info@fqechecs.qc.ca
www.fqechecs.qc.ca
www.facebook.com/eqechecs
twitter.com/fqechecs
Aperçu: *Dimension:* moyenne; *Envergure:* provinciale; Organisme sans but lucratif; fondée en 1967
Mission: Promouvoir l'étude, l'enseignement et la pratique du jeu d'échecs au Québec
Membre de: Regroupement Loisir-Québec
Membre(s) du bureau directeur:
Richard Bérubé, Directeur Général, 514-727-3133
dirgen@fqechecs.qc.ca
Finances: *Budget de fonctionnement annuel:* $100,000-$250,000
Membre(s) du personnel: 3; 7 bénévole(s)
Membre: 2 000 individu; 45 clubs; *Montant de la cotisation:* 45$ adulte; 35$ junior; 25$ cadet
Activités: Publication du Magazine Bimestriel Echec+Championnats Nationaux D'Echecs; *Service de conférenciers:* Oui

Fédération Québécoise des Intervenants en Sécurité Incendie (FQISI)

CP 40025, Granby QC J2G 9SI
Tél: 514-990-1338; *Téléc:* 514-666-9119
info@fqisi.org
www.fqisi.org
www.linkedin.com/company/fqisi—f-d-ration-qu-b-coise-des-intervenant
www.facebook.com/FQISI.org
Nom précédent: Association Québécoise des Pompiers Volontaires et Permanents
Aperçu: *Dimension:* moyenne; *Envergure:* provinciale; fondée en 1978
Mission: Aider à promouvoir la prévention des incendies; aider, soutenir et susciter des efforts en vue de réduire les pertes de vie; favoriser le perfectionnement en vue de combattre plus efficacement les incendies; promouvoir l'éducation populaire en général sur la protection et la prévention des incendies; faire des recommandations auprès des corps politiques et gouvernementaux
Membre(s) du bureau directeur:
Jocelyn Lussier, Président
president@fqisi.org
Alain Richard, Directeur Éxécutif
directeur.executif@fqisi.org
Membre(s) du personnel: 4
Membre: 500-999; *Montant de la cotisation:* Barème; *Critères d'admissibilite:* Actif, oeuvrant dans le domaine de la protection contre les incendies et ayant acquitté sa cotisation; *Comités:* Consultatif
Activités: *Stagiaires:* Oui; *Service de conférenciers:* Oui

Fédération québécoise des jeux récréatifs (FQJR)

4545, av Pierre-de Coubertin, Montréal QC H1V 0B2
Tél: 514-252-3032
info@quebecjeux.org
www.quebecjeux.org
www.facebook.com/355560369062
www.youtube.com/user/FQJRJeux
Aperçu: *Dimension:* moyenne; *Envergure:* provinciale; fondée en 1975
Mission: De promouvoir les sports de loisirs et jeux
Membre(s) du bureau directeur:
Dominic Robitaille, Président
Membre: 23 organismes; *Montant de la cotisation:* Barème

Fédération québécoise des laryngectomisés / Quebec Federation of Laryngectomees

5565, rue Sherbrooke est, Montréal QC H1N 1A2
Tél: 514-259-5113; *Téléc:* 514-259-8946
fqlar@fqlar.qc.ca
www.fqlar.qc.ca/index.htm
Nom précédent: Association des laryngectomisés de Montréal
Aperçu: *Dimension:* moyenne; *Envergure:* provinciale; Organisme sans but lucratif; fondée en 1979
Mission: Etre la voix de l'ensemble des personnes laryngectomisées, glossectomisées et trachéotomisées du Québec; assurer une meilleure connaissance des besoins particuliers de ces personnes et promouvoir la satisfaction de ces besoins
Affliation(s): Société canadienne du Cancer; International Association of Laryngectomy
Membre(s) du bureau directeur:
Lorne Germain, Président
Finances: *Budget de fonctionnement annuel:* $50,000-$100,000
Membre: 500-999; *Montant de la cotisation:* 5$; *Critères d'admissibilite:* Personne laryngectomisée, glossectomisée ou trachéotomisée; toute autre personne désireuse d'offrir son aide bénévole

Fédération québécoise des massothérapeutes (FQM)

#400, 4428, boul St-Laurent, Montréal QC H2W 1Z5
Tél: 514-597-0505; *Téléc:* 514-597-0141
Ligne sans frais: 800-363-9609
administration@fqm.qc.ca
www.fqm.qc.ca
www.facebook.com/massotherapie.FQM
twitter.com/FederationFQM
www.youtube.com/user/FQMmassotherapie
Aperçu: *Dimension:* moyenne; *Envergure:* provinciale; Organisme sans but lucratif; Organisme de réglementation; fondée en 1979
Mission: Regrouper les massothérapeutes afin de promouvoir la massothérapie sous l'intérêt public et de valoriser la profession de la massothérapie
Membre(s) du bureau directeur:
Sylvie Bédard, Directrice générale
sylvie.bedard@fqm.qc.ca
Finances: *Budget de fonctionnement annuel:* $500,000-$1.5 Million
Membre(s) du personnel: 11
Membre: 5 500; *Montant de la cotisation:* 240$; *Comités:* Discipline, inspection professionelle, syndic

Fédération Québécoise des Municipalités (FQM)

#560, 2954, boul Laurier, Sainte-Foy QC G1V 4T2
Tél: 418-651-3343; *Téléc:* 418-651-1127
Ligne sans frais: 866-951-3343
info@fqm.ca
www.fqm.ca
www.facebook.com/FQMenligne
twitter.com/fqmenligne
Nom précédent: Union des municipalités régionales de comté et des municipalités locales du Québec
Aperçu: *Dimension:* moyenne; *Envergure:* provinciale; fondée en 1944
Mission: Etre la porte-parole des régions; défendre les intérêts de ses membres
Membre(s) du bureau directeur:
Bernard Généreux, Président
Ann Bourget, Directrice générale
Membre: 1000 municipalités et presque la totalité des MRC; *Critères d'admissibilite:* Municipalites
Activités: *Service de conférenciers:* Oui

La Fédération québécoise des organismes communautaires Famille (FQOCF)

222, av Victoria, Saint-Lambert QC J4P 2H6
Tél: 450-466-2538; *Téléc:* 450-466-4196
Ligne sans frais: 866-982-9990
accueil@fqocf.org
www.fqocf.org
Nom précédent: Fédération des unions de familles inc.
Aperçu: *Dimension:* moyenne; *Envergure:* provinciale; fondée en 1961
Mission: Contribuer au développement d'une politique familiale; promouvoir le mieux-être des familles et la compétence parentale; soutenir les familles dans leur quotidien, leur réflexion et leurs actions; aider les familles à se regrouper; informer, assister et stimuler les groupes membres dans leurs initiatives
Membre de: Union internationale des organismes familiaux
Affliation(s): Institut Vanier de la Famille
Membre(s) du bureau directeur:
Louisane Côté, Directrice générale
Membre: 200; *Montant de la cotisation:* 200$; *Critères d'admissibilite:* Organismes communautaires famille
Activités: Représentation; animation; formation; carrefour d'échanges

Fédération québécoise des professeures et professeurs d'université (FQPPU) / Québec Federation of University Professors

#405, 4446, boul St-Laurent, Montréal QC H2W 1Z5
Tél: 514-843-5953; *Téléc:* 514-843-6928
Ligne sans frais: 888-843-5953
federation@fqppu.org
www.fqppu.org
Aperçu: *Dimension:* moyenne; *Envergure:* provinciale surveillé par Canadian Association of University Teachers
Mission: La Fédération québécoise des professeures et professeurs d'université (FQPPU) est un organisme à vocation politique dont la mission globale est d'ouvrer au maintien, à la défense, à la promotion et au développement de l'université comme service public et de défendre une université accessible et de qualité.
Membre de: Canadian Association of University Teachers
Membre(s) du bureau directeur:
Max Roy, Président
presidence@fqppu.org
Sylvain Beaudry, Secrétaire-trésorier
Sylvain_Beaudry@uqtr.ca

Fédération québécoise des revêtements de sol (FQRS)

#410, 7400, boul. Les Galeries d'Anjou, Anjou QC H1M 3M2
Tél: 514-355-8001; *Téléc:* 514-355-4159
fqrs@spg.qc.ca
www.fqrs.ca
Aperçu: *Dimension:* petite; *Envergure:* provinciale; Organisme sans but lucratif; fondée en 1960
Mission: Se consacrer en permanence et en exclusivité à la promotion et à la défense des intérêts professionnels et commerciaux se ses membres
Membre(s) du bureau directeur:
Jean-Marc Couture, Secrétaire-trésorier
Membre: *Montant de la cotisation:* Barème; *Critères d'admissibilite:* Entreprises dans le revêtement de sol
Activités: Tournois de golf; soirée Méritas; colloque; déjenner-causerie; *Service de conférenciers:* Oui

Fédération québécoise des revêtements de sol (FQRS) / Québec Institute of Floor Covering

#410, 7400 boul Les Galeries d'Anjou, Anjou QC H1M 3M2
Tél: 514-355-8001; *Téléc:* 514-355-4159
fqrs@spg.qc.ca
www.fqrs.ca
Nom précédent: Institut québécois des revêtements de sol inc.
Aperçu: *Dimension:* moyenne; *Envergure:* provinciale; fondée en 1972
Mission: Regrouper les gens de l'industrie des revêtements de sol pour les aider dans les différents domaines
Membre de: National Floor Covering Association
Membre(s) du bureau directeur:
Jacques Cloutier, Président
Membre(s) du personnel: 2
Membre: *Critères d'admissibilite:* Opérer dans l'industrie du couvre-planchers ou dans un secteur connexe

Fédération québécoise des sociétés Alzheimer (FQSA) / Federation of Québec Alzheimer Societies

#211, 5165, rue Sherbrooke ouest, Montréal QC H4A 1T6
Tél: 514-369-7891; *Téléc:* 514-369-7900
Ligne sans frais: 888-636-6473
info@alzheimerquebec.ca
www.alzheimerquebec.ca
Aperçu: *Dimension:* grande; *Envergure:* provinciale; Organisme sans but lucratif; fondée en 1985 surveillé par Alzheimer Society of Canada
Mission: Alléger les conséquences personnelles et sociales de la maladie d'Alzheimer; diffuser l'information auprès du public sur la maladie d'Alzheimer et sur les services offerts par notre réseau; soutenir les sociétés qui offrent aide et formation;

promouvoir et encourager la recherche sur la maladie d'Alzheimer entre autres par la gestion d'un fonds provincial de la recherche; établir des relations et faire des représentations auprès des autorités concernées
Membre(s) du bureau directeur:
Réal Leahey, Président
Finances: *Budget de fonctionnement annuel:* $100,000-$250,000
Membre(s) du personnel: 3; 4 bénévole(s)
Membre: 21; *Comités:* Hébergement; Levée de fonds; Normes et Standards; Recherche; Sensibilisation; Soutien aux Sociétés; Financement; Stratégie Alzheimer de Soins; Communications; Planification Stratégique
Activités: *Evénements de sensibilisation:* Mois de sensibilisation, jan.; *Bibliothèque:* Centre d'information; rendez-vous

Bas St-Laurent
Légion canadienne, 114, av St-Jérôme, Matane QC G4W 3A2
Tél: 418-562-2144; *Téléc:* 418-562-7449
Ligne sans frais: 877-446-2144
info@alzheimer-bsl.com
www.alzheimer-bsl.com
www.facebook.com/societealzheimer.bassaintlaurent
Membre(s) du bureau directeur:
Denis Bond, Président

Centre du Québec
880, rue Côté, St-Charles-de-Drummond QC J2C 4Z7
Tél: 819-474-3666; *Téléc:* 819-474-3133
myosotis@aide-internet.org
www.alzheimer-centre-du-quebec.org
Membre(s) du bureau directeur:
Nagui Habashi, Directeur général

Chaudière-Appalaches
CP 1, 440, boul Vachon Sud, Sainte-Marie QC G6E 3B4
Tél: 418-387-1230; *Téléc:* 418-387-1360
Ligne sans frais: 888-387-1230
sachap@globetrotter.net
www.alzheimerchap.qc.ca
Membre(s) du bureau directeur:
Sonia Nadeau, Directrice générale

Côte-Nord
373, av Jolliet, Sept-Iles QC G4R 2B1
Tél: 418-968-4673; *Téléc:* 418-962-4161
Ligne sans frais: 866-366-4673
sacotenord@globetrotter.net

Estrie
#112, 740, rue Galt Ouest, Sherbrooke QC J1H 1Z3
Tél: 819-821-5127; *Téléc:* 819-820-8649
info@alzheimerestrie.com
www.alzheimerestrie.com
www.facebook.com/saeestrie
twitter.com/AlzheimerEstrie
Membre(s) du bureau directeur:
Caroline Giguère, Directrice générale
carolinegiguere@alzheimerestrie.com

Gaspésie/Iles-De-La-Madeleine
114C, av Grand-Pré, Bonaventure QC G0C 1E0
Tel: 418-534-1313; *Fax:* 418-534-1312
www.alzheimer.ca/fr/gim
Membre(s) du bureau directeur:
Bernard Babin, Directeur général
bernard.sagim@navigue.com

Granby et Région
#3, 356, rue Principale, Granby QC J2G 2W6
Tél: 450-777-3363; *Téléc:* 450-777-8677
sagrinfo@videotron.ca
www.alzheimergranby.ca

Haut-Richelieu
#2, 125, Jacques Cartier nord, Saint-Jean-sur-Richelieu QC J3B 8C9
Tél: 450-347-5500; *Téléc:* 450-347-7370
info@sahr.ca
www.sahr.ca

Lanaudière
190, rue Montcalm, Joliette QC J6E 5G4
Tél: 450-759-3057; *Téléc:* 450-760-2633
Ligne sans frais: 877-759-3077
info@sadl.org
www.sadl.org
www.facebook.com/alzheimerlanaudiere
Membre(s) du bureau directeur:
Janie Duval, Directrice générale

Laurentides
CP 276, #100, 31, rue Principale, Sainte-Agathe-des-Monts QC J8C 3A3
Tél: 819-326-7136; *Téléc:* 819-326-9664
Ligne sans frais: 800-978-7881
admin@salaurentides.ca
www.alzheimerlaurentides.com
www.facebook.com/361627480558344
Membre(s) du bureau directeur:
Catherine Vaudry, Directrice générale
direction@salaurentides.ca

Laval
2525, boul. René-Laennec, Laval QC H7K 0B2
Tél: 450-629-0966; *Téléc:* 450-975-0517
info@alzheimerlaval.org
www.alzheimerlaval.ca
Membre(s) du bureau directeur:
Lise Lalande, Directrice générale
llalande@alzheimerlaval.org

Maskoutains-Vallée des Patriotes
650, rue Girouard Est, Saint-Hyacinthe QC J2S 2Y2
Tél: 450-768-6616; *Téléc:* 450-768-3716
info@alzheimermvp.com
www.alzheimermvp.com
www.facebook.com/alzheimer.mvp
Membre(s) du bureau directeur:
Flore Barrière, Directrice générale

MRC de La Matapédia
123 Desbiens, Amqui QC G5J 3P9
Tél: 418-629-6200
www.alzheimerquebec.ca/indexEn.asp?numero=99&numero2=16
www.facebook.com/group.php?gid=21548021978
Membre(s) du bureau directeur:
Réal Leahey, Président
Lisette Joly, Vice-Présidente

Outaouais québécois
380, boul St-Raymond, Gatineau QC J9A 1V9
Tél: 819-777-4232; *Téléc:* 819-777-0728
Ligne sans frais: 877-777-0888
saoq@saoq.org
www.saoq.org
www.linkedin.com/company/1079874
www.facebook.com/saoq.org
twitter.com/AlzOutaouais
www.youtube.com/channel/UC1rMYxu-ZqK6FTGwHRJ4ecQ
Membre(s) du bureau directeur:
Marie-Josée Williams, Directrice
mjwilliams@saoq.org

Québec
#312, 1040, av Belvédère, Québec QC G1S 3G3
Tél: 418-527-4294; *Téléc:* 418-527-9966
Ligne sans frais: 866-350-4294
info@societealzheimerdequebec.com
www.societealzheimerdequebec.com
www.facebook.com/311740120513
Membre(s) du bureau directeur:
Hélène Thibault, Directrice générale

Rive-Sud
1160, boul Nobert, Longueuil QC J4K 2P1
Tél: 450-442-3333; *Téléc:* 450-442-9271
info@alzheimerrivesud.ca
www.alzheimerrivesud.ca
Membre(s) du bureau directeur:
Geneviève Grégoire, Directrice générale
ggregoire@alzheimerrivesud.ca

Rouyn-Noranda
CP 336, 58, Monseigneur Tessier Est, Rouyn-Noranda QC J9X 5C3
Tél: 819-764-3554; *Téléc:* 819-764-3534
sarn@cablevision.qc.ca

Sagamie
1657, av du Pont Nord, Alma QC G8B 5G2
Tél: 418-668-0161; *Téléc:* 418-668-2639
alzheimersag@bellnet.ca
www.alzheimersagamie.com
Membre(s) du bureau directeur:
Josée Pearson, Coordonnatrice régionale

Société Alzheimer Society Montréal
#410, 5165, rue Sherbrooke ouest, Montréal QC H4A 1T6
Tél: 514-369-0800; *Téléc:* 514-369-4103
info@alzheimermontreal.ca
www.alzheimer.ca/montreal
www.facebook.com/Montreal.Alzheimer
twitter.com/AlzMtl
www.youtube.com/user/montrealalzheimer
Membre(s) du bureau directeur:
Gérald Hubert, Directeur général
ghubert@alzheimermontreal.ca

Suroît
#101, 340, boul du Havre, Salaberry-de-Valleyfield QC J6S 1S6
Tél: 450-373-0303; *Téléc:* 450-373-0388
Ligne sans frais: 877-773-0303
info@alzheimersuroit.com
www.alzheimersuroit.com
Membre(s) du bureau directeur:
Ian Worthington, Président

Val d'or
734, 4e Ave., Val-d'Or QC J9P 1J2
Tél: 819-825-7444; *Téléc:* 819-825-7448
sco.alz.valdor@tlb.sympatico.ca

Fédération québécoise des sociétés de généalogie (FQSG)

CP 9454, Succ. Sainte-Foy, 1055, av du Séminaire, Québec QC G1V 4B8
Tél: 418-653-3940; *Téléc:* 418-653-3940
federationgenealogie@bellnet.ca
www.federationgenealogie.qc.ca
Aperçu: *Dimension:* moyenne; *Envergure:* provinciale; Organisme sans but lucratif; fondée en 1984
Mission: Représenter les sociétés de généalogie locales et régionales; la promotion et l'épanouissement de la généalogie au Québec et son rayonnement à l'étranger sont les buts visés
Membre de: Confédération internationale de généalogie et d'héraldique
Membre(s) du bureau directeur:
Albert J. Cyr, Président
Finances: *Budget de fonctionnement annuel:* $50,000-$100,000; *Fonds:* Ministère de la Culture et des Communications
Membre(s) du personnel: 2; 9 bénévole(s)
Membre: 54 sociétés; *Montant de la cotisation:* Barème; *Critères d'admissibilite:* Tout organisme de généalogie sans but lucratif dont le siège social est situé sur le territoire du Québec ou à l'extérieur; *Comités:* Portail; Attestation de compétence; CISGH 2008
Prix, Bouses:
- Le prix Septentrion (Prix)
- Le prix Cyprien-Tanguay (Prix)
- Le prix Jeunéalogie (Prix)

Fédération québécoise des sports cyclistes (FQSC) / Québec Cycling Sports Federation

4545, av Pierre-de Coubertin, Montréal QC H1V 3R2
Tél: 514-252-3071; *Téléc:* 514-252-3165
info@fqsc.net
www.fqsc.net
www.facebook.com/176077399110320
Nom précédent: Fédération cycliste du Québec
Aperçu: *Dimension:* moyenne; *Envergure:* provinciale; Organisme sans but lucratif; fondée en 1971 surveillé par Cycling Canada Cyclisme
Mission: Régie et promotion des sports cyclistes au Québec
Membre de: Cycling Canada Cyclisme
Affliation(s): Union cycliste internationale; Sports-Québec; Regroupement loisir Québec
Membre(s) du bureau directeur:
Louis Barbeau, Directeur général
lbarbeau@fqsc.net
Bruno Vachon, Directeur technique, Hors-Route
bvachon@fqsc.net
Finances: *Budget de fonctionnement annuel:* $500,000-$1.5 Million
Membre(s) du personnel: 5; 57 bénévole(s)
Membre: 5 000 individus; 150 clubs; *Montant de la cotisation:* 10-130
Activités: Temple de la Renommée du Cyclisme Québécois; mérite cycliste québécois; *Bibliothèque*

Fédération québécoise du canot camping inc *Voir* Fédération québécoise du canot et du kayak

Fédération québécoise du canot et du kayak (FQCK)

CP 1000, Succ. M, 4545, av Pierre-de Coubertin, Montréal QC H1V 3R2
Tél: 514-252-3001; *Téléc:* 514-252-3091
info@canot-kayak.qc.ca

www.canot-kayak.qc.ca
www.facebook.com/group.php?gid=254842564559812
Nom précédent: Fédération québécoise du canot camping inc
Aperçu: *Dimension:* moyenne; *Envergure:* provinciale; Organisme sans but lucratif; fondée en 1976
Mission: Regrouper les organismes et individus intéressés à la pratique du canotage récréatif et du canot-camping et de promouvoir la pratique de ces activités en utilisant le canot ouvert de type amérindien autrement appelé Canot Canadien
Membre(s) du bureau directeur:
Philippe Pelland, Directeur général
ppelland@canot-kayak.qc.ca
Jean A. Plamondon, Président
Bernard Hugonnier, Directeur, Technique
bhugonnier@canot-kayak.qc.ca
Émilie Bisson, Agent, Information et aux communications
ebisson@canot-kayak.qc.ca
15 bénévole(s)
Membre: 4 000; *Montant de la cotisation:* 40$; *Comités:* Cartographie; Formation
Activités: *Stagiaires:* Oui; *Service de conférenciers:* Oui

Fédération québécoise du cerf-volant (FQCV)
a/s Fédération québécoise des jeux récréatifs, CP 1000, Succ. M, 4545, av Pierre-de Coubertin, Montréal QC H1V 3R2
Tél: 514-252-3032; *Téléc:* 514-251-8038
info@fqcv.org
www.fqcv.org
Aperçu: *Dimension:* moyenne; *Envergure:* provinciale; Organisme sans but lucratif; fondée en 1983
Mission: Former un regroupement de membres; favoriser le développement, la création, la fabrication et l'utilisation des cerfs-volants; informer et éduquer membres et public; organiser des activités; encourager et favoriser la recherche et l'évolution du cerf-volant; normaliser la pratique; proposer une réglementation appropriée aux autorités compétentes
Affiliation(s): Fédération québécoise des jeux récréatifs; American Kiteliers Association
Finances: *Budget de fonctionnement annuel:* Moins de $50,000
6 bénévole(s)
Membre: 5 institutionnel; 300 individu; 6 corporatif; *Montant de la cotisation:* 10$ étudiant; 20$ individu; 35$ corporatif
Activités: Festivals

La Fédération Québécoise du Cricket Inc. / The Quebec Cricket Federation Inc. (QCF)
7037, boul Acadie, Montréal QC H3N 2V5
www.cricketstar.net/qcf
Aperçu: *Dimension:* petite; *Envergure:* provinciale surveillé par Cricket Canada
Membre de: Cricket Canada
Membre(s) du bureau directeur:
Charles Pais, President
charles_pais@hotmail.com
Dalip Kirpaul, Secretary
dalip@hotmail.com
Membre: *Comités:* School Program; Umpiring Association; Disciplinary; Senior Selection; Junior Selection; Umpiring Co-ordinator; Statisticians; Development Co-ordinators; Publication; Woman Co-ordinator

Fédération québécoise du loisir littéraire (FQLL)
CP 1000, Succ. M, 4545, av Pierre-de Coubertin, Montréal QC H1V 3R2
Tél: 514-252-3033
Ligne sans frais: 866-533-3755
www.litteraire.ca
Nom précédent: Loisir littéraire du Québec
Aperçu: *Dimension:* moyenne; *Envergure:* provinciale; Organisme sans but lucratif; fondée en 1962
Mission: Offre au grand public l'accès à toutes les formes de l'expression littéraire et artistique dans un contexte de loisir, d'éducation et de perfectionnement
Membre(s) du bureau directeur:
Diane Robert, Présidente
Finances: *Budget de fonctionnement annuel:* Moins de $50,000
Membre(s) du personnel: 2; 5 bénévole(s)
Membre: 700; *Montant de la cotisation:* 40$ individuel, 25$ étudiant, 35$ âge d'or, 50$ corporatif
Activités: Ateliers pour lire, dire et écrire, concours littéraire annuel, soirées de lecture; *Événements de sensibilisation:* Je vous entends écrire - spectacle littéraire annuel; *Service de conférenciers:* Oui

Fédération québécoise du scoutisme *Voir* Association des Scouts du Canada

Fédération québécoise du sport étudiant *Voir* Réseau du sport étudiant du Québec

Fédération québécoise du théâtre amateur (FQTA)
CP 211, Succ. Saint-Élie-d'Orford, Sherbrooke QC J1R 1A1
Tél: 819-571-9358
Ligne sans frais: 877-752-2501
info@fqta.ca
www.fqta.ca
Nom précédent: Association québécoise du théâtre amateur inc.
Aperçu: *Dimension:* petite; *Envergure:* provinciale; Organisme sans but lucratif; fondée en 1958
Mission: Promouvoir le théâtre amateur en réunissant tous les individus et les groupes de théâtre pour contribuer à l'éducation artistique, esthétique et sociale de la population; établir un contact permanent entre les individus; fournir des occasions d'échange, de travaux, de recherches, de méthodes, de matériel et d'information ayant trait au théâtre
Membre de: Association Internationale du Théâtre Amateur; Conseil québécois du loisir; Regroupement Loisir Québec; Théâtre Canada
Affiliation(s): Académie théâtrale l'Envol de Laval; AQAD; Art Neuf; Cabotins de Thetford Mines; Café-Théâtre de Chambly; Catherine Chevrot; CEAD - Centre des auteurs dramatiques; Frasqc Productions; Collège Notre-Dame-de-Lourdes; Commission Scolaire du Lac-Témiscamingue; Compagnie de théâtre Sauvageau; Corporation Les Amis de la musique de Richmond et Festival de Richmond; CQL - Conseil Québécois du loisir; Double Défi; École Nationale de théâtre du Canada; Festival de Richmond & Les Amis de la Musique de Richmond; Festival de théâtre amateur Esprit-Saint; Festival des Molières; Groupe de la Veillée
Membre(s) du bureau directeur:
Yoland Roy, Directeur général
Membre: 86; *Critères d'admissibilite:* Troupe et individus
Activités: Concours création-production-théâtre; festival international de théâtre amateur; *Événements de sensibilisation:* Concours Création-Production-Théâtre, 25 juin; *Bibliothèque* Bibliothèque publique

Fédération québécoise pour le saumon atlantique (FQSA)
42B, rue Racine, Québec QC G2B 1C6
Tél: 418-847-9191; *Téléc:* 418-847-9279
Ligne sans frais: 888-847-9191
secretariat@saumon-fqsa.qc.ca
www.FQSA.ca
www.facebook.com/85717316801?fref=ts
twitter.com/SaumonFQSA
instagram.com/fqsa_saumon
Aperçu: *Dimension:* moyenne; *Envergure:* provinciale; fondée en 1984 surveillé par Atlantic Salmon Federation
Mission: Organisme à but non lucratif dont la raison d'être est d'unir et de représenter les intérêts de l'ensemble des saumoniers du Québec
Membre(s) du bureau directeur:
Michel Jean, Directeur général
mjean@saumon-fqsa.qc.ca
Membre: 1 000; *Montant de la cotisation:* 40$
Activités: *Service de conférenciers:* Oui

La fédération sioniste canadienne *See* Canadian Zionist Federation

Fédération ski nautique et planche Québec
CP 1000, Succ. M, 4545, av Pierre-de Coubertin, Montréal QC H1V 3R2
Tél: 514-252-3092; *Téléc:* 514-252-3186
info@skinautiqueetplanchequebec.qc.ca
www.skinautiqueetplanchequebec.qc.ca
Aperçu: *Dimension:* petite; *Envergure:* provinciale
Membre(s) du bureau directeur:
Louis Simard, Président
Membre: 600; *Montant de la cotisation:* 45$ individuelle; 70$ familiale

Fédération sportive de ringuette du Québec
4545, av Pierre-de Coubertin, Montréal QC H1V 3R2
Tél: 514-252-3085; *Téléc:* 514-254-1069
ringuette@ringuette-quebec.qc.ca
www.ringuette-quebec.qc.ca
Aperçu: *Dimension:* petite; *Envergure:* provinciale; fondée en 1973
Mission: Promouvoir le sport de la ringuette au Québec
Membre de: Ringuette-Canada
Membre(s) du bureau directeur:
Florent Gravel, Président
florent.gravel@ringuette-quebec.qc.ca
Membre(s) du personnel: 3

Fédération vietnamienne du Canada *See* Vietnamese Canadian Federation

Fédérations de l'UPA de Lévis Bellechasse, Rive Nord, Lotbinière-Mégantic
5185, rue Rideau, Québec QC G2E 5H5
Tél: 418-872-0770; *Téléc:* 418-872-3386
Aperçu: *Dimension:* petite; *Envergure:* locale; fondée en 1924
Mission: Défendre l'intérêt des membres auprès des corps publics; négociation collective pour obtenir de meilleurs prix pour les produits; gestion d'organismes de producteurs
Affiliation(s): Confédération de l'U.P.A.
Membre(s) du bureau directeur:
Luce Bisson, Présidente
Finances: *Budget de fonctionnement annuel:* $3 Million-$5 Million
Membre(s) du personnel: 64
Membre: 6 500; *Montant de la cotisation:* 281,81$; *Critères d'admissibilite:* Productrice ou producteur agricole
Activités: *Listes de destinataires:* Oui

Feed Nova Scotia (FNS)
213 Bedford Hwy., Halifax NS B3M 2J9
Tel: 902-457-1900; *Fax:* 902-457-4500
communications@feednovascotia.ca
www.feednovascotia.ca
www.facebook.com/feednovascotia
twitter.com/feednovascotia
www.youtube.com/user/feednovascotia
Also Known As: Metro Food Bank Society-Nova Scotia
Previous Name: Metro Food Bank Society
Overview: A small provincial charitable organization founded in 1984
Mission: To help feed the hungry by collecting & distributing food.
Member of: Canadian Association of Food Banks
Chief Officer(s):
Paul Kidston, Chair
Dianne Swinemar, Executive Director
dswinemar@feednovascotia.ca
Membership: 150+; *Member Profile:* Food banks; shelters; soup kitchens
Activities: Client support services; food distribution; job training for the food industry; *Awareness Events:* Hunger Awareness Week, June; *Internships:* Yes; *Speaker Service:* Yes; *Library* by appointment
Publications:
• Foodchain
Type: Newsletter; *Frequency:* Monthly

FEESA - An Environmental Education Society *See* Inside Education

Fellowship of Evangelical Baptist Churches in Canada
PO Box 457, 351 Elizabeth St., Guelph ON N1H 6K9
Tel: 519-821-4830; *Fax:* 519-821-9829
www.fellowship.ca
Also Known As: The Fellowship
Overview: A large national organization
Mission: To glorify God & to proclaim the good news of Jesus Christ, evangelizing our generation & producing healthy, growing churches in Canada & around the world
Member of: The Evangelical Fellowship of Canada
Affliation(s): Association d'églises baptistes évangéliques au québec
Chief Officer(s):
Steven Jones, President, 519-821-4830 Ext. 231
sjones@fellowship.ca
Finances: *Annual Operating Budget:* Greater than $5 Million
Staff Member(s): 16
Membership: 500+ churches
Activities: *Library:* Archives;

FEB Central
175 Holiday Inn Dr., Cambridge ON N3C 3T2
Tel: 519-654-9555; *Fax:* 519-654-9991
admin@febcentral.ca
www.febcentral.ca
www.facebook.com/febcentral
Chief Officer(s):
Ed F. Fontaine, Chair, 905-887-5651
edfontaine@springvale.ca

Bob Flemming, Regional Director, 519-591-7756
bob@febcentral.ca

Fellowship Atlantic
39 Olive Ave., Bedford NS B4B 1C7
Tel: 902-482-4132; *Fax:* 902-482-4669
www.fellowshipatlantic.com
Chief Officer(s):
Glenn Goode, Regional Director
gagoode@gmail.com
• Fellowship Atlantic Newsletter
Type: Newsletter; *Frequency:* Weekly

Fellowship Pacific
PO Box 1107, 9111 Church St., Fort Langley BC V1M 2S4
Tel: 778-298-8887; *Fax:* 866-888-1670
fellowship@shaw.ca
www.bcfellowship.ca
Chief Officer(s):
Colin Van der Vuur, Church Planting Director
colin.fellowship@shaw.ca

Fellowship Prairies
Taylor College Seminary, Benke Hall, Room 207/208, PO Box 168, 11525 - 23 Ave., Edmonton AB T6J 4T3
Tel: 780-451-4878; *Fax:* 780-436-4871
www.fellowshipprairies.ca
Chief Officer(s):
Laurie Kennedy, Regional Director
febcastrd@shaw.ca

Feminine Association for Education & Social Action *Voir* Association féminine d'éducation et d'action sociale

Femmes autochtones du Québec inc. (FAQ) / Québec Native Women Inc.
CP 1989, Kahnawake QC J0L 1B0
Tél: 450-632-0088; *Téléc:* 450-632-9280
info@faq-qnw.org
www.faq-qnw.org
www.facebook.com/FAQQNW
twitter.com/FAQQNW
vimeo.com/user14258370
Aperçu: *Dimension:* moyenne; *Envergure:* provinciale; Organisme sans but lucratif; fondée en 1974 surveillé par Native Women's Association of Canada
Mission: Appuyer les efforts des femmes autochtones pour l'amélioration de leurs conditions de vie par la promotion de la non-violence, de la justice et de l'égalité des droits et de les soutenir dans leur engagement au sein de leur communauté.
Membre(s) du bureau directeur:
Aurelie Arnaud, Contact, Médias
communication@faq-qnw.org
Activités: *Bibliothèque:* Centre de Documentation; Bibliothèque publique rendez-vous

Les femmes sur les marchés financiers *See* Women in Capital Markets

Fencing - Escrime New Brunswick (FENB)
c/o Mark Dobson, 20 Branch Cres., Quispamsis NB E2E 0A9
Tel: 506-847-4204
www.fencingnb.ca
Previous Name: New Brunswick Fencing Association
Overview: A small provincial organization overseen by Canadian Fencing Federation
Mission: To promote & develop the sport of fencing in New Brunswick
Member of: Canadian Fencing Federation; Sport New Brunswick
Chief Officer(s):
Diane Raiche-Phillips, President
Mark Dobson, Membership Registrar
dobsonmarkr@yahoo.ca
Membership: *Fees:* $20 associate; $25 first-time member; $60 fencing member

Fencing Association of Nova Scotia (FANS) / Association d'escrime de la Nouvelle-Écosse
c/o Sport Nova Scotia, 5516 Spring Garden Rd., 4th Fl., Halifax NS B3J 3G6
Fax: 902-425-5606
www.chebucto.ns.ca/SportFit/Fencing
www.facebook.com/246284375433922
Overview: A small provincial organization overseen by Canadian Fencing Federation
Mission: To develop & promote the sport of fencing in Nova Scotia
Member of: Canadian Fencing Federation
Chief Officer(s):
DeAnna Paul, President
drpaul@hotmail.ca
Trudy Sangster, Treasurer, 902-457-1309
20tlsangster@auracom.com
Derek McPhee, Registrar
dmcphee@ns.sympatico.ca
Membership: *Member Profile:* National fencing competitors; Provincial fencing competitors; Recreational fencers; Persons who wish to promote fencing
Activities: Providing information about tournaments

Fenelon Falls & District Chamber of Commerce
PO Box 28, 15 Oak St., Fenelon Falls ON K0M 1N0
Tel: 705-887-3409; *Fax:* 705-887-6912
info@fenelonfallschamber.com
www.fenelonfallschamber.com
twitter.com/ffdchamber
Previous Name: Fenelon Falls North Kawartha District Chamber of Commerce
Overview: A small local organization founded in 1956
Mission: To promote economic confidence for the business community; To attract people to live & play in the area on a year-round basis by providing products, programs, events, & services for the benefit of members, visitors & residents
Member of: Ontario Chamber of Commerce
Chief Officer(s):
Chris Handley, President
Finances: *Annual Operating Budget:* Less than $50,000; *Funding Sources:* Membership dues; home show
Staff Member(s): 1; 8 volunteer(s)
Membership: 113; *Fees:* $56.50 associate; $137.70 regular

Fenelon Falls North Kawartha District Chamber of Commerce *See* Fenelon Falls & District Chamber of Commerce

Fenelon Falls Stamp Club
Fenlon Falls ON
Tel: 705-324-7577
Overview: A small local organization founded in 1985
Mission: To promote the study and interest in philately in Fenelon Falls.
Member of: Royal Philatelic Society of Canada
Chief Officer(s):
Lloyd McEwan, President
lmccewan@sympatico.ca
Activities: Meetings 2nd Monday, every month; *Speaker Service:* Yes

Fenestration Association of BC (FEN-BC)
#101, 20351 Duncan Way, Langley BC V3A 7N3
Tel: 778-571-0245; *Fax:* 866-253-9979
info@fen-bc.org
www.fen-bc.org
www.facebook.com/pages/Fen-Bc/561853500522221?ref=ts&fref=ts
twitter.com/fenbc
www.youtube.com/user/FenBC?feature=mhee
Merged from: Glazing Contractors Association of BC (GCABC); Window and Door Manufacturers Association of BC
Overview: A medium-sized provincial organization
Mission: A nonprofit trade association representing the interests of businesses engaged in the fenestration industry in BC.
Chief Officer(s):
Zana Gordon, Executive Director, 604-855-0245
zgordon@fen-bc.org
Membership: *Member Profile:* Western Canadian companies involved with the fenestration industry.; *Committees:* Marketing; Membership; Technical
Meetings/Conferences: • Fenestration West Annual Conference 2015, 2015, BC
Scope: Provincial
Publications:
• Fenestration West Magazine
Type: Magazine; *Frequency:* Quarterly

Fenestration Canada
#1208, 130 Albert St., Ottawa ON K1P 5G4
Tel: 613-235-5511; *Fax:* 613-235-4664
info@fenestrationcanada.ca
www.fenestrationcanada.ca
Previous Name: Canadian Window & Door Manufacturers Association
Overview: A medium-sized national organization founded in 1967
Mission: To represents its members in all aspects of the window & door manufacturing industry, including formulating & promoting high standards of quality in manufacturing, design, marketing, distribution, sales, & application of all types of window & door products
Chief Officer(s):
Yvan Banman, President
yhoule@portesetfenetrepresident.com
Eva Ryterband, Treasurer
eva@screenco.ca
Membership: 150+; *Fees:* Schedule available; *Member Profile:* Manufacturers of all types & classes of window & door products; Suppliers of raw materials & processing machinery; Research & testing facilities; *Committees:* Win-Door Show; Membership & Marketing; Meetings; Technical; Government Relations; Education
Activities: Representing industry views to the federal & provincial governments & crown corporations; Scheduling meetings, activities, plant tours, & discussions encouraging a healthy exchange of ideas on product & marketing strategies; Providing information on the industry, government regulations, building codes, & standards; Distributing newsletters, special bulletins & memos to keep members aware of the latest developments facing the industry & the association
Meetings/Conferences: • Fenestration Canada's 2015 Annual General Meeting, June, 2015, Fairmont Hotel Vancouver, Vancouver, BC
Scope: National
Description: A business meeting to keep current with industry trends & opportunities
• Win-Door North America 2015 (an event owned & produced by Fenestration Canada), November, 2015, Metro Toronto Convention Centre, Toronto, ON
Scope: International
Attendance: 3,500+
Description: Meetings, demonstrations, & seminars, plus an opportunity for suppliers to show their products & services to manufacturers & fabricators from across Canada, the United States, & international destinations
• Win-Door North America 2016 (an event owned & produced by Fenestration Canada), 2016
Scope: International
Description: Meetings, demonstrations, & seminars, plus an opportunity for suppliers to show their products & services to manufacturers & fabricators from across Canada, the United States, & international destinations

Fernie & District Arts Council (FDAC)
PO Box 1453, 601 - 1 Ave., Fernie BC V0B 1M0
Tel: 250-423-4842; *Fax:* 250-423-4842
info@theartsstation.com
www.theartsstation.com
www.facebook.com/45966352567
twitter.com/artsstation
vimeo.com/ferniearts
Also Known As: The Arts Station
Overview: A small local charitable organization founded in 1973
Mission: To encourage appreciation of the arts & artistic expression throughout community
Member of: Assembly of BC Arts Councils; Fernie Chamber of Commerce; Tourism Fernie
Affliation(s): Cultural Network of the Rockies; Columbia Kootenay Cultural Alliance
Chief Officer(s):
Courtney Baker, Administrator, 250-423-4842, Fax: 450-423-4842
info@theartsstation.com
Finances: *Annual Operating Budget:* $100,000-$250,000; *Funding Sources:* Municipal, provincial & federal government; Private
Staff Member(s): 2; 300 volunteer(s)
Membership: 300+; *Fees:* $35 adult; $15 youth; $20 Senior; *Member Profile:* Artists; crafts people; businesses; *Committees:* Gallery; Concert; Garden; Film; Volunteer; Human Resources; Strategic Planning; Programming
Activities: Creative workshops; Concerts; Plays; Children's art camps; Rental spaces available; Film festivals; *Internships:* Yes

Fernie & District Historical Society
PO Box 1527, Fernie BC V0B 1M0
Tel: 250-423-7016
www.ferniemuseum.com
Overview: A small local organization founded in 1964
Mission: To preserve & present the history of Fernie by collecting & displaying photographs, artifacts & documents relating to the town's development.
Membership: *Fees:* $10 individual; $15 family

Publications:
• Fernie, A Celebration of 100 Years
Type: book; *Price:* $31

Fernie Chamber of Commerce

102 Commerce Rd., Fernie BC V0B 1M5
Tel: 250-423-6868; *Fax:* 250-423-3811
Toll-Free: 877-433-7643
office@ferniechamber.com
www.ferniechamber.com
twitter.com/FernieChamber
Overview: A small local organization founded in 1902
Mission: To promote & improve the economy & the social quality of life in Fernie & area
Member of: Canadian Chamber of Commerce; BC Chamber of Commerce
Affliation(s): Economic Development Association of BC
Chief Officer(s):
Todd Fyle, President
Sarah Perry, Executive Director
Finances: *Annual Operating Budget:* $100,000-$250,000; *Funding Sources:* Membership dues; fee-for-service contracts
Staff Member(s): 2; 25 volunteer(s)
Membership: 300; *Fees:* $100 home-based business; $125 non-profit; $45 individual; $162-$375 business
Activities: Visitor information centre; economic development centre; commercial info; marketing; tourism promotions; events coordination; *Library:* Business Information Centre; Open to public

Fertilizer Safety & Security Council (FSSC) / Conseil de la sécurité en fertilisation (CSF)

#907, 350 Sparks St., Ottawa ON K1N 7S8
Tel: 613-230-2600
info@fssc.ca
www.fssc.ca
Overview: A small national organization founded in 2003
Mission: To promote the safe and secure manufacturing, handling, storage, transportation and application of commercial fertilizers thereby protecting employees, transportation workers, first responders, farmers and the general public from risk due to accidental release, environmental emergency, or criminal misuse of fertilizer products.
Chief Officer(s):
Giulia Brutesco, Director, Scientific & Regulatory Affairs
gbrutesco@cfi.ca

Festival Chorus of Calgary

EPCOR Centre for Performing Arts, 205 - 8 Ave. SE, Calgary AB T2G 0K9
Tel: 403-294-7400
info@festivalchorus.ca
www.festivalchorus.ca
www.facebook.com/182865794560
Overview: A small local charitable organization founded in 1959
Mission: To present two concerts per year for the Marblehead community
Chief Officer(s):
Mel Kirby, Artistic Director
artisticdirector@festivalchorus.ca
Finances: *Funding Sources:* Private & corporate donations; ticket sales; membership fees; government grants
Membership: 80
Activities: *Internships:* Yes

Festival d'été de Québec / Québec City Summer Festival

#150, 683, rue Saint-Joseph est, Québec QC G1K 3C1
Tél: 418-523-4540; *Téléc:* 418-523-0194
Ligne sans frais: 888-992-5200
infofestival@infofestival.com
www.infofestival.com
www.facebook.com/FestivaldetedeQuebec
twitter.com/FestivalEteQc
www.youtube.com/user/infofestival;
www.flickr.com/photos/infofestival
Aperçu: *Dimension:* petite; *Envergure:* locale; fondée en 1968
Membre(s) du bureau directeur:
Nancy Florence Savard, Présidente
Gélinas Daniel, Directeur général
Prix, Bouses:
• Prix Miroir (Prix)

Festival de concours du Québec *See* Québec Competitive Festival of Music

Festivals & Events Ontario (FEO)

#301, 5 Graham St., Woodstock ON N4S 6J5
Tel: 519-537-2226; *Fax:* 519-537-2226
info@festivalsandeventsontario.ca
www.festivalsandeventsontario.ca
www.facebook.com/FestivalsandEventsOntario
twitter.com/FEOntario
Overview: A small provincial organization founded in 1987
Mission: Festivals & Events Ontario (FEO) is an association devoted to the growth and stability of the festival and event industry in Ontario. FEO provides festival and event organizers across the province with a networking forum offering professional development opportunities and resources aimed to encourage professionalism and excellence in the delivery of festivals and special events.
Chief Officer(s):
Debbie Mann, Interim Executive Director
debbie@festivalsandeventsontario.ca
Martha Cookson, Administrative Coordinator
martha@festivalsandeventsontario.ca
Staff Member(s): 4
Meetings/Conferences: • Festivals & Events Ontario 2015 Conference, March, 2015, Sheraton on the Falls, Niagara Falls, ON
Scope: Provincial
Contact Information: URL: www.feo2015.com

Festivals et Événements Québec (FEQ)

CP 1000, Succ. M, 4545, av Pierre-de Coubertin, Montréal QC H1V 3R2
Tél: 514-252-3037; *Téléc:* 514-254-1617
Ligne sans frais: 800-361-7688
info@satqfeq.com
www.evenementsquebec.qc.ca
Également appelé: Société des fêtes et festivals du Québec
Aperçu: *Dimension:* moyenne; *Envergure:* provinciale; fondée en 1976
Mission: Regrouper les fêtes, festivals et événements, de les promouvoir et de leur offrir des services qui favorisent leur développement
Membre de: Regroupement Loisir Québec
Affliation(s): International Festivals Association
Membre(s) du bureau directeur:
Pierre-Paul Leduc, Directeur general
Luc Martineau, Directeur marketing
Sylvain Martineau, Dir. Ventes
Lyne Voyer, Dir. Communications
Sylvie Theberge, Dir. Services Membres
Robert Aucoin, Dir. recherche
Claude Latour, Dir. web
Finances: *Budget de fonctionnement annuel:* $500,000-$1.5 Million
Membre(s) du personnel: 4; 15 bénévole(s)
Membre: 248; *Montant de la cotisation:* 305-950
Activités: *Listes de destinataires:* Oui

Fibromyalgia Association of Saskatchewan (FMAS)

PO Box 7525, Saskatoon SK S7K 4L4
Tel: 306-343-3627
Overview: A small provincial charitable organization founded in 1994
Mission: To improve the quality of life for those directly or indirectly affected by fibromyalgia syndrome (FMS) & chronic fatigue syndrome (CFS).
Affliation(s): FM-CFS Canada
Activities: Annual fall seminar/conference; information sharing; public awareness; self-help groups;

Fibromyalgia Support Group of Winnipeg, Inc.

c/o SMD Clearinghouse, 825 Sherbrooke St., Winnipeg MB R3A 1M5
Tel: 204-975-3037
info@fmswinnipeg.com
fmswinnipeg.com
Also Known As: Fibromyalgia Syndrome Winnipeg
Overview: A small provincial charitable organization founded in 1992
Mission: To sponsor & promote educational services to all persons with Fibromyalgia, families, friends, health-care professionals & the general public; To promote & sponsor scientific & clinical research as to causes, treatments & cure of Fibromyalgia
Member of: SMD Self-Help Clearinghouse
Finances: *Annual Operating Budget:* Less than $50,000
Staff Member(s): 6; 8 volunteer(s)
Membership: 120; *Fees:* $20 regular; $30 professional; *Member Profile:* People with fibromyalgia; *Committees:* Membership; Finance; Newsletter; Library; Education Course; Public Relations; Phoning
Activities: Monthly meetings; educational program; neighbourhood groups; *Library:* Lending Library

Fibrose Kystique Canada *See* Cystic Fibrosis Canada

Fibrose kystique Québec (FKQ) / Cystic Fibrosis Québec (CFQ)

625 av du Président-Kennedy, Montréal QC H3A 1K2
Tél: 514-877-6161; *Téléc:* 514-877-6116
Ligne sans frais: 800-363-7711
www.fibrosekystiquequebec.com
www.facebook.com/group.php?gid=162576157129896
twitter.com/FKQuebec
plus.google.com/106908476349956061911
Nom précédent: Association québécoise de la fibrose kystique (AQFK)
Aperçu: *Dimension:* moyenne; *Envergure:* provinciale; Organisme sans but lucratif; fondée en 1981
Mission: Sensibiliser la population sur la fibrose kystique; amasser des fonds pour la recherche médicale; améliorer la qualité de vie des personnes atteintes de FK; découvrir un remède ou un moyen de contrôler la fibrose kystique.
Membre de: Cystic Fibrosis Canada
Membre(s) du bureau directeur:
Benoit Vigneau, Président-directeur général
bvigneau@fibrosekystiquequebec.ca
Finances: *Budget de fonctionnement annuel:* $3 Million-$5 Million
Membre(s) du personnel: 9; 1000 bénévole(s)
Activités: Grand bal de la FK; spectacle bénéfice; tirage provincial; recueillir des fonds servant à financer un réseau de centres de recherche intensive et de thérapie à travers le Québec, où les personnes atteintes de fibrose kystique peuvent recevoir des soins appropriés; *Événements de sensibilisation:* Marchethon de Montréal, mai; Mois de la fibrose kystique, mai; *Stagiaires:* Oui; *Bibliothèque*

Section Bas St-Laurent/Gaspésie
Rimouski QC
info@fibrosekystiquequebec.ca
www.fibrosekystiquequebec.com/fr/association/les-sections-locales

Section Charlevoix-ouest
Baie-Saint-Paul QC
www.fibrosekystiquequebec.com/fr/association/les-sections-locales
Membre(s) du bureau directeur:
Sylvian Lajoie, Président
lajoie300@hotmail.com

Section Côte-Nord
Baie-Comeau QC
www.fibrosekystiquequebec.com/fr/association/les-sections-locales
Membre(s) du bureau directeur:
Sophie Girard, Présidente
sofaca@globetrotter.net

Section Estrie
Sherbrooke QC
www.fibrosekystiquequebec.com/fr/association/les-sections-locales
Membre(s) du bureau directeur:
Michael Roy, Président
michel.roy@usherbrooke.ca

Section La Malbaie
La Malbaie QC
www.fibrosekystiquequebec.com/fr/association/les-sections-locales
Membre(s) du bureau directeur:
Girard Dorothée, Présidente
dorotheefk@live.ca

Section Lac-St-Jean
Alma QC
www.fibrosekystiquequebec.com/fr/association/les-sections-locales
Membre(s) du bureau directeur:
Monique Gobeil, Présidente
monique.gobeil@cgocable.ca

Section Mauricie/Centre-du-Québec
Trois-Rivières QC
www.fibrosekystiquequebec.com/fr/association/les-sections-locales
Membre(s) du bureau directeur:

Lisette Tremblay, Présidente
lisette.tremblay@uqtr.ca
Section Montréal
#510, rue Viger ouest, Montréal QC H2Z 1X2
Tél: 514-877-6161; *Téléc:* 514-877-6116
Ligne sans frais: 800-363-7711
sectionmontreal@fibrosekystiquequebec.ca
www.fibrosekystiquequebec.com/fr/association/les-sections-locales
Membre(s) du bureau directeur:
Francine Bernier, Présidente
Section Outaouais
Gatineau QC
www.fibrosekystiquequebec.com/fr/association/les-sections-locales
Membre(s) du bureau directeur:
Lyne Lacroix, Présidente
lyne.r.lacroix@aexp.com
Section Québec
#227, 2750, ch Sainte-Foy, Québec QC G1V 1V6
Tél: 418-653-2086; *Téléc:* 418-653-1152
Ligne sans frais: 877-653-2086
www.fkquebec.com
Membre(s) du bureau directeur:
Denise Johnson, Présidente
denisejaqfk@gmail.com
Section Saguenay
Chicoutimi QC
www.fibrosekystiquequebec.com/fr/association/les-sections-locales
Membre(s) du bureau directeur:
Éric Gaudreault, Président
erico.gaud@sympatico.ca

Fiducie du patrimoine ontarien *See* Ontario Heritage Trust

Fiducie foncière Vallée de Ruiter *See* Ruiter Valley Land Trust

Field Botanists of Ontario (FBO)
c/o W.D. McIlveen, RR#1, Acton ON L7J 2L7
www.trentu.ca/fbo
Overview: A small provincial organization founded in 1983
Mission: To increase documentation of the flora of Ontario; To encourage interest in botany & conservation in the province of Ontario
Chief Officer(s):
Mike McMurtry, President
michael.mcmurtry@sympatico.ca
Bill Westerhof, Vice-President
dwesterhof@beaconenviro.com
Nancy Falkenberg, Secretary
falken@rogers.ca
Bill Draper, Treasurer
william.draper@sympatico.ca
Bill McIlveen, Chair, Membership
wmcilveen@sympatico.ca
Membership: *Fees:* $20 individuals; $25 families; $350 life memberships; *Member Profile:* Amateur & professional botanists of all ages
Activities: Offering field trips; Providing education & workshops; Offering botanical expertise; Encouraging the exchange of botanical information; Facilitating networking opportunities
Meetings/Conferences: • Field Botanists of Ontario Annual General Meeting, 2015, ON
Scope: Provincial
Publications:
• Field Botanists of Ontario Newsletter
Type: Newsletter; *Frequency:* Quarterly; *Editor:* Cheryl Hendrickson
Profile: Articles, meeting information, & field trip reports

Field Hockey Alberta (FHA)
#1, 2135 Westmount Rd. NW, Calgary AB T2N 3N3
Tel: 403-670-0014; *Fax:* 403-670-0018
Toll-Free: 888-670-0018
info@fieldhockey.ab.ca
www.fieldhockey.ab.ca
www.facebook.com/group.php?gid=21871703180
Merged from: Alberta Field Hockey Association
Overview: A small provincial charitable organization founded in 1974 overseen by Field Hockey Canada
Mission: To develop field hockey for all in Alberta; To provide & facilitate provincial field hockey teams
Member of: Field Hockey Canada
Chief Officer(s):
Burgundy Biletski, Executive Director
burgundy@fieldhockey.ab.ca
Staff Member(s): 2; 50 volunteer(s)
Membership: 800; *Fees:* $30 senior player; $20 junior player; $50 associate member; $0 coach/umpire; *Committees:* High Performance; Umpiring; South/North Alberta
Activities: School programs, clinics, festivals, equipment rentals; *Speaker Service:* Yes; *Library* Open to public by appointment

Field Hockey BC (FHBC) / Hockey sur gazon C-B
#202, 210 Broadway West, Vancouver BC V5Y 3W2
Tel: 604-737-3046; *Fax:* 604-737-6488
info@fieldhockeybc.com
www.fieldhockeybc.com
www.facebook.com/465853180146750
twitter.com/FieldHockeyBC
www.youtube.com/user/fieldhockeybc
Merged from: British Columbia Field Hockey Association; British Columbia Women's Field Hockey Federation
Overview: A medium-sized provincial organization founded in 1992 overseen by Field Hockey Canada
Mission: To foster, promote & encourage the development & organization of field hockey in BC at all levels
Member of: Field Hockey Canada
Chief Officer(s):
Mark Saunders, Executive Director, 604-737-3045
mark@fieldhockeybc.com
Finances: *Annual Operating Budget:* $500,000-$1.5 Million; *Funding Sources:* Provincial government; membership fees
Staff Member(s): 5
Membership: 7,275; *Fees:* $33-$66; *Committees:* High Performance; Finance

Field Hockey Canada (FHC) / Hockey sur gazon Canada
311 West 1st St., North Vancouver BC V7M 1B5
Other Communication: Media, E-mail: communications@fieldhockey.ca
fhc@fieldhockey.ca
www.fieldhockey.ca
www.facebook.com/FHCanada
twitter.com/FieldHockeyCan
www.youtube.com/user/hockeysurgazoncanada
Previous Name: Canadian Field Hockey Association
Overview: A medium-sized national charitable organization founded in 1991
Mission: To promote the development & growth of field hockey in Canada; To provide coaching, training, & competitive opportunities to prepare Canada's national teams
Member of: International Hockey Federation (FIH); Pan American Hockey Federation (PAHF)
Chief Officer(s):
Jeff Sauvé, CEO, 778-228-9564
jsauve@fieldhockey.ca
Connor Meakin, Coordinator, Communications
cmeakin@fieldhockey.ca
Finances: *Funding Sources:* Sponsorships; Donations
Membership: 7 provincial associations; *Fees:* $20; *Member Profile:* Members of Field Hockey Canada member clubs
Activities: Hosting world class field hockey events in Canada; Seeking partnerships with corporations; Offering technical programs

Field Hockey Manitoba (FHM)
145 Pacific Ave., Winnipeg MB R3B 2Z6
Tel: 204-925-5794; *Fax:* 204-925-5792
info@fieldhockeymb.org
www.facebook.com/fieldhockey.manitoba
Overview: A small provincial organization overseen by Field Hockey Canada
Mission: The Association fosters growth & development of field hockey & indoor hockey in Manitoba.
Member of: Field Hockey Canada
Chief Officer(s):
Kim Knowles, President
Staff Member(s): 2
Membership: 100; *Fees:* $55 adult; $20 under 18; $10 associate/coach/umpire/volunteer; $55 affliate

Field Hockey Nova Scotia
5516 Spring Garden Rd., 4th Fl., Halifax NS B3J 1G6
e-mail: administration@fieldhockey.ns.ca
www.fieldhockey.ns.ca
www.facebook.com/groups/39499666567
Overview: A small provincial organization founded in 1971 overseen by Field Hockey Canada
Mission: The Association promotes the sport of field hockey for both men & women in the province of Nova Scotia.
Member of: Field Hockey Canada
Chief Officer(s):
Brianna Holmes, Contact, Administration

Field Hockey Ontario (FHO)
PO Box 80030, Stn. Appleby, Burlington ON L7L 6B1
Tel: 905-492-1680
info@fieldhockeyontario.com
www.fieldhockeyontario.com
www.facebook.com/FieldHockeyOntario
Merged from: Ontario Field Hockey Association; Women's Field Hockey Association
Overview: A medium-sized provincial organization founded in 1985 overseen by Field Hockey Canada
Mission: To promote the sport of field hockey for both men & women in the province of Ontario.
Member of: Field Hockey Canada
Chief Officer(s):
Bill Baring, President
Finances: *Annual Operating Budget:* $100,000-$250,000; *Funding Sources:* Sponsorship; government grants; membership fees
Staff Member(s): 3; 180 volunteer(s)
Membership: 6,000; *Fees:* $50 team
Activities: *Internships:* Yes

Fife House
490 Sherburne St., 2nd Fl., Toronto ON M4X 1K9
Tel: 416-205-9888; *Fax:* 416-205-9919
info@fifehouse.org
www.fifehouse.org
www.facebook.com/FifeHouse
twitter.com/FifeHouse
Overview: A medium-sized local charitable organization founded in 1988 overseen by Canadian AIDS Society
Mission: To provide secure, affordable, supportive housing & support services to people living with HIV/AIDS
Member of: Ontario AIDS Network; Ontario Non-Profit Housing Association
Chief Officer(s):
Keith Hambly, Executive Director
khambly@fifehouse.org
Finances: *Annual Operating Budget:* $3 Million-$5 Million; *Funding Sources:* Federal, provincial & municipal government; Toronto Central Local Health Integration Network; Ontario HIV Treatment Network

15th Field Artillery Regiment Museum & Archives Society
2025 - 11th Ave. West, Vancouver BC V6J 2C7
Tel: 604-666-4370; *Fax:* 604-666-4083
Overview: A small local charitable organization founded in 1983
Mission: To collect & preserve artifacts, photos & documents related to artillery units in the Greater Vancouver region; to restore World War II Point Grey Battery
Member of: Canadian Museums Association; BC Museums Association; Organization of Military Museums of Canada
Chief Officer(s):
Stuart McDonald, President, 604-886-6847
P.N. Moogk, Curator, 604-228-9445
moogk@mail.ubc.ca
Finances: *Annual Operating Budget:* Less than $50,000; *Funding Sources:* Public donations; government grants
5 volunteer(s)
Membership: 27; *Fees:* $15
Activities: *Library:* 15th Field Regiment Archives; Open to public by appointment

50 & Piu Enasco
#103, 3939 Hastings St., Burnaby BC V5C 2H8
Tel: 604-294-2023; *Fax:* 604-294-2118
Toll-Free: 800-269-0065
canada1@enasco.it
www.50epiucanadaenasco.com
Previous Name: Enasco - Institute of Social Service for Workers of Italian Origin
Overview: A small national organization founded in 1967
Mission: ENASCO is an agency assisting people free of charge in applying to receive social security benefits from Italy, Canada & other countries.
Chief Officer(s):
Leonara Perizzolo, Contact
l.perizzolo@enasco.it

Hamilton Office
#12, 1001 Rymal Rd. East, Hamilton ON L8W 3M2
Tel: 905-318-4488; *Fax:* 905-385-4823
canada1@enasco.it
Chief Officer(s):
Catia Squartecchia, Contact
c.squartecchia@enasco.it
St. Catharines Office
30 Facer St., St. Catharines ON L2M 5H3
Tel: 905-646-6555; *Fax:* 905-935-1572
Chief Officer(s):
Vilma Vergalito, Contact
v.vergalito@enasco.it
Toronto Office
1337 St. Clair Ave. West, Toronto ON M6E 1C3
Tel: 416-652-3759; *Fax:* 888-888-2465
canada1@enasco.it
Chief Officer(s):
Diego Zuccarelli, Contact
d.zuccarelli@enasco.it
Woodbridge Office
Market Lane, #201, 140 Woodbridge Ave., Woodbridge ON L4L 4K9
Tel: 905-266-1866; *Fax:* 905-266-1867
Chief Officer(s):
Vincenzo Ghiandoni, Contact
v.ghiandoni@enasco.it

Filarmónica Portuguesa de Montreal / Philharmonique Portugais de Montréal
260, rue Rachel Est, Montréal QC H2W 1E6
Tél: 514-982-0688; *Téléc:* 514-982-0607
www.filarmonicaportuguesa.com
Également appelé: Montreal Portuguese Philharmonic
Aperçu: *Dimension:* petite; *Envergure:* locale; fondée en 1972
Mission: Un orchestre avec des musiciens canadiens-portugais
Membre(s) du bureau directeur:
Joao Balança, Président, 514-465-3230
Activités: Concerts; Festivals de musique

Filipino Association of Nova Scotia (FANS)
152 Rosedale Ave., Halifax NS B3N 2J8
Tel: 902-445-5549
www.filipinonovascotia.org
twitter.com/FilipinoNS
Overview: A small local organization founded in 1964
Mission: To promote understanding between Filipinos & people from all nations
Chief Officer(s):
Leni Van der jagt, President
Nimfa P. Oakley, Secretary
Rosie Dorey, Treasurer
Sally Martinez, Business Manager
Amado G. Foronda, Officer, Public Relations
Membership: *Member Profile:* Filipinos in Nova Scotia & the Atlantic Region
Activities: Participating in cultural events; Arranging social activities; *Awareness Events:* Fiesta Filipino

Filipino Canadian Association of London & District (FCALD)
London ON
Overview: A small local organization
Mission: To promote Filipino heritage & culture in London, Ontario & the surrounding region
Membership: *Member Profile:* Filipino Canadian children & adults from the London, Ontario area
Activities: Organizing cultural, educational, & social activities
Publications:
• Filipino Canadian Association of London & District Newsletter
Type: Newsletter
Profile: Association activities available for members

Filipino Canadian Association of Vaughan (FCAV)
Vaughan ON
Tel: 905-881-1600
fcav@rogers.com
www.fcav.ca
www.facebook.com/fcaov
Overview: A small local organization founded in 1990
Mission: To assist Filipino Canadians in Vaughan, Ontario; To promote community spirit among Filipinos; To assimilate Filipino culture into Canadian society
Chief Officer(s):
Erlinda Insigne, Chair
Gloria Pasildo, Vice-President
Lily Miranda, Secretary, 647-886-8223
lilyleo2750@yahoo.com
Mina Benesa, Treasurer
Finances: *Funding Sources:* Membership fees; Grants; Fundraising
Membership: *Member Profile:* Filipino Canadians in Vaughan, Ontario
Activities: Helping new Filipino immigrants to Vaughan; Participating in civic & community events; Offering educational & recreational programs, such as English tutorials, heritage classes, & cultural dancing; Providing seminars on topics such as immigration & caregiving; Participating in a Friendship Agreement with Baguio City in the Philippines, to promote economic opportunities & cultural, social, & educational exchanges; *Awareness Events:* Philippine Independence Day Parade (Filipino Day)

Filipino Canadian Catholic Charismatic Prayer Communities (FCCCPC)
53 Belvedere Cres., Richmond Hill ON L4C 8VA
Tel: 416-903-3453
fcccpc@yahoo.com
www.fcccpc.com
Overview: A small national organization founded in 1992
Mission: To defend the Word; To advocate righteousness, through witnessing & instructions; To provide refuge to the weak, needy, & persecuted
Affliation(s): Archdiocese of Toronto
Chief Officer(s):
Ben Ebcas, Spiritual Director
Don Quilao, Head Servant
cbquilao@rogers.com
Teresita P. Gutierrez, Secretary & Director, 416-456-0381
terigutierrez@yahoo.ca
Caring Labindao, Treasurer
Membership: 10+ charismatic prayer communities; *Member Profile:* Individuals are members of a Catholic prayer community (majority of members are of Filipino heritage)
Activities: Counselling; Providing faith instruction & prayer groups; Offering renewal programs, general assemblies, & fellowship; Presenting spiritual formation seminars

Filipino Canadian Technical Professionals Association of Manitoba, Inc. (FCTPAM)
c/o CCI Cadpower Canada Inc., #3, 1680 Dublin Ave., Winnipeg MB R3H 1AB
Tel: 204-988-9100; *Fax:* 204-786-3033
directors@fctpam.net
www.fctpam.net
Previous Name: Filipino Technical Professionals Association of Manitoba, Inc.
Overview: A small provincial organization founded in 1992
Mission: To guide graduates of engineering, architecture, & other technical courses from the Philippines in the recognition & accreditation of foreign credentials
Finances: *Funding Sources:* Membership fees; Fundraising
Membership: *Member Profile:* Filipinos who reside in Canada, & Canadian born Filipinos, who are engineers, architects, technicians, or technologists & who are registered or practise in Manitoba
Activities: Assisting newly arrived immigrants to integrate to life in Canada; Organizing cultural, social, & recreational activities; Providing skills & technical development programs

Filipino Students' Association of Toronto (FSAT)
12 Hart House Circle, Toronto ON M5S 3J9
Tel: 289-200-3438
fsat.fsat@gmail.com
fsat.sa.utoronto.ca
twitter.com/FSAT
Overview: A small local organization
Mission: To encourage Filipino young people to further their education; To promote awareness of the Filipino community & the Filipino culture at the University of Toronto; To represent Filipino students & the Filipino culture at the University of Toronto's St. George Campus
Chief Officer(s):
Jannel Fontz, Coordinator, Internal & University Affairs
Liza Caringal, Coordinator, Internal & University Affairs
Finances: *Funding Sources:* Fundraising; Sponsorships
Membership: *Member Profile:* Filipino students, faculty, alumni, & staff from the University of Toronto; Interested non-Filipino students, faculty, alumni, & staff from the University of Toronto
Activities: Liaising between the University of Toronto & the Filipino community; Speaking to high school students; Awarding scholarships to high school students; Offering mentorship programs; Providing academic events, featuring lectures by professors & Filipino speakers; Organizing cultural workshops; Participating in multicultual fairs; Offering social activities within the campus community; Sponsoring a child's tuition in the Philippines; Organizing a homework club at The Filipino Centre

Filipino Technical Professionals Association of Manitoba, Inc. *See* Filipino Canadian Technical Professionals Association of Manitoba, Inc.

Film & Video Arts Society Alberta (FAVA)
Ortona Armoury Arts Building, 9722 - 102 St., 2nd Fl., Edmonton AB T5K 0X4
Tel: 780-429-1671; *Fax:* 780-429-3636
Other Communication: Rentals Phone: 780-424-4368
info@fava.ca
www.fava.ca
www.facebook.com/fava.love.75
twitter.com/FAVA_Love
Overview: A small provincial charitable organization founded in 1982
Mission: Independent artists willing to challenge & explore through their creativity; all members contribute through some combination of financial support, talents, skills & experience; in return, FAVA provides an open atmosphere & access to resources - equipment, peer support & shared information
Member of: Independent Media Arts Alliance; Alberta Media Arts Alliance; Edmonton Arts Council
Affliation(s): Independent Film & Video Alliance; Alberta Media Arts Alliance
Chief Officer(s):
Dylan Pearce, President
Dave Cunningham, Executive Director
ed@fava.ca
Finances: *Annual Operating Budget:* $250,000-$500,000; *Funding Sources:* Grants; Classes & Workshops; Equipment Rental; Member Fees
Staff Member(s): 5; 200 volunteer(s)
Membership: 300; *Fees:* $42 producer; $68.25 general; $89.25 associate
Activities: Monthly screenings; participation in Global Visions; Edmonton International Film Festival; workshops; *Speaker Service:* Yes; *Library* by appointment

Film Studies Association of Canada (FSAC/ACÉC) / Association canadienne des études cinématographiques (ACEC)
c/o Peter Lester, Brock University, 500 Glenridge Ave., St Catharines ON L2S 3A1
e-mail: fsac@filmstudies.ca
www.filmstudies.ca
www.facebook.com/FSAC.ACEC
twitter.com/_filmstudies
Overview: A small national organization founded in 1977 overseen by Canadian Federation for Humanities & Social Sciences
Mission: To foster & advance the study of the history & art of film & its related fields.
Affliation(s): Association for the Study of Canadian Radio & Television; Association québécoise des études cinématographiques
Chief Officer(s):
Liz Czach, President
Peter Lester, Secretary
membership@filmstudies.ca
Finances: *Funding Sources:* Membership fees; award from SSHRC
Membership: *Fees:* $110 regular; $50 associate; $40 retired; $30 student/contract instructors; $100 sustaining
Awards:
• Gerald Pratley Award (Award)
Meetings/Conferences: • Film Studies Association of Canada 2015 Annual Conference, June, 2015, University of Ottawa, Ottawa, ON
Soopc: National
Contact Information: conference2015@filmstudies.ca
Publications:
• Canadian Journal of Film Studies
Type: Journal; *Frequency:* Quarterly; *Editor:* William C. Wees
• Continuity
Type: Newsletter; *Frequency:* Irregular; *Editor:* Jean Charles Bellemare

FilmOntario
625 Church St., 2nd Fl., Toronto ON M4Y 2G1
Tel: 416-642-6704
www.filmontario.ca

Overview: A large provincial organization
Mission: To market Ontario as a creator of film content & a location for film & television production
Chief Officer(s):
Sarah Ker-Hornell, Executive Director & CEO
sarah@filmontario.ca
Membership: 30,000

Financial & Consumer Affairs Authority of Saskatchewan (FCAA)

#601, 1919 Saskatchewan Dr., Regina SK S4P 4H2
Tel: 306-787-5645; *Fax:* 306-787-5899
consumerprotection@gov.sk.ca
www.fcaa.gov.sk.ca
Overview: A medium-sized provincial organization overseen by Canadian Securities Administrators
Mission: To strengthen Saskatchewan's financial marketplace & protect consumers
Member of: Canadian Securities Administrators
Chief Officer(s):
Dave Wild, Chair
Activities: Regulating providers of financial products & services
Publications:
• FCAA [Financial & Consumer Affairs Authority of Saskatchewan] Annual Report
Type: Report; *Frequency:* Annually
• FCAA [Financial & Consumer Affairs Authority of Saskatchewan] Strategic Plan
Type: Report; *Frequency:* Annually
• A Statistical Perspective on Pension Plans Registered in Saskatchewan
Type: Report; *Frequency:* Annually
• Statistical Report of the Superintendent of Insurance
Type: Report; *Frequency:* Annually

Financial & Consumer Services Commission (FCNB) / Commission des services financiers et des services aux consommateurs

#300, 85 Charlotte St., Saint John NB E2L 2J2
Fax: 506-658-3059
Toll-Free: 866-933-2222
info@fcnb.ca
www.fcnb.ca
www.facebook.com/FCNB.ca
twitter.com/FCNB_
www.youtube.com/NBSC2008
Previous Name: New Brunswick Securities Commission
Overview: A medium-sized provincial organization founded in 2013 overseen by Canadian Securities Administrators
Mission: To administer & enforce provincial legislation pertaining to the following sectors: securities, insurance, pensions, credit unions, caisses populaires, trust & loan companies, co-operatives, & other consumer legislation
Member of: Canadian Securities Administrators; Council of Securities Regulators of the Americas; North American Securities Administrators Association
Affliation(s): International Forum for Investor Education (IFIE); International Organization of Securities Commissions; Securities & Exchange Commission (USA)
Chief Officer(s):
Peter Klohn, Chair, 506-643-7311
Peter.Klohn@fcnb.ca
Rick Hancox, Chief Executive Officer, 506-658-3119
rick.hancox@fcnb.ca
Manon Losier, General Counsel & Secretary, 506-643-7690
manon.losier@fcnb.ca
Jake van der Laan, Chief Information Officer & Director, Enforcement, 506-658-6637
jake.vanderLaan@fcnb.ca
Kevin Hoyt, Director, Securities, 506-643-7691
kevin.hoyt@fcnb.ca
Andrew Nicholson, Director, Education & Communications, 506-658-3021
andrew.nicholson@fcnb.ca
Finances: *Funding Sources:* By investors, through the securities industry
Activities: Developing securities regulation; Registering persons & companies operating in New Brunswick's securities industry; Providing educational resources to New Brunswick residents who are interested in the investing process; Reviewing prospectuses; Considering exemption applications; Taking enforcement action when securities laws have been contravened
Publications:
• Financial & Consumer Services Commission Annual Report
Type: Report; *Frequency:* Annually
• Financial & Consumer Services Commission Governance Policy
Number of Pages: 47
Profile: An outline of the governance policy of the Commission

Financial Executives Institute Canada *See* Financial Executives International Canada

Financial Executives International Canada (FEIC)

#1201, 170 University Ave., Toronto ON M5H 3B3
Tel: 416-366-3007; *Fax:* 416-366-3008
Toll-Free: 866-677-3007
www.feicanada.org
www.linkedin.com/company/fei-canada
twitter.com/financial_execs
Also Known As: FEI Canada
Previous Name: Financial Executives Institute Canada
Overview: A medium-sized national organization founded in 1931
Mission: To promote ethical conduct in the practice of financial management; To contribute to the legal & policy making process in Canada
Chief Officer(s):
William G. Ross, Chair
bill.ross@enbridge.com
Tim Zahavich, Vice-Chair
tjklaz@aol.com
Michael Conway, President & CEO, 416-366-3007 Ext. 5106
mconway@feicanada.org
Line Trudeau, Chief Financial Officer & Secretary, 416-366-3007 Ext. 5115
ltrudeau@feicanada.org
Don Comish, Director, Sponsorship, 416-366-3007 Ext. 5108
dcomish@feicanada.org
Liz Bowell, Coordinator, Membership, 416-366-3007 Ext. 5110
lbowell@feicanada.org
Finances: *Funding Sources:* Sponsorship
Membership: 2,000+; *Member Profile:* Senior financial officers of medium to large organizations; *Committees:* Corporate Reporting; Issues & Policy Advisory
Activities: Providing seminars, conferences, professional development events, & networking opportunities; Offering advocacy services
Awards:
• Canada's Chief Financial Officer of the Year (Award)
Meetings/Conferences: • Financial Executives International Canada 2015 Conference, June, 2015, RBC Convention Centre Winnipeg, Winnipeg, MB
Scope: National
Publications:
• Finance & Accounting Review
Type: Journal; *Frequency:* Monthly; *Price:* Free to members of Financial Executives International Canada
Profile: Domestic & international happenings in the industry
• Financial Executives International Canada Annual Report
Type: Yearbook; *Frequency:* Annually
• Xpress
Type: Newsletter; *Frequency:* Monthly; *Price:* Free to members of Financial Executives International Canada
Profile: Happenings at FEI Canada plus forthcoming professional development activitie, new members, & job postings

Atlantic Provinces Chapter
Chief Officer(s):
Tyrone Cotie, President, 902-457-8181
tcotie@clearwater.ca
Ray McCormick, Treasurer, 902-493-3510
ray.mccormick@impgroup.com

Calgary Chapter
Chief Officer(s):
Grant McNeil, President, 403-242-7177
grant.mcneil@imcprojects.ca
Brian Callaghan, Treasurer
bcallaghan@telus.net
• Calgary Newsletter
Editor: Tariq Malik
Profile: News & committee reports for members

Edmonton Chapter
Chief Officer(s):
Darren Buma, President, 780-466-6204
dbuma@kwbllp.com
Hans Lung, Treasurer
hlung@gss.org

National Capital Region Chapter
Chief Officer(s):
Dean Cosman, President, 613-996-9043
dcosman@cdic.ca
Ernie Briard, Vice-President & Treasurer
erniebriard@rogers.com

Québec Chapter
Tel: 514-399-4784; *Fax:* 514-399-8604
fei.quebec@sympatico.ca
Chief Officer(s):
Louis Marcotte, President
louis.marcotte@intact.net
David Anderson, Treasurer
david.anderson@cgi.com

Regina Chapter
Chief Officer(s):
Gail Kruger, President, 306-777-6060
gkruger@reginalibrary.ca
Jeff Stepan, Treasurer
bhoffart@cma-sask.org

Southern Golden Horseshoe Chapter
Tel: 289-828-0200
FEI.SGH@gmail.com
Chief Officer(s):
Elysia Estee, President
elysia.estee@softchoice.com
Dan Bowes, Treasurer
dbowes@wattscanada.ca

Southwestern Ontario Chapter
Chief Officer(s):
Nicole Archibald, President, 519-680-0707 Ext. 264
nicole@tribemedical.com
Dawn Butler, Treasurer
butlerd@highstreet.ca
• Financial Executives International Southwestern Ontario Chapter Newsletter
Type: Newsletter; *Frequency:* Annually
Profile: Chapter news for members, including upcoming events & reviews of conferences & activities

Toronto Chapter
Tel: 905-330-5055
Toronto.Chapter@feicanada.org
Chief Officer(s):
Russell Wong, President
rwong3618@gmail.com
Leah Halpenny, Secretary & Treasurer
lhalpenny@execurisk.com
• Financial Executives International Canada Toronto Newsletter
Type: Newsletter; *Frequency:* 3 pa
Profile: Chapter news & committee reports

Vancouver Chapter
Chief Officer(s):
Jeff Shickele, President, 604-602-7735
jeff@shickele.com
Alan Wong, Treasurer
alanlwong@telus.net
• Financial Executives International Canada Vancouver Chapter Newsletter
Type: Newsletter; *Frequency:* 11 pa
Profile: News, upcoming events, & committee reports for members

Winnipeg Chapter
Chief Officer(s):
Beverley Szaura, President
beverley_szaura@cwb.ca
Dana Thiessen, Treasurer
dana.thiessen@shaw.ca

Financial Executives International Canada Hamilton Chapter *See* Financial Executives International Canada

Financial Fitness Centre

420 Devonshire Rd., Windsor ON N8Y 4T6
Tel: 519-258-2030
Toll-Free: 877-777-9218
info@financialfitnesswindsor.com
www.ccswindsor.com
www.facebook.com/122761461101338
twitter.com/FinancialFitWin
Previous Name: Credit Counselling Services of Southwestern Ontario
Overview: A small local charitable organization overseen by Ontario Association of Credit Counselling Services
Mission: To assist persons in southwestern Ontario to solve their money problems; To provide confidential credit, debt, bankruptcy, & budget counselling
Member of: Credit Counselling Canada; Ontario Association of

Credit Counselling Services
Affliation(s): Family Services Credit Counselling Employee Assistance Programs
Finances: *Funding Sources:* United Way of Windsor / Essex; Creditors
Activities: Teaching budgeting & money management skills; Presenting workshops & community education; Contacting creditors to negotiate payment plans

Financial Management Institute of Canada (FMI) / Institut de la gestion financière (IFG)

#1107, 200 Elgin St., Ottawa ON K2P 1L5
Tel: 613-569-1158; *Fax:* 613-569-4532
Other Communication: French URL: www.igf.ca
national@fmi.ca
www.fmi.ca
www.linkedin.com/groups?gid=2350339
www.facebook.com/fmiigf
twitter.com/FMI_IGF
www.youtube.com/user/FMIIGF
Overview: A medium-sized national organization founded in 1962
Mission: To be the source for professional development on topical issues & best practices to public sector financial management stakeholders; To facilitate the dissemination of information on managing public sector resources
Chief Officer(s):
Marcel Boulianne, President
marcel.boulianne@fmi.ca
Yvonne Samson, Vice-President
yvonne.samson@gnb.ca
Shawn Johnson, Secretary-Treasurer
shawn.johnson@gnb.ca
Cheryl Munro, Acting Managing Director
cmunro@fmi.ca
Cheryl Elliott, Manager, Marketing & Communications
cheryl@fmi.ca
Finances: *Funding Sources:* Membership fees; Sponsorships
Membership: 2,240; *Member Profile:* Professionals in the finance field throughout Canada
Activities: Offering seminars & learning events for both members & non-members, as well as a Professional Development Week; Providing networking opportunities
Meetings/Conferences: • Public Sector Management Workshop 2015, May, 2015, Victoria, BC
Scope: National
Publications:
• Community Report
Type: Report; *Frequency:* Annually
Profile: An overview of the Financial Management Institute of Canada
• Financial Management Institute of Canada Annual Report
Type: Yearbook; *Frequency:* Annually
• FMI / IGF Journal
Type: Magazine; *Frequency:* 3 pa; *Accepts Advertising; Editor:* Rocky J. Dwyer, PhD, CMA
Profile: News, articles, & columns of interest to public sector professionals in the field of public sector financial management

Financial Markets Association of Canada (FMAC) / Association des marchés financiers du Canada

#301, 250 Consumers Rd., Toronto ON M2J 4V6
Tel: 416-773-0584; *Fax:* 416-495-8723
fmac@fmac.ca
www.fmac.ca
Previous Name: Foreign Exchange Association of Canada
Overview: A medium-sized national organization founded in 1972
Mission: To promote the educational & professional interests of participants in the Canadian wholesale financial markets; To ensure members adhere to international principles of professional conduct
Affliation(s): Association Cambiste Internationale (ACI); Canadian Foreign Exchange Committee; Canadian Committee for Professionalism
Chief Officer(s):
Jean-François Gratton, President
Maria Jones, Secretary
Blake Jsespersen, Treasurer & Past President
Membership: 350+; *Member Profile:* A professional who deals in money markets, foreign exchange, captital markets, & derivatives, & whose institution is registered with & regulated by at least one of the following authorities: Office of the Superintendent of Financial Institutions, Securities & Exchange Commission, Investment Dealers Association, Financial Services Commission of Ontario, & the Ontario Securities Commission
Activities: Hosting business functions with speakers; Providing networking opportunities
Publications:
• Market Maker [a publication of the Financial Markets Association of Canada]
Type: Newsletter; *Frequency:* Quarterly
Profile: Activities of the association

Financial Planners Standards Council *See* Financial Planning Standards Council

Financial Planning Standards Council (FPSC)

#902, 375 University Ave., Toronto ON M5G 2J5
Tel: 416-593-8587; *Fax:* 416-593-6903
Toll-Free: 800-305-9886
Other Communication: communications@fpsc.ca
inform@fpsc.ca
www.fpsc.ca
www.linkedin.com/company/100790
www.facebook.com/FPSC.Canada
twitter.com/FPSC_Canada
www.youtube.com/user/FPVision2020
Previous Name: Financial Planners Standards Council
Overview: A medium-sized national licensing organization founded in 1995
Mission: To develop, enforce, & promote competency & ethical standards in financial planning by those who have earned the designation of Certified Financial Planner (CFP)
Affliation(s): The Financial Advisors Association of Canada; The Canadian Institute of Chartered Accountants; The Canadian Institute of Financial Planning; Certified General Accountants Association of Canada; Certified Management Accountants of Canada; Credit Union Institute of Canada
Chief Officer(s):
Lisa Pflieger, Chair
Dawn Hawley, Vice-Chair
Cary List, President & Chief Executive Officer
Kimberley Ney, Vice-President, Communications & Program Development
Stephen Rotstein, Vice-President, Policy & Regulatory Affairs
Heather Terrence, Vice-President, Operations
Joan Yudelson, Vice-President, Professional Practice
Isabelle Gonthier, Director, Certification Process & Examinations
Membership: *Committees:* Recognition & Awards; Panel of Examiners; Governance; Compensation; Audit; Certification; Enforcement; Nominating
Activities: Increasing awareness of the importance of financial planning; Presenting honours & awards; Hosting financial planning seminars; Conducting surveys; Collecting statistics; *Awareness Events:* Financial Planning Week Canada
Publications:
• CFP Code of Ethics
Type: Booklet; *Number of Pages:* 10
Profile: The Code of Ethics that Certified Financial Planner professionals must abide by to maintain their Certified Financial Planner license
• CFP Financial Planning Practice Standards
Type: Booklet; *Number of Pages:* 14
Profile: An outline of practice standards to which Certified Financial Planner professionals must adhere
• CFP Professional Competency Profile
Number of Pages: 54
Profile: An outline of the competencies that all Certified Financial Planner professionals must possess
• Do I need help with my financial planning?
Type: Booklet; *Number of Pages:* 4
Profile: Information for clients on working with a financial planner
• Financial Planners Standards Council Strategic Plan
Profile: A guide for the organization's future
• Financial Planners Standards Council Annual Report
Type: Yearbook; *Frequency:* Annually
• FPSC [Financial Planning Standards Council] Bulletin
Type: Newsletter; *Editor:* Tamara Smith
Profile: Information for Certified Financial Planner professionals & their clients, including a report on disciplinary action, interviews, & upcoming events
• What assurance do I have that financial planning is working for me?
Type: Booklet; *Number of Pages:* 4
Profile: A guide for clients to understanding the Certified Financial Planner Code of Ethics & Standards of Practice & Competency
• What makes CFP certification trustworthy?
Type: Booklet; *Number of Pages:* 8
Profile: An overview of Certified Financial Planner certification for consumers

Financial Services Commission of Ontario (FSCO) / Commission des services financiers de l'Ontario (CSFO)

PO Box 85, 5160 Yonge St., 17th Fl., Toronto ON M2N 6L9
Tel: 416-250-7250; *Fax:* 416-590-7070
Toll-Free: 800-668-0128; *TTY:* 800-387-0584
contactcentre@fsco.gov.on.ca
www.fsco.gov.on.ca
Previous Name: Canadian Council of Insurance Regulators
Overview: A small provincial organization founded in 1998
Mission: To regulate the following sectors in Ontario: insurance; pension plans; loan & trust companies; credit unions & caisses populaires; mortgage brokering; co-operative corporations in Ontario; & service providers who invoice auto insurers for statutory accident benefits claims.
Chief Officer(s):
Brian Mills, Interim Chief Executive Officer

Findhelp Information Services

PO Box 203, #125, 543 Richmond St. W., Toronto ON M5V 1Y6
Tel: 416-392-4605; *Fax:* 416-392-4404
Toll-Free: 800-836-3238
info@findhelp.ca
www.211toronto.ca
www.facebook.com/pages/211-Central/137803876305769?sk=wall
twitter.com/211Central
Also Known As: 211 Toronto
Overview: A small local charitable organization founded in 1971 overseen by InformOntario
Mission: To provide comprehensive information & referral services in English, French & other languages; resources for information & referral professionals; call centre; newcomer services; Possibilities online employment resource centre; training & outreach
Member of: Alliance of Information & Referral Systems
Affliation(s): United Way of Greater Toronto
Chief Officer(s):
Janice Hayes, Executive Director
Jane Henderson, President
Finances: *Annual Operating Budget:* $1.5 Million-$3 Million; *Funding Sources:* United Way of Greater Toronto; provincial & city funding
Staff Member(s): 65; 5 volunteer(s)
Activities: Database of over 4,000 community services & programs; training & staff development programs for direct service providers working in information & referral environments; information & referral on a wide range of community, social services, health & government programs; *Rents Mailing List:* Yes

Finnish Canadian Cultural Federation / Fédération culturelle finno-canadienne

128 Quartz Ave., Timmins ON P4N 4L6
finnsincanada.org
Overview: A small international organization founded in 1971
Mission: To act as non-political coordinator between associations, congregations, clubs & other groups of Finnish ethnic background; To promote Finland & Canadians of Finnish origin; To promote Canada & its Finnish ethnic community in Finland; To support Annual Finnish Canadian Grand Festival
Member of: Canadian Ethnocultural Council
Affliation(s): Finland Society, R.Y.; Finn Fest USA, Inc.
Chief Officer(s):
Margaret Kangas, Treasurer
Finances: *Annual Operating Budget:* Less than $50,000; *Funding Sources:* Membership fees
12 volunteer(s)
Membership: 57 corporate; *Fees:* Schedule available; *Member Profile:* Canadian non-political organizations, clubs, congregations & other groups of Finnish ethnic origin; *Committees:* Finnish-Canadian Grand Festival; Archives
Activities: *Awareness Events:* Finn Thunder, July

Finnish Canadian Rest Home Association

2288 Harrison Dr., Vancouver BC V5P 2P6
Tel: 604-325-8241; *Fax:* 604-325-2394
info@finncare.ca
finncare.ca
Overview: A small local organization founded in 1958
Mission: To represent a number of Finnish Canadian rest homes & seniors apartments in the Vancouver Area
Chief Officer(s):
Tanya Rautava, Administrator
finnishhome@telus.net

Staff Member(s): 11
Membership: *Fees:* $20; $200 lifetime

Fire Fighters Historical Society of Winnipeg, Inc.
56 Maple St., Winnipeg MB R3B 0Y8
Tel: 204-942-4817; *Fax:* 204-885-1306
firemuseum@gatewest.net
www.winnipegfiremuseum.ca
Overview: A small local charitable organization founded in 1982
Mission: To preserve & display equipment, historical records & photos related to the history of the Winnipeg Fire Department
Finances: *Annual Operating Budget:* Less than $50,000; *Funding Sources:* Membership dues; donations
11 volunteer(s)
Membership: 300; *Fees:* $15
Activities: *Library* by appointment

Fire Prevention Canada (FPC)
PO Box 37009, 3332 McCarthy Rd., Ottawa ON K1V 0W0
Tel: 613-749-3844
info@fiprecan.ca
www.fiprecan.ca
Also Known As: Fiprecan
Overview: A medium-sized national charitable organization
Mission: To work with the public & private sectors to achieve fire safety through education.
Chief Officer(s):
Peter Adamakos, National Manager
padamakos@fiprecan.ca
Staff Member(s): 1

Firefighters Burn Fund Inc. (FFBF)
#303, 83 Garry St., Winnipeg MB R3C 4J9
Tel: 204-783-1733; *Fax:* 204-772-2531
inquiries@firefightersburnfund.mb.ca
www.firefightersburnfund.mb.ca
Overview: A medium-sized provincial charitable organization founded in 1978
Mission: To improve health care available to adults & children in Manitoba who suffer burn injuries; To develop & support fire/burn prevention initiatives so that needless injuries & deaths are prevented
Member of: American Burn Association, Canadian Association of Fire Chiefs
Chief Officer(s):
Martin Johnson, Chairman
Finances: *Annual Operating Budget:* $100,000-$250,000; *Funding Sources:* Fundraising
6 volunteer(s)
Membership: 950; *Fees:* $1; *Committees:* Executive
Activities: Sponsors a burn camp for children who have been patients in the burn unit; promotes Learn Not To Burn curriculum throughout province; *Speaker Service:* Yes

Firefly
820 Lakeview Dr., Kenora ON P9N 3P7
Tel: 807-467-5437; *Fax:* 807-467-5444
Toll-Free: 800-465-7203
www.fireflynw.ca
Merged from: Lake of the Woods Child Development Centre; Patricia Centre for Children and Youth
Overview: A small local organization founded in 2011
Mission: To provide services & programs that help children develop emotionally & physically
Chief Officer(s):
Karen Ingebrigtson, Chief Executive Officer, 807-467-5440
kingebrigtson@fireflynw.ca
Activities: Assessment, counselling & training programs

First Nation Lands Managers Association of Québec & Labrador (FNLMAQ&L)
c/o Gino Clement, 17 Riverside West, Listiguj First Nationl QC E3E 1K3
Tel: 418-788-2136
Overview: A small provincial organization founded in 2002 overseen by National Aboriginal Lands Managers Association
Chief Officer(s):
Gino Clement, Chair
gclement@listuguj.ca
Staff Member(s): 1

First Nations Agricultural Association (FNAA)
PO Box 1186, Stn. Main, 7410 Dallas Dr., Kamloops BC V2C 6H3
Tel: 778-469-5040; *Fax:* 778-469-5030
info@fnala.com
www.fnala.com
Overview: A small provincial charitable organization founded in 1978
Mission: To further the social & economic well-being of Aboriginal agricultural businesses
Affliation(s): First Nations Agricultural Lending Association; Aboriginal Agricultural Education Society of British Columbia
Chief Officer(s):
Harold Aljam, President
Activities: Conferences; workshops;

First Nations Agricultural Lending Association (FNALA)
PO Box 1186, Stn. Main, 7410 Dallas Dr., Kamloops BC V2C 6H3
Tel: 778-469-5040; *Fax:* 778-469-5030
info@fnala.com
www.fnala.com/fnala.php
Overview: A small provincial organization founded in 1988
Mission: To provide loans of up to up to $350,000 to Aboriginal agricultural & agri-food businesses (on & off-reserve projects); to provide First Citizen's Fund loans & mortgages
Affliation(s): First Nations Agricultural Association; Aboriginal Agricultural Education Society of British Columbia
Finances: *Funding Sources:* Government

First Nations Breast Cancer Society
#309, 1333 East 7th Ave., Vancouver BC V5N 1R6
Tel: 604-872-4390; *Fax:* 604-875-0779
echoes@fnbreastcancer.bc.ca
www.fnbreastcancer.bc.ca
Overview: A small national organization founded in 1995
Mission: Offers breast cancer education and support to First Nations women.
Chief Officer(s):
Jacqueline Davis, President
jdavis@fnbreastcancer.bc.ca
Finances: *Funding Sources:* Donations; member fees
Membership: *Fees:* $15 regualr; $0 for breast cancer survivors

First Nations Chiefs of Police Association (FNCPA)
c/o Six Nations Police, PO Box 157, Ohsweken ON N0A 1M0
Tel: 519-445-4191
dale13@allstream.net
www.fncpa.ca
Overview: A small national organization
Mission: To serve First Nation police services & First Nation territories across Canada by facilitating the highest level of professionalism & accountability in their police services, all in a manner that reflects the unique cultures, constitutional status, social circumstances, traditions, & aspirations of First Nations
Chief Officer(s):
Stan Grier, President
stan.grier@tsuutinapolice.com
John Syrette, Vice-President
jsyrette@apscops.org
Lee Boyd, Secretary
lee.boyd@bloodtribepolice.com
William Moffat, Treasurer
lpdchief@listiguj.ca
Dave Whitlow, Executive Director
dave.whitlow@fncpa.ca
Membership: 72; *Fees:* $150 active, associate, sustaining; *Committees:* Credentials; By-Laws; Training Assessment; S.I.U. Protocol; Recruitment & Retnetion; APD Evaluation
Awards:
• National Youth Justice Policing Award (Award)

First Nations Child & Family Caring Society of Canada
#401, 309 Cooper St., Ottawa ON K2P 0G5
Tel: 613-230-5885; *Fax:* 613-230-3080
info@fncaringsociety.com
www.fncaringsociety.com
www.facebook.com/CaringSociety
twitter.com/Caringsociety
www.youtube.com/user/fncaringsociety
Overview: A small national organization founded in 2003
Chief Officer(s):
Cindy Blackstock, Executive Director
Membership: *Fees:* $75 individual; $25 student; $350-$600 associate/agency

First Nations Confederacy of Cultural Education Centres
#302, 666 Kirkwood Ave., Ottawa ON K1Z 5X9
Tel: 613-728-5999; *Fax:* 613-728-2247
www.fnccec.com
www.facebook.com/134419529944964
twitter.com/fnccec
Overview: A medium-sized provincial organization
Mission: To advocate for the recovery, maintenance, enhancement & preservation of First Nations languages, cultures & traditions
Chief Officer(s):
Claudette Commanda, Executive Director
Donna Goodleaf, National President
Tiffany Sark-Carr, Vice-President
Dorothy Myo, Secretary-Treasurer
Membership: 87 First Nations cultural centres & programs; *Member Profile:* Canadian First Nations cultural centres & programs
Activities: Providing programs & technical support to member centres; Developing projects; Offering public education; Increasing cultural awarness; Liaising with government, museums, academic institutions, & professional groups; Establishing partnerships; Assisting in the establishment of First Nations cultural centres

First Nations Education Council (FNEC)
95, rue De l'Ours, Wendake QC G0A 4V0
Tel: 418-842-7672; *Fax:* 418-842-9988
info@cepn-fnec.com
www.cepn-fnec.com
www.facebook.com/cepn.fnec
www.youtube.com/user/CEPNFNEC
Overview: A small national organization
Mission: To achieve full jurisdiction over education. This will be accomplished through mutual collaboration, in providing mandates to the Education Secretariat in Assembly, to support, promote, inform and defend the interests and actions of members in regards to all matters of education, while respecting our unique cultural identities and common beliefs, and promoting our languages, values and traditions.
Chief Officer(s):
Lise Bastien, Director
lbastien@cepn-fnec.com
Publications:
• The Journal
Type: Newsletter; *Frequency:* 2 pa

First Nations Environmental Network
PO Box 394, Tofino BC V0R 2Z0
Tel: 250-726-5265; *Fax:* 250-725-2357
councilfire@hotmail.com
www.fnen.org
Overview: A small national organization overseen by Canadian Environmental Network
Mission: The First Nations Environmental Network is a circle of First Nations people committed to protecting, defending, and restoring the balance of all life by honouring traditional Indigenous values and the path of our ancestors. We encourage the work of protecting, defending and healing Mother Earth. We desire and need to link grassroots Indigenous people nationally and internationally to support each other on environmental struggles and concerns. We are obligated to leave footprints for our children to follow by striving to live our life with traditional values.
Membership: 20;

First Nations Friendship Centre (FNFC)
2904 - 29th Ave., Vernon BC V1T 1Y7
Tel: 250-542-1247
fnfc@shawcable.com
fnfcvernon.com
Also Known As: First Nations Friendship Centre Society
Overview: A small local charitable organization founded in 1975
Mission: To improve the quality of life for Native People in a welcome environment, by supporting self-determined activities which encourage equal access to & participation in Canadian society & which respect Native cultural distinctiveness
Activities: Programs for children, youth & adults; health programs

First Nations SchoolNet (FNS)
Indian & Northern Affairs Canada, Education Program Directorate, 10 Wellington St., North Tower, Gatineau QC K1A 0H4
Toll-Free: 800-567-9604; *TTY:* 866-553-0554
pnr-fns@ainc-inac.gc.ca
www.ainc-inac.gc.ca/edu/ep/index1-eng.asp
Overview: A medium-sized national organization founded in 1996
Mission: Established by the federal government, FNS provides internet access, computer equipment & technical support to First

Nations schools on reserves across the country. Students can connect with each other, develop new skills, & participate in national & international events. Six non-profit, regional management organizations deliver the program in their respective region, working with Indian & Northern Affairs Canada.
Membership: *Member Profile:* All First Nations schools
Atlantic Region
c/o Mi'kmaw Kina'matnewey, 47 Maillard St., Membertou NS B1S 2P5
Tel: 902-567-0842; *Fax:* 902-567-0337
Toll-Free: 877-484-7606
admin@firstnationhelp.com
www.firstnationhelp.com
www.facebook.com/firstnationhelp
twitter.com/firstnationhelp
Chief Officer(s):
Kevin Burton, Director
Jetta Denny, Communications & Youth Coordinator
jetta@firstnationhelp.com
British Columbia Region
c/o First Nations Education Steering Committee, #113, 100 Park Royal South, West Vancouver BC V7T 1A2
Tel: 604-925-6087; *Fax:* 604-925-6097
Toll-Free: 877-422-3672
info@fnesc.ca
www.fnesc.ca
twitter.com/FNESC
Chief Officer(s):
Deborah Jeffrey, Executive Director
djeffrey@fnesc.ca
Manitoba Region
c/o Keewatin Tribal Council, #26, 30 Fort St., Winnipeg MB R3C 1C4
Fax: 204-949-4015
Toll-Free: 866-397-5446
info@mfns.ca
www.mfns.ca
Ontario Region
PO Box 1439, Sioux Lookout ON P8T 1B9
Tel: 807-737-1135; *Fax:* 807-737-1720
Toll-Free: 877-737-5638
www.knet.ca
Québec Region
a/s Conseil en Éducation des Premières Nations, 95, rue de l'Ours, Wendake QC G0A 4V0
Tél: 418-842-7672; *Téléc:* 418-842-9988
info@cepn-fnec.com
www.cepn-fnec.com
www.facebook.com/people/cepn-fnec/100001611305347
www.youtube.com/user/CEPNFNEC
Chief Officer(s):
Lise Bastien, Directrice générale
lbastien@cepn-fnec.com
Josée Goulet, Directeur adjoint
jgoulet@cepn-fnec.com
Saskatchewan & Alberta Region
c/o Keewatin Career Development Corporation, 135 Finlayson St., La Ronge SK S0J 1L0
Tel: 306-425-4778; *Fax:* 306-425-4780
Toll-Free: 866-966-5232
office@kcdc.ca
www.kcdc.ca
• PRISM International
Price: $28 individual subscription; $46 library/institution subscription
Profile: Contemporary writing journal; published quarterly

First Pacific Theatre Society
1440 West 12 Ave., Vancouver BC V6H 1M8
Tel: 604-731-5483
info@pacifictheatre.org
www.pacifictheatre.org
www.facebook.com/pacifictheatre
twittor.com/pacifictheatre
Also Known As: Pacific Theatre
Overview: A small local charitable organization founded in 1984
Mission: To produce high quality theatre; to operate with artistic, spiritual, relational & financial integrity
Member of: Greater Vancouver Professional Theatre Alliance; Alliance for Arts & Culture
Affliation(s): Professional Association of Canadian Theatres
Chief Officer(s):
Ron Reed, Artistic & Executive Director
Alison Chisholm, Senior Operations Manager
Frank Nickel, Senior Business Manager
Andrea Loewen, Communications Manager
Finances: *Funding Sources:* Private; corporate; government
Staff Member(s): 6
Activities: Performances; workshops; theatre rental; *Internships:* Yes

First Portuguese Canadian Cultural Centre
60 Caledonia Rd., Toronto ON M6E 4S3
Tel: 416-531-9971; *Fax:* 416-658-3553
fpccc@firstportuguese.com
www.firstportuguese.com
www.linkedin.com/company/first-portuguese-canadian-cultural-centre
www.facebook.com/212725188833941
Overview: A small national organization founded in 1956
Mission: To provide assistance to individuals, institutions, associations or any other type of organization so as to enhance health, welfare, education, knowledge & well-being of the Portuguese-speaking community & of the Canadian community as a whole; to provide theory & practice of the principles of good citizenship; to unite members in the bonds of friendship, good fellowship & mutual understanding; to provide facilities for education & instruction in the laws of Canada, the English language & the cultures of Portugal & Canada; to receive & maintain funds for charitable, educational or any other purposes beneficial to the community
Member of: Canadian Ethnocultural Council
Chief Officer(s):
Maria Tavares, Contact
mariatavares@firstportuguese.com
Finances: *Funding Sources:* Citizenship & Immigration Canada; City of Toronto; Trillium Foundation
Membership: *Member Profile:* Portuguese-speaking
Activities: Portuguese Seniors' Centre offers social, cultural & educational programs; LINC - Language Instruction for Newcomers to Canada

FIRST Robotics Canada
PO Box 518, Stn. Main, Pickering ON L1V 2R7
Tel: 416-396-5907
info@firstroboticscanada.org
www.firstroboticscanada.org
www.linkedin.com/groups?gid=4554063
www.facebook.com/FIRSTRoboticsCanada
twitter.com/CANFIRST
www.youtube.com/user/FIRSTRoboticsCanada
Also Known As: For Inspiration & Recognition of Science & Technology
Previous Name: Canadian Association for Student Robotics
Overview: A small national organization
Mission: To create a world where science & technology are celebrated, where young people dream of becoming science & technology heroes
Chief Officer(s):
Mark Breadner, Executive Director
mark.breadner@firstroboticscanada.org

First Unitarian Congregation of Toronto
175 St. Clair Ave. West, Toronto ON M4V 1P7
Tel: 416-924-9654; *Fax:* 416-924-9655
administrator@firstunitariantoronto.org
www.firstunitariantoronto.org
www.facebook.com/223855447667879
Overview: A small national charitable organization founded in 1845
Mission: To serve the religious needs of those who embrace Unitarian Universalist principles, who respect the free exercise of private judgment in all matters of belief & who live in the Metropolitan Toronto area.
Member of: Canadian Unitarian Council
Chief Officer(s):
Shawn Newton, Minister, 416-924-9654 Ext. 222, Fax: 416-924-9655
ShawnNewton@FirstUnitarianToronto.org
Finances: *Annual Operating Budget:* $250,000-$500,000
Staff Member(s): 9; 25 volunteer(s)
Membership: 306 individuals
Activities: Monthly newcomers' orientation, weekly service, library, bookstore, social justice & community outreach, small group activities; *Internships:* Yes; *Library* by appointment
Publications:
• First Light
Type: Electronic newsletter; *Frequency:* Weekly
• Horizons
Type: Newsletter; *Frequency:* Monthly

First Vancouver Theatre Space Society (FVTS)
PO Box 203, 1398 Cartwright St., Vancouver BC V6H 3R8
Tel: 604-257-0350
communications@vancouverfringe.com
www.vancouverfringe.com
Also Known As: Theatre Space
Overview: A small local organization founded in 1983
Mission: To promoting interest in the arts in Vancouver; to nurture & support artists
Member of: CAFF
Chief Officer(s):
Eduardo Ottoni, Production Manager
David Jordan, Executive Director
Staff Member(s): 14
Activities: Produces, promotes, operates the Vancouver Fringe Festival; manages the Festival Box Office; *Awareness Events:* Vancouver Fringe Festival, Sept.

Fiscal & Financial Planning Association *Voir* Association de planification fiscale et financière

Fish Harvesters Resource Centres (FRC)
PO Box 1242, Stn. C, 368 Hamilton Ave., St. John's NL A1C 5M9
Tel: 709-576-0292; *Fax:* 709-576-0339
www.frc.nf.ca
Overview: A small provincial organization founded in 1993
Mission: The Centres assist & support the restructuring of the Newfoundland & Labrador fishing industry by providing information & resources to fish harvesters in the province. They offer business counselling & technical assistance to encourage entrepreneurship among harvesters.
Affliation(s): FFAW/CAW Fish; Food & Allied Workers Union; Atlantic Canada Opportunities Agency (ACOA)
Chief Officer(s):
Liz Smith, Executive Director
lizsmith@frc.nf.ca
Staff Member(s): 7; 330 volunteer(s)

Fish, Food & Allied Workers (FFAW)
PO Box 10, Stn. C, 368 Hamilton Ave., 2nd. Fl., St. John's NL A1C 5H5
Tel: 709-576-7276; *Fax:* 709-576-1962
president@ffaw.net
www.ffaw.nf.ca
Overview: A medium-sized provincial organization
Mission: To represent employees in the fishing industry in Newfoundland and Labrador
Member of: Canadian Auto Workers
Affliation(s): Canadian Council of Professional Fish Harvesters; National Seafood Sector Council
Chief Officer(s):
Keith Sullivan, President
president@ffaw.net
David Decker, Secretary-Treasurer
ddecker@ffaw.nfld.net
Staff Member(s): 7
Membership: 15,000; *Committees:* Community; Regional; Fleet; Fish Plants; Brewery; Metal Fabrication; Window Manufacturing; Hotel; Retail; Trawlers; Oil Tankers; Tug Boats

Fisher Branch & District Chamber of Commerce
PO Box 566, Fisher Branch MB R0C 0Z0
Tel: 204-372-8585; *Fax:* 204-372-6504
fisherchamber@gmail.com
www.facebook.com/fisherbranchchamberofcommerce
Overview: A small local organization
Chief Officer(s):
Darcy Plett, President
Membership: 30; *Fees:* $75

Fisheries Council of British Columbia *See* Fisheries Council of Canada - British Columbia Representative

Fisheries Council of Canada (FCC)
#900, 170 Laurier Ave. West, Ottawa ON K1P 5V5
Tel: 613-727-7450; *Fax:* 613-727-7453
info@fisheriescouncil.org
www.fisheriescouncil.ca
Previous Name: Canadian Fisheries Association
Overview: A large national organization founded in 1915
Mission: To represent Canada's fish & seafood industry
Chief Officer(s):
Patrick McGuinness, President
pmcguinness@fisheriescouncil.org
Membership: *Fees:* $600 associate members; $5000 special purpose associations; *Member Profile:* Enterprises &

associations that harvest, handle, process, distribute, & market fish & seafood; Associate institutions & firms that provide a product or service to the fish & seafood industry
Activities: Developing an economically sound & competitive industry; Liaising with government departments & agencies
Meetings/Conferences: • Fisheries Council of Canada 2015 70th Annual Conference, 2015
Scope: National
Description: Educational sessions, opportunities to network, & social programs
Contact Information: E-mail: info@fisheriescouncil.org
Publications:
• Building a Fishery that Works: Ottawa Update
Type: Newsletter; *Frequency:* Monthly
Profile: Updates on the Council's activities, environmental issues, Canadian & international fisheries issues, & market reports
• Fisheries Council of Canada Annual Fish & Seafood Products & Services Directory
Type: Directory; *Frequency:* Annually
Profile: Listings to promote members' products & services

Fisheries Council of Canada - British Columbia Representative
4214 - 199A St., Langley BC V3A 4V6
Tel: 604-530-7258; *Fax:* 604-530-2015
gjconsult@telus.net
Previous Name: Fisheries Council of British Columbia
Overview: A medium-sized provincial organization
Member of: Fisheries Council of Canada
Chief Officer(s):
Patrick McGuinness, President

Fishermen & Scientists Research Society (FSRS)
PO Box 25125, Halifax NS B3M 4H4
Tel: 902-876-1160; *Fax:* 902-876-1320
www.fsrs.ns.ca
Overview: A medium-sized provincial organization
Mission: To establish and maintain a network of fishermen and scientific personnel that are concerned with the long-term sustainability of the marine fishing industry in the Atlantic Region.
Chief Officer(s):
Patricia King, General Manager, 902-876-1160
pmdservices@bellaliant.net
Membership: *Member Profile:* Fishermen; Research scientists; *Committees:* Communications; Scientific Program; Shellfish Working Group;Groundfish Working Group; Nearshore Temperature Monitoring Project Working Group

Fitness New Brunswick (NBCFAL) / Conditionnement physique Noueau-Brunswick (CCPVANB)
Lady Beaverbrook Gym, University of New Brunswick, PO Box 4400, #A112A, 2 Peter Kelly Dr., Fredericton NB E3B 5A3
Tel: 506-453-1094; *Fax:* 506-453-1099
Toll-Free: 888-790-1411
membershipservices@fitnessnb.ca
www.fitnessnb.ca
www.facebook.com/Fitness.New.Brunswick
Previous Name: New Brunswick Council for Fitness & Active Living (NBCFAL); New Brunswick Fitness Council
Overview: A small provincial organization founded in 1988
Mission: To certify fitness professionals in New Brunswick; to promote professionalism in the fitness industry; To offer standardization & consistency in training programs; To uphold professional ethics through the Code of Conduct for fitness service providers
Member of: Coalition for Active Living (CCAL)
Affliation(s): Atlantic Canadian Society for Exercise Physiology (CSEP) Health & Fitness Program (H&FP); National Fitness Leadership Alliance (NFLA)
Chief Officer(s):
Eric Porcellato, President
Marilynn Georgas, Executive Director
executivedirector@fitnessnb.ca
Membership: *Fees:* $50; *Committees:* Professional Development; Marketing & Communications; Human Resources; Translation; Conference
Activities: Providing fitness education in New Brunswick; Raising public awareness of safe & effective practices for fitness professionals
Publications:
• Fitness New Brunswick Member Handbook
Type: Handbook
• Fitness New Brunswick Monthly Update
Type: Newsletter; *Frequency:* Monthly
Profile: Fitness New Brunswick activities, articles, job opportunities, & equipment sales
• Inside Fitness
Type: Newsletter
Profile: Information for fitness professionals in New Brunswick, including articles & forthcoming professional development opportunities

The 519 Church St. Community Centre
519 Church St., Toronto ON M4Y 2C9
Tel: 416-392-6874; *Fax:* 416-392-0519
info@the519.org
www.the519.org
www.facebook.com/The519
twitter.com/The519
www.youtube.com/The519Toronto
Overview: A medium-sized local charitable organization founded in 1975
Mission: The 519 is a meeting place and focal point for its diverse downtown communities working to respond to the needs of the local neighbourhood and the broader Lesbian, Gay, Bisexual, Transsexual, Transgender, and Queer community.
Chief Officer(s):
Maura Lawless, Executive Director
Finances: *Annual Operating Budget:* $3 Million-$5 Million; *Funding Sources:* Federal, provincial & municipal governments; United Way; individual & corporate donors

Flamborough Chamber of Commerce (FCC)
#227, 7 Innovation Dr., Flamborough ON L9H 7H9
Tel: 905-689-7650; *Fax:* 905-689-1313
admin@flamboroughchamber.ca
flamboroughchamber.ca
Overview: A small local organization founded in 1982
Mission: To recognize & encourage good corporate citizenship, defending & promoting private enterprise; To contribute to the growth of a healthy local economy & continual improvement to the quality of life in Flamborough
Affliation(s): Ontario & Canadian Chamber of Commerce
Chief Officer(s):
Jason Small, President
Arend Kersten, Executive Director
arend@flamboroughchamber.ca
Finances: *Funding Sources:* Membership fees
Staff Member(s): 2
Membership: *Fees:* Schedule available depending on number of employees
Activities: *Awareness Events:* Awards ceremony
Awards:
• Outstanding Business Achievement Awards (Award)
• Lifetime Achievement Award (Award)
Publications:
• Bottom Line [a publication of the Flamborough Chamber of Commerce]
Type: Newspaper
• Flamborough Community Guide & Business Directory
Type: Directory

Flamborough Information & Community Services (FICS)
Millgrove Library, PO Box 240, 857 Millgrove Side Rd., Waterdown ON L0R 2H0
Tel: 905-689-7880; *Fax:* 905-689-6828
Toll-Free: 800-297-3427
fics@infoflam.on.ca
www.infoflam.on.ca
Overview: A small local charitable organization founded in 1977 overseen by InformOntario
Mission: To empower residents through information & referral services; to enhance quality of life by identifying unmet needs, liaising with the community & facilitating social services
Member of: Inform Hamilton
Chief Officer(s):
Shelley Scott, Executive Director
sscott@hpl.ca
Finances: *Annual Operating Budget:* $50,000-$100,000
Staff Member(s): 2; 5 volunteer(s)

Flavour Manufacturers Association of Canada (FMAC) / Association canadienne de fabricants des arômes
#600, 100 Sheppard Ave. East, Toronto ON M2N 5N6
Tel: 416-510-8036; *Fax:* 416-510-8043
info@flavourcanada.ca
www.flavorcanada.com
Overview: A medium-sized national organization founded in 1990
Mission: To serve the needs of the Canadian flavour industry by providing a forum for the examination of industry problems, assisting in the implementation of solutions, & fostering a global perspective for creativity, innovation & competition.
Membership: *Member Profile:* Flavour manufacturers; flavour ingredient suppliers; others with interest in the Canadian flavour industry

Flax Canada 2015 Inc.
#465, 167 Lombard Ave., Winnipeg MB R3B 0T6
Tel: 204-942-2115; *Fax:* 204-982-2128
kelley@fc2015.ca
www.fc2015.ca
Overview: A small national organization
Mission: To position flax as one of the main drivers of the Canadian bio-economy by the year 2015; To develop health care strategies based on flaxseed; To increase research & commercialization of new products from flax; To ensure utilization of value-added components from seed & straw; To develop a "branding strategy" for flax; To capture opportunities provided by the multiple end-uses of flax to increase net farm income; To improve agricultural sustainability & to enhance Canada's rural communities
Chief Officer(s):
Kelley C. Fitzpatrick, Director
kelleyf@shaw.ca

Flax Council of Canada
#465, 167 Lombard Ave., Winnipeg MB R3B 0T6
Tel: 204-982-2115; *Fax:* 204-982-2128
flax@flaxcouncil.ca
www.flaxcouncil.ca
Overview: A medium-sized national organization founded in 1985
Mission: To provide a central focus for industry, producers, government, research institutions & marketing organizations; to promote flax worldwide through crop, market & product development.
Chief Officer(s):
William Hill, President
Staff Member(s): 4
Membership: *Committees:* Communications; Market Development; Research & Technical; Member Relations; Value Added Processing; Finance
Activities: *Library* Open to public

Flemingdon Community Legal Services
#1, 1 Leaside Park Dr., Toronto ON M4H 1R1
Tel: 416-441-1764; *Fax:* 416-441-0269
www.flemingdonlegal.com
Overview: A small local organization founded in 1980
Mission: The agency provides free legal assistance to low income people who live within their geographical catchbasin. Cases taken involve: landlord/tenant law; employment & income; immigration matters. There is also a satellite office at 5 Massey Square Toronto, ON, M4C 5L3, 416-461-0969. Walk-ins are welcome.
Chief Officer(s):
Marjorie Hiley, Executive Director
Finances: *Funding Sources:* Legal Aid Ontario
Staff Member(s): 14

Flemingdon Neighbourhood Services
#104, 10 Gateway Blvd., Toronto ON M3C 3A1
Tel: 416-424-2900; *Fax:* 416-424-3455
info@fnservices.org
www.fnservices.org
Overview: A medium-sized local charitable organization
Mission: To enhance the over-all quality of life for residents of Flemingdon Park and the City of Toronto by increasing access to information and community resources for our clients through advocacy, empowerment and education.
Chief Officer(s):
John Carey, Executive Director
Finances: *Annual Operating Budget:* $500,000-$1.5 Million; *Funding Sources:* Government, United Way
Staff Member(s): 21
Membership: *Fees:* Free

A fleur de sein
313 3e Rue, Chibougamau QC G8P 1N4
Tél: 418-748-7914; *Téléc:* 418-748-4422
Aperçu: *Dimension:* petite; *Envergure:* locale; fondée en 1987
Mission: Offrir solidarité, présence, écoute & entraide à ceux & celles qui sont atteints d'un cancer, quel qu'il soit

Membre de: Regroupement Provincial des Organismes et Groupes d'entraide Communautaire en Oncologie; Vie Nouvelle
Affiliation(s): Réseau québécoise pour la santé du sein
Membre(s) du bureau directeur:
Suzanne Hamel Migneaul, Présidente, A fleur de sein
Membre: 75 individus

Fleurs Canada *See* Flowers Canada

Flin Flon & District Chamber of Commerce
#235, 35 Main St., Flin Flon MB R8A 1J7
Tel: 204-687-4518; *Fax:* 204-687-4456
flinflonchamber@mts.net
www.cityofflinflon.com/chamber
Overview: A medium-sized local organization founded in 1948
Mission: To promote & improve trade & commerce & the economic, civic & social welfare of the district; the Chamber represents the communities of Flin Flon, Creighton, Denare Beach, & Cranberry Portage.
Chief Officer(s):
Kory Eastman, President
Tom Therien, President Elect
Finances: *Funding Sources:* City Map; postcards; gala; membership
Staff Member(s): 1
Membership: 105; *Fees:* Based on number of employees; *Committees:* Fundraising; Government Liaison; Education & Training
Activities: *Speaker Service:* Yes

Flin Flon Indian & Metis Friendship Centre
57 Church St., Flin Flon MB R8A 1K8
Tel: 204-687-3900
Also Known As: Flin Flon Indian-Metis Friendship Association Inc.
Overview: A small local organization founded in 1966
Mission: To encourage active participation of Aboriginal people in Canadian society, promoting awareness of Aboriginal cultural; to provide culturally sensitive programs & services to members of the community.
Activities: Sweetgrass Aboriginal Head Start Initiative; Community Youth Resource Centre; Partners For Careers; Parent/Child Centred Initiative;

Floorball Canada (FC)
347 Brunswick Ave., Toronto ON M5R 2Z1
Tel: 416-970-2529
info@floorballcanada.org
www.floorballcanada.org
www.facebook.com/CanadaFloorball
twitter.com/CanadaFloorball
Overview: A small national organization
Mission: To be the official governing body of the sport of floorball in Canada.
Member of: International Floorball Federation
Affiliation(s): International Olympic Committee
Chief Officer(s):
Randy Sa'd, President

Floorball Nova Scotia
NS
playfloorball.weebly.com
www.linkedin.com/pub/floorball-nova-scotia/5a/831/b28
www.facebook.com/256739071063733
Overview: A small provincial organization overseen by Floorball Canada
Mission: To be the provincial governing body for the sport of floorball in Nova Scotia.
Member of: Floorball Canada
Membership: 5 provincial leagues

Floorball Ontario (FO)
ON
e-mail: info@floorballontario.com
www.floorballontario.com
Overview: A small provincial organization overseen by Floorball Canada
Mission: To be the provincial governing body for the sport of floorball in Ontario.
Member of: Floorball Canada
Chief Officer(s):
Kultar Singh, President
David Thomas, Director, Corporate Relations

Floorball Québec
2105 Guerin St., Laval QC H7E 1R7
Tel: 514-567-8449
info@floorballqc.ca
www.floorballqc.ca
www.facebook.com/floorballqc
twitter.com/floorballqc
www.youtube.com/user/iffchannel
Overview: A small provincial organization founded in 2014 overseen by Floorball Canada
Mission: To promote floorball in Quebec
Member of: Floorball Canada

Floorcovering Institute of Ontario (FIO)
#101, 987 Clarkson Rd. South, Mississauga ON L5J 2V8
Tel: 905-822-2280; *Fax:* 905-822-2494
Toll-Free: 877-604-4384
info@thefio.ca
www.thefio.ca
Overview: A medium-sized provincial organization overseen by National Floor Covering Association
Chief Officer(s):
Jason Walker, President
Membership: 500; *Fees:* $295-$555

FLORA Community WEB
www.flora.org
Overview: A small local organization
Mission: To promote the use of the internet & other electronic communications tools to help build stronger communities
Member of: Telecommunities Canada; OX
Affiliation(s): Ottawa Peace & Environment Research Centre; Auto-Free Ottawa; Citizens for Safe Cycling; Ottawa News Administrative Group
Chief Officer(s):
Russell McOrmond, Coordinator
Finances: *Annual Operating Budget:* Less than $50,000; *Funding Sources:* Sponsors
Activities: Research; lobbying; networking

FloraQuebeca
4101, rue Sherbrooke Est, Montréal QC H1X 2B2
Tél: 450-258-0448
floraquebeca@hotmail.com
www.floraquebeca.qc.ca
Aperçu: *Dimension:* petite; *Envergure:* locale; Organisme sans but lucratif; fondée en 1996
Mission: Vouée à la connaissance, à la promotion et surtout à la protection de la flore et des paysages végétaux du Québec
Membre(s) du bureau directeur:
André Lapointe, Président
Finances: *Budget de fonctionnement annuel:* Moins de $50,000
5 bénévole(s)
Membre: 105; *Montant de la cotisation:* 15$ individuel; 20$ familial; *Comités:* Bulletin; Flore québécoise; Bryologie; Flore photographique

Florenceville-Bristol Chamber of Commerce
PO Box 601, Florenceville-Bristol NB E7L 1Y7
Tel: 506-392-0900; *Fax:* 506-392-5211
chamber@florencevillebristol.ca
www.florencevillebristol.ca/html/chamber.html
Overview: A small local organization
Chief Officer(s):
Doug Thomson, Treasurer

Flowercart
9412 Commercial St., New Minas NS B4N 3E9
Tel: 902-681-0120; *Fax:* 902-681-0922
reception@flowercart.ca
www.flowercart.ca
www.facebook.com/Flowercart
Overview: A small local charitable organization founded in 1970
Mission: To provide supported training & employment for adults with intellectual disabilities
Member of: DIRECTIONS Council for Vocational Services Society
Chief Officer(s):
David Cameron, Chair
Roger Tatlock, Executive Director/Manager
Membership: *Committees:* Budget
Publications:
- FlowercartNEWS

Type: Newsletter; *Frequency:* 3 pa

Flowers Canada (FC) / Fleurs Canada
Retail & Distribution Sector, #305, 99 Fifth Ave., Ottawa ON K1S 5P5
Fax: 866-671-8091
Toll-Free: 800-447-5147
flowers@flowerscanada.org
www.flowerscanada.org
Also Known As: Association of the Canadian Floral Industry
Overview: A medium-sized national organization founded in 1897
Mission: To act as the voice of the Canadian floriculture industry; To improve the Canadian floriculture industry
Chief Officer(s):
James Fuller, Chairman
Membership: 1,000; *Fees:* $200 associates; $265 retailers; $500 distributors & wholesalers; *Member Profile:* Flower growers; Distributors; Retailers; Educators; Associates
Activities: Establishing partnerships; Researching; Developing consumers; Taking legislative action; Encouraging professional accreditation; Providing education; Offering business services; Giving sales & marketing support; Organizing conferences; Communicating with members; Developing standards; Conducting research; Identifying & sharing best practices; Promoting e-business; Presenting awards; *Library:* Flowers Canada Library

Flowers Canada Growers (FCA)
#7, 45 Speedvale Ave. East, Guelph ON N1H 1J2
Tel: 519-836-5495; *Fax:* 519-836-7529
Toll-Free: 800-698-0113
flowers@fco.on.ca
www.flowerscanadagrowers.com
Overview: A medium-sized national organization
Mission: To help members increase their exposure & sales by addressing issues pertaining to the industry
Chief Officer(s):
Dean Shoemaker, Executive Director
Staff Member(s): 12
Membership: 357

Foam Lake & District Chamber of Commerce
PO Box 238, Foam Lake SK S0A 1A0
Tel: 306-272-4578
Overview: A small local organization

Focolare Movement - Work of Mary / Mouvement des Focolari
PO Box 69523, 5845 Yonge St., Toronto ON M2M 4K3
Tel: 416-250-6606
toronto@focolare.ca
www.focolare.ca
www.facebook.com/pages/focolareorg/190678934277979
twitter.com/Focolare_org
vimeo.com/focolareorg
Overview: A small local charitable organization founded in 1943
Mission: To fulfill Jesus' last will & testament: "That all may be one"; To strive for the Focolare spirituality to have an impact on family life, youth, & all areas of ecclesial & secular life; To promote the ideals of unity & universal brotherhood
Affiliation(s): Archdiocese of Toronto
Chief Officer(s):
Brigitte Sass, Contact, Women's Branch
Jacques Maillet, Contact, Men's Branch
Finances: *Funding Sources:* Donations
Membership: *Member Profile:* Individuals of all ages, walks of life, & vocations; Churches of religions & convictions that differ from Catholicism
Activities: Providing gatherings for families, youth, children, & various branches
Publications:
- Living World

Type: Magazine; *Frequency:* Monthly
Profile: Articles on religion & culture

Focus for Ethnic Women (FEW)
#9, 145 Columbia St. West, Waterloo ON N2L 3L2
Tel: 519-746-3411; *Fax:* 519-746-6799
ffew@golden.net
www.few.on.ca
www.facebook.com/Focusforethnicwomen
twitter.com/Focus4EthnicWmn
Overview: A small local organization founded in 1987
Mission: To enhance the participation of immigrant & visible minority women in Canadian society, through innovative & collaborative efforts among the board, staff, participants, funders & community partners
Chief Officer(s):
Leanne Casey, Executive Director
leanne@few.on.ca
Maryam Naji, Job Developer
maryam@few.on.ca

Jane Sparks, Employment Specialist
jane@few.on.ca
Staff Member(s): 13; 9 volunteer(s)
Membership: 19
Activities: Career exploration & counselling; Skills training; Job search assistance; Resume- & cover letter-building workshops; Industrial sewing training; Leadership & personal development workshops; Interview preparation; Computer training; *Awareness Events:* Focus on Friends Fundraising; *Library:* Learner Resource Centre

Focus on the Family Canada

19946 - 80A Ave., Langley BC V2Y 0J8
Tel: 604-455-7900; *Fax:* 604-455-7999
Toll-Free: 800-661-9800
Other Communication: events@fotf.ca; hr@fotf.ca; volunteers@fotf.ca
letters@fotf.ca
www.focusonthefamily.ca
www.facebook.com/fotfcanada
twitter.com/fotfcanada
Overview: A large national charitable organization founded in 1982
Mission: To strengthen & encourage the Canadian family through education & resources
Member of: Canadian Council of Christian Charities
Chief Officer(s):
Terence Rolston, President
Finances: *Funding Sources:* Donations
250 volunteer(s)
Activities: *Library*
Publications:
• inFocus
Type: Newsletter
• Thriving Family
Type: Magazine

Fogo Island Folk Alliance

PO Box 146, Fogo NL A0G 2B0
Tel: 709-266-2403
Brimstonehead_festival@yahoo.ca
brimstoneheadfestival.com
www.facebook.com/BrimstoneHeadFolkFestival
Overview: A small local organization founded in 1985
Mission: To promote traditional Newfoundland & Irish music
Finances: *Funding Sources:* Provincial
Activities: The Brimstone Head Folk Festival;

FogQuest

448 Monarch Pl., Kamloops BC V2E 2B2
Tel: 250-374-1745; *Fax:* 250-374-1746
info@fogquest.org
www.fogquest.org
Overview: A small international charitable organization founded in 1987
Mission: To plan & implement water projects for rural communities located in developing countries
Chief Officer(s):
Robert Schemenauer, Executive Director
Melissa Rosato, Associate Executive Director
Finances: *Funding Sources:* Grants; donations; membership fees
Membership: *Fees:* $40
Meetings/Conferences: • 7th International Conference on Fog, Fog Collection and Dew, 2016, University of Wroclaw, Wroclaw
Scope: International
Contact Information: Mietek Sobik; sobikmie@meteo.uni.wroc.pl

Foire agricole royale d'hiver *See* Royal Agricultural Winter Fair Association

Folk Arts Council of St Catharines

85 Church St., St Catharines ON L2R 3C7
Tel: 905-685-6589; *Fax:* 905-685-8376
www.folk-arts.ca
Also Known As: Niagara Folk Arts Multicultural Centre
Overview: A small local charitable organization founded in 1970
Mission: To support the community of newcomers in the Niagara region
Member of: Regional Association of Volunteer Administrators; Festival & Event Ontario; Niagara North Community Legal Assistance; Ontario Council of Agencies Serving Immigrants; Community Development & Race Relations
Affliation(s): Canadian Council of Refugees; St. Catharines & Area Arts Council
Chief Officer(s):
Salvatore Sorrento, President
Finances: *Annual Operating Budget:* $500,000-$1.5 Million
Staff Member(s): 25; 300 volunteer(s)
Membership: 35 associations, organizations & individuals; *Fees:* $75 ethnocultural groups; $25 community groups; $15 individuals
Activities: Youth services; skills training programs; settlement services; job search programs; English classes; Crossroads self-employment program; Community Connections for Newcomers to Canada; Childminding; *Library:* Resource Centre; Open to public

Folk Arts Council of Winnipeg *See* Folklorama

Folk Festival Society of Calgary

1215 - 10 Ave. SE, Calgary AB T2G 0W6
Tel: 403-233-0904; *Fax:* 403-266-3373
www.calgaryfolkfest.com
www.facebook.com/calgaryfolkfest
Also Known As: Calgary Folk Music Festival
Overview: A medium-sized local charitable organization founded in 1989
Mission: Promotes folk music and folk artists from several genres including blues, Celtic, traditional music, roots, global grooves, cutting-edge sounds, dub, bluegrass, funk, country, hip-hop, R& B, old-timey, spoken word, and alternative.
Chief Officer(s):
Talia Potter, Acting General Manager
talia@calgaryfolkfest.com
Kerry Clarke, Artistic Director
kerry@calgaryfolkfest.com
Dean Warnock, Production Manager
dean@calgaryfolkfest.com
Finances: *Funding Sources:* Municipal government; national government; provincial government
Staff Member(s): 11; 1350 volunteer(s)
Activities: *Speaker Service:* Yes; *Rents Mailing List:* Yes

Folklorama

183 Kennedy St., 2nd Fl., Winnipeg MB R3C 1S6
Tel: 204-982-6210; *Fax:* 204-943-1956
Toll-Free: 800-665-0234
info@folklorama.ca
www.folklorama.ca
www.facebook.com/Folklorama
twitter.com/folklorama
Previous Name: Folk Arts Council of Winnipeg
Overview: A large local organization founded in 1970
Mission: To celebrate diversity; To promote cultural understanding
Chief Officer(s):
Debra Zoerb, Executive Director
zoerbd@folklorama.ca
Finances: *Annual Operating Budget:* $1.5 Million-$3 Million
Staff Member(s): 13; 2000 volunteer(s)
Membership: 200; *Fees:* Schedule available
Activities: *Library* by appointment

Folklore Canada International (FCI)

2040, rue Alexandre-de-Sève, Montréal QC H2L 2W4
Tel: 514-524-8552; *Fax:* 514-524-0262
patrimoine@qc.aira.com
www.folklore-canada.org
Overview: A small international charitable organization founded in 1986
Mission: To promote folk arts; to organize cultural exhanges between groups at national & international levels; to organize international folk arts festivals.
Member of: Conseil international des organisations de festivals de folklore et d'arts traditionels.
Finances: *Funding Sources:* Membership dues; projects
Membership: *Member Profile:* Folk groups & festivals
Activities: Consultant expertise; training; international relations & invitations; *Speaker Service:* Yes; *Library* by appointment

Folklore Studies Association of Canada (FSAC) / Association canadienne d'ethnologie et de folklore (ACEF)

CÉLAT - Faculté des lettres, Pavillon Charles-De-Koninck, 1030 ave des Sciences humaines, Université Laval, Québec QC G1V 0A6
Tel: 418-656-2131
cfc@celat.ulaval.ca
www.acef-fsac.ulaval.ca
Overview: A small national charitable organization founded in 1976
Mission: To increase education & research in the field of folklore studies
Affliation(s): Humanities & Social Sciences Federation of Canada
Chief Officer(s):
Habib Saidi, President
habib.saidi@hst.ulaval.ca
Finances: *Annual Operating Budget:* Less than $50,000
Staff Member(s): 1; 50 volunteer(s)
Membership: 200; *Fees:* $65 organization; $50 join + $45 regular; $25 student/unwaged; *Member Profile:* University faculty, students, researchers, museum/archivist
Activities: *Speaker Service:* Yes; *Rents Mailing List:* Yes
Awards:
• Luc Lacourcière Memorial Scholarship (Scholarship)
• Marius Barbeau Medal (Award)
Publications:
• Ethnologies
Editor: Dr. Diane Tye
Profile: Annual journal

Fondation Alfred Dallaire

1111, av Laurier ouest, Montréal QC H2V 2L3
Tél: 514-277-7778
Ligne sans frais: 866-277-7778
info@memoria.ca
www.memoria.ca
Aperçu: *Dimension:* petite; *Envergure:* nationale; Organisme sans but lucratif

Fondation André Sénécal pour la recherche sur la moelle épinière *Voir* Fondation pour la recherche sur la moelle épinière

Fondation Asie Pacifique du Canada *See* Asia Pacific Foundation of Canada

Fondation autochtone nationale de partenariat pour la lutte contre les dépendances *See* National Native Addictions Partnership Foundation

Fondation Canada-Scandinavie *See* Canadian-Scandinavian Foundation

La Fondation canadienne d'ergothérapie *See* Canadian Occupational Therapy Foundation

La Fondation canadienne de l'ouïe *See* Hearing Foundation of Canada

Fondation canadienne de la maladie de lyme *See* Canadian Lyme Disease Foundation

La Fondation canadienne de la porphyrie *See* Canadian Porphyria Foundation Inc.

Fondation canadienne de la recherche dur l'alcoolisation foetale *See* Canadian Foundation on Fetal Alcohol Research

La Fondation canadienne de la Thyroïde *See* Thyroid Foundation of Canada

La fondation canadienne de pédiatrie *See* Canadian Pediatric Foundation

La Fondation canadienne de recherche de l'anémie de Fanconi *See* Canadian Fanconi Anemia Research Fund

Fondation canadienne de recherche en psychiatrie *See* Canadian Psychiatric Research Foundation

Fondation canadienne de recherche en publicité *See* Canadian Advertising Research Foundation

Fondation canadienne de recherche sur le cancer de la prostate *See* Prostate Cancer Research Foundation of Canada

Fondation canadienne de recherche sur le SIDA *See* Canadian Foundation for AIDS Research

Fondation Canadienne des 3c *See* The 3C Foundation of Canada

Fondation canadienne des echanges educatifs *See* Canadian Education Exchange Foundation

Fondation canadienne des études ukrainiennes *See* Canadian Foundation for Ukrainian Studies

Fondation canadienne des femmes *See* Canadian Women's Foundation

Fondation canadienne des maladies inflammatoires de l'intestin *Voir* Crohn's & Colitis Foundation of Canada

Fondation canadienne des plantes ornementales *See* Canadian Ornamental Plant Foundation

Fondation canadienne des pompiers morts en service *See* Canadian Fallen Firefighters Foundation

Fondation canadienne Donner *See* Donner Canadian Foundation

Fondation canadienne du foie *See* Canadian Liver Foundation

Fondation canadienne du rein *See* Kidney Foundation of Canada

La Fondation canadienne du rein, section Chibougamau

CP 462, Chibougamau QC G8P 2Y8
Aperçu: *Dimension:* petite; *Envergure:* locale surveillé par The Kidney Foundation of Canada
Membre(s) du bureau directeur:
Hélène Ross-Arseneault

Fondation canadienne du service social *See* Canadian Social Work Foundation

La Fondation canadienne du syndrome de Tourette *See* Tourette Syndrome Foundation of Canada

Fondation canadienne for la promotion de la santé digestive *See* Canadian Digestive Health Foundation

Fondation canadienne MedicAlert *See* Canadian MedicAlert Foundation

Fondation canadienne pour l'amélioration des services de santé *See* Canadian Foundation for Healthcare Improvement

Fondation canadienne pour l'étude de la mortalité infantile *See* Canadian Foundation for the Study of Infant Deaths

Fondation canadienne pour l'innovation *See* Canada Foundation for Innovation

Fondation canadienne pour la pharmacie *See* Canadian Foundation for Pharmacy

La Fondation canadienne pour la recherche en chiropratique *See* Canadian Chiropractic Research Foundation

Fondation Canadienne pour le Cancer du Sein *See* Canadian Breast Cancer Foundation

Fondation canadienne pour le développement de carrière *See* Canadian Career Development Foundation

Fondation canadienne pour les Amériques *See* Canadian Foundation for the Americas

Fondation canadienne pour les sciences du climat et de l'atmosphère *See* Canadian Foundation for Climate & Atmospheric Sciences

Fondation canadienne rêves d'enfants *See* Children's Wish Foundation of Canada

La Fondation canadienne sur les tumeurs cérébrales *See* Brain Tumour Foundation of Canada

La Fondation canadienne un monde de rêves *See* A World of Dreams Foundation Canada

Fondation canadienne-polonaise *See* Canadian Polish Foundation

Fondation Cardinal-Villeneuve

#C-500, 2975, ch Saint-Louis, Sainte-Foy QC G1W 1P9
Tél: 418-529-9141; *Téléc:* 418-266-5751
fondation.cardinal-villeneuve@irdpq.qc.ca
www.irdpq.qc.ca
Aperçu: *Dimension:* petite; *Envergure:* provinciale; fondée en 1970
Mission: L'institut de réadaptation en déficience physique de Québec (IRDPQ) est un institut universitaire qui offre des services d'adaptation, de réadaptation, de soutien à l'intégration sociale, d'accompagnement et de soutien à l'entourage. Ces services s'adressent aux personnes de tout âge ayant une déficience auditive, motrice, neurologique, visuelle, de la parole ou du langage.
Membre(s) du bureau directeur:
Claude Goulet, Président
Membre(s) du personnel: 5; 200 bénévole(s)
Membre: 13
Activités: Soirée bénéfice; loterie; tournois golf; campagne de la "Pomme"; *Service de conférenciers:* Oui

Fondation Cardio-Montérégienne (FOCAM)

#230, 1750, boul Marie-Victorin, Longueuil QC J4G 1A5
Tél: 450-468-3333; *Téléc:* 450-468-3334
Aperçu: *Dimension:* petite; *Envergure:* locale
Mission: Encourager et soutenir l'avancement de la science médicale au moyen de dons permettant l'acquisition d'équipements reliés à la médecine cardiaque.

Fondation Caritas-Sherbrooke inc.

110, rue Ozias-Leduc, Sherbrooke QC J1H 1M7
Tél: 819-566-6345; *Téléc:* 819-566-6181
Info@caritas-estrie.org
www.caritas-estrie.org/organismes-connexes/fondation-caritas
Également appelé: Caritas
Aperçu: *Dimension:* petite; *Envergure:* locale; Organisme sans but lucratif; fondée en 1969
Mission: Venir en aide à Caritas Sherbrooke qui supporte des services et des organismes qui viennent répondre aux besoins des défavorisés en Estrie
Membre(s) du bureau directeur:
Yvon Couture, Directeur général
yrcouture@caritas-estrie.org
Finances: *Budget de fonctionnement annuel:* Moins de $50,000
Membre(s) du personnel: 1; 11 bénévole(s)
Membre: 10
Activités: Campagnes de financement

Fondation catholique du Manitoba *See* The Catholic Foundation of Manitoba

Fondation Centre de cancérologie Charles-Bruneau

4515, rue de Rouen, Montréal QC H1V 1H1
Tél: 514-256-0404; *Téléc:* 514-256-2116
Ligne sans frais: 877-256-0404
fondation@charlesbruneau.qc.ca
charlesbruneau.qc.ca
www.facebook.com/fcharlesbruneau
twitter.com/fcharlesbruneau
www.youtube.com/fcharlesbruneau
Aperçu: *Dimension:* petite; *Envergure:* locale; Organisme sans but lucratif
Mission: Pour amasser des fonds qui finance la recherche sur le cancer pédiatrique
Membre(s) du bureau directeur:
Rébecca Dumont, Directrice générale
rdumont@charlesbruneau.qc.ca
Membre(s) du personnel: 13

Fondation Charles LeMoyne *Voir* Fondation Hôpital Charles-LeMoyne

Fondation CHU de Québec

Hôpital Saint-François d'Assise, #E1-152, 10, rue de l'Espinay, Québec QC G1L 3L5
Tél: 418-525-4385; *Téléc:* 418-525-4393
info@fondationduchum.com
fondationduchum.com
twitter.com/FCHUQ
Aperçu: *Dimension:* petite; *Envergure:* locale; Organisme sans but lucratif
Mission: Pour augmenter des fonds sur le compte de 5 hôpitaux pour améliorer les services offerts aux patients et à financer la recherche
Membre(s) du bureau directeur:
Denis Rhéaume, Président et chef de la direction
denis.rheaume@chuq.qc.ca
Membre(s) du personnel: 24
Membre: *Comités:* Organisateur du Bal des Grands romantiques; Organisateur du Tournoi de golf; Organisateur du Loto-Voyages et cadeaux de rêve; Communications

Fondation CHU Dumont Foundation

330 University Ave., Moncton NB E1C 2Z3
Tel: 506-862-4285
Toll-Free: 800-862-6775
info@fondationdumont.ca
www.chudumont.ca
www.facebook.com/ChuDumont
Overview: A small local charitable organization
Mission: To raise money on behalf of the Dr. Georges L. Dumont Hospital to improve the services offered to patients & to fund research
Chief Officer(s):
Jacques B. LeBlanc, Executive Director
jacquesB.leblanc@fondationdumont.ca
Staff Member(s): 8

Fondation CHU Sainte-Justine

#335, 5757, av Decelles, Montréal QC H3S 2C3
Tél: 514-345-4710; *Téléc:* 514-345-4718
Ligne sans frais: 888-235-3667
fondation@sainte-justine.org
www.fondation-sainte-justine.org
Aperçu: *Dimension:* petite; *Envergure:* locale; Organisme sans but lucratif; fondée en 1987
Mission: Pour amasser des fonds pour le compte de le CHU Sainte-Justine que aident à améliorer les services offerts aux patients et à financer la recherche
Membre(s) du bureau directeur:
Anièle Lecoq, Présidente et directrice générale

Fondation communautaire d'Ottawa *See* Community Foundation of Ottawa

Fondation communautaire du Grand-Québec (FCG-Q) / Community Foundation of Greater Québec

#150, 3100, av du Bourg Royal, Québec QC G1C 5S7
Tél: 418-521-6664; *Téléc:* 418-521-6668
info@fcommunautaire.com
www.fcommunautaire.com
www.facebook.com/FCdGQ
twitter.com/FCGQ
Aperçu: *Dimension:* petite; *Envergure:* locale; Organisme sans but lucratif; fondée en 1993
Mission: La mission de la Fondation est d'améliorer la qualité de vie de la communauté en offrant à des donateurs la possibilité de créer des fonds qui constituent des capitaux perpétuels et inaliénables dont les revenus sont redistribués principalement selon les fins que poursuit chaque fonds; la FCGQ offre aux entreprises privées, aux organismes à but non lucratif, aux fondations caritatives, aux fiducies, aux individus et aux familles de l'aide et des ressources pour créer des fonds qui porteront leur nom ou celui d'êtres chers; les revenus découlant de la gestion des fonds sont répartis sous forme de subventions à toute une gamme d'organismes oeuvrant dans les domaines des services sociaux, de l'action communautaire, des arts et de la culture, de l'éducation, de l'aide internationale, de la santé et de l'environnement
Membre de: Fondation communautaire du Canada
Affliation(s): Association canadienne des professionnels en dons planifiés; Un héritage à partager
Membre(s) du bureau directeur:
Nataly Rae, Directrice générale
nrae@fcommunautaire.com
Robert Tanguay, Président
Daniel Doucet, 1er Vice-président
Diane Bélanger, 2e Vice-présidente
Membre(s) du personnel: 5
Membre: *Critères d'admissibilite:* Les membres sont actifs dans le milieu et proviennent de sphères professionnelles variées pour assurer l'équilibre dans la représentation; *Comités:* Placement; Audit; Promotion et développement; Attribution d'aide financière; Gouvernance et ressources humaines
Activités: *Stagiaires:* Oui; *Service de conférenciers:* Oui

Fondation communautaire juive de Montréal *See* Jewish Community Foundation of Montréal

Fondation culturelle Canada-Israël *See* Canada-Israel Cultural Foundation

Fondation d'aide aux personnes incontinentes (Canada) *See* The Canadian Continence Foundation

Fondation d'Alzheimer pour les proches aidants au Canada inc. *See* Alzheimer's Foundation for Caregiving in Canada, Inc.

Fondation d'art Inuit *See* Inuit Art Foundation

Fondation d'éducation économique *See* Canadian Foundation for Economic Education

La fondation de basketball Dr James Naismith *See* Dr. James Naismith Basketball Foundation

Fondation de danse Margie Gillis *See* Margie Gillis Dance Foundation

La Fondation de Jerusalem du Canada Inc *See* Jerusalem Foundation of Canada Inc

Fondation de l'Ataxie Charlevoix-Saguenay / Ataxia of Charlevoix-Saguenay Foundation

1, Place Ville-Marie, 39e étage, Montréal QC H3B 4M7

Tél: 514-878-8851; *Téléc:* 514-866-2241
ataxia@arsacs.com
www.arsacs.com
Aperçu: *Dimension:* moyenne; *Envergure:* provinciale; fondée en 2006
Mission: Financer la recherche scientifique sur l'ataxie récessive spastique autosomique de Charlevoix-Saguenay
Membre(s) du bureau directeur:
Jean Groleau, Président, Conseil d'administration

Fondation de l'entrepreneurship

#201, 55, rue Marie-de-l'Incarnation, Québec QC G1N 3E9
Tél: 418-646-1994; *Téléc:* 418-646-2246
Ligne sans frais: 800-661-2160
fondation@entrepreneurship.qc.ca
www.entrepreneurship.qc.ca
www.linkedin.com/groups/Fondation-lentrepreneurship-135631
www.facebook.com/fondationdelentrepreneurship
twitter.com/entreprendreinc
www.youtube.com/FondEntrepreneurship
Nom précédent: Fondation de l'entrepreneurship du Québec
Aperçu: *Dimension:* moyenne; *Envergure:* provinciale; Organisme sans but lucratif; fondée en 1980
Mission: Promouvoir la culture entrepreneuriale, dans toutes ses formes d'expression, comme moyen privilégié pour assurer le développement économique et social de toutes les régions
Membre(s) du bureau directeur:
Alain Aubut, Président-directeur général
aaubut@entrepreneurship.qc.ca
Pierre Karl Péladeau, Président du Conseil
Finances: *Budget de fonctionnement annuel:* $1.5 Million-$3 Million; *Fonds:* Gouvernements fédéral et provincial et entreprises privées
Membre(s) du personnel: 20; 1200 bénévole(s)
Membre: 400 institutionnel; *Montant de la cotisation:* 100$
Activités: *Stagiaires:* Oui; *Listes de destinataires:* Oui

Fondation de l'entrepreneurship du Québec *Voir* Fondation de l'entrepreneurship

Fondation de l'Hôpital de Montréal pour enfants / Montréal Children's Hospital Foundation

#1420, 3400, boul de Maisonneuve Ouest, Montréal QC H3Z 3B8
Tel: 514-934-4846; *Fax:* 514-939-3551
Toll-Free: 866-934-4846
info@fhme.com
fondationduchildren.com
www.facebook.com/lechildren
twitter.com/hopitalchildren
www.youtube.com/montrealchildrens
Overview: A small local charitable organization
Mission: Pour amasser des fonds au nom de l'Hôpital de Montréal pour enfants afin de financer la recherche et améliorer les soins aux patients
Chief Officer(s):
Marie-Josée Gariépy, Présidente
mgar@fhme.com
Finances: *Annual Operating Budget:* Greater than $5 Million
Staff Member(s): 32

Fondation de l'Hôpital du Sacré-Coeur de Montréal

5400, boul Gouin Ouest, Montréal QC H4J 1C5
Tél: 514-338-2303; *Téléc:* 514-338-3153
Ligne sans frais: 866-453-3666
fondation.hsc@ssss.gouv.qc.ca
www.fhscm.com
www.linkedin.com/company/5323549
www.facebook.com/HopitalHSCM
twitter.com/fhscm
www.youtube.com/user/HSCM2009
Aperçu: *Dimension:* petite; *Envergure:* locale; Organisme sans but lucratif; fondée en 1976
Mission: Pour amasser des fonds au nom du Hôpital du Sacré-Coeur de Montréal afin de financer la recherche et améliorer les soins aux patients
Membre(s) du bureau directeur:
Benoit Tremblay, Directeur général
benoit.tremblay.hsc@ssss.gouv.qc.ca
Membre(s) du personnel: 12

Fondation de l'Hôpital Général de Montréal / Montréal General Hospital Foundation

#E6-129, 1650, av Cedar, Montréal QC H3G 1A4
Tel: 514-934-8230; *Fax:* 514-937-7683
info@mghfoundation.com
www.mghfoundation.com
Overview: A small local charitable organization founded in 1973
Mission: Pour amasser des fonds au nom de l'Hôpital Général de Montréal afin de financer la recherche et améliorer les soins aux patients
Chief Officer(s):
Jean-Guy Gourdeau, Président et directeur exécutif
jggourdeau@mghfoundation.com%20
Staff Member(s): 10

Fondation de l'Hôpital Maisonneuve-Rosemont

#270, 5345, boul de L'Assomption, Montréal QC H1T 4B3
Tél: 514-252-3435; *Téléc:* 514-252-3943
info@fondationhmr.ca
fondationhmr.ca
www.facebook.com/fondationhmr
twitter.com/fondationhmr
www.youtube.com/user/FondationHMR
Aperçu: *Dimension:* petite; *Envergure:* locale; Organisme sans but lucratif
Mission: Pour amasser des fonds pour le compte de l'Hôpital Maisonneuve-Rosemont que contribuent à améliorer les services offerts aux patients et à financer la recherche
Membre(s) du bureau directeur:
Lucie Drapeau, Directrice générale
Membre(s) du personnel: 17; 122 bénévole(s)

Fondation de la banque d'yeux du Québec inc. / Québec Eye Bank Foundation

5415, boul de l'Assomption, Montréal QC H1T 2M4
Tél: 514-252-3886; *Téléc:* 514-252-3821
Aperçu: *Dimension:* petite; *Envergure:* provinciale; Organisme sans but lucratif; fondée en 1976
Mission: Financement de la recherche sur les maladies de l'oeil et plus particulièment de la cornée (greffe)
Membre(s) du bureau directeur:
Daniel Michaluk, Coordonnatrice administrative
Finances: *Budget de fonctionnement annuel:* $50,000-$100,000
Activités: *Service de conférenciers:* Oui

Fondation de la famille Birks *See* Birks Family Foundation

La fondation de la famille J.W. McConnell *See* The J.W. McConnell Family Foundation

Fondation de la famille Samuel et Saidye Bronfman *See* Samuel & Saidye Bronfman Family Foundation

Fondation de la faune du Québec (FFQ)

#420, 1175, av Lavigerie, Sainte-Foy QC G1V 4P1
Tél: 418-644-7926; *Téléc:* 418-643-7655
Ligne sans frais: 877-639-0742
ffq@fondationdelafaune.qc.ca
www.fondationdelafaune.qc.ca
www.facebook.com/fondationdelafauneduquebec
Aperçu: *Dimension:* moyenne; *Envergure:* provinciale; Organisme sans but lucratif; fondée en 1985
Mission: Promouvoir la conservation et la mise en valeur de la faune et de son habitat
Membre(s) du bureau directeur:
André Martin, Président-directeur général
direction@fondationdelafaune.qc.ca
Finances: *Budget de fonctionnement annuel:* $3 Million-$5 Million
Membre(s) du personnel: 17
Membre: 4 500; *Montant de la cotisation:* 20$
Activités: Programmes de subvention: amélioration de la qualité des habitats aquatiques; faire connaître nos habitats fauniques; programme d'aide à la protection des habitats; pêche en herbe, faune en danger; programme de mise en valeur des cours d'eau en milieu agricole

Fondation de la greffe de moelle osseuse de l'Est du Québec (FGMOEQ)

1433, 4e av, Québec QC G1J 3B9
Tél: 418-529-5580; *Téléc:* 418-529-4004
Ligne sans frais: 877-520-3466
info@fondation-moelle-osseuse.org
www.fondation-moelle-osseuse.org
Aperçu: *Dimension:* petite; *Envergure:* locale; Organisme sans but lucratif; fondée en 1996
Mission: Venir en aide aux personnes greffées et à leurs proches en fournissant des services gratuits ou à coût modique
Membre(s) du bureau directeur:
Pierre Drolet, Président
Activités: Service d'écoute; réseau d'entraide; service de consultation psychologique; facilités d'hébergement et service de transport; centre de documentation; *Service de conférenciers:* Oui; *Bibliothèque* rendez-vous

Fondation de la radio française en Saskatchewan *Voir* Fondation fransaskoise

Fondation de recherche de l'Institut canadien des valeurs mobilières *See* Canadian Securities Institute Research Foundation

Fondation de recherche en sciences infirmières du Québec (FRESIQ)

4200, boul Dorchester ouest, Montréal QC H3Z 1V4
Tél: 514-935-2505; *Téléc:* 514-935-2055
Ligne sans frais: 800-363-6048
info@fresiq.org
www.fresiq.org
Aperçu: *Dimension:* petite; *Envergure:* provinciale; Organisme sans but lucratif; fondée en 1987
Mission: Promouvoir l'avancement des sciences infirmières et l'amélioration continue des soins infirmiers au Québec par le soutien à la recherche et le transfert de connaissances; son but ultime demeure l'amélioration de la santé et du bien-être des Québécoises et des Québécois
Membre(s) du bureau directeur:
Gyslaine Desrosiers, Présidente
Finances: *Budget de fonctionnement annuel:* $250,000-$500,000
Membre(s) du personnel: 1; 20 bénévole(s)
Membre: 1000; *Montant de la cotisation:* 25$; *Critères d'admissibilite:* Infirmière, infirmier ou personne intéressée à la recherche en soins infirmiers; *Comités:* Scientifique; développement; promotion
Activités: Collecte de fonds; subventionner des projets cliniques soumis par des infirmières; Tournoi annuel de golf, sept.; Soirée Inspiration, mai;

Fondation de recherches médicales sur la dystonie *See* Dystonia Medical Research Foundation Canada

Fondation de recherches sur les blessures de la route *See* Traffic Injury Research Foundation

Fondation des amis de l'environnement TD *See* TD Friends of the Environment Foundation

La Fondation des Amis de la généalogie du Québec

275, rue Dufferin, Sherbrooke QC J1H 4M5
FondationAG@GMail.com
Aperçu: *Dimension:* petite; *Envergure:* locale; fondée en 1980
Membre(s) du bureau directeur:
Lise Leblanc, Présidente

Fondation des aveugles du Québec (FAQ)

5112, rue Bellechasse, Montréal QC H1T 2A4
Tél: 514-259-9470; *Téléc:* 514-254-5079
Ligne sans frais: 855-249-5112
www.aveugles.org
www.linkedin.com/company/2968845
www.facebook.com/aveugles
twitter.com/Aveugles_Qc
www.youtube.com/user/fondationaveuglesqc
Aperçu: *Dimension:* petite; *Envergure:* provinciale
Mission: Soutenir les personnes handicapées de la vue, les conseiller et les aider à mener la vie la plus autonome possible à la maison, au travail et dans les loisirs; informer le public sur l'importance de la prévention quotidienne afin de conserver une bonne vision
Membre(s) du bureau directeur:
Ronald Beauregard, Directeur général
Membre(s) du personnel: 7
Activités: Sorties éducatives; camps d'été; ski alpin

Fondation des Clubs Garçons et Filles du Canada *See* Boys & Girls Clubs of Canada Foundation

La Fondation des écrivains canadiens inc. *See* The Canadian Writers' Foundation Inc.

Fondation des étoiles / Foundation of Stars

#20S, 370, rue Guy, Montréal QC H3S 1S6
Tél: 514-595-5730; *Téléc:* 514-595-5745
Ligne sans frais: 800-665-2358
info@fondationdesetoiles.ca
www.fondationdesetoiles.ca
www.facebook.com/FondationDesEtoiles
twitter.com/EnfantsEtoiles
www.youtube.com/user/FondationdesEtoiles
Aperçu: *Dimension:* moyenne; *Envergure:* provinciale; fondée en 1963
Mission: Amasser des fonds pour la recherche sur les maladies infantiles au Québec; ces fonds sont distribués aux quatre

centres de recherche suivants: Centre de recherche de l'Hôpital Ste-Justine, Institut de recherche de l'Hôpital de Montréal pour enfants, Centre Hospitalier Universitaire de Québec et Centre Hospitalier Universitaire de Sherbrooke
Membre(s) du bureau directeur:
Josée Saint-Pierre, Présidente-directrice générale
jsaint-pierre@fondationdesetoiles.ca
David Merlo, Coordonnateur, Gestion des dons et marketing
dmerlo@fondationdesetoiles.ca
Membre(s) du personnel: 12; 200 bénévole(s)

Fondation des infirmières et infirmiers du Canada ***See*** Canadian Nurses Foundation

Fondation des maladies du coeur de la Saskatchewan ***See*** Heart & Stroke Foundation of Saskatchewan

Fondation des maladies du coeur du Canada ***See*** Heart & Stroke Foundation of Canada

Fondation des maladies du coeur du Nouveau-Brunswick ***See*** Heart & Stroke Foundation of New Brunswick

Fondation des maladies du coeur du Québec (FMCQ) / Heart & Stroke Foundation of Québec

#500, 1434, rue Sainte-Catherine ouest, Montréal QC H3G 1R4
Tél: 514-871-1551; *Téléc:* 514-871-9385
Ligne sans frais: 800-567-8563
www.fmcoeur.qc.ca
www.facebook.com/fmcoeur
www.twitter.com/FMCoeur
www.youtube.com/heartandstrokefdn
Nom précédent: Fondation du Québec des maladies du coeur
Aperçu: *Dimension:* grande; *Envergure:* provinciale; Organisme sans but lucratif; fondée en 1955 surveillé par Heart & Stroke Foundation of Canada
Mission: Forte de l'engagement de ses donateurs, de ses bénévoles et de ses employés, a pour mission de contribuer à l'avancement de la recherche et de promouvoir la santé du coeur, afin de réduire les invalidités et les décès dus aux maladies cardiovasculaires et aux accidents vasculaires cérébraux
Membre(s) du bureau directeur:
Edmée Métivier, CEO
Richard Légaré, Président du conseil
Finances: *Budget de fonctionnement annuel:* Plus de $5 Million
Membre(s) du personnel: 70
Membre: 1-99
Activités: *Stagiaires:* Oui; *Service de conférenciers:* Oui

Bas St-Laurent et Gaspésie
33, boul René-Lepage est, Rimouski QC G5L 1N8
Tél: 418-869-1022; *Téléc:* 418-869-2748
Ligne sans frais: 888-473-4636
Membre(s) du bureau directeur:
Louiselle Bérubé, Directrice régionale

Côte-Nord
1, rue Arnaud, Les Escoumins QC G0T 1K0
Tél: 418-233-2119; *Téléc:* 418-233-3771
Membre(s) du bureau directeur:
Liliane Larouche, Personne responsable

Estrie
#100, 2630, rue King ouest, Sherbrooke QC J1J 2H1
Tél: 819-562-7942; *Téléc:* 819-564-0690
Membre(s) du bureau directeur:
Manon Thibodeau, Directrice régionale

La Capitale
#261, 4715, av des Replats, Québec QC G2J 1B8
Tél: 418-682-6387; *Téléc:* 418-682-8214
Membre(s) du bureau directeur:
Jocelyn Thémens, Directeur régional

Laval/Laurentides/Lanaudière
Tour A, #410, 1600, boul Saint-Martin est, Laval QC H7G 4R8
Tél: 450-669-6909; *Téléc:* 450-669-8987
Membre(s) du bureau directeur:
Carol Pincox, Directrice régionale

Mauricie/Centre du Québec
137, rue Radisson, Trois-Rivières QC G9A 2C5
Tél: 819-375-9565; *Téléc:* 819-375-0233

Ouest de Montréal
#18, 795, av Carson, Dorval QC H9S 1L7
Tél: 514-636-4599; *Téléc:* 514-636-8576
Membre(s) du bureau directeur:
Dalia Solo, Directrice régionale

Outaouais
#007, 109, rue Wright, Gatineau QC J8X 2G7
Tél: 819-771-8595; *Téléc:* 819-771-7070
Membre(s) du bureau directeur:
Gabrielle Ouzilleau, Directrice régionale

Rive-Sud/Montérégie
#200, 1194, ch de Chambly, Longueuil QC J4J 2W6
Tél: 450-442-6387; *Téléc:* 450-442-3329
Membre(s) du bureau directeur:
Hélène Gagné, Directrice régionale

Saguenay/Lac Saint-Jean
#251, 152, rue Racine est, Chicoutimi QC G7H 1R8
Tél: 418-543-8959; *Téléc:* 418-543-5872
Membre(s) du bureau directeur:
Martine Paradis, Directrice régionale

Fondation des maladies mentales / Mental Illness Foundation

#804, 55, av du Mont-Royal West, Montréal QC H2T 2S6
Tél: 514-529-5354; *Téléc:* 514-529-9877
Ligne sans frais: 888-529-5354
info@fondationdesmaladiesmentales.org
www.fondationdesmaladiesmentales.org
Nom précédent: Fondation québécoise des maladies mentales
Aperçu: *Dimension:* petite; *Envergure:* provinciale; fondée en 1980
Mission: Pour mettre des services cliniques en place et les maintenir
Membre(s) du bureau directeur:
Brigitte Germain, Directrice générale
bgermain@fondationdesmaladiesmentales.org
Membre(s) du personnel: 13
Activités: *Listes de destinataires:* Oui

Fondation des pompiers du Québec pour les grands brûlés

1050, ch Ste-Foy, Québec QC G1S 4L8
Tél: 418-682-7709; *Téléc:* 418-682-7800
Ligne sans frais: 877-682-7709
info@fondationdespompiers.ca
www.fondationdespompiers.ca
www.facebook.com/FondationDesPompiers
www.youtube.com/user/FondationPompiers
Aperçu: *Dimension:* petite; *Envergure:* provinciale
Mission: Venir en aide aux grands brûlés de la province en améliorant la qualité des soins dont ils doivent bénéficier, via les centres de traitement et de recherche du Québec
Membre(s) du bureau directeur:
Michel Crevier, Président
Sylvie Tremblay, Directrice exécutive
Finances: *Fonds:* Dons; Lotopompiers; Lotovoyages; calendriers des pompiers
Membre(s) du personnel: 4; 700+ bénévole(s)
Activités: Tournoi de golf; soirée des bénévoles; tombolas; carting

Montréal
2600, boul St-Joseph Est, Montréal QC H1Y 2A4
Tél: 514-523-5325; *Téléc:* 514-523-3348
Ligne sans frais: 888-523-5325
info@fondationdespompiers.ca
www.fondationdespompiers.ca
Mission: La Fondation des pompiers du Québec pour les grands brûlés est un organisme sans but lucratif qui vise à venir en aide aux grands brûlés de la province en améliorant la qualité des soins dont ils doivent bénéficier, via les centres de traitement et de recherche du Québec.
Membre(s) du bureau directeur:
Denis Deschamps, Président

Québec
1050, ch Ste-Foy, Québec QC G1S 4L8
Tél: 418-682-7709; *Téléc:* 418-682-7800
Ligne sans frais: 877-682-7709
info@fondationdespompiers.ca
Mission: La Fondation des pompiers du Québec pour les grands brûlés est un organisme sans but lucratif qui vise à venir en aide aux grands brûlés de la province en améliorant la qualité des soins dont ils doivent bénéficier, via les centres de traitement et de recherche du Québec.
Membre(s) du bureau directeur:
Denis Deschamps, Président

Fondation des Prix Ernest C. Manning ***See*** Ernest C. Manning Awards Foundation

La fondation des soins avancés en urgence coronarienne du Canada ***See*** Advanced Coronary Treatment (ACT) Foundation of Canada

Fondation des sourds du Québec inc.

3348, boul Mgr-Gauthier, Beauport QC G1E 2W2
Tél: 418-660-6800; *Téléc:* 418-666-0123
Ligne sans frais: 800-463-5617
www.fondationdessourds.net
Aperçu: *Dimension:* petite; *Envergure:* provinciale; Organisme sans but lucratif; fondée en 1986
Mission: Aider les sourds dans leurs activités quotidiennes afin de contribuer à l'amélioration de la qualité de vie, dans une société d'entendants
Membre(s) du bureau directeur:
Daniel Forgues, Président
Activités: Assistance dans la recherche d'emploi; financement d'equipement; cours de LSQ; *Stagiaires:* Oui

Fondation Desjardins

1, Complexe Desjardins, CP 7, Succ. Desjardins, Montréal QC H5B 1B2
Tél: 514-281-7171; *Téléc:* 514-281-2391
Ligne sans frais: 800-443-8611
desjardins.foundation@desjardins.com
www.desjardins.com
Aperçu: *Dimension:* petite; *Envergure:* provinciale; Organisme sans but lucratif; fondée en 1970
Mission: Supporter l'éducation et la recherche en coopération, économie, administration, sciences humaines et arts
Membre(s) du bureau directeur:
Diane Derome, Directrice générale
Membre(s) du personnel: 9
Membre: *Critères d'admissibilite:* Résidents du Québec
Activités: Bourses universitaires; *Stagiaires:* Oui

Fondation Diane Hébert Inc

132, rue Blainville est, Sainte-Thérèse-de-Blainville QC J7E 1M2
Tél: 450-971-1112; *Téléc:* 450-971-1818
Ligne sans frais: 877-971-1110
fdh@macten.net
Aperçu: *Dimension:* moyenne; *Envergure:* nationale; Organisme sans but lucratif; fondée en 1987
Mission: Services directs offerts aux patients en attente de greffes, aux greffés et à leur famille autant sur le plan moral, physique ou financier; prêt d'équipements médicaux tels que chaises roulantes électriques; la Fondation vise aussi à sensibiliser la population au don d'organes
Membre de: Info Don D'Organes; Québec Transplant; Canadian Transplant Association
Membre(s) du bureau directeur:
Diane Hébert, Présidente fondatrice
Finances: *Budget de fonctionnement annuel:* $100,000-$250,000
Membre(s) du personnel: 3; 20 bénévole(s)
Membre: 20 000 individu
Activités: *Evénements de sensibilisation:* Semaine du don d'organes, dernière semaine d'avril (du L au V); *Service de conférenciers:* Oui

Fondation du barreau du Québec

Maison du Barreau, 445, boul Saint-Laurent, Montréal QC H2Y 3T8
Tél: 514-954-3400
Ligne sans frais: 800-361-8495
information@barreau.qc.ca
www.barreau.qc.ca
www.linkedin.com/groups?gid=2206718
www.facebook.com/barreauduquebec
twitter.com/BarreauduQuebec
plus.google.com/101349996276959545722
Aperçu: *Dimension:* petite; *Envergure:* provinciale; fondée en 1978
Mission: Subventionner, primer et supporter des travaux axés vers l'intérêt public et utiles à la pratique du droit.
Membre(s) du bureau directeur:
Bernard Synnott, Président
Membre: *Comités:* Accès à la profession; Arbitrage des comptes d'honoraires des avocats; Discipline, Équivalences; Exécutif; Fonds d'études juridiques; Fonds d'indemnisation; Formation continue obligatoire; Formation des avocats; Formation professionnelle des avocats; Inspection professionnelle; Médiation civile et commerciale et aux petites créances; Médiation familiale; Requêtes; Révision des plaintes; Sténographie

Fondation du bien-être animal du Canada ***See*** Animal Welfare Foundation of Canada

Fondation du CHUM

#1405, 500, place d'Armes, Montréal QC H2Y 2W2

Tél: 514-890-8077; *Téléc:* 514-412-7393
Ligne sans frais: 877-570-0797
info@fondationduchum.com
fondationduchum.com
www.facebook.com/FondationCHUM
twitter.com/FondationCHUM
www.youtube.com/user/fondationduchum
Aperçu: *Dimension:* petite; *Envergure:* locale; Organisme sans but lucratif
Mission: Pour amasser des fonds pour le compte de le Centre hospitalier de l'Université de Montréal pour améliorer les services offerts aux patients et à financer la recherche
Membre(s) du bureau directeur:
Ékram Antoine Rabbat, Président-directeur général
Membre(s) du personnel: 12

Fondation du conseil des gouverneurs du centre de recherche et de développement sur les aliments inc ***Voir*** Fondation Initia

La fondation du droit de l'Ontario ***See*** Law Foundation of Ontario

Fondation du Québec des maladies du coeur ***Voir*** Fondation des maladies du coeur du Québec

Fondation du sentier transcanadian ***See*** Trans Canada Trail Foundation

Fondation Edward Assh

80, av du Collège, Beauport QC G1E 2Y1
Aperçu: *Dimension:* petite; *Envergure:* internationale; Organisme sans but lucratif; fondée en 1989
Mission: Fondation charitable pour venir en aide aux plus démunis, orphelins, personnes âgées, infirmes dans les pays du Tiers-monde

Fondation Elizabeth Greenshields ***See*** Elizabeth Greenshields Foundation

La Fondation Émile-Nelligan

#202, 100, rue Sherbrooke est, Montréal QC H2X 1C3
Tél: 514-278-4657; *Téléc:* 514-278-1943
info@fondation-nelligan.org
www.fondation-nelligan.org
Aperçu: *Dimension:* petite; *Envergure:* provinciale; Organisme sans but lucratif; fondée en 1979
Membre(s) du bureau directeur:
Manon Gagnon, Directrice générale
Michel Dallaire, Président
Prix, Bouses:
• Prix Ozias-Leduc (Prix)
Prix triennal en arts visuels (peinture, sculpture, gravure, installations, 'land art'). Décerné à un artiste citoyen du Canada né au Québec ou à un artiste citoyen du Canada ayant sa résidence principale au Québec depuis au moins dix ans
Amount: 25 000$
• Prix Serge-Garant (Prix)
Prix triennal de composition musicale décerné à un compositeur citoyen du Canada né au Québec ou à un compositeur citoyen du Canada ayant sa résidence principale au Québec depuis au moins dix ans*Amount:* 25 000$
• Prix Émile-Nelligan (Prix)
Prix annuel. Il s'agit d'un prix de poésie décerné à un poète de moins de 35 ans, pour un recueil publié au cours de l'année
Amount: 7 500$ et une médaille en bronze frappée à l'effigie d'Émile Nelligan
• Prix Gilles-Corbeil (Prix)
Prix triennal en littérature (poésie, roman, nouvelles, récits, théâtre ou essai littéraire). Décerné à un écrivain citoyen du Canada ou des États-Unis, pour une oeuvre écrite en langue française*Amount:* 100 000$

Fondation Famille Molson ***See*** The Molson Family Foundation

La Fondation Farha ***See*** The Farha Foundation

Fondation fiduciaire canadienne de bourses d'études ***See*** Canadian Scholarship Trust Foundation

Fondation franco-ontarienne (FFO)

CP 7340, Ottawa ON K1L 8E4
Tél: 613-565-4720; *Téléc:* 613-565-8539
info@fondationfranco-ontarienne.ca
www.fondationfranco-ontarienne.ca
www.facebook.com/Fondationfranco
twitter.com/fondationfranco
Aperçu: *Dimension:* petite; *Envergure:* provinciale; Organisme sans but lucratif; fondée en 1986
Mission: La Fondation franco-ontarienne appuie financièrement la réalisation d'initiatives qui assurent la vitalité de la communauté franco-ontarienne
Membre(s) du bureau directeur:
Marie-Michèle Laferrière, Directrice générale
mmlaferriere@fondationfranco-ontarienne.ca
Membre(s) du personnel: 5
Membre: *Critères d'admissibilite:* Professionnels; commerçants
Activités: Vin et fromage; programme d'appuis financiers

Fondation fransaskoise

#205, 1440, 9e av, Regina SK S4R 8B1
Tél: 306-566-6000
Ligne sans frais: 800-670-0879
fondationfransaskoise@ccs-sk.ca
www.fondationfransaskoise.ca
Nom précédent: Fondation de la radio française en Saskatchewan
Aperçu: *Dimension:* petite; *Envergure:* provinciale; Organisme sans but lucratif; fondée en 1998
Mission: Octroi de bourses d'études en français - enseignement ou communication - en plus de subventions de projets et de programmes susceptibles à faciliter la survivance de la langue française en Saskatchewan
Membre(s) du bureau directeur:
Roger Lepage, Président
Laurette Lefol, Vice-présidente
Michel Vézina, Secrétaire
Activités: L'octroi de subventions aux communautés locales francophones pour le financement d'activités susceptibles d'améliorer la qualité de vie en français dans ses communautés

Fondation Frontière ***See*** Frontiers Foundation

La fondation Gustav Levinschi ***See*** Gustav Levinschi Foundation

Fondation Harmonie du Canada ***See*** Harmony Foundation of Canada

Fondation Héritage Canada ***See*** Heritage Canada Foundation

Fondation Hôpital Charles-LeMoyne (FHCLM)

3120, boul Taschereau, Greenfield Park QC J4V 2H1
Tél: 450-466-5487; *Téléc:* 450-672-1716
www.fhclm.ca
Nom précédent: Fondation Charles LeMoyne
Aperçu: *Dimension:* petite; *Envergure:* locale; Organisme sans but lucratif; fondée en 1964
Mission: S'occuper de réunir les fonds pour que l'Hôpital Charles LeMoyne puisse acheter et remplacer de l'équipement spécialisé et pour permettre la recherche médicale
Membre(s) du bureau directeur:
Danièle J. Martin, Directrice générale
Finances: *Budget de fonctionnement annuel:* $3 Million-$5 Million
Membre(s) du personnel: 4; 100 bénévole(s)
Membre: 100-499
Activités: Tournoi de golf mixte et féminin; grand bal; bingo; tirage-voyages; dégustation homard;

Fondation Hydro-Québec pour l'environnement / Hydro-Québec Foundation for the Environment

740, rue Notre-Dame Ouest, 8e étage, Montréal QC H3C 3X6
Tél: 514-289-5384; *Téléc:* 514-289-2079
fondation_environnement@hydro.qc.ca
www.hydroquebec.com/fondation_environnement
Aperçu: *Dimension:* petite; *Envergure:* provinciale
Mission: Promouvoir la conservation, la restauration et la mise en valeur de la faune, de la flore et des habitats naturels; soutenir les besoins locaux en matière de prise en charge de l'environnement; contribuer à l'utilisation responsable et durable des ressources naturelles
Membre(s) du bureau directeur:
Stella Leney, Présidente

Fondation Initia

3600, boul Casavant ouest, Saint-Hyacinthe QC J2S 8E3
Tél: 450-768-3340; *Téléc:* 450-773-8461
info@initia.org
www.initia.org
www.linkedin.com/groups/Professionnels-lagroalimentaire-4008965
twitter.com/initiaorg
vimeo.com/initia
Nom précédent: Fondation du conseil des gouverneurs du centre de recherche et de développement sur les aliments inc
Aperçu: *Dimension:* petite; *Envergure:* nationale; Organisme sans but lucratif; fondée en 1991
Mission: Les activités de la Fondation INITIA sont au service de tous les acteurs de la transformation des aliments et ont pour objectif de: favoriser le dialogue et l'échange; encourager l'innovation; transférer les connaissances; disséminer l'information; et faciliter la globalisation.
Membre(s) du bureau directeur:
Véronique Fournier, Directrice exécutive, Affaires scientifiques
veronique@initia.org
Membre(s) du personnel: 3
Membre: *Montant de la cotisation:* 100$ individu; 500$ institutionnel; *Critères d'admissibilité:* Secteur de la transformation des aliments
Activités: Transfert de connaissances scientifiques; *Bibliothèque:* CRDA
Prix, Bouses:
• Prix Innovation André-Latour (Prix)
Souligner les efforts soutenus en recherche et développement des intervenants du milieu *Amount:* 5 000$

Fondation Institut de Cardiologie de Montréal / Montréal Heart Institute Foundation

5000, rue Bélanger, Montréal QC H1T 1C8
Tel: 514-593-2525; *Fax:* 514-376-5400
Toll-Free: 877-518-2525
ficmdon@icm-mhi.org
www.icm-mhi.org
www.facebook.com/institutcardiologiemontreal
twitter.com/ICMtl
www.youtube.com/user/InstitutdeCardioMtl
Overview: A small local charitable organization founded in 1977
Mission: Pour amasser des fonds au nom de l'Institut de Cardiologie de Montréal afin de financer la recherche
Chief Officer(s):
Mélanie La Couture, Directrice générale
melanie.lacouture@icm-mhi.org
Staff Member(s): 20
Membership: *Committees:* Relève

Fondation Jeanne-Crevier

151, rue de Muy, Boucherville QC J4B 4W7
Tél: 450-655-8587
Aperçu: *Dimension:* petite; *Envergure:* provinciale

La Fondation Jeux Canada Games Saint John, Inc. ***See*** Saint John Jeux Canada Games Foundation Inc.

Fondation Jules et Paul-Émile Léger

130, av de l'Épée, Outremont QC H2V 3T2
Tél: 514-495-2409; *Téléc:* 514-495-2059
Autres numéros: www.flickr.com/photos/72235893@N02
info@leger.org
www.leger.org
www.facebook.com/LOEUVRELEGER
twitter.com/LOEUVRELEGER
www.youtube.com/user/LOEUVRELEGER
Également appelé: L'Oeuvre Léger
Nom précédent: Institut Cardinal Léger contre la lèpre
Aperçu: *Dimension:* grande; *Envergure:* internationale; Organisme sans but lucratif; fondée en 1981
Mission: La Fondation Jules et Paul-Émile Léger est constituée de six filiales pour mener à bien les différents aspects de sa mission. A l'international: Institut Cardinal Léger pour la santé (contre la lèpre et les grandes pendémies); La Croix d'or (enfants), le Cardinal Léger et ses oeuvres (développement durable). Les autres filiales sont au Canada: Secours aux aînés; les Partenaires contre la violence et la faim; Recours des sans-abris
Membre de: Chambre de commerce de Montréal Métropolitain
Affliation(s): Anonyme; Association l'amitié n'a pas d'âge; Centre d'action bénévole St-Siméon/Port-Daniel; Fondation de la Visite; Foyer des jeunes travailleurs et travailleuses de Montréal; Le regroupement communautaire L'itinéraire; Maison des enfants Marie-Rose; Présence Amie De La Montérégie; Programme d'aide aux jeunes mères célibataires en difficulté: l'envol
Membre(s) du bureau directeur:
André Dostie, Président
Norman MacIsaac, Directeur général
Gary Béliveau, Directeur, Finances et de l'administration
Lucie Lauzon, Directrice, Développement et programmes
Finances: *Budget de fonctionnement annuel:* Plus de $5 Million*Fonds:* Gouvernement international
Membre(s) du personnel: 30

Membre: 40; *Comités:* Direction; Consultatif honoraire
Activités: Omnium de Golf; Concert Cardinal Léger; Nourrir un Enfant
Publications:
• Au présent [a publication of the Fondation Jules et Paul-Émile Léger]
Type: Bulletin

Fondation Les oiseleurs du Québec inc.
CP 351, Succ. Lévis, Lévis QC G6V 6P1
Tél: 418-835-4066; *Téléc:* 418-835-7476
oiseleurs@oiseleurs.ca
www.oiseleurs.ca
Aperçu: *Dimension:* moyenne; *Envergure:* provinciale; Organisme sans but lucratif; fondée en 1986
Mission: Promouvoir et développer les connaissances et les recherches permettant de mieux gérer les ressources naturelles dans un contexte de développement durable; renseigner et sensibiliser le public; le conscientiser sur l'importance de la préservation des ressources naturelles dans un contexte de développement durable
Membre de: Association canadienne-française pour l'avancement des sciences; Conseil régional de l'environnement Chaudière-Appalaches
5 bénévole(s)
Membre: 1-99; *Montant de la cotisation:* 50$
Activités: *Service de conférenciers:* Oui

Fondation Lionel-Groulx (FLG)
261, av Bloomfield, Montréal QC H2V 3R6
Tél: 514-271-4759; *Téléc:* 514-271-6369
www.fondationlionelgroulx.org
www.facebook.com/fondationlionelgroulx
twitter.com/fondlgroulx
twitter.com/fondlgroulx
Aperçu: *Dimension:* petite; *Envergure:* nationale; Organisme sans but lucratif; fondée en 1956
Mission: Encourager et soutenir la recherche et les publications en histoire de l'Amérique française; entretenir l'intérêt pour l'histoire nationale; et contribuer à développer l'enseignement de l'histoire
Affliation(s): Centre de recherche Lionel-Groulx
Membre(s) du bureau directeur:
Pierre Graveline, Directeur général, 514-271-4759 Ext. 222
Finances: *Budget de fonctionnement annuel:* $250,000-$500,000
Membre(s) du personnel: 6
Membre: 100-499
Activités: Concours Lionel-Groulx pour les écoles secondaires; *Stagiaires:* Oui
Prix, Bouses:
• Prix Jean-Éthier-Blais de critique littéraire (Prix)
• Prix Maxime-Raymond (Prix)

Fondation Lucie et André Chagnon / Lucie & André Chagnon Foundation
#1000, 2001, av McGill College, Montréal QC H3A 1G1
Tél: 514-380-2001; *Téléc:* 514-340-8434
info@fondationchagnon.org
www.fondationchagnon.org
Aperçu: *Dimension:* moyenne; *Envergure:* nationale
Mission: Contribuer au développement et à l'amélioration de la santé par la prévention de la pauvreté et de la maladie en agissant principalement auprès des enfants et de leurs parents
Membre(s) du bureau directeur:
André Chagnon, Président du conseil

Fondation manitobaine de lutte contre les dépendances *See* Addictions Foundation of Manitoba

La Fondation manitobaine du droit *See* The Manitoba Law Foundation

Fondation Marie-Ève Saulnier
1125, rue Murray, St-Hubert QC J4T 3M1
Tél: 450-926-9000; *Téléc:* 450-656-5437
lindasaulnier@videotron.ca
www.fondationmarieevesaulnier.qc.ca
Aperçu: *Dimension:* petite; *Envergure:* provinciale
Mission: La Fondation Marie-Ève Saulnier améliore au jour le jour la qualité de vie des enfants atteints de cancer.

Fondation Mario-Racine / Mario Racine Foundation
#110, 2075, rue Plessis, Montréal QC H2L 2Y4
Tél: 514-528-5940
fondationmarioracine99@gmail.com
www.algi.qc.ca/asso/fmr
Aperçu: *Dimension:* petite; *Envergure:* locale
Mission: A pour mission de favoriser le développement communautaire et culturel des gais et lesbiennes à Montréal; est engagée dans la réalisation du Centre communautaire des gais et lesbiennes de Montréal.
Membre(s) du bureau directeur:
Michel Durocher, Président

La Fondation médicale canadienne *See* Canadian Medical Foundation

Fondation nationale des prix du magazine canadien *See* National Magazine Awards Foundation

Fondation orthopédique du Canada *See* Canadian Orthopaedic Foundation

Fondation Père-Ménard
1195, rue Sauvé est, Montréal QC H2C 1Z8
Tél: 514-274-7645; *Téléc:* 514-274-7647
Ligne sans frais: 800-665-7645
info@fondationperemenard.org
www.fondationperemenard.org
www.facebook.com/pages/Fondation-P%C3%A8re-M%C3%A9nard/145827832121166
Aperçu: *Dimension:* petite; *Envergure:* internationale; Organisme sans but lucratif; fondée en 1970
Mission: Améliorer de façon durable la qualité de vie des populations défavorisées des pays en développement, principalement en Amérique du sud, en encourageant et soutenant l'établissement et la gestion de projets communautaires en santé, éducation, eau et alimentation ainsi que la formation de leaders spirituels locaux
Membre(s) du bureau directeur:
Miriam Castro Herrera, Directrice générale
mcastro@fondationperemenard.org
Finances: *Budget de fonctionnement annuel:* $1.5 Million-$3 Million
Membre(s) du personnel: 3; 10 bénévole(s)
Membre: 15 000+

La Fondation pour l'avancement du droit au Nouveau-Brunswick *See* New Brunswick Law Foundation

Fondation pour la protection des sites naturels du Nouveau-Brunswick *See* Nature Trust of New Brunswick

Fondation pour la recherche sur la moelle épinière
#400, 6020 rue Jean-Talon Est, Montréal QC H1S 3B1
Tél: 514-341-7272; *Téléc:* 514-341-8884
Ligne sans frais: 877-341-7272
info@moelleepiniere.com
www.moelleepiniere.com
Nom précédent: Fondation André Sénécal pour la recherche sur la moelle épinière
Aperçu: *Dimension:* moyenne; *Envergure:* provinciale; fondée en 1994
Mission: A pour but de récolter des fonds pour financer, principalement, la recherche scientifique et médicale sur les lésions médullaires
Membre(s) du bureau directeur:
Walter Zelaya, Directeur général
wzelaya@moelleepiniere.com
Membre(s) du personnel: 18

Fondation pour le développement de la jeunesse T.R.E.E. *See* T.R.E.E. Foundation for Youth Development

La Fondation pour le journalisme canadien *See* Canadian Journalism Foundation

Fondation Québec Labrador du (Canada) inc. *See* Québec-Labrador Foundation (Canada) Inc.

Fondation québécoise de la déficience intellectuelle (FQDI)
6275, boul des Grandes-Prairies, Montréal QC H1P 1A5
Tél: 514-725-9797; *Téléc:* 514-725-3530
www.fqdi.ca
www.facebook.com/pages/FQDI/473133932730673
Aperçu: *Dimension:* petite; *Envergure:* provinciale; Organisme sans but lucratif; fondée en 1988
Mission: Amasse des fonds pour venir en aide aux organismes oeuvrant à l'intégration et à l'amélioration de la qualité de vie des personnes présentant une déficience intellectuelle
Affliation(s): Association du Québec pour l'intégration sociale
Membre(s) du bureau directeur:
Philippe Siebes, Directeur général
Activités: Collecte d'articles et de vêtements usagés par le biais de boîtes; collectes à domicile; *Stagiaires:* Oui

Fondation québécoise de la maladie coeliaque (FQMC) / Québec Celiac Foundation
#230, 4837, rue Boyer, Montréal QC H2J 3E6
Tél: 514-529-8806; *Téléc:* 514-529-2046
info@fqmc.org
www.fqmc.org
Aperçu: *Dimension:* petite; *Envergure:* provinciale; Organisme sans but lucratif; fondée en 1983
Mission: Diffuser de l'information sur la maladie et le régime sans gluten; faciliter l'approvisionnement; encourager les initiatives des membres; supporter les membres et défendre leurs droits; favoriser la recherche; solliciter des fonds pour réaliser ses mandats
Membre(s) du bureau directeur:
Suzanne Laurencelle, Directrice Générale
Finances: *Budget de fonctionnement annuel:* $100,000-$250,000
Membre(s) du personnel: 2; 60 bénévole(s)
Membre: 1 650; *Montant de la cotisation:* 75$ adhésion; 90$ professionnel de la santé; *Critères d'admissibilite:* Atteint de la maladie coeliaque; *Comités:* Club des 100 Gluten; Documentation; Communication; Financement; Info-Voyage; Médical; Support psychologique; Nutrition; Liaisons avec les régions; Colloque; Conseiller juridique; Siège social de la fondation
Activités: *Bibliothèque:* Centre de documentation; rendez-vous

Fondation québécoise des maladies mentales *Voir* Fondation des maladies mentales

Fondation québécoise du cancer
2075, rue de Champlain, Montréal QC H2L 2T1
Tél: 514-527-2194; *Téléc:* 514-527-1943
Ligne sans frais: 877-336-4443
cancerquebec.mtl@fqc.qc.ca
www.fqc.qc.ca
www.facebook.com/fqcancer
Aperçu: *Dimension:* petite; *Envergure:* provinciale; Organisme sans but lucratif; fondée en 1979
Mission: Vouée à l'amélioration de la condition de la personne atteinte de cancer et de ses proches; offrir des services d'hôtellerie, d'écoute et d'information pour gens atteints du cancer; améliorer la qualité de vie des patients et celle de leurs proches.
Membre(s) du bureau directeur:
Pierre-Yves Gagnon, Directeur général
Finances: *Budget de fonctionnement annuel:* Plus de $5 Million*Fonds:* Dons individuels; Hôtelleries; Activités-bénéfice; Entreprises; Legs testamentaires; Dons In memoriam; Fondations
1600 bénévole(s)
Activités: *Stagiaires:* Oui; *Bibliothèque* Bibliothèque publique

Hôtellerie de l'Estrie
3001, 12e av nord, Sherbrooke QC J1H 5N4
Tél: 819-822-2125; *Téléc:* 819-822-1392
cancerquebec.she@fqc.qc.ca
www.fqc.qc.ca
Membre(s) du bureau directeur:
Marie Toupin, Directrice

Hôtellerie de l'Outaouais
Pavillon Michael J. MacGivney, 555, boul de l'Hôpital, Gatineau QC J8V 3T4
Tél: 819-561-2262; *Téléc:* 819-561-1727
cancerquebec.gat@fqc.qc.ca
www.fqc.qc.ca
Membre(s) du bureau directeur:
Corinne Lorman, Directrice

Hôtellerie de la Mauricie
3110, rue Louis-Pasteur, Trois-Rivières QC G8Z 4E3
Tél: 819-693-4242; *Téléc:* 819-693-4243
cancerquebec.trv@fqc.qc.ca
www.fqc.qc.ca
Membre(s) du bureau directeur:
Luce Girard, Directrice

Hôtellerie de Montréal
2075, rue de Champlain, Montréal QC H2L 2T1
Tél: 514-527-2194; *Téléc:* 514-527-1943
Ligne sans frais: 877-336-4443
cancerquebec.mtl@fqc.qc.ca
www.fqc.qc.ca
Membre(s) du bureau directeur:
Pierre-Yves Gagnon, Directeur

Fondation québécoise en environnement / Québec Environment Foundation
#706, 1255 carré Phillips, Montréal QC H3B 3G1

Tél: 514-849-3323; *Téléc:* 514-849-0028
Ligne sans frais: 800-361-2503
info@fqe.qc.ca
www.fqe.qc.ca
www.facebook.com/FQEnvironnement
twitter.com/fqe
Aperçu: *Dimension:* moyenne; *Envergure:* provinciale; Organisme sans but lucratif; fondée en 1987
Mission: Sensibiliser les Québécoises et les Québécois à l'égard de l'environnement par l'information et l'éducation; créer une synergie entre l'économie et l'écologie; favoriser la recherche et la mise en place de solutions concrètes et efficaces
Membre(s) du bureau directeur:
Louis-Paul Allard, Président
Claude Hill, Directeur général
chill@fqe.qc.ca
Finances: *Budget de fonctionnement annuel:* $500,000-$1.5 Million
Membre(s) du personnel: 5; 35 bénévole(s)
Membre: 210 membres; 10 000 ami(e)s; *Montant de la cotisation:* 25$; *Comités:* Environnement
Activités: Journées éducatives, colloques, conférences, plantations d'arbres; *Service de conférenciers:* Oui

Fondation québécoise pour l'alphabétisation
#200, 5420, boul Saint-Laurent, Montréal QC H2T 1S1
Tél: 514-289-1178; *Téléc:* 514-289-9286
Ligne sans frais: 800-361-9142
www.fondationalphabetisation.org
www.facebook.com/fondationalphabetisation
twitter.com/fondationalpha
Aperçu: *Dimension:* petite; *Envergure:* provinciale; Organisme sans but lucratif; fondée en 1989
Mission: Faire en sorte que tous, adultes et enfants, aient accès à la lecture et à l'écriture.
Membre(s) du bureau directeur:
Nancy Leggett-Bachand, Présidente-Directrice Générale
Membre(s) du personnel: 7
Activités: Campagnes médias; *Stagiaires:* Oui; *Service de conférenciers:* Oui

Fondation Ressources-Jeunesse (FRJ)
#300, 1001, boul de Maisonneuve Ouest, Montréal QC H3A 3C8
Tél: 514-982-0577; *Téléc:* 514-286-7554
info@frj.qc.ca
www.frj.qc.ca
www.linkedin.com/company/fondation-ressources-jeunesse
www.facebook.com/480926321968659
twitter.com/FondationRJ
Aperçu: *Dimension:* petite; *Envergure:* provinciale; fondée en 1979
Mission: Intégration des jeunes (18-30 ans) sans emploi au marché du travail et la prise en main de leur carrière
Membre(s) du bureau directeur:
Francine Giguère, Présidente-directrice générale
fgiguere@frj.qc.ca
Membre(s) du personnel: 14
Activités: *Stagiaires:* Oui

Fondation Rêves d'Enfants, div. Nord-du-Québec
CP 553, 14, chemin Lac Cumming, Chibougamau QC G8P 2Y8
beaudoinmarca@hotmail.com
Aperçu: *Dimension:* petite; *Envergure:* locale surveillé par The Children's Wish Foundation of Canada
Membre(s) du bureau directeur:
Marc-André Beaudoin, Responsable

Fondation Richelieu International (FRI)
#25, 1010 rue Polytek, Ottawa ON K1J 9J1
Tél: 613-742-6911; *Téléc:* 613-742-6916
Ligne sans frais: 800-267-6525
international@richelieu.org
www.fondationrichelieu.org
www.facebook.com/pages/Le-Richelieu-International/277906642896
Aperçu: *Dimension:* petite; *Envergure:* internationale; fondée en 1944
Mission: Recueillir des dons auprès de ses membres et du grand public en général afin d'appuyer des services, des projets et des programmes visant le mieux-être des jeunes
Membre(s) du bureau directeur:
Mélanie Raymond, Directeur général
Membre(s) du personnel: 3
Membre: 250 clubs
Activités: Réseau Ado;

Fondation roumaine de Montréal / Tribuna Noastra
#RC90, 3550, ch Côte-des-Neiges, Montréal QC H3H 1V4
Tél: 514-937-4473; *Téléc:* 514-937-0049
tribunanoastra@hotmail.com
www.fundatiaromana.org
Nom précédent: Fédération des associations roumaines du Canada
Aperçu: *Dimension:* petite; *Envergure:* locale; Organisme sans but lucratif; fondée en 2005
Mission: Service d'accueil et d'intégration des immigrants
Membre(s) du bureau directeur:
Basile Gliga, Président
Finances: *Budget de fonctionnement annuel:* $50,000-$100,000
Membre(s) du personnel: 16; 50 bénévole(s)
Membre: *Comités:* Mutuelles entre les gens d'affaires canadiens et roumains
Activités: Faciliter les liaisons; *Stagiaires:* Oui; *Service de conférenciers:* Oui; *Listes de destinataires:* Oui; *Bibliothèque:* Bibliothèque de langue roumaine

Fondation Santé Gatineau
Pavillon Desjardins, #B-202, 116, boul Lionel-Émond, Gatineau QC J8Y 1W7
Tél: 819-966-6108; *Téléc:* 819-966-6012
csssgatineau_info_fondation@ssss.gouv.qc.ca
www.fondationsantegatineau.ca
www.facebook.com/FondationSanteGatineau
twitter.com/FondSanteGat
Aperçu: *Dimension:* petite; *Envergure:* locale; Organisme sans but lucratif
Mission: Pour augmenter des fonds sur le compte du CSSS de Gatineau pour améliorer les services offerts aux patients et à financer la recherche
Membre(s) du bureau directeur:
Marc Villeneuve, Directeur général
Membre(s) du personnel: 19
Membre: *Comités:* Dons Majeurs; Audit; Aviseur des Dons Planifiés; Nominations; Conjoint; Activités Publiques; Communications; Ressources Humaines; Placement

Fondation Savoy Inc. ***Voir*** Savoy Foundation Inc.

Fondation Sommeil: Association de personnes atteintes de déficiences reliées au sommeil
1600, av de Lorimier, Montréal QC H2K 3W5
Tél: 514-522-3901
Ligne sans frais: 888-622-3901
www.fondationsommeil.com
www.facebook.com/119979448083302
Également appelé: Fondation Sommeil
Aperçu: *Dimension:* moyenne; *Envergure:* provinciale; Organisme sans but lucratif; fondée en 1990
Mission: Rejoindre les gens touchés par des troubles du sommeil et les appuyer dans leur démarche
Membre de: Confédération des organismes de personnes handicapées du Québec
Affliation(s): Regroupement des organismes de promotion du Montréal Métropolitain
Membre: *Montant de la cotisation:* 25$; *Critères d'admissibilite:* Adolescents 15 - adultes
Activités: Rencontres d'échange et d'information; congrès; *Bibliothèque:* Centre de documentation; rendez-vous

Fondation sport pur ***See*** True Sport Foundation

La Fondation Terry Fox ***See*** The Terry Fox Foundation

Fondation Tourisme Jeunesse
3514, av Lacombe, Montréal QC H3T 1M1
Tél: 514-252-3208; *Téléc:* 514-252-3024
fondationtourismejeunesse@gmail.com
www.tourismejeunesse.org
Nom précédent: Organisation pour le tourisme étudiant au Québec et Fédération québécoise d'ajisme
Aperçu: *Dimension:* grande; *Envergure:* provinciale; Organisme sans but lucratif; fondée en 1989
Mission: Rendre accessible le tourisme aux jeunes, en développant divers outils et services, notamment par le biais des bureaux d'information voyages et des auberges de jeunesse du Québec
Membre de: Hostelling International - Canada
Affliation(s): Fédération internationale des auberges de jeunesse; Regroupement loisir Québec; Bureau canadien de l'éducation internationale; Bureau international du tourisme social
Membre(s) du bureau directeur:
Veronica Gomez, Directrice de la Fondation
Finances: *Fonds:* Gouvernement du Québec
500 bénévole(s)
Membre: 65 sociétés + 500 doyens/membres à vie + 9500 particuliers; *Montant de la cotisation:* 35$; *Critères d'admissibilite:* Détenir une carte de membre Hostelling International
Activités: Bureaux d'information sur les voyages; Auberges de jeunesse; Voyages Tourisme Jeunesse; Boutiques Tourisme Jeunesse; Conférences sur travail à l'étranger; Fondation Tourisme Jeunesse; *Stagiaires:* Oui; *Service de conférenciers:* Oui

La Fondation Trillium de l'Ontario ***See*** The Ontario Trillium Foundation

Fondation Wellspring pour les personnes atteintes de cancer ***See*** Wellspring Cancer Support Foundation

Fondations philanthropiques Canada ***See*** Philanthropic Foundations Canada

Fonds canadien de protection des épargnants ***See*** Canadian Investor Protection Fund

Fonds d'action et d'éducation juridiques pour les femmes ***See*** Women's Legal Education & Action Fund

Fonds d'études académiques pour les Noirs ***See*** Black Academic Scholarship Fund

Fonds des Athlétes Canadiens ***See*** Canadian Athletes Now Fund

Le fonds du Primat pour le secours et le développement mondial ***See*** The Primate's World Relief & Development Fund

Fonds du Souvenir ***See*** Last Post Fund

Fonds indépendant de production ***See*** Independent Production Fund

Fonds international pour la protection des animaux ***See*** International Fund for Animal Welfare Canada

Fonds mondial pour la nature ***See*** World Wildlife Fund - Canada

Food & Consumer Products of Canada (FCPC) / Produits alimentaires et de consommation du Canada (PACC)
100 Sheppard Ave. East, Toronto ON M2N 6Z1
Tel: 416-510-8024; *Fax:* 416-510-8043
info@fcpc.ca
www.fcpc.ca
www.linkedin.com/company/2609609?trk=tyah
twitter.com/FCPC1
Previous Name: Grocery Products Manufacturers of Canada; Food & Consumer Products Manufacturers of Canada
Overview: A large national organization founded in 1959
Mission: To represent the food & consumer products industry, from small privately-owned companies to big glboal multinationals
Chief Officer(s):
Nancy Croitoru, President & Chief Executive Officer
Glenda Costa, Vice-President, Finance & Administration
Errol Cerit, Senior Director, Industry Affairs & Membership
Rachel Kagan, Vice-President, Environment & Sustainability Policy
Janice Emery-Carter, Manager, Education Centre
Derek Nighbor, Senior Vice-President, Public & Regulatory Affairs
Heather Spencer, Coordinator, Member Services
Heather.Spencer@fcpc.ca
Jami Nirenberg, Coordinator, Events
Membership: *Member Profile:* Companies that make & market retailer & national brands
Activities: Offering educational opportunities; Engaging in advocacy activities; Advising members about government policy changes; Offering networking opportunities
Meetings/Conferences: • Food & Consumer Products of Canada 3rd Annual Health & Wellness Forum - The Science of Sugar & Sugar Substitutes, April, 2015
Scope: National

Food Bank Moncton Inc. ***See*** Food Depot Alimentaire, Inc.

Food Bank of Waterloo Region (FBWR)
50 Alpine Ct., Kitchener ON N2E 2M7
Tel: 519-743-5576; *Fax:* 519-743-8965
www.thefoodbank.ca

www.facebook.com/10150145973860618
twitter.com/FoodBankWatReg
Overview: A small local charitable organization founded in 1984
Mission: To support the well-being of low-income persons
Member of: Ontario Association of Food Banks; Food Banks Canada
Affliation(s): Dairy Farmers of Ontario
Chief Officer(s):
Wendi Campbell, Executive Director
Staff Member(s): 17
Membership: 100+; *Member Profile:* Agencies that distribute food to the less fortunate in Waterloo Region
Activities: *Internships:* Yes; *Speaker Service:* Yes

Food Banks British Columbia (FBBC)
13595 King George Blvd., Surrey BC V3T 2V1
Tel: 604-489-1798; *Fax:* 604-498-1795
info@foodbanksbc.com
www.foodbanksbc.ca
www.facebook.com/FoodBanksBC
twitter.com/RealFoodBanksBC
Overview: A small provincial charitable organization
Mission: To work to reduce hunger across BC
Member of: Food Banks Canada
Chief Officer(s):
Laura Lansink, Executive Director
laura@foodbanksbc.com
Finances: *Funding Sources:* Corporate sponsors; private donors
Staff Member(s): 2
Membership: 93; *Member Profile:* Small, medium & large food banks across the province
Activities: Coordination of product from Food Bank Canada; coordination of provincial fundraising; liaising between local food banks & national agency

Food Banks Canada / Banques alimentaires Canada
Bldg. 2, #400, 5025 Orbitor Dr., Mississauga ON L4W 4Y5
Tel: 905-602-5234; *Fax:* 905-602-5614
Toll-Free: 877-535-0958
www.foodbankscanada.ca
www.facebook.com/FoodBanksCanada
twitter.com/foodbankscanada
www.youtube.com/user/FoodBanksCanada1
Previous Name: Canadian Association of Food Banks
Overview: A medium-sized national charitable organization founded in 1988
Mission: To act as the voice for the hungry in Canada; To find short term & long term solutions for Canadians who are assisted by food banks
Member of: Global FoodBanking Network
Chief Officer(s):
Katharine Schmidt, Executive Director, 416-203-9241 Ext. 222
Brian Fraser, Chair
Marc Guay, Vice-Chair
Monica Donahue, Secretary
Allan Cosman, Treasurer
Finances: *Funding Sources:* Donations; Sponsorships
Staff Member(s): 19
Membership: 10 provincial food bank associations + 450+ food banks; *Member Profile:* Provincial food bank associations; Food banks & their associated agencies
Activities: Collecting & sharing donations of food with members; Sharing donated funds; Collecting statistics about hunger in Canada; Raising awareness of hunger; Lobbying government to establish policies to reduce hunger; Promoting the dignity of food bank clients & the ethical stewardship of food donations; *Awareness Events:* National Hunger Awareness Day
Publications:
• HungerCount
Type: Yearbook; *Frequency:* Annually
Profile: A national survey of emergency food programs in Canada
• Provisions
Type: Newsletter
Profile: Featuring statistics, advocacy efforts, & event results

Food Beverage Canada (FBC)
#201, 17914 - 105 Ave., Edmonton AB T5S 2H5
Tel: 780-486-9679; *Fax:* 780-484-0985
Toll-Free: 800-493-9767
www.foodbeveragecanada.com
Overview: A small national organization founded in 1994
Mission: To develop export strategies & programs that will strengthen & increase our members' share of global food & beverage markets

Food Depot Alimentaire, Inc.
330 MacNaughton Ave., Moncton NB E1H 2K1
Tel: 506-383-4281; *Fax:* 506-388-5822
info@fooddepot.ca
www.fooddepotalimentaire.ca
www.facebook.com/268995153176974
Previous Name: Food Bank Moncton Inc.
Overview: A small local charitable organization founded in 1986
Mission: To collect & supply food to food banks in the province
Member of: Association of Food Banks & C.V.A.s for New Brunswick; Canadian Association of Food Banks
Finances: *Annual Operating Budget:* $50,000-$100,000; *Funding Sources:* City; province; donations
20 volunteer(s)
Membership: 20 food banks

Food for Life Canada
2258 Mountainside Dr., Burlington ON L7P 1B7
Tel: 905-510-5724
info@foodforlife.ca
www.foodforlife.ca
Overview: A small local charitable organization
Mission: To collect & distribute fresh food to people in need in the Halton region
Chief Officer(s):
Ian Gibbons, Director, Operations
ian@foodforlife.ca
Staff Member(s): 7; 800 volunteer(s)

Food Institute of Canada *See* Food Processors of Canada

Food Processors of Canada (FPC) / Fabricants de produits alimentaires du Canada
#900, 350 Sparks St., Ottawa ON K1R 7S8
Tel: 613-722-1000; *Fax:* 613-722-1404
Other Communication: conferences@foodprocessors.ca
fpc@foodprocessors.ca
www.foodnet.fic.ca
Previous Name: Food Institute of Canada
Overview: A medium-sized national organization founded in 1989
Mission: To provide professional services & advice to members on matters such as manufacturing, trade, & commerce
Chief Officer(s):
Christopher J. Kyte, President
Mel Fruitman, Vice-President
Membership: *Member Profile:* Canadian food industry executives who own or manage food processing companies
Activities: Maintaining relationships with government departments to affect policies, programs, & regulations; Organizing conferences; Providing networking opportunities
Meetings/Conferences: • Food Processors of Canada Annual Executives Meeting 2015, 2015
Scope: National

Foodservice Consultants Society International - Canadian Chapter
c/o CRS Management Services Ltd., 524 Beresford Ave., Toronto ON M6S 3C1
Tel: 416-769-8097; *Fax:* 416-769-0217
canada@fcsi.org
www.fcsi.org
www.facebook.com/FCSI.Canadachapter
twitter.com/FCSIcdn
Overview: A small national organization founded in 1984
Mission: To maintain & advance a professional standard in the food service & hospitality industry
Member of: FCSI Worldwide
Chief Officer(s):
Cathy Sommers, Administrator
Activities: Fundraisers; Meetings; Educational Programs

Foodshare (Metro) Toronto *See* Foodshare Toronto

Foodshare Toronto
90 Croatia St., Toronto ON M6H 1K9
Tel: 416-363-6441; *Fax:* 416-363-0474
info@foodshare.net
www.foodshare.net
Previous Name: Foodshare (Metro) Toronto
Overview: A medium-sized local charitable organization founded in 1985
Mission: Working with communities to improve access to affordable & healthy food, from field to table
Chief Officer(s):
Debbie Field, Executive Director
debbie@foodshare.net
Zahra Parvinian, Director, Social Enterprise
zahra@foodshare.net
Finances: *Annual Operating Budget:* $3 Million-$5 Million; *Funding Sources:* Private donors; government; foundations
Staff Member(s): 15; 14 volunteer(s)
Membership: 4,000
Activities: Operates fresh fruit & vegetable distribution system, the Good Food Box; Toronto Kitchen Incubator, an industrial kitchen available for rent to entrepreneurs & community groups; Field to Table Catering Co., a CED project specializing in healthy, seasonal food; education & training on community kitchens & gardens; baby nutrition workshops; advocacy on hunger & food security; operates FoodLink Hotline: a food bank & alternative food project referral service;

Foosball Québec
QC
Tél: 418-906-0977
foosballquebec@gmail.com
www.foosballquebec.com
www.facebook.com/foosballquebec
Aperçu: *Dimension:* petite; *Envergure:* provinciale
Membre(s) du bureau directeur:
Lévesque Olivier, Président

Foot Care Canada *See* Canadian Association of Foot Care Nurses

Football BC
#434, 6939 Hastings St., Burnaby BC V5B 4Z5
Tel: 604-677-1025
communications@playfootball.bc.ca
www.playfootball.bc.ca
www.facebook.com/footballbc
twitter.com/Football_BC
Also Known As: British Columbia Amateur Football Association
Overview: A medium-sized provincial organization
Mission: To operate as the governing body for amateur football in British Columbia
Chief Officer(s):
Daniel Fung, Director, Communications
Patrick Waslen, Executive Director
Staff Member(s): 3
Membership: 6 associations; *Member Profile:* Football leagues, coaches & officials
Activities: Clnics; Camp; Education sessions

Football Canada
#100, 2255 St. Laurent Blvd., Ottawa ON K1G 4K3
Tel: 613-564-0003; *Fax:* 613-564-6309
info@footballcanada.com
footballcanada.com
www.facebook.com/FootballCanada
twitter.com/FootballCanada
Also Known As: Canadian Amateur Football Association
Previous Name: Canadian Rugby Union
Overview: A medium-sized national charitable organization founded in 1882
Mission: Through its members, to initate, regulate, & manage the programs, services & activities that promote participation & excellence in Canadian Amateur Football.
Chief Officer(s):
Shannon Donovan, Executive Director
operations@footballcanada.com
Rick Sowieta, Director, High Performance
gridiron@footballcanada.com
Patrick DeLottinville, Coordinator, Communications
communications@footballcanada.com
Aaron Geisler, Coordinator, Technical
development@footballcanada.com
Christine Piché, Administrative Coordinator
admin@footballcanada.com
Finances: *Annual Operating Budget:* $250,000-$500,000; *Funding Sources:* Membership fees; government; corporate sponsors
Membership: 110,000
Activities: Football Canada Cup; Touch Bowl;

Football Nova Scotia Association
5516 Spring Garden Rd., Halifax NS B3J 1G6
Tel: 902-425-5450; *Fax:* 902-425-5606
footballns@ns.aliantzinc.ca
www.footballnovascotia.ca
www.facebook.com/footballnovascotia
twitter.com/footballns

Overview: A small provincial organization founded in 1974
Mission: To promote amateur football in Nova Scotia, at both the competitive & recreational levels, to assist members with their programs, & to develop the sport in new areas of the province
Affiliation(s): Canadian Amateur Football Association
Chief Officer(s):
Richard MacLean, President
football@eastlink.ca
Rob Manson, Vice-President
rmanson@oceansecurities.com
Finances: *Funding Sources:* Provincial Government
Staff Member(s): 1; 14 volunteer(s)
Membership: 1,000 individual
Activities: *Rents Mailing List:* Yes

Football Ontario *See* Ontario Football Alliance

Football PEI
40 Enman Cres., Charlottetown PE C1E 1E6
Tel: 902-368-4262; *Fax:* 902-368-4548
www.peifootball.ca
twitter.com/footballpei
Overview: A large provincial organization
Mission: To operate as the provincial sport governing body for amateur football in Prince Edward Island; To promote & further the development of the sport in its three forms - flag, tackle, & touch
Chief Officer(s):
Glen Flood, Executive Director
gflood@sportpei.pe.ca
Shaun Matheson, President
matheson_shaun@yahoo.com

Football Québec (FFAQ) / Fédération de football amateur de Québec
4545, av Pierre-de Coubertin, Montréal QC H1V 0B2
Tél: 514-252-3059; *Téléc:* 514-252-5216
footballquebec.com
www.facebook.com/footballquebec
twitter.com/footballquebec
www.youtube.com/profile?user=footballqc
Aperçu: *Dimension:* moyenne; *Envergure:* provinciale; fondée en 1882
Mission: Régir le développement du football au Québec, avec règlement de securité, formation des entraîneurs et des officiels, et les championnats provinciaux
Membre de: Sport Québec
Affiliation(s): National Football Federation of Canada
Membre(s) du bureau directeur:
René Robillard, Président
Jean-Charles Meffe, Directeur Général
jeancharles@football.qc.ca
Finances: *Budget de fonctionnement annuel:* $250,000-$500,000; *Fonds:* Gouvernement provincial
Membre(s) du personnel: 3; 3000 bénévole(s)
Membre: 15 000; *Montant de la cotisation:* 15$ individu

Foothills Forage & Grazing Association (FFGA)
PO Box 5145, High River AB T1V 1M3
Tel: 403-652-4900; *Fax:* 403-652-4090
www.foothillsforage.com
www.facebook.com/166272723417016
twitter.com/FoothillsForage
Overview: A small local organization founded in 1972 overseen by Agricultural Research & Extension Council of Alberta
Mission: To provide forage & livestock information to producers; to partner with industry, government & the agricultural community
Member of: Agricultural Research & Extension Council of Alberta
Chief Officer(s):
Laura Gibney, Manager
laura@foothillsforage.com
Membership: *Foos:* $31.50; *Member Profile:* Any individual or firm involved in the production of forage
Publications:
• Grassroots News & Views [a publication of Foothills Forage & Grazing Association]
Type: Newsletter

Foothills Library Association (FLA)
PO Box 2985, Stn. M, Calgary AB T2P 3C3
e-mail: flapresident@fla.org
www.fla.org
Overview: A small local organization founded in 1975
Mission: To share & promote the concerns of libraries & information professionals in the Calgary area
Chief Officer(s):
Jerremie Clyde, President, 403-220-7391
flapresident@fla.org
Katharine Barrette, Vice-President, 403-440-6126
flavp@fla.org
Francine May, Secretary, 403-217-3202
secretary@fla.org
Julia Brewster, Treasurer, 403-260-2717
treasurer@fla.org
Kathryn Ranjit, Contact, Membership, 403-943-4736
memberships@fla.org
Membership: *Fees:* $25; *Member Profile:* People interested in the information professions in the Foothills region of Alberta; Institutions & organizations interested in the objects of the association
Activities: Facilitating networking opportunities within the Calgary library community; Offering presentations & discussions on prominent issues in libraries in the region; Organizing seminars, lectures, & tours to contribute to the professional development of members
Meetings/Conferences: • Foothills Library Association 2015 Calgary Libraries in Action, 2015, AB
Scope: Local
Description: Prominent issues for librarians are explored through presentations & discussions.
Contact Information: Events Line Contact: Inesia Adolph, E-mail: events@fla.org
• Foothills Library Association 2015 Annual General Meeting, September, 2015, AB
Scope: Local
Description: A general meeting & social event.
Contact Information: Events Line Contact: Inesia Adolph, E-mail: events@fla.org
Publications:
• Foothills Library Association Gazette (FLAG)
Type: Newsletter; *Frequency:* Quarterly; *Price:* Free with membership in the Foothills Library Association
Profile: Foothills Library Association business & activities
• Foothills Library Association Membership Directory
Type: Directory; *Editor:* John Wright; Katie Edwards
Profile: Listings of members' names & affiations

Foothills Model Forest *See* Foothills Research Institute

Foothills Orchid Society
PO Box 22111, Stn. Bankers Hall, Calgary AB T2P 4J5
e-mail: calgaryorchidsociety@shaw.ca
www.foothillsorchidsociety.com
Overview: A small local organization
Member of: Canadian Orchid Congress
Affiliation(s): American Orchid Society; Orchid Digest; Orchid Society of Alberta
Membership: *Fees:* $30

Foothills Research Institute
PO Box 6330, Hinton AB T7V 1X6
Tel: 780-865-8330; *Fax:* 780-865-8331
foothillsresearchinstitute.ca
Previous Name: Foothills Model Forest
Overview: A small local organization founded in 1992
Mission: Plays a key role in establishing Alberta & Canada's reputation as a world leader in sustainable forest management
Member of: Canadian Model Forest Network
Chief Officer(s):
Bill Tinge, General Manager
btinge@foothillsri.ca
Rick Bonar, President
rick.bonar@westfraser.com
Finances: *Annual Operating Budget:* $3 Million-$5 Million
Membership: 1-99; *Member Profile:* Industry, government, environmental non-governmental offices, academics, aboriginals, researchers

Footprints Dance Project Society of Alberta
3935 Varsity Dr. SW, Calgary AB T3A 0Z3
Tel: 587-228-5440
calgaryfootprintsdance@gmail.com
www.footprintsdance.com
www.facebook.com/pages/Footprints-Dance-Project/220966381324107
www.youtube.com/user/CalgaryFootprints
Overview: A small provincial organization founded in 1999
Mission: To ensure children and youth have opportunities to explore and express the creativities inside their hearts and minds, and to level the performing arts field for the disadvantaged and disabled, to build a caring community, and to democratize participation in the arts.
Chief Officer(s):
Andrea Pass, Artistic Producer

For Ed BC
#213, 4438 - 10th Ave. West, Vancouver BC V6R 4R8
Tel: 604-737-8555; *Fax:* 604-737-8598
info@foredbc.org
www.landscapesmag.com
Previous Name: Canadian Forestry Association of BC; British Columbia Forestry Association
Overview: A medium-sized provincial charitable organization founded in 1925 overseen by Canadian Forestry Association
Mission: To provide education to lifelong learners in all segments of society about the environment & its resources to achieve better environmental decisions & health outcomes; To engage citizens, communities, & volunteers to rehabilitate, protect, & enhance the environment
Chief Officer(s):
Cheryl Ziola, President
cheryl@foredbc.org
Sandra Ulmer, Contact, Education
education@foredbc.org
Helen Sutherland, Contact, Administration
admin@foredbc.org
Finances: *Funding Sources:* Donations
Activities: Offering field service programs; Providing information resources about sustainability; Supporting youth volunteer groups; Providing community participation models for First Nations; Increasing public awareness about conservation, stewardship, economic diversification, & volunteerism; Providing resource packages to community groups, youth leaders, teachers, & volunteers involved in environmental activities; Giving workshops; Consulting with communities & youth groups; *Awareness Events:* National Forest Week, September

Force Jeunesse
#322, 1000, rue Saint-Antoine ouest, Montréal QC H3C 3R7
Tél: 514-384-8666; *Téléc:* 514-384-6442
info@forcejeunesse.qc.ca
www.forcejeunesse.qc.ca
Aperçu: *Dimension:* moyenne; *Envergure:* provinciale; fondée en 1998
Mission: Force Jeunesse est un regroupement de jeunes travailleurs issus de différents milieux dont le principe fondateur est l'équité intergénérationnelle; agit concrètement en revendiquant des mesures qui améliorent la situation économique et sociale des jeunes.
Membre(s) du bureau directeur:
Jonathan Plamondon, Président
Membre: 9 associations; *Montant de la cotisation:* 10$ membre individuel; 50$ membre associatif; *Critères d'admissibilite:* Associations et individus

Foreign Agricultural Resource Management Services (FARMS)
#706, 5995 Avebury Rd., Mississauga ON L5R 3P9
Tel: 905-568-4500
Toll-Free: 866-271-0826
www.farmsontario.ca
www.facebook.com/FARMSCANADA
twitter.com/FARMSCanada
Overview: A medium-sized international organization founded in 1987 overseen by Canadian Federation of Agriculture
Mission: To facilitate & coordinate requests for foreign seasonal agricultural workers
Member of: Canadian Federation of Agriculture
Chief Officer(s):
Ken Forth, President
Sue Williams, General Manager
Membership: *Member Profile:* Participating countries: Barbados, Eastern Caribbean, Jamaica, Mexico & Trinidad & Tobago
Activities: Operating CanAg Travel Services; providing forms & information online

Foreign Exchange Association of Canada *See* Financial Markets Association of Canada

Foreign Service Community Association (FSCA) / Association de la communauté du service extérieur (ACSE)
L.B. Pearson Building, 125 Sussex Dr., Ottawa ON K1A 0G2
Tel: 613-944-5729; *Fax:* 613-995-9335
fsca.acse@international.gc.ca
www.fsca-acse.org

Overview: A medium-sized international organization founded in 1976
Mission: To support the employees, spouses, & dependants of Canadian foreign service departments; To act as a liaison between families of the Canadian Foreign Service & Foreign Affairs Canada (FAC), the Canadian International Development Agency (CIDA), International Trade Canada (ITCan), Citizenship & Immigration Canada (CIC), & the Department National Defence (DND)
Chief Officer(s):
Helen Boutilier-Inglis, President
Membership: *Fees:* $25; *Member Profile:* Foreign service employees; Family members of foreign service employees & retired employees; Retired employees; Widows, widowers, & ex-spouses; *Committees:* Spousal Employment; Membership; Foreign Service Alumni Group; Ex-spouses; Lesbian, Bisexual, Transsexual, & Gay; Education; Life on the Move
Activities: Acting on behalf of foreign service families; Monitoring government policies; Consulting for changes beneficial to the foreign service community; Providing information to members; Organizing events;

Foremost & District Chamber of Commerce
PO Box 272, Foremost AB T0K 0X0
Tel: 403-867-3077; *Fax:* 403-867-2700
cofc4mst@shockware.com
www.foremostalberta.com
Overview: A small local organization
Mission: We have numerous entrepreneurs and businesses with friendly outgoing staff that are always willing to go the extra mile for you, the consumer. Our business people are very supportive of our community and in return our residents support their businesses. Shopping local has always been a way to support ones community and the #1 reason why businesses succeed in a small town such as Foremost
Chief Officer(s):
Lorne Buis, President

Forest Action Network (FAN)
PO Box 625, Bella Coola BC V0T 1C0
e-mail: info@fanweb.org
fanweb.org
Overview: A small local organization founded in 1993
Mission: To campaign to save British Columbia's coastal temperate rainforest & other ancient forests
Finances: *Annual Operating Budget:* Less than $50,000
Membership: 100-499
Activities: Public education & civil disobedience against clearcutting & other industrial deforestation

Forest Engineering Research Institute of Canada, A Division of FPInnovations *See* FPInnovations

Forest Products Association of Canada (FPAC) / Association des produits forestiers du Canada
#410, 99 Bank St., Ottawa ON K1P 6B9
Tel: 613-563-1441; *Fax:* 613-563-4720
ottawa@fpac.ca
www.fpac.ca
www.facebook.com/FPAC.APFC
twitter.com/FPAC_APFC
www.youtube.com/ForestProdsAssocCan
Previous Name: Canadian Pulp & Paper Association
Overview: A medium-sized national organization founded in 1913
Mission: To be the voice of Canada's wood, pulp & paper producers nationally & internationally in the areas of government, trade, & environmental affairs; To advance the Canadian forest products industry's global competitiveness & sustainable stewardship; To operate in a mannner which is economically viable, environmentally responsible, & socially desirable
Chief Officer(s):
David Lindsay, President & Chief Executive Officer
Susan Murray, Executive Director, Public Relations
smurray@fpac.ca
Membership: *Member Profile:* Canadian producers of forest products, with third-party certification of member companies' forest practices
Activities: Liaising with governments, non-governmental organizations (NGOs), & multi-stakeholder groups; Conducting advertising campaigns; *Library:* Forest Products Association of Canada Resource Centre
Publications:
• A Buyers' Guide to Canada's Sustainable Forest Products
Type: Guide; *Number of Pages:* 32
Profile: Contents include sustainable procurement, key issues related to sustainable procurement, sample forest products procurement, green building with Canada's forestproducts, FPAC member companies, a glossary, useful links, reference guides, & standards, & environmental performance data
• Canadian Wood, Renewable by Nature, Sustainable by Design
Type: Report; *Number of Pages:* 22
Profile: Information about sustainable forest management in Canada
• Forest Certification in Canada: The Programs, Similarities, & Achievements
Type: Report; *Number of Pages:* 26
Profile: Contents include an introduction to certification, Canada, a world leader in forest certification, & key elements of certification programs
• Forest Products Association of Canada Annual Report
Type: Yearbook; *Frequency:* Annually
• FPAC [Forest Products Association of Canada] Sustainability Report
Type: Report; *Frequency:* Biennially
• The New Face of the Canadian Forest Industry: The Emerging Bio-revolution (The Bio-pathways Project)
Type: Report
Profile: An examination of the market potential of emerging bio-energy, bio-chemical, & bio-products
• Tackle Climate Change, Use Wood
Type: Report; *Number of Pages:* 22
Profile: Managing forests to mitigate climate change
• Transforming Canada's Forest Products Industry: Summary of Findings from the Future Bio-Pathways Project
Type: Report
Profile: Forest Products Association of Canada investigators & their partner, FPInnovations, examine traditional & emergingbio-industries to assess how wood fibre can create bio-products such as bio-energy & bio-chemicals
• Woodland Caribou Recovery: Audit of Operatinig Practices & Mitigation Measures Employed within Woodland Caribou Ranges
Type: Report; *Author:* Golder Associates
Profile: An audit commissioned by the Forest Products Association of Canada & the CaribouLandscape Management Association

Forest Products Association of Nova Scotia (FPANS)
PO Box 696, Truro NS B2N 5E5
Tel: 902-895-1179; *Fax:* 902-893-1197
www.fpans.ca
Previous Name: Nova Scotia Forest Products Association
Overview: A medium-sized provincial organization founded in 1934
Mission: To act as the voice of the forest industry in Nova Scotia; To cooperate with industry, federal, provincial, & municipal governments, & other stakeholders to ensure adherence to forest management & stewardship policies; To promote sustainable management & viability of the forest industry
Chief Officer(s):
Steve Talbot, Executive Director
stalbot@fpans.ca
Jeff Bishop, Coordinator, Communications
jbishop@fpans.ca
Membership: 500-999; *Fees:* Schedule available; *Member Profile:* Representatives from the logging sector of the trucking industry; Pulp & paper manufacturers; Sawmill operators; Forest equipment operators; Woodlot owners; Small & large landowners; Maple product producers; Silviculture & harvesting contractors; Christmas tree producers; *Committees:* Forest management; Gas tax access road; Annual meeting; Communications; Energy; Environment; Safety training & worker's compensation; Transportation; Ad hoc gypsy moth
Activities: Enhancing training standards; Providing educational programs in schools; *Awareness Events:* National Forest Week
Meetings/Conferences: • Forest Products Association of Nova Scotia 2015 81st Annual Meeting, January, 2015, Marriott Harbourfront Hotel, Halifax, NS
Scope: Provincial
Description: A yearly gathering of association members
Contact Information: Contact: Brenda Archibald, Phone: 902-895-1179, E-mail: barchibald@fpans.ca
Publications:
• Forest Products Association of Nova Scotia Newsletter
Type: Newsletter
Profile: Updates for association members

Foresters
Forester House, 789 Don Mills Rd., Toronto ON M3C 1T9
Tel: 416-429-3000; *Fax:* 416-467-2518
Toll-Free: 800-828-1540
service@foresters.com
www.foresters.com
www.facebook.com/Foresters
www.youtube.com/user/forestersmembership
Previous Name: The Independent Order of Foresters
Overview: A large national organization founded in 1874
Mission: A fraternal benefit society which provides life insurance & other financial products to its members
Affliation(s): Children's Miracle Network; Barnardo's Children's Charity (U.K.)
Chief Officer(s):
George Mohacsi, CEO & President
Membership: 735,000+
Activities: Children's Miracle Network; Prevention of Child Abuse Funds; Foresters Fund for Children;
Awards:
• Foresters Competitive Scholarships (Scholarship)
Eligibility: Students of any age with a minimum 40 hours community service and a GPA of at least 2.8% or 70% *Amount:* Up to $11,000 (250)
• Orphan Scholarships (Scholarship)
Amount: Up to $6,000
• Project Grants (Grant)
Eligibility: Members

Burlington
#402, 3027 Harvester Rd., Burlington ON L7N 3G7
Tel: 905-637-5119

Edmonton
#100, 10637 - 124 St., Edmonton AB T5J 3G1
Tel: 780-425-2948; *Fax:* 780-425-9124

Markham
#401, 3000 Steeles Ave. East, Markham ON L3R 4T9
Tel: 905-474-3665

Forests Ontario
#700, 144 Front St. West, Toronto ON MSJ 2L7
Tel: 416-646-1193; *Fax:* 416-493-4608
Toll-Free: 877-646-1193
info@treesontario.ca
www.forestsontario.ca
www.linkedin.com/company/1243400?trkInfo=tas%3Aontario+fores%2Cidx%3A1
www.facebook.com/Forests.Ontario?ref=ts
twitter.com/Forests_Ontario
www.youtube.com/user/ontforest
Merged from: Trees Ontario & Ontario Forestry Association
Overview: A medium-sized provincial charitable organization founded in 1949 overseen by Canadian Forestry Association
Mission: To promote sound land use & full development protection & utilization of Ontario's forest resources for maximum public advantage; to increase public awareness, school education & natural appreciation of forests; to bring about better understanding of forests to people of all ages & backgrounds
Chief Officer(s):
Rob Keen, CEO
Al Corlett, Director of Programs
Shelley McKay, Director of Communications & Development
Finances: *Annual Operating Budget:* $250,000-$500,000
Staff Member(s): 4; 100 volunteer(s)
Membership: 1000; *Fees:* $50 individual, $25 student, $150 group, $85 educational institution, $1000 life
Activities: 50 Million Tree Program; Forest Recovery Canada; Workshops; Tree Planting; Landowner Resources; Educational Programs; *Speaker Service:* Yes
Awards:
• James S. Miller Memorial Scholarship (Scholarship)
Eligibility: Student in Northern Ontario in final year of high school entering first year of post-secondary education in natural resources or related field*Deadline:* February *Contact:* Tracey Cooke
• John Wesley Beaver Memorial Awards (Scholarship)
Eligibility: Student of Native ancestry entering Ontario college or university for engineering, technology, environmental studies, forestry, biology, land use & environmental planning, or business *Amount:* $4000
• Bentley Cropping Systems Fellowship (Scholarship)
Eligibility: Student in graduate studies doing research related to agriculture, forestry or biology in developing countries *Amount:* $30,000
• William Peyton Hubbard Award (Scholarship)
Eligibility: African-Canadian student in 2nd, 3rd or 4th year in engineering, computer science, forestry or business *Amount:* $2,000-4,000

Meetings/Conferences: • 66th Annual Forests Ontario Conference 2015, February, 2015, Nottawasaga Inn, Alliston, ON
Scope: Provincial

Forever Young Seniors Society (FYSS)
Vancouver BC
Tel: 604-454-9907
contact@foreveryoungseniorssociety.com
www.foreveryoungseniorssociety.com
www.youtube.com/user/fysscanada
Overview: A small local organization
Mission: To preserve the Filipino heritage & cultural traditions; To serve Filipino Canadian seniors in the Vancouver area
Chief Officer(s):
Romeo Mercado, President
Juanita Lamothe, Vice-President
Adel Johanson, Secretary
Angie Jimenez, Treasurer
Membership: *Fees:* $10 regular members; $8 associate members; *Member Profile:* Filipino Canadian seniors, over 50 years of age, in the Vancouver area; Associate members range in age from 20 to 49 years
Activities: Hosting Filipino traditional cultural events; Offering social & recreational activities for Filipino seniors in the Vancouver area; Organizing an annual general meeting; Raising public awareness of the Filipino community, through participation in community events; Offering assistance to members
Publications:
• Forever Young Journal
Type: Newsletter
Profile: Society activities, membership news, & forthcoming events

Formation juridique permanente du Nouveau-Brunswick
See New Brunswick Continuing Legal Education

Fort Calgary Society
PO Box 2100, Stn. M, Calgary AB T2P 2M5
Tel: 403-290-1875; *Fax:* 403-265-6534
info@fortcalgary.com
www.fortcalgary.com
www.facebook.com/fortcalgary
twitter.com/fortcalgary
www.instagram.com/fortcalgary
Overview: A small local organization founded in 1977
Mission: To preserve, interpret & promote the early history of the Mounted Police at Fort Calgary & to communicate Calgary's early cultural heritage & diversity through its interactive programs, services & exhibits.
Member of: Alberta Museums Association; Alliance for Historic Landscape Preservation; Old Forts Trail
Chief Officer(s):
Cecilia Gossen, Chair
Sara-Jane Gruetzner, President & CEO
Finances: *Annual Operating Budget:* $1.5 Million-$3 Million; *Funding Sources:* City of Calgary; province of Alberta; private
203 volunteer(s)
Activities: *Library:* Resource Centre

Fort Edmonton Foundation
PO Box 67112, Stn. Meadowlark, Edmonton AB T5R 5Y3
Tel: 780-496-6977; *Fax:* 780-496-6979
Other Communication: www.flickr.com/photos/fortedmontonpark
info@fortedmontonfoundation.org
www.fortedmontonpark.ca/about-us/foundation.aspx
www.facebook.com/fortedmontonpark
twitter.com/fortedpark
www.youtube.com/fortedmontonpark
Previous Name: Fort Edmonton Historical Foundation
Overview: A small local charitable organization founded in 1969
Mission: To raise capital funding for the ongoing development of Fort Edmonton Park; To recreate as historically accurate as possible the history of the city of Edmonton; To create & promote FEF as an internationally acclaimed living history experience
Member of: Museums Alberta; Alberta Association of Fundraising Executives
Chief Officer(s):
Sue Currie, President
Ray Marshall, Executive Director
Finances: *Annual Operating Budget:* $100,000-$250,000; *Funding Sources:* Fundraising; donations
Staff Member(s): 2; 100 volunteer(s)
Membership: 100 individual
Activities: *Library:* Resource Centre

Fort Edmonton Historical Foundation *See* Fort Edmonton Foundation

Fort Erie Native Friendship Centre
796 Buffalo Rd., Fort Erie ON L2A 5H2
Tel: 905-871-8931; *Fax:* 905-871-9655
www.fenfc.org
Overview: A small local organization
Mission: To enhance all aspects of Native life through such programs as day care services & the distribution of business attire & advice to those seeking employment.
Chief Officer(s):
Bernie LaFontaine, President
Staff Member(s): 28
Membership: *Fees:* $2 organization/honourary/elder/senior; $3 adult; $5 family
Activities: Aboriginal Alcohol & Drug Worker Program (ADDWP)

Fort Frances & District Labour Council
140 - 4 St. West, Fort Frances ON P9A 3B8
Tel: 807-274-7411
Overview: A small local organization overseen by Ontario Federation of Labour
Member of: Ontario Federation of Labour

Fort Frances Chamber of Commerce (FFCC)
601 Mowat Ave., Fort Frances ON P9A 1Z2
Tel: 807-274-5773; *Fax:* 807-274-8706
Toll-Free: 800-820-3678
thefort@fortfranceschamber.com
www.fortfranceschamber.com
Overview: A small local charitable organization founded in 1909
Mission: To improve trade & commerce & the economic, civic & social welfare of the district; To promote tourism, agriculture & labour
Member of: Ontario's Sunset Country Travel Association; Northwestern Ontario Tourism Association; Northwestern Ontario Associated Chambers of Commerce
Affliation(s): Ontario Chamber of Commerce; Canadian Chamber of Commerce
Chief Officer(s):
Mark Caron, President
mlcaron@bellnet.ca
Finances: *Annual Operating Budget:* $100,000-$250,000; *Funding Sources:* Membership dues; fundraising
Staff Member(s): 2; 50 volunteer(s)
Membership: 182; *Fees:* Schedule available; *Committees:* By-Law; Events & Projects; Executive, Finance & Personnel; Government Relations; Home & Leisure Show; Membership & Marketing; Nominations
Activities: Business Awards; Trade Show; Quest for the Best
Awards:
• Two Scholarships for the Fort Frances High School (Scholarship)
Amount: $250
• Business of the Year Award (Award)
• Community Safety Award (Award)

Fort Macleod & District Chamber of Commerce
PO Box 178, Fort MacLeod AB T0L 0Z0
Tel: 403-553-3355
EDO@FortMacleod.com
www.fortmacleod.com/business/chamber_commerce.cfm
Overview: A small local organization
Mission: The Chamber's function is to promote and assist local businesses and as part of a larger provincial organization draw on resources to strengthen economic development in the local community.
Chief Officer(s):
Emily McTighe, President, 403-553-3391

Fort Macleod Historical Association
PO Box 776, 219 Jerry Potts Blvd., Fort MacLeod AB T0L 0Z0
Tel: 403-553-4703; *Fax:* 403-553-3451
Toll-Free: 866-273-6841
info@nwmpmuseum.com
www.nwmpmuseum.com
Also Known As: The Fort Museum
Overview: A small local charitable organization founded in 1957
Mission: To preserve, educate, inform & entertain visitors with collection of North West Mounted Police, Royal Canadian Mounted Police, Native & pioneer artifacts; To aim to keep North West Mounted Police tradition alive through musical ride by Fort Mounted Patrol
Member of: Alberta Museums Association

Finances: *Annual Operating Budget:* $100,000-$250,000; *Funding Sources:* Admission fees; gift shop sales; student grants
Staff Member(s): 40; 15 volunteer(s)
Membership: 100; *Fees:* $25 business; $5 senior; single $10; family $15; *Member Profile:* 200 memberships sold annually (individual, family, business); *Committees:* Finance; Programs; Archives; Personnel; Grounds; Mounted Patrol
Activities: *Awareness Events:* Museum's Day, July 1; Heritage Fest

Fort McMurray Association for Community Living (FMACL)
10010 Franklin Ave., Fort McMurray AB T9H 2K6
Tel: 780-791-3009; *Fax:* 780-791-7506
fmacl@shawlink.ca
Overview: A small local charitable organization founded in 1969
Mission: To provide service to individuals with physical & mental challenges, to seniors & to newcomers
Member of: Alberta Association for Community Living
Activities: Career & employment counseling; training & skill enhancement programs; immigrant assessment services

Fort McMurray Chamber of Commerce
#304, 9612 Franklin Ave., Fort McMurray AB T9H 2J9
Tel: 780-743-3100; *Fax:* 780-790-9757
fmcoc@telus.net
www.fortmcmurraychamber.ca
Overview: A small local organization founded in 1914 overseen by Alberta Chambers of Commerce
Mission: To promote & strengthen the economy of Fort McMurray & region
Member of: Canadian Chamber of Commerce
Chief Officer(s):
Jack Bonville, President
Diane Slater, Executive Director
Finances: *Annual Operating Budget:* $100,000-$250,000; *Funding Sources:* Membership dues; fundraising
Staff Member(s): 3; 15 volunteer(s)
Membership: 541; *Fees:* Schedule available; *Member Profile:* Interest in trade, commerce or the economic & social welfare of the district; *Committees:* Governments Affairs; Education; Marketing & Tourism; Retail; Business Development; Oil Sands Development; Technology
Activities: *Awareness Events:* Small Business Week
Awards:
• Business of the Year (Award)
• Small Business of the Year (Award)
• Environmental Leadership of the Year (Award)
• Family Friendly Business Award of Distinction (Award)
• X-ceptional kidz (Award)
• Leader of Tomorrow Award (Award)
• Sustainable Communities Recognition Award (Award)
• Public Service Award of Excellence (Award)

Fort McMurray Construction Association (FMCA)
#304, 9612 Franklin Ave., Fort McMurray AB T9H 2J9
Tel: 780-791-9288; *Fax:* 780-790-9757
fmca@telus.net
www.fmca.net
Overview: A small local organization founded in 1987 overseen by Canadian Construction Association
Mission: To serve it's members by displaying plans and information on current projects in the industry; to act as their collective voice on issues of concern to promote standards, education, and communication in an effort to benefit the industry and society.
Member of: Alberta Construction Association
Chief Officer(s):
Charles Iggulden, President
Diane Slater, CAO
Staff Member(s): 3
Membership: *Fees:* $1510 full; $1000 corporate; $550 associate
Activities: Golf tournament

Fort McMurray Food Bank
10117 King St., Fort McMurray AB T9H 3J1
Tel: 780-743-1125; *Fax:* 780-743-9156
www.woodbuffalofoodbank.com
facebook.com/profile.php?id=149900681755337
twitter.com/fmmfoodbank
Previous Name: Wood Buffalo Food Bank
Overview: A small local charitable organization founded in 1983
Member of: Alberta Association of Food Banks
Chief Officer(s):
Kathy Flett, Chair

Arianna Johnson, Executive Director
Finances: *Annual Operating Budget:* $100,000-$250,000
Staff Member(s): 2; 35 volunteer(s)
Membership: 1-99
Activities: *Awareness Events:* Food Bank Drive, Dec.; Hunger Awareness Week, May; *Speaker Service:* Yes

Fort McMurray Genealogical Study Group *See* Alberta Genealogical Society

Fort McMurray Historical Society
1 Tolen Dr., Fort McMurray AB T9H 1G7
Tel: 780-791-7575; *Fax:* 780-791-5180
heritage@fortmcmurrayhistory.com
www.fortmcmurrayhistory.com
www.facebook.com/260650299824
twitter.com/McMurrayHistory
Also Known As: Heritage Park
Previous Name: Historical Society of Fort McMurray
Overview: A small local charitable organization founded in 1974
Mission: To encourage & participate in collecting, preserving, researching & interpreting artifacts, documents, buildings & sites; To preserve & maintain an ongoing record of the history of the region; To inform & educate the public regarding the social & cultural history
Member of: Fort McMurray Tourism; Chamber of Commerce; Alberta Museums; Canadian Museums
Affliation(s): Travel Alberta; Chevron Canada
Chief Officer(s):
Roseann Davidson, Executive Director
execdirector@fortmcmurrayhistory.com
Finances: *Funding Sources:* Donations; Federal, provincial, & municipal funding; Sale of goods & services
Staff Member(s): 10; 20+ volunteer(s)
Membership: 51+; *Fees:* $20
Activities: Informing & educating the public regarding social & cultural history, through school programs, summer camps, & special events such as Pioneer Days & Celtic Day in the Park; Providing photo reproduction; Supporting research projects; *Awareness Events:* National Aboriginal Day, June; Heritage Day, August; Old Fashioned Christmas, November; *Library:* Fort McMurray Historical Society Library; Open to public by appointment

Fort McMurray Realtors Association
9909 Sutherland St., Fort McMurray AB T9H 1V3
Tel: 780-791-1124; *Fax:* 780-743-4724
boards.mls.ca/fortmcmurray
Overview: A small local organization overseen by Alberta Real Estate Association
Member of: Alberta Real Estate Association; The Canadian Real Estate Association
Chief Officer(s):
Chris Moskalyk, Executive Officer
moskalykc@shaw.ca

Fort McMurray Society for the Prevention of Cruelty to Animals
155 MacAlpine Cres., Fort McMurray AB T9H 4A5
Tel: 780-743-8997; *Fax:* 780-791-3772
info@fortmcmurrayspca.ca
www.fortmcmurrayspca.ca
www.facebook.com/307296965992025
Also Known As: Fort McMurray SPCA
Overview: A small local charitable organization founded in 1978 overseen by Canadian Federation of Humane Societies
Mission: To ensure the humane treatment of all animals in the regional municipality of Wood Buffalo.
Member of: Alberta Society for the Prevention of Cruelty to Animals; Canadian Federation of Humane Societies
Chief Officer(s):
Tara Clarke, Executive Director
ed@fortmcmurrayspca.ca
Finances: *Funding Sources:* United Way; fundraising
Staff Member(s): 19

Fort McMurray Youth Soccer Association (FMYSA)
PO Box 10, 8115 Franklin Ave., Fort McMurray AB T9H 2H7
Tel: 780-791-7090; *Fax:* 780-791-1446
www.fmyouthsoccer.com
Overview: A small local organization overseen by Alberta Soccer Association
Member of: Alberta Soccer Association
Chief Officer(s):
Martha Maddalena, Office Manager
Bill Carr, President
president.fmysa@shaw.ca

Fort Nelson & District Chamber of Commerce
PO Box 196, 5500 Alaska Hwy., Fort Nelson BC V0C 1R0
Tel: 250-774-2956; *Fax:* 250-774-2958
info@fortnelsonchamber.com
www.fortnelsonchamber.com
www.facebook.com/151418621591719
twitter.com/FNchamber
Overview: A small local organization founded in 1959
Mission: To be the collective voice for business in the Northern Rockies Regional District; To promote & enhance trade & commerce for the benefit of the region
Member of: British Columbia Chamber of Commerce; Canadian Chamber of Commerce
Chief Officer(s):
Jeremy Cote, President, 250-774-7494
Bev Vandersteen, Executive Director
Finances: *Funding Sources:* Fundraising activities
Staff Member(s): 2
Membership: *Fees:* Schedule available; *Member Profile:* Business person & companies
Activities: Community & Business Awards; *Library:* Business Information; Open to public

Fort Nelson Aboriginal Friendship Society
PO Box 1266, 5012 - 49th Ave., Fort Nelson BC V0C 1R0
Tel: 250-774-2993
friendshipecoviety@northwestel.net
Also Known As: Fort Nelson Friendship Centre
Previous Name: Fort Nelson-Liard Friendship Society
Overview: A small local charitable organization founded in 1975
Mission: Committed to assisting in the transition of Aboriginal people to the urban community; provides programs & events that enhance self-esteem & positive growth for Aboriginal & Non-Aboriginal
Activities: Youth activities; dances; elders luncheons; A&D counselling; fashion shows; fundraising

Fort Nelson-Liard Friendship Society *See* Fort Nelson Aboriginal Friendship Society

Fort Qu'Appelle & District Chamber of Commerce
PO Box 1273, Fort Qu'Appelle SK S0G 1S0
Tel: 306-332-5717; *Fax:* 306-332-1287
FQChamber@hotmail.com
Overview: A small local organization
Mission: To act as the voice of business in Fort Qu-Appelle Saskatchewan & the surrounding area
Member of: Saskatchewan Chamber of Commerce
Chief Officer(s):
Kelly Nattern, Contact

Fort St. James Chamber of Commerce
PO Box 1164, 115 Douglas Ave., Fort St. James BC V0J 1P0
Tel: 250-996-7023; *Fax:* 250-996-7047
fsjchamb@fsjames.com
www.fortstjameschamber.ca
Overview: A small local organization founded in 1985
Member of: BC Chamber of Commerce
Finances: *Annual Operating Budget:* Less than $50,000; *Funding Sources:* Fishing Derby; Business Directory; Thunder On Ice
Staff Member(s): 2
Membership: 99; *Fees:* $45-$295; *Committees:* 6 Standing
Activities: Fishing Derby; Thunder On Ice; *Awareness Events:* Chamber Week; *Library* Open to public

Fort St. John & District Chamber of Commerce
#100, 9907 - 99 Ave., Fort St John BC V1J 1V1
Tel: 250-785-6037; *Fax:* 250-785-6050
info@fsjchamber.com
www.fsjchamber.com
www.facebook.com/122497777819790
twitter.com/fsjchamber
Overview: A small local organization founded in 1961
Mission: To promote the economic & social well-being of the businesses & community within the Fort St. John District; To continue to provide & enhance services & information to the members of the Chamber of Commerce
Member of: BC Chamber of Commerce; Canadian Chamber of Commerce; Northern Rockies Alaska Highway Tourism Association
Chief Officer(s):
Annette Oak, Chamber Manager
Brent Hodson, President
Finances: *Annual Operating Budget:* $100,000-$250,000; *Funding Sources:* Membership fees; fees for service
Staff Member(s): 1; 15 volunteer(s)

Membership: 406; *Fees:* Schedule available
Activities: Special Improvement project program; district enhancement programs for existing & new business opportunities; *Library:* Northpeace Business Resource Centre

Fort St. John Association for Community Living (FSJACL)
10251 - 100 Ave., Fort St John BC V1J 1Y8
Tel: 250-787-9262; *Fax:* 250-787-9224
info@fsjacl.com
www.fsjacl.com
Overview: A small local charitable organization founded in 1960
Mission: To educate, advocate & provide quality services for those with mental disabilities to ensure opportunities in all areas of their lives
Member of: British Columbia Association for Community Living
Chief Officer(s):
Cindy Mohr, Executive Director
cindy.mohr@fsjacl.com
Membership: *Fees:* $10; *Member Profile:* All who believe that all individuals with a developmental disability have the right to the same opportunities as other citizens to live in a manner consistent with their needs & capabilities
Activities: Residential Services include: a Street House - community living for adults; Dee Jay's Place - community living for adults; 10th Avenue House - community living for adults; apartment support program; Community Connections Program - support & skills development for handicapped adults in the community; Careers - pre-employment preparation, job training & support for people facing challenging circumstances; *Awareness Events:* Pay it Forward Day, June; *Library:* Professional Resource Program

Fort St. John Community Arts Council
PO Box 6474, Fort St John BC V1J 4H9
Tel: 250-787-2781; *Fax:* 250-787-9781
info@fsjarts.org
fsjarts.org
www.facebook.com/fsjarts.council
twitter.com/fsjarts
Overview: A small local organization founded in 1970
Mission: To increase & broaden the opportunities for Fort St. John & district citizens to enjoy & to participate in cultural activities; to help coordinate the work & programmes of cultural groups in the area; to stimulate & encourage the development of cultural project & to render service to all participating groups
Member of: BC Arts Council
Finances: *Funding Sources:* Provincial government; City of Fort St. John; BC Arts Council
Awards:
• The Lindsay Dumaine Memorial Music Scholarship Fund (Scholarship)
Publications:
• The Reflection
Type: Newsletter; *Frequency:* Quarterly

Fort Saskatchewan Chamber of Commerce
PO Box 3072, 10030 - 99 Ave., Fort Saskatchewan AB T8L 2T1
Tel: 780-998-4355; *Fax:* 780-998-1515
chamber@fortsaskchamber.com
www.fortsaskchamber.com
www.facebook.com/fortsaskchamber
twitter.com/FtSaskChamber
Overview: A small local organization founded in 1954
Mission: While remembering the hard-working, forward thinking, community-minded people of the past, the Chamber looks forward with enthusiasm and optimism to the challenging years ahead.
Affliation(s): Alberta Chamber of Commerce; Canadian Chamber of Commerce
Chief Officer(s):
Michelle Gamache, President
Conal MacMillan, Executive Director
cmacmillan@fortsaskchamber.com
Finances: *Annual Operating Budget:* $100,000-$250,000
Membership: 300+

Fort Saskatchewan Fish & Game Association
PO Box 3038, Fort Saskatchewan AB T8L 2T1
Tel: 780-998-0062
fortfishngame@hotmail.com
www.fsfga.com
Overview: A small local organization founded in 1958
Mission: To promote through education, lobbying & programs the conservation & utilization of fish & wildlife; protect & enhance the habitat they depend on
Member of: Alberta Fish & Game Association

Chief Officer(s):
Gord Blize, President
Finances: *Funding Sources:* Fundraising
500 volunteer(s)
Membership: 500; *Fees:* $25
Activities: Monthly club meetings; various events for members & families; *Awareness Events:* Kid's Ice Fishing Derby, March; Fishing Derby, June; Family Fun Day & Fishing Derby, Dec.

Fort Saskatchewan Historical Society
10006 - 100 Ave., Fort Saskatchewan AB T8L 1V9
Tel: 780-998-1783
fortsaskhistoricalsociety@gmail.com
www.facebook.com/522313361151571
Also Known As: Fort Saskatchewan Museum
Overview: A small local charitable organization founded in 1958
Mission: To collect, preserve, document & display artifacts pertaining to local history by means of operating a community museum
Member of: Alberta Museums Association; Canadian Museums Association
Activities: *Library:* Resource Centre; Open to public by appointment

Fort Saskatchewan Minor Sports Association (FSMSA)
Jubilee Recreation Center, PO Box 3071, Fort Saskchatewan AB T8L 2T1
Tel: 780-998-1835
fsmsa@telus.net
www.fsmsa.net
Overview: A small local organization
Mission: To govern minor sports in Fort Saskatchewan
Chief Officer(s):
Vaughan McGrath, President, 780-992-1735
vmcgrath@telusplanet.net
Membership: *Committees:* Bylaw Review; Disciplinary; Minor Sport Executive

Fort Simpson Chamber of Commerce
PO Box 244, Fort Simpson NT X0E 0N0
Tel: 867-695-6538; *Fax:* 867-695-3551
Other Communication:
www.flickr.com/photos/fortsimpsonchamber
fscofc@gmail.com
www.fortsimpsonchamber.ca
www.linkedin.com/pub/kirby-groat/44/6a8/719
www.facebook.com/216513448425813
twitter.com/FortSChamber
www.youtube.com/user/FortSimpsonChamber
Overview: A small local organization founded in 1970
Member of: Canadian Chamber of Commerce; NWT Chamber of Commerce
Chief Officer(s):
Angela Fiebelkorn, President
Finances: *Annual Operating Budget:* Less than $50,000
Membership: 60; *Fees:* $75-$125 regular; $75-$300 associate; *Committees:* Tourism; Mackenzie Hwy.

Fort Smith Chamber of Commerce
PO Box 121, Fort Smith NT X0E 0P0
Tel: 867-872-8400; *Fax:* 867-872-8401
www.fortsmith.ca/cms/webcontent/business-services
Overview: A small local organization
Membership: 52

Fort Vermilion & Area Board of Trade
PO Box 456, Fort Vermilion AB T0H 1N0
Tel: 780-927-3505
Overview: A small local organization founded in 1914
Member of: Alberta Chamber of Commerce
Membership: 1-99
Activities: *Speaker Service:* Yes; *Library:* Resource Centre
Awards:
- Citizen of the Year (Award)
- Senior of the Year (Award)
- Farm Family of the Year (Award)
- Volunteer of the Year (Award)

Fort Whoop-up Interpretive Society
PO Box 1074, 200 Indian Battle Park Rd., Lethbridge AB T1J 5B3
Tel: 403-329-0444; *Fax:* 403-329-0645
info@fortwhoopup.com
www.fortwhoopup.com
www.facebook.com/WhoopUp
twitter.com/FortWhoopUp
Overview: A small local charitable organization founded in 1973
Mission: To operate the Fort Whoop-Up National Historic Site
Chief Officer(s):
Doran Degenstein, Contact
Finances: *Funding Sources:* Donations; Fundraising; Admission
Activities: Providing information about Blackfoot culture

Fort William Trades & Labour Council *See* Thunder Bay & District Labour Council

Fort York Food Bank (FYFB)
797 Dundas St. West, Toronto ON M6J 1V2
Tel: 416-203-3011; *Fax:* 416-203-3275
info@fyfb.com
www.fyfb.com
Overview: A small local charitable organization
Mission: To collect & distribute a 3 day supply of food to people in need in downton Toronto
Chief Officer(s):
Mike Schoonheyt, Program Manager
Staff Member(s): 1
Membership: *Committees:* Steering

Fortier Danse-Création
#301, 2022, rue Sherbrooke Est, Montréal QC H2K 1B9
Tél: 514-529-8158; *Téléc:* 514-529-1222
admin@fortier-danse.com
www.fortier-danse.com
www.facebook.com/fortier.dansecreation
twitter.com/FortierDanse
vimeo.com/user8490850
Aperçu: *Dimension:* petite; *Envergure:* locale; Organisme sans but lucratif; fondée en 1981
Mission: Création et diffusion des oeuvres du chorégraphe Paul-André Fortier
Membre de: Regroupement québécois de la danse; Conférence canadienne des arts
Membre(s) du bureau directeur:
Paul-André Fortier, Directeur artistique
Gilles Savary, Directeur général
Membre(s) du personnel: 10

Fortress Louisbourg Association
265 Park Service Rd., Louisbourg NS B1C 2L2
Tel: 902-733-3548; *Fax:* 902-733-3046
Other Communication: Events & Programs Phone: 902-733-3548
info@fortressoflouisbourg.ca
www.fortressoflouisbourg.ca
www.facebook.com/216181515095381
twitter.com/FortressAssoc
www.youtube.com/FortressLouisbourg
Overview: A small local charitable organization
Mission: To foster an appreciation for the history of Canada in regards to the Fortress of Louisbourg
Chief Officer(s):
Paul Gartland, President
Mitch McNutt, General Manager
mmcnutt@fortressoflouisbourg.ca
Activities: Operating the Fortress of Louisbourg

FortWhyte Alive
1961 McCreary Rd., Winnipeg MB R3P 2K9
Tel: 204-989-8355; *Fax:* 204-895-4700
info@fortwhyte.org
www.fortwhyte.org
www.facebook.com/pages/FortWhyte-Alive/471614835647?ref=ts
twitter.com/fortwhytealive
Previous Name: Wildlife Foundation of Manitoba; Fort Whyte Centre for Environmental Education
Overview: A small local organization founded in 1966
Mission: FortWhyte Alive is dedicated to providing programming, natural settings and facilities for environmental education and outdoor recreation. In so doing, FortWhyte promotes awareness and understanding of the natural world and actions leading to sustainable living.
Chief Officer(s):
Bill Elliott, President/CEO
Membership: 2,000; *Fees:* Schedule available

Forum canadien des opérations forestières *See* The Canadian Woodlands Forum

Forum canadien sur l'apprentissage *See* Canadian Apprenticeship Forum

Forum conjoint des autorités de réglementation du marché financier *See* Joint Forum of Financial Market Regulators

Le forum des églises canadiennes pour les ministères globaux *See* The Canadian Churches' Forum for Global Ministries

Forum des fédérations *See* Forum of Federations

Forum des politiques publiques du Canada *See* Canada's Public Policy Forum

Forum for International Trade Training (FITT) / Forum pour la formation en commerce international
#300, 116 Lisgar St., Ottawa ON K2P 0C2
Tel: 613-230-3553; *Fax:* 613-230-6808
Toll-Free: 800-561-3488
info@fitt.ca
www.fitt.ca
www.linkedin.com/company/fitt-forum-for-international-trade-training-
www.facebook.com/FITTNews
twitter.com/FITTNews
Overview: A small international licensing organization founded in 1992
Mission: To provide quality programs' training & certification in international trade designed to prepare businesses & individuals to compete successfully in world markets.
Affliation(s): Founding Partners: Canadian Manufacturers & Exporters Association; Canadian Chamber of Commerce; Rounding Partners: Canadian Association of Importers & Exporters; Canadian Professional Logistics Institute; World Trade Centres of Canada; Industry Canada; DFAIT; HRDC; Canadian Professional Sales Association; Canadian Federation of Labour
Chief Officer(s):
Caroline Tompkins, President
Membership: *Fees:* $40 student; $100 general; $695 corporate
Activities: *Rents Mailing List:* Yes

Forum francophone des affaires (FFA-CNC)
6256, av Henri-Julien, Montréal QC H2S 2T8
Tél: 514-717-5610
www.ffacnc.qc.ca
Aperçu: *Dimension:* moyenne; *Envergure:* internationale; Organisme sans but lucratif; fondée en 1987
Mission: Planifier, organiser et réaliser toutes formes d'activités (colloques, missions, réseautage, publications, etc.) susceptibles de permettre aux dirigeants francophones d'entreprises et d'organisations canadiennes de faire plus et mieux sur les marchés du monde entier
Membre de: FFA International
Affiliation(s): FFA Atlantique
Membre: *Montant de la cotisation:* 10$ étudiant; 75$ individuel; 150$ ONBL; 350$ corporatif
Activités: Bourse de réseautage; déjeuners/causeries; tables rondes; missions commerciales; séances d'information

Forum of Federations / Forum des fédérations
#700, 325 Dalhousie St., Ottawa ON K1N 7G2
Tel: 613-244-3360; *Fax:* 613-244-3372
forum@forumfed.org
www.forumfed.org
Also Known As: An International Network of Federalism
Overview: A medium-sized international charitable organization founded in 2000
Mission: The Forum is concerned with the contribution that federalism makes & can make to the maintenance & construction of democratic societies & governments
Chief Officer(s):
Rupak Chattopadhyay, President & CEO
Activities: *Internships:* Yes; *Library* by appointment
Publications:
- Federations

Editor: Rod MacDonell; *Price:* $25 subscription
Profile: Magazine, published three times annually in multiple languages

Forum pour la formation en commerce international *See* Forum for International Trade Training

Foster Parent Support Services Society (FPSS)
#145, 735 Goldstream Ave., Victoria BC V9B 2X4
Tel: 778-430-5459; *Fax:* 778-430-5463
Toll-Free: 888-922-8437
admin@fpsss.com
www.fpsss.com

www.facebook.com/fpsssociety
twitter.com/FPSSSociety
Overview: A small local charitable organization
Mission: To provide meaningful and accessible support, education and networking services which will continually enhance the skills and abilities of foster parents to deliver the best care possible to the children in their homes.
Chief Officer(s):
Dan Malone, Executive Director
execdirect@fpsss.com

Foster Parents Association of Ottawa
1602 Telesat Ct., Ottawa ON K1B 1B1
Tel: 613-747-7800
ottawafpa@casott.on.ca
Previous Name: Ottawa & District Foster Parent Association
Overview: A small local organization founded in 1975
Mission: A local organization providing mutual support to families caring for foster children. During monthly meetings, members share their concerns & information on parenting skills through discussions & guest speakers
Chief Officer(s):
Peter Fortier, President
Finances: *Funding Sources:* Children's Aid Society

Foster Parents Plan Canada *See* Plan Canada

Foundation Assisting Canadian Talent on Recordings (FACTOR)
247 Spadina Ave., 3rd Fl., Toronto ON M5T 3A8
Tel: 416-696-2215; *Fax:* 416-351-7311
Toll-Free: 877-696-2215
general.info@factor.ca
www.factor.ca
www.facebook.com/FACTORCanada
www.twitter.com/FACTORCanada
Previous Name: Foundation to Assist Canadian Talent on Records
Overview: A large national organization founded in 1982
Mission: To provide financial assistance for production of sound recordings, videos, syndicated radio programs & international tour support; English-language counterpart of Musicaction
Chief Officer(s):
Duncan McKie, President
duncan.mckie@factor.ca
Phil Gumbley, Director of Operations
phil.gumbley@factor.ca
Finances: *Annual Operating Budget:* Greater than $5 Million; *Funding Sources:* Dept. of Canadian Heritage; Private Radio Broadcasting
Staff Member(s): 16
Activities: *Speaker Service:* Yes; *Rents Mailing List:* Yes
Awards:
• FACTOR Grants (Grant)
Available to Artists for Sound Recordings, Marketing & Promotion, Videos, Touring and Showcasing. There are also programs supporting Record Labels, Distributors, Music Publishers, Artist Managers, Songwriters, Music Industry Associations, Music Industry events and Collective Digital Initiatives.

Foundation canadienne de fiscalité *See* Canadian Tax Foundation

The Foundation Fighting Blindness (FFB)
890 Yonge St., 12th Fl., Toronto ON M4W 3P4
Tel: 416-360-4200; *Fax:* 416-360-0060
Toll-Free: 800-461-3331
info@ffb.ca
www.ffb.ca
www.facebook.com/187447074652378
twitter.com/FFBCanada
Previous Name: RP Research Foundation - Fighting Blindness
Overview: A medium-sized national charitable organization founded in 1974
Mission: To support & promote research directed to finding the causes, treatments & ultimately the cures for retinitis pigmentosa, macular degeneration & related retinal diseases
Member of: International RP Association
Affliation(s): US RP Foundation
Chief Officer(s):
Sharon M. Colle, President & CEO
scolle@ffb.ca
Rahn Dodick, Treasurer
Andrew Burke, Secretary
Finances: *Annual Operating Budget:* $500,000-$1.5 Million; *Funding Sources:* Individual donations
Staff Member(s): 6
Membership: 100,000; *Committees:* Fundraising; RP Network; Ride for Sight; RP Golf Classic
Activities: *Awareness Events:* Ride for Sight; Forever Yonge Run; RP Golf Classic; *Speaker Service:* Yes

The Foundation for Active Healthy Kids *See* Active Healthy Kids Canada

Foundation for Education Perth Huron
62 Chalk St. North, Seaforth ON N0K 1W0
Tel: 519-527-0111; *Fax:* 519-527-0444
Toll-Free: 800-592-5437
foundationforeducation@gmail.com
www.foundationforeducation.ca
www.facebook.com/pages/Foundation-For-Education/11119114 8910133
twitter.com/found4education
www.youtube.com/user/foundation4education
Previous Name: Foundation for Enriching Education Perth Huron; Perth Foundation for the Enrichment of Education
Overview: A small local charitable organization founded in 1988
Mission: To develop, support & encourage the integration of the rich & unique cultural, corporate, industrial & agricultural resources of Huron & Perth counties into the school system
Chief Officer(s):
Wes MacVicar, Executive Director
wesmacv@fc.amdsb.ca
Lynda McGregor, Director, Development
Finances: *Annual Operating Budget:* $250,000-$500,000; *Funding Sources:* Government; foundations; corporate; community; special events
Staff Member(s): 6; 12 volunteer(s)
Membership: 50 corporate + 30 individual; *Fees:* $50 sustaining; $100 Founder's Club; $25 associate
Activities: Arts-based programs; fundraising; consultant to schools; life skill mentorship; *Awareness Events:* Charity Auction, Nov.

Foundation for Educational Exchange Between Canada & the United States of America
#2015, 350 Albert St., Ottawa ON K1R 1A4
Tel: 613-688-5540; *Fax:* 613-237-2029
info@fulbright.ca
www.fulbright.ca
www.facebook.com/pages/Fulbright-Canada/193768967190
twitter.com/FulbrightPrgrm
www.youtube.com/user/FulbrightCanada
Also Known As: Canada-U.S. Fulbright Program
Overview: A medium-sized international charitable organization founded in 1990
Mission: To support outstanding graduate students, faculty, professionals, & independent researchers in order to enhance understanding between the people of Canada & the United States
Chief Officer(s):
Michael K. Hawes, Executive Director
mhawes@fulbright.ca
Ava Kovats, Sr. Finance Officer
akovats@fulbright.ca
Finances: *Funding Sources:* Department of Foreign Affairs and International Trade Canada; United States Department of State; Public sector partners; Private sector partners
Activities: Presenting grants & scholarships to Canadian & American scholars, post-doctoral researchers, experienced professionals, junior professionals, executives of the Government of Canada, & Canadian & American teachers; *Internships:* Yes

Foundation for Enriching Education Perth Huron; Perth Foundation for the Enrichment of Education *See* Foundation for Education Perth Huron

Foundation for International Training (FIT)
#110, 7181 Woodbine Ave., Markham ON L3R 1A3
Tel: 416-305-8680; *Fax:* 905-305-8681
info@ffit.org
www.ffit.org
www.facebook.com/171697116212687
Overview: A large international charitable organization founded in 1976
Mission: To strengthen human & social capital in developing countries
Chief Officer(s):
Richard Beattie, Chair
Mirabelle Rodrigues, Executive Director

Foundation for Legal Research (FLR) / La foundation pour la recherche juridique
Cour d'appel du Québec, 100 rue Notre-Dame E., Montreal QC H2Y 4B6
Toll-Free: 800-267-8860
foundationforlegalresearch.org
Overview: A small local charitable organization founded in 1957
Mission: To support & maintain scholarships, bursaries & prizes in the field of legal research
Affliation(s): Canadian Bar Association
Chief Officer(s):
Nicholas Kasirer, Chair, 514-393-4862
nkasirer@judicom.ca
Francois Letourneaux, Secretary
Stephen Bresolin, Treasurer
stephenb@cba.org
Finances: *Annual Operating Budget:* $100,000-$250,000
Membership: 500; *Fees:* $2,000
Awards:
• Walter Owen Book Prize (Award)
Amount: $10,000 *Contact:* John N. Davis, jdavis@osgoode.yorku.ca

Foundation for Prader-Willi Research in Canada (FPWR Canada)
#370, 19 - 13085 Yonge St., Richmond Hill ON L4E 0K2
Toll-Free: 866-993-7972
opwsa@rogers.com
www.pwsacanada.com
www.facebook.com/78626677947
twitter.com/keeganj
www.youtube.com/user/fpwrcanada
Previous Name: Canadian Prader-Willi Syndrome Association
Overview: A small national charitable organization founded in 2006
Mission: To educate families & inform community services on behalf of individuals with Prader-Willi Syndrome, about the special needs of persons with this condition in Canada
Member of: International Prader-Willi Syndrome Organization
Affliation(s): Ontario Prader-Willi Syndrome Association; British Columbia Prader-Willi Syndrome Association; Alberta Prader-Willi Association; Foundation for Prader Willi Research
Chief Officer(s):
Keegan Johnson, President & Chair
Susan James, Contact, Member Services
susan.james@fpwr.ca
Finances: *Annual Operating Budget:* Less than $50,000
Membership: *Member Profile:* People with a special interest in the syndrome
Activities: Provides counselling & up-to-date scientific information on PWS; *Library:* Research Centre; Open to public by appointment

Foundation for Rural Living
Ontario Agricentre, #109, 100 Stone Rd. West, Guelph ON N1G 5L3
Tel: 519-826-4126; *Fax:* 519-826-3408
foundationruralliving@gmail.com
www.frl.on.ca
Overview: A small provincial charitable organization
Mission: To act as a catalyst in building healthy sustainable rural communities & enhancing the agricultural industry in Ontario
Chief Officer(s):
Anita Hayes, Executive Director
Finances: *Annual Operating Budget:* $50,000-$100,000
Membership: 1-99
Activities: *Internships:* Yes; *Speaker Service:* Yes

Foundation for the Study of Objective Art
80 Gerrard St. East, Toronto ON M5B 1G6
Tel: 416-977-1077; *Fax:* 416-977-1066
ob-art@arcturus.ca
www.arcturus.ca
Also Known As: Gallery Arcturus
Overview: A small local organization founded in 1994
Mission: To acquire a permanent collection of works by contemporary North American artists; To make the collection available to the public; To further understanding of objective art by offering study materials & educational programs
Member of: Art Gallery of Ontario; Ontario Association of Art Galleries
Affliation(s): Art Gallery of Ontario; Ontario Museum Association
Chief Officer(s):
James S. Anthony, President

Cathy Stilo, Vice-President
Finances: *Funding Sources:* Private
Staff Member(s): 2
Activities: *Library*

Foundation of Catholic Community Services Inc (FCCS)

#310, 1857, boul de Maisonneuve ouest, Montréal QC H3H 1J9
Tel: 514-934-1326; *Fax:* 514-934-0453
info@fccsmontreal.org
www.fccsmontreal.org
Overview: A small local organization founded in 1932
Chief Officer(s):
Andrea Bobkowicz, President
Staff Member(s): 2
Membership: 100 individual;

Foundation of Stars *Voir* Fondation des étoiles

La foundation pour la recherche juridique *See* Foundation for Legal Research

Foundation to Assist Canadian Talent on Records *See* Foundation Assisting Canadian Talent on Recordings

Foundation to Underwrite New Drama for Pay Television (FUND) *See* The Harold Greenberg Fund

Fountain of Love & Life (FLL)

#10A, 9033 Leslie St., Richmond Hill ON L4B 4K3
Tel: 905-707-7800; *Fax:* 416-900-2270
Toll-Free: 888-606-4808
info@fll.cc
www.fll.cc
Overview: A small local organization founded in 2004
Mission: To use the media to spread the Good Word of Christ, as taught by the Roman Catholic Church, to Chinese communities; FLL is the Chinese Programming Ministry of Salt + Light Television
Affliation(s): Archdiocese of Toronto
Chief Officer(s):
Paul Yeung, Contact
paulyeung@fll.cc
Finances: *Funding Sources:* Donations
Activities: Television & radio programs
Publications:
• FLL [Fountain of Love & Life] Spotlight
Type: Newsletter; *Frequency:* 3 pa

4Cs Foundation

#104, 5663 Cornwallis St., Halifax NS B3K 1B6
Tel: 902-422-4805
info@4csfoundation.com
www.4csfoundation.com
Overview: A small local organization founded in 1999
Mission: To support meaningful relationships between children, youth, artists & other community members through engagement in collaborative, arts-based community development (community arts) projects
Chief Officer(s):
Terri Whetstone, Executive Director
Staff Member(s): 1
Activities: Provides grants for arts-based community development in the Halifax Regional Municipality

4Korners Family Resource Center

1906 d'Oka St., Deux Montagnes QC J7R 1N4
Tel: 450-974-3940; *Fax:* 450-974-0147
info@4kornerscenter.org
4kornerscenter.org
www.facebook.com/4KornersCenter
Overview: A small local charitable organization
Mission: To provide day care support & create a community of English speaking residents of Laurentians
Chief Officer(s):
Rola Helou, Executive Director
rola@4kornerscenter.org
Kim Nymark, Communications Director
kim@4kornerscenter.org
Peter Andreozzi, President, Board of Directors
president@4kornerscenter.org
Membership: *Fees:* $25 per member
Activities: *Internships:* Yes

Foursquare Gospel Church of Canada

#307, 2099 Lougheed Hwy., Port Coquitlam BC V3B 1A8
Tel: 604-941-8414; *Fax:* 604-941-8415
Toll-Free: 866-941-8414
info@foursquare.ca
www.foursquare.ca
Overview: A medium-sized national charitable organization founded in 1981
Member of: Evangelical Fellowship of Canada
Chief Officer(s):
Steve Falkiner, President
Finances: *Annual Operating Budget:* $250,000-$500,000
Staff Member(s): 3
Membership: 67 churches

Fox Creek Chamber of Commerce

PO Box 774, Fox Creek AB T0H 1P0
Tel: 780-622-2670
admin@foxcreek.ca
www.foxcreek.ca/index.php/doing-business/chamber-of-commerce
www.facebook.com/143047395735293
Overview: A small local organization
Finances: *Funding Sources:* Membership; advertising; donations
Staff Member(s): 1; 7 volunteer(s)
Membership: 1-99

Fox Valley Chamber of Commerce

PO Box 133, Fox Valley SK S0N 0V0
Tel: 306-666-4447; *Fax:* 306-666-4448
Overview: A small local organization
Chief Officer(s):
Lester N Lodoen, President
Delia E. Hughes, Secretary

FPInnovations

570, boul Saint-Jean, Pointe-Claire QC H9R 3J9
Tel: 514-630-4100; *Fax:* 514-630-4134
info@fpinnovations.ca
fpinnovations.ca
twitter.com/fpinnovations
Previous Name: Forest Engineering Research Institute of Canada, A Division of FPInnovations
Overview: A medium-sized national organization founded in 1975
Mission: To develop & assist with the implementation of innovative & safe forest operational solutions, which encompass areas such as the engineering, environmental, & human aspects of forestry & wildland fire operations; To improve sustainable forest operations in Canada; To provide members with knowledge & technology, based on research, to conduct cost-competitive, quality forest operations
Chief Officer(s):
Pierre Lapointe, President & CEO
Hervé Deschênes, Vice-President, Business Development
herve.deschenes@fpinnovations.ca
Finances: *Funding Sources:* Forestry companies; Government of Canada; Provincial & territorial governments
Staff Member(s): 100
Membership: *Member Profile:* Forestry companies; Canadian forestry equipment manufacturers & distributors (CFEMD); *Committees:* Strategic Advisory; Advisory Committeeon Forest Engineering Research; Advisory Committee on Wildland Fire Operations Research
Activities: Researching, in consultation with members & partners, which focuses on silvicultural operations, harvesting, wildland fire operations, transportation & roads, & precision forestry; Providing Feric workshops & seminars; *Library:* FERIC Library;

Edmonton Division
11810, Kingsway NW, Edmonton AB T5G 0X5
Tel: 780-413-9031

Québec Division
319 Franquet, Québec QC G1P 4R4
Tel: 418-659-2647

Vancouver Division
2601 East Mall, Vancouver BC V6T 1Z4
Tel: 604-224-3221
Chief Officer(s):
John W. Mann, Vice-President, Western Region

Fragile X Research Foundation of Canada (FXRFC)

167 Queen St. West, Brampton ON L6Y 1M5
Tel: 905-453-9366
info@fragilexcanada.ca
www.fragilexcanada.ca
Overview: A small national charitable organization founded in 1997
Mission: To raise public awareness of Fragile X; to raise money for Fragile X research & support services; to establish a support system for those with & affected by Fragile X
Chief Officer(s):
Carlo Paribello, President / Medical Director
medical@fragilexcanada.ca
Membership: *Committees:* National Fundraising and Volunteer; Marketing; Scientific

Francofonds inc.

#101, 205, boul Provencher, Winnipeg MB R2H 0G4
Tél: 204-237-5852; *Téléc:* 204-233-6405
Ligne sans frais: 866-237-5852
frds@francofonds.org
www.francofonds.org
Aperçu: *Dimension:* petite; *Envergure:* provinciale; Organisme sans but lucratif; fondée en 1978
Mission: Promouvoir et appuyer le développement de la communauté franco-manitobaine
Membre(s) du bureau directeur:
Aimée Craft, Présidente
Finances: *Budget de fonctionnement annuel:* $50,000-$100,000
Membre(s) du personnel: 2; 10 bénévole(s)
Membre: 1,000-4,999

Franco-Jeunes de Terre-Neuve et du Labrador (FJTNL)

#233, 65, ch Ridge, St. John's NL A1B 4P5
Tél: 709-722-8302; *Téléc:* 709-722-9904
coord@fjtnl.ca
www.fjtnl.ca
Aperçu: *Dimension:* petite; *Envergure:* provinciale; fondée en 1988
Mission: Sauvegarder, promouvoir et assurer l'épanouissement de la langue et la culture française auprès des jeunes francophones et acadiens qui résident à Terre-Neuve et au Labrador; maximiser les expériences langagières chez la clientèle jeunesse qu'elle dessert
Membre de: Fédération de la jeunesse canadienne-française inc.; Société nationale de l'Acadie, inc.
Affliation(s): Féderation des francophones de Terre-Neuve et du Labrador
Membre(s) du bureau directeur:
Jeffrey Young, Président
presidence@fjtnl.ca
Finances: *Budget de fonctionnement annuel:* $50,000-$100,000
Membre(s) du personnel: 4
Membre: 80; *Montant de la cotisation:* 1$; *Critères d'admissibilite:* Jeunes de 13 ans à 21 ans résidant dans l'une des 3 régions francophone de TNL
Activités: Jeux de l'Acadie; Festival jeunesse de l'atlantique; formation; loisirs; arts; direction;

Franco-Ontarian Teachers' Association *Voir* Association des enseignantes et des enseignants franco-ontariens

Francophone Association of Municipalities of Ontario *Voir* L'Association française des municipalités de l'Ontario

Francophonie jeunesse de l'Alberta (FJA) / French Youth Association of Alberta

#306, 8627 Marie-Anne Gaboury St., Edmonton AB T6C 3N1
Tél: 780-469-1344; *Téléc:* 780-469-0014
fja@fja.ab.ca
www.fja.ab.ca
www.facebook.com/francophoniejeunesse.delalberta
twitter.com/FJAlberta
Aperçu: *Dimension:* petite; *Envergure:* provinciale; Organisme sans but lucratif; fondée en 1972
Mission: Stimuler la jeunesse albertaine d'expression française à se découvrir et à vivre son plein potentiel
Membre de: Fédération de la jeunesse canadienne-française inc.
Affliation(s): Association canadienne-française de l'Alberta
Membre(s) du bureau directeur:
Rhéal Poirier, Directeur général
r.poirier@fja.ab.ca
Finances: *Budget de fonctionnement annuel:* $250,000-$500,000
Membre(s) du personnel: 3; 75 bénévole(s)
Membre: 700; *Critères d'admissibilite:* Jeunes d'expression française âgés de 14 à 25 ans résidant en Alberta
Activités: Stages de leadership, regroupements jeunesses; parlement jeunesse et formation aux conseils d'étudiants; fête franco-albertaine; congrès provincial; le RaJe; Jeux de la francophonie; *Evénements de sensibilisation:* Fête franco-albertaine, août; *Stagiaires:* Oui

Frank Gerstein Charitable Foundation
PO Box 430, Stn. First Canadian, 130 King ST. West, 20th Fl., Toronto ON M5X 1K1
Tel: 416-933-2228
Overview: A small local charitable organization
Mission: Grants are not open to application
Chief Officer(s):
Amy Loh, Contact
amy.loh@scotiatrust.com

Fransaskois Cultural Council *Voir* Conseil culturel fransaskois

Fransaskois Parents Association *Voir* Association des parents fransaskois

Fraser Basin Council (FBC)
Basin-Wide Office, 470 Granville St., 1st Fl., Vancouver BC V6C 1V5
Tel: 604-488-5350; *Fax:* 604-488-5351
info@fraserbasin.bc.ca
www.fraserbasin.bc.ca
Overview: A medium-sized local organization founded in 1997
Mission: To advance sustainability in the Fraser River Basin & across British Columbia
Chief Officer(s):
David Marshall, Executive Director
dmarshall@fraserbasin.bc.ca
Charlotte Argue, Assistant Manager, Climate Change & Air Quality Program
cargue@fraserbasin.bc.ca
Awards:
• Sustainability Awards (Award)
Publications:
• Basin News [a publication of the Fraser Basin Council]
Type: Newsletter; *Frequency:* 2 pa

Cariboo-Chilcotin Regional Office
#104, 197 Second Ave. North, Williams Lake BC V2G 1Z5
Tel: 250-392-1400; *Fax:* 250-305-1004
Chief Officer(s):
Maureen LeBourdais, Regional Manager & Sr. Program Manager, Smart Planning for Communities
mlebourdais@fraserbasin.bc.ca

Fraser Valley Regional Office
PO Box 3006, Mission BC V2V 4J3
Tel: 604-826-1661; *Fax:* 604-826-6848
Chief Officer(s):
Marion Town, Senior Regional Manager, GVSS & Fraser Valley
mtown@fraserbasin.bc.ca
Marion Robinson, Regional Manager
mrobinson@fraserbasin.bc.ca

Greater Vancouver Sea to Sky Regional Office (GVSS)
470 Granville St., 1st Fl., Vancouver BC V6C 1V5
Tel: 604-488-5365; *Fax:* 604-488-5351
Chief Officer(s):
Marion Town, Senior Regional Manager, GVSS & Fraser Valley
mtown@fraserbasin.bc.ca

Thompson Regional Office
#200A, 1383 McGill Rd., Kamloops BC V2C 6K7
Tel: 250-314-9660; *Fax:* 250-828-2597
Chief Officer(s):
Mike Simpson, Senior Regional Manager
msimpson@fraserbasin.bc.ca

Upper Fraser Regional Office
#207, 155 George St., Prince George BC V2L 1P8
Tel: 250-612-0252; *Fax:* 250-564-6514
Chief Officer(s):
Terry Robert, Regional Manager & Program Manager, Climate Change & Air Quality
trobert@fraserbasin.bc.ca

The Fraser Institute
1770 Burrard St., 4th Fl., Vancouver BC V6J 3G7
Tel: 604-688-0221; *Fax:* 604-688-8539
info@fraserinstitute.ca
www.fraserinstitute.ca
www.linkedin.com/company/the-fraser-institute
www.facebook.com/fraserinstitute
twitter.com/FraserInstitute
www.youtube.com/FraserInstitute
Overview: A medium-sized national charitable organization founded in 1974
Mission: To redirect public attention to the role competitive markets play in the economic well-being of all Canadians
Affiliation(s): Organizations in 57 countries
Chief Officer(s):
Peter Brown, Chair
Niels Veldhuis, President
niels.veldhuis@fraserinstitute.org
Kenneth P. Green, Senior Director, Centre for Natural Resources
ken.green@fraserinstitute.org
Finances: *Funding Sources:* Donations; sale of publications; grants from foundations
Activities: *Internships:* Yes; *Library* by appointment

Calgary Office
#403, 525 - 11th Ave. SW, Calgary AB T2R 0C9
Tel: 403-216-7175; *Fax:* 403-234-9010

Montréal Office
#252, 1470, rue Peel, Montréal QC H3A 1T1
Tél: 514-281-9550; *Téléc:* 514-281-9464

Toronto Office
#401, 1491 Yonge St., Toronto ON M4T 1Z4
Tel: 416-363-6575; *Fax:* 416-934-1639

Fraser Lake Chamber of Commerce
PO Box 1059, Fraser Lake BC V0J 1S0
Tel: 250-699-6605; *Fax:* 250-699-6469
www.fraserlake.ca
www.facebook.com/fraserlake
Overview: A small local organization
Chief Officer(s):
Maureen Olson, President, 250-699-6605
Finances: *Funding Sources:* Membership dues
Membership: 8

Fraser Valley Egg Producers' Association
c/o Agir Labour Pool, #307, 34252 Marshall Rd., Abbotsford BC V2S 5E4
Tel: 604-853-3556; *Fax:* 604-853-7471
Overview: A small local organization
Chief Officer(s):
Garth Bean, Secretary
Dan Kampen, President

Fraser Valley Labour Council
#202, 9292 - 200th St., Langley BC V1M 3A6
Tel: 604-314-9867; *Fax:* 604-430-6762
bharder@usw.ca
www.fvlc.ca
www.facebook.com/group.php?gid=242003131602&ref=mf
Overview: A small local organization founded in 2007 overseen by British Columbia Federation of Labour
Mission: To advance the economic, social, & political life of persons in British Columbia's Fraser Valley; To act as the unified voice for workers to ensure workers' rights, such as fair wages & safe working conditions
Chief Officer(s):
Brian Harder, President
bharder@usw.ca
Pamela Willingshofer, Secretary
kidogo@shaw.ca
Karen Porter, Treasurer
kporter64@shaw.ca
Membership: 12,000; *Member Profile:* Members of unions from the Fraser Valley region of British Columbia, such as Chilliwack, Hope, Abbotsford, Mission, Lytton, & Harrison
Activities: Lobbying governments about worker's issues; Providing labour education; Conducting campaigns to support the issues of working families; Supporting local organizations, such as the United Way
Meetings/Conferences: • Fraser Valley Labour Council 2015 Annual General Meeting, 2015, BC
Scope: Local
Contact Information: Secretary: Pamela Willingshofer, Phone: 604-837-3426

Fraser Valley Real Estate Board
15463 - 104 Ave., Surrey BC V3R 1N9
Tel: 604-930-7600; *Fax:* 604-588-0325
Toll-Free: 877-286-5685
mls@fvreb.bc.ca
www.fvreb.bc.ca
www.linkedin.com/company/fraser-valley-real-estate-board
www.facebook.com/FVREB
twitter.com/FVREB
Overview: A medium-sized local organization founded in 1955 overseen by British Columbia Real Estate Association
Mission: To provide the most efficient real estate marketing service.
Member of: The Canadian Real Estate Association
Chief Officer(s):
Ron Todson, President
Rob Philipp, Chief Executive Officer
Finances: *Funding Sources:* Membership dues; service fees
Membership: 3,000; *Member Profile:* Licensed real estate sales
Activities: *Library*

Fraser Valley Rock & Gem Club
#109, 22015 - 48 Ave., Langley BC V3A 8L3
Tel: 604-532-8734
Overview: A small local charitable organization founded in 1959
Mission: To promote & encourage the lapidary/rockhound hobby, which includes collecting minerals & other geological materials; to encourage camaraderie & cooperation within the club & with other lapidary clubs & organizations.
Member of: Lapidary Rock & Mineral Society of British Columbia; Gem & Mineral Federation of Canada
Chief Officer(s):
Karen Archibald, Contact
karchiba@telus.net
Activities: Rockhounding; lapidary; silversmithing; jewellery; fossils; field trips; monthly meetings; *Library*

Fraser Valley Square & Round Dance Association
c/o Secretary, 2687 Grant St., Vancouver BC V5K 3G8
Tel: 604-253-5467
region2.squaredance.bc.ca/fvsrdaexec.html
Overview: A small local organization founded in 1959
Member of: BC Square & Round Dance Federation
Affliation(s): Canadian Square & Round Dance Society
Chief Officer(s):
Barbara & Guy Tryssenaar, President, 604-466-5091
btryssenaar@telus.net
45 volunteer(s)
Membership: under 3,000 in 43 clubs; *Fees:* $1
Activities: *Speaker Service:* Yes; *Rents Mailing List:* Yes

Fraser Valley Symphony Society
PO Box 122, Abbotsford BC V2S 4N8
Tel: 604-859-3877
info@fraservalleysymphony.org
www.fraservalleysymphony.org
Overview: A small local organization founded in 1984 overseen by Orchestras Canada
Activities: Concerts & rehearsals

Fraserside Community Services Society
519 - 7th St., 2nd Fl., New Westminster BC V3M 6A7
Tel: 604-522-3722; *Fax:* 604-522-4031
info@fraserside.bc.ca
www.fraserside.bc.ca
Overview: A small local charitable organization founded in 1972
Mission: To provide a range of services assisting people to overcome challenging conditions; Maximize their quality of life; Offer programs that inform, motivate & facilitate self-help
Affliation(s): British Columbia Association for Community Living; Federation of Child & Family Services
Chief Officer(s):
Linda Edmonds, Chief Executive Officer
ledmonds@fraserside.bc.ca
Membership: *Fees:* $2 senior/student; $10 individual; $25 family/organization

Frasier Valley Orchid Society
George Preston Recreation Centre, 20699 - 42 Ave., Langley BC V3A 2G5
Tel: 604-530-1323
www.fraservalleyorchidsociety.com
www.facebook.com/FraserValleyOrchidSociety
www.twitter.com/wix
plus.google.com/117167403531518744294
Overview: A small local organization founded in 1978
Chief Officer(s):
Dianne Gillis, President

Fraternité des Indiens de la Colombie-Britannique *See* Native Brotherhood of British Columbia

Fraternité des Policiers et Policières de la Ville de Québec (FPPVQ)
#210, 600 boul Pierre-Bertrand, Québec QC G1M 3W5
Tél: 418-683-8558; *Téléc:* 418-683-4637
info@fppvq.qc.ca
www.fppvq.qc.ca

Nom précédent: Syndicat professionnel de la police municipale de Québec
Aperçu: *Dimension:* petite; *Envergure:* locale
Membre(s) du bureau directeur:
Bernard Lerhe, Président
president@fppvq.qc.ca
Membre: 440

Fraternite des prisons du Canada *See* Prison Fellowship Canada

Fraternité interprovinciale des ouvriers en électricité (CTC) (FIPOE) / Interprovincial Brotherhood of Electrical Workers (CLC)
#11100, 565, boul Crémazie est, Montréal QC H2M 2W2
Tél: 514-385-3476; *Téléc:* 514-385-9298
info@fipoe.org
www.fipoe.org
www.facebook.com/FIPOE
twitter.com/fipoeorg
www.youtube.com/fipoeorg
Aperçu: *Dimension:* grande; *Envergure:* provinciale
Mission: Regrouper des électriciens de construction, des installateurs de systèmes d'alarmes et des monteurs de ligne.
Membre(s) du bureau directeur:
Styve Grenier, Président
styve.grenier@fipoe.org
Arnold Guérin, Directeur général
arnold.guerin@fipoe.org
Membre: 12 000 individus + 10 sections locales
Publications:
• La FIPOE
Type: Journal

Fraternité nationale des forestiers et travailleurs d'usine (CTC) / National Brotherhood of Foresters & Industrial Workers (CLC)
Locale 299, #101, 2, boul Desaulniers, Saint-Lambert QC J4P 1L2
Tél: 450-465-2218; *Téléc:* 450-465-1301
Ligne sans frais: 800-317-1818
fnftu@qc.aira.com
Aperçu: *Dimension:* grande; *Envergure:* nationale; Organisme sans but lucratif; fondée en 1981
Mission: L'étude, la sauvegarde et le développement des intérêts économiques, et l'application de conventions collectives
Affiliation(s): Fédération des travailleurs et travailleuses de Québec
Membre(s) du bureau directeur:
Sylvie Labelle, Adjointe au président
Yves Guérette, Président
Membre(s) du personnel: 5
Membre: 5 000; *Montant de la cotisation:* 2% du salaire brut; *Critères d'admissibilite:* Doit être salarié qui a signé sa formule d'adhésion à la fraternité et qui a payé la cotisation requise durant six mois consécutifs
Activités: *Bibliothèque*

Fred Victor Centre
59 Adelaide St. East, 6th Fl., Toronto ON M5C 1K6
Tel: 416-364-8228; *Fax:* 416-364-4728
www.fredvictor.org
Overview: A medium-sized local charitable organization founded in 1894
Mission: To offer a continuum of community services, housing options and advocacy for adults who are experiencing homelessness, marginalization and poverty. Over 150 beds and spaces are available across 6 sites and programs.
Chief Officer(s):
Mark Aston, Executive Director
maston@fredvictor.org
Finances: *Annual Operating Budget:* Greater than $5 Million; *Funding Sources:* Federal, provincial & municipal government; Toronto United Church Council; foundations; individual & corporate donations

The Freda Centre for Research on Violence Against Women & Children
Simon Fraser University, 515 West Hastings St., Vancouver BC V6B 5K3
Tel: 778-782-5197
freda@sfu.ca
fredacentre.com
twitter.com/FREDA_Centre
Overview: A small provincial organization founded in 1992
Mission: To facilitate & conduct research on violence against women & children, in order to raise awareness & effect policy
Chief Officer(s):
Margaret A. Jackson, Director
Staff Member(s): 8

Fredericton Anti-Poverty Association (FAPO)
242 Gibson St., Fredericton NB E3A 4E3
Tel: 506-458-9102
fapo@antipoverty.com
antipoverty.com
www.facebook.com/185812278109170
Overview: A small provincial charitable organization founded in 1991
Affliation(s): National Anti-Poverty Organization
Membership: *Member Profile:* Must have received social assistance at one time
Activities: Presentations to municipal & provincial government; speakers panel; observer attendance at Civic Board & committees including police, hospital & city council; sponsors Anti-Poverty Legal Clinic; undertaking a study of operation of food banks

Fredericton Area Moms of Multiples (FAMOM)
Fredericton NB
Other Communication: fredericton@multiplebirthscanada.org
frederictonareamoms@gmail.com
www.multiplebirthscanada.org/~fredericton
Overview: A small local organization overseen by Multiple Births Canada

Fredericton Board of Trade *See* Fredericton Chamber of Commerce

Fredericton Chamber of Commerce / La Chambre de Commerce de Fredericton
PO Box 275, 270 Rookwood Ave., Fredericton NB E3B 4Y9
Tel: 506-458-8006; *Fax:* 506-451-1119
fchamber@frederictonchamber.ca
www.frederictonchamber.ca
Previous Name: Fredericton Board of Trade
Overview: A medium-sized local organization founded in 1874
Mission: To contribute to the economic development of the community by being the advocate of business in the Greater Fredericton area
Chief Officer(s):
Andrew Steeves, President
Jennifer English, Coordinator, Research & Communications
jennifere@frederictonchamber.ca
Membership: 910+; *Member Profile:* Small, medium & large businesses in the Fredericton area; *Committees:* Executive; Management; Provincial/Federal Government Affairs; Municipal Government Affairs; Economic Development; Ambassadors; Business Excellence Awards Selection; Distinguished Citizens Awards Selection
Activities: Working with economic development organizations & government on behalf of Chamber members; Providing networking opportunities; Offering education sessions
Awards:
• Distinguished Citizen Awards (Award)
• Business Excellence Awards (Award)

Fredericton Community Services Inc.
686 Riverside Dr., Fredericton NB E3A 8R6
Tel: 506-459-7461
Overview: A small local organization founded in 1983
Mission: To provide food & clothing to those in need
Member of: Canadian Association of Food Banks
Chief Officer(s):
Elizabeth Thurber, Contact
Staff Member(s): 4; 15 volunteer(s)

Fredericton Fish & Game Association (FFGA)
PO Box 1083, Stn. A, Fredericton NB E3B 5C2
Tel: 506-474-0458
www.freewebs.com/fishandgame
www.facebook.com/165642576892091
Overview: A small local organization founded in 1924
Mission: To foster sound management & wise use of natural resources so that economic, recreational & aesthetic values may continue to benefit future generations
Member of: New Brunswick Wildlife Federation
Chief Officer(s):
Rod Currie, President
president@frederictonfishandgame.org
Finances: *Annual Operating Budget:* Less than $50,000
30 volunteer(s)
Membership: 140; *Fees:* $25 single; $40 family; *Member Profile:* Individuals concerned about natural resources & willing to assist in conservation; *Committees:* Jr. Branch; Education; Environment; Conservation Lottery; Wildlife; Newsletter
Activities: Adopt-A-Stream; Youth Fishing Tournament; Fishing & Hunting Enhancement Project; education & speakers

Fredericton Northwest Construction Association Inc. (FNWCA)
59 Avonlea Ct., Fredericton NB E3C 1N8
Tel: 506-458-1086; *Fax:* 506-453-1958
fnwca@nbnet.nb.ca
www.fnwca.ca
Overview: A small local organization founded in 1951 overseen by Canadian Construction Association
Member of: Construction Association of New Brunswick
Chief Officer(s):
Brian Dingle, President
Susan McDonald, Office Manager
Finances: *Funding Sources:* Membership dues
Membership: 150+

Fredericton Numismatic Society
89 Bellflower St., New Maryland NB E3C 1C2
Overview: A small local organization
Member of: Royal Canadian Numismatic Association

Fredericton Police Association / Association des policiers de Fredericton
311 Queen St., Fredericton NB E3B 1B1
Tel: 506-460-2300; *Fax:* 506-460-2316
Overview: A small local organization

Fredericton Rape Crisis Centre *See* Fredericton Sexual Assault Crisis Centre

Fredericton Sexual Assault Crisis Centre (FSACC) / Centre pour les victimes d'agression sexuelle de Fredericton
PO Box 174, Fredericton NB E3B 4Y9
Tel: 506-454-0460; *Fax:* 506-457-2780; *Crisis Hot-Line:* 506-454-0437
fsacc@nbnet.nb.ca
www.fsacc.ca
Previous Name: Fredericton Rape Crisis Centre
Overview: A small local charitable organization founded in 1975 overseen by Canadian Association of Sexual Assault Centres
Mission: To eradicate violence against women & children through public education & direct services to victims of incest, sexual assault, sexual harassment & dating violence
Member of: National Action Committee on the Status of Women
Finances: *Funding Sources:* United Way; Project Grants; Donations; Fundraising; Corporations
Membership: *Member Profile:* Women; 18 years & older
Activities: Crisis Line Program; Public Education Program; Dating Violence Program; Sexual Assault Counselling Program; Self-Protection Program; *Speaker Service:* Yes; *Library* Open to public by appointment

Fredericton Society for the Prevention of Cruelty to Animals
165 Hilton Rd., Fredericton NB E3B 4Y9
Tel: 506-459-1555
info@frederictonspca.ca
www.frederictonspca.ca
www.facebook.com/frederictonspca
twitter.com/frederictonspca
www.youtube.com/user/frederictonspca
Also Known As: Fredericton SPCA
Overview: A small local charitable organization founded in 1914
Mission: To investigate allegations of cruelty to animals under the SPCA Act & the Criminal Code; to promote the welfare of animals
Member of: Canadian Federation of Humane Societies
Chief Officer(s):
Scott Elliot, President
Annette James, Director, Operations
Finances: *Funding Sources:* Donations; fundraising
Staff Member(s): 11
Membership: *Fees:* $15 individual; $30 family; $100 corporate

Fredericton Tourism
11 Carleton St., Fredericton NB E3B 3T1
Tel: 506-460-2041; *Fax:* 506-460-2474
Toll-Free: 888-888-4768
tourism@fredericton.ca
www.tourismfredericton.ca
www.facebook.com/FrederictonTourism
twitter.com/FredTourism
www.youtube.com/user/FrederictonTourism

Also Known As: Fredericton Visitor & Convention Bureau
Overview: A small local organization overseen by Tourism Industry Association of New Brunswick
Mission: To develop & run a variety of cultural programs largely focused in the Historic Garrison District; to operate 2 municipal Visitor Information Centres, Lighthouse on the Green, & River Valley Crafts retail shop.
Member of: Tourism Industry Association of Canada; Tourism Industry Association of New Brunswick
Affliation(s): Canadian Association of Visitor & Convention Bureaux
Chief Officer(s):
Ken Forrest, Director, Growth & Community Planning, 506-460-2696
Finances: *Funding Sources:* Municipal government
Staff Member(s): 10

Free Methodist Church in Canada (FMCIC) / Église méthodiste libre du Canada

4315 Village Centre Ct., Mississauga ON L4Z 1S2
Tel: 905-848-2600; *Fax:* 905-848-2603
ministrycentre@fmc-canada.org
www.fmc-canada.org
www.facebook.com/137599632927885
twitter.com/FMCIC
Overview: A medium-sized national organization founded in 1880
Mission: To make known to people everywhere God's call to wholeness through forgiveness & holiness in Jesus Christ & to invite into membership & to equip for ministry all who respond in faith; to see healthy churches within the reach of all people in Canada & beyond.
Member of: Free Methodist World Conference
Affliation(s): Evangelical Fellowship of Canada; Canadian Council of Christian Charities; World Relief Canada
Chief Officer(s):
Daniel Sheffield, Director, Global & Intercultural Ministries
Jared Siebert, Director, Growth Ministries
Mark Molczanski, Director, Administrative Services
Keith A. Elford
Kim Henderson, Director, Personnel
Finances: *Annual Operating Budget:* $1.5 Million-$3 Million
Staff Member(s): 11
Membership: 12,000+ attendees at 144 churches
Activities: *Internships:* Yes; *Speaker Service:* Yes

Free Vietnamese Association of Manitoba

#100, 458 Balmoral St., Winnipeg MB R3B 2P8
Tel: 204-774-3214
banguyen@hotmail.com
Overview: A medium-sized provincial organization
Member of: Vietnamese Canadian Federation

Freedom Party of Ontario (FPO)

240 Commissioners Rd. West, London ON N6J 1Y1
Tel: 519-681-3999; *Fax:* 519-681-2857
Toll-Free: 800-830-3301
feedback@freedomparty.org
www.freedomparty.on.ca
www.facebook.com/fpontario
twitter.com/fpontario
www.youtube.com/fpontario
Overview: A small provincial organization founded in 1984
Mission: To provide a capitalist political alternative in Ontario, & to form an elected government in Ontario, based on the principles of fundamental rights & freedoms
Chief Officer(s):
Paul McKeever, Leader, 905-721-9772
pmckeever@freedomparty.on.ca
Finances: *Annual Operating Budget:* $50,000-$100,000
100 volunteer(s)
Membership: 500 individual; *Fees:* $10 individual
Activities: Political lobbying; fielding candidates in Ontario provincial elections; *Speaker Service:* Yes

Freelance Editors' Association of Canada *See* Editors' Association of Canada

Freestyle Ski Nova Scotia (FSNS)

c/o Alpine Ski Nova Scotia, 5516 Spring Garden Rd., 4th Fl., Halifax NS B3J 1G6
Tel: 902-425-5450; *Fax:* 902-425-5606
alpinens@sportnovascotia.ca
freestylenovascotia.ca
Overview: A small provincial organization overseen by Canadian Freestyle Ski Association
Mission: To govern the sport of freestyle skiing in Nova Scotia.
Member of: Canadian Freestyle Ski Association; Alpine Ski Nova Scotia
Chief Officer(s):
Lorraine Burch, Executive Director
Membership: *Committees:* Competitions; Marketing & Communications; High Performance; Sport Development

Freestyle Skiing Ontario (FSO)

#214A, 3 Concorde Gate, Toronto ON M3C 3N7
Tel: 416-670-8239
info@ontariofreestyle.com
www.ontariofreestyle.com
www.facebook.com/156749758280
Overview: A small provincial organization overseen by Canadian Freestyle Ski Association
Mission: To direct the sport of freestyle skiing in Ontario.
Member of: Canadian Freestyle Ski Association
Chief Officer(s):
Jeff Ord, Executive Director
jefford@ontariofreestyle.com

Freight Carriers Association of Canada (FCA)

#3-4, 427 Garrison Rd., Fort Erie ON L2A 6E6
Fax: 905-994-0117
Toll-Free: 800-559-7421
info@fca-natc.org
www.fca-natc.org
Previous Name: Canadian Transport Tariff Bureau Association
Overview: A medium-sized national organization
Mission: To provide quality information, products & services to users, providers & third parties involved in motor carrier transportation
Affliation(s): North American Transportation Council
Chief Officer(s):
David J. Sirgey, President, 800-559-7421 Ext. 214
dsirgey@natc.com
Ken Leising, Manager Rate Research/Development, 800-559-7421 Ext. 203
kleising@natc.com
Diane Sheppard, Accountant, 800-559-7421 Ext. 207
dsheppard@natc.com
Jon Ainsworth, Senior Analyst/Programmer, 800-559-7421 Ext. 217
jda@natc.com
Mary Anne Vehrs, Sales/Marketing, 800-559-7421 Ext. 212
mvehrs@natc.com
Finances: *Annual Operating Budget:* $1.5 Million-$3 Million; *Funding Sources:* Membership fees; sales of publications & software
Membership: *Member Profile:* For-hire motor carriers
Activities: Carrier meetings; seminars; research; info gathering & dissemination; *Speaker Service:* Yes

Freight Management Association of Canada (FMA) / Association canadienne de gestion du fret (AGF)

#405, 580 Terry Fox Dr., Ottawa ON K2L 4C2
Tel: 613-599-3283; *Fax:* 613-599-1295
info@fma-agf.ca
www.cita-acti.ca
www.linkedin.com/company/canadian-industrial-transportation-associatio
twitter.com/CITA_ACTI
Previous Name: Canadian Industrial Transportation Association
Overview: A medium-sized national organization founded in 1916
Mission: To promote a competitive & cost effective North American transportation system serving Canada and its NAFTA allies.
Chief Officer(s):
Bob Ballantyne, President
ballantyne@fma-agf.ca
Kelsey Lemieux, Manger, Marketing
lemieux@fma-agf.ca
Cindy Hick, Vice-President
hick@fma-agf.ca
Finances: *Funding Sources:* Membership dues
Membership: 86; *Fees:* Schedule available; *Member Profile:* Companies involved in the shipping industry
Activities: Advocacy; education; *Speaker Service:* Yes
Meetings/Conferences: • Canadian Industrial Transportation Association 58th Annual Convention & Golf Tournament, 2015
Scope: National

French Chamber of Commerce *Voir* Chambre de commerce française au canada

French Jurists Association of Saskatchewan *Voir* Association des juristes d'expression française de la Saskatchewan

French Youth Association of Alberta *Voir* Francophonie jeunesse de l'Alberta

Frequency Co-ordination System Association (FCSA) / Association pour la coordination des fréquences

#700, 1 Nicholas St., Ottawa ON K1N 7B7
Tel: 613-241-3080; *Fax:* 613-241-9632
www.fcsa.ca
Previous Name: Canadian Telecommunication Carriers Association
Overview: A medium-sized national organization founded in 1983
Mission: To operate & administer computerized Microwave Information & Coordination System (MICS); to provide cost-effective, timely & high quality centralized administrative & technical services to allow members to be able to effectively plan & coordinate frequencies for microwave communication systems on national basis.
Chief Officer(s):
Alejandro Moreno, General Manager/Secretary-Treasurer
amoreno.fcsa@sympatico.ca
Finances: *Funding Sources:* Member organizations
Staff Member(s): 5
Membership: 23 organizations; *Member Profile:* Telecommunications service providers; *Committees:* MICS Management; MICS Technical Group

Frères de Notre-Dame de la Miséricorde / Brothers of Our Lady of Mercy

1149, ch Tour du Lac nord, Lac-Sergent QC G0A 2J0
Tél: 418-875-2792; *Téléc:* 418-875-4829
fndm@cite.net
Aperçu: *Dimension:* petite; *Envergure:* internationale; Organisme sans but lucratif; fondée en 1839
Mission: Rassembler des personnes en vue d'un travail apostolique auprès des jeunes et particulièrement auprès des personnes éprouvant des difficultés
Membre(s) du bureau directeur:
Omer Beaulieu, Délégué du Supérieur général
Finances: *Budget de fonctionnement annuel:* Moins de $50,000
Membre(s) du personnel: 1; 6 bénévole(s)
Membre: 9

Fresh Outlook Foundation (FOF)

12510 Ponderosa Rd., Lake Country BC V4V 2G9
Tel: 250-766-1777; *Fax:* 250-766-1767
www.freshoutlookfoundation.org
www.facebook.com/FreshOutlookFoundation?ref=website
www.twitter.com/FreshOutlook
Overview: A small national charitable organization founded in 2007
Mission: The Fresh Outlook Foundation (FOF) builds sustainable communities through a focus on the social, cultural, environmental, and economic aspects of community sustainability.
Chief Officer(s):
Joanne de Vries, CEO
jo@freshoutlookfoundation.org
Finances: *Funding Sources:* Donations (industry, business); government (federal/provincial, less than 5%); private foundations
Activities: Green School Program, environmental action program for elementary school students; Challenge Programs; Water & Clean Air; Writing & Bird challenges for elementary & junior high school students; Creating a Climate of Change Multimedia Program; Energy Literacy Series; Taking Action on Climate Change
Meetings/Conferences: • 2015 Building SustainABLE Communities Conference, 2015
Scope: National

Freshwater Fisheries Society of British Columbia (FFSBC)

#101, 80 Regatta Landing, Victoria BC V9A 7S2
Tel: 250-414-4200; *Fax:* 250-414-4211
Toll-Free: 888-601-4200
fish@gofishbc.com
www.gofishbc.com
www.facebook.com/gofishbc
twitter.com/go_fish_bc
www.youtube.com/gofishbc
Overview: A medium-sized provincial organization

Mission: To stock eggs & fish into lakes & streams across British Columbia; To support sturgeon & steelhead recovery programs; To operate hatcheries & visitor's centres
Chief Officer(s):
Don Peterson, President
Jonathan Pew, Chair
James Gordon, Secretary-Treasurer
Activities: Providing information related to freshwater fishing & freshwater ecosystems in British Columbia; Partnering with organizations such as the Ministry of Environment to offer the Go Fish program so that children can experience fishing & foster an appreciation for the environment

The Friends of Algonquin Park
PO Box 248, Whitney ON K0J 2M0
Tel: 613-637-2828; *Fax:* 613-637-2138
www.algonquinpark.on.ca/friends
Overview: A small local charitable organization founded in 1983
Mission: To further the educational & interpretive programs in Algonquin Park
Affiliation(s): Canadian Parks Partnership; Ontario Parks
Chief Officer(s):
Lee Pauzé, General Manager
Finances: *Annual Operating Budget:* $500,000-$1.5 Million
Staff Member(s): 7; 197 volunteer(s)
Membership: 3,000; *Fees:* $7 student; $12 individual; $17 family
Activities: *Speaker Service:* Yes

The Friends of Awenda Park / Les Amis du Parc Awenda
c/o Awenda Provincial Park, PO Box 5004, Penetanguishene ON L9M 2G2
Tel: 705-549-6378
Other Communication: 705-549-2231 (Awenda Provincial Park)
awenda@csolve.net
www.awendapark.ca
Overview: A small local organization founded in 1991
Mission: Dedicated to the preservation, understanding & interpretation of Awenda's biological, geological & cultural treasurers

The Friends of Bon Echo Park
16151 Highway 41, RR#1, Cloyne ON K0H 1K0
Tel: 613-336-0830; *Fax:* 613-336-2712
logistics@bonechofriends.ca
www.bonechofriends.ca
www.facebook.com/bonechofriends
Overview: A small local charitable organization
Mission: To preserve the natural & cultural heritage of Bon Echo Provincial Park
Chief Officer(s):
Ernest Lapchinski, President
Derek Maggs, Executive Director
Finances: *Annual Operating Budget:* $100,000-$250,000
90 volunteer(s)
Membership: 200; *Fees:* $15 individual; $25 family; $150 life
Activities: Annual Art Show & Sale, July;

The Friends of Bonnechere Parks
RR#5, 4024 Round Lake Rd., Killaloe ON K0J 2A0
Tel: 613-732-9273
bettyb@nrtco.net
www.bonnecherepark.on.ca
www.facebook.com/bonnecherepark
twitter.com/bonnechere
Overview: A small local organization founded in 1992
Mission: To encourage & support programs for interpretive, educational, scientific, historical, protection & preservation purposes related to the natural & historic resources of the Little Bonnechere River in the Ottawa Valley
Chief Officer(s):
Betty Biesenthal, Director of Publicity

Friends of Canadian Broadcasting (FCB)
#200-238, 131 Bloor St. West, Toronto ON M5S 1R8
Tel: 416-968-7496; *Fax:* 416-968-7406
friends@friends.ca
www.friends.ca
www.facebook.com/sharer.php?u=/&t=*Welcome
twitter.com/friendscb
www.youtube.com/user/FriendsCB
Overview: A large national organization founded in 1985
Mission: To defend & enhance the quality & quantity of Canadian programming in the Canadian audio-visual system
Chief Officer(s):
Ian Morrison, Spokesperson
Finances: *Annual Operating Budget:* $1.5 Million-$3 Million; *Funding Sources:* Membership fees
Membership: 66,000 households
Awards:
• The Dalton Camp Award (Award)
Award will go to the winner of an essay competition on the link between democracy and the media in Canada. *Amount:* $5,000

Friends of Canadian Libraries (FOCAL)
PO Box 2843, Stony Plain AB T7J 1A0
Tel: 780-963-7816
focal@accessola.com
www.accessola.com/focal
www.facebook.com/174088412634167
Overview: A medium-sized national charitable organization founded in 1998
Mission: To provide a national support & resource network to assist in the formation & promotion of Friends of Libraries groups throughout the library community in Canada; Friends of Libraries are volunteers acting collectively & independently to preserve, promote & strengthen library services in harmony with library management & policies
Affiliation(s): Friends of Libraries USA; Friends of Libraries Australia
Chief Officer(s):
Dorothy Macnaughton, President
Jocelyn MacNiel, Secretary
Jami van Haaften, Treasurer
Finances: *Annual Operating Budget:* Less than $50,000
Membership: 160; *Fees:* $25-$75; *Member Profile:* Friends of the library groups; library foundations; public libraries; school & university libraries; public & private corporations & individual friends
Activities: Conferences; education; seminars; networking; Friends' Day at Ontario Library Association & Canadian Library Association conferences; *Library:* Lending Library

Friends of Chamber Music
PO Box 38046, RPO Edward Mall, Vancouver BC V5Z 4L9
Tel: 604-437-5747; *Fax:* 604-437-4769
fcmtickets@yahoo.com
www.friendsofchambermusic.ca
www.facebook.com/focm.org
Overview: A small local charitable organization founded in 1948
Mission: To present the best in chamber music
Member of: Vancouver Cultural Alliance
Chief Officer(s):
Eric Wilson, Program Chair
Finances: *Annual Operating Budget:* $100,000-$250,000; *Funding Sources:* Donations; Subscriptions; Ticket sales
24 volunteer(s)
Membership: 350; *Fees:* Schedule available; *Member Profile:* Mature music lovers
Activities: Season of ten concerts; competition for young musicians; *Awareness Events:* Chamber Music Competition for Young Musicians, March

The Friends of Charleston Lake Park
148 Woodvale Rd., RR#4, Lansdowne ON K0E 1L0
e-mail: info@friendsofcharlestonlake.ca
www.friendsofcharlestonlake.ca
Overview: A small local organization
Mission: To help people enjoy Charleston Lake Park, this unique & beautiful place & to help keep it that way
Chief Officer(s):
Steve Psge, Chair

Friends of Clayoquot Sound (FOCS)
PO Box 489, 331 Neill St., Tofino BC V0R 2Z0
Tel: 250-725-4218
info@focs.ca
www.focs.ca
Overview: A medium-sized local charitable organization founded in 1979
Mission: To be peaceful & courageous advocates for the earth, air & waters of Clayoquot Sound & all temperate rainforests; To dramatically reduce economic reliance upon raw resource extraction by developing sustainability in rural & urban cultures; To oppose logging on ancient temperate rainforests, as well as the export of raw (unprocessed) logs; To support ecoforestry in second growth forest; To promote reduced wood & paper consumption & support the use of ecologically sustainable, tree-free alternatives to wood & wood-fibre products; To advocate taking fish farms out of wild waters & putting them in on-land closed containment systems
Member of: BC Environmental Network; Coastal Alliance for Aquaculture Reform (CAAR)
Affiliation(s): Greenpeace; Sierra Club; Natural Resources Defence Council; Western Canada Wilderness Committee (WCWC)
Chief Officer(s):
Dan Lewis, Executive Director
dan@focs.ca
Finances: *Annual Operating Budget:* $100,000-$250,000; *Funding Sources:* Individual donors; foundation grants
Staff Member(s): 4
Membership: 3,000; *Fees:* $25
Activities: *Speaker Service:* Yes; *Library:* FOCS Resource Centre

Friends of Devonian Botanic Garden
PO Box 69227, Stn. skyview, 13040 - 137 Ave. NW, Edmonton AB T8N 2H2
Tel: 780-221-6467
info@friends-devonianbotanicgarden.org
www.friends-devonianbotanicgarden.org
www.facebook.com/FriendsOfTheDevonianBotanicGarden
twitter.com/FriendsofDBG
www.pinterest.com/devonianbotanic/pins
Overview: A small local charitable organization founded in 1971
Mission: To promote a wider educational use & public appreciation of the scientific & cultural values of the Devonian Botanic Garden by the larger Edmonton community & beyond
Chief Officer(s):
Brenda Harvey, President
brendaharvey@telus.net
Finances: *Annual Operating Budget:* $50,000-$100,000; *Funding Sources:* Membership fees; donations; grants
Staff Member(s): 1; 15 volunteer(s)
Membership: 375; *Fees:* $75 families; $50 individuals; $40 seniors/students
Activities: Promote & finance construction of gardens, paths, signs, structures & other facilities; raise funds for projects of the society; promote volunteerism;

Friends of Dismas
PO Box 117, Markham ON L3P 3J5
Tel: 416-525-8967
friendsofdismas@gmail.com
www.friendsofdismas.com
twitter.com/friendsofdismas
Overview: A small local organization
Mission: To help people affected by crime through the building of a creative & healing community
Affiliation(s): Archdiocese of Toronto
Chief Officer(s):
Michael Walsh, Contact
Finances: *Funding Sources:* Donations

Friends of Ecological Reserves (FER)
PO Box 8477, Stn. Central, Victoria BC V8W 3S1
Tel: 250-361-1694
ecoreserves@hotmail.com
www.ecoreserves.bc.ca
Overview: A small local charitable organization founded in 1982
Mission: To promote the interests of British Columbia's ecological reserves program
Chief Officer(s):
Michael Fenger, President
Stephen Ruttan, Vice-President
Finances: *Funding Sources:* Donations; Fundraising
Membership: *Fees:* $15 students & seniors; $20 individuals; $25 families & institutions
Activities: Supporting research in the area of ecological reserves; Organizing field trips
Publications:
• The Log [a publication of the Friends of Ecological Reserves]
Type: Newsletter; *Frequency:* Semiannually; *Editor:* Louise Beinhauer; *Price:* Free to members of Friends ofEcological Reserves
Profile: Information about the establishment, management, & maintenance of ecological reserves in British Columbia

Friends of Ferris Provincial Park
PO Box 504, Campbellford ON K0L 1L0
Tel: 705-653-3575
info@friendsofferris.ca
www.friendsofferris.ca
www.facebook.com/138273219576405
Overview: A small local organization founded in 1994
Mission: The Friends of Ferris is a non-profit group of volunteers who are hard at work, constantly bringing to Ferris special events and promotions unique to the Provincial Park.
Chief Officer(s):

Doreen Sharpe, President
Membership: *Fees:* $10 individual; $17 family

The Friends of Fort York & Garrison Common

PO Box 183, Toronto ON M5A 1N1
e-mail: info@fortyork.ca
www.fortyork.ca
www.facebook.com/fortyork
twitter.com/fortyork
Overview: A small local charitable organization founded in 1994
Mission: To enhance the reputation & financial security of Historic Fort York
Affliation(s): Heritage Toronto
Chief Officer(s):
Harriet De Koven, Co-Chair
Stephen Otto, Co-Chair
Membership: *Fees:* $40 individual; $60 family; $100-$249 special friend of Fort York; $250 patron

The Friends of Frontenac Park

PO Box 2237, Kingston ON K7L 5J8
e-mail: frontenacpark@frontenacpark.ca
www.frontenacpark.ca
www.facebook.com/frontenacpark
twitter.com/frontenacpark
Overview: A small local organization

The Friends of Killarney Park

c/o Killarney Provincial Park, Killarney ON P0M 2A0
Tel: 705-287-2800; *Fax:* 705-287-2922
friendsofkillarneypark.ca
www.facebook.com/group.php?gid=9103598236
www.youtube.com/user/friendsofkillarney
Overview: A small local organization founded in 1986
Mission: To enhance the interpretive, educational & recreational objectives of Killarney Park
Chief Officer(s):
Kris Puhvel, Executive Director

The Friends of Library & Archives Canada / Les Amis de Bibliothèque et archives Canada

395 Wellington St., Ottawa ON K1A 0N4
Tel: 613-943-1544; *Fax:* 613-943-2343
Other Communication: Alternate Phone: 613-992-8304
friends.amis@lac-bac.gc.ca
www.friendsoflibraryandarchivescanada.ca
Merged from: Friends of the National Archives of Canada; Friends of the National Library of Canada
Overview: A small national charitable organization founded in 2003
Mission: To promote & encourage public interest in & support for the work of Library & Archives Canada in fulfilling its role as a preserver of the national published & unpublished heritage; to provide interested persons & organizations with the opportunity to share in the activities of Library & Archives; to attract collections of Canadiana as gifts to the Library & Archives; to organize fundraising events in support of a variety of its endeavours, including special acquisitions
Affliation(s): Friends of Canadian Libraries
Chief Officer(s):
Marianne Scott, President
Kathleen Shaw, Vice-President
Michael Gnarowski, Treasurer
Georgia Ellis, Executive Director
Finances: *Annual Operating Budget:* Less than $50,000; *Funding Sources:* Membership fees; donations; fundraising events
Staff Member(s): 1; 105 volunteer(s)
Membership: 500; *Fees:* $35 individual; $20 senior/student; $50 family; $100 sustaining; $250 protecting; $1000 lifetime
Activities: Cultural programs; fundraising for the National Library

The Friends of MacGregor Point

c/o MacGregor Point Provincial Park, RR#1, Port Elgin ON N0H 2C5
Tel: 519-389-6232; *Fax:* 519-389-2444
fompp@bmts.com
www.friendsofmacgregor.org
www.facebook.com/101912730956
www.twitter.com/fompp
Overview: A small local organization
Mission: To supplement & enhance the interpretive & educational programs in the park; to stimulate community interest in & understanding of the park & its resources; to support research of the park's natural & cultural resources
Membership: *Fees:* $15 individual; $20 family; $30 corporate

Friends of Mashkinonje Park

Site 8, Box 1, 99 Langs Landing, Monetville ON P0M 2K0
e-mail: friendsofmashkinonje@yahoo.ca
www.mashkinonje.com
Overview: A small local organization founded in 2000
Mission: To maintain & share the beauty of this unique area of scenic shorelines & wonderful wetlands
Chief Officer(s):
Angela Martin, President
Membership: *Fees:* $15 individual; $25 family; $50 organization
Publications:
• The Wetlands Observer
Type: Newsletter; *Frequency:* Semiannually

The Friends of Nancy Island Historic Site & Wasaga Beach Park

11 - 22nd St. North, Wasaga Beach ON L9Z 2V9
Tel: 705-429-2516; *Fax:* 705-429-7983
www.wasagabeachpark.com
Overview: A small local organization
Mission: To further the educational & interpretive programs of Wasaga Beach Provincial Park & Nancy Island Historic Site

Friends of Nature Conservation Society

PO Box 281, Chester NS B0J 1J0
Tel: 902-275-3361
info@friends-of-nature.ca
www.friends-of-nature.ca
Overview: A small local organization founded in 1954
Mission: To preserve the balance of nature for the mutual benefit of people & their plant & animal friends
Member of: Nova Scotia Environmental Network; Nova Scotia Public Lands Coalition
Affliation(s): Nature Canada; Friends of Nature, Incorporated
Chief Officer(s):
Martin R. Haase, Executive Secretary
Finances: *Annual Operating Budget:* Less than $50,000
Membership: 100-499; *Fees:* $10
Activities: *Library:* Friends of Nature: Environmental Library

The Friends of Pinery Park

c/o The Visitor Centre, Pinery Provincial Park, RR#2, Grand Bend ON N0M 1T0
Tel: 519-243-2220
www.pinerypark.on.ca/friends.html
Overview: A small local organization founded in 1989
Mission: Dedicated to the development of interpretive, educational, historical & scientific projects & programs to ensure that Pinery Provincial Park's natural legacy will remain for future generations

The Friends of Presqu'ile Park

PO Box 1442, Brighton ON K0K 1H0
Tel: 613-475-2209
info@friendsofpresquile.on.ca
www.friendsofpresquile.on.ca
Overview: A small local organization
Mission: To enhance the educational, interpretive, & scientific research programs at Presqu'ile Provincial Park

Friends of Red Hill Valley

PO Box 61536, Hamilton ON L8T 5A1
Tel: 905-664-8796
redhill@hwcn.org
Overview: A medium-sized local organization founded in 1991
Mission: To protect & enhance the Red Hill Valley in Hamilton, Ontario
Chief Officer(s):
Don McLean, Chair
don.mclean@cogeco.ca
Membership: 800; *Fees:* $5

The Friends of Rondeau Park

RR#1, Morpeth ON N0P 1X0
Tel: 519-674-1777
Info@rondeauprovincialpark.ca
www.rondeauprovincialpark.ca
www.facebook.com/pantsgloydi
Overview: A small local organization
Mission: To raise funds on a continuing basis in order to encourage & support programs for interpretive, educational, scientific, historical, protection & preservation purposes related to the natural & historical resources of Rondeau Provincial Park & other Ontario Provincial Parks

The Friends of Sandbanks Park

PO Box 20007, 97 Main St., Picton ON K0K 0A0
e-mail: friends@friendsofsandbanks.org
friendsofsandbanks.org
Overview: A small local organization founded in 1993
Mission: To protect & preserve the natural & cultural history of provincial park through interpretation, education, & scientific & historic research
Publications:
• Between Friends
Type: Newsletter

Friends of Short Hills Park

PO Box 236, Fonthill ON L0S 1E0
e-mail: shorthillspark@gmail.com
www.friendsofshorthillspark.ca
www.facebook.com/group.php?gid=8166876669
www.youtube.com/user/friendsofshorthills?feature=mhum
Overview: A small local organization
Mission: To preserve the cultural & natural integrity of Short Hills Provincial Park through liaison with Ontario Parks, volunteer work, public education & fundraising activities
Membership: *Fees:* $20

Friends of Simon Wiesenthal Centre for Holocaust Studies - Canada

#902, 5075 Yonge St., Toronto ON M2N 6C6
Tel: 416-864-9735; *Fax:* 416-864-1083
Toll-Free: 866-864-9735
swcmain@fswc.ca
www.friendsofsimonwiesenthalcenter.com
www.linkedin.com/pub/avi-benlolo/10/173/131
www.facebook.com/244499848933801
twitter.com/avibenlolo
www.youtube.com/profile?user=FSWC2009#g/u
Overview: A small national charitable organization founded in 1980
Mission: To carry out in Canada the work of the Wiesenthal Center in California, by bringing antisemitism, bigotry, racial hatred, & ethnic intolerance to the attention of the Canadian government, the public & media
Chief Officer(s):
Avi Benlolo, President & CEO
president@fswc.ca
Staff Member(s): 7
Activities: *Internships:* Yes; *Speaker Service:* Yes; *Library* Open to public by appointment

The Friends of Sleeping Giant

PO Box 29031, Thunder Bay ON P7B 6P9
e-mail: info@thefriendsofsleepinggiant.ca
www.thefriendsofsleepinggiant.ca
Overview: A small local organization founded in 1993
Mission: To assist in conserving & fostering an appreciation for Sleeping Giant Provincial Park

Friends of SOS Children's Villages, Canada Inc. *See* SOS Children's Villages Canada

Friends of the Archibald

Archibald Library, Briercrest College and Seminary, 510 College Dr., Caronport SK S0H 0S0
Tel: 306-756-3252
library@briercrest.ca
www.briercrest.ca/library/databases/FAL
Overview: A small local organization
Mission: Promotes the library as a place that fosters learning community through the sharing of literary and academic works created within the BCS learning community.
Chief Officer(s):
Brad Doerksen, Library Director
bdoerksen@briercrest.ca
Membership: *Fees:* $15

Friends of the Canadian Centre for Architecture *See* Les Amis du centre canadien d'architecture

Friends of The Canadian War Museum (FCWM) / Les Amis du Musée canadien de la guerre (AMCG)

1 Vimy Pl., Ottawa ON K1A 0M8
Tel: 819-776-8618; *Fax:* 819-776-8623
fcwm-amcg@magma.ca
www.friends-amis.org
www.facebook.com/warmuseum
twitter.com/FCWMCanada
Overview: A medium-sized national organization founded in 1987
Mission: To promote & stimulate interest in & give support to the Canadian War Museum by promoting & organizing special events compatible with the approved themes & objectives of the

Museum; to provide volunteers to the Museum, raise funds & promote understanding, communication & cooperation between the people of Canada & military museums of Canada.
Member of: Council of Heritage Organizations in Ottawa (CHOO)
Chief Officer(s):
Douglas C. Rowland, President
Linda Colwell, Vice President
Helen McKiernan, Secretary
David Parr, Treasurer
Finances: *Funding Sources:* Membership and Donations
Membership: 600; *Fees:* $25 individual; *Committees:* Events, Research, Membership, Communications, Resources
Activities: Guides for the Canadian War Museum; silent auctions; book sales; fundraising; *Internships:* Yes; *Speaker Service:* Yes
Publications:
• The Torch
Type: Newsletter; *Frequency:* Quarterly; *Editor:* Bon Margeson

Friends of the Central Experimental Farm (FCEF)
Building 72, Central Experimental Farm, Ottawa ON K1A 0C6
Tel: 613-230-3276; *Fax:* 613-230-1238
info@friendsofthefarm.ca
www.friendsofthefarm.ca
www.facebook.com/FCEFOttawa
www.twitter.com/FCEFOttawa
www.flickr.com/groups/aogcef
Overview: A small local charitable organization
Mission: To preserve, maintain, protect and enhance the Arboretum, the Ornamental Gardens and other public areas of the Central Experimental Farm in Ottawa, Ontario, Canada.
Chief Officer(s):
Eric Jones, President
Finances: *Funding Sources:* Membership fees; Government grants
Membership: *Fees:* $25 adult; $45 family; $20 student/senior; $250 corporate

Friends of the Coves Subwatershed Inc. (FOTCSI)
111 Elmwood Ave. East, London ON N6C 1J4
Tel: 519-640-5397; *Fax:* 519-640-5780
contact@thecoves.ca
www.thecoves.ca
Overview: A small local organization
Mission: A group supporting the protection, conservation & stewardship of the Coves Environmentally Significant Area and surrounding watershed
Chief Officer(s):
Heather Popham, Program Manager
Staff Member(s): 1
Membership: *Fees:* $25, individual; $35, family; $75, non-profit organization; $200, corporate
Activities: *Awareness Events:* Christmas Bird Count, December

Friends of the Delta Marsh Field Station
c/o University Field Station, University of Manitoba, 239 Machray Hall, Winnipeg MB R3T 2N2
Tel: 204-474-9297
delta_marsh@umanitoba.ca
www.umanitoba.ca/faculties/science/delta_marsh/friends
Previous Name: Friends of the Field Station (Delta Marsh)
Overview: A small local organization founded in 1992
Mission: To further the development & use of the University of Manitoba field stations
Chief Officer(s):
Harry Duckworth, President
harry_duckworth@umanitoba.ca
Gordon Goldsborough, Director, Field Station
ggoldsb@cc.umanitoba.ca
Finances: *Annual Operating Budget:* Less than $50,000
Staff Member(s): 3; 10 volunteer(s)
Membership: 1-99; *Fees:* $15 individual; $25 family; $40 three years; $150 lifetime

Friends of the Earth Canada (FoE) / Les Ami(e)s de la Terre Canada
#300, 260 St. Patrick St., Ottawa ON K1N 5K5
Tel: 613-241-0085; *Fax:* 613-241-7998
Toll-Free: 888-385-4444
foe@foecanada.org
www.foecanada.org
www.facebook.com/foe.canada
twitter.com/FoE_Canada
www.flickr.com/photos/foecanada
Overview: A large international charitable organization founded in 1978
Mission: To serve as a national voice for the environment, working with others to inspire the renewal of our communities & the earth, through research, education, advocacy & cooperation
Member of: Friends of the Earth International; Canadian Council for International Cooperation
Affliation(s): Canadian Environmental Network
Chief Officer(s):
Beatrice Olivastri, CEO
Geoff Love, President
Finances: *Annual Operating Budget:* $250,000-$500,000; *Funding Sources:* 52% individuals; 19% corporate; 5% foundation; 11% government; 13% earned income/merchandise
Staff Member(s): 6; 10 volunteer(s)
Membership: 1,000-4,999; *Committees:* Campaigns: Stop Global Warming; Universal Water Security; Stop Devils Lake Outlet; Environmental Justice
Activities: *Speaker Service:* Yes

Friends of the Environment Foundation *See* TD Friends of the Environment Foundation

Friends of the Field Station (Delta Marsh) *See* Friends of the Delta Marsh Field Station

Friends of the Forestry Farm House Inc. (FFFH)
1903 Forestry Farm Dr., Saskatoon SK S7N 1G9
Tel: 306-249-1315
www.fffh.ca
Overview: A small local charitable organization founded in 1996
Mission: To restore the superintendent's residence of the Sutherland Forest Nursery Station which, from 1913 to 1965, distributed millions of trees to prairie farmers, who planted these trees on their land to create the miles of shelterbelts
Affliation(s): Saskatoon Tourism; Saskatchewan Tourism
Chief Officer(s):
Bernie Cruikshank, President
maxic@yourlink
Finances: *Annual Operating Budget:* Less than $50,000; *Funding Sources:* Saskatchewan Heritage Foundation; City of Saskatoon Heritage Conservation Program
Staff Member(s): 3; 20 volunteer(s)
Membership: 1-99; *Fees:* $10
Activities: Historical walking tour brochure; Victoria Day High Tea; Haunted House Program; Old Fashioned Christmas Party; *Speaker Service:* Yes

Friends of the Greater Sudbury Public Library
Greater Sudbury Public Library, 74 MacKenzie St., Sudbury ON P3C 4XB
Tel: 705-673-1155
www.sudburylibraries.ca/en/aboutus/Friends.asp
Overview: A small local charitable organization founded in 1997
Mission: Administers the Write the Next Chapter fundraising campaign, and engaging the community to make the new South End Library a truly remarkable space.
Chief Officer(s):
Jessica Watts, Contact
jessica.watts@greatersudbury.ca
Finances: *Annual Operating Budget:* Less than $50,000
12 volunteer(s)
Membership: 12; *Fees:* $5 senior/student; $10 individual; $15 family; $100 corporations/clubs

Friends of the Greenbelt Foundation
#500, 661 Yonge St., Toronto ON M4Y 1Z9
Tel: 416-960-0001; *Fax:* 416-960-0030
info@greenbelt.ca
www.greenbelt.ca
www.facebook.com/ontariogreenbelt
twitter.com/greenbeltca
www.youtube.com/user/OntarioGreenbelt
Overview: A large provincial organization
Mission: The Foundation was created to help foster the Greenbelt's living countryside by nurturing and supporting activities that preserve its environmental and agricultural integrity.
Chief Officer(s):
Burkhard Mausberg, CEO
Rodney V. Northey, Chair
Finances: *Annual Operating Budget:* $3 Million-$5 Million
Awards:
• Friends of the Greenbelt Foundation Grant (Grant)

Friends of the Haileybury Heritage Museum
PO Box 911, 575 Main St., Haileybury ON P0J 1K0
Tel: 705-672-1922; *Fax:* 705-672-2551
hhmuseum@hotmail.com
www.haileyburyheritagemuseum.ca
Overview: A small local organization founded in 1983
Mission: To preserve & develop heritage tourism in Haileybury; to stimulate public interest in Haileybury's history; to disseminate heritage information; to provide support to the Museum's operations
Affliation(s): Ontario Historical Society
Chief Officer(s):
Allan Bellaire, Coordinator, Museum Operations
Finances: *Annual Operating Budget:* $50,000-$100,000
Staff Member(s): 2; 20 volunteer(s)
Membership: 200; *Fees:* $15 individual; $25 family; $30 corporate
Activities: Operates Haileybury Heritage Museum; *Library:* Sehldon Dobbs Memorial Research Room; Open to public

Friends of the Land of the Wine *See* Amici dell'Enotria Toronto

Friends of the McCreary Centre Society *See* McCreary Centre Society

Friends of The Moncton Hospital Foundation
135 MacBeath Ave., Moncton NB E1C 6Z8
Tel: 506-857-5488; *Fax:* 506-857-5753
friends@horizonnb.ca
www.friendsfoundation.ca
www.facebook.com/FriendsofTMH
twitter.com/FriendsofTMH
www.youtube.com/user/FriendsofTMH
Overview: A small local charitable organization founded in 1965
Mission: To raise money on behalf of the Moncton Hospital in order to improve the services offered to patients & fund research
Chief Officer(s):
Linda Saunders, Regional Director of Development
linda.saunders@horizonnb.ca
Staff Member(s): 9

Friends of the Montréal Botanical Garden *Voir* Les Amis du Jardin botanique de Montréal

Friends of the Oldman River (FOR)
615 Deer Croft Way SE, Calgary AB T2J 5V4
Tel: 403-271-1408
Overview: A small local organization founded in 1987
Mission: To defend the Oldman River from environmentally destructive activities; to protect the Oldman River & decommission the Oldman Dam
Member of: Alberta Environmental Network
Affliation(s): Canadian Environmental Network
Finances: *Annual Operating Budget:* Less than $50,000; *Funding Sources:* Membership dues; donations
8 volunteer(s)
Membership: 1,000; *Fees:* $5
Activities: Sustainable community/watershed project in Cameroon; legal actions on water issues; *Speaker Service:* Yes

Friends of the Orphans, Canada
470 Industrial Ave., Woodstock ON N4S 7L1
Tel: 519-421-1992; *Fax:* 519-421-7593
Toll-Free: 855-741-4033
info@fotocan.org
www.fotocan.org
Also Known As: Nuestros Peque¤os Hermanos International
Overview: A medium-sized international charitable organization founded in 1977
Mission: To provide a home, education, shelter & nourishment for orphans in Mexico, Honduras, Haiti, Nicaragua, Guatemala & El Salvador
Affliation(s): Nuestros Paquenos Hermanos
Chief Officer(s):
Margaret Blair, Executive Director
Finances: *Funding Sources:* Donations; sponsorship
Staff Member(s): 2

Friends of the Third World
6207 - 144 St., Edmonton AB T6H 4H8
Tel: 780-434-0671; *Fax:* 780-495-2201
Overview: A small international organization
Mission: To establish links with southern & northern NGOs working in the areas of environment & development; provides expertise in the fields of environment, natural resources, communication, women in development & education
Chief Officer(s):
Prem Kumar, Secretary

Friends of the Ukrainian Village Society
c/o 8820 - 112 St., Edmonton AB T6G 2P8
Tel: 780-662-3640; *Fax:* 780-662-3273
info@friendsukrainianvillage.com
www.friendsukrainianvillage.com
www.facebook.com/164545290238894
Overview: A small local organization
Chief Officer(s):
Nick Fedchyshyn, President

Ukrainian Museum & Village Society Inc.
5302 PR#209, Gardenton MB R0A 0M0
Tel: 204-425-3072
Mission: To provide the rural communities with activities & to preserve the history of the area; Museum includes exhibit of churches, Ukrainian clothing & artifacts of late 1800s & early 1900s; site includes museum, one room school, thatched roof house & a campground

The Friends of West Kootenay Parks Society (FWKP)
PO Box 212, Nelson BC V1L 5P9
e-mail: fwkp@kics.bc.ca
www.fwkp.kics.bc.ca
Overview: A small local organization founded in 1988
Mission: To promote conservationist & recreational use of British Columbia parks in the West Kootenay area
Chief Officer(s):
Bill Bryce, Chair
Membership: *Fees:* $10
Activities: Kokanee Glacier Alpine Campaign; advocacy for parks; construction projects; fundraising; publicizing parks issues

Friendship Centre of Québec *Voir* Centre d'amitié autochtone du Québec

Friendship House Association of Prince Rupert
744 Fraser St., Prince Rupert BC V8J 1P9
Tel: 250-627-1717
www.friendshiphouse.ca
Overview: A small local organization founded in 1958
Mission: To provide educational & cultural programs to the First Nations community in Prince Rupert

From Grief To Action (FGTA)
c/o St. Mary's Anglican Church, 2490 West 37th Ave., Vancouver BC V6M 1P5
Tel: 604-454-1484
info@fgta.ca
fgta.ca
Overview: A small local charitable organization founded in 1999
Mission: Support group for those affected by drug addiction in a family member or friend; Promotes the recognition of drug addiction as a health issue; Supports a comprehensive continuum of care for drug users, including harm reduction, detoxification, treatment & rehabilitation in order that they acheive & maintain healthy, productive lives
Chief Officer(s):
Ray Hall, President
Finances: *Funding Sources:* United Way; Donations
Membership: *Fees:* $25 individual; $45 family: $100 organization

Front commun des personnes assistées sociales du Québec
2000, boul St-Joseph est, Montréal QC H2H 1E4
Tél: 514-987-1989; *Téléc:* 514-987-1918
sol@fcpasq.qc.ca
www.fcpasq.qc.ca
Aperçu: *Dimension:* petite; *Envergure:* nationale; fondée en 1977
Mission: Défendre les droits des personnes assistées sociales; regrouper et mobiliser les personnes assistées sociales; informer les personnes assistées sociales; améliorer les conditions de vie des personnes assistées sociales
Membre(s) du bureau directeur:
Nicole jetté, Porte-parole
Finances: *Budget de fonctionnement annuel:* $100,000-$250,000; *Fonds:* Les Communautés religieuses du Québec; les groupes syndicaux du Québec
Membre: 34

Le Front des artistes canadiens *See* Canadian Artists' Representation

Le Front des artistes canadiens de l'Ontario *See* Canadian Artists' Representation Ontario

Le Front des artistes canadiens de Manitoba *See* Canadian Artists' Representation Manitoba

Frontenac Children's Aid Society *See* Children's Aid Society of the City of Kingston & County of Frontenac

Frontenac County Schools Museum Association
PO Box 2146, Kingston ON K7L 5J9
Tel: 613-544-9113
fcschoolsmuseum@gmail.com
www.fcsmuseum.com
www.facebook.com/SchoolsMuseum
Overview: A small local organization founded in 1977
Mission: To establish & run the Frontenac County Schools Museum; to research & compile the history of Frontenac County schools; to collect & preserve the artifacts & archival records from the schools & to present this material to the general public & the educational community
Member of: Ontario Museum Association; Canadian Museum Association; Kingston Association of Museums, Historic Sites & Galleries
Membership: *Fees:* $30
Activities: Exhibits; tours; education; archival assistance; *Library*

Frontenac Law Association
Frontenac County Courthouse, 5 Court St., Kingston ON K7L 2N4
Tel: 613-542-0034; *Fax:* 613-531-9764
library@cfla.on.ca
www.cfla.on.ca
Overview: A small local organization
Chief Officer(s):
Leanne Wight, President
president@cfla.on.ca
Activities: *Library:* Frontenac Law Association Library;

Frontier Duty Free Association (FDFA) / Association Frontière Hors Taxes
#600, 116 Lisgar St., Ottawa ON K2P 0C2
Tel: 613-233-1946; *Fax:* 613-238-3878
www.fdfa.ca
www.facebook.com/dutyfreecanada
twitter.com/CanadaDutyFree
Overview: A small local organization founded in 1984
Chief Officer(s):
Abe Taqtaq, President
Laurie Karson, Executive Director
lkarson@fdfa.ca
Membership: 35 active + 110 associate members; *Member Profile:* Land Border duty free shops in Canada; Duty free shops in the U.S. & in Canadian Airports

Frontière électronique du Canada *See* Electronic Frontier Canada Inc.

Frontiers Foundation (FF/OB) / Fondation Frontière
419 Coxwell Ave., Toronto ON M4L 3B9
Tel: 416-690-3930; *Fax:* 416-690-3934
www.frontiersfoundation.ca
www.facebook.com/pages/Frontiers-Foundation/66661443145
Also Known As: Operation Beaver
Overview: A medium-sized international charitable organization founded in 1968
Mission: To implement the enduring relief of human poverty throughout Canada & also abroad in tangible advancement projects.
Member of: Canadian Council for International Organization; Coordinating Committee for International Voluntary Service
Affliation(s): Native Council of Canada
Chief Officer(s):
Marco A. Guzman, Executive Director
marcoguzman@frontiersfoundation.ca
Lawrence Gladue, President
Activities: Housing projects in 30 communities annually + seven educational projects in Northern communities
Awards:
• Volunteer of the Year (Award)

Manitoba Office
201 Portage Ave., 18th Fl., Winnipeg MB R3B 3K6
Tel: 204-221-5209; *Fax:* 204-926-8501
admin@frontiersmb.ca
frontiersmb.ca

North Western Office
9781 - 127 St., Surrey BC V3V 5J1
Tel: 604-585-6646; *Fax:* 604-585-6647
fronwest@shaw.ca
northernfrontiers.org
Chief Officer(s):
Don Irving, Coordinator

Québec Office
11A - 5th Ave. West, Cadillac QC J0Y 1C0
Tel: 819-760-3476
Chief Officer(s):
Lylas Polson, Coordinator
lylas.polson@hotmail.com

FTQ Laurentides-Lanaudière
330, rue Parent, 2e étage, Saint-Jérôme QC J7Z 2A2
Tél: 450-431-6659; *Téléc:* 450-438-0567
ftql-l@qc.aira.com
www.ftql-l.ftq.qc.ca
Aperçu: *Dimension:* petite; *Envergure:* locale surveillé par Fédération des travailleurs et travailleuses du Québec

Fujiwara Dance Inventions
PO Box 8039, Toronto ON M2R 1Z1
Tel: 416-593-8455
info@fujiwaradance.com
www.fujiwaradance.com
www.facebook.com/fujiwaradance
twitter.com/fujiwaradance
www.youtube.com/user/fujiwaradance
Overview: A small local organization
Mission: To dance into insight, through the creation, performance, & teaching of dance; To encounter & express the mysteries of human nature as they are manifest in the body, before words
Chief Officer(s):
Denise Fujiwara, Artistic Director

Full Gospel Business Men's Fellowship in Canada (FGBMFI)
#403, 50 Gervais Dr., Toronto ON M3C 1Z3
Tel: 416-449-7272; *Fax:* 416-449-9743
fgbmfi@allstream.net
www.fgbmfi.ca
www.facebook.com/groups/5807578145/
Overview: A medium-sized national charitable organization founded in 1964
Mission: To reach men at all levels of our modern society, calling them to God, & releasing them into their respective gifts & talents through the Holy Spirit
Member of: Full Gospel Business Men's Fellowship International
Finances: *Annual Operating Budget:* $100,000-$250,000
Staff Member(s): 2; 2 volunteer(s)
Membership: 1,000-4,999; *Fees:* $60 individual
Activities: National convention; *Internships:* Yes; *Speaker Service:* Yes

Fundy Model Forest Network
13 Drury's Cover Rd., Lower Cove NB E4E 4E4
Tel: 506-432-7575; *Fax:* 506-432-7562
info@fundymodelforest.net
www.fundymodelforest.net
www.facebook.com/pages/Fundy-Model-Forest/101162803270718
Overview: A small local organization
Member of: Canadian Model Forest Network
Chief Officer(s):
Nairn Hay, General Manager
nairn@fundymodelforest.net
Membership: 30

Fundy Stamp Collectors Club
c/o 37 Saunders St., Riverview NB E1B 4N8
e-mail: info@fundystampclub.ca
www.fundystampclub.ca
Overview: A small provincial organization founded in 1997
Mission: To promote & foster stamp collecting
Chief Officer(s):
Art Gillard, President
Membership: *Fees:* $20; *Member Profile:* Sponsored by current members

Fundy Trail Beagle Club
540 Garnett Settlement Rd., Saint John NB E2S 1S6
Tel: 506-652-2272
Overview: A small local organization
Member of: New Brunswick Wildlife Federation
Chief Officer(s):

Michael Hicks, President

Funeral & Cremation Services Council of Saskatchewan (FCSCS)
3847C Albert St., Regina SK S4S 3R4
Tel: 306-584-1575; *Fax:* 306-584-1576
Toll-Free: 800-892-0116
administration@fcscs.ca
www.fcscs.ca
Previous Name: Saskatchewan Funeral Service Association
Overview: A small provincial licensing organization founded in 2001
Mission: To outline standard practices for the funeral industry for the benefit of the public
Affliation(s): Funeral Service Association of Canada
Chief Officer(s):
Phil Fredette, Chair
pfredette@arbormemorial.com
Sandy Mahon, Registrar
registrar@fcscs.ca
Finances: *Annual Operating Budget:* $250,000-$500,000; *Funding Sources:* Licenses; Regulatory fees
Staff Member(s): 4
Membership: *Committees:* Audit/Finance; Communications; Education & Professional development; Legislative & Governance; Licensing; Pandemic Planning; INvestigation Panel; Discipline Panel
Activities: *Internships:* Yes; *Library* Open to public by appointment

Funeral Advisory & Memorial Society (FAMS)
55 St. Phillips Rd., Toronto ON M9P 2N8
Tel: 416-241-6274
info@fams.ca
www.fams.ca
Also Known As: Toronto Memorial Society
Overview: A medium-sized local charitable organization founded in 1956
Mission: To provide unbiased consumer advice on funeral planning
Member of: Federation of Ontario Memorial Societies - Funeral Consumers Alliance
Chief Officer(s):
Margaret Adamson, Chair
Paul Siemens, Vice-Chair & Secretary
Johanna Ntiforo, Office Administrator
Membership: *Fees:* $40 single; $35 additional family members over 18 years old; $15 persons of limited means
Activities: Helping members pre-arrange simple & inexpensive funerals; Providing information about funeral planning

Funeral Advisory & Memorial Society of Saskatchewan (FAMSS)
PO Box 1846, Saskatoon SK S7K 3S2
Tel: 306-374-5190
Toll-Free: 866-283-2677
info@famss.ca
www.famss.ca
Previous Name: Memorial Society of Saskatchewan
Overview: A small provincial organization founded in 1969
Mission: To provide simplicity in obtaining affordable funeral plans through membership from certified funeral service provider in the major urban areas of the province; to provide an information kit to guide a person to make an informed decision on pre-planning a funeral
Member of: Federation of Ontario Memorial Societies - Funeral Consumers Alliance
Membership: *Fees:* $25
Activities: *Speaker Service:* Yes

Funeral Information & Memorial Society of Guelph
PO Box 1784, Guelph ON N1H 7A1
Tel: 519-835-9603
memorialsociety_guelph@hotmail.com
www myfuneralplan.org/guelph.htm
Also Known As: Memorial Society of Guelph
Overview: A small local organization founded in 1970
Mission: To assist people in planning & arranging simple, inexpensive & dignified funerals by providing information
Member of: Federation of Ontario Memorial Societies - Funeral Consumers Alliance
Chief Officer(s):
Kevin Mooney, Contact
Finances: *Annual Operating Budget:* Less than $50,000
8 volunteer(s)
Membership: *Fees:* $15 life
Activities: *Speaker Service:* Yes

Funeral Information Society of Ottawa (FISO) / Société de l'information funéraire d'Ottawa
PO Box 32057, 1386 Richmond Rd., Ottawa ON K2B 1A1
Tel: 613-828-4926
fiso@ncf.ca
fiso.ncf.ca
Overview: A small local organization founded in 1958
Mission: To support simple, dignified & affordable funerals
Member of: Federation of Ontario Memorial Societies - Funeral Consumers Alliance
Chief Officer(s):
Mary Nash, President
Membership: *Fees:* $25 individual; #35 family
Publications:
• Funeral Information Society of Ottawa Newsletter
Type: Newsletter

Funeral Planning & Memorial Society of Manitoba
613 St. Mary's Rd., Winnipeg MB R2M 3L8
Tel: 204-452-7999
FPMSInfo@mts.net
www.funeralsocietymb.org
Overview: A small provincial organization
Mission: To help Manitobans when having to make funeral arrangements
Member of: Memorial Society Association of Canada
Membership: *Fees:* $15 lifetime; $25 family lifetime

Funeral Service Association of Canada (FSAC) / L'Association des services funéraires du Canada
#304, 555 Legget Dr., Ottawa ON K2K 2K3
Tel: 613-271-2107; *Fax:* 613-271-3737
Toll-Free: 866-841-7779
info@fsac.ca
www.fsac.ca
www.facebook.com/FuneralAssociation
Overview: A medium-sized national organization founded in 1921
Mission: To provide a collective voice for the Canadian funeral professional; To provide high quality professional services with dignity & competence; To ensure compliance with all provisions of the law; To provide information about services
Chief Officer(s):
Faye Doucette, President
belvederefh@eastlink.ca
Phil Fredette, Vice-President
pfredette@arbormemorial.com
Finances: *Funding Sources:* Membership fee
Membership: *Member Profile:* Canadian funeral professionals; Suppliers; *Committees:* Education; Government Relations; Health & Pandemic Planning; Communications; Membership Growth & Strategic Development; Executive; Coalition
Activities: Cooperating with related professions; Offering continuing education; Organizing conventions
Meetings/Conferences: • Funeral Service Association of Canada 2015 Convention, May, 2015, St. John's, NL
Scope: National

Fung Loy Kok Institute of Taoism
134 D'Arcy St., Toronto ON M5T 1K3
Tel: 416-656-2110; *Fax:* 416-654-3937
fungloykok@taoist.org
www.taoist.org
Overview: A small international organization
Mission: Observes the unified teachings of the three religions of Confucianism, Buddhism and Taoism.
Activities: Tai Chi arts; Taoist meditation

FunTeam Alberta
11759 Groat Rd., Edmonton AB T5M 3K6
Tel: 780-490-0242; *Fax:* 780-485-0262
www.funteamalberta.com
www.facebook.com/145733822158095
Overview: A small provincial organization founded in 1990
Mission: To provide the opportunity for children, youth, & adults in Alberta to engage in sporting activities at low cost; to foster leadership skills
Chief Officer(s):
Randy Gregg, President
Finances: *Funding Sources:* Government of Alberta
Activities: FunTeam (12 & under); RecTeam (13+); Family Try-Athlon; Mini Try-Athlon; FunTeam Young Leaders
Awards:
• FunTeam Family Try-athlon Grant (Grant)
• FunTeam Mini Try-athlon Grant (Grant)
• RecTeam Event Grant (Grant)
• FunTeam Equipment & Facilities Grant (Grant)
• FunTeam Membership Grant (Grant)
• RBC Sereda Hockey Grant (Grant)
• FunTeam Alberta Outstanding Participant Award (Grant)
• Randy Gregg Volunteer Award (Grant)

The Fur Council of Canada (FCC) / Conseil canadien de la fourrure
#1270, 1435 St. Alexandre Rd., Montréal QC H3A 2G4
Tel: 514-844-1945; *Fax:* 514-844-8593
info@furcouncil.com
www.furcouncil.com
www.youtube.com/user/EcoFurs
Overview: A medium-sized national organization founded in 1964
Mission: To promote all aspects of the fur trade
Activities: Public education; fashion promotion & advertising; market development

Fur Institute of Canada (FIC) / Institut de la fourrure du Canada (IFC)
#701, 331 Cooper St., Ottawa ON K2P 0G5
Tel: 613-231-7099; *Fax:* 613-231-7940
info@fur.ca
www.fur.ca
Overview: A medium-sized national organization founded in 1983
Mission: To promote the sustainable & wise use of Canadian fur resources
Member of: International Fur Trade Federation; World Conservation Union; International Association of Fish & Wildlife Agencies
Chief Officer(s):
Robert B. Cahill, Executive Director
rcahill@fur.ca
Bruce Williams, Chair
Mary Baskin, Manager, Corporate & Communications
mbaskin@fur.ca
Finances: *Funding Sources:* Membership dues; Donations
Membership: *Member Profile:* Trappers; Fur Farmers; Wholesale Fur Dealers; Fur Manufacturers & Processors; Fur Retailers; Aboriginal Organizations; Conservation Organizations; Animal Welfare Associations; Support Industries; Government of Canada; Provincial & Territorial Governments; *Committees:* Trap Research & Development; National Communications; Aboriginal Communications; External Communications
Activities: Coordinating the implementation of the Agreement on International Humane Trapping Standards in Canada; Presenting awards; Offering programs such as trap research & testing, conservation, international relations, communication, aboriginal communications, & funding; Researching; Promoting conservation efforts

Fur-Bearer Defenders (FBD)
179 West Broadway, Vancouver BC V5Y 1P4
Tel: 604-435-1850
fbd@furbearerdefenders.com
furbearerdefenders.com
ca.linkedin.com/pub/fur-bearer-s-assoc/20/52/587
www.facebook.com/FurFree
twitter.com/FurBearers
www.youtube.com/furbearerdefenders
Also Known As: The Association for the Protection of Fur-Bearing Animals
Previous Name: The Fur-Bearers
Overview: A medium-sized national charitable organization founded in 1944
Mission: To stop trapping cruelty & protect fur-bearing animals
Chief Officer(s):
Lesley Fox, Executive Director
Finances: *Funding Sources:* Donations; Membership dues
Staff Member(s): 5
Membership: *Fees:* $25
Activities: Providing information to government, media, activists, & the public; Launching campaigns to create awareness
Meetings/Conferences: • 5th Annual Living with Wildlife 2015, September, 2015, Vancouver, BC
Scope: National
Description: Living With Wildlife conference brings together experts in their field to discuss a wide variety of solutions of how we can co-exist with urban wildlif
Contact Information: info@furbearerdefenders.com

The Fur-Bearers *See* Fur-Bearer Defenders

Furriers Guild of Canada
#211, 4174 Dundas St. West, Toronto ON M8X 1X3

Tel: 416-234-9494; *Fax:* 416-234-2244
furriersguildca@ica.net
Merged from: Fur Trade Association of Canada (Ontario) Inc.; Retail Furriers Guild of Canada
Overview: A medium-sized national organization
Mission: To promote Canadian fur retailers
Membership: *Member Profile:* Canadian fur retailers
Activities: Providing programs such as community outreach

Further Poultry Processors Association of Canada (FPPAC)

#206, 1545 Carling Ave., Ottawa ON K1Z 8P9
Tel: 613-738-1175
www.fppac.ca
Overview: A medium-sized national organization founded in 1984
Mission: To promote, foster, develop & represent the interests of corporations engaged in the further processing of poultry
Affliation(s): Further Poultry Processors Association of Ontario
Chief Officer(s):
Blair Shier, Chair
Ian Hesketh, Vice-Chair
Bruce McCullagh, Secretary-Treasurer
Finances: *Funding Sources:* Membership dues
Membership: 1-99; *Fees:* Sliding scale; *Member Profile:* Manufacturers of poultry products
Activities: *Library* by appointment

Fusion: The Ontario Clay & Glass Association

1444 Queen St. East, Toronto ON M4L 1E1
Tel: 416-438-8946; *Fax:* 416-438-0192
fusion@clayandglass.on.ca
www.clayandglass.on.ca
Previous Name: Ontario Potters Association
Overview: A medium-sized provincial charitable organization
Mission: To encourage & promote excellence & quality in clay & glass; to provide opportunities for fellowship & a sense of community involvement; to provide continuing education resources for members & people interested in clay & glass; to reach out, demonstrating tolerance, caring & acceptance for the diverse aspects of expression in clay & glass.
Affliation(s): Ontario Crafts Council; Canadian Clay & Glass Gallery; National Council on Education for the Ceramic Art; Studio Potter Network
Chief Officer(s):
Jenanne Longman, Office Administrator
Finances: *Funding Sources:* Ontario Arts Council
Membership: *Fees:* Schedule available; *Member Profile:* People who enjoy handmade clay & glass objects
Activities: "Fireworks", biennial juried exhibition of the finest works of members; silent auction, annual fundraiser; conference, regional workshops & weekend demonstrations; permanent art collection at Burlington Arts Centre

FutureWatch Environment & Development Education Partners

3101 Dundas St. West, Toronto ON M6P 1Z9
Tel: 416-926-1985; *Fax:* 416-926-0618
info@futurewatch.net
www.futurewatch.net
Also Known As: FutureWatch
Overview: A small local charitable organization founded in 1993
Mission: To foster the creation of healthy & sustainable communities locally & internationally
Chief Officer(s):
Lidia Ferreira, Executive Director
lidiaf@futurewatch.net
Staff Member(s): 6

Futurpreneur Canada

#700, 133 Richmond St. West, Toronto ON M5H 2L3
Fax: 877-408-3234
Toll-Free: 866-646-2922
www.futurpreneur.ca
www.linkedin.com/company/futurpreneur-canada
www.facebook.com/futurpreneur
twitter.com/@Futurpreneur
www.youtube.com/user/CYBF
Previous Name: Canadian Youth Business Foundation
Overview: A medium-sized national organization founded in 1996
Mission: A national, non-profit organization that provides financing, mentoring and support tools to aspiring business owners aged 18-39.
Chief Officer(s):
Julia Deans, CEO, 416-408-2923 Ext. 3001
jdeans@futurpreneur.ca
Rebecca Dew, CFO, 416-408-2923 Ext. 2102
rdew@futurpreneur.ca
Membership: 6,900
Activities: Pre-Launch Coaching; Online Resources; Financing; Mentoring
Awards:
• BDC Mentorship Award (Award)

Alberta Office
Willow Park Centre, #418, 10325 Bonaventure Dr. SE, Calgary AB T2J 7E4
Tel: 403-265-2923; *Fax:* 403-265-2343
www.facebook.com/FuturpreneurAB
twitter.com/@FuturpreneurAB
Chief Officer(s):
Kathy McReynolds, Contact, 403-265-3228, Fax: 403-265-2343
kmcreynolds@cybf.ca

Atlantic Office
#204, 540 Southgate Dr., Bedford NS B4A 0C9
Tel: 902-407-7709
www.facebook.com/futurpreneurATL
twitter.com/@futurpreneurATL
Chief Officer(s):
Christian Perron

British Columbia Office
#580, 425 Carrall St., Vancouver BC V6B 6E3
Tel: 604-598-2923
www.facebook.com/FuturpreneurBC
twitter.com/@FuturpreneurBC

Manitoba Office
#500, 321 McDermot Ave., Winnipeg MB R3A 0A3
Tel: 204-480-8481
www.facebook.com/futurpreneurMB
twitter.com/@futurpreneurMB

Québec Office
#402, 5605, av De Gaspé, Montréal QC H2T 2A4
Tel: 514-225-7035
www.facebook.com/futurpreneurQC
twitter.com/@futurpreneurQC

Saskatchewan Office
#113, 220 - 20th St., Saskatoon SK S7M 0W9
Tel: 306-717-9216
www.facebook.com/futurpreneurSK
twitter.com/@futurpreneurSK

Gabriola Island Chamber of Commerce

PO Box 249, Gabriola BC V0R 1X0
Tel: 250-247-9332
giccmanager@shaw.ca
www.gabriolaisland.org
www.facebook.com/pages/Gabriola-Island/243621859026542
Overview: A small local charitable organization founded in 1984
Mission: To promote & improve trade & commerce & the economic, civic & social welfare of Gabriola.
Member of: BC Chamber of Commerce
Affliation(s): Tourism Association of Vancouver Island
Chief Officer(s):
Ken Gurr, President
Liz Rey, Manager
Membership: 115; *Fees:* Schedule available; *Member Profile:* Local businesses
Activities: *Library*

Gagetown & Area Chamber of Commerce

c/o Village Office, 68 Babbit St., Gagetown NB E5M 1C8
Tel: 506-488-2020
Overview: A small local organization founded in 1992
Mission: To promote local businesses & help them grow
Member of: Atlantic Chamber of Commerce; New Brunswick Chamber of Commerce
Chief Officer(s):
Leone Pippard, President
Finances: *Funding Sources:* Membership dues; provincial government
Membership: *Member Profile:* Small businesses; crafts; artists; retailers; B&B

Gai Écoute inc.

CP 1006, Succ. C, Montréal QC H2L 4V2
Tél: 514-866-6788; *Téléc:* 514-866-8157
courrier@gaiecoute.org
www.gaiecoute.org
www.facebook.com/gaiecoute
www.twitter.com/gaiecoute
www.youtube.com/gaiecoute
Aperçu: *Dimension:* petite; *Envergure:* locale; Organisme sans but lucratif; fondée en 1980
Mission: Offrir un soutien aux personnes homosexuelles en difficulté, ainsi qu'à leurs proches; offrir une écoute attentive à ces personnes, ainsi qu'une information générale sur le milieu gai et lesbien; faciliter l'intégration des personnes homosexuelles dans leur communauté et dans la société et contribuer à leur bien-être; combattre les préjugés
Membre(s) du bureau directeur:
Laurent McCutcheon, Président
Finances: *Budget de fonctionnement annuel:* $100,000-$250,000
Membre(s) du personnel: 3; 60 bénévole(s)
Membre: 1-99
Activités: *Service de conférenciers:* Oui; *Bibliothèque*

The Gairdner Foundation

4 Devonshire Place, Toronto ON M5S 2E1
Tel: 416-596-9996; *Fax:* 416-596-9992
thegairdner@gairdner.org
www.gairdner.org
Overview: A small national charitable organization founded in 1957
Mission: To recognize individuals whose work or contribution constitutes tangible achievement in the field of medical science
Chief Officer(s):
John Dirks, President
john.dirks@gairdner.org
Finances: *Annual Operating Budget:* $50,000-$100,000
Staff Member(s): 1; 1 volunteer(s)
Membership: *Committees:* Board of Trustees; Medical Advisory Board; Medical Review Panel

Galiano Island Chamber of Commerce

PO Box 73, Galiano BC V0N 1P0
Tel: 250-539-2233
info@galianoisland.com
www.galianoisland.com
www.facebook.com/GalianoChamberOfCommerce
Also Known As: Galiano Travel Infocentre
Overview: A small local organization
Mission: To strengthen the community & protect the environment by developing local business.
Member of: BC Chamber of Commerce; Tourism Victoria
Chief Officer(s):
Connie Nordin, President
president@galianoisland.com
Finances: *Annual Operating Budget:* Less than $50,000
Staff Member(s): 1; 8 volunteer(s)
Membership: 104; *Fees:* $40; *Committees:* Brochure; Tourism; Booth; Communication; Social
Activities: Tourist booth; services directory; chamber socials twice a year; *Internships:* Yes; *Library:* Infocentre; Open to public

Galiano Rod & Gun Club

#2, 594 Porlier Pass Rd., Galiano Island BC V0N 1P0
Tel: 250-539-2113
Overview: A small local organization

Galt and District Real Estate Board; Real Estate Board of Cambridge *See* Cambridge Association of Realtors

GAMA International Canada / GAMA International du Canada

#209, 390 Queens Quay West, Toronto ON M4V 3A2
Tel: 416-444-5251; *Fax:* 416-444-8031
Toll-Free: 800-563-5822
info@gamacanada.com
www.gamacanada.com
www.linkedin.com/groups/GAMA-International-Canada-1952201
twitter.com/Advocis
www.youtube.com/user/AdvocisTFAAC
Previous Name: Managers Association of Financial Advisors of Canada
Overview: A medium-sized national organization founded in 1974
Mission: To focus on professional development for leaders involved in the distribution of financial services
Chief Officer(s):
Rob Popazzi, President
robert.popazzi@sunflie.com
Celia Ciotola, Director
cciotola@advocis.ca
Finances: *Annual Operating Budget:* $250,000-$500,000; *Funding Sources:* Membership dues; corporate sponsorship
Staff Member(s): 1

Membership: 24 chapters; *Fees:* Schedule available; *Member Profile:* Leaders in distribution management in financial services; individuals in activities related to financial services with an interest in management; companies that wish to be sponsors or supporters
Activities: Teleconferences, newsletters & articles, annual awards
Awards:
- Agency Builder Award (ABA) (Award)
- Agency Achievement Award (AAA) (Award)
- National Management Award (NMA) (Award)

GAMA International du Canada *See* GAMA International Canada

Gananoque Food Bank
c/o Gananoque Legion, 55 King St. East, Gananoque ON K7G 1E8
Tel: 613-382-4434
ganfoodbank@gmail.com
Also Known As: Gananoque & District Food Bank
Overview: A small local charitable organization founded in 1987
Member of: Ontario Association of Food Banks
Chief Officer(s):
Cliff Weir, President
c_weir@sympatico.ca
Staff Member(s): 1; 50 volunteer(s)
Membership: 1-99
Activities: Spring Appreciation Day for Volunteers; Annual Food Drive; Santa Claus parade

Ganaraska Hiking Trail Association (GHTA)
PO Box 693, Orillia ON L3V 6K7
e-mail: admin@ganaraska-hiking-trail.ca
www.ganaraska-hiking-trail.ca
Overview: A small local charitable organization founded in 1969
Mission: To construct & maintain a hiking trail from Port Hope to Glen Huron; to encourage recreational hiking & respect for the environment
Member of: Hike Ontario; Ontario Nature
Chief Officer(s):
Bob Bowles, President
rbowles@rogers.com
Finances: *Funding Sources:* Membership dues; donations
Membership: *Fees:* $25
Activities: On the edge of the Laurentian Shield, within reach of Ontario's major cities, the trail forms a vital link in the National Trail network (500 km)

Gander & Area Chamber of Commerce (GACC)
109 Trans Canada Hwy., Gander NL A1V 1P6
Tel: 709-256-7110; *Fax:* 709-256-4794
ganderchamber@ganderchamber.nf.ca
www.ganderchamber.nf.ca
Overview: A small local charitable organization founded in 1959
Mission: To promote & improve the economic climate of the area; to support the needs & concerns of the business community; to enhance the civic & social well-being of the community
Member of: Newfoundland & Labrador Chamber of Commerce; Atlantic Provinces Chamber of Commerce
Chief Officer(s):
Darrin Murray, President
darrin.murray@olddutchfoods.com
Hazel Bishop, Executive Director
Finances: *Annual Operating Budget:* $100,000-$250,000; *Funding Sources:* Membership fees
Staff Member(s): 2; 11 volunteer(s)
Membership: 200+ businesses; *Fees:* Schedule available
Activities: Home, garden & outdoor show; annual golf tournament; *Library:* Business Library

Gander & Area Society for the Prevention of Cruelty to Animals
36 McCurdy Dr., Gander NL A1V 1A2
Tel: 709-651-3002
ganderspca@hotmail.com
www.envision.ca/webs/ganderandareaspca
www.facebook.com/home.php#!/group.php?gid=53600827073
Also Known As: Gander & Area SPCA
Overview: A small local organization founded in 1985
Finances: *Annual Operating Budget:* Less than $50,000; *Funding Sources:* Fundraising
Membership: 30

The Garden Clubs of Ontario (GCO)
PO Box 399, Hamilton ON L8N 3H8
www.gardenclubsofontario.ca
www.facebook.com/GardenClubsOfOntario
Overview: A small provincial organization founded in 1954
Mission: To stimulate knowledge & love of gardening amongst amateurs; to aid in the protection of native plants, trees, birds & soil; to encourage civic planning
Member of: Ontario Horticultural Association; World Association of Flower Arrangers
Chief Officer(s):
Janice Middleton, Contact
Finances: *Annual Operating Budget:* $50,000-$100,000
15 volunteer(s)
Membership: 1,500 individual; *Committees:* Archives; Judges; National & International Liaison
Activities: Coordinates activities of 12 Garden Clubs in Ontario; Tour of Summer Gardens

Burlington
PO Box 85185, Stn. Brant Plaza, Burlington ON L7R 4K4
Tel: 905-632-0561
Chief Officer(s):
Heather Medley, President

Dundas
101 King St. East, Dundas ON L9H 1B9
Tel: 905-627-0884
dundas@gardenclubsofontario.ca
Chief Officer(s):
June Solntseff, President

Georgian Bay
Grey Sauble Conservation Authority, 237897 Inglis Falls Rd., RR #4, Owen Sound ON N4K 5N6
Tel: 519-414-4564
georgianbay@gardenclubsofontario.ca
georgianbaygardenclubowensound.com
Chief Officer(s):
Marsha Barrow, President

Hamilton
180 Dalewood Cres., Hamilton ON L8S 4C1
Tel: 905-528-7441
hamilton@gardenclubsofontario.ca
Chief Officer(s):
Wendy Downing, President

Kitchener-Waterloo
27 Autumn Ridge Trail, Kitchener ON N2P 2J6
Tel: 519-578-8682
kitchenerwaterloo@gardenclubsofontario.ca
Chief Officer(s):
Geri Laughlen, President

London
Civic Garden Complex, 625 Springbank Dr., London ON N6K 4T1
Tel: 519-471-6200
www.gardenclubofiondon.ca
www.facebook.com/GardenClubOfLondon
Chief Officer(s):
Jeanne Anne Goldrick, President

Milne House
The Toronto Botanical Garden, 777 Lawrence Ave. East, Toronto ON M3C 1P2
e-mail: milnehouse@gardenclubsofontario.ca
Chief Officer(s):
Patrisha Galiana, President

Niagara
565 Niagara Pkwy., Niagara Falls ON L2E 6T2
Tel: 905-937-1427
niagara@gardenclubsofontario.ca
Chief Officer(s):
Anne Lemon, President, 905-295-4228

Toronto
777 Lawrence Ave. East, Toronto ON M3C 1P2
Tel: 416-447-5218; *Fax:* 416-447-2154
gardenclauboftoronto@on.aibn.com
www.thegardenclauboftoronto.ca
www.facebook.com/groups/14742407967
Chief Officer(s):
Janet Kennish, President

Toronto Japanese Garden
1063 Pape Ave., Toronto ON M4K 3W4
Tel: 416-425-3161
tjgc@rogers.com
tjgc.awardspace.com
Chief Officer(s):
Toshi Oikawa, President

Garderie du Carrefour *Voir* CPE du Carrefour

Gardiner Centre
Business Administration Bldg., Memorial University of Newfoundland, St. John's NL A1B 3X5
Tel: 709-864-7977; *Fax:* 709-864-7999
gardinercentre@mun.ca
www.busi.mun.ca/gardinercentre
www.linkedin.com/company/gardinercentrememorialuniversity
twitter.com/GardinerCentre
www.youtube.com/user/GardinerCentre
Merged from: **P.J. Gardiner Institute (PJG); Centre for Management Development (CMD)**
Overview: A small local organization
Mission: To connect Memorial University of Newfoundland's Faculty of Business with Newfoundland & Labrador's business community; To advance business knowledge & skills in the public & private sectors
Chief Officer(s):
Brian Hurley, Director, 709-864-8893
bhurley@mun.ca
Activities: Offering professional development programs & customized training;

Garth Homer Society
813 Darwin Ave, Victoria BC V8X 2X7
Tel: 250-475-2270; *Fax:* 250-475-2279
ghsinquiries@garthhomersociety.org
www.garthhomersociety.org
www.facebook.com/garthhomer
twitter.com/garthhomer1
Overview: A small local organization founded in 1979
Mission: To create opportunities for independance, growth & community participation for people who strive to overcome developmental & physical obstacles
Member of: B.C. Association for Community Living
Chief Officer(s):
Bruce Homer, Chair
chair@garthhomersociety.org
Mitchell Temkin, Chief Executive Officer
Finances: *Annual Operating Budget:* $3 Million-$5 Million; *Funding Sources:* Provincial government
Staff Member(s): 52; 25 volunteer(s)
Membership: 110 individuals; *Fees:* $20 individual
Activities: Day program & supported employment services for adults with developmental disabilities

Gas Processing Association Canada (GPAC)
#400, 1040 - 7th Ave. SW, Calgary AB T2P 3G9
Tel: 403-244-4487; *Fax:* 403-244-2340
info@gpacanada.com
www.gpacanada.com
www.linkedin.com/groups/Gas-Processing-Association-Canada-4334615
twitter.com/GPACanada
Previous Name: Canadian Gas Processors Association
Overview: A medium-sized national organization founded in 1960
Mission: To promote interaction & exchange of ideas & technology that will add value to those who are involved with or affected by the hydrocarbon processing industry
Affliation(s): Gas Processors Association (USA)
Chief Officer(s):
Josh Carter, President
josh.carter@zedi.ca
Cheryl Lafond, Director, Safety
crlafond@shaw.ca
Rob Nadalutti, Director, Academic
rob.nadalutti@megenergy.com
Brenda Hong, Coordinator, Events
brendah@associationsplus.ca
Finances: *Funding Sources:* Membership dues
17 volunteer(s)
Membership: 750 individuals; *Fees:* $75 Regular, $9 Retired; $20 student; *Member Profile:* Open to those employed in companies processing gaseous & liquid hydrocarbons; *Committees:* Safety; Research; Environment; Membership; Publications; Northern
Activities: *Library*
Meetings/Conferences: • Gas Processing Association Canada 2015 Safety Conference & Awards Banquet, 2015, AB
Scope: National
Contact Information: conference@gpacanada.com

Gateway Association for Community Living (GACL)
#104, 18304 - 105 Ave., Edmonton AB T5S 0C6
Tel: 780-454-0701; *Fax:* 780-454-0843
info@gatewayassociation.ca

www.gatewayassociation.ca
www.facebook.com/GatewayAssociation
twitter.com/gatewayassocedm
Overview: A small local charitable organization founded in 1975
Mission: To promote the welfare of people with handicaps & their families
Member of: Alberta Association for Community Living
Chief Officer(s):
Cindy de Bruijn, Executive Director
Finances: *Funding Sources:* United Way; City of Edmonton; Alberta Lottery Fund; Grants
Staff Member(s): 17
Membership: *Member Profile:* Families; professionals; agencies; schools
Activities: Provides support & advocacy assistance to individuals with developmental disabilities & their families; transitional planning workshops; sibling seminars; women's retreat; family support; *Speaker Service:* Yes; *Library:* Family Resource Centre; Open to public
Awards:
• Arbor Awards (Award)

GATEWAY Centre For Learning
488 Dominion Ave., Midland ON L4R 1P6
Tel: 705-527-1522; *Fax:* 705-527-0693
admin@gatewaycentreforlearning.ca
www.gatewaycentreforlearning.ca
www.facebook.com/GatewayCentreForLearningMidland
Overview: A small local charitable organization founded in 1982
Mission: To train volunteers to work one-to-one with adults to help them acquire basic reading, writing, numeracy & computer skills; To offer small group classes; To raise awareness of literacy needs in local community; To promote a literate society
Member of: Laubach Literacy of Canada-Ontario; Simco/Musford Literacy Network
Affliation(s): Laubach Literacy of Canada-Ontario
Chief Officer(s):
Jennifer Ellis, Executive Director
jellis@csolve.net
Gunter Kuch, President
gunter@rogers.com
Finances: *Funding Sources:* Provincial government; Fundraising
Staff Member(s): 7
Activities: Hockey Challenge, Feb.; Books 4 Brunch, Sept.; *Awareness Events:* Bruce Stanton Fish Fry Fundraiser, May; *Speaker Service:* Yes; *Library* Open to public

Gateway Research Organization (GRO)
PO Box 5865, 10336 - 106 St., Westlock AB T7P 2G1
Tel: 780-349-4546; *Fax:* 780-349-5399
Other Communication: Forage e-mail: groforage@telus.net
grohome@telus.net
www.areca.ab.ca/grohome.html
www.facebook.com/GatewayResearchOrganizationgro
twitter.com/gatewayresearch
Overview: A small local organization founded in 1979 overseen by Agricultural Research & Extension Council of Alberta
Mission: To meet the changing needs of the agriculture industry in Alberta by working with producers & industry stakeholders
Member of: Agricultural Research & Extension Council of Alberta
Chief Officer(s):
Keith Taylor, Chair
Michelle Holden, Manager, 780-349-4546, Fax: 780-349-5399
grocrops@telus.net
Staff Member(s): 1
Membership: *Fees:* $30
Publications:
• Hayshaker [a publication of the Gateway Research Organization]
Type: Newsletter; *Frequency:* 2 pa

The Gathering Place *See* Ma-Mow-We-Tak Friendship Centre Inc.

Gatineau Gliding Club (GGC)
PO Box 8145, Stn. T, Ottawa ON K1G 3H6
Tel: 613-673-5386
ggc@gatineaugliding club.ca
www.gatineauglidingclub.ca
Overview: A small local organization
Member of: Soaring Association of Canada
Membership: 100;

Gatineau Valley Historical Society (GVHS) / Société historique de la Vallée de la Gatineau
CP 1803, Chelsea QC J9B 1A1
Tél: 819-827-6224
info@gvhs.ca
www.gvhs.ca
Aperçu: *Dimension:* petite; *Envergure:* locale; Organisme sans but lucratif; fondée en 1962
Mission: To promote matters of historical significance in the Gatineau Valley region of Québec; To provide historical resources, such as newspapers, photographs, & oral histories
Membre(s) du bureau directeur:
Marc Cockburn, President, 819-459-2004
cockburn.marc@gmail.com
Linda Bardell, Secretary, 819-827-0095
lbard@sympatico.ca
David Yuill, Treasurer, 819-827-0851
david.yuill@sympatico.ca
Finances: *Fonds:* Donations; Fundraising
Membre: 300
Activités: Maintaining the Chelsea Pioneer Cemetery; Hosting speakers who are experts on history & heritage subjects; Offering tours to points of historic interest; *Bibliothèque:* Gatineau Valley Historical Society Archives; Bibliothèque publique
Prix, Bouses:
• Arthur Davison Award for the Best Article (Prix)
Publications:
• Gatineau Valley Historical Society Newsletter
Type: Newsletter; *Frequency:* Quarterly; *Editor:* Shirley Brown
Profile: Information about the society's forthcoming meetings & events
• Up the Gatineau
Type: Journal; *Frequency:* Annually
Profile: Local history articles

Gay & Lesbian Community Centre of Edmonton *See* Pride Centre of Edmonton

Gay Fathers of Montréal Inc. *Voir* Association des pères gais de Montréal inc.

Gay Fathers of Toronto
PO Box 43, Stn. F, Toronto ON M4Y 2L4
Tel: 416-925-9872
info@gayfathers-toronto.com
www.gayfathers-toronto.com
Overview: A small local organization founded in 1987
Mission: To offer a supportive environment to fathers who are gay-oriented by providing assistance in building a positive self-image & by encouraging them to be loving & responsible
Chief Officer(s):
Paul Leuschner, Coordinator
Finances: *Annual Operating Budget:* Less than $50,000
20 volunteer(s)
Membership: 50; *Fees:* $25
Activities: *Library*

Gay Line *See* CAEO Québec

Gays & Lesbians of the First Nations *See* 2-Spirited People of the First Nations

Les Gédéons - L'Association Internationale des Gédéons au Canada *See* Gideons International in Canada

Gelbvieh Association of Alberta/BC (GAA/BC)
PO Box 11, Tatla Lake BC V0L 1V0
Tel: 250-476-1221; *Fax:* 250-476-1280
halfwayranch2000@hotmail.com
Overview: A small provincial organization founded in 1974
Mission: To promote the Gelbvieh breed in Alberta & British Columbia through a newsletter & information booth displayed at livestock expositions
Member of: Canadian Gelbvieh Association
Chief Officer(s):
Romacordelia Cox, President
cordy_cox@hotmail.com
Finances: *Funding Sources:* Membership dues; fundraising; advertising
Membership: 64
Activities: National Gelbvieh Show & Sale; Annual Field Day

Gem & Mineral Club of Scarborough (GMCS)
#1B, 10 Chichester Pl., Toronto ON M1T 1G5
e-mail: scarbgemclub@gmail.com
www.scarbgemclub.ca
www.facebook.com/group.php?gid=181294731911802
Overview: A small local organization founded in 1963
Mission: To promote collecting & studying rocks, minerals, fossils, & lapidary work
Member of: Central Canadian Federation of Mineralogical Societies (CCFMS)
Membership: *Fees:* $15 single members; $20 families; *Member Profile:* Collectors & mineral enthusiasts in Scarborough, Ontario
Activities: Hosting monthly meetings from September to June; Exchanging information about the hobby; Organizing exhibits; Presenting auctions; Planning mineral & fossil collecting field trips; Providing workshops; *Awareness Events:* Gem Show, September; *Library:* Gem & Mineral Club of Scarborough Library
Publications:
• Strata Data: GMCS [Gem & Mineral Club of Scarborough] Newsletter
Type: Newsletter; *Frequency:* 10 pa
Profile: Upcoming events & articles about the hobby

Gem & Mineral Federation of Canada (GMFC) / Fédération canadienne des gemmes et des minéraux
PO Box 42015, RPO North, Winfield BC V4V 1Z8
Tel: 250-766-4353
president@gmfc.ca
www.gmfc.ca
Overview: A small national organization founded in 1977
Mission: To promote earth sciences; to protect collecting sites; to educate collectors; to foster good will, friendship & rapport among all
Chief Officer(s):
Peter Hagar, President
madpete@accesscomm.ca
Membership: *Committees:* Communications; Education; Membership/Directory/Supplies; Public Relatiosn & Show Registry; Field Trips

Alberta Federation of Rock Clubs
c/o Pauline Zeschuk, 2073 Blackmud Creek Dr. SW, Edmonton AB T6W 1G8
Tel: 780-430-6694
www.afrc.ca
Chief Officer(s):
Pauline Zeschuk, Secretary

British Columbia Lapidary Society
c/o Georgina Selinger, PO Box 10072, Abbotsford BC V4X 2M0
Tel: 604-852-1307
bcls10072@hotmail.com
www.lapidary.bc.ca
Chief Officer(s):
Georgina Selinger, Exec. Secretary

Mid Pro Rock & Gem Society
1010 Central Ave., Prince Albert SK S6V 4V5
Tel: 306-764-1049
Chief Officer(s):
Douglas Hodgins, Secretary

Nova Scotia Mineral & Gem Society
c/o Nova Scotia Museum of Natural History, 1747 Summer St., Halifax NS B3H 3A6
www.nsmgs.ca

Rock of Ages Lapidary Club
#142, 505 Chalmers Ave., Winnipeg MB R2L 0G4
Tel: 204-832-1109
Chief Officer(s):
Joan Turner, Secretary

Genealogical Association of Nova Scotia (GANS) / Association généalogique de la Nouvelle-Écosse
PO Box 333, 3045 Robie St., Halifax NS B3K 4P6
Tel: 902-454-0322
info@novascotiaancestors.ca
www.novascotiaancestors.ca
www.facebook.com/NovaScotiaAncestors
twitter.com/NSAncestors
Overview: A small provincial charitable organization founded in 1982
Mission: To encourage interest in & to raise standards of research in genealogy through workshops & publications; to acquaint members with research materials & methods to serve as medium of exchange for genealogical information; to support the collection & preservation of documents & other genealogical materials; to foster recognition of the value of genealogy to a proper study of the social sciences.

Member of: Federation of Nova Scotian Heritage; Canadian Federation of Genealogical & Family History Societies Inc.
Affliation(s): Genealogical Institute of the Maritimes; Council of Nova Scotia Archives
Chief Officer(s):
Allan Marble, President
Finances: *Funding Sources:* Membership fees; donations; sale of publications
Membership: 600; *Fees:* $30; $750 lifetime

Genealogical Institute of The Maritimes (GIM) / Institut généalogique des Provinces Maritimes
PO Box 36022, 5675 Spring Garden Rd., Halifax NS B3J 1G0
nsgna.ednet.ns.ca/gim
Overview: A medium-sized provincial licensing organization founded in 1983
Mission: To pursue geneaology; to upgrade the quality of professional family history research in the Maritimes
Member of: Nova Scotia Genealogical Network Association
Chief Officer(s):
Allen Marble, Contact
allan.marble@ns.sympatico.ca
Finances: *Funding Sources:* Membership & accreditation fees
Membership: 23; *Fees:* $15
Activities: Professional accreditation of genealogical researchers;

Généalogie Abitibi-Témiscamingue
CP 371, Rouyn-Noranda QC J9X 5C4
genat@genat.org
www.genat.org
Aperçu: *Dimension:* petite; *Envergure:* locale; fondée en 1995
Membre(s) du bureau directeur:
Serge Pétrin, Président
Membre: *Montant de la cotisation:* 30$
Publications:
• Le Lien
Type: Newsletter; *Frequency:* Quarterly

General Church of the New Jerusalem in Canada (GCIC)
c/o Olivet Church of the New Jerusalem, 279 Burnhamthorpe Rd., Toronto ON M9B 1Z6
Tel: 416-239-3054; *Fax:* 416-239-4935
assistant@olivetnewchurch.org
www.newchurch.ca
Overview: A small national organization founded in 1971
Mission: An incorporated national organization of individual church members, groups and congregations devoted to the Christian life and teaching expounded in the works of Emanuel Swedenborg.
Chief Officer(s):
James Cooper, Pastor
Nathan Cole, Assistant Pastor

General Conference of the Canadian Assemblies of God / Conférence générale des assemblées de dieu canadiennes
PO Box 37315, Stn. Marquette, 6724 Fabre St., Montréal QC H2E 3B5
Tel: 514-279-1100; *Fax:* 514-279-1131
info@caogonline.org
www.caogonline.org
Previous Name: Italian Pentecostal Church of Canada
Overview: A small national charitable organization founded in 1912
Mission: To provide distinctive ministry to the Italian community, extending to all Canadians, regardless of language, nationality, or race; To proclaim the gospel of Jesus Christ in the power of the Holy Spirit throughout Canada & the world, based on the biblical standard of ministry in the New Testament
Member of: The Evangelical Fellowship of Canada; Canadian Council of Christian Charities
Chief Officer(s):
Dino Cianflone, General Treasurer
Daniel Ippolito, Overseer Emeritus
David Di Staulo, General Superintendent
Raymond Narula, General Secretary
Giulio Gabeli, Overseer
Finances: *Annual Operating Budget:* $100,000-$250,000
Staff Member(s): 2; 3 volunteer(s)
Membership: 6,000 + 21 affiliated churches
Activities: Hosting an annual conference; *Internships:* Yes
Meetings/Conferences: • Annual General Conference

General Insurance OmbudService (GIO) / Service de conciliation en assurance de dommages (SCAD)
#701, 10 Milner Business Ct., Toronto ON M1B 3C6
Fax: 416-299-4261
Toll-Free: 877-225-0446
www.giocanada.org
Overview: A medium-sized national organization founded in 2002
Mission: To provide dispute resolution services for consumers of home, automobile, & business insurance in Canada; To ensure that services are provided in a cost-free, confidential, impartial, knowledgeable, timely, & courteous manner
Member of: Financial Services OmbudsNetwork (FSON)
Chief Officer(s):
Brian Maltman, Executive Director
Staff Member(s): 7
Publications:
• General Insurance OmbudService Annual Report
Type: Yearbook; *Frequency:* Annually

General Practice Psychotherapy Association (GPPA)
312 Oakwood Court, Newmarket ON L3Y 3C8
Tel: 416-410-6644; *Fax:* 866-328-7974
info@gppaonline.ca
www.gppaonline.ca
Overview: A small national organization founded in 1984
Mission: To support & encourage quality psychotherapy by physicians in Canada; To promote professional development through ongoing education & collegial interaction
Chief Officer(s):
Howard Schneider, MD, CGPP, CCFP, Chair
Muriel J. van Lierop, MGPP, President
Finances: *Annual Operating Budget:* $100,000-$250,000; *Funding Sources:* Membership fees; educational fees, conference
Staff Member(s): 1; 10 volunteer(s)
Membership: 225; *Fees:* $250 clinical, certificant or mentor member; $175 associate member; *Member Profile:* Doctors who practice psychotherapy, either full-time or part-time; *Committees:* Education; Membership; Newsletter; Professional Development, Conference; Finance
Activities: Annual conference; workshops & seminars

Générations Unies Ontario *See* United Generations Ontario

Genesis Research Foundation
92 College St., 3rd Fl., Toronto ON M5G 1L4
Fax: 416-978-8350
genesis@genesisresearch.org
www.genesisresearch.org
www.linkedin.com/company/genesis-research-foundation
twitter.com/GenesisOrg
Overview: A small provincial charitable organization founded in 1983
Mission: To fund & promote research & understanding in women's health in the areas of obstetrics & gynaecology
Chief Officer(s):
Alan Bocking, MD, FRCSC, Chair
Finances: *Annual Operating Budget:* $100,000-$250,000
Staff Member(s): 2; 20 volunteer(s)
Membership: *Member Profile:* Women
Activities: *Speaker Service:* Yes

Geneva Centre for Autism (GCA)
112 Merton St., Toronto ON M4S 2Z8
Tel: 416-322-7877; *Fax:* 416-322-5894
Toll-Free: 866-436-3829
info@autism.net
www.autism.net
www.linkedin.com/company/geneva-centre-for-autism
www.facebook.com/genevacentre
twitter.com/geneva_centre
Overview: A medium-sized national charitable organization founded in 1974
Mission: To empower individuals with autism & other related disorders & their families, to fully participate in their communities
Member of: Autism Society of Canada; Autism Society of Ontario; Autism Society of America
Chief Officer(s):
Debbie Irish, Chief Executive Officer
Jim Gilmour, Chief Financial Officer
Debbie Drewett, Director, Development
foundation@autism.net
Finances: *Annual Operating Budget:* $3 Million-$5 Million
Staff Member(s): 170; 50 volunteer(s)
Membership: 1,200; *Fees:* Level 1: $40 professionals, $25 parents & students; Level 2: $80 professionals, $50 parents & students; *Member Profile:* Parents & professionals
Activities: Services to families of children with autism; training events & workshops; international symposium on autism; *Awareness Events:* The Autists, a fundraising gala in support of children, youth & adults with autism.; Butterfly Classic Charity Golf Tournament; Trailblazers Track & Field Championships, a track & field competition for children & youth with autism; *Internships:* Yes; *Speaker Service:* Yes; *Library:* Resource Library (for members); by appointment

Genome Canada
#2100, 150 Metcalfe St., Ottawa ON K2P 1P1
Tel: 613-751-4460; *Fax:* 613-751-4474
info@genomecanada.ca
www.genomecanada.ca
www.facebook.com/GenomeCanada
twitter.com/genomecanada
www.youtube.com/genomecanada
Overview: A medium-sized national organization
Mission: To develop & implement a national strategy in genomics & proteomics research for the benefit of all Canadians; to enable Canada to become a world leader in genomics & proteomics research in key selected areas as agriculture, environment, fisheries, forestry & health
Chief Officer(s):
Pierre Meulien, President & CEO
pmeulien@genomecanada.ca

Genome Alberta
#200, 3215 - 33 St. NW, Calgary AB T2L 2A6
Tel: 403-210-5275; *Fax:* 403-503-5225
info@genomealberta.ca
www.genomealberta.ca
Chief Officer(s):
David Bailey, President/CEO
dbailey@genomealberta.ca
Mike Spear, Director, Corporate Communications
mspear@genomealberta.ca

Genome Atlantic
#123, 1344 Summer St., Halifax NS B3H 0A8
Tel: 902-421-5683; *Fax:* 902-421-2733
info@genomeatlantic.ca
www.genomeatlantic.ca
www.facebook.com/pages/Genome-Atlantic/113846955323882
twitter.com/GenomeAtlantic
Chief Officer(s):
Steven Armstrong, President/CEO
sarmstrong@genomeatlantic.ca
Sue Coueslan, Director, Communications & Government Relations
sue@genomeatlantic.ca

Genome British Columbia
#400, 575 West 8th Ave., Vancouver BC V5Z 0C4
Tel: 604-738-8072; *Fax:* 604-738-8597
info@genomebc.ca
www.genomebc.ca
www.linkedin.com/company/genome-british-columbia
www.facebook.com/genomebc
twitter.com/genomebc
www.youtube.com/user/genomicseducation
Chief Officer(s):
Alan E. Winter, President & CEO
Sally Greenwood, Vice-President, Communication & Education

Genome Prairie
Innovation Place, Atrium Bldg., #101, 111 Research Dr., Saskatoon SK S7N 3R2
Tel: 306-668-3570; *Fax:* 306-668-3580
info@genomeprairie.ca
www.genomeprairie.ca
Chief Officer(s):
David Gauthier, President/CEO
dgauthier@genomeprairie.ca

Génome Québec
#2660, 630, boul. René-Lévesque ouest, Montréal QC H3B 1S6
Tél: 514-398-0668; *Téléc:* 514-398-0883
gqinfo@genomequebec.com
www.genomequebec.com
www.linkedin.com/company/genome-quebec?trk=NUS_CMP_TWIT
www.facebook.com/GenomeQc
twitter.com/GenomeQuebec

www.youtube.com/channel/UCPN6xorJnmYU_SBUdkwoW6Q?feature=plcp
Chief Officer(s):
Marc LePage, Président-directeur général

Ontario Genomics Institute
MaRS Centre, West Tower, #490, 661 University Ave., Toronto ON M5G 1M1
Tel: 416-977-9582; *Fax:* 416-977-8342
info@ontariogenomics.ca
www.ontariogenomics.ca
Chief Officer(s):
Mark J. Poznansky, President/CEO
mpoznansky@OntarioGenomics.ca

Geogrian Bay Association

ON
www.gbabaptist.org
Overview: A small local organization overseen by Canadian Baptists of Ontario and Quebec
Mission: To support their members in achieving their goals
Member of: Canadian Baptists of Ontario & Quebec
Chief Officer(s):
Steve Barker, Moderator
office@hopecommunitysite.com
Membership: 15 churches; *Member Profile:* Baptist churches in Georgian Bay

Geological Association of Canada (GAC) / Association géologique du Canada (AGC)

Department of Earth Sciences, Memorial University of Newfoundland, #ER4063, Alexander Murray Bldg., St. John's NL A1B 3X5
Tel: 709-737-7660; *Fax:* 709-737-2532
gac@mun.ca
www.gac.ca
Overview: A large national organization founded in 1947
Mission: To advance the wise use of geoscience in academic, professional, & public circles
Member of: Canadian Federation of Earth Sciences
Affliation(s): American Geophysical Union; Atlantic Geoscience Society; Canadian Geophysical Union; Canadian Quaternary Association; Canadian Society of Petroleum Geologists; Toronto Geological Discussion Group
Chief Officer(s):
Peter Bobrowsky, President, 613-947-0333
pbobrows@nrcan.gc.ca
Richard Wardle, Vice-President, 709-753-2074
richwardle@nl.rogers.com
Toby Rivers, Secretary-Treasurer, 709-864-8392
trivers@mun.ca
Karen Johnston, Manager, Finance & Administration, 709-864-2399
kajohnston@mun.ca
Karen Dawe, Director, Publications, 709-864-2151
kfmdawe@mun.ca
Finances: *Funding Sources:* Membership fees; Publication sales
Membership: 1,000-4,999; *Fees:* $10 students & teachers; $20 spousal; $70 - $80 seniors & unemployed; $105 - $120 full members; $250 universities; $500 supporters; $1000 sponsors; *Committees:* Science Program; Finance; Publications; Communications
Activities: Providing professional development opportunities for members; Disseminating information about geoscience; Offering networking opportunities; *Internships:* Yes; *Speaker Service:* Yes
Awards:
• Logan Medal (Award)
To honour an individual for sustained distinguished achievement in Canadian earth science *Contact:* Stephen Johnston, E-mail: stj@uvic.ca
• W.W. Hutchison Medal (Award)
To recognize a young person for exceptional advances in Canadian earth science research *Contact:* Daniel Lebel, E-mail: Daniel.lebel@ec.gc.ca
• E.R. Ward Neale Medal (Award)
To honour an individual for sustained outstanding efforts in sharing earth science with Canadians *Contact:* Tim Corkery, E-mail: timothy.corkery@gov.mb.ca
• J. Willis Ambrose Medal (Award)
To recognize a person for dedicated service to the Canadian earth science community *Contact:* Stephen Rowins, E-mail: stephen.rowins@gov.bc.ca
• Yves O. Fortier Earth Science Journalism Award (Award)
To honour excellence in journalistic presentation of earth science in the newsprint media *Contact:* Eileen van der Flier-Keller, E-mail: fkeller@uvic.ca
• CJES Best Paper Award (Award)
Presented jointly by the Geological Association of Canada & the National Research Council Press for the best paper published in the Canadian Journal of Earth Sciences
• Distinguished Member Award (Award)
A service award of the Geological Association of Canada *Contact:* Carolyn Relf, Phone: 867-667-8892; E-mail: carolyn.relf@gov.yk.ca
• Distinguished Service Award (Award)
To recognize outstanding contributions to the Geological Association of Canada through volunteer work *Contact:* Tim Corkery, Phone: 204-945-6554; E-mail: timothy.corkery@gov.mb.ca
• Voluntary Service Award (Award)
Awarded to members or non-members for significant voluntary contributions to the Geological Association of Canada *Contact:* Tim Corkery, Phone: 204-945-6554; E-mail: timothy.corkery@gov.mb.ca
• Honorary Life Members (Award)
To honour individuals for long-term distinguished service to the Geological Association of Canada *Contact:* Tim Corkery, Phone: 204-945-6554; E-mail: timothy.corkery@gov.mb.ca
• Certificate of Appreciation (Award)
To recognize both members of the Geological Association of Canada & non-members for voluntary service to the association
• Mary-Claire Ward Geoscience Award (Award)
Awarded to a graduate student at a Canadian university whose thesis incorporates geoscience mapping *Contact:* Lisa McDonald, E-mail: lmcdonald@pdac.ca
• Jerome H. Remick Poster Awards (Award)
Awards & certificates of merit given to outstanding poster presenters at each Geological Association of Canada Annual Meeting
Meetings/Conferences: • Geological Association of Canada (GAC) & the Mineralogical Association of Canada (MAC) 2015 Joint Annual Meeting, May, 2015, Palais des congrès de Montréal, Montréal, QC
Scope: National
Description: Featuring exhibits, a technical program, & special events
Contact Information: Communications Chair, Mike Villeneuve, E-mail: mike.villeneuve@nrcan.gc.ca; URL: ja.agu.org/2015
Publications:
• Geolog
Type: Magazine; *Frequency:* Quarterly; *Accepts Advertising*; *Price:* Free with membership in the Geological Association of Canada
Profile: News items & short articles of interest to Geological Association of Canada members
• Geological Association of Canada Membership Directory
Type: Directory
• Geoscience Canada
Type: Journal; *Frequency:* Quarterly; *Accepts Advertising*; *Editor:* R.A. Wilson (reg.wilson@gnb.ca); *Price:* Free with membership in the GeologicalAssociation of Canada
Profile: A general interest, earth-science journal featuring review papers, topical articles, conference reports, book reviews, & commentary

Edmonton Section
c/o Matt Grobe, Alberta Geological Survey, 4999 - 98 Ave., 4th Fl., Edmonton AB T6B 2X3
Tel: 780-427-2843
www.egs.ab.ca
Mission: To facilitate communication between earth scientists in Edmonton, Alberta & the surrounding area; To promote the science of geology
Chief Officer(s):
Marilyn Huff, President
huff@ualberta.ca
Rob L'Heureux, Treasurer
Matt Grobe, Manager, Publications, 780-427-2843
matt.grobe@ercb.ca
• Edmonton Beneath Our Feet: A Guide to the Geology of the Edmonton Area
Type: Book; *Price:* $12.95
Profile: A guide, containing walking routes
• EGS Notices
Type: Newsletter; *Price:* Free with membership in the Edmonton Geological Society
Profile: Information about field trips & other events of the Edmonton section of the Geological Association of Canada
• Report on the Great Landslide at Frank, Alta., 1903
Type: Book; *Price:* $9.95
• The Valley Beneath Our Feet: An Earth Science Walk Across Edmonton's River
Price: $6.95
Profile: A guide to the North Saskatchewan River Valley

Newfoundland & Labrador Section
c/o Heather Rafuse, Department of Natural Resources, Geological Survey, PO Box 8700, St. John's NL A1B 4J6
gac.esd.mun.ca/nl/nfsection.htm
Chief Officer(s):
Sam Bentley, President
sbentley@mun.ca
Joe McQuaker, Vice-President
jmacquaker@mun.ca
Larry Hicks, Secretary-Treasurer
larryhicks@gov.nl.ca
Andrew Kerr, Chair, Technical Program
andykerr@gov.nl.ca
• Field Trip
Type: Guide
Profile: Guides from the section's annual field trips
• Travellers Guide to the Geology of Newfoundland & Labrador
Type: Guidebook
Profile: Including a list of geological localities & a highway geology map

Québec Section
QC
gac.esd.mun.ca/AQUEST/index_anglais.htm
Mission: To promote geoscience throughout Québec
Chief Officer(s):
Robert Marquis, Contact, Membership
robert.marquis@mrnf.gouv.qc.ca
• AQUEST Newsletter
Type: Newsletter
Profile: Information about current activities for members of the Québec section of the Geological Association of Canada

Vancouver (Cordilleran) Section
Bentall Centre, PO Box 398, Stn. A, Vancouver BC V6C 2N2
e-mail: webmaster@gac-cs.ca
www.gac-cs.ca
Chief Officer(s):
Thomas Bissig, President
Peter Friz, Treasurer
• Garibaldi Geology
Type: Guide; *Number of Pages:* 48; *Author:* W.H Matthews; *Price:* $4.95 members; $9 non-members
Profile: The geology of the Garibaldi Lake region
• Geological Association of Canada, Cordilleran Section Newsletter
Type: Newsletter; *Editor:* Stuart Sutherland
Profile: Articles & announcements of interest to members of the section
• Geological Field Trips in Southern British Columbia
Type: Guide
• Geology Tours of Vancouver's Buildings & Monuments
Type: Guide; *Number of Pages:* 143; *Author:* P. Mustard; Z.D. Hora; C. Hansen; *ISBN:* 10: 0-919216-85-4; *Price:* $11.22 members; $20.40 non-members
• Guidebook for Geological Field Trips in Southwestern British Columbia & Northern Washington
Type: Guide
Profile: A guidebook edited by G.J. Woodsworth, L.E. Jackson, J.L. Nelson, & B.C. Ward
• A Transect of the Southern Canadian Cordillera from Calgary to Vancouver
Type: Guide; *Number of Pages:* 165; *Author:* R.A. Price; J.W.H. Monger; *ISBN:* 10: 0-9687005-3-5; *Price:* $24.75 members; $45 non-members
Profile: A field trip

Winnipeg Section
#360, 1395 Ellice Ave., Winnipeg MB R3G 3P2
Tel: 204-945-6561; *Fax:* 204-945-1406
wgs-gac@hotmail.com
www.umanitoba.ca/faculties/science/geological_sciences/gac wpg/
Mission: To promote geoscience in Winnipeg, Manitoba & the surrounding area
Chief Officer(s):
Scott Anderson, President
scott.anderson@gov.mb.ca

Geomatics for Informed Decisions Network

Pavillon Louis-Jacques-Casault, Cité Universitaire, #2306, 1055, av du Séminaire, Québec QC G1V 0A6

Tel: 418-656-7758; *Fax:* 418-656-2611
info@geoide.ulaval.ca
www.geoide.ulaval.ca
Also Known As: GEOIDE
Overview: A medium-sized national organization
Member of: Networks of Centres of Excellence
Chief Officer(s):
Chantal Arguin, President
Nicholas Chrisman, Scientific Director
Nicholas.Chrisman@geoide.ulaval.ca

Geomatics Industry Association of Canada (GIAC) / Association canadienne des entreprises de géomatique
1460 Merivale Rd., Ottawa ON K2E 1B1
Tel: 613-851-1256
Previous Name: Canadian Association of Aerial Surveyors
Overview: A medium-sized national organization founded in 1961
Mission: To strengthen business climate; to maintain cooperative relations with government; to promote expanded role for members in provision of geomatics products & services; to encourage adoption by governments of improved policies & practices for procurement of geomatics products & services; to promote member firms as source of high quality, professional services; to promote Canadian geomatics industry abroad.
Member of: Alliance of Manufacturers & Exporters Canada
Finances: *Funding Sources:* Membership fees

Géomètres professionnels du Canada *See* Professional Surveyors Canada

George Bray Sports Association (GBSA)
9606 Tower Rd., RR#3, St. Thomas ON N5P 3S7
Tel: 519-633-9411
www.georgebraysports.ca
www.facebook.com/pages/George-Bray-Sports-Association/563729230361725
Overview: A small local organization founded in 1968
Mission: To organize hockey games for children with learning disabilities
Chief Officer(s):
Murray Howard, President
murrayhoward@execulink.com

George Cedric Metcalf Charitable Foundation
38 Madison Ave., Toronto ON M5R 2S1
Tel: 416-926-0366; *Fax:* 416-926-0370
info@metcalffoundation.com
www.metcalffoundation.com
twitter.com/metcalf_ca
Also Known As: Metcalf Foundation
Overview: A small local organization founded in 1967
Chief Officer(s):
Sandy Houston, President
shouston@metcalffoundation.com
Staff Member(s): 9

George Morris Centre
#107, 100 Stone Rd. West, Guelph ON N1G 5L3
Tel: 519-822-3929; *Fax:* 855-482-3245
info@georgemorris.org
www.georgemorris.org
www.linkedin.com/company/george-morris-centre
www.facebook.com/georgemorriscentre
twitter.com/GMCagrifood
Overview: A small provincial charitable organization founded in 1990
Mission: To provoke quality dialogue on relevant policies & issues & to encourage innovations that enhance insight & excellence in the agriculture & food sector
Chief Officer(s):
Bob Funk, Chair
Bob Funk, Chair
Frank Ingratta, Vice-Chair
Bob Hunsberger, Sec.-Treas.
John F.T. Scott, Managing Director, 519-822-3929 Ext. 205
Finances: *Funding Sources:* Membership fees, sales of goods & services
Staff Member(s): 5
Membership: *Fees:* $250 individual; $1,000 association; $2,500 corporate
Activities: Canadian AgriFood Executive Development Program; Introduction to Commodity Risk Management Using Futures & Options; Designing Hedging Strategies Using Technical Analysis, Futures & Options; Workshop on Strategic Alliances; Canadian Total Excellence in Agricultural Management; *Library*
Publications:
• Agri-food for Thought
Type: Newsletter; *Frequency:* Quarterly

Georgeville Historical Society / Société d'histoire de Georgeville
4600 Georgeville Rd., Georgeville QC J0B 1T0
Tel: 819-562-8036
Overview: A small local organization founded in 1992
Mission: Documents the history of the village of Georgeville, Québec.
Chief Officer(s):
Steve Moore, Contact
Publications:
• The Georgevill Enterprise
Type: Newsletter; *Frequency:* Semiannually; *Price:* Free for members

Georgian Bay Country Tourism Association (GBC)
#3, 70 Church St., Parry Sound ON P2A 1Y9
Tel: 705-746-4213; *Fax:* 705-746-6537
Toll-Free: 888-229-7257
touristinfo@gbcountry.com
www.gbcountry.com
www.facebook.com/GeorgianBayCountry
twitter.com/gbcountry
www.foursquare.com/venue/19127087
Overview: A small local organization
Mission: To increase tourism in the Georgian Bay area
Affliation(s): Tourism Industry Association of Ontario; Ontario Accommodation Association; Attractions Ontario
Chief Officer(s):
Anna Marie Harris, Manager, 705-746-4213
annamarie@gbcountry.com

Georgian Bay Folk Society (GBFS)
PO Box 521, Owen Sound ON N4K 5R1
Tel: 519-371-2995; *Fax:* 519-371-2973
gbfs@bmts.com
summerfolk.org
twitter.com/GeorgianBayFolk
ww.flickr.com/photos/gbfs
Overview: A small local charitable organization founded in 1978
Member of: Ontario Council of Folk Festivals; North American Folk Alliance
Chief Officer(s):
James Keelaghan, Artistic Director
artisticdirector@summerfolk.org
Finances: *Funding Sources:* Corporate & private donations; fundraising concerts; government grants
Staff Member(s): 2
Membership: *Fees:* $15 folkie; $25 student; $40 individual; $70 family; $500 lifetime
Activities: Winterfolk year round concert series; *Awareness Events:* Summerfolk Music & Craft Festival, August

Georgian Bay Native Friendship Centre
175 Yonge St., Midland ON L4R 2A7
Tel: 705-526-5589
reception@gbnfc.com
www.gbnfc.com
Overview: A small local charitable organization founded in 1984
Mission: To provide youth activities & programs, to create opportunities for them to have a voice & participate in the community.
Member of: Ontario Federation of Indian Friendship Centres
Chief Officer(s):
Bruce Sandy, President
Compton Khan, Executive Director
edirector@gbnfc.com
Staff Member(s): 16
Activities: L'il Beavers; youth social/recreation program; arts & crafts; drug & alcohol intervention programming; child & family services; life long care; native language program; tenant counsellor; employment & training; healing & wellness; desktop publishing services; *Internships:* Yes; *Speaker Service:* Yes

Georgian Bay Steam & Antique Association
c/o Grace Priest, 224 Cundles Rd. East, Barrie ON L4M 6L1
Tel: 705-728-7649
info@steamshow.ca
www.steamshow.ca
Also Known As: Georgian Bay Steam Show
Previous Name: Georgian Bay Steam Association
Overview: A small local organization
Chief Officer(s):
Tim Anderson, President, 705-834-8142
Finances: *Annual Operating Budget:* Less than $50,000
500 volunteer(s)
Membership: 500
Activities: Heritage & farm-related displays of antiques

Georgian Bay Steam Association *See* Georgian Bay Steam & Antique Association

Georgian Bay Symphony (GBS)
PO Box 133, Owen Sound ON N4K 5P1
Tel: 519-372-0212; *Fax:* 519-372-9023
gbs@bmts.com
www.georgianbaysymphony.ca
www.facebook.com/pages/Georgian-Bay-Symphony/41551049364
twitter.com/GeorgianBaySymp
Overview: A small local charitable organization founded in 1972 overseen by Orchestras Canada
Mission: To enhance appreciation of music which includes growth & development of regional orchestra
Affliation(s): Owen Sound Chamber of Commerce
Chief Officer(s):
John Barnum, Music Director
Finances: *Funding Sources:* Ticket sales; donations; private & corporate sponsorship; fundraising; endowment fund; OAC grant
Membership: *Member Profile:* Subscribers & musicians in the orchestra
Activities: Wine-tasting fundraiser; four string quartet outings annually; three chamber music concerts; five symphony concerts annually; *Library:* GBS Library

The Georgian Triangle Tourist Association & Tourist Information Centre
45 St. Paul St., Collingwood ON L9Y 3P1
Tel: 705-445-7722; *Fax:* 705-444-6158
Toll-Free: 888-227-8667
info@georgiantriangle.com
www.georgiantriangle.com
www.facebook.com/114000537662
twitter.com/SGeorgianBay
Overview: A small local organization founded in 1979
Mission: To promote tourism & convention industries in the Georgian Triangle
Member of: Tourism Industry Association of Canada
Staff Member(s): 4
Membership: *Fees:* Schedule available dependant on business type & size; *Member Profile:* Tourism or tourism-related businesses, municipalities, counties
Activities: *Internships:* Yes

Georgina Association for Business *See* South Lake Community Futures Development Corporation

Georgina Association for Community Living
PO Box 68, 26943 Hwy. 48, Sutton West ON L0E 1R0
Tel: 905-722-8947; *Fax:* 905-722-9591
admin@communitylivinggeorgina.com
communitylivinggeorgina.com
Overview: A small local organization
Mission: To provide services & support to people with developmental disabilities
Member of: Community Living Ontario
Chief Officer(s):
Susan Rome, Executive Director
srome@communitylivinggeorgina.com
Staff Member(s): 6
Membership: *Fees:* $10 single; $15 family; $50 group/business; *Committees:* Administration; Finance & Property; Public Relations & Fundraising
Publications:
• Communicator
Type: Newsletter; *Frequency:* Quarterly; *Accepts Advertising*

Georgina Chamber of Commerce
430 The Queensway South, Keswick ON L4P 2E1
Tel: 905-476-7870; *Fax:* 905-476-6700
Toll-Free: 888-436-7446
admin@georginachamber.com
www.georginachamber.com
Overview: A small local organization founded in 1990
Mission: To focus on the current & future success of its members
Member of: Ontario Chamber of Commerce
Chief Officer(s):
Christine Thomas, General Manager

Dan Fellini, President
Finances: *Annual Operating Budget:* Less than $50,000; *Funding Sources:* Membership fees; golf tournament; trade show
Staff Member(s): 2; 13 volunteer(s)
Membership: 275; *Fees:* $150; *Member Profile:* Entrepreneur, voice of business in Georgina; *Committees:* Business Development & Tourism; Economic Development; Membership; General Meetings
Activities: *Rents Mailing List:* Yes

Georgina Family Life Centre *See* Family Services York Region

Geotechnical Society of Edmonton (GSE)
c/o City of Edmonton, Engineering Services Section, 11004 - 190 St. NW, Edmonton AB T5S 0G9
Tel: 780-944-7653
gse@geotechnical.ca
www.geotechnical.ca
Overview: A small local organization founded in 1969
Chief Officer(s):
Kristen Tappenden, President
Membership: 190; *Fees:* $15
Activities: Student presentations; lecture series & talks; professional development events; Reinforced Soil Wall Competition
Awards:
• Morgenstern Student Award (Award)

Gerald Hardy Memorial Society
PO Box 131, 22657 Hwy. 7, Sheet Harbour NS B0J 3B0
Tel: 902-885-2300; *Fax:* 902-885-2054
ghms@ns.sympatico.ca
geraldhardymemorialsociety.webs.com
Overview: A small local organization
Mission: To provide intellectually disabled adults with job skills & work experience
Member of: DIRECTIONS Council for Vocational Services Society
Chief Officer(s):
Deanna Currie, Executive Director/Manager
Activities: Operates a thrift store & the Rainbow Food Bank

Geraldton & District Chamber of Commerce *See* Geraldton Chamber of Commerce

Geraldton Chamber of Commerce
PO Box 128, Geraldton ON P0T 1M0
Tel: 807-986-3617
www.gdcc-on.ca
Previous Name: Geraldton & District Chamber of Commerce
Overview: A small local organization
Member of: Northwestern Ontario Associated Chambers of Commerce
Chief Officer(s):
Eric Pietsch, President
eric.pietsch@geraldtonchamber.com
Kathy Beaupre, Secretary, 807-854-1217
kathy.beaupre@geraldtonchamber.com
Membership: 1-99

German Canadian Association of Nova Scotia
c/o Anthony L. Chapman, Q.C., Tower 1, Cox & Palmer Purdy's Wharf, PO Box 2380, Stn. Central, #1100, 1959 Upper Water St., Halifax NS B3J 3E5
Tel: 902-401-6409
info@germancanadianassociation.ca
www.germancanadianassociation.ca
www.facebook.com/gcanovascotia
twitter.com/gca_ns
Overview: A small provincial organization founded in 1972
Mission: To preserve the cultural heritage of German speaking immigrants & descendants in Nova Scotia; To promote the understanding & appreciation of the German language & culture in Nova Scotia
Chief Officer(s):
René Bulzenhardt, President
Joerg Kanehl, Vice-President
Jessica Wyss, Membership Secretary
Bianca Krueger, Treasurer
Finances: *Funding Sources:* Membership fees; Sponsorships
Membership: *Fees:* $15 students; $20 seniors; $30 singles; $40 families; $50 businesses
Activities: Providing cultural & educational activities; Supporting the teaching of the German language; Facilitating networking opportunities among German speaking persons; *Awareness Events:* Halifax Oktoberfest; Family Sommerfest

German Canadian Business Association
PO Box 91462, West Vancouver BC V7V 3P2
Tel: 604-925-2664
rebecca@germancanadianbusinessassociation.com
www.germancanadianbusinessassociation.com
Previous Name: German-Canadian Business Association of British Columbia
Overview: A small provincial organization founded in 1963
Mission: To actively promote & foster professional & social relationships; to contribute to the enhancement of our European heritage
Chief Officer(s):
Rebecca Lees, Secretary, 604-925-2664
rebecca@germancanadianbusinessassociation.com
Finances: *Funding Sources:* Membership fees
7 volunteer(s)
Membership: 70; *Fees:* $385; *Member Profile:* German speaking business in Canada
Activities: Monthly dinner meetings

German Canadian Cultural Association
German Canadian Cultural Centre, 8310 Roper Rd., Edmonton AB T6E 6E3
Tel: 780-466-4000; *Fax:* 780-440-6963
gcca@shaw.ca
www.gcca.ca
Overview: A small local organization founded in 1983
Member of: German-Canadian Association of Alberta
Finances: *Annual Operating Budget:* $500,000-$1.5 Million
Staff Member(s): 25; 11 volunteer(s)
Membership: 750; *Fees:* $30 single; $60 family; *Member Profile:* To preserve & promote the heritage & culture of all persons of German language origin
Activities: *Library* Open to public

German Canadian Cultural Association of Manitoba Inc.
#15, 1110 Henderson Hwy., Winnipeg MB R2G 1L1
Tel: 204-334-8491
Overview: A small provincial organization founded in 1983
Membership: *Member Profile:* Interest in German language & culture
Activities: *Library* by appointment

German Society of Winnipeg
285 Flora Ave., Winnipeg MB R2W 5H7
Tel: 204-589-7724; *Fax:* 204-589-0030
gswmb@mymts.net
gswmb.ca
Overview: A small local organization founded in 1892
Membership: *Fees:* $160 regular; $140 seniors; *Member Profile:* German Canadians living in Manitoba
Activities: *Library*

German-Canadian Association of Alberta (GCAA)
8310 Roper Rd., Edmonton AB T6E 6E3
Tel: 780-465-7466
mail@gcaa.ca
www.gcaa.ca
Overview: A medium-sized provincial organization founded in 1958
Mission: To keep up German culture in Alberta
Chief Officer(s):
Heinz Kleist, President
Finances: *Funding Sources:* Membership fees
15 volunteer(s)

German-Canadian Business & Professional Association of Kitchener-Waterloo
332 Charles St. East, Kitchener ON N2G 2P9
Tel: 519-744-3586; *Fax:* 519-744-3587
info@german-canadian-business.ca
german-canadian-business.com
twitter.com/GermanCdnBusPro
Overview: A small local organization
Mission: To represent business owners & other professionals of German-Canadian heritage in the K-W area
Membership: *Member Profile:* Business owner/operators, entrepreneurs, professionals, & academics with basic German language knowledge & fluency; prospective members must be sponsored by current members
Activities: Bitzer Award & German-Canadian Education Fund; *Awareness Events:* German Pioneers Day, October; Christkindl Market; Christmas Celebration

German-Canadian Business Association of British Columbia *See* German Canadian Business Association

German-Canadian Congress (GCC) / Congrès germano-canadien
#58, 81 Garry St., Winnipeg MB R3C 4J9
Tel: 204-989-8300
gccmb@hotmail.com
www.gccmb.com
Overview: A medium-sized national organization founded in 1985
Mission: To serve as official voice for 2.7 million Canadians of German-speaking background
Member of: Canadian Ethnocultural Council
Finances: *Annual Operating Budget:* $100,000-$250,000
Staff Member(s): 2; 100 volunteer(s)
Activities: *Speaker Service:* Yes

German-Canadian Congress (Manitoba) Inc.
#58, 81 Garry St., Winnipeg MB R3C 4J9
Tel: 204-989-8300; *Fax:* 204-989-8304
gccmb@hotmail.com
www.gccmb.ca
Also Known As: Deutschkanadischer Kongress
Overview: A large provincial organization founded in 1985 overseen by German-Canadian Congress
Mission: To cultivate & promote language, culture, customs & traditions of German Canadians within scope of Canadian multiculturalism
Chief Officer(s):
Carola Lange, President
Werner Klinger, Secretary
Finances: *Annual Operating Budget:* Less than $50,000
Staff Member(s): 2; 10 volunteer(s)
Membership: 170; *Fees:* $20 individual; $35 family; $10 student; $15 senior; $100 corporate; *Committees:* Media; German-Canadian Studies Foundation; Seniors
Activities: Representation of members; conventions, workshops & forum discussions; national network of pension counsellors for German pension; educational material on German-Canadian history; cooperation with other ethnic groups; student exchange program to Germany; *Library:* Office Library; Open to public
Publications:
• Infoblatt
Type: Newsletter; *Frequency:* Quarterly

German-Canadian Congress (Ontario) (GCC)
41B River Rd. East, Kitchener ON N2B 2G3
Tel: 519-571-8980
info@germancanadiancongress.com
www.germancanadiancongress.com
Overview: A small provincial organization founded in 1984
Mission: To cultivate & promote the language, culture & customs of German speaking Canadians
Chief Officer(s):
Wayne Wettlaufer, President
Staff Member(s): 1
Membership: 1,400; 44 clubs; *Fees:* $15-$200; *Committees:* Financial Audit; Liaison; Event Management; Cultural & Heritage Related Affairs; Corporate Communications; Youth Related Affairs; Charitable Foundation of the German-Canadian Congress (Ontario); Liaison with Other Similar Organizations; Fundraising; Membership; Nominating

German-Canadian Historical Association Inc. (GCHA)
Department of Modern Languages, University of Prince Edward Island, Charlottetown PE C1A 4P3
Fax: 902-566-0359
german-canadian.ca
Overview: A small provincial organization founded in 1973
Mission: To collect, promote & disseminate information regarding the development & contributions of the German-speaking groups in Canada.
Chief Officer(s):
Lothar Zimmermann, Contact
zimmermann@upei.ca
Membership: *Fees:* $14 student/pensioners; $28 individual; $42 sustaining; $400 life
Publications:
• Canadiana Germanica
Type: Journal; *Frequency:* Quarterly; *Number of Pages:* 45
Profile: Presents original articles, reprints of relevant material & announcements concerning new publications & upcoming meetings

German-Canadian Mardi Gras Association Inc. (BDKK) / Bund Deutscher Karnevalsgesellschaften Kanada
119 Glendonwynne Rd., Toronto ON M6P 3E7

Overview: A small local organization founded in 1963
Chief Officer(s):
Herbert H. Wittig, Contact
Membership: 19 institutional; 1,200 individual
Activities: *Rents Mailing List:* Yes

Germans from Russia Heritage Society - British Columbia Chapter (GRHS-BCC)
2400 - 25 St., Vernon BC V1T 4P5
Tel: 604-542-2110
Overview: A small provincial organization
Chief Officer(s):
Pat Hagel, President
Bergetta Mercer, Secretary

Gerontological Nursing Association of British Columbia (GNABC)
c/o 328 Nootka St., New Westminster, BC V3L 4X4
Tel: 604-484-5698; *Fax:* 604-874-4378
gnabc@shaw.ca
gnabc.com
Overview: A medium-sized provincial organization founded in 1981 overseen by Canadian Gerontological Nursing Association
Mission: To promote a high standard of nursing care & related health services for older adults; To enhance professionalism in the practice of gerontological nursing
Chief Officer(s):
Kim Martin, President
k_martin@shaw.ca
Membership: *Fees:* $32.50 student; $45 RPN/LPN (affiliate); $65 RN; *Member Profile:* Registered Nurses, Registered Psychiatric Nurses, & Licensed Practical Nurses within the province of BC; *Committees:* Membership & Local Group Development; Education; Media
Activities: Offering professional networking opportunities; Providing professional development; Advocating for comprehensive services for older adults; Supporting research related to gerontological nursing; Promoting gerontological nursing to the public
Meetings/Conferences: • Gerontological Nursing Association of British Columbia 2015 Conference, April, 2015, Coast Capri Hotel, Kelowna, BC
Scope: Provincial

Gerontological Nursing Association of Ontario (GNAO)
PO Box 368, Stn. K, Toronto ON M4P 2E0
e-mail: info@gnaontario.org
www.gnaontario.org
Overview: A medium-sized provincial charitable organization founded in 1974 overseen by Canadian Gerontological Nursing Association
Mission: To promote a high standard of nursing care & related health services for older adults; To enhance professionalism in the practice of gerontological nursing
Affiliation(s): Registered Nurses Association of Ontario
Chief Officer(s):
Julie Rubel, President
julie.rubel@gmail.com
Gwen Harris, Treasurer
gcharris@ebtech.net
Membership: 1,200+; *Fees:* $55 Regular; $40 Associate; $20 Student/Retired; *Member Profile:* Registered Nurses; Registered Practical Nurses; Full time students enrolled in a nursing program; Associate members interested in the GNA
Activities: Offering professional networking opportunities; Providing professional development; Advocating for comprehensive services for older adults; Supporting research related to gerontological nursing; Promoting gerontological nursing to the public
Awards:
• Education & Research Funding Grant (Grant)
For educational or research initiatives related to gerontological nursing practice
Meetings/Conferences: • Gerontological Nursing Association of Ontario 2015 Annual General Meeting, April, 2015, Toronto, ON
Scope: Provincial
Description: Conference Theme: Aging 2015: Innovations, Networks and Communities

The Gershon Iskowitz Foundation
19 Whiterock Dr., Toronto ON M1C 3N3
Tel: 416-530-4133
Overview: A small local organization
Mission: To provide grants in order to promote the development of artists in Canada
Chief Officer(s):
Nancy Hushion, Executive Director
nlh@hushion.ca
Awards:
• Gershon Iskowitz Prize (Award)
$25,000 to recognize achievements in visual art

Gethsemane Ministries
ON
Tel: 905-789-9909
gethsemaneministries@yahoo.ca
www.gethsemaneministries.com
Overview: A small local charitable organization founded in 1997
Mission: To offer evangelization through proclamation of the "Word," evangelization outreaches, & personal testimonies; To strengthen Catholic faith & family values through sacraments, personal prayer, reflection of scriptures, & fellowship; To renew commitment to the Church; To protect & uphold the sanctity of life, & the teachings of the Catholic Church on life & family; To undertake charitable acts to serve the community
Chief Officer(s):
Stan Rodrigo, Contact
stan.rodrigo@gmail.com
Finances: *Funding Sources:* Donations
Membership: *Fees:* Free; *Member Profile:* All age groups
Activities: Counselling; Providing faith instruction & spiritual guidance; Participating in sacramental life; Offering prayer groups, with Rosary, praise & worship, intercession, & fellowship; Assisting the ill, elderly, & needy; Helping youth in their Catholic faith formation, including catechism classes for grades 1-8; Providing youth programs, retreats, & summer camps; Offering retreats for married couples, mainly conducted by preachers; Supporting other parish & diocesan activities; Offering adult & youth music ministry
Publications:
• The Gethsemane Newsletter
Type: Newsletter; *Editor:* Agnello Desa
Profile: Articles, testimonies, & forthcoming activities

GI (Gastrointestinal) Society
855 - 12th Ave., Vancouver BC V5Z 1M9
Tel: 604-875-4875; *Fax:* 604-875-4429
Toll-Free: 866-600-4875
info@badgut.org
www.badgut.org
www.facebook.com/CISociety
twitter.com/GISociety
Overview: A medium-sized national organization
Mission: To improve the lives of people with GI and liver conditions, support research, advocate for appropriate patient access to healthcare & promote gastrointestinal & liver health
Chief Officer(s):
Gilles Larose, Chairperson
Gail Attara, Co-Founder & President/CEO
Finances: *Funding Sources:* Subscription fees; donations; fundraising events
Membership: *Committees:* Board of Directors; Medical Advisory Council
Activities: Support Groups; Lectures; Information on: Constipation, Celiac Disease, Crohn's Disease, Diverticular Disease, GERD, Hemorrhoids, Hiatus Hernia, Inflammatory Bowel Disease, Intestinal Gas, IBS, Functional Dyspepsia, Liver conditions, Pancreatitis, Stress Management, Ulcer Disease, Ulcerative Colitis, Ulcerative Proctitis; *Awareness Events:* IBS Awareness Month, April; Crohn's disease Awareness Month, November; Celiac disease awareness month, May

Gibsons & District Chamber of Commerce
PO Box 1190, #21, 900 Gibsons Way, Gibsons BC V0N 1V0
Tel: 604-886-2325; *Fax:* 604-886-2379
www.gibsonschamber.com
Overview: A small local organization founded in 1947
Member of: BC Chamber of Commerce
Chief Officer(s):
Dean Walford, President
Donna McMahon, Executive Director
Staff Member(s): 2

Gideons International in Canada / Les Gédéons - L'Association Internationale des Gédéons au Canada
PO Box 3619, 501 Imperial Rd. North, Guelph ON N1H 7A2
Tel: 519-823-1140; *Fax:* 519-767-1913
Toll-Free: 888-482-4253
info@gideons.ca
www.gideons.ca
www.linkedin.com/company/the-gideons-international-in-canada
www.facebook.com/group.php?gid=177253638952857
twitter.com/GideonsCanada
Overview: A medium-sized international charitable organization founded in 1911
Mission: The interdenominational lay association communicates/gives away freecopies of God's Word in Canada & around the world.
Chief Officer(s):
Paul Mercer, Executive Director
Finances: *Annual Operating Budget:* Greater than $5 Million; *Funding Sources:* Membership fees; voluntary donations; funds from other registered charities
Membership: 4,500; *Fees:* $100; *Member Profile:* Christian business & professional people
Activities: Sharing faith; Placing Bibles & New Testaments to the public; Distributing New Testaments to selected groups
Publications:
• The Canadian Gideon: The Official Publication of The Gideons International in Canada
Type: Magazine; *Editor:* Neil Bramble; *Price:* $15
Profile: Information & resources for Gideon & Auxiliary members
• Gideon News
Type: Newsletter

Gilbert Plains & District Chamber of Commerce
PO Box 670, Gilbert Plains MB R0L 0X0
Tel: 204-548-2682; *Fax:* 204-548-2682
Overview: A small local organization
Chief Officer(s):
Brenda Kerns, President

Gillam Chamber of Commerce
PO Box 366, Gillam MB R0B 0L0
Tel: 204-652-5135; *Fax:* 204-652-5155
www.townofgillam.com
Overview: A small local organization
Mission: The Gillam Chamber of Commerce is dedicated to business in the community.
Member of: The Manitoba Chambers of Commerce
Chief Officer(s):
Ken Hill, President
Membership: *Fees:* #25

Gina Lori Riley Dance Enterprises
Jackman Dramatic Art Centre, #210, 401 Sunset Ave., Windsor ON N9B 3P4
Tel: 519-253-3000
www.ginaloririleydanceenterprises.com
Overview: A small local organization founded in 1979
Mission: To advance the art of dance through the development of new work, performance & through community education in an exemplary manner as a contemporary modern professional Canadian dance company
Chief Officer(s):
Gina Lori Riley, Artistic Director
riley2@uwindsor.ca
Finances: *Funding Sources:* Private & public; box office; fundraising
Awards:
• Civic Recognition Award (Award)

Gioventù Studentesca (Student Youth) *See* Communion & Liberation Canada

Girl Guides of Canada (GGC) / Guides du Canada
50 Merton St., Toronto ON M4S 1A3
Tel: 416-487-5281; *Fax:* 416-487-5570
Other Communication: www.flickr.com/photos/girlguidesofcan
www.girlguides.ca
www.linkedin.com/groups/Girl-Guides-Canada-Guides-du-3598633
www.facebook.com/GirlGuidesofCanada.GuidesduCanada
twitter.com/girlguidesofcan
www.youtube.com/user/ggcanada
Overview: A large national charitable organization founded in 1910
Mission: To prepare girls to meet the challenges of life, in a safe environment, by teaching them such skills as bandaging wounds & coping with bullies; to encourage girls to foster friendships & develop a sense of leadership; to make girls. It is part of a global organization of 145 countries, the largest for girls in the world
Member of: World Association of Girl Guides & Girl Scouts
Affliation(s): World Association of Girl Guides & Girl Scouts
Chief Officer(s):
Pamela Rice, Chief Commissioner
Sharron Callahan, International Commissioner
Deborah Del Duca, CEO

Finances: *Annual Operating Budget:* $3 Million-$5 Million
Staff Member(s): 50; 18,0 volunteer(s)
Membership: 70,000+ individual; *Committees:* Finance; Provincial; National Audit; Program Stewardship
Activities: Programs for: Sparks, Brownies; Guides; Pathfinders; Rangers; Women 18+; *Awareness Events:* Annual Cookie Campaign, Oct. to June; *Library:* Resource Centre; Open to public by appointment
Publications:
• Canadian Guider [a publication of Girl Guides of Canada]
Type: Magazine; *Frequency:* 3 pa.; *Editor:* Stephanie Bangarth
ISSN: 0300-435X; *Price:* $4.25 each
• Guiding Matters [a publication of Girl Guides of Canada]
Type: Newsletter

Alberta, Northwest Terrirories & Yukon Council
11055 - 107 St. NW, Edmonton AB T5H 2Z6
Tel: 780-424-5510; *Fax:* 780-426-1715
info@albertagirlguides.com
www.albertagirlguides.com
twitter.com/GGCAlberta
Chief Officer(s):
Margaret Utgoff, Provincial Commissioner

British Columbia Council
1476 West 8th Ave., Vancouver BC V6H 1E1
Tel: 604-714-6636; *Fax:* 604-714-6645
Toll-Free: 800-565-8111
info@bc-girlguides.org
www.bc-girlguides.org
Chief Officer(s):
Dawnette Humphrey, Provincial Commissioner

Manitoba Council
#213, 530 Century St., Winnipeg MB R3H 0Y4
Tel: 204-774-4475; *Fax:* 204-774-9271
Toll-Free: 800-565-8111
info@girlguides.mb.ca
www.girlguides.mb.ca
Chief Officer(s):
Elaine Cullingham, Executive Director
ecullingham@girlguides.mb.ca

New Brunswick & Prince Edward Island Council
55 Rothesay Ave., Saint John NB E2J 2B2
Tel: 506-634-0808; *Fax:* 506-634-0908
Toll-Free: 800-565-8111
ggcnbc@nb.aibn.com
www.girlguides.nb.ca
www.facebook.com/NBPEI.GirlGuides
Chief Officer(s):
Brenda Malcolm, Provincial Commissioner
pc.ggcnbc@gmail.com

Newfoundland & Labrador Council
63 Roosevelt Ave., St. John's NL A1A 0E8
Tel: 709-726-1116; *Fax:* 709-726-4045
Toll-Free: 800-565-8111
provoffice@ggcnf.org
www.ggcnf.org
twitter.com/GGCNL
Chief Officer(s):
Kay Penney, Provincial Commissioner

Nova Scotia Council
3581 Dutch Village Rd., Halifax NS B3N 2S9
Tel: 902-423-3735; *Fax:* 902-423-5347
Toll-Free: 800-565-8111
ggcns@girlguides.ns.ca
www.girlguides.ns.ca
twitter.com/GGCNovaScotia
Chief Officer(s):
Holly Thompson, Provincial Commissioner
holly.thompson@girlguides.ns.ca

Ontario Council
14 Birch Ave., Toronto ON M4V 1C8
Tel: 416-926-2351; *Fax:* 416-920-1440
Toll-Free: 877-323-4545
executive.coord@guidesontario.org
www.guidesontario.org
Chief Officer(s):
Marcia Powers-Dunlop, Provincial Commissioner
provincial.commissioner@guidesontario.org

Québec Council
#270, 100 boul Alexis-Nihon, Saint-Laurent QC H4M 2N7
Tel: 514-933-5839; *Fax:* 514-933-7591
Toll-Free: 800-565-8111
info@guidesquebec.ca
www.guidesquebec.ca
twitter.com/guidesquebec
Chief Officer(s):
Pamela Rice, Provincial Commissioner
pc.cp@guidesquebec.ca

Saskatchewan Council
#200, 1530 Broadway Ave., Regina SK S4P 1E2
Tel: 306-757-4102; *Fax:* 205-347-0995
Toll-Free: 877-694-0383
provincial@girlguides.sk.ca
www.girlguides.sk.ca

Gitxsan Treaty Office (GTO)
PO Box 229, Hazelton BC V0J 2N0
Fax: 250-842-6709
Toll-Free: 866-842-6780
www.gitxsan.com
www.facebook.com/GitxsanDevelopmentCorporation
Overview: A medium-sized local organization founded in 1975
Mission: To support the Gitxsan people in their treaty & other negotiations, & in their economic & social initiatives
Finances: *Funding Sources:* National & provincial government

Glace Bay Food Bank Society
PO Box 552, 2 Hector St., Glace Bay NS B1A 6G4
Tel: 902-849-0750
glacebayfoodbank@gmail.com
www.facebook.com/GlaceBayFoodBankSociety
Overview: A small local charitable organization
Member of: Nova Scotia Food Bank Association; Atlantic Alliance of Food Banks & C.V.A.'s
Chief Officer(s):
Sandra MacPherson, Coordinator

Glace Bay Literacy Council
c/o Citizen Service League, 150 Commercial St., Glace Bay NS B1A 3C1
Tel: 902-849-2449
Overview: A small local organization
Mission: To promote literacy in the Glace Bay area.
Chief Officer(s):
Leah Skanes, Contact

The Gladys & Merrill Muttart Foundation *See* The Muttart Foundation

Glanbrook Heritage Society
4280 Binbrook Rd., Binbrook ON L0R 1C0
Tel: 905-679-0245
glanbrookheritage@yahoo.ca
www.glanbrookheritage.ca
Previous Name: Glanford Heritage Society
Overview: A small local charitable organization founded in 1995 overseen by Ontario Historical Society
Mission: To collect, maintain & preserve the creation & history of the former Townships of Binbrook & Glanford, now amalgamated into the Township of Glanbrook.
Member of: Hamilton-Wentworth Heritage Association
Chief Officer(s):
Ron Sinclair, President
Marianne Brown, Secretary
Finances: *Funding Sources:* Donations; book sales
Membership: *Fees:* $15 family
Activities: *Speaker Service:* Yes; *Library:* Archives; Open to public

Glanford Heritage Society *See* Glanbrook Heritage Society

Glass & Architectural Metals Association (GAMA)
c/o Calgary Construction Association, 2725 - 12 St. NE, Calgary AB T2E 7J2
www.pgaa.ca/gama
Overview: A small local organization
Mission: To advance the glass & architectural metals industry
Chief Officer(s):
Al Ryland, President
Becky McLaughlin, Treasurer & Contact, Membership
Membership: *Member Profile:* Glass contractors, suppliers, & educators from western Canada
Activities: Supporting the glass & architectural metals industry; Providing information about safety; Assisting the apprenticeship training program; Offering networking opportunities
Meetings/Conferences: • Glass & Architectural Metals Association 2015 Annual General Meeting, March, 2015, Red Deer, AB
Scope: Provincial
Description: The yearly business meeting of the association
Publications:
• Glass & Architectural Metals Association Member Directory
Type: Directory
Profile: Contact information for association members
• Glass & Architectural Metals Association Newsletter
Type: Newsletter; *Editor:* Jeff Vitale
Profile: Updates from the association of interest to persons interested in or engaged in the glass & architectural metals industry

Glass Art Association of Canada (GAAC) / Association du verre d'art du Canada (AVAC)
c/o Marcia DeVicque, Treasurer, 9840 Porlier Pass Dr., Galiano Island BC V0N 1P0
e-mail: gaacanada@gmail.com
www.glassartcanada.ca
www.facebook.com/89639673869
www.youtube.com/gaacanada
Overview: A large international organization
Mission: To connect a geographically diverse community of artists, craftspeople, educators, curators, collectors, gallerists & students passionate about glass
Chief Officer(s):
Jamie Gray, President
gaacpresident@gmail.com
Marcia DeVicque, Treasurer
devicque@shaw.ca
Membership: 400 worldwide; *Fees:* $35-$145
Activities: Directory of Glass Artists; project grants; workshops; conferences; e-zine; scholarships; exhibitions
Publications:
• Contemporary Canadian Glass [a publication of the Glass Art Association of Canada]
Type: Magazine; *Editor:* Sally McCubbin

Glaucoma Research Society of Canada / Société canadienne de recherche sur le glaucome
#215E, 1929 Bayview Ave., Toronto ON M4G 3E8
Tel: 416-483-0200
Toll-Free: 877-483-0204
info@glaucomaresearch.ca
www.glaucomaresearch.ca
Overview: A small national charitable organization founded in 1988
Mission: The Glaucoma Research Society of Canada is a national registered charity committed to funding research into the causes, diagnosis, prevention and treatment of glaucoma.
Chief Officer(s):
Martin Chasson, President
Finances: *Funding Sources:* Donations
Membership: *Committees:* Scientific Advisory

Gleaners Food Bank
PO Box 20029, 25 Wallbridge Cres., Belleville ON K8N 5V1
Tel: 613-962-9043; *Fax:* 613-962-8627
info@gleanersfoodbank.ca
www.gleanersfoodbank.ca
www.facebook.com/profile.php?id=1789039726
ja.twitter.com/GleanersFB/status/194866801438507009
Overview: A small local charitable organization founded in 1986
Mission: To work together to improve the quality of life in Quinte & surrounding area
Member of: Ontario Association of Food Banks; Canadian Association of Food Banks; Tri-County Regional Food Network
Affiliation(s): Quinte Coalition for Social Justice; Quinte Region Food Share Shelter
Chief Officer(s):
Susanne Quinlan, Director of Operations
Staff Member(s): 2; 30 volunteer(s)
Membership: *Member Profile:* Food banks from region: Trenton, Madoc, Marmora, Stirling, Deseronto, Picton & Gleaners of Belleville
Activities: Registered site for the Canada Wide Think Food & Phones for Food Recycling Program; School Breakfast & Snack programs; emergency hamper delivery; meal programs; child care; *Awareness Events:* Fall Food Drive, Oct.; Grocery Industry Food Drives, Spring, Fall & Christmas

Glendon & District Chamber
PO Box 300, Glendon AB T0A 1P0
Tel: 780-635-2557
Overview: A small local organization

Glengarry Association for Community Living *See* Community Living Glengarry

Global Business Travel Association (Canada) (GBTA)
#919, 105-150 Crowfoot Cres. NW, Calgary AB T3G 3T2

Fax: 403-719-6336
membercare@gbta.org
www.gbta.org/canada
www.linkedin.com/groups?gid=697547
www.facebook.com/NBTAonFB
twitter.com/NBTA
www.youtube.com/gbtatv
Previous Name: National Business Travel Association (Canada)
Overview: A large international organization
Mission: To be the the leading organization for corporate travel professionals in Canada
Chief Officer(s):
Craig Banikowski, CCTE, C.P.M., C, Chair, GBTA
craig.banikowski@hilton.com
Jim McMullan, President & CEO, GBTA
jmcmullan@gbta.org
Tanya Racz, CTE, CCTE, President, GBTA Canada, 703-684-0836 Ext. 187
tracz@gbta.org
Membership: 5,000 worldwide; *Committees:* Leadership Advisory
Activities: Networking & professional development; advocacy; educational programs; *Library:* Resource Library
Meetings/Conferences: • Global Business Travel Association Canada Conference 2015, April, 2015, Toronto, ON
Scope: National
Description: Featuring over 50 exhibitors, 12 concurrent education sessions & 4 general session featured speakers
• Global Business Travel Association Canada Conference 2016, 2016
Scope: National
Description: Featuring over 50 exhibitors, 12 concurrent education sessions & 4 general session featured speakers

Global Food Bank Association Inc. ***See*** The World Job & Food Bank Inc.

Global Outreach Mission Inc.
PO Box 1210, St. Catharines ON L2R 7A7
Tel: 905-684-1401; *Fax:* 905-684-3069
Toll-Free: 866-483-5787
glmiss@on.aibn.com
www.missiongo.org
www.facebook.com/168935979827368
twitter.com/GlobalOutreachM
www.youtube.com/user/missiongo
Previous Name: European Evangelistic Crusade, Inc.
Overview: A small international organization founded in 1943
Affliation(s): Interdenominational Foreign Mission Association
Chief Officer(s):
Constable Greg, Vice-President, Candidates/Personnel
gconstable@missiongo.org

Global Village Nanaimo (GVN)
2695 Camcrest Dr., Nanaimo BC V9T 4V8
e-mail: gvnanaimo@gmail.com
globalvillagenanaimo.com
www.facebook.com/pages/Global-Village-Nanaimo/1167867106 8
Also Known As: The Fair Trade Store
Overview: A small international charitable organization founded in 1975
Mission: GVN is an independent, non-profit society selling fair trade goods in the Central Vancouver Island region. The society is run by entirely by volunteers.
Member of: BC Council for International Cooperation
Chief Officer(s):
Marjorie Stewart, Board Director
stewartm@island.net
Finances: *Annual Operating Budget:* Less than $50,000
40 volunteer(s)
Membership: 150; *Fees:* $5; *Member Profile:* General public
Activities: Store is open Oct.-Dec.

Global Youth Network ***See*** Global Youth Volunteer Network

Global Youth Volunteer Network (GYVN)
PO Box 40053, Stn. Waterloo Square, Waterloo ON N2J 4V1
Tel: 519-742-9383; *Fax:* 519-742-9383
Toll-Free: 888-411-0330
info@gyvn.ca
en.gyvn.ca
www.facebook.com/pages/Global-Youth-Network/113231510753
twitter.com/GlobalYouthNet
Previous Name: Global Youth Network
Overview: A small international organization
Mission: An international, youth-driven, grass-roots organization working to educate and mobilize young people towards making positive change.
Chief Officer(s):
Dave Skene, Founder
Nicole Ward, Director
Membership: *Fees:* $30; *Committees:* Global Sustainability; Global Education; Global Fundraising; Global Membership
Activities: Global Team program; volunteer engagement programs; summer leadership camps; community action; social justice; child sponsorship; malaria detection clinics

Global, Environmental & Outdoor Education Council (GEOEC)
c/o Barnett House, Alberta Teachers' Association, 11010 - 142 St. NW, Edmonton AB T5N 2R1
Tel: 780-987-7315; *Fax:* 780-455-6481
Toll-Free: 800-232-7208
Other Communication: membership@geoec.org
info@geoec.org
www.geoec.org
www.facebook.com/geoecalberta
www.twitter.com/geoec
Previous Name: Environmental & Outdoor Education Council of Alberta
Overview: A small provincial organization founded in 1976
Mission: To encourage professional development for teachers in the area of global, environmental, & outdoor education
Member of: Alberta Teachers' Association
Chief Officer(s):
Don McLaughlin, President
president@geoec.org
Chenoa Marcotte, Secretary
secretary@geoec.org
Suzanna Wong, Treasurer
treasurer@geoec.org
Membership: *Fees:* $12.50 students; $25 regular & life memberships; $30 subscription; *Member Profile:* Active members of the Alberta Teachers' Association; Students members of the Alberta Teachers' Association; Individuals or corporations ineligible for active or associate membership in the Alberta Teachers' Association, such as teaching assistants, parents, & libraries
Activities: Providing workshops
Awards:
• Appreciation of Serivce (Award)
• Award of Merit (Award)
• Distinguished Service (Award)
Publications:
• Connections [a publication of the Global, Environmental & Outdoor Education Council]
Type: Newsletter; *Frequency:* Quarterly; *Editor:* Noel Jantzie;
Price: Free with membership in the Global,Environmental & Outdoor Education Council
Profile: Articles & features related to global, environmental, & outdoor education

GLOBE Foundation
World Trade Centre, #578, 999 Canada Pl., Vancouver BC V6C 3E1
Tel: 604-695-5001; *Fax:* 604-695-5019
Toll-Free: 800-274-6097
info@globe.ca
www.globe.ca
Overview: A medium-sized national organization founded in 1993
Mission: To strive to find practical business-oriented solutions to environmental problems; To assist companies & individuals realize the value of economically viable environmental business opportunities
Chief Officer(s):
John D. Wiebe, President & Chief Executive Officer
ceo@globe.ca
Freddie Frankling, Vice-President, International Relations
freddie.frankling@globe.ca
Nancy Wright, Vice-President, Marketing
nancy.wright@globe.ca
Cindy Leung, Director, Finance & Administration
cindy.leung@globe.ca
John Gough, Manager, Information Technology
john.gough@globe.ca
Zahida Kanani, Manager, Registration & Database
zahida.kanani@globe.ca
Finances: *Funding Sources:* Sponsorships
Activities: Researching & consulting; Managing projects; Providing opportunities for communication; Developing partnerships
Awards:
• The GLOBE Awards for Environmental Excellence: The Award for Corporate Environmental Excellence (Award)
Presented to a Canadian corporation with a record of environmental stewardship & sustainability practices *Contact:* Carine Vindeirinho, GLOBE Awards Coordinator, Phone: 604-695-5002, Fax: 604-695-5019, E-mail: carine@globe.ca
• The GLOBE Awards for Environmental Excellence: The Award for Technology Innovation & Application (Award)
Awarded to a Canadian company or group of companies that have developed or applied an innovative technology with a significant environmental application *Contact:* Carine Vindeirinho, GLOBE Awards Coordinator, Phone: 604-695-5002, Fax: 604-695-5019, E-mail: carine@globe.ca
• The GLOBE Awards for Environmental Excellence: The Award for Excellence in Urban Sustainability (Award)
To honour a local government, private sector company, or consortium that has developed & applied beneficial urban sustainability principles *Contact:* Carine Vindeirinho, GLOBE Awards Coordinator, Phone: 604-695-5002, Fax: 604-695-5019, E-mail: carine@globe.ca
• The GLOBE Awards for Environmental Excellence: The Award for Best Green Consumer Product (Award)
To recognize a Canadian company or group of companies that is pursing new & emerging technologies, or has advanced current environmental technologies *Contact:* Carine Vindeirinho, GLOBE Awards Coordinator, Phone: 604-695-5002, Fax: 604-695-5019, E-mail: carine@globe.ca
• The GLOBE Awards for Environmental Excellence: The Finance Award for Sustainability (Award)
To recognize a North American fund manager, a global fund manager, a commercial bank, an investment bank, a private bank, an investment broker, an asset management company, a venture capital firm, or an investment advisor who developed portfolios, investment instruments, analytical tools, or funds for Canadian environmental markets *Contact:* Carine Vindeirinho, GLOBE Awards Coordinator, Phone: 604-695-5002, Fax: 604-695-5019, E-mail: carine@globe.ca
Meetings/Conferences: • GLOBE 2016 13th Biennial Conference & Trade Fair on Business & the Environment, March, 2016, Vancouver Convention Centre - East Building, Vancouver, BC
Scope: International
Attendance: 10,000+
Description: A global gathering of government leaders, senior executives, & NGO representatives, from more than seventy countries, to share experiences & explore new opportunities during conference sessions & interactive networking opportunities, & to see the most recent environmental & clean technologies at the international trade show
Contact Information: General Information: Phone: 604-695-5001, Toll-Free Phone: 1-800-274-6097, E-mail: info@globeseries.com; Exhibiting Information, E-mail: sales@globeseries.com; URL: www.globeseries.com
Publications:
• GLOBE-Net Environmental Business E-Newsletter
Type: Newsletter; *Frequency:* Weekly

Globe Theatre Society
Globe Theatre, Prince Edward Bldg., 1801 Scarth St., Regina SK S4P 2G9
Tel: 306-525-9553; *Fax:* 306-352-4194
Toll-Free: 866-954-5623
onstage@globetheatrelive.com
www.globetheatrelive.com
www.facebook.com/globetheatrelive
twitter.com/GlobeRegina
www.youtube.com/user/GlobeTheatreRegina
Overview: A small local charitable organization founded in 1966
Mission: To create & produce professional theatre & make it accessible with a view to entertain, educate & challenge
Member of: Professional Association of Canadian Theatres
Affliation(s): Canadian Actors' Equity
Chief Officer(s):
Ruth Smillie, Artistic Director
ruths@globetheatrelive.com
Finances: *Funding Sources:* Canada Council; Saskatchewan Arts Board; City of Regina
Staff Member(s): 18
Activities: *Speaker Service:* Yes

Gloucester Arts Council ***See*** Arts Ottawa East-Est

Gloucester Chamber of Commerce *See* Eastern Ottawa Chamber of Commerce

Gloucester Historical Society / Société historique de Gloucester
4550B Bank St., Gloucester ON K1T 3W6
Tel: 613-822-2076
english@gloucesterhistory.com
www.gloucesterhistory.com
Overview: A small local organization
Mission: To research, collect, preserve & promote the history of Gloucester & its environs through its publications & historical documents & photographs.
Finances: *Funding Sources:* Municipal government; donations
Membership: *Fees:* $20 annual; $150 life
Activities: *Library:* Research Room; Open to public

GO Rowing & Paddling Association of Canada
#105, 2940 Jutland Rd., Victoria BC V8T 5K6
Tel: 250-658-6333; *Fax:* 250-658-6340
Toll-Free: 866-658-6333
info@gorowandpaddle.org
www.gorowandpaddle.org
www.facebook.com/gorowandpaddle
twitter.com/gorowandpaddle
Also Known As: GO
Overview: A small national charitable organization founded in 1996
Mission: To promote & advance rowing & paddling sports in Canada.
Activities: Operating rowing & paddling centres; program development; fundraising; sponsorship; community based programs

God, Sex, & the Meaning of Life Ministry (GSML Ministry)
889 Finley Ave., Ajax ON L1S 3S5
Tel: 905-427-6137
gsmlministry@gmail.com
www.godsexandthemeaningoflife.com
Also Known As: Theology of the Body Team
Overview: A small national organization founded in 2006
Mission: To provide Catholic Church teaching in areas of sexuality for married, single, & celibate people, based on Pope John Paul II's "Theology of the Body"
Affliation(s): Archdiocese of Toronto
Chief Officer(s):
Susan Kennedy, Primary Contact
Rose Heron, Contact, 905-683-9055
Jan Noonan, Contact, 905-420-8696
Membership: *Member Profile:* Lay volunteers help in all areas of the ministry; Trained volunteer facilitators offer workshops
Activities: Offering faith instruction workshops & resources for youth, singles, couples, & seniors
Publications:
• God, Sex, & the Meaning of Life Newsletter
Type: Newsletter

Goderich & District Chamber of Commerce *See* Huron Chamber of Commerce - Goderich, Central & North Huron

Goethe-Institut (Montréal)
#100, 1626, boul St-Laurent, Montréal QC H2X 2T1
Tel: 514-499-0159; *Fax:* 514-499-0905
info@montreal.goethe.org
www.goethe.de/montreal
www.facebook.com/GoetheInstitutMontreal
twitter.com/GI_Montreal
Overview: A small local organization
Mission: The Goethe-Institur is the cultural institue of the Federal Republic of Germany with a global reach. They promote knowledge of the German language abroad and foster international cultural cooperation. They convey a comprehensive picture of Germany by providing information on Germany's cultural, social, and political life. They perform the principle talks of cultural and educational policy, they work in partnership with public and private cultural bodies, the German federal states and municipalities, and the corporate sector.

Goethe-Institut (Toronto)
North Tower, PO Box 136, #201, 100 University Ave., Toronto ON M5J 1V6
Tel: 416-593-5257; *Fax:* 416-593-5145
info@toronto.goethe.org
www.goethe.de/toronto
www.facebook.com/GoetheToronto
twitter.com/GoetheToronto
Also Known As: German Cultural Centre
Overview: A medium-sized local organization founded in 1962
Mission: To provide cultural programs, international cultural cooperation, German language teaching, & library & information services
Chief Officer(s):
Uwe Rau, Director
director@toronto.goethe.org
Venuta Recio, Deputy Director
language@toronto.goethe.org
Hannah Day, Program & Office Assistant
office@toronto.goethe.org
Finances: *Annual Operating Budget:* $500,000-$1.5 Million; *Funding Sources:* Foreign Affairs Dept. of the Federal Republic of Germany
Staff Member(s): 9
Activities: Film series spring/fall; exhibitions of art & photography; language courses; pedagogic development; information services on Germany; *Internships:* Yes; *Library* Open to public

Gogama Chamber of Commerce
c/o Gogama CAP Committee, PO Box 116, Gogama ON P0M 1W0
Tel: 705-894-2111
gogamachamber@vianet.ca
www.gogama.ca/organizations.html#chamber
Overview: A small local organization

Goh Ballet Society
2345 Main St., Vancouver BC V5T 3C9
Tel: 604-872-4014; *Fax:* 604-872-4011
admin@gohballet.com
www.gohballet.com
www.facebook.com/pages/Goh-Ballet/105951356102489
twitter.com/GohBallet
www.youtube.com/user/GohBallet
Overview: A small local organization founded in 1978
Mission: To prepare aspiring dancers for professional careers by providing rigorous training in the vocabulary & artistry of classical ballet.
Chief Officer(s):
Chan Hon Goh, Director
Membership: *Committees:* Volunteer

Gold River Chamber of Commerce
PO Box 39, Gold River BC V0P 1G0
Tel: 250-285-2724
goldriverchamber@gmail.com
www.goldriver.ca
Overview: A small local organization
Chief Officer(s):
Dawn Dakin, President
Norm Cowie, Vice-President
15 volunteer(s)
Membership: 51; *Fees:* $60

Golden & District Chamber of Commerce *See* Kicking Horse Country Chamber of Commerce

Golden Age Society
4061A - 4th Ave., Whitehorse YT Y1A 1H1
Tel: 867-668-5538
goldenagesociety@gmail.com
yukon-seniors-and-elders.org/goldenage/goldenage.home.htm
Overview: A small provincial organization founded in 1976
Mission: To promote & give opportunity for social, recreational activities for seniors in the Yukon
Membership: *Fees:* $20

Golden District Arts Council
PO Box 228, Golden BC V0A 1H0
Tel: 250-344-6186
info@kickinghorseculture.ca
www.kickinghorseculture.ca
twitter.com/goldenculture
www.youtube.com/user/khcgdac
Also Known As: Kicking Horse Culture
Overview: A small local organization founded in 1970
Mission: To stimulate and encourage the development of the arts in the Golden area through interaction with the public
Member of: Assembly of BC Arts Councils; Kootenay Cultural Network of the Rockies
Chief Officer(s):
Bill Usher, Executive Director
director@kickinghorseculture.ca
Monica Parkinson, Chair
Finances: *Funding Sources:* Private; government
Membership: 800; *Fees:* $10 adults/seniors; $20 family
Activities: Performance Series; Children's Festival; Art Gallery; Student Art Show; X-mas Craft Fair; Summer Music Series; *Internships:* Yes

Golden Food Bank
PO Box 1047, #102, 115 - 9th St. South, Golden BC V0A 1H0
Tel: 250-344-2113
info@goldenfoodbank.ca
goldenfoodbank.ca
Overview: A small local charitable organization founded in 1981 overseen by Food Banks British Columbia
Mission: The agency provides food for the needy in the local area
Member of: Food Banks British Columbia
Chief Officer(s):
Barb Davies, Director

Golden Horseshoe Beekeepers' Association
Brantford ON
Tel: 519-752-8766
www.goldenhorseshoebeekeepers.ca
Overview: A small local organization founded in 1980
Mission: To provide educational information to Hamilton & Halton Region's beekeepers
Member of: Ontario Beekeepers' Association
Chief Officer(s):
Jim Henderson, President
jimhenderson93@hotmail.com
Membership: *Member Profile:* Professional & hobbyist beekeepers in Hamilton & the surrounding region
Activities: Organizing meetings at the Marritt Hall in Jerseyville, Ontario; Providing opportunities to network; Removing swarms of honey bees

Golden Horseshoe Co-operative Housing Federation (GHCHF)
#1A, 36 Keefer Crt., Hamilton ON L8E 4V4
Tel: 905-561-2667; *Fax:* 905-561-1153
ghchf@primus.ca
www.ghchf.ca
Overview: A small local organization founded in 1986
Mission: To act as a collective voice for housing co-ops & associated organizations in the Hamilton/Niagara regions.
Membership: 52; 44 housing cooperatives; *Member Profile:* Housing co-operatives; service managers; property management companies
Activities: Workshops & training for co-op members & staff

Golden Opportunities Vocational Rehabilitation Centre Workshop
PO Box 887, 32 Industrial Park, Springhill NS B0M 1X0
Tel: 902-597-3158
www.nsnet.org/govrc
Also Known As: GOVRC Workshop
Overview: A small local organization
Mission: To offer vocational training for mentally challenged adults
Member of: DIRECTIONS Council for Vocational Services Society
Chief Officer(s):
Joanne Hunter, Executive Director/Manager
Activities: Woodworking; packaging; ornaments; flyers; fundraising kits; assembling; collating & sorting; wreaths & bow making; gardening

Golden Prairie Arts Council (GPAC)
PO Box 2103, 38 Centre Ave. West, Carman MB R0G 0J0
Tel: 204-745-6568
gpaccarman@gmail.com
www.gparts.ca
www.facebook.com/group.php?gid=43647958167
Overview: A small local organization founded in 1996
Mission: To support fine arts in Manitoba's south central region
Chief Officer(s):
Larry Jeffers, Chair
Kathy Wikdahl, Treasurer
Finances: *Funding Sources:* Manitoba Arts Council; Grants; Fundraising
Activities: Operating a gallery; Hosting art shows; Mentoring artists; Organizing programs, such as "Artists in the School"; Offering an annual members' art sale; Providing music classes; Hosting musical performances; Offering workshops;

Golden Rock & Fossil Club
PO Box 2542, Golden BC V0A 1H0

Tel: 250-344-2108
goldenrockandfossilclub@gmail.com
Overview: A small local organization
Member of: Lapidary, Rock & Mineral Society of British Columbia
Chief Officer(s):
Stan Walker, Contact
Activities: Hunting for rocks & minerals, lapidary

The Golden Triangle Parrot Club

ON
e-mail: info@gtpc.ca
www.gtpc.ca
Overview: A small local organization
Mission: To provide an informative and entertaining environment for lovers of Psittacines
Member of: Avicultural Advancement Council of Canada

Golden Women's Resource Centre Society (GWRCS)

PO Box 2343, 419C - 9th Ave. North, Golden BC V0H 1H0
Tel: 250-344-5317; *Fax:* 750-344-2565; *Crisis Hot-Line:* 250-344-2101
gwrced@uniserve.com
www.goldenwomencentre.ca
www.facebook.com/groups/gwrcfriends
twitter.com/gwrc1
Overview: A small local charitable organization founded in 1978
Mission: GWRCS operates the Golden Women's Resource Centre which provides a safe, non-judgmental, welcoming environment for women to gather, relax, share ideas & get support. It is actively engaged in efforts to end violence against women & their children, & strives to improve the economic, social & legal situation of women in the home, workplace, community & world at large. It is a registered charity, BN: 107438996RR0001.
Affliation(s): British Columbia/Yukon Society of Transition Houses; British Columbia Coalition of Women's Centres
Chief Officer(s):
Melanie Myers, Outreach Coordinator & ED
Roni Beauregard, Safehomes Coordinator
safehomes@redshift.bc.ca
Finances: *Annual Operating Budget:* $50,000-$100,000; *Funding Sources:* National & provincial government; Status of Women Canada; Ministry of Women's Equality
Membership: 100 individual
Activities: Counselling; educational workshops, internet access; *Awareness Events:* International Women's Day, March 8; Prevention of Violence Against Women Week, April; Take Back the Night, Sept.; Women's History Month, Oct.

Goldstream Food Bank Society

PO Box 28122, Stn. Westshore Town Centre, Victoria BC V9B 6K8
Tel: 250-474-4443
foodbank.islandnet.com
Overview: A small local charitable organization founded in 1983 overseen by Food Banks British Columbia
Mission: To provide food hampers & advocacy to community members in need.
Member of: Food Banks British Columbia
Membership: *Fees:* $5

Golf Association of Ontario (GAO)

PO Box 970, Uxbridge ON L9P 1N3
Tel: 905-852-1101; *Fax:* 905-852-8893
administration@gao.ca
www.gao.ca
www.facebook.com/GAOGolf
twitter.com/GAOGolf
instagram.com/gaogolf
Merged from: Ontario Golf Association; Ontario Ladies Golf Association
Overview: A large provincial organization founded in 2001 overseen by Royal Canadian Golf Association
Mission: To develop & promote golf in the province
Chief Officer(s):
Jim King, President
Steve Carroll, Executive Director
scarroll@gao.ca
Dave Colling, Director, Rules & Competitions
dcolling@gao.ca
Mike Kelly, Managing Director, Sport Development
mkelly@gao.ca
Craig Loughryne, Director, Handicapping & Course Rating
cloughry@gao.ca
Kyle McFarlane, Director, Marketing & Communications
kmcfarlane@gao.ca
Kate Sheldon, Director, Administration
ksheldon@gao.ca
Finances: *Funding Sources:* Membership dues; Tournament entry fees
Staff Member(s): 19
Membership: 115,000 individuals, 420 member clubs; *Fees:* $27.50 Adult; $18 Junior; *Member Profile:* Golfers who are members of private, semi-private or public golf courses; *Committees:* Governance & Nominating; Finance & Risk Management; Hall of Fame; Handicap & Course Rating; Sport; Membership; Marketing & Sponsorship; Scholarship; District Coordinators; Human Resources & Compensation
Activities: Offering tournaments, junior camps, & programming; *Internships:* Yes
Awards:
• Marlene Streit Award Fund (Award)
• Ken Trowbridge Legacy Fund (Award)
• GAO Scholarship Program (Scholarship)

Golf Canada Foundation

#1, 1333 Dorval Dr., Oakville ON L6M 4X7
Tel: 905-849-9700; *Fax:* 905-845-7040
Toll-Free: 800-263-0009
www.golfcanadafoundation.com
Also Known As: RCGA Foundation
Previous Name: Canadian Golf Foundation
Overview: A medium-sized national charitable organization founded in 1979
Mission: To raise & grant funds for the betterment of golf in Canada
Chief Officer(s):
Spencer Snell, Operations Manager, Golf Canada Foundation
ssnell@golfcanada.ca
Finances: *Funding Sources:* Private & corporate donations
Staff Member(s): 2
Activities: *Internships:* Yes

Golf Manitoba Inc.

#420, 145 Pacific Ave., Winnipeg MB R3B 2Z6
Tel: 204-925-5730; *Fax:* 204-925-5731
golfmb@golfmanitoba.mb.ca
golfmanitoba.mb.ca
www.facebook.com/217256961725416
twitter.com/golf_manitoba
Previous Name: Manitoba Golf Association Inc.
Overview: A small provincial organization founded in 1915 overseen by Royal Canadian Golf Association
Mission: The Association determines policies & standards relating to the development & promotion of golf in the province.
Chief Officer(s):
Rob MacDonald, President
Dave Comaskey, Executive Director, 204-295-5729
dcomaskey@golfmanitoba.mb.ca
Awards:
• Manitoba Golf Scholarship Fund (Scholarship)
The fund has its own board of directors & is a registered charity, BN: 898823539RR0001. Eligibility: Young golfers entering or continuing in a post-secondary educational institution in Canada *Amount:* $1000, but depends on fund size

Golf Newfoundland & Labrador (GNL)

6 Lester St., St. John's NL A1E 2P6
Tel: 709-364-3534
golf@hnl.ca
www.golfnewfoundland.ca
www.facebook.com/pages/Golf-NL/178044602356289
Previous Name: Newfoundland & Labrador Golf Association
Overview: A medium-sized provincial organization overseen by Royal Canadian Golf Association
Chief Officer(s):
Greg Hillier, Executive Director
Membership: 20 clubs
Activities: Providing information about golf courses in Newfoundland & Labrador; Promoting golf in the province

Good Jobs Coalition *See* Good Jobs for All Coalition

Good Jobs for All Coalition

Toronto ON
Tel: 416-937-9378
communications@goodjobsforall.ca
goodjobsforall.ca
www.facebook.com/groups/goodjobs
twitter.com/goodjobsforall
Previous Name: Good Jobs Coalition
Overview: A medium-sized local organization founded in 2008
Mission: The Good Jobs for All Coalition is an alliance of community, labour, social justice, youth and environmental organizations in the Toronto region. It was formed in 2008 to start a focused dialogue on how to improve living and working conditions in Canada's largest urban centre.
Chief Officer(s):
Preethy Sivakumar, Coordinator
Publications:
• L'ACELF en Action
Type: Newsletter; *Frequency:* Monthly

Good News Broadcasting Association of Canada

PO Box 246, Stn. A, Abbotsford BC V2T 6Z6
Toll-Free: 800-663-2425
bttb@backtothebible.ca
www.backtothebible.ca
www.facebook.com/BTTBCanada
twitter.com/BTTBC
Also Known As: Back to the Bible Canada
Overview: A small local charitable organization
Member of: Canadian Council of Christian Charities; Evangelican Fellowship of Canada
Chief Officer(s):
Byron Reaume, CFO & Director of Stewardship
Bob Beasley, CEO
Staff Member(s): 6
Meetings/Conferences: • 2nd Annual Back to the Bible Canada / Laugh Again ministry cruise, March, 2015, Various, Caribbean
Scope: National
Description: Cruise conference including Bible teaching & engagement; inspirational speaking, worship & special music

Good Shepherd Refuge *See* Good Shepherd Refuge Social Ministries

Good Shepherd Refuge Social Ministries

412 Queen St. East, Toronto ON M5A 1T3
Tel: 416-869-6319; *Fax:* 416-869-0510
info@goodshepherd.ca
www.goodshepherd.ca
www.linkedin.com/company/good-shepherd-ministries
www.facebook.com/285444011485206
twitter.com/goodshepherd_to
Also Known As: Good Shepherd Ministries
Previous Name: Good Shepherd Refuge
Overview: A small local charitable organization founded in 1963
Mission: To provide services to homeless, disadvantaged, marginalized people; to provide the basic necessities of food, shelter & a host of ancillary services, ensuring each client justice, equality, dignity & acceptance; to provide human services that will assist clients in regaining freedom from homelessness
Member of: Ontario Hostels Association
Chief Officer(s):
Werner (Vern) Frank Zapfe, Chair
David Lynch, Executive Director
Aklilu Wendaferew, Assistant Executive Director
Finances: *Annual Operating Budget:* Greater than $5 Million; *Funding Sources:* Donations; government grants
Staff Member(s): 70; 7000 volunteer(s)
Membership: *Committees:* Fundraising
Activities: Operates Good Shepherd Centre: provides shelter, clothing, daily meals, drop-in, medical & housing services; Barrett House: residence for people living with HIV/AIDS; St. Joseph's Residence: longterm care supportive housing for elderly homeless men with physical &/or mental health problems
Publications:
• Good Shepherd Journal
Type: Newsletter; *Frequency:* Bi-annual; *Editor:* Adrienne Urquhart; *Price:* Free to supporters
Profile: Provides client, service & donor updates.

Goodsoil & District Chamber of Commerce

PO Box 88, Goodsoil SK S0M 1A0
Tel: 306-238-2033; *Fax:* 306-238-4441
Overview: A small local organization

Goodwill Industries

255 Horton St., London ON N6B 1L1
Tel: 519-850-9000; *Fax:* 519-645-8610
info@goodwillindustries.ca
www.goodwillindustries.ca
twitter.com/Goodwill_OGL
www.youtube.com/user/GoodwillOGLakes
Previous Name: London Goodwill Industries Association
Overview: A medium-sized local organization founded in 1943

Mission: To provide programs & services that enhance the employability of people with barriers or diminished opportunities; to provide & recycle goods
Member of: Goodwill Industries International Inc.
Chief Officer(s):
Michelle Quintyn, President & CEO
mquintyn@goodwillindustries.ca
Finances: *Funding Sources:* Retail; government
Activities: Collects donations of clothing & house wares; operates retail stores; administers three career centres; *Speaker Service:* Yes

Goodwill Industries Essex Kent Lambton
1121 Wellington St., Sarnia ON N7S 6J7
Tel: 519-332-0440
info@goodwillekl.com
www.goodwillekl.com
www.facebook.com/GoodwillEKL
Overview: A small local charitable organization founded in 1933
Mission: To promote dignity & independence; To provide employment & training programs to assist people with employment barriers; To help people develop life skills
Chief Officer(s):
Kevin Smith, Chief Executive Officer
ksmith@goodwillekl.com
Maryam Foroughian, Chief Financial Officer
mforoughian@goodwillekl.com
Christopher Chartrand, Director, Marketing & Fund Development
cchartrand@goodwillekl.com
Janine Downes, Director, Human Resources
jdownes@goodwillekl.com
Kevin Neill, Director, Operations & Retail
kneill@goodwillekl.com
Michelle Repuski, Director, Workforce Development
mrepuski@goodwillccc.com
Benica Barton, Manager, Operations / Retail
bbarton@goodwillekl.com
John Rooke, Manager, Accounting
jrooke@goodwillekl.com
Finances: *Funding Sources:* Donations
Activities: Operating stores

Goodwill Industries of Alberta
8761 - 51 Ave., Edmonton AB T6E 5H1
Tel: 780-944-1414
Toll-Free: 866-927-1414
media@goodwill.ab.ca
www.goodwill.ab.ca
www.facebook.com/GoodwillAB
twitter.com/goodwillab
www.youtube.com/GoodwillAB
Overview: A medium-sized provincial charitable organization founded in 1951
Mission: To help persons with disabilities & disadvantages; To build a strong future through rehabilitation & training
Member of: Goodwill Industries International
Affliation(s): United Way of the Capital Region
Chief Officer(s):
Larry Brownoff, Chair
Dale Monaghan, President & CEO
Finances: *Funding Sources:* Revenue from retail thrift stores; United Way; Alberta Family & Social Services
Membership: *Committees:* Review; Governance
Activities: *Awareness Events:* Goodwill Week, 1st week of May

Goodwill Industries of Toronto
#1400, 365 Bloor St. East, Toronto ON M4W 3L4
Tel: 416-362-4711; *Fax:* 416-362-0720; *TTY:* 416-815-4791
info@goodwill.on.ca
www.goodwill.on.ca
Previous Name: Goodwill Toronto
Overview: A large local charitable organization founded in 1935
Mission: To provide effective vocational programs & services to people who face employment barriers to enable them to become as independent as possible
Member of: Goodwill Industries International
Chief Officer(s):
Keiko Nakamura, CEO
Finances: *Annual Operating Budget:* Greater than $5 Million; *Funding Sources:* 86% self-generated, mostly by collection & sale of donated goods
Staff Member(s): 930; 250 volunteer(s)
Activities: Employment services include: vocational assessment, work tolerance assessment, placement services, transitional/supported employment; Work training includes: computer skills, customer service, janitorial & maintenance, small engine repair; *Speaker Service:* Yes

Goodwill Toronto *See* Goodwill Industries of Toronto

Goodwill, The Amity Group
225 King William St., Hamilton ON L8R 1B1
Tel: 905-526-8482
www.goodwillonline.ca
www.facebook.com/GoodwillIntl
twitter.com/JobsGoodwill
www.youtube.com/GoodwillIntl
Previous Name: Amity Goodwill Industries
Overview: A large national organization founded in 1935
Mission: To enrich the community by providing vocational rehabilitation programmes & services to assist people challenged by disabilities & special needs to achieve maximum employment, community participations & self-fulfilment
Affliation(s): Canadian Association of Goodwill Industries; Goodwill Industries International
Chief Officer(s):
Jean Anne Farmilo, Chair
Paul Chapin, President & CEO, 905-526-8482 Ext. 222
Albert Deveau, Vice-President, Retail & Donated Goods, 905-338-6240
Finances: *Annual Operating Budget:* Greater than $5 Million; *Funding Sources:* Provincial government; donations
Staff Member(s): 230; 53 volunteer(s)
Membership: 18 associate
Activities: Accepting donations of household & business goods; operating Value Centre locations around the GTA; offering contract services; providing employment opportunities; *Awareness Events:* Tastes of Downtown Walking Restaurant Tour
Awards:
• Annual Outstanding Achievement Awards (Award)
Publications:
• Goodwill, The Amity Group Newsletter
Type: Newsletter

Gorsebrook Research Institute for Atlantic Canada Studies
Saint Mary's University, 5960 Inglis St., Halifax NS B3H 3C3
Tel: 902-420-5668; *Fax:* 902-496-8135
gorsebrook@smu.ca
www.smu.ca/administration/gorsebrook/
Overview: A small local organization founded in 1982
Mission: The Institute administers an interdisciplinary research centre concerned with social, economic, & cultural issues specific to Canada's Atlantic Region. It encourages research pertaining to the region, its culture, history, etc.
Chief Officer(s):
John Reid, Chair
Peter L. Twohig, Executive Director, 902-420-5447
peter.twohig@smu.ca
Finances: *Funding Sources:* Federal government; projects; The Austin Willis Moving Images Research Centre
Staff Member(s): 3
Activities: Ongoing Fisheries & Coastal Seminar series; Labrador Project; James Bay Project; conferences, symposia, workshops; Community Seascapes; History of Moving Images in Nova Scotia; Literacy Project

Gospel Tract & Bible Society
PO Box 180, Ste. Anne MB R5H 1R1
Tel: 204-355-4975
info@gospeltract.ca
e-menno.org/tracts.htm
Overview: A small national organization
Mission: Publishes Christian religious tracts; affiliated with Church of God in Christ, Mennonite.

Governing Board of Dental Technicians of Ontario *See* College of Dental Technologists of Ontario

Government Finance Officers Association of British Columbia (GFOABC)
#408 - 612 View St., Victoria BC V8W 1J5
Tel: 250-382-6871
office@gfoabc.ca
www.gfoabc.ca
twitter.com/GFOABC
Overview: A medium-sized provincial organization founded in 1989 overseen by Government Finance Officers Association
Mission: A not-for-profit organization that represents local government finance officers in BC.
Chief Officer(s):
Rob Bullock, Executive Director
rbullock@gfoabc.ca
Membership: 1000
Meetings/Conferences: • 2015 Government Finance Officers Association of British Columbia Annual Conference, May, 2015, Penticton, BC
Scope: Provincial

Government Services Union (GSU) / Syndicat des services gouvernementaux
#705, 233 Gilmour St., Ottawa ON K2P 0P2
Tel: 613-560-4395; *Fax:* 613-230-6774
www.gsu-ssg.ca
Merged from: Supply & Services Union; Union of Public Works Employees
Overview: A medium-sized national organization founded in 1999 overseen by Public Service Alliance of Canada (CLC)
Mission: Their members provide compensation, audit, procurement, disposal telecommunications and informatics, translation, real property and reciever general services to some 100 federal government departments and agencies. They also provide information about government programmes and research the opinions of Canadians.
Chief Officer(s):
Donna Lackie, President, 613-560-4395
lackied@psac-afpc.com
Staff Member(s): 9
Membership: 7,000 in 32 locals; *Member Profile:* Employees at Public Works & Government Services Canada, Shared Services Canada, the Royal Canadian Mint & Metcalfe Realty

Governor General's Performing Arts Awards Foundation (GGPAAF) / Les Prix du Gouverneur Général pour les arts de la scène
#804, 130 Albert St., Ottawa ON K1P 5G4
Tel: 613-241-5297; *Fax:* 613-238-4849
www.bell.ca/ggawards
Overview: A medium-sized national charitable organization founded in 1992
Mission: To celebrate outstanding lifetime achievement in various performing arts disciplines in Canada; To raise awareness of the contributions of Canadian performing artists; To foster awareness of Francophone artists in English Canada & Anglophone artists in French Canada; To inspire future performing artists
Chief Officer(s):
Whitney Taylor, Director
whitneytaylor@ggpaa.ca
Peter Herrndorf, President/CEO
Harold Redekopp, Co-Chair
Albert Millaire, Co-Chair
Finances: *Funding Sources:* Fundraising; Sponsorships
Activities: Coordinating the nomination & selection processes; Organizing events related the the awards presentation; Forming partnerhips
Awards:
• Governor General's Performing Arts Awards (Award)
Established in 1992; honours six performing artists for their lifetime achievement & contribution to the cultural enrichment of Canada; each recipient is awarded $15,000 & a commemorative medal
• The National Arts Centre Award (Award)
Recognizes work of an extraordinary nature & significance in the performing arts by an individual artist &/or company in the past performance year; recipients receive a $15,000 cash award donated by the NAC Foundation & an original sculpture by Wei Yew
• Ramon John Hnatyshyn Award for Voluntarism in the Performing Arts (Award)
Recognizes outstanding service to the performing arts; the recipient is presented with a specially commissioned artwork by Canadian glass artist Naoko Takenouchi

Grace Communion International Canada
#101, 5668 - 192 St., Surrey BC V3S 2V7
Tel: 604-575-2705; *Fax:* 604-575-2758
info@gcicanada.ca
www.gcicanada.ca/welcome.php
Previous Name: Worldwide Church of God Canada
Overview: A small national organization
Mission: To proclaim the gospel of Jesus Christ around the world & to help members grow spiritually
Chief Officer(s):
Gary Moore, National Director
gmoore@telus.net

Publications:
• Northern Light
Type: Magazine; *Frequency:* Quarterly

Grahamdale Chamber of Commerce
R.M. Of Grahamdale Administration Office, PO Box 160, 23 Government Rd., Moosehorn MB R0C 2E0
Tel: 204-768-2858; *Fax:* 204-768-3374
info@grahamdale.ca
www.grahamdale.ca
Overview: A small local organization
Mission: Creating and supporting business in Grahamdale and surrounding areas.
Chief Officer(s):
Karen Bittner, President
krbittner@mb.sympatico.ca

Grain Farmers of Ontario
Ontario AgriCentre, #201, 100 Stone Rd. West, Guelph ON N1G 5L3
Fax: 519-767-9713
Toll-Free: 800-265-0550
info@gfo.ca
www.gfo.ca
Merged from: Ontario Soybean Growers; Ontario Corn Producers' Association; Ontario Wheat Producers' Marketing Bd.
Overview: A medium-sized provincial organization
Mission: To develop an innovative & successful business environment to benefit farmer members; To promote the Ontario grain industry to become a global leader
Chief Officer(s):
Barry Senft, Chief Executive Officer
bsenft@gfo.ca
Ryan Brown, Vice-President, Operations
rbrown@gfo.ca
John Cowan, Vice-President, Strategic Development
jcowan@gfo.ca
Todd Austin, Manager, Marketing
taustin@gfo.ca
Crosby Devitt, Manager, Research & Market Development
cdevitt@gfo.ca
Tom Farfaras, Manager, Finance & Administration
tfarfaras@gfo.ca
Erin Fletcher, Manager, Public Affairs & Communications
efletcher@gfo.ca
Brenda Miller-Sanford, Manager, Projects
bmsanford@gfo.ca
Membership: 15,000-49,999; *Member Profile:* Ontario's growers of soybeans, corn, & wheat
Activities: Researching; Expanding markets; Encouraging new uses for Ontario grains; Engaging in advocacy activities
Meetings/Conferences: • Grain Farmers of Ontario 2015 March Classic, March, 2015, ON
Scope: Provincial
Attendance: 500+
Description: A gathering of representatives from government, industry, & farms throughout Ontario to attend presentations about trade, world markets, & new oppotunities
Contact Information: E-mail: info@gfo.ca

Grain Growers of Canada (GGC)
#912, 350 Sparks St., Ottawa ON K1R 7S8
Tel: 613-233-9954; *Fax:* 613-236-3590
office@ggc-pgc.ca
www.ggc-pgc.ca
Overview: A small national organization
Mission: To supprt policies that allow for a competitive global farming industry
Affliation(s): Alberta Barley Commission; Alberta Oat, Rye & Triticale Association; Alberta Pulse Growers; Alberta Wheat Commission; Atlantic Grains Council; British Columbia Grain Producers Association; Canadian Canola Growers Association; Canadian Young Farmers Forum; Manitoba Corn Growers Association; Prairie Oat Growers Association; Western Barley Growers Association; Western Canadian Wheat Growers Association
Chief Officer(s):
Stephen Vandervalk, President
Janet Krayden, Manager, Public Affairs
Membership: 14; *Member Profile:* Groups involved in the grain, pulse & oilseed industries

Grain Services Union (CLC) (GSU) / Syndicat des services du grain (CTC)
2334 McIntyre St., Regina SK S4P 2S2
Tel: 306-522-6686; *Fax:* 306-565-3430
Toll-Free: 866-522-6686
gsu.regina@sasktel.net
www.gsu.ca
Overview: A medium-sized national organization founded in 1936
Mission: They represent Saskatchewan Wheat Pool Workers and represent members working for a variety of companies within Canada.
Affliation(s): Interntaionl Longshore and Warehouse Union
Chief Officer(s):
Carolyn Illerbrun, President
Hugh J. Wagner, Secretary/Manager
Membership: 1,500

Grain Workers' Union, Local 333 (GWU)
#103- 3989 Henning Dr., Vancouver BC V5C 6P8
Tel: 604-254-8635; *Fax:* 604-254-6254
local333@telus.net
www.grainworkersunion.com
Overview: A small provincial organization
Mission: A Canadian Union representing members in the Ports of Vancouver and Prince Rupert.
Member of: National Union of Public and General Employees
Affliation(s): BC Government & Service Employees' Union; Canadian Labour Congress
Chief Officer(s):
Gerry Gault, President
gerryis@telus.net
Kevin Ling, Sec.-Treas.
Staff Member(s): 2
Membership: 800+

Grand Bend & Area Chamber of Commerce
PO Box 248, #1, 81 Crescent St., Grand Bend ON N0M 1T0
Tel: 519-238-2001; *Fax:* 519-238-5201
Toll-Free: 888-338-2001
info@grandbendtourism.com
www.grandbendtourism.com
Overview: A small local organization founded in 1975
Chief Officer(s):
Susan Mills, Manager
Finances: *Annual Operating Budget:* Less than $50,000; *Funding Sources:* Membership dues
Staff Member(s): 2
Membership: 190
Activities: *Library*

Grand Centre Canadian Native Friendship Centre ***See*** Cold Lake Native Friendship Centre

Grand Chapitre des Maçons de l'Arche Royale du Québec ***See*** Grand Chapter, Royal Arch Masons of Québec

Grand Chapter, R.A.M. of Nova Scotia
www.grandchapterram.org
Overview: A medium-sized provincial organization founded in 1869
Chief Officer(s):
Frederick W. Richard, Grand Secretary
Finances: *Annual Operating Budget:* Less than $50,000
Staff Member(s): 1
Membership: 988

Grand Chapter, Royal Arch Masons of Québec / Grand Chapitre des Maçons de l'Arche Royale du Québec
#404B, 2295 St. Marc Rd., Montréal QC H3H 2G9
e-mail: admin@royalarchmasonsofquebec.ca
www.royalarchmasonsofquebec.ca
Overview: A small provincial organization
Mission: To pursue excellence in masonry
Chief Officer(s):
Paul Arturi, M.Ex.Comp.
Membership: *Member Profile:* Master Masons in good standing of a Craft Lodge; *Committees:* Jurisprudence, Grievances & Appeals; State of the Order; Finance; Ritual, Rites & Ceremonies; Credentials; Grand Convocation Social Affair

Grand Conseil des Cris ***See*** Grand Council of the Crees

Grand Council of the Crees / Grand Conseil des Cris
2, rue Lakeshore, Nemaska QC J0Y 3B0
Tel: 819-673-2600; *Fax:* 819-673-2606
cree@cra.qc.ca
www.gcc.ca
www.linkedin.com/companies/grand-council-of-the-crees
www.facebook.com/gcccra
twitter.com/gcccra
Overview: A medium-sized provincial organization founded in 1974
Mission: To representg the Cree people; to foster, promote, protect & assist in preserving the way of life, values & traditions of the Cree people of Quebec.
Chief Officer(s):
Mathew Coon Come, Grand Chief
Bill Namagoose, Executive Director, 613-761-1655, Fax: 613-761-1388

Bureau de Montréal
#100, 277, rue Duke, Montréal QC H3C 2M2
Tel: 514-861-5837; *Fax:* 514-861-0760
cra@gcc.ca

Bureau de Ottawa
#900, 81 Metcalfe St., Ottawa ON K1P 6K7
Tel: 613-761-1655; *Fax:* 613-761-1388
cree@gcc.ca

Bureau de Québec
200, Grande Alleé est, Québec QC G1R 2H9
Tel: 418-691-1111; *Fax:* 418-523-8478
cree.embassy@gcc.ca

Grand Falls, Saint-André & Drummond Chamber of Commerce; Grand Falls & Region Chamber of Commerce ***See*** Valley Chamber of Commerce

Grand Falls-Windsor Chamber of Commerce ***See*** Exploits Regional Chamber of Commerce

Grand Lodge of Alberta ***See*** Grand Orange Lodge of Canada

Grand Lodge of Québec - Ancient, Free & Accepted Masons (GLQ) / Grande Loge du Québec
2295, rue Saint-Marc, Montréal QC H3H 2G9
Tel: 514-933-6739; *Fax:* 514-933-6730
Other Communication: info@glquebec.org
admin@glquebec.ca
www.glquebec.org
Previous Name: Ancient, Free & Accepted Masons of Canada - Grand Lodge of Québec
Overview: A medium-sized provincial organization founded in 1869
Chief Officer(s):
Marc Andre Sicard, Grand Secretary
Staff Member(s): 1; 5 volunteer(s)

Grand Manan Chamber of Commerce ***See*** Grand Manan Tourism Association & Chamber of Commerce

Grand Manan Fishermen's Association (GMFA)
PO Box 907, Grand Manan NB E5G 3M1
Tel: 506-662-8481; *Fax:* 506-662-8336
gmfa@nb.aibn.com
www.gmfa.nb.ca
Overview: A small local organization founded in 1981
Mission: To provide advice to the government on fishery management issues; to operate the Fundy Marine Service Center for fishermen to repair, paint & store boats; To manage the Grand Manon Harbour Authority, responsible for the wharves.
Chief Officer(s):
Brian Guptill, President
Membership: *Fees:* $100 captain/associate; $50 crew member; $25 retired; *Committees:* Lobster; Weir Sector

Grand Manan Museum Inc.
1141, Rte. 776, Grand Manan NB E5G 4E9
Tel: 506-662-3524
gmadmin@grandmananmuseum.ca
www.grandmananmuseum.ca
Overview: A small local organization founded in 1962
Mission: To collect, store, display, & interpret Grand Manan's social & natural history with special emphasis on her marine tradition
Affliation(s): AMNB, CMA
Chief Officer(s):
Otis Green, President
Finances: *Annual Operating Budget:* Less than $50,000; *Funding Sources:* Provincial & national governments; donations, fundraising; gift shop
Membership: *Fees:* $20-$1000
Activities: Exhibits, archives, slide shows, nature school, tours, tourism information, fundraising; publications on aspects of

Grand Manan; *Library:* Grand Manan Museum Research Library; Open to public by appointment

Grand Manan Tourism Association & Chamber of Commerce
1141 Rte. 776, Grand Manan NB E5G 4K9
Tel: 506-662-3442
Toll-Free: 888-525-1655
info@grandmanannb.com
www.grandmanannb.com
Previous Name: Grand Manan Chamber of Commerce
Overview: A small local organization
Mission: To promote and expand business in the Grand Manan and White Head Islands area.
Member of: Atlantic Provinces Chamber of Commerce
Finances: *Annual Operating Budget:* Less than $50,000
Membership: 84; *Fees:* $130 business; $10 individual

Grand Manan Whale & Seabird Research Station (GMWSRS) / Centre de recherche sur la vie marine de Grand Manan
24 Rte. 776, Grand Manan NB E5G 1A1
Tel: 506-662-3804
info@gmwsrs.org
www.gmwsrs.org
www.facebook.com/122376994520768
twitter.com/GMWSRS
Overview: A small local charitable organization founded in 1981
Mission: To conduct research on the Bay of Fundy ecosystem, concentrating on marine mammals & seabirds; To operate a public display of Bay of Fundy Marine Fauna
Member of: New Brunswick Environmental Network
Chief Officer(s):
Laurie Murison, Managing Director
Finances: *Annual Operating Budget:* $50,000-$100,000
4 volunteer(s)
Activities: *Speaker Service:* Yes; *Library:* Gaskin Memorial Library; by appointment

Grand Masters Curling Association Ontario
c/o Art Lobel, 106 Kirk Dr., Thornhill ON L3T 3L2
Tel: 905-881-0547
grandmasterscurling.com
Overview: A medium-sized provincial organization founded in 2007
Affliation(s): Ontario Curling Association
Chief Officer(s):
Art Lobel, President
asobel@sympatico.ca
Membership: 28 teams; *Member Profile:* Curlers 70 & older; *Committees:* Executive

The Grand Orange Lodge of British America *See* Grand Orange Lodge of Canada

Grand Orange Lodge of Canada
94 Sheppard Ave. West, Toronto ON M2N 1M5
Tel: 416-223-1690; *Fax:* 416-223-1324
Toll-Free: 800-565-6248
www.grandorangelodge.ca
Also Known As: Loyal Orange Association
Previous Name: The Grand Orange Lodge of British America
Overview: A large national organization founded in 1830
Mission: To encourage its members to actively participate in the Protestant church of their choice; to actively support the Canadian system of government; to anticipate legislation & its impact on the civil & religious liberties of all Canadians; to provide social activities which will enrich the lives of its members; to participate in benevolent activities which will enrich our communities & our country
Member of: Imperial Orange Council of the World
Chief Officer(s):
John Chalmers, Grand Secretary
Jodachal@yahoo.ca
Roy Dawe, Grand Master & Sovereign
Finances: *Annual Operating Budget:* Less than $50,000; *Funding Sources:* Membership dues
Staff Member(s): 8
Membership: 100,000; *Member Profile:* Protestant faith
Activities: *Awareness Events:* Annual Golf Tournament

Grand Lodge of Newfoundland-Labrador
NL
Chief Officer(s):
Clyde Crane, Grand Secretary
clyde.crane@hotmail.com

Grand Orange Lodge of New Brunswick
553 Hwy. 104, Burtts Corner NB E6L 2B2
Tel: 506-363-2827
Chief Officer(s):
Daniel Grasse, Grand Secretary
danielgrasse@outlook.com

Grand Orange Lodge of Ontario East
PO Box 284, Brockville ON K6V 5V5
Tel: 613-342-7353
www.orangelodge.com
Chief Officer(s):
Art Duncan, Grand Master
arthurduncan@sympatico.ca

Grand Orange Lodge of Ontario West
ON
e-mail: gm@orangeontario.org
www.orangeontario.org
Chief Officer(s):
Keith Wright, Grand Master

Grand Orange Lodge of Québec
3081 Allan Rd., Kinnear's Mills QC G0N 1K0
Tel: 418-424-0912
Chief Officer(s):
James Allan, Grand Master

Grand Orange Lodge of Western Canada
407 Falconridge Gardens NE, Calgary AB T3J 2B9
Tel: 587-968-1519
info@grandorangelodgeofwesterncanada.com
grandorangelodgeofwesterncanada.com
Chief Officer(s):
Adrian Cotter, Grand Secretary

Grand River Beekeepers' Association
Branchton ON
Tel: 519-740-1416
grandriverbee@gmail.com
Overview: A small local organization
Mission: To develop the beekeeping skills of members
Member of: Ontario Beekeepers' Association
Chief Officer(s):
Vince Nevidon, President
Membership: *Member Profile:* Beekeepers who have between one & fifty hives
Activities: Organizing meetings at the Christian Fellowship Church in Waterloo; Providing opportunities for beekeepers to network;

Grand River Conservation Foundation (GRCF)
PO Box 729, 400 Clyde Rd., Cambridge ON N1R 5W6
Tel: 519-621-2761; *Fax:* 519-621-4844
Toll-Free: 877-294-7263
foundation@grandriver.ca
www.grandriver.ca
www.facebook.com/grandriverconservation
twitter.com/grandriverca
www.youtube.com/user/grandriverca
Previous Name: Grand River Foundation
Overview: A small local charitable organization founded in 1965
Mission: To provide leadership & support within the community of the Valley of the Grand River for the protection, conservation, responsible use & management of its natural resources, in response to the needs & wishes & for the ongoing enjoyment of its residents, as well as of the broader community of our province & country
Chief Officer(s):
Joe Farwell, P.Eng, CAO
jfarwell@grandriver.ca
Sara Wilbur, Executive Director, Development
swilbur@grandriver.ca
Finances: *Annual Operating Budget:* Less than $50,000; *Funding Sources:* Individuals, groups & corporations
Staff Member(s): 1; 22 volunteer(s)
Membership: 1-99
Activities: *Speaker Service:* Yes
Awards:
• S.C. Johnson & Son Ltd. Environmental Scholarship (Scholarship)
Annual award for a student enrolled in an environmental sciences program with an emphasis on manufacturing, eocnomics, business, chemistry or related applications at a university in the Grand River watershed area *Amount:* $1,500

Grand River Foundation *See* Grand River Conservation Foundation

GRAND Society
c/o #509, 14 Spadina Rd., Toronto ON M5R 3M4
Tel: 416-513-9404
Also Known As: Grandparents Requesting Access & Dignity
Overview: A medium-sized national organization founded in 1983
Mission: To provide emotional support to grandparents who have been denied access to their grandchildren; to make the public & professionals aware of this problem; to influence provincial family law to recognize the rights of grandparents
Chief Officer(s):
Joan Brooks, President/Chair
Finances: *Funding Sources:* New Horizons Program; federal government
Membership: *Fees:* $20 individual; $35 a couple

Hamilton Chapter
#19, 317 Limeridge Rd. West, Hamilton ON L9C 7C8
Tel: 905-385-6561
Chief Officer(s):
Sylvia Chappell, President

Ottawa Chapter
1516 Boutier Dr., Ottawa ON K1E 3J5
Tel: 613-837-8371; *Fax:* 613-837-8371
Chief Officer(s):
Liliane George, Contact

Grand Valley Construction Association (GVCA)
25 Sheldon Dr., Cambridge ON N1R 6R8
Tel: 519-622-4822; *Fax:* 519-621-3289
staff@gvca.org
www.gvca.org
www.facebook.com/GVCA25
twitter.com/_GVCA
Overview: A medium-sized local organization founded in 1974 overseen by Canadian Construction Association
Chief Officer(s):
Martha George, President
mgeorge@gvca.org
Finances: *Annual Operating Budget:* $250,000-$500,000
Staff Member(s): 6; 13 volunteer(s)
Membership: 680; *Fees:* $650
Publications:
• Grand Valley Construction Association Journal
Type: Journal

Grand Valley Trails Association (GVTA)
PO Box 40068, Waterloo ON N2J 4V1
Tel: 519-576-6156
info@gvta.on.ca
www.gvta.on.ca
www.facebook.com/20610893171
twitter.com/GrandVTrails
Overview: A small local charitable organization founded in 1973
Mission: To establish & maintain a public trail along or adjacent to the Grand River watershed & to engage in & promote year-round hiking
Member of: Hike Ontario
Chief Officer(s):
Nicholas Dinka, President
president@gvta.on.ca
Membership: *Fees:* $30 per household; $300 life
Activities: Trail follows the Grand River north from Dunnville on Lake Erie to Alton; connects to the Bruce by sidetrail (255 km)

Grande Cache Chamber of Commerce
PO Box 1342, 4600 Pine Plaza, Grande Cache AB T0E 0Y0
Tel: 780-827-0100
info@grandecachechamber.com
www.grandecachechamber.com
www.facebook.com/gchamber1
twitter.com/gcchamber1
Overview: A small local organization
Affliation(s): Alberta Chamber of Commerce; Canadian Chamber of Commerce
Chief Officer(s):
Susan Feddema-Leonard, President
Finances: *Annual Operating Budget:* Less than $50,000; *Funding Sources:* Membership fees; grants
50 volunteer(s)
Membership: 41; *Fees:* Schedule available; *Committees:* Tourism; Membership; Trade Fair; 25th Anniversary; Programs

Grande Loge du Québec *See* Grand Lodge of Québec - Ancient, Free & Accepted Masons

Grande Prairie & Area Association of Realtors (GPAAR)
10106 - 102 St., Grande Prairie AB T8V 2V7
Tel: 780-532-3508; *Fax:* 780-539-3515
eo@gpaar.ca

www.grandeprairie-mls.ca
www.facebook.com/GPAAR
Overview: A small local organization overseen by Alberta Real Estate Association
Member of: Alberta Real Estate Association; The Canadian Real Estate Association
Chief Officer(s):
Susan Rankin, President
Membership: 260+; *Member Profile:* Real estate industry members & partners
Activities: Operating an MLS system for the region;

Grande Prairie & District Association for Persons with Developmental Disabilities (GPDAPDD)
8702 - 113 St., Grande Prairie AB T8V 6K5
Tel: 780-532-8436; *Fax:* 780-532-5144
www.gpdapdd.org
Previous Name: Grande Prairie & District Association for the Mentally Handicapped
Overview: A small local organization founded in 1956
Mission: To serve the needs of persons with developmental disabilities, both adults & children, & their families, in the City of Grande Prairie & throughout the northwest region of Alberta
Member of: Alberta Council of Disability Services; Alberta Association for Community Living; Alberta Association for Supported Employment
Chief Officer(s):
Darrin Stubbs, Executive Director
dstubbs@gpdapdd.org
Activities: Residential services; day programs; after-school programs

Grande Prairie & District Association for the Mentally Handicapped ***See*** Grande Prairie & District Association for Persons with Developmental Disabilities

Grande Prairie & District Chamber of Commerce
#217, 11330 - 106 St., Grande Prairie AB T8V 7X9
Tel: 780-532-5340; *Fax:* 780-532-2926
Other Communication: membership@gpchamber.com
info@gpchamber.com
www.grandeprairiechamber.com
www.facebook.com/303922827273
twitter.com/grprchamber
Overview: A small local organization founded in 1915
Mission: To enhance the economic well-being of our members, community & region
Chief Officer(s):
Dan Pearcy, CEO
dan@gpchamber.com
Karen Kluyt, Office Manager
Finances: *Funding Sources:* Membership dues; trade shows
Staff Member(s): 4; 920 volunteer(s)
Membership: 900+; *Fees:* Schedule available; *Committees:* Membership; Advocacy; Policy; Health Action
Activities: *Speaker Service:* Yes; *Library* Open to public

Grande Prairie & Region United Way
#213, 11330 - 106 St., Grande Prairie AB T8V 7X9
Tel: 780-532-1105; *Fax:* 780-532-3532
info@gpunitedway.org
www.gpunitedway.org
www.facebook.com/GPUnited
twitter.com/GPUnited
www.youtube.com/user/GrowUnitedBreakfast
Overview: A small local organization overseen by United Way of Canada - Centraide Canada
Mission: United Ways brings people together to strenghten our community- nuturing health and well being, building self-sufficiency, reducing barriers to independence, creating oppourtunities for children and youth, promoting understanding, dignity and respect. All dollars are raised locally are allotted to local and regional agencies.
Chief Officer(s):
Gladys Blackmore, President/Executive Director
gladys@gpunitedway.org

Grande Prairie Construction Association (GPCA)
9607 - 102 St., Grande Prairie AB T8V 2T8
Tel: 780-532-4548; *Fax:* 780-539-4100
office@gpca.ca
www.gpca.ca
Overview: A small local organization
Member of: Canadian Construction Association; Alberta Construction Association
Chief Officer(s):
Lanny Brown, President
lanny@t-west.ca
Carmen Lemay, Chief Operating Officer
gpca@telusplanet.net
Staff Member(s): 2
Membership: 161; *Fees:* $840-$1,155; *Committees:* ACA Director; ACSA/WCB/Safety; Government Action; Standard & Practices; Online Plan Room; Research & Technology; Social; City Representative
Activities: Courses related to construction, with an emphasis on safety

Grande Prairie Food Bank
9615 - 102 St., Grande Prairie AB T8V 2T8
Tel: 780-532-3720; *Fax:* 780-532-1960
Overview: A small local organization founded in 1978
Mission: To provide food bank family services; To try to help people help themselves & become self-sufficient
Member of: The Salvation Army
Chief Officer(s):
Jo Sobool, Contact
Dale Sobool, Contact
Staff Member(s): 6; 500 volunteer(s)

Grande Prairie Friendship Centre
10507 - 98 Ave., Grande Prairie AB T8V 4L1
Tel: 780-532-5722; *Fax:* 780-539-5121
gpfriend@telusplanet.net
anfca.com/friendship-centres/grande-prairie
Overview: A small local organization overseen by Alberta Native Friendship Centres Association
Member of: Alberta Native Friendship Centres Association

Grande Prairie Museum
10329 - 101 Ave., Grande Prairie AB T8V 6V3
Tel: 780-830-7090
info@grandeprairiemuseum.org
www.facebook.com/G.P.Museum
Overview: A small local charitable organization founded in 1961
Mission: To maintain a high standard of collection activity & preserve the historical objects that represent the community
Member of: Alberta Museum Association; Canadian Museum Association; Chamber of Commerce
Affliation(s): Society of the Peace Museums Network; Pioneer Museum Society of Grande Prairie & District
Finances: *Funding Sources:* Sales; donations; grants
Activities: Educational programs & tours

Grande Prairie Regional College Academic Staff Association (GPRC) / Association des enseignants du collège régional de Grande Prairie
10726 - 106 Ave., Grande Prairie AB T8V 4C4
Tel: 780-539-2992; *Fax:* 780-539-2214
Toll-Free: 888-539-4772
asaoffice@gprc.ab.ca
www.gprc.ab.ca/departments/asa
Overview: A small local organization
Member of: Alberta Colleges & Institutes Faculty Association
Chief Officer(s):
Libero Ficocelli, President
LFicocelli@gprc.ab.ca
Gavin Winter, Vice-President
gwinter@gprc.ab.ca
Bill Corcoran, Treasurer
BCorcoran@GPRC.ab.ca
Finances: *Annual Operating Budget:* $50,000-$100,000; *Funding Sources:* Membership dues
Staff Member(s): 150
Membership: 250; *Member Profile:* College instructors; *Committees:* Art Acquisition; College Foundation; Degree Equivalence; Early Retirement; Environment; Evaluations; Food Service; Grievance; Negotiating; Nominating; Professional Growth; Professional Standards; Retirement; Staff Development; Tenure; Tribute; Writing Centre Coordinating

Grande Prairie Soaring Society
PO Box 64, Hythe AB T0H 2C0
soaring.ab.ca/gpss
Overview: A small local organization
Member of: Soaring Association of Canada
Chief Officer(s):
Lloyd Sherk, President, 780-354-8769
lsherk@telusplanet.net
Terry Hatfield, Secretary-Treasurer, 780-356-3870
tdrlk@995.ca
Membership: *Fees:* $300 single; $150 add. for family member; $120 youth; $80 cadet

Grande Prairie Society for the Prevention of Cruelty to Animals (GPSPCA)
12220 - 104th Ave., Grande Prairie AB T8V 8A8
Tel: 780-538-4030; *Fax:* 780-532-7275
adopt@gpspca.com
www.gpspca.com
www.facebook.com/gpspca
www.youtube.com/GPSPCA
Also Known As: Grande Prairie & District S.P.C.A.
Overview: A small local charitable organization founded in 1984
Mission: To promote respect, humane treatment & compassion toward animals
Member of: Alberta Society for the Prevention of Cruelty to Animals
Chief Officer(s):
Laureen Harcourt, Executive Director
Staff Member(s): 6
Membership: *Fees:* $25 individual; $50 family; $100 corporate
Activities: Adoption; humane education programs

Grandparents Raising Grandchildren - British Columbia
c/o Parent Support Services Society of BC, #204, 5623 Imperial St., Burnaby BC V5J 1G1
Tel: 604-669-1616; *Fax:* 604-669-1636
Toll-Free: 877-345-9777
Other Communication: Support Line: 1-855-474-9777
GRGline@parentsupportbc.ca
www.parentsupportbc.ca/grandparents_raising_grandchildren
Overview: A small local organization
Mission: To provide answers & assistance to grandparents & other relatives who are raising a family member's child.

Les Grands Ballets Canadiens de Montréal (GBCM)
4816, rue Rivard, Montréal QC H2J 2N6
Tél: 514-849-8681
info@grandsballets.com
www.grandsballets.com
www.facebook.com/lesgrandsballets
twitter.com/grandsballets
Aperçu: *Dimension:* moyenne; *Envergure:* locale; Organisme sans but lucratif; fondée en 1957
Mission: Maintenir la tradition du ballet classique et élargir le champ d'expression de cette forme artistique par la création; faire connaître et apprécier la danse à tous les publics grâce à la qualité de nos presentations et de nos productions
Membre(s) du bureau directeur:
Alain Dancyger, Directeur général
Gradimir Pankov, Directeur artistique
Membre(s) du personnel: 40
Activités: *Service de conférenciers:* Oui

Grands Frères Grandes Soeurs d'Ottawa ***See*** Big Brothers Big Sisters Ottawa

Les Grands Frères Grandes Soeurs du Canada ***See*** Big Brothers Big Sisters of Canada

Grands-Parents Tendresse
374, rue Laviotte, Saint-Jérôme QC J7Y 2S9
Tél: 450-436-6664; *Téléc:* 450-436-9885
info@grandsparentstendresse.org
www.grandsparentstendresse.org
Aperçu: *Dimension:* petite; *Envergure:* locale
Mission: D'offrir des activités aux personnes âgées, afin d'affirmer leurs compétences physiques et mentales.
Membre(s) du bureau directeur:
Marlene Girard, Coordonatrice
Membre: *Critères d'admissibilite:* Personnes 45 ans et plus; *Comités:* Bibliothèque; Causerie; Cuisine; Intergénération; Journal; Marrainage; Représentation; Social; Tricot

Grandview & District Chamber of Commerce
PO Box 28, Grandview MB R0L 0Y0
Tel: 204-546-2501
www.grandviewmanitoba.com
Overview: A small local organization
Mission: Promotion of the town of Grandview & area.
Chief Officer(s):
Pierce Cairns, President, 204-546-2626
Robyn Dingwall, Secretary/Treasurer
Finances: *Annual Operating Budget:* Less than $50,000; *Funding Sources:* Municipal government
20 volunteer(s)
Membership: 41 individual; *Fees:* $25 individual; $100 business
Activities: Beautification of town; tourism; business

Grant MacEwan College Faculty Association (GMCFA) / Association des professeurs du Collège Grant MacEwan
City Centre Campus, #7-102, 10700 - 104 Ave., Edmonton AB T5J 4S2
Tel: 780-497-5068; *Fax:* 780-497-5065
macewanfa.ca
Previous Name: Grant MacEwan Community College Faculty Association
Overview: A small local organization founded in 1972
Member of: Alberta College-Institutes Faculties Association
Chief Officer(s):
Aimee Skye, President, 780-633-3302
skyea2@macewan.ca
Finances: *Annual Operating Budget:* $100,000-$250,000
Staff Member(s): 3
Membership: 877 individual; *Fees:* 1% of gross salary

Grant MacEwan College Non-Academic Staff Association *See* MacEwan Staff Association

Grant MacEwan Community College Faculty Association *See* Grant MacEwan College Faculty Association

Grape Growers of Ontario
PO Box 100, Vineland Station ON L0R 2E0
Tel: 905-688-0990; *Fax:* 905-688-3211
info@grapegrowersofontario.com
www.grapegrowersofontario.com
www.facebook.com/174946032541143
twitter.com/grapegrowersont
www.pinterest.com/grapegrowers
Previous Name: Ontario Grape Growers' Marketing Board
Overview: A medium-sized provincial organization
Mission: To implement innovations in the grape growing industry in order to improve the product
Chief Officer(s):
Debbie Zimmerman, Chief Executive Officer
d.zimmerman@grapegrowersofontario.com
Staff Member(s): 8
Membership: *Member Profile:* Grape growers & viticulturalists; *Committees:* Growers'

Graphic Arts Industries Association; Canadian Printing & Imaging Association *See* Canadian Printing Industries Association

Grasslands Naturalists (GN)
Police Point Park Nature Centre, PO Box 2491, Police Point Dr. NE, Medicine Hat AB T1A 8G8
Tel: 403-529-6225; *Fax:* 403-526-6408
www.natureline.info/gn/index.php
Also Known As: Society of Grasslands Naturalists
Overview: A small local charitable organization founded in 1991
Member of: Nature Alberta
Affiliation(s): Canadian Nature Federation
Chief Officer(s):
Marty Drut, Contact
Staff Member(s): 1; 25 volunteer(s)
Membership: 140; *Fees:* $20 individuals; $25 families; *Committees:* Land; Wildlife
Activities: Offering educational opportunities, such as field trips & lectures; Publishing a bi-weekly newspaper column; *Library:* Police Point Park Nature Centre Resource Centre

Gravelbourg Chamber of Commerce
PO Box 85, Gravelbourg SK S0H 1X0
Tel: 306-648-3182; *Fax:* 306-648-2311
Overview: A small local organization
Member of: Saskatchewan Chamber of Commerce
Chief Officer(s):
Maria Lepage, Contact, 306-648-2562
Cees Brouwer, President
Finances: *Annual Operating Budget:* Less than $50,000; *Funding Sources:* Membership fees
Membership: 52; *Fees:* $50; *Member Profile:* Businesses

Gravenhurst Board of Trade *See* Gravenhurst Chamber of Commerce/Visitors Bureau

Gravenhurst Chamber of Commerce/Visitors Bureau
#685, 2 Muskoka Rd. North, Gravenhurst ON P1P 1N5
Tel: 705-687-4432; *Fax:* 705-687-4382
info@gravenhurstchamber.com
www.gravenhurstchamber.com
www.facebook.com/TheGravenhurstChamberOfCommerce
Previous Name: Gravenhurst Board of Trade
Overview: A small local organization founded in 1948
Mission: To work together to advance the commercial, financial, & investment interests of the community
Member of: Ontario Chamber of Commerce
Chief Officer(s):
Dap Thach, President
president@gravenhurstchamber.com
Danielle Millar, Manager
manager@gravenhurstchamber.com
Finances: *Annual Operating Budget:* $100,000-$250,000; *Funding Sources:* Membership fees; Special events
Staff Member(s): 3; 200 volunteer(s)
Membership: 180; *Fees:* $145-$200; *Member Profile:* Individuals; Businesses

The Great Herd of Bisons of the Fertile Plains
6 Melness Bay, Winnipeg MB R2K 2T5
Overview: A small local organization founded in 1984
Affiliation(s): The Bootmakers of Toronto
Chief Officer(s):
Ihor Mayba, Contact
Finances: *Annual Operating Budget:* Less than $50,000
Membership: 32; *Fees:* $10

Great Lakes Gliding Club (GLGC)
7272 - 6 Line, RR#3, Tottenham ON L0G 1W0
Tel: 416-466-7016
postmaster@greatlakesgliding.com
www.greatlakesgliding.com
www.facebook.com/flyglgc
Overview: A small local organization founded in 1998
Mission: The club offers license training as well as flying competitions
Membership: 35; *Fees:* $149 air cadets; $375 students; $550 full; *Member Profile:* Students; Licenced pilots

Great Lakes Institute for Environmental Research (GLIER)
401 Sunset Ave., Windsor ON N9B 3P4
Tel: 519-253-3000; *Fax:* 519-971-3616
glier@uwindsor.ca
www.uwindsor.ca/glier
Overview: A small provincial organization founded in 1981
Mission: Multidisciplinary facility with members from many disciplines, including biology, geology, chemistry, engineering, marine biology, molecular biology, genetics and ecology.
Chief Officer(s):
Brian Fryer, Contact
bfryer@uwindsor.ca

The Great Lakes Marine Heritage Foundation
55 Ontario St., Kingston ON K7L 2Y2
Tel: 613-542-2261; *Fax:* 613-542-0043
marmus@marmuseum.ca
www.marmuseum.ca
Overview: A small local charitable organization founded in 1991
Chief Officer(s):
Doug Cowie, Manager
manager@marmuseum.ca
Staff Member(s): 1

Great Lakes United (GLU) / Union Saint Laurent Grands Lacs
#302, 260 Patrick St., Ottawa ON K1N 5K5
Tel: 519-591-7503
Other Communication: usgl@glu.org (Montréal)
glu@glu.org
www.glu.org
Overview: A small international charitable organization founded in 1982
Mission: To ensure a healthy, safe, & sustainable St. Lawrence River & Great Lakes region
Chief Officer(s):
John Jackson, Executive Director & Director, Clean Production & Toxics
jjackson@glu.org
Bonnie Danni, Director, Finance & Development
bonnie@glu.org
Jennifer Nalbone, Director, Navigation & Invasive Species
jen@glu.org
Sylvie Trudel, Director, Québec Operations
sylvie@glu.org
Lauren Cheal, Contractor, Communications
lcheal@glu.org
Brent Gibson, Contact, Press Inquiries, 613-482-1324 Ext. 509
Finances: *Funding Sources:* Donations; Membership fees
Membership: *Fees:* $50 individuals; $75 supporting individuals; $35 - $125 organizations (based upon annual budget)
Activities: Engaging in advocacy activities; Conducting campaigns around issues such as invasive species, navigation, restoration, energy, & water levels & flows

Great Lakes Waterways Development Association *See* Chamber of Marine Commerce

Great Northern Ski Society
c/o Mt. Sima Alpine Adventure Park, PO Box 30103, 777 Mt. Sima Rd., Whitehorse YT Y1A 0A8
Tel: 867-668-4557; *Fax:* 867-633-6340
greatnorthernskisociety@gmail.com
mountsima.com
www.facebook.com/GreatNorthernSkiSociety
Overview: A small provincial organization
Mission: To operate Mt. Sima Alpine Adventure Park.
Chief Officer(s):
Craig Hougen, President

Great Slave Snowmobile Association
4209 - 49A Ave., Yellowknife NT X1A 1B3
Tel: 867-766-4353
Also Known As: GSSA Trail Riders
Overview: A small provincial organization founded in 1988
Mission: The Association is a non-profit organization that is dedicated to promoting safe, responsible snowmobiling in Yellowknife.
Affiliation(s): Canadian Council of Snowmobile Organizations; International Snowmobile Council
Chief Officer(s):
Bill Braden, President
Finances: *Annual Operating Budget:* Less than $50,000
6 volunteer(s)
Membership: 300 individual; *Fees:* $35 single; $50 family
Activities: Community fund-raising; clearing trails; adding signage along trail system

Greater Arnprior Chamber of Commerce (GACC)
#111, 16 Edward St., Arnprior ON K7S 3W4
Tel: 613-623-6817; *Fax:* 613-623-6826
info@gacc.ca
www.gacc.ca
Overview: A small local organization founded in 1995
Mission: The mission of the Greater Arnprior Chamber of Commerce is to act as an independent and non-partisan, member-driven business orgniazation that enhances economic prosperity and quality of life in Arnprior and McNab/Braeside by creating a positive business environment and contributing to the success of communities through leadership, representation, information and networking oppourtunities.
Member of: Ontario Chamber of Commerce
Chief Officer(s):
Cheryl Sparling, Administrative Assistant, 613-623-6817
Wes Schnob, President, 613-878-0808
wes@nerdsonsite.com
Finances: *Funding Sources:* Membership fees
Staff Member(s): 1
Membership: 150; *Fees:* $100
Activities: Networking; speaker meetings; Canada Day events; golf tournament

Greater Barrie Chamber of Commerce
97 Toronto St., Barrie ON L4N 1V1
Tel: 705-721-5000; *Fax:* 705-726-0973
chadmin@barriechamber.com
barriechamber.com
www.facebook.com/BarrieChamber
twitter.com/barriechamber
www.youtube.com/barriechamber
Overview: A small local organization
Mission: To assist new & existing businesses with their promotional/advertising needs of their product or products; to provide effective administrative functions to carry out the policies & procedures of the Board for the continual enhancement of the membership.
Chief Officer(s):
Sybil Goruk, Executive Director, 705-721-5000 Ext. 23
chexec@barriechamber.com
Finances: *Annual Operating Budget:* $250,000-$500,000; *Funding Sources:* Membership dues; events
Staff Member(s): 3; 100 volunteer(s)
Membership: 1,250; *Fees:* Based on number of employees; *Committees:* Membership; Marketing; Governmental Affairs
Activities: Gala Awards; business breakfast networking; seminars;

Greater Bathurst Chamber of Commerce / Chambre de commerce du Grand Bathurst
CEI Bldg., 725 College St., Bathurst NB E2A 4B9
Tel: 506-548-8498; *Fax:* 506-548-2200
info@bathurstchamber.ca
www.bathurstchamber.ca
www.facebook.com/335718759975
twitter.com/bathurstchamber
Overview: A medium-sized local organization founded in 1913
Mission: To facilitate economic growth in the Chaleur area; To advocate for the business community of Greater Bathurst
Affliation(s): Canadian Chamber of Commerce
Chief Officer(s):
Danielle Gaudet, General Manager
danielle.gaudet@bathurstchamber.ca
Vilma Glidden, President
Gilles Deveaux, Treasurer
Membership: 300+; *Fees:* Schedule available based upon number of employees; *Member Profile:* Business & professional individuals of the Chaleur business community, from Allardville to Belledune
Activities: Providing resources; Offering networking opportunities; Providing education for members

Greater Charlottetown & Area Chamber of Commerce
National Bank Tower, 134 Kent St., Charlottetown PE C1A 7K2
Tel: 902-628-2000; *Fax:* 902-368-3570
chamber@charlottetownchamber.com
www.charlottetownchamber.com
www.facebook.com/117356628329546
Previous Name: Charlottetown Board of Trade
Overview: A large local organization founded in 1887
Mission: To be the voice of business on economic issues; to provide services & opportunities for members to enhance their ability to do business
Member of: Canadian Chamber of Commerce
Affliation(s): Atlantic Provinces Chamber of Commerce
Chief Officer(s):
Keith Lambe, President
keith.lambe@aliant.ca
Kathy Hambly, Executive Director
khambly@charlottetownchamber.com
Cate Proctor, Executive Director
cproctor@charlottetownchamber.com
Finances: *Annual Operating Budget:* $250,000-$500,000; *Funding Sources:* Membership dues; fundraising
Staff Member(s): 6
Membership: 800; *Fees:* $220-$1,050 based on number of employees; *Committees:* Policy; Business Development; Human Resources; Communications; Business Under Forty; Event; Immigration; Stratford Business Community Forum; Cornwall Business Community Forum; Bonding By
Awards:
• Entrepreneurial Award of Excellence (Award)
Publications:
• Greater Charlottetown & Area Chamber of Commerce E-Newsletter
Type: Newsletter

Greater Corner Brook Board of Trade (GCBBT)
PO Box 475, 11 Confederation Dr., Corner Brook NL A2H 6E6
Tel: 709-634-5831; *Fax:* 709-639-9710
sherry@gcbbt.com
www.gcbbt.com
www.facebook.com/groups/116751161670496
twitter.com/cornerbrookbot
Previous Name: Corner Brook Chamber of Commerce
Overview: A small local organization
Chief Officer(s):
Keith Goulding, President
Staff Member(s): 1
Membership: 165; *Fees:* $80-$825 business; $50 individual; $25 charity; $10 student; *Committees:* Tourism; Finance; Government
Activities: Seminars; luncheons, workshops

Greater Dufferin Area Chamber of Commerce
PO Box 101, Orangeville ON L9W 2Z5
Tel: 519-941-0490; *Fax:* 519-941-0492
info@gdacc.ca
www.gdacc.ca
www.facebook.com/GDACC
twitter.com/TheChamberGDACC
www.youtube.com/TheChamberGDACC
Previous Name: Orangeville & District Chamber of Commerce
Overview: A small local organization
Mission: To provide value added services & benefits for members
Affliation(s): Ontario Chamber of Commerce; Canadian Chamber of Commerce
Chief Officer(s):
Pete Renshaw, President
Anita Sequeira, Director
anita@gdacc.ca
Membership: 450; *Fees:* $173.25-$546; *Committees:* Membership; Golf; Business Excellence Awards; Home & Lifestyle Show; Get Involved; Homebuilders Association; Dufferin Women in Business (DWIB); Education & Training
Awards:
• Business Excellence Awards (Award)

Greater Edmonton Library Association (GELA)
PO Box 60104, Stn. U of A Postal Outlet, Edmonton AB T6G 2S4
e-mail: gelaweb@gela.ca
www.gela.ca
twitter.com/gela_edmonton
Previous Name: Edmonton Library Association
Overview: A small local organization founded in 1945
Mission: To support library workers in the city of Edmonton & the surrounding region
Chief Officer(s):
Jordan Smith, President
Sean Lyuk, Vice-President/President Elect
Cam Laforest, Secretary
Eric An, Treasurer
Membership: *Fees:* Free, student membership; $25 personal membership; $50 institutional membership; *Member Profile:* Librarians, library technicians, library staff, students, & others who are interested in library activities in Edmonton & the surrounding area
Activities: Offering programs addressing library issues in the Greater Edmonton area; Promoting continuing education opportunities; Providing professional development activities; Organizing community outreach initiatives, through the Women's Prison & Reintegration Subcommittee & the Community Bookshelf Subcommittee; Facilitating the exchange of ideas between local library workers; Offering networking opportunities

Greater Fort Erie Chamber of Commerce
#1, 660 Garrison Rd., Fort Erie ON L2A 6E2
Tel: 905-871-3803; *Fax:* 905-871-1561
info@forteriechamber.com
www.forteriechamber.com
www.facebook.com/groups/2402319873
Overview: A small local organization founded in 1947
Chief Officer(s):
Dean Demizio, President
Karen Audet, Operations Manager
Finances: *Annual Operating Budget:* $100,000-$250,000
Staff Member(s): 2
Membership: 381; *Fees:* $124-$576; *Member Profile:* Local businesses; organizations; *Committees:* Human Resources; Government Action & All Candidates; Member Recruitment; Education; Directory; Bursary; AGM; Golf; International Women's Day
Activities: Business networking; social outings; professional workshops & seminars; annual general meetings

Greater Halifax Conventions & Meetings Bureau *See* Destination Halifax

Greater Hamilton Technology Enterprise Centre *See* Hamilton Technology Centre

Greater Hamilton Tourism & Convention Services *See* Tourism Hamilton

Greater Hillsborough Chamber of Commerce
PO Box 3051, Hillsborough NB E4H 4W5
Tel: 506-734-3773; *Fax:* 506-734-2244
Overview: A small local organization
Chief Officer(s):
Carole Coleman, Director

Greater Innisfil Chamber of Commerce (GICC)
7896 Yonge St., Innisfil ON L9S 1L5
Tel: 705-431-4199; *Fax:* 705-431-6628
info@innisfilchamber.com
www.innisfilchamber.com
Previous Name: Innisfil Chamber of Commerce
Overview: A small local organization founded in 1973
Mission: To provide one voice for a prosperous Innisfil
Member of: Canadian Chamber of Commerce; Ontario Chamber of Commerce
Affliation(s): Alcona Business Association; South Innisfil Business & Community Association; Cookstown Chamber of Commerce; 400 Industrial Group
Chief Officer(s):
Deb Webster, Secretary
Shannon MacIntyre, President
Finances: *Annual Operating Budget:* Less than $50,000; *Funding Sources:* Membership fees; fundraising; municipal grant
Staff Member(s): 1; 18 volunteer(s)
Membership: 150; *Fees:* $115.50; *Member Profile:* Business leaders; *Committees:* Membership; Golf; Gala; Canada Day; Fundraising; Business Luncheon Seminar Series; After 5's
Activities: Hosting the Annual Business Awards & an annual golf tournament; Promoting existing business; Attracting & welcoming new business; Communicating between business, community, & government; *Speaker Service:* Yes

Greater Kamloops Chamber of Commerce
1290 Trans-Canada Hwy., Kamloops BC V2C 6R3
Tel: 250-372-7722; *Fax:* 250-828-9500
www.kamloopschamber.ca
Also Known As: Kamloops Chamber of Commerce
Overview: A small local organization founded in 1896
Mission: To create an environment that ensures the greatest opportunity for the success of our members.
Member of: BC Chamber of Commerce; Canadian Chamber of Commerce
Chief Officer(s):
Maurice Hindle, President
Deb McClelland, Executive Director
deb@kamloopschamber.ca
Finances: *Annual Operating Budget:* $250,000-$500,000; *Funding Sources:* Membership; fundraising
Staff Member(s): 5; 10 volunteer(s)
Membership: 715
Activities: Business Awards Gala; luncheons; seminars; socials; *Awareness Events:* Chamber Week; Small Business Week; *Library:* Business Information Centre; Open to public
Awards:
• Technology Innovator Award (Award)
• Service Provider Award (Award)
• Resource Industry Award (Award)
• Business Person of the Year (Award)
• Business of the Year (Award)
• First Nations Business of the Year (Award)
• Young Entrepreneur of the Year (Award)
• Project of the Year (Award)
• Retailer Award (Award)
• Manufacturer Award (Award)
• Tourism Award (Award)
• Home-Based Business Award (Award)

Greater Kingston Chamber of Commerce (GKCC)
945 Princess St., Kingston ON K7L 3N6
Tel: 613-548-4453; *Fax:* 613-548-4743
info@kingstonchamber.on.ca
www.kingstonchamber.on.ca
www.facebook.com/greaterkingstonchamber
twitter.com/kingstonchamber
Previous Name: Kingston Board of Trade
Overview: A medium-sized local organization founded in 1841
Mission: To advance economic progress, free enterprise, & the quality of life
Member of: Canadian Chamber of Commerce; Ontario Chamber of Commerce
Chief Officer(s):
John Ryce, President
David Phillips, Coordinator, New Membership
Finances: *Annual Operating Budget:* $500,000-$1.5 Million; *Funding Sources:* Membership dues; programs; events
Staff Member(s): 6; 200 volunteer(s)
Membership: 950; *Committees:* Golf Tournament; Tour Trolley; Special Events; Task Forces: Finance; Ways & Means; Community Development; Networking
Activities: Offering a group benefits plan & a discount program; Organizing business mixers, breakfast clubs, & a golf tournament; *Awareness Events:* Tourism Awareness Week; Small Business Week; *Rents Mailing List:* Yes

Greater Kitchener & Waterloo Chamber of Commerce
PO Box 2367, 80 Queen St. North, Kitchener ON N2H 6L4

Tel: 519-576-5000; *Fax:* 519-742-4760
Toll-Free: 888-672-4282
admin@greaterkwchamber.com
www.greaterkwchamber.com
www.linkedin.com/groups/Greater-KW-Chamber-Commerce-2056325
www.facebook.com/GKWCC
twitter.com/gkwcc
Overview: A medium-sized local charitable organization founded in 2001
Mission: To serve business in the Greater Kitchener Waterloo area & be its voice in the betterment of the community
Member of: Canadian Chamber of Commerce; Ontario Chamber of Commerce
Chief Officer(s):
Ian McLean, President & CEO, 519-749-6038
Finances: *Annual Operating Budget:* $500,000-$1.5 Million; *Funding Sources:* Membership fees; special projects
Staff Member(s): 10; 200 volunteer(s)
Membership: 1,600; *Fees:* Based on number of employees; *Committees:* Business After 5; Communications; Environment; Federal/Provincial Affairs; Membership; Networking & Breakfast Club; Regional/Municipal Affairs; Special Projects; Training & Education
Activities: *Rents Mailing List:* Yes; *Library:* Chamber of Commerce Resource Centre; Open to public

Greater Langley Chamber of Commerce
#1, 5761 Glover Rd., Langley BC V3A 8M8
Tel: 604-530-6656; *Fax:* 604-530-7066
info@langleychamber.com
www.langleychamber.com
www.linkedin.com/pub/jaclyn-van-den-berg/24/854/766
www.facebook.com/langleychamber
twitter.com/LangleyChamber
Overview: A small local organization
Chief Officer(s):
Angie Quaale, President
Lynn Whitehouse, Executive Director
Membership: 1,100+; *Fees:* Schedule available
Publications:
• Greater Langley Chamber of Commerce Newsletter
Type: Newsletter; *Frequency:* Monthly

Greater Miramichi Chamber of Commerce *See* Miramichi Chamber of Commerce

Greater Moncton Chamber of Commerce (GMCC) / Chambre de commerce du Grand Moncton
#200, 1273 Main St., Moncton NB E1C 0P4
Tel: 506-857-2883; *Fax:* 506-857-9209
npelligrew@gmcc.nb.ca
www.gmcc.nb.ca
www.linkedin.com/company/greater-moncton-chamber-of-commerce
www.facebook.com/GreaterMonctonChamberOfCommerce
twitter.com/MonctonChamber
www.youtube.com/user/GreaterMonctonCham?feature=guide
Overview: A medium-sized local organization founded in 1891
Mission: To strengthen business & community in the Greater Moncton area through leadership, member services, & advocacy on business issues at the municipal, provincial, & national levels
Member of: Atlantic Provinces Chamber of Commerce (APCC); New Brunswick Chamber of Commerce; Canadian Chamber of Commerce
Chief Officer(s):
Nancy Whipp, CEO, 506-856-4000
nwhipp@gmcc.nb.ca
Tom Badger, Chair
Finances: *Funding Sources:* Membership dues and events
Staff Member(s): 5; 50 volunteer(s)
Membership: 810; *Fees:* Schedule available based upon number of employees; *Member Profile:* Businesses in the Greater Moncton area; *Committees:* Ambassador; Appreciation; Chairman's Gala; Curling Funspiel; ecoRevolution; Education & Training; Golf; Greater Moncton Excellence Awards; Marketing & Communication; Membership; Networking
Activities: Offering training sessions; Providing networking opportunities; advocacy
Awards:
• Greater Moncton Excellence Awards (Award)
Categories include the following: Excellence in Business, Emerging Business, Marketing, Innovation, Service Excellence, & Community Service

Greater Moncton Chinese Cultural Association (GMCCA)
Moncton NB
www.gmcca.ca
Previous Name: Moncton Chinese Friendship Association (MCFA)
Overview: A small local organization founded in 1981
Mission: To promote the appreciation & understanding of Chinese culture among both members of the Chinese community & general public in the Greater Moncton area
Member of: Chinese Canadian National Council
Chief Officer(s):
Mingkun Gu, President

Greater Moncton Real Estate Board Inc.
541 St. George Blvd., Moncton NB E1E 2B6
Tel: 506-857-8200; *Fax:* 506-857-1760
gmreb@nb.aibn.com
www.monctonrealestateboard.com
Overview: A small local organization overseen by New Brunswick Real Estate Association
Mission: To provide its members with the strcuture & services to enhance REALTOR professionalism, standards of business practice and ethics in meeting the real estate needs of the community.
Member of: Canadian Real Estate Association
Chief Officer(s):
Kerry Rakuson, Executive Officer
Roxanne Maillet, President, 506-866-6295
Staff Member(s): 3
Membership: 310; *Committees:* Arbitration; Audit & Finance; Governance; Nominating; Rules & Regulations

Greater Moncton Society for the Prevention of Cruelty to Animals (GMSPCA) / Société de protection des animaux du Grand Moncton (SPAGM)
116 Greenock St., Moncton NB E1H 2J7
Tel: 506-857-8698; *Fax:* 506-854-1473
info@monctonspca.ca
www.monctonspca.ca
www.facebook.com/gmspca.spagm
twitter.com/GrMonctonSPCA
www.youtube.com/monctonspca
Overview: A small local charitable organization founded in 1956
Mission: To provide a safe haven for unwanted & abused animals until which time they can be adopted into loving homes
Member of: Canadian Federation of Humane Societies
Affliation(s): New Brunswick Society for the Prevention of Cruelty to Animals
Chief Officer(s):
Karen Nelson, Executive Director
Activities: Education/Awareness Program; Pets & People (Therapy Program); Dog Jog; radio spots with pet tips;

Greater Montreal Athletic Association (GMAA) / Association régionale du sport scolaire
#101, 5925, av Monkland, Montréal QC H4A 1G7
Tel: 514-482-8555; *Fax:* 514-487-0121
gmaa@gmaa.ca
www.gmaa.ca
Overview: A small local charitable organization founded in 1975
Mission: Devoted to the promotion of athletics in the English schools of the greater Montreal region.
Member of: Réseau du sport étudiant du Québec
Chief Officer(s):
Don McEwen, Executive Director
don@gmaa.ca
Finances: *Annual Operating Budget:* $250,000-$500,000
Staff Member(s): 3
Membership: 152; *Fees:* User fees by activity; *Member Profile:* Principals of elementary & secondary schools
Activities: Organize & run sports activities & leagues for English schools on the Island of Montréal

Greater Montréal Convention & Tourism Bureau *Voir* Tourisme Montréal/Office des congrès et du tourisme du Grand Montréal

Greater Montréal Real Estate Board *Voir* Chambre immobilière du Grand Montréal

Greater Nanaimo Chamber of Commerce
2133 Bowen Rd., Nanaimo BC V9S 1H8
Tel: 250-756-1191; *Fax:* 250-756-1584
info@nanaimochamber.bc.ca
www.nanaimochamber.bc.ca
Overview: A medium-sized local organization founded in 1889
Mission: To act as the voice of business in Greater Nanaimo; To ensure a healthy economic base & socio-economic structure to benefit the central Vancouver Island area
Chief Officer(s):
Lee Mason, CEO
Donna Hais, President
Scott Thomson, Treasurer
Finances: *Funding Sources:* Membership dues; Fundraising
Membership: 850+; *Fees:* Schedule available based upon number of employees; *Member Profile:* Businesses, professionals, & community groups in Greater Nanaimo; *Committees:* Executive; Finance & Budget; Nomination; Professional Development Group; Membership; Chamber Ambassador; Special Events; Sterling Community Awards; Kidventures Business Fair; Leadership BC - Nanaimo Advisory Team
Activities: Promoting business in Nanaimo; Encouraging investment; Researching business issues; Liaising with politicians to benefit the business environment; Providing information about the community to newcomers; Offering educational seminars & training sessions; *Speaker Service:* Yes
Awards:
• Sterling Awards (Award)
To recognize excellence in business & customer service in Greater Nanaimo

Greater Nepean Chamber of Commerce
#1175, 2720 Queensview Dr., Ottawa ON K2B 1A5
Tel: 613-828-5556; *Fax:* 613-828-8022
gm@nepeanchamber.com
www.nepeanchamber.com
Overview: A small local organization
Chief Officer(s):
Virginia Boro, Chair
Membership: 300;

Greater Niagara Chamber of Commerce (GNCC)
PO Box 940, #103, 1 St. Paul St., St Catharines ON L2R 6Z4
Tel: 905-684-2361; *Fax:* 905-684-2100
info@gncc.ca
www.greaterniagarachamber.com
www.linkedin.com/groups/Greater-Niagara-Chamber-Commerce-4151488
www.facebook.com/NiagaraChamber
twitter.com/NiagaraCoC
Previous Name: St Catharines-Thorold Chamber of Commerce; St Catharines Chamber of Commerce
Overview: A medium-sized local organization founded in 1867
Mission: The Greater Niagara Chamber of Commerce is a non-partisan, non-sectarian association of businesses, groups and individuals who support business growth and effective government fostering a sustainable and vibrant Niagara.
Member of: Ontario Chamber of Commerce; Canadian Chamber of Commerce
Chief Officer(s):
Kithio Mwanzia, Interim CEO, 905-684-2361
policy@gncc.ca
Walter Sendzik, CEO, 905-684-2361
ceo@gncc.ca
Finances: *Annual Operating Budget:* $500,000-$1.5 Million; *Funding Sources:* Membership dues; special events; programs
Staff Member(s): 8
Membership: 1,500+; *Fees:* $175-$3,200; *Committees:* For Social Profit Council, Women In Niagara Council, NEXTNiagara Council, Small Business Niagara Council, St. Catharines Business Council, Thorold Business Council.
Activities: Business After 5, Niagara Business Achievement Awards, NEXTNiagara and Women In Niagara Events, Small Business Trade Show, Cabinet Minister's Luncheons, State of the City, State of the Region; *Internships:* Yes; *Speaker Service:* Yes; *Library:* Chamber Education Centre

Greater Oshawa Chamber of Commerce
#100, 44 Richmond St. West, Oshawa ON L1G 1C7
Tel: 905-728-1683; *Fax:* 905-432-1259
info@oshawachamber.com
www.oshawachamber.com
www.facebook.com/oshawachamber
twitter.com/oshawachamber
www.youtube.com/oshawachamber
Previous Name: Oshawa/Clarington Chamber of Commerce
Overview: A small local organization founded in 1928
Mission: To be the voice of business or Greater Oshawa, by providing positive leadership in support of members, business & the private enterprise system.

Affiliation(s): Ontario Chamber of Commerce; Canadian Chamber of Commerce
Chief Officer(s):
Dan Carter, President
president@oshawachamber.com
Bob Malcolmson, CEO & General Manager
ceo@oshawachamber.com
Finances: *Annual Operating Budget:* $250,000-$500,000; *Funding Sources:* Membership dues
Staff Member(s): 4; 70 volunteer(s)
Membership: 890; *Fees:* As per number of employees; *Committees:* Ambassador; Awards; Economic Development/Government Affairs; Events
Activities: Seminars; training; networking

Greater Peterborough Chamber of Commerce (GPCC)
175 George St. North, Peterborough ON K9J 3G6
Tel: 705-748-9771; *Fax:* 705-743-2331
Toll-Free: 887-640-4037
info@peterboroughchamber.ca
www.peterboroughchamber.ca
Previous Name: Peterborough Chamber of Commerce
Overview: A medium-sized local organization founded in 1889
Mission: To create a prosperous community by promoting the free enterprise system, a healthy business environment, & acting as the voice of business
Member of: Ontario Chamber of Commerce; Canadian Chamber of Commerce
Chief Officer(s):
Stuart Harrison, General Manager Ext. 202
stuart@peterboroughchamber.ca
Finances: *Annual Operating Budget:* $500,000-$1.5 Million; *Funding Sources:* Members fees
Staff Member(s): 11; 25 volunteer(s)
Membership: 850; *Fees:* $200; *Committees:* Program/Awards; Membership; Communications; Economic Development; Policy/Government Relations
Activities: *Speaker Service:* Yes; *Rents Mailing List:* Yes

Greater Sackville Chamber of Commerce (GSCC)
#87, 8 Main St., Sackville NB E4L 4A9
Tel: 506-364-8911; *Fax:* 506-364-8082
gscc@eastlink.ca
sackvillechamber.com
Overview: A small local organization founded in 1991
Mission: To enhance economic prosperity & quality of life in Greater Sackville
Chief Officer(s):
Laura Landriault, President
Lori Ann Roness, Executive Director
Susan Tower, Secretary
Finances: *Annual Operating Budget:* Less than $50,000; *Funding Sources:* Membership fees; fundraising events; administration of Mainstreet Redevelopment Sackville Inc.
Staff Member(s): 1
Membership: 61
Activities: *Library* Open to public
Awards:
• Business Recognition Award (Award)
Excellence in innovation & creativity, management skills, growth, job creation & contributions to the community

Greater Saskatoon Chamber of Commerce
#104, 202 - 4th Ave. North, Saskatoon SK S7K 0K1
Tel: 306-244-2151; *Fax:* 306-244-8366
chamber@saskatoonchamber.com
www.saskatoonchamber.com
www.facebook.com/saskatoonchamber
Previous Name: Saskatoon & District Chamber of Commerce
Overview: A small local organization founded in 1903
Mission: To build the business climate, thereby creating a city of opportunity
Member of: Saskatchewan Chamber of Commerce; Canadian Chamber of Commerce; World Chambers
Affiliation(s): Enterprise Centre; Leadership Saskatoon; Raj Manek Mentorship Program; Saskatchewan Agrivision Corporation; Saskatchewan Economic Development Authority; Saskatchewan Young Professionals & Entrepreneurs; Saskatoon Aboriginal Employment & Business Opportunities Inc., Saskatoon Air Services; Saskatoon Regional Economic Development Authority; Tourism Saskatoon; United Way of Saskatoon; Vision 2000
Chief Officer(s):
Kent Smith-Windsor, Executive Director
Christian Braid, President
Finances: *Annual Operating Budget:* $500,000-$1.5 Million
Staff Member(s): 8; 100 volunteer(s)
Membership: 1,600; *Fees:* Schedule available; *Member Profile:* Local businesses; *Committees:* Aboriginal Opportunities; Agribusiness Development; Knowledge Industry; Government Affairs; Health Care Opportunities; Transportation; Junior Chamber of Commerce; Celebrate Success; Future Opportunities
Activities: Advocating for business; Hosting business luncheons & community & other chamber events
Awards:
• SABEX New Product (Award)
Awarded to a company that has launched a new Saskatchewan made product or service that is original & currently available to consumers
• SABEX Innovation (Award)
Awarded to a business that has demonstrated the application of knowledge or ability to create new forms and/or ways of doing things that provide a competitive advantage; may include involvement of people or new technology to successfully compete in a changing marketplace
• SABEX Marketing (Award)
Awarded to a company that has development and implemented a marketing strategy which has contributed to the success of an operation
• SABEX New Business Venture (Award)
Awarded to a business that has been in existence for 3 years or less & has shown positive performance in terms of current or expected profitability, job creation or entrance into new markets
• SABEX Customer Service (Award)
Awarded to a company providing excellent customer services to customers
• SABEX Export (Award)
Awarded to a company exporting Saskatchewan goods or services nationally or internationally
• SABEX Growth & Expansion (Award)
Awarded to a business that has made changes resulting in growth or expansion of markets, creation of jobs, increases in physical size, that enhance its ability to increase revenues, investments & profits
• SABEX Hall of Fame (Award)
One individual, or business, will be inducted into the Hall of Fame each year; the recipient will abe a long-standing member of the Saskatoon Business community
• SABEX Business of the Year (Award)
Awarded to a business which has demonstrated excellence in areas they consider key to their success
• SABEX Community Involvement (Award)
Awarded to a business demonstrating exceptional performanc in its support of the arts, culture, amateur sports, education or volunteer groups within the community

Greater Shediac Chamber of Commerce / Chambre de commerce du Grand Shediac
#302, 290 Main St., Shediac NB E4P 2E3
Tel: 506-532-7000; *Fax:* 506-532-6556
www.greatershediacchamber.com
Overview: A small local organization
Chief Officer(s):
Ronald Cormier, President
Membership: 61; *Fees:* $55 individual/non-profit; $125 1-10 employees; $200 11-50 employees; $350 51-100 employees; 450 101+ employees

Greater Sudbury Association for Community Living *See* Community Living Greater Sudbury

Greater Sudbury Chamber of Commerce / Chambre de commerce du Grand Sudbury
#1, 40 Elm St., Sudbury ON P3C 1S8
Tel: 705-673-7133; *Fax:* 705-673-1951
cofc@sudburychamber.ca
www.sudburychamber.ca
www.linkedin.com/company/1025331
www.facebook.com/greatersudburychamber
twitter.com/sudburycofc
Overview: A small local organization founded in 1895
Mission: To act as the voice of business in Ontario's Greater Sudbury area; To advocate for business & community prosperity
Chief Officer(s):
Debbi Nicholson, President & Chief Executive Officer, 705-673-7133 Ext. 225
debbi@sudburychamber.ca
Staff Member(s): 15
Membership: 1,000; *Fees:* Schedule available

Greater Summerside Chamber of Commerce (GSCC)
#10, 263 Harbour Dr., Summerside PE C1N 5P1
Tel: 902-436-9651; *Fax:* 902-436-8320
info@chamber.summerside.ca
www.chamber.summerside.ca
www.facebook.com/120850442004
Overview: A medium-sized local organization founded in 1900
Mission: To provide a voice on behalf of business in the City of Summerside & area; To work towards the prosperity & betterment of Greater Summerside
Member of: Atlantic Provinces Chamber of Commerce; Canadian Chamber of Commerce
Chief Officer(s):
Bill Schurman, Executive Director, 902-439-9651
bill@chamber.summerside.ca
Garth Doiron, President
garth.doiron@nbpcd.com
Heather Matheson, Secretary
heather@pchcare.com
Patrick McSweeney, Treasurer
patrick@arsenaultmcsweeney.ca
Finances: *Funding Sources:* Membership dues; Sponsorships
Membership: *Fees:* Schedule available based on number of employees; *Member Profile:* Professional & business people in the Greater Summerside area; *Committees:* Education / Training; Business; Membership / Public Relations; Transportation; Government Relations; Special Projects; Primary Resources; City of Summerside; Business
Activities: Promoting trade & commerce; Providing networking opportunities; Creating business opportunities; Advocating of behalf of members' concerns to municipal, provincial, national, & international governments
Awards:
• Wendell J. Gallant Memorial Scholarship (Scholarship)
• Excellence In Business Awards (Award)

Greater Toronto Al-Anon Information Services (GTAIS)
PO Box 1304, 145 The West Mall, Toronto ON M9C 1C0
Tel: 416-410-3809
Toll-Free: 888-425-2666
gtais.updates@gmail.com
al-anon.alateen.on.ca/gtais
Overview: A small local organization
Mission: The group provides a forum for the Al-Anon & Alateen groups within the Toronto geographic area to exchange information. It also offers a variety of services, such as lists of meeting schedules, post office box, telephone answering.
Affiliation(s): Toronto Al-Anon Family Groups Public Outreach
Activities: Public outreach

Greater Toronto Apartment Association (GTAA)
#103, 20 Upjohn Rd., Toronto ON M3B 2V9
Tel: 416-385-3435
info@gtaaonline.com
www.gtaaonline.com
twitter.com/GTAAONLINE
Previous Name: Metropolitan Toronto Apartment Builders Association
Overview: A medium-sized local organization founded in 1969
Mission: To promote the well-being & interests of the apartment development industry; to regulate relations between employers & employees & to promote new development
Affiliation(s): Joint Construction Council
Chief Officer(s):
Mitch Rasussen, Secretary
Ivan Murgic, Chair
Membership: 200+ companies; *Fees:* $2 per suite, $325 minimum, owner/property manager membership; $1,500 millennium membership; *Member Profile:* Firms involved in multifamily rental housing industry; *Committees:* Executive; Education & Training; Members' Services & Fundraising; Political & Municipal Liaison; Policy, Finance & Administration; Utilities, Environment & Communications

Greater Toronto CivicAction Alliance
#1800, 110 Yonge St., Toronto ON M5C 1T6
Tel: 416-309-4480; *Fax:* 416-309-4481
www.civicaction.ca
www.linkedin.com/companies/civicaction
www.facebook.com/civicactiongta
twitter.com/civicactiongta
www.youtube.com/civicactiongta
Overview: A large S organization
Chief Officer(s):

Mina Mawani, Chief Development Officer
mina.mawani@civicaction.ca

Greater Toronto Electrical Contractors Association
#207, 23 Lesmill Rd., Toronto ON M3B 3P6
Tel: 416-391-3226; *Fax:* 416-391-3926
mail@greatertorontoeca.org
www.greatertorontoeca.org
Overview: A small local organization founded in 1970
Mission: To represent electrical contractors for industrial, commercial, institutional, residential, line/utility, & communications construction & service markets within the Greater Toronto Area; to advocate for its members in labour relations matters, commercial & tendering practices, & government & regulatory issues
Affliation(s): International Brotherhood of Electrical Workers (IBEW)
Chief Officer(s):
Paul Sheridan, President
Activities: Supplementary training courses & seminars; funding for the Joint Apprenticeship Council; apprentice recruiting

Greater Toronto Hotel Association (GTHA)
#404, 207 Queens Quay West, Toronto ON M5J 1A7
Tel: 416-351-1276; *Fax:* 416-351-7749
gtha@gtha.com
www.gtha.com
Previous Name: Hotel Association of Metropolitan Toronto
Overview: A medium-sized local organization founded in 1925
Mission: To provide the membership with a proactive, informative & cohesive service-oriented organization whose objective is to raise the profile & prosperity of its members
Chief Officer(s):
Terry Mundell, President
Staff Member(s): 3
Activities: *Speaker Service:* Yes

Greater Toronto Marketing Alliance (GTMA)
#1200, 350 Bay St., Toronto ON M5H 2S6
Tel: 416-360-7320; *Fax:* 416-360-7331
www.greatertoronto.org
www.linkedin.com/company/greater-toronto-marketing-alliance
twitter.com/gtmatoronto
www.flickr.com/photos/gtmatoronto
Overview: A small local organization founded in 1998
Mission: To attract international investment & employment to the Greater Toronto Area
Member of: Toronto Board of Trade; EDCO; Canadian Urban Institute; World Teleport Association; EDAC; CoreNet
Chief Officer(s):
George Hanus, President & CEO
ghanus@greatertoronto.org
Gerald Pisarzowski, Vice-President, Business Development
gpisarzowski@greatertoronto.org
Tony Romano, Vice-President, Corporate & Investor Services
tromano@greatertoronto.org
Finances: *Annual Operating Budget:* Greater than $5 Million
Staff Member(s): 6
Membership: 80; *Member Profile:* Municipalities; boards of trade; chambers of commerce; government; private sector; NGO; *Committees:* Automotive; Information Technology; Energy Environment; Call Centres; Aerospace; Industrial Design
Activities: GTA Luncheon series; Council Investment missions; Corporate call programs; Incoming delegation hosting; *Speaker Service:* Yes
Awards:
- GTA International Awards of Distinction (Award)

Greater Toronto Rose & Garden Horticultural Society
9 Tarlton Rd., Toronto ON M5P 2M5
Tel: 416-485-5907
GTRoses@aol.com
www.gardenontario.org/site.php/rosegarden
Also Known As: Toronto Rose
Previous Name: York Rose & Garden Society
Overview: A small local organization founded in 1979 overseen by Ontario Horticultural Association
Mission: Dedicated to cultivation & enjoyment of roses
Member of: Canadian Rose Society, American Rose Society, Ontario Horticultural Association
Chief Officer(s):
Iris Hazen, Contact
Membership: 150; *Fees:* $10 regular; $15 family
Activities: Annual "Roses" garden tour; lectures; public meetings

Greater Toronto Water Garden & Horticultural Society (GTWGHS)
4691 Hwy. 7A, RR#1, Nestleton Station ON L0B 1L0
Tel: 416-438-4862
info@onwatergarden.com
www.onwatergarden.com
Previous Name: Ontario Water Garden Society
Overview: A small provincial organization
Member of: Ontario Horticultural Association
Chief Officer(s):
Laura Grant, Contact, 416-422-2164, Fax: 416-422-2820
Joachim G. Doehler, President
Peter Poot, Secretary
Membership: *Fees:* $20 single; $25 family

Greater Vancouver Apartment Owners Association *See* British Columbia Apartment Owners & Managers Association

Greater Vancouver Association of the Deaf (GVAD)
2125 West 7th Ave., Vancouver BC V6K 1X9
Fax: 604-738-4645; *TTY:* 604-738-4644
gvadoffice@gmail.com
www.gvad.com
Overview: A small local charitable organization founded in 1926
Mission: To promote all matters of the welfare of the deaf; to foster the social, cultural, educational & recreational activities of the deaf; To affiliate & serve with provincial, regional & national organizations of the deaf & hard of hearing; To ensure that the activities of the society always be intended to contribute positively to the Greater Vancouver area or to any other district within the society's areas of operation
Affliation(s): BC Deaf Sports Federation
Chief Officer(s):
Leanor Vlug, President
Finances: *Funding Sources:* Grants, members, donation
Membership: 1-99; *Fees:* $0 youth/seniors; $10 regular
Activities: Annual Corn Party; Talent Night
Awards:
- Annual GVAD Student Scholarship (Scholarship)
Amount: $500

Greater Vancouver Community Services Society (GVCSS)
#500, 1212 West Broadway, Vancouver BC V6H 3V1
Tel: 604-737-4900; *Fax:* 604-737-2922
info@gvcss.bc.ca
www.gvcss.bc.ca
Overview: A small provincial organization
Mission: Non-profit provider of in-home health care services to the elderly and individuals with physical and/or developmental disabilities
Chief Officer(s):
Ron McLeod, CEO
Membership: 100 agencies
Activities: Home support; assisted living

Greater Vancouver Food Bank Society (GVFBS)
1150 Raymur Ave., Vancouver BC V6A 3T2
Tel: 604-876-3601; *Fax:* 604-876-7323
www.foodbank.bc.ca
www.facebook.com/VanFoodBank
twitter.com/vanfoodbank
Overview: A small local charitable organization founded in 1982 overseen by Food Banks British Columbia
Mission: The agency provides food & related assistance to those in need in the local area. It is a registered charity, BN: 107449787RR0001.
Member of: Food Banks British Columbia; Food Banks Canada; Foodchain; Burnaby Chamber of Commerce; Vancouver Board of Trade; Vancouver Food Policy Organization; Volunteer Vancouver
Finances: *Annual Operating Budget:* $1.5 Million-$3 Million; *Funding Sources:* Donations
Staff Member(s): 10; 500 volunteer(s)
Membership: 250; *Fees:* $10; *Committees:* Advisory; Audit; Executive; Finance; Fundraising
Activities: 18 direct food distribution centres; *Awareness Events:* Annual Christmas in July; Christmas Campaign

Greater Vancouver Home Builders' Association (GVHBA)
#1003, 7495 - 132 St., Surrey BC V3W 1J8
Tel: 778-565-4288; *Fax:* 778-565-4289
www.gvhba.org
ca.linkedin.com/groups?gid=5069902
www.facebook.com/gvhba/
twitter.com/GVHBA
www.youtube.com/GreaterVancouverHBA
Overview: A small local organization founded in 1974 overseen by Canadian Home Builders' Association
Mission: To promote professionalism in the homebuilding industry & committed to providing timely new home & renovation information to consumers
Member of: Canadian Home Builders' Association
Chief Officer(s):
Robert de Wit, Chief Executive Officers
bob@gvhba.org
Staff Member(s): 7
Membership: 740+; *Member Profile:* Home builders, renovators, architects, manufacturers, suppliers, sub-contractors, government agencies, utilities, publishers, bankers, lawyers & other professionals
Activities: Certification courses & industry workshops; consumer seminars; monthly dinner meetings

Greater Vancouver International Film Festival Society (VIFF)
1181 Seymour St., Vancouver BC V6B 3M7
Tel: 604-685-0260; *Fax:* 604-688-8221
viff@viff.org
viff.org
www.facebook.com/pages/Vancouver-Film-and-TV-Forum/9991 0045387
twitter.com/VIFForum
Also Known As: Vancouver International Film Festival
Overview: A small international charitable organization founded in 1982
Mission: To operate the Annual Vancouver International Film Festival, bringing to British Columbia the best in current art cinema from around the world as well as buried treasures from past international cinema
Chief Officer(s):
Alan Franey, Festival Director
Finances: *Annual Operating Budget:* $1.5 Million-$3 Million; *Funding Sources:* 45% corporate sponsorship; 35% box office; 20% government funding
Staff Member(s): 7; 750 volunteer(s)
Membership: 42,000; *Fees:* $2
Activities: *Awareness Events:* Vancouver International Film Festival; VIFF Film + TV Forum; *Internships:* Yes
Awards:
- Rogers People's Choice Award for Most Popular Film (Award)
- The VIFF Award for Most Popular Canadian Film (Award)
- The Dragons & Tigers Award for Young Cinema (Award)
Amount: $10,000
- The CityTV Award for Best Western Canadian Film (Award)
Amount: $12,000
- The National Film Board of Canada Awards for Best Documentary Feature (Award)
Amount: $2,500
- VIFF Environmental Film Award (Award)

Greater Vancouver Japanese Canadian Citizens' Association (JCCA)
Nikkei Heritage Centre, #200, 6688 Southoaks Cres., Burnaby BC V5E 4M7
Tel: 604-777-5222; *Fax:* 604-777-5223
jccabulletin-geppo.ca/about-2/jcca-bulletin
Previous Name: Japanese Canadian Citizens Association
Overview: A small local organization founded in 1949
Member of: National Association of Japanese Canadians
Chief Officer(s):
Ron Nishimura, President
romini@shaw.ca
Membership: *Fees:* $35 regular; $25 senior
Activities: "Keirokai"; Powell Street Festival; music festival; movie festival; workshops
Publications:
- The Bulletin
Type: Journal; *Editor:* John Endo Greenaway

Greater Vancouver Professional Theatre Alliance (GVPTA)
1405 Anderson St., 3rd Fl., Vancouver BC V6H 3R5
Tel: 604-608-6799; *Fax:* 604-608-6923
info@gvpta.ca
www.gvpta.ca
www.facebook.com/GVPTA
twitter.com/gvptatheatre
Previous Name: Vancouver Professional Theatre Alliance
Overview: A medium-sized local organization founded in 1987

Mission: To promote live theatre & foster a thriving environment for the continued growth & development of theatre in Greater Vancouver
Member of: Alliance for Arts & Culture; Granville Island Business and Community Association; Tourism Vancouver; Vantage Point
Chief Officer(s):
Dawn Brennan, Director
director@gvpta.ca
Finances: *Funding Sources:* Self-generated; government grants
Staff Member(s): 3
Membership: *Member Profile:* Theatre companies & venues; *Committees:* Marketing; Membership Development; Conferences & Meetings; Fundraising
Activities: Membership program; workshops; guest speakers; *Internships:* Yes

Greater Vancouver Regional District Employees' Union (GVRDEU)
#102, 3060 Norland Ave., Burnaby BC V5B 3A6
Tel: 604-220-7052
gvrdeu@telus.net
www.gvrdeu.org
Overview: A small local organization founded in 1946
Mission: The Union serves the outside workers of Metro Vancouver & is their sole bargaining agent in collective agreements.
Chief Officer(s):
Bob Beaumont, Secretary
Membership: 500+; *Member Profile:* Workers in water distribution & disinfection, watershed management, watershed security, social housing across the region, regional parks, wastewater collection & treatment, construction, including temporary summer workers

Greater Vernon Chamber of Commerce (GVCC)
#102, 2901 - 32nd St., Vernon BC V1B 3W4
Tel: 250-545-0771; *Fax:* 250-545-3114
info@vernonchamber.ca
www.vernonchamber.ca
twitter.com/VernonChamber
Also Known As: Vernon Chamber of Commerce
Overview: A small local organization founded in 1897
Mission: To facilitate, enhance & improve the region's unique quality of life; To support positive & sustainable development; To encourage growth in commerce & industry for the prosperity of its members & the Greater Vernon area
Member of: BC Chamber of Commerce
Affliation(s): Canadian Chamber of Commerce
Chief Officer(s):
George Duffy, General Manager
manager@vernonchamber.ca
David Fletcher, President
Finances: *Annual Operating Budget:* $250,000-$500,000; *Funding Sources:* Membership dues; sponsors; banner ads on website
Staff Member(s): 3; 25 volunteer(s)
Membership: 500; *Fees:* $175-$525; *Member Profile:* Businesses in Vernon & area; *Committees:* Executive; Membership; Events
Activities: Annual Business Excellence Awards; luncheons; Business After 5; seminars; *Internships:* Yes; *Speaker Service:* Yes

Greater Victoria Chamber of Commerce (GVCC)
#100, 852 Fort St., Victoria BC V8W 1H8
Tel: 250-383-7191; *Fax:* 250-385-3552
chamber@gvcc.org
www.victoriachamber.ca
www.facebook.com/VictoriaChamber
twitter.com/ChamberVictoria
www.youtube.com/user/victoriachamber
Also Known As: Victoria Chamber of Commerce
Overview: A medium-sized local organization founded in 1863
Mission: To act as the voice of business for the Greater Victoria region; To ensure that the area maintains & enhances its prosperous & vibrant business climate
Member of: BC Chamber of Commerce; Canadian Chamber of Commerce
Chief Officer(s):
Bruce Carter, CEO, 250-360-3470
bcarter@gvcc.org
Margaret Lucas, Chair
David Marshall, Treasurer
Finances: *Funding Sources:* Membership fees; Sponsorships
Membership: 1,500+; *Fees:* Schedule available based upon number of employees; *Member Profile:* Businesses in the Greater Victoria region; *Committees:* Greater Victoria Development Agency; Prodigy Group; Ambassadors; Regional Planning Group; Leadership Group; Crime Reduction Working Group
Activities: Influencing public policy to support a healthy enterprise system; Advancing existing business; Attracting new economic opportunities to Greater Victoria; Forming partnerships; Hosting events; Offering networking opportunities; Providing educational programs;

Greater Victoria Hospitals Foundation *See* Victoria Hospitals Foundation

Greater Victoria Philatelic Society (GVPS)
928 Claremont Ave., Victoria BC V8Y 1K3
e-mail: gvps@vicstamps.com
www.vicstamps.com/gvps.htm
Overview: A small local organization
Member of: Royal Canadian Philatelic Society; Northwest Federation of Stamp Clubs
Activities: Annual local stamp show, Oct. & May; PIPEX International Show; meetings 3rd Fri. every month

Greater Victoria Youth Orchestra (GVYO)
1611 Quadra St., Victoria BC V8W 2L5
Tel: 250-360-1121; *Fax:* 250-381-3573
gvyo@telus.net
www.gvyo.org
Overview: A small local charitable organization founded in 1986 overseen by Orchestras Canada
Mission: To affirm & nourish the love of music in young people; to foster musical development of orchestra members; to serve as musical resource to the community at large
Affliation(s): Community Arts Council of Greater Victoria
Chief Officer(s):
Yariv Aloni, Music Director
Sheila Redhead, Manager
Finances: *Funding Sources:* Provincial & municipal government; individual & corporate donations; fundraising; player fees; box office
Membership: *Member Profile:* By audition; *Committees:* Parents; Music
Activities: *Speaker Service:* Yes; *Library* by appointment
Awards:
- Annual Music Scholarships (Scholarship)
- Bursary Awards (Award)

Greater Woodstock Chamber of Commerce
#2, 220 King St., Woodstock NB E7M 1Z8
Tel: 506-325-9049; *Fax:* 506-328-4683
info@gwcc.ca
www.gwcc.ca
Overview: A small local organization
Mission: To promote & improve tourism, trade & commerce & the economic, civic & social welfare of the district
Member of: Atlantic Provinces Chamber of Commerce
Chief Officer(s):
Allison McLellan, President
allison@mclellanscountrywide.ca
Finances: *Annual Operating Budget:* Less than $50,000
Membership: 140; *Fees:* $180-$360 business; $84 non-profit
Activities: *Awareness Events:* Small Business Week, Oct.

Greek Community of Metropolitan Toronto Inc.
30 Thorncliffe Park Dr., Toronto ON M4H 1H8
Tel: 416-425-2485; *Fax:* 416-425-2954
info@greekcommunity.org
www.greekcommunity.org
Overview: A medium-sized local organization
Chief Officer(s):
Nikona (Nick) Georgakopoulos, President
Membership: *Fees:* $100 individual/family; $40 seniors; $20 student; $1000 lifetime

Greek Orthodox Church (Canada) *See* Greek Orthodox Metropolis of Toronto (Canada)

Greek Orthodox Community of East Vancouver
C/O Saints Nicholas & Dimitrios Greek Orthodox Church, 4641 Boundary Rd., Vancouver BC V7C 1B9
Tel: 604-438-6432; *Fax:* 604-438-6400
father@saintsnicholasanddimitrios.org
www.saintsnicholasanddimitrios.org
Overview: A small local organization
Member of: Greek Orthodox Church
Chief Officer(s):
Kostas Rokanas, President
Membership: 100-499; *Member Profile:* Orthodox Christians living in conformity with the canons of the Church

Greek Orthodox Metropolis of Toronto (Canada)
86 Overlea Blvd., Toronto ON M4H 1C6
Tel: 416-429-5757; *Fax:* 416-429-4588
metropolis@gometropolis.org
www.gometropolis.org
twitter.com/GO_Metropolis
www.youtube.com/user/GOMetropolisToronto
Previous Name: Greek Orthodox Church (Canada)
Overview: A large national organization
Mission: There are 76 Greek Orthodox Communities in Canada under the jurisdiction of the Greek Orthodox Metropolis of Toronto (Canada)
Member of: The Canadian Council of Churches
Staff Member(s): 21
Membership: Over 50,000
Activities: *Library*

Greek-Canadian Cultural Centre (GCCA)
2349 Portage Rd., Niagara Falls ON L2E 6S4
Tel: 905-374-7044
Also Known As: Greek-Canadian Community Association
Overview: A small local charitable organization founded in 1977
Mission: To promote Greek heritage & culture; to support local community charities.
Affliation(s): Greek Canadian Community Association of Niagara
Finances: *Funding Sources:* Bingo/Nevada; hall rentals; dances; donations

Green Acres Art Centre
PO Box 545, Teulon MB R0C 3B0
Tel: 204-886-3192
gaac@mymts.net
www.greenacresartcentre.org
Overview: A small local organization founded in 1976
Mission: To provide arts, music & cultural actvities for the Town of Teulon & environs.
Member of: Manitoba Association of Community Arts Councils Inc.
Chief Officer(s):
Lana Knor, President
gaacpresident@mymts.net
Staff Member(s): 1
Activities: Dance, music, oil painting, & yoga classes; astronomy club;

Green Action Centre (RCM)
303 Portage Ave., 3rd Fl., Winnipeg MB R3B 2B4
Tel: 204-925-3777; *Fax:* 204-942-4207
Toll-Free: 866-394-8880
info@greenactioncentre.ca
greenactioncentre.ca
www.facebook.com/group.php?gid=134760813229244
twitter.com/greenactionctr
www.pinterest.com/gacentre/
Previous Name: Recycling Council of Manitoba; Resource Conservation Manitoba Inc.
Overview: A medium-sized provincial organization founded in 1985
Mission: To promote ecological sustainability by developing alternatives to currently unsustainable practices; our principal activity is environmental education; our partners & clients include businesses, schools, non-profit groups, governments, recyclers, home gardeners & general public
Member of: Canadian Environment Network; Manitoba Eco-Network; Manitoba Environmental Industries Association
Chief Officer(s):
Tracy Hucul, Executive Director, 204-925-3770
tracy@greenactioncentre.ca
Finances: *Annual Operating Budget:* $100,000-$250,000; *Funding Sources:* 3 levels of government; corporate; private foundations; membership dues
Staff Member(s): 11; 20 volunteer(s)
Membership: 200; *Committees:* Membership; Policy
Activities: Public Infoline; Environmental Speaker's Bureau; The R-Report; Public Forums; Green Commuting Program; Composting Education Program; *Speaker Service:* Yes; *Library:* Resource Centre

Green Calgary
#100, 301 - 14th St. NW, Calgary AB T2N 2A1
Tel: 403-230-1443; *Fax:* 403-230-1458
Other Communication: products@greencalgary.org

info@greencalgary.org
www.greencalgary.org
www.facebook.com/home.php#!/pages/Green-Calgary/136497856363082
twitter.com/greencalgary
Previous Name: Clean Calgary Association
Overview: A medium-sized local charitable organization founded in 1978
Mission: To provide educational programs which assist Calgarians to develop an environmentally friendly lifestyle
Member of: Alberta Environmental Network; Ecotrust; City of Calgary Environment Advisory Committee
Chief Officer(s):
Patricia Cameron, Executive Director
patricia@greencalgary.org
Finances: *Annual Operating Budget:* $250,000-$500,000; *Funding Sources:* Municipal government; corporate; casino; goods & services
Staff Member(s): 8; 125 volunteer(s)
Membership: 90; *Fees:* $15 low-income/student; $50 individual; $75 non-profit; $200 business; *Member Profile:* Concern for environment & positive, proactive programs
Activities: Waste reduction & water conservation; *Speaker Service:* Yes

Green Communities Association *See* Green Communities Canada

Green Communities Canada (GCC)

PO Box 928, 416 Chambers St., 2nd Fl., Peterborough ON K9J 7A5
Tel: 705-745-7479; *Fax:* 705-745-7294
info@greencommunitiescanada.org
www.gca.ca
www.facebook.com/125118647578545
twitter.com/GCCCanada
Previous Name: Green Communities Association
Overview: A small national organization founded in 1995
Mission: To support member organizations in achieving environmental sustainability
Member of: Canadian Renewable Energy Alliance
Chief Officer(s):
Clifford Maynes, Executive Director, 705-745-7479 Ext. 118
cmaynes@greencommunitiescanada.org
Sé Keohane, Manager, Finance, 705-745-7479 Ext. 112
finance@greencommunitiescanada.org
Jacky Kennedy, Director, Canada Walks, 416-488-7263, Fax: 416-488-2296
info@saferoutestoschool.ca
Sharyn Inward, Director, Water Programs, 705-745-7479 Ext. 113
sharyn@greencommunitiescanada.org
Bruce Roxburgh, Manager, Green Information Technology, 705-745-7479 Ext. 117
broxburgh@greencommunitiescanada.org
Membership: *Fees:* $500 full membership; $250 associate membership; *Member Profile:* Non-profit community-based organizations that deliver environmental programs
Activities: Sharing information & resources; joint member projects; Water Programs; Energy Programs; Walking Programs/Safe Routes to School; Green IT
Publications:
• Green Community News
Type: Newsletter; *Frequency:* Weekly
Profile: Association activities, resources, & events

Green Kids Inc.

#251, 162-2025 Corydon Ave., Winnipeg MB R3P 0N5
Tel: 204-940-4745; *Fax:* 204-201-0676
Toll-Free: 800-441-6751
www.greenkids.com
www.facebook.com/pages/Green-Kids/133450756699837
Overview: A small national charitable organization founded in 1991
Mission: To empower children to take positive action & change the world
Chief Officer(s):
Jeff Golfman, Volunteer President
Membership: *Committees:* Honorary Advisory; Technical Advisory
Activities: Educates children (K-8) about environmental issues in schools using interactive theatre

The Green Party of Alberta

PO Box 45066, Stn. Brentwood, #319, 3630 Brentwood Rd. NW, Calgary AB T2L 1Y4
Tel: 403-293-4593
information@evergreenparty.ca
albertagreens.ca
www.facebook.com/EverGreenParty
twitter.com/evergreenparty
www.youtube.com/channel/UCDThlj1s25MXizher-qXRWg
Also Known As: Evergreen Party of Alberta
Overview: A small provincial organization founded in 1990 overseen by Green Party of Canada
Mission: To encourage the development of an attitude that everyone is part of the land; to encourage strict control of all forms of pollution; to promote programs teaching consensus & facilitation; to facilitate the process of all interested community members becoming involved in education, both learning & teaching, guided by the long-term sustainability of the Earth community; to create the opportunity for Albertans to become involved in the strategic planning process
Chief Officer(s):
Janet Keeping, Party Leader
leader@greenpartyofalberta.ca
Susan Stratton, President
president@greenpartyofalberta.ca
Matt Burnett, Chief Financial Officer
cfo@greenpartyofalberta.ca
Finances: *Funding Sources:* Donations; membership
Membership: *Member Profile:* Environmentally & socially concerned Albertans
Activities: Organizing for provincial elections; education; raising awareness of issues; *Speaker Service:* Yes

Green Party of Canada (GPC) / Parti vert du Canada

PO Box 997, Stn. B, #204, 396 Cooper St., Ottawa ON K1P 5R1
Tel: 613-562-4916; *Fax:* 613-482-4632
Toll-Free: 888-868-3447
info@greenparty.ca
www.greenparty.ca
www.facebook.com/GreenPartyofCanada
twitter.com/canadiangreens
www.youtube.com/user/canadiangreenparty
Overview: A medium-sized national organization founded in 1983
Mission: To promote a platform that includes debt reduction, eco-jobs, saving Canada's forests, supporting small business, use of soft energies, sovereignty for First Nations, & a guarantee of full rights for women
Member of: CanAmex; World Greens Coordination
Chief Officer(s):
Elizabeth May, Leader
leader@greenparty.ca
Adriane Carr, Deputy Leader
Paul Estrin, President
Finances: *Annual Operating Budget:* $50,000-$100,000; *Funding Sources:* Individual contributions
Staff Member(s): 1; 40 volunteer(s)
Membership: 4,000; *Fees:* $10+; *Committees:* Election Coordinating; Officer/Functionary Review; Finance/Administration; Green Convenors
Activities: *Speaker Service:* Yes

The Green Party of Manitoba

PO Box 26023, Stn. Maryland, 120 Sherbrook St., Winnipeg MB R3C 3R3
Tel: 204-488-2831
Toll-Free: 866-742-4292
info@greenparty.mb.ca
www.greenparty.mb.ca
facebook.com/profile.php?id=43307539939
twitter.com/Green_Party_MB
www.youtube.com/user/GreenPartyofManitoba
Also Known As: Manitoba Greens
Overview: A medium-sized provincial organization founded in 1996 overseen by Green Party of Canada
Chief Officer(s):
James R. Beddome, Party Leader
Membership: *Fees:* $5

Green Party of New Brunswick / Parti Vert du Nouveau Brunswick

PO Box 3723, Stn. B, 403 Regent St., Bottom Fl., Fredericton NB E3A 5L8
Tel: 506-447-8499; *Fax:* 506-447-8489
Toll-Free: 888-662-8683
info@greenpartynb.ca
www.greenpartynb.ca
Overview: A small provincial organization overseen by Green Party of Canada
Chief Officer(s):
David Coon, Party Leader

Green Party of Nova Scotia

PO Box 36044, 5665 Spring Garden Rd., Halifax NS B3J 3S9
e-mail: gpns@greenparty.ns.ca
www.greenparty.ns.ca
Overview: A small provincial organization overseen by Green Party of Canada
Chief Officer(s):
John Percy, Party Leader
leader@greenparty.ns.ca

The Green Party of Ontario (GPO) / Parti Vert d'Ontario

PO Box 1132, Stn. F, #035, 67 Mowat Ave., Toronto ON M4Y 2T8
Tel: 416-977-7476; *Fax:* 416-977-5476
Toll-Free: 888-647-3366
admin@gpo.ca
www.gpo.ca
Previous Name: The Ontario Greens
Overview: A small provincial organization founded in 1983 overseen by Green Party of Canada
Chief Officer(s):
Mike Schreiner, Leader
Becky Smit, Executive Director, 647-830-6486
Finances: *Funding Sources:* Membership dues
Staff Member(s): 1; 900 volunteer(s)
Membership: 1,000; *Fees:* $25; *Committees:* Policy; Candidate Facilitation
Activities: Annual Fall Meeting; *Library* by appointment

Green Party of Prince Edward Island

PO Box 104, 101 Kent St., Charlottetown PE C1A 7K2
Tel: 902-569-2068
info@greenparty.pe.ca
greenparty.pe.ca
www.facebook.com/109519535816769
Overview: A small provincial organization overseen by Green Party of Canada
Chief Officer(s):
Peter Bevan Baker, Party Leader, 902-393-8101
leader@greenparty.pe.ca

Green Party of Québec *Voir* Parti Vert du Québec

Green Party Political Association of British Columbia (GPBC)

PO Box 8088, Stn. Central, Victoria BC V8W 3R7
Tel: 250-590-4537; *Fax:* 250-590-4537
Toll-Free: 888-473-3686
office@greenparty.bc.ca
www.greenparty.bc.ca
www.facebook.com/groups/bcgreens
twitter.com/janesterk
Also Known As: Green Party of BC
Overview: A medium-sized provincial charitable organization founded in 1983 overseen by Green Party of Canada
Mission: To form healthy communities with diverse economies by involving the citizens of British Columbia in the political process; To offer voters in British Columbia fiscal responsibility, socially progressive policies, & environmental sustainability
Chief Officer(s):
Adam Olsen, Interim Leader
leader@greenparty.bc.ca
Andrew Weaver, Deputy Leader
David Pearce, Treasurer & Financial Agent
Finances: *Funding Sources:* Donations
Membership: 4,000; *Fees:* Donation; *Member Profile:* Residents of British Columbia, fourteen years of age & older, who are not members of any other provincial political party; *Committees:* Fundraising; Administration; Media; Organizing; Membership

Green Roofs for Healthy Cities (GRHC)

406 King St. East, Toronto ON M5A 1L1
Tel: 416-971-4494; *Fax:* 416-971-9844
www.greenroofs.org
Overview: A medium-sized international organization founded in 1999
Mission: To promote the green roof industry throughout North America
Chief Officer(s):
Jeffrey Bruce, Chair
Steven Peck, President
speck@greenroofs.org
Dan Slone, Secretary

Paul Sheehy, Treasurer
Membership: *Member Profile:* Corporate suppliers & manufacturers; Individuals who practise the art of living architecture; Supporters (LAM subscribers); *Committees:* Research; Policy; Membership; Training & Accreditation; Corporate Members; Technical; GreenSave Calculator; Conference; Green Walls; Integrated Building Water Management; Growing Medium
Activities: Increasing awareness of the environmental, economic, & social benefits of green roofs & green walls; Providing education; Offering networking opportunities
Publications:
• Living Architecture Monitor
Type: Magazine; *Frequency:* Quarterly; *Accepts Advertising*; *Editor:* Caroline Nolan
Profile: For Green Roofs for Healthy Cities members only

Green Thumb Theatre for Young People

#210, 49 Dunlevy Ave., Vancouver BC V6A 3A3
Tel: 604-254-4055; *Fax:* 604-251-7002
info@greenthumb.bc.ca
www.greenthumb.bc.ca
www.facebook.com/GreenThumbTheatre
twitter.com/gr_thumbtheatre
Also Known As: Green Thumb Players Society
Overview: A small international organization founded in 1975
Mission: To tour schools, festivals & theatres across Canada & the world with productions which explore contemporary issues for young audiences
Affliation(s): Professional Association of Canadian Theatres
Chief Officer(s):
Victoria Henderson, President
Patrick McDonald, Artistic Director
pmcdonald@greenthumb.bc.ca
Nadine Carew, General Manager
nadine.carew@greenthumb.bc.ca
Finances: *Annual Operating Budget:* $500,000-$1.5 Million; *Funding Sources:* Canada Council for the Arts; City of Vancouver; BC Arts Council
Staff Member(s): 8; 50 volunteer(s)

Greenest City

220 Cowan Ave., Toronto ON M6K 2N6
Tel: 647-438-0038
info@greenestcity.ca
www.greenestcity.ca
www.facebook.com/GreenestCityToronto
www.twitter.com/Greenest_City
pinterest.com/greenestcity
Overview: A small local organization
Mission: To reduce pollution; To regenerate urban life; To promote social equity
Chief Officer(s):
Sandi Trillo, Secretary
Activities: Walk to School Day; Active & Safe Routes to School; Walking School Bus; projects & campaigns embrace community diversity & engage people in finding locally appropriate solutions to global environmental problems

Greenpeace Canada

33 Cecil St., Toronto ON M5T 1N1
Tel: 416-597-8408; *Fax:* 416-597-8422
Toll-Free: 800-320-7183
supporter.ca@greenpeace.org
www.greenpeace.org/canada
www.facebook.com/greenpeace.canada
twitter.com/greenpeaceCA
www.youtube.com/user/GreenpeaceCanada
Overview: A large international charitable organization founded in 1971
Mission: Greenpeace is an independent, non-profit organization best known for non-violent direct actions to raise awareness on issues such as biodiversity, pollution of the Earth, nuclear threats & disarmament; it brings public opinion to bear on decisions makers. Public protest is only one of many Greenpeace strategies; it conducts scientific, economic & political research, publicizes environmental problems, recommends environmentally sound solutions & lobbies for change.
Member of: Greenpeace International; Canadian Renewable Energy Alliance
Chief Officer(s):
Joanna Kerr, Executive Director
Ann Rowan, Chair
Finances: *Annual Operating Budget:* $1.5 Million-$3 Million; *Funding Sources:* Donations; shop sales
Staff Member(s): 35
Membership: 100,000+ in Canada + over 2.5 million internationally; *Fees:* $30
Activities: Communications; e-news; reports; *Speaker Service:* Yes; *Library:* Information Office; Open to public
Publications:
• Forest Views [a publication of Greenpeace Canada]
Type: Newsletter
• Greenpeace Canada Annual Report
Type: Yearbook
• Greenpeace Canada E-News
Type: Newsletter

Edmonton Office
6328 - 104 St. NW, Edmonton AB T6H 2K9
Tel: 780-430-9202; *Fax:* 780-430-9282

Montréal Office
454, Laurier est, 3e étage, Montréal QC H2J 1E7
Tel: 514-933-0021; *Fax:* 514-933-1017

Vancouver Office
1726 Commercial Dr., Vancouver BC V5N 4A3
Tel: 604-253-7701; *Fax:* 604-253-0114

Greenspace Alliance of Canada's Capital

PO Box 55085, 240 Sparks St., Ottawa ON K1P 1A1
e-mail: greenspace@greenspace-alliance.ca
www.greenspace-alliance.ca
Overview: A medium-sized local organization founded in 1997
Mission: To preserve green spaces in the National Capital area.
Chief Officer(s):
Amy Kempster, Chair, 613-722-6039
Membership: *Fees:* $15 group; $5 student; $30 associate

Greenwood Board of Trade

c/o City of Greenwood, PO Box 129, 202 South Government Ave., Greenwood BC V0H 1J0
Tel: 250-445-6644; *Fax:* 250-445-6441
greenwoodbot@gmail.com
www.greenwoodbot.com
www.facebook.com/100003967639871
Overview: A small local organization founded in 1899
Mission: To promote Greenwood & enhance it with the aid of grants.
Member of: Canadian Chamber of Commerce; BC Chamber of Commerce; Thompson Okanagan Tourist Association
Chief Officer(s):
Dave Evans, President
Finances: *Funding Sources:* Municipal grants
Membership: 86
Activities: Demolition Car Derby, June; operates City Campground;

Greniers de Joseph

#300, 4975, boul. Sir Wilfred Laurier, Saint-Hubert QC J3Y 7R6
Tél: 450-445-3511; *Téléc:* 450-445-2812
info@greniersdejoseph.com
greniersdejoseph.com
www.facebook.com/181077338602972
Aperçu: *Dimension:* petite; *Envergure:* locale
Mission: Pour aider les familles défavorisées en leur fournissant de la nourriture, des meubles et des vêtements
Membre(s) du bureau directeur:
Denise Dubuc, Administrateur
Christiane Poisson, Administrateur
Activités: Coin des enfants; Événements de collecte de fonds

Grenville County Historical Society (GCHS)

Grand Trunk / CN Railway Station, PO Box 982, 500 Railway Ave., Prescott ON K0E 1T0
Tel: 613-925-0489
gchs@ripnet.com
web.ripnet.com/~gchs
Overview: A small local charitable organization founded in 1891
Mission: To collect, preserve, exhibit, & publish material about Ontario's Grenville County; To provide historical records for research, such as local birth, marriage, & death records, microfilmed newspapers, & census, church, & cemetery records; To promote the preservation of historical buildings & monuments
Chief Officer(s):
Gini Leonard, President
Bonnie Gaylord, Chair, Research
Valerie Schulz, Manager, Collections
Finances: *Funding Sources:* Archive & research fees; Fundraising; Sale of publications
Membership: *Fees:* $20 individuals; $200 life memberships
Activities: Offering research for a fee; *Library:* Grenville County Historical Society Archival Resource Centre; Open to public
Publications:
• The Grenville Sentinel
Type: Newsletter; *Frequency:* 6 pa; *Editor:* Sandra Shouldice; *Price:* Free with membership in the Grenville County Historical Society

Grey Bruce Beekeepers' Association

ON
Tel: 519-794-3335
Overview: A small local organization
Mission: To provide education about beekeeping skills
Member of: Ontario Beekeepers' Association
Chief Officer(s):
Toby Bruce, President
tobyjcbruce@gmail.com
Membership: *Member Profile:* Beekeepers from the Grey Bruce region of Ontario
Activities: Assisting local beekeepers with the challenges of the industry;

Grey Bruce Real Estate Board; Grey Bruce Owen Sound Real Estate Board *See* REALTORS Association of Grey Bruce Owen Sound

Grey County Kiwanis Festival of Music

PO Box 456, Owen Sound ON N4K 5P7
www.kiwanismusicfestival.net
Previous Name: Grey County Kiwanis Music Festival
Overview: A small local organization founded in 1932
Affliation(s): Federation of Canadian Music Festivals
Chief Officer(s):
Becky Azzano, Festival Coordinator
festivalcoordinator@kiwanismusicfestival.net
Kevin Dandeno, Chair
Finances: *Funding Sources:* Kiwanis Club of Owen Sound; Kiwanis Club of Meaford; Golden "K"; fundraising; private donations
Staff Member(s): 1
Activities: Producing an annual competition music festival

Grey County Kiwanis Music Festival *See* Grey County Kiwanis Festival of Music

Grey County Law Association

611 - 9th Ave. East, Owen Sound ON N4K 6Z4
Tel: 519-371-5495; *Fax:* 519-371-4606
Toll-Free: 866-578-5841
Overview: A small local organization
Member of: Law Society of Upper Canada; Ontario Courthouse Librarians Association
Chief Officer(s):
Ronn Cheney, Librarian
Finances: *Annual Operating Budget:* $50,000-$100,000; *Funding Sources:* Law Foundation of Ontario
Staff Member(s): 1
Membership: 80; *Member Profile:* Practising lawyers; *Committees:* Executive; Library
Activities: *Library:* Courthouse Library

Grey Highlands Chamber of Commerce

PO Box 177, 19 Toronto St. North, Markdale ON N0C 1H0
Tel: 519-986-4612
Toll-Free: 888-986-4612
info@greyhighlandschamber.com
greyhighlandschamber.com
Previous Name: Markdale Chamber of Commerce
Overview: A small local organization
Mission: To promote business and tourism in the area of Markdale.
Member of: Ontario Chamber of Commerce
Chief Officer(s):
Doug Crawford, Co-President
David Turner, Co-President
Kate FitzPatrick, Office Administrator
Finances: *Annual Operating Budget:* Less than $50,000; *Funding Sources:* Membership dues; donations; grants
Membership: 100; *Fees:* $125
Activities: Tourist Booth; Ice Cream Festival, Aug.;

Grey Wooded Forage Association (GWFA)

PO Box 1448, 5039 - 45 St., Rocky Mountain House AB T4T 1B1
Tel: 403-844-2645; *Fax:* 403-844-2642
gwfa1@telus.net
www.greywoodedforageassociation.com
www.facebook.com/342501612491987
Overview: A small local organization overseen by Agricultural Research & Extension Council of Alberta

Mission: To create awareness about the uses of forages; to help the agricultural community be more environmentaly & economically sustainable through knowledge & innovation
Member of: Agricultural Research & Extension Council of Alberta
Chief Officer(s):
Albert Kuipers, Manager
gwfa2@telus.net
Muriel Finkbeiner, Office Manager
gwfa1@telus.net
Staff Member(s): 2
Membership: *Fees:* $20; *Member Profile:* Those interested in forage production & grazing management
Publications:
• The Blade [a publication of the Grey Wooded Forage Association]
Type: Newsletter; *Frequency:* Monthly
• The Newsletter [a publication of the Grey Wooded Forage Association]
Type: Newsletter; *Frequency:* 2 pa

Grey, Bruce, Dufferin, & Simcoe Postal History Study Group (PHSC)

PO Box 163, Stn. C, Kitchener ON N2G 3X9
e-mail: phscdb@postalhistorycanada.net.
www.postalhistorycanada.net/php/StudyGroups/GreyBruce/
Overview: A small local organization founded in 1998
Mission: To study the postal history of the Ontario counties of Grey, Bruce, Dufferin, & Simcoe
Affliation(s): Postal History Society of Canada
Chief Officer(s):
Justus (Gus) Knierim, Contact
Membership: *Fees:* $12; *Member Profile:* Individuals interested in the postal history of the Grey, Bruce, Dufferin, & Simcoe region of Ontario
Publications:
• Grey, Bruce, Dufferin, & Simcoe Postal History Study Group Newsletter
Type: Newsletter; *Frequency:* Quarterly; *Editor:* Justus (Gus) Knierim
Profile: Local postal history information

Greyhound Pets of Atlantic Canada Society (GPACS)

343 West Petpeswick Rd., Musquodoboit Harbour NS B0J 2L0
Tel: 902-889-2214; *Fax:* 902-443-7731
greyhnd@ns.sympatico.ca
www.gpac.ca
Overview: A small local charitable organization
Mission: To rehoming retired greyhounds across Atlantic Canada.
Chief Officer(s):
Jeanette Reynolds, President
Jennifer Melanson, Vice-President & Director, Marketing
jen_wagner77@yahoo.ca
Finances: *Funding Sources:* Corporate sponsors; private donations

Grieving Children at Seasons Centre

38 McDonald St., Barrie ON L4M 1P1
Tel: 705-721-5437; *Fax:* 705-737-5683
norma@grievingchildren.com
www.grievingchildren.com
Also Known As: Grieving Children Centre
Previous Name: Seasons Centre for Grieving Children
Overview: A small local charitable organization founded in 1995
Mission: Founded on the belief that every child deserves an opportunity to grieve in an opportune & understanding environment
Member of: Bridges in the Community
Chief Officer(s):
Patricia Copeland, Executive Director
Greg Ferguson, President
Finances: *Annual Operating Budget:* $250,000 $500,000
Staff Member(s): 4; 50 volunteer(s)
Membership: 185; *Member Profile:* Children & families who have experienced the death of someone they love
Activities: Community events; fundraising events; Healing Hearts Golf Tournament; Tender Hearts Valentines Dance; *Internships:* Yes; *Speaker Service:* Yes; *Library:* Resource Centre; by appointment

Grimsby & District Chamber of Commerce

15 Main St. East, Grimsby ON L3M 1M7
Tel: 905-945-8319; *Fax:* 905-945-1615
info@grimsbychamber.com
www.grimsbychamber.com
www.facebook.com/grimsbychamberofcommerce
Overview: A medium-sized local organization
Mission: To promote commerce in the community
Chief Officer(s):
Naomi Beirnes, President
president@grimsbychamber.com
Membership: *Fees:* Schedule available; *Committees:* Annual Events; Golf Tournaments; Trade Show; Information Services - Gateway; Budget & Finance; Sponsorship/Partners; Communications; Programs & Education; Membership; Human Resources; Liaison

Grimsby/Lincoln & District Association for Community Living Inc. *See* Community Living Grimsby, Lincoln & West Lincoln

Grimshaw & District Chamber of Commerce

PO Box 919, Grimshaw AB T0H 1W0
Tel: 780-332-4370; *Fax:* 780-332-4375
www.grimshawchamber.com
Overview: A small local organization
Member of: Alberta Chamber of Commerce
Chief Officer(s):
Theresa Bruce, President
Jenny Borys, Secretary
Finances: *Annual Operating Budget:* Less than $50,000
Staff Member(s): 1; 12 volunteer(s)
Membership: 52; *Fees:* $50-150
Activities: Trade Show, June; Business Awards Banquet, Oct.;

GRIS-Mauricie/Centre-du-Québec

#232, 255 rue Brock, Drummondville QC J2C 1M5
Tél: 819-445-0007
Ligne sans frais: 877-745-0007
info@grismcdq.org
www.grismcdq.org
Nom précédent: L'Association des gais, lesbiennes et bisexuel(le)s du Québec
Aperçu: *Dimension:* petite; *Envergure:* locale; fondée en 1998
Mission: De promouvoir la diversité de l'acceptation
Membre(s) du bureau directeur:
Nathalie Niquette, Directrice générale
Membre(s) du personnel: 3
Membre: *Montant de la cotisation:* 10$

Grocery Products Manufacturers of Canada; Food & Consumer Products Manufacturers of Canada *See* Food & Consumer Products of Canada

Grotto Cerebral Palsy Foundation Inc.

97 Guildwood Pkwy., Toronto ON M1E 5G5
Tel: 416-264-7500
Overview: A small local charitable organization
Mission: To sponsor cerebral palsy research at the Hospital for Sick Children & full sponsorship of a Dentistry for Handicapped Children Program at that hospital; special equipment for education & medical support for schools & individuals

Groundfish Enterprise Allocation Council

1362 Revell Rd., Manotick ON K4M K84
Tel: 613-692-8249; *Fax:* 613-692-8250
bchapman@sympatico.ca
www.geaconline.com
Overview: A medium-sized national organization founded in 1997
Mission: To generally promote the common interests of its members; to promote the wise use, development & conservation of the Atlantic Canadian groundfish resource; To provide an organization that permits Atlantic groundfish enterprise allocation license holders to speak with a unified voice to the general public & all levels of government on matters of broad concern to the members; To provide an organization that permits groundfish enterprise allocation license holders to interface with similar organizations in Canada; To conduct research that has the potential to produce information & data that will be helpful or useful to the members; to monitor regional, national & international corporate & political activities which have a bearing on the members; To provide a platform for the views of members with regard to these activities
Chief Officer(s):
Bruce Chapman, Executive Director

Group 25 Model Car Builders' Club

Toronto ON
Tel: 416-781-0757
www.group25.org
Overview: A small local organization founded in 1976
Chief Officer(s):
Douglas Mawson, Secretary/Treasurer
KeepemFlyingDM@yahoo.ca

The Group Halifax

Halifax NS
e-mail: info@thegrouphalifax.com
thegrouphalifax.com
www.linkedin.com/groups/Group-Professional-Networking-Association-2403
www.facebook.com/TheGroupHalifax
twitter.com/TheGroupHalifax
Overview: A medium-sized local organization founded in 2008
Mission: A Halifax Metro-based business networking association with the aim of bringing together professionals in different sectors and industries to develop new skills, expand business networks, and promote the growth of their businesses.
Membership: *Fees:* $300
Activities: Weekly meetings

Group of 78 / Groupe des 78

#244, 211 Bronson Ave., Ottawa ON K1R 6H5
Tel: 613-230-0860; *Fax:* 613-563-0017
group78@web.net
www.web.net/~group78
www.facebook.com/groupof78/info
Overview: A small international charitable organization founded in 1980
Mission: To advocate for peace, disarmament, sustainable development & strengthening of the United Nations.
Chief Officer(s):
Richard Harmston, Chair
Membership: *Fees:* $125 regular; $180 family; $50 limited income; $25 student
Activities: Annual policy conference with guest speakers

Groupe Brosse Art

8245, rue St-Laurent, Brossard QC J4X 2A6
Tel: 450-656-6610
www.groupebrosseart.com
Overview: A small local organization
Mission: D'unir les artistes de Montérégie en tant que groupe, afin de promouvoir et vendre leur art.
Chief Officer(s):
Louise Lacasse, Présidente, Conseil d'administration
louloulacasse@hotmail.com
Staff Member(s): 6
Membership: 30; *Member Profile:* Artistes amateurs et semi-professionnels
Activities: Expositions

Groupe canadien d'aphérèse *See* Canadian Apheresis Group

Groupe canadien d'endocrinologie pédiatrique *See* Canadian Pediatric Endocrine Group

Groupe CDH

#201, 1000, rue Amherst, Montréal QC H2L 3K5
Tél: 514-849-7800; *Téléc:* 514-849-1495
info@groupecdh.com
www.groupecdh.com
Aperçu: *Dimension:* petite; *Envergure:* locale; fondée en 1976
Mission: Pour créer des logements abordables qui est détenue par les locataires

Groupe CTT Group

3000, rue Boullé, Saint-Hyacinthe QC J2S 1H9
Tél: 450-778-1870; *Téléc:* 450-778-3901
Ligne sans frais: 877-288-8378
info@gcttg.com
www.groupecttgroup.com
Nom précédent: CTT Group Centre for Textile & Geosynthetic Technologies
Aperçu: *Dimension:* grande; *Envergure:* nationale; Organisme sans but lucratif; fondée en 1987
Mission: Favoriser le développement des matériaux textiles et de stimuler l'avancement technologique de l'industrie textile et géosynthétique par des activités telles que la recherche et le développement, l'assistance technique, la formation sur mesure, l'information spécialisé et l'animation du milieu
Affliation(s): Fédération canadienne du textile; Association canadienne des coloristes et chimistes du textile; Société des textiles du Canada; Association des textiles des Cantons de l'Est; Institut canadien du tapis; Institut canadien des textiles; Institut québécois des revêtements de sol; Société des diplômés en textile
Membre(s) du bureau directeur:

Jacek Mlynarek, Président & PDG
jmlynarek@gcttg.com
Martin Filteau, Vice-Président
mfilteau@gcttg.com
Finances: *Budget de fonctionnement annuel:* $3 Million-$5 Million
Membre(s) du personnel: 40
Membre: 80+; *Montant de la cotisation:* 250$; *Critères d'admissibilité:* Industriel
Activités: Expo-Hightex; Forum Geosynthetiques; *Service de conférenciers:* Oui
Meetings/Conferences: • Expo Hightex 2015, March, 2015, Boucherville, QC
Scope: National

Groupe d'action pour la prévention de la transmission du VIH et l'éradication du Sida (GAP-VIES)

#300, 7355, boul Saint-Michel, Montréal QC H2A 2Z9
Tél: 514-722-5655; *Téléc:* 514-722-0063
gapvies@gapvies.ca
www.gapvies.ca
Nom précédent: Groupe haïtien pour la prévention du sida; Groupe d'action pour la prévention du sida
Aperçu: *Dimension:* petite; *Envergure:* provinciale; fondée en 1987 surveillé par Canadian AIDS Society
Mission: Prévenir la transmission du VIH/sida et d'aider les personnes atteintes du virus de l'immunodéficience humaine dans la population en général et dans la communauté haïtienne en particulier; informer et d'éduquer sur les implications de la maladie et les moyens de la prévenir; accompagner les personnes atteintes ainsi que leurs proches
Membre de: Coalition des organismes communautaires québécois de lutte contre le sida
Membre(s) du bureau directeur:
Joseph Jean-Gilles, Coordonnateur
Finances: *Budget de fonctionnement annuel:* $50,000-$100,000
Membre(s) du personnel: 6; 36 bénévole(s)
Membre: 68; *Montant de la cotisation:* 5$ individuel; 20$ institutionnel; *Critères d'admissibilite:* Professionnels; individus; institutions
Activités: Kiosques; conférences; ateliers; *Bibliothèque*

Le groupe d'action sida ***See*** AIDS Action Now

Groupe d'aide et d'information sur le harcèlement sexuel au travail de la province de Québec (GAIHST)

2231, rue Bélanger, Montréal QC H2G 1C5
Tél: 514-526-0789; *Téléc:* 514-526-8891
info@gaihst.qc.ca
www.gaihst.qc.ca
Aperçu: *Dimension:* petite; *Envergure:* provinciale; Organisme sans but lucratif; fondée en 1980
Mission: Briser le mur du silence entourant les victimes d'harcèlement sexuel; éduquer la population sur le harcèlement sexuel au travail; conseiller les femmes sur les démarches à suivre, pour tenter de régler le problème d'harcèlement sexuel au travail; aider les femmes à surmonter le problème dont elles ont été victimes; rédiger, publier et diffuser des documents, manuels, et périodiques sur la problématique
Finances: *Budget de fonctionnement annuel:* $100,000-$250,000; *Fonds:* Municipal Government
Membre(s) du personnel: 4; 11 bénévole(s)
Membre: 25
Activités: *Stagiaires:* Oui; *Service de conférenciers:* Oui

Groupe d'entraide à l'intention des personnes itinérantes et séropositives (GEIPSI)

1223, rue Ontario Est, Montréal QC H2L 1R5
Tél: 514-523-0979; *Téléc:* 514-523-3075
info@geipsi.ca
www.geipsi.ca
Aperçu: *Dimension:* petite; *Envergure:* locale; fondée en 1992
Mission: Pour apporter soutien et assistance aux personnes qui sont séropositives
Membre(s) du bureau directeur:
Yvon Coulliard, Directuer général
Olivier Lourdel, Président, Conseil d'administration
Membre: *Critères d'admissibilité:* Les personnes qui sont séropositives
Activités: Dîners communautaires; Sorties; Ateliers éducatifs;
Publications:
• Le Sans-Mots

Groupe d'entraide G.E.M.E.

Tél: 450-332-4463
Ligne sans frais: 866-443-4363
info@geme.qc.ca
geme.qc.ca
www.facebook.com/281207001891651
Aperçu: *Dimension:* moyenne; *Envergure:* locale; fondée en 1996
Mission: Pour fournir un soutien aux personnes souffrant de maladies mentales et les troubles anxieux
Membre: 6,500+; *Montant de la cotisation:* 20$
Activités: Méditation; Conférences

Groupe de droit collaboratif du Québec

445, boul. Saint-laurent, 5e étage, Montréal QC H2Y 3T8
Tél: 514-954-3471; *Téléc:* 514-954-3451
info@quebeccollaborativelaw.ca
www.droitcollaboratifquebec.ca
Aperçu: *Dimension:* petite; *Envergure:* provinciale; fondée en 2002
Mission: Pour promouvoir la pratique du droit collaboratif
Membre(s) du bureau directeur:
Diane Chartrand, Présidente, Conseil d'administraion, 514-847-8989 Ext. 238
Membre: *Montant de la cotisation:* 169,31$
Activités: Conférences; Formation

Groupe de recherche d'intérêt public de l'Ontario ***See*** Ontario Public Interest Research Group

Groupe de recherche d'intérêt public du Québec - McGill *Voir* Québec Public Interest Research Group - McGill

Groupe de recherche en animation et planification économique (GRAPE)

#280, 4765, 1e av, Québec QC G1J 3B9
Tél: 418-522-7356; *Téléc:* 418-522-0845
Aperçu: *Dimension:* petite; *Envergure:* locale; Organisme sans but lucratif; fondée en 1979
Mission: Intervenir en consultation budgétaire individuelle particulièrement auprès des gens à faibles revenus du Grand Québec
Membre de: Coalition des associations de consommateurs du Québec
Membre(s) du bureau directeur:
Laurence Marget, Coordonnatrice
Finances: *Budget de fonctionnement annuel:* $100,000-$250,000
Membre(s) du personnel: 7; 15 bénévole(s)
Membre: 99; *Critères d'admissibilité:* Habitant du Grand Québec intéressé à ce qui touche la consommation
Activités: Consultations budgétaires individuelles; ateliers budget; défense des droits du consommateur; *Stagiaires:* Oui; *Bibliothèque:* Centre de documentation; Bibliothèque publique rendez-vous

Groupe de recherche en écologie sociale (GRESOC) / Social Ecology Research Group (SERG)

Dépt. de Sociologie, Université de Montréal, CP 6128, Succ. Centre, Montréal QC H3C 3J7
Tél: 514-343-5959; *Téléc:* 514-343-5722
Aperçu: *Dimension:* petite; *Envergure:* locale; Organisme sans but lucratif; fondée en 1978
Mission: Le GRESOC est constitué de chercheurs universitaires qui s'intéressent à l'écologie sociale, à l'écosociologie et à la sociologie de l'environnement; les recherches en cours portent sur le mouvement vert (écologisme et environnementalisme), le développement durable, les pluies acides, les déchets, et les aspects sociaux des changements environnementaux globaux; plusieurs rapports de recherches, livres, chapitres et articles ont été publiés
Membre de: Réseau des Groupes Écologistes Québécois; Conseil Régional de l'Environnement de Montréal
Membre(s) du bureau directeur:
Jean-Guy Vaillancourt, Directeur
Finances: *Budget de fonctionnement annuel:* Moins de $50,000; *Fonds:* Hydro-Québec; Agence de l'efficacité énergétique; étalez votre science
2 bénévole(s)
Membre: 25; *Critères d'admissibilité:* Chercheurs universitaires
Activités: *Stagiaires:* Oui; *Bibliothèque*

Groupe de recherche et d'intervention sociale (GRIS-Montréal)

CP 476, Succ. C, Montréal QC H2L 4K4
Tél: 514-590-0016; *Téléc:* 514-590-0764
info@gris.ca
www.gris.ca
www.facebook.com/grismontreal
twitter.com/GRISmontreal
Aperçu: *Dimension:* petite; *Envergure:* locale
Mission: Favoriser un meilleure connaissance des réalités homosexuelles et de faciliter l'intégration des gais, lesbiennes et bisexuel(les) dans la société
Membre(s) du bureau directeur:
David Platts, Président
Membre(s) du personnel: 6
Membre: *Comités:* Appartenance; Formation; Démystification; Communications; Financement; Recherche

Groupe de recherche informatique et droit (GRID)

UQAM, CP 8888, Succ. Centre-Ville, Montréal QC H3C 3P8
Tél: 514-987-3000; *Téléc:* 514-987-4784
Aperçu: *Dimension:* petite; *Envergure:* locale
Membre(s) du bureau directeur:
Pierre Mackay, Directeur

Groupe de recherches sur les transports au Canada ***See*** Canadian Transportation Research Forum

Groupe des 78 ***See*** Group of 78

Groupe export agroalimentaire Québec - Canada (GEAQC) / Agri-Food Export Group Québec - Canada

1971, rue Léonard-De Vinci, Sainte-Julie QC J3E 1Y9
Tél: 450-649-6266; *Téléc:* 450-461-6255
Ligne sans frais: 800-563-9767
info@groupexport.ca
www.groupexport.ca
www.linkedin.com/company/1742471
Nom précédent: Club export agro-alimentaire du Québec
Aperçu: *Dimension:* moyenne; *Envergure:* provinciale; Organisme sans but lucratif; fondée en 1990
Mission: Développer des services adaptés aux besoins réels de nos membres afin d'augmenter leurs ventes sur les marchés internationaux; faciliter l'accès aux programmes gouvernementaux dont nous avons la gestion.
Membre de: SIAL Group; Chambre de commerce de Montréal
Membre(s) du bureau directeur:
André A. Coutu, Président-directeur général
andrecoutu@groupexport.ca
Francine Lapointe, Directrice, Programme et affaires gouvernemntale
francinelapointe@groupexport.ca
Finances: *Budget de fonctionnement annuel:* Plus de $5 Million*Fonds:* Services offerts aux membres; Agriculture Canada; Ministère de l'Agriculture des pêcheries et de l'alimentation du Québec
Membre(s) du personnel: 12
Membre: 400; *Montant de la cotisation:* 675$; *Critères d'admissibilite:* Exportateurs alimentaires
Activités: Conférence annuelle; Encadrement à l'exportation agroalimentaire; salon internationaux; accueil d'acheteur; Programme d'aide financière; *Stagiaires:* Oui; *Service de conférenciers:* Oui
Publications:
• Répertoire des exportateurs agroalienntaire du Québec
Type: Newsletter; *Editor:* Dominique Girard
Profile: Liste détaillée des entreprises membre du Groupe Export qui sont actifs sur les différents marchés

Groupe familiaux Al-Anon ***See*** Al-Anon Family Groups (Canada), Inc.

Groupe gai de l'Outaouais

#003, 109, rue Wright, Gatineau QC J8X 2G7
Tél: 819-776-2727; *Téléc:* 819-776-2001
Ligne sans frais: 877-376-2727
info@lebras.qc.ca
www.algi.qc.ca/asso/gdhgfo/
Aperçu: *Dimension:* petite; *Envergure:* locale; fondée en 1991
Mission: Discussions, rencontres, activités sociales; les rencontres ont lieu les mercredis soir à 19h30, au Bureau régional d'action sida, 109, rue Wright, local 003 (Gatineau, secteur Hull).

Groupe gai de l'Université Laval (GGUL)

Pavillon Mauice-Pollack, #2223, 2305, rue de l'Université, Québec QC G1V 0A6
Tél: 418-656-2131
ggul@public.ulaval.ca
www.ggul.org
ca.linkedin.com/pub/ggul-ulaval/28/37a/23
twitter.com/ggul_ulaval
www.youtube.com/user/GGULULAVAL
Aperçu: *Dimension:* petite; *Envergure:* locale; fondée en 1978

Groupe haïtien pour la prévention du sida; Groupe d'action pour la prévention du sida *Voir* Groupe d'action pour la prévention de la transmission du VIH et l'éradication du Sida

Groupe intervention vidéo (GIV)

#105, 4001, rue Berri, Montréal QC H2L 4H2
Tél: 514-271-5506; *Téléc:* 514-271-6890
info@givideo.org
www.givideo.org
Aperçu: *Dimension:* petite; *Envergure:* internationale; Organisme sans but lucratif; fondée en 1975
Mission: Nous privilégions sensibilisation et de discussion sur la condition féminine; le GIV organise des visionnements publics et offre des formations en vidéo légère de montage aux femmes
Membre de: Alliance du film et vidéo indépendent du Canada
Finances: *Budget de fonctionnement annuel:* $100,000-$250,000
Membre(s) du personnel: 4
Membre: 60; *Montant de la cotisation:* 25-35
Activités: Visionnement publiques; ateliers; *Stagiaires:* Oui; *Service de conférenciers:* Oui; *Bibliothèque* rendez-vous

Le groupe multimédia du Canada / The Multimedia Group of Canada

261, rue Saint-Sacrement, Montréal QC H2Y 3V2
Tél: 514-844-3636; *Téléc:* 514-844-4990
Aperçu: *Dimension:* petite; *Envergure:* internationale
Membre(s) du personnel: 2

Groupe régional d'intervention social - Québec (GRIS-Québec)

#202, 363, rue de la Couronne, Québec QC G1K 6E9
Tél: 418-523-5572
info@grisquebec.org
www.grisquebec.org
www.facebook.com/GrisQuebec
Aperçu: *Dimension:* petite; *Envergure:* locale
Membre(s) du bureau directeur:
André Tardiff, Directeur général
direction@grisquebec.org
Finances: *Budget de fonctionnement annuel:* $100,000-$250,000
Membre(s) du personnel: 3
Membre: *Montant de la cotisation:* 10$ individuel bénévole; 15$ individuel régulier
Activités: Activités sportives, sociales et culturelles; groupes de discussion; ateliers d'information;

Groupement des assureurs automobiles (GAA)

Tour de la Bourse, CP 336, #2410, 800 Place-Victoria, Montréal QC H3A 3C6
Tél: 514-288-4321
Ligne sans frais: 877-288-4321
cinfo@gaa.qc.ca
www.gaa.qc.ca
Aperçu: *Dimension:* moyenne; *Envergure:* provinciale; fondée en 1978
Mission: Administrer, de façon efficace et selon les décisions du conseil d'administration, tous les mandats certifiés au Groupement des assureurs automobiles par la Loi sur l'assurance automobile du Québec
Membre de: Chambre de commerce du Québec
Membre(s) du bureau directeur:
Patricia St-Jean, Présidente
Johanne Lamanque, Directrice générale
Finances: *Budget de fonctionnement annuel:* $1.5 Million-$3 Million
Membre(s) du personnel: 46
Membre: 100-499; *Critères d'admissibilité:* Regroupe tous les assureurs privés autorisés à pratiquer l'assurance automobile au Québec; *Comités:* Exécutif; Candidatures; Audit; Actuariat; Normes et pratiques en assurance automobile; Discipline des estimateurs; Arbitrage
Activités: *Service de conférenciers:* Oui; *Bibliothèque:* Centre de documentation

Grunthal & District Chamber of Commerce

PO Box 451, Grunthal MB R0A 0R0
Tel: 204-434-6750
grunthal.ca/chamber.php
Overview: A small local organization
Chief Officer(s):
Leonard Hiebert, President

GS1 Canada

#800, 1500 Don Mills Rd., Toronto ON M3B 3L1
Tel: 416-510-8039; *Fax:* 416-510-1916
Toll-Free: 800-567-7084
info@gs1ca.org
www.gs1ca.org
Also Known As: Electronic Data Interchange Council of Canada
Previous Name: Electronic Commerce Council of Canada
Overview: A medium-sized national organization founded in 1985
Mission: To act as a facilitator for the use of electronic information transactions in support of Canadian users.
Chief Officer(s):
N. Arthur Smith, President/CEO
Finances: *Funding Sources:* Membership dues; conferences; education courses; books
Membership: 20,000; *Fees:* $60 individual; $150 basic; $500 limited; $900 advanced; $1500 corporate; *Member Profile:* Businesses; *Committees:* Standards & Services Governance; Carenet Healthcare Sector; Foodservice Service Sector; Grocery Sector; General Merchandise, Appeal & Hardlines Sector; Healthcare Pharmacy
Activities: Provides a standard for company-to-company exchange of business transactions; *Speaker Service:* Yes; *Rents Mailing List:* Yes; *Library* Open to public

Calgary Office
#110, 720 - 28th St. NE, Calgary AB T2A 6R3
Tel: 403-291-2235
images@gs1ca.org

Montréal Office
9200 Golf Blvd., Montreal QC H1J 3A1
Tel: 514-355-8929; *Fax:* 514-356-3235
ECCnetlandV@gs1ca.org

Guaranteed Funeral Deposits of Canada (GFD)

#408, 701 Evans Ave., Toronto ON M9C 1A3
Tel: 416-626-7225; *Fax:* 416-626-1766
Toll-Free: 800-268-2466
info@gfd.org
www.gfd.org
Overview: A small national organization founded in 1961
Chief Officer(s):
Heather Kiteley, Manager, 416-407-9343

Guelph & District Multicultural Centre *See* Immigrant Services - Guelph Wellington

Guelph & District Real Estate Board

400 Woolwich St., Guelph ON N1H 3X1
Tel: 519-824-7270
info@gdar.ca
www.gdar.ca
Overview: A small local organization founded in 1959 overseen by Ontario Real Estate Association
Member of: The Canadian Real Estate Association
Finances: *Funding Sources:* Membership dues

Guelph & Wellington United Way Social Planning Council *See* United Way of Guelph, Wellington & Dufferin

Guelph Arts Council (GAC)

#404, 147 Wyndham St., Guelph ON N1H 4E9
Tel: 519-836-3280; *Fax:* 519-766-9212
administration@guelpharts.ca
guelpharts.ca/guelphartscouncil
www.facebook.com/GuelphArtsCouncil
twitter.com/guelpharts
Overview: A small local charitable organization founded in 1975
Mission: To foster & coordinate the development of the arts in the region
Affliation(s): Community Arts Ontario; Canadian Conference of the Arts; Theatre Ontario; Visual Arts Ontario; Canadian Artists Representation; Ontario Crafts Council; Dance Ontario; Ontario Historical Society; Surfacing; Arts Education Council of Ontario
Chief Officer(s):
Brad E. Hutton, President
Sonya Poweska, Executive Director
Finances: *Funding Sources:* Ontario Arts Council; City of Guelph; membership fees; donations; fundraising; Ontario Trillium Foundation
Staff Member(s): 3
Membership: 450; *Fees:* $20 youth; $30 family/individual; $45 not-for-profit; $60 business
Activities: Doors Open Guelph; Historical Walking Tours; Artist Workshops; Resource Centre; *Library* Open to public

Guelph Chamber of Commerce (GCC)

PO Box 1268, 111 Farquhar St., Guelph ON N1H 3N4
Tel: 519-822-8081; *Fax:* 519-822-8451
chamber@guelphchamber.com
www.guelphchamber.com
www.linkedin.com/groups/Guelph-Chamber-Commerce-2053342?trk=myg_ugrp_
www.facebook.com/192083367496898?sk=info
www.youtube.com/user/GuelphChamberComerc1
Overview: A medium-sized local organization founded in 1868
Mission: To serve as the voice of the business community in Guelph; to help strengthen the economy of Guelph & adjacent townships; provide a forum for the development of discussion & programs that will contribute to the social, economic & physical quality of life in Guelph; to promote Guelph as a good place to live, work & visit
Member of: Canadian Chamber of Commerce; Ontario Chamber of Commerce
Affliation(s): Guelph Business Enterprise Centre; Guelph Partnership for Innovation
Chief Officer(s):
Rob McLean, Chair & CEO
Lloyd Longfield, President & CAO
lloyd@guelphchamber.com
Finances: *Annual Operating Budget:* $500,000-$1.5 Million
Staff Member(s): 7; 200 volunteer(s)
Membership: 775; *Fees:* Based on number of employees; *Member Profile:* Businesses; *Committees:* Business Resource; Education; Environment; Industrial; Government Liaison; Marketing & Membership
Awards:
• Guelph Quality Awards (Award)

Guelph Coin Club *See* South Wellington Coin Society

Guelph District Labour Council

PO Box 293, Guelph ON N1H 6J9
Tel: 519-823-1030; *Fax:* 519-823-0102
office@guelphlabourcouncil.ca
www.guelphlabourcouncil.ca
Overview: A small local organization
Chief Officer(s):
Janice Folk-Dawson, President
jfd@members.cupe.ca
Terry O'Connor, Vice-President
terryo3@hotmail.com

Guelph Equine Area Rescue Stables

RR#3, Hanover ON N4N 3B9
Tel: 519-369-3330
info@gearstables.com
Overview: A small local organization
Mission: To give equines in hardship the opportunity at life they deserve, whether they are unwanted, retired, abused, neglected, abandoned, heading to auction or slaughter; to assess, vet and retrain these horses to make them fit for reintegration to the general public; to put all proceeds from adoption back into the mission

Guelph Food Bank

#12C, 100 Crimea St., Guelph ON N1H 2Y6
Tel: 519-767-1380; *Fax:* 519-824-1640
gfb@spiritwind.ca
spiritwind-christian-centre.ca/guelphfoodbank.html
Overview: A small local charitable organization founded in 1989
Mission: To supply food to the less fortunate in the community; to help people to become self-sufficient by offering a number of social programs.
Member of: Spiritwind Christian Centre
Affliation(s): Ontario Association of Food Banks; Canadian Association of Food Banks
Activities: Job & placement programs; skills training; credit counselling; clothing exchange

Guelph Hiking Trail Club (GHTC)

PO Box 1, Guelph ON N1H 6J6
Tel: 519-822-3672
www.guelphhiking.com
Overview: A small local organization founded in 1972
Member of: Hike Ontario
Chief Officer(s):
Kathy Somers, President, 519-836-9147
Finances: *Annual Operating Budget:* Less than $50,000
300 volunteer(s)
Membership: 200; *Fees:* $25
Activities: Guelph Radial Trail runs along an abandoned electric railway route from the Bruce Trail to Guelph; the Speed River Trail follows river southwest to the Grand Valley; The Kissing Bridge Trail runs from Guelph to Midland;

Guelph Historical Society (GHS)
#A102, 100 Crimea St., Guelph ON N1H 2Y6
e-mail: inquiries@guelphhistoricalsociety.ca
www.guelphhistoricalsociety.ca
twitter.com/GlphHistoricSoc
Overview: A small local charitable organization founded in 1961
Mission: To bring together individuals interested in the research, preservation, promotion & advancement of the history of Guelph
Member of: Guelph Arts Council; Guelph Museums
Affliation(s): Ontario Historical Society; Wellington County Historical Society
Chief Officer(s):
Betty Lou Clark, Co-President, 519-821-6191
blouclark@rlproyalcity.com
Libby Walker, Co-President, 519-763-8280
libbyw@wcm.on.ca
Finances: *Annual Operating Budget:* Less than $50,000
16 volunteer(s)
Membership: 275; *Fees:* $30 individual/institutional; $40 family; $15 student; $200 lifetime (individual); $300 lifetime (family)
Activities: Lectures; bus trip; journal; newsletter; essay contest; plaques; *Library* by appointment
Awards:
• Vern McIlwraith Essay Contest (Award)
Publications:
• Historic Guelph [a publication of Guelph Historical Society]
Type: Journal; *Frequency:* Annual

Guelph Information *See* Volunteer Centre of Guelph/Wellington

Guelph International Resource Centre (GIRC)
123 Woolwich St., Guelph ON N1H 3V1
Tel: 519-822-3110; *Fax:* 519-822-7089
info@girc.org
Overview: A small local organization
Mission: To promote awareness, analysis & action on issues of social justice & global sustainability; to help Canadians understand their connection to people in Asia, Africa & the Americas
Member of: Global Education Centres of Ontario
Finances: *Annual Operating Budget:* $100,000-$250,000; *Funding Sources:* Membership fees; donations; fundraising
Staff Member(s): 4
Membership: 1-99; *Fees:* $15
Activities: Sponsors speakers; seminars; workshops; offers educational programs; *Speaker Service:* Yes; *Library:* Resource Centre; Open to public

Guelph Musicfest
521 Kortright Rd. West, Guelph ON N1G 3R5
Tel: 519-993-7591
musicfest@artset.net
artset.net/guelphmusicfest
www.facebook.com/guelphmusicfest
twitter.com/guelphmusicfest
Overview: A small local organization
Mission: To provide an annual creative celebration of the performing arts (primarily classical music)
Chief Officer(s):
Ken Gee, Artistic Director
Finances: *Funding Sources:* Sponsorship
Membership: *Member Profile:* Members of the community interested in classical music & the status of arts in Guelph

Guelph Police Association Inc. / Association de la police de Guelph inc.
PO Box 472, Stn. Main, Guelph ON N1H 6K9
Tel: 519-763-0111
www.guelphpa.ca
twitter.com/gpapres
Overview: A small local organization
Chief Officer(s):
Matthew Jotham, President
Membership: 100-499

Guelph Symphony Orchestra (GSO)
10 Carden St., Guelph ON N1H 3A2
Tel: 519-820-4111
info@guelphsymphony.com
www.guelphsymphony.com
www.facebook.com/GuelphSymphony
twitter.com/GuelphSymphony
Overview: A small local organization founded in 2001 overseen by Orchestras Canada
Chief Officer(s):
Judith Yan, Artistic Director
Staff Member(s): 2

Guelph-Wellington Counselling Centre *See* Family Counselling & Support Services for Guelph-Wellington

Guelph-Wellington Women in Crisis
PO Box 1451, Guelph ON N1H 6N9
Tel: 519-836-1110; *Fax:* 519-836-1979; *Crisis Hot-Line:* 519-836-5710
adminrec@gwwomenincrisis.org
www.gwwomenincrisis.org
www.facebook.com/pages/Guelph-Wellington-Women-in-Crisis/47696722728
twitter.com/gwwic
www.youtube.com/user/gwwic
Previous Name: Sexual Assault Centre of Guelph
Overview: A small local organization founded in 1979
Mission: To end violence against women & children in all its forms
Member of: Ontario Association of Interval & Transition Houses; Ontario Coalition of Rape Crisis Center
Staff Member(s): 40; 160 volunteer(s)
Activities: Operating Marianne's Place, a shelter for women & their children who have been physically, emotionally, mentally, financially, or sexually abused (Phone 519-836-5710 or 1-800-265-7233); Providing the Rural Women's Support Program (Phone 519-833-2301 in Erin; 519-843-6834 in Fergus; 519-323-3638 in Mount Forest; or 519-519-5192 or 1-800-661-6041 in Palmerston); *Awareness Events:* Dec. 6 Vigil; Take Back the Night

Guid'amies franco-manitobaines
273, av Taché, Winnipeg MB
Tél: 204-237-6217
guidesfm@mymts.net
www.guidamiesfm.wix.com/guidamies
Nom précédent: Guides franco-manitobaines
Aperçu: *Dimension:* petite; *Envergure:* provinciale; Organisme sans but lucratif; fondée en 1935
Mission: Notre association constitue un organisme visant à l'éducation et à l'épanouissement des filles de 5 à 13 ans et des femmes d'expression francaise du Canada.
Membre de: Guides franco-canadiennes
Membre(s) du bureau directeur:
Paulette Hamilton, Présidente
Finances: *Budget de fonctionnement annuel:* Moins de $50,000; *Fonds:* Centraide; Francofonds
Membre(s) du personnel: 1; 10 bénévole(s)
Membre: 60; *Montant de la cotisation:* 135$; *Comités:* United Way Winnipeg
Activités: Travail en équipe; bonnes actions; service; la vie dans la nature;

Guide Outfitters Association of British Columbia (GOABC)
#103, 19140 - 28th Ave., Surrey BC V3S 6M3
Tel: 604-541-6332; *Fax:* 604-541-6339
info@goabc.org
www.goabc.org
www.twitter.com/GOABC
Overview: A small provincial organization founded in 1966
Affliation(s): Council of Tourism Associations of British Columbia
Chief Officer(s):
Dale Drown, General Manager
Finances: *Annual Operating Budget:* $500,000-$1.5 Million
Staff Member(s): 5
Membership: 200; *Fees:* $395.90; *Member Profile:* Licensed guide outfitter; angling guide
Activities: *Speaker Service:* Yes
Publications:
• Mountain Hunter Magazine
Type: Magazine; *Frequency:* 3 times pa

Guides du Canada *See* Girl Guides of Canada

Guides franco-manitobaines *Voir* Guid'amies franco-manitobaines

Guild of Industrial, Commercial & Institutional Accountants / Guilde des comptables industriels, commerciaux et institutionnels
36 Tandian Ct., Woodbridge ON L4L 8Z9
Tel: 905-264-2713; *Fax:* 905-264-1043
iciaguild@aol.com
www.guildoficia.ca
Also Known As: Guild of ICIA
Overview: A medium-sized national organization founded in 1961
Mission: To support & promote interest in vocational accountancy; To encourage acceptance of modern accounting methods & procedures
Finances: *Funding Sources:* Membership fees
Membership: *Fees:* $150 accredited; $75 associate; *Member Profile:* Graduates of accounting programs or related fields, who have also finished the requisite practical work & administrative experience; Individuals who possess bookkeeping basic skills & general accounting skills, & who work in the accounting field, may be associate members; Students in accounting or a related field
Activities: Presenting seminars on accounting & other matters of interest to Guild members; Offering an educational program in association with the Granton Institute of Technology
Publications:
• The Journal
Type: Newsletter; *Frequency:* Quarterly
Profile: Recent & forthcoming activities of the Guild available to members

The Guild Society
27 - 14th Ave., Whitehorse YT Y1A 5A7
Tel: 867-633-3550
guildhall@northwestel.net
www.guildhall.ca
Overview: A small local organization
Mission: Produces community theatre productions in Whitehorse.
Chief Officer(s):
Katherine McCallum, Artistic Director & Production Manager
Jenny Hamilton, General Manager
Activities: Produces three to four plays a season between September and May;

La Guilde canadienne des médias *See* Canadian Media Guild

Guilde canadienne des métiers d'art *See* Canadian Guild of Crafts

La Guilde canadienne des réalisateurs *See* Directors Guild of Canada

Guilde canadienne des relieurs et des artisans du livre *See* Canadian Bookbinders & Book Artists Guild

Guilde de la marine marchande du Canada *See* Canadian Merchant Service Guild

Guilde des comptables industriels, commerciaux et institutionnels *See* Guild of Industrial, Commercial & Institutional Accountants

La Guilde des Musiciens/Musiciennes du Quebec
#900, 505, boul René-Lévesque ouest, Montréal QC H2Z 1Y7
Tél: 514-842-2866; *Téléc:* 514-842-0917
Ligne sans frais: 800-363-6688
info@gmmq.com
www.gmmq.com
www.facebook.com/327272200684984
twitter.com/GMMQ
Aperçu: *Dimension:* petite; *Envergure:* provinciale; fondée en 1897
Mission: To promote the economic, social, moral & professional interests of its members & all other musicians in general; To negotiate collective agreements; to establish favourable tariff-of-fees & working conditions
Membre(s) du bureau directeur:
Mylène Cyr, Directrice générale
mcyr@gmmq.com

Guillain-Barré Syndrome Foundation of Canada (GBSFCI)
PO Box 80060 RPO Rossland Garden, 3100 Garden St., Whitby ON L1R 0H1
Tel: 647-560-6842
Toll-Free: 866-224-3301
info@gbs-cidp.org
www.gbs-cidp.org/canada/
www.facebook.com/gbscidp
twitter.com/GBS_CIDP
Overview: A medium-sized national organization founded in 1985
Mission: The Foundation provides information about, & offers moral & practical support to individuals, families & friends affected by this inflammatory disorder of the peripheral nerves

outside the brain & spinal cord. It is a registered charity, BN: 887327906RR0001.
Affliation(s): Guillain-Barré Syndrome Foundation International
Chief Officer(s):
Kenneth T. Singleton, Executive Director
Finances: *Annual Operating Budget:* Less than $50,000
12 volunteer(s)
Membership: 1-99

Guitar Society of Toronto
Toronto ON
Tel: 416-964-8298
info@GuitarSocietyofToronto.com
www.guitarsocietyoftoronto.com
www.facebook.com/GuitarToronto
twitter.com/GuitarToronto
Overview: A small local organization founded in 1956
Mission: To further the study & appreciation of the classical guitar (predominately but not exclusively)
Chief Officer(s):
Jack Silver, President
Timothy Smith, Communications Officer
Finances: *Annual Operating Budget:* Less than $50,000
Membership: *Fees:* $80; *Committees:* Concert; Promotion & Publicity; Development; Finance; Outreach & Education; Communications; 2016 GFA; Eli Kassner's 90th; By-laws

Gulf of Maine Council on the Marine Environment
c/o New Brunswick Dept. of Environment & Local Government, PO Box 6000, 850 Lincoln Rd., Fredericton NB E3B 5H1
Tel: 506-457-8946; *Fax:* 506-457-7823
www.gulfofmaine.org
Mission: This U.S.-Canadian partnership of government & non-government organizations works to maintain & enhance environmental quality in the Gulf of Maine to allow for sustainable resource use. The Council organizes conferences & workshops; offers grants & recognition awards; conducts environmental monitoring; provides science translation to management; raises public awareness about the Gulf. The secretariat rotates annually among the member jurisdictions. Initiatives include: Gulf of Maine Mapping Initiative (GOMMI), comprehensive seafloor imaging, mapping & biological & geological surveys; habitat restoration grants program (U.S. only); Action Plan grants program; Gulf of Maine Times, a quarterly newspaper; Gulfwatch Monitoring Program, which helps to assess the fate & impacts of toxic contaminants in the Gulf of Maine.
Affliation(s): ME State Planning Office; NB Department of Environment; naturesource communications, NH; NH Department of Environmental Services; NS Department of Fisheries & Aquaculture
Chief Officer(s):
Robert Capozi, New Brunswick Contact
robert.capozi@gnb.ca
Sophia Foley, Nova Scotia Contact
foleysm@gov.ns.ca

Gustav Levinschi Foundation / La fondation Gustav Levinschi
#110, 1820, av Dr Penfield, Montréal QC H3H 1B4
Tel: 514-932-2595
Overview: A small provincial charitable organization founded in 1967
Mission: To improve physical & mental health & alleviate poverty with special focus on children, adolescents & the elderly, by supporting institutions & organization in this area
Activities: Grants are made mainly for seed money, program funding, special projects, equipment funds, research projects & scholarships as agreed by the board of directors

Guyana Cultural Association of Montréal (GCAM)
PO Box 29640, Stn. CSP Prom du Parc, St. Hubert QC J3Y 9A9
Tel: 450-445-0747
gcaminfo@yahoo.com
www.gcaom.org
Overview: A small local organization founded in 1967
Mission: To help the Guyanese community in Montreal
Chief Officer(s):
U. Leebert Sancho, President
Membership: *Committees:* Benevolent; Information; Entertainment; Youth

Guysborough Antigonish Pictou Arts & Culture Council *See* Antigonish Culture Alive

Guysborough County Historical Society (GCHA)
PO Box 49, Guysborough NS B0H 1N0
Tel: 902-533-4008
guysborough.historical@ns.sympatico.ca
www.guysboroughcountyheritage.ca
Also Known As: Old Court House Museum
Overview: A small local charitable organization founded in 1972
Mission: To collect, preserve, study & exhibit these objects that serve to illustrate the story of Guysborough county & its people
Chief Officer(s):
Dan Armstrong, President
Finances: *Annual Operating Budget:* Less than $50,000
8 volunteer(s)
Membership: 60; *Fees:* $25/family
Activities: Operates Old Court House Museum;

Guysborough County Inshore Fishermen's Association (GCIFA)
PO Box 98, 990 Union St., Canso NS B0H 1H0
Tel: 902-366-2266; *Fax:* 902-366-2679
gcifa@gcifa.ns.ca
www.gcifa.ns.ca
www.facebook.com/GuysboroughCountyInshoreFishermensAssociation
Overview: A small local organization
Mission: To provide community based management of the fishing resource & to ensure a sustainable resource fishery & habitat, healthy fish stocks & act as an information liaison between inshore fishermen & the Dept. of Fisheries, as well as provide effective representation within the industry & other associations.
Chief Officer(s):
Eugene O'Leary, President
Virginia Boudreau, Manager
Katherine Newell, Lab Technician/Researcher
knewell@gcifa.ns.ca
Staff Member(s): 2
Membership: 134

Gymnastics B.C. (GBC)
#268, 828 West 8 Ave., Vancouver BC V5Z 1E2
Tel: 604-333-3496; *Fax:* 604-333-3499
Toll-Free: 800-556-2242
info@gymnastics.bc.ca
www.gymnastics.bc.ca
www.linkedin.com/groups/Gymnastics-BC-3800514
www.facebook.com/GymnasticsBC
twitter.com/GymnasticsBC
www.youtube.com/user/gymnasticsbc1
Also Known As: British Columbia Gymnastics Association
Overview: A large provincial organization founded in 1969
Mission: To provide, promote & guide positive lifelong gymnastics experiences by: directing the development & delivery of quality, comprehensive provincial programs; promoting the benefits of gymnastics as a foundation for human movement, sport, health, wellness & enjoyment; coordinating, suppporting & promoting programs in the pursuit of national & international excellence in consultation with Gymnastics Canada Gymnastique
Member of: Gymnastics Canada Gymnastique
Chief Officer(s):
Brian Forrester, CEO
bforrester@gymbc.org
Twyla Ryan, President
evolveconsulting@telus.net
Finances: *Annual Operating Budget:* $1.5 Million-$3 Million; *Funding Sources:* Membership dues; sponsorship; programs
Staff Member(s): 13
Membership: 46,000; *Committees:* Men's Technical; Women's Technical; Trampoline & Tumbling; Gymnastics for All; Provincial Advisory
Activities: Provincial championships, Fall congress, Gymnaestrada; *Library:* Resource Library
Awards:
- Volunteer Awards (Award)
- Judging Awards (Award)
- Artistic Women's Program Awards (Award)
- Artistic Men's Program Awards (Award)
- Recreational Awards (Award)
- Trampoline & Tumbling Awards (Award)
- Recognition Awards (Award)

Gymnastics Canada Gymnastique (GCG)
#120, 1900 Promenade City Park Dr., Ottawa ON K1J 1A3
Tel: 613-748-5637; *Fax:* 613-748-5691
info@gymcan.org
www.gymcan.org
www.facebook.com/gymcan
twitter.com/GymnasticsCan
www.youtube.com/user/gymnasticscanada
Previous Name: Canadian Gymnastics Federation
Overview: A large national charitable organization founded in 1969
Mission: To lead, promote, facilitate & guide gymnastics in Canada as a sport for the pursuit of excellence & world prominence, & as an activity for lifelong participation; To act as the national umbrella organization for provincial & territorial associations which are members; To publish & enforce a standard set of rules & regulations to serve as guidelines for all members; To represent Canadian gymnastics as a member of national & international agencies & federations; To coordinate application of regulations in Canada; To promote, develop & direct high performance gymnastics programs; To promote, facilitate & guide development of national gymnastics programs; To promote, guide & encourage general gymnastics activities; to promote gymnastics as a healthy & safe sport/activity
Affliation(s): Fédération internationale de gymnastique
Chief Officer(s):
Richard Crepin, Chair
Peter Nicol, Acting President & CEO
pnicol@gymcan.org
Cathy Haines, Chief Technical Officer
chaines@gymcan.org
Stephan Duchesne, Director, High Performance
sduchesne@gymcan.org
Marieve Millaire, Director, Event
mmillaire@gymcan.org
Finances: *Funding Sources:* Sport Canada; Membership; Marketing; Fundraising
Staff Member(s): 20
Membership: 250,000 individuals; *Committees:* Audit; Nominating; Human Resources; Awards; By-Law & Policy Review; Women's Artistic Gymnastics; Men's Artistic Gymnastics; Trampoline Gymnastics Program; Rhythmic Gymnastics Program; National Development/Education Program
Activities: National & international programs & competitions; *Awareness Events:* National Gymnastics Week; *Internships:* Yes
Awards:
- Life Membership (Award)
- Jay Goold Memorial Award (Award)
- Malcolm Hogarth Leadership Award (Award)
- Ed Brougham Club Awards (Award)
- Dr. Gene Sutton Memorial Award (Award)

Gymnastics Newfoundland & Labrador Inc.
PO Box 21248, Stn. MacDonald Dr., St. John's NL A1A 5B2
Tel: 709-576-0146; *Fax:* 709-576-7493
Other Communication: Alt. Phone: 709-576-0144
gymnastics@sportnl.ca
www.gymnastics.nl.ca
Overview: A small provincial organization
Mission: GNL promotes & supports the development of gymnastics throughout the province.
Member of: Canadian Gymnastics Federation
Chief Officer(s):
Bob Godden, President
Natelle Tulk, Executive Director
Membership: 8 clubs

Gymnastics Nova Scotia (GNS)
5516 Spring Garden Rd., 4th Fl., Halifax NS B3J 1G6
Tel: 902-425-5450; *Fax:* 902-425-5606
gns@sportnovascotia.ca
www.gymns.ca
Previous Name: Nova Scotia Gymnastics Association
Overview: A small provincial organization
Mission: To operate as the governing body of gymnastics in Nova Scotia; To promote gymnastics, from the recreational level to the high performance level; To encourage participation, fitness, & well-being; To promote safe & positive gymnastics environments
Chief Officer(s):
Byron Topp, President
Angela Gallant, Executive Director
Vaughn Arthur, Chair, Fair Play & Equity
Nick Lenehan, Chair, Competition
Eleanor Melrose, Chair, Education & Recreation
Cathy Huntington, Secretary
Steve Lowe, Treasurer
Membership: *Fees:* $15 recreational coaches & gymnasts & trampolinists; $25 competitive coaches & judges; $55 competitive gymnasts & trampolinists; $200 active clubs; *Member Profile:* Active & associatte gymnastics clubs throughout Nova Scotia; Judges; Recreational & competitive

coaches; Pre-school, recreational, & competitive gymnasts & trampolinists; *Committees:* Men's Program; Trampoline Program; Women's Program; Education & Recreation; Fair Play & Equity; Competition
Activities: Training & certifying coaches, officials, & judges; Organizing & sanctioning gymnastics competitions; Providing resources about gymnastics; Offering the introductory Tumblebugs progam for children from 3.5 to 5 years of age
Meetings/Conferences: • Gymnastics Nova Scotia 2015 Annual General Meeting, June, 2015, Ottawa, ON
Scope: Provincial
Description: A yearly gathering to establish the general policy & direction of the association, consider committee reports, & elect the new executive committee
Contact Information: E-mail: gns@sportnovascotia.ca
Publications:
• Gymnastics Nova Scotia Newsletter
Type: Newsletter; *Price:* Free for Gymnastics Nova Scotia members
Profile: Updates of the association's activities
• Gymnastics Nova Scotia Policy Manual
Type: Manual; *Number of Pages:* 107
Profile: Information about the association's structure, registration, meetings, elections, financials, travel, competitions, fair play, & awards

Gymnastics PEI
Sport PEI, PO Box 302, Charlottetown PE C1A 7K7
Tel: 902-368-4262; *Fax:* 902-368-4548
www.gymnasticspei.ca
Overview: A small provincial organization
Chief Officer(s):
Valerie Vuillemot, Executive Director
cgcrozier@sportpei.pe.ca

Gymnastics Saskatchewan
1870 Lorne St., Regina SK S4P 2L7
Tel: 306-780-9229; *Fax:* 306-780-9475
info@gymsask.com
www.gymsask.com
www.facebook.com/192174240806986
twitter.com/GYMSASK
Previous Name: Saskatchewan Gymnastics Association
Overview: A medium-sized provincial organization
Member of: Sask Sport Inc.; Canadian Gymnastics Federation
Chief Officer(s):
Klara Miller, CEO
Finances: *Annual Operating Budget:* $250,000-$500,000; *Funding Sources:* Grants; self-generated revenues
Staff Member(s): 5
Membership: 9,000
Activities: *Awareness Events:* Gymnastics Awareness Week

Gymn-eau Laval inc
2465, rue Honoré-Mercier, Laval QC H7C 1H6
Tél: 450-625-2674; *Téléc:* 450-625-3698
info@gymn-eau.org
www.gymn-eau.org
Aperçu: *Dimension:* petite; *Envergure:* locale; Organisme sans but lucratif; fondée en 1978
Membre(s) du personnel: 22; 10 bénévole(s)
Membre: 424; *Critères d'admissibilite:* Parents utilisateurs
Activités: Loisirs adaptés aux enfants ayant des difficultés d'apprentissage; 8 programmes d'activités sont offerts annuellement dont des camps de jour et de séjour

Habitat Acquisition Trust (HAT)
PO Box 8552, Victoria BC V8W 3S2
Tel: 250-995-2428; *Fax:* 250-920-7975
hatmail@hat.bc.ca
www.hat.bc.ca
www.facebook.com/HabitatAcqTrust
twitter.com/HabitatAcqTrust
Overview: A small local charitable organization founded in 1996
Mission: To promote the preservation of the natural environment on Southern Vancouver Island & the Southern Gulf Island by: conserving habitats by acquisition, conservation coverants or other legal mechanisms; & promoting habitat stewardship, education & research
Member of: Land Trust Alliance of British Columbia
Affliation(s): Victoria Natural History Society
Chief Officer(s):
Adam Taylor, Executive Director
Finances: *Annual Operating Budget:* $250,000-$500,000; *Funding Sources:* Private; foundations; provincial & municipal government
Staff Member(s): 4; 100 volunteer(s)
Membership: 100-499; *Fees:* $30 regular; $45 family; $100 corporate; $20 Victoria Natural History Society member
Activities: Land purchase; conservation covenants (easements); environmental education; *Library:* Bob Ogilvie Bioregional Resource Library; Open to public by appointment

Habitat faunique Canada *See* Wildlife Habitat Canada

Habitat for Humanity Canada (HFHC) / Habitat pour l'Humanité Canada
40 Albert St., Waterloo ON N2L 3S2
Tel: 519-885-4565; *Fax:* 519-885-5225
Toll-Free: 800-667-5137
habitat@habitat.ca
www.habitat.ca
www.facebook.com/HabitatforHumanityCanada
twitter.com/HabitatCanada
www.youtube.com/user/HabitatCDA?feature=mhee
Overview: A large national charitable organization founded in 1985
Mission: To provide affordable & adequate housing for God's people in need by mobilizing local communities, volunteers & material & financial resources in wide-ranging, inclusive partnerships; to support, encourage, facilitate & empower those affiliates to build affordable homes in partnership with needy families.
Member of: Habitat for Humanity International
Chief Officer(s):
Stewart Hardacre, President & CEO
Finances: *Annual Operating Budget:* $3 Million-$5 Million; *Funding Sources:* Corporate & individual donations of cash & building materials
Staff Member(s): 20; 15 volunteer(s)
Membership: 72 local affiliates
Activities: Ed Schreyer Work Project; All Women Build Project; *Speaker Service:* Yes

Alberta - Camrose Region
5007 - 46th St., Camrose AB T4V 3G3
Tel: 780-672-4484; *Fax:* 780-672-4453
hfhc@habitatcamrose.com
www.habitatcamrose.com
www.facebook.com/HabitatCamrose
twitter.com/HabitatCamrose
Chief Officer(s):
Cody McCarroll, Executive Director

Alberta - Edmonton
8210 Yellowhead Trail NW, Edmonton AB T5B 1G5
Tel: 780-479-3566; *Fax:* 780-479-0762
habitat@hfh.org
www.hfh.org
www.facebook.com/Habitatedm
www.twitter.com/Habitatedm
www.youtube.com/user/HabitatEdmGuy
Chief Officer(s):
Alfred Nikolai, President/CEO
anikolai@edmonton.hfh.org
Steve Hertzog, COO
shertzog@edmonton.hfh.org

Alberta - Lethbridge
20 Rocky Mountain Blvd. West, Lethbridge AB T1K 8E1
Tel: 403-327-6612; *Fax:* 403-331-2195
lhfh@theboss.net
www.habitatlethbridge.ca
www.facebook.com/pages/Habitat-for-Humanity-Lethbridge/440548125961345
twitter.com/HFHLethbridge
Chief Officer(s):
Dan Shapiro, Chair

Alberta - Red Deer Region
4732 - 78A St. Close, Red Deer AB T4P 2J2
Tel: 403-309-0998; *Fax:* 403-309-0915
info@habitatreddeer.ca
www.habitatreddeer.ca
www.facebook.com/restorereddeer?ref=ts
Chief Officer(s):
Hans Wiesner, Chair

Alberta - South Peace
PO Box 21114, Grande Prairie AB T8V 6W7
Tel: 780-513-0100
habitatsouthpeace@gpwins.ca
www.hfhsouthpeace.com
Chief Officer(s):
Paula Laver, Contact

Alberta - Southern Alberta
#210, 805 Manning Rd. NE, Calgary AB T2E 7M8
Tel: 403-253-9331; *Fax:* 403-253-9335
info@habitatcalgary.ca
www.habitatcalgary.ca
www.facebook.com/136402523147235?sk=wall
twitter@restorecalgary
Chief Officer(s):
Leslie Tamogi, President & CEO
Scott Graham, CFO
scott@habitatcalgary.ca

Alberta - Wood Buffalo
PO Box 6346, Fort McMurray AB T9H 5N3
Tel: 780-714-9414
info@habitatwoodbuffalo.org

British Columbia - Boundary
PO Box 1088, Grand Forks BC V0H 1H0
Tel: 250-442-0705
hfhboundary@hughes.net
www.habitatboundary.com
www.facebook.com/pages/Habitat-for-Humanity-Boundary/169898626390980
Chief Officer(s):
Rick Friesen, Executive Director

British Columbia - Greater Vancouver
69 West 69th Ave., Vancouver BC V6H 4B9
Tel: 604-681-5618; *Fax:* 604-326-0122
info@vancouverhabitat.bc.ca
www.vancouverhabitat.bc.ca
Chief Officer(s):
Anneke Rees, CEO

British Columbia - Kamloops
28-1425 Cariboo Pl., Kamloops BC V2C 5Z3
Tel: 250-314-6783; *Fax:* 250-374-9370
info@habitatkamloops.com
www.habitatkamloops.com
Chief Officer(s):
Ziggy Morash, Chair
+ziggym@telus.net

British Columbia - Kelowna
PO Box 25031, Stn. Mission Park, Kelowna BC V1W 4P2
Tel: 250-762-7303; *Fax:* 250-762-7303
habitatforhumanitykelowna@telus.net
habitatforhumanitykelowna.ca
www.facebook.com/HabitatforHumanityKelowna
twitter.com/hfhkelowna
Chief Officer(s):
Bob Wiebe, Executive Director

British Columbia - Mid-Vancouver Island Society
#1, 4128 Mostar Rd., Nanaimo BC V9T 6C9
Tel: 250-758-8078; *Fax:* 250-758-8096
info@habitatmvi.org
www.habitatmvi.org
www.facebook.com/205667832791866
Chief Officer(s):
Mark Drysdale, President
Teresa Pring, Executive Director
tpring@habitatmvi.org

British Columbia - Prince George
220 Queensway, Prince George BC V2L 1L2
Tel: 250-564-1188; *Fax:* 250-564-1132
info@habitatpg.org
www.habitatpg.org
www.facebook.com/group.php?gid=4000043586
Chief Officer(s):
Christina Wall, President

British Columbia - South Okanagan
PO Box 23021, Penticton BC V2A 8L7
Tel: 250-487-4888; *Fax:* 250-770-1654
info@habitatsouthokanagan.ca
www.habitatsouthokanagan.ca
Chief Officer(s):
Florence Barton, Chair

British Columbia - Sunshine Coast
PO Box 2356, 1494 Hilltop Rd., Sechelt BC V0N 3A0
Tel: 604-885-6773; *Fax:* 604-885-0298
info@habitatsc.ca
www.habitatsc.ca
Chief Officer(s):
Ron Pepper, Executive Director

British Columbia - Upper Fraser Valley Society
#2, 34220 South Fraser Way, Abbotsford BC V2T 1T9
Tel: 604-557-1020; *Fax:* 604-557-9991
Toll-Free: 866-856-2434
www.habitatufv.ca
www.facebook.com/403131583068845

Chief Officer(s):
Doug Rempell, Executive Director
executive@habitatufv.ca

British Columbia - Vancouver Island North Society
1755 - 13th St., Courtenay BC V9N 7B6
Tel: 250-334-3777; *Fax:* 250-334-2528
info@HabitatNorthIsland.com
www.habitatnorthisland.com
www.facebook.com/HabitatVin
Chief Officer(s):
Deb Roth, Executive Director
exdvin@gmail.com

British Columbia - Victoria
849 Orono Ave., Victoria BC V8B 2T9
Tel: 250-480-7688; *Fax:* 250-480-7648
info@habitatvictoria.com
www.habitatvictoria.com
www.facebook.com/HabitatVictoria
Chief Officer(s):
Jennifer Burgis, President

British Columbia - West Kootenay
#809, 622 Front St., Nelson BC V1L 4B7
Tel: 250-352-9778
info@habitatwk.ca
www.habitatwk.ca
www.facebook.com/habitatwk
Chief Officer(s):
Darril Beninger, Contact

Manitoba - Winnipeg
60 Archibald St., Winnipeg MB R2J 0V8
Tel: 204-233-5160; *Fax:* 204-233-5271
info@habitat.mb.ca
www.habitat.mb.ca
www.facebook.com/pages/Habitat-for-Humanity-Winnipeg/11 6555538378744
twitter.com/habitat_MB
www.youtube.com/user/HFHWPG
Chief Officer(s):
Sandy Hopkins, CEO
shopkins@habitat.mb.ca

New Brunswick - Fredericton Area Inc.
PO Box 643, Fredericton NB E3B 5A6
Tel: 506-474-1520; *Fax:* 506-452-7213
info@habitatfredericton.com
www.habitatfredericton.com
www.facebook.com/group.php?gid=2366761401
Chief Officer(s):
Doug Swan, Chair

New Brunswick - Moncton Area/Région de Moncton
175 Barker St., Moncton NB E1C 9T8
Tel: 506-384-4663; *Fax:* 506-384-4661
hfhma@nb.aibn.com
Chief Officer(s):
Gayle Milburn, Executive Director

New Brunswick - Saint John
388 Rothesay Ave., Saint John NB E2J 2C4
Tel: 506-635-7867; *Fax:* 506-635-0206
info@habitatsaintjohn.ca
www.habitatsaintjohn.ca
www.facebook.com/SJHabitat
www.twitter.com/SJHabitat
Chief Officer(s):
Tim Ryan, Contact

Newfoundland & Labrador
PO Box 8910, 55 Kenmount Rd., St. John's NL A1B 3P6
Tel: 709-737-2823; *Fax:* 709-737-5832
contact@habitatnl.ca
www.cabothabitat.ca
www.facebook.com/cabothabitat
twitter.com/HabitatNLCA
www.youtube.com/user/CabotHabitat
Chief Officer(s):
Nelson White, Executive Director

Northwest Territories
YK Centre Mall, Lower Level, PO Box 243, Yellowknife NT X1A 2N2
Tel: 867-920-4010
admin@habitatnwt.ca
www.habitatnwt.ca
www.facebook.com/pages/Habitat-for-Humanity-NWT/132151 686903893
twitter.com/HabitatNWT
Chief Officer(s):
Dave Hurley, President

Nova Scotia - Halifax Regional Municipality Association
121 Ilsley Ave., #U, Dartmouth NS B3B 1S4
Tel: 902-464-0274; *Fax:* 902-464-0089
info@habitathrm.com
www.habitathrm.com
ca.linkedin.com/pub/habitat-for-humanity-nova-scotia/31/7ba/ 699
www.facebook.com/HabitatNovaScotia
twitter.com/habitatns
Chief Officer(s):
Anne Connolly, Executive Director
AConnolly@HabitatHRM.com

Nunavut - Iqaluit
PO Box 1989, Iqaluit NU X0A 0H0
Tel: 867-979-7810
admin@habitaiqaluit.ca
habitatiqaluit.ca
www.facebook.com/pages/Habitat-for-Humanity-Iqaluit/67619 634416
www.twitter.com/habitatiqaluit

Ontario - Brampton
#3, 268 Rutherford Rd. South, Brampton ON L6W 3N3
Tel: 905-455-0883; *Fax:* 905-455-2622
www.habitatbrampton.com
www.linkedin.com/company/habitat-for-humanity-brampton
www.facebook.com/HabitatforHumanityBrampton
twitter.com/HFH_Brampton
Chief Officer(s):
Janice McNabbs, Contact
janice@janicmcnabb.ca

Ontario - Brant
408 Henry St., Brantford ON N3S 7W1
Tel: 519-759-8600; *Fax:* 519-751-2032
info@habitatbrant.org
www.habitatbrant.org
www.facebook.com/pages/Habitat-for-Humanity-Brant/10942 4489092063
twitter.com/@habitatbrant
www.youtube.com/watch?v=GC2eVBGAm2g
Chief Officer(s):
Kathy Poirier, Contact
kpoirier@habitatbrant.org

Ontario - Chatham-Kent
PO Box 606, 425 McNaughton Ave. West, Chatham ON N7M 5K8
Tel: 519-354-0506
info@habitatchatham-kent.ca
www.habitatchatham-kent.ca

Ontario - Durham
#7, 85 Chambers Dr., Ajax ON L1Z 1E2
Tel: 905-428-7434; *Fax:* 905-428-7494
info@habitatdurham.com
www.habitatdurham.com
www.facebook.com/148296605229034
twitter.com/HFHDurham
Chief Officer(s):
Mary Bone, Executive Director
mary@habitatdurham.com

Ontario - Greater Kingston & Frontenac
323 Bath Rd., Kingston ON K7M 2X6
Tel: 613-548-8763; *Fax:* 613-547-4119
volunteer@habitatkingston.com
www.habitatkingston.com
www.facebook.com/273145579362995
twitter.com/HabitatKingston
Chief Officer(s):
Tim Jamieson, CEO
tjamieson@habitatkingston.com

Ontario - Grey-Bruce
458344 Grey Rd. 11, RR#8, Owen Sound ON N4K 5W4
Tel: 519-371-6776; *Fax:* 519-371-2642
Toll-Free: 866-771-6776
info@habitatgreybruce.ca
www.habitatgreybruce.com
www.facebook.com/habitatgreybruce
Chief Officer(s):
Greg Fryer, Executive Director

Ontario - Halton
#10, 1800 Appleby Line, Burlington ON L7L 6A1
Tel: 905-637-4446; *Fax:* 905-637-1540
Toll-Free: 866-314-4344
office@habitathalton.ca
www.habitathalton.ca
www.facebook.com/HabitatHalton
www.twitter.com/HabitatHalton
www.youtube.com/habitathalton#p/u
Chief Officer(s):
John Gerrard, Executive Director
jgerrard@habitathalton.ca

Ontario - Hamilton
#1, 285 Nash Rd. North, Hamilton ON L8H 7P4
Tel: 905-560-6707; *Fax:* 905-560-6703
info@habitathamilton.ca
www.habitathamilton.ca
www.twitter.com/HabitatHamilton
Chief Officer(s):
Robert McConkey, Chief Executive Officer
bob@habitathamilton.ca

Ontario - Huron County
PO Box 453, Goderich ON N7A 4C7
Tel: 519-612-1614
info@habitathuroncounty.ca
www.habitathuroncounty.ca

Ontario - Huronia
128 Brock St., Barrie ON L4N 2M2
Tel: 705-727-0802; *Fax:* 705-727-0214
Melody@habitathuronia.com
www.habitathuronia.com

Ontario - Mississauga
#10-12, 1705 Argentia Rd., Mississauga ON L5N 3A9
Tel: 905-828-0987
info@habitatmississauga.ca
www.habitatmississauga.ca
www.facebook.com/114930171916967
twitter.com/HFHMississauga
Chief Officer(s):
John Gardner, Chair

Ontario - Muskoka
1964 Muskoka Beach Rd., RR#1, Gravenhurst ON P1P 1R1
Tel: 705-646-0106; *Fax:* 705-646-2948
info@habitatmuskoka.com
www.habitatmuskoka.ca
www.facebook.com/115892231780907?ref=ts
twitter.com/HabitatMuskoka
www.youtube.com/user/habitatmuskoka?feature=mhee
Chief Officer(s):
Linda Acton-Riddle, President

Ontario - National Capital Region
#170, 2370 Walkley Rd., Ottawa ON K1G 4H9
Tel: 613-749-9950; *Fax:* 613-749-8991
habitat@habitatncr.com
www.habitatncr.com
www.facebook.com/HabitatForHumanityNCR
Chief Officer(s):
Donna Hicks, CEO
donna@habitatncr.com

Ontario - Niagara
150 Bunting Rd., St Catharines ON L2P 3G5
Tel: 905-685-7395; *Fax:* 905-685-7396
habitat@habitatniagara.ca
www.habitatniagara.on.ca
Chief Officer(s):
Alastair Davis, CEO
alastair@habitatniagara.ca

Ontario - North Bay & Blue Sky Region
#206, 289 Main St. West, North Bay ON P1B 2H3
Tel: 705-495-6244; *Fax:* 866-393-6785
info@habitatnorthbay.com
www.habitatnorthbay.com
Chief Officer(s):
Monique Verschelden, Présidente

Ontario - North Simcoe
PO Box 703, 253 Whitfield Cres., Midland ON L4R 4P4
Tel: 705-528-0681
habitatnorthsimcoe@gmail.com
www.habitatnorthsimcoe.on.ca
twitter.com/HFHNorthSimcoe
Chief Officer(s):
Louise Daigneault, Présidente

Ontario - Northumberland
PO Box 222, 45 Ewart St., Cobourg ON K9A 4K5
Tel: 905-373-4663; *Fax:* 905-373-1459
info@habitatnorthumberland.ca
www.habitatnorthumberland.ca
www.facebook.com/HabitatNorthumberland
twitter.com/hfhnrestore
Chief Officer(s):

Canadian Associations

Meaghan Macdonald, Executive Director
mmacdonald@habitatnorthumberland.ca
Ontario - Orilla Lake Country
3835 Campbell Rd., RR#3, Orilla ON L3V 6H3
Tel: 705-327-3207
info@habitatorillia.ca
www.habitatorillia.ca
www.facebook.com/HabitatOrilliaLakeCountry
Chief Officer(s):
Marlene Mattson, President
Ontario - Oxford/Middlesex/Elgin
#2, 40 Pacific Crt., London ON N5V 3K4
Tel: 519-455-6623; *Fax:* 519-455-8479
info@habitat4home.ca
habitat4home.ca
www.facebook.com/Habitat.For.Humanity.London.Ontario
twitter.com/Habitat4HOME
www.youtube.com/user/HabitatLondonON
Chief Officer(s):
Jeff Duncan, CEO
jduncan@habitat.london.on.ca
Ontario - Peterborough & District
PO Box 298, 161 Sherbrooke St., Peterborough ON K9J 5T9
Tel: 705-750-1456; *Fax:* 705-775-0621
info@habitatpeterborough.ca
www.habitatpeterborough.ca
www.facebook.com/group.php?gid=26011007054
twitter.com/habitatpd
Chief Officer(s):
Sarah Tate, Executive Director
sarahtate@habitatpeterborough.ca
Ontario - Prince Edward-Hastings
365 Bell Blvd., Belleville ON K8P 5N9
Tel: 613-969-1415; *Fax:* 613-962-7526
info@habitatpeh.org
www.habitatpeh.org
www.facebook.com/113997471993077
twitter.com/HFH_PEH
Chief Officer(s):
Norah Buckley, President
norahbuckley@yahoo.ca
Melanie Flynn, Executive Director
Ontario - Sarnia/Lambton
460 Christina St. North, Sarnia ON N7T 5W4
Tel: 519-336-7075
habitatsarnia@xcelco.on.ca
www.habitatsarnia.org
www.facebook.com/255991847841581
Chief Officer(s):
David K. Butler, Chair
Ontario - Sault Ste Marie
32 White Oak Dr. East, Sault Ste Marie ON P6B 4J8
Tel: 705-942-7443; *Fax:* 705-941-9100
hfhadmin@habitatsault.ca
Ontario - Seaway Valley
17335 Myers Rd., Bonville ON K0C 2A0
Tel: 613-938-0413; *Fax:* 613-938-0446
info@habitatseawayvalley.org
www.habitatseawayvalley.org
Chief Officer(s):
Leigh Taggart, Executive Director
leightaggart@habitatseawayvalley.org
Ontario - South Georgian Bay
155 Sandford Fleming Dr., Collingwood ON L9Y 5A6
Tel: 705-446-9740; *Fax:* 705-446-3210
info@habitatgeorgianbay.ca
www.habitatgeorgianbay.ca
Chief Officer(s):
Iona Tough, Chair
chair@habitatgeorgianbay.ca
Ontario - Stratford-Perth
PO Box 21027, 32 Erie St., Stratford ON N5A 7V4
Tel: 519-814-0022; *Fax:* 519-273-9350
volunteer@habitatstratfordperth.ca
www.habitatstratfordperth.ca
www.facebook.com/135822856428772
twitter.com/HabitatSP/
Chief Officer(s):
Ric McGratten, President
Ontario - Sudbury District
444 Barrydowne Rd., Sudbury ON P3A 3T3
Tel: 705-669-0624; *Fax:* 705-669-1187
www.habitatsudbury.com
Chief Officer(s):
Lise Rheault, Executive Director
lrheault.hfhs@persona.ca
Ontario - Thousand Islands
PO Box 383, Brockville ON K6V 5V6
Tel: 613-342-3521; *Fax:* 613-342-3501
info@Habitat1000islands.ca
www.habitat1000islands.com
Chief Officer(s):
Ron Stembridge, Executive Director
Ron.Stembridge@Habitat1000Islands.com
Ontario - Thunder Bay
660 Squier St., Thunder Bay ON P7B 4A8
Tel: 807-345-5520; *Fax:* 807-346-4401
office@habitattbay.com
www.habitattbay.com
www.facebook.com/group.php?gid=52292660611
Chief Officer(s):
Andrew Campbell, Chair
andrew@brickhost.com
Ontario - Toronto
155 Bermondsey Rd., Toronto ON M4A 1X9
Tel: 416-755-7353; *Fax:* 416-916-2333
info@torontohabitat.ca
www.torontohabitat.on.ca
www.facebook.com/HabitatforHumanityToronto
twitter.com/HabitatToronto
www.youtube.com/watch?v=MmMSr3hxlsw&feature=player_embedded
Chief Officer(s):
Neil Hetherington, CEO
Ontario - Waterloo Region
120 Northfield Dr. East, Waterloo ON N2J 4G8
Tel: 519-747-0664; *Fax:* 519-747-2153
mail@hfhwr.ca
www.habitatwaterlooregion.on.ca
www.facebook.com/HFHWR
twitter.com/habitatwaterloo
www.flickr.com/photos/hfhwr
Chief Officer(s):
Karen Redman, COO
kredman@hfhwr.ca
Ontario - Wellington County
#300, 104 Dawson Rd., Guelph ON N1H 1A7
Tel: 519-767-9752; *Fax:* 519-767-9096
info@habitatwellington.on.ca
www.habitatwellington.on.ca
twitter.com/HFHWC
www.youtube.com/user/HFHWC99?feature=mhee
Chief Officer(s):
Diane Nelson, Executive Director
d.nelson@habitatwellington.on.ca
Ontario - Windsor-Essex
3064 Devon Dr., Windsor ON N8X 4L2
Tel: 519-969-3762; *Fax:* 519-969-7832
www.habitatwindsor.org
www.facebook.com/HabitatForHumanityWindsorEssex
twitter.com/HFHWindsorEssex
Chief Officer(s):
Ed Link, President
Ontario - York Region
449 Eagle St., Newmarket ON L3Y 1K7
Tel: 905-868-8722; *Fax:* 905-868-8724
Toll-Free: 866-638-7242
info@habitatyork.ca
www.habitatyork.ca
www.linkedin.com/companies/habitat-for-humanity-york-region
www.facebook.com/HabitatforHumanityYorkRegion
twitter.com/HabitatYork/
Chief Officer(s):
Tom Taylor, Acting Executive Director
executivedirector@habitatyork.ca
Prince Edward Island
365 Mount Edward Rd., Charlottetown PE C1A 2A1
Tel: 902-368-7539; *Fax:* 902-368-3951
www.habitatpei.ca
Chief Officer(s):
Susan Zambonin, Executive Director
executivedirector@habitatpei.ca
Québec - Montréal Region
4399, rue Notre-Dame Ouest, Montréal QC H4C 1R9
Tel: 514-907-8991; *Fax:* 514-907-8991
info@habitatmontreal.qc.ca
www.habitatmontreal.qc.ca
ca.linkedin.com/pub/isabel-stgermain-singh/17/195/1b5
www.facebook.com/habitatmontreal
twitter.com/HabitatMontreal
Chief Officer(s):
Isabel St Germain Singh, President & CEO
Québec - Region des Deux-Montagnes
1002, ch d'Oka, Deux-Montagnes QC JTR 1L7
Tél: 514-842-7007
www.habitatrdm.org
www.facebook.com/280338171985748
Québec - Sherbrooke
610, rue King est, Sherbrooke QC J1G 5K2
www.habitatsherbrooke.org
www.facebook.com/habitatmontreal
Chief Officer(s):
Diane Desrosiers, Directrice générale
Saskatchewan - On the Border, Lloydminster
PO Box 143, Lloydminster SK S9V 0Y1
Tel: 306-825-4611
hab4hum@sasktel.net
www.habitatlloydminster.ca
Saskatchewan - Prince Albert
PO Box 644, Prince Albert SK S6V 5S2
Tel: 306-764-4663
habitatpa@sasktel.net
Saskatchewan - Regina
1740 Broder St., Regina SK S4N 2H7
Tel: 306-522-9700; *Fax:* 306-522-9703
www.habitatregina.ca
www.facebook.com/Habitatregina
twitter.com/habitatregina
www.youtube.com/user/habitatregina
Chief Officer(s):
Kelly Holmes-Binns, CEO
kholmes-binns@habitatregina.ca
Saskatchewan - Saskatoon
320 21st St. West, Saskatoon SK S7M 4E6
Tel: 306-343-7772; *Fax:* 306-343-7801
www.habitatsaskatoon.ca
Chief Officer(s):
Barb Cox-Lloyd, Executive Director
barb@habitatsaskatoon.ca
Yukon
PO Box 31118, Whitehorse YT Y1A 5P7
Tel: 867-456-4349
info@habitatyukon.org
www.habitatyukon.org
Chief Officer(s):
Arthur Mitchell, President

Habitat pour l'Humanité Canada ***See*** Habitat for Humanity Canada

Hagersville & District Chamber of Commerce
PO Box 1090, Hagersville ON N0A 1H0
Tel: 905-768-0422; *Fax:* 905-768-0422
Overview: A small local organization
Chief Officer(s):
Robert C. Phillips, Secretary-Treasurer
rcpca@sprint.ca
Membership: 72; *Fees:* $75 business; $25 individual

Haida Gwaii Arts Council
PO Box 35, Queen Charlotte BC V0T 1S0
Tel: 250-559-4691
info@hgartscouncil.ca
www.hgartscouncil.ca
Previous Name: Queen Charlotte Islands Arts Council
Overview: A small local organization
Member of: Assembly of BC Arts Councils
Chief Officer(s):
Astrid Egger, President
abegger@haidagwaii.net

Haines Junction Chamber of Commerce ***See*** St. Elias Chamber of Commerce

Hal Jackman Foundation
165 University AVe., 10th Fl., Toronto ON M5H 3BS
Tel: 416-350-5877; *Fax:* 416-362-7961
www.haljackmanfoundation.org
Overview: A small national charitable organization founded in 1964
Mission: Focuses on increasing access to and appreciation of arts and culture, as well as building the audiences of the future.
Chief Officer(s):

Victoria Jackman, Executive Director
victoria@jackman.org

HALCO
#400, 65 Wellesley St. East, Toronto ON M4Y 1G7
Tel: 416-340-7790; *Fax:* 416-340-7248
Toll-Free: 888-705-8889; *TTY:* 866-513-9883
talklaw@halco.org
www.halco.org
Also Known As: HIV & AIDS Legal Clinic of Ontario
Overview: A small provincial organization founded in 1995
Mission: Community-based legal clinic that provides free legal services to people living with HIV/AIDS in Ontario
Chief Officer(s):
Ryan Peck, Executive Director

Haldimand Association for the Developmentally Challenged *See* Community Living Haldimand

Haldimand Community Support Centre *See* Community Support Centre Haldimand-Norfolk

Haldimand-Norfolk District Beekeepers' Association
Simcoe ON
Tel: 519-428-5386
Overview: A small local organization
Mission: To develop the beekeeping skills of interested persons in Haldimand-Norfolk
Chief Officer(s):
David Bowen, President
president@halnorbeekeepers.com
Membership: *Member Profile:* Beekeepers in Ontario's Haldimand-Norfolk District
Activities: Providing a forum for networking for district beekeepers;

Haldimand-Norfolk Information Centre (HNIC)
Brantford ON
haldimand.cioc.ca
Overview: A small local charitable organization founded in 1974 overseen by InformOntario
Mission: To provide human service information to community
Member of: On-Line Ontario
Chief Officer(s):
Valerie A. Spours, Executive Director
Finances: *Annual Operating Budget:* $50,000-$100,000
Staff Member(s): 4; 15 volunteer(s)
Membership: *Fees:* $10
Activities: Electronic Data-Bases; Public Access Terminal; Ontario Business Connects Workstation; Provincial government forms & resources; *Speaker Service:* Yes; *Rents Mailing List:* Yes; *Library* Open to public

Haldimand-Norfolk Literacy Council (HNLC)
200 West St., Simcoe ON N3Y 1S9
Tel: 519-428-0064
Toll-Free: 866-973-7323
info@hnliteracy.com
www.hnliteracy.com
Overview: A small local charitable organization founded in 1986
Mission: To work with adults to upgrade their literacy & math skills.
Affiliation(s): Laubach Literacy of Canada - Ontario
Chief Officer(s):
Anita Hillis-Krause, Interim Executive Director
ed@hnliteracy.com
Sherry Black-Schrubb, Coordinator, Norfolk
sherry@hnliteracy.com
Finances: *Funding Sources:* United Way; provincial government; private donations
Activities: ESL classes, in small groups & 1-to-1, free to adults over 18

Dunnville Office & Adult Learning Centre
227 Queen St., Dunnville ON N1A 2X5
Tel: 905-774-9141
Chief Officer(s):
Gina McIntee, Coordinator
hc@hnliteracy.com

Haley Street Adult Services Centre Society
26 Haley St., North Sydney NS B2A 3L3
Tel: 902-794-3517; *Fax:* 902-794-9650
haleystreet@ns.sympatico.ca
www.haleystreet.ca
Overview: A small local organization
Mission: To provide vocational training for adults with disabilities
Member of: DIRECTIONS Council for Vocational Services Society
Chief Officer(s):
Judy Gouthro Snow, President
Debra MacLean, Executive Director/Manager
Membership: 60+ individuals
Activities: Nora's New to You thrift store; woodworking; recreation & leisure program;

Haliburton County Association for Community Living *See* Community Living Haliburton County

Haliburton Highlands Chamber of Commerce (HHCofC)
PO Box 670, 195 Highland St., #L1, Haliburton ON K0M 1S0
Tel: 705-457-4700; *Fax:* 705-457-4702
Toll-Free: 877-811-6111
admin@haliburtonchamber.com
www.haliburtonchmaber.com
www.facebook.com/HaliburtonChamberofCommerce
twitter.com/HHCofC
Overview: A small local organization founded in 1964 overseen by Ontario Chamber of Commerce
Mission: To act as the voice of business for Haliburton County
Chief Officer(s):
Eric Thompson, President
president@haliburtonchamber.com
Jerry Walker, Vice-President
Rosemarie Jung, Chamber Manager
rosemarie@haliburtonchamber.com
Finances: *Annual Operating Budget:* $50,000-$100,000; *Funding Sources:* Membership dues
Staff Member(s): 2; 25 volunteer(s)
Membership: 350; *Fees:* $75-$400; *Committees:* Member Services; Networking & Special Events; Public Affairs
Activities: Support & development of business in the Haliburton County; *Internships:* Yes
Awards:
• Business of the Year (Award)
• Highlander of the Year (Award)

Haliburton Highlands Guild of Fine Arts (HHGFA)
PO Box 912, 23 York St., Haliburton ON K0M 1S0
Tel: 705-457-2330
info@railsendgallery.com
www.railsendgallery.com
www.facebook.com/railsend
twitter.com/RailsEnd
www.pinterest.com/railsend
Also Known As: Rails End Gallery & Arts Centre
Overview: A small local charitable organization founded in 1966
Mission: To maintain a not-for-profit, public art gallery & arts centre which focuses on contemporary art of the region; to offer programs open to the public to foster exploration, appreciation, expression & exchange of creativity.
Finances: *Funding Sources:* Municipal government
Membership: *Fees:* $28.25 adult/artist; $45.20 family/studio; $22.60 senior; $11.30 student

Halifax Amateur Radio Club (HARC)
PO Box 8895, Halifax NS B3K 5M5
Tel: 902-490-6421
www.halifax-arc.org
Overview: A small local organization founded in 1932
Mission: To promote amateur radio and Ham radio and provide a forum for the exchange of ideas and information related to radio communications and technical experimentation in Nova Scotia.
Chief Officer(s):
Scott Wood, President
ve1qd@rac.ca
Membership: 125; *Fees:* $30 full; $15 associate; $45 family; *Committees:* Government & Media Relations; Membership; Web page; Basic ham course

Halifax Area Leisure & Therapeutic Riding Association
The Stables, 1690 Bell Rd., Halifax NS B3H 2Z3
Tel: 902-423-6723
hjbl@ns.sympatico.ca
www.bengallancers.com/haltr.html
www.facebook.com/pages/Halifax-Junior-Bengal-Lancers/14695 17326609058
twitter.com/hfxbengalancers
Previous Name: Lancer Rehab Riders
Overview: A small local charitable organization
Mission: HALTR is a volunteer-run group that provides horse-riding & driving programs for people with special needs. It is a registered charity, BN: 890783947RR0001.
Member of: Canadian Therapeutic Riding Association
Affliation(s): Sport Canada; Equine Canada
Chief Officer(s):
Jill Barker, Manager, 902-423-6723
hjblmanager@bellaliant.com
Membership: *Member Profile:* Mostly children & young adults with disabilities

Halifax Association of Vegetarians (HAV)
PO Box 3087, Tantallon NS B3Z 4G9
e-mail: halifaxvegetarians@gmail.com
www.halifaxvegetarians.ca
Overview: A medium-sized local organization
Mission: To promote a vegetarian lifestyle, and unite vegetarians and those interested in vegetarianism in the Halifax area and throughout Nova Scotia.
Member of: International Vegetarian Union
Membership: *Fees:* $20 individual; $25 family; $15 senior/student

Halifax Chamber of Commerce
#200, 656 Windmill Rd., Dartmouth NS B3B 1B8
Tel: 902-468-7111; *Fax:* 902-468-7333
info@halifaxchamber.com
www.halifaxchamber.com
www.linkedin.com/groups/Lnkdln-Group-Halifax-Chamber-Commerce-1865797
www.facebook.com/halifaxchamberofcommerce
twitter.com/halifaxchamber
Previous Name: Metropolitan Halifax Chamber of Commerce
Merged from: Bedford Board of Trade; Halifax Board of Trade; Dartmouth Chamber of Commerce; Sackville Chamber of
Overview: A large local organization founded in 1995
Mission: The Chamber builds & strengthens the business culture in Metro Halifax through advocacy, networking & leadership
Member of: Canadian Chamber of Commerce
Chief Officer(s):
Paula Gallagher, Chair
Valerie Payn, President, 902-481-1229
valerie@halifaxchamber.com
Finances: *Funding Sources:* Membership dues; event revenue
Staff Member(s): 14; 400 volunteer(s)
Membership: 1,500+; *Fees:* Based on number of employees; *Committees:* Provincial Government Affairs; Municipal Government Affairs; Transportation; Energy Advisory Group; Ambassadors; Chamber Councils; Small Business
Activities: *Awareness Events:* Annual Golf Tournament; Annual Spring & Fall Dinners; Halifax Business Awards; *Speaker Service:* Yes; *Library:* Policy Work Library; Open to public
Publications:
• Business Voice Online [a publication of the Halifax Chamber of Commerce]
Type: Newsletter; *Frequency:* Biweekly
• Business Voice [a publication of the Halifax Chamber of Commerce]
Type: Magazine; *Frequency:* 10 pa
• Business Voice Outlook [a publication of the Halifax Chamber of Commerce]
Type: Magazine; *Frequency:* Annually
Profile: Special issue of BV that gives a preview of the year ahead
• Chamber Events Online [a publication of the Halifax Chamber of Commerce]
Type: Newsletter; *Frequency:* Biweekly
• Profile [a publication of the Halifax Chamber of Commerce]
Profile: Ongoing series examining various business sectors & matters of interest to the Halifax business community

Halifax Chebucto Ringette Association
c/o Simon Lee, 1425 John Brackett Dr., Herring Cove NS B3V 1G6
chebucto.goalline.ca
Overview: A small local organization overseen by Ringette Nova Scotia
Member of: Ringette Nova Scotia
Chief Officer(s):
Ernest Dupres, President
hcrapresident@gmail.com
Membership: 14 teams; *Fees:* Schedule available

Halifax Citadel Regimental Association (HCRA)
PO Box 9080, Stn. A, Halifax NS B3K 5M7

Tel: 902-426-1990; *Fax:* 902-426-7806
info@regimental.com
www.citadel.colourdigital.to
Overview: A small local organization founded in 1993
Mission: To assist Parks Canada in the administration & delivery of the historical interpretive program & associated activities at the Halifax Citadel National Historic Site of Canada and raise funds in support of that program.
Chief Officer(s):
James Bruce, President

Halifax County United Soccer Club
#7, 102 Chain Lake Dr., Halifax NS B3S 1A7
Tel: 902-876-8784; *Fax:* 902-446-3620
info@hcusoccer.ca
www.hcusoccer.ca
Overview: A medium-sized local organization founded in 1998
Mission: To foster a love of soccer & help individuals of all ages achieve their full potential.
Chief Officer(s):
Glen Herbert, President
herbertglen@hotmail.com
Laura Yost, Administrator
Membership: 1,600 players; *Fees:* $125-$250 depending on age group

Halifax Elizabeth Fry Society *See* Canadian Association of Elizabeth Fry Societies

Halifax Employers Association (HEA)
#200, 5121 Sackville St., Halifax NS B3J 1K1
Tel: 902-422-4471; *Fax:* 902-422-7550
hea@hfxemp.ca
www.halifaxemployers.com
Overview: A medium-sized local organization founded in 1996
Mission: To negotiate efficient labour agreements on behalf of its members and to develop and maintain positive employer/employee work relations and oversee the training of employees in the Longshore industry in the port of Halifax.
Chief Officer(s):
Fritz Burns King, Chair
Membership: 12 corporate

Halifax Field Naturalists (HFN)
c/o Nova Scotia Museum of Natural History, 1747 Summer St., Halifax NS B3H 3A6
e-mail: hfninfo@yahoo.ca
halifaxfieldnaturalists.ca/hfnWP
Overview: A small local charitable organization founded in 1975
Mission: To promote the enjoyment & preservation of Nova Scotia's history & natural areas through education, discussion & fellowship
Member of: Federation of Nova Scotia Naturalists
Affliation(s): Canadian Nature Federation; Canadian Parks & Wilderness Society; The Nature Conservancy of Canada
Chief Officer(s):
Janet Dalton, President
Finances: *Annual Operating Budget:* Less than $50,000; *Funding Sources:* Membership dues; sales; donations
Membership: 120; *Fees:* $15 student; $20 individual; $25 family; $30 supporting/institutional; $5 Nature Nova Scotia; *Committees:* Programme; Newsletter; Conservation; Colin Stewart Conservation Award; Membership; Socials; Web Site
Activities: Presentations, field trips; *Speaker Service:* Yes
Publications:
• The Halifax Field Naturalist
Type: Newsletter; *Frequency:* Quarterly

Halifax Foundation
PO Box 2635, Stn. CPO, Halifax NS B3J 3A5
e-mail: halifax_foundation@hotmail.com
www.halifax.ca/foundation
Overview: A small local charitable organization
Chief Officer(s):
Jack Keith, Chair

Halifax Library Association
c/o 5940 South St., Halifax NS B3H 1S6
e-mail: halifaxlibraryassociation@gmail.com
halifaxla.wordpress.com
www.facebook.com/group.php?gid=20160077946
Overview: A medium-sized local organization
Mission: To promote libraries and their services, and to encourage more extensive cooperation and interdependence among libraries in the geographic area of Halifax Regional Municipality.
Chief Officer(s):
Denise Parrott, President
Membership: *Fees:* $10
Meetings/Conferences: • Halifax Library Association 2015 Annual General Meeting, 2015, Halifax, NS
Scope: Local

Halifax North West Trails Association (HNWTA)
c/o 27 Warwick Lane, Halifax NS B3M 4J3
Tel: 902-443-5051
info@halifaxnorthwesttrails.ca
www.halifaxnorthwesttrails.ca
www.facebook.com/124497311008207
twitter.com/HalifaxNWTrails
Overview: A medium-sized local organization
Mission: To promote the creation, protection and maintenance of trails within the Halifax Mainland North area.
Chief Officer(s):
Todd Beal, Chair

Halifax Professional Fire Fighters Association
PO Box 2330, Dartmouth NS B2W 3Y4
Tel: 902-453-5242; *Fax:* 902-453-1812
secretary@hpff.ca
www.hpff.ca
www.facebook.com/460302050722807
twitter.com/HFXFirefighters
Also Known As: IAFF Local 268
Overview: A medium-sized local organization

Halifax Regional CAP Association (HRC@P)
Halifax NS
Tel: 902-293-8122
admin@halifaxcap.ca
www.halifaxcap.ca
www.facebook.com/HRCAP
twitter.com/hrcap
Overview: A small provincial organization founded in 2000
Mission: To deliver quality service to communities through their locally operated Community Access Program (CAP) sites.
Chief Officer(s):
Paul Hudson, Chair

Halifax Regional Cerebral Palsy Association
PO Box 33075, Stn. Quinpool, Halifax NS B3L 4T6
Tel: 902-479-0963
cerebral.palsy@ns.sympatico.ca
www.hrcpa.ca
Overview: A small local organization
Mission: The Association offers social events, financial assistance & education for members & the general public to improve the lives of those with Cerebral Palsy in the area. It is a registered charity, BN :118951029RR0001.
Finances: *Annual Operating Budget:* Less than $50,000
Membership: 100-499; *Fees:* $10; $20 household; $30 5 people or more household

Halifax Regional Coin Club
c/o Dartmouth Seniors' Service Centre, 45 Ochterloney St., Dartmouth NS B2Y 4M7
Overview: A small local organization
Member of: Royal Canadian Numismatic Association

Halifax Regional Police Association (HRPA)
103 Thorne Ave., Dartmouth NS B3B 0A4
Tel: 902-490-5234; *Fax:* 902-490-4188
unifiedstrengthhalifax.ca
Overview: A small local organization founded in 1990
Mission: To protect the rights & interests of the men & women who protect & serve the citizens of the Halifax Regional Municipality
Affliation(s): Canadian Professional Police Association
Chief Officer(s):
Mark Hartlen, President
hartlema@halifax.ca

Halifax Sexual Health Centre
#201, 6009 Quinpool Rd., Halifax NS B3K 5J7
Tel: 902-455-9656; *Fax:* 902-429-3853
info@halifaxsexualhealth.ca
www.halifaxsexualhealth.ca
www.facebook.com/HSHCNS
www.twitter.com/HfxSexualHealth
www.youtube.com/HSHCTV
Previous Name: Planned Parenthood Metro Clinic
Overview: A small local charitable organization founded in 1970
Mission: To promote sexual & reproductive health within an environment that respects & supports individual choice
Member of: Canadian Federation for Sexual Health
Chief Officer(s):
Kelly Grover, Executive Director
Finances: *Annual Operating Budget:* $500,000-$1.5 Million
Staff Member(s): 6; 30 volunteer(s)
Membership: 300; *Fees:* Donations $10+
Activities: Sexual health clinic; annonymous HIV testing; education; *Awareness Events:* Sexual & Reproductive Health Day; *Speaker Service:* Yes; *Library* Open to public by appointment

Halifax Sport & Social Club (HSSC)
PO Box 8821, Halifax NS B3K 5M5
Tel: 902-431-8326
info@halifaxsport.ca
www.halifaxsport.ca
www.facebook.com/HalifaxSSC
twitter.com/HalifaxSSC
Overview: A medium-sized local organization
Mission: To offer co-ed recreational sport leagues, tournaments & social events for adults.
Chief Officer(s):
Lael Morgan, Executive Director
Staff Member(s): 5

Halifax Transition House Association - Bryony House
3358 Connaught Ave., Halifax NS B3L 3B5
Tel: 902-429-9002; *Fax:* 902-429-0954; *Crisis Hot-Line:* 902-422-7650
info@bryonyhouse.ca
www.bryonyhouse.ca
www.facebook.com/pages/Bryony-House/159269017458704
twitter.com/BryonyHouse
Overview: A small provincial charitable organization founded in 1978
Mission: To operate a 24-bed shelter for abused women & their children; to advocate for legislative, social & economic change to end violence against women & their children.
Finances: *Funding Sources:* Provincial government
Activities: Counselling service

Halifax-Dartmouth Automobile Dealers' Association (HDADA)
PO Box 9410, Stn. A, Halifax NS B3K 5S3
Tel: 902-425-2445; *Fax:* 902-425-2441
association@pathfinder-group.com
Overview: A small local organization
Member of: Nova Scotia Automobile Dealers' Association
Chief Officer(s):
John K. Sutherland, Executive Vice-President
Membership: 30; *Committees:* Executive

Halifax-St. Margaret's Ringette Association
12 Westwood Blvd., Upper Tantallon NS B3Z 1H3
e-mail: registrar@hsmringette.com
hsmringette.com
Also Known As: HSM Ringette Association
Overview: A small local organization overseen by Ringette Nova Scotia
Member of: Ringette Nova Scotia
Chief Officer(s):
Terry Teal, President
president@hsmringette.com
Membership: 12 teams; *Fees:* Schedule available

Halton Children's Aid Society
1445 Norjohn Ct., Burlington ON L7L 0E6
Tel: 905-333-4441; *Fax:* 905-333-1844
Toll-Free: 866-607-5437
www.haltoncas.ca
Overview: A large local charitable organization founded in 1914
Member of: Ontario Association of Children's Aid Societies
Chief Officer(s):
Scott Waterhouse, President
Finances: *Annual Operating Budget:* Greater than $5 Million
50 volunteer(s)
Membership: 14 senior/lifetime + 80 individual; *Fees:* Schedule available
Activities: *Internships:* Yes

Halton District Educational Assistants Association (HDEAA)
#202, 3425 Harvester Rd., Burlington ON L7N 3N1
Tel: 905-639-3680; *Fax:* 905-639-8517
www.hdeaa.com
Previous Name: Halton Instructional Assistants Association
Overview: A small local organization founded in 1995

Membership: 600; *Member Profile:* 95% Female Educational Assistants; special education support staff

Halton Family Services (HFS)

235 Lakeshore Rd. East, Oakville ON L6J 7R4
Tel: 905-845-3811; *Fax:* 905-845-3537
info@haltonfamilyservices.org
www.haltonfamilyservices.org
Overview: A small local charitable organization founded in 1954 overseen by Ontario Association of Credit Counselling Services
Mission: To assist individuals, couples, & families in Oakville & the Halton region cope with challenges, by providing a professional counselling service; To operate the Halton-Peel Consumer Credit Counselling Service, to help persons find solutions to their financial problems
Member of: Ontario Association of Credit Counselling Services
Finances: *Funding Sources:* United Ways in Halton; Ministry of Community and Social Services; Donations; Fees, on a sliding scale, for some programs
Activities: Providing individual, couple, family, bereavement, & credit & debt counselling; Offering services for children, men, & abused women; Providing the Employee Assistance Program; Presenting seminars & workshops on topics such as separtation & divorce, healthy relationships, & anger management
Publications:
• Halton Family Services Annual Report
Type: Yearbook; *Frequency:* Annually

Halton Foundation *See* Conservation Halton Foundation

Halton Hills Chamber of Commerce

328 Guelph St., Halton Hills ON L7G 4B5
Tel: 905-877-7119
tourism@haltonhillschamber.on.ca
www.haltonhillschamber.on.ca
www.facebook.com/HaltonHillsChamberOfCommerce
twitter.com/HHCoC
Overview: A small local organization founded in 1918
Mission: To promote economic prosperity & sustainable development in Halton Hills.
Member of: Ontario Chamber of Commerce; Canadian Chamber of Commerce
Chief Officer(s):
Sue Walker, President & CEO
sue@haltonhillschamber.on.ca
Finances: *Annual Operating Budget:* $100,000-$250,000; *Funding Sources:* Private sector; memberships
Staff Member(s): 3; 60 volunteer(s)
Membership: 495; *Fees:* Schedule available; *Committees:* Business Education; Economic Development; Government Issues; Marketing; Membership Services; Tourism; Visitor Info. Centre
Activities: Business & tourist information; annual golf day; after business networking; municipal lobbying; business development seminars; *Speaker Service:* Yes; *Rents Mailing List:* Yes

Halton Instructional Assistants Association *See* Halton District Educational Assistants Association

Halton Mississauga Youth Orchestra (HMYO)

159 Cavendish Ct., Oakville ON L6J 5S3
Tel: 905-842-5569
info@hmyo.ca
www.hmyo.ca
www.facebook.com/haltonmississaugayouthorchestra
twitter.com/HMYOmusic
Merged from: Halton Youth Symphony; Mississauga Youth Orchestr
Overview: A small local charitable organization founded in 2014 overseen by Orchestras Canada
Mission: To inspire, encourage & challenge young musicians to build their musical skills through the experience of various forms of orchestral music; to create an enjoyable environment that promotes teamwork, leadership & community involvement
Chief Officer(s):
Gregory Burton, Music Director
Finances: *Funding Sources:* Grants; fundraising drives; membership fees
Staff Member(s): 10
Membership: 130; *Member Profile:* Musicians

Halton Multicultural Council (HMC)

1092 Speers Rd., Oakville ON L6L 2X4
Tel: 905-842-2486; *Fax:* 905-842-8807
info@halton-multicultural.org
www.halton-multicultural.org
www.facebook.com/HaltonMC
Overview: A small local organization founded in 1979 overseen by Ontario Council of Agencies Serving Immigrants
Mission: To offer settlement services, employment & language training, interpretation & translation services, TOEFL testing, social & cultural programs, transitional housing consultation.
Affiliation(s): United Way of Oakville; Ontario Trillium Foundation
Chief Officer(s):
Trivi Mehendale, President
Activities: Host Match program; programs for youth, seniors, individuals and families; Transracial Parenting Initiative; *Speaker Service:* Yes

Halton Peel Hispanic Association

1092 Speers Rd., Oakville ON L6L 2X4
Tel: 905-842-2486
information@hphispanicassociation.org
www.hispaniccanadian.or
ca.linkedin.com/in/hphassociation
www.facebook.com/halton.peel
Overview: A small local organization founded in 2008
Mission: To preserve & promote Hispanic culture & identity in Canada
Chief Officer(s):
Alberto Rincon, President, Board of Directors
Membership: *Fees:* $20 Individual; *Member Profile:* Individuals as well as organizations; *Committees:* Events; Web Master; Legal; Translation; Library Advisory
Activities: Cultural festivals

Halton Regional Police Association (HRPA)

#6, 2333 Wyecroft Rd., Oakville ON L6L 6L4
Tel: 905-825-8789; *Fax:* 905-825-0826
Toll-Free: 866-843-9993
info@hrpa.com
www.hrpa.com
Overview: A small local organization founded in 1974
Mission: To promote the interests of members & raise the standards of policing; to promote the individual rights of members, including working conditions, wages, benefits & pensions
Chief Officer(s):
Duncan Foot, President
Paul Lacourse, Chief Administrator
Staff Member(s): 2
Membership: *Member Profile:* Members of Burlington, Oakville, Milton & Halton Hills police

Halton Social Planning Council & Volunteer Centre *See* Community Development Halton

Halton Trauma Centre

60 Lakeshore Rd. West, Oakville ON L6K 1E1
Tel: 905-825-3242; *Fax:* 905-825-3276
Toll-Free: 800-663-9888
info@haltontraumacentre.ca
www.haltontraumacentre.ca
www.facebook.com/TheHaltonTraumaCentre
Overview: A small local organization founded in 1983
Mission: Provides clinical assessment and treatment services to children, adolescents and families affected by child abuse.
Chief Officer(s):
John Herald, President
Darryll Hall, Executive Director

Halton/Peel Region *See* B'nai Brith Canada

Hamber Foundation

Toronto Dominion Tower, PO Box 10083, Stn. Pacific Centre, 700 West Georgia St., 18th Fl., Vancouver BC V7Y 1B6
Tel: 604-659-7448; *Fax:* 604-659-7469
www.hamberfoundation.ca
Overview: A small provincial charitable organization
Mission: To award grants to organizations registered as charitable or educational & projects arising & undertaken in the province of British Columbia
Membership: 1-99

Hamilton & District Health Library Network

c/o Debra Wingfield, Hamilton Health Sciences, 293 Wellington St. North, Hamilton ON L8L 8E7
Tel: 905-521-2100; *Fax:* 905-527-8458
hsl.mcmaster.ca/network
Overview: A small local organization founded in 1970
Mission: The Network promotes resource sharing & cooperation to enhance the quality of library & information services within the healthcare community.
Chief Officer(s):
Debra Wingfield, Contact
wingfdeb@hhsc.ca
Finances: *Funding Sources:* Members cost sharing basis
Membership: *Member Profile:* Health-related libraries & library resource centres

Hamilton & Region Arts Council *See* Hamilton Arts Council

Hamilton AIDS Network (HAN)

#101, 140 King St. East, Hamilton ON L8N 1B2
Tel: 905-528-0854; *Fax:* 905-528-6311
Toll-Free: 866-563-0563
info@aidsnetwork.ca
www.aidsnetwork.ca
www.facebook.com/TheAIDSNetwork
Previous Name: Hamilton AIDS Network for Dialogue & Support
Overview: A medium-sized local organization founded in 1986 overseen by Canadian AIDS Society
Mission: To help mobilize community-based responses to the needs created & exacerbated by the HIV epidemic in Hamilton & the surrounding community
Member of: Ontario AIDS Network; Canadian AIDS Society
Chief Officer(s):
Ruthann Tucker, Executive Director
rtucker@aidsnetwork.ca
Finances: *Funding Sources:* Ontario Ministry of Health; Health Canada; Region of Hamilton-Wentworth
Staff Member(s): 11
Activities: *Library:* Hamilton AIDS Network Resource Centre

Hamilton AIDS Network for Dialogue & Support *See* Hamilton AIDS Network

Hamilton Arts Council

22 Wilson St., Hamilton ON L8R 1C5
Tel: 905-481-3218; *Fax:* 905-529-9738
info@hamiltonartscouncil.ca
www.artshamilton.ca
www.facebook.com/people/Arts-Hamilton/1266965869
twitter.com/hamartscouncil
Previous Name: Hamilton & Region Arts Council
Overview: A small local charitable organization founded in 1969
Mission: To serve the community & its artists as an advocate for the arts & as a forum for promoting the arts in Hamilton & region
Member of: Community Arts Ontario; Ontario Crafts Council; Canadian Artists' Representation Ontario; Canadian Conference of the Arts; Theatre Ontario
Chief Officer(s):
Stephanie Vegh, Executive Director
stephanie@hamiltonartscouncil.ca
Finances: *Annual Operating Budget:* $100,000-$250,000; *Funding Sources:* City of Hamilton; membership; Ontario Arts Council; donations; Trillium Foundation
Staff Member(s): 4; 55 volunteer(s)
Membership: 400; *Fees:* $25; *Member Profile:* Artists; arts organizations; educators; businesses; individuals; *Committees:* Craft; Fundraising; Literary; Music; Theatre; Visual Arts
Activities: Lit Awards; Designer Crafts; Crafts Award; designer crafts exhibition; Lit Chats; Photophobia; Monologic; Gallery in the Mall; studio walking tour; Class & Trash; *Speaker Service:* Yes; *Library* Open to public

Hamilton Association for Community Living *See* Community Living Hamilton

Hamilton Baseball Umpires' Association (HBUA)

Hamilton ON
Tel: 905-538-6071
hbua@hotmail.ca
hbua.ca
www.facebook.com/190866890945303
Overview: A small local organization
Chief Officer(s):
Bill Tunney, President & Assignor

Hamilton Chamber of Commerce (HCC)

Plaza Level, #507, 120 King St. West, Hamilton ON L8P 4V2
Tel: 905-522-1151; *Fax:* 905-522-1154
hcc@hamiltonchamber.ca
www.hamiltonchamber.ca
www.linkedin.com/company/hamilton-chamber-of-commerce
www.facebook.com/140038556040986
twitter.com/hamiltonchamber
Overview: A medium-sized local licensing organization founded in 1845

Mission: To make greater Hamilton a great place to live, work, play, visit & invest; & to recognize the importance of the individual as the most significant contributor to achieving community objectives
Member of: Ontario Chamber of Commerce; Canadian Chamber of Commerce
Chief Officer(s):
Diane Stephenson, Manager, Advertising & Promotions
d.stephenson@hamiltonchamber.ca
Finances: *Annual Operating Budget:* $1.5 Million-$3 Million; *Funding Sources:* Membership dues; special events; publications
Staff Member(s): 12; 100 volunteer(s)
Membership: 1,650; *Fees:* Based on number of employees; *Member Profile:* Businesses; *Committees:* Ambassador; Business Development; Finance; Government; Hospitality; Human Resources; Science & Technology; Transportation; Dundas & Ancaster Divisions
Activities: General business networking & seminars; Business After Business; orientation breakfasts; *Speaker Service:* Yes; *Rents Mailing List:* Yes; *Library:* Business Reference Library; Open to public
Awards:
• Outstanding Business Achievement Awards (OBAA) (Award)
• Dundas, Ancaster & Hamilton Citizen of the Year & Youth Volunteer (Award)
• Athena Award (Award)

Hamilton Community Foundation
#700, 120 King St. West, Hamilton ON L8P 4V2
Tel: 905-523-5600; *Fax:* 905-523-0741
information@hamiltoncommunityfoundation.ca
hamiltoncommunityfoundation.ca
www.facebook.com/pages/Hamilton-Community-Foundation/141724739930
twitter.com/HamCommFdn
Overview: A small local charitable organization founded in 1954
Mission: To distribute grants in perpetuity to those of Hamilton/Wentworth & Burlington region. Grants in the past have been for adult basic education, theatre arts, residential redevelopment, environment, poverty reduction, youth activities, preschool, sexual assault centre, community healthcare.
Member of: Canadian Centre for Philanthropy; Council on Foundations; Community Foundations of Canada
Chief Officer(s):
Justin Cooper, Chair
Terry Cooke, President & CEO Ext. 224
terry.cooke@hamiltoncommunityfoundation.ca
Finances: *Annual Operating Budget:* Greater than $5 Million; *Funding Sources:* Estate gifts; private sector donations; investment revenue
Staff Member(s): 17
Membership: 191 foundations
Activities: *Speaker Service:* Yes

Hamilton District Society for Disabled Children (HDSDC)
Holbrook Bldg., Chedoke Site, PO Box 2000, Hamilton ON L8N 3Z5
Tel: 905-385-5391; *Fax:* 905-521-2636
disabledchildren@bellnet.ca
Overview: A small local organization founded in 1951
Mission: To assist in addressing the needs of children (under 21 years of age) who have physical disabilities that affect gross or fine motor control & that limit their ability to function in activities of daily living, by providing financial assistance to projects not funded by other agencies or government
Chief Officer(s):
Mark Matson, President
Paula Kerlew, Executive Director
Finances: *Annual Operating Budget:* $50,000-$100,000
Staff Member(s): 1
Membership: 10 individual
Activities: *Speaker Service:* Yes

Hamilton Folk Arts Heritage Council
#1, 12 Walnut St. South, Hamilton ON L8N 2K7
Tel: 905-525-2297
www.hamiltonfolkarts.org
Overview: A small local charitable organization founded in 1969
Mission: To promote ethnic awareness among the communities through the avenues of arts, crafts, food & entertainment; to provide activity & fun that are essential to a healthy lifestyle; to promote cultural heritage & public awareness of the diversity of cultures & ethnic lifestyle throughout Canada
Member of: Greater Hamilton Tourism Committee; Ontario Craft Council; Hamilton & Region Art Council
Affliation(s): Festival & Events Ontario
Chief Officer(s):
Harnald Toomsalu, Acting President
Membership: *Member Profile:* Non-commercial & non-political organizations
Activities: Art exhibitions; theatrical presentation; exhibits; cultural events; "It's Your Festival" multi-arts celebration;

Hamilton Food Share
339 Barton St., Stoney Creek ON L8E 2L2
Tel: 905-664-9065; *Fax:* 905-664-2108
www.hamiltonfoodshare.org
Overview: A small local charitable organization
Mission: To collect & distribute food to people in need in the Hamilton region; to reduce hunger in the community
Chief Officer(s):
Joanne Santucci, Executive Director
Staff Member(s): 3

Hamilton Industrial Environmental Association (HIEA)
PO Box 35545, Hamilton ON L8H 7S6
Tel: 905-561-4432
info@hiea.org
www.hiea.org
Overview: A medium-sized local organization
Mission: To improve the local environment - air, land and water - through joint and individual activities, and by partnering with the community to enhance future understanding of environmental issues and help establish priorities for action.
Chief Officer(s):
Jim Stirling, Chair
Membership: 15 companies

Hamilton Jewish Federation
PO Box 81203, 1030 Lower Lions Club Rd., Ancaster ON L9G 3N6
Tel: 905-648-0605
www.jewishhamilton.org
twitter.com/JewishHamilton
Also Known As: Jewish Hamilton
Overview: A small local charitable organization founded in 1932
Mission: To govern & represent the Jewish community of Hamilton
Affliation(s): UIA Federations Canada
Chief Officer(s):
Barb Babij, Chief Executive Officer, 905-648-0605 Ext. 305
bbabij@jewishhamilton.org
Staff Member(s): 7
Activities: *Speaker Service:* Yes; *Library:* Holocaust Library; by appointment

Hamilton Law Association (HLA)
John Sopinka Court House, #500, 45 Main St. East, Hamilton ON L8N 2B7
Tel: 905-522-1563; *Fax:* 905-572-1188
hla@hamiltonlaw.on.ca
www.hamiltonlaw.on.ca
www.linkedin.com/company/hamilton-law-association
www.facebook.com/hamiltonlawassociation
twitter.com/HLAlibrary
Overview: A small local organization founded in 1879
Mission: To educate & support its members in the practice of law, as well as to advocate their interests as lawyers.
Member of: County & District Law Presidents' Association
Chief Officer(s):
David W. Howell, President, 905-572-5830, Fax: 905-526-0732
dhowell@rossmcbride.com
Rebecca Bentham, Executive Director, 905-522-7992
rbentham@hamiltonlaw.on.ca
Staff Member(s): 10
Membership: 832; *Fees:* Schedule available; *Member Profile:* Lawyers; judges; articling students; *Committees:* Family Law; Real Estate; Continuing Professional Development; Corporate Commercial; New Lawyers
Activities: Maintaining library; legal seminars; lobbying for professional issues; social functions; *Speaker Service:* Yes; *Library:* Anthony Pepe Memorial Law Library;
Awards:
• Emilius Irving Award (Award)
Awarded for outstanding contribution to association
Publications:
• Hamilton Law Association Journal
Type: Journal; *Frequency:* Bimonthly; *Price:* $30 pa, non-members

Hamilton Naturalists' Club (HNC)
PO Box 89052, Hamilton ON L8S 4R5
Tel: 905-381-0329
info@hamiltonnature.org
www.hamiltonnature.org
www.facebook.com/386408715600
Overview: A small local charitable organization founded in 1919
Mission: To promote the enjoyment of nature through environmental appreciation & conservation; To foster public interest & education in the appreciation & study of nature; To encourage wise use & conservation of natural resources; to promote environmental protection
Member of: Federation of Ontario Naturalists
Affliation(s): Canadian Nature Federation
Chief Officer(s):
Michael Fischer, President, 905-526-0325
fischermj@sympatico.ca
Finances: *Annual Operating Budget:* Less than $50,000; *Funding Sources:* Donations; membership dues; grants
80 volunteer(s)
Membership: 500; *Fees:* $30 senior/student; $35 individual/institution; $40 family; $750 lifetime; *Committees:* Bird Study Group; Conservation; Hamilton Bird Records; Education; Sanctuary; Newsletter; Plant Study Group
Activities: Monthly public meetings from Sept.-May; public hikes; *Speaker Service:* Yes

Hamilton Niagara Haldimand Brant Community Care Access Centre (HNHB CCAC)
#4, 195 Henry St., Bldg. 4, Brantford ON N3S 5C9
Tel: 519-759-7752
Toll-Free: 800-810-0000
www.hamilton.ccac-ont.ca
Overview: A small local organization
Mission: To provide access to community care services
Chief Officer(s):
Melody Miles, CEO
Finances: *Funding Sources:* Government of Ontario

Hamilton Philharmonic Orchestra
#501, 105 Main St. East, Hamilton ON L8N 1G6
Tel: 905-526-1677
communications@hpo.org
www.hpo.org
www.facebook.com/HamiltonPhilharmonic
twitter.com/h_p_o/
www.youtube.com/user/HamiltonPhilharmonic
Previous Name: New Hamilton Orchestra
Overview: A medium-sized local charitable organization founded in 1996 overseen by Orchestras Canada
Mission: To provide artistically excellent music to patrons
Chief Officer(s):
James Sommerville, Music Director
Carol Kehoe, Executive Director
ckehoe@hpo.org
Finances: *Funding Sources:* Ticket revenue; municipal & regional funding; federal & provincial arts councils
Staff Member(s): 11
Activities: *Library*

Hamilton Philharmonic Youth Orchestra (HPYO)
299 Fennell Ave. West, Hamilton ON L9C 1G3
e-mail: info@hpyo.com
www.hpyo.com
www.facebook.com/HamiltonPhilharmonicYouthOrchestra
Overview: A small local charitable organization founded in 1965 overseen by Orchestras Canada
Chief Officer(s):
Colin Clarke, Music Director
Finances: *Funding Sources:* Donations; Membership fees; Fundraising
Membership: *Member Profile:* Persons from ages 12 to 23
Activities: Providing Orchestra-in-Residence at Hillfield Strathallan College; Offering 10 concerts each year; *Library*

Hamilton Police Association (HPA) / Association de la police de Hamilton
555 Upper Wellington St., Hamilton ON L9A 3P8
Tel: 905-574-6044; *Fax:* 905-574-3223
hpa@hpa.on.ca
www.hpa.on.ca
Previous Name: Hamilton-Wentworth Police Association
Overview: A medium-sized local organization founded in 1974
Mission: To promote high quality professional policing through labour relations & political activity
Affliation(s): Police Association of Ontario; Canadian Police Association

Chief Officer(s):
Brad Boyce, Administrator
bboyce@hpa.on.ca
Mike Cruse, Executive Officer
mcruse@hpa.on.ca
Finances: *Funding Sources:* Membership dues
Staff Member(s): 6
Activities: *Speaker Service:* Yes

Hamilton Program for Schizophrenia (HPS)
#102, 350 King St. East, Hamilton ON L8N 3Y3
Tel: 905-525-2832; *Fax:* 905-546-0055
info@hpfs.on.ca
www.hpfs.on.ca
Overview: A small local organization founded in 1979
Mission: The organization is a comprehensive, community-based treatment & rehabilitation program for adults with schizophrenia. It promotes an understanding of schizophrenia in the community.
Affliation(s): McMaster University Clinical Teaching Unit
Chief Officer(s):
Peter E. Cook, Executive Director
Finances: *Annual Operating Budget:* $1.5 Million-$3 Million; *Funding Sources:* Provincial government
Staff Member(s): 22
Activities: Social gatherings

Hamilton Regional Indian Centre
34 Ottawa St. North, Hamilton ON L8H 3Y7
Tel: 905-548-9593; *Fax:* 905-545-4077
support@hric.ca
www.hric.ca
www.facebook.com/hric.hamilton
twitter.com/hric2013
Overview: A small local organization founded in 1972
Mission: To serve the needs of the Native People in Hamilton & surrounding areas; to assist those in an urban environment by sponsoring programs that maintain Native traditions & culture.
Member of: Ontario Federation of Indian Friendship Centres
Affliation(s): National Association of Friendship Centres
Chief Officer(s):
Carol Hill, President
Susan Barberstock, Executive Director
sbarberstock@hric.ca
Staff Member(s): 25
Membership: *Fees:* $2 elder; $3 individual; $5 family; $10 organization
Activities: *Library:* Resource Library

Hamilton Right to Life
166 Bay St. North, Hamilton ON L8R 2P7
Tel: 905-528-3065; *Fax:* 905-528-5593
hamiltonrighttolife.org
Overview: A small local charitable organization founded in 1972
Mission: To promote public awareness of the sanctity of all life from conception to natural death, of the impact of abortion on women's health, of parent's rights, & of the medical professionals' responsibility to patients & to society
Affliation(s): Alliance for Life
Chief Officer(s):
Barry Mombourquette, President
Sandra Dykstra, Office Manager
Finances: *Annual Operating Budget:* $50,000-$100,000; *Funding Sources:* Membership dues; donations
Staff Member(s): 1; 7 volunteer(s)
Membership: 100 student + 15 lifetime + 1,900 individual; *Fees:* Schedule available; *Committees:* Speakers Bureau; Membership; Public Advocacy
Activities: *Speaker Service:* Yes; *Library* Open to public

Hamilton Stamp Club (HSC)
65 Glen Rd., Hamilton ON L8S 3M6
e-mail: elsaclare@cogeco.ca
www.hamiltonstampclub.com
Overview: A small local organization founded in 1897
Member of: Royal Philatelic Society of Canada; American Philatelic Society
Affliation(s): Grand River Valley Philatelic Association
Chief Officer(s):
Wuchow Than, President
wthan@cogeco.ca
Finances: *Annual Operating Budget:* Less than $50,000
20 volunteer(s)
Membership: 140; *Fees:* $15; *Member Profile:* Family
Activities: *Awareness Events:* Fall Show, 1st weekend in Nov.; Springpex, 4th weekend in April; *Speaker Service:* Yes; *Library* Open to public

Hamilton Technology Centre (HIT)
#200, 7 Innovation Dr., Flamborough ON L9H 7H9
Tel: 905-689-2400; *Fax:* 905-689-2200
www.hitcentre.ca
Previous Name: Greater Hamilton Technology Enterprise Centre
Overview: A small local organization founded in 1977
Mission: To create wealth-generating jobs by helping form & grow technology-focussed business
Member of: City of Hamilton
Chief Officer(s):
Penny Gardiner, Facilities Director
penny.gardiner@hamilton.ca
Finances: *Funding Sources:* City of Hamilton
Activities: Incubating, mentoring & coaching tech business start-ups;

Hamilton-Brantford Building & Construction Trades Council
#213, 1104 Fennell Ave. East, Hamilton ON L8T 1R9
Tel: 905-389-1574; *Fax:* 905-389-2207
Overview: A small local organization
Chief Officer(s):
Joseph Beattie, Business Manager
jbeattiehbbt@shaw.ca

Hamilton-Burlington & District Real Estate Board (HBDREB)
505 York Blvd., Hamilton ON L8R 3K4
Tel: 905-529-8101; *Fax:* 905-529-4349
info@rahb.ca
www.rahb.ca
Also Known As: REALTORS Association of Hamilton-Burlington
Previous Name: Metropolitan Hamilton Real Estate Board
Overview: A medium-sized local organization founded in 1921 overseen by Ontario Real Estate Association
Mission: To pursue excellence & professionalism in real estate through commitment & service
Member of: The Canadian Real Estate Association; Real Estate Council of Ontario
Finances: *Funding Sources:* Membership dues; fees for service
Membership: 1,000-4,999

Hamilton-Halton Construction Association (HHCA)
#100, 370 York Blvd., Hamilton ON L8R 3L1
Tel: 905-522-5220; *Fax:* 905-572-9166
www.hhca.ca
Overview: A small local organization founded in 1921 overseen by Canadian Construction Association
Mission: To promote excellence in structures & safety for commercial & industrial enterprises
Affliation(s): Council of Ontario Construction Associations
Chief Officer(s):
Sandy Alyman, General Manager
sandy@hhca.ca
Judith Mosel, Executive Assistant/Bookkeeper
judith@hhca.ca
Finances: *Annual Operating Budget:* $250,000-$500,000; *Funding Sources:* Membership dues; Program revenue
Staff Member(s): 5
Membership: 370; *Fees:* Schedule available
Publications:
• The Exchange
Type: Newsletter; *Frequency:* Monthly

Hamilton-Wentworth Police Association ***See*** Hamilton Police Association

Hamiota Chamber of Commerce
PO Box 403, Hamiota MB R0J 1Z0
www.hamiota.com/business.html
Overview: A small local organization
Mission: To participate in community fundraisers, the Hamiota Agricultural Fair & Hamiota's Millennium Park; To act as liaison between the Manitoba Chamber of Commerce, the Manitoba Government, & local entrepreneurs
Chief Officer(s):
Larry Oakden, President
Bonnie Michaudville, Secretary

Hampton Area Chamber of Commerce (HACC)
PO Box 1829, #2, 17 Centennial Rd., Hampton NB E5N 6N3
Tel: 506-832-2559; *Fax:* 506-832-2559
hacc@nbnet.nb.ca
www.hamptonareachamber.org
www.facebook.com/HamptonACC
Overview: A small local organization founded in 1979
Member of: New Brunswick Chamber of Commerce; Atlantic Provinces Chamber of Commerce
Chief Officer(s):
Barb Curry, President
Gail Kilpatrick, Secretary
Finances: *Annual Operating Budget:* Less than $50,000
Staff Member(s): 1; 10 volunteer(s)
Membership: 81; *Fees:* $60-$96

Hampton Food Basket & Clothing Centre Inc.
#2, 39 Tilley St., Hampton NB E5N 5B4
Tel: 506-832-4340
Overview: A small local charitable organization founded in 1985
Mission: To help the poor as commanded by Jesus Christ
Member of: Association of Food Banks & C.V.A.'s for New Brunswick; Atlantic Alliance of Food Banks & C.V.A.'s
Chief Officer(s):
Janice Titus, Coordinator
Betty Kennett, Secretary/Founder
Sally Evans, Treasurer
Finances: *Annual Operating Budget:* Less than $50,000; *Funding Sources:* Private donations; churches; service clubs; government grants
30 volunteer(s)
Activities: Distribution of food, clothes, small appliances & bedding to the needy; fundraisers; yard sale

Handball Association of Newfoundland & Labrador
St. John's NL
www.nlhandballontherock.com
www.facebook.com/nlhandballontherock
Also Known As: NL Handball Association; Handball on the Rock
Overview: A small provincial organization
Mission: To promote & develop the sport of handball in Newfoundland & Labrador, with emphasis on junior programs
Chief Officer(s):
Wayne Amminson, President

Handball Association of Nova Scotia (HANS)
NS
nshandball.com
twitter.com/nshandball
Overview: A small provincial organization
Mission: To promote & develop the sport of handball in Nova Scotia
Chief Officer(s):
Daniel Marcil, President & CEO
dan@nshandball.com
Activities: Tournaments; junior program

Handicapped Organization Promoting Equality
PO Box 562, 84 Main St., Yarmouth NS B5A 4B4
Tel: 902-742-8910; *Fax:* 902-742-1281
Toll-Free: 877-305-7433
hopecentre@ns.sympatico.ca
Also Known As: HOPE
Overview: A small local charitable organization founded in 1981
Mission: The organization offers life skill courses for adults & programs for children with special needs. It is a registered charity, BN: 118952282RR0001.
Affliation(s): Nova Scotia League for Equal Opportunities
Finances: *Funding Sources:* Federal, provincial governments

Handidactis ***See*** Disability Awareness Consultants

Hands on Summer Camp Society
1309 Hillside Ave., Victoria BC V8T 2B3
Tel: 250-995-6425; *Fax:* 250-995-6428
Other Communication: Alternate e-mail: ebssec@live.ca
laurieweaye@gmail.com
www.handsonsummercamp.com
Also Known As: Elizabeth Buckley School
Overview: A small national charitable organization
Mission: To foster & promote recreational & educational opportunities for all children; To meet their individual communication needs, with an emphasis on Sign Language
Finances: *Annual Operating Budget:* $100,000-$250,000; *Funding Sources:* Fundraising; fees
Staff Member(s): 10
Membership: 1-99
Activities: Operates the Elizabeth Buckley School & the Hands on Summer Camp

The Hanen Centre
#515, 1075 Bay St., Toronto ON M5S 2B1

Tel: 416-921-1073; *Fax:* 416-921-1225
Toll-Free: 877-426-3655
info@hanen.org
www.hanen.org
www.facebook.com/thehanencentre
twitter.com/TheHanenCentre
Overview: A medium-sized local licensing charitable organization founded in 1975
Mission: To provide specialized services & resources to parents, teachers & caregivers of language delayed children, & to provide training to speech-language pathologists
Affliation(s): Canadian Association of Speech-Language Pathologists & Audiologists; American Speech & Hearing Association
Chief Officer(s):
Elaine Weitzman, Executive Director
elaine.weitzman@hanen.org
Finances: *Funding Sources:* Provincial government
Membership: *Member Profile:* Hanen certified speech-language pathologists
Activities: *Speaker Service:* Yes

Hang Gliding & Paragliding Association of Atlantic Canada (HPAAC)
hpaac.ca
www.facebook.com/HPAAC
Previous Name: Hang Gliding Association of Newfoundland
Overview: A small local organization founded in 1979
Mission: To develop & promote the sports of hang glinding & paragliding in Atlantic Canada
Affliation(s): Hang Gliding & Paragliding Association of Canada
Chief Officer(s):
Michael Fuller, President
Membership: 1-99; *Fees:* $140
Activities: Paragliding & hang gliding at coastal cities in Nova Scotia, Prince Edward Island, New Brunswick & Newfoundland & Labrador; *Awareness Events:* Atlantic Annual Paragliding/Hang Gliding Festival, May

Hang Gliding & Paragliding Association of Canada (HPAC) / Association canadienne de vol libre (ACVL)
#308, 1978 Vine St., Vancouver BC V6K 4S1
Fax: 604-731-4407
Toll-Free: 877-370-2078
admin@hpac.ca
www.hpac.ca
Overview: A medium-sized national organization founded in 1977
Mission: To promote unpowered foot-launched flight in hang gliders & paragliders.
Member of: Aero Club of Canada; Fédération aéronautique internationale
Chief Officer(s):
Domagoj Juretic, President
Margit Nance, Executive Director
Finances: *Annual Operating Budget:* $50,000-$100,000; *Funding Sources:* Membership fees
Staff Member(s): 1
Membership: 890; *Fees:* Schedule available; *Committees:* Safety

Hang Gliding Association of British Columbia *See* British Columbia Hang Gliding & Paragliding Association

Hang Gliding Association of Newfoundland *See* Hang Gliding & Paragliding Association of Atlantic Canada

Hanley Agricultural Society
Hanley SK
e-mail: hanleyagsociety@gmail.com
Overview: A small local organization founded in 1982
Mission: To improve agriculture & the quality of life in the community by providing a forum for discussion of agricultural issues
Member of: Saskatchewan Association of Agricultural Societies & Exhibitions
Chief Officer(s):
Patti Prosofsky, President, 306-544-2226
Activities: Agricultural & domestic displays; beef show; light horse show; co-ed slow pitch; men's fastball; children's activities

Hanna & District Chamber of Commerce
PO Box 2248, Hanna AB T0J 1P0
Tel: 403-854-4004
info@hannachamber.ca
www.hannachamber.ca
Overview: A small local organization
Member of: Alberta Chamber of Commerce; Canadian Chamber of Commerce
Chief Officer(s):
Harlan Boss, President
Staff Member(s): 1
Membership: 80
Activities: *Library:* The Learning Centre; Open to public

Hanna Museum & Pioneer Village
PO Box 1528, Hanna AB T0J 1P0
Tel: 403-854-4244
Overview: A small local charitable organization founded in 1965
Mission: To preserve the history of the rural pioneer of this area & of Western Canada; To operate Hanna Pioneer Village & Museum
Chief Officer(s):
Bill McFalls, Contact
Finances: *Annual Operating Budget:* Less than $50,000
Staff Member(s): 1; 10 volunteer(s)
Membership: 25; *Fees:* $1; *Committees:* Building; Machinery; Membership; Archives
Activities: Conducts visiting patrons tours; *Library:* Archives; by appointment

Hanover Chamber of Commerce
214 - 10th St., Hanover ON N4N 1N7
Tel: 519-364-5777; *Fax:* 519-364-6949
info@hanoverchamber.ca
www.hanoverchamber.ca
Overview: A small local organization
Member of: Ontario Chamber of Commerce
Chief Officer(s):
Michele Hettrick, President, 519-369-5563
Finances: *Annual Operating Budget:* Less than $50,000; *Funding Sources:* Membership fees
Staff Member(s): 1; 11 volunteer(s)
Membership: 119; *Fees:* $145

Hantsport & Area Historical Society
PO Box 525, Hantsport NS B0P 1P0
nsgna.ednet.ns.ca/hantsport/index.html
Overview: A small local charitable organization founded in 1977
Mission: To preserve history of area & make it accessible to the public; To provide index for genealogy
Member of: Federation of Nova Scotia Heritage
Chief Officer(s):
John Harvie, Contact
john.harvie@eastlink.ca
Finances: *Annual Operating Budget:* Less than $50,000
Membership: 50; *Fees:* $3 individual; $5 family
Activities: *Library* Open to public

Harbourfront Centre
235 Queens Quay West, Toronto ON M5J 2G8
Tel: 416-973-4600; *Fax:* 416-973-6055
info@harbourfrontcentre.com
www.harbourfrontcentre.com
www.facebook.com/HarbourfrontTO
twitter.com/HarbourfrontTO
Overview: A medium-sized local charitable organization founded in 1974
Mission: To nurture the growth of new cultural expression; to stimulte Canadian & international interchange; to provide a dynamic, accessible environment for the public to experience the marvels of the creative imagination
Chief Officer(s):
William J.S. Boyle, CEO
Finances: *Funding Sources:* Corporate; government; individual donations
2000 volunteer(s)

Harbourfront Community Centre (HCC)
627 Queen's Quay West, Toronto ON M5V 3G3
Tel: 416-392-1509; *Fax:* 416-392-1512
hcc@harbourfrontcc.ca
www.harbourfrontcc.ca
Overview: A medium-sized local charitable organization founded in 1991
Mission: To advocate for provision of necessary services to the community, provide a range of responsive programs and services in an atmosphere of belonging and meet the needs of a diverse and changing multicultural community.
Chief Officer(s):
Leona Rodall, Executive Director
leona@harbourfrontcc.ca
Finances: *Funding Sources:* City of Toronto
Membership: *Fees:* Schedule available

Harmony Foundation of Canada / Fondation Harmonie du Canada
PO Box 50022, #15, 1594 Fairfield Rd., Victoria BC V8S 1G1
Tel: 250-380-3001; *Fax:* 250-380-0887
harmony@islandnet.com
www.harmonyfdn.ca
www.facebook.com/117724434937243
www.youtube.com/user/harmonyfdn
Overview: A medium-sized international charitable organization founded in 1985
Mission: To encourage development which is socially & environmentally sustainable; To strive towards ecological stability, long-term prosperity, & social harmony
Chief Officer(s):
Michael Bloomfield, Founder & Executive Director
Robert Bateman, Honorary Chair
Jean-Pierre Soublière, President
Nick Mosky, Secretary
Robert Van Tongerloo, Treasurer
Finances: *Funding Sources:* Donations; Sponsorships
Activities: Working with organizations & individuals around the world through the Building Sustainable Societies Program; Improving environmental practices in workplaces; Providing community service opportunities for young people; Publishing action guides for homes, workplaces, & communities; Implementing training programs; Forming partnerships to establish meaningful results around environment & development issues; Educating about sustainable development & global change

Harmony, Inc.
Toll-Free: 855-750-3341
info@harmonyinc.org
www.harmonyinc.org
www.facebook.com/HarmonyIncorporated
Also Known As: International Organization of Women Barbershop Singers
Overview: A small international organization founded in 1959
Mission: To perform & promote four-part a cappella harmony in the barbershop style; To promote personal growth & development through education & the practice of democratic principles
Chief Officer(s):
Jeanne O'Connor, International President
president@harmonyinc.org
Denise Dyer, Executive Secretary
exsecretary@harmonyinc.org
45 volunteer(s)
Membership: 2,500 individual
Meetings/Conferences: • Harmony, Inc. 2017 International Convention & Contests, November, 2017, Halifax Convention Centre, Halifax, NS
Attendance: 1,000

Harold Crabtree Foundation
Varette Building, #603, 130 Albert St., Ottawa ON K1P 5G4
Tel: 613-563-4589; *Fax:* 613-563-2819
Overview: A small local charitable organization founded in 1951
Mission: To support education, health & social services in Ontario, Quebec, & Atlantic provinces; does not support individual requests or annual compaigns
Chief Officer(s):
Sandra Crabtree, President

The Harold Greenberg Fund
Astral Media, Brookfield Place, PO Box 787, #100, 181 Bay St., Toronto ON M5J 2T3
Tel: 416-956-5432; *Fax:* 416-956-2087
hgfund@astral.com
www.astral.com/en/about-astral/astrals-harold-greenberg-fund
Previous Name: Foundation to Underwrite New Drama for Pay Television (FUND)
Overview: A small national organization founded in 1986
Mission: To foster the development & production of feature-length movies written by Canadians & the production of family television series
Chief Officer(s):
John Galway, President
Finances: *Annual Operating Budget:* $3 Million-$5 Million; *Funding Sources:* The Movie Network; Viewer's Choice Canada; Family Channel
Staff Member(s): 4

Harrison Agassiz Chamber of Commerce
PO Box 429, Harrison Hot Springs BC V0M 1K0

Tel: 604-796-1133; *Fax:* 604-796-3694
www.harrison.ca
twitter.com/HAChamber
Overview: A small local organization founded in 1982
Mission: To actively explain, promote & support the free enterprise system & democratic principle in order to improve trade, commerce & the economic, social & human welfare of the people
Chief Officer(s):
Robert Reyerse, President
Staff Member(s): 1; 12 volunteer(s)
Membership: 15; *Fees:* $65-215

Harriston-Minto & District Chamber of Commerce *See* Minto Chamber of Commerce

Harrow & Colchester Chamber of Commerce
PO Box 888, Harrow ON N0R 1G0
Tel: 519-974-3200; *Fax:* 519-974-2222
www.harrowchamber.ca
Overview: A small local organization
Chief Officer(s):
Murdo Mclean, President
Membership: *Fees:* $75-$125 business; $25 individual; $15 retired

Harrow Early Immigrant Research Society (HEIRS)
PO Box 53, Harrow ON N0R 1G0
Tel: 519-738-3700
www.heirs.ca
Overview: A small local charitable organization founded in 1971
Mission: To collect & safeguard local historical information & genealogical data relating to Harrow & Colchester South areas of Essex County, Ontario; to act as a link for other researchers in the field and strives to foster community interest in local history & promotes conservation of historical artifacts
Member of: Southwestern Heritage Association (Essex County)
Affliation(s): Ontario Historical Society; Ontario Genealogical Society
Chief Officer(s):
Richard Herniman, President
Finances: *Funding Sources:* Sale of books; donations; provincial grants; federal student employment grants
Membership: *Fees:* $20; *Member Profile:* Interest in local & family history
Activities: *Speaker Service:* Yes; *Library* by appointment

Harrowsmith Beekeepers Guild *See* Limestone Beekeepers Guild

Harry A. Newman Memorial Foundation
#423, 157 Adelaide St. West, Toronto ON M5H 4E7
Tel: 416-862-8669
Overview: A small local organization
Mission: To supply funds to develop leadership potential in the community
Affliation(s): Lions Club
Chief Officer(s):
William DeLaurentis, Chairman
Finances: *Annual Operating Budget:* Less than $50,000
Membership: 8

Harry E. Foster Foundation
PO Box 20029, Newcastle ON L1B 1M3
www.harryefosterfoundation.org
Overview: A small provincial charitable organization founded in 1954
Mission: As a primary focus, the Foundation offers grants to programs & projects for people with intellectual disabilities, but it is also interested in Alzheimers' disease & community organizations for the disadvantaged. There is an office at: 60 St. Clair Ave. East, Toronto, M4T 1N5. It is a registered charity, BN: 132116914RR0001.
Chief Officer(s):
James P. Thompson, President
Carol Davis-Kerr, Administrator
c.davis-kerr@rogers.com

Hart House Orchestra
University of Toronto, 7 Hart House Circle, Toronto ON M5S 3H3
www.harthouseorchestra.ca
Overview: A small local organization overseen by Orchestras Canada
Chief Officer(s):
Zoe Dille, Programme Advisor
zoe.dille@utoronto.ca
Henry Janzen, Director, Music

Membership: 80-90; *Fees:* $50 students; $225.60 non students; $184.28 seniors; *Member Profile:* Students, alumni, senior members
Activities: Three concerts per year

Hartney & District Chamber of Commerce
PO Box 224, Hartney MB R0M 0X0
Overview: A small local organization

Hashomer Hatzair / Young Guard
#2, 4700 Bathurst St., Toronto ON M2R 1W8
Tel: 416-736-1339; *Fax:* 647-693-7359
mail@campshomria.ca
www.hashomerhatzair.ca
www.facebook.com/groups/155999800078
Overview: A small international charitable organization founded in 1912
Mission: To promote Jewish cultural identity & social justice, participation & commitment to Israel & the Jewish community
Member of: Canadian Jewish Congress
Chief Officer(s):
Carmi Daniel, Director, Shaliach & Camp
carmidaniel@gmail.com
Staff Member(s): 2; 30 volunteer(s)
Membership: 400; *Fees:* $180 individual
Activities: Weekly meetings; special outings; educational activities; residential camps; Purim Ball; Chanukah Party; Passover Seder; Rabin Memorial; 8-week leadership training; *Internships:* Yes; *Speaker Service:* Yes; *Rents Mailing List:* Yes

Hastings Centre Rockhounds
c/o Hastings Community Centre, 3096 East Hastings St., Vancouver BC V5K 2A3
Tel: 604-718-6222; *Fax:* 604-718-6226
Previous Name: Hastings Community Centre Rockhounds
Overview: A small local organization
Member of: Lapidary, Rock & Mineral Society of British Columbia

Hastings Children's Aid Society (HCAS)
363 Dundas St. West, Belleville ON K8P 1B3
Tel: 613-962-9291; *Fax:* 613-966-3868
Toll-Free: 800-267-0570
info@highlandshorescas.com
www.highlandshorescas.com
Overview: A small local charitable organization founded in 1907
Member of: Ontario Association of Children's Aid Societies
Chief Officer(s):
Len Kennedy, Executive Director
Finances: *Annual Operating Budget:* Greater than $5 Million
Staff Member(s): 189
Membership: 53; *Fees:* $5; *Member Profile:* Individuals, 18 or older; corporations who do business in the area served by the society
Activities: *Awareness Events:* Purple Ribbon Campaign, Oct.; Adoption Awareness Month, Nov.
Awards:
- Outstanding Leadership in Child Welfare Award (Award)

Cobourg Location
1005 Burnham St., Cobourg ON K9A 5J6
Tel: 905-372-1821; *Fax:* 905-372-5284
Toll-Free: 800-267-0570

North Hastings Location
PO Box 837, 16 Billa St., Bancroft ON K0L 1C0
Tel: 613-332-2425; *Fax:* 613-332-5686
Toll-Free: 866-532-2269

Quinte West Location
469 Dundas St. West, Trenton ON K8V 3S4
Tel: 613-965-6261; *Fax:* 613-965-0930
Toll-Free: 800-267-0570

Hastings Community Centre Rockhounds *See* Hastings Centre Rockhounds

Hastings County Historical Society
154 Cannifton Rd. North, Cannifton ON K0K 1K0
Tel: 613-962-1110
info@hastingshistory.ca
www.hastingshistory.ca
Overview: A small local charitable organization founded in 1957
Mission: To promote & conduct research into the history of Hastings County. It maintains archives on historical documents & encourages community interest in the preservation of local history.
Member of: Ontario Historical Society
Chief Officer(s):
Richard Hughes, President
president@hastingshistory.ca
Membership: *Fees:* $25 individual; $30 family; $20 senior/student; $25 non-profit organization; $100 corporate; $150 lifetime
Activities: Monthly meetings with speaker, open to public; *Library:* Resource Centre; by appointment

Hastings County Law Association (HCLA)
Quinte Consolidated Courthouse, #2900, 15 Bridge St. West, Belleville ON K8P 0C7
Tel: 613-962-2280; *Fax:* 613-962-1611
hcla@on.aibn.com
www.communitylegalcentre.ca/hcla
www.facebook.com/HastingsCountyLawAssociation
twitter.com/HastingsCty_Law
Overview: A small local organization
Mission: To act as a lobbying voice for its members & provides research resources through its library.
Chief Officer(s):
Judith Dale, Librarian
Membership: *Committees:* Library; Social
Activities: *Library:* Courthouse Library

Haute Yamaska Real Estate Board *Voir* Chambre immobilière de la Haute Yamaska Inc.

Hautes études internationales (IQHEI)
Pavillon Charles de Koninck, Université Laval, #5456, 1030 av des Sciences-Humaines, Québec QC G1V 0A6
Tél: 418-656-7771
hei@hei.ulaval.ca
www.hei.ulaval.ca
www.linkedin.com/groups?mostRecent=&gid=4487818
www.facebook.com/HEIulaval
twitter.com/hei_ulaval
Nom précédent: Institut québécois des hautes études internationales
Aperçu: *Dimension:* petite; *Envergure:* internationale; fondée en 1994
Mission: Assurer à la société des services spécialisés d'information, d'animation et d'expertise sur les problèmes internationaux ainsi que sur les sociétés et cultures étrangères et leur signification dans un context canadien et québécois
Affiliation(s): Université Laval; Défense nationale; Ministère étrangères et du Commerce international; Le Devoir; Canal Savoir
Membre(s) du bureau directeur:
Louis Bélanger, Directeur
Membre(s) du personnel: 12
Membre: 60; *Comités:* Directeur; Programmes
Activités: Études et de recherches sur l'Asie contemporaine; recherches sur les aspects juridiques internationaux et transitionaux de l'intégration économique; programme de maîtrise en relations internationales; programme pluridisciplinaire incluant un stage pratique de fin d'études au Canada ou à l'étranger; centre d'études interaméricaines; cercle Europe; programme paix et sécurité internationale; chaîne de recherche du Canada en sécurité, en droit de l'environnement, maghrébines Rabah-Bitat; *Stagiaires:* Oui; *Service de conférenciers:* Oui

Havelock, Belmont, Methuen & District Chamber of Commerce
PO Box 779, Havelock ON K0L 1Z0
Tel: 705-778-2182; *Fax:* 866-822-2182
havelockchamber@hotmail.com
www.havelockchamber.com
Overview: A small local organization
Mission: To promote Havelock Belmont Methuen & District Chamber of Commerce
Chief Officer(s):
Phil Higgins, President, 705-778-7873
Membership: *Fees:* $30-$100

Le Havre *See* Our Harbour

Hawkesbury & Region Chamber of Commerce / Chambre de Commerce de Hawkesbury et région
PO Box 36, #5A, 151 Main St. East, Hawkesbury ON K6A 2R4
Tel: 613-632-8066
info@hawkesburychamberofcommerce.ca
www.hawkesburychamberofcommerce.ca
www.facebook.com/190878677617612
Overview: A small local organization founded in 1930
Mission: To promote tourism, commerce & industries
Chief Officer(s):

Yves Robert, President
yves.robert@sunlife.ca
Finances: *Annual Operating Budget:* Less than $50,000; *Funding Sources:* Membership dues
Staff Member(s): 1; 13 volunteer(s)
Membership: 225
Activities: Promotion of business

Hay River Chamber of Commerce
10K Gagnier St., Hay River NT X0E 1G1
Tel: 867-874-2565; *Fax:* 867-874-3631
www.hayriverchamber.com
Overview: A small local organization
Chief Officer(s):
Janet-Marie Fizer, President
Membership: 70; *Fees:* $77.75-$735; *Committees:* Public Relations & Tourism; Finance, Admin & Education; Member Services; Special Events; Business & Government Affairs; Taxes & Utilities; Retail Business; Chamber Park; Business, Home & Leisure Show

Head & Hands / A deux mains
5833, rue Sherbrooke ouest, Montréal QC H4A 1X4
Tel: 514-481-0277; *Fax:* 514-481-2336
info@headandhands.ca
www.headandhands.ca
www.facebook.com/headandhands
twitter.com/#!/headandhands
www.youtube.com/user/HeadandHands
Overview: A small local charitable organization founded in 1970
Mission: Medical, social, and legal services with an approach that is harm-reductive, holistic, and non-judgmental.
Chief Officer(s):
Jon McPhedran Waitzer, Director
admin@headandhands.ca
Juniper Belshaw, Contact, Fundraising and Development
membres@headandhands.ca
Membership: *Member Profile:* Anyone who makes a donation within a given year
Activities: Jeunesse 2000 drop-in centre; Community Workshops; Street Work; Young Parents Program; Sense Project

Headache Network Canada (HNC)
210 Georgian Drive, Oakville ON L6H 6T8
Tel: 905-330-9657
headachenetwork.ca
Overview: A large national charitable organization
Mission: To raise awareness about headache disorders in Canada; To encourage government assistance to the field; To educate the public about headache disorders
Affliation(s): Neurological Health Charities Canada
Publications:
• Canadian Headache Society Guideline for Migraine Prophylaxis
Profile: To assist the doctor in recommending the appropriate medication for a migraine sufferer

Headingley Chamber of Commerce
#1, 126 Bridge Rd., Headingley MB R4H 1G9
Tel: 204-837-5766; *Fax:* 204-831-7207
www.headingleychamber.ca
Overview: A small local organization founded in 1993
Mission: To promote & improve trade & commerce & the economic, civic & social welfare of the district
Member of: Manitoba Chamber of Commerce
Affliation(s): Central Plains Development Corporation; White Horse Plains Development Corporation; Headingley Heritage Centre
Chief Officer(s):
Jill Ruth, President
jillruth@headingleysport.mb.ca
Barb McEachern, Secretary
mceachern1963@hotmail.com
Dave White, Executive Director
dwhite@rmofheadingley.ca
Finances: *Annual Operating Budget:* Less than $50,000; *Funding Sources:* Membership dues; local government grant; fundraisers
Staff Member(s): 1; 13 volunteer(s)
Membership: 90; *Fees:* $100; *Member Profile:* Business owners, associate members, honorary members
Activities: Annual dinner dance; awards night; annual golf tournament; summer tourist booth; family fun day; *Library*
Awards:
• Corporate Citizen Award (Award)
• Community Volunteer Award (Award)
• Member Appreciation Award (Award)

Head-of-the-Lake Historical Society
PO Box 896, Hamilton ON L8N 3P6
Tel: 905-524-0805
contactus@headofthelake.ca
www.headofthelake.ca
Overview: A small local organization founded in 1944
Chief Officer(s):
Margaret E. Houghton, President
Staff Member(s): 11
Membership: 215; *Fees:* $20 individual; $35 family; $500 life
Publications:
• The Herald [a publication of the Head-of-the-Lake Historical Society]
Type: Newsletter; *Frequency:* Quarterly; *Price:* Free with membership in the Head-of-the-Lake Historical Society

Healing Our Nations (HON)
31 Gloster Ct., Dartmouth NS B3B 1X9
Tel: 902-492-4255
ea@accesswave.ca
www.hon93.ca
www.facebook.com/Healing.Our.Nations
Also Known As: Atlantic First Nations AIDS Task Force
Overview: A small local organization founded in 1991 overseen by Canadian AIDS Society
Mission: To educate First Nation people about HIV/AIDS; to improve the community by elimiating family violence, substance abuse, mental & spiritual malaise leading to depression & suicide.
Member of: Canadian HIV/AIDS Legal Network
Affliation(s): Union of NS Indians; Union of NB Indians; Atlantic Policy Congress; Mawiw Council; Confederacy of Mainland Mi'Kmaq
Chief Officer(s):
Julie Thomas, Program Manager
Staff Member(s): 7
Activities: HIV/AIDS education & awareness workshops & training; *Speaker Service:* Yes; *Library:* Resource Centre

Healing Our Spirit BC Aboriginal HIV/AIDS Society
137 East 4 Ave., Vancouver BC V5T 1G4
Tel: 604-879-8884; *Fax:* 604-879-9926
Toll-Free: 866-745-8884
info@healingourspirit.org
www.healingourspirit.org
Overview: A medium-sized local charitable organization founded in 1992
Mission: To prevent & reduce the spread of HIV infection in First Nation communities & to support those affected by HIV/AIDS.
Member of: Canadian Aboriginal AIDS Network
Affliation(s): Red Road HIV/AIDS Network; BC Aboriginal AIDS Awareness Program; AIDS Vancouver; BC Persons with AIDS
Chief Officer(s):
Winston Thompson, Executive Director
winston@healingourspirit.org
Leonard George, President
Finances: *Annual Operating Budget:* $500,000-$1.5 Million; *Funding Sources:* Ministry of Health; Health Canada; Healing Foundation; fundraising
Staff Member(s): 19; 57 volunteer(s)
Membership: 150; *Fees:* full membership: $5; association membership:$15; *Member Profile:* Clients, family, friends, societies, organizations; *Committees:* Conference
Activities: Preventive HIV educational workshops; housing subsidy program; community health programs; advocacy; peer support; volunteer & fundraising programs; speakers bureau; research & community development; healing project-residential schools; *Awareness Events:* Aboriginal AIDS Awareness Week, Nov./Dec.; *Speaker Service:* Yes

Health & Safety Conference Society of Alberta (HSCSA)
PO Box 38009, Calgary AB T3K 5G9
Tel: 403-236-2225; *Fax:* 780-455-1120
Other Communication: Trade Fair Information e-mail: tradefair@hsconference.com
info@hsconference.com
www.hsconference.com
Overview: A small provincial organization
Mission: To promote the importance of health & safety for safer workplaces
Chief Officer(s):
Guy Clyne, President
Arlene Ledi-Thom, Vice-President
Dianne Paulson, Secretary
Jerald Richelhoff, Treasurer
Finances: *Funding Sources:* Sponsorships
Membership: 1-99; *Member Profile:* Health & safety associations; Professional societies; Employer associations
Activities: Hosting an annual multi-partner conference; Providing health & safety education;
Meetings/Conferences: • Alberta Health & Safety 2015 14th Annual Conference & Trade Fair, 2015
Scope: Provincial

Health Action Network Society (HANS)
#202, 5262 Rumble St., Burnaby BC V5J 2B6
Tel: 604-435-0512; *Fax:* 604-435-1561
hans@hans.org
www.hans.org
twitter.com/JoinHANS
Overview: A medium-sized national charitable organization founded in 1984
Mission: To support complementary & alternative health care; To provide resources about preventive medicine & natural therapeutics; To facilitate delivery of integrated health care; To act as a voice for natural health consumers in Canada
Chief Officer(s):
Lorna Hancock, Director
Finances: *Funding Sources:* Donations
Membership: *Fees:* $35 Regular membership; $50 Family membership; $180 Professional membership; *Member Profile:* Lay & professional individuals with an interest in a natural approach to health care
Activities: Providing educational seminars; Organizing events & workshops; Enabling change at the regulatory level; *Library:* HANS Reference Library

Health Association Nova Scotia
2 Dartmouth Rd., Halifax NS B4A 2K7
Tel: 902-832-8500; *Fax:* 902-832-8505
contactus@healthassociation.ns.ca
www.healthassociation.ns.ca
twitter.com/HealthAssnNS
Previous Name: Nova Scotia Association of Health Organizations
Overview: A medium-sized provincial organization founded in 1960 overseen by Canadian Healthcare Association
Mission: To promote an effective, efficient & integrated quality health system for all Nova Scotians through leadership in influencing the development of public policy, representing & advocating members' interests & providing services to assist its members meet the health care needs of their communities
Member of: Canadian Alliance for Long Term Care
Chief Officer(s):
Gerald Pottier, Chair
Mary Lee, President/CEO, 902-832-8500 Ext. 236
Alex Cross, Communications Assistant, 902-832-8500 Ext. 295
alex.cross@healthassociation.ns.ca
Membership: 1-99; *Member Profile:* Health care & community services providers, including nursing care facilities, adult residential centres, rehabilitation centres, home care organizations, group homes, foundations, regulatory bodies & community-based health care providers; individuals active or interested in the provision of health care services
Activities: *Rents Mailing List:* Yes; *Library* by appointment

Bedford Office
Clinical Engineering, 2 Datmouth Rd., Bedford NS B4A 2K7
Tel: 902-832-8500; *Fax:* 902-832-8507
Chief Officer(s):
Steve Smith, Director, Clinical Engineering
steve.smith@healthassociation.ns.ca

Central Region Office
Clinical Engineering, 150 Exhibition St., Kentville NS B4N 5E3
Tel: 902-678-7090; *Fax:* 902-578-0565
Chief Officer(s):
Ed Ezekiel, Coordinator, Central Region
edward.ezekiel@healthassociation.ns.ca

Northern Region Office
Clinical Engineering, 835 East River Rd., New Glasgow NS B2H 3S6
Tel: 902-752-5487; *Fax:* 902-755-6297
Chief Officer(s):
John Inch, CET, CBET, Coordinator, Northern Region
john.inch@healthassociation.ns.ca

Southern Region Office
Clinical Engineering, 90 Glenn Allen Dr., Bridgewater NS B4V 3S6
Tel: 902-527-5234; *Fax:* 902-543-1662

Chief Officer(s):
Philip Bradfield, CET, CBET, Coordinator, Southern Region
phil.bradfield@healthassociation.ns.ca

Health Association of African Canadians (HAAC)

c/o Black Cultural Centre for Nova Scotia, 10 Cherry Brook Rd., Cherry Brook NS B2Z 1A8
Tel: 902-405-4222
info@africancanadianhealth.ca
africancanadianhealth.ca
Overview: A medium-sized provincial organization founded in 2000
Mission: To promote and improve the health of African Canadians in Nova Scotia through community engagement, education, policy recommendations, partnerships, and research participation.
Chief Officer(s):
Donna Smith Darrell, President/Treasurer
Staff Member(s): 4

Health Association of PEI (HAPEI)

10 Pownal St., Charlottetown PE C1A 3V6
Tel: 902-368-3901
Previous Name: Hospital Association of PEI
Overview: A small provincial organization founded in 1961 overseen by Canadian Healthcare Association
Mission: To influence the change & development of the health delivery system; to provide services which assist members in managing their human, financial & physical resources.
Finances: *Funding Sources:* Membership dues
Activities: *Library*

Health Care Public Relations Association (HCPRA) / Association des relations publiques des organismes de la santé (ARPOS)

PO Box 36029, 1106 Wellington St., Ottawa ON K1Y 4V3
Tel: 613-729-2102; *Fax:* 613-729-7708
info@hcpra.org
www.hcpra.org
www.linkedin.com/HCPRA
www.facebook.com/165490196835523
twitter.com/HCPRA
Overview: A medium-sized national organization founded in 1973
Mission: To address the concerns of the public relations professionals in Canadian health care settings
Affliation(s): Association for Healthcare Philanthropy
Chief Officer(s):
Jane Adams, National Coordinator
Judy Brown, HCPRA President
jbrown@qch.on.ca
Staff Member(s): 1
Membership: 300; *Member Profile:* Health care communicators from across Canada with responsibilities for the public relations of a health region, institution or organization, or a national, provincial, or community health delivery organization; Students pursuing a full-time course of study in public relations with an interest in health care communications; *Committees:* Professional Development; Recognition; Membership; Communications
Activities: Providing professional development opportunities; Sharing research & best practices; Offering networking opportunities; *Speaker Service:* Yes
Awards:
• The Hollobon Awards (Award)
Presented to members of the media whose work has contributed significantly to the public's understanding of health care*Eligibility:* Media representatives whose work has appeared in print or television with a health care focus
• HYGEIA Awards (Award)
Awarded for excellence in health care communications

Health Charities Coalition of Canada (HCCC) / Coalition canadienne des organismes bénévoles en santé

41 Empress Ave., Annex D, Ottawa ON K1R 7E9
Tel: 613-232-7266; *Fax:* 613-569-3278
www.healthcharities.ca
Overview: A small national organization founded in 2000
Mission: To provide health policy leadership for the health of all people of Canada; To act as a collective authoritative voice of national health charities in public policy & health research issues that affect the lives of the people of Canada
Chief Officer(s):
Bev Heim-Myers, Executive Director/CEO
Finances: *Annual Operating Budget:* $100,000-$250,000
Staff Member(s): 1; 200 volunteer(s)
Membership: 19; *Fees:* Sliding scale; *Member Profile:* Amyotrophic Lateral Sclerosis Society of Canada; Canadian Breast Cancer Fdn.; Canadian Cancer Society; Canadian Cystic Fibrosis Fdn.; Canadian Diabetes Assn.; Canadian Hospice Palliative Care Assn.; Canadian Lung Assn.; Canadian Mental Health Assn.; The Fdn. Fighting Blindness - Canada; Heart & Stroke Fdn. of Canada; The Kidney Fdn. of Canada; Muscular Dystrophy Canada; Multiple Sclerosis Society of Canada; Osteoporosis Canada; Parkinson Society Canada; Schizophrenia Society of Canada; Sick Kids Fdn.; The Arthritis Society
Awards:
• Health Charities Coalition of Canada's Award of Distinction (Award)

Health Employers Association of British Columbia (HEABC)

#200, 1333 West Broadway, Vancouver BC V6H 4C6
Tel: 604-736-5909; *Fax:* 604-736-2715
contact@heabc.bc.ca
www.heabc.bc.ca
Overview: A medium-sized provincial organization founded in 1993 overseen by Canadian Healthcare Association
Mission: To serve a diverse group of over 250 publicly funded healthcare employers; To represent the entire spectrum of healthcare employers
Chief Officer(s):
Michael Marchbank, President & CEO
Roy Thorpe-Dorward, Executive Director, Communications, 604-714-2285
royt@heabc.bc.ca
Membership: 250 employers

Health Food Dealers Association *See* Canadian Health Food Association

Health Law Institute (HLI)

Law Centre, 4th Floor, University of Alberta, Edmonton AB T6G 2H5
Tel: 780-248-1175; *Fax:* 780-492-9575
hli@law.ualberta.ca
www.law.ualberta.ca/centres/hli
Overview: A small international organization founded in 1977
Mission: To research needs & be proactive to emerging health law issues; To disseminate research findings & information through publications; To provide public lectures & educational presentations
Chief Officer(s):
Tracey M. Bailey, Executive Director, 780-492-6127
tbailey@law.ualberta.ca
Finances: *Annual Operating Budget:* $100,000-$250,000; *Funding Sources:* Alberta Law Foundation; Alberta Heritage Foundation for Medical Research; Federal government; grants
Staff Member(s): 5
Membership: *Fees:* $75
Activities: *Library* by appointment
Publications:
• Health Law Journal
Type: Journal; *Frequency:* Annually
Profile: Papers that explore innovative and original issues in the interdisciplinary area of health law. The HLJ is a peer-reviewed publication.

Health Libraries Association of British Columbia (HLABC)

c/o Devon Greyson, UBC Centre for Health Services & Policy Research, #201, 2206 East Mall, Vancouver BC V6T 1Z3
Tel: 604-822-7353; *Fax:* 604-822-5690
hlabc.exec@gmail.com
chla-absc.ca/hlabc/
www.facebook.com/group.php?gid=2347253553
Overview: A small provincial organization founded in 1980 overseen by Canadian Health Libraries Association
Mission: To support the work of health librarians throughout British Columbia
Chief Officer(s):
Megan L. Crouch, President, 778-782-4962
mcrouch@sfu.ca
Leigh Anne Palmer, Vice-President
leighannep@ehlbc.ca
Chantelle Jack, Secretary
chantelle.jack@vch.ca
Antje Helmuth, Treasurer & Contact, Membership
antje.helmuth@gov.bc.ca
Membership: *Fees:* $25 regular members; $15 students (after free first year); *Member Profile:* Librarians working in health services throughout British Columbia
Activities: Delivering continuing education programs for librarians
Publications:
• Health Libraries Association of British Columbia Directory
Type: Directory
Profile: Detailed listing of association members

Health Record Association of British Columbia (HRABC)

c/o Shirley Sirkia, Nanaimo Regional General Hospital, 1200 Dufferin Cres., Nanaimo BC V9S 2B7
www.hrabc.net
Overview: A small provincial organization founded in 1949
Mission: To contribute to the promotion of wellness & the provision of quality healthcare through excellence in information management
Member of: National Health Information Management Alliance
Affliation(s): Canadian Health Information Management Association
Chief Officer(s):
Linda Penner, President
hrabc.president@gmail.com
Shirley Sirkia, Treasurer
hrabc.treasurer@gmail.com
Finances: *Annual Operating Budget:* Less than $50,000
9 volunteer(s)
Membership: 320; *Fees:* $70 active; $175 corporate; $40 inactive/associate; *Member Profile:* Health information management professionals; *Committees:* Data Quality; Membership & Credentials; Program & Arrangements; Nominating; Policy; Constitution & Bylaws; Archives
Awards:
• Academic Award (Award)
• Leadership Award (Award)

Health Sciences Association of Alberta (HSAA) / Association des sciences de la santé de l'Alberta (ind.)

10212 - 112 St., Edmonton AB T5K 1M4
Tel: 780-488-0168; *Fax:* 780-488-0534
Toll-Free: 800-252-7904
www.hsaa.ca
Overview: A medium-sized provincial organization founded in 1971
Mission: To conduct activities as a labour union to enhance the quality of life for HSAA members & society
Member of: National Union of Public and General Employees
Chief Officer(s):
Elisabeth Ballermann, President
elisabethb@hsaa.ca
Patricia Heffel, Director, Administrative Services
patriciah@hsaa.ca
Lynette McAvoy, Director, Labour Relations
lynettem@hsaa.ca
Roni Hermanutz, Manager, Human Resources
ronih@hsaa.ca
Joanne Monro, Officer, Occupational Health & Safety
joannem@hsaa.ca
Scott Pattison, Officer, Communications, 780-405-4684
scottpat@hsaa.ca
Finances: *Funding Sources:* Membership dues; Merchandise sales
Membership: 17,000; *Member Profile:* Professional, paramedical technical, general support, & EMS employees in the public & private health care sectors of Alberta; *Committees:* Bylaws & Resolutions; Community Relations; Elections/Credentials; EMAC; Environmental; Finance; Human Rights & Equality; Labour Relations Appeals; Members' Benefits; OHS&W; Political Action / Education
Activities: Offering educational workshops; Awarding bursaries
Awards:
• Barb Mikulin Award (Award)
To honour an HSAA member who has made extraordinary efforts to improve the world
Meetings/Conferences: • Health Sciences Association of Alberta 2015 44th Annual General Meeting, 2015, AB
Scope: Provincial
Contact Information: Communications Officer: Kim Adonyi-Keegan, E-mail: kima@hsaa.ca
Publications:
• HSAA Challenger
Type: Magazine; *Frequency:* Quarterly; *Accepts Advertising*; *Editor:* Scott Pattison (scottpat@hsaa.ca)
Profile: Feature articles, labour relations updates, HSAA activities, affiliate & member news, forthcoming workshops & events

Health Sciences Association of British Columbia (HSABC)

180 East Columbia St., New Westminster BC V3L 0G7
Tel: 604-517-0994; *Fax:* 604-515-8889
Toll-Free: 800-663-2017
www.hsabc.org
www.facebook.com/HSABC
twitter.com/hsabc
www.youtube.com/user/healthsciencesbc
Overview: A large provincial organization founded in 1971
Mission: To negotiate collective agreements for members; To preserve & promote public health care in Canada
Member of: National Union of Public and General Employees
Chief Officer(s):
Reid Johnson, President
webpres@hsabc.org
Jeanne Meyers, Executive Director, Labour Relations & Legal Services
jmeyers@hsabc.org
Bruce MacDonald, Secretary-Treasurer
Miriam Sobrino, Director, Communications
msobrino@hsabc.org
Finances: *Annual Operating Budget:* Greater than $5 Million; *Funding Sources:* Union dues
Membership: 16,000+; *Member Profile:* Health Care & Social services professionals; *Committees:* Education; Equality & Social Action; Occupational Health & Safety; Political Action; Run for the Cure; Women
Meetings/Conferences: • Health Sciences Association 2015 Convention, April, 2015, Hyatt Regency, Vancouver, BC
Scope: Provincial
Description: A gathering of health care & social services professionals
Contact Information: Director of Communications: Miriam Sobrino, E-mail: msobrino@hsabc.org

Health Sciences Association of Saskatchewan (HSAS) / Association des sciences de la santé de la Saskatchewan (ind.)

#42, 1736 Quebec Ave., Saskatoon SK S7K 1V9
Tel: 306-955-3399; *Fax:* 306-955-3396
Toll-Free: 888-565-3399
hsasstoon@sasktel.net
www.hsa-sk.com
www.facebook.com/124779960928913
Overview: A medium-sized provincial organization founded in 1972
Mission: To conduct activities as an independent union representing its members who are health sciences professionals in Saskatchewan
Chief Officer(s):
Karen Wasylenko, President
president@hsa-sk.com
Anne Robins, Vice-President
mt@hsa-sk.com
Cara McDavid, Secretary
sw3@hsa-sk.com
Karen Kinar, Treasurer
respiratory@hsa-sk.com
Bill Craik, Executive Director, 306-585-7757
bill@hsa-sk.com
Membership: 2,900+; *Member Profile:* Health professionals from all health regions in Saskatchewan; *Committees:* Annual Convention; Constitutional; Emergency Fund; Grievance; Charitable Donations / Professional Contributions; Communications; Education Fund; Regional Council Development; Provincial Negotiating; Finance
Activities: Conducting public relations campaigns to increase public awareness about the profession; Presenting bursaries & scholarships

Health Sciences Centre Foundation (HSCF)

Thorlakson Building, 820 Sherbrook St., #MS107, Winnipeg MB R3A 1R9
Tel: 204-787-2022; *Fax:* 204-787-2804
Toll-Free: 800-679-8493
hsc_foundation@hsc.mb.ca
www.hscfoundation.mb.ca
www.facebook.com/hscfdn
twitter.com/hscfoundation
Also Known As: HSC Foundation
Previous Name: Health Sciences Centre Research Foundation
Overview: A small national charitable organization founded in 1981
Mission: HSC Foundation supports the men and women who provide health care at Health Sciences Centre Winnipeg by funding research, education, advanced technology and infrastructure enhancements.
Member of: Association of Healthcare Philanthropy; Association of Fundraising Professionals
Affliation(s): Health Sciences Centre; Foundations for Health; Breakthrough!
Chief Officer(s):
Jonathon Lyon, President & CEO, 204-787-4391
jlyon@hsc.mb.ca
Sue Graham, Vice-President, 204-787-2273
sgraham5@hsc.mb.ca
Finances: *Annual Operating Budget:* Greater than $5 Million; *Funding Sources:* Donations, Events, Lottery revenue
Staff Member(s): 11; 12 volunteer(s)
Membership: 40; *Committees:* Executive, Donor Development, Finance & Audit, Grants & Allocations, Marketing & Communications, Nominating & Governance, Honourary Directors, Lottery
Activities: *Speaker Service:* Yes
Awards:
• Grants for Research & Patient Care (Grant)
Provision of grants for research & patient care locally*Location:* Local

Health Sciences Centre Research Foundation *See* Health Sciences Centre Foundation

HealthBridge Foundation of Canada

#1105, 1 Nicholas St., Ottawa ON K1N 7B7
Tel: 613-241-3927; *Fax:* 613-241-7988
admin@healthbridge.ca
www.healthbridge.ca
Previous Name: PATH Canada
Overview: A small national organization founded in 1982
Mission: Works with partners worldwide to improve health & health equity through research, policy & action
Chief Officer(s):
Sian Fitzgerald, Executive Director
sfitzgerald@healthbridge.ca
Finances: *Annual Operating Budget:* $3 Million-$5 Million
Staff Member(s): 6; 12 volunteer(s)

HealthCareCAN

#100, 17 York St., Ottawa ON K1N 9J6
Tel: 613-241-8005; *Fax:* 613-241-5055
info@healthcarecan.ca
www.healthcarecan.ca
www.linkedin.com/company/1363724?trk=cws-btn-overview-0-0
www.facebook.com/healthcarecan.soinssantecan
twitter.com/healthcarecan
Merged from: Canadian Healthcare Association; Association of Canadian Academic Healthcare Organizations
Overview: A large national charitable organization
Mission: To improve the delivery of health services in Canada through policy development, advocacy & leadership
Affliation(s): American Hospital Association; Canadian Council on Health Services Accreditation
Chief Officer(s):
Bill Tholl, President/CEO, 613-241-8005 Ext. 202
Finances: *Annual Operating Budget:* $1.5 Million-$3 Million; *Funding Sources:* Membership fees; Services
Staff Member(s): 22
Membership: 13; *Fees:* Schedule available; *Member Profile:* Federation of 13 provinicial & territorial hospital/health associations & serves as a voice for over 1,200 health care facilities & health service agencies
Activities: *Rents Mailing List:* Yes
Awards:
• CHA Award of Excellence for Distinguished Service (Award)
To honour achievements in the administration & governance in the healthcare sector*Deadline:* January
• Marion Stephenson Award (Award)
To recognize outstanding contributions to community care*Deadline:* January
Meetings/Conferences: • Canadian Healthcare Association 2015 Annual General Meeting, 2015
Scope: National
Description: The association's business meeting, including the presentation of the Marion Stephenson Award & the CHA Award for Distinguished Service by the Boarrd of Directors
Contact Information: Communications Specialist: Teresa Neuman, E-mail: tneuman@cha.ca
• Canadian Healthcare Assn & Canadian College of Health Leaders 2015 National Health Leadership Conference, 2015
Scope: National
Description: A meeting of health system decision-makers, such as chief executive officers, trustees, directors, managers, & department heads. The theme this year is "From rhetoric to action: Achieving person & family-centred health systems."
Contact Information: Coordinator, Conference Services: Laurie Oman, Phone: 613-235-7218, Toll-Free: 1-800-363-9056, ext. 237, E-mail: loman@cchl-ccls.ca

Healthy Indoors Partnership (HIP) / Partenariat pour des environnements intérieurs sains

2699 Priscilla St., Ottawa ON K2B 7E1
Tel: 613-224-3800
mail@cullbridge.com
www.cullbridge.com/Projects/Healthy_Indoors.htm
Overview: A small national organization
Mission: To involve private, public & not-for-profit organizations & individuals in the development, implementation & financing of a broad range of collaborative actions to improve indoor environments in Canada
Chief Officer(s):
Jay Kassirer, President
kassirer@healthyindoors.com
Membership: *Fees:* $100

Healthy Minds Canada

#500, 2 Toronto St., Toronto ON M5C 2B6
Tel: 416-351-7757; *Fax:* 416-351-7765
Toll-Free: 800-915-2773
admin@healthymindscanada.ca
www.healthymindscanada.ca
www.facebook.com/healthymindscanada
twitter.com/Healthy_Minds
Overview: A medium-sized national charitable organization founded in 1980
Chief Officer(s):
Katie W. Robinette, Executive Director
krobinette@healthymindscanada.ca
Finances: *Funding Sources:* Grants, fundraising
Activities: *Awareness Events:* Anti-Stigma Youth Summits; Silver Dinner; Open Minds Across Canada

Hearing Foundation of Canada / La Fondation canadienne de l'ouïe

20 Bay St. 11th Floor, Toronto ON M5J 2N8
Tel: 416-364-4060; *Fax:* 416-369-0515
Toll-Free: 866-432-7968
info@hearingfoundation.ca
www.hearingfoundation.ca
twitter.com/HearFdnCan
Previous Name: Canadian Hearing Society Foundation
Overview: A medium-sized national charitable organization founded in 1979
Mission: To eliminate the devastating effects of hearing loss on the quality of life of Canadians by promoting prevention, early diagnosis, leading edge medical research & successful intervention
Member of: Association of Development Professionals; Canadian Society of Association Executives
Chief Officer(s):
John Pepperell, Chair Ext. 2
Dino Sophocleous, President Ext. 2
Janice Eales, Manager, Development & Programs Ext. 2
Finances: *Annual Operating Budget:* $500,000-$1.5 Million; *Funding Sources:* Individual & corporate donations; foundations; service clubs
Staff Member(s): 8; 70 volunteer(s)
Membership: *Committees:* Special Events; Finance; Governance; Executive; Programming; Major Gifts; Medical Research; Grant Review; Music Industry Advisory
Activities: Infant Hearing Screening Awareness Program; Medical Research Program; Sound Sense: Save Your Hearing for the Music; *Speaker Service:* Yes

Hearst & Area Association for Community Living / Association de Hearst et de la région pour l'intégration communautaire

PO Box 12000, 923 Edward St., Hearst ON P0L 1N0
Tel: 705-362-5758; *Fax:* 705-362-8093
Overview: A small local charitable organization founded in 1970
Mission: To promote & realize the well-being & integration of developmentally challenged persons
Member of: Community Living Ontario
Chief Officer(s):
Katrina Carrera, President
Chantal G. Dillon, Executive Director
Finances: *Annual Operating Budget:* $500,000-$1.5 Million; *Funding Sources:* Fundraising; MCSS

Staff Member(s): 12; 30 volunteer(s)
Membership: 200; *Fees:* $2; *Committees:* Personnel; Admission; Social Activities
Activities: *Awareness Events:* Access Awareness Week; Community Living Month

Hearst, Mattice - Val Côté & Area Chamber of Commerce

PO Box 987, #60, 9th St., Hearst ON P0L 1N0
Tel: 705-362-5880
info@hearstcommerce.ca
hearstcommerce.ca
Previous Name: Hearst, Mattice Chamber of Commerce
Overview: A small local organization founded in 1994
Mission: The Chamber of Commerce is the spokesperson of the commercial, industrial and professional community to ensure economic prosperity to the Hearst, Mattice-Val Côté area.
Member of: Chambre économique de l'Ontario; James Bay Frontier Travel Association; Northeastern Ontario Chamber of Commerce
Chief Officer(s):
Lise Joanis, President, 705-362-4325
Finances: *Annual Operating Budget:* Less than $50,000; *Funding Sources:* Membership
15 volunteer(s)
Membership: 80; *Fees:* $110-610; *Committees:* Tourism; Economic Development

Hearst, Mattice Chamber of Commerce *See* Hearst, Mattice - Val Côté & Area Chamber of Commerce

Heart & Stroke Foundation of Alberta *See* Heart & Stroke Foundation of Alberta, NWT & Nunavut

Heart & Stroke Foundation of Alberta, NWT & Nunavut (HSFA)

#100, 119 - 14 St. NW, Calgary AB T2N 1Z6
Tel: 403-351-7030; *Fax:* 403-237-0803
Toll-Free: 888-473-4636
www.hsf.ab.ca
Previous Name: Heart & Stroke Foundation of Alberta
Overview: A medium-sized provincial charitable organization founded in 1956 overseen by Heart & Stroke Foundation of Canada
Mission: To disseminate information about heart disease & stroke; to promote research into new drugs, therapies, treatments in disorders leading to heart disease & stroke; to conduct several events to campaign for funds.
Chief Officer(s):
Michael Hill, Chair
Donna Hastings, CEO
Finances: *Annual Operating Budget:* $100,000-$250,000
Activities: Advocating in areas such as the promotion of a smoke-free world & eqaual access to quality stroke care; *Awareness Events:* Jump Rope for Heart; Ski for Heart; Heart & Stroke Month

Edmonton Office
10985 - 124 St., Edmonton AB T5M 0H9
Tel: 780-451-4545; *Fax:* 780-454-1593

Grande Prairie Office
#109, 10126 - 120 Ave., Grande Prairie AB T8V 8H9
Tel: 780-513-0439; *Fax:* 780-513-0941

Lethbridge Office
PO Box 2211, Lethbridge AB T1J 4K7
Tel: 403-327-3239; *Fax:* 403-327-9928

Medicine Hat Office
#124, 430 - 6 Ave. SE, Medicine Hat AB T1A 2S8
Tel: 403-527-0028; *Fax:* 403-526-9655

Red Deer Office
#202, 5913 - 50 Ave., Red Deer AB T4N 4C4
Tel: 403-342-4435; *Fax:* 403-342-7088

Heart & Stroke Foundation of British Columbia & Yukon (HSFBCY)

1212 West Broadway, Vancouver BC V6H 3V2
Tel: 604-736-4404; *Fax:* 604-736-8732
Toll-Free: 888-473-4636
info@hsf.bc.ca
www.heartandstroke.bc.ca
Previous Name: BC & Yukon Heart Foundation
Overview: A large provincial charitable organization founded in 1955 overseen by Heart & Stroke Foundation of Canada
Mission: To further the study, prevention & relief of cardiovascular disease
Chief Officer(s):
Bobbe Wood, CEO
Finances: *Annual Operating Budget:* Greater than $5 Million
Staff Member(s): 70; 1500 volunteer(s)
Membership: 94; *Fees:* $5 annual; $100 lifetime
Activities: Information Line 1-800-473-4636; *Awareness Events:* Heart Month, Feb.; Stroke Month, June; *Speaker Service:* Yes

Coastal Vancouver Area Office - Richmond/South Delta
#260, 7000 Minoru Blvd., Richmond BC V6Y 3Z5
Tel: 604-279-7130; *Fax:* 604-279-7134
Chief Officer(s):
Joan Mann, Area Manager
jmann@hsf.bc.ca

Coastal Vancouver Area Office - Vancouver/North Shore
1216 West Broadway, Vancouver BC V6H 1G6
Tel: 604-736-4088; *Fax:* 604-736-4087
Chief Officer(s):
Shanitha Rifayee, Area Administrator

Fraser North & East Area Office - Tri-Cities/Fraser Valley/Burnaby/New Westminster
2239C McAllister Ave., Port Coquitlam BC V3C 2A5
Tel: 604-472-0045; *Fax:* 604-472-0055
Toll-Free: 877-472-0045
Chief Officer(s):
Gillian Yardley, Area Manager

Kamloops Area Office - Kamloops/Cariboo
729 Victoria St., Kamloops BC V2C 2B5
Tel: 250-372-3938; *Fax:* 250-372-3940
Chief Officer(s):
Teresa Moore, Area Manager
tmoore@hsf.bc.ca

Kelowna Area Office - Okanagan/Kootenays
#4, 1551 Sutherland Ave., Kelowna BC V1Y 9M9
Tel: 250-860-6275; *Fax:* 250-860-8790
Toll-Free: 866-432-7833
Chief Officer(s):
Diana Barker, Area Manager
dbarker@hsf.bc.ca

Prince George Area Office Northern BC/Yukon
1480 Seventh Ave., Prince George BC V2L 3P2
Tel: 250-562-8611; *Fax:* 250-562-8614
Chief Officer(s):
Suzanne Anderson, Area Manager
sanderson@hsf.bc.ca

Surrey Area Office - Surrey/Langley/Whiterock/Cloverdale/Aldergrove/North Delta
#101, 13569 - 76th Ave., Surrey BC V3W 2W3
Tel: 604-591-1955; *Fax:* 604-591-2624
Chief Officer(s):
Karen Reid-Sidhu, Area Manager

Vancouver Island Area Office - Nanaimo
#401, 495 Dunsmuir Street, Nanaimo BC V9R 6B9
Tel: 250-754-5274; *Fax:* 250-754-2575
Chief Officer(s):
Donya Fiske, Area Manager
dfiske@hsf.bc.ca

Victoria Office
#107, 1001 Cloverdale Ave., Victoria BC V8X 4C9
Tel: 250-382-4035; *Fax:* 250-382-0231
Chief Officer(s):
Victoria Newstead, Area Manager
vnewstead@hsf.bc.ca

Heart & Stroke Foundation of Canada (HSFC) / Fondation des maladies du coeur du Canada

#1402, 222 Queen St., Ottawa ON K1P 5V9
Tel: 613-569-4361; *Fax:* 613-569-3278
www.heartandstroke.ca
www.facebook.com/heartandstroke
twitter.com/TheHSF
www.youtube.com/heartandstrokefdn
Overview: A medium-sized national charitable organization founded in 1983
Mission: To further the study, prevention & reduction of disability & death from heart disease & stroke through research, education & the promotion of healthy lifestyles
Member of: Imagine Canada
Affliation(s): International Society & Federation of Cardiology; Canadian Coalition for High Blood Pressure Prevention & Control
Chief Officer(s):
David Sculthorpe, CEO
Douglas B. Clement, Chair
Finances: *Funding Sources:* Personal & corporate donations
Staff Member(s): 620; 1400 volunteer(s)
Activities: The Foundation provides more than 60% of non-industry funding for cardiovascular research in Canada as well as supporting successful education programs for healthy living; *Awareness Events:* Stroke Month, Feb.; Heart Month, Feb.; CPR Awareness Month, Nov.; *Speaker Service:* Yes

Heart & Stroke Foundation of Manitoba (HSFM)

The Heart & Stroke Bldg., #200, 6 Donald St., Winnipeg MB R3L 0K6
Tel: 204-949-2000; *Fax:* 204-957-1365
www.heartandstroke.mb.ca
Previous Name: Manitoba Heart Foundation
Overview: A medium-sized provincial charitable organization founded in 1957 overseen by Heart & Stroke Foundation of Canada
Mission: To eliminate heart disease & stroke through education, advocacy, & research
Chief Officer(s):
Debbie Brown, CEO
Finances: *Funding Sources:* Donations; Fundraising

Heart & Stroke Foundation of New Brunswick / Fondation des maladies du coeur du Nouveau-Brunswick

#606, 133 Prince William St., Saint John NB E2L 2B5
Tel: 506-634-1620; *Fax:* 506-648-0098
Toll-Free: 800-663-3600
www.heartandstroke.nb.ca
Previous Name: New Brunswick Heart Foundation
Overview: A medium-sized provincial organization founded in 1967 overseen by Heart & Stroke Foundation of Canada
Mission: To improve the health of residents of New Brunswick by preventing & reducing disability & death from heart disease & stroke, through research, health promotion & advocacy
Chief Officer(s):
Daniel Connolly, CEO
Finances: *Funding Sources:* Donations; Fundraising
Activities: Organizing the Hearts in Motion Walking Club to improve heart health; Establishing the Wellness at Heart Award for New Brunswick businesses; Coordingating the Heart & Stroke Big Bike fundraising event across New Brunswick; Developing the New Brunswick Food Bank Project; Providing health information resources available free of charge; *Awareness Events:* Bruce Hadley Memorial Relay Run for Heart, August; Heart & Stroke Golf for Heart, July; Heart & Stroke Skate for Heart, February; *Library:* Video Library

Heart & Stroke Foundation of Newfoundland & Labrador

PO Box 670, 1037 Topsail Rd., Mount Pearl NL A1C 5X3
Tel: 709-753-8521; *Fax:* 709-753-3117
info@heartandstroke.nf.net
www.heartandstroke.nf.ca
Overview: A medium-sized provincial organization overseen by Heart & Stroke Foundation of Canada
Mission: To work in Newfoundland & Labrador to advance research, advocate, & promote healthy lifestyles so that heart disease & stroke will be eliminated & their impact reduced
Chief Officer(s):
George Tilley, CEO
Activities: Supporting the Active School program in the central Newfoundland area; Offering the Heart to Heart Cardiac Rehabilitation program for patients & their families; Providing pillows to cardiac patients through the Heart Pillow program, in partnership with Aliant Telephone Pioneers; Introducing the product known as CPR Anytime: Family & Friends to assist in teaching resuscitation; Ensuring that the quality of care is high through the Provincial Integrated Stroke Strategy; *Awareness Events:* Mayor's March on Heart Disease & Stroke

Heart & Stroke Foundation of Nova Scotia (HSFNS)

Park Lane - Mall Level 3, PO Box 245, 5657 Spring Garden Rd., Halifax NS B3J 3R4
Tel: 902-423-7530; *Fax:* 902-492-1464
Toll-Free: 800-423-4432
contactus@heartandstroke.ns.ca
www.heartandstroke.ns.ca
Previous Name: Nova Scotia Heart Foundation
Overview: A medium-sized provincial charitable organization founded in 1958 overseen by Heart & Stroke Foundation of Canada
Mission: To eliminate heart disease & stroke; To advance research; To promote healthy living; To engage in advocacy activities
Member of: The Heart and Stroke Foundation of Canada
Chief Officer(s):

Jane Farquharson, CEO
Finances: *Funding Sources:* Donations
4 volunteer(s)
Activities: Funding research; Helping Nova Scotians to be more active & healthy; Offering CPR programs; Providing healthy living information, including multilingual & multicultural resources; Liaising with Nova Scotia's provincial & municipal governments; Delivering patient programs; *Library:* Resource Centre;

Heart & Stroke Foundation of Ontario (HSFO)
PO Box 2414, #1300, 2300 Yonge St., Toronto ON M4P 1E4
Tel: 416-489-7111; *Fax:* 416-489-6885
www.heartandstroke.on.ca
Previous Name: Ontario Heart Foundation
Overview: A medium-sized provincial charitable organization founded in 1952 overseen by Heart & Stroke Foundation of Canada
Mission: To eliminate heart disease & stroke by advancing research & promoting healthy living; To advocate in areas such as a smoke-free world, equal access to quality stroke care, obesity targeting, elimination of trans-fat, & resuscitation/CPR
Member of: Heart & Stroke Foundation of Canada
Chief Officer(s):
Barry Cracower, Chair
Finances: *Funding Sources:* Donations
Activities: Funding research; Providing health information; *Awareness Events:* Polo for Heart

Barrie Office
#1, 112 Commerce Park Dr., Barrie ON L4N 8W8
Tel: 705-737-1020; *Fax:* 705-737-0902
www.heartandstroke.on.ca

Belleville Office
#106A, 121 Dundas St. East, Belleville ON K8N 1C3
Tel: 613-962-2502; *Fax:* 613-962-6080
www.heartandstroke.on.ca

Brantford Office
442 Grey St., #A, Brantford ON N3S 7N3
Tel: 519-752-1301; *Fax:* 519-752-5554
www.heartandstroke.on.ca

Brockville Office
#310, 51 King St. East, Brockville ON K6V 1A8
Tel: 613-345-6183; *Fax:* 613-345-3037
www.heartandstroke.on.ca

Chatham-Kent Office
214 Queen St., Chatham ON N7M 2H1
Tel: 519-354-6232; *Fax:* 519-354-6351
www.heartandstroke.on.ca

Chinese Canadian Council
PO Box 2414, #1300, 2300 Yonge St., Toronto ON M4P 1E4
Tel: 416-489-7111; *Fax:* 416-489-9179
www.heartandstroke.on.ca

Cornwall Office
36 - 2nd St. East, Cornwall ON K6H 1Y3
Tel: 613-938-8933; *Fax:* 613-938-0655
www.heartandstroke.on.ca

Durham Regional Office
#2, 105 Consumers Dr., Whitby ON L1N 1C4
Tel: 905-666-3777; *Fax:* 905-666-9956
www.heartandstroke.on.ca

Guelph Office
#204, 21 Surrey St. West, Guelph ON N1H 3R3
Tel: 519-837-4858; *Fax:* 519-837-9209
www.heartandstroke.on.ca

Halton Region Office
#7, 4391 Harvester Rd., Burlington ON L7L 4X1
Tel: 905-634-7732; *Fax:* 905-634-1353
www.heartandstroke.on.ca

Hamilton Office
#7, 1439 Upper Ottawa St., Hamilton ON L8W 3J6
Tel: 905-574-4105; *Fax:* 905-574-4380
www.heartandstroke.on.ca

Kingston Office
720 Progress Ave., Kingston ON K7M 4W9
Tel: 613-384-2871; *Fax:* 613-384-2899
www.heartandstroke.on.ca

Kitchener Office
#2A, 1373 Victoria St. North, Kitchener ON N2B 3R6
Tel: 519-571-9600; *Fax:* 519-571-9832
www.heartandstroke.on.ca

London Office
#180, 633 Colborne St., London ON N6B 2V3
Tel: 519-679-0641; *Fax:* 519-679-6898
www.heartandstroke.on.ca

Niagara District Office
#3, 300 Bunting Rd., St Catharines ON L2M 7X3
Tel: 905-938-8800; *Fax:* 905-938-8811
www.heartandstroke.on.ca

Ottawa Office
#100, 1101 Prince of Wales Dr., Ottawa ON K2C 3W7
Tel: 613-727-5060; *Fax:* 613-727-1895
www.heartandstroke.on.ca

Owen Sound Office
795 - 1st Ave. East, Owen Sound ON N4K 2C6
Tel: 519-371-0083; *Fax:* 519-371-8164
www.heartandstroke.on.ca

Peel Office
#306, 201 County Court Blvd., Brampton ON L6W 4L2
Tel: 905-451-0021; *Fax:* 905-452-0503
www.heartandstroke.on.ca

Peterborough Office
#3, 824 Clonsilla Ave., Peterborough ON K9J 5Y3
Tel: 705-749-1044; *Fax:* 705-749-1470
www.heartandstroke.on.ca

Sarnia Office
774 London Rd., Sarnia ON N7T 4Y1
Tel: 519-332-1415; *Fax:* 519-332-3139
www.heartandstroke.on.ca

Sault Ste. Marie Office
59 Great Northern Rd., Sault Ste Marie ON P6B 4Y7
Tel: 705-253-3775; *Fax:* 705-946-5760
www.heartandstroke.on.ca

Stratford Office
556 Huron St., Stratford ON N5A 5T9
Tel: 519-273-5212; *Fax:* 519-273-7024
www.heartandstroke.on.ca

Sudbury Office
#130, 43 Elm St., Sudbury ON P3C 1S4
Tel: 705-673-2228; *Fax:* 705-673-7406
www.heartandstroke.on.ca

Thunder Bay Office
#104, 979 Alloy Dr., Thunder Bay ON P7B 5Z8
Tel: 807-623-1118; *Fax:* 807-622-9914
www.heartandstroke.on.ca

Timmins Office
#301, 60 Wilson Ave., Timmins ON P4N 2S7
Tel: 705-267-4645; *Fax:* 705-268-6721
www.heartandstroke.on.ca

Toronto Office
#1300, 2300 Yonge St., Toronto ON M4P 1E4
Tel: 416-489-7111; *Fax:* 416-489-6885
www.heartandstroke.on.ca

Windsor Office
#350, 4570 Rhodes Dr., Windsor ON N8W 5C2
Tel: 519-254-4345; *Fax:* 519-254-4215
www.heartandstroke.on.ca

York Region North Office
#29, 17665 Leslie St., Newmarket ON L3Y 3E3
Tel: 905-853-6355; *Fax:* 905-853-7961
www.heartandstroke.on.ca

York South Office
#204, 9251 Yonge St., Richmond Hill ON L4C 9T3
Tel: 905-709-4899; *Fax:* 905-709-0883
www.heartandstroke.on.ca

Heart & Stroke Foundation of Prince Edward Island Inc.
PO Box 279, 180 Kent St., Charlottetown PE C1A 7K4
Tel: 902-892-7441; *Fax:* 902-368-7068
www.heartandstroke.pe.ca
Overview: A medium-sized provincial charitable organization overseen by Heart & Stroke Foundation of Canada
Mission: To improve the health of Islanders through the funding of heart disease & stroke research & the provision of heart & stroke education & programs
Chief Officer(s):
Charlotte Comrie, CEO
ccomrie@hsfpei.ca
Sharon Hollingsworth, Manager, Communications
shollingsworth@hsfpei.ca
Sarah Crozier, Manager, Health Promotion
healthpromotion@hsfpei.ca
Finances: *Funding Sources:* Donations
Activities: Delivering programs, such as Live Life Well, to create heart-healthy workplaces on PEI; Providing professional development grants; Initiating community-based strategies, such as the Healthy Living Strategy, to address chronic disease risk factors; *Awareness Events:* Stroke Month, June

Heart & Stroke Foundation of Québec *Voir* Fondation des maladies du coeur du Québec

Heart & Stroke Foundation of Saskatchewan (HSFS) / Fondation des maladies du coeur de la Saskatchewan
279 - 3 Ave. North, Saskatoon SK S7K 2H8
Tel: 306-244-2124; *Fax:* 306-664-4016
Toll-Free: 888-473-4636
heart.stroke@hsf.sk.ca
www.heartandstroke.sk.ca
www.linkedin.com/company/heart-and-stroke-foundation-saskatchewan
www.facebook.com/heartandstrokesask
www.youtube.com/saskheart
Overview: A medium-sized provincial charitable organization founded in 1956 overseen by Heart & Stroke Foundation of Canada
Mission: To eliminate & reduce the impact of heart disease & stroke; to advance research, promote healthy living, & advocates a healthy public policy.
Finances: *Funding Sources:* Donations
Activities: Providing the Saskatchewan Integrated Stoke Strategy website (www.hsf.sk.ca/siss); Liaising with government; Engaging in fund development activities; *Awareness Events:* Heart Month, Feb.; Stroke Month, June

Hearth Stet Association of Canada *See* Hearth, Patio & Barbecue Association of Canada

Hearth, Patio & Barbecue Association of Canada (HPBAC)
PO Box 5422, Huntsville ON P1H 2K8
Tel: 705-788-2221; *Fax:* 705-788-0255
Toll-Free: 800-792-5284
hpbac@bellnet.ca
www.hpbacanada.org
Previous Name: Hearth Stet Association of Canada
Overview: A small national organization founded in 1994
Mission: HPBAC provides a lobbying voice for its members & promotes the interests of those in the industry. It also offers a forum for its members to network.
Member of: HPBA
Affliation(s): Association des Professionels du Chauffage
Chief Officer(s):
Alan Murphy, President
alan@blackrockdistributing.com
Tony Gottschalk, Manager
tonyhpbac@bellnet.ca
Laura Litchfield, Administrator
hpbac@bellnet.ca
Finances: *Annual Operating Budget:* $100,000-$250,000
Staff Member(s): 3; 18 volunteer(s)
Membership: 502; *Fees:* varies; *Member Profile:* Hearth Patio and Barbecue product manufacturers, distributors & retailers and associated suppliers; *Committees:* Government Affairs, Member Services, Education, Communications
Activities: *Awareness Events:* Great Woodstove Changeout; Ener Choice
Publications:
• The Voice
Type: Newsletter; *Frequency:* 3 pa

Heartwood Centre for Community Youth Development
#202, 5516 Spring Garden Rd., Halifax NS B3J 1G6
Tel: 902-444-5885; *Fax:* 902-444-3140
home-place@heartwood.ns.ca
www.heartwood.ns.ca
www.facebook.com/heartwood.centre
twitter.com/HeartWoodNS
www.youtube.com/heartwoodcentre
Previous Name: Heartwood Institute for Leadership in Youth Development
Overview: A small local charitable organization founded in 1989
Mission: To nurture personal leadership qualities through adventure, teamwork, environmental appreciation & service to others.
Chief Officer(s):
Christopher Hayes, Co-Chair
Laura Swaine, Executive Director
Staff Member(s): 8
Activities: Youth leadership camp; professional development services for adults & organizations; *Internships:* Yes

Heartwood Institute for Leadership in Youth Development *See* Heartwood Centre for Community Youth Development

Heatherton Activity Centre (HAC)
PO Box 114, Heatherton NS B0H 1R0
Tel: 902-386-2808; *Fax:* 902-386-2808
hac@ns.sympatico.ca
Overview: A small local organization
Member of: DIRECTIONS Council for Vocational Services Society
Chief Officer(s):
Treena Grace, Executive Director/Manager

Heating, Refrigeration & Air Conditioning Institute of Canada (HRAI) / Institut canadien du chauffage, de la climatisation et de la réfrigération (ICCCR)
Bldg. 1, #201, 2800 Skymark Ave., Mississauga ON L4W 5A6
Tel: 905-602-4700; *Fax:* 905-602-1197
Toll-Free: 800-267-2231
hraimail@hrai.ca
www.hrai.ca
www.facebook.com/pages/HRAI/322711681086830
twitter.com/HRAI_Canada
www.youtube.com/hraichannel
Overview: A large national organization founded in 1969
Mission: To serve the HRAI membership & HVACR industry in Canada by facilitating industry solutions, coordinating a strong national membership, representing the industry to their publics, conducting accountable association activities, providing quality member/customer services, & educating & training industry members
Chief Officer(s):
Warren J. Heeley, President
Martin Luymes, Vice-President
Andrew Hall, Director, Energy Conservation/Demand Management Programs
Joanne Spurrell, Director, Education & Market Development
Heather Grimoldby-Campbell, Manager, Administration & Wholesalers Division
Daisy Del Prado, Communications Coordinator
Finances: *Annual Operating Budget:* $1.5 Million-$3 Million; *Funding Sources:* Membership dues; education programs
Staff Member(s): 24
Membership: 900 corporate; *Fees:* $342-$5,250; *Member Profile:* Voting members divided into three divisions based on industry sector - manufacturers, wholesalers & contractors; Associate members include utilities, municipalities, manufacturers' agents & distributors, builders, educational institutions, building maintenance, other associations, & consultants; *Committees:* C.M.X. Show; Technical; Education
Activities: Owns the Canadian Mechanicals Exposition (C.M.X.), a national trade show held every two years in Toronto at the end of March; educational programs provide industry members with the technical & management competence required to design & install HVAC systems & operate successful HVAC businesses

British Columbia - Regional Chapter
Refrigeration & Air Conditioning Contractors Assn. of BC, 26121 Fraser Hwy., Aldergrove BC V4X 2E3
Tel: 604-856-8644; *Fax:* 604-856-7768
raccabc@hrai.ca
Chief Officer(s):
Blair Mastlezav, Chapter President

Manitoba - Regional Chapter
c/o Refrigeration & Air Conditioning Contractors Assn. of Manitoba, 807 McLeod Ave., Winnipeg MB R2G 0Y4
Chief Officer(s):
Ryan Dalgleish, Regional Manager, 204-956-5888
rdalgleish@hrai.ca

Ontario - Brant/Haldimand/Norfolk Chapter
c/o Bowser Technical Ltd., 200 St. George St., Brantford ON N3R 1W4
e-mail: brant@hrac.ca
www.hracbrant.com
Chief Officer(s):
Dave Murtland, President, 519-428-4000, Fax: 519-428-2591
Dara Bowser, Secretary, 519-756-9116, Fax: 519-756-9227

Ontario - Essex/Kent/Lambton Chapter
c/o Ideal Heating & Cooling Ltd, PO Box 1030, Stn. A, 1900 North Talbot Rd., Windsor ON N9A 6P4
e-mail: essex_kent_lambton@hrai.ca
Chief Officer(s):
Peter Steffes, Chapter President, 519-737-6797

Ontario - Golden Horseshoe Chapter
c/o Arvin Air Systems, 331 Glover Rd., Stoney Creek ON L8E 5M2
e-mail: goldenhorseshoe@hrai.ca

Ontario - Greater Toronto Area Chapter
c/o Carrier Canada Ltd., 1515 Drew Rd., Mississauga ON L5S 1Y8
Chief Officer(s):
Marisa Soulis, Chapter Meeting Manager, 905-405-3201

Ontario - Huronia Chapter
c/o LifeBreath Indoor Air Systems, 511 McCormick Blvd., Oro Station ON N5W 4C8
Chief Officer(s):
Wayne Fischer, Chapter President, 705-791-3418
wfischer@airiabrands.com

Ontario - Kawartha Lakes Chapter
c/o Coulter Heating & Air Conditioning, 89 West St., Fenelon Falls ON K0M 1N0
Chief Officer(s):
Laverne Coulter, Chapter President, 705-887-5559

Ontario - Loyalist Chapter
c/o McKeown & Wood Ltd., 373 Centre St. North, Napanee ON K7R 1P7

Ontario - National Capital Region Chapter
c/o E.N. Blue Ltd., PO Box 535, Stittsville ON K2S 1A6
Chief Officer(s):
Darrell McCagg, Chapter President, 613-831-1430, Fax: 613-831-2969
enblue@enblue.com

Ontario - Waterloo/Wellington Chapter
c/o BRC Mechanical Inc., 92 Woolwich St. South, Breslau ON N0B 1M0

Québec - Montréal Chapter
c/o Corporation des maîtres mécaniciens en tuyauterie du Québec, 8175, boul Saint-Laurent, Montréal QC H2P 2M1

Heaven Can Wait Equine Rescue
c/o Claire Malcolm, 95 Cameron Rd., Cameron ON K0M 1G0
Tel: 705-359-3766; *Fax:* 705-359-3769
HCWEquineRescue@sympatico.ca
www.heavencanwaitequinerescue.org
Overview: A small local organization founded in 1997
Mission: To help save horses & ponies from slaughter, & take in any unwanted horse or pony & find them a new, loving home
Chief Officer(s):
Claire Malcolm, Founder

Heavy Civil Association of Newfoundland & Labrador, Inc. (HCANL)
PO Box 23038, St. John's NL A1B 4J9
Tel: 709-364-8811; *Fax:* 709-364-8812
heavycivilnl.ca
Overview: A small provincial organization founded in 1968 overseen by Canadian Construction Association
Mission: To act as the voice of the heavy construction industries in Newfoundland & Labrador; To develop standard tendering & contractual practices & procedures
Chief Officer(s):
Jim Organ, Executive Director
jorgan.hcanl@gmail.com
Lorraine Richards, Manager, Operations
nlrbhca@nf.aibn.com
Membership: *Fees:* $1,243 road builders & water & sewer members; $847.50 associate members; *Member Profile:* Individuals in the highway construction & paving, concrete structure construction, & the marine construction industries; Persons engaged in water & sewer, civil construction, & municipal infrastructure projects; *Committees:* Annual General Meeting; Associate Member Contact; Dispute Resolution; Employers' Council; Front End Documents; Funding; Labour Shortage; Labour Shortage; Occupational Health & Safety; Pits & Quarries; Scholarship; Specifications & Equipment Rental Rates; Blaster Advisory; Charity; Education & Training; Government Liaison; Honours & Awards; Membership; Seminars
Activities: Liaising with provincial government departments & agencies, municipal councils, engineering consultants, & the public; Assisting in the development of occupational health & safety regulations; Developing rental rates for equipment; Awarding scholarships
Publications:
• Newfoundland & Labrador Road Builders / Heavy Civil Association Membership Directory
Type: Directory
• NLRB/HCA Newsletter
Type: Newsletter
Profile: Association activities & accomplishments, committee reports & updates on the industry
• Road Builders Bulletin
Type: Newsletter; *Frequency:* Weekly; *Accepts Advertising;* *Editor:* Cliff Wight; *Price:* $700
Profile: Bulletin sections include the notebook, open tender report, closed tender report, & advertising

Heavy Equipment & Aggregate Truckers Association of Manitoba (HEAT)
2215 Henderson Hwy., East St. Paul MB R2E 0B8
Tel: 204-654-9426; *Fax:* 204-224-4907
heatmb.ca
Overview: A small provincial organization
Mission: To raise awareness about the the heavy equipment industry & to set standards for the companies & people who are involved in the business
Chief Officer(s):
Ken McKeen, President
Membership: 185

Les Hebdos du Québec inc. *Voir* Hebdos Québec

Hebdos Québec
2572, Daniel-Johnson, 2e étage, Laval QC H7T 2R3
Tél: 514-861-2088; *Téléc:* 514-221-3769
communications@hebdos.com
www.hebdos.com
www.facebook.com/hebdosqc
twitter.com/HebdosQuebec
Nom précédent: Les Hebdos du Québec inc.
Aperçu: *Dimension:* moyenne; *Envergure:* provinciale; fondée en 1932
Mission: Favoriser et stimuler le développement du secteur des hebdomadaires en offrant à ses membres divers services en matière de recherche, de marketing et de formation; projeter une image crédible de la presse hebdomadaire, de la défendre, et de la rendre plus visible et plus accessible
Affliation(s): Association des professionels de la communication et du marketing
Membre(s) du bureau directeur:
Angèle Marcoux-Prévost, Présidente
Gilber Paquette, Directeur général
gpaquette@ehbdos.com
Finances: *Budget de fonctionnement annuel:* $250,000-$500,000
Membre(s) du personnel: 4
Membre: 30 journaux; *Critères d'admissibilité:* Journal hebdomadaire francophone à tirage certifié
Activités: Porte-parole; recherches; échanges; occasions d'affaires; économies et rabais; plaques de presse; alliances stratégiques; *Stagiaires:* Oui; *Listes de destinataires:* Oui
Prix, Bouses:
• Les Grands prix des hebdos (Prix)
18 Prix des Hebdos, des prix d'excellence décernés selon trois catégories d'hebdomadaires, dont le prix de l'hebdo de l'année dans chaque catégoire; et 10 Prix du Jury couronnant les artisans des hebdos

Hébergement la casa Bernard-Hubert
La Casa, 1215, boul. Ste-Foy, Longueuil QC J4K 1X4
Tél: 450-442-4777
casa.bernardhubert@videotron.ca
www.la-casa-bernard-hubert.org
Aperçu: *Dimension:* petite; *Envergure:* locale; fondée en 1988
Mission: Pour aider les hommes sans-abri restructurer leur vie et de se réinsérer dans la société
Membre de: L'Association des intervenants en Toxicomanie du Québec; La Fédération des OSBL, d'Habitation Roussillon, Jardins du Québec, Suroît; e Regroupement pour la valorisation de la paternité; Le Réseau d'aide aux personnes seules et itinérantes de Montréal; Le Réseau Solidarité Itinérance du Québec
Affliation(s): La Fondation Les Amis de La Casa; L'Abri de la Rive-Sud; La Corporation de développement communautaire de Longueuil; La table Itinérance Rive-Sud
Membre(s) du bureau directeur:
Claire Desrosiers, Directrice générale
Lucie Pelletier, Présidente, Conseil d'administration
Activités: Ateliers et séances de groupe; Encadrement psychosicial; Interventions

Hébergements de l'envol
6984, rue Fabre, Montréal QC H2E 2B2
Tél: 514-374-1614; *Téléc:* 514-593-9227
hebergementlenvol@hotmail.com
pages.infinit.net/lenvol2/
Aperçu: *Dimension:* petite; *Envergure:* locale
Mission: Foyer collectif pour personnes en perte d'autonomie
Affliation(s): Coalition des organismes communautaires québécois de lutte contre le sida

Heiltsuk Tribal Council

PO Box 880, Bella Bella BC V0T 1Z0
Tel: 250-957-2381; *Fax:* 250-957-2544
Toll-Free: 877-957-2381
Overview: A small local organization
Chief Officer(s):
Marilyn Slett, Executive Director
mslett@bellabella.net
Wilfred Hunchitt, Contact
whumchitt@heiltsuk.com

HeliCat Canada

PO Box 968, Revelstoke BC V0E 2S1
Tel: 250-837-5770
info@helicatcanada.com
www.helicatcanada.com
www.youtube.com/channel/UCmMNdyDIRkF3Udowcl5R-2A
Previous Name: BC Helicopter & Snowcat Skiing Operators Association
Overview: A small provincial organization founded in 1975
Member of: Council of Tourism Associations BC; Wilderness Tourism Association
Chief Officer(s):
Rob Rohn, President
Ian Tomm, Executive Director
ed@helicatcanada.com
Membership: *Committees:* Environmental; Standards; Communications; Conduct Review; Government Relations

Helicopter Association of Canada (HAC)

#500, 130 Albert St., Ottawa ON K1P 5G4
Tel: 613-231-1110; *Fax:* 613-369-5097
www.h-a-c.ca
Overview: A small national organization
Mission: To ensure the financial viability of the Canadian civil helicopter industry; To promote flight safety; To expand utilization of helicopter transport
Chief Officer(s):
Teri Northcott, Chair
teri_northcott@telus.net
Fred L. Jones, BA LLB, President & Chief Executive Officer, 613-231-1110 Ext. 239, Fax: 613-236-2361
Fred.Jones@h-a-c.ca
Sylvain Seguin, Vice-President & Director, Marketing
sseguin@canadianhelicopters.com
Gary McDermid, Secretary
gary.mcdermid@helifor.com
Maureen Crockett, Treasurer
mcrockett@dt-avn.com
Membership: *Member Profile:* Individuals who operate helicopters in Canada; Non-operator organizations; *Committees:* Air Taxi; Finance; Flight Training Units; Heli Logging; IFR / EMS; Law Enforcement; Maintenance & Manufacturing; Oil & Gas Producers; Safety; Utility Flight Operations
Activities: Educating members, civil servants, & the public about issues important to the industry; Providing opportunities for members to exchange maintenance practices & common issues
Awards:
• Helicopter Association of Canada Carl Agar / Alf Stringer Award (Award)
To honour a leader in the helicopter industry*Deadline:* February
Contact: Barb Priestley, Office Manager, Fax: 613-369-5097; E-mail: barb.priestley@h-a-c.ca
Meetings/Conferences: • Helicopter Association of Canada 2015 20th Annual Convention & Trade Show, November, 2015, Vancouver Convention Centre, Vancouver, BC
Scope: National
Attendance: 800+
Description: Professional development programs & information sessions to help Helicopter Association of Canada members achieve in the present economic & regulatory climate
Contact Information: Office Manager & Contact, Member Services: Barb Priestley, Phone: 613-231-1110, ext. 237, Fax: 613-369-5097, E-mail: barb.priestley@h-a-c.ca
• Helicopter Association of Canada 2016 21st Annual Convention & Trade Show, November, 2016, Shaw Convention Centre, Edmonton, AB
Scope: National
Attendance: 800+
Description: Professional development programs & information sessions to help Helicopter Association of Canada members achieve in the present economic & regulatory climate
Contact Information: Office Manager & Contact, Member Services: Barb Priestley, Phone: 613-231-1110, ext. 237, Fax: 613-369-5097, E-mail: barb.priestley@h-a-c.ca
• Helicopter Association of Canada 2017 22nd Annual Convention & Trade Show, November, 2017, Westin Ottawa, Ottawa, ON
Scope: National
Attendance: 800+
Description: Professional development programs & information sessions to help Helicopter Association of Canada members achieve in the present economic & regulatory climate
Contact Information: Office Manager & Contact, Member Services: Barb Priestley, Phone: 613-231-1110, ext. 237, Fax: 613-369-5097, E-mail: barb.priestley@h-a-c.ca
Publications:
• Class "D" External Loads Training Guidelines
Type: Guide
Profile: An outline of industry training guidelines to support operations specifications allowing carriage of class D external loads
• HAC [Helicopter Association of Canada] Newsletter
Type: Newsletter
Profile: Association & general information updates
• Helicopter Association of Canada Utility Flight Operations Committee Best Practices Safety Guide for Helicopter Operators
Type: Guide; *Number of Pages:* 90
Profile: Chapters include background information, basic utility infrastructure, helicopter patrol safeguidelines, power line construction & maintenance, safety guide for utilities in evaluating & selecting qualified helicopter contractors, & safety guide for utilities performing utility flight operations
• Helicopter Guidelines for Canadian Onshore Seismic Operations
Type: Guide; *Number of Pages:* 89
Profile: Sections include safety management systems (SMS), program operations, training, competency, & staffing levels, personal protective equipment (PPE), helicopterperformance & role equipment standards, & base camp / staging area / helipad requirements
• Heli-skiing Guidelines
Type: Guide
Profile: Information about performance, weight management, ski baskets, pilot flight & duty time, weather, training, safety briefings, & flagging
• Mountain Flying Training Guidelines
Type: Guide
Profile: Helicopter Association of Canada recommended guidelines for mountain fluying training
• Pilot Competencies for Helicopter Wildfire Operations - Best Practices Training & Evaluation
Type: Guide; *Number of Pages:* 26
Profile: Guidance for members of the Helicopter Association of Canada, prepared by the Air Tax Committee, Pilot Qualifications WorkingGroup

Helios Nudist Association (HNA)

Box 8, Site 1, RR#2, Tofield AB T0B 4J0
Tel: 587-986-5522
membership@heliosnudistassociation.ca
heliosnudistassociation.ca
Overview: A small local organization founded in 1964
Mission: To promote the practice of social nudism & recreation in 27 acres of natural setting.
Affliation(s): Federation of Canadian Naturists; International Naturist Federation; American Association of Nude Recreation
Finances: *Funding Sources:* Membership dues
Membership: 165; *Fees:* Full: $325 single, $500 couple; Associate: $120 single, $180 couple; *Member Profile:* Couples & single adults; board reserves the right to maintain the family-oriented environment
Activities: Dances, dinners, barbecues, swimming, hiking; camping

Hellenic Canadian Congress of BC (HCC(BC))

PO Box 129, 4500 Arbutus St., Vancouver BC V6J 4A2
Tel: 604-780-2460
info@helleniccongressbc.ca
www.helleniccongressbc.ca
www.facebook.com/124766634268645
Overview: A medium-sized national organization
Mission: Fosters education, communication, and cooperation between Hellenic Canadians and other ethnic groups, and promotes the development of just and equitable policies and legislation concerning all citizens.
Chief Officer(s):
Jimmy Sidiropoulos, President

Hellenic Community of Vancouver

St. George Greek Orthodox Cathedral, 4500 Arbutus St., Vancouver BC V6J 4A2
Tel: 604-266-7148; *Fax:* 604-266-7140
hellenic@telus.net
www.helleniccommunity.org
Overview: A small local organization founded in 1927
Mission: To serve as a spiritual, cultural & social gathering place for all Greeks of Vancouver and the Lower Mainland.
Chief Officer(s):
Effie Kerasiotis, President
Membership: *Fees:* $150 family; $75 individual; $40 senior/student
Activities: Greek language classes; traditional dance instruction; book club; cooking lessons; arts & crafts; a variety of sports; rental/catering; *Library* Open to public

Hellenic-Canadian Board of Trade

PO Box 801, 31 Adelaide St. East, Toronto ON M4C 2K1
Tel: 416-410-4228
membership@hcbt.com
www.hcbt.com
Overview: A medium-sized international organization
Chief Officer(s):
Aggy Agostolopoulos, President
president@hcbt.com
Membership: *Fees:* $110 individual; $150 corporate

Help Fill a Dream Foundation of Canada

4085 Qunadra St., #D, Victoria BC V8X 1K5
Tel: 250-382-3135; *Fax:* 250-382-2711
Toll-Free: 866-382-2711
info@helpfilladream.com
helpfilladream.com
www.facebook.com/195114740510608
twitter.com/helpfilladream
Overview: A small national charitable organization founded in 1986
Mission: To fill the dreams of children under 19 years of age who have life-threatening illness in BC
Chief Officer(s):
Denyse Koo, President
Craig Smith, Executive Director
Finances: *Funding Sources:* Telephone campaign; various events
Activities: *Speaker Service:* Yes

Help for Headaches (HFH)

PO Box 1568, Stn. B, 515 Richmond St., London ON N6A 5M3
Tel: 519-434-0008
Other Communication: www.helpforheadaches.org
brent@helpforheadaches.org
www.headache-help.org
Also Known As: Headache Support Group
Overview: A small local charitable organization founded in 1995
Mission: A volunteer registered charity that provide research, education, advocacy & support for head pain suffers & the public at large.
Member of: World Headache Alliance; Canadian Pain Society
Chief Officer(s):
Brent Lucas, Managing Director
brent@helpforheadaches.org
Finances: *Annual Operating Budget:* Less than $50,000
Staff Member(s): 2; 9 volunteer(s)
Membership: 3 student; 20 individual; 5 associate
Activities: Presentations; newsletter; factsheets; brochures; headache library for members - free online website programs; seminars; awareness displays; *Speaker Service:* Yes; *Library* by appointment
Publications:
• Chronic Daily Headache
Type: Book; *Price:* $25.25

Help Honduras Foundation *See* Horizons of Friendship

Help the Aged (Canada) (HTA) / Aide aux aînés (Canada)

#205, 1300 Carling Ave., Ottawa ON K1Z 7L2
Tel: 613-232-0727; *Fax:* 613-232-7625
Toll-Free: 800-648-1111
Other Communication: adoptagran@helptheaged.ca
info@helptheaged.ca
www.helptheaged.ca
Overview: A medium-sized international charitable organization founded in 1975
Mission: To meet the needs of poor or destitute elderly people in Canada & the developing world

Membership: *Fees:* $5 student; $15 single; $20 family; $10 senior; $15 senior couple; $25 group/institutions; $500 life membership; *Member Profile:* Individuals & groups who are committed to the protection & rehabilitation of Nova Scotia's heritage; *Committees:* Buildings-at-Risk; Communities; Education; Events/Programs; HRM; Quarterly; Painted Rooms; Publications; Public Relations; Tax Incentives; Places of Worship; Awards
Activities: Providing a public lecture series; Offering input on legislative policy at the municipal & provincial levels; *Speaker Service:* Yes; *Library* Open to public
Awards:
• Heritage Trust of Nova Scotia Built Heritage Award (Award)
Presented for outstanding contribution to building restoration
Contact: Joyce McCulloch, HTNS Awards Chair
Publications:
• The Griffin [a publication of the Heritage Trust of Nova Scotia]
Type: Newsletter; *Frequency:* Quarterly; *Price:* Free with Heritage Trust of Nova Scotia membership

Heritage Winnipeg Corp. (HW)
#509, 63 Albert St., Winnipeg MB R3B 1G4
Tel: 204-942-2663; *Fax:* 204-942-2094
info@heritagewinnipeg.com
www.heritagewinnipeg.com
Overview: A small local charitable organization founded in 1978
Mission: To promote & encourage preservation of historic sites & structures in Winnipeg; To educate the public on heritage issues & make them aware of the richness of their material culture; To advocate & lobby on behalf of heritage related issues
Member of: Heritage Canada; Manitoba Historical Society; St. Boniface Historical Society; Manitoba Heritage Federation
Affliation(s): Downtown Biz; Exchange Biz, Destination Winnipeg; Parks Canada; City of Winnipeg; Province of Manitoba
Chief Officer(s):
Cindy Tugwell, Executive Director
Penny McMillan, President
Finances: *Annual Operating Budget:* Less than $50,000; *Funding Sources:* Private donations; provincial government; city of Winnipeg; membership dues; fundraisers
Staff Member(s): 1
Membership: 170; *Fees:* $20 individual; $15 student/senior; $30 family/organization; corporate $100-$1,000; *Committees:* Public Service & Information; Legal & Economic Instruments; Advocacy; Preservation Awards; Education
Activities: Museum & Heritage Exposition; heritage auctions; annual preservation awards; school presentations; walking tours; Manitoba Day events; heritage fairs; Doors Open Winnipeg; *Awareness Events:* Heritage Preservation Awards; Doors Open Winnipeg; 3rd Mon. in Feb.; *Speaker Service:* Yes; *Library* Open to public by appointment
Awards:
• Architectural Conservation Award (Award)
• Institutional Architectural Conservation Award (Award)
• Residential Architectural Conservation Award (Award)
• Distinguished Service Award (Award)
• Youth Awards (Award)
Publications:
• Illustrated Guide to Winnipeg's Exchange District
Type: Brochure

Heritage York
Lambton House, 4066 Old Dundas St., Toronto ON M6S 2R6
Tel: 416-767-5472; *Fax:* 416-767-7191
admin@lambtonhouse.org
www.lambtonhouse.org
Overview: A small local charitable organization founded in 1991
Mission: To preserve & restore the historical heritage of the City of York, starting with the 1847 landmark building, Lambton House.
Affliation(s): Ontario Historical Society
Finances: *Funding Sources:* Private; various government sources
Membership: *Fees:* $25 family; $15 adult; $10 junior (under 14)
Activities: At Lambton House - lecture series; annual carol singing; dinners; pub night; room rental; *Speaker Service:* Yes
Publications:
• The Heritage York Reporter
Type: newsletter

High Level & District Chamber of Commerce
10803 - 96 St., High Level AB T0H 1Z0
Tel: 780-926-2470; *Fax:* 780-926-4017
hlchambr@incentre.net
highlevelchamber.com
Overview: A small local charitable organization founded in 1962
Mission: To promote the economic & social well-being of High Level & district as a unified voice of free enterprise.
Member of: Alberta Chamber of Commerce; Canadian Chamber of Commerce
Chief Officer(s):
Don Warman, President
Finances: *Funding Sources:* Membership fees
Membership: 117; *Fees:* Schedule available; *Committees:* Policy; MacKenzie Crossroads; REDI; Health Services; Merchants; Executive

High Level Native Friendship Centre
PO Box 1735, 11000-95 Street, High Level AB T0H 1Z0
Tel: 780-926-3355; *Fax:* 780-926-2038
garycallihoo@yahoo.ca
anfca.com/friendship-centres/high-level
Overview: A small local organization overseen by Alberta Native Friendship Centres Association
Member of: Alberta Native Friendship Centres Association

High Prairie & Area Chamber of Commerce
PO Box 3600, High Prairie AB T0G 1E0
Tel: 780-507-1565
office@hpchamber.net
hpchamber.net
Overview: A small local organization
Affliation(s): Alberta Chamber of Commerce; Canadian Chamber of Commerce
Chief Officer(s):
Gordon Olson, President
gordolson@hotmail.com
Membership: 70

High Prairie Association for Community Living
PO Box 345, High Prairie AB T0G 1E0
Tel: 780-523-2254
Overview: A small local charitable organization founded in 1971
Mission: To improve & enhance the lives of people with handicaps; To advocate for those who need support, as well as providing support for them & their families.
Member of: Alberta Association for Community Living

High Prairie Native Friendship Centre
PO Box 1448, 4919 - 51 Ave., High Prairie AB T0G 1E0
Tel: 780-523-4511; *Fax:* 780-523-3055
grammerlyanne@yahoo.com
anfca.com
Overview: A small local organization founded in 1975 overseen by Alberta Native Friendship Centres Association
Mission: To improve the quality of life for Aboriginal people in urban areas by supporting self-determined activities that encourage: the development of human and community resources; the improvement of socio-economic and physical conditions; better understanding and relationships between Aboriginal and non-Aboriginal citizens; and the enhancement of Aboriginal culture among Aboriginal people and the communities they reside in.
Member of: Alberta Native Friendship Centres Association
Chief Officer(s):
Anne Grammerly
Activities: friendship centre facilitation; health & wellness; arts & culture; elders; youth

High River & District Chamber of Commerce
PO Box 5244, 149B Macleod Trail SW, High River AB T1V 1M4
Tel: 403-652-3336; *Fax:* 403-652-7660
hrdcc@telus.net
www.hrchamber.ca
Overview: A small local organization founded in 1968
Mission: To enhance the economy in High River & district for the benefit of the community
Member of: High River Agricultural Society; Kinsmen Club of High River
Chief Officer(s):
Yousra Jomha, President, 403-652-1997, Fax: 403-652-4296
yjomha@shaw.ca
Lynette McCracken, Executive Director
Finances: *Annual Operating Budget:* $50,000-$100,000; *Funding Sources:* Fundraising; membership fees
Staff Member(s): 1; 235 volunteer(s)
Membership: 190; *Fees:* $125-$300
Activities: Operates a year-round tourist information centre; annual trade fair; parades, rodeo; *Awareness Events:* Santa Parade, Dec. 1; Rodeo Parade, May; *Speaker Service:* Yes

Hiiye'yu Lelum Society House of Friendship
PO Box 1015, Duncan BC V9L 3Y2
Tel: 250-748-2242; *Fax:* 250-748-2238
hofduncan.org
Previous Name: Valley Native Friendship Centre Society
Overview: A small local organization
Mission: To develop Aboriginal leadership in the community, as well as provide a bridge between cultures in the Cowichan Valley; to promote well-being in the community by offering counselling, information & referral services, in addition to a centre for communal recreation, education & meetings.
Chief Officer(s):
Debbie Williams, Executive Director
DebbieWilliams@hofduncan.org
Staff Member(s): 38

Hike Ontario
#800, 165 Dundas St. West, Mississauga ON L5B 2N6
Tel: 905-277-4453
Toll-Free: 800-894-7249
info@hikeontario.com
www.hikeontario.com
Overview: A medium-sized provincial charitable organization founded in 1974
Mission: To act as the voice for hikers & walkers in Ontario; To encourage hiking, walking & trail development in Ontario; To promote trail maintenance. best practices, & safe hiking; To enhance environmental awareness, conservation & sustainable trails
Affliation(s): Ontario Trails Council (OTC); Hike Canada En Marche
Chief Officer(s):
Bill Wilson, President
Fran Rawlings, Secretary
Asvin Parsad, Treasurer
Finances: *Funding Sources:* Membership dues; Grants; Sponsorships; Donations
Membership: *Member Profile:* Not-for-profit trail building & hiking organizations; Individuals; Corporations, government agencies, & organizations other than hiking or trail building organizations
Activities: Providing hiking information & services throughout Ontario; Offering the Hike Leader Certification Program & the Young Hikers Program; Supporting trails across the province; Advocating for clubs; Liaising with government; Promoting research & education into the health benefits of walking & hiking; Presenting awards to celebrate dedicated hikers; *Awareness Events:* Ontario Hiking Week, September

Hilal Committee of Metropolitan Toronto & Vicinity
1015 Danforth Ave., Toronto ON M4J 1M1
Tel: 416-230-5229; *Fax:* 416-467-9787
Other Communication: Alt. Phone: 416-970-5786
info@hilaalcommittee.com
www.hilalcommittee.com
twitter.com/HilalCommittee
Overview: A small local organization
Mission: To coordinate the beginnings of Islamic months & holidays through local sightings of the moon.
Chief Officer(s):
Khalil Sufi, Chair
Membership: 90; *Member Profile:* Islamic & masjid centres & organizations
Activities: Publishing an Islamic calendar based on calculations of the moon's visibility

Hillel of Greater Toronto
Wolfond Centre, University of Toronto, 36 Harbord St., Toronto ON M5S 1G2
Tel: 416-913-2424
info@hilleltoronto.org
www.hilleltoronto.org
twitter.com/HillelTO
Previous Name: University of Toronto Menorah Society
Overview: A small local organization founded in 1917
Mission: To promote Jewish identity, religious & political diversity, & student leadership
Chief Officer(s):
Zac Kaye, Executive Director, 416-913-2426
zac.kaye@hilleltoronto.org
Shirin Ezekiel, Director, Israel Affairs, 416-913-2428
shirin.ezekiel@hilleltoronto.org
Aaron Greenberg, Director, Jewish Learning Initiative, 416-736-5179
aaron.greenberg@hilleltoronto.org
Finances: *Funding Sources:* Donations

Membership: *Member Profile:* Jewish students who attend universities & community colleges throughout the Greater Toronto Area
Activities: Offering programming & events

Hillfield-Strathallan College Foundation
299 Fennell Ave. West, Hamilton ON L9C 1G3
Tel: 905-389-1367; *Fax:* 905-389-6366
www.hsc.on.ca
Overview: A small local organization
Chief Officer(s):
Tom Matthews, Contact
headmaster@hillstrath.on.ca

Hincks-Dellcrest Treatment Centre & Foundation
440 Jarvis St., Toronto ON M4Y 2H4
Tel: 416-924-1164; *Fax:* 416-924-8208
Toll-Free: 855-944-4673
info@hincksdellcrest.org
www.hincksdellcrest.org
www.facebook.com/hincksdellcrest
twitter.com/hincksdellcrest
www.youtube.com/thehincksdellcrest
Overview: A small local organization founded in 1998
Mission: To offer a comprehensive range of mental health services to infants, children, youth, & their families; to provide a variety of programs, including prevention & early intervention, outpatient & residential treatment.
Affliation(s): University of Toronto
Chief Officer(s):
Ian Smith, Chair
Donna Duncan, President & CEO
Finances: *Annual Operating Budget:* Greater than $5 Million

Gail Appel Institute
114 Maitland St., Toronto ON M4Y 1E1
Tel: 416-924-1164; *Fax:* 416-924-9808

Treatment Centre
1645 Sheppard Ave. West, Toronto ON M3M 2X4
Tel: 416-924-1164; *Fax:* 416-633-7141

Hindu Society of Alberta
14225 - 133 Ave., Edmonton AB T5L 4W3
Tel: 780-451-5130
hindu.society@hotmail.com
www.hindusociety.ab.ca
www.facebook.com/441978332488940
twitter.com/Hindu_Society
Overview: A small provincial charitable organization founded in 1967
Mission: The Society is a cultural, social & religious institute catering to the needs of those influenced by Hinduism.
Chief Officer(s):
Amar Bhasin, President
Activities: Classes in yoga & meditation; language classes; lectures & seminars on history & religion; religious celebrations; music & dance performances; hall rentals; *Library:* library

Hinton & District Chamber of Commerce
309 Gregg Ave., Hinton AB T7V 2A7
Tel: 780-865-2777; *Fax:* 888-533-3145
hintoncc@telus.net
www.hintonchamber.com
Overview: A small local organization founded in 1957
Chief Officer(s):
Mike Smith, President
Risa Croken, Office Manager
Staff Member(s): 1; 13 volunteer(s)
Membership: 132; *Fees:* Schedule available
Activities: Business Awards Gala, Oct.;

Hinton Friendship Centre
PO Box 6720, Stn. Main, 965 Switzer Dr., Hinton AB T7V 1X6
Tel: 780-865-5189; *Fax:* 780-865-1756
main@fchinton.com
anfca.com/friendship-centres/hinton
Overview: A small local organization overseen by Alberta Native Friendship Centres Association
Member of: Alberta Native Friendship Centres Association
Chief Officer(s):
Yvonne Oshanyk, Executive Director

Hinton-Edson & District Real Estate Board *See* West Central Alberta Real Estate Board

Hispanic Canadian Arts & Culture Association (HCACA)
ON
e-mail: info@hispaniccanadianarts.org
www.hispaniccanadianarts.org
www.facebook.com/HispanicCanadianArts
twitter.com/hcaca_info
Overview: A small local organization founded in 2010
Mission: To promote Hispanic culture in the Greater Toronto Area
Chief Officer(s):
Carlos Bastidas, Executive Director
Roger Marles, President, Board of Directors
Staff Member(s): 3; 5 volunteer(s)
Activities: Exhibitions; Music festivals

Hispanic Development Council (HDC)
#201, 326 Adelaide St. West, Toronto ON M5V 1R3
Tel: 416-516-0851; *Fax:* 647-346-3707
info@hispaniccouncil.net
Overview: A small national organization
Mission: To serve the local Hispano/Latin community, forming a network of member organizations & individuals to assist with such services as immigrant settlement & youth counselling, the ultimate goal being a strengthening of community & a chance for all to integrate & participate fully in society.
Chief Officer(s):
Juan Carranza, President
Duberlis Ramos, Executive Director

Hispanic-Canadian Alliance of Ontario *See* Alianza Hispano-Canadiense Ontario

Histoire Canada *See* Canada's History

Historic Restoration Society of Annapolis County (HRS)
PO Box 503, 136 St George St., Annapolis Royal NS B0S 1A0
Tel: 902-532-7754; *Fax:* 902-532-0700
Other Communication:
www.annapolisroyalheritage.blogspot.com
historic@ns.aliantzinc.ca
www.annapolisheritagesociety.com
twitter.com/odellmuseum
Also Known As: Annapolis Heritage Society
Overview: A small local charitable organization founded in 1967
Mission: To preserve local heritage; To strive to be a leader in preserving heritage through the rehabilitation of buildings, through direct example or advocacy; To be responsible for the operation of museums &/or resource centres; To support relevant community & provincial aims
Chief Officer(s):
Ryan Scranton, Executive Director
Finances: *Funding Sources:* Provincial Government
Activities: Owns & operates O'Dell & Sinclair Inn Museums; operates North Hills Museum; *Library:* Archives; Open to public

Historic Sites Association of Newfoundland & Labrador (HSANL)
PO Box 5542, 10 Barter's Hill, 5th Fl., St. John's NL A1C 5W4
Tel: 709-753-2566; *Fax:* 709-753-0879
Toll-Free: 877-753-9262
info@historicsites.ca
www.historicsites.ca
www.facebook.com//131036186980761
twitter.com/historicsitesnl
Overview: A small provincial charitable organization founded in 1984
Mission: To preserve, promote, & interpret the history & heritage of Newfoundland & Labrador, in partnership with Parks Canada
Affliation(s): Parks Canada; Museum Association of Newfoundland & Labrador; Canadian Museum Association
Chief Officer(s):
Catherine Dempsey, Executive Director
Finances: *Annual Operating Budget:* $1.5 Million-$3 Million; *Funding Sources:* Operation of Heritage Shops of NL
Staff Member(s): 10; 30 volunteer(s)
Membership: 15; *Member Profile:* Board of Directors & Members Emeritus
Activities: Manning Awards; Joan Woods Exhibition; Book launches; Heritage Fairs; Bartlett Lectures; Operates the Hawthorne Cottage
Awards:
• The Manning Award (Award)
To recognize community heritage projects and the work of heritage champions.*Deadline:* February 15th
• History and Heritage Writer's Award (Award)
• Paul O'Neill Scholarship (Scholarship)
Eligibility: Undergraduate student at Memorial University enrolled in the Bachelor of Arts program. *Amount:* $1000
• The Craft Award (Award)
Recognizing artisans in the province who preserve traditional crafts or use their work to interpret Provincial History

Historic Theatres' Trust (HTT) / Société des salles historiques
PO Box 387, Stn. Victoria Station, Montréal QC H3Z 2V8
Tel: 514-933-8077; *Fax:* 514-933-8012
theatres@total.net
Previous Name: Theatres' Trust
Overview: A medium-sized national charitable organization founded in 1989
Mission: To develop an increased appreciation within the Canadian public concerning the preservation of historic Canadian theatres; To provide technical documentation & expertise to encourage improved methods of preserving, restoring, maintaining, operating & researching historic theatres
Chief Officer(s):
Janet MacKinnon, President
Finances: *Annual Operating Budget:* Less than $50,000
5 volunteer(s)
Membership: 100; *Fees:* $35 individual; $60 institutional; $20 seniors/students
Activities: *Awareness Events:* Local tours of theatres; *Speaker Service:* Yes; *Rents Mailing List:* Yes; *Library* by appointment

Historic Vehicle Society of Ontario (HVSO)
c/o Canadian Transportation Museum & Heritage Village, 6155 Arner Town Line, RR#2, Kingsville ON N9Y 2E5
Tel: 519-776-6909; *Fax:* 519-776-8321
Toll-Free: 886-776-6909
info@ctmhv.com
www.ctmhv.com
Overview: A medium-sized provincial charitable organization founded in 1959
Mission: To collect, restore & display vehicles, buildings & artifacts that serve to demonstrate the founding settlement of Essex County; to preserve the past to enhance the future.
Chief Officer(s):
Kim Brimner, Contact
Finances: *Annual Operating Budget:* $250,000-$500,000
Staff Member(s): 7; 100 volunteer(s)
Membership: 140; *Fees:* $35; *Member Profile:* Lovers of history, antiques, old cars

Historica Canada
East Mezzanine, 2 Carlton St., Toronto ON M5B 1J3
Tel: 416-506-1867; *Fax:* 416-506-0300
Toll-Free: 866-701-1867
info@historicacanada.ca
www.historicacanada.ca
www.facebook.com/Historica.Canada
twitter.com/HistoricaCanada
www.youtube.com/TheHDInstitute
Previous Name: Historica-Dominion Institute
Merged from: The Historica Foundation of Canada; The Dominion Institute
Overview: A small national charitable organization founded in 2009
Mission: To conduct original research into Canadians' knowledge of the country's past & to build innovative programs that broaden appreciation of the richness & complexity of Canadian history
Chief Officer(s):
Anthony Wilson-Smith, President
Staff Member(s): 61
Activities: Lectures; articles; TV documentaries; interactive websites; teaching tools; publications; operates www.blackhistorycanada.ca

Historica-Dominion Institute *See* Historica Canada

Historical Association of Annapolis Royal
PO Box 659, Annapolis Royal NS B0S 1A0
Tel: 902-532-3035; *Fax:* 902-532-2911
tours@tourannapolisroyal.com
www.tourannapolisroyal.com
www.facebook.com/CandlelightGraveyardTours
twitter.com/explorerguide
www.youtube.com/user/TourAnnapolisRoyal
Overview: A small local organization founded in 1919
Mission: The Association is known, not only for its walking tours through historic areas of the city, where history is presented in fun, accessible fashion, but also for its work in designating local

sites with heritage plaques.
Affliation(s): Royal Nova Scotia Historical Society
Chief Officer(s):
Durline Melanson, President
Lorna McLagan, Secretary
Membership: *Fees:* $5 regular; $100 lifetime
Activities: Candlelight Graveyard Tours; National Historic District Tours; Acadian Heritage Tours; maintenance of local lighthouse

Historical Automobile Society of Canada, Inc. (HASC)

c/o D. Hemmings, 146 Bellefontaine St., Toronto ON M1S 4E6
e-mail: hascweb@hotmail.com
www.historical-automobile-society.ca
Overview: A small local organization founded in 1963
Mission: To collect, restore & operate an antique, classic & special interest automobiles, motorcycles, trucks, etc. & to preserve related materials
Chief Officer(s):
D. Hemmings, National Membership Chair
dhemmings@yahoo.com
Finances: *Annual Operating Budget:* Less than $50,000; *Funding Sources:* Membership fees
Membership: 1,135; *Fees:* $8 regional; $42 national
Activities: *Awareness Events:* The Family Picnic, July; Normoska, Aug.; *Library:* HASC Library
Publications:
• The Canadian Klaxon [a publication of the Historical Automobile Society of Canada]
Type: Magazine; *Frequency:* 5 pa; *Price:* Free to members of the HASC.

Historical Society of Alberta (HSA)

PO Box 4035, Stn. C, Calgary AB T2T 5M9
Tel: 403-261-3662; *Fax:* 403-269-6029
info@albertahistory.org
www.albertahistory.org
Overview: A medium-sized provincial charitable organization founded in 1907
Mission: To preserve & promote the history of Alberta; to encourage the study & preservation of Canadian & Albertan history; to rescue from oblivion the memories, experiences & knowledge of early inhabitants.
Affliation(s): Heritage Canada; Alberta Heritage Council
Chief Officer(s):
Belinda Crowson, President
Finances: *Funding Sources:* Membership fees; donations; provincial government grant
Membership: *Fees:* $15 individual; $25 family; $55 affiliate; $120 associate
Activities: Historic Edmonton Week, Historic Calgary Week & Doors Open, Historic Red Deer Week & Doors Open, Historic Lethbridge Week & Doors, summer; monthly meetings held by four chapters, fall & winter
Awards:
• Award of Merit & Lifetime Membership (Award)

Central Alberta Historical Society
4525 - 47A Ave., Red Deer AB T4N 6Z6
Tel: 403-347-7873; *Fax:* 403-340-7521
contact@centralalbertahistory.org
centralalbertahistory.org
www.facebook.com/ca.history
Chief Officer(s):
Lianne Kruger, President

Chinook Country Historical Society
#311, 223 - 12 Ave. SW, Calgary AB T2R 0G9
Tel: 403-261-4667
www.chinookcountry.org
www.facebook.com/ChinookCountryHistoricalSociety
Chief Officer(s):
Donna Zwicker, President
donnazwicker@shaw.ca
David Sztain, Treasurer
david.sztain@replicon.com

Edmonton & District Historical Society
7730 - 106 St., 3rd Fl., Edmonton AB T6E 4W3
Tel: 780-439-2797; *Fax:* 888-692-9019
info@historicedmonton.ca
www.historicedmonton.ca
www.facebook.com/HistoricEdmonton
twitter.com/EdmontonDHS
Chief Officer(s):
Dean Wood, President

Lethbridge Historical Society
PO Box 974, Lethbridge AB T1J 4A2
Tel: 403-320-4994
lhs@albertahistory.org
albertahistory.org/lethbridge
Chief Officer(s):
Belinda Crowson, President, 403-381-4316

Peace Country Historical Society
PO Box 23394, RPO Prairie Mall, Grande Prairie AB T8V 7G7
e-mail: contactus@pc-hs.ca
www.pc-hs.ca
Chief Officer(s):
Daryl White, President

Historical Society of Fort McMurray *See* Fort McMurray Historical Society

Historical Society of Ottawa / Société historique d'Ottawa

PO Box 523, Stn. B, Ottawa ON K1P 5P6
e-mail: hsottawa@storm.ca
hsottawa.ncf.ca
Previous Name: Women's Canadian Historical Society of Ottawa
Overview: A small local charitable organization founded in 1898
Mission: To encourage the study of Canadian history & literature; to collect, preserve, exhibit & publish Canadian historical records & artifacts, especially those that illustrate the origin, growth & development of Ottawa; to foster Canadian loyalty & patriotism
Member of: Canadian Museums Association; Ontario Museum Association; Ontario Historical Society
Chief Officer(s):
George Neville, President, 613-729-0579
george.neville@ncf.ca
Margaret Back, Secretary, 613-236-7166
ea590@freenet.carleton.ca
Membership: *Fees:* $10 student; $35 individual; $50 family; $350 single lifetime; *Committees:* Awards; Library/Archives; Membership; Nominations; Newsletter; Publications; Telephone
Activities: *Internships:* Yes; *Speaker Service:* Yes; *Library* by appointment

Historical Society of St. Boniface & Maryhill Community

1338 Maryhill Rd., #B, Maryhill ON N0B 2B0
e-mail: info@maryhillroots.com
www.maryhillroots.com
Also Known As: Maryhill Historical Society
Overview: A small local organization founded in 1977
Mission: To collect, preserve, exhibit & publishe historical material pertaining to the parish, school & Maryhill community.
Member of: Ontario Historical Society
Chief Officer(s):
Marlene Bruckhardt, President
Finances: *Funding Sources:* Membership, donations, publications, research
Membership: *Fees:* $5; $25 life individual; $40 life couple; *Committees:* St. Boniface Church; St. Boniface School; Building Maintenance; Community; Resource Centre; Fundraising; Wayside Shrines; Birthday Club; Geneology; Publications; Program; Membership
Activities: *Awareness Events:* Heritage Day, 3rd Sun. in Sept.; *Library:* Resource Centre (summer); by appointment

Historical Society of St. Catharines

Pen Centre, PO Box 25017, 221 Glendale AVe., St Catharines ON L2T 4O4
Tel: 905-227-5120
stcatharineshistory.wordpress.com
Overview: A small local organization founded in 1927
Mission: To increase the knowledge & appreciation of the history of St Catharines & vicinity
Member of: Ontario Historical Sociaty
Chief Officer(s):
Brenda Zadoroznij, Secretary
brendaz@cogeco.ca
Elizabeth Finnie, President
finnies@sympatico.ca
Finances: *Annual Operating Budget:* Less than $50,000; *Funding Sources:* Membership fees; Ontario Ministry of Culture, Tourism & Recreation
11 volunteer(s)
Membership: 100-499; *Fees:* $10 singles; $15 family; *Committees:* Programme
Activities: Spring & fall walking tours; Oille Fountain Potting Ceremony; sponsors research on the history of the St Catharines Grand Opera House; monthly meetings; presentation of history awards to a student at each of nine local high schools; workshops; *Awareness Events:* Observance of the birthday of William Hamilton Merritt, July 3

Historical Society of Sherbrooke *Voir* Société d'histoire de Sherbrooke

HIV Network of Edmonton Society

9702 - 111 Ave. NW, Edmonton AB T5G 0B1
Tel: 780-488-5742; *Fax:* 780-488-3735
Toll-Free: 877-388-5742
contact@hivedmonton.com
www.hivedmonton.com
www.facebook.com/home.php#!/hiv.edmonton?fref=ts
twitter.com/HIVEdmonton
www.youtube.com/user/hivedmontonvideo
Also Known As: HIV Edmonton
Previous Name: AIDS Network of Edmonton Society
Overview: A small local charitable organization founded in 1986
Mission: HIV Edmonton is a community-based, not-for-profit organization that works to reduce HIV/AIDS related stigma & discrimination. It works to educate, support & advocate on behalf of those infected & affected by HIV & related conditions.
Member of: Canadian AIDS Society; Canadian Centre for Philanthropy Canadian HIV/AIDS Legal Network; Canadian Palliative Care Association; Chamber of Commerce
Affliation(s): Alberta Community Council on HIV
Chief Officer(s):
James Mabey, Chair
John Gee, Director, Operations
john.g@hivedmonton.com
Finances: *Annual Operating Budget:* $500,000-$1.5 Million; *Funding Sources:* Government; foundations; fundraising
Staff Member(s): 7; 150 volunteer(s)
Membership: 1-99; *Committees:* Capital Development; Bylaws & Policy; Finance
Activities: Support; health promotion; harm reduction; advocacy; *Awareness Events:* AIDS Walk; The Art of Healing; AIDS Awareness Week; *Internships:* Yes; *Speaker Service:* Yes
Awards:
• Bob Mills Community Leadership Award (Award)

HIV North Society

Co-Operators Square, #303, 9804 - 100 Ave., Grande Prairie AB T8V OT8
Tel: 780-538-3388; *Fax:* 780-538-3368
info@hivnorth.org
www.hivnorth.org
Also Known As: HIV North
Previous Name: South Peace AIDS Council of Grande Prairie; Society of the South Peace AIDS Council
Overview: A small local charitable organization founded in 1987 overseen by Canadian AIDS Society
Mission: To provide outreach, education, harm reduction & support programs & services, working collaboratively with other agencies, to fight against HIV/AIDS
Member of: Alberta Community Council on AIDS
Chief Officer(s):
Brenda Yamkowy, Executive Director
director@hivnorth.org
Finances: *Funding Sources:* Health Canada; Alberta Health; fundraising
Staff Member(s): 7
Membership: *Member Profile:* Interest in & knowledge of AIDS/HIV
Activities: *Speaker Service:* Yes; *Library* Open to public

HIV West Yellowhead Society

#105, 612 Connaught Dr., Jasper AB T0E 1E0
Tel: 780-852-5274; *Fax:* 780-852-5273
Toll-Free: 877-291-8811
hivdirector@incentre.net
www.hivwestyellowhead.com
www.facebook.com/pages/HIV-West-Yellowhead/115352815214838
Previous Name: AIDS Jasper Society
Overview: A small local organization founded in 1988 overseen by Canadian AIDS Society
Mission: To promote healthy lifestyles & relationships & prevent the spread of HIV
Member of: Alberta Community Council on HIV
Chief Officer(s):
Nancy Robbins, Project Coordinator
nancypat@telus.net

Finances: *Annual Operating Budget:* $50,000-$100,000; *Funding Sources:* Health Canada; Alberta Health; community donations
Staff Member(s): 2; 15 volunteer(s)
Membership: 10; *Fees:* $5; *Member Profile:* Community members
Activities: Prevention education & awareness; information & referral; community outreach; *Awareness Events:* AIDS Walk; National AIDS Awareness Week; World AIDS Day

HIV/AIDS Regional Services (HARS)
844A Princess St., Kingston ON K7L 1G5
Tel: 613-545-3698; *Fax:* 613-545-9809
Toll-Free: 800-565-2209
hars@kingston.net
www.hars.ca
www.facebook.com/382928277418
Previous Name: Kingston AIDS Project
Overview: A medium-sized local charitable organization founded in 1986
Mission: To prevent spread of Human Immunodeficiency Virus (HIV); to educate people about AIDS & HIV; to support people affected by AIDS & HIV infection
Affliation(s): Ontario AIDS Network; Canadian AIDS Society; Canadian HIV/AIDS Legal Network
Chief Officer(s):
John McTavish, Executive Director
Joseph Babcock, Chair
Finances: *Funding Sources:* Federal, provincial & city governments & fundraising
Staff Member(s): 8
Membership: *Fees:* $15 regular; $5 Senior/Student; $0 Person with HIV/AIDS
Activities: *Awareness Events:* AIDS Vigil, May; Red Ribbon Campaign, Dec.; *Library* Open to public

HMWN (Holy Mother World Networks) Radio Maria
1247 Lawrence Ave. West, Toronto ON M6L 1A1
Tel: 416-245-7117; *Fax:* 416-245-2668
info@hmwn.net
www.hmwn.net
Also Known As: Radio Maria Canada
Overview: A small local charitable organization
Mission: To promote the Gospel message of joy & hope for the family, the sick, & the lonely, in accordance with the teaching of the Roman Catholic Church; to provide 24-hour Catholic radio broadcasting services as part of an evangelization project
Affliation(s): Archdiocese of Toronto; World Family of Radio Maria
Finances: *Funding Sources:* Donations
Membership: *Member Profile:* Religious & lay volunteers, devoted to the Holy Mother, to operate HMWN Radio Maria
Activities: Offering programming in faith instruction & prayer

Hockey Alberta / Hockey l'Alberta
PO Box 5005, #2606, 100 College Blvd., Red Deer AB T4N 5H5
Tel: 403-342-6777; *Fax:* 403-346-4277
info@hockeyalberta.ca
www.hockeyalberta.ca
www.facebook.com/HockeyAlberta
twitter.com/HockeyAlberta
Overview: A large provincial organization founded in 1907 overseen by Hockey Canada
Mission: To serve those who serve the athletes by providing good governance, quality services, programs & education
Member of: Hockey Canada
Chief Officer(s):
Terry Engen, Chair, 403-746-5466
tengen@hockeyalberta.ca
Rob Litwinski, Executive Director
rlitwinski@hockeyalberta.ca
Tim Leer, Senior Manager, Hockey Development
tleer@hockeyalberta.ca
Mike Olesen, Senior Manager, Operations & Administration
molesen@hockeyalberta.ca
Staff Member(s): 37; 500+ volunteer(s)
Membership: 450 organizations + 90,000+ individual members
Activities: *Internships:* Yes; *Speaker Service:* Yes; *Rents Mailing List:* Yes
Publications:
• Hockey Alberta Magazine
Type: Magazine

Hockey Canada
801 King Edward Ave., #N204, Ottawa ON K1N 6N5
Tel: 613-562-5677; *Fax:* 613-562-5676
www.hockeycanada.ca
www.linkedin.com/company/hockey-canada
www.facebook.com/HockeyCanada
twitter.com/hockeycanada
www.youtube.com/hockeycanadavideos
Also Known As: Canadian Hockey Association
Merged from: Canadian Amateur Hockey Association; Hockey Canada
Overview: A large national organization founded in 1914
Mission: To advance amateur hockey for all individuals through progressive leadership, ensuring meaningful opportunities & enjoyable experiences in a safe, sustainable environment
Affliation(s): International Ice Hockey Federation
Chief Officer(s):
Jim Hornell, Chair
Tony Renney, President
André Brin, Contact, Communications & Media Relations
abrin@hockeycanada.ca
Finances: *Funding Sources:* Government; Sponsorship; Sales; Fundraising
Awards:
• Female Hockey Breakthrough Award (Award)
• Liz MacKinnon Award (Award)
• Hal Lewis Award (Award)
• Gordon Juckes Award (Award)
• Officiating Award (Award)
• Hockey Canada Award of Merit (East) (Award)
• Hockey Canada Award of Merit (West) (Award)
• Hockey Canada Award of Merit (Central) (Award)
• Outstanding Volunteer Award (Award)

Calgary Office
#201, 151 Canada Olympic Rd. SW, Calgary AB T3B 6B7
Tel: 403-777-3636; *Fax:* 403-777-3635
info@canadianhockey.ca
www.canadianhockey.ca

Hockey Canada Foundation
#N204, 801 King Edward Ave., Ottawa ON K1N 6N5
Tel: 613-562-5677; *Fax:* 613-562-5676
foundation@hockeycanada.ca
www.hockeycanada.ca
Overview: A large national charitable organization
Mission: To establish & grow endowment & general purpose funds for Hockey Canada
Chief Officer(s):
Chris Bright, Executive Director
cbright@hockeycanada.ca
Finances: *Funding Sources:* Donations; fundraising
Activities: Focus areas: Skill Development & Qualified Coaching; Accessibility & Diversity; Health & Wellness; Athlete & Alumni Support; Facilities; *Awareness Events:* Golf Gala

Hockey Development Centre for Ontario (HDCO)
#312, 3 Concorde Gate, Toronto ON M3C 3N7
Tel: 416-426-7252; *Fax:* 416-426-7348
Toll-Free: 888-843-4326
hockey@hdco.on.ca
www.hdco.on.ca
Overview: A medium-sized provincial organization founded in 1984
Mission: To provide educational, developmental & financial opportunities for amateur hockey participants in Ontario
Chief Officer(s):
Wayne Dillon, Executive Director
wdillon@hdco.on.ca
Finances: *Annual Operating Budget:* $500,000-$1.5 Million; *Funding Sources:* Provincial government; sponsorships
Staff Member(s): 3
Membership: 11 institutional; 2 associate
Activities: Hockey Trainers Certification Program; *Rents Mailing List:* Yes; *Library:* Hockey Resources; Open to public

Hockey Eastern Ontario (HEO)
#D300, 1247 Kilborn Pl., Ottawa ON K1H 6K9
Tel: 613-224-7686; *Fax:* 613-224-6079
info@hockeyeasternontario.ca
www.odha.com
www.facebook.com/HockeyEasternOntario
twitter.com/HEOhockey
Overview: A medium-sized provincial organization founded in 1920 overseen by Hockey Canada
Mission: To advance amateur hockey players
Member of: Hockey Canada
Chief Officer(s):
Debbie Rambeau, Executive Director
drambeau@hockeyeasternontario.ca
Staff Member(s): 5

Hockey l'Alberta *See* Hockey Alberta

Hockey Manitoba
145 Pacific Ave., Winnipeg MB R3B 2Z6
Tel: 204-925-5755; *Fax:* 204-925-5761
info@hockeymanitoba.mb.ca
www.hockeymanitoba.ca
www.facebook.com/hockeymanitoba
twitter.com/hockeymanitoba
www.youtube.com/hockeymanitoba
Also Known As: Manitoba Amateur Hockey Association
Overview: A medium-sized provincial organization founded in 1914 overseen by Hockey Canada
Mission: To foster, develop, & promote amateur hockey throughout Manitoba; To encourage fair play; To secure the enforcement of rules as adopted by by the assosication; To conduct games between member clubs to determine provincial champions
Member of: Hockey Canada
Chief Officer(s):
Bill Whitehead, President
bwhitney@cici.mb.ca
Peter Woods, Executive Director
peter@hockeymanitoba.ca
Bernie Reichardt, Director, Hockey Development
bernie@hockeymanitoba.ca
Staff Member(s): 6
Membership: 30,000; *Committees:* Officials Development; Athlete Development
Activities: Administering clinics & skills camps; To collaborate in development programs for players, coaches & officials

Hockey New Brunswick (HNB) / Hockey Nouveau-Brunswick
PO Box 456, 861 Woodstock Rd., Fredericton NB E3B 4Z9
Tel: 506-453-0089; *Fax:* 506-453-0868
www.hnb.ca
www.facebook.com/148777865135246
twitter.com/HockeyNB
Previous Name: New Brunswick Amateur Hockey Association
Overview: A medium-sized provincial organization founded in 1968 overseen by Hockey Canada
Member of: Hockey Canada
Chief Officer(s):
Brian Whitehead, Executive Director
bwhitehead@hnb.ca
Staff Member(s): 5; 120 volunteer(s)
Membership: 15,000-49,999

Hockey Newfoundland & Labrador (NLHA) / Association de hockey de Terre-Neuve et Labrador
PO Box 176, 32 Queensway, Grand Falls-Windsor NL A2A 2J4
Tel: 709-489-5512; *Fax:* 709-489-2273
office@hockeynl.ca
www.hockeynl.ca
twitter.com/Hkynl
Overview: A medium-sized provincial organization founded in 1935 overseen by Hockey Canada
Mission: Support for hockey in Canada including minor, junior, senior, female and development.
Member of: Hockey Canada
Chief Officer(s):
Craig Tulk, Executive Director
ctulk@hockeynl.ca
Tamar Hobbs, Administrative Assistant
thobbs@hockeynl.ca
Staff Member(s): 2

Hockey North
PO Box 62, Fort Smith NT X0E 0P0
Tel: 867-872-3383; *Fax:* 867-872-7724
www.hockeynorth.ca
Overview: A small provincial organization overseen by Hockey Canada
Member of: Hockey Canada
Chief Officer(s):
Mike Gravel, Executive Director
ed@hockeynorth.ca

Hockey Northwestern Ontario (HNO)
#100, 216 Red River Rd., Thunder Bay ON P7B 1A6
Tel: 807-623-1542; *Fax:* 807-623-0037
info@hockeyhno.com
www.hockeyhno.com
www.facebook.com/HNOHockey
twitter.com/HNOHockey
Previous Name: Thunder Bay Amateur Hockey Association

Overview: A small provincial organization overseen by Hockey Canada
Member of: Hockey Canada
Chief Officer(s):
Trevor Hosanna, General Manager
manager@hockeyhno.com
Ron MacKinnon, Development Coordinator
mackinnonr@hockeyhno.com
Staff Member(s): 3

Hockey Nouveau-Brunswick *See* Hockey New Brunswick

Hockey Nova Scotia
#17, 7 Mellor Ave., Dartmouth NS B3B 0E8
Tel: 902-454-9400; *Fax:* 902-454-3883
www.hockeynovascotia.ca
www.facebook.com/hockeynovascotia
twitter.com/HockeyNS
www.youtube.com/channel/UC8gbE0o_HAAQ6bj2c8S6kdg
Previous Name: Nova Scotia Hockey Association
Overview: A medium-sized provincial organization founded in 1974 overseen by Hockey Canada
Member of: Hockey Canada
Chief Officer(s):
Darren Cossar, Executive Director
dcossar@hockeynovascotia.ca
Finances: *Funding Sources:* Government; registration fees; fundraising
Staff Member(s): 6
Membership: 20,000

Hockey PEI
PO Box 302, 40 Enman Cres., Charlottetown PE C1A 7K7
Tel: 902-368-4334; *Fax:* 902-368-4337
info@hockeypei.com
hockeypei.com
www.facebook.com/210191735702089
twitter.com/hockeypei
Previous Name: Prince Edward Island Hockey Association
Overview: A medium-sized provincial organization founded in 1974 overseen by Hockey Canada
Member of: Hockey Canada
Chief Officer(s):
Rob Newson, Executive Director
rob@hockeypei.com
Finances: *Annual Operating Budget:* $250,000-$500,000
Staff Member(s): 3; 100 volunteer(s)
Membership: 6,000;

Hockey Québec (FQHG)
#210, 7450, boul. les Galeries d'Anjou, Montréal QC H1M 3M3
Tél: 514-252-3079; *Téléc:* 514-252-3158
communication@hockey.qc.ca
www.hockey.qc.ca
www.facebook.com/HockeyQuebec
twitter.com/HockeyQuebec
www.youtube.com/channel/UCjHSK9n17ccFJca_wbfJakQ
Nom précédent: Fédération québécoise de hockey sur glace
Aperçu: *Dimension:* grande; *Envergure:* provinciale; fondée en 1976 surveillé par Hockey Canada
Mission: Assurer l'encadrement du hockey sur glace; favoriser la promotion et le développement de la personne qui pratique le hockey
Membre de: Hockey Canada
Membre(s) du bureau directeur:
Sylvain B. Lalonde, Directeur général
sblalonde@hockey.qc.ca
Membre(s) du personnel: 23
Activités: La Méthode d'apprentissage de hockey sur glace; excellence; développement régional; entraîneurs et officiels; formation des administrateurs bénévoles; hockey féminin; franc jeu; sports-études; *Service de conférenciers:* Oui; *Listes de destinataires:* Oui

Hockey sur gazon Canada *See* Field Hockey Canada

Hockey sur gazon C-B *See* Field Hockey BC

Hola
c/o 519 Church Street Community Centre, 519 Church St., Toronto ON M4Y 2C9
Tel: 416-925-9872
latinogrouphola@gmail.com
Overview: A small local organization founded in 1991
Mission: Hola offers opportunities to socialize, runs workshops on HIV/AIDS prevention, takes part in immigration panels, holds drug and alcohol abuse seminars, and battles homophobia.
Finances: *Funding Sources:* Grants and fundraisers
Membership: 65

Holland Centre *See* Jeffery Hale Community Services in English

Holocaust Education Centre
Lipa Green Centre, Sherman Campus, 4600 Bathurst St., 4th Fl., Toronto ON M2R 3V2
Tel: 416-635-2883; *Fax:* 416-635-0925
neuberger@ujafed.org
www.holocaustcentre.com
twitter.com/Holocaust_Ed
Also Known As: Sarah & Chaim Neuberger Holocaust Education Centre
Overview: A small international organization founded in 1985
Member of: UJA Federation of Greater Toronto
Chief Officer(s):
Mira Goldfarb, Executive Director
Carson Phillips, Head, Education
Mary Siklos, Manager, Operations
Anna Skorupsky, Librarian
Staff Member(s): 2; 150 volunteer(s)
Membership: 5,000-14,999; *Committees:* Christian Outreach; Education; Holocaust Education Week; Child Survivor / Hidden Children; Holocaust Resource Centre & Memorial Museum; Survivor Support Services; Youth for Youth
Activities: Providing professional aid & support groups for survivors, child survivors, & the second generation; Offering forums for discussion; Organizing conferences; Establishing the oral history project; *Awareness Events:* Raoul Wallenberg Day, January 17; International Holocaust Remembrance Day, January 27; Holocaust Education Week, November; *Internships:* Yes; *Speaker Service:* Yes; *Library:* Holocaust Resource Centre; Open to public by appointment

Holstein Canada
PO Box 610, 20 Corporate Pl., Brantford ON N3T 5R4
Tel: 519-756-8300; *Fax:* 519-756-3502
www.holstein.ca
www.facebook.com/HolsteinCanada
Overview: A large national organization founded in 1884
Mission: To improve the Holstein breed by ascertaining the most desirable characteristics of the breed for current & prospective conditions in Canada; To prepare, maintain & make available a genealogical record of the breed; To promote the best interests of breeders & owners of Holstein cattle
Member of: Canadian Agricultural Hall of Fame; Canadian Livestock Genetics Association; Dairy Farmers of Canada
Chief Officer(s):
Ann Louise Carson, Chief Executive Officer, 519-756-8300 Ext. 240
annlouise@holstein.ca
Glen McNeil, President, 519-524-4696, Fax: 519-524-8063
heaholme@hurontel.on.ca
Finances: *Funding Sources:* Service & membership fees
Staff Member(s): 90
Membership: 12,000 regular, affiliate, honorary life, & junior members; *Fees:* $25
Activities: Animal identification; Conformation analysis; Performance data; Research
Awards:
• Cow of the Year Award (Award)
• Superior Production Award (Award)
• Superior Production Award (Award)
• Holstein Canada Education Awards (Award)
Deadline: Nov. 30 *Amount:* $750 (6) *Contact:* Janet Walker, jwalker@holstein.ca
Publications:
• Info Holstein
Frequency: Bimonthly; *Editor:* Jane Whaley

Alberta Branch
Alberta Holstein Association Office, RR#1, Didsbury AB T0M 0W0
Tel: 403-335-5916; *Fax:* 403-335-4751
info@albertaholstein.ca
www.albertaholstein.ca
www.facebook.com/270585993034177
www.youtube.com/user/mountainsab
Chief Officer(s):
Heidi Voegeli-Bleiker, Contact

British Columbia Branch
c/o Secretary, 847 Garnett Rd., Cobble Hill BC V0R 1L0
Tel: 250-743-8690; *Fax:* 250-743-8691
bcbranch@telus.net
www.bcholsteins.com
Chief Officer(s):
Joan Wikkerink, Secretary

Manitoba Branch
PO Box 750, Blumenort MB R0C 0H0
Tel: 204-326-6539
info@manitobaholsteins.ca
www.manitobaholsteins.ca
Chief Officer(s):
Darcy Heapy, President
dheapy@mymts.net

New Brunswick Branch
c/o Secretary, 436 Route 616, Keswick Ridge NB E6L 1S5
Tel: 506-363-2534; *Fax:* 506-363-3701
kitkat@nb.sympatico.ca
www.facebook.com/300481096665386
Chief Officer(s):
Lorraine Allen, Secretary

Nova Scotia & Newfoundland Branch
PO Box 2155, RR#1, Corner Brook NL A2H 2N2
Tel: 709-660-0434
Chief Officer(s):
Dave Simmons, President
simmons_david@hotmail.com

Ontario Branch
285 Fountain St. South, Cambridge ON N3H 1J2
Tel: 519-653-6180; *Fax:* 519-653-2129
branch@ontario.holstein.ca
www.ontario.holstein.ca
Chief Officer(s):
Jason French, General Manager

Prince Edward Island Branch
487 Frenchfort Rd., Frenchfort PE C1C 0G9
Tel: 902-368-2804; *Fax:* 902-566-4264
www.holsteinpei.com
Chief Officer(s):
Tom Robinson, President
bluediamondfarm@live.ca

Saskatchewan Branch
c/o Tricia Flaman, PO Box 40, Vibank SK S0G 4Y0
Tel: 306-762-2241
saskbranch@sasktel.net
Chief Officer(s):
Tymen Vanzessen, President
vanzessendairy@hotmail.com

Section de Québec
3955, boul Laurier ouest, Saint-Hyacinthe QC J2S 3T8
Tél: 450-778-9636; *Téléc:* 450-778-9637
info@holsteinquebec.com
www.holsteinquebec.com
www.facebook.com/holstein.quebec
twitter.com/holstein_quebec
vimeo.com/holsteinquebec
Chief Officer(s):
James Peel, Directeur général
jpeel@holsteinquebec.com

Holy Childhood Association (HCA)
2219 Kennedy Rd., Toronto ON M1T 3G5
Tel: 416-699-7077; *Fax:* 416-699-9019
Toll-Free: 800-897-8865
hca@missionsocieties.ca
www.missionsocieties.ca
www.facebook.com/pontificalmissionsocieties
www.youtube.com/user/WorldMissionTV
Also Known As: Children Helping Children
Overview: A medium-sized international charitable organization founded in 1843
Mission: To develop mission awareness through a school program for elementary Catholic school children; to provide aid to children in developing countries.
Member of: Pontificial Mission Societies
Chief Officer(s):
Osei Alex, National Director
Finances: *Funding Sources:* Donations
Staff Member(s): 8

Holy Face Association / Association de la Sainte Face
PO Box 100, Stn. St. Jacques, Montréal QC H3C 1C5
Tel: 514-747-0357; *Fax:* 514-747-9147
holyface@holyface.com
www.holyface.com
Overview: A small national charitable organization founded in 1976

Mission: The goal of this apostolate is reparation to God (Father, Son & Holy Spirit) through contemplative devotion to the Holy Face of Jesus
Finances: *Annual Operating Budget:* $250,000-$500,000; *Funding Sources:* Donations
20 volunteer(s)
Membership: 15,000-49,999
Activities: *Speaker Service:* Yes; *Library* by appointment
Publications:
• Holy Face Association Newsletter
Type: Newsletter
• The Holy Face of Jesus Christ, Discovery, Journey, Destination [a publication of the Holy Face Association]
Type: Book

Holy Trinity Community - North America (HTCNA)
2 Aberfeldy Cres., Markham ON L3T 4C2
Tel: 647-669-7524; *Fax:* 905-763-1522
www.holytrinitycarmel.com
www.facebook.com/sahabatktm
twitter.com/sahabatktm
www.youtube.com/user/sahabatktm
Overview: A large international organization
Mission: To experience the Holy Spirit & bring that experience to others
Affliation(s): Archdiocese of Toronto
Chief Officer(s):
Pauline Susanto, Contact
pauline.susanto@gmail.com

Home Business Association of the National Capital Region *See* Small Business Association

Home Care Program for Metropolitan Toronto *See* Toronto Community Care Access Centre

Home Child Care Association of Ontario (HCCAO)
756 Ossington Ave., Toronto ON M6G 3T9
Tel: 416-233-1506; *Fax:* 416-530-1924
info@hccao.com
www.hccao.com
Previous Name: Private Home Day Care Association of Ontario
Overview: A small provincial organization founded in 1983
Mission: To promote, develop & support home-based child care services for families through licensed agencies
Chief Officer(s):
Marni Flaherty, President
mflaherty@todaysfamily.ca
Janene Parr, Secretary
jparr@ccrconnect.ca
JoAnn Gillan, Treasurer
gjoann@region.waterloo.on.ca
Membership: 70 home child care agencies; *Fees:* Schedule available; *Member Profile:* Child care staff; educators; providers; parents; students
Publications:
• Liason
Type: Newsletter; *Frequency:* Quarterly

Home School Legal Defence Association of Canada (HSLDA)
#32B, 980 Adelaide St. South, London ON N6E 1R3
Tel: 519-913-0318; *Fax:* 519-913-0321
info@hslda.ca
www.hslda.ca
www.facebook.com/pages/HsldaCanada/289196517815387
twitter.com/hsldacanada
pinterest.com/hsldacanada
Overview: A small national organization
Mission: To promote home education & protect parent educators
Chief Officer(s):
Gerald Huebner, Chair
Paul D. Faris, President & Legal Counsel
Staff Member(s): 8
Membership: *Fees:* $135.60 full time pastor/missionary/single parent; $162.72 regular

H.O.M.E. Society
31726 South Fraser Way, Abbotsford BC V2T 1T9
Tel: 604-852-7888; *Fax:* 604-852-7801
www.homesociety.com
Also Known As: Healthy Opportunities for Meaningful Experience Society
Overview: A small local organization
Chief Officer(s):
Cam Doré, Executive Director
cam.dore@homesociety.ca
Dave Lappin, Executive Director
dave.lappin@homesociety.ca

HomeLink International Home Exchange (HLCA)
1707 Platt Cres., North Vancouver BC V7J 1X9
Tel: 604-987-3262
info@homelink.ca
www.homelink.org/canada/
www.facebook.com/HomeLink.CA
Also Known As: HomeLink Canada
Previous Name: West World Holiday Exchange; WorldHomes Holiday Exchange
Overview: A small international organization founded in 1986
Mission: To produce directories listing homes for vacation exchange worldwide
Member of: HomeLink International Associates Inc.
Chief Officer(s):
Jack Graber, Director
Finances: *Annual Operating Budget:* $100,000-$250,000; *Funding Sources:* Membership fees
Staff Member(s): 2
Membership: 13,000 international; 24 affiliates; *Fees:* $170 basic; *Member Profile:* Home/apartment/condo owners

Homeopathic College of Canada (HCC)
e-mail: info@homeopathy.edu
www.homeopathy.edu
Also Known As: International Academy of Homeopathy
Overview: A small national organization founded in 1995
Mission: To maintain the highest professional standards of homeopathy; To provide international leadership in the fields of homeopathy & complementary medicine; To promote homeopathy as an alternative & complement within the health care system; To provide treatment effectively & economically within the health care system
Member of: Ontario Homeopathic Association; Homeopathic Medical Council of Canada
Chief Officer(s):
John Crellin, M.D., Ph.D., Dean
Idoia Ania, Contact, Student Affairs
Finances: *Annual Operating Budget:* $500,000-$1.5 Million; *Funding Sources:* Tuition
Staff Member(s): 30
Membership: 180; *Fees:* $495-$7,500; *Member Profile:* Homeopath professionals; full-time homeopathy students
Activities: *Speaker Service:* Yes; *Library:* The Homeopathic Library

Homeopathic Medical Association Of Canada (HMAC)
2649 Islington Ave., Toronto ON M9V 2X6
Tel: 647-505-6992
info@hmac.ca
www.hmac.ca
Overview: A small national organization
Mission: To serve homeopathic practitioners across Canada; To uphold the code of ethics
Chief Officer(s):
Syed Arif Hussain, Vice-President
drarif11@yahoo.ca
Membership: *Fees:* $200 professionals; $75 students; *Member Profile:* Homeopathic doctors throughout Canada; Homeopathic students
Activities: Maintaining the National Homeopathic Doctor's Resgistry; Offering educational seminars & practice management sessions
Publications:
• Homeopathic Medical Council of Canada Journal
Type: Journal
Profile: Featuring a list of homeopathic doctors who are members of the council

Homestead Christian Care
249 Caroline St. South, #A, Hamilton ON L8P 3L6
Tel: 905-529-0454; *Fax:* 905-529-0355
Toll-Free: 866-529-0454
info@hscc.ca
homesteadchristiancare.ca
www.facebook.com/homesteadchristiancare
Overview: A small local charitable organization founded in 1974
Mission: To assist those with mental illness, through affordable housing & rehabilitation services, in order to help them reach personal recovery goals
Chief Officer(s):
Jeffrey Neven, Executive Director
Finances: *Funding Sources:* Donations; Funding through churches

Hominum
#401, 55 Blackberry Dr., New Westminster BC V3L 5S7
Tel: 604-329-9760
hominumformen@yahoo.ca
www.hominum.ca
Overview: A small local organization founded in 1982
Mission: To serve as support group for gay men presently or previously married
Membership: 50; *Fees:* $15; *Member Profile:* Married men coming out as gay seeking support

Honey Harbour/Port Severn District Chamber of Commerce *See* Southeast Georgian Bay Chamber of Commerce

Hong Fook Mental Health Association (HFMHA)
#201, 3320 Midland Ave., Toronto ON M1V 5E6
Tel: 416-493-4242; *Fax:* 416-493-2214
www.hongfook.ca
Overview: A small local charitable organization founded in 1982 overseen by Ontario Council of Agencies Serving Immigrants
Mission: To empower Canadians, including those of Cambodian, Chinese, Korean & Vietnamese, & other Asian communities, who reside within the Greater Toronto Area; to obtain ethno-racial equity in the mental health system & to achieve optimal mental health status through activities of direct services, promotion & prevention & system advocacy.
Affliation(s): Ontario Federation of Community Mental Health & Addiction Programs; Canadian Mental Health Association
Chief Officer(s):
Bonnie Wong, Executive Director
Finances: *Annual Operating Budget:* $3 Million-$5 Million; *Funding Sources:* Ministry of Health & Long-Term Care; United Way; fundraising
432 volunteer(s)
Membership: *Fees:* $5 student; $10 individual; $250 silver life membership; $1,000 gold membership
Activities: Case management & supportive housing services; family initiatives; prevention & promotion; volunteer development; community outreach; collaborative efforts with other mental health providers; ESL classes;; *Library:* Resource Centre; by appointment

Downton Branch
130 Dundas St. West, 3rd Fl., Toronto ON M5G 1C3
Tel: 416-493-4242; *Fax:* 416-595-6332

Hong Kong Trade Development Council
Hong Kong Convention & Exhibition Centre, 1 Expo Dr., Wanchai Hong Kong
Tel: 852-1830-668; *Fax:* 852-2824-0249
hktdc@hktdc.org
www.hktdc.com
Overview: A medium-sized international organization founded in 1966
Mission: To promote external trade in goods & services; to create & facilitate opportunities in international trade for Hong Kong companies; to strengthen Hong Kong as the global trade platform of Asia; to assist manufacturers, traders & service providers through marketing opportunities, trade contacts, market knowledge & competitive skills
Chief Officer(s):
Fred Lam, Executive Director
Activities: *Library:* Business Information Centre; Open to public

Toronto Office
Hong Kong Trade Centre, 1st Fl., 9 Temperance St., Toronto ON M5H 1Y6
Tel: 416-366-3594; *Fax:* 416-366-1569
toronto.office@tdc.org.hk
Chief Officer(s):
Andrew Yui, Director

Hong Kong-Canada Business Association (HKCBA) / L'Association commerciale Hong Kong-Canada
#600, 1285 West Broadway, Vancouver BC V6H 3X8
Tel: 604-684-2410; *Fax:* 604-684-6208
nationaled@hkcba.com
national.hkcba.com
Overview: A medium-sized international organization founded in 1984
Mission: To encourage & promote trade & commercial activities across a broad range of industries between Canada & Hong Kong, & through Hong Kong to China & the Asia Pacific Region.
Member of: Federation of Hong Kong Business Associations Worldwide
Affliation(s): Hong Kong Trade Development Council; Hong

Kong Economic & Trade Office, HKSAR Government; Hong Kong Tourism Board; Invest HK; Canadian Chamber of Commerce in Hong Kong; Federation of Hong Kong Business Associations Worldwide; Canadian Consulate General in Hong Kong; Cathay Pacific Airways
Chief Officer(s):
Wayne Berg, National Chair
Joyce Chung, Executive Director
vancouver@hkcba.com
Finances: *Funding Sources:* Membership dues
Staff Member(s): 1
Membership: 1,300 corporate
Activities: *Internships:* Yes; *Speaker Service:* Yes

Atlantic Office
PO Box 29086, 7001 Mumford Rd., Halifax NS B3L 4T8
www.hkcba.com/halifax
Mission: To help its members conduct business between Canada and Hong Kong and encourage Canadian companies to utilize Hong Kong as their business "Smart Link"- to China and the rest of the world.
Chief Officer(s):
Bill Bu, President

Calgary Section Office
PO Box 22308, Stn. Bankers Hall, Calgary AB T2P 4J1
e-mail: admin@calgaryhkcba.com
calgaryhkcba.com
Mission: To help its members conduct business between Canada and Hong Kong and encourage Canadian companies to utilize Hong Kong as their business "Smart Link"- to China and the rest of the world.
Chief Officer(s):
Tim Onyett, President
Kit Koon, Executive Director
kit@hkcba.com

Edmonton Section Office
#90, 11215 Jasper Ave., Edmonton AB T5K 0L5
e-mail: hkcba.edmonton@gmail.com
www.edmontonhkcba.com
www.facebook.com/331342930211327
twitter.com/HKCBAEdmonton
Mission: To help its members conduct business between Canada and Hong Kong and encourage Canadian companies to utilize Hong Kong as their business "Smart Link"- to China and the rest of the world.
Chief Officer(s):
David Tam, President
Monica Barclay, Interim Executive Director

London Section Office
c/o Q Integrators, 42 Chalfont Cres., London ON N6H 4Y4
Tel: 519-473-6227; *Fax:* 519-657-4499
ctse@qint.com
www.hkcba.com/london
Mission: To help its members conduct business between Canada and Hong Kong and encourage Canadian companies to utilize Hong Kong as their business "Smart Link"- to China and the rest of the world. It also facilitates business relationships amongst its membership in Canada.

Montréal Section Office
#200, 1010 Gauchetière Rd. West, Montréal QC H3B 2N2
Tel: 514-931-6333; *Fax:* 450-227-9164
montreal@hkcba.com
montreal.hkcba.com
www.linkedin.com/profile/view?id=167781838
www.facebook.com/239670779452083
Mission: To help its members conduct business between Canada and Hong Kong and encourage Canadian companies to utilize Hong Kong as their business "Smart Link"- to China and the rest of the world.
Chief Officer(s):
Geoffrey Bush, Executive Director

Ottawa Section Office
c/o Virginia Lock, 131 Queen St., Ottawa ON K1P 0A1
Fax: 613-238-3553
hkcbaottawa@hkcba.com
national.hkcba.com/ottawa.html
Mission: To help its members conduct business between Canada and Hong Kong and encourage Canadian companies to utilize Hong Kong as their business "Smart Link"- to China and the rest of the world.
Chief Officer(s):
Ruby Williams, President

Saskatchewan Section Office
c/o Saskatchewan Trade & Export Partnership, PO Box 1787, Regina SK S4P 3C6
Tel: 306-787-1550; *Fax:* 306-787-6666
www.hkcba.com/saskatchewan
Mission: To help its members conduct business between Canada and Hong Kong and encourage Canadian companies to utilize Hong Kong as their business "Smart Link"- to China and the rest of the world. It also facilitates business relationships amongst its membership in Canada.
Chief Officer(s):
John Treleaven, Representative
jtreleaven@sasktrade.sk.ca

Toronto Section Office
9 Temperance St., 2nd Fl., Toronto ON M5H 1Y6
Tel: 416-366-2642; *Fax:* 416-366-1569
toronto@hkcba.com
www.toronto.hkcba.com
www.facebook.com/HKCBAToronto
twitter.com/HKCBATO
Mission: To help its members conduct business between Canada and Hong Kong and encourage Canadian companies to utilize Hong Kong as their business "Smart Link"- to China and the rest of the world. It also facilitates business relationships amongst its membership in Canada.
Chief Officer(s):
Robert Brown, Executive Director
bob@hkcba.com

Vancouver Section Office
#600, 1285 West Broadway, Vancouver BC V6H 3X8
Tel: 604-684-2410; *Fax:* 604-684-6208
vancouver@hkcba.com
vancouver.hkcba.com
www.linkedin.com/groups?gid=2644089
twitter.com/HKCBA
www.youtube.com/user/hkcbavancouver
Mission: To help its members conduct business between Canada and Hong Kong and encourage Canadian companies to utilize Hong Kong as their business "Smart Link"- to China and the rest of the world. It also facilitates business relationships amongst its membership in Canada.
Chief Officer(s):
Carmen Lee, Executive Director

Winnipeg Section Office
c/o 201 Alexander Ave., Winnipeg MB R3B 3C1
Tel: 613-789-8388
hkcba-winnipeg@mts.net
national.hkcba.com/Winnipeg_Section_Home.html
Mission: To help its members conduct business between Canada and Hong Kong and encourage Canadian companies to utilize Hong Kong as their business "Smart Link"- to China and the rest of the world.
Chief Officer(s):
Dave Speirs, President

Hope & District Chamber of Commerce
PO Box 588, 419 Wallace St., Hope BC V0X 1L0
Tel: 604-869-3111; *Fax:* 604-869-8208
info@hopechamber.bc.ca
hopechamber.net
www.facebook.com/HopeChamberofCommerce
Overview: A small local organization founded in 1923
Mission: To improve & promote trade, economic, civic & social welfare of Hope & the scenic Fraser Canyon
Member of: BC Chamber of Commerce; Canadian Chamber of Commerce; Vancouver Coast & Mountains Tourism Association
Chief Officer(s):
Glen Ogren, President
Finances: *Annual Operating Budget:* $100,000-$250,000; *Funding Sources:* Provincial government; District of Hope; fundraising; membership dues; retail sales
Staff Member(s): 2; 13 volunteer(s)
Membership: 108; *Fees:* $50-$300; *Member Profile:* Business, organization or individual wishing to improve or promote trade, economic, civic & social welfare in Hope & the Fraser Canyon
Activities: Hope Business Info. Centre & Visitor Info. Centre; *Awareness Events:* Chamber of Commerce Week, Feb.

Hope Air / Vols d'espoir
#207, 124 Merton St., Toronto ON M4S 2Z2
Tel: 416-222-6335; *Fax:* 416-222-6930
Toll-Free: 877-346-4673
mail@hopeair.ca
www.hopeair.ca
www.facebook.com/pages/Hope-Air
twitter.com/Hope_Air
Previous Name: Mission Air Transportation Network
Overview: A small national charitable organization founded in 1986
Mission: To provide free air transportation to Canadians in financial need who must travel between their own communities & recognized facilities for medical care
Chief Officer(s):
Doug Keller-Hobson, Executive Director
Wayne Twaits, Chair
Robert Reeves, Vice-Chair
Finances: *Annual Operating Budget:* $250,000-$500,000; *Funding Sources:* Corporate; private donations; government
Staff Member(s): 6; 30 volunteer(s)
Membership: 1-99; *Fees:* N/A; *Committees:* Air Coordination; Funding; Finance; Office Administrations; Planning; Public Relations

Hope Association for Community Living *See* Tillicum Centre - Hope Association for Community Living

Hope Food Bank
PO Box 74, Hope BC V0X 1L0
Tel: 604-869-2466; *Fax:* 604-869-3317
info@hopecommunityservices.com
www.hopecommunityservices.com
Also Known As: Hope Community Services
Overview: A small local organization founded in 1979 overseen by Food Banks British Columbia
Mission: The food bank is run by Hope Community Services which offers a range of social services to seniors, children, youth, & families in the Hope & Fraser Canyon region of BC. The organization also operates a volunteer bureau, thrift store, emergency shelter, emergency social services, drug & alcohol addiction programs.
Member of: Food Banks British Columbia; Food Banks Canada
Finances: *Funding Sources:* Thrift store sales; private donations

Hope for the Nations
#222, 1889 Springfield Rd., Kelowna BC V1Y 5V5
Tel: 250-712-2007; *Fax:* 250-862-2942
community@hopeforthenations.com
www.hopeforthenations.com
www.linkedin.com/company/hope-for-the-nations
www.facebook.com/thisishopeforthenations
twitter.com/nations4hope
Overview: A medium-sized international charitable organization founded in 1994
Mission: An international organization established to help address the needs of exploited children around the world; participates in community development, poverty reduction & gender equity in areas where these issues affect children
Affliation(s): HFTN Children's Charity (UK), HFTN USA (Western Division, AZ)
Chief Officer(s):
Ralph Bromley, President
Patrick Elaschuk, Executive Director
patrick@hopeforthenations.com
Finances: *Funding Sources:* Donations; funds from other charities
Staff Member(s): 5

Hope for Wildlife Society
5909 Hwy. 207, Seaforth NS B0J 1N0
Tel: 902-452-3339; *Crisis Hot-Line:* 902-407-9453
info@hopeforwildlife.net
www.hopeforwildlife.net
www.facebook.com/hopeforwildlife
twitter.com/hopeforwildlife
Overview: A small provincial organization founded in 1997
Mission: Specializing in the care, treatment and rehabilitation of injured or orphaned native fur bearing mammals, sea birds and songbirds both indigenous to the Nova Scotia area as well as non-indigenous species and pets.
Chief Officer(s):
Hope Swinimer, Founder & Director
70 volunteer(s)

HOPE International Development Agency
214 Sixth St., New Westminster BC V3L 3A2
Tel: 604-525-5481; *Fax:* 604-525-3471
Toll-Free: 866-525-4673
hope@hope-international.com
www.hope-international.com
twitter.com/HOPEInt
Overview: A large international charitable organization founded in 1975

Mission: To help the poverty-stricken section of Third World people to attain the basic necessities of life; To inform Canadians regarding issues related to the developing world & HOPE's activities; To provide alternative technological & educational support to people in developing countries where enviornmental, economic, &/or social circumstances have interfered with the ability of local communities to sustain themselves by using traditional methods. Other offices in Afghanistan, Australia, Cambodia, Ethiopia, Japan, Myanmar, New Zealand, the U.K., & the U.S.
Member of: Canadian Council of Christian Charities
Chief Officer(s):
David S. McKenzie, Executive Director
Aklilu Mulat, COO
John King, Director of Development
Finances: *Annual Operating Budget:* Greater than $5 Million; *Funding Sources:* Government; coalitions; general public
Staff Member(s): 10; 50 volunteer(s)
Activities: *Internships:* Yes; *Speaker Service:* Yes

Hope Studies Central
11032 - 89 Ave., Edmonton AB T6G 0Z6
Tel: 780-492-5897; *Fax:* 780-492-1318
www.ualberta.ca/hope/
www.youtube.com/user/HopeStudiesCentral
Overview: A small provincial charitable organization
Mission: To increase understanding of the role of hope in human life so that people can be intentional in using hope to enhance quality of life
Chief Officer(s):
Denise Larsen, Team Lead
denise.larsen@ualberta.ca

Hôpital général juif fondation *See* Jewish General Hospital Foundation

Horizon Achievement Centre
780 Upper Prince St., Sydney NS B1P 5N6
Tel: 902-539-8553; *Fax:* 902-567-0415
www.horizon-ns.ca
www.facebook.com/HorizonAchievement
Overview: A small local charitable organization founded in 1984
Mission: Providing services & employment opportunities to people with disabilities
Member of: DIRECTIONS Council for Vocational Services Society
Chief Officer(s):
Carol Pendergast, Executive Director/Manager
Activities: Services include: banquets, catering, baking, mail services & printing, assembly & promotions, & job placements

Horizons of Friendship (HOF)
PO Box 402, 50 Covert St., Cobourg ON K9A 4L1
Tel: 905-372-5483; *Fax:* 905-372-7095
Toll-Free: 888-729-9928
info@horizons.ca
www.horizons.ca
www.facebook.com/horizonsoffriendship
twitter.com/HorizonsFriends
www.youtube.com/user/HorizonsofFriendship
Also Known As: Horizons
Previous Name: Help Honduras Foundation
Overview: A medium-sized international charitable organization founded in 1973
Mission: To address the root causes of poverty & injustice through the cooperation of people from the south & north; To support Central American & Mexican partner organizations which undertake local initiatives; To raise awareness in Canada of global issues; To work with Canadian organizations at the local & national levels
Member of: Canadian Council for International Cooperation
Affliation(s): Americas Policy Group
Chief Officer(s):
Patricia Rebolledo, Executive Director
Finances: *Annual Operating Budget:* $500,000-$1.5 Million; *Funding Sources:* Private donations; government grants
Staff Member(s): 9; 80 volunteer(s)
Membership: *Committees:* Executive; Nominating
Activities: 2 thrift shops; Special Events; Education Sessions; *Awareness Events:* International Development Week, Feb.; Writers & Friends, November; *Speaker Service:* Yes; *Rents Mailing List:* Yes; *Library* Open to public

Hornby Island Food Bank
3130 Cannon Rd., Hornby Island BC V0R 1Z0
Tel: 250-335-1629
hornby@valleylinks.net
Overview: A small local organization overseen by Food Banks British Columbia
Mission: The agency provides food to the needy in the local area.
Member of: Food Banks British Columbia
Chief Officer(s):
Susan Crowe, Contact
crosusan@yahoo.ca

Hors sentiers
10229, rue Chambord, Montréal QC H2C 2R3
Tél: 450-433-7508
sentiers@hotmail.ca
www.algi.qc.ca/asso/horssentiers/
Également appelé: Groupe de plein air Hors sentiers
Aperçu: *Dimension:* petite; *Envergure:* locale
Mission: Groupe de plein air
Affliation(s): Équipe Montréal
Membre: *Montant de la cotisation:* 15$

Horse Council British Columbia (HCBC)
27336 Fraser Hwy., Aldergrove BC V4W 3N5
Tel: 604-856-4304; *Fax:* 604-856-4302
Toll-Free: 800-345-8055
reception@hcbc.ca
www.hcbc.ca
www.facebook.com/pages/Horse-Council-BC/116275438383133?ref=sgm
www.twitter.com/horsecouncilbc/
www.youtube.com/user/HorseCouncilBC/
Overview: A medium-sized provincial organization founded in 1980
Mission: To represent members & work on behalf of their equine interests in British Columbia; To preserve equestrian use of public lands; To foster & promote participation in equine activities; To ensure the well-being of horses
Chief Officer(s):
Lisa Laycock, Executive Director
administration@hcbc.ca
Orville Smith, President, 250-964-2269
orsmith@telus.net
Carol Cody, Secretary, 604-855-6890
crazycreek@telus.net
Carolyn Farris, Treasurer, 250-546-6083
farrisfarms@xplornet.com
Finances: *Funding Sources:* Membership dues; Province of British Columbia
Membership: 21,000+; *Member Profile:* Clubs; Individuals & families; Businesses; Affiliates
Activities: Collaborating with individuals, professionals, industry, businesses, & governments to improve education, safety, & communication; Representing the industry in areas of sport, recreation, agriculture, & industry; Providing education; Granting funds & supporting clubs; Presenting awards; *Awareness Events:* Horse Week, June
Awards:
• Horse Council BC Post Secondary Scholarships (Scholarship)
Eligibility: Horse Council BC members in good standing, who are a BC graduate from grade 12 and entering into a accredited College or University Study program.*Deadline:* June 30 *Amount:* $1000.00 (5)

Horse Industry Association of Alberta (HIAA)
97 East Lake Ramp NE, Airdrie AB T4A 0C3
Tel: 403-420-5949; *Fax:* 403-948-2069
www.albertahorseindustry.ca
Overview: A small provincial organization founded in 1982
Mission: To act as a unified voice for the Alberta horse industry to foster a growing & profitable industry
Chief Officer(s):
Peter Fraser, President
Darrell Dalton, Vice-President
Doug Milligan, Secretary
Bruce Roy, Treasurer
Teresa van Bryce, Manager
tvanbryce@albertahorseindustry.ca
Heather Mitchell-Matheson, Program Assistant
heathermm@albertahorseindustry.ca
Activities: Advocating for the horse industry in Alberta; Engaging in research; Presenting educational seminars, such as "Getting Started with Horses"
Awards:
• Alberta Horse Industry Distinguished Service Award (Award)
In recognition of an individual who has provided a significant contribution toward the development of the horse industry in Alberta *Contact:* Teresa van Bryce, tvanbryce@albertahorseindustry.ca
Meetings/Conferences: • Horse Breeders & Owners 33rd Annual Conference, January, 2015, Red Deer, AB
Scope: Provincial
Description: Internationally recognized speakers of interest to horse breeders, owners, & professionals
• Horse Breeders & Owners 34th Annual Conference, 2016
Scope: Provincial
Description: Internationally recognized speakers of interest to horse breeders, owners, & professionals
Publications:
• HIAA eNews
Type: Newsletter; *Frequency:* Monthly
Profile: Information about the association & horses, plus upcoming events

Horse Trials New Brunswick
c/o Pam Nierlich, 47 Millstream Dr., Charters Settlement NB E3C 1W9
www.htnb.org
www.facebook.com/groups/179253845513282
Overview: A small provincial organization
Affiliation(s): Horse Trials Canada
Chief Officer(s):
Lori Leach, President
Rien Erichsen-Meesters, Secretary
Finances: *Annual Operating Budget:* Less than $50,000; *Funding Sources:* Provincial government; membership fees
Membership: 35; *Fees:* $25-$55

Horse Trials Nova Scotia (HTNS)
c/o Pam Macintosh, 53 Normandy Ave., Truro NS B2N 3J6
Tel: 902-893-2042
www.htns.org
www.facebook.com/groups/290523457701524
Overview: A small provincial organization
Mission: To foster & encourage safe & fun enjoyment of the sport of Horse Trials (eventing) through regular training & education of riders, coaches, horses & officials
Member of: Canadian Equestrian Federation
Affiliation(s): Horse Trials Canada; Nova Scotia Equestrian Federation
Chief Officer(s):
Pam Macintosh, President
pmacintosh@bellaliant.net
Finances: *Annual Operating Budget:* Less than $50,000
Staff Member(s): 7
Membership: 1-99; *Fees:* $45 senior; $40 junior; $65 family; *Committees:* Athlete Development; Coaching; Competitions; Officials & Technical Delegate; Crosss Country Course Advisors Panel; Eventing Rules
Activities: Clinics (lessons); course design seminars; competitions; booth & brochures; seminars

Horseshoe Canada
Hatchet Lake NS
Tel: 902-852-3231
www.horseshoecanada.ca
Overview: A medium-sized national organization founded in 1979
Mission: To promote & foster the sport of horseshoe pitching in Canada.
Chief Officer(s):
Cecil Mitchell, President
cmitchell@rainbownetrigging.com
Tom Moffatt, Vice-President, 250-474-1785
xpostie@shaw.ca
Lia Snell, Secretary, 519-237-3495
sydsnell@hay.net
Sheryl Arnold, Treasurer, 905-779-3409
walter.arnold@sympatico.ca
Membership: 10 member associations with 3,500 individual members
Activities: *Awareness Events:* Canadian Horseshoe Pitching Championship

Horseshoe New Brunswick
c/o Jason Rideout, 14 Nicholas Dr., Old Ridge NB E3L 4Y6
Tel: 506-467-9100
Other Communication: Alt. Phone: 506-467-1129
www.horseshoenb.com
www.facebook.com/HorseshoeNB
twitter.com/SSHPC
Overview: A small provincial organization overseen by Horseshoe Canada

Mission: To promote the sport of horseshoe pitching in New Brunswick.
Member of: Horseshoe Canada
Chief Officer(s):
Jason Rideout, President
jrideout.tp@gmail.com

Horseshoe Ontario
48 Erie Ave. North, Fisherville ON N0A 1G0
www.horseshoeontario.com
Overview: A small provincial organization overseen by Horseshoe Canada
Mission: To promote the sport of horseshoe pitching in Ontario.
Member of: Horseshoe Canada
Chief Officer(s):
Roy Hartman, President
hcanadianeh@rogers.com
Membership: 450; *Fees:* $20 regular; $1 junior

Horseshoe Saskatchewan Inc.
PO Box 29029, Saskatoon SK S7N 4Y2
e-mail: info@saskhorseshoe.ca
www.horseshoesask.ca
Overview: A small provincial organization founded in 1973 overseen by Horseshoe Canada
Mission: Clubs in this horseshoe-pitching association represent areas in Saskatchewan, Alberta & Manitoba.
Member of: Horseshoe Canada
Chief Officer(s):
Tammy Christensen, President, 306-565-1409
Denise Squires, Executive Coordinator, 306-374-8233
squires_denise@hotmail.com
Finances: *Annual Operating Budget:* Less than $50,000; *Funding Sources:* Raffles; merchandise sales; Saskatchewan Lotteries
Staff Member(s): 2; 30 volunteer(s)
Membership: 13 clubs; *Fees:* $10 regular & group; $8 junior; $2 associate
Activities: Annual Western Classics Tournament

Horticulture Nova Scotia (HORT NS)
Kentville Agricultural Centre, 32 Main St., Kentville NS B4N 1J5
Tel: 902-678-9335; *Fax:* 902-678-1280
info@horticulturens.ca
www.hortns.com
Previous Name: Vegetable & Potato Producers' Association of Nova Scotia
Merged from: Vegetables NS and Berries NS
Overview: A small provincial organization founded in 1998
Mission: To enhance collaborative efforts among members which will strengthen & provide leadership to the horticultural industry
Affliation(s): Nova Scotia Potato Marketing Board
Chief Officer(s):
Marlene Huntley, Executive Director
Marlene@horticulturens.ca
Mark Sawler, President
Finances: *Funding Sources:* Membership fees
Staff Member(s): 2
Membership: *Fees:* Schedule available; *Member Profile:* Vegetable & berry growers; agribusiness
Activities: Administers NS Potato Marketing Board
Meetings/Conferences: • Scotia Horticultural Congress 2015, January, 2015, Old Orchard Inn, Greenwich, NS
Scope: Provincial

Hospice & Palliative Care Manitoba (HPCM)
2109 Portage Ave., Winnipeg MB R3J 0L3
Tel: 204-889-8525; *Fax:* 204-888-8874
Toll-Free: 800-539-0295
info@manitobahospice.mb.ca
www.manitobahospice.ca
www.facebook.com/group.php?gid=127684137242311
Overview: A medium-sized provincial charitable organization founded in 1983
Mission: To champion the development of hospice palliative care for the people of Manitoba through education, information, advocacy & support to service delivery
Member of: Canadian Hospice Palliative Care Association
Chief Officer(s):
Mary Williams, Executive Director
mwilliams@manitobahospice.mb.ca
Lynda Wolf, President
Bob Brennan, Treasurer
Kelly Morris, Vice-President
Finances: *Annual Operating Budget:* $250,000-$500,000; *Funding Sources:* Donations; Foundation grants; Fundraising; United Way
Staff Member(s): 8; 275 volunteer(s)
Membership: 200 individuals; 60 agencies; *Fees:* $45 Individual; $100 Agency
Activities: Providing a Community Hospice Volunteer Program & Volunteer Education Programs; *Awareness Events:* Celebrate Life Breakfast, April; Hike for Hospice, May; Poinsettias for the Holidays, December; *Speaker Service:* Yes; *Library* Open to public
Meetings/Conferences: • Hospice & Palliative Care Manitoba 2015 24th Provincial Conference, September, 2015, Victoria Inn, Winnipeg, MB
Scope: Provincial
Attendance: 400+
Description: An opportunity to for persons working in the field of palliative care to advance their knowledge & skills, to network with others in the field, & to view displays by approximately 30 exhibitors
Contact Information: Conference Coordinator: Andrea Firth, E-mail: afirth2@manitobahospice.mb.ca
Publications:
• Hospice & Palliative Care Manitoba Annual Report
Type: Yearbook; *Frequency:* Annually
Profile: Highlights of the year plus financial statements
• The Hospice Companion
Type: Newsletter; *Frequency:* Semiannually; *Price:* Free with membership in Hospice & Palliative Care Manitoba
Profile: Information about volunteering, upcoming events, news from regions, & membership news

Hospice Niagara
#2, 403 Ontario St., St Catharines ON L2N 1L5
Tel: 905-984-8766; *Fax:* 905-984-8242
info@hospiceniagara.ca
www.hospiceniagara.ca
www.facebook.com/group.php?gid=157424072710
twitter.com/HospiceNiagara
Overview: A small local charitable organization founded in 1993
Member of: Hospice Palliative Care Ontario
Chief Officer(s):
Alicia Merry, Manager, Community Relations
amerry@hospiceniagara.ca
Margaret Jarrell, Executive Director
mjarrell@hospiceniagara.ca
Finances: *Funding Sources:* Provincial funding; Donations; Fundraising
Staff Member(s): 55; 400 volunteer(s)

Hospice of Waterloo Region
298 Lawrence Ave., Kitchener ON N2M 1Y4
Tel: 519-743-4114; *Fax:* 519-743-7021
hospice@hospicewaterloo.ca
www.hospicewaterloo.ca
Overview: A small local charitable organization
Mission: Volunteer organization dedicated to providing comfort, care & support to people affected by life-threatening illness; Services provided in hospitals, long-term care facilities or in the home
150 volunteer(s)

Hospice Palliative Care Association of Prince Edward Island
c/o Prince Edward Home, 5 Brighton Rd., Charlottetown PE C1A 8T6
Tel: 902-368-4498; *Fax:* 902-368-4498
hpca@hospicepei.ca
www.hospicepei.ca
Previous Name: Island Hospice Association
Overview: A medium-sized provincial organization founded in 1985
Mission: To provide care & support to the terminally ill & their families & to those who are bereaved
Member of: Canadian Hospice Palliative Care Association
Chief Officer(s):
Jodi Swan, Chair
Finances: *Annual Operating Budget:* $50,000-$100,000
Staff Member(s): 2; 250 volunteer(s)
Membership: 200; *Fees:* $10-30
Activities: *Awareness Events:* Let Their Lights Shine; Hospice Dog Walk

Hospice Palliative Care Ontario (HPCO)
#707, 2 Carlton St., Toronto ON M5B 1J3
Tel: 416-304-1477; *Fax:* 416-304-1479
Toll-Free: 800-349-3111
info@hpco.ca
www.hpco.ca
www.facebook.com/profile.php?id=176702165712316
twitter.com/hpcontario
www.youtube.com/user/hpcotube?sub_confirmation=1
Merged from: Hospice Association of Ontario; Ontario Palliative Care Association
Overview: A medium-sized provincial charitable organization founded in 2011
Mission: To act as a voice on issues related to the provision of quality end-of-life care for Ontarian; To advance palliative care standards of practice
Member of: Canadian Hospice Palliative Care Association (CHPCA)
Chief Officer(s):
Rick Firth, President & CEO, 416-304-1477 Ext. 24
rfirth@hpco.ca
Paula Neil, Director of Operations
pneil@hpco.ca
Finances: *Funding Sources:* Donations; Fundraising
Membership: *Member Profile:* Individuals from the interdisciplinary field of hospice palliative care; Family representatives; Persons with an interest in hospice palliative care
Activities: Providing educational opportunities; Offering information; Increasing public awareness of end-of-life care; Liaising with local, regional, provincial, & national palliative care organizations; Engaging in advocacy activities; Providing networking opportunities with colleagues
Awards:
• Dorothy Ley Award of Excellence in Hospice Palliative Care (Award)
• The Dr. S. Lawrence Librach Award for Palliative Medicine in the Community (Award)
• Hospice Palliative Care Ontario Outstanding Philanthropist Award (Award)
• June Callwood Circle of Outstanding Volunteers (Award)
• The Richard R. Walker Visionary Award (Award)
• The Marilyn Lundy Hospice Palliative Care Award (Award)
• The Joan Lesmond Scholarship (Scholarship)
Amount: $2,000
• The Frances Montgomery Personal Support Worker Hospice Palliative Care Award (Scholarship)
Meetings/Conferences: • 2015 Annual Hospice Palliative Care Ontario Conference, April, 2015, Sheraton Parkway Toronto North Hotel & Convention Centre, Richmond Hill, ON
Scope: Provincial
Attendance: 500
Publications:
• The Flame
Type: Newsletter
Profile: Association reports, conferences, & articles
• Ontario Palliative Care Association Annual Report
Type: Yearbook; *Frequency:* Annually

Hospital Association of PEI *See* Health Association of PEI

Hospital Auxiliaries Association of Ontario (HAAO)
#2800, 200 Front St. West, Toronto ON M5V 3L1
Tel: 416-205-1407; *Fax:* 416-205-1337
Toll-Free: 800-598-8002
jroth@haao.com
www.haao.com
www.facebook.com/193203857388754
Overview: A medium-sized provincial charitable organization founded in 1910
Mission: To advocate for community partnerships to support health care in Ontario; To promote volunteer services
Chief Officer(s):
Elayne Meharg, President
Joan Farlinger, Vice-President
Janet Simms-Baldwin, Secretary
Margaret Anne Robertson, Treasurer
Membership: *Member Profile:* Auxiliaries & associations in healthcare facilities throughout Ontario; *Committees:* Convention; Finance; Public Relations; Nominating; Advisory
Activities: Fund-raising; Providing education; Offering networking opportunities; Disseminating resource materials; Organizing conventions; *Speaker Service:* Yes
Awards:
• HAAO Student Award (Award)

Hospital Employees' Union (HEU) / Syndicat des employés d'hôpitaux
5000 North Fraser Way, Burnaby BC V5J 5M3

Tel: 604-438-5000; *Fax:* 604-739-1510
Toll-Free: 800-663-5813
Other Communication: info@heu.org
heu@heu.org
www.heu.org
twitter.com/HospEmpUnion
Overview: A large provincial organization founded in 1944
Mission: To unite & associate together all employees employed in hospital, medical or related work for the purpose of securing concerted action in whatever may be regarded as conducive to their best interests; to embrace the concept of equality of treatment for all in hospital, medical or related employment, with respect to wages & job opportunities, recognizing their obligation to provide high-quality care; to defend & preserve the right of all persons to high standards of medical & hospital treatment
Member of: CUPE; Canadian & BC Health Coalitions; BC Federation of Labour
Affiliation(s): Labour Councils
Chief Officer(s):
Ken Robinson, President
Bonnie Pearson, Secretary & Business Manager
Finances: *Annual Operating Budget:* Greater than $5 Million
Staff Member(s): 140
Membership: 43,000 + 250 locals; *Fees:* $5 initiation fee; *Member Profile:* LPNS; care aids; clerical; food service workers & supervisors; technical support; trades people; laundry housekeeping; maintenance; stores; transportation; *Committees:* Women's; Political Action; Equity; International Solidarity
Activities: *Internships:* Yes
Awards:
• HEU Bursaries (Scholarship)
Eligibility: HEU members, their children and spouses, including common-law and same-sex partners. *Amount:* $350-$1,000
Publications:
• The Guardian
Type: Magazine; *Frequency:* 3-4 pa

Hospital for Sick Children Foundation (HSCF)

525 University Ave., 14th Fl., Toronto ON M5G 2L3
Tel: 416-813-6166; *Fax:* 416-813-5024
Toll-Free: 800-661-1083
www.sickkidsfoundation.com
www.facebook.com/sickkidsfoundation
twitter.com/sickkids
www.youtube.com/sickkidsfoundation
Overview: A medium-sized national charitable organization founded in 1972
Mission: To invest contributions in paediatric care, research & education to help children at The Hospital for Sick Children, throughout Canada, & around the world
Chief Officer(s):
Ted Garrard, President/CEO
Kathleen Taylor, Chair
Staff Member(s): 22
Activities: Sick Kids Miracle Weekend Telethon

Hospitality Food Service Employees Association ***See*** University of Guelph Food Service Employees Association

Hospitality New Brunswick ***See*** Tourism Industry Association of New Brunswick Inc.

Hospitality Newfoundland & Labrador (HNL)

#102, 71 Goldstone St., St. John's NL A1B 5C3
Tel: 709-722-2000; *Fax:* 709-722-8104
Toll-Free: 800-563-0700
hnl@hnl.ca
hnl.ca
www.facebook.com/HospitalityNL
twitter.com/hospitalitynl
Also Known As: Tourism Industry Association of Newfoundland & Labrador
Overview: A medium-sized provincial organization founded in 1983
Mission: To develop & promote tourism & hospitality industry throughout Newfoundland & Labrador.
Member of: Atlantic Canada Tourism Partnership; Canadian Tourism Human Resources Council; Hotel Association of Canada; Tourism Industry Association of Canada
Chief Officer(s):
Carol-Ann Gilliard, Chief Executive Officer, 709-722-2000 Ext. 229
cgilliard@hnl.ca
Finances: *Funding Sources:* Membership dues; fees for service; government grants; fundraising
Staff Member(s): 12
Membership: 508; *Fees:* Schedule available; *Member Profile:* Person, business or organization directly or indirectly related to the tourism industry; *Committees:* Policy; Finance; Governance; Professional Development; Membership

Central Office
#102, 71 Goldstone St., St. John's NL A1B 5C3
Tel: 709-632-3395
esheppard@hnl.ca
www.hnl.ca
www.linkedin.com/profile/view?id=105793543
www.facebook.com/HospitalityNL
twitter.com/hospitalitynl/
Affiliation(s): Canadian Academy of Travel & Tourism; Discover Tourism; Emerit
Chief Officer(s):
Rex Avery, Chair, Finance
John Dicks, Chair, Governance
Annette Parsons, Chair, Membership
Rod Pike, Chair, Policy
Darlene Thomas, Chair, Professional Development
Rod Pike, Vice-Chair, Governance

Western Office
Millbrook Mall, Corner Brook NL A2H 1A1
Tel: 709-634-7050
Toll-Free: 800-563-0700
hnl@hnl.ca
www.hnl.ca
Chief Officer(s):
Scott Penney, Regional Coordinator

Hostelling International - Canada (HI-C)

#400, 205 Catherine St., Ottawa ON K2P 1C3
Tel: 613-237-7884; *Fax:* 613-237-7868
info@hihostels.ca
www.hihostels.ca
www.facebook.com/hostelling.canada
twitter.com/HIcanadahostels
www.youtube.com/canadahostels
Overview: A medium-sized international charitable organization
Chief Officer(s):
Joël Marier, Executive Director

Atlantic Region
1253 Barrington St., Halifax NS B3J 1Y3
Tel: 902-422-3863; *Fax:* 902-422-0116
atlantic@hihostels.ca
www.hihostels.ca
Chief Officer(s):
Kevin Murphy, President

Manitoba Region
330 Kennedy St., Winnipeg MB R3B 2M6
Tel: 204-943-5581
info@hihostels.ca
www.hihostels.ca
Chief Officer(s):
Evelyn Riggs, President

Pacific Mountain Region
#200, 761 Cardero St., Vancouver BC V6G 2G3
Tel: 604-684-7111
Toll-Free: 800-661-0020
info@hihostels.ca
www.hihostels.ca

Saskatchewan Region
2310 McIntyre St., Regina SK S4P 2S2
Tel: 306-791-8160; *Fax:* 306-721-2667
info.asl@hihostels.ca
www.hihostels.ca

St-Lawrence Region
3514, ave Lacombe, Montréal QC H3T 1M1
Tel: 514-731-1015; *Fax:* 514-731-1715
Toll-Free: 866-754-1015
info.asl@hihostels.ca
www.hihostels.ca

Hotel & Restaurant Suppliers Association Inc. ***See*** Association des fournisseurs d'hôtels et restaurants inc.

Hotel Association of Canada Inc. (HAC) / Association des hôtels du Canada

#1206, 130 Albert St., Ottawa ON K1P 5G4
Tel: 613-237-7149; *Fax:* 613-237-8928
info@hotelassociation.ca
www.hotelassociation.ca
www.facebook.com/pages/Hotel-Association-of-Canada/133966226704876
twitter.com/hotelassoc
Overview: A large national organization founded in 1913
Mission: To represent members both nationally & internationally; to provide cost-effective services which stimulate & encourage a free market accommodation industry
Affiliation(s): American Hotel & Lodging Association; International Hotel & Restaurant Association; Canadian Tourism Commission; Tourism Industry Association of Canada; Meeting Planners International
Chief Officer(s):
Anthony Pollard, President, 613-237-7149 Ext. 105
pollard@hotelassociation.ca
Andrea Myers, Director, Member Programs
myers@hotelassociation.ca
Finances: *Annual Operating Budget:* $500,000-$1.5 Million; *Funding Sources:* Membership fees; program sales; contract trade shows
Staff Member(s): 5; 60 volunteer(s)
Membership: 8,400+ hotels; *Fees:* $525; *Member Profile:* Hotel corporations, provincial hotel associations
Activities: Access Canada Training Program; Asia Pacific Program for Canadian Hotels; Certified Rooms Division Executive designation; Certified Hospitality Housekeeping Executive designation; Research & Data; Resource center; Trade show; Government relations; *Speaker Service:* Yes; *Rents Mailing List:* Yes; *Library* by appointment
Awards:
• The Humanitarian Award (Award)
• The Human Resources Award (Award)
• The Energy & Environment Award (Award)
Meetings/Conferences: • Hotel Association of Canada 2015 Annual Conference, February, 2015, Hilton Toronto, Toronto, ON
Scope: National
Contact Information: Orie Berlasso, Director; Phone: 416-924-2002; orieberlasso@bigpictureconferences.ca
Publications:
• Roomers
Type: Newsletter; *Frequency:* 6 times a year

Hotel Association of Metropolitan Toronto ***See*** Greater Toronto Hotel Association

Hotel Association of Nova Scotia (HANS)

PO Box 473, Stn. M, Halifax NS B3J 2P8
Tel: 902-425-4890
admin@novascotiahotels.ca
www.novascotiahotels.ca
Overview: A medium-sized provincial organization founded in 1993 overseen by Hotel Association of Canada Inc.
Mission: To make Nova Scotia a year-round travel destination; To act as the official voice of the collective member hotels; To provide support for appropriate advisory boards & committees; To develop & encourage a coordinated joint marketing effort
Chief Officer(s):
Scott Travis, President
Membership: 36; *Fees:* $500 hotels with less than 100 rooms; $5 per room for hotels with more than 100 rooms
Activities: Informing members on issues important to the industry

Hotel Association of Prince Edward Island

c/o Murphy Hospitality Group, 96 Kensington Rd., Charlottetown PE C1A 5J4
Tel: 902-566-3137
Overview: A medium-sized provincial organization overseen by Hotel Association of Canada Inc.
Chief Officer(s):
Kevin Murphy, President

Hotel Association of Québec ***Voir*** Association des hôteliers du Québec

Hotel Association of Vancouver (HAV)

30045 - 8602 Granville St., Vancouver BC V6P 6S3
Tel: 778-574-1954
hotelassocvan@shaw.ca
hotelassociationofvancouver.com
Overview: A small local organization founded in 1986
Mission: The Vancouver Hotel Association strives to promote the benefits of the hotel industry to all levels of government, the media and public
Member of: BC & Yukon Hotels Association; Hotel Association of Canada
Chief Officer(s):
Jonas Melin, Chair
Staff Member(s): 1

Membership: 60; *Member Profile:* Full-service hotels in Greater Vancouver

Hotels Association of Saskatchewan *See* Saskatchewan Hotel & Hospitality Association

House of Commons Security Services Employees Association / Association des employés du Service de sécurité de la Chambre des communes

PO Box 903, Confederation Bldg., Ottawa ON K1A 0A6
Tel: 613-992-9802
Overview: A small local organization founded in 1987
Chief Officer(s):
Roch Lapensée, President
Membership: 203

Housing & Urban Development Association of Canada *See* Canadian Home Builders' Association

Houston & District Chamber of Commerce *See* Houston Chamber of Commerce

Houston Chamber of Commerce

PO Box 396, 3289 Hwy. 16, Houston BC V0J 1Z0
Tel: 250-845-7640; *Fax:* 250-845-3682
info@houstonchamber.ca
www.houstonchamber.ca
Previous Name: Houston & District Chamber of Commerce
Overview: A small local organization founded in 1961
Mission: To enable the local businesses to achieve that which they could not do alone
Member of: BC Chamber of Commerce; Canadian Chamber of Commerce
Chief Officer(s):
John Sullivan, President
Maureen Czirfusz, Manager
Finances: *Annual Operating Budget:* $100,000-$250,000
Staff Member(s): 3; 10 volunteer(s)
Membership: 102; *Fees:* $75-$750
Activities: Operates the Visitor Info. Centre; provides business & volunteer community awards; *Speaker Service:* Yes

Houston Friendship Centre Society

PO Box 640, Houston BC V0J 1Z0
Tel: 250-845-2131; *Fax:* 250-845-2136
hfcs@mail.bulkley.net
Overview: A small local charitable organization
Mission: A community-based Aboriginal organization that encourages healthy lifestyles and learning opportunities, through quality programs and services.
Member of: British Columbia Association of Aboriginal Friendship Centres; National Association of Friendship Centres
Activities: Youth programs; counselling; income tax preparation for low income families

Houston Link to Learning (HLL)

PO Box 1294, Houston BC V0J 1Z0
Tel: 250-845-2727; *Fax:* 250-845-5629
www.facebook.com/237646302964028
Overview: A small local charitable organization founded in 1990
Mission: To ensure that all adults in Houston area have the opportunity to develop the literacy skills they need to lead satisfying & productive lives in the community
Finances: *Funding Sources:* National government; provincial government

H.R. MacMillan Space Centre Society (HRMSC)

1100 Chestnut St., Vancouver BC V6J 3J9
Tel: 604-738-7827; *Fax:* 604-736-5665
info@spacecentre.ca
www.spacecentre.ca
www.facebook.com/MacMillanSpaceCentre
twitter.com/AskAnAstronomer
www.youtube.com/user/MacMillanSpaceCentre
Also Known As: H.R. MacMillan Planetarium
Previous Name: Pacific Space Centre Society
Overview: A medium-sized local charitable organization founded in 1968
Mission: To educate, inspire & evoke a sense of wonder about the universe, our planet & space exploration
Member of: Canadian Association of Science Centres
Affliation(s): Canadian Museums Association
Chief Officer(s):
Raylene Marchand, Interim Executive Director
Lisa McIntosh, Director, Learning
Finances: *Annual Operating Budget:* $1.5 Million-$3 Million; *Funding Sources:* Government; foundations; corporate sponsors; individuals; admissions to facility
Staff Member(s): 50; 30 volunteer(s)
Membership: 700; *Fees:* $20 general membership
Activities: New star show productions; teacher workshops; classroom activities; community astronomy; Starlab; video-conferences

HRMS Professionals Association (HRMSP) / Association des professionnels en SGRH (PSGRH)

#301, 250 Consumers Rd., Toronto ON M2J 4V6
Tel: 416-221-4559; *Fax:* 416-495-8723
Toll-Free: 866-878-3899
info@hrmsp.org
www.hrmscanada.com
Overview: A medium-sized national organization
Mission: To serve human resource management systems professionals by sharing knowledge, best practices, & industry trends
Chief Officer(s):
Richard Rousseau, President
richard.rousseau@hrmsp.org
Martine Castellani, Vice-President & Treasurer
martine.castellani@hrmsp.org
John Allen Doran, Secretary
aldoran@pmihrm.com
Membership: *Fees:* $160 Individual; $35 Student; *Member Profile:* Professionals, practitioners, consultants, & product & service vendors from the human resources & payroll fields
Activities: Offering networking opportunities; Providing educational programs; Facilitating communication between users of technology in the business sector, vendors, & consultants;

HUDAM *See* Manitoba Home Builders' Association

Hudson Bay Chamber of Commerce

PO Box 730, Hudson Bay SK S0E 0Y0
Tel: 306-865-2288; *Fax:* 306-865-2177
www.townofhudsonbay.com
Overview: A small local organization
Chief Officer(s):
Corinne Reine, President
Janice Dyck, Secretary
Activities: *Awareness Events:* Annual Golf Tournament, May

Hudson's Hope Museum

PO Box 98, 9510 Beattie Dr., Hudson's Hope BC V0C 1V0
Tel: 250-783-5735; *Fax:* 250-783-5770
Other Communication: hhmuseum@gmail.com
hhmuseum@pris.ca
www.hudsonshopemuseum.com
twitter.com/hhmuseum
Also Known As: Hudson's Hope Historical Society
Overview: A small local charitable organization founded in 1967
Mission: To preserve & display the history of Hudson's Hope & area through artifacts collection, oral histories & records
Member of: Canadian Museums Association; BC Museums Association; BC Heritage Society
Chief Officer(s):
Rosaleen Ward, Contact
Finances: *Annual Operating Budget:* Less than $50,000
Staff Member(s): 2; 3 volunteer(s)
Membership: 25; *Fees:* $20
Activities: Operates museum; *Library:* Resource Centre; by appointment

Human Concern International (HCI)

PO Box 3984, Stn. C, Ottawa ON K1Y 4P2
Tel: 613-742-5948
Toll-Free: 800-587-6424
info@humanconcern.org
www.humanconcern.org
www.facebook.com/HCICanada
twitter.com/humanconcernint
www.youtube.com/user/HumanConcernInt
Overview: A small national organization founded in 1980
Mission: To help alleviate human suffering by investing in humanity, through long-term development projects for sustainability, & emergency relief assistance during times of dire need
Chief Officer(s):
Kaleem Akhtar, Executive Director
kaleem@humanconcern.org
Garnayl Abdi, Program Officer
Staff Member(s): 10
Activities: Sustainable development projects; Emergency relief assistance; Child sponsorship program; Education/school support; Higher education; Scholarship; Human resource development; Micro-enterprise; Skill development training

Human Factors Association of Canada *See* Association of Canadian Ergonomists

Human Parts Banks of Canada *See* Organ Donors Canada

Human Resource Management Association of Manitoba (HRMAM)

#1810, 275 Portage Ave., Winnipeg MB R3B 2B3
Tel: 204-943-2836; *Fax:* 204-943-1109
hrmam@hrmam.org
www.hrmam.org
Overview: A small provincial organization founded in 1943
Mission: To enhance & promote the value of the human resource profession & practices across Manitoba
Member of: Canadian Council of Human Resource Association
Chief Officer(s):
Ron Gauthier, Executive Director, 204-943-0884
rgauthier@hrmam.org
Finances: *Annual Operating Budget:* $100,000-$250,000
Staff Member(s): 2
Membership: 1,200; *Fees:* $65-$367
Activities: *Internships:* Yes; *Speaker Service:* Yes
Meetings/Conferences: • Human Resource Management Association of Manitoba Human Resource & Leadership Conference 2015, 2015, MB
Scope: Provincial
Publications:
• HRmatters
Type: Magazine; *Frequency:* Fall and spring; *Editor:* Laura Haines

Human Resources Association of New Brunswick (HRANB) / Association des ressources humaines du Nouveau-Brunswick (ARHNB)

PO Box 23128, Moncton NB E1A 6S8
Tel: 506-855-4466; *Fax:* 506-855-4424
Toll-Free: 888-803-4466
solange@hranb.org
www.hranb.org
www.linkedin.com/company/hranb-arhnb
Overview: A medium-sized provincial organization founded in 1996
Mission: Promotes a professional standard of knowledge and proficiency in Human Resources.
Member of: Canadian Council of Human Resources Associations
Chief Officer(s):
Pierre Simoneau, President
simoneap@nbnet.nb.ca
Membership: *Fees:* $100 + HST: regular & associate; $35 + HST: student & retired.

Human Resources Association of Nova Scotia (HRANS)

#102, 84 Chain Lake Dr., Halifax NS B3J 1A2
Tel: 902-446-3660; *Fax:* 902-446-3677
bffice@hrans.org
www.hrans.org
Overview: A small provincial organization founded in 1945
Mission: Dedicated to providing leadership and advocacy in the human resource profession. We will enhance the contribution of the human resource profession to humanity by developing our members and through partnerships with business and society.
Member of: Canadian Council of Human Resources Associations
Chief Officer(s):
Sheila Oyler, Chief Executive Officer
Steve Ashton, President
Staff Member(s): 3
Membership: 1,100+; *Fees:* $140 + tax full & association members; $40 + tax students
Meetings/Conferences: • Human Resources Association of Nova Scotia 2015 Conference, May, 2015, World Trade and Convention Centre, Halifax, NS
Scope: Provincial

Human Resources Institute of Alberta (HRIA)

#410, 1111 - 11 Ave. SW, Calgary AB T2R 0G5
Tel: 403-209-2420; *Fax:* 403-209-2401
Toll-Free: 800-668-6125
info@hria.ca
humanresourcesalberta.com
www.linkedin.com/groups/HRIA-Human-Resources-Institute-Alberta-3951073
twitter.com/HRIA
Overview: A small provincial organization founded in 1984

Mission: To promote & encourage maintenance of the professional standards in the field of human resources management & to set out the standard & process for certification as a Certified Human Resources Professional
Member of: Canadian Council of Human Resources Associations
Chief Officer(s):
Janice MacPherson, Interim Executive Director
jmacpherson@hria.ca
Leslie Henkel, Chair
chair@hria.ca
Finances: *Funding Sources:* Membership fees
Membership: 3,000+; *Fees:* $60 + GST student; $200 + GST associate, general; $225 CHRP candidate; $350 + GST certified; *Member Profile:* Certified professionals
Activities: Annual conference
Meetings/Conferences: • 2015 Human Resources Institute of Alberta Conference, April, 2015, Shaw Conference Centre, Edmonton, AB
Scope: Provincial

Human Resources Professionals Association (HRPA)

#200, 150 Bloor St. West, Toronto ON M5S 2X9
Tel: 416-923-2324; *Fax:* 416-923-7264
Toll-Free: 800-387-1311; *TTY:* 866-620-3848
info@hrpa.org
www.hrpa.ca
www.linkedin.com/company/HRPA
www.facebook.com/pages/HRPA/192819190690
twitter.com/HRPA
www.youtube.com/user/HRPATV
Previous Name: Personnel Association of Ontario
Overview: A medium-sized provincial organization founded in 1954
Mission: To empower human resources professionals by providing management & leadership support, through information resources, events, professional development, & networking opportunities.
Member of: Canadian Council of Human Resources Associations
Chief Officer(s):
Philip C. Wilson, Chair
William (Bill) Greenhalgh, CEO
ceo@hrpa.ca
Louise Tagliacozzo, Manager, Board Relations & Administration
ltagliacozzo@hrpa.ca
Membership: 20,000+ members in 28 Ontario chapters & internationally; *Fees:* Schedule available; *Member Profile:* Human resources practitioners; Students; Individuals interested in the practice of human resources, such as lawyers, specialists, consultants, retirees, academics, & line managers; *Committees:* Appeals; Audit & Finance; Awards; Academic Standards; Complaints & Investigation; Discipline; Editorial Advisory; Experience Assessment; Board Nominating; Governance & Nominating; Human Resources & Compensation; Professional Development; Annual Conference; Professional Regulation & Standards; Continuing Professional Development; Summit Awards Judges; Registration; SHRP Review; Ethos; Health & Safety
Activities: Granting the Certified Human Resources Professional (CHRP) designation; promoting the profession; engaging in government relations; *Library:* HRPAO Resource Centre; by appointment
Awards:
• Honourary Life Award (Award)
• TOSI/HRPAO Scholarship (Scholarship)
• Ross A. Hennigar Memorial Award (Award)
Presented each year to the outstanding CHRM (Certificate in Human Resources Management) candidate who has completed the program in the current year; it was established to encourage participants of the CHRM program to achieve a high standard in their studies, their human resources careers, & their personal & community endeavours*Eligibility:* Recipients must be at a professional or supervisory level for at least one year & show evidence of growth or the potential for growth & achievement
• HRPAO Outstanding CHRP Achievement Award (Award)
• HRPAO Professional Leadership Award (Award)
• HRPAO Volunteer Leadership Awards (Award)
Meetings/Conferences: • Human Resources Professionals Association 2015 Annual Conference & Trade Show, January, 2015, Metro Toronto Convention Centre, Toronto, ON
Scope: Provincial
Publications:
• HR Professional
Type: Magazine; *Frequency:* Bimonthly; *Accepts Advertising*; *Editor:* Meredith Birchall-Spencer; *Price:* Free for members; $29 non-members in Canada; $49 non-members in U.S.A
Profile: A membership magazine for HRPAO, with events & products of interest to HR professionals

Algoma Chapter
Algoma ON
www.hrpa.ca/algoma
Chief Officer(s):
Lorri Kennis, President
lorri.kennis@ssmpuc.com

Barrie & District Chapter
#124, 92 Caplan Ave., Barrie ON L4N 0Z7
Chief Officer(s):
Bonnie Firth, President
president@hrpabarrie.ca

Brockville Chapter
Brockville ON
Tel: 613-340-4427
info@hrpabrockville.ca
Chief Officer(s):
Leah Wales, President, 613-533-6000 Ext. 75435
leah.wales@queensu.ca

Durham Chapter
105 Consumers Dr., Whitby ON L1N 1C4
Tel: 905-721-9564; *Fax:* 647-689-2264
hrpad@adminedge.com
twitter.com/HRPADurham
Chief Officer(s):
Tracey Starrett, President
Rebecca Lauzon, Administrator

Grand Valley Chapter
PO Box 40043, RPO Waterloo Square, Waterloo ON N2J 4V1
Tel: 519-747-8102; *Fax:* 519-489-2736
office@gvhrpa.on.ca
www.linkedin.com/groups?gid=3689596
www.facebook.com/HRPAGV
twitter.com/HRPA_GV
Chief Officer(s):
Anna Aceto-Guerin, President

Grey Bruce Chapter
Owen Sound ON
Chief Officer(s):
Audrey Bross, President, 519-367-3174
audreyb@wightman.ca

Guelph & District Chapter
Guelph ON
www.gdhrpa.ca
Chief Officer(s):
Stephen Goodwin, President
sgoodwin@gdhrpa.ca

Halton Chapter
ON
e-mail: communications@hrpahalton.org
www.linkedin.com/Human-Resources-Professionals-Association-Halton
twitter.com/HRPAHalton
Chief Officer(s):
Rebecca Weber, President
president@hrpahalton.org

Hamilton Chapter
PO Box 73010, Hamilton ON L9A 4X0
Tel: 905-667-6622
info@hamiltonhrpa.ca
Chief Officer(s):
Silvia Stankovic, President
president@hamiltonhrpa.ca

Chatham-Kent Chapter
Chatham-Kent ON
Chief Officer(s):
Elise Marentette, President, 519-682-0470 Ext. 1229
emarentette@anchordanly.com

Kingston & District
PO Box 1709, Kingston ON K7L 5J7
Tel: 613-547-2962; *Fax:* 613-547-8265
admin@hrpakingston.ca
www.hrpa.ca
Mission: To advance relationships between employees & management & to educate HR professionals
Chief Officer(s):
Emily Koolen, President
president@hrpakingston.ca

London & District Chapter
#321, 509 Commissioners Rd. West, London ON N6J 1Y5
Tel: 519-645-7741
info@hrpld.ca
Chief Officer(s):
Stephen Sesar, President
president@hrpld.ca

Niagara Chapter
PO Box 30084, RPO Ridley Square, St Catharines ON L2S 4A1
e-mail: admin@hrpaniagara.ca
www.hrpan.ca
Chief Officer(s):
Marcey Saunders, President
msaunders@hrpaniagara.ca
Jodi Fitzgerald, Communications Director
jfitzgerald@hrpaniagara.ca

North Bay Chapter
North Bay ON
Chief Officer(s):
Marsha Cresswell, President
cresswellm@sympatico.ca

Northumberland Chapter
e-mail: northumberlandhrpa@gmail.com
Chief Officer(s):
Wendy Perry, President
wperry@nhh.ca

Northwestern Ontario Chapter
#421, 1100 Memorial Ave., Thunder Bay ON P7B 4A3
e-mail: executive@hrpano.org
Chief Officer(s):
Allane Danchuk, President, 807-684-1892
allane@tbaycounselling.com

Ottawa Chapter
PO Box 315, Stn. Main, Stittsville ON K2S 1A4
Tel: 613-224-6477; *Fax:* 613-369-4347
infohr@hrpaottawa.ca
www.hrpaottawa.ca
Chief Officer(s):
Elizabeth Roberts, President

Peel Chapter
PO Box 538, #6, 2400 Dundas St. West, Mississauga ON L5K 2R8
Tel: 905-337-7141
info@hrpapeel.ca
www.linkedin.com/groups?gid=2219644
twitter.com/HRPA_Peel
Member of: Human Resources Professionals Association of Ontario
Chief Officer(s):
Jeannette Schepp, President
president@hrpapeel.ca

Peterborough Chapter
www.hrpapeterborough.ca
Chief Officer(s):
Pat Cole, President

Quinte Chapter
e-mail: info@hrpaquinte.ca
Chief Officer(s):
Barb Frederick, President
barbf@pathwaysind.com

Sarnia & District Chapter
Chief Officer(s):
Rebecca Mitchell, President, 519-869-2679
rebeccawmitchell@sympatico.ca

Stormont, Dundas & Glengarry Chapter
Chief Officer(s):
Dora Cameron, President

Sudbury Chapter
Sudbury ON
Chief Officer(s):
Peter Bonish, President
peter@petesrental.ca

Timmins & District Chapter
Timmins ON
Chief Officer(s):
Jamie Klomp, President, 705-360-7502
jklomp@dumasmining.com

Toronto Chapter
Toronto ON
e-mail: communications@hrpatoronto.ca
www.hrpa.ca/toronto
www.linkedin.com/groups?home=&gid=4112691

www.facebook.com/HRPATO
twitter.com/HRPATO
Andrea Fraser, President
West Toronto Chapter
Toronto ON
e-mail: communications@hrpwt.com
hrpwt.com
twitter.com/WestTorontoHRPA
Chief Officer(s):
Heather Wannamaker, President
president@hrpwt.com
Windsor & District Chapter
Windsor ON
e-mail: info@hrpawindsor.ca
www.hrpawindsor.ca
Chief Officer(s):
Jody Merritt, President
jmerritt@stclaircollege.ca
York Region Chapter
#256, 14845-6 Yonge St., Aurora ON L4G 6H8
Tel: 416-483-2070
Toll-Free: 866-977-9975
public_relations@hrpyr.org
www.hrpyr.org
www.linkedin.com/groups?gid=132598
Chief Officer(s):
Jodi Zigelstein-Yip, President
president@hrpyr.org

Human Resources Professionals of Durham (HRPAD)
105 Consumers Dr., Whitby ON L1N 1C4
Tel: 905-721-9564; *Fax:* 647-689-2264
hrpad@adminedge.com
www.hrpad.org
twitter.com/HRPADurham
Overview: A small local organization
Mission: Advocates excellence in the leadership of Human Resources; provides opportunities for professional development and advancement; and promoting the Human Resources profession and designation.
Member of: Human Resources Professionals Association of Ontario
Chief Officer(s):
Tracey Starrett, President
Morgan Kerby, Vice-President
Membership: *Committees:* Professional Development; Membership; Communications; Education
Activities: *Awareness Events:* Annual Social, Dec.

Human Resources Professionals of Newfoundland & Labrador (HRPNL)
PO Box 21454, St. John's NL A1A 5G6
Tel: 709-351-4134
hrpnl@hrpnl.ca
www.hrpnl.ca
www.linkedin.com/groups/Human-Resources-Professionals-Newfoundland-Lab
Overview: A medium-sized provincial organization founded in 1994
Mission: Serves as a community of HR interest with a commitment to promoting the HR profession and advancing HR professionals.
Member of: Canadian Council of Human Resources Associations
Chief Officer(s):
Neil Coombs, President
president@hrpnl.ca
Leroy Murphy, Vice-President
vicepresident@hrpnl.ca
Kelly Gould, Contact, Administration
Membership: *Fees:* $120 annual; $60 half-year; $25 student

Human Rights & Race Relations Centre (HRRRC) / Centre des droits de la personne et des relations inter-raciales
#500, 120 Eglinton Ave. East, Toronto ON M4P 1E2
Tel: 416-481-7793
Toll-Free: 888-667-5877
humanrights@sympatico.ca
Overview: A medium-sized national organization founded in 1989
Mission: To uphold & protect human rights everywhere; to promote multiculturalism; To promote employment equity; to recognize & acknowledge excellence in race relations
Affiliation(s): Employment Equity Council; Canadian Association of Lawyers of Foreign Jurisdiction; Canada Flag & Unity Centre
Chief Officer(s):
Ismat Pasha, Secretary
Hasanat Ahmad Syed, President
Finances: *Annual Operating Budget:* $50,000-$100,000; *Funding Sources:* Donations
Staff Member(s): 4; 10 volunteer(s)
Membership: 1,000; *Fees:* $15; *Member Profile:* Mainly Canadian immigrants; *Committees:* Essay Competition
Activities: *Awareness Events:* Race Relations Day, March 21 & Oct. 15; *Speaker Service:* Yes; *Rents Mailing List:* Yes
Awards:
• Race Relations Gold Medals (Award)
• Essay Competition on How to Fight Racism (Award)
Publications:
• New Canada
Type: Newspaper; *Frequency:* Weekly
Profile: One of the oldest ethnic newspapers in Toronto, published since 1988

Human Rights & Race Relations Centre
#500, 120 Eglinton Ave. East, Toronto ON M4P 1E2
Tel: 416-481-7793
Toll-Free: 888-667-5877
humanrights@sympatico.ca
Previous Name: The South Journalists Club
Overview: A small local organization founded in 1994
Mission: To protect & work for the rights of journalists of South Asian origin
Chief Officer(s):
Hasanat Ahmad Syed, President
Finances: *Annual Operating Budget:* Less than $50,000
Staff Member(s): 1; 10 volunteer(s)
Membership: 40 individual; 5 associate; *Fees:* $10 student; $20 individual/associate
Activities: *Speaker Service:* Yes

Human Rights Internet (HRI) / Internet des droits humains
#1105, 1 Nicholas St., Ottawa ON K1N 7B7
Tel: 613-789-7407
info@hri.ca
www.hri.ca
Overview: A medium-sized international charitable organization founded in 1976
Mission: Consulting & capacity building organization committed to the promotion of human rights in the areas of social justice, good governance & conflict prevention
Affiliation(s): Network on International Human Rights
Chief Officer(s):
Hazel Postma, Chair
Finances: *Funding Sources:* International government
Membership: *Member Profile:* Non-governmental, inter-governmental organizations worldwide
Activities: *Internships:* Yes

Human Rights Research & Education Centre (HRREC) / Centre de recherche et d'enseignement sur les droits de la personne
University of Ottawa, Fauteux Hall, #550, 57 Louis Pasteur, Ottawa ON K1N 6N5
Tel: 613-562-5775; *Fax:* 613-562-5125
hrrec@uottawa.ca
www.cdp-hrc.uottawa.ca
www.facebook.com/265881216771281
Also Known As: Human Rights Centre
Overview: A medium-sized international organization founded in 1981
Mission: To further the discussion of the linkages between human rights, governance, legal reform & development; to support national human rights institutions; to improve social justice institutions/programs
Affiliation(s): University of Ottawa; Canadian Centre for International Justice; Canadian Civil Liberties Association; Canadian Commission for UNESCO; Canadian Red Cross; Interdisciplinary Research Laboratory on the Rights of the Child; Lique des droits et libertés; Office of the Prosecutor of the International Criminal Court
Chief Officer(s):
Penelope Simons, Acting Research Director
penelope.simons@uOttawa.ca
Finances: *Annual Operating Budget:* $1.5 Million-$3 Million; *Funding Sources:* University of Ottawa
Staff Member(s): 4; 3 volunteer(s)
Membership: 33
Activities: *Library:* HRREC Documentation Centre; Open to public

Humane Society International/Canada (HSI Canada)
#506, 460, rue St. Catherine ouest, Montréal ON H3B 1A7
Tel: 514-395-2914
info@hsicanada.ca
www.hsi.org/world/canada
www.facebook.com/hsiglobal
twitter.com/HSI_Canada
Overview: A large international organization
Mission: To protect all animals, including companion animals, farm animals, animals in the wild
Chief Officer(s):
Bruce Fogle, Chair, Humane Society International
Andrew Rowan, Ph.D., President & CEO, Humane Society International
Rebecca Aldworth, Executive Director, Humane Society International/Canada
Finances: *Funding Sources:* Donations
Activities: Engagging in advocacy, education, investigation, litigation & field work; programs including habitat protection, marine mammal preservation & farm animal welfare; projects to stop puppy mills, commercial sealing, confinement of farm animals, horse slaughter, trophy hunting & dog & cat fur; Animal Rescue Fund

Humane Society of Ottawa-Carleton *See* Ottawa Humane Society

Humane Society Yukon
126 Tlingit Rd., Whitehorse YT Y1A 6J2
Tel: 867-633-6019; *Fax:* 867-633-2210
shelter@northwestel.net
www.humanesocietyyukon.ca
www.facebook.com/153522391419947
Also Known As: Mae Bachur Animal Shelter
Overview: A medium-sized provincial organization founded in 1989 overseen by Canadian Federation of Humane Societies
Mission: To foster a caring, compassionate atmosphere; to promote a humane ethic & responsible pet ownership; to prevent & suppress cruelty to animals.
Chief Officer(s):
Hoby Irwin, President
Finances: *Funding Sources:* Public donations
Membership: *Fees:* $20 individual; $200 corporate
Activities: Public education; animal shelter; pet adoptions & rescue

Humanist Canada (HC) / Humaniste Canada (HC)
#1150, 45 O'Connor St., Ottawa ON K1P 1A4
Fax: 613-739-5969
Toll-Free: 877-486-2671
info@humanistcanada.com
www.humanistcanada.com
Also Known As: Humanist Association of Canada
Overview: A medium-sized national charitable organization founded in 1968
Mission: To bring together people who share a non-theistic view of the world; to educate the public about humanism & its ethics & values
Member of: Coalition for Secular Humanism & Free Thought
Affliation(s): International Humanist & Ethical Union (UK)
Finances: *Annual Operating Budget:* Less than $50,000; *Funding Sources:* Membership fees & donations
12 volunteer(s)
Membership: 800; *Fees:* $500 life; $50 household; $40 individual
Activities: Licensed officiants to perform legal marriages, funeral services; *Awareness Events:* Humanist of the Year; *Library:* HAC Library; by appointment
Awards:
• Humanist of the Year (Award)

Humaniste Canada *See* Humanist Canada

Humanities & Social Sciences Federation of Canada *See* Canadian Federation for Humanities & Social Sciences

Humanity First Canada
#40, 600 Bowes Rd., Concord ON L6A 4A3
Tel: 416-440-0346; *Fax:* 416-440-0346
info@humanityfirst.ca
www.humanityfirst.ca
Overview: A small international charitable organization founded in 2004
Mission: to provide hunmanitarian aid and to arrange response to disasters and help restore communities and help them build a

future in addition to relieve poverty by establishing, operating and maintaining training centres in developing countries.
Chief Officer(s):
Aslam Daud, President
Ejaz Khan, Secretary
Publications:
• Humanity Matters
Type: Newsletter; *Frequency:* Quarterly; *Accepts Advertising*; *Price:* Free
Profile: Articles about disasters & assistance provided, plus information about local events & fundraising efforts

Humboldt & District Chamber of Commerce
PO Box 1440, 201 - 8th Ave., Humboldt SK S0K 2A0
Tel: 306-682-4990; *Fax:* 306-682-5203
humboldtchamber@sasktel.net
www.humboldtchamber.ca
www.facebook.com/humboldtchamber
www.youtube.com/user/humboldtchamber
Overview: A small local organization
Member of: Saskatchewan Chamber of Commerce
Chief Officer(s):
Jodi Smith, President
DonnaLyn Thorsteinson, Executive Director
donnalyn@humboldtchamber.ca
Finances: *Annual Operating Budget:* $100,000-$250,000; *Funding Sources:* Membership dues
Membership: 120; *Committees:* Executive; Public Relations & Promotions; Business Retention & Expansion; Campground & Tourist Booth

Humboldt & District Labour Council
PO Box 4089, Humboldt SK S0K 2A0
Tel: 306-682-5253
Overview: A small local organization overseen by Saskatchewan Federation of Labour
Mission: To support union members & workers in Humboldt, Saskatchewan & the surrounding area; To advance the economic & social welfare of workers; To act as the voice of labour
Affiliation(s): Canadian Labour Congress (CLC)
Chief Officer(s):
Sandy Weyland, President
dsweyland@sasktel.net
Activities: Promoting the interests of affiliates; Liaising with local elected officials to ensure the issues of workers are heard; Offering educational programs, such as farm safety seminars;

Hungarian Canadian Cultural Centre
1170 Sheppard Ave. West, Toronto ON M3K 2A3
Tel: 416-654-4926
office@hccc.org
www.hccc-e.org
Also Known As: Hungarian House
Previous Name: Hungarian Canadian Federation
Overview: A small national charitable organization founded in 1945
Mission: To preserve & showcase Hungarian heritage in the Canadian mosaic.
Activities: Provides space, guidance & funding to several cultural & sports groups; *Library:* Hungarian Library; by appointment

Hungarian Canadian Engineers' Association (HCEA)
57 Drew Kelly Way, Markham ON L3R 5R2
Tel: 905-474-9225
magyar_mernok@kmme.org
kmme.org
Overview: A small national charitable organization founded in 1953
Finances: *Annual Operating Budget:* Less than $50,000
10 volunteer(s)
Membership: 165; *Fees:* $20-$50; *Member Profile:* Engineers; technicians, etc.
Activities: Monthly meetings

Hungarian Canadian Federation *See* Hungarian Canadian Cultural Centre

Hungarian Studies Association of Canada (HSAC) / Association canadienne des études hongroises
c/o Margit Lovrics, #1804, 75 Graydon Hall Dr., Toronto ON M3A 3M5
www.hungarianstudies.org
Also Known As: Kanadai Magyarsagtudományi Társaság
Overview: A small national organization founded in 1985
Mission: To study Hungarian culture & history at the academic level
Chief Officer(s):
Agatha Schwartz, Acting President
agathas@uottawa.ca
Nandor Dreisziger, Vice-President
nandor@kingston.net
Margit Lovrics, Treasurer
margitlovrics@gmail.com
Finances: *Funding Sources:* Membership fees
Membership: *Fees:* $45 regular; $30 retired & students; $75 family; *Member Profile:* Interested academics & professionals; *Committees:* Conference Program; Planning & Nominations; Publications
Activities: Annual conference; occasional special events
Awards:
• F. Harcsar Award (Award)
Meetings/Conferences: • 2015 Conference of the Hungarian Studies Association of Canada, May, 2015, University of Ottawa, Ottawa, ON
Description: Held in conjunction with the Congress of the Humanities & Social Sciences

The Hunger Project Canada / Le Projet Faim
11 O'Connor Dr., Toronto ON M4K 2K3
Tel: 416-429-0023
www.thehungerproject.ca
www.facebook.com/TheHungerProjectCanada
Also Known As: THP-Canada
Overview: A medium-sized international charitable organization founded in 1977
Mission: Committed to the sustainable end of world hunger
Member of: Canadian Council for International Cooperation
Chief Officer(s):
Malgorzata Smelkowska, Director

Huntington Society of Canada / Société Huntington du Canada
#400, 151 Frederick St., Kitchener ON N2H 2M2
Tel: 519-749-7063; *Fax:* 519-749-8965
Toll-Free: 800-998-7398
info@huntingtonsociety.ca
www.huntingtonsociety.ca
www.facebook.com/HuntingtonSC
twitter.com/HuntingtonSC
Overview: A medium-sized national charitable organization founded in 1973
Mission: To aspire for a world free of Huntington disease; To maximize the quality of life of people living with HD
Chief Officer(s):
Anne Brace, Chair
Sean Dewart, Secretary
Glenda Rowein, Treasurer
Bev Heim-Myers, Executive Director & CEO
bheimmyers@huntingtonsociety.ca
Cyndy Moffat Forsyth, Director, Development & Marketing
cmoffatforsyth@huntingtonsociety.ca
Finances: *Funding Sources:* Donations; Fundraising; Sponsorships
Staff Member(s): 32; 1000 volunteer(s)
Activities: Delivering services; Increasing understanding of the disease; Furthering research; *Awareness Events:* Amaryllis Month, Nov.; Annual Indy Go-Kart Challenge, September; Huntington Disease Awareness Month, May

British Columbia Chapter
c/o Centre for Huntington Disease, #S179, 2211 Wesbrook Mall, Vancouver BC V6T 2B5
Tel: 604-682-3269
britishcolumbiahd@gmail.com
www.britishcolumbiahd.ca
Chief Officer(s):
Manny Abecia, Co-President
mabecia@gmail.com
Graham Cook, Co-President
grahamc@sfu.ca

East Central Ontario Resource Centre
PO Box 103, 71 Old Kingston Rd., Ajax ON L1T 3A6
Tel: 905-426-4333
Toll-Free: 855-426-4333
Chief Officer(s):
Marilyn Mitchell, Director
mmitchell@huntingtonsociety.ca

Individual & Family Services
PO Box 32539, Richmond Hill ON L4C 9V0
Tel: 905-787-1645
Toll-Free: 877-573-7011
Chief Officer(s):
Rozi Andrejas, Director
randrejas@huntingtonsociety.ca

Manitoba Chapters
c/o Sandra Funk, 200 Woodlawn St., Winnipeg MB R3J 2H7
Tel: 204-772-4617; *Fax:* 204-940-8414
www.hdmanitoba.ca
Chief Officer(s):
Sandy Funk, Brandon Contact, 204-726-8323
sandson10@hotmail.com
Vern Barrett, Winnipeg Contact, 204-694-1779
vbarrett@mts.net

Manitoba Resource Centre
200 Woodlawn St., Winnipeg MB R3J 2H7
Tel: 204-772-4617; *Fax:* 204-940-8414
www.hdmanitoba.ca
Chief Officer(s):
Sandra Funk, Director
sfunk@huntingtonsociety.ca

Newfoundland/Labrador Resource Centre
NL
Tel: 709-745-1155
Toll-Free: 877-745-1155
Chief Officer(s):
Elaine Smith, Director
esmith@huntingtonsociety.ca

Northern Alberta Chapter - Peace Country
Peace Country AB
peacecountryhd.ca
Chief Officer(s):
Mack Erno, President, 780-897-8048
mack@jadecash.com
Candi Diepdael, Secretary/Treasurer, 780-402-8680
karlyn@telusplanet.net

Northern Alberta Resource Centre
c/o St. Joseph's Auxiliary Hospital, 10707 - 29th Ave., Edmonton AB T6J 6W1
Tel: 780-434-3229
Chief Officer(s):
Bernadette Modrovsky, Director
bmodrovsky@huntingtonsociety.ca

Northern Ontario Resource Centre
PO Box 1072, Chelmsford ON P0M 1L0
Tel: 705-897-1969; *Fax:* 705-897-3026
Toll-Free: 855-897-1969
Chief Officer(s):
Angèle Bénard, Director
abenard@huntingtonsociety.ca

Nova Scotia & PEI Chapters - Atlantic
Halifax NS
Chief Officer(s):
Jim Russell, President, Nova Scotia, 902-576-5660
jimrussell@eastlink.ca
Danny Drouin, President, PEI, 902-853-3066
ddrouin@pei.sympatico.ca

Nova Scotia & PEI Resource Centre
West End Mall, #2077, 6960 Mumford Rd., Halifax NS B3L 4P1
Tel: 902-446-4803
Chief Officer(s):
Barbara Horner, Director
bhorner@huntingtonsociety.ca

Saskatoon & Area
PO Box 23079, 2325 Preston Ave., Saskatoon SK S7J 3H5
Tel: 306-979-9111
hdsaskatoon@gmail.com
www.facebook.com/HuntingtonSocietyOfCanadaSaskatoon
Chief Officer(s):
Cam Heintz, President

Southern Alberta Chapter
AB
www.southernalbertahd.ca

Southern Alberta Resource Centre
Westech Bldg., #102, 5636 Burbank Cres. SE, Calgary AB T2H 1Z6
Tel: 403-532-0609
Chief Officer(s):
Shannon MacKinnon, Director
smackinnon@huntingtonsociety.ca

Toronto Chapter
c/o HSC National Office, #400, 151 Frederick St., Kitchener ON N2H 2M2

Toll-Free: 800-998-7398
info@hdtoronto.org
www.hdtoronto.org
Chief Officer(s):
Tim Irwin, President
West Central Ontario Resource Centre
#400, 151 Frederick St., Kitchener ON N2H 2M2
Tel: 519-576-6102
Toll-Free: 866-796-8016
Chief Officer(s):
Maike Zinabou, Director
mzinabou@huntingtonsociety.ca

Huntington Society of Québec *Voir* Société Huntington du Québec

Huntley Township Historical Society
PO Box 313, Carp ON K0A 1L0
e-mail: HuntleyHistory@gmx.net
www.huntleyhistory.ca
Overview: A small local charitable organization founded in 1987
Mission: To gather, preserve & display to the public information pertaining to the history of the former Huntley Township & its people
Affiliation(s): Ontario Historical Society
Finances: *Funding Sources:* Membership dues; grants; book sales; provincial & municipal funding
Membership: *Fees:* $25 regular; US$25 foreign; *Member Profile:* Interest in local history
Activities: *Library:* Resource Centre at Carp Branch, Ottawa Public Library; Open to public

Huntsville & District Association for the Mentally Retarded *See* Community Living Huntsville

Huntsville & Lake of Bays Railway Society
88 Brunel Rd., Huntsville ON P1H 1R1
Tel: 705-789-7576; *Fax:* 705-789-6169
www.portageflyer.org
Also Known As: The Portage Railway
Overview: A small local charitable organization founded in 1984
Mission: Maintains & displays original artifacts of the old Huntsville & Lake of Bays Railway, plus vintage railway equipment of the turn of the century
Affliation(s): Muskoka Heritage Place
Chief Officer(s):
David Topps, President
president@portageflyer.org
Finances: *Funding Sources:* Fundraising; Rotary Club; local industry; donations
Membership: *Fees:* $35 regular; $45 foreign
Activities: A fully functional operating railway

Huntsville, Lake of Bays Chamber of Commerce
8 West St. North, Huntsville ON P1H 2B6
Tel: 705-789-4771; *Fax:* 705-789-6191
chamber@huntsvillelakeofbays.on.ca
huntsvillelakeofbays.on.ca
www.facebook.com/HLOBChamber
twitter.com/HuntsvilleChamb
Overview: A small local organization
Mission: To help with the economic growth of their members
Member of: Canadian Chamber of Commerce
Chief Officer(s):
Kelly Haywood, Executive Director, 705-789-4771 Ext. 22
kelly@huntsvillelakeofbays.on.ca
Staff Member(s): 8
Membership: *Fees:* $75 non-profit; $178 1 employee; $230 2-10 employees; $288 11-40 employees; $558 40+ employees

Huron Chamber of Commerce - Goderich, Central & North Huron
36 North St., Goderich ON N7A 2T4
Tel: 519-440-0176; *Fax:* 519-440-0305
www.goderichchamber.ca
www.facebook.com/huronchamber
twitter.com/huronchamber
Previous Name: Goderich & District Chamber of Commerce
Overview: A small local organization
Mission: To promote & improve trade & commerce & the economic, civic & social welfare of the Goderich, Central & North Huron regions
Member of: Ontario Chamber of Commerce
Chief Officer(s):
Laura Herman, President
Judy Crawford, CEO
judy@huronchamber.ca
Finances: *Annual Operating Budget:* Less than $50,000; *Funding Sources:* Membership fees
Membership: 70; *Fees:* Schedule available

Huron East Chamber of Commerce
c/o Ralph Laviolette, PO Box 433, Seaforth ON N0K 1W0
Tel: 519-440-6206
www.huroneastcc.ca
Overview: A small local organization
Mission: To act as a voice for its members
Member of: Canadian Chamber of Commerce
Chief Officer(s):
Ralph Laviolette, Secretary
Membership: 67

Huron Perth Association of Realtors
#6, 55 Lorne Ave. East, Stratford ON N5A 6S4
Tel: 519-271-6870; *Fax:* 519-271-3040
www.hpar.ca
Merged from: Huron Real Estate Board; Perth County Real Estate Board
Overview: A small local organization overseen by Ontario Real Estate Association
Mission: To maintain a professional standard among its members in order to better serve the public
Member of: The Canadian Real Estate Association
Chief Officer(s):
Gwen Kirkpatrick, Executive Officer
gwen@wightman.ca
Membership: 252

Huronia & District Beekeepers' Association (HDBA)
c/o Peter Dickey, Dickey Bee Honey Inc., 4031 - 3rd Line., Cookstown ON L0L 1L0
Tel: 705-458-1258
www.huroniabeekeepers.com
www.facebook.com/huroniabeekeepers
Overview: A small local organization
Mission: To inform members of current developments in beekeeping
Member of: Ontario Beekeepers' Association
Chief Officer(s):
Peter Dickey, President
Membership: *Fees:* $30; *Member Profile:* Persons from the Huronia area who are dedicated to the practice of keeping honey bees
Activities: Organizing lectures, meetings, beekeeping field trips, seminars, & demonstrations; Providing networking opportunities with professional & amateur beekeepers; Recommending literature about beekeeping to members; Offering beekeeping mentors to teach beginners interested in beekeeping
Publications:
• Bee Talker
Type: Newsletter

Huronia Symphony Orchestra (HSO)
PO Box 904, Stn. Main, Barrie ON L4M 4Y6
Tel: 705-721-4752
office@huroniasymphony.ca
www.huroniasymphony.ca
www.facebook.com/huroniasymphony
twitter.com/huroniasymphony
Overview: A small local charitable organization founded in 1966 overseen by Orchestras Canada
Mission: To operate & support a symphony orchestra in Simcoe County; to provide symphonic music for people of the area as well as an opportunity for children & youth to receive instruction in orchestral music
Chief Officer(s):
John Hemsted, President
Don MacLeod, General Manager
Finances: *Funding Sources:* Donations; ticket revenue; grants
Membership: 55; *Committees:* Logistics; Marketing; Human Resources; Youth Program; Artistic Advisory
Activities: *Awareness Events:* Huronia Golf Classic, Sept.; Viennese Gala, Oct.

Huronia Tourism Association *See* Tourism Simcoe County

Huron-Perth Beekeepers' Association
Wingham ON
Tel: 519-395-0248
Overview: A small local organization
Mission: To provide education about beekeeping; To promote the beekeeping industry in Huron-Perth
Member of: Ontario Beekeepers' Association
Chief Officer(s):
Bill Higgins, Contact
whiggins@sympatico.ca
Membership: *Member Profile:* Beekeepers in the Huron-Perth area of Ontario
Activities: Offering networking opportunities for members; Helping local beekeepers deal with problems that arise for beekeepers

Hussar Fish & Game Association
c/o Alberta Fish & Game Association, 6924 - 104th St., Edmonton AB T6H 2L7
Tel: 780-437-2342; *Fax:* 780-438-6872
office@afga.org
www.afga.org/html/content/clubandzones
Overview: A small local organization
Member of: Alberta Fish & Game Association
Chief Officer(s):
Deb Clarke, Director, Zone 2, Alberta Fish & Game Association

Hydro-Québec Foundation for the Environment *Voir* Fondation Hydro-Québec pour l'environnement

Hydro-Québec Professional Engineers Union (Ind.) *Voir* Syndicat professionnel des ingénieurs d'Hydro-Québec (ind.)

Hypertension Canada
c/o Judi Farrell, #211, 3780 - 14th Ave., Markham ON L3R 9Y5
Tel: 905-943-9400; *Fax:* 905-943-9401
www.hypertension.ca
twitter.com/HTNCANADA
www.youtube.com/user/hypertensioncanada
Merged from: Blood Pressure Canada; Canadian Hypertension Society; & Canadian Hypertension Education Program
Overview: A medium-sized national organization
Mission: To advance health by preventing & controlling high blood presseure
Chief Officer(s):
Ernesto Schiffrin, President
Angelique Berg, Chief Executive Officer
Laura Syron, Vice-President
Robert Brooks, Treasurer
Finances: *Funding Sources:* Membership fees: Donations; Sponsorships
Membership: *Fees:* $25 associates (fellows, residents, medical student, or graduate students); $100 individuals; *Member Profile:* Professionals who support goals of Hypertension Canada; Individuals in training for practice in the field of hypertension; Pharmaceutical industries & other companies with an interest in hypertension
Activities: Supporting research; Engaging in advocacy activities; Providing education
Meetings/Conferences: • Canadian Hypertension Congress 2015, October, 2015, Hilton Toronto Airport Hotel and Suites, Toronto, ON
Scope: National
Publications:
• Hypertension Therapeutic Guide
Type: Textbook
Profile: A reference tool to help physicians, nurses, & pharmacistsin the management of hypertension

IAB Internet Advertising Bureau of Canada *See* Interactive Advertising Bureau of Canada

IAESTE Canada (International Association for the Exchange of Students for Technical Experience) (IAESTE)
c/o Gordon Hall, Queens University, 74 Union St., Kingston ON K7L 3N6
Tel: 613-533-2992; *Fax:* 613-533-2535
canada@iaeste.org
www.queensu.ca/iaeste
Overview: A small international organization founded in 1953
Mission: To provide technical students with international work experience related to their studies
Member of: IAESTE International
Affiliation(s): International Association for the Exchange of Students for Technical Experience
Chief Officer(s):
Michele Lee, National Secretary
Finances: *Annual Operating Budget:* $100,000-$250,000
Staff Member(s): 2; 4 volunteer(s)
Membership: 80+ countries

IAMAW District 78
#102, 557 Dixon Rd., Etobicoke ON M9W 6K1

Tel: 416-225-9003
iamdl78.org
Previous Name: Northern Independent Union
Overview: A small provincial organization
Member of: International Association of Machinists & Aerospace Workers
Chief Officer(s):
Terry Rennette, President

I.C.C. Foundation
#1001, 75 Albert St., Ottawa ON K1P 5E7
Tel: 613-563-2642; *Fax:* 613-565-3089
icc@inuitcircumpolar.com
www.inuitcircumpolar.com
Also Known As: Inuit Circumpolar Council
Overview: A small national charitable organization
Mission: To promote Inuit culture in Canada & the circumpolar region, & the knowledge of its members concerning social, economic & cultural studies of same
Chief Officer(s):
Corinne Gray, Executive Director
cgray@inuitcircumpolar.com

Ice Skating Association of Ontario *See* Ontario Speed Skating Association

Icelandic National League of North America (INL/NA)
#103, 94 - 1st Ave., Gimli MB R0C 1B1
Tel: 204-642-5897
inl@mymts.net
www.inlofna.org
www.facebook.com/115047545201629
Overview: A medium-sized national organization founded in 1918
Mission: To foster & promote good citizenship among people of Icelandic descent; to foster & strengthen a mutual understanding of kinship, language, literature & cultural bonds among people of Icelandic origin & descent in North America & the people of Iceland; to cooperate with organizations which have similar purposes & objectives; to actively support various cultural & ethnic developments including education, history, publishing & the arts
Chief Officer(s):
Gail Einarson-McCleery, President
arsonmccleery@gmail.com
Gwen Grattan, Executive Secretary
Finances: *Annual Operating Budget:* Less than $50,000; *Funding Sources:* Membership fees; donations
Membership: 2,000; *Fees:* $25 individual; $100 affiliate club; chapters - formula

ICOM Musées Canada *See* ICOM Museums Canada

ICOM Museums Canada / ICOM Musées Canada
#400, 280 Metcalfe St., Ottawa ON K2P 1R7
Tel: 613-567-0099
www.linkedin.com/groups/ICOM-Canada-4263110
www.facebook.com/150364635019516
twitter.com/ICOMCanada
Also Known As: International Council of Museums
Overview: A medium-sized national charitable organization founded in 1946
Mission: To advance the cause of museums throughout the world & in Canada; to provide liaison with International Council of Museums in Paris; to hold annual meeting in conjunction with Canadian Museums Association.
Member of: Canadian Museums Association & Société des musées québécois
Chief Officer(s):
Audrey Vermette, Director, Programs & Public Affairs
avermette@museums.ca
Finances: *Funding Sources:* Membership dues
Membership: *Member Profile:* Museologists
Activities: *Library* Open to public

ICOMOS Canada
PO Box 737, Stn. B, Ottawa ON K1P 5P8
Tel: 613-749-0971; *Fax:* 613-749-0971
canada@icomos.org
canada.icomos.org
Also Known As: International Council on Monuments & Sites Canada
Overview: A medium-sized international organization founded in 1975
Mission: To further the conservation, protection, rehabilitation, & enhancement of monuments, groups of buildings & sites; To encourage primary research in many important fields
Affiliation(s): UNESCO; International Centre for the Study of the Preservation & Restoration of Cultural Property (ICCROM)
Chief Officer(s):
Dinu Bumbaru, President
Alain Dejeans, Vice-président, Comité francophone
John Ward, Vice President, English Speaking Committee
Finances: *Annual Operating Budget:* Less than $50,000
Staff Member(s): 1
Membership: 500; *Fees:* $85 individual; $30 students & friends; institutional available; *Member Profile:* Conservation professionals & advocates concerned with developing & promoting, through international exchange, the highest professional standards of practice in the conservation of the built environment; *Committees:* National Committees which bring together professionals in each country
Activities: Researching; Communicating; Providing professional services
Publications:
• eCOMoS [a publication of the ICOMOS Canada]
Type: Newsletter

Ikaluktutiak Paddling Association
PO Box 125, Cambridge Bay NU X0B 0C0
Tel: 867-983-2068
ipanorth69@gmail.com
Overview: A small provincial organization
Member of: Paddle Canada
Chief Officer(s):
Rob Harmer, President

Ile-a-la-Crosse Friendship Centre
PO Box 160, Lajeunesse Ave., Ile-a-la-Crosse SK S0M 1C0
Tel: 306-833-2313; *Fax:* 306-833-2216
ilx.friendctr.inc@sasktel.net
www.facebook.com/4925553507971
Overview: A small local organization founded in 1992
Mission: The Centre provides referrals, information, social, cultural, health awareness & sports & recreational programs to help ensure a better quality of life for the community & area.
Member of: Aboriginal Friendship Centres of Saskatchewan; National Association of Friendship Centres
Chief Officer(s):
Martin Durocher, Contact

Ileostomy & Colostomy Association of Montréal (ICAM) / Association d'iléostomie et colostomie de Montréal (AICM)
5151, boul de l'Assomption, Montréal QC H1T 4A9
Tel: 514-255-3041; *Fax:* 514-645-5464
www.aicm-montreal.org
Overview: A small local charitable organization founded in 1958
Mission: To act for the welfare for ostomates & their families
Affiliation(s): United Ostomy Association of Canada Inc.
Chief Officer(s):
Jean-Pierre Lapointe, President & Treasurer, 514-645-4023
Nancy Brockwell, Vice-President, 450-824-1858
Huguette Fortier, Secretary, 514-355-1245
Finances: *Funding Sources:* Donations; Sponsorships
Membership: *Fees:* $20 regular members
Activities: Hosting monthly meetings; Providing information to members & the public; Organizing social activities

Imagine Canada
#600, 2 Carlton St., Toronto ON M5B 1J3
Tel: 416-597-2293; *Fax:* 416-597-2294
Toll-Free: 800-263-1178
info@imaginecanada.ca
www.imaginecanada.ca
www.linkedin.com/groups/Imagine-Canada-1866345
www.facebook.com/ImagineCanada
twitter.com/ImagineCanada
www.youtube.com/ImagineCanada
Merged from: Canadian Centre for Philanthropy; Coalition of National Voluntary Organizations
Overview: A large national charitable organization founded in 1980
Mission: To support Canada's charities, non-profit organizations, & socially conscious businesses
Chief Officer(s):
Faye Wightman, Chair
Marcel Lauzière, President & CEO
mlauziere@imaginecanada.ca
Cathy Barr, Senior Vice-President
cbarr@imaginecanada.ca
Stephen Faul, Vice-President, Strategic Communications & Business Development
Michelle Gauthier, Vice-President, Public Policy & Community Engagement, 613-238-7555
mgauthier@imaginecanada.ca
Marnie Grona, Director, Marketing & Communications, 416-597-2293 Ext. 244
mgrona@imaginecanada.ca
Finances: *Funding Sources:* Foundations; Corporations; Government; Earned income; Donations
20 volunteer(s)
Membership: 1,250; *Fees:* $100-$1,000 depending on type & size of organization; *Member Profile:* Charities, foundations & businesses
Activities: Conducting research about the charitable sector; Providing information resources; *Library:* John Hodgson Library; by appointment

Calgary
#600, 635 Eighth Ave. SW, Calgary AB T2P 3M3
Tel: 800-263-1178

Ottawa
#1705, 130 Albert St., Ottawa ON K1P 5G4
Tel: 613-238-7555; *Fax:* 613-238-9300
Toll-Free: 800-263-1178

Québec
Tel: 800-263-1178

Immigrant & Multicultural Services Society (IMSS)
1270 - 2nd Ave., Prince George BC V2L 3B3
Tel: 250-562-2900; *Fax:* 250-563-4852
Toll-Free: 877-562-2977
imss.pg@shawcable.com
www.imss.ca
www.facebook.com/274005189316931
Overview: A small provincial charitable organization founded in 1976
Mission: The Society works to promote multiculturalism & to develop cross-cultural understanding in the community. It acts as a central resource & information center for smaller agencies & professionals, & the agency also provides orientation counselling & assistance to immigrants in this northern region of the province. It is a registered charity, BN: 107504045RR0001.
Member of: Affiliation of Multicultural Societies & Service Agencies of BC
Chief Officer(s):
Ben Levine, President
Baljit Sethi, Executive Director
baljit.imss@shawcable.com
Ann Saa, Settlement Practitioner/Executive Assistant
ann@imss.ca
Finances: *Annual Operating Budget:* $500,000-$1.5 Million; *Funding Sources:* Provincial and Federal government
Staff Member(s): 25; 30 volunteer(s)
Membership: 80; *Fees:* $10
Activities: English Language Services for Adults; Youth Against Racism; Employment Assistance Program; Settlement Program; Women's Program; information & referral services; computer classes; *Awareness Events:* BC Multicultural Week, November

Immigrant & Visible Minority Women Against Abuse *See* Immigrant Women Services Ottawa

Immigrant Centre Manitoba Inc.
100 Adelaide St., Winnipeg MB R3A 0W2
Tel: 204-943-9158; *Fax:* 204-949-0734
info@icmanitoba.com
icmanitoba.com
Also Known As: International Centre of Winnipeg
Previous Name: Citizenship Council of Manitoba Inc.
Overview: A medium-sized provincial charitable organization founded in 1965
Mission: To encourage pride in Canada & appreciation of Canadian citizenship; to encourage intercultural understanding in multicultural Canada; to support immigration & provide caring services to newcomers.
Member of: Canadian Citizenship Federation
Affiliation(s): Canadian Council for Refugees; Canadian Citizenship Federation
Chief Officer(s):
Cec Hanec, President
Finances: *Annual Operating Budget:* $1.5 Million-$3 Million; *Funding Sources:* Federal government; Provincial government; United Way
Staff Member(s): 34; 300 volunteer(s)
Membership: 70 corporate + 130 individual; *Fees:* $10 individual; $25 group
Activities: Immigrant serving agency; multicultural centre; hostels & residences

Immigrant Services - Guelph Wellington
#4 & 5, 926 Paisley Rd., Guelph ON N1K 1X5
Tel: 519-836-2222
info@is-gw.ca
www.is-gw.ca
Previous Name: Guelph & District Multicultural Centre
Overview: A small local organization founded in 1976 overseen by Ontario Council of Agencies Serving Immigrants
Mission: To help settle & integrate newcomers into their community; to encourage individuals to participate fully in all aspects of society, social, economic, political & cultural.
Chief Officer(s):
Roger Manning, President
Roya Rabbani, Executive Director
Finances: *Annual Operating Budget:* $500,000-$1.5 Million; *Funding Sources:* Citizenship & Immigration Canada; Canadian Heritage; National Crime Prevention Centre; United Way of Guelph & Wellington; City of Guelph
Staff Member(s): 21
Activities: Settlement integration; citizenship program; interpreter & translation services; anti-racism program; employment services; language assessment; *Awareness Events:* Guelph Multicultural Festival

Immigrant Services Association of Nova Scotia (ISANS)
Mumford Professional Centre, #2120, 6960 Mumford Rd., Halifax NS B3L 4P1
Tel: 902-423-3607; *Fax:* 902-423-3154
Toll-Free: 866-431-6472
info@isans.ca
www.isans.ca
facebook.com/isans.ca
www.twitter.com/isans_ca
vimeo.com/isans
Previous Name: Immigrant Settlement & Integration Services (ISIS)
Merged from: Metropolitan Immigrant Settlement Association (MISA); Halifax Immigrant Learning Centre (HILC)
Overview: A medium-sized provincial organization founded in 1980
Mission: To assist immigrants settling in Nova Scotia
Chief Officer(s):
Catharine Penney, Chair
Colin MacLean, Vice-Chair
Merlin Fownes, Secretary-Treasurer
Finances: *Annual Operating Budget:* Greater than $5 Million; *Funding Sources:* Provincial & federal government grants; United Way; Family Learning Initiative Endowment Fund
Staff Member(s): 115
Activities: Refugee resettlement; Professional programs; Family counselling; English in the Workplace;

Immigrant Services Calgary (CIAS)
#1200, 910 - 7th Ave. SW., Calgary AB T2P 3N8
Tel: 403-265-1120; *Fax:* 403-266-2486
info@calgaryimmigrantaid.ca
www.immigrantservicescalgary.ca
www.linkedin.com/company/immigrant-services-calgary
www.facebook.com/ImmigrantServicesCalgary
twitter.com/askISCmmigrantServicesCalgary
Previous Name: Calgary Immigrant Aid Society
Overview: A small local charitable organization founded in 1977
Mission: To offer information to newcomers & helps them to settle in, find employment, access language training, send children to Canadian schools, & become a part of the Calgary community.
Member of: Canadian Citizenship Federation
Chief Officer(s):
Wilson Ho, Chair
Krystyna Biel, CEO
Finances: *Funding Sources:* Federal/provincial/local government; foundations; IDA & casino
Staff Member(s): 150; 730 volunteer(s)
Membership: *Fees:* $5
Activities: Certified translation; interpretation services; language assessment; career counseling
Awards:
• Immigrants of Distinction Awards (Award)
Publications:
• ESL Directory
Type: guide
Profile: A general guide to ESL programs & services offered around Calgary

Immigrant Services Society of BC (ISSofBC)
#501, 333 Terminal Ave., Vancouver BC V6A 2L7
Tel: 604-684-2561; *Fax:* 604-684-2266
iss@issbc.org
www.issbc.org
www.facebook.com/issbc
Overview: A small provincial charitable organization founded in 1972
Mission: To be a leader in identifying the needs of immigrants & refugees & in developing, demonstrating & delivering effective, quality programs & services which serve those needs; to provide integration services; to deliver educational programs; to advocate for our clients & communities
Member of: Affiliation of Multicultural Societies & Service Agencies of BC; Assn. of Service Providers for Employability & Career Training; Better Business Bureau; Canadian Council for Refugees; Volunteer Vancouver; Vancouver Refugee Council
Chief Officer(s):
Manchan Sonachansingh, President
Finances: *Annual Operating Budget:* Greater than $5 Million
Staff Member(s): 220; 600 volunteer(s)
Membership: 150; *Fees:* $10 individual; $50-$1,000 corporate; $25 non-profit; *Committees:* Bursary; Community Relations; Executive; Finance; Governance; Membership; Nominations; Personnel; Premises
Activities: *Awareness Events:* Refugee Children's Christmas Party
Awards:
• Susan Paulson Bursary Award (Award)

Burnaby - Settlement Services
#207, 7355 Canada Way, Burnaby BC V3N 4Z6
Tel: 604-395-8000; *Fax:* 604-395-8003
settlement@issbc.org

Coquitlam - Career & Settlement Services
#240A, 3020 Lincoln Ave., Coquitlam BC V3B 6B4
Tel: 778-284-7026; *Fax:* 604-942-1730
employment.outreach@issbc.org

Coquitlam - ELSA
#136, 3030 Lincoln Ave., Coquitlam BC V3B 6B4
Tel: 604-942-1777; *Fax:* 604-942-1780
elsa.tricities@issbc.org

Langley - Settlement Services
#204, 20621 Logan Ave., Langley BC V3A 3Y9
Tel: 604-510-5136
settlement@issbc.org

Maple Ridge - ELSA & Settlement Services
#320, 22470 Dewdney Trunk Rd., Maple Ridge BC V2X 5Z6
Tel: 604-942-1777; *Fax:* 604-477-1154
settlement@issbc.org

New Westminster - ELSA & Settlement Services
#200, 620 Roayl Ave., New Westminster BC V3M 1J2
Tel: 604-522-5902; *Fax:* 604-522-5908
elsa.nwest@issbc.org

Port Coquitlam - ELSA & Career Services
#204, 3242 Westwood St., Port Coquitlam BC V3C 3L8
Tel: 604-942-1777; *Fax:* 604-942-1780
elsa.tricities@issbc.org

Richmond - ELSA
#150, 8400 Alexandra Rd., Richmond BC V6X 3I4
Tel: 604-233-7077; *Fax:* 604-233-7046
elsa.richmond@issbc.org

Richmond - ELSA
#110, 5751 Cedarbridge Way, Richmond BC V6X 2A*
Tel: 604-233-7077; *Fax:* 604-303-8711
elsa.richmond@issbc.org

Squamish - ELSA
38085 - 2nd Ave., 1st Fl., Squamish BC V8B 0C3
Tel: 604-567-4490
zoriana.fry@issbc.org

Surrey - Career Services
#303, 7337 - 137th St., Surrey BC V3W 1A4
Tel: 604-595-4021; *Fax:* 604-595-4028
joboptions@issbc.org

Vancouver - Welcome House & Settlement Services
530 Drake St., Vancouver BC V6B 2H3
Tel: 604-684-7498; *Fax:* 604-684-5683
settlement@issbc.org

Immigrant Settlement & Integration Services (ISIS) ***See*** Immigrant Services Association of Nova Scotia

Immigrant Women of Saskatchewan ***See*** Regina Immigrant Women Centre

Immigrant Women of Saskatchewan, Saskatoon Chapter
See International Women of Saskatoon

Immigrant Women Services Ottawa (IWSO) / Services pour femmes immigrantes d'Ottawa
#400, 219 Argyle St., Ottawa ON K2P 2H4
Tel: 613-729-3145; *Fax:* 613-729-9308
infomail@immigrantwomenservices.com
www.immigrantwomenservices.com
www.facebook.com/immigrantwomenservicesottawa
twitter.com/ImmigrantWomen
Previous Name: Immigrant & Visible Minority Women Against Abuse
Overview: A small local organization founded in 1989
Mission: To empower & enable immigrant women in the Ottawa region to participate in the elimination of all forms of abuse against women; to raise awareness among immigrant women who are abused, in order to break down their isolation & enable them to advocate on their own behalf; to develop a crisis service for immigrant women who are abused to give them full access to mainstream resources; to develop cross-cultural training for shelters & mainstream agencies regarding the special needs of immigrant women in order to ensure that existing services are accessible & appropriate to them & their families; to educate immigrant communities to work toward ending violence against women.
Activities: Information & referrals to services; crisis counselling & group support; cultural interpretation to communicate with service agencies;

Immigrant Women's Health Centre (IWHC)
#200, 489 College St., Toronto ON M6G 1A5
Tel: 416-323-9986; *Fax:* 416-323-0447
info@immigranthealth.info
immigranthealth.info
Overview: A small local charitable organization founded in 1975 overseen by Ontario Council of Agencies Serving Immigrants
Mission: To help immigrant & refugee women who have difficulty accessing health services due to cultural, physical, economic, linguistic, political, racial, sexual orientation, age & religious barriers.
Member of: Ontario Sexual Health Network; Metro Network for Social Justice; Toronto Health Coalition
Chief Officer(s):
Ayesha Adhami, Administrative Coordinator
aadhami@immigranthealth.info
Activities: Free clinical services; workshops at ESL classes, factories, schools, support groups, etc.; mobile clinic

Immigrant Women's Job Placement Centre ***See*** Toronto Community Employment Services

Immunisation Canada ***See*** Immunize Canada

Immunize Canada / Immunisation Canada
#404, 1525 Carling Ave., Ottawa ON K1Z 8R9
Tel: 613-725-3769; *Fax:* 613-725-9826
immunize@cpha.ca
immunize.ca
www.facebook.com/ImmunizeCanada
twitter.com/immunizedotca
www.youtube.com/user/ImmunizeCanada
Previous Name: Canadian Coalition for Immunization Awareness & Promotion
Overview: A small national organization founded in 2004
Mission: To contribute to the control/elimination/eradication of vaccine preventable diseases in Canada by increasing awareness of the benefits & risks of immunization for all ages.
Chief Officer(s):
Susan Bowles, BSc, Phm, Pharm, Chair
Shelly McNeil, MD, FRCPC, Vice-Chair
Finances: *Annual Operating Budget:* $250,000-$500,000; *Funding Sources:* NGOs; federal government; private sector
Staff Member(s): 2
Membership: 31; *Member Profile:* NGOs; federal government; private sector
Activities: *Awareness Events:* National Immunization Awareness Week, April; Influenza Awareness Month, Oct.

Impact Society
5050A Skyline Way NE, Calgary AB T2E 6v1
Tel: 403-280-1856; *Fax:* 403-250-1905
Toll-Free: 888-224-3762
info@impactsociety.com
www.impactsociety.com
www.facebook.com/157828990911059

twitter.com/Impact_Society
www.youtube.com/heroesimpact
Overview: A small national organization
Mission: To provide leadership & innovation for character development across Canada; To offer a framework of support for youth & the persons who influence them
Chief Officer(s):
Jack Toth, Chief Executive Officer, 403-280-1856 Ext. 15
Jeff Sterzuk, Vice President, Development & External Relations, 403-280-1856 Ext. 22
John Bullock, Manager, New Program Initiatives, 403-280-1856 Ext. 24
Jaralyn Monkman, Director, Programs, 403-280-1856 Ext. 16
Finances: *Funding Sources:* United Way; Donations; Grants; Sponsorships; Agencies; Fundraising
Activities: Offer experiential-learning programs, such as the HEROES Across Canada program, to help youth discover what's already inside them—greatness. Focus on every student's unique skills & abilities.; *Awareness Events:* Night of Impact gala fund; *Speaker Service:* Yes
Publications:
• Impact Update
Type: Newsletter
Profile: Reports of the Society's work across Canada

Imperial Order Daughters of the Empire *See* IODE Canada

IMS Health Canada
16720 Route Transcanadienne, Kirkland QC H9H 5M3
Tel: 514-428-6000; *Fax:* 514-428-6086
imshealth@ca.imshealth.com
www.imshealthcanada.com
Overview: A small national organization founded in 1960
Mission: A provider of business intelligence and strategic consulting services for the pharmaceutical and healthcare industries.
Chief Officer(s):
Murray Aitken, Executive Director

The In Community
#110, 1150 Morrison Dr., Ottawa ON K2H 8S9
Tel: 613-724-5886; *Fax:* 613-724-5889
Other Communication: Online resource centre, URL: www.disabilityinfo.ca
info@theincommunity.ca
www.theincommunity.ca
Previous Name: Disabled Persons Community Resources
Overview: A small local charitable organization founded in 1957
Mission: To provide programs & servces that maximize opportunities for the contribution, participation & inclusion of people with physical disabilities within the city of Ottawa
Chief Officer(s):
Matthew Cole, President
Teena Tomlinson, Executive Director
ttomlinson@theincommunity.ca
Finances: *Annual Operating Budget:* $1.5 Million-$3 Million; *Funding Sources:* Provincial government
Staff Member(s): 120; 30 volunteer(s)
Membership: 15; *Fees:* $15

In Kind Canada
#165, 215 Spadina Rd., Toronto ON M5T 2C7
Tel: 416-628-9173
www.inkindcanada.ca
twitter.com/inkindcanada
Overview: A medium-sized national charitable organization
Mission: Matches surplus goods & services from within Canadian businesses with needs within Canadian charities
Chief Officer(s):
John Page, Executive Director
Membership: 1200; *Member Profile:* Charitable organizations

INAS (Canada) *See* Patronato INAS (Canada)

INCA *See* Canadian National Institute for the Blind

Incident Prevention Association of Manitoba (IPAM)
#51, 162 - 2025 Corydon Ave., Winnipeg MB R3P 0N5
Tel: 204-275-3727
office@ipam-manitoba.com
ipam-manitoba.com
Overview: A small provincial organization founded in 1961
Chief Officer(s):
Karen Turner, President, 204-582-3932
protec1@mymts.net
Membership: *Member Profile:* Government & individuals in the Province of Manitoba, who are interested in health and safety
Meetings/Conferences: • Safety Saves Conference & Tradeshow 2015, October, 2015, Canad Inns Polo Park, MB
Scope: Provincial
Contact Information: Kristin Petaski; Kristin@workengsolutions.ca

Inclusion BC
227 - 6th St., New Westminster BC V3L 3A5
Tel: 604-777-9100; *Fax:* 604-777-9394
Toll-Free: 800-618-1119
info@inclusionbc.org
www.inclusionbc.org
www.facebook.com/pages/Inclusion-BC/112557852110381
twitter.com/InclusionBC
www.youtube.com/user/BCACL
Previous Name: British Columbia Association for Community Living; British Columbians for Mentally Handicapped People
Overview: A medium-sized provincial charitable organization founded in 1955 overseen by Canadian Association for Community Living
Mission: To enhance the lives of persons with developmental disabilities & their families; To promote the participation of people with developmental disabilities in all aspects of community life; To support activities dedicated to building inclusive communities that value the diverse abilities of all people
Member of: Canadian Association for Community Living; United Way of Lower Mainland
Chief Officer(s):
Annette Delaplace, President
Faith Bodnar, Executive Director, 604-777-9100 Ext. 516
fbodnar@inclusionbc.org
Karen De Long, Director, Community Development, 604-777-9100 Ext. 530
kdelong@inclusionbc.org
Rick O'Brien, Director, Resource Development, 604-777-9100 Ext. 507
robrien@inclusionbc.org
Frank Peng, Director, Finance & Administration, 604-777-9100 Ext. 513
fpeng@inclusionbc.org
Charlotte Kates, Coordinator, Communications, 604-777-9100 Ext. 527
ckates@inclusionbc.org
Finances: *Funding Sources:* Donations
Membership: *Member Profile:* Individuals; Families; Volunteers; Associations
Activities: Advocating for children, youth, & adults with developmental disabilities & their families; Ensuring justice, rights & opportunities for people with developmental disabilities; Presenting scholarships for personal & professional development opportunities; Communicating through social media (www.twitter.com/bcacl); *Speaker Service:* Yes; *Rents Mailing List:* Yes; *Library:* British Columbia Association for Community Living Library
Meetings/Conferences: • 2015 Inclusion BC Conference, May, 2015, Vancouver, BC
Scope: Provincial
Publications:
• BACL Update
Type: Newsletter
Profile: Information about issues, campaigns, & events of interest to British Columbia Association for Community Living members
• British Columbia Association for Community Living Membership Directory
Type: Directory
Profile: Information on programs & services provided by British Columbia Association for Community Living & its member associations
• British Columbia Association for Community Living Annual Report
Type: Yearbook; *Frequency:* Annually

In-Definite Arts Society (IDAS)
8038 Fairmount Dr. SE, Calgary AB T2H 0Y1
Tel: 403-253-3174; *Fax:* 403-255-2234
ida@indefinitearts.com
www.indefinitearts.com
www.facebook.com/pages/IDAS-Community-Art/118800698139342
Overview: A small local charitable organization founded in 1975
Mission: To provide opportunities for people with developmental disabilities to express themselves & to grow, through their involvement in art; to strive to increase community awareness of the talents & diversity of artists with disabilities. It has been certified by the Alberta Council of Disability Services.
Chief Officer(s):
John Lee, Chair
Darlene Murphy, Executive Director
Finances: *Funding Sources:* Provincial government
Staff Member(s): 9
Activities: Programs in fiberarts, ceramics, drawing, painting, sculpture & woodworking; *Speaker Service:* Yes

Independence Plus Inc.
#115, 66 Waterloo St., Saint John NB E2L 3P4
Tel: 506-643-7004; *Fax:* 506-643-7009
Overview: A small local charitable organization
Mission: To provide residential service for persons who are physically or mentally challenged & operates a Handi-Bus transit service for people with mobility concerns.
Chief Officer(s):
David Black, Executive Director
DavidBlack@nb.aibn.com
Finances: *Funding Sources:* Saint John Transit Commission

Independent Assemblies of God International - Canada
PO Box 653, Chatham ON N7M 5K8
Tel: 519-352-1743; *Fax:* 519-351-6070
pmcphail@ciaccess.com
www.iaogcan.com
Also Known As: IAOGI Canada
Overview: A small national charitable organization founded in 1918
Member of: Independent Assemblies of God International
Chief Officer(s):
Paul McPhail, General Secretary
pmcphail@ciaccess.com
Finances: *Annual Operating Budget:* $100,000-$250,000; *Funding Sources:* Membership fees; offerings
Staff Member(s): 2; 12 volunteer(s)
Membership: 500 churches/ministries; *Fees:* $100; *Member Profile:* Must be called by God to preach His Word
Activities: *Awareness Events:* National Convention, May; *Speaker Service:* Yes
Publications:
• The Canadian Mantle
Type: Newsletter; *Frequency:* 3 pa

Independent Association of Support Staff (IASS) / Association indépendante des employés de soutien
121, av Summerhill, Pointe-Claire QC H9R 2L8
Tel: 514-426-1003; *Fax:* 514-426-5814
office-info@iass.ca
www.iass.ca
Overview: A medium-sized local organization
Chief Officer(s):
Luce Pattison, President
Staff Member(s): 3
Membership: 1,600; *Committees:* Professional Development; Labour Relations; Executive
Activities: Secretarial; classroom; librarians; daycare; supervisor; computer techs

Independent Canadian Extrusion Workers Union (CNFIU)
836 Fuller Ave., Penetanguishene ON L9M 1G8
Tel: 705-549-8728
Overview: A small national organization
Chief Officer(s):
David Miller, President
Membership: 165 + 1 local

Independent Contractors & Businesses Association of British Columbia (ICBA)
#211, 3823 Henning Dr., Burnaby BC V5C 6P3
Tel: 604-298-7795; *Fax:* 604-298-2246
Toll-Free: 800-663-2865
info@icba.bc.ca
www.icba.bc.ca
Overview: A medium-sized provincial organization founded in 1975 overseen by Merit Canada
Mission: To market & raise profile of open shop sector; to provide members with construction information & programs which assist them in labour relations efforts; to promote ongoing improvement of skills & knowledge of new entrants to the construction industry (scholarships, apprenticeships, grants)
Member of: Coalition of BC Businesses
Affliation(s): Merit Contractors Group
Chief Officer(s):

Philip Hochstein, President
philip@icba.ca
Finances: *Annual Operating Budget:* $500,000-$1.5 Million
Staff Member(s): 16
Membership: 700; *Fees:* $400-$1425 based on annual volume; *Member Profile:* Companies active in the construction industry

Independent Federation of Autonomous Unions *Voir* Fédération indépendante des syndicats autonomes

Independent Film & Video Alliance *See* Independent Media Arts Alliance

Independent Filmmakers' Co-operative of Ottawa (IFCO)
#140, 2 Daly Ave., Ottawa ON K1N 6E2
Tel: 613-569-1789; *Fax:* 613-564-4428
admin@ifco.ca
www.ifco.ca
Overview: A small local organization founded in 1992
Mission: To promote independent filmmaking in the Ottawa region; to foster film production by providing access to training programs, equipment rentals, on-site facilities, & grants.
Member of: Independent Media Arts Alliance
Affliation(s): Ottawa Arts Court Tenants (City of Ottawa)
Chief Officer(s):
Deniz Berkin, President
Patrice James, Executive Director
director@ifco.ca
Staff Member(s): 3
Membership: *Fees:* $80; $25 student; *Member Profile:* Independent filmmakers
Activities: Training; exhibition of film; news/communications; technical support; equipment rentals; open house; premiere of members' films; *Internships:* Yes; *Library* Open to public

Independent Financial Brokers of Canada (IFB) / Courtiers indépendants en sécurité financière du Canada (CISF)
#740, 30 Eglinton Ave. West, Mississauga ON L5R 3E7
Tel: 905-279-2727; *Fax:* 905-276-7295
Toll-Free: 888-654-3333
general@ifbc.ca
www.ifbc.ca
www.linkedin.com/company/independent-financial-brokers-of-canada
twitter.com/IFBcanada
Previous Name: Independent Life Insurance Brokers of Canada
Overview: A small national organization founded in 1985
Mission: To enhance & protect businesses of members; to support consumer choice
Chief Officer(s):
John Dargie, Chair & President
Scott Findlay, Vice-Chair
Marie Jose (MJ) Comtois, Treasurer
Finances: *Annual Operating Budget:* $500,000-$1.5 Million; *Funding Sources:* Membership fees; conference registration
Membership: 4,000; *Fees:* Schedule available; *Member Profile:* Independent insurance, mutual fund & other financial service brokers & professionals; *Committees:* Executive; Nominating
Activities: Frequent Educational Summits

Independent First Nations' Alliance (IFNA)
PO Box 5010, 98 King St., Sioux Lookout ON P8T 1K6
Tel: 807-737-1902; *Fax:* 807-737-3501
Toll-Free: 888-253-4362
receptionist@ifna.ca
www.ifna.ca
Overview: A small local organization
Mission: IFNA provides its member communities with technical support & community development programs. The Alliance tries to meet the needs & aspirations of its First Nations on a collective basis, while each member First Nation maintains its autonomy.
Chief Officer(s):
Gerry McKay, CEO
gmckay@ifna.ca
Staff Member(s): 7
Membership: *Member Profile:* 4 communities: Lac Seul First Nation, Muskrat Dam First Nation, Pikangikum First Nation, & Kitchenubmaykossib First Nation

Independent Life Insurance Brokers of Canada *See* Independent Financial Brokers of Canada

Independent Living Canada (ILC) / Vie autonome Canada (VAC)
#402, 214 Montréal Rd., Ottawa ON K1L 8L8
Tel: 613-563-2581; *Fax:* 613-563-3861; *TTY:* 613-563-4215
info@ilc-vac.ca
www.ilcanada.ca
Previous Name: Canadian Association of Independent Living Centres
Overview: A medium-sized national charitable organization founded in 1986
Mission: To represent & coordinate the network of independent living centres; To guide & support independent living centres in the delivery of programs & services
Chief Officer(s):
Cecilia Carroll, National Chair
Steve Lind, Financial Officer
Finances: *Funding Sources:* Membership fees; Sponsorships; Fundraising
Membership: *Committees:* Centre Development & Accreditation; Communications & Marketing; External Relations; Governance Policy & Structure; Resosurces & Fund Development
Activities: Developing policies to support programs offered by independent living centres; Providing training & resources; Creating networking opportunities for the exchange of information & ideas; Liaising with government & other organizations; Raising public awareness of independent living centres; Offering information about independent living centres to the public, the media, & governments; *Library:* Independent Living Library;
Awards:
- John Lord Award (Award)
- Canada Consumer Award of Excellence (Award)
- The Allan Simpson Award for Programming (Award)
- Canada Volunteer Award (Award)

Publications:
- Independent Living Canada Annual Report

Type: Yearbook; *Frequency:* Annually
- The Perspective: The National Independent Living News Bulletin

Type: Newsletter
Profile: Organizational updates, current events, articles, social policy & research, & fundraising intiatives

Independent Living Nova Scotia (ILNS)
#212, 2786 Agricola St., Halifax NS B3K 4E1
Tel: 902-453-0004; *Fax:* 902-455-5287
ilnsadmin@ilns.ca
www.ilns.ca
Overview: A medium-sized local organization
Mission: To support persons with disabilities make informed choices about their lives by providing programs and services that support independent living.
Chief Officer(s):
Lois Miller, Executive Director
Staff Member(s): 5
Membership: 300; *Fees:* $5
Activities: *Library* Open to public

Independent Lumber Dealers Co-operative (ILDC)
#100, 596 Kingston Rd. West, Ajax ON L1T 3A2
Tel: 905-428-0690; *Fax:* 905-428-0690
ildc@ildc.com
www.ildc.com
Overview: A small local organization founded in 1964
Member of: SPANCAN
Chief Officer(s):
A. Battagliotti, General Manager
P. Bonhomme, President
Finances: *Annual Operating Budget:* $250,000-$500,000
Membership: 20; *Member Profile:* Independent home improvement chains

Independent Media Arts Alliance (IMAA) / Alliance des arts médiatiques indépendants (AAMI)
#200-A, 4067 boul Saint-Laurent, Montréal QC H2W 1Y7
Tel: 514-522-8240; *Fax:* 514-987-1862
info@imaa.ca
www.imaa.ca
www.facebook.com/imaa.aami
twitter.com/IMAA_AAMI
www.youtube.com/channel/UC4dulDEsR21dbEg_0hTqNiw?feature=mhee
Previous Name: Independent Film & Video Alliance
Overview: A small national organization founded in 1980
Mission: To promote discussion among media art centres; To coordinate independent film & video centres
Chief Officer(s):
Jennifer Dorner, National Director
dir@imaa.ca
Finances: *Annual Operating Budget:* $100,000-$250,000; *Funding Sources:* Canada Council; Canadian Heritage; Telefilm; NFB
Staff Member(s): 2; 11 volunteer(s)
Membership: 80 organizations, 12,000 individuals; *Fees:* $100-300; *Member Profile:* Independent film, video, audio & new media organizations
Activities: Annual meetings; newsletter; lobbying; *Internships:* Yes

Independent Meeting Planners Association of Canada, Inc. *See* Canadian Society of Professional Event Planners

The Independent Order of Foresters *See* Foresters

Independent Power Association of BC *See* Clean Energy BC

Independent Power Producers Society of Alberta (IPPSA)
#2600, 144 - 4th Ave. SW, Calgary AB T2P 3N4
Fax: 403-256-8342
www.ippsa.com
Overview: A small provincial organization founded in 1993
Mission: To represent Alberta's major power producers; To encourage dialogue among power producers in Alberta
Chief Officer(s):
Evan Bahry, Executive Director, 403-282-8811, Fax: 403-256-8342
Evan.Bahry@ippsa.com
Joe Novecosky, Contact, Membership & Events, 403-256-1587, Fax: 403-256-8342
joeno@telusplanet.net
Membership: 100+; *Fees:* $10,000 power member; $5,000 junior power member; $1,000 corporate member; $250 associate member; *Member Profile:* Operators of Alberta's power supply
Activities: Engaging with Alberta's government & its agencies in policy development; Reviewing legislation, regulations, & market rules; Promoting competition in Alberta's electrical market; Providing news about the industry; Sponsoring a bursary for a student at the University of Calgary's Schulich School of Engineering (Electricity Department)
Meetings/Conferences: • Independent Power Producers Society of Alberta 2015 21st Annual Conference, March, 2015, AB
Scope: Provincial
Attendance: 500+
Description: An event featuring guest speakers, panel discussions, debates, a trade show, social events, & networking opportunities
Contact Information: Executive Director: Evan Bahry, Phone: 403-282-8811, E-mail: Evan.Bahry@ippsa.com
Publications:
- IPPSA [Independent Power Producer Society of Alberta] News

Type: Newsletter; *Frequency:* 5 pa
Profile: Industry happenings for IPPSA members

Independent Power Producers Society of Ontario (IPPSO) *See* Association of Power Producers of Ontario

Independent Practice Nurses Interest Group (IPNIG)
Attn: RNAO Membership Services, 158 Pearl St., Toronto ON M5H 1L3
Tel: 416-599-1925; *Fax:* 416-599-1926
Toll-Free: 800-268-7199
admin@ipnig.ca
www.ipnig.ca
Previous Name: Ontario Association of Nurses in Independent Practice
Overview: A small national organization
Mission: To facilitate unity within our diverse profession by supporting our members through educational & networking opportunities; To promote direct access to independent nursing services through political & social action, public awareness & professional liaisons
Member of: Registered Nurses Association of Ontario
Affliation(s): Canadian Nurses Association
Chief Officer(s):
Lynne Browning, Chair
lbrowning@ipnig.ca
Betty Franklin, Contact, Membership/Recruitment
bfranklin@ipnig.ca
Finances: *Annual Operating Budget:* Less than $50,000; *Funding Sources:* Membership fees
5 volunteer(s)

Membership: 100-499; *Fees:* Schedule available; *Member Profile:* Must be Registered Nurse & member of RNAO; *Committees:* Professional Nursing Practice/Best Practice Guidelines; Research & Education; Policy & Political Action; Public Relations/Networking; Finance/Secretary; Membership/Recruitment; Newsletter/Membership Communication
Activities: *Speaker Service:* Yes; *Rents Mailing List:* Yes; *Library* by appointment

Independent Production Fund (IPF) / Fonds indépendant de production

#1709, 2 Carlton St., Toronto ON M5B 1J3
Tel: 416-977-8966; *Fax:* 416-977-0694
info@ipf.ca
ipf.ca
Previous Name: Canadian Television Series Development Foundation
Overview: A small national charitable organization founded in 1989
Mission: To support the production of Canadian dramatic television series by independent producers through financial investment.
Chief Officer(s):
Charles Ohayon, Chair
Andra Sheffer, Executive Director
Carly McGowan, Program Manager
Finances: *Funding Sources:* Mountain Cablevision Ltd.; Broadcast Distribution Undertaking (BDU) contributions
Staff Member(s): 9
Activities: Funding Canadian dramatic television series & pilots; awarding special project grants for professional development activities, training & promotional programs

Québec Office
#503, 4200, boul St-Laurent, Montréal QC H2W 2R2
Tel: 514-845-4334; *Fax:* 514-845-5498
fipinfo@ipf.ca
Chief Officer(s):
Claire Dion, Associate Director

Independent Telecommunications Providers Association (ITPA)

29 Peevers Cres., Newmarket ON L3Y 7T5
Tel: 519-595-3975; *Fax:* 519-595-3976
www.ota.on.ca
Previous Name: Ontario Telecommunications Association
Overview: A small provincial organization
Mission: Assists its members to successfully provide state-of-the-art telecommunications services to the benefit of their customers.
Chief Officer(s):
Jonathan Holmes, Executive Director
jonathan.holmes@ota.on.ca
Finances: *Funding Sources:* Membership dues
Staff Member(s): 1
Membership: 20; *Member Profile:* Independent Local Exchange Carriers in British Columbia and Ontario.
Activities: Liaising with government departments & agencies & industry associates, such as Bell Canada; Setting policies & compliance guidelines; Offering a forum to share expertise
Meetings/Conferences: • Independent Telecommunications Providers Association 2015 50th Annual Convention, June, 2015, Taboo Muskoka Resort, Gravenhurst, ON
Scope: Provincial
Description: An event featuring guest speakers, informative seminars, the annual general meeting, social events, & opportunities to meet with telecommunications industry representatives

Indexing & Abstracting Society of Canada / Société canadienne pour l'analyse de documents *See* Indexing Society of Canada

Indexing Society of Canada / Société canadienne d'indexation

133 Major St., Toronto ON M5S 2K9
www.indexers.ca
twitter.com/indexerscanada
Previous Name: Indexing & Abstracting Society of Canada / Société canadienne pour l'analyse de documents
Overview: A medium-sized national organization founded in 1977
Mission: To encourage the production & use of indexes & abstracts; to promote the recognition of indexers & abstractors; to improve indexing & abstracting techniques; to improve communication among individual indexers & abstractors.
Affliation(s): American Society of Indexers; Association of Southern African Indexers and Bibliographers; Australian and New Zealand Society of Indexers; China Society of Indexers; Deutsches Netzwerk der Indexer; International Committee of Representatives of Indexing Societies; Netherlands Indexing Network; Society of Indexers; Publishing Technology Group of SI; Editors' Association of Canada; Society for Editors and Proofreaders; Editorial Freelancers Association; Canadian Library Association; American Library Association; American Society for Information Science and Technology; Canadian Publishers' Council
Chief Officer(s):
Mary Newberry, Co-President
mary.newberry@rogers.com
Jennifer Hedges, Co-President
jennifer.hedges@sympatico.ca
Audrey McClellan, Membership Secretary
amcclellan@shaw.ca
Gillian Watts, Treasurer
treasurer@indexers.ca
Isabel Steurer, Representative, British Columbia
isabelsteurer@yahoo.ca
Margaret de Boer, Representative, Central Canada
mtdeboer@sympatico.ca
Stéphanie Bilodeau, Representative, Eastern Canada
Stephanie.Bilodeau@gmail.com
Judy Dunlop, Representative, Prairies & Northern Canada
judy@dunlopinfo.ca
Finances: *Funding Sources:* Membership fees
Membership: *Fees:* $145 institutional; $140 individuals; $110 student; *Member Profile:* Any institution, service or individual interested in promotion of the society's objectives
Activities: Annual conference & AGM

India Rainbow Community Services of Peel (IRCS)

#206 & Unit 1, 3038 Hurontario St., Mississauga ON L5B 3B9
Tel: 905-275-2369; *Fax:* 905-275-6799
info@indiarainbow.org
www.indiarainbow.org
Overview: A small local charitable organization founded in 1985
Mission: To provide non-religious & non-political services for integration into Canadian society; To meet the need for social services & training in the Peel immigrant community
Affliation(s): Multicultural Inter-Agency Group; Volunteer Centre of Peel; Mayors Breakfast Group; Peel Community Against Woman Abuse; Caregivers of Peel Network
Chief Officer(s):
Samuel Malvea, President
Finances: *Annual Operating Budget:* $500,000-$1.5 Million; *Funding Sources:* CIC/OASIS; COSTI/OCASI; Ministry of Health; Ministry of Community & Social Services; United Way of Peel Region
Staff Member(s): 40; 80 volunteer(s)
Membership: 200; *Fees:* $10 individual; $15 family
Activities: Job search workshops in Mississauga 905/275-1976; English language training in Mississauga 905/273-4932; Adult Day Centre for Long Term Care; English Language Training Brampton; Job Search Brampton; LINC Brampton; Mississauga Training Centre; Rainbow Long Term Care Centre;

Indian & Inuit Nurses of Canada *See* Aboriginal Nurses Association of Canada

Indian & Metis Friendship Centre of Prince Albert (IMFCPA)

94 - 15th St. East, Prince Albert SK S6V 1E8
Tel: 306-764-3431; *Fax:* 306-764-3205
www.imfcpa.com
Previous Name: Prince Albert Indian & Métis Friendship Centre
Overview: A small local organization founded in 1964
Mission: To promote understanding, cooperation, & trust; To recognize the social, cultural, & recreational needs of aboriginal people in Prince Albert & the surrounding area
Affliation(s): Aboriginal Friendship Centres of Saskatchewan
Chief Officer(s):
George Sayese, President
Connie Farber, Executive Director
paimfc.ed@sasktel.net
Membership: *Fees:* $2
Activities: Information & referral services; home visits; advocacy; housing; income tax services; transient aid, elder & youth programming; fine option program; native court-workers program
Publications:
• Prince Albert Indian & Métis Friendship Centre Newsletter
Type: Newsletter; *Frequency:* Monthly

Indian & Metis Friendship Centre of Winnipeg Inc. (IMFC)

45 Robinson St., Winnipeg MB R2W 5H5
Tel: 204-586-8441; *Fax:* 204-582-8261
general@imfc.net
www.imfc.net
Overview: A small local organization
Chief Officer(s):
Mark Fleming, Executive Director
ed@imfc.net
Membership: *Fees:* $1

Indian Agricultural Program of Ontario (IAPO)

PO Box 100, 220 North St., Stirling ON K0K 3E0
Tel: 613-395-5505; *Fax:* 613-395-5510
Toll-Free: 800-363-0329
iapo-lambeth@on.aibn.com
www.indianag.on.ca
Overview: A small provincial organization founded in 1984
Mission: IAPO is a non-profit corporation that fosters sustainable economic growth of Ontario First Nations People through agricultural programs involved in all sectors, including dairy, beef, swine, poultry, crops, farm retail, repair, & agri-forestry.
Chief Officer(s):
William J. Brant, Chair
Beth Wismer, General Manager
beth@indianag.on.ca
Membership: *Member Profile:* Status Indians registered in Ontario with businesses on or off reserve
Activities: Loans program; agriculture advisory service; seminars; conferences
Publications:
• Native Agri Update
Type: Newsletter; *Frequency:* Monthly

Western/Southern Office
PO Box 83, Stn. Lambeth, 6453 Hamlyn St., London ON N6P 1P9
Tel: 519-652-2440; *Fax:* 519-652-0085
Toll-Free: 800-663-6912
Chief Officer(s):
Mary McFarlane, Agricultural Programs Officer
mary@indianag.on.ca

Indian Friendship Centre in Sault Ste Marie

122 East St., Sault Ste Marie ON P6A 3C7
Tel: 705-256-5634; *Fax:* 705-942-3227
info@ssmifc.ca
www.ssmifc.com
www.facebook.com/ssm.ifc
twitter.com/ssmifc
Overview: A small local organization founded in 1972
Mission: To provide a comprehensive range of social programs to improve the overall well-being of its community; to nurture Indian self-expression & leadership, & it encourages the study of Indian needs, the planning of services from both public & private agencies. 2nd location: 29 Welington St., East, Sault Ste. Marie.
Member of: Ontario Federation of Indian Friendship Centres
Affliation(s): National Association of Friendship Centres
Chief Officer(s):
Cathy Syrette, Executive Director
director@ssmifc.ca
Finances: *Funding Sources:* Provincial & federal funding; fundraising
Staff Member(s): 39
Membership: *Fees:* $2 single; $5 family; elders - free; *Member Profile:* Urban aboriginal
Activities: A wide variety of services & programs, including employment unit, crisis intervention, life long care, literacy, alternative school, Ojibway language, family support, foster care, healing & wellness, alcohol/drug prevention, homeless initiative, health access centre

Indian Métis Christian Fellowship (IMCF)

3131 Dewdney Ave., Regina SK S4T 0Y5
Tel: 306-359-1096; *Fax:* 306-359-0103
imcfr@sasktel.net
Overview: A small local organization founded in 1978
Mission: IMCF is an urban aboriginal ministry supported by the Christian Reformed Church in North America - Canada. Its mission is to develop a worshipping, working community through serving the spiritual & social needs of aboriginal people in

Regina.
Affliation(s): Canadian Ministry Board; Indian Family Center, Winnipeg; Native Healing Centre, Edmonton
Chief Officer(s):
Ben Vandezande, Interim Director
Finances: *Annual Operating Budget:* $100,000-$250,000
Membership: 30 individual
Activities: Drop-in ministry; daily prayer circle; soup & bannock lunch; computer club

Indigenous Bar Association
70 Pineglen Cres., Ottawa ON K2G 0G8
Tel: 613-224-1529
www.indigenousbar.ca
Overview: A medium-sized national organization
Mission: To recognize & respect the spiritual basis of our Indigenous laws, customs & traditions; to promote the advancement of legal & social justice for Indigenous peoples in Canada; to promote reform of policies & laws affecting Indigenous peoples in Canada; to foster public awareness within the legal community, the Indigenous community & the general public in respect of legal & social issues of concern to Indigenous peoples in Canada; to provide a forum & network amongst Indigenous lawyers
Chief Officer(s):
Koren Lightning-Earle, President
klightning-earle@indigenousbar.ca
Drew Lafond, Secretary
dlafond@indigenousbar.ca
Anne Chalmers, Administrative Support
achalmers@indigenousbar.ca
Membership: *Fees:* $200 law graduates; $50 students; *Member Profile:* Full - Indigenous person who is a member of the Bar or law society of any province or territory in Canada; Indigenous person who is a judge or a retired judge of any Court of Record in Canada; Indigenous person in Canada who has graduated from a recognized law school; Student - Indigenous person in Canada who is enrolled in a recognized law school; Honourary - person who has distinguished himself/herself in the field of Indigenous law, or has made a significant contribution to the advancement of justice for Indigenous peoples in Canada

Indigenous Physicians Association of Canada (IPAC)
#305, 323 Portage Ave., Winnipeg MB R3B 2C1
Tel: 204-219-0099; *Fax:* 204-940-2560
info@ipac-amic.org
www.ipac-amic.org
Overview: A small national organization
Mission: To serve the interests of Indigenous physicians, medical students & the health related interests of Indigenous people in Canada
Chief Officer(s):
Kandice Léonard, Executive Director
Marcia Anderson, President

Indo-Canada Chamber of Commerce (ICCC) / Chambre de commerce Indo-Canada
#940, 45 Sheppard Ave. East, Toronto ON M2N 5W9
Tel: 416-224-0090; *Fax:* 416-224-0089
iccc@iccc.org
www.iccc.org
Overview: A small international organization founded in 1977
Mission: To promote Indo-Canadian professionals & businesses; to facilitate business & trade between Canada & India & the Indian diaspora throughout the world; to highlight Indo-Canadian contributions in the economic, cultural & social fabric of Canada
Member of: Toronto Board of Trade; Ontario Chamber of commerce
Chief Officer(s):
Naval Bajaj, President
Puneet S. Kohli, Vice-President & Corp. Secretary
Mayank Bhatt, Contact, 416-224-0090 Ext. 541
Finances: *Funding Sources:* Sponsorships
Staff Member(s): 1
Membership: 850; *Fees:* $100 regular; $250 corporate; $40 student; $1,150 lifetime; *Member Profile:* Business; *Committees:* Business Development: Events; Energy; Finance; Golf; iCATS; IT; New Immigrants; SME; Trade
Activities: Business seminars; IT seminars; social events; *Awareness Events:* Cricket Tournament & Festival; Golf Tournament; Annual Awards & Gala Nite
Awards:
• ICCC Awards Nomination (Award)
Recognizes achievements through awards to the Professional Woman/Man of the year; Business Woman/Man of the year; Lifetime Achievement; Outstanding Achievement; Youth Achievement; Humanitarian; Technology Achievement

Indspire
Six Nations of the Grand River, PO Box 5, #100, 50 Generations Dr., Ohsweken ON N0A 1M0
Tel: 519-445-3021; *Fax:* 866-433-3159
communications@indspire.ca
indspire.ca
www.facebook.com/Indspire
twitter.com/Indspire
Overview: A small local charitable organization
Mission: To provide scholarships to Indigenous people that help them pay for a post-secondary educations
Chief Officer(s):
Roberta L. Jamieson, President & CEO
Finances: *Annual Operating Budget:* Greater than $5 Million
Staff Member(s): 34

Indspire
Six Nations of the Grand River, PO Box 759, 50 Generations Dr., Oshweken ON N0A 1M0
Tel: 416-926-0775; *Fax:* 866-433-3159
Toll-Free: 855-463-7747
www.indspire.ca
Previous Name: National Aboriginal Achievement Foundation
Overview: A small national charitable organization founded in 1985
Chief Officer(s):
Roberta Jamieson, CEO
Finances: *Annual Operating Budget:* Greater than $5 Million
Staff Member(s): 13
Activities: Educational programs; "Blueprint for the Future" - a series of Aboriginal youth career fairs; financial assistance to Aboriginal Youth; *Internships:* Yes; *Speaker Service:* Yes
Awards:
• National Aboriginal Achievement Foundation Scholarships (Scholarship)
Established 1985; provides scholarships to Aboriginal students for post-secondary education
• National Aboriginal Achievement Awards (Award)
Established in 1993 & awarded to 14 aboriginal achievers from the First Nations, Inuit & Metis communities; nominees are outstanding achievers working in any occupational area

Toronto Office
#450, 215 Spadina Ave., Toronto ON M5T 2C7
Tel: 416-926-7554; *Fax:* 416-977-1764
Toll-Free: 855-463-7747

Industrial Accident Victims Group of Ontario (IAVGO)
#203, 489 College St., Toronto ON M6G 1A5
Tel: 416-924-6477
Toll-Free: 877-230-6311
www.iavgo.org
www.facebook.com/167369409975545
Overview: A medium-sized provincial charitable organization founded in 1975
Mission: Our community legal clinic provides free services to injured workers in Ontario including legal advice, legal representation, public legal education, advocacy training and community development.
Chief Officer(s):
Mary DiNucci, Coordinator
Finances: *Annual Operating Budget:* $100,000-$250,000
Staff Member(s): 8
Membership: *Fees:* $10
Activities: *Library* by appointment

Industrial Developers Association of Canada *See* Economic Developers Association of Canada

Industrial Fabrics Association International Canada (IFAI Canada)
1485 Laperriere Ave., Ottawa ON K1Z 7S8
Tel: 613-792-1218; *Fax:* 613-729-6206
Toll-Free: 800-225-4324
Other Communication: membership@ifai.com
ifaicanada@ifai.com
www.ifaicanada.com
Overview: A small national organization overseen by Industrial Fabrics Association International
Mission: To promote the welfare of the Canadian technical textile industry; To work towards solutions to common industry problems; To improve efficiency, quality, & maintenance within the Canadian industrial textile industry; To ensure ethical business practices; To benefit users of Canadian textile products
Chief Officer(s):
Kathy Jones, Executive Director
Frank Braeuer, Chair
Craig Fawcett, Vice-Chair
Membership: *Fees:* $285 affiliate membership; $385 sponsoring membership; $435 - $985 end product manufacturing companies (fee based on sales range); $1,135 supplier; *Member Profile:* Canadian corporations, proprietorships, or partnerships involved in the manufacture or sale of industrial textile products; Suppliers of goods or services to the industrial fabrics industry in Canada; Canadian designers & architects, who are involved in the textile industry
Activities: Directing work towards standardizing materials & production methods; Liaising with related organizations; Representing members before legislative bodies; Informing members of new & better materials & techniques; Creating networking opportunities with industry peers & experts; Offering training & educational opportunities
Meetings/Conferences: • IFAI (Industrial Fabrics Association International) Canada Expo 2015, March, 2015, Vancouver, BC
Scope: International
Description: Featuring how-to workshops, technical symposiums, business & professional development sessions, & product launches
Contact Information: Ashleigh Esselman; aeesselman@ifai.com; Phone: 1 651 225 6934
Publications:
• Industrial Fabrics Association International Membership Directory
Type: Directory

Industrial First Aid Attendants Association of British Columbia *See* Occupational First Aid Attendants Association of British Columbia

Industrial Gas Users Association Inc. (IGUA) / Association des consommateurs industriels de gaz (ACIG)
#502, 350 Sparks St., Ottawa ON K1R 7S8
Tel: 613-236-8021; *Fax:* 613-230-9531
info@igua.ca
www.igua.ca
Overview: A medium-sized national organization founded in 1973
Mission: To provide a coordinated & effective voice for industrial firms depending on natural gas as fuel or feedstock; to represent industrial users of natural gas before regulatory boards & governments
Chief Officer(s):
Shahrzad Rahbar, President
srahbar@igua.ca
Martin Phipps, Chair
Finances: *Annual Operating Budget:* $500,000-$1.5 Million; *Funding Sources:* Membership dues
Staff Member(s): 3
Membership: 39 corporate; *Fees:* Based on gas consumption, $1,200-$36,099; *Member Profile:* Open to end users of natural gas
Meetings/Conferences: • 2015 Industrial Gas User's Association Spring Seminar, 2015
Scope: National

Industrial Instrument Manufacturers Association *See* Canadian Process Control Association

l'Industrie forestière de l'Ontario *See* Ontario Forest Industries Association

Industry Training Authority (ITA)
8100 Granville Ave., 8th Fl., Richmond BC V6Y 3T6
Tel: 778-328-8700; *Fax:* 778-328-8701
Toll-Free: 866-660-6011
customerservice@itabc.ca
www.itabc.ca
www.facebook.com/IndustryTrainingAuthority
twitter.com/ita_bc
Overview: A small provincial organization founded in 2004
Mission: A provincial government agency with legislated responsibility to govern and develop the industry training system in B.C.

Infant & Toddler Safety Association (ITSA) / Association pour la sécurité des bébés et des tout petits
#154, 23 - 500 Fairway Rd. South, Kitchener ON N2C 1X3

Tel: 519-570-0181; *Fax:* 519-570-1078
Toll-Free: 888-570-0181
www.infantandtoddlersafety.ca
Overview: A small national charitable organization founded in 1980
Mission: To provide information & resource materials to increase safety awareness & knowledge, in order to reduce early childhood unintentional injuries & death
Finances: *Annual Operating Budget:* Less than $50,000
25 volunteer(s)
Membership: 1-99
Activities: Child car seat clinics, safety workshops, speakers service; *Speaker Service:* Yes

Infant Development Program of BC (IDP)
c/o Infant & Child Development Association of BC, 426 Anderson St., Nelson BC V1L 3Y3
Tel: 250-352-5546
info@idpofbc.ca
www.idpofbc.ca
Overview: A medium-sized provincial organization founded in 1975
Mission: Funded by the BC Ministry of Children & Family Development, the Infant Development Program of BC provides opportunities for parents to learn about child development, meet other parents to discuss parenting & child development issues, & to link to other community resources & activities. The Program serves children from birth to 3 years old, who are at risk for or who already have a delay in development
Affliation(s): Aboriginal Infant Development; BC Family Hearing Resource Centre; Deaf Children's Society; Snuneymuxw First Nation
Finances: *Annual Operating Budget:* $3 Million-$5 Million
Staff Member(s): 120
Membership: 100-499
Activities: Provides support information & developmental assessment programming

Infant Feeding Action Coalition
6 Trinity Sq., Toronto ON M5G 1B1
Tel: 416-595-9819; *Fax:* 416-591-9355
info@infactcanada.ca
www.infactcanada.ca
Also Known As: INFACT Canada
Previous Name: Infant/Maternal Nutrition Education Association
Overview: A small local organization
Mission: To protect, promote & support breastfeeding in Canada & globally; to promote better infant & maternal health; to foster appropriate mother & infant nutrition
Member of: Canadian Council for International Cooperation
Chief Officer(s):
Elisabeth Sterken, National Director
esterken@infactcanada.ca
Finances: *Funding Sources:* Membership dues; foundations; government
Membership: 3,000; *Fees:* $55
Activities: *Awareness Events:* World Breastfeeding Week, 1st week of Oct.; *Speaker Service:* Yes; *Library:* Breastfeeding Information Resource Centre; by appointment

Infant/Maternal Nutrition Education Association ***See*** Infant Feeding Action Coalition

Infertility Awareness Association of Canada (IAAC) / Association canadienne de sensibilisation à l'infertilité (ACSI)
2160 av Nightingale, Montréal QC H9S 1E4
Tel: 514-484-2891; *Fax:* 514-484-0454
Toll-Free: 800-263-2929
info@iaac.ca
www.iaac.ca
www.facebook.com/57435550753
Overview: A medium-sized national charitable organization founded in 1990
Mission: To offer assistance, support & education to individuals with infertility concerns; to increase the awareness & understanding of the causes, treatments & the emotional impact of infertility through the development of educational programs.
Member of: International Federation of Infertility Patient Associations (IFIPA)
Affliation(s): Canadian Fertility & Andrology Society; Society of Obstetricians & Gynaecologists of Canada
Chief Officer(s):
Jocelyn Smith, President
Finances: *Annual Operating Budget:* Less than $50,000; *Funding Sources:* Government; membership dues; donations
25 volunteer(s)
Membership: 400; *Fees:* $40 individual; *Committees:* Executive; Membership; Publications & Education; Chapter Development; Fundraising
Activities: Chapter Establishment Program (assists individuals who wish to contact existing chapters or who wish to establish an IAAC chapter in their area); information seminars; support groups; resource centres; telephone assistance programs; information package; *Awareness Events:* National Infertility Awareness Week; *Library* by appointment

Infertility Network
160 Pickering St., Toronto ON M4E 3J7
Tel: 416-691-3611; *Fax:* 416-690-8015
Info@InfertilityNetwork.org
www.infertilitynetwork.org
Overview: A small national charitable organization founded in 1990
Mission: Provides information, support & referral on infertility & related issues, helps people make informed choices for family-building options, & advocates for reform of gamete donation practices
Chief Officer(s):
Patricia Silver, President
Finances: *Annual Operating Budget:* $50,000-$100,000
Staff Member(s): 2; 10 volunteer(s)
Membership: 7,000; *Fees:* $10
Activities: Seminars & support groups

Infirmières de l'Ordre de Victoria du Canada ***See*** Victorian Order of Nurses for Canada

Infirmières et infirmiers en santé communautaire au Canada ***See*** Community Health Nurses of Canada

Infirmières unies de l'Alberta ***See*** United Nurses of Alberta

Info Northumberland
#700, 600 William St., Cobourg ON K9A 5J4
Tel: 905-372-8913; *Fax:* 905-372-4417
Toll-Free: 800-396-6626
Northumberland@fourinfo.com
www.fourinfo.com
twitter.com/fourinfo2
Also Known As: SHARE INFO Community Information Centre Inc.
Previous Name: Cobourg Community Information Centre Inc.
Overview: A small local charitable organization founded in 1979 overseen by InformOntario
Mission: To aid all citizens of Northumberland County giving them, upon request, information &/or referring them to the proper organization or service; To assess trends which meet needs of the community by careful evaluation of demands made by citizens
Member of: Community Information Online Consortium
Finances: *Annual Operating Budget:* $50,000-$100,000; *Funding Sources:* United Way; fundraising; Ministry of Community, Family & Children's Services; Trillium Foundation
Staff Member(s): 2; 10 volunteer(s)
Membership: 1-99; *Fees:* $25 organization; $5 individual

Information & Communication Technologies Association of Manitoba (ICTAM)
#412, 435 Ellice Ave., Winnipeg MB R3B 1Y6
Tel: 204-943-7133; *Fax:* 204-957-5628
www.ictam.ca
www.linkedin.com/company/information-&-communication-technologies-asso
www.facebook.com/ICTAMMB?ref=hl
twitter.com/ICTAM
Overview: A medium-sized provincial organization
Mission: To provide programming, advocacy & collaboration to the information & communication technologies industry in Manitoba, in order to accelerate growth, prosperity & sustainability
Chief Officer(s):
Charles Loewen, President
Kathy Knight, CEO
kathy.knight@ictam.ca
Membership: 85; *Fees:* $75-$3,000
Publications:
• The HUB [a publication of the Information & Communication Technologies Association of Manitoba]
Type: Newsletter

Information & Communications Technology Council of Canada (ICTC) / Conseil des technologies de l'information et des communications du Canada (CTIC)
#300, 116 Lisgar St., Ottawa ON K2P 0C2
Tel: 613-237-8551; *Fax:* 613-230-3490
info@ictc-ctic.ca
www.ictc-ctic.ca
Previous Name: Software Human Resource Council (Canada) Inc.
Overview: A medium-sized national organization
Mission: To serve the software development profession by developing joint ventures in courseware design & delivery, by integrating training & education processes, by helping to ensure sufficient supply & quality of new entrants to the profession & by promoting an attractive image & definition of software workers
Member of: Canadian Advanced Technology Association (CATA); Information Technology Association of Canada (ITAC); Canadian Information Processing Society (CIPS)
Chief Officer(s):
Faye West, Chair
Finances: *Annual Operating Budget:* Greater than $5 Million; *Funding Sources:* Private
Staff Member(s): 10
Membership: 1,000-4,999; *Fees:* Schedule available
Activities: *Internships:* Yes; *Speaker Service:* Yes

Information Agincourt; Information Scarborough ***See*** Agincourt Community Services Association

Information Barrie
Barrie Public Library, 60 Worsley St., Barrie ON L4M 1L6
Tel: 705-728-1010; *Fax:* 705-728-4322
infobarrie@barrie.ca
www.library.barrie.on.ca/infobarrie
Overview: A small local organization founded in 1977 overseen by InformOntario
Mission: To provide community information & referral; To work with other community agencies
Member of: Inform Canada; InformOntario
Affliation(s): Information Providers Coalition (Simcoe County); 211 Simcoe County; Community Connection (Collingwood & Dist.); Information Orillia; Contact (Alliston)
Chief Officer(s):
Cathy Bodle, Coordinator
Finances: *Annual Operating Budget:* $50,000-$100,000
Staff Member(s): 3

Information Brock
30 Allan St., Cannington ON L0E 1E0
Tel: 705-432-2636
Previous Name: Brock Information Centre
Overview: A small local organization founded in 1963 overseen by InformOntario
Mission: Free & confidential information & referral service; on-site thrift shop
Member of: InformOntario
Chief Officer(s):
Deneen Dixon, Coordinator
Staff Member(s): 2; 6 volunteer(s)
Membership: 7

Information Burlington
c/o Burlington Public Library, 2331 New St., 2nd Floor, Burlington ON L7R 1J4
Tel: 905-639-4212; *Fax:* 905-681-7277
informationburlington@bpl.on.ca
www.bpl.on.ca/community_information
twitter.com/InfoBurlington
Overview: A small local organization founded in 1971 overseen by InformOntario
Mission: To offer a free, confidential information service to the citizens of Burlington; To connect people with the community & government services they need; To ensure that the public is aware of the programmes & services offered in the community
Member of: InformOntario
Affliation(s): Halton Information Providers
Chief Officer(s):
Nina Truscott, Manager
Finances: *Annual Operating Budget:* $50,000-$100,000; *Funding Sources:* City of Burlington
Activities: Database: www.halinet.on.ca/hcd/sql/start.asp; *Library* Open to public

Information Durham
144 Old Kingston Rd., Ajax ON L1T 2Z9
Tel: 905-434-4636; *Fax:* 905-686-0606
Toll-Free: 866-463-6910

informdurham@bellnet.ca
www.informdurham.com
Also Known As: United Way Information Services
Overview: A small local organization overseen by InformOntario
Member of: InformOntario
Affliation(s): United Way of Oshawa/Whitby/Clarington/Brock & Scugog; United Way of Ajax/Pickering/Uxbridge
Chief Officer(s):
Cathy Gowland, Manager
Finances: *Annual Operating Budget:* $50,000-$100,000
Staff Member(s): 1; 5 volunteer(s)
Activities: Provides information on & referral to community, social & government services

Information Markham
101 Town Centre Blvd., Markham ON L3R 9W3
Tel: 905-415-7500
imarkham@markham.ca
www.informationmarkham.ca
Overview: A small local organization founded in 1974 overseen by InformOntario
Mission: To deliver quality information services to our clients; To enhance community life & promote Markham & York Region
Affliation(s): Community Information & Volunteer Centre - York Region
Chief Officer(s):
Dianne Martin, Executive Director
Finances: *Annual Operating Budget:* Less than $50,000
Staff Member(s): 5; 30 volunteer(s)
Membership: 35; *Committees:* Community Relations; Finance & Management; Human Relations

Information Niagara
#10, 235 Martindale Rd., St Catharines ON L2W 1A5
Tel: 905-682-6611; *Fax:* 905-682-4314
Toll-Free: 800-263-3695
info@informationniagara.com
www.informationniagara.com
www.facebook.com/InformationNiagara
twitter.com/211CentralSouth
Also Known As: 211 Central South
Overview: A small local organization founded in 1974 overseen by InformOntario
Mission: The organization offers community information & referral services, including an online searchable information database & another database of volunteers. It also maintains an interpretation service for a wide range of languages. It is a registered charity, BN: 118968346RR0001.
Member of: United Way
Chief Officer(s):
Terri Bruce, Information Services Manager, 905-682-1900 Ext. 221
terri@informationniagara.com
Finances: *Annual Operating Budget:* $100,000-$250,000; *Funding Sources:* Ontario Trillium Foundation
Staff Member(s): 9; 15 volunteer(s)
Membership: 1-99

Information Oakville
c/o Oakville Public Library, Central Branch, 120 Navy St., Oakville ON L6J 2Z4
Tel: 905-815-2046
Other Communication: Editorial e-mail: informationoakville@oakville.ca
oplreference@oakville.ca
www.informationoakville.org
Also Known As: Community Information Service of the Oakville Public Library
Overview: A small local organization founded in 1980
Mission: To provide accurate information on the community of Oakville; information & referral services. Information Oakville is a founding member of Halton Information Providers, & Community Information Online Consortium (CIOC). Halton Community Services Database URL: halton.cioc.ca.
Member of: Inform Canada; Inform Ontario; Oakville Public Library
Chief Officer(s):
Michael Hodgins, Manager of Community Information
mhodgins@oakville.ca
Finances: *Annual Operating Budget:* $50,000-$100,000; *Funding Sources:* Library
Staff Member(s): 3
Activities: *Library:* Resource Centre; Open to public

Information Orillia
33 Mississauga St. East, Orillia ON L3V 1V4
Tel: 705-326-7743; *Fax:* 705-326-6064
info@informationorillia.org
www.informationorillia.org
www.facebook.com/groups/43448477416
Overview: A small local organization founded in 1969 overseen by InformOntario
Mission: To bring people & services together in Orillia & surrounding townships by information & referral
Member of: InformCanada; InformOntario
Affliation(s): Coalition of Information Providers of Simcoe County
Chief Officer(s):
Shannon O'Donnell, Executive Director
sodonnell@informationorillia.org
Finances: *Annual Operating Budget:* $50,000-$100,000; *Funding Sources:* City of Orillia; publications; bazaars; public donations
Staff Member(s): 2; 70 volunteer(s)
Membership: 100; *Fees:* Donations
Activities: *Library:* Resource Centre

Information Resource Management Association of Canada (IRMAC)
PO Box 5639, Stn. A, Toronto ON M5W 1N8
Tel: 416-712-9932
www.irmac.ca
Also Known As: Database Association of Ontario
Overview: A medium-sized national organization founded in 1971
Mission: To provide a forum for members to exchange information about data administration & information resource management
Affliation(s): DAMA International; British Columbia Data Management Association
Chief Officer(s):
Ron Klein, President, 416-777-8721
Ruxandra Petolescu, Vice-President
Jonathan Pinchefsky, Secretary
Rezelline Tan, Treasurer
Finances: *Funding Sources:* Membership dues
Membership: 100-150 individuals; *Member Profile:* Information management professionals, such as systems professionals; Industry suppliers
Activities: Sponsoring conferences, seminars, & workshops; Organizing the Data Warehouse Special Interest Group; *Speaker Service:* Yes

Information Sarnia Lambton
PO Box 354, Sarnia ON N7T 7J2
Tel: 519-542-1949; *Fax:* 519-542-4566
www.informationsarnialambton.org
Overview: A small local organization founded in 1960 overseen by InformOntario
Mission: To maintain a database of social & human service organizations in Lambton County
Chief Officer(s):
Norm Lamoureux, Database Manager
Finances: *Annual Operating Budget:* Less than $50,000
10 volunteer(s)
Membership: 1-99; *Committees:* Publications; Updating; Electronic

Information Services Vancouver
#330, 111 West Hastings St., Vancouver BC V6B 1H4
Tel: 604-875-6431; *Fax:* 604-660-9415; *TTY:* 604-875-0885; *Crisis Hot-Line:* 800-563-0808
info@bc211.ca
www.bc211.ca
www.facebook.com/pages/Bc211-we-can-help/166932003317984
Also Known As: BC211
Overview: A small local charitable organization founded in 1953
Mission: Information & referral to community, social & government agencies
Member of: BC Alliance of Information & Referral Services, InformCanada
Affliation(s): Alliance of Information & Referral Systems (AIRS)
Chief Officer(s):
Myrna Holman, Executive Director, 604-708-3200
Myrna@bc211.ca
Michele Pye, President
Finances: *Annual Operating Budget:* $500,000-$1.5 Million; *Funding Sources:* United Way; provincial government; City of Vancouver
Staff Member(s): 31; 2 volunteer(s)
Membership: 39; *Fees:* $25
Activities: Free & confidential assistance; links to more than 4,000 social, community & government agencies & services across the Lower Mainland & British Columbia; *Library* by appointment

Information Technology Association of Canada (ITAC) / Association canadienne de la technologie de l'information
#801, 5090 Explorer Dr., Mississauga ON L4W 4T9
Tel: 905-602-8345; *Fax:* 905-602-8346
info@itac.ca
www.itac.ca
Merged from: Strategic Microelectronics Council; Strategic Microelectronics Consortium
Overview: A medium-sized national organization founded in 1997
Mission: Represents 1,300 companies in the computing & telecommunications hardware, software, services & electronic content sectors; identifies & leads on issues that affect the industry; advocates initiatives to enable continued growth & development.
Chief Officer(s):
Karna Gupta, President
Bill Munson, Vice President
Carlo Viola, Director, Finance
Alberta Fraccaro, Accounting Coordinator
Staff Member(s): 17
Membership: 1,300 companies

Montréal Office
#401, 465 St-Jean, Montréal QC H2Y 2R6
Tel: 514-287-0449
Chief Officer(s):
Claude Lemay, Vice-President, Quebec Region
clemay@itac.ca

Ottawa Office
#1120, 220 Laurier Ave. West, Ottawa ON K1P 5Z9
Tel: 613-238-4822; *Fax:* 613-238-7967
info@itac.ca
www.itac.ca
Chief Officer(s):
Lynda Leonard, Senior Vice President
leonard@itac.ca

Information Technology Industry Alliance of Nova Scotia; Software Industry Association of Nova Scotia *See* Digital Nova Scotia

Information Tilbury & Help Centre
PO Box 309, 20 Queen St., Tilbury ON N0P 2L0
Tel: 519-682-2268; *Fax:* 519-682-3771
rose-anne@unitedway.chatham-kent.on.ca
Overview: A small local charitable organization founded in 1982 overseen by InformOntario
Mission: To act as a "middle person" connecting people with services or volunteers who can help & to become involved with the community when & where needed; to provide the community with mediation information & referrals to community services by accessing individual & community needs by formulating programs services & resources in cooperation with existing organizations
Chief Officer(s):
Karen Kirkwood-Whyte, Executive Director
karen@unitedway.chatham-kent.on.ca
Finances: *Annual Operating Budget:* Less than $50,000; *Funding Sources:* United Way
Staff Member(s): 3; 200 volunteer(s)
Activities: Food bank; community outreach; resume writing; emergency clothing; *Library* Open to public

Information Tillsonburg *See* Tillsonburg & District Multi-Service Centre

Information Windsor *See* 211 Southwest Ontario

InformCanada (ICF)
#10, 235 Martindale Rd., St. Catharines ON L2W 1A5
Fax: 905-682-4314
info@informcanada.ca
www.informcanada.ca
Also Known As: Inform Canada Federation
Overview: A medium-sized national organization
Mission: To act as a resource for our members; to develop & promote national standards in our field, strengthen a national I&R network, & represent information & referral at a national level
Chief Officer(s):
Rosanna Thoms, President

Membership: *Member Profile:* Public, not-for-profit & government information & referral services & practitioners
Activities: *Awareness Events:* Annual General Meeting

InformOntario (IO)
c/o 3010 Forest Glade Dr., Windsor ON N8R 1L5
Tel: 519-735-9344
info@informontario.on.ca
www.informontario.on.ca
Also Known As: Association of Community Information Centres in Ontario
Overview: A medium-sized provincial charitable organization founded in 1980
Mission: To provide leadership to the organizations it represents so that they are able to best serve their members
Chief Officer(s):
Sylvia Mueller, President
Barbara McLachlan, Coordinator
Finances: *Funding Sources:* Membership fees
Membership: 60 community information centres; *Committees:* Standards

Inforoute Santé du Canada *See* Canada Health Infoway

Infrastructure Health & Safety Association (IHSA)
Centre for Health & Safety Innovation, #400, 5110 Creekbank Rd., Mississauga ON L4W 0A1
Tel: 905-625-0100; *Fax:* 905-625-8998
Toll-Free: 800-263-5024
info@ihsa.ca
www.ihsa.ca
ca.linkedin.com/pub/ihsa-news/41/986/aa3
twitter.com/IHSAnews
Merged from: CSAO; E&USA; THSAO
Overview: A medium-sized provincial organization founded in 2010
Mission: To serve the utilities, electrical, natural gas, aggregates, ready-mix, construction, & transportation industries in Ontario; To develop prevention solutions for work environments
Chief Officer(s):
Al Beattie, Chief Executive Officer & President
Membership: *Committees:* Advisory Councils; CVOR Review Panel; Fleet Safety Council; Labour - Management Committees; Section 21 Committees
Activities: Providing training that meets regulatory requirements & compliance standards
Meetings/Conferences: • Infrastructure Health & Safety Association 2015 Annual General Meeting, 2015, ON
Scope: Provincial
Description: A business meeting featuring a guest speaker & the presentation of awards
Contact Information: E-mail: info@ihsa.ca
Publications:
• IHSA.ca Magazine
Type: Magazine; *Frequency:* Quarterly
• Infrastructure Health & Safety Association Annual Report
Type: Yearbook; *Frequency:* Annually
Profile: Departmental updates & financial statements

Ingénieurs Canada *See* Engineers Canada

Ingénieurs sans Frontières *See* Engineers Without Borders

Ingersoll Coin Club
Ingersoll ON
Tel: 519-643-6541
woodydoesit-icc@yahoo.ca
Overview: A small local organization
Chief Officer(s):
Lorne Barnes, Contact

Ingersoll District Chamber of Commerce
132 Thames St. South, Ingersoll ON N5C 2T4
Tel: 519-485-7333; *Fax:* 519-485-6606
info@ingersollchamber.com
ingersollchamber.com
Overview: A small local organization founded in 1960
Chief Officer(s):
Kevin Homewood, President
Ann Campbell, General Manager
anncampbell@ingersollchamber.com
Membership: 118

Ingersoll District Nature Club
205 George St., Ingersoll ON N5C 1Z5
Tel: 519-485-2645
wwalden@sympatico.ca
www.ingersollnature.ca
www.facebook.com/pages/Ingersoll-District-Nature-Club/230279593830908
twitter.com/IngersollDNC
Overview: A small local charitable organization founded in 1952
Mission: To promote the enjoyment of nature through environmental appreciation & conservation; To encourage wise use & conservation of natural resources; to promote environmental protection
Member of: Federation of Ontario Naturalists
Chief Officer(s):
Sheila Fleming, Contact
sheila.fleming@lawsonresearch.com
Ken Whiteford, Contact, 519-539-5234
kenwhiteford@sympatico
John Bomans, Contact, 519-485-7575
bomansj@msn.com
Finances: *Annual Operating Budget:* Less than $50,000; *Funding Sources:* Donations
Membership: 45; *Fees:* $10 youth; $15 single; $25 family
Activities: Adopt-a-Bird program

Ininew Friendship Centre
PO Box 1499, Cochrane ON P0L 1C0
Tel: 705-272-4497; *Fax:* 705-272-3597
reception@ininewfriendshipcentre.ca
www.ininewfriendshipcentre.ca
www.facebook.com/pages/ininew-friendship-centre/115600240820
Overview: A small local organization
Mission: To improve the quality of life for everyone in the community by offering a wide variety of programs, covering health management, social work, sports & other communal activities.
Chief Officer(s):
Jeremy Girard, President
Jack Solomon, Executive Director
executive@ininewfriendshipcentre.ca
Activities: Programs & services include life-long care, community development, drug & alcohol counselling, family support, a 10-bed facility for young offenders, employment counselling & continuous training programs

Initiative nationale pour le soin des personnes âgées *See* National Initiative for the Care of the Elderly

L'Initiative torontoise de biotechnologie *See* Toronto Biotechnology Initiative

Initiatives canadiennes oecuméniques pour la justice *See* KAIROS: Canadian Ecumenical Justice Initiatives

Inland Refugee Society of BC
#615, 525 Seymour St., Vancouver BC V6B 3K4
Tel: 778-328-8888; *Fax:* 604-873-6620
inlandrefugeesociety@live.ca
inlandrefugeesociety.ca
Overview: A small provincial organization founded in 1984
Mission: To assist asylum seekers with basic necessities
Member of: Affiliation of Multicultural Societies & Service Agencies of BC; Canadian Council for Refugees
Affliation(s): Vancouver Refugee Council
Chief Officer(s):
Mario Ayala, Director
Finances: *Annual Operating Budget:* $100,000-$250,000; *Funding Sources:* Private donation; provincial & municipal grants; gaming
Staff Member(s): 2; 35 volunteer(s)
Membership: 250; *Fees:* $5 individual; $20 organization; *Member Profile:* Friends & supporters; *Committees:* Nominations; Finances; Program; Personnel
Activities: Food bank, clothing & household items distribution; information & referral; orientation & advocacy; ESL classes

Inland Terminal Association of Canada (ITAC)
PO Box 283, Elbow SK S0H 1J0
Tel: 306-854-4554
www.inlandterminal.ca
Overview: A small national organization founded in 1995
Mission: To supprt & promote the interests of people working with inland terminals
Chief Officer(s):
Kevin Hursh, Executive Director, 306-933-0138
kevin@hursh.ca
Staff Member(s): 2
Membership: 9; *Member Profile:* Inland terminal grain handling facilities

Inn From the Cold Society
110 - 11 Ave. SE, Calgary AB T2G 0X5
Tel: 403-263-8384; *Fax:* 403-263-9067
inn@innfromthecold.org
innfromthecold.org
www.linkedin.com/company/inn-from-the-cold
www.facebook.com/innfromthecold
twitter.com/innfromthecold
www.youtube.com/user/innfromthecoldyyc
Overview: A small local charitable organization
Mission: To provide shelter & programs to homeless people in hopes that they can become self-sufficient
Chief Officer(s):
Linda McLean, Executive Director
Staff Member(s): 60

Inner City Angels (ICA)
Distillery Historic District, #203, 15 Case Goods Lane, Toronto ON M5A 3C4
Tel: 416-598-0242; *Fax:* 416-598-9338
innercityangels@mac.com
www.innercityangels.ca
www.facebook.com/pages/Inner-City-Angels/109852662439384?sk=wall
Overview: A small local organization founded in 1969
Mission: To provide quality arts education opportunities in diverse & innovative ways for children & youth who would otherwise have little opportunity for them; the organization believes that the arts play an integral role in the personal growth & creative potential of all people & that equal access to arts experiences & opportunities is a shared social responsibility of all sectors of society
Chief Officer(s):
Jane Howard Baker, Executive Director
Finances: *Annual Operating Budget:* $250,000-$500,000; *Funding Sources:* Ontario Arts Council; Toronto Arts Council; Ontario Trillium Foundation; donations
Staff Member(s): 3; 15 volunteer(s)
Membership: 400; *Committees:* Artist & Board Development; Fundraising
Activities: Over 400 visits annually by Angels artists to Toronto priority community schools; *Internships:* Yes

Inner City Home of Sudbury (ICHOS)
251 Elm St., Sudbury ON P3C 1V5
Tel: 705-675-7550; *Fax:* 705-675-1652
ichos1986@gmail.com
www.innercityhomesudbury.ca
Overview: A small local charitable organization
Mission: To provide food & counselling to the less fortunate
Chief Officer(s):
Mary Ali, Executive Director
Staff Member(s): 3

Inner Peace Movement of Canada
PO Box 1138, Stn. B, Ottawa ON K1R 5R2
Tel: 613-238-7844
Toll-Free: 877-969-0095
www.innerpeacemovementptyltd.com
Overview: A small national organization founded in 1969
Mission: To promote self-help techniques by following 4 steps, each step providing tools to allow for a deeper self-awareness as a spiritual being

Innisfail & District Chamber of Commerce
5031 - 40th St., Innisfail AB T4G 1H8
Tel: 403-227-1177; *Fax:* 403-227-6749
ichamber@telusplanet.net
www.innisfailchamber.ca
Overview: A small local organization founded in 1939
Mission: To support and encourage business and members of the Innisfail community.
Member of: Alberta Chamber of Commerce
Chief Officer(s):
Doug Bos, President
Joelle Czuy, Secretary
Finances: *Annual Operating Budget:* Less than $50,000; *Funding Sources:* Membership dues; fundraising
Staff Member(s): 1; 17 volunteer(s)
Membership: 210; *Fees:* $52-$315
Activities: Junior 4-H Show; Trade Show; Christmas promotion; Small Business Week; rodeo; parade; car show & shine; *Speaker Service:* Yes

Innisfil Chamber of Commerce *See* Greater Innisfil Chamber of Commerce

Innkeepers Guild of Nova Scotia (IGNS)
PO Box 66, Tatamagouche NS BOK 1V0
Tel: 902-496-7478
www.innkeeperguild.com
www.facebook.com/groups/42158824863
Overview: A small provincial charitable organization founded in 1939
Mission: To work toward improved standards & facilities to better serve the travelling public
Affliation(s): American Hotel/Motel Association
Chief Officer(s):
Peter Sheehan, President
ocean.haven@ns.sympatico.ca
Finances: *Annual Operating Budget:* Less than $50,000; *Funding Sources:* Membership dues
30 volunteer(s)
Membership: 240 corporate + 25 associate + 5 senior/lifetime; *Fees:* Schedule available; *Member Profile:* Licensed fixed roof accommodation operations & suppliers
Activities: *Speaker Service:* Yes; *Library* Open to public

Innkeepers of Ontario *See* Ontario's Finest Inns & Spas

Innovate Calgary
Alastair Ross Technology Centre, 3553 - 31 St. NW, Calgary AB T2L 2K7
Tel: 403-284-6400; *Fax:* 403-267-5699
info@innovatecalgary.com
www.innovatecalgary.com
www.linkedin.com/company/innovate-calgary
www.facebook.com/innovatecalgary
twitter.com/innovatecalgary
Overview: A medium-sized local organization founded in 2010
Mission: To aid in acceleration & innovation in the technology sector
Chief Officer(s):
Peter Garrett, Interim President, 403-284-6424
pgarrett@innovatecalgary.com

Innovation & Technology Association of Prince Edward Island (ITAP)
PO Box 241, Charlottetown PE C1A 7K4
Tel: 902-894-4827; *Fax:* 902-894-4867
itap@itap.ca
www.itap.ca
www.facebook.com/pages/ITAP/229205927166908
twitter.com/itapei
Overview: A medium-sized provincial organization
Mission: To provide advocacy and support to our members, through projects in the key areas of export development, communication and leadership development.
Chief Officer(s):
Daniel Lazaratos, President
Mike Gillis, Innovation Director
mike.gillis@itap.ca
Membership: 70

Innovation Management Association of Canada (IMAC) / Association canadienne de la gestion de l'innovation (ACGI)
c/o CATAAlliance, #416, 207 Bank St., Ottawa ON K2P 2N2
Tel: 613-236-6550; *Fax:* 613-236-8189
info@cata.ca
www.cata.ca/imac/
Previous Name: Canadian Research Management Association
Overview: A small national organization founded in 1996
Mission: To enhance the productivity & effectiveness of Canadian research development & technology-based innovations
Chief Officer(s):
Cathi Malette, Membership Coordinator
cmalette@cata.ca
Finances: *Annual Operating Budget:* $50,000-$100,000
Membership: 240; *Fees:* $225 individual; *Member Profile:* Research, technology management & innovation leaders; *Committees:* Program; Research Practices

Innovation Norway
#2120, 2 Bloor St. West, Toronto ON M4W 3E2
Tel: 416-920-0434; *Fax:* 416-920-5982
toronto@innovationnorway.no
www.innovasjonnorge.no/canada
Previous Name: Norwegian Trade Council
Overview: A small international organization
Mission: To promote industrial development beneficial to both Norway & local businesses; to encourage alliances & partnerships between Norwegian & Canadian enterprises.
Chief Officer(s):
Rolf H. Sorland, Trade Commissioner & Manager, 416-920-0434 Ext. 123
rolf.h.sorland@innovasjonnorge.no
Staff Member(s): 5

INO / Institut national d'optique
2740, rue Einstein, Québec QC G1P 4S4
Tel: 418-657-7006; *Fax:* 418-657-7009
Toll-Free: 866-657-7406
info@ino.ca
www.ino.ca
Also Known As: National Optics Institute
Overview: A large national licensing organization founded in 1985
Mission: To be an international leader in optics & photonics R&D, promoting economic expansion in the country by providing assistance to companies seeking to be more competitive
Member of: Canadian Advanced Technology Association
Chief Officer(s):
Jean-Yves Roy, President & CEO
Finances: *Annual Operating Budget:* Greater than $5 Million; *Funding Sources:* 70% self-supporting; 30% government
Staff Member(s): 235
Membership: 11 affiliate + 19 associate + 4 individual; *Fees:* $10,000 affiliate; $1,000 associate; $100 individual; *Member Profile:* Company, individual, organization interested in photonics research & development; *Committees:* Executive; Health & Safety; R&D Advisory; ISO 9001
Activities: Provides a full range of R&D services in optics & photonics; *Internships:* Yes
Awards:
• INO Fellowship Program (Scholarship)

InScribe Christian Writers' Fellowship (ICWF)
PO Box 6201, Wetaskiwin AB T9A 2E9
Tel: 780-542-7950
query@inscribe.org
www.inscribe.org
www.facebook.com/CanadianWriters
twitter.com/InscribeCWF
Overview: A small national organization
Mission: To stimulate, encourage & support Christians across Canada who write; to advance effective Christian writing; to promote the availability & influence of all Christians who write
Chief Officer(s):
Jack Popjes, President
jack_popjes@wycliffe.ca
Leanne Vanderveen, Secretary
inscribe.mail@gmail.com
Finances: *Annual Operating Budget:* Less than $50,000
Membership: 160; *Fees:* $40
Activities: Fall Conference; Spring Workshop; InSpiration Groups; *Speaker Service:* Yes

Inside Education
11428 - 100 Ave., Edmonton AB T5K 0J4
Tel: 780-421-1497; *Fax:* 780-425-4506
Toll-Free: 888-421-1497
info@insideeducation.ca
www.insideeducation.ca
www.linkedin.com/company/1409777
www.facebook.com/InsideEducation
twitter.com/insideeducation
www.youtube.com/user/InsideEducation
Previous Name: FEESA - An Environmental Education Society
Overview: A medium-sized provincial charitable organization founded in 1985
Mission: To empower all Albertans to make informed choices about the environment by providing bias-balanced environmental education; to communicate, coordinate & initiate the development & support of bias-balanced environmental education in Alberta through a variety of programs & services; to ensure that the views of business, industry, government, the environment & community sector are represented in any programming or communication
Member of: Environmental Outdoor Education Council; Alberta Environmental Network; Canadian Environmental Network
Affliation(s): North American Association for Environmental Education; EECOM
Chief Officer(s):
Steve McIsaac, Executive Director
smcisaac@insideeducation.ca
Finances: *Annual Operating Budget:* $500,000-$1.5 Million; *Funding Sources:* Industry 50%; government 40%; private/users 10%
Staff Member(s): 9; 1000 volunteer(s)
Membership: 300 associates; 18 members (Board); *Fees:* $15 student; $25 individual; $50 institution; $250 corporate
Activities: Promotion of environmental education in formal & public education areas; presentations, conferences & conventions; coordination & development of education resources that focus on a variety of environmental & educational needs; teacher-training institutes focusing on a variety of environmental issues; *Awareness Events:* Environment Week, 1st week of June

Calgary
#205, 1117 - 1st St. SW, Calgary AB T2R 0T9
Tel: 403-263-7720; *Fax:* 403-263-7709

Inside Out Lesbian & Gay Film & Video Festival *See* Inside Out Toronto LGBT Film & Video Festival

Inside Out Toronto LGBT Film & Video Festival
#219, 401 Richmond St. West, Toronto ON M5V 3A8
Tel: 416-977-6847; *Fax:* 416-977-8025
insideout@insideout.ca
www.insideout.ca
twitter.com/InsideOutTO
www.youtube.com/InsideOutToronto
Previous Name: Inside Out Lesbian & Gay Film & Video Festival
Overview: A small international organization founded in 1991
Mission: To host the largest lesbian & gay festival in Canada & one of the largest in the world
Chief Officer(s):
Scott Ferguson, Executive Director
scott@insideout.ca
Staff Member(s): 20; 100 volunteer(s)
Membership: 350+; *Fees:* $35 basic; $100 supporter; $175 associate; $350 benefactor; $600 patron; $2,500 deluxe
Activities: *Awareness Events:* Inside Out Toronto LGBT Film & Video Festival, May
Awards:
• Mark S. Bonham Scholarship for Queer Studies in Film and Video (Scholarship)
Eligibility: Individual who identifies as part of the LGBT community; pursuing undergraduate studies in film; Canadian citizen*Deadline:* May 30

Insitut canadien des économistes en construction - Québec
8615, rue Lafrenaie, St-Léonard QC H1P 2B6
Tél: 514-324-0968; *Téléc:* 514-324-2807
info@ocec-quebec.org
www.ciqs.org
Également appelé: ICÉC - Québec
Nom précédent: Association des Estimateurs et Économistes en Construction du Québec
Aperçu: *Dimension:* petite; *Envergure:* provinciale; fondée en 1973
Mission: Promouvoir et avancer le statut professionnel des Économistes en construction; établir et maintenir un haut degré de compétence professionnelle et d'intégrité en limitant l'adhésion à ceux rencontrant les critères de l'Association; assurer la solidarité et servir d'intermédiaire dans les échanges de connaissance en matière de construction afin de promouvoir l'avancement de la profession
Membre(s) du bureau directeur:
Jean Paradis, Président
André Lavoie, Vice-président
Hervé Couture, Trésorier
Bernard Mercier, Secrétaire
Isabelle Buisson, Coordonnatrice administrative
Finances: *Budget de fonctionnement annuel:* Moins de $50,000
Membre: 180
Activités: *Service de conférenciers:* Oui

Inspirit Foundation
Centre for Social Innovation, #417, 215 Spadina Ave., Toronto ON M5T 2C7
Tel: 416-644-3600
www.inspiritfoundation.ca
www.facebook.com/pages/Inspirit-Foundation/29940300013279 3
twitter.com/InspiritFdn
Overview: A medium-sized national organization
Mission: A national grant-making organization that supports Canadians, particularly young adults, in building a more inclusive and pluralist Canada.
Chief Officer(s):

Andrea Nemtin, President & CEO
anemtin@inspiritfoundation.ca
Awards:
• Inspirit Bridge Building Grants (Grant)
Support projects that bring together young Canadians of different religious, spiritual, and secular beliefs for a common goal at the community level. Eligibility: Canadian; aged 18-30
Amount: $5,000-$25,000

Installation, Maintenance & Repair Sector Council & Trade Association (IMR)

#300, 180 Attwell Dr., Toronto ON M9W 6A9
Tel: 905-602-8877; *Fax:* 416-679-9234
Toll-Free: 866-602-8877
info@electrofed.com
www.electrofed.com/imr
www.linkedin.com/company/1458895?trk=tyah
twitter.com/EFC_Tweets
Overview: A medium-sized national organization
Mission: To ensure that there is an adequate supply of trained people with the skills required for today's appliances & electronics
Chief Officer(s):
Jeff Miller, Executive Director, 647-258-7478
jmiller@electrofed.com

Instit du Chrysotile ***See*** Chrysotile Institute

Institut aéronautique et spatial du Canada ***See*** Canadian Aeronautics & Space Institute

Institut agréé de la logistique et des transports Amérique du Nord ***See*** The Chartered Institute of Logistics & Transport in North America

Institut agricole du Canada ***See*** Agricultural Institute of Canada

L'Institut canadien ***See*** The Canadian Institute

Institut canadien d'administration de la justice ***See*** Canadian Institute for the Administration of Justice

Institut canadien d'éducation des adultes ***Voir*** Institut de coopération pour l'éducation des adultes

Institut canadien d'études méditerranéennes ***See*** Canadian Institute for Mediterranean Studies

Institut canadien d'études ukrainiennes ***See*** Canadian Institute of Ukrainian Studies

Institut canadien d'information sur la santé ***See*** Canadian Institute for Health Information

Institut canadien de conservation ***See*** Canadian Conservation Institute

Institut canadien de formation ***See*** Canadian Training Institute

Institut canadien de formation de l'énergie ***See*** Canadian Institute for Energy Training

Institut canadien de gemmologie ***See*** Canadian Institute of Gemmology

Institut canadien de gestion ***See*** Canadian Institute of Management

Institut canadien de l'immeuble ***See*** Real Estate Institute of Canada

Institut canadien de la construction en acier ***See*** Canadian Institute of Steel Construction

Institut canadien de la recherche sur la condition physique et le mode de vie ***See*** Canadian Fitness & Lifestyle Research Institute

Institut canadien de la retraite et des avantages sociaux ***See*** Canadian Pension & Benefits Institute

Institut canadien de la santé animale ***See*** Canadian Animal Health Institute

Institut canadien de la santé infantile ***See*** Canadian Institute of Child Health

Institut canadien de la tôle d'acier pour le bâtiment ***See*** Canadian Sheet Steel Building Institute

Institut canadien de plomberie et de chauffage ***See*** Canadian Institute of Plumbing & Heating

L'Institut canadien de Québec (ICQ)

350, rue Saint-Joseph est, 4e étage, Québec QC G1K 3B2
Tél: 418-641-6788; *Téléc:* 418-641-6787
courrier@institutcanadien.qc.ca
www.institutcanadien.qc.ca
www.linkedin.com/company/l'institut-canadien-de-qu-bec
www.facebook.com/176468254731
twitter.com/ICQ_Quebec
Aperçu: *Dimension:* grande; *Envergure:* nationale; fondée en 1848
Mission: Démocratiser l'accès au savoir et aux oeuvres d'imagination par un service de bibliothèque universellement accessible; sensibiliser le public aux arts et à la culture; gestion de bibliothèques publiques de la Ville de Québec.
Membre de: Association des Bibliothèques publiques du Québec
Membre(s) du bureau directeur:
Marie-Claire Lévesque, Présidente
Sylvie Fortin, Secrétaire
Jean Payeur, Directeur général
jpayeur@institutcanadien.qc.ca
Finances: *Budget de fonctionnement annuel:* Plus de $5 Million
Membre(s) du personnel: 150
Membre: Over 50,000
Activités: *Bibliothèque:* Bibliothèque de Québec;
Publications:
• Lettre de la Maison de la littérature [a publication of L'Institut canadien de Québec]
Type: Bulletin

Institut canadien de recherche sur le Judaïsme ***See*** Canadian Institute for Jewish Research

Institut canadien de recherches avancées ***See*** Canadian Institute for Advanced Research

Institut canadien de recherches sur les femmes ***See*** Canadian Research Institute for the Advancement of Women

Institut canadien de relations avec les investisseurs ***See*** Canadian Investor Relations Institute

Institut canadien de science et technologie alimentaires ***See*** Canadian Institute of Food Science & Technology

Institut canadien des actuaires ***See*** Canadian Institute of Actuaries

Institut canadien des affaires culturelles ***See*** Canadian Institute of Cultural Affairs

Institut canadien des engrais ***See*** Canadian Fertilizer Institute

Institut canadien des évaluateurs ***See*** Appraisal Institute of Canada

L'Institut canadien des experts en évaluation d'entreprises ***See*** Canadian Institute of Chartered Business Valuators

L'Institut canadien des ingénieurs ***See*** The Engineering Institute of Canada

Institut Canadien des inspecteurs en santé publique ***See*** Canadian Institute of Public Health Inspectors

Institut canadien des mines, de la métallurgie et du pétrole ***See*** Canadian Institute of Mining, Metallurgy & Petroleum

L'Institut Canadien des Technologies Scénographiques ***See*** Canadian Institute for Theatre Technology

Institut canadien des urbanistes ***See*** Canadian Institute of Planners

L'Institut canadien des valeurs mobilières ***See*** Canadian Securities Institute

Institut canadien du béton préfabriqué et précontraint ***See*** Canadian Precast / Prestressed Concrete Institute

Institut canadien du chauffage, de la climatisation et de la réfrigération ***See*** Heating, Refrigeration & Air Conditioning Institute of Canada

L'Institut canadien du crédit ***See*** Credit Institute of Canada

Institut canadien du droit des ressources ***See*** Canadian Institute of Resources Law

Institut canadien du film ***See*** Canadian Film Institute

Institut canadien du marketing ***See*** Canadian Institute of Marketing

Institut canadien du sucre ***See*** Canadian Sugar Institute

Institut canadien du tapis ***See*** Canadian Carpet Institute

Institut canadien du trafic et du transport ***See*** Canadian Institute of Traffic & Transportation

Institut canadien pour la résolution des conflits ***See*** Canadian Institute for Conflict Resolution

Institut canadien pour la sécurité des patients ***See*** Canadian Patient Safety Institute

Institut Cardinal Léger contre la lèpre ***Voir*** Fondation Jules et Paul-Émile Léger

Institut C.D. Howe ***See*** C.D. Howe Institute

Institut circumpolaire canadien ***See*** Canadian Circumpolar Institute

L'Institut Cooper ***See*** Cooper Institute

Institut culturel et éducatif montagnais (ICEM)

1034, av Brochu, Sept-Iles QC G4R 2Z1
Tél: 418-968-4424; *Téléc:* 418-968-1841
Ligne sans frais: 800-391-4424
www.icem.ca
Nom précédent: Institut éducatif et culturel Attikamek-Montagnais
Aperçu: *Dimension:* moyenne; *Envergure:* locale; fondée en 1978
Mission: Préserver le patrimoine montagnais; sauvegarder la langue montagnaise; promouvoir l'éducation des montagnais
Membre de: Confédération des centres éducatifs et culturels des Premières Nations
Membre(s) du bureau directeur:
Jean-Pierre Donat, Président
Finances: *Budget de fonctionnement annuel:* $500,000-$1.5 Million
Membre(s) du personnel: 12
Membre: 8
Activités: *Bibliothèque* rendez-vous

Institut d'administration publique du Canada ***See*** Institute of Public Administration of Canada

Institut d'arbitrage et de médiation du Canada ***See*** ADR Institute of Canada

L'Institut d'assurance de dommages du Québec (IADQ)

#2230, 1200, av McGill College, Montréal QC H3B 4G7
Tél: 514-393-8156; *Téléc:* 514-393-9222
Autres numéros: quebeccourriel@institutdassurance.ca
montrealcourriel@institutdassurance.ca
www.iadq.qc.ca/informa/
Nom précédent: L'Institut d'assurance du Québec
Aperçu: *Dimension:* moyenne; *Envergure:* provinciale; Organisme sans but lucratif; fondée en 1927 surveillé par Insurance Institute of Canada
Mission: Organiser des cours, des séminaires et des conférences; promouvoir le rayonnement des titres professionnels PAA et FPAA d'assurance du Canada (AIAC & FIAC). Organisme sans but lucratif, qui a été mis sur pied par l'industrie de l'assurance de dommages pour donner la formation professionnelle à tous ceux qui oeuvrent dans ce secteur au Québec
Membre(s) du bureau directeur:
François Houle, Directeur général
Finances: *Budget de fonctionnement annuel:* $500,000-$1.5 Million
Membre(s) du personnel: 6
Membre: 6 000; *Montant de la cotisation:* 64,91$
Activités: Formation professionnelle en assurance de dommages; *Evénements de sensibilisation:* Gala; Tournoi de golf; *Service de conférenciers:* Oui

Bureau de Québec
#1300, 2875, boul Laurier, Sainte-Foy QC G1V 2M2
Tél: 418-623-3688; *Téléc:* 418-623-6935
quebeccourriel@institutdassurance.ca

Institut d'assurance du Canada ***See*** Insurance Institute of Canada

L'Institut d'assurance du Québec ***Voir*** L'Institut d'assurance de dommages du Québec

Institut d'éthiques mondiales (Canada) ***See*** Institute for Global Ethics (Canada)

L'Institut d'études canadiennes de McGill *See* McGill Institute for the Study of Canada

Institut d'histoire de l'Amérique française (IHAF)
a/s Département d'histoire, Université de Montréal, CP 6128, Succ. Centre-Ville, #6097c, 3150, rue Jean-Brillant, Montréal QC H3C 3J7
Tél: 514-343-6111; *Téléc:* 514-343-2483
ihaf@ihaf.qc.ca
www.ihaf.qc.ca
Aperçu: *Dimension:* petite; *Envergure:* nationale; Organisme sans but lucratif; fondée en 1946
Membre(s) du bureau directeur:
Alain Beaulieu, Président
beaulieu.alain@uqam.ca
Ollivier Hubert, Vice-président
ollivier.hubert@umontreal.ca
Brigitte Caulier, Secrétaire
Brigitte.Caulier@hst.ulaval.ca
Dominique Marquis, Trésorière
marquis.dominique@uqam.ca
Membre: *Critères d'admissibilité:* Professeurs, porfessionnels, et amateurs d'histoire
Publications:
• Revue d'histoire de l'Amérique française
Type: Journal; *Editor:* Louise Bienvenue

L'Institut d'Ingénierie Simultanée *Voir* L'Institut de développement de produits

Institut de cardiologie de Montréal (ICM) / Montréal Heart Institute (MHI)
5000, rue Bélanger est, Montréal QC H1T 1C8
Tél: 514-376-3330
Ligne sans frais: 855-922-6387
www.icm-mhi.org
Aperçu: *Dimension:* petite; *Envergure:* locale; fondée en 1954
Mission: Un centre uniquement consacré au développement des traitements des maladies cardiovasculaires
Membre(s) du bureau directeur:
Pierre Anctil, Président
Robert Busilacchi, Directeur général
Activités: *Bibliothèque*

Institut de chimie du Canada *See* Chemical Institute of Canada

Institut de coopération pour l'éducation des adultes (ICEA)
#303, 55, ave Mont-Royal ouest, Montréal QC H2T 2S6
Tél: 514-948-2044; *Téléc:* 514-948-2046
Ligne sans frais: 877-948-2044
icea@icea.qc.ca
www.icea.qc.ca
Nom précédent: Institut canadien d'éducation des adultes
Aperçu: *Dimension:* petite; *Envergure:* nationale; Organisme sans but lucratif; fondée en 1946
Mission: Promouvoir l'exercice du droit des adultes à l'éducation tout au long de la vie
Membre de: Centre de documentation sur l'éducation des adultes et la condition féminine; Communautique; Conseil international de l'éducation des adultes;
Membre(s) du bureau directeur:
Diane Dupuis, Directrice générale
Finances: *Budget de fonctionnement annuel:* $1.5 Million-$3 Million
Membre(s) du personnel: 15
Membre: 160; *Montant de la cotisation:* $500 nationale; $350 régionale; $150 locale; *Comités:* Politiques et éducation des adultes; Coordination; Éducation populaire automone; Besoin éducatif des adultes du 3ième âge
Activités: Recherche et analyse stratégiques; intervention publique; concertation; réalisation, production d'outils; *Evénements de sensibilisation:* Semaine québécoise des adultes en formation, mars/avril; *Bibliothèque:* CDEACF

L'Institut de développement de produits (IDP) / Institute for Product Development (IPD)
4805, rue Molson, Montréal QC H1Y 0A2
Tél: 514-383-3209; *Téléc:* 514-383-3266
info@idp-ipd.com
www.idp-ipd.com
Nom précédent: L'Institut d'Ingénierie Simultanée
Aperçu: *Dimension:* petite; *Envergure:* provinciale; Organisme sans but lucratif; fondée en 1995
Mission: Accélérer l'adoption des meilleures pratiques développement de produits au sein des entreprises québécoises afin de les rendre nos performantes
Membre de: Reseau canadien de technologie
Membre(s) du bureau directeur:
Bertrand Derome, Directeur général
Membre(s) du personnel: 11
Membre: *Montant de la cotisation:* Barème; *Critères d'admissibilite:* Manufacturier
Activités: Atelier visite en entreprise; séminaire de sensibilisation aux meilleures pratiques en développement de produits

Institut de développement urbain du Canada *See* Urban Development Institute of Canada

Institut de l'énergie et de l'environnement de la Francophonie (IEPF)
56, rue St-Pierre, 3e étage, Québec QC G1K 4A1
Tél: 418-692-5727; *Téléc:* 418-692-5644
www.iepf.org
Aperçu: *Dimension:* moyenne; *Envergure:* internationale; Organisme sans but lucratif; fondée en 1988
Mission: Contribuer au renforcement des capacités nationales et au développement des partenariats dans les domaines de l'énergie et de l'environnement
Membre de: Agence de la Francophonie
Membre(s) du bureau directeur:
Fatimata Dia Touré, Directrice
Finances: *Budget de fonctionnement annuel:* $3 Million-$5 Million
Membre(s) du personnel: 17
Activités: *Bibliothèque:* Service information et documentation

Institut de la fondation d'acupuncture du Canada *See* Acupuncture Foundation of Canada Institute

Institut de la fourrure du Canada *See* Fur Institute of Canada

Institut de la gestion financière *See* Financial Management Institute of Canada

Institut de la Propriété Intellectuelle du Canada *See* Intellectual Property Institute of Canada

Institut de médiation et d'arbitrage du Québec (IMAQ)
CP 874, Succ. B, Montréal QC H3B 3k5
Tél: 514-282-3327; *Téléc:* 514-282-2214
info@imaq.org
www.imaq.org
Aperçu: *Dimension:* petite; *Envergure:* provinciale; fondée en 1977
Mission: Promouvoir les méthodes alternatives de résolution de conflits (médiation, arbitrage); donner accès par internet à la population et aux entreprises à une banque de médiateurs et d'arbitres accrédités selon leur: spécialité (médiateur ou arbitre), région, langue de communication, catégorie de membre, profession, domaine d'expertise
Membre(s) du bureau directeur:
Thierry Bériault, Président
Pierre D. Grenier, Vice-président

Institut de prévention des sinistres catastrophiques *See* Institute for Catastrophic Loss Reduction

Institut de radioprotection du Canada *See* Radiation Safety Institute of Canada

Institut de réadaptation en déficience physique de Québec (IRDPQ)
525, boul Wilfrid-Hamel, Québec QC G1M 2S8
Tél: 418-529-9141; *TTY:* 418-649-3733
communications@irdpq.qc.ca
www.irdpq.qc.ca
www.facebook.com/IRDPQ
www.youtube.com/user/VideosIRDPQ
Nom précédent: Institut de réadaptation physique de Québec
Aperçu: *Dimension:* petite; *Envergure:* provinciale; fondée en 1996
Mission: Offrir des services de réadaptation, d'adaptation et de soutien à l'intégration sociale aux enfants, adultes et ainés qui ont des incapacités et vivent des situations de handicap en raison de leur déficience auditive, motrice, neurologique, visuelle, de la parole ou du langage, de même que des services d'accompagnement et de soutien à l'entourage
Membre de: Association des établissements de réadaptation en déficience physique du Québec
Membre(s) du bureau directeur:
Marc Prenevost, Directeur général
Finances: *Budget de fonctionnement annuel:* Plus de $5 Million
Membre(s) du personnel: 1300; 200 bénévole(s)
Membre: *Comités:* Administratif; Évaluation du directeur général; Orientation et de planification stratégique; Éthique clinique; Usagers; Gestion des risques; Vigilance et de la qualité; Gouvernance et d'éthique; Révision; Vérification et d'utilisation des ressources; Éthique de la recherche
Activités: *Stagiaires:* Oui; *Bibliothèque:* Centre de documentation

Institut de réadaptation physique de Québec *Voir* Institut de réadaptation en déficience physique de Québec

Institut de recherche - brassage et orge de maltage *See* Brewing & Malting Barley Research Institute

Institut de recherche en biologie végétale (IRBV) / Plant Biology Research Institute (PBRI)
4101, rue Sherbrooke est, Montréal QC H1X 2B2
Tél: 514-343-2121; *Téléc:* 514-343-2288
irbv@irbv.umontreal.ca
www.irbv.umontreal.ca
Aperçu: *Dimension:* petite; *Envergure:* locale; Organisme sans but lucratif; fondée en 1990
Mission: To develop a centre of excellence in plant biology; both in fundamental research and its applicaitons; train students in plant biology at the master, doctoral, and post-doctoral levels; further training and knowledge of its researchers and technical personnel; promote the technological transfer of its scientific research results to users; provide complementary services to the community in fields relevant to plant biology, where expertise in the field is lacking.
Membre(s) du bureau directeur:
Anne Bruneau, Directrice, 514-343-2121
Finances: *Budget de fonctionnement annuel:* $1.5 Million-$3 Million
Membre(s) du personnel: 100
Membre: 200
Activités: *Service de conférenciers:* Oui; *Bibliothèque*

Institut de recherche en politiques publiques *See* Institute for Research on Public Policy

Institut de recherche en services de santé *See* Institute for Clinical Evaluative Sciences

Institut de recherche et de développement en agroenvironnement *See* Research & Development Institute for the Agri-Environment

Institut de recherche Robert-Sauvé en santé et en sécurité du travail (IRSST) / Robert Sauvé Occupational Health & Safety Research Institute
505, boul de Maisonneuve ouest, 15e étage, Montréal QC H3A 3C2
Tél: 514-288-1551; *Téléc:* 514-288-7636
communications@irsst.qc.ca
www.irsst.qc.ca
www.facebook.com//207703664186
twitter.com/IRSST
Aperçu: *Dimension:* moyenne; *Envergure:* provinciale; fondée en 1980
Mission: Contribuer par la recherche et le développement à l'amélioration de la santé et de la sécurité des travailleurs et plus spécifiquement, à l'élimination à la source des dangers pour leur santé, leur sécurité et leur intégrité physique ainsi qu'à la réadaptation des travailleurs victimes d'accidents ou de maladies professionnelles; fournir au Réseau public québécois de la prévention en santé et en sécurité du travail - composé de CSST, des Centres locaux de services communautaires, des Régies de la santé et des services sociaux et des associations sectorielles paritaires - les services et l'expertise nécessaires à leur action; diffuser les connaissances issues de ces recherches et de ces expertises auprès des milieux de travail et en favoriser le transfert; accorder des bourses d'études supérieures en santé et en sécurité du travail; agir comme laboratoire de référence au Québec, dans le domaine de l'hygiene industrielle.
Affiliation(s): International Occupational Safety & Health Information Centre
Membre(s) du bureau directeur:
Michel Després, Président/Directeur général
Finances: *Budget de fonctionnement annuel:* Plus de $5 Million*Fonds:* Près de 85 % des revenus proviennent d'une subvention de la Commission de la santé et de la sécurité du travail du Québec (CSST)
Membre(s) du personnel: 130
Membre: *Comités:* Executive Committee; Follow-up Committee
Activités: Mène des recherches dans les domaines jugés prioritaires; Fait la promotion du développement de nouvelles

connaissances en santé et en sécurité du travail en collaboration avec la communauté scientifique; Contribue à la formation de chercheurs en santé et en sécurité du travail; Contribue au développement de normes et règlements touchant la santé et la sécurité du travail; Diffuse les connaissances issues des recherches auprès du monde du travail et de la communauté scientifique; *Bibliothèque* Bibliothèque publique
Prix, Bouses:
• Bourse de maîtrise (Bourse d études)
Deadline: octobre *Amount:* 14 100$ *Contact:* Michel Asselin, Téléphone: 514-288-1551 poste 377; Courriel: bourses@irsst.qc.ca
• Bourse de doctorat (Bourse d études)
Deadline: octobre *Amount:* 18 000$ *Contact:* Michel Asselin, Téléphone: 514-288-1551 poste 377; Courriel: bourses@irsst.qc.ca
• Bourse de doctorat hors du Québec (Bourse d études)
Deadline: octobre *Amount:* 24 000$ *Contact:* Michel Asselin, Téléphone: 514-288-1551 poste 377; Courriel: bourses@irsst.qc.ca
• Bourse de formation postdoctorale au Québec (Bourse d études)
Deadline: octobre *Amount:* 30 000$ *Contact:* Michel Asselin, Téléphone: 514-288-1551 poste 377; Courriel: bourses@irsst.qc.ca
• Bourse de stagiaire postdoctoral invité à l'IRSST (Bourse d études)
Deadline: octobre *Amount:* 30 000$ *Contact:* Michel Asselin, Téléphone: 514-288-1551 poste 377; Courriel: bourses@irsst.qc.ca
• Bourse de formation postdoctorale hors du Québec (Bourse d études)
Deadline: octobre *Amount:* 36 000$ *Contact:* Michel Asselin, Téléphone: 514-288-1551 poste 377; Courriel: bourses@irsst.qc.ca
• Programme de subvention de recherche par concours (Brouse)
• Programme de subvention de recherche concertée (Brouse)
• Programme de subvention d'activité concertée (Brouse)
Publications:
• Bulletin d'information du REM
Type: Bulletin électronique; *Frequency:* semi-annuel
Profile: Un bulletin qui constitue un moyen d'échanges entre les membres du Réseau d'échange sur la manutention (REM)
• INFO LABO - Des nouvelles de nos laboratoires
Type: Bulletin électronique
Profile: Un bulletin qui contient des communiqués, des avis ainsi que des recommandations s'adressant plus spécifiquement aux intervenants du réseau québécois de la santéet de la sécurité du travail
• infoIRSST - Des nouvelles de la recherche
Type: Bulletin électronique; *Frequency:* 10 fois par an
Profile: Un bulletin qui présente toute l'actualité de la recherche réalisée ou financée par l'IRSST : les communiqués, les dernières parutions et les nouveaux projets derecherche, les colloques et les conférences et les dernières nouvelles de nos laboratoires
• Prévention au travail
Type: Magazine; *Frequency:* trimestriel; *Number of Pages:* 31
Profile: Un magazine qui vise à fournir une information utile pour prévenir les accidents du travail et les maladies professionnelles

Institut de recherche sur le cancer Populomix *See* Populomix Cancer Research Institute

Institut de recherche sur le travail et la santé *See* Institute for Work & Health

Institut de recherches cliniques de Montréal (IRCM)
110, av des Pins Ouest, Montréal QC H2W 1R7
Tél: 514-987-5500; *Téléc:* 514-987-5532
info@ircm.qc.ca
www.ircm.qc.ca
www.facebook.com/IRCM.Montreal
Aperçu: *Dimension:* petite; *Envergure:* locale; fondée en 1967
Mission: Pour comprendre les causes et les mécanismes des maladies; Pour découvrir des outils diagnostiques et des moyens de prévention et traitement des maladies; Pour faciliter le développement commercial de nouvelles découvertes
Membre(s) du bureau directeur:
Tarik Möröy, President & Scientific Director
André Veillette, Executive Director, Academic Affairs
Louis-Gilles Durand, Executive Director, Administration & Research Services
Yves Berthiaume, Executive Director, Clinic & Clinical Research
Stéphane Létourneau, Executive Director, Corporate & Legal Affairs
Membre(s) du personnel: 425
Membre: *Comités:* Direction; Direction scientifique; Scientifique; Consultatif scientifique
Activités: Former les scientifiques; Favoriser les collaborations nationales et internationales pour faire avancer la science

Institut de tourisme et d'hôtellerie du Québec (ITHQ)
3535, rue Saint-Denis, Montréal QC H2X 3P1
Tél: 514-282-5111; *Téléc:* 514-873-4529
Ligne sans frais: 800-361-5111
info@ithq.qc.ca
www.ithq.qc.ca
www.linkedin.com/company/ithq-montreal---canada?trk=biz-companies-cym
www.facebook.com/ecoleITHQ
twitter.com/ITHQ
Aperçu: *Dimension:* grande; *Envergure:* provinciale; fondée en 1968
Mission: l'ITHQ est la plus importante école de gestion hôtelière au Canada spécialisée en tourisme, hôtellerie, restauration et sommellerie.
Membre(s) du bureau directeur:
Lucille Daoust, Directrice générale
Paolo Di Pietrantonio, Président
Finances: *Budget de fonctionnement annuel:* Plus de $5 Million
Membre(s) du personnel: 280
Activités: *Stagiaires:* Oui; *Bibliothèque:* Bibliothèque; Bibliothèque publique

Institut des administrateurs de sociétés *See* Institute of Corporate Directors

Institut des Affaires Culturelles International *See* Institute of Cultural Affairs International

L'Institut des agronomes du Nouveau-Brunswick *See* New Brunswick Institute of Agrologists

Institut des communications et de la publicité *See* Institute of Communication Agencies

Institut des comptables agréés du Nouveau-Brunswick *See* New Brunswick Institute of Chartered Accountants

L'Institut des fonds d'investissement du Canada *See* Investment Funds Institute of Canada

Institut des manufacturiers du vêtement du Québec (IMVQ) / Apparel Manufacturers Institute of Québec (AMIQ)
#1514 555, rue Chabanel ouest, Montréal QC H2N 2J2
Tél: 514-382-3846; *Téléc:* 514-383-1689
sc@vetementquebec.com
www.vetementquebec.com
Également appelé: Vêtement Québec
Aperçu: *Dimension:* moyenne; *Envergure:* provinciale; fondée en 1974
Mission: Vêtement Québec (IMVQ) joue des rôles multiples - elle est une source, notamment, d'information, de formation, d'inspiration et de motivation. Toutefois, d'abord et avant tout, c'est une association. Vêtement Québec est le regroupement professionnel des hommes et des femmes qui dirigent un grand nombre des entreprises de vêtements les plus progressives du pays, ainsi que d'entreprises qui offrent des produits et des services essentiels au secteur.
Membre(s) du bureau directeur:
Patrick Thomas, Directrice générale

Membre(s) du personnel: 3
Membre: 350

Institut des planificateurs professionnels de l'Ontario *See* Ontario Professional Planners Institute

Institut des sciences textiles *See* Institute of Textile Science

Institut des secrétaires et administrateurs agréés au Canada *See* Institute of Chartered Secretaries & Administrators - Canadian Division

Institut des Urbanistes de l'atlantique *See* Atlantic Planners Institute

Institut du cancer de Montréal (ICM) / Montréal Cancer Institute
900, rue St-Denis, Montréal QC H2X 0X9
Tél: 514-890-8213; *Téléc:* 514-412-7591
info@icm.qc.ca
www.icm.qc.ca
www.facebook.com/cancermtl
twitter.com/cancermtl
Aperçu: *Dimension:* petite; *Envergure:* locale; fondée en 1942
Mission: Favoriser la recherche fondamentale et clinique sur le cancer et de préparer la relève dans ce domaine par le biais de l'enseignement et de la formation
Affiliation(s): CHUM, Université de Montréal
Membre(s) du bureau directeur:
André Boulanger, Président
Maral Tersakian, Directrice générale
maral.tersakian@icm.qc.ca

Institut éducatif et culturel Attikamek-Montagnais *Voir* Institut culturel et éducatif montagnais

Institut féminin francophone du Nouveau-Brunswick
737, rte 133, Grand-Barachois NB E4P 8J1
Tél: 506-388-9604
Aperçu: *Dimension:* petite; *Envergure:* provinciale
Mission: Le mandat est de regrouper les femmes francophones du Nouveau-Brunswick dans le but de promouvoir les intérêts & de défendre les droits des femmes & des francophones
Membre de: Alliance des femmes de la francophonie canadienne
Membre(s) du bureau directeur:
Francine Gallant, Présidente
fgallant@cott.com

Institut forestier du Canada *See* Canadian Institute of Forestry

Institut généalogique des Provinces Maritimes *See* Genealogical Institute of The Maritimes

L'Institut international canadien de la négociation pratique *See* Canadian International Institute of Applied Negotiation

Institut international des sciences humaines intégrales *See* International Institute of Integral Human Sciences

Institut international du développement durable *See* International Institute for Sustainable Development

Institut manitobain des conseillers en administration agréés *See* Institute of Certified Management Consultants of Manitoba

Institut national d'optique *See* INO

Institut national de la magistrature *See* National Judicial Institute

Institut national de la qualité *See* National Quality Institute

Institut national de recherche et de gestion de l'incapacité au travail *See* National Institute of Disability Management & Research

Institut Nazareth et Louis-Braille (INLB)
1111, rue St-Charles Ouest, Longueuil QC J4K 5G4
Tél: 450-463-1710; *Téléc:* 450-463-0243
Ligne sans frais: 800-361-7063
info.inlb@ssss.gouv.qc.ca
inlb.qc.ca
www.facebook.com/InstitutNazarethEtLouisBraille
Aperçu: *Dimension:* petite; *Envergure:* locale; fondée en 1861
Mission: Pour trouver de nouvelles façons d'aider les personnes ayant une déficience visuelle deviennent autonomes
Membre(s) du bureau directeur:
Jean Bouchard, Président, Conseil d'administration
Annie Hulmann, Responsable des communications
annie.hulmann.inlb@ssss.gouv.qc.ca
Line Ampleman, Directrice générale
Membre: *Critères d'admissibilite:* Les personnes ayant une déficience visuelle ou ont de graves dommages à vue
Activités: *Stagiaires:* Oui

L'Institut Nord-Sud *See* The North-South Institute

Institut pour tuyaux de tôle ondulée *See* Corrugated Steel Pipe Institute

Institut professionnel de la fonction publique du Canada *See* The Professional Institute of the Public Service of Canada

L'Institut professionnel du personnel municipal *See* Civic Institute of Professional Personnel

Institut québécois de planification financière (IQPF)
#501, 3, place du Commerce, Montréal QC H3E 1H7
Tél: 514-767-4040; *Téléc:* 514-767-2845
Ligne sans frais: 800-640-4050
www.iqpf.org

www.facebook.com/IQPF.Planification.Financiere
twitter.com/IQPF
www.youtube.com/user/IQPFplanification
Aperçu: *Dimension:* petite; *Envergure:* provinciale; Organisme sans but lucratif; fondée en 1989
Mission: Contribuer à la protection et au mieux-être économique des consommateurs québécois, en veillant sur la formation et la qualification des professionnels regroupés en un réseau de planificateurs financiers solidaires d'une approche intégrée de la planification financière
Membre(s) du bureau directeur:
Jocelyne Houle-LeSarge, Présidente/Directrice Générale
Finances: *Budget de fonctionnement annuel:* $1.5 Million-$3 Million
Membre(s) du personnel: 19
Membre: 5 000; *Critères d'admissibilite:* Planificateur financier; *Comités:* Comité développement professionnel; comité d'audit; comité de gouvernance; comité du meilleur formateur; comité bourse de recherche; groupe de travail sur le congrès 2014; groupe des mentors; groupe de rédaction de la cible
Activités: Formation professionnelle des planificateurs financiers du Québec

Institut québécois des hautes études internationales *Voir* Hautes études internationales

Institut québécois des revêtements de sol inc. *Voir* Fédération québécoise des revêtements de sol

Institut royal d'architecture du Canada *See* Royal Architectural Institute of Canada

Institut Séculier Pie X (ISPX) / Pius X Secular Institute

CP 87731, Succ. Succ. Charlesbourg, 1645, boul Louis-XIV, Québec QC G1G 5W6
Tél: 418-626-5882; *Téléc:* 418-624-2277
info@ispx.org
www.ispx.org
Aperçu: *Dimension:* petite; *Envergure:* internationale; Organisme sans but lucratif; fondée en 1939
Mission: Évangéliser les milieux populaires par la présence et par des activités apostoliques
Membre de: Conférence canadienne des instituts séculiers; Conférence mondiale des instituts séculiers
Membre(s) du bureau directeur:
Gérald Cyprien Lacroix, Directeur général
Finances: *Budget de fonctionnement annuel:* $100,000-$250,000
Membre: 17 consacrés + 250 associés
Activités: Apostolat catholique; évangélisation; présence au monde; *Service de conférenciers:* Oui

Institut sur la gouvernance *See* Institute On Governance

Institut Vanier de la famille *See* Vanier Institute of The Family

Institut Voluntas Dei / Voluntas Dei Institute

7385, boul Parent, Trois-Rivières QC G9A 5E1
Tél: 819-375-7933; *Téléc:* 819-691-1841
ivd.cent@cgocable.ca
www.voluntasdei.org
www.facebook.com/voluntasdei
twitter.com/voluntasdei
www.youtube.com/voluntasdeis?feature=mhee#p/u/22/
Également appelé: I.V. Dei
Aperçu: *Dimension:* petite; *Envergure:* internationale; Organisme sans but lucratif; fondée en 1958
Mission: To make known & communicate God's love for all to all people; To be present in every milieu; apostolic objective is "to create peace & brotherhood in Jesus Christ"
Membre de: Roman Catholic Church
Finances: *Budget de fonctionnement annuel:* $100,000-$250,000
Membre(s) du personnel: 3
Membre: 752; *Critères d'admissibilite:* Clerics & laymen who commit their lives to the service of Jesus Christ; married people as associate members who live out the same ideal & same apostolic project as the celibate members
Activités: *Stagiaires:* Oui

Institute for Catastrophic Loss Reduction (ICLR) / Institut de prévention des sinistres catastrophiques (IPSC)

#210, 20 Richmond St. East, Toronto ON M5C 2R9
Tel: 416-364-8677; *Fax:* 416-364-5889
info@iclr.org
www.iclr.org
www.facebook.com/instituteforcatastrophiclossreduction
twitter.com/ICLRCanada
www.youtube.com/user/ICLRinfo
Overview: A small national licensing organization founded in 1998
Mission: Reduce the loss of life & property caused by severe weather & earthquakes through the identification & support of sustained actions that improve society's capacity to adapt to, anticipate, mitigate, withstand & recover from natural disasters
Affliation(s): The University of Western Ontario
Chief Officer(s):
Paul Kovacs, Executive Director
pkovacs@iclr.org
Finances: *Annual Operating Budget:* $250,000-$500,000
Membership: 50; *Fees:* $2,000 associate; *Member Profile:* Organizations interested in disaster prevention
Activities: Protecting Kids from Disaster Program; Safety Upgrades for Child Care Centres; *Speaker Service:* Yes

London Office
Boundary Layer Wind Tunnel Laboratory, Univ. of Western Ontario, 1151 Richmond St., London ON N6A 5B9
Tel: 519-661-3234; *Fax:* 519-661-4273

Institute for Clinical Evaluative Sciences (ICES) / Institut de recherche en services de santé

#G1 06, 2075 Bayview Ave., Toronto ON M4N 3M5
Tel: 416-480-4055; *Fax:* 416-480-6048
info@ices.on.ca
www.ices.on.ca
www.facebook.com/105181509564479
twitter.com/ICESOntario
www.youtube.com/user/ICESOntario
Overview: A small provincial organization founded in 1992
Mission: Conducts research that contributes to the effectiveness, quality, equity & efficiency of health care in Ontario
Chief Officer(s):
Michael Baker, Chair, 416-480-4297
David Henry, President & CEO
Finances: *Annual Operating Budget:* $3 Million-$5 Million
Staff Member(s): 94
Membership: 1-99
Activities: *Library:* Resource Centre
Publications:
• At A Glance [a publication of the Institute for Clinical Evaluative Sciences]
Type: Bulletin; *Frequency:* Monthly; *Number of Pages:* 2

Institute for Global Ethics (Canada) / Institut d'éthiques mondiales (Canada)

#208 - 431 Pacific St., Vancouver BC V6Z 2P5
Tel: 604-688-6216
Toll-Free: 800-729-2613
canada@globalethics.org
www.globalethics.org/canada.php
Overview: A small national organization founded in 1997
Mission: To promote ethical action in a global context; to explore the global common ground of shared values, elevate awareness of ethics & provide practical tools for making ethical decisions
Chief Officer(s):
Rushworth M. Kidder, President, 800-729-2615 Ext. 133
rush.kidder@globalethics.org
Membership: *Fees:* $100-$1,000

Institute for Optimizing Health Outcomes

#600, 151 Bloor St. West, Toronto ON M5S 1S4
Tel: 416-969-7431; *Fax:* 416-969-7420
Toll-Free: 877-992-6364
info@optimizinghealth.org
www.optimizinghealth.org
Previous Name: Anemia Institute for Research & Education
Overview: A small national organization
Mission: Promotes patient-centred programs, education, research & advocacy to improve care & support for persons at risk for, or living with, health conditions (including, but not limited to, anemia)
Affliation(s): Ontario Patient Self-Management Network

Institute for Policy Analysis *See* Rotman Institute for International Business

Institute for Product Development *Voir* L'Institut de développement de produits

Institute for Research on Public Policy / Institut de recherche en politiques publiques

#200, 1470, rue Peel, Montréal QC H3A 1T1
Tel: 514-985-2461; *Fax:* 514-985-2559
irpp@irpp.org
www.irpp.org
Overview: A medium-sized national organization founded in 1972
Mission: To improve public policy in Canada by generating research, providing insight, & sparking debate that will contribute to the public policy decision-making process & strengthen the quality of public policy decisions made by Canadian governments, citizens, institutions, & organizations
Chief Officer(s):
Graham Fox, President, 514-787-0741
gfox@irpp.org
Finances: *Funding Sources:* Government; general donations
Staff Member(s): 15
Activities: *Library*

Institute for Risk Research (IRR)

University of Waterloo, 200 University Ave. West, Waterloo ON N2L 3G1
Tel: 519-885-4027; *Fax:* 519-725-4834
irr-neram@uwaterloo.ca
www.irr-neram.ca
Overview: A small local organization founded in 1982
Mission: To promote safety for Canadians by improving the understanding of risk & risk policy decisions
Chief Officer(s):
John Shortreed, Director
shortree@uwaterloo.ca
Finances: *Funding Sources:* Corporations; government grants & contracts
Membership: 146
Activities: Includes Environmental Risk Management shortcourse; environmental conferences; *Speaker Service:* Yes; *Library* Open to public by appointment

Institute for Stuttering Treatment & Research & the Communication Improvement Program (ISTAR, CIP)

College Plaza, #1500, 8215 - 112 St., Edmonton AB T6G 2C8
Tel: 780-492-2619; *Fax:* 780-492-8457
istar@ualberta.ca
www.istar.ualberta.ca
twitter.com/ISTAR_UofA
Overview: A small international charitable organization founded in 1986
Member of: Institute Faculty of Rehabilitation Medicine, University of Alberta
Affliation(s): The University of Alberta; Alberta College of Speech-Language Pathologists & Audiologists; Canadian Association of Speech-Language Pathology & Audiology
Chief Officer(s):
Deryk Beal, Executive Director
Finances: *Funding Sources:* Elks of Alberta; Elks & Royal Purple Fund for Children; Clinic fees; Donations
Staff Member(s): 10; 40 volunteer(s)
Membership: 7
Activities: Providing treatment for stuttering; Conducting research into the nature & treatment of stuttering; Providing advanced professional training for speech pathologists; Offering presentations to university students, teachers, parents, speech-language pathologists, & the general public; Publishing;
Awards:
• Scholarships (Scholarship)
Available to clients depending on need

Institute for Sustainable Energy, Economy & Environment Student's Association (ISEEESA)

Scrubfield Hall, #199B, 2500 University Dr., Calgary AB T2N 1N4
e-mail: info@iseeesa.ca
www.iseeesa.ca
www.facebook.com/groups/iseeesa
twitter.com/iseeesa
flickr.com/iseeesa
Overview: A large national organization founded in 2006
Mission: To promote and create initiatives that reflect the growing movement to obtain a cleaner energy supply, healthy environment, and efficient economy.
Chief Officer(s):
Pasley Weeks, President

Institute for the Study & Treatment of Pain (ISTOP)

5655 Cambie St., Lower Fl., Vancouver BC V5Z 3A4

Tel: 604-264-7867; *Fax:* 604-264-7860
istop@istop.org
www.istop.org
Overview: A small international charitable organization founded in 1995
Mission: A non-profit organization dedicated to the understanding & treatment of soft tissue pain
Chief Officer(s):
Chan Gunn, President
Allan Lam, Clinic Director
Finances: *Annual Operating Budget:* $250,000-$500,000
Staff Member(s): 3
Membership: 500-999
Activities: *Internships:* Yes

Institute for Work & Health (IWH) / Institut de recherche sur le travail et la santé

#800, 481 University Ave., Toronto ON M5G 2E9
Tel: 416-927-2027; *Fax:* 416-927-4167
info@iwh.on.ca
www.iwh.on.ca
Previous Name: Ontario Workers' Compensation Institute
Overview: A medium-sized provincial organization founded in 1990
Mission: To conduct & share research with workers, labour, employers, clinicians & policy-makers to promote, protect & improve the health of working people
Chief Officer(s):
Cameron Mustard, President & Senior Scientist
Ian Anderson, Chair
Finances: *Annual Operating Budget:* $3 Million-$5 Million; *Funding Sources:* Public & private sector; research grants
Staff Member(s): 75
Activities: *Awareness Events:* Alf Nachemson Memorial Lecture
Awards:
• Mustard Fellowship in Work Environment & Health (Scholarship)
Deadline: April

Institute of Air & Space Law (IASL)

3690 Peel St., Montréal QC H3A 1W9
Tel: 514-398-5095; *Fax:* 514-398-8197
maria.damico@mcgill.ca
www.mcgill.ca/iasl/
Overview: A small national organization
Mission: To educate air & space lawyers to serve the needs of the air & space community worldwide; To publish interdisciplinary research of value to governments & multinational institutions, the airline & aerospace industries, & the legal profession; To create a global network for faculty, students & subject experts
Chief Officer(s):
Paul Stephen Dempsey, Director
Membership: 500-999
Activities: *Speaker Service:* Yes
Publications:
• Annals of Air & Space Law / Annales de droit aérien et spatial
Type: Journal; *Frequency:* Annually

Institute of Asian & Slavonic Studies ***See*** Institute of Asian Research

Institute of Asian Research (IAR)

C.K. Choi Building, University of British Columbia, 1855 West Mall, Vancouver BC V6T 1Z2
Tel: 604-822-4688; *Fax:* 604-822-5207
iar@mail.ubc.ca
www.iar.ubc.ca
Previous Name: Institute of Asian & Slavonic Studies
Overview: A medium-sized international organization founded in 1978
Mission: To promote interdisciplinary research on the Asia Pacific region through its programs of research, training, information & public policy; To collaborate with other Asian researchers in documenting the processes of cultural, economic, political, social & technological change in the region
Member of: CANCAPS; Canadian-Asian Studies Association; American Oriental Society
Chief Officer(s):
Marietta Lao, Manager, Administration
mlao@exchange.ubc.ca
Finances: *Funding Sources:* Provincial government; grants; contracts; endowments
Staff Member(s): 20
Activities: International Associates Forum; Research Associates & Visiting Scholars Program; Program in inter-cultural studies in Asia; China Program for Integrative Research & Development (CPIRD); Program on Canada-Asia Policy Studies; China Transport & Communication Systems Project; *Library:* Asian Library; Open to public

Institute of Association Executives ***See*** Canadian Society of Association Executives

Institute of Canadian Advertising; Institute of Communications & Advertising ***See*** Institute of Communication Agencies

Institute of Canadian Bankers ***See*** Canadian Securities Institute

Institute of Certified Management Consultants of Alberta (CMC-Alberta)

c/o CMC-Canada National Office, PO Box 20, #2004, 410 Bay St., Toronto ON M5H 2Y4
Tel: 416-860-1515; *Fax:* 416-860-1535
Toll-Free: 800-268-1148
consulting@cmc-canada.ca
www.cmc-canada.ca/provincial_institutes.cfm?Portal_ID=1
Overview: A medium-sized provincial organization founded in 1991 overseen by Canadian Association of Management Consultants
Mission: To act under the regulations of the Professional & Occupational Associations Registration Act; To work as the regulatory authority for provisional registrants, certified management consultants, & fellow certified management consultants in Alberta; To ensure that members abide by professional & ethical standards
Chief Officer(s):
Greg McIntyre, Vice-President
Jeff Griffiths, Registrar
Membership: *Member Profile:* Certified management consultants; Fellow certified management consultants; *Committees:* Membership
Activities: Offering professional development opportunities;

Institute of Certified Management Consultants of Atlantic Canada

c/o CMC-Canada National Office, PO Box 20, #2004, 401 Bay St., Toronto ON M5H 2Y4
Tel: 416-860-1515; *Fax:* 416-860-1535
Toll-Free: 800-268-1148
consulting@cmc-canada.ca
www.cmc-canada.ca/provincial_institutes.cfm?Portal_ID=2
Also Known As: CMC-Atlantic Canada
Overview: A small provincial organization founded in 1982 overseen by Canadian Association of Management Consultants
Mission: To foster excellence & integrity in the management consulting profession.
Chief Officer(s):
Jerrold White, President
Blaine Atkinson, Registrar
Finances: *Funding Sources:* Membership fees
Membership: *Member Profile:* University graduation; 3 years full-time consulting experience; completion of 8 exams or equivalent

Institute of Certified Management Consultants of British Columbia (CMC-BC)

c/o CMC-Canada National Office, PO Box 20, #2004, 401 Bay St., Toronto ON M5H 2Y4
Tel: 416-860-1515; *Fax:* 416-860-1535
Toll-Free: 800-268-1148
Other Communication: cmc-bc@shaw.ca
consulting@camc.com
www.cmc-canada.ca/provincial_institutes.cfm?Portal_ID=3
Previous Name: Institute of Management Consultants of BC
Overview: A medium-sized provincial organization founded in 1973 overseen by Canadian Association of Management Consultants
Mission: To protect the general public & clients by ensuring that the Institute's Code of Professional Conduct is followed by the certified management consultant profession; To ensure that certified members comply with all applicable legislation & laws
Chief Officer(s):
Stephen Spooner, President
Lyn Blanchard, Vice-President
Shayda Kassam, Treasurer
Finances: *Annual Operating Budget:* Less than $50,000
Membership: *Member Profile:* Persons primarily engaged in management consulting in British Columbia
Activities: Presenting awards; Organizing annual general meetings; Ensuring that members are aware of all legislation & laws that affect the profession

Institute of Certified Management Consultants of Canada ***See*** Canadian Association of Management Consultants

Institute of Certified Management Consultants of Manitoba (CMC-Manitoba) / Institut manitobain des conseillers en administration agréés

c/o CMC-Canada National Office, PO Box 20, #2004, 401 Bay St., Toronto ON M5H 2Y4
Tel: 416-860-1515; *Fax:* 416-860-1535
Toll-Free: 800-268-1148
consulting@cmc-canada.ca
www.cmc-canada.ca/provincial_institutes.cfm?Portal_ID=4
Overview: A small provincial organization founded in 1977 overseen by Canadian Association of Management Consultants
Mission: To foster & promote the development & acceptance of the profession of management consulting; to promote excellence in the practice of the profession for the benefit of members, clients & the community at large.
Chief Officer(s):
Timothy Wildman, President
Warren Thompson, Registrar
Finances: *Annual Operating Budget:* Less than $50,000; *Funding Sources:* Membership fees; exams
6 volunteer(s)
Membership: *Member Profile:* Consultants (full-time) with a university degree, three years consulting experience & completing exam process
Activities: *Speaker Service:* Yes

Institute of Certified Management Consultants of Saskatchewan

c/o CMC-Canada National Office, PO Box 20, #2004, 401 Bay St., Toronto ON M5H 2Y4
Tel: 416-860-1515; *Fax:* 416-860-1535
Toll-Free: 800-662-2972
consulting@cmc-canada.ca
www.cmc-canada.ca/provincial_institutes.cfm?Portal_ID=7
www.facebook.com/CMC.Saskatchewan
Also Known As: CMC-Saskatchewan
Overview: A medium-sized provincial licensing charitable organization founded in 1990 overseen by Canadian Association of Management Consultants
Chief Officer(s):
Richmond Graham, President
Jeremy Hall, Registrar

Institute of Chartered Accountants of Alberta (ICAA)

Manulife Place, #580, 10180 - 101 St., Edmonton AB T5J 4R2
Tel: 780-424-7391; *Fax:* 780-425-8766
Toll-Free: 800-232-9406
info@icaa.ab.ca
www.albertacas.ca
Overview: A medium-sized provincial licensing organization founded in 1910 overseen by Alberta Accountants Unification Agency
Mission: To protect the public interest by setting & enforcing high professional & ethical standards
Chief Officer(s):
Rachel Miller, FCA, CEO & Executive Director
Membership: 14,875; *Member Profile:* Chartered accountants, chartered acccountant students, accounting firms & corporations in Alberta
Activities: Providing professional development opportunities to enhance the competencies of chartered accountants (note the ICAA will integrate under the CPA banner); *Speaker Service:* Yes

Institute of Chartered Accountants of British Columbia (ICABC)

One Bentall Centre, PO Box 22, #500, 505 Burrard St., Vancouver BC V7X 1M4
Tel: 604-681-3264; *Fax:* 604-681-1523
Toll-Free: 800-663-2677
www.ica.bc.ca
www.linkedin.com/company/2129203
twitter.com/icabc
www.youtube.com/user/CAsofBCvideo
Overview: A large provincial licensing organization founded in 1905 overseen by Chartered Professional Accountants of British Columbia
Mission: To protect & serve the public, members, & students by providing exceptional education, regulation & member services programs so that chartered accountants may provide the highest quality of professional services
Chief Officer(s):
Richard Rees, Chief Executive Officer
rees@ica.bc.ca

Finances: *Annual Operating Budget:* Greater than $5 Million; *Funding Sources:* Membership dues
Membership: 11,000; *Fees:* Schedule available; *Member Profile:* 30-month service term & successful completion of national uniform final exam (UFE)
Activities: Professional development (note that the ICABC will integrate under the CPA banner); *Speaker Service:* Yes
Awards:
• Community Service Award (Award)
Eligibility: Members of ICABC who have been involved in volunteer activities in their communities*Deadline:* January *Contact:* Jennifer Weintraub, Tel: 604-681-1523
• Early Achievement Award (Award)
Eligibility: Members of ICABC who have received their designation in the last ten years & have shown professional achievement*Deadline:* January *Contact:* Jennifer Weintraub, weintraub@ica.bc.ca
• Fellowship Designation Award (Award)
Eligibility: Members of ICABC who have shown leadership & outstanding performance in at least two of these areas: work of government, an association, a business, service, or researching/teaching*Deadline:* January *Contact:* Sandy Parcher, parcher@ica.bc.ca
• Lifetime Achievement Award (Award)
Deadline: January *Contact:* Sandy Parcher, parcher@ica.bc.ca

Institute of Chartered Accountants of Manitoba (ICAM)
#1675, 1 Lombard Pl., Winnipeg MB R3B 0X3
Tel: 204-942-8248; *Fax:* 204-943-7119
Toll-Free: 888-942-8248
cpamb@cpamb.ca
www.icam.mb.ca
Also Known As: Chartered Accountants of Manitoba
Overview: A medium-sized provincial licensing organization founded in 1886 overseen by Chartered Professional Accountants of Manitoba
Mission: To protect the public by acting as the governing body of the profession of chartered accountancy in Manitoba; To ensure the profession observes established professional practice standards, rules of professional conduct, bylaws, & regulations
Chief Officer(s):
Gary Hannaford, Chief Executive Officer
ghannaford@cpamb.ca
Activities: Providing an advisory service to assist members; Recognizing members by presenting awards; Offering professional development opportunies (note that CA Manitoba will integrate under the CPA banner)

Institute of Chartered Accountants of Newfoundland (ICANL)
#501, 95 Bonaventure Ave., St. John's NL A1B 2X5
Tel: 709-753-7566; *Fax:* 709-753-3609
www.icanl.ca
Also Known As: CA Newfoundland
Overview: A medium-sized provincial organization founded in 1949 overseen by Chartered Professional Accountants of Newfoundland & Labrador
Mission: To serve the interests of society & the membership by providing leadership; To uphold the professional standards, integrity & preeminence of chartered accountants in Newfoundland & Labrador
Chief Officer(s):
Frank Kennedy, CA, Chief Executive Officer
fkennedy@icanl.ca
Membership: 755; *Member Profile:* Persons engaged in the practice of public accounting in Newfoundland & Labrador & accounting students
Activities: Offering professional development opportunities (note that ICANL will integrate under the CPA banner)

Institute of Chartered Accountants of Nova Scotia (ICANS)
#502, 5151 George St., Halifax NS B3J 1M5
Tel: 902-425-3291; *Fax:* 902-423-4505
icans@icans.ns.ca
www.icans.ns.ca
Overview: A medium-sized provincial licensing organization founded in 1900 overseen by Chartered Professional Accountants Canada
Mission: To protect & serve the public & our members by providing exceptional services & resources within a well-regulated profession
Chief Officer(s):
Michele A. Wood-Tweel, FCA, CFP, TEP, CEO/Executive Director
mwood-tweel@icans.ns.ca
Kathie Slaunwhite, Office Administrator & Director, Professional Development
kslaunwhite@icans.ns.ca
Finances: *Annual Operating Budget:* $500,000-$1.5 Million
Membership: 2,000+
Activities: Professional development (note that ICANS will integrate under the CPA banner once new legislation is approved)

Institute of Chartered Accountants of Prince Edward Island (ICAPEI)
Dominion Building, #600, 97 Queen St., Charlottetown PE C1A 4A9
Tel: 902-894-4290; *Fax:* 902-894-4791
www.icapei.com
Overview: A medium-sized provincial licensing organization founded in 1921 overseen by Chartered Professional Accountants of Prince Edward Island
Mission: To foster public confidence in the profession of chartered accountancy in Prince Edward Island; To act in the public interest; To assist members to excel in their role as leaders in senior management, advisory, finance, tax & assurance
Chief Officer(s):
Albert M. Ferris, Executive Director
amferris@icapei.com
Membership: *Fees:* Schedule available; *Member Profile:* Members of the CA profession in Prince Edward Island
Activities: Offering professional development opportunities (note that ICAPEI will integrate under the CPA banner)

Institute of Chartered Accountants of Saskatchewan (ICAS)
#101, 4581 Parliament Ave., Regina SK S4W 0G3
Tel: 306-359-0272; *Fax:* 306-347-8580
info@cpask.ca
www.icas.sk.ca
Overview: A medium-sized provincial licensing organization overseen by Chartered Professional Accountants of Saskatchewan
Mission: Represents CA's & CA students in Saskatchewan; protects the public by ensuring members adhere to high professional & ethical standards of practice
Chief Officer(s):
Shelley Thiel, FCA, Chief Executive Officer, 306-791-4135
s.thiel@icas.sk.ca
Membership: 2,000
Activities: Member services; professional development (note that ICAS will integrate under the CPA banner)

Institute of Chartered Accountants of the Northwest Territories & Nunavut (ICANTNU)
PO Box 2433, Yellowknife NT X1A 2P8
Tel: 867-873-3680; *Fax:* 867-873-6387
info@icanwt.nt.ca
www.icanwt.nt.ca
Overview: A small provincial organization founded in 1977 overseen by Chartered Professional Accountants Canada
Mission: To use financial management in order to improve the function of businesses
Chief Officer(s):
Tara Clowes, CA, CFP, President
Membership: *Fees:* Schedule available
Activities: Providing professional development opportunities (note that ICANTNU will integrate under the CPA banner once legislation is approved)

Institute of Chartered Accountants of the Yukon (ICAYT)
c/o Institute of Chartered Accountants of British Columbia, PO Box 22, #500, 505 Burrard St., One Bentall Centre, Vancouver BC V7X 1M4
Tel: 604-681-3264; *Fax:* 604-681-1523
Toll-Free: 800-663-2677
www.icayt.ca
Overview: A large provincial licensing organization founded in 1977 overseen by Chartered Professional Accountants of the Yukon
Chief Officer(s):
Jason C. Bilsky, CA, President
Activities: Providing professionl development opportunities (note the ICAYT will integrate under the CPA banner)

Institute of Chartered Secretaries & Administrators - Canadian Division (ICSA Canada) / Institut des secrétaires et administrateurs agréés au Canada
#202, 300 March Rd., Ottawa ON K2K 2E2
Tel: 613-595-1151; *Fax:* 613-595-1155
Toll-Free: 800-501-3440
info@icsacanada.org
www.icsacanada.org
Also Known As: Chartered Secretaries Canada
Previous Name: Chartered Institute of Secretaries
Overview: A medium-sized national organization founded in 1920
Mission: The organization represents and serves Chartered Secretaries & Administrators, professionals who are hired by organizations to administer key areas such as corporate governance, director/officer/shareholder matters, compliance & regulatory matters, & financial matters.
Affliation(s): International Institute of Chartered Secretaries & Administrators
Chief Officer(s):
Nancy Barrett, Executive Director
Finances: *Annual Operating Budget:* $250,000-$500,000
Staff Member(s): 3; 20 volunteer(s)
Membership: 1200; *Fees:* Schedule available; *Member Profile:* By examination; entry by academic pre-qualification & professional experience; *Committees:* Education; Editorial; Marketing
Activities: Training courses in corporate governance & corporate law are available at the head office as well as through its branch offices nationally;

Institute of Communication Agencies (ICA) / Institut des communications et de la publicité (ICP)
#3002, 2300 Yonge St., Toronto ON M4P 1E4
Tel: 416-482-1396; *Fax:* 416-482-1856
Toll-Free: 800-567-7422
ica@icacanada.ca
www.icacanada.ca
Previous Name: Institute of Canadian Advertising; Institute of Communications & Advertising
Overview: A small national organization founded in 1905
Mission: To anticipate, serve & promote the collective interests of ICA members, with regard to defining, developing & helping to maintain the highest possible standards of professional practice
Chief Officer(s):
Jani Yates, President
Gillian Graham, CEO
Activities: Canadian Advertising Agency Practitioners program, a two-year course open to those already in the business; *Library* by appointment
Awards:
• Cassie Awards (Award)
Established 1993; jointly administered with the Association of Canadian Advertisers; Cassies - an acronym for Canadian Advertising Success Stories - are judged on their effectiveness in attaining the advertiser's objectives; 10 gold awards presented bi-annually

Institute of Corporate Directors (ICD) / Institut des administrateurs de sociétés
#2701, 250 Yonge St., Toronto ON M5B 2L7
Tel: 416-593-7741; *Fax:* 416-593-0636
Toll-Free: 877-593-7741
info@icd.ca
www.icd.ca
Overview: A medium-sized national organization founded in 1980
Mission: To enhance the quality of corporate governance in Canada
Affiliation(s): Institute of Directors
Chief Officer(s):
Stan Magidson, President & CEO
Maliha Aqeel, Director, Communications
maqeel@icd.ca
Al-Azhar Khalfan, Director, Marketing & Sales
akhalfan@icd.ca
Finances: *Annual Operating Budget:* $500,000-$1.5 Million; *Funding Sources:* Membership fees
Staff Member(s): 20
Membership: 7,800 individual & corporate; *Fees:* Schedule available; *Member Profile:* Full - corporate director; associate - senior executive or professional; *Committees:* Membership; Communications; Education; Accreditation; Audit; Finance; Governance
Activities: Monthly luncheons/breakfast seminars; annual conference; Fellowship Awards Dinner; education programs

Institute of Cultural Affairs International (ICAI) / Institut des Affaires Culturelles International

c/o ICA Canada, 655 Queen St. East, Toronto ON M4M 1G4
Tel: 416-691-2316; *Fax:* 416-691-2491
icai@ica-international.org
ica-international.org
www.facebook.com/icainternational
twitter.com/icai
Also Known As: ICA International
Overview: A small international charitable organization founded in 1977
Mission: ICAI is an association of legally recognized ICAs & affiliated organizations engaged in human development activities globally. It supports work in four major areas: promoting global ecological perspectives, facilitating organizational change, enabling sustainable development efforts, advancing lifelong learning & training.
Affiliation(s): Has Category II consultative status with The United Nations Economic & Social Council (ECOSOC) & consultative status with UNICEF; liaison status with the Food & Agricultural Organization (FAO) & a working relationship with the World Health Organization (WHO); consultative status with the United Nations Children's Fund (UNICEF); Service on the Non Governmental Organisation Consultative Group for the International Fund of Agriculture Development (IFAD); membership in CIVICUS, the World Alliance for Citizen Participation
Chief Officer(s):
Lawrence Philbrook, President
icalarry@gmail.com
Gerald Gomani, Secretary
icazim@africaonline.co.zw
Nan Hudson, Executive Director, ICA Canada
nhudson@icacan.org
Finances: *Annual Operating Budget:* $500,000-$1.5 Million; *Funding Sources:* Membership dues, individual/family donations, institutional/program support (grants)
Staff Member(s): 5; 5 volunteer(s)
Membership: 30 national member organizations, global network of individual and family members; *Fees:* $1,050 statutory; $525 provisional statutory; $330 associate; $150 individual; $250 family; $500 facilitator; $1,000 supporter
Publications:
• Winds & Waves [a publication of the Institute of Cultural Affairs International]
Type: Magazine; *Editor:* John Miesen

ICA Canada
655 Queen St. East, Toronto ON M4M 1G4
Tel: 416-691-2316; *Fax:* 416-691-2491
Toll-Free: 877-691-1422
ica@icacan.org
www.icacan.org
Chief Officer(s):
Jeanette Standfield, Chair
Nan Hudson, Executive Director
nhudson@icacan.org

Institute of Electrical & Electronics Engineers Inc. - Canada

PO Box 63005, Stn. University, 102 Plaza Dr., Dundas ON L9H 4H0
Tel: 905-628-9554
www.ieee.ca
Also Known As: IEEE Canada
Overview: A medium-sized national charitable organization founded in 1884
Mission: To advance the theory & practice of electrical, electronics, & computer engineering & computer science
Member of: Institute of Electrical and Electronics Engineers (IEEE)
Affiliation(s): The Engineering Institute of Canada
Chief Officer(s):
Cathie Lowell, IEEE Canada Administrator
cathie.lowell@gmail.com
Keith Brown, President
Amir Aghdam, President Elect
Ashfaq Husain, Treasurer
Finances: *Funding Sources:* Membership dues; Publications; Sponsorship; Sale of products & services
Membership: *Member Profile:* Professional engineers or technologists; *Committees:* Awards & Recognition; Conferences; Humanitarian
Activities: Sponsoring technical conferences, symposia & local meetings worldwide; Providing resources to assist members in increasing their professional skills; Facilitating networking capabilities
Awards:
• A.G.L. McNaughton Gold Medal (Award)
• R.A. Fessenden Award (Award)
• Power Engineering Award (Award)
• Computer Award (Award)
• Outstanding Engineer Award (Award)
• Outstanding Engineering Educator Award (Award)
• W.S. Read Outstanding Service Award (Award)
• J.J. Archambault Eastern Canada Merit Award (Award)
• M.B. Broughton Central Canada Merit Award (Award)
• E.F. Glass Western Canada Merit Award (Award)
• RAB Achievement Award (Award)
• RAB Innovation Award (Award)
• RAB Leadership Award (Award)
• RAB Larry K. Wilson Transnational Award (Award)
• RAB GOLD Achievement Award (Award)
• William W. Middleton Distinguished Service Award (Award)
• Friend of IEEE Regional Activities Award (Award)
• RAB Section Recognition Awards (Award)
Publications:
• Canadian Journal of Electrical & Computer Engineering
Type: Journal; *Frequency:* Quarterly; *Editor:* Witold Kinsner; Xavier Maldague *ISSN:* 0840-8688; *Price:* $30 IEEE member; $60 other individual; $90institution
Profile: Refereed scientific papers in all areas of electrical & computer engineering
• IEEE [Institute of Electrical & Electronics Engineers Inc.] Canada Newsletter / Bulletin de IEEE Canada
Type: Newsletter; *Frequency:* Monthly; *Editor:* Alex Bot
Profile: IEEE activities & industry trends
• IEEE [Institute of Electrical & Electronics Engineers Inc.] Canadian Review / La revue canadienne de l'IEEE
Type: Magazine; *Frequency:* 3 pa; *Accepts Advertising*; *Editor:* Eric Holdrinet *ISSN:* 1481-2002; *Price:* Free to members in Canada; $35 non-members; $37.50 corporations & libraries

Institute of Health Economics (IHE)

#1200, 10405 Jasper Ave., Edmonton AB T5J 3N4
Tel: 780-448-4881; *Fax:* 780-448-0018
info@ihe.ca
www.ihe.ca
Previous Name: Institute of Pharmaco-Economics
Overview: A small local organization founded in 1996
Mission: To deliver outstanding health economics, health outcomes, health policy research & related services to governments, health care providers, the health industry & universities
Affiliation(s): Health Technology Assessment International; University of Alberta; University of Calgary; Canadian Association for Health Services & Policy Research; International Health Economics Association; Health Technology Assessment International
Chief Officer(s):
Egon Jonsson, Executive Director & CEO
ejonsson@ihe.ca
Staff Member(s): 16
Membership: *Member Profile:* Government, academia, pharmaceutical industry
Activities: Research; training; knowledge transfer; *Library* by appointment

Institute of Housing Management (IHM)

#310, 2175 Sheppard Ave. East, Toronto ON M2J 1W8
Tel: 416-493-7382; *Fax:* 416-491-1670
Toll-Free: 866-212-4377
ihm@taylorenterprises.com
ihm-canada.com
Overview: A small provincial organization founded in 1976
Mission: To promote the art & science of property management & the education & training of people engaged in the management & operations of private & public rental housing
Chief Officer(s):
Kevin O'Hara, President
kohara@regionofwaterloo.ca
Carolyne Vigon, Administrator
carolyne@taylorenterprises.com
Staff Member(s): 1; 11 volunteer(s)
Membership: *Fees:* $69-$307; *Member Profile:* Practising property managers & those with an interest in property management issues

Institute of Law Clerks of Ontario (ILCO)

#502, 20 Adelaide St. East, Toronto ON M5C 2T6
Tel: 416-214-6252; *Fax:* 416-214-6255
reception@ilco.on.ca
www.ilco.on.ca
Overview: A medium-sized provincial organization founded in 1968
Mission: To provide an organized network for promoting unity, cooperation & mutual assistance among law clerks in Ontario; to advance & protect their status & interests; to promote their education for the purpose of increasing their knowledge, efficiency & professional ability.
Member of: Canadian Association of Legal Assistants
Chief Officer(s):
Rose Kottis, President
Elsie Karulas, Vice-President
Finances: *Annual Operating Budget:* $250,000-$500,000; *Funding Sources:* Membership fees
Staff Member(s): 4; 50 volunteer(s)
Membership: 1,700+; *Fees:* $145 ordinary; $170 associate; $195 fellow; $60 student
Activities: Courses for law clerks available at a number of community colleges throughout Ontario; seminars & workshops;

Institute of Management Consultants of BC *See* Institute of Certified Management Consultants of British Columbia

Institute of Municipal Assessors

#206, 10720 Yonge St., Richmond Hill ON L4C 3C9
Tel: 905-884-1959; *Fax:* 905-884-9263
Toll-Free: 877-877-8703
info@assessorsinstitute.ca
www.assessorsinstitute.ca
Overview: A medium-sized provincial organization founded in 1957
Mission: The IMA is the largest Canadian professional association representing members that practice in the field of Property Assessment and related Property Taxation functions.
Chief Officer(s):
Terry Tomkins, President
Colleen Vercouteren, 1st Vice President
Finances: *Annual Operating Budget:* $250,000-$500,000
Staff Member(s): 2
Membership: 1,250; *Committees:* Accreditation; Education; Bylaw & Legislation Review; Communications; Nominating; Professional Conduct; Scholarship Trust Fund; Professional Association Liaison
Activities: *Library* by appointment

Institute of Pharmaco-Economics *See* Institute of Health Economics

Institute of Power Engineers (IPE)

PO Box 878, Burlington ON L7R 3Y7
Tel: 905-333-3348; *Fax:* 905-333-9328
ipenat@nipe.ca
www.nipe.ca
Overview: A medium-sized national organization founded in 1940
Mission: To promote business relations, social activities & mutual understanding among power engineers
Chief Officer(s):
Jude Rankin, National President
Bruce King, 1st National Vice President
Don Purser, National Secretary
Finances: *Annual Operating Budget:* $50,000-$100,000
1400 volunteer(s)
Membership: 1,420; *Fees:* $105; *Member Profile:* Persons holding certificates of qualification as recognized by the Institute; persons enrolled in recognized power engineering courses; persons engaged in any pursuit identified or allied with power engineering

Institute of Professional Bookkeepers of Canada (IPBC)

10185 - 164 St., Surrey BC V4N 2K4
Toll-Free: 866-616-4722
info@ipbc.ca
www.ipbc.ca
www.linkedin.com/groups?gid=3759620
www.facebook.com/ipbc.ca
twitter.com/ipbc_canada
Overview: A medium-sized national organization
Mission: To increase excellence in the bookkeeping industry in Canada; To strengthen the credentials & professional standing of bookkeepers
Chief Officer(s):
Dianne Mueller, Chair
Peter Lindop, Secretary

Louie Prosperi, Chief Executive Officer
Membership: *Fees:* $415 bookkeeper & accountant; $149.95 student; *Member Profile:* Bookkeepers & accountants throughout Canada
Activities: Providing timely information; Coordinating continuing education events; Offering networking opportunities with other industry professionals; Organizing national phone conferences; Increasing recognition of the bookkeeping profession
Publications:
• Tips & Topics Newsletter
Type: Newsletter; *Frequency:* Semiannually; *Price:* Free
Profile: Industry news articles & advice from experts in the industry

Institute of Professional Management (IPM)

#2210, 1081 Ambleside Dr., Ottawa ON K2B 8C8
Tel: 613-721-5957; *Fax:* 613-721-5850
info@workplace.ca
www.workplace.ca
www.facebook.com/InstituteofProfessionalManagement
Overview: A small national organization founded in 1984
Affiliation(s): Association of Professional Recruiters of Canada; Canadian Management Professional Association
Staff Member(s): 8
Activities: Management training & development; workplace.ca gateway to management and workplace resources; publications; *Speaker Service:* Yes
Publications:
• Workplace Today
Type: Journal; *Frequency:* Monthly

Institute of Public Administration of Canada (IPAC) / Institut d'administration publique du Canada (IAPC)

#401, 1075 Bay St., Toronto ON M5S 2B1
Tel: 416-924-8787; *Fax:* 416-924-4992
www.ipac.ca
Overview: A medium-sized national charitable organization founded in 1947
Mission: To advance public service excellence, by sharing effective practices & policy in public administration; To lead public administration research in Canada; To further professional, non-artisan public service
Chief Officer(s):
Michael Fenn, Executive Director, 416-924-8787 Ext. 230
mfenn@ipac.ca
Gabriella Ciampini, Director, Special Events, 416-924-8787 Ext. 223
gciampini@ipac.ca
Wendy Feldman, Director, Research, 416-924-8787 Ext. 228
wfeldman@ipac.ca
Carole Humphries, Director, Membership & Marketing, 416-924-8787 Ext. 234
chumphries@ipac.ca
Ann Masson, Director, International Programs, 416-924-8787 Ext. 229
amasson@ipac.ca
Jehan Contractor, Coordinator, Finance & Administration, Special Projects, 416-924-8787 Ext. 224
jcontractor@ipac.ca
Jennifer Dany Aubé, Coordinator, Member Services, 416-924-8787 Ext. 225
jaube@ipac.ca
Elisabeth Laviolette, Managing Editor & Manager, Public Sector Management Magazine, 416-924-8787 Ext. 227
elaviolette@ipac.ca
Megan Sproule-Jones, Managing Editor, Canadian Public Administration Journal, 705-523-9192
msproule-jones@ipac.ca
Membership: *Member Profile:* Public servants; Academics; Persons interested in public administration
Activities: Offering learning opportunities; Encouraging research; Providing networking activities; *Speaker Service:* Yes
Awards:
• IPAC / Deloitte Public Sector Leadership Awards (Award)
To recognize organizations that have demonstrated outstanding leadership by advancing public policy & management *Contact:* Carole Humphries, IPAC, Phone: 416-924-8787, ext. 234, E-mail: chumphries@ipac.ca
• IPAC Promising New Professional Award (Award)
To recognize a promising new public service professional*Deadline:* June 18 *Contact:* Carole Humphries, Dir, Membership & Marketing, Phone: 416-924-8787, ext 234; E-mail: chumphries@ipac.ca
• Innovative Management Award (Award)
To recognize exceptional management within the public sector of Canada
• Vanier Award (Award)
Awarded annually to a person who has shown leadership in public administration & public service in Canada, or who, by his or her writings or other endeavours, has made a significant contribution in the field of public administration or public service
• Regional Group Excellence Award (Award)
Awarded to a Regional IPAC group that exhibits excellence
• J.E. Hodgetts Award (Award)
Awarded annually for the best article in English appearing in the journal Canadian Public Administration
• IPAC Pierre De Celles Award for Excellence in Teaching Public Administration (Award)
• Roland Parenteau Award (Award)
Awarded annually for the best article in French appearing in the journal Canadian Public Administration
• National Student & Thought Leadership Awards in Public Administration (Award)
To recognize talent in Canadian schools at the regional & national levels
Meetings/Conferences: • Institute of Public Administration of Canada 2015 10th National Leadership Conference & Awards, February, 2015, King Edward Hotel, Toronto, ON
Scope: National
Contact Information: URL: www.ipac.ca/Leadership2015, ntl@ipac.ca
• Institute of Public Administration of Canada 2015 67th National Annual Conference: Governing in the Now, August, 2015, Halifax, NS
Scope: National
Attendance: 500+
Description: Conference participants & speakers include Canadian public decison makers from both municipal, provincial, & federal jurisdictions, as well as members of academia, senior policy advisors, & heads of schools of pubic policy
Contact Information: URL: www.ipac.ca/2015
• Institute of Public Administration of Canada 2015 Annual Book Colloquium, 2015
Scope: Provincial
• Institute of Public Administration of Canada 2015 Annual General Meeting, 2015
Scope: National
Description: A yearly business meeting, presenting reports from the national president, treasurer, & secretary
Publications:
• Canadian Public Administration Journal
Type: Journal; *Frequency:* Quarterly; *Editor:* Megan Sproule-Jones
Profile: A refereed scholary publication to examine the structures & processes of public management & public policy at all three level of Canadian government
• Case Studies Program
Editor: Andrew Graham
Profile: Descriptions of situations which public administrators made or influenced
• Collection IPAC en Management Public et Gouvernance
Profile: A French language series, published with the Presses de l'Université Laval, to broaden discussion around policy, governance, & administration
• Institute of Public Administration of Canada Annual Report
Type: Yearbook; *Frequency:* Annually
• IPAC E-newsletter
Type: Newsletter
Profile: Happenings at IPAC, including membership information, research, awards, & forthcoming conferences
• IPAC Series in Public Management & Governance
Editor: Patrice Dutil
Profile: Published in collaboration with the University of Toronto Press to promote excellent scholarship in the field of public sector management
• New Directions Series
Profile: Results of issue-oriented working goups of public servants & academics, such as "Managing Service Transformation Relationships Between Government & Industry: Best Practices"
• Public Sector Management Magazine
Type: Magazine; *Editor:* Elisabeth Laviolette
Profile: Feature articles on topics such as IPAC international programs & country profiles

Institute of Space & Atmospheric Studies (ISAS)

University of Saskatchewan, 116 Science Pl., Saskatoon SK S7N 5E2
Tel: 306-966-6401; *Fax:* 306-966-6428
isas.office@usask.ca
www.usask.ca/physics/isas
Overview: A small national organization
Mission: Focus is on space & atmospheric studies, solar terrestrial physics, space weather, & atmospheric change
Chief Officer(s):
J.-P. St-Maurice, Chair, 306-966-2906
jp.stmaurice@usask.ca
Alan Manson, Executive Secretary, 306-966-6449
alan.manson@usask.ca
Staff Member(s): 35
Membership: 1-99; *Member Profile:* Professors, research associates, post-doctoral fellow, research engineers

Institute of Textile Science (ITS) / Institut des sciences textiles

c/o Jerry Bauerle, #105, 4575 Lakeshore Rd., Burlington ON L7L 1E1
Tel: 905-822-4111; *Fax:* 905-823-1446
info@textilescience.ca
www.textilescience.ca
Overview: A small national organization founded in 1956
Mission: To promote the dissemination & interchange of knowledge concerning textile science; to encourage research & development related to textile science & technology, including the establishment & granting of awards
Member of: Textile Federation of Canada
Chief Officer(s):
Aldjia Begriche, President
Finances: *Annual Operating Budget:* Less than $50,000; *Funding Sources:* Membership fees; scientific sessions
Membership: 180; *Fees:* $40

Institute of Urban Studies (IUS)

University of Winnipeg, #103, 520 Portage Ave., Winnipeg MB R3C 0G2
Tel: 204-982-1140; *Fax:* 204-943-4695
ius@uwinnipeg.ca
ius.uwinnipeg.ca
Overview: A medium-sized national organization founded in 1969
Mission: To undertake policy-oriented research in the field of Urban Studies; to serve as a resource centre for the community; to provide educational services to the University community & the community-at-large.
Member of: National Housing Research Committee
Chief Officer(s):
Jino Distasio, Director
j.distasio@uwinnipeg.ca
Finances: *Funding Sources:* University of Winnipeg; contracts
Staff Member(s): 5
Activities: Areas of expertise include: housing, planning, urban Aboriginal issues, sustainable development, municipal government & finance, & socio-economic & demographic analysis; Research services include: trend analysis, market analysis, cost/benefit analysis, database development, survey & data analysis, community needs assessment, program/policy development & evaluation, community consultation & consensus building, & literature search & review, bibliography development; conference, workshop & publishing services; *Library* by appointment

Institute On Governance (IOG) / Institut sur la gouvernance

60 George St., Ottawa ON K1N 1J4
Tel: 613-562-0090; *Fax:* 613-562-0087
info@iog.ca
www.iog.ca
www.linkedin.com/groups/Institute-On-Governance-4179557
www.facebook.com/IOGca
twitter.com/IOGca
Overview: A medium-sized national charitable organization founded in 1990
Mission: To explore, share & promote responsible & responsive governance in Canada & abroad
Chief Officer(s):
Maryantonett Flumian, President
mflumian@iog.ca
Philip Bolger, Vice-President, Operations
pbolger@iog.ca
Todd Cain, Vice-President, Crown & Organization Governance
tcain@iog.ca
Laura Edgar, Vice-President, Partnerships & International Programming
ledgar@iog.ca

Toby Fyfe, Vice-President, Learning Lab
tfyfe@iog.ca
Marion Lefebvre, Vice-President, Aboriginal Governance
mlefebvre@iog.ca
Finances: *Funding Sources:* Public & private sector organizations
Membership: 1-99
Activities: Building policy capacity; Providing advice to public organizations on governance matters in Canada & internationally; Offering professional development activities to promote learning & dialogue on governance issues;; *Library:* Information Resource Centre

Institutional Limited Partners Association (ILPA)

#1200, 55 Yonge St., Toronto ON M5J 1R7
Tel: 416-941-9393; *Fax:* 416-941-9307
info@ilpa.org
www.ilpa.org
Overview: A medium-sized national organization
Mission: To serve limited partner investors in the global private equity industry
Chief Officer(s):
Kathy Jeramaz-Larson, Executive Director
Michael Mazzola, Chair
Richard Hall, Vice Chair
Jennifer Kerr, Treasurer
Staff Member(s): 15
Membership: 300; *Fees:* US$3,000 1-5 member organization; US$3,500 6-10 member organization; US$4,000 11+ member organization; *Committees:* Audit & Finance; Membership; Education; Research, Benchmarking and Standards; Nominating; GP Summit

Insurance Agents Association of Manitoba *See* Insurance Brokers Association of Manitoba

Insurance Brokers Association of Alberta (IBAA)

3010 Calgary Trail NW, Edmonton AB T6J 6V4
Tel: 780-424-3320; *Fax:* 780-424-7418
Toll-Free: 800-318-0197
Other Communication: education@ibaa.ca
ibaa@ibaa.ca
www.ibaa.ca
www.facebook.com/24855482207166
twitter.com/IBAAI
Overview: A medium-sized provincial organization founded in 1925 overseen by Insurance Brokers Association of Canada
Mission: To preserve & strengthen insurance brokers
Chief Officer(s):
George Hodgson, Chief Executive Officer
ghodgson@ibaa.ca
Rikki McBridge, Director
rmcbride@ibaa.ca
Karen Bushie, Director, Professional Development
kbushie@ibaa.ca
Staff Member(s): 11
Membership: 4,400+; *Member Profile:* Insurance brokers in Alberta
Activities: Lobbying on behalf of member brokers; Offering educational services to members; Providing marketing support; Organizing conventions
Meetings/Conferences: • Insurance Brokers Association of Alberta Fall Conference 2015, 2015, AB
Scope: Provincial
• Insurance Brokers Association of Alberta 2015 Convention, May, 2015, The Fairmont Chateau Lake Louise, Lake Louise, AB
Scope: Provincial
Contact Information: Margaret Buhay;convention@ibaa.ca; Tel: 780-569-5121

Insurance Brokers Association of British Columbia (IBABC)

#1300, 1095 West Pender St., Vancouver BC V6E 2M6
Tel: 604-606-8000; *Fax:* 604-683-7831
www.ibabc.org
twitter.com/ibabc
Overview: A small provincial organization founded in 1920 overseen by Insurance Brokers Association of Canada
Mission: To promote the member insurance broker as the premiere distributor of general insurance products & services in British Columbia
Chief Officer(s):
Charles (Chuck) Byrne, Executive Director
cbyrne@ibabc.org
Trudy Lancelyn, Deputy Executive Director
tlancelyn@ibabc.org
Staff Member(s): 10
Membership: 822 corporate; *Fees:* Schedule available
Activities: Licensing courses; continuing education
Meetings/Conferences: • Insurance Brokers Association of British Columbia 67th Annual Conference & Trade Show, 2015, BC
Scope: Provincial

Insurance Brokers Association of Canada (IBAC) / Association des courtiers d'assurances du Canada (ACAC)

#1210, 18 King St. East, Toronto ON M5C 1C4
Tel: 416-367-1831; *Fax:* 416-367-3687
ibac@ibac.ca
www.ibac.ca
Overview: A medium-sized national organization founded in 1922
Mission: The national voice of p&c insurance brokers & an advocate for insurance consumers. IBAC represents their interests to the government of Canada.
Chief Officer(s):
Dan Danyluk, Chief Executive Officer
ddanyluk@ibac.ca
Staff Member(s): 7

Insurance Brokers Association of Manitoba (IBAM)

#600, 1445 Portage Ave., Winnipeg MB R3G 3P4
Tel: 204-488-1857; *Fax:* 204-489-0316
Toll-Free: 800-204-5649
info@ibam.mb.ca
www.ibam.mb.ca
www.linkedin.com/company/insurance-brokers-association-of-manitoba-iba
www.facebook.com/IBAManitoba
twitter.com/IBAManitoba
Previous Name: Insurance Agents Association of Manitoba
Overview: A medium-sized provincial organization founded in 1951 overseen by Insurance Brokers Association of Canada
Mission: To promote insurance brokers as the primary providers of insurance products & services in Manitoba
Chief Officer(s):
David Schioler, Chief Executive Officer
davidschioler@ibam.mb.ca
Finances: *Funding Sources:* Membership dues
Staff Member(s): 5
Membership: 2,000 brokers; *Member Profile:* Independent property & casualty insurance brokers in Manitoba; *Committees:* Young Brokers' Committee
Meetings/Conferences: • 2015 Insurance Brokers Association of Manitoba Convention, April, 2015, Fairmont Winnipeg, Winnipeg, MB
Scope: Provincial

Insurance Brokers Association of New Brunswick (IBANB) / Association des courtiers d'assurances du Nouveau-Brunswick

PO Box 1523, #201, 590 Brunswick St., Fredericton NB E3B 5G2
Tel: 506-450-2898; *Fax:* 506-450-1494
ibanb@nbinsurancebrokers.ca
www.nbinsurancebrokers.ca
www.youtube.com/nbbrokerstv
Overview: A small provincial organization overseen by Insurance Brokers Association of Canada
Mission: To champion the professional, independent insurance broker system in New Brunswick
Chief Officer(s):
Geordie Lamb, Chair
Andrew McNair, Chief Executive Officer
amcnair@nbinsurancebrokers.ca

Insurance Brokers Association of Newfoundland (IBAN)

Chimo Bldg., 151 Crosbie Rd., 3rd Floor, St. John's NL A1B 4B4
Tel: 709-726-4450; *Fax:* 709-754-4399
iban@nfld.net
www.iban.ca
Overview: A small local organization overseen by Insurance Brokers Association of Canada
Mission: Association of insurance brokers in Newfoundland. Insurance brokers work on behalf of clients to secure the best coverage in the market from federally regulated insurance companies
Chief Officer(s):
CJ Nolan, President, 709-757-0505, Fax: 709-726-5041
cjnolan@munninsurance.com
Staff Member(s): 1; 15 volunteer(s)
Membership: 772; *Committees:* Young Brokers' Committee
Activities: Professional development, including online learning
Awards:
• Rus Rice Memorial Bursary (Scholarship)
Eligibility: Full-time student pursuing undergraduate studies at a recognized degree-granting institution; dependent of a broker or a staff member of a brokerage in the Atlantic Provinces.*Deadline:* June *Amount:* $1,000
• IBAN Scholarship (Scholarship)
Eligibility: Either high school student entering first-year studies or currently enrolled in first year studies at an accredited university or post-secondary college; dependant of an employee of an IBAN-member company, or an employee of such a brokerage.*Deadline:* October *Amount:* $1,000
• Broker Identity Program (BIP) Scholarships (Scholarship)
Eligibility: Either high school student entering first-year studies or currently enrolled in first year studies at an accredited university or post-secondary college; must not be a dependant of an employee of an IBAN-member company, or an employee of such a brokerage.*Deadline:* October *Amount:* $500.00 each

Insurance Brokers Association of Nova Scotia (IBANS)

380 Bedford Hwy, Halifax NS B3M 2L4
Tel: 902-876-0526; *Fax:* 902-876-0527
info@ibans.com
www.ibans.com
www.linkedin.com/company/3485745
twitter.com/InsuranceNS
Overview: A small provincial organization founded in 1949 overseen by Insurance Brokers Association of Canada
Mission: To promote the independent insurance broker as the premier distributor of property & casualty insurance products & other related insurance services in Nova Scotia
Chief Officer(s):
Karen Slaunwhite, Executive Director
Staff Member(s): 3; 12 volunteer(s)
Membership: 1,100+; *Member Profile:* Independent property & casualty insurance brokers in Nova Scotia; *Committees:* Public Affairs/Liaison; Professional Development; Member Services; Technology

Insurance Brokers Association of Ontario (IBAO)

#700, 1 Eglinton Ave. East, Toronto ON M4P 3A1
Tel: 416-488-7422; *Fax:* 416-488-7526
Toll-Free: 800-268-8845
contact@ibao.com
www.ibao.org
www.linkedin.com/groups/Insurance-Brokers-Association-Ontario-3976676
www.facebook.com/IBAO1
twitter.com/IBAOntario
www.youtube.com/user/IBAOntario
Overview: A medium-sized provincial organization founded in 1920 overseen by Insurance Brokers Association of Canada
Mission: To act as the authoritative voice of independent brokers in Ontario; To serve the interests of member brokers; To preserve & enhance the value & integrity of the independent broker insurance distribution system
Member of: Insurance Brokers Association of Canada (IBAC)
Chief Officer(s):
Randy Carroll, CEO
rcarroll@ibao.on.ca
Debbie Thompson, President
dthompson@beyondins.net
Rick Orr, Chair
rorr@orrinsurance.net
Membership: 12,000+; *Member Profile:* Independent insurance brokers throughout Ontario who have passed a licensing exam as set by the Registered Insurance Brokers of Ontario (RIBO)
Activities: Liaising with government ministries & regulatory bodies & insurance industry commissions & associations; Offering continuing education programs & training seminars for members; Providing networking opportunities; Offering marketing & business management support; Organizing annual conventions; Presenting annual awards
Meetings/Conferences: • 95th Annual Insurance Brokers Association of Ontario Convention, 2015, ON
Scope: Provincial
• Young Brokers Council 2015 Annual Conference, June, 2015, Sheraton On The Falls Hotel & Conference Centre, Niagara Falls, ON
Scope: Provincial

Insurance Brokers Association of Prince Edward Island
c/o Hyndman & Co. Limited, PO Box 790, 57 Queen St., Charlottetown PE C1A 4A5
Tel: 902-566-4244; *Fax:* 902-566-5990
hyndmaninsurance@anchorgroup.com
Overview: A small provincial organization overseen by Insurance Brokers Association of Canada
Chief Officer(s):
Helen Hyndman, Contact
helen.hyndman@hyndmaninsurance.ca

Insurance Brokers Association of Québec - Assembly *Voir* Regroupement des cabinets de courtage d'assurance du Québec

Insurance Brokers' Association of Saskatchewan (IBAS)
#305, 2631 - 28 Ave., Regina SK S4S 6X3
Tel: 306-525-5900; *Fax:* 306-569-3018
IBASinfo@ibas.ca
www.ibas.ca
www.facebook.com/270988899613418
twitter.com/SKbrokers
Overview: A medium-sized provincial organization
Mission: To promote & preserve the independent insurance brokerage system as a secure, knowledgeable, cost-effective, customer-oriented, professional method of insurance delivery
Member of: Insurance Brokers Association of Canada
Chief Officer(s):
Garth Neher, President
southeyagencies@sasktel.net
Ernie Gaschler, Executive Director
ernie.gaschler@ibas.ca
Staff Member(s): 5; 11 volunteer(s)
Membership: 360; *Member Profile:* Independent insurance brokerages
Activities: Information; licensing courses & education programs

Insurance Council of British Columbia
PO Box 7, #300, 1040 West Georgia St., Vancouver BC V6E 4H1
Tel: 604-688-0321; *Fax:* 604-662-7767
Toll-Free: 877-688-0321
info@insurancecouncilofbc.com
www.insurancecouncilofbc.com
Overview: A medium-sized provincial licensing organization founded in 1930
Mission: Has the authority to license insurance agents, salespersons, & adjusters, & to investigate & discipline licensees. The Council is accountable to the provincial government & reports to the Minister of Finance.
Chief Officer(s):
Gerald Matier, Executive Director
Finances: *Annual Operating Budget:* $1.5 Million-$3 Million
Staff Member(s): 30
Membership: *Member Profile:* Insurance agents, salespersons, & adjusters

Insurance Council of Canada *See* Insurance Bureau of Canada

Insurance Council of Manitoba (ICM)
#466, 167 Lombard Ave., Winnipeg MB R3B 0T6
Tel: 204-988-6800; *Fax:* 204-988-6801
contactus@icm.mb.ca
www.icm.mb.ca
Overview: A small provincial licensing organization founded in 1992
Mission: The Council's role is to administer the regulatory legislation governing insurance agents/brokers operating in Manitoba
Chief Officer(s):
Erin Pearson, Executive Director
epearson@icm.mb.ca
Staff Member(s): 6
Membership: 5,000-14,999;

Insurance Councils of Saskatchewan (ICS)
#310, 2631 - 28th Ave., Regina SK S4S 6X3
Tel: 306-347-0862; *Fax:* 306-569-3018
info@skcouncil.sk.ca
www.insurancecouncils.sk.ca
Overview: A small provincial licensing organization founded in 1986
Mission: Comprising the General Insurance Council, the Life Insurance Council, & the Hail Insurance Council, Insurance Councils of Saskatchewan are committed to promoting a fair, ethical & professional industry, & responsible advice to consumers
Chief Officer(s):
Ron Fullan, Executive Director
Membership: 5,000-14,999

Insurance Institute of British Columbia (IIBC)
#1110, 800 West Pender St., Vancouver BC V6C 2V6
Tel: 604-681-5491; *Fax:* 604-681-5479
Toll-Free: 888-681-5491
IIBCmail@insuranceinstitute.ca
www.iibc.org
Overview: A medium-sized provincial organization overseen by Insurance Institute of Canada
Chief Officer(s):
Danielle Bolduc, Manager, 604-681-5491 Ext. 22
Membership: *Fees:* $60; *Committees:* Career Connections; Education; Future Directions; Marketing & Communications; Operations; Seminars & Events
Activities: Offering educational opportunities

Insurance Institute of Canada (IIC) / Institut d'assurance du Canada (IAC)
18 King St. East, 6th Fl., Toronto ON M5C 1C4
Tel: 416-362-8586; *Fax:* 416-362-1126
Toll-Free: 866-362-8585
IICmail@insuranceinstitute.ca
www.insuranceinstitute.ca
Overview: A large national licensing organization founded in 1952
Mission: To design, develop, & delivers insurance educational programs & texts; To prepare examinations & awards diplomas; To provide a graduate society; To develop career information on behalf of the property/casualty insurance industry
Member of: Institute for Global Insurance Education
Affliation(s): Insurance Institute of America; Chartered Insurance Institute; Australian Insurance Institute; Insurance Institute of India; Insurance Institute of Malaysia
Chief Officer(s):
Peter G. Hohman, MBA, FCIP, ICD., President & CEO
Finances: *Annual Operating Budget:* Greater than $5 Million; *Funding Sources:* Fees for services & voluntary corporate subscriptions
Staff Member(s): 28; 100 volunteer(s)
Membership: 36,000 individuals; *Fees:* $50; $95 CIP Society; *Member Profile:* Employed in property/casualty insurance industry; *Committees:* Academic Council; Professionals' Council; Executive
Activities: Offers education programs through local institutes (Chartered Insurance Professionals Program - CIP) & through participating Canadian universities, including the University of Toronto, School of Continuing Studies (Fellowship Program - FCIP), parent organization of the Chartered Insurance Professional Society; *Internships:* Yes; *Speaker Service:* Yes

Insurance Institute of Manitoba (IIM)
#303, 175 Hargrave St., Winnipeg MB R3C 3R8
Tel: 204-956-1702; *Fax:* 204-956-0758
IIMmail@insuranceinstitute.ca
www.insuranceinstitute.ca
Overview: A medium-sized provincial organization founded in 1923 overseen by Insurance Institute of Canada
Mission: To provide educational services in the general insurance industry in both English and French, such as the Chartered Insurance Professional (CIP), & Fellow Chartered Insurance Professional (FCIP) programs
Chief Officer(s):
Margaret Rempel, Manager
Membership: *Member Profile:* Individuals in Manitoba who want to acquire or expand their knowledge of the insurance industry through educational programs provided by the Institute
Activities: Offering continuing educational seminars;

Insurance Institute of New Brunswick (IINB)
#101, 1010 St-George Blvd., Moncton NB E1E 4R5
Tel: 506-386-5896; *Fax:* 506-386-1130
IINBmail@insuranceinstitute.ca
www.insuranceinstitute.ca
Overview: A medium-sized provincial organization founded in 1952 overseen by Insurance Institute of Canada
Chief Officer(s):
Monique LeBlanc, Manager
mleblanc@insuranceinstitute.ca
Membership: 500-999
Activities: *Library*

Insurance Institute of Newfoundland & Labrador Inc. (IINL)
Chimo Bldg., 151 Crosbie Rd., St. John's NL A1B 4B4
Tel: 709-754-4398; *Fax:* 709-754-4399
IINLmail@insuranceinstitute.ca
www.insuranceinstitute.ca
Overview: A medium-sized provincial organization founded in 1956 overseen by Insurance Institute of Canada
Chief Officer(s):
Leona Rowsell, Manager
Finances: *Annual Operating Budget:* $50,000-$100,000
Staff Member(s): 1; 5 volunteer(s)
Membership: 400
Activities: *Speaker Service:* Yes

Insurance Institute of Northern Alberta (IINA)
#204, 10109 - 106 St., Edmonton AB T5J 3L7
Tel: 780-424-1268; *Fax:* 780-420-1940
IINAmail@insuranceinstitute.ca
www.insuranceinstitute.ca
Overview: A medium-sized local charitable organization overseen by Insurance Institute of Canada
Mission: The Insurance Institute of Northern Alberta provides products and sevices to the general insurance industry, and ensures the maintenance of a uniform standard of education for the general Insurance Business throughout Canada
Affiliation(s): CIP Society of Canada
Chief Officer(s):
Dawn Horne, Manager
Finances: *Annual Operating Budget:* $100,000-$250,000
Staff Member(s): 2; 12 volunteer(s)
Membership: 2,300; *Fees:* $50; *Committees:* Education; Seminars; Operations; CIP Society
Activities: Seminars; fundraising; social events

Insurance Institute of Nova Scotia (IINS)
#220, 250 Baker Dr., Dartmouth NS B2W 6L4
Tel: 902-433-0070; *Fax:* 902-433-0072
IINSmail@insuranceinstitute.ca
www.insuranceinstitute.ca
Overview: A medium-sized provincial organization founded in 1953 overseen by Insurance Institute of Canada
Mission: To provide educational products & services to the general insurance industry, such as the Chartered Insurance Professional (CIP) & the Fellow Chartered Insurance Professional (FCIP) designation programs
Chief Officer(s):
Jenny Renyo, Manager
jreyno@insuranceinstitute.ca
Membership: *Member Profile:* Any individual in Nova Scotia who wants to acquire or expand their knowledge of the general insurance industry
Activities: Presenting continuing education seminars; Supervising examinations; Providing networking opportunities;

Insurance Institute of Ontario (IIO)
18 King St. East, 16th Fl., Toronto ON M5C 1C4
Tel: 416-362-8586; *Fax:* 416-362-8081
iiomail@insuranceinstitute.ca
insuranceinstitute.ca/en/institutes-and-chapters/Ontario.aspx
Overview: A medium-sized provincial organization founded in 1899 overseen by Insurance Institute of Canada
Mission: To deliver general insurance educational services in English & French, which are consistent with the standardized curriculum offered throughout Canada, such as the Fellow Chartered Insurance Professional (FCIP) & the Fellow Chartered Insurance Professional (FCIP) designation programs
Chief Officer(s):
Dawna Matton, BA, FCIP, Senior Director
Membership: *Member Profile:* Any person in Ontario who would like to acquire or expand their knowledge of the insurance industry
Activities: Arranging instruction; Supervising examinations; Presenting continuing education seminars; Presenting scholarships

Cambrian Shield Chapter
18 King St. East, 16th Fl., Toronto ON M5C 1C4
Tel: 416-362-8585; *Fax:* 416-362-8081
cambrianshieldmail@insuranceinstitute.ca
twitter.com/IIOCambrian
Chief Officer(s):
Livia Tersigni, Chapter Manager

Conestoga Chapter
#101, 515 Riverbend Dr., Kitchener ON N2K 3S3

Tel: 519-579-0184; *Fax:* 519-579-1692
conestogamail@insuranceinstitute.ca
twitter.com/IIOConestoga
Chief Officer(s):
Heather Graham, B.Ed, FCIP, CRM, Chapter Manager
Hamilton/Niagara Chapter
#4-5, 1439 Upper Ottawa St., Hamilton ON L8W 3J6
Tel: 905-574-1820; *Fax:* 905-574-8457
hamiltonniagaramail@insuranceinstitute.ca
twitter.com/IIOHam_Nia
Chief Officer(s):
Dawn Cant Elliott, FCIP, CRM, ACS, Chapter Manager
Kawartha/Durham Chapter
18 King St. East, 16th Fl., Toronto ON M5C 1C4
Fax: 416-362-8081
Toll-Free: 866-362-8585
kawarthadurhammail@insuranceinstitute.ca
twitter.com/IIOKaw_Dur
Chief Officer(s):
Livia Tersigni, Chapter Manager
Ottawa Chapter
#300, 1335 Carling Ave., Ottawa ON K1Z 8N8
Tel: 613-722-7870; *Fax:* 613-722-3544
ottawamail@insuranceinstitute.ca
twitter.com/IIOOttawa
Chief Officer(s):
Ellen Legault, BA, FCIP, Chapter Manager
Southwestern Ontario Chapter
#101, 200 Queens Ave., London ON N6A 1J3
Tel: 519-432-3666; *Fax:* 519-432-5919
southwesternmail@insuranceinstitute.ca
twitter.com/IIOSouthWest
Chief Officer(s):
Robert Munford, BA, CIP, Chapter Manager

Insurance Institute of Prince Edward Island (IIPEI)
c/o The Insurance Institute of Canada, 18 King St. East, 6th Fl., Toronto ON M5C 1C4
Tel: 902-892-1692; *Fax:* 902-368-7305
IIPEImail@insuranceinstitute.ca
www.insuranceinstitute.ca
Overview: A small provincial organization founded in 1960 overseen by Insurance Institute of Canada
Chief Officer(s):
Kent Hudson, Marketing Coordinator
khudson@insuranceinstitute.ca
Finances: *Funding Sources:* Membership fees; seminar fees
Membership: 100-499; *Fees:* $25
Activities: Courses; seminars

Insurance Institute of Saskatchewan (IIS)
#310, 2631 - 28 Ave., Regina SK S4S 6X3
Tel: 306-525-9799; *Fax:* 306-525-8169
IISmail@insuranceinstitute.ca
www.insuranceinstitute.ca
Overview: A medium-sized provincial organization overseen by Insurance Institute of Canada
Mission: To offer educational products & services to the general insurance industry in both English & French, such as the Fellow Chartered Insurance Professional (FCIP) & the Chartered Insurance Professional (CIP) designation programs
Chief Officer(s):
Seti Mazaheri, Manager
Membership: *Member Profile:* Any person in Saskatchewan who wishes to attain or expand their knowledge of the insurance industry by registering for Insurance Institute courses; *Committees:* Executive; Academic; Seminar
Activities: Providing continuing education credits for persons who have completed CIP courses

Insurance Institute of Southern Alberta (IISA)
#1110, 833 - 4 Ave. SW, Calgary AB T2P 3T5
Tel: 403-266-3427; *Fax:* 403-269-3199
IISAmail@insuranceinstitute.ca
www.insuranceinstitute.ca
Overview: A medium-sized local organization founded in 1954 overseen by Insurance Institute of Canada
Mission: To advance the efficiency, expertise & ability of people employed in the insurance & financial services industry
Chief Officer(s):
Caroline Logan, Manager
Finances: *Annual Operating Budget:* $100,000-$250,000; *Funding Sources:* Membership dues; industry
Staff Member(s): 2
Membership: 3,540; *Fees:* $50; *Committees:* Education; Professional; Seminars; Newsletter

Insurance Professionals of Calgary
c/o Orla McGregor - Intact Insurance, #1200, 321 - 6 Ave. SW, Calgary AB T2P 4W7
Tel: 403-269-7961; *Fax:* 403-263-1839
www.ipcalgary.ca
www.facebook.com/108424839228674
twitter.com/ipcalgary
Previous Name: Calgary Insurance Women
Overview: A small local organization
Mission: Association of individuals employed in the insurance industry or related service providers
Member of: Canadian Association of Insurance Women
Chief Officer(s):
Orla McGregor, President
president@ipcalgary.org
Evanne Shepherdson, Vice-President
vpresident@ipcalgary.org
Julie Ann Gauthier, Treasurer
treasurer@ipcalgary.org

Insurance Women of Edmonton ***See*** Edmonton Insurance Association

Insurance Women's Association of Manitoba ***See*** Manitoba Association of Insurance Professionals

Insurance Women's Association of Western Manitoba
c/o Portage Mutual, 749 Saskatchewan Ave. East, Portage la Prairie MB R1N 2B8
Tel: 204-857-3415; *Fax:* 204-239-6655
www.caiw-acfa.com/member_associations/iwawm
Overview: A medium-sized local organization founded in 1988
Mission: To encourage & foster education programs for members; to foster & cultivate good fellowship & loyalty among members; to make members more responsive to requirements of the Canadian insurance industry as a whole
Member of: Canadian Association of Insurance Women
Chief Officer(s):
Andrea Mitchell, President
amitchell@portagemutual.com
Lori Penner, Director
lpenner@portagemutual.com
Finances: *Annual Operating Budget:* Less than $50,000
30 volunteer(s)
Membership: 30; *Fees:* $45 individual; *Member Profile:* Those employed in the insurance industry
Activities: Monthly meeetings; seminars; golf tournament, Aug.; Wine & Cheese, April; *Awareness Events:* Insurance Information Week

Integrated Vegetation Management Association of British Columbia (IVMA of BC)
#720, 999 West Broadway, Vancouver BC V5Z 1K5
e-mail: reception@ivma.com
www.ivma.com
Overview: A small provincial organization
Mission: The organization is dedicated to the responsible practice of all aspects of vegetation management
Chief Officer(s):
Gwen Shrimpton, President
Membership: *Member Profile:* Independent contractors, consultants, manufacturers, suppliers

Intégration communautaire Chapleau Community Living
PO Box 1377, Chapleau ON P0M 1K0
Tel: 705-864-2932
chapleau.aclhousing@bellnet.ca
Overview: A small local organization
Member of: Community Living Ontario

Intégration communautaire Cochrane Association for Community Living
PO Box 2330, 18 - 2nd Ave., Cochrane ON P0L 1C0
Tel: 705-272-2999; *Fax:* 705-272-4983
Also Known As: Community Living
Overview: A small local charitable organization founded in 1970
Mission: To ensure that all persons live in a state of dignity, share all elements of living, have equal opportunity to maximize inividual potential for personal growth & independence in the community
Member of: Community Living Ontario
Chief Officer(s):
Mac Hiltz, Executive Director
Finances: *Annual Operating Budget:* $500,000-$1.5 Million
Staff Member(s): 40; 11 volunteer(s)

Membership: 25; *Fees:* $5
Activities: Adult retraining; accommodations services; developmental services

Intégration communautaire comté de Stormont ***See*** Community Living Stormont County

Intégration communautaire de Nipissing ouest ***See*** Community Living West Nipissing

Integration Communautaire Grand Sudbury ***See*** Community Living Greater Sudbury

Intégration Communautaire Kingston ***See*** Community Living Kingston

Intégration Communautaire North Bay ***See*** Community Living North Bay

Intégration communautaire Ontario ***See*** Community Living Ontario

Integrity Toronto
PO Box 873, Stn. F, Toronto ON M4Y 2N9
Tel: 416-925-9872
toronto@integritycanada.org
www.toronto.integritycanada.org
Overview: A small local organization founded in 1975
Mission: International organization of gay & lesbian Anglicans & their friends; to help its members discover & affirm that we can be both Christian & gay/lesbian/bisexual/transgender
Affliation(s): Integrity Inc. - USA
Chief Officer(s):
Chris Ambidge, Co-Convener
Finances: *Annual Operating Budget:* Less than $50,000; *Funding Sources:* Donations
6 volunteer(s)
Membership: 100 individual; *Fees:* $15 single, $20 couple

Integrity Vancouver
PO Box 3016, Stn. Terminal, Vancouver BC V6B 3X5
Tel: 604-432-1230
www.vancouver.integritycanada.org
www.facebook.com/203812556325704
Overview: A small local charitable organization
Affliation(s): Integrity Inc. - USA
Finances: *Annual Operating Budget:* Less than $50,000
14 volunteer(s)
Membership: 50-100; *Fees:* $15 single, $20 couple; *Member Profile:* Gay, lesbian, bisexual, transgendered Anglicans
Activities: Monthly services on first Sunday, St. Paul's Anglican Church; monthly potluck dinners at members' homes; *Speaker Service:* Yes

IntegrityLink
#302, 880 Ouellette Ave., Windsor ON N9A 1C7
Tel: 519-258-7222; *Fax:* 519-258-1198
Other Communication: Complaints, E-mail: complaints@integritylink.ca
info@integritylink.ca
www.integritylink.ca
Previous Name: Better Business Bureau of Windsor & Southwestern Ontario
Overview: A medium-sized local organization
Mission: Their mission is to promote & foster the highest ethical relationship between businesses & the public through voluntary self-regulation, consumer & business education & service education.
Chief Officer(s):
Joe Amort, President & CEO

Intellectual Property Institute of Canada (IPIC) / Institut de la Propriété Intellectuelle du Canada (IPIC)
#606, 60 Queen St., Ottawa ON K1P 5Y7
Tel: 613-234-0516; *Fax:* 613-234-0671
info@ipic.ca
www.ipic.ca
Previous Name: Patent & Trademark Institute of Canada
Overview: A medium-sized national organization founded in 1926
Mission: To promote the protection of intellectual property in Canada & abroad in order to enhance Canada's economic prospects as a sovereign nation & to foster cooperation between Canada & its trading partners around the world.
Affiliation(s): Industry Canada
Finances: *Annual Operating Budget:* $250,000-$500,000; *Funding Sources:* Membership dues; meetings
Staff Member(s): 3; 27 volunteer(s)

Membership: 1,700+; *Member Profile:* Professionals who specialize in intellectual property: patents for inventions, trademarks, copyrights, & industrial designs; *Committees:* Patent Legislation; Trade Mark Legislation; Copyright Legislation; Industrial Design Legislation
Activities: *Rents Mailing List:* Yes

Inter Pares / Among Equals
221 Laurier Ave. East, Ottawa ON K1N 6P1
Tel: 613-563-4801; *Fax:* 613-594-4704
Toll-Free: 866-563-4801
info@interpares.ca
www.interpares.ca
Overview: A medium-sized international charitable organization
Mission: To build equality of people, North & South, by collaborating with & supporting justice for people around the world; Inter Pares applies 4 principles: Leadership by Women, Participation, Sustainability & Respect for Cultural Values
Member of: Canadian Council for International Cooperation
Chief Officer(s):
Rita Morbia, Executive Director
Finances: *Annual Operating Budget:* $3 Million-$5 Million
Staff Member(s): 12
Membership: 1-99
Activities: *Rents Mailing List:* Yes

Inter University Committee on Canadian Slavs (IUCCS) *See* Canadian Ethnic Studies Association

Interac Association / L'Association Interac
Royal Bank Plaza, North Tower, #2400, 200 Bay St., Toronto ON M5J 2J1
Tel: 416-362-8550
Toll-Free: 855-789-2979
info@interac.org
www.interac.org
www.linkedin.com/companies/1328202/Interac+Association
www.facebook.com/interac
twitter.com/interac
youtube.ca/InteracBrand
Overview: A medium-sized national organization founded in 1984
Mission: The Association is a recognized leader in debit card services in Canada
Chief Officer(s):
Mark O'Connell, President & CEO
Membership: 80+ organizations; *Member Profile:* Banks; trust companies; credit unions; caisses populaires; technology & payment related companies
Activities: Responsible for the development of a national network of two shared electronic financial services: Shared Cash Dispensing Service at automated banking machines, & Interac Direct Payment Services, a national debit service;

Interactive Advertising Bureau of Canada
#602, 2 St. Clair Ave. West, Toronto ON M4V 1L5
Tel: 416-598-3400; *Fax:* 416-598-3500
Other Communication: quebec@iabcanada.com; west@iabcanada.com
information@iabcanada.com
www.iabcanada.com
www.linkedin.com/groups?home=&gid=4942473&trk=groups_guest_about-h-log
www.facebook.com/IABCanada
twitter.com/iabcanada
www.youtube.com/iabcanada
Also Known As: IAB Canada
Previous Name: IAB Internet Advertising Bureau of Canada
Overview: A small national organization
Mission: To establish & communicate interactive advertising best practices that optimize advertising investment, leading to increased stakeholder value
Chief Officer(s):
Chris Williams, President
Julie Ford, Vice President, Operations
Membership: *Member Profile:* Publishers, advertisers, advertising agencies & service associates in the Canadian interactive marketing industry; *Committees:* Ad Operations; Big Data; Content Marketing; Emerging Platforms; Mobile; Research; Programmatic Trading; Search; Social Media; Video

Interactive Gaming Council (IGC)
#175, 2906 West Broadway, Vancouver BC V6K 2G8
Tel: 604-732-3833; *Fax:* 604-677-5785
www.igcouncil.org
Overview: A small national organization founded in 1996
Mission: To provide a forum for interested parties to address issues & advance common interests in the global interactive gaming industry; to establish fair & responsible trade guidelines & practices that enhance consumer confidence in interactive gaming products & services; to serve as the industry's public policy advocate & information clearinghouse
Chief Officer(s):
Keith Furlong, Chief Executive
keithf@igcouncil.org
John Anderson, Chair
Staff Member(s): 3

Interactive Ontario (IO)
#600, 431 King St. West, Toronto ON M5V 1K4
Tel: 416-516-0077
Other Communication: Membership E-mail: membership@interactiveontario.com
info@interactiveontario.com
www.interactiveontario.com
www.linkedin.com/groups?about=&gid=2096721&trk=anet_ug_grppro
www.facebook.com/28971906704
www.twitter.com/ionews
www.flickr.com/photos/32406922@N04/
Previous Name: New Media Business Alliance
Overview: A medium-sized provincial organization
Mission: To advance the digital media industry in Ontario, including e-Learning, video & online games, mobile, television & social media.
Member of: Canadian Interactive Alliance
Chief Officer(s):
Peter Miller, Chair
Lucie Lalumière, Vice-Chair
Spence McDonnell, Treasurer
David Dembroski, Secretary
Christa Dickenson, Executive Director
christa@interactiveontario.com
Membership: *Fees:* Based on size of company

Inter-American Commercial Arbitration Commission (IACAC)
Canadian Arbitration Centre & Amicable Composition Center, Inc., c/o Faculty of Law, University of Ottawa, Ottawa ON
Tel: 613-232-1476
sice@sice.oas.org
www.sice.oas.org/dispute/comarb/iacac/iacac1e.asp
Overview: A medium-sized international organization founded in 1934
Mission: To promote conciliation, amicable composition & arbitration in the international commercial settling of disputes in the Western hemisphere
Member of: International Federation of Commercial Arbitration Institutions
Chief Officer(s):
Julio Gonzales Soria, President
Paul J. Davidson, Director, Canada
Finances: *Annual Operating Budget:* $50,000-$100,000; *Funding Sources:* Case fees; grants
Staff Member(s): 2
Membership: 15
Activities: *Internships:* Yes; *Speaker Service:* Yes

Canadian National Section
Canadian Arbitration Centre & Amicable Composition Centre, Inc., 57 Louis-Pasteur St., Fauteux Hall, University of Ottawa, Ottawa ON K1N 6N5
Tel: 613-232-1476; *Fax:* 613-564-9800
Chief Officer(s):
Paul J. Davidson, Contact

Intercede International
201 Stanton St., Fort Erie ON L2A 3N8
Tel: 905-871-1773; *Fax:* 905-871-5165
Toll-Free: 800-871-0882
friends@intercedenow.ca
www.intercedenow.ca
Previous Name: Christian Aid Mission
Overview: A medium-sized international charitable organization founded in 1953
Mission: To aid, encourage, & strengthen indigenous New Testament Christianity, particularly where Christians are impoverished, few, or persecuted; to encourage Christian witness & ministry to the international community in North America
Member of: Canadian Council of Christian Charities
Affliation(s): Evangelical Fellowship of Canada
Chief Officer(s):
James S. Eagles, President
Finances: *Annual Operating Budget:* $500,000-$1.5 Million; *Funding Sources:* Private donations
Staff Member(s): 10; 50 volunteer(s)
Membership: 10; *Committees:* Audit Review
Activities: Sponsorship programs; relief aid; equipment & materials provisions; Missions cafe held in major cities; *Speaker Service:* Yes; *Library* by appointment
Publications:
• Mission Gateway
Type: Magazine; *Frequency:* 3x/yr.; *Editor:* Alan Doerksen
Profile: Publication keeping churches, friends and donors current on indigenous mission work at various global sites.

Inter-Cultural Association of Greater Victoria (ICA)
930 Balmoral Rd., Victoria BC V8T 1A8
Tel: 250-388-4728; *Fax:* 250-386-4395
www.icavictoria.org
www.linkedin.com/company/intercultural-association-of-victoria
www.facebook.com/ICAVictoria
twitter.com/ICAVictoria
www.youtube.com/user/icagreatervictoria
Overview: A small local charitable organization founded in 1971
Mission: To encourage sensitivity, appreciation & respect for individuals of all cultures in our changing community; to assist newcomers to settle in the Greater Victoria area & to facilitate their inclusion & full participation in the community; to advocate for the human rights of people of all cultures; to animate cultural awareness by promoting public multicultural events within Greater Victoria
Member of: Affiliation of Multicultural Societies & Service Agencies of BC
Chief Officer(s):
Jean McRae, Executive Director
Staff Member(s): 62
Membership: *Member Profile:* Individuals & ethnic member groups
Activities: FolkFest - festival of music, dance & food; ESL; citizenship classes; parenting programs; Women's & Youth Groups; family counselling; interpretation & translation; employment services; Host Family

Intercultural Heritage Association
70 Lancaster Rd., Moncton NB E1C 7P6
e-mail: interculturalheri.association@gmail.com
www.facebook.com/231828396947539
Overview: A small local organization
Mission: To increase the participation & contribution of immigrants & minorities to the social & economic fibres of the New Brunswick community
Chief Officer(s):
JoAnne Gittens, President

Interfaith Food Bank Society of Lethbridge
1103 - 3 Ave. North, Lethbridge AB T1H 0H7
Tel: 403-320-8779; *Fax:* 403-328-0521
info@interfaithfoodbank.ca
www.interfaithfoodbank.ca
www.facebook.com/lethbridgeinterfaith
www.twitter.com/IFBLethbridge
www.youtube.com/playlist?list=PL7AE96D1025B75C6B&feature=plcp
Overview: A medium-sized local charitable organization founded in 1989 overseen by Alberta Food Bank Network Association
Mission: Providing food and access to services and resources for those in need.
Member of: Food Banks Canada
Chief Officer(s):
Danielle McIntyre, Executive Director
danielle@interfaithfoodbank.ca

Intergovernmental Committee on Urban & Regional Research (ICURR) / Comité intergouvernemental de recherches urbaines et régionales (CIRUR)
#210, 40 Wynford Dr., Toronto ON M3C 1J5
Fax: 647-345-7004
www.muniscope.ca
Overview: A medium-sized national organization founded in 1967
Mission: ICURR supports local and regional governments, as well as private and non-profit companies through subsidized information and networking services. Muniscope is Canada's national resource on municipal issues, with subscription-based research and library services available on economic development, finance and taxation, housing and infrastructure, transportation, planning, and sustainability.

Chief Officer(s):
Mathieu Rivard, Director
mrivard@icurr.org
Finances: *Funding Sources:* Canadian Mortgage & Housing Corporation
Staff Member(s): 4
Activities: Information exchange & research; *Rents Mailing List:* Yes

Interior Designers Association of Saskatchewan (IDAS)

PO Box 32005, Stn. Erindale, Saskatoon SK S7S 1N8
Tel: 306-343-3311
idasadmin@idas.ca
www.idas.ca
Overview: A small provincial organization overseen by Interior Designers of Canada
Mission: To promote an understanding of the profession to the public & to support members in their profession through continuing education & networking
Chief Officer(s):
Kenda Owens, President
kenda.owens@siast.sk.ca
Finances: *Funding Sources:* Auction
Membership: 54; *Fees:* $26.25 student; $156.06 retired; $411.08 registered; $227.23 provisional/out of province; *Member Profile:* 7 years combined education & experience; successful completion of NCIDQ exam; *Committees:* CEU; Events
Activities: Lunch & Learn, monthly

Interior Designers Institute of British Columbia (IDIBC)

#400, 601 West Broadway, Vancouver BC V5Z 4C2
Tel: 604-298-5211; *Fax:* 604-421-5211
info@idibc.org
www.idibc.org
Overview: A medium-sized provincial organization founded in 1950 overseen by Interior Designers of Canada
Mission: To act as the single representative voice of the Interior Design profession in British Columbia; to advance the profession through public recognition & provide leadership & services to members through programs, communication & education; to benefit public health, safety & welfare, contribute to the enhancement of the environment & increase the perception, appreciation & value of design in the community.
Affliation(s): Design Resource Association
Chief Officer(s):
Alyssa Myshok, President
Finances: *Annual Operating Budget:* $100,000-$250,000; *Funding Sources:* Corporate; fundraising
Staff Member(s): 1
Membership: 230; *Fees:* $424 professional; $201 associate; $69 pre-professional; $275 affiliate; $32 student; *Member Profile:* Professional; Associate; Pre-Professional; Fellow; Charter; Honorary; Inactive; Student; *Committees:* Newsletter; Fundraising; Design Awards; Special Projects; Education; Membership Services; Programs
Activities: Continuing education; Awards of Excellence Design Competition; professional recognition; seminars; *Rents Mailing List:* Yes

Interior Designers of Alberta (IDA)

PO Box 21171, #202, 5404 - 99 St., Edmonton AB T6R 2V4
Tel: 780-413-0013; *Fax:* 780-413-0076
info@idalberta.ca
www.idalberta.ca
Also Known As: Registered Interior Designers of Alberta
Overview: A small provincial organization founded in 1960 overseen by Interior Designers of Canada
Mission: To ensure that its members receive up to date information so that they can best serve their clients
Affliation(s): Interior Designers of Canada; National Council for Interior Design Qualification; Council for Interior Design Accreditation; Interior Design Continuing Education Council Inc.; Interior Designers Institute of British Columbia; Interior Designers Association of Saskatchewan; Professional Interior Designers Institute of Manitoba; Association of Registered Interior Designers of Ontario; Association professionnelle des designers d'interieur du Quebec; Association of Registered Interior Designers of New Brunswick; Association of Interior Designers of Nova Scotia
Chief Officer(s):
Kelly Vander Hooft, President
Adele Bonetti, Registrar
Membership: 160; *Fees:* $25 student; $290 provisional; $345 registered-licensed; $395 registered; $380 associate; *Member Profile:* People involved with the interior design profession & students

Interior Designers of Alberta (IDA)

PO Box 21171, #202, 5405 - 99 St., Edmonton AB T6R 2V4
Tel: 780-413-0013; *Fax:* 780-413-0076
info@idalberta.ca
www.idalberta.ca
Overview: A small provincial organization founded in 1960
Mission: To develop and maintain standards of practice of interior design; to encourage excellence in interior design; to develop standards of and encourage continuing education of practicing designers; and to provide a liaison between the profession and the general public.
Affliation(s): Interior Designers of Canada; Interior Designers Institute of British Columbia; Professional Interior Designers Institute of Manitoba; Association of Registered Interior Designers of Ontario; Association of Registered Interior Designers of New Brunswick; Association of Interior Designers of Nova Scotia; National Council for Interior Design Qualifications; Council for Interior Design Accreditation; International Interior Design Education Council
Chief Officer(s):
Kelly Vander Hooft, President
Membership: *Fees:* $345 Registered Licensed Member; $395 Registered, $380 Associate Member; $290 Provisional Member; $25 Student Member

Interior Designers of Canada (IDC) / Designers d'intérieur du Canada

#220, 6 Adelaide St. East, Toronto ON M5C 1H6
Tel: 416-649-4425; *Fax:* 416-921-3660
Toll-Free: 877-443-4425
www.idcanada.org
www.facebook.com/147037918674277?v=info
twitter.com/IDCanadaTweets
Overview: A medium-sized national organization founded in 1972
Mission: To advance the interior design industry in Canada through high standards of education for the profession, professional responsibility, professional development, & communication
Chief Officer(s):
Susan Wiggins, Executive Director
Finances: *Funding Sources:* Sponsorships
Activities: Providing educational programs & professional qualifications; Offering national liability insurance; Liaising with federal government committees to represent the interior design profession; Promoting environmental consciousness; Initiating The Interior Designers of Canada Foundation to provide scholarships, bursaries, & fellowships to interior design students & practitioners

Interior Designers of New Brunswick *See* Association of Registered Interior Designers of New Brunswick

Interior Designers of Ontario (IDO) *See* Association of Registered Interior Designers of Ontario

Interior Indian Friendship Society

125 Palm St., Kamloops BC V2B 8J7
Tel: 250-376-1296; *Fax:* 250-376-2275
www.iifs.ca
Overview: A small local charitable organization founded in 1972
Mission: To improve the quality of life for Aboriginal People
Chief Officer(s):
Delphine Terbasket, Executive Director
Finances: *Annual Operating Budget:* $500,000-$1.5 Million
Staff Member(s): 28
Membership: 30-80; *Fees:* $2; *Member Profile:* Urban Aboriginal People; *Committees:* Education; Personnel
Activities: Social programs; Mental Health programs; Alcohol and Drug Counseling; Family Preservation & Roots; Life Skills Housing programs; *Awareness Events:* Aboriginal Day; *Library* Open to public

Interior Miniature Horse Club

c/o Joan McNaughton, 822 Quesnel Canyon Rd., Quesnel BC V2J 6S4
Tel: 250-992-2748
minipg@telus.net
www.bcminiaturehorseclubs.com/interior.htm
Overview: A small local organization
Chief Officer(s):
Lori Standeven, President
lstandeven@gmail.com
Kari Robinson, Vice-President
Kimi Robinson, Secretary
Joan McNaughton, Treasurer, 250-992-7485
joan_geo_mcnaug@shaw.ca
Membership: *Member Profile:* Miniature horse owners & breeders from the interior of British Columbia
Activities: Organizing monthly meetings at the Prince George Agriplex; Hosting educational clinics or workshops about miniature horses; Participating in parades; Hosting annual American Miniature Horse Registry & American Miniature Horse Association sanctioned shows
Publications:
• Interior Miniature Horse Club Newsletter
Type: Newsletter
Profile: Club information for members

Interior Running Association

Kamloops BC
Tel: 250-374-1652
www.interiorrunningassociation.com
www.facebook.com/InteriorRunningAssociation
twitter.com/interiorrunning
Overview: A small national organization
Mission: To promote fitness & running in the Southern Interior of British Columbia.
Chief Officer(s):
Rick Jenkner, President
ultramanrick@yahoo.ca
Peter Pollhammer, Vice-President, 250-491-9414
ppollham@pmp-software.com
Linda Conrad, Secretary, 250-558-7823
conrad@junction.net
Activities: Road & trail races

Inter-loge

1503, rue La Fontaine, Montréal QC H2L 1T7
Tél: 514-522-2107; *Téléc:* 514-522-7070
www.linkedin.com/company/inter-loge
www.facebook.com/Interloge
twitter.com/interloge
Aperçu: *Dimension:* petite; *Envergure:* locale; fondée en 1978
Mission: Pour fournir des logements abordables pour les locataires à faible revenu et d'aide à la reconversion de la communauté

International Academy of Energy, Minerals, & Materials (AEMM)

Esprit Dr., Ottawa ON K4A 4Z1
Tel: 613-322-1029; *Fax:* 613-830-8371
info@iaemm.com
iaemm.com
Overview: A medium-sized international organization
Mission: To provide information about technological advancements in the fields of energy, minerals, & materials to academia & industry
Chief Officer(s):
Lyne Bourgault, Adjointe administrative
Meetings/Conferences: • International Academy of Energy, Minerals, & Materials 2015 International Conference on Clean Energy, September, 2015, Ottawa, ON
Scope: International
Description: Conference topics include the following: Biomass energy, materials & technologies; Hydro energy, materials & technologies; Wind energy resources & technologies; Solar cells energy, materials & technologies; Fuel cells materials & hydrogen energy; Battery materials & technologies; Energy storage techniques; Nanotechnology & energy; Green buildings; Energy process & system simulation, modelling & optimization; & more
Contact Information: URL: icce2015.iaemm.com
• International Academy of Energy, Minerals, & Materials 2015 International Conference & Exhibition on advanced and nano materials, August, 2015, Ottawa, ON
Scope: International
Contact Information: URL: icanm2015.iaemm.com
• International Academy of Energy, Minerals, & Materials 2015 International Conference on Mining, Material and Metallurgical Education, 2015
Scope: International
Publications:
• Additives & Surfactants
Price: $185
• Anode Materials for Lithium Ion Batteries — Patent Review, Market Trends, & Mmore
Price: $350
• Hard Metal Process, Application & Analysis
Price: $235

• Hydrometallurgy
Price: $225
• Ore Analysis, Handling, & Preparation
Price: $225
• Physical & Chemical Separation
Price: $225
• Plant Optimisation & Control
Price: $225
• Pyrometallurgy
Price: $225

International Academy of Law & Mental Health (IALMH) / Académie internationale de droit et de santé mentale (AIDSM)

c/o Philippe Pinel, Faculty of Medicine, University of Montreal, PO Box 6128, Stn. Centre-Ville, Montréal QC H3C 3J7
Tel: 514-343-5938; *Fax:* 514-343-2452
admin@ialmh.org
www.ialmh.org
Overview: A small international organization founded in 1981
Chief Officer(s):
Thomas Gutheil, President
Membership: *Fees:* US$100 regular; US$50 student

International Academy of Science, Engineering & Technology

#414, 1376 Bank St., Ottawa ON K1H 7Y3
Tel: 613-695-3040
info@international-aset.com
www.international-aset.com
www.linkedin.com/company/1169039
www.facebook.com/207827708283
twitter.com/ASET_INC
www.youtube.com/user/InternationalASET
Also Known As: International ASET Inc.
Overview: A medium-sized international organization
Mission: The International Academy of Science, Engineering and Technology (International ASET Inc.) is a young, growing and independent institution created to serve in the matters of education involving science and engineering.
Meetings/Conferences: • HTFF 2015: International Conference on Heat Transfer and Fluid Flow, July, 2015, Bracelona
Scope: International
• MVML 2015: International Conference on Machine Vision and Machine Learning, July, 2015, Bracelona
Scope: International
• ICCSTE 2015: International Conference on Civil, Structural and Transportation Engineering, May, 2015, Ottawa, ON
Scope: International
Description: Conference topics focus on the areas of civil, structural & transportation engineering
Contact Information: URL: iccste.com
• CDSR 2015: International Conference of Control, Dynamic Systems, and Robotics, May, 2015, Ottawa, ON
Scope: National
Description: Annual conference in fields related to traditional and modern control and dynamic systems.
Contact Information: Website: dscconference.com
• MMME 2015: International Conference on Mining, Material and Metallurgical Engineering, July, 2015, Barcelona
Scope: International
• ICEPR 2015: 5th International Conference on Environmental Pollution and Remediation, July, 2015, Barcelona
Scope: International
Contact Information: URL: icepr.org
• ICMIE 2015: 4th International Conference on Mechanics & Industrial Engineering, July, 2015, Barcelona
Scope: International
Contact Information: URL: icmie.net
• ICNFA 2015: 6th International Conference on Nanotechnology: Fundamentals and Applications, July, 2015, Barcelona
Scope: International
Contact Information: URL: icnfa.com

International Agricultural Exchange Association ***See*** AgriVenture International Rural Placements

International Air Transport Association (IATA) / Association du transport aérien international

PO Box 113, 800, Place Victoria, Montréal QC H4Z 1M1
Tel: 514-874-0202; *Fax:* 514-874-1753
www.iata.org
www.linkedin.com/groups?mostPopular=&gid=3315879
twitter.com/iata
www.youtube.com/iatatv
Overview: A small international organization founded in 1945
Mission: To promote safe, regular & economical air transport for the benefit of the peoples of the world; to foster air commerce; to study the problems connected with air transport; to provide a means for collaboration among the air transport enterprises engaged directly or indirectly in international air transport service; to cooperate with the International Civil Aviation Organization & other international organizations; to furnish for governments a forum for developing industry working standards &, as appropriate, coordinating international fares & rates; to simplify the travelling process for the general public
Affiliation(s): International Civil Aviation Organization
Chief Officer(s):
Tony Tyler, Director General
Membership: *Committees:* Avionics & Telecommunications; Engineering & Environment; Airports; Flight Operations; Medical; Security; Air Law; Financial; Traffic Coordination; Traffic Services

International Airborne Geophysics Safety Association (IAGSA)

144 Harry MacKay Rd., Woodland ON K0A 2M0
Tel: 613-832-1646
www.iagsa.ca
Overview: A small international organization founded in 1995
Mission: To promote & enhance safety in airborne geophysics
Finances: *Funding Sources:* Membership fees
Membership: 98; *Fees:* Schedule available based on number of employees; *Member Profile:* Companies involved in airborne geophysics
Activities: *Library*

International Alliance of Breast Cancer Organizations ***See*** Alliance of Cancer Consultants

International Alliance of Theatrical Stage Employees, Moving Picture Technicians, Artists & Allied Crafts of the U.S. ***Voir*** Alliance internationale des employé(e)s de scène, de théâtre et de cinéma

International Association for Educational & Vocational Guidance (IAEVG) / Association internationale d'orientation scolaire et professionnelle (AIOSP)

c/o University of Calgary, Division of Applied Psychology, #202, 119 Ross Ave., Ottawa ON K1Y 0N6
Tel: 613-729-6164; *Fax:* 613-729-3515
membership@iaevg.org
www.iaevg.org
Overview: A small international organization founded in 1951
Mission: To promote communication between persons & organizations active in educational & vocational guidance; to encourage the permanent development of ideas, practice & research in this field on national & international levels; to advise governments on the development of guidance & counselling programs
Affliation(s): Canadian Career Development Foundation; Centre de recherche sur l'éducation au travail (CRET); National Life/Work Centre; Canada WorkInfoNet Partnership
Chief Officer(s):
Lester Oakes, President
lester.oakes@clear.net.nz
Suzanne Bultheel, Secretary General
Suzanne.Bultheel@gmail.com
Finances: *Annual Operating Budget:* $100,000-$250,000
Membership: 400 individuals + 50 national associations; *Fees:* US$84

International Association for Impact Assessment - Western & Northern Canada

2215 - 19th St. SW, Calgary AB T2T 4X1
Tel: 403-245-6404
IAIA-WNC@praxis.ca
www.iaia-wnc.ca
Overview: A small local organization
Chief Officer(s):
Susan P. Wilkins, President

International Association for Literary Journalism Studies (IALJS)

c/o Ryerson University School of Journalism (Attn: Bill Reynolds), 350 Victoria St., Toronto ON M5B 2K3
Tel: 416-979-5000
www.ialjs.org
Overview: A small international organization founded in 2006
Mission: To promote scholarly research & education in literary journalism (narrative journalism, creative non-fiction, or journalism as literature)
Chief Officer(s):
Bill Reynolds, First Vice President-Treasurer
reynolds@ryerson.ca
Membership: *Fees:* $25-$100 USD
Activities: Online newsletter; blog
Publications:
• Literary Journalism Studies
Type: Journal; *Editor:* John C. Hartsock *ISSN:* 1994-897X

International Association for Medical Assistance to Travellers (IAMAT)

#036, 67 Mowat Ave., Toronto ON M6K 3E3
Tel: 416-652-0137; *Fax:* 416-652-1983
www.iamat.org
www.facebook.com/IAMATHealth
twitter.com/IAMAT_Travel
Overview: A medium-sized international charitable organization founded in 1960
Mission: To make competent care available to the traveller around the world; to make direct grants to medical institutions
Member of: Foundation for the Support of International Medical Training (Canada)
Chief Officer(s):
Assunta Uffer-Marcolongo, President
Tullia Marcolongo, Director, Programs & Development
Nadia Sallete, Director, Membership Services
Finances: *Annual Operating Budget:* $250,000-$500,000; *Funding Sources:* Donations
Staff Member(s): 10
Membership: 6,000,000 worldwide; *Fees:* Donation appreciated
Activities: World directory of IAMAT physicians; traveller clinical record; world immunization, malaria & schistosomiasis risk & climate charts; scholarship & grant funding in the field of travel medicine; *Speaker Service:* Yes; *Library:* Online Library;

Guelph Office
2162 Gordon St., Guelph ON N1L 1G6
Tel: 519-836-0102; *Fax:* 519-836-3412
Chief Officer(s):
Nadia Sallese, Contact

International Association of Educators for World Peace (IAEWP Canada)

#100-209, 2 Bloor St. West, Toronto ON M4W 3E2
Tel: 416-924-4449; *Fax:* 416-924-4094
Other Communication: Alternate Fax: 416-921-4365
www.homeplanet.org
Overview: A large international organization founded in 1969
Mission: To promote peace through education; to promote a universal declaration of human rights & responsibilities; to promote global citizenship; to promote World Water Day; to promote the Vision Changer Project, TOPS Program & homeplanet.org
Affiliation(s): NGO status with UNESCO, UNICEF, UNDPI, UNCED & United Nations
Chief Officer(s):
Mitchell Gold, Secretary General & Executive Director, Homeplanet Alliance
mgold@homeplanet.org
Finances: *Annual Operating Budget:* $50,000-$100,000; *Funding Sources:* Programs; grants
Staff Member(s): 1; 200 volunteer(s)
Membership: 35,000 worldwide; *Fees:* $50
Activities: Regional workshops; exchanges; community outreach projects; UNESCO clubs; lectures; seminars; Home Planet Alliance; TOPS Program; *Awareness Events:* Vision Changer Project; *Speaker Service:* Yes

International Association of Hydrogeologists - Canadian National Chapter (IAH-CNC)

c/o WESA, 3108 Carp Rd., Carp ON K0A 1L0
Tel: 613-839-3053
www.iah.ca
Overview: A medium-sized national organization founded in 1972
Mission: To advance the science of hydrogeology & exchange hydrogeologic information internationally
Member of: Canadian Geoscience Council
Affliation(s): International Union of Geological Congresses
Chief Officer(s):
Nell van Walsum, Secretary
Finances: *Annual Operating Budget:* Less than $50,000
Membership: 300 across Canada; *Fees:* $120; schedule
Activities: *Speaker Service:* Yes

International Association of Infant Massage Canada
Toll-Free: 877-532-2323
aimbiaim@gmail.com
www.iaim-aimbcanada.org
Overview: A small national organization
Mission: To promote the nuturing touch and communication through training, education and research.
Chief Officer(s):
Manon Salois, President
Membership: *Fees:* $80

International Association of Science & Technology for Development (IASTED)
Bldg B6, #101, 2509 Dieppe Ave. SW, Calgary AB T3E 7J9
Tel: 403-288-1195; *Fax:* 403-247-6851
calgary@iasted.com
www.iasted.org
www.facebook.com/pages/IASTED/130963346917239
twitter.com/IASTED_Calgary
Overview: A medium-sized international organization founded in 1977
Mission: To further economic development by promoting science & technology
Membership: *Fees:* $110 individual; $190 corporate; $20 developping country; *Committees:* Technical
Activities: Interchange & circulation of information on science & technology; organizing international conferences, symposia, courses
Publications:
• Control & Intelligent Systems
Type: Journal; *Frequency:* Quarterly; *Editor:* Prof. Clarence W. de Silva
• International Journal of Computational Bioscience
Type: Journal; *Frequency:* Quarterly; *Editor:* Dr. L. Elnitski; Prof. L.R. Welch
• International Journal of Computers and Applications
Type: Journal; *Frequency:* Quarterly; *Editor:* Dr. L. Monticone
• International Journal of Modelling and Simulation
Type: Journal; *Frequency:* Quarterly; *Editor:* Prof. A. Houshyar
• International Journal of Power and Energy Systems
Type: Journal; *Frequency:* Quarterly; *Editor:* Dr. A/ Domijan, Jr.
• International Journal of Robotics and Automation
Type: Journal; *Frequency:* Quarterly

International Atomic Energy Agency: Canadian Regional Office
PO Box 20, #1702, 365 Bloor St. East, Toronto ON M4W 3L4
Tel: 416-928-9149; *Fax:* 416-928-0046
official.mail@iaea.org
www.iaea.org
www.facebook.com/iaeaorg
Overview: A large international organization founded in 1957
Mission: Serves as the global focal point for nuclear cooperation
Activities: Develops nuclear safety standards
Publications:
• IAEA Bulletin
Type: Bulletin

International Board on Books for Young People - Canadian Section (IBBY - Canada) / Union internationale pour les livres de jeunesse
c/o Canadian Children's Book Centre, #217, 40 Orchard View Blvd., Toronto ON M4R 1B9
Tel: 416-975-0010; *Fax:* 416-975-8970
info@ibby-canada.org
www.ibby-canada.org
www.facebook.com/ibbycanada
twitter.com/IBBYCanada
flickr.com/photos/50914640@N08
Overview: A small international organization founded in 1980
Mission: To promote the belief that all children everywhere should have the ability to read a wide & rich selection of books at the level of their needs & interests; To build bridges of understanding & tolerance through children's books
Affliation(s): Canadian Children's Book Centre
Chief Officer(s):
Susane Duchesne, President
president@ibby-canada.org
Stephanie Dror, Secretary, Membership
membership@ibby-canada.org
Finances: *Funding Sources:* Private donations & membership fees
Membership: *Fees:* $15 student; $50 individual; $125 supporter; $250 donor; $750 patron; *Member Profile:* General interest in children's literature
Awards:
• Elizabeth Mrazik-Cleaver Picture Book Award (Award)
Awarded for distinguished Canadian picture book illustration; submissions to Children's Literature Service, National Library of Canada, 395 Wellington St., Ottawa, ON K1A 0N4 *Amount:* $1,000
• Frances E. Russell Award (Award)
Awarded to initiate & encourage research in children's literature in Canada *Amount:* $1,000
• Claude Aubry Award (Award)
Awarded biennially for distinguished contributions to Canadian children's literature by a librarian, teacher, author, illustrator, publisher, bookseller, or editor *Amount:* $1,000

International Catholic Deaf Association (ICDA)
71 Gough Ave., Toronto ON M4K 3N9
Tel: 647-328-7631
Other Communication: www.icdacanadasection.wordpress.com
www.deafcatholic.ca
Also Known As: ICDA-Canada
Overview: A small local organization founded in 1949
Mission: To promote religion, religious education, fellowship & leadership among deaf people of all ages; to promote in Canada & the ICDA various programs in foreign countries with a view to enhancing the life of deaf people
Chief Officer(s):
Carol L. Stokes, Co-ordinator
cstokes@archtoronto.org
Kevin Brockerville, Deacon
kevinbr@rogers.com
Wanda Berrette, President
wberrette@rogers.com
Giuliana Grobelski, Vice-President
julianamusso3@hotmail.com
John Shores, Treasurer
jshores@shaw.ca
Finances: *Annual Operating Budget:* Less than $50,000
40 volunteer(s)
Membership: 150 + 5,000 non-members; 16 Canadian chapters; *Fees:* $10 single; $15 couple; *Member Profile:* Practicing Catholics; deaf diaconates; lay ministries
Activities: National conference/workshop; Canadian Catholic Pastoral Workers for the Deaf meetings; fundraising; retreats; signed Mass; assists the Pastoral Workers, seminarians to learn sign languages; spreads the knowledge of the deaf culture among the hearing parishioners
Awards:
• The Frank Crough Award (Award)
For the outstanding member of the year
• The Sr. Columbiere Award (Award)
For the outstanding pastoral worker of the year

International Centre *See* Queen's University International Centre

International Centre for Comparative Criminology *Voir* Centre international de criminologie comparée

International Centre for Criminal Law Reform & Criminal Justice Policy (ICCLR)
1822 East Mall, Vancouver BC V6T 1Z1
Tel: 604-822-9875; *Fax:* 604-822-9317
icclr@law.ubc.ca
www.icclr.law.ubc.ca
Overview: A medium-sized national charitable organization founded in 1991
Mission: To improve the quality of justice through reform of criminal law, policy & practice; to provide advice, information, research & proposals for policy development & legislation
Affliation(s): UN Crime Prevention & Criminal Justice Programme
Chief Officer(s):
Kathleen Macdonald, Executive Director
Staff Member(s): 10
Membership: 1-99
Activities: Publications; *Speaker Service:* Yes

International Centre for Sustainable Cities (ICSC)
#210, 128 West Hastings St., Vancouver BC V6B 1G8
Tel: 778-712-0965
sustainablecities.net
Overview: A small international charitable organization founded in 1993
Mission: To support sustainable city projects around the world through demonstration projects using Canadian experience & expertise
Chief Officer(s):
Jane McRae, CEO
jcmcrae@icsc.ca
Beth Johnson, Chair
Finances: *Funding Sources:* Projects
Membership: 40 member cities; *Committees:* Executive
Activities: Supports sustainable urban development demonstration projects in India, China, Columbia, Thailand, SE Asia (Thailand, Indonesia, Philippines), Turkey, Poland, Slovakia, Hungary: Plus-30 Network; *Internships:* Yes; *Library* by appointment

International Centre for the Prevention of Crime *Voir* Centre international pour la prévention de la criminalité

International Cheese Council of Canada (ICCC)
c/o Canadian Association of Importers & Exporters, PO Box 189, Toronto ON M3C 2S2
Overview: A medium-sized national organization founded in 1976 overseen by The Canadian Association of Importers & Exporters
Mission: To act as the representative voice of Canadian importers of cheese, with respect to the activities of the federal & provincial governments & agencies & all other bodies affecting the commercial interests of cheese importers in Canada; To monitor & analyze all developments relating to the importation of cheese into Canada; To contribute to the formulation, revision & amendment of government policy relating to the commercial regulatory framework within which Canadian cheese importers operate their businesses; To promote the commercial interests of members in a public relations capacity; To liaise with other industry & trade associations working in cheese-related sectors
Chief Officer(s):
Amesika Baëta, Director, Member Relations & Development, 613-595-5333 Ext. 41
abaeta@iecanada.com
Finances: *Funding Sources:* Membership fees
Membership: 100-499; *Member Profile:* Executive Committee - 12 firms elected by voting membership at annual meetings; Voting Members - importers of cheese, financial contributors to the Council & members of the Canadian Importers Association; Non-Voting Members - governmental trade-promoting organizations & representatives who have an active interest in the work of the Council; Non-Association Member ICCC Contributors

International Civil Aviation Organization: Legal Affairs & External Relations Bureau
999, rue Université, Montréal QC H3C 5H7
Tel: 514-954-8219; *Fax:* 514-954-6077
Other Communication: sales@icao.int
icaohq@icao.int
www.icao.int
twitter.com/icao
www.youtube.com/icaovideo
Overview: A large international organization
Mission: To promote the safe & orderly development of civil aviation in the world; to set international standards & regulations necessary for the safety, security, efficiency & regularity of air transport & to serve as the medium for cooperation in all fields of civil aviation.
Chief Officer(s):
Roberto Kobeh González, President
Raymond Benjamin, Secretary General
Activities: *Library:* ICAO Library; by appointment

International College of Traditional Chinese Medicine of Vancouver (ICTCMV)
#201, 1508 West Broadway, Vancouver BC V6J 1W8
Tel: 604-731-2926; *Fax:* 604-731-2964
info@tcmcollege.com
www.tcmcollege.com
Overview: A medium-sized provincial organization founded in 1986
Mission: To foster the most effective & ethical TCM doctors by providing deep & wide training in TCM; promoting medical ethics; helping students to develop an interest in life-long learning; & cultivating TCM research.
Chief Officer(s):
Henry Lu, President
Membership: *Committees:* Program Advisory

International Commission of Jurists (Canadian Section) (ICJ) / La Commission internationale de juristes (section canadienne) (CIJ)
#500, 865 Carling Ave., Ottawa ON K1S 5S8

Tel: 613-237-2925; *Fax:* 613-237-0185
patw@cba.org
www.icjcanada.org
Also Known As: ICJ Canada
Overview: A small international organization founded in 1952
Mission: To works internationally with the parent organization to monitor & promote the rule of law & the impartiality & independence of the judiciary in countries where these are threatened or non-existent; to act nationally & locally to promote awareness of these issues & human rights generally
Member of: International Commission of Jurists, Geneva
Chief Officer(s):
Paul D.K. Fraser, President
Pat Whiting, Executive Director
Finances: *Annual Operating Budget:* Less than $50,000; *Funding Sources:* Membership fees
Staff Member(s): 2
Membership: 600; *Fees:* $75; *Member Profile:* Judges, lawyers & law professionals
Activities: *Library*
Awards:
• Walter S. Tarnopolsky Award for Human Rights (Award)

International Commission on Irrigation & Drainage - Canadian National Committee *See* Canadian National Committee for Irrigation & Drainage

International Commission on Radiological Protection (ICRP)

PO Box 1046, Stn. B, 280 Slater St., Ottawa ON K1P 5S9
Tel: 613-947-9750
admin@icrp.org
www.icrp.org
Overview: A small international charitable organization founded in 1928
Mission: To advance for the public benefit the science of radiological protection, in particular by providing recommendations & guidance on all aspects of protection against ionisary radiation
Chief Officer(s):
Christopher Clement, Scientific Secretary
Finances: *Annual Operating Budget:* $250,000-$500,000; *Funding Sources:* Grants from intergovernmental/governmental organizations & national sources
Staff Member(s): 2; 100 volunteer(s)
Membership: 1-99; *Committees:* Radiation Effects; Doses from Exposures; Protection in Medicine; Application of the Commission's Recommendations; Radiological Protection of the Environment
Meetings/Conferences: • ICRP 2015, October, 2015, Mayfield Hotel & Resort, Seoul
Scope: International
Contact Information: ICRP Scientific Secretary Christopher Clement, sci.sec@icrp.org

International Community for the Relief of Suffering & Starvation Canada (ICROSS)

PO Box 3, Stn. Main, Saanichton BC V8M 2C3
Tel: 250-652-4137
icross-canada.com
Overview: A small national charitable organization founded in 1998
Mission: A Canadian Humanitarian NGO with a goal to sending life-saving and ease-suffering medical supplies to the poorest of the poor in the Global Village.
Chief Officer(s):
Billy Willbond, CEO & President
billywillbond@shaw.ca
Finances: *Funding Sources:* Donations

International Council for Canadian Studies (ICCS) / Conseil international d'études canadiennes (CIEC)

#303, 250 City Centre Ave., Ottawa ON K1R 6K7
Tel: 613-789-7834; *Fax:* 613-789-7830
lise.nichol@iccs-ciec.ca
www.iccs-ciec.ca
www.facebook.com/ICCS.CIEC.page
twitter.com/ICCS_CIEC
Overview: A medium-sized international organization founded in 1981
Mission: To promote scholarly study, research, teaching & publication about Canada in all disciplines & all countries; to enhance communications among its members to facilitate & develop such scholarly activities; to disseminate research results & to publicize researchers' activities in the area of Canadian Studies; to encourage the development of an international community of Canadianists.
Affiliation(s): Assn. for Cdn. Studies in the US; Assn. for Cdn. Studies; British Assn. of Cdn. Studies; Assn. française d'études canadiennes; Associazione Italiana di Studi Canadesi; Japanese Assn. for Cdn. Studies; Gesellschaft für Kanada-Studien; Assn. for Cdn. Studies in Australia & New Zealand; Assn. of Cdn. Studies in Ireland; Nordic Assn. for Cdn. Studies; Assn. for Cdn. Studies in China; Assn. for Cdn. Studies in The Netherlands; Indian Assn. for Cdn. Studies; Israel Assn. for Cdn. Studies; Asociacion Espanola de Estudios Canadienses; Russian Assn. for Cdn. Studies; Associacao Brasileira de Estudios
Chief Officer(s):
Patrick James, President
patrickj@usc.edu
Susan Hodgett, Secretary
sl.hodgett@ulster.ac.uk
Finances: *Annual Operating Budget:* $500,000-$1.5 Million
Staff Member(s): 7
Membership: 21 Canadian Studies associations, 6 associate members in 39 countries; *Member Profile:* Full - national or multi-national Canadian Studies association, anywhere in the world; associate - Canadian Studies centres or organizations
Activities: *Speaker Service:* Yes; *Library* Open to public
Awards:
• ICCS Award of Merit (Award)
• Governor General's International Award in Canadian Studies (Award)
• Graduate Student Thesis/Dissertation Scholarship (Scholarship)
• ICCS-NCC National Capital Research Scholarship (Scholarship)
Publications:
• International Journal of Canadian Studies
Type: Journal; *Frequency:* 2

International Council of AIDS Service Organizations (ICASO) / Le Conseil international des organisations de lutte contre le SIDA

#403, 65 Wellesley St. East, Toronto ON M4Y 1G7
Tel: 416-921-0018; *Fax:* 416-921-9979
icaso@icaso.org
www.icaso.org
Overview: A small international organization founded in 1990
Mission: To promote & support the work of community-based organizations around the world in the prevention of AIDS, & care & treatment for people living with HIV/AIDS, with particular emphasis on strengthening the response in communities with fewer resources; to accomplish these objectives through information sharing, advocacy & network building
Chief Officer(s):
Mary Ann Torres, Executive Director
maryannt@icaso.org

International Council of Graphic Design Associations (ICOGRADA) / Conseil international des associations de design graphique

455, rue Saint-Antoine ouest, #SS10, Montréal QC H2Z 1J1
Tel: 514-448-4949; *Fax:* 514-448-4948
info@icograda.org
www.icograda.org
www.facebook.com/Icograda
twitter.com/icograda
www.flickr.com/photos/icograda
Overview: A medium-sized international organization founded in 1963
Mission: To raise internationally the standards of graphic design & its professional practice, & the professional status of the graphic designer; to improve & expand the contribution of graphic design towards a greater understanding between people everywhere & towards a better solution of social, cultural, economic & environmental problems; to promote cooperation & exchange of information & research between designers & with professionals in related fields; to contribute to the theory & practice of graphic design education & research; to establish international standards
Affiliation(s): Society of Graphic Designers of Canada; Société des graphistes du Québec
Chief Officer(s):
Marilena Farruggia, Managing Director
mfarruggia@icograda.org
Iva Babaja, President
ibabaja@icograda.org
Staff Member(s): 4
Membership: 200 associations in 67 countries; *Fees:* Schedule available; *Member Profile:* National professional associations; national design promotional organizations
Activities: Icograda Foundation advances worldwide understanding & education through the effective use of graphic design; ICOGRADA gathers young designers to exchange knowledge on issues of interest to them; promotes standards in liaison with the International Chamber of Commerce, the International Standards Organization, World Intellectual Property Organization & the International Federation for Reproduction Rights; Annual International Student Seminars; competitions; exhibitions; archives; international congresses & meetings; *Library:* Icograda Library at the Design Museum in London; Open to public by appointment
Awards:
• Icograda Excellence Award (Award)
• ICOGRADA Presidents Award (Award)
Meetings/Conferences: • 2017 International Council of Graphic Design Associations World Congress, October, 2017, Palais des congrès de Montréal, Montreal, QC
Scope: International

International Council on Active Aging (ICAA)

3307 Trutch St., Vancouver BC V6L 2T3
Tel: 604-734-4466; *Fax:* 604-708-4464
Toll-Free: 866-335-9777
info@icaa.cc
www.icaa.cc
www.linkedin.com/groups?gid=2294475
www.facebook.com/ICAAhome
Overview: A small international organization founded in 2001
Mission: Dedicated to changing the way we age by uniting professionals in the retirement, assisted living, fitness, recreation, rehabilitation, & wellness fields to help dispel society's myths about aging; to help these professionals to empower aging Baby Boomers & older adults to improve their quality of life & maintain their dignity.
Chief Officer(s):
Colin Milner, CEO
colinmilner@icaa.cc
Julie Milner, COO
juliemilner@icaa.cc
Membership: 9,200 organizations; *Fees:* $209 regular; $619 organizations

International Credential Assessment Service of Canada (ICAS) / Service canadien d'évaluation de documents scolaires internationaux

Ontario AgriCentre, #102, 100 Stone Rd. West, Guelph ON N1G 5L3
Tel: 519-763-7282; *Fax:* 519-763-6964
Toll-Free: 800-321-6021
info@icascanada.ca
www.icascanada.ca
Overview: A medium-sized international organization founded in 1958
Mission: Committed to providing reliable information that will help individuals achieve personal, career and educational goals and help employers, educational institutions, immigration authorities, community agencies and other organizations to understand international credentials.
Member of: Canadian Education Association; Ontario School Counsellors' Association; Association of International Educators; America-Mideast Educational Training Service; European Association of International Educators; Canadian Association of Prior Learning Assessment; Canadian Bureau of International Educatio

International Criminal Defence Attorneys Association (ICDAA) / Association Internationale des Avocats de la Défense (AIAD)

#W-3345, 455 René Lévesque Blvd. East, Montreal QC H2L 4Y2
Tel: 514-285-1055
admin@aiad-icdaa.org
www.aiad-icdaa.org
Overview: A large international organization founded in 1997
Mission: De s'assurer que les gens qui sont accusés de crimes dans tous les pays disposent d'un procès équitable
Affliation(s): Organization of American States; Organisation internationale de la francophonie; ECOSOC
Chief Officer(s):
Elise Groulx, Présidente, Board of Directors
Activities: Advocacy - enforcing fair trial rights; Legal training; Strengthening the Rule of Law in developping countries

International Curling Information Network Group (ICING)

73 Appleford Rd., Hamilton ON L9C 6B5

Tel: 905-389-7781
www.icing.org
Overview: A small international organization founded in 1995
Mission: To provide information about the sport of curling worldwide
Chief Officer(s):
Peter M. Smith, Contact
psmith@icing.org
Staff Member(s): 2; 4 volunteer(s)

Canadian Associations

International Development & Relief Foundation (IDRF)

908 The East Mall, 1st Fl., Toronto ON M9B 6K2
Tel: 416-497-0818; *Fax:* 416-497-0686
Toll-Free: 866-497-4373
office@idrf.ca
www.idrf.ca
www.linkedin.com/pub/idrf-canada
www.facebook.com/IDRFCANADA
twitter.com/IDRF
www.youtube.com/IDRFCANADA
Overview: A small international organization founded in 1984
Mission: To empower the disadvantaged peoples of the world, through emergency relief & participatory development programs based on the Islamic principles of human dignity, self-reliance, & social justice
Affliation(s): Canadian Council for International Cooperation
Chief Officer(s):
Winston Shyam Liaquat Kassim, Chair
Finances: *Annual Operating Budget:* $500,000-$1.5 Million
Staff Member(s): 9
Membership: *Member Profile:* People who regularly donate $100 or more yearly
Activities: Providing relief, rehabilitation & development aid to communities in need, both overseas & in Canada; *Speaker Service:* Yes

International Development Research Centre (IDRC) / Centre de recherches pour le développement international

PO Box 8500, 150 Kent St., Ottawa ON K1G 3H9
Tel: 613-236-6163; *Fax:* 613-238-7230
Other Communication: www.flickr.com/photos/idrccrdi
info@idrc.ca
www.idrc.ca
www.facebook.com/IDRC.CRDI
twitter.com/idrc_crdi
www.youtube.com/user/IDRCCRDI
Overview: A large international organization founded in 1970
Mission: To help scientists in developing countries identify long-term, practical solutions to pressing development problems; support is given directly to scientists in universities, private enterprise, government & non-profit organizations; priority given to equitable & sustainable development; projects are designed to maximize the use of local materials & to strengthen human & institutional capacity; research is undertaken by Third World recipients independently or in collaboration with Canadian partners
Affliation(s): Regional offices in Asia & Africa
Chief Officer(s):
David M. Malone, President
Aboudou Karim Adjibade, Regional Director, Middle East & North Africa, Cairo, Egypt
Federico Burone, Regional Director, Latin America & the Caribbean, Montevideo, Uruguay
Simon Carter, Regional Director, Eastern & Southern Africa, Nairobi, Kenya
Kathryn Touré, Regional Director, West & Central Africa, Dakar, Senegal
Finances: *Annual Operating Budget:* Greater than $5 Million
Staff Member(s): 408
Activities: Environment & natural resource management; social & economic equity; information & communication technologies for development; innovation, policy & science; *Internships:* Yes; *Library:* IDRC Library; Open to public
Awards:
• AGROPOLIS-Farming in the City (Scholarship)
Awards programme that supports innovative master's & doctoral level research. It aims to add to the body of knowledge of urban & peri-urban agriculture, & thereby to support interventions that address critical areas in the industry*Eligibility:* Award intended primarily for researchers from developing countries, including those studying in a developed country & returning to the South after their studies. However, up to a third of all awards may be granted to citizens or permanent residents of a developed country (currently only Canada). The research must be for a master's or a doctoral thesis. Researchers must be registered at a university-in the South or the North-that *Amount:* Maximum of $20,000 per year *Contact:* AGROPOLIS International & Graduate Research, 613-236-6163; Fax: 567-7749; Email AGROPOLIS@irdc.ca
• Ecosystem Approaches to Human Health Training Awards (Award)
Supports research that focuses on ecosystem management interventions leading to the improvement of human health & well-being while simultaneously maintaining or improving the condition of the ecosystem as a whole. Awards will be granted for training & research linked to the Ecosystem Approaches to Human Health Program Initiatives of the Centre. Priority will be give to proposals for research on ecosystems that are stressed through agriculture, urbanization or mining activities*Eligibility:* Citizens of developing countries &/or Canadian citizens or landed immigrants students currently enrolled in a graduate programme at a recognized university in Canada or in a developing country. Relevant language proficiency for site of study*Deadline:* May 31 *Amount:* Up to 6 awards for a maximum of $15,000 *Contact:* Centre Training & Awards Unit, 613/236-6163 ext 2098; Fax: 563-0815; cta@idrc.da
• IDRC Doctoral Research Awards (IDRA) (Scholarship)
Supports the field research of Canadian graduate students enrolled in a Canadian university for doctoral research on a topic of relevance to sustainable & equitable development*Eligibility:* Applicants must hold Canadian citizenship or permanent residency status; be registered at a Canadian university; research proposal is for a doctoral thesis; provide evidence of affiliation with an institution or organization in the region in which the research will take place; have completed course work & passed comprehensive examinations by the time of award tenure*Deadline:* May *Amount:* Maximum of $20,000 per year *Contact:* Centre Training & Awards Unit, 613/236-6163 ext 2098; Fax: 613/563-0815; cta@irdc.ca
• John G. Bene Fellowship: Community Forestry, Trees & People (Award)
Contributes to the expenses of Canadian graduate students undertaking field research in social forestry in a developing country*Eligibility:* Applicants must be Canadian citizens or hold permanent residency status; be registered in a Canadian university at the master's or doctoral level; have an academic background that combines forestry or agroforestry with social sciences. Applicants from interdisciplinary programs (e.g. environmental studies) may also be eligible, provided their programs contain the specified elements*Deadline:* March *Amount:* $15,000 per year *Contact:* Centre Training & Awards Unit, 613/236-6163 ext. 2098; Fax: 613/563-0815; Emails cta@irdc.ca
• Canadian Window on International Development Awards (Scholarship)
Award offered for doctoral research that explores the relationship between Canadian aid, trade, immigration & diplomatic policy, & international development & the alleviation of global policy*Eligibility:* Applicants must hold Canadian citizenship or permanent residency status; be registered at a Canadian university; be conducting the proposed research for a doctoral dissertation & have completed course work & passed comprehensive examinations by the time of the award tenure*Deadline:* April *Amount:* $20,000 per year *Contact:* Centre Training & Awards Unit, 613/236-6163 ext 2098; Fax: 613/563-0815; cta@idrc.ca
• Bentley Fellowship: Use of Fertility Enhancing Food, Forage & Cover Crops in Sustainably Managed Agroecosystems (Award)
Supports applied research of Canadian graduate students on how increased use of forage crops in cropping systems can improve agricultural production by farmers in developing countries*Eligibility:* Applicants must be Canadian citizens or hold permanent residency status; be registered in a Canadian university at the master's or doctoral level; have an academic background in agriculture or biology undertaking research on the role of forage crops in improved sustainable tropical farming. Applicants from interdisciplinary programs (e.g. environmental studies) may be eligible provided their programs contain the specified elements*Deadline:* October *Amount:* $20,000 *Contact:* Centre Training & Awards Unit, 613/236-6163 ext 2098; Fax: 613/563-0815; cta@idrc.ca
Publications:
• IDRC [International Development Research Centre] Bulletin
Type: Newsletter

International Economuseum Network Society ***Voir*** **Société internationale du réseau ÉCONOMUSÉE et Société ÉCONOMUSÉE du Québec**

International Electrotechnical Commission - Canadian National Committee (IEC-CNC) / Commission Électrotechnique Internationale - Comité National du Canada (CEI-CNC)

c/o Standards Council of Canada, #200, 270 Albert St., Ottawa ON K1P 6n7
Tel: 613-238-3222; *Fax:* 613-569-7808
scc.ca
Overview: A medium-sized international organization founded in 1912
Mission: The Standards Council of Canada (SCC) sponsors the Canadian National Committee of the International Electrotechnical Commission, an SCC advisory committee which is the Canadian member body at IEC. It promotes international cooperation on all questions of electrotechnical standardization & related matters, such as the assessment of conformity to standards, in the fields of electricity, electronics & related technologies.
Member of: Standards Council of Canada
Chief Officer(s):
Keith L. Rodel, President
Lynne M. Gibbens, Secretary
Finances: *Funding Sources:* Parliamentary appropriation; corporate sponsors; individuals
Staff Member(s): 2; 1000 volunteer(s)
Membership: 16; *Committees:* Approx. 100, paralleling the IEC committee structure

International Energy Foundation (IEF)

Clear Mountain Estates, PO Box 64, Site 8, RR#1, Okotoks AB T1S 1A1
Tel: 403-938-6210; *Fax:* 403-938-6210
www.ief-energy.org
Overview: A medium-sized international charitable organization founded in 1989
Mission: To facilitate the transfer of research & technology in all areas of energy with special emphasis on developing countries; interested in better ways to produce, transmit & conserve energy; to sponsor & conduct research studies, surveys & state-of-the-art studies; to undertake consulting projects & organize training programs for the interchange of knowledge & expertise amongst the international community; to provide scholarships for the education of students in fields of interest consistent with the objectives of the Foundation; to administer awards for the purpose of recognition & encouragement of outstanding achievement in areas of study consistent with objectives of the Foundation; to recommend standards to existing national & international associations & promote adoption of such approved standards for energy consumption, production & conservation
Member of: International Standards Organization
Chief Officer(s):
Peter J. Catania, Chair
Finances: *Annual Operating Budget:* $100,000-$250,000; *Funding Sources:* Contributions, donations, subventions, aids & grants made by donors & benefactors; fees for membership
50 volunteer(s)
Membership: fellows in 49 countries, committee members in 175 countries; *Member Profile:* Open to all professionals, educational institutes, industries, governmental or quasi-governmental bodies operating in the field of energy; *Committees:* Constitution & Bylaws; External Administrative Centres; External & Internal Meetings; Finance; Goals & Objectives; Membership; Publications & Public Relations
Activities: Conferences, symposiums, workshops; *Speaker Service:* Yes

International Federation of Bodybuilders (IFBB) / Fédération Internationale des Culturistes

2875 Bates Rd., Montréal QC H3S 1B7
Tel: 514-731-3783; *Fax:* 514-731-9026
info@ifbb.com
www.ifbb.com
Overview: A large international charitable organization founded in 1946
Mission: To promote fitness & a healthy lifestyle through the sport of bodybuilding
Member of: General Association of International Sports Federations
Chief Officer(s):
Rafael Santonja, President
Pamela Kagan, Executive Director
William Tierney, General Secretary
Staff Member(s): 3

Membership: 182 countries affiliated; *Fees:* $300 (national federations only); *Committees:* Judges; Medical & Doping Commission; Technical; Women's; Research & Development
Activities: Professional & amateur championships held worldwide; *Speaker Service:* Yes
Publications:
• International Federation of Bodybuilders Newsletter
Type: Newsletter

International Federation on Aging (IFA) / Fédération internationale du vieillissement (FIV)
Castleview Wichwood Towers, 351 Christie St., Toronto ON M6G 3C3
Tel: 416-342-1655; *Fax:* 416-392-4157
www.ifa-fiv.org
Overview: A medium-sized international organization founded in 1973
Mission: To provide a worldwide forum for ageing issues & concerns; to foster the development of associations & agencies that serve or represent older people; to develop a universal charter of rights & responsibilities for the elderly; to advocate for the rights & respect of older people
Affliation(s): World Health Organization; International Labour Organization; United Nations Educational, Scientific & Cultural Organization
Chief Officer(s):
Irene Hoskins, President
Jane Barratt, Secretary General
jbarratt@ifa-fiv.org
Finances: *Annual Operating Budget:* $250,000-$500,000; *Funding Sources:* Membership fees; service fees; grants; special projects
Staff Member(s): 4; 6 volunteer(s)
Membership: 300; *Fees:* Sliding scale US$75-2,000; *Member Profile:* Full - reserved for national voluntary organizations either representing or serving older people; Associate - several categories of international organizations, governmental agencies, professional associations, voluntary organizations whose activities are less than national in scope; Individual; Corporate - any business interested in or providing products & services for older persons; Government associate; Professional associate
Activities: *Internships:* Yes; *Speaker Service:* Yes; *Rents Mailing List:* Yes

International Fellowship of Christians & Jews of Canada
Corporate Office, #218, 449 The Queensway South, Keswick ON L4P 2C9
Tel: 416-596-9307; *Fax:* 416-981-7293
Toll-Free: 888-988-4325
info@IFCJ.ca
www.ifcj.ca
www.facebook.com/FellowshipFan
Overview: A medium-sized international charitable organization
Mission: To encourage improved understanding between Christian & Jewish people; To promote cooperation between Christian & Jewish communities
Chief Officer(s):
Yechiel Eckstein, Founder & Chair
Activities: Accepting donations to support the work of the organization (c/o Donation Centre, PO Box 670, Station K, Toronto, ON M4P 2H1). Supporting Israel & Jewish people in need

International Finance Club of Montréal *Voir* Cercle de la finance internationale de Montréal

International Financial Centre of Montréal (IFC) / Le Centre Financier International - Montréal (CFI)
c/o Finance Montreal, #1600, 1130, Sherbrooke ouest, Montréal QC H3A 2M8
Tel: 514-287-1477; *Fax:* 514-287-1694
info@cfimontreal.com
www.cfimontreal.com
Also Known As: IFC Montréal
Overview: A small local organization founded in 1986
Mission: To facilitate the establishment, development & preservation in the Montréal City region of companies specializing in international financial transactions
Chief Officer(s):
Jacques Girard, CEO
Staff Member(s): 5
Membership: 65 companies

International Fiscal Association Canada
#310, 4 Cataraqui St., Kingston ON K7K 1Z7
Tel: 613-531-8292; *Fax:* 613-531-0626
office@ifacanada.org
www.ifacanada.org
Also Known As: IFA Canada
Overview: A small national organization
Mission: To study & advance international & comparative law in regard to public finance, specifically international & comparative fiscal law & the financial & economic aspects of taxation
Affliation(s): International Fiscal Association
Chief Officer(s):
Nick Pantaleo, President
Membership: 850; *Fees:* $135 + GST

International Fund for Animal Welfare Canada (IFAW) / Fonds international pour la protection des animaux
#2, 301 1/2 Bank St., Ottawa ON K2P 1X7
Tel: 613-241-8996; *Fax:* 613-241-0641
Toll-Free: 888-500-4329
info-ca@ifaw.org
www.ifaw.org
www.facebook.com/ifaw
twitter.com/IFAWCanada
www.youtube.com/ifawvideo
Overview: A small international organization founded in 1969
Mission: Works to improve the welfare of wild & domestic animals throughout the world by reducing the commercial exploitation of animals, protecting wildlife habitats & assisting animals in distress; seeks to motivate the public to prevent cruelty to animals; promotes animal welfare & conservation policies that advance the well-being of animals & people
Chief Officer(s):
Azzedine Downes, President & Chief Executive Officer
Patricia Zaat, Canadian Director
Finances: *Annual Operating Budget:* $500,000-$1.5 Million
Staff Member(s): 12
Membership: 45,000
Activities: Campaigns against the commercial seal hunt in Canada, supporting anti-cruelty legislations for Canada
Publications:
• Gaining Ground: In Pursuit of Ecological Sustainability
Type: Book; *Number of Pages:* 425; *Editor:* Lavigne, D.M.
Profile: 26 chapters written by a variety of conservationists, spanning the fields of conservation biology, fishery science, wildlife biology, ethics,economics, engineering, and the social sciences.
• World of Animals
Type: Magazine; *Frequency:* Bi-Annual

International Geographical Union - Canadian Committee
Dept. of Geography & Environmental Management, University of Waterloo, 200 University Ave. West, Waterloo ON N2L 3G1
Tel: 519-504-7985; *Fax:* 519-746-0658
www.igu-net.org
Overview: A small national organization
Mission: To promote international programs in geography within Canada; to promote activities within IGU programs relevant to Canada & to coordinate Canadian participation; to formulate Canadian position & advise the National Research Council on Canadian participation in IGU activities
Chief Officer(s):
Jean Andrey, Contact
jandrey@uwaterloo.ca
Finances: *Funding Sources:* National Research Council; SSHRCC

The International Grenfell Association (IGA)
81 Kenmount Rd., 2nd Fl., St. John's NL A1B 3P8
Tel: 709-745-6162; *Fax:* 709-745-6163
www.grenfellassociation.org
Overview: A small provincial charitable organization founded in 1914
Mission: To provide funds in support of initiatives that benefit the health, education, social & cultural well-being of the people of Northern Newfoundland & Coastal Labrador, working in partnership with government & other agencies
Chief Officer(s):
Norman Pinder, Chair
Finances: *Funding Sources:* Investments; endowments
Activities: Grant program; scholarships; bursaries

International Hockey Hall of Fame & Museum; International Ice Hockey Federation Museum Inc. *See* Original Hockey Hall of Fame & Museum

International Institute for Sustainable Development (IISD) / Institut international du développement durable (IIDD)
161 Portage Ave. East, 6th Fl., Winnipeg MB R3B 0Y4
Tel: 204-958-7700; *Fax:* 204-958-7710
info@iisd.ca
www.iisd.org
www.facebook.com/IISDnews
twitter.com/IISD_news
Overview: A large international organization founded in 1990
Mission: To promote sustainable development in decision-making in Canada & abroad by undertaking sustainable development research, advising government, business & organizations, analyzing & reporting on issues & events, & publishing & disseminating sustainable development information. Offices in Winnipeg, Ottawa, New York, & Geneva.
Chief Officer(s):
Scott Vaughan, President/CEO
Grace Mota, Treasurer and Chief Financial Officer
Janice Gair, VP, Human Resources & Corporate Services
Joel Trenaman, Director, Communications & Publishing
Finances: *Annual Operating Budget:* Greater than $5 Million; *Funding Sources:* Federal & provincial government; government of other countries; philanthropic foundations
Staff Member(s): 80
Activities: Trade & sustainable development; community adaptation & sustainable livelihoods; greening national budgets; business & industry accountability; Great Plains Sustainable Development; sustainable development measurement & indicators; *Internships:* Yes; *Speaker Service:* Yes; *Library* Open to public by appointment
Awards:
• IISD Scholar (Scholarship)
To assist post-secondary students (up to the Ph.D. level) studying issues related to sustainable development *Amount:* $5,000

International Institute for Transportation & Ocean Policy Studies; Oceans Institute of Canada *See* International Oceans Institute of Canada

International Institute of Concern for Public Health (IICPH)
PO Box 40017, 292 Dupont St., Toronto ON M5R 0A2
Tel: 905-906-6128
info@iicph.org
www.iicph.org
Overview: A medium-sized international charitable organization founded in 1984
Mission: To engage in advocacy on health issues; to assist in promoting & protecting people in their work & living environment in Ontario; to provide expertise on health, scientific & environmental issues
Member of: Ontario Environment Network; Earth Appeal; Nuclear Waste Watch
Chief Officer(s):
Marion Odell, Contact
Finances: *Annual Operating Budget:* Less than $50,000; *Funding Sources:* Private donations
7 volunteer(s)
Activities: *Speaker Service:* Yes

International Institute of Integral Human Sciences (IIIHS) / Institut international des sciences humaines intégrales
PO Box 1387, Stn. H, Montréal QC H3G 2N3
Tel: 514-937-8359; *Fax:* 514-937-5380
info@iiihs.org
www.iiihs.org
Overview: A medium-sized international organization
Mission: An interdisciplinary, professional association for scientists, scholars, and spiritual leaders worldwide, who are involved in the sciences of human consciousness & healing, paradigms for the convergence of science, spirituality & humane values in the world, & new insights into the potential of the human spirit.
Chief Officer(s):
John Rossner
jrossner@iiihs.org
Marilyn Rossner
mrossner@iiihs.org
Membership: 10,000; *Fees:* $15
Activities: Corporate Divisions: SSF-IIIHS National & Regional Chapters; International College of Human Sciences; International Academy for Research & Advanced Studies;

International Council of World Religions & Cultures; The Order of the Transfiguration; *Library*
Meetings/Conferences: • The 39th Annual SSF-IIIHS Int'l Conference, July, 2015, Montreal, QC
Scope: International

International Law Association - Canadian Branch
c/o Bloomfield & Associés, #1720, 1080, Côte du Beaver Hall Hill, Montréal QC H2Z 1S8
Tel: 514-871-9571; *Fax:* 514-397-0816
ila@fieldbloom.com
www.ila-canada.ca
Overview: A medium-sized national organization founded in 1967
Mission: Is a body for the study & advancement of international law in all its forms, commercial & interpersonal. Membership of the Association which is at present over 3,500 is spread among 50 Branches in every continent.
Chief Officer(s):
Bernard Colas, President
president@ila-canada.ca
Finances: *Annual Operating Budget:* Less than $50,000
Membership: *Committees:* International Committees
Activities: *Awareness Events:* Biennial Conference

International Log Builders' Association
PO Box 775, Lumby BC V0E 2G0
Tel: 250-547-8776; *Fax:* 250-547-8775
info@logassociation.org
www.logassociation.org
Previous Name: American/Canadian Log Builders' Association
Overview: A medium-sized international organization founded in 1974
Mission: To further the craft of handcrafted log building & the advancement of log builders, & to promote the highest standards of the trade
Chief Officer(s):
Higgs Murphy, President, 250-631-7839
logdoggies@yahoo.com

International Machine Cancel Research Society of Canada (IMCRSC)
39 Silver Trail, Barrie ON L4N 3K2
www.postalhistorycanada.net/php/StudyGroups/IMCRSC
Overview: A small national organization
Mission: To study the uses of the International Postal Supply Company of New York's rapid cancelling machine models in Canada; To investigate related areas of historical interest, such as the relationship between the Canada Post Office Department & the International Postal Supply Company
Affliation(s): Postal History Society of Canada
Chief Officer(s):
David Collver, Contact
Membership: *Member Profile:* Individuals interested in the history of the machine cancellations of Canada & Newfoundland, & especially the International machine era
Activities: Undertaking research projects, such as the identification of individual daters in Canadian post offices with an International machine; Publishing the results of research activities involving International machines; Developing a database of International machines; *Library:* International Machine Cancel Research Society of Canada Library

International Mennonite Health Association Inc. (IMHA)
15 Coleridge Park Dr., Winnipeg MB R3K 0B2
Tel: 204-831-1699; *Fax:* 204-985-3226
info@africancanadianhealth.ca
www.intermenno.net
Overview: A small international charitable organization
Mission: Providing resources and services to Mennonite and Brethren in Christ health programs in developing countries.
Chief Officer(s):
Murray Nickel, President
nickel.murray@gmail.com

International Napoleonic Society (INS) / Société Napoléonienne Internationale
#3315, 81 Navy Wharf Crt., Toronto ON M5V 3S2
Other Communication: www.societenapoleonienne.com
ins@napoleonicsociety.com
www.napoleonicsociety.com
Overview: A small international organization founded in 1995
Mission: To promote the study of the Napoleonic Era in accordance with proper academic standards; to gather the leading minds in this field for the purpose of creating, reviewing, commenting, awarding & financially supporting Napoleonic scholarship; to encourage the publication of works of academic merit; to make available original documents, as well as material available only in languages not commmonly read by western scholars; to encourage & support the translation &/or publication of such materials; to encourage the creation & expansion of programs of study in the Napoleonic Era at accredited institutions of learning
Chief Officer(s):
Rowayda Guirguis, Executive Secretary & Webmaster
J. David Markham, President
Rafe Blaufarb, Chair, Awards Committee
Finances: *Annual Operating Budget:* $100,000-$250,000
Staff Member(s): 6; 6 volunteer(s)
Membership: 650; *Member Profile:* Napoleonic historians; *Committees:* Literary; Awards
Activities: International congress
Awards:
• Literary Award (Award)
• Legion of Merit Medal (Award)

International Network for Cultural Diversity / Réseau international pour la diversité culturelle
5 Brulé Cres., Toronto ON M6S 4H8
Tel: 416-268-5665
incd@neilcraigassociates.com
www.incd.net
Overview: A small national organization
Mission: INCD is a worldwide network working to counter the adverse affects of globalization on world cultures.
Chief Officer(s):
Garry Neil, Executive Director

International Oceans Institute of Canada (IOIC)
c/o Dalhousie Univ., PO Box 15000, 6414 Coburg Rd., Halifax NS B3H 4R2
Tel: 902-494-1977; *Fax:* 902-494-1334
ioi@dal.ca
internationaloceaninstitute.dal.ca
Previous Name: International Institute for Transportation & Ocean Policy Studies; Oceans Institute of Canada
Overview: A small national organization founded in 1976
Mission: To promote responsible management of the world's oceans & sustainable development of marine resources; to protect the integrity of the ocean environment; to promote sustainable resource development; to improve the quality of ocean-dependent human life, including health & safety of maritime communities; to further these objectives, all aspects of the ocean environment are pursued - resource management & development, marine environmental quality, ocean law & policy, high seas management, coastal zone management, marine transportation, ocean science & technology, tourism & recreation, ocean industries & maritime boundary delimitation
Affliation(s): International Oceans Institute; Atlantic Coastal Zone Information Steering Committee
Chief Officer(s):
Michael J.A. Butler, Director
michael.butler@dal.ca
Staff Member(s): 4
Activities: Services of the institute are available nationally & internationally for governments, organizations & private sector concerns, including industry, special interest groups & foundations; services include project development & management, policy development, education & training, conference & workshop coordination, research & information

International Peat Society - Canadian National Committee
c/o Canadian Society for Peat and Peatlands, 196 - 15 St., Shippagan NB E8S 1E8
Tel: 506-336-6600; *Fax:* 506-336-6601
www.peatsociety.org
Overview: A small national organization founded in 1970
Mission: To foster the advancement, exchange and communication of scientific, technical and social knowledge and understanding for the wise use of peatlands and peat.
Affliation(s): International Peat Society
Chief Officer(s):
Jean-Yves Daigle, Chair
jydaigle@nb.sympatico.ca
Paul Short, Secretary
cspma@peatmoss.com
Finances: *Annual Operating Budget:* Less than $50,000; *Funding Sources:* Membership fees
Activities: *Rents Mailing List:* Yes

International Personnel Management Association - Canada (IPMA-Canada)
National Office, 20 Edwards Pl., Mount Pearl NL A1N 3V5
Fax: 613-226-2298
Toll-Free: 888-226-5002
national@ipma-aigp.ca
ipma-aigp.ca
www.facebook.com/IPMACanada
Previous Name: Canadian Public Personnel Management Association
Overview: A medium-sized national organization founded in 1906
Mission: To promote excellence in the practice of human resource management; to promote & enhance the HR profession in Canada & globally; to provide professional development & training for the HR community; to maintain a code of ethics & standards of practice; to recognize excellence through national & local awards programs
Affliation(s): IPMA-HR
Chief Officer(s):
Glenn Saunders, Executive Director
national@ipma-aigp.ca
Rick Brick, President
Rick.Brick@gov.ab.ca
Heather Bowser, Director, Communications
bowserha@gov.ns.ca
Finances: *Annual Operating Budget:* $100,000-$250,000
Membership: 1,000; *Member Profile:* Human resources managers & practitioners across the country
Activities: Provides local courses & speakers programs; national & local newsletters; national & local awards program; Certification Program; National Human Resource Management Certificate Program; *Rents Mailing List:* Yes
Meetings/Conferences: • International Personnel Management Association - Canada 2015 Leadership Summit, 2015
Scope: National

Alberta & North Chapter
#154, 21 - 10405 Jasper Ave., Edmonton AB T5J 3S2
e-mail: ipma.abn@shaw.ca
www.linkedin.com/groups?gid=3647281
www.facebook.com/164286233597783

Manitoba Chapter
c/o Prairie Rose School Division, 45 Main St. South, Carman MB R0G 0J0
Tel: 204-745-2003; *Fax:* 204-745-3699
olabossiere@prsdmb.ca
www.ipma-aigp.ca/chapters/manitoba/index.htm
Chief Officer(s):
Ken Kowalski, President
kkowalsk@mts.net

National Capital Region Chapter
c/o Herzig College, Ottawa Campus, PO Box 225, 1200 St. Laurent Blvd., Ottawa ON K1K 3B8
Tel: 613-216-5201; *Fax:* 613-742-8336
www.ipma-aigp.ca
Chief Officer(s):
Michel Nadeau, President
michael.n.nadeau@servicecanada.gc.ca
Maureen Meaney, President Elect
maureenmeaney@yahoo.ca
Ian Widgett, Treasurer
ian.widgett@agr.gc.ca

New Brunswick Chapter
c/o Peter Trask, Centennial Bldg., PO Box 6000, Fredericton NB E3B 5H1
Chief Officer(s):
Peter Trask, Contact, 506-444-5099, Fax: 506-444-4724
peter.trask@gnb.ca

Newfoundland & Labrador Chapter
Chief Officer(s):
John Peddle, President
john.peddle@nl.rogers.com

Nova Scotia Chapter
c/o Service Nova Scotia & Municipal Relations, PO Box 2513, 10th Fl., Maritime Centre, Halifax NS B3J 3N5
Tel: 902-424-7802; *Fax:* 902-424-8136
burgessml@gov.ns.ca
www.ipma-aigp.ca/chapters/novascotia/index.htm
Chief Officer(s):
Dale Rushton, President
rushtodl@gov.ns.ca
Margan Dawson, Executive Director
awens@eastlink.ca

Saskatchewan Chapter
PO Box 601, Regina SK S4P 3A3
www.saskatchewanipma.com
www.facebook.com/373753279756
Chief Officer(s):
Alison Biese, President, 306-787-9161
alison.biese@gov.sk.ca

International PhotoTherapy Association
Photo Therapy Centre, #607, 1027 Davie St., Vancouver BC V6E 4L2
Tel: 604-689-9709; *Fax:* 604-676-2245
jweiser@phototherapy-centre.com
www.phototherapy-centre.com
Overview: A small international organization
Mission: To educate about therapeutic uses of still & video photography
Finances: *Annual Operating Budget:* Less than $50,000
Staff Member(s): 3
Membership: 100-499
Activities: *Library* Open to public by appointment

International Political Science Association (IPSA) / Association internationale de science politique (AISP)
#331, 1590, av Docteur-Penfield, Montréal QC H3G 1C5
Tel: 514-848-8717; *Fax:* 514-848-4095
info@ipsa.org
www.ipsa.org
www.facebook.com/IPSA.AISP
twitter.com/IPSN_AISP
Overview: A medium-sized international charitable organization founded in 1949
Mission: To promote the advancement of political science through the collaboration of scholars in different parts of the world; IPSA has consultative status with the Economic & Social Council of the United Nations & with UNESCO
Member of: International Social Sciences Council
Chief Officer(s):
Guy Lachapelle, Secretary General
guy.lachapelle@concordia.ca
Helen Milner, President
Mathieu St-Laurent, Manager, Membership Services & External Relations
Finances: *Annual Operating Budget:* $250,000-$500,000; *Funding Sources:* Member fees; royalties
Staff Member(s): 7
Membership: 4,045 individuals; 53 associations
Activities: Congress; symposiums; publications; research; *Rents Mailing List:* Yes

International Relief Agency Inc. (IRA)
#84, 95 Wood St., Toronto ON M4Y 2Z3
Tel: 416-928-0901
ira@ica.net
Overview: A medium-sized international organization founded in 1979
Mission: To promote free enterprise, national freedoms & democracy
Affiliation(s): Best of 7 Continents Inc.; International Hippocrates Foundation; Council of Nations
Activities: Foreign aid & relief; international investment; health care services; overseas adoption services; *Library* Open to public by appointment

International Schizophrenia Foundation
16 Florence Ave., Toronto ON M2N 1E9
Tel: 416-733-2117; *Fax:* 416-733-2352
centre@orthomed.org
www.orthomed.org/isf/isf.html
Previous Name: Canadian Schizophrenia Foundation
Overview: A medium-sized international charitable organization founded in 1969
Mission: To raise the levels of diagnosis, treatment & prevention of the schizophrenias & related disorders; to reduce the fear & stigma; to provide the best possible treatment & rehabilitation services.
Member of: International Society for Orthomolecular Medicine
Finances: *Annual Operating Budget:* $100,000-$250,000; *Funding Sources:* Donations; literature sales; membership fees
Staff Member(s): 2
Membership: 1,000; *Fees:* $35
Activities: *Speaker Service:* Yes; *Library* Open to public by appointment

International Social Service Canada (ISSC) / Service Social International Canada (SSIC)
#201, 1376 Bank St., Ottawa ON K1H 7Y3
Tel: 613-733-9938; *Fax:* 613-733-4868
www.issc-ssic.ca
Overview: A small international charitable organization founded in 1979
Mission: To provide linkages to social service organizations worldwide; To help resolve individual & family problems resulting from the movement of people across national borders
Member of: Canadian Council for Refugees; Canadian Coalition for the Rights of Children; Family Service Canada; Child Welfare League of Canada; United Nations Association in Canada; Canadian Society of Association Executives
Affiliation(s): International Social Service - Geneva, Switzerland
Chief Officer(s):
Sylvie J. Lapointe, Director, Services
lapointesylvie71@sympatico.ca
Finances: *Annual Operating Budget:* $100,000-$250,000; *Funding Sources:* Federal & provincial contracts; fees for service; membership fees; donations
Staff Member(s): 4; 25 volunteer(s)
Membership: 100; *Fees:* Schedule available; *Member Profile:* Residents of Canada
Activities: Provides a professional social work liaison to social service agencies & government departments in Canada when assistance is required in other countries to help resolve a client's individual & family problems (divorce, custody, placement, visiting rights, abandonment, abduction, family reunification, child welfare investigations & service of child welfare documents overseas); also provides assistance in matters relating to health & other relevant social services requiring intercountry linkages; *Speaker Service:* Yes

International Society for Augmentative & Alternative Communication (ISAAC) / Société internationale de communication non-orale
East Building, #100, 3800 Steels Ave. West, Woodbridge ON L4L 4G9
Tel: 905-850-6848; *Fax:* 905-850-6852
info@isaac-online.org
www.isaac-online.org
Overview: A small international charitable organization founded in 1983
Mission: To promote the best possible communication for people with complex communication needs
Chief Officer(s):
Jeffrey K. Riley, President
jriley@cayabc.org
Franklin Smith, Executive Director
franklin@isaac-online.org
Teraiz El-Deir, Coordinator, Membership
Membership: 1,000-4,999; *Fees:* Schedule available; *Member Profile:* People who use AAC, families, researchers, providers & manufacturers of communication devices; *Committees:* Committee for People Who Use AAC; Emerging AAC Countries; Research; Nominations
Activities: *Rents Mailing List:* Yes
Awards:
- Ablenet Distinguished Lecture (Award)
- Sherri Johnson/ISAAC Travel Scholarship (Scholarship)
- Words+ /ISAAC Consumer Scholarship (Scholarship)
- Words+ /ISAAC Consumer Lecture Award (Award)
- The ISAAC Distinguished Service Award (Award)
- The Shirley McNaughton Exemplary Communication Award (Award)
- AAC Journal Editor's Awards (Award)
- The President's Award (Award)

International Society for Cellular Therapy (ISCT)
#201, 375 West 5th Ave., Vancouver BC V5Y 1J6
Tel: 604-874-4366; *Fax:* 604-874-4378
isct@celltherapysociety.org
www.celltherapysociety.org
Previous Name: International Society for Hematotherapy & Graft Engineering
Overview: A medium-sized international organization founded in 1992
Mission: To serve as a voice for investigators, clinicians & technical personnel working in cell therapies & research
Chief Officer(s):
Queenie Jang, Executive Director
queenie@celltherapysociety.org
Membership: 1,100; *Fees:* Schedule available
Activities: Cord blood; Ex Vivo Expansion; Gene Therapy; Graft Evaluation; Immunotherapy & Dendritic Cells; Nonhematopoietic Mesenchymal Stem Cells; Transplantation; Tumor Evaluation; Legal & Regulatory Affairs

International Society for Evolutionary Protistology (ISEP)
c/o Andrew J. Roger, President, Dalhousie University, 5850 College St., #8B1, Halifax NS B3H 1X5
Tel: 902-494-2620; *Fax:* 902-494-1355
www.isepsociety.com
Overview: A small international organization
Chief Officer(s):
Andrew Roger, President
Membership: *Fees:* $35 per 2-year period

International Society for Hematotherapy & Graft Engineering ***See*** International Society for Cellular Therapy

International Society for Krishna Consciousness (Toronto Branch) (ISKCON) / Subuddhi Deri Dasi
243 Avenue Rd., Toronto ON M5R 2J6
Tel: 416-922-5415; *Fax:* 416-922-1021
info@torontokrishna.com
www.torontokrishna.com
Also Known As: ISKCON Toronto - Hare Krishna Movement
Overview: A medium-sized local charitable organization founded in 1966
Mission: To preach Krishna Consciousness around the world, following in the footsteps of the founder & spiritual master, His Divine Grace A.C. Bhaktivedanta Swami Prabhupada.
Chief Officer(s):
Subuddhi Dasi, President
Finances: *Annual Operating Budget:* $3 Million-$5 Million; *Funding Sources:* Donations from congregations & festivals
Staff Member(s): 10; 20 volunteer(s)
Membership: 700 institutional; 2,000 individual; *Fees:* $1,100
Activities: Distribution of free food; taking care of seniors & youth; *Internships:* Yes

International Society for Labour & Social Security Law - Canadian Chapter (ISLSSL) / Société internationale de droit du travail et de la sécurité sociale
Faculty of Law, University of Montreal, Maximilien-Caron Pavillon, PO Box 6128, Stn. Centre-Ville, Montreal QC H3C 3J7
Tel: 514-343-6124; *Fax:* 514-343-2199
islssl.org
Overview: A small international organization founded in 1958
Mission: To promote the study of labour law & social security law both at national & international levels; to promote the exchange of ideas & information, & collaboration between jurists & other experts in the fields of labour law & social security
Chief Officer(s):
Gilles Trudeau, Contact
gilles.trudeau@umontreal.ca

International Society for Research in Palmistry Inc. / Société internationale de recherches en chirologie inc.
576 rte 315, ChénéVille QC J0V 1E0
Tel: 819-428-4298; *Fax:* 819-428-4495
Toll-Free: 866-428-3799
info@birlacenter.com
www.birlacenter.com/palmistry
Also Known As: Birla Center for Hast Jyotish
Overview: A small international organization founded in 1977
Mission: The Society offers individual & group counselling through palmistry & astrology based on Eastern Vedic System.

Consultation Center
351 Victoria Ave., Westmount QC H3Z 2N1
Tel: 514-488-2292; *Fax:* 514-488-3822

International Society for the History of Medicine - Canadian Section (ISHM) / Société internationale d'histoire de la médecine (SIHM)
c/o Isabelle Perreault, Université d'Ottawa, Pavillon FSS, #14022, 120 Université ON K1N 6N5
Tel: 613-562-5700
iperreault@uottawa.ca
Overview: A small international charitable organization founded in 1921
Mission: To hold biennial conferences; to publish proceedings, abstracts & periodical
Chief Officer(s):
Isabelle Perreault, PhD, Secretary-Treasurer, Canada
Staff Member(s): 2
Membership: 15 Canadian members; 300 internationally; *Fees:* Regular: $60; Corporate: $75; Retired & students: $30; *Member*

Profile: Professional historians (medical) & physician historians of medicine; *Committees:* Administrative; Executive
Meetings/Conferences: • Annual Conference
Publications:
• Canadian Bulletin of Medical History
Type: Journal; *Frequency:* Semiannually; *Editor:* Kristin Burnett, Jayne Elliott; *Price:* Free to members

International Special Events Society - Toronto Chapter (ISES)
312 Oakwood Ct., Newmarket ON L3Y 3C8
Tel: 905-898-7434; *Fax:* 905-895-1630
Toll-Free: 866-729-4737
info@isestoronto.com
www.isestoronto.com
www.linkedin.com/company/international-special-events-society-toronto-
www.facebook.com/ISESToronto
twitter.com/isestoronto
Also Known As: ISES Toronto
Overview: A small local organization founded in 1979
Mission: To educate, advance & promote the special events industry & its network of professionals along with related industries; to uphold the integrity of the special events profession to the public through "Principles of Professional Conduct & Ethics"; to acquire & disseminate useful business information; to foster a spirit of cooperation among members & other special events professionals
Chief Officer(s):
Aaron Kaufman, President
aaron@5thelementevents.com
Finances: *Funding Sources:* Membership dues
Membership: *Fees:* $299 non-profit; $300 individual/corporate; *Member Profile:* Individuals who currently hold a position in the special events industry, who have had 3 consecutive years experience in the industry & who are sponsored by an ISES member in good standing
Activities: Administers "Certified Special Events Professional" (CSEP) designation through professional accreditation program; monthly dinner meetings; annual gala auction
Awards:
• Toronto Chapter Awards (Award)
Honours leaders in the industry for the Toronto chapter

International Special Events Society - Vancouver Chapter (ISES)
PO Box 166, #101, 1001 West Broadway, Vancouver BC V6H 4E4
www.isesvancouver.com
ca.linkedin.com/pub/ises-vancouver-ises/57/8a6/bbb
www.facebook.com/pages/ISES-Vancouver/143263959021798
twitter.com/isesvancouver
Previous Name: International Special Events Society Pacific Northwest
Overview: A small local organization founded in 1993
Mission: To educate, advance and promote the special events industry and its network of professionals along with related industries.
Chief Officer(s):
Shelley Johnston, President
president@isesvancouver.com
Membership: *Fees:* $225 corporate primary; $175 additional corporate; $225 regular; $175 non-profit; all new memberships have a one-time $55 fee

International Special Events Society Pacific Northwest *See* International Special Events Society - Vancouver Chapter

International Symphony Orchestra of Sarnia, Ontario & Port Huron, Michigan
225 Davis St., Sarnia ON N7T 1B2
Tel: 519-337-7775; *Fax:* 519-337-1822
iso@rivernet.net
www.theiso.org
Overview: A small local charitable organization founded in 1957 overseen by Orchestras Canada
Mission: To provide cultural enrichment within the community by providing high calibre choral & symphonic performances
Member of: Choirs Ontario
Affliation(s): American Federation of Symphony Orchestras; Michigan Orchestra Association
Chief Officer(s):
Anne Brown, Executive Director
Activities: *Speaker Service:* Yes; *Rents Mailing List:* Yes

International Symphony Orchestra Youth String Ensemble
225 Davis St., Sarnia ON N7T 1B2
Tel: 519-337-7775; *Fax:* 519-337-1822
iso@rivernet.net
Overview: A small local organization
Member of: Association of Canadian Youth Orchestras
Chief Officer(s):
Anne Brown, Executive Director
Finances: *Annual Operating Budget:* Less than $50,000
Membership: 34; *Fees:* $120; *Member Profile:* Musicians 6 to 18
Activities: Workshops; string education programs in schools

International Telecommunications Society (ITS)
Bohdan (Don) Romaniuk, ITS Secretariat, 416 Wilverside Way SE, Calgary AB T2J 1Z7
e-mail: secretariat@itsworld.org
www.itsworld.org
Overview: A small international organization
Mission: To address issues in telecommunications & related industries, such as public policy, user requirements, & industry changes
Chief Officer(s):
Erik Bohlin, Chair
erik.bohlin@chalmers.se
Bronwyn Howell, Secretary
Bronwyn.Howell@vuw.ac.nz
Leland W. Schmidt, Treasurer
lschmidt@metrocast.net
Membership: 400; *Fees:* $125 USD individual; $6000 USD corporate; $3000 USD international; $l500 USD society; $500 USD government/not-for-profit; *Member Profile:* Professionals from the communications, technology, & information sectors; *Committees:* Strategic Planning; Conference & Seminars; Publications; Membership & Nominations; Finance; Marketing & Promotions; Web Development
Activities: Organizing courses, seminars, & workshops; Disseminating research results & news to members & the public
Publications:
• Interconnect [a publication of the International Telecommunications Society]
Type: Newsletter; *Editor:* Don Romaniuk
Profile: Member profiles, conference information, committee reports, & society news

International Union of Food Science & Technology (IUFoST)
IUFoST Secretariat, PO Box 61021, #19, 511 Maple Grove Dr., Oakville ON L6J 6X0
Tel: 905-815-1926; *Fax:* 905-815-1574
secretariat@iufost.org
www.iufost.org
www.linkedin.com/company/2754293
www.facebook.com/437738436247543
Overview: A large international organization
Mission: To improve the distribution & conservation of the world's food supply; To promote international cooperation among food technologists & scientists
Affliation(s): Institute of Food Technologists
Chief Officer(s):
Pingfan Rao, President
Rickey Yada, President-Elect
Judith Meech, Secretary-General & Treasurer
Gustavo Barbosa-Canovas, Chair, Scientific Council
Membership: *Member Profile:* Food scientists, technologists, & engineers from around the world; *Committees:* Food Safety; Food Security Task Force
Activities: Promoting training in food science & technology; Sponsoring international conferences & workshops; Fostering the international exchange of knowledge in the food science & technology community
Publications:
• International Union of Food Science & Technology Scientific Information Bulletins (SIBs)
Type: Bulletin
Profile: Food science issues, presented by scientific experts & reviewed & approved by the IUFoST Scientific Council, for members of IUFoSTadhering bodies, legislators, food scientists & technologists, & consumers
• IUFoST [International Union of Food Science & Technology] Newsline
Type: Newsletter; *Frequency:* Irregular
Profile: The official newsletter of the International Union of Food Science & Technology, featuring activities of the General Assembly, theBoard, the Governing Council, the International Academy, & adhering bodies, for adhering bodies in more than 100 countries around the world
• Sustainable Development at Risk: Ignoring the Past
Type: Book; *Author:* Robert D. Reichert; *ISBN:* 9788175965218
Profile: The challenge of improving third world nations, while conserving critical resources & protecting the environment
• The Textbook of Food Science & Technology
Type: Book; *Editor:* Geoffrey Campbell-Platt; *ISBN:* 978-0-632-06421-2
Profile: Chapters from international industry researchers, experts, & teachers, written for students, teachers, & professionals in the food industry
• Trends in Food Science & Technology [a publication of the International Union of Food Science & Technology]
Type: Journal *ISSN:* 0924-2244
Profile: A peer-reviewed journal, featuring critical synopses of advances in food research
• Using Food Science & Technology to Improve Nutrition & Promote National Development: Selected Case Studies
Type: Book; *Editor:* Gordon Robertson & John Lupien; *ISBN:* 978-0-9810247-0-7
Profile: A handbook about the application of food science & technology toimprove nutrition & promote national development in developing countries
• World of Food Science [a publication of the International Union of Food Science & Technology]
Profile: A joint publication of the IUFoST & the Institute of Food Technologists (IFT)

International Women of Saskatoon
#412, 230 Ave. R South, Saskatoon SK S7M 2Z1
Tel: 306-978-6611; *Fax:* 306-978-6614
iwssaskatoon@sasktel.net
www.internationalwomenofsaskatoon.org
Previous Name: Immigrant Women of Saskatchewan, Saskatoon Chapter
Overview: A small local organization
Member of: Regina Immigrant Women Centre
Chief Officer(s):
April Sora, President
Ijeoma Udemgba, Executive Director

Internet des droits humains *See* Human Rights Internet

Interpretation Canada - A Professional Association for Heritage Interpretation (IC)
c/o Kerry Wood Nature Centre, 6300 - 45 Ave., Red Deer AB T4N 3M4
Tel: 604-947-0483
membership@interpscan.ca
www.interpcan.ca
Previous Name: Canadian Association for Interpretation
Overview: A small national organization founded in 1974
Mission: To foster greater public appreciation, understanding & enjoyment of Canadian heritage & its resources through interpretation; to reveal meanings & relationships of our cultural & natural heritage to the public through first-hand experience with an object, artifact, landscape or site
Chief Officer(s):
Chris Mathieson, Chair
chris.mathieson@interpscan.ca
Sue Ellen Fast, Executive Director
editor@interpcan.ca
Stephanie Yuill, Secretary
stephanie.yuill@interpscan.ca
Finances: *Funding Sources:* Membership dues
Membership: *Fees:* $50 student/volunteer; $65 individual; $75 subscription; $95 small institution/consultant; $190 company; *Member Profile:* Heritage interpreters & heritage interpretation institutions
Activities: Professional development; networking; workshops & conferences; service & product suppliers; employment opportunities & recruitment; awards; on-line discussion; training; advertising; fun activities; *Library*
Awards:
• Annual Awards of Excellence (Award)

Interpreting Services of Newfoundland & Labrador Inc. (ISNL)
The Viking Building, #100A, 136 Crosbie Rd., St. John's NL A1B 3K3
Tel: 709-753-5621; *Fax:* 709-753-5682; *TTY:* 709-753-5620
info@isnl.ca
www.isnl.ca
Previous Name: Newfoundland & Labrador Interpreting Service
Overview: A small provincial charitable organization founded in 2001

Mission: To provide interpretive services for Newfoundland & Labrador residents
Affiliation(s): Canadian Hard of Hearing Association
Finances: *Annual Operating Budget:* $50,000-$100,000; *Funding Sources:* Provincial government
Staff Member(s): 10
Membership: 200; *Fees:* $10; *Member Profile:* Deaf, deafened & hard of hearing people
Activities: *Awareness Events:* Deaf Culture Month, Sept.; *Library* Open to public

Inter-Provincial Association on Native Employment (IANE)

#316, 35-2855 Pembina Hwy., Winnipeg MB R3T 2H5
Tel: 204-257-2754; *Fax:* 204-255-1182
www.ianeinc.ca
Overview: A small national organization
Mission: To reflect the needs of Native peoples regarding employment; to provide advice & assistance; to assist companies & other groups employing or assisting Native persons; to provide information about pertinent government policies & programs to industry & labour groups; to encourage development of education & training programs
Chief Officer(s):
Lynda Highway, Event Coordinator
lhighway@shaw.ca

Interprovincial Brotherhood of Electrical Workers (CLC) ***Voir*** Fraternité interprovinciale des ouvriers en électricité (CTC)

Interprovincial Denturist Societies *See* Denturist Association of Canada

Interprovincial School Development Association (ISDA)

5940 South St., Halifax NS B3H 1S6
Tel: 902-424-8500; *Fax:* 902-424-0543
apsea@apsea.ca
www.apsea.ca
Overview: A small provincial organization
Mission: To provide & extend opportunities, activities & experiences for children who are deaf or hard of hearing in Atlantic Canada up to the age of 21 years; To achieve these goals by administering funds for post-secondary scholarships, graduation awards & prizes, research grants & grants to support recreational, social & cultural activities
Chief Officer(s):
Heather Conrad, Director, Finance & Administration
Heather_Conrad@apsea.ca

Interval House

#200, 131 Bloor St., Toronto ON M5S 1R8
Tel: 416-924-1411; *Fax:* 416-928-9020; *TTY:* 416-924-0899; *Crisis Hot-Line:* 416-924-1491
info@intervalhouse.ca
www.intervalhouse.ca
www.facebook.com/pages/Interval-House/112483398798217
twitter.com/interval_house
Overview: A small local charitable organization
Mission: To provide a continuum of services that enable abused women & children to have access to safe shelter & responsive services that help them establish lives free from violence; To provide integrated & specialized services related to counselling, advocacy, outreach, legal & housing support, as well as programs to help build economic self-sufficiency

Inter-Varsity Christian Fellowship (IVCF)

1 International Blvd., Toronto ON M9W 6H3
Tel: 416-443-1170; *Fax:* 416-443-1499
Toll-Free: 800-668-9766
info@ivcf.ca
www.ivcf.ca
Overview: A medium-sized national charitable organization founded in 1929
Mission: To help young people live a transformed life in Jesus Christ
Chief Officer(s):
Geri Rodman, President
Finances: *Funding Sources:* Donations
Activities: Offering Pioneer Camps across Canada; Providing ministry at university & college campuses; Offering travel opportunities through Inter-Varsity's World Services' Global Partnerships; Participating in the Urbana Student Mission Convention

Intervention régionale et information sur le sida en Estrie

505, rue Wellington Sud, Sherbrooke QC J1H 5E2
Tél: 819-823-6704
iris.estrie@videotron.ca
www.iris-estrie.com
Également appelé: IRIS/Estrie
Aperçu: *Dimension:* petite; *Envergure:* locale; Organisme sans but lucratif; fondée en 1988
Mission: Stimuler et développer une action communautaire pour faire face à la problématique du Sida dans la région de l'Estrie; pour remplir sa mission, l'organisme a regroupé ses actions dans trois programmes spécifiques: Soutien, Prévention, Intervention
Affiliation(s): Coalition québécoise des organismes communautaires de lutte contre le sida
Membre(s) du bureau directeur:
Susan Garand, Directrice générale
Membre(s) du personnel: 9
Membre: *Comités:* Ressources Humaines; Levée de Fonds; Gestion Interne; Activités de l'Organisme; Action Bénévole; Communication, Développement et Marketing social régional et provincial; Santé Sexuelle régional et provincial; Femmes Vulnérables régional et provincial; HARSAH régional et provincial; Ethnoculturelle régional et provincial; UDI régional et provincial; Droit pronvincial
Activités: *Stagiaires:* Oui; *Service de conférenciers:* Oui; *Listes de destinataires:* Oui; *Bibliothèque:* Centre de documentation; Bibliothèque publique

Intrepid Theatre Co. Society

#2, 1609 Blanshard St., Victoria BC V8W 2J5
Tel: 250-383-2663
www.intrepidtheatre.com
Also Known As: Victoria Fringe Festival; UNO Festival of Solo Performance
Overview: A small local charitable organization founded in 1986
Mission: To educate & enhance the public's awareness & aesthetic appreciation of contemporary & progressive styles of modern theatre by encouraging, developing & producing new or experimental works for public performance; by coordinating & producing the annual Fringe Theatre Festival in Victoria
Member of: Canadian Association of Fringe Festivals
Affliation(s): ProArt Alliance of Vancouver, Arts Action BC
Chief Officer(s):
Janet Munsil, Artistic Director/Producer
Heather Lindsay, General Manager
gm@intrepidtheatre.com
Finances: *Funding Sources:* Government; sponsors; bingo/casino; box office
Staff Member(s): 5
Activities: Victoria Fringe Theatre Festival; Uno Festival of Solo Performance; Intrepid Theatre Presentation Series; *Rents Mailing List:* Yes

Inuit Art Foundation (IAF) / Fondation d'art Inuit

2081 Merivale Rd., Ottawa ON K2G 1G9
Tel: 613-224-8189; *Fax:* 613-224-2907
Toll-Free: 800-830-3293
iaf@inuitart.org
www.inuitart.org
Overview: A medium-sized national charitable organization founded in 1985
Mission: To facilitate the creative expression of Inuit artists; To foster an increased understanding of this expression in a local & global context; To assist in the marketing of Inuit art; To promote Inuit art through exhibits, publications & public events
Chief Officer(s):
Marybelle Mitchell, Executive Director
Finances: *Funding Sources:* Donations
Membership: *Member Profile:* Inuit artists
Activities: Managing the Inuit Artists' Shop; Assisting organizations to obtain copyright permission; Providing marketing brochures for dealers & artists

Inuit Community Centre

604 Laurier Ave. West, Ottawa ON K1R 6L1
Tel: 613-565-5885; *Fax:* 613-563-4136
info@tungasuvvingatinuit.ca
www.tungasuvvingatinuit.ca
Also Known As: Tungasuvvingat Inuit
Overview: A small local organization founded in 1987
Mission: A social, cultural & counselling organization serving the Inuit
Chief Officer(s):
Kevin Kablutsiak, President
Finances: *Annual Operating Budget:* $3 Million-$5 Million
Activities: Programs: Addiction treatment; lunch; homeless support; employment support; head start; youth; diabetes prevention & awareness; community support

Inuit Tapiriit Kanatami (ITK)

#1101, 75 Albert St., Ottawa ON K1P 5E7
Tel: 613-238-8181; *Fax:* 613-234-1991
Toll-Free: 866-262-8181
info@itk.ca
www.itk.ca
www.facebook.com/group.php?gid=149359161748927
twitter.com/ITK_CanadaInuit
www.youtube.com/inuitofcanada
Previous Name: Inuit Tapirisat of Canada
Overview: A large local organization founded in 1971
Mission: To ensure the survival of Inuit culture in Canada
Chief Officer(s):
Terry Audia, President
Jim Moore, Executive Director
Stephen Hendrie, Communications Director
Staff Member(s): 38
Membership: Represents 55,000 Inuit; *Member Profile:* Members come from 4 geographic regions: Nunatsiavut (Labrador), Nunavik (Québec), Nunavut, and the Inuvialuit Settlement Region (NWT)
Activities: *Library*

Inuit Tapirisat of Canada *See* Inuit Tapiriit Kanatami

Inuvik Chamber of Commerce

PO Box 3039, Inuvik NT X0E 0T0
inuvikchamber.com
Overview: A small local organization founded in 1971
Mission: To improve & promote commerce in Inuvik
Member of: Canadian Chamber of Commerce
Chief Officer(s):
Lee Smallwood, President
president@inuvikchamber.com
Membership: 49; *Fees:* $100

Inventors Association of Ottawa

PO Box 4028, Stn. E, Ottawa ON K1S 5B1
Tel: 613-788-0688
Overview: A small local organization
Chief Officer(s):
Gene Shershen, President

Inverness Cottage Workshop (ICW)

PO Box 485, 46 Lower Railway St., Inverness NS B0E 1N0
Tel: 902-258-3316; *Fax:* 902-258-3351
www.invernesscottageworkshop.ca
Overview: A small local organization founded in 1981
Member of: DIRECTIONS Council for Vocational Services Society
Chief Officer(s):
Donna MacLean, President
Cindy O'Neill, Executive Director/Manager
Staff Member(s): 5
Activities: Daily programs include: Bakery, Used Clothing Store, Shredding, Recycling, Bags-n-Tags, & Village Market;

Inverness County Centre for the Arts (ICCA)

PO Box 709, 16080 Hwy. 19, Inverness NS B0E 1N0
Tel: 902-258-2533; *Fax:* 902-258-2277
manager@invernessarts.ca
www.invernessarts.ca
Overview: A small local organization founded in 1984
Mission: The Inverness County Council of the Arts is a charitable organization, dedicated to promoting exhibitions and cultural events that showcase artists in the community and creating awareness of the opportunities and benefits associated with the arts
Chief Officer(s):
Kathy Hannigan, Executive Director
Membership: *Fees:* $10-$50
Activities: Annual visual art shows

Invest in Kids Foundation

425 Adelaide St. West, 6th Fl., Toronto ON M5V 3C1
Tel: 416-977-1222; *Fax:* 416-977-9655
Toll-Free: 877-583-5437
www.investinkids.ca
www.facebook.com/group.php?gid=10479882324
Overview: A small national charitable organization
Mission: To help parents become the parents they want & need to be; to strengthen the parenting knowledge, skills & confidence of all those who touch healthy social, emotional & intellectual development of children from birth to age five

Chief Officer(s):
Nancy Birnbaum, President/CEO
Activities: Research; public education; parent education; professional education & support

Invest Ottawa / Investir Ottawa
#100, 80 Aberdeen St., Ottawa ON K1S 5R5
Tel: 613-828-6274; *Fax:* 613-726-3440
worldclass@investottawa.ca
investottawa.ca
www.facebook.com/InvestOttawa
twitter.com/Invest_Ottawa
www.linkedin.com/company/invest-ottawa
Previous Name: Ottawa Centre for Research & Innovation; Ottawa Carleton Research Institute
Overview: A small local organization founded in 1983
Mission: To foster the advancement of Ottawa & area's globally competitive knowledge-based industries & institutions
Chief Officer(s):
David Ritonja, Co-Chair
Jim Watson, Co-Chair
Bruce Lazenby, President & CEO, 613-828-6274 Ext. 267
blazenby@investottawa.ca
Kevin Carroll, Managing Director, Innovation, 613-828-6274 Ext. 287
kcarroll@investottawa.ca
Walt Hutchings, Managing Director, Investment & Trade, 613-828-6274 Ext. 240
whutchings@investottawa.ca
Jon Milne, Director, Marketing, 613-828-6274 Ext. 201
jmilne@investottawa.ca
Finances: *Funding Sources:* Membership fees; Professional development programs; Municipal, provincial & federal governments; Private sector contributions
Membership: 500-999
Activities: Connecting business, research, education, government, & talent; Marketing Ottawa to business; Offering access to market research;

Investir Ottawa *See* Invest Ottawa

Investment Counsel Association of Canada *See* Portfolio Management Association of Canada

Investment Funds Institute of Canada (IFIC) / L'Institut des fonds d'investissement du Canada
11 King St. West, 4th Fl., Toronto ON M5H 4C7
Tel: 416-363-2150
Toll-Free: 866-347-1961
member-services@ific.ca
www.ific.ca
www.linkedin.com/company/266541
twitter.com/ific
Previous Name: Canadian Mutual Fund Association
Overview: A medium-sized national organization founded in 1962
Mission: To act as the voice of the investment funds industry in Canada; To enhance the integrity & growth of the Canadian mutual fund industry
Affliation(s): The Canadian Institute of Financial Planning
Chief Officer(s):
Brian Peters, Chair
Sian Burgess, 1st Vice-Chair
Joanne De Laurentiis, President & CEO
Membership: 150; *Member Profile:* Fund managers; Distributors; Industry service organizations; *Committees:* Governance; Regulatory Watch; Compliance; Operations; Communications
Activities: Advocating on industry issues; Providing an investor resource centre; Improving members' knowledge & proficiency; Communicating with members; Providing a job board & networking opportunities; *Library:* Advisor Resource Centre

Bureau du Québec - Le Conseil des fonds d'investissement du Québec
#1800, 1010, rue Sherbrooke ouest, Montréal QC H3A 2R7
Tel: 514-985-7025
cfiqinfo@ific.ca

Investment Industry Association of Canada (IIAC) / Association canadienne du commerce des valeurs mobilières (AACVM)
#1600, 11 King St. West, Toronto ON M5H 4C7
Tel: 416-364-2754; *Fax:* 416-364-4861
info@iiac.ca
www.iiac.ca
Overview: A small national organization founded in 2006
Mission: Advances the growth and development of the Canadian investment industry; acts as a proactive voice for the industry; endeavours to create efficient and competitive capital markets, stimulate the savings and investment process, and provide support and services that contribute to member success. Montreal Office: Place Montreal Trust, 1800, av McGill College, bureau 2112, Montreal QC H3A 3J6, Ph. 514-843-8380. Vancouver Office: 888 Dunsmuir St., Suite 1230, Vancouver BC V6C 3K4, Ph. 604-482-1790.
Chief Officer(s):
Ian Russell, President
Membership: *Member Profile:* Bank-owned securities firms; independent integrated firms; institutional boutiques; *Committees:* Compliance; Debt Markets; Equity Markets; Insurance; Institutional Boutiques; Investment Banking; Private Client; Qualified Intermediary; Regional; Tax Reporting; Tax Policy
Activities: Continuing education; publications; job search resources

Investment Industry Regulatory Organization of Canada (IIROC) / Organisme canadien de réglementation du commerce des valeurs mobilières (OCRCVM)
#2000, 121 King St. West, Toronto ON M5H 3T9
Tel: 416-364-6133; *Fax:* 416-364-0753
Toll-Free: 877-442-4322
Other Communication: Enforcement Matters, Fax: 416-364-2998
publicaffairs@iiroc.ca
www.iiroc.ca
Merged from: Investment Dealers Association of Canada; Canada & Market Regulation Services Inc.
Overview: A large national licensing organization founded in 2008
Mission: To oversee investment dealers & trading activity on debt & equity marketplaces in Canada; To focus on regulatory & investment industry standards, protecting investors & strengthening market integrity
Chief Officer(s):
Andrew J. Kriegler, President & CEO
Membership: 100-499; *Member Profile:* Investment dealer firms & their employees; *Committees:* Corporate Governance; Finance & Audit; Human Resources & Pension
Activities: Providing continuing education & member events

Bureau de Montréal
#1550, 5, Place Ville-Marie, Montréal QC H3B 2G2
Tél: 514-878-2854; *Téléc:* 514-878-3860

Calgary Office
Bow Valley Square 3, #800, 255 - 5 Ave. SW, Calgary AB T2P 3G6
Tel: 403-262-6393; *Fax:* 403-234-0861
Chief Officer(s):
Warren Funt, Vice-President, Western Canada

Vancouver Office
Royal Centre, PO Box 11164, #2800, 1055 West Georgia St., Vancouver BC V6E 3R5
Tel: 604-683-6222; *Fax:* 604-683-3491

Investment Property Owners Association of Cape Breton (IPOACB)
105 Bentinck St., Sydney NS B1P 1G3
Tel: 902-562-1813
ipoacb@syd.eastlink.ca
www.ipoacb.ca
www.facebook.com/IPOACB
www.twitter.com/IPOACB
Overview: A medium-sized local organization founded in 1978
Mission: To represent owners of residential properties in the Cape Breton area while providing members with services.
Affliation(s): Investment Property Owners Association of Nova Scotia
Chief Officer(s):
Priscilla Lotherington, President
Membership: 300+

Investment Property Owners Association of Nova Scotia Ltd. (IPOANS)
Vantage Business Centre, #208-209, 102 Chain Lake Dr., Halifax NS B3S 1A7
Tel: 902-425-3572; *Fax:* 902-422-0700
association@ipoans.ca
www.ipoans.ca
www.linkedin.com/groups/Investment-Property-Owners-Association-Nova-66
www.facebook.com/ipoansca
twitter.com/ipoans
Overview: A medium-sized provincial organization founded in 1979
Mission: To protect, enhance & contribute to the ability of rental housing owners & operators to profit from their investments; to provide educational programs for members; to serve as an information centre
Member of: Canadian Society of Association Executives; Canadian Federation of Apartment Associations
Affliation(s): National Apartment Association
Chief Officer(s):
Rose Marie Howell, Executive Director
Finances: *Annual Operating Budget:* $50,000-$100,000; *Funding Sources:* Membership fees; education
Staff Member(s): 2
Membership: 100-499; *Member Profile:* Must own or operate rental/commercial property; *Committees:* Education; Legislative; Membership; Public Relations
Activities: Lobbying; legislative task forces; Certified Management Program discounts; property management advice; *Speaker Service:* Yes; *Rents Mailing List:* Yes

Investor Learning Centre of Canada *See* Canadian Securities Institute Research Foundation

IODE Canada (IODE)
#219, 40 Orchard View Blvd., Toronto ON M4R 1B9
Tel: 416-487-4416; *Fax:* 416-487-4417
iodecanada@bellnet.ca
www.iode.ca
Previous Name: Imperial Order Daughters of the Empire
Overview: A medium-sized national charitable organization founded in 1900
Mission: To operate as a women's charitable organization
Chief Officer(s):
A. Mason, Contact
Finances: *Funding Sources:* Membership fees; Donations; Foundations
Staff Member(s): 2; 4,00 volunteer(s)
Membership: *Fees:* $30; *Committees:* Education; Social Services; Citizenship
Activities: *Library:* The National Chapter of Canada IODE Resource Centre; by appointment
Awards:
• Labrador Bursary (Scholarship)
Amount: $1,000
• IODE 100th Anniversary Grant to Child Protection Workers (Grant)
Amount: $20,000
• The National Chapter of Canada IODE Violet Downey Book Award (Award)
Awarded annually for the best English-language book, containing at least 500 words of text, preferably with Canadian content, in any category suitable for children aged 13 & under
Amount: $3,000
• IODE War Memorial Doctoral Scholarships (Scholarship)
• National IODE (RCMP) Police Community Relations Award (Award)

Iqaluit Chamber of Commerce
PO Box 1107, Iqaluit NU X0A 0H0
Tel: 867-979-4095; *Fax:* 867-979-2929
Overview: A small local organization

Iranian Community Association of Ontario
#205, 5330 Yonge St., Toronto ON M2N 5P9
Tel: 416-441-2656; *Fax:* 416-691-8466
info@iranianassociation.ca
www.iranianassociation.ca
Overview: A small local organization founded in 1986
Mission: To provide basic orientation for Iranian newcomers in Ontario; To refer clients to appropriate governmental organizations; To help newcomers find a place to live & a job
Chief Officer(s):
Mohammad Asari, Chief of the Board
Finances: *Annual Operating Budget:* $50,000-$100,000
Staff Member(s): 5
Membership: 800
Activities: *Library* Open to public

Iraqi Canadian Society of Ontario
1057 McNicoll Ave., Toronto ON M1W 3W6
Tel: 416-494-1438; *Fax:* 416-494-1438
Overview: A small provincial organization founded in 1991
Mission: To create a healthy & friendly environment so that Iraqis regardless of their race, religion, age & background, can come together, cooperate & unite

Iraqi Jewish Association of Ontario
7026 Bathurst, Thornhill ON L4J 8K3
Tel: 416-488-6262
info@ijao.ca
ijao.ca
Overview: A small provincial organization
Chief Officer(s):
Reuven Ahron, President

The Ireland Fund of Canada
#401, 67 Yonge St., Toronto ON M5E 1J8
Tel: 416-367-8311; *Fax:* 416-367-5931
theirelandfunds.org/canada
twitter.com/IrelandFundCda
Overview: A medium-sized international charitable organization
Mission: A non-political, non-sectarian Canadian charity that funds community level projects in Ireland, North & South, & Irish projects here in Canada; the Ireland Funds are dedicated to raising funds to support programs of peace & reconciliation, arts & culture, education & community development
Chief Officer(s):
Jane Noonan, Executive Director
jnoonan@irlfunds.org

Ireland-Canada Chamber of Commerce (ICCC)
121 Decarie Circle, Toronto ON M9B 3J6
e-mail: info@iccto.com
www.iccto.com
www.facebook.com/1417845151804118
twitter.com/iccto
Overview: A small international organization founded in 1991
Mission: To bring together individuals & corporations interested in the development & enhancement of commercial relations between Ireland & Canada; to provide a forum for its members to network within the business community in Vancouver & Ireland.
Chief Officer(s):
Matthew Cotter, President
Finances: *Funding Sources:* Membership dues
Membership: *Fees:* $25 under 25/new member; $30 under 30/over 65; $100 standard; $500 gold
Activities: Speakers; networking

Iridologists' Association of Canada
PO Box 421, Stn. D, Toronto ON M9A 4X4
Tel: 416-233-9837; *Fax:* 905-824-0063
Overview: A small provincial organization founded in 1994

Irish Canadian Cultural Association of New Brunswick (ICCA NB)
c/o Patricia O'Leary-Coughlan, 189 Carlisle Rd., Douglas NB E3A 7M8
e-mail: info@newirelandnb.ca
www.newirelandnb.ca
Overview: A small provincial organization founded in 1983
Mission: To recognize & honour the contributions made by our ancestors to Canada by holding an annual Irish Festival, promoting an Irish Studies program at universities & sponsoring Irish cultural & social programs & events
Chief Officer(s):
Patricia O'Leary-Coughlan, Contact
Finances: *Funding Sources:* Membership dues
Membership: *Fees:* $20 individuals; $25 families

Irish Dance Teacher's Association of Eastern Canada
c/o Ryan Carroll, Goggin-Carroll School of Irish Dance, 1040 South Service Rd. East, Oakville ON L6J 2X7
www.irishdancecanada.com
Overview: A small local organization
Mission: To promote Irish dance throughout eastern Canada
Chief Officer(s):
Ryan Carroll, Regional Director
ryan@goggin-carroll.com
Bernadette Short, Vice Regional Director
Fiona Cunningham, Treasurer
Membership: *Member Profile:* Registered teachers (TCRG) & adjudicators (ADCRG) in eastern Canada
Activities: Regulating Feiseanna in the eastern Canadian region; Maintaining a standardized syllabus of competitions & rules

Irish Loop Chamber of Commerce
PO Box 139, Ferryland NL A0A 2H0
Tel: 709-432-3104; *Fax:* 709-432-3056
info@IrishLoopChamber.com
irishloopchamber.com
twitter.com/IrishLoopCofC
Overview: A small local organization
Chief Officer(s):
Jeff Marshall, President

Irma & District Chamber of Commerce
PO Box 284, Irma AB T0B 2H0
Tel: 780-754-3996
Overview: A small local organization
Chief Officer(s):
Claudia Williams, President

Irma Fish & Game Association
General Delivery, Irma AB T0B 2H0
Tel: 780-754-3937
Overview: A small local organization
Member of: Alberta Fish & Game Association; National Firearms Association
Chief Officer(s):
Brad Hill, Contact
Ken Veer, Contact, 780-754-3969
Finances: *Annual Operating Budget:* Less than $50,000
Membership: 75
Activities: Hide collection program;

Iroquois Falls & District Chamber of Commerce
727 Synagogue Ave., Iroquois Falls ON P0K 1G0
Tel: 705-232-4656; *Fax:* 705-232-4656
ifchamber@hotmail.com
www.iroquoisfallschamber.com
Overview: A small local organization founded in 1924
Member of: Canadian & Ontario Chambers of Commerce; James Bay Frontier
Chief Officer(s):
Dale Romain, President
Finances: *Annual Operating Budget:* Less than $50,000; *Funding Sources:* Membership fees
Staff Member(s): 2; 16 volunteer(s)
Membership: 71; *Fees:* $60-$658; *Member Profile:* Business promotor & economic development; *Committees:* Business & Commerce; Community Programs; Economic Development; Tourism
Activities: *Speaker Service:* Yes; *Library:* Tourism & Info Centre; Open to public

Iroquois Falls Association for Community Living
PO Box 310, 9 Vetrans Dr., Iroquois Falls ON P0K 1E0
Tel: 705-258-3971
ifacl@onlink.net
Overview: A small local organization
Member of: Community Living Ontario
Chief Officer(s):
Carol Gauthier, Executive Director
carol_ifacl@onlink.net

Iroquois Falls Historical Society
245 Devonshire Ave., Iroquois Falls ON P0K 1E0
Tel: 705-258-3730; *Fax:* 705-258-3730
ifpioneermuseum@outlook.com
iroquoisfallschamber.com/web-content/Pages/historicalsociety.html
Overview: A small local charitable organization
Mission: To preserve the local history of the area
Member of: Ontario Historical Society; Ontario Museum Association
Affliation(s): Cochrane Temiskaming Museum & Galleries Assoc.
Chief Officer(s):
Denis Charette, President
Finances: *Funding Sources:* Grants; admissions; gift shop; membership fees
Membership: *Fees:* $5 single; $10 family; $25 corporate
Activities: Operates a Pioneer Museum; *Library* Open to public

Irritable Bowel Syndrome Self Help & Support Group
PO Box 94074, Toronto ON M4N 3R1
Tel: 416-932-3311; *Fax:* 416-932-8909
ibs@ibsgroup.org
www.ibsgroup.org
Also Known As: IBS Self Help Group
Overview: A medium-sized international organization founded in 1987
Mission: To educate & provide support for people who have IBS; To use membership to encourage both medical & pharmaceutical research to make the lives of those with IBS easier
Member of: Self Help Resource Centre; American Self-Help Clearinghouse
Affliation(s): IBS Association
Chief Officer(s):
Jeffrey Roberts, Founder & President
Finances: *Funding Sources:* Membership dues; industry sponsors
Activities: *Rents Mailing List:* Yes

Is Five Foundation
#302, 161 Eglinton Ave. East, Toronto ON M4P 1J5
Tel: 416-480-2408; *Fax:* 416-480-2546
Overview: A small local organization

ISIS Canada Research Network (ISIS)
Agricultural & Civil Engineering Building, University of Manitoba, #A250, 96 Dafoe Rd., Winnipeg MB R3T 2N2
e-mail: muftia@cc.umanitoba.ca
www.isiscanada.com
Also Known As: Intelligent Sensing for Innovative Structures; ISIS Canada
Overview: A medium-sized national organization founded in 1995
Mission: To advance civil engineering in Canada to a world leadership position through the development & application of fibre-reinforced polymers & integrated intelligent fibre optic sensing technologies, for the benefit of all Canadians
Member of: Networks of Centres of Excellence
Chief Officer(s):
Donald Whitmore, Chair
donw@vectorgroup.com
Aftab Mufti, President & Scientific Director, 204-474-8506, Fax: 204-474-7519
muftia@cc.umanitoba.ca
Edward Pentland, Chair, Technology Transfer & Commercialization Committee
edward_pentland@telus.net
Finances: *Funding Sources:* NSERC
Membership: 100-499
Activities: *Speaker Service:* Yes

Islamic Association of Nova Scotia (IANS)
PO Box 103-136, 287 Lacewood Dr., Dartmouth NS B3M 3Y7
Tel: 902-469-9490
info@islamnovascotia.ca
www.islamnovascotia.ca
Previous Name: Islamic Association of the Maritimes
Overview: A small local organization founded in 1966
Chief Officer(s):
Mohsin Rashid, President
rashid@eastlink.ca
Mohammed Amin Aliyar, Secretary
Membership: *Fees:* $50 single; $100 family; $25 student

Islamic Association of Saskatchewan (Saskatoon)
222 Copland Cres., Saskatoon SK S7H 2Z5
Tel: 306-665-6424
info@islamiccenter.sk.ca
www.islamiccenter.sk.ca
Overview: A small provincial organization founded in 1968
Affliation(s): Multi-Faith Group; Saskatchewan Organization for Heritage Language; Saskatchewan Intercultural Association; Saskatchewan Forum for "Racialized" Canadians; Saskatchewan Council for International Cooperation
Chief Officer(s):
Omaer Jamil, President
president@islamiccenter.sk.ca
Areeb Faruqi, Secretary
Membership: *Fees:* $40 family; $25 single; *Committees:* The Muslim Communications and Outreach Committee (MCOC); The Takaful Fund Committee (TFC); The Strategic Planning Committee (SPC); The Constitution Review Committee (CRC)
Activities: Operates Islamic Centre; represents Muslims; provides activities; responsible for Muslim Cemetery

Islamic Association of the Maritimes *See* Islamic Association of Nova Scotia

Islamic Care Centre (ICC)
312 Lisgar St., Ottawa ON K2P 0E2
Tel: 613-232-0210; *Fax:* 613-232-0210
info@islamcare.ca
www.islamcare.ca
Also Known As: Daw'ah Centre
Overview: A small national charitable organization founded in 1999

Mission: Islam Care Centre provides the Canadian (Ottawa) Muslim community with resources to meet religious and social needs with the objective of establishing a better relationship with the larger Canadian society.
Member of: Muslim Community Council of Ottawa
Affliation(s): Islam Care Centre
Chief Officer(s):
Omar Mahfoudhi, Executive Director
Finances: *Annual Operating Budget:* $50,000-$100,000
Staff Member(s): 2; 10 volunteer(s)
Membership: 35; *Fees:* $50; *Committees:* Business; Conference; Daw'ah; Membership; Newsletter
Activities: *Speaker Service:* Yes; *Library:* Islamic Information; Open to public

Islamic Foundation of Toronto (IFT)
441 Nugget Ave., Toronto ON M1S 5E1
Tel: 416-321-0909; *Fax:* 416-321-1995
info@islamicfoundation.ca
www.islamicfoundation.ca
Also Known As: Nugget Mosque
Overview: A small local charitable organization founded in 1969
Chief Officer(s):
Shakil Akhter, Administrator
Zaib Mirza, Social Services Coordinator
Finances: *Annual Operating Budget:* $3 Million-$5 Million
Staff Member(s): 72
Membership: 1,000-4,999; *Committees:* Dawah; Library; School Board; Social Services
Activities: Full time Islamic school, JK to Grade 10; part-time evening Islamic school; Arabic language centre for adults; Friday & Sunday schools

Islamic Information Foundation (IIF)
8 Laurel Lane, Halifax NS B3M 2P6
Tel: 902-445-2494; *Fax:* 902-445-2494
jamalbadawi@hotmail.com
www.facebook.com/296700910341355
Overview: A small national charitable organization founded in 1981
Mission: To promote better understanding of Islam among Muslims & Christians through information provided in print, audio & video forms & through lecture, seminars & interfaith dialogues
Chief Officer(s):
Jamal Badawi, Chairperson
Finances: *Annual Operating Budget:* $100,000-$250,000; *Funding Sources:* Sale of religious material; donations
4 volunteer(s)
Membership: 40 individuals
Activities: *Speaker Service:* Yes

Islamic Propagation Centre International (Canada) (IPCI (Canada))
5761 Coopers Ave., Mississauga ON L4Z 1R9
Tel: 905-507-3323; *Fax:* 905-507-3323
Secretary@jamemasjid.org
www.jamemasjid.org
Also Known As: Jama Masjid Mississauga
Overview: A small local charitable organization founded in 1984
Mission: The Centre offers a selection of resource material for those interested in learning about Islam. Topics covered include comparative religion, history, culture, lifestyle, politics, law & women in Islam. It is a registered charity, BN: 886810191RR0001.
Finances: *Annual Operating Budget:* $50,000-$100,000
Staff Member(s): 2; 100 volunteer(s)
Membership: 100 student; 1,000 individual; *Fees:* $200 individual; *Committees:* Fundraising; Eid & Ramadhan; Executive
Activities: Congregation; marriages; family counselling; summer & evening school for kids; *Speaker Service:* Yes; *Library:* IPC Office Library; Open to public by appointment

Islamic Relief Canada
3506 Mainway, Burlington ON L7M 1A8
Tel: 905-332-4673
Toll-Free: 855-377-4673
info@islamicreliefcanada.org
islamicreliefcanada.org
www.facebook.com/islamicrelief.canada
twitter.com/IRCanada
www.youtube.com/user/IslamicReliefC
Overview: A small international charitable organization founded in 1984
Mission: To provide food & supplies to people in developing countries in order to help them establish better living situations for themselves
Affliation(s): Islamic Relief Worldwide; People in Aid
Finances: *Annual Operating Budget:* Greater than $5 Million
Staff Member(s): 3

Island Deaf & Hard of Hearing Centre (IDHHC)
#201-754 Broughton St., Victoria BC V8W 1E1
Tel: 250-592-8144; *Fax:* 250-592-8199
Toll-Free: 800-667-5448; *TTY:* 250-592-8147
victoria@idhhc.ca
www.idhhc.ca
www.facebook.com/145668377075
twitter.com/IDHHC
Overview: A small local charitable organization founded in 1991
Mission: To enable individuals who are deaf, hard of hearing or deafened, their supporters & the communities they represent, to have full & active access, recognition & involvement in society
Chief Officer(s):
Denise Robertson, Executive Director
Finances: *Annual Operating Budget:* $500,000-$1.5 Million; *Funding Sources:* Government; contract; donations; United Way
Staff Member(s): 14; 50 volunteer(s)
Membership: 200; *Fees:* $15-40
Activities: Counselling; interpreting; employment services; technical aids; family services; Spring Family Celebration; aural rehabilitation; support groups; *Awareness Events:* Sound & Silence Run/Walk, Aug.; *Internships:* Yes; *Speaker Service:* Yes; *Rents Mailing List:* Yes

Nanaimo Branch Office
#101, 75 Front St., Nanaimo BC V9R 5G9
Tel: 250-753-0999; *Fax:* 250-753-9601
Toll-Free: 877-424-3323; *TTY:* 250-753-0977
nanaimo@idhhc.ca
www.idhhc.ca
Chief Officer(s):
Alexandra Walker, Office Manager
alex@idhhc.ca

Island Fishermen Cooperative Association Ltd. *Voir* Association coopérative des pêcheurs de l'île ltée

Island Fitness Council
Sport PEI, PO Box 302, Charlottetown PE C1A 7K7
Tel: 902-368-4110; *Fax:* 902-368-4548
Toll-Free: 800-247-6712
sports@sportpei.pe.ca
Overview: A small provincial organization
Mission: A volunteer driven organization that is committed to developing a competent and enthusiastic core of active living leaders through leadership programs and standards which have been designed to establish professional competency and credibility, and ultimately enhance the health of all Islanders.
Affliation(s): National Fitness Leadership Alliance
Finances: *Funding Sources:* Provincial government
Activities: Fitness Leader Certification;

Island Horse Council (IHC)
c/o Sport PEI, 40 Enman Cres., Charlottetown PE C1E 1E6
www.islandhorsecouncil.ca
www.facebook.com/islandhorsecouncil
twitter.com/pei_IHC
Overview: A small provincial organization overseen by Sport PEI Inc.
Mission: The objectives of Island Horse Council are: to promote, conduct and manage a Council for the benefit of Prince Edward Island equestrians; to provide a unified voice for the horse industry on Prince Edward Island; to establish a liaison with any authorities, including federal, provincial, and municipal governments, and provincial or national Horse Councils or Equestrian Federations; and to encourage the development of all aspects of horsemanship, health, education, training, competition, breeding, facilities and humane practices.
Member of: Sport PEI
Affliation(s): Equine Canada
Chief Officer(s):
Gary Evans, Chair
gevans@upei.ca
Frank Szentmiklossy, Treasurer
frank.szentmiklossy@systronix.net
Finances: *Funding Sources:* Sponsorships; PEI Provincial Government, Community & Cultural Affairs
Membership: 600+ individuals & 12 clubs; *Fees:* $35; *Committees:* Insurance/Membership; Provincial Coaching; Strathgartney; Trails & Recreation
Activities: Offering seminars, on topics such as first aid; Liaising with governments & other authorities; Encouraging the certification of coaches
Awards:
• Annual Volunteer of the Year (Award)
Publications:
• Business Directory
Type: Directory
• Island Horse Council Newsletter
Type: Newsletter; *Accepts Advertising*
Profile: Council activities & upcoming shows & event

Island Hospice Association *See* Hospice Palliative Care Association of Prince Edward Island

Island Lake Tribal Council
338 Broadway Ave., 4th Fl., Winnipeg MB R3C 0T2
Tel: 204-982-3300
wpgsuboffice@iltc.ca
www.iltc.ca
Overview: A small local organization
Mission: To generally unify, maintain and expand the interests, lives and identity of the Membership in every manner and respect whatsoever by facilitating leadership of all Island Lake Tribal Council communities; strengthening first nations communities; and working with first nations staff to bring in resources to strengthen skills and knowledge.
Affliation(s): Assembly of Manitoba Chiefs; Manitoba Keewatinowi Okimakanak; Assembly of First Nations
Chief Officer(s):
Jonathan Flett, Executive Director
jflett@iltc.ca
Staff Member(s): 17
Membership: *Member Profile:* Represents four member reserves: Garden Hill; Red Sucker Lake; St. Theresa Point; Wasagamack
Activities: Education Advisory Services; Financial Advisory Services; First Nation Child Care Program; Social Development Advisory Services; Technical Services

Island Media Arts Co-op (IMAC)
PO Box 2726, Charlottetown PE C1A 8C3
Tel: 902-892-3131
director@imac.coop
www.islandmedia.pe.ca
Overview: A small provincial organization founded in 1982
Mission: To provide support & equipment for independent films produced on Prince Edward Island
Member of: Independent Film & Video Alliance
Chief Officer(s):
Renee Laprise, Executive Director
Staff Member(s): 1
Membership: *Fees:* $25 general; $40 producer
Activities: Film & video training workshops; *Awareness Events:* Reel Island Film Festival

Island Nature Trust (INT)
PO Box 265, Charlottetown PE C1A 7K4
Tel: 902-566-9150; *Fax:* 902-628-6331
admin@islandnaturetrust.ca
www.islandnaturetrust.ca
www.facebook.com/pages/Island-Nature-Trust/190787204315860
Also Known As: Prince Edward Island Nature Trust
Overview: A small provincial charitable organization founded in 1979
Mission: To acquire & manage natural areas on PEI
Member of: Tourism Industry Association of PEI
Affliation(s): Canadian Nature Federation; Tree Canada Foundation
Finances: *Funding Sources:* Donations; fundraising; contract work
Membership: *Fees:* $20 single; $25 family; $10 student; $50 sustaining; $100 active; $250 supporting; $500 membership
Activities: Educational programs; acquisition, protection & management of natural areas; *Speaker Service:* Yes

The Island Party of Prince Edward Island
1254 Peakes Rd., RR#5, Mount Stewart PE C0A 1T0
Tel: 902-583-2145
theislandparty@yahoo.com
Also Known As: The Island Party of P.E.I.
Overview: A small provincial organization
Mission: Representing the Liberal Party of PEI.
Chief Officer(s):
Sandra Sharpe, President

Island Writers' Association (P.E.I.)
c/o Debbie Gamble, 1320 Pownal Rd., RR#1, Alexandra, Charlottetown PE C1A 7J6
Tel: 902-569-3913
Overview: A small provincial organization founded in 1979
Mission: To facilitate information for P.E.I. freelance writers
Chief Officer(s):
Debbie Gamble, Contact
debbiegamble@pei.sympatico.ca
Membership: *Member Profile:* Writer or aspiring writer
Activities: Writers & photographers workshops; conferences

Islands Historical Society
PO Box 67, Freeport NS B0V 1B0
Tel: 902-839-2034; *Fax:* 902-839-2018
islandshistorical@cwswireless.ca
www.islandshistoricalsociety.com
Overview: A small local organization founded in 1984
Mission: To preserve, protect and promote the social history of Long and Brier Islands.
Member of: Association of Nova Scotia Museums; Council of Nova Scotia Archives; Canadian Heritage Information Network; Nova Scotia Lighthouse Preservation Society; Federation of the Nova Scotian Heritage

Islands Organic Producers Association (IOPA)
3490 Glenora Rd., Duncan BC V9L 6S2
Tel: 250-748-2791; *Fax:* 250-748-2741
admin@iopa.ca
www.iopa.ca
Overview: A small local organization founded in 1990
Affiliation(s): Certified Organic Associations of BC
Finances: *Funding Sources:* Membership fees
30 volunteer(s)
Membership: 60; *Member Profile:* Organic farmers

Israel Aliyah Center
#210, 4600 Bathurst St., Toronto ON M2R 3V3
Tel: 416-633-4766; *Fax:* 416-633-2758
aliyahto@jafi.org
www.aliyah.org
Overview: A small local organization
Mission: Committed towards maintaining Israel as a prominent focus of Jews everywhere and of stimulating interest in Israel as a viable living option.
Member of: Jewish Agency for Israel

Montréal Office
#206, 1 Cummings Sq., Montréal QC H3W 1M6
Tel: 514-739-7300; *Fax:* 514-739-9412
mtlaliyah@jafi.org
www.aliyah.org
Mission: To promote Aliyah and prepare potential Olim to make their Aliyah and Absorption a success.
Member of: Jewish Agency for Israel
Chief Officer(s):
Yvonne Margo, Aliyah Coordinator & Office Manager

Israel Cancer Research Fund (ICRF)
PO Box 29, #616, 1881 Yonge St., Toronto ON M4S 3C4
Tel: 416-487-5246; *Fax:* 416-487-8932
Toll-Free: 866-207-4949
research@icrf.ca
www.icrf.ca
www.facebook.com/ICRFToronto
twitter.com/icrftoronto
www.youtube.com/user/ICRFOnline
Overview: A small international charitable organization founded in 1975
Mission: To support scientists who are conducting cancer research in Israel
Chief Officer(s):
Bryna Goldberg, President
Joy Wagner Arbus, Executive Director
joy.wagner@icrf.ca
Staff Member(s): 3
Membership: *Member Profile:* Those committed to finding the cures for cancer; *Committees:* Scientific Advisory
Activities: Postdoctoral fellowships; project grants; Research Career Development Awards (RCDAs) & professorships; Women of Action Luncheon; The ICRF Gala; *Speaker Service:* Yes

The Israel Economic Mission to Canada
#700, 180 Bloor St. West, Toronto ON M5S 2V6
Tel: 416-847-0227
itrade.gov.il/canada
ca.linkedin.com/pub/israel-economic-mission-to-canada/35/530/410
facebook.com/112558825499912
twitter.com/IsraelFTA
Overview: A small international organization
Mission: To forge trade & investment relations between Israel & Canada
Chief Officer(s):
Ephraim Shoham, Trade Commissioner
Activities: *Library*

Montréal
#650, 1 Westmount Square, Montréal QC H3Z 2P9
Tel: 514-940-8518
Chief Officer(s):
Sandra Winston, Deputy Trade Commissioner

Israel Medical Association-Canadian Chapter (IMA)
#309, 788 Marlee Ave., Toronto ON M6B 3K1
Tel: 416-781-9562; *Fax:* 416-781-3166
Overview: A small international charitable organization founded in 1958
Mission: Devoted to promotion of professional & cultural ties between physicians in Israel & their colleagues abroad
Affiliation(s): Israel Medical Association World Fellowship
Chief Officer(s):
Rose Geist, President
rgeist@thc.on.ca
Activities: *Speaker Service:* Yes

Italian Canadian Benevolent Corporation (Toronto District)
See Villa Charities Inc. (Toronto District)

Italian Canadian Cultural Association of Nova Scotia (ICCA NS)
PO Box 9044, Stn. A, 2629 Agricola St., Halifax NS B3K 5M7
Tel: 902-453-5327; *Fax:* 902-453-1852
icca@eastlink.ca
www.iccans.org
Overview: A small provincial organization
Mission: To enrich & share Italian Canadian culture throughout Nova Scotia; To honour Italian heritage
Membership: *Fees:* $25 students (full time, from age 18 to 25) & seniors (over 65 years of age); $35 single members; $70 fammilies; *Member Profile:* Persons of Italian heritage; Individuals of non-Italian heritage, who have an interest in Italian history & culture
Activities: Providing educational services, such as instruction in the Italian language; Organizing social, cultural, & recreational events which build family & community ties; Offering a forum for members to share their experiences; *Library:* Italian Canadian Cultural Association of Nova Scotia Library
Publications:
• La Voce
Type: Newsletter; *Accepts Advertising; Editor:* Giovanni Da Ros
Profile: Announcements of upcoming events in the Italian community

Italian Chamber of Commerce in Canada (ICCC)
#1150, 550 Sherbrooke St. West, Montréal QC H3A 1B9
Tel: 514-844-4249; *Fax:* 514-844-4875
info.montreal@italchamber.qc.ca
www.italchamber.qc.ca
twitter.com/CCICmontreal
Overview: A small international organization
Mission: ICCC is a private, non-profit organization that nurtures economic ties between Italy & Canada, with a special focus on Quebec. It encourages the development of business relations between major public & private economic players, & provides a range of services that contribute to clients' internationalization projects. It has experience in advanced technology sectors, such as aeronautics, biotechnology, telecommunications, genomics, nanotechnology & chemical industries.
Chief Officer(s):
Emanuele Triassi, President
Danielle Virone, Executive Director
virone.montreal@italchamber.qc.ca
Staff Member(s): 7
Membership: *Fees:* $450 corporate; $1200 sustaining
Activities: Trade shows in Canada & Italy

Italian Chamber of Commerce in Canada - West
#405, 889 West Pender St., Vancouver BC V6C 3B2
Tel: 604-682-1410; *Fax:* 604-682-2997
iccbc@iccbc.com
www.iccbc.com
www.facebook.com/group.php?gid=139358149347600
twitter.com/Italian_Chamber
Overview: A small international organization founded in 1992
Mission: The Chamber is private, non-profit, membership organization with the mandate of promoting & enhancing business, trade & investment exchanges between Italy & Western Canada
Chief Officer(s):
Celso Boscariol, President
Giorgio Puppin, Executive Director
Staff Member(s): 7
Membership: *Fees:* $100 friend; $200 associate; $350 business; $550 corporate; *Member Profile:* Open to all individuals & companies with an interest in business links between BC, Alberta & Italy
Activities: Trade shows; seminars
Publications:
• Conexus
Type: Magazine; *Frequency:* Quarterly
Profile: www.conexusmagazine.ca

Calgary Office
#9, 3927 Edmonton Trail NE, Calgary AB T2E 6T1
Tel: 403-283-0453; *Fax:* 403-283-0484
calgary@iccbc.com
Chief Officer(s):
Petra Saccani, Contact

Italian Chamber of Commerce of Ontario (ICCO)
201, 622 College St., Toronto ON M6G 1B6
Tel: 416-789-7169; *Fax:* 416-789-7160
info@italchambers.ca
www.italchambers.ca
www.linkedin.com/company/icco-italian-chamber-of-commerce-of-ontario
www.facebook.com/IccoItalianChamberOfCommerceOfOntario
twitter.com/Italchambers
Previous Name: Italian Chamber of Commerce of Toronto
Overview: A medium-sized international organization founded in 1961
Mission: To enhance & promote business, trade & cultural relations between Canada & Italy.
Member of: European Union Chambers of Commerce; Greater Toronto Business Alliance
Chief Officer(s):
George Visintin, President
Corrado Paina, Executive Director
paina@italchambers.ca
Membership: *Fees:* $50 student; $100 forward; $200 individual; $1000 business; $3000 partner 3 star; $5000 partner 4 star; $10000 partner 5 star
Activities: *Library*
Publications:
• Partners Magazine
Type: trade journal

Italian Chamber of Commerce of Toronto *See* Italian Chamber of Commerce of Ontario

Italian Cultural Centre Society
3075 Slocan St., Vancouver BC V5M 3E4
Tel: 604-430-3337; *Fax:* 604-430-3331
info@iccvancouver.ca
italianculturalcentre.ca
www.facebook.com/ilcentrovan
twitter.com/IlCentroVan
Overview: A small local organization founded in 1978
Mission: To promote Italian culture and bring together Italians in Vancouver
Member of: BC Chamber of Commerce; Business in Vancouver; Commercial Drive BIA; Tourism Vancouver; Vancouver Board of Trade
Chief Officer(s):
Mauro Vescera, Executive Director, 604-430-3337 Ext. 226
executivedirector@iccvancouver.ca
Activities: Italian Language Classses; Italian Sports; Bingo;

Italian Cultural Institute (Istituto Italiano di Cultura)
496 Huron St., Toronto ON M5R 2R3
Tel: 416-921-3802; *Fax:* 416-962-2503
Other Communication: Courses, E-mail: corsi.iictoronto@esteri.it
iicToronto@esteri.it
www.iictoronto.esteri.it
www.facebook.com/iictoronto
twitter.com/IICToronto
www.youtube.com/user/IICCulturalToronto
Overview: A medium-sized international organization founded in 1976
Mission: To promote Italian culture & language in its many expressions in a spirit of vital interaction with the host country;

To provide information on Italy's cultural heritage & contemporary cultural production
Chief Officer(s):
Adriana Frisenna, Director, 416-921-3802 Ext. 221
adriana.frisenna@esteri.it
Carlo Settembrini, Technical Manager, 416-921-3802 Ext. 222
carlo.settembrini@esteri.it
Tiziana Miano brini, Assistant to the Manager, 416-921-3802 Ext. 221
tiziana.miano@esteri.it
Finances: *Funding Sources:* Italian Ministry of Foreign Affairs; Private sponsors
Membership: 5,000-14,999
Activities: *Speaker Service:* Yes; *Rents Mailing List:* Yes; *Library* Open to public by appointment

Italian Cultural Society of Edmonton
14230 - 133 Ave. NW, Edmonton AB T5L 4W4
Tel: 780-453-6182; *Fax:* 780-451-0669
Overview: A small local organization
Mission: To foster retention of Italian cultural heritage; to operate a Cultural Centre in order to provide its members and other community organizations with facilities for carrying out their activities; To initiate and undertake activities which bring closer ties between the Italian community and the Canadian community at large.
Chief Officer(s):
Alfredo Pitrini, Contact
Activities: Annual Senior's dinner; monthly dinner dances; annual banquets

Italian Pentecostal Church of Canada *See* General Conference of the Canadian Assemblies of God

ITAP
PO Box 241, Charlottetown PE C1A 7K4
Tel: 902-894-4827
itap@itap.ca
www.itap.ca
www.facebook.com/pages/ITAP/229205927166908
twitter.com/itapei
Also Known As: Innovation & Technology Association of PEI
Overview: A small provincial organization founded in 1997
Mission: To promote the technology industry in PEI; to act as a liaison with the government, providing information needed to foster growth, & maintains a comprehensive database on its members which can be accessed to show their skills, products & services; to assess future market requirements to develop training initiatives, internships & apprenticeships for school graduates.
Member of: Software Human Resource Council; Canadian ICT Federation; Canadian Interactive Alliance
Chief Officer(s):
Paul Lypaczewski, Innovation Director
paul.lypaczewski@itap.ca
Staff Member(s): 3
Membership: 70; *Member Profile:* Businesses in the technology sector; suppliers; public sector representatives; students
Activities: Professional development workshops; mentoring programs; *Library* by appointment
Awards:
• Premier's Entrepreneurship Award (Award)
Honours the achievements of an ITAP member for a significant contribution to the Island economy by establishing & maintaining a successful independent IT business
• Most Valuable Employee Award (Award)

iTaxiworkers Association
25 Cecil St., Toronto ON M5T 1N1
Tel: 416-597-6838; *Fax:* 416-597-2195
info@itaxiworkers.ca
www.itaxiworkers.ca
Overview: A medium-sized provincial organization
Mission: To improve the rights & working conditions of Ontario taxi drivers
Membership: *Fees:* $35/month; *Member Profile:* Taxi drivers

IWK Health Centre Foundation (IWKF)
#B220, 5855 Spring Garden Rd., Halifax NS B3H 4S2
Tel: 902-470-8085
Toll-Free: 800-595-2266
foundationmail@iwk.nshealth.ca
iwkfoundation.org
www.facebook.com/iwkfoundation
twitter.com/IWKFoundation
www.youtube.com/theiwkfoundation
Overview: A small local charitable organization
Mission: To raise money on behalf of the IWK Health Centre that helps fund research & improve patient care
Chief Officer(s):
Jennifer Gillivan, President & CEO
Finances: *Annual Operating Budget:* Greater than $5 Million
Staff Member(s): 32

Iyengar Yoga Association of Canada
c/o Theresa McDiarmid, 22 Langley Ave., Toronto ON M4K 1B5
e-mail: info@iyengaryogacanada.com
www.iyengaryogacanada.com
www.facebook.com/IYAC.ACYI
twitter.com/Canadalyengar
Overview: A small national organization
Chief Officer(s):
Theresa McDiarmid, Membership
Membership: *Fees:* $42-$173.25

J. Douglas Ferguson Historical Research Foundation
PO Box 5079, Shediac NB E4P 8T8
Tel: 506-532-6025
www.nunet.ca/jdfhrf/main.php
Overview: A small national charitable organization founded in 1971
Mission: To give financial support to a broad range of activities aimed at preserving the heritage of early historical currency, banks & other issuers of money, coins, tokens & paper money issued throughout Canada since the 18th century.
Chief Officer(s):
Geoffrey G. Bell, Deputy Chair
gbel@nb.sympatico.ca
Chris Faulkner, Chairman
Len Buth, Treasurer
Finances: *Funding Sources:* Bequests; donation
Activities: Undergraduate/Graduate Essay Contests;
Awards:
• Rev. Dr. Bernard O'Connor Scholarship (Scholarship)
Eligibility: Applicants must be numismatic students, advanced collectors, university students & educators wishing to pursue post-graduate studies in Canadian numismatics, banking history, economics, currency development & related studies *Amount:* Up to $10,000 *Contact:* Graham Esler, 56 Glass Ave., London, ON

Jack Miner Migratory Bird Foundation, Inc.
PO Box 39, 360 RR#3 WeEst, Kingsville ON N9Y 2E5
Tel: 519-733-4034
Toll-Free: 877-289-8328
info@jackminer.com
www.jackminer.com
www.facebook.com/JackMinerMigratoryBirdSanctuary
Overview: A small local charitable organization founded in 1904
Mission: The sanctuary provides food, shelter & protection to migratory water fowl, tags birds & tracks migration patterns
Chief Officer(s):
Kirk W. Miner, Executive Director
Finances: *Funding Sources:* Private
Staff Member(s): 3; 12 volunteer(s)

Jake Thomas Learning Centre
7575 Townline Rd., Site 1, RR#1, Wilsonville ON N0E 1Z0
Tel: 519-445-0779; *Fax:* 519-445-0802
www.jakethomaslearningcentre.ca
www.facebook.com/jake.centre?fref=ts
Also Known As: The Friends of the Jake Thomas Learning Centre
Overview: A small local charitable organization founded in 1993
Mission: To raise funds both on & off Six Nations Reserve to enhance & support the Jake Thomas Learning Centre which is dedicated to preserve & promote Iroquoian Heritage & the traditional way of life; fundraising for the Jake Thomas Learning Centre building & the Friends of the Jake Thomas Learning Centre organization to be able to operate all events to the aims stated above
Chief Officer(s):
Phyllis Hill, Treasurer
Dan Longboat, Director
Ken Maracle, Director
Yvonne Thomas, Executive Director
Finances: *Annual Operating Budget:* $50,000-$100,000
Staff Member(s): 2; 8 volunteer(s)
Membership: *Committees:* Archive; Building
Activities: Workshops: Wampum-bead making, Cornhusk weaving; Tutoring languages: Mohawk, Cayuga, Onondaga; *Library* Open to public by appointment

Jaku Konbit
211 Bronson Ave., Ottawa ON K1R 6H5
Tel: 613-567-0600
www.jakukonbit.com
Overview: A small local organization founded in 2000
Mission: To enhance the quality of life for underpriviledged youth & minority groups, particularly those of African & Caribbean descent.
Chief Officer(s):
Kenneth Campbell, President

Jamaica Association of Montréal Inc.
4065, Jean-Talon ouest, Montréal QC H4P 1W6
Tel: 514-737-8229
www.jam-montreal.com
www.facebook.com/JamaicaAssociationOfMontrealInc
Overview: A small local organization
Mission: Educational, cultural & social activities for the Jamaican community; after-school & evening classes & programs for youth & adults; Saturday morning program for children; restaurant on site

Jamaican Canadian Association (JCA)
995 Arrow Rd., Toronto ON M9M 2Z5
Tel: 416-746-5772; *Fax:* 416-746-7035
info@jcaontario.org
jcaontario.org
Overview: A small international charitable organization founded in 1962
Mission: To provide social interaction among members & to facilitate desirable relations with Canadian society; to represent the Caribbean community on public matters; to respond to the diverse social service needs of members; to facilitate economic, social & cultural integration of Caribbean people within Canadian society
Chief Officer(s):
Audrey Campbell, President
Membership: *Member Profile:* People of Jamaican & Caribbean descent
Activities: Immigrant Settlement & Adaption Program (ISAP); Caribbean Canadian Seniors' Club; Program for Abused & Assaulted Black Women; Pal Program (provides supportive, one-on-one relationship between Caribbean/Black children ages 7-16 & caring adults); Caribbean Youth & Family Services; Youth Development Programs; Multicultural Community Outreach; Parenting/Healthy Babies; Meals on Wheels; Job Assistance; Computer Training; Teen Drop-In; Spring & Summer Camp; Under 12 Program on Delinquency; *Library:* Marcus Garvey Resource Library; Open to public
Awards:
• "I Have a Dream" Scholarship (Scholarship)
• Marcus Mosiah Garvey Scholarship (Scholarship)
• Dr. Ezra Nesbeth Scholarship (Scholarship)

Jamaican Ottawa Community Association (JOCA)
211 Bronson Ave., Ottawa ON K1R 6H5
Tel: 613-523-9085
jamaicanottawaassn@yahoo.com
www.jakukonbit.com
www.facebook.com/136531216361229
Overview: A small local organization
Mission: To enhance the quality of life for the Jamaican communtiy in Ottawa
Chief Officer(s):
Joanne Robinson, President
Membership: *Fees:* $20 student/associate; $25 senior; $30 general; $50 family; *Committees:* Jamday; Youth; Brunch; Education; Heroes Gala; Building Fund; Variety Concert; Christmas Party; Seniors; Fundraising

Jamaican Self-Help Organization (JSH)
PO Box 1992, #9, 129« Hunter St. West, Peterborough ON K9J 7X7
Tel: 705-743-1671; *Fax:* 705-743-4020
jshcanada.org
Overview: A small international charitable organization founded in 1981 overseen by Ontario Council for International Cooperation
Mission: To foster the development of healthy Jamaican communities through partnership based on mutual respect, understanding & a shared vision of self determination; to foster an understanding of global forces North & South & their interconnectedness
Member of: Canadian Council for International Cooperation
Chief Officer(s):
Marisa Kaczmarczyk, Executive Director
marisa@jshcanada.org

Tuucker Barton, President
Finances: *Annual Operating Budget:* $250,000-$500,000; *Funding Sources:* Donations; CIDA matches every dollar raised; foundations; religious groups
100 volunteer(s)
Membership: 25; *Committees:* Finance; Fundraising; Personnel; Strategic Planning; Global Education; Jamaican Program
Activities: One World Dinner; *Speaker Service:* Yes

James Bay Association for Community Living
PO Box 460, #18, 4 St., Moosonee ON P0L 1Y0
Tel: 705-336-2378
www.jbacl.org
Previous Name: Moosonee-Moose Factory Association for Community Living
Overview: A small local charitable organization
Mission: To integrate developmentally handicapped adult Cree Indians into their home communities; to work toward supported employment & independent living (area covers west coast of James Bay) so that all persons live in a state of dignity, share in all elements of living in the community & have the opportunity to participate effectively
Member of: Community Living Ontario
Chief Officer(s):
Barbara Louttit, President
Lynn Gray, Executive Director
lynn.gray@jbacl.org
Finances: *Annual Operating Budget:* $250,000-$500,000; *Funding Sources:* Ministry of Community & Social Services; Ministry of Municipal Affairs & Housing
Staff Member(s): 13
Membership: 1-99
Activities: *Awareness Events:* Community Living Month, May

James Bay Tourism *Voir* Tourisme Baie-James

Jane Austen Society of North America (JASNA)
#105, 195 Wynford Dr., Toronto ON M3C 3P3
Toll-Free: 800-836-3911
info@jasna.org
www.jasna.org
www.facebook.com/285332054855712
Overview: A medium-sized international organization founded in 1979
Mission: To promote an appreciation of Jane Austen & her writings
Chief Officer(s):
Nancy Stokes, Canadian Membership Secretary
naristo@rogers.com
Finances: *Funding Sources:* Membership dues; contributions
Membership: 4,500; *Fees:* $18 student; $30 individual; $45 family; $60 sustaining; $500 life; $700 family life
Activities: Tours of Austen sites in England; scholarly publishing; student essay contest; lectures; teas; Jane Austen's birthday Dec. 16; *Speaker Service:* Yes
Publications:
• Persuasions: The Jane Austen Journal
Type: Journal; *Frequency:* Annually *ISSN:* 0821-0314

Alberta - Calgary Chapter
e-mail: jasnacalgary@jasnacalgary.ca
www.jasnacalgary.ca
Chief Officer(s):
Catherine Gardner, Regional Coordinator, 403-242-5016
c.gardner@shaw.ca

Alberta - Edmonton Chapter
Edmonton AB
Tel: 780-451-9243
Chief Officer(s):
Bridget Toms, Contact
twolegsgood@telus.net

British Columbia - Vancouver Chapter
698 Wellington Place, North Vancouver BC V7K 3A1
Tel: 604-988-6806
www.jaonavancouver.ca
Chief Officer(s):
Phyllis Bottomer, Coordinator
pmfb.jasna@gmail.com

British Columbia - Victoria Chapter
Victoria BC
Tel: 250-384-0193
Chief Officer(s):
Joan Millar, Contact
sophycroft-at-sea@shaw.ca

Manitoba Region
Winnipeg MB
Tel: 204-475-3200
Chief Officer(s):
Celine Kear, Contact
Lorna Pyrih, Contact

Nova Scotia Region
NS
janeausteninnovascotia.wordpress.com
Chief Officer(s):
Anne Thompson, Regional Coordinator, 902-477-2341
anne_thompson@ns.sympatico.ca

Ontario - London Chapter
12569 Boston Dr., RR#41, London ON N6H 5L2
Tel: 519-657-3994
jasnalondonchapter@hotmail.com
Chief Officer(s):
Nancy Johnson, Contact

Ontario - Ottawa Chapter
Ottawa ON
Tel: 613-523-1485
Chief Officer(s):
Emily Arrowsmith, Coordinator
emily_arrowsmith@caf-fca.org

Ontario - Toronto Chapter
Toronto ON
Chief Officer(s):
Louise Yearwood, Coordinator
lyearwood@havergal.on.ca

Québec - Montréal & Québec Chapters
Montréal QC
Tel: 514-481-4555
jasna.montrealqc@gmail.com
jasna-mtl.weebly.com
Chief Officer(s):
Elaine Bander, Coordinator

Saskatchewan - Moose Jaw Chapter
Chief Officer(s):
Brenda Babich, 306-692-3224
babich.brenda@sasktel.net

Jane Finch Community & Family Centre
#108, 440 Jane St., Toronto ON M3N 2K4
Tel: 416-663-2733; *Fax:* 416-663-3816
admin@janefinchcentre.org
www.janefinchcentre.org
www.facebook.com/people/Jane-Finch-Centre/1518951464
Overview: A medium-sized local charitable organization
Mission: To operate with a strong commitment to social justice, community engagement, & collaboration
Chief Officer(s):
Michelle Dagnino, Executive Director
Membership: *Fees:* $3 individual; $5 non-resident; $10 group

The Jane Goodal Institute of Canada (JGI)
c/o University of Toronto Mailroom, 565 Spadina Cres., Toronto ON M5S 2J7
Tel: 416-978-3711; *Fax:* 416-978-3713
Toll-Free: 888-882-4467
Other Communication: roots_shoots@janegoodall.ca
info@janegoodall.ca
www.janegoodall.ca/roots-shoots.php
www.facebook.com/rootsandshoots.canada
twitter.com/JaneGoodallCAN
www.youtube.com/user/RootsanShoots
Also Known As: Roots & Shoots
Overview: A small local organization founded in 1994
Mission: To support wildlife research, education, & conservation
Chief Officer(s):
Jane Lawton, CEO
Jane Goodall, Founder
Finances: *Funding Sources:* Donations
Activities: Providing training in environmental & humanitarian education; Raising awareness of endangered animals; Promoting activities to aid the well-being of wild & captive chimpanzees
Publications:
• Jane Goodall Institute of Canada eNewsletter
Type: Newsletter
Profile: Canadian news, news from the field, & ways to become involved
• Roots & Shoots Canada eNewsletter
Type: Newsletter
Profile: Events, activities, parnerships, & resources

The Jane Goodall Institute of Canada
c/o University of Toronto Mailroom, 563 Spadina Cres., Toronto ON M5S 2J7
Tel: 416-978-3711; *Fax:* 416-978-3713
Toll-Free: 888-882-4467
info@janegoodall.ca
www.janegoodall.ca
www.facebook.com/JaneGoodallCAN
twitter.com/JaneGoodallCAN
www.youtube.com/user/jgicanada
Overview: A small national charitable organization founded in 1994
Mission: To support wildlife research, education & conservation; to promote informed & compassionate action to improve the environment shared by all Earth's living creatures
Affliation(s): The Jane Goodall Institute - USA; The Jane Goodall Institute - UK
Chief Officer(s):
John Wall, Chair
Jane Lawton, Executive Director
Finances: *Annual Operating Budget:* $250,000-$500,000; *Funding Sources:* Private donations; lecture honorariums
Staff Member(s): 8; 32 volunteer(s)
Membership: 100-499
Activities: Chimp Guardian Program - sponsor orphan chimpanzees; Roots & Shoots - Jane Goodall Institute's global environmental & humanitarian program; *Awareness Events:* Earth Day, April 22; Peace Day, Sept. 21; *Internships:* Yes
Publications:
• Jane Goodall Institute of Canada eNewsletter
Type: Newsletter; *Frequency:* 2 pa; *Price:* Free online
• Roots & Shoots Canada eNewsletter [a publication of the Jane Goodall Institute of Canada]
Type: Newsletter; *Price:* Free online

Janeway Children's Hospital Foundation
300 Prince Philip Dr., St. John's NL A1B 3V6
Tel: 709-777-4640; *Fax:* 709-777-4489
janewayfoundation@easternhealth.ca
www.janewayfoundation.nf.ca
www.facebook.com/JanewayNL
twitter.com/JanewayNL
www.youtube.com/user/janewayfoundation
Overview: A small local charitable organization
Mission: To raise money on behalf of the Janeway Childnren's Hospital that helps fund research & improve patient care
Chief Officer(s):
Lynn Sparkes, Executive Director
Staff Member(s): 8

Japan Automobile Manufacturers Association of Canada
#460, 151 Bloor St. West, Toronto ON M5S 1S4
Tel: 416-968-0150; *Fax:* 416-968-7095
jama@jama.ca
www.jama.ca
Also Known As: JAMA Canada
Overview: A medium-sized international organization founded in 1984
Mission: To promote increased understanding of economic & trade matters pertaining to the motor vehicle industry; To encourage closer cooperation between Canada & Japan; To represent the interests of members
Chief Officer(s):
Takashi Sekiguchi, Chairman
Activities: Providing information about the Japanese-affiliated auto industry in Canada; Producing statistics on Japanese-affiliated motor vehicle production, imports & expors & sales in Canada

The Japan Foundation, Toronto / Kokosai Koryu Kikin Toronto Nihon Bunka Centre
#213, 131 Bloor St. West, Toronto ON M5S 1R1
Tel: 416-966-1600; *Fax:* 416-966-9773
info@jftor.org
www.japanfoundationcanada.org
www.facebook.com/pages/The-Japan-Foundation-Toronto/280213815446606
twitter.com/JFToronto
Overview: A medium-sized international organization founded in 1972
Mission: To promote Japanese culture abroad; to offer a broad range of programs designed to further cultural exchange with Japan, with an emphasis on Japanese studies at the post-secondary level & Japanese language study
Chief Officer(s):

Ishida Takashi, Executive Director
Chieko Kono, Director
Finances: *Funding Sources:* Japanese Ministry of Foreign Affairs
Staff Member(s): 14
Activities: *Library* Open to public
Awards:
• The Japan Foundation Fellowships (Scholarship)
Scholars, researchers, artists & other professionals are provided an opportunity to conduct research or pursue projects in Japan. Term of award is from two to 14 months, depending on category; annual application deadline is Dec. 1 for funding year beginning the following April 1
• The Japan Foundation Scholarships & Programs (Scholarship)
The Foundation offers a wide range of programs in more than 180 countries, including the following: exchange of persons (fellowships); support for Japanese-language instruction; support for Japanese studies; support for arts-related exchange; support for media exchange

The Japan Society Canada
#604, 157 Adelaide St. West, Toronto ON M5H 4E7
Tel: 416-366-4196; *Fax:* 416-366-4176
www.japansocietycanada.com
Overview: A small international organization founded in 1989
Mission: To enable Canadian & Japanese executives & academic leaders to meet on a continuing basis to discuss matters of mutual interest; To further economic relationships between Canada & Japan; To acquire greater cultural understanding; To support business, educational, & cultural exchanges
Member of: Canadian Society of Association Executives
Affliation(s): National Association of Japan-America Societies
Chief Officer(s):
John Craig, Chair, 416-865-7128
Ben Ciprietti, President
ben@japansocietycanada.com
Finances: *Funding Sources:* Membership fees
Membership: 100-499

Japanese Canadian Association of Yukon (JCAY)
531 Grove St., Whitehorse YT Y1A 5J9
Tel: 867-393-2588
jcayukon@gmail.com
Overview: A medium-sized provincial organization
Chief Officer(s):
Fumi Torigai, President
ftorigai@gmail.com

Japanese Canadian Citizens Association *See* Greater Vancouver Japanese Canadian Citizens' Association

Japanese Canadian Cultural Centre (JCCC)
6 Garamond Ct., Toronto ON M3C 1Z5
Tel: 416-441-2345; *Fax:* 416-441-2347
jccc@jccc.on.ca
www.jccc.on.ca
twitter.com/jccc_toronto
www.youtube.com/jccctoronto
Overview: A small national charitable organization founded in 1964
Mission: To serve as a gathering place for Japanese-Canadians & those interested in Japanese culture.
Chief Officer(s):
James Heron, Executive Director
Gary Kawaguchi, President
Sharon Marubashi, Secretary
Finances: *Funding Sources:* Membership fees; donations; space rental; class fees; special events
Staff Member(s): 9
Membership: 4,300; *Fees:* Schedule available
Activities: Cultural & martial arts classes & performances; festivals; *Awareness Events:* Spring Festival, March; Natsu Matsuri, July; Issei Day, Oct.; *Speaker Service:* Yes

Japanese Cultural Association of Manitoba (JCAM)
180 McPhillips Ave., Winnipeg MB R3E 2J9
Tel: 204-774-5909; *Fax:* 204-775-6029
m.jccc@shaw.ca
www.mjccc.org
Merged from: Manitoba Japanese Canadian Citizens' Association; Manitoba Japanese Canadian Cultural Centre
Overview: A small local organization
Mission: To promote a strong Japanese Canadian identity in Manitoba; To advocate for equal rights for all persons
Member of: National Association of Japanese Canadians (NAJC)
Chief Officer(s):
Art Miki, President
Membership: *Fees:* Family $30; Individual $20
Activities: Raising funds for the Canadian Museum of Human Rights; Presenting events to celebrate Japanese Canadian arts & culture; Sponsoring workshops related to Japanese culture, heritage, & history; *Library:* MJCCC Library
Awards:
• Harold Hirose Education Fund (Scholarship)
Eligibility: Student *Amount:* $1,500
Publications:
• The History of Japanese Canadians in Manitoba
Type: Book

Les jardins botaniques royaux *See* Royal Botanical Gardens

Jasper Environmental Association (JEA)
PO Box 2198, Jasper AB T0E 1E0
Tel: 780-852-4152
jea2@telus.net
www.jasperenvironmental.org
Overview: A medium-sized local organization
Mission: To support Parks Canada in administering Jasper National Park in accordance with Canadian legislation, Parks Canada principles and policies and the wishes of the Canadian public.
Finances: *Funding Sources:* Membership fees
Membership: *Fees:* $5

Jasper Park Chamber of Commerce
PO Box 98, Jasper AB T0B 1E0
Tel: 780-852-4621
admin@jpcc.ca
www.jaspercanadianrockies.com
www.facebook.com/JasperParkChamber
twitter.com/JasperParkChamb
Overview: A small local organization founded in 1952
Mission: To advocate on behalf of its members
Chief Officer(s):
Wayne Hnatyshin, President
Pattie Pavlov, General Manager
Staff Member(s): 3
Membership: 180; *Member Profile:* Local businesses

Jazz Yukon
PO Box 31307, Whitehorse YT Y1A 5P7
Tel: 867-633-3300
info@jazzyukon.ca
www.jazzyukon.ca
Overview: A medium-sized provincial charitable organization
Mission: To promote & present jazz in the Yukon through an annual integrated program of live jazz presentations & jazz education outreach
Membership: *Member Profile:* Jazz musicians & fans
Activities: Offering the Jazz on the Wing concert series

JE de la Republique du Madawaska *See* Junior Achievement of Canada

Jean Tweed Treatment Centre (JTC)
215 Evans Ave., Toronto ON M8Z 1J5
Tel: 416-255-7359; *Fax:* 416-255-9021
info@jeantweed.com
www.jeantweed.com
www.facebook.com/pages/The-Jean-Tweed-Centre/213119005385114
twitter.com/jeantweedcentre
Overview: A small provincial charitable organization founded in 1983
Mission: To provide services for women with substance abuse or gambling problems & their families with a focus on children 0-6
Member of: Federation of Community Mental Health & Addictions Programs; Toronto Area Addictions Services Committee; Residential Addiction Services of Ontario
Chief Officer(s):
Nancy Bradley, Executive Director
Katherine Devlin, Chair
Erin MacRae, Vice Chair/ Treas.
Finances: *Annual Operating Budget:* $3 Million-$5 Million
Staff Member(s): 98; 30 volunteer(s)
Activities: Child care; parenting services; *Awareness Events:* Staying on Course Charity Golf Classic, Sept.; *Internships:* Yes

Jeffery Hale Community Services in English
1250, ch Sainte-Foy, Québec QC G1S 2M6
Tel: 418-684-5333; *Fax:* 418-681-9265
www.jefferyhale.org
Previous Name: Holland Centre
Overview: A small local organization
Staff Member(s): 35

The Jerrahi Sufi Order of Canada
Canadian Sufi Cultural Centre, 270 Birmingham St., Toronto ON M8V 2E4
e-mail: jerrahi@jerrahi.ca
www.jerrahi.ca
Overview: A medium-sized local organization
Mission: The Jerrahi Sufi Order of Canada holds weekly gatherings where attendees come to gain knowledge about Islam by participating in discourses & discussions, observing the art of Sufi music & poetry, & celebrating the praises of God through prayer & Zikrullah (Sufi remembrance ceremony).
Activities: *Library*

Jersey Canada (JC)
#9, 350 Speedvale Ave. West, Guelph ON N1H 7M7
Tel: 519-821-1020; *Fax:* 519-821-2723
info@jerseycanada.com
www.jerseycanada.com
Previous Name: Jersey Cattle Association of Canada
Overview: A medium-sized national organization founded in 1901
Mission: To represent & promote the Jersey breed & encourage market development domestically & internationally; To provide & maintain a registration system, catalogues, & pedigree information; To update classification & milk production records
Member of: Canadian Livestock Genetics Association
Chief Officer(s):
Mathieu Larose, President, 514-444-0069
laroselait@hotmail.com
Brian Raymer, First Vice-President, 519-462-2267
brilin@cwisp.ca
Mark Anderson, Second Vice-President, 506-433-1423
cococreekfarm@yahoo.ca
Kathryn Kyle, General Manager, 519-821-1020 Ext. 23
kathryn@jerseycanada.com
Jill Dann, Registrar Ext. 22
jill@jerseycanada.com
Finances: *Funding Sources:* Membership fees; The Jersey Store; Federal government
Membership: *Committees:* Executive; Finance; Youth; Genetic Improvement; Marketing; Milk Marketing; Strategic Planning; Publications; Joint Classification Representatives; Show; Disciplinary; Awards Review
Activities: Communicating with members & liaising with industry; Providing classification & herdbook services; Presenting awards & scholarships

Atlantic
10032 Hwy. 224, Middle Musquodoboit NS B0N 1X0
Tel: 902-568-2211
Chief Officer(s):
David Cole, Secretary
dhcole2010@gmail.com

British Columbia
27336 River Rd., Langley BC V1M 3L7
Tel: 604-857-5445
Chief Officer(s):
Caryl Fair, Secretary
caryl.fair@ledalite.com

Manitoba
PO Box 7, St. Alphonse MB R0K 1Z0
Tel: 204-836-2072; *Fax:* 204-836-2371
Chief Officer(s):
Henry Delichte, Secretary
clubmilk@xplornet.com

Ontario
#9, 350 Speedvale West, Guelph ON N1H 7M7
Tel: 519-766-9980; *Fax:* 519-766-9981
ontario@jerseycanada.com
www.jerseyontario.ca
Chief Officer(s):
Kristie Rivington, Secretary

Québec
4685, boul. Laurier Ouest, Saint-Hyacinthe QC J2S 3T8
Tel: 450-771-2227; *Fax:* 450-778-9637
quebec@jerseycanada.com
Chief Officer(s):
Sandra Berthiaume, Provincial Secretary

West
RR#2, Didsbury AB T0M 0W0
Tel: 403-335-3028
Chief Officer(s):

Adrian Haeni, Co-Secretary
lonepinej@xplornet.com

Jersey Cattle Association of Canada ***See*** Jersey Canada

Jersey West
c/o Adrian Haeni, Didsbury AB
Tel: 403-335-3028
www.jerseycanada.com/jerseywest
www.facebook.com/pages/Jersey-West/298887860267644
Overview: A small provincial organization overseen by Jersey Canada
Chief Officer(s):
Adrian Haeni, Contact
lonepine@cciwireless.ca
Activities: Promoting Jersey cattle; Organizing showcase sales

Jerusalem Foundation of Canada Inc / La Fondation de Jerusalem du Canada Inc
#1040, 2 Place Alexis Nihon, Montréal QC H3Z 3C1
Tel: 514-484-1289; *Fax:* 514-482-9640
Toll-Free: 877-484-1289
www.jerusalemfoundation.ca
Overview: A small national organization founded in 1970
Mission: To enhance & enrich the quality of life for all residents of the city of Jerusalem
Chief Officer(s):
Monica E. Berger, National Executive Director
Membership: *Committees:* Gala Tribute
Activities: Funds are raised in Canada to support a host of programs which span the arts, social services, health care, historical preservation & beautification

Jessie's - The June Callwood Centre for Young Women
205 Parliament St., Toronto ON M6A 2Z4
Tel: 416-365-1888; *Fax:* 416-365-1944
mail@jessiescentre.org
jessiescentre.org
www.facebook.com/jessiescentre
Overview: A small local charitable organization
Mission: To provide help & social services to pregnant teenagers, young parents & their children
Chief Officer(s):
Maritza Sanchez, Executive Director
Finances: *Annual Operating Budget:* $500,000-$1.5 Million
Staff Member(s): 21

Jessie's Hope Society
#400, 601 West Broadway St., Vancouver BC V5Z 4C2
Tel: 604-466-4877; *Fax:* 604-466-4897
Toll-Free: 877-288-0877
www.jessieshope.org
www.facebook.com/group.php?gid=2536011953
Previous Name: Association for Awareness & Networking around Disordered Eating
Overview: A small national organization founded in 1985
Chief Officer(s):
Heather Quick Rajala
Staff Member(s): 2

Jesuit Development Office (JDO)
c/o Jesuit in English Canada, Provincial Office, 43 Queen's Park Cres. East, Toronto ON M5S 2C3
Tel: 416-481-9154; *Fax:* 416-920-5799
jdo@jesuits.ca
www.jesuits.ca
Overview: A medium-sized international charitable organization founded in 1940
Mission: To raise & provide the funds necessary for the support of Jesuit brothers & priests in formation, in ministry & in their senior years
Member of: Jesuit Fathers & Brothers of Upper Canada
Chief Officer(s):
Robert Wong, National Director
Barbara DeCarlo, Director, Development & Administration
bdecarlo@jesuits.ca
Staff Member(s): 6
Membership: under 200

Jesus Youth Canada
e-mail: canada@jesusyouth.org
canada.jesusyouth.org
www.facebook.com/280977068632989
twitter.com/jycanada
Overview: A small international organization
Mission: To reach out to other young people as witnesses of the joy of life in Christ & in service of the Catholic Church; To offer ministries of youth, intercession, prayer, & Angel's Army; To provide a focus on a Jesus-centred life; To take guidance from the international Jesus Youth International Team which coordinates worldwide activities
Affiliation(s): Toronto Archdiocese
Chief Officer(s):
Soby Joseph, East Area Coordinator, 647-459-9360
Xavier Mathew, Central Area Coordinator, 647-988-2659
Thomas Varghese, West Area Coordinator, 416-456-7050
Membership: *Member Profile:* Open to young people
Activities: Offering prayer programs, the sacraments, & worship programs; Working with youth in local parishes in faith & leadership development; Providing monthly youth meetings, fellowship, efellowship, youth camps, & retreats
Publications:
• Jesus Youth International Newsletter
Type: Newsletter; *Frequency:* Quarterly
Profile: Global JY initiatives & activities

Jeune Barreau de Québec
#RC-21, #300, boul. Jean-Lesage, Québec QC G1K 8K6
Tél: 418-802-5816; *Téléc:* 418-522-4560
jbq@jeunebarreaudequebec.ca
jeunebarreaudequebec.ca
www.facebook.com/379908232065460
twitter.com/JBQ_Quebec
Aperçu: *Dimension:* petite; *Envergure:* provinciale; fondée en 1914
Mission: Pour représenter les intérêts de ses membres au niveau national et international
Affliation(s): Barreau de Québec; Desjardins; Juris Concept; SOQUIJ; Médicassurance
Membre(s) du bureau directeur:
Jad-Patrick Barsoum, Président, Conseil d'administration
Membre: 1000+; *Critères d'admissibilite:* Les avocats qui exercent au Québec qui ont moins de 10 ans d'expérience; *Comités:* La formation; les services aux membres; Service de consultations à la Cour du Québec, Division des petites créances; Tournoi de hockey bottines; Concours oratoire; Tournoi de soccer; Tournoi de balle-molle; Cocktail de Noël; Journée Noël des enfants; Relations extérieures
Activités: Formations; Consultations pro bono; Tournoi de balle-molle; Concours oratoire; Tournoi de soccer; Tournoi de Hockey;

Jeune chambre de commerce de Montréal (JCCM)
#1220, 1010, rue Sherbrooke ouest, Montréal QC H3A 2R7
Tél: 514-845-4951; *Téléc:* 514-845-0587
www.jccm.org
www.linkedin.com/groups?gid=121393
www.facebook.com/jeunechambremtl
twitter.com/jccm_mtl
Aperçu: *Dimension:* petite; *Envergure:* locale; fondée en 1931
Mission: De favoriser le développement professionnel et personnel des jeunes gens d'affaires de Montréal, de promouvoir leurs intérêts et de contribuer à l'essor du milieu dans lequel ils évoluent.
Membre de: Chambre de commerce du Québec
Membre(s) du bureau directeur:
Véronique St-Germain, Directrice générale
vstgermain@jccm.org
Membre: *Montant de la cotisation:* 70$ étudiant; 150$ individuel; 120$ 3 à 10 membres corporatif; 95$ 11 à 20 membres; 85$ 21 membres et plus; *Critères d'admissibilite:* Être âgé entre 18 et 40 ans; *Comités:* Gestion

Jeune chambre de commerce de Québec
#249, 4600, boul Henri-Bourassa, Québec QC G1H 3A5
Tél: 418-622-6937; *Téléc:* 418-628-7777
jccq@jccq.qc.ca
www.jccq.qc.ca
www.linkedin.com/groupInvitation?gid=1043997
www.facebook.com/group.php?gid=6715149631
twitter.com/jccdequebec
www.youtube.com/user/JeunechambredeQuebec
Aperçu: *Dimension:* petite; *Envergure:* locale
Mission: La Jeune chambre de commerce de Québec (JCCQ) regroupe plus de 500 membres animés d'une vision d'avenir et surtout de la volonté de bâtir, maintenant, le Québec de demain.
Membre(s) du bureau directeur:
Marie-Eve Goulet, Présidente
Sophie Gingras, Directrice générale, 418-622-6937
sgingras@jccq.qc.ca
Membre(s) du personnel: 3
Membre: 600; *Montant de la cotisation:* 66$ étudiant; 66-120 corporatif

Jeune chambre internationale du Canada ***See*** Junior Chamber International Canada

Jeunes canadiens pour une civilisation chrétienne
880 av Louis Fréchette, Québec QC G1S 3N3
Aperçu: *Dimension:* petite; *Envergure:* locale; fondée en 1977
Mission: Travailler avec la jeunesse pour préserver les principes catholiques et éducatifs
Membre(s) du bureau directeur:
Frank Murphy, President
Finances: *Budget de fonctionnement annuel:* Moins de $50,000

Jeunes en forme Canada ***See*** Active Healthy Kids Canada

Jeunes en partage
CP 441, Chibougamau QC G8P 2X8
Tél: 418-748-2935
Aperçu: *Dimension:* petite; *Envergure:* locale
Membre(s) du bureau directeur:
Dany Larouche, Responsable

Jeunes Entreprises du Canada ***See*** Junior Achievement Canada

Jeunes entreprises du Québec inc. (JEQ)
187, rue Ste-Catherine est, Montréal QC H2X 1K8
Tél: 514-285-8944; *Téléc:* 514-285-1035
info@jeq.org
www.jequebec.org
Également appelé: Junior Achievement of Quebec
Aperçu: *Dimension:* moyenne; *Envergure:* provinciale; fondée en 1962
Mission: Diffusion de programmes d'éducation économique pour étudiants du secondaire et du collégial
Membre de: Junior Achievement of Canada
Membre(s) du bureau directeur:
Jean-Pierre Gaumont, Président et directeur général
jpgaumont@jeq.org
Stéphanie Bangs, Directrice aux programmes
sbangs@jeq.org
Julie Mongrain, Directrice au développement régional
jmongrain@jeq.org
Lise Ann Bigras, Coordonnatrice aux programmes
lbigras@jeq.org
250 bénévole(s)

Jeunesse Acadienne (JA)
5, av Marie-Stella, Summerside PE C1N 6M9
Tél: 902-888-1682; *Téléc:* 902-436-6936
coord1@ssta.org
www.jeunesseacadienne.ca
www.facebook.com/group.php?gid=2459928159
twitter.com/JeunesseAcadie
Aperçu: *Dimension:* petite; *Envergure:* provinciale; Organisme sans but lucratif; fondée en 1976
Mission: Permettre aux jeunes acadiens et francophones de la province à vivre et s'épanouir en français
Membre de: Fédération de la jeunesse canadienne-française inc; Société Nationale de l'Acadie
Membre(s) du bureau directeur:
Myranda Kelly, Présidente
myranda_4@hotmail.com
Katelyn Gill, Vice-Président
Kelly McGrath, Secrétaire-trésoriaire
Finances: *Budget de fonctionnement annuel:* $50,000-$100,000
Membre(s) du personnel: 1; 20 bénévole(s)
Membre: 150+; *Montant de la cotisation:* 10$
Activités: Regroupements de jeunes pour promouvoir des activités en sports, éducation, économie, politique et communications; promouvoir la langue française et la culture acadienne auprès des jeunes

Jeunesse Canada Monde ***See*** Canada World Youth

Jeunesse du Monde
920, rue Richelieu, Québec QC G1R 1L2
Tél: 410-694-1222; *Téléc:* 410-094-1227
Aperçu: *Dimension:* petite; *Envergure:* internationale; Organisme sans but lucratif; fondée en 1959
Mission: Former des jeunes à devenir des citoyens responsables et à s'engager dans la lutte contre toutes les formes de racisme, l'éducation à la paix, le respect des droits humains, la création de rapports de justice entre les peuples, le développement durable; proposer des programmes d'éducation planétaire dans les institutions scolaires et dans les groupes communautaires; appuyer des projets de développement durable menés par des partenaires en Amérique latine, en

Afrique, en Asie; offrir aux jeunes la possibilité de vivre des stages au sud et au nord
Membre(s) du bureau directeur:
Nicole Riberdy, Directrice
Finances: *Budget de fonctionnement annuel:* $500,000-$1.5 Million
Membre(s) du personnel: 9; 200 bénévole(s)

Jeunesse j'écoute ***See*** Kids Help Phone

Jeunesse Lambda
CP 321125, Succ. Saint-André, Montréal QC H2L 4Y5
Tél: 514-528-7535
info@jeunesselambda.org
www.algi.qc.ca/asso/jlambda/
www.facebook.com/pages/Jeunesse-Lambda/139443476158956
Aperçu: *Dimension:* petite; *Envergure:* locale
Mission: Groupe d'accueil francophone de discussion et d'activités par et pour les jeunes gais, lesbiennes, bisexuel(les).
Membre: 60

La Jeunesse Youth Orchestra (LJYO)
PO Box 134, Port Hope ON L1A 3W3
Toll-Free: 866-460-5596
info@ljyo.ca
www.ljyo.ca
Previous Name: North York Symphony Youth Orchestra
Overview: A small local organization overseen by Orchestras Canada
Chief Officer(s):
Michael Lyons, Music Director

Jeunesses Musicales du Canada (JMC) / Jeunesses Musicales of Canada (JMC)
305, av du Mont-Royal est, Montréal QC H2T 1P8
Tél: 514-845-4108; *Téléc:* 514-845-8241
Ligne sans frais: 877-377-7951
info@jeunessesmusicales.com
www.jeunessesmusicales.com
Aperçu: *Dimension:* moyenne; *Envergure:* nationale; Organisme sans but lucratif; fondée en 1949
Mission: To promote Canadian musical artists & develop audiences
Membre de: Jeunesses Musicales International; Conseil québécois de la musique
Membre(s) du bureau directeur:
Jacques Marquis, Directeur général et artistique Ext. 226
jmarquis@jmcanada.ca
Claudia Morissette, Directrice, Concerts Ext. 250
cmorissette@jmcanada.ca
Nathalie Allen, Directrice, Services financiers Ext. 248
nallen@jmcanada.ca
Isabelle Ligot, Directrice, Communications JMC/CMIM/FJMC Ext. 236
iligot@jmcanada.ca
Finances: *Budget de fonctionnement annuel:* $500,000-$1.5 Million
Membre(s) du personnel: 15; 400 bénévole(s)
Membre: 40 member centres in Ontario, Québec & New Brunswick; *Montant de la cotisation:* Schedule available
Activités: Family concerts; school concerts; touring artists (Ovation Series); Jeunesses Musicales World Orchestra (Orchestre mondial des jeunesses musicales) held each summer in a different member country of the JMI; *Stagiaires:* Oui; *Bibliothèque* Bibliothèque publique rendez-vous

Jeunesses Musicales of Canada ***Voir*** Jeunesses Musicales du Canada

Jeux du Commonwealth Canada ***See*** Commonwealth Games Canada

Jeux Olympiques Spéciaux du Québec Inc. (OSQ) / Québec Special Olympics
5311, boul. de Maisonneuve ouest, 2e étage, Montréal QC H4A 1Z5
Tél: 514-843-8778; *Téléc:* 514-843-8223
Ligne sans frais: 877-743-8778
www.olympiquesspeciaux.qc.ca
www.facebook.com/olympiquesspeciauxquebec
twitter.com/athletesOSQ
Aperçu: *Dimension:* petite; *Envergure:* provinciale; fondée en 1981 surveillé par Special Olympics Canada
Mission: Les Olympiques spéciaux, actifs dans plus de 170 pays, ont pour mission d'enrichir, par le sport, la vie des personnes présentant une déficience intellectuelle. Plus de 3.7 millions d'athlètes spéciaux, de tous âges, sont inscrits dans le monde dont plus de 31,000 au Canada et 4,850 aux programmes récréatifs scolaine ou compétitifs offerts dans toutes les régions du Québec. Les 14 sports officiels sont pratiqués à l'intérieur d'un réseau de compétitions annuelles, comptant plus de 80 événements conçus pour tous les niveaux d'habiletés.
Membre de: Special Olympics Canada
Membre(s) du bureau directeur:
Daniel Granger, Président
Membre: *Comités:* Comité provincial des programmes

Les Jeux Olympiques Spéciaux du Yukon ***See*** Special Olympics Yukon

Jewellers Vigilance Canada Inc. (JVC)
#600, 27 Queen St. East, Toronto ON M5C 2M6
Tel: 416-368-4840; *Fax:* 416-368-5552
Toll-Free: 800-636-9536
info@jewellersvigilance.ca
www.jewellersvigilance.ca
Overview: A small national organization founded in 1987
Mission: To advance ethical practices, establish a level playing field for the Canadian jewellery industry & provide crime prevention education for the trade.

Jewish Advisory Committee on Scouting & Guiding
265 Yorkland Blvd., 2nd Fl., Toronto ON M2J 5C7
Tel: 416-490-6364; *Fax:* 416-490-6911
Overview: A small local organization
Mission: Assists Scouts Canada & Girl Guides of Canada in meeting the religious & cultural needs of Jewish youth & adults in groups chartered to Jewish & non-Jewish organizations; promotes the use of scouting programs as an educational tool to strengthen Jewish values in a multicultural society
Affiliation(s): Canadian Jewish Congress; Scouts Canada; Girl Guides of Canada.
Finances: *Annual Operating Budget:* Less than $50,000
Membership: 1-99

Jewish Chamber of Commerce / Chambre de commerce juive
#400, 1 Cummings Square, Montréal QC H3W 1M6
Tel: 514-345-2645
info@jccmontreal.com
www.jccmontreal.com
www.linkedin.com/groups?home=&gid=3063
www.facebook.com/jccmontreal
Overview: A small local organization founded in 1995
Mission: To provide a network for Jewish business people in Montréal
Member of: A division of Federation CJA
Membre(s) du bureau directeur:
Michel Ohayon, Co-president
Stacey Stivaletti, Co-president

Jewish Child & Family Services (JCFS)
123 Doncaster St., #C200, Winnipeg MB R3N 2B2
Tel: 204-477-7430; *Fax:* 204-477-7450; *Crisis Hot-Line:* 204-946-9510
jcfs@jcfswinnipeg.org
www.jcfswinnipeg.org
www.linkedin.com/company/2869417
Overview: A small local charitable organization founded in 1952
Mission: To provide social services that focus on 3 areas: care of children, family problems, & concern for the needs of recent immigrants.
Chief Officer(s):
Bruce Caplan, President
Emily Shane, Executive Director
Finances: *Funding Sources:* Jewish Federation of Winnipeg/Combined Jewish Appeal; United Way; provincial governmnt; Jewish Foundation of Manitoba
Staff Member(s): 40
Activities: Counselling; services to the older adult; child welfare services; newcomer services; volunteer program; family life education: workshops on contemporary family issues; mental health program; homemaker registry;

Jewish Community Centre of Greater Vancouver
950 West 41 Ave., Vancouver BC V5Z 2N7
Tel: 604-257-5111; *Fax:* 604-257-5119
reception@jccgv.bc.ca
www.jccgv.com
www.facebook.com/256610085406
Overview: A small local organization founded in 1928
Mission: To bring together the Jewish community in Vancouver & provide activities & programs to the population
Member of: Vancouver Cultural Alliance
Chief Officer(s):
Eldad Goldfarb, Executive Director
eldad@jccgv.bc.ca
Membership: *Fees:* Schedule available
Activities: *Library:* Isaac Waldman Jewish Public Library; Open to public

Jewish Community Centre of Winnipeg ***See*** Rose & Max Rady Jewish Community Centre

Jewish Community Council of Montreal
6825 Decarie Blvd., Montréal QC H3W 3E4
Tel: 514-739-6363; *Fax:* 514-739-7024
Toll-Free: 866-739-6363
info@mk.ca
www.mk.ca
Also Known As: Montréal Kosher
Overview: A small local licensing organization founded in 1922
Affliation(s): Synagogues, Jewish organisations
Activities: Kosher supervision, counselling, divorces, disputes, community work

Jewish Community Foundation of Montréal / Fondation communautaire juive de Montréal
1 Cummings Square, Montréal QC H3W 1M6
Tel: 514-345-6414; *Fax:* 514-345-6410
info@jcfmontreal.org
www.jcfmontreal.org
Overview: A small local organization founded in 1971
Chief Officer(s):
Robert A. Kleinman, FCA, Executive Director
robert.kleinman@jcfmontreal.org
Joel Segal, President
president@jcfmontreal.org
Brenda Gewurz, Vice-President
seniorvp@jcfmontreal.org
Marlene Gerson, Director, Marketing
marlene.gerson@jcfmontreal.org
Joelle Mamane, Director, Finance
joelle.mamane@jcfmontreal.org
Finances: *Funding Sources:* Donations

Jewish Family & Child Service (JFCS)
4600 Bathurst St., 1st Fl., Toronto ON M2R 3V3
Tel: 416-638-7800; *Fax:* 416-638-7943
info@jfandcs.com
www.jfandcs.com
www.facebook.com/pages/Jewish-Family-Child/136955996482
Overview: A small local charitable organization founded in 1868
Mission: To support the healthy development of individuals, families & communities in the Greater Toronto Area through prevention, protection, counselling, education & advocacy services, within the context of Jewish values
Affiliation(s): Family Service Ontario; Association of Jewish Family & Children's Agencies; Canadian Family Services Accreditation Program; Children's Mental Health Ontario; Council on Accreditation; Ontario Association of Children's Aid Societies; Ontario Association of Social Workers; Ontario College of Social Workers and Social Service Workers
Chief Officer(s):
Richard L. Cummings, Executive Director
Staff Member(s): 120
Activities: *Internships:* Yes; *Speaker Service:* Yes

Jewish Family Services - Calgary (JESC)
#420, 5920 - 1A St. SW, Calgary AB T2H 0G3
Tel: 403-287-3510; *Fax:* 403-287-3735
info@jfsc.org
www.jfsc.org
Overview: A medium-sized local charitable organization founded in 1961
Mission: To strengthen the community by helping people in the spirit of Jewish tradition & values
Member of: Association of Jewish Family & Children's Agencies; Family Service Canada
Chief Officer(s):
Marty Hornstein, Executive Director
Finances: *Annual Operating Budget:* $500,000-$1.5 Million; *Funding Sources:* United Way; Calgary Foundation; Jewish Community Council; City of Calgary; B'Nai B'Rith Lodge; Mazon Canada
Staff Member(s): 21; 70 volunteer(s)
Activities: *Library* by appointment

Jewish Family Services Edmonton
#200, 10235 - 124 St., Edmonton AB T5N 1P9
Tel: 780-454-1194; *Fax:* 780-482-4784
info@jfse.org
www.jfse.org
twitter.com/JFS_Edmonton
Overview: A small local charitable organization founded in 1955
Mission: To provide strength & support to individuals & families in need, in a manner sensitive to Jewish values
Member of: Association of Jewish Family & Children's Agencies
Chief Officer(s):
Larry Derkach, Executive Director
tikunolam@jfse.org
Finances: *Annual Operating Budget:* $500,000-$1.5 Million; *Funding Sources:* United Way; United Jewish Appeal; donors; Jewish Immigrant Aid Services; Family & Community Support
Staff Member(s): 33
Activities: Bereavement support; counselling; immigrant support advocacy; *Library:* Edmonton Bereavement Centre

Jewish Family Services of Ottawa-Carleton (JFSOC)
#300, 2255 Carling Ave., Ottawa ON K2B 7Z5
Tel: 613-722-2225; *Fax:* 613-722-7570
info@jfsottawa.com
www.jfsottawa.com
Also Known As: Jewish Social Service Agency of Ottawa-Carleton
Overview: A small local charitable organization founded in 1979
Mission: Through Jewish traditions, values & culture, to build a community where people can learn to care for themselves & each other with dignity, respect & compassion
Affliation(s): Family Service Ontario Agencies; Family Service Canada Agencies
Chief Officer(s):
Mark Zarecki, Executive Director
mzarecki@jfsottawa.com
Activities: Social services; seniors services; settlement services; employment services; *Internships:* Yes; *Library:* Resource Centre

The Jewish Federation of Greater Toronto *See* UJA Federation of Greater Toronto

Jewish Federation of Greater Vancouver (JFGV)
#200, 950 West 41 Ave., Vancouver BC V5Z 2N7
Tel: 604-257-5100; *Fax:* 604-257-5110
reception@jewishvancouver.com
www.jewishvancouver.com
www.facebook.com/jewishvancouver
twitter.com/JewishVancouver
Overview: A medium-sized local charitable organization founded in 1932
Mission: Committed to building a strong, vibrant & enduring Jewish community in the Lower Mainland, in Israel & throughout the world by nurturing those values, practices & traditions which sustain & enrich Judaism & the Jewish people; to serve the Greater Vancouver Jewish community by working in partnership with community members & other agencies to: identify & plan for community needs; enhance mutual cooperation; raise & allocate funds for programs & services locally, nationally, in Israel & worldwide; develop & sustain leadership; encourage involvement in Jewish communal life
Affliation(s): United Israel Appeal Federations Canada; United Jewish Communities
Chief Officer(s):
Ezra S. Shanken, Chief Executive Officer
eshanken@jewishvancouver.com
Finances: *Annual Operating Budget:* Greater than $5 Million
Staff Member(s): 21
Membership: *Committees:* Executive; Finance; Allocations Planning; Israel & Overseas Affairs; Yom Hazikaron; High School Debate; Axis Steering

Jewish Federation of Ottawa
21 Nadolny Sachs Private, Ottawa ON K2A 1R9
Tel: 613-798-4696; *Fax:* 613-798-4695
infocentre@jewishottawa.com
jewishottawa.com
www.facebook.com/JFedOttawa
twitter.com/JewishOttawa
Overview: A medium-sized local organization founded in 1934
Mission: Promoting & preserving the Jewish community in Ottawa
Chief Officer(s):
Andrea Freedman, President & CEO
afreedman@jewishottawa.com
Staff Member(s): 11
Membership: *Committees:* Resource Development; Outreach; Supplemental Schools; Communications & Community Relations; Finance, Audit & Administration; Planning; Grants & Evaluations; Ottawa Jewish Archives; Shoah; Hillel Ottawa; Partnership 2Gether
Activities: Golf tournament; Missions; Mitzvah Day; Walkathon; Dragon Boat Team

Jewish Federations of Canada - UIA (JFC-UIA)
#315, 4600 Bathurst St., Toronto ON M2R 3V3
Tel: 416-636-7655; *Fax:* 416-636-9897
info@jfcuia.org
www.jewishcanada.org
www.facebook.com/JewishFederationsofCanadaUIA
twitter.com/jfcuia
www.youtube.com/user/JewishFedofCanada
Also Known As: United Israel Appeal of Canada
Overview: A small international organization founded in 1967
Mission: To raise money for Canadian Jewish organizations & to promote their efforts
Chief Officer(s):
Linda Kislowicz, President & CEO
lkislowicz@jfcuia.org

Jewish Foundation of Manitoba
#C400, 123 Doncaster St., Winnipeg MB R3N 2B2
Tel: 204-477-7520; *Fax:* 204-477-7527
Toll-Free: 855-284-1918
info@jewishfoundation.org
www.jewishfoundation.org
twitter.com/jfm_mb
Overview: A small provincial charitable organization
Mission: To provide funding to organizations that are involved with education, arts & culture, health & social services, Jewish life, recreation & religion
Chief Officer(s):
Marsha Cowan, Chief Executive Officer
mcowan@jewishfoundation.org
Staff Member(s): 10
Membership: *Committees:* Audit; Endowment Book of Life; Grants; Investment; Special Awards; Special Grants; Scholarship; Women's Endowment Fund Grants; Women's Endowment Fund

Jewish Free Loan Toronto (JFLT)
#340, 4600 Bathurst St., Toronto ON M2R 3V3
Tel: 416-635-1217; *Fax:* 416-635-8926
tjflc.com
Previous Name: Toronto Jewish Free Loan Cassa
Overview: A small local charitable organization founded in 1924
Mission: Offering interest-free loans to needy individuals of the Jewish community in the Greater Toronto Area.
Chief Officer(s):
David Sefton, President
Staff Member(s): 3

Jewish Genealogical Institute of British Columbia
c/o 950 West 41 Ave., Vancouver BC V5Z 2N7
Tel: 604-321-9870
jgibc@yahoo.com
jgibc.shutterfly.com
Overview: A small provincial organization founded in 1992
Mission: To research genealogy & encourage the exploration of the community's Jewish heritage.
Membership: *Fees:* $30 individual; $45 family

Jewish Genealogical Society of Canada (JGSC)
PO Box 91006, 2901 Bayview Ave., Toronto ON M2K 2Y6
Tel: 647-247-6414
info@jgstoronto.ca
www.jgstoronto.ca
Previous Name: Jewish Genealogical Society of Toronto
Overview: A medium-sized national charitable organization founded in 1985
Mission: To foster interest in Jewish genealogical research; To facilitate the pursuit of Jewish genealogical research domestically & internationally; To provide a forum for the exchange of knowledge & information among people interested in Jewish genealogy
Member of: International Association of Jewish Genealogical Societies (IAJGS)
Chief Officer(s):
Harvey Glasner, President
president@jgstoronto.ca
Faye Blum, Secretary
secretary@jgstoronto.ca
Sid Disenhouse, Treasurer
treasurer@jgstoronto.ca
Finances: *Funding Sources:* Membership fees; Donations
Membership: *Fees:* $36 individual; $18 student
Activities: Offering workshops & guest lectures; Conducting the Cemetery Digital Photography Project; *Library:* Canadiana Room, North York Central Library

Jewish Genealogical Society of Toronto *See* Jewish Genealogical Society of Canada

Jewish General Hospital Foundation (JGHF) / Hôpital général juif fondation (HGJF)
#A107, 3755 Côte-Sainte-Catherine Rd., Montréal QC H3T 1E2
Tel: 514-340-8251; *Fax:* 514-340-8220
info@jghfoundation.org
www.jghfoundation.org
www.facebook.com/FHGJ.JGHF
Overview: A small local charitable organization founded in 1969
Mission: To raise money on behalf of the Jewish General Hospital in order to fund research & improve patient care
Chief Officer(s):
Myer Bick, President & CEO
Finances: *Annual Operating Budget:* Greater than $5 Million
Staff Member(s): 25
Membership: *Committees:* Executive; Invesment & Finance; Audit; Corporate Governance; Strategic Planning; Human Resources; Nominating

Jewish Heritage Centre of Western Canada Inc. (JHC)
123 Doncaster St., #C140, Winnipeg MB R3N 2B2
Tel: 204-477-7460; *Fax:* 204-477-7465
jewishheritage@jhcwc.org
www.jhcwc.org
Also Known As: Jewish Heritage Centre
Previous Name: Jewish Historical Society of Western Canada
Overview: A small local charitable organization founded in 1999
Mission: The Jewish Heritage Centre is composed of The Jewish Historical Society of Western Canada, Marion & Ed Vickar Jewish Museum of Western Canada, Freeman Foundation Holocaust Education Centre & Genealogical Institute
Finances: *Annual Operating Budget:* $250,000-$500,000
Staff Member(s): 5; 63 volunteer(s)
Membership: 300; *Fees:* $50; *Committees:* Finance; Membership; Holocaust Education Program; Exhibition; Acquisition
Activities: Research; Holocaust education; preservation of documents, photos, sound; *Speaker Service:* Yes; *Library:* Archives

Jewish Historical Society of BC (JHS)
c/o Jewish Museum & Archives of BC, 6184 Ash St., Vancouver BC V5Z 3G9
Tel: 604-257-5199
info@jewishmuseum.ca
www.jewishmuseum.ca
Overview: A small provincial charitable organization founded in 1971
Mission: To document & preserve the history of the Jewish community in BC & its contribution to the development of BC
Member of: Vancouver Historical Society; Canadian Jewish Historical Society; British Columbia Museum Association; Association for Canadian Jewish Studies; BC Historical Federation
Chief Officer(s):
Perry Seidelman, President
Finances: *Funding Sources:* Membership dues; donations; sale of books, videos, cards; government & foundation grants
Membership: *Fees:* $54 basic; $75 institutions; *Member Profile:* Members of the British Columbia Jewish Community
Activities: Lecture series; exhibits & displays; archival reference service; *Library:* Nemetz Jewish Community Archives; by appointment

Jewish Historical Society of Southern Alberta (JHSSA)
1607 - 90 Ave. SW, Calgary AB T2V 4V7
Tel: 403-444-3171; *Fax:* 403-253-7915
jhssa@shaw.ca
www.jhssa.org
twitter.com/JHSSA1
Overview: A small local charitable organization founded in 1990
Mission: To preserve the history of Jewish individuals, businesses, organizations & activities of southern Alberta
Chief Officer(s):
Betty Sherwood, President

Finances: *Funding Sources:* Fundraising; private donations; membership fees
Staff Member(s): 1
Membership: *Fees:* $18 individual; $36 family; $50 patrons; $100 benefactors
Activities: Oral history interviews; gathering of museum & archival material; *Library:* Harry & Martha Cohen Library; Open to public by appointment

Jewish Historical Society of Western Canada *See* Jewish Heritage Centre of Western Canada Inc.

Jewish Immigrant Aid Services of Canada (JIAS) / Services canadiens d'assistance aux immigrants juifs

#300, 2255 Carling Ave., Ottawa ON K2B 7Z5
Tel: 613-722-2225; *Fax:* 613-722-5750
national@jias.org
www.jias.org
Overview: A medium-sized international charitable organization founded in 1922
Mission: To serve the needs of Jewish immigrants & refugees; to facilitate the legal entry of Jewish immigrants to Canada; to provide services about immigration, naturalization, resettlement & integration.
Chief Officer(s):
Mark Zarecki, Executive Director
mzarecki@jfsottawa.com
Finances: *Funding Sources:* Jewish community; government grants
Activities: Scholarship Fund; *Speaker Service:* Yes

Agence Ometz
Cummings Square, #1, 51 Côte Ste-Catherine Rd., Montréal QC H3W 1M6
Tel: 514-342-0000; *Fax:* 514-342-2371
info@ometz.ca
www.ometz.ca
www.linkedin.com/company/agence-ometz
www.facebook.com/AgenceOmetz
twitter.com/ometz
www.youtube.com/agenceometz
Mission: To provide employment, family, and immigration services to the Montreal Jewish Community.
Chief Officer(s):
Howard Berger, Co-Executive Director
Gail Small, Co-Executive Director

Jewish Immigrant Aid Services of Canada - Montreal *See* Jewish Immigrant Aid Services of Canada

Jewish Information Referral Service Montréal (JIRS) / Le Service juif d'information et de référence

1 Cummings Square, Montréal QC H3W 1M6
Tel: 514-735-3541; *Fax:* 514-735-8972
fcja@federationcja.org
www.federationcja.org
www.facebook.com/federationcja
twitter.com/federationcja
www.youtube.com/federationcja
Previous Name: Jewish Information Service Montreal
Overview: A small local organization
Mission: To bring together the Jewish community in Montréal
Affliation(s): Alliance of Information & Referral Systems Inc.
Chief Officer(s):
Deborah Corber, CEO
Finances: *Annual Operating Budget:* Greater than $5 Million
Membership: *Committees:* Allocations & Community Relations; Audit; Budget & Finance; Compensation; Development; Governance & Ethics
Activities: *Rents Mailing List:* Yes

Jewish Information Service Montreal *See* Jewish Information Referral Service Montréal

Jewish Information Service of Greater Toronto (JIST)

4600 Bathurst St., Toronto ON M2R 3V3
Tel: 416-635-5600; *Fax:* 416-849-1005
jinfo@ujafed.org
www.jewishtoronto.com
Overview: A small local organization founded in 1973
Mission: To offer information & referral to walk-ins, by phone, & by e-mail; To support & maintain "Doing Jewish in Toronto"
Member of: UJA Federation of Greater Toronto
Affliation(s): Latner Centre for Jewish Knowledge & Heritage of UJA Federation

Jews for Jesus

#402, 1315 Lawrence Ave. East, Toronto ON M3A 3R3
Tel: 416-444-7020; *Fax:* 416-444-1028
toronto@jewsforjesus.ca
www.jewsforjesus.ca
Overview: A small local charitable organization founded in 1981
Mission: Jews for Jesus Canada is a Jewish evangelistic agency dedicated to bringing the Gospel into places where a significantly Jewish testimony is needed.
Member of: Canadian Council of Christian Charities; Evangelical Fellowship of Canada; Interdenominational Foreign Mission Association
Chief Officer(s):
Andrew Barron, Canadian Director
Staff Member(s): 6; 10 volunteer(s)

Jews for Judaism

PO Box 41032, 2795 Bathurst St., Toronto ON M6B 4J6
Tel: 416-789-0020; *Fax:* 416-789-0030
Toll-Free: 866-307-4362
toronto@jewsforjudaism.ca
www.jewsforjudaism.ca
www.facebook.com/jewsforjudaismcanada
twitter.com/JewsforJudaism1
www.youtube.com/user/JewsforJudaismCanada
Overview: A small international organization
Mission: To counteract the multi-million dollar efforts of numerous cults & missionary groups who target Jews for conversion
Chief Officer(s):
Julius Ciss, Executive Director
juliusciss@bellnet.ca
Finances: *Funding Sources:* Corporate sponsorship, donations

JMJ Children's Fund of Canada Inc

PO Box 20051, 390 Rideau St. East, Ottawa ON K1N 9N5
Tel: 613-565-4779
www.jmjchildren.ca
Overview: A small national organization founded in 1972
Mission: To assist children in need of food, medication & schooling; to provide physiotherapy for the physically disabled
Chief Officer(s):
Frank Pantano, President
Activities: sponsoring students in schools in Malawi, Zaire, Haiti, and the Dominican Republic; supporting medical clinics that treat children for malnutrition, tuberculosis, tropical diseases and AIDS; Providing support to children so that the family unit stays together in difficult times; Emergency relief to children in crisis situations; providing food, clothing and medical assistance when required

Jobs Unlimited

1079 York St., Fredericton NB E3B 3S4
Tel: 506-458-9380
www.jobsunlimited.nb.ca
Overview: A small local charitable organization
Mission: To facilitate work placement for individuals who face barriers to employment
Affliation(s): United Way
Chief Officer(s):
Maynard Shore, Chair
Abdel Belhadjsalah, Executive Director
Staff Member(s): 45
Activities: *Awareness Events:* Employers Appreciation Night, Oct.; *Internships:* Yes; *Speaker Service:* Yes

Jockey Club du Canada *See* Jockey Club of Canada

Jockey Club of Canada / Jockey Club du Canada

PO Box 66, Stn. B, Toronto ON M9W 5K9
Tel: 416-675-7756; *Fax:* 416-675-6378
jockeyclub@bellnet.ca
www.jockeyclubcanada.com
twitter.com/jockeyclubofCAN
Overview: A small national licensing organization founded in 1973
Mission: Promote good quality racing throughout Canada
Member of: Thoroughbred Racing Industry participants in Canada
Affliation(s): The Jockey Club (New York)
Chief Officer(s):
James Lawson, Chief Steward
Stacie Roberts, Executive Director
Membership: *Member Profile:* Liaises with foreign Jockey Clubs; promotes Thoroughbred ownership; and represents Canada at international racing conferences.
Activities: *Library* Open to public by appointment

Jockeys Benefit Association of Canada (JBAC)

c/o Thoroughbred Race Office, 555 Rexdale Blvd., Toronto ON M9W 5L2
Tel: 416-798-8715
jbacmanager@mac.com
jbac.ca/trainers/jbac
Overview: A small national organization
Mission: The Jockey's Benefit Association of Canada (JBAC) has been in operation for over 40 years as a non profit corporation which operates to assist & represent jockeys as a group across Canada. Operated under a number of directors across the country, the JBAC is the official spokesperson of jockeys in Canada.
Chief Officer(s):
Emma-Jayne Wilson, President
Robert King Jr., National Manager
Membership: 150

Jodo Shinshu Buddhist Temples of Canada

11786 Fentiman Pl., Richmond BC V7E 6M6
Tel: 604-272-3330; *Fax:* 604-272-6865
jsbtcheadquarters@shaw.ca
www.bcc.ca
www.youtube.com/user/livingdharmacentre
Previous Name: Buddhist Churches of Canada
Overview: A medium-sized national charitable organization founded in 1933
Mission: Propagation of Buddhism
Affliation(s): Jodo Shinshu Hongwanji, Kyoto
Chief Officer(s):
Leslie Kawamura, Director, Living Dharma Centre
Finances: *Annual Operating Budget:* $100,000-$250,000
Staff Member(s): 9
Membership: 2,500; *Fees:* $45
Activities: *Speaker Service:* Yes; *Library* by appointment

The Joe Brain Foundation

609 Holland Blvd., Winnipeg MB R3P 1X1
Tel: 204-771-4583
Overview: A small provincial charitable organization founded in 1977
Mission: To advance education, with particular emphasis on mining research & education, medical research & relief of poverty
Finances: *Annual Operating Budget:* $50,000-$100,000; *Funding Sources:* Investment income
4 volunteer(s)
Membership: 1-99

John Gordon Home

596 Pall Mall St., London ON N5Y 2Z9
Tel: 519-433-3951; *Fax:* 519-433-1314
johngordonhome@lrah.ca
www.johngordonhome.ca
Also Known As: London Regional AIDS Hospice
Overview: A small local organization founded in 1991 overseen by Canadian AIDS Society
Mission: To provide compassionate care to people with AIDS & HIV in a comforting, non-discriminatory, homeike environment; to provide medical, psychosocial, spiritual & personal support
Member of: Ontario AIDS Network; Canadian AIDS Society; Ontario Non-Profit Housing Association
Chief Officer(s):
Bruce Rankin, Executive Director
brucerankin@lrah.ca
Finances: *Annual Operating Budget:* $250,000-$500,000; *Funding Sources:* Donations; Ministry of Health - Long-Term Care Division
Membership: 200; *Fees:* $10
Activities: Personal care; palliative care; psychological support; supportive housing; *Internships:* Yes; *Speaker Service:* Yes

The John Howard Society of British Columbia

763 Kingsway, Vancouver BC V5V 3C2
Tel: 604-872-5651; *Fax:* 604-872-8737
jhsed@jhslmbc.ca
www.johnhowardbc.ca
Overview: A medium-sized provincial organization founded in 1931
Mission: To prevent crime & reform the justice system through alternative programming
Affliation(s): John Howard Society of Canada
Chief Officer(s):
Tim Veresh, Executive Director
Finances: *Funding Sources:* Government; Foundations; Non-profit Organizations; Donations

The John Howard Society of Canada / Société John Howard du Canada
809 Blackburn Mews, Kingston ON K7P 2N6
Tel: 613-384-6272; *Fax:* 613-384-1847
national@johnhoward.ca
www.johnhoward.ca
twitter.com/JohnHoward_Can
Overview: A medium-sized national charitable organization founded in 1978
Mission: To promote effective, just, & humane responses to the causes & consequences of crime
Chief Officer(s):
Catherine Latimer, Executive Director
Trish Cheverie, President
Finances: *Annual Operating Budget:* $250,000-$500,000; *Funding Sources:* Federal Grant; Donations; Project Contracts
Staff Member(s): 2; 15 volunteer(s)
Membership: *Fees:* Schedule available; *Member Profile:* Provincial/territorial society
Activities: *Speaker Service:* Yes

John Howard Society of Kawartha Lakes & Haliburton Outreach Literacy Program
31 Peel St., Lindsay ON K9V 3L9
Tel: 705-328-0472; *Fax:* 705-328-2549
www.jhscklh.on.ca
Previous Name: Outreach Literacy Program of the John Howard Society of Victoria / Haliburton / Simcoe & Muskoka
Overview: A small local charitable organization founded in 1987
Mission: To prevent crime by offering services such as community education, reform, & advocacy
Finances: *Funding Sources:* Government; United Way
Activities: Providing tutoring & small classes for adults in basic skills, such as readign & writing

The John Howard Society of Manitoba, Inc. (JHSMB)
583 Ellice Ave., Winnipeg MB R3B 1Z7
Tel: 204-775-1514; *Fax:* 204-775-1670
office@johnhoward.mb.ca
www.johnhoward.mb.ca
www.facebook.com/137026123009646
twitter.com/JHSofMB
Previous Name: Manitoba Prisoner's Aid Group
Overview: A medium-sized provincial organization founded in 1957
Mission: To achieve restorative justice through measures that resolve conflicts, repair them, & restore peaceful relations in society
Member of: John Howard Society of Canada
Chief Officer(s):
John Hutton, Executive Director, 204-775-1514
jhutton@johnhoward.mb.ca
Finances: *Funding Sources:* Solicitor General of Canada; United Way; Manitoba Department of Justice
Staff Member(s): 13
Activities: *Library:* Justice Resource Centre; Open to public
Publications:
• The Inside Scoop [a publication of The John Howard Society of Manitoba, Inc.]
Type: Newsletter
Profile: Prison literacy & art, created by inmates for inmates
• The John Howard Society of Manitoba, Inc. Annual Report
Type: Yearbook; *Frequency:* Annually
Profile: Reports on the society's key areas, such as reintegration, literacy, volunteers, & finances

The John Howard Society of New Brunswick
68 Carleton St., Saint John NB E2L 2Z4
Tel: 506-657-5547; *Fax:* 506-649-2006
info@jhssj.nb.ca
www.johnhowardnb.ca
Overview: A small provincial organization
Mission: To promote peace through understanding & reaction of problems with the criminal disciplinary system
Chief Officer(s):
William Bastarache, Executive Director
Staff Member(s): 5
Activities: Advocacy; reseach; communication; community education; coalition building; resource development; stewardship

The John Howard Society of Newfoundland & Labrador (JHSNL)
426 Water St., St. John's NL A1C 1E2
Tel: 709-726-5500; *Fax:* 709-726-5509
info@jhsnl.ca
www.johnhowardnl.ca
Overview: A medium-sized provincial charitable organization founded in 1951
Mission: To reduce crime primarily by providing program opportunities for the rehabilitation of offenders
Member of: John Howard Society of Canada
Chief Officer(s):
Bryan Purcell, President
Finances: *Annual Operating Budget:* $500,000-$1.5 Million
Membership: *Committees:* Executive; Personnel; Scholarship; Nomination
Activities: Group homes for young offenders; public education & reform activities; prison services; counselling services; employment/training services; *Awareness Events:* John Howard Society Week, Feb.

Loretta Bartlett Home for Youth
278 Curling St., Corner Brook NL A2H 6G1
Tel: 709-785-7656; *Fax:* 709-785-2927
www.johnhowardnl.ca/services/loretta.html
Chief Officer(s):
Rosemary Mullins, Coordinator

West Bridge House
92 West St., Stephenville NL A2N 1E4
Tel: 709-643-2903; *Fax:* 709-643-3084
www.johnhowardnl.ca/services/wb.html
Chief Officer(s):
Audrey Gracie, Director
audreygracie@nf.aibn.com

The John Howard Society of Northwest Territories
4901 - 48th St., Yellowknife NT X1A 3S3
Tel: 867-920-4276; *Fax:* 867-669-9715
Overview: A small local charitable organization founded in 1992
Member of: John Howard Society of Canada
Chief Officer(s):
Lydia Bardak, Executive Director
Finances: *Funding Sources:* Dept. of Justice; revenue
Activities: Diversion program; fine options; community service hours; public education; services to offenders & families of offenders; counselling; after care

The John Howard Society of Nova Scotia
#1, 541 Sackville Dr., Lr sackville NS B4C 1S2
Tel: 902-429-6429
contact@ns.johnhoward.ca
ns.johnhoward.ca
Overview: A small provincial organization
Chief Officer(s):
Janis Atkin, President
Activities: Public education; work resource centre; research; after care; parole supervision

The John Howard Society of Ontario
#603, 111 Peter St., Toronto ON M5V 2H1
Tel: 416-408-4282; *Fax:* 416-408-2991
jhso@johnhoward.on.ca
www.johnhoward.on.ca
Overview: A medium-sized provincial charitable organization founded in 1929
Mission: To promote effective, just, & humane responses to crime & its causes
Member of: John Howard Society of Canada; Criminal Justice Association
Chief Officer(s):
Paula Osmok, Executive Director
Finances: *Annual Operating Budget:* $500,000-$1.5 Million
Staff Member(s): 7
Activities: *Rents Mailing List:* Yes; *Library* Open to public

The John Howard Society of Prince Edward Island
PO Box 1211, 163 Queen St., Charlottetown PE C1A 7M8
Tel: 902-566-5425; *Fax:* 902-628-6842
johnhowardsociety@pei.aibn.com
pei.johnhoward.ca
Overview: A small provincial charitable organization founded in 1960
Chief Officer(s):
Donna Hartley, Executive Director
Finances: *Annual Operating Budget:* $100,000-$250,000
Staff Member(s): 8; 9 volunteer(s)

The John Howard Society of Saskatchewan
1801 Toronto St., Regina SK S4P 1M7
Tel: 306-584-2115; *Fax:* 306-347-0707
Toll-Free: 877-584-2115
jhsinfo@sk.johnhoward.ca
www.sk.johnhoward.ca
www.facebook.com/218360001561654
twitter.com/JHSocietySask
Overview: A small provincial charitable organization
Chief Officer(s):
Greg Fleet, Executive Director
g.fleet@sk.johnhoward.ca

John Milton Society for the Blind in Canada
#202, 40 St. Clair Ave. East, Toronto ON M4T 1M9
Tel: 416-960-3953; *Fax:* 416-960-3570
Overview: A small national charitable organization
Mission: To provide Christian materials in alternative formats to blind, deafblind, & visually impaired Canadians
Chief Officer(s):
Barry Brown, Executive Director
bbrown@jmsblind.ca

Joint Centre for Bioethics
University of Toronto, #754, 155 College St., Toronto ON M5T 1P8
Tel: 416-978-2709; *Fax:* 416-978-1911
jcb.info@utoronto.ca
www.jointcentreforbioethics.ca
www.facebook.com/164894946861612
twitter.com/utjcb
Overview: A small national organization founded in 1995
Mission: A network of individuals and institutions committed to improving healthcare through leadership in bioethics research, education, practice, and public engagement.
Chief Officer(s):
Jennifer L. Gibson, Interim Director
Carmen Alfred, Academic Secretary, 416-978-0871
carmen.alfred@utoronto.ca
Rhonda Martin, Executive Assistant
Finances: *Funding Sources:* Government (56%), academic institutions (37%), individuals and foundations (4%), and private sector (3%)
Membership: 215

Joint Forum of Financial Market Regulators / Forum conjoint des autorités de réglementation du marché financier
c/o Joint Forum Secretariat, 5160 Yonge St., 17th Fl., Box 85, Toronto ON M2N 6L9
Tel: 416-590-7526; *Fax:* 416-590-7070
jointforum@fsco.gov.on.ca
www.jointforum.ca
Overview: A small national organization founded in 1999
Mission: Established as a mechanism through which pension, securities and insurance regulators could co-ordinate, harmonize and streamline the regulation of financial products and services in Canada.
Affliation(s): Canadian Council of Insurance Regulators (CCIR); the Canadian Securities Administrators (CSA); Canadian Association of Pension Supervisory Authorities (CAPSA)
Chief Officer(s):
Sabitha Kanagasabai, Acting Policy Manager, 416-226-7781
sabitha.kanagasabai@fsco.gov.on.ca
Activities: Strategic planning; publications; meetings;

Joint Regional Library Boards Association of Nova Scotia *See* Library Boards Association of Nova Scotia

Jour de la terre Canada *See* Earth Day Canada

Journalistes canadiens pour la liberté d'expression *See* Canadian Journalists for Free Expression

Judo Alberta
Percy Page Centre, 11759 Groat Rd., Edmonton AB T5M 3K6
Tel: 780-427-8379; *Fax:* 780-447-1915
Toll-Free: 866-919-5836
judo@judoalberta.com
www.judoalberta.com
www.facebook.com/judoalberta
twitter.com/JudoAlberta
Also Known As: Alberta Kodokan Black Belt Association - AKBBA
Overview: A small provincial organization founded in 1960 overseen by Judo Canada
Mission: To promote the principles & teachings of the sport of kodokan judo to all levels in all parts of Alberta; to have qualified facilities & equipment in places throughout Alberta; to promote judo as a lifelong interest; to develop competitive opportunities throughout Alberta; to promote greater public awareness of the sport; to increase the number of participants in the sport; to develop & maintain qualified judo officials & coaches throughout Alberta; to develop high performance athletes; to develop

recreational opportunities throughout Alberta
Member of: Judo Canada
Affliation(s): International Judo Federation
Chief Officer(s):
Kelly Thornton, President
Finances: *Annual Operating Budget:* $100,000-$250,000
Staff Member(s): 2; 200 volunteer(s)
Membership: 1,200; *Fees:* $40; *Committees:* Grading; Technical; Referee; Coaching; Women's Ctee
Activities: *Library:* Video Library; Open to public

Judo BC

#523, 4438 West 10th Ave., Vancouver BC V6R 4R8
Tel: 604-333-3513; *Fax:* 604-333-3514
www.judobc.ca
twitter.com/OfficialJudoBC
Overview: A medium-sized provincial organization founded in 1952 overseen by Judo Canada
Mission: Provincial sport governing body working to promote & support the development of all aspects of Judo in the province; to inform & report on all aspects of Judo & planned activities in BC & elsewhere; to promote Judo & public awareness of the sport; to increase the number of participants in the sport; to keep close liaison with Judo clubs in BC in order to share all things of common interest to members
Member of: Judo Canada; Sport BC; Pan-American Confederation of Judo; International Judo Federation; Kodokan Judo Institute
Chief Officer(s):
Sandy Kent, President
president@judobc.ca
Finances: *Annual Operating Budget:* $100,000-$250,000; *Funding Sources:* Provincial government; self-generated revenue; gaming
Staff Member(s): 1
Membership: 2,200; *Fees:* $20-$50; *Member Profile:* Clubs must go through a one-year probationary period; *Committees:* Technical; Grading & Kata Board; Referee; NCCP; Membership
Activities: Coaching clinics; tournaments; insurance; referee training; athlete training; awareness campaign; referrals; policy manual; referee book; *Awareness Events:* Judo Awareness Week, 3rd week of Sept.; *Library* by appointment

Judo Canada

#212, 1725 St. Laurent Blvd., Ottawa ON K1G 3V4
Tel: 613-738-1200; *Fax:* 613-738-1299
Toll-Free: 877-738-5836
Other Communication: www.livestream.com/judocanada
info@judocanada.org
www.judocanada.org
www.facebook.com/judocanada
twitter.com/judocanada
www.youtube.com/judocanada2012
Also Known As: Canadian Kodokan Black Belt Association
Overview: A large national charitable organization founded in 1956
Mission: To promote the principles & teachings of the sport of Kodokan Judo; To work towards the advancement of Judo throughout Canada
Member of: Pan American Judo Union
Affliation(s): International Judo Federation
Chief Officer(s):
Mike Tamura, President
Andrien Landry, Executive Director
ed@judocanada.org
Andrzej Sadej, Director, Sports
andrzej@judocanada.org
Gosselin Nathalie, Coordinator, Project
ngosselin@rogers.com
Francine Latreille, Office Manager
Finances: *Funding Sources:* Sport Canada; Membership dues; Sponsorships
Staff Member(s): 9
Membership: *Member Profile:* Black belt & provincial members; *Committees:* High Performance; NCCP/LTAD; Women's Programs; Grading; Kata; Referee; Aboriginal & Territorial Affairs; Tournament; Legal; Awards; Finance & Audit
Activities: Providing Rendez-Vous Canada & the Canadian Championships; *Library* by appointment

National Training Centre
5319, av Notre-Dame-de-Grâce, Montréal QC H4A 1L2
Toll-Free: 877-738-5836
hp@judocanada.org
Chief Officer(s):
Nicolas Gill, Director, High Performance
Isabelle Pearson, Chief Therapist

Judo Manitoba

c/o Sport Manitoba, #311, 145 Pacific Ave., Winnipeg MB R3B 2Z6
Tel: 204-925-5691; *Fax:* 204-925-5703
judo@sportmanitoba.ca
www.judomanitoba.mb.ca
Also Known As: Manitoba Judo Black Belt Association Inc.
Overview: A small provincial organization founded in 1963 overseen by Judo Canada
Mission: To propagate & perpetuate the sport of Judo; to improve the calibre of athletes, referees & coaches
Member of: Judo Canada; Sport Manitoba; International Judo Federation; Canadian Olympic Committee
Chief Officer(s):
Oscar Li, Executive Director
David Minuk, President
Finances: *Annual Operating Budget:* $100,000-$250,000
Staff Member(s): 2
Membership: 86 Black Belts + 594 others; *Fees:* $50; *Committees:* Fundraising; Officials; Grading; Bingo; NCCP; Grassroots; Awards
Activities: *Library*

Judo New Brunswick / Judo Nouveau Brunswick

#13, 900 Hanwell Rd., Fredericton NB E3B 6A3
Tel: 506-451-1322
www.judonb.org
Also Known As: Judo NB
Overview: A small local organization overseen by Judo Canada
Mission: To promote judo in New Brunswick
Member of: Judo Canada
Membership: 500; *Committees:* Grading

Judo Nouveau Brunswick *See* Judo New Brunswick

Judo Nova Scotia

10 Mystic Ridge, Brookside NS B3T 1S9
Tel: 902-223-7574
admin@judons.ca
www.judons.ca
www.facebook.com/judons
Overview: A small provincial organization overseen by Judo Canada
Mission: To promote the principles of judo &, in collaboration with members & interested parties, to work towards the advancement of judo, at all levels & areas of Nova Scotia.
Member of: Judo Canada
Chief Officer(s):
Dave Anderson, President
dave@judons.ca
Scott Tanner, Provincial Coach, 902-223-7574
scott@judons.ca
Gordon Brown, Administrative Manager

Judo Nunavut

PO Box 2135, Iqaluit NU X0A 0H0
Tel: 867-979-4540
judo.nunavut@gmail.com
www.facebook.com/NunavutJudo
Overview: A small provincial organization overseen by Judo Canada
Member of: Judo Canada

Judo Ontario

6 Garamond Crt., Toronto ON M3C 1Z5
Tel: 416-447-5836; *Fax:* 416-449-5836
Toll-Free: 866-553-5836
info@judoontario.ca
www.judoontario.ca
www.facebook.com/JudoOntario
Overview: A small provincial organization founded in 1959 overseen by Judo Canada
Mission: To govern the sport of Judo in Ontario
Member of: Judo Canada; International Judo Federation
Chief Officer(s):
Brian Kalsen, President, 613-852-2206
briank@judoontario.ca
Kevin Doherty, First Vice-President & Director, Judo Canada - Ontario Region, 613-852-2206
Pedro Guedes, Technical Coach & Director
pedrog@judoontario.ca
Finances: *Annual Operating Budget:* $250,000-$500,000
Staff Member(s): 2; 100 volunteer(s)
Membership: 1,000-4,999; *Fees:* Schedule available; *Committees:* HPC; Grading Board; Referee; LTAD; NCCP; Aboriginal; Differently Abled; Quest for Gold; Website; Membership
Awards:
• Judo Ontario Recognition Awards (Award)
Publications:
• The Gentle Way [a publication of Judo Ontario]
Type: Newsletter; *Frequency:* Quarterly

Judo Prince Edward Island

PO Box 302, 40 Enman Cres., Charlottetown PE C1A 7K7
Tel: 902-368-4262
www.facebook.com/JUDOPEI
Overview: A small provincial organization overseen by Judo Canada
Mission: To promote and govern the sport of Judo in Prince Edward Island.
Member of: Sport PEI Inc.; Judo Canada
Chief Officer(s):
John Wilbert, President

Judo Saskatchewan

c/o Registrar, PO Box 271, Vibank SK S0G 4Y0
Tel: 306-762-4629
www.judosask.ca
Also Known As: Saskatchewan Kodokan Black Belt Association
Overview: A small provincial licensing organization founded in 1950 overseen by Judo Canada
Mission: To govern the sport of Judo in Saskatchewan
Member of: Judo Canada; Pan-American Judo Federation
Affliation(s): International Judo Federation
Chief Officer(s):
T.V. Taylor, President
tvtaylor@sasktel.net
Kate Schneider, Registrar
judomom.kate@sasktel.net
Finances: *Annual Operating Budget:* $100,000-$250,000
Staff Member(s): 1; 10 volunteer(s)
Membership: 300+; *Fees:* $25-$65

Judo Yukon

4061 - 4th Ave., Whitehorse YT Y1A 1H1
Tel: 867-668-4236; *Fax:* 867-667-4237
judoyukon@gmail.com
www.judoyukon.ca
Overview: A small provincial charitable organization founded in 1995 overseen by Judo Canada
Mission: To govern the sport of Judo in the Yukon
Member of: Judo Canada; Sport Yukon; True Sport; Sport Officials Canada
Chief Officer(s):
Dan Poelman, President
Finances: *Annual Operating Budget:* Less than $50,000
Membership: 100+; *Fees:* $105; *Member Profile:* Juniors & seniors; ages 8 & up; *Committees:* NCCP; Officials
Activities: Kodokan Judo practise; competition; demonstrations; *Awareness Events:* Judo Yukon Open Tournament, April; *Library:* Resource Library

Judo-Québec inc

4545, av Pierre-de Coubertin, Montréal QC H1V 0B2
Tél: 514-252-3040; *Téléc:* 514-254-5184
info@judo-quebec.qc.ca
www.judo-quebec.qc.ca
www.facebook.com/JudoQuebec
www.youtube.com/user/judoquebec
Également appelé: Association québécoise de judo-kodokan
Aperçu: *Dimension:* moyenne; *Envergure:* provinciale; Organisme sans but lucratif; fondée en 1966 surveillé par Judo Canada
Mission: Assurer la promotion et le développement du judo au Québec; éduquer, développer et servir nos membres
Membre de: Judo Canada; Sport Québec
Affliation(s): Fédération internationale de Judo; Union panaméricaine du Judo
Membre(s) du bureau directeur:
Daniel De Angelis, Président
daniel.deangelis@csp.qc.ca
Jean-François Marceau, Directeur général
jfmarceau@judo-quebec.qc.ca
Patrick Vesin, Coordonnateur technique
pvesin@judo-quebec.qc.ca
Finances: *Budget de fonctionnement annuel:* $500,000-$1.5 Million; *Fonds:* Secrétariat au loisirs et aux sports
Membre(s) du personnel: 6; 200 bénévole(s)
Membre: 10 000; *Montant de la cotisation:* barème; *Critères d'admissibilite:* Personne de 7 à 77 ans; *Comités:* Arbitrage; excellence; développement; grade; éthique; ju-jutsu

Activités: Competition; stage; colloque; gala; formation; *Stagiaires:* Oui; *Service de conférenciers:* Oui; *Bibliothèque*

Jump Alberta
#132, 250 Shawville Blvd. SE, Calgary AB T2Y 2Y7
e-mail: jumpalberta@gmail.com
www.jumpalberta.com
Overview: A small provincial organization
Affliation(s): Alberta Equestrian Federation
Chief Officer(s):
Kristi Beunder, President

Junior Achievement Canada (JACAN) / Jeunes Entreprises du Canada
#218, 1 Eva Rd., Toronto ON M9C 4Z5
Tel: 416-622-4602; *Fax:* 416-622-6861
Toll-Free: 800-265-0699
www.jacan.org
www.linkedin.com/groups?mostPopular=&gid=3027142
www.facebook.com/JAchievement
Overview: A large national charitable organization founded in 1967
Mission: To provide practical business & economic education programs & experience for young people, through partnerships with business & education communities
Member of: Junior Achievement Worldwide
Affliation(s): Temple de la renommée de l'entreprise canadienne
Chief Officer(s):
Stephen Ashworth, President & CEO
Jim Doherty, Chair
Erin Filey, Director, Development Ext. 223
Aliya Ansari, Director, Development & Events
Claudia Bishop, CFO Ext. 225
Finances: *Annual Operating Budget:* $500,000-$1.5 Million; *Funding Sources:* Corporate contributions
Staff Member(s): 10; 150 volunteer(s)
Membership: 250,000 students; *Member Profile:* Senior business representatives; *Committees:* Finance; Canadian Business Hall of Fame; Strategic Planning; Marketing; Programs
Activities: Operates in 114 countries around the world; programs delivered by experienced business people through a network of 40 chartered organizations across Canada; *Awareness Events:* Junior Achievement Month, Feb.; *Speaker Service:* Yes

Junior Achievement Nova Scotia
#2068, 6960 Mumford Rd., Halifax NS B3L 4P1
Tel: 902-425-4564; *Fax:* 902-454-4514
info@janovascotia.org
www.janovascotia.org
www.linkedin.com/company/junior-achievement-nova-scotia
www.facebook.com/janovascotia
twitter.com/janovascotia
www.youtube.com/user/janovascotia
Chief Officer(s):
Kristin Williams, President & CEO
kwilliams@janovascotia.org

Junior Achievement of British Columbia
#110, 475 West Georgia St., Vancouver BC V6B 4M9
Tel: 604-688-3887; *Fax:* 604-689-5299
info@jabc.org
british-columbia.jacan.org
ca.linkedin.com/in/juniorachievementbc
www.facebook.com/jabc.page
twitter.com/JA_of_BC
www.youtube.com/user/JuniorAchievementBC
Chief Officer(s):
Jan Bell-Irving, President
jan.bell-irving@jabc.org

Junior Achievement of Central Ontario
#405, 133 Richmond St. West, Toronto ON M5H 2L3
Tel: 416-360-5252; *Fax:* 416-366-5252
info@jacentralontario.org
central-ontario.jacan.org
ca.linkedin.com/pub/junior-achievement-of-central-ontario/2b/8a4/690
www.facebook.com/JACOCompanyProgram
twitter.com/JACO_CP
Mission: To inspire and educate young Canadians to experience free enterprise, understand business and economics and develop entrepreneurial and leadership skills.
Chief Officer(s):
Jane Eisbrenner, President & CEO

Junior Achievement of Chaleur, Restigouche & Miramichi
PO Box 455, Bathurst NB E2A 6L9
Tel: 506-548-3700
jaje@nb.aibn.com
new-brunswick.jacan.org
Chief Officer(s):
Sharon Jagoe, Program Manager

Junior Achievement of Fredericton
PO Box 631, Stn. A, Fredericton NB E3B 5A6
Tel: 506-455-6552; *Fax:* 506-454-5752
jafrednb@nb.aibn.com
new-brunswick.jacan.org
Chief Officer(s):
Connie Woodside, President & CEO

Junior Achievement of Guelph-Wellington
#3, 15 Surrey St. West, Guelph ON N1H 3R3
Tel: 519-835-1140; *Fax:* 519-837-0438
info@jaguelphwellington.org
guelph-wellington.jacan.org

Junior Achievement of London & District
15 Wharncliffe Rd. North, London ON N6H 2A1
Tel: 519-439-4201; *Fax:* 519-438-2331
Toll-Free: 877-229-9925
info@jalondon.org
london-and-district.jacan.org
www.linkedin.com/groups?mostPopular=&gid=3027142
www.facebook.com/pages/Junior-Achievement-London/131713956572
twitter.com/JA_London
www.youtube.com/user/JALondonTV
Chief Officer(s):
Bev Robinson, President & CEO
brobinson@jalondon.org

Junior Achievement of Manitoba
1149 St. Matthews Ave., Winnipeg MB R3G 0J8
Tel: 204-956-6088; *Fax:* 204-831-5284
manitoba.jacan.org
www.facebook.com/pages/Junior-Achievement-of-Manitoba/191061872629
twitter.com/JAManitoba
Mission: To inspire and educate young Canadians to experience free enterprise, understand business and economics, and develop entrepreneurial and leadership skills.
Chief Officer(s):
Greg Leipsic, President & CEO
gleipsic@jamanitoba.org

Junior Achievement of Newfoundland and Labrador
Delgado Bldg., PO Box 7468, 171 Water St., 3rd Fl., St. John's NL A1E 4V8
Tel: 709-753-9533; *Fax:* 709-753-2612
info@janl.org
newfoundland-and-labrador.jacan.org
Chief Officer(s):
Sandra Patterson, President & CEO
spatterson@janl.org

Junior Achievement of Northern Alberta & Northwest Territories
World Trade Centre Edmonton, #200, 9990 Jasper Ave., Edmonton AB T5J 1P7
Tel: 780-428-1421; *Fax:* 780-428-1031
Toll-Free: 877-626-7666
northern-alberta-and-nwt.jacan.org
www.facebook.com/JANorthernAlberta
twitter.com/JA_northalberta
www.youtube.com/user/JANorthernAlberta
Chief Officer(s):
Jen Panteluk, President & CEO
jpanteluk@janorthalberta.org

Junior Achievement of Northwestern New Brunswick
PO Box 391, Edmundston NB E3V 3L1
Tel: 506-739-6354; *Fax:* 506-736-6511
jaedm@nb.aibn.com
new-brunswick.jacan.org
Chief Officer(s):
Jeanne Ouellette, Program Manager

Junior Achievement of P.E.I.
PO Box 21, Charlottetown PE C1A 7K2
Tel: 902-892-6066; *Fax:* 902-892-1993
prince-edward-island.jacan.org
Chief Officer(s):
Betty Ferguson, President & Director, Operations
bferguson@japei.org

Junior Achievement of Sarnia-Lambton
556 Christina St. North, Sarnia ON N7T 5W6
Tel: 519-336-1484; *Fax:* 519-336-2815
south-western-ontario.jacan.org
Chief Officer(s):
Marci Palframan, Program Manager
mpalframan@jaswont.org

Junior Achievement of Saskatchewan
#1110, 450 - 22nd St. East, Saskatoon SK S7K 5T6
Tel: 306-955-5267; *Fax:* 306-653-1507
info@jasask.org
saskatchewan.jacan.org
www.facebook.com/JASask
twitter.com/JASask
Chief Officer(s):
Darren Hill, President & CEO

Junior Achievement of Southeastern New Brunswick
PO Box 631, Stn. A, Frederickton NB E3B 5A6
Tel: 506-457-7420; *Fax:* 506-454-5752
jamtn@nb.aibn.com
new-brunswick.jacan.org
Chief Officer(s):
Ryan Richard, Program Manager

Junior Achievement of Southern Alberta
#870, 105 - 12 Ave. SE, Calgary AB T2G 1A1
Tel: 403-237-5252; *Fax:* 403-261-6988
info@jasouthalberta.org
southern-alberta.jacan.org
www.linkedin.com/groups?mostPopular=&gid=3027142
www.facebook.com/JASouthAlberta
twitter.com/jasouthalberta
www.youtube.com/user/JASouthAlberta
Chief Officer(s):
Scott Hillier, President & CEO, 403-781-2578
shillier@jasouthalberta.org

Junior Achievement of Southwestern New Brunswick
PO Box 22009, Stn. Landsdowne Postal Outlet, Saint John NB E2K 4T7
Tel: 506-634-8409; *Fax:* 506-634-8495
jastj@nb.aibn.com
new-brunswick.jacan.org
Chief Officer(s):
Dave Evans, Program Manager

Junior Achievement of Southwestern Ontario
PO Box 353, 60 William St. South, Chatham ON N7M 5K4
Tel: 519-352-0151; *Fax:* 519-352-6180
info@jaswont.org
www.south-western-ontario.jacan.org
www.facebook.com/group.php?gid=2233505751
Chief Officer(s):
Scott McGeachy, Chair

Junior Achievement of the Waterloo Region
29 King St. East, #B, Kitchener ON N2G 2K4
Tel: 519-576-6610; *Fax:* 519-576-3210
admin@jawaterlooregion.org
www.jawaterlooregion.com
www.linkedin.com/groups?home=&gid=4241803
www.facebook.com/JAWaterlooRegion
twitter.com/JAWatRegion
www.youtube.com/user/JAWaterlooRegion
Chief Officer(s):
Karen Gallant, President & CEO
kgallant@jawaterlooregion.org

Junior Achievement Mainland Nova Scotia ***See*** Junior Achievement of Canada

Junior Achievement of Chatham-Kent ***See*** Junior Achievement of Canada

Junior Achievement of Eastern Newfoundland ***See*** Junior Achievement of Canada

Junior Achievement of Greater Moncton Inc. ***See*** Junior Achievement of Canada

Junior Achievement of Guelph ***See*** Junior Achievement of Canada

Junior Achievement of Northern Saskatchewan ***See*** Junior Achievement of Canada

Junior Achievement of Saint John ***See*** Junior Achievement of Canada

Junior Chamber International Canada / Jeune chambre internationale du Canada
14 Bruce Farm Dr., Toronto ON M2H 1G3
Tel: 416-226-9756; *Fax:* 416-221-9389
Toll-Free: 800-265-0484

administration@jcicanada.com
www.jcicanada.com
Also Known As: JAYCEES
Previous Name: Canadian Junior Chamber
Overview: A medium-sized national organization
Mission: To contribute to the advancement of the global community by providing the opportunity for young people to develop the leadership skills, social responsibility & fellowship necessary to create positive change. Chapters across Canada.
Affliation(s): Junior Chamber International
Chief Officer(s):
Francois Begin, Chairman of the Board
fbegin@jci.cc
Jason Ranchoux, National President
president@jcicanada.com
Finances: *Funding Sources:* Membership fees; fundraising; sponsorship
Membership: *Member Profile:* Ages 18-40

Junior Farmers' Association of Ontario (JFAO)

Ontario AgriCentre, #206, 100 Stone Rd. West, Guelph ON N1G 5L3
Tel: 519-780-5326; *Fax:* 519-821-8810
info@jfao.on.ca
www.jfao.on.ca
www.facebook.com/547606885270544
Overview: A medium-sized provincial organization founded in 1944
Mission: To build future rural leaders through self-help & community betterment
Chief Officer(s):
Sarah McLaren, President
president@jfao.on.ca
Membership: *Member Profile:* People ages 15-29

Junior League of Calgary (JLC)

511 - 22 Ave. SW, Calgary AB T2S 0H5
Tel: 403-244-5355; *Fax:* 403-244-2217
jlc@juniorleaguecalgary.com
www.juniorleaguecalgary.com
www.facebook.com/121206674567702
twitter.com/JLeagueCalgary
www.youtube.com/juniorleaguecalgary
Overview: A small local charitable organization founded in 1950
Mission: Organization of women committed to promoting voluntarism, developing the potential of women, & improving communities through the effective action & leadership of trained volunteers.
Member of: Canadian Federation of Junior Leagues; Association of Junior Leagues International
Chief Officer(s):
Lynne Christensen, President
Finances: *Annual Operating Budget:* $50,000-$100,000; *Funding Sources:* Membership fees; Fund-raising events
Staff Member(s): 2; 98 volunteer(s)
Membership: 300; *Fees:* $155; *Member Profile:* Women 18 & over; *Committees:* Junior Chefs; Distribution Centre; Training
Activities: Moms U Matter (MUM); Treasure Trunk; Teen Holiday Totes; Kids In The Kitchen; Done in a Day (DIAD)

Junior League of Edmonton (JLE)

10447 - 86 Ave. NW, Edmonton AB T6E 2M4
Tel: 780-433-9739; *Fax:* 780-431-0138
kjristen@jledmonton.org
www.jledmonton.org
Overview: A small local charitable organization founded in 1928
Mission: An organization of women committed to promoting voluntarism, developing the potential of women, & improving the community through the effective action & leadership of trained volunteers
Member of: Canadian Federation of Junior Leagues; Association of Junior Leagues International
Chief Officer(s):
Heather MacDonald, President
Megan Demers, President-Elect
Finances: *Annual Operating Budget:* $50,000-$100,000; *Funding Sources:* Fundraising; grants; donations; casinos
Staff Member(s): 1; 163 volunteer(s)
Membership: 120+ active & sustaining members; *Fees:* $85; $70
Activities: Huggies Every Little Bottom; Done-in-a-Day projects; Kids in the Kitchen; Clear out your closet with Talbots; Junior Chefs; Community Assistance Fund; Calgary & Edmonton Railway Station Museum; *Awareness Events:* Indulgence: A Canadian Epic of Food & Wine, June; Homes for the Holidays, Nov.
Awards:
• Janet Blair Miller Memorial Scholarship (Award)
• Community Assistance Fund Grant (Award)
Publications:
• Telegraph [a publication of the Junior League of Edmonton]
Type: Newsletter

Junior League of Halifax

PO Box 8011, Stn. A, Halifax NS B3K 5L8
Tel: 902-429-9437
info@juniorleagueofhalifax.org
www.juniorleagueofhalifax.org
Overview: A small local charitable organization founded in 1934
Mission: To promote voluntarism; to develop the potential of women & to improve communities through effective action & leadership of trained volunteers
Member of: Canadian Federation of Junior Leagues; Association of Junior Leagues International
Affliation(s): Supportive Housing for Young Mothers
Chief Officer(s):
Catherine Gunn, President
Jocelyn Jackson, President-Elect
Finances: *Annual Operating Budget:* Less than $50,000
150 volunteer(s)
Membership: 150; *Member Profile:* Female over 19 years of age
Activities: Backpacks for Kids; Laing House; Kids in the Kitchen; Healthy Families; Youth Run Club; Amanda's Gift; *Awareness Events:* Homes for the Holidays, Nov.

Junior League of Hamilton-Burlington, Inc. (JLHB)

1424 Plains Rd. West, Burlington ON L7T 1H6
Tel: 905-525-1077; *Fax:* 905-525-4996
info@juniorleague.ca
www.juniorleague.ca
www.facebook.com/JuniorLeagueHamiltonBurlington
www.youtube.com/watch?v=s_MVUCnjcNs
Overview: A small local charitable organization founded in 1934
Mission: To promote voluntarism, to develop the potential of women & to improve the community through the effective action & leadership of trained volunteers
Member of: Canadian Federation of Junior Leagues; Association of Junior Leagues International
Chief Officer(s):
Ellen McWhinnie, President
president@juniorleague.ca
Finances: *Annual Operating Budget:* $100,000-$250,000
Staff Member(s): 1; 166 volunteer(s)
Membership: 166; *Fees:* $125; *Committees:* Kids on the Block; House Tour; PR; New Member; Community Research Link; Nominating; Member Placement & Development
Activities: Empowerment Hour; Discretionary Fund; Kids in the Kitchen; Kids on the Block puppet troupe (currently on hiatus); *Awareness Events:* Holiday House Tour of Distinctive Homes, Nov.

Junior League of Toronto

539A Mount Pleasant Rd., Toronto ON M4S 2M5
Tel: 416-485-4218; *Fax:* 416-485-5949
info@jlt.org
www.jlt.org
www.facebook.com/JuniorLeagueOfToronto
twitter.com/jrleaguetoronto
Also Known As: JLT
Overview: A small local charitable organization founded in 1926
Mission: A woman's organization committed to promoting voluntarism, developing the potential of women & improving communities through effective action & leadership of trained volunteers; purpose is educational & charitable.
Member of: Canadian Federation of Junior Leagues; Associaton of Junior Leagues International Inc.
Chief Officer(s):
Nadine Spencer, President
Selby Kostuik, President-Elect
Stephanie Knox, Treasurer
Finances: *Annual Operating Budget:* $250,000-$500,000
Staff Member(s): 1; 450 volunteer(s)
Membership: 100-499; *Fees:* $135
Activities: Healthy Living Project

Junior Symphony Society *See* Vancouver Youth Symphony Orchestra Society

Justice Centre for Constitutional Freedoms (JCCF)

#253, 7620 Elbow Dr. SW, Calgary AB T2V 1K2
Tel: 403-475-3622
www.facebook.com/165911043462459
twitter.com/JCCFCanada
www.youtube.com/user/JCCFdotCA
Overview: A small national organization founded in 2010
Mission: To defend constitutional freedoms through litigation & education
Chief Officer(s):
John Carpay, President

Justice for Children & Youth (JFCY)

#1203, 415 Yonge St., Toronto ON M5B 2E7
Tel: 416-920-1633; *Fax:* 416-920-5855
Toll-Free: 866-999-5329
info@jfcy.org
www.jfcy.org
Also Known As: Canadian Foundation for Children, Youth & the Law
Overview: A medium-sized provincial charitable organization founded in 1978
Mission: To assist & empower children & youth in obtaining fair & equal access to legal, educational, medical & social resources; to provide direct legal assistance in all areas of children's law to eligible children & youth of Metro Toronto & vicinity; to provide summary legal advice, information & assistance to young people, parents, professionals & community groups on a province-wide basis; to advocate for law & policy reform; to monitor & respond to developments & changes to the laws which affect children
Chief Officer(s):
Mary Birdsell, Executive Director
Emily Chan, Community Development Lawyer
Finances: *Annual Operating Budget:* $250,000-$500,000
Staff Member(s): 6; 20 volunteer(s)
Membership: 40 institutional + 150 individual; *Fees:* $20 individual; $50 organization; $100 sustaining member; *Committees:* Legal Services; Policy; Community Development; Personnel; Youth Advisory
Activities: *Internships:* Yes; *Speaker Service:* Yes; *Library:* Resource Centre; Open to public

Justice for Girls

Tel: 604-689-7887; *Fax:* 604-689-5600
justiceforgirls@justiceforgirls.org
www.justiceforgirls.org
Overview: A small national organization
Mission: To promote support, justice & equality for homeless, low income & street-involved teenage girls who have experienced violence
Chief Officer(s):
Annabel Webb, Director
annabel@justiceforgirls.org
Activities: Court monitoring; public education; advocacy & legal education; internship for young women;

Justice Institute of British Columbia (JIBC)

715 McBride Blvd., New Westminster BC V3L 5T4
Tel: 604-525-5422; *Fax:* 604-528-5518
Toll-Free: 888-865-7764
infodesk@jibc.ca
www.jibc.ca
www.linkedin.com/company/justice-institute-of-british-columbia
www.facebook.com/justiceinstitute
twitter.com/JIBCnews
www.youtube.com/user/JusticeInstitute
Overview: A small provincial organization
Chief Officer(s):
Michel Tarko, President
Activities: *Library* Open to public

Juvenile Diabetes Research Foundation Canada (JDRF)

#800, 2550 Victoria Park Ave., Toronto ON M2J 5A9
Tel: 647-789-2000; *Fax:* 416-491-2111
Toll-Free: 877-287-3533
general@jdrf.ca
www.jdrf.ca
Previous Name: Diabetes Research Foundation
Overview: A medium-sized national charitable organization founded in 1974
Mission: To support research to find a cure for diabetes & its complications; To increase awareness of diabetes, particularly Juvenile (Type 1) diabetes
Chief Officer(s):
Aubrey Baillie, Chair
Andrew McKee, President/CEO
David Kozloff, Secretary
Alex Davidson, Treasurer
Finances: *Funding Sources:* Donations

Activities: Liaising with government; Advocating for diabetes research; *Awareness Events:* Walk to Cure Diabetes; Ride for Diabetes Research

Calgary
#204, 1608 - 17th Ave. SW, Calgary AB T2T 0E3
Tel: 403-255-7100; *Fax:* 403-253-6683
calgary@jdrf.ca
Chief Officer(s):
Randy Diddams, Regional Manager, Fundraising and Development

Edmonton
#17321, 108 Ave. NW, Edmonton AB T5S 1G2
Tel: 780-428-0343; *Fax:* 780-428-0348
edmonton@jdrf.ca

Halifax Region
Bedford Place Mall, 1658 Bedford Hwy., Bedford NS B4A 2X9
Tel: 902-453-1009; *Fax:* 902-453-2528
Toll-Free: 888-439-5373
halifax@jdrf.ca

Hamilton
#202, 180 James St. South, Hamilton ON L8P 4V1
Tel: 905-524-5638; *Fax:* 905-524-1611
burlham@jdrf.ca

London
309 Commissioners Rd. West, Unit A, London ON N6J 1Y4
Tel: 519-641-7006; *Fax:* 519-641-7837
london@jdrf.ca

Québec
#330, 615 Blvd. Rene-Levesque W., Montréal QC H3B 1P5
Tel: 514-744-5537; *Fax:* 514-744-0516
Toll-Free: 877-634-2238
montreal@jdrf.ca
Chief Officer(s):
Agathe Grinberg, 514-744-0516 Ext. 243
agrinberg@jdrf.ca

Saskatoon
PO Box 30055, 1624 - 33rd St. West, Saskatoon SK S7L 7M6
Tel: 306-955-2284; *Fax:* 306-955-2140
saskatoon@jdrf.ca

South Saskatchewan
PO Box 3924, Regina SK S4P 3S9
Tel: 306-789-8474
regina@jdrf.ca
www.facebook.com/group.php?gid=196565697030951
Chief Officer(s):
Susan Clarkson, Chair

Toronto-York
#800, 2550 Victoria Park Ave., Toronto ON M2J 5A9
Tel: 647-789-2000; *Fax:* 416-491-2111
Toll-Free: 877-944-0800
toronto@jdrf.ca
www.facebook.com/group.php?gid=144016148944613
Chief Officer(s):
Marla Ingles, Regional Manager
mingles@jdrf.ca

Vancouver
Sperling Plaza II, #150, 6450 Roberts St., Burnaby BC V5G 4E1
Tel: 604-320-1937; *Fax:* 604-320-1938
twitter.com/jdrf_bc

Waterloo-Wellington
#103, 684 Belmont Ave., Kitchener ON N2M 1N6
Tel: 519-745-2426; *Fax:* 519-745-2626
waterloo@jdrf.ca

Winnipeg
#1101, 191 Lombard Ave., Winnipeg MB R3B 0X1
Tel: 204-953-4477; *Fax:* 204-953-4470
winnipeg@jdrf.ca

JVS of Greater Toronto
74 Tycos Dr., Toronto ON M6B 1V9
Tel: 416-787-1151; *Fax:* 416-785-7529
services@jvstoronto.org
www.jvstoronto.org
www.linkedin.com/company/jvs-toronto
www.facebook.com/pages/JVS-Toronto/159022368653
twitter.com/JVSToronto
www.youtube.com/JVSTorontoOnline
Also Known As: Jewish Vocational Service
Overview: A small local charitable organization founded in 1947
Mission: To provide leadership in the development & delivery of educational & vocational services of the highest quality in order to assist clients to identify educational & vocational goals & to develop the skills & knowledge to achieve those goals; to deal effectively with educational or vocational barriers
Member of: International Association of Counselling Services; International Association of JVS
Affliation(s): United Way; Agency of UJA
Chief Officer(s):
Paul Habert, Chair
Staff Member(s): 220
Activities: *Library* Open to public

Employment Resources Centre
Atria 1, #120, 2255 Sheppard Ave. East, Toronto ON M2J 4Y1
Tel: 416-756-0202; *Fax:* 416-756-0211
ERCatria@jvstoronto.org
www.jvstoronto.org
Chief Officer(s):
Terri Hylton, Project Coordinator

Jane-Finch
Jane Finch Mall, #3, 1911 Finch Ave. West, Toronto ON M3N 2V2
Tel: 416-636-2481; *Fax:* 416-636-6416
youthinc@jvstoronto.org
www.jvstoronto.org
Chief Officer(s):
Deborah Lewis, Coordinator

JVS North
#607, 1280 Finch Ave. West, Toronto ON M3J 3K6
Tel: 416-661-3010; *Fax:* 416-661-5716
jcei@jvstoronto.org
www.jvstoronto.org
Chief Officer(s):
Doreen Cort

Project Job Search
74 Tycos Dr., Toronto ON M6B 1V9
Tel: 416-787-1151; *Fax:* 416-785-7529
pjs@jvstoronto.org
www.jvstoronto.org
Chief Officer(s):
Ken Percy

The J.W. McConnell Family Foundation / La fondation de la famille J.W. McConnell
#1800, 1002, rue Sherbrooke ouest, Montréal QC H3A 3L6
Tel: 514-288-2133; *Fax:* 514-288-1479
information@mcconnellfoundation.ca
www.mcconnellfoundation.ca
Overview: A small national charitable organization founded in 1937
Mission: To fund initiatives of national significance, which address challenges for Canadian society, by engaging people & by developing a strong knowledge base for the work supported
Member of: Private Foundations Canada; Council on Foundations; Canadian Centre for Philanthropy
Chief Officer(s):
Stephen Huddart, President & Chief Executive Officer
John Cawley, Director, Programs & Operations
jcawley@mcconnellfoundation.ca
Brianna Hunter, Officer, Communications
bhunter@mcconnellfoundation.ca
Membership: 1-99

K3C Community Counselling Centres / Centre de Conseil Communautaire
Unison Place, 417 Bagot St., Kingston ON K7K 3C1
Tel: 613-549-7850; *Fax:* 613-544-8138
Toll-Free: 800-379-5556
info@k3c.org
www.k3c.org
www.facebook.com/1394815584088014
Previous Name: Kingston Community Counselling Centre
Overview: A medium-sized local charitable organization founded in 1968 overseen by Ontario Association of Credit Counselling Services
Mission: To assist persons in Kingston & the surrounding area to solve their debt & money management troubles for free, or a small fee; To provide a variety of educational presentations about financial matters
Member of: Canadian Association of Credit Counselling Services; Ontario Association of Credit Counselling Services; United Way
Chief Officer(s):
Danielle Brown, Administrator
Finances: *Annual Operating Budget:* $3 Million-$5 Million
Activities: Counselling persons in a confidential & unbiased manner about credit concerns; Offering debt management programs; Liaising with creditors; Teaching budgeting & money management skills; Offering alternatives to declaring bankruptcy; *Speaker Service:* Yes
Publications:
• K3C Newsletter
Type: Newsletter; *Frequency:* bi-monthly
Profile: Information about agency & topical articles.

K3C Credit Counselling Belleville
235 Bridge St. East, Belleville ON K8N 1P2
Tel: 613-966-3556
Toll-Free: 800-379-5556
belleville@k3c.org
Mission: To provide confidential, unbiased professional counselling & support to persons in Quinte Region
Member of: Canadian Association of Credit Counselling Services; Ontario Association of Credit Counselling Services

K3C Credit Counselling Brockville
7B Perth St., Brockville ON K6V 6C5
Tel: 613-341-8788
Toll-Free: 800-379-5556
brockville@k3c.org
Mission: To assist individuals & families in Brockville & the surrounding area who are experiencing financial problems
Member of: Canadian Association of Credit Counselling Services; Ontario Association of Credit Counselling Services; United Way

K3C Credit Counselling Cornwall
26 Montreal Rd., Cornwall ON K6H 1B1
Toll-Free: 866-202-0425
cornwall@k3c.org
Mission: To offer free, qualified, & confidential financial advice to persons in the Cornwall area
Member of: Canadian Association of Credit Counselling Services; Ontario Association of Credit Counselling Services; United Way

K3C Credit Counselling Oshawa
Oshawa Executive Centre, 203A, 419 King St. West, Oshawa ON L1J 2K5
Tel: 905-665-6204
Toll-Free: 800-379-5556
oshawa@k3c.org
Mission: To provide confidential credit counselling services to individuals & families, in Whitby & Oshawa, who are experiencing financial concerns; To offer education about financial well-being
Member of: Canadian Association of Credit Counselling Services; Ontario Association of Credit Counselling Services; United Way

K3C Credit Counselling Ottawa - Carling Ave.
#209, 1300 Carling Ave., Ottawa ON K1Z 7L2
Tel: 613-728-2041
Toll-Free: 866-202-0425
ottawa@k3c.org
Mission: To help persons in Ottawa & area find solutions to their debt difficulties
Member of: Canadian Association of Credit Counselling Services; Ontario Association of Credit Counselling Services; United Way

K3C Credit Counselling Ottawa - McArthur Ave.
311 McArthur St., Ottawa ON K1L 8M3
Tel: 613-728-2041
Toll-Free: 866-202-0425
ottawa@k3c.org
Mission: To offer free, qualified, & confidential financial advice to persons in the Ottawa area
Member of: Canadian Association of Credit Counselling Services; Ontario Association of Credit Counselling Services; United Way

Kababayan Community Centre *See* Kababayan Multicultural Centre

Kababayan Multicultural Centre
#133, 1313 Queen St. West, Toronto ON M6K 1L8
Tel: 416-532-3888; *Fax:* 416-532-0037
office@kababayan.org
www.kababayan.org
www.facebook.com/KababayanCommunity
Previous Name: Kababayan Community Centre
Overview: A small local charitable organization founded in 1977 overseen by Ontario Council of Agencies Serving Immigrants
Mission: To develop a strong immigrant community in Canada
Chief Officer(s):
Flordeliz M. Dandal, Executive Director
Staff Member(s): 7

Kabuki Syndrome Network Inc. (KSN)
8060 Struthers Cres., Regina SK S4Y 1J3
Tel: 306-543-8715
margot@kabukisyndrome.com
kabukisyndrome.com
Overview: A small national charitable organization founded in 1997
Mission: To provide information on Kabuki syndrome
Chief Officer(s):
Dean Schmiedge, Contact
Margot Schmiedge, Contact
Finances: *Annual Operating Budget:* Less than $50,000
Membership: 200; *Fees:* $20

Kainai Chamber of Commerce
PO Box 350, Stand Off AB T0L 1Y0
Tel: 403-737-8124; *Fax:* 403-737-2116
chamber@bloodtribe.org
Overview: A small local organization founded in 1999

KAIROS: Canadian Ecumenical Justice Initiatives / Initiatives canadiennes oecuméniques pour la justice
#200, 310 Dupont St., Toronto ON M5R 1V9
Tel: 416-463-5312; *Fax:* 416-463-5569
Toll-Free: 877-403-8933
info@kairoscanada.org
www.kairoscanada.org
twitter.com/kairoscanada
Previous Name: Ecumenical Coalition for Economic Justice; GATT-Fly
Overview: A small national organization founded in 1973
Mission: To undertake a program of research & action with churches & popular groups emphasizing coalition-building & social transformation; five churches have participated in the Coalition since its inception: the Anglican Church of Canada, the Canadian Conference of Catholic Bishops, the Evangelical Lutheran Church in Canada, the Presbyterian Church in Canada, the United Church of Canada
Member of: Action Canada Network
Affliation(s): Canadian Council of Churches
Chief Officer(s):
Jennifer Henry, Executive Director
Sara Stratton, Program Coordinator, Education & Campaigns
Finances: *Annual Operating Budget:* $100,000-$250,000
Staff Member(s): 4
Membership: *Fees:* $100
Activities: *Speaker Service:* Yes

Kaleidoscope Theatre Productions Society (KTPS)
3130 Jutland Rd., Victoria BC V8T 2T3
Tel: 250-383-8124; *Fax:* 250-383-8911
Toll-Free: 800-811-5777
info@kaleidoscope.bc.ca
www.kaleidoscope.bc.ca
facebook.com/kaleidoscopetheatre
twitter.com/kaleidoscope_ca
youtube.com/kaleidoscopetps
Also Known As: Kaleidoscope Theatre
Overview: A medium-sized national charitable organization founded in 1974
Mission: To create & present original, innovative & relevant theatre that stimulates & inspires the minds & imaginations of families & young people, using a style of presentation that emphasizes timeless & universal themes, is centered on the lives of young people & is enhanced by the integration of visuals, music & movement
Member of: ProArt; Greater Victoria Community Arts Council; Artstarts in Schools; BC Touring Council
Affliation(s): Canadian Actors' Equity Association
Chief Officer(s):
Roderick Glanville, Artistic Director
David Ferguson, General Manager
Finances: *Annual Operating Budget:* $250,000-$500,000; *Funding Sources:* Federal, provincial & regional governments; performance fees; fundraising
Staff Member(s): 3
Membership: 40
Activities: Annual theatre productions; local, national & international touring; Annual Family Concert Series; Annual Young Playwright's Competition & Festival

Kali-Shiva AIDS Services
646 Logan Ave., Winnipeg MB R3A 0S7
Tel: 204-783-8565; *Fax:* 204-772-7237
kalishiv@mts.net
kalishiva.wix.com/shiva
Overview: A small local charitable organization founded in 1987 overseen by Canadian AIDS Society
Mission: To provide community-based home support, home care & home hospice for persons with HIV/AIDS
Activities: *Speaker Service:* Yes

Kamloops & District Labour Council (KDLC)
PO Box 369, Stn. Main, 929 Laval Cres., Kamloops BC V2C 5K9
Tel: 250-374-7310; *Fax:* 250-374-7304
karencerniuk@hotmail.com
www.facebook.com/group.php?gid=38547037157
Overview: A medium-sized local organization overseen by British Columbia Federation of Labour
Mission: To promote the interests of affiliates in Kamloops & the surrounding area; To advance the economic & social welfare of workers
Chief Officer(s):
Karen Cerniuk, President
karencerniuk@hotmail.com
Peter Kerek, First Vice-President
peterkerek@shaw.ca
Cathy Hamilton, Second Vice-President
jh3500@telus.net
Membership: 10,000; *Member Profile:* Unionized workers in British Columbia's Kamloops area, including Clearwater, Merritt, Ashcroft, & Chase
Activities: Raising awareness of issues, such as the Northern Gateway Pipeline Project & offshore oil exploration; Promoting social justice & human rights; Organizing Day of Mourning ceremonies, to remember persons who were injured or died on the job; Contributing to the community by participating in the Day of Caring
Awards:
• Kamloops & District Labour Council Bursaries (Grant)
Amount: $1,000

Kamloops & District Real Estate Association (KADREA)
#101, 418 St. Paul St., Kamloops BC V2C 2J6
Tel: 250-372-9411
kadrea.realtyserver.com
Overview: A small local organization founded in 1973 overseen by British Columbia Real Estate Association
Member of: Canadian Real Estate Association

Kamloops Exploration Group
#1100, 235 First Ave., Kamloops BC V2C 3J4
Tel: 250-828-2585
info@keg.bc.ca
www.keg.bc.ca
www.facebook.com/107234792716213
twitter.com/#%21/KamloopsExplora
Overview: A small local organization
Mission: To generally promote the interests of mining & prospecting for minerals, metals, & petroleum to the general public; to further the member's knowledge of mineral exploration & mining by offering informational lectures to members & the general public; to hold prospecting classes & promote other educational projects in connection with mining & prospecting;to further the general public's knowledge on the subject of Geoscience
Chief Officer(s):
Colin Russell, President, 250-578-2068
russellgeoscience@gmail.com

Kamloops Foodbank & Outreach Society
PO Box 1513, Stn. Main, 171 Wilson St., Kamloops BC V2C 6L8
Tel: 250-376-2252
Other Communication: www.flickr.com/photos/kamloopsfoodbank
kamloopsfoodbank.org
www.facebook.com/kamloopsfoodbank
twitter.com/kamfoodbank
www.youtube.com/user/kamloopsfoodbank
Overview: A small local organization founded in 1985
Mission: To provide & support programs & services that feed the hungry, promote long-term food security & improve the social well-being of people in our community
Affliation(s): Canadian Association of Food Banks
Finances: *Annual Operating Budget:* $500,000-$1.5 Million
Staff Member(s): 6; 70 volunteer(s)
Membership: 17; *Fees:* $1; *Committees:* Health Promotion; Fundraising; Maintenance; Personnel; Public Relations; Food Bank
Activities: Confidential services; hamper distribution on a monthly basis; hampers to last 3-58 days; nutritionally designed hampers; bread & bread products on a daily basis; birthday packages for children; pre-natal hampers; hampers for special needs diets; school snacks for students & children; free clothing when available; referrals to alternate agencies when needed; *Awareness Events:* Food Bank Month, Dec.

Kamloops Immigrant Services (KIS)
448 Tranquille Rd., Kamloops BC V2B 3H2
Tel: 778-470-6101; *Fax:* 778-470-6102
Toll-Free: 866-672-0855
kis@immigrantservices.ca
www.immigrantservices.ca
Overview: A small local organization founded in 1982
Mission: To assist immigrants, visible minorities & new Canadians to be full & equal participants in Canadian society; to promote positive race relations & organizational change in diversity
Member of: Affiliation of Multicultural Societies & Service Agencies of BC
Chief Officer(s):
David Cruz, Chair
Paul Lagace, Executive Director, 778-470-6101 Ext. 101
kcris@shaw.ca
Finances: *Annual Operating Budget:* $500,000-$1.5 Million; *Funding Sources:* Federal & provincial government; United Way; fundraising
Staff Member(s): 16; 60 volunteer(s)
Membership: *Committees:* Race Relations
Activities: Direct settlement; integration services; employment programs; ESL programs; counselling; interpretation/translation; diversity training & organizational change training; Safe Harbour Program; *Speaker Service:* Yes; *Rents Mailing List:* Yes; *Library:* ESL Library

Kamloops Multicultural Society (KMS)
PO Box 1515, Stn. Main, Kamloops BC V2C 6L8
Tel: 250-682-0289
info@kmsociety.ca
www.kmsociety.ca
Overview: A small local organization
Mission: To increase public awareness about issues surrounding multiculturalism
Member of: Affiliation of Multicultural Societies & Service Agencies of BC
Chief Officer(s):
Ray Dhaliwal, President
Membership: 30 member groups; *Fees:* $50 group; $10 individual; *Member Profile:* Cultural organizations & interested individuals from Kamloops & area
Activities: Educational programmes in schools, festivals; *Speaker Service:* Yes

Kamloops Naturalist Club (KNC)
PO Box 625, Kamloops BC V2C 5L7
Tel: 250-554-1285
marggraham@shaw.ca
www.kamloopsnaturalistclub.ca
Overview: A small local charitable organization founded in 1981 overseen by Federation of BC Naturalists
Mission: To promote the enjoyment of nature through environmental appreciation & conservation; to encourage wise use & conservation of natural resources & environmental protection
Member of: Canadian Nature Federation
Affliation(s): Nature Canada
Finances: *Annual Operating Budget:* Less than $50,000; *Funding Sources:* Membership fees; grants; raffles
Membership: 1-99; *Fees:* $25 single; $35 family; *Member Profile:* All ages, but predominately retired
Activities: Field trips; workshops; monthly meetings; speakers

Kamloops Society for Community Living (KSCL)
521 Seymour St., Kamloops BC V2C 2G8
Tel: 250-374-3245; *Fax:* 250-374-2133
www.kscl.ca
Overview: A small local charitable organization founded in 1956
Mission: To provide opportunities for persons with a developmental disability to experience a full life in as many aspects as they so choose by providing supports and services.
Member of: British Columbia Association for Community Living
Chief Officer(s):
Gail Saunders, Executive Director
gsaunders@kscl.ca
Finances: *Funding Sources:* Public support
Staff Member(s): 3

Kamloops Symphony (KSO)
PO Box 57, Kamloops BC V2C 5K3

Tel: 250-372-5000; *Fax:* 250-372-5089
info@kamloopssymphony.com
www.kamloopssymphony.com
www.facebook.com/kamloopssymphony
Also Known As: Kamloops Symphony Society
Overview: A small local charitable organization founded in 1976 overseen by Orchestras Canada
Mission: To operate & promote a symphony orchestra for the Kamloops region
Chief Officer(s):
Bruce Dunn, Music Director
Finances: *Funding Sources:* Provincial, federal & municipal government; ticket sales; donations; fundraising
Staff Member(s): 6
Activities: *Library:* Music Library

Kamloops Wildlife Park Society
9077 Dallas Dr., Kamloops BC V2C 6V1
Tel: 250-573-3242; *Fax:* 250-573-2406
info@bczoo.org
www.bczoo.org
www.facebook.com/group.php?gid=21639298837447З
Also Known As: BC Wildlife Park
Overview: A small local charitable organization founded in 1965
Mission: To encourage the appreciation of & respect for BC's wildlife; to assist in preserving biodiversity through education, research, captive breeding & rehabilitation service
Affliation(s): Canadian Association of Zoos & Aquariums
Chief Officer(s):
Glenn Grant, General Manager, 250-573-3242 Ext. 231
glenn@bczoo.org
Jeff Stone, President
Jack Madryga, 1st Vice-President
Rod Simmons, 2nd Vice-President
Don Bogie, Treasurer
Finances: *Annual Operating Budget:* $500,000-$1.5 Million; *Funding Sources:* Regional government; self-generated revenue
Staff Member(s): 15; 200 volunteer(s)
Membership: 2,000; *Fees:* $32 adults; $24 seniors; $20 children (age 3-17); $99 family (up to 5 members); *Member Profile:* Families from Kamloops region
Activities: Captive breeding for release endangered Burrowing Owls; *Awareness Events:* BC Hydro Wildlights, Dec.-Jan.; Family Farm, May-Sept.; BC Wildlife Day, Ist Mon. in Aug.; *Internships:* Yes; *Speaker Service:* Yes; *Library* by appointment

Kamloops, Revelstoke, Okanagan & District Building & Construction Trades Council
785 Tranquille Rd., Kamloops BC V2B 3J3
Tel: 250-554-2278; *Fax:* 250-554-1766
Overview: A small local organization
Member of: AFL-CIO
Chief Officer(s):
Leroy Vollans, Secretary-Treasurer
Andy Semenoff, Vice-President
Gary Kinnear, President

Kamsack & District Arts Council
PO Box 1496, Kamsack SK S0A 1S0
Tel: 306-590-0196
clachambre@aol.com
kamsackarts.weebly.com
www.facebook.com/KamsackArt
Overview: A small local charitable organization founded in 1981
Mission: To promote enjoyment & education in visual & performing arts
Member of: Organization of Saskatchewan Arts Councils
Finances: *Annual Operating Budget:* Less than $50,000; *Funding Sources:* Trust Initiatives Program; Saskatchewan Lotteries
7 volunteer(s)
Membership: 7; *Committees:* Visual Arts; Performing Arts

Kamsack & District Chamber of Commerce
PO Box 817, Kamsack SK S0A 1S0
Tel: 306-542-3553; *Fax:* 306-542-3553
Overview: A small local organization

Kanadsko-Hrvatski Kongres *See* Canadian-Croatian Congress

Kanata Chamber of Commerce
#107, 555 Legget Dr., Kanata ON K2K 2X3
Tel: 613-592-8343; *Fax:* 613-592-1157
manager@kanatachamber.com
kanatachamber.com
Overview: A small local organization founded in 1991
Mission: To help with the success of its members by providing leadership & information
Member of: Canadian Chamber of Commerce
Chief Officer(s):
Rosemary Leu, Executive Director
rosemaryleu@kanatachamber.com
Staff Member(s): 3
Membership: 473; *Fees:* $200 non-profit; $240 1-3 employees; $265 4-9 employees; $445 10-25 employees; $730 26-50 employees; $815 50+ employees; *Committees:* Economic & Business Development; Women Only Event; Food & Wine Show; Communications; Membership; Business Advisory; Golf Tournament Organizing; People's Choice Business Awards Organizing

Kanien'kehaka Onkwawen'na Raotitiohkwa *See* Kanien'kehaka Onkwawen'na Raotitiohkwa Language & Cultural Centre

Kanien'kehaka Onkwawen'na Raotitiohkwa Language & Cultural Centre (KORLCC)
PO Box 969, Kahnawake QC J0L 1B0
Tel: 450-638-0880; *Fax:* 450-638-0920
kor@korkahnawake.org
www.korkahnawake.org
Previous Name: Kanien'kehaka Onkwawen'na Raotitiohkwa
Overview: A small local charitable organization founded in 1978
Mission: To lead & support all Kanien'kehaka; to practice, maintain, respect, renew & enhance Kanien'kehaka language, beliefs, values, customs & traditions through the development, delivery & sharing with all peoples; to provide cultural & educational activities which will ensure the continued existence of present & future generations of Kanien'kehaka
Member of: First Nations Confederacy of Cultural Education Centres
Chief Officer(s):
Reaghan Tarbell, Executive Director
Joe Deom, Chair
Staff Member(s): 12
Activities: Kanien'keha language courses; cultural workshops; translation services; *Library* Open to public

Kapuskasing & District Association for Community Living
12 Kimberly Dr., Kapuskasing ON P5N 1L5
Tel: 705-337-1417; *Fax:* 705-337-6538
kdacl@nt.net
www.kdacl.com
Overview: A small local organization
Member of: Community Living Ontario
Chief Officer(s):
Joelle Rancourt, President
Carole Theriault, Executive Director
ctheriault@kdacl.com

Kapuskasing & District Chamber of Commerce
25 Millview St., Kapuskasing ON P5N 2X6
Tel: 705-335-2332
info@kapchamber.ca
www.kapchamber.ca
Overview: A medium-sized local organization
Mission: To help businesses & the community thrive & grow
Chief Officer(s):
Martin Proulx, President
Jammy Pouliot, Contact, Administration
Activities: *Awareness Events:* Business Drive Golf Tournament, June

Kapuskasing Indian Friendship Centre
41 Murdock St., Kapuskasing ON P5N 1H9
Tel: 705-337-1935; *Fax:* 705-335-6789
kifc@ntl.sympatico.ca
Overview: A small local organization
Mission: To help improve the lives of the Aboriginal community in the Kapuskasing area through participation in Canadian society which values Native culture
Member of: Ontario Federation of Indian Friendship Centres
Chief Officer(s):
Francis Matthews, Executive Director

Karate Alberta Association (KAA)
c/o Stewart Price, 56 Auburn Crest Park, Calgary AB T3M 0Z3
Tel: 403-389-5072
www.karateab.org
Overview: A small provincial organization overseen by Karate Canada
Mission: To be the provincial governing organization for karate in Alberta.
Member of: Karate Canada
Finances: *Funding Sources:* Government of Alberta
Membership: *Committees:* Bylaws; casino; coaching; communications; officials; tournament; technical

Karate BC (KBC)
Fortius Athlete Development Centre, Sydney Landing, #2002A, 3713 Kensington Ave., Burnaby BC V5B 0A7
Tel: 604-333-3610; *Fax:* 604-333-3612
www.karatebc.org
www.facebook.com/340127472723273
twitter.com/KarateBC
www.youtube.com/user/KarateBCVideos
Overview: A small provincial charitable organization founded in 1974 overseen by Karate Canada
Mission: To promote the traditions & integrity of karate-do; to improve opportunities to excel in a competitive environment; to be the governing body of the sport of karate in British Columbia.
Member of: Karate Canada; BC Recreation & Parks Association; BC Coaches Association; Sport BC
Chief Officer(s):
Charles La Vertu, President
charleslavertu@gmail.com
Ken Corrigan, Treasurer
kenjan6@telus.net
Dan Wallis, Executive Director
dwallis@karatebc.org
Finances: *Annual Operating Budget:* $250,000-$500,000; *Funding Sources:* Provincial government; gaming; fundraising
Staff Member(s): 2
Membership: 4,000; *Fees:* $150 club; $25 juniors; $45 adults; $65 black belts; *Member Profile:* Instructor must hold bona-fide Dan certificate, be certified at level I NCCP & pass a criminal records check; *Committees:* Executive; Officials; Technical; Tournament; Marketing; Newsletter; High Performance
Activities: Tournaments; coaching clinics; officials seminars; athlete assistance program; coaching grants; first aid clinics; BC Winter Games; mall demos; annual recognition banquet for outstanding athletes & volunteers; *Internships:* Yes; *Speaker Service:* Yes; *Library* by appointment

Karate Canada
4545, av Pierre-de Coubertin, Montréal QC H1V 0B2
Tel: 514-252-3209; *Fax:* 514-252-3211
info@karatecanada.org
www.karatecanada.org
www.facebook.com/459465044133223
Previous Name: National Karate Association of Canada
Overview: A medium-sized national organization founded in 1963
Mission: To be the national governing body for the sport of karate in Canada.
Member of: Sport Canada; Canadian Olympic Committee; World Karate Federation
Chief Officer(s):
Olivier Pineau, Executive Director
olivier@karatecanada.org
Membership: 10 provincial & territorial associations; 13,000 individuals; *Committees:* Finance; Communications & Marketing; Governance & Policy; Domestic Development; Events; High Performance; Officials; NCCP / LTAD; Technical; AWAD

Karate Manitoba
PO Box 2519, 266 Graham Ave., Winnipeg MB R3C 4A7
Tel: 204-925-5605; *Fax:* 204-925-5916
info@karatemanitoba.ca
www.karatemanitoba.ca
www.facebook.com/KarateManitobaWKF
twitter.com/KarateManitoba
www.youtube.com/user/KarateManitoba
Also Known As: Manitoba Karate Association
Overview: A small provincial organization founded in 1974 overseen by Karate Canada
Mission: To promote & develop karate in the province of Manitoba at all levels (grassroots to elite athlete) & as recreation.
Member of: Karate Canada; World Karate Federation; Sport Manitoba
Chief Officer(s):
Debra Kofsky, President
Clive Hinds, Secretary
Membership: 600; *Committees:* NCCP; Officials; Athlete Development; Finance; Grassroots

Karate New Brunswick
c/o Joe Hatfield, 87 Winslow St., Saint John NB E2M 1W4
Tel: 506-650-7748
karatenb.com
Previous Name: New Brunswick Karate Association
Overview: A small provincial organization overseen by Karate Canada
Member of: Karate Canada
Chief Officer(s):
Paul Oliver, President
ollie@nbnet.nb.ca
Joe Hatfield, Secretary
kosephmivyotlh@hotmail.com
Rick MacMichael, Treasurer
suerick@nbnet.nb.ca
Finances: *Funding Sources:* Provincial government
Staff Member(s): 1; 15 volunteer(s)
Membership: 600 individual
Activities: *Rents Mailing List:* Yes

Karate Newfoundland & Labrador
388 Pine Line, Torbay NL A1K 1A2
e-mail: karatenl@gmail.com
www.karatenl.ca
Overview: A small provincial organization overseen by Karate Canada
Mission: To be the provincial governing organization for karate in Newfoundland & Labrador.
Member of: Karate Canada
Chief Officer(s):
Derek J. Ryan, President

Karate Nova Scotia
5516 Spring Garden Rd., 4th Fl., Halifax ON B3J 3G6
e-mail: info@novascotiakarate.com
www.novascotiakarate.com
www.facebook.com/groups/NSKarate
Overview: A small provincial organization overseen by Karate Canada
Mission: To be the official governing body for the sport of karate in Nova Scotia.
Member of: Karate Canada

Karate Ontario (KAO)
#160, 2 County Court Blvd., Brampton ON L6W 4V1
Tel: 647-706-4835
info@karate-ontario.com
karate-ontario.com
www.facebook.com/309961174058
twitter.com/KarateOntario
Overview: A medium-sized provincial organization overseen by Karate Canada
Mission: To promote & perpetuate karate as a martial art & lifetime activity; to promote karate for physical fitness, mental fitness, & as a way of life; to develop provincial standards & programs; to encourage all participants in safely achieving their maximum at the recreational or competitive level; to provide safe competitive opportunities for karate-ka wishing to participate in the sport aspect of karate; to govern the amateur sport of karate & the conduct of all karate-ka under its jurisdiction
Member of: Karate Canada
Affliation(s): World Karate Federation; Sport Alliance of Ontario; Coaches Association of Ontario
Chief Officer(s):
Dragan Kljenak, President, 905-274-7852
Membership: *Committees:* Technical; Referee; Coaching; Constitution; Dispute Resolution; Medical; Women's Affairs; Communications; Awards
Activities: *Awareness Events:* Sport Science Karate Symposium, June
Publications:
- Black Belt Journal
- Karate Masters

Frequency: Quarterly
Profile: The methods, masters, philosophy and training skills of Martial Arts.

Karaté Québec
CP 1000, Succ. M, 4545, av Pierre-de Coubertin, Montréal QC H1V 3R2
Tél: 514-252-3161; *Téléc:* 514-252-3036
Ligne sans frais: 877-527-2835
info@karatequebec.com
www.karatequebec.com
www.facebook.com/karatequebec
Aperçu: *Dimension:* moyenne; *Envergure:* provinciale; fondée en 1995 surveillé par Karate Canada
Mission: Karaté Québec est une organisation structurée et démocratique qui vise à promouvoir, à organiser et à administrer la pratique du karaté au Québec de manière à ce que cet art martial ne perde jamais son sens premier : favoriser une progression saine et équilibrée des karatékas dans une société en mouvance perpétuelle
Membre de: Karate Canada
Membre(s) du bureau directeur:
Jean-Pierre Gendron, Président
jpg1956@hotmail.com
Georges Struthers, Directeur des activités
dg@karatequebec.com

Kashmiri Canadian Council (KCC)
#44516, 2376 Eglinton Ave. East, Toronto ON M1K 5K3
Tel: 416-282-6933; *Fax:* 416-282-7488
kcc@kashmiri-cc.ca
www.kashmiri-cc.ca
Overview: A small international organization
Finances: *Annual Operating Budget:* $100,000-$250,000
Staff Member(s): 3

Kashruth Council of Canada
#308, 3200 Dufferin St., Toronto ON M6A 3B2
Tel: 416-635-9550; *Fax:* 416-635-8760
questions@cor.ca
www.cor.ca
www.facebook.com/CORKosher
twitter.com/CORKosher
Also Known As: COR
Previous Name: Kashruth Council of Toronto
Overview: A small local organization founded in 1956
Mission: To promote awareness among consumers and manufacturers about kosher products.
Affliation(s): Vaad Harabonim of Toronto
Chief Officer(s):
Tuvia Basser, Chief Executive Officer
Staff Member(s): 20
Activities: Kosher cooking demos; holiday recipes & updates; kosher food supervision;

Kashruth Council of Toronto *See* Kashruth Council of Canada

Kaslo & Area Chamber of Commerce
PO Box 329, Kaslo BC V0G 1M0
Toll-Free: 866-276-3212
info@kaslochamber.com
www.kaslochamber.com
www.facebook.com/kaslochamber
Previous Name: Kaslo Chamber of Commerce
Overview: A small local organization founded in 1897
Mission: To promote & improve trade & commerce & the economic, civic & social welfare of the district.
Chief Officer(s):
Steve Hoffart, President
Finances: *Annual Operating Budget:* Less than $50,000; *Funding Sources:* Membership dues
Membership: 65; *Fees:* $55-$80
Awards:
- Kaslo Citizen of the Year Award (Award)
- Business Excellence Awards (Award)

Publications:
- Kaslo & Area Chamber of Commerce Newsletter

Type: Newsletter

Kaslo Arts Counci *See* Langham Cultural Society

Kaslo Chamber of Commerce *See* Kaslo & Area Chamber of Commerce

Katarokwi Native Friendship Centre
50 Hickson Ave., Kingston ON K7K 2N6
Tel: 613-548-1500; *Fax:* 613-548-1847
Overview: A small local charitable organization founded in 1992
Mission: Committed to bringing positive changes to the daily lives of the Aboriginal community in the Kingston and surrounding rural areas. Provides Aboriginal people with a safe and enjoyable venue to stay in touch with their communities, and assist them by allowing them to receive culturally appropriate programs for individual and family needs.
Member of: Ontario Federation of Indian Friendship Centres; National Federation of Friendship Centres
Activities: Provide support to urban Aboriginal status; non-status; self identified

Katimavik
429, av Viger est, Montréal QC H2L 2N9
Tel: 514-868-0898; *Fax:* 514-868-0901
Toll-Free: 888-525-1503
info@katimavik.org
www.katimavik.org
www.facebook.com/group.php?gid=24093459546
Overview: A small national organization founded in 1977
Mission: To engage youth in volunteer service and foster sustainable communities through challenging national youth service programs.
Chief Officer(s):
Robert Landry, Executive Director
Andréanne Sylvestre, Coordinator, Communications

Kawartha Baseball Umpires Association (KBUA)
Peterborough ON
www.kbua.net
Overview: A small local organization
Chief Officer(s):
Jim McMillan, President
jimmymcmillan@hotmail.com
Kevin Fitzgerald, Vice-President
k_lfitzgerald@hotmail.com

Kawartha Chamber of Commerce & Tourism
PO Box 537, 12 Queen St., Lakefield ON K0L 2H0
Tel: 705-652-6963; *Fax:* 705-652-9140
Toll-Free: 888-565-9140
info@kawarthachamber.ca
www.kawarthachamber.ca
www.linkedin.com/company/kawarthachamberofcommerce&tourism
www.facebook.com/KawarthaChamber
twitter.com/KawarthaChamber
Previous Name: Kawartha Lakes Chamber of Commerce
Overview: A small local organization founded in 1947
Mission: To promote the commercial, industrial, agricultural & civic welfare of the community; to maintain just & equitable principles in business & the professions
Member of: Canadian Chamber of Commerce; Ontario Chamber of Commerce; Canadian Society of Association Executives
Chief Officer(s):
Scott Davidson, President
sdavidson@hendrenfuneralhome.com
Sherry Boyce-Found, General Manager
generalmanager@kawarthachamber.ca
Finances: *Annual Operating Budget:* $50,000-$100,000
Staff Member(s): 4; 14 volunteer(s)
Membership: 350; *Fees:* $165-$595; *Committees:* Marketing; Membership; Programs & Events; Public Policy; Human Resources; Finance; Governance; Nominating
Activities: *Library*

Kawartha Lakes Chamber of Commerce *See* Kawartha Chamber of Commerce & Tourism

Kawartha Lakes Real Estate Association
31 Kent St. East, Lindsay ON K9V 2C3
Tel: 705-324-4515; *Fax:* 705-324-3916
www.kawarthalakes-mls.ca
Previous Name: Lindsay & District Real Estate Board
Overview: A small local organization founded in 1958 overseen by Ontario Real Estate Association
Mission: To provide its members with resources that allow them to grow within the profession
Member of: The Canadian Real Estate Association
Chief Officer(s):
Susan Schell, Executive Officer
sschell@kawarthalakes-mls.ca

Kawartha Sexual Assault Centre
#102, 411 Water St., Peterborough ON K9H 3L9
Tel: 705-748-5901; *Fax:* 705-741-0405
Toll-Free: 866-298-7778; *Crisis Hot-Line:* 705-741-0260
ksac@nexicom.net
www.kawarthasexualassaultcentre.com
www.facebook.com/125032707554367
twitter.com/KSACstaff
Previous Name: Sexual Violence Support & Information Centre of the Kawarthas
Overview: A small local charitable organization founded in 1977
Mission: To provide sexual assault services & public education for the community
Finances: *Funding Sources:* Ministry of the Attorney General; City of Peterborough; Trent University Student Levy
Activities: 24-hour crisis line; outreach counselling; in-house counselling; public education; *Speaker Service:* Yes

Kawartha World Issues Centre (KWIC)
PO Box 895, Peterborough ON K9J 7A2
Tel: 705-748-1680; *Fax:* 705-748-1681
info@kwic.info
www.kwic.info
www.facebook.com/KWICPeterborough
twitter.com/KWICnews
www.youtube.com/user/KWICpeterborough
Overview: A small international charitable organization founded in 1988
Mission: To further an understanding of global issues; to create links between global & local community development; to promote analysis & action for positive social change
Member of: Eastern Ontario Coalition of Internationally-Minded NGOs; Ontario Council for International Cooperation
Chief Officer(s):
Julie Cosgrove, Coordinator
Finances: *Funding Sources:* Public donations; Trent student donations; CIDA; special grants
Staff Member(s): 2
Membership: *Fees:* Donations
Activities: Public Programming on global issues; skills training; networking; special projects: Person's Day Breakfast, International Development Week; One World (Vegetarian) Dinner; Global Youth Day, Volunteer Recruitment & Training, Annual Secondary School Symposium; *Speaker Service:* Yes; *Library* Open to public

Kawartha-Haliburton Children's Aid Society
1100 Chemong Rd., Peterborough ON K9H 7S2
Tel: 705-743-9751
Toll-Free: 800-661-2843
www.khcas.on.ca
Overview: A small local organization
Member of: Ontario Association of Children's Aid Societies
Chief Officer(s):
Deirdre Thomas, President
Finances: *Annual Operating Budget:* Greater than $5 Million
Staff Member(s): 100; 50 volunteer(s)
Activities: *Speaker Service:* Yes

Haliburton
HALCO Plaza, PO Box 958, 1 Maple Ave., Haliburton ON K0M 1S0
Tel: 705-457-1661
Toll-Free: 800-661-1979

Lindsay
42 Victoria Ave. North, Lindsay ON K9V 4G2
Tel: 705-324-3594
Toll-Free: 800-567-9136

Kaye Nickerson Adult Service Centre
PO Box 3, 87 Parade St., Yarmouth NS B0H 1R0
Tel: 902-742-2238; *Fax:* 902-386-2808
kayenick@ns.aliantzinc.ca
www.facebook.com/102076771951
Overview: A small local organization
Mission: To provide mentally challenged adults in Yarmouth with vocational training & work experience
Chief Officer(s):
Darrell Foster, Executive Director/Manager
Membership: 32; *Member Profile:* Adults with special needs, aged 18+
Activities: Provides services involving pallets, lawn furniture, survey stakes, rough boxes, garbage bins, kindling wood & buttons, as well as special orders;

Keewatin Chamber of Commerce *See* Kivalliq Chamber of Commerce

Keewatin Tribal Council (KTC)
23 Nickel Rd., Thompson MB R8N 0Y4
Tel: 204-677-2341; *Fax:* 204-677-0256
www.ktc.ca
Previous Name: Winnipeg Tribal Council
Overview: A small provincial organization
Chief Officer(s):
Irvin Sinclair, Grand Chief
Walter Spence, Chair
Gilbert G. Andrews, Vice-Chair
Peter Thorassie, Sec.-Treas.

Kelowna & District Arts Council *See* Arts Council of the Central Okanagan

Kelowna & District Society for Community Living (KDSCL)
555 Fuller Ave., Kelowna BC V1Y 7W8
Tel: 250-763-4484; *Fax:* 250-763-4488
cdaley@kdscl.bc.ca
www.kdscl.bc.ca
www.facebook.com/KDSCL
Overview: A small local organization
Member of: BC Association for Community Living
Chief Officer(s):
Gail Meier, President

Kelowna & District Stamp Club
4740 Parkridge Dr., Kelowna BC V1W 3A5
Overview: A small local organization
Mission: To provide an opportunity for stamp collectors to exhibit, buy & sell stamps & to share their knowledge of philately
Activities: Monthly meetings, every 1st Wed. at Odd Fellows Hall

Kelowna Chamber of Commerce
544 Harvey Ave., Kelowna BC V1Y 6C9
Tel: 250-861-3627; *Fax:* 250-861-3624
info@kelownachamber.org
www.kelownachamber.org
www.linkedin.com/groups/Kelowna-Chamber-Commerce-3972388
www.facebook.com/KelownaChamberofCommerce
twitter.com/KelownaChamber
Overview: A medium-sized local organization
Mission: To improve trade & commerce & the economic, civic & social welfare of the city of Kelowna
Affiliation(s): BC Chamber of Commerce
Chief Officer(s):
Dave Bond, President
Caroline Grover, Chief Executive Officer
Staff Member(s): 8
Membership: *Fees:* Schedule available; *Committees:* Advocacy; Member Care; Municipal Affairs; Federal Policy; Provincial Policy; Ambassadors; Governance; Young Professionals; Volunteer
Activities: *Rents Mailing List:* Yes; *Library* Open to public

Kelowna Community Development Society (KCDS)
#2, 1441 St. Paul St., Kelowna BC V1Y 2E4
Tel: 250-763-6696; *Fax:* 250-763-6694
www.kcds.info
www.linkedin.com/company/kelowna-community-development-society
www.facebook.com/KelownaCommunityDevelopmentSociety
Overview: A small local organization founded in 1983
Mission: To improve the quality of life of people with developmental disabilities so that they will be accepted and valued citizens; accomplish personal goals; and benefit from active involvement of family and friends.
Member of: British Columbia Association of Community Living
Chief Officer(s):
Daryle Roberts, Executive Director
droberts@kcds.info
Staff Member(s): 3
Activities: Services to people with developmental disabilites

Kelowna Community Food Bank
1265 Ellis St., Kelowna BC V1Y 1Z7
Tel: 250-763-7161; *Fax:* 250-763-9116
info@kcfb.ca
www.kelownafoodbank.com
www.facebook.com/kelownafoodbank
twitter.com/kcfbank
www.youtube.com/user/KelownaFoodBank
Overview: A small local charitable organization founded in 1983
Mission: To assist low income persons by providing food
Member of: Canadian Association of Food Banks
Affiliation(s): Canadian Association of Food Banks - Western Branch
Chief Officer(s):
Vonnie Lavers, Executive Director
vonnie@kcfb.ca
Lenetta Parry, Associate Executive Director
lenetta@kcfb.ca
Finances: *Annual Operating Budget:* $250,000-$500,000; *Funding Sources:* Public donations
Staff Member(s): 4; 125 volunteer(s)
Membership: 23

Kelowna Visitor & Convention Bureau *See* Tourism Kelowna

Kemptville & District Chamber of Commerce *See* North Grenville Chamber of Commerce

Kenaston & District Chamber of Commerce
PO Box 70, Kenaston SK S0G 2N0
Tel: 306-252-2236; *Fax:* 306-252-2089
www.kenaston.ca/pages/chamber.htm
Overview: A small local organization
Chief Officer(s):
Susan Anbolt, Sec.-Treas.
Mary Lou Whittles, President
r.m.whittles@sasktel.net

Kennebecasis Naturalists' Society
c/o Ms. H. Folkins, 827 Main St., Sussex NB E4E 2N1
www.macbe.com/kns/
Overview: A small local organization
Chief Officer(s):
Gart Bishop, Chair
5 volunteer(s)
Membership: 80
Activities: Field trips

Kennebecasis Valley Chamber of Commerce
PO Box 4455, 140L Hampton Rd., Rothesay NB E2E 5X2
Tel: 506-849-2860; *Fax:* 506-848-0121
kvchambr@nbnet.nb.ca
www.intellis.net/kvchamber
Overview: A small local organization
Mission: To represent the interests & aspirations of the local business community; to make the communities of the Kennebecasis Valley a preferred location in which to live, work & do business
Member of: Canadian Chamber of Commerce; New Brunswick Chamber of Commerce; Atlantic Provinces Chambers of Commerce
Chief Officer(s):
Michael F Cole, President
Catherine Selkirk, Executive Director, 506-849-2860
Finances: *Annual Operating Budget:* Less than $50,000
Staff Member(s): 1; 120 volunteer(s)
Membership: 155; *Fees:* $100-250

Kenora & District Chamber of Commerce (KDCC)
PO Box 471, Kenora ON P9N 3X5
Tel: 807-467-4646; *Fax:* 807-468-3056
kenorachamber@kmts.ca
www.kenorachamber.com
www.facebook.com/KenoraChamber
Overview: A small local organization founded in 1888
Mission: To promote a favourable business climate, quality of life & the growth & prosperity of our members
Member of: Northwestern Ontario Associated Chambers of Commerce; Canadian Chamber of Commerce
Chief Officer(s):
Carol Leduc, Chamber Manager
Membership: 230+; *Fees:* Schedule available based on number of employees; *Committees:* Membership/Membership Services; Education; Constitution/By-laws; Special Events/After Hours; Home & Leisure Show; AGM; Government Affairs & Tendering

Kenora Association for Community Living (KACL)
501 - 8th Ave. South, Kenora ON P9N 3Z9
Tel: 807-467-5225; *Fax:* 807-467-5247
central@kacl.ca
www.kacl.ca
www.facebook.com/kenora.acl
twitter.com/KenoraACL
www.youtube.com/user/KenoraACL
Overview: A medium-sized local charitable organization founded in 1961
Mission: To ensure that all people with special needs have the opportunity to enjoy a meaningful & satisfying lifestyle & to interact as an equal in their community by providing continuing opportunities for personal growth through education, training, support, advocacy & an informed public
Member of: Community Living Ontario
Chief Officer(s):
Deborah Everley, Executive Director, 807-467-5251
debbie.everley@kacl.ca
Sharon White, Director, Human Resources / Intake, 807-467-5237
sharon.white@kacl.ca
Lisa Thomassen, Director, Finance and Administration, 807-467-5205
lisa.thomassen@kacl.ca
Finances: *Annual Operating Budget:* $3 Million-$5 Million
Staff Member(s): 160; 20 volunteer(s)
Membership: 50; *Fees:* $10
Activities: *Speaker Service:* Yes; *Library* Open to public

Kenora District Labour Council
PO Box 388, Kenora ON P9N 3X4
Previous Name: Kenora-Keewatin & District Labour Council
Overview: A small local organization overseen by Ontario Federation of Labour
Chief Officer(s):
Donna Wiebe, President
Membership: 2,700; *Fees:* $22

Kenora Fellowship Centre
PO Box 447, Kenora ON P9N 3X4
Tel: 807-467-8205; *Fax:* 807-468-9063
kenorafellowship@kmts.ca
www.kenorafellowshipcentre.ca
Overview: A small local charitable organization
Mission: To offer emergency shelter to the less fortunate
Chief Officer(s):
Henry Hildebrandt, Executive Director
Staff Member(s): 20

Kenora-Keewatin & District Labour Council ***See*** Kenora District Labour Council

Kensington & Area Chamber of Commerce
PO Box 234, Kensington PE C0B 1M0
Tel: 902-836-3209; *Fax:* 902-836-3206
kensingtonchamber.ca
www.linkedin.com/groups/Kensington-Area-Chamber-Commerce-3837839
www.facebook.com/Kensington.Chamber
twitter.com/KTownChamber
www.youtube.com/user/KtownChamber
Overview: A small local organization founded in 1960
Member of: PEI Chamber of Commerce; Atlantic Provinces Chambers of Commerce
Chief Officer(s):
Ryan Cochrane, President
Glenna Lohnes, Executive Director
glenna@kensingtonchamber.ca
Finances: *Annual Operating Budget:* Less than $50,000; *Funding Sources:* Membership fees
Membership: 129; *Fees:* $85

Kensington & Area Tourist Association
PO Box 600, Kensington PE C0B 1M0
Tel: 902-836-3031; *Fax:* 902-836-3674
mail@kata.pe.ca
www.kata.pe.ca
Overview: A small local organization
Staff Member(s): 3; 6 volunteer(s)
Membership: *Fees:* $26+

Kensington Cooperative Association Ltd
48 Victoria St. East, Kensington PE C0B 1M0
Tel: 902-836-3116; *Fax:* 902-836-3770
Overview: A small local organization

Kensington Foundation
25 Brunswick Ave., Toronto ON M5S 2L9
Tel: 416-964-3636; *Fax:* 416-963-9811
www.kensingtonhealth.org/Kensington-Foundation
Overview: A small local charitable organization
Mission: To raise money of behalf of Kensington Health, a long term care organization
Chief Officer(s):
Brian McFarlane, Executive Director
Finances: *Annual Operating Budget:* Greater than $5 Million
Membership: *Committees:* Audit; Investment; Kensington Golf; Grants/Donations; Strategic Planning

Kent Centre Chamber of Commerce
#1, 9235 rue Main, Richibucto NB E4W 4B4
Tel: 506-523-7870; *Fax:* 506-523-7850
www.kentcentre.com
www.facebook.com/groups/714368781928494/
Previous Name: Richibouctou chambre de commerce
Overview: A small local organization
Mission: Chambre de Commerce Kent Centre Chamber of Commerce, under the direction of an organized and responsible Board of Directors, governed by a set of by-laws, is a non-profit organization serving the needs and interest of local entrepreneurs by giving them a voice in issues affecting local business and community.
Member of: Atlantic Chamber of Commerce
Chief Officer(s):
Bobby Johnson, Président
Finances: *Annual Operating Budget:* Less than $50,000
10 volunteer(s)
Membership: 100; *Fees:* $25
Activities: *Speaker Service:* Yes

Kent Coin Club
27 Peter St., Chatham ON N7M 5B2
Tel: 519-352-5477
Overview: A small local organization founded in 1963
Mission: To encourage & promote the collection and study of coins, tokens, paper money, medals, badges, trade money, and other currency related collectibles; to cultivate fraternal relations among collectors.
Chief Officer(s):
Lucien Wagenaer, President
Finances: *Funding Sources:* Membership fees
Membership: *Fees:* $2 child; $5 adult; $7 family
Activities: Annual Coin Show;

Kent County Cattlemen's Association
7189 - 9th Line, RR#6, Chatham ON N7M 5J6
Tel: 519-436-0701
Overview: A small local organization
Affliation(s): Ontario Cattlemen's Association
Chief Officer(s):
Mike Buis, President

Kent County Community Volunteer Action Organization
PO Box 2706, #4, 9358 Main St., Richibucto NB E4W 4C8
Tel: 506-523-7580; *Fax:* 506-523-4086
Also Known As: Kent County C.V.A. Organization
Overview: A small local organization
Member of: Association of Food Banks & C.V.A.'s for New Brunswick

Kent County Stamp Club
43 Sudbury Dr., Chatham ON N7L 2K1
Tel: 519-354-1845
Overview: A small local organization founded in 1960
Mission: Provides an opportunity for members & guests to trade, deal & learn about stamps in a friendly, informal setting
Member of: Royal Philatelic Society of Canada
Chief Officer(s):
Allan Burk, Contact
Membership: *Fees:* $10
Activities: *Awareness Events:* KENTPEX, annual Stamp Exhibition & Bourse

Kentville & Area Board of Trade; Eastern Kings Chamber of Commerce ***See*** Annapolis Valley Chamber of Commerce

Kerby Centre for the 55 Plus
1133 - 7th Ave. SW, Calgary AB T2P 1B2
Tel: 403-265-0661; *Fax:* 403-705-3211
information@kerbycentre.com
kerbycentre.com
www.facebook.com/pages/Kerby-Centre-for-the-55/514905501859242
twitter.com/KerbyCentre
www.youtube.com/user/hheerema29
Overview: A medium-sized local charitable organization founded in 1976
Mission: To assist older people to live as well as possible for as long as possible as residents in the community. Services include Adult Day Support, grocery delivery, food services, housing registry, wellness centre
Chief Officer(s):
Luanne Whitmarsh, CEO
Hank Heerema, President
Finances: *Annual Operating Budget:* $3 Million-$5 Million; *Funding Sources:* Provincial & regional government (38%); remaining funds are self-generated
Membership: 2,997 individual; *Member Profile:* Anyone age 55 and over
Activities: Sr. Multi Service Centre; *Library:* Resource Centre for the Aging Family; Open to public

Kermode Friendship Centre ***See*** Kermode Friendship Society

Kermode Friendship Society
#201, 3240 Kalum St., Terrace BC V8G 2N4
Tel: 250-635-1476; *Fax:* 250-635-7696
Toll-Free: 877-635-1476
info@kermode-fs.ca
kermodefriendship.ca
www.facebook.com/KermodeFS
Previous Name: Kermode Friendship Centre
Overview: A small local charitable organization founded in 1976
Mission: To provide cultural services & programs to the Aboriginal community in the Terrace area
Chief Officer(s):
Calvin Albright, Executive Director
execdir@kermode-fs.ca
Staff Member(s): 38
Activities: Health; education; parenting; youth

Keroul, Tourism & culture for people with restricted physical ability ***Voir*** Kéroul, Tourisme pour personnes à capacité physique restreinte

Kéroul, Tourisme pour personnes à capacité physique restreinte / Keroul, Tourism & culture for people with restricted physical ability
CP 1000, Succ. M, 4545, av Pierre-de Coubertin, Montréal QC H1V 3R2
Tél: 514-252-3104; *Téléc:* 514-254-0766
infos@keroul.qc.ca
www.keroul.qc.ca
www.facebook.com/pages/K%C3%A9roul/201239641037?v=info
Aperçu: *Dimension:* moyenne; *Envergure:* provinciale; Organisme sans but lucratif; fondée en 1979
Mission: Rendre le tourisme et la culture accessibles aux personnes à capacité physique restreinte
Affiliation(s): Regroupement loisir Québec
Membre(s) du bureau directeur:
André Leclerc, Président-directeur général et fondateur
aleclerc@keroul.qc.ca
Lyne Ménard, Directrice adjointe
lmenard@keroul.qc.ca
Finances: *Budget de fonctionnement annuel:* $250,000-$500,000
Membre(s) du personnel: 7; 9 bénévole(s)
Membre: 400 individus; 40 institutionnel; *Montant de la cotisation:* 20$ individus; 50$ organismes
Activités: Représentation; information et promotion; recherche; formation; organisation d'événements; *Stagiaires:* Oui; *Service de conférenciers:* Oui

Kerrobert Chamber of Commerce
PO Box 408, Kerrobert SK S0L 1R0
Tel: 306-834-5423
kerrobert@sasktel.net
www.kerrobertsk.com
Overview: A small local organization
Member of: Saskatchewan Chamber of Commerce
Chief Officer(s):
Darryl Morris, President
Finances: *Annual Operating Budget:* Less than $50,000
Membership: 35; *Fees:* $100

Kerry's Place Autism Services
34 Berczy St., Aurora ON L4G 1W9
Tel: 905-841-6611; *Fax:* 905-841-1461
info@kerrysplace.org
www.kerrysplace.org
www.facebook.com/pages/Kerrys-Place-Autism-Services/106809869347752
twitter.com/kerrysplace
Overview: A medium-sized local charitable organization founded in 1974
Mission: To enhance the quality of life of individuals with Autism Spectrum Disorder, through innovative personalized supports, expertise, collaboration & advocacy
Chief Officer(s):
Sally Ginter, President & CEO
Finances: *Annual Operating Budget:* Greater than $5 Million; *Funding Sources:* Donations, Fundraising events
Staff Member(s): 1000
Membership: *Fees:* $20 individual/associate; $15 people with autism/seniors/students; $60 corporate; *Member Profile:* Parents; professionals
Activities: *Library:* Resource Centre; by appointment

Central East
c/o #201, 34 Berczy St., Aurora ON L4G 1W9
Tel: 905-713-6808; *Fax:* 905-841-1461
cjohnson@kerrysplace.org
twitter.com/kerrysplace
Chief Officer(s):
Brenda Scott, Regional Executive Director, 905-713-6808 Ext. 318

Kerry's Place Central West
#3, 25 Van Kirk Dr., Brampton ON L7A 1A6
Tel: 905-457-8711; *Fax:* 905-457-8462
peelhaltoninquiry@kerrysplace.org

Chief Officer(s):
Jim Preston, Regional Executive Director
Kerry's Place Toronto
#12A, 219 Dufferin St., Toronto ON M6K 3J1
Tel: 416-537-2000; *Fax:* 416-537-7715
rock@kerrysplace.org
Chief Officer(s):
Joe Persaud, Regional Executive Director
jpersaud@kerrysplace.org
South East Regional Office
189 Victoria Ave., Belleville ON K8N 2B9
Tel: 613-968-5554; *Fax:* 613-962-6003
Chief Officer(s):
Christine Johnson, Regional Executive Director
cjohnson@kerrysplace.org

Kerry's Place Hastings *See* Kerry's Place Autism Services

Kerry's Place South East *See* Kerry's Place Autism Services

Keyano College Faculty Association (KCFA) / Association des professeurs du Collège Keyano
8115 Franklin Ave., Fort McMurray AB T9H 2H7
Tel: 780-791-4800
Overview: A small local organization
Chief Officer(s):
C. Vincella Thompson, Contact
vincella.thompson@keyano.ca

Keystone Agricultural Producers (KAP)
#203, 1700 Ellice Ave., Winnipeg MB R3H 0B1
Tel: 204-697-1140; *Fax:* 204-697-1109
kap@kap.mb.ca
www.kap.mb.ca
Previous Name: Manitoba Farm Bureau
Overview: A medium-sized provincial organization founded in 1985 overseen by Canadian Federation of Agriculture
Mission: To be a democratic & effective policy organization, promoting the social, economic & physical well-being of all Manitoban agricultural producers
Chief Officer(s):
James Battershill, General Manager
james.battershill@kap.mb.ca
Doug Chorney, President
Staff Member(s): 6
Membership: *Fees:* $210 farm unit/associate
Meetings/Conferences: • Keystone Agricultural Producers 2015 Annual Meeting, January, 2015, Delta Hotel, Winnipeg, MB
Scope: National
Publications:
• Manitoba Farmers' Voice
Type: Journal; *Frequency:* Quarterly

Khalsa Diwan Society
c/o Sikh Temple, 8000 Ross St., Vancouver BC V5X 4C5
Tel: 604-324-2010
Other Communication: World Gurudwara Database URL: www.worldgurudwara.com
www.worldgurudwara.com/V4/641.asp
Also Known As: Gurdwara Sahib Ross Street
Overview: A large local organization founded in 1906
Finances: *Annual Operating Budget:* $500,000-$1.5 Million
Membership: *Fees:* $25/3 years

Kicking Horse Country Chamber of Commerce (KHCCC)
PO Box 1320, #500, 10 North Ave., Golden BC V0A 1H0
Tel: 250-344-7125; *Fax:* 250-344-6688
Toll-Free: 800-622-4653
info@goldenchamber.bc.ca
www.goldenchamber.bc.ca
www.facebook.com/KHCCC
Previous Name: Golden & District Chamber of Commerce
Overview: A small local organization
Mission: To actively encourage, develop & represent the business community of Golden & District
Member of: BC Chamber of Commerce; Tourism Rockies
Chief Officer(s):
Ruth Kowalski, Manager
Lori Baxendale, President
Finances: *Annual Operating Budget:* $50,000-$100,000; *Funding Sources:* Membership dues
Staff Member(s): 2
Membership: 174; *Fees:* $150-$942; *Committees:* Policy & Advocacy; Events; Education & Training; Finance; Membership

KickStart Disability Arts & Culture
PO Box 2749, Stn. Terminal, Vancouver BC V6B 3X2
Tel: 604-559-6626
info@kickstart-arts.ca
www.kickstart-arts.ca
www.facebook.com/318968627521
Previous Name: Society for Disability Arts & Culture
Overview: A small national organization founded in 1998
Mission: Kickstart's mission is to produce and present works by artists with disabilities and to promote artistic excellence among artists with disabilities working in a variety of disciplines.
Chief Officer(s):
Nisse Gustafson, Operations Director
Emma Kivisild, Artistic Director

Kidney Cancer Canada (KCC)
PO Box 25034, 411 The Queensway Ave. South, Keswick ON L4P 4C2
Tel: 905-476-1935; *Fax:* 866-806-1720
Toll-Free: 866-598-7166
www.kidneycancercanada.ca
www.facebook.com/KidneyCancerCanada
twitter.com/KidneyCancer_Ca
www.youtube.com/KidneyCancerCanada
Overview: A medium-sized national charitable organization founded in 2006
Mission: To support & improve the lives of patients & families living with kidney cancer
Chief Officer(s):
Deb Maskens, Chair
debmaskens@kidneycancercanada.ca
Catherine Madden, Executive Director
cmadden@kidneycancercanada.ca
Finances: *Funding Sources:* Donations
Membership: 2,000+

Kidney Foundation of Canada (KFOC) / Fondation canadienne du rein
#300, 5165, rue Sherbrooke ouest, Montréal QC H4A 1T6
Tel: 514-369-4806; *Fax:* 514-369-2472
Toll-Free: 800-361-7494
Other Communication: webmaster@kidney.ca
info@kidney.ca
www.kidney.ca
www.facebook.com/kidneyfoundation
twitter.com/kidneycanada
www.youtube.com/kidneycanada
Overview: A large national charitable organization founded in 1964
Mission: To improve the health & quality of life of people living with kidney disease; To fund research & related clinical education; To provide services for the special needs of individuals living with kidney disease; To advocate for access to high quality health care; To actively promote awareness of & commitment to organ donation
Member of: National Voluntary Organization; Healthpartners; Canadian Centre for Philanthrophy; Health Charities Coalition
Chief Officer(s):
Julian Midgley, National President
Andrew MacRitchie, National Vice President
Finances: *Annual Operating Budget:* Greater than $5 Million; *Funding Sources:* Fundraising programs
Staff Member(s): 145
Membership: 5,000; *Fees:* $10; *Committees:* National Medical Advisory Board; Executive; Board of Directors; Finance; Fundraising; Patient Services & Organ Donation; Human Resources; Research; Allied Health Scientific; Public Policy; Biomedical Scientific; Fellowship & Scholarship
Activities: Offering monthly support group meetings in Ontario, in Kitchener, Brantford, Thunder Bay, Mississauga & Oshawa-Whitby; *Awareness Events:* Kidney Month, March; Organ Donor Awareness Week, 3rd week in April; *Speaker Service:* Yes
Awards:
• Breslinger Award of Excellence (Award)
• Medal for Research Excellence (Award)
• The Gavin Turley Scholarship for Civic Engagement (Scholarship)
Meetings/Conferences: • Kidney Foundation of Canada / Fondation canadienne du rein 2015 Kidney Care Conference, 2015
Scope: National
Contact Information: Kidney Care Coordinator: Molly Diamond, Phone: 780-451-6900, ext. 222, E-mail: molly.diamond@kidney.ab.ca
Publications:
• Living with Kidney Disease
Type: Manual
Profile: Published in English, French, Italian, Chinese, & Punjabi
Atlantic Canada Branch
#204, 56 Avonlea Ct., Fredericton NB E3C 1N8
Tel: 506-453-0533; *Fax:* 506-454-3639
Toll-Free: 877-453-0533
kidneyatlantic@kidney.ca
www.kidney.ca/atlantic
Chief Officer(s):
Tracy Durkee Jones, Executive Director
tracy.durkee-jones@kidney.ca
British Columbia Branch
#200, 4940 Canada Way, Burnaby BC V5G 4K6
Tel: 604-736-9775; *Fax:* 604-736-9703
Toll-Free: 800-567-8112
info@kidney.bc.ca
www.kidney.ca/BC
Chief Officer(s):
Karen Philip, Executive Director, 604-736-9775 Ext. 224
kphilp@kidney.bc.ca
Division du Québec
2300, boul René-Lévesque Ouest, Montréal QC H3H 2R5
Tél: 514-938-4515; *Téléc:* 514-938-4757
Ligne sans frais: 800-565-4515
infoquebec@kidney.ca
www.kidney.ca/quebec
Chief Officer(s):
Martin Munger, Directeur général
martin.munger@kidney.ca
Eastern Ontario Chapter
#401, 1376 Bank St., Ottawa ON K1H 7Y3
Tel: 613-724-9953; *Fax:* 613-722-5907
Toll-Free: 800-724-9953
Chief Officer(s):
Suzanne Laniel, Administrative Assistant
slaniel@kidney.on.ca
Hamilton & District Chapter
#201, 1599 Hurontario St., Mississauga ON L5G 4S1
Fax: 905-271-4990
Toll-Free: 800-387-4474
michelle@kidney.ca
Chief Officer(s):
Natalie Charette, Chapter Manager
ncharette@kidney.on.ca
Kingston Chapter
c/o Kidd House, 100 Stuart St., Kingston ON K7L 2V6
Tel: 613-542-2121; *Fax:* 613-542-7258
Chief Officer(s):
Ann LaBrash, Administrative Assistant
alabrash@kidney.on.ca
Manitoba Branch
#1, 452 Dovercourt Dr., Winnipeg MB R3Y 1G4
Tel: 204-989-0800
Toll-Free: 800-729-7176
info@kidney.mb.ca
www.kidney.ca/manitoba
twitter.com/KidneyFdnMB
Chief Officer(s):
Valerie Dunphy, Executive Director
vdunphy@kidney.mb.ca
Niagara District Chapter
#201, 1599 Hurontario St., Mississauga ON L5G 4S1
Fax: 905-271-4990
Toll-Free: 800-387-4474
Chief Officer(s):
Natalie Charette, Chapter Manager
ncharette@kidney.on.ca
Northern Alberta & The Territories Branch
#202, 11227 Jasper Ave. NW, Edmonton AB T5K 0L5
Tel: 780-451-6900; *Fax:* 780-451-7592
Toll-Free: 800-461-9063
info@kidney.ab.ca
www.kidney.ca/Page.aspx?pid=266
Chief Officer(s):
Flavia Robles, Executive Director
Northern Superior Chapter - Thunder Bay
605 Hewitson St., Thunder Bay ON P7B 5V5
Tel: 807-624-2680; *Fax:* 807-623-9137
Chief Officer(s):
Riley Winter, Interim Chapter Coordinator
kidney@tbaytel.net

Ontario Branch
#201, 1599 Hurontario St., Mississauga ON L5G 4S1
Tel: 905-278-3003; *Fax:* 905-271-4990
Toll-Free: 800-387-4474
kidney@kidney.on.ca
www.kidney.ca/ontario
Chief Officer(s):
Jim O'Brien, Executive Director, 905-278-3003 Ext. 4950

Outaouais-Québécois Chapter
CP 89027, Succ. Cité des jeunes, 207, boul Mont-Bleu, Gatineau QC J8Z 3G3
Tél: 819-682-2830
Ligne sans frais: 800-565-4515
Chief Officer(s):
Laureen Bureau, Contact

Prince Edward Island Chapter
565 North River Rd., Charlottetown NB C1E 1J7
Tel: 902-892-9009; *Fax:* 902-626-3753
Toll-Free: 877-892-9009
kidneypei@kidney.ca
www.kidney.ca/page.aspx?pid=607
Chief Officer(s):
Crystal Fall, Contact
crystal.fall@kidney.ca

Québec Chapter
#101, 1675, ch Ste-Foy, Québec QC G1S 2P7
Tél: 418-683-1449; *Téléc:* 418-683-7079
Chief Officer(s):
Maryse Neron, Coordonnatrice
maryse.neron@oricom.ca

Regina & District Chapter
1545C McAra St., Regina SK S4N 6H4
Tel: 306-347-0711; *Fax:* 306-586-8287
regina@kidney.sk.ca

Saguenay/Lac Saint-Jean Chapter
#301, 23, rue Racine est, Chicoutimi QC G7H 1P4
Tél: 418-543-9644; *Téléc:* 418-543-2839
Chief Officer(s):
Nathalie Sauliner, Coordinatrice
nathalie.saulnier@kidney.ca

Sarnia-Lambton Chapter
546 Christina St. North, Main Fl., Sarnia ON N7T 5W6
Tel: 519-344-3462; *Fax:* 519-344-4038
Chief Officer(s):
Elaine Hayter, Senior Development Manager
ehayter@kidney.on.ca

Saskatchewan Branch
#1, 2217 Hanselman Ct., Saskatoon SK S7L 6A8
Tel: 306-664-8588; *Fax:* 306-653-4883
Toll-Free: 888-664-8588
info@kidney.sk.ca
www.kidney.ca/sk
Chief Officer(s):
Joyce VanDeurzen, Executive Director
executivedirector@kidney.sk.ca

Sault Ste Marie Chapter
#1, 514 Queen St. East, 2nd Fl., Sault Ste Marie ON P6A 2A1
Tel: 705-949-0400; *Fax:* 705-949-0030
Chief Officer(s):
Penny Marquis, Campaign Coordinator
ssmkidney@shaw.ca

Southern Alberta Branch
6007 - 1A St. SW, Calgary AB T2H 0G5
Tel: 403-255-6108; *Fax:* 403-255-9590
Toll-Free: 800-268-1177
info@kidneyfoundation.ab.ca
www.kidney.ca/southernalberta
Chief Officer(s):
Joyce Van Deurzen, Executive Director
joyce.vandeurzen@kidneyfoundation.ab.ca

Southwestern Ontario Chapter
#119, 379 Dundas St., London ON N6B 1V5
Tel: 519-850-5362; *Fax:* 519-850-5360
Chief Officer(s):
Kim Pritchard, Manager, Fund Development
kpritchard@kidney.on.ca

Timmins-Porcupine Chapter
11357 Hwy. 101 East, Connaught ON P0N 1A0
Tel: 705-235-3233; *Fax:* 705-235-3237
treasurer@tcba.ca
Marlene Smith, President

Western Ontario Chapter
#4, 569 Lancaster St. West, Kitchener ON N2K 3M9
Tel: 519-742-2023; *Fax:* 519-742-3082

Windsor & District Chapter
#310, 1368 Ouellette Ave., Windsor ON N8X 1J9
Tel: 519-977-9211; *Fax:* 519-977-9768
Chief Officer(s):
Mike Brennan, Chapter Manager
mbrennan@mdirect.net

Kids Can Free the Children

233 Carlton St., Toronto ON M5A 2L2
Tel: 416-925-5894; *Fax:* 416-925-8242
info@freethechildren.com
www.freethechildren.org
www.facebook.com/freethechildren
twitter.com/freethechildren
www.youtube.com/freethechildrenintl
Also Known As: Free the Children
Overview: A large international charitable organization founded in 1995
Mission: To free young people from the idea that they are powerless to bring about positive social change, to encourage them to act now to improve the lives of young people everywhere
Affliation(s): Free the Children International
Chief Officer(s):
Scott Baker, Executive Director
scott@freethechildren.com
Finances: *Annual Operating Budget:* Greater than $5 Million
400 volunteer(s)
Membership: 100,000+
Activities: Education; peacebuilding & leadership; *Internships:* Yes; *Speaker Service:* Yes
Awards:
- World of Children Founders Award (Award)
- World's Children's Prize for the Rights of the Child (Award)
- Human Rights Award from the United Nations/World Association of Non-Government Organizations (Award)
- Skoll Award for Social Entrepreneurship (Award)
- World Economic Forum Medal (Award)

Kids Cancer Care Foundation of Alberta

#302, 609 - 14 St. NW, Calgary AB T2N 2A1
Tel: 403-216-9210; *Fax:* 403-216-9215
Toll-Free: 888-554-2267
staff@kidscancercare.ab.ca
www.kidscancercare.ab.ca
www.facebook.com/KCCFA
twitter.com/KidsCancerCare
instagram.com/kidscancercare
Overview: A small local charitable organization
Mission: To help improve the lives of children who are suffering from cancer
Chief Officer(s):
Christine McIver, Founder & CEO
Finances: *Annual Operating Budget:* Greater than $5 Million
Staff Member(s): 23

Kids First Parent Association of Canada

8337 Shaske Cres., Edmonton AB T6R 0B4
Tel: 604-291-0088
info@kidsfirstcanada.org
www.kidsfirstcanada.org
Overview: A medium-sized national charitable organization founded in 1987
Mission: To lobby to protect their right & choice to raise children in a family setting; to provide support to anyone wanting to further this cause in other communities
Chief Officer(s):
Helen Ward, President
Finances: *Funding Sources:* Donations; membership fees
Activities: Political lobbying; public information meetings; parenting workshops; *Speaker Service:* Yes; *Library* Open to public by appointment

Kids Help Phone (KHP) / Jeunesse j'écoute

#300, 439 University Ave., Toronto ON M5G 1Y8
Tel: 416-586-5437; *Fax:* 416-586-0651
Toll-Free: 800-668-6868
info@kidshelpphone.ca
kidshelpphone.ca
www.facebook.com/KidsHelpPhone
twitter.com/kidshelpphone
Overview: A medium-sized national charitable organization founded in 1989
Mission: To provide a national, bilingual, 24-hours a day, 365 days of the year, toll-free, professionally staffed, confidential counselling service to young people; To help young people deal with concerns large or small; To contribute to awareness of children's issues & the development of policies & practices to help Canadian children
Member of: Child Helpline International; Alliance of Information & Referral Systems
Chief Officer(s):
Sharon Wood, President
Finances: *Funding Sources:* Donations; Sponsorships
Activities: *Awareness Events:* Walk for Kids Help Phone; Boolathon, October; *Internships:* Yes; *Library* by appointment

Alberta/Northwest Territories
#290, 115 - 9th Ave. SE, Calgary AB T2G 0P5
Tel: 403-476-0386; *Fax:* 403-645-4020
alberta@kidshelpphone.ca
www.org.kidshelpphone.ca
Chief Officer(s):
Sherrie Cameron, Manager
Community Fundraising & Corporate Development

Atlantic Region
3433 Dutch Village Rd., Halifax NS B3N 2S7
Tel: 902-457-4779
Toll-Free: 888-470-8880
atlantic@kidshelpphone.ca
Chief Officer(s):
Shelley Richardson, Regional Director
shelley.richardson@kidshelpphone.ca

British Columbia/Yukon
#1100, 1200 West 73 Ave., Vancouver BC V6P 6G5
Tel: 604-267-7057; *Fax:* 604-267-7058
Toll-Free: 877-267-7057
bc@kidshelpphone.ca
Chief Officer(s):
Marcia Harrison, Regional Director

Manitoba
#120, 2150 Scarth St., Regina SK S4P 2H7
Tel: 204-925-5675; *Fax:* 306-780-9497
Toll-Free: 866-321-4125
manitoba@kidshelpphone.ca
Chief Officer(s):
Cindy Kobayashi, Regional Director

Ontario
#300, 439 University Ave., Toronto ON M5G 1Y8
Tel: 416-586-5437; *Fax:* 416-581-1744
Toll-Free: 800-268-3062
ontario@kidshelpphone.ca
Chief Officer(s):
Jenny Yuen, Director, Signature Events & Community Fundraising
jenny.yuen@kidshelpphone.ca

Québec
#323, 911, rue Jean-Talon est, Montréal QC H2R 1V5
Tel: 514-273-7007; *Fax:* 514-273-0589
quebec@kidshelpphone.ca
Chief Officer(s):
Patrick Bourassa, Regional Chair

Saskatchewan
#120, 2150 Scarth St., Regina SK S4P 2H7
Tel: 306-780-9492; *Fax:* 306-780-9497
Toll-Free: 866-321-4125
sask@kidshelpphone.ca

Kids Kottage Foundation

10107 - 134 Ave., Edmonton AB T5E 1J2
Tel: 780-448-1752; *Crisis Hot-Line:* 780-944-2888
info@kidskottage.org
www.kidskottage.org
www.facebook.com/pages/Kids-Kottage/291808499947
twitter.com/KidsKottageEDM
Previous Name: Canadian Foundation for the Love of Children
Overview: A medium-sized local charitable organization founded in 1987
Mission: To promote the health & well-being of children & their families; to prevent child abuse & neglect by supporting families in crisis
Chief Officer(s):
Lori Reiter, Executive Director
Activities: *Awareness Events:* Premier's Breakfast; Radiothon

Kids Now

PO Box 1314, 1500 Avenue Rd., Toronto ON M5M 0A1
Tel: 416-488-4848; *Fax:* 647-436-3126
Toll-Free: 877-407-4848
info@kidsnowcanada.org
www.kidsnowcanada.org

www.linkedin.com/company/kids.now
www.facebook.com/kidsnow
twitter.com/kids_now
www.youtube.com/mentorkidsnow
Overview: A small local charitable organization founded in 1999
Mission: To provide guidance & counselling to students in grades 7 & 8 in order to give them more skills & confidence to help their future
Chief Officer(s):
Janet King, President & Founder
Staff Member(s): 8
Membership: *Committees:* Advisory

Kids Up Front
Corus Quay, 25 Dockside Dr., Toronto ON M5A 0B5
www.kidsupfronttoronto.com
www.facebook.com/kidsupfrontto
twitter.com/kidsupfrontto
Overview: A medium-sized national charitable organization
Mission: Provides access to arts, culture, sport and recreation for children who otherwise do not have the opportunity.
Chief Officer(s):
Lindsay Oughtred, Executive Director, 416-479-6926
lindsay@kidsupfronttoronto.com
Finances: *Funding Sources:* Donations
Activities: Ticket donations; CIBC Theatre of ALL; Kids Count

Kidsfest *See* Start2Finish

KidSport Alberta
11759 Groat Rd., Edmonton AB T5M 3K6
Tel: 780-644-1815; *Fax:* 780-644-1896
www.kidsport.ab.ca
www.facebook.com/KidSportAlberta
twitter.com/KidSportAlberta
Overview: A small provincial organization overseen by KidSport Canada
Mission: To provide financial assistance to children in Alberta, aged 18 & under, who are interested in playing sports; help with registration fees & equipment
Member of: KidSport Canada
Chief Officer(s):
Carole Holt, Executive Director
cholt@kidsport.ab.ca
Membership: *Member Profile:* Local chapters
Activities: Providing grants from $100-$500

KidSport British Columbia
#260, 3820 Cessna Dr., Richmond BC V7B 0A2
Tel: 604-333-3430; *Fax:* 604-333-3401
Pete.Quevillon@sportbc.com
www.kidsportcanada.ca
twitter.com/kidsport
Overview: A small provincial organization overseen by KidSport Canada
Mission: To provide financial assistance to children in British Columbia, aged 18 & under, who are interested in playing sports; help with registration fees & equipment
Member of: KidSport Canada; Sport BC
Membership: *Member Profile:* Local chapters
Activities: Providing grants from $100-$500

KidSport Canada
Sport for Life Centre, #423, 145 Pacific Ave., Winnipeg MB R3B 2Z6
Tel: 204-925-5914; *Fax:* 204-925-5916
www.kidsportcanada.ca
twitter.com/KidSportCA
Overview: A medium-sized national organization founded in 2005
Mission: To provide financial assistance to children aged 18 & under who are interested in playing sports; help with registration fees & equipment
Chief Officer(s):
Bryan Ezako, Manager
bezako@kidsportcanada.ca
3600 volunteer(s)
Membership: 11 provincial/territorial chapters + 177 community chapters
Activities: Providing grants from $100-$500

KidSport Manitoba
145 Pacific Ave., Winnipeg MB R3B 2Z6
Tel: 204-925-5600; *Fax:* 204-925-5916
Toll-Free: 866-774-2220
kidsport@sportmanitoba.ca
www.kidsportcanada.ca
www.facebook.com/sportmb
twitter.com/SportManitoba
Overview: A small provincial organization overseen by KidSport Canada
Mission: To provide financial assistance to children in Manitoba, aged 18 & under, who are interested in playing sports; help with registration fees & equipment
Member of: KidSport Canada; Sport Manitoba
Membership: *Member Profile:* Local chapters
Activities: Providing grants from $100-$500;

KidSport New Brunswick
#13, Hanwell Rd., Fredericton NB E3B 6A2
Tel: 506-451-1320; *Fax:* 506-451-1325
programs@sportnb.com
www.kidsportcanada.ca
www.facebook.com/groups/53868967454
twitter.com/KidSportNB
Overview: A small provincial organization overseen by KidSport Canada
Mission: To provide financial assistance to children in New Brunswick, aged 18 & under, who are interested in playing sports; help with registration fees & equipment
Member of: KidSport Canada; Sport New Brunswick
Membership: *Member Profile:* Local chapters
Activities: Providing grants from $100-$500

KidSport Newfoundland & Labrador
1296A Kenmount Rd., Paradise NL A1L 1N3
Tel: 709-579-5977; *Fax:* 709-576-7493
kidsport@sportnl.ca
www.kidsport.nl.ca
Overview: A small provincial organization overseen by KidSport Canada
Mission: To provide financial assistance to children in Newfoundland & Labrador, aged 18 & under, who are interested in playing sports; help with registration fees & equipment
Member of: KidSport Canada; Sport Newfoundland & Labrador
Chief Officer(s):
Rosie Stead, Coordinator, Events & Marketing, Sport NL
rstead@sportnl.ca
Membership: *Member Profile:* Local chapters
Activities: Providing grants from $100-$500

KidSport Northwest Territories
Don Cooper Bldg., 4908 - 49th St., 3rd Fl., Yellowknife NT X1A 3X7
Tel: 867-669-8332; *Fax:* 867-669-8327
mkornacki@sportnorth.com
www.kidsportcanada.ca
www.facebook.com/279234862113396
twitter.com/SportNorth
www.youtube.com/user/SportNorthFederation
Overview: A small provincial organization overseen by KidSport Canada
Mission: To provide financial assistance to children in the Northwest Territories, aged 18 & under, who are interested in playing sports; help with registration fees & equipment
Member of: KidSport Canada; Sport North Federation
Membership: *Member Profile:* Local chapters
Activities: Providing grants from $100-$500

KidSport Nova Scotia
5516 Spring Garden Rd., 4th Fl., Halifax NS B3J 1G6
Tel: 902-425-5454; *Fax:* 902-425-5606
kidsport@sportnovascotia.ca
www.sportnovascotia.ca/KidSport
Overview: A small provincial organization overseen by KidSport Canada
Mission: To provide financial assistance to children in Nova Scotia, aged 18 & under, who are interested in playing sports; help with registration fees & equipment
Member of: KidSport Canada; Sport Nova Scotia
Membership: *Member Profile:* Local chapters
Activities: Providing grants from $100-$500

KidSport Ontario
#313, 3 Concorde Gate, Toronto ON M3C 3N7
Tel: 416-426-7177; *Fax:* 416-426-7177
Toll-Free: 866-641-7767
adamv@kidsportcanada.ca
www.kidsportcanada.ca/ontario
www.facebook.com/KidSportOntario
twitter.com/KidSportOntario
Overview: A small provincial organization overseen by KidSport Canada
Mission: To provide financial assistance to children in Ontario, aged 18 & under, who are interested in playing sports; help with registration fees & equipment
Member of: KidSport Canada
Membership: *Member Profile:* Local chapters
Activities: Providing grants from $100-$500;

KidSport PEI
PO Box 302, Charlottetown PE C1A 7K7
Tel: 902-368-4110; *Fax:* 902-368-4548
sports@sportpei.pe.ca
www.kidsportcanada.ca
www.facebook.com/176050449103403
Overview: A small provincial organization overseen by KidSport Canada
Mission: To provide financial assistance to children in Prince Edward Island, aged 18 & under, who are interested in playing sports; help with registration fees & equipment
Member of: KidSport Canada; Sport PEI Inc.
Membership: *Member Profile:* Local chapters
Activities: Providing grants from $100-$500

KidSport Québec *Voir* Sport Jeunesse

KidSport Saskatchewan
1870 Lorne St., Regina SK S4P 2L7
Tel: 306-780-9345; *Fax:* 306-781-6021
Toll-Free: 800-319-4263
kidsport@sasksport.sk.ca
www.kidsportsask.ca
Overview: A small provincial organization overseen by KidSport Canada
Mission: To provide financial assistance to children in Saskatchewan, aged 18 & under, who are interested in playing sports; help with registration fees & equipment
Member of: KidSport Canada; Sask Sport Inc.
Membership: *Member Profile:* Local chapters
Activities: Providing grants from $100-$500

Kikinahk Friendship Centre
PO Box 254, 320 Boardman St., La Ronge SK S0J 1L0
Tel: 306-425-2051; *Fax:* 306-425-3359
Previous Name: Neginuk Friendship Centre
Overview: A small local organization founded in 1976
Mission: To provide a cultural centre for Indian, Métis & non-status Indian persons
Chief Officer(s):
Ron Woytowich, Executive Director
Activities: Social welfare services; recreational activities; job training; leadership skills programs

Killam & District Chamber of Commerce
PO Box 272, Killam AB T0B 2L0
Tel: 780-385-7052; *Fax:* 780-385-2413
Overview: A small local organization
Member of: Canadian Chamber of Commerce; Alberta Chamber of Commerce
Chief Officer(s):
Rob Hutchison, President
Chris Raab, Treasurer
Finances: *Annual Operating Budget:* Less than $50,000; *Funding Sources:* Fundraising; membership fees
5 volunteer(s)
Membership: 31; *Fees:* $30-70

Killarney & District Chamber of Commerce
PO Box 809, Killarney MB R0K 1G0
Tel: 204-523-4202
killarneychamber@hotmail.com
Overview: A small local organization
Chief Officer(s):
Mark Witherspoon, Chair
Dale Banman, Executive Director

Les Kilomaîtres de LaSalle
CP 3022, Succ. Succursale Lapierre, LaSalle QC H8N 3H2
Tél. 514-582-5494
www.kilomaitreslasalle.com
Aperçu: *Dimension:* petite; *Envergure:* locale
Mission: Pour offrir un moyen à faible coût pour l'exercice et le rester en bonne santé
Membre(s) du bureau directeur:
Richard Proulx, Président, Conseil d'administration
Membre: *Montant de la cotisation:* $115 Adultes; 40$ Jeunes

Ki-Low-Na Friendship Society (KFS)
442 Leon Ave., Kelowna BC V1Y 6J3

Canadian Associations

Tel: 250-763-4905; *Fax:* 250-861-5514
reception@kfs.bc.ca
www.kfs.bc.ca
Previous Name: Central Okanagan Indian Friendship Society
Overview: A small national charitable organization founded in 1974
Mission: To promote total well-being for Native people in all human dimensions: physical, spiritual, mental & emotional
Member of: United Way
Chief Officer(s):
Edna Terbasket, Executive Director
Finances: *Annual Operating Budget:* $500,000-$1.5 Million
Staff Member(s): 15
Membership: 236; *Fees:* $5
Activities: Recreational activities; advocacy; employment & educational services; counselling in alcohol & drugs, family violence & other topics

Kimberley Arts Council *See* Kimberley Arts Council - Centre 64 Society

Kimberley Arts Council - Centre 64 Society

64 Deer Park Ave., Kimberley BC V1A 2J2
Tel: 250-427-4919; *Fax:* 250-427-4920
kimberleyarts@telus.net
www.kimberleyarts.com
Also Known As: Centre 64
Previous Name: Kimberley Arts Council
Overview: A small local organization founded in 1977
Mission: To increase & broaden the opportunities of Kimberley citizens to enjoy & participate in cultural activities & arts & crafts
Member of: Assembly of BC Arts Councils
Finances: *Annual Operating Budget:* $50,000-$100,000; *Funding Sources:* City of Kimberley; cultural services; lotteries
Staff Member(s): 1; 50 volunteer(s)
Membership: 150; *Fees:* $20
Activities: Art gallery; theatre; fibrearts studio; concerts; workshops;

Kimberley Bavarian Society Chamber of Commerce (KBSCC)

270 Kimberley Ave., Kimberley BC V1A 3N3
Tel: 250-427-3666
Toll-Free: 866-913-3666
info@kimberleychamber.com
www.kimberleychamber.com
www.linkedin.com/groups/Kimberley-District-Chamber-Commerce-3678646
www.facebook.com/KimberleyChamber
twitter.com/KimberleyCofC
Overview: A small local organization founded in 1925
Mission: To play a leadership role in the promotion, development, growth & prosperity of businesses in the community
Member of: British Columbia Chamber of Commerce; Canadian Chamber of Commerce
Chief Officer(s):
Darren Close, President
president@kimberleychamber.com
Finances: *Annual Operating Budget:* $100,000-$250,000; *Funding Sources:* City of Kimberly; Tourism BC
Staff Member(s): 3; 40 volunteer(s)
Membership: 185; *Fees:* $150-$300
Activities: Julyfest; *Speaker Service:* Yes; *Rents Mailing List:* Yes; *Library* Open to public

Kimberley Helping Hands Food Bank

All Saint's Anglican Church, 340 Leadenhall St., Kimberley BC V1A 2X6
Tel: 250-427-5522
allaboutkimberley.com/foodbankhours.html
Overview: A small local organization founded in 1985
Mission: To supply food to individuals & families in need
Activities: *Awareness Events:* Canada Day Duck Race, July

Kin Canada

PO Box 3460, 1920 Rogers Dr., Cambridge ON N3H 5C6
Tel: 519-653-1920; *Fax:* 519-650-1091
Toll-Free: 800-742-5546
kinhq@kincanada.ca
www.kincanada.ca
www.facebook.com/kincanada
twitter.com/kincanada
Also Known As: Association of Kinsmen, Kinette & Kin Clubs
Previous Name: Kinsmen & Kinette Clubs of Canada; The Association of Kin Clubs
Overview: A large national organization founded in 1920
Mission: To enrich communities through service, while embracing national pride, positive values, personal development, & lasting friendships; To support Cystic Fibrosis research & care in Canada
Affiliation(s): Cystic Fibrosis Canada
Chief Officer(s):
Ric McDonald, Executive Director & CEO
rmcdonald@kincanada.ca
Finances: *Annual Operating Budget:* $500,000-$1.5 Million; *Funding Sources:* Membership dues; sponsorship; sales of items to members
Staff Member(s): 9
Membership: 7,000 individuals in 500 clubs; *Fees:* Schedule available; *Member Profile:* Men & women over ages of 19; *Committees:* Awards; Kin Education; Membership; Risk Management; Charter & Expansion; Service; Committee Volunteer; Hal Rogers Endowment Fund
Activities: *Awareness Events:* Great Strides Walk; *Speaker Service:* Yes
Awards:
• National Awards & Recognition Program (Award)
• Hal Rogers Endowment Fund (Scholarship)
Amount: $1,000
• Bill Skelly Awards (Award)
In support of Cystic Fibrosis Canada
Meetings/Conferences: • Kin Canada 2015 National Convention, August, 2015, Brandon, MB
Scope: National
Publications:
• KIN Magazine [a publication of Kin Canada]
Type: Magazine; *Frequency:* 5 pa.; *Price:* $10 non-member

Kin Canada Foundation

PO Box 3460, 1920 Rogers Dr., Cambridge ON N3H 5C6
Tel: 519-653-1920; *Fax:* 519-650-1091
Toll-Free: 800-742-5546
kinhq@kincanada.ca
www.kincanada.ca
www.facebook.com/kincanada
twitter.com/kincanada
Overview: A large national charitable organization founded in 2005
Mission: To support Kin clubs across Canada
Chief Officer(s):
Curtis Kimpton, President

Kinark Child & Family Services

#200, 500 Hood Rd., Markham ON L3R 9Z3
Tel: 905-944-7086; *Fax:* 905-474-1448
Toll-Free: 800-230-8533
info@kinarkfoundation.org
www.kinarkfoundation.org
www.facebook.com/kinark
twitter.com/mykinark
Overview: A small provincial organization founded in 1972
Mission: To strengthen the well-being of children & their families, thereby contributing to safe & healthy communities; we seek to achieve this goal by being a provider of choice in the delivery of the highest quality services to our clients in partnership with community resources
Affliation(s): Children's Mental Health Ontario
Chief Officer(s):
Cheri Smith, Director, Development
cheri.smith@kinarkfoundation.org
Finances: *Funding Sources:* Provincial government; donations

Kincardine & District Chamber of Commerce

PO Box 115, 717 Queen St., Kincardine ON N2Z 2Y6
Tel: 519-396-9333; *Fax:* 519-396-5529
www.kincardinechamber.com
Overview: A small local organization
Mission: To promote business and tourism in the Kincardine area.
Member of: Ontario Chamber of Commerce
Chief Officer(s):
Linda Bowers, President
Jackie Pawlikowski, Office Manager
Finances: *Funding Sources:* Membership dues
Staff Member(s): 1
Membership: 140; *Fees:* $110

Kindersley Chamber of Commerce

PO Box 1537, 605 Main St., Kindersley SK S0L 1S0
Tel: 306-463-2320; *Fax:* 306-463-2312
kindersleychamber@sasktel.net
www.kindersleychamber.com
www.facebook.com/kindersleychamber.ofcommerce
twitter.com/kindersleycoc
Overview: A small local organization founded in 1989
Mission: To promote town of Kindersley & local business.
Member of: Saskatchewan Chamber of Commerce; Sask Tourism
Chief Officer(s):
Tolanda Baker, President
Finances: *Annual Operating Budget:* Less than $50,000; *Funding Sources:* Membership fees; Trade show
Staff Member(s): 1; 10+ volunteer(s)
Membership: 105; *Fees:* $175-$275; *Committees:* Tourism; Business Development; Membership; Promotion
Activities: *Awareness Events:* Kindersley Chamber of Commerce Annual Trade Show, June; Goose Festival, Sept.; Winter Wonderland, Dec.

The Kindness Club / Le Cercle Saint-François

#142, 527 Dundonald St., Fredericton NB E3B 1X5
Tel: 506-459-3379
info@kindnessclub.ca
www.kindnessclub.nb.ca
Overview: A small international charitable organization founded in 1959
Mission: To educate children to be kind to animals & people & to respect the environment
Member of: Canadian Federation of Humane Societies; World Society for the Protection of Animals; Nature Canada; Zoocheck Canada
Affliation(s): New Brunswick Naturalists
Finances: *Funding Sources:* Donations; interest from small capital
Membership: *Fees:* $5 child; $10 adult
Activities: Essay contest for students, grades 4-8; pet shows; displays; weekly column in 6 New Brunswick newspapers; liaison teacher program; *Library*

Kinesis Dance Society

Scotia Bank Dance Centre, 677 Davie St., Level 7, Vancouver BC V6B 2G6
Tel: 604-684-7844; *Fax:* 604-684-7834
admin@kinesisdance.org
www.kinesisdance.org
Overview: A small local charitable organization founded in 1986
Mission: To contribute new & provocative works of contemporary dance to the local, national & international dance scene; to educate through workshops & cultural exchanges & to collaborate with other media, such as film, video & theatre
Chief Officer(s):
Paras Terezakis, Artistic Director
Finances: *Funding Sources:* Canada Council; BC Arts Council; BC Gaming
Staff Member(s): 2
Membership: *Member Profile:* Women & men; urban; ages 26-45; university degree/certificate
Activities: *Library* Open to public

King Chamber of Commerce

PO Box 381, Schomberg ON L0G 1T0
Tel: 905-717-7199; *Fax:* 416-981-7174
info@kingchamber.ca
kingchamber.ca
Overview: A small local organization founded in 2008
Mission: To act as a voice for its members & to help them promote their business
Member of: Canadian Chamber of Commerce; Ontario Chamber of Commerce
Chief Officer(s):
Lucy Belperio, President
Helen Neville, Administrator
Staff Member(s): 1
Membership: 200; *Fees:* $85 associate; $110 non-profit; $100 1 employee; $135 2-10 employees; $225 11-25 employees; $300 26-50 employees; $400 51+ employees; *Committees:* Events; Communications; Tourism; Educational Outreach

King's County Historical Society

27 Centennial Rd., Hampton NB E5N 6N3
Tel: 506-832-6009
kingscm@nbnet.nb.ca
www.kingscountymuseum.com
www.facebook.com/434926949879214
Also Known As: King's County Museum
Overview: A small local charitable organization founded in 1968
Mission: To preserve the history of archives; to make history alive; to collect artifacts that reflect the County lifestyle
Member of: Museums New Brunswick; New Brunswick

Historical Society; Canadian Heritage Information Network; New Burnswick Genealogical Society; Queen's County Historical Society
Finances: *Funding Sources:* Municipal government
Membership: *Fees:* $20 single; $25 couple

Kings Historical Society

Kings County Museum, 37 Cornwallis St., Kentville NS B4N 2E2
Tel: 902-678-6237; *Fax:* 902-678-2764
museum@okcm.ca
www.okcm.ca
www.facebook.com/kingscountymuseum
twitter.com/Kings_Co_Museum
www.youtube.com/embed/JBOKCFM_Do8
Overview: A small local charitable organization founded in 1979
Mission: To preserve the cultural & natural history of Kings County, Nova Scotia
Member of: Federation of the Nova Scotian Heritage; Council of Nova Scotia Archives; Heritage Canada; Genealogical Association of Nova Scotia
Affliation(s): Kings Historical Scoeity
Chief Officer(s):
Bria Stokesbury, Curator
Finances: *Annual Operating Budget:* $50,000-$100,000; *Funding Sources:* Government; private
Staff Member(s): 3; 25 volunteer(s)
Membership: 400; *Fees:* $20 adult; $25 family/organizations; *Committees:* Family History
Activities: Administrative & financial support to Kings County Museum; Christmas Homes Tour & Tea; Heritage Homes Tours; Heritage Fashion Shows; *Awareness Events:* Heritage Day; *Internships:* Yes; *Speaker Service:* Yes; *Library:* Kings County Museum; Open to public

Kingston & Area Real Estate Association

720 Arlington Park Pl., Kingston ON K7M 8H9
Tel: 613-384-0880; *Fax:* 613-384-0863
info@karea.ca
www.karea.ca
Overview: A small local organization overseen by Ontario Real Estate Association
Member of: The Canadian Real Estate Association and the Ontario Real Estate Association (OREA)
Membership: 550+

Kingston & District Association for Community Living *See* Community Living Kingston

Kingston & District Labour Council

105 Sutherland Dr., Kingston ON K7K 5V6
Tel: 613-548-4952; *Fax:* 613-545-1659
kingstonlabourcouncil@gmail.com
kingstonlabourcouncil.wordpress.com
Overview: A small local organization
Chief Officer(s):
Lisa Marion, President
unionlisa@gmail.com

Kingston AIDS Project *See* HIV/AIDS Regional Services

Kingston Area Economic Development Commission *See* Kingston Economic Development Corporation

Kingston Arts Council (KAC)

PO Box 1005, Kingston ON K7L 4X8
Tel: 613-546-2787
info@artskingston.com
www.artskingston.com
www.facebook.com/kingstonartscouncil
twitter.com/artsking
www.youtube.com/kingstonartscouncil
Overview: A small local charitable organization founded in 1961
Mission: To serve as an advocate for the arts & arts education; To sponsor, encourage, & foster the visual, performing & literary arts; To encourage excellence in artistic expression; To coordinate & facilitate the exchange of information about the arts; To educate & encourage public interest in the arts & to actively seek partnership opportunities with governments, business, the community & the media
Member of: Ontario Arts Council; Community Arts Ontario
Chief Officer(s):
Karen Dolan, Executive Director
karen@artskingston.ca
Finances: *Annual Operating Budget:* $50,000-$100,000
Staff Member(s): 2; 20 volunteer(s)
Membership: 300 individual + 75 groups; *Fees:* Schedule available; *Member Profile:* Individual or group interested in supporting the arts & arts-related activities in the Kingston region; *Committees:* Executive; Advancement & Development; Nominating; Human Resources; Advocacy; Arts Salon; Arts Events; Membership; Marketing
Activities: Art workshops, community conferences on arts; juried arts salon; Town & Country Studio Tour; student art contest; Beat Bethoven foundraising run (annual); Timepieces Dance Festival (annual); *Library* by appointment
Awards:
• Kingston Prize for Contemporary Canadian Portraiture (Award)
Amount: $3,000
• Kingston Art Awards (Award)
• Student Art Contest (Award)

Kingston Association of Museums, Art Galleries & Historic Sites (KAM)

PO Box 1921, Stn. Main, Kingston ON K7L 5J7
Tel: 613-538-4014
www.kingstonmuseums.ca
Overview: A medium-sized local organization founded in 1978
Mission: To work for the promotion & growth of museums & museum-based tourism in the Kingston area
Chief Officer(s):
Ann Blake, Managing Director
managing.director@kingstonmuseums.ca
Staff Member(s): 2
Membership: 26 institutional; *Member Profile:* Museums, art galleries & historic sites in Kingston, ON; *Committees:* Education; Governance; Marketing; Professional Development
Activities: Monthly meetings; group advertising & promotional projects; coordinate/partner on many diverse projects

Kingston Board of Trade *See* Greater Kingston Chamber of Commerce

Kingston Community Counselling Centre *See* K3C Community Counselling Centres

Kingston Construction Association (KCA)

1575 John Counter Blvd., Kingston ON K7M 3L5
Tel: 613-542-9431; *Fax:* 613-542-2417
staff@kca.on.ca
www.kca.on.ca
Overview: A small local organization founded in 1950 overseen by Canadian Construction Association
Mission: To foster and advance the interests of those engaged in, or who are directly or indirectly connected with, or affected by the construction industry (ICI sector), in the Province of Ontario.
Member of: Council of Ontario Construction Associations; Business Association Alliance
Chief Officer(s):
Harry Sullivan, Executive Director
harry.sullivan@kca.on.ca
Staff Member(s): 3
Membership: 400+; *Member Profile:* Firms working in the industrial, commercial & institutional construction industry
Activities: *Library*

Kingston Economic Development Corporation (KEDCO)

945 Princess St., Kingston ON K7L 3N6
Tel: 613-544-2725; *Fax:* 613-546-2882
Toll-Free: 866-665-3326
business@kingstoncanada.com
business.kingstoncanada.com
www.linkedin.com/company/kingston-economic-development-corporation
www.facebook.com/KingstonEconomicDevelopmentCorporation
twitter.com/kingstoncanada
Previous Name: Kingston Area Economic Development Commission
Overview: A small local organization founded in 1997
Mission: To work with the community to develop world-class products & services that are competitive in global markets; to enhance economic development partnerships including private/public initiatives related to economic development policy; to position Kingston as an innovative jurisdiction, a place for new models of wealth creation; to expand the private sector in the tourism, culture, advance materials, biotechnology, information technology & environmental cluster; to stimulate entrepreneurship
Member of: Economic Development Council of Ontario
Affliation(s): Canadian Manufacturing & Exporters
Chief Officer(s):
Jeff Garrah, Chief Executive Officer, 613-544-2725 Ext. 7230
garrah@kingstoncanada.com
Rob Carnegie, Director, Tourism & Marketing Development, 613-544-2725 Ext. 7245
carnegie@kingstoncanada.com
Cyril Cooper, Director, Business Development, 613-544-2725 Ext. 7242
cooper@kingstoncanada.com
Finances: *Annual Operating Budget:* $1.5 Million-$3 Million; *Funding Sources:* Municipal government; private sector; provincial & federal government on a per project basis
Staff Member(s): 20
Activities: Small Business Self-Help Office; KANnet; provides on-line searchable Business directory, the Jobs & Prosperity Guide, on-line searchable Available Property Guide, on-line media releases, & downloadable Community Profile; *Library:* Entrepreneurship Centre/Self-Help Resource Centre; Open to public

Kingston Field Naturalists (KFN)

PO Box 831, Kingston ON K7L 4X6
e-mail: info@kingstonfieldnaturalists.org
kingstonfieldnaturalists.org
Overview: A small local charitable organization founded in 1949
Mission: To acquire, record & disseminate knowledge of natural history; To stimulate public interest in nature & in the protection & preservation of wildlife
Member of: Ontario Nature
Affliation(s): Canadian Nature Federation; Thousand Islands-Frontenac Arch Biosphere Reserve Network
Chief Officer(s):
Gaye Beckwith, President, 613-376-3716
Finances: *Annual Operating Budget:* Less than $50,000; *Funding Sources:* Membership fees
Membership: 500; *Fees:* $30 individual; $32 family; $20 young adult/junior; $800 life; *Committees:* Conservation; Education; Bird Records; Field Trips; Nature Reserves
Activities: Junior naturalists club (6-12); bird counts; Helen Quillam Sanctuary; Amherst Island Reserve; teen naturalists (13-17); habitat protection projects; *Awareness Events:* Spring/Fall Leisure Shows - Kingston
Awards:
• Scholarship (Scholarship)
For junior members to attend camp

Kingston Historical Society (KHS)

PO Box 54, Kingston ON K7L 4V6
Tel: 613-544-9925
kingstonhs@gmail.com
www.kingstonhistoricalsociety.ca
Overview: A small local organization founded in 1893
Mission: To preserve, promote & publicize local history & heritage through the presentation/publication of learned papers & the commemoration & celebration of people, events, institutions & the military related to local heritage; to operate Murney Tower Museum
Member of: Ontario Historical Society
Chief Officer(s):
Gordon Sinclair, President
Finances: *Annual Operating Budget:* Less than $50,000; *Funding Sources:* Membership dues; grants
20 volunteer(s)
Membership: 250+; *Fees:* $40 individual; $50 family; $25 student
Activities: Operates museum at Murney Tower National Historic Site May-Sept.; Military Day; *Speaker Service:* Yes; *Library:* Resource Centre - Queen's University Archives

Kingston Independent Nylon Workers Union (KINWU)

662D Progress Ave., Kingston ON K7M 4W9
Tel: 613-389-5255; *Fax:* 613-389-8265
www.kinwu.com
Overview: A small local organization founded in 1968
Mission: To represent workers in the nylon industry.
Chief Officer(s):
Larry Garrah, President
Sean Foley, Treasurer

Kingston Kiwanis Music Festival

PO Box 883, Kingston ON K7L 4X8
Tel: 613-876-3577
info@kiwaniskingston.ca
www.kiwaniskingston.ca
Overview: A small local charitable organization founded in 1972
Mission: To nurture a friendly, mainly non-competitive atmosphere where amateur musicians of all ages can enjoy performing & hearing others perform, while at the same time

gaining new artistic insights from experienced adjudicators
Affliation(s): Ontario Music Festivals Association
Chief Officer(s):
Philip Wilson, President
Finances: *Funding Sources:* Entry fees; donations; grants
Membership: *Member Profile:* Parents, teachers, students, general public interested in performing arts
Activities: Planning & organizing a 10-day performing arts festival annually

Kingston Lapidary & Mineral Club
623 King St. West, Kingston ON K7M 2E7
www.mineralclub.ca
Overview: A small local organization founded in 1962
Mission: To encourage the growth of silversmithing work, & mineral, fossil, & crystal collecting
Member of: The Central Canadian Federation of Mineralogical Societies (CCFMS)
Chief Officer(s):
Paul Blaney, President, 613-544-5138
paulrichardblaney@hotmail.com
Eileen Moss, Vice-President, Social & Publicity, 613-384-4439
emoss@cogeco.net
Wendy Dawes, Secretary, 613-876-2505
wdawes1@cogeco.ca
Membership: *Fees:* $10 junior; $15 adult; $20 family; *Member Profile:* Rockhounds; Lapidary enthusiasts; Silversmiths
Activities: Hosting meetings & workshops; Organizing field trips; *Library:* Kingston Lapidary & Mineral Club Library
Publications:
• The Streak Plate: The Kingston Lapidary & Mineral Club Newsletter
Type: Newsletter; *Frequency:* 5 pa; *Editor:* John Casnig
Profile: Upcoming events & articles about the hobby

Kingston Orchid Society (KOS)
c/o Gian Frontini, 66 Earl St., Kingston ON K7L 2G6
e-mail: kingstonorchidsociety@yahoo.ca
www.kingstonorchidsociety.ca
www.facebook.com/456078307817916
Overview: A small local organization founded in 1988
Member of: Canadian Orchid Congress; American Orchid Society
Chief Officer(s):
Gian Frontini, President
gianfrontini@bell.net
Membership: 60; *Fees:* $20 single; $25 family

Kingston Police Association / Association de la police de Kingston
705 Division St., Kingston ON K7K 4C2
Tel: 613-549-4660; *Fax:* 613-549-7111
kpf.ca
Overview: A small local organization
Mission: To represent all members of the Kingston Police Force.
Chief Officer(s):
Sean Bambrick, President
sbambrick@kpf.ca

Kingston Stamp Club
c/o Ongwanada Resource Centre, 191 Portsmouth Ave., Kingaston ON K0H 1G0
Tel: 613-389-6536
www.kingstonstampclub.ca
Overview: A small local organization founded in 1975
Member of: Royal Philatelic Society of Canada
Chief Officer(s):
Richard Weigand, President, 613-352-8775
rweigand@kos.net
Finances: *Annual Operating Budget:* Less than $50,000
10 volunteer(s)
Membership: 80; *Fees:* $8
Activities: Kingston Stamp Festival, Oct.; bi-monthly meetings; auctions

Kingston Symphony Association (KSA)
PO Box 1616, #206, 11 Princess St., Kingston ON K7L 5C8
Tel: 613-546-9729; *Fax:* 613-546-8580
info@kingstonsymphony.on.ca
www.kingstonsymphony.on.ca
www.facebook.com/KingstonSymphonyAssociation
twitter.com/KingstonSymph
www.youtube.com/user/Kingstonsymphony
Overview: A small local charitable organization founded in 1956 overseen by Orchestras Canada
Mission: To maintain & produce professional orchestral & symphonic music in the Kingston area
Chief Officer(s):
Andrea Haughton, General Manager
ahaughton@kingstonsymphony.on.ca
Finances: *Funding Sources:* Government; private; grants; ticket sales
Staff Member(s): 6
Membership: 55; *Committees:* KSA Volunteer Committee
Activities: Concerts; youth training; *Internships:* Yes

Kingston Youth Orchestra
c/o Kingston Symphony Association, PO Box 1616, Kingston ON K7L 5C8
Tel: 613-546-9729; *Fax:* 613-546-8580
info@kingstonsymphony.on.ca
www.kingstonsymphony.on.ca/youth.cfm
Overview: A small local organization founded in 1968 overseen by Orchestras Canada
Affiliation(s): Kingston Symphony Association
Chief Officer(s):
Linda Craig, Manager
Activities: Performs at least 2 concerts per year

Kinistino & District Chamber of Commerce
PO Box 803, Kinistino SK S0J 1H0
Tel: 306-864-2275
Overview: A small local organization

Kinsmen & Kinette Clubs of Canada; The Association of Kin Clubs *See* Kin Canada

Kinsmen Foundation of British Columbia & Yukon (KRF)
#3, 33361 Wren Cres., Abbotsford BC V2S 5V9
Tel: 604-644-2771; *Fax:* 604-852-4501
Toll-Free: 800-335-1234
kinsmenfoundationofbc@shaw.ca
www.kinsmenfoundationofbc.ca
Overview: A medium-sized provincial charitable organization founded in 1952 overseen by Easter Seals Canada
Mission: Committed to providing funding for services & technologies empowering British Columbians with physical disabilities to live more independently
Chief Officer(s):
David Owen, Volunteer CEO
daveowen@kinsmenfoundationofbc.ca
Finances: *Annual Operating Budget:* $50,000-$100,000; *Funding Sources:* Annual Kinsmen Tag Day; direct mail appeals; special events
25 volunteer(s)
Membership: 500-999; *Fees:* $5; *Member Profile:* Kinsmen & kinette clubs of BC & Yukon; *Committees:* Executive; Programs; Finance
Activities: Supports Technology for Independent Living division that assists persons with severe physical disabilities by providing assistive technology; supports disability awareness to elementary school children through the "Kids on the Block" educational puppetry program; *Awareness Events:* Disability Tag Day, Apr. 2; *Speaker Service:* Yes
Awards:
• Simon Cox Award of Excellence (Award)
Recognizes the achievements of teenagers in overcoming disabilities & other obstacles to achieve excellence

Kipling Chamber of Commerce
PO Box 700, Kipling SK S0G 2S0
Tel: 306-736-8520; *Fax:* 306-736-2260
www.townofkipling.ca/business/chamber-of-commerce
Overview: A small local organization
Chief Officer(s):
Buck Bright, Secretary
Tammy Frater, Chair
Finances: *Annual Operating Budget:* Less than $50,000

Kirkland & District Association for the Developmentally Handicapped *See* Kirkland Lake Association for Community Living

Kirkland Lake Association for Community Living
PO Box 274, 51 Government Rd. West, Kirkland Lake ON P2N 2H7
Tel: 705-567-9331; *Fax:* 705-567-5005
www.communitylivingkl.com
Previous Name: Kirkland & District Association for the Developmentally Handicapped
Overview: A small local organization
Member of: Community Living Ontario
Chief Officer(s):
Annice Tilley, President
Heather Topliss, Executive Director
heather.topliss@communitylivingkl.com

Kirkland Lake District Chamber of Commerce (KLCC)
PO Box 966, 400 Government Rd. West, Kirkland Lake ON P2N 3N1
Tel: 705-567-5444; *Fax:* 705-567-1666
Other Communication: Alternate e-mail: kirklandchamber@ntl.sympatico.ca
klcofc@ntl.sympatico.ca
www.kirklandlakechamberofcommerce.com
Overview: A small local organization founded in 1920
Member of: Canadian Chamber of Commerce
Affiliation(s): Ontario Chamber of Commerce
Chief Officer(s):
David Gorman, President
Jennifer Verge, Office Coordinator
Finances: *Annual Operating Budget:* Less than $50,000; *Funding Sources:* Membership dues
Staff Member(s): 2; 20 volunteer(s)
Membership: 120; *Committees:* Retail; Annual Meeting; Exposition; Membership; Municipal & Government Affairs
Activities: Northern College Business Program

Kitchener *See* Juvenile Diabetes Research Foundation

The Kitchener & Waterloo Community Foundation (KWCF)
29 King St. East, #B, Kitchener ON N2G 2K4
Tel: 519-725-1806; *Fax:* 519-725-3851
info@kwcf.ca
www.kwcf.ca
www.facebook.com/TheKWCF
twitter.com/thekwcf
Overview: A small local charitable organization founded in 1984
Mission: To improve the quality of life in Kitchener-Waterloo & area, now & for generations to come, by building community endowment, addressing needs through grant-making & providing leadership on key community issues
Member of: Community Foundations of Canada; Canadian Association of Gift Planners
Chief Officer(s):
Rosemary Smith, Chief Executive Officer
rsmith@kwcf.ca
Finances: *Funding Sources:* Donations
Staff Member(s): 9
Membership: *Committees:* Grants; Investment; Audit; Leadership Identification; Nominating; Ontario Endowment for Children and Youth in Recreation Fund; Random Act of Kindness Day
Activities: Town Hall Meeting; *Library* by appointment

Kitchener Sports Association (KSA)
50 Ottawa St. South, Kitchener ON N2G 3S7
Tel: 519-208-9302
www.kitchenersports.ca
www.facebook.com/pages/Kitchener-Sports-Association/492371234132957
twitter.com/KitchenerSA
Overview: A small local organization founded in 1944
Mission: To govern sports & sporting facilities in Kitchener
Chief Officer(s):
Bill Pegg, President
ksapresident@kitchenersports.ca
Membership: *Committees:* Operating

Kitchener-Waterloo Building & Construction Trades Council *See* Waterloo, Wellington, Dufferin & Grey Building & Construction Trades Council

Kitchener-Waterloo Chamber Music Society (KWCMS)
57 Young St. West, Waterloo ON N2L 2Z4
Tel: 519-886-1673
kwcms@yahoo.ca
www.k-wcms.com
www.facebook.com/group.php?gid=203443633010012
Overview: A small local charitable organization founded in 1974
Mission: To put on good concerts of chamber music
Affliation(s): Faculty of Music, Wilfrid Laurier University
Chief Officer(s):
Jan Narveson, President
jnarveso@uwaterloo.ca
Stanley Lipshitz, Vice-President, 519-884-2049

Finances: *Annual Operating Budget:* $100,000-$250,000; *Funding Sources:* Private donors
15 volunteer(s)
Membership: 100; *Fees:* Full: $390 regular; $225 student; $360 senior
Activities: Presents 50-60 concerts per year; radio program "The World of Chamber Music"; *Speaker Service:* Yes

Kitchener-Waterloo Chamber Orchestra (KWCO)
F-168 Lexington Ct., Waterloo ON N2J 4R9
e-mail: info@kwchamberorchestra.ca
www.kwchamberorchestra.ca
www.facebook.com/75294799995
twitter.com/KW_Chamber
Overview: A small local organization founded in 1985 overseen by Orchestras Canada
Chief Officer(s):
Matthew Jones, Music Director
Activities: *Library*

Kitchener-Waterloo Field Naturalists
317 Highland Rd. East, Kitchener ON N2M 3W6
www.kwfn.ca
Overview: A small local charitable organization founded in 1934
Mission: To promote the enjoyment of nature through environmental appreciation & conservation; To encourage wise use & conservation of natural resources
Member of: Federation of Ontario Naturalists
Chief Officer(s):
Janet Ozaruk, President, 519-893-0490
janeto@golden.net
Finances: *Annual Operating Budget:* Less than $50,000
Membership: 250; *Fees:* $20
Activities: Walks; speakers; social; photography; plant study; *Library*

Kitchener-Waterloo Kiwanis Music Festival
#193, 55 Northfield Dr. East, Waterloo ON N2K 3T6
Tel: 519-496-7085
admin@kwkiwanismusicfestival.org
www.kwkiwanismusicfestival.org
www.facebook.com/kwmusicfestival
twitter.com/KWKMF
Overview: A small local organization
Chief Officer(s):
Heidi Wall, Coordinator

Kitchener-Waterloo Multicultural Centre
102 King St. West, Kitchener ON N2G 1A6
Tel: 519-745-2531; *Fax:* 519-745-5857
kwmc@kwmc-on.com
www.kwmc.on.ca
www.facebook.com/128710583884871
twitter.com/kwmcED
Overview: A small local organization founded in 1970 overseen by Ontario Council of Agencies Serving Immigrants
Mission: To foster diversity & encourage participation in community life
Chief Officer(s):
Lucia Harrison, Executive Director
lucia@kwmc-on.com
Finances: *Funding Sources:* Federal, provincial & municipal government
Staff Member(s): 19
Membership: 40 groups; *Member Profile:* Multicultural groups & social service providers
Activities: *Speaker Service:* Yes

Kitchener-Waterloo Parents of Multiple Births Association
PO Box 48001, Stn. Williamsburg, Kitchener ON N2E 4K6
e-mail: kitchenerwaterloo@multiplebirthscanada.org
www.multiplebirthscanada.org/~kwpomba
Also Known As: K-W POMBA
Overview: A small local organization overseen by Multiple Births Canada
Mission: Providing support services for parents of multiple birth children in Durham Region.
Chief Officer(s):
Jenna Aylott, President
Membership: *Fees:* $25-$30
Activities: *Library*

Kitchener-Waterloo Philatelic Society (KWPS)
c/o C. Pinchen, PO Box 904, Stn. C, Kitchener ON N2G 4C5
e-mail: kwps-president@kwstampclub.org
www.kwstampclub.org
Also Known As: K-W Philatelic Society
Overview: A small local organization founded in 1935
Member of: Royal Philatelic Society of Canada; Grand River Valley Philatelic Association
Chief Officer(s):
George Pepall, Treasurer
treasurer@kwstampclub.org
Membership: *Fees:* $15 adult; $20 family; $8 associate
Activities: Monthly meetings; annual exhibition; *Awareness Events:* Stampfest, March; *Speaker Service:* Yes

Kitchener-Waterloo Symphony Orchestra Association Inc. (KWSOA)
36 King St. West, Kitchener ON N2G 1A3
Tel: 519-745-4711; *Fax:* 519-745-4474
Toll-Free: 888-745-4717
info@kwsymphony.on.ca
kwsymphony.on.ca
www.facebook.com/kwsymphony
twitter.com/kw_symphony
www.youtube.com/user/kwsymphony
Overview: A small local charitable organization founded in 1945 overseen by Orchestras Canada
Mission: To cultivate the tradition of live performance through the presentation of classical orchestral & popular music for the edification, enrichment, education & excitement of our community & beyond
Chief Officer(s):
Amy Higgins, Manager, Administration
ahiggins@kwsymphony.on.ca
Finances: *Funding Sources:* Government; individuals; companies
Staff Member(s): 28
Membership: *Fees:* Schedule available; *Member Profile:* Individuals & companies; *Committees:* Volunteer
Activities: Concerts; Educational programs; Special Events; *Library:* KWS Music Library

Kitchener-Waterloo Symphony Youth Orchestra (KWSYO)
36 King St. West, Kitchener ON N2G 1A3
Tel: 519-745-4711; *Fax:* 519-745-4474
Toll-Free: 888-745-4717
info@kwsymphony.on.ca
www.kwsymphony.on.ca
Overview: A small local charitable organization founded in 1975 overseen by Orchestras Canada
Chief Officer(s):
Barbara Kaplanek, Education & Community Programs Manager, Youth Orchestra & Schools
bkaplanek@kwsymphony.on.ca
Evan Mitchell, Youth Orchestra Conductor
Membership: *Fees:* $470
Activities: Offers the following ensembles: Youth Orchestra; Youth Strings; Senior Youth Sinfonia; Valhalla Brass; Chamber Music

Kitikmeot Regional Board of Trade (KRBT)
Kugaaruk NU
www.krbt.ca
twitter.com/kitikmeotgrowth
Overview: A small local organization
Mission: To represent businesses in the Kitikmeot region
Chief Officer(s):
Greg Holitzki, Director
Membership: *Committees:* Governance; Urban/rural Planning; Resource Development; Workforce Development; Funding Models; Marketing & Branding; Membership Development; Governance

Kitimat Chamber of Commerce
PO Box 214, 2109 Forest Ave., Kitimat BC V8C 2G7
Tel: 250-632-6294; *Fax:* 250-632-4685
Toll-Free: 800-664-6554
info@kitimatchamber.ca
www.kitimatchamber.ca
www.facebook.com/tourismkitimat
twitter.com/KitimatChamber
Overview: A small local organization founded in 1955
Member of: BC Chamber of Commerce; Canadian Chamber of Commerce
Chief Officer(s):
Derick Stinson, President
Trish Parsons, Executive Director
tparsons@kitimatchamber.ca
Finances: *Annual Operating Budget:* $100,000-$250,000
Staff Member(s): 3; 16 volunteer(s)
Membership: 200+; *Fees:* $130+
Activities: *Rents Mailing List:* Yes; *Library:* Resource Centre; Open to public

Kitimat Child Development Centre
1515 Kingfisher Ave., Kitimat BC V8C 1S5
Tel: 250-632-3144; *Fax:* 250-632-3120
info@kitimatcdc.ca
www.kitimatcdc.ca
Overview: A small local organization founded in 1974
Mission: To ensure that special needs children have equal opportunities to be the best that they can be
Member of: BC Association for Community Living; Canadian Council for Exceptional Children; Spina Bifida Association of BC; Child Development & Rehabilitation Network; Association for the Care of Children's Health
Finances: *Annual Operating Budget:* $500,000-$1.5 Million; *Funding Sources:* Fundraising; donations; government funding
Staff Member(s): 32; 75 volunteer(s)
Membership: 60; *Fees:* $5
Activities: Children's & Family Resource Centre; prenatal program; car seat program; Building Healthier Babies; family resources programs; physiotherapy; occupational therapy; speech-language therapy; preschool; school-aged programs; parenting classes; *Awareness Events:* Walk-for-Kids, June; *Library* Open to public

Kitimat Community Services Society
#102, 170 City Centre, Kitimat BC V8C 1T6
Tel: 250-632-9107; *Fax:* 250-632-6599
Toll-Free: 877-632-9101
kcss@telus.net
www.kitimatcommunityservices.ca
Overview: A small local charitable organization founded in 1989
Affliation(s): Literacy BC
Chief Officer(s):
Janette Camazzola, Contact
Denise O'Neil, Executive Director
Finances: *Annual Operating Budget:* Less than $50,000; *Funding Sources:* Regional government; donations; BC gaming
Staff Member(s): 1; 15 volunteer(s)
Membership: 27; *Fees:* $5; *Member Profile:* Residents of Kitimat area
Activities: Conversation groups; one-to-one tutoring; upgrading; *Awareness Events:* National Literacy Day

Kitimat Food Bank
14 Morgan St., Kitimat BC V8C 1J3
Tel: 250-632-6611
Overview: A small local organization
Chief Officer(s):
Marjorie Phelps, Contact
marjon@citywest.ca

Kitimat Valley Naturalists
12 Farrow St., Kitimat BC V8C 1E2
Tel: 250-632-7632
Overview: A small local organization
Mission: Interests include birding, wildflowers, ecology, & environmental issues related to wildlife.
Chief Officer(s):
Walter Thorne, Contact
swthorne.@telus.net
Membership: 10; *Fees:* $16.10

Kitimat, Terrace & District Labour Council
PO Box 741, Terrace BC V8G 4C3
Tel: 250-635-5080; *Fax:* 250-635-5083
ktdlc@telus.net
Overview: A small local organization overseen by British Columbia Federation of Labour
Mission: To advance the economic & social welfare of workers in Kitimat, Terrace & the surrounding area in British Columbia
Affliation(s): Canadian Labour Congress (CLC)
Chief Officer(s):
Rob Goffinet, President
goffinet@telus.net
Tom LaPorte, First Vice-President
tom_laporte@hotmail.com
William Knox, Second Vice-President
wknox@telus.net
Benilde Gomes, Secretary-Treasurer
BGomes@citywest.ca
Activities: Promoting the interests of affiliates; Providing training, in areas such as campaign organizing, women & leadership, & problem solving; Raising awareness of local issues, such as the Northen Gateway project to transport oil;

Hosting a ceremony for the annual Day of Mourning for Workers Killed or Injured On the Job;

Kitsilano Chamber of Commerce (KCC)
#400, 1681 Chestnut St., Vancouver BC V6J 4M6
Tel: 604-731-4454; *Fax:* 877-312-1898
office@kitsilanochamber.com
www.kitsilanochamber.com
www.linkedin.com/groups/Kitsilano-Chamber-Commerce-3254358
www.facebook.com/kitschamberofcommerce
twitter.com/KitsChamber
Also Known As: Kitsilano Business Association
Overview: A small local organization founded in 1934
Mission: To promote local businesses & to act as a liason between members, government & the public
Member of: BC Chamber of Commerce
Chief Officer(s):
Christian Johannsen, Chair
Cheryl Ziola, Executive Director
office@kitsilanochamber.com
Finances: *Annual Operating Budget:* $100,000-$250,000; *Funding Sources:* Membership dues; donations
Staff Member(s): 1; 15 volunteer(s)
Membership: 500+; *Fees:* $75-$1200; *Committees:* Membership; Events; Policy; Executive
Activities: Business after hours; Meetups; Westside Business Awards; Annual general meeting

Kitsilano Showboat Society
PO Box 74526, 2300 Cornwall Ave., Vancouver BC V6K 4P9
Tel: 604-734-7332
kitsilanoshowboat@hotmail.com
www.kitsilanoshowboat.com
Overview: A small local organization
Mission: To showcase talent during the summer season
Chief Officer(s):
Bea Leinbach, President

Kivalliq Chamber of Commerce
PO Box 819, Rankin Inlet NU X0C 0G0
Tel: 867-645-2823; *Fax:* 867-645-2082
Previous Name: Keewatin Chamber of Commerce
Overview: A small local organization
Chief Officer(s):
Paul Delany, Contact

Kivalliq Inuit Association
PO Box 340, #164, 1 Mivvik Ave., Rankin Inlet NU X0C 0G0
Tel: 867-645-5725; *Fax:* 867-645-2348
reception@kivalliqinuit.ca
www.kivalliqinuit.ca
Overview: A small local organization
Mission: To promote the interests of Inuit liiving in the Kivalliq Region
Chief Officer(s):
Steve Hartman, Executive Director
shartman@kivalliqinuit.ca
Staff Member(s): 19

Kiwanis Music Festival ***See*** Sault Ste. Marie Music Festival

Kiwanis Music Festival Association of Greater Toronto
1422 Bayview Ave., #A, Toronto ON M4G 3A7
Tel: 416-487-5885; *Fax:* 416-487-5784
kiwanismusic@bellnet.ca
kiwanismusictoronto.org
Overview: A small local charitable organization
Mission: To bring together various choirs in music competitions
Member of: Ontario Music Festivals Association; The Federation of Canadian Music Festivals
Chief Officer(s):
Pam Allen, General Manager
Staff Member(s): 3

Kiwanis Music Festival of Windsor/Essex County
PO Box 941, Windsor ON N9A 6P2
Tel: 226-783-9686
info@wkmf.ca
www.wkmf.ca
www.facebook.com/131126860274386
twitter.com/WKMFestival
Overview: A small local organization founded in 1947
Chief Officer(s):
Kim Beneteau, Contact
150+ volunteer(s)

Kiwassa Neighbourhood Services Association
2425 Oxford St., Vancouver BC V5K 1M7
Tel: 604-254-5401; *Fax:* 604-254-7673
info@kiwassa.bc.ca
www.kiwassa.bc.ca
Overview: A small local organization
Mission: To bring the community together
Member of: Affiliation of Multicultural Societies & Service Agencies of BC
Chief Officer(s):
Nancy McRitchie, Executive Director
nancym@kiwassa.ca
Staff Member(s): 18
Activities: Social, recreational & educational services for youth, families, seniors & the unemployed

Klondike Placer Miners' Association
3151B Third Ave., Whitehorse YT Y1A 1G1
Tel: 867-667-2267; *Fax:* 867-668-7127
kpma@kpma.ca
www.kpma.ca
Overview: A small provincial organization founded in 1974
Chief Officer(s):
Mike McDougall, President
Membership: *Fees:* $159-$3210

Klondike Snowmobile Association (KSA)
4061 - 4th Ave., Whitehorse YT Y1A 1H1
Tel: 867-667-7680
klonsnow@yknet.ca
www.ksa.yk.ca
www.facebook.com/253094448062816
Overview: A small local organization
Member of: Canadian Council of Snowmobile Organizations
Affliation(s): Trans Canada Trail - Yukon
Chief Officer(s):
Mark Daniels, President
mnd@northwestel.net
Membership: 500; *Fees:* $20-30; $100 corporate

Klondike Visitors Association (KVA)
PO Box 389, Dawson City YT Y0B 1G0
Tel: 867-993-5575; *Fax:* 867-993-6415
Toll-Free: 877-465-3006
kva@dawson.net
www.dawsoncity.ca
www.facebook.com/dawsoncity
Overview: A small local organization founded in 1952 overseen by Tourism Industry Association of the Yukon
Mission: To respond to visitor information requests & liaises with municipal & territorial governments to encourage Tourism-related initiatives; to promote Dawson City, Yukon & the Klondike Region as a year-round tourist destination.
Chief Officer(s):
Gary Parker, Executive Director
Finances: *Funding Sources:* Casino gaming; entertainment venue
Membership: *Fees:* $210 corporate
Activities: Diamond Tooth Gerties Gambling Hall; Thaw-di-Gras Spring Carnival; Klondike Outhouse Races; Yukon Goldpanning; Gaslight Follies; Jack London Interpretive Centre

Kneehill Historical Society
PO Box 653, 1301 2nd St. North, Three Hills AB T0M 2A0
Tel: 403-443-2092; *Fax:* 403-443-7941
www.threehills.ca
Overview: A small local charitable organization founded in 1975
Mission: To collect, preserve & display artifacts pertaining to local history
Affliation(s): Big Country Tourist Association
Chief Officer(s):
Gordon Park, President
Alice Park, Secretary
George Boles, Vice-President
Finances: *Funding Sources:* Alberta Museum Association; Alberta Lotteries; local support
Staff Member(s): 2; 10 volunteer(s)
Membership: 30; *Fees:* $15
Activities: Operates Three Hills Museum

Knights Hospitallers, Sovereign Order of St. John of Jerusalem, Knights of Malta, Grand Priory of Canada (OSJ)
#301, 2800 Hwy. 7 West, Concord ON L4K 1W8
Also Known As: Knights Hospitallers of Cyprus, Rhodes, Malta & Russia
Overview: A medium-sized international charitable organization founded in 1048
Mission: To propagate the principles of chivalry; care for the sick, aged, invalid, poor & children in need; protect & defend Christianity throughout the world; combat errors; champion the truth; promote & encourage the spirit of Brotherhood & charity within the order; members are expected to be united in brotherhood & charity
Member of: International Chivalric Congress
Affliation(s): United Nations - Canada, participant
Chief Officer(s):
Mario Cortellucci, Contact
Finances: *Funding Sources:* Members' donations
Membership: *Member Profile:* Exemplary Christians of any official denomination, active in community charitable works
Activities: Supreme Council; Priory Councils; Hospitaller Service; *Awareness Events:* Feast of St. John, June 24; Great Siege Day, Sept. 8; *Internships:* Yes; *Speaker Service:* Yes; *Library:* Gr. Priory OSJ Library; by appointment
Awards:
• Cross of Merit (Award)
Amount: Pro merito medal for volunteer work

Knights of Columbus of Québec ***Voir*** Les Chevaliers de Colomb du Québec

Knights of Pythias - Domain of British Columbia
BC
knightsofpythiasbritishcolumbia.ca
Overview: A small provincial organization founded in 1880
Affliation(s): Supreme Lodge Knights of Pythias
Chief Officer(s):
Roger Murray, Chancellor
Activities: *Rents Mailing List:* Yes

Knights of St. John International - Canada
c/o Jerome Catholic Church, 8530 Chinguacousy Rd., Brampton ON L6Y 5G4
Tel: 647-220-5115
info@knightsofstjohncanada.org
www.ksjcanada.org
Also Known As: Knights of St. John International Commandery 710
Overview: A large international organization founded in 2010
Mission: To advance the interests of the Roman Catholic Church; to foster fraternity & fellowship among members; to promote undiscriminating charity
Affliation(s): Archdiocese of Toronto
Chief Officer(s):
Jan Kolodynski, Spiritual Leader
Membership: *Member Profile:* Catholic males aged 16 & above

Kokosai Koryu Kikin Toronto Nihon Bunka Centre ***See*** The Japan Foundation, Toronto

Kolbe Eucharistic Apostolate
c/o St. Brigid's Church, 300 Wolverleigh Blvd., Toronto ON M4C 1S6
www.kolbeapostolate.com
Overview: A small local organization founded in 1996
Mission: To make the Eucharistic Christ the heart of lives, through Eucharistic Adoration
Affliation(s): Archdiocese of Toronto
Chief Officer(s):
Maria De Manche, Event Co-Coordinator & Animator
Therese De Manche, Event Co-Coordinator & Animator
Charles Anang, Spiritual Advisor
Membership: *Member Profile:* Any Catholic individual who lives in accordance with the teaching of the Catholic Church, & who wishes to deepen his or her knowledge of God
Activities: Developing faith formation; Providing mini-retreats, prayer groups, Bible study, & catechesis;

Kootenay Lake Chamber of Commerce
PO Box 120, Crawford Bay BC V0B 1E0
Tel: 250-227-9655
info@kootenaylake.bc.ca
www.kootenaylake.bc.ca
Overview: A small local organization
Chief Officer(s):
Jamie Cox, President
jcox@theeastshore.net
Lois Wakelin, Vice-President
thelakeview@xplornet.com
Membership: 46; *Fees:* $70

Tel: 709-931-2073; *Fax:* 709-931-2073
Overview: A small local organization

Labrador West Association for Community Living *See* Newfoundland & Labrador Association for Community Living

Labrador West Chamber of Commerce
PO Box 273, 118 Humphrey Rd., Labrador City NL A2V 2K5
Tel: 709-944-3723; *Fax:* 709-944-4699
lwc@crrstv.net
www.labradorwestchamber.ca
Overview: A small local organization
Chief Officer(s):
Brian Brace, President, 709-944-5444
bbrace@crrstv.net
Patsy Ralph, Business Manager

Lac du Bonnet & District Chamber of Commerce
PO Box 598, Lac du Bonnet MB R0E 1A0
Tel: 204-340-0497
ldbchamberofcommerce@gmail.com
www.lacdubonnetchamber.com
www.facebook.com/LdBChamberOfCommerce
Overview: A small local organization
Mission: To promote economic development & tourism marketing in & around Lac du Bonnet, Manitoba
Affliation(s): Manitoba Chambers of Commerce
Chief Officer(s):
Marie Hiebert, President
Jennifer Hudson Stewart, Administrator
Finances: *Funding Sources:* Town; Rural Municipality; Membership dues
Membership: 137; *Fees:* $80 1-2 employees; $105 3-10 employees; $177 11 or more employees; $80 non-profit; *Member Profile:* Retail; Services; Individuals

Lac La Biche & District Chamber of Commerce
PO Box 804, Lac La Biche AB T0A 2C0
Tel: 780-623-2818; *Fax:* 780-623-7217
info@llbchamber.ca
www.llbchamber.ca
www.facebook.com/127175950658710
twitter.com/LLBCHAMBER
Overview: A small local organization founded in 1922
Mission: To help promote business and tourism in the area.
Affliation(s): Alberta Chamber of Commerce
Chief Officer(s):
Reuel Thomas, President
Finances: *Funding Sources:* Membership fees; events
Membership: *Member Profile:* Local businesses

Lac La Biche Canadian Native Friendship Centre
PO Box 2338, 10105 Churchill Dr., Lac La Biche AB T0A 2C0
Tel: 780-623-3249; *Fax:* 780-623-1846
ed@nativefriendship.ca
anfca.com/friendship-centres/lac-la-biche
Overview: A small local organization overseen by Alberta Native Friendship Centres Association
Mission: Dedicated to providing culturally-based programs and services that respond to the distinct needs of urban Aboriginal people in their communities and bridging the gaps that occur between Aboriginal and non-Aboriginal peoples in urban areas.
Member of: Alberta Native Friendship Centres Association
Chief Officer(s):
Richard Cloutier, Executive Director
Lorraine Deschambeau, President
Staff Member(s): 4

Lac La Biche Disability Services
PO Box 2078, 10018 - 103 Ave., Lac La Biche AB T0A 2C0
Tel: 780-623-2800; *Fax:* 780-623-3874
llbds@telus.net
www.llbds.com
Previous Name: Community Living Association for the Little Divide; Lac La Biche & District Association for the Handicapped
Overview: A small local charitable organization founded in 1979 overseen by Alberta Association for Community Living
Mission: The Association is a not-for-profit organization that assists people with developmental disabilities to contribute & participate fully in the community.
Member of: Alberta Association for Community Living; Alberta Association of Rehabilitation Centres
Chief Officer(s):
Gwen Bilodeau, Executive Director
gwen@llbds.com
Finances: *Funding Sources:* Government funds
Staff Member(s): 3

Activities: *Internships:* Yes; *Speaker Service:* Yes; *Library* Open to public

Lachine Black Community Association
PO Box 34042, Lachine QC H8S 4H4
Tel: 514-634-1862
Overview: A small local organization
Chief Officer(s):
Marcia Babb, Contact
msmbabb@sympatico.ca

LaCloche Foothills Chamber of Commerce
PO Box 5292, 133 Barber St., Espanola ON P5E 1S3
Tel: 705-869-7671
www.laclochefoothillschamber.com
Previous Name: Espanola & District Chamber of Commerce
Overview: A small local organization
Mission: To represent Espanola, Sable-Spanish, Baldwin, & Nairn & Hyman
Chief Officer(s):
Cheryl Kay, President
cheryl@laclochefoothillschamber.com
Membership: *Fees:* $28.25

Lacombe & District Chamber of Commerce
6005 - 50 Ave., Lacombe AB T4L 1K7
Tel: 403-782-4300; *Fax:* 403-782-4302
info@lacombechamber.ca
www.lacombechamber.ca
Overview: A small local organization founded in 1924
Mission: To promote & enhance the economic well-being of Lacombe & district businesses, industries & residents.
Member of: Alberta Chamber of Commerce; Canadian Chamber of Commerce
Chief Officer(s):
Keith Meyers, President
k.meyers@reddeercoop.com
Finances: *Annual Operating Budget:* $100,000-$250,000; *Funding Sources:* Trade show; membership fees; events; grants
Staff Member(s): 1
Membership: 254; *Fees:* Schedule available

Lacombe Handicraft & Lapidary Guild
c/o Bea Ganter, 5539 - 53 Ave., Lacombe AB T4L 1L3
Tel: 403-782-6221
Previous Name: Lacombe Lapidary Club
Overview: A small local organization
Member of: Alberta Federation of Rock Clubs
Chief Officer(s):
Bea Ganter, Contact

Lacombe Lapidary Club *See* Lacombe Handicraft & Lapidary Guild

Lacrosse New Brunswick
850 Old Black River Rd., Saint John NB E2J 4T3
Tel: 506-632-9188
www.laxnb.ca
www.facebook.com/128267803907009
Also Known As: Lacrosse NB
Overview: A small provincial organization overseen by Canadian Lacrosse Association
Mission: To oversee the sport of lacrosse in the province of New Brunswick.
Member of: Canadian Lacrosse Association
Chief Officer(s):
Dave Higdon, President
davehigdon@rogers.com
Dave Arsenault, Technical Director, 506-648-1098
majorlac@nbnet.nb.ca
Libby O'Brien, Director, Administration, 506-849-9081
obriend@nb.sympatico.ca

Lacrosse Nova Scotia
5516 Spring Garden Rd., 4th Fl., Halifax NS B3J 1G6
Tel: 902-425-5450; *Fax:* 902-425-5606
lacrosse@sportnovascotia.ca
lacrossens.ca
www.facebook.com/421011914655642
Overview: A small provincial organization founded in 1971 overseen by Canadian Lacrosse Association
Member of: Canadian Lacrosse Association; Sport Nova Scotia
Chief Officer(s):
Mike Hayes, President
president@lacrossens.ca
Greg Knight, Administrative Coordinator
Lawrence Taylor, Technical Director
lacrossetechdirector@sportnovascotia.ca

Finances: *Funding Sources:* Provincial government

The Ladies of the Lake
ON
Tel: 905-476-4045
Other Communication: sponsorship@lakeladies.ca
ladies@lakeladies.ca
www.lakeladies.ca
Overview: A small local organization founded in 2005
Mission: To promote a greater sense of connection with Lake Simcoe; to get people involved in what the future brings - both in terms of the lake itself & for those who share it; to offer a set of possible actions to restore the Lake to health for the communities around the Lake & watershed
Chief Officer(s):
Annabel Slaight, President
Membership: 100+; *Member Profile:* Women of all ages who are working to rescue Lake Simcoe and its watershed.
Activities: Calendar; "Naked Truth" series of events

Ladies' Morning Musical Club (LMMC) / Les Matinées de musique de chambre
#12, 1410 Guy St., Montréal QC H3H 2L7
Tel: 514-932-6796; *Fax:* 514-932-0510
lmmc@qc.aibn.com
www.lmmc.ca
Also Known As: LMMC Concerts
Overview: A small local charitable organization founded in 1892
Member of: Conseil québecois de la musique
Chief Officer(s):
Constance V. Pathy, President
Rosemary Neville, Secretary-Treasurer
Finances: *Annual Operating Budget:* $100,000-$250,000
Staff Member(s): 1; 10 volunteer(s)
Membership: 480; *Fees:* $80 student subscription; $250 adult subscription; *Member Profile:* Men & women
Activities: Chamber music concerts;

Ladies' Orange Benevolent Association of Canada (LOBA)
c/o Grand Orange Lodge of Canada, 94 Sheppard Ave. West, Toronto ON M2N 1M5
Tel: 416-223-1690; *Fax:* 416-223-1324
Toll-Free: 800-565-6248
Overview: A medium-sized national organization founded in 1894 overseen by Grand Orange Lodge of Canada
Mission: To provide women with an opportunity to practice Orange beliefs & participate in benevolent activities
Chief Officer(s):
John Chalmers, Grand Secretary, Grand Lodge of Canada

Ladysmith Chamber of Commerce
441B - 1st Ave., Ladysmith BC V9G 1A4
Tel: 250-245-2112; *Fax:* 250-245-2124
info@ladysmithcofc.com
www.ladysmithcofc.com
Overview: A small local organization founded in 1930
Mission: To promote & improve the commercial, industrial, civic & social welfare of the Town of Ladysmith & its trade area
Member of: BC Chamber of Commerce
Affliation(s): Cowichan Regional Valley
Chief Officer(s):
Rob Waters, President
Finances: *Annual Operating Budget:* $100,000-$250,000; *Funding Sources:* Membership fees; Town of Ladysmith; fundraising
Staff Member(s): 2; 200 volunteer(s)
Membership: 220; *Fees:* $100-$175; *Member Profile:* Local businesses & services

Ladysmith Food Bank
PO Box 1653, 721 First Ave., Ladysmith BC V9G 1B2
Tel: 250-245-3079; *Fax:* 250-245-3798
info@lrca.bc.ca
www.lrca.bc.ca/food_bank.htm
Overview: A small local organization founded in 1998 overseen by Food Banks British Columbia
Mission: To provide food and service to those in need in the Ladysmith area.
Member of: Food Banks British Columbia
Chief Officer(s):
Kit Willmot, Contact

LaHave Islands Marine Museum Society (LIMM)
PO Box 69, 100 LaHave Islands Rd., LaHave NS B0R 1C0

Tel: 902-688-2973
www.lahaveislandsmarinemuseum.ca
www.facebook.com/179807478711382
Overview: A small local charitable organization founded in 1979
Mission: To maintain & preserve the history & culture of the LaHave Islands & the Inshore Fisheries
Member of: Federation of the Nova Scotian Heritage; South Shore Tourism Association; LaHave River Valley Association
Chief Officer(s):
Douglas Berrigan, President
Mary Fulleman, Treasurer
Finances: *Annual Operating Budget:* Less than $50,000; *Funding Sources:* Membership fees; donations
40 volunteer(s)
Membership: 70; *Fees:* $5
Activities: Manage LaHave Islands Marine Museum; Municipal Heritage Church; *Awareness Events:* Fishermen's Memorial Service, Aug.

Laidlaw Foundation
#2000, 365 Bloor St. East, Toronto ON M4W 3L4
Tel: 416-964-3614; *Fax:* 416-975-1428
www.laidlawfdn.org
www.facebook.com/LaidlawFoundation
twitter.com/laidlawfdn
www.youtube.com/user/LaidlawFdn
Overview: A medium-sized national charitable organization founded in 1949
Mission: Committed to a Canada where communities are inclusive, creative & answerable, where all children & families are valued for their capacities & potential; to fund ideas, convince shareholders & advocate for change
Affliation(s): Canadian Environmental Grantmakers Network; FUNDERS Alliance for Children & Youth; Grantmakers for Children Youth & Families; Grantmakers in the Arts; Philanthropic Foundation Canada
Chief Officer(s):
Jehad Aliweiwi, Executive Director, 416-964-3614 Ext. 304
Finances: *Annual Operating Budget:* $3 Million-$5 Million; *Funding Sources:* Private endowment
Staff Member(s): 8; 100 volunteer(s)
Membership: 1-99; *Committees:* Youth Engagement; Youth Arts; Contaminants & Child Health; Inclusive Communication for Children, Youth & Family
Activities: *Internships:* Yes; *Speaker Service:* Yes; *Library:* Laidlaw Foundation Library; by appointment

Lake Abitibi Model Forest
PO Box 129, Cochrane ON P0L 1C0
Tel: 705-272-7800; *Fax:* 705-272-2744
Overview: A small local organization
Member of: Canadian Model Forest Network
Chief Officer(s):
Sue Parton, General Manager, 705-272-8449
parton.sue@gmail.com

Lake Country Chamber of Commerce
Winfield Professional Building, #106, 3121 Hill Rd., Lake Country BC V4V Gg1
Tel: 250-766-5670; *Fax:* 250-766-0170
Toll-Free: 888-766-5670
manager@lakecountrychamber.com
www.lakecountrychamber.com
Overview: A small local organization
Mission: The Lake Country Chamber of Commerce is an organization that is mandated to serve its membership, the business community and the community at large.
Chief Officer(s):
Garth McKay, President
Corrinne Cross, Manager

Lake Country Food Assistance Society
3130C Berry Rd., Winfield BC V4V 1Z7
Tel: 250-766-0125
Overview: A small local organization overseen by Food Banks British Columbia
Member of: Food Banks British Columbia
Chief Officer(s):
Phyllis MacPherson, Contact
pmacpher@shaw.ca

Lake of the Woods Adult Learning Line
#203, 115 Chipman St., Kenora ON P9N 1V7
Tel: 807-468-8202; *Fax:* 807-468-3921
Overview: A small local organization founded in 1980
Member of: Ontario Council of Agencies Serving Immigrants
Chief Officer(s):
Bonnie Boucha, Program Coordinator
bonnie.boucha@shaw.ca

Lake of the Woods Ojibway Cultural Centre
237 Airport Rd., Kenora ON P9N 0A2
Tel: 807-548-5744; *Fax:* 807-548-1591
Other Communication: lowocc@gmail.com
ojibwaycrafts@shaw.ca
www.ojibwayculturalcentre.com
www.facebook.com/467406369968488
Overview: A small local organization founded in 1977
Activities: Craft display; job search assistance; *Library* Open to public

Lake Simcoe Region Conservation Foundation
PO Box 282, 120 Bayview Pkwy., Newmarket ON L3Y 4X1
Tel: 905-895-1281
Toll-Free: 800-465-0437
lakesimcoefoundation.ca
Overview: A small local organization
Mission: The Lake Simcoe Conservation Foundation (LSCF) invests in projects designed to protect and restore Lake Simcoe. Working in partnership with the Lake Simcoe Region Conservation Authority (LSRCA), watershed municipalities and other partners, they enable vital work to be done that maintains the natural environment, and in many places return the land and the rivers and the streams to a natural state.
Chief Officer(s):
Cheryl Taylor, Executive Director
Activities: Undertaken a million dollar fundraising campaign to help restore the lake

Lake Superior Coin Club
PO Box 10245, Thunder Bay ON P7B 6T7
Tel: 807-577-5416
Overview: A small local organization founded in 1980
Member of: Royal Canadian Numismatic Association
Chief Officer(s):
Germain Tremblay, Treasurer

LakeCity Employment Services Association
386 Windmill Rd., Dartmouth NS B3A 1J5
Tel: 902-465-5000; *Fax:* 902-465-5009
lesa@lakecityemployment.com
www.lakecityemployment.com
Also Known As: LakeCity Woodworkers
Overview: A small local organization founded in 1982
Mission: To assist mental health consumers in improving their quality of life by helping them to assume responsibility & independence through work
Member of: DIRECTIONS Council for Vocational Services Society
Affliation(s): Workshop Council of Nova Scotia; Teamwork Co-Operative Ltd.
Chief Officer(s):
Andre McConnell, Chair
Chris Fyles, Executive Director
Finances: *Annual Operating Budget:* $500,000-$1.5 Million; *Funding Sources:* Provincial government
Staff Member(s): 25; 10 volunteer(s)
Membership: 10 individual

Lakehead Association for Community Living *See* Community Living Thunder Bay

Lakehead Japanese Cultural Association (LJCA)
West Thunder Community Centre, 915 Edward St. South, Thunder Bay ON P7E 6R2
Tel: 807-475-9396; *Fax:* 807-473-9055
westthunder@tbaytel.net
my.tbaytel.net/westthunder/Lakehead_Japanese_Cultural_Association
Overview: A small local organization
Chief Officer(s):
Steve Sellar, President

Lakehead Social Planning Council (LSPC)
Victoria Mall, #28, 125 Syndicate Ave. South, Thunder Bay ON P7E 6H8
Tel: 807-624-1720; *Fax:* 807-625-9427
Toll-Free: 866-624-1729; *TTY:* 888-622-4651
info@lspc.ca
lspc-circ.on.ca
Overview: A small local charitable organization founded in 1963
Mission: To strengthen Thunder Bay by providing collaborative community responses to social issues, research & access to human service information; to bring people together, promote social & economic justice, develop programs & services, link people to services; to research social, economic, environmental & health issues
Member of: Inform Ontario; Ontario Social Development Council; Canadian Council on Social Development
Chief Officer(s):
Marie Klassen, Director, Services
Finances: *Funding Sources:* All levels of government; sale of goods & services; fundraising
Staff Member(s): 10
Membership: *Fees:* $20 individual; $40 organizations
Activities: *Speaker Service:* Yes; *Library* Open to public

Lakehead Stamp Club
c/o Daryl Lein, 232 Dease St., Thunder Bay ON P7C 2H8
Tel: 807-623-2179
Overview: A small local organization founded in 1947
Member of: Royal Philatelic Society of Canada
Chief Officer(s):
Daryl Lein, Secretary
daryl_j@shaw.ca
Finances: *Funding Sources:* Membership fees

Lakehead University Faculty Association (LUFA) / Association des professeurs de l'Université Lakehead
#CB-4108, Lakehead University, 855 Oliver Rd., Thunder Bay ON P7B 5E1
Tel: 807-343-8789; *Fax:* 807-766-7142
LUFA@lakeheadu.ca
www.lufa.org
www.linkedin.com/company/lakehead-university-faculty-association
www.facebook.com/136377669839280
Overview: A small local organization founded in 1960
Chief Officer(s):
Glenna Knutson, President
glenna.knutson@lakeheadu.ca
Finances: *Annual Operating Budget:* $100,000-$250,000
Membership: 290;

Lakeland Agricultural Research Association (LARA)
PO Box 7068, Bonnyville AB T9N 2H4
Tel: 780-826-7260; *Fax:* 780-826-7099
livestock.lara@mcsnet.ca
www.areca.ab.ca/larahome.html
Overview: A small local organization overseen by Agricultural Research & Extension Council of Alberta
Mission: To achieve a profitable & sustainable future for agricultural producers by conducting agricultural research programs
Member of: Agricultural Research & Extension Council of Alberta
Chief Officer(s):
Janet Montgomery, Manager
manager.lara@mcsnet.ca
Kellie Nichiporik, Coordinator, Conservation
sustainag.lara@mscnet.ca
Publications:
• LARA [Lakeland Agricultural Research Association] Newsletter
Type: Newsletter

Lakeland College Faculty Association (LCFA) / Association des professeurs du Collège de Lakeland
c/o Lakeland College, 5707 College Dr., Vermilion AB T9X 1K5
Overview: A small local organization
Chief Officer(s):
Neil Maclean, President, 780-853-8561
neil.maclean@lakelandcollege.ca
Membership: 100-499

Lakeland District Soccer Association (LDSA)
c/o Paula Whynot, 5901 Labrador Rd., Cold Lake AB T9M 0C6
Tel: 780-573-4704; *Fax:* 780-594-1656
lakelandsoccer.ca
Overview: A small local organization overseen by Alberta Soccer Association
Member of: Alberta Soccer Association
Membership: 17 teams

Lakeland Industry & Community Association (LICA)
PO Box 8237, 5107W - 50 St., Bonnyville AB T9N 2J5
Tel: 780-812-2182; *Fax:* 780-812-2186
Toll-Free: 877-737-2182
lica2@lica.ca
www.lica.ca
Overview: A small local organization

Mission: To protect the environment by collecting ecological information about the Lakeland area and using it to further their cause
Chief Officer(s):
Delano Tolley, Chairman, Board of Directors
Membership: *Fees:* $0 - $1,000; *Member Profile:* People who are of legal age & who live or work in the LICA area; Corporations; Non-profit organizations; *Committees:* Education & Info; Governance; Resolution; Airshed Zone; Beaver River Watershed Alliance
Activities: Commitee meetings

Lakeland United Way
Marina Mall, PO Box 8125, #3, 901 - 10 St., Cold Lake AB T9M 1N1
Tel: 780-826-0045; *Fax:* 780-639-2699
www.lakelandunitedway.com
Overview: A small local charitable organization founded in 1987 overseen by United Way of Canada - Centraide Canada
Mission: Umbrella fundraising organization for a variety of local charities & social services.
Chief Officer(s):
Ajaz Quraishi, President
ajaz@telus.net
Finances: *Annual Operating Budget:* Less than $50,000
Staff Member(s): 1; 8 volunteer(s)

Lakelands Association of Realtors (MHAR)
34 Cairns Cres., Huntsville ON P1H 1Y3
Tel: 705-788-1504; *Fax:* 705-788-2040
comms@thelakelands.ca
www.thelakelands.ca
www.facebook.com/179085482158066
twitter.com/TheLakelands
Overview: A small local organization overseen by Ontario Real Estate Association
Mission: To provide realtors within the Muskoka, Haliburton & Orillia with information & services that allow them to better serve their customers
Membership: 700

Lakes District Festival Association
c/o Jana Epkens-Shaffer, PO Box 202, Francois Lake BC V0J 1R0
Tel: 250-695-6400
www.ldfestival.com
Overview: A small local organization founded in 1957
Mission: To celebrate each spring with competitions in piano, band, speech arts, instrumental, strings, highland dance, modern dance, ballet, jazz, ethnic dance & musical theatre
Chief Officer(s):
Lois Koop, President, 250-695-6699
Membership: *Member Profile:* Interest in music, drama or dance & willingness to work as on festival & planning committee & during festival; *Committees:* Awards; Advertising; Publicity; Hospitality
Activities: Annual Festival competitions in the performing arts; *Awareness Events:* Lake District Festival of the Performing Arts

Lakeshore Area Multi-Service Project (LAMP)
185 - 5th St., Toronto ON M8V 2Z5
Tel: 416-252-6471; *Fax:* 416-252-4474
www.lampchc.org
www.facebook.com/LAMPCHEALTHC
Overview: A medium-sized local charitable organization
Mission: To offer community health centre services in South Etobicoke, Toronto West
Chief Officer(s):
Russ Ford, Executive Director
Finances: *Annual Operating Budget:* Greater than $5 Million; *Funding Sources:* Government; Donations; United Way
Staff Member(s): 6
Membership: *Fees:* $3
Activities: Offering a variety of integrated programs & services to meet the health needs of the community

Lakeshore Coin Club
PO Box 46004, Pointe-Claire QC H9R 5R4
Tel: 514-289-9761
medievalcoins@gmail.com
Overview: A small local organization founded in 1962
Member of: Canadian Numismatic Association; Ontario Numismatic Association
Chief Officer(s):
Michael Joffre, President
Activities: *Library:* Lakeshore Coin Club Library at City of Pointe Claire, Stewart Hal;

Lakeshore Community Services (LCS)
PO Box 885, 571B Notre Dame St., Belle River ON N0R 1A0
Tel: 519-728-1435; *Fax:* 519-728-4713
info@communitysupportcentre.ca
www.lakeshorecommunity.net
Previous Name: Community Information Centre Belle River
Overview: A small local organization overseen by InformOntario
Mission: The Mission of LCS is to service the Community of Lakeshore responsibly by providing information about and access to health, government, and community and support services and through this research social needs.
Chief Officer(s):
Tracey Bailey, Executive Director
Activities: Meals on Wheels; vistor services; transit bus; Coats for Kids; job bank; Keep the Heat; income tax clinic

Lakeshore Stamp Club Inc.
PO Box 1, Stn. Pointe-Claire, Dorval QC H9R 4N5
www.lakeshorestampclub.ca
Overview: A small local organization founded in 1961
Mission: To promote stamp collecting
Affliation(s): American Philatelic Society; Fédération québécoise de philatélie; Royal Philatelic Society of Canada; The American Association of Philatelic Exhibitors; The American Topical Association
Chief Officer(s):
Chuck Colomb, President
president@lakeshorestampclub.ca
Robert Carswell, Secretary
secretary@lakeshorestampclub.ca
Finances: *Funding Sources:* Membership dues
Membership: 180; *Fees:* $30 adults; $1 juniors; *Committees:* Philatelic Study Group; Bourse; Exhibitions; House; Library; Publicity; Shoebox; Social Events
Activities: Exchange & exhibition of philatelic items; annual exhibition

Lambton County Association for the Mentally Handicapped
See Lambton County Developmental Services

Lambton County Developmental Services (LCDS)
PO Box 1210, 339 Centre St., Petrolia ON N0N 1R0
Tel: 519-882-0933; *Fax:* 519-882-3386
administration@lcds.on.ca
lcdspetrolia.ca
Previous Name: Lambton County Association for the Mentally Handicapped
Overview: A large local organization founded in 1955
Mission: Support services for children & adults with developmental disabilities in Sarnia-Lambton
Affliation(s): Ontario Agencies Serving Individuals with Special Needs
Chief Officer(s):
Frank Huybers, President
Patrick O'Malley, Executive Director
pomalley@lcds.on.ca
Finances: *Funding Sources:* Ministry of Community & Social Services; fundraising; donations
Staff Member(s): 250; 300 volunteer(s)
Membership: 200; *Fees:* $25; *Committees:* Residential Services; Nominating
Activities: Businesses include Petrolia Enterprises, Kitchen Creations Catering, Evoke Performance Consultants, Oil Town Suds & Duds, Olde Post Office Gift Shoppe, Olde Post Parlour, & The Wicket; supported employment services; community skills development program; adult residential services; supported independent living services; respite care; drop-in centre; recreation & leisure resources
Publications:
- LCDS [Lambton County Developmental Services] Focus Newsletter
Type: Newsletter; *Frequency:* 3 pa

Lambton County Historical Society (LCHS)
3775 Shiloh Line, #RR4, Petrolia ON N0N 1R0
Tel: 519-882-0881
Overview: A small local charitable organization founded in 1960
Mission: To encourage the preservation of the history of the county by publication, exhibition & collection of books, manuscripts, artifacts
Affliation(s): Ontario Historical Society
Chief Officer(s):
Betty Lou Snetselaar, Secretary
Finances: *Annual Operating Budget:* Less than $50,000; *Funding Sources:* Membership fees; book sales
Staff Member(s): 5; 65 volunteer(s)
Membership: 60; *Fees:* $10 corporate; $5 individual; *Committees:* Publication; Special Events
Activities: *Library:* Lambton County Library; Open to public

Lambton Industrial Society: An Environmental Co-operative
See Sarnia-Lambton Environmental Association

Lambton Wildlife Inc. (LWI)
PO Box 681, Sarnia ON N7T 7J7
Tel: 519-542-7914
info@lambtonwildlife.com
www.lambtonwildlife.com
Overview: A small local charitable organization founded in 1966
Mission: To preserve our natural heritage for present & future generations; Particularly concerned with the natural history of Lambton County & the establishment & care of conservation areas & wildlife sanctuaries therein
Member of: Federation of Ontario Naturalists
Affliation(s): Canadian Nature Federation
Chief Officer(s):
Janet Bremner, President
Finances: *Annual Operating Budget:* Less than $50,000; *Funding Sources:* Membership fees; donations
75 volunteer(s)
Membership: 210; *Fees:* $20 individual; $25 family; *Committees:* Adopt-a-Highway; Arbor Week; Ausable Trail; Binational Public Advisory; Bluebird Nesting; Conservation; Education; Environment; Indoor; Mandaumin Woods; Outdoor; Rural Lambton Stewardship; Wawanosh Wetlands Management; Wildlife Inventory; Woodlot Protection; Howard Watson Nature Trail; Port Franks Property Management
Activities: Education programs in environmental studies & natural history; lectures in natural history at Lambton County schools & other organizations; special public lectures; regular field trips; sponsors the annual Audubon Christmas Bird census in Lambton area; purchase & management of Mandaumin Woods Nature Reserve; establishment of Ausable Trail; sponsorship of the World Wildlife studies of the Port Franks Karner Blue Butterfly & the Walpole Island Life Science Inventory

LAMP Community Health Centre
185 - 5th St., Toronto ON M8V 2Z5
Tel: 416-252-6471; *Fax:* 416-252-4474
volunteering@lampchc.org
www.lampchc.org
www.facebook.com/groups/111947859235
Also Known As: Lakeshore Area Multi-Services Project Inc.
Overview: A large local charitable organization founded in 1976
Mission: To meet the community's health needs through integrated programs & services
Chief Officer(s):
Barbara Pidcock, Chair
Russ Ford, Executive Director
Staff Member(s): 7
Membership: *Fees:* $3; *Committees:* Community Relations & Membership
Activities: Occupational health & safety program; primary health care; speech & language program; "Equally Healthy Kids" program; chiropody; adult literacy; community development; mental health program; child psychiatry; community information centre; *Library:* Toy Lending Library & Parenting Library; Open to public
Awards:
- Awards of Merit (Award)

Publications:
- LAMP Community Health Centre Newsletter
Type: Newsletter

Lanark County Beekeepers' Association (LCBA)
c/o Paul Lacelle, 126 Bruce St., Carleton Place ON K7C 3P1
Tel: 613-253-0566
lanarkcountybeekeepers@gmail.com
sites.google.com/site/lanarkcountybeekeepers
Overview: A small local organization founded in 1998
Mission: To promote the beekeeping & honey industry in Lanark County; To provide information about beekeeping to members
Member of: Ontario Beekeepers' Association
Chief Officer(s):
Paul Lacelle, President
Membership: *Fees:* $15; *Member Profile:* Individuals interested in beekeeping from Ontario's Lanark County; *Committees:* Membership; Library
Activities: Organizing four meetings each year at the McMartin House in Perth; Assisting new beekeepers through a mentoring program; Showing honey & honey bee products, such as displays at the Perth Fair; Capturing swarms of honey bees

Lanark County Food Bank
5 Allan St., Carleton Place ON K7C 1T1
Tel: 613-257-8546
Overview: A small local charitable organization
Member of: Ontario Association of Food Banks
Chief Officer(s):
Nadine Kennedy, Executive Director
30 volunteer(s)

The Lanark County Museums Network (LCMN)
c/o Carleton Place & Beckwith Heritage Museum, 267 Edmund St., Carleton Place ON K7C 3E8
Tel: 613-253-7013
www.lanarkcountymuseums.ca
Overview: A small local organization founded in 1991
Mission: To offer self-help in every phase of museum activity; to promote all twelve museums & the Lanark County Archives in Lanark County
Member of: Ontario Museums Association
Affliation(s): Lanark County Tourism Association
Finances: *Funding Sources:* Donations; membership dues
Membership: 12; *Member Profile:* Community museums in Lanark County: Lanark & District Museum; Mill of Kintail Conservation Area; Mississippi Valley Textile Museum; Middleville & District Museum; North Lanark Historical Society; Naismith Museum & Hall of Fame; Matheson House; Heritage House Museum; Inge-Va

Lanark County Therapeutic Riding Programme (LCTRP)
30 Bennett St., Carleton Place ON K7C 4J9
e-mail: info@therapeuticriding.ca
www.therapeuticriding.ca
Overview: A small local charitable organization founded in 1986
Mission: To provide individuals a holistic approach to therapy, rehabilitation & recreation; the opportunity to experience freedom & movement astride a horse
Member of: Canadian Therapeutic Riding Association; Ontario Therapeutic Riding Association; Lanark Health & Community Services
Chief Officer(s):
Amy Booth, Contact
Finances: *Annual Operating Budget:* $50,000-$100,000; *Funding Sources:* Local fundraising events; fees for service
Staff Member(s): 1; 45 volunteer(s)
Membership: 105 riders; *Committees:* Advisory; Fundraising
Activities: Provides individuals a holistic approach to therapy, rehabilitation & recreation & the opportunity to experience freedom when riding a horse; *Internships:* Yes

Lancer Rehab Riders *See* Halifax Area Leisure & Therapeutic Riding Association

Land Improvement Contractors of Ontario
231 Dimson Rd., Guelph ON N1G 3C7
Tel: 519-836-1386; *Fax:* 519-836-4059
john.johnston@gto.net
www.drainage.org
Overview: A small provincial organization founded in 1995
Mission: An association of professional contractors, suppliers of drainage pipe and equipment, engineers and municipal drainage superintendents principally concerned with agriculture and the land drainage industry of Ontario, Canada.
Chief Officer(s):
Gerald Neeb, President, 519-656-2618
John Johnston, Sec.-Treas.
Finances: *Annual Operating Budget:* Less than $50,000
Membership: *Fees:* $146.90 general membership

Landis & District Chamber of Commerce
PO Box 400, Landis SK S0K 2K0
Tel: 306-658-2100; *Fax:* 306-658-4455
Overview: A small local organization

Landlord's Self-Help Centre
425 Adelaide St. West, 4th Fl., Toronto ON M5V 3C1
Tel: 416-504-5190; *Fax:* 416-504-1932
Toll-Free: 800-730-3218
info@landlordselfhelp.com
www.landlordselfhelp.com
www.facebook.com/landlordselfhelp
twitter.com/LSHC1
Overview: A small local organization founded in 1975
Mission: To provide information, assistance & educational programs to Ontario's small scale landlords free of charge
Chief Officer(s):
Jonathan Lau, President

LandlordBC
830B Pembroke St., Victoria BC V8T 1J9
Tel: 250-382-6324; *Fax:* 877-382-6006
Toll-Free: 888-330-6707
info@landlordbc.ca
www.landlordbc.ca
www.linkedin.com/company/landlordbc
www.facebook.com/landlordBC
twitter.com/LandlordBC
Previous Name: Rental Owners & Managers Society of British Columbia; Apartment Owners & Property Managers Association of Vancouver Island
Overview: A small provincial organization founded in 1971
Mission: To serve & represent our members & enhance the residential rental industry in B.C.
Member of: Canadian Federation of Apartment Associations
Chief Officer(s):
David Hutniak, CEO
Staff Member(s): 7
Membership: 3,200+; *Member Profile:* Owners & managers of residential rental properties in B.C.
Activities: Lobbying, service;

Landmark & Community Chamber of Commerce
PO Box 469, Landmark MB R0A 0X0
Tel: 204-355-4035; *Fax:* 204-355-4800
office@landmarkonline.ca
Overview: A small local organization
Chief Officer(s):
Randy Wolgemuth, President

Landscape Alberta Nursery Trades Association (LANTA)
#200, 10331 - 178 St. NW, Edmonton AB T5S 1R5
Tel: 780-489-1991; *Fax:* 780-444-2152
Toll-Free: 800-378-3198
admin@landscape-alberta.com
www.landscape-alberta.com
twitter.com/LandscapeAB
Overview: A medium-sized provincial organization founded in 1957 overseen by Canadian Nursery Landscape Association
Mission: To advance the Alberta ornamental horticulture industry through unity, education & professionalism
Affliation(s): Saskatchewan Nursery Landscape Association
Chief Officer(s):
Nigel Bowles, Executive Director
nigel.bowles@landscape-alberta.com
Finances: *Funding Sources:* Membership fees; fundraising programs
Staff Member(s): 6
Membership: 256; *Fees:* Schedule available; *Member Profile:* Must be engaged in the horticultural industry or a supplier

Landscape New Brunswick Horticultural Trades Association (LNBHTA)
PO Box 742, Saint John NB E2L 4B3
Fax: 866-595-5467
Toll-Free: 866-752-6862
lnb@nbnet.nb.ca
www.landscapenbmember.com
www.facebook.com/Landscapenewbrunswick
Overview: A small provincial organization
Mission: To further the development of the ornamental horticulture industry by focusing on the environment, education, promotion & professionalism; to represent members & to help them achieve their goals
Chief Officer(s):
Joe Wynberg, President
Membership: *Fees:* $375 active; $425 commercial; $225 out-of-province; $25 affiliate; *Committees:* Environment; Education; Landscape Horticulture Training Institute; Awards; Membership; All Commodity Education Sessions; Certification; Garden Centre Canada; HortEast; Summer Tour

Landscape Newfoundland & Labrador (LNL)
PO Box 8062, St. John's NL A1B 3M9
Fax: 866-833-8603
Toll-Free: 855-872-8722
lnl@landscapenl.com
members.landscapenl.com
facebook.com/landscapenlevents
www.twitter.com/@landscapeNL
pinterest.com/landscapenl/
Overview: A small provincial organization founded in 1992 overseen by Canadian Nursery Landscape Association
Mission: Our vision is one that promotes professionalism at all levels of the Industry, and achieves the highest standards of excellence in delivery of services and products across all sectors of our industry.
Chief Officer(s):
David Kiell, Executive Director
Membership: 75; *Fees:* $50 individual; $125 affiliated; $310 associate/active
Meetings/Conferences: • Landscape NL Annual General Meeting 2015, 2015
Scope: Provincial

Landscape Nova Scotia
Executive Plus Business Centre, Burnside Industrial Park, #44, 201 Brownlow Ave., Dartmouth NS B3B 1W2
Tel: 902-463-0519; *Fax:* 902-446-8104
Toll-Free: 877-567-4769
info@landscapenovascotia.ca
www.landscapenovascotia.ca
www.facebook.com/199135136822813
Overview: A medium-sized provincial organization overseen by Canadian Nursery Landscape Association
Mission: To promote high standards in product quality, professional service and conduct in the landscape and horticulture industry
Chief Officer(s):
Pam Woodman, Executive Director
pam@landscapenovascotia.ca
Staff Member(s): 1
Membership: 3,700 companies; *Fees:* $452 active; $78 affiliate; $130 out of province

Landscape Ontario Horticultural Trades Association (LOHTA)
7856 - 5th Line South, RR#4, Milton ON L9T 2X8
Tel: 416-848-7575; *Fax:* 905-875-3942
Toll-Free: 800-265-5656
www.horttrades.com
Overview: A medium-sized provincial organization founded in 1973 overseen by Canadian Nursery Landscape Association
Mission: To be a leader in representing, promoting & fostering a favourable environment for the advancement of the horticultural industry in Ontario
Affliation(s): American Nursery Landscape Association; Canadian Nursery Landsape Association; Canadian Ornamental Plant Foundation; Communities in Bloom; International Association of Horticultural Producers; International Garden Centre Association; Irrigation Association; North American Plant Protection Organization; Ontario Parks Association; Professional Landcare Network; Trees for Life; Vineland Research and Innovation Centre
Chief Officer(s):
Tony DiGiovanni, Executive Director
tonydigiovanni@landscapeontario.com
Finances: *Funding Sources:* Membership dues; congress
Staff Member(s): 28
Membership: 2,000+; *Member Profile:* Active - firms with at least 3 years experience in the field; Interim/Active - firms with at least 1 year but less than 3 years experience in the field; Associate - suppliers to the industry & the association
Activities: *Speaker Service:* Yes
Awards:
• The Landscape Awards Program (Award)
Publications:
• Landscape Ontario
Type: Magazine; *Frequency:* Monthly; *Editor:* Lee Ann Knudsen
Profile: Industry news, association news, industry issue features, profiles, event announcements, extension bulletins and more.

Langara Faculty Association / Association des professeurs de Langara
100 - West 49th Ave., Vancouver BC V5Y 2Z6
Tel: 604-323-5343
langarafacultyassociation@lfaweb.ca
www.lfaweb.ca
Overview: A small local organization
Mission: To facilitate collective bargaining agreements for the faculty of Langara College in Vancouver, BC.

Langdon & District Chamber of Commerce
PO Box 18, Langdon AB T0J 1X0
Tel: 403-369-1590
membership@langdonchamber.ca
www.langdonchamber.ca
Overview: A small local organization
Affliation(s): Alberta Chamber of Commerce; Canadian Chamber of Commerce
Chief Officer(s):

Gerard Lucyshyn, President
president@langdonchamber.ca
Membership: 184; *Fees:* $75

Langenburg & District Chamber of Commerce
PO Box 610, Langenburg SK S0A 2A0
Tel: 306-743-2231; *Fax:* 306-743-2873
Overview: A small local organization
Mission: To promote the Town of Langenburg & District
Chief Officer(s):
R.J. Buchberger, President
Janice Fogg, Secretary
djfogg@sasktel.net
Finances: *Funding Sources:* Membership fees

Langham Cultural Society
PO Box 1000, 447A Ave., Kaslo BC V0G 1M0
Tel: 250-353-2661; *Fax:* 250-353-2671
langham@netidea.com
www.thelangham.ca
Previous Name: Kaslo Arts Counci
Overview: A small local charitable organization founded in 1974
Mission: To preserve Langham Building, Kaslo; To stimulate educational & cultural awareness of the community & surrounding area through the introduction of works in performing & visual arts; To foster interest & pride in cultural heritage of community of Kaslo & the West Kootenay region
Member of: North Kootenay Lake Arts & Heritage Council
Chief Officer(s):
Alice Windsor, Administrator
Brent Bukowski, Curator
Finances: *Annual Operating Budget:* $50,000-$100,000; *Funding Sources:* Provincial & federal government; private foundation grants; memberships; donations
Membership: 200; *Fees:* $12 single; $20 family; $450 lifetime; *Committees:* Building; Windows; Contracts
Activities: Operates Langham Gallery & gallery programs, The Langham Theatre & the Japanese Canadian Museum; *Library:* Langham Arts Instruction Library; Open to public

Langley & Aldergrove Food Bank
5768 - 203 St., Langley BC V3A 1W3
Tel: 604-533-0671; *Fax:* 604-533-0891
info@langleyfoodbank.com
www.langleyfoodbank.com
Overview: A small local organization
Mission: Dedicated to helping bring food and services to the needy in the Langley area.
Finances: *Funding Sources:* donations from local churches, organizations and individuals

Langley Arts Council (LAC)
#206, 20641 Logan Ave., Langley BC V3R 7R3
Tel: 604-534-0781; *Fax:* 604-534-0781
administrator@langleyartscouncil.com
www.langleyartscouncil.com
www.facebook.com/pages/Langley-Arts-Council/238568312822173
Overview: A small local organization founded in 1968
Mission: To promote & support the Arts by participating in cultural & multicultural events; To solicit funds from private & government sources; to support heritage conservation; To continue to campaign for community cultural affairs; to act as a resource centre for information on the Arts; To help to initiate new arts groups & activities; To act as a liaison between government & arts organizations
Member of: Assembly of BC Arts Councils; Langley Chamber of Commerce
Chief Officer(s):
Don Shilton, Interim General Manager
Membership: *Member Profile:* Interest in supporting & promoting the arts
Activities: *Speaker Service:* Yes; *Library* Open to public

Langley Association for Community Living (LACL)
23535 - 44th Ave., Langley BC V2Z 2V2
Tel: 604-534-8611; *Fax:* 604-534-4763
main@langleyacl.com
www.langleyacl.com
www.facebook.com/392209904180351
twitter.com/LangleyACL
Overview: A small local organization founded in 1959
Mission: To support the participation & inclusion of people with developmental disabilities in the community; To provide quality services
Member of: British Columbia Association for Community Living
Affliation(s): Canadian Association for Community Living
Chief Officer(s):
Dan Collins, Executive Director
dcollins@langleyacl.com
Finances: *Funding Sources:* Government; fundraising
Membership: *Fees:* $5
Activities: *Speaker Service:* Yes

Langley District Help Network
5768 - 203 St., Langley BC V3A 1W3
Tel: 604-533-0671; *Fax:* 604-533-0891
info@langleyfoodbank.com
www.langleyfoodbank.com
Overview: A small local organization
Chief Officer(s):

Langley Field Naturalists Society (LFN)
PO Box 56052, Stn. Valley Centre, Langley BC V3A 8B3
e-mail: Langleyfieldnaturalists@shaw.ca
www.langleyfieldnaturalists.org
Overview: A small local organization founded in 1973
Mission: To promote the enjoyment of nature; to learn about natural history; to promote preservation of the environment through active participation in conservation projects
Member of: The Federation of BC Naturalists; Canadian Nature Federation
Finances: *Annual Operating Budget:* Less than $50,000; *Funding Sources:* Langley Arts Council Grant; membership fees
Membership: 60-70; *Fees:* $25 single; $30 family; *Committees:* Conservation education; Watson nature reserve
Activities: Monthly field trips from Sept.-June, weekly walks July-Aug.; Maintenance of Brydan Lagoon & Irene Pearce Trail; *Awareness Events:* Rivers Day; Earth Day; Campbell Valley Country Celebration

Langley Heritage Society (LHS)
PO Box 982, Fort Langley BC V1M 2S3
Tel: 604-513-8787
info@langleyheritage.ca
www.langleyheritage.ca
www.facebook.com/LangleyHeritageSociety
Overview: A small local charitable organization founded in 1979
Mission: To plan for restoration & ongoing use for Langley's heritage buildings & sites
Member of: BC Heritage Society; Langley Arts Council
Chief Officer(s):
Fred Pepin, President
Membership: *Fees:* $8 individual; $15 family; $50 contributing; $100 sustaining

Language Industry Association (AILIA) / Association de l'industrie de la langue
PO Box 1250, Stn. Hull, #F0239, 283, boul. Alexandre-Taché, Gatineau QC J8X 3X7
Tel: 819-595-3849; *Fax:* 613-822-4988
communication@ailia.ca
www.ailia.ca
www.linkedin.com/groups?gid=3026714
www.facebook.com/106697719417820
twitter.com/AILIA_LANG
www.youtube.com/user/AILIALang
Overview: A small national organization founded in 2003
Mission: To promote and increase the competitiveness of the Canadian language industry nationally & internationally throug advocacy, accreditation & information sharing
Chief Officer(s):
Ann Rutledge, Chair
Loïc Le Bihan, Director, Operations
llebihan@ailia.ca
Finances: *Annual Operating Budget:* $1.5 Million-$3 Million
Staff Member(s): 3; 11 volunteer(s)
Membership: 150; *Fees:* Schedule available; *Member Profile:* Enterprises; individuals in translation, language training, language technologies; *Committees:* Technology Roadmap; Human Resources; Communications; Translation
Activities: Canadian Annual Tour in seven cities, Jan. - Mar.

Languages Canada / Langues Canada
5886 - 169A St., Surrey BC V3S 6Z8
Tel: 604-574-1532; *Fax:* 888-277-0522
Other Communication: Executive Director Phone: 613-324-8409 (Ottawa)
info@languagescanada.ca
www.languagescanada.ca
www.facebook.com/languagescanada
twitter.com/LangCanada
Merged from: Canadian Association of Private Language Schools; Canada Language Council
Overview: A large national organization founded in 2008
Mission: To promote quality, accredited English & French language training in Canada, & to represent Canada as a destination for excellent English & French language training
Chief Officer(s):
Michael Armour, Contact
Staff Member(s): 5; 16 volunteer(s)
Membership: 204 programs; *Member Profile:* Language schools which meet the rigorous standards of the association
Meetings/Conferences: • Languages Canada 2015 8th Annual Conference & Annual General Meeting, March, 2015, Hilton Lac-Leamy Hotel, Gatineau, QC
Scope: National
Contact Information: conference@languagescanada.ca

Langues Canada *See* Languages Canada

Lansdowne Outdoor Recreational Development Association (LORDA)
PO Box 591, Westville NS B0K 2A0
Tel: 902-396-4470; *Fax:* 902-396-1399
contact@lorda.org
www.lorda.org
www.facebook.com/LORDAPark
Overview: A small local organization
Chief Officer(s):
Dave Leese, Contact
dave@lorda.org
Activities: Operates senior citizen & disabled persons park; facilities: fishing ponds, nature trails, bocce court, trailer parking, picnic benches, screened gazebo, croquet court, tenting area

Lao Association of Ontario
956 Wilson Ave., Toronto ON M3K 1E7
Tel: 416-398-3057
info@laoweb.org
www.laoweb.org
www.facebook.com/249069225233477
Overview: A small provincial charitable organization founded in 1979
Mission: To assist Lao people settle into Canadian society; to promote Lao culture
Member of: Canadian Multiculturalism Council; Ontario Council of Agencies Serving Immigrants; Laotian Federation of Canada
Activities: Information exchange; interpretation & translation services; supportive counselling

Lao Community of Québec *Voir* Communauté Laotienne du Québec

Lapidary Club of West Vancouver
PO Box 91233, West Vancouver BC V7V 2N6
Tel: 604-922-0072
Overview: A small local organization
Member of: Lapidary, Rock & Mineral Society of British Columbia

Last Post Fund (LPF) / Fonds du Souvenir
#401, 505, boul René-Lévesque ouest, Montréal QC H2Z 1Y7
Tel: 514-866-2727; *Fax:* 514-866-1471
Toll-Free: 800-465-7113
info@lastpost.ca
www.lastpostfund.ca
Overview: A medium-sized national charitable organization founded in 1909
Mission: To ensure that no war veterans, or certain other persons who meet the wartime service eligibility criteria, are denied a funeral & burial due to lack of funds
Chief Officer(s):
Douglas Briscoe, President
Charles Keple, Vice-President, West
Barry Keeler, Vice President (East)
Jean-Pierre Goyer, Executive Director
Finances: *Funding Sources:* Donations
Activities: Conveying Last Post Fund resolutions to Veterans Affairs Canada; *Awareness Events:* Annual Commemorative Ceremonies, Last Post Fund National Field of Honour, Pointe-Claire, Québec, first Sunday each June

Alberta Branch
Canada Place, #1130, 9700 Jasper Ave., Edmonton AB T5J 4C3
Tel: 780-495-3766; *Fax:* 780-495-6960
Toll-Free: 888-495-3766
www.lastpostfund.ca

Mission: The Last Post Fund is dedicated to ensure, in so far as possible, that no war veterans, military disability pensioners or civilians who meet wartime service eligibility criteria are denied a dignified funeral and burial for lack of sufficient funds.
Chief Officer(s):
Hans Brink, President

British Columbia Branch
#307, 7337 - 137th St., Surrey BC V3W 1A4
Tel: 604-572-3242; *Fax:* 604-572-3306
Toll-Free: 800-268-0248
www.lastpostfund.ca
Mission: The Last Post Fund is dedicated to ensure, in so far as possible, that no war veterans, military disability pensioners or civilians who meet wartime service eligibility criteria are denied a dignified funeral and burial for lack of sufficient funds.
Chief Officer(s):
Ike Hall, President

Newfoundland-Labrador Branch
Prudential Bldg., 49 Elizabeth Ave., St. John's NL A1A 1W9
Tel: 709-579-4288; *Fax:* 709-579-0966
Toll-Free: 888-579-4288
www.lastpostfund.ca
Mission: The Last Post Fund is dedicated to ensure, in so far as possible, that no war veterans, military disability pensioners or civilians who meet wartime service eligibility criteria are denied a dignified funeral and burial for lack of sufficient funds.
Chief Officer(s):
Donald Newell, President

Nova Scotia Branch
Chebucto Place, #200A, 7105 Chebucto Rd., Halifax NS B3L 4W8
Tel: 902-455-5283; *Fax:* 902-455-4058
Toll-Free: 800-565-4777
www.lastpostfund.ca
Mission: The Last Post Fund is dedicated to ensure, in so far as possible, that no war veterans, military disability pensioners or civilians who meet wartime service eligibility criteria are denied a dignified funeral and burial for lack of sufficient funds.
Chief Officer(s):
Roderick Morrison, President

Ontario Branch
#905, 55 St. Clair Ave. East, Toronto ON M4T 1M2
Tel: 416-923-1608
info@lastpost.ca
www.lastpostfund.ca
Mission: The Last Post Fund is dedicated to ensure, in so far as possible, that no war veterans, military disability pensioners or civilians who meet wartime service eligibility criteria are denied a dignified funeral and burial for lack of sufficient funds.
Chief Officer(s):
Edward S. Fitch, National President

Saskatchewan Branch
Federal Building, #403, 101 - 22 St. East, Saskatoon SK S7K 0E1
Tel: 306-975-6045; *Fax:* 306-975-6678
Toll-Free: 800-667-3668
lastpost@sasktel.net
www.lastpostfund.ca
Mission: The Last Post Fund is dedicated to ensure, in so far as possible, that no war veterans, military disability pensioners or civilians who meet wartime service eligibility criteria are denied a dignified funeral and burial for lack of sufficient funds.
Chief Officer(s):
Charles Keple, CD, SVM, President

United Kingdom Representative
Veteran Affairs Divison- High Commission of Canada, MacDonald House, 1 Grosvenor Sq., London W1X 0AB United Kingdom
Tel: 44(0)20-7258-6339; *Fax:* 44(0)20-7258-6645
www.lastpostfund.ca
Mission: The Last Post Fund is dedicated to ensure, in so far as possible, that no war veterans, military disability pensioners or civilians who meet wartime service eligibility criteria are denied a dignified funeral and burial for lack of sufficient funds.
Chief Officer(s):
Suzanne Happe, Representative
suzanne.happe@dfait-maeci.gc.ca

Latin American Mission Program (LAMP)
81 Prince St., Charlottetown PE C1A 4R3
Tel: 902-368-7337; *Fax:* 902-368-7180
www.dioceseofcharlottetown.com
www.facebook.com/dioceseofcharlottetown
twitter.com/chtowndiocese
Overview: A small international organization founded in 1967
Mission: To send out & receive back missionaries; to learn from the dispossessed & oppressed & to stand with them in building a society of justice; to develop & encourage a Faith response based on the life & struggle of dispossessed peoples; to participate in "return mission" by working with groups committed to social justice in Canada & developing education programs in PEI which analyze the causes of exploitation of the poor & which expose the reality of their lives
Affliation(s): Diocese of Charlottetown; Les missionnaires du Sacre-Coeur; Scarboro Foreign Mission Society
Finances: *Annual Operating Budget:* $50,000-$100,000; *Funding Sources:* Share Lent collections taken up annually in all parishes
Membership: 20
Activities: Educational events; orientation & support for missionaries

Latino Canadian Cultural Association (LCCA) / Association Culturelle Latino Canadienne (ACLC)
#254, 601 Christie St., Toronto ON M6G 4C7
e-mail: info@lccatoronto.com
www.lccatoronto.com
Also Known As: Asociacion Cultural Latino Canadiense
Overview: A small local organization
Mission: To support Latino artists & help them connect to the Canadian community
Chief Officer(s):
Dinoi Toledo, President, Board of Directors
Alejandro Freeland, Executive Director
Activities: Exhibitions; Cultural events

Latvian Canadian Cultural Centre (LCCC)
4 Credit Union Dr., Toronto ON M4A 2N8
Tel: 416-759-4900; *Fax:* 416-759-9311
office@latviancentre.org
www.latviancentre.org
www.facebook.com/143970339032047
Overview: A small national charitable organization founded in 1977
Mission: To acquire, maintain & operate a Centre; to foster & sustain the Latvian heritage & cultural tradition; to provide social & cultural exchange with the various cultural communities in Canada; to provide facilities for meetings, concerts, dances, seminars, theatre & film shows & similar social/recreational activities for the general public & members
Chief Officer(s):
Sylvia Shedden, President & CEO
Finances: *Annual Operating Budget:* $250,000-$500,000
Staff Member(s): 10; 60 volunteer(s)
Membership: 800; *Fees:* $1,000; *Member Profile:* Latvian or Latvian background
Activities: *Library:* Latvian Centre Library; Open to public

Latvian National Federation in Canada / Fédération nationale lettone au Canada
4 Credit Union Dr., Toronto ON M4A 2N8
Tel: 416-755-2353
lnak@lnak.org
www.lnak.org
Overview: A small national organization overseen by Baltic Federation in Canada
Mission: To represent the interests of Latvian Canadians at the city, provincial & federal levels; to maintain contact with other Canadian non-governmental organizations & expedites projects both in Canada & in Latvia.
Member of: Canadian Ethnocultural Council
Chief Officer(s):
Andris Kesteris, Chair, 613-837-4928
akestr0542@rogers.com
Vilnis Pētersons, Administrator, 416-491-0560
vilnispetersons@yahoo.ca
Activities: Participation in Toronto Museum Project; Tribute to Liberty, a memorial establishing project

Latviesu Dailamatnieku Savieniba *See* Association of Latvian Craftsmen in Canada

Laubach Literacy New Brunswick
347 Mountain Rd., Moncton NB E1C 2M7
Tel: 506-384-6371; *Fax:* 506-388-9314
laubachliteracynb@nb.aibn.com
www.llnb.ca
Overview: A medium-sized provincial organization
Chief Officer(s):
Deanna Allen, Executive Director
Staff Member(s): 2

Laubach Literacy Ontario
#8A, 65 Noecker St., Waterloo ON N2J 2R6
Tel: 519-743-3309; *Fax:* 519-743-7520
Toll-Free: 866-608-2574
literacy@laubach-on.ca
www.laubach-on.ca
www.facebook.com/LaubachLiteracyOntario
twitter.com/LLOntario
Overview: A medium-sized provincial organization
Mission: To provide their students with skills in order to combat illiteracy in Ontario
Affliation(s): Lauback Literacy of Canada is the Canadian affiliate of ProLiteracy Worldwide (formerly Laubach Literacy International)
Chief Officer(s):
Gary Porter, President
Lana Faessler, Executive Director
Staff Member(s): 3
Membership: 80; *Fees:* $50 organizational; $75 associate; *Committees:* Social Enterprise; Student

LAUDEM, L'Association des musiciens liturgiques du Canada
1085, rue de la Cathédrale, Montréal QC H3B 2V3
Tél: 514-321-3644
Autres numéros: Adresse électronique: laudem.canada@gmail.com
info@laudem.org
www.laudem.org
www.facebook.com/laudemcanada
Nom précédent: L'Association des organistes liturgiques du Canada
Aperçu: *Dimension:* petite; *Envergure:* nationale; fondée en 1992
Mission: De réunir les organistes liturgiques pour la promotion et le développement de leur ministère dans l'Église catholique romaine
Membre de: Fédération francophone des amis de l'orgue
Membre(s) du bureau directeur:
Jean-Pierre Couturier, Président, 514-321-3644
jpcouturier@montréal.net
Paul Cadrin, Vice-Président, 438-381-5048
paulcadrin@hotmail.com
Samuel Croteau, Secrétaire-trésorier, 514-663-4729
samuel.croteau@gmail.com
Membre: 45

Laurentian Tourist Association *Voir* Association touristique des Laurentides

Laurentian University Faculty Association (LUFA) / Association des professeurs de l'Université Laurentienne
#C105, Laurentian University, 935 Ramsey Lake Rd., Sudbury ON P3E 2C6
Tel: 705-675-1151; *Fax:* 705-673-6536
lufa@laurentian.ca
www.lufapul.ca
Overview: A small local organization
Affliation(s): Canadian Association of University Teachers; Ontario Confederation of University Faculty Associations; Sudbury and District Labour Council; Ontario Federation of Labor; Canadian Labor Congress
Chief Officer(s):
Anis Farah, President
AFarah@laurentienne.ca
Finances: *Annual Operating Budget:* $100,000-$250,000
Staff Member(s): 1
Membership: 391 individual; *Fees:* Based on salary; *Member Profile:* Professors; librarians

Laurentian University Staff Union (LUSU) / Syndicat des employé(es) de l'Université Laurentienne (SEUL)
Laurentian University, 935 Ramsey Lake Rd., Sudbury ON P3E 2C6
Tel: 705-675-1151
www.lusu-seul.ca
Overview: A small local organization founded in 1973

Member of: Confederation of Canadian Unions
Affliation(s): Confederation of Ontario University Staff Associations
Chief Officer(s):
Tom Fenske, President
tc_fenske@laurentian.ca
Membership: 270
Awards:
• Lynn McGlade Memorial Bursary (Scholarship)
• Dan MacLean Memorial Bursary (Scholarship)
• Evelyn Ham/LUSU Bursary (Scholarship)

The Laurier Institution
UBC Robson Square, #1600, 800 Robson St., Vancouver BC V6Z 2C5
Tel: 604-822-2054
Other Communication: www.facebook.com/thelaurier
info@thelaurier.ca
www.thelaurier.ca
www.youtube.com/user/thelaurierca
Overview: A small national charitable organization founded in 1989
Mission: To provide research & educational projects on Canada's cultural diversity
Chief Officer(s):
Farid Rohani, Board Member
Finances: *Funding Sources:* Membership fees; Donations
Membership: 100-499; *Member Profile:* Individuals & students
Activities: Conducting research studies; Providing education; Offering support services; *Library* by appointment

Laurier Teachers Union (LTU) / Syndicat des enseignantes et enseignants Laurier
#210, 2292, Industriel, Laval QC H7S 1P9
Tel: 450-667-7037; *Fax:* 450-667-9506
Toll-Free: 800-301-1351
laurierteachersunion@ltu.ca
www.ltu.ca
Previous Name: North Island Laurentian Teachers' Union
Overview: A small local organization founded in 1998
Mission: To promote & defend the interests of teachers & public education
Member of: Québec Provincial Association of Teachers
Chief Officer(s):
Theresa Kralik, President
Finances: *Annual Operating Budget:* $250,000-$500,000
Staff Member(s): 4; 50 volunteer(s)
Membership: 840 individual; *Fees:* $650 individual

Laval University Faculty Union *Voir* Syndicat des professeurs de l'Université Laval

Law Foundation of British Columbia
#1340, 605 Robson St., Vancouver BC V6B 5J3
Tel: 604-688-2337; *Fax:* 604-688-4586
info@lawfoundationbc.org
www.lawfoundationbc.org
Overview: A medium-sized provincial charitable organization founded in 1969
Mission: To allocate funds to programs that will benefit the general public of British Columbia; To act in accordance with The Legal Profession Act & distribute income in areas that promote & advance a just society & the rule of law, such as legal aid, law libraries, legal education, legal research, & law reform; To conduct operations with recognition of the diverse population of British Columbia
Chief Officer(s):
Wayne Robertson, Executive Director
Margaret Sasges, Chair
Jo-Anne Kaulius, Director, Finance
Finances: *Funding Sources:* Income is the result of interest on client's funds that are held in lawyers' pooled trust accounts maintained in financial institutions
Activities: Accepting grant applications from non-profit organizations; Funding projects

Law Foundation of Newfoundland & Labrador
Murray Premises, 2nd Fl., PO Box 5907, #49, 55 Elizabeth Ave., St. John's NL A1C 5X4
Tel: 709-754-4424; *Fax:* 709-754-4320
www.atyp.com/lawfoundationnl
Overview: A medium-sized provincial organization founded in 1980
Mission: To provide grants for the following services in Newfoundland & Labrador that advance public understanding of the law & access to legal services: the Legal Aid Commission as established under the Legal Aid Act; law libraries; legal research; legal education; scholarships for studies relevant to law; law reform; & legal referral services
Activities: Accepting & reviewing application & sponsoring programs

Law Foundation of Nova Scotia
Cogswell Tower, #1305, 2000 Barrington St., Halifax NS B3J 3K1
Tel: 902-422-8335; *Fax:* 902-492-0424
nslawfd@nslawfd.ca
www.nslawfd.ca
Overview: A small provincial organization founded in 1976
Mission: To establish & maintain a fund to be used for the examination, research, revision & reform of & public access to the law, legal education, the administration of justice in the province & any other purposes incidental or conducive to or consequential upon the attainment of any such objects
Chief Officer(s):
Kerry L. Oliver, Executive Director
Finances: *Funding Sources:* Interest acquired from lawyers' general trust accounts
Staff Member(s): 1

Law Foundation of Ontario (LFO) / La fondation du droit de l'Ontario
PO Box 19, #3002, 20 Queen St. West, Toronto ON M5H 3R3
Tel: 416-598-1550; *Fax:* 416-598-1526
Other Communication: grants@lawfoundation.on.ca
general@lawfoundation.on.ca
www.lawfoundation.on.ca
www.facebook.com/pages/The-Law-Foundation-of-Ontario/222748937889770
twitter.com/LawFoundationOn
Overview: A small provincial charitable organization founded in 1974
Mission: An organization that provides funding to a wide range of organizations to foster excellence in the work of lawyers, paralegals and other legal professionals.
Chief Officer(s):
Mark J. Sandler, Chair
Elizabeth Goldberg, Chief Executive Officer
egoldberg@lawfoundation.on.ca
Awards:
• Guthrie Award (Award)
The Guthrie Award recognizes outstanding individuals and organizations for their contributions to access to justice and excellence in the legal profession.
• Roy and Ria McMurtry Endowment (Scholarship)
The Guthrie Award recognizes outstanding individuals and organizations for their contributions to access to justice and excellence in the legal profession. Eligibility: Students who are enrolled in courses related to law.

Law Foundation of Prince Edward Island
49 Water St., Charlottetown PE C1A 7K2
Tel: 902-620-1763
info@lawfoundationpei.ca
www.lawfoundationpei.ca
Overview: A small provincial organization founded in 1973
Mission: To establish & maintain a fund & use the proceeds for the purposes of: legal education & research on law reform; the editing & printing of decisions of the Supreme Court & the Provincial Court of PEI; the promotion of legal aid; aid in the establishment, operation & maintenance of law libraries in PEI
Affliation(s): Association of Canadian Law Foundations
Chief Officer(s):
Sheila Lund MacDonald, Executive Director
5 volunteer(s)
Membership: 5

Law Foundation of Saskatchewan
#200, 2208 Scarth St., Regina SK S4P 2J6
Tel: 306-352-1121; *Fax:* 306-522-6222
lfsk@virtusgroup.ca
www.lawfoundation.sk.ca
Overview: A medium-sized provincial organization founded in 1971
Mission: To maintain a fund to support legal aid, law reform, law libraries, legal education, & legal research
Chief Officer(s):
Robert Arscott, Secretary
Patricia Quaroni, Chair
Bob Watt, Treasurer
Finances: *Funding Sources:* Fund results from interest on the sums in lawyers' mixed trust accounts in chartered banks & other financial institutions in Saskatchewan
Activities: Meeting on a quarterly basis to consider grant applications

Law Society of Alberta (LSA)
#500, 919 - 11th Ave. SW, Calgary AB T2R 1P3
Tel: 403-229-4700; *Fax:* 403-228-1728
Toll-Free: 800-661-9003
www.lawsocietyalberta.com
Overview: A large provincial licensing organization founded in 1907
Mission: To serve the public by promoting a high standard of legal services & professional conduct through the governance & regulation of an independent legal profession; to govern all lawyers who practise law in Alberta; responsible for admitting lawyers to the Bar, professional conduct & discipline of lawyers
Affliation(s): Federation of Law Societies of Canada
Chief Officer(s):
Don Thompson, Executive Director
Carsten Jensen, President
Finances: *Funding Sources:* Membership fees
Staff Member(s): 85
Membership: 5,000-14,999; *Fees:* Schedule available; *Committees:* Access to Justice; Appeal; Audit; Civil Practice Advisory; Conduct; Continuing Competence; Corporate & Commercial Advisory; Credentials & Education; Criminal Practice ADvisory; Executive; Family Law Advisory; Finance; Governance; Insurance & Claims; Joint Library; Practice Review; Professional Responsibility; Re-Engagment & Retention; Third Party Funding Policy; Trust Safety
Awards:
• Distinguished Service Awards (Award)
• The Viscount Bennett Scholarship (Scholarship)
Amount: Up to $20,000
• Peter Freeman, QC, Bursary for Indigenous Students in Law. (Scholarship)
Meetings/Conferences: • Alberta LAw Conference 2015, January, 2015, Fairmont Hotel Macdonald, Edmonton, AB
Scope: Provincial

Edmonton Office
Bell Tower, 10104 - 103 Ave., Edmonton AB T5J OH8
Tel: 780-429-3343; *Fax:* 780-424-1620
Toll-Free: 800-272-8839
Mission: To serve the public interest by promoting a high standard of legal services and professional conduct through the governance and regulation of an independent legal profession
Chief Officer(s):
Don Thompson, QC, Executive Director, 403-229-4700

Law Society of British Columbia
845 Cambie St., 8th Fl., Vancouver BC V6B 4Z9
Tel: 604-669-2533; *Fax:* 604-669-5232
Toll-Free: 800-902-5300; *TTY:* 604-443-5700
communications@lsbc.org
www.lawsociety.bc.ca
twitter.com/LawSocietyofBC
Overview: A large provincial licensing organization founded in 1884
Mission: To ensure that the public is well served by a competent, honourable & independent legal profession
Affliation(s): Federation of Law Societies of Canada
Chief Officer(s):
Timothy E. McGee, CEO & Executive Director
Bruce A. LeRose, President
Finances: *Annual Operating Budget:* Greater than $5 Million; *Funding Sources:* Membership dues
50 volunteer(s)
Membership: 10,210 practising; 1,298 non-practising; *Fees:* $855 practising; $180 non-practising; *Member Profile:* Completed requirement for call to B.C. Bar; *Committees:* Benchers; Executive; Treasurer's; Audit; Competency; Credentials; Discipline; Audit; Ethics; Special Compensation Fund; Finance
Activities: *Speaker Service:* Yes
Awards:
• The Law Society Award (Award)
• Law Society Gold Medals (Award)
• Law Society Scholarship for Graduate Legal Studies (Scholarship)
• Jack Webster Award for Excellence in Legal Journalism (Scholarship)
Publications:
• Benchers' Bulletins
Type: Bulletin

Law Society of Manitoba (LSM) / La Société du Barreau du Manitoba

219 Kennedy St., Winnipeg MB R3C 1S8
Tel: 204-942-5571; *Fax:* 204-956-0624
admin@lawsociety.mb.ca
www.lawsociety.mb.ca
Overview: A medium-sized provincial licensing organization founded in 1877
Mission: To ensure the public in Manitoba is well served by the legal profession
Member of: Canadian Lawyers Insurance Association (CLIA)
Chief Officer(s):
Allan Fineblit, CEO
afineblit@lawsociety.mb.ca
Marilyn Billinkoff, Deputy CEO
Membership: *Committees:* Executive & Administration; Admissions & Education; Complaints Investigation, Competence, & Discipline; Spot Audit Program; Professional Liability Insurance Program; Practice & Ethics Issues; Equity Issues
Activities: Admitting persons to the Bar; Providing continuing professional education; Conducting investigations of complaints, & disciplinary procedures; Auditing of law firms; Offering professional liability insurance; Publishing legal studies
Awards:
• Scholarships (Scholarship)
1st, 2nd, 3rd & 4th highest standing in third year law

Law Society of New Brunswick / Barreau du Nouveau-Brunswick

68 Avonlea Court, Fredericton NB E3C 1N8
Tel: 506-458-8540; *Fax:* 506-451-1421
general@lawsociety-barreau.nb.ca
www.lawsociety-barreau.nb.ca
Overview: A medium-sized provincial licensing organization founded in 1846
Mission: The Law Society was officially created in 1846. The Provincial Legislative Assembly adopted Chapter 48 of the Provincial Statutes which in effect incorporated what was then called the "Barristers' Society" for the "purpose of securing in the Province a learned and honourable legal profession, for establishing order and good conduct among its members and for promoting knowledgeable development and reform of the law".
Affliation(s): Federation of Law Societies of Canada
Chief Officer(s):
Mark Canty, President
Marc L. Richard, Executive Director
mrichard@lawsociety-barreau.nb.ca
Membership: 1,000-4,999; *Member Profile:* Open to individuals in accordance with the criteria & procedures established in the Law Society Act & the regulations under that Act; *Committees:* Articling; Admissions; Competence; Complaints; Insurance; New Brunswick Law Foundation; Property Law Advisory; Discipline; Legal Aid; Bar Admission Course; Examining; Compensation Fund; Provincial Libraries
Activities: *Library*

Law Society of Newfoundland & Labrador

PO Box 1028, 196-198 Water St., St. John's NL A1C 5M3
Tel: 709-722-4740; *Fax:* 709-722-8902
thelawsociety@lawsociety.nf.ca
www.lawsociety.nf.ca
Overview: A medium-sized provincial licensing organization founded in 1826
Mission: To ensure that law students are appropriately educated and trained through articling and Bar Admission programs and exams, and provides continuing legal education to practititoners.
Affliation(s): Federation of Law Societies of Canada
Chief Officer(s):
Brenda B. Grimes, Executive Director
brenda.grimes@lawsociety.nf.ca
Staff Member(s): 16
Membership: 719; *Committees:* Executive; Accounts and Finance; Archives; Bar Admission; Claims Review; Complaints Authorization; Custodianship; Discipline; Education; Honours & Awards; Insurance; Law Society Act & Rules; Law Society of Newfoundland & Labrador Medical Legal Liason; Legislation; Library; Life Membership; Practice Rules Compliance; Professional Law Corporations; Professionals' Assistance; Real Estate; The SS Daisy Legal History; Student Awards; Unauthorized Practice
Activities: *Library* Open to public by appointment

Law Society of Nunavut (LSNU)

PO Box 149, Iqaluit NU X0A 0H0
Tel: 867-979-2330; *Fax:* 867-979-2333
administrator@lawsociety.nu.ca
lawsociety.nu.ca
Overview: A medium-sized provincial licensing organization founded in 1999
Mission: To govern its membership & protect the public
Member of: Federation of Law Societies of Canada
Chief Officer(s):
Nalini Vaddapalli, CEO
Staff Member(s): 5
Membership: 262; *Committees:* Executive; Membership & Admissions; Discipline; Ethics & Unauthorized Practice; Finance

Law Society of Prince Edward Island

PO Box 128, 49 Water St., Charlottetown PE C1A 7K2
Tel: 902-566-1666; *Fax:* 902-368-7557
lawsociety@lspei.pe.ca
www.lspei.pe.ca
Overview: A small provincial licensing organization founded in 1876
Mission: To uphold & protect the public interest in the administration of justice; to establish standards for the education, professional responsibility & competence of members & applicants for membership; to ensure the independence, integrity & honour of the society & its members; to regulate the practice of law; to uphold & protect the interests of members.
Affiliation(s): Federation of Law Societies of Canada
Chief Officer(s):
Susan M. Robinson, Executive Director & Sec.-Treas.
Finances: *Funding Sources:* Membership fees
Staff Member(s): 5
Membership: Law firm members: 152; government members: 59; corporate members: 19; *Committees:* Annual and Mid-Winter Meeting; Articling & Admissions/ Board of Examiners; Continuing Legal Education; Credentials; Discipline; Discipline Policies and Procedure; Ethics; Insurance; Law Foundation; Legislation; Library, Court House; Nominating; Practice Standards/Competence; Real Property; Scholarship; Unauthorized Practice
Activities: *Internships:* Yes; *Library:* Law Library; Open to public

Law Society of Saskatchewan

#1100, 2002 Victoria Ave., Regina SK S4P 0R7
Tel: 306-569-8242; *Fax:* 306-352-2989
reception@lawsociety.sk.ca
www.lawsociety.sk.ca
Overview: A small provincial licensing organization founded in 1907
Mission: To govern the legal profession by upholding high standards of competence & integrity; ensuring the independence of the profession; advancing the administration of justice, the profession & the rule of law, all in the public interest
Affliation(s): Federation of Law Societies of Canada
Chief Officer(s):
Tom Schonhoffer, Executive Director
tom@lawsociety.sk.ca
Tim Huber, Counsel
tim@lawsociety.sk.ca
Staff Member(s): 29
Membership: *Committees:* Admission & Education; Discipline; Insurance; Ethics; Professional Standards

Law Society of the Northwest Territories / Le Barreau des Territoires du Nord-Ouest

PO Box 1298, Stn. Main, Yellowknife NT X1A 2N9
Tel: 867-873-3828; *Fax:* 867-873-6344
info@lawsociety.nt.ca
www.lawsociety.nt.ca
twitter.com/LawSocietyNWT
Overview: A small provincial licensing organization founded in 1978
Mission: To serve the public by an independent, responsible & responsive legal profession.
Affliation(s): Federation of Law Societies of Canada
Chief Officer(s):
Pamela Naylor, Executive Director
pamela.naylor@lawsociety.nt.ca
Finances: *Funding Sources:* Membership fees
Staff Member(s): 3
Membership: 547 individuals; *Fees:* $1,470 practising member; $236.25 non practising member; *Member Profile:* Graduate of common law faculty of Canadian law school or equivalent; *Committees:* Admissions; Continuing Professional Development; Discipline; Finance; Insurance; Legal Ethics & Practice; Rules; Social
Activities: Referral service; *Internships:* Yes

Law Society of Upper Canada / Barreau du Haut-Canada

Osgoode Hall, 130 Queen St. West, Toronto ON M5H 2N6
Tel: 416-947-3300; *Fax:* 416-947-3924
Toll-Free: 800-668-7380; *TTY:* 416-644-4886
lawsociety@lsuc.on.ca
www.lsuc.on.ca
www.linkedin.com/company/the-law-society-of-upper-canada
www.facebook.com/pages/Law-Society-of-Upper-Canada/110214529001232
twitter.com/LawsocietyLSUC
www.youtube.com/lawsocietylsuc
Overview: A large provincial licensing organization founded in 1797
Mission: To govern the legal profession in the public interest by ensuring that the people of Ontario are served by lawyers who meet high standards of learning, competence & professional conduct.
Affliation(s): Federation of Law Societies of Canada
Chief Officer(s):
Robert G. W. Lapper, CEO
Diana Miles, Director, Professional Development & Competence
Finances: *Annual Operating Budget:* $3 Million-$5 Million; *Funding Sources:* Membership fees; Law Foundation of Ontario
Membership: 27,500; *Committees:* Access to Justice; Appeal Panel; Audit & Finance; Compensation; Compensation Fund; Equity and Aboriginal Issues; Government Relations; Hearing Panel; Heritage; Inter-Jurisdictional Mobility; Law Society Awards; Litigation; Paralegal Standing; Priority Planning; Proceedings Authorization; Professional Development and Competence; Professional Regulation; Summary Disposition; Tribunals
Activities: Complaints: 1-800-268-7568, 416-947-3310; Law Society Referral Service (LSRS): 1-800-268-8326; *Library:* Great Library
Awards:
• The Law Society Medal (Award)
• Distinguished Paralegal Award (Award)
• The Lincoln Alexander Award (Award)
To recognize an Ontario lawyer who has demonstrated a commitment to the public through community service.
• The Laura Legge Award (Award)
Recognizes woman lawyers from Ontario who have exemplified leadership within the profession.
Meetings/Conferences: • Law Society of Upper Canada / Barreau du Haut-Canada 2015 Annual General Meeting, 2015
Scope: Provincial
Contact Information: E-mail: lawsociety@lsuc.on.ca

Law Society of Yukon (LSY)

#202, 302 Steele St., Whitehorse YT Y1A 2C5
Tel: 867-668-4231; *Fax:* 867-667-7556
info@lawsocietyyukon.com
www.lawsocietyyukon.com
Also Known As: Yukon Law Society
Overview: A small provincial licensing organization founded in 1985
Mission: To govern legal profession in the Yukon.
Affliation(s): Federation of Law Societies of Canada
Chief Officer(s):
Lynn Daffe, Executive Director
Staff Member(s): 1
Membership: 329; *Fees:* Schedule available
Activities: *Library:* Law Library; Open to public

Law Union of Ontario

31 Prince Arthur Ave., Toronto ON M5R 1B2
Tel: 416-927-9662; *Fax:* 416-960-5456
law.union.of.ontario@gmail.com
www.lawunion.ca
Overview: A small provincial organization founded in 1974
Mission: Coalition of progressive & socialist lawyers, law students & legal workers providing an alternative bar in Ontario which seeks to counter the traditional protections afforded by the legal system to social, political & economic privilege
Membership: 200
Meetings/Conferences: • Law Union of Ontario 2015 Annual Conference, 2015, ON
Scope: Provincial

Lawn Bowls Association of Alberta

11759 Groat Rd., Edmonton AB T5M 3K6
Tel: 780-427-8119
office@bowls.ab.ca
www.bowls.ab.ca

Overview: A small provincial organization founded in 1989 overseen by Bowls Canada Boulingrin
Affliation(s): Commonwealth; Highlands; Royal Lawn Bowling Club; Edmonton Indoor Lawn Bowling Club; Bow Valley; Calgary Lawn; Rotary Park; Stanley Park; Ted Petrunia Lawn Bowling Green; Medicine Hat Lawn Bowling Green
Chief Officer(s):
Anthony Peter Spencer, President
Dave Cox, Vice-President
Laura Lochanski, Vice-President
Staff Member(s): 1

Lawn Bowls Canada Boulingrin *See* Bowls Canada Boulingrin

Lawyers for Social Responsibility (LSR) / Avocats en faveur d'une conscience sociale (AFCS)
Calgary AB
Tel: 403-282-8260
www.peacelawyers.ca
Overview: A small national organization founded in 1984
Mission: To advise the public, politicians, & government officials on the application of the law to foreign & defence policies; To call for use of law, not use of force, to resolve conflicts
Affliation(s): International Association of Lawyers Against Nuclear Arms; Mines Action Canada; Canadian Network to Abolish Nuclear Weapons
Chief Officer(s):
Beverley Delong, President
bevdelong@shaw.ca
Finances: *Funding Sources:* Donations
Membership: *Member Profile:* Lawyers; professors; law students; law librarians
Activities: Chapters in major cities & on university campuses across Canada; *Speaker Service:* Yes

Lawyers Without Borders Canada *See* Avocats sans frontières Canada

Lay Missionaries of Charity - Canada (LMC)
c/o Odette C.-Duggan, #45, 25 Pebble Byway, Toronto ON M2H 3J6
Tel: 416-498-5842
www.laymc.com
Also Known As: Lay Missionaries of Charity of Mother Teresa
Overview: A large international organization
Mission: To advance the interests of the Roman Catholic Church; to foster fraternity & fellowship among members; to promote undiscriminating charity
Affliation(s): Archdiocese of Toronto
Chief Officer(s):
Chuck Stevens, National Spiritual Director
cstevens@dol.ca
Odette C. Duggan, LMC Canadian National Link
ocd.lmc@gmail.com
Membership: *Member Profile:* Catholic males aged 16 & above

LC Line Contractors' Association of BC
#222, 7455 - 132 St., Surrey BC V3W 1J8
Tel: 604-599-9228; *Fax:* 604-599-4433
Toll-Free: 877-439-9827
info@lca.ca
www.lca.ca
Also Known As: LCA of BC
Overview: A small provincial organization founded in 1999
Member of: Mining, Suppliers, Contractors & Consultants Association of British Columbia
Affliation(s): Electrical Industry Training Institute; IBEW Local 258
Chief Officer(s):
Jeff Skosnik, CEO
jeff@lca.ca
Activities: Safety Program; Skills Upgrading; Safety Database; *Internships:* Yes
Awards:
• Annual Safety Awards (Award)

LEAD Canada Inc.
PO Box 250, 3202 Tullochgorum, Ormstown QC J0S 1K0
Toll-Free: 866-532-3539
office@leadcanada.net
www.leadcanada.net
Also Known As: Leadership for Environment & Development Canada
Overview: A small national organization
Chief Officer(s):
John Lewis, President
john@intelligentfutures.ca

Membership: *Fees:* $15

Leader Board of Trade
PO Box 104, Leader SK S0N 1H0
Tel: 306-628-3687; *Fax:* 306-628-3674
Overview: A small local organization
Chief Officer(s):
K. Wagman, Secretary
Gordon Stueck, President
gstueck@sasktel.net
Membership: 23; *Fees:* $50

Leaf Rapids Chamber of Commerce
c/o Town of Leaf Rapids, Town Centre Mall, PO Box 340, Leaf Rapids MB R0B 1W0
Tel: 204-473-2436; *Fax:* 204-473-2566
www.townofleafrapids.ca
Overview: A small local organization founded in 1974
Mission: To promote tourism, business in Leaf Rapids as well as helping to attract new members of the community as well.
Member of: Manitoba Chamber of Commerce
Chief Officer(s):
Lianna Anderson, Community Economic Development Officer, 204-473-2436 Ext. 5
cedo@townofleafrapids.ca
Finances: *Annual Operating Budget:* Less than $50,000; *Funding Sources:* Membership dues
6 volunteer(s)
Membership: 1-99; *Fees:* Schedule available; *Member Profile:* Businesses, Non-governmental offices, educators, artists; *Committees:* Tourism
Activities: Economic & social development; *Library* by appointment

League for Human Rights of B'nai Brith Canada / Ligue des droits de la personne de B'nai Brith Canada
15 Hove St., Toronto ON M3H 4Y8
Tel: 416-633-6224; *Fax:* 416-630-2159
Toll-Free: 800-892-2624; *Crisis Hot-Line:* 800-892-2624
league@bnaibrith.ca
www.bnaibrith.ca/league
Previous Name: Anti-Defamation League of B'nai Brith
Overview: A medium-sized national charitable organization founded in 1965
Mission: To strive for human rights for all Canadians; to improve inter-community relations; to combat racism & racial discrimination; to prevent bigotry & anti-Semitism.
Member of: B'nai Brith Canada
Affliation(s): Anti-Defamation League
Chief Officer(s):
Frank Dimant, CEO
Finances: *Funding Sources:* Private donations; B'nai Brith Foundation; grants
Membership: *Committees:* Legal/Legislative; Community Action; Intercultural Dialogue; Education; Holocaust & Hope; Human Rights Youth League; Young Leadership Network
Activities: Multicultural anti-racist workshops for students, teachers & administrators, police services, businesses, government, health services, community organizations; intercultural & interfaith dialogue programs; monitoring hate group activity & etc.; *Internships:* Yes; *Speaker Service:* Yes; *Library:* Education & Training Centre; by appointment
Awards:
• Student Human Rights Achievement Award (Award)
• Special Human Rights Award (Award)
• Friend of the League (Award)
• Media Human Rights Awards (Award)
Eligibility: Awards for "alerting, informing, sensitizing the public with regard to the nature & value of human rights"; one major award & one honourable mention is presented to organizations in each of press, television, advertising

Manitoba Office
#C403, 123 Doncaster St., Winnipeg MB R3N 2B2
Tel: 204-487-9623; *Fax:* 204-487-9648
wbb@bnaibrith.ca
Chief Officer(s):
Alan Yusim, Midwest Region Director

National Capital Region Office
Fuller Bldg., #212, 75 Albert St., Ottawa ON K1P 5E7
Tel: 613-598-0060; *Fax:* 613-598-0059
ParliamentHill@bnaibrith.ca
Chief Officer(s):
Michael Mostyn, Director, Government Relations

Ontario Region Office
15 Hove St., Toronto ON M3H 4Y8
Tel: 416-633-6224; *Fax:* 416-630-2159
bnb@bnaibrith.ca

Québec/Eastern Office
#202, 7155 Cote St. Luc Rd., Montréal QC H4V 1J2
Tel: 514-733-5377; *Fax:* 514-342-9632
chershon@bnaibrith.ca
www.bnaibrith.ca/quebec
Chief Officer(s):
Cindy Hershon, Quebec Region Director

Western Region - Calgary Office
1607-90 Ave. SW, Calgary AB T2V 4V7
Tel: 403-262-9255
calgary@bnaibrith.ca
Chief Officer(s):
Joyce Aster, Regional Director

Western Region - Edmonton Office
PO Box 67306, Stn. Hawkstone R.P.O., Edmonton AB T6M 0J5
Tel: 780-483-6939
bnaibrith.westcan@shaw.ca

The League of Canadian Poets (LCP)
#312, 192 Spadina Ave., Toronto ON M5T 2C2
Tel: 416-504-1657; *Fax:* 416-504-0096
admin@poets.ca
www.poets.ca
Overview: A medium-sized national organization founded in 1966
Mission: To develop the art of poetry; to enhance the status of poets & nurture a professional poetic community; to facilitate the teaching of Canadian poetry at all levels of education; to enlarge the audience for poetry by encouraging publication, performance & recognition of poetry nationally & internationally; to uphold freedom of expression
Member of: Canadian Conference of the Arts
Affliation(s): Book & Periodical Council
Chief Officer(s):
Joanna Poblocka, Executive Director
joanna@poets.ca
Finances: *Annual Operating Budget:* $250,000-$500,000; *Funding Sources:* Canada Council; Ontario Arts Council; Toronto Arts Council; Metro Cultural Affairs
Staff Member(s): 3; 50 volunteer(s)
Membership: 600; *Fees:* $175 full membership; $100 supporting; $60 associate; $20 student; *Member Profile:* Full - poets who have published at least one book of poetry or two chapbooks & have substantial publication credits in periodicals; associate - poets who have begun publishing in magazines but are not ready for full membership; students; supporting; *Committees:* Freedom of Expression; Education; International; Feminist; Communications
Activities: Poetry webstore; *Awareness Events:* Writes of Spring Readings; National Poetry Month, April; *Library:* Poetry Library; Open to public
Awards:
• Canadian Youth Poetry Competition (Award)
Entry fee $5 per poem
• Gerald Lampert Memorial Award (Award)
Established 1979; awarded annually for excellence in a first book of poetry, written by a Canadian citizen or landed immigrant, & published in the preceding year *Amount:* $1,000
• Pat Lowther Memorial Award (Award)
$1,000 awarded annually for excellence in a book of poetry, written by a Canadian female citizen or landed immigrant, & published in the preceding year

The League of Canadian Theatres *See* Professional Association of Canadian Theatres

League of Ukrainian Canadians
9 Plastics Ave., Toronto ON M8Z 4B6
Tel: 416-516-8223; *Fax:* 416-516-4033
luc@lucorg.com
www.lucorg.com
www.facebook.com/LeagueofUkrainianCanadians
Overview: A medium-sized national organization
Mission: To aid Ukrainian people living in Canada & in Ukraine; dedicated to the continued growth & development of a prosperous Ukrainian community in Canada.
Member of: Ukrainian Canadian Congress
Affliation(s): Ukrainian World Congress
Chief Officer(s):
Orest Steciw, President
Activities: Education projects; cultural events; research; publications; networking

Leamington District Chamber of Commerce
PO Box 321, 21 Talbot St., Leamington ON N8H 1L1
Tel: 519-326-2721; *Fax:* 519-326-3204
Toll-Free: 800-250-3336
sally@leamingtonchamber.com
www.leamingtonchamber.com
Overview: A small local organization founded in 1936
Chief Officer(s):
Sally McDonald, General Manager
Finances: *Annual Operating Budget:* $50,000-$100,000
Staff Member(s): 2; 15 volunteer(s)
Membership: 300

Learning Assistance Teachers' Association (LATA)
c/o BC Teachers' Federation, #100, 550 West 6th Ave., Vancouver BC V5Z 4P2
Fax: 250-377-0860
www.latabc.com
www.facebook.com/LATABC
twitter.com/latabc
Overview: A small provincial organization
Mission: To provide equal access to the educational system, a position that supports the opportunity for students to pursue their goals in all aspects of education; To work together with parents and the community, and give all students the best opportunities for success
Member of: BC Teachers' Federation
Chief Officer(s):
Janice Neden, President
jneden@sd73.bc.ca
Gail Bailey, Vice-President
gailbailey@shaw.ca
Membership: *Fees:* $35 BCTF member; $54.50 non-BCTF member; *Member Profile:* Classroom teachers; learning assistance specialists; administrators; parents

Learning Centre for Georgina (LCG)
23324 Woodbine Ave., Keswick ON L4P 3E9
Tel: 905-476-9900; *Fax:* 905-476-3085
info@lcgeorgina.org
www.lcgeorgina.org
www.facebook.com/learningcentregeorgina
Overview: A small local charitable organization founded in 1985
Mission: To help people (must be 16 years of age or older to access cost free services & not in full-time attendance in school) improve their basic reading, writing, spelling, & math skills
Member of: Georgina Board of Trade; United Way
Affliation(s): Metro Toronto Movement for Literacy; Ontario Literacy Coalition; Community Literacy Ontario
Chief Officer(s):
Yvonne Parker, President
Grant Peckford, Executive Director
grantp@lcgeorgina.org
Finances: *Funding Sources:* Provincial government; United Way; fundraising events; Trillium Foundation
Staff Member(s): 5

Learning Disabilities Association of Alberta (LDAA) / Troubles d'apprentissage - Association de l'Alberta
PO Box 29011, Stn. Lendrum, Edmonton AB T6H 5Z6
Tel: 780-448-0360; *Fax:* 780-438-0665
www.ldalberta.ca
www.facebook.com/group.php?gid=136125872711
twitter.com/@LDAssocAb
Overview: A medium-sized provincial charitable organization founded in 1968 overseen by Learning Disabilities Association of Canada
Mission: Supporting people with learning disabilities so that they develop to their full potential. Chapters in Calgary, Red Deer & Edmonton.
Chief Officer(s):
Kathryn Burke, Executive Director, 780-977-5549
execdir@ldaa.ca
Finances: *Annual Operating Budget:* $100,000-$250,000; *Funding Sources:* Government
Staff Member(s): 3; 8 volunteer(s)
Membership: 300 + 3 provincial chapters; *Fees:* $40
Activities: *Awareness Events:* Learning Disabilities Month, March
Awards:
- Siobhan Isabella Reid Memorial Scholarship (Scholarship)
- Mandin Memorial Education Fund (Award)

Calgary Chapter
#340, 1202 Centre St. SE, Calgary AB T2G 5A5
Tel: 403-283-6606; *Fax:* 403-270-4043
info@ldaa.net
www.ldaa.net

Edmonton Chapter
St. Gabriel's School, 5540 - 106 Ave., Edmonton AB T6A 1G3
Tel: 780-466-1011; *Fax:* 780-466-1095
ldae@compusmart.ab.ca

Red Deer Chapter
3757 - 43 Ave, Red Deer AB T4N 3B7
Tel: 403-340-3885; *Fax:* 403-340-3884
sue.ldard@shawbiz.ca

Learning Disabilities Association of Canada (LDAC) / L'association Canadienne des troubles d'apprentissage (ACTA)
#20, 2420 Bank St., Ottawa ON K1V 8S1
Tel: 613-238-5721
Toll-Free: 877-238-5332
info@ldac-acta.ca
www.ldac-acta.ca
www.facebook.com/ldacacta
twitter.com/ldacacta
www.youtube.com/ldacacta
Overview: A large national charitable organization founded in 1971
Mission: To advance the education, employment, social development, legal rights & general well-being of people with learning disabilities; to create a greater public awareness & understanding of learning disabilities; to promote & develop early recognition, diagnosis, treatment & appropriate educational, social, recreational & career-oriented programs for people with learning disabilities; to promote legislation, research & training of personnel in the field of learning disabilities
Chief Officer(s):
Claudette Larocque, Executive Director
claudette@ldac-acta.ca
Thealzel Lee, Chair
Finances: *Funding Sources:* Direct mail; publications; sales; government
Staff Member(s): 2
Membership: *Fees:* $20-$50; *Member Profile:* Parents; teachers; individuals with learning disabilities; buyers; physicians
Activities: LDAC represents people with learning disabilities at national meetings, & through briefs & position papers to the federal government & agencies; acts as a clearinghouse for information, communication & joint action; *Awareness Events:* Learning Disabilities Awareness Month, Oct.; *Library* by appointment
Publications:
- National

Type: Newsletter; *Frequency:* Quarterly

Learning Disabilities Association of Manitoba (LDAM) / Troubles d'apprentissage - Association de Manitoba
617 Erin St., Winnipeg MB R3G 2W1
Tel: 204-774-1821; *Fax:* 204-788-4090
ldamb@mts.net
www.ldamanitoba.org
Also Known As: LDA Manitoba
Overview: A medium-sized provincial charitable organization founded in 1966 overseen by Learning Disabilities Association of Canada
Mission: To provide support to all those who are concerned with learning disabilities; To represent individuals & families with learning disabilities
Affliation(s): Learning Disabilities Association of Canada
Chief Officer(s):
Marilyn MacKinnon, Executive Director
ldamanitoba4@mts.net
Finances: *Funding Sources:* The City of Winnipeg; United Way of Winnipeg; Manitoba Lotteries; Sponsorships; Fundraising
Membership: *Fees:* $25 individual; $15 student; *Member Profile:* Parents; Professionals; Persons with learning disabilities &/or attention deficit disorders; Individuals interested in learning disabilities
Activities: Providing educational workshops, courses, & seminars, such as parenting courses; Offering programs, such as Destination Employment & a literacy tutoring program; Providing information about learning disabilities & attention deficit disorders; Giving referrals to community, government, & private services; *Awareness Events:* Learning Disabilities Month, March; Annual Mercer Learning Disabilities Golf Classic; *Library:* LDAM Resource Library; by appointment

Learning Disabilities Association of New Brunswick (LDANB) / Troubles d'apprentissage - Association du Nouveau-Brunswick (TA-ANB)
#203, 403 Regent St., Fredericton NB E3B 3X6
Tel: 506-459-7852; *Fax:* 506-455-9300
Toll-Free: 877-544-7852
ldanb_taanb@nb.aibn.com
www.ldanb-taanb.ca
www.facebook.com/groups/112870582480
Also Known As: LDA New Brunswick
Overview: A medium-sized provincial charitable organization founded in 1980 overseen by Learning Disabilities Association of Canada
Mission: Promotes the understanding & acceptance of the ability of persons with learning disabilities to lead meaningful & successful lives. Satellite office in Saint John.
Finances: *Annual Operating Budget:* Less than $50,000; *Funding Sources:* Membership fees; Human Resources Development Canada
Membership: 48; *Fees:* $25
Activities: *Awareness Events:* Learning Disabilities Month, March; *Speaker Service:* Yes; *Library:* LDANB Resource Library & ADHD Resource Centre; Open to public by appointment
Awards:
- Tia Klarissa Rickard Memorial Award (Award)

Publications:
- Reflexions [a publication of the Learning Disabilities Association of New Brunswick]

Type: Newsletter

Moncton Chapter
Chief Officer(s):
Millie LeBlanc, Board Contact
wbook@nbnet.nb.ca

Saint John Chapter (LDASJ)
c/o St. John The Baptist/King Edward School, 223 St. James St., Saint John NB E2L 1W3
Tel: 506-642-4956
ldasj@nb.aibn.com
www.ldasj.ca
Chief Officer(s):
Fabienne McKay, Office Coordinator

Learning Disabilities Association of Newfoundland & Labrador Inc. (LDANL)
The Board of Trade Bldg., #301, 66 Kenmount Rd., St. John's NL A1B 3V7
Tel: 709-753-1445; *Fax:* 709-753-4747
info@ldanl.ca
www.ldanl.ca
www.facebook.com/103104129749204
twitter.com/ldanl
Also Known As: LDA Newfoundland & Labrador
Overview: A medium-sized provincial charitable organization founded in 2001 overseen by Learning Disabilities Association of Canada
Mission: To work towards to the advancement of legal rights, social development, education, employment, & the general well-being of people with learning disabilities
Member of: Learning Disabilities Association of Canada (LDAC)
Chief Officer(s):
David Banfield, Executive Director
david@ldanl.ca
Finances: *Funding Sources:* Donations; Fundraising; Sponsorships
Membership: *Fees:* $30 individual & family; $100 schools & associated organizations; *Member Profile:* Individuals & organizations wishing support services & resources
Activities: Increasing public awareness & understanding of learning disabilities; Liaising with all levels of government & the community; Providing information & support services; Offering assistive technology demonstrations; Advocating on behalf of people with learning disabilities & parents; Organizing conferences; *Library:* Resource Library

Learning Disabilities Association of Ontario (LDAO) / Troubles d'apprentissage - Association de l'Ontario
#202, 365 Evans Ave., Toronto ON M8Z 1K2
Tel: 416-929-4311; *Fax:* 416-929-3905
resource@ldao.ca
www.ldao.ca
www.facebook.com/LDAOntario
twitter.com/ldaofontario
Overview: A medium-sized provincial charitable organization founded in 1964 overseen by Learning Disabilities Association of Canada

Mission: To provide leadership in learning disabilities advocacy, research, education & services; to advance the full participation of children, youth & adults with learning disabilites in today's society
Chief Officer(s):
Lawrence Barns, President & CEO
lawrence@ldao.ca
Karen Quinn, Director, Operations
karenq@ldao.ca
Finances: *Annual Operating Budget:* $1.5 Million-$3 Million; *Funding Sources:* Public & private donations
Staff Member(s): 6; 30 volunteer(s)
Membership: 1,000 in 18 chapters; *Fees:* $50 individual/family; $20 student; $75 professional; $125 institutional; *Member Profile:* Open to all who are interested in the needs & interests of people with learning disabilities; *Committees:* Legislation & Policy; Fundraising/Finance
Activities: 18 local chapters provide information & services to individuals & families; *Awareness Events:* Learning Disabilities Month, Oct.; *Library:* LDAO Resource Library; by appointment
Awards:
• Gloria Landis Memorial Bursary (Grant)
For adult student with a learning disability returning to school for further education
• Roy Cooper Scholarship (Scholarship)

Learning Disabilities Association of Prince Edward Island (LADPEI)

#149, 40 Enman Cres., Charlottetown PE C1E 1E6
Tel: 902-894-5032
info@ldapei.ca
www.ldapei.ca
www.facebook.com/ldapei
twitter.com/LDAPEI
Overview: A medium-sized provincial charitable organization founded in 1975 overseen by Learning Disabilities Association of Canada
Mission: To advance the interests of people with learning disabilities; To act as a voice for learning disabled people of Prince Edward Island
Member of: Prince Edward Island Literacy Alliance Inc.
Affliation(s): Learning Disabilities Association of Canada (LDAC)
Chief Officer(s):
Nils Ling, Executive Director
nils@ldapei.ca
Finances: *Funding Sources:* Donations
Membership: *Fees:* $25 individuals & families; $50 schools & associated organizations; *Member Profile:* Individuals & organizations who wish support services & resources
Activities: Advocating for improved education, health & employment opportunities; Offering programs, such a job-readiness program for adults with learning disabilities & strategies for caregivers; Organizing educational workshops; Offering monthly support groups; Increasing public awareness; Presenting awards; *Awareness Events:* Annual Blind Date with a Star fundraising event; *Library:* LDAPEI Resource Library;

Learning Disabilities Association of Québec *Voir* Association québécoise des troubles d'apprentissage

Learning Disabilities Association of Saskatchewan (LDAS) / Troubles d'apprentissage - Association de la Saskatchewan

221 Hanselman Ct., Saskatoon SK S7L 6A8
Tel: 306-652-4114; *Fax:* 306-652-3220
reception@ldas.org
www.ldas.org
Overview: A medium-sized provincial charitable organization founded in 1973 overseen by Learning Disabilities Association of Canada
Mission: To advance the education, employment, social development, legal rights & general well-being of people with learning disabilities. Branches in Regina & Prince Albert.
Member of: The United Way of Saskatoon
Chief Officer(s):
Dale Rempel, Provincial Executive Director, 306-652-4116
dale.rempel@ldas.org
Finances: *Annual Operating Budget:* $500,000-$1.5 Million
Staff Member(s): 20; 30 volunteer(s)
Membership: 300; *Fees:* $35
Activities: *Awareness Events:* Learning Disabilities Month, October; *Speaker Service:* Yes; *Library:* Kinsmen Resource Centre; Open to public
Awards:
• Memorial Scholarship (Scholarship)
Amount: $250
• High Voltage Scholarship (Scholarship)
Amount: $200

Prince Albert Branch
1106 Central Ave., Prince Albert SK S6V 4V6
Tel: 306-922-1071; *Fax:* 306-922-1073
pabranch1@sasktel.net
Chief Officer(s):
Prema Arsiradam, Director

Regina Branch
438 Victoria Ave. East, Regina SK S4N 0N7
Tel: 306-352-5327; *Fax:* 306-352-2260
ldas.reginabranch@sasktel.net
ldas.saskatelwebsite.net
Chief Officer(s):
Shelley Kemp, Branch Director

Learning Disabilities Association of The Northwest Territories (LDA-NWT)

PO Box 242, Yellowknife NT X1A 2N2
Tel: 867-873-6378; *Fax:* 867-873-6378
lda-nwt@arcticdata.ca
www.nald.ca/contacts?f=76
Previous Name: The Northwest Territories Association for Children (& Adults) with Learning Disabilities
Overview: A medium-sized provincial organization founded in 1981 overseen by Learning Disabilities Association of Canada
Mission: To help people with learning disabilities achieve their potential in school, the workplace, & in society
Chief Officer(s):
Nancy Galway, Contact
Membership: *Fees:* $20 individual & agencies
Activities: Offering information & workshop; Advocating for children & adults with learning disabilities; *Library:* Resource Centre;

Learning Disabilities Association of Yukon Territory (LDAY)

107 Main St., Whitehorse YT Y1A 2A7
Tel: 867-668-5167; *Fax:* 867-668-6504
ldayoffice@northwestel.net
www.ldayukon.com
Also Known As: LDA Yukon
Previous Name: Yukon Association for Children & Adults with Learning Disabilities
Overview: A medium-sized provincial charitable organization founded in 1973 overseen by Learning Disabilities Association of Canada
Mission: To provide services & programs for Yukoners with learning disabilities so that they reach their potential & become productive members of society
Chief Officer(s):
Stephanie Hammond, Executive Director
ldayexecutivedirector@northwestel.net
Esther Chasse, President
Finances: *Funding Sources:* City of Whitehorse, Yukon, & Federal Government; Corporate sponsorships; Service clubs & organizations; Individual donations
Membership: *Member Profile:* Parents; Adults; Professionals; Persons with Learning Disabilities
Activities: Presenting tutorials & demonstations for assistive technologies; Offering a computer lab to assist the public; Mentoring & tutoring; Offering learning disability assessments; Organizing summer & winter camps; Providing workshops; *Library:* The LDAY Library
Awards:
• Roland Sanders Boone Scholarship (Scholarship)
For students attending the Learning for Success Course at Yukon College
• Tutoring Bursary (Grant)
For children, youth, or adults in need of tutoring

Learning Enrichment Foundation (LEF)

116 Industry St., Toronto ON M6M 4L8
Tel: 416-769-0830; *Fax:* 416-769-9912
info@lefca.org
www.lefca.org
Overview: A medium-sized local charitable organization founded in 1978
Mission: To provide programs & services to help individuals become contributors to their community's social & economic development
Chief Officer(s):
Ed Lamoureux, President
James McLeod, Vice-President
Kathleen Macdonald, Secretary
Activities: Offering workshops, training programs; Providing employment services; Presenting language instruction for newcomers to Canada & literacy & numeracy classes; Operating LEF's licensed Child Care Centres, child care consulting, & after care programs

Learning for a Sustainable Future (LSF)

York University, 343 York Lanes, Toronto ON M3J 1P3
Toll-Free: 877-250-8202
info@lsf-lst.ca
www.lsf-lst.ca
www.facebook.com/lsf.lst.ca
twitter.com/LSF_LST
Overview: A medium-sized national charitable organization founded in 1991
Mission: LSF is a non-profit Canadian organization that was created to integrate sustainability education into Canada's education system.
Chief Officer(s):
Lisa Roy, Chair
liseroy@health.nb.ca

Leave Out Violence (LOVE)

#202, 3130 Bathurst St., Toronto ON M6A 2A1
Tel: 416-785-8411
toronto@leaveoutviolence.org
www.leaveoutviolence.com
www.facebook.com/leaveoutviolence
twitter.com/love_ontario
Overview: A small local organization founded in 1993
Mission: Leave Out Violence (LOVE) is a not-for-profit, grass roots youth organization that is an effective means of social change, providing hope, motivation and opportunity to thousands of young people.
Membership: *Committees:* In-School Violence Prevention
Activities: Media Arts Program; Leadership Training; School and Community Violence Prevention Outreach Program

British Columbia
#103, 2780 East Broadway, Vancouver BC V5M 1Y8
Tel: 604-709-5728
vancouver@leaveoutviolence.org

Nova Scotia
#106, 1657 Barrington St., Halifax NS B3J 2A1
Tel: 902-429-6616; *Fax:* 902-429-0097
love@eastlink.ca

Québec
#300, 400, rue Saint Jacques, Montréal QC H2Y 1S1
Tel: 514-938-0006; *Fax:* 514-938-2377
info@vivresansviolence.org

La Leche League Canada (LLLC) / Ligue La Leche Canada

PO Box 700, Winchester ON K0C 2K0
Tel: 613-774-4900; *Fax:* 613-774-2798
ofm@LLLC.ca
www.lllc.ca
Overview: A medium-sized national charitable organization founded in 1961
Mission: To act as a support network for breastfeeding mothers; To promote the importance of breastfeeding in Canada; To disseminate information on how to help mothers succeed in breastfeeding
Affliation(s): La Leche League International
Chief Officer(s):
Fiona Audy, Chair
Lisa Loeppky, Secretary
Wendy Dale, Treasurer
Finances: *Funding Sources:* Membership fees; Donations
Membership: *Committees:* Nominations & Board Development; By-Laws & Policies; Finance; Human Resources; Programs & Innovations; Financial Resource Development
Activities: Providing educational seminars for the public & health professionals; *Awareness Events:* Annual Walk for Breastfeeding

Leduc & District Chamber of Commerce *See* Leduc Regional Chamber of Commerce

Leduc & District Food Bank Association

PO Box 5008, Leduc AB T9E 6L5
Tel: 780-986-5333; *Fax:* 780-986-4803
leducfb@shaw.ca
www.leducfoodbank.ca
www.facebook.com/LeducFoodBank
twitter.com/leducfoodbank

Overview: A small local charitable organization overseen by Alberta Food Bank Network Association
Mission: To provide for Leduc & the surrounding areas of Beaumont, Calmar, Devon, New Sarepta, Thorsby, Warburg & Leduc County
Affliation(s): Canadian Association of Food Banks; Alberta Food Bank Network Association
Chief Officer(s):
Gert Reynar, Executive Director
gert@ldfb.ca
Staff Member(s): 4
Activities: Fall Food Round Up;

Leduc Regional Chamber of Commerce
6420 - 50 St., Leduc AB T9E 7K9
Tel: 780-986-5454; *Fax:* 780-986-8108
info@leduc-chamber.com
www.leduc-chamber.com
www.linkedin.com/groups/Leduc-Regional-Chamber-Commerce-4904841
www.facebook.com/252602708089872
twitter.com/LeducChamber
www.youtube.com/user/LeducChamber
Previous Name: Leduc & District Chamber of Commerce
Overview: A small local organization founded in 1906
Mission: To be the premier business organization in the region; To be a business advocate for members, to strengthen the economic climate & to promite the free enterprise system
Member of: Alberta Chambers of Commerce; Edmonton Tourism; Greater Edmonton Regional Chambers of Commerce; Canadian Chamber of Commerce
Chief Officer(s):
Shaun Green, Executive Director
sgreen@leduc-chamber.com
Jessica Roth, Coordinator, Communications & Marketing
jroth@leduc-chamber.com
Finances: *Funding Sources:* Membership dues; Special events; Mixers
Staff Member(s): 6
Membership: 713; *Fees:* Schedule available
Activities: Trade shows; Seminars; Promotional & tourism services; Parade; Directory; Policy & advocacy

Legal & District Chamber of Commerce
PO Box 338, General Delivery, Legal AB T0G 1L0
Tel: 780-456-3424
www.legalchamberofcommerce.ca
Overview: A small local organization
Mission: To promote local business & community
Affliation(s): Greater Edmonton Regional Chambers of Commerce
Chief Officer(s):
Ken Evans, President
Carol Tremblay, Secretary
Staff Member(s): 1
Membership: 100; *Fees:* $30-$60; *Committees:* Membership; "Legal-Lerie"; Tourism; Trade & Craft Fair; Nominations

Legal Aid New Brunswick
PO Box 20026, Saint John NB E2L 5B2
Tel: 506-633-6030; *Fax:* 506-633-8994
www.sjfn.nb.ca/community_hall/L/lega6030.html
Overview: A small provincial organization
Mission: Provides Duty Counsel lawyers at Provincial Court in Sussex, Hampton, Saint John & St. Stephen in adult & youth courts; provides lawyers for trials to successful applicants for serious crimincal charges & for parents when the Dept. of Health & Community Services is applying for permanent custody of the child/children
Chief Officer(s):
Charlotte Fowler, Area Administrator

Legal Aid Ontario (LAO) / Aide juridique Ontario
#200, 40 Dundas St. West, Toronto ON M5G 2H1
Tel: 416-979-1446; *Fax:* 416-979-8669
Toll-Free: 800-668-8258
info@lao.on.ca
www.legalaid.on.ca
twitter.com/legalaidontario
www.youtube.com/user/LegalAidOntario
Overview: A small provincial organization founded in 1998
Mission: To promote access to justice throughout Ontario for low income individuals by means of providing consistently high quality legal aid services in a cost-effective & efficient manner
Chief Officer(s):
John McCamus, Chair
Bob Ward, President/CEO

Legal Aid Society of Alberta (LAA)
Revillion Building, #400, 10320 - 102 Ave., Edmonton AB T5J 4A1
Tel: 780-644-4971; *Fax:* 780-415-2618
Toll-Free: 888-845-3342
Other Communication: Tollfree fax: 1-866-382-7253
lsc@legalaid.ab.ca
www.legalaid.ab.ca
Also Known As: Legal Aid Alberta
Overview: A small provincial organization founded in 1970
Mission: To provide a continuum of innovative & cost-effective legal services for people in need throughout Alberta
Chief Officer(s):
Suzanne Polkosnik, President/CEO
Finances: *Annual Operating Budget:* $50,000-$100,000; *Funding Sources:* Government of Alberta; Federal Government; Alberta Law Foundation; Client contributions; Interest
Activities: Five offices in Alberta; *Speaker Service:* Yes

Legal Archives Society of Alberta (LASA)
#510, 919 - 11 Ave. SW, Calgary AB T2R 1P3
Tel: 403-244-5510; *Fax:* 403-541-9102
lasa@legalarchives.ca
legalarchives.ca
Overview: A small provincial charitable organization founded in 1990
Mission: To preserve complete and acuurate documentation and provide resources for research on the evaluation of law and society in Alberta
Affliation(s): Archives Society of Alberta; Association of Canadian Archivists
Chief Officer(s):
Stacy Kaufeld, Executive Director
Ken Mills, Acting President
Finances: *Annual Operating Budget:* $250,000-$500,000; *Funding Sources:* Donations; a Grant from the Law Society of Alberta
Staff Member(s): 3; 2 volunteer(s)
Membership: 450 individual; *Fees:* $10 student; $25 individual; *Member Profile:* Members of Alberta's legal profession; *Committees:* Oral History; Advisory; Editorial
Activities: Direct mail campaigns; Historical dinners; Auctions; Book launches; dDisplay openings; *Library:* Legal History Library; Open to public by appointment

Legal Education Society of Alberta (LESA)
#2610, 10104 - 103 Ave., Edmonton AB T5J 0H8
Tel: 780-420-1987; *Fax:* 780-425-0885
Toll-Free: 800-282-3900
lesa@lesa.org
www.lesaonline.org
www.linkedin.com/company/legal-education-society-of-alberta
www.facebook.com/lesaonline
twitter.com/lesaonline
Overview: A medium-sized provincial organization founded in 1975
Mission: To educate providers of legal services in Alberta; To increase awareness of issues affecting the legal profession; To maintain & increase professional responsibility & competence; To develop & provide education in law, skills, & ethics
Chief Officer(s):
Tamara Buckwold, Chair
Aaron D. Martens, Secretary-Treasurer
Jennifer Flynn, Executive Director & Director, Canadian Centre for Professional Legal Education (CPLED) Alberta, 780-420-1988
Activities: Providing continuing legal education seminars for lawyers & support staff; Publishing seminar materials, practice manuals, & Canadian Centre for Professional Legal Education (CPLED) materials;

Legal Information Society of Nova Scotia (LISNS)
5523B Young St., Halifax NS B3K 1Z7
Tel: 902-454-2198; *Fax:* 902-455-3105
Toll-Free: 800-665-9779
lisns@legalinfo.org
www.legalinfo.org
Previous Name: Public Legal Education Society of Nova Scotia
Overview: A medium-sized provincial charitable organization founded in 1982
Mission: To provide Nova Scotians easy access to information & resources about the law
Chief Officer(s):
Kevin A. MacDonald, President
Finances: *Funding Sources:* Law Foundation of Nova Scotia; Department of Justice Canada; Nova Scotia Department of Justice; Donations
Activities: Providing legal information through online resources, publications on various topics, dial-a-law, a legal information line, the lawyer referral service, workshops, & training sessions; Fundraising; *Awareness Events:* Annual Law Day Lunch, April; *Speaker Service:* Yes

A Legal Resource Centre for Persons with Disabilities *See* ARCH Disability Law Centre

Legal Services Society (LSS)
#400, 510 Burrard St., Vancouver BC V6C 3A8
Tel: 604-601-6000; *Fax:* 604-682-7967
www.lss.bc.ca
www.facebook.com/legalaidbc
twitter.com/legalaidbc
Also Known As: Legal Aid
Overview: A large provincial organization founded in 1979
Mission: To assist low income individuals to resolve their legal problems by providing a spectrum of services that promote their effective participation in the justice system
Chief Officer(s):
E. David Crossin, Chair
Mark Benton, Executive Director
Finances: *Annual Operating Budget:* Greater than $5 Million; *Funding Sources:* Provincial government; Law Foundation of BC; Notary Foundation
Publications:
- The Elan
Type: Newsletter
Profile: Brings current legal aid-related news to community workers, other intermediaries, librarians, and the general public.

Kamloops Regional Centre
#208, 300 Columbia St., Kamloops BC V2C 3N3
Tel: 250-314-1900; *Fax:* 250-314-1605

Kelowna Regional Centre
#210, 347 Leon Ave., Kelowna BC V1Y 8N3
Tel: 250-763-8613; *Fax:* 250-763-3594

Prince George Regional Centre
1057 Third Ave., Prince George BC V2L 3E3
Tel: 250-564-9717; *Fax:* 250-564-8636

Surrey Legal Regional Centre
#102, 10706 King George Blvd., Surrey BC V3T 5X3
Tel: 604-585-6595; *Fax:* 604-585-7898

Terrace Regional Centre
#207, 3228 Kalum St., Terrace BC V8G 2N1
Tel: 250-635-2133; *Fax:* 250-635-9085
Toll-Free: 800-787-2511

Vancouver Regional Centre
#400, 510 Burrard St., Vancouver BC V6C 3A8
Tel: 604-601-6206; *Fax:* 604-681-2719

Victoria Regional Centre
#218, 852 Fort St., Victoria BC V8W 1H8
Tel: 250-388-4516; *Fax:* 250-388-4664

Legion of Mary - Senatus of Montréal *Voir* Légion de Marie - Senatus de Montréal

La Légion royale canadienne *See* The Royal Canadian Legion

Legislative Recording & Broadcast Association
c/o Broadcasting & Recording Service, Queen's Park, Toronto ON M7A 1A2
Tel: 416-325-7900; *Fax:* 416-325-7916
Overview: A small provincial organization
Member of: Legislative Assemblies
Finances: *Annual Operating Budget:* Less than $50,000
2 volunteer(s)
Membership: 16; *Member Profile:* Employees of Canadian legislative assemblies

Lennox & Addington Association for Community Living
99 Richmond Blvd., Napanee ON K7R 3S3
Tel: 613-354-2185; *Fax:* 613-354-0815
Previous Name: Lennox & Addington Association for the Mentally Retarded
Overview: A small local organization
Mission: To offer day support & services to people with disabilities as well as family support
Member of: Community Living Ontario
Chief Officer(s):
Barb Fabius, Executive Director

Lennox & Addington Association for the Mentally Retarded *See* Lennox & Addington Association for Community Living

Lennox & Addington County Law Association
97 Thomas St. East, Napanee ON K7R 4B9
Tel: 613-654-5469
Toll-Free: 866-603-6383
lalaw@kingston.net
Overview: A small local organization founded in 1953
Membership: 30 individual
Activities: *Library*

Lennox & Addington Historical Society
PO Box 392, Napanee ON K7R 3P5
Tel: 613-354-3027; *Fax:* 613-354-1005
Membership@LennoxandAddingtonHistoricalSociety.ca
www.lennoxandaddingtonhistoricalsociety.ca
Also Known As: Macpherson House & Park
Overview: A small local organization founded in 1907
Mission: To promote the study, practice, knowledge & preservation of the history of the county of Lennox & Addington
Member of: Ontario Historical Society; Ontario Museums Association
Chief Officer(s):
Jane Foster, Manager, Museum
jfoster@lennox-addington.on.ca
Membership: *Fees:* $25 single; $30 corporate; $35 family; $525 lifetime
Activities: Operates Lennox & Addington County Museum & Archives & MacPherson House; *Library:* Archives; Open to public

Lennoxville-Ascot Historical & Museum Society (LAHMS) / Société d'histoire et de musée de Lennoxville-Ascot
9, rue Speid, Sherbrooke QC J1M 1R9
Tél: 819-564-0409; *Téléc:* 819-564-8951
lahms@uplands.ca
www.uplands.ca
www.facebook.com/pages/Uplands/138071916264187
twitter.com/Uplands1
Aperçu: *Dimension:* petite; *Envergure:* locale; fondée en 1970
Mission: To collect, preserve, & exhibit material from the Lennoxville-Ascot region of Québec; To provide genealogical & historical information
Membre(s) du bureau directeur:
Nancy Barnett, Contact
Finances: *Fonds:* Donations; Fundraising
Activités: Displaying local antiques at the Uplands Cultural & Heritage Centre; Promoting local history; *Service de conférenciers:* Oui; *Bibliothèque:* Lennoxville-Ascot Historical & Museum Society Reference Library

The Leon & Thea Koerner Foundation
PO Box 39209, Stn. Point Grey, 3695 West 10th Ave., Vancouver BC V6R 4P1
Tel: 604-224-2611
www.koernerfoundation.ca
Overview: A small provincial charitable organization founded in 1955
Mission: To assist & support development projects by registered charitable organizations in cultural & creative arts & social services areas in BC

Leprosy Relief (Canada) Inc. *Voir* Secours aux lépreux (Canada) inc.

Lesbian & Gay Community Appeal Foundation *See* Community One Foundation

Lesbian & Gay Immigration Task Force
1170 Bute St., Vancouver BC V6E 1Z6
e-mail: vancouver@legit.ca
www.legit.ca
Overview: A small local organization
Mission: Provides immigration information and support to queer, lesbian, gay, bisexual, and transgendered people while working to end discrimination in Canada's immigration regulations.

LEGIT - Toronto
PO Box 111, Stn. F, Toronto ON M4Y 2L4
Tel: 416-392-6874
toronto@legit.ca
www.legit.ca
Mission: Provides immigration information and support to queer, lesbian, gay, bisexual, and transgendered people while working to end discrimination in Canada's immigration regulations.

Lésions Médullaires Canada *See* Spinal Cord Injury Canada

Lesser Slave Lake Indian Regional Council (LSLIRC)
PO Box 269, Slave Lake AB T0G 2A0
Tel: 780-849-4943; *Fax:* 780-849-4975
www.lslirc.com
Overview: A small local organization founded in 1971
Mission: To help improve the ecnominic, social & educational well being of its member First Nations
Finances: *Funding Sources:* Federal & provincial government
Membership: 5; *Member Profile:* First Nations band governments

Let's Talk Science
1584 North Routledge Park, London ON N6H 5L6
Tel: 519-474-4081; *Fax:* 519-474-4085
Toll-Free: 877-474-4081
www.letstalkscience.ca
www.facebook.com/LetsTalkScience
twitter.com/LetsTalkScience
Overview: A medium-sized national organization
Mission: Strives to improve Science literacy through leadership, innovative educational programs, research and advocacy. It motivates and empowers youth to use science, technology and engineering to develop critical skills, knowledge and attitudes needed to thrive in our world.
Chief Officer(s):
Bonnie Schmidt, President
Finances: *Funding Sources:* Public & private sponsorship

Lethbridge & District Association of Realtors
522 - 6 St. South, Lethbridge AB T1J 2E2
Tel: 403-328-8838; *Fax:* 403-328-8906
eo@ldar.ca
www.ldar.ca
twitter.com/LDAR2013
Previous Name: Lethbridge Real Estate Board
Overview: A small local organization overseen by Alberta Real Estate Association
Mission: To provide real estate information on the Lethbridge area; to serve as a forum to network & build connections within the real estate community.
Member of: Alberta Real Estate Association; Canadian Real Estate Association
Membership: 291; *Member Profile:* Brokers; associate brokers
Activities: Training & educational courses & seminars; advocacy at all levels of government, regulatory bodies, CREA & AREA

Lethbridge & District Humane Society
PO Box 783, 2920 - 16th Ave. North, Lethbridge AB T1J 3Z6
Tel: 403-320-8991
pets4you2@hotmail.com
www.humanehaven.ab.ca
Overview: A small local charitable organization founded in 1970
Mission: To spay/neuter all adult animals prior to adoption; To shelter, protect & provide for stray, abandoned, orphaned & unwanted cats & dogs & to place them in the best possible homes; To provide information, advice & counsel to help people understand the fundamentals of responsible pet ownership
Member of: Canadian Federation of Humane Societies; Alberta Society for the Prevention of Cruelty to Animals
Chief Officer(s):
Sherry VanderGriendt, Contact
Finances: *Annual Operating Budget:* Less than $50,000; *Funding Sources:* Adoption fees; donations; fundraising; sale of promotional items
Staff Member(s): 1; 80 volunteer(s)
Membership: 275; *Fees:* $15 single; $20 family; $10 senior/child; *Committees:* Shelter; Adoption; Office & Cleaning; Fundraising; Public Relations; Building Maintenance & Office Supply; Dogwalking; Youth Group; Statistician; Building
Activities: *Awareness Events:* Annual Dog Jog

Lethbridge & District Japanese Garden Society
PO Box 751, Lethbridge AB T1J 3Z6
Tel: 403-328-3511; *Fax:* 403-328-0511
info@nikkayuko.com
www.nikkayuko.com
www.facebook.com/123765594310823
twitter.com/NikkaYuko
Also Known As: Nikka Yuko Japanese Garden
Overview: A small local organization founded in 1965
Mission: To acquaint visitors with cultural & historical background; to create support for garden philosophy of authenticity & meditative/contemplative setting; to create a unique attraction drawing large numbers to foster economic betterment of the community; to contribute to education fields such as arts, botany & general gardening
Member of: Lethbridge Chamber of Commerce
Affliation(s): Chinook Tourist Association; Community Volunteer Centre
Chief Officer(s):
John Harding, President
Membership: *Fees:* $30 single; $40 family

Lethbridge & District Pro-Life Association
#1805 - 9 Ave. North, Lethbridge AB T1H 1H8
Tel: 403-320-5433; *Fax:* 403-380-2827
lprolife@shaw.ca
www.lifelethbridge.org
www.facebook.com/127238990668890
Overview: A small local charitable organization founded in 1977 overseen by Alliance for Life
Mission: To increase public awareness concerning life issues; to recognize the right to life; to maintain the principle of the intrinsic value of human life
Finances: *Funding Sources:* Membership dues; churches; Knights of Columbus; individual donors; Hike for Life
Membership: *Fees:* $10 students; $20 regular
Activities: Speaker's Forum; *Speaker Service:* Yes; *Library* Open to public
Awards:
• Elsie Alexander Pro-Life Scholarship (Scholarship)
Amount: $1,000

Lethbridge AIDS Connection Society *See* Lethbridge HIV Connection

Lethbridge Association for Community Living (LACL)
527 - 6 St. South, Lethbridge AB T1J 2E1
Tel: 403-327-2911; *Fax:* 403-320-7054
mail@lacl.ca
www.lacl.ca
Overview: A small local charitable organization founded in 1957
Mission: To advocate for & to provide support to individuals with developmental disabilities & their families/guardians; to assist in gaining full inclusion in the community
Chief Officer(s):
Dave Lawson, Executive Director
dave.lawson@lacl.ca
Finances: *Annual Operating Budget:* $100,000-$250,000
Staff Member(s): 3; 40 volunteer(s)
Membership: 75; *Fees:* $10 individual; $20 family; *Member Profile:* Individuals; families/guardians
Activities: *Speaker Service:* Yes

Lethbridge Chamber of Commerce
#200, 529 - 6 St. South, Lethbridge AB T1J 2E1
Tel: 403-327-1586; *Fax:* 403-327-1001
office@lethbridgechamber.com
www.lethbridgechamber.com
www.facebook.com/LethbridgeChamber
twitter.com/lethchamber
www.youtube.com/lethchamber
Overview: A medium-sized local organization founded in 1889
Mission: To serve and represent the interests of its members by promoting and enhancing free enterprise, for the benefit of the social and economic environment of the City of Lethbridge
Member of: Alberta Chamber of Commerce; Canadian Chamber of Commerce
Chief Officer(s):
Bruce Galts, President
Stephanie Palecheck, General Manager
stephanie@lethbridgechamber.com
Kevin Farrell, Coordinator, Communications & Events
kevin@lethbridgechamber.com
Finances: *Annual Operating Budget:* $50,000-$100,000; *Funding Sources:* Membership
Staff Member(s): 3; 150 volunteer(s)
Membership: 750 businesses; *Fees:* Based on number of employees; *Member Profile:* Representatives from all business sectors; *Committees:* Business Affairs; Special Events; Business & Education; Finance; Government Relations; Member Services; Tourism Connection
Activities: Workshops; seminars; speakers; business education; partnerships; career fair; trade shows; *Speaker Service:* Yes

Lethbridge Community College Faculty Association (LCCFA)
3000 College Dr. South, Lethbridge AB T1K 1L6
Tel: 403-320-3217
Overview: A small local organization

Canadian Associations

Member of: Alberta Colleges Institute Faculty Association
Chief Officer(s):
Rika Snip, Acting President
Rika.Snip@LethbridgeCollege.ca
Staff Member(s): 1

Lethbridge Construction Association (LCA)

2918 - 7 Ave. North, Lethbridge AB T1H 5C6
Tel: 403-328-2474; *Fax:* 403-329-0971
lca3@telus.net
www.lethconst.ca
Overview: A small local licensing organization founded in 1954
Mission: The Lethbridge Construction Association is a respected and influential voice for the commercial, industrial and institutional construction industry. They gather information, communicate, and advocate for our membership on common issues and the public well-being. They promote safety, quality work, training, construction standards, apprenticeship and business ethics.
Member of: Alberta Construction Association
Chief Officer(s):
Lorrie Vos, Executive Director
Neil Nunweiler, President
Simpson Roger, 1st Vice-President
Nathan Neudorf, 2nd Vice-President
Finances: *Funding Sources:* Membership fees
Staff Member(s): 1
Membership: 125; *Fees:* $950 general; $850 trade; $775 manufacturer/supplier; $250 associte; *Member Profile:* Generals; Sub-Trades; Suppliers; *Committees:* ACA/Communications; ACSA; Government; EDL; Safety/WCB; Standard Practices; Coolnet
Activities: Golf; Casino Night; Meet N' Greet; *Awareness Events:* Scholarship Awards, May; *Library:* ACSA Video Library
Publications:
• Lethbridge Construction Association Magazine
Type: Magazine; *Frequency:* Annual
Profile: Construction stories, advertisements, editorials

Lethbridge Fish & Game Association (LFGA)

PO Box 495, Lethbridge AB T1J 3Z1
Tel: 403-308-3541
lfga.info@gmail.com
www.lfga.org
Overview: A small local organization founded in 1923
Mission: To promote, through education, lobbying and programs, the conservation & utilization of fish & wildlife & to protect & enhance the habitat upon which they depend
Member of: Alberta Fish & Game Association
Chief Officer(s):
Brian Dingreville, President
brianad@shaw.ca
Finances: *Annual Operating Budget:* Less than $50,000
900 volunteer(s)
Membership: 1,300; *Fees:* $15 youth; $35 regular; $60 family; *Committees:* Big Game; Bird Game; Casino; Outdoor Education; Political Action; Publicity

Lethbridge Handicraft Guild

Bowman Art Centre, 811 - 5 Ave. South, Lethbridge AB T1J 0V2
Tel: 403-328-7488
Overview: A small local organization
Affliation(s): Handweavers, Spinners & Dyers of Alberta
Finances: *Annual Operating Budget:* $250,000-$500,000
Staff Member(s): 40

Lethbridge HIV Connection (LHC)

1206 - 6th Ave. South, Lethbridge AB T1J 1A4
Tel: 403-328-8186; *Fax:* 403-328-8564
lethhiv@telusplanet.net
www.lethbridgehiv.com
Previous Name: Lethbridge AIDS Connection Society
Overview: A medium-sized local charitable organization founded in 1986 overseen by Canadian AIDS Society
Mission: To support, educate, advocate & facilitate compassionate & effective community responses to HIV
Member of: Alberta Community Council on HIV; United Way of Southwestern Alberta
Chief Officer(s):
Charleen Davidson, Executive Director
Finances: *Funding Sources:* Alberta Community HIV Fund; Alberta Community Council on HIV; Health Canada; Alberta Health & Wellness; Public Health Agency of Canada; Donations
Activities: Information line; educational presentations; support groups; counselling; advocacy; volunteer program; *Awareness Events:* World AIDS Day Candlelight Vigil, Dec; *Speaker Service:* Yes; *Library* Open to public

Lethbridge Lacrosse Association

PO Box 874, Lethbridge AB T1J 3Z8
Tel: 403-715-3291
www.lethbridgelacrosse.com
www.facebook.com/lethbridge.lacrosse
twitter.com/lethlax
Overview: A small local organization
Mission: To promote lacrosse in southern Alberta
Chief Officer(s):
Mark Stewart, Program Director
progdirector@lethbridgelacrosse.com

Lethbridge Naturalists' Society

PO Box 1691, Stn. Main, Lethbridge AB T1J 4K4
Overview: A small local organization founded in 1966
Mission: To encourage knowledge & appreciation of natural history & understanding of ecological processes; To organize lectures, visual presentations & field trips; to conduct research on natural history; To become involved in environmental issues relating to conservation of the natural environment
Member of: Federation of Alberta Naturalists
Chief Officer(s):
Becky Little, Contact
becky.little@lethbridge.ca
Finances: *Funding Sources:* Membership fees
Activities: Winter programs; summer field trips

Lethbridge Network for Peace (LNFP)

1002 - 15 St. South, Lethbridge AB T1K 1V3
Tel: 403-328-1066
groups.yahoo.com/group/lethpeacenet/
Overview: A small local organization founded in 1984
Mission: To educate and promote citizen action for nuclear disarmament and peace.
Member of: Canadian Peace Alliance
Chief Officer(s):
Anne Williams, Contact
willae@uleth.ca
Finances: *Funding Sources:* Donations
Membership: 55 individuals
Activities: Educational programs; advocacy; *Library* Open to public

Lethbridge Oldtimers Sports Association (LOSA)

PO Box 84, Lethbridge AB T1J 3Y3
www.losa.ca
Overview: A small local organization
Mission: To organize recreational hockey games for adults
Chief Officer(s):
Brian Wright, President
Membership: *Fees:* $50

Lethbridge Real Estate Board *See* Lethbridge & District Association of Realtors

Lethbridge Soccer Association

2501 - 28 St. South, Lethbridge AB T1K 7L6
Tel: 403-320-5425
admin@lethbridgesoccer.com
lethbridgesoccer.com
www.facebook.com/LethbridgeSoccerAssociation
twitter.com/LethSoccer
Overview: A small local organization overseen by Alberta Soccer Association
Member of: Alberta Soccer Association
Chief Officer(s):
Steven Dudas, General Manager

Lethbridge Soup Kitchen Association

802 - 2A Ave. North, Lethbridge AB T1H 0C9
Tel: 403-320-8688
www.soupbridge.org
Overview: A small local charitable organization founded in 1984
Mission: To feed the hungry of Lethbridge & area
Chief Officer(s):
Joyce Crittenden, Executive Director
Staff Member(s): 1
Activities: Provision of hot lunch meals; referrals to other agencies

Lethbridge Symphony Orchestra (LSO)

PO Box 1101, Lethbridge AB T1J 4A2
Tel: 403-328-6808; *Fax:* 403-380-4418
Toll-Free: 855-328-6808
info@lethbridgesymphony.org
www.lethbridgesymphony.org
ca.linkedin.com/company/lethbridge-symphony-orchestra
www.facebook.com/lethbridgesymphony
twitter.com/LethSymphony
pinterest.com/lethsymphony
Also Known As: Lethbridge Symphony Association
Overview: A small local charitable organization founded in 1961 overseen by Orchestras Canada
Mission: To promote the orchestra & provide memorable musical experiences for their audiences.
Member of: Allied Arts Council of Lethbridge; Orchestras Canada; League of American Orchestras
Chief Officer(s):
Melanie Gattiker, Operations Manager
melanie@lethbridgesymphony.org
David Shefsiek, Executive Director
david@lethbridgesymphony.org
Finances: *Annual Operating Budget:* $250,000-$500,000; *Funding Sources:* Box office; donations; government grants; advertising
Staff Member(s): 12; 250 volunteer(s)
Membership: 500; *Fees:* $25
Activities: *Awareness Events:* Sentimental Journey, Oct.; *Internships:* Yes
Publications:
• Opus '61
Type: Newsletter
Profile: Information about musicians & events held by the symphony

Lethbridge Therapeutic Riding Association (LTRA)

RR#8-24-6, Lethbridge AB T1J 4P4
Tel: 403-328-2165
ltra@platinum.ca
www.ltra.ca
www.facebook.com/202084159822253
Also Known As: Rainbow Riding Centre
Overview: A small local charitable organization founded in 1977
Mission: To provide the opportunity for improved physical & emotional well-being for people of all ages & abilities who participate in therapeutic, recreational, educational & competitive riding programs at Rainbow Riding Centre
Member of: Canadian Therapeutic Riding Association
Finances: *Annual Operating Budget:* $100,000-$250,000
Staff Member(s): 2; 200 volunteer(s)
Membership: 260; *Fees:* $10 individual; $25 family; *Committees:* Facility; Program; Fundraising; Public relations; Foundation
Activities: 5-6 riding sessions per year; summer Ride On camp; Easter clinic

Leucan - Association for Children with Cancer *Voir* Leucan - Association pour les enfants atteints de cancer

Leucan - Association pour les enfants atteints de cancer / Leucan - Association for Children with Cancer

#505, 5800, rue St-Denis, Montréal QC H2S 3L5
Tél: 514-731-3696; *Téléc:* 514-731-2667
Ligne sans frais: 800-361-9643
info@leucan.qc.ca
www.leucan.qc.ca
www.linkedin.com/company/1115189
www.facebook.com/leucanpageprovinciale
twitter.com/Leucan_Org
www.youtube.com/user/associationleucan
Aperçu: *Dimension:* moyenne; *Envergure:* provinciale; fondée en 1978
Mission: Accroître la confiance en l'avenir des enfants atteints de cancer et de leurs familles
Membre de: Imagine Canada; Association des camps certifiés du Québec; Children's Oncology Camp Association International; Association canadienne des camps pédiatriques en oncologie
Membre(s) du bureau directeur:
Sandro Di Cori, Directeur général
sandro.dicori@leucan.qc.ca
Finances: *Budget de fonctionnement annuel:* Plus de $5 Million*Fonds:* Campagnes; dons
Membre(s) du personnel: 70; 2000 bénévole(s)
Membre: 3600 familles; *Montant de la cotisation:* Barème
Activités: Camp Vol d'été Leucan-CSN; Fête de Noël; Karting; Défi têtes rasées; Marche et course à la fête des Mères; Camp d'Halloween Leucan-Simple Plan; Fins de semaine de répit; Cueillette de pommes; Cabane à sucre; *Événements de sensibilisation:* Omnium Michel Blouin; Campagne de tirelires; Défi ski 12 h Leucan; L'Expérience Leucan; Défi Loïc 12 h vélo; *Stagiaires:* Oui; *Bibliothèque:* Centre d'information Leucan; Bibliothèque publique rendez-vous

Prix, Bouses:
• Prix femmes d'affaires du Québec (Prix)

The Leukemia & Lymphoma Society of Canada (LLSC) / Société de leucémie et lymphome du Canada

#804, 2 Lansing Square, Toronto ON M2J 4P8
Fax: 416-661-7799
Toll-Free: 877-668-8326
donatecanada@lls.org
www.llscanada.org
www.facebook.com/LLSCanada
twitter.com/llscanada
www.youtube.com/llscanada; www.flickr.com/photos/llscanada
Previous Name: Leukemia Research Fund of Canada
Overview: A medium-sized national charitable organization founded in 1955
Mission: To cure leukemia, lymphoma, Hodgkin's disease & myeloma, & to improve the quality of life of patients & their families
Affliation(s): Canadian Centre for Philanthropy
Chief Officer(s):
Adrian Hartog, Chair
Finances: *Annual Operating Budget:* $3 Million-$5 Million; *Funding Sources:* Fundraising
Staff Member(s): 31; 1400 volunteer(s)
Membership: 600; *Fees:* $25 branch
Activities: *Awareness Events:* Leukemia Awareness Month, June; *Internships:* Yes

Atlantic Canada Branch
#H2, 1660 Hollis St., Halifax NS B3J 1V7
Tel: 902-422-5999; *Fax:* 902-422-5968
Toll-Free: 855-515-5572
Chief Officer(s):
Cheryl Easter, Executive Director

British Columbia/Yukon Branch
#310, 1662 West 7th Ave., Vancouver BC V6J 4S6
Tel: 604-733-2873
Chief Officer(s):
Davidrine Swan, Executive Director
david.swan@lls.org

Ontario Branch - Ottawa
#701, 116 Albert St., Ottawa ON K1P 5G3
Tel: 613-234-1274

Ontario Branch - Toronto
#1502, 480 University Ave., Toronto ON M5G 1V2
Tel: 416-661-2873; *Fax:* 416-661-3840
Toll-Free: 877-668-8326
Chief Officer(s):
Andrea Swinton, Executive Director
andrea.swinton@lls.org

Prairies/Territories Branch - Calgary
2020 - 10th St. NW, Calgary AB T2M 3M2
Tel: 403-263-5300
Chief Officer(s):
Jason Campbell, Executive Director

Prairies/Territories Branch - Edmonton
#208, 10240 - 124th St., Edmonton AB T5N 3W6
Tel: 780-758-4261

Prairies/Territories Branch - Saskatoon
#202, 402 - 21st St. East, Saskatoon SK S7K 0C3
Tel: 306-242-6611

Québec Branch
#705, 1255, rue Universite, Montréal QC H3B 3W1
Tel: 514-875-1000

Leukemia Research Fund of Canada *See* The Leukemia & Lymphoma Society of Canada

Lewisporte & Area Chamber of Commerce

PO Box 953, Lewisporte NL A0G 3A0
Tel: 709-535-2500; *Fax:* 709-535-2482
lacc@superweb.ca
www.lewisporteareachamberofcommerce.ca
Overview: A small local organization
Chief Officer(s):
Cynthia Aylward, Executive Assistant

LGBT Family Coalition *Voir* Coalition des familles LGBT

Liaison of Independent Filmmakers of Toronto (LIFT)

1137 Dupont St., Toronto ON M6K 3P6
Tel: 416-588-6444; *Fax:* 416-588-7017
lift.ca
www.facebook.com/LIFT.ca
twitter.com/LIFTfilm
Overview: A small local charitable organization founded in 1979
Mission: To support & encourage independent filmmaking through the exchange of information, access to film production equipment & post-production facilities, regular series of workshops & regular public film exhibitions
Member of: Independent Media Arts Alliance; Artist-run Centres & Collectives of Ontario
Affliation(s): Independent Film & Video Alliance; Association of National Non-Profit Artist-Run Centres; Artist Run Centres Toronto
Chief Officer(s):
Kathryn MacKay, Chair
Ben Donoghue, Executive Director
Finances: *Annual Operating Budget:* $500,000-$1.5 Million
Staff Member(s): 5
Membership: 600+ individual; *Fees:* $60 individual; $70 associate; $130 full; *Member Profile:* Three levels of membership: affiliate, associate, full; all new members join at affiliate level & upgrade (via volunteer hours & an additional fee) to associate or full status, if desired; *Committees:* Workshops; Equipment; Lobbying; Programming; Magazine
Activities: *Library*

The Liberal Party of Canada (LPC) / Le Parti Libéral du Canada (PLC)

#600, 81 Metcalfe St., Ottawa ON K1P 6M8
Tel: 613-237-0740; *Fax:* 613-235-7208
info@liberal.ca
www.liberal.ca
www.facebook.com/LiberalCA
twitter.com/Liberal_party
www.youtube.com/user/liberalvideo
Previous Name: The National Liberal Federation
Overview: A large national organization founded in 1867
Mission: To seek a common ground of understanding among the people of the provinces & territories of Canada; To advocate liberal philosophies, principles & policies; To promote the election of candidates of the Liberal Party to the Parliament of Canada
Affliation(s): Liberal International
Chief Officer(s):
Justin Trudeau, Party Leader
Anna Gainey, National President
Jeremy Broadhurst, National Director
Chris MacInnes, National Vice-President, English
cmacinnes@liberal.ca
Geneviève Hinse, National Vice-President, French
Finances: *Annual Operating Budget:* Greater than $5 Million; *Funding Sources:* Donations
Staff Member(s): 30
Membership: Over 50,000; *Fees:* $5-10; *Committees:* Policy Development; Organization; Constitutional & Legal; Communications & Publicity; Multiculturalism; Platform; National Campaign; Permanent Appeal; Management; Financial Management; Young Liberals of Canada; National Women's Liberal Commission; Aboriginal Peoples' Commission; Seniors' Commission
Activities: *Speaker Service:* Yes
Meetings/Conferences: • Liberal Party of Canada 2016 Biennial Convention, 2016
Scope: National
Description: An opportunity for Liberals across Canada to engage in preparations for the next election, to elect the Party's new executive, and to discuss policy resolutions that shape the party's next electoral platform.

The Liberal Party of Canada (British Columbia) (LPCBC) / Parti libéral du Canada (Colombie-Britannique)

#460, 580 Hornby St., Vancouver BC V6C 3B6
Tel: 604-664-3777; *Fax:* 604-874-8966
Toll-Free: 888-411-6511
assistance@liberal.ca
bc.liberal.ca
www.facebook.com//LPCBC
twitter.com/lpcbc
www.youtube.com/user/liberalvideo
Overview: A medium-sized provincial organization overseen by The Liberal Party of Canada
Chief Officer(s):
Braeden Caley, President
Finances: *Funding Sources:* Donations; fundraising
Staff Member(s): 5; 10 volunteer(s)
Membership: 15,000; *Fees:* $10
Activities: *Internships:* Yes; *Speaker Service:* Yes

The Liberal Party of Canada (Manitoba)

Molgat Place, 635 Broadway, Winnipeg MB R3C 0X1
Tel: 204-988-9540; *Fax:* 204-988-9549
manitoba.liberal.ca
www.facebook.com/LPCMB.PLCMB
Overview: A medium-sized provincial organization overseen by The Liberal Party of Canada
Chief Officer(s):
Don Fletcher, President
David Johnson, Executive Director
david@lpcm.ca

Liberal Party of Canada (Ontario) (LPC(O)) / Parti libéral du Canada (Ontario)

#420, 10 St. Mary St., Toronto ON M4Y 1P9
Tel: 416-921-2844; *Fax:* 416-921-3880
Toll-Free: 800-361-3881
Other Communication: communications@lpco.ca
admin@lpco.ca
ontario.liberal.ca
www.facebook.com/LPCO.PLCO
twitter.com/lpc_o
Overview: A medium-sized provincial organization overseen by The Liberal Party of Canada
Mission: The Liberal Party of Canada (Ontario) represents the Federal Liberal Party and its 106 Electoral District Associations in Ontario. LPC(O) works with the thousands of members and volunteers in Ontario to ensure that it is a healthy and vibrant political organization.
Chief Officer(s):
Tyler Banham, President
president@lpco.ca
Brett Thalmann, Director, Operations
bthalmann@liberal.ca
Staff Member(s): 10

Liberal Party of Canada in Alberta (LPC(A))

#308, 10247 - 124 St., Edmonton AB T5N 3W6
Fax: 613-235-7208
Toll-Free: 888-542-3725
assistance@liberal.ca
alberta.liberal.ca
Overview: A medium-sized provincial organization overseen by The Liberal Party of Canada
Chief Officer(s):
Robbie Schuett, President
Finances: *Funding Sources:* Donations

Liberal Party of Newfoundland & Labrador / Parti libéral de Terre-Neuve et du Labrador

Beothuk Bldg., #205, 20 Crosbie Place, St. John's NL A1B 3Y8
Tel: 709-754-1813; *Fax:* 709-754-0820
Toll-Free: 866-726-7116
info@nlliberals.ca
nlliberals.ca
www.facebook.com/nlliberals
twitter.com/nlliberals
www.youtube.com/nlliberals
Overview: A medium-sized provincial organization overseen by The Liberal Party of Canada
Mission: The Liberal Party in Newfoundland and Labrador has been the dominant political party since confederation in 1949 and are responsible for many of the major social transformations that has occurred in this province in the last half century. Those developments, which include Memorial University, countless new schools across the province and an greatly improved standard of living, have made the Liberal Party the voice of social development in Newfoundland and Labrador.
Chief Officer(s):
Dwight Ball, Leader, 709-729-3011
dwightball@gov.nl.ca
John Allan, President
jda@nf.aibn.com

Liberal Party of Nova Scotia

PO Box 723, #1400, 5151 George St., Halifax NS B3J 1M5
Tel: 902-429-1993; *Fax:* 902-423-1624; *TTY:* 902-429-1772
office@liberal.ns.ca
www.liberal.ns.ca
www.facebook.com/pages/Stephen-McNeil/19853187485
twitter.com/NSLiberal
www.youtube.com/nsliberalparty
Also Known As: Nova Scotia Liberal Party
Overview: A small provincial organization overseen by The Liberal Party of Canada

Chief Officer(s):
Stephen McNeil, Leader
mcneilsr@gov.ns.ca
Michael Mercer, Executive Director, 902-429-7666
mmercer@liberal.ns.ca
John Gillis, President
Staff Member(s): 4

Liberal Party of Prince Edward Island / Parti libéral de l'Ile du Prince Édouard

PO Box 2559, #205, 129 Kent St., Charlottetown PE C1A 8C2
Tel: 902-368-3449; *Fax:* 902-368-3687
Toll-Free: 877-740-3449
reception@liberal.pe.ca
www.liberal.pe.ca
www.facebook.com/pages/PEI-Liberals/183212951743526
twitter.com/PEILiberalWire
www.youtube.com/user/peiliberals?feature=mhee
Overview: A medium-sized provincial organization overseen by The Liberal Party of Canada
Mission: Representing the Liberal Party of PEI.
Chief Officer(s):
Robert Ghiz, Party Leader
Jamie McPhail, Executive Director
jamie@liberal.pe.ca

The Libertarian Party of Canada

#205, 372 Rideau St., Ottawa ON K1N 1G7
Tel: 613-288-9089
info@libertarian.ca
www.libertarian.ca
www.facebook.com/groups/lpcanada/
twitter.com/Clibrtrn
www.youtube.com/user/CLibrtrn?feature=guide
Overview: A small national organization
Chief Officer(s):
Katrina Chowne, Party Leader
kchowne@libertarian.ca
Meetings/Conferences: • Libertarian Party of Canada 2015 Convention, 2015
Scope: National

Libertel de la Capitale Nationale *See* National Capital FreeNet

Libra House Inc.

PO Box 449, Stn. B, Happy Valley-Goose Bay NL A0P 1E0
Tel: 709-896-8022; *Fax:* 709-896-8223
Toll-Free: 877-896-3014; *Crisis Hot-Line:* 709-896-3014
librahouse@nf.aibn.com
www.librahouse.ca
Overview: A small local organization founded in 1983
Mission: To provide crisis shelter for abused women & their children; to offer support & education to women
Member of: Provincial Association Against Family Violence
Staff Member(s): 7
Activities: 24-hour crisis support line

Librarians Without Borders (LWB)

PO Box 47015, Stn. UCC, 1151 Richmond St. North, London ON N6G 6G6
e-mail: info@lwb-online.org
www.lwb-online.org
www.facebook.com/librarianswithoutborders
twitter.com/LWB_Online
www.flickr.com/photos/librarians-without-borders
Overview: A small international organization founded in 2005
Mission: To address the information resource inequity in different regions of the world; To improve access to information, regardless of geography, language, or religion; To build sustainable libraries & support their librarians
Chief Officer(s):
Melanie Sellar, Co-Executive Director
melanie.sellar@lwb-online.org
Mark Gelsomino, Co-Executive Director
mark.gelsomino@lwb-online.org
Erika Heesen, Director, Membership
erika.heesen@lwb-online.org
Laura George, Secretary
laura.george@lwb-online.org
Nalini Battu, Treasurer
nalini.battu@lwb-online.org
Finances: *Funding Sources:* Donations; Fundraising
Membership: *Fees:* Free; *Committees:* Dalhousie University; McGill University; University of British Columbia; University of Toronto; University of Western Ontario; University of Ottawa
Activities: Partnering with community organizations in developing regions
Publications:
• The Compass
Type: Newsletter
Profile: Updates about the progress of Librarians without Borders' projects, plus future plans & events

Library Association of Alberta (LAA)

80 Baker Cres. NW, Calgary AB T2L 1R4
Tel: 403-284-5818; *Fax:* 403-282-6646
Toll-Free: 877-522-5550
info@laa.ca
www.laa.ca
www.linkedin.com/groups/Library-Association-Alberta-4735949
www.facebook.com/LibraryAssociationOfAlberta
twitter.com/Lib_Assn_AB
plus.google.com/114726559596090866928
Previous Name: Alberta Library Association
Overview: A medium-sized provincial organization founded in 1931
Mission: To facilitate the improvement of library services in Alberta; To promote library service throughout Alberta; To encourage cooperation among libraries & information centres across the province; To promote intellectual freedom in Alberta
Chief Officer(s):
Karen Hildebrandt, President
president@laa.ca
Jason Openo, 1st Vice-President
1stvicepresident@laa.ca
Norene James, 2nd Vice-President
2ndvicepresident@laa.ca
Jackie Flowers, Treasurer
treasurer@laa.ca
Finances: *Funding Sources:* Sponsorships
Membership: 490; *Member Profile:* Individuals, institutions, & organizations involved in library service; *Committees:* Advocacy; Association Governance; Continuing Education; Personnel; Finance; Intellectual Freedom; Member Services; Nominations & Elections
Activities: Liaising with other library organizations; Engaging in advocacy activities; Influencing government policy & legislation regarding library services; Providing continuing education opportunities; Facilitating communication among persons concerned with libary & information services in Alberta
Meetings/Conferences: • Library Association of Alberta Annual Conference 2015, April, 2015, AB
Scope: Provincial
Description: A conference held each spring for members of the Alberta library community, featuring association annual general meetings, session presentations, networking opportunities, & a trade show. Beginning this year, the conference is no longer held jointly with the Alberta Library Trustees Association (ALTA).
Contact Information: Library Association of Alberta, Phone: 403-284-5818, Toll-Free Phone: 1-877-522-5550, Fax: 403-282-6646, E-mail: info@laa.ca, info@albertalibraryconference.com
• Library Association of Alberta Annual Conference 2016, April, 2016, AB
Scope: Provincial
Description: A conference held each spring for members of the Alberta library community, featuring association annual general meetings, session presentations, networking opportunities, & a trade show. Beginning this year, the conference is no longer held jointly with the Alberta Library Trustees Association (ALTA).
Contact Information: Library Association of Alberta, Phone: 403-284-5818, Toll-Free Phone: 1-877-522-5550, Fax: 403-282-6646, E-mail: info@laa.ca, info@albertalibraryconference.com
• Library Association of Alberta Annual Conference 2017, April, 2017, AB
Scope: Provincial
Description: A conference held each spring for members of the Alberta library community, featuring association annual general meetings, session presentations, networking opportunities, & a trade show. Beginning this year, the conference is no longer held jointly with the Alberta Library Trustees Association (ALTA).
Contact Information: Library Association of Alberta, Phone: 403-284-5818, Toll-Free Phone: 1-877-522-5550, Fax: 403-282-6646, E-mail: info@laa.ca, info@albertalibraryconference.com
• Library Association of Alberta Annual Conference 2018, April, 2018, AB
Scope: Provincial
Description: A conference held each spring for members of the Alberta library community, featuring association annual general meetings, session presentations, networking opportunities, & a trade show. Beginning this year, the conference is no longer held jointly with the Alberta Library Trustees Association (ALTA).
Contact Information: Library Association of Alberta, Phone: 403-284-5818, Toll-Free Phone: 1-877-522-5550, Fax: 403-282-6646, E-mail: info@laa.ca, info@albertalibraryconference.com
• Library Association of Alberta Annual Conference 2019, April, 2019, AB
Scope: Provincial
Description: A conference held each spring for members of the Alberta library community, featuring association annual general meetings, session presentations, networking opportunities, & a trade show. Beginning this year, the conference is no longer held jointly with the Alberta Library Trustees Association (ALTA).
Contact Information: Library Association of Alberta, Phone: 403-284-5818, Toll-Free Phone: 1-877-522-5550, Fax: 403-282-6646, E-mail: info@laa.ca, info@albertalibraryconference.com
• Library Association of Alberta Annual Conference 2020, April, 2020, AB
Scope: Provincial
Description: A conference held each spring for members of the Alberta library community, featuring association annual general meetings, session presentations, networking opportunities, & a trade show. Beginning this year, the conference is no longer held jointly with the Alberta Library Trustees Association (ALTA).
Contact Information: Library Association of Alberta, Phone: 403-284-5818, Toll-Free Phone: 1-877-522-5550, Fax: 403-282-6646, E-mail: info@laa.ca, info@albertalibraryconference.com
Publications:
• Letter of the LAA
Type: Newsletter; *Accepts Advertising*; *Price:* Free with membership in the Library Association of Alberta
Profile: Library Association of Alberta activities
• Library Association of Alberta Membership Directory
Type: Directory; *Price:* Free with membership in the Library Association of Alberta
Profile: Contact information, place of work, & position for association members

Library Association of the National Capital Region (LANCR) / Association des bibliothèques de la région de la capitale nationale

PO Box 924, Stn. B, Ottawa ON K1P 5P9
e-mail: lancrinfo@gmail.com
lancr.wordpress.com
Overview: A small local organization
Mission: To create a forum for library personnel & friends of libraries from the Ottawa-Hull region, where members can discuss library issues of general interest, share information related to library matters, promote an esprit de corps among librarians, library technicians, & all others interested in libraries & library work.
Chief Officer(s):
Laura May, President

Library Boards Association of Nova Scotia (LBANS)

c/o Janet Ness, Secretary, Library Boards Association of Nova Scotia, 53 Sherwood Dr., Wolfville NS B4P 2K5
Tel: 902-542-7386
janet_ness@hotmail.com
www.standupforlibraries.ca
Previous Name: Joint Regional Library Boards Association of Nova Scotia
Overview: A small provincial organization founded in 1976
Mission: To preserve & support quality public library service throughout Nova Scotia
Chief Officer(s):
Gary Archibald, Executive Director
archibaldg@eastlink.ca
Mary MacLellan, President
mmaclellan@antigonishcounty.ns.ca
Shirley McNamara, Vice-President
smcnamara@richmondcounty.ca
Janet Ness, Secretary
janet_ness@hotmail.com
Marie Hogan Loker, Treasurer
mariebarry@ns.sympatico.ca
Membership: *Member Profile:* Appointed persons from the nine regional library boards in Nova Scotia, such as elected councillors or volunteers with an interest in public libraries & their services
Activities: Promoting public library services across Nova Scotia; Offering a forum for the exchange of ideas; Encouraging cooperation between regional library boards: Advocating on

behalf of public libraries; Liaising with government & other stakeholders
Meetings/Conferences: • Library Boards Association of Nova Scotia 2015 Annual Conference, 2015, NS
Scope: Provincial
Description: An annual autumn meeting for anyone with an interest in public libraries in Nova Scotia
Contact Information: Library Boards Association of Nova Scotia Executive Assistant: Christina Pottie, cpottie@southshorepubliclibraries.ca
• Library Boards Association of Nova Scotia 2016 Annual Conference, 2016, NS
Scope: Provincial
Description: An annual autumn meeting for anyone with an interest in public libraries in Nova Scotia
Contact Information: Library Boards Association of Nova Scotia Executive Assistant: Christina Pottie, cpottie@southshorepubliclibraries.ca

Library Technicians' & Assistants' Section
#150, 900 Howe St., Vancouver BC V6Z 2M4
Other Communication: www.ltaig.proboards.com
www.bcla.bc.ca/ltaig
www.facebook.com/groups/11830528766
twitter.com/ltaig
Overview: A small provincial organization overseen by British Columbia Library Association (BCLA)
Mission: To establish an inclusive, province-wide organization which supports &promotes the role of library technicians & assistants, regardless of formal training or certification, through education, communication & advocacy.
Chief Officer(s):
Tamarack Hockin, Chair
ltaschair@gmail.com

Licensed Practical Nurses Association & Regulatory Board of PEI
#204, 155 Belvedere Ave., Charlottetown PE C1A 2Y9
Tel: 902-566-1512; *Fax:* 902-892-6315
info@lpna.ca
www.lpna.ca
Overview: A medium-sized provincial organization overseen by Canadian Council of Practical Nurse Regulators
Mission: To represent practical nurses within the health care system
Chief Officer(s):
Alana Essery, Executive Director/Registrar
aessery@lpna.ca

Licensed Practical Nurses Association of British Columbia (LPNABC)
#211, 3030 Lincoln Ave., Coquitlam BC V3B 6B4
Tel: 604-434-1972
info@lpnabc.ca
www.lpnabc.ca
www.facebook.com/group.php?gid=104192534883
twitter.com/LPNABC
www.youtube.com/user/LPNABC
Overview: A small provincial organization founded in 1951 overseen by Practical Nurses Canada
Mission: To promote professional excellence among the licensed practical nurses of British Columbia; To offer a unified voice for the province's licensed practical nurses
Member of: Practical Nurses Canada
Chief Officer(s):
Teresa McFadyen, President
Membership: *Fees:* $25 students & retired persons; $60 active members; *Member Profile:* Licensed practical nurses in British Columbia; Retired persons; Students; *Committees:* Communications; Conference; Finance; Legislation and Bylaw; Nominations; Promotions
Activities: Supporting licensed practical nurses in British Columbia; Lobbying for the profession; Liaising with the government & employers; Promoting the profession to the public; Organizing educational & mentoring opportunities; Facilitating provincial & national networking opportunities; Awarding education bursaries
Meetings/Conferences: • Licensed Practical Nurses Association of British Columbia 2015 Conference and AGM, 2015, BC
Scope: Provincial
Publications:
• In Touch
Type: Newsletter; *Frequency:* 3 pa; *Price:* Free with membership in Licensed Practical Nurses Association of British Columbia
Profile: Association activities

Licensed Practical Nurses Association of Nova Scotia; Nova Scotia Certified Nursing Assistants Association *See* College of Licensed Practical Nurses of Nova Scotia

Lieutenant Governor's Circle on Mental Health & Addiction
PO Box 62072, Edmonton AB T5M 4B5
Tel: 780-850-0533; *Fax:* 780-466-1095
www.mhpa.ab.ca/LGCircle
Overview: A small provincial organization
Chief Officer(s):
Dennis Anderson, Co-Chair
Fay Orr, Co-Chair
Awards:
• True Grit (Award), True Awards
An individual who has made use of mental health &/or addictions services & inspired others to get help in the management of mental illness; or who has helped to further mental health & addictions programmes
• True Compassion (Award), True Awards
An individual who has provided guidance in effecting the improvement of mental health & addictions programmes
• True Leadership (Award), True Awards
An individual who has provided exceptional leadership in improving mental health & addictions programmes
• True Service (Award), True Awards
A public body that has provided service in the improvement of mental health & addictions reduction
• True Imagination (Award), True Awards
An individual, group or organization that has used treatment or programmes in the imaginative improvement of mental health or reduction of addictions

Life Foundation
www.poderofprayer.com
Also Known As: Poder of Prayer
Overview: A small international organization founded in 1967
Mission: To promote devotion of Divine Mercy through Our Lady of Guadalupe; To encourage prayer for the right of human life from conception until natural death
Affliation(s): Archdiocese of Toronto
Chief Officer(s):
Gustavo Rico, Contact
gus@poderofprayer.com
Finances: *Funding Sources:* Donations
Membership: *Member Profile:* Individuals who are followers of Jesus Christ, under obediance of the Holy Father & the local bishop
Activities: Offering counselling, faith instruction, & prayer groups

Life Insurance Institute of Canada *See* LOMA Canada

Life Science Association of Manitoba (LSAM)
1000 Waverley St., Winnipeg MB R3T 0P3
Tel: 204-272-5095; *Fax:* 204-272-2961
info@lsam.ca
www.lsam.ca
www.linkedin.com/groups?about=&gid=3753791&trk=anet_ug_grppro
www.facebook.com/123001494423036
twitter.com/LifeScienceMB
www.youtube.com/user/LifeScienceMB
Overview: A medium-sized provincial organization founded in 1990
Mission: To represent the life science industry in Manitoba; to provide services for companies in the industry; to promote economic development
Affliation(s): BIOTECanada; BioTalent Canada; Life Sciences British Columbia; BioAlberta; Ag-West Biotech Inc.; Ontario Agri-Food Technologies; MaRS; Ottawa Life Sciences Council; Toronto Biotechnology Initiative; TechAlliance; The Golden Horseshoe Biosciences Network; York Biotech; BioQuebec; BioAtlantech; BioNova; PEI BioAlliance; Newfoundland & Labrador Assn of Technology Industries
Chief Officer(s):
Tracey Maconachie, President, 204-272-5096
tmaconachie@lsam.ca
Finances: *Funding Sources:* Membership dues
Staff Member(s): 4
Membership: 107 member organizations; *Fees:* Schedule available; *Member Profile:* Corporations involved in the manufacturing & research health care industries

Life Underwriters Association of Canada *See* Advocis

Life's Vision
#5, 130 Marion St., Winnipeg MB R2H 0T4
Tel: 204-233-8047; *Fax:* 204-233-0523
lifesvision@shaw.ca
lifesvision.ca
Also Known As: League for Life in Manitoba, Inc.
Overview: A medium-sized provincial charitable organization founded in 1974
Mission: To engage in non-sectarian educational activities in order to encourage & promote among the general public an understanding & awareness of the dignity & worth of each individual human life, whatever its state & circumstances; to foster respect for all human life. Life's Vision provides information & referral services dealing with pregnancy & end of life issues, such as abortion, euthanasia & assisted suicide, & provides a voice for those opposed to abortion.
Chief Officer(s):
Heather White, Executive Director
Finances: *Annual Operating Budget:* $100,000-$250,000; *Funding Sources:* Membership dues; private donations; fundraising
Membership: 5,000-14,999; *Committees:* Education; Membership
Activities: Field calls from people in crisis pregnancies 1-800-665-0570; Create awareness in community with truth booth display; Presentations for schools, youth groups on pre-natal development, abortion & post-abortion healing resources; *Awareness Events:* Life Hike; Respect for Life Week, Feb.; Annual Banquet; *Speaker Service:* Yes; *Library* Open to public

LifeCanada / VieCanada
PO Box 500, Ottawa ON K0A 3P0
Tel: 613-722-1552; *Fax:* 613-482-4937
Toll-Free: 866-780-5433
Other Communication: Local BC: 778-805-2171
info@lifecanada.org
www.lifecanada.org
www.facebook.com/pages/LifeCanada/261835447215975
twitter.com/LifeCanadaOrg
Overview: A medium-sized national organization
Mission: A national association of local and provincial educational pro-life groups across Canada for the purpose of promoting the respect and dignity of all human life.
Membership: *Fees:* $25 individual; $50 supporting; $5 per member, affliate/associate
Meetings/Conferences: • LifeCanada / VieCanada 2015 National Conference, 2015
Scope: National
Description: A 3-day national gathering of experts and pro-life professionals from across the country and abroad.
Publications:
• LifeCanada Journal
Type: Journal; *Frequency:* Bi-Monthly; *Price:* $20 for 6 issues
Profile: Sent to every Member of Parliament and Senator as well as to pro-life organizations, supporters and benefactors.

Lifeforce Foundation
PO Box 3117, Vancouver BC V6B 3X6
Tel: 604-649-5258
lifeforcesociety@hotmail.com
www.lifeforcefoundation.org
www.facebook.com/196062246185
Also Known As: Lifeforce
Overview: A small international charitable organization founded in 1981
Mission: To raise public awareness of the interrelationship of human, animal & environmental problems; to urge society to address & solve problems by taking into consideration the long-term effects on all parts of the ecosystem
Finances: *Funding Sources:* Donations; membership fees; bequests
Activities: Whale & dolphin hotline; Orca research; Lifewatch program distributes whale watching regulations & stops boaters who harass marine mammals; Marine Wildlife Rescue; educational materials & displays; all animal rights & issues

Lifesaving Society / Société de sauvetage
287 McArthur Ave., Ottawa ON K1L 6P3
Tel: 613-746-5694; *Fax:* 613-746-9929
experts@lifesaving.ca
www.lifesaving.ca
Previous Name: Royal Life Saving Society Canada
Overview: A large national charitable organization founded in 1908

Mission: The Society is a volunteer organization that works to prevent drowning & water-related incidents by providing lifesaving, lifeguarding & leadership education. It is a registered charity, BN: 119129088RR0001.
Affliation(s): Canadian Armed Forces; Canadian Parks & Recreation Association; Canadian Red Cross Society; L'Institut Maritime du Québec; Professional Association of Diving Instructors Canada; Royal Canadian Mounted Police; St. John Ambulance; Swimming Canada; YMCA Canada
Chief Officer(s):
Paul Dawe, President
Yvan Chalifour, Executive Director, 613-746-5694 Ext. 28
ychalifour@lifesaving.ca
Finances: *Annual Operating Budget:* $500,000-$1.5 Million
Staff Member(s): 8; 100 volunteer(s)
Membership: 87 organizations in Canada; *Committees:* Strategic Units - Communications & Marketing; Behavioural Change/Injury Prevention; Education; Lifeguarding; Research & Development; International Affairs
Activities: Certifications (Accredited Boat Certification Course, Water Rescue Awards, Life Saving Fitness Awards, Resuscitation & Emergency Care Awards, Specialized Life Saving Awards, Leadership Training); Canadian Life Saving Manual; films & publications on life saving; demonstrations; competitions; *Awareness Events:* National Drowning Prevention Day, July; *Library:* Resource Centre; by appointment
Awards:
• M.G. Griffiths Award Plaque (Award)
Acknowledges significant acts of bravery while performing an exceptional rescue, by an individual who hase been taught rescue methods through the Society's proficiency award program.

Alberta & NWT Branch
13123 - 156 St., Edmonton AB T5V 1V2
Tel: 780-415-1755; *Fax:* 780-427-9334
experts@lifesaving.org
www.lifesaving.org
Chief Officer(s):
Martin Evers, President
Barbara Costache, Chief Administrative Officer

British Columbia & Yukon Branch
#112, 3989 Henning Dr., Burnaby BC V5C 6N5
Tel: 604-299-5450; *Fax:* 604-299-5795
www.lifesaving.bc.ca
www.facebook.com/LifesavingBCYK
Chief Officer(s):
Dale Miller, Executive Director

Manitoba Branch
#100, 383 Provencher Blvd., Winnipeg MB R2H 0G9
Tel: 204-956-2124; *Fax:* 204-944-8546
aquatics@lifesaving.mb.ca
www.lifesaving.mb.ca
Chief Officer(s):
Michael Limerick, Chair
Carl Shier, CEO
cshier@lifesaving.mb.ca

New Brunswick Branch
#34, 55 Whiting Rd., Fredericton NB E3B 5Y5
Tel: 506-455-5762; *Fax:* 506-450-7946
www.lifesavingnb.ca
Doug Ferguson, Chief Executive Officer

Newfoundland & Labrador Branch
PO Box 8065, Stn. A, 11 Austin St., St. John's NL A1B 3M9
Tel: 709-576-1953; *Fax:* 709-738-1475
lifeguard@bellaliant.com
www.lifesavingnl.ca
www.facebook.com/182894758427066
twitter.com/LifesavingNL
Chief Officer(s):
Jeanette Jobson, Executive Director
lifeguard@bellaliant.com

Nova Scotia Branch
5516 Spring Garden Rd., 4th Fl., Halifax NS B3J 1G6
Tel: 902-425-5450; *Fax:* 902-425-5606
experts@lifesavingsociety.ns.ca
www.lifesavingsociety.ns.ca
www.facebook.com/NovaScotiaLifesavingSociety
twitter.com/NSLifesaving
Chief Officer(s):
Mike Melenchuk, President
Gordon Richardson, Executive Director
gordonr@lifesavingsociety.ns.ca

Ontario & Nunavut Branch
400 Consumers Rd., Toronto ON M2J 1P8
Tel: 416-490-8844; *Fax:* 416-490-8766
www.lifesavingsociety.com
www.facebook.com/lifesavingsocietyON
twitter.com/LifesavingON
Chief Officer(s):
Doug Ferguson, Executive Director

Prince Edward Island Branch
40 Enman Cres., Charlottetown PE C1E 1E6
Tel: 902-368-7757; *Fax:* 902-368-1593
info@lifesavingsocietypei.ca
lifesavingsocietypei.ca
www.facebook.com/pages/Lifesaving-Society-PEI/152048238151395
twitter.com/lifesavingpei
www.youtube.com/user/OntarioLifesaving
Chief Officer(s):
Halbert Pratt, Executive Director & President

Québec Branch
CP 1000, Succ. M, 4545, av Pierre-de Coubertin, Montréal QC H1V 3R2
Tél: 514-252-3100; *Téléc:* 514-254-6232
Ligne sans frais: 800-265-3093
alerte@sauvetage.qc.ca
www.sauvetage.qc.ca
Chief Officer(s):
Raynald Hawkins, Directeur général
rhawkins@sauvetage.qc.ca

Saskatchewan Branch
2224 Smith St., Regina SK S4P 2P4
Tel: 306-780-9255
lifesaving@sasktel.net
www.lifesavingsociety.sk.ca
www.facebook.com/207169849327920
twitter.com/sklifesaving
plus.google.com/+LifesavingsocietySkCa

LifeSciences British Columbia
#900, 1188 West Georgia St., Vancouver BC V6E 4A2
Tel: 604-669-9909; *Fax:* 604-669-9912
info@lifesciencesbc.ca
www.lifesciencesbc.ca/
www.facebook.com/lifesciencesbc
twitter.com/lifesciences_bc
Previous Name: BC Biotech
Overview: A medium-sized provincial organization founded in 1991
Mission: To improve the climate in which the business of biotechnology is conducted in BC; To be an advocate for the industry; To improve the level of awareness & understanding of biotechnology
Chief Officer(s):
Don Enns, President
denns@lifesciencesbc.ca
Karimah Es Sabar, President
Finances: *Annual Operating Budget:* $250,000-$500,000; *Funding Sources:* Membership fees
Staff Member(s): 4
Membership: 260; *Fees:* $50 students; $250 individuals; $750+ corporations, depending on membership categories; *Member Profile:* Producers & users of biotechnology, including companies, colleges & universities, government agencies & students; *Committees:* Communications; Finance; Human Resources; Public Policies; Research & Development
Awards:
• Annual BC Biotechnology Awards (Award)

Lifestyle Information Network (LIN) / Réseau Info Style de Vie
#302, 1 Concorde Gate, Toronto ON M3C 3N6
Tel: 416-426-7176; *Fax:* 416-426-7371
info@lin.ca
www.lin.ca
Overview: A small national organization founded in 1995
Mission: To help individuals & organizations that care about individual & community well-being, parks, recreation, sport & culture, use interract technology effectively to exchange knowledge
Member of: Coalition for Active Living
Affliation(s): Canadian Health Network
Chief Officer(s):
Clem Pelot, CEO
Staff Member(s): 6; 20 volunteer(s)
Membership: 3,500

Lifewater Canada
#194, 307 Euclid Ave., Thunder Bay ON P7E 6G6
Tel: 807-622-4848; *Fax:* 807-577-9798
Toll-Free: 888-543-3426
www.lifewater.ca
Overview: A small international organization
Mission: Christian organization dedicated to ensuring that people everywhere have access to adequate supplies of safe water; to train & equip nationals with drill rigs & hand pumps so they can solve their own water problems; to place as many technical documents on-line as possible so they can benefit people everywhere, regardless of affiliation
Chief Officer(s):
Alanna Drost, Contact
Membership: *Member Profile:* Hydrogeologists, well drillers, educators, engineers, environmental scientists, businessmen & many other people with diverse skills & training

Lighthouse Food Bank Society
PO Box 179, Chester NS B0J 1J0
Tel: 902-275-5304
Overview: A small local charitable organization founded in 1986
Member of: Nova Scotia Food Bank Association
Chief Officer(s):
Madge Cook, Chair
Finances: *Annual Operating Budget:* Less than $50,000
10 volunteer(s)
Membership: *Fees:* $25

Lighthouse Mission
669 Main St., Winnipeg MB R3B 1E3
Tel: 204-943-9669; *Fax:* 204-949-9479
info@lighthousemission.ca
www.lighthousemission.ca
Overview: A small local organization founded in 1911
Mission: Provides food and services to the needy in Winnipeg.
Chief Officer(s):
Joel Cormie, Operations Manager
Staff Member(s): 3
Activities: Operates a soup kitchen; distributes clothing to the needy

La Ligue canadienne de compositeurs *See* Canadian League of Composers

Ligue canadienne de football *See* Canadian Football League

Ligue de dards Ungava
331, 2e Rue, Chibougamau QC G8P 1M4
Tél: 418-748-8060
Aperçu: *Dimension:* petite; *Envergure:* locale
Membre(s) du bureau directeur:
Claude Patoine, Président

Ligue de sécurité de l'Ontario *See* Ontario Safety League

Ligue des cadets de l'air du Canada *See* Air Cadet League of Canada

Ligue des cadets de l'armée du Canada *See* Army Cadet League of Canada

Ligue des droits de la personne de B'nai Brith Canada *See* League for Human Rights of B'nai Brith Canada

La Ligue des Noirs du Québec *See* Black Coalition of Québec

Ligue des propriétaires de Montréal / Property Owners League of Montréal
8565, rue St-Denis, Montréal QC H2P 2H4
Tél: 514-381-1182; *Téléc:* 514-381-2214
Ligne sans frais: 888-381-1182
ligue@liguedesproprietaires.ca
www.liguedesproprietaires.ca
Aperçu: *Dimension:* petite; *Envergure:* locale; Organisme sans but lucratif; fondée en 1921
Mission: Promouvoir les droits des propriétaires d'immeuble de logements locatifs
Membre(s) du bureau directeur:
Pierre Aubry, Président, 514-381-1182
Jeanne-Mance Calvé, Secretariat
Membre: *Montant de la cotisation:* Barème; *Critères d'admissibilite:* Être propriétaire d'un immeuble à logements locatifs
Activités: *Bibliothèque* Bibliothèque publique

Ligue La Leche Canada *See* La Leche League Canada

Ligue Monarchiste du Canada *See* Monarchist League of Canada

Ligue navale du Canada ***See*** Navy League of Canada

Ligue pour le bien-être de l'enfance du Canada ***See*** Child Welfare League of Canada

Ligue trotskyste du Canada ***See*** Trotskyist League of Canada

Likely & District Chamber of Commerce
PO Box 29, Likely BC V0L 1N0
Tel: 250-790-2127; *Fax:* 250-790-2323
chamber@likely-bc.ca
www.likely-bc.ca
Overview: A small local organization founded in 1965
Member of: BC Chamber of Commerce
Finances: *Annual Operating Budget:* Less than $50,000; *Funding Sources:* Fundraising
Membership: 50; *Fees:* $10-$25; $100 corporate; *Member Profile:* Business & community members; *Committees:* Community Forest; Community School; Likely Cemetary; Seniors; Likely Community Hall

Lillooet & District Chamber of Commerce
PO Box 650, Lillooet BC V0K 1V0
Tel: 250-256-3578; *Fax:* 250-256-4882
info@lillooetchamberofcommerce.com
www.lillooetchamberofcommerce.com
Overview: A small local organization
Chief Officer(s):
Scott Hutchinson, President
Staff Member(s): 2
Membership: 87

Lillooet Food Bank
PO Box 2170, 357 Main St., Lillooet BC V0K 1V0
Tel: 250-256-4146; *Fax:* 250-256-7928
lillooetfriendshipcentre.org
Overview: A small local organization overseen by Food Banks British Columbia
Mission: Provides food to the needy in the Lillooet area.
Member of: Food Banks British Columbia
Chief Officer(s):
Justin Kane, Contact

Lillooet Tribal Council
PO Box 1420, 80 Seton Lake Rd., Lillooet BC V0K 1V0
Tel: 250-256-7523; *Fax:* 250-256-7119
lillooet_tribal_council@yahoo.ca
Overview: A small local organization
Chief Officer(s):
Susan James, Data Provider
Membership: *Member Profile:* Bridge River Indian Band; Cayoose Creek Band; Mount Currie Band Council; Seton Lake Band; T'it'q'et Administration; Ts'kw'aylaxw First Nation

Limestone Beekeepers Guild
c/o Bill Lake, 2712 Round Lake Rd., Battersea ON K0H 1H0
Tel: 613-353-6768
betsybhoney@hotmail.com
www3.sympatico.ca/lovegrove1//bees/index.htm
Previous Name: Harrowsmith Beekeepers Guild
Overview: A small local organization founded in 1987
Mission: To promote apiculture in the Kingston, Ontario region; To provide education about beekeeping
Member of: Ontario Beekeepers' Association
Chief Officer(s):
Bill Lake, President, 613-353-6768
Membership: *Fees:* $15 individuals; $20 families; *Member Profile:* Beekeepers from Kingston & area, with one to several hundred hives
Activities: Organizing meetings with guest speakers; Hosting an annual honey contest; Supporting the Ontario Bee Research Fund; *Speaker Service:* Yes
Publications:
- Bee Space: The Limestone Beekeepers Guild Newsletter
Type: Newsletter
Profile: Guild information, including upcoming meetings & honey contests

Lincoln Chamber of Commerce
PO Box 493, 4961 King St., #T2, Beamsville ON L0R 1B0
Tel: 905-563-5044; *Fax:* 905-563-7098
info@lincolnchamber.ca
www.lincolnchamber.ca
www.facebook.com/LCOCbusiness
twitter.com/LCOCbusiness
Overview: A small local organization
Chief Officer(s):
Cathy McNiven, Office Manager

Lincoln County Humane Society
160 - 4th Ave., St Catharines ON L2S 0B6
Tel: 905-682-0767; *Fax:* 905-682-8133
myconnect@lchs.ca
www.lchs.ca
Overview: A small local charitable organization founded in 1927
Mission: Cruelty investigation & prosecution; animal rescue & protection; to promote humane treatment of animals; to provide shelter to animals & pet therapy
Affliation(s): Ontario Humane Society
Chief Officer(s):
Kevin Strooband, Executive Director
Finances: *Funding Sources:* Regional government

Lincoln County Law Association
59 Church St., St Catharines ON L2R 3C3
Tel: 905-685-9094; *Fax:* 905-685-0981
Toll-Free: 866-637-6829
library@thelcla.ca
Overview: A small local organization
Mission: To provide information for lawyers practicing in the Niagara North area
Chief Officer(s):
Keith Newell, Librarian
Membership: 220 individual

Lindsay & District Chamber of Commerce
20 Lindsay St. South, Lindsay ON K9V 2L6
Tel: 705-324-2393; *Fax:* 705-324-2473
info@lindsaychamber.com
www.lindsaychamber.com
www.facebook.com/lindsay.chamber
twitter.com/LDChamber
Overview: A medium-sized local organization
Chief Officer(s):
Ann Gibbons, President
Gayle Jones, General Manager
gayle@lindsaychamber.com
Membership: *Fees:* Schedule available; *Committees:* Advocacy; Audit; Executive; Membership; Programs & Events; Policy Review; Kawartha Lakes Associated Chambers of Commerce

Lindsay & District Real Estate Board ***See*** Kawartha Lakes Real Estate Association

Lions Eye Bank of Manitoba & Northwest Ontario, Incorporated
320 Sherbrook St., Winnipeg MB R3B 2W6
Tel: 204-772-1899; *Fax:* 204-943-6823
Toll-Free: 800-552-6820
lfmnoi@mts.net
www.eyebankmanitoba.com
Overview: A small provincial charitable organization founded in 1984
Mission: To maintain professional staff to procure, process, & distribute human donor eye tissue for surgical transplantation in recipients of Manitoba & Norhwest Ontario
Member of: Eye Bank Association of America
Affiliation(s): Lions Eye Bank
Staff Member(s): 1; 2 volunteer(s)
Membership: *Member Profile:* Lions clubs of Manitoba & northwestern Ontario; *Committees:* Funding Assistance; Awards; Fundraising
Activities: Increasing public awareness; Arranging funding assistance; *Awareness Events:* Eye Bank Awareness Week, November
Awards:
- Stew Peever Memorial Award (Award)

Lions Foundation of Canada
152 Wilson St., Oakville ON L6J 5E8
Tel: 905-842-2891; *Fax:* 905-842-3373
Toll-Free: 800-768-3030; *TTY:* 905-842-1585
info@dogguides.com
www.dogguides.com
www.facebook.com/LFCDogGuides
twitter.com/LFCDogGuides
Overview: A small national charitable organization founded in 1983
Mission: To provide service to physically challenged Canadians in the areas of mobility, safety & independence
Affliation(s): Lions Clubs of Canada
Chief Officer(s):
Sandy Turney, Executive Director
sandyturney@dogguides.com
Julie Jelinek, Director of Development
Finances: *Annual Operating Budget:* $3 Million-$5 Million; *Funding Sources:* Donations; fundraising; gift shop
Staff Member(s): 40
Activities: Canine Vision Canada; Hearing Ear Dogs of Canada; Special Skills Dogs of Canada; *Awareness Events:* Walk for Dog Guides; *Speaker Service:* Yes

Lions Gate Hospice Society ***See*** North Shore Hospice Society

Lions Gate Hospital Foundation
231 East 15th St., North Vancouver BC V7L 2L7
Tel: 604-984-5785; *Fax:* 604-984-5786
info@lghfoundation.com
www.lghfoundation.com
www.facebook.com/lghfoundation
twitter.com/LGHFoundation
Overview: A small local charitable organization
Mission: To help raise money on behalf of 10 health care centres to fund research & improve patient care
Chief Officer(s):
Judy Savage, President
judy.savage@vch.ca
Finances: *Annual Operating Budget:* Greater than $5 Million
Staff Member(s): 8

Lions Quest Canada - The Centre for Positive Youth Development
#1, 427 Elgin St. North, Cambridge ON N1R 8G4
Tel: 519-624-1170; *Fax:* 519-624-3354
Toll-Free: 800-265-2680
qbear@lionsquest.ca
www.lionsquest.ca
Overview: A medium-sized national organization founded in 1988
Mission: To provide leadership, knowledge and resources to develop capable young Canadians of positive character.
Chief Officer(s):
Joanne McQuiggan, Executive Director
Finances: *Funding Sources:* Private sponsorship
Staff Member(s): 3

Listowel Chamber of Commerce ***See*** North Perth Chamber of Commerce

Literacy Alberta
3060 - 17 Ave. SW, Calgary AB T3E 7G8
Tel: 403-410-6990; *Fax:* 403-410-9024
Toll-Free: 800-410-6584
office@literacyalberta.ca
www.literacyalberta.ca
www.linkedin.com/company/1511757
www.facebook.com/literacyalberta
twitter.com/literacyalberta
Previous Name: Literacy Co-ordinators of Alberta
Overview: A small provincial charitable organization founded in 2003
Mission: To support people involved in literacy activities; to influence public policy on literacy issues
Member of: Movement for Canadian Literacy
Chief Officer(s):
Phillip Hoffmann, Executive Director
Staff Member(s): 10
Membership: 300+; *Fees:* $5 student; $50 individual; $150 small organization; $250 large organization; *Member Profile:* Literacy program coordinators, tutors, students, professionals & general public
Activities: To conceive & administrate projects that provide funding, resources & professional development opportunities for literacy programs in Alberta; *Speaker Service:* Yes; *Library:* Literacy Alberta Library; Open to public by appointment
Awards:
- Literacy Awards of Excellence (Award)

Literacy Alliance of West Nipissing
210 Holditch St., Sturgeon Falls ON P2B 1S6
Tel: 705-753-0537; *Fax:* 705-753-7942
yes2literacy.ca
www.facebook.com/1406891759532704
Previous Name: Sturgeon Falls Literacy Alliance
Overview: A small local organization
Mission: To provide free service to adults in the West Nipissing area who wish assistance in upgrading their English literacy skills
Chief Officer(s):

Isabel Mosseler, Contact
Finances: *Funding Sources:* National government
Staff Member(s): 1; 15 volunteer(s)
Membership: 9 institutional; 10 student; 15 individual
Activities: Workshops; literary events

Literacy Central Vancouver Island

19 Commercial St., Nanaimo BC V9R 5G3
Tel: 250-754-8988; *Fax:* 250-754-8114
info@literacycentralvi.org
www.literacynanaimo.org
www.facebook.com/literacycentralvi
Also Known As: Literacy Central VI
Previous Name: Nanaimo Literacy Association
Overview: A small local charitable organization founded in 1990
Mission: To promote literacy for all individuals
Member of: Literacy BC
Affliation(s): National Adult Literacy Database
Chief Officer(s):
Rebecca Kirk, Cheif Executive Officer
Staff Member(s): 8; 200 volunteer(s)
Activities: Volunteer Tutor Program; Computer Recycling Program; Computer learning centre; Used book store; Book fair; Community access internet site; Adult learning centre; *Library:* Tutor Resource Centre; Open to public by appointment

Literacy Coalition of New Brunswick (LCNB) / Coalition pour l'alphabétisme du Nouveau-Brunswick

921 College Hill Rd., Fredericton NB E3B 6Z9
Tel: 506-457-1227; *Fax:* 506-458-1352
Toll-Free: 800-563-2211
lcnb@nb.literacy.ca
www.nb.literacy.ca
www.facebook.com/35154741794
twitter.com/LiteracyNB
www.youtube.com/channel/UCfeWUS_xRj6Fm5lWviK61iA
Previous Name: New Brunswick Coalition for Literacy
Overview: A small provincial charitable organization founded in 1988
Mission: To increase literacy in partnership with others; to maintain &/or extend network of NB Literacy groups & stakeholders; to increase public understanding of the literacy issue & its impact on every facet of society; to facilitate & mobilize activities which will result in opportunites for higher levels of literacy among the people of New Brunswick
Member of: Movement for Canadian Literacy
Affliation(s): National Adult Literacy Database, Frontier College, ABC Canada, Laubach Literacy New Brunswick, Literacy New Brunswick Inc., La Fédération d'alphbétisation du Nouveau-Brunswick, Provincial Partners for Literacy; Learning Disabilities Association of New Brunswick
Chief Officer(s):
Natasha Bozek, Executive Director
natasha@nb.literacy.ca
Finances: *Annual Operating Budget:* $250,000-$500,000; *Funding Sources:* National Literacy Secretariat; corporate donations
Staff Member(s): 2
Membership: *Member Profile:* Persons with a high interest in promoting, supporting & delivering literacy services; family, adult & workplace; *Committees:* Executive; Family Literacy & Lifelong Learning; Adult/Workplace Literacy & Essential Skills; Communications & Government Relations
Activities: Refer learners to programs; collection & distribution of new & used reading materials for adults & children; promote literacy through television & radio campaigns; continue to form partnerships with groups which have an interest in literacy; continue to build a literacy "community"; participate in policy discussions provincially & nationally; *Awareness Events:* Peter Gzowski Invitational Golf Tournament, May

Literacy Co-ordinators of Alberta *See* Literacy Alberta

Literacy Council of Brantford & District

173 Colborne St., Brantford ON N3T 2G8
Tel: 519-758-1664; *Fax:* 519-758-9394
info-literacy@bfree.on.ca
Overview: A small local charitable organization founded in 1984
Mission: To teach adults & older youth who request help in learning to read, to write & to understand numbers
Member of: Laubach Literacy of Canada, Ontario
Chief Officer(s):
Lori Bruner, Executive Director
lbruner-literacy@bfree.on.ca
Finances: *Annual Operating Budget:* $50,000-$100,000
Staff Member(s): 3; 88 volunteer(s)
Membership: 1-99

The Literacy Council of Burlington

Upper Canada Place, #21, 460 Brant St., Burlington ON L7R 4B6
Tel: 905-631-1770; *Fax:* 905-631-5533
info@literacycouncil.ca
www.literacycouncil.ca
Overview: A small local charitable organization founded in 1980
Mission: To assist adults in Burlington, Ontario to improve their quality of life, by offering individual tutoring & small classes in reading, writing, mathematics, & computer literacy
Member of: Employment Ontario; Laubach Literacy of Ontario; Peel-Halton-Dufferin Adult Learning Network
Chief Officer(s):
Janet Campbell, Executive Director
janet@literacycouncil.ca
Kathy Hall, Manager, Skills Training
kathy@literacycouncil.ca
Tina Koschate, Case Manager
tina@literacycouncil.ca
Eileen Neale-Attzs, Group Instructor
eileen@literacycouncil.ca
Finances: *Funding Sources:* Ministry of Training, Colleges & Universities; Donations
Membership: *Fees:* $5

Literacy Council of Durham Region (LCDR)

115 Simcoe St. South, 2nd Fl., Oshawa ON L1H 4G7
Tel: 905-434-5441; *Fax:* 905-725-6015
lcdr@bellnet.ca
www.literacydurham.ca
Overview: A small local charitable organization
Mission: To tutor adults to read & write in the Durham region; to recruit & train adult volunteers to become literacy tutors
Member of: Laubach Literacy of Canada - Ontario
Chief Officer(s):
Brad Cook, Executive Director
Finances: *Annual Operating Budget:* $50,000-$100,000; *Funding Sources:* Ministry of Training, Colleges & Universities
Staff Member(s): 1; 100 volunteer(s)
Membership: 1-99
Activities: *Speaker Service:* Yes

Literacy Council of Lincoln *See* Niagara West Employment & Learning Resource Centres

Literacy Council York-Simcoe (LCYS)

#15, 1100 Gorham St., Newmarket ON L3Y 8Y8
Tel: 905-853-6279; *Fax:* 905-836-7323
info@lcys.ca
www.lcys.ca
www.facebook.com/LCYorkS
twitter.com/LCYorkS
Overview: A small local charitable organization founded in 1987
Mission: To promote adult literacy in York Region & South Simcoe & provide a free tutoring service; to recruit & train volunteer tutors to help non-literate adults become fully functioning members of our community
Affliation(s): Laubach Literacy International; Laubach Literacy of Canada; Laubach Literacy Ontario; Newmarket Chamber of Commerce; Community Literacy of Ontario; Ontario Literacy Coalition
Chief Officer(s):
Trisha Patrick, Executive Director
trishap@lcys.ca
Natalie Cholewa, Coordinator, Learning
nataliec@lcys.ca
Finances: *Funding Sources:* Provincial government; fundraising
Staff Member(s): 6
Membership: *Fees:* $15
Activities: *Speaker Service:* Yes; *Library* by appointment

The Literacy Group of Waterloo Region

#1, 89 Main St., Cambridge ON N1R 1W1
Tel: 519-621-7993; *Fax:* 519-621-1145
Cambridge@theliteracygroup.com
www.theliteracygroup.com
www.facebook.com/323565181054788
Previous Name: Cambridge Literacy Council; Literacy Council of Kitchener-Waterloo
Overview: A small local charitable organization founded in 1980
Mission: To improve basic reading, writing & math skills of adults (16 years of age & older) in our community by providing trained volunteers & staff & to help students meet their goals
Member of: Laubach Literacy of Canada; Laubauch Literacy Ontario; Ontario Literacy Coalition; Community Literacy Ontario; Project Read Literacy Network
Chief Officer(s):
Carol Risidore, Executive Director
carol@theliteracygroup.com
Finances: *Annual Operating Budget:* $250,000-$500,000
Staff Member(s): 7; 150 volunteer(s)
Membership: 150; *Fees:* $20; *Committees:* Program Development; Community Relations; Executive; Programming
Activities: *Awareness Events:* International Literacy Day, Sept.; *Speaker Service:* Yes

Kitchener Branch
#200, 151 Frederick St., Kitchener ON N2H 2M2
Tel: 519-743-6090; *Fax:* 519-743-0474
Kitchener@theliteracygroup.com
Chief Officer(s):
Carol Risidore, Executive Director

Literacy Link South Central (LLSC)

255 Horton St., 3rd Fl., London ON N6B 1L1
Tel: 519-681-7307; *Fax:* 519-681-7310
Toll-Free: 800-561-6896
literacylink@bellnet.ca
www.llsc.on.ca
Previous Name: Southwestern Ontario Adult Literacy Network
Overview: A small local charitable organization founded in 1991
Mission: To support all literacy programs equally & inclusively, respecting diversities in service delivery based on their individual community needs in counties of Brant, Haldimand/Norfolk, Elgin, Middlesex & Oxford
Member of: Ontario Literacy Coalition; Community Literacy of Ontario; London Council for Adult Education
Chief Officer(s):
Tamara Kaattari, Executive Director
Finances: *Annual Operating Budget:* $100,000-$250,000
Staff Member(s): 4
Membership: 15; *Fees:* $20 individual voting & non-voting; $40 organizational; *Member Profile:* Literacy programs; adult educators; employment service organizations; youth service organizations
Activities: Provide ongoing support for literacy agencies to deliver quality programming; support lifelong learning through a variety of community planning activities; enchance communication among literacy deliverers & funders; participate in the regional plan for information & referral services; support literacy initiatives through regional coordination of training; coordinate & manage literacy development projects; educate the public about literacy; network/link with other regional, provincial & national organizations; *Awareness Events:* Literacy Awareness Workshops; Clear Writing Workshops

Literacy New Brunswick Inc. (LNBI) / Alphabétisation Nouveau-Brunswick Inc.

#400, 500 Beaverbrook Crt Suite 400, Fredericton NB E3B 5X4
Tel: 506-457-7323
Overview: A small provincial charitable organization founded in 1991
Mission: To marshall the full resources of New Brunswick to increase literacy by bringing learning to the people through partnerships with government, communities, the voluntary & private sectors
Chief Officer(s):
Lillian Linton, Chair
Maryanne Bourgeois, Executive Director
Daniel Coulombe, Treasurer
Staff Member(s): 12; 1 volunteer(s)

Literacy Nova Scotia (LNS)

NSCC Truro Campus, Forrester Hall, PO Box 1516, #125, 36 Arthur St., Truro NS B2N 5V2
Tel: 902-897-2444; *Fax:* 902-897-4020
Toll-Free: 800-255-5203
literacyns@nscc.ca
www.ns.literacy.ca
www.facebook.com/LiteracyNovaScotia
twitter.com/literacyns1
www.youtube.com/LiteracyNS
Previous Name: Nova Scotia Provincial Literacy Coalition
Overview: A small provincial organization founded in 1992
Mission: To provide Nova Scotians with access to literacy, skills, & learning opportunities
Chief Officer(s):
Marlene Duckworth, Chair
queenslearning@ns.aliantzinc.ca
Jayne Hunter, Executive Director

Membership: *Fees:* $5 individual; $50 organizational; *Committees:* Executive; NS PGI; PGI Grant Selection; Scholarship/Bursary
Activities: *Awareness Events:* International Literacy Day, Sept.; The Word On The Street Halifax, Sept.; Literacy Action Week, Nov.
Awards:
• Learner Recognition Awards (Award)
Publications:
• Literacy Nova Scotia News
Type: Newsletter

Literacy Ontario Central South (LOCS)
#203, 113 Park St. South, Peterborough ON K9J 3R8
Tel: 705-749-0675; *Fax:* 705-749-1883
www.locs.on.ca
www.facebook.com/179735928825157
twitter.com/LOCSLiteracy
Overview: A small local organization founded in 1990
Mission: To serve literacy programs in the counties of Haliburton, Northumberland, Peterborough, Renfrew & the City of Kawartha Lakes
Affliation(s): Ontario Literacy Coalition
Chief Officer(s):
Joan Connolly, Executive Director
joan@locs.on.ca
Finances: *Funding Sources:* National & provincial government
Staff Member(s): 3; 6 volunteer(s)
Activities: Literacy programs; information & referral; resources & reference material

Literacy Partners of Manitoba (LPM) / Les Partenaires en alphabétisation du Manitoba (LPAM)
#401, 321 McDermot Ave., Winnipeg MB R3A 0A3
Tel: 204-947-5757; *Fax:* 204-956-9315
Toll-Free: 866-947-5757
literacy@mb.literacy.ca
www.mb.literacy.ca
Overview: A small provincial charitable organization founded in 1987
Mission: To promote literacy in Manitoba
Member of: Movement for Canadian Literacy
Affliation(s): ABC Canada; Canadian Libary Association; National Adult Literacy Database
Chief Officer(s):
Wendy Bulloch, Executive Director
wbulloch@mb.literacy.ca
Finances: *Annual Operating Budget:* $250,000-$500,000
Staff Member(s): 7; 30 volunteer(s)
Membership: 320; *Fees:* $5 student/senior; $40 individual; *Member Profile:* Practitioners; tutors; learners; business supporters; *Committees:* Executive; Finance & Administration; Operations, Services & Programs; Resource Development; Public Relations; Nominating
Activities: Public awareness; advocacy; member networking & professional development; LEARN Helpline; learners circle; PGI Golf Tournament; *Awareness Events:* International Literacy Day, Jan. 27; Family Literacy Day; *Library:* Resource Centre; Open to public
Awards:
• Community Partnership Award (Award)

Interlake Region
PO Box 394, Stn. Group 346, R.R. 3, Selkirk MB R1A 2A8
Tel: 204-482-6248
carol_gossen@hotmail.com
Chief Officer(s):
Carol Goossen, Coordinator

Northern Region
PO Box 714, Thompson MB R8N 1N5
Tel: 204-677-2872; *Fax:* 204-677-5008
www.nald.ca/litpman.htm
Chief Officer(s):
Wendy Lindblad, Coordinator

Western Region
Box 22076, Brandon MB R7A 6Y9
Tel: 204-727-1407
alanna_hillis@elit.ca
Chief Officer(s):
Alanna Hillis, Coordinator

Literacy Partners of Québec
4855 Kensington Ave., Montréal QC H3X 3S6
Tel: 514-369-7962; *Fax:* 514-489-5302
jbrandeis@nald.ca
www.nald.ca/lpq.htm
Overview: A small provincial charitable organization founded in 1992
Member of: Movement for Canadian Literacy
Chief Officer(s):
Judy Brandeis, Executive Director
Finances: *Annual Operating Budget:* $50,000-$100,000; *Funding Sources:* National Literacy Secretariat
Staff Member(s): 3; 9 volunteer(s)
Membership: 35; *Fees:* $50
Activities: Research; public awareness; operates LEARN line for referrals; professional development

Literacy Society of South Muskoka Inc. (LSSM)
#690, 2 Muskoka Rd. South, Gravenhurst ON P1P 1K2
Tel: 705-687-9323; *Fax:* 705-687-2020
Toll-Free: 800-293-9020
lssm@bellnet.ca
www.literacysocietysouthmuskoka.org
Overview: A small local charitable organization founded in 1982
Mission: To provide one-to-one literacy training & small group tutoring; to promote awareness of literacy
Member of: Simcoe Literacy Network; Ontario Literacy Coalition; Community Literacy of Ontario
Affliation(s): Laubach Literacy of Ontario; Laubach Literacy Canada
Chief Officer(s):
Gail Oakley, President
Finances: *Annual Operating Budget:* $50,000-$100,000; *Funding Sources:* Provincial government
Staff Member(s): 2; 35 volunteer(s)
Membership: 50; *Fees:* $10 individual
Activities: Family literacy; ESL tutoring; one-to-one tutoring; small groups tutoring; *Awareness Events:* Tee-off for Literacy, Labour Day Weekend

Literacy Volunteers of Quebec (LVQ)
#230A, 1001 Lenoir St., Montréal QC H4C 2Z6
Tel: 514-508-6805; *Fax:* 514-508-4985
Toll-Free: 855-890-1587
info@literacyvolunteersquebec.org
www.literacyquebec.org
www.facebook.com/pages/Literacy-Volunteers-of-Quebec/20575 0747010
Overview: A medium-sized provincial organization founded in 1980
Mission: A coalition of volunteer groups offering literacy services to the Anglophone population of Quebec.
Chief Officer(s):
Margo Legault, Executive Director
margolegault@literacyvolunteersquebec.org
Staff Member(s): 3
Membership: 13; *Fees:* $50; *Member Profile:* Literacy organizations

Literary & Historical Society of Québec (LHSQ) / Société littéraire et historique de Québec
44 Chaussée des Écossais, Québec QC G1R 4H3
Tel: 418-694-9147; *Fax:* 418-694-0754
info@morrin.org
www.morrin.org
Overview: A small provincial charitable organization founded in 1824
Mission: To preserve, develop & share the diverse cultural life of the Québec City region's English-speaking community through innovative, responsive & effective services
Member of: Heritage Canada Foundation; Champlain Society; Québec Anglophone Heritage Network
Chief Officer(s):
Barry McCullough, Executive Director
barrymccullough@morrin.org
Staff Member(s): 7
Membership: *Fees:* $20 student; $45 individual; $60 family; $100 friend of LHSQ; $250 corporate
Activities: Lectures; courses (poetry, social history); readings; bake sale; raffle; *Library* Open to public

The Literary Press Group of Canada (LPG)
#501, 192 Spadina Ave., Toronto ON M5T 2C2
Tel: 416-483-1321; *Fax:* 416-483-2510
info@lpg.ca
www.lpg.ca
Overview: A medium-sized national organization founded in 1976
Mission: A not-for-profit association of Canadian literary book publishers, with a mandate to advocate on behalf of its members, & to foster the survival, growth & maintenance of strong Canadian-owned & controlled literary book publishing houses
Member of: Book & Periodical Council
Affliation(s): Association of Canadian Publishers
Chief Officer(s):
Jack Illingworth, Executive Director Ext. 1
Petra Morin, Sales & Marketing Manager
Finances: *Annual Operating Budget:* $500,000-$1.5 Million; *Funding Sources:* Membership fees & commissions; federal & provincial grants
Staff Member(s): 8; 7 volunteer(s)
Membership: 51 corporate; *Fees:* $450; *Member Profile:* Minimum requirements: 5 books in print; 80% Canadian owned; in business at least 2 years; 50% of books in categories of fiction, poetry, literary criticism, drama or creative non-fiction or juvenile/young adult literature
Activities: Cooperative sales & marketing projects

Literary Translators' Association of Canada (LTAC) / Association des traducteurs et traductrices littéraires du Canada (ATTLC)
Concordia University LB 601, 1455 Maisonneuve Blvd. West, Montréal QC H3G 1M8
Tel: 514-848-2424
info@attlc-ltac.org
www.attlc-ltac.org
www.facebook.com/111956408910924
Overview: A small national organization founded in 1975
Mission: To promote literary translation & interests of literary translators.
Member of: Fédération internationale des Traducteurs
Chief Officer(s):
Nicola Danby, President
Finances: *Funding Sources:* Membership dues; Canada Council
Membership: *Fees:* $130 full; $60 associate; $25 student; *Member Profile:* Canadian citizen or landed immigrant; published one book-length work of literary translation or equivalent
Activities: Brings together Canadian translators of literature (fiction, non-fiction, film, theatre, poetry, juvenile); provides members with sample contracts; lobbies & liaises with cultural & government agencies & literary associations
Awards:
• Glassco Translation Prize (Award)
Awarded annually for a translator's first work in book-length literary translation into French or English, published in Canada during the previous calendar year*Deadline:* June *Amount:* $1,000 & one year's membership in the association

The Lithuanian Canadian Community / La Communauté lithuanienne du Canada
1 Resurrection Rd., Toronto ON M9A 5G1
Tel: 416-533-3292; *Fax:* 416-533-2282
info@klb.org
www.klb.org
Overview: A medium-sized national organization founded in 1952 overseen by Baltic Federation in Canada
Mission: To promote, maintain, & encourage the survival of the Lithuanian culture & language in Canada & abroad
Member of: Canadian Ethnocultural Council
Chief Officer(s):
Joana Kuraite-Lasiene, President
Membership: *Member Profile:* Some Lithuanian heritage

Lithuanian Community Association of Toronto
1573 Bloor St. West, Toronto ON M6P 1A6
Tel: 416-955-4810; *Fax:* 416-532-4745
Other Communication: Alternate Phone: 416-532-3311
litn@rogers.com
www.lithuanianbanquethalls.ca
www.facebook.com/LithuanianBanquetHalls
Also Known As: Lithuanian House
Overview: A small local organization founded in 1952
Mission: To promote, support & fund Lithuanian organizations
Affliation(s): Labdara Foundation
Membership: 1,000-4,999

The Lithuanian Society of Edmonton
11629 - 83 St., Edmonton AB T5B 2Y7
Tel: 780-474-0350
Overview: A small local organization founded in 1953
Affliation(s): Lithuanian Canadian Community
Finances: *Annual Operating Budget:* Less than $50,000; *Funding Sources:* Membership fees; shares; donations
Membership: 100

Lithuanian-Canadian Foundation (LCF)
1 Resurrection Rd., Toronto ON M9A 5G1
Tel: 416-889-5531

Overview: A small national charitable organization

Little Bits Therapeutic Riding Association

PO Box 29016, Stn. Lendrum, Edmonton AB T6H 5Z6
Tel: 780-476-1233; *Fax:* 780-476-7252
info@littlebits.ca
www.littlebits.ca
www.facebook.com/LittleBitsVolunteers
Overview: A small local charitable organization founded in 1978
Mission: To provide recreational riding programs that have therapeutic benefits for disabled children & adults in Edmonton & surrounding area
Member of: Central Canadian Therapeutic Riding Association; North American Riding for the Handicapped Association
Chief Officer(s):
Linda Rault, Riding Administrator
200 volunteer(s)
Membership: 200; *Fees:* $15; *Committees:* Finance; Fundraising; Public Relations; Riding Program; Camp Horseshoe

Little Brothers of the Good Shepherd / Petits Frères du Bon-Pasteur

Good Shepherd Centre, PO Box 1003, 10 Delaware Ave., Hamilton ON L8N 3R1
Tel: 905-572-6435; *Fax:* 905-528-6967
info@goodshepherdcentres.ca
www.goodshepherdcentres.ca
www.facebook.com/goodshepherdhamilton
twitter.com/goodshepherdham
Overview: A small local charitable organization founded in 1951
Chief Officer(s):
Richard MacPhee, Executive Director
Finances: *Annual Operating Budget:* $500,000-$1.5 Million
Activities: Housing for battered women & children; residence for homeless youth; men's hostel; food bank & food line; speakers on topics dealing with violence & abuse; *Speaker Service:* Yes

Little Burgundy Sports Centre *See* Centre Sportif de la Petite Bourgogne

Little Faces of Panama Association

#1202, 2177 Sherobee Rd., Mississauga ON L5A 3G9
Tel: 647-262-2353
www.littlefacesofpanama-association.com
www.facebook.com/littlefacesofpanama
Overview: A small local organization
Mission: To promote the culture of Panama and raise funds for impoverished children in the country
Chief Officer(s):
Waldy Marcucci, President, Board of Directors
Activities: Carnival; Dance recitals

Little League Canada / Petite ligue Canada

235 Dale Ave., Ottawa ON K1G 0H6
Tel: 613-731-3301; *Fax:* 613-731-2829
Other Communication: media@littleleague.ca
canada@littleleague.org
www.littleleague.ca
www.facebook.com/pages/Little-League-Baseball-Canada/1375 89529592785
twitter.com/LittleLgeCanada
www.youtube.com/DugoutTheMascot
Overview: A large national charitable organization founded in 1951
Mission: To provide baseball & softball programs to every boy or girl wishing to participate
Member of: Little League Baseball International
Chief Officer(s):
Roy Bergerman, President & Chair
rbergerman@littleleague.ca
Joe Shea, Regional Director
Wendy Thomson, Assistant Regional Director
Finances: *Funding Sources:* Membership dues; corporate
Staff Member(s): 2
Membership: 35,000
Publications:
• The 7th Inning Stretch
Type: Newsletter

Little People of Manitoba (LPM)

4 Lakepoint Rd., Winnipeg MB R3T 4R4
Tel: 204-226-0110
www.lpmanitoba.ca
Overview: A small provincial charitable organization founded in 1981
Mission: Dedicated to helping people of small stature become useful members of society through education, employment and social adjustment, and to focus public attention to the fact that the magnitude of any physical limitation is a function of attitude of both the small and the average-sized person and desire to assist in these matters.
Chief Officer(s):
Connie Magalhaes, President
Finances: *Annual Operating Budget:* Less than $50,000
25 volunteer(s)
Membership: 60; *Fees:* $25 family; $15 single
Activities: Monthly meetings; socials; fundraising

Little People of Ontario (LPO)

PO Box 43058, 4841 Yonge St., Toronto ON M2N 6N1
e-mail: lpo@bfree.on.ca
www.lpo.on.ca
Overview: A small provincial organization founded in 1965
Mission: The organization provides fellowship, support & information to people of short stature, their families & friends, & raises awareness about dwarfism
Chief Officer(s):
Sue Berzins, President
Finances: *Annual Operating Budget:* Less than $50,000
6 volunteer(s)
Membership: 100; *Fees:* $25 single; $35 family; $15 newsletter subscription
Activities: Social events; newsletter; education; *Library*

Living Bible Explorers (LBE)

600 Burnell St., Winnipeg MB R3G 2B7
Tel: 204-786-8667; *Fax:* 204-775-7525
Toll-Free: 866-786-8667
lbe@mymts.net
livingbibleexplorers.com
www.facebook.com/livingbibleexplorers
Overview: A small local charitable organization founded in 1969
Mission: To develop relationships with children & teens from inner city homes in an effort to evangelize them & to promote discipleship with a view to integrating them into the life & care of Bible-believing churches
Member of: Canadian Council of Christian Charities
Chief Officer(s):
George Hill, General Manager
george_t_hill@hotmail.com
MaryAnn Funk, Girls Program Coordinator
Michelle MacGibbon, Teen Girls Coordinator
Mark Henkleman, Teen Boys Coordinator
Ben Krocker, Childrens Program Coordinator
Diana Cuthbertson, Volunteer Coordinator
Randal Moroski, Ministry Worker
Finances: *Annual Operating Budget:* $250,000-$500,000; *Funding Sources:* Individual and cooperate donations; Provincial government; individual churches; foundations
Staff Member(s): 10; 200 volunteer(s)
Membership: 700 individual; *Member Profile:* Manitobans who have a tangible interest by working, volunteering or giving to the work; *Committees:* New Bible Camp; Board of Directors
Activities: Boys & Girls Clubs; summer camps; weekend camps; weekly kids church; teens church; food distribution; weekly home visitation; annual banquet, Mar. Currently constructing a New Bible Camp for children in Hadoshville, Manitoba.; *Awareness Events:* Mission Fest - Feb; Annual Fundraising Banquet - Mar; Garage Sale - May; *Internships:* Yes; *Speaker Service:* Yes; *Library:* Resource Library;

Living Positive

#50, 9912 - 106 St., Edmonton AB T5K 1C5
Tel: 780-488-5768
livepos@telusplanet.net
www.facebook.com/LivingPoz
Previous Name: Edmonton Persons Living with HIV Society
Overview: A small local charitable organization founded in 1990 overseen by Canadian AIDS Society
Mission: To provide persons living with HIV infection nurturing, supportive environments in which to develop positive attitudes & self image
Member of: Alberta Community Council on HIV
Chief Officer(s):
Randy Sampert, Executive Director
Finances: *Annual Operating Budget:* Less than $50,000; *Funding Sources:* Provincial AIDS Program; Alberta Health
Staff Member(s): 1
Membership: 100-499; *Member Profile:* HIV positive persons & their supporters
Activities: *Awareness Events:* AIDS Walk; *Internships:* Yes; *Speaker Service:* Yes; *Library* Open to public

Living Positive Resource Centre, Okanagan (LPRC)

168 Asher Rd., Kelowna BC V1X 3H6
Tel: 778-753-5830; *Fax:* 778-753-5832
Toll-Free: 800-616-2437
info@lprc.ca
www.livingpositive.ca
www.facebook.com/lprcokanagen
Previous Name: ARC, AIDS Resource Centre, Okanagan & Region
Overview: A small local charitable organization founded in 1992
Mission: To educate & inform the public about HIV/AIDS & hepatitis, its transmission, prevention, treatment & care, providing the most accurate & up-to-date information available; to develop & promote community based partnerships for the delivery of education & support; to dispel the myths & misunderstandings & to promote awareness of the discrimination & marginalization of persons infected & affected by HIV/AIDS & hepatitis & to advocate for change; to advocate & lobby for programs & services, necessary to promote wellness & quality of life of persons infected & affected by HIV/AIDS & hepatitis; to facilitate access to emotional, spiritual, social & practical support for persons infected & affected by HIV/AIDS & hepatitis, respectful of their right to determine the direction of their lives; to provide accessible services in non-judgmental, safe, confidential environments; to identify & seek solutions to existing gaps in services
Member of: Canadian AIDS Society; Pacific AIDS Network
Affliation(s): Central Okanagan Hospice Society; Vernon Hospice; Salmon Arm Hospice; North Okanagan Youth & Family Services; Columbia-Shuswap HIV/AIDS Project; Outreach Health Services
Chief Officer(s):
Clare Overton, Executive Director
coverton@lprc.ca
Finances: *Annual Operating Budget:* $250,000-$500,000; *Funding Sources:* Provincial government; Ministry of Health; fundraising; HRDC
Staff Member(s): 6; 45 volunteer(s)
Membership: 60; *Fees:* $12; *Committees:* Fund Development; Special Events; Board of Directors
Activities: Information & referral telephone service; counselling & education; support groups & wellness workshops; *Awareness Events:* MDS Walk; World AIDS Day; AIDS Walk; Annual Candlelight Vigil; *Speaker Service:* Yes; *Library:* LPRC; Open to public

Livres Canada Books

#504, 1 Nicholas St., Ottawa ON K1N 7B7
Tel: 613-562-2324; *Fax:* 613-562-2329
info@livrescanadabooks.com
www.livrescanadabooks.com
www.facebook.com/groups/108847509155281
Previous Name: Association for the Export of Canadian Books
Overview: A medium-sized international organization founded in 1972
Mission: The association defends the interests of Canadian book publishers by providing market intelligence products and services, information and resources on digital publishing, as well as financial, promotion and logisitical support; the association administers the Foreign Rights Marketing Assistance Program, a component of the Canada Book Fund, as well as mentoring programs and other funding initiatives
Affliation(s): Association of Canadian Publishers; Canadian Publishers Council; Association of Canadian University Presses; Association nationale des éditeurs de livres
Chief Officer(s):
Caroline Fortin, Chair
François Charette, Executive Director
Finances: *Annual Operating Budget:* $3 Million-$5 Million
Staff Member(s): 6
Membership: *Committees:* Export Expertise; Nominating & Governance
Activities: Provides financial assistance to Canadian book publishers through the Export Marketing Assistance Program & the Foreign Rights Marketing Assistance Program; coordinates Canada's collective presence at international book fairs; conducts workshops on foreign markets; provides information on foreign markets & on opportunities for export sales;

Lloydminster & District Fish & Game Association (LDFGA)

PO Box 116, Lloydminster AB T9V 0X9

Tel: 780-875-5100
admin@lloydfishandgame.org
www.lloydfishandgame.org
Overview: A medium-sized local organization founded in 1927
Mission: To advocate for & assist in the conservation & management of fish, wildlife & habitat for the continuing benefit of association members & the general public
Affliation(s): Saskatchewan Wildlife Federation; Alberta Fish & Game Association
Chief Officer(s):
Bill Armstrong, President
Membership: 650; *Fees:* $30
Activities: Recreational hunting & fishing; trout ponds; outdoor rifle range & Pistol Club; archery; gun show

Lloydminster & District United Way
4419 - 52nd Ave., Lloydminster AB T9V 0Y8
Tel: 780-875-3743; *Fax:* 780-875-3793
Other Communication: office@lloydminster.unitedway.ca
luw@telusplanet.net
www.lloydminster.unitedway.ca
Overview: A small local organization overseen by United Way of Canada - Centraide Canada

Lloydminster Agricultural Exhibition Association (LAEA)
PO Box 690, 5521 - 49 Ave., Lloydminster SK S9V 0Y7
Tel: 306-825-5571; *Fax:* 306-825-7017
lloydexh@lloydexh.com
www.lloydexh.com
www.facebook.com/pages/Lloydminster-Exhibition-Association/56114974626
Overview: A small local charitable organization founded in 1904
Mission: Dedicated in continuing to foster and develop the tourism industry of Lloydminster, and providing support to the business, social and cultural sectors of the reason.
Member of: Saskatchewan Association of Agricultural Societies & Exhibitions
Affliation(s): Alberta Association of Agricultural Associations; Canadian Association of Fairs & Exhibitions; International Association of Fairs & Exhibitions
Chief Officer(s):
Michael Sidoryk, Manager
Owen Noble, President
Finances: *Annual Operating Budget:* $1.5 Million-$3 Million
Staff Member(s): 15; 300 volunteer(s)
Membership: 100-499; *Fees:* $10 with $40 on demand
Activities: Agricultural activities; rentals; seminars; livestock sales & shows; social receptions

Lloydminster Chamber of Commerce
4419 - 52 Ave., Lloydminster AB T9V 0Y8
Tel: 780-875-9013; *Fax:* 780-875-0755
contact_lcc@lloydminsterchamber.com
www.lloydminsterchamber.com
www.facebook.com/LloydChamber
twitter.com/LloydChamber
www.youtube.com/user/LloydminsterChamber
Overview: A medium-sized local organization founded in 1934
Mission: To enhance private enterprise in Lloydminster & surrounding area
Member of: Canadian Chamber of Commerce; Alberta Chamber of Commerce; Saskatchewan Chamber of Commerce
Chief Officer(s):
Pat Tenney, Executive Director
Michael Holden, President
Finances: *Funding Sources:* Membership fees; fundraising
Staff Member(s): 7
Membership: 584; *Fees:* Schedule available
Activities: Christmas Preview Trade Show; Business Week; Service with a Smile Program; *Library:* Chamber Reference Library; Open to public
Awards:
• J.A. McLean Memorial (Award)
Amount: $500
• Chamber of Commerce Scholarship (Scholarship)
Amount: $500

Lloydminster Construction Association
4419 - 52 Ave., Lloydminster AB T9V 0Y8
Tel: 780-875-8875; *Fax:* 780-875-8874
lloydca@telusplanet.net
www.lloydconstruction.ca
Overview: A small local organization
Mission: To work on behalf of all companies involved in the construction industry
Member of: Alberta Construction Association; Canadian Construction Association
Affliation(s): Saskatchewan Construction Association
Chief Officer(s):
Dorothy Carson, Executive Director
Staff Member(s): 1; 14 volunteer(s)
Membership: 70; *Fees:* $850-$1050 Full Members; $650 Affiliate; $500 Associate; $500 Bulletin

Lloydminster Early Childhood Intervention Program ***See*** Early Childhood Intervention Program (ECIP) Sask. Inc.

Lloydminster German Heritage Society Inc.
4708 - 49 St., Lloydminster SK S9V 0L8
Tel: 306-825-3177
Overview: A small local organization
Member of: German-Canadian Association of Alberta; Saskatchewan German Council

Lloydminster Interval Home Society
PO Box 1523, Lloydminster SK S9V 1K5
Tel: 780-808-5282; *Fax:* 780-875-0609
lihsi@telusplanet.net
www.intervalhome.ab.ca
Overview: A small local organization founded in 1980
Mission: To provide safe short-term accommodation & supportive counselling for women & their children who are in a family violence or crisis situation
Chief Officer(s):
Angela Rooks-Trotzuk, Executive Director
Finances: *Funding Sources:* Community donations; fundraising; government; Sask Lotteries; United Way
Staff Member(s): 38
Membership: *Fees:* $5

Lloydminster Native Friendship Centre (LNFC)
PO Box 1364, 4602 - 49 Ave., Lloydminster SK S9V 1K4
Tel: 306-825-6558; *Fax:* 306-825-6565
reception@LNFC.org
www.lnfc.org
Overview: A small local charitable organization founded in 1982 overseen by Alberta Native Friendship Centres Association
Mission: To provide services to residents from SK & AB, within an approximate 11 km radius; to promote better understanding & relations between the different cultures within our community; to develop wellness, education, cultural & social programs & activities for children & their families; to promote the well-being & enhancement of quality of life for all people within the community through partnership with community & government agencies; to seek avenues of financial security to ensure viable & sustainable operation
Member of: Alberta Native Friendship Centres Association
Chief Officer(s):
Audrey Parke, President
president@lnfc.org
Staff Member(s): 9; 50 volunteer(s)
Membership: 200; *Fees:* $2; *Member Profile:* Aboriginal & non-Aboriginal of all ages
Activities: Teen & young parent program; extrajudicial sanctions program; day program for youth; planting the seeds of tolerance program; soup & bannock weekly program; skill enhancement & pre-employment preparedness; help n' hand youth centre; Cree conversational classes; young ladies self-esteem program; family craft classes; elder socials; summer day camp for children; healing circles; tutor services; educational opportunities workshops; Métis culture awareness campaign; family dances, drumming & drama; *Awareness Events:* National Aboriginal Day, June 21

Lloydminster Real Estate Board ***See*** Realtors Association of Lloydminster & District

Lloydminster Region Health Foundation (LRHF)
#116, 4910 - 50 St., Lloydminster SK S9V 0Y5
Tel: 306-820-6161
lrhf.ca
www.facebook.com/LloydRHF
Overview: A small local charitable organization founded in 1983
Mission: To help raise money on behalf of 4 health care centres to fund research & improve patient care
Chief Officer(s):
Dave Schneider, Chair

Lloydminster Rock & Gem Club
PO Box 781, Lloydminster AB S9V 1C1
Tel: 306-825-2837
Overview: A small local organization
Member of: Alberta Federation of Rock Clubs
Affliation(s): Gem & Mineral Federation of Canada
Chief Officer(s):
Bert Smith, Contact
Activities: Hosting regular meetings at the Community Services Center in Lloydminster

Lloydminster Society for the Prevention of Cruelty to Animals
PO Box 566, Lloydminster SK S9V 0Y6
Tel: 780-875-2809; *Fax:* 780-875-2819
www.lloydminsterspca.org
www.facebook.com/280509945522
twitter.com/LloydSPCA
Also Known As: Lloydminster & District SPCA
Overview: A small local charitable organization founded in 1972
Mission: To provide shelter & care to unwanted & neglected companion animals; To investigate & enact laws in the prevention of cruelty to animals; To educate the community about the proper care & maintenance of animals towards the goal of reducing the number of unwanted & neglected animals in Lloydminster & area
Member of: Alberta SPCA; Saskatchewan SPCA
Chief Officer(s):
Shelly Zimmerman, Executive Director
execetivedirector@lloydminsterspca.org
Finances: *Annual Operating Budget:* $100,000-$250,000; *Funding Sources:* Donations; fundraising
Staff Member(s): 6; 100 volunteer(s)
Membership: 10
Activities: *Awareness Events:* Dog Jog; Dinner Theatre; Garage Sale

Loaves & Fishes Community Food Bank
1009 Farquhar St., Nanaimo BC V9R 2G2
Tel: 250-754-8347; *Fax:* 250-754-8349
info@nanaimoloavesandfishes.org
www.nanaimoloavesandfishes.org
www.facebook.com/NanLoavesFishes
twitter.com/nanaimofoodbank
Overview: A small local organization founded in 1996 overseen by Food Banks British Columbia
Member of: Food Banks British Columbia
Chief Officer(s):
Peter Sinclair, Executive Director

Local Government Management Association of British Columbia (LGMA)
Central Building, 620 View St., 7th Fl., Victoria BC V8W 1J6
Tel: 250-383-7032; *Fax:* 250-384-4879
Other Communication: editor@lgma.ca (magazine);
ads@lgma.ca
office@lgma.ca
www.lgma.ca
Previous Name: Municipal Officers' Association of British Columbia
Overview: A medium-sized provincial organization founded in 1919
Mission: To promote professional management & leadership excellence in local government; To create awareness of local government officers' roles in the community
Chief Officer(s):
Tom MacDonald, Executive Director, 250-383-7032 Ext. 223, Fax: 250-383-4879
tmacdonald@lgma.ca
Elizabeth Brennan, Coordinator, Internship Program, 250-383-7032 Ext. 231, Fax: 250-383-4879
ebrennan@lgma.ca
Ana Fuller, Coordinator, Program, 250-383-7032 Ext. 227, Fax: 250-383-4879
afuller@lgma.ca
Renee Johansson, Accountant, 250-383-7032, Fax: 250-383-4879
rjohansson@lgma.ca
Finances: *Funding Sources:* Membership dues; Conference fees; Workshop fees; Sponsorships
Membership: *Fees:* $125 retired; $275 regular; $325 affiliate; fee for corporate membership based on number of members; *Member Profile:* Municipal & regional district managers, administrators, clerks, treasurers, & other local government officials in the province of British Columbia; Persons with an interest in local government administration may be affiliate members; *Committees:* Operations & Member Services; Education; Special Initiatives & External Relations; LGMA Policy 004
Activities: Providing educational programs for local government professionals to encourage fellowship & networking; Offering

career transition counselling services; Providing personal pension & retirement planning counselling services for members
Meetings/Conferences: • Local Government Management Association of British Columbia 2015 Annual General Meeting & Conference, June, 2015, Prince George Civic Centre, Prince George, BC
Scope: Provincial
Attendance: 400-500
Description: A meeting & tradeshow held each year in May or June in British Columbia for members of the Local Government Management Association of British Columbia
Contact Information: Program Coordinator: Ana Fuller, Phone: 250-383-7032, ext. 227, Fax: 250-383-4879, E-mail: afuller@lgma.ca
• Local Government Management Association of British Columbia 2016 Annual General Meeting & Conference, June, 2016, Vancouver Island Conference Centre, Nanaimo, BC
Scope: Provincial
Attendance: 400-500
Description: A meeting & tradeshow held each year in May or June in British Columbia for members of the Local Government Management Association of British Columbia
Contact Information: Program Coordinator: Ana Fuller, Phone: 250-383-7032, ext. 227, Fax: 250-383-4879, E-mail: afuller@lgma.ca
• Local Government Management Association of British Columbia 2015 Annual General Meeting & Conference, May, 2017, Penticton Trade & Convention Centre, Penticton, BC
Scope: Provincial
Description: A conference & tradeshow held in May or June each year for members of the Local Government Management Association of British Columbia
Contact Information: Program Coordinator: Ana Fuller, Phone: 250-383-7032, ext. 227, Fax: 250-383-4879, E-mail: afuller@lgma.ca
Publications:
• Exchange
Type: Magazine; *Frequency:* Quarterly; *Accepts Advertising*
Profile: A magazine, featuring best practices, ideas, & professional development, distributed to more than 1,000 local government managers, mayors, & regional district chairs throughout British Columbia, as well asbusiness affiliates
• Local Government Elections Manual
Type: Manual; *Price:* $175
Profile: Ready-to-use forms, plus a CD ROM with sample bylaws
• Local Government Management Association of British Columbia Annual Report
Type: Yearbook; *Frequency:* Annually
Profile: A review of the year's activities, including chapter reports & financial statements
• Local Government Management Association of British Columbia Guide for Approving Officers
Type: Manual; *Price:* $150 CD ROM; $225 print version, including the CD ROM
Profile: An updated edition to reflect new & amended legislation & court decisions
• Local Government Management Association of British Columbia Records Management Manual for Local Government
Type: Manual; *Price:* $150 CD ROM; $225 print version, including the CD ROM
Profile: Standards & best practices for records management

Lower Mainland Chapter
BC
Chief Officer(s):
Susan Rauh, President, 604-927-5413, Fax: 604-927-5360
rauhs@portcoquitlam.ca

North Central Chapter
BC
Chief Officer(s):
Ron Bowles, President, 250-638-4725, Fax: 250-638-4777
rbowles@terrace.ca
Eliana Clements, Secretary, 250-569-2229, Fax: 250-569-3276
eliana@mcbride.ca
Karla Jensen, Treasurer, 250-960-4444, Fax: 250-563-7520
kjensen@rdffg.bc.ca

Rocky Mountain Chapter
c/o Raeleen Manjak, District of Sparwood, PO Box 520, 136 Spruce Ave., Sparwood BC V0B 2G0
Chief Officer(s):
Curtis Helgesen, President & Treasurer, 250-865-4000, Fax: 250-865-4001
chelgesen@elkford.ca
Jon Wilsgard, Vice-President, 250-344-2271 Ext. 237, Fax: 250-344-6577
jon.wilsgard@golden.ca

Thompson Okanagan Chapter
BC
Chief Officer(s):
Stephen Fleming, President, 250-469-8660, Fax: 250-862-3399
sfleming@kelowna.ca
Ian Wilson, Vice-President, 250-469-8500, Fax: 250-862-3399
iwilson@kelowna.ca
Stephen Banmen, Treasurer, 250-766-5650, Fax: 250-766-0116
sbanmen@lakecountry.bc.ca

Vancouver Island Chapter
BC
Chief Officer(s):
Don Schaffer, President, 250-361-0549, Fax: 250-361-0348
dschaffer@victoria.ca
Andrew Hicik, Vice-President, 250-665-5410, Fax: 250-665-4508
ahicik@sidney.ca
Anja Nurvo, Secretary, 250-414-7135, Fax: 250-414-7111
anja.nurvo@esquimalt.ca
Michael Dillabaugh, Treasurer, 250-642-1634, Fax: 250-642-0541
mdillabaugh@sooke.ca

West Kootenay Boundary Chapter
BC
Chief Officer(s):
Theresa Lenardon, President, 250-368-0225, Fax: 250-368-3990
tlenardon@rdkb.com
Bryan Teasdale, Vice-President, 250-368-9148, Fax: 250-368-3990
bteasdale@rdkb.com
Amy Gurnett, Secretary-Treasurer, 250-367-7234, Fax: 250-367-7288
montvill@telus.net

Locomotive & Railway Historical Society of Western Canada
87 Chelsea St. NW, Calgary AB T2K 1P1
Tel: 403-282-3485
Overview: A small local charitable organization founded in 1985
Mission: To promote the preservation of railway equipment integral to the history of Western Canada; to act in a consultative capacity on heritage rail projects
Member of: Canadian Council for Railway Heritage
Chief Officer(s):
James E. Lanigan, President
Finances: *Annual Operating Budget:* Less than $50,000
9 volunteer(s)
Membership: 9
Activities: Preservation & restoration of important historic Canadian railway equipment; *Speaker Service:* Yes

LOFT Community Services (LOFT)
15 Toronto St., 9th Floor, Toronto ON M5C 2E3
Tel: 416-979-1994; *Fax:* 416-979-3028
info@loftcs.org
www.loftcs.org
www.facebook.com/loftcs
Previous Name: Anglican Houses
Overview: A large local organization founded in 1953
Mission: To promote recovery & independence for people marginalized by mental illness, addiction & homelessness; To offer housing & support services that are respectful, voluntary & responsive to individual needs
Member of: CARF Canada
Chief Officer(s):
Terry McCullum, CEO
tmccullum@loftcs.org
Jim Nason, Director, Operations
jnason@loftcs.org
Rosa Galluzzo, Director, Finance
rgalluzzo@loftcs.org
Jane Corbett, Director, Development
jcorbett@loftcs.org
Finances: *Annual Operating Budget:* Greater than $5 Million; *Funding Sources:* Donations
Staff Member(s): 350; 50 volunteer(s)
Activities: Community outreach & supportive housing services to over 4,000 vulnerable & homeless people at 50 sites in Toronto, York Region & South Simcoe Region; *Awareness Events:* Annual Holiday Benefit Concert, December; *Speaker Service:* Yes

Logan Lake Arts Council (LLAC)
PO Box 299, Logan Lake BC V0K 1W0
Tel: 250-523-2390
llac@ocis.net
llac.d3ross.info
Overview: A small local organization founded in 1983
Mission: To promote arts & culture in community
Member of: Assembly of BC Arts Councils
Chief Officer(s):
Joan Wankel, President
Membership: 1-99
Activities: *Library*

The Logistics Institute
#501, 20 Maud St., Toronto ON M5V 2M5
Tel: 416-363-3005; *Fax:* 416-363-5598
loginfo@loginstitute.ca
www.loginstitute.ca
www.linkedin.com/groups?home=&gid=1581887
www.facebook.com/groups/47876774880
twitter.com/CdnProfLogInst
Overview: A medium-sized national organization founded in 1990
Chief Officer(s):
Victor S. Deyglio, Founding President, 416-363-3005 Ext. 1200
vdeyglio@loginstitute.ca
Ben Avery, Coordinator, Technology & Administrative Support, 416-363-3005 Ext. 1500
bavery@loginstitute.ca
Jasmine Gill, Coordinator, Program & Membership, 416-363-3005 Ext. 1700
jgill@loginstitute.ca

Logos Education Society of Alberta
3239 Oakwood Dr. SW, Calgary AB T2V 0K4
Tel: 403-281-2188; *Fax:* 403-238-3033
jspicer@furthered.ca
www.nald.ca/fesa
Overview: A small provincial charitable organization founded in 1976
Chief Officer(s):
Wally Shoults, President
Finances: *Annual Operating Budget:* Less than $50,000
4 volunteer(s)
Membership: 30 individual; *Fees:* $15
Activities: Provision of student scholarships (post-secondary); *Speaker Service:* Yes

Loisir littéraire du Québec *Voir* Fédération québécoise du loisir littéraire

LOMA Canada
675 Cochrane Dr., East Tower, 6th Floor, Markham ON L3R 0B8
Tel: 905-530-2309; *Fax:* 905-530-2001
lomacanada@loma.org
www.loma.org/canada
Previous Name: Life Insurance Institute of Canada
Overview: A medium-sized national organization founded in 2002
Mission: To serve its member companies by encouraging & assisting individuals to acquire knowledge & understanding of business of life & health insurance & related financial services.
Member of: Life Office Management Association
Chief Officer(s):
Brent Lemanski, Resident Director, Canada
blemanski@limra.com
Staff Member(s): 1; 100 volunteer(s)
Membership: 40 corporate; *Member Profile:* Chartered life & health insurance companies, with their head or a branch office operating in Canada; organizations that provide services to life & health insurance companies; academic institutions that provide education in & outside the life & health insurance industry
Meetings/Conferences: • LIMRA and LOMA Canada 2015 Annual Conference, 2015
Scope: National
Description: This full-day event connects corporate leaders with industry pundits and innovative thinkers to examine current challenges, share strategic insights and get cutting-edge solutions for an unpredictable business environment.
Contact Information: askloma@loma.org

London & District Construction Association
331 Aberdeen Dr., London ON N5V 4S4

Tel: 519-453-5322; *Fax:* 519-453-5335
admin@ldca.on.ca
www.ldca.on.ca
Overview: A small local organization founded in 1898 overseen by Canadian Construction Association
Mission: To bring together contractors, manufacturers, suppliers, & many other firms associated with the construction industry
Chief Officer(s):
Dave Baxter, Executive Director
dbaxter@ldca.on.ca
Staff Member(s): 5
Membership: 562; *Member Profile:* Contractors; manufacturers; suppliers; professionals

London & District Distress Centre
PO Box 801, Stn. B, London ON N6A 4Z3
Tel: 519-667-6710; *Crisis Hot-Line:* 519-667-6711
www.londondistresscentre.com
www.linkedin.com/company/london-&-district-distress-centre
www.facebook.com/LondonDistressCentre
twitter.com/LondonDistress
Overview: A small local charitable organization founded in 1968 overseen by Distress Centres Ontario
Mission: To provide an opportunity for people to be listened to when they are distressed
Chief Officer(s):
Cheryl Legate, Executive Director
cheryl@londondistresscentre.com
Finances: *Funding Sources:* United Way; Grants; Donations
Staff Member(s): 5
Activities: 24-hour crisis intervention; Distress management; Emotional support; Information & referral; Crisis response line 519-433-2023; Senior's helpline 519-667-6600; *Speaker Service:* Yes

London & District Labour Council
#1, 380 Adelaide St. North, London ON N6B 3P6
Tel: 519-432-3188; *Fax:* 519-642-7834
ldlc@execulink.com
www.ldlc.on.ca
twitter.com/ldnlabour
Overview: A small local organization overseen by Ontario Federation of Labour
Member of: Ontario Federation of Labour
Chief Officer(s):
Patti Dalton, President

London & Middlesex Historical Society (LMHS)
PO Box 303, Stn. B, London ON N6A 4W1
www.londonheritage.ca/LondonMiddlesexHistoricalSociety
Overview: A small local charitable organization founded in 1901
Mission: To promote awareness of local heritage through public meetings, historical tours & demonstrations; to encourage the preservation of records, documents, pictures, buildings & sites relating to history of London & Middlesex
Member of: Ontario Historical Society
Chief Officer(s):
Sandy McRae, President
smcrae@gtn.on.ca
Finances: *Funding Sources:* Membership fees; donations; grants
Membership: *Fees:* $20 single; $15 senior/student
Activities: Meetings; bus tours; displays

London & St. Thomas Association of Realtors
342 Commissioners Rd. West, London ON N6J 1Y3
Tel: 519-641-1400; *Fax:* 519-641-4613
info@lstar.ca
www.lstar.ca
www.facebook.com/LSTAR.REALTORS
twitter.com/LSTARtweets
www.youtube.com/user/LSTARMembers
Overview: A small local organization overseen by Ontario Real Estate Association
Mission: To provide its members with the necessary tools that enable them to deliver excellent service to the community
Member of: The Canadian Real Estate Association
Chief Officer(s):
Doug Pedlar, President
Betty Doré, Executive Vice President
Membership: 1,500
Activities: Education; political action; statistical reports; *Library*

London Building & Construction Trades Council
56 Firestone Blvd., London ON N5W 5L4
Tel: 519-455-8083; *Fax:* 519-455-0712
Overview: A small local organization founded in 1946
Member of: AFL-CIO
Chief Officer(s):
Jim MacKinnon, Contact
jmackinnon@liuna1059.ca
Finances: *Annual Operating Budget:* $50,000-$100,000
Membership: 6,000+; *Member Profile:* Skilled construction trades
Activities: Trade shows; career days; volunteer labour for community projects; *Speaker Service:* Yes

London Chamber of Commerce
#101, 244 Pall Mall St., London ON N6A 5P6
Tel: 519-432-7551; *Fax:* 519-432-8163
info@londonchamber.com
www.londonchamber.com
Overview: A small local organization founded in 1857
Mission: To serve as the voice of business committed to the enhancement of economic prosperity & quality of life in London.
Member of: Ontario Chamber of Commerce; Canadian Chamber of Commerce
Chief Officer(s):
Gus Kotsiomitis, President
Gerry MacCartney, General Manager & CEO
gerry@londonchamber.com
Finances: *Funding Sources:* Membership dues; fundraising
Staff Member(s): 7; 1500 volunteer(s)
Membership: 980; *Fees:* Schedule available; *Committees:* Marketing & Communications; Federal & Provincial Affairs; Municipal Affairs; Special Events & Networking; Membership Sales & Services; Asian Business Opportunities; Hispanic Business Opportunities
Activities: Business After Five; Business Before Business; Breakfast with the Mayor; Comedy Auction; Corporate Challenge; Past Presidents' Golf Classic; Volunteer Appreciation Night; Speed Networking; *Speaker Service:* Yes; *Rents Mailing List:* Yes; *Library* Open to public
Awards:
- Innovation Award (Award)
- Environment Award (Award)
- Business of the Year (Award)
- E-Business Award (Award)
- London Quality Award (Award)

London Community Foundation (LCF)
Covent Garden Market, 130 King St., London ON N6A 1C5
Tel: 519-667-1600; *Fax:* 519-667-1615
info@lcf.on.ca
www.lcf.on.ca
twitter.com/LdnCommFdn
www.youtube.com/user/Ldncommfdn
Overview: A small local charitable organization founded in 1954
Mission: To create a vibrant & caring community; To strengthen the community by making strategic & effective grants; To build & manage a permanent endowment; To serve the community as a resource & partner so that each member has the opportunity for an enriched quality of life
Chief Officer(s):
Martha Powell, Chief Executive Officer, 519-667-1600 Ext. 101
mpowell@lcf.on.ca
Ulyana Kordyuk, Finance & Administrative Assistant, 519-667-1600 Ext. 108
ukordyuk@lcf.on.ca
Staff Member(s): 5; 50 volunteer(s)

London Community Orchestra (LCO)
482 Dundas St., London ON N6B 1W6
e-mail: info@lco-on.ca
lco-on.ca
www.facebook.com/LondonCommunityOrchestra
twitter.com/LCO_ON
Previous Name: Fanshawe Community Orchestra
Overview: A small local charitable organization founded in 1974 overseen by Orchestras Canada
Mission: To give concerts & to sponsor local young artists as soloists
Chief Officer(s):
Leonard Ingrao, Music Director
Pam Gregory, Manager
Sally Vernon, President
Finances: *Funding Sources:* Membership fees; donations; ticket sales; playing by invitation
Activities: 4 symphony concerts per season

London District Chief's Council *See* Southern First Nations Secretariat

London Food Bank
926 Leathorne St., London ON N5Z 3M5
Tel: 519-659-4045; *Fax:* 519-680-1627
londonfb@web.net
www.londonfoodbank.net
www.facebook.com/LondonFoodBank
twitter.com/LondonFoodBank1
Overview: A small local charitable organization founded in 1987
Mission: To help a caring community share its food resources
Member of: Ontario Association of Food Banks; Canadian Association of Food Banks
Chief Officer(s):
Brian Ratcliffe, General Manager
Glen Peason, Director
Jane Roy, Director
Finances: *Annual Operating Budget:* $100,000-$250,000
Staff Member(s): 3; 200 volunteer(s)
Membership: 100-499
Activities: *Internships:* Yes; *Speaker Service:* Yes

London Goodwill Industries Association *See* Goodwill Industries

London Health Sciences Foundation (LHSF)
747 Base Line Rd. East, London ON N6C 2R6
Tel: 519-685-8409; *Fax:* 519-685-8265
foundation@lhsc.on.ca
www.lhsf.ca
www.facebook.com/lhsf.ca
twitter.com/LHSFCanada
www.youtube.com/LHSFCanada
Overview: A small local charitable organization
Mission: To help raise money on behalf of the London Health Sciences Centre to fund research & improve patient care
Chief Officer(s):
John H. MacFarlane, President
Staff Member(s): 51

London Humane Society (LHS)
624 Clarke Rd., London ON N5V 3K5
Tel: 519-451-0630; *Fax:* 519-451-8995
administration@londonhumane.ca
www.londonhumanesociety.ca
www.facebook.com/londonhumanesociety
twitter.com/LondonHumaneS
Overview: A small local charitable organization founded in 1899 overseen by Canadian Federation of Humane Societies
Mission: To monitor animal welfare & treatment in London & Middlesex County; to afford our community's animals who have been abandoned, abused, neglected or injured with a facility dedicated to their well-being; to act as their advocate relating to animal welfare; to educate our community
Member of: Ontario SPCA
Affliation(s): OSPCA
Finances: *Funding Sources:* Donations; fundraising
Activities: *Awareness Events:* Bark in the Park; Christmas Pet Gifts, Dec.

London Insurance Professionals Association
c/o Preferred Insurance Group, 217 Whamcliffe Rd. South, London ON N6J 2L2
Tel: 519-661-0200
www.caiw-acfa.com
Overview: A small local organization
Member of: Canadian Association of Insurance Women
Chief Officer(s):
Mary Hooper, President
mhooper@preferred-ins.com

London Jewish Community Council; London Jewish Community Foundation *See* London Jewish Federation

London Jewish Federation
536 Huron St., London ON N5Y 4J5
Tel: 519-673-3310; *Fax:* 519-673-1161
ljf@ljf.on.ca
www.jewishlondon.ca
www.facebook.com/jcclondonontario
twitter.com/jcclondonon
Previous Name: London Jewish Community Council; London Jewish Community Foundation
Overview: A medium-sized local charitable organization founded in 1974 overseen by Ontario Council of Agencies Serving Immigrants
Mission: To support & enrich the quality of Jewish life in London; to assist in enhancing Jewish values in Israel & throughout the world

Member of: Council of Jewish Federations; Jewish Community Centre Association
Affliation(s): United Israel Appeal of Canada
Chief Officer(s):
Esther Marcus, Executive Director
jccexec@ljf.on.ca
Finances: *Funding Sources:* United Jewish Appeal; United Way
Staff Member(s): 11
Activities: Annual Holocaust program; Israel Day; Special Event programs at Chanukah, Purim, etc.; Speaker series; *Internships:* Yes; *Speaker Service:* Yes

London Memorial Society; Memorial & Funeral Advisory Society of London *See* Memorial Society of London

London Multiple Births Association (LMBA)
PO Box 52031, RPO Commissioners Road E., London ON N6C 0A1
e-mail: london@multiplebirthscanada.org
www.londonmultiples.com
Overview: A small local organization founded in 1977 overseen by Multiple Births Canada
Chief Officer(s):
Tammy Langendyk, Co-President
lmba.president@rogers.com
Erika Kafka, Co-President
lmba.president@rogers.com
Membership: *Committees:* Sales; Social; Parent Outreach

London Musicians' Association
c/o kowork London, 352 Talbot St., London ON N6A 2R6
Tel: 519-685-2540; *Fax:* 519-685-2690
Other Communication: Booking e-mail: bookingreferral@londonmusicians.com
admin@londonmusicians.com
www.londonmusicians.com
Also Known As: American Federation of Musicians, Local 279
Overview: A small local organization founded in 1903
Mission: Local 279 of the American Federation of Musicians of the U.S. & Canada represents professional musicians in the London area
Affliation(s): American Federation of Musicians
Membership: 300+; *Fees:* $100 initiation; $180 annual; *Committees:* By-Laws; Finance; Membership/Diversity
Activities: Booking referral service; legal assistance; immigration/travel assistance; *Library*

London Numismatic Society
543 Kininvie Dr., London ON N6G 1P1
Tel: 519-472-9679
Overview: A small local organization founded in 1951
Mission: To study coins, discuss purchases, present educational material, and auction items
Chief Officer(s):
Ted Leitch, Contact
12 volunteer(s)
Activities: *Awareness Events:* Numismatic Society Annual Coin Show, September

London Orchid Society
#162, 509 Commissioners Rd. West, London ON N6J 1Y5
los.lon.imag.net
Overview: A small local organization founded in 1976
Mission: To promote the cultivation of orchids
Member of: Canadian Orchid Congress; American Orchid Society
Chief Officer(s):
Sean Moore, President
spmoore@rogers.com
Membership: *Fees:* $20 single; $25 family

London Philatelic Society
1738 Gore Rd, London ON N5W 5L5
e-mail: rstanlick@sympatico.ca
www.londonphilatelicsociety.com
Overview: A small local organization founded in 1892
Mission: To promote the study and collecting of stamps in the London area
Chief Officer(s):
Leff Sherwin, President
Finances: *Annual Operating Budget:* Less than $50,000; *Funding Sources:* Membership dues
Staff Member(s): 6
Membership: 100; *Fees:* $10; *Member Profile:* Stamp collecting
Activities: *Library*

London Police Association (LPA) / Association de la police de London
330 William St., London ON N6B 3C7
Tel: 519-661-5360; *Fax:* 519-660-6018
carolyn@lpa.on.ca
www.lpa.on.ca
Overview: A small local organization founded in 1947 overseen by Police Association of Ontario
Mission: To represent all police & civilian members of the London Police Service; To promote the mutual interests of members
Member of: Police Association of Ontario
Chief Officer(s):
Rick Terrio, Vice-President
rterrio@lpa.on.ca
Brian Urquhart, President
Dan Axford, Administrator
lpa@lpa.on.ca
Finances: *Funding Sources:* LPA facility rental fees
Membership: 801; *Member Profile:* Police & civilian members of London Ontario's police service
Activities: Supporting charities

London Regional Art & Historical Museums *See* Museum London

London Regional Resource Centre for Heritage & the Environment
1017 Western Rd., London ON N6G 1G5
Tel: 519-645-2845; *Fax:* 519-645-0981
info@grosvenorlodge.com
www.heritagelondonfoundation.org/Grosvenor/indexgrosvenor.html
www.facebook.com/events/1431960477024890
Also Known As: Grosvenor Lodge
Overview: A small local organization founded in 1992
Mission: To promote heritage & environmental activities & organizations in the London area
Member of: Heritage London Foundation
Staff Member(s): 3

London Soaring Club
34 Mark Cres., Woodstock ON N4S 7V6
Tel: 519-661-7844
info@londonsoaringclub.ca
www.londonsoaringclub.ca
Overview: A small local organization
Member of: Soaring Association of Canada
Chief Officer(s):
Bill Vollmar, President
Mike Luckham, Secretary
mluckham54@gmail.com

London Youth Symphony (LYS)
PO Box 553, Stn. B, London ON N6A 4W8
Tel: 519-686-8070
manager@londonyouthsymphony.org
www.londonyouthsymphony.org
www.facebook.com/169142799797422
Overview: A small local organization overseen by Orchestras Canada
Mission: To provide the region's most talented young musicians with the opportunity to build self-discipline, confidence & team spirit within an outstanding symphonic environment that offers professional directorship & coaching
Chief Officer(s):
Len Ingrao, Conductor
conductor@londonyouthsymphony.org
Joan Mortimer, Manager
Finances: *Funding Sources:* Tuition; grant; fundraising
Staff Member(s): 3
Membership: *Fees:* $475; *Member Profile:* Orchestral musicians ages 13 to 23

London-Middlesex Children's Aid Society
PO Box 7010, 1680 Oxford St. East, London ON N5Y 5R8
Tel: 519-455-9000; *Fax:* 519-455-4355
Toll-Free: 888-661-6167; *TTY:* 519-455-6498
info@caslondon.on.ca
www.caslondon.on.ca
Overview: A small local organization
Mission: To protect & care for children at risk; committed to the healthy development of children & the strengthening of families
Member of: Ontario Association of Childrens' Aid Societies
Chief Officer(s):
Walter LeGrow, President
Jane Fitzgerald, Executive Director
196 volunteer(s)
Membership: *Fees:* $10
Activities: *Speaker Service:* Yes

Long Point Bird Observatory *See* Bird Studies Canada

Long Term & Continuing Care Association of Manitoba (LTCAM)
#103, 1483 Pembina Hwy., Winnipeg MB R3T 2C6
Tel: 204-477-9888; *Fax:* 204-477-9889
Toll-Free: 855-477-9888
info@ltcam.mb.ca
www.ltcam.mb.ca
www.facebook.com/ltcam
twitter.com/LTCAManitoba
www.youtube.com/LTCAManitoba
Overview: A small provincial organization founded in 1959 overseen by Canadian Alliance for Long Term Care
Mission: To advance long term & continuing care by promoting awareness to government, regional health authorities, health agencies & the community
Chief Officer(s):
Linda Sundevic, President
Membership: *Member Profile:* Long term & continuing care organizations in Manitoba

Longlac Chamber of Commerce
PO Box 203, 110 Lake St., Longlac ON P0T 2A0
Tel: 807-876-4562
info@longlacchamber.com
www.facebook.com/pages/Longlac-Chamber-of-Commerce/219883008040164
Overview: A small local organization
Mission: To promote local businesses & help them grow.
Chief Officer(s):
Martin Boucher, Vice-President
burcheron86@hotmail.com

Lookout Emergency Aid Society
429 Alexander St., Vancouver BC V6A 1C6
Tel: 604-255-0340; *Fax:* 604-255-0790
info@lookoutsociety.bc.ca
www.lookoutsociety.bc.ca
www.facebook.com/LookoutSociety
www.twitter.com/LookoutSociety
www.youtube.com/user/LookoutSociety
Also Known As: Lookout Society
Overview: A medium-sized local charitable organization founded in 1971
Mission: To provides housing and a range of support services to adults with low or no income who have few, if any, housing or support optionss. Operating in 4 municipalities within Metro Vancouver, Lookout serves the homeless popoulation by providing 4 permanent emergency shelters, 3 temporary extreme weather shelters, 6 tranitional and 14 permanent supported residences as well as a drop in activity centre for people living with mental illness within Vancouver's Downtown Eastside.
Member of: Shelter Net BC; Home & Homeless Network; Health Employers Association of BC; Greater Vancouver Shelter Strategy; Burnaby Homeless Task Force; Vancouver Urban Core Community Workers Association; Surrey Board of Trade
Affliation(s): Vancouver Urban Care Community Workers Association; Adult Mental Health Service Providers Committee
Chief Officer(s):
Shayne Williams, Executive Director, 604-255-0340
shaynew@lookoutsociety.ca
Leonard Levy, Director of Operations
leonardl@lookoutsociety.ca
Finances: *Annual Operating Budget:* Greater than $5 Million; *Funding Sources:* Provincial government; federal grants; donations; health authorities
Staff Member(s): 360; 5231 volunteer(s)
Membership: 11; *Fees:* $11; *Committees:* Board of Directors; H'Arts Annual Gala Committee
Activities: Housing & support services; Blanket drive in December; *Awareness Events:* Coins for Change; *Internships:* Yes; *Speaker Service:* Yes

Lord Reading Law Society / Association de droit Lord Reading
5161 Décarie Blvd., Montréal QC H2X 2H9
e-mail: info@lordreading.org
lordreading.org
Overview: A small local organization founded in 1948
Mission: Pour faire avancer les droits de l'homme et des libertés des juristes juifs

Chief Officer(s):
Morris Chaikelson, Executive Director
Heather Michelin, President, Board of Directors
president@lordreading.org
Membership: *Member Profile:* Jewish jurists; *Committees:* Communications; Careers; Membership; Sponsorship; Program; Young Bar

The Lord Selkirk Association of Rupert's Land (TLSARL)
Winnipeg MB
www.lordselkirk.ca
Overview: A small local organization founded in 1908
Mission: To serve as a link to bind together the descendants of the hardy men & women who first settled on the bank of the Red River in the early 1800s; to perpetuate the memory & preserve the spirit, traditions & history of those first agricultural settlers
Finances: *Funding Sources:* Membership fees
Membership: *Member Profile:* Descendants of settlers resident at Red River prior to 1835

The Lord's Flock Charismatic Community
c/o Our Lady of Fatima Shrine, 3170 St. Clair Ave. East, Toronto ON M1L 1V6
e-mail: lordsflock.intl@gmail.com
www.lordsflock.org
www.facebook.com/TechieRodriguez
www.youtube.com/user/lordsflockorg
Overview: A medium-sized international organization
Mission: To promote the Christian faith while preserving culture & heritage for future generations
Affliation(s): Archdiocese of Toronto
Chief Officer(s):
Jun Silva, Contact, 416-916-1577
Cynthia Silva, Contact, 416-916-1577
Georgia Gaceta, Contact, 416-317-9599
Finances: *Annual Operating Budget:* Less than $50,000
Activities: Pilgrimages; Christian holiday celebrations; seminars

Lorne Agricultural & Industrial Society *See* Prince Albert Exhibition Association

Lorraine Kimsa Theatre for Young People *See* Young People's Theatre

Lost Villages Historical Society
PO Box 306, Ingleside ON K0C 1M0
Tel: 613-534-2197
lostvillages.ca
Overview: A small local charitable organization founded in 1977
Mission: To collect, preserve & display the heritage of the Lost Villages, the communities which were inundated in the Hydro & Seaway flooding of July 1, 1958; to operate the Lost Villages Museum, open mid-June to late Sept.
Membership: *Fees:* $10 individual; $15 family; $50 life
Activities: Historical tours of St. Lawrence Seaway & Lost Villages area; *Library* by appointment

Lo-Se-Ca Foundation
#215, 1 Carnegie Dr., St Albert AB T8N 5B1
Tel: 780-460-1400; *Fax:* 780-459-1380
lo-se-ca@telusplanet.net
www.loseca.ca
www.facebook.com/115663645142959
Overview: A small local charitable organization founded in 1988
Mission: To promote the quality of life of families & individuals by providing services within a Christian environment; to enhance human well-being, worth & dignity of life for all persons with disabilities
Member of: Alberta Association of Rehabilitation Centres; Persons with Developmental Disabilities
Chief Officer(s):
Marie Renaud, Executive Director, 780-460-1400 Ext. 231
Finances: *Annual Operating Budget:* $1.5 Million-$3 Million
Staff Member(s): 100; 150 volunteer(s)
Membership: 58; *Fees:* $10 individual
Activities: Day service; thrift shop; in-services; seminars; respite care

Lotus Car Club of Canada
15 Citation Cres., Whitby ON L1N 6X2
www.lotusclubcanada.ca/Public/Welcome.html
Overview: A small national charitable organization founded in 1977
Member of: British Car Council
Affliation(s): Specialty Vehicle Association of Ontario
Chief Officer(s):
Duncan Lamb, President
duncan.lamb@sympatico.ca
Chris Happé, Membership
chris@happe.ca
Membership: 141; *Fees:* $20; *Member Profile:* Lotus car owners & enthusiasts

Louise Bédard Danse
#300, 2022, rue Sherbrooke Est, Montréal QC H2K 1B9
Tél: 514-982-4580
infos@lbdanse.org
www.lbdanse.org
www.facebook.com/lbdanse
twitter.com/lbdanse
www.youtube.com/lbdanse
Aperçu: *Dimension:* petite; *Envergure:* locale; fondée en 1990
Mission: De poursuivre les activités modernes création de danse, de sensibilisation et d'éducation, et en offrant des créations chorégraphiques originales pour le grand public.
Membre de: Circuit-Est centre chorégraphique; Regroupement québécois de la danse; La danse sur les routes du Québec
Membre(s) du bureau directeur:
Louise Bédard, Directrice artistique
Membre(s) du personnel: 4

Lower Mainland Independent Secondary School Athletic Association (LMISSAA)
BC
e-mail: athletics@yorkhouse.ca
www.lmissaa.com
Overview: A small local organization
Member of: BC School Sports
Chief Officer(s):
Carm Renzullo, President

Lower Mainland Local Government Association (LMLGA)
#60, 10551 Shellbridge Way, Richmond BC V6X 2W9
Tel: 250-356-5122; *Fax:* 604-270-9116
www.lmlga.ca
Overview: A small local organization
Mission: To enhance & improve the level of services provided by local governments; To promote the welfare of residents of member governments; To advance proposed changes to legislation, regulations, or government policies
Chief Officer(s):
Iris Hesketh-Boles, Executive Coordinator
Iris@lmlga.bc.ca
James Atebe, President
Sav Dhaliwal, 1st Vice President
Barbara Steele, 2nd Vice President
Membership: 31 local governments + 3 regional districts; *Member Profile:* Local governments from Lillooet to Hope, British Columbia; Regional districts
Activities: Offering information & educational activities; Providing networking opportunities
Meetings/Conferences: • Lower Mainland Local Government Association 2015 Annual General Meeting & Conference, May, 2015, Harrison Hot Springs Resort and Spa, Harrison, BC
Scope: Local
Description: Tradeshow, workshops, & seminars for persons involved in local government
• Lower Mainland Local Government Association 2016 Annual General Meeting & Conference, May, 2016, Fairmont Chateau Whistler, Whistler, BC
Scope: Local
Description: Tradeshow, workshops, & seminars for persons involved in local government
• Lower Mainland Local Government Association 2017 Annual General Meeting & Conference, 2017
Scope: Local
Description: Tradeshow, workshops, & seminars for persons involved in local government

Lower Mainland Spina Bifida Association *See* Spina Bifida & Hydrocephalus Association of British Columbia

Lower Mainland Wildlife Rescue Association *See* Wildlife Rescue Association of British Columbia

Lu'ma Native Housing Society (LNHS)
25 West 6th Ave., Vancouver BC V5Y 1K2
Tel: 604-876-0811; *Fax:* 604-876-0999
www.lnhs.ca
Also Known As: New Beginnings Native Housing Society
Overview: A small provincial organization founded in 1981
Mission: To provide affordable, adequate & accessible housing to meet the needs of Aboriginal people; To assist tenants with the transition to urban living
Member of: National Aboriginal Housing Association
Affliation(s): First Funds Society
Chief Officer(s):
Marcel Swain, Consultant
Finances: *Annual Operating Budget:* $3 Million-$5 Million; *Funding Sources:* Canada Mortgage & Housing Society; BC Housing Management Commission
Staff Member(s): 29; 10 volunteer(s)
Membership: 100; *Fees:* $1; *Committees:* Membership; Finance; Development; AGM
Activities: Advocates for low-cost afforable housing to Aboriginal peoples & finding best practice methods in providing housing services & homelessness initiatives

Lucie & André Chagnon Foundation *Voir* Fondation Lucie et André Chagnon

Lucie Grégoire Danse
6811, rue de Laundière, Montréal QC H2G 3B2
Tél: 514-278-1620
luciegregoire3@sympatico.ca
www.luciegregoire.ca
Aperçu: *Dimension:* petite; *Envergure:* locale; fondée en 1981
Membre de: Regroupement québécois de la danse
Membre(s) du bureau directeur:
Lucie Grégoire, Directrice artistique
Finances: *Fonds:* Conseil des Arts du Canada; Conseil des arts et des lettres du Québec

Lucknow & District Chamber of Commerce
PO Box 313, Lucknow ON N0G 2H0
Tel: 519-357-8454
info@lucknowchamber.ca
www.lucknowchamber.ca
www.facebook.com/pages/Lucknow-Ontario/422493221143383
twitter.com/LucknowChamber
Overview: A small local organization founded in 1993
Mission: To enhance the economic prosperity & quality of life in Lucknow & the surrounding district
Member of: Ontario Chamber of Commerce
Chief Officer(s):
Morten Jokbsen, President
Finances: *Funding Sources:* Membership dues
Membership: *Fees:* $80; *Member Profile:* Local businesses
Activities: Promotion of the business community;
Awards:
• Citizen of the Year (Award)

Luggage, Leathergoods, Handbags & Accessories Association of Canada (LLHA)
PO Box 144, Stn. A, Toronto ON M9C 4V2
Fax: 519-624-6408
Toll-Free: 866-872-2420
info@llha.ca
www.llha.ca
Overview: A medium-sized national organization
Mission: To promote the growth of the industry in Canada; To foster the interchange of ideas
Chief Officer(s):
Catherine Genge, Executive Administrator
Membership: *Member Profile:* Manufacturers; Distributors; Importers; Wholesalers; Agents; Retailers
Activities: Presenting educational speakers & seminars; *Awareness Events:* Trade Show, April

Lumber & Building Materials Association of Ontario (LBMAO)
#27, 5155 Spectrum Way, Mississauga ON L4W 5A1
Tel: 905-625-1084; *Fax:* 905-625-3006
Toll-Free: 888-365-2626
www.lbmao.on.ca
Previous Name: Ontario Retail Lumber Dealers Association
Overview: A medium-sized provincial organization founded in 1917
Mission: To promote the welfare of members so that they are able to build a competitive advantage & remain at the leading edge of the lumber & building materials industry
Chief Officer(s):
David W. Campbell, President
dwcampbell@lbmao.on.ca
Bob Lockwood, Chair
lockwoodbc@hotmail.com
Dwayne Sprague, Vice-Chair

Canadian Associations

Membership: *Member Profile:* Manufacturers; Distributors; Purchasing organizations; Wholesalers; Service firm
Activities: Providing educational opportunities; Offering support services; Engaging in advocacy activities

Lumby Chamber of Commerce
PO Box 534, 1882 Vernon St., Lumby BC V0E 2G0
Tel: 250-547-2300; *Fax:* 250-547-2300
lumbychamber@shaw.ca
www.monasheetourism.com
Overview: A small local organization founded in 1979
Mission: To facilitate, enhance & improve Lumby's unique quality of life; to support positive & sustainable development; to encourage growth in commerce & industry for the prosperity of members & the Lumby area
Member of: BC Chamber of Commerce
Chief Officer(s):
Stephanie Sexsmith, Manager
Bill Maltman, President
Finances: *Annual Operating Budget:* Less than $50,000; *Funding Sources:* Memberships; fee for service
Staff Member(s): 3; 10 volunteer(s)
Membership: 90; *Fees:* $95-$255; *Member Profile:* Business; tourism; service groups; *Committees:* Arts & Parks; Business Development; Tourism
Activities: Downtown Revitalization; Mural Project; Lumby Visitor Infocentre; *Speaker Service:* Yes

Lumsden & District Chamber of Commerce
PO Box 114, Lumsden SK S0G 3C0
Tel: 306-731-2862
info@lumsdenchamber.ca
www.lumsdenchamber.ca
Overview: A small local organization founded in 1985
Chief Officer(s):
Wendy Joorisity, President
Membership: *Fees:* $100

Lundy's Lane Historical Society (LLHS)
5810 Ferry St., Niagara Falls ON L2G 1S9
Tel: 905-358-5082
Overview: A small local organization founded in 1887
Mission: To arouse & stimulate interest in the history of Niagara Falls, the Battle of Lundy's Lane, the Niagara Peninsula & Ontario by means of public lectures, field trips & publications
Member of: Ontario Historical Society
Chief Officer(s):
Bill Houston, President
Marg Lamb, Contact, 905-227-1632
Finances: *Annual Operating Budget:* Less than $50,000; *Funding Sources:* Membership fees; sale of books; donations
Membership: 140; *Fees:* $8 individual; $10 family; *Committees:* Executive; Publications; Museum
Activities: Monthly meetings; two walking tours; annual commemorative service

Lunenburg Board of Trade
PO Box 1300, Lunenburg NS B0J 2C0
Tel: 902-634-3170; *Fax:* 902-634-3194
Toll-Free: 888-615-8305
lbt@ns.aliantzinc.ca
www.lunenburgns.com/board-of-trade
Overview: A small local organization
Chief Officer(s):
Mike Smith, President

Lunenburg County Historical Society (LCHS)
PO Box 99, La Have NS B0R 1C0
Tel: 902-688-1632; *Fax:* 902-688-1632
Other Communication: fortpointmuseum.wordpress.com
lchsftpt@gmail.com
www.fortpointmuseum.com
www.facebook.com/fort.point.5
twitter.com/fortpointmuseum
Also Known As: Fort Point Museum
Overview: A small local organization founded in 1969
Mission: To preserve the LeHave River Estuary cultural & historical heritage while educating & learning
Member of: Federation of the Nova Scotian Heritage
Finances: *Annual Operating Budget:* Less than $50,000; *Funding Sources:* Membership fees; donations
Staff Member(s): 1; 50 volunteer(s)
Membership: 105; *Fees:* $10
Activities: Fort Point Museum; concerts; art events; workshop;

Lunenburg Heritage Society
PO Box 674, 125 Pelham St., Lunenburg NS B0J 2C0
Tel: 902-634-3498; *Fax:* 902-634-3194
lunenburgheritagesociety@hotmail.com
www.lunenburgheritagesociety.ca
www.facebook.com/lunenburg.heritage.9
twitter.com/lunenburghs
Overview: A small local charitable organization founded in 1972
Mission: To promote & preserve the architectural & cultural heritage of the Town of Lunenburg
Member of: Heritage Trust of Nova Scotia; National Historic Site(Knaut-Rhuland House Museum)
Affliation(s): Heritage Advisory - Town of Lunenburg; South Shore Tourism Association; Lunenburg Board of Trade
Chief Officer(s):
Don Wilson, President
Finances: *Annual Operating Budget:* Less than $50,000; *Funding Sources:* Fundraising
Staff Member(s): 1; 10 volunteer(s)
Membership: 100-200; *Fees:* $10 individual; $15 family; *Committees:* Marketing; Cabaret; Bandstand; House Tour; Knaut-Rhuland House Museum; NS Folk Art Festival
Activities: Heritage House Tour; Knaut-Rhuland House Museum; NS Folk Art Festival; Bandstand Summer Concerts; Christmas Cabaret

Lunenburg Marine Museum Society
PO Box 1363, 68 Bluenose Dr., Lunenburg NS B0J 2C0
Tel: 902-634-4794; *Fax:* 902-634-8990
Toll-Free: 866-579-4909
fma@gov.ns.ca
www.fisheries.museum.gov.ns.ca
Also Known As: Fisheries Museum of the Atlantic
Overview: A small local organization founded in 1965
Mission: To protect, enhance & celebrate the heritage of the Atlantic Canada Fishery; to collect, interpret & share this valuable heritage with special emphasis on the traditional Nova Scotia fisheries for all Atlantic Canadians & our visitors
Member of: Canadian Museums Association
Chief Officer(s):
Angela Saunders, General Manager
Finances: *Annual Operating Budget:* $500,000-$1.5 Million; *Funding Sources:* Nova Scotia Museum; admissions; gift shop
Staff Member(s): 9; 21 volunteer(s)
Membership: 184; *Fees:* $10
Activities: Programs & demonstrations during open season, first weekend in May - last weekend in October; *Library* Open to public

The Lung Association of Nova Scotia (LANS)
6331 Lady Hammond Rd., Halifax NS B3K 2S2
Tel: 902-443-8141; *Fax:* 902-445-2573
Toll-Free: 888-566-5864
info@ns.lung.ca
www.ns.lung.ca
www.linkedin.com/company/the-lung-association-of-nova-scotia
www.facebook.com/LungNS
twitter.com/NSLung
www.youtube.com/LungNovaScotia
Overview: A small provincial charitable organization founded in 1909 overseen by Canadian Lung Association
Mission: To control & prevent lung disease in Nova Scotia; To help people who live with lung disease
Chief Officer(s):
Louis Brill, President & Chief Executive Officer, 902-443-8141 Ext. 22
louisbrill@ns.lung.ca
Jayne Norrie, Manager, Health Initiatives
jaynenorrie@ns.lung.ca
Lesley Dunn, Manager, Resource Development
lesleydunn@ns.lung.ca
Hamza Haneef, Manager, Finance
hamzahaneef@ns.lung.ca
Paige Hoveling, Manager, Communications
paigehoveling@ns.lung.ca
Lynette Hollett, Coordinator, Donor Relations
lynettehollett@ns.lung.ca
Jonathan Dyer, Manager, Health Initiatives
jonathandyer@ns.lung.ca
Robert MacDonald, Manager, Health Initiatives
robertmacdonald@ns.lung.ca
Finances: *Funding Sources:* Donations; Fundraising; Sponsorships
Staff Member(s): 8; 10+ volunteer(s)
Activities: Offering lung health education to Nova Scotians; Supporting research; Engaging in advocacy activities; Providing information & peer support to help people with COPD & lung disease; Offering a camp for children with asthma; *Library:* Nova Scotia Lung Association Resource Library; Open to public

Lupus Canada
#14, 3555 14th Ave., Markham ON L3R 0H5
Tel: 905-513-0004; *Fax:* 905-513-9516
Toll-Free: 800-661-1468
info@lupuscanada.org
www.lupuscanada.org
www.facebook.com/group.php?gid=69263929055&ref=ts
Overview: A medium-sized national charitable organization founded in 1987
Mission: To improve the lives of people living with lupus; To encourage cooperation among the lupus organizations in Canada
Chief Officer(s):
Catherine Madden, Executive Director, 905-513-0004 Ext. 222
catherine.madden@lupuscanada.org
Kendra MacDonald, President
Karen Chow, Vice-President
Leanne Mielczarek, Manager, National Operations
leanne.mielczarek@lupuscanada.org
Finances: *Funding Sources:* Individual & corporate donations; Fundraising; Bequests; Memorials; Grants; Contributions from member organization
Staff Member(s): 2
Membership: *Member Profile:* Provincial & regional organizations
Activities: Promoting public awareness; Providing general education about lupus; Engaging in advocacy activities; Encouraging research; Offering support to people living with lupus; Organizing annual patient symposia; *Awareness Events:* Lupus Awareness Month, Oct.; World Lupus Day, May 10

Lupus Foundation of Ontario (LFO)
PO Box 687, 294 Ridge Rd. North, Ridgeway ON L0S 1N0
Tel: 905-894-4611; *Fax:* 905-894-4616
Toll-Free: 800-368-8377
lupusont@vaxxine.com
www.lupusfoundationofontario.com
Overview: A medium-sized provincial charitable organization founded in 1977 overseen by Lupus Canada
Mission: To serve the lupus patient community as a charitable organization
Chief Officer(s):
Laurie Kroeker, President, 905-894-4611, Fax: 905-894-4616
Finances: *Funding Sources:* Donations; Member support; Fundraising
Staff Member(s): 1; 94 volunteer(s)
Membership: *Fees:* $25 yearly
Activities: Raising public awareness & understanding of lupus; Providing support services; Encouraging research; Engaging in advocacy activitiesl Offering educational opportunities to learn about lupus & develop coping strategies; Providing literature about lupus; Donating funds to research projects & treatment facilities; *Awareness Events:* Walk for Lupus, May; World Lupus Day, May 10; Lupus Awareness Month, October; *Speaker Service:* Yes; *Library:* The Lupus Foundation of Ontario Library

Lupus New Brunswick
#17, 55 Grant St., Moncton NB E1A 3R3
Toll-Free: 877-303-8080
lupins@rogers.com
www.lupusnb.ca
Overview: A small provincial organization founded in 1986 overseen by Lupus Canada
Mission: To promote eduction & public awarness of lupus; to bring together lupus patients, friends, family, & other interested persons for a network of support.
Member of: Lupus Canada
Membership: *Fees:* $25
Activities: *Awareness Events:* Walk for Lupus, May

Lupus Newfoundland & Labrador
PO Box 8121, Stn. A, Konmount Rd., St. John's NL A1B 3M9
Tel: 709-368-8130
lupus.nl.ca@gmail.com
www.envision.ca/webs/lupusnfldlab
Previous Name: Lupus Society of Newfoundland
Overview: A small provincial charitable organization overseen by Lupus Canada
Mission: To support individuals with lupus; to promote education & awareness of lupus; to support research & treatment of the disease
Chief Officer(s):
Dale Williams, President
Membership: *Fees:* $10

Activities: *Awareness Events:* Walk for Lupus, June; Diane Bartlett Memorial Ride, Sept.

Lupus Nova Scotia
PO Box 38038, Dartmouth NS B3B 1X2
Tel: 902-425-0358; *Fax:* 902-798-0772
Toll-Free: 800-394-0125
info@lupusns.org
www.lupuscanada.org/novascotia
www.facebook.com/208993942462906
www.flickr.com/photos/65268085@N06
Previous Name: Lupus Society of Nova Scotia
Overview: A small provincial charitable organization founded in 1989 overseen by Lupus Canada
Mission: To inform, educate & support all those afflicted with lupus; to promote public & professional awareness of the disease as a prevalent & controllable one, as well as funding research for its cure.
Member of: Lupus Canada; Lupus Foundation of America
Finances: *Funding Sources:* Membership; Donations; Memorial Funds; Item Sales; Fundraising Events
Membership: *Fees:* $20 single; $30 family
Activities: *Library* by appointment

Lupus Ontario
#301, 2900 John St., Markham ON L3R 5G3
Tel: 905-415-1099; *Fax:* 905-415-9874
Toll-Free: 877-240-1099
info@lupusontario.org
www.lupusontario.org
twitter.com/LupusON
Merged from: Ontario Lupus Association; Lupus Society of Hamilton
Overview: A medium-sized provincial charitable organization founded in 2004 overseen by Lupus Canada
Mission: To serve the needs of Lupus sufferers in Ontario
Member of: Lupus Canada
Chief Officer(s):
Michael Stewart, President
Karen Furlotte, Coordinator
kfurlotte@lupusontario.org
Finances: *Funding Sources:* Donations; Memberships; Memorials; Item Sales; Special Events
Staff Member(s): 3
Membership: *Fees:* $25
Activities: Providing information about lupus; Offering support groups; Increasing public awareness; Encouraging research; Organizing annual general meetings & clinical updates; *Awareness Events:* Lupus Awareness Month, Oct.; Annual Walk a Block for Lupus in Ontario, May (Part of Walk the World for Lupus event); World Lupus Dat, May

Kingston Branch
c/o 127 Kings Court Ave., Kingston ON K7K 4P4
Tel: 613-530-2129

Kitchener Branch
47 Blackwalnut Dr., Kitchener ON N2P 1N9
Tel: 519-748-1266

London Branch
PO Box 43003, London ON N6C 6A2
Tel: 519-641-3788; *Fax:* 519-641-4182

Mississauga/Oakville/Brampton/West Toronto Branch
253 Huntington Ridge Dr., Mississauga ON L5R 1S2
Tel: 905-501-7795
wellness_group@hotmail.com
Chief Officer(s):
Jacquie Tetrault, President

Ottawa Branch
#200, 1701 Woodward Dr., Ottawa ON K2C 0R4
Tel: 613-723-1083
Chief Officer(s):
David Boal, Contact
David.boal@sympatico.ca

Sudbury Branch
PO Box 365, Sudbury ON P3E 4P2
Tel: 705-983-4343
Chief Officer(s):
Brenda Seguin, President

Thunder Bay Branch
1256 Lakeshore Dr,. RR#13, Thunder Bay ON P7B 5E4
Chief Officer(s):
Sylvia Randall, President

Timmins Branch
1331 Richard Cres., Timmins ON P4R 1K9
Tel: 705-268-5299

Windsor Branch
1395 Albert Rd., Windsor ON N8Y 3R1
Tel: 519-974-7869
Chief Officer(s):
Kevin Stannard, President
kgsmailbox1@gmail.com

Lupus PEI
PO Box 23002, Charlottetown PE C1E 1Z6
Tel: 902-892-3875; *Fax:* 902-626-3585
Toll-Free: 800-661-1468
info@lupuscanada.org
www.lupuscanada.org/pei
Overview: A small provincial organization founded in 1993 overseen by Lupus Canada
Mission: To promote public awareness of lupus on PEI, while offering support & educational materials to lupus patients, their families & friends.
Finances: *Funding Sources:* Donations
Activities: *Speaker Service:* Yes

Lupus SK Society
c/o Royal University Hospital, PO Box 88, 103 Hospital Dr., Saskatoon SK S7N 0W0
Toll-Free: 877-566-6123
lupus@lupussk.com
www.lupussk.com
www.facebook.com/pages/Lupus-SK/254959414545218
twitter.com/Lupus_SK
www.youtube.com/user/sasklupus?
Overview: A small provincial charitable organization founded in 1981 overseen by Lupus Canada
Mission: To provide support for those affected by lupus through understanding, education, public awareness & research
Chief Officer(s):
Lloyd Driedger, President
Finances: *Funding Sources:* Donations
Membership: *Fees:* $20
Activities: *Library*

Lupus Society of Alberta (LESA)
#202, 1055 - 20 Ave. NW, Calgary AB T2M 1E7
Tel: 403-228-7956; *Fax:* 403-228-7853
Toll-Free: 888-242-9182
lupuslsa@shaw.ca
www.lupus.ab.ca
www.youtube.com/user/LupusSocietyofAB
Overview: A small provincial charitable organization founded in 1973 overseen by Lupus Canada
Mission: To provide education & support on lupus issues & enable research to find a cure.
Member of: Imagine Canada; Leave a Legacy Calgary; Volunteer Calgary
Chief Officer(s):
Rosemary E. Church, Executive Director
Mike Sewell, President
Finances: *Funding Sources:* Membership dues; corporate; individual; casino
Membership: *Fees:* $25; *Committees:* Communications & Public Awareness; Fund Development; Education & Support; Nominating
Activities: *Awareness Events:* Lupus Awareness Month, Oct.; *Speaker Service:* Yes

Lupus Society of Manitoba
#105, 386 Broadway Ave., Winnipeg MB R3C 3R6
Tel: 204-942-6825; *Fax:* 204-942-4894
Toll-Free: 888-942-6825
lupus@mts.net
www.lupusmanitoba.com
www.facebook.com/lupus.manitoba
Overview: A small provincial charitable organization founded in 1988 overseen by Lupus Canada
Mission: To provide support, encouragement & education to lupus patients & their families
Chief Officer(s):
Debbie Dohan, President
Finances: *Annual Operating Budget:* Less than $50,000; *Funding Sources:* Fundraising; donations
Membership: 200 individual; *Fees:* Schedule available; *Committees:* Fundraising; Public Awareness; Education; Support
Activities: *Awareness Events:* Lupus Awareness Month, Oct.; Golf Tournament, June; Walk For Lupus, May; *Library* Open to public

Lupus Society of Newfoundland *See* Lupus Newfoundland & Labrador

Lupus Society of Nova Scotia *See* Lupus Nova Scotia

Lutheran Association of Missionaries & Pilots (LAMP)
4966 - 92 Ave. NW, Edmonton AB T6B 2V4
Tel: 780-466-8507; *Fax:* 780-466-6733
Toll-Free: 800-307-4036
Other Communication: www.mistyriverministries.blogspot.ca
office@lampministry.org
www.lampministry.org
www.facebook.com/233505351133
www.youtube.com/user/LAMPMinistry/videos
Overview: A small international organization founded in 1970
Mission: To share Jesus Christ with the people of remote areas of Canada
Affliation(s): Lutheran Church Canada; Evangelical Lutheran Church in Canada
Chief Officer(s):
Ron Ludke, Executive Director
Finances: *Annual Operating Budget:* $500,000-$1.5 Million
300 volunteer(s)
Activities: *Speaker Service:* Yes

Lutheran Bible Translators of Canada Inc. (LBTC)
137 Queen St. South, Kitchener ON N2G 1W2
Tel: 519-742-3361; *Fax:* 519-742-5989
Toll-Free: 866-518-7071
info@lbtc.ca
www.lbtc.ca
Overview: A small international charitable organization founded in 1974
Mission: To bring people to faith in Jesus Christ through Bible translations & literacy work
Affliation(s): Canadian Council of Christian Charities
Chief Officer(s):
James Keller, Executive Director
JKeller@lbtc.ca
Finances: *Annual Operating Budget:* $250,000-$500,000
Staff Member(s): 5
Membership: 1-99
Activities: *Speaker Service:* Yes

Lutheran Church - Canada (LCC) / Église Luthérienne du Canada
3074 Portage Ave., Winnipeg MB R3K 0Y2
Tel: 204-895-3433; *Fax:* 204-832-3018
Toll-Free: 800-588-4226
Other Communication: communications@lutheranchurch.ca
info@lutheranchurch.ca
www.lutheranchurch.ca
www.facebook.com/117026825048861
twitter.com/CanLutheran
Overview: A medium-sized national organization founded in 1988
Mission: To share the Gospel of Jesus Christ; To proclaim the Lutheran belief & faith in word & deed
Affliation(s): Canadian Lutheran World Relief; Lutheran Women's Missionary League - Canada; Lutheran Laymen's League; Concordia Lutheran Mission Society
Chief Officer(s):
Robert Bugbee, President
president@lutheranchurch.ca
Dwayne Cleave, Treasurer
treasurer@lutheranchurch.ca
Finances: *Funding Sources:* Donations
Membership: 75,000+ members in 319 congregations
Activities: Supporting LCC missionaries in other countries; Working with Canadian Lutheran World Relief; Responding to social needs in local communities, such as establishing food banks & offering English as a Second Language classes; Education children through Sunday schools, Vacation Bible Schools, & confirmation classes; Offering various resources, such as congregation resources, statistical data, & theological documents; Organizing Synod conventions; *Awareness Events:* National Lutheran Open House; National Youth Gathering
Publications:
- The Canadian Lutheran
Type: Magazine; *Frequency:* Bimonthly; *Editor:* Mathew Block
ISSN: 0383-4247; *Price:* $20/yr.

Alberta-British Columbia District
7100 Ada Blvd. NW, Edmonton AB T5B 4E4
Tel: 780-474-0063; *Fax:* 780-477-9829
Toll-Free: 888-474-0063
info@lccabc.ca
www.lccabc.ca
Chief Officer(s):

Don Schiemann, District President
president@lccabc.ca
Central District
3074 Portage Ave., Winnipeg MB R3K 0Y2
Tel: 204-832-7242; *Fax:* 204-897-4319
Toll-Free: 800-663-5673
www.lcccentral.ca
Chief Officer(s):
Thomas Prachar, District President
tprachar@lutheranchurch.ca
East District
275 Lawrence Ave., Kitchener ON N2M 1Y3
Tel: 519-578-6500; *Fax:* 519-578-3369
Toll-Free: 800-465-8179
info@lcceastdistrict.ca
www.lcceastdistrict.ca
www.facebook.com/pages/Mr-ED-Missions/357998197548521
Chief Officer(s):
Allen Maleske, District President

Lutheran Laymen's League of Canada (LLL-C)
270 Lawrence Ave., Kitchener ON N2M 1Y4
Tel: 519-578-7420; *Fax:* 519-742-8091
Toll-Free: 800-555-6236
helpful@lll.ca
www.lll.ca
www.facebook.com/162406453805301
Also Known As: Lutheran Hour Ministries
Overview: A small national charitable organization founded in 1967
Mission: To proclaim gospel of Jesus Christ through the use of media; To bring Christ to the nations & the nation to the Christ
Affliation(s): International Lutheran Layman's League
Chief Officer(s):
Klinck Stephen, Managing Director
director@lll.ca
Finances: *Annual Operating Budget:* $500,000-$1.5 Million; *Funding Sources:* Donations
Staff Member(s): 2; 200 volunteer(s)
Membership: 1,000-4,999
Activities: Christian radio & TV programs; print & Internet resources; communication workshops
Publications:
• Media Matters [a publication of the Lutheran Layman's League of Canada]
Type: Newsletter

Lutsel K'E Development Corporation *See* Denesoline Corporation Ltd.

Lutte NB Wrestling (LNBW)
NB
www.luttenbwrestling.com
Overview: A small provincial organization overseen by Wrestling Lutte Canada
Mission: Lutte New Brunswick Wrestling (LNBW) is a non-profit, equal opportunity organization, dedicated to the development, administration and promotion of amateur wrestling throughout the Province.
Chief Officer(s):
Mary Singh, Executive Director
exec@luttenbwrestling.com
Chris Falconer, President
Staff Member(s): 2

Lymphedema Association of Québec *Voir* Association Québécoise du Lymphoedème

Lymphoma Canada
#351, 7111 Syntex Dr., Mississauga ON L5N 8C3
Tel: 905-822-5135; *Fax:* 905-822-5135
Toll-Free: 866-659-5556
info@lymphoma.ca
www.lymphoma.ca
www.facebook.com/LymphomaCanada
twitter.com/lymphomacanada
www.youtube.com/user/LymphomaTV
Previous Name: Lymphoma Foundation Canada
Merged from: Lymphoma Research Foundation of Canada (LRFC); Canadian Lymphoma Foundation (CLF)
Overview: A medium-sized national charitable organization founded in 2000
Mission: To provide education & support for individuals with lymphoma & their support network; To fund medical research to find a cure for lymphatic cancer; to advocate for the best treatment & care for lymphoma patients; To promote further research & new treatments in lymphoma & to promote rapid access to new developments
Chief Officer(s):
Paul Weingarten, Chair
Finances: *Annual Operating Budget:* $500,000-$1.5 Million; *Funding Sources:* Donations; Fundraising
Activities: *Awareness Events:* World Lymphoma Awareness Day, Sept.
Publications:
• Lymphoma & You: A Guide for Patients Living with Hodgkin's & Non-Hodgkin's Lymphoma
Type: Guide; *Editor:* C. Tom Kouroukis
Profile: Contents include an overview of lymphoma, Non-Hodgkin's & Hodgkin's Lymphoma, new developments in treatment, living withcancer, & a glossary
• Lymphoma Patient Resource
Type: Manual; *Number of Pages:* 146
Profile: A useful resource for patients recently diagnosed with lymphoma
La Fondation Lymphome Canada - Bureau du Québec
Montréal QC
Tél: 514-607-5967
www.lymphoma.ca
Chief Officer(s):
Tracy-Anne Curtis, Directrice générale, Québec
traceyann@lymphoma.ca

Lymphoma Foundation Canada *See* Lymphoma Canada

Lymphovenous Association of Ontario (LAO)
#203, 4800 Dundas Street West, Toronto ON M9A 1B1
Tel: 416-410-2250; *Fax:* 416-546-8991
Toll-Free: 877-723-0033
lymphontario@yahoo.com
www.lymphontario.org
Overview: A small provincial charitable organization founded in 1996
Mission: To educate the public; To promote improved treatments for lymphovenous disorders; To support research for a cure
Affliation(s): Canadian Disability Organization; Canadian Organization for Rare Disorders
Chief Officer(s):
Denise Lang, President
Anne Blair, Vice-Chair
Finances: *Annual Operating Budget:* Less than $50,000; *Funding Sources:* fundraising
15 volunteer(s)
Membership: 200; *Fees:* $50 individual; $150 professional; $200 business; *Member Profile:* Family or individual suffering lymphodema or lymphovenous disorder; *Committees:* Education; Newsletter; Conference; Fundraising; Research
Activities: Providing public education; Supporting research; Offering workshops;

Lymphovenous Canada
151 Rothsay Ave., Hamilton ON L8M 3G5
e-mail: info@lymphovenous-canada.ca
www.lymphovenous-canada.ca
Overview: A small national organization founded in 1996
Mission: The association links Canadians with lymphedema or dysfunctioning lymphatic systems with health care professionals & support groups locally & internationally. Lymphovenous Canada strives to provide information about the latest developments in scientific research & treatment in the field.
Member of: National Organization for Rare Disorders; Canadian Organization for Rare Disorders
Affliation(s): Canadian Health Network
Chief Officer(s):
C.J. McPherson, Administrator
Finances: *Funding Sources:* Donations
Activities: *Library:* Lymphovenous Canada Library

Lyndhurst Seeleys Bay & District Chamber of Commerce
PO Box 89, Lyndhurst ON K0E 1N0
Tel: 613-928-2382
info@lyndhurstseeleysbaychamber.com
www.lyndhurstseeleysbaychamber.com
Overview: A small local organization founded in 1993
Mission: To promote local businesses & help them grow
Member of: Ontario Chamber of Commerce
Chief Officer(s):
John Sederis, Vice-President
Finances: *Funding Sources:* Membership dues
Membership: 83; *Fees:* $75; *Member Profile:* Local businesses

Lynn Canyon Ecology Centre
3663 Park Rd., North Vancouver BC V7J 3G3
Tel: 604-990-3755
ecocentre@dnv.org
www.dnv.org/ecology/
Overview: A small local organization founded in 1971
Mission: To educate people about ecology
Chief Officer(s):
S.A. Kissinger
D. Robertson
Finances: *Funding Sources:* District of North Vancouver
Staff Member(s): 3; 12 volunteer(s)
Membership: 1,000-4,999; *Committees:* Stream Keepers - Maplewood Conservation Area
Activities: School & public education program; displays; leaflets

Lynn Lake Friendship Centre
PO Box 460, Lynn Lake MB R0B 0W0
Tel: 204-356-2407; *Fax:* 204-356-8223
www.mac.mb.ca/LynnL/home.htm
Overview: A small local organization
Mission: Provides programs and services to meet the needs of the Aboriginal and Non Aboriginal people in Lynn Lake and surrounding area.
Chief Officer(s):
Marilyn Hunt, Executive Director
Staff Member(s): 20
Activities: Family First Project; Partners for Careers; Eagle Feather Youth Council;

Lytton & District Chamber of Commerce
PO Box 460, 400 Fraser St., Lytton BC V0K 1Z0
Tel: 250-455-2523
Other Communication: Visitor Centre e-mail: visitorcentre@lyttonchamber.com
info@lyttonchamber.com
lyttonchamber.com
Also Known As: Lytton Infocentre
Overview: A small local organization founded in 1949
Mission: To encourage social & economic development in our area
Member of: BC Chamber of Commerce
Affliation(s): Vancouver Coast & Mountains Tourism Region
Chief Officer(s):
Bernie Fandrich, President
Sheila Maguire, Secretary
secretary@lyttonchamber.com
Finances: *Annual Operating Budget:* Less than $50,000; *Funding Sources:* Membership fees
Staff Member(s): 4; 4 volunteer(s)
Membership: 69; *Fees:* $50-150
Activities: Harvest Wine & Cheese, Oct.; Pizza Night - April

Lytton Community Food Bank
PO Box 86, Lytton BC V0K 1Z0
Tel: 250-455-2316; *Fax:* 250-455-6669
Overview: A small local organization overseen by Food Banks British Columbia
Member of: Food Banks British Columbia
Chief Officer(s):
Peggy Chute, Contact
Esther Brown, Contact

M2/W2 Association - Restorative Christian Ministries (M2/W2)
#208, 2825 Clearbrook Rd., Abbotsford BC V2T 6S3
Tel: 604-859-3215; *Fax:* 604-859-1216
Toll-Free: 800-298-1777
info@m2w2.com
www.m2w2.com
www.linkedin.com/groups/M2-W2-Association-5100601/about?trk=anet_ug_gr
www.facebook.com/M2W2Association?ref=hl
twitter.com/M2W2Association
Also Known As: Man-to-Man/Woman-to-Woman
Overview: A small provincial charitable organization founded in 1966
Mission: To mutually transform lives - one relationship at a time; To see individuals & communities in British Columbia safer, transformed, reconciled, & restored through justice, accountability, partnerships, mutual support, mediation, education & prevention; To provide one-to-one volunteers for men & women in British Columbia prisons, combined with pre- & post-release support & resources; To counsel prisoners, ex-prisoners, & their families; To prevent crime through one-to-one support for parents of young children at risk
Member of: Canadian Council of Christian Charities

Chief Officer(s):
Wayne Northey, Executive Director
northey@m2w2.com
Finances: *Annual Operating Budget:* $250,000-$500,000; *Funding Sources:* 65% community fundraising; 35% federal & provincial government contracts
Staff Member(s): 11; 400 volunteer(s)
Membership: 190; *Fees:* $10; *Member Profile:* Wide range of people whose common interest is the focus of M2/W2; *Committees:* Finance/Promotion; Program/New Initiatives; Personnel
Activities: Organizing annual promotion dinners; *Speaker Service:* Yes

Maccabi Canada
#418, 1881 Steeles Ave. West, Toronto ON M3H 0A1
Tel: 416-398-0515; *Fax:* 647-547-1699
info@maccabicanada.com
www.maccabicanada.com
www.facebook.com/213044145375553
twitter.com/MaccabiCanada
Overview: A small national organization
Mission: To promote Jewish identity & traditions through athletic, cultural, social & educational activities
Member of: Maccabi World Union
Chief Officer(s):
Tommy Bacher, President
tommybacher@rogers.com
Tali Dubrovsky, Executive Director
tali@maccabicanada.com
Membership: *Fees:* $18 student/youth; $216 adult; $300 family; *Committees:* National Athletic
Activities: *Awareness Events:* Maccabiah Games: every 4 years, in Israel; Pan-American Maccabiah Games: every 4 years in South America

British Columbia Region
Chief Officer(s):
Phil Levinson, Regional Chair
plevinson@zlc.net

Calgary South Region
Chief Officer(s):
Barb Krell, Regional Chair
b.krell@maccabicanada.com

Manitoba Region
Chief Officer(s):
Al Greenberg, Regional Chair

Ottawa-Hull Region
Ottawa-Hull QC
Chief Officer(s):
Bill Izso, Regional Chair
b.izso@maccabicanada.com

Québec Region
5400, Westbury, Montréal QC H3W 2W9
Tél: 514-736-6776; *Téléc:* 514-736-2176
Chief Officer(s):
Teddy Miller, Président
t.miller@maccabicanada.com

Macedonian Human Rights Movement of Canada (MHRMC) / Mouvement canadien de défense des droits de la personne dans la communauté macédonienne
#434, 157 Adelaide St., Toronto ON M5H 4E7
Tel: 416-850-7125; *Fax:* 416-850-7127
info@mhrmi.org
www.mhrmi.org
www.facebook.com/group.php?gid=24826968928
twitter.com/mhrmi
Overview: A small national organization founded in 1986
Mission: To secure & maintain the human rights of all Macedonians wherever they live through advocacy & education
Member of: Macedonian World Congress; Canadian Macedonian Federation
Chief Officer(s):
Bill Nicholov, President
Luby Vidinovski, Vice-President
Mark Opashinov, Secretary
Andy Plukov, Treasurer
Finances: *Annual Operating Budget:* $50,000-$100,000; *Funding Sources:* Donations; publications sales; membership fees
Staff Member(s): 2; 25 volunteer(s)
Membership: 600; *Fees:* $10; *Committees:* Data Collection; Executive; Fundraising; Membership; Publication; Public Relations
Activities: *Library* by appointment

MacEwan Staff Association (MSA)
MacEwan University, City Centre Campus, #7-102D, 10700 - 104 Ave., Edmonton AB T5J 2P2
Tel: 780-497-5697; *Fax:* 780-497-5696
msa@macewan.ca
www.macewanstaff.ca
www.facebook.com/macewanstaffassociation
twitter.com/MacEwanMSA
Previous Name: Grant MacEwan College Non-Academic Staff Association
Overview: A small local organization founded in 1982
Mission: To enhance the work environment; to advocate the interests of its members while contributing to the success of the college
Affliation(s): Non-Academic Staff Association, Univ. of Alberta
Chief Officer(s):
Donna-Mae Winquist, President
WinquistD@MacEwan.ca
Finances: *Funding Sources:* Membership fees
Staff Member(s): 4
Membership: *Member Profile:* Support or supervisory employees of Grant MacEwan College; *Committees:* Academic Governance Council; Admissions & Selections; Bylaw; Job Evaluation & Classification Review; Negotiations; Performance Management; Professional Development; Sick Leave & Disability Management; Social; MSA Financial; Health & Wellness; Employee Benefits; MSA Human Resources

MacGregor Chamber of Commerce
PO Box 220, MacGregor MB R0H 0R0
Tel: 204-685-2390
Overview: A small local organization
Mission: To facilitate the creation of an economic & social base in MacGregor & District that will encourage development & promotion in all sectors of the community
Member of: Manitoba Chamber of Commerce; Canadian Chamber of Commerce
Chief Officer(s):
Jason McKelvy, President
mckelv@mts.net
Finances: *Annual Operating Budget:* Less than $50,000; *Funding Sources:* Membership dues
Staff Member(s): 1
Membership: 165; *Fees:* $50; *Committees:* Promotion; Lobby
Activities: Certificate of Merit to new businesses; Sponsor of Communities in BLPOM & Pancake Breakfast; townwide garage sale; MacGregor & District Rodeo; *Library*
Awards:
• Citizen of the Year (Award)

Mackenzie & District Museum Society
PO Box 934, 86 Centennial Dr., Mackenzie BC V0J 2C0
Tel: 250-997-3021
museum@mackbc.com
www.mackenziemuseum.ca
www.facebook.com/mackenziemuseum
Overview: A small local charitable organization founded in 1991
Mission: To ensure the public has the opportunity to learn history & have fun while doing it
Member of: British Columbia Museums Association
Affliation(s): Fraser-Fort George Regional Museum
Chief Officer(s):
Christopher Johansen, President
Finances: *Annual Operating Budget:* Less than $50,000
Staff Member(s): 1; 7 volunteer(s)
Membership: 19; *Fees:* $10 individual; $15 family; *Member Profile:* Residents of Mackenzie
Activities: Displays are borrowed from residents & other museums; communication with schools & public advertising display; participates in Mackenzie Children's Festival; leisure fair; school tours; *Library:* Archives; Open to public by appointment

Mackenzie Applied Research Assciation (MARA)
PO Box 646, 1 River Road Experimental Farm, Fort Vermilion AB T0H 1N0
Tel: 780-927-3776; *Fax:* 780-927-4747
mara3@telus.net
www.areca.ab.ca/marahome.html
Overview: A small local organization overseen by Agricultural Research & Extension Council of Alberta
Mission: To conduct agricultural research, trials & rural extension in Northern Alberta's Mackenzie county
Chief Officer(s):
Jim Ludwig, Coordinator/Manager, 780-285-0843
ludwig41@telus.net

Mackenzie Chamber of Commerce
PO Box 880, 88 Centennial Dr., Mackenzie BC V0J 2C0
Tel: 250-997-5459; *Fax:* 250-997-6117
office@mackenziechamber.bc.ca
www.mackenziechamber.bc.ca
Overview: A small local charitable organization founded in 1984
Mission: To promote & support business; to improve trade & commerce; to enhance civic & social welfare in Mackenzie & area
Member of: BC Chamber of Commerce; Canadian Chamber of Commerce
Affliation(s): Retail Merchants Association of BC
Chief Officer(s):
Peter McGaffin, President
Finances: *Annual Operating Budget:* $100,000-$250,000; *Funding Sources:* District of Mackenzie; Community Futures; trade show; contract service fees; fundraising
Staff Member(s): 4; 23 volunteer(s)
Membership: 77; *Fees:* $94.76-$355.35 business; $39.65 individual; $71.07 non-profit
Activities: Info Centre; Civic Night; Self-Employed Business Funding; Referrals; Trade Show; Community Events; *Library* Open to public by appointment

Mackenzie Community Arts Council
Ernie Bodine Centre, PO Box 301, 86 Centennial Dr., Mackenzie BC V0J 2C0
Tel: 250-997-5818
Overview: A small local charitable organization founded in 1974
Mission: To support, encourage & promote arts & culture in the community through education, coordination of programs & raising public awareness
Member of: Assembly of BC Arts Councils; Central Interior Regional Arts Council; Canadian Artists Representation-CARFAC
Affliation(s): Mackenzie Potters Guild
Chief Officer(s):
Michele Gillespie, President
Finances: *Annual Operating Budget:* Less than $50,000
Staff Member(s): 1; 20 volunteer(s)
Membership: 111; *Fees:* $15 individual; $25 family; *Member Profile:* Potters, painters; artists; crafters & supporters; *Committees:* Advocacy; Finance; Programs; Festival of Bells; Mountain Gifts 'n Gallery; Children's Festival
Activities: Children's & adult programming; craft fair; children's festival; gift store; art gallery; monthly meetings; *Library:* Resource Centre; Open to public by appointment
Awards:
• Mackenzie Secondary School Scholarship (Scholarship)
• Mackenzie Secondary School Bursary (Grant)

The Mackenzie Institute
PO Box 338, Stn. Adelaide, Toronto ON M5C 2J4
Tel: 416-686-4063
institute@mackenzieinstitute.com
www.mackenzieinstitute.com
Overview: A small international charitable organization founded in 1986
Mission: To provide comment on terrorism, organized crime, political extremism, propaganda, conflict & other such matters
Finances: *Annual Operating Budget:* $100,000-$250,000
Staff Member(s): 3; 2 volunteer(s)
Membership: 500-999; *Fees:* $60 minimum annual donation
Activities: *Speaker Service:* Yes

Macklin Chamber of Commerce
PO Box 642, Macklin SK S0L 2C0
Tel: 306-753-2221; *Fax:* 306-753-3585
Other Communication: Alternate Phone: 306-753-2333
Overview: A small local organization
Finances: *Annual Operating Budget:* Less than $50,000
Membership: *Fees:* $50

Macleod Institute
#223, 20 Coachway Rd. SW, Calgary AB T3H 1E6
Tel: 403-240-2573; *Fax:* 403-246-1852
Toll-Free: 866-204-6123
macleod@macleodinstitute.com
www.macleodinstitute.com
Previous Name: Macleod Institute for Environmental Analysis
Overview: A small national organization founded in 1995
Mission: To provide impartial advice on regulatory & environmental issues
Affliation(s): University of Calgary

Chief Officer(s):
Elaine McCoy, President
Finances: *Annual Operating Budget:* $100,000-$250,000; *Funding Sources:* Contract
Staff Member(s): 5
Membership: 1-99

Macleod Institute for Environmental Analysis *See* Macleod Institute

Mactaquac County Chamber of Commerce
PO Box 1163, Nackawic NB E6G 2N1
Tel: 506-575-9622; *Fax:* 506-575-2035
mccc@mactaquaccountry.com
www.mactaquaccountry.com
Overview: A small local organization founded in 1997
Chief Officer(s):
Melanie Sloat, President
Dora Boudreau, Secretary
Finances: *Annual Operating Budget:* Less than $50,000
Membership: 75; *Fees:* $75; *Committees:* Awards Banquet; Artisans Sale; Charity Casino

Madawaska Forest Products Marketing Board / Office de vente des produits forestiers du Madawaska
PO Box 5, 870 Canada St., Edmundston NB E3V 3X3
Tel: 506-739-9585; *Fax:* 506-739-0859
odvdm@nbnet.nb.ca
Overview: A small local charitable organization founded in 1962
Mission: Mise en marché des produits forestiers bruts; encourager les bonnes pratiques d'aménagement forestier
Member of: La Fédération des Propriétaires de Lots Boissés du Nouveau Brunswick
Chief Officer(s):
Claude A. Pelletier, Manager
Finances: *Annual Operating Budget:* $100,000-$250,000
Staff Member(s): 7
Membership: 2 200 individu; 400 associé

Madawaska Valley Association for Community Living *See* Community Living Madawaska Valley

MADD Canada / Les mères contre l'alcool auvolant
#500, 2010 Winston Park Dr., Oakville ON L6H 5R7
Tel: 905-829-8805; *Fax:* 905-829-8860
Toll-Free: 800-665-6233
info@madd.ca
www.madd.ca
www.facebook.com/maddcanada.ca
twitter.com/maddcanada
Also Known As: Mothers Against Drunk Driving
Previous Name: PRIDE - People to Reduce Impaired Driving Everywhere (Ontario)
Overview: A medium-sized national charitable organization founded in 1982
Mission: To stop death & injury caused by impaired driving; To support victims of this crime
Chief Officer(s):
Andrew Murie, CEO
amurie@madd.ca
Wayne Kauffeldt, Chairperson
Denise Dubyk, President
Finances: *Funding Sources:* Donations; Sponsorships
7 volunteer(s)
Activities: Increasing public awareness about the dangers of drinking & driving; Offering programs such youth / school outreach; Engaging in legislative & public policy advocacy; Providing education; Offering support services to victims; Publishing & distributing brochures, statistics, & research papers; *Awareness Events:* Annual MADD Canada National Victims' Weekend & Candlelight Vigil of Hope and Remembrance; *Rents Mailing List:* Yes; *Library:* MADD Canada Research Library

Madoc & District Chamber of Commerce
PO Box 669, 20 Davidson St., Madoc ON K0K 2K0
Tel: 613-473-1616; *Fax:* 613-473-0860
cocmadoc@bellnet.ca
www.centrehastings.com/chamber_of_commerce.htm
Overview: A small local organization
Mission: To act as a voice for its members
Member of: Canadian Chamber of Commerce
Chief Officer(s):
Rob Price, President, 613-473-2131
rob@spotteddogbandb.ca
Leigh Anne Lavender, Coordinator
Staff Member(s): 1
Membership: *Fees:* $50

Madonna House Apostolate
2888 Dafoe Rd., RR#2, Combermere ON K0J 1L0
Tel: 613-756-3713; *Fax:* 613-756-0211
Other Communication: publications@madonnahouse.org
combermere@madonnahouse.org
www.madonnahouse.org
www.facebook.com/MadonnaHouse
twitter.com/madonnahouse
www.youtube.com/MadonnaHouseCanada
Overview: A small national charitable organization founded in 1947
Affliation(s): Roman Catholic Church; Diocese of Pembroke
Chief Officer(s):
David May, Director General
Susanne Stubbs, Director General
Mark Schlingerman, Director General
Finances: *Funding Sources:* Donations
Membership: 200+; *Member Profile:* Christian lay men, women, & priests, who are dedicated to promises of poverty, chastity, & obedience
Activities: Offering the Cana Colony summer program for families; Distributing gooods to the poor; Operating a gift shop, flea market, & used book shop to raise funds
Publications:
• Friends of Madonna House
Type: Newsletter; *Frequency:* Monthly; *Price:* Free
• Restoration: The Madonna House Catholic Newspaper
Type: Newspaper; *Frequency:* 10 pa; *Number of Pages:* 8 *ISSN:* 0708-2177

Edmonton
Marian Centre, 10528 - 98th St., Edmonton AB T5H 2N4
Tel: 780-424-3544
MCEEdmonton@shaw.ca
Mission: To offer friendship & hospitality to all who visit
Affliation(s): Archdiocese of Edmonton

Ottawa
440 Kensington Ave., Ottawa ON K1Z 6G8
Tel: 613-729-0956
Mission: To pray for salvation, the world, & for the people of the Archdiocese of Ottawa
Affliation(s): Archdiocese of Ottawa

Regina
Marian Centre, 1835 Halifax St., Regina SK S4P 1T4
Tel: 306-757-0073
Mission: To care for the poor; To pray for those who serve, benefactors, all those who enter the doors of Madonna House Apostolate, & for the people of the Regina area
Affliation(s): Archdiocese of Regina

Toronto
501 Parkside Dr., Toronto ON M6R 2Z9
Tel: 416-761-9965
mht@ca.inter.net
www.madonnahouse.org/field/toronto.html
Mission: To form a community of love; to be a house of hospitality, with a focus on evangelization; To provide availability to persons of every walk of life
Affliation(s): Archdiocese of Toronto

Vancouver
5450 Trafalgar St., Vancouver BC V6N 1B9
Tel: 604-267-1757
madonna02@shaw.ca
Mission: To be a place of welcome and friendship; To proclaim the Gospel of Jesus Christ; To provide an evangelizing presence in the Archdiocese of Vancouver
Affliation(s): Archdiocese of Vancouver

Whitehorse
Maryhouse, 506 Cook St., Whitehorse YT Y1A 2R4
Tel: 867-667-7146
Mission: To provide for the needs of the poor; To aim to preach the Gospel

Windsor
1374 Benjamin Ave., Windsor ON N8X 4M9
Tel: 519-252-9236
Mission: To offer a prayer-listening house to serve the Diocese of London; To pray & fast in support of priestly vocations
Affliation(s): Diocese of London

Magazines Canada
#700, 425 Adelaide St. West, Toronto ON M5V 3C1
Tel: 416-504-0274; *Fax:* 416-504-0437
info@magazinescanada.ca
www.magazinescanada.ca
www.linkedin.com/company/magazines-canada
www.facebook.com/MagazinesCanada
twitter.com/magscanada
www.youtube.com/magazinescanada
Previous Name: Canadian Periodical Publishers' Association; Canadian Magazine Publishers Association (CMPA)
Overview: A medium-sized national organization founded in 1973
Chief Officer(s):
Mark Jamison, Chief Executive Officer, 416-504-0274 Ext. 223, Fax: 416-504-0437
mjamison@magazinescanada.ca
Barbara Zatyko, General Manager, 416-504-0274 Ext. 222, Fax: 416-504-0437
bzatyko@magazinescanada.ca
Barbara Bates, Executive Director, Circulation Marketing, 416-504-0274 Ext. 229, Fax: 416-504-0437
bbates@magazinescanada.ca
Jim Everson, Executive Director, Public Affairs, 613-488-9916, Fax: 613-488-2861
jeverson@magazinescanada.ca
Gary Garland, Executive Director, Advertising Services, 416-504-0274 Ext. 245, Fax: 416-504-0437
ggarland@magazinescanada.ca
Finances: *Funding Sources:* Dept. of Canadian Heritage; ON Media Development Corp.; ON Arts Council; ON Ministry of Culture; Canada Council for the Arts; Private sponsorships
Membership: 350+; *Committees:* Advertising Services; Circulation Services; Executive; Government Relations; Market Intelligence; Membership
Activities: Offering member services such as direct-to-retail distribution, marketing, & advertising services; Providing professional development opportunities; Liaising with all levels of government; *Internships:* Yes

Magen David Adom canadien pour Israël *See* Canadian Magen David Adom for Israel

Maggie's: The Toronto Prostitutes' Community Service Project; Prostitute's Safe Sex Project *See* Maggie's: The Toronto Sex Workers Action Project

Maggie's: The Toronto Sex Workers Action Project
298A Gerrard St. East, 2nd Fl., Toronto ON M5A 2G7
Tel: 416-964-0150
maggiescoord@gmail.com
www.maggiestoronto.ca
www.facebook.com/Maggiestoronto
Also Known As: Maggie's
Previous Name: Maggie's: The Toronto Prostitutes' Community Service Project; Prostitute's Safe Sex Project
Overview: A small local charitable organization founded in 1991
Mission: To provide education & support to assist sex workers in our efforts to live & work with safety & dignity
Member of: Ontario AIDS Network
Finances: *Funding Sources:* Ontario Ministry of Health; AIDS Bureau; Donations
Membership: *Member Profile:* Sex trade workers
Activities: *Speaker Service:* Yes

The Magic of Christmas
PO Box 76097, Stn. Millrise, 9136 - 52 St., Calgary AB T2Y 2Z9
Tel: 403-803-1619; *Fax:* 403-256-8443
info@themagicofchristmas.org
www.themagicofchristmas.org
Also Known As: The Spirit of Christmas
Overview: A small local charitable organization founded in 1980
Mission: To spread the love, caring & sharing associated with the most joyous time of year
Finances: *Annual Operating Budget:* Less than $50,000
200 volunteer(s)
Membership: 200; *Member Profile:* People of all ages bringing love, care & sharing at Christmas; *Committees:* Transportation; Beneficiaries; Pickups; Sewing & Repairs; Media & Newsletter; Fundraising; Santa Shows; Phone; Office & Sorting; Decorating
Activities: Visiting private homes, hospitals, shelters, nursing homes on Christmas Eve; *Awareness Events:* Santa Clause Parade, Dec.; Christmas Eve Run, Dec. 24

Magnificat Charismatic Prayer Community
19309 Warden Ave., Queensville ON L0G 1R0
Tel: 905-478-4264
sanctuary-magnificat@rogers.com
reginamundimagnificat.com
Also Known As: Regina Mundi Retreat Centre
Overview: A small local organization founded in 1990

Mission: To provide spiritual care to all community members
Affliation(s): Regina Mundi Retreat Centre
Chief Officer(s):
Lita Malixi, Treasurer

Magog Historical Society *Voir* Société d'histoire de Magog

Magrath & District Chamber of Commerce
Magarath AB
www.magrathchamber.com
www.facebook.com/magrathchamber
twitter.com/magrathchamber
Overview: A small local organization
Affiliation(s): Alberta Chamber of Commerce; Canadian Chamber of Commerce
Chief Officer(s):
Jay Mackenzie, President
Membership: 46; *Fees:* $50 1-4 employees; $60 5-10 employees; $70 11-15 employees; $75 16+ employees; *Committees:* Membership/Budget; Business Development/Planning/Beautification; Public Relations/Communication/Education; Programs/Events

Mahatma Gandhi Canadian Foundation for World Peace
PO Box 60002, RPO University of Alberta, Edmonton AB T6G 2S4
Tel: 780-492-5504; *Fax:* 780-492-0113
gandhifoundationcanada@gmail.com
www.gandhi.ca
Overview: A small local charitable organization founded in 1986
Mission: To conduct programs & activities that promote the teachings & philosophy of Mahatma Gandhi in order to advance peace & understanding amongst peoples of the world
Chief Officer(s):
Jaime Beck, Educational Coordinator
Finances: *Annual Operating Budget:* Less than $50,000; *Funding Sources:* Banquet; casino funds
28 volunteer(s)
Membership: 40; *Fees:* $10
Activities: Speakers; public lectures; banquet; annual debate in school; summer institute; *Awareness Events:* Gandhi Memorial Day, Jan. 30; *Speaker Service:* Yes; *Library* by appointment
Awards:
• Mahatma Gandhi Scholarship (Scholarship)
Amount: $1,000

Mahone Bay & Area Chamber of Commerce
PO Box 59, Mahone Bay NS B0J 2E0
Tel: 902-624-6151; *Fax:* 902-624-6152
Toll-Free: 888-624-6151
info@mahonebay.com
www.mahonebay.com
Overview: A small local organization
Chief Officer(s):
Andrew Parrott, President, 902-531-5433
Ray Morin, Secretary
Marie Raymond, Staff

Maidstone & District Chamber of Commerce
PO Box 300, Maidstone SK S0M 1M0
Tel: 306-893-2461; *Fax:* 306-893-4222
Overview: A small local organization
Membership: *Fees:* $50

Mainland Nova Scotia Building & Construction Trades Council
#205, 14 McQuade Lake Cres., Halifax NS B3S 1B6
Tel: 902-450-1012; *Fax:* 902-450-1013
info@mainlandbuildingtrades.ca
www.mainlandbuildingtrades.ca
Overview: A small local organization
Mission: Committed to providing easy access to highly trained, safe working industrial tradesmen; to forge partnerships with owners & developers to become synonymous with sound investment & industrial growth in mainland Nova Scotia
Member of: AFL-CIO
Chief Officer(s):
Brad Smith, Executive Director
Finances: *Annual Operating Budget:* $100,000-$250,000
Staff Member(s): 1; 5 volunteer(s)
Membership: 12,000; *Member Profile:* Construction, maintenance & service

Mainland South Heritage Society (MSHS)
16 Sussex St., Halifax NS B3R 1N9
Tel: 902-868-2553
www.rootsweb.ancestry.com/~nsmshs/index.html
Overview: A small local charitable organization
Mission: To preserve the heritage of Mainland South
Chief Officer(s):
Leslie Harnish, President, 902-686-2553
harnish@hfx.eastlink.ca
Membership: *Fees:* $10; $15 senior couples

Mainstream Association for Proactive Community Living *See* posAbilities Association of BC

Maintenance, Engineering & Reliability (MER) Society (MER)
c/o Secretary, Marcel M. Djivre, 2058 Latimer Cres., Sudbury ON P3E 5L6
Tel: 705-621-1945
www.cim.org
Previous Name: Mechanical-Electrical Division of The Canadian Institute of Mining, Metallurgy & Petroleum
Overview: A medium-sized national organization overseen by Canadian Institute of Mining, Metallurgy & Petroleum
Mission: To advance the theory & practice of electrical & mechanical arts & sciences in the mining industry; To improve mechanical-electrical standards
Chief Officer(s):
Jo-Anne Boucher, Chair, 705-675-7720 Ext. 214
jo-anne_boucher@bestech.com
R.A. (Dick) McIvor, Treasurer
dmcivor@sympatico.ca
Activities: Facilitating the exchange of information & data on electrical & mechanical subjects; Publishing technical papers; Providing educational assistance; Promoting methods & devices to increase safety;
Awards:
• The McParland Memorial Medal (Award)
• JD (Pat) Patterson Memorial Scholarship (Scholarship)
• The CIM Fellow-ship Award (Award)
• Centennial Scholarship (Scholarship)
• Distinguished Lecturer (Award)
Meetings/Conferences: • Maintenance & Engineering Society of The Canadian Institute of Mining, Metallurgy & Petroleum 2015 Maintenance Engineering/Mine Operators' Conference, 2015
Scope: National
Description: A technical conference of interest to persons involved in maintenance & engineering in the mining industry
• Maintenance & Engineering Society of The Canadian Institute of Mining, Metallurgy & Petroleum 2016 Maintenance Engineering/Mine Operators' Conference, 2015
Scope: National
Description: A technical conference of interest to persons involved in maintenance & engineering in the mining industry

Maison Amaryllis
1462, rue Panet, Montréal QC H2L 2Z3
Tél: 514-526-3635; *Téléc:* 514-521-9209
maison.amaryllis@sympatico.ca
Aperçu: *Dimension:* petite; *Envergure:* locale; Organisme sans but lucratif; fondée en 1990 surveillé par Canadian AIDS Society
Affliation(s): Coalition des organismes communautaires québécois de lutte contre le sida
Finances: *Budget de fonctionnement annuel:* $250,000-$500,000
Membre(s) du personnel: 10; 7 bénévole(s)
Membre: 1-99
Activités: Maison d'hébergement pour personnes vivant avec le VIH/Sida, sans-abri et polytoxicomanes; *Événements de sensibilisation:* Souper bénéfice

Maison D'Haiti (MH)
8883, boul Saint-Michel, Montréal QC H1Z 3G3
Tél: 514-326-3022; *Téléc:* 514-326-3024
mhaiti@mhaiti.org
www.mhaiti.org
www.facebook.com/maison.haiti.1
Aperçu: *Dimension:* petite; *Envergure:* locale; fondée en 1972
Mission: L'organisme a pour missions, la promotion, l'intégration, l'amélioration des conditions de vie et la défense des droits des québécois d'origine haïtienne et des personnes immigrantes ainsi que la promotion de leur participation au développement de la société d'accueil.
Membre de: Issu de la communauté, issu des organisations, membres sympathisants et amis de la Maison d'Haïti
Membre(s) du bureau directeur:
Marjorie Villefranche, Directrice générale
dg@mhaiti.org
Finances: *Budget de fonctionnement annuel:* $1.5 Million-$3 Million; *Fonds:* MELS, MIDI, MSP, MSSS, Santé Canada, DRHC, Lutte à la pauvreté, Centraide, Québec jeunes, Dufresne Gauthier
Membre(s) du personnel: 19; 65 bénévole(s)
Membre: 125; *Montant de la cotisation:* 5$
Activités: Volet Éducation:alphabétisation, francisation, persévérance scolaire, camps éducatifs; Volet Femmes:sécurité alimentaire des familles, Réseau de jeunes parents, insertion des mères adolescentes; Volet Jeunesse: Animations culturelles et sportives, prévention contre la violence les les gangs de rue et l'exploitation sexuelle; Volet Intégration et insertion sociale: Accueil des nouveaux immigrants, orientation, recherche d'emploi

Maison de Campagne & d'Entraide Communautaire du Lac
Succ. 184, 2915, rte du Lac ouest, Alma QC G8B 5V6
Tél: 418-662-2102; *Téléc:* 418-662-6471
Nom précédent: Association des citoyennes averties Alma
Aperçu: *Dimension:* petite; *Envergure:* locale; fondée en 1976
Mission: Vise à informer, sensibiliser, et conscientiser les personnes à faible revenu de leurs droits; offrir une maison communautaire sans but lucratif, et permettre des vacances aux familles à faible revenu, un lieu privilégié pour des rencontres familiales, sessions de formation et d'éducation populaire, session de cuisine collective
Membre(s) du bureau directeur:
Germaine Gauthier, Coordonnatrice
maicam@cgocable.ca
Finances: *Budget de fonctionnement annuel:* $100,000-$250,000; *Fonds:* Gouvernements régional et provincial
Membre(s) du personnel: 7; 20 bénévole(s)
Membre: 77; *Montant de la cotisation:* 5$
Activités: *Listes de destinataires:* Oui

La Maison de jeunes Kekpart
1000, boul Roland-Therrien, Longueuil QC J4J 5H3
Tél: 450-677-3821; *Téléc:* 450-677-1907
maisonkekpart@videotron.ca
www.kekpart.com
www.facebook.com/pages/Maison-de-jeunes-Kekpart/414977215229908
twitter.com/Kekpart
Également appelé: Action jeunesse St-Pie X de Longueuil, inc.
Aperçu: *Dimension:* petite; *Envergure:* locale; Organisme sans but lucratif; fondée en 1981
Mission: Favoriser, chez les 12 à 18 ans, l'accessibilité à un statut de citoyen critique, actif et responsable; offre un lieu de rencontre animé où les jeunes peuvent choisir, organiser et participer à des activités de groupe
Membre de: Boys & Girls Clubs of Canada (Québec Region)
Membre(s) du bureau directeur:
Richard Desjardins, Directeur général et coordonnateur
Activités: Bowling; spectacle extérieur; cueuillette de pommes; marche en montagne; équitation; ateliers; soupers communautaires; conférences

La Maison de la culture inc. (MC)
#123, 218, boul J.D. Gauthier, Shippagan NB E8S 1P6
Tél: 506-336-3423; *Téléc:* 506-336-3434
mculture@umcs.ca
www.maisonculture.ca
Aperçu: *Dimension:* petite; *Envergure:* locale; Organisme sans but lucratif; fondée en 1983
Mission: Viser le développement et le rayonnement culturel communautaire, en français, dans toute la région, de Pokemouche à Miscou
Membre de: Conseil de promotion de diffusion de la culture
Affliation(s): Conseil provincial des sociétés culturelles; Réseau atlantique de diffusion des arts de la scène
Membre(s) du bureau directeur:
Carole Savoie, Présidente
Denise Haché, Secrétaire
Finances: *Budget de fonctionnement annuel:* Moins de $50,000; *Fonds:* Patrimoine canadien
Membre(s) du personnel: 2; 9 bénévole(s)
Membre: 84 individuels; 9 familles; 2 entreprise; *Montant de la cotisation:* 3$ étudiant(e)/aîné(e); $5 individuel; $15 famille; 30$ organisme; *Comités:* Bureau de direction; Conseillières-Conseillers
Activités: Spectacle, pièces de théâtre; expositions, ventes; ateliers; camp musical et artistique; revendications; lancement de disques et de livres

Maison de la famille de la Vallée du Richelieu
91, boul. Cartier, Beloeil QC J3G 6R4

Tél: 450-446-0852
famillevr@videotron.ca
mfvr.ca
Aperçu: *Dimension:* petite; *Envergure:* locale
Mission: Pour aider les parents à apprendre plus de compétences parentales pour aider à améliorer leur vie et celle de leurs enfants
Membre: *Montant de la cotisation:* 15$
Activités: Ateliers; Conférences; Halte-garderie; Services de soutien; *Stagiaires:* Oui

Maison de Ribatejo *Voir* Casa do Ribatejo

La Maison des Açores du Québec *Voir* La Maison des Açores du Québec

La Maison des Açores du Québec / La Maison des Açores du Québec

229, rue Fleury Ouest, Montréal QC H3L 1T8
Tél: 514-388-4129; *Téléc:* 514-388-2813
casadosacoresdoquebeque@hotmail.com
casadosacores.org
Également appelé: Quebec Acores House
Aperçu: *Dimension:* petite; *Envergure:* internationale; fondée en 1978
Mission: Maintenir la communauté açores et la culture açores et préserver leur indentité
Membre(s) du bureau directeur:
Damiao Sousa, Président, Consil d'administration
José Machado, Vice-Président, Consil d'administration
Maria Alice Macedo, Trésorière, Consil d'administration

Maison des femmes de Québec inc.

CP 48023, Québec QC G1R 5R5
Tél: 418-522-0042; *Téléc:* 418-522-8034
maisondesfemmes.qc@videotron.ca
www.lamaisondesfemmesdequebec.com
Aperçu: *Dimension:* petite; *Envergure:* locale; Organisme sans but lucratif; fondée en 1980
Mission: Pourvoir hébergement gratuit & protection pour femmes et enfants victomes de violence conjugale; assurer un lieu sécuritaire d'intervention
Membre de: Regroupement provincial des maisons d'hébergement
Finances: *Budget de fonctionnement annuel:* $250,000-$500,000; *Fonds:* Gouvernement provincial
Membre(s) du personnel: 7; 25 bénévole(s)
Membre: 25; *Montant de la cotisation:* 2$
Activités: Représentation extérieure (écoles, universités, etc.); écoute téléphonique consultation à l'externe; support et accompagnement dans les démarchers; intervention individuelle et de groupe; *Stagiaires:* Oui; *Service de conférenciers:* Oui

Maison des marins de Montréal *See* Mariners' House of Montréal

Maison du Parc

1287, rue Rachel est, Montréal QC H2J 2J9
Tél: 514-523-6467; *Téléc:* 514-523-6800
info@maisonduparc.org
www.maisonduparc.org
Aperçu: *Dimension:* petite; *Envergure:* locale; fondée en 1991 surveillé par Canadian AIDS Society
Membre de: Coalition des Organismes Communautaires Québécois-Sida
Membre(s) du bureau directeur:
Catherine Breton, Directrice générale
Membre(s) du personnel: 15; 15 bénévole(s)
Activités: Centre d'hébergement pour personnes vivant avec le VIH-Sida (12 places); repas préparés sont distribués;

Maison du Tourisme

892, rte 111 est, Amos QC J9T 2K4
Tél: 819-727-1242; *Téléc:* 819-727-3437
www.ville.amos.qc.ca/tourisme
Également appelé: Tourism Harricana
Nom précédent: Tourisme Harricana
Aperçu: *Dimension:* petite; *Envergure:* locale; Organisme sans but lucratif; fondée en 1995
Mission: Accueil; promotion; développement
Finances: *Budget de fonctionnement annuel:* $100,000-$250,000
Membre(s) du personnel: 2

Maison Elizabeth *See* Elizabeth House

Maison internationale de la Rive-Sud (MIRS)

#220, 2152, boul Lapinière, Brossard QC J4W 1L9
Tél: 450-445-8777; *Téléc:* 450-445-1222
info@mirs.qc.ca
www.mirs.qc.ca
Aperçu: *Dimension:* petite; *Envergure:* locale; fondée en 1975
Membre(s) du bureau directeur:
Gérard Deschênes, Président
Nicole Diessenes, Vice-présidente
Miguel Del Rio, Trésorier
Pierre Faubert, Secrétaire
Noureddine Belhocine, Directeur général
Membre(s) du personnel: 10

Maison Plein Coeur

1611, rue Dorion, Montréal QC H2K 4A5
Tél: 514-597-0554; *Téléc:* 514-597-2788
infompc@maisonpleincoeur.org
www.maisonpleincoeur.org
Aperçu: *Dimension:* petite; *Envergure:* locale; fondée en 1991
Mission: Contribuer à prévenir le VIH-SIDA, et à promouvoir la santé chez les personnes vivant avec la maladie; offrir des services sans aucune discrimination
Membre(s) du bureau directeur:
Gary Lacasse, Directeur général, 514-597-0554 Ext. 222
gary@maisonpleincoeur.org
Elaine Mayrand, Présidente

Maisons Adrianna

2500, rue Ste-Catherine Est, Montréal QC H2K 2K2
Tél: 514-527-9233
info@maisons-adrianna.org
maisons-adrianna.org
Aperçu: *Dimension:* petite; *Envergure:* locale; fondée en 1988
Mission: Pour aider à améliorer la qualité de vie des personnes défavorisées vivant dans la région centre-sud et de leur offrir une éducation sur la malnutrition
Membre(s) du bureau directeur:
Reynald Leboeuf, Directeur général
Activités: Bazar; Friperie; Librairie; Bingo

The Maitland Trail Association (MTA)

PO Box 443, Goderich ON N7A 4C7
e-mail: mta.goderich@gmail.com
www.maitlandtrail.cjb.net
Overview: A small local organization founded in 1975
Mission: To develop & maintain low impact recreational trails in the natural areas of the Maitland River Valley
Member of: Hike Ontario
Chief Officer(s):
Susanna Reid, President
Finances: *Funding Sources:* Membership dues; donations; grants; Nevada outlet funding
Membership: *Fees:* $20 individual; $25 family
Activities: Trail follows the north side of the Maitland River from Lake Huron at Goderich to the Village of Auburn; developed & maintains the Goderich to Auburn Rail Trail (GART) in cooperation with the Colborne Snowmobile Club, a 2.5 km trail in the Maitland Woods (owned by Town of Goderich); work on new trail on the south bank of the Maitland River, called the Millennium Trail

Make-A-Wish Canada / Fais-Un-Voeu Canada

#520, 211 Yonge St., Toronto ON M2P 2A9
Tel: 416-224-9474; *Fax:* 416-224-8795
Toll-Free: 888-822-9474
nationaloffice@makeawish.ca
makeawish.ca
www.linkedin.com/company/422218
www.facebook.com/makeawish.ca
twitter.com/MakeAWishCA
www.youtube.com/user/makeawishcanada
Overview: A large national charitable organization founded in 1980
Mission: The Foundation grants wishes to children suffering from a high risk, life-threatening illnesses
Chief Officer(s):
Jennifer Klotz-Ritter, Chief Executive Officer
Finances: *Annual Operating Budget:* Greater than $5 Million; *Funding Sources:* Donations
Staff Member(s): 15

Maker Kids

2241 Dundas St. West, Toronto ON M6R 1X6
Tel: 416-534-4560
info@makerkids.ca
www.makerkids.ca
www.facebook.com/MakerKids
twitter.com/Maker_Kids
Overview: A small local charitable organization
Mission: To help children & adults become more creative using physical tools & materials in areas including electronics, cooking, crafts & woodworking
Chief Officer(s):
Andy Forest, Co-Founder & Chief Investigator
Marianne Mader, Co-Founder
Staff Member(s): 7; 4 volunteer(s)
Activities: *Internships:* Yes

Makivik Corporation / Société Makivik

PO Box 179, Kuujjuaq QC J0M 1C0
Tel: 819-964-2925
Toll-Free: 877-625-4825
info@makivik.org
www.makivik.org
Previous Name: Northern Quebec Inuit Association
Overview: A large local charitable organization founded in 1978
Mission: A non-profit organization owned by the Inuit of Nunavik, the Corporation promotes the social & economic interests of the Inuit people; receives, administers & invests Inuit compensation funds received under the James Bay & Northern Québec Agreement, & promotes the political, social & economic development of the Nunavik region. Offices in Kuujjuaq, Montreal, Ottawa, Quebec City
Member of: Inuit Tapirisat Kanatami; Inuit Circumpolar Conference
Chief Officer(s):
Jobie Tukkiapik, President
Anthony Ittoshat, Treasurer
Andy Moorhouse, Corporate Secretary
Finances: *Annual Operating Budget:* Greater than $5 Million; *Funding Sources:* JBNQA compensation; investments; subsidiary corporations
Staff Member(s): 83
Membership: 9,838; *Member Profile:* Inuit as defined in James Bay Agreement
Activities: *Awareness Events:* Signing of James Bay & Northern Québec Agreement, Nov. 11, 1975; *Speaker Service:* Yes
Publications:
- Makivik Magazine [a publication of the Makivik Corporation]
Type: Magazine; *Frequency:* Quarterly
- Nunavik Newsletter [a publication of the Makivik Corporation]
Type: Newsletter

Inukjuak Office
Inukjuak QC J0M 1M0
Tél: 819-254-1173; *Téléc:* 819-254-1040

Kuujjuaraapik Office
Kuujjuaraapik QC J0M 1G0
Tél: 819-929-3925; *Téléc:* 819-929-3982

Montréal Office
1111, boul Dr. Frederic-Philips, 3e étage, Saint-Laurent QC H4M 2X6
Tél: 514-745-8880
Ligne sans frais: 800-361-7052

Québec City Office
555, Grande-Allée est, Québec QC G1R 2J5
Tél: 418-522-2224

Malaspina Printmakers Society (MPS)

1555 Duranleau St., Vancouver BC V6H 3S3
Tel: 604-688-1724
www.malaspinaprintmakers.com
www.facebook.com/malaspinaprintmakers
twitter.com/malaspinaprint
www.youtube.com/malaspinaprintmakers
Overview: A small international charitable organization founded in 1975
Mission: To support the development of printmaking as a contemporary art form and promotes and preserves traditional print practice; to advance knowledge of printmaking in the community; to facilitate the critical and technical exploration of printmaking in contemporary visual art practice.
Member of: Vancouver Cultural Alliance
Chief Officer(s):
Justin Muir, Executive Director
Finances: *Funding Sources:* All levels of government; membership fees; fundraising; sales; studio rent
Membership: *Fees:* $35 individual; $50 friend; $150 patron; $300-$599 supporter; $600+ benefactor
Activities: *Internships:* Yes; *Library:* Resource Centre; Open to public

Mallaig Chamber of Commerce

PO Box 144, Mallaig AB T0A 2K0
Tel: 780-635-3952

Overview: A small local organization
Member of: Alberta Chambers of Commerce

Malloch Foundation
c/o Lazier Hickey LLP, 25 Main St. West, 15th Fl., Hamilton ON L8P 1H1
Tel: 905-525-3652; *Fax:* 905-525-6278
www.mallochfoundation.ca
Previous Name: F. David Malloch Memorial Foundation
Overview: A small local charitable organization founded in 1964
Mission: To provide funds in fields of child development, conservation, treatment of animals, education, medicine, adult & adolescent rehabilitation & reform with preference given to charities in Hamilton area
Chief Officer(s):
Colin G. Lazier, Secretary-Treasurer
laziercg@lazierhickey.com

Malta Band Club, Inc.
5745 Coopers Ave., Mississauga ON L4Z 1R9
Tel: 905-890-8507; *Fax:* 905-890-1306
maltabandclub@bellnet.ca
www.maltabandclub.net
Overview: A medium-sized local organization founded in 1971
Mission: To promote Maltese culture
Affliation(s): Maltese Canadian Federation
Chief Officer(s):
Anthony Vella, President
Activities: Musical instruction; *Library* Open to public

Maltese Veterans Association of Canada
3 Baby Point Cres., Toronto ON M6S 2B7
Tel: 416-767-8185
Overview: A small national organization founded in 1975
Member of: Maltese-Canadian Federation
Membership: *Member Profile:* Maltese-Canadians

Maltese-Canadian Federation Inc.
c/o St. Paul the Apostle Church, 3223 Dundas St. West, Toronto ON M6P 2A4
Overview: A small national organization
Affliation(s): Maltese Veterans Association of Canada
Chief Officer(s):
Joe Sherri, President
joesherri21@gmail.com
Membership: *Member Profile:* Maltese-Canadians

Maltese-Canadian Society of Toronto, Inc. (MCST)
3132 Dundas St. West, Toronto ON M6P 2A1
Tel: 416-767-3645
Also Known As: The Maltese Society
Overview: A small local organization founded in 1922
Mission: The organization strives for the betterment of the Maltese community in Toronto. It also preserves & promotes the Maltese language & culture in Canada.
Affliation(s): Maltese-Canadian Federation Inc.
Finances: *Annual Operating Budget:* Less than $50,000
9 volunteer(s)
Membership: *Member Profile:* Persons of Maltese-Canadian background
Activities: Outings; social events; Miss Malta of Canada Pageant

Malton Neighbourhood Services
3540 Morning Star Dr., Mississauga ON L4T 1Y2
Tel: 905-677-6270; *Fax:* 905-677-6281
www.mnsinfo.org
www.facebook.com/181976788507092
Overview: A small local charitable organization founded in 1978 overseen by Ontario Council of Agencies Serving Immigrants
Mission: To identify community needs; to promote community participation in planning; to ensure services are accessible & available to Malton residents; to promote community pride
Affliation(s): City of Mississauga Recreation Department
Chief Officer(s):
Joyce Temple-Smith, Executive Director
Tony Patey, Chair
Membership: *Member Profile:* Resident/worker in ward 5, Mississauga
Activities: Malton Community Information Service; *Speaker Service:* Yes; *Library* Open to public
Awards:
• Citizenship & Immigration Citation for Citizenship (Award)

Mamawehetowin Crisis Centre
PO Box 133, Pukatawagan MB R0B 1G0
Tel: 204-553-2198; *Fax:* 204-553-2302; *Crisis Hot-Line:* 866-432-1041
Previous Name: Mamawehetowin Crisis Centre for Abused Women & Children
Overview: A small local organization
Mission: To provide shelter & servies to battered aboriginal women & their children
Member of: National Aboriginal Circle Against Family Violence
Activities: Emergency shelter; Support groups; Crisis counselling & intervention; Referrals to medical, legal & social service agencies; Follow-up services

Mamawehetowin Crisis Centre for Abused Women & Children *See* Mamawehetowin Crisis Centre

Mamingwey Burn Survivor Society
#303, 83 Garry St., Winnipeg MB R3C 4J9
Tel: 204-272-0945
info@mamingwey.ca
www.mamingwey.ca
Overview: A small local organization
Mission: To offer support to persons with burn injuries
Chief Officer(s):
Barbara-Anne Hodge, Chair & Occupational Therapist
Membership: *Member Profile:* Burn survivors; Family members & friends of burn survivors; Persons who work with burn victims
Activities: Providing networking opportunities;

Ma-Mow-We-Tak Friendship Centre Inc. / The Gathering Place
122 Hemlock Cres., Thompson MB R8N 0R6
Tel: 204-677-0950; *Fax:* 204-677-0970
reception@mamowwetak.mb.ca
www.mamowwetak.mb.ca
Overview: A small local organization founded in 1976
Mission: To support Aboriginal people making the transition from life on the reserve or isolated communities to urban life in Thompson, Manitoba; To operate as a non-sectarian, non-political, non-profit, charitable organization, geared to meeting the needs of Aboriginal people in Thompson and the surrounding area
Chief Officer(s):
Anita Campbell, Executive Director
Activities: Northern Council of Youth; Youth Employment Assistant Services; Parent/Child Centre Initiative; New Beginnings

Managers Association of Financial Advisors of Canada *See* GAMA International Canada

Manitoba 5 Pin Bowlers' Association (M5PBA)
#432, 145 Pacific Ave., Winnipeg MB R3B 2Z6
Tel: 204-925-5766; *Fax:* 204-925-5792
Toll-Free: 800-282-8069
www.m5pba.com
twitter.com/M5PBA
Overview: A small provincial organization overseen by Manitoba Five Pin Bowling Federation, Inc.
Member of: Manitoba Five Pin Bowling Federation, Inc.
Chief Officer(s):
Marilyn McMullan, President
mgmc.hdqtrs@shaw.ca

Manitoba Aboriginal Education Counselling Association Inc.
#305, 352 Donald St., Winnipeg MB R3B 2H8
Tel: 204-947-0421
Overview: A small provincial organization founded in 1989
Awards:
• Abraham McPherson Scholarship Award (Scholarship)
Eligibility: High school graduate with an overall average of 70% upon graduation *Amount:* $250

Manitoba Amateur Bodybuilding Association (MABBA)
23 Forestgate Ave., Winnipeg MB R3P 2L2
e-mail: mabba@shaw.ca
www.bodybuilding.ca
Overview: A small provincial organization overseen by Canadian Bodybuilding Federation
Mission: To govern the sport of amateur bodybuilding, fitness & figure in Manitoba.
Member of: Canadian Bodybuilding Federation; International Federation of Bodybuilding; Sport Manitoba
Chief Officer(s):
Tom Heffner, President
mabbapres@mymts.net
Chris McKee, Executive Director
mabba@shaw.ca
Membership: *Committees:* Fitness; Figure; Bikini; Bodybuilding; Physique

Manitoba Amateur Boxing Association *See* Boxing Manitoba

Manitoba Amateur Broomball Association (MABA)
145 Pacific Ave., Winnipeg MB R3B 2Z6
Tel: 204-925-5668; *Fax:* 204-925-9792
broomballmb@shaw.ca
www.mbbroomball.com
Overview: A medium-sized provincial organization founded in 1982 overseen by Ballon sur glace Broomball Canada
Mission: To promote the sport of broomball in Manitoba; to offer opportunities to members in competing in provincial & national championships
Member of: Ballon sur glace Broomball Canada; Sport Manitoba
Staff Member(s): 1
Membership: 500
Activities: School clinics; competitions; tournaments; provincials

Manitoba Amateur Wrestling Association (MAWA)
c/o Sport Manitoba, 145 Pacific Ave., Winnipeg MB R3B 2Z6
e-mail: mawawrestling@mts.net
www.mawawrestling.ca
Overview: A small provincial organization founded in 2007 overseen by Canadian Amateur Wrestling Association
Mission: The Manitoba Amateur Wrestling Association (MAWA) is the recognised provincial sport organization (PSO) for the sport of wrestling in Manitoba. MAWA is dedicated to the continuing development of wrestling across the province and to maintain a safe, fun environment for all its members. MAWA is an organization that promotes teamwork, leadership and healthy lifestyles through wrestling in Manitoba for all ages.
Chief Officer(s):
Sally McNabb, President
Membership: *Fees:* Schedule available; *Member Profile:* Individual wrestlers & clubs; *Committees:* Tournament; Athlete Development; Marketing

Manitoba Animal Health Technologists Association (MAHTA)
1590 Inkster Blvd., Winnipeg MB R2X 2W4
Tel: 204-832-1394; *Fax:* 204-896-6756
office@mahta.ca
www.mahta.ca
Overview: A small provincial organization
Member of: Canadian Association of Animal Health Technologists & Technicians
Membership: *Fees:* Schedule available

Manitoba Antique Association
PO Box 2881, Winnipeg MB R3C 4B4
e-mail: manitobaantique@gmail.com
www.manitobaantiqueassociation.com
Overview: A medium-sized provincial organization founded in 1967
Mission: To preserve & restore antiques; To promote the admiration of all antiques
Chief Officer(s):
Frank Coelho, President, 204-389-3639
fjosecoelho@gmail.com
Finances: *Annual Operating Budget:* Less than $50,000
Membership: 300; *Fees:* $25 individual; $35 family
Activities: Organizing educational programs; Presenting shows & sales; *Speaker Service:* Yes

Manitoba Arm Wrestling Association (MAWA)
MB
Tel: 204-509-9896
info@manitobaarmwrestling.com
www.manitobaarmwrestling.com
www.facebook.com/groups/375248869203923
Overview: A small provincial organization overseen by Canadian Arm Wrestling Federation
Mission: To oversee & promote the sport of arm wrestling in Manitoba.
Member of: Canadian Arm Wrestling Federation
Chief Officer(s):
Darrell Steffenson, Contact

Manitoba Arts Council (MAC) / Conseil des arts du Manitoba (CAM)
#525, 93 Lombard Ave., Winnipeg MB R3B 3B1
Tel: 204-945-2237; *Fax:* 204-945-5925
Toll-Free: 866-994-2787
info@artscouncil.mb.ca
artscouncil.mb.ca
www.facebook.com/190664875839

Overview: A medium-sized provincial organization founded in 1969
Mission: An arms-length agency of the provincial government dedicated to artistic excellence; offers a broad based grant program for professional artists & arts organizations; promotes, preserves, supports & advocates for the arts as essential to the quality of life of all people of Manitoba.
Chief Officer(s):
Keith Bellamy, Chair
Douglas Riske, Executive Director, 204-945-2239
driske@artscouncil.mb.ca
Finances: *Annual Operating Budget:* Greater than $5 Million; *Funding Sources:* Dept. of Culture, Heritage & Tourism
Staff Member(s): 18
Activities: *Speaker Service:* Yes
Awards:
- Performing Arts (Grant)
- Arts Development (Grant)
- Writing & Publishing (Grant)
- Aboriginal Arts (Grant)
- Visual Arts (Grant)
- Multidisciplinary (Grant)

Manitoba Arts Network
#203, 100 Arthur St., Winnipeg MB R3B 1H3
Tel: 204-943-0036; *Fax:* 204-943-1126
Toll-Free: 866-919-2787
info@communityarts.mb.ca
www.manitobaartsnetwork.ca
www.facebook.com/pages/Manitoba-Arts-Network/77135232619
twitter.com/search/manitoba%20arts
www.flickr.com/search/?q=manitoba+arts
Also Known As: Manitoba Association of Community Arts Councils Inc.
Overview: A small provincial charitable organization founded in 1984
Mission: To represent community arts councils & community arts programming organizations throughout Manitoba; to enhance community life by providing opportunities for individuals in rural & remote communities to participate in & gain knowlege from arts & cultural activities that enrich their lives; to provide support for the growth & development of community arts councils throughout Manitoba; to provide programs & services designed to foster the development of arts & cultural activity in rural & remote communities
Chief Officer(s):
Rose-Ann Harder, Director
director@mbartsnet.ca
Staff Member(s): 5; 50 volunteer(s)
Membership: 150; *Member Profile:* Arts organizations & individual artists; *Committees:* Visual Arts; Northern Touring; Southern Touring
Activities: Tour Visual arts exhibitions; arrange block booking for performance tours; *Library*

Manitoba Association for Art Education (MAAE)
Winnipeg MB
maae.weebly.com
Overview: A small provincial organization
Mission: To promote & improve visual art education in Manitoba
Affliation(s): Manitoba Teachers' Society; Canadian Society for Education through Art
Chief Officer(s):
Dawn Knight, President
dknight@pembinatrails.ca
Membership: *Fees:* $20; $10 (student); *Member Profile:* Teachers; artists; students; *Committees:* Grants; SAGE Conference

Manitoba Association for Behaviour Analysis (MABA)
PO Box 53017, Stn. South St. Vital, Winnipeg MB R2N 3X2
e-mail: president@maba.ca
www.maba.ca
Overview: A small provincial organization
Chief Officer(s):
Genevieve Roy-Wsiaki, President
president@maba.ca
Membership: *Committees:* Executive Public Relations; Newsletter; Membership; Conference
Meetings/Conferences: • 10th Annual Manitoba Association for Behaviour Analysis 2015 Conference, 2015, MB
Scope: Provincial

Manitoba Association for Business Economics (MABE)
MB
www.cabe.ca/jmv3/index.php/cabe-chapters/mabe
Overview: A small provincial organization overseen by Canadian Association for Business Economics
Mission: To provide a forum for people in Manitoba who are interested in economics; to foster education in the field of economics
Member of: Canadian Association for Business Economics
Chief Officer(s):
Sarah Piercy, President, 204-947-1379 Ext. 16
sarah.piercy@mhca.mb.ca
Stephen Verhaeghe, President, 204-945-1479
stephen.verhaeghe@gov.mb.ca
Finances: *Funding Sources:* Membership

Manitoba Association for Medical Laboratory Science (MAMLS)
585 London St., Winnipeg MB R2K 2Z6
Tel: 204-669-9050; *Fax:* 204-667-1747
mamlsprez1@gmail.com
www.mamls.ca
Previous Name: Manitoba Society of Medical Laboratory Science; Manitoba Society of Medical Laboratory Technologists
Overview: A medium-sized provincial organization overseen by Canadian Society for Medical Laboratory Science
Mission: To protect public safety by maintaining & improving standards of medical laboratory technology practice in Manitoba, & promoting closer cooperation between its members & other health care professionals to more effectively aid in the diagnosis of disease
Affliation(s): Canadian Society for Medical Laboratory Science
Chief Officer(s):
Michele Sykes, President
Finances: *Funding Sources:* Member fees
Membership: *Member Profile:* Certified technologists & trainees

Manitoba Association for Volunteer Administration (MAVA)
PO Box 3099, Winnipeg MB R3C 4B3
e-mail: MAVAmanitoba@gmail.com
www.mavamanitoba.ca
www.facebook.com/840199486025116
twitter.com/MAVA_MB
Overview: A small provincial organization
Mission: To unite individuals involved in the administration of volunteer services & programs in a professional association; promotes volunteer administration as a profession; provides opportunities for the exchange of knowledge & experience in the administration of volunteer services & programs; promotes professional standards, education, growth & development
Member of: Canadian Administrators of Volunteer Resources
Chief Officer(s):
Lesley Camaso-Catalan, President
Membership: *Fees:* $35 student; $65 adult
Meetings/Conferences: • Manitoba Association for Volunteer Administration Biennial Conference 2015, 2015, MB
Scope: Provincial

Manitoba Association of Architects (MAA)
137 Bannatyne Ave., 2nd Fl., Winnipeg MB R3B 0R3
Tel: 204-925-4620; *Fax:* 204-925-4624
info@mbarchitects.org
www.mbarchitects.org
Overview: A medium-sized provincial licensing organization founded in 1914
Mission: To protect the public interest and advance the profession of architecture.
Chief Officer(s):
Judy Pestrak, Executive Director
Finances: *Funding Sources:* Membership dues
Staff Member(s): 2
Membership: *Fees:* Schedule available; *Committees:* Registration; Executive; Practice; Education; Public Affairs; Investigation; Inquiry; Internship in Architecture
Activities: *Internships:* Yes; *Rents Mailing List:* Yes

Manitoba Association of Cheerleading (MAC)
MB
Tel: 204-888-0317
info@cheermanitoba.ca
www.cheermanitoba.ca
www.facebook.com/ManitobaAssociationofCheerleading
twitter.com/MAC_Cheer_MB
Overview: A small provincial organization founded in 1986 overseen by Cheer Canada
Mission: To be the official regulating body for cheerleading in Manitoba.
Member of: Cheer Canada
Chief Officer(s):
Patricia McNeill, President

Manitoba Association of Christian Home Schools (MACHS)
PO Box 13 RPO SO St Vital, Winnipeg MB R2N 3X9
e-mail: info@machs.ca
www.machs.mb.ca
Overview: A small provincial organization founded in 1983
Mission: MACHS is a non-profit, volunteer provincial organization that seeks to connect, support and equip all those who are involved in Christian Home Education in the Province of Manitoba.
Chief Officer(s):
Edgar Donelle, Président
Activities: *Library:* MACHS Library;
Meetings/Conferences: • Homeschool Conference 2015, March, 2015, Calvary Temple, Winnipeg, MB
Scope: Provincial

Manitoba Association of Fire Chiefs (MAFC)
PO Box 1208, Portage La Prairie MB R1N 3J9
Tel: 204-857-6249
mb.firechiefs@mymts.net
mafc.ca
Overview: A small provincial organization founded in 1950
Chief Officer(s):
Martin Haller, President
Membership: *Fees:* $150 regular; *Committees:* Annual Conference; Finance & Audit; Nominating; Resolutions
Meetings/Conferences: • 2015 Manitoba Association of Fire Chiefs Annual Conference & Trade Show, June, 2015, South Beach Casino & Resort, Winnipeg, MB
Scope: Provincial

Manitoba Association of Friendship Centres (MAC)
#11, 150 Henry Ave., Winnipeg MB R3B 0J7
Tel: 204-942-6299; *Fax:* 204-942-6308
www.mac.mb.ca
www.facebook.com/FriendshipCentres
Overview: A medium-sized provincial charitable organization founded in 1971 overseen by National Association of Friendship Centres
Mission: To assist friendship centres in communication, funding & training.
Chief Officer(s):
Joan Church, President
Adam Blanchard, Executive Director
Finances: *Funding Sources:* Provincial & federal government
Membership: 11 centres; *Committees:* Personnel & Finance; Constitution & Policy; National Issues

Manitoba Association of Health Care Professionals (MAHCP) / Association des professionnels de la santé du Manitoba
#101, 1500 Notre Dame Ave., Winnipeg MB R3E 0P9
Tel: 204-772-0425; *Fax:* 204-775-6829
info@mahcp.ca
mahcp.com
Overview: A medium-sized provincial organization
Mission: To protect, advocate for & advance the rights of its members through labour relations activities.
Chief Officer(s):
Bob Moroz, President
bobm@mahcp.ca
Staff Member(s): 12
Membership: *Committees:* Communication; Governance; Management; Oversight; Social Action & Strategic Partnership; Strike Readiness
Activities: *Library*

Manitoba Association of Health Information Providers (MAHIP)
c/o Neil John Maclean Health Sciences Library, University of Manitoba, 727 McDermott Ave., Winnipeg MB R3E 3P5
www.chla-absc.ca/mahip/
Previous Name: Manitoba Health Libraries Association
Overview: A small provincial organization founded in 1979 overseen by Canadian Health Libraries Association
Mission: To promote the provision of quality library service to the health community in Manitoba by communication & mutual assistance.
Chief Officer(s):
Orvie Dingwall, President
orvie.dingwall@ad.umanitoba.ca
Membership: *Fees:* $50 institution; $30 professional librarian; $20 library technician/assistant; $10 student

Meetings/Conferences: • 2015 Manitoba Association of Health Information Providers Annual General Meeting, 2015, MB
Scope: Provincial

Manitoba Association of Home Economists (MAHE)
PO Box 582, Stn. Main, Winnipeg MB R3C 2J3
Tel: 204-885-0718
Toll-Free: 866-261-0707
Other Communication: Home & Family URL: www.homefamily.net
mahe@mahe.ca
www.mahe.ca
www.facebook.com/HomeAndFamily.net
twitter.com/HomeFamily_PHEc
Overview: A small provincial organization
Mission: To enable families, both as individual units & generally as a social institution, to build & maintain systems of action which lead to maturing in individual self-formation & enlightened, co-operative participation in the critique & formulation of social goals & means for accomplishing them.
Chief Officer(s):
Debra Durnin-Richards, President

Manitoba Association of Insolvency & Restructuring Professionals (MAIRP)
c/o Ernst & Young Inc., Commodity Exchnage Tower, #2700, 360 Main St., Winnipeg MB R3C 4G9
Tel: 204-954-5568; *Fax:* 204-956-0138
Previous Name: Manitoba Insolvency Association
Overview: A small provincial organization overseen by Canadian Association of Insolvency & Restructuring Professionals
Member of: Canadian Association of Insolvency & Restructuring Professionals
Chief Officer(s):
Joseph Healey, President
joe.a.healey@ca.ey.com

Manitoba Association of Insurance Professionals (MAIP)
PO Box 66, Winnipeg MB R3C 2G1
Tel: 204-330-6842; *Fax:* 204-953-4862
www.caiw-acfa.com
Previous Name: Insurance Women's Association of Manitoba
Overview: A small provincial organization founded in 1966
Mission: To preserve and enhance the value of its members through education and networking, and to foster personal growth
Member of: Canadian Association of Insurance Women
Chief Officer(s):
Katherine Morgan Clark, President
katherine.morganclark@intact.net
Activities: Monthly dinner meetings & speakers; continuing education, awards; *Awareness Events:* Annual Golf Tournament; Annual Wine & Cheese; Annual Public Speaking Contest

Manitoba Association of Landscape Architects (MALA)
131 Callum Cres., Winnipeg MB R2G 2C7
Tel: 204-663-4863; *Fax:* 204-668-5662
www.mala.net
Overview: A medium-sized provincial organization founded in 1973
Mission: To promote, improve & advance the profession; to maintain standards of professional practice & conduct consistent with the need to serve & protect public interest; to support improvement &/or conservation of the natural, cultural, social & built environment
Member of: Canadian Society of Landscape Architects
Chief Officer(s):
Emeka Nnadi, President
Finances: *Annual Operating Budget:* Less than $50,000
Staff Member(s): 1
Membership: 49 individual + 5 honorary + 28 associate + 40 student affiliates + 4 friend; *Committees:* CSLA Awards/Annual Symposium; Communications; Examining Board; Ethics; University Liaison
Activities: *Internships:* Yes; *Rents Mailing List:* Yes

Manitoba Association of Library Technicians (MALT)
PO Box 1872, Winnipeg MB R3C 3R1
e-mail: malt.mb.ca@gmail.com
www.malt.mb.ca
www.facebook.com/malt.mb.ca
Overview: A medium-sized provincial organization founded in 1971
Mission: To promote & advance the role of library technicians throughout Manitoba; To respond to issues that relate to the library & information services community
Chief Officer(s):
Catherine Taylor, President
Marge Dyck, Secretary
Elizabeth Stregger, Treasurer
Katie McKee, Coordinator, Communications
Candice Phillips, Coordinator, Membership
Eric Wesselius, Editor, Newsletter
Membership: *Fees:* $12.50 students & unemployed members; $25 regular membership; $40 institutions; *Member Profile:* Library technician students throughout Manitoba; Individuals from all types of libraries in Manitoba; Institutions
Activities: Offering workshops; Sponsoring programs; Maintaining a job bank to advertise library positions; Promoting libraries in Manitoba
Meetings/Conferences: • Manitoba Association of Library Technicians 2015 Annual General Meeting, May, 2015, MB
Scope: Provincial
Description: Each year between May 1st & May 31st, reports of the association's executive are presented & officers are elected
• Manitoba Association of Library Technicians 2016 Annual General Meeting, May, 2016, MB
Scope: Provincial
Description: Each year between May 1st & May 31st, reports of the association's executive are presented & officers are elected
Publications:
• Manitoba Association of Library Technicians Newsletter
Type: Newsletter; *Frequency:* Quarterly; *Editor:* Eric Wesselius
ISSN: 1489-4920
Profile: Continuing education information, meeting highlights, association business, & awards

Manitoba Association of Medical Radiation Technologists (MAMRT)
#202, 819 Sargent Ave., Winnipeg MB R3E 0B9
Tel: 204-774-5346; *Fax:* 204-774-5346
admin@mamrt.ca
www.mamrt.ca
Overview: A small provincial organization founded in 1929 overseen by Canadian Association of Medical Radiation Technologists
Mission: To support medical radiation technologists & therapists throughout Manitoba
Chief Officer(s):
Sandra Iftody, President
Tracy Jackman, Executive Director
exec@mamrt.ca
Nishala Goolcharan, Director, Communications
Julie Love, Director, Finance & Administration
Finances: *Funding Sources:* Membership dues; Sponsorships
Membership: *Member Profile:* Medical radiation technologists & therapists in Manitoba
Activities: Providing continuing education to members; *Library:* MAMRT Lending Library
Awards:
• Colin Maxwell Memorial Award (Award)
• Bill Doern Service Award (Award)
• Claude Bodle Memorial Lecture Award (Award)
Meetings/Conferences: • Manitoba Association of Medical Radiation Technologists 2015 Annual General Conference, 2015
Scope: Provincial
Description: A conference providing educational sessions, held each spring
Publications:
• MAMRT News: A Newsletter of the Manitoba Association of Medical Radiation Technologists
Type: Newsletter; *Frequency:* 3 pa; *Accepts Advertising*
Profile: Information from the association for members

Manitoba Association of Native Fire Fighters Inc. (MANFF)
Sub Office, #102, 1555 St. James St., Winnipeg MB R3H 1B5
Tel: 204-953-2920; *Fax:* 204-953-2929
Toll-Free: 888-356-8959
manffin1@mts.net
www.manff.ca
Overview: A small provincial organization founded in 1991
Mission: To promote a greater awareness of fire safety & emergency preparedness on First Nation communities
Affliation(s): Assembly of Manitoba Chiefs
Chief Officer(s):
Daren Mini, Executive Director
Krissy Paul, Administration Officer
Finances: *Annual Operating Budget:* $250,000-$500,000; *Funding Sources:* Federal government; fundraising
Staff Member(s): 4
Membership: 62; *Member Profile:* First Nations fire chiefs
Activities: Technical support to First Nation communities leadership & fire/emergency services; annual Manitoba First Nation Fire Fighter Rodeo & Conference; annual fire fighter competition; *Internships:* Yes; *Speaker Service:* Yes

Manitoba Association of Non-Teaching Employees (MANTE) / Association des employés non enseignants du Manitoba
#210, 2281 Portage Ave., Winnipeg MB R3J 0M1
Tel: 204-931-2397
mante@mante.ca
mante.ca
Overview: A small provincial organization founded in 1978
Chief Officer(s):
Joan McEachern, President

Manitoba Association of Optometrists (MAO)
#200B, 392 Academy Rd., Winnipeg MB R3N 0B8
Tel: 204-943-9811; *Fax:* 204-943-1208
mao@optometrists.mb.ca
www.optometrists.mb.ca
Previous Name: Manitoba Optometric Society
Overview: A medium-sized provincial organization founded in 1909 overseen by Canadian Association of Optometrists
Mission: To regulate the practice of optometry in Manitoba, in accordance with The Optometry Act & Regulation; To represent optometrists in Manitoba; To protect & promote the vision care needs & eye health of Manitobans
Member of: Canadian Association of Optometrists (CAO)
Chief Officer(s):
Michelle Georgi, President
Laureen Goodridge, Executive Director
Lorne Ryall, Registrar
Membership: *Member Profile:* Doctors of optometry in Manitoba
Activities: Registering practitioners; Establishing & ensuring standards of practice; Communicating the role of optometrists' in the health care system; Answering inquiries & concerns from patients & the public; Encouraging regular, preventitive eye examinations

Manitoba Association of Parent Councils (MAPC)
#1005, 401 York Ave., Winnipeg MB R3C 0P8
Tel: 204-956-1770; *Fax:* 204-948-2855
Toll-Free: 877-290-4702
info@mapc.mb.ca
www.mapc.mb.ca
www.facebook.com/mapcmb
twitter.com/mapcmb
www.youtube.com/MBParentCouncils
Overview: A small provincial charitable organization overseen by Canadian Home & School Federation
Mission: An organization of school-based parent groups throughout Manitoba.
Chief Officer(s):
Naomi Kruse, Executive Director
Finances: *Annual Operating Budget:* Less than $50,000; *Funding Sources:* Grants; membership dues; donations
Staff Member(s): 1; 14 volunteer(s)
Membership: 295; *Fees:* $50; *Member Profile:* Parent groups involved in their child's school
Activities: *Speaker Service:* Yes; *Library* Open to public
Meetings/Conferences: • 2015 MAPC Annual General Meeting and Conference, May, 2015, Victoria Inn and Conference Centre, Winnipeg, MB
Scope: Provincial

Manitoba Association of Personal Care Home Social Workers (MAPCHSW)
PO Box 2591, Stn. Main, Winnipeg MB R3C 4B3
www.mapchsw.com
Overview: A small provincial organization founded in 1972
Mission: To provide a forum for discussion of topics pertinent to social workers in long-term care settings
Chief Officer(s):
Lori Orford, Contact
Finances: *Funding Sources:* Membership dues
Membership: *Fees:* $30

Manitoba Association of Playwrights (MAP)
#503, 100 Arthur St., Winnipeg MB R3B 1H3
Tel: 204-942-8941
mbplay@mts.net

www.mbplays.ca
www.facebook.com/mbplaywrights
Overview: A small provincial charitable organization founded in 1979
Mission: To provide support for playwrights in Manitoba through the operation of programs for emerging & established playwrights
Chief Officer(s):
James Durham, President
Membership: *Fees:* $50; $25 student; *Member Profile:* Directors, actors & anyone interested in the continuing health of playwriting & the production of new plays in Manitoba theatres
Activities: Playwrights Development & Workshop; Open Door; Workshops & Seminars; Young Emerging Playwrights Program; Mentorship; Resource Centre & Archives; Play Reading Service; *Speaker Service:* Yes; *Library* Open to public

Manitoba Association of Prosthetists & Orthotists
c/o Canadian Association for Prosthetics & Orthotics, #605, 294 Portage Ave., Winnipeg MB R3C 0B9
Overview: A small provincial organization overseen by Canadian Association for Prosthetics & Orthotics
Mission: To promote quality care for prosthetic & orthotic patients in Manitoba; To encourage professionalism in Manitoba's prosthetic & orthotic field
Chief Officer(s):
Eric Kuhl, President
Peter Ten Krooden, Vice-President
Daniel Mazur, Secretary
Doug Paulsen, Treasurer
Membership: *Member Profile:* Certified prosthetic & orthotic practitioners, registered technicians, allied health professionals, students, & retired persons in Manitoba
Activities: Promoting continuing education; Liaising with related organizations in Manitoba

Manitoba Association of Registered Nurses *See* College of Registered Nurses of Manitoba

Manitoba Association of Registered Respiratory Therapists, Inc. (MARRT) / L'Association des thérapeutes respiratoires du Manitoba, inc.
PO Box 2087, Winnipeg MB R3C 3R4
Tel: 204-944-8081
info@marrt.org
www.marrt.org
Overview: A medium-sized provincial licensing organization founded in 1981
Affliation(s): Canadian Society of Respiratory Therapists
Chief Officer(s):
Tracy Simcoe, President
Finances: *Annual Operating Budget:* Less than $50,000
8 volunteer(s)
Membership: 200; *Fees:* $80-$130; *Member Profile:* Respiratory therapists; student respiratory therapists
Activities: *Speaker Service:* Yes

Manitoba Association of School Business Officials (MASBO)
PO Box 547, Morris MB R0G 1K0
Tel: 204-254-7570; *Fax:* 204-254-3606
www.masbo.ca
Overview: A small provincial organization founded in 1965
Mission: To provide leadership in the areas of finance, maintenance & transportation
Chief Officer(s):
Roy Seidler, Executive Director
Membership: 160; *Fees:* $318

Manitoba Association of School Psychologists Inc.
#562, 162 - 2025 Corydon Ave., Winnipeg MB R3P 0N5
www.masp.mb.ca
Overview: A small provincial organization founded in 1981
Mission: To promote & support school psychology in Manitoba; to develop a network of communication among practitioners of school psychology in Manitoba; to encourage & provide information to educators & the public regarding the practice of school psychololgy & other related educational issues
Chief Officer(s):
Barry Mallin, President
Membership: *Fees:* $100 full; $50 affiliate; $50 retired; $18 student; *Committees:* Issues; Membership; Professional Development; Publications/Communications; Website

Manitoba Association of School Superintendents (MASS)
375 Jefferson Ave., Winnipeg MB R2V 0N3
Tel: 204-487-7972; *Fax:* 204-487-7974
www.mass.mb.ca
Overview: A small provincial organization founded in 1956
Mission: To provide leadership for public education by advocating in the best interest of learners, & supports its members through professional services.
Affliation(s): Canadian Association of School Administrators
Chief Officer(s):
Ken Klassen, Executive Director
ken.klassen@7oaks.org
Finances: *Funding Sources:* Membership fees
Staff Member(s): 2
Membership: 110; *Member Profile:* Senior professional administrator in education; *Committees:* Curriculum; Education Finance; ICT; Legislation/Policy; Professional Learning; Public Relations/Membership Services; Research; Aboriginal Education Advisory
Activities: *Library* by appointment

Manitoba Association of School Trustees *See* Manitoba School Boards Association

Manitoba Association of Sheet Metal & Air Handling Contractors Inc. (MASMAHC)
24 Trottier Bay, Winnipeg MB R3T 3Y5
Tel: 204-774-3459
Overview: A medium-sized provincial organization
Mission: To improve the industry & image of the sheet metal contractor; To upgrade procedures & workmanship; To address mutual problems of trade contractors & construction; To educate members on government regulations
Affliation(s): Sheet Metal & Air Conditioning Contractors' National Association, Inc.
Finances: *Annual Operating Budget:* Less than $50,000; *Funding Sources:* Membership dues
Membership: 30
Activities: *Library*

Manitoba Association of the Appraisal Institute of Canada (MB AIC)
#193, 162 - 2025 Corydon Ave., Winnipeg MB R3P 0N5
Tel: 204-771-2982; *Fax:* 204-654-9583
mbaic@mts.net
www.aicanada.ca
Overview: A small provincial organization founded in 1978 overseen by Appraisal Institute of Canada
Member of: Winnipeg Real Estate Board (Business Partner)
Chief Officer(s):
Eric Krueger, President
elkrueger@shaw.ca
Pamela Wylie, Executive Director
Finances: *Annual Operating Budget:* $50,000-$100,000; *Funding Sources:* Membership dues; courses & seminars
Staff Member(s): 1; 25 volunteer(s)
Membership: 167; *Fees:* Schedule available; *Member Profile:* Residential & commercial real estate appraisers; *Committees:* Professional Development; Communications
Activities: Winnipeg Free Press home section articles; annual fall meeting

Manitoba Association of Visual Language Interpreters (MAVLI)
PO Box 68056, Stn. Osborne Village, Winnipeg MB R3L 2V9
www.mavli.com
Overview: A small provincial organization founded in 1976 overseen by Association of Visual Language Interpreters of Canada
Mission: To promote the profession of visual language interpretation through advocacy & education
Member of: Association of Visual Language Interpreters of Canada (AVLIC)
Affliation(s): Winnipeg Community Centre of the Deaf
Chief Officer(s):
Mandy MacDonald, President
president@mavli.com
Membership: *Member Profile:* Those involved in the provision of sign language interpretation or who support the aims of the organization; *Committees:* Education

Manitoba Association of Women's Shelters (MAWS)
c/o Genesis House, PO Box 389, Winkler MB R6W 4A6
Tel: 204-325-9957; *Crisis Hot-Line:* 877-977-0007
maws@maws.mb.ca
www.maws.mb.ca
Overview: A medium-sized provincial organization founded in 1991
Mission: To eliminate violence against women; To provide support to member shelters for abused women & their children; To share information & resources with its member shelters, increase training of staff & increase services for clients.
Chief Officer(s):
Karen Peto, Co-Chair
Sharon Morgan, Co-Chair
Finances: *Funding Sources:* Provincial government; private donations
Membership: 9 provincially funded shelters & several affliate members; *Member Profile:* Shelters for abused women & children
Activities: *Speaker Service:* Yes

Agape House
PO Box 3130, Steinbach MB R0A 2A0
Tel: 204-326-6062; *Fax:* 204-326-2359; *Crisis Hot-Line:* 204-346-0028
agapehouse@mts.net
agapehouse.shelternet.ca
Chief Officer(s):
Tracie Rigby, Executive Director

Aurora House
PO Box 3779, The Pas MB R9A 1S4
Tel: 204-623-7427; *Fax:* 204-623-3901; *Crisis Hot-Line:* 204-623-5497
auroratp@mts.net
aurorahouse.shelternet.ca
Chief Officer(s):
Dianne Kandt, Executive Director

Genesis House
PO Box 389, Winkler MB R6W 4A6
Tel: 204-325-9957; *Fax:* 204-325-5889; *Crisis Hot-Line:* 204-325-9800
sccfv@mts.net
genesishouse.shelternet.ca
Chief Officer(s):
Ang Braun, Executive Director

Ikwe-Widdjitiwin Inc.
PO Box 1056, Winnipeg MB R3C 2X4
Tel: 204-987-2780; *Crisis Hot-Line:* 800-362-3344
diane.ikwe@shawcable.com
ikwe.shelternet.ca
Chief Officer(s):
Sharon Morgan, Executive Director, 204-987-2794

Nova House
PO Box 337, Selkirk MB R1A 2B3
Tel: 204-482-7882
novahous@mts.net
novahouse.shelternet.ca
Chief Officer(s):
Debra Jenkins, Chair

Osborne House
PO Box 397, Winnipeg MB R3C 2H6
Tel: 204-942-7373; *Crisis Hot-Line:* 204-942-3052
osbornehouse.shelternet.ca
Chief Officer(s):
Barbara Judt, Executive Director Ext. 230
execdirector@osbornehouse.org

Parkland Crisis Centre & Women's Shelter
PO Box 651, Dauphin MB R7N 3B3
Tel: 204-638-9484; *Fax:* 204-622-4625
pkndcris@mts.net
www.mts.net/~pkndcris

Portage Family Abuse Prevention Centre
PO Box 1541, Portage la Prairie MB R1N 3P1
Tel: 204-239-5234; *Fax:* 204-239-6710; *Crisis Hot-Line:* 204-239-5233
pwsheltr@mts.net
www.abuseprevention.ca

Thompson Crisis Centre
PO Box 1266, Thompson MB R8N 1P1
Tel: 204-677-9668; *Fax:* 204-677-8376
tcc9668@mts.net
thompson.shelternet.ca
Chief Officer(s):
Leslie Allen, Executive Director

YWCA Westman Women's Shelter
c/o 148 - 11th St., Brandon MB R7A 4J4
Tel: 204-727-3644
ywcawws@westman.wave.ca
westman.shelternet.ca
Chief Officer(s):
Jodi Wyman, President

Manitoba Athletic Therapists Association Inc. (MATA)
145 Pacific Ave., Winnipeg MB R3B 2Z6
Tel: 204-925-5930; *Fax:* 204-925-5624
www.mata.mb.ca
www.facebook.com/162809277115285
twitter.com/MATATherapist
Overview: A small provincial organization founded in 1983
Mission: Committed to the prevention and care of activity-related injuries, at all levels of sport and recreation, ranging from the grass roots level to the elite athlete, throughout Manitoba.
Member of: Canadian Athletic Therapists Association; Sports Medicine Council of Manitoba; Sport Manitoba
Chief Officer(s):
Melissa Skrabek-Senecal, President
Finances: *Annual Operating Budget:* $50,000-$100,000
Staff Member(s): 2
Membership: 200; *Fees:* Schedule available
Activities: Athletic First Aid Programs; medical coverage for sport & recreation; *Library* Open to public

Manitoba Audio Recording Industry Association *See* Manitoba Music

Manitoba Badminton Association (MBA)
#323, 145 Pacific Ave., Winnipeg MB R3B 2Z6
Tel: 204-925-5679; *Fax:* 204-925-5703
admin.assistant@badminton.mb.ca
www.badminton.mb.ca
www.youtube.com/user/badmintonmb
Overview: A small local organization overseen by Badminton Canada
Mission: To provide the leadership that promotes the growth of badminton throughout Manitoba as a lifelong sport.
Chief Officer(s):
Don Snider, President
Ryan Giesbrecht, Executive Director, 204-925-5621
ed@badminton.mb.ca
Staff Member(s): 3
Membership: *Member Profile:* Athletes, coaches, officials & badminton clubs

Manitoba Ball Hockey Association (MBHA)
#306, 145 Pacific Ave., Winnipeg MB R3B 2Z6
Tel: 204-925-5602
mbha1@hotmail.com
www.winnipegballhockey.com
www.facebook.com/groups/50027852199
Overview: A small provincial organization founded in 1978
Mission: To promote & encourage the development of competitive & recreational ball hockey in Manitoba
Member of: Sport Manitoba
Chief Officer(s):
Kelly Huff, Executive League Director
Membership: 2,500+;

Manitoba Band Association
#305, 1820 Henderson Hwy., Winnipeg MB R2G 1P2
Tel: 204-663-1226
mbband@shaw.ca
www.mbband.org
Previous Name: Manitoba Instrumental Music Association
Overview: A small provincial charitable organization founded in 1977 overseen by Canadian Band Association
Mission: To promote growth & development of bands in Manitoba
Affliation(s): Canadian Band Association; Manitoba Music Educators' Association; Coalition for Music Education in Canada
Chief Officer(s):
Janet Yochim, President
jyochim@flbsd.mb.ca
Finances: *Annual Operating Budget:* $50,000-$100,000
Membership: 350; *Fees:* $50 general; $20 student; $25 senior; $85 corporate; *Member Profile:* Music teachers; music students; music dealers; others who share the goals of the association

Manitoba Bar Association (MBA) / Association du barreau du Manitoba
#1450, 363 Broadway, Winnipeg MB R3C 3N9
Tel: 204-927-1210; *Fax:* 204-927-1212
admin@cba-mb.ca
www.cba.org/manitoba
Overview: A medium-sized provincial organization founded in 1896
Member of: Canadian Bar Association
Chief Officer(s):
Josh A. Weinstein, President
jweinstein@myersfirm.com
Finances: *Funding Sources:* Membership fees; member services
Staff Member(s): 2; 17 volunteer(s)
Membership: 1,200; *Fees:* Schedule available; *Member Profile:* Lawyer; Law Student; Law Professor; Judiciary
Activities: *Awareness Events:* Law Day, April 17; *Speaker Service:* Yes
Meetings/Conferences: • Manitoba Bar Association 2015 Mid-Winter Conference, January, 2015, Winnipeg, MB
Scope: Provincial

Manitoba Baseball Association
145 Pacific Ave., Winnipeg MB R3B 2Z6
Tel: 204-925-5763; *Fax:* 204-925-5928
baseball.info@sportmanitoba.ca
www.baseballmanitoba.ca
www.facebook.com/171229052909245
twitter.com/BaseballMB
Also Known As: Baseball Manitoba
Overview: A small provincial organization founded in 1968 overseen by Baseball Canada
Mission: To foster the participation, development & competition of amateur baseball in Manitoba
Chief Officer(s):
Morgan de Peña, Executive Director
baseball.morgan@sportmanitoba.ca
Membership: 15,000; *Committees:* Management

Manitoba Baton Twirling Sportive Association (MBTSA)
MB
www.manitobabaton.com
Overview: A small provincial organization overseen by Canadian Baton Twirling Federation
Mission: To oversee the sport of baton twirling in Manitoba.
Member of: Canadian Baton Twirling Federation

Manitoba Beef Cattle Performance Association (MBCPA)
PO Box 1190, Carberry MB R0K 0H0
Tel: 204-763-4696; *Fax:* 204-763-4102
bulltest@mts.net
www.manitobabulltest.com
Also Known As: Douglas Bull Test Station
Overview: A small provincial organization founded in 1964
Chief Officer(s):
Ivan Ahntholz, Manager
Tod Wallace, President
Staff Member(s): 2
Membership: 215; *Fees:* $10

Manitoba Beekeepers' Association (MBA)
c/o Hilary Stewart, PO Box 192, Baldur MB R0K 0B0
Tel: 204-535-2167
manitobabeekeepers@mts.net
www.manitobabee.org
Overview: A small provincial organization founded in 1903
Mission: To represent the interests of Manitoba honey producers
Affliation(s): Canadian Honey Council
Chief Officer(s):
Allan Campbell, President, 204-638-6515
allan.campbell@durstonhoneyfarms.com
Jake Maendel, Vice-Chair, 204-513-0529, Fax: 204-886-2215
jake@destinyroad.ca
Jim Campbell, Secretary, 204-467-5246
mbasecretary@mts.net
Hilary Stewart, Treasurer, 204-535-2167
Finances: *Funding Sources:* Membership fees; Donations
Membership: *Fees:* $60 associate members; $200 + $.40 colony levy (maximum 1,000 colonies) or $.13 (1,001 colonies or more); *Member Profile:* Manitoba honey producers, who are sole proprietors, with 50 or more colonies; Honey producers in Manitoba who represent a Hutterite colony, partnership, or corporation; Associate members include out-of-province beekeepers, industry supporters, or volunteers; *Committees:* Convention & Annual General Meeting; Fee/Levy; Finance; Foreign Worker; KAP; Newsletter; Nomination; Pests & Pest Management; Pollination; Promotion/Education; Resolution; Research; Safety Nets; Stock Replacement
Activities: Supporting bee research projects in Manitoba; Facilitating networking opportunities to discuss industry issues
Publications:
• Manitoba Beekeeper
Type: Newsletter; *Frequency:* Quarterly; *Accepts Advertising;* *Editor:* Dan Lecocq; *Price:* Free with membership in the Manitoba Beekeepers'Association
Profile: Reports from the Manitoba Beekeepers' Association, CHC, & the provincial apiarist, plus honey prices, honey shows, & beekeeping issues

Manitoba Bison Association (MBA)
PO Box 64, Inwood MB R0C 1P0
Tel: 204-278-3302; *Fax:* 204-278-3737
vwdyck@mts.net
www.manitobabison.ca
Overview: A small provincial organization
Member of: Canadian Bison Association
Chief Officer(s):
Len Epp, President
sepp@mts.net

Manitoba Blind Sports Association (MBSA)
145 Pacific Ave., Winnipeg MB R3B 2Z6
Tel: 204-925-5694; *Fax:* 204-925-5792
blindsport@shawbiz.ca
www.blindsport.mb.ca
Previous Name: Manitoba Sport & Recreation Association for the Blind
Overview: A medium-sized provincial organization founded in 1976 overseen by Canadian Blind Sports Association Inc.
Mission: To provide blind & visually impaired Manitobans with the opportunity to participate in sport at all levels of skill & ability
Finances: *Annual Operating Budget:* Less than $50,000
20 volunteer(s)
Membership: 45; *Fees:* $10 for membership, $40 program fee, $50 refundable fundraising fee
Activities: *Awareness Events:* Run for Light; *Speaker Service:* Yes; *Library* by appointment

Manitoba Block Parent Program *See* Block Parent Program of Winnipeg Inc.

Manitoba Blues Society Inc. (MBS)
PO Box 56036, Stn. Portage Place, Winnipeg MB R3B 0G9
Tel: 204-667-3491
info@bluesmb.ca
www.bluesmb.ca
Overview: A small provincial organization founded in 1995
Mission: To foster an understanding of & appreciation for the music form known as The Blues
Chief Officer(s):
Lee Wenaus, Chair
Ted Shorten, Treasurer
Eleanor Reimer, Secretary
Finances: *Funding Sources:* Membership dues; fundraising events
Membership: 1-99; *Committees:* Advertising; Communications; Education; Events; Marketing; Volunteers/Membership; Jams
Activities: Blues jams; blues events
Publications:
• Blues News [a publication of the Manitoba Blues Society Inc.]
Type: Journal

Manitoba Boxing Commission *See* Manitoba Combative Sports Commission

Manitoba Brain Injury Association Inc.
#204, 825 Sherbrook St., Winnipeg MB R3A 1M5
Tel: 204-975-3280; *Fax:* 204-975-3027
Toll-Free: 866-327-1998
mbia@mts.net
www.mbia.ca
Also Known As: MBIA
Overview: A small provincial charitable organization founded in 1987 overseen by Brain Injury Association of Canada
Mission: To improve the quality of life & give hope to those affected by acquired brain injury; To support persons affected by acquired brain injury in Manitoba
Chief Officer(s):
David Sullivan, Executive Director
Clark Brownlee, President
Finances: *Funding Sources:* Membership fees; Donations; Fundraising; Sponsorships
Membership: 400+; *Fees:* $15 individuals; $20 families; $30 non-profit organizations; $50 corporate members; *Member Profile:* Survivors of brain injuries & their families throughout Manitoba
Activities: Preparing prevention programs; Raising awareness of acquired brain injury in Manitoba; Engaging in advocacy activities on behalf of those with acquired brain injury; Offering peer support programs & support groups in Dauphin & Parkland

region, Winnipeg, Steinbach & area, & Brandon; Providing education, such as a lecture series called the Empowerment Series & discussion groups; Planning social & recreational activities for members & other acquired brain injury survivors; *Library:* Manitoba Brain Injury Association Inc. Library;
Publications:
• MBIA News
Type: Newsletter; *Frequency:* Quarterly
Profile: Association activities, provincial news, meetings, events, & programs, plus member information

Manitoba Brown Swiss Association
PO Box 428, Austin MB R0H 0C0
Tel: 204-637-2589
Overview: A small provincial organization
Member of: Canadian Brown Swiss Association
Chief Officer(s):
Linda Doerksen, Provincial Secretary

Manitoba Building & Construction Trades Council (MBCTC)
#508, 138 Portage Ave. East, Winnipeg MB R3C 0A1
Tel: 204-956-7425; *Fax:* 204-956-7427
office@mbctc.mb.ca
www.mbtrades.ca
Previous Name: Winnipeg Building & Construction Trades Council
Overview: A small provincial organization founded in 1908
Member of: AFL-CIO
Chief Officer(s):
Ron Stecy, Executive Director
rstecy@mbctc.mb.ca
Staff Member(s): 3
Membership: 6,000

Manitoba Building Envelope Council (MBEC)
PO Box 2052, Winnipeg MB R3C 3R3
www.mb-bec.ca
Overview: A small provincial organization founded in 1983
Mission: To promote excellence in the building envelope through technology transfer.
Member of: National Building Envelope Council
Chief Officer(s):
Ryan Dalgleish, President
rdalgleish@buildingprofessionals.com
Membership: *Fees:* $150 corporate; $35 individual

Manitoba Building Officials Association
PO Box 2063, Winnipeg MB R3C 3R4
Tel: 204-832-1512; *Fax:* 204-897-8094
info@mboa.mb.ca
www.mboa.mb.ca
Overview: A small provincial organization
Mission: To promote building safety through training & awareness in order to help their members
Chief Officer(s):
Rick Grimshaw, President
rgrimshaw@gov.mb.ca
Membership: 200; *Fees:* $60 government; $500 government group; $70 associate; $600 associate group; $25 student

Manitoba Call Centre Association ***See*** **Manitoba Customer Contact Association, Inc.**

Manitoba Camping Association (MCA)
#302, 960 Portage Ave., Winnipeg MB R3G 0R4
Tel: 204-784-1134; *Fax:* 204-784-4177
sunshinefund@mbcamping.ca
www.mbcamping.ca
www.facebook.com/sunshinefundmb
Overview: A medium-sized provincial organization founded in 1937 overseen by Canadian Camping Association
Mission: To act as a coordinating body for organized camping in Manitoba; To promote organized camping as an educational and recreational experience
Member of: Canadian Camping Association
Chief Officer(s):
Bryan Ezako, Executive Director
executivedirector@mbcamping.ca
Janis Banman, Coordinator, General Office Administration & Sunshine Fund Program, 204-784-1130, Fax: 204-784-4177
Finances: *Funding Sources:* Donations; Membership dues
Membership: *Member Profile:* Organizations & individuals who support organized childrens & family camps & the mission of the MCA
Activities: Developing standards for organized camping in Manitoba; Communicating information about regulations & developments that affect organized camping; Representing member camps to government agencies & to the public; Administering the Winnipeg Free Press Sunshine Fund which allows financially disadvantaged children to attend camps; Offering workshops; Providing networking opportunities; *Awareness Events:* Manitoba Parade of Camps

Manitoba Cardiac Institute (Reh-Fit) Inc.
1390 Taylor Ave., Winnipeg MB R3M 3V8
Tel: 204-488-8023; *Fax:* 204-488-4819
reh-fit@reh-fit.com
www.reh-fit.com
Also Known As: Kinsmen Reh-Fit Centre
Overview: A small provincial organization
Mission: To enhance the health and well-being of its members and the community by providing innovative health and fitness services through assessment, education, and exercise in a suportive environment.
Chief Officer(s):
Rosanna Buonpensiere, Director

Manitoba Cattle Producers Association (MCPA)
154 Paramount Rd., Winnipeg MB R2X 2W3
Tel: 204-772-4542; *Fax:* 204-774-3264
Toll-Free: 800-772-0458
www.mcpa.net
www.facebook.com/ManitobaBeefProducers
twitter.com/ManitobaBeef
www.youtube.com/user/mcpacom
Overview: A medium-sized provincial organization
Mission: To act as the voice of the cattle industry in Manitoba; To ensure a sustainable future for the industry
Member of: Canadian Cattlemen's Association
Chief Officer(s):
Trevor Atchison, President
pvsf@rfnow.com
Cam Dahl, General Manager
cdahl@mbbeef.ca
Kristen Lucyshyn, Coordinator, Communications
klucyshyn@mbbeef.ca
Staff Member(s): 8
Membership: 8,000; *Member Profile:* Cattle producers in Manitoba; *Committees:* Executive; Animal Health; Annual Meeting; Communications; Crown Lands; Environment; Finance; Production Management; Research; Resolutions; Nomination; Domestic Agriculture Programs; Governance; Community Pastures
Activities: Engaging in advocacy activities; Researching; Providing education; *Awareness Events:* Manitoba Beef Week
Awards:
• Environmental Stewardship Award (Award)
Meetings/Conferences: • 2015 Manitoba Cattle Producers Association Annual General Meeting, February, 2015, Victoria Inn Hotel & Convention Centre, Brandon, MB
Scope: Provincial
Publications:
• Cattle Country: The Voice of Manitoba's Cattle Industry
Type: Magazine; *Frequency:* 8 pa; *Accepts Advertising*; *Editor:* Karen Emilson; *Price:* Free
Profile: Information for cattle producers & industry supporters in Manitoba & eastern Saskatchewan

Manitoba Cerebral Palsy Sports Association (MCPSA)
200 Main St., Winnipeg MB R3C 4M2
Other Communication: Alt. E-mail: mcpsa-swim@hotmail.com
mcpsa-boccia@hotmail.com
Overview: A small provincial organization overseen by Canadian Cerebral Palsy Sports Association
Mission: To assist in the development of sport for the disabled in Manitoba by providing an opportunity for a wider participation for persons with cerebral palsy & other neuromuscular disorders
Member of: Canadian Cerebral Palsy Sports Association
Membership: 60
Activities: Track; Field; Swimming; Boccia

Manitoba CGIT Association
PO Box 52073, Winnipeg MB R2M 5P9
Tel: 204-254-2378
cgit@cgitmanitoba.ca
www.cgitmanitoba.ca
Also Known As: Canadian Girls in Training - Manitoba
Previous Name: National CGIT Association - Manitoba & Northwestern Ontario
Overview: A small provincial organization

Manitoba Chamber Orchestra (MCO)
Portage Place, 393 Portage Ave., #Y300, Winnipeg MB R3B 3H6
Tel: 204-783-7377; *Fax:* 204-783-7383
mco@mts.net
www.manitobachamberorchestra.org
Overview: A small provincial charitable organization founded in 1972 overseen by Orchestras Canada
Mission: To perform chamber orchestra repertoire with emphasis on premiering new Canadian works & Canadian soloists
Chief Officer(s):
Anne Manson, Music Director
Vicki Young, General Manager
Finances: *Annual Operating Budget:* $500,000-$1.5 Million; *Funding Sources:* Government grants (3 levels)
Staff Member(s): 3; 60 volunteer(s)
Membership: 728; *Fees:* $133.75; $65 student
Activities: 8 concert subscription series; Education programs; Chamber music agency; *Speaker Service:* Yes

The Manitoba Chambers of Commerce
227 Portage Ave., Winnipeg MB R3B 2A6
Tel: 204-948-0100; *Fax:* 204-948-0110
Toll-Free: 877-444-5222
mbchamber@mbchamber.mb.ca
www.mbchamber.mb.ca
www.linkedin.com/company/manitoba-chambers-of-commerce
www.facebook.com/118694504008
twitter.com/mbchambersofcom
Overview: A medium-sized provincial organization founded in 1930
Member of: Canadian Chamber of Commerce
Chief Officer(s):
Graham Starmer, President, 204-948-0107
gstarmer@mbchamber.mb.ca
Finances: *Annual Operating Budget:* $250,000-$500,000; *Funding Sources:* Membership dues; advertising; special events
Staff Member(s): 4; 20 volunteer(s)
Membership: 275 corporate + 77 chambers + 9,500 businesses; *Member Profile:* Registered business or organization; *Committees:* Tourism; Trade; Transportation; Education; Finance; Government Relations
Activities: Small Business Week; Youth Business Institute; Rural Forum; Invest in Manitoba; Forum for International Trade; *Internships:* Yes; *Speaker Service:* Yes; *Rents Mailing List:* Yes; *Library* by appointment

Manitoba Cheer Federation Inc. (MCF)
PO Box 42010, 1881 Portage Ave., Winnipeg MB R3J 0J0
e-mail: info@mbcheer.ca
www.mbcheer.ca
Overview: A small provincial organization founded in 2010 overseen by Cheer Canada
Mission: To regulate, promote & develop cheerleading in Manitoba.
Member of: Cheer Canada
Chief Officer(s):
Patricia Tomczyk, President
Kait Allen, Director, Judging
Marian Henry, Director, Event
Carrie Robson, Director, Communications

Manitoba Chicken Producer Board ***See*** **Manitoba Chicken Producers**

Manitoba Chicken Producers (MCP)
1357 Kenaston Blvd., Winnipeg MB R3P 2P2
Tel: 204-489-4603; *Fax:* 204-488-1163
chicken@chicken.mb.ca
www.chicken.mb.ca
Previous Name: Manitoba Chicken Producer Board
Overview: A medium-sized provincial organization founded in 1968 overseen by Chicken Farmers of Canada
Mission: To represent the needs of hatching egg & chicken producers of Manitoba by providing leadership in maintaining a viable & stable hatching egg & chicken production industry
Member of: Canadian Hatching Egg Producers; Chicken Farmers of Canada
Chief Officer(s):
Wayne Hiltz, Executive Director
whiltz@chicken.mb.ca
Staff Member(s): 6

Manitoba Child Care Association (MCCA)
2350 McPhillips St., 2nd Fl., Winnipeg MB R2V 4J6

Tel: 204-586-8587; *Fax:* 204-589-5613
Toll-Free: 888-323-4676
info@mccahouse.org
www.mccahouse.org
Overview: A medium-sized provincial organization founded in 1974
Mission: To act as the voice of child care in Manitoba; To advocate for a quality system of child care; To advance early childhood education as a profession
Affliation(s): Canadian Child Care Federation
Chief Officer(s):
Julie Skaftfeld, President
Pat Wege, Executive Director
patwege@mccahouse.org
Karen Gander, Manager, Professional Development
karengander@mccahouse.org
Monique Sutherland, Manager, Finance & Accounting
msutherland@mccahouse.org
Tami Karsin, Director, Branch Services
Laurinda Neyron, Director, Public Policy & Professionalism
Finances: *Funding Sources:* Membership dues
Membership: 3,800+; *Member Profile:* Early childhood educators; Child care assistants; Centre administrators; Academics; Licensed family child care providers; Parents who volunteer on boards of their children's programs; Students; *Committees:* Child Care Benefits; Conference; Editorial; Public Policy & Professionalism; Finance; Ethics; Family Child Care; School Age; Board Operations & Development
Activities: Informing members about issues; Providing professional development opportunities; Offering networking occasions; Presenting awards; Building broad coalitions; Encouraging research; Participating in the development of standards & guidelines to maintain quality child care services; Organizing conferences; *Awareness Events:* Week of the ECE; *Library:* Manitoba Child Care Association Resource Library
Meetings/Conferences: • Manitoba Child Care Association 2015 38th Annual Early Childhood Educator Provincial Conference, May, 2015, MB
Scope: Provincial
Description: Keynote speakers, a trade show, & an awards banquet
Contact Information: Manager, Professional Development: Karen Houdayer, Phone: 204-336-5062, Toll-Free: 1-888-323-4676, ext. 224, E-mail: khoudayer@mccahouse.org

Manitoba Chiropractors' Association (MCA)
#610, 1445 Portage Ave., Winnipeg MB R3G 3P4
Tel: 204-942-3000; *Fax:* 204-942-3010
www.mbchiro.org
Overview: A medium-sized provincial licensing organization founded in 1945 overseen by Canadian Chiropractic Association
Mission: To act as both a regulatory body & a professional association to serve the public & the chiropractors of Manitoba; To foster high standards of chiropractic health care for Manitobans; To ensure that safe, ethical, & competent servicew are provided by Manitoba chiropractors
Chief Officer(s):
Taras Luchak, Executive Director
Ernie Miron, Registrar
registrar@mbchiro.org
Finances: *Funding Sources:* Membership dues
Activities: Licensing Manitoba chiropractors; Enforcing a Code of Ethics & Standards of Practice; Investigating & resolving complaints; Advocating for accessible & affordable health care

Manitoba Choral Association (MCA)
#5, 276 Marion St., Winnipeg MB R2H 0T7
Tel: 204-942-6037; *Fax:* 204-947-3105
mca@manitobasings.org
www.manitobasings.org
Overview: A small provincial charitable organization founded in 1976
Mission: To advance knowledge & appreciation of, & to stimulate interest in the choral arts
Affliation(s): Manitoba Music Educators Association; American Choral Directors Association; International Federation for Choral Music; Manitoba Opera; Association of Canadian Choral Conductors; Chorus America; Arts & Cultural Industries Association of Manitoba
Chief Officer(s):
Robert Neufeld, Executive Director
Finances: *Annual Operating Budget:* $100,000-$250,000
Staff Member(s): 1; 300 volunteer(s)
Membership: 63 individuals; 168 choirs; *Fees:* $40 individual; $80 choirs; *Member Profile:* Choirs choral directors; *Committees:* Choral Fest; Provincial Honour Choir; Manitoba Youth Choir; Professional Development; Volunteer Coordination; 30th Anniversary
Activities: Diversity Sings Project; *Library:* MCA Choral Library

Manitoba Christmas Tree Growers Association (MCTGA)
900 Corydon Ave., Winnipeg MB R3M 0Y4
Tel: 204-453-3128
mctga@realchristmastrees.mb.ca
www.realchristmastrees.mb.ca
Overview: A small provincial organization
Mission: To assist membership in promoting benefits of Christmas trees
Chief Officer(s):
Cliff Freund, President
Dorothy Freund, Treasurer

Manitoba Clearinghouse Concerning Disabilities Inc. *See* Society for Manitobans with Disabilities Inc.

Manitoba Coin Club
PO Box 321, Stn. Main, Winnipeg MB R3C 2H6
Tel: 204-260-9717
manitobacoinclub@hotmail.com
www.manitobacoinclub.org
Overview: A small provincial organization founded in 1954
Mission: To promote numismatics in the province of Manitoba
Chief Officer(s):
Landon Taraschuk, President
Membership: *Fees:* $2 youth; $10 adult; $15 family
Activities: Shows; Auctions; Guest speakers; Videos; Show-and-tell nights; Grading challenges

Manitoba Combative Sports Commission (MCSC)
#420, 213 Notre Dame Ave., Winnipeg MB R3B 1N3
Tel: 204-945-1788; *Fax:* 204-948-3649
www.manitobaboxingcommission.com
twitter.com/MBCombatSports
Previous Name: Manitoba Boxing Commission
Overview: A small provincial licensing organization founded in 1993 overseen by Canadian Professional Boxing Federation
Mission: The Manitoba Combative Sports Commission (MCSC) regulates professional boxing, kickboxing and mixed martial arts throughout the Province by licensing all participants, promoters, athletes, and supervising events.
Member of: Canadian Professional Boxing Federation
Chief Officer(s):
Dan Vandal, Chair
Joel Fingard, Executive Director
joel.fingard@gov.mb.ca

Manitoba Community Newspapers Association (MCNA)
943 McPhillips St., Winnipeg MB R2X 2J9
Tel: 204-947-1691; *Fax:* 204-947-1919
Toll-Free: 800-782-0051
www.mcna.com
Overview: A medium-sized provincial organization founded in 1919 overseen by Canadian Community Newspapers Association
Mission: To serve community newspaper publishers in Manitoba; To act as the industry voice for the issues of community newspaper publishers; To encourage high standards in publishing
Affliation(s): Canadian Community Newspapers Association (CCNA); Atlantic Community Newspapers Association
Chief Officer(s):
Tanis Hutchinson, Manager, Display Ad Sales
tanis@mcna.com
Membership: 46 newspapers; *Member Profile:* Community newspaper publishers throughout Manitoba which meet MCNA publishing standards
Activities: Liaising with the federal, provincial, & municipal levels of government; Providing education & training opportunities for the betterment of the industry; Communicating recent publishing trends & technological advancements to members; Representing the industry to advertisers
Awards:
• Better Newspapers Competition Awards (Award)

Manitoba Conservation Districts Association (MCDA)
#4, 940 Princess Ave., Brandon MB R7A 0P6
Tel: 204-570-0164
info@mcda.ca
www.mcda.ca
www.facebook.com/176771465790644
twitter.com/MBConsDistAssoc
www.youtube.com/channel/UCNM4SLi9ZNTxurTbQcYWWpQ
Overview: A small provincial organization
Mission: Manitoba Conservation Districts Association (MCDA) is a non-profit organization which represents the 18 Conservation Districts (CD's) within Manitoba.
Chief Officer(s):
Shane Robins, Executive Director, 204-570-0164
Meetings/Conferences: • Manitoba Conservation Districts Association 40th Annual Conservation Conference, 2015, MB
Scope: Provincial

Manitoba Cooperative Association (MCA) Inc.
#400, 317 Donald St., Winnipeg MB R3B 2H6
Tel: 204-989-5930
info@manitoba.coop
www.manitoba.coop
www.facebook.com/290929227626052
twitter.com/MBIYC
Overview: A medium-sized provincial organization
Mission: To promote a united, growing & influential co-operative movement through focussed, collective energies & resources
Chief Officer(s):
Dale Ward, President
Membership: 11 representing 150 co-ops
Awards:
• Cooperative Awards (Award)

Manitoba Cooperative Honey Producers Ltd.
625 Roseberry St., Winnipeg MB R3H 0T4
Tel: 204-786-8977; *Fax:* 204-783-8468
Toll-Free: 866-788-8030
www.beemaid.com
www.facebook.com/BeeMaidHoney
Overview: A small provincial organization
Chief Officer(s):
Ida MacLeod, Contact

Manitoba Council for International Cooperation (MCIC) / Conseil du Manitoba pour la coopération internationale
#302, 280 Smith St., Winnipeg MB R3C 1K2
Tel: 204-987-6420; *Fax:* 204-956-0031
Other Communication: mcic@web.ca
info@mcic.ca
www.mcic.ca
www.facebook.com/mcic.ca
twitter.com/MCIC_CA
Overview: A medium-sized international charitable organization founded in 1974
Mission: To promote international development that protects the environment; To coordinate the development work of member agencies
Member of: Canadian Council for International Cooperation (CCIC)
Chief Officer(s):
Janice Hamilton, Executive Director
janice@mcic.ca
Finances: *Funding Sources:* Federal & provincial Government; Members; Winnipeg Foundation; Assiniboine Credit Union
Staff Member(s): 8
Membership: 40+ non-governmental organizations; *Member Profile:* Non-governmental organizations working in Manitoba which support international development cooperation
Activities: Administering funds for international development through the Manitoba Government Matching Grant Program (MGMGP); Supporting overseas projects that deal with development, community solidarity or relief & rehabilitation of countries in Africa, Asia & Latin America; Providing development education in Manitoba; Increasing awareness of international issues through youth conferences & public engagement groups; Fostering member interaction; Building solidarity with the developing world through the Fair Trade Manitoba Program; *Awareness Events:* International Development Week
Awards:
• Paul LeJeune Volunteer Service Award (Award)
• Global Citizenship Award for Graduating Grade 12 Students (Award)
Eligibility: Grade 12 students in Manitoba who have engaged in meaningful global citizenship activities aimed at making a more just and sustainable world*Location:* Manitoba*Deadline:* February *Amount:* $250
• Global Citizenship Award for Educators (Award)
Eligibility: Manitoba teachers and administrators who have been leaders in promoting global citizenship*Location:* Manitoba*Deadline:* February

Meetings/Conferences: • Manitoba Council for International Cooperation's Annual General Meeting 2015, 2015
Scope: Provincial
Description: Featuring a panel discussion, nominations for the board, bylaw changes, & the presentation of the Global Citizenship Awards for graduating Grade 12 students & Educators.
Contact Information: info@mcic.ca; Phone: 204-987-6420

Manitoba Council of Archives ***See*** Association for Manitoba Archives

Manitoba Crafts Council (MCC)
#553, 70 Arthur St., Winnipeg MB R3B 1G7
Tel: 204-946-0803
media@manitobacraft.ca
manitobacraft.ca
www.facebook.com/ManitobaCraftCouncil
twitter.com/mbcraftcouncil
pinterest.com/manitobacraft/
Also Known As: Council of Manitoba Artisans Inc.
Overview: A medium-sized provincial charitable organization founded in 1978
Mission: To promote the development & appreciation of fine craft; to facilitate a supportive environment in which fine, contemporary craft may flourish.
Member of: Canadian Crafts Federation
Chief Officer(s):
Alison Norberg, President
Finances: *Funding Sources:* Manitoba Arts Council; Winnipeg Arts Council; Canada Council for the Arts; WH & SE Loewen Foundation; Art Gallery of Southwestern Manitoba
Membership: *Fees:* $45 individual; $25 student/low income/friend; *Member Profile:* Craft artists & those with an interest in contemporary craft
Activities: *Internships:* Yes; *Speaker Service:* Yes; *Library* Open to public
Awards:
• Judith Ryan Award for Best in Show (Award)
• Marilyn Levitt Award for Excellence in Clay (Award)
• Jurors Awards for Excellence & Innovation (Award)

Manitoba Cricket Association (MCA)
#327, 145 Pacific Ave., Winnipeg MB R3B 2Z6
Tel: 204-925-5672; *Fax:* 204-925-5703
www.cricket.mb.ca
Overview: A small provincial organization founded in 1937 overseen by Cricket Canada
Mission: To make cricket available to all Manitobans.
Member of: Cricket Canada
Chief Officer(s):
Garvin Budhoo, President
garvin.budhoo@shaw.ca
Ron Dipchand, Executive Director
rondipchand@shawbiz.ca
Finances: *Annual Operating Budget:* $50,000-$100,000; *Funding Sources:* Manitoba government; Lotteries Foundation
Staff Member(s): 1; 10 volunteer(s)
Membership: 362; *Fees:* $900 per team
Activities: *Library*

Manitoba Criminal Justice Association (MCJA)
#510, 405 Broadway, Winnipeg MB R3C 3L6
Tel: 204-945-8547; *Fax:* 204-945-1260
info@mcja.ca
www.mcja.ca
Previous Name: Manitoba Society of Criminology Inc.
Overview: A small provincial organization founded in 1969
Mission: The MCJA reflects the views of people from all areas of the criminal justice system, and to addresses problems arising within this system.
Affiliation(s): Canadian Criminal Justice Association; Alberta Criminal Justice Association; British Columbia Criminal Justice Association; Criminal Justice Association of Ontario; New Brunswick/Prince Edward Island Criminal Justice Association; Newfoundland & Labrador Criminology & Corrections Association; Nova Scotia Criminal Justice Association; Société de Criminologie du Québec; Saskatchewan Justice Institute
Chief Officer(s):
Mike Cook, President
Membership: *Fees:* Student $25; Individual $60-$145; Patron $200; Corporate $500

Manitoba Cultural Society of the Deaf (MCSD)
101-285 Pembina Hwy., Winnipeg MB R3L 2E1
Tel: 204-284-0802; *Fax:* 204-284-0802; *TTY:* 204-284-0802
www.deafmanitoba.org
Overview: A small provincial organization
Affliation(s): Winnipeg Community Centre of the Deaf; Canadian Cultural Society of the Deaf
Chief Officer(s):
Sheila Montney, Executive Director
Finances: *Annual Operating Budget:* Less than $50,000
Membership: 60+; *Fees:* $10
Activities: Deaf entertainment; Forrest C. Nickerson Day; *Speaker Service:* Yes

Manitoba Customer Contact Association, Inc. (MCCA)
1000 Waverley St., Winnipeg MB R2T 0P3
Tel: 204-975-6464; *Fax:* 204-975-6460
info@mcca.mb.ca
www.mcca.mb.ca
Previous Name: Manitoba Call Centre Association
Overview: A small provincial organization founded in 1997
Mission: To promote the development & sustainability of a growing, healthy & dynamic contact centre industry
Member of: Manitoba & Winnipeg Chambers of Commerce, CSAE; Alliance of MB Sector Councils; Contact Centre Canada
Chief Officer(s):
Cheryl Barsalou, CEO
ceo@mcca.mb.ca
Lisa Dabrowski, Program Manager
Sherry Woods, Project Assistant
Jean Ruppel, Administrative Coordinator
Finances: *Annual Operating Budget:* $250,000-$500,000; *Funding Sources:* Government; Membership fees; Events
Staff Member(s): 4; 20 volunteer(s)
Membership: *Fees:* $250 - $1,500 various levels; *Committees:* Human Resources; Events; Advisory; Training & Development; Conference Planning; Awards; Membership Survey; Website Review; MECCA Promotion; Decorations/Mementoes; Sponsorship; Judging; Representative Workforce Strategy
Activities: MECCA Awards; *Awareness Events:* March Forum; AGM, May; MECCA Awards, November (Manitoba Excellence in Contact Centre Achievement

Manitoba Cycling Association (MCA)
145 Pacific Ave., Winnipeg MB R3B 2Z6
Tel: 204-925-5686
mbcycling.ca
www.facebook.com/182495551800883
twitter.com/ManitobaCycling
Overview: A small provincial organization overseen by Cycling Canada Cyclisme
Mission: To be the provincial organizing body for the sport of cycling in Manitoba.
Member of: Cycling Canada Cyclisme
Chief Officer(s):
Andy Romanovych, President
tpeabody@shaw.ca
Twila Pitcher, Executive Director
cycling.ed@sportmanitoba.ca
Membership: *Fees:* $59

Manitoba Darts Association Inc. (MDAI)
c/o MDAI Membership, 720 Consol Ave., Winnipeg MB R2K 1T2
e-mail: info@manitobadarts.com
www.manitobadarts.com
www.facebook.com/419900691404805
Overview: A small provincial organization overseen by National Darts Federation of Canada
Member of: National Darts Federation of Canada
Chief Officer(s):
Gerry Convery, President, 204-694-5909
tconvery@mts.net
Glen Walker, Treasurer, 204-667-3577
walk720@shaw.ca
Lisa Loe, Secretary, 204-338-9763
lloe37@yahoo.com
Kim Clawson, Provincial & Tournament Director
kimmyclawson@live.com
Membership: *Fees:* $30

Manitoba Deaf Sports Association Inc. (MDSA)
18 Aylmer St., Winnipeg MB R2R 2G8
Other Communication: Alt. E-mail: bdstanley@shaw.ca
deafeagle@hotmail.com
Overview: A small provincial organization overseen by Canadian Deaf Sports Association
Mission: To govern fitness, amateur sports & recreation for deaf people in Manitoba.
Member of: Canadian Deaf Sports Association
Chief Officer(s):
Cliff Beaulieu, President

Manitoba Dental Assistants Association
#17, 595 Clifton St., Winnipeg MB R3G 2X5
Tel: 204-586-7378; *Fax:* 204-783-9631
mdaa@mdaa.ca
www.mdaa.ca
Overview: A small provincial organization overseen by Canadian Dental Assistants Association
Meetings/Conferences: • Manitoba Dental Assistants Association 2015 Annual General Meeting, February, 2015, Caboto Centre, Winnipeg, MB
Scope: Provincial
Description: A review of the year & bylaws & results of the MDAA Wage Survey
Contact Information: E-mail: mdaa@mdaa.ca
Publications:
• Manitoba Dental Assistants Association Newsletter
Type: Newsletter; *Accepts Advertising*; *Price:* Free with membership in the Manitoba Dental Assistants Association
Profile: Association updates, including notice of professional development courses & Dental Assisting Week events, plus information from the Manitoba DentalAssociation regulatory body

Manitoba Dental Association (MDA)
#103, 698 Corydon Ave., Winnipeg MB R3M 0X9
Tel: 204-988-5300; *Fax:* 204-988-5310
office@manitobadentist.ca
www.manitobadentist.ca
Overview: A medium-sized provincial licensing organization founded in 1883 overseen by Canadian Dental Association
Mission: To act as the governing body for dentists & dental assistants in Manitoba; To ensure that that the oral health of Manitobans is met
Chief Officer(s):
Joel Antel, President
Allan Cogan, Vice-President
Rafi Mohammed, Sec.-Treas.
Activities: Carrying out the requirements of The Dental Association Act; Developing clinical standards; Ensuring professional & ethical standards; Encouraging continuing dental education
Meetings/Conferences: • Manitoba Dental Association 2015 131st Annual Meeting & Convention, April, 2015, Keystone Centre, Brandon, MB
Scope: Provincial
Description: A conference & trade show, with business meetings, educational presentations, & networking opportunities, for dentists, dental hygienists, the oral health team, lab personnel, practice consultants, & dental students
Contact Information: E-mail: office@manitobadentist.ca

Manitoba Dental Hygienists Association (MDHA)
#200E, 1215 Henderson Hwy., Winnipeg MB R2G 1L8
Tel: 204-981-7327
info@mdha.ca
www.mdha.ca
www.facebook.com/208495962663337
twitter.com/MDHA_MB
Overview: A small provincial organization founded in 1966
Mission: To cultivate, promote & sustain the art & science of dental hygiene; To represent, maintain & safeguard the honour & common interests of members; To promote closer communication, unity & social intercourse among members; To contribute toward the education & the improvement of public health
Affliation(s): Canadian Dental Hygienists Association
Chief Officer(s):
Kim Wozniak, Executive Director
Membership: *Committees:* Mentorship; U of M Endowment Fund Advisory; Membership; Sponsorship

Manitoba Diving Association
145 Pacific Ave., Winnipeg MB R3B 2Z6
Tel: 204-925-5654; *Fax:* 204-925-5703
www.manitobadiving.com
Overview: A small provincial organization
Mission: Provides strong ethical and values driven foundation for diving throughout Manitoba and Canada, and supports athletic development, personal growth and community awareness through excellence in leadership
Member of: Diving Plongeon Canada
Chief Officer(s):
Jim Lambie, Contact
jimlambie@yahoo.com

Manitoba Down Syndrome Society (MDSS)

#204, 825 Sherbrook St., Winnipeg MB R3A 1M5
Tel: 204-992-2731; *Fax:* 204-975-3027
www.manitobadownsyndromesociety.com
www.facebook.com/ManitobaDownSyndromeSociety
twitter.com/manitobadss
Overview: A small provincial charitable organization founded in 1991
Mission: To provide support, information & opportunities for individuals with Down Syndrome, parents, professionals and other interested persons; To seek resolutions to issues of concern
Affliation(s): Canadian Down Syndrome Society
Chief Officer(s):
Lorraine Baydack, President
Val Surbey, Vice-President
Finances: *Funding Sources:* Donations; Fundraising
Membership: *Fees:* $30 family/individual; $55 organization
Activities: Visiting Parents Program; Parent Networking Evenings; Family Fun Days; *Awareness Events:* World Down Syndrome Day, March

Manitoba Eco-Network Inc. (MEN) / Réseau écologique du Manitoba inc.

#3, 303 Portage Ave., Winnipeg MB R3B 2B4
Tel: 204-947-6511; *Fax:* 866-237-3130
info@mbeconetwork.org
www.mbeconetwork.org
www.facebook.com/Manitoba.Eco.Network
twitter.com/MB_EcoNetwork
www.youtube.com/user/ManitobaEcoNetwork
Also Known As: Manitoba Environmental Network
Overview: A small provincial charitable organization founded in 1988 overseen by Canadian Environmental Network
Mission: To educate the public on environmental issues; to conduct research on environmental issues; to facilitate communications between environmental groups & the general public
Member of: Canadian Environmental Network
Chief Officer(s):
Kristine Koster, Executive Director
kristine@mbeconetwork.org
Finances: *Funding Sources:* Project work; donations; membership dues; grants
Staff Member(s): 11
Membership: 80; *Fees:* $100 associate; $50 group; $30 individual; *Member Profile:* Open to any non-profit non-governmental group which has as one of its objectives the enhancing or furthering of environmental quality, protecting the environment or environmental education
Activities: Sponsors public forums, speakers, workshops on a broad variety of issues; operates projects regarding climate change, water issues & organic lawn care; offers GIS & mapping services to environmental projects; meets regularly with officials of the provincial government; *Speaker Service:* Yes; *Library:* Alice Chambers Memorial Library; Open to public
Awards:
• Annual Environmental Awards (Award)

Manitoba Egg Farmers

Waverley Square, #18, 5 Scurfield Blvd., Winnipeg MB R3Y 1G3
Tel: 204-488-4888; *Fax:* 204-488-3544
www.eggs.mb.ca
Previous Name: Manitoba Egg Producers
Overview: A small provincial organization
Mission: To provide an adequate supply of eggs to the marketplace at a fair price to the consumer & equitable return to the producer
Chief Officer(s):
Ed Kleinsasser, Chair
Cory Rybuck, General Manager
Membership: 170; *Member Profile:* Egg & pullet farmers

Manitoba Egg Producers *See* Manitoba Egg Farmers

Manitoba Electrical League Inc. (MEL)

#104, 1780 Wellington Ave., Winnipeg MB R3H 1B3
Tel: 204-783-4125; *Fax:* 204-783-4216
www.meleague.net
Also Known As: ME League
Overview: A medium-sized provincial organization founded in 1957
Mission: To advise & inform all people of Manitoba on effective use of electricity toward maintenance & betterment of standards of living; to encourage cooperation of various branches of electrical industry in developing programs in support of common marketing objectives.
Chief Officer(s):
Gord Macpherson, Executive Director
gordmeleague@gmail.com
Staff Member(s): 2
Membership: 211 corporate; *Fees:* Schedule available; *Committees:* Education; Finance; Membership; Contractor; Sports; Marketing; Policy & Governance; AGM; Ethics & Standards Liaison
Activities: *Rents Mailing List:* Yes

Manitoba Environment Officers Association Inc. (MEOA)

147 Norcross Cres., Winnipeg MB R3X 1J2
e-mail: meoa@mts.net
www.meoa.ca
Overview: A medium-sized provincial organization
Mission: To enhance the public health and safety of Manitobans and to protect, maintain and rehabilitate Manitoba's environment ecosystems through the diligent duties of educated Environment Officers and to obtain for Environment Officers continued education and recognition of their efforts.
Chief Officer(s):
Bill Barr, President
Membership: *Fees:* $25

Manitoba Environmental Industries Association Inc. (MEIA)

#100, 62 Albert St., Winnipeg MB R3B 1E9
Tel: 204-783-7090; *Fax:* 204-783-6501
admin@meia.mb.ca
www.meia.mb.ca
Overview: A medium-sized provincial organization founded in 1991
Mission: To assist members in the business of the environment; To connect business, government, & stakeholders with environmental issues
Chief Officer(s):
John Fjeldsted, Executive Director
Vaughn Bullough, President
Rosemary Deans, Coordinator, Education & Training
Deb Tardiff, Coordinator, Education & Training
Sheldon McLeod, Secretary
John Pikel, Treasurer
Finances: *Funding Sources:* Membership fees; Sponsorships
Membership: *Fees:* Schedule available, based upon number of employees & number of representatives; *Member Profile:* Professionals, companies, & organizations in Manitoba who practise in the area of environment & sustainable development; *Committees:* Executive; Member Services; Legislation & Regulation; Programs Development
Activities: Providing professional development training, including courses, MEIA learning sessions, & environment industry workshops; Collaborating with other organizations; Providing networking opportunities;
Meetings/Conferences: • Manitoba Environmental Industries Association Inc. 2015 Remediation & Renewal Conference, February, 2015, Victoria Inn, Winnipeg, MB
Scope: Provincial
Description: An annual one day conference with information about recent changes in provincial & federal environmental legislation & regulatory affairs
Contact Information: Coordinator, Education & Training: Rosemary Deans, Phone: 204-783-7090
• Manitoba Environmental Industries Association Inc. 2015 Conference, 2015
Scope: Provincial
Description: An annual one day conference to inform participants about recent environmental legislation & regulatory affairs at the provincial & federal levels
Contact Information: Coordinator, Education & Training: Rosemary Deans, Phone: 204-783-7090
• Manitoba Environmental Industries Association Inc. 2015 Annual General Meeting, 2015, MB
Scope: Provincial
Description: A gathering of members to address the business of the association & to provide networking opportunities
Contact Information: Executive Director: Margo Shaw, Phone: 204-783-7090
Publications:
• Manitoba Environmental Industries Association Inc. Members' Directory
Type: Directory
Profile: Contact information for association members
• MEIA [Manitoba Environmental Industries Association Inc.] Information Bulletin
Type: Newsletter; *Frequency:* Biweekly
Profile: Information for Manitoba Environmental Industries Association Inc. members about events, technology updates, & emerging regulatory & policyissues

Manitoba Farm Bureau *See* Keystone Agricultural Producers

Manitoba Farm Vacations Association; Manitoba Country Vacations Association Inc *See* Manitoba Rural Tourism Association Inc.

Manitoba Federation of Independent Schools Inc. (MFIS)

630 Westminster Ave., Winnipeg MB R3C 3S1
Tel: 204-783-4481
www.mfis.ca
Overview: A medium-sized provincial organization founded in 1974 overseen by Federation of Independent Schools in Canada
Mission: To support & encourage high educational standards & values unique to our various school communities; to represent interests & concerns of member independent schools in Manitoba
Chief Officer(s):
Susan Eberhard, Executive Director
execdir@mfis.ca
Robert Praznik, President
Finances: *Annual Operating Budget:* $100,000-$250,000; *Funding Sources:* Membership fees
Membership: 51; *Fees:* $8.25 full-time-equivalent student; *Committees:* Education; Government Liaison; Public Relations; Membership

Manitoba Federation of Labour / Fédération du travail du Manitoba

#303, 275 Broadway, Winnipeg MB R3C 4M6
Tel: 204-947-1400; *Fax:* 204-943-4276
www.mfl.mb.ca
Overview: A medium-sized provincial organization founded in 1956 overseen by Canadian Labour Congress
Mission: To advance economic & social welfare of working people in Manitoba; To encourage workers to vote & exercise full rights & responsibilities
Chief Officer(s):
Darlene Dziewit, President
Finances: *Annual Operating Budget:* $500,000-$1.5 Million; *Funding Sources:* Membership dues
Staff Member(s): 7
Membership: 90,000; *Member Profile:* Members of affiliated unions; Sectors include manufacturing, government, business, retail, health care, schools, tourism industry, agriculture, transportation; *Committees:* Occupational Health & Safety; Workers Compensation; Environment; Women; Human Rights; Political Education; Education
Activities: *Internships:* Yes; *Speaker Service:* Yes; *Library:* Occupational Health Centre;
Meetings/Conferences: • Manitoba Federation of Labour 2015 Convention, May, 2015, Keystone Centre, Brandon, MB
Scope: Provincial
Contact Information: Communications Coordinator: John Doyle, Phone: 204-782-8465, E-mail: jdoyle@mfl.mb.ca

Manitoba Fencing Association (MFA)

#308, 145 Pacific Ave., Winnipeg MB R3B 2Z6
Tel: 204-925-5696; *Fax:* 204-925-5703
fencing@sportmanitoba
www.fencing.mb.ca
www.facebook.com/pages/Manitoba-Fencing-Association/19989 8656787720
Overview: A small provincial organization founded in 1978 overseen by Canadian Fencing Federation
Mission: To promote & develop the sport of fencing in Manitoba
Member of: Canadian Fencing Federation
Chief Officer(s):
Monika Feist, President
Travis Paskaruk, Executive Director
Finances: *Funding Sources:* Fundraising
Staff Member(s): 2
Membership: *Member Profile:* Fencing clubs in Manitoba
Activities: Organizing training programs for high level athletes; Offering coaching training opportunities & clinics; Providing certification opportunities for officials; Conducting school & community outreach programs

Manitoba Five Pin Bowling Federation, Inc. (MFPBF)

145 Pacific Ave., Winnipeg MB R3B 2Z6
Tel: 204-925-5766; *Fax:* 204-925-5767
www.mfpbf.com

Overview: A small provincial organization overseen by Sport Manitoba
Mission: To provide services & resources to its members which enable them to increase membership & promote bowling as a lifetime sport through effective programs at all levels of participation
Member of: Canadian 5 Pin Bowlers' Association; Sport Manitoba
Affliation(s): Manitoba 5 Pin Bowlers' Association; Master Bowlers Association of Manitoba; Youth Bowling Canada - Manitoba Divisio
Chief Officer(s):
Deanne Zilinsky, Executive Director
Staff Member(s): 2

Manitoba Food Processors Association (MFPA)
#12, 59 Scurfield Blvd., Winnipeg MB R3Y 1V2
Tel: 204-982-6372; *Fax:* 204-632-5143
mfpa@mfpa.mb.ca
www.mfpa.mb.ca
Overview: A small provincial organization founded in 1993
Mission: To act as the voice of the food processing industry in Maniboba; To promote food products made in Manitoba to both local & international markets; To increase awareness of locally grown & processed food products
Chief Officer(s):
Dave Shambrock, Executive Director
Dave_Shambrock@mfpa.mb.ca
Carly McGregor, Coordinator, Communications
Carly_McGregor@mfpa.mb.ca
Membership: 260+ companies; *Fees:* Schedule available, based upon number of employees; *Member Profile:* Food processing companies in Manitoba, ranging from start-up operations to multi-national companies; Food growers; Suppliers; Retailers; Marketing boards; Government agencies
Activities: Providing continuing education & networking opportunities; Liaising with government
Awards:
• Industry Excellence Awards (Award)
To recognize Manitoba food industry leaders
Publications:
• Entrepreneur's Technical Guide To New Product Development & Manufacture
Type: Guide
Profile: Information for managers
• Food Processors' Reference Manual
Type: Manual
Profile: Information for business establishment & expansion
• In The Process
Type: Newsletter; *Frequency:* Monthly
Profile: Member profiles, forthcoming events, market information, & industry news
• Manitoba Food Processors Association Membership Directory & Product Guide
Type: Directory
• Shoppers' Guide: Manitoba Made Brand Names
Type: Guide
Profile: Information for consumers

Manitoba Forestry Association Inc.
900 Corydon Ave., Winnipeg MB R3M 0Y4
Tel: 204-453-3182; *Fax:* 204-477-5765
www.thinktrees.org
Previous Name: Prairie Provinces Forestry Association
Overview: A medium-sized provincial charitable organization founded in 1972 overseen by Canadian Forestry Association
Mission: To promote the wise use & management of all natural renewable resources, with emphasis on forests; to promote the planting of trees; to promote private land forestry (woodlots); to act as liaison among government, industry & the general public.
Chief Officer(s):
Patricia Pohrebnuk, Executive Director
Christina McDonald, President
Finances: *Funding Sources:* Government; industry; individuals
Staff Member(s): 8
Membership: *Fees:* $25 individual; $250 corporate
Activities: School programs; forest centres; Private Land Forests Program; operates Forest Museum; conservation kits for use by teachers; wildfire prevention campaigns; *Speaker Service:* Yes
Awards:
• Alan B. Beaven Forestry Scholarship (Scholarship)
Manitoba resident; must be a recent graduate of high school, entering a Canadian university or technical school in forestry or an allied field*Deadline:* July *Amount:* $500

Manitoba Freestyle Ski Association
200 Main St., Winnipeg MB R3C 4M2
Tel: 204-795-9754
info@mbfreestyle.com
www.mbfreestyle.com
Overview: A small provincial organization overseen by Canadian Freestyle Ski Association
Mission: To promote the sport of freestyle skiing in Manitoba.
Member of: Canadian Freestyle Ski Association
Chief Officer(s):
Frank Berg, President
twoicebergs@yahoo.com

Manitoba Funeral Service Association (MFSA)
#610, 55 Garry St., Winnipeg MB R3C 4H4
Tel: 204-947-0927
info@mfsa.mb.ca
www.mfsa.mb.ca
Overview: A small provincial organization founded in 1964
Mission: To serve funeral directors & funeral homes throughout Manitoba; To advance funeral service; To uphold a code of ethics
Affliation(s): Western Canada Cemetery Association
Chief Officer(s):
Owen McKenzie, President, 204-857-4021
mckpfc@gmail.com
Thorunn Petursdottir, Executive Director, 204-947-0927
mfsa63@gmail.com
Matt Nichol, Secretary-Treasurer, 204-523-7791
matt@wheatlandfs.com
Membership: 38; *Member Profile:* Funeral homes in Manitoba; Organizations which serve funeral homes; *Committees:* Government Affairs; FSAC; Member & Public Affairs; Continuing Education; Finance
Activities: Providing educational opportunities

Manitoba Genealogical Society Inc. (MGS)
1045 St. James St., #E, Winnipeg MB R3H 1B1
Tel: 204-783-9139; *Fax:* 204-783-0190
contact@mbgenealogy.com
www.mbgenealogy.com
www.facebook.com/group.php?gid=8750026759
twitter.com/MbGenealogy
Overview: A small provincial charitable organization founded in 1976
Mission: To collect & preserve local genealogical & historical records & materials; To foster education in genealogical research through society workshops & seminars; To encourage production of genealogical publications relating especially to Manitoba
Member of: Manitoba Heritage Federation Inc.
Chief Officer(s):
Kathy Stokes, President
Mary Bole, Library Chair
library@mbgenealogy.com
Finances: *Funding Sources:* Membership fees; Government grants; Fundraising; Donations
Membership: 18 institutional + 25 associate + 61 lifetime + 441 individual; *Fees:* $20 associate; $40 individual & institutional; $115 corporate; *Committees:* Education; Membership; Library; Research; Special Projects
Activities: Seminars & workshops; Genealogical research; *Library:* Resource Centre; Open to public

Beautiful Plains
PO Box 2620, Neepawa MB R0J 1H0
Tel: 204-476-5131
djmcg@mts.net
www.mbgenealogy.com/index.php?page=beautiful-plains-branch
Chief Officer(s):
Don McGillivray, President
djmcg@mts.net

Dauphin Branch
c/o Tammy Zurba, 6th Ave. Southeast, Dauphin MB R7N 2C3
e-mail: dauphinbranch@yahoo.ca
www.sitescapers.com/Webpages
Chief Officer(s):
Tammy Zurba, Contact

South West Branch
Knox United Church, 451 - 18th St., Brandon MB R7A 5A9
e-mail: info@swmanitobagenealogy.ca
www.swmanitobagenealogy.ca
Chief Officer(s):
Eleanor Burch, President

Southeast & Winnipeg Branch
1045 St. James St., #E, Winnipeg MB R3H 1B1
Tel: 204-453-1431
www.mbgenealogy.com/index.php?page=southeast-and-winnipeg-branch
Virginia Braid, President
vbraid@mts.net
Gord McBean, Vice-President
glmcbean@mts.net

Swan Valley Branch
PO Box 6, Swan River MB R0L 1Z0
Tel: 204-734-2170
www.mbgenealogy.com/index.php?page=swan-valley-branch
Chief Officer(s):
Eric Neufeld, Contact
eneufeld@mts.net

Manitoba Gerontological Nurses' Association (MGNA)
c/o Leslie Dryburgh, 300 Booth Dr., Winnipeg MB R3J 3M7
Tel: 204-831-2547
info@mbgna.com
mbgna.ca
Overview: A medium-sized provincial organization overseen by Canadian Gerontological Nursing Association
Mission: To promote a high standard of nursing care & related health services for older adults; To enhance professionalism in the practice of gerontological nursing
Chief Officer(s):
Poh Lin Lim, President
plim@vgh.mb.ca
Membership: *Fees:* $27.50 associate; $70 regular; *Member Profile:* Nurses interested in gerontology; *Committees:* Membership; Education; Media
Activities: Offering professional networking opportunities; Providing professional development; Advocating for comprehensive services for older adults; Supporting research related to gerontological nursing; Promoting gerontological nursing to the public
Awards:
• MGNA Nursing Distinction Award - Clinical Category (Award)
• MGNA Nursing Distinction Award - Education/Research/Administration (Award)

Manitoba Golf Association Inc. *See* Golf Manitoba Inc.

Manitoba Government & General Employees' Union (MGEU)
#601, 275 Broadway, Winnipeg MB R3C 4M6
Tel: 204-982-6438; *Fax:* 204-942-2146
Toll-Free: 866-982-6438; *TTY:* 204-982-6599
resourcecentre@mgeu.ca
www.mgeu.ca
www.facebook.com/174238299256105
twitter.com/MGEUnion
www.youtube.com/user/mgeulogin
Overview: A medium-sized provincial organization
Member of: National Union of Public and General Employees
Chief Officer(s):
Michelle Gawronsky, President
Debbie O'Hare, Executive Assistant
Membership: 40,000
Activities: *Library*

Manitoba Gymnastics Association (MGA)
145 Pacific Ave., Winnipeg MB R3B 2Z6
Tel: 204-925-5781; *Fax:* 204-925-5932
mga@sportmanitoba.ca
www.gymnastics.mb.ca
www.facebook.com/pages/Manitoba-Gymnastics/427931587283744
twitter.com/GymnasticsMB
Overview: A small provincial organization founded in 1968
Mission: To develop, promote & guide gymnastics as a lifetime activity in Manitoba
Member of: Canadian Gymnastics Federation
Chief Officer(s):
Kathy Stoesz, Executive Director
mga.kathy@sportmanitoba.ca
Staff Member(s): 2
Membership: *Committees:* Women's Technical; Men's Technical; Development; Trampoline & Trumbling Technical

Manitoba Hairstylists' Association
PO Box 12, Stn. L, Winnipeg MB R3H 0Z4
Tel: 204-775-8633
www.manitobahairstylists.com

Overview: A small provincial organization
Chief Officer(s):
Mary Elliott, President
Membership: *Member Profile:* Hairstylists in Manitoba
Activities: Educational seminars, workshops, guest speakers, and platform artists; *Library:* Video Library
Publications:
• Clippings
Type: Newsletter

Manitoba Handball Association Inc.
c/o Sport Manitoba, 145 Pacific Ave., Winnipeg MB R3B 2Z6
Tel: 204-925-5667
www.manitobahandballassociation.com
www.facebook.com/groups/2390949216
Overview: A small provincial organization
Mission: To promote & develop the sport of handball in Manitoba
Chief Officer(s):
Abbie Bajon, Executive Director
abbiebajon@hotmail.com
Membership: *Fees:* $10 associate; $15 individual; $25 family

Manitoba Hang Gliding Association (MHGA)
c/o Sport Manitoba, 145 Pacific Ave., Winnipeg MB R3B 2Z6
mhga.ca
Overview: A small provincial organization founded in 1980 overseen by Hang Gliding & Paragliding Association of Canada
Mission: To promote safety, excellence & public awareness of the sport of hang gliding.
Member of: Hang Gliding & Paragliding Association of Canada

Manitoba Health Information Management Association (MHIMA)
PO Box 1544, Winnipeg MB R3C 2Z4
Tel: 204-632-3413
www.mhima.ca
Overview: A small provincial organization
Mission: To advance health information in Manitoba; To ensure the ethical management of health information; To promote the profession of health information management
Member of: Canadian Health Information Management Association (CHIMA)
Chief Officer(s):
Lee Bassett, President
lbassett@rha-central.mb.ca
Alice le Cuff, Secretary
alecunff@stamant.mb.ca; alecunff@shaw.ca
Mandy Prange, Treasurer
mprange@brha.mb.ca
Membership: *Member Profile:* Health information management professionals in Manitoba
Activities: Providing information about health information practices & advances in technology; Liaising with government & other organizations; Offering continuing education & networking opportunities;
Awards:
• Manitoba Health Information Management Association Bursary (Scholarship)
Eligibility: Manitoba students in the health information management program, year one & two *Amount:* 2 awards of $250 each
• Manitoba Health Information Management Association Academic Achievement Awards (Award)
Eligibility: Students in the RRC health information management program, year one & two

Manitoba Health Libraries Association *See* Manitoba Association of Health Information Providers

Manitoba Health Organizations *See* The Regional Health Authorities of Manitoba

Manitoba Heart Foundation *See* Heart & Stroke Foundation of Manitoba

Manitoba Heavy Construction Association (MHCA)
#3, 1680 Ellice Ave., Winnipeg MB R3G 0Z2
Tel: 204-947-1379; *Fax:* 204-943-2279
info@mhca.mb.ca
www.mhca.mb.ca
twitter.com/ManitobaHeavy
Overview: A small provincial organization founded in 1943 overseen by Canadian Construction Association
Mission: To promote a safe workplace for employees in Manitoba's heavy construction industry; To represent the heavy construction industry in Manitoba
Chief Officer(s):
Christopher Lorenc, President
Wendy Greund Summerfield, Manager, Finance
Greg Huff, Manager, MHC Training Academy
Christine Miller, Manager, Events & Membership, 204-947-1379
Jason Rosin, Manager, Communications
Membership: 340+ organizations & businesses; *Member Profile:* Heavy construction (heavy civil) & related industries in Manitoba; *Committees:* Safety Program; Winnipeg; Aggregate Producers; Highways; Events; Equipment Rental Rates; Education, Training, Education, Training, & Gold Seal; Membership
Activities: Providing government approved career & vocational training; Liaising with government; Facilitating networking opportunities
Meetings/Conferences: • Manitoba Heavy Construction Association 2015 4th Annual Expo, March, 2015, Winnipeg, MB
Scope: Provincial
Description: An educational event, to help train & educate workers in the heavy construction industry
Contact Information: Manager, Events & Membership: Christine Miller, Phone: 204-947-1379
Publications:
• Heavy News Weekly
Type: Newsletter; *Frequency:* Weekly
Profile: Articles about the heavy construction industry & association activities
• Manitoba Heavy Construction Association Annual Report
Type: Yearbook; *Frequency:* Annually
• Manitoba Heavy Construction Association Directory
Type: Directory; *Frequency:* Annually
Profile: Listings of Manitoba Heavy Construction Association member & a guide to equipment rental rates in Manitoba
• Perspectives [a publication of the Manitoba Heavy Construction Association]
Type: Magazine; *Frequency:* Annually; *Accepts Advertising*
Profile: Information about public policy, industry positions, & safety & environment related issues

Manitoba Hereford Association
PO Box 7, Stn. Site 520, Brandon MB R7A 5Y5
Tel: 204-769-4459
www.mbhereford.ca
www.facebook.com/255808637782090
www.youtube.com/mbhereford
Overview: A small provincial organization founded in 1990
Mission: To promote the hereford breed of cattle in Manitoba.
Member of: Canadian Hereford Association
Chief Officer(s):
Brent Blaine, President
bblaine2002@yahoo.ca
Kailey Penner, Contact
kjpenner@hotmail.ca
Membership: 75

Manitoba High Schools Athletic Association (MHSAA)
145 Pacific Ave., Winnipeg MB R3B 2Z6
Tel: 204-925-5640; *Fax:* 204-925-5624
www.mhsaa.mb.ca
www.facebook.com/MBHighSchoolsAthleticsAssociation
twitter.com/MHSAA_
Overview: A medium-sized provincial charitable organization founded in 1962 overseen by School Sport Canada
Mission: To promote the value of sports in Manitoba secondary schools; To provide athletic & educational opportunities so that students reach their full potential
Member of: School Sport Canada
Chief Officer(s):
Morris Glimcher, Executive Director
morris@mhsaa.mb.ca
Scott Kwasnitza, President
skwasnitza@lssd.ca
Finances: *Funding Sources:* Sport Manitoba grants; Membership fees; Corporate support; Revenues from admissions to provincial championships; Fundraising
Membership: 192 schools + 37,000 athletes; *Fees:* Schedule available based on school size; *Member Profile:* Secondary schools in Manitoba
Activities: Encouraging participation in high school sports; Assisting in running equitable & fair sporting events for high schools; Presenting awards & scholarships for athletes, coaches, & volunteeers; Promoting volunteer involvement; Seeking support for the association; Providing educational materials for coaches & teachers

Manitoba Historical Society (MHS)
61 Carlton St., Winnipeg MB R3C 1N7
Tel: 204-947-0559; *Fax:* 204-943-2565
info@mhs.mb.ca
www.mhs.mb.ca
Overview: A medium-sized provincial organization founded in 1879
Mission: To promote public interest in, and preservation of Manitoba's historical resources; To encourage research relating to the history of Manitoba
Chief Officer(s):
Annabelle Mays, President
president@mhs.mb.ca
James Kostuchuk, First Vice-President
homes@mhs.mb.ca
Victor Sawelo, Manager, Ross House
rosshouse@mhs.mb.ca
Finances: *Funding Sources:* Donations
Membership: *Member Profile:* Individuals, families, students, organizations, & businesses interested in the history of Manitoba & Western Canada; *Committees:* Centennial Business; Centennial Farm; Centennial Organization; McWilliams; Young Historians; Field Trip; Finance; Publications; Membership; Program; Macdonald Dinner; Historic Preservation; Heritage Trust; Dalnavert Museum Management; Ross House Management
Activities: Assisting in the work of local historical societies; Organizing field trips; Preserving heritage buildings & historical landmarks; Operating Dalnavert Museum & Ross House Museum; Hosting programs with historical themes; Organizing annual general meetings & conferences; *Library:* The Edwin Nix Memorial Library
Awards:
• Centennial Farm Award (Award)
• Centennial Business Award (Award)
• Margaret McWilliams Award (Award)
• Young Historians Award (Award)

Manitoba Holiday Festival of the Arts Inc.
PO Box 147, Neepawa MB R0J 1H0
Tel: 204-476-3232
mhfa@mts.net
www.mts.net/~mhfa
Overview: A small provincial charitable organization founded in 1967
Mission: To provide art opportunities to all members of a family, regardless of age or experience
Chief Officer(s):
Greg Heschuk, Administrator
Moira Woods, President
Finances: *Funding Sources:* Regional Government; Manitoba Culture, Heritage and Tourism
Staff Member(s): 1; 7 volunteer(s)

Manitoba Home Builders' Association (MHBA)
#1, 1420 Clarence Ave., Winnipeg MB R3T 1T6
Tel: 204-925-2560; *Fax:* 204-925-2567
info@homebuilders.mb.ca
www.homebuilders.mb.ca
Previous Name: HUDAM
Overview: A small provincial organization founded in 1937 overseen by Canadian Home Builders' Association
Mission: To act as the voice of Manitoba's residential construction industry; To promote affordability & choice in housing in Manitoba; To uphold the MHBA Code of Ethics & the Code of Discipline
Affiliation(s): Canadian Home Builders' Association
Chief Officer(s):
Mike Moore, President
mmoore@homebuilders.mb.ca
Janet Constable, Coordinator, Special Events & Membership, 204-925-2578
jconstable@homebuilders.mb.ca
Jan Currier, Coordinator, Show, 204-925-2566
jcurrier@homebuilders.mb.ca
James Murphy, Coordinator, Training Program, 204-925-2572
jmurphy@homebuilders.mb.ca
Membership: *Member Profile:* Builders, conducting business in Manitoba, who have been members of a new home warranty program for two years, & who have completed COR registration, or have a Simplified Safety certificate; Renovators, conducting business in Manitoba, for at least two years, who are members of a new home warranty program, if they build complete new homes; Developers in Manitoba; Professionals registered to provide services to the housing industry; Sub-contractors; Suppliers to the housing industry; Manufacturers; Government;

Persons employed by or enrolled in any educational institution, in study related to the housing industry; *Committees:* Government Liaison; Technical Research; Show Management; Education & Training; Workplace Safety & Health; Parade of Homes; Renovators; Nominating; Marketing; Membership Services; Past Chairman's Advisory
Activities: Offering information about the housing industry in Manitoba; Providing educational opportunities; Supporting Habitat for Humanity
Meetings/Conferences: • Manitoba Home Builders' Association 2015 14th Annual Kitchen, Bath, & Renovation Show, 2015
Scope: Provincial
Description: A showcase of products & services, where appointments can be made with members of the Manitoba Home Builders' Association's Renovation Council to learn solutions to renovation dilemmas
• Manitoba Home Builders' Association 2015 Spring Parade of Homes, 2015
Scope: Provincial
• Manitoba Home Builders' Association 2015 41th Annual Home Expressions Home & Garden Show, 2015
Scope: Provincial
Description: A consumer show owned & managed by the Manitoba Home Builders' Association
Publications:
• Builders' Voice
Type: Newsletter
Profile: Association activities & forthcoming events

Manitoba Horse Council Inc.
145 Pacific Ave., Winnipeg MB R3B 2Z6
Tel: 204-925-5719; *Fax:* 204-925-5703
mhc.admin@sportmanitoba.ca
www.manitobahorsecouncil.ca
www.facebook.com/pages/Manitoba-Horse-Council/587153197974798
Overview: A medium-sized provincial organization founded in 1974
Mission: To represent clubs & individuals involved with equestrian
Member of: Canadian Equestrian Federation
Chief Officer(s):
Geri Sweet, President
Bruce Rose, Executive Director
mhc.exec@sportmanitoba.ca
Finances: *Funding Sources:* Manitoba Lotteries Foundation; membership dues
Staff Member(s): 3
Membership: *Fees:* $60.50 senior; $49.50 junior; $121 family; friends of Horses $27.50; *Committees:* Athlete Development; Bingo; Breeds & Industry; Coaching; Competitions; Equestrian Centre; Officials; Recreation; Special Events; Marketing
Activities: *Rents Mailing List:* Yes; *Library* Open to public

Manitoba Hotel Association (MHA)
#200, 1534 Gamble Pl., Winnipeg MB
Tel: 204-942-0671; *Fax:* 204-942-6719
Toll-Free: 888-859-9976
www.manitobahotelassociation.ca
Overview: A small provincial organization founded in 1927
Mission: To serve the needs of the hotel & accommodation industry in Manitoba; To promote the interests of the industry; To encourage growth & excellence in Manitoba's hospitality industry
Chief Officer(s):
Reid Kelner, Chair
Jim Baker, President & Chief Executive Officer
jbaker@manitobahotelassociation.ca
Jerry Weir, Executive Director
jweir@manitobahotelassociation.ca
Ryan Kirkness, Manager, Membership & Corporate Relations
rkirkness@manitobahotelassociation.ca
Jeremy Leroux, Manager, Communications
jleroux@manitobahotelassociation.ca
Membership: *Member Profile:* Members of the hotel & accommodation industry from Manitoba, including hotels & suppliers
Activities: Promoting professionalism, accountability, & ethical principles in Manitoba's hotel & accommodation industry; Organizing regional meetings throughout Manitoba; Liaising with government organizations, regarding changes to legislation & regulations that affect the hotel industry; Arranging networking opportunities; Awarding bursaries to students in Red River College's Hotel Restaurant Administration program
Awards:
• Alexander Campbell Scholarship Fund (Scholarship)
To assist Manitoba students who are enrolled in a four year degree course in hotel management
Meetings/Conferences: • Manitoba Hotel Association 2015 Annual General Meeting, Convention, & Tradeshow, 2015, MB
Scope: Provincial
Description: Presentations from government ministers, educational speakers, & others from the hospitality industry
Contact Information: Phone: 204-942-0671; Fax: 204-942-6719
Publications:
• Manitoba Hotel Association Newsletter
Type: Newsletter; *Frequency:* Monthly; *Accepts Advertising*; *Editor:* Ryan Kirkness
Profile: Hotel & accommodation industry issues, programs, & information for association members

Manitoba Independent Insurance Adjusters' Association
c/o Timothy W. Bromley, J.P. Hamilton Adjusters Ltd., 125 Enfield Cres., Winnipeg MB R2H 1A8
www.ciaa-adjusters.ca
Overview: A small provincial organization overseen by Canadian Independent Adjusters' Association
Member of: Canadian Independent Adjusters' Association
Chief Officer(s):
Timothy W. Bromley, President, 204-944-1057, Fax: 204-944-1606
tbromley@mts.net

Manitoba Indian Cultural Education Centre (MICEC)
119 Sutherland Ave., Winnipeg MB R2W 3C9
Tel: 204-942-0228; *Fax:* 204-947-6564
info@micec.com
www.micec.com
www.facebook.com/micec.mb
Overview: A medium-sized provincial charitable organization founded in 1975
Mission: To stimulate, reidentify, maintain, expand & promote the cultural interests, lives & identity of Manitoba First Nations in every manner & respect whatsoever, & to promote an awareness of the traditional history of the First Nation Peoples of Manitoba; to advance the interests of First Nation Peoples who are registered members of the reserves within Manitoba, whether residing on or outside them; to cooperate with other organizations concerned with the interests of First Nation Peoples; to establish & promote research services; to assist in the development of accurate curriculum for use in schools within Manitoba; to produce audio, visual, & written materials relevant to cultural education development
Member of: First Nations Confederacy of Cultural Education Centres
Finances: *Funding Sources:* Federal government
Activities: Library; video & television production & editing services & equipment; community school liaison programme; *Speaker Service:* Yes; *Library:* People's Library; Open to public

Manitoba Indian Education Association Inc. (MIW)
PO Box 1250, Lake Manitoba First Nation MB R0C 3K0
Tel: 204-947-0421; *Fax:* 204-942-3067
www.miea.ca
Overview: A small provincial organization founded in 1981
Activities: Providing a student services office (#200, 70 Albert St., Winnipeg, MB, R3C 1E7); Offering support programs in academic, social, & financial counselling, tutorial services, orientation, & recreation; Providing a computer lab with internet access; Engaging in community relations; Offering referrals

Manitoba Insolvency Association *See* Manitoba Association of Insolvency & Restructuring Professionals

Manitoba Institute of Agrologists (MIA)
#201, 38 Dafoe Ave., Winnipeg MB R3T 2N2
Tel: 204-275-3721; *Fax:* 888-315-6661
mia@mts.net
www.mia.mb.ca
Overview: A small provincial organization founded in 1950 overseen by Agricultural Institute of Canada
Mission: To act in accordance with the Agrologists Act of Manitoba; To regulate the practice of agrology in Manitoba; To ensure the knowledge, competence, & integrity of institute members, in order to protect the public interest; To act as the voice of the agrology profession
Chief Officer(s):
Richard Kieper, P.Ag., President
miapresident@mia.mb.ca
Jim Weir, Executive Director & Registrar
miaweir@mia.mb.ca ca
Estel Facundo, Officer, Administration
miaadmin@mia.mb.ca
Membership: *Member Profile:* Agricultural professionals in Manitoba; *Committees:* Finance; Education; Admission & Registration
Activities: Licensing agrologists; Promoting high standards in research; Advancing the professional status of members; Providing educational & networking opportunities;
Meetings/Conferences: • Manitoba Institute of Agrologists 2015 65th Annual General Meeting & Professional Development Event, 2015, MB
Scope: Provincial
Description: The business meeting of the institute, plus presentations & networking opportunities
Publications:
• MIA [Manitoba Institute of Agrologists] Bulletin
Type: Newsletter
Profile: Institute activities, member news, & events

Manitoba Institute of Registered Social Workers (MIRSW)
#101, 2033 Portage Ave., Winnipeg MB R3J 0K6
Tel: 204-888-9477; *Fax:* 204-831-6359
www.mirsw.mb.ca
Overview: A medium-sized provincial organization founded in 1963
Mission: To certify members; To act as the regulatory arm of the social work profession; To encourage ethical standards of practice to protect the public
Chief Officer(s):
Liz McLeod, President
Membership: *Member Profile:* Individuals with a Bachelor of Social Work degree or a Master of Social Work degree from a school accredited by the Canadian Association of Schools of Social Work or the Council of Social Work Education
Activities: Investigating public complaints in its role as a disciplinary body; Ensuring registrants maintain current knowledge

Manitoba Institute of the Purhcasing Management Association of Canada; NPurchasing Management Association of Canada - Manitoba Institute *See* Supply Chain Management Association - Manitoba

Manitoba Instrumental Music Association *See* Manitoba Band Association

Manitoba Interfaith Welcome Place
521 Bannatyne Ave., Winnipeg MB R3A 0E4
Tel: 204-977-1000; *Fax:* 204-956-7548
www.miic.ca
Overview: A small provincial organization
Mission: To welcome & extend hospitality to all refugees/immigrants & to serve them as brothers & sisters
Chief Officer(s):
Rita Chahal, Executive Director
Ruth Magnuson, Chair
Finances: *Annual Operating Budget:* $1.5 Million-$3 Million
Membership: *Committees:* Finance; Funding Diversification; Governance; Property; Human Resources

Manitoba Islamic Association (MIA)
2445 Waverley St., Winnipeg MB R3Y 1S3
Tel: 204-256-1347
www.miaonline.org
www.facebook.com/ManitobaIslamicAssociation
Overview: A small provincial organization founded in 1976
Mission: Large collection of English and Arabic books on major Islamic sciences & theology
Chief Officer(s):
Ismael Mukhtar, President
Khaled Al-Nahar, Office Manager
Membership: *Fees:* $30; *Member Profile:* Muslim persons in Manitoba who abide by the association's rules & regulations; *Committees:* Takaful Fund
Activities: Accepting applications for financial assistance, through the Takaful Fund; Providing funeral services to the Muslim community, through partnership with Cropo Funeral Services; Offering services for marriage; Conducting Sunday Qur'an classes for children & the MIA Al Nur Weekend Islamic School; Sponsoring the Al-Hamd Learning Center, which offers an Arabic & Islamic educational program for preschoolers; *Library:* Al-Hikmah (Wisdom) Library; by appointment
Awards:
• MIA / MSA University Scholarships (Scholarship)
Publications:
• Manitoba Muslim

Type: Newsletter; *Accepts Advertising*
Profile: Editorials, reports, articles, announcements, community news, & local events

Manitoba Lacrosse Association
145 Pacific Ave., Winnipeg MB R3B 2Z6
Tel: 204-925-5684; *Fax:* 204-925-5792
lacrosse@sportmanitoba.ca
manitobalacrosse.mb.ca
www.facebook.com/groups/2238712736
twitter.com/MBLacrosse
Overview: A small provincial organization overseen by Canadian Lacrosse Association
Mission: To oversee the sport of lacrosse in the province of New Brunswick.
Member of: Canadian Lacrosse Association
Chief Officer(s):
Paul Magnan, President
pmagnan@sunrisesd.ca
Don Jacks, Executive Director

The Manitoba Law Foundation / La Fondation manitobaine du droit
412 McDermot Ave., Winnipeg MB R3A 0A9
Tel: 204-947-3142; *Fax:* 204-942-3221
bpalace@gatewest.net
Overview: A medium-sized provincial organization founded in 1986
Mission: To provide funds for legal education, legal research, legal aid, law reform & the establishment, operation & maintenance of law libraries
Chief Officer(s):
Barbara Palace, Executive Director

Manitoba Lawn Bowling Association ***See*** Bowls Manitoba

Manitoba League of Persons with Disabilities (MLPD)
#105, 500 Portage Ave., Winnipeg MB R3C 3X1
Tel: 204-943-6099; *Fax:* 204-943-6654
Toll-Free: 888-330-1932
www.mlpd.mb.ca
Overview: A medium-sized provincial charitable organization founded in 1974
Mission: To remove systemic barriers to community participation for people with disabilities
Member of: Council of Canadians with Disabilities
Affliation(s): Disabled Peoples' International
Chief Officer(s):
Jess Turner, Co-Chair
Carlos Sosa, Co-Chair
Finances: *Annual Operating Budget:* $100,000-$250,000
Staff Member(s): 5
Membership: *Fees:* $5 individuals; *Member Profile:* People with disabilities; *Committees:* Ethics; Fundraising; Housing; Transportation
Activities: Advocacy; Great Obstacle Race; *Library* Open to public
Awards:
• Access Awareness Achievement Award (Award)

Brandon Branch
#407, 121 - 4th St., Brandon MB R7A 3G5
Tel: 204-725-2767
Chief Officer(s):
Don Butler, Chair
butler@prairie.ca

Souris & District Branch
PO Box 213, Souris MB R0K 2C0
Tel: 204-483-2269
Chief Officer(s):
Mary Ann Carlisle, Branch Representative

Thompson Branch
100 Greenway Cres., Thompson MB R8N 0R4
Tel: 204-677-3398
Chief Officer(s):
Audrey Beaton, Chair

Manitoba Liberal Party (MLP)
635 Broadway, Winnipeg MB R3C 0X1
Tel: 204-988-9380; *Fax:* 204-284-1492
Toll-Free: 800-567-5746
manager@manitobaliberals.ca
mlp.manitobaliberals.ca
www.facebook.com/manitobaliberals
www.youtube.com/user/manitobaliberals
Overview: A medium-sized provincial organization
Chief Officer(s):
Rana Bokhari, Leader of the Party
Membership: 14,000; *Fees:* $10

Manitoba Library Association (MLA)
#606, 100 Arthur St., Winnipeg MB R3B 1H3
Tel: 204-943-4567; *Fax:* 866-202-4567
manitobalibrary@gmail.com
www.mla.mb.ca
www.facebook.com/group.php?gid=6003904478
Overview: A medium-sized provincial charitable organization founded in 1936
Mission: To develop, support, & promote library & information services in Manitoba for the benefit of the library community & Manitoba residents
Member of: Canadian Library Association
Chief Officer(s):
Emma Hill Kepron, President, 204-474-6710
emma_kepron@umanitoba.ca
Alex Homanchuk, Vice-President, 204-786-9940
a.homanchuk@uwinnipeg.ca
Katherine Penner, Secretary, 204-474-6846
katherine_penner@umanitoba.ca
Kathy Rusnak, Treasurer, 204-474-8858
Kathy_Rusnak@UManitoba.ca
Dawn Bassett, Director, Professional Development, 204-474-8858
dbassett69@gmail.com
Lesley Mackie, Director, Membership, 204-788-8108
mackiel@cc.umanitoba.ca
Evelyn Bruneau, Director, Fund Development
Evelyn_bruneau@umanitoba.ca
Stephen Carney, Director, Communications
stephen.carney@humanrightsmuseum.ca
Ian Fraser, Director, Advocacy
i.fraser@uwinnipeg.ca
Vera Keown, Director, Conferences
vera_keown@umanitoba.ca
Alison Pattern, Director, Membership
alisonpattern@gmail.com
Membership: *Fees:* Schedule available, based on the annual salary for individuals & the operating budget for institutions; *Member Profile:* Persons in Manitoba, representing all types of libraries & information services
Activities: Advocating for the development of accessible & comprehensive library & information services; Increasing public awareness of library services in Manitoba; Providing professional development activities; Offering up-to-date information about professional issues; Fostering cooperation between the library community & the information resource management sector; Facilitating interaction with members of Manitoba's libary & information services field
Awards:
• John Edwin Bissett Scholarship (Scholarship)
Deadline: June
• Jean Thorunn Law Scholarship (Scholarship)
Deadline: June 1
• Website of the Year Awards (Award)
• Manitoba Library Service Award (Award)
Meetings/Conferences: • Manitoba Library Association 2015 Annual General Meeting, 2015, MB
Scope: Provincial
Description: A meeting of association members held each year between March 1st & May 31st, featuring reports from the president, treasurer, & each person chairing a standing or ad hoc committee established by the executive committee. Theme: Unlimited Potential
Contact Information: Co-Chair MLC Program Committee: Sarah Clark, Sarah.Clark@umanitoba.ca
• Manitoba Libraries 2016 Bi-annual Conference, 2016, MB
Scope: Provincial
Description: Informative presentations, guest speakers, & a trade show for members of Manitoba's library community
Contact Information: Professional Development Director: Katherine Penner, Phone: 204-474-6846, E-mail: katherine_penner@umanitoba.ca
• Manitoba Libraries 2018 Bi-annual Conference, 2018, MB
Scope: Provincial
Description: Informative presentations, guest speakers, & a trade show for members of Manitoba's library community
Contact Information: Professional Development Director: Katherine Penner, Phone: 204-474-6846, E-mail: katherine_penner@umanitoba.ca
Publications:
• MALT Newsletter
Type: Newsletter; *Frequency:* Quarterly *ISSN:* 0070-3684
Profile: Manitoba Association of Library Technicians activities

Manitoba Library Consortium Inc. (MLCI) / Consortium de bibliothèques du Manitoba
c/o Library Administration, University of Winnipeg, 515 Portage Ave., Winnipeg MB R3B 2E9
Fax: 204-783-8910
manitobalibraryconsortium@gmail.com
www.mlcinc.mb.ca
Overview: A medium-sized provincial organization
Mission: To facilitate resource sharing among the libraries in Manitoba; To build a public information network to contribute to a community's economic goals; to strengthen library services for the residents of Manitoba; To promote the exchange of information related to preservation
Chief Officer(s):
Paddy Burt, Chair, 204-632-2382
Colleen Slight, Secretary, 204-775-9741
Linwood Delong, Treasurer, 204-786-9124
Membership: *Fees:* Schedule available, based upon library's annual budget; *Member Profile:* Library systems or libraries in Manitoba, which support the purposes of the Manitoba Library Consortium
Activities: Planning & managing cooperative projects, to enable efficient & equitable access to library resources for Manitobans; Initiating the Manitobia.ca project, to gather & to provide access to historically significant documents & publications; Offering "Library Express", to provide timely delivery of materials to clients; Arranging consortial licensing; Creating a Manitoba Union List of Serials

Manitoba Lung Association
629 McDermot Ave., Winnipeg MB R3A 1P6
Tel: 204-774-5501; *Fax:* 204-772-5083
Toll-Free: 888-566-5864
info@mb.lung.ca
www.mb.lung.ca
www.facebook.com/manitobalungassociation
twitter.com/ManitobaLung
www.youtube.com/user/ManitobaLung
Overview: A small provincial charitable organization founded in 1904 overseen by Canadian Lung Association
Mission: To improve lung health
Member of: Sanatorium Board of Manitoba
Chief Officer(s):
Margaret Bernhardt-Lowdon, Executive Director
margaret.bernhardt-lowdon@mb.lung.ca
Tracy Fehr, Director, Tobacco Reduction Initiatives
tracy.fehr@mb.lung.ca
Kris Kamenz, Director, Finance
kristopher.kamenz@mb.lung.ca
Finances: *Funding Sources:* Donations; Fundraising; Sponsorships
Staff Member(s): 17
Activities: Providing information about lung health; Supporting & promoting research; Offering education programs in areas such as asthma, chronic obstructive pulmonary disease (COPD), & air quality
Publications:
• Manitoba Lung Association Annual Report
Type: Yearbook; *Frequency:* Annually

Manitoba Magazine Publishers Association (MMPA)
#606 - 100 Arthur St., Winnipeg MB R3B 1H3
Tel: 204-942-0189; *Fax:* 204-257-2467
exedir@manitobamagazines.ca
manitobamagazines.ca
www.linkedin.com/pub/manitoba-magazine-publishers-association-inc/80/5
www.facebook.com/553448658032785?fref=ts
plus.google.com/111826288530235237421
Overview: A small provincial organization founded in 1988
Mission: The Manitoba Magazine Publishers' Association (MMPA) aims to represent and promote Manitoba magazines.
Chief Officer(s):
Brenda Johnstone, President
bjj@convenienceandcarwash.com
Meetings/Conferences: • Manitoba Magazine Publishers Association 2015 Conference, May, 2015, Viscount Gort, Winnipeg, MB
Scope: Provincial

Manitoba Medical Association ***See*** Doctors Manitoba

Manitoba Medical Service Foundation Inc. (MMSF)
599 Empress St., Winnipeg MB R3G 3P3

Tel: 204-788-6801; Fax: 204-774-1761
info@mmsf.ca
www.mmsf.ca
Overview: A medium-sized provincial organization founded in 1971
Mission: To consider the provision of funds for the advancement of scientific, educational, & other activities to maintain & improve the health & welfare of the citizens of Manitoba
Affliation(s): Manitoba Blue Cross
Chief Officer(s):
Greg Hammond, Executive Director
Allen Rouse, Chair
Activities: Supporting medical research in Manitoba by awarding grants to researchers in the health care field
Awards:
• The Norman and Margaret Corne Memorial Scholarship (Scholarship)
To recognize research excellence
• The Morris Neaman Memorial Award (Scholarship)
To recognize research excellence
• The Richard Hoeschen Memorial Award (Award)
To permit students in clinical chemistry to travel to national & international meetings
• Basic Science Career Development Research Award (Scholarship)

Manitoba Medical Students' Association (MMSA)
c/o Faculty of Medicine, University of Manitoba, #270, 727 McDermot Ave., Winnipeg MB R3E 3P5
Tel: 204-789-3424; *Fax:* 204-789-3929
umlipsom@cc.umanitoba.ca
umanitoba.ca/medicine/mmsa
Overview: A small provincial organization
Chief Officer(s):
Sarah van Gaalen, Contact, Communications
Membership: *Committees:* Curriculum; Clerkship; Pre-Clerkship; Pre-Clerkship Organizing; Clinical; Evaluation; Admissions; Bachelor of Science (Medicine); Academic Standing; Faculty Executive Council; Manitoba Medical College Foundation; Student Affairs Awards; Introduction to Clerkship; Manitoba Medical College Foundation; Association of Canadian Medical Colleges; Internal Medicine Undergraduate; Curriculum Evaluation Seminar

Manitoba Mennonite Historical Society (MMHS)
c/o Mennonite Heritage Centre, 600 Shaftesbury Blvd., Winnipeg MB R3P 0M4
Tel: 204-888-6781; *Fax:* 204-831-5675
Toll-Free: 866-888-6785
mmhs@mmhs.org
www.mmhs.org
Overview: A small provincial organization founded in 1958
Mission: To foster interest in Manitoba's Mennonite heritage & culture; To preserve Mennonite stories
Chief Officer(s):
Conrad Stoesz, President
Membership: 150; *Fees:* $15 students; $40 regular; $65 couples
Activities: Conducting workshops & seminars in Mennonite studies
Publications:
• Heritage Postings
Type: Newsletter; *Frequency:* Quarterly
Profile: Reports about members' historical interests

Manitoba Métis Federation / Fédération des Métis du Manitoba
Head Office, #300, 150 Henry Ave., Winnipeg MB R3B 0J7
Tel: 204-586-8474; *Fax:* 204-947-1816
mmf@mmf.mb.ca
www.mmf.mb.ca
www.facebook.com/ManitobaMetisFederationOfficial
twitter.com/MBMetis_MMF
www.youtube.com/ManitobaMetisMMF
Overview: A medium-sized provincial organization
Mission: To promote & instill pride in the history & culture of the Métis people; to educate members with respect to their legal, political, social & other rights; to promote the participation & represention of the Métis people in key political & economic bodies & organizations; to promote the political, legal, social and economic interests & rights of its members.
Affliation(s): Infinity Women; Louis Riel Capital Corporation; Louis Riel Institute; Metis Child and Family Services; Metis Economic Development Organization; Metis Economic Development Fund; Metis Generation Fund; Pemmican Publications
Chief Officer(s):
David Chartrand, President
Membership: *Member Profile:* People who have Métis ancestors

Manitoba Milk Prices Review Commission
Norquay Building, #812, 401 York Ave., Winnipeg MB R3C 0P8
Tel: 204-945-3854; *Fax:* 204-948-2844
Overview: A small provincial organization founded in 1980
Mission: To set a price for producers of fluid milk; to monitor & control wholesale & retail milk prices
Chief Officer(s):
Randy Ozunko, Chair
randy.ozunko@gov.mb.ca
Finances: *Funding Sources:* Provincial government

Manitoba Milk Producers *See* Dairy Farmers of Manitoba

Manitoba Model Forest
PO Box 6500, 3 Walnut St., Pine Falls MB R0E 1M0
Tel: 204-367-4541; *Fax:* 204-367-4768
admin@manitobamodelforest.net
www.manitobamodelforest.net
Overview: A small provincial organization founded in 1992
Member of: Canadian Model Forest Network
Chief Officer(s):
Brian Kotak, General Manager
gm@manitobamodelforest.net

Manitoba Motion Picture Industries Association *See* On Screen Manitoba

Manitoba Motor Dealers Association (MMDA)
#230, 530 Century St., Winnipeg MB R3H 0Y4
Tel: 204-985-4200; *Fax:* 204-775-9125
Toll-Free: 800-949-6632
info@mmda.mb.ca
www.mmda.mb.ca
Overview: A medium-sized provincial organization founded in 1944
Mission: To represent franchised automobile & truck dealers in Manitoba by dealing with provincial issues that affect this membership; To advance the automotive industry in Manitoba; To uphold the code of ethics
Chief Officer(s):
Neil Metcalfe, President
Geoff Sine, Executive Director
Membership: *Member Profile:* Regular members consist of franchised automobile dealerships in Manitoba that sell new cars & trucks; Associate members consist of companies that supply products & services to dealers; *Committees:* Driver's Ed Revitalization
Activities: Offering a Sales Certification Program; Providing professional development programs; Liaising wtih other companies & organizations;
Publications:
• Advertising & Marketing Guidelines
Type: Guide
Profile: Distributed to Manitoba Motor Dealers Association members, in order to improve relations between dealers & customers
• Manitoba Motor Dealers Association Newsletter
Type: Newsletter; *Frequency:* Bimonthly

Manitoba Municipal Administrators' Association Inc.
533 Buckingham Rd., Winnipeg MB R3R 1B9
Tel: 204-255-4883; *Crisis Hot-Line:* 800-668-9920
mmaa@mts.net
www.mmaa.mb.ca
Overview: A medium-sized provincial organization
Mission: To promote the needs of membership & their professional development.
Chief Officer(s):
Mel Nott, Executive Director
mnott@qworks.biz
Membership: *Committees:* Certificate Advisory; Conference; Executive; Finance; Professional Development

Manitoba Music
#1, 376 Donald St., Winnipeg MB R3B 2J2
Tel: 204-942-8650; *Fax:* 204-942-6083
info@manitobamusic.com
www.manitobamusic.com
www.facebook.com/manitobamusic
twitter.com/manitobamusic
Previous Name: Manitoba Audio Recording Industry Association
Overview: A medium-sized provincial organization founded in 1987
Mission: To develop and sustain the Manitoba music community and industry to their fullest potential
Affliation(s): Foundation to Assist Canadian Talent on Records; Manitoba Film & Music; Aboriginal Music Program
Chief Officer(s):
Sara Stasiuk, Executive Director, 204-975-0147
sara@manitobamusic.com
Finances: *Funding Sources:* Member fees; government funding
Staff Member(s): 9
Membership: 700+; *Fees:* $50 individual; $200 corporate; $35 youth; $75 band; *Member Profile:* Members of the music industry, including artists; bands; studios; managers; agents; songwriters; venues; promoters; producers
Activities: Promotion, education & lobbying for Manitoba's recording industry

Manitoba Naturopathic Association (MNA)
PO Box 434, 971 Corydon Ave., Winnipeg MB R3M 0Y0
Tel: 204-947-0381
info@mbnd.ca
www.mbnd.ca
Overview: A small provincial licensing organization founded in 1946 overseen by The Canadian Association of Naturopathic Doctors
Mission: To act as a regulatory body for the profession of naturopathy, in accordance with The Naturopathic Act of Manitoba
Chief Officer(s):
Lesley Phimister, Executive Director/Registrar
Staff Member(s): 1
Membership: 28; *Fees:* $2000; *Member Profile:* Licensed naturopathic physicians in Manitoba, who employ natural methods of healing in their treatment
Activities: Licensing naturopathic doctors in Manitoba

Manitoba Non-Profit Housing Association (MNPHA)
#200A, 1215 Henderson Hwy., Winnipeg MB R2G 1L8
Tel: 204-797-6746; *Fax:* 204-336-3809
info@mnpha.com
mnpha.com
www.facebook.com/380849451979226?ref=ts&fref=ts
twitter.com/mnpha_
Overview: A small provincial organization
Mission: To build, support and strengthen its members who are diverse non-profit housing providers in Manitoba through services, educational opportunities and advocacy.
Chief Officer(s):
Menno Peters, President, 204-949-2886
mpeters@whrc.ca
Membership: *Committees:* Aboriginal Housing; Conference; Membership; Government; Sponsorship; Policy
Activities: Training and workshops
Meetings/Conferences: • Manitoba Non-Profit Housing Association 2015 Conference, February, 2015, Victoria Inn Hotel & Convention Centre, Winnipeg, MB
Scope: Provincial

Manitoba Nurses' Union (MNU) / Syndicat des infirmières du Manitoba
#301, 275 Broadway, Winnipeg MB R3C 4M6
Tel: 204-942-1320; *Fax:* 204-942-0958
Toll-Free: 800-665-0043
manitobanurses.ca
www.facebook.com/ManitobaNurses
twitter.com/ManitobaNurses
www.youtube.com/user/mbnursesunion
Previous Name: Manitoba Organization of Nurses' Associations (MONA); Manitoba Staff Nurses' Council
Overview: A medium-sized provincial organization founded in 1975
Mission: To represent & support all categories of licensed nurses in Manitoba; To safeguard the role of nurses in the health care system of Manitoba
Member of: Canadian Federation of Nurses' Unions; Manitoba Council of Health Care Unions; Canadian Labour Congress
Chief Officer(s):
Sandi Mowat, President
Kirsten Andersson, Director, Labour Relations
kandersson@manitobanurses.ca
Bill Crawford, Director, Communications & Government Relations
bcrawford@manitobanurses.ca

Janice Grift, Director, Operations
jgrift@manitobanurses.ca
Staff Member(s): 32
Membership: 11,000; *Member Profile:* Unionized nurses in Manitoba, including Registered Nurses, Registered Psychiatric Nurses, Licensed Practical Nurses, & Operating Room Technicians; *Committees:* Executive; Finance; Nominations; Provincial Collective Bargaining; Resolutions & Constitution; Discipline
Activities: Liaising with registering & licensing bodies; Organizing an annual general meeting; Preparing briefs & reports about issues relevant to members

Manitoba Opera Association Inc.

#1060, 555 Main St., Winnipeg MB R3B 1C3
Tel: 204-942-7479; *Fax:* 204-949-0377
mbopera@manitobaopera.mb.ca
www.manitobaopera.mb.ca
www.facebook.com/ManitobaOpera
twitter.com/ManitobaOpera
www.youtube.com/user/ManitobaOpera
Overview: A small provincial charitable organization founded in 1969
Mission: To present & develop appreciation for art of opera in Manitoba; to assist in development of Canadian talent, with emphasis on Manitobans
Affliation(s): Opera America; Canadian Actor's Equity; Opera.ca
Chief Officer(s):
Larry Desrochers, General Director & CEO
Finances: *Funding Sources:* Ticket Sales; Government; Donations
Staff Member(s): 10
Activities: Presents two full operation productions & one concert per season;

Manitoba Operating Room Nurses Association (MORNA)

MB
Overview: A medium-sized provincial organization overseen by Operating Room Nurses Association of Canada
Chief Officer(s):
Karen Sagness, President, 204-787-3364
Membership: *Member Profile:* Registered Nurses in Manitoba who are engaged in operating room nursing or involved in the Perioperative setting.; *Committees:* Communications Committee & Newsletter; Constitution & By-Laws; Education; Nominations
Activities: *Awareness Events:* Perioperative Nurses Week, November
Meetings/Conferences: • Manitoba Operating Room Nurses Association 2015 Annual General Meeting, May, 2015, Norwood Hotel, Winnipeg, MB
Scope: Provincial

Manitoba Optometric Society *See* Manitoba Association of Optometrists

Manitoba Orchid Society (MOS)

c/o Harvey Keselman, 8 Vassar Rd., Winnipeg MB R3T 3M9
www.manitobaorchidsociety.ca
www.facebook.com/126535720751112
Overview: A small provincial organization founded in 1970
Member of: Canadian Orchid Congress
Chief Officer(s):
Harvey Keselman, President
president@manitobaorchidsociety.ca
Membership: *Fees:* $25 single; $35 family
Activities: *Library*

Manitoba Organization of Disc Sports (MODS)

145 Pacific Ave., Winnipeg MB R3B 2Z6
Tel: 204-925-5665; *Fax:* 204-925-5916
mods.mb.ca
twitter.com/modsmbca
Overview: A small provincial organization founded in 1988
Mission: To organize & govern disc sports in Manitoba, including ultimate, disc golf & Goaltimate.
Member of: Sport Manitoba
Chief Officer(s):
Corey Draper, Executive Director
director@mods.mb.ca
Josh Drury, Program Coordinator
programcoordinator@mods.mb.ca

Manitoba Organization of Nurses' Associations (MONA); Manitoba Staff Nurses' Council *See* Manitoba Nurses' Union

Manitoba Orienteering Association Inc. (MOA)

145 Pacific Ave., Winnipeg MB R3B 2Z6
Tel: 204-925-5706; *Fax:* 204-925-5792
info@orienteering.mb.ca
www.orienteering.mb.ca
Overview: A medium-sized provincial organization
Mission: Promotes and supports orienteering in Manitoba.
Member of: Canadian Orienteering Federation
Affliation(s): Sports Manitoba
Membership: *Fees:* $5 adult; $3 junior

Manitoba Ozone Protection Industry Association (MOPIA)

1980B Main St., Winnipeg MB R2V 2B6
Tel: 204-338-0804; *Fax:* 204-338-0810
Toll-Free: 888-667-4203
mopia@mts.net
www.mopia.ca
Overview: A medium-sized provincial organization
Mission: To work towards protection of the stratospheric ozone layer; To control, reduce, & eventually eliminate emissions of ozone depleting substances
Chief Officer(s):
Mark E. Miller, Executive Director
George Kurowski, Chair
John Kub, Secretary
Laverne Dalgleish, Treasurer
Activities: Liaising with industry, interest groups, & Manitoba Environment; Raising public awareness of the impact of ozone depleting substances
Meetings/Conferences: • Manitoba Ozone Protection Industry Association 2015 22nd Annual General Meeting, 2015, Winnipeg, MB
Scope: Provincial
Description: The presentation of the annual report, featuring financial & executive reports
Publications:
• Environmental Awareness Training for Ozone Depleting Substances (ODS) & Other Halocarbons
Type: Manual; *Price:* $45
Profile: A training manual for persons working on refrigeration or air conditioning equipment that contains a regulated substance
• Manitoba Ozone Protection Industry Association Annual Report
Type: Yearbook; *Frequency:* Annually
Profile: Featuring messages from the Chair of the Board of Directors & the Executive Director, reports from the treasurer & auditor, as well as highlights of the year
• MOPIA [Manitoba Ozone Protection Industry Association] E-Bulletin
Type: Newsletter; *Frequency:* Monthly; *Editor:* Mark Miller; Vanessa Krahn
Profile: Information for Manitoba Ozone Protection Industry Association members & select stakeholders

Manitoba Paddling Association Inc. (MPA)

145 Pacific Ave., Winnipeg MB R3B 2Z6
Tel: 204-925-5681; *Fax:* 204-925-5792
mpa@sportmanitoba.ca
www.mpa.mb.ca
Overview: A medium-sized provincial organization founded in 1982 overseen by CanoeKayak Canada
Mission: To act as the governing body for all competitive paddling sports in Manitoba, including kayak, canoe, & dragon boat; To develop high performance athletes to compete for Manitoba nationally & to qualify for the national team; To develop coaches to coach from the grassroots to the high performance levels; To service paddlers from beginners to elite athletes; To ensure the existence of paddling clubs in Manitoba
Member of: CanoeKayak Canada; Sport Manitoba
Finances: *Funding Sources:* Sport Manitoba
Membership: *Member Profile:* Paddling clubs & athletes from Manitoba
Activities: Hosting paddling events; Promoting paddling

Manitoba Paraplegia Foundation Inc.

825 Sherbrook St., Winnipeg MB R3A 1M5
Tel: 204-786-4753; *Fax:* 204-786-1140
winnipeg@canparaplegic.org
www.cpamanitoba.ca/mpf
Overview: A small provincial organization founded in 1980
Mission: To provide support for research & prevention activities; to provide direct aid to paraplegics & quadriplegics for home modifications, vocational aid & other items to assist spinal cord injured Manitobans to lead independent lives within the community; to provide support for special projects undertaken on behalf of spinal cord injured persons in Manitoba

Chief Officer(s):
Doug Finkbeiner, President
Finances: *Annual Operating Budget:* $50,000-$100,000
Staff Member(s): 2; 12 volunteer(s)
Membership: *Member Profile:* Interest in spinal cord research
Activities: *Library* by appointment

Manitoba Percheron & Belgian Club

c/o Brenda Hunter, PO Box 159, Kenton MB R0M 0Z0
Tel: 204-764-3789
bhunterphoto@gmail.com
www.manpercheronbelgianclub.com
Overview: A small provincial organization
Mission: To promote the Percheron & Belgian horse breeds throughout Manitoba & eastern Saskatchewan
Chief Officer(s):
Robert Berry, President
Rod Delaquis, Vice-President
Brenda Hunter, Secretary
Jodi Denbrok, Treasurer
Janice Rutherford, Coordinator, Youth Program
Finances: *Funding Sources:* Membership fees; Sponsorships; Fundraising
Membership: 80; *Fees:* $35 individuals; $50 families; *Member Profile:* Heavy horse enthusiasts from Manitoba & eastern Saskatchewan; *Committees:* Executive; Futurity
Activities: Hosting shows; Sponsoring various events; Offering youth clinics; Presenting awards
Meetings/Conferences: • Manitoba Percheron & Belgian Club 2015 Annual General Meeting, January, 2015, Royal Oak Inn, Brandon, MB
Scope: Provincial
Description: Featuring a joint banquet & auction with the Clyde Club
Publications:
• Manitoba Percheron & Belgian Club Breeder Directory
Type: Directory
• Manitoba Percheron & Belgian Club Breeder Directory
Type: Newsletter; *Frequency:* Semiannually

Manitoba Pharmaceutical Association *See* College of Pharmacists of Manitoba

Manitoba Physical Education Teachers Association (MPETA)

c/o Sport for Life Centre, #319, 145 Pacific Ave., Winnipeg MB R3B 2Z6
Tel: 204-926-8357; *Fax:* 204-925-5703
mpeta@sportmanitoba.ca
mpeta.ca
twitter.com/MPETA_news
Overview: A small provincial organization
Mission: MPETA is an educational and professional organization which is dedicated to serve physical education in Manitoba Schools.
Affliation(s): Manitoba Teacher's Society
Chief Officer(s):
Ray Agostino, President
Membership: *Fees:* $25 full; $15 student/retired/associate
Meetings/Conferences: • Manitoba Physical Education Teachers Association 2015 SAGE Conference, 2015, MB
Scope: Provincial

Manitoba Physiotheraphy Association (MPA)

145 Pacific Ave., Winnipeg MB R3B 2Z6
Tel: 204-925-5701; *Fax:* 204-925-5624
Toll-Free: 877-925-5701
ptassociation@mbphysio.org
www.mbphysio.org
www.facebook.com/MBPhysiotherapy
twitter.com/MBPhysiotherapy
Overview: A medium-sized provincial organization overseen by Canadian Physiotherapy Association
Mission: To provide leadership & direction to the physiotherapy profession; To foster excellence in practice, education & research
Member of: Canadian Physiotherapy Association
Chief Officer(s):
Allison Guerico, President
Finances: *Funding Sources:* Membership dues; Educational activities
Membership: 500; *Committees:* Professional Development; Business Affairs Private Practice; Awards; Communications

Manitoba Poison Control Centre

Children's Hospital Health Sciences Centre, 840 Sherbrook St., Winnipeg MB R3A 1S1

Tel: 204-787-2444; *Crisis Hot-Line:* 204-787-2591
Overview: A small provincial organization
Mission: To provide poison information, by physicians, for the public & health care advisers
Member of: Canadian Association of Poison Control Centres
Activities: Providing poison control phones, answered by physicians; Offering treatment advice, toxicology information, & veterinary toxicology information

Manitoba Pork Council
28 Terracon Place, Winnipeg MB R2J 4G7
Tel: 204-237-7447; *Fax:* 204-237-9831
Toll-Free: 888-893-7447
info@manitobapork.com
www.manitobapork.com
www.facebook.com/mbpork
twitter.com/MBPork
www.youtube.com/user/MBPorkfan
Overview: A small provincial organization founded in 1964
Mission: To represent Manitoba hog producers in related associations; To conduct promotion & market development campaigns for Manitoba Pork Marketing Agency
Chief Officer(s):
Andrew Dickson, General Manager
adickson@manitobapork.com
Staff Member(s): 13
Membership: *Committees:* Public Relations; Sustainable Development & Research; Industry Performance & Services

Manitoba Powerlifting Association (MPA)
MB
manitobapowerlifting.ca
Overview: A small provincial organization founded in 1967 overseen by Canadian Powerlifting Union
Member of: Manitoba Sports Federation; Manitoba Sports Directorate; Canadian Powerlifting Union; International Powerlifting Federation

Manitoba Printmakers Association
11 Martha St., Winnipeg MB R3B 1A2
Tel: 204-779-6253; *Fax:* 204-944-1804
printmakers@mymts.net
www.printmakers.mb.ca
www.facebook.com/marthastreet
Also Known As: Martha Street Studio
Overview: A small provincial organization founded in 1984
Mission: To promote printmaking & digital & photographic art in Manitoba
Chief Officer(s):
Larry Glawson, Executive Director
director.printmakers@mymts.net
Finances: *Funding Sources:* Membership dues; Donations
Membership: *Fees:* $35 regular; $20 student

Manitoba Prisoner's Aid Group *See* The John Howard Society of Manitoba, Inc.

Manitoba Professional Painting Contractors Association (MPPCA)
1447 Waverley St., Winnipeg MB R3T 0P7
Tel: 204-479-8279; *Fax:* 204-958-5740
Overview: A small provincial organization
Mission: To elevate & promote professionalism & quality in the industry of painting contracting, paint & wall covering suppliers, & the related paint industry business

Manitoba Professional Planners Institute (MPPI)
137 Bannatyne Ave., 2nd Fl., Winnipeg MB R3B 0R3
Tel: 204-943-3637; *Fax:* 204-925-4624
mppiadmin@shaw.ca
www.mppi.mb.ca
Overview: A medium-sized provincial organization overseen by Canadian Institute of Planners
Mission: To handle membership applications & services & to enforce the Code of Professional Conduct
Member of: Canadian Institute of Planners (CIP)
Chief Officer(s):
Valdene Buckley, President
Kari MacKinnon, Administrator
Membership: 147; *Fees:* Schedule available; *Member Profile:* University graduates working in planning & student planners; *Committees:* Continuous Professional Learning; Events; Membership; Communications & Events
Meetings/Conferences: • Manitoba Professional Planners Institute 2015 Annual General Meeting, 2015
Scope: Provincial

Manitoba Provincial Handgun Association (MPHA)
PO Box 314, Stn. Corydon Ave., Winnipeg MB R3M 3S7
Tel: 204-925-5682; *Fax:* 204-925-5703
mbhndgn@shaw.ca
www.handgunmb.ca
Overview: A small provincial organization
Mission: To provide opportunities & programming for handgun athletes, coaches & officials; to help participants learn, practice & develop skills in the sport of handgun shooting.
Member of: Sport Manitoba
Chief Officer(s):
Randy Myrdal, President
Membership: *Fees:* $10 individual; $25 club

Manitoba Provincial Rifle Association Inc. (MPRA)
795 Valour Rd., Winnipeg MB R3G 3B3
Tel: 204-783-0768
www.manitobarifle.ca
Overview: A medium-sized provincial organization founded in 1872
Mission: To promote & encourage safe firearm handling & competitive target shooting in Manitoba
Member of: Shooting Federation of Canada; Dominion of Canada Rifle Association
Affliation(s): Sports Manitoba
Membership: *Fees:* $40 full member; $25 associate member/under 25; $65 family; $350 lifetime; *Member Profile:* Individuals & clubs interested in rifle target shooting
Activities: Shooting practices & competitions

Manitoba Public Health Association (MPHA)
c/o Klinic Community Health Centre, 870 Portage Ave., Winnipeg MB R3G 0P1
e-mail: manitobapha@mts.net
www.manitobapha.ca
Overview: A small provincial organization founded in 1940 overseen by Canadian Public Health Association
Mission: To influence health, social, environmental, & economic policy decisions, in order to improve the well-being of people in Manitoba; To ensure that health promotion, health protection, & disease protection are part of services
Member of: Canadian Public Health Association (CPHA)
Chief Officer(s):
Barb Wasilewski, President
Membership: *Fees:* Schedule available
Activities: Advocating for healthy public policies; Liaising with community & professional associations & the government

Manitoba Pulse Growers Association Inc.
PO Box 1760, 38 - 4th Ave. NE, Carman MB R0G 0J0
Tel: 204-745-6488; *Fax:* 204-745-6213
Toll-Free: 866-226-9442
www.manitobapulse.ca
Overview: A medium-sized provincial organization founded in 1984
Mission: To provide production knowledge to members of the Manitoba pulse growers industry
Chief Officer(s):
Kyle Friesen, President
Roxanne Lewko, Executive Director, 204-745-6488
Membership: 3,000; *Member Profile:* Farmers in Manitoba who grow edible beans, peas, lentils, chickpeas, faba beans & soybeans; *Committees:* Executive; Edible Bean; Finance; Market Development; MASC; Peas, Faba beans, Lentils & Chickpeas; Soybean; Variety Trial Results
Awards:
• Manitoba Pulse Growers Association Degree Scholarship (Scholarship)
Amount: $500
• Manitoba Pulse Growers Association Diploma Scholarship (Scholarship)
Amount: $500
• Manitoba Pulse Growers Association Agribusiness Bridging Award (Award)
Amount: $750

Manitoba Quality Network
#660, 175 Hargrave St., Winnipeg MB R3C 3R8
Tel: 204-949-4999; *Fax:* 204-949-4990
www.qnet.ca
Also Known As: QNET
Overview: A medium-sized provincial organization
Mission: To help organizations pursue continuous excellence & improvement
Chief Officer(s):
Trish Wainikka, Executive Director
Membership: 400 individuals + 200 businesses; *Fees:* $135-$2,000; *Member Profile:* Members of various sectors, including: manufacturing, service, health care, government, education, consultant & non-profit

Manitoba Reading Association
c/o Child Guidance Clinic, Winnipeg School Division, 700 Elgin Ave., Winnipeg MB R2E 1B2
Tel: 204-786-7841
www.readingmanitoba.org
Also Known As: Council No: CG150
Overview: A medium-sized provincial organization overseen by International Reading Association
Chief Officer(s):
Carol Hryniuk-Adamov, Coordinator
cadamov@shaw.ca
Meetings/Conferences: • 3rd Annual Adolescent Literacy Summit, April, 2015, Victoria Inn, Winnipeg, MB
Scope: Provincial

Brandon Reading Council
Brandon MB
www2.brandonsd.mb.ca/brc/
Chief Officer(s):
Carole McCurry, President
mccurry.carole@bsd.ca

Manitoba Council of Reading Clinicians
MB
www.mcrc-online.ca

Pembina Escarpment Reading Council
MB
pereadingcouncil.pbworks.com/w/page/30555408/FrontPage

Manitoba Ready Mixed Concrete Association Inc. (MRMCA)
3 Park Ridge Dr., East St. Paul MB R2E 1H7
Tel: 204-667-8539; *Fax:* 204-668-9740
info@mrmca.com
www.mrmca.com
Overview: A small provincial organization founded in 1971 overseen by Canadian Ready Mixed Concrete Association
Mission: To represent the concrete industry in Manitoba; To advance the quality of concrete in Manitoba
Chief Officer(s):
Jayson Chale, President
jchale@citymixinc.com
Finances: *Funding Sources:* Membership
Membership: 52 companies; *Fees:* $225 + $22.50 per truck to a maximum of $750, for concrete producers; $250 associate members; $200 cement suppliers; *Member Profile:* Professionals in Manitoba's concrete industry, such as producers & cement manufacturers
Activities: Engaging in lobbying activities; Promoting the use of concrete; Providing networking opportunities; Offering eductional programs, such as safety & technical seminars & concrete workshops; Awarding scholarships;; *Library:* MRMCA Technical Information Library
Publications:
• Manitoba Ready-Mixed Concrete Association Inc. Membership Directory
Type: Directory
• Manitoba Ready-Mixed Concrete Association Inc. Newsletter
Type: Newsletter

Manitoba Real Estate Association (MREA)
1873 Inkster Blvd., Winnipeg MB R2R 2A6
Tel: 204-772-0405; *Fax:* 204-775-3781
Toll-Free: 800-267-6019
cduheme@mrea.mb.ca
www.realestatemanitoba.com
www.facebook.com/144040815612760
Overview: A medium-sized provincial organization founded in 1949
Mission: To represent the interest of Manitoba's licensed realtors
Chief Officer(s):
Brian M. Collie, Executive Director
bcollie@mrea.mb.ca
Membership: 1,700 real estate professionals + 4 real estate boards; *Member Profile:* Real estate professionals & real estate boards in Manitoba
Activities: Training real estate agents; Advocating for improvements to government policies & programs in Manitoba

Manitoba Recreational Canoeing Association *See* Paddle Manitoba

Manitoba Regional Lily Society
PO Box 846, Neepawa MB R0J 1H0
e-mail: nigel@lilynook.mb.ca
www.manitobalilies.ca
Overview: A small provincial organization
Mission: To promote the growing and care of lillies in Manitoba.
Chief Officer(s):
Deborah Petrie, President
petrie@mymts.net
Membership: *Fees:* $10

Manitoba Restaurant & Food Services Association (MRFA)
103-D Scurfield Blvd., Winnipeg MB R3Y 1M6
Tel: 204-783-9955; *Fax:* 204-783-9909
Toll-Free: 877-296-2909
info@mrfa.mb.ca
www.mrfa.mb.ca
www.facebook.com/105407752852372
twitter.com/ManRFA
Overview: A medium-sized provincial organization founded in 1947
Mission: To lobby government and other regulatory bodies on issues affecting you and your business; to present educational seminars and social programs; to provide member services such as insurance programs and credit card savings; to represent the restaurant and foodservice industry effectively through a large membership.
Chief Officer(s):
Scott Jocelyn, Executive Director
Finances: *Funding Sources:* Membership; seminars; special events
Staff Member(s): 2
Membership: 500; *Fees:* $225 restaurant/food service; $275 associate; *Member Profile:* Organizations in the restaurant/food service industry & suppliers; *Committees:* Membership; Finance; Government Affairs; Events
Meetings/Conferences: • Manitoba Restaurant & Foodservices Association LocalFare Trade Show, January, 2015, RBC Convnetion Centre, Winnipeg, MB
Scope: Provincial

Manitoba Rhythmic Sportive Gymnastics Association *See* Rhythmic Gymnastics Manitoba Inc.

Manitoba Riding for the Disabled Association Inc. (MRDA)
145 Pacific Ave., Winnipeg MB R3B 2Z6
Tel: 204-925-5905; *Fax:* 204-925-5792
exedir@mrda.cc
www.mrda.cc
www.facebook.com/105010909544565
Overview: A small provincial charitable organization founded in 1977
Mission: To provide a therapeutic horseback riding program for children with disabilities.
Member of: Canadian Therapeutic Riding Association
Chief Officer(s):
Peter Manastyrsky, Executive Director
Finances: *Funding Sources:* corporate sponsors
100 volunteer(s)

Manitoba Ringette Association (MRA) / Association de ringuette du Manitoba
145 Pacific Ave., Winnipeg MB R3B 2Z6
Tel: 204-925-5710; *Fax:* 204-925-5925
ringette.admin@sportmanitoba.ca
www.manitobaringette.ca
twitter.com/MBRingette
Overview: A medium-sized provincial organization founded in 1970 overseen by Ringette Canada
Mission: To develop, encourage and promote Ringette for the enjoyment of all Manitobans through the provision of programs, services and resources that inform, educate and teach skills.
Member of: International Ringette Federation
Affliation(s): Sport Manitoba
Chief Officer(s):
Laralie Higginson, Executive Director
edringette@sportmanitoba.ca
Melanie Reimer, Coordinator, Program
ringette@sportmanitoba.ca
Finances: *Funding Sources:* Sponsorship; grants & registration fees
Staff Member(s): 4
Activities: Tournaments; provincial competitions; national competitions; world competitions; *Library* Open to public

Manitoba Rowing Association
Sport for Life Centre, 145 Pacific Ave., Winnipeg MB R3B 2Z6
Tel: 204-925-5653
rowing@sportmanitoba.ca
rowingmanitoba.ca
www.facebook.com/167216186659194
Overview: A medium-sized provincial organization overseen by Rowing Canada Aviron
Mission: To govern the sport of rowing in Manitoba.
Member of: Rowing Canada Aviron
Chief Officer(s):
Andrea Katz, Executive Director
Brent Figg, Provincial Head Coach
rowingcoach@sportmanitoba.ca

Manitoba Runners' Association (MRA)
1046 Clarence Ave., Winnipeg MB R3T 1S4
Tel: 204-477-5185
office@mraweb.ca
www.mraweb.ca
www.facebook.com/188241213063
Overview: A small provincial organization
Mission: To encourage road running in Manitoba.
Chief Officer(s):
Campbell Leni, Executive Director
Membership: *Fees:* Schedule available
Activities: Fun runs; races

Manitoba Rural Tourism Association Inc. (MRTA)
PO Box 11, Lake Audy MB R0J 0Z0
Tel: 204-848-7354
info@countryvacations.mb.ca
www.countryvacations.mb.ca
Previous Name: Manitoba Farm Vacations Association; Manitoba Country Vacations Association Inc
Overview: A small provincial organization founded in 1972
Mission: To provide a quality, rural alternative to tourism
Chief Officer(s):
Jim Irwin, Contact
Membership: 15; *Fees:* $125

Manitoba Safety Council *See* Safety Services Manitoba

Manitoba Sailing Association Inc. *See* Sail Manitoba

Manitoba Schizophrenia Society, Inc. (MSS)
#100, 4 Fort St., Winnipeg MB R3C 1C4
Tel: 204-786-1616; *Fax:* 204-783-4898
info@mss.mb.ca
www.mss.mb.ca
www.facebook.com/ManitobaSchizophreniaSociety
twitter.com/mbschizophrenia
www.youtube.com/user/recoverytree?
Overview: A medium-sized provincial charitable organization founded in 1979
Mission: To improve the quality of life for individuals affected by schizophrenia / psychosis & co-occurring disorders
Chief Officer(s):
Chris Summerville, Executive Director
chris@mss.mb.ca
Finances: *Funding Sources:* Donations; Fundraising; Sponsorships
Staff Member(s): 6; 40 volunteer(s)
Membership: *Fees:* $15 single members; $25 families; $50 corporate members; *Committees:* Gala; Golf; Walk
Activities: Engaging in advocacy activities; Raising public awareness; Providing public educational opportunities; Offering the "Name That Feeling" program, for children who have a family member with a mental illness; Providing peer support programs; *Awareness Events:* Journey of Hope Walk for People with Schizophrenia; Iris Gala; Golf for Schizophrenia Tournament; *Library:* Mental Health Education Resource Centre (MHERC); Open to public
Publications:
• Reasons for Hope
Type: Newsletter; *Frequency:* Quarterly; *Editor:* Chris Summerville
• The Sensitive Scoop: A Consumer Newsletter
Type: Newsletter; *Frequency:* Bimonthly; *Editor:* Jo-Ann Paley

Manitoba School Boards Association
191 Provencher Blvd., Winnipeg MB R2H 0G4
Tel: 204-233-1595; *Fax:* 204-231-1356
Toll-Free: 800-262-8836
webmaster@mbschoolboards.ca
www.mbschoolboards.ca
Previous Name: Manitoba Association of School Trustees
Overview: A medium-sized provincial organization overseen by Canadian School Boards Association
Mission: To provide services to school boards in Manitoba; To advocate for public education
Member of: Manitoba Chamber of Commerce; Manitoba Council for Leadership in Education; Physical Activity Coalition of Manitoba; Social Planning Council of Winnipeg; Winnipeg Chamber of Commerce
Chief Officer(s):
Carolyn Duhamel, Executive Director
cduhamel@mbschoolboards.ca
Heather Demetrioff, Associate Director, Education and Communication Services
hdemetrioff@mbschoolboards.ca
George Coupland, Director, Labour Relations and Human Resource Services
Staff Member(s): 16
Membership: 38 public school boards; *Member Profile:* Public school boards in Manitoba; *Committees:* Aboriginal Education; Convention Planning; MB Public School Employees Dental & Extended Health Care Plan Trust; Finance/Audit; General Insurance Management; Group Life Insurance; MSBA Universal Standards Trust Fund; Nominating; Pension; Resolutions & Policy
Activities: Providing labour relations & personnel services to member school boards; Administering benefit programs; Offering guidance in risk management areas; Assisting school boards to obtain insurance through the Manitoba Schools Insurance (MSI) program; Providing professional development opportunities for trustees & senior administrators
Awards:
• Student Citizenship Awards (Award)
• Presidents' Council Award (Award)
• Premier Award for School Board Innovation (Award)
Meetings/Conferences: • Manitoba School Boards Association Convention 2015: Building Partnerships for Student Success, March, 2015, Delta Winnipeg, Winnipeg, MB
Scope: Provincial

Manitoba School Counsellors' Association (MSCA) / Association manitobaine des conseillers d'Orientation
c/o Manitoba Teachers' Society, 77 John Forsyth Rd., Winnipeg MB R2N 1R3
Tel: 204-254-0120; *Fax:* 204-253-7981
www.msca.mb.ca
Previous Name: School Counsellors' Association of Manitoba
Overview: A small provincial organization founded in 1965
Mission: To promote & develop guidance & counselling services for children & youth; To provide a forum & a voice for those interested in promoting the personal, social, educational & career development of young Manitobans
Member of: Manitoba Teachers' Society
Chief Officer(s):
Carla Bennett, President
Charu Gupta, President-Elect
Finances: *Annual Operating Budget:* $50,000-$100,000
22 volunteer(s)
Membership: 340; *Fees:* $25 regular; $15 student; *Member Profile:* Individual involved in, or interested in counselling; *Committees:* Awards; Career Symposium; Ethics; Membership; Professional Development; Public Relations; Social

Manitoba School Library Association (MSLA)
c/o Claudia Klausen, Emerson Elementary School, 323 Emerson Ave., Winnipeg MB R2G 1V3
www.manitobaschoollibraries.com
Previous Name: Manitoba School Library Audio-Visual Association
Overview: A small provincial organization
Mission: To advocate for school library programs in Manitoba; To provide professional development opportunities for members
Chief Officer(s):
Joyce Riddell, President
mslapresident@gmail.com
Heather Eby, Secretary, 204-489-0799
heby@pembinatrails.ca
Rhonda Morrissette, Webmaster
mikisew@shaw.ca
Claudia Klausen, Treasurer, 204-669-4430
cklausen@retsd.mb.ca
Jeff Anderson, Co-Chair, Conferences, 204-786-1401
jeffanderson@wsd1.org
Lorie Battershill, Chair, Publications, 204-663-5073
lbattershill@retsd.mb.ca

Jo-Anne Gibson, Chair, Awards, 204-269-6210
jagibson@pembinatrails.ca
Kim Marr, Chair, Membership, 204-989-6730
kmarr@lindenchristian.org
Christine Robinson, Co-Chair, Conferences, 204-668-9442
crobinson@retsd.mb.ca
Membership: *Fees:* $25; *Member Profile:* School librarians in Manitoba
Activities: Liaising with the Department of Education, as well as provincial, national, & international associations;
Meetings/Conferences: • Manitoba School Library Association SAGE Conference: 2015 - Canadian Literature, 2015, MB
Scope: Provincial
Description: A business meeting for school librarians from Manitoba
Contact Information: President, E-mail: mslapresident@gmail.com
• Manitoba School Library Association 2016 Annual General Meeting, 2016, MB
Scope: Provincial
Contact Information: President, E-mail: mslapresident@gmail.com
Publications:
• Manitoba School Library Association Journal
Frequency: 3 pa; *Price:* Free for all members of the Manitoba School Library Association Journal
Profile: Current research & topics about school libraries in Manitoba, Canada, & around the world

Manitoba School Library Audio-Visual Association ***See*** Manitoba School Library Association

Manitoba Schools' Orchestra ***See*** Winnipeg Youth Orchestras

Manitoba Securities Commission (MSC)
#500, 400 St. Mary Ave., Winnipeg MB R3C 4K5
Tel: 204-945-2548; *Fax:* 204-945-0330
Toll-Free: 800-655-5244
Other Communication: Real Estate Division Phone: 204-945-2562; Fax: 204-948-4627
securities@gov.mb.ca
www.msc.gov.mb.ca
Overview: A medium-sized provincial organization founded in 1968 overseen by Canadian Securities Administrators
Mission: To regulate securities trading in Manitoba, through the administration of the Securities Act; To report to the Legislature, through the minister responsible for the administration of the Securities Act; To foster a fair & competitive securities market; To protect investors & market integrity
Member of: Canadian Securities Administrators
Chief Officer(s):
Donald Murray, Chair & Chief Executive Officer
Don.Murray@gov.mb.ca
Finances: *Funding Sources:* Fees collected from market participants under the legislation
Membership: *Committees:* Securities Advisory; Real Estate Advisory Council
Publications:
• Manitoba Securities Commission Annual Report
Type: Report; *Frequency:* Annually

Manitoba Sign Association
850 Main St., Steinbach MB R5G 2H4
Tel: 204-326-4282; *Fax:* 204-326-5572
Toll-Free: 877-938-7446
mansa.ca
Overview: A small provincial organization
Mission: To promote the welfare of the sign industry in Manitoba; to benefit the users of signs
Member of: Sign Association of Canada / Association canadienne de l'enseigne
Chief Officer(s):
Andrew Wrolstad, President
Matt Voth, Vice-President
Rona Jackson, Secretary/Treasurer
Membership: *Committees:* Events; Regulatory

Manitoba Simmental Association (MSA)
PO Box 142, Cartwright MB R0K 0L0
Tel: 204-529-2444
mbsimmental.com
Overview: A small provincial organization founded in 1971
Mission: To assist in and promote the breeding of the Simmental breed of cattle in Manitoba.
Member of: Canadian Simmental Association
Chief Officer(s):
Everett Olson, President
everettolson@hotmail.com
Donalee Jones, Secretary-Treasurer
donalee@midcan.com
Membership: *Fees:* $50; *Member Profile:* Purebred simmental cattle breeders; *Committees:* Test Station; Show/Sale; Advertising; 4H/YCS

Manitoba Soaring Council
200 Main St., Winnipeg MB R3C 4M2
www.wgc.mb.ca/msc/Manitoba_Soaring_Council_Home_Page.htm
Overview: A small provincial organization founded in 1970 overseen by Soaring Association of Canada
Mission: To foster the art of soaring as an environmentally friendly safe & competitive life sport accessible to all Manitobans
Membership: 1,000-4,999

Manitoba Society of Artists (MSA)
c/o Luba Olesky, 2018 Henderson Hwy., Winnipeg MB R2G 1P2
www.mbsa.ca
Overview: A small provincial charitable organization founded in 1902
Mission: To foster & promote professional visual arts in Manitoba
Chief Officer(s):
Bonnie Taylor, President
president@mbsa.ca
Heather Robbins, Vice-President
John Mills, Secretary
Jack Watts, Treasurer
Luba Olesky, Chair, Membership
rlo@mts.net
Lori Zebiere, Chair, Publicity
lori@zebiereart.com
Membership: 90+; *Fees:* $50
Activities: Hosting workshops, lectures, & slide presentations; Sponsoring juried exhibitions; Organizing rotating exhibits for members; Arranging social activities
Awards:
• Brian J. Hyslop Memorial Award (Award)
Presented at the Manitoba Society of Artists Provincial Annual Open Juried Exhibition
• Lynn Sisson Watercolour Award (Award)
Awarded at the Manitoba Society of Artists Provincial Annual Open Juried Exhibition
• W. Cliff Packer Memorial Award (Award)
An award presented at the Annual Open Juried Exhibition of the Manitoba Society of Artists
Meetings/Conferences: • Manitoba Society of Artists 2015 83rd Provincial Annual Open Juried Competition & Exhibition, 2015, MB
Scope: Provincial
Description: A major exhibition & the presentation of awards for both professional & amateur artists
Contact Information: Chairs, Juried Exhibition: Pat McCullough & Bonnie Taylor
• Manitoba Society of Artists 2015 Art History Conference & Annual General Meeting, 2015, MB
Scope: Provincial
Contact Information: E-mail: president@mbsa.ca
Publications:
• Manitoba Society of Artists Newsletter
Type: Newsletter; *Editor:* Rachel Ines; Tom Andrich

Manitoba Society of Certified Engineering Technicians & Technologists Inc. ***See*** Certified Technicians & Technologists Association of Manitoba

Manitoba Society of Criminology Inc. ***See*** Manitoba Criminal Justice Association

Manitoba Society of Medical Laboratory Science; Manitoba Society of Medical Laboratory Technologists ***See*** Manitoba Association for Medical Laboratory Science

Manitoba Society of Occupational Therapists (MSOT)
#7, 120 Maryland St., Winnipeg MB R3G 1L1
Tel: 204-957-1214; *Fax:* 204-775-2340
msot@msot.mb.ca
www.msot.mb.ca
www.facebook.com/TheMSOT
Overview: A medium-sized provincial organization founded in 1963
Mission: To build & strengthen occupational therapy in Manitoba
Chief Officer(s):
Pearl Soltys, Executive Officer
Katie Kitchen, President
Esther Hawn, Secretary
Kathy Kelly, Treasurer
Membership: *Fees:* $100 active; $37.50 associate & affiliate; $45 out of province; Free, first year students; $50 new grad; *Member Profile:* Occupational therapists, students & people working in occupational therapy in a support role; *Committees:* Executive; Communications; Newsletter; Website; Nominating & Awards; Public Relations; Professional Development; Special Events; Archives
Activities: Providing professional representation to government & professional groups; Promoting occupational therapy in Manitoba; Offering networking opportunities; Providing continuing education courses; *Library:* MSOT Resource Library
Awards:
• MSOT Book Prize (Award)
Awarded to the student with the second highest standing in the final year of the Master of Occupational Therapy program at the University of Manitoba
• Outstanding Occupational Therapists Award (Award)
To honour an MSOT member who has made an outstanding contribution to the profession
• 25 Year Membership Acknowledgement (Award)
• MSOT Award for Professional Excellence in Fieldwork (Award)
For the graduating student of the Masters of Occupational Therapy program at the University of Manitoba who has demonstrated excellence in fieldwork
• MSOT Student Research Award (Award)
To honour the University of Manitoba Occupational Therapy student with the highest marks in Statistics & Research Methods
• OT Memorial Bursary (Grant)
Eligibility: All students in the Masters of Occupational Therapy program at the University of Manitoba
Publications:
• MSOT Update
Type: Newsletter; *Frequency:* Bimonthly; *Accepts Advertising*
Profile: MSOT executive functions, current projects, & forthcoming events

Manitoba Society of Pharmacists Inc. (MSP)
#202, 90 Garry St., Winnipeg MB R3C 4H1
Tel: 204-956-6681; *Fax:* 204-956-6686
Toll-Free: 800-677-7170
info@msp.mb.ca
www.msp.mb.ca
Previous Name: Manitoba Society of Professional Pharmacists Inc.
Overview: A small provincial organization founded in 1973
Mission: To act as the voice of pharmacists in Manitoba on economic & professional issuess
Chief Officer(s):
Brenna Shearer, Executive Director
bshearer@msp.mb.ca
Scott McFeetors, President
scott.mcfeetors@loblaw.ca
Barret Procyshyn, Vice-President
barret@dcp.ca
Sharon Smith, Secretary-Treasurer
vercaigne@mts.net
Finances: *Funding Sources:* Membership fees; Sponsorships
Membership: *Fees:* $682.50-$718.20 active members & Canadian Society of Hospital Pharmacists members; $603.75-$628.95 new graduate members; $288.75-$304.50 associates; *Member Profile:* Licensed, practising pharmacists in Manitoba, who are in good standing under the Pharmaceutical Act; Licensed, practising new graduates in Manitoba, who are in good standing under the Pharmaceutical Act; Canadian Society of Hospital Pharmacists members, whose practice is hospital-based; Non-practising & retired members are associate members of the society; *Committees:* Government Relations; Membership Services; Public Relations; Finance & Compensation; Professional Relations; Good Governance
Activities: Engaging in advocacy activities; Promoting pharmacists & their services
Meetings/Conferences: • Manitoba Society of Pharmacists Conference 2015, April, 2015, RBC Convention Centre, Winnipeg, MB
Scope: Provincial
Publications:
• Communication
Type: Journal; *Frequency:* Bimonthly; *Accepts Advertising*; *Price:* Free with membership in the Manitoba Society of Pharmacists; $72 non-members

Profile: Includes accredited & non-accredited continuing education units
• Communication Plus
Type: Newsletter; *Price:* Free with membership in the Manitoba Society of Pharmacists
Profile: Updated information for society members

Manitoba Society of Professional Pharmacists Inc. ***See*** Manitoba Society of Pharmacists Inc.

Manitoba Special Olympics ***See*** Special Olympics Manitoba

Manitoba Speech & Hearing Association (MSHA) / Association des orthophonistes et des audiologistes du Manitoba

#2, 333 Vaughan St., Winnipeg MB R3B 3J9
Tel: 204-453-4539; *Fax:* 204-477-1881
office@msha.ca
www.msha.ca
Overview: A small provincial licensing organization founded in 1958
Mission: To ensure that members of the association provide high quality speech-language pathology & audiology services to persons with commmunication disorders & their families
Chief Officer(s):
Maureen Penko, President
president@msha.ca
Frank A. Pisa, Executive Director, 204-453-4539 Ext. 4
frankpisa@msha.ca
Erin Crawford, Vice-President, Public Relations
prwebsite@msha.ca
Sharon Halldorson, Vice-President, Government Affairs
govaffairs@msha.ca
Reesa Daun, Secretary & Registrar
office@msha.ca
Membership: *Fees:* Schedule available; *Member Profile:* Speech-language pathologists & audiologists who work in Manitoba; Individuals who practice in another regulated province in Canada who apply for membership under the Labour Mobility Act & Chapter 7 (Labour Mobility) of the Agreement on Internal Trade; Affiliate members who are interested in speech-language pathology / audiology; Students studying speech-language pathology / audiology
Activities: *Awareness Events:* Speech & Hearing Month, May
Meetings/Conferences: • Manitoba Speech & Hearing Association 2015 Annual Conference, 2015
Scope: Provincial
Description: A continuting education event, with speaker & poster presentations, & exbibits, as well as networking & social activities
Contact Information: E-mail: office@msha.ca
Publications:
• Hearsay
Type: Newsletter; *Editor:* Janine Ennis
Profile: Activities of the Manitoba Speech & Hearing Association, such as meetings, as well as informative articles about speech & hearing
• Manitoba Speech & Hearing Association Annual Report
Type: Yearbook; *Frequency:* Annually
Profile: A review of the association's activities, as well as financial statements

Manitoba Speed Skating Association

145 Pacific Ave., Winnipeg MB R3B 2Z6
Tel: 204-925-5657; *Fax:* 204-925-5792
Toll-Free: 888-628-9921
office@mbspeedskating.ca
www.mbspeedskating.org
Overview: A small provincial organization overseen by Speed Skating Canada
Mission: The MSSA is dedicated to the development, growth & effective administration of the sport of speed skating in Manitoba through the provision of leadership, support & promotion of its members & clubs.
Member of: Speed Skating Canada
Chief Officer(s):
Caroline Slegers-Boyd, President
Membership: *Committees:* Finance; High Performance; Coaching; Officials; Competitions
Activities: Short-track, long-track speed skating

Manitoba Sport & Recreation Association for the Blind ***See*** Manitoba Blind Sports Association

Manitoba Sport Parachute Association (MSPA)

145 Pacific Ave., Winnipeg MB R3B 2Z6
Other Communication: Events E-mail: events@mspa.mb.ca; Marketing: marketing@mspa.mb.ca
membership@mspa.mb.ca
www.mspa.mb.ca
Overview: A small provincial organization founded in 1978 overseen by Canadian Sport Parachuting Association
Mission: To promote awareness & participation in skydiving in Manitoba
Member of: Canadian Sport Parachuting Association
Chief Officer(s):
Kelly Parker, President
president@mspa.mb.ca
Finances: *Funding Sources:* Manitoba Sports Federation; Manitoba Lotteries; Sport Directorate
Membership: *Fees:* $15

Manitoba Sports Federation Inc. ***See*** Sport Manitoba

Manitoba Sports Hall of Fame & Museum (MSHF&M)

145 Pacific Ave., Winnipeg MB R3B 2Z6
Tel: 204-925-5735; *Fax:* 204-925-5916
halloffame@sportmanitoba.ca
www.halloffame.mb.ca
www.facebook.com/sportmb
twitter.com/SportManitoba
www.youtube.com/user/sportmanitoba
Overview: A small provincial charitable organization founded in 1980
Mission: The mandate of the Manitoba Sports Hall of Fame is to recognize and honour those people who have made their mark in Manitoba's rich sports history through their activities and achievements. The core business of the Hall of Fame is to honour people by telling their story through articles and exhibits, or right here on this website.
Member of: Association of Manitoba Museums (AMM), the Association of Manitoba Archives (AMA), the Canadian Association for Sport Heritage (CASH) and the Canadian Heritage Information Network (CHIN).
Affliation(s): Association of Manitoba Museums; Association of Manitoba Archives; Canadian Association for Sport Heritage; Canadian Heritage Information Network
Chief Officer(s):
Rick Brownlee, Sport Heritage Manager
Finances: *Funding Sources:* Fundraising; lotteries; provincial government
Activities: Casino Fun Nite; Stanley Cup Nite; Induction Dinner

Manitoba Square & Round Dance Federation

c/o President, #2, 297 Enfield Cres., Winnipeg MB R2H 1C1
Tel: 204-224-3742
www.squaredancemb.com
Overview: A medium-sized provincial organization overseen by Canadian Square & Round Dance Society
Mission: To promote and govern square, round, clog, and line dancing in Manitoba
Chief Officer(s):
Sam Dunn, Co-President
Anne Wiebe, Co-President
Finances: *Funding Sources:* Member fees
Membership: *Member Profile:* Organizations & individuals participating in square, round, line, contra, clog, country/western, or related dancing

Manitoba Table Tennis Association (MTTA)

145 Pacific Ave., Winnipeg MB R3B 2Z6
Tel: 204-925-5690; *Fax:* 204-925-5916
table.tennis@sportmanitoba.ca
www.mtta.ca
Overview: A small provincial organization founded in 1959 overseen by Table Tennis Canada
Mission: To develop & promote the sport of table tennis at all levels within Manitoba
Member of: Table Tennis Canada; Sport Manitoba
Affliation(s): International Table Tennis Federation
Chief Officer(s):
Mark Lehmann, President
lehmann@ca.ibm.com
Ron Edwards, Executive Director
Finances: *Annual Operating Budget:* $100,000-$250,000; *Funding Sources:* Sport Manitoba; Manitoba Lotteries; program revenue
Staff Member(s): 2; 25 volunteer(s)
Membership: 504; *Fees:* $25 active; $10 associate; *Committees:* Tournaments; Leagues; Athlete Development; Grass Roots & Regional Developments; Coaching Development; Officials Development; Facilities & Equipment; Special Events; Finance & Administration; Bylaws & Policy Review; Privacy Officer; Fundraising & Bingos; Publicity & Promotion; Membership, Stats & Ranking; Banquets & Awards; Disciplinary; Nominations
Activities: *Library:* MTTA Resource Library; Open to public

Manitoba Tae Kwon-Do Association ***See*** Taekwondo Manitoba

Manitoba Teachers' Society (MTS)

McMaster House, 191 Harcourt St., Winnipeg MB R3J 3H2
Tel: 204-888-7961; *Fax:* 204-831-0877
Toll-Free: 800-262-8803
www.mbteach.org
www.facebook.com/manitobateachers
twitter.com/mbteachers
Overview: A large provincial organization founded in 1919 overseen by Canadian Teachers' Federation
Mission: Envisions a public education system that provides equal accessibility & equal opportunity for all children, that optimizes the potential of all students as individuals & citizens, that fosters lifelong learning & that ensures a safe learning environment respectful of diversity & human dignity
Chief Officer(s):
Dave Tate, CEO
Finances: *Annual Operating Budget:* Greater than $5 Million; *Funding Sources:* Membership fees
Staff Member(s): 70; 500 volunteer(s)
Membership: 15,000; *Fees:* $755; *Member Profile:* Manitoba public school teachers
Meetings/Conferences: • Manitoba Teachers' Society 2015 Annual General Meeting, 2015, MB
Scope: Provincial

Manitoba Team Handball Federation

MB
Overview: A small provincial organization
Mission: Promotes team handball, by establishing & developing participative & competitive programs for Manitobans throughout Manitoba
Member of: Canadian Team Handball Federation

Manitoba Tenpin Federation

#407, 145 Pacific Ave., Winnipeg MB R3B 2Z6
Tel: 613-925-5705; *Fax:* 613-925-5792
man10pin@mts.net
www.mbtenpinfed.com
Overview: A small provincial organization overseen by Canadian Tenpin Federation, Inc.
Mission: To oversee the sport of tenpin bowling in Manitoba.
Member of: Canadian Tenpin Federation, Inc.

Manitoba Theatre Centre (MTC)

174 Market Ave., Winnipeg MB R3B 0P8
Tel: 204-942-6537; *Fax:* 204-947-3741
Toll-Free: 877-446-4500
patronservices@mtc.mb.ca
www.mtc.mb.ca
www.facebook.com/MTCwinnipeg
www.twitter.com/MTCWinnipeg
Overview: A medium-sized provincial charitable organization founded in 1957
Mission: Canada's first English-language regional theatre, with a mandate to study, practise & promote all aspects of the dramatic arts, with particular emphasis on professional production
Member of: Professional Association of Canadian Theatres (PACT); Canadian Institute for Theatre Technology
Chief Officer(s):
Steven Schipper, Artistic Director
Camilla Holland, General Manager
Finances: *Annual Operating Budget:* Greater than $5 Million; *Funding Sources:* Canada Council; Manitoba Arts Council; City of Winnipeg; The Winnipeg Foundation
Staff Member(s): 29; 450 volunteer(s)
Activities: *Awareness Events:* Master Playwright Festival; Winnipeg Fringe Theatre Festival; *Internships:* Yes; *Library* by appointment

Manitoba Tobacco Reduction Alliance

192 Goulet St., Winnipeg MB R2H 0R8
Tel: 204-784-7030; *Fax:* 204-784-7039
info@mantrainc.ca
www.mantrainc.ca
Also Known As: ManTRA
Previous Name: Council for a Tobacco-Free Manitoba
Overview: A small provincial organization founded in 1977

Mission: To strive for a tobacco-free society for Manitobans; to encourage & support legislation to restrict smoking in public places & workplaces; to maintain awareness of the hazards of tobacco consumption to identified high-risk target groups
Member of: Canadian Council on Smoking & Health
Chief Officer(s):
Rick Lambert, Chair
Murray Gibson, Executive Director
Finances: *Annual Operating Budget:* $250,000-$500,000
Membership: *Member Profile:* Open to organizations which are interested in achieving a tobacco-free society for Manitobans; associate - available for those who wish to receive minutes only at a reduced fee

The Manitoba Tourism Education Council (MTEC)

#3, 75 Scurfield Blvd., Winnipeg MB R3Y 1P6
Tel: 204-957-7437; *Fax:* 204-956-1700
Toll-Free: 800-820-6832
www.mtec.mb.ca
Overview: A medium-sized provincial organization founded in 1989
Mission: To build the quality and performance of Manitoba's tourism and hospitality industry through excellence in training, education and recognition.
Chief Officer(s):
Shannon Fontaine, Chief Executive Officer
Staff Member(s): 11

Manitoba Trail Riding Club Inc. (MTRC)

838 Alfred Ave., Winnipeg MB R2X 0T6
www.mbtrailridingclub.ca
Overview: A small provincial organization founded in 1979
Mission: To meet the needs of a growing number of horse people who wanted a type of riding other than in the show ring which could demonstrate good horsemanship and promote sound, sensible trail horses
Member of: Manitoba Horse Council
Affliation(s): Canadian Long Distance Riding Association
Chief Officer(s):
Iris Oleksuk, President
irisolek@yahoo.com
Mary Anne Kirk, Treasurer, 204-955-7388
yaknow3@hotmail.com
Membership: *Fees:* $25 individual; $40 family

Manitoba Trucking Association (MTA)

25 Bunting St., Winnipeg MB R2X 2P5
Tel: 204-632-6600; *Fax:* 204-694-7134
info@trucking.mb.ca
www.trucking.mb.ca
www.linkedin.com/manitobatruckingassociation
www.facebook.com/manitobatruckingassociation
twitter.com/truckingmb
www.youtube.com/manitobatruckingassociation
Overview: A medium-sized provincial organization founded in 1932 overseen by Canadian Trucking Alliance
Mission: To develop & maintain a safe and healthy business environment for its members
Affliation(s): Canadian Trucking Alliance; Canadian Council of Motor Transport Administrators; Canadian Trucking Human Resource Council; Winnipeg Chamber of Commerce; Manitoba Chamber of Commerce; Infrastructure Council of Manitoba; Employers' Task Force on Workers' Compensation; Manitoba Employers' Council
Chief Officer(s):
Norm Blagden, President
Greg Arndt, 1st Vice President
Gary Arnold, 2nd Vice President
Terry Shaw, General Manager
Bob Dolyniuk, Executive Director
Finances: *Funding Sources:* Membership dues & fundraising through services
Staff Member(s): 6
Membership: 250 organizations; *Member Profile:* PSV Carriers; City Transportation; Private Fleet; Household Goods Carriers; Associated Trades; Vehicle Maintenance; *Committees:* Safety; Professional Truck Driving Championships; Scholarship Fund; Human Resources; Workers Compensation
Activities: *Speaker Service:* Yes; *Library* Open to public by appointment
Awards:
• MTA Scholarships (Scholarship)
Open to employees & dependants of member companies
• Driver of the Month Award (Award)
• Provincial & National Driver of the Year Awards (Award)
• Trailmobile Service to Industry Award (Award)
• Maxim Transportation Services Associate of the Year Award (Award)
Publications:
• Western Canada Highway News
Type: Journal; *Frequency:* Quarterly

Manitoba Underwater Council (MUC)

PO Box 711, Winnipeg MB R3C 2K3
Tel: 204-632-8508
info@manunderwater.com
www.manunderwater.com
Overview: A medium-sized provincial charitable organization founded in 1962
Mission: To coordinate, preserve, support & promote sport diving clubs & associations; to promote safety in diving; to exchange & disseminate information concerning the sport of skin & scuba diving & to foster conservation
Member of: Sport Manitoba
Chief Officer(s):
Ronals Hempel, President
president@manunderwater.com
Finances: *Annual Operating Budget:* Less than $50,000; *Funding Sources:* Provincial Government & membership fees
Staff Member(s): 10; 10 volunteer(s)
Membership: 27 institutional + 150 individual; *Fees:* $20; *Member Profile:* Certified scuba divers, divers in training
Activities: Spear fishing competition, pumpkin dive, super dive, underwater football competition

Manitoba UNIX User Group (MUUG)

PO Box 130, Stn. St-Boniface, Winnipeg MB R2H 3B4
Tel: 204-474-8161; *Fax:* 204-474-7609
Other Communication: membership@muug.mb.ca
info@muug.mb.ca
www.muug.mb.ca
Overview: A small provincial organization founded in 1986
Mission: To provide a forum for sharing ideas & information about open systems & their applications
Member of: Computer User Groups of Manitoba Inc.
Chief Officer(s):
Gilbert Detillieux, Contact
Finances: *Annual Operating Budget:* Less than $50,000; *Funding Sources:* Membership fees; corporate sponsorships & donations
Membership: 65; *Fees:* $20

Manitoba Uske

c/o Gord Bluesky, Brokenhead Ojibway First Nation, PO Box 180, Scanterbury MB R0E 1W0
Tel: 204-766-2494
Overview: A small provincial organization founded in 1998 overseen by National Aboriginal Lands Managers Association
Chief Officer(s):
Gord Bluesky, Chair
gordbluesky@gmail.com
Staff Member(s): 1

Manitoba Veterinary Medical Association (MVMA)

1590 Inkster Blvd., Winnipeg MB R2X 2W4
Tel: 204-832-1276; *Fax:* 204-832-1382
Toll-Free: 866-338-6862
www.mvma.ca
Overview: A small provincial organization overseen by Canadian Veterinary Medical Association
Mission: To enhance professional excellence for the health & welfare of animals & Manitobans.
Chief Officer(s):
Andrea Lear, Executive Director
alear@mvma.ca
Finances: *Funding Sources:* Membership fees
Staff Member(s): 4
Membership: 300; *Fees:* Schedule available; *Committees:* Council Advisory
Activities: *Internships:* Yes; *Rents Mailing List:* Yes

Manitoba Volleyball Association (MVA)

#412, 145 Pacific Ave., Winnipeg MB R3B 2Z6
Tel: 204-925-5783; *Fax:* 204-925-5786
volleyball.ed@sportmanitoba.ca
www.volleyballmanitoba.ca
www.facebook.com/150460355015535
Overview: A small provincial organization founded in 1977 overseen by Volleyball Canada
Mission: To govern the sport of volleyball in Manitoba; To promote the development & growth of volleyball in the province
Affliation(s): Volleyball Canada
Chief Officer(s):
John Blacher, Executive Director
volleyball.ed@sportmanitoba.ca
Finances: *Funding Sources:* Fundraising
Staff Member(s): 5
Membership: *Member Profile:* Elite & recreational athletes; Coaches; Officials; *Committees:* Grassroots Development; Competitions; Finance & Audit; Marketing; Awards & Recognition; Conduct & Ethics; Nominations; Governance; High Performance Development; Hall of Fame
Activities: Offering coaching clinics; Training & certifying officials; Providing competitive programs; Conducting Youth Talent Identification Camps; *Library:* Manitoba Volleyball Association Resource Library
Awards:
• Nikki Redekop Memorial Camp Scholarship (Scholarship), Manitoba Volleyball Association
Eligibility: Manitoba residents, female and male Jr High and High School students (under 19) who want to participate in a summer volleyball camp.*Location:* Manitoba*Deadline:* March 31st *Amount:* $50-$200
• Dale Iwanoczko Scholarship (Scholarship), Manitoba Volleyball Association
Eligibility: Manitoba residents, 2 female and 2 male students currently attending highschool and pursuing post-secondary studies after graduation; academic excellence (min. 65 average); volleyball ability and leadership; extra-curricular activities*Location:* Manitoba *Amount:* $750 per student
• Stefan Savoie Scholarship (Scholarship), Manitoba Volleyball Association
Eligibility: Manitoba residents, 1 female and 1 male grade 12 student*Location:* Manitoba*Deadline:* November 18 *Amount:* $550 per student *Contact:* Catherine-Grace Peters, 145 Pacific Avenue, Winnipeg, MB R3B 2Z6

Manitoba Wall & Ceiling Association (MWCA)

1447 Waverley St., Winnipeg MB R3T 0P7
Tel: 204-772-1700
info@mwca.ca
mwca.ca
www.facebook.com/568487016545116
Overview: A small provincial organization
Chief Officer(s):
Tom Robson, President
Membership: 25; *Member Profile:* Contractors, manufacturers & dealers

Manitoba Water & Wastewater Association (MWWA)

PO Box 1600, #215, 9 Saskatchewan Ave. West, 2nd Fl., Portage la Prairie MB R1N 3P1
Tel: 204-239-6868; *Fax:* 204-239-6872
Toll-Free: 866-396-2549
mwwa@mts.net
www.mwwa.net
www.facebook.com/group.php?gid=167933616574016
Overview: A small provincial organization founded in 1975
Mission: To provide operator members with educational opportunities for operating & maintaining water & wastewater treatment facilities & water distribution & wastewater collection systems; To promote operator certification & facility classification
Member of: Western Canada Water & Wastewater Association
Chief Officer(s):
Dale Scott, Chair
Iva Last, Executive Director
Activities: Exchnaging information & experiences
Meetings/Conferences: • Manitoba Water & Wastewater Association 2015 Annual Conference & Trade Show, January, 2015, Keystone Centre/Canad Inn, Brandon, MB
Scope: Provincial
Description: The presentation of technical papers plus the opportunity to view industry products & services
Contact Information: Executive Director: Iva Last: Phone: 204-239-6868, Toll-Free Phone: 1-866-396-2549, Fax: 204-239-6872, E-mail: mwwa@mts.net
• Manitoba Water & Wastewater Association 2016 Annual Conference & Trade Show, January, 2016, Victoria Inn, Winnipeg, MB
Scope: Provincial
Description: The presentation of technical papers plus the opportunity to view industry products & services
Contact Information: Executive Director: Iva Last: Phone: 204-239-6868, Toll-Free Phone: 1-866-396-2549, Fax: 204-239-6872, E-mail: mwwa@mts.net
Publications:
• Waterways [a publication of the Manitoba Water & Wastewater Association]
Type: Newsletter

Profile: Information for members about upcoming conferences & educational opportunities

Manitoba Water Polo Association Inc.
#307, 145 Pacific Ave., Winnipeg MB R3B 2Z6
Tel: 204-925-5777; *Fax:* 204-925-5730
mwpa@shaw.ca
www.mbwaterpolo.com
Overview: A small provincial organization overseen by Water Polo Canada
Mission: To promote & govern the sport of water polo in Manitoba
Member of: Water Polo Canada
Affliation(s): Sport Manitoba
Chief Officer(s):
Bruce Rose, Executive Director
Cindra Leclerc, President

Manitoba Water Well Association (MWWA)
PO Box 1648, Winnipeg MB R3C 2Z6
Tel: 204-479-3777
info@mwwa.ca
www.mwwa.ca
Overview: A medium-sized provincial organization founded in 1958 overseen by Canadian Ground Water Association
Mission: To promote & support the water well industry in Manitoba
Chief Officer(s):
Jeff Bell, President
Ray Ford, Vice-President
Lynn Giersch, Business Manager
Marilyn Schneider, Secretary-Treasurer
Membership: *Member Profile:* Manufacturers; Technicians; Suppliers; Contractors
Activities: Offering workshops & seminars; Providing networking opportunities; Fostering & promoting scientific education, research, & standards
Meetings/Conferences: • 2015 Manitoba Water Well Association Annual Conference & Trade Show, January, 2015, Keystone Centre/Canad Inn, Brandon, MB
Scope: Provincial
Description: A review of the year's highlights & an opportunity to address new business
Contact Information: E-mail: info@mwwa.ca
• 2016 Manitoba Water Well Association Annual Conference & Trade Show, January, 2016, Victoria Inn, Winnipeg, MB
Scope: Provincial
Description: A review of the year's highlights & an opportunity to address new business
Contact Information: E-mail: info@mwwa.ca
Publications:
• Manitoba Water Well Association Newsletter
Type: Newsletter; *Frequency:* Quarterly
Profile: Featuring the president's report, membership information

Manitoba Welsh Pony & Cob Association
c/o Donna Hunter, PO Box 135, Kenton MB R0M 0Z0
Tel: 204-848-2411
mwpca.webs.com
Overview: A small provincial organization founded in 1975 overseen by Welsh Pony & Cob Society of Canada
Mission: To promote & develop the Welsh pony breed in Manitoba
Chief Officer(s):
Marg Allen, President, 204-352-4324
Donna Hunter, Secretary, 204-838-2411
kenview@inethome.ca
Membership: *Member Profile:* Welsh pony breeders & other interested persons in Manitoba
Activities: Increasing public awareness of the Welsh pony breed; Hosting annual shows

Keystone Region
c/o Norman Kalinski, PO Box 45, Carroll MB R0K 0K0
Tel: 204-483-2222; *Fax:* 204-483-3687
kalinski@mts.net
Mission: To promote the Welsh ponies & Cobs in Manitoba's Keystone area
Chief Officer(s):
Norman Kalinski, Contact, 204-483-2222

Manitoba Wheelchair Sports Association
145 Pacific Ave., Winnipeg MB R3B 2Z6
Tel: 204-925-5790; *Fax:* 204-925-5792
mwsa@sportmanitoba.ca
www.mwsa.ca
www.facebook.com/manitobawheelchairsports
Overview: A small provincial organization founded in 1962
Mission: Committed to leadership in the promotion of well being and a healthy lifestyle through the development of sport and fitness related opportunities for physically disabled Manitobans.
Member of: Canadian Wheelchair Sports Association
Chief Officer(s):
Angela Lloyd, Executive Director
Staff Member(s): 2
Membership: *Fees:* $5

Manitoba Wildlife Federation (MWF)
70 Stevenson Rd., Winnipeg MB R3H 0W7
Tel: 204-633-5967
Toll-Free: 877-633-4868
info@mwf.mb.ca
www.mwf.mb.ca
Overview: A medium-sized provincial charitable organization founded in 1944 overseen by Canadian Wildlife Federation
Mission: To devote members to the causes of conservation & the participation in the wise use of natural resources; To encourage the propagation of game & fish; To promote the enforcement of game laws; To cooperate with government departments
Chief Officer(s):
Brian Strauman, President
Beverly Sawchuck, Director, Administration
Finances: *Funding Sources:* Membership fees; Donations; Sponsorships
Staff Member(s): 5
Membership: 14,000+; *Fees:* $9 youth (12 to 17 years of age); $30 individuals; $40 families; *Member Profile:* Anglers; Hunters; Outdoor enthusiasts
Activities: Offering hunting skills & firearms training programs; Developing the Hunters Sharing the Harvest program; Supporting the MWF Habitat Foundation
Publications:
• Outdoor Edge [a publication of the Manitoba Wildlife Federation]
Type: Magazine; *Frequency:* Bimonthly; *Price:* Free with Manitoba Wildlife Federation membership
Profile: Information for Manitoba's hunters & anglers

Manitoba Wildlife Rehabilitation Organization *See* Wildlife Haven Rehabilitation Centre

Manitoba Women's Enterprise Centre *See* Women's Enterprise Centre of Manitoba

Manitoba Women's Institutes (MWI)
1129 Queens Ave., Brandon MB R7A 1L9
Tel: 204-726-7135; *Fax:* 204-726-6260
mbwi.org
www.facebook.com/557282304320877
twitter.com/manitobawomen
Overview: A medium-sized provincial charitable organization founded in 1910 overseen by Federated Women's Institutes of Canada
Mission: Focuses on personal development, the family, agriculture, rural development & community action, locally & globally
Member of: Federated Women's Institutes of Canada; Associated Country Women of the World
Chief Officer(s):
Patricia Dyck, Executive Administrator
Finances: *Funding Sources:* Government; membership fees
Membership: *Member Profile:* Any woman 18 years of age & older
Activities: Networking; personal development; advocacy; health issues; culture & education; family life; farm issues; local & regional action; bursaries; conventions & seminars
Awards:
• Myrtle A. Rose Bursary (Scholarship)
Awarded to a mature student wishing to upgrade skills & re-enter the work force
• Manitoba Women's Institute Bursary (Scholarship)

Manitoba Writers' Guild Inc. (MWG)
#218, 100 Arthur St., Winnipeg MB R3B 1H3
Tel: 204-944-8013
info@mbwriter.mb.ca
www.mbwriter.mb.ca
Overview: A medium-sized provincial charitable organization founded in 1981
Mission: To provide services & support writers in Manitoba
Chief Officer(s):
Darcia Senft, President
Sharron Arksey, Secretary
Mickey Cuthbert, Treasurer
Membership: 100-499; *Fees:* $50 regular; $25 seniors, students, & persons on a fixed income; *Member Profile:* Manitoba writers at all stages of their writing careers; *Committees:* Administration & Finance; Advocacy & Promotion; Education & Youth; Membership & Outreach; Programming & Professional Development; Rural Outreach; Ad hoc / Special Projects
Activities: Offering a wide range of programs, such as the Blue Pencil Sessions & Master Classes; Providing manuscript evaluation services; Offering writing contests; *Awareness Events:* Winnipeg International Writers Festival; *Library:* Writers Resource Library
Awards:
• McNally Robinson Book of the Year (Award)
To the Manitoba author judged to have written the best book in the calendar year
• John Hirsch Award for Most Promising Manitoba Writer (Award)
Awarded annually to the most promising Manitoba writer working in poetry, fiction, creative non-fiction or drama
• Alexander Kennedy Isbister Award for Non-Fiction (Award)
Presented to the Manitoba writer whose book is judged the best book of adult non-fiction written in English
• Margaret Laurence Award for Fiction (Award)
Presented to the Manitoba writer whose book is judged the best book of adult fiction written in English
• McNally Robinson Book for Young People Awards (Award)
Awarded annually to the writer whose young person's book is judged the best written by a Manitoba author; two categories: children's & young adult
• Le Prix littéraire Rue des Chambeault (Award)
Biennial award presented to the author whose published book or play is judged to be the best French language work by a Manitoba author
• Carol Shields City of Winnipeg Award (Award)
To honour books that evoke the special caracter of & contribute to the appreciation & understanding of the City of Winnipeg
• Eileen McTavish Sykes Award for Best First Book (Award)
Awarded annually to a Manitoba author whose first professionally published book is deemed the best written*Eligibility:* Must have been written in the previous year
• Mary Scorer Award for Best Book by a Manitoba Publisher (Award)
Awarded to the best book published by a Manitoba publisher & written for the trade, bookstore, educational, academic or scholarly market
• Manitoba Book Design of the Year Awards (Award)
For the best overall design in Manitoba book publishing in two categories: book design for adults; book design for children

Manitoba/Saskatchewan Gelbvieh Association *See* Saskatchewan/Manitoba Gelbvieh Association

Manitoba-Saskatchewan Prospectors & Developers Association (MSPDA)
PO Box 306, 12 Mitchell Rd., Flin Flon MB R8N 1N1
Tel: 204-687-3500; *Fax:* 204-687-4762
more@mts.net
Overview: A medium-sized provincial organization founded in 1950
Mission: To act on behalf of individuals & firms engaged in mineral exploration in Manitoba & Saskatchewan in their dealings with government with respect to acts & regulations; to promote interest in mineral exploration in these provinces; to provide members with access to technical improvement
Chief Officer(s):
Steve Masson, President
Membership: *Member Profile:* Geoscientists; prospectors; suppliers
Activities: Participation in provincial committees (Manitoba, Saskatchewan) dealing with land access, aboriginal concerns, mining, exploration & development; arrange technical speakers

Manitoulin Chamber of Commerce
PO Box 307, 6062 Hwy. 542, Mindemoya ON P0P 1S0
Tel: 705-377-7501
Toll-Free: 800-698-6681
office@manitoulinchamber.com
www.manitoulinchamber.com
Overview: A small local organization
Mission: The voice of business providing leadership, service, education & communication in making Manitoulin prosper.
Member of: Ontario Chamber of Commerce

Chief Officer(s):
Owen Legge, President
manlegg@amtelecom.net
Finances: *Annual Operating Budget:* Less than $50,000;
Funding Sources: Membership; Fundraising
Staff Member(s): 1; 16 volunteer(s)
Membership: 200+; *Fees:* $100 1-10 employees & non-for-profit; $200 11-24 employees; $367 25+ employees;
Member Profile: Businesses located in Manitoulin; *Committees:* Networking; Education; Four Seasons; Membership; Office; Fundraising; Signage; Business Award; Lobby; Office; Shop Manitoulin

Manitoulin District Association for Community Living *See* Community Living Manitoulin

Manitouwadge Chamber of Commerce *See* Manitouwadge Economic Development Corporation

Manitouwadge Economic Development Corporation
c/o Township of Manitouwadge, 1 Mississauga Dr.,
Manitouwadge ON P0T 2C0
Tel: 807-826-3227; *Fax:* 807-826-4592
Toll-Free: 877-826-7529
www.manitouwadge.ca
Previous Name: Manitouwadge Chamber of Commerce
Overview: A small local organization
Chief Officer(s):
Anthony Friedrich, Economic Development Officer,
807-826-3227 Ext. 234
afriedrich@manitouwadge.ca
Activities: Education seminars; community & special events; supports local organizations; information booth; represents the community to the provincial government

Mannawanis Native Friendship Centre
PO Box 1358, 4901 - 50 St., St Paul AB T0A 3A0
Tel: 780-645-4630; *Fax:* 780-645-1980
mnfc@mcsnet.ca
www.anfca.com/stpaul.html
Overview: A small local charitable organization overseen by Alberta Native Friendship Centres Association
Mission: "With the help of our Creator we will remember & maintain the strength of spirituality & our traditions to create opportunities for self-sufficiency"; To co-exist in a safe & unified environment that supports the development of healthy aboriginal families, providers & members of the community
Member of: Alberta Native Friendship Centres Association
Affliation(s): Alberta Food Bank Association; Canadian Food Bank Association
Chief Officer(s):
Theresa Whiskeyjack, Executive Director
Linda Boudreau, President
Judi Malone, Sec.-Treas.
Membership: 100-499
Activities: Annual talent show; Family day celebration; National Addictions Awareness Powerwalk; Monthly soup & bannock day for general public; *Library* Open to public

Manning & District Chamber of Commerce
PO Box 130, Manning AB T0H 2M0
Tel: 780-836-4045; *Fax:* 780-836-4048
manningchamber@gmail.com
www.facebook.com/Manningchamber
Overview: A small local organization
Member of: Alberta Chamber of Commerce
Chief Officer(s):
Kevin Albright, Chair
Finances: *Funding Sources:* Membership fees
Membership: *Member Profile:* To promote & enhance the business community through creation, participation & support of innovative programs

Mannville & District Chamber of Commerce
PO Box 54, Mannville AB T0B 2W0
Tel: 780-763-2499; *Fax:* 780-763-2218
www.mannvillechamber.com
Overview: A small local organization
Mission: Serving our local businesses & surrounding districts & community
Chief Officer(s):
Verner Thompson, President
Finances: *Annual Operating Budget:* Less than $50,000
Membership: 20; *Fees:* $20 business; $10 single
Activities: Parade; Hollydaze; Agricultural Fair

Manufacturiers et Exportateurs Canada *See* Canadian Manufacturers & Exporters

Many Rivers Counselling & Support Services
4071 - 4th Ave., Whitehorse YT Y1A 1H3
Tel: 867-667-2970; *Fax:* 867-633-3557
info@manyrivers.yk.ca
www.manyrivers.yk.ca
Previous Name: Yukon Family Services Association
Overview: A small provincial charitable organization founded in 1969
Mission: To support & strengthen families & individuals throughout the Yukon while striving for supportive & responsive communities
Member of: Family Service Canada
Chief Officer(s):
Brent Ramsay, Executive Director
bramsay@manyrivers.yk.ca
Finances: *Annual Operating Budget:* $1.5 Million-$3 Million;
Funding Sources: Yukon government; Membership fees; Contracts; Donations
Staff Member(s): 19
Membership: *Fees:* $10
Activities: Counselling; Psycho-educational groups; Workshops; Parenting programs; Youth outreach; Intervention workers;
Awareness Events: National Family Week, Oct.; *Library* Open to public

Dawson City
Waterfront Bldg., PO Box 595, 1085 Front St., Dawson YT Y0B 1G0
Tel: 867-993-6455; *Fax:* 867-993-6456
dawson@manyrivers.yk.ca

Haines Junction
PO Box 2109, 108 Auriol St., Haines Junction YT Y0B 1L0
Tel: 867-634-2111; *Fax:* 867-634-2333
hainesjunction@manyrivers.yk.ca

Watson Lake
Holt Agencies Bldg., PO Box 537, 714 Adela Trail, Watson Lake YT Y0A 1C0
Tel: 867-536-2330; *Fax:* 867-536-7854
watson@manyrivers.yk.ca
www.manyrivers.yk.ca/contactus.html

Maple Creek Chamber of Commerce
Tel: 306-662-4005
Other Communication: Alternate Phone: 306-662-3333
info@maplecreekchamber.ca
www.maplecreekchamber.ca
Overview: A small local organization
Member of: Saskatchewan Chamber of Commerce; Canadian Chamber of Commerce
Chief Officer(s):
Tina Cresswell, President
Wayne Litke, Secretary
Finances: *Annual Operating Budget:* Less than $50,000;
Funding Sources: Membership fees
6 volunteer(s)
Membership: 25

Maple Ridge Lapidary Club
23750 Fern Cres., Maple Ridge BC V4R 2S9
Tel: 604-466-4938
m.ridge_lapiclub@yahoo.ca
www.mrlclub.com
Overview: A small local organization founded in 1958
Mission: To provide a venue to develop appreciation of & skill in the lapidary & mineral arts
Member of: Lapidary, Rock & Mineral Society of British Columbia; Gem & Mineral Association of Canada
Chief Officer(s):
Carol Kostachuk, President
Finances: *Funding Sources:* Membership fees; workshop fees; annual gem show
Membership: *Fees:* $25 single; $45 family
Activities: Silversmithing; gem cutting; stone carving; enamelling; classroom discussions; workshops; displays;
Speaker Service: Yes

Maple Ridge Pitt Meadows Arts Council
11944 Haney Pl., Maple Ridge BC V2X 6G1
Tel: 604-476-2787; *Fax:* 604-476-2187
info@mract.org
www.theactmapleridge.org
Previous Name: Community Arts Council of T'Lagunna
Overview: A small local charitable organization founded in 1971
Mission: To serve the artistic & cultural needs of the Maple Ridge & Pitt Meadows area; To act as a voice for arts & culture in Maple Ridge & Pitt Meadows; To encourage appreciation for the arts
Affliation(s): Assembly of British Columbia Arts Councils
Chief Officer(s):
Lindy Sisson, Executive Director
Karen Pighin, Communications Manager
karenp@mract.org
Finances: *Funding Sources:* Membership; Fundraising; Grants
Membership: *Member Profile:* Individuals; Families; Corporations; Groups
Activities: Operating & managing The Arts Centre & Theatre (The Act); Promoting all disciplines of the arts; Organizing arts programs, such as arts & crafts classes; *Awareness Events:* Annual Family Arts Fair

Maple Ridge Pitt Meadows Chamber of Commerce
22238 Lougheed Hwy., Maple Ridge BC V2X 2T2
Tel: 604-463-3366; *Fax:* 604-463-3201
carrisa@ridgemeadowschamber.com
www.ridgemeadowschamber.com
Overview: A medium-sized local organization founded in 1910
Affliation(s): BC Chamber Executive; Canadian Chamber of Commerce; Southwestern BC Tourism
Chief Officer(s):
Jeff Cerpenter, President
Finances: *Annual Operating Budget:* $100,000-$250,000;
Funding Sources: Membership fees
Membership: 587
Activities: *Library* Open to public

Marathon canadien de ski *See* Canadian Ski Marathon

Marathon Chamber of Commerce
PO Box 1439, Marathon ON P0T 2E0
Tel: 807-229-1340
marathonchamberofcommerce@gmail.com
www.marathon.ca
Overview: A small local organization founded in 1962
Mission: To preserve & promote entrepreneurial spirit & the free enterprise system; to provide an alliance, a framework to help members expand their business, practice or service
Member of: Ontario Chamber of Commerce
Affliation(s): Northwestern Ontario Associated Chambers of Commerce
Chief Officer(s):
George Macey, President
Finances: *Annual Operating Budget:* Less than $50,000
Staff Member(s): 1; 20 volunteer(s)
Membership: 35; *Fees:* $75
Activities: Business education; professional & social network;
Internships: Yes

March of Dimes Canada (MODC) / Mars de dix sous du Canada
10 Overlea Blvd., Toronto ON M4H 1A4
Tel: 416-425-3463; *Fax:* 416-425-1920
Toll-Free: 800-263-3463
info@marchofdimes.ca
www.marchofdimes.ca
www.facebook.com/marchofdimescanada
twitter.com/modcanada
www.youtube.com/user/marchofdimescda
Also Known As: Rehabilitation Foundation for Disabled Persons, Canada
Overview: A large national charitable organization founded in 2001
Mission: To provide support services to people with disabilities, their families & caregivers across Canada
Affliation(s): Ontario March of Dimes; Ontario March of Dimes Non-Profit Housing Corporation (NPHC); OMOD Independence Non-Profit Corporation; Rehabilitation Foundation for Disabled Persons Inc., U.S.; Polio Canada; Stroke Recovery Canada
Chief Officer(s):
John Humphries, Chair
Andria Spindel, President & CEO
Finances: *Annual Operating Budget:* Greater than $5 Million
Staff Member(s): 4; 10 volunteer(s)
Membership: *Member Profile:* Board members of Ontario March of Dimes
Activities: Advocating; Researching; Offering information & peer support services; *Awareness Events:* Polio Awareness Month, March; Stroke Awareness Month, May
Awards:
- Vocational Rehabilitation Award (Award)
- Jeannette Shannon Post-Polio Program Volunteer Award (Award)
- Award of Merit for Barrier-Free Design (Award)
- Judge George Ferguson Award (Award)

• Rick Hansen Award of Excellence (Award)
• Vocational Rehabilitation Award (Award)
• Jonas Salk Award (Award)
Presented annually to a Canadian scientist, physician or researcher who has made a new and outstanding contribution in science or medicine to prevent, alleviate or eliminate a physical disability. *Contact:* Awards Selection Committee, Phone: 416-425-3463; E-mail: awardscommittee@Marchofdimes.ca
Meetings/Conferences: • 2015 Annual Breaking the ICE Conference, 2015
Scope: Provincial
Description: A consumer-centered conference aimed at helping people who use Alternative and Augmentative Communication (AAC) systems to develop their lives to the best of their abilities
Contact Information: Phone: 800-263-3463
• 2015 Annual Breaking the ICE West Conference, October, 2015, Burnaby, BC
Scope: Provincial
Description: A consumer-centered conference aimed at helping people who use Alternative and Augmentative Communication (AAC) systems to develop their lives to the best of their abilities
Contact Information: Phone: 800-263-3463
• 2015 L.I.V.E. Conference, 2015
Scope: Provincial
Description: The Leadership in Volunteer Education (L.I.V.E) Conference is Peer Support's annual 3-day training and networking event for active members, current and future volunteer leaders in stroke, polio and caregiver support groups across Canada.
Contact Information: Phone: 800-263-3463

March of Dimes Non-Profit Housing Corporation (NPHC)
10 Overlea Blvd., Toronto ON M4H 1A4
Tel: 416-425-3463; *Fax:* 905-845-0957
Toll-Free: 800-263-3463
info@marchofdimes.ca
www.marchofdimes.ca/dimes
Overview: A small national charitable organization founded in 1992
Mission: To develop & promote affordable supportive housing for people with physical disabilities
Affiliation(s): March of Dimes Canada
Chief Officer(s):
Cameron Whale, Chair
Karima Manji, Property Manager
Finances: *Annual Operating Budget:* $500,000-$1.5 Million
Staff Member(s): 2; 32 volunteer(s)
Membership: *Member Profile:* Consumers; donors; sustaining & volunteers
Activities: Operates supportive housing projects.
Publications:
• Ontario March of Dimes Non-Profit Housing Corporation Annual Report
Type: Yearbook; *Frequency:* Annually

Marche des dix sous de l'Ontario ***See*** Ontario March of Dimes

Les Marchés agricoles Canada ***See*** Farmers' Markets Canada

Margaree Salmon Association
PO Box 108, Margaree Centre NS B0E 1Z0
Tel: 902-248-2578; *Fax:* 902-248-2578
margareesalmon@gmail.com
www.margareesalmon.ca
Overview: A small local organization founded in 1982
Mission: Dedicated to the conservation, protection & enhancement of Atlantic salmon, trout & their habitat
Affiliation(s): Atlantic Salmon Federation; Nova Scotia Salmon Association
Chief Officer(s):
Lester Wood, President
Membership: *Fees:* $30 regular; $50 family; $10 junior; $300 lifetime

Margaret Laurence Home, Inc.
PO Box 2099, 312 First Ave., Neepawa MB R0J 1H0
Tel: 204-476-3612
mlhome@mts.net
www.mts.net/~mlhome
Overview: A small local charitable organization founded in 1986
Mission: To operate as a Provincial Heritage Site & museum; To preserve & display the possessions of Margaret Laurence
Finances: *Funding Sources:* Admission fees; Grants; Donations
Activities: Providing books, magazines, letters & tapes for research; Hosting writers' workshops, book launchings, & Elder Hostel education programs; Offering meeting space; *Awareness Events:* Annual Margaret Laurence Home Antiques & Collectibles Sale

Margaret M. Allemang Centre for the History of Nursing
c/o Judith Young, Treasurer, 355 Millwood Rd., Toronto ON M4S 1J9
Tel: 416-488-0597
secretary@allemang.on.ca
www.allemang.on.ca
Previous Name: Ontario Society for the History of Nursing
Overview: A small provincial organization founded in 1994
Mission: To promote the study of the history of nursing; to establish & maintain a collection of archival resources relating to the history of nursing
Chief Officer(s):
Judith Young, Treasurer
Finances: *Annual Operating Budget:* Less than $50,000; *Funding Sources:* Membership dues
Membership: 86 nurses; *Fees:* $50; $15 retired, student or associate; *Committees:* Archives; Acquisition
Activities: Public lectures; collection of nursing archival material (Ontario focus); oral history; *Speaker Service:* Yes

Margaret Morris Method (Canada) (MMM)
Tel: 613-938-7066
www.mmmcanada.ca
Also Known As: MMM (Canada)
Overview: A small national organization founded in 1951
Mission: To promote Margaret Morris exercise & dance methods & techniques
Affliation(s): International Association of M.M.M. Ltd.
Chief Officer(s):
Marie Paquette-Rivard, Contact
mariepr.mmm@gmail.com
Finances: *Annual Operating Budget:* Less than $50,000
50 volunteer(s)
Membership: 200; *Fees:* $20 individual; $10 junior; $50 registered teacher
Activities: *Library*
Awards:
• Special Junior Achievement Award (Award)
• Outstanding Contribution to MMM (Award)
Bronze trophy awarded annually

Margie Gillis Dance Foundation / Fondation de danse Margie Gillis
#304, 1908, rue Panet, Montréal QC H2L 3A2
Tel: 514-845-3115; *Fax:* 514-845-4526
info@margiegillis.org
www.margiegillis.org
www.facebook.com/pages/Margie-Gillis/63111821500
twitter.com/fdmargiegillis
Overview: A small local charitable organization founded in 1981
Mission: To reach as large a public as possible with a dance program of physical & emotional integrity; to make the audience aware of the potential of their own lives.
Chief Officer(s):
Margie Gillis, Artistic Director
Valerie Buddle, General Manager
Staff Member(s): 7

Marguerite Bourgeoys Family Centre Fertility Care Programme (MBFC)
#100, 688 Coxwell Ave., Toronto ON M4C 3B7
Tel: 416-465-2868; *Fax:* 416-465-3538
info@fertilitycare.ca
www.fertilitycare.ca
www.facebook.com/groups/123576671007676
Overview: A small national charitable organization
Mission: To help families manage & care for their reproductive health, by providing health care & resources; To educate women, couples, & youth about sexuality, fertility, & family relationships, in the framework of Catholic values; To respect the dignity & differences of people
Member of: ShareLife Catholic Charities
Affiliation(s): Archdiocese of Toronto
Chief Officer(s):
Thomas J. Murray, B.A., F.R.I., President & Treasurer
Hemingway Karen, CFCS, Executive Director
Finances: *Funding Sources:* Donations
Activities: Offering marriage preparation & family planning services

Marigold Enterprises Rehabilitation Services Society
PO Box 2207, 4724 - 53 Ave., High Prairie AB T0G 1E0
Tel: 780-523-4588; *Fax:* 780-523-5350
hpmari@telusplanet.net
Overview: A small local organization
Mission: To serve & support both adults & children with developmental disabilities in High Prairie
Member of: Alberta Council of Disability Services
Affliation(s): Alberta Association for Community Living
Chief Officer(s):
Vivian Cox, Executive Director
Activities: Offering vocational training; Encouraging supported & independent living

Marijuana Party
5535 Bourbonnière Ave., Montréal QC H1X 2N3
Tel: 514-507-5188
info@marijuanaparty.ca
www.marijuanaparty.ca
Overview: A small national organization founded in 2000
Chief Officer(s):
Blair T. Longley, Leader

Marine Insurance Association of British Columbia (MIABC)
c/o Marsh Canda, #800, 550 Burrard St., Vancouver BC V6C 2K1
Tel: 604-443-3519; *Fax:* 604-685-3112
marineinsuranceassociationbc.ca
Previous Name: Association of Marine Underwriters of British Columbia
Overview: A medium-sized provincial organization
Mission: To represent the goals & interests of the marine insurance industry in British Columbia
Chief Officer(s):
Jodi Gardner, President
jodi.gardner@marsh.com
Finances: *Funding Sources:* Membership fees
Membership: *Fees:* $200 associate; $350 full; *Member Profile:* Marine underwriters, brokers, surveyors & lawyers; *Committees:* Education; Legislative; Underwriting; Social; Claims; Communications
Activities: Educational courses; drafting of clauses for industry use

Marine Renewables Canada
121 Bird Sanctuary Dr., Nanaimo BC V9R 6H1
www.marinerenewables.ca
www.linkedin.com/groups/Marine-Renewables-Canada-2689413?home=&gid=268
www.facebook.com/marinerenewablescanada
twitter.com/Canadian_MRE
Previous Name: Ocean Renewable Energy Group
Overview: A medium-sized national charitable organization founded in 2004
Mission: Marine Renewables Canada aligns industry, academia and government to ensure that Canada is a leader in providing ocean energy solutions to a world market.
Chief Officer(s):
Chris Campbell, Exective Director, 250-754-0040
chris@marinerenewables.ca
Membership: *Fees:* $50 student; $300 individual; $500 organization; $1,000 government dept.; $2,500-$10,000 Ocean Energy Leader
Activities: Conferences
Meetings/Conferences: • Marine Renewables Canada 2015 Annual Conference, 2015
Scope: National
Description: Multiple networking opportunities to meet leaders and experts from business, government, and academia that will help build connections and support emerging industry needs.
• 6th International Conference on Ocean Energy (ICOE) 2015, 2015
Scope: International
Description: Global marine renewable energy event focused on the industrial development of marine renewable energy.

Atlantic Office
PO Box 34066, #400, 1533 Barrington St., Halifax NS B3J 3S1
Chief Officer(s):
Elisa Obermann, Atlantic Director, 902-817-4317
elisa@marinerenewables.ca

Mariners' House of Montréal / Maison des marins de Montréal
PO Box 128, Stn. Place d'Armes, Montréal QC H2Y 3E9

Tel: 514-849-3234; *Fax:* 514-849-2874
manager@marinershouse.ca
www.marinershouse.ca
Also Known As: Montréal Seafarers Centre
Previous Name: Montreal Sailors' Institute & Catholic Sailors' Club
Overview: A small local charitable organization founded in 1862
Mission: To aid & assist seafarers temporarily in the City of Montréal & surrounding vicinity; to provide a place of repose for such seafarers & to provide for their spiritual, moral & social welfare
Chief Officer(s):
Carolyn Osborne, Manager
Finances: *Annual Operating Budget:* $100,000-$250,000
Staff Member(s): 5; 8 volunteer(s)
Membership: 1-99
Activities: A home away from home for some 15,000 seafarers annually; services include local & overseas calls, currency exchange, postal services, recreation, library & snack bar

Mario Racine Foundation ***Voir*** Fondation Mario-Racine

Mariposa Folk Foundation
PO Box 383, Orillia ON L3V 6J8
Tel: 705-326-3655; *Fax:* 705-326-5963
officemanager@mariposafolk.com
www.mariposafolk.com
www.facebook.com/MariposaFolkFestivalOfficial
twitter.com/mariposafolk
www.youtube.com/mariposafolk
Overview: A medium-sized national organization founded in 1961
Mission: To promote & preserve folk arts in Canada through song, story, dance, & craft.
Member of: North America Folk Alliance; Ontario Council of Folk Festivals; Archives Association of Ontario; Orillia & District Arts Council
Chief Officer(s):
Pam Carter, President
Staff Member(s): 6
Membership: *Fees:* $20 regular; $5 student/unwaged/accredited volunteer voting; *Committees:* Festival
Activities: Festivals & concerts; *Library* by appointment

Maritime Aboriginal Peoples Council (MAPC)
172 Truro Heights Rd., Truro NS B6L 1X1
Tel: 902-895-2982; *Fax:* 902-895-3844
mapcorg.ca
Overview: A medium-sized provincial organization
Mission: Represents the Traditional Ancestral Homeland Mi'Kmaq, Maliseet, and Passamaquoddy Aboriginal Peoples of Canada.

Maritime Angus Association (MAA)
RR#1, Salt Springs Pictou NS B0K 1P0
Tel: 902-925-2057; *Fax:* 902-925-2655
windcrest.farm@ns.sympatico.ca
Overview: A small local organization founded in 1963
Mission: To provide services that enhance the growth & position of the Angus breed in the Maritime provinces
Affliation(s): Canadian Angus Association
Chief Officer(s):
Betty Lou Scott, General Manager
windcrest.farm@ns.sympatico.ca
Membership: 60+; *Fees:* $100

Maritime Appaloosa Horse Club ***See*** Appaloosa Horse Club of Canada

Maritime Association of Professional Sign Language Interpreters (MAPSLI)
PO Box 2625, Halifax NS B3J 1P7
www.mapsli.ca
www.facebook.com/367468123385697
twitter.com/MAPSLI_Canada
Overview: A small local organization founded in 1992 overseen by Association of Visual Language Interpreters of Canada
Member of: Association of Visual Language Interpreters of Canada (AVLIC)
Chief Officer(s):
Brenna D'Arcy, Acting President
president@mapsli.ca
Jessica Bezanson, Secretary
secretary@mapsli.ca
Membership: *Committees:* Newsletter; Membership; Professional Development

Maritime Auto Wreckers Association ***See*** Automotive Recyclers Association of Atlantic Canada

Maritime Board of Traide; Atlantic Provinces Chamber of Commerce ***See*** Atlantic Chamber of Commerce

Maritime Breeders Association (MBA)
c/o PEI Harness Racing Industry Association, #204A, 420 University Ave., Charlottetown PE C1A 7Z5
Tel: 902-569-1682; *Fax:* 902-569-1827
peracing@eastlink.ca
Overview: A small local organization founded in 1982
Member of: Prince Edward Island Harness Racing Industry Association
Chief Officer(s):
Wayne Pike, Executive Director, PEI Harness Racing Industry Association
Membership: *Member Profile:* Maritime stallion owners
Activities: Sponsoring the Maritime Breeders Association championship series; Registering stallions

Maritime Fire Chiefs' Association (MFCA)
PO Box 6, Dartmouth NS B2Y 3Y2
www.mfca.ca
Overview: A medium-sized local organization founded in 1914
Mission: To advance the science of the fire service in the Atlantic provinces
Chief Officer(s):
Neville Wheaton, President
nwheaton@cornerbrook.com
Al Duchesne, First Vice-President
duchesa@halifax.ca
Vince Mackenzie, Second Vice-President
firechief@grandfallswindsor.com
Charles Kavanaugh, Sergeant at Arms
charles.kavanaugh@inspection.gc.ca
Membership: *Member Profile:* Persons in the position of fire chief, deputy fire chief, assistant fire chief, platoon fire chief, division fire chief, district fire chief, fire marshal, deputy fire marshal, fire commissioner, deputy fire commissioner, & individuals with an equivalent rank; *Committees:* Constitution & Bylaws; Resolutions; Training & Education; Conference; Finance; Nominating; Honours
Activities: Advocating & supporting educational programs for fire chiefs in fire protection & prevention, firefighting, administration, & training; Liaising with government; Rendering financial assistance to families of deceased members
Meetings/Conferences: • Maritime Fire Chiefs' Association 2015 101st Annual Conference, July, 2015, Summerside, PE
Scope: Provincial
Description: Information about the latest trends & innovations within the fire service

Maritime Fishermen's Union (CLC) (MFU) / Union des pêcheurs des Maritimes (CTC) (UPM)
408 Main St., Shediac NB E4P 2G1
Tel: 506-532-2485; *Fax:* 506-532-2487
shediac@mfu-upm.com
www.mfu-upm.com
Overview: A medium-sized local organization founded in 1977
Mission: To maintain a sustainable inshore fishery & defend the principal of the fishermen/owner-operator.
Chief Officer(s):
Christian Brun, Executive Secretary
christian@mfu-upm.com
Membership: 1,300+

Maritime Hereford Association
RR#1, New Ross NS B0J 2M0
Tel: 902-425-7427; *Fax:* 902-425-7427
Overview: A small local organization
Mission: To increase the demand for Hereford & Hereford-influence cattle in the Maritime provinces
Member of: Canadian Hereford Association
Chief Officer(s):
Bobby Jo Hickey, Secretary-Manager, 506-523-7543
bobjhickey@hotmail.com
Philip Thorne, President
philshel@yahoo.ca
Gordie Raymond, Vice-President
garay@nb.sympatico.ca
Activities: Encouraging the breeding of purebred Hereford cattle in the Maritimes

Maritime Library Association ***See*** Atlantic Provinces Library Association

Maritime Limousin Association
c/o Sandra Othberg, Summerfield NB
Tel: 506-433-5245
www.maritimelimousin.com
Overview: A small provincial organization
Mission: To promote the limousin breed in the Maritime provinces
Member of: Canadian Limousin Association
Chief Officer(s):
Michael Byrne, President, 902-485-6731
Sandra Othberg, Secretary-Treasurer
Membership: *Member Profile:* Breeders of limousine cattle in the Maritimes
Activities: Providing member services

Maritime Lumber Bureau (MLB) / Bureau de bois de sciage des Maritimes
PO Box 459, Amherst NS B4H 4A1
Tel: 902-667-3889; *Fax:* 902-667-0401
Toll-Free: 800-667-9192
info@mlb.ca
www.mlb.ca
Overview: A medium-sized local organization founded in 1938
Mission: An accredited quality control agency for the lumber industry in the region.
Member of: Canadian Lumber Standards Accreditation Board; Canadian Wood Council
Chief Officer(s):
Diana L. Blenkhorn, President & CEO
Staff Member(s): 12
Activities: *Speaker Service:* Yes

Maritime Lumber Dealers Association ***See*** Atlantic Building Supply Dealers Association

Maritime Model Horse Collectors & Showers Association (MMHC&SA)
c/o Debbie Gamble-Arsenault, Alexandra RR#1, Charlottetown PE C1A 7J6
Overview: A small local organization
Mission: To bring together people who collect model horses & to foster growth in the hobby
Affliation(s): Canadian Model Club & Registry
Chief Officer(s):
Debbie Gamble-Arsenault, Contact
dgamble@isn.net
Membership: *Fees:* $1; *Member Profile:* Residents of the Maritimes who collect model horses

Maritime Professional Photographers Association (MPPA) ***See*** Professional Photographers Association of Canada - Atlantic / Atlantique

Maritime Regional CGIT Committee
PO Box 383, Pictou NS B0K 1H0
Tel: 902-485-4011
Also Known As: Canadian Girls in Training - Maritimes
Previous Name: National CGIT Association - Maritime Regional Committee
Overview: A small provincial organization
Chief Officer(s):
Chris MacDonald, Contact

Maritime Shorthorn Association
9011 Moose River Rd., Middle Musquodoboit NS B0N 1X0
Tel: 902-384-2964
Overview: A small local organization
Mission: To promote the use & breeding of Canadian Shorthorn cattle
Member of: Canadian Shorthorn Association
Chief Officer(s):
Lynn Poole, Secretary
James Poole, President
jpoole@nssympatico.ca

Maritime Sikh Society (MSS)
10 Parkhill Rd., Halifax NS B3P 1R3
Tel: 902-477-0008
www.maritimesikhsociety.com
Overview: A small local organization founded in 1968
Member of: Multicultural Association of Nova Scotia
Chief Officer(s):
S. Major Singh Jassal, President, 902-405-1237
jatinderbhupa@hotmail.com
Finances: *Annual Operating Budget:* Less than $50,000
Membership: 46; *Fees:* $12
Activities: *Library* by appointment

The Maritimes Energy Association
Cambridge Tower 1, #305, 202 Brownlow Ave., Dartmouth NS B3B 1T5
Tel: 902-425-4774; *Fax:* 902-422-2332
info@maritimesenergy.com
www.maritimesenergy.com
twitter.com/MEnergyAssoc
Previous Name: Offshore / Onshore Technologies Association of Nova Scotia (OTANS)
Overview: A small provincial organization founded in 1982
Mission: To represent companies that offer goods & services to the maritime energy industry; To identify, promote, & support opportunities in the energy industry on Canada's east coast for member businesses
Chief Officer(s):
Sue Ritter, Chair
Barbara Pike, Chief Executive Officer
barbara@maritimesenergy.com
Sara Colburne, Director, Stakeholder Engagement
sara@maritimesenergy.com
Lori Peddle, Manager, Business & Operations
lori@maritimesenergy.com
Paula Broaders, Coordinator, Member Relations
Paula@MaritimesEnergy.com
Membership: 300+; *Fees:* $30 student membership; $498 companies with 1-10 employees; $760.50 businesses with 11-50 employees; $998 for companies with 51 or more employees; *Member Profile:* Businesses throughout Atlantic Canada that supply goods & services to the energy sector, including the gas, oil, wind, tidal, & solar industries; *Committees:* Audit; Executive; Membership; Oil & Gas; Core Energy Conference Organizing; Government Relations; Nominations; Renewable Energy
Activities: Collaborating with provincial & federal governments & regulatory authories; Facilitating trade missions to investigate export opportunities; Advocating for the interests of the energy industry; Conducting policy research; Offering industry history & news; Organizing sessions with guest speakers who address current topics of interest in the energy industry; Providing networking opportunities
Meetings/Conferences: • The Maritimes Energy Association 2015 Annual General Meeting & Dinner, February, 2015, The Marriott Harbourfront, Halifax, NS
Scope: Provincial
Description: An event featuring the induction of new members to the board of directors, plus a keynote speaker & networking opportunities
• The Maritimes Energy Association 2015 Core Energy Conference & Trade Show, September, 2015, Halifax, NS
Scope: Provincial
Description: A gathering of interest to decision makers in the offshore & onshore & the renewable & non-renewable energy sectors to participate in roundtable discussions & networking events
• The Maritimes Energy Association 2016 Annual General Meeting & Dinner, 2016
Scope: Provincial
Description: Focus on innovation, leadership and connecting with the WIT to get it done.
• The Maritimes Energy Association 2016 Core Energy Conference & Trade Show, 2015
Scope: Provincial
Description: An annual event during the first week of October for stakeholders in the onshore, offshore, wind, tidal, & policy sectors of the Maritime energy industry
Publications:
• The Maritimes Energy Association Annual Report with Financials
Type: Yearbook; *Frequency:* Annually
Profile: Contents include messages from the chair, executive committee, & board of directors, as well as industry activity in the maritime region, events, &committees
• The Maritimes Energy Association Daily Energy Bulletin
Type: Newsletter; *Frequency:* Daily
Profile: Current events of interest to members of the energy industry in Eastern Canada, such as notices of trade shows, association events, news releases from membercompanies, & procurement opportunities
• The Maritimes Energy Association Directory
Type: Directory
Profile: A listing of association members with company profiles & contact information

Maritimes Health Libraries Association (MHLA) / Association des bibliothèques de la santé des Maritimes (ABSM)
c/o Robin Parker, W.K. Kellogg Health Sciences Library, Dalhousie Uni., PO Box 1500, Halifax NS B3H 4R2
www.chla-absc.ca/mhla/
Overview: A medium-sized provincial organization overseen by Canadian Health Libraries Association
Mission: To support members in the provision of quality information services for the health care community in the maritime provinces
Member of: Canadian Health Libraries Association / Association des bibliothèques de la santé du Canada
Chief Officer(s):
Michelle Helliwell, President, 902-542-2347, Fax: 902-542-4619
mhelliwell@avdha.nshealth.ca
Membership: 31; *Fees:* $25; *Member Profile:* Health library specialists in the maritime provinces
Activities: Advocating for the value of health library specialists & health libraries; Providing educational opportunities; Communicating with members

Markdale Chamber of Commerce *See* Grey Highlands Chamber of Commerce

Marketing Research & Intelligence Association (MRIA) / L'Association de la recherche et de l'intelligence marketing (ARIM)
Bldg. 4, #104, 2600 Skymark Ave., Mississauga ON L4W 5B2
Tel: 905-602-6854; *Fax:* 905-602-6855
Toll-Free: 888-602-6742
info@mria-arim.ca
mria-arim.ca
www.linkedin.com/groups/MRIA-113690
www.facebook.com/MRIAARIM
twitter.com/MRIAARIM
Merged from: Canadian Association of Marketing Research Organizations; Canadian Survey Research Council
Overview: A medium-sized national licensing organization founded in 2004
Mission: To benefit the public & its members by developing & delivering ethical, professional practice standards, promoting the industry, & advocating for public policy that balances the need for research with privacy & consumer rights.
Chief Officer(s):
Anastasia Arabia, President
anastasia@trendresearch.ca
John Ball, Interin Executive Director, 905-602-6854 Ext. 8724
jball@mria-arim.ca
Tricia Benn, Secretary-Treasurer
tricia.benn@rci.rogers.com
Finances: *Funding Sources:* Member fees
Staff Member(s): 6
Membership: 2,000+; *Fees:* Schedule available; *Member Profile:* Members represent all aspects of the market intelligence & survey research industry, including practitioners, research houses, & buyers of research services, such as financial institutions, retailers, insurance companies, & manufacturers.; *Committees:* Certification Advisory; Communications; Conference; Fellowship Review; Litigation & Regulatory Resources; Membership; Research & Development; Field Management Group
Activities: Advancing the industry through education & accreditation; Offering industry surveys & reports; *Library*
Awards:
• Excellence in Research Awards (Award)
• Blankenship Award (Award)
• John F. Graydon Award (Award)
• Joseph Doyle Award (Award)
• Commins Award (Award)
For best paper in the Canadian Journal of Marketing Research
Publications:
• Canadian Journal of Marketing Research
Type: Journal; *Editor:* Cam Davis; *Price:* $50
Profile: Articles by Canadian researchers
• The Research Buyers Guide
Type: Directory; *Frequency:* Annually; *Accepts Advertising*; *Editor:* Barbara Justason; *Price:* Free to members
Profile: Listing of companies & organizations that provide marketing research services & products in Canada
• Vue Magazine
Type: Magazine; *Frequency:* Monthly; *Accepts Advertising*; *Editor:* Stephen Popiel
Profile: Articles relating to research methods & practices, book reviews, industry conference reviews, upcoming events, & member news

Markham Board of Trade (MBT)
Markham Convergence Centre, 7271 Warden Ave., Markham ON L3R 5X5
Tel: 905-474-0730; *Fax:* 905-474-0685
info@markhamboard.com
www.markhamboard.com
Also Known As: Markham Chamber of Commerce
Overview: A medium-sized local organization founded in 1982
Mission: To enhance the success of members & the Markham business community
Member of: Ontario Chamber of Commerce; Canadian Chamber of Commerce
Affliation(s): Scarborough York Region Chinese Business Association
Chief Officer(s):
Richard Cunningham, President/CEO
Mary Ann Quagliara, Director, Member Services
Finances: *Annual Operating Budget:* $500,000-$1.5 Million; *Funding Sources:* Membership dues; programs & services
Staff Member(s): 6; 100 volunteer(s)
Membership: 800; *Fees:* Schedule available; *Committees:* Leaders/Nominating; Strategic Planning; Breakfast Committee; Government Affairs; Annual Awards Selection; Membership; Youth; International Business
Activities: Luncheons; golf tournaments
Awards:
• Business Excellence Awards (Award)

Markham District Historical Society
c/o Markham District Historical Museum, 9350 Hwy. 48, Markham ON L3P 3J3
Tel: 905-294-4576; *Fax:* 905-294-4590
Overview: A small local charitable organization founded in 1969
Mission: To research, record & preserve Markham's history & to present a series of programs for its members
Affliation(s): Ontario Historical Society
Chief Officer(s):
Lorne R. Smith, Historian
lorne.smith@sympatico.ca
Finances: *Funding Sources:* Membership dues; Provincial government; Dinners; Festival days
Activities: Museum activities; Meetings; Bus tours; *Speaker Service:* Yes

Markham Federation of Filipino Canadians
#10 & 11, 1151 Denison St., Markham ON L3R 3Y4
Tel: 905-305-1320; *Fax:* 905-284-6191
www.mffc.ca
Overview: A small local organization founded in 1989
Mission: To promote & preserve the Filipino culture & heritage through dialogue & activites
Affliation(s): National Council of Canadian Filipino Associations
Chief Officer(s):
Ester Toribio, Secretary
Yoly Ladines, President
Finances: *Funding Sources:* Membership dues; Fundraising
Membership: *Fees:* $10 individual; $20 family; $50 organizations

Markham Stouffville Hospital Foundation
PO Box 1800, 381 Church St., Markham ON L3P 7P3
Tel: 905-472-7171; *Fax:* 905-472-7018
mshfoundation@msh.on.ca
www.mshf.on.ca
Overview: A small local charitable organization
Mission: To raise money on behalf of the Markham Stouffville Hospital in order to fund research & improve patient care
Chief Officer(s):
Suzette Strong, Chief Executive Officer
suzette@msh.on.ca
Finances: *Funding Sources:* Donations
Staff Member(s): 17

Markland Homes Association (MHA)
PO Box 11, Toronto ON M9C 4V2
e-mail: mhapresident@marklandwood.org
www.marklandwood.org
Overview: A small local organization
Mission: To create, foster & maintain a community spirit
Chief Officer(s):
Anna Schaefer, President
Membership: *Fees:* $20; *Member Profile:* Residents of the Markland Wood neighbourwood in Toronto's west end.; *Committees:* Environmental; Government Relations; Positively Promoting Markland; Safety; Social; Youth Awards

Marmot Recovery Foundation
PO Box 2332, Stn. A, Nanaimo BC V9R 6X6
Tel: 250-390-0006
Toll-Free: 877-462-7668
marmots@telus.net
www.marmots.org
Overview: A small local organization founded in 1998
Mission: To manage the recovery effort for one of North America's most endangered mammals: the Vancouver Island marmot (Marmota vancouverensis)
Affliation(s): Vancouver Island Marmot Recovery Team
Chief Officer(s):
Viki Jackson, Executive Director

The Marquis Project, Inc.
PO Box 50045, Brandon MB R7A 7E4
Tel: 204-727-5675; *Fax:* 204-727-5683
marquis@marquisproject.com
www.marquisproject.com
www.facebook.com/group.php?gid=57146899285&
Overview: A small international charitable organization founded in 1979
Mission: To inform rural Manitobans of global issues; to link concerns to those of Third World peoples; to encourage concrete positive action in response to global concerns
Affliation(s): Canadian Council for International Cooperation; Manitoba Council for International Cooperation; Partnership Africa-Canada; Canadian Peace Alliance; Manitoba Eco-Network
Chief Officer(s):
Al Friesen, President
Finances: *Annual Operating Budget:* $100,000-$250,000; *Funding Sources:* Government; membership dues; donations; foundations
Staff Member(s): 3; 100 volunteer(s)
Membership: 30 institutional + 25 student + 50 senior/lifetime + 450 individual; *Fees:* $30; *Committees:* Overseas Projects; Education; Program; Finance
Activities: Operates a 3rd world craft store "Worldly Goods"; *Internships:* Yes; *Speaker Service:* Yes; *Library:* Laura Delamater Resource Centre; Open to public

Mars de dix sous du Canada *See* March of Dimes Canada

Marsh Collection Society
235A Dalhousie St., Amherstburg ON N9V 1W6
Tel: 519-736-9191
research@marshcollection.org
www.marshcollection.org
Overview: A small local charitable organization founded in 1983
Mission: To collect, preserve & encourage research into the heritage of Amherstburg & the lower Detroit River
Member of: Ontario Museum Association; Ontario Historical Society; Ontario Genealogical Society; Archives Association of Ontario; Amherstburg Museums & Galleries; Association for Great Lakes Maritime History; Essex County Historical Society
Activities: *Library* Open to public

The Martello Tower Society *See* Community Foundation for Kingston & Area

Marwayne & District Chamber of Commerce
PO Box 183, Marwayne AB T0B 2X0
Tel: 780-847-3784; *Fax:* 780-847-4144
www.village.marwayne.ab.ca
Overview: A small local organization
Member of: Alberta Chamber of Commerce
Chief Officer(s):
Sharon Kneen, President
jskneen@hmsinet.ca
Finances: *Annual Operating Budget:* Less than $50,000
Staff Member(s): 6; 20 volunteer(s)
Membership: 1-99

Mary Undoer of Knots
#1, 271 Richvale Dr. South, Brampton ON L6Z 4W6
Tel: 905-495-4614
novena@maryundoerofknots.com
www.maryundoerofknots.com
Overview: A small local organization
Mission: To be devoted to Mary Undoer of Knots; To pray, as described in the Novena booklet, which is translated in 19 languages & Braille
Affliation(s): Archdiocese of Toronto
Activities: Providing faith instruction; Offering prayer groups for youth, singles, & seniors

Masaryk Memorial Institute Inc. / The New Homeland
450 Scarborough Golf Club Rd., Toronto ON M1G 1H1
Tel: 416-439-4354
office@masaryktown.org
masaryktown.ca
Also Known As: Masarykuv Ustav
Overview: A small national charitable organization founded in 1945 overseen by Czech & Slovak Association of Canada
Mission: To keep tradition alive; to maintain heritage
Chief Officer(s):
Frantisek Jecmen, President
Membership: *Fees:* $20; *Member Profile:* Canadians of Czech or Slovak origins & people with an interest in Czech culture
Activities: Newspaper, library, school, courses, cultural events; *Library:* MMI Library; Open to public

Mascall Dance
1130 Jervis St., Vancouver BC V6E 2C7
Tel: 604-669-9337
admin@mascalldance.ca
www.mascalldance.ca
twitter.com/MascallDance
Overview: A small local organization founded in 1989
Mission: To provide a forum for research, creation, performance, education, documentation & dissemination of contemporary dance & related disciplines
Member of: Dance Centre; Alliance for Arts & Culture; Shape; CADA
Chief Officer(s):
Jennifer Mascall, Artistic Director
Finances: *Funding Sources:* The Canadian Council; BC Arts Council; City of Vancouver; fundraising
Staff Member(s): 3
Activities: Modern Dance; workshops; summer school; programs; educational tours

Masonic Foundation of Manitoba Inc.
420 Corydon Ave., Winnipeg MB R3L 0N8
Tel: 204-453-7410
Overview: A small provincial charitable organization founded in 1976
Chief Officer(s):
C.R. Haldane-Wilsone, Secretary-Treasurer

Masonic Foundation of Ontario
361 King St. West, Hamilton ON L8P 1B4
Tel: 905-527-9105; *Fax:* 905-527-8859
www.masonicfoundation.on.ca
Overview: A small provincial charitable organization founded in 1964
Mission: To provide bursaries for needy students attending universities & colleges in Ontario
Chief Officer(s):
Mel Duke, Secretary
mel_duke@masonicfoundation.on.ca
Finances: *Annual Operating Budget:* Greater than $5 Million

Masonry Industry Employers Council of Ontario (MIECO)
360 Superior Blvd., Mississauga ON L5T 2N7
Tel: 905-564-6622; *Fax:* 905-564-5744
www.canadamasonrycentre.com/mieco
Overview: A small provincial organization
Mission: To maintain a fair working relationship with local & provincial unions across Ontario
Member of: Ontario Masonry Contractors Association
Chief Officer(s):
D. Webb, Contact
dwebb@canadamasonrycentre.com
Staff Member(s): 7
Membership: 500-999
Activities: *Library:* Canada Masonry Centre; Open to public

MasonryWorx
#10, 150 Jardin Dr., Concord ON L4K 3P9
Tel: 905-760-9679; *Fax:* 866-700-4974
info@masonryworx.com
www.masonryworx.com
www.facebook.com/MasonryWorx
twitter.com/masonryworx
www.youtube.com/user/MasonryWorx1
Overview: A small local organization
Mission: To create beautiful communities across the Greater Toronto Area, that will increase in value & stand the test of time; To promote the use, understanding & benefits of masonry professionals, masonry products & masonry systems in the design & construction of our communities throughout the GTA

Massage Therapist Association of Alberta (MTAA)
#2, 7429 - 49 St., Red Deer AB T4P 1N2
Tel: 403-340-1913; *Fax:* 403-346-2269
info@mtaalberta.com
www.mtaalberta.com
www.facebook.com/MTAAlberta
Overview: A small provincial organization founded in 1953
Mission: To promote massage therapy through member services, education, professional standards & advocacy
Member of: Canadian Massage Therapist Alliance
Membership: *Fees:* $575 active

Massage Therapist Association of Saskatchewan (MTAS)
#16, 1724 Quebec Ave., Saskatoon SK S7K 1V9
Tel: 306-384-7077; *Fax:* 306-384-7175
mtas@sasktel.net
www.saskmassagetherapy.com
Overview: A small provincial organization founded in 1965
Member of: Canadian Massage Therapist Alliance
Chief Officer(s):
Lori Green, Executive Director, 306-382-7225, Fax: 306-384-7175
execdir.mtas@sasktel.net
Jayne Little, Manager, Member Services
Staff Member(s): 2
Membership: 825; *Fees:* $177.50 non-practicing; $355 practicing; *Member Profile:* Registered massage therapists; *Committees:* Continuing Education; Membership; Finance; Legislation
Activities: *Awareness Events:* Massage Therapy Awareness Week, October

Massage Therapists' Association of Nova Scotia (MTANS)
PO Box 9410, Stn. A, Halifax NS B3K 5S3
Tel: 902-429-2190; *Fax:* 902-425-2441
info@mtans.ca
www.mtans.ca
Overview: A small provincial organization founded in 1990
Mission: To promote the science, art & philosophy of Massage Therapy for the betterment of public health & in the public interest; to represent membership before governmental & regulating bodies concerned with Massage Therapy; to foster & encourage professional & ethical standards among its members; to encourage high standards of education for students of Massage Therapy; to increase the awareness & knowledge of the general public concerning the benefits of Massage Therapy; to liaise with & recommend potential students to recognized schools of Massage Therapy which meet the standards of the Association; to offer post-graduate education & to set post-graduate standards
Member of: Canadian Massage Therapist Alliance
Affliation(s): Alliance of Complemeniary Health Professions
Chief Officer(s):
Kelly Carrington, President
Donna Noddin, Executive Director
Finances: *Funding Sources:* Membership dues
Membership: *Fees:* $400 regular; $100 associate/inactive; $0 student; *Member Profile:* Massage therapists; *Committees:* Public Relations; Complaints; Continuing Education; Examination & Education Standards; Conference & Tradeshow; Legislation
Activities: Annual booth at Labatt's 24-Hour Relay, a fundraiser for Abilities Foundation of Nova Scotia

Massage Therapy Alliance of Canada (MTAC) / Alliance canadienne de massothérapeutes
c/o Massage.ca, 581 Huron St., Toronto ON M5R 2R6
Tel: 416-929-9759
www.massage.ca
Previous Name: Canadian Massage Therapist Alliance (CMTA)
Overview: A medium-sized national organization founded in 1991
Mission: To foster & advance the art, science & philosophy of massage therapy through nationwide cooperation in a professional, ethical & practical manner for the betterment of health care in Canada
Finances: *Funding Sources:* Membership dues
Activities: *Awareness Events:* National Massage Therapy Awareness Week, Sept.

Massage Therapy Association of Manitoba Inc. (MTAM)
#611, 428 Portage Ave., Winnipeg MB R3C 0E2
Tel: 204-927-7979; *Fax:* 204-927-7978
Toll-Free: 866-605-1433

info@mtam.mb.ca
www.mtam.mb.ca
www.linkedin.com/company/2511272?trk=tyah
www.facebook.com/MTAManitoba
twitter.com/MTAManitoba
Overview: A small provincial organization founded in 1973
Mission: To promote and enhance the art, science and philosophy of massage therapy in a professional and ethical manner to ensure the highest level of competency-based practice for massage therapy within the province of Manitoba.
Chief Officer(s):
George Fraser, Executive Director
gfraser@mtam.mb.ca
Membership: *Fees:* $550; *Member Profile:* Massage Therapists who have successfully completed two years of study from a recognized school/college of massage therapy and who have attained a minimum grade point average of 75%.

Massey Centre for Women
1102 Broadview Ave., Toronto ON M4K 2S5
Tel: 416-425-6348; *Fax:* 416-425-4056
giving@massey.ca
www.massey.ca
www.facebook.com/pages/Massey-Centre-for-Women/219366904794546
twitter.com/MasseyCentre
Overview: A small local charitable organization founded in 1901
Mission: To improve the lives of disadvantaged young women & their children
Affliation(s): The United Church of Canada
Chief Officer(s):
Ekua Asabea Blair, CEO
Finances: *Annual Operating Budget:* $3 Million-$5 Million; *Funding Sources:* Donations; Municipal, provincial & federal government grants; Fundraising
Staff Member(s): 81; 57 volunteer(s)
Activities: *Speaker Service:* Yes

Master Bowlers' Association of Alberta
1 Oxbow St., Red Deer AB T4N 5C3
Tel: 403-309-6916
mbaofa@shaw.ca
mbaofa.ca
Also Known As: MBA of A
Overview: A small provincial organization overseen by Master Bowlers' Association of Canada
Member of: Master Bowlers' Association of Canada
Chief Officer(s):
Brian Rossetti, President

Master Bowlers' Association of British Columbia
712 Colinet St., Coquitlam BC V3J 4X8
www.mbaofbc.com
Overview: A small provincial organization overseen by Master Bowlers' Association of Canada
Member of: Master Bowlers' Association of Canada
Chief Officer(s):
Joan Ritchie, President
jwritchie@gmail.com
Kelly Gorsek, Director, Membership, 778-574-6048
kgorsek@hotmail.com

Master Bowlers' Association of Canada
c/o Master Bowlers' Association of Alberta, 1 Oxbow St., Red Deer AB T4N 5C3
www.mastersbowling.ca
www.facebook.com/MBAofCanada
twitter.com/MBA_Calgary2013
Overview: A medium-sized national organization founded in 1970
Mission: To connect master bowlers across Canada
Membership: *Member Profile:* NCCP certified coaches & athletes competing as Teaching Masters, Tournament Masters & Senior Masters
Activities: Annual National Championships

Master Bowlers' Association of Manitoba (MBAM)
c/o Manitoba Five Pin Bowling Federation, 145 Pacific Ave., Winnipeg MB R3B 2Z6
Tel: 204-925-5766; *Fax:* 204-925-5792
www.manitobamasterbowlers.com
Overview: A small provincial organization overseen by Master Bowlers' Association of Canada
Member of: Manitoba Five Pin Bowling Federation, Inc.; Master Bowlers' Association of Canada
Chief Officer(s):
Doug Wood, President
doug_wood@manitobamasterbowlers.com

Master Bowlers' Association of Ontario (MBAO)
#302, 3 Concorde Gate, Toronto ON M3C 3N7
Tel: 416-426-7165; *Fax:* 416-426-7387
office@mbao.ca
mbao.ca
www.facebook.com/185964874757498
Overview: A small provincial organization overseen by Master Bowlers' Association of Canada
Member of: Master Bowlers' Association of Canada
Chief Officer(s):
Brenda Walters, President
Dave Johnson, Director, Operations

Master Insulators' Association of Ontario Inc.
Building 1, #101, 2600 Skymark Ave., Mississauga ON L4W 5B2
Tel: 905-279-6426; *Fax:* 905-279-6422
miapublic1@miaontario.org
www.miaontario.org
Overview: A small provincial organization founded in 1942
Mission: To promote & advance the insulation industry
Chief Officer(s):
Caroline O'Keeffe, Office Manager
Membership: 102; *Member Profile:* Companies who install thermal insulation; suppliers, distributors & manufacturers of thermal insulation; *Committees:* Joint Apprentice; Labour Advisory; Charity Golf; Health & Safety

Master Painters & Decorators Association (MPDA)
2800 Ingleton Ave., Burnaby BC V5C 6G7
Tel: 604-298-7578; *Fax:* 604-298-5183
Toll-Free: 888-674-8708
info@paintinfo.com
www.paintinfo.com/assoc/mpda/
Previous Name: Master Painters & Decorators Association of British Columbia
Overview: A medium-sized provincial organization founded in 1899
Mission: To set & raise standards of industrial organizations
Affliation(s): Master Painters Institute
Chief Officer(s):
Greg Boshard, President
Alan Kelly, Vice President
Finances: *Annual Operating Budget:* $250,000-$500,000
Staff Member(s): 4
Membership: 1-99; *Committees:* Technical
Activities: *Speaker Service:* Yes

Master Painters & Decorators Association of British Columbia *See* Master Painters & Decorators Association

Matane Historical & Genealogical Society *Voir* Société d'histoire et de généalogie de Matane

MATCH International Centre / Centre international Match
1404 Scott St., Ottawa ON K1Y 4M8
e-mail: info@matchinternational.org
www.matchinternational.org
www.facebook.com/matchinternational
twitter.com/MatchIntCentre
Overview: A small international organization founded in 1977
Mission: Guided by a feminist vision of sustainable development which recognizes the diversity of women & respects their efforts toward self-determination; works in partnership with women's groups in Africa, Asia, the Caribbean, & South America toward the empowerment of women through political, economic, social, & cultural justice.
Member of: Canadian Council for International Cooperation; South Asia Partnership
Chief Officer(s):
Patricia Harewood, Chair
Jessica Tomlin, Executive Director, 613-761-3695
kbulger@matchinternational.org
Nuala Nazarko, Coordinator, Fundraising, 613-761-3661
kbulger@matchinternational.org
Finances: *Annual Operating Budget:* $500,000-$1.5 Million; *Funding Sources:* Government; donations; foundations
Staff Member(s): 10; 40 volunteer(s)
Membership: 5,000 supporters; *Fees:* Donation; *Committees:* Program; Administrative
Activities: Eliminating Violence Against Women; Words of Women; Women & Sustainable Human Development; Africa; South America; Asia; Caribbean; *Awareness Events:* International Women's Day, March 8; *Speaker Service:* Yes; *Library:* Resource Clearing Centre; Open to public by appointment
Awards:
• Norma Walmsley Award (Award)

Mathematics of Information Technology & Complex Systems (MITACS)
Technology Enterprise Facility, University of British Columbia, #301, 6190 Agronomy Rd., Vancouver BC V6T 1Z3
Tel: 604-822-9189; *Fax:* 604-822-3689
mitacs@mitacs.ca
www.mitacs.math.ca
www.linkedin.com/company/mitacs
www.facebook.com/MITACS
twitter.com/DiscoverMITACS
Also Known As: MITACS Inc.
Overview: A medium-sized national organization
Mission: MITACS leads Canada's effort in the generation, application and commercialization of new mathematical tools and methodologies within a world-class research program. The network initiates and fosters linkages with industrial, governmental, and not-for-profit organizations that require mathematical technologies to deal with problems of strategic importance to Canada. MITACS is driving the recruiting, training, and placement of a new generation of highly mathematically skilled personnel that is vital to Canada's future social and economic wellbeing. Offices in Vancouver, Toronto, Montréal, St. John's & Fredericton.
Member of: Networks of Centres of Excellence
Chief Officer(s):
Arvind Gupta, CEO & Scientific Director

Les Matinées de musique de chambre *See* Ladies' Morning Musical Club

Matsqui Sumas Abbotsford Museum Society
2313 Ware St., Abbotsford BC V2S 3C6
Tel: 604-853-0313; *Fax:* 866-373-2771
info@msamuseum.ca
www.msamuseum.ca
Also Known As: MSA Museum
Overview: A small local charitable organization founded in 1969
Mission: To be the memory of the community by preserving & interpreting its history
Member of: Abbotsford Chamber of Commerce; BC Museums Association; Canadian Museum Association
Affliation(s): Abbotsford Public Art
Chief Officer(s):
Dororthy van der Ree, Executive Director
Staff Member(s): 4
Membership: *Fees:* $5 student; $10 senior; $20 individual; $30 family; $30+ club; $50 corporate
Activities: Halloween House; Easter Egg Hunt; school programs; tours; av production & presentations; *Awareness Events:* International Museums Day, May; *Speaker Service:* Yes

Matsqui-Abbotsford Food Bank *See* Abbotsford Food Bank & Christmas Bureau

Maxville & District Chamber of Commerce
PO Box 279, Maxville ON K0C 1T0
e-mail: postmaster@maxvillechamber.ca
www.maxvillechamber.ca
Overview: A small local organization founded in 1991
Mission: To promote its members
Member of: Canadian Chamber of Commerce
Chief Officer(s):
Debbie Gaulin, President
debbie@maxvillechamber.ca
Membership: 25; *Fees:* $25 individual; $50 business

Mayne Island Community Chamber of Commerce (MICCC)
PO Box 2, Mayne Island BC V0N 2J0
e-mail: executiveofficer@mayneislandchamber.ca
www.mayneislandchamber.ca
www.facebook.com/mayneislandcommunitychamberofcommerce
Overview: A small local organization
Chief Officer(s):
Millie Leathers, Chair, 250-539-5526
millieleathers@shaw.ca
Lauren Underhill, Executive Officer
Membership: 60; *Fees:* $5 community; $60 business

Mazda Sportscar Owners Club (MSOC)
3327 Charmaine Heights, Mississauga ON L5A 3C2

Tel: 416-625-1532
thelimit@rogers.com
www.wiredmotorsports.com/pitl
Previous Name: RX-7 Club of Toronto
Overview: A small provincial organization
Mission: To provide a car club for all Mazda sportscar owners; officially recognized by Mazda Canada Inc.
Affiliation(s): Canadian Automobile Sportscar Club
Chief Officer(s):
Darryl Dimitroff, President
Finances: *Annual Operating Budget:* Less than $50,000; *Funding Sources:* Advertising; membership fees
8 volunteer(s)
Membership: 50; *Fees:* $40
Activities: Caravans; autoslalom racing; "Push it to the Limit" performance driving competitions

MB Mission (MBMSI) / Mennonite Brethren Mission & Service International

International & Western Canada (BC), #300, 32040 Downes Rd., Abbotsford BC V4X 1X5
Tel: 604-859-6267; *Fax:* 604-859-6422
Toll-Free: 866-964-7627
mbmission@mbmission.org
www.mbmission.org
www.facebook.com/211465999015576
twitter.com/MBMission_EC
www.youtube.com/MBMissionVideos
Also Known As: Board of Missions & Services of the Mennonite Brethren Churches of North America
Previous Name: MBMS International
Overview: A medium-sized local charitable organization founded in 1900 overseen by Canadian Conference of Mennonite Brethren Churches
Mission: To make disciples & plant churches globally through church planting & envangelism, discipleship & leadership training & social ministry
Member of: Evangelical Fellowship of Mission Agencies
Chief Officer(s):
Brent Warkentin, Chair
Randy Friesen, General Director
randyf@mbmsi.org
Finances: *Funding Sources:* Voluntary contributions; grants
Activities: Cross-cultural mission agency of Mennonite Brethren churches in Canada & the US; *Internships:* Yes; *Speaker Service:* Yes

Central Canada (Alta., Sask. & Man.)
83 Henderson Hwy., Winnipeg MB R2L 1L2
Tel: 204-415-0670; *Fax:* 204-415-2249
Toll-Free: 888-866-6267
winnipeg@mbmsi.org
Chief Officer(s):
Lloyd Letkeman, Regional Mobilizer
lloydl@mbmsi.org

Eastern Canada (Ont., Qué., Maritimes)
#3B, 236 Victoria St. North, Kitchener ON N2H 5C8
Tel: 519-886-4378; *Fax:* 519-571-5059
Toll-Free: 888-866-6267
waterloo@mbmsi.org
Chief Officer(s):
Philip Serez, Regional Mobilizer
philipserez@gmail.com

MBMS International *See* MB Mission

MBTelehealth Network

John Buhler Research Centre, #772, 715 McDermot Ave., Winnipeg MB R3E 3P4
Tel: 204-272-3063; *Fax:* 204-975-7787
Toll-Free: 866-667-9891
www.mbtelehealth.ca
Overview: A small provincial organization
Mission: To promote the use of information technology to link people to health care expertise at a distance
Chief Officer(s):
Liz Loewen, Director, Coordination of Care
Finances: *Funding Sources:* Provincial Government
Staff Member(s): 28

McBride & District Chamber of Commerce

PO Box 2, McBride BC V0J 2E0
Tel: 250-569-3366; *Fax:* 250-569-2376
Toll-Free: 866-569-3366
come2mcbride@telus.net
www.mcbridebc.info
Overview: A small local organization
Member of: BC Chamber of Commerce
Chief Officer(s):
Vincent de Niet, President
Finances: *Annual Operating Budget:* Less than $50,000
Membership: 72

McCord Museum of Canadian History / Musée McCord d'histoire canadienne

690, rue Sherbrooke ouest, Montréal QC H3A 1E9
Tel: 514-398-7100
info@mccord.mcgill.ca
www.mccord-museum.qc.ca
www.facebook.com/museemccord
twitter.com/MuseeMcCord
www.youtube.com/user/MuseeMcCordMuseum
Also Known As: The McCord
Overview: A small local charitable organization founded in 1921
Mission: To preserve, study, diffuse & appreciate Canadian history; to make available to the general public & specialized researchers collections of artifacts & documents which record all facets of Canadian history, with special focus on the history of Montréal & Québec.
Member of: Canadian Museums Association; Société des directeurs des musées montréalais
Affliation(s): Société des musées québécois
Chief Officer(s):
Suzanne Sauvage, President & CEO
Cynthia Cooper, Head, Collections & Research
Pascale Grignon, Director, Marketing & Communications
Finances: *Annual Operating Budget:* Greater than $5 Million; *Funding Sources:* National government
Staff Member(s): 57
Membership: *Committees:* Ball; Wine & Food; Development; Marketing & Communications; Sugar Ball
Activities: Permanent & temporary exhibitions; educational, cultural & native programs; WEB exhibitions; research databases & pedagogical resources; hall rental service; bookstore & giftshop café; annual conference; *Internships:* Yes; *Library:* Archive & Documentation Centre; by appointment

McCreary Centre Society (MCS)

3552 Hastings St. East, Vancouver BC V5K 2A7
Tel: 604-291-1996; *Fax:* 604-291-7308
mccreary@mcs.bc.ca
www.mcs.bc.ca
Previous Name: Friends of the McCreary Centre Society
Overview: A small local charitable organization founded in 1977
Mission: To foster wider understanding of the importance of youth health; to increase knowledge about youth health needs & issues; to promote a continuing commitment to youth health issues; to initiate & implement innovative projects which directly address unmet health needs of young people
Member of: Canadian Health Network
Chief Officer(s):
R. Tonkin, Chair
Finances: *Annual Operating Budget:* $250,000-$500,000; *Funding Sources:* Membership fees; donations; grants; contracts
Staff Member(s): 6; 25 volunteer(s)
Membership: 48; *Fees:* $20; *Member Profile:* Open
Activities: Community-based research; education; youth participation projects; *Library:* ERC; by appointment

McGill Chamber Orchestra / Orchestre de chambre McGill

5459 Earnscliffe Ave., Montréal QC H3X 2P8
Tel: 514-487-5190; *Fax:* 514-487-7390
info@ocm-mco.org
www.ocm-mco.org
www.facebook.com/ocm.mco.montreal
twitter.com/ocm_mco
Overview: A small local charitable organization founded in 1939
Member of: Association of Canadian Orchestras
Chief Officer(s):
Boris Brott, Artistic Director
Taras Kulish, Executive Director
taraskulish@ocm-mco.org
Staff Member(s): 5

McGill Institute for the Study of Canada (MISC) / L'Institut d'études canadiennes de McGill

3463 Peel St., Montréal QC H3A 1W7
Tel: 514-398-8346; *Fax:* 514-398-7336
misc.iecm@mcgill.ca
www.mcgill.ca/misc
www.facebook.com/150347341735712
twitter.com/MISCCAN
Overview: A small national charitable organization founded in 1994
Mission: To promote a better understanding of Canada through the study & appreciation of our heritage; to provide new understanding about our social, political & economic future; to identify & explore the benefits that a pluralistic society offers; to breathe new life into the field of Canadian studies
Member of: Association for Canadian Studies
Chief Officer(s):
Will Straw, Director
Finances: *Funding Sources:* Charles & Andrea Bronfman Foundation; McGill University; Seagram Co. Ltd.
Staff Member(s): 19
Activities: Seminars, conferences & publications on a wide range of issues; Interdisciplinary courses in Canadian studies at McGill University; Graduate fellowships; *Library:* MISC Reading Room; Open to public by appointment

McGill University Health Centre Foundation

#900, 2155, rue Guy, Montréal QC H3H 2R9
Tel: 514-931-5656; *Fax:* 514-931-5696
www.muhcfoundation.com
Also Known As: MUHC Foundation
Overview: A small local charitable organization
Mission: To raise money on behalf of the McGill University Health Centre in order to fund research & improve patient care
Chief Officer(s):
David Boucher, Executive Director
david.boucher@muhc.mcgill.ca
Finances: *Funding Sources:* Donations
Staff Member(s): 7

McGill University Non Academic Certified Association (MUNACA) / Association accréditée du personnel non enseignant de l'université McGill

3483, rue Peel, Montréal QC H3A 1W7
Tel: 514-398-6565; *Fax:* 514-398-6892
reception@munaca.com
www.munaca.com
www.facebook.com/McGillStrike
Overview: A small local organization founded in 1994
Chief Officer(s):
Kevin Whittaker, President
president@munaca.com
Membership: *Member Profile:* Technical, clerical & library assistants; *Committees:* Communications; Health & Safety; Social Justice

McGill University Sexual Identity Centre *Voir* Centre d'orientation sexuelle de l'université McGill

McGregor Model Forest

PO Box 2640, Prince George BC V2N 4T5
Tel: 250-612-5840; *Fax:* 250-612-5848
Overview: A small local organization
Member of: Canadian Model Forest Network
Chief Officer(s):
Al Gorley, President
Dan Adamson, General Manager
dan.adamson@mcgregor.bc.ca

McIlwraith Field Naturalists

PO Box 24008, London ON N6H 5C4
Tel: 519-457-4593
info@mcilwraith.ca
www.mcilwraith.ca
Overview: A small local organization founded in 1890
Mission: To promote the enjoyment of nature through environmental appreciation & conservation; to encourage wise use & conservation of natural resources; to promote environmental protection
Affliation(s): Canadian Nature Federation; Federation of Ontario Naturalists
Finances: *Annual Operating Budget:* $50,000-$100,000
Membership: 5 institutional + 400 individual; *Fees:* $30 individual; $10 student; $50 contributing, $100 sustaining; *Member Profile:* Interest in natural world; *Committees:* Conservation; Education; Birding; Junior Naturalists
Activities: Field trips; tree & wild flower plantings; nature reserve; life science inventories; *Speaker Service:* Yes

The McLean Foundation

#1008, 2 St. Clair Ave. West, Toronto ON M4V 1L5
Tel: 416-964-6802; *Fax:* 416-964-2804
info@mcleanfoundation.ca
mcleanfoundation.ca

Overview: A small national charitable organization founded in 1945
Mission: To provide grants to registered charitable organizations in Canada
Chief Officer(s):
Paul McLean, President
Ev McTaggart, Secretary
Finances: *Annual Operating Budget:* $500,000-$1.5 Million
Staff Member(s): 2

McLennan Chamber of Commerce
PO Box 90, McLennan AB T0H 2L0
Tel: 780-324-2279
mclennanchamber@serbernet.com
mclennan.ca/town-a-government/businesses/chamber-of-commerce
Overview: A small local organization
Chief Officer(s):
Ray Johnson, President

McMan Youth, Family & Community Services Association
11016 - 127 St., Edmonton AB T5M 0T2
Tel: 780-482-4461; *Fax:* 780-409-9419
mcman@mcman.ca
www.mcman.ca
Also Known As: McMan Community Services
Overview: A medium-sized local charitable organization founded in 1975
Mission: To help individuals & families across Alberta develop the skills & supports to function effectively as members of their communities; to exercise advocacy & leadership in the community
Affiliation(s): Alberta Association of Services for Children & Families; Alberta Association of Rehabilitation Centres
Chief Officer(s):
Mikk Peek, President
Finances: *Annual Operating Budget:* Greater than $5 Million; *Funding Sources:* Provincial Government
Staff Member(s): 800; 100 volunteer(s)
Membership: 1-99; *Fees:* $10 individual; *Committees:* Fund Development; Edmonton & North
Activities: *Library:* McMan Library Services

Calgary
#1, 4004 - 19 St. NW, Calgary AB T2L 2B6
Tel: 403-508-6259; *Fax:* 403-508-7757
Chief Officer(s):
Carolyn Koltutsky, President
Jason Stone, Acting Executive Director
Laura Foster, Office Administrator
laura.foster@mcman.ca

Central Alberta
#121, 4804 - 50 St., Innisfail AB T4G 1C2
Tel: 403-227-5580; *Fax:* 403-227-5541
Chief Officer(s):
Luba Rusyn, President
Sherri McAllister, Executive Director
sherri.mcallister@mcman.ca

Southern Alberta
#4, 941 South Railway St. Southeast, Medicine Hat AB T1A 2W3
Tel: 403-527-1588; *Fax:* 403-526-8249
Chief Officer(s):
Tom Coulter, President
Chris Christie, Executive Director
chris.christie@mcman.ca

McMaster Symphony Orchestra; Greater Hamilton Symphony Association *See* Symphony on the Bay

McMaster University Faculty Association (MUFA) / Association des professeurs de l'Université McMaster
McMaster University, Hamilton Hall, #103A, 1280 Main St. West., Hamilton ON L8S 4K1
Tel: 905-525-9140; *Fax:* 905-522-8320
mufa@mcmaster.ca
www.mcmaster.ca/mufa
Overview: A small local organization founded in 1951
Mission: To protect the interests & negotiate terms & conditions of employment for the faculty members & librarians of McMaster University
Member of: Ontario Confederation of University Faculty Associations; Canadian Association of University Teachers
Chief Officer(s):
Phyllis DeRosa Koetting, Executive Director
Martin Dooley, President
dooley@mcmaster.ca
Finances: *Annual Operating Budget:* $250,000-$500,000; *Funding Sources:* Membership fees
Staff Member(s): 2; 13 volunteer(s)
Membership: 900; *Committees:* Academic Affairs; Grievance; Human Rights; Library; Membership; Pension; Public Relations; Renumerations; Tenure
Awards:
• MUFA Service Award (Award)

McMaster University Retirees Association (MURA)
c/o McMaster University, Gilmour Hall, #B108, 1280 Main St. W, Hamilton ON L8S 4L8
Tel: 905-525-9140
mura@mcmaster.ca
mura.mcmaster.ca
Overview: A medium-sized local organization founded in 1984
Mission: The McMaster University Retirees Association seeks to contribute in as many ways as possible to the welfare, prestige, and excellence of the University and to encourage and promote a spirit of fraternity and unity among the members of the Association, and to provide means for continuing the associations which retirees enjoyed as employees of the University.
Membership: 1685; *Member Profile:* Retired McMaster University faculty and staff

McMaster University Staff Association (MUSA)
Gilmour Hall, #B111, 1280 Main St. West, Hamilton ON L8S 4L8
Tel: 905-525-9140; *Fax:* 905-524-3111
caw555@cawlocal555.ca
www.cawlocal555.ca
Also Known As: CAW Local 555
Overview: A small local organization
Chief Officer(s):
Maggie Wilson, Administrative Assistant
Membership: 2,220+; *Member Profile:* Support staff, regional medical associates, parking & transit services staff & special constables working at McMaster University; *Committees:* Bylaws; Community Services; Elections; Education; Environment; Health & Safety; Human Rights; Recreation; Social Justice; Union in Politics; Women's; WSIB

Meadow Lake & District Chamber of Commerce
PO Box 847, Meadow Lake SK S9X 1Y6
Tel: 306-236-4061
mlchamberofcommerce@sasktel.net
www.meadowchamber.com
Overview: A small local organization
Member of: Saskatchewan Chamber of Commerce
Affliation(s): Northwest Regional Economic Development Authority
Finances: *Annual Operating Budget:* Less than $50,000; *Funding Sources:* Membership dues; local government
Staff Member(s): 1; 30 volunteer(s)
Membership: 100; *Fees:* $25-160

Meadow Lake Tribal Council (MLTC)
8003 Flying Dust Reserve, Meadow Lake SK S9X 1T8
Tel: 306-236-5654; *Fax:* 306-236-6301
www.mltc.ca
Overview: A small local organization founded in 1981
Mission: To create & improve programs & services that meet the needs of the member First Nations
Chief Officer(s):
Eric Sylvestre, Tribal Chief
Dwayne Lasas, Vice-Chief
Membership: 9 First Nations; *Member Profile:* Birch Narrows Dene Nation; Buffalo River Dene Nation; Canoe Lake Cree Nation; Clearwater River Dene Nation; English River First Nation; Flying Dust First Nation; Island Lake First Nation; Makwa Sahgaiehcan First Nation; & Waterhen Lake First Nation.
Activities: Economic development programs

Meaford Chamber of Commerce (MDCC)
#1, 16 Trowbridge St. West, Meaford ON N4L 1N2
Tel: 519-538-1640; *Fax:* 519-538-5493
Toll-Free: 888-632-3673
info@mcofc.ca
mcofc.ca
Previous Name: Meaford Community Partners
Overview: A small local organization founded in 1857
Mission: To be the voice of businesses in Meaford & the body through which all the members work in order to achieve their goals
Member of: Ontario Chamber of Commerce; Canadian Chamber of Commerce
Chief Officer(s):
Shirley Keaveney, President
shirlkeaveney@rogers.com
Donna Earl, Manager
business@mdcc.ca
Finances: *Funding Sources:* Municipal; Membership dues; Grants
Staff Member(s): 2
Membership: *Fees:* Schedule available
Activities: Info Nights; After 5's; Business seminars; Communityawards; Community Christmas party

Meaford Community Partners *See* Meaford Chamber of Commerce

Meals on Wheels Ontario Inc. *See* Ontario Community Support Association

Meanskinisht Village Historical Association
PO Box 155, Kitwanga BC V0J 2A0
Tel: 250-849-5732
Overview: A small local organization founded in 1979
Chief Officer(s):
Mary Dalen, Contact
6 volunteer(s)
Membership: *Member Profile:* Descendents of original inhabitants
Activities: Operates Cedarvale Museum; looks after graveyard of original inhabitants & descendants;

Meat Packers Council of Canada *See* Canadian Meat Council

Mechanical Contractors Association of Alberta
#204, 2725 - 12 St. NE, Calgary AB T2E 7J2
Tel: 403-250-7237; *Fax:* 403-291-0551
Toll-Free: 800-251-0620
vicky@mca-ab.com
www.mca-ab.com
Overview: A small provincial organization overseen by Mechanical Contractors Association of Canada
Mission: To promote plumbing & mechanical contractors; to provide educational programs to foster improved management & productivity in mechanical contracting; to represent mechanical contractors with their various publics - governments, design authorities, labour; to foster professional advancement & profitability of the plumbing, heating & mechanical contracting industry through its member services
Chief Officer(s):
Hans Tiedemann, Executive Director
hans@mcaalberta.com
Finances: *Annual Operating Budget:* $250,000-$500,000
Staff Member(s): 3
Membership: 100-499; *Fees:* $530 contractor; $424 affiliate

Mechanical Contractors Association of British Columbia (MCABC)
#223, 3989 Henning Dr., Burnaby BC V5C 6N5
Tel: 604-205-5058; *Fax:* 604-205-5075
Toll-Free: 800-663-8473
www.mcabc.org
www.linkedin.com/company/mechanical-contractors-association-of-bc
twitter.com/mcabc
www.flickr.com/photos/mcabc
Previous Name: Canadian Plumbing & Mechanical Contractors Association, BC Branch
Overview: A medium-sized provincial organization founded in 1905 overseen by Mechanical Contractors Association of Canada
Mission: To encourage, support & promote the advancement of the mechanical contracting industry; to provide leadership, assistance & training to members.
Chief Officer(s):
Dana Taylor, Executive Vice President
danat@mcabc.org
Staff Member(s): 6
Membership: 192; *Member Profile:* Licensed contractors in the mechanical trades; suppliers; manufacturers; distributors; servce providers
Activities: *Speaker Service:* Yes

Mechanical Contractors Association of Canada (MCAC) / Association des entrepreneurs en mécanique du Canada
#601, 280 Albert St., Ottawa ON K1P 5G8

Tel: 613-232-0492; *Fax:* 613-235-2793
mcac@mcac.ca
www.mcac.ca
Overview: A medium-sized national organization founded in 1895
Mission: To promote plumbing & mechanical contractors; to provide educational programs to foster improved management & productivity in mechanical contracting; to represent mechanical contractors to their various publics - governments, design authorities, labour.
Affliation(s): Council of Construction Trade Associations
Chief Officer(s):
Richard McKeagan, President
rick@mcac.ca
Membership: 800
Meetings/Conferences: • Mechanical Contractors Association of Canada (MCAC) 74th Annual National Conference 2015, November, 2015, Omni Ranco las Palmas Resort & Spa, Palm Springs, CA
Scope: National
• Mechanical Contractors Association of Canada (MCAC) 75th Annual National Conference 2016, 2016
Scope: National

Mechanical Contractors Association of Manitoba (MCAM)
#1, 860 Bradford St., Winnipeg MB R3H 0N5
Tel: 204-774-2404; *Fax:* 204-772-0233
mcam@mts.net
www.mca-mb.com
Overview: A medium-sized provincial organization founded in 1970 overseen by Mechanical Contractors Association of Canada
Mission: To continually improve mechanical industry standards while providing a high level of value performance & customer service for our members
Chief Officer(s):
Betty McInerney, Executive Director
bmcinerney@mts.net
Staff Member(s): 2
Membership: 77; *Member Profile:* Plumbing & heating contractors; *Committees:* Associate Members; Education; Finance; Government Liaison; Long Range Planning; MCAM Golf Tournament; Mechanical Service Contractors; Pipe Trades Pre-Employment Advisory; Social; Membership

Mechanical Contractors Association of New Brunswick / Association des entrepreneurs en mécanique du N.-B.
c/o Moncton Northeast Construction Association, 297 Collishaw St., Moncton NB E1C 9R2
Tel: 506-857-4128; *Fax:* 506-857-8861
bdixon@mneca.ca
www.mneca.ca
Also Known As: MCA New Brunswick Inc.
Previous Name: Plumbing & Mechanical Contractors Association of New Brunswick
Overview: A small provincial organization founded in 1976 overseen by Mechanical Contractors Association of Canada
Mission: To provide leadership & service to members; to act on behalf of members in labour relations matters, including collective bargaining; to advance & develop the industry, primarily in New Brunswick; to endeavour to improve legislation affecting the industry; to promote sound labour relations
Affliation(s): Canadian Construction Association
Chief Officer(s):
Bill Dixon, Executive Director
Finances: *Annual Operating Budget:* $100,000-$250,000; *Funding Sources:* Membership fees
Staff Member(s): 1
Membership: 28; *Fees:* $1,017 contractor/sub-contractor/supplier; $491.55 associate; *Member Profile:* Open to individual firms engaged in plumbing & related trades

Mechanical Contractors Association of Newfoundland & Labrador
PO Box 745, Stn. Mount Pearl, Mount Pearl NL A1N 2Y2
Tel: 709-747-5577; *Fax:* 709-368-5342
ddawe@nfld.net
Overview: A small provincial organization overseen by Mechanical Contractors Association of Canada
Chief Officer(s):
David Dawe, Executive Director

Mechanical Contractors Association of Nova Scotia
c/o Construction Association of Nova Scotia, #3, 260 Brownlow Ave., Dartmouth NS B3B 1V9
Tel: 902-468-2267; *Fax:* 902-468-2470
cans@cans.ns.ca
www.cans.ns.ca
Also Known As: Mechanical Contractors Section of The Construction Association of Nova Scotia (CANS)
Overview: A small provincial organization overseen by Mechanical Contractors Association of Canada
Chief Officer(s):
Donna Cruickshank, Manager

Mechanical Contractors Association of Ontario (MCAO)
#103, 10 Director Ct., Woodbridge ON L4L 7E8
Tel: 905-856-0342; *Fax:* 905-856-0385
mcao@mcao.org
www.mcao.org
Overview: A medium-sized provincial organization overseen by Mechanical Contractors Association of Canada
Chief Officer(s):
Steve Coleman, Executive Vice-President
steve@mcao.org

Mechanical Contractors Association of Ottawa / Association des entrepreneurs en mécanique d'Ottawa
#401, 39 Robertson Rd., Nepean ON K2H 8R2
Tel: 613-237-1491; *Fax:* 613-567-3177
mcaottawa@on.aibn.com
www.mcaottawa.ca
Overview: A small local organization founded in 1966
Mission: To advance the unionized trades in the mechanical contracting industry; To improve working conditions & safety laws for the mechanical trades; To promote improved relations between employer & employee
Chief Officer(s):
Robert Martel, General Manager
Membership: *Member Profile:* Trade contractors (sheet metal, pipefitting & plumbing); Manufacturers, suppliers, & dealers
Activities: Providing information & education programs to members; Conducting trade promotion activities; Upholding a code of ethics
Publications:
• Safety Matters
Type: Newsletter

Mechanical Contractors Association of Saskatchewan Inc. (MCAS)
Heritage Business Park, #105, 2750 Faithfull Ave., Saskatoon SK S7K 6M6
Tel: 306-664-2154; *Fax:* 306-653-7233
admin@mca-sask.com
www.mca-sask.com
Overview: A small provincial organization founded in 1919 overseen by Mechanical Contractors Association of Canada
Mission: To represent plumbing & heating contractors in relation to the construction industry, legislative departments of municipal & provincial government & other industry-related bodies.
Affliation(s): Mechanical Contractors Association of Canada
Chief Officer(s):
Ryan Tynning, President, 306-778-2830, Fax: 306-778-2833
Carolyn Bagnell, Executive Director
carolyn@mca-sask.com
Finances: *Funding Sources:* Membership fees
Staff Member(s): 3
Membership: 251; *Fees:* $450; *Member Profile:* Mechanical contractors

Mechanical Industrial Relations Association (MIRA)
#223, 3989 Henning Dr., Burnaby BC V5C 6P8
Tel: 604-205-5058; *Fax:* 604-205-5075
Toll-Free: 800-663-8473
www.mcabc.org/mira
Overview: A medium-sized provincial organization founded in 1960
Mission: To represent mechanical contractors; to achieve improved labour relations & productivity
Chief Officer(s):
Dana Taylor, Executive Vice President
3 volunteer(s)
Membership: 104 companies; *Committees:* Executive; Negotiating
Activities: *Library*

Mechanical Service Contractors of Canada (MSCC)
#601, 280 Albert St., Ottawa ON K1P 5G8
Tel: 613-232-0492; *Fax:* 613-235-2793
Toll-Free: 877-622-2668
daryl@mcac.ca
www.servicecontractor.ca
Overview: A medium-sized national organization overseen by Mechanical Contractors Association of Canada
Mission: The Mechanical Service Contractors of Canada (MSCC), a division of the Mechanical Contractors Association of Canada, is dedicated to mechanical service, repair and retrofit contractors.
Chief Officer(s):
Daryl Sharkey, Chief Operating Officer

Mechanical-Electrical Division of The Canadian Institute of Mining, Metallurgy & Petroleum *See* Maintenance, Engineering & Reliability (MER) Society

Médecins francophones du Canada
8355, boul Saint-Laurent, Montréal QC H2P 2Z6
Tél: 514-388-2228; *Téléc:* 514-388-5335
Ligne sans frais: 800-387-2228
www.medecinsfrancophones.ca
Nom précédent: Association des médecins de langue française du Canada
Aperçu: *Dimension:* moyenne; *Envergure:* nationale; fondée en 1902
Membre(s) du bureau directeur:
Conrad L. Pelletier, Président
Membre: 5 000

Médecins pour la survie mondiale (Canada) *See* Physicians for Global Survival (Canada)

Médecins pour un Canada sans fumée *See* Physicians for a Smoke-Free Canada

Médecins sans frontières Canada *See* Doctors without Borders Canada

Media Awareness Network *See* Media Smarts

Media Smarts
#120, 950 Gladstone Ave., Ottawa ON K1Y 3E6
Tel: 613-224-7721; *Fax:* 613-761-9024
Toll-Free: 800-896-3342
info@mediasmarts.ca
mediasmarts.ca
www.facebook.com/MediaSmarts
twitter.com/MediaSmarts
Previous Name: Media Awareness Network
Overview: A small national organization
Mission: To ensure children and youth possess the necessary critical thinking skills and tools to understand and safely and actively engage with media, and to be the leading Canadian provider of media education resources and awareness programs for educators, parents, children and youth.
Chief Officer(s):
Cathy Wing, Co-Executive Director
Jane Tallim, Co-Executive Director

Mediate BC Society
#177, 800 Hornby St., Vancouver BC V6Z 2C5
Tel: 604-684-1300; *Fax:* 604-684-1306
Toll-Free: 877-656-1300
info@mediatebc.com
www.mediatebc.com
Merged from: D.R. Innovation Society; B.C. Mediator Roster Society
Overview: A small provincial organization founded in 2010
Mission: To provide practical, accessible, & affordable dispute resolution choices
Affliation(s): Family Mediation Canada
Chief Officer(s):
Peter C.P. Behie, President
Kari D. Boyle, Executive Director
Finances: *Funding Sources:* Ministry of Attorney General; Law Foundation of British Columbia; Ministry of Children & Family Development; training fees; membership fees
Activities: Training; mediator roster

Médiation Familiale Canada *See* Family Mediation Canada

Mediation PEI Inc.
c/o Elizabeth S. Reagh, 17 West St., Charlottetown PE C1A 3S3
Tel: 902-892-7667; *Fax:* 902-368-8629
mediationpei.com
Overview: A small provincial organization founded in 1988

Affliation(s): Family Mediation Canada
Chief Officer(s):
Frank Bulger, Mediator
fpbulger@hotmail.com
Viola Evans-Murley, Mediator
vaevans-murley@ihis.org
Elizabeth S. Reagh, Q.C., Mediator
ereagh@eastlink.ca

Mediation Saskatchewan *See* Conflict Resolution Saskatchewan Inc.

Mediation Yukon Society
PO Box 31102, Whitehorse YT Y1A 5P7
e-mail: mediationyukon@gmail.com
mediationyukon.com
Overview: A small provincial organization
Mission: To encourage alternate methods for dispute resolution
Affiliation(s): Family Mediation Canada
Chief Officer(s):
Christiane Boisjoly, Mediator, 867-668-6794, Fax: 867-668-6795
boisjoly@northwestel.net

Medical Council of Canada (MCC) / Le Conseil médical du Canada (CMC)
PO Box 8234, Stn. T, #100, 2283 St. Laurent Blvd., Ottawa ON K1G 3H7
Tel: 613-521-6012; *Fax:* 613-521-9509
MCC_Admin@mcc.ca
www.mcc.ca
www.linkedin.com/company/medical-council-of-canada
www.facebook.com/MedicalCouncilOfCanada
twitter.com/MedCouncilCan
www.youtube.com/user/medicalcouncilcanada
Overview: A large national licensing organization founded in 1912
Mission: To establish & promote a qualification in medicine, known as the Licentiate of the Medical Council of Canada, such that the holders thereof are acceptable to medical licensing authorities for the issuance of a licence to practise medicine
Chief Officer(s):
Ian Bowmer, Executive Director
Finances: *Annual Operating Budget:* $3 Million-$5 Million; *Funding Sources:* Examination & related service fees
Staff Member(s): 40
Awards:
• Outstanding Achievement Award (Award)
• Louis Levasseur Award (Award)
• Medical Council of Canada Grants (Grant)
Eligibility: To interested faculty members, staff members or graduate students of Canadian medical faculties *Amount:* Up to $37,500
Meetings/Conferences: • 2015 Canadian Conference on Medical Education (CCME), April, 2015, Fairmont Vancouver & Hyatt Regency Vancouver, Vancouver, BC
Scope: National
Contact Information: www.mededconference.ca/ccme2015
• Medical Council of Canada's 2015 Annual General Meeting, 2015
Scope: National
Publications:
• The Echo
Type: Newsletter; *Frequency:* Bi-Annual

Medical Council of Prince Edward Island *See* College of Physicians & Surgeons of Prince Edward Island

Medical Devices Canada
#900, 405 The West Mall, Toronto ON M9C 5J1
Tel: 416-620-1915; *Fax:* 416-620-1595
Toll-Free: 866-586-3332
info@medec.org
www.medec.org
Also Known As: MEDEC
Previous Name: Canadian Association of Manufacturers of Medical Devices; Canada's Medical Device Technology Companies
Overview: A large national organization founded in 1973
Mission: To achieve a business & regulatory environment favourable to the growth of the industry & ensuring the availability of new cost-effective medical technologies that benefit Canadians
Chief Officer(s):
Peter Robertson, Chair
Brian Lewis, President & CEO
ceo@medec.org
Finances: *Annual Operating Budget:* $500,000-$1.5 Million; *Funding Sources:* Membership fees
Staff Member(s): 4
Membership: 100 manufacturers & distributors; *Fees:* Based on sales volume; *Committees:* Cardiac; Diabetes Care; Diagnostic; Vision Care; Orthopaedic; Medical Imaging; Wound Care; Ontario; Quebec; Western Canada; Federal Affairs; Human Resources; Policy & Issues; Procurement; Regulatory Affairs; Value of Technology; Code of Conduct
Activities: 3 Action Groups - Regulatory, Marketing & Health Care Policy; Re-use Task Force; Certificate Program for Medical/Surgical Supply Consultants (in conjunction with Humber College); *Library*
Awards:
• MEDEC Award for Medical Achievement (Award)
To recognize & encourage scientific excellence & reward contributions to health care by focusing national & international attention on Canadian medical achievements
Publications:
• Pulse
Type: Newsletter

Medical Group Management Association of Canada
c/o Associate Medical Centre, 5016 - 48th Ave., Taber AB T1G 1R8
Tel: 403-223-3525; *Fax:* 403-223-9020
info@mgmac.org
www.mgmac.org
Overview: A small national organization
Chief Officer(s):
Bernadette Kieley, President
Tom Malone, Treasurer

Medical Laboratory Science Association of Yukon (MLSAY)
c/o Laboratory, Whitehorse General Hospital, 5 Hospital Rd., Whitehorse YT Y1A 3H7
Overview: A medium-sized provincial organization overseen by Canadian Society for Medical Laboratory Science

Medical Services Association; CU&C Health Services Society *See* Canadian Association of Blue Cross Plans

Medical Society of Nova Scotia *See* Doctors Nova Scotia

Medical Society of Prince Edward Island (MSPEI)
2 Myrtle St., Stratford PE C1B 2W2
Tel: 902-368-7303; *Fax:* 902-566-3934
Toll-Free: 888-368-7303
www.mspei.org
twitter.com/MSPEI_Docs
Overview: A medium-sized provincial organization founded in 1855 overseen by Canadian Medical Association
Mission: To promote health & improvement of medical services; to prevent disease; to represent members at national bodies & government; to consider all matters concerning the professional welfare of members.
Chief Officer(s):
Kathy Maher, Director, Operations & Communications
kathy@mspei.org
Finances: *Funding Sources:* Membership dues
Staff Member(s): 4
Membership: 400 physicians; *Member Profile:* Individuals licensed to practise medicine in PEI; *Committees:* Executive; Medical Society; Finance; Nominating; Human Resources; Continuing Medical Education; Physician Support; Health Care & Promotion; Economics
Activities: *Internships:* Yes; *Library* by appointment

Medical Women's International Association (MWIA)
7555 Morley Dr., Burnaby BC V5E 3Y2
Tel: 604-439-8993; *Fax:* 604-439-8994
secretariat@mwia.net
www.mwia.net
Overview: A small international organization founded in 1919
Mission: To offer medical women the opportunity to meet so as to confer upon questions concerning the health & well-being of humanity; to overcome gender-related differences in health & healthcare between women & men, girls & boys throughout the world; to overcome gender-related inequalities in the medical profession; to promote health for all throughout the world with particular interest in women, health & development
Affiliation(s): Federation of Medical Women of Canada
Chief Officer(s):
Shelley Ross, Secretary General
Finances: *Funding Sources:* Membership dues & donations
Staff Member(s): 2
Membership: 20,000 in 46 national associations + 74 individual members in 45 countries; *Member Profile:* Fully-qualified women doctors; *Committees:* Finance; Ethics & Resolution; Scientific & Research

Medicine Hat & District Chamber of Commerce
413 - 6th Ave. SE, Medicine Hat AB T1A 2S7
Tel: 403-527-5214; *Fax:* 403-527-5182
info@medicinehatchamber.com
www.medicinehatchamber.com
www.linkedin.com/company/medicine-hat-and-district-chamber-of-commerce
www.facebook.com/MHChamber
twitter.com/mhdchamber
Overview: A medium-sized local organization founded in 1900
Mission: To promote a healthy business environment
Member of: Canadian Society of Association Executives; National Association of Member Development
Affiliation(s): Alberta Chamber of Commerce; Canadian Chamber of Commerce
Chief Officer(s):
Milvia Bauman, Chair
Jason Melhoff, Chair
Finances: *Annual Operating Budget:* $100,000-$250,000; *Funding Sources:* Trade shows; events
Staff Member(s): 5; 75 volunteer(s)
Membership: 900; *Fees:* Determined by number of full-time employees; *Member Profile:* Small 1-10 employess; Large 50+ employes; *Committees:* Policy & Advocacy; Membership; Governance
Activities: Trade shows; tourism; President's Ball; membership networking; speaking series; *Speaker Service:* Yes
Awards:
• Hospitality/Tourism Award (Award)
• Business of the Year Award (Award)
• Industry of the Year Award (Award)
• Citizen of the Year Award (Award)
• Keeper of the Gates Award (Award)
• Silver Spade Award (Award)
• Athlete of the Year Award (Award)

Medicine Hat & District Food Bank
532 South Railway St. SE, Medicine Hat AB T1A 2V6
Tel: 403-528-4313; *Fax:* 403-528-4381
www.mhfoodbank.com
Overview: A medium-sized local charitable organization overseen by Alberta Food Bank Network Association
Member of: Food Banks Canada
Chief Officer(s):
Jim Turner, Executive Director
jim_mhfbank@telus.net

Medicine Hat Coin & Stamp Club
c/o Ron Schmidt, #324, 2800 - 13 Ave. SE, Medicine Hat AB T1A 3P9
Tel: 403-526-5158
medhatcsc@live.com
www.mhcasc.ca
Overview: A small local organization
Chief Officer(s):
Ron Schmidt, Secretary

Medicine Hat Construction Association
914 - 16 St. SW, Medicine Hat AB T1A 8A4
Tel: 403-527-9700; *Fax:* 403-526-0520
mhca@telusplanet.net
www.telusplanet.net/public/mhca
Overview: A small local charitable organization founded in 1955 overseen by Canadian Construction Association
Mission: To represent the interests of employees working in the construction industry.
Member of: Alberta Construction Association
Chief Officer(s):
Barry Bitz, President
barryb@swmw.net
Lori Breum, Executive Director
Staff Member(s): 2
Membership: 135; *Fees:* $1,150 full member; $600 associate
Activities: *Library* Open to public

Medicine Hat Fibre Arts Society
c/o Cultural Centre, Medicine Hat College, 299 College Dr. SE, Medicine Hat AB T1A 3Y6
Tel: 403-529-1174
Overview: A small local organization
Affiliation(s): Handweavers, Spinners & Dyers of Alberta
Chief Officer(s):

Sharon Regehr, Vice-President

Medicine Hat Fish & Game Association

PO Box 883, Medicine Hat AB T1A 7G8
Tel: 403-526-9261
mhfga1@gmail.com
www.mhfishandgame.com
Overview: A small local organization founded in 1973
Member of: Alberta Fish & Game Association
Chief Officer(s):
Glen Heather, President
Finances: *Annual Operating Budget:* Less than $50,000; *Funding Sources:* Donations; fundraising
14 volunteer(s)
Membership: 250+; *Fees:* $25; *Committees:* Fish; Big Game; Membership; Habitat; Bird; Fundraising; Environment
Activities: Stocking fish; releasing pheasants; planting shelterbelt trees & securing habitat; *Awareness Events:* Sportsmen's Trade Show, Jan.

Medicine Hat Police Association / Association des policiers de Medicine Hat

884 - 2 St. SE, Medicine Hat AB T1A 8H2
Tel: 403-529-8400
www.mhpoliceassociation.com
twitter.com/medhatpa
Overview: A small local organization
Chief Officer(s):
Brent Secondiak, President

Medicine Hat Real Estate Board Co-operative Ltd.

403 - 4 St. SE, Medicine Hat AB T1A 0K5
Tel: 403-526-2879; *Fax:* 403-526-0307
www.mhreb.ca
Overview: A small local organization overseen by Alberta Real Estate Association
Member of: Alberta Real Estate Association; The Canadian Real Estate Association
Chief Officer(s):
Murray Schlenker, President
Randeen Bray, Executive Officer
Membership: 140

Medicine Hat Rock & Lapidary Club

826 - 11th St. SE, Medicine Hat AB T1A 1T7
Tel: 403-526-8113
www.afrc.ca/medicinehat.htm
Overview: A small local charitable organization founded in 1989
Member of: Alberta Federation of Rock Clubs; Gem & Mineral Federation of Canada
Chief Officer(s):
Marilyn Jetyter, President
Finances: *Funding Sources:* Membership fees; Casino revenues
Membership: *Fees:* $20 individual; $25 family or couple
Activities: Workshops & training seminars

Medicine Hat Soccer Association

59 Tweed Ave. NW, Medicine Hat AB T1A 6W3
Tel: 403-529-6931
mhsa@telusplanet.net
www.medicinehatsoccer.com
www.facebook.com/128594980557868
Overview: A small local organization founded in 1971 overseen by Alberta Soccer Association
Member of: Alberta Soccer Association
Chief Officer(s):
Jim Loughlin, District Head Coach, 403-866-1289
Nanette Newton, Officer Manager, 403-529-6931
Membership: 2,700

Medicine Hat Society for the Prevention of Cruelty to Animals (MHSPCA)

55 Southwest Dr. SW, Medicine Hat AB T1A 8E8
Tel: 403-526-7722; *Fax:* 403-504-5740
contact@medhatspca.ca
www.medhatspca.ca
Also Known As: Medicine Hat SPCA
Overview: A small local charitable organization founded in 1979
Mission: To provide protective care for sick, injured, homeless & unwanted animals; to promote humane attitudes & responsible pet ownership; to promote wildlife conservation
Member of: Canadian Federation of Humane Societies
Affliation(s): Alberta SPCA
Finances: *Funding Sources:* Bingos; raffles; membership dues; coin banks; dog jog; bequests; donations
Activities: Open house; mall displays; garage sale; dog jogs; Christmas Party for the Animals

Medico-Legal Society of Toronto

#1700, 438 University Ave., Toronto ON M5G 2L9
Tel: 416-523-4469; *Fax:* 416-585-7860
mlst@mlst.ca
www.mlst.ca
ca.linkedin.com/pub/medico-legal-society-of-toronto/62/747/8a3
www.facebook.com/pages/Medico-Legal-Society-of-Toronto/220520598037210
twitter.com/MLSTExDir
Overview: A small local organization founded in 1950
Mission: To promote the medical & legal professions as well as information involving those subjects.
Chief Officer(s):
Clare Samworth, Executive Director
Phillipa Samworth, President
Membership: *Fees:* $45 student/senior; $260 full; *Committees:* Submissions; Outreach; Membership; Program

Meetings & Conventions Prince Edward Island (MCPEI)

9 Queen St., Charlottetown PE C1A 4A2
Tel: 902-629-1655
Toll-Free: 855-368-3688
info@peimc.com
www.meetingsandconventionspei.com
www.facebook.com/meetinpei
twitter.com/MeetInPEI
www.youtube.com/user/MeetOnPEI;
www.flickr.com/photos/64609093@N05
Previous Name: Prince Edward Island Convention Partnership; Meetings Prince Edward Island; Prince Edward Island Convention Bureau
Overview: A medium-sized provincial organization founded in 1987
Mission: To promote & confirm PEI as the destination for meetings, conferences & special events
Affliation(s): Canadian Society of Professional Event Planners; Canadian Society of Association Executives; Prince Edward Island Business Women's Association; Tourism Industry Association of Prince Edward Island; Meeting Professionals International; Religious Conference Management Association; Destination Management Association of Canada
Chief Officer(s):
Michael Matthews, Executive Director
mmatthews@peimc.com
Jo-Ann Thomsen, Director, Business Development, 902-368-2191
jthomsen@peimc.com
Finances: *Funding Sources:* Government funding
Staff Member(s): 10
Membership: *Fees:* Schedule available; *Member Profile:* Meetings & conventions industry

Meewasin Valley Authority (MVA)

402 - 3rd Ave. South, Saskatoon SK S7K 3G5
Tel: 306-665-6887; *Fax:* 306-665-6117
meewasin@meewasin.com
www.meewasin.com
www.facebook.com/Meewasin
twitter.com/meewasin
Overview: A small local organization founded in 1979
Mission: To ensure a healthy & vibrant river valley with a balance between human use & conservation by: providing leadership in the management of its resources; promoting understanding, conservation & beneficial use of the valley; undertaking programs & projects in river valley development & conservation for the benefit of present & future generations
Chief Officer(s):
Lloyd Isaak, CEO
Finances: *Funding Sources:* Donations; Government of Saskatchewan; City of Saskatoon; University of Saskatchewan
Staff Member(s): 6
Membership: *Committees:* Development Review; Resource Conservation Advisory; Design Advisory; Education Advisory; Fund Development
Activities: Clean-up Campaign; Stewardship Program; Dragon Boat Races

MEFM Myalgic Encephalomyelitis & Fibromyalgia Society of British Columbia

PO Box 462, 916 West Broadway Ave., Vancouver BC V5Z 1K7
Tel: 604-878-7707
Toll-Free: 888-353-6322
info@mefm.bc.ca
www.mefm.bc.ca
Merged from: British Columbia Fibromyalgia Society; Myalgic Encephalomyelitis Society of British Columbia
Overview: A medium-sized provincial organization
Mission: To provide support to people with (ME) Myalgic Encephalomyelitis, (Chronic Fatique Syndrome) & (FM) Fibromyalgia & their families; to help educate physicians, paramedical professionals, family members & the community at large regarding ME & FM; to promote research aimed at improving treatment & ultimately finding a cure; to help to encourage early diagnosis & effective treatment
Chief Officer(s):
Wendy Snelgrove, President
Membership: 600; *Fees:* $25

Megantic County Historical Society

#701, 6550 Sherbrooke St. West, Montréal QC H4R 1N6
Tel: 514-489-8354
Other Communication: Alt Phone: 418-424-3258
Overview: A small local organization founded in 1971
Chief Officer(s):
Sheila Allan, President

Melfort & District Chamber of Commerce

PO Box 2002, 102 Spruce Haven Rd., Melfort SK S0E 1A0
Tel: 306-752-4636; *Fax:* 306-752-9505
melfortchamber@sasktel.net
www.melfortchamber.com
Overview: A small local organization founded in 1907
Mission: To identify & fulfill development needs through communication, implementation of strategies, & promotion, for the growth of the business community in an accountable & equitable manner to our membership
Member of: Saskatchewan Chamber of Commerce; CANAM International Highway Association
Chief Officer(s):
Grant Schutte, President
Nicole Gagné, Executive Director
Finances: *Annual Operating Budget:* $50,000-$100,000
Staff Member(s): 3; 50 volunteer(s)
Membership: 173; *Fees:* $75-310
Activities: *Awareness Events:* Northern Lights Showcase, Oct.; *Rents Mailing List:* Yes

Melfort Agricultural Society

PO Box 816, Melfort SK S0E 1A0
Tel: 306-752-2240; *Fax:* 306-752-2240
info@melfortex.com
www.melfortex.com
Overview: A small local charitable organization founded in 1906
Mission: To improve agriculture & the quality of life in the community by educating members & the community; to provide a community forum for discussing agricultural issues; to foster community development & community spirit; to help provide markets for Saskatchewan products; to encourage conservation of natural resources, including soil conservation, reforestation, rural & urban beautification
Member of: Saskatchewan Association of Agricultural Societies & Exhibitions; Canadian Association of Fairs & Exhibitions
Chief Officer(s):
Christy Vodicka, President
Finances: *Annual Operating Budget:* $100,000-$250,000; *Funding Sources:* Bingo; flea markets; exhibition; grants
Staff Member(s): 1; 101 volunteer(s)
Membership: 101; *Fees:* $5

Melfort Real Estate Board

PO Box 3157, Melfort SK S0E 1A0
Tel: 306-752-5751; *Fax:* 306-752-5754
Overview: A small local organization overseen by Saskatchewan Real Estate Association
Member of: The Canadian Real Estate Association
Chief Officer(s):
Derwood Dodds, President
derwooddodds@royallepage.ca

Melita & District Chamber of Commerce

PO Box 666, Melita MB R0M 1L0
Tel: 204-522-2490
www.melitamb.ca
Overview: A small local organization founded in 1902
Mission: To promote tourism & trade in the town of Melita
Chief Officer(s):
Bill Warren, President, 204-522-5361
wjwarren@hotmail.com

Melville & District Agri-Park Association Inc.
PO Box 2678, Melville SK S0A 2P0
Tel: 306-728-5277; *Fax:* 306-728-4544
agripark@sasktel.net
www.melvilleagripark.com
Also Known As: Melville Agri-Park
Overview: A small local organization founded in 1981
Mission: To promote agriculture events in Melville & surrounding district
Member of: Saskatchewan Association of Agricultural Societies & Exhibitions; Canadian Association of Exhibitions; Saskatchewan Horse Federation
Chief Officer(s):
Jamie D. McDonald, Manager
Finances: *Annual Operating Budget:* $50,000-$100,000
Staff Member(s): 1; 100 volunteer(s)
Membership: 200 senior/lifetime; *Fees:* $100; *Committees:* 4-H Organization; Horse Show; Showstoppers ATV; Archery Club; Homecrafts; Horse Racing; Rodeo; Cattle, Team Roping; Barrel Racing
Activities: *Internships:* Yes; *Rents Mailing List:* Yes

Melville & District Chamber of Commerce
PO Box 429, 430 Main St., Melville SK S0A 2P0
Tel: 306-728-4177
melvillechamber@sasktel.net
www.melvillechamber.com
Overview: A small local charitable organization founded in 1988
Mission: To promote business for Melville & district
Chief Officer(s):
Ron Walton, Executive Director
Terry Sieffert, President, 306-728-5425
terry.sieffert@horizoncu.ca
Finances: *Annual Operating Budget:* Less than $50,000; *Funding Sources:* City grants; memberships; proceeds from Bingo
Staff Member(s): 1; 20 volunteer(s)
Membership: 60; *Committees:* Tourism

Melville Arts Council
PO Box 309, 800 Prince Edward St., Melville SK S0A 2P0
Tel: 306-728-4494
mcworks@accesscomm.ca
www.melvillecommunityworks.ca
www.facebook.com/MelvilleCommunityWorks
Also Known As: Melville Community Works
Overview: A small local charitable organization founded in 2001
Mission: To foster & promote opportunities for Melville & district citizens to enjoy & participate in cultural & artistic activities; to stimulate & encourage development of cultural projects & activities; to make a available high standard of performing & visual arts events; to encourage municipal government, private corporations & individuals to participate & assist in growth, development & appreciation of the arts
Member of: Organization of Saskatchewan Arts Councils
Chief Officer(s):
Lorie Dietz-Rathgeber, Administrator
Finances: *Annual Operating Budget:* $50,000-$100,000
Staff Member(s): 4; 12 volunteer(s)
Membership: 12 senior + 100 subscribers; *Fees:* $20; *Member Profile:* Interest in performing &/or visual arts; willing volunteer &/or leader; *Committees:* Membership; Volunteer; Reception
Activities: *Internships:* Yes

Melville Dance Association
PO Box 1101, Melville SK S0A 2P0
www.melvilledance.citymax.com
www.facebook.com/pages/Melville-Dance-Association/135585143159414
Overview: A small local organization founded in 1985
Mission: To encourage friendships & self confidence in our youth by promoting the art of dance through various styles & music
Member of: Multicultural Council of Saskatchewan; Dance Saskatchewan Inc.
Chief Officer(s):
Shannon Bell, President
4bells@sasktel.net
Membership: *Member Profile:* Students 4-18
Activities: Annual dance recital; ballet examinations through Royal Academy of Dance; *Rents Mailing List:* Yes

Memberane Structures Manufacturers Association Inc. (MSMA)
e-mail: admin@msma.ca
www.msma.ca
Overview: A small national organization
Mission: To serve as an information resource for members of the membrane structures industry; to represent the industry's interests & concerns; to promote the use & growth of membrane structures
Chief Officer(s):
Ron Bryant, President
Bill Heemskerk, Vice-President
Patrice Harnois, Secretary
Carey Ewanik, Treasurer
Jerome Bosch, Administrator
Membership: 10; *Fees:* Schedule available; *Committees:* Industry Standards; Membership; Membrane Standards
Activities: Insurance; information for members

Memorial Society of British Columbia (MSBC)
#205, 640 West Broadway, Vancouver BC V5Z 1G4
Tel: 604-733-7705; *Fax:* 604-733-7730
Toll-Free: 888-816-5902
mail@memsoc.org
www.memorialsocietybc.org
www.facebook.com/MemorialSocietyBC
Overview: A large provincial organization founded in 1956
Mission: To promote simple, dignified funeral rites through education; to assist members in pre-recording the kind of funeral arrangements preferred through a written record; to ensure availability of suitable low-cost funeral arrangements through written contracts with selected funeral homes
Member of: Better Business Bureau
Chief Officer(s):
Barbara Beach, President
Nicole Renwick, Executive Director
Finances: *Annual Operating Budget:* $250,000-$500,000; *Funding Sources:* Membership fees + $35 records fee at time of death
Staff Member(s): 3; 30 volunteer(s)
Membership: 200,000; *Fees:* $40 Individual lifetime; $50 Individual sustaining; *Member Profile:* Individuals join by completing an application & paying $20 lifetime membership fee; issued arrangement form where he/she records his/her wishes regarding funeral arrangements, & some vital statistic information necessary for the registration of the death; *Committees:* Green Burial
Activities: *Speaker Service:* Yes

Memorial Society of Calgary *See* Calgary Co-operative Memorial Society

Memorial Society of Edmonton & District (MSED)
#1108, 10235 - 124 St., Edmonton AB T5N 1P9
Tel: 780-944-0196; *Fax:* 780-944-0791
info@memorialsocietyedmonton.ca
www.memorialsocietyedmonton.ca
Overview: A small local charitable organization founded in 1958
Chief Officer(s):
Yvonne Racine, Board President
Finances: *Annual Operating Budget:* Less than $50,000
Staff Member(s): 1; 10 volunteer(s)
Membership: 8; *Fees:* $25; *Member Profile:* General public
Activities: Pre-planning simple, low-cost funeral arrangements; public consumer education

Memorial Society of Kitchener-Waterloo & Area
PO Box 23032, 537 Frederick St., Kitchener ON N2B 3V1
Tel: 519-662-6576
kwmemsoc@gmail.com
www.kwmemsoc.ca
Also Known As: KW Memorial Society; Kitchener-Waterloo Memorial Society
Overview: A small local organization founded in 1971
Mission: To promote & ensure affordable funerals; to monitor practices & performances of funeral providers; to promote environmentally sound disposal of human remains
Member of: Federation of Ontario Memorial Societies - Funeral Consumers Alliance
Chief Officer(s):
Allan Grose, President
Membership: *Fees:* $30
Publications:
• Perspective [a publication of the Memorial Society of Kitchener-Waterloo & Area]
Type: Newsletter; *Frequency:* Annual

Memorial Society of London
PO Box 1729, London ON N6A 5H9
Tel: 519-649-1014
whunter@uwo.ca
www.londonmemorialsociety.com
Previous Name: London Memorial Society; Memorial & Funeral Advisory Society of London
Overview: A small local organization founded in 1963
Member of: Federation of Ontario Memorial Societies - Funeral Consumers Alliance
Chief Officer(s):
Don McCuaig, Chair
joyhyde@rogers.com
Amelia Wehlau, Secretary
Finances: *Annual Operating Budget:* Less than $50,000; *Funding Sources:* Member donations
Staff Member(s): 7; 7 volunteer(s)
Membership: 850; *Fees:* $20/member; *Member Profile:* Those interested in preplanning, simplicity & dignity; *Committees:* Outreach; Liaison; Visitation; Research
Activities: Educational presentations; information service; *Speaker Service:* Yes

Memorial Society of Northern Ontario (MSNO)
PO Box 1355, Stn. B, Sudbury ON P3E 5K4
Tel: 705-671-1229
Toll-Free: 866-203-5139
msnont@gmail.com
www.memorialsociety.ca
Overview: A small local organization founded in 1979
Mission: To promote simple, dignified funerals at moderate cost; to educate the public with respect to funeral arrangements; to advise members concerning funeral arrangements & funeral planning
Member of: Federation of Ontario Memorial Societies - Funeral Consumers Alliance
Chief Officer(s):
Robin Bolton
Finances: *Annual Operating Budget:* Less than $50,000
25 volunteer(s)
Membership: 2,300; *Fees:* $40; *Committees:* Executive; Promotion; Membership; Nominations
Activities: Board & committee meeting; public presentations; media promotions; *Speaker Service:* Yes
Publications:
• Memorial Society of Northern Ontario Newsletter
Type: Newsletter

Memorial Society of Red Deer & District
3030 - 55 St., Red Deer AB T4P 3S6
Tel: 403-340-3898
info@memorialsocietyrd.ca
www.memorialsocietyrd.ca
Overview: A small local charitable organization founded in 1978
Mission: To provide pre-planned, dignified, reasonably priced funerals to our members & to offer personal assistance to their families
Affliation(s): Continental Association of Funeral & Memorial Societies, Inc.
Finances: *Funding Sources:* Membership fees; donations; record fees
Membership: 2,500; *Fees:* $25

Memorial Society of Saskatchewan *See* Funeral Advisory & Memorial Society of Saskatchewan

Memorial Society of Thunder Bay
316 Talbot St., Thunder Bay ON P7A 1J7
Tel: 807-683-3051
www.myfuneralplan.org/thunderbay.htm
Overview: A small local organization founded in 1972
Mission: To create a climate of public opinion in which simplicity, dignity & moderate expense in funerals are acceptable; to encourage individuals & families, in consultation with their clergy or other advisors, to give prior thought to funeral arrangements; to provide consultative services concerning funeral arrangements & costs, cremation & bequeathals; to encourage memorials which serve the living while honouring the dead (such as scholarships, bursaries, donations to medical research, or to a charity in which the deceased was interested); to enlist the understanding & cooperation of funeral directors
Member of: Federation of Ontario Memorial Societies - Funeral Consumers Alliance
Affliation(s): Funeral & Memorial Societies of America
Chief Officer(s):
Pat Zimsak, Executive Secretary
Peter Cloke, President
Finances: *Annual Operating Budget:* Less than $50,000; *Funding Sources:* Membership dues; donations
12 volunteer(s)
Membership: 2,700 individual; *Fees:* $20 individual
Activities: *Speaker Service:* Yes

Memorial Society of Windsor & District
PO Box 481, Windsor ON N9A 6M6
Tel: 519-969-6767
memsoc2@sympatico.ca
www3.sympatico.ca/stanmcdo/memsoc
Overview: A small local organization founded in 1973
Mission: To encourage making simple & dignified funeral arrangements, burials, cremations & organ/whole body donations
Member of: Federation of Ontario Memorial Societies - Funeral Consumers Alliance
Chief Officer(s):
Stan McDowall, Contact, 519-969-6767
Ron Ewing, Contact, 519-945-1901
Finances: *Annual Operating Budget:* Less than $50,000; *Funding Sources:* Fees & donations
10 volunteer(s)
Membership: 980 individual; *Fees:* $10 life
Activities: *Speaker Service:* Yes

Men for Change (M4C)
PO Box 33005, Halifax NS B3L 4T6
Tel: 902-492-4104
www.chebucto.ns.ca/CommunitySupport/Men4Change
Overview: A small local organization
Mission: To promote positive masculinity; To end sexism & violence

Meningitis Research Foundation of Canada
PO Box 28015, Stn. Parkdale, Waterloo ON N2L 6J8
Tel: 519-664-0244
Toll-Free: 800-643-1303
fund@meningitis.ca
www.meningitis.ca
www.facebook.com/175290785814598
twitter.com/meningitisCA
Overview: A small national charitable organization
Mission: To raise funds to promote education & research in order to prevent death & disability from meningitis & other infections of the central nervous system; to provide support & education to patients & their families affected by meningitis; to increase public awareness of meningitis; to promote better understanding of the disease among healthcare professionals; to provide funds for research into improved diagnosis, treatment, & prevention of meningitis

Mennonite Brethren Mission & Service International *See* MB Mission

Mennonite Central Committee Canada (MCCC)
134 Plaza Dr., Winnipeg MB
Tel: 204-261-6381; *Fax:* 204-269-9875
Toll-Free: 888-622-6337
canada@mennonitecc.ca
mcccanada.ca
www.facebook.com/289561555567
twitter.com/MCCCan
Overview: A large national charitable organization founded in 1920
Mission: To operate as a relief & development service agency; To promote relief, development, & peace
Member of: Mennonite Central Committee
Chief Officer(s):
Don Peters, Executive Director
Publications:
• A Common Place
Type: Magazine; *Frequency:* Quarterly

Mennonite Central Committee Supportive Care Services Society *See* Communitas Supportive Care Society

Mennonite Church Canada (MC Canada)
600 Shaftesbury Blvd., Winnipeg MB R3P 0M4
Tel: 204-888-6781; *Fax:* 204-831-5675
Toll-Free: 866-888-6785
office@mennonitechurch.ca
www.mennonitechurch.ca
Also Known As: Conference of Mennonites in Canada
Overview: A medium-sized national charitable organization founded in 1903
Mission: To form a people of God; To become a global church; To grow leaders
Chief Officer(s):
Willard Metzger, General Secretary
Finances: *Funding Sources:* Donations
Staff Member(s): 40
Membership: 31,000 baptized believers in 225 congregations & 5 area conferences
Activities: *Library:* Resource Centre

Mennonite Church Alberta
Box 43037, RPO Deer Valley, Calgary AB T2J 7A7
Tel: 403-275-6935; *Fax:* 403-275-3711
info@mennonitechurch.ab.ca
www.mennonitechurch.ab.ca
Chief Officer(s):
Linden Willms, Moderator

Mennonite Church British Columbia
#305, 32025 George Ferguson Way, Abbotsford BC V2T 2K7
Tel: 604-850-6658; *Fax:* 604-850-9372
admin@mcbc.ca
www.mcbc.ca
Chief Officer(s):
Garry Janzen, Executive Minister, 778-242-1185
garryjanzen@mcbc.ca

Mennonite Church Eastern Canada
4489 King St. East, Kitchener ON N2P 2G2
Tel: 519-650-3806; *Fax:* 519-650-3947
Toll-Free: 800-206-9356
mcec@mcec.ca
www.mcec.ca
Chief Officer(s):
David Martin, Executive Minister
dmartin@mcec.ca

Mennonite Church Manitoba
#200, 600 Shaftesbury Blvd., Winnipeg MB R3P 2J1
Tel: 204-896-1616; *Fax:* 204-832-7804
office@mennochurch.mb.ca
www.mennochurch.mb.ca
Mission: Their vision is to be a community of congregrations unified in Jesus Christ, living a biblical Anabaptist faith, together presenting Jesus Christ to the world. Their mission is to resource and empower each other, and to facilitate spiritual growth, service, and evangelism.
Member of: Mennonite Church Canada
Chief Officer(s):
Ken Warkentin, Executive Director
kwarkentin@mennochurch.mb.ca

Mennonite Church Saskatchewan
#101A, 301 Pawka Place, Saskatoon SK S7L 6A3
Tel: 306-249-4844; *Fax:* 306-249-4441
mcsask@mcsask.ca
www.mcsask.ca
Chief Officer(s):
Henry Block, Moderator

Mennonite Economic Development Associates Canada
#I-106, 155 Frobisher Dr., Waterloo ON N2V 2E1
Tel: 519-725-1633; *Fax:* 519-725-9083
Toll-Free: 800-665-7026
meda@meda.org
www.meda.org
Also Known As: MEDA Canada
Overview: A medium-sized international charitable organization founded in 1953 overseen by Manitoba Council for International Cooperation
Mission: To be committed to the nurture & expression of Christian faith in a business setting; To enable members to integrate biblical values & business principles in their daily lives; To address the needs of the disadvantaged through programs of economic development
Chief Officer(s):
Allan Sauder, President
Finances: *Annual Operating Budget:* $1.5 Million-$3 Million
Membership: 3,000 Canada & US
Activities: *Library* by appointment
Publications:
• The Marketplace
Type: Magazine; *Frequency:* Bimonthly; *Editor:* Wally Kroeker
ISSN: 0199-7130

Mennonite Foundation of Canada (MFC)
#12, 1325 Markham Rd., Winnipeg MB R3T 4J6
Tel: 204-488-1985; *Fax:* 204-488-1986
Toll-Free: 800-772-3257
contact@mennofoundation.ca
www.mennofoundation.ca
Overview: A medium-sized national charitable organization founded in 1974
Mission: The Foundation was established to accumulate, manage & distribute financial resources exclusively for charitable purposes, as a means, for example, of supporting the Mennonite Community by providing loans to churches & related organizations. Resources provide stewardship education & service from an Anabaptist perspective. It is a registered charity, BN: 129253308RR0001.
Affliation(s): Mennonite Church Canada; Evangelical Mennonite Mission Conference; Mennonite Church Eastern Canada; Northwest Mennonite Conference; Evangelical Mennonite Conference; Chortitzer Mennonite Conference; Evangelical Missionary Church of Canada
Chief Officer(s):
Lloyd Plett, Chair
Darren Pries-Klassen, Executive Director, 905-934-0484 Ext. 23, Fax: 905-935-0153
dpklassen@mennofoundation.ca
Milly Siderius, Director, Stewardship Services
msiderius@mennofoundation.ca
Finances: *Annual Operating Budget:* $500,000-$1.5 Million
Staff Member(s): 12
Membership: 24; *Member Profile:* Representatives of 7 conferences
Activities: *Speaker Service:* Yes; *Library* Open to public

Abbotsford Office
#102, 2825 Clearbrook Rd., Abbotsford BC V2T 6S3
Tel: 604-850-9613; *Fax:* 604-859-5574
Toll-Free: 888-212-8608
mfcabbot@mennofoundation.ca
Chief Officer(s):
Arnie Friesen, Stewardship Consultant
afriesen@mennofoundation.ca

Calgary Office
#220, 2946 - 32 St. NE, Calgary AB T1Y 6J7
Tel: 403-717-0331; *Fax:* 403-717-0335
Toll-Free: 800-772-3257
mfccgy@mennofoundation.ca
Chief Officer(s):
Kevin Davidson, Stewardship Consultant
kdavidson@mennofoundation.ca

Kitchener Office
50 Kent Ave., Kitchener ON N2G 3R1
Tel: 519-745-7821; *Fax:* 519-745-8940
Toll-Free: 888-212-7759
mfceast@mennofoundation.ca
Chief Officer(s):
Mike Strathdee, Stewardship Consultant
mstrathdee@mennofoundation.ca

St Catharines Office
#4, 595 Carlton St., St Catharines ON L2M 4Y2
Tel: 905-934-0484; *Fax:* 905-935-0153
Toll-Free: 800-772-3257
mfcniagara@mennofoundation.ca
Chief Officer(s):
Donald Brooker, Stewardship Consultant
dbrooker@mennofoundation.ca

Mennonite Historical Society of Canada (MHSC)
c/o La Société Mennonite d'histoire du Québec, 1326, rue St-Zotique est, Montréal ON H2G 1G5
e-mail: info@mhsc.ca
www.mhsc.ca
Overview: A small local organization
Mission: To produce publications about Mennonite history & to coordinate provincial historical & archival societies
Chief Officer(s):
Lucille Marr, President

Mensa Canada Society / La Société Mensa Canada
PO Box 1570, Kingston ON K7L 5C8
Tel: 613-547-0824; *Fax:* 613-531-0626
mensa@eventsmgt.com
www.canada.mensa.org
Also Known As: The High IQ Society
Overview: A medium-sized national organization founded in 1967
Mission: To identify & foster human intelligence for the benefit of humanity; To encourage research; To provide an intellectual & social environment for members
Member of: Mensa International Inc.
Chief Officer(s):
Millie Norry, President
Finances: *Funding Sources:* Membership dues
Membership: *Fees:* $60 individual; $38 student; $82 family; *Member Profile:* Individuals who have shown that they have an IQ higher than 98% of the world's population

Activities: Offering networking opportunities & international contacts; Presenting annual scholarships; Providing assistance for gifted children; Administering the Mensa Supervised Entrance Examination

Mental Illness Foundation *Voir* Fondation des maladies mentales

Mercaz-Canada

#508, 1000 Finch Ave. West, Toronto ON M3J 2V5
Tel: 416-667-1717
Toll-Free: 866-357-3384
info@mercaz.ca
www.mercaz.ca
Also Known As: Movement to Reaffirm Conservative Zionism
Overview: A medium-sized international organization founded in 1994
Mission: To support the State of Israel as a democratic & pluralistic national home for all Jews, secure & at peace with its Arab neighbours, committed to protecting the rights of all its citizens & supporting all streams of Jewish practices; in Canada, to promote Aliyah, trips to Israel & local Zionist programming
Member of: Canadian Zionist Federation; World Zionist Organization; Mercaz-Olami
Affliation(s): United Synagogues of Conservative Judaism
Chief Officer(s):
Rabbi Jennifer Gorman, Executive Director
Marion Mayman, President
Philip Scheim, Vice President
Staff Member(s): 3
Membership: *Fees:* $9 adult

Mères avec pouvoir (MAP)

2015A, rue Fullum, Montréal QC H2K 3N5
Tél: 514-282-1882
info@mapmontreal.org
www.mapmontreal.org
www.facebook.com/meresavecpouvoir
www.youtube.com/user/mapmontreal
Aperçu: *Dimension:* petite; *Envergure:* locale; fondée en 2001
Mission: Pour aider les mères célibataires à trouver un travail ou poursuivre leurs études grâce à des logements abordables et de garderie
Affliation(s): Inter-lodge; CPE du Carrefour
Membre: *Critères d'admissibilite:* Femmes qui habitent à Montréal, qui sont monoparentale avec un enfant de la naissance à cinq ans et avoir un manumim de deux enfants, qui ont la garde pour plus de 50% du temps, qui terminent leurs études ou qui travaillent ou cherchent du travail

Les mères contre l'alcool auvolant *See* MADD Canada

Merit Canada

Toll-Free: 877-416-3748
info@meritcanada.ca
meritcanada.ca
Overview: A small national organization founded in 2008
Mission: A united national voice for eight different provincial Open Shop construction associations.
Finances: *Annual Operating Budget:* Less than $50,000
Staff Member(s): 1
Membership: *Member Profile:* Construction contractors
Activities: Training and education programs

Merit Contractors Association of Alberta

#103, 13025 St. Albert Trail, Edmonton AB T5L 4H5
Tel: 780-455-5999; *Fax:* 780-455-2109
Toll-Free: 888-816-9991
meritedm@meritalberta.com
www.meritalberta.com
www.facebook.com/meritalberta
twitter.com/merit_ab
www.youtube.com/user/meritalberta
Overview: A small provincial organization overseen by Merit Canada
Mission: Merit Contractors Association provides the construction industry with benefits and benefit programs, industry specific training programs, employee education support, human resource tools and advocacy specifically related to open shop contractors.
Chief Officer(s):
Stephen Kushner, President
Membership: *Member Profile:* Construction contractors

Merit Contractors Association of Manitoba

#112, 131 Provencher Blvd., Winnipeg MB R2H 0G2
Tel: 204-888-6202; *Fax:* 204-888-6204
info@meritmb.com
www.meritmb.com
Overview: A small provincial organization founded in 1994 overseen by Merit Canada
Chief Officer(s):
Harvey Millier, Executive Director
hmiller@meritmb.com
Finances: *Annual Operating Budget:* Less than $50,000
Staff Member(s): 1
Membership: 83; *Member Profile:* Construction contractors

Merit Contractors Association of Newfoundland & Labrador

#213, 446 Newfoundland Dr., St. John's NL A1A 4G7
Tel: 709-576-3748; *Fax:* 709-576-3749
Toll-Free: 877-544-3748
merit@merit-nl.ca
www.merit-nl.ca
Overview: A small provincial organization overseen by Merit Canada
Mission: Merit Contractors Association is the voice of the open shop construction industry in Newfoundland and Labrador.
Chief Officer(s):
Paul Dubé, Executive Director
paul@merit-nl.ca
Membership: *Member Profile:* Construction contractors

Merit Contractors Association of Nova Scotia

#216, 30 Damascus Rd., Bedford NL B4A 0C1
Tel: 902-453-6248; *Fax:* 902-453-0689
Toll-Free: 877-525-9205
info@meritns.com
meritns.com
www.facebook.com/MeritNovaScotia?ref=hl
twitter.com/MeritNS
Also Known As: Merit Nova Scotia
Overview: A small provincial organization overseen by Merit Canada
Mission: To support open shop contractors seeking fair opportunities to compete and do business in Nova Scotia.
Chief Officer(s):
Bill McLellan, Executive Director, 902-453-6248
Membership: 135 companies (2,000 employees); *Member Profile:* Construction contractors

Merit Contractors Association of Saskatchewan

#102, 70 - 17th St. West, Prince Albert SK S6V 3X3
Tel: 306-764-4380; *Fax:* 306-764-4390
info@meritsask.com
www.meritcontractors.sk.ca
www.twitter.com/meritsask
Overview: A small provincial organization founded in 1988 overseen by Merit Canada
Mission: An open shop association in Saskatchewan
Chief Officer(s):
Karen Low, Executive Director
Membership: 200; *Member Profile:* Construction contractors

Merit OpenShop Contractors Association of Ontario

11 Kodiak Cres., Toronto ON M3J 3E5
Toll-Free: 888-303-9878
www.meritontario.com
www.twitter.com/meritontario
Also Known As: Merit Ontario
Previous Name: United Independent Contractors' Group of Ontario
Overview: A small provincial organization founded in 1990 overseen by Merit Canada
Mission: To represent and support the growth of open shop construction by encouraging sound business practices and ensuring a fair and competitive marketplace for construction in Ontario.
Chief Officer(s):
Gordon Sproule, Chair
Membership: 3,500; *Member Profile:* Construction contractors

Merritt & District Chamber of Commerce

PO Box 1649, 2058B Granite Ave., Merritt BC V1K 1B8
Tel: 250-378-5634; *Fax:* 250-378-6561
manager@merrittchamber.com
www.merrittchamber.com
Overview: A small local organization founded in 1914
Mission: To support our members & our community by strengthening the business climate & to create public awareness of our activities
Staff Member(s): 4
Membership: 198; *Fees:* $100 individual; $175 business
Activities: Merritt Mountain Music Festival; trade shows; street malls; business awards dinner; parades; shopping events

Merry Go Round Children's Foundation

#410, 463 King St. West, Toronto ON M5V 1K4
Tel: 647-426-1252; *Fax:* 416-849-2514
www.kidscopscomputers.org
www.facebook.com/KidsCopsComputers
twitter.com/KidCopComputer
www.youtube.com/user/kidscopscomputers
Overview: A small local organization founded in 1997
Mission: To help children who do not have access to computers or internet, by providing them with laptops, internet connections & police mentorship
Affliation(s): Toronto District School Board; Toronto Catholic District School Board; Toronto Police Service
Chief Officer(s):
Clayton Shold, Executive Director, 647-426-1280
clayton@merrygoround.ca
Staff Member(s): 3
Membership: *Member Profile:* Underpriviledged children in grades 7 - 12

Messagères de Notre-Dame de l'Assomption (MNDA)

#4, 45, rue de la Sapiniere-dorion, Québec QC G1L 1A3
Tél: 418-626-7492
Aperçu: *Dimension:* petite; *Envergure:* locale; Organisme sans but lucratif; fondée en 1964
Membre(s) du bureau directeur:
Lucie Dorval, Présidente
Finances: *Budget de fonctionnement annuel:* $50,000-$100,000
Membre: 100-499

Méta d'âme

2250, rue Florian, Montréal QC H2X 2P5
Tél: 514-528-9000; *Téléc:* 514-527-6999
administration@metadame.org
metadame.org
Aperçu: *Dimension:* petite; *Envergure:* locale
Mission: Pour prodiguer des soins médicaux aux personnes souffrant de dépendance aux médicaments d'ordonnance et à faciliter leur réinsertion dans la société
Membre: *Critères d'admissibilite:* Les personnes qui sont accro aux médicaments d'ordonnance

The Metal Arts Guild of Canada (MAGC)

151 Marion St., Toronto ON M6R 1E6
e-mail: communications@metalartsguild.ca
www.metalartsguild.ca
twitter.com/MAGcanada
Overview: A medium-sized national charitable organization founded in 1946
Mission: To be committed to the exchange of information & ideas encouraging appreciation for the metal arts; To promote & develop the metal arts; To further education in the metal arts; To encourage members to experiment with all the forms that metal takes
Affliation(s): Ontario Crafts Council
Chief Officer(s):
Delane Cooper, President
president@metalartsguild.ca
Finances: *Funding Sources:* Membership; Ontario Arts Council; private funding; corporate sponsorship
Membership: *Fees:* Schedule available
Activities: Workshops; lectures & seminars; *Internships:* Yes; *Speaker Service:* Yes; *Library:* Archives & Resource Centre; Open to public by appointment

Metal Industries Association *See* Western Employers Labour Relations Association

The Metal Working Association of New Brunswick (MWANB) / Association des entreprises métallurgiques du Nouveau-Brunswick

PO Box 7129, #12, 567 Coverdale Rd., Riverview NB E1B 4T8
Tel: 506-861-9071; *Fax:* 506-857-3059
nb@cme-mec.ca
www.mwanb.com
Overview: A small provincial organization founded in 1976
Mission: To be a voice for the metal working sector in New Brunswick; to be a forum for members to network discuss opportunities
Affliation(s): Canadian Manufacturers & Exporters
Chief Officer(s):
Marco Gagnon, President

David Plante, Manager
Membership: *Fees:* $300
Publications:
• Metal Working Matters [a publication of The Metal Working Association of New Brunswick]
Type: Newsletter

Metallurgy & Materials Society of the Canadian Institute of Mining, Metallurgy & Petroleum (MetSoc)

#1250, 3500, boul de Maisonneuve ouest, Montréal QC H3Z 3C1
Tel: 514-939-2710
www.metsoc.org
www.facebook.com/group.php?gid=77992627143
Overview: A medium-sized national organization founded in 1967 overseen by Canadian Institute of Mining, Metallurgy & Petroleum
Mission: To expand the professional horizons of society members in order to serve the metals & materials industry
Chief Officer(s):
Greg Richards, President
greg.richards@teck.com
Brigitte Farah, Manager, Administration & Meetings, 514-939-2710 Ext. 1329, Fax: 514-939-2714
bfarah@cim.org
Ronona Saunders, Contact, Publications, Web, & Marketing, 514-939-2710 Ext. 1327, Fax: 514-939-2714
rsaunders@cim.org
Membership: *Member Profile:* Persons involved in the development & application of technologies for the extraction, fabrication, & utilization of metals & materials in Canada; *Committees:* CIM Journal; Student Activities; Historical Metallurgy; Membership Services; Publications; Trustees
Activities: Providing information to the government & the public; Offering continuing education; Recognizing excellence; Providing networking opportunities
Meetings/Conferences: • Metallurgy & Materials Society of the Canadian Institute of Mining, Metallurgy & Petroleum COM 2015: 54th Annual Conference of Metallurgists, August, 2015, Fairmont Royal York Hotel, Toronto, ON
Scope: International
Description: A technical program, with short courses & industrial tours, plus a metals trade show, the poster session, plenary sessions, & student activities
Contact Information: E-mail: metsoc@cim.org
• Metallurgy & Materials Society of the Canadian Institute of Mining, Metallurgy & Petroleum World Gold 2015 5th International Conference, September, 2015, Misty Hills, Gauteng
Scope: International
Description: Jointly convened by the Canadian Institute of Mining, Metallurgy & Petroleum (CIM), the Australasian Institute of Mining & Metallurgy (AusIMM), & the Southern African Institute of Mining & Metallurgy (SAIMM)
• Metallurgy & Materials Society of the Canadian Institute of Mining, Metallurgy & Petroleum COM 2016: 55th Annual Conference of Metallurgists, 2016
Scope: International
Description: A conference featuring short courses, industrial tours, a metals trade show, a poster session, plenary sessions, & student activities
Contact Information: E-mail: metsoc@cim.org
Publications:
• Canadian Metallurgical Quarterly: The Canadian Journal of Metallurgy & Materials Science
Type: Journal; *Frequency:* Quarterly; *Accepts Advertising*; *Editor:* Doug Boyd *ISSN:* 0008-4433
Profile: Research in the areas of mineral processing, extraction, synthesis, processing, characterization properties, &performance of metals & materials
• mLink: The The Electronic Newsletter of the METSOC of CIM
Type: Newsletter
Profile: News for members & students about MetSoc meetings & publications

Métis Child & Family Services Society (Edmonton)

10437 - 123rd St., Edmonton AB T5N 1N8
Tel: 780-452-6100; *Fax:* 780-452-8944
www.metischild.com
Overview: A small local organization
Mission: To promote the health & well-being of Aboriginal children & families by building the capacity of the Métis community through the provision of culturally sensitive & appropriate services & programs
Chief Officer(s):
Don Langford, Executive Director
ed1@metischild.com
Staff Member(s): 28

Métis Nation - Saskatchewan

231 Robin Cres., Saskatoon SK S7L 6M8
Tel: 306-343-8285; *Fax:* 306-343-0171
Toll-Free: 888-343-6667
reception@mn-s.ca
www.mn-s.ca
www.facebook.com/metisnationsaskatchewan
twitter.com/metisnationsask
www.youtube.com/user/MetisSK2012
Overview: A medium-sized provincial organization
Mission: To represent Saskatchewan Métis & act as its legislative assembley
Affliation(s): Métis National Council; Métis Women of Saskatchewan; Métis Nation of Saskatchewan Youth Council
Membership: *Committees:* CDC; Woodland Caribou Recovery Strategy; Sturgeon River Plains Bison Management; North Saskatchewan River Basin Council
Activities: *Awareness Events:* Louis Riel Day, Nov.; Back to Batoche Days

Métis Nation of Alberta

Delia Gray Bldg., #100, 41738 Kingsway Ave., Edmonton AB T5G 0X5
Tel: 780-455-2200; *Fax:* 780-452-8948
Toll-Free: 800-252-7553
www.albertametis.com
www.facebook.com/pages/Metis-Nation-of-Alberta/339682308115
twitter.com/AlbertaMetis
Overview: A medium-sized provincial organization founded in 1932
Mission: To represent the interests of the Métis people of Alberta & ensure the advancement of their culture & well-being
Affliation(s): Métis Urban Housing; Métis Child & Family Services; Métis Development Inc.
Chief Officer(s):
Audrey Poitras, President
Finances: *Funding Sources:* Donations
Membership: *Fees:* $40 replacement card fee
Activities: *Awareness Events:* Louis Riel Week; *Library:* Culture & Resource Centre; Open to public by appointment

Regional Office - Zone 1
PO Box 1350, Lac La Biche AB T0A 2C0
Tel: 780-623-3039; *Fax:* 780-623-2733
Chief Officer(s):
William Landstrom, President

Regional Office - Zone 2
PO Box 6497, Bonnyville AB T9N 2H1
Tel: 780-826-7483; *Fax:* 780-826-7603
Chief Officer(s):
Karen (KC) Collins, President

Regional Office - Zone 3
1415 - 28th St. NE, Calgary AB T2A 2P6
Tel: 403-569-8800; *Fax:* 403-569-8959
Toll-Free: 800-267-5844
Chief Officer(s):
Marlene Lanz, President

Regional Office - Zone 4
11724 - 95 St., Edmonton AB T5G 1L9
Tel: 780-944-9288; *Fax:* 780-455-5546
Toll-Free: 888-588-4088
Chief Officer(s):
Cecil Bellrose, President

Regional Office - Zone 5
353 Main St. North, Slave Lake AB T0G 2A3
Tel: 780-849-4654; *Fax:* 780-849-2890
Toll-Free: 866-849-4660
Chief Officer(s):
Bev New, President

Regional Office - Zone 6
9621 - 90 Ave., Peace River AB T8S 1G8
Tel: 780-624-4219; *Fax:* 780-624-3477
Toll-Free: 800-668-5319
Chief Officer(s):
Sylvia Johnson, President

Métis Nation of Ontario

#3, 500 Old St. Patrick St., Ottawa ON K1N 9G4
Tel: 613-798-1488; *Fax:* 613-722-4225
Toll-Free: 800-263-4889
www.metisnation.org
www.facebook.com/147602041992683
Overview: A medium-sized provincial organization
Mission: To bring Métis people together to celebrate and share their rich culture and heritage and to forward the aspirations of the Métis people in Ontario as a collective.
Affliation(s): Métis National Council
Chief Officer(s):
Gary Lipinski, President
garyl@metisnation.org
Staff Member(s): 150
Membership: 15,000;

Métis National Council (MNC) / Ralliement national des Métis

#4, 340 MacLaren St., Ottawa ON K2P 0M6
Tel: 613-232-3216; *Fax:* 613-232-4262
Toll-Free: 800-928-6330
info@metisnation.ca
www.metisnation.ca
Overview: A medium-sized provincial organization founded in 1983
Mission: To represent the Métis both nationally & internationally; To secure a healthy space for the Métis Nation's existence within Canada
Chief Officer(s):
Clément Chartier, President
Finances: *Funding Sources:* Government of Canada

Métis National Council of Women (MNCW) / Conseil national des femmes métisses, inc. (CNFM)

PO Box 293, Woodlawn ON K0A 3M0
Tel: 613-567-4287; *Fax:* 613-567-9644
Toll-Free: 888-867-2635
info@metiswomen.ca
www.metiswomen.ca
Overview: A medium-sized national organization founded in 1992
Mission: To unite & organize Métis women in Canada and to maintain & promote respect for the individual rights, freedoms & gender equality of Métis women.
Chief Officer(s):
Sheila D. Genaille, President
Finances: *Annual Operating Budget:* $100,000-$250,000
Activities: Youth programs; research & publishing; *Speaker Service:* Yes

Métis Provincial Council of British Columbia

30691 Simpson Rd., Abbotsfrod BC V2T 2C7
Tel: 604-557-5851; *Fax:* 604-557-2024
Toll-Free: 800-940-1150
reception@mnbc.ca
www.mnbc.ca
www.facebook.com/metisnationbc
Also Known As: Métis Nation BC
Overview: A medium-sized provincial organization founded in 1996
Mission: To support the Métis population in British Columbia.
Affliation(s): Métis National Council
Chief Officer(s):
Bruce Dumont, President
bdumont@mnbc.ca
Dale Drown, Chief Executive Officer
Staff Member(s): 18
Membership: 35 Métis communities; *Committees:* Operations & Finance; Priorities & Planning; Governance; Human Resource

Métis Settlements General Council

#101, 10335 - 172 St., Edmonton AB T5S 1K9
Tel: 780-822-4096; *Fax:* 780-489-9558
Toll-Free: 888-213-4400
reception@msgc.ca
www.msgc.ca
www.facebook.com/alberta.settlements
www.youtube.com/user/MSGCHistoryOnline
Also Known As: Alberta Federation of Métis Settlement Associations
Overview: A medium-sized provincial organization
Mission: To represent settlements & address socio-economic issues on their behalf; to promote good governance & community involvement
Chief Officer(s):
Randy Hardy, President

Métis Women's Council of Edmonton *See* Edmonton Aboriginal Senior Centre

Metro (Toronto) Association of Family Resource Programs (MAFRP)

1117 Gerrard St. East, Toronto ON M4M 1Z9

Tel: 416-463-7974; *Fax:* 416-463-0316
mafrp@web.net
Overview: A small local organization founded in 1993
Mission: To encourage the healthy growth & development of young children, their families & care givers; we collaborate with family resource programes to develop the networks & resources necessary to enhance & maintain a high level of program quality
Chief Officer(s):
Cheryl Lajoie, Contact
Finances: *Annual Operating Budget:* Less than $50,000
Staff Member(s): 1
Membership: 1-99
Activities: *Rents Mailing List:* Yes

Metro Action Committee on Public Violence Against Women & Children *See* Metropolitan Action Committee on Violence Against Women & Children

Metro Food Bank Society *See* Feed Nova Scotia

Metro Toronto Chinese & Southeast Asian Legal Clinic (MCSA)

#1701, 180 Dundas St. West, Toronto ON M5G 1Z8
Tel: 416-971-9674; *Fax:* 416-971-6780
mtcsalc.org
www.facebook.com/mcsalegal
twitter.com/mcsalegalclinic
plus.google.com/116850532419152142411
Overview: A small local organization founded in 1987
Mission: To provide free legal services to low income Torontonians who do not speak English & are originally from China, Vietnam, Loas or Cambodia.
Staff Member(s): 5
Membership: *Fees:* Free

Metro Toronto Movement for Literacy (MTML) / Rassemblement pour l'alphabétisation de la communauté urbaine de Toronto

#405, 344 Bloor St. West, Toronto ON M5S 3A7
Tel: 416-961-4013; *Fax:* 416-961-8138
admin@mtml.ca
www.mtml.ca
Overview: A small local charitable organization founded in 1978
Mission: To provide leadership & work actively to develop & promote adult literacy in Toronto & York Region
Member of: Ontario Literacy Coalition
Chief Officer(s):
Chris Beesley, Executive Director
chrisb@mtml.ca
Stephanie Gris, Community Planner
stephanieg@mtml.ca
Finances: *Annual Operating Budget:* $100,000-$250,000; *Funding Sources:* Ontario Ministry of Training, Colleges & Universities; National Literacy Secretariat; Ontario Trillium Foundation; City of Toronto; Canada Post
Staff Member(s): 3
Membership: 100-499; *Fees:* $15-$50 individual (pay what you can); $60-$240 organization; $30 subscriber; *Member Profile:* Community groups; school boards; libraries; workplaces; community colleges; individual members: literacy workers, volunteer tutors & learners
Activities: Public education; information & referral services to learners & volunteers through the Literacy Access Network hotline; community planning coordination; professional development for literacy workers & volunteers; *Awareness Events:* The Word On The Street; International Literacy Day; CBC Book Sale

Metro United Way (Halifax-Dartmouth) *See* United Way of Halifax Region

Metronome Canada

118 Sherbourne St., Toronto ON M5A 2R2
Tel: 416-367-0162; *Fax:* 416-367-1569
Toll-Free: 877-411-7456
info@metronomecanada.com
www.metronomecanada.com
www.facebook.com/MetronomeCanada?ref=search&sid=6
Overview: A small local charitable organization
Mission: To transform the historic Canada Malting Silo Complex on Toronto's waterfront into a facility to integrate, educate, celebrate & promote all facets of the Canadian music industry
Chief Officer(s):
John Harris, Contact
johnharris@metronomecanada.com
Activities: *Internships:* Yes; *Speaker Service:* Yes

Metropolitan Action Committee on Violence Against Women & Children (METRAC)

158 Spadina Rd., Toronto ON M5R 2T8
Tel: 416-392-3135; *Fax:* 416-392-3136
Toll-Free: 877-558-5570; *TTY:* 416-392-3031
info@metrac.org
www.metrac.org
www.facebook.com/pages/Metrac/193631320655070
www.twitter.com/metracorg
www.youtube.com/user/metracorg
Previous Name: Metro Action Committee on Public Violence Against Women & Children
Overview: A small local charitable organization founded in 1984
Mission: To promote the rights of women & children to live free of violence; to decrease & finally eliminate all forms of violence against women & children; to work with agents of change at the municipal, provincial & federal levels; to work with other community-based organizations & with educators, urban planners, police, health & legal professionals; to seek to identify the need for action & to determine appropriate solutions to violence against women & children; to promote education of the public, of professionals & of public officials on the causes of, & appropriate solutions to, violence against women & children
Member of: National Association of Women & the Law
Affliation(s): Ontario Women's Justice Network (OWJN)
Chief Officer(s):
Wendy Komiotis, Executive Director
executivedirector@metrac.org
Finances: *Annual Operating Budget:* $250,000-$500,000
Staff Member(s): 9; 20 volunteer(s)
Membership: 200; *Fees:* Sliding scale; *Member Profile:* Violence against women organizations; community activists; researchers; students; *Committees:* Fundraising; Finance; HR & Nominations; Communications; Planning & Evaluation; Social Action; Executive
Activities: Consultations; research; public education; workshops; annual meeting; training; violence prevention; "Night out with a Difference" event; handbooks; pamphlets; kits & links; *Awareness Events:* Women's Safety Audit Night; *Speaker Service:* Yes; *Library* by appointment

Metropolitan Halifax Chamber of Commerce *See* Halifax Chamber of Commerce

Metropolitan Hamilton Real Estate Board *See* Hamilton-Burlington & District Real Estate Board

The Metropolitan Toronto & Region Conservation Foundation; The Conservation Foundation of Greater Toronto *See* Conservation Foundation of Greater Toronto

Metropolitan Toronto Apartment Builders Association *See* Greater Toronto Apartment Association

Metropolitan Toronto Convention & Visitors Association *See* Tourism Toronto

Metropolitan Toronto Lawyers Association; County of York Law Association *See* Toronto Lawyers Association

Metropolitan Toronto Police Association *See* Toronto Police Association

Mi'Kmaq Association for Cultural Studies (MACS)

PO Box 243, Sydney NS B1P 6H1
Tel: 902-567-1752; *Fax:* 902-567-0776
macs@mikmaq-assoc.ca
www.mikmaqculture.com
Overview: A medium-sized local organization founded in 1974
Mission: To promote, maintain & protect the customs, language, history, tradition & culture of the Mi'Kmaq people; to facilitate & promote understanding & awareness of our culture among the public; to teach the culture, language & history of the Mi'Kmaq people to others
Chief Officer(s):
Deborah Ginnish, Executive Director
Membership: *Member Profile:* All registered Mi'Kmaq in 12 First Nations communities

Mi'kmaq Native Friendship Centre

2158 Gottingen St., Halifax NS B3K 3B4
Tel: 902-420-1576; *Fax:* 902-423-6130
www.mymnfc.com
www.facebook.com/121366117945828
Overview: A small local charitable organization founded in 1973 overseen by National Association of Friendship Centres
Mission: To promote the educational & cultural advancement of native people in & about the Halifax/Dartmouth area; to assist people of native descent who have newly arrived in the area to settle in; to strive to create & improve mutual understanding between people of native descent & others.
Chief Officer(s):
Pam Glode-Desrochers, Executive Director
Staff Member(s): 17
Activities: Alcohol & Drug Counselling; Community & Cultural Development Program; Crisis Intervention Program; DayCare Program; Employment & Education Program; Justice Program; Micmac Native Learning Centre; Mainline Needle Exchange Program

Micah House

c/o 333 King St. East, Hamilton ON L8N 1C1
Tel: 905-296-4387
info@micahhouse.ca
www.micahhouse.ca
www.facebook.com/MicahHouseHamilton
twitter.com/micah_house
Overview: A small local organization founded in 2006
Mission: To demonstrate God's love to newly arrived refugees in Hamilton, Ontario
Chief Officer(s):
Ian Innis, Chair
Scott Jones, Executive Director
scott@micahhouse.ca
Finances: *Funding Sources:* Donations
Staff Member(s): 6
Membership: *Member Profile:* Christians from a variety of churches & organizations in Hamilton, Ontario
Activities: *Awareness Events:* Walkathon

Michael Smith Foundation for Health Research (MSFHR)

#200, 1285 West Broadway, Vancouver BC V6H 3X8
Tel: 604-730-8322; *Fax:* 604-730-0524
Toll-Free: 866-673-4722
info@msfhr.org
www.msfhr.org
www.linkedin.com/MichaelSmithFoundationforHealthReserath
twitter.com/msfhr
www.youtube.com/themsfhr
Overview: A medium-sized provincial organization founded in 2001
Mission: To build British Columbia's capacity for excellence in clinical, biomedical, health services & population health research
Chief Officer(s):
Diane Finegood, President & CEO
Bev Holmes, Vice-President
Gordon Schwark, Vice-President, Finance & Administration
Staff Member(s): 35

The Michener Institute for Applied Health Sciences

222 St. Patrick St., Toronto ON M5T 1V4
Tel: 416-596-3101; *Fax:* 416-596-3168
Toll-Free: 800-387-9066
info@michener.ca
www.michener.ca
Previous Name: Toronto Institute of Medical Technology
Overview: A medium-sized national organization founded in 1967
Mission: To design, develop & deliver the best educational programs, products & services in applied health sciences
Affliation(s): 170 hospitals, labs, & clinics across Canada
Chief Officer(s):
Paul Bertin, Chair
Paul Gamble, Secretary/President & CEO
Finances: *Annual Operating Budget:* Greater than $5 Million; *Funding Sources:* Ontario Ministry of Health
Staff Member(s): 97
Activities: *Library* by appointment

Microscopical Society of Canada (MSC) / Société de Microscopie du Canada

Brockhouse Inst. of Mat.Res., McMaster Univ., 1280 Main St. West, Hamilton ON L8S 4M1
Tel: 905-525-9140; *Fax:* 905-521-2773
butcher@mcmaster.ca
msc.rsvs.ulaval.ca
Overview: A medium-sized national organization founded in 1973
Chief Officer(s):
Randy Mikula, President
Chris Butcher, Treasurer
Frances Leggett, Executive Secretary
leggett@agr.gc.ca
Membership: *Fees:* $45 individual; $28 retired; $15 student

Middle River & Area Historical Society
sites.google.com/site/middleriverhistoricalsociety
Overview: A small local organization founded in 1984
Member of: Federation of the Nova Scotian Heritage
Chief Officer(s):
Shirley Hart, Contact, 902-295-2686
mrhs844@ns.sympatico.ca
Peggy MacLeod, Contact, 902-295-2669
pegnsandy@ns.sympatico.ca
Finances: *Annual Operating Budget:* Less than $50,000; *Funding Sources:* Donations; sale of books; fundraising
15 volunteer(s)
Membership: 13; *Fees:* $2; *Committees:* Auditing

Middlesex Community Living
82 Front St. West, Strathroy ON N7G 1X7
Tel: 519-245-1301; *Fax:* 519-245-5654
www.middlesexcl.on.ca
Overview: A small local organization
Member of: Community Living Ontario
Chief Officer(s):
Sherri Kroll, Executive Director
skroll@middlesexcl.on.ca

Middlesex Federation of Agriculture (MFA)
PO Box 820, 633 Lions Park Dr., Mount Brydges ON N0L 1W0
Tel: 519-457-8444; *Fax:* 519-264-9173
mfa4h@bellnet.ca
www.ofa.on.ca/about/county-federation-sites/middlesex.aspx
Overview: A small local organization founded in 1939 overseen by Ontario Federation of Agriculture
Mission: To advance agriculture & the rural community through partnerships, education & advocacy
Chief Officer(s):
Lucia Lilbourne, Coordinator
Finances: *Annual Operating Budget:* $50,000-$100,000
Staff Member(s): 1; 50 volunteer(s)
Membership: 2500; *Committees:* Education; Communication; Special Events; Political Awareness

Middlesex Law Association (MLA)
80 Dundas St., #N, Gr. Fl., London ON N6A 6A1
Tel: 519-679-7046; *Fax:* 519-672-5917
Toll-Free: 866-556-5570
library@middlaw.on.ca
www.middlaw.on.ca
Overview: A small local organization founded in 1879
Chief Officer(s):
Bill Woodward, President, 519-673-1100, Fax: 519-679-6108
wwoodward@dyerbrownlaw.com
Finances: *Funding Sources:* Law Society of Upper Canada; membership dues
Staff Member(s): 3
Membership: 850; *Fees:* $125 regular member; $60 first-year member & retired member; *Member Profile:* Hold a L.L.B.
Activities: *Library*

Middlesex, Oxford, Elgin Beekeepers' Association
c/o Bob Crowhurst, 21977 Wonderland Rd. North, RR#1, Arva ON N0M 1C0
Tel: 519-666-1670
www.moebeea.com
Overview: A small local organization
Mission: To educate & assist local beekeepers
Member of: Ontario Beekeepers' Association
Chief Officer(s):
Bob Crowhurst, President
robert.crowhurst@sympatico.ca
Membership: *Member Profile:* Persons interested in beekeeping in Middlesex, Oxford, & Elgin, Ontario
Activities: Organizing meetings for members to provide timely information about beekeeping techniques & issues;

Middlesex-Lambton-Huron Association of Baptist Churches
ON
www.mlha.ca
Overview: A small local organization overseen by Canadian Baptists of Ontario and Quebec
Member of: Canadian Baptists of Ontario & Quebec
Chief Officer(s):
Harvey Park, Moderator
hpcon@rogers.com
Membership: 19 churches; *Member Profile:* Baptist churches in Southwestern Ontario
Activities: Camp site; Golf tournament; Annual Picnic

Mid-Island Coin Club
c/o West Coast Stamp & Coin, 4061 Norwell Dr., Nanaimo BC V9T 1Y8
Tel: 250-758-5896
relmcoin@shaw.ca
Overview: A small local organization

Mid-Pro Rock & Gem Society
c/o Prince Albert Arts Centre, 1010 Central Ave., Prince Albert SK S6V 4V5
Tel: 306-763-6581
Overview: A small local organization
Affliation(s): Gem & Mineral Federation of Canada
Membership: *Fees:* $20 individual; $30 family

Mid-Toronto Community Services (MTCS)
192 Carlton St., 2nd Fl., Toronto ON M5A 2K8
Tel: 416-962-9449; *Fax:* 416-962-5541
admin@midtoronto.com
www.midtoronto.com
Overview: A small local charitable organization founded in 1965
Mission: Provides programs & services to support the independence of seniors & adults with disabilities to continue living in their own homes
Member of: Ontario Community Support Association
Chief Officer(s):
Kaarina Luoma, Executive Director
kluoma@midtoronto.com
Susan Burns, Chair
Finances: *Funding Sources:* Provincial government, municipal Government; United Way
Membership: *Fees:* Free
Activities: Alzheimer Day Program; Adult Day Program; Adult Enrichment & Wellness Program; Meals on Wheels; critical housing support; community transportation; volunteer opportunities; social work services; Korean social work; *Internships:* Yes; *Speaker Service:* Yes; *Rents Mailing List:* Yes

Midwives Association of British Columbia
#2, 175 - 15th Ave. East, Vancouver BC V5T 2P6
Tel: 604-736-5976; *Fax:* 604-736-5957
mabc@telus.net
www.bcmidwives.com
www.facebook.com/196300877987
www.twitter.com/bcmidwives
Overview: A small provincial organization founded in 1980
Mission: Supports the profession of midwifery in British Columbia
Member of: International Confederation of Midwives; Canadian Association of Midwives
Chief Officer(s):
Ganga Jolicoeur, Executive Director
Finances: *Funding Sources:* Membership dues

Midwives Association of Saskatchewan (MAS)
c/o Birdene Keefe, 439 Assiniboia St., Weyburn SK S4H 0R5
e-mail: glk@sasktel.net
www.saskatchewanmidwives.com
Overview: A small provincial organization founded in 1987
Mission: To support midwives working in Saskatchewan; To promote midwifery in the province
Chief Officer(s):
Birdene Keefe, Treasurer
Finances: *Funding Sources:* Membership fees
Membership: *Fees:* $50 non-voting members, such as students & others interested in midwifery; $100 voting members; *Member Profile:* Practicing & non-practicing persons in Saskatchewan with midwifery training & experience
Activities: Providing education about midwifery

Midwives Collective of Toronto
1203 Bloor St. West, Toronto ON M6H 1N3
Tel: 416-963-8842; *Fax:* 416-963-4398
midwivescollective@bellnet.ca
www.midwivescollective.ca
Overview: A small local organization founded in 1983
Chief Officer(s):
Heather Douglas, Administrator
Finances: *Funding Sources:* Provincial government
Staff Member(s): 3; 1 volunteer(s)
Activities: Prenatal care; birth care; postnatal care

The Mighty Pen
PO Box 46108, Stn. College Park, 777 Bay St., Toronto ON M5G 2P6
www.themightypen.org
www.facebook.com/pages/The-Mighty-Pen/143250992392760
twitter.com/the_mighty_pen
Previous Name: Tempus International
Overview: A large international charitable organization founded in 2003
Mission: To promote sustainable development by organizing literacy & education projects that provide opportunities for underprivileged youth
Chief Officer(s):
Jeff Zajac, Chair
jeff@themightypen.org
Chris de Eyre, Founder & Vice-Chair
chris@themightypen.org
Nikolas MacLean, Executive Director
nik@themightypen.org
Finances: *Funding Sources:* Donations
Activities: The Mighty Pen bi-annual writing competition (Nepal) & related scholarships; *Awareness Events:* Give the Gift of Literacy

Military Collectors Club of Canada (MCC of Canada)
c/o John Zabarylo, Secretary-treasurer, PO Box 64009, 525 London St., Winnipeg MB R2K 3Y4
Tel: 204-669-0871
militarycollectorsclubofcanada@yahoo.ca
www.mccofc.org
Overview: A medium-sized national organization founded in 1963
Chief Officer(s):
John Zabarylo, Sec.-Treas.
Sectreas@mccofc.org
Jim Simmons, President
jsimmons36@shaw.ca
Membership: 500+; *Member Profile:* Canadian, U.S.A. & overseas individuals interested in militaria, military history, & research
Activities: Preserving military artifacts; Researching military history; Organizing conventions

Militia of the Immaculata Canada (M.I.)
PO Box 21003, 314 Harwood Ave. South, Ajax ON L1S 2J0
Tel: 416-465-9466
immaculatacanada@yahoo.com
consecration.ca
Overview: A small local organization founded in 1922
Mission: To recognize the consecration to God through the Immaculata the primacy of vocation to sanctity; to bring together spiritual life & action; To live out its ecclesial dimension, by taking on pastoral programs of the bishops' conferences; To listen to the needs of the New Evangelization
Affliation(s): Archdiocese of Toronto
Membership: *Member Profile:* Members of the Militia of the Immaculata Canada live consecration in the Church, love the Church, & recognize & profess their Catholic faith; Individuals are called to work with creativity & unity, while combining Church teaching, Kolbean inspiration, & environmental concerns
Activities: Contributing in all areas in the form of catechesis, social work, humanitarian initiatives, & cultural proposals; Participating in the apostolate of the Church, in the spirit of our Marian consecration

Mill Woods Society for Community Living (MSCL)
1911 - 42 St., Edmonton AB T6L 5P8
Tel: 780-450-9884; *Fax:* 780-465-3897
mscl@shaw.ca
Previous Name: Millwoods Society for Community Living
Overview: A small local charitable organization founded in 1986
Mission: To support & advocate for individuals with multiple disabilites in their home & their community; to enhance awareness & understanging for all individuals with disabilities
Member of: Alberta Association of Rehabilitation Centres; Alberta Council of Disability Services
Chief Officer(s):
Henriette Groeneveld, Executive Director
Finances: *Annual Operating Budget:* $250,000-$500,000; *Funding Sources:* Provincial government
Staff Member(s): 18
Membership: 60

Millarville Racing & Agricultural Society (MRAS)
PO Box 68, Millarville AB T0L 1K0
Tel: 403-931-3411; *Fax:* 403-931-3485
www.millarvilleracetrack.com
www.facebook.com/131119606994283
twitter.com/MillarvilleFM
Overview: A small local organization founded in 1907

Mission: To build a strong community
Member of: Alberta Association of Agricultural Societies
Chief Officer(s):
Barb Castell, Staff
Don Stewart, President
Finances: *Annual Operating Budget:* $250,000-$500,000
Staff Member(s): 3; 300 volunteer(s)
Membership: 500; *Fees:* $38.50 individual; $44 family; $26.25 student/senior
Activities: Organizing rodeos, races, farmers' markets, & fairs

Millbrook & Cavan Historical Society

PO Box 334, Millbrook ON L0A 1G0
Tel: 705-932-2713
millbrookcavanhs@gmail.com
www.millbrookcavanhs.com
Overview: A small local organization
Mission: To preserve & promote local history
Member of: Ontario Historical Society
Membership: *Fees:* $15 single; $25 family; $5 student

Millbrook & District Chamber of Commerce

PO Box 271, 46 King St. East, Millbrook ON L0A 1G0
Tel: 705-932-7007
info@millbrook.ca
www.millbrook.ca
www.facebook.com/107078996075141
twitter.com/millbrookon
Overview: A small local organization founded in 1953
Chief Officer(s):
Angela Beal, President, 705-749-1259
beal@hrsgroup.com
Diane Moore, Office Manager
Membership: *Fees:* $100

Millet & District Chamber of Commerce

PO Box 389, Millet AB T0C 1Z0
Tel: 780-387-4554; *Fax:* 780-387-4459
Overview: A small local organization
Mission: To promote business and tourism in the Millet area.

Millet & District Historical Society (MDHS)

PO Box 178, Millet AB T0C 1Z0
Tel: 780-387-5558
info@milletmuseum.ca
www.milletmuseum.ca
Overview: A small local charitable organization founded in 1977
Mission: To maintain, preserve, further develop & expand Millet's cultural resources; & ensure them for future generations; to operate Millet & District Museum & Archives
Member of: Museums Alberta; Archives Society of Alberta; Central Alberta Regional Museums Network
Chief Officer(s):
Tracey Leavitt, Executive Director
Finances: *Funding Sources:* Bingos; Grants; Donations
Membership: *Member Profile:* Interested in preserving Millet history
Activities: School curriculum tours; Interpretation guided tours; Trade show; Parade; Conservation; *Library:* Museum Archives; by appointment

Millwoods Society for Community Living *See* Mill Woods Society for Community Living

Milton Chamber of Commerce

#104, 251 Main St. East, Milton ON L9T 1P1
Tel: 905-878-0581; *Fax:* 905-878-4972
info@miltonchamber.ca
www.miltonchamber.ca
www.linkedin.com/groups/Milton-Chamber-Commerce-44704?trk=myg_ugrp_ovr
www.facebook.com/miltonchamber
www.twitter.com/miltonchamber
www.youtube.com/miltonchamber
Overview: A small local organization founded in 1888
Chief Officer(s):
Sandy Martin, Executive Director
sandy@miltonchamber.ca

Milton Historical Society (MHS)

16 James St., Milton ON L9T 2P4
Tel: 905-875-4156
miltonhistoricalsociety@bellnet.ca
www.miltonhistoricalsociety.ca
www.facebook.com/pages/Milton-Historical-Society/349295522254
twitter.com/miltonsoldiers
Overview: A small local charitable organization founded in 1977
Mission: To provide a friendly forum for those interested in the Milton community; to search out Milton's heritage & make it known to the community; to recognize those who have helped preserve our heritage; to cooperate with other heritage organizations & Town Council on heritage projects & concerns; to stimulate public interest in Milton's historic people & places; to encourage & assist educational heritage programs
Member of: Ontario Historical Society
Chief Officer(s):
Jan Mowbray, President
Finances: *Funding Sources:* Membership dues; government grants; plaquing; books
15 volunteer(s)
Membership: 50; *Fees:* $20
Activities: Awards; 10 monthly meetings; outreach; research; publishing; community displays; Mayor's Levee; *Library:* Milton Historical Society Collection; by appointment
Awards:
• Heritage Awards for Visual Arts, Education, & Writing (Award)
• President's Award (Award)
Given to a home owner who has preserved & maintained an older home

Minalliance

#2200, 1250, boul René-Lévesque ouest, Montréal QC H3B 4W8
Tel: 514-983-1382; *Fax:* 514-989-3136
minalliance.ca
www.linkedin.com/company/minalliance
Overview: A medium-sized provincial organization founded in 2010
Mission: Minalliance is the Quebec mining industry's communications fund that brings together Quebec and Canadian mining exploration and production companies, suppliers of goods and services, industry associations and other partners.
Chief Officer(s):
Isabelle Poirier, Executive Director

La Mine d'Or, entreprise d'insertion sociale

542, 3e Rue, Chibougamau QC G8P 1N9
Tél: 418-748-4183
dglaminedor@outlook.com
Aperçu: *Dimension:* petite; *Envergure:* provinciale
Mission: Organisme sans but lucratif, qui a pour mission l'insertion sociale & professionnelle des personnes en situation d'exclusion; offre une passerelle aux participants vers le marché du travail, la formation ou d'autres alternatives
Membre de: Collectif des entreprises d'insertion du Québec
Membre(s) du bureau directeur:
France Bureau, Présidente

The Mineral & Gem Society of Nova Scotia *See* The Nova Scotia Mineral & Gem Society

Mineral Society of Manitoba (MSM)

c/o The Manitoba Museum, 190 Rupert Ave., Winnipeg MB R3B 0N2
e-mail: ysearle@mts.net
www.umanitoba.ca/geoscience/mineralsociety/index.htm
Overview: A small provincial organization founded in 1971
Mission: To promote the study of minerals, rocks, & fossils for both scientific & recreational purposes
Chief Officer(s):
Jack Bauer, Contact, Membership, 204-632-6934
jebauer@mts.net
Marion Foster, Contact, General Information, 204-775-0625
2mandm@mts.net
Yvonne Searle, Contact, School Programs, 204-663-6637
wsearle@mts.net
Membership: *Fees:* $15 individuals; $20 families
Activities: Hosting monthly meetings at the Manitoba Museum; organizing field trips; planning educational exhibits; guest speakers
Publications:
• The Mineral Vein: The Mineral Society of Manitoba Newsletter
Type: Newsletter; *Frequency:* 9 pa; *Editor:* Tony Smith
Profile: Upcoming events, presentation summaries, & articles about rockhounding & mineralogy

Mineralogical Association of Canada (MAC) / Association minéralogique du Canada

490, rue de la Couronne, Québec QC G1K 9A9
Tel: 418-653-0333; *Fax:* 418-653-0777
office@mineralogicalassociation.ca
www.mineralogicalassociation.ca
Overview: A medium-sized national charitable organization founded in 1955
Mission: To promote & advance knowledge of mineralogy & the allied disciplines of petrology, crystallography, mineral deposits, & geochemistry
Chief Officer(s):
Lee A. Groat, President
lgroat@eos.ubc.ca
Johanne Coran, Manager, Business
jcaron@mineralogicalassociation.ca
Membership: *Member Profile:* Individuals or organizations engaged or interested in mineralogy, crystallography, petrology, geochemistry, & economic geology; *Committees:* Finance
Activities: Organizing annual meetings & symposia; Providing short courses; Disseminating information about mineralogy; Providing reference books & textbooks in the mineral sciences; Presenting awards & scholarships; Increasing public awareness of science
Publications:
• The Canadian Mineralogist: The Journal of the Mineralogical Association of Canada
Type: Journal; *Frequency:* Bimonthly; *Editor:* Robert F. Martin
Profile: Subjects include mineralogy, mineral deposits, petrology, crystallography, & geochemistry
• Elements: An International Magazine of Mineralogy, Geochemistry, & Petrology
Type: Magazine; *Frequency:* Bimonthly; *Accepts Advertising*; *Editor:* Pierrette Tremblay *ISSN:* 1811-5209; *Price:* Free with membership in the Mineralogical Association of Canada
Profile: An international magazine published by organizations such as the Mineralogical Association of Canada, theMineralogical Society of America, the Mineralogical Society of Great Britain & Ireland, the European Association of Geochemistry, the Clay Minerals Society, & the Geochemical Society

Mines Alerte Canada *See* MiningWatch Canada

Miniature Horse Association of Canada

c/o David Trus, #316, 1305 Baseline Rd., Tower 5, Ottawa ON K1A 0C5
Tel: 613-773-0229; *Fax:* 613-759-6316
Overview: A small national organization founded in 1992
Mission: To establish standards of breeding for miniature horses; To encourage the breeding, exhibiting, & uses of miniature horses
Affliation(s): Canadian Livestock Records Corporation
Chief Officer(s):
Mavis MacDonald, Registrar, 613-731-7110 Ext. 311, Fax: 613-731-0704
David Trus, Officer, Animal Registration, 613-773-0229, Fax: 613-759-6316
Membership: *Fees:* $45 initiation fee for persons other than juniors; $25 / year Canadian & foreign members; $5 junior members; *Member Profile:* Owners, associations, clubs, & enthusiasts of miniature horses
Activities: Publicizing miniature horses to increase public awareness; Providing educational programs for miniature horse owners & enthusiasts; Liaising with similar organizations

Miniature Horse Association of Nova Scotia (MHANS)

NS
Tel: 902-783-2251
www.freewebs.com/mhansweb
Overview: A small provincial organization founded in 2003
Mission: To promote the miniature horse breed in Nova Scotia
Chief Officer(s):
Roger Gouchie, President, 902-667-8917
mffargouchie02@hotmail.com
Brenda Green, Vice-President, 902-783-2251
brenda.darryl@gmail.com
Lon Balderston, Secretary
balderston.lori@gmai.com
Kim Horton, Treasurer, 902-364-2258
horton.rk@ns.sympatico.ca
Membership: 100-499; *Member Profile:* Persons involved in the miniature horse industry in Nova Scotia
Activities: Presenting educational clinics about showing miniature horses; Sanctioning & participating in shows; Increasing public awareness of miniature horses in Nova Scotia; Organizing regular meetings; Providing information about the breed for members; Offering networking opportunities; Liaising with similar organizations
Publications:
• Miniature Horse Association of Nova Scotia Newsletter

Type: Newsletter
Profile: Association notices, meeting information, upcoming sales, show results, & registration information

Miniature Horse Club of Ontario (MHCO)
c/o Carolyn Aarup, PO Box 2, RR#1, Meaford ON N4L 1W5
Tel: 519-538-3114
mhco@mhco.ca
www.mhco.ca
www.facebook.com/120325871333053
Overview: A small provincial organization
Mission: To provide information & opportunity for those in Ontario who are interested in the miniature horse breed; To encourage improvement of miniature horse stock through proper breeding programs
Member of: Ontario Equestrian Federation
Affliation(s): American Miniature Horse Registry
Chief Officer(s):
Doug Savage, President, 905-936-6873
savagemoor@hotmail.com
John McCallum, Vice-President, 519-285-5683
ajmccallum@rogers.com
Angie Trumpler, Secretary
trumpler56@gmail.com
Carolyn Aarup, Treasurer & Coordinator, Promotions
kacahana@sympatico.ca
Membership: *Fees:* $20 youth members, age 17 & under; $35 single members; $45 families; $55 farms; *Member Profile:* Miniature horse enthusiasts of any age in Ontario; *Committees:* Advertising, Promotion & Public Relation; MHCO Club Point Shows; AMHR Sanction Show; Social; Fundraising; MHCO Awards; Administration, Rules, & By-Laws; Youth Club Plus; Electronic Media
Activities: Promoting the miniature horse breed in Ontario at various public events, such as equine events; Providing educational clinics on topics such as show preparation, conformation, & driving principles; Participating in competitions for miniature horses; Hosting shows, such as the annual American Miniature Horse Registry sanctioned show; Presenting awards; Offering recreational activities; Hosting two general meetings each year to plan club activities; Planning fun days for members & their horses, such as pleasure drives;

Mining Association of British Columbia (MABC)
#900, 808 West Hastings St., Vancouver BC V6C 2X4
Tel: 604-681-4321; *Fax:* 604-681-5305
mabcinfo@mining.bc.ca
www.mining.bc.ca
www.facebook.com/MABCMining
twitter.com/ma_bc
Overview: A medium-sized provincial organization founded in 1901 overseen by Mining Association of Canada
Mission: To speak on behalf of mineral producers; To represent the interests of British Columbia's mining industry; To communicate with senior government decision-makers, communities, NGOs, First Nations, & the media; To act as the industry's voice regarding issues such as environmental regulations, taxation, infrastructure demands, labour issues, health & safety, & international trade
Chief Officer(s):
Karina Brino, President & CEO
kbrino@mining.bc.ca
Zoe Younger, Vice-President, Corporate Affairs
zyounger@mining.bc.ca
David Ewing, Vice-President, Environmental & Technical Affairs
dewing@mining.bc.ca
Staff Member(s): 8
Membership: 48; *Member Profile:* Members include corporate members with producing operations within BC, service & supply organizations, institutions, & non-profit organizations.
Activities: Liaising with government legislators; Lobbying for regulatory advancement; Promoting the economic & social value of mining; Updating members on regulatory change; Facilitating exchange of information among members
Publications:
• Daily News [a publication of the Mining Association of British Columbia]
Type: Newsletter; *Frequency:* Daily
Profile: Mining related news, on provincial, national, & international levels, for members

Mining Association of Canada (MAC) / Association minière du Canada
#1105, 350 Sparks St., Ottawa ON K1R 7S8
Tel: 613-233-9392; *Fax:* 613-233-8897
communications@mining.ca
www.mining.ca
www.facebook.com/group.php?gid=193636270672849
twitter.com/theminingstory
Overview: A large national organization founded in 1935
Mission: To represent the interests of member companies engaged in mineral exploration, extraction & refining; To work with governments on public policy pertaining to minerals
Chief Officer(s):
Pierre Gratton, President & CEO
Marilyn Fortin, Office Manager & Member Services
Monique Laflèche, Executive Assistant
Finances: *Annual Operating Budget:* $1.5 Million-$3 Million; *Funding Sources:* Membership dues
Staff Member(s): 10
Membership: 55
Activities: *Awareness Events:* National Mining Week, May; Mining Weeks in Canada, April - June
Awards:
• Paul Stothart Memorial Scholarship in Mineral Economics (Scholarship)
Eligibility: Candidates must be enrolled full-time in their second, third or fourth year of a Bachelors of Economics degree or in their first or second year of a Master of Economics or MBA program; must demonstrate an interest, supported by current or intended course work, in mineral economics or mining commerce.*Deadline:* April 15 *Amount:* $3,500 *Contact:* Marilyn Fortin, mfortin@mining.ca

Mining Association of Manitoba Inc. (MAMI)
#700, 305 Broadway Ave., Winnipeg MB R3C 3J7
Tel: 204-989-1890; *Fax:* 204-989-1899
www.mines.ca
Overview: A medium-sized provincial organization founded in 1940 overseen by Mining Association of Canada
Mission: To represent mining & exploration companies in Manitoba.
Chief Officer(s):
Barrie Simoneau, Director, Risk Management
bsimoneau@mines.ca
Finances: *Funding Sources:* Membership dues
Membership: *Member Profile:* Mining companies with more than 50 employees
Activities: *Speaker Service:* Yes; *Library* by appointment

Mining Association of Nova Scotia (MANS)
7744 St. Margaret's Bay Rd., Ingramport NS B3Z 3Z8
Tel: 902-820-2115
info@tmans.ca
tmans.ca
www.facebook.com/MiningNS
twitter.com/MiningNS
Overview: A medium-sized provincial organization founded in 1981
Mission: To ensure Nova Scotia is recognized internationally as having mineral resources worthy of investment; to develop mineral deposits; to work for government policies that provide a framework for a competitive mining industry within the global marketplace; to promote mining as a corporate industry creating wealth & long-term stable employment, with responsible environmental & social attitudes
Affliation(s): Mining Association of Canada
Chief Officer(s):
Sean Kirby, Executive Director
sean@tmans.ca
Staff Member(s): 2
Membership: 90; *Fees:* Schedule available
Activities: *Library* by appointment

Mining Industry Human Resources Council (MIHR) / Conseil des ressources humaines de l'industrie minière (RHIM)
#401, 260 Hearst Way, Kanata ON K2L 3H1
Tel: 613-270-9696; *Fax:* 613-270-9399
info@mihr.ca
www.mihr.ca
www.facebook.com/group.php?gid=103398309715163
Overview: A medium-sized national organization
Mission: Contributes to the strength, competitiveness & sustainability of the Canadian mining industry by collaborating with all communities of interest in the development & implementation of solutions to the industry's national human resource challenges
Chief Officer(s):
Patricia Dillon, Chair
Ryan Montpellier, Executive Director
Finances: *Annual Operating Budget:* $3 Million-$5 Million; *Funding Sources:* Government; Industry

Mining Industry NL
Prince Charles Bldg., PO Box 21463, #W280, 120 Torbay Rd., St. John's NL A1A 2G8
Tel: 709-722-9542; *Fax:* 709-722-8588
info@miningnl.com
www.miningnl.com
Overview: A medium-sized provincial organization
Mission: To represent all sectors of the mineral industry in the province; to be a central contact for government, media & the public
Chief Officer(s):
Ed Moriarity, Executive Director
edmoriarity@miningnl.com
Jennifer Kelly, Communications Advisor
jkelly@miningnl.com
Membership: 60 corporate; *Fees:* Schedule available; *Member Profile:* Exploration companies, mine operators, service & supply companies

Mining Society of Nova Scotia
88 Leeside Dr., Sydney NS B1R 1S6
Tel: 902-567-2147; *Fax:* 902-567-2147
www.miningsocietyns.ca
Overview: A small provincial organization founded in 1887 overseen by Mining Association of Canada
Mission: To provide services in order to help & improve the mining industry
Affliation(s): Canadian Institute of Mining, Metallurgy & Petroleum
Chief Officer(s):
Willie McNeil, President
Staff Member(s): 2

Mining Suppliers, Contractors & Consultants Association of BC (MSCCA)
#900, 808 West Hastings St., Vancouver BC V6C 2X4
Tel: 604-681-4321; *Fax:* 604-681-5305
tmulligan@mining.bc.ca
miningsuppliersbc.ca/
Overview: A medium-sized provincial licensing organization founded in 1986
Mission: To promote the development of a sustainable mining industry in BC
Affliation(s): Mining Association of British Columbia
Chief Officer(s):
Terry B. Mulligan, Executive Director Ext. 111
Finances: *Annual Operating Budget:* $100,000-$250,000; *Funding Sources:* Membership dues; special events
Staff Member(s): 1; 3 volunteer(s)
Membership: 225 companies; *Fees:* Based on sales to BC mining
Activities: Networking functions with the mining industry

MiningWatch Canada / Mines Alerte Canada
City Centre Building, #508, 250 City Centre Ave., Ottawa ON K1R 6K7
Tel: 613-569-3439; *Fax:* 613-569-5138
info@miningwatch.ca
www.miningwatch.ca
www.facebook.com/MiningWatch
twitter.com/MiningWatch
www.youtube.com/miningwatch
Overview: A small national organization founded in 1999
Mission: To address the urgent need for a coordinated public interest response to the threats to public health, water & air quality, fish & wildlife habitat & community interests posed by irresponsible mineral policies & practices in Canada & around the world
Member of: Canadian Environmental Network; Canadian Council for International Cooperation; Halifax Initiative
Chief Officer(s):
Catherine Coumans, Research Coordinator
Staff Member(s): 5
Membership: 1-99; *Fees:* Sliding scale; *Member Profile:* Aboriginal, labour, environmental, international groups

Minnedosa Chamber of Commerce
PO Box 857, Minnedosa MB R0J 1E0
Tel: 204-867-2951; *Fax:* 204-867-3641
minnedosachamber@gmail.com
www.discoverminnedosa.ca
Overview: A small local organization

Mission: To be the voice of the business community & enhance trade & commerce in the Minnedosa area
Member of: Manitoba Chamber of Commerce
Chief Officer(s):
Don Farr, President
Callie Mashtoler, Secretary
Finances: *Annual Operating Budget:* Less than $50,000; *Funding Sources:* Membership fees & fundraising
4 volunteer(s)
Membership: 140; *Fees:* $30-160; *Committees:* Retail; Business Improvement; Membership; Executive
Activities: Community events; parade; town clean-up; tourism; economic development; educational features;
Awards:
• Business of the Year (Award)
• Lifetime Achievement Award (Award)

Minor Hockey Alliance of Ontario
71 Albert St., Stratford ON N5A 3K2
Tel: 519-273-7209; *Fax:* 519-273-2114
alliance@alliancehockey.com
www.alliancehockey.com
www.facebook.com/114981545258512
twitter.com/ALLIANCE_Hockey
Also Known As: Alliance Hockey
Overview: A small provincial organization founded in 1993
Mission: To organize, coordinate & develop hockey programs for all ages
Member of: Canadian Hockey Association; Ontario Hockey Federation
Chief Officer(s):
Tony Martindale, Executive Director
tmartindale@alliancehockey.com
Staff Member(s): 5
Membership: 29,734; *Committees:* Development; Constitution; House League & Select; Minor Development; Group Structure; Insurance & Risk Management; Discipline & Suspension; Championship; Overseas; AGM

Minto Chamber of Commerce
PO Box 864, Harriston ON N0G 1Z0
Tel: 519-327-9619
info@mintochamber.on.ca
www.mintochamber.on.ca
www.facebook.com/mintochamberofcommerce
Previous Name: Harriston-Minto & District Chamber of Commerce
Overview: A small local organization
Chief Officer(s):
John Mock, President
Membership: 56; *Fees:* $65

Mirabel Morgan Special Riding Centre
1201 - 2nd Line South, RR#1, Bailieboro ON K0L 1B0
e-mail: mirabelmf@gmail.com
Overview: A small local organization
Mission: Year round program for anyone who wishes to ride who has medical, physical, or emotional needs; for those who enjoy the outdoors & animals, want to improve flexibility, balance, joint, muscle & nerve stimulation; designed to meet unique needs, limitations & abilities of the rider
Member of: Canadian Therapeutic Riding Association
Chief Officer(s):
Colleen Baptist, Contact

Miramichi Board of Trade
6506 Rte. 8, Boiestown NB E6A 1Z7
Tel: 506-369-8889; *Fax:* 506-369-2468
Overview: A small local organization founded in 1953

Miramichi Chamber of Commerce (MCC)
PO Box 342, #2, 120 Newcastle Blvd., Miramichi NB E1N 3A7
Tel: 506-622-5522; *Fax:* 506-622-5959
mirchamber@nb.aibn.com
www.miramichichamber.com
Previous Name: Greater Miramichi Chamber of Commerce
Overview: A small local organization founded in 1981
Affliation(s): New Brunswick Chamber of Commerce; Atlantic Provinces Chamber of Commerce; Canadian Chamber of Commerce
Chief Officer(s):
Wally McLean, President
Brooke Hamilton, Executive Director, 506-622-5522
Membership: *Fees:* $125-$450 business; $55 retired; $25 student
Activities: Golf Tournament; Lunch and Learns

Miramichi Historical Society, Inc.
2224 King George Hwy., Miramichi NB E1V 6N3
Tel: 506-733-3448
Overview: A small local organization founded in 1959
Mission: To acquire & preserve papers, articles & artifacts of historical or architectural interest; to maintain archives of genealogical & historical information
Finances: *Funding Sources:* Provincial government; public donations
Activities: Operates Rankin House Museum

Miramichi Salmon Association
485 Rte. 420, South Esk NB E1V 4L9
Tel: 506-622-4000
nola@miramichisalmon.ca
www.miramichisalmon.ca
www.facebook.com/MiramichiSalmonAssociation
Overview: A small local organization founded in 1953
Mission: To preserve, protect & propagate the Atlantic salmon
Member of: Atlantic Salmon Federation
Chief Officer(s):
Mark Hambrook, President
mark@miramichisalmon.ca
Kenneth Kyle, Secretary-Treasurer
Finances: *Annual Operating Budget:* $500,000-$1.5 Million; *Funding Sources:* Fundraising; Membership dues; Donations; Government grants
Staff Member(s): 6
Membership: *Fees:* $10 junior/guide/camp staff; $50 regular; $100 sustaining; $250-$500 Corporations; $1000 lifetime

Mirror & District Museum Association
PO Box 246, Mirror AB T0B 3C0
Tel: 403-788-3828; *Fax:* 403-788-3828
mmuseum@telus.net
Overview: A small local charitable organization founded in 1977
Mission: To collect & display artifacts & specimens that depict the district's past in terms of natural resources, native peoples, exploration, transportation, settlement, education, cultural achievements, agriculture, petroleum, mining, manufacturing & with special emphasis of the contribution made by the railroad as an important factor in its economic base
Member of: Museum's Alberta
Chief Officer(s):
Ernie Schafer, President

Miss G Project
PO Box 557, Stn. A, Toronto ON K1N 9H1
e-mail: missg@themissgproject.org
themissgproject.wix.com
www.facebook.com/missgproject
twitter.com/missgproject
Overview: A small provincial organization
Mission: The Miss G Project for Equity in Education is a grassroots feminist organization working to combat all forms of oppression in and through education.
Chief Officer(s):
Sarah Ghabrial, Political Action & Communications
sarah@themissgproject.org
Dilani Mohan, Finances & Events Coordinator
dilani@themissgproject.org
Sheetal Rawal, Research & High School Coordinator
sheetal@themissgproject.org
Lara Shkordoff, Education & University Coordinator
lara@themissgproject.org

Missing Children Quebec *Voir* Enfant-Retour Québec

Missing Children Society of Canada (MCSC)
#219, 3501 - 23 St. NE, Calgary AB T2E 6V8
Tel: 403-291-0705; *Fax:* 403-291-9728
Toll-Free: 800-661-6160
info@mcsc.ca
www.mcsc.ca
www.facebook.com/MissingChildrenSocietyofCanada
twitter.com/MCSCanada
www.youtube.com//MissingChildCanada
Overview: A medium-sized national charitable organization founded in 1986
Mission: To reunite abducted & runaway children with their searching families
Chief Officer(s):
Amanda Pick, Executive Director
apick@mcsc.ca
Darcy Tuer, Chair
Jeff Davison, Vice-Chair
David Grout, Secretary
Finances: *Funding Sources:* Donations
Staff Member(s): 6
Activities: Facilitating searches nationally & internationally through professional investigations & public awareness; Offering family support programs; Organizing fundraising activities; *Awareness Events:* "Light the Way Home"; National Missing Children's Day, May 25

Ontario Office
#814, 99 Bronte Rd., Oakville ON L6K 3B7
Tel: 905-469-8826; *Fax:* 905-469-8828
missingchildren@mcsc.ca
Chief Officer(s):
Barb Snider, Case Director

Mission à l'intérieur de l'Afrique (Canada) *See* Africa Inland Mission International (Canada)

Mission Air Transportation Network *See* Hope Air

Mission Association for Community Living (MACL)
33345 - 2nd Ave., Mission BC V2V 1K4
Tel: 604-826-9080; *Fax:* 604-826-9611
macl@macl.bc.ca
www.macl.bc.ca
Overview: A small local charitable organization founded in 1958
Mission: To advocate for & build an inclusive & caring community where the empowerment & rights of all individuals are realized
Member of: British Columbian Association for Community Living
Chief Officer(s):
Bob Ingram, President
Finances: *Annual Operating Budget:* $3 Million-$5 Million; *Funding Sources:* Provincial government; bingo & gaming revenue
Staff Member(s): 120; 15 volunteer(s)
Membership: 75; *Fees:* $10; $5 self advocates; $1 non-voting staff memberships; *Member Profile:* People with developmental disabilities; their families; staff; *Committees:* Advocacy; Public Relations; Executive
Activities: *Awareness Events:* Illuminaria, 3rd Sat. of Sept.; *Library:* MACL Library
Awards:
• Annual Student Bursaries (Grant)

Mission Aviation Fellowship of Canada (MAFC)
264 Woodlawn Rd. West, Guelph ON N1H 1B6
Tel: 519-821-3914; *Fax:* 519-823-1650
Toll-Free: 877-351-9344
info@mafc.org
www.mafc.org
www.facebook.com/mafcanada
twitter.com/mafcanada
www.youtube.com/MAFCanada
Overview: A small international charitable organization founded in 1973
Mission: To provide aviation & communications help to overseas missions; To operate approximately 145 aircraft in over 30 developing countries
Member of: Canadian Council of Christian Charities
Affliation(s): Mission Aviation US; Mission Aviation Australia; Mission Aviation Europe; Mission Aviation South Africa; Asas de Socorro, Brazil
Chief Officer(s):
Robert Roebuck, Chair
Finances: *Annual Operating Budget:* $1.5 Million-$3 Million; *Funding Sources:* Donations
Staff Member(s): 60; 20 volunteer(s)
Membership: 1-99
Activities: *Awareness Events:* Charity Air Fair, last weekend in May

Mission Bon Accueil / Welcome Hall Mission
606, rue de Courcell, Montréal QC M4C 3C1
Tel: 514-523-5288; *Fax:* 514-523-6456
info@missionba.com
www.missionbonaccueil.com
www.linkedin.com/company/welcome-hall-mission-mission-bon-accueil
www.facebook.com/MissionBonAccueil
twitter.com/whmba
www.youtube.com/user/whmba
Overview: A small local charitable organization founded in 1982
Mission: Pour fournir les moins fortunés à Montréal avec des services essentiels tels que le logement, le traitement de la toxicomanie, de la nourriture, des conseils et éducation
Chief Officer(s):
Cyril Morgan, Directeur exécutif

Finances: *Annual Operating Budget:* Less than $50,000
Staff Member(s): 110

Mission Community Services Food Bank *See* Mission Community Services Food Centre

Mission Community Services Food Centre (MCSS)
32646 Logan Ave., Mission BC V2V 6C7
Tel: 604-814-3333
missionfoodcentre@hotmail.ca
www.missionfoodcentre.com
Previous Name: Mission Community Services Food Bank
Overview: A small local charitable organization founded in 1972
Mission: To identify & respond to the needs of individuals, families, & the community
Member of: Mission Community Services Society
Finances: *Annual Operating Budget:* Less than $50,000
10 volunteer(s)
Membership: *Committees:* Mission Food Coalition
Activities: *Awareness Events:* Christmas in July

Mission Heritage Association (MHA)
PO Box 3341, Mission BC V2V 4J5
Tel: 604-826-0277; *Fax:* 604-826-0333
mhadmin@telus.net
www.heritagepark-mission.ca
www.facebook.com/FraserRiverHeritagePark
Overview: A small local organization founded in 1979

Mission Indian Friendship Centre (MIFC)
33150A - 1st Ave., Mission BC V2V 1G4
Tel: 604-826-1281; *Fax:* 604-826-4056
Toll-Free: 888-826-1281
www.mifcs.org
www.facebook.com/missionfriendshipcentresociety
Overview: A small local charitable organization founded in 1973
Mission: To provide acceptable assistance & services to the community, without prejudice from an aboriginal perspective
Affliation(s): all First Nations organizations
Chief Officer(s):
Grace Cunningham, Executive Director
director@mifcs.bc.ca
Finances: *Funding Sources:* Federal & provincial government
Staff Member(s): 14
Activities: *Awareness Events:* National Aboriginal Day, June; *Library:* Resource Centre; Open to public

Mission Regional Chamber of Commerce
34033 Lougheed Hwy., Mission BC V2V 5X8
Tel: 604-826-6914; *Fax:* 604-826-5916
info@missionchamber.bc.ca
www.missionchamber.bc.ca
www.facebook.com/Mission.Business.Network
twitter.com/MissionCommerce
www.youtube.com/TheMissionChamber
Overview: A medium-sized local organization founded in 1893
Mission: To foster a network for entrepreneurial leaders to partner in education, communication & representation.
Member of: aC Chamber of Commerce; Vancouver Coast Mountains Tourism Association
Chief Officer(s):
Sean Melia, President
smelia@prospera.ca
Membership: 444; *Fees:* Schedule available; *Committees:* Membership; Events; Government Affairs; Tourism
Activities: *Awareness Events:* Annual Business Excellence Awards

The Mission to Lepers *See* effect:hope

Missionaires de la Royauté du Christ / Missionaries of the Kingship of Christ
5750, boul Rosemont, Montréal QC H1T 2H2
Tél: 514-259-2542; *Téléc:* 514-259-6911
andre.comtois@bellnet.ca
www.simkc.org
Aperçu: *Dimension:* petite; *Envergure:* locale

Missionaries of the Kingship of Christ *Voir* Missionaires de la Royauté du Christ

Missionary Sisters of Our Lady of the Angels *Voir* Soeurs missionnaires Notre-Dame des Anges

Missionary Sisters of The Precious Blood of North America
St Bernard's Convent, 685 Finch Ave. West, Toronto ON M2R 1P2
Tel: 416-630-3298; *Fax:* 416-630-9114
www.preciousbloodsisters.com
www.facebook.com/156106151112902
Overview: A small international organization founded in 1885
Mission: Involved in early childhood education & teaching at the elementary, secondary, & college levels. Also work in health care services as nurses, doctors, administrators, physical & occupational therapists, hospital chaplains, caregivers for the elderly, with AIDs patients & in nutrition education. Serves in social work, parish ministry, domestic work, gardening, religious education, work with the mentally & physically handicapped, retreat work, art, & in ministry to the Hispanic & First Nations people.
Finances: *Funding Sources:* donations
Staff Member(s): 60

Missions catholiques au Canada *See* Catholic Missions in Canada

Les Missions des Soeurs Missionnaires du Christ-Roi
4730, boul Lévesque ouest, Chomedey QC H7W 2R4
Tél: 450-687-2100
missionsmcr@hotmail.com
Également appelé: Missions MCR
Aperçu: *Dimension:* moyenne; *Envergure:* internationale; Organisme sans but lucratif; fondée en 1979
Mission: Organiser, administrer, maintenir une oeuvre dont les fins sont la religion, la charité; promouvoir l'éducation et le bien-être, particulièrement en ce qui a trait aux différents buts qu'il s'est fixé; aide internationale
Membre(s) du bureau directeur:
Maekawa Harumi, Présidente
Finances: *Budget de fonctionnement annuel:* $100,000-$250,000; *Fonds:* Fondations; Subventions
Membre(s) du personnel: 1
Membre: 213 institutionnel
Activités: *Bibliothèque*

Missisquoi Historical Society / Société d'histoire de Missisquoi
2, rue River, Stanbridge East QC J0J 2H0
Tel: 450-248-3153; *Fax:* 450-248-0420
info@missisquoimuseum.ca
www.missisquoimuseum.ca
Overview: A small local charitable organization founded in 1899
Mission: To administer the Missisquoi Museum, including the Cornell Mill, Hodge's Store & Bill's Barn; UEL archives & to collect, preserve, research, exhibit & publish items of historical interest
Chief Officer(s):
Pamela Realffe, Executive Secretary
Finances: *Annual Operating Budget:* $100,000-$250,000
Staff Member(s): 3; 75 volunteer(s)
Membership: 600; *Fees:* $10 single; $15 family; $125 life
Activities: Apple Pie Festival; *Library:* Archives; by appointment

Mississauga Arts Council (MAC)
#1055, 300 City Centre Dr., Ground Fl., Mississauga ON L5B 3C9
Tel: 905-615-4278; *Fax:* 905-615-4171
info@mississaugaartscouncil.com
www.mississaugaartscouncil.com
www.facebook.com/missartscouncil?ref=ts
twitter.com/missartscouncil
Overview: A small local charitable organization founded in 1981
Mission: To foster & develop, support & champion a vibrant, dynamic arts comminity in the city of Mississauga through services; to enrich the lives of its citizens
Affliation(s): Ontario Arts Council; City of Mississauga; Boards of Education in Peel; Mississauga Board of Trade
Chief Officer(s):
Linda Thomas, Executive Director
linda@mississaugaartscouncil.com
Benjamin Thornton, President
Finances: *Annual Operating Budget:* $500,000-$1.5 Million; *Funding Sources:* City of Mississauga; sponsors; donors; membership fees; The Ontario Trillium Foundation; foundations
Staff Member(s): 4; 60 volunteer(s)
Membership: 250 groups + 250 corporate + 700 individuals; *Fees:* $25 individual; $30 family; $35 arts organizations (non-profit); *Member Profile:* Individuals; organizations; corporations; *Committees:* Grants; Membership; Executive; Development; Projects; Special Events; Ad Hoc; Communications
Activities: Member breakfasts; networking events; workshops; advocacy; *Library* by appointment
Awards:
• Mississauga Arts Awards (Award)

The Mississauga Astronomical Society *See* Royal Astronomical Society of Canada

Mississauga Board of Trade (MBOT)
#701, 77 City Centre Dr., Mississauga ON L5B 1M5
Tel: 905-273-6151; *Fax:* 905-273-4937
info@mbot.com
www.mbot.com
www.linkedin.com/groups/Mississauga-Board-Trade-1851210
www.facebook.com/MississaugaBoardofTrade
twitter.com/MBOTOntario
www.youtube.com/user/MBOTMississauga
Overview: A small local organization founded in 1976
Mission: To provide a forum for business; To work together to influence public policy; To promote a better understanding of the marketplace among policy makers, educators, & the general public
Member of: Ontario Chamber of Commerce; Canadian Chamber of Commerce
Chief Officer(s):
Sheldon Leiba, President & CEO
sleiba@mbot.com
Finances: *Funding Sources:* Membership fees
Staff Member(s): 9
Membership: 1,500; *Committees:* Ambassadors; Environment; Health & Safety; Human Resources; Independent Business; Technology; International Trade; Education & Training; Transportation, Supply, Chain
Activities: *Speaker Service:* Yes; *Rents Mailing List:* Yes

Mississauga Choral Society (MCS)
PO Box 59505, Mississauga ON L5H 1G9
Tel: 905-278-7059
Other Communication: www.youtube.com/embed/UdTF-yu9oYM
info@mcschorus.ca
www.mcschorus.ca
www.facebook.com/pages/Mississauga-Choral-Society/273190841879
Overview: A small local organization founded in 1975
Mission: To present to its audiences the major works of the choral repertoire from the 16th to 21st century; to provide choristers an opportunity to improve vocal skills while learning & performing works
Member of: Mississauga Arts Council
Affliation(s): Oakville Arts Council; Choirs Ontario
Chief Officer(s):
Mervin William Fick, Artistic Director & Conductor
Rosanne Caruso, Administrator
George Hrubecky, President
Finances: *Annual Operating Budget:* $100,000-$250,000; *Funding Sources:* Government
Staff Member(s): 3; 8 volunteer(s)
Membership: 90 individual + 12 associate; *Fees:* $10; *Member Profile:* Volunteer choir with paid section leads; *Committees:* Marketing; Programming; Finance; Fundraising
Activities: Resident choir of the Living Arts Centre, Missisauga; concert series;

Mississauga Food Bank
3121 Universal Dr., Mississauga ON L4X 2E2
Tel: 905-270-5589; *Fax:* 905-270-4076
info@themississaugafoodbank.org
www.themississaugafoodbank.org
www.facebook.com/themississaugafoodbank
twitter.com/food_bank
Overview: A small local charitable organization
Mission: To distribute to food to the less fortunate in Mississauga
Chief Officer(s):
Christopher Hatch, Executive Director
chris@themississaugafoodbank.org
Staff Member(s): 8
Membership: *Fees:* $50

Mississauga Heritage Foundation Inc. (MHF)
1921 Dundas St. West, Mississauga ON L5K 1R2
Tel: 905-828-8411; *Fax:* 905-828-8176
info@heritagemississauga.org
www.heritagemississauga.com
Also Known As: Heritage Mississauga
Overview: A small local charitable organization founded in 1960
Mission: To identify, research, interpret, promote & encourage awareness of the heritage resources relating to the city of Mississauga

Member of: Heritage Canada
Affiliation(s): City of Mississauga
Chief Officer(s):
Jayme Gaspar, Executive Director
jgaspar@heritagemississauga.org
Finances: *Funding Sources:* City of Mississauga grant; service fees; fundraising
Staff Member(s): 4
Membership: *Fees:* $30 individual; $50 family/small business; $10 senior/students; $35 school/non-profit; *Committees:* Marketing
Activities: Tours; lectures; outreach; exhibits; events; Heritage Mississauga Showcase; awards dinner; *Internships:* Yes; *Speaker Service:* Yes; *Library:* Resource Centre; by appointment
Awards:
• MHF Heritage Award (Award)
• Lifetime Member Award (Award)
• Special Recognition Certificate (Award)

Mississauga Real Estate Board
#1, 3450 Ridgeway Dr., Mississauga ON L5L 0A2
Tel: 905-608-6732; *Fax:* 905-608-9988
www.mreb.ca
twitter.com/MREBca
Overview: A small local organization founded in 1954 overseen by Ontario Real Estate Association
Mission: To represent its members & keep them informed about events involving real estate so that they are able to provide knowledgable service to the public
Member of: The Canadian Real Estate Association
Chief Officer(s):
Donna Metcalfe, Executive Director
executiveofficer@mreb.ca
Gay Napper, Manager, Events & Membership Services
events@mreb.ca
Staff Member(s): 5
Membership: 1,000-4,999; *Fees:* $160; *Committees:* CMC; Communications; Education; Finance; Golf; Governance; Government Relations; Membership; Nominations; Related Services

Mississauga-Etobicoke Coin Stamp & Collectibles Club (MECSCC)
5261 Naskapi Ct., Mississauga ON L5R 2P4
Tel: 905-677-3765
info@gta-collects.ca
www.gta-collects.ca
Previous Name: Thistletown Coin & Stamp Club
Overview: A small local organization
Mission: To promote collectors in various numismatic & related groups
Member of: Ontario Numismatic Association; Royal Canadian Numismatic Association
Chief Officer(s):
Bob Wilson, Chair
Membership: 25+
Activities: Monthly meetings

Mississippi Mills Chamber of Commerce
PO Box 1244, Almonte ON K0A 1A0
Tel: 613-256-7886
www.mississippimills.com
www.facebook.com/MMChamber
Overview: A small local organization founded in 1996
Mission: To host networking events for its members
Member of: Canadian Chamber of Commerce
Membership: 109; *Fees:* $100 1-3 employees; $150 4-5 employees

Mittimatalik Hunters' & Trappers' Organization
PO Box 189, Pond Inlet NU X0A 0S0
Tel: 867-899-8856; *Fax:* 867-899-8095
Overview: A small local organization founded in 1974

Mizrachi Organization of Canada
296 Wilson Ave., Toronto ON M3H 1S8
Tel: 416-630-9266; *Fax:* 416-630-2305
mizrachi@rogers.com
www.mizrachi.ca
www.facebook.com/186778775014
twitter.com/MizrachiCanada
Also Known As: Mizrachi-Hapoel Hamizrachi Men's Organization
Overview: A medium-sized international charitable organization
Mission: To coordinate Zionist-oriented programming for the Orthodox Jewish communities in Canada; to raise funds for educational & social welfare institutions in Israel
Member of: Canadian Zionist Federation; World Religious Zionist Movement; World Mizrachi Organization
Chief Officer(s):
Meir Rosenberh, Executive Director
mizrachi@rogers.com
Finances: *Funding Sources:* Private donations
Staff Member(s): 4
Activities: Adult educational programs; *Speaker Service:* Yes; *Library* Open to public by appointment

Mobilité Électrique Canada ***See*** Electric Mobility Canada

Model "A" Owners of Canada Inc. (MAOC)
PO Box 31, Stn. A, Toronto ON M1K 5B9
e-mail: maocinc@rogers.com
www.modelaowners.com
www.youtube.com/user/ModelAOwners
Overview: A small national organization founded in 1959
Mission: To grow & maintain enthusiasm about the Ford Model A car
Chief Officer(s):
Ross Walter, President
rosswalter@cogeco.ca
Finances: *Funding Sources:* Membership fees
Membership: 350+
Activities: Meetings held the first Tues. of every month

Model Aeronautics Association of Canada Inc. (MAAC) / Modélistes Aéronautiques Associés du Canada
#9, 5100 South Service Rd., Burlington ON L7L 6A5
Tel: 905-632-9808; *Fax:* 905-632-3304
Toll-Free: 855-359-6222
www.maac.ca
www.facebook.com/group.php?gid=112219502126070
Overview: A medium-sized national organization founded in 1949
Mission: To foster, enhance, assist, aid & engage in scientific development; To provide central organization to record & disseminate information relating to model aeronautics; To guide & direct national model aviation activities; To direct technical organization of national & international model aircraft contests
Affiliation(s): Aero Club of Canada; Fédération aeronautique internationale
Chief Officer(s):
Ronald R. Dodd, President, 604-824-2976
Linda Patrick, Secretary-Treasurer
Finances: *Funding Sources:* Membership fees
Membership: 13,000+; *Fees:* Schedule available; *Member Profile:* Aircraft modelling enthousiasts; *Committees:* Over 30 committees including all disciplines of model aviation
Activities: *Library:* Archives; by appointment
Awards:
• MAAC [Model Aeronautics Association of Canada] Hall of Fame Award (Award)
To recognize a significant contribution to model aviation in Canada
Meetings/Conferences: • Model Aeronautics Association of Canada 2015 Annual Meetings, April, 2015, Delta Edmonton Centre, Edmonton, AB
Scope: National
Contact Information: Phone: 780-429-3900

Alberta Zone
PO Box 1245, 328 Harrison Ct., Crossfield AB T0M 0S0
Tel: 403-946-9939
zone-a@maac.ca
Chief Officer(s):
Don G. McGowan, Zone Director

Atlantic Zone
11665 Hwy. 11, Pokemouche NB E8P 1J4
Tel: 506-727-5225; *Fax:* 506-727-7788
Chief Officer(s):
Regis Landry, Zone Director

British Columbia & Yukon Zone
#39, 844 Hutley Rd., Armstrong BC V0E 1B7
Tel: 250-546-0612; *Fax:* 250-546-0618
Chief Officer(s):
Steve Hughes, Zone Director

British Columbia Coastal Zone
PO Box 1376, Parksville BC V9P 2H3
Tel: 250-248-5545
Chief Officer(s):
William (Bill) Rollins, Zone Director

Manitoba/Northwestern Ontario Zone
1256 Heenan Pl., Kenora ON P9N 2Y8
Tel: 807-468-7507
Chief Officer(s):
Peter Schaffer, Zone Director

Middle Ontario Zone
1546 - 8th Ave., St Catharines ON L2R 6P7
Tel: 905-685-1170; *Fax:* 905-641-1082
Chief Officer(s):
Roy R.R. Rymer, Zone Director

Northern Ontario Zone
40 Parkshore Ct., Sault Ste Marie ON P6A 5Z3
Tel: 705-759-1670
Chief Officer(s):
Kevin McGrath, Zone Director

Ottawa Valley Zone
3104 County Rd. 29, Brockville ON K6V 5T4
Tel: 613-802-5000; *Fax:* 613-342-1029
Chief Officer(s):
Claude R. Melbourne, Zone Director

Quebec Zone
1272 av LaVigerie, Québec QC G1W 3X2
Tel: 418-650-3150
Chief Officer(s):
Rodger A. Williams, Zone Director

St. Lawrence Zone
5763, av McAlear, Côte Saint-Luc QC H4W 2H2
Tel: 514-486-1898
Chief Officer(s):
Steve Woloz, Zone Director

Saskatchewan Zone
1116 Horace St., Regina SK S4T 5L4
Tel: 306-781-7400
Chief Officer(s):
Heinz U. Pantel, Zone Director

Southeast Ontario Zone
#RR1, 15390 - 8th Conc., Schomberg ON L0G IT0
Tel: 905-939-2928
Chief Officer(s):
Clair B. Murray, Zone Director

Southwest Ontario Zone
450 Broadway St., Tillsonburg ON N4G 3S7
Tel: 519-842-8242
Chief Officer(s):
Frank Klenk, Zone Director

Model Forest of Newfoundland & Labrador (MFNL)
Humber Trust Building, PO Box 68, #11, 19 - 21 West St., Corner Brook NL A2H 6C3
Tel: 709-637-7300
Previous Name: Western Newfoundland Model Forest
Overview: A small local organization
Mission: The Model Forest is a not-for-profit corporation formed as a partnership of organizations & individuals working on the implementation of activities that advance their abilities to practice sustainable forest management & community-based economic development utilizing forest resources
Member of: Canadian Model Forest Network
Chief Officer(s):
Sean Dolter, General Manager
seandolter@mfnl.ca

Modélistes Aéronautiques Associés du Canada ***See*** Model Aeronautics Association of Canada Inc.

Modern Baroque Opera Society
1895 Venables St., Vancouver BC V5L 2H6
Tel: 604-216-1114
Overview: A small local organization

Modular Housing Association Prairie Provinces (MMHA)
PO Box 3538, Stn. main, Sherwood Park AB T8H 2T4
Tel: 780-429-1798; *Fax:* 780-429-1871
mha@shawlink.ca
mhaprairies.ca
www.linkedin.com/profile/view?id=67115543&trk=tab_pro
www.facebook.com/ModularHousingAssociationPrairieProvinces
Also Known As: Modular Housing Association
Previous Name: Modular Manufactured Housing Association - Alberta & Saskatchewan
Overview: A small provincial organization founded in 1975
Mission: A regional trade association responsible for the interests of the manufactured housing industry in Alberta, Manitoba and Saskatchewan.
Chief Officer(s):
Sandra Nigro, Executive Director, 780-429-1798, Fax: 780-429-1871

Hank Starno, Director, Technical & Government Relations, 780-429-1798, Fax: 780-429-1871
Finances: *Annual Operating Budget:* $100,000-$250,000; *Funding Sources:* Industry-funded
Staff Member(s): 1
Membership: 150; *Committees:* Finance; membership; advertising
Activities: Building green and sustainable housing; *Speaker Service:* Yes
Meetings/Conferences: • Modular Housing Association - Prairie Provinces 9th Annual Saskatchewan Industry Meeting, February, 2015, Executive Hotel & Resorts, Regina, SK
Scope: Provincial

Modular Manufactured Housing Association - Alberta & Saskatchewan *See* Modular Housing Association Prairie Provinces

Moelle Épinière et Motricité Québec
#400, 6020, rue Jean-Talon est, Montréal QC H1S 3B1
Tél: 514-341-7272; *Téléc:* 514-341-8884
Ligne sans frais: 877-341-7272
info@moelleepiniere.com
www.moelleepiniere.com
www.facebook.com/MEMOQuebec
twitter.com/MEMOQuebec
Aperçu: *Dimension:* moyenne; *Envergure:* provinciale; fondée en 2010 surveillé par Spinal Cord Injury Canada
Membre(s) du bureau directeur:
Martine St-Yves, Présidente
Guylaine Beaulac, Trésorière
Walter Zelaya, Directeur général
wzelaya@paraquad.qc.ca
Finances: *Fonds:* Emploi-Québec
Membre: 2,000
Activités: Intégration sociale; employabilité; défense des droits; sensibilisation et prévention; recherche scientifique

Mohawk Council of Akwesasne
PO Box 579, Cornwall ON K6H 5T3
Tel: 613-575-2250; *Fax:* 613-575-2181
info@akwesasne.ca
www.akwesasne.ca
Overview: A small local organization
Chief Officer(s):
Russell Roundpoint, CAO

Moisson Laurentides
25, rue Rolland-Brière, Blainville QC J7C 5R8
Tél: 450-434-0790; *Téléc:* 450-434-9235
reception@moissonlaurentides.org
www.moissonlaurentides.org
Aperçu: *Dimension:* petite; *Envergure:* locale; Organisme sans but lucratif; fondée en 1987
Mission: Une banque alimentaire dont le rôle est la récupération gratuite des surplus de l'industrie alimentaire et la distribution gratuite d'aliments aux plus démunis par l'intermédiaire d'organismes communautaires
Membre de: Reseau banques alimentaires du Québec; Banques alimentaires Canada
Membre(s) du bureau directeur:
Anne Bélanger, Directrice générale
direction@moissonlaurentides.org
Josée Lamy, Chef, Distribution
distribution@moissonlaurentides.org
Mireille Corbeil, Coordonnatrice, Ressources financières
comptabilite@moissonlaurentides.org
Finances: *Budget de fonctionnement annuel:* $250,000-$500,000
Membre(s) du personnel: 3; 500 bénévole(s)
Activités: Tournoi du golf

Moisson Mauricie/Centre-du-Québec
630, rue Poisson, Trois-Rivières QC G9A 2V5
Tél. 819-377-7778; *Téléc:* 819-377-7718
moisson.mauricie@tr.cgocable.ca
www.moisson-mcdq.org
www.facebook.com/moissonmcdq
Aperçu: *Dimension:* petite; *Envergure:* locale; Organisme sans but lucratif; fondée en 1988
Mission: Récupération et distribution d'aliments aux personnes économiquement défavorisées; lutte contre la pauvreté avec les organismes partenaires; utilisation de divers moyens pour favoriser la prise en mains des personnes démunies et développer leur autonomie
Membre de: Association québécoise des banques alimentaires et des moissons; Association canadienne des banques alimentaires
Membre(s) du bureau directeur:
Chantal Paquin, Directrice générale
Finances: *Budget de fonctionnement annuel:* $250,000-$500,000; *Fonds:* Centraide; Régie Régionale de la Santé et des Services Sociaux
Membre(s) du personnel: 6; 250 bénévole(s)
Membre: 60; *Critères d'admissibilité:* Organismes d'aide alimentaire; *Comités:* De soutien; d'accréditation des organismes; de bénévolat
Activités: Deux grandes collectes annuelles; Fête des bénévoles; Rencontres annuelle des organismes; *Evénements de sensibilisation:* Grande collecte de denrées; *Stagiaires:* Oui; *Service de conférenciers:* Oui

Moisson Québec / Québec Harvest
2125, rue Hertz, Sainte-Foy QC G1N 4E1
Tél: 418-682-5061; *Téléc:* 418-682-3549
info@moissonquebec.com
www.moissonquebec.com
Aperçu: *Dimension:* moyenne; *Envergure:* locale; Organisme sans but lucratif; fondée en 1986
Mission: Enrayer la faim et la pauvreté; récupérer et redistribuer gratuitement aux organismes communautaires les surplus agro-alimentaires; sensibiliser la population et les instances concernées à la faim et à la pauvreté; implanter des solutions favorisant l'autonomie des personnes en difficulté
Membre de: Fédération québécoise des banques alimentaires; Association canadienne des banques alimentaires
Affliation(s): Centraide Québec & Chaudière-Appalaches
Membre(s) du bureau directeur:
Elaine Côté, Directrice générale
Finances: *Budget de fonctionnement annuel:* $500,000-$1.5 Million
Membre(s) du personnel: 8; 100 bénévole(s)
Membre: 80
Activités: *Evénements de sensibilisation:* Soupe Populaire, sep.; Grande Collecte, mai; Récolte de l'Amitié; *Stagiaires:* Oui; *Service de conférenciers:* Oui; *Bibliothèque:* Centre de ressources éducatives; rendez-vous

The Molson Family Foundation / Fondation Famille Molson
1555, rue Notre Dame est, Montréal QC H2L 2R5
Tel: 514-521-1786; *Fax:* 514-599-5396
Previous Name: The Molson Foundation
Overview: A small national charitable organization
Mission: To support innovative projects in fields of health & welfare, education, social development, national development & the humanities; registered Canadian charitable organizations only

The Molson Foundation *See* The Molson Family Foundation

Mon Réseau Plus, Association professionnelle des massothérapeutes spécialisés du Québec inc.
2285, rue St-Pierre, Drummondville QC J2C 5A7
Téléc: 819-472-2900
Ligne sans frais: 800-461-1312
info@monreseauplus.com
www.monreseauplus.com
www.linkedin.com/company/mon-r-seau-plus
www.facebook.com/pages/Mon-Réseau-Plus/122150035971
Également appelé: Mon Réseau +
Merged from: AMOC; CMA; CMAPPAC
Aperçu: *Dimension:* petite; *Envergure:* provinciale; fondée en 2008
Membre(s) du bureau directeur:
Danielle Kenney, Présidente
Membre: *Montant de la cotisation:* 45.99$

Mon Sheong Foundation
11199 Yonge St., Richmond Hill ON L4S 1L2
Tel: 905-883-9288; *Fax:* 905-883-9855
Toll-Free: 866-708-0002
msf@monsheong.org
www.monsheong.org
Overview: A medium-sized local organization founded in 1964
Mission: To recognize the Chinese language & philosophy through caring for the elderly & edifying the young; To provide programs & services which respond to the needs of communities
Member of: Ontario Association of Nonprofit Homes & Services for Seniors
Affliation(s): Ontario Hospital Association
Chief Officer(s):
Fiona Cho, Marketing & Communication Director
Finances: *Annual Operating Budget:* $1.5 Million-$3 Million; *Funding Sources:* Ministry of Health; Donations; Membership fees
Staff Member(s): 28; 100 volunteer(s)
Membership: 250+; *Fees:* $10
Activities: Operating the Mon Sheong Home for the Aged, the Mon Sheong Foundation Chinese Schools, & the Mon Sheong Youth Group

Monarchist League of Canada (MLC) / Ligue Monarchiste du Canada
PO Box 1057, Stn. Lakeshore West, Oakville ON L6K 0B2
Tel: 905-912-0916
Other Communication: youth@monarchist.ca (Young Monarchists)
domsec@monarchist.ca
www.monarchist.ca
www.facebook.com/canadamonarchist
twitter.com/monarchist
www.youtube.com/LigueMonarchLeague?hl=en-GB
Overview: A large national organization founded in 1970
Mission: To promote loyalty to the Sovereign & a broader understanding of constitutional monarchy as part of Canada's parliament, history, social fabric, culture & traditions
Affliation(s): Canadian Royal Heritage Trust
Chief Officer(s):
Robert Finch, Dominion Chairman
chairman@monarchist.ca
Keith Roy, Vice-Chairman
homes@keithroy.com.
Finances: *Annual Operating Budget:* $250,000-$500,000; *Funding Sources:* Membership fees; donations
Staff Member(s): 2; 15 volunteer(s)
Membership: 25 institutional + 500 student + 13,500 individual + 3,000 other; *Fees:* $24; *Member Profile:* Loyalty to Crown
Activities: Promotion of education & support for the Canadian Crown; "Red Boxes" for schools & youth groups; *Awareness Events:* Royal Week, 3rd week of May; *Library:* King George III Library; by appointment
Publications:
• Canadian Monarchist News
Type: Newsletter

Moncton Archers & Bowhunters Association *See* Tir-à-l'arc Moncton Archers Inc.

Moncton Area Lawyers' Association (MALA) / Association des avocats et avocates de la région de Moncton (AAARM)
145 Assomption blvd., Moncton NB E1C 0R2
Tel: 506-389-1649; *Fax:* 506-856-6031
mala@nbnet.nb.ca
Previous Name: Moncton Barristers' Society
Overview: A small provincial organization founded in 1937
Mission: To procure & maintain a law library; to advance the science of jurisprudence; to promote the administration of justice; to uphold the honour of the profession of the law; to foster relations & cooperation among members; to encourage a high standard of legal education, training & ethics; to foster goodwill & better understanding of the legal system in the community
Chief Officer(s):
Jacqueline A. Cormier, Librarian
Finances: *Annual Operating Budget:* $50,000-$100,000; *Funding Sources:* Law Society of N.B.
Staff Member(s): 1
Membership: 204; *Fees:* $160
Activities: *Library:* Law Library; Open to public

Moncton Barristers' Society *See* Moncton Area Lawyers' Association

Moncton Chinese Friendship Association (MCFA) *See* Greater Moncton Chinese Cultural Association

Moncton Coin Club
PO Box 54, Moncton NB E1C 8R9
e-mail: coincbnt@nbnet.nb.ca
Overview: A small local organization founded in 1961
Member of: Canadian Numismatic Association

Moncton Northeast Construction Association (MNECA)
297 Collishaw St., Moncton NB E1C 9R2
Tel: 506-857-4038; *Fax:* 506-857-8861
info@mneca.ca
www.mneca.ca

Overview: A small local organization founded in 1942 overseen by Canadian Construction Association
Mission: To represent & advocate for employees of the construction industry
Chief Officer(s):
Bill Dixon, President
bdixon@mneca.ca
Staff Member(s): 3
Membership: 300+; *Fees:* $910 contractors/sub-contractor/manufacturer/supplier; $500 associate

Moncton Retriever Club
434 Charles Lutes Rd., Lutes Mountain NB E1G 2T4
Tel: 506-852-7107; *Fax:* 506-852-7107
yeloros@nb.sympatico.ca
Overview: A small local organization
Member of: New Brunswick Wildlife Federation
Chief Officer(s):
Brian Dempsey, President
Evelyn Hoyt, Secretary
5 volunteer(s)
Membership: 20 individual

Moncton University Employees Association ***Voir*** Association des employés de l'Université de Moncton

Monde des mots ***See*** People, Words & Change

Money Mentors
Airstate Bldg., #150, 1200 - 59 Ave. SE, Calgary AB T2H 2M4
Fax: 403-265-2240
Toll-Free: 888-294-0076
info@moneymentors.ca
www.moneymentors.ca
www.facebook.com/MoneyMentors
twitter.com/MoneyMentors
www.youtube.com/user/moneymentors?ob=0
Previous Name: Credit Counselling Services of Alberta
Overview: A small provincial organization founded in 1997
Mission: Not-for-profit credit counselling agency helping consumers resolve debt & money problems & gain control over their finances
Member of: Credit Counselling Canada
Chief Officer(s):
Jim Thorne, Executive Director
Activities: Offices in Red Deer, Lethbridge, Medicine Hat, Edmonton and Grande Prairie.

Montreal Advocates' Mutual Assistance Association ***Voir*** Association d'entraide des avocats de Montréal

Montréal Association for the Blind (MAB) / Association montréalaise pour les aveugles
Head Office, 7000 Sherbrooke Rd. West, Montréal QC H4B 1R3
Tel: 514-488-5552; *Fax:* 514-489-3477
info@mabmackay.ca
www.mabmackay.ca
Overview: A medium-sized local organization founded in 1908
Mission: To offer rehabilitation services (low vision, social work, occupational therapy, activites of daily living, orientation & mobility, computer adaptation, early intervention etc.) to blind & visually impaired persons; to offer residential services to blind & visually impaired seniors. The MAB-Mackay Rehabilitation Centre, located at 3500, boul Decarie in Montréal, provides family-centred adaptation, rehabilitation & social integration services to persons with a visual disability, and/or deaf or hard of hearing.
Finances: *Funding Sources:* Provincial government
Membership: *Member Profile:* Blind & visually impaired persons; *Committees:* Users'
Activities: *Internships:* Yes; *Speaker Service:* Yes

Montreal Association for the Intellectually Handicapped ***Voir*** Association de Montréal pour la déficience intellectuelle

Montréal Association of Insurance Women ***Voir*** Association des femmes d'assurance de Montréal

Montréal Association of Law Libraries ***Voir*** Association des bibliothèques de droit de Montréal

Montréal Cancer Institute ***Voir*** Institut du cancer de Montréal

Montreal CFA Society ***Voir*** Association CFA Montréal

Montréal Chamber Orchestra ***Voir*** Orchestre de chambre de Montréal

Montréal Children's Hospital Foundation ***See*** Fondation de l'Hôpital de Montréal pour enfants

Montréal Council of Women (MCW) / Le Conseil des femmes de Montréal (CFM)
1195 Sherbrooke St. West, Montréal QC H3A 1H9
Tel: 514-932-1154; *Fax:* 514-271-8914
mcwcfm@gmail.com
www.mcw-cfm.org
www.facebook.com/175809462469517
Overview: A small local organization founded in 1893
Mission: To improve the quality of life for women & their families in Québec
Affiliation(s): Canadian National Council of Women; Quebec Provincial Council of Women
Membership: 30,000; *Member Profile:* 70 federated societies
Activities: Monthly meetings; *Awareness Events:* Intl. Woman's Day (UN Day for Women's Rights & Intl. Peace), March 8
Awards:
- Woman of the Year Award (Award)

Montréal Danse
#109, 372, rue Sainte-Catherine ouest, Montréal QC H3B 1A2
Tél: 514-871-4005
questions@montrealdanse.com
www.montrealdanse.com
www.facebook.com/pages/Montreal-Danse/100944976616149
Aperçu: *Dimension:* petite; *Envergure:* locale; Organisme sans but lucratif; fondée en 1986
Mission: Se voue à la création de vibrantes oeuvres chorégraphiques avec le concours de plusieurs chorégraphes nationaux et internationaux
Membre de: Regroupement québécois de la danse
Membre(s) du bureau directeur:
Kathy Casey, Directrice artistique
Finances: *Fonds:* Conseil des Arts du Canada; Conseil des Arts et des Lettres du Québec; Conseil des Arts de Montréal
Membre(s) du personnel: 6

Montréal Federation of Housing Cooperatives ***Voir*** Fédération des coopératives d'habitation intermunicipale du Montréal métropolitain

Montréal Field Naturalists Club
42, av Ballantyne nord, Montréal QC H4X 2B8
Tel: 514-769-1542
montrealfieldnaturalists.wordpress.com
Overview: A small local organization founded in 1971
Mission: To increase knowledge of nature through outdoor & indoor activities; to act when nature seems to be threatened, by expressing protests, participating in meetings
Chief Officer(s):
Pat Borlace, President
p.borlace@yahoo.ca
10 volunteer(s)
Membership: 150 individual; *Fees:* $15 individual

Montréal Firefighters' Association Inc. ***Voir*** Association des Pompiers de Montréal inc.

Montréal Gem & Mineral Club (MGMC) / Le Club de gemmologie et de minérlogie de Montréal
CP 32522, Succ. B, 2445 ch Lucern, Montréal QC H3R 2K5
Tél: 514-878-9110
geminews@gmail.com
www.montrealgemmineralclub.ca
Aperçu: *Dimension:* petite; *Envergure:* locale; fondée en 1957
Mission: To provide information about gems & minerals
Membre de: Central Canadian Federation of Mineralogical Societies
Membre(s) du bureau directeur:
Mike Rooney, Contact
Membre: *Montant de la cotisation:* $20 individuals; $30 familiesy; *Critères d'admissibilite:* Rockhounds, collectors lapidaries, jewelers, & persons interested in learning about gems & minerals in the Montréal area
Activités: Organizing programs & field trips; Planning workshops; *Evénements de sensibilisation:* Annual Gem & Mineral Show; *Bibliothèque:* Montréal Gem & Mineral Club Library
Publications:
- Geminews

Type: Newsletter; *Frequency:* Monthly; *Price:* Free for Montréal Gem & Mineral Club members
Profile: Club activities & forthcoming events

Montréal General Hospital Foundation ***See*** Fondation de l'Hôpital Général de Montréal

Montréal Heart Institute ***Voir*** Institut de cardiologie de Montréal

Montréal Heart Institute Foundation ***See*** Fondation Institut de Cardiologie de Montréal

The Montréal Holocaust Memorial Centre (MHMC) / Le Centre commémoratif de l'Holocauste à Montréal
Cummings House, 5151, chemin de la Côte-Sainte-Catherine, Montréal QC H3W 1M6
Tel: 514-345-2605; *Fax:* 514-344-2651
info@mhmc.ca
www.mhmc.ca
www.facebook.com/78382729139
Overview: A medium-sized local organization founded in 1979
Mission: To provide services & programs for survivors of the Holocaust, their children & the general public (Jewish & non-Jewish, English & French speaking); to collect, document & preserve the record of Jewish life in Europe before, during & after the Holocaust
Member of: Canadian Museum Association; Societé des musées québécois; International Council of Museums; American Association of Museums; American Association of State & Local History; Association of Holocaust Organizations; Canadian Jewish Historical Society
Chief Officer(s):
Alice Herscovitch, Executive Director
Helen Malkin, President
Staff Member(s): 10; 180 volunteer(s)
Membership: *Committees:* Education; Finance; Remembrance; Holocause Education Series; Human Rights; Kristallnacht; Museum; 35th Anniversary Event; Public Position; Rememberance; Yom Hashoah
Activities: Museum open throughout the year; provides guided tours, three major travelling exhibits; exhibits & museum, education & outreach are based on art, culture, historical reference & testimony & artifacts collected in Montréal; provides docent training, archives; Community Outreach - commemoration, testimonies, lectures/films, interfaith programs; Educational Resources - seminars/workshops, roundtable discussions, teachers' training, instructional material, speakers' bureau; CEGEP Holocaust Symposium; *Internships:* Yes; *Speaker Service:* Yes; *Library:* MHMC Library; Open to public

Montreal Numismatic Society
c/o Michael Joffre, #900, 1117 St-Catherine St. West, Montréal QC H3B 1H9
Tel: 514-289-9761
medievalcoins@gmail.com
Overview: A small local organization
Chief Officer(s):
Michael Joffre, President

Montréal Opera ***Voir*** L'Opéra de Montréal

Montréal Print Collectors' Society ***Voir*** Société des collectionneurs d'estampes de Montréal

Montreal Sailors' Institute & Catholic Sailors' Club ***See*** Mariners' House of Montreal

Montréal Science Fiction & Fantasy Association / Association montréalaise de science-fiction et de fantastique
4456, boul Ste-Rose, Laval QC H7R 1Y6
e-mail: president@monsffa.com
www.monsffa.com
Also Known As: MonSFFA
Overview: A small local organization founded in 1987
Membership: *Fees:* $25 standard; $35 platinum; $40 family; *Member Profile:* Fans of the science fiction & fantasy genres in literature, movies, television, comics, gaming, art, animation, scale-model building, costuming, memorabilia collecting, & film & video production
Activities: Hosting meetings, lectures, & hands-on demonstrationc

Montréal Soaring Council (MSC) / Club de Vol à Voile MSC
PO Box 147, Saint-Laurent QC H4L 4V4
Tel: 613-632-5438
flymsc.info@gmail.com
www.flymsc.org
Overview: A small local organization founded in 1946
Mission: To promote the sport of soaring & gliding, including the provision of gliding training
Member of: Soaring Association of Canada
Chief Officer(s):

Wouter Beerman, Director, Publicity & Membership
Finances: *Annual Operating Budget:* $100,000-$250,000
Staff Member(s): 11; 30 volunteer(s)
Membership: 100; *Fees:* $713.25; *Member Profile:* Open to individuals interested in soaring

Montréal SPCA
5215, rue Jean-Talon Ouest, Montréal QC H4P 1X4
Tél: 514-735-2711; *Téléc:* 514-735-7448
admin@spcamontreal.com
www.spcamontreal.com
www.facebook.com/SPCAMontreal
twitter.com/SPCAMontreal
Également appelé: Société pour la prévention de la cruauté envers les animaux
Aperçu: *Dimension:* petite; *Envergure:* locale; fondée en 1869 surveillé par Canadian Federation of Humane Societies
Mission: Recueillir, héberger et soigner les animaux errants ou abandonnés; rendre les animaux perdus à leurs propriétaires; mettre en adoption les animaux en santé; inspecter et enquêter sur les plaintes de cruauté.
Membre de: Canadian Federation of Humane Societies
Membre(s) du bureau directeur:
Isabelle Brodeur, Présidente
ca@spcamontreal.com

Monument canadien pour les droits de la personne *See* Canadian Tribute to Human Rights

Mood Disorders Association of British Columbia (MDA)
#200, 460 Nanaimo St., Vancouver BC V5L 4W3
Tel: 604-873-0103; *Fax:* 604-873-3095
info@mdabc.net
www.mdabc.net
www.facebook.com/mdasupport
twitter.com/MDA_BC
Overview: A small provincial charitable organization founded in 1982
Mission: To provide support & education for people with a mood disorder, & those around them, in order to help them live a healthy & active life
Chief Officer(s):
Sophia Van Norden, Operations Manager, 604-873-0103, Fax: 604-873-3095
sophia.vannorden@mdabc.net
Staff Member(s): 5; 50+ volunteer(s)
Membership: 4000+; *Fees:* $15 consumer; $25 professional/agency/supporter
Activities: *Awareness Events:* National Mental Health Week; May; *Speaker Service:* Yes

Mood Disorders Association of Manitoba (MDAM)
#100, 4 Fort St., Winnipeg MB R3C 1C4
Tel: 204-786-0987; *Fax:* 201-786-1906
Toll-Free: 800-263-1460
info@mooddisordersmanitoba.ca
www.mooddisordersmanitoba.ca
www.facebook.com/MoodDisordersMB
twitter.com/MoodDisordersMB
Overview: A small provincial charitable organization
Mission: To help others through peer support, education & advocacy; to increase public awareness about mood disorders & empower people to develop & manage mental wellness
Chief Officer(s):
Tara Brousseau, Executive Director
TaraS@mooddisordersmanitoba.ca
Membership: *Fees:* $15

Mood Disorders Association of Ontario (MDAO)
#602, 36 Eglinton Ave., Toronto ON M4R 1A1
Tel: 416-486-8046; *Fax:* 416-486-8127
Toll-Free: 888-486-8236
www.mooddisorders.on.ca
Overview: A small provincial charitable organization founded in 1985
Mission: To provide information, education & support to those affected by depression & manic depression, their families & friends; to develop & maintain a network of supportive self-help groups; to improve the quality of life of people who experience mood disorders, their families & friends; to advocate for a flexible & responsive system of care
Member of: Federation of Community Mental Health & Addictions; Consumer Survivor Development Initiative
Chief Officer(s):
Anne Davis, President & Chair
Ann Marie MacDonald, Executive Director
Finances: *Annual Operating Budget:* $250,000-$500,000
Staff Member(s): 6; 150 volunteer(s)
Membership: 1,500; *Fees:* $25 individual; *Member Profile:* Consumers/families with mood disorders; community mental health professionals; *Committees:* Conference; Nominating
Activities: Support groups; telephone information; information meetings; resource centre; public outreach; conferences; workshops; resource materials for group development; Distinguished Speakers Series; *Speaker Service:* Yes; *Library:* Paul Horner Resource Centre; Open to public

Mood Disorders Society of Canada (MDSC) / La Société pour les troubles de l'humeur du Canada
#736, 3-304 Stone Rd. West, Guelph ON N1G 4W4
Tel: 519-824-5565; *Fax:* 519-824-9569
info@mooddisorderscanada.ca
www.mooddisorderscanada.ca
www.facebook.com/MoodDisordersSocietyCanada
twitter.com/MoodDisordersCa
www.youtube.com/user/MDSofC?
Overview: A large national organization
Mission: The MDSC works nationally to ensure that issues related to mood disorders are understood and considered in the setting of research priorities, the development of treatment strategies, and the creation of government programs and policies. The Mood Disorders Society of Canada is one of the leading national, voluntary health organizations in the fields of depression, bipolar illness, and associated mood disorders
Chief Officer(s):
Phil Upshall, National Executive Director
John Starzynski, President

Mooredale Youth Concert Orchestra
c/o Mooredale House, 146 Crescent Rd., Toronto ON M4W 1V2
Tel: 416-922-3714
orchestras@mooredaleconcerts.com
www.mooredaleconcerts.com/youth.html
www.linkedin.com/MooredaleConcerts
www.facebook.com/MooredaleConcerts
Overview: A small local organization founded in 1989 overseen by Orchestras Canada
Chief Officer(s):
Christina A. Cavanagh, Managing Director
marketing@mooredaleconcerts.com
8 volunteer(s)
Membership: 120; *Member Profile:* Junior, intermediate & senior string orchestras
Activities: Three performances per season

Moorelands Community Services
#501, 250 Merton St., Toronto ON M4S 1B1
Tel: 416-466-9987; *Fax:* 416-466-0727
info@moorelands.ca
www.moorelands.org
www.facebook.com/moorelandscommunityservices
twitter.com/MoorelandsCS
www.youtube.com/user/MoorelandsCommunity?feature=mhee
Previous Name: The Downtown Churchworkers' Association
Overview: A small local charitable organization founded in 1912
Chief Officer(s):
Patricia Jacobs, Executive Director
pjacobs@moorelands.ca
Dagmar Schroeder, Director, Development & Communications
dschroeder@moorelands.ca
Finances: *Funding Sources:* Donations; Foundations; Corporations; Churches; Individuals
Staff Member(s): 9
Membership: 1-99; *Committees:* Fundraising; Finance & Programs
Activities: Offering a summer camp; Providing year-round city programs for youth from ages six to eighteen; Arranging assistance for new mothers; Organizing a Christmas relief program; Raising public awareness; *Speaker Service:* Yes

Moose Jaw & District Chamber of Commerce
88 Saskatchewan St. East, Moose Jaw SK S6H 0V4
Tel: 306-692-6414
www.mjchamber.com
www.facebook.com/185971824814293
Overview: A small local licensing organization founded in 1888
Mission: To act as the voice of business in Moose Jaw on matters affecting its membership & concerning the economic climate & directly related to social well-being of Moose Jaw & trading area
Member of: Canadian Chamber of Commerce; Saskatchewan Chamber of Commerce
Chief Officer(s):
Chris Aparicio, President
Brian Martynook, CEO
Finances: *Annual Operating Budget:* $100,000-$250,000; *Funding Sources:* Membership dues; special events
Staff Member(s): 2; 20 volunteer(s)
Membership: 485; *Fees:* $105-$787.50; *Member Profile:* Businesses & individuals; *Committees:* Focus on Trade; Business Excellence Awards; Golf Tour
Activities: Business information & promotion; *Library:* Business Resource Centre; Open to public

Moose Jaw & District Food Bank
350 Fairford St. West, Moose Jaw SK S6H 1V8
Tel: 306-692-2911
Overview: A small local organization
Member of: Food Banks of Saskatchewan Inc.

Moose Jaw & District Labour Council
1402 Caribou St. West, Moose Jaw SK S6H 7S9
Tel: 306-693-6507
Overview: A small local organization overseen by Saskatchewan Federation of Labour
Mission: To support union members & workers in Moose Jaw, Saskatchewan & the surrounding region; To advance the the economic & social welfare of workers
Affliation(s): Canadian Labour Congress (CLC)
Chief Officer(s):
Stacey Landin, President
staceylandin@sasktel.net
Activities: Presenting educational seminars; Liaising with local elected officials to present workers' issues; Promoting the interests of affiliates; Increasing awareness of the plight of workers, by organizing events such as a ceremony on the Day of Mourning to remember workers who were killed & injured on the job; Supporting local community organizations, such as the Moose Jaw Health Foundation & the Transition House

Moose Jaw Construction Association
610 - 1 Ave. NW, Moose Jaw SK S6H 3M6
Tel: 306-693-1232; *Fax:* 306-694-1766
mjca3@shaw.ca
www.mjcaonline.ca
Overview: A small local organization overseen by Canadian Construction Association
Chief Officer(s):
Brad Duncan, President
droofing@sasktel.net
Membership: *Fees:* $305 associate; $460 affiliate; $865 full; *Committees:* Finance; Safety; Bid Depository; Social; Membership

Moose Jaw Exhibition Association
250 Thatcher Dr. East, Moose Jaw SK S6J 1L7
Tel: 306-692-2723; *Fax:* 306-692-2762
www.moosejawex.com
Overview: A small local organization founded in 1884
Mission: To provide quality entertainment, recreation & education for rural & urban communities
Member of: Saskatchewan Association of Agricultural Societies & Exhibitions
Affliation(s): Canadian Association of Exhibitions; Western Canada Fair Association
Finances: *Annual Operating Budget:* $1.5 Million-$3 Million
Staff Member(s): 20; 200 volunteer(s)
Membership: 100; *Fees:* $5; *Member Profile:* Rural & urban
Activities: Spring & fall rodeo; Hometown Fair; *Awareness Events:* Moose Jaw Hometown Fair, June

Moose Jaw Humane Society Inc.
PO Box 1658, Stn. Main, 1755 Stadacona St. West, Moose Jaw SK S6H 7K7
Tel: 306-692-1517; *Fax:* 306-694-0720
contact@mjhs.ca
www.mjhs.ca
Overview: A small local organization founded in 1966
Mission: To promote the belief that all animals have intrinsic value, deserving humane & compassionate treatment
Member of: Canadian Federation of Humane Societies
Chief Officer(s):
Kristyn McEwen, Executive Director
kmcewen@mjhs.ca
Staff Member(s): 13
Membership: *Fees:* $20 senior; $25 regular; $500 lifetime/corporate
Activities: Provide shelter & care for lost & abandoned animals;

Moose Jaw Multicultural Council (MJMC)
60 Athabasca St. East, Moose Jaw SK S6H 0L2
Tel: 306-693-4677; *Fax:* 306-694-0477
reception@mjmcinc.ca
www.mjmcinc.ca
Overview: A small local organization founded in 1974
Mission: Welcomes & integrates newcomers to Canada & develops harmonious relations among Canadians, through programs & activities that recognize, respect & promote the positive aspects of cultural diversity & that seek seek to discover, encourage & develop commmonalities among peoples
Member of: Multicultural Council of Saskatchewan
Affliation(s): Saskatchewan Organization of Heritage Languages; Moose Jaw Chamber of Commerce; Saskatchewan Cultural Exchange Society; Saskatchewan Literacy Network
Membership: 15 organizations
Activities: Immigrant settlement & adaptation; *Awareness Events:* Motif, Moose Jaw Multicultural Festival, July; *Library:* Moose Jaw Multicultural Council Library; Open to public

Moose Jaw Music Festival
1437 Duffield St. West, Moose Jaw SK S6H 5K5
Tel: 306-694-0953
moosejawmusicfestival@hotmail.com
www.smfa.ca/festivals/MooseJaw.php
Overview: A small local organization
Member of: Saskatchewan Music Festival Association
Chief Officer(s):
Marcie Carswell, Corresponding & Recording Secretary

Moose Jaw Real Estate Board
88 Saskatechewan St. East, Moose Jaw SK S6H 0V4
Tel: 306-693-9544; *Fax:* 306-692-4463
eo.mjreb@sasktel.net
www.moosejawrealestateboard.com
Overview: A small local organization overseen by Saskatchewan Real Estate Association
Mission: To promote the real estate sector in the area & provides a forum for local realtors to exchange information.
Member of: The Canadian Real Estate Association
Chief Officer(s):
Jami Thorn, President
jamithorn@royallepage.ca
Jim Millar, Executive Officer
Membership: *Committees:* Finance; Advertising & Public Relations; Membership & Education; Professional Standards; MLS Legislation & Standard Forms; Social
Activities: Fundraising for local charities

Moose Mountain Friendship Centre
PO Box 207, 112 Main St., Carlyle SK S0M OJO
Tel: 306-453-2425; *Fax:* 306-453-6777
Overview: A small local organization

Moosomin Chamber of Commerce
Moosomin SK S0G 3N0
Tel: 306-435-2445
world_spectator@sasktel.net
www.moosomin.com/chamber
Overview: A small local organization
Member of: Saskatchewan Chamber of Commerce
Chief Officer(s):
Ed Hildebrandt, President
Kevin Weedmark, Treasurer
Finances: *Annual Operating Budget:* Less than $50,000; *Funding Sources:* Membership fees; projects
15 volunteer(s)
Membership: 93; *Fees:* $26.50-$254.40

Moosonee Native Friendship Centre
PO Box 478, Moosonee ON P0L 1Y0
Tel: 705-336-2808; *Fax:* 705-336-2929
www.onlink.net/~mcap
Overview: A small local organization founded in 1982
Mission: To assist the Aboriginal population of Moosonee with establishing a better quality of life, spiritually, culturally, socially & economically
Member of: Ontario Federation of Indian Friendship Centres

Moosonee-Moose Factory Association for Community Living *See* James Bay Association for Community Living

Morden & District Chamber of Commerce
#100, 379 Stephen St., Morden MB R6M 1V1
Tel: 204-822-5630
marketing@mordenchamber.com
www.mordenchamber.com
www.facebook.com/167405713285498
twitter.com/MordenChamber
Previous Name: Morden Chamber of Commerce
Overview: A small local organization founded in 1890
Mission: To make Morden a better place to live & work
Member of: Manitoba Chamber of Commerce; Canadian Chamber of Commerce, Canadian Taxpayers Association
Chief Officer(s):
Ross Ariss, President
Pamela Hiebert, Director, Marketing & Promotions
Finances: *Annual Operating Budget:* $50,000-$100,000; *Funding Sources:* Membership dues; grants; fundraising
Staff Member(s): 1; 8 volunteer(s)
Membership: 235; *Fees:* Based on number of employees; *Member Profile:* Small business; home-based business; individuals; *Committees:* Executive; Advocacy; Farmer's Market; Marketing & Communications; Programming; Information & Technology; Tourism; Board Development; Human Resource; Fundraising; Membership; Governance
Activities: Annual meeting; spring golf tournament; seminars; farmer's market; *Library:* Canada/Manitoba Business Service Centre; Open to public

Morden Chamber of Commerce *See* Morden & District Chamber of Commerce

Morgan Sports Car Club of Canada (MSCCC)
21 Penn Dr., Burlington ON L7N 2B6
www.morgansportscarclubofcanada.com
Overview: A small national organization founded in 1965
Chief Officer(s):
Martin Beer, President
Finances: *Annual Operating Budget:* Less than $50,000; *Funding Sources:* Membership dues; membership
Membership: 100; *Fees:* $25; *Member Profile:* Owners of Morgan sports cars or otherw with an interest in Morgans
Activities: Participation in British car events

Morinville & District Chamber of Commerce
10113 - 100 Ave., Morinville AB T8R 1P8
Tel: 780-939-9462
chamber@morinvillechamber.com
www.morinvillechamber.com
twitter.com/MoriChamber
Overview: A small local organization
Mission: The Morinville & District Chamber of Commerce is committed to promoting the Morinville District as a leading business centre and in co-operation with others, to support, expand, and diversify business opportunities.
Chief Officer(s):
Heather Folkins, President
Membership: 89; *Fees:* $75-$200

Morning Light Ministry
c/o St. Mary Star of the Sea Church, 11 Peter St. South, Mississauga ON L5H 2G1
Tel: 416-765-2155
morninglightministry@yahoo.ca
www.morninglightministry.org
Overview: A small local organization founded in 1996
Mission: To provide Catholic ministry for bereaved parents who have experienced the death of a baby through ectopic pregnancy, miscarriage, stillbirth, or infant death up to two years of age; To help families who have received an adverse prenatal diagnosis; To offer suuport to couples who are experiencing infertility
Affliation(s): Archdiocese of Toronto
Chief Officer(s):
Bernadette Zambri, Contact
Membership: *Member Profile:* Bereaved Catholic parents, as well as bereaved parents of other Christian denominations, other faiths, & those with no religious affiliation who struggle with the notion of faith
Activities: Providing information at no cost; Counselling; Offering faith instruction; Providing support by e-mail, telephone, & individual & group meetings; Conducting an annual memorial Mass

Moroccan Association of Toronto (AMDT) / Association Marocaine de Toronto
44 Plum Treeway, Toronto ON M9C 2Y3
Tel: 647-407-4809
info@amdt.ca
www.amdt.ca
Overview: A small provincial organization
Mission: To promote & defend the cultural interests of Moroccans in Toronto
Chief Officer(s):
Mohamed Smyej, AMDT President
Mohamed Bouchama, Vice-President
Hassan Douelrachad, Treasurer
Amine Ouahi, Secretary
Hassane Rifai, Executive Director
Membership: *Member Profile:* Persons of Moroccan origin who reside in the Greater Toronto Area
Activities: Establishing traditional events & services to link the Moroccan community of Toronto; Providing information to newcomers to Toronto from Morocco; *Awareness Events:* Annual Cultural Party
Publications:
• Moroccan Association of Toronto Report of Activities
Type: Yearbook; *Frequency:* Annually

Morris & District Chamber of Commerce
141 Main St. South, Morris MB R0G 1K0
Tel: 204-746-6275
info@morrischamberofcommerce.com
morrischamberofcommerce.com
www.facebook.com/143472332424547
Overview: A small local organization founded in 1974 overseen by The Manitoba Chambers of Commerce
Mission: To promote & enhance business in the community; To promote tourism & recreational activities
Member of: Manitoba Chambers of Commerce
Chief Officer(s):
Mabel Maxim, President
president@morrischamberofcommerce.com
Andy Anderson, Secretary
secretary@morrischamberofcommerce.com
Finances: *Annual Operating Budget:* Less than $50,000; *Funding Sources:* Membership fees; Municipal levy
6 volunteer(s)
Membership: 77; *Fees:* $50; *Member Profile:* Business & services
Activities: *Awareness Events:* Moonlight Madness, Dec.; Stampede Kickoff, July

Morrisburg & District Chamber of Commerce *See* South Dundas Chamber of Commerce

Mortgage Investment Association of British Columbia (MIABC)
The Marine Bldg., #1000, 355 Burrard St., Vancouver BC V6C 2G8
Tel: 604-380-1107
contactus@miabc.com
www.miabc.com
Overview: A small provincial organization founded in 1917
Chief Officer(s):
Jeff Puhl, President, 604-406-6004
jeff.puhl@centract.com
Michelle Holst, Executive Coordinator, 778-245-9559
michelle_holst@miabc.com
Membership: 200+; *Fees:* $346.50 corporate; *Member Profile:* Commercial & residential lenders; banks; trust companies; life insurance companies; mortgage companies & credit unions; mortgage insurers; appraisers; law firms; accountants; environmental consultants; mortgage brokers; technology suppliers
Activities: Dealing with the government & public regarding matters of concern; networking opportunities; *Awareness Events:* Annual Golf Tournament, Summer; Summer Social

Mosaic Counselling & Family Services
400 Queen St. South, Kitchener ON N2G 1W7
Tel: 519-743-6333
info@mosaiconline.ca
www.mosaiconline.ca
www.facebook.com/MosaicCounselling
twitter.com/MosaicUpdates
Previous Name: Catholic Family Counselling Centre; Catholic Social Services; Catholic Welfare Bureau
Overview: A small local charitable organization founded in 1952 overseen by Ontario Association of Credit Counselling Services
Mission: To provide full-service professional counselling services in Kitchener & the surrounding region
Member of: Canadian Association of Credit Counselling Services; Ontario Association of Credit Counselling Services; United Way of Kitchener-Waterloo & Area; Family Service Ontario
Chief Officer(s):
Cathy Brothers, Executive Director, 519-743-6333 Ext. 232
Jennifer Berry, Director, Communications, 519-743-6333 Ext. 303

Canadian Associations

Megan Conway, Director, Pathways to Education, 519-743-6333 Ext. 306
Peter Fisher, Director, Clinical Services, 519-743-6333 Ext. 223
Sandy Hoy, Director, Research & Evaluation, 519-743-6333 Ext. 267
Nancy Kyle, Director, Community Services, 519-743-6333 Ext. 229
Kathie Must, Director, Workplace Programs, 519-743-6333 Ext. 231
Judy Nairn, Director, Business, 519-743-6333 Ext. 328
Karin Voisin, Director, Volunteers & Community Relations, 519-743-6333 Ext. 243
Andrew Wilding, Director, Resource Development, 519-743-6333 Ext. 307
Heather Cudmore, Manager, Credit Counselling Program, 519-743-6333 Ext. 236
Finances: *Annual Operating Budget:* $3 Million-$5 Million; *Funding Sources:* United Way; Government of Canada; Province of Ontario; Regional Municipality of Waterloo; Foundations, such as Pathways to Education Canada
Activities: Offering individual, group, & credit counselling; Providing workplace & employee assistance programs; Offering community outreach services; *Library:* Mosaic Counselling & Family Services Library
Awards:
• Leadership Award (Award)
For exceptional contribution to the well being of families in Canada

Mosaïque centre d'action bénévole et communautaire
1650, av de l'Église, Le Moyne QC J4P 2C8
Tél: 450-465-1803; *Téléc:* 450-465-5440
info@lamosaique.qc.ca
lamosaique.org
Aperçu: *Dimension:* petite; *Envergure:* locale; fondée en 1985
Mission: De renforcer la communauté et aider à l'autonomie et l'intégration des personnes défavorisées dans la communauté
Membre(s) du bureau directeur:
Danielle Lavigne, Directrice générale
Lyse Summerside, Présidente, Conseil d'administration
Activités: *Evénements de sensibilisation:* Donner pour changer leur vie collecte de fonds (novembre)

Mossley Post Heritage & Citizenship Society (MPH&CS)
4006 Elgin Rd., Mossley ON N0L 1V0
e-mail: mossleypost@hotmail.com
www.mossleyheritagesociety.com
Overview: A small local charitable organization founded in 1987
Mission: Provides educational scholarships, bursaries & prizes for Canadian citizens under the age of 19; Nurtures an appreciation of aesthetic matters; Provides a social & cultural facility for the benefit of the Mossley area community
Member of: Ontario Historical Society
Finances: *Funding Sources:* Fundraising; Donations; Government
Membership: *Member Profile:* People interested in Mossley's heritage
Activities: Monthly meetings; Social events; Addressing & assisting in producing heritage events when needed

Mother of Red Nations Women's Council of Manitoba (MORN)
#300, 141 Bannatyne Ave., Winnipeg MB R3B 0R3
Tel: 204-942-6676; *Fax:* 204-942-7639
Toll-Free: 866-258-6726
morn.cimnet.ca
Previous Name: Aboriginal Women of Manitoba
Overview: A small provincial organization overseen by Native Women's Association of Canada
Mission: To represent Aboriginal women in Manitoba & serve as their primary political & advocacy organization; to promote, protect & support the spiritual, emotional, physical & mental well-being of all Aboriginal women & children in the province.
Affliation(s): Native Woman's Association of Canada
Chief Officer(s):
Rita Lynn Emerson, Executive Director
remerson@morn.ca
Staff Member(s): 5
Membership: 1,200; *Member Profile:* Girl or woman 14 years of age or older; of the Aboriginal Peoples of Canada, as defined in the Constitution Act of 1982; and a resident of Manitoba.

Motion Picture Association - Canada / Association Cinématographique - Canada
#210, 55 St. Clair Ave. West, Toronto ON M4V 2Y7
Tel: 416-961-1888; *Fax:* 416-968-1016
info@mpa-canada.org
mpa-canada.org
twitter.com/mpacanada
Previous Name: Canadian Motion Picture Distributors Association
Overview: A small national organization founded in 1920
Mission: To act as the voice of U.S.A. studios who market feature films, prime time entertainment programming for television & pay TV, & pre-recorded videos & DVDs in Canada; To coordinate recommendations on matters affecting national distributors of feature films, pre-recorded videocassettes, & television programs; To protect the rights of copyright owners
Affliation(s): Motion Picture Association of America; Motion Picture Association
Chief Officer(s):
Katherine Ward, Director, Public Affairs, 416-355-7459
katherine_ward@mpa-canada.org
Membership: *Member Profile:* Associations in the motion picture, video, & television programming industry
Activities: Promoting the interests of the industry; Liaising with federal & provincial government departments & ministries; Directign an anti-piracy program to protect films, videos, & television programs

Motion Picture Theatre Association of Alberta
#400, 2555 - 32nd St. NE, Calgary AB T1Y 7J6
Tel: 403-381-1251
Overview: A small provincial organization
Mission: To help sustain the general welfare & prosperity of motion picture exhibitors
Member of: The Motion Picture Theatre Associations of Canada
Membership: *Member Profile:* Theatre exhibitors, owners, executives & managers

Motion Picture Theatre Association of British Columbia
20090 - 91A Ave., Langley BC V1M 3Y9
Overview: A small provincial organization
Member of: The Motion Picture Theatre Associations of Canada

Motion Picture Theatre Association of Central Canada
www.mptaccentral.ca
Also Known As: MPTAC Central
Overview: A small provincial organization
Member of: The Motion Picture Theatre Associations of Canada
Chief Officer(s):
Kellen Jasper, President

Motion Picture Theatre Association of Manitoba
c/o Empire Theatres, #127, 1120 Grant Ave., Winnipeg MB R2C 4J2
Tel: 204-453-4536; *Fax:* 204-470-3104
et084-gm@empiretheatres.com
Overview: A small provincial organization
Member of: The Motion Picture Theatre Associations of Canada
Chief Officer(s):
Kellen Jasper, President
Membership: 672
Meetings/Conferences: • Motion Picture Theatre Associations of Canada ShowCanada 2015, June, 2015, Fairmont Le Château Frontenac, Québec City, QC
Scope: National
Description: A program featuring speakers, seminars, information about digital issues & new technologies, the presentation of awards, a trade show, film screenings, & social & networking events
Contact Information: Head Coordinator, ShowCanada: Patricia Gariepy, Phone: 450-668-1346, E-mail: registration@showcanada.ca; URL: www.showcanada.ca

Motor Carrier Passenger Council of Canada (MCPCC) / Conseil canadien du transport de passages
#306, 9555 Yonge St., Richmond Hill ON L4C 9M5
Tel: 905-884-7782; *Fax:* 905-884-8335
Toll-Free: 866-271-1107
info@buscouncil.ca
www.buscouncil.ca
Overview: A small national organization
Mission: To develop, promote & enhance human capability by sharing resources, talents & best practices resulting in business & personal growth within the motor carrier passenger industry
Chief Officer(s):
Joan Crawford, Executive Director & CEO
Finances: *Funding Sources:* Government of Canada's Sector Council Program

Motor Coach Canada (MCC) / L'Association des autocaristes Canadiens (AAC)
#505, 555 Burnhamthorpe Rd., Toronto ON M9C 2Y3
Tel: 416-229-9305; *Fax:* 416-229-6281
info@motorcoachcanada.com
www.motorcoachcanada.com
Overview: A medium-sized international organization
Mission: To provide a united voice at the national level for motor coach tour operators & bus operators & to create an environment that supports members investments & growth
Chief Officer(s):
Réal Boissonneault, Chair
Doug Switzer, President & CEO, 416-229-9305 Ext. 222
doug@motorcoachcanada.com
Finances: *Funding Sources:* Membership dues; services
Staff Member(s): 7
Membership: *Fees:* Schedule available; *Member Profile:* Bus operators; tour operators; product & service members

Motor Dealers' Association of Alberta (MDA)
9249 - 48 St., Edmonton AB T6B 2R9
Tel: 780-468-9552; *Fax:* 780-465-6201
info@mdaalberta.com
www.mdaalberta.com
www.facebook.com/MDAofAlberta
Overview: A medium-sized provincial charitable organization founded in 1950
Mission: To serve the collective interest of all its members and promote positive relationships with government, industry, suppliers, consumers and media, by offering needed and effective programs and services.
Member of: Canadian Automobile Dealers' Association
Chief Officer(s):
Denis Ducharme, President
dducharme@mdaalberta.com
Finances: *Funding Sources:* Membership dues; training program; endorsements
Staff Member(s): 2
Membership: *Member Profile:* New vehicle franchise dealers
Activities: Annual celebrity golf classic in support of special olympics; staff training programs; *Library*
Awards:
• Alberta Dealer of Excellence (Award)

Motor Dealers' Association of BC; BC Automobile Dealers' Association *See* BCADA - The New Car Dealers of BC

Motorcycle & Moped Industry Council (MMIC) / Le Conseil de l'industrie de la motocyclette et du cyclomoteur (CIMC)
#201, 3000 Steeles Ave. East, Markham ON L3R 4T9
Tel: 416-491-4449; *Fax:* 416-493-1985
Toll-Free: 877-470-6642
info@mmic.ca
www.mmic.ca
Overview: A small national organization founded in 1971
Mission: To represent the manufacturers & distributors of street legal motorcycles and related products and services in Canada.
Chief Officer(s):
Jo-Anne Farquhar, Director, Communications & Public Affairs
jfarquhar@mmic.ca
Luc Fournier, Director, Policy & Government Relations
lfournier@mmic.ca
Tim Stover, Director, Operations
tstover@mmic.ca
Staff Member(s): 10
Membership: 12; *Fees:* Schedule available; *Member Profile:* Companies involved in the manufacturing or distribution of motorcycles, mopeds or scooters

Motorsport Club of Ottawa (MCO) / Club des sports moteur d'Ottawa
PO Box 65006, Stn. Merivale Post Office, Nepean ON K2G 5Y3
e-mail: registrar@mco.org
www.mco.org
Previous Name: Ottawa Light Car Club
Overview: A small local organization founded in 1949
Mission: To foster a spirit of unity & comradership among car owners; to encourage courtesy both to other drivers & to pedestrians; To provide information which may be of aid & interest to car owners; to organize & to encourage the organization of legitimate sporting events
Affliation(s): ASN Canada FIA; CASC-OR; Rallysport Ontario
Chief Officer(s):

Steve Greiner, President
Finances: *Annual Operating Budget:* $50,000-$100,000
10 volunteer(s)
Membership: 380; *Fees:* $60 single; $75 family; *Member Profile:* Road racing participants; enthusiasts; all involved at grassroots level; *Committees:* Race; Rally; Solo; Social
Activities: Winter & Summer Solo II; winter driving school; go-karting; rallying; road racing; summer high-performance driving school; Canaska Cup; group tours

Mount Allison Faculty Association (MAFA) / Association des professeurs de Mount Allison
PO Box 6314, Sackville NB E4L 1G6
Tel: 506-364-2289; *Fax:* 506-364-2288
mafa@mta.ca
www.mafa.ca
Overview: A small local organization founded in 1839
Member of: Canadian Association of University Teachers
Chief Officer(s):
Stephen Law, President
slaw@mta.ca
Membership: 117

Mount Forest District Chamber of Commerce
514 Main St. North, Mount Forest ON N0G 2L0
Tel: 519-323-4480; *Fax:* 519-323-1557
mfchamber@wightman.ca
www.mountforest.ca
www.facebook.com/mountforest
Overview: A small local organization
Mission: To promote the civic, commercial & industrial progress of the district served by this organization
Member of: Ontario Chamber of Commerce
Chief Officer(s):
Ron Forrest, President
Finances: *Annual Operating Budget:* $50,000-$100,000; *Funding Sources:* Membership dues; advertising sales
Membership: 130; *Fees:* $185
Activities: Community awareness; festivals;

Mount Pearl Chamber of Commerce
39 Commonwealth Ave., Mount Pearl NL A1N 1W7
Tel: 709-364-8513; *Fax:* 709-364-8500
info@mtpearlparadisechamber.com
www.mtpearlchamber.com
Overview: A small local organization
Mission: To promote economic development & provide an information base for all employees & employers in the area; to represent the membership to local & provincial governments
Member of: Canadian Chamber of Commerce; Atlantic Provinces Chamber of Commerce; Newfoundland & Labrador Chamber of Commerce
Finances: *Annual Operating Budget:* $50,000-$100,000; *Funding Sources:* Membership dues; special projects; annual auction; fundraising
Staff Member(s): 1; 25 volunteer(s)
Membership: 200; *Fees:* $149.50-$299
Activities: *Speaker Service:* Yes; *Library* Open to public

Mount Pleasant Group
e-mail: info@mountpleasantgroup.com
www.mountpleasantgroup.com
Previous Name: Mt. Pleasant Group of Cemeteries; Commemorative Services of Ontario
Overview: A small local organization founded in 1826
Chief Officer(s):
Diane Chabot, President & CEO, Mount Pleasant Memorial Services
Eileen Fitzpatrick, President, Funeral Company
Glenn McClary, President, Cemetery Company
Activities: Operates Mount Pleasant Memorial Services, Mount Pleasant Group of Cemeteries, & Canadian Memorial Services.

Mount Royal Staff Association (MRSA)
#W301, 4825 Mount Royal Gate SW, Calgary AB T3E 6K6
Tel: 403-440-5993; *Fax:* 403-440-6763
mrsa@mtroyal.ca
www.mrssa.ca
Previous Name: Mount Royal Support Staff Association
Overview: A small local organization founded in 1976
Mission: To ensure Mount Royal University staff work in a fair environment
Chief Officer(s):
Baset Zarrugr, President
bzarrug@mtroyal.ca
Finances: *Annual Operating Budget:* $50,000-$100,000
Staff Member(s): 1
Membership: 650; *Committees:* Education, Development & Training; Develop, Train & Learn; Professional Development Days; Policies & Procedures; Negotiating; Audit & Finance; Labour Relations; Social Engagement & Communications

Mount Royal Support Staff Association *See* Mount Royal Staff Association

Mount Saint Vincent University Faculty Association (MSVUFA) / Association des professeurs de l'Université Mount Saint Vincent
166 Bedford Hwy., Halifax NS B3M 2J5
Tel: 902-457-6265; *Fax:* 902-457-2118
msvufa@msvu.ca
www.msvufa.ca
Overview: A small local organization founded in 1987
Chief Officer(s):
Linda Mann, President
Membership: 150; *Fees:* 1.15% of gross annual salary

Mount Sinai Hospital Foundation
1001 - 522 University Ave., Toronto ON M5G 1W7
Tel: 416-586-8203; *Fax:* 416-586-8639
Toll-Free: 877-565-8555
foundation@mtsinai.on.ca
www.mshfoundation.ca
Overview: A small local charitable organization founded in 1923
Mission: The Foundation raises & stewards funds to support the Mount Sinai Hospital's patient care, research & education. In 2008, more than $344 million has been raised to fund The Best Medicine Campaign, to support research, innovative programs, improved facilities & technology. Mount Sinai Hospital's Centres of Excellence include: the Samuel Lunenfeld Research Institute, Women's & Infants' Health, Oncology, Acute & Chronic Medicine, & Laboratory Medicine & Infection Control
Chief Officer(s):
Brent S. Belzberg, Chair
Joseph Mapa, President & CEO
Activities: *Awareness Events:* Mount Sinai Annual Golf Classic; Unicorn Gala; Mother Daughter Tea
Publications:
• The Best Medicine Matters [a publication of the Mount Sinai Hospital Foundation]
Type: Newsletter; *Frequency:* q.

Mount View Special Riding Association (MVSRA)
5629, 49 Ave., Olds AB T4H 1G5
Tel: 403-556-7247
www.mountviewriding.com
Previous Name: Mountview Handicapped Riding Association
Overview: A small local charitable organization founded in 1983
Mission: To provide recreational & therapeutic riding to specially abled adults & children with mental &/or physical disabilities
Member of: Canadian Therapeutic Riding Association
Chief Officer(s):
Kathy Owens, President
Finances: *Annual Operating Budget:* Less than $50,000
40 volunteer(s)
Membership: 75; *Fees:* $5

Mountview Handicapped Riding Association *See* Mount View Special Riding Association

Mourir dans la dignité *See* Dying with Dignity

Mouvement action chômage de Longueuil
1194, av Marquette, Longueuil QC J4K 4H8
Tél: 450-670-7615; *Téléc:* 450-670-1347
macl@videotron.ca
www.macl.org
Aperçu: *Dimension:* petite; *Envergure:* locale

Mouvement ATD Quart Monde Canada / ATD Fourth World Movement Canada
6747, rue Drolet, Montréal QC H2S 2T1
Tél: 514-279-0468; *Téléc:* 514-279-7759
www.atdquartmonde.ca
www.facebook.com/AtdQMCanada
Nom précédent: Association des Amis d'ATD Quart-Monde
Aperçu: *Dimension:* moyenne; *Envergure:* nationale; fondée en 1982
Mission: Développer un courant de refus de la misère en donnant la priorité aux plus pauvres, dans le respect des droits et de la dignité de la personne; contribuer à l'action du Mouvement dans le monde
Affiliation(s): Mouvement international ATD Quart-Monde (France)
Membre: 1,000-4,999; *Montant de la cotisation:* 3$
Activités: Soirées Quart Monde thématiques, groupes de travail avec différents intervenants sociaux (groupes communautaires, travailleurs sociaux, syndicats, écoles) participation à différents collectifs de lutte contre la pauvreté, recrutement et formation de volontaires-permanents (pour le Canada et des équipes du Mouvement dans le monde); *Evénements de sensibilisation:* Journée mondiale pour l'élimination de la pauvreté, 17 oct.; *Stagiaires:* Oui; *Service de conférenciers:* Oui
Publications:
• Actualités Quart Monde
Type: Newsletter

Mouvement canadien de défense des droits de la personne dans la communauté macédonienne *See* Macedonian Human Rights Movement of Canada

Mouvement contre le viol et l'inceste (MCVI)
CP 50009, Succ. Jarry, Montréal QC H2P 0A1
Tél: 514-278-9383; *Téléc:* 514-278-9385
mcvi@contreleviol.org
contreleviol.wordpress.com
Aperçu: *Dimension:* petite; *Envergure:* locale; Organisme sans but lucratif; fondée en 1976
Mission: Contrer la violence sexuelle dont sont victimes les femmes et les enfants
Affliation(s): Regroupement québécois des Centre d'aide et de lutte contre les agressions à caractère sexuel
Activités: Counselling individuel; Groupes de soutien; informations et références médico-légales; ateliers de sensibilisation et de prévention; *Bibliothèque:* Centre de documentation

Mouvement d'éducation et de défense des actionnaires (MÉDAC)
82, rue Sherbrooke ouest, Montréal QC H2X 1X3
Tél: 514-286-1155; *Téléc:* 514-286-1154
Ligne sans frais: 866-332-7347
admin@medac.qc.ca
www.medac.qc.ca
twitter.com/MEDACtionnaires
Nom précédent: Association de protection des épargnants et investisseurs du Québec
Aperçu: *Dimension:* moyenne; *Envergure:* provinciale; Organisme sans but lucratif; fondée en 1994
Mission: Le MÉDAC a pour mission: faire valoir auprès des gouvernements le point de vue des membres sur le fonctionnement des marchés financiers; promouvoir une meilleure représentation des actionnaires aux conseils d'administration des entreprises; favoriser une plus grande transparence dans la gestion des sociétés par actions; constituer un espace de débats et d'échanges; et assurer la formation des membres
Membre de: International Corporate Governance Network
Membre(s) du bureau directeur:
Daniel Thouin, Président
Membre(s) du personnel: 1; 9 bénévole(s)
Membre: 1,000-4,999; *Montant de la cotisation:* 35$ individuel; 250$ institutionnel

Mouvement d'éducation populaire et d'action communautaire du Québec (MÉPACQ)
#396, 1600, av De Lorimier, Montréal QC H2K 3W5
Tél: 514-843-3236; *Téléc:* 514-843-6512
coordination@mepacq.qc.ca
www.mepacq.qc.ca
Aperçu: *Dimension:* moyenne; *Envergure:* provinciale
Mission: Mouvement national et multisectoriel qui travaille à la transformation sociale dans une perspective de justice sociale. Il regroupe 11 Tables régionales en éducation populaire autonome (ÉPA) qui regroupent 333 groupes populaires et communautaires autonomes
Membre: 11
Activités: Publications

Mouvement d'étudiant(e)s chrétien(ne)s *See* Student Christian Movement of Canada

Mouvement d'information et d'entraide dans la lutte contre le sida à Québec
625, av Chouinard, Québec QC G1S 3E3
Tél: 418-649-1720; *Téléc:* 418-649-1256
miels@miels.org
www.miels.org
www.facebook.com/mielsQC
Également appelé: MIELS-Québec
Aperçu: *Dimension:* petite; *Envergure:* provinciale; fondée en 1986 surveillé par Canadian AIDS Society

Mission: Soutenir les personnes vivant avec le VIH/sida et leurs proches; prévenir la transmission du VIH; accueillir et héberger personnes vivant avec le sida
Affliation(s): Société canadienne du sida
Membre(s) du bureau directeur:
Donald Careau, Président
dgmiels@miels.org
Thérèse Richer, Directrice générale
Finances: *Budget de fonctionnement annuel:* $500,000-$1.5 Million
Membre(s) du personnel: 9; 150 bénévole(s)
Membre: 250; *Montant de la cotisation:* 5$
Activités: *Evénements de sensibilisation:* Soirée Tangô; Party de Noël; *Bibliothèque* Bibliothèque publique

Mouvement d'information, d'éducation et d'entraide dans la lutte contre le sida (MIENS)

CP 723, Chicoutimi QC G7H 5E1
Tél: 418-693-8983; *Téléc:* 418-693-0409
Ligne sans frais: 800-463-3764
lemiens@lemiens.com
www.lemiens.com
Aperçu: *Dimension:* petite; *Envergure:* provinciale; Organisme sans but lucratif; fondée en 1988
Mission: Pour fournir des informations sur la prévention du VIH ainsi que de soutenir et d'aider les personnes infectées par le VIH et à leurs proches
Affiliation(s): Coalition des organismes québécois de lutte contre le sida
Membre: *Critères d'admissibilite:* Avoir un intérêt particulier pour la problématique de l'infection au VIH et le sida
Activités: Information; éducation; entraide

Mouvement de sainteté biblique *See* The Bible Holiness Movement

Mouvement des Focolari *See* Focolare Movement - Work of Mary

Mouvement du Renouveau charismatique

#102, 161, rue du Parc, Chibougamau QC G8P 2H3
Tél: 418-748-4951
Aperçu: *Dimension:* petite; *Envergure:* locale
Membre(s) du bureau directeur:
Réjeanne Lalancette, Responsable

Mouvement national des québécoises et québécois (MNQ)

2207, rue Fullum, Montréal QC H2K 3P1
Tél: 514-527-9891; *Téléc:* 514-527-9460
mnq@mnq.qc.ca
www.mnq.qc.ca
www.facebook.com/MouvementnationaldesQuebecois
twitter.com/mouvnatqc
www.youtube.com/channel/UCcTnAaXg-22JCesXIXHbqAQ
Aperçu: *Dimension:* moyenne; *Envergure:* nationale; fondée en 1947
Mission: Regroupe dix-neuf sociétés nationales et Saint-Jean-Baptiste réparties dans les régions du Québec; défendre, promouvoir la langue française, la souveraineté du Québec et la fierté nationale; est coordonnateur de la Fête à échelle du Québec
Membre(s) du bureau directeur:
Gilles Laporte, Président
Gilles Grondin, Directeur général
Membre(s) du personnel: 9
Membre: 18 institutionnel; *Critères d'admissibilite:* Société nationale ou Société Saint-Jean-Baptiste
Activités: Fête nationale du Québec;

SN de l'Est du Québec
75, boul Arthur-Buies ouest, Rimouski QC G5L 5C2
Tél: 418-723-9259; *Téléc:* 418-724-7201
sneq@globetrotter.net
www.sneq.qc.ca
Membre(s) du bureau directeur:
Alain Martineau, Président

SN Gaspésie/Iles-de-la-Madeleine
#2, 14, rue Comeau, Carleton-sur-Mer QC G0C 1J0
Tél: 418-364-6313; *Téléc:* 418-364-2005
snatgim@hotmail.com
Membre(s) du bureau directeur:
Marcel Landry, Président

SNQ d'Abitibi-Témiscamingue et du Nord-du-Québec inc.
CP 308, 127, 8e Rue, Rouyn-Noranda QC J9X 5C3
Tél: 819-764-4556
info@snqat-nq.com
www.snqat-nq.com
Membre(s) du bureau directeur:
Chantal Tremblay, Directrice générale
ctremblay@snqat-nq.com

SNQ de Chaudière-Appalaches
2217, ch du Fleuve, Saint-Romuald QC G6W 5P7
Tél: 418-834-1160
snqca@bellnet.ca
Membre(s) du bureau directeur:
Pierre-Paul Sénéchal, Président

SNQ de l'Outaouais
30A, rue Bourque, Gatineau QC J8Y 1X1
Tél: 819-773-2221
snqoutaouais@gmail.com
Membre(s) du bureau directeur:
Mathieu-Henri Jetté, Président par intérim

SNQ de la Capitale
#222, 157, rue Des Chênes Ouest, Québec QC G1L 1K6
Tél: 418-640-0799; *Téléc:* 418-640-0880
snqc@snqc.qc.ca
www.snqc.qc.ca
www.facebook.com/pages/SNQC/217255374961031
twitter.com/SNQCapitale
Membre(s) du bureau directeur:
Anne Beaulieu, Présidente

SNQ de la Côte-Nord
126, av Laval, Baie-Comeau QC G4Z 1R2
Tél: 418-296-4158
Membre(s) du bureau directeur:
Viviane Richard, Présidente
v-richard@globetrotter.net

SNQ de la région de Thetford
479, rue des Rosiers, Thetford Mines QC G6G 1B3
Tél: 418-755-1251
Membre(s) du bureau directeur:
Gaston St-Jacques, Président
gastonstjac@hotmail.com

SNQ de Lanaudière
414, rue Beaudry nord, Joliette QC J6E 6A8
Tél: 450-759-0100; *Téléc:* 450-759-9238
info@snql.com
www.snql.com
Membre(s) du bureau directeur:
Yvon Blanchet, Président

SNQ des Hautes-Rivières
#201, 332, rue de la Madone, Mont-Laurier QC J9L 1R9
Tél: 819-623-3617; *Téléc:* 819-623-6464
snqhr@tlb.sympatico.ca
www.snqhr.com
Membre(s) du bureau directeur:
Richard Gagnon, Président

SNQ des Laurentides
487, rue Laviolette, Saint-Jérôme QC J7Y 2T8
Tél: 450-438-4129; *Téléc:* 450-438-8895
info@snql.qc.ca
www.snql.qc.ca
Membre(s) du bureau directeur:
Gilles Broué, Président

SNQ du Saguenay/Lac-Saint-Jean
CP 308, 512, boul Auger Est, Alma QC G8B 5V8
Tél: 418-668-2357; *Téléc:* 418-668-2313
snqalma@cgocable.ca
Membre(s) du bureau directeur:
Claire Bouchard, Présidente

SNQ du Suroît
2898, rue Honoré-Mercier, Vaudreuil-Dorion QC J7V 8P5
Tél: 450-455-3636; *Téléc:* 450-455-3636
Membre(s) du bureau directeur:
Lise Dandurand, Présidente

SNQ Richelieu/Saint-Laurent
219, rue Jacques-Cartier nord, Saint-Jean-sur-Richelieu QC J3B 6T3
Tél: 450-346-1141; *Téléc:* 450-346-2953
information@snqrsl.qc.ca
www.snqrsl.qc.ca
Membre(s) du bureau directeur:
Christian Haché, Président

SSJB de la Mauricie
CP 1059, 3239, rue Papineau, Trois-Rivières QC G9A 5K5
Tél: 819-375-4881; *Téléc:* 819-375-5854
ssjbm@ssjbmauricie.qc.ca
www.ssjbmauricie.qc.ca
Membre(s) du bureau directeur:
Sandra Dessureault, Présidente

SSJB de Montréal
82, rue Sherbrooke ouest, Montréal QC H2X 1X3
Tél: 514-843-8851; *Téléc:* 514-844-6369
reception@ssjb.com
www.ssjb.com
Membre(s) du bureau directeur:
Mario Beaulieu, Président

SSJB de Richelieu/Yamaska
515, av Robert, Saint-Hyacinthe QC J2S 4L7
Tél: 450-773-8535; *Téléc:* 450-773-8262
ssjb@maskatel.net
www.ssjbry.org
Membre(s) du bureau directeur:
Lise Lavoir, Présidente

SSJB du Centre-du-Québec
449, rue Notre-Dame, Drummondville QC J2B 2K9
Tél: 819-478-2519; *Téléc:* 819-472-7460
info@ssjbcq.qc.ca
www.ssjbcq.qc.ca
www.facebook.com/ssjbcq
Membre(s) du bureau directeur:
Gisèle Denoncourt, Directeur général

Mouvement québécois de la qualité (MQQ)

#1710, 360, rue Saint-Jacques ouest, Montréal QC H2Y 1P5
Tél: 514-874-9933; *Téléc:* 514-866-4600
Ligne sans frais: 888-874-9933
mqq@qualite.qc.ca
www.qualite.qc.ca
www.facebook.com/MouvementQuebecoisQualite
Aperçu: *Dimension:* moyenne; *Envergure:* provinciale
Mission: Promouvoir et rendre accessibles aux organisations les meilleures pratiques d'affaire pour accroître leur performance et leur compétitivité
Membre(s) du bureau directeur:
Roch Dubé, Président
Finances: *Budget de fonctionnement annuel:* $250,000-$500,000
Membre(s) du personnel: 10
Membre: 1 600
Activités: *Bibliothèque:* Centre de documentation; Bibliothèque publique rendez-vous

Mouvement québécois des camps familiaux inc. *Voir* Mouvement québécois des vacances familiales inc.

Mouvement québécois des chantiers jeunesse *Voir* Chantiers jeunesse

Mouvement québécois des vacances familiales inc. (MQVF)

4545, av Pierre-de Coubertin, Montréal QC H1V 3R2
Tél: 514-252-3118; *Téléc:* 514-252-4302
mqvf@vacancesfamiliales.qc.ca
www.vacancesfamiliales.qc.ca
www.facebook.com/Vacancesfamiliales
Nom précédent: Mouvement québécois des camps familiaux inc.
Aperçu: *Dimension:* moyenne; *Envergure:* provinciale; Organisme sans but lucratif; fondée en 1982
Mission: Le Mouvement vise à favoriser l'accessibilité aux loisirs et aux vacances pour les familles à faible revenu en particulier et soutenir les organismes oeuvrant dans ce domaine
Membre(s) du bureau directeur:
Colette Casavant, Présidente
Robert Rodrigue, Directeur général
Finances: *Fonds:* Gouvernement provincial
Membre(s) du personnel: 3

Mouvement Retrouvailles

#201, 150, rue Grant, Longueuil QC J4H 3H6
Tél: 450-646-1060; *Téléc:* 450-646-7401
Ligne sans frais: 888-646-1060
mouvement-retrouvailles.qc.ca
Aperçu: *Dimension:* petite; *Envergure:* locale; fondée en 1983
Mission: Pour réunir les parents biologiques avec les enfants qu'ils avaient donnés en adoption
Membre(s) du bureau directeur:
Caroline Fortin, Présidente, Conseil d'administration
cfortin@mouvement-retrouvailles.qc.ca
Membre: 13,000+; *Montant de la cotisation:* 35$; *Critères d'admissibilite:* Les enfants adoptés; Les parents de naissance; Les parents adoptifs

Movement for Marriage Enrichment (MME)

57 Spiers Cres., Ajax ON L1S 6Z1

Tel: 905-428-6137
mmeenrich.tripod.com
Overview: A small local organization founded in 1992
Mission: To enrich the lives of married couples within the Filipino community in Toronto by caring for the spiritual, moral & temporal needs of members
Affliation(s): Archdiocese of Toronto
Chief Officer(s):
Jorge Isidro, Coordinator
jorgeisidro57@yahoo.ca
Elsa Isidro, Coordinator
Activities: Weekend activites; mass; pilgrimages

Moving Images Distribution
#103, 511 - 14th Ave., Vancouver BC V5Z 1P5
Tel: 604-684-3014; *Fax:* 604-684-7165
Toll-Free: 800-684-3014
mailbox@movingimages.ca
www.movingimages.ca
Overview: A small local organization
Mission: To promote Canadian culture & the recognition of film as an art form through the distribution of film & video created by its membership of Canadian independent producers
Chief Officer(s):
Sylvia Jonescu Lisitza, Executive Director

Mr. & Mrs. P.A. Woodward's Foundation
c/o Medical Advisor, #710, 1155 West Pender St., Vancouver BC V6E 2E9
Tel: 604-682-8116; *Fax:* 604-682-8153
pawoodwardfoundation@gmail.com
www.woodwardfoundation.ca
Overview: A medium-sized provincial charitable organization founded in 1951
Mission: To assist in projects that would contribute to better health care for British Columbians
Chief Officer(s):
J. Wm. Ibbott, Contact & Medical Advisor
Christine Alexander, Sec.-Treas.
Leo P. Sauve, President
Staff Member(s): 2
Membership: 8

MSA Society for Community Living
2391 Crescent Way, Abbotsford BC V2S 3M1
Tel: 604-852-6800; *Fax:* 604-852-2856
info@msasociety.com
www.msasociety.com
Also Known As: MSA Society
Overview: A medium-sized local charitable organization founded in 1957
Mission: To promotes active participation of people with disabilities in the community; To support those people & their families to maximize their potential for growth & community participation
Member of: British Columbia Association for Community Living
Chief Officer(s):
Richard Ashton, Executive Director, 604-852-6800 Ext. 102
ashton@msasociety.com
Finances: *Annual Operating Budget:* $1.5 Million-$3 Million; *Funding Sources:* Government; Donations; Fundraising
Staff Member(s): 43; 14 volunteer(s)
Membership: 153; *Member Profile:* Open (full, associate, & organizational)
Activities: Offering residential & day services

The M.S.I. Foundation
12230 - 106 Ave. NW, Edmonton AB T5N 3Z1
Tel: 780-421-7532; *Fax:* 780-425-4467
info@msifoundation.ca
www.msifoundation.ca
Also Known As: Medical Services Incorporated
Overview: A small provincial charitable organization founded in 1971
Mission: To foster & support research into any aspect of the provision of medical & allied health services to the people of Alberta
Chief Officer(s):
Doug Wilson, Chairperson
Finances: *Funding Sources:* Interest from invested capital
Activities: Supports medical research through universities & hospitals in Alberta

Mt. Pleasant Group of Cemeteries; Commemorative Services of Ontario *See* **Mount Pleasant Group**

MuchFACT
299 Queen St. West, Toronto ON M5V 2Z5
Tel: 416-384-5000; *Fax:* 416-384-2791
info@muchfact.ca
muchfact.ca
www.facebook.com/muchfact
twitter.com/muchfact
Previous Name: VideoFACT, A Foundation to Assist Canadian Talent
Overview: A small national charitable organization founded in 1984
Mission: To stimulate production of Canadian music videos, websites & electronic press kits
Chief Officer(s):
Tiffany Ferguson, Program Manager, 416-384-2616
tiffany.ferguson@bellmedia.ca
David Kines, Chairperson
Finances: *Funding Sources:* Sponsored by MuchMusic/MuchMoreMusic/MusiquePlus Network
Activities: *Library:* Resource Centre; Open to public by appointment

Mulgrave Road Theatre Foundation (MRT)
PO Box 219, Guysborough NS B0H 1N0
Tel: 902-533-2092; *Fax:* 902-533-3320
admin@mulgraveroad.ca
www.mulgraveroad.ca
www.facebook.com/pages/Mulgrave-Road-Theatre-Official-Site/22341319917
Overview: A small local charitable organization founded in 1977
Mission: To create theatre that is inspired by the Atlantic Canadian experience
Member of: Theatre Nova Scotia; Playwrights Atlantic Resource Centre; Professional Association of Canadian Theatres; Guysborough Antigonish Pictou Arts & Culture Council
Chief Officer(s):
Emmy Alcorn, Artistic Director
emmy@mulgraveroad.ca
Finances: *Funding Sources:* Canada Council for the Arts; Nova Scotia Department of Communities, Culture & Heritage
Staff Member(s): 2
Activities: Touring Theatre; Script Development
Awards:
• Fogarty's Cove Scholarship (Scholarship)

Multicultural Association of Carleton County Inc.
#4, 330 Centreville Rd., Florenceville NB E7L 3K6
Tel: 506-392-6011; *Fax:* 506-392-6411
admin@maccnb.ca
www.maccnb.ca
www.facebook.com/108327792575549
Overview: A small local organization
Mission: To help newcomers adapt to our rural area as well as to promote intercultural respect & awareness
Activities: English as a Second Language Training (E.S.L.); job counseling; social activities; neighborhood liaison; Canadian lifestyle guidance

Multicultural Association of Fredericton (MCAF) / Association multiculturelle de Fredericton Inc.
28 Saunders St., Fredericton NB E3B 1N1
Tel: 506-454-8292; *Fax:* 506-450-9033
www.mcaf.nb.ca
Overview: A small local organization founded in 1974
Mission: To establish communication & to foster understanding between the community, settled immigrants & newcomers
Chief Officer(s):
Arthur Jaucian, President
Lisa Bamford De Gante, Executive Director
bamford@mcaf.nb.ca
Membership: *Fees:* $5 student; $10 individual; $15 family; $25 organization

Multicultural Association of Kenora & District
136 Main St. South, Kenora ON P9N 1S9
Tel: 807-468-7140; *Fax:* 807-468-3895
makd@kmts.ca
www.kenoramulticultural.com
Overview: A small local organization
Mission: To promote the concept of multiculturalism; to encourage cultural awareness, appreciation & cooperation; to preserve cultural freedom, heritage & cultural identity; to work toward anti-racism & cultural diversity within the community
Member of: Multicultural Association of Northwestern Ontario
Chief Officer(s):
Darlene Smeaton, Contact
Activities: Settlement & interpreter service

Multicultural Association of Northwestern Ontario (MANWO)
511 East Victoria Ave., Thunder Bay ON P7C 1A8
Tel: 807-622-4666; *Fax:* 807-622-7271
Toll-Free: 800-692-7692
manwoyc@tbaytel.net
Overview: A small local organization founded in 1981
Mission: To promote the concept of multiculturalism; to provide information, training & resources on citizenship, multiculturalism & race relations.
Affliation(s): Other multicultural associations; Native Friendship Centres; Race Relations Committees; Association des Francophones du Nord-Ouest de L'Ontario
Activities: *Internships:* Yes; *Speaker Service:* Yes; *Rents Mailing List:* Yes; *Library* Open to public

Multicultural Association of Nova Scotia (MANS) / Association multiculturelle de la Nouvelle-Écosse
1113 Marginal Rd., Halifax NS B3H 4P7
Tel: 902-423-6534; *Fax:* 902-422-0881
Other Communication: communications@mans.ns.ca
admin@mans.ns.ca
www.mans.ns.ca
Overview: A medium-sized provincial organization founded in 1975
Mission: To develop & influence multicultural policy & to promote equality; To create a sense of belonging & respect for all cultures
Chief Officer(s):
Sylvia Parris, Vice-President
Membership: *Committees:* Education & Programming; Festival Management; Finance; Fundraising; Membership; Nomination; Personnel; Advisory; By-Laws; Immigration
Activities: Partnering with community agencies & stakeholders; Providing resources & education to members & the public; Presenting awards for exemplary services to multiculturalism; Advocating for multicultural issues; Initiating the development of legislation that reflects multiculturalism; Delivering multicultural programs; *Awareness Events:* Multicultural Festival; *Internships:* Yes; *Library:* MANS Library

Multicultural Association of Saint John Inc.
5 Bartlett Rd., Rothesay NB E2H 2W8
Tel: 506-849-8778
masjinc@gmail.com
Overview: A small local organization founded in 1984
Member of: Canadian Citizenship Federation; New Brunswick Multicultural Council
Chief Officer(s):
Melana Iverson, Executive Director
daba@rogers.com
Finances: *Funding Sources:* Fundraising; provincial government
Membership: *Fees:* $5 Senior/student; $20 individual; $25 family; $35 not for profit; $175 corporation; *Member Profile:* People of all races & diverse ethnic backgrounds
Activities: *Speaker Service:* Yes; *Library* Open to public

Multicultural Association of the Greater Moncton Area (MAGMA) / Association multiculturelle, Grand Moncton (AMGM)
#C170, 22 Church St., Moncton NB E1C 0P7
Tel: 506-858-9659; *Fax:* 506-857-9430
info@magma-amgm.org
www.magma-amgm.org
www.facebook.com/people/Magma-Amgmorg-Moncton/746910498
Overview: A small local organization founded in 1980
Mission: To promote & protect human rights; to assist various groups to develop & preserve their cultural identities; to foster harmonious relations among people of all cultures; to create cultural awareness & encourage sharing for the benefit of all Canadians; to be the medium of contact & communications between the members & the various ethnic, cultural & affiliated groups
Member of: New Brunswick Multicultural Council
Chief Officer(s):
Tradina Meadows Forgeron, Executive Director
Paul Vautour, President
Finances: *Funding Sources:* Municipal, provincial & federal government; United Nations Association in Canada
Staff Member(s): 23
Activities: Multicultural dinner;

Multicultural Council of Windsor & Essex County (MCC)
245 Janette Ave., Windsor ON N9A 4Z2

Tel: 519-255-1127; *Fax:* 519-255-1435
contact@themcc.com
www.themcc.com
www.facebook.com/pages/413981915289052
twitter.com/MultiCulturalCl
www.youtube.com/user/MCCWEC
Overview: A small local organization founded in 1973
Mission: To create a harmonious multicultural society
Chief Officer(s):
Kathleen Thomas, Executive Director
kthomas@themcc.com
Lisa Kolody, Director, Programs & Services
lkolody@themcc.com
Finances: *Annual Operating Budget:* $100,000-$250,000
Staff Member(s): 60; 200 volunteer(s)
Membership: 50; *Fees:* $20; *Committees:* Human Rights; Race Relations; Education; Carousel of the Nations; Folk Arts
Activities: *Awareness Events:* Carrousel of the Nations; Herb Gray Harmony Award Gala; Harmony Ribbon Campaign; *Internships:* Yes; *Library* Open to public by appointment
Awards:
• Herb Gray Harmony & Champion Award (Award)
Eligibility: Individuals, businesses & organizations that act as champions & role models and aid in creating and sustaining a community that is multicultural and works toward social equality of cultures*Location:* Windsor-Essex*Deadline:* December

Multicultural History Society of Ontario (MHSO)
c/o Oral History Museum, #307, 901 Lawrence Ave. West, Toronto ON M5S 1C3
Tel: 416-979-2973; *Fax:* 416-979-7947
mhso.mail@utoronto.ca
www.mhso.ca
www.facebook.com/multiculturalhistorysociety
www.youtube.com/user/MulticulturalHistory
Overview: A medium-sized provincial organization founded in 1976
Mission: Working with communities, schools, cultural agencies and institutions to preserve, record and make accessible archival and other material which demonstrate the role of immigration and ethnicity in shaping the culture and economic growth of Ontario and Canada. Library is located at St. Michael's College, University of Toronto.
Chief Officer(s):
Cathy Leekam, Program Manager
cathy.leekam@mhso.ca
Finances: *Annual Operating Budget:* $250,000-$500,000; *Funding Sources:* Government; corporate; private
Staff Member(s): 3; 25 volunteer(s)
Membership: 250; *Fees:* Schedule available; *Member Profile:* Interest in multiculturalism
Activities: *Speaker Service:* Yes; *Rents Mailing List:* Yes; *Library:* Resource Centre; by appointment

Multicultural Marketing Society of Canada
c/o Gautam Nath, Monsoon Communications, 37 Bulwer St., Toronto ON M5T 1A1
Tel: 647-477-3167
www.linkedin.com/groups/Multicultural-Marketing-Society-Canada-3853327
Overview: A small national organization
Chief Officer(s):
Gautam Nath, Founder
gautam@monsooncommunications.ca

Multi-Ethnic Association for the Integration of Persons with Disabilities *Voir* Association multi-ethnique pour l'intégration des personnes handicapées

Multifaith Action Society (MAS)
#5, 305 West 41 Ave., Vancouver BC V5Y 2S5
Tel: 604-321-1302
admin@multifaithaction.org
www.multifaithaction.org
www.facebook.com/113668295376729
Previous Name: Canadian Ecumenical Action
Overview: A small national charitable organization founded in 1972
Mission: To promote interfaith & multifaith dialogue & understanding; To provides information & resources on world religions to the community & develops community service programs
Chief Officer(s):
Derek LaCroix, President
Marcus Hynes, Operations Coordinator
Staff Member(s): 1
Membership: *Fees:* Schedule available
Activities: Lectures & conferences promoting interreligious dialogue; forums on faith; environmental awareness programs within religious communities; faith centre visits; *Speaker Service:* Yes

Multilingual Association of Regina, Inc. (MLAR)
2144 Cornwall St., Regina SK S4P 2K7
Tel: 306-757-3171; *Fax:* 306-757-3172
mlar@accesscomm.ca
www.mlar.ca
Overview: A small local organization founded in 1978
Mission: To advance education in heritage languages, other than the official languages of Canada, in Regina & the surrounding areas; To promote cultural diversity
Chief Officer(s):
Jim Leskun, President
Emile Carignan, Coordinator, Office
Finances: *Funding Sources:* Saskatchewan Organization for Heritage Languages; SaskCulture; Saskatchewan Ministry of Education; Saskatchewan Lotteries
Membership: 35 language schools; *Member Profile:* Non-profit heritage language schools in the Regina region
Activities: Developing heritage language curriculum & resource materials; Organizing training workshops for heritage language teachers; Providing materials, such as teaching aids, course materials, & technology; Conducting heritage language school visitations; Negotiating with the City of Regina, the Public School Board, & individual collegiates, for access to public school facilities; Assisting members to secure funding for schools; Promoting literature written in heritage languages
Publications:
• The Multilingual Association of Regina Newsletter
Type: Newsletter; *Frequency:* Quarterly *ISSN:* 1483-9660
Profile: Executive reports, meeting summaries, & reports from schools

Multilingual Orientation Service Association for Immigrant Communities (MOSAIC)
1720 Grant St., 2nd Fl., Vancouver BC V5L 2Y7
Tel: 604-254-9626; *Fax:* 604-254-3932
mosaic@mosaicbc.com
www.mosaicbc.com
www.linkedin.com/in/mosaicbc
www.facebook.com/mosaicbc
twitter.com/mosaicbc
www.youtube.com/mosaicbc
Overview: A small local charitable organization founded in 1976
Mission: To empower immigrants & refugees with settlement & immigration needs; to promote respect for people of different cultures, beliefs & abilities; to advocate for social justice & equality for all
Affiliation(s): Canadian Council for Refugees
Chief Officer(s):
Gabrielle Smith, President
Eyob Naizghi, Executive Director
Finances: *Funding Sources:* Federal, provincial & municipal governments; donations; translation fees; foundation grants
46 volunteer(s)
Membership: *Member Profile:* Staff, volunteers, organizations, business, individuals
Activities: Interpretation; translation; settlement support; employment services; family support services; English training for adults
Awards:
• MOSAIC Human Rights Award (Award)
• Dr. Kes Chetty Education Award (Award)
• Employer Recognition Award (Award)
• Britannia Scholarship Award (Award)

The Multimedia Group of Canada *Voir* Le groupe multimédia du Canada

Multiple Birth Families Association (MBFA)
PO Box 5532, Stn. F, Ottawa ON K2C 3M1
Tel: 613-860-6565
www.mbfa.ca
Previous Name: Ottawa Twins' Parents Association
Overview: A small local charitable organization founded in 1961
Mission: Giving parents an opportunity to get together & share ideas on raising multiples - the joys & the pitfalls
Chief Officer(s):
Olga Kutikov, President
president@mbfa.ca
Finances: *Funding Sources:* Membership dues; Advertising in newsletter
Membership: 350; *Fees:* $45; *Member Profile:* Parents & expectant parents of twins, triplets, quadruplets & higher order multiples

Multiple Births Canada (MBC) / Naissances multiples Canada
PO Box 432, Wasaga Beach ON L0L 2P0
Tel: 613-834-8946
Toll-Free: 866-228-8824
office@multiplebirthscanada.org
www.multiplebirthscanada.org
www.facebook.com/MultipleBirthsCanada
twitter.com/Multiple_Births
Previous Name: Parents of Multiple Births Association of Canada Inc.
Overview: A small national organization founded in 1978
Mission: To improve the quality of life for multiple birth individuals & their families through research, education, service & advocacy
Member of: International Society for Twin Studies
Finances: *Annual Operating Budget:* Less than $50,000
10 volunteer(s)
Membership: 60 corporate + 10 institutional + 50 individual; *Fees:* $20-$30; *Member Profile:* Individual & multiple birth families; caregivers; professionals; healthcare; *Committees:* Single Parents of Multiple Births; Parents of Multiples With Special Needs; Parents of Triplets; Quads & Quints; Loss of Multiples Registry
Activities: Speakers seminars; workshops; publications; referrals; *Awareness Events:* National Multiple Births Awareness Day, May 28

Multiple Births Guelph-Wellington
PO Box 21012, 35 Harvard Rd., Guelph ON N1G 4T3
Tel: 519-829-5337
Other Communication: guelphmultiples@live.ca
guelph@multiplebirthscanada.org
www.multiplebirthscanada.org/~guelphwellington
twitter.com/guelphmultiples
Overview: A small local organization founded in 1977 overseen by Multiple Births Canada
Mission: To offer support and encouragement to families in our area who are experiencing the joys and challenges of raising multiple-birth children.
Chief Officer(s):
Ruth Morton, President
Membership: *Fees:* $20-$30

Multiple Organ Retrieval & Exchange Program of Ontario *See* Trillium Gift of Life Network

Multiple Sclerosis Society of Canada (MS) / Société canadienne de la sclérose en plaques
North Tower, #500, 250 Dundas St. West, Toronto ON M5T 2Z5
Tel: 416-922-6065; *Fax:* 416-922-7538
Toll-Free: 800-268-7582
info@mssociety.ca
www.mssociety.ca
www.linkedin.com/company/ms-society-of-canada
www.facebook.com/MSSocietyCanada
twitter.com/mssocietycanada
www.youtube.com/MSSocietyCanada
Also Known As: MS Society
Overview: A medium-sized national charitable organization founded in 1948
Mission: To be a leader in finding a cure for multiple sclerosis & enabling people affected by MS to enhance their quality of life
Member of: Multiple Sclerosis International Federation
Affiliation(s): Canadian Medical Association
Chief Officer(s):
Charles Ford, Chair
Yves Savoie, President & CEO
Finances: *Funding Sources:* Fundraising; Donations; Membership fees
1350 volunteer(s)
Membership: 28,000; *Member Profile:* People with MS & their families
Activities: Funding of MS medical research; Providing services for persons with MS; Offering education; *Awareness Events:* MS Carnation Campaign, May; RONA MS Bike Tours, July-Sept.; *Internships:* Yes; *Speaker Service:* Yes; *Library:* Information Resource Centre; by appointment
Publications:
• MS Canada
Type: Magazine; *Frequency:* Quarterly; *Editor:* Jody Fiorino; Tiffany Regaudie *ISSN:* 0315-1131; *Price:* Free with membership in the Multiple Sclerosis Society of Canada

Profile: MS Society programs & services, plus the latest advance in MS research & treatments

Alberta & Northwest Territories Division
#150, 9405 - 50 St., Edmonton AB T6B 2T4
Tel: 403-463-1190; *Fax:* 403-479-1001
Toll-Free: 800-268-7582
info.alberta@mssociety.ca
mssociety.ca/alberta
www.facebook.com/mssocietyalberta
twitter.com/MS_Society_AB
www.youtube.com/mssocietyAB
Chief Officer(s):
Carey Mogdan, Chair
Neil Pierce, President
neil.pierce@mssociety.ca

Atlantic Division
#1, 109 Ilsley Ave., Dartmouth NS B3B 1S8
Tel: 902-468-8230; *Fax:* 902-468-5328
Toll-Free: 800-268-7582
info.atlantic@mssociety.ca
mssociety.ca/atlantic
www.facebook.com/170182879748684
twitter.com/MSAtlantic
Chief Officer(s):
Sean FitzGerald, Chair
Dena Simon, President
dena.simon@mssociety.ca

British Columbia & Yukon Division
#1501, 4330 Kingsway, Burnaby BC V5H 4G7
Tel: 604-689-3144; *Fax:* 604-689-0377
Toll-Free: 866-991-0577
info.bc@mssociety.ca
mssociety.ca/bc
www.facebook.com/mssocietybcy
twitter.com/mssocietybc
www.flickr.com/photos/mssociety_bcyukon
Chief Officer(s):
John Folka, Chair
Tania Vrionis, President, 604-602-3214 Ext. 241
tania.vrionis@mssociety.ca

Calgary & Area Chapter
Emerson Bldg., #150, 110 Quarry Park Blvd. SE, Calgary AB T2C 3G3
Tel: 403-250-7090; *Fax:* 403-250-8937
info.calgary@mssociety.ca
www.mssociety.ca/calgary
www.facebook.com/MSSocietyCalgary
twitter.com/MS_Calgary
www.youtube.com/user/calgaryms
Chief Officer(s):
Darrel Gregory, Southern Regional Director
darrel.gregory@mssociety.ca

Division du Québec
Tour Est, #1010, 550, rue Sherbrooke ouest, Montréal QC H3A 1B9
Tél: 514-849-7591; *Téléc:* 514-849-8914
Ligne sans frais: 800-268-7582
info.qc@mssociety.ca
mssociety.ca/qc
www.linkedin.com/company/soci-t-canadienne-de-la-scl-rose-en-plaques-d
www.facebook.com/SocieteSPCanada
twitter.com/SocCanDeLaSP
www.flickr.com/photos/societesp-quebec
Louis Adam, Executive Director

Manitoba Division
#100, 1465 Buffalo Pl., Winnipeg MB R3T 1L8
Tel: 204-943-9595; *Fax:* 204-988-0915
Toll-Free: 800-268-7582
info.manitoba@mssociety.ca
mssociety.ca/manitoba
www.facebook.com/mssocietymanitoba
twitter.com/mssocietyMB
Chief Officer(s):
Keith McConnell, Chair
Donna Boyd, President
donna.boyd@mssociety.ca

Ontario & Nunavut Division
#500, 250 Dundas St. West, Toronto ON M5T 2Z5
Tel: 416-922-6065; *Fax:* 416-922-7538
Toll-Free: 800-268-7582
info.ontario@mssociety.ca
www.mssociety.ca/ontario
twitter.com/MSSocietyON
Chief Officer(s):
Marie Vaillant, Chair

Saskatchewan Division
150 Albert St., Regina SK S4R 2N2
Tel: 306-522-5600; *Fax:* 306-565-0477
Toll-Free: 800-268-7582
info.sask@mssociety.ca
mssociety.ca/sask
twitter.com/MSSocietySK
www.flickr.com/photos/mssocietysask/
Chief Officer(s):
Brian Duck, Chair
Jack Aldcorn, President

Multiple Sclerosis Society of Canada (Québec Division) *Voir* Société canadienne de la sclérose en plaques (Division du Québec)

The Municipal Chapter of Toronto IODE

#219, 40 Orchard View Blvd., Toronto ON M4R 1B9
Tel: 416-925-5078
iodetoronto@bellnet.ca
Overview: A small local charitable organization founded in 1912
Mission: To improve the quality of life for children, youth & those in need through educational, social service & citizenship programs
Member of: The National Chapter of Canada IODE; The Provincial Chapter of Ontario IODE
Chief Officer(s):
Mary K. Anderson, President
Finances: *Funding Sources:* Donations; special programs; trusts
Awards:
• IODE Book Award (Award)
Established in 1975; an inscribed scroll & not less than $1,000 awarded annually to the author or illustrator of the best children's book written or illustrated by a Canadian resident in Toronto or surrounding area & published by a Canadian publisher within the preceding 12 months
• Music Awards (Award)
• Education Bursaries (Scholarship)

Municipal Electric Association *See* Electricity Distributors Association

---

Municipal Engineers Association (MEA)

#2, 6355 Kennedy Rd., Mississauga ON L5T 2L5
Tel: 905-795-2555; *Fax:* 905-795-2660
info@municipalengineers.on.ca
www.municipalengineers.on.ca
Overview: A medium-sized provincial organization founded in 1974
Mission: To provide focus & unity for licensed engineers employed by municipalities in Ontario; To address issues of common concern to members; To facilitate the dissemination of information
Chief Officer(s):
Rick A. Kester, President, 905-795-2555, Fax: 905-795-2660
J. David Shantz, Executive Director
Gary Carroll, Vice-President
Trevor D. Lewis, Treasurer
Membership: *Member Profile:* Public sector professional engineers in full time employment of municipalities, who perform functions in the field of municipal engineering; *Committees:* Administrative & Seconded; Municipal Transportation Advisory; MEA/CEO Liaison; Development Engineering; MEA/MNR/CO Liaison; MEA Training; MEA/MOE Liaison; Ontario Works Network; Tri-Committee Board
Activities: Organizing training events; Advocating for sound municipal engineering; Championing positions on municipal engineering issues; Recognizing achievements of municipal engineers
Meetings/Conferences: • Municipal Engineers Association 2015 Annual General Meeting & Workshop, November, 2015, ON
Scope: Provincial
Description: A workshop & business meeting during three days each November
Publications:
• Annual Report of the Municipal Engineers Association Administrative & Standing Committees
Type: Yearbook; *Frequency:* Annually
Profile: A review of the year's activities
• Municipal Engineers Association Members Directory
Type: Directory

Municipal Equipment & Operations Association (Ontario) Inc.

38 Summit Ave., Kitchener ON N2M 4W2
Tel: 519-741-2600; *Fax:* 519-741-2750
Other Communication: stcc@meoa.org (safety matters)
admin@meoa.org
www.meoa.org
Also Known As: MEOA
Overview: A small provincial organization founded in 1965
Mission: To promote high standards & cost effectiveness in public services across Ontario
Chief Officer(s):
Mike Beattie, President
Finances: *Funding Sources:* Annual membership dues
Membership: 250; *Member Profile:* Supervisory employees & management support staff from any government body; Suppliers of equipment & services used by municipal corporate organizations; Honorary members who have been beneficial to the association; Affiliate members who have an interest in the association
Activities: Offering education & training; Organizing field trips; Facilitating the exchange of information; Providing networking opportunities
Meetings/Conferences: • Municipal Equipment & Operations Association (Ontario) Inc. 2015 Annual Spring Meeting, April, 2015, Waterloo Motor Inn, Waterloo, ON
Scope: Provincial
Description: An event to elect the new executive, to address the business of the association, to participate in a plant tour, to hear guest speakers, & to attend educational presentations
• Municipal Equipment & Operations Association (Ontario) Inc. 2015 Annual Professional Development Day, May, 2015, Forest City GC, London, ON
Scope: Provincial
Description: A learning opportunity for members of the association
• Municipal Equipment & Operations Association (Ontario) Inc. 2015 Annual Municipal & Contractor Fall Equipment Show, 2015
Scope: Provincial
Description: An opportunity for suppliers to promote & demonstrate their products & services

---

Municipal finance & development agency for emergency 9-1-1 call centres in Quebec *Voir* Agence municipale de financement et de développement des centres d'urgence 9-1-1 du Québec

---

Municipal Finance Officers' Association of Ontario (MFOA)

2169 Queen St. East, 2nd Fl., Toronto ON M4L 1J1
Tel: 416-362-9001; *Fax:* 416-362-9226
office@mfoa.on.ca
www.mfoa.on.ca
Overview: A medium-sized provincial organization founded in 1989
Mission: To represent the interests of municipal finance officers throughout Ontario; To promote the interests of members
Affliation(s): Association of Municipalities of Ontario (AMO)
Chief Officer(s):
Dan Cowin, Executive Director, 416-362-9001 Ext. 223
dan@mfoa.on.ca
Ron Kaufman, President
ron.kaufman@caledon.ca
Mona Monkman, Vice-President
mona.monkman@ottawa.ca
Finances: *Funding Sources:* Sponsorships
Staff Member(s): 8
Membership: 2,000+ individuals representing 350+ municipalities; *Member Profile:* Municipalities; Provincial Employees; Corporate individuals; *Committees:* Accounting & Financial Reporting; Finance Policy; Professional Development; Provincial Offences Act
Activities: Organizing annual meetings; Presenting awards; Sponsoring seminars; Initiating studies; Developing positions on policy & financial management issues
Meetings/Conferences: • 2015 Municipal Finance Officers' Association of Ontario Annual Conference, September, 2015, ON
Scope: Provincial

Municipal Information Systems Association of Canada

#309, 14845-6 Yonge St., Aurora ON L4G 6H8
Tel: 416-662-3950; *Fax:* 905-602-4295
info@misa.on.ca
www.misa-asim.ca

Overview: A small provincial organization
Mission: To promote the efficient & effective use of municipal information systems & technology; to provide a medium of communication for interchange of information between members & interested persons or groups leading to a more efficient use of information systems.
Chief Officer(s):
Kathryn Bulko, President
kbulko@toronto.ca
Roy Wiseman, Executive Director
roy.wiseman@rogers.com

Municipal Law Departments Association of Ontario (MLDAO)
c/o The City of Greater Sudbury, PO Box 5000, Stn. A, Sudbury ON P3A 5P3
Tel: 705-671-2489
www.mldao.ca
Previous Name: Regional Solicitors' Association of Ontario
Overview: A small provincial organization founded in 2002
Mission: To exchange information & advice on municipal issues; to hold meetings & seminars as a forum for sharing information & education of members; to advocate reform of legislation to the benefit of municipalities; to participate in consultation with governments & other associations interested in matters affecting municipalities
Member of: Association of Municipalities of Ontario
Chief Officer(s):
Jamie M. Canapini, Chair
jamie.canapini@greatersudbury.ca
Alan Barber, Vice-Chair
abarber@peterborough.ca
Jennifer A. Smout, Vice-Chair
jsmout@london.ca
Elizabeth Waight, Vice-Chair
elizabeth.waight@mississauga.ca
Membership: 45 departments; *Member Profile:* Municipal law departments of all those municipalities in Ontario that maintain in-house legal services
Activities: Five plenary meetings/seminars annually; Annual conference

Municipal Law Enforcement Officers' Association (Ontario) Inc.
c/o j. Popple, PO Box 100, #7-8. 100 Dissett St., Bradford ON L3Z 2A7
Tel: 905-775-5366; *Fax:* 905-775-0153
mleo@mleoa.ca
www.mleoa.ca
www.facebook.com/group.php?gid=215037141887694
Overview: A medium-sized provincial organization founded in 1979
Mission: To bring members into helpful association with each other to maintain professional standards; to encourage & assist in the education & training programs for Municipal Law Enforcement Officers
Chief Officer(s):
Randy Berg, President
randy.berg@sympatico.ca
Finances: *Annual Operating Budget:* $50,000-$100,000; *Funding Sources:* Membership fees
9 volunteer(s)
Membership: 1,500; *Fees:* $17 retired; $83 associate & student; $110 individual; *Committees:* Education; Communications; Government Liaison; Strategic Planning; By-Law Registry; Procedures & Elections; Certification; Membership; Inventory; 2012 Conference
Activities: Annual training seminars; training courses; *Speaker Service:* Yes

Municipal Officers' Association of British Columbia *See* Local Government Management Association of British Columbia

Municipal Pension Retirees Association (MPRA)
Unit 22, #525, 2475 Dobbin Rd., West Kelowna BC V4T 2E9
Tel: 250-768-1519
mpra@shawbiz.ca
www.mpra.ca
Overview: A small national organization
Chief Officer(s):
Steven Polak, President
Membership: 32 districts + 1 out of province; *Fees:* $20 individual; $35 couples; *Member Profile:* Individuals who recieve a Municipal Pension
Activities: Networking; newsletters; access to travel & home insurance; discounts at select retailers;

Municipal Police Authorities *See* Ontario Association of Police Services Boards

Municipal Waste Association (MWA)
#100, 127 Wyndham St. North, Guelph ON N1H 4E9
Tel: 519-823-1990; *Fax:* 519-823-0084
carrie@municipalwaste.ca
www.municipalwaste.ca
Previous Name: Association of Municipal Recycling Coordinators
Overview: A medium-sized provincial organization founded in 1987
Mission: To expedite the flow of information regarding 3R programs to municipalities & other community & government groups; To act as an information forum for municipal recycling coordinators; To allow member municipalities to act as a unified voice in promoting progressive waste reduction & recycling alternatives
Member of: Recycling Council of Ontario
Chief Officer(s):
Vivian De Giovanni, Executive Director
vivian@municipalwaste.ca
Ben Bennett, Manager, Projects & Communications
ben@municipalwaste.ca
Finances: *Funding Sources:* Membership fees; Project sponsorship
Membership: 100-499; *Fees:* $85 - $995, based on population; *Committees:* Household Hazardous Waste; Markets Operation & Contracts; Organic Waste Diversion; Policy & Program
Activities: *Speaker Service:* Yes
Meetings/Conferences: • Municipal Waste Association 2015 Annual General Meeting, 2015, ON
Scope: Provincial
Description: A yearly event featuring a business meeting, trade show, & networking opportunities
Contact Information: Executive Director: Ben Bennett, E-mail: ben@municipalwaste.ca

Municipalities Newfoundland & Labrador
460 Torbay Rd., St. John's NL A1A 5J3
Tel: 709-753-6820; *Fax:* 709-738-0071
Toll-Free: 800-440-6536
info@municipalnl.ca
www.municipalitiesnl.com
Previous Name: Newfoundland & Labrador Federation of Municipalities
Overview: A medium-sized provincial charitable organization founded in 1951
Mission: To assist communities in their endeavour to achieve & sustain strong & effective local government thereby improving the quality of life for all the people of this province.
Member of: Federation of Canadian Municipalities
Chief Officer(s):
Terry Taylor, General Manager
Churence Rogers, President
president@municipalnl.ca
Membership: 281 municipalities; *Fees:* Sliding scale based on population; *Member Profile:* Incorporated municipal governments in Newfoundland
Activities: *Internships:* Yes; *Rents Mailing List:* Yes

Municipality of Port Hope Historical Society (EDHS)
PO Box 116, Port Hope ON L1A 3V9
Tel: 905-885-2981
info@porthopehistorical.ca
www.porthopehistorical.ca
Previous Name: East Durham Historical Society
Overview: A small local organization founded in 1964
Mission: Responsible for Dorothy's House Museum & preserving local history
Chief Officer(s):
Joan Parrott, President
Membership: 100; *Fees:* $15 single; $25 family; $40 business; $75 lifetime

The Murphy Foundation Incorporated
#919, 167 Lombard Ave., Winnipeg MB R3B 0V3
Tel: 204-942-5281
Overview: A small provincial charitable organization founded in 1969
Mission: To fund medical research, education, & wildlife
Chief Officer(s):
Art W. Van de Vijsel, Secretary-Treasurer
Finances: *Funding Sources:* Bequests
Membership: *Member Profile:* Nominated by directors

Murray Grey International, Incorporated (MGI)
c/o Canadian Livestock Records Coroporation, 2417 Holly Lane, Ottawa ON K1V 0M7
Tel: 613-731-7110; *Fax:* 613-731-0704
clrc@clrc.ca
www.murraygrey.org
Also Known As: Murray Grey International Association
Overview: A small international organization
Mission: To promote the Murray Grey breed; To provide a registry of Murray Grey breeding
Affliation(s): Canadian Livestock Records Corporation
Chief Officer(s):
Terry Anderson, Contact, 819-632-7352
Membership: *Fees:* Schedule available based on number of bulls; *Member Profile:* Murray Grey breeders in North America & South America, & other areas of the world
Publications:
• Breeder Directory
Type: Directory; *Frequency:* Annually
• Murray Grey International, Incorporated Newsletter
Type: Newsletter

Musagetes Foundation
6 Dublin St. South, Guelph ON N1H 4L5
Tel: 519-836-7300; *Fax:* 519-836-7320
info@musagetes.ca
www.musagetes.ca
www.facebook.com/musagetesfoundation
twitter.com/musagetesf
Overview: A small international organization
Mission: To function as a catalyst to generate ideas & actions that bring artistic creativity into daily life. It sponsors Cafés, multi-year projects which occur at comfortable, social places where people with common interests can explore & apply creative ideas for community change & development.
Chief Officer(s):
Joy Roberts, President
Shawn Van Sluys, Executive Director
Staff Member(s): 4
Activities: Café meetings in Barcelona (Spain), Lecce (Italy), London (UK), Rijeka (Croatia), Sudbury (Canada)

Muscular Dystrophy Canada (MDC) / Dystrophie musculaire Canada (DMC)
#900, 2345 Yonge St., Toronto ON M4P 2E5
Tel: 416-488-0030; *Fax:* 416-488-7523
Toll-Free: 866-687-2538
info@muscle.ca
www.muscle.ca
www.linkedin.com/company/466761
www.facebook.com/muscle.ca
twitter.com/md_canada
www.youtube.com/user/musculardystrophycan
Overview: A large national charitable organization founded in 1954
Mission: To improve the quality of life of persons who have muscular dystrophy through a broad range of programs, education, support of research & the delivery of needed services to people with muscular dystrophy & their families
Chief Officer(s):
Nancy Cumming, Chair
Catherine Sherrard, CEO
Melanie Towell, CFO
Finances: *Annual Operating Budget:* Greater than $5 Million
Staff Member(s): 53
Membership: *Committees:* Executive; Marketing & Communications; Services & Advocacy; Human Resources; Chapter Relations; Medical & Scientific Advisory; National Fire Fighter Relations; Governance & Mandate
Activities: *Awareness Events:* Walk for Muscular Dystrophy; Muscular Dystrophy Month, Sept.
Awards:
• Courage to Inspire Award (Award)
• Dr. George Karpati Award (Award)
• Fire Department of the Year Award (Award)
• Fire Fighter of the Year Award (Award)
• Mary Ann Wickham Award for Volunteer of the Year (Award)
• Michel Louvain Award for Client of the Year (Award)

Atlantic Regional Office
#47, 201 Brownlow Ave., Dartmouth NS B3B 1W2
Tel: 902-429-6322; *Fax:* 902-425-4226
Toll-Free: 800-884-6322
infoatlantic@muscle.ca

Ontario & Nunavut Regional Office
#901, 2345 Yonge St., Toronto ON M4P 2E5

Tel: 416-488-2699; *Fax:* 416-488-0107
Toll-Free: 800-567-2873
infoontario@muscle.ca
Québec Regional Office
#506, 1425, René-Lévesque ouest, Montréal QC H3G 1T7
Tel: 514-393-3522; *Fax:* 514-393-8113
Toll-Free: 800-567-2236
infoquebec@muscle.ca
Western Canada Regional Office
1401 West Broadway, 7th Fl., Vancouver BC V6H 1H6
Tel: 604-732-8799; *Fax:* 604-731-6127
Toll-Free: 800-336-8166
infowest@muscle.ca
Chief Officer(s):
Darren Soy, Executive Director
darren.soy@muscle.ca

Musée Colby-Curtis *See* Stanstead Historical Society

Le Musée de chemin de fer de Sydney à Louisburg *See* Sydney & Louisburg Railway Historical Society

Le Musée et la fondation du patrimoine de l'Ile-du-Prince-Édouard *See* Prince Edward Island Museum & Heritage Foundation

Musée et Temple canadien de la renommée du golf *See* Canadian Golf Hall of Fame & Museum

Musée McCord d'histoire canadienne *See* McCord Museum of Canadian History

Musée minéralogique et minier de Thetford Mines
711, boul Frontenac ouest, Thetford Mines QC G6G 7Y8
Tél: 418-335-2123; *Téléc:* 418-335-5605
Ligne sans frais: 855-335-2123
Autres numéros: communication@museemineralogique.com
secretariat@museemineralogique.com
www.museemineralogique.com
www.facebook.com/333048121773
Aperçu: *Dimension:* petite; *Envergure:* nationale; Organisme sans but lucratif; fondée en 1976
Mission: Le Musée vise à faire connaître la région de L'Amiante, son patrimoine minier, géologique et minéralogique; collectionner et présenter des minéraux et roches du monde entier; conserver, présenter et interpréter les témoins du patrimoine minier régional; initier jeunes et moins jeunes aux sciences de la terre; et, favoriser les échanges avec d'autres musées du Québec, du Canada et de l'étranger
Membre de: Société des musées québécois; Association des musées canadiens
Membre(s) du bureau directeur:
Yvan Faucher, Président
François Cinq-Mars, Directeur
f.cinq-mars@museemineralogique.com
Monique Laberge, Secrétaire
Finances: *Budget de fonctionnement annuel:* $250,000-$500,000; *Fonds:* Ministère de la culture et des communications du québec
Membre(s) du personnel: 10; 35 bénévole(s)
Membre: 13 institutionnel; 181 individu; *Montant de la cotisation:* 50$ institutionnel; 75$ commerce; 9,20$ étudiant; 20$ individuel; 30$ familial; *Critères d'admissibilite:* 18 ans et plus
Activités: Expositions; excursions géologiques; forfait mine-musée en été; boutique souvenirs; 8 livres ont été publiés par le Musée; collections de roches et de minéraux produites par les musée pour la vente; Jounrées de la Culture; Expo-Cadeaux

Museum Association of Newfoundland & Labrador (MANL)
PO Box 5785, St. John's NL A1C 5X3
Tel: 709-722-9034; *Fax:* 709-722-9035
manl@nf.aibn.com
www.manl.nf.ca
Overview: A medium-sized provincial charitable organization founded in 1980
Mission: To protect & preserve the cultural & natural heritage of Newfoundland & Labrador; To unite, support & promote members; To improve & promote museums
Member of: Canadian Museums Association
Chief Officer(s):
Teresita McCarthy, President
teresita_mccarthy@hotmail.com
John Griffin, Vice-President
Angela Noseworthy, Treasurer
anoseworthy@gmail.com
Diane Curtis, Secretary
jacksonsarmheritagesociety@live.ca
Finances: *Funding Sources:* Donations
Staff Member(s): 2
Membership: 115 individuals; 150 museums & heritage societies; *Member Profile:* Individuals, museums, & heritage groups of Newfoundland & Labrador interested in the preservation & promotion of the province's material & cultural heritage
Activities: Providing training; Advocating for members; Encouraging standards of excellence; Connecting with other provincial & national associations & organizations to provide members with up-to-date information; Disseminating information to museums & concerned individuals; Presenting awards; Organizing conferences; *Awareness Events:* Museum Week, June; *Library:* Resource Centre;

Museum London
421 Ridout St. North, London ON N6A 5H4
Tel: 519-661-0333
www.museumlondon.ca
Previous Name: London Regional Art & Historical Museums
Overview: A medium-sized local charitable organization founded in 1989
Mission: To enrich public knowledge & enjoyment of the art & history of the London region & Canada
Member of: Ontario Museums Association; Ontario Association of Art Galleries; Canadian Museums Association
Chief Officer(s):
Brian Meehan, Executive Director
bmeehan@museumlondon.ca
Finances: *Annual Operating Budget:* $3 Million-$5 Million; *Funding Sources:* All levels of government; Fees; Fundraising; Sponsorship; Revenues
Staff Member(s): 20
Membership: *Committees:* Property & Finance; Art Collection; Material Culture; Policy; Marketing & Development; Museum Underground
Activities: Exhibitions of art & artifacts with related programs & special events

Museums Association of Saskatchewan (MAS)
424 McDonald St., Regina SK S4N 6E1
Tel: 306-780-9279; *Fax:* 306-780-9463
Toll-Free: 866-568-7386
mas@saskmuseums.org
www.saskmuseums.org
www.facebook.com/saskmuseums
twitter.com/saskmuseums
Previous Name: Saskatchewan Museums Association
Overview: A medium-sized provincial charitable organization founded in 1967
Mission: To work for the advancement of strong & vibrant museums in Saskatchewan; To encourage the preservation & understanding of the province's cultural & natural heritage; To serve Saskatchewan museums
Chief Officer(s):
Wendy Fitch, Executive Director, 306-780-9280
wendy.fitch@saskmuseums.org
Robert Hubick, President
Finances: *Funding Sources:* Department of Canadian Heritage Museums Assistance Program; Saskatchewan Lotteries Trust for Sport, Culture & Recreation
Staff Member(s): 6
Membership: 400+; *Fees:* Schedule available; *Member Profile:* Individuals; Museums; Associate organizations
Activities: Offering training opportunities; Providing support to First Nations & Métis communities; Advising museums through an information & referral service & on-site visits; Administering grants; *Library:* MAS Resources Library

Museums of Niagara Association (MONA)
c/o Helen Booth, Jordan Historical Museum of the Twenty, 3800 Main St., Jordan ON L0R 1S0
Tel: 905-562-5242; *Fax:* 905-562-7786
Overview: A small local organization founded in 1979
Mission: To advocate, educate & cooperate with Niagara's cultural facilities
Membership: *Member Profile:* Museums & art galleries of Niagara
Activities: Production of area brochure of member institutions; meetings featuring workshops & speakers on current & relevant issues; *Speaker Service:* Yes

Musgamagw Tsawataineuk Tribal Council
#1-2, 2005 Eagle Dr., Campbell River BC V9H 1V8
Tel: 250-914-3402; *Fax:* 250-914-3406
Overview: A small local organization

Mushrooms Canada (CMGA)
7660 Mill Rd., RR#4, Guelph ON N1H 6J1
Tel: 519-829-4125; *Fax:* 519-837-0729
info@canadianmushroom.com
www.mushrooms.ca
www.facebook.com/mushroomscanada
twitter.com/mushroomscanada
www.youtube.com/cdnmushroom
Previous Name: Canadian Mushroom Growers' Association
Overview: A medium-sized national organization founded in 1955
Mission: To encourage cooperation & communication within the Canadian industry, with various levels of government, & with related organizations internationally; To promote mushroom consumption
Affliation(s): International Society for Mushroom Science (ISMS)
Finances: *Funding Sources:* Membership dues
Membership: *Fees:* Schedule available; *Member Profile:* Mushroom growers; Consultants; Suppliers to the industry; Research scientists
Activities: Researching in mushroom cultivation; Marketing

Music BC Industry Association (PMIA)
#100, 938 Howe St., Vancouver BC V6Z 1N9
Tel: 604-873-1914; *Fax:* 604-873-9686
Toll-Free: 888-866-8570
info@musicbc.org
www.musicbc.org
www.facebook.com/MusicBC
twitter.com/musicbc
Previous Name: Pacific Music Industry Association
Overview: A medium-sized provincial organization founded in 1990
Mission: To address key issues; to implement positive change by presenting a strong voice to government, business & community; To enhance the profile of the BC music industry in the international marketplace; To promote communication; To stimulate activity & employment
Member of: Western Canadian Music Alliance
Affliation(s): FACTOR; MROC
Chief Officer(s):
Bob D'Eith, Executive Director
bob@musicbc.org
Finances: *Funding Sources:* Provincial government; membership dues; events; Socan Foundation
Staff Member(s): 4
Membership: *Fees:* schedule
Activities: Professional development sessions throughout the province; *Library* by appointment
Awards:
• West Coast Music Awards (Award)

Music Canada
85 Mowat Ave., Toronto ON M6K 3E3
Tel: 416-967-7272; *Fax:* 416-967-9415
info@musiccanada.com
www.musiccanada.com
www.facebook.com/MusicCanada
twitter.com/music_canada
Previous Name: Canadian Recording Industry Association
Overview: A medium-sized national organization
Mission: To develop & promote high ethical standards in the creation, manufacture and marketing of sound recordings.
Affliation(s): EMI Music Canada; Sony Music Entertainment Canada, Inc.; Universal Music Canada, Inc.; Warner Music Canada, Co.
Chief Officer(s):
Jennifer Hardy, Contact
jhardy@musiccanada.com
Membership: 20

Music for Young Children (MYC) / Musique pour jeunes enfants
39 Leacock Way, Kanata ON K2K 1T1
Tel: 613-592-7565; *Fax:* 613-592-9353
Toll-Free: 800-561-1692
myc@myc.com
www.myc.com
www.facebook.com/Music.for.Young.Children.MYC
www.youtube.com/user/MYCKanata
Overview: A medium-sized local licensing organization founded in 1980

Mission: To develop, deliver & support comprehensive entry level music education programs of the finest quality
Member of: Registered Music Teachers Association
Chief Officer(s):
Janice Reade, Manager, Public Relations
janice@myc.com
Finances: *Funding Sources:* Private
Membership: 900 individual; *Fees:* Schedule available; *Member Profile:* Teachers must have completed a training seminar
Activities: *Library* by appointment
Awards:
• Helena Evans Memorial Scholarship (Scholarship)
Awarded annually to an MYC graduate pursuing music at the post-secondary level

Alberta
326 Superior Ave. SW, Calgary AB T3C 2J2
Tel: 403-244-9080
Toll-Free: 866-244-9008
Chief Officer(s):
Judy Causgrove, Coordinator
j.causgrove@myc.com

British Columbia & Western United States
4350 - 13th St. South, Cranbrook BC V1C 7A6
Tel: 250-489-1746
Chief Officer(s):
Wendy Guimont, Coordinator
w.guimont@myc.com

Manitoba
2735 Hallama Dr., Grande Pointe MB R5A 1H5
Tel: 204-257-1071; *Fax:* 204-257-1071
www.facebook.com/MYC.MB.NWON
Chief Officer(s):
Marilyn Unrau, Coordinator
m.unrau@myc.com

New Brunswick & Prince Edward Island
34 Llangollen Rd., Moncton NB E1E 3W5
Tel: 506-382-0280; *Fax:* 506-382-0280
Toll-Free: 888-371-5577
Chief Officer(s):
Doris Sabean, Coordinator
d.sabean@myc.com

Newfoundland & Labrador
21 Connemara Pl., St. John's NL A1A 3E3
Tel: 709-753-0218
Chief Officer(s):
Heather Meaney, Coordinator
h.meaney@myc.com

Nova Scotia
49 Charles St., Timberlea NS B3T 1J7
Tel: 902-434-3929
Chief Officer(s):
Megan Henley, Coordinator
m.henley@myc.com

Ontario - Central
c/o Muskoka Music Centre, 36 Lorne St. South, Huntsville ON P1H 1V7
Tel: 705-224-0070
Toll-Free: 866-999-1091
play@muskokamusiccentre.com
Chief Officer(s):
Frank Berg, Coordinator
f.berg@myc.com

Ontario - Eastern
1599 Winterport Way, Ottawa ON K4A 4C2
Tel: 613-841-5811
Chief Officer(s):
Eileen Leversedge, Coordinator
e.leversedge@myc.com

Ontario - Southern
Elmira ON
Tel: 519-669-8941
Toll-Free: 866-884-3080
Chief Officer(s):
Sandra Poolton, Coordinator
s.poolton@myc.com

Prince Edward Island Sunrise Program
Wildon St., Summerside PE C1N 4H6
Tel: 902-436-2674
Chief Officer(s):
Nancy Rogerson, Coordinator
n.rogerson@myc.com

Québec
Montréal QC
Tel: 514-696-0008
www.facebook.com/MYC.Quebec.MJE
Chief Officer(s):
Cathy Morabito, Coordinator
c.morabito@myc.com

Saskatchewan
493 Willow Bay, Estevan SK S4A 2G3
Tel: 306-636-2692
Chief Officer(s):
Anita Kuntz, Coordinator
a.kuntz@myc.com

Music Industries Association of Canada (MIAC) / Association canadienne des industries de la musique
#310, 3-1750 The Queensway, Toronto ON M9C 5H5
Tel: 416-490-1871; *Fax:* 866-524-0037
Toll-Free: 877-480-6422
info@miac.net
www.miac.net
www.facebook.com/pages/MIAC-Show/127195590711806
twitter.com/MIAC_Show
Overview: A medium-sized national organization founded in 1972
Mission: To represent Canadian manufacturers, distributors, retailers & wholesalers of musical instruments & accessories, sound reinforcement/lighting products, published music & computer music software
Affliation(s): Music Distributors Association - USA; National Association of Music Merchants - USA
Chief Officer(s):
Dale Kroke, President, 905-896-3001 Ext. 329
dale@miac.net
Finances: *Funding Sources:* Membership dues; trade show revenue
Staff Member(s): 6
Membership: 170 manufacturers & distributors; 150 retailers; *Fees:* $350+GST; *Committees:* Retail; PAL
Activities: *Awareness Events:* Trade Show

Music Industry Association of Newfoundland & Labrador
See MusicNL

Music Managers Forum Canada
1731 Lawrence Ave. East, Toronto ON M1R 2X7
Tel: 416-462-9160
Other Communication: Toll-Free Fax: 1-866-766-4255
info@musicmanagersforum.ca
musicmanagersforum.ca
Also Known As: MMF Canada
Overview: A small national organization
Mission: To be a source of information for Canadian musicians, artists & managers
Affliation(s): International Music Managers Forum
Chief Officer(s):
Ryhna Thompson, President
Jamie New Johnson, Manager, Operations
jamie@musicmanagersforum.ca
Membership: 150+ members serving 300+ Canadian & international acts

Music Nova Scotia
2157 Gottingen St., 2nd Fl., Halifax NS B3K 3B5
Tel: 902-423-6271; *Fax:* 902-423-8841
Toll-Free: 888-343-6426
info@musicnovascotia.ca
www.musicnovascotia.ca
www.facebook.com/MusicNovaScotia
twitter.com/musicnovascotia
musicnovascotia.tumblr.com; www.youtube.com/user/MusicNS
Overview: A large provincial organization founded in 1989
Mission: To encourage the creation, development, growth and promotion of Nova Scotia's music industry.
Chief Officer(s):
Scott Long, Executive Director
scott@musicnovascotia.ca
Staff Member(s): 9
Membership: *Fees:* $20 student; $50 individual; $60 band; $70 small business/non-profit/venue; $135 corporate

Music NWT
PO Box 127, Yellowknife NT X1A 2N1
www.musicnwt.ca
twitter.com/musicnwt
Overview: A medium-sized provincial organization
Mission: To bring together musicians, offers workshops & other resources, & provides networking opportunities
Chief Officer(s):
Mike Filipowitsch, Executive Director
mike@musicnwt.ca
Staff Member(s): 2
Membership: *Fees:* $10 supporter; $15 senior/youth; $30 individual; $250 venue; $500 corporate; *Member Profile:* Musicians, including bands; music-related associations & corporations

Music PEI
PO Box 2371, 220 Kent St., Charlottetown PE C1A 8C4
Tel: 902-894-6734; *Fax:* 902-894-4404
music@musicpei.com
www.musicpei.com
www.facebook.com/MusicPEI
twitter.com/MusicPEI
Overview: A large provincial organization founded in 2001
Mission: To promote, foster and develop artists and the music industry on PEI.
Chief Officer(s):
Jim Hornby, President
Rob Oakie, Executive Director
roboakie@musicpei.com
Membership: 200+; *Fees:* $25 artist; $50 band; $65 corporate; $15 student; $20 music lover
Activities: *Awareness Events:* Music PEI Week, February
Awards:
• Achievement in Classical Music (Award)

Music Yukon
#416, 108 Elliott St., Whitehorse YT Y1A 6C4
Tel: 867-456-8742
office@musicyukon.com
www.musicyukon.com
www.facebook.com/musicyukon
twitter.com/musicyukon
Overview: A medium-sized provincial organization
Mission: To promote the Yukon music industry
Affliation(s): Canadian Academy of Recording Arts & Sciences; Yukon Film & Sound Commission; Canadian Independent Record Production Association; Folk Alliance Canada; Foundation to Assist Canadian Talent on Records; Songwriters Association of Canada; Society of Composers, Authors & Music Publishers of Canada
Chief Officer(s):
Stephen Clarke, President
frasercanyon51@yahoo.ca
Michael Brooks, Interim Executive Director
Finances: *Funding Sources:* Member fees; Government grants
Membership: *Fees:* $200 corporate; $40 full service; $20 associate; No fee for affiliates or supporting cast members; *Member Profile:* Individuals, groups, organizations, companies & entities involved in the Yukon's music industry

Music/Musique NB
#9, 140 Botsford St., Moncton NB E1C 4X4
Tel: 506-383-4662; *Fax:* 506-383-6171
contact@musicnb.org
musicnb.org
Also Known As: Music New Brunswick
Overview: A medium-sized provincial organization
Mission: To support musicians, managers & businesses involved in the music industry in New Brunswick.
Affliation(s): The Foundation Assisting Canadian Talent on Recordings
Chief Officer(s):
Richard Hornsby, President
richard@musicnb.org
David Adams, Vice-President
Shawn Bostick, Vice-President
Jean Surette, Executive Director
jean@musicnb.org
Membership: *Fees:* $5 Student; $25 Individual; $50 Group; $55 Festivals/Venues/Publicists; $100 Corporate

Musicaction
#2, 4385, rue Saint-Hubert, Montréal QC H2J 2X1
Tél: 514-861-8444; *Téléc:* 514-861-4423
Ligne sans frais: 800-861-5561
info@musicaction.ca
www.musicaction.ca
www.facebook.com/musicaction.ca
Aperçu: *Dimension:* petite; *Envergure:* nationale; Organisme sans but lucratif; fondée en 1985
Mission: Développement de la musique vocale francophone au Canada
Membre(s) du bureau directeur:

Louise Chenail, Directrice générale
lchenail@musicaction.ca
Finances: *Budget de fonctionnement annuel:* Plus de $5 Million
Membre(s) du personnel: 15
Activités: *Service de conférenciers:* Oui

Musicians' Association of Victoria & the Islands, Local 247, AFM
#201, 732 Princess Ave., Victoria BC V8T 1K6
Tel: 250-385-3954; *Fax:* 250-480-1518
afm247.com
Previous Name: Victoria Musicians' Association
Overview: A small local organization founded in 1902
Mission: To organize professional musicians within our jurisdiction in order to provide services & work towards the betterment of their working conditions & benefits
Member of: American Federation of Musicians of the United States & Canada
Affliation(s): Canadian Labour Congress
Chief Officer(s):
Paul Wainwright, President
Finances: *Annual Operating Budget:* $50,000-$100,000; *Funding Sources:* Membership dues
Staff Member(s): 2
Membership: 120; *Fees:* $110
Activities: *Speaker Service:* Yes

Musiciens amateurs du Canada *See* Canadian Amateur Musicians

MusicNL
186 Duckworth St., St. John's NL A1C 1G5
Tel: 709-754-2574; *Fax:* 709-754-5758
info@musicnl.ca
www.musicnl.ca
www.facebook.com/MusicNL
twitter.com/_MusicNL_
Previous Name: Music Industry Association of Newfoundland & Labrador
Overview: A small provincial organization founded in 1992
Mission: To promote, encourage & develop the music from Newfoundland & Labrador, in all its forms, whether written, recorded or in live performances
Affliation(s): Foundation to Assist Canadian Talent on Records (FACTOR)
Chief Officer(s):
David Chafe, President
dbchafe@gmail.com
Denis Parker, Executive Director
Finances: *Funding Sources:* Provincial government
Staff Member(s): 1
Membership: 700;

Musique pour jeunes enfants *See* Music for Young Children

Muskoka Arts & Crafts Inc. (MAC)
PO Box 376, Bracebridge ON P1L 1T7
Tel: 705-645-5501; *Fax:* 705-645-0385
info@muskokaartsandcrafts.com
www.muskokaartsandcrafts.com
www.facebook.com/MuskokaArtsandCraftsInc
Overview: A small local organization founded in 1963
Mission: To assure the strength & vitality of the arts & crafts community in Muskoka
Member of: Ontario Crafts Council
Chief Officer(s):
Elene J. Freer, Executive Director
Finances: *Funding Sources:* Fundraising; Membership fees
Staff Member(s): 1
Membership: *Fees:* $39.55 individual; $32.77 senior; $20.34 student; $53.11 family
Activities: Craft shows, workshops, lectures, special events, public art gallery

Muskoka Community Futures Development Corporation
111 Manitoba St., Bracebridge ON P1L 2B6
Tel: 705-646-9511; *Fax:* 705-646-9522
Toll-Free: 800-414-6570
www.muskokafutures.ca
www.facebook.com/652906441425560
twitter.com/MuskokaFutures
www.youtube.com/channel/UCY-VoZwDpkVPTVKeKTwys2w
Also Known As: Muskoka Futures
Overview: A small local organization
Mission: To enable long-term employment & economic growth by providing professionally guided access to business information, counselling, mentoring & business financing for start-up, maintenance & expansion; facilitation services for community economic development projects & activities taking place throughout the region
Chief Officer(s):
David Brushey, Executive Director, 705-646-9511 Ext. 220
Finances: *Annual Operating Budget:* $250,000-$500,000
Staff Member(s): 4
Activities: *Internships:* Yes; *Speaker Service:* Yes; *Library* Open to public

Muskoka Lakes Association
PO Box 289, 65 Joseph St., 2nd Fl., Port Carling ON P0B 1J0
Tel: 705-765-5723; *Fax:* 705-765-3203
info@mla.on.ca
www.mla.on.ca
www.facebook.com/muskokalakesassociation
twitter.com/MuskokaLakes
Overview: A medium-sized local organization founded in 1894
Mission: To represent the interests of lakeshore residents in preserving the unique beauty of Muskoka
Chief Officer(s):
Lisa Noonan, Senior Manager
lisa@mla.on.ca
Staff Member(s): 2; 104 volunteer(s)
Membership: 2,458 members; *Fees:* $95 family; *Member Profile:* Permanent & seasonal residents of the Muskoka Lakes & area; anyone interested in the preservation & safety of the lakes

Muskoka Lakes Chamber of Commerce
PO Box 536, 3181 Muskoka Rd. 169, Bala ON P0C 1A0
Tel: 705-762-5663; *Fax:* 705-762-5664
info@muskokalakeschamber.com
www.muskokalakeschamber.com
www.linkedin.com/company/muskoka-lakes-chamber-of-commerce
www.facebook.com/group.php?gid=152472788107902
twitter.com/muskokalkscc
Previous Name: West Muskoka Chamber of Commerce
Overview: A small local organization
Member of: Ontario Chamber of Commerce
Chief Officer(s):
Jane Templeton, Manager, 705-762-5663
info@muskokalakeschamber.com
Kailey Luker, Consultant, Event & Tourism
kailey@muskokalakeschamber.com
Tracy Owen, President, 705-765-0200
info@thedrawingboard.ca
Walter Moon, Vice-President, 705-765-2050
wmoon@clublink.ca
Susan McEachern, Treasurer, 705-762-3335 Ext. 250
mceacs@tdbank.ca
Finances: *Annual Operating Budget:* Less than $50,000
10 volunteer(s)
Membership: 325; *Fees:* $160
Activities: *Internships:* Yes; *Speaker Service:* Yes

Muskoka Pioneer Power Association
PO Box 2256, Bracebridge ON P1L 1W2
Tel: 705-645-6546
www.bracebridgechamber.com/mppa/
Overview: A small local organization founded in 1984
Mission: To preserve the farming & logging artifacts of Muskoka & to provide a demonstration show each year
Chief Officer(s):
Ray Leng, President
Activities: Annual show second weekend of July; participate at local fall fair in Sept.

Muskoka Ratepayers' Association (MRA)
PO Box 336, Port Carling ON P0B 1J0
Tel: 705-765-0022; *Fax:* 705-765-0023
muskokaratepayers@vianet.ca
www.tmlra.on.ca
Overview: A small local organization founded in 1976
Mission: Preservation, fairness & enhancement for & with property owners in the Township of Muskoka Lakes & beyond
Chief Officer(s):
J. Douglas Bryden, President

Muskoka Steamship & Historical Society
c/o Muskoka Boat & Heritage Centre, 275 Steamship Bay Rd., Gravenhurst ON P1P 1Z9
Tel: 705-687-2115; *Fax:* 705-687-9408
membership@realmuskoka.com
www.segwun.com
www.facebook.com/pages/Muskoka-Steamships/119101791445311
twitter.com/rmssegwun
www.youtube.com/user/muskokasteamships
Overview: A small local charitable organization founded in 1973
Mission: To preserve & promote the traditions of boat building & steamships in the Muskoka region of Ontario
Chief Officer(s):
John Miller, General Manager
Ann Curley, Manager, Muskoka Boat & Heritage Centre Operations
Christi Gardner, Manager, Sales
Cathy Tait, Director, Sales & Marketing
Molly Rivers, Comptroller
Finances: *Funding Sources:* Ship ticket sales; Muskoka Boat & Heritage Centre admissions & room rentals; Membership fees; Government grants; Donations; Fundraising
Staff Member(s): 71; 100 volunteer(s)
Membership: 600; *Fees:* $10 juniors; $52 individual; $63 family; $150 corporate; *Committees:* Fundraising; Communciations / Newsletter; Membership; Marketing; Muskoka Boat & Heritage Centre Management; Archives & Curatorial; Education; Collections; Program; Heritage Boatworks; Volunteer; Muskoka Steamships Management; Safety & Technical Standards
Activities: Providing education about boat building & steamships; Operating the Muskoka Boat & Heritage Centre as well as the Royal Mail Ship Segwun, Wenonah II, & Wanda III
Publications:
• The Real Muskoka Story
Type: Newsletter; *Frequency:* Quarterly; *Price:* Free with membership
Profile: News & events from the Muskoka Steamship & Historical Society

Muskoka Tourism
1342 Hwy. 11 North, RR#2, Kilworthy ON P0E 1G0
Tel: 705-689-0660; *Fax:* 705-689-9118
Toll-Free: 800-267-9700
info@muskokatourism.ca
www.discovermuskoka.ca
www.facebook.com/discovermuskoka
twitter.com/DiscoverMuskoka
www.youtube.com/user/MuskokaTourism
Also Known As: Muskoka Tourism Marketing Agency
Overview: A medium-sized local organization founded in 1984
Mission: To market the region's tourism resources to the public, media & group tour travel markets
Member of: Ontario Motor Coach Association; Tourism Industry Association of Canada; Meeting Professionals International
Chief Officer(s):
Michael Lawley, Executive Director
mlawley@muskokatourism.ca
Finances: *Funding Sources:* Municipal
Membership: *Fees:* Schedule available
Activities: Travel counselling; event planning; *Speaker Service:* Yes; *Rents Mailing List:* Yes; *Library* by appointment

Muskoka-Parry Sound Beekeepers' Association
c/o Cathy Crowder, 87 Denniss Dr., Bracebridge ON P1L 1L7
Tel: 705-645-6180
MuskokaBeesmith@gmail.com
Overview: A small local organization
Mission: To provide education & information about beekeeping in the Muskoka - Parry Sound region; To assist local beekeepers with problems encountered
Member of: Ontario Beekeepers' Association
Chief Officer(s):
Cathy Crowder, President
Membership: *Member Profile:* Persons working in apiculture in the Muskoka - Parry Sound area of Ontario
Activities: Hosting meetings for members; Offering networking opportunities to exchange information about beekeeping

Muslim Association of Canada (MAC)
2270 Speakman Dr., mississauga ON L5K 1B4
Tel: 905-822-2626; *Fax:* 905-822-2727
mac@macnet.ca
www.macnet.ca
Overview: A medium-sized national organization
Mission: Seeks to promote a balanced, constructive & integrated Islamic presence in Canada; operates in 11 Canadian cities
Activities: Schools & community centres; educational & other projects; youth projects; outreach;

Muslim Association of New Brunswick (MANB)
1100 Rothesay Rd., Saint John NB E2H 2H8

Tel: 506-633-1675
info@manb.ca
www.manb.ca
Overview: A medium-sized provincial organization
Mission: The Muslim Association of New Brunswick (MANB) is a Saint John-based, nonprofit organization found to present, serve, & educate the Muslim community in the Saint John Area. MANB aims to strengthen access to Islamic education, facilitate community outreach & interaction with other religious organizations & community groups, consolidate the social fabric of the community, & sustain Islamic work by encouraging & building endowments.
Chief Officer(s):
Husni Abou El Niaj, President
Activities: *Library*

Muslim Community of Québec (MCQ) / Communauté musulmane du Québec
7445, av Chester, Montréal QC H4V 1M4
Tel: 514-484-2967; *Fax:* 514-484-3802
muslimcommunity@hotmail.ca
www.muslimcommunityofquebec.com
Also Known As: Mosque of Montréal
Overview: A small local organization founded in 1979
Mission: To facilitate Muslim religious life
Chief Officer(s):
Mohammed M. Amin, Founder
Finances: *Annual Operating Budget:* $500,000-$1.5 Million
Membership: 500
Activities: *Speaker Service:* Yes

Muslim Council of Montreal (MCM)
PO Box 180, Stn. St-Laurent, Montreal QC H4L 4Z8
Tel: 514-748-8427
info@muslimcouncil.org
www.muslimcouncil.org
Overview: A small local organization
Mission: Seeks effective cooperation among Islamic organizations & Muslims of all nationalities or schools of thought; seeks better understanding of Islam; assists media by open discussion; takes part in multicultural activities
Finances: *Annual Operating Budget:* Less than $50,000
5 volunteer(s)
Membership: 40 Muslim institutions

Muslim Education & Welfare Foundation of Canada (MEWFC)
Southbourne Centre, 2580 McGill St., Vancouver BC V5K 1H1
Tel: 604-255-9941
al.iman.education.metrotown@gmail.com
Also Known As: Al Iman Education
Overview: A medium-sized national charitable organization founded in 1987
Mission: To provide for the educational, religious & welfare needs of the Muslim community
Activities: *Library:* Jannat Bibi Library
Awards:
• Jannat Bibi Award of Educational Excellence (Award)

Muslim World League - Canada
#7, 2630 Royal Windsor Dr., Mississauga ON L5J 1K7
Tel: 905-542-1050; *Fax:* 905-542-1054
mwl@mwlcanada.org
www.mwlcanada.org
Overview: A small national organization founded in 1985
Mission: The League is a non-profit, non-governmental organization that serves the religious needs of Muslims in Canada. It promotes Islam & Islamic teachings among Canadian Muslims & helps non-Muslims grasp an accurate understanding of the religion. It also serves as a resource centre, publishing booklets & flyers on current issues.
Affliation(s): Muslim World League, Makkah, Saudia Arabia
Chief Officer(s):
Mohamad Khatib, Director
abusinan@yahoo.com
Staff Member(s): 4
Membership: *Member Profile:* Muslims
Activities: *Rents Mailing List:* Yes; *Library* Open to public

Musquodoboit Trailways Association
PO Box 336, Musquodoboit Harbour NS B0J 2L0
Tel: 902-889-3447
www.mta-ns.ca
Overview: A small local organization founded in 1997
Mission: To provide world-class hiking & cycling trails while preserving the ecosystem & wildlife habitats of the area
Member of: Nova Scotia Regional Trails Federation; Trans Canada Trail
Chief Officer(s):
Stanley Van Dyke, Chair
stanley.vandyke@gmail.com
Membership: *Fees:* $10 individual; $15 family; $25 corporate
Activities: Manages & maintains 40 kms of non-motorized trails

Mustard Seed Food Bank
625 Queens Ave., Victoria BC V8T 1L9
Tel: 250-953-1575; *Fax:* 250-953-1588
contact@mustardseed.ca
www.mustardseed.ca
www.facebook.com/mustardseed
twitter.com/mustardseedvic
mustardseed.ca/blog
Overview: A small local charitable organization overseen by Food Banks British Columbia
Mission: To provide good nutritional food to people in need
Member of: Food Banks British Columbia; Food Banks Canada
Chief Officer(s):
Brent A. Palmer, Vice-President
brentpalmer@mustardseed.ca
Staff Member(s): 2; 52 volunteer(s)
Publications:
• Street Beat
Frequency: Monthly
Profile: Newsletter

The Muttart Foundation
Scotia Place, #1150, 10060 Jasper Ave., Edmonton AB T5J 3R8
Tel: 780-425-9616; *Fax:* 780-425-0282
Toll-Free: 877-788-5437
www.muttart.org
Previous Name: The Gladys & Merrill Muttart Foundation
Overview: A small local charitable organization founded in 1953
Mission: To support projects that improve the effectiveness of the charitable sector; funding limited to Alberta, Saskatchewan, NWT & the Yukon
Affliation(s): Canadian Centre for Philanthropy; Council on Foundations; Association of Canadian Foundations
Chief Officer(s):
Bob Wyatt, Executive Director
bwyatt@muttart.org
Marion Gracey, President
Finances: *Annual Operating Budget:* $500,000-$1.5 Million; *Funding Sources:* Private endowment
Staff Member(s): 8; 12 volunteer(s)
Activities: *Speaker Service:* Yes

Mutual Fund Dealers Association of Canada (MFDA) / Association canadienne des courtiers de fonds mutuels
#1000, 121 King St. West, Toronto ON M5H 3T9
Tel: 416-361-6332
Toll-Free: 888-466-6332
Other Communication: Member Fax: 416-943-1218; HR Fax: 416-361-6381
mfda@mfda.ca
www.mfda.ca
Overview: A large national organization founded in 1998
Mission: To be the national self-regulatory organization (SRO) for the distribution side of the Canadian mutual fund industry
Chief Officer(s):
Roderick M. McLeod, Q.C., Chair
Mark T. Gordon, LLB, President & CEO
Shaun Devlin, Senior Vice-President, Member Regulation - Enforcement
Karen L. McGuinness, Senior Vice-President, Member Regulation - Compliance
Paige L. Ward, General Counsel, Corporate Secretary & VP, Policy
Membership: *Fees:* Schedule available; *Committees:* Audit & Finance; Governance; Regulatory Issues; Policy Advisory
Publications:
• MFDA [Mutual Fund Dealers Association of Canada] Bulletins
Type: Bulletin

Pacific Regional Office
PO Box 11603, #1220, 650 West Georgia St., Vancouver BC V6B 4N9
Tel: 604-694-8840; *Fax:* 604-683-6577
PacificOffice@mfda.ca
Chief Officer(s):
Jeff Mount, Vice-President, Pacific Region

Prairie Regional Office
#850, 800 - 6th Ave. SW, Calgary AB T2P 3G3
Tel: 403-266-8826; *Fax:* 403-266-8858
PrairieOffice@mfda.ca
Chief Officer(s):
Mark Stott, Vice-President, Prairie Region

Myalgic Encephalomyelitis Association of Halton/Hamilton-Wentworth
#5, 2230 Mountainside Dr., Burlington ON L7P 1B5
Tel: 905-319-7966
Overview: A small local charitable organization
Chief Officer(s):
Sally Hansen, President
Finances: *Funding Sources:* Membership fees; private donations
Activities: Public awareness; fundraising; support group; *Library:* Resource Centre; Open to public

Myalgic Encephalomyelitis Association of Ontario (MEAO)
#370, 170 Donway West, Toronto ON M3C 2G3
Tel: 416-222-8820
Toll-Free: 877-632-6682
info@meao.ca
www.meao.ca
Overview: A small provincial charitable organization founded in 1992
Mission: To support individuals who have Myalgic Encephalomyelitis/Chronic Fatigue Syndrome & their families; to provide medical professionals, government & the general public with information on the illness & its effects & consequences
Finances: *Funding Sources:* Membership dues; Donations; City of Toronto; Trillium Foundation
Membership: *Fees:* $25

Myasthenia Gravis Association of British Columbia (MGABC)
2805 Kingsway, Vancouver BC V5R 5H9
Tel: 604-451-5511; *Fax:* 604-451-5651
mgabc@centreforability.bc.ca
www.myastheniagravis.ca
Overview: A small provincial charitable organization founded in 1955
Mission: To provide information & support to British Columbians who suffer from Myasthenia Gravis (Grave Muscular Disease) & to their caregivers; to increase public awareness of the disease; to gather & disseminate specific information on Myasthenia Gravis to healthcare providers in British Columbia; to foster & support research into the causes & treatment of Myasthenia Gravis
Chief Officer(s):
Brenda Kelsey, President
Finances: *Funding Sources:* Donations; Membership; Charity gaming funds
Membership: *Member Profile:* People with Myasthenia Gravis; friends; family; health professionals
Activities: *Speaker Service:* Yes; *Library* Open to public by appointment

North Island MG Association
BC
Chief Officer(s):
John Skalos, Contact
lisaandjohn@shaw.ca

Victoria
Victoria BC
Chief Officer(s):
Dennis Shpeley, Contact
shpeley@shaw.ca

Mycological Society of Toronto (MST)
c/o 42 Eastwood Cres., Markham ON L3P 5Z7
e-mail: info@myctor.org
www.myctor.org
Overview: A small local organization
Mission: To provide opportunities for members to develop their interest in mycology through discussions, exhibits, lectures, forays, field trips & contacts with professional mycologists; to stimulate public interest & awareness in the broad area of mycology; and to foster a responsible & caring attitude towards the natural environment
Affliation(s): North American Mycological Association
Chief Officer(s):
Margaret Faye, Membership Director
Kevin McAuslan, President
Membership: *Fees:* $30
Activities: *Speaker Service:* Yes

Myeloma Canada / Myélome Canada
PO Box 326, Kirkland QC H9H 0A4
Tel: 514-570-9769; *Fax:* 514-505-1055
Toll-Free: 888-798-5771
info@myeloma.ca
www.myelomacanada.ca
Overview: A small national organization founded in 2004
Mission: To support persons living with multiple myeloma; To promote clinical research & improved access to drug trials in Canada
Member of: Canadian Cancer Action Network
Affliation(s): International Myeloma Foundation
Chief Officer(s):
John F. Lemieux, President & Co-Founder
Aldo E. Del Col, Vice-President & Co-Founder
Aldo E. Papillon, Secretary & Treasurer
Andrew R. Belch, Chair, Scientific Advisory Board
Finances: *Funding Sources:* Fundraising; Donations
Activities: Increasing awareness of myeloma; Providing educational information about myeloma; Facilitating access to new treatment options; Offering emotional support; Liaising with support groups across Canada
Publications:
• Multiple Myeloma Patient Handbook
Type: Handbook; *Price:* Free
Profile: Education for myeloma patients & their loved ones, so that they can be an active partner in their care
• Myeloma Canada Today
Type: Newsletter; *Frequency:* Quarterly
Profile: News & developments related to the disease, plus upcoming meetings & fundraisers

Myélome Canada *See* Myeloma Canada

N'Amerind (London) Friendship Centre
260 Colbourne St., London ON N6B 2S6
Tel: 519-672-0131; *Fax:* 519-672-0717
www.namerind.on.ca
www.facebook.com/332001323499406
Overview: A small local organization founded in 1967
Mission: To promote the intellectual, spiritual & physical well being of Native people, with a focus on Urban Natives
Member of: Ontario Federation of Indian Friendship Centres
Chief Officer(s):
Al Day, Executive Director
aday@namerind.on.ca
Julie Peters, Secretary
Luke Nicholas, President
Staff Member(s): 30

N'swakamok Native Friendship Centre
110 Elm St., Sudbury ON P3C 1T5
Tel: 705-674-2128; *Fax:* 705-671-3539
nnfcadmin@on.aibn.com
www.nfcsudbury.org
Overview: A small local organization founded in 1967
Mission: To provide social programs & services to the Native population
Chief Officer(s):
Marie Meawasige, Executive Director

Na'amat Canada Inc.
#6, 7005 Kildare Rd., Montréal QC H4W 1C1
Tel: 514-488-0792; *Fax:* 514-487-6727
Toll-Free: 888-278-0792
naamat@naamatcanada.org
www.naamat.com
www.facebook.com/NaamatCanada
twitter.com/NaamatCanada
www.youtube.com/user/NaamatCanada
Previous Name: Pioneer Women Organization of Canada Inc.
Overview: A medium-sized national charitable organization founded in 1925
Mission: To support social programs in Canada & Israel; to help protect women, children & families in both nations; to support the state of Israel
Member of: Canadian Zionist Federation; National Council of Women of Canada
Affliation(s): National Action Committee on the Status of Women
Chief Officer(s):
Orit Tobe, President
Staff Member(s): 6; 3,00 volunteer(s)
Membership: 2,000; *Fees:* Schedule available; *Committees:* Israel Information; Leadership Development; Social Action; Status of Women
Activities: Social program for seniors; daycare; events for children; legal aid; women's rights support
Meetings/Conferences: • Na'amat Canada National Triennial Convention, 2017

Edmonton Council
e-mail: naamatedmonton@yahoo.ca
Chief Officer(s):
Darlene Bushewsky, President

Montréal Council
#4, 7005, Kildare Rd., Montréal QC H4W 1C1
Tel: 514-484-0252; *Fax:* 514-487-6727
info@naamat-mtl.ca
Chief Officer(s):
Mindy Spiegel, President

Ottawa Council
#204, 11 Nadolny Sachs Private, Ottawa ON K2A 1R9
Tel: 613-722-2932; *Fax:* 613-722-0873
naamat.ottawa@sympatico.ca
Chief Officer(s):
Eileen Barak, President

Toronto Council
272 Codsell Ave., Toronto ON M3H 3X2
Tel: 416-636-5425; *Fax:* 416-636-5248
Toll-Free: 888-622-6280
info@naamattoronto.ca
Chief Officer(s):
Laurel Wiseman, President

Vancouver Council
#303, 950 - 41st Ave. West, Vancouver BC V5Z 2N7
Tel: 604-257-5177; *Fax:* 604-266-2561
naamat@telus.net
Chief Officer(s):
Karen Rabinovitch, President

Windsor Council
e-mail: naamatwindsor@gmail.com

Winnipeg Council
1010 Sinclair St., Winnipeg MB R2V 3H7
Tel: 204-334-3637; *Fax:* 204-338-4500
naamatw@mts.net

NABET 700 CEP
#203, 100 Lombard St., Toronto ON M5C 1M3
Tel: 416-536-4827; *Fax:* 416-536-0859
info@nabet700.com
www.nabet700.com
Overview: A medium-sized local organization founded in 1970
Mission: To be a union serving television & film technicians in Toronto; in 1994 NABET 700 merged with the Communications, Energy & Paperworkers Union of Canada (CEP).
Chief Officer(s):
Jonathan Ahee, President
Craig Steele, Senior Vice-President
Frank Iacobucci, Secretary-Treasurer
Membership: 1,000; *Member Profile:* Television & film technicians

NAID Canada
95 King St. East, 4th Fl., Toronto ON M5C 1G4
Toll-Free: 800-825-0864
info@naidcanada.org
www.naidcanada.org
Also Known As: National Association for Information Destruction Canada
Overview: A small national organization
Mission: To raise awareness & understanding of the importance of secure information & document destruction; to ensure that private personal & business information is not used for purposes other than originally intended; to develop & implement industry standards & certification; to provide a range of member services which include advocacy, communication, education & professional development
Member of: National Association for Information Destruction in United States
Chief Officer(s):
Kevin Perry, Chair
Membership: *Member Profile:* Companies that specialize in secure information & document destruction

NAIMA Canada
#500, 150 Laurier Ave. West, Ottawa ON K1P 5J4
Tel: 613-232-8093; *Fax:* 613-232-9149
contact@naimacanada.ca
www.naimacanada.ca
twitter.com/NAIMACanada
www.youtube.com/user/NAIMAVideo
Overview: A small national organization founded in 2004
Mission: To promote energy efficiency & sustainable building while promoting safe use of members products; to support standardization in insulation systems & installation
Affliation(s): North American Insulation Manufacturers Association, USA
Chief Officer(s):
Michelle Bunch, Director, Finance & Administration
Angus Crane, Secretary
Jay Nordenstrom, Executive Director
Finances: *Funding Sources:* Membership
Membership: 7 companies; *Committees:* Steering; Government Affairs; Technical/Product
Activities: *Speaker Service:* Yes

NAIOP Greater Toronto
#300, 1100 Burloak Dr., Burlington ON L7L 6B2
Tel: 905-332-2322; *Fax:* 905-331-1768
Toll-Free: 877-331-9668
info@torontonaiop.org
www.torontonaiop.org
www.linkedin.com/company/naiop-greater-toronto-chapter
www.facebook.com/146718738715302?v=wall
twitter.com/torontonaiop
Also Known As: National Association of Industrial & Office Properties
Overview: A small local organization founded in 1977
Mission: To serve owners & developers of industrial & office properties in the Greater Toronto
Chief Officer(s):
Constance Wrigley-Thomas, Executive Director
constance@torontonaiop.org
Membership: 1,000; *Committees:* Programs; Real Estate Excellence (REX) Awards; Membership; Developing Leaders; Government Affairs; Education; Sustainability; Sponsorship; Annual Ski Day; Annual Golf Tournament

Naissances multiples Canada *See* Multiple Births Canada

Naissances multiples Temiskaming *See* Temiskaming Multiple Births

Nakiska Alpine Ski Association (NASA)
PO Box 68080, Stn. Crowfoot, Calgary AB T3G 3N8
Tel: 403-613-5935
www.skinasa.org
www.facebook.com/122652134004
Overview: A small local organization founded in 2009
Mission: To train athletes in alpine ski racing.
Chief Officer(s):
Scott Zahn, Director, Program & Technical
szahn@skinasa.org
Membership: 6 clubs + 300 individual

Nakusp & District Chamber of Commerce
PO Box 387, 92 - 6th Ave. NW, Nakusp BC V0G 1R0
Tel: 250-265-4234; *Fax:* 250-265-3808
Toll-Free: 800-909-8819
nakusp@telus.net
www.nakusparrowlakes.com
www.facebook.com/nakusp.bc
Overview: A small local organization
Mission: To promote & improve trade & commerce & the economic welfare of the area
Member of: British Columbia Chamber of Commerce; Kootenay Rockies Tourism
Affliation(s): Tourism British Columbia
Chief Officer(s):
Dawn Devlin, President
reawake@telus.net
Finances: *Annual Operating Budget:* Less than $50,000; *Funding Sources:* Fee for service
Staff Member(s): 1; 2 volunteer(s)
Membership: 140; *Fees:* $93.80 - $175.56 business; $52.64 individual; $70.28 non-profit; $79.24 associate
Activities: *Awareness Events:* Nakusp Celebration of Light, July

Nanaimo Association for Community Living (NACL)
#201, 96 Cavan St., Nanaimo BC V9L 2V1
Tel: 250-741-0224; *Fax:* 250-741-0227
info@nanaimoacl.com
www.nanaimoacl.com
www.facebook.com/nanaimoacl
Overview: A medium-sized local organization founded in 1986
Mission: To support all people with disabilities to achieve the highest quality of life through participation, independence,

inclusion & education
Member of: British Columbia Association for Community Living
Chief Officer(s):
Graham Morry, Executive Director, 250-741-0224 Ext. 60
graham.morry@nanaimoacl.com
Finances: *Funding Sources:* Donations; provincial & municipal funding
Membership: *Fees:* By donation
Activities: Actions Day Program; 7 residential programs: Hammond Bay Home, Jingle Pot Home, Kennedy Home, Morningside Home, Portsmouth Road Home, Turner Connection Home, McCauley Drive Home; annual general meeting; Community Living event; *Library:* NACL Resource Library

Nanaimo Community Foundation
#106, 619 Comox Rd., Nanaimo BC V9R 5V8
Tel: 250-714-0047
administrator@nanaimocommunityfoundation.com
www.nanaimocommunityfoundation.com
Overview: A small local charitable organization founded in 1982
Finances: *Funding Sources:* Bequests; Public & private donations
Membership: 1-99

Nanaimo District Museum (NDM)
100 Museum Way, Nanaimo BC V9R 5J8
Tel: 250-753-1821
admin@nanaimomuseum.ca
www.nanaimomuseum.ca
www.facebook.com/NanaimoMuseum
Also Known As: Nanaimo & District Museum Society
Overview: A small local charitable organization founded in 1967
Mission: To promote & engage the community & visitor in meaningful experiences to the cultural heritage of the City of Nanaimo & its surrounding district
Member of: BC Museums Association
Chief Officer(s):
Debbie Trueman, General Manager
debbie@nanaimomuseum.ca
David Hill-Turner, Curator
david@nanaimomuseum.ca
Finances: *Annual Operating Budget:* $250,000-$500,000; *Funding Sources:* Municipal & provincial government; earned revenue
Staff Member(s): 7; 50 volunteer(s)
Membership: 350; *Fees:* $5-$30; *Member Profile:* Community based; *Committees:* Finance; Personal Collection; Marketing; Volunteer
Activities: Coal mine bus tours; photo contest; exhibits; special events; educational programs; daily summer cannon firing; outreach; *Awareness Events:* Chinese New Year, Jan./Feb.; Heritage Week, Feb.
Awards:
- Don Sale Annual Scholarship for Excellence in History (Award)

Nanaimo Family Life Association (NFLA)
1070 Townsite Rd., Nanaimo BC V9S 1M6
Tel: 250-754-3331; *Fax:* 250-753-0268
reception@nflabc.org
www.nflabc.org
www.facebook.com/447668528623973
twitter.com/NanaimoFamLife
Overview: A medium-sized local charitable organization founded in 1967
Mission: To provide counselling & support services to individuals & families in Nanaimo
Chief Officer(s):
Deborah Hollins, Executive Director
Finances: *Funding Sources:* Provincial government; foundations
Staff Member(s): 6
Membership: *Fees:* $10

Nanaimo Historical Society (NHS)
PO Box 933, Nanaimo BC V9R 5N2
Overview: A small local organization founded in 1953
Mission: To collect, preserve & disseminate local & BC history
Member of: British Columbia Historical Federation
Activities: Monthly meetings; field trips; historic gatherings; book publications; *Library:* Historical Society Archives; by appointment
Awards:
- Annual Award to Student in the History Course at Malaspina University College (Award)

Nanaimo Literacy Association *See* Literacy Central Vancouver Island

Nanaimo, Duncan & District Labour Council (NDDLC)
PO Box 822, Nanaimo BC V9R 5N2
Tel: 250-760-0547; *Fax:* 250-760-0548
labour@telus.net
www.nddlc.ca
Overview: A small local organization founded in 1958 overseen by British Columbia Federation Of Labour
Mission: To represent 65 affiliated local unions from British Columbia's Nanaimo, Duncan, & district; To build a strong labour movement & community; To promote quality social programs & public services
Affliation(s): Canadian Labour Congress (CLC)
Chief Officer(s):
Ellen Oxman, President
eoxman@shaw.ca
Jennifer Duggan, First Vice-President
yoduggan@telus.net
Jim Sadlemyer, Second Vice-President
jsadlemyer@hotmail.com
John Little, Third Vice-President
littlehome@telus.net
Debbie Fraess, Secretary
dfraess@shaw.ca
Betty Smits, Treasurer
betty@rsmits.ca
Membership: 14,000; *Member Profile:* Male & female trade unionists from the central area of Vancouver Island & the Gulf Islands north of Saltspring; *Committees:* Mid Island Health Coalition; Budget; Education; Political Action; Social; Social Justice; Strike / Labour Support; Union Label
Activities: Organizing workers; Providing education to members, such as labour & social justice education courses; Promoting workers' issues, such as pay equity & employment equity; Lobbying government; Raising awareness of local issues, such as the Ban Log Rally in Nanaimo; Supporting striking or locked out workers; Campaigning for economic & social justice; Supporting the community, by working with local organizations, such as the United Way; Offering networking opportunities; Providing labour news; Hosting monthly meetings

Nanton & District Chamber of Commerce
PO Box 711, Nanton AB T0L 1R0
Tel: 403-646-2111
www.nantonchamber.com
Overview: A small local organization
Chief Officer(s):
Pam Woodall, President
president@nantonchamber.com
Finances: *Annual Operating Budget:* Less than $50,000
Membership: 66;

Napanee & District Chamber of Commerce
Napanee Business Centre, 47 Dundas St. East, Napanee ON K7R 1H7
Tel: 613-354-6601
Toll-Free: 877-354-6601
inquiry@napaneechamber.ca
www.napaneechamber.ca
www.facebook.com/137245796288349
twitter.com/NapaneeChamber
Overview: A small local organization founded in 1995 overseen by Ontario Chamber of Commerce
Mission: To advocate on behalf of local businesses & promote their members
Chief Officer(s):
Janet Flynn, President
Membership: *Fees:* Schedule available

Napanee Sports Association
16 McPherson Dr., Napanee ON K7R 3L1
Tel: 613-354-4423; *Fax:* 613-354-2212
info@napaneesportsassociation.com
www.losa.ca
Overview: A small local organization founded in 2006
Mission: To provide funding to local sports teams
Chief Officer(s):
Chuck Airhart, Chair

Napi Friendship Association
PO Box 657, 622 Charlotte St., Pincher Creek AB T0K 1K0
Tel: 403-627-4224; *Fax:* 403-627-2564
executivedirector@okinapi.com
www.okinapi.com
Overview: A small provincial charitable organization overseen by Alberta Native Friendship Centres Association
Mission: To create better communication & understanding between the residents of Pincher Creek & the Peigan Nation
Member of: Alberta Native Friendship Centres Association
Chief Officer(s):
Kevin Provost

Nar-Anon Family Groups of Ontario
PO Box 20046, 2900 Warden Ave., Toronto ON M1W 3Y9
Tel: 416-239-0096
Toll-Free: 877-239-0096
info@naranonontario.com
www.naranonontario.com
Overview: A medium-sized provincial organization
Mission: The Nar-Anon Family Group is for those who know or have known a feeling of desperation due to the addiction problem of someone close to them. Nar-Anon members share their experiences, strength, & hope at weekly meetings

Narcotics Anonymous *See* Canadian Assembly of Narcotics Anonymous

Narcotiques Anonymes
Chibougamau QC
Ligne sans frais: 800-463-0162
www.naquebec.org
Aperçu: *Dimension:* petite; *Envergure:* locale

Natation Canada *See* Swimming Canada

Natation Nouveau-Brunswick *See* Swimming New Brunswick

National & Provincial Parks Association (NPPAC) *See* Canadian Parks & Wilderness Society

National Aboriginal Achievement Foundation *See* Indspire

National Aboriginal Capital Corporation Association (NACCA)
#605, 75 Albert St., Ottawa ON K1P 5E7
Tel: 613-688-0894; *Fax:* 613-688-0895
office@nacca.net
www.nacca.net
Overview: A small national organization founded in 1996
Mission: To promote the growth of aboriginal business by providing products & services to aboriginal financial institutions & aboriginal focused organizations including institutional capacity, building, training, access to capital, advocacy, partnerships & member services with quality & accountability
Chief Officer(s):
Lucy Pelletier, Chair
lucy.pelletier@sasktel.net
Tim Zehr, CEO
tim@nacca.net
Finances: *Annual Operating Budget:* $1.5 Million-$3 Million
Staff Member(s): 6; 13 volunteer(s)
Membership: 56 corporate; *Member Profile:* Aboriginal financial institutions; Aboriginal Capital Corporations; Community Future Development Centres; Development Corporations
Activities: Business loans; financial consulting services; aftercare; start-up support; Youth Entrepreneur Symposium

National Aboriginal Circle Against Family Violence
Kahnawake Business Complex, PO Box 2169, Kahnawake QC J0L 1B0
Tel: 450-638-2968; *Fax:* 450-638-9415
www.nacafv.ca
Overview: A medium-sized national organization
Mission: To reduce & eliminate family violence in our Aboriginal communities; programs are culturally appropriate, & support shelters & family violence prevention centres
Chief Officer(s):
Brenda Combs, Chair, 705-941-9054, Fax: 705-941-9055
bcombs@nimkii@shaw.ca
Activities: Advocacy; research; promotion of public awareness

National Aboriginal Diabetes Association Inc. (NADA)
#B1, 90 Garry St, Winnipeg MB R3C 4H1
Tel: 204-927-1220; *Fax:* 204-927-1222
Toll-Free: 877-232-6232
diabetes@nada.ca
www.nada.ca
www.facebook.com/nadasugarfree
twitter.com/nadasugarfree
Overview: A small national organization founded in 1995
Mission: To be the driving force in addressing diabetes & Aboriginal people as a priority health issue by working together with people, Aboriginal communities & organizations in the

prevention to combat increasing rates of obesity, cancer, diabetes & cardiovascular disease

National Association of Women & the Law (NAWL) / Association nationale de la femme et du droit (ANFD)

PO Box 46008, 2339 Ogilvie Rd., Gloucester ON K1J 9M7
Tel: 613-241-7570
www.nawl.ca
Overview: A medium-sized national charitable organization founded in 1974
Mission: To promote the equality rights of women through legal education, research & law reform advocacy; to improve the legal status of women in Canada through law reform; to dismantle barriers to all women's equality
Member of: National Action Committee on the Status of Women; Women's Future Fund
Chief Officer(s):
Alison Dewar, Chair, National Steering Committee
Jane Bailey, Member, National Steering Committee
Samantha Henrickson, Member, National Steering Committee
Finances: *Annual Operating Budget:* $250,000-$500,000; *Funding Sources:* Women's Program; Status of Women Canada; donations; projects
Staff Member(s): 4; 100 volunteer(s)
Membership: 1,000; *Fees:* $55; $75 institution; *Member Profile:* Supports goals of the association
Activities: Education; research & advocacy; membership support; *Library* by appointment
Awards:
• Charitable Trust for Research & Education (Scholarship)

National Automobile, Aerospace, Transportation & General Workers Union of Canada, Canadian Auto Workers, Communications, Energy & Paperworkers *See* UNIFOR

National Automotive Trades Association of Canada

#1, 8980 Fraserwood Ct., Burnaby BC V5J 5H7
Tel: 604-432-7987; *Fax:* 604-432-1756
www.natacanada.ca
Overview: A small national organization
Mission: To act as the unified voice for the Canadian Automotive Trades industry
Chief Officer(s):
Rene Young, Executive Vice-President
Rob Lang, President

National Ballet of Canada

Walter Carsen Centre, 470 Queens Quay West, Toronto ON M5V 3K4
Tel: 416-345-9686; *Fax:* 416-345-8323
info@national.ballet.ca
national.ballet.ca
www.facebook.com/nationalballet
twitter.com/nationalballet
www.youtube.com/user/nationalballetcanada
Overview: A medium-sized national organization
Chief Officer(s):
Karen Kain, Artistic Director
Barry Hughson, Executive Director
David Briskin, Music Director/Principal Conductor

National Brotherhood of Foresters & Industrial Workers (CLC) *Voir* Fraternité nationale des forestiers et travailleurs d'usine (CTC)

National Building Envelope Council (NBEC) / Conseil National de l'Enveloppe du Bâtiment (CNEB)

c/o 5041 Regent St., Burnaby BC V5C 4H4
Tel: 604-473-9587
nbec@cebq.org
www.nbec.net
Overview: A small national organization
Mission: To pursue excellence in the design, construction & performance of the building envelope
Chief Officer(s):
Dominique Derome, President Elect
Meetings/Conferences: • 15th Canadian Conference on Building Science and Technology, 2015
Scope: National
Description: Provides a forum for the presentation, discussion and sharing of practical building science research, knowledge and field experience.

National Business Travel Association (Canada) *See* Global Business Travel Association (Canada)

National Campus & Community Radio Association (NCRA) / Association nationale des radio étudiantes et communautaires (ANREC)

#230, 325 Dalhousie, Ottawa ON K1N 7G2
Tel: 613-321-1440; *Fax:* 613-321-1442
Toll-Free: 866-859-8086
office@ncra.ca
www.ncra.ca
Overview: A medium-sized national organization founded in 1981
Mission: To encourage development of community & student radio in Canada by providing core services to community-oriented radios & representing them to government, industry & the public
Affiliation(s): World Association of Community Radio Broadcasters (AMARC); Canadian Radio-Television & Telecommunications Commission (CRTC); Canadian Society of Independent Radio Producers
Chief Officer(s):
Catherine Fisher, President
president@ncra.ca
Shelley Robinson, Executive Director
shelley@ncra.ca
Finances: *Annual Operating Budget:* $100,000-$250,000; *Funding Sources:* Membership fees; corporate sponsors; government funding
Staff Member(s): 7; 30 volunteer(s)
Membership: 40 radio stations; *Fees:* % of expenses, $.50 first time & associates; *Member Profile:* Community &/or student-oriented broadcasting enterprise; *Committees:* Development; Fundraising; Publications
Activities: Represents campus & community radio in Canada; *Awareness Events:* Dig Your Roots; *Library:* Documentation Centre; by appointment

National Cancer Institute of Canada *See* Canadian Cancer Society Research Institute

National Capital FreeNet (NCF) / Libertel de la Capitale Nationale

Trailhead Building, #302, 1960 Scott St., Ottawa ON K1Z 8L8
Tel: 613-520-9001; *Fax:* 613-520-3524
ncf@ncf.ca
www.ncf.ca
Overview: A medium-sized local organization founded in 1993
Mission: Free, computer-based information sharing network; links the people & organization of the National Capital region; provides useful information & enables an open exchange of ideas with the world; prepares people for full participation in a rapidly changing communications environment
Member of: Telecommunities Canada
Finances: *Funding Sources:* Member donations
500 volunteer(s)
Membership: 7,500; *Fees:* Donations requested; *Committees:* Complaints; Finance; Francophone

National Capital Sports Council of the Disabled Inc. (NCSCD) / Le Conseil des sports des handicapées de la capitale nationale inc. (CSHCN)

#104, 720 Belfast Rd., Ottawa ON K1G 0Z5
Tel: 613-569-7632; *Fax:* 613-244-4857
ncscd@ncscd.ca
www.ncscd.ca
Overview: A medium-sized national charitable organization founded in 1985
Mission: To promote sporting opportunities for amputee, blind, cerebral palsy, deaf & wheelchair athletes in the National Capital Region; to promote the development of new sporting activities & athletic training opportunities for junior athletes with physical disabilities
Chief Officer(s):
Dana Chenette, Office Manager
Finances: *Annual Operating Budget:* $100,000-$250,000
Staff Member(s): 1; 50 volunteer(s)
Membership: 16 institutional + 350 individual; *Fees:* Schedule available; *Member Profile:* Involved in sports for physically disabled athletes
Activities: Wheel-a-thon fundraiser & awareness campaign; Junior Development Program to introduce children with a physical disability to a variety of sporting opportunities; *Library* Open to public by appointment

National CGIT Association - BC Provincial Board *See* Provincial CGIT Board of BC

National CGIT Association - Manitoba & Northwestern Ontario *See* Manitoba CGIT Association

National CGIT Association - Maritime Regional Committee *See* Maritime Regional CGIT Committee

National CGIT Association - Ontario *See* Ontario CGIT Association

National CGIT Association - Saskatchewan Committee *See* Saskatchewan CGIT Committee

National Chinchilla Breeders of Canada (NCBC)

9575 Winston Churchill Blvd., Brampton ON L6X 0A4
Tel: 905-451-8736; *Fax:* 905-457-5326
ncbc@idirect.com
Overview: A small national organization founded in 1946
Affiliation(s): Agriculture Canada; Canadian National Livestock Records
Chief Officer(s):
Marie Riedstra, Secretary-Manager
Membership: *Fees:* $30 resident; $12.50 non-resident

The National Citizens Coalition / Coalition nationale des citoyens inc.

#501, 27 Queen St. East, Toronto ON M5C 2M6
Tel: 416-869-3838; *Fax:* 416-869-1891
Toll-Free: 888-703-5553
ncc@nationalcitizens.ca
www.nationalcitizens.ca
twitter.com/PeterNCC
Overview: A small national organization founded in 1967
Mission: To promote free markets, individual freedom & responsibility under limited government & a strong defence
Chief Officer(s):
Colin T. Brown, Chair
Peter Coleman, President & CEO
pcoleman@ncc-on.org
Finances: *Annual Operating Budget:* $1.5 Million-$3 Million
Staff Member(s): 16
Membership: 40,000
Activities: Political advocacy; *Speaker Service:* Yes
Publications:
• Freedom Watch
Type: Newsletter; *Frequency:* Monthly; *Price:* Free with membership
Profile: Updates on NCC activities & commentary on current events.
• National Citizens Review
Frequency: Quarterly; *Price:* Free with membership
Profile: Analysis & commentary on national & international issues.

National Colorectal Cancer Campaign *See* Colon Cancer Canada

National Committee of Schools of Social Work; Canadian Association of Schools of Social Work (CASSW) *See* Canadian Association for Social Work Education

National Congress of Italian Canadians (NCIC) / Congrès national des italo-canadiens

#202, 340 Falstaff Ave., Toronto ON M6L 3E8
Tel: 416-531-9964; *Fax:* 416-531-9966
Other Communication: Alternate Phone: 416-809-5564
www.canadese.org
Also Known As: NCIC Toronto District
Overview: A medium-sized international organization founded in 1974
Member of: Canadian Ethnocultural Council
Chief Officer(s):
Michael Tibollo, President
Catherine Tinaburri, Coordinator
Membership: Over 50,000
Activities: *Speaker Service:* Yes; *Library* by appointment

Québec Region
#302, 8370 boul Lacordaire, Saint-Léonard QC H1R 3Y6
Tel: 514-279-6357; *Fax:* 514-955-8527
info@italcongresso.qc.ca
www.italcongresso.qc.ca
Mission: Promotion de la culture et de la langue et patrimoine.
Chief Officer(s):
Antonio Sciascia, President

National Contingency Fund *See* Canadian Investor Protection Fund

National Convenience Stores Distributors Association *See* Association nationale des distributeurs aux petites surfaces alimentaires

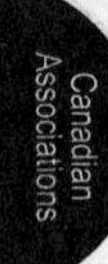

National Council of Barbadian Associations in Canada (NCBAC) / Conseil national des associations barbadiennes au Canada
#300, 211 Consumers Rd., Toronto ON M2J 4G8
www.ncbac.ca
Overview: A small national organization founded in 1984
Mission: To incorporate Barbadians into Canadian society
Member of: Canadian Ethnocultural Council
Chief Officer(s):
Malcolm Flatts, President
presidentncbacmflatts@hotmail.com

National Council of Canadian Filipino Associations / Conseil national des associations canadiennes des Philippines
180 Larkin Dr., Ottawa ON K2J 1H9
Tel: 613-815-6314
Overview: A small national organization

National Council of Canadian Muslims (NCCM)
PO Box 13219, Ottawa ON K2K 1X4
Tel: 613-254-9704; *Fax:* 613-254-9810
Toll-Free: 866-524-0004
info@nccm.ca
www.nccm.ca
www.facebook.com/NCCMuslims
www.twitter.com/NCCM
www.youtube.com/NCCMtv
Previous Name: Council on American-Islamic Relations Canada
Overview: A small international organization founded in 2000
Mission: National Council of Canadian Muslims is a nonprofit organization promoting the civic engagement of Canadian Muslims, the protection of their human rights, & the education of non-Muslims so they may hold an accurate understanding of Islam. It is active in the areas of media relations, anti-discrimination & political advocacy.
Chief Officer(s):
Kashif A. Ahmed, Chair
Ihsaan Gardee, Executive Director, 613-853-4111
Activities: Seminars & workshops; publication of guides, handbooks & media resource kits

National Council of Jamaicans & Supportive Organizations in Canada
4065, rue Jean Talon Ouest, Montréal QC H4P 1W6
Tel: 514-737-8299; *Fax:* 514-737-4861
Overview: A small national organization founded in 1987
Activities: *Speaker Service:* Yes

National Council of Jewish Women of Canada (NCJWC)
#118, 1588 Main St., Winnipeg MB R2V 1Y3
Tel: 204-339-9700; *Fax:* 204-334-3779
Toll-Free: 866-625-9274
info@ncjwc-ts.org
www.ncjwc.org
Overview: A medium-sized national charitable organization founded in 1897
Mission: To further human welfare in the Jewish & general communities; To help fulfill unmet needs & to serve the individual & the community
Affiliation(s): International Council of Jewish Women; UNESCO Sub commission on the Status of Women; Coalition of Jewish Women against Domestic Violence and the Coalition for Agunot Rights
Membership: *Fees:* $36

Edmonton Section
7200 - 156 St., Edmonton AB T5R 1X3

Montréal Section
Decor Decarie Office Tower, #348, 6900, boul Décarie, Montréal QC H3X 2T8
Tel: 514-733-7589; *Fax:* 514-733-3217
chesed@generation.net

Toronto Section
4700 Bathurst St., Toronto ON M2R 1W8
Tel: 416-633-5100; *Fax:* 416-633-1956
info@ncjwc-ts.org
www.ncjwc-ts.org
Chief Officer(s):
Ena Cord, President

Vancouver Section
#302, 950 - West 41st Ave., Vancouver BC V5Z 2N7
Tel: 604-339-5180; *Fax:* 604-339-5158
ncjwvan@telus.net

Winnipeg Section
1588 Main St., Winnipeg MB R2V 1Y3
Tel: 204-339-7291; *Fax:* 204-334-3779
ncjwws@mts.net

National Council of Trinidad & Tobago Organizations in Canada (NCTTOC)
66 Oakmeadow Blvd., Toronto ON M1E 4G5
Tel: 416-283-9672; *Fax:* 416-283-9672
Overview: A small national organization founded in 1983
Mission: To provide a national focus for representing the concerns of Trinidad & Tobago Nationals; to advocate on behalf of Trinidad & Tobago Nationals & their families in Canada; to develop & maintain a system of communication, information sharing & networking among Trinidad & Tobago organizations; to provide information, referrals, advocacy & support to new arrivals from Trinidad & Tobago
Member of: Canadian Ethnocultural Council
Affliation(s): National Visible Minority Council on Labour Force Development
Chief Officer(s):
Emmanuel Dick, Contact
Finances: *Funding Sources:* Government projects; contributions
Membership: *Member Profile:* Trinidad & Tobago provincial organizations
Activities: *Speaker Service:* Yes

National Council of Veteran Associations (NCVA) / Conseil national des associations d'anciens combattants au Canada (CNAAC)
2827 Riverside Dr., Ottawa ON K1V 0C4
Tel: 613-731-3821; *Fax:* 613-731-3234
Toll-Free: 800-465-2677
ncva@waramps.ca
www.ncva-cnaac.ca
www.twitter.com/NCVACanada
Overview: A medium-sized national organization
Mission: The National Council of Veteran Associations is an umbrella organization of some 60 distinct Veterans' Associations formed to ensure a strong and independent voice on issues which are of significant interest to the Veterans' community at large.
Chief Officer(s):
Brian N. Forbes, Chair
Membership: 55;

The National Council of Women of Canada (NCWC) / Le Conseil national des femmes du Canada
PO Box 67099, Ottawa ON K2A 4E4
Tel: 613-232-5025; *Fax:* 613-232-8419
Toll-Free: 877-319-0993
ncwc@magma.ca
www.ncwc.ca
www.facebook.com/thencwc
Overview: A large national organization founded in 1893
Mission: To empower all women to work together towards improving the quality of life for women, families & society through a forum of member organizations & individuals
Member of: International Council of Women
Chief Officer(s):
Denise Mattok, President
Catherine Tillsley, Executive Director
Finances: *Annual Operating Budget:* $100,000-$250,000
Staff Member(s): 3; 100 volunteer(s)
Membership: 20 local + 5 provincial councils; *Committees:* Citizenship & Immigration; Culture & Heritage; Environment; Global Affairs; Health; Social Issues; Senior Issues

National Council on Canada-Arab Relations (NCCAR) / Conseil National des Relations Canado-Arabes
116 Promenade du Portage, Gatineau QC J8X 2K1
Tel: 613-238-3795; *Fax:* 613-235-9185
nccar@nccar.ca
www.nccar.ca
www.facebook.com/Connecting.Canadians.Arabs
Overview: A small national organization
Mission: The National Council on Canada-Arab Relations (NCCAR) is a charitable organization whose mission is to build ties between Canadians and people of the Arab World in order to develop stronger relations and cooperation between them, as well as raise an appreciation of their common values.
Chief Officer(s):
Bahija Reghai, President
Membership: *Fees:* $35 youth; $100 regular; $500 sustaining; $1000 corporate

National Council on Ethics in Human Research / Conseil national d'éthique en recherche chez l'humain
#208, 240 Catherine St., Ottawa ON K2P 2G8
Tel: 613-233-5445; *Fax:* 613-233-0658
www.ncehr-cnerh.org
Overview: A small national organization
Mission: To advance the protection & promotion of the well-being of human participants in research; to foster high ethical standards for the conduct of research involving humans
Chief Officer(s):
Richard Carpentier, Executive Director
Staff Member(s): 4

National Crowdfunding Association of Canada (NCFA)
#1801, 1 Yonge St., Toronto ON M5E 1W7
Tel: 416-618-0254
www.ncfacanada.org
www.linkedin.com/groups/NCFA-Canada-4657887?gid=4657887&mostPopular=&t
www.facebook.com/NCFACanada.org?ref=hl
twitter.com/NCFACanada
Overview: A medium-sized national organization
Mission: NCFA Canada works closely with industry groups, government, academia, other business associations and affiliates to create a strong and vibrant crowdfunding industry and voice across Canada.
Member of: World Crowdfund Federation
Chief Officer(s):
Craig Asano, Executive Director
casano@ncfacanada.org
Publications:
• Canadian Crowdfunding Directory
Type: Directory

National Darts Federation of Canada (NDFC) / Fédération nationale de dards du Canada
2417, rue Montante, Ascot QC J1H 6M3
Tel: 819-823-1392; *Fax:* 819-821-3539
secretary@ndfc.ca
www.ndfc.ca
www.facebook.com/groups/113225318718761
www.livestream.com/ndfctv
Overview: A medium-sized national organization founded in 1977
Mission: To promote & organize darts events & promote the betterment of the game
Affliation(s): World Darts Federation
Chief Officer(s):
Bill Hatter, President
president@ndfc.ca
Mary Dezan, General Secretary
Finances: *Annual Operating Budget:* $50,000-$100,000
Staff Member(s): 7
Membership: 5,000-14,999
Activities: Provincial/national championships; international events

National Dental Assisting Examining Board (NDAEB) / Bureau national d'examen d'assistance dentaire (BNEAD)
#205, 2255 St. Laurent Blvd., Ottawa ON K1G 4K3
Tel: 613-526-3424; *Fax:* 613-526-5560
office@ndaeb.ca
www.ndaeb.ca
Overview: A medium-sized national organization founded in 1997
Mission: To assure that individuals entering the practice of dental assisting have met a national baseline standard in the knowledge, skills and attitudes necessary to practice as a dental assistant.
Chief Officer(s):
Jennifer Tewes, President

National Dental Examining Board of Canada / Le bureau national d'examen dentaire du Canada
80 Elgin St., 2nd Fl., Ottawa ON K1P 6R2
Tel: 613-236-5912; *Fax:* 613-236-8386
director@ndeb.ca
www.ndeb.ca
Overview: A small national organization
Mission: To establish qualifying conditions for a national standard of dental competence for general practitioners; to establish & maintain an examination facility to test for this national standard of dental competence; to issue certificates to dentists who successfully meet this national standard.

Chief Officer(s):
W. Judson, President

National Dental Hygiene Certification Board
#322, 1929 Russell Rd., Ottawa ON K1G 4G3
Tel: 613-260-8156; *Fax:* 613-260-8511
exam@ndhcb.ca
www.ndhcb.ca
Overview: A small national licensing organization founded in 1994
Mission: To issue the National Dental Hygiene Certification Examination (NDHCE)
Chief Officer(s):
Doris Lavoie, Executive Director
dlavoie@ndhcb.ca

National Eating Disorder Information Centre (NEDIC)
ES 7-421, 200 Elizabeth St., Toronto ON M5G 2C4
Tel: 416-340-4156; *Fax:* 416-340-4736
Toll-Free: 866-633-4220
nedic@uhn.ca
www.nedic.ca
www.facebook.com/267097966860
twitter.com/NEDIC85
Overview: A small national charitable organization founded in 1985
Mission: The National Eating Disorder Information Centre (NEDIC) is a non-profit organization founded in 1985 to provide information and resources on eating disorders and food and weight preoccupation. One of their main goals is to inform the public about eating disorders and related issues.
Member of: Toronto General Hospital
Chief Officer(s):
Merryl Bear, Director
Finances: *Annual Operating Budget:* $100,000-$250,000; *Funding Sources:* Community Mental Health Branch, Ontario Ministry of Health; donations; sales of materials
Staff Member(s): 3; 7 volunteer(s)
Membership: 1-99
Activities: Lectures & workshops for schools, community groups & individuals; support groups; information & consultation for public health professionals & interested individuals to enable them to start support groups; national referral to treatment; *Awareness Events:* Eating Disorder Awareness Week, 1st full week in Feb.; International No Diet Day, May 6; *Speaker Service:* Yes

National Educational Association of Disabled Students (NEADS) / Association nationale des étudiant(e)s handicapé(e)s au niveau postsecondaire
Carleton University, Unicentre, #426, 1125 Colonel By Dr., Ottawa ON K1S 5B6
Tel: 613-380-8065; *Fax:* 613-369-4391
Toll-Free: 877-670-1256
info@neads.ca
www.neads.ca
Overview: A small national organization founded in 1986
Mission: To encourage the self-empowerment of post-secondary students with disabilities; to advocate for increased accessibility at all levels so that disabled students may gain equal access to a college or university education; to provide an information resource base on services for disabled students nationwide according to a file of material from post-secondary institutions
Affiliation(s): Association québécoise des étudiant(e)s handicapé(e)s au post-secondaire; Council of Canadians with Disabilites
Chief Officer(s):
Frank Smith, National Coordinator, 613-380-8065 Ext. 201
frank.smith@neads.ca
Membership: 400; *Fees:* $10 regular & associate; $20 institutional; *Member Profile:* Disabled persons; regular - student; associate - professional; institutional - business
Activities: *Library* Open to public by appointment

National Electricity Roundtable (NER)
c/o Bryan Simonson, 148 Park Estates Pl. SE, Calgary AB T2J 3W5
Tel: 403-619-8967
nationaler@shaw.ca
www.nationalelectricityroundtable.com
Overview: A medium-sized national organization founded in 1994
Mission: To act as a forum for companies operating in the Canadian electric power industry; to work with government to develop a sustainable industry
Chief Officer(s):
Richard Wunderlich, Chair, 416-294-5861
richard.wunderlich@siemens.com
Bryan Simonson, President
Membership: 20 companies + 6 federal departments

National Elevator & Escalator Association (NEEA)
#708, 6299 Airport Rd., Mississauga ON L4V 1N3
Tel: 905-678-9940
Overview: A medium-sized national organization founded in 1977
Chief Officer(s):
Andrew Reistetter, Executive Director

National Emergency Nurses Affiliation (NENA) / Affiliation des infirmières et infirmiers d'urgence
112 Old River Rd., RR#2, Mallorytown ON K0E 1R0
www.nena.ca
www.facebook.com/103455173059386
Overview: A medium-sized national organization
Mission: To represent the Canadian emergency nursing specialty.
Affiliation(s): Canadian Nurses Association
Chief Officer(s):
Landon James, President
Membership: 1,158; *Fees:* $20; *Committees:* Nominations/Awards; Certification; Nursing Practice
Meetings/Conferences: • National Emergency Nurses Affiliation 2015 Conference, April, 2015, Edmonton, AB
Scope: National
Description: Theme: Prepare For The Unexpected
Contact Information: conference2015@nena.ca; Phone: 604-594-5407

National Energy Conservation Association Inc. (NECA) / Association nationale pour la conservation de l'énergie
#400, 283 Bannatyne Ave., Winnipeg MB R3B 3B2
Tel: 204-956-5888; *Fax:* 204-956-5819
Toll-Free: 800-263-5974
neca@neca.ca
Previous Name: National Insulation & Energy Conservation Contractors Association
Overview: A medium-sized national organization founded in 1983
Mission: To promote energy efficiency in the building sector; To work towards a sustainable future

National Farmers Foundation
2717 Wentz Ave., Saskatoon SK S7K 4B6
Tel: 306-652-9465; *Fax:* 306-664-6226
nationalfarmersfoundation@gmail.com
www.nfu.ca/about/national-farmers-foundation
Overview: A large national charitable organization founded in 1987
Mission: To stimulate rural/urban cooperation; to fund education & research that will further the progressive farm movement in Canada
Affiliation(s): National Farmers Union
Chief Officer(s):
Jim Phelps, President
Finances: *Funding Sources:* Fundraising; donations

National Farmers Union (NFU) / Syndicat national des cultivateurs
2717 Wentz Ave., Saskatoon SK S7K 4B6
Tel: 306-652-9465; *Fax:* 306-664-6226
nfu@nfu.ca
www.nfu.ca
www.facebook.com/nfuCanada
twitter.com/NFUcanada
Overview: A large national organization founded in 1969
Mission: To improve economic & social well-being of rural people & rural communities
Member of: Rural Dignity of Canada
Affiliation(s): Action Canada Network
Chief Officer(s):
Terry Boehm, President
centaur2@sasktel.net
Joan Brady, Women's President
jbbrady@eastlink.ca
Cammie Harbottle, Youth President
cammie@waldegrave.org
Finances: *Annual Operating Budget:* $500,000-$1.5 Million; *Funding Sources:* Membership dues; fundraising; donations
Staff Member(s): 7; 300 volunteer(s)
Membership: *Fees:* $195 family; $97 youth; $65 associate; *Committees:* Women's Advisory; Youth Advisory; International Program
Activities: *Speaker Service:* Yes
Awards:
• The Paul Beingessner Award for Excellence in Writing (Award)
Amount: $500
Publications:
• Union Farmer Monthly [a publication of the National Farmers Union]
Type: Newsletter; *Frequency:* Monthly
• Union Farmer Quarterly [a publication of the National Farmers Union]
Type: Magazine; *Frequency:* q.

Manitoba - Taxation Office
Newdale Shopping Centre, 2999B Pembina Hwy., Winnipeg MB R3T 2H5
Tel: 204-261-0500

Maritimes - NFU Financial Services
120 Bishop Dr., Summerside PE C1N 5Z8
Tel: 902-436-1872
Chief Officer(s):
Gayle Read, Contact

Maritimes - Taxation Office
559 Rte. 390, Rowena NB E7N 4N2
Tel: 506-273-4328; *Fax:* 506-273-4328
Chief Officer(s):
Judy Barr, Contact

Ontario Office
5420 Hwy. 6 North, RR#5, Guelph ON N1H 6J2
Tel: 705-738-3993
Toll-Free: 888-832-9638
office@nfuontario.ca
nfuontario.ca
Chief Officer(s):
Ann Slater, Ontario NFU Coordinator
Sarah Bakker, Regional Office Administrator

National Federation for the Sports of Triathlon, Duathlon & Aquathlon in Canada *See* Triathlon Canada

National Federation of Communication Workers (CNTU) *Voir* Fédération nationale des communications (CSN)

National Federation of Nurses' Unions *See* Canadian Federation of Nurses Unions

National Federation of Pakistani Canadians Inc. (NFPC)
#1100, 251 Laurier Ave. W, Ottawa ON K1P 5J6
Tel: 613-232-5346; *Fax:* 613-232-6607
www.cool.mb.ca/nfpc
Overview: A medium-sized national organization founded in 1982
Mission: To preserve & promote the heritage, culture & language of Pakistani Canadians; to generate goodwill & understanding among ethnic & mainstream communities; to provide support to new immigrants; to create awareness of Canadian issues in the Pakistani community
Member of: Canadian Ethnocultural Council
Finances: *Annual Operating Budget:* Less than $50,000; *Funding Sources:* Grants; contributions from community; membership fee
Membership: 25 institutions
Activities: *Library* Open to public

National Federation of Québec Teachers *Voir* Fédération nationale des enseignants et des enseignantes du Québec

National Federation of the Blind: Advocates for Equality *See* Alliance for Equality of Blind Canadians

National Firearms Association *See* Canada's National Firearms Association

National Floor Covering Association (NFCA) / Association nationale des revêtements de sol
987 Clarkson Rd. South, Mississauga ON L5J 2V8
Tel: 905-822-2280; *Fax:* 905-822-2494
www.nfcaonline.ca
Overview: A small national organization founded in 1987
Mission: To unite the Canadian regional & provincial associations in a spirit of cooperation; to improve & enhance the floorcovering industry; to share information & ideas; to undertake & support programs which will improve communications at all levels of the industry
Finances: *Annual Operating Budget:* $50,000-$100,000; *Funding Sources:* Membership fees

Staff Member(s): 1; 10 volunteer(s)
Membership: 4 provincial/regional floor covering associations

National Golf Course Owners Association Canada (NGCOA) / L'Association nationale des propriétaires de terrains de golf du Canada (ANPTG)

#105, 955 Green Valley Cres., Ottawa ON K2C 3V4
Tel: 613-226-3616; *Fax:* 613-226-4148
Toll-Free: 866-626-4262
ngcoa@ngcoa.ca
www.ngcoa.ca
Overview: A large national organization
Mission: Provides business support to Canadian golf course operators & related stakeholders, networking opportunities, purchasing programs, & education
Chief Officer(s):
Jeff Calderwood, CEO
jcalderwood@ngcoa.ca
Nathalie Lavallée, COO
nlavallee@ngcoa.ca
Membership: *Fees:* Schedule available; *Member Profile:* Golf course owner/operators
Activities: Golfmax Purchasing Program, Golfmax Online Tradeshow, Golf Research Centre; *Awareness Events:* Take a Kid to the Course Week, July; GolfBusiness Canada Conference & Trade Show; NGCOA Canada Golf Invitationals
Meetings/Conferences: • Golf Business Canada Conference & Trade Show 2015, 2015
Scope: National
Publications:
• Golf Business Canada
Type: Magazine

Alberta Chapter
AB
Tel: 403-335-2834
Chief Officer(s):
Brent Hutcheon, Regional Director
bhutcheon@ngcoa.ca

Atlantic Chapter
NB
Toll-Free: 866-626-4262
Chief Officer(s):
Jim Thompson, Interim Regional Director
jthompson@ngcoa.ca

British Columbia Chapter
BC
Tel: 778-808-6711
Toll-Free: 866-262-4262
Chief Officer(s):
Erica Beck, Regional Director
ebeck@ngcoa.ca

Central Ontario Chapter
ON
Tel: 705-812-1254
Toll-Free: 866-626-4262
Chief Officer(s):
Mike Bell, Regional Director
mbell@ngcoa.ca

Eastern Ontario / Outaouais Chapter
ON
Tel: 613-528-1994
Toll-Free: 866-626-4262
Chief Officer(s):
Carol Ann Campbell, Regional Director
cacampbell@ngcoa.ca

Prairie Chapter
MB
Tel: 204-282-6422
Toll-Free: 866-626-4262
Chief Officer(s):
Kevin O'Donovan, Regional Director
kodonovan@ngcoa.ca

Québec Chapter
QC
Toll-Free: 866-626-4262
Chief Officer(s):
Mark Fraser, Regional Director
mfraser@ngcoa.ca

Southwestern Ontario Chapter
ON
Tel: 519-637-3361
Chief Officer(s):
Shawn Hunter, Regional Director
shunter@ngcoa.ca

National Health Union (NHU) / Syndicat national de la santé (SNS)

#1202, 233 Gilmour St., Ottawa ON K2P 0P2
Tel: 613-237-2732; *Fax:* 613-237-6954
Toll-Free: 888-454-6305
Www.nhu-sns.ca
Overview: A medium-sized national organization overseen by Public Service Alliance of Canada (CLC)
Mission: To protect their members by ensuring safe working conditions & fair wage rights & benefits
Chief Officer(s):
Tony Tilley, President
Membership: 5,000 + 24 Locals; *Member Profile:* Employees at Health Canada & Public Health Agency of Canada; *Committees:* Finance; Health & Safety; Honours & Awards; Organization & Structure

National Hockey League Alumni Association (NHLA)

400 Kipling Ave., Toronto ON M8V 3L1
Tel: 416-798-2586; *Fax:* 416-798-2582
info@nhlalumni.net
nhlalumni.net
la.linkedin.com/groups?gid=1039337
www.facebook.com/nhlalumni
www.twitter.com/NHLAlumni
Also Known As: NHL Alumni Association
Overview: A medium-sized national charitable organization founded in 1999
Mission: Provides programs and assistance for all retired NHL players, including career transition with the BreakAway Program.
Affiliation(s): National Hockey League (NHL); National Hockey League Players' Association
Chief Officer(s):
Mark Napier, Executive Director
mark@nhlalumni.net
Mike Pelyk, Chair
Staff Member(s): 7
Membership: 28 chapters + 2,500 members
Activities: *Speaker Service:* Yes; *Rents Mailing List:* Yes
Awards:
• NHL Alumni 'Man of the Year' (Award)
• Keith McCreary '7th Man Award' (Award)
• Ace Bailey 'Award of Courage' (Award)
• Scholarships for Members (Scholarship)
• Scholarships for Members Descendants (Scholarship)

National Hockey League Players' Association (NHLPA)

#1700, 20 Bay St., Toronto ON M5J 2N8
www.nhlpa.com
www.facebook.com/nhlpa
twitter.com/nhlpa
www.youtube.com/user/NHLPA
Overview: A medium-sized national organization founded in 1967
Mission: The union for professional hockey players in the National Hockey League (NHL).
Affiliation(s): National Hockey League (NHL); National Hockey League Players' Association
Chief Officer(s):
Don Fehr, Executive Director
Membership: *Committees:* Competition

National Indian & Inuit Community Health Representatives Organization (NIICHRO)

PO Box 1019, 1 Roy Montour Rd., Kahnawake QC J0L 1B0
Tel: 450-632-0892; *Fax:* 450-632-2111
NIICHRO@NIICHRO.com
www.niichro.com
Overview: A small national organization founded in 1986
Mission: To upgrade the quality of health care of First Nation & Inuit people to the standard of health enjoyed by the rest of the population; to provide a forum for CHRs to communicate & exchange information; To promote awareness & understanding of the community health representative program thoughout Canada
Chief Officer(s):
Debbie Dedam-Montour, Executive Director
debbiedm@niichro.com
Staff Member(s): 9
Membership: *Fees:* $75 regular; $100 associate; $0 retired CHR; *Member Profile:* Community Health Representatives

National Indian Brotherhood *See* Assembly of First Nations

National Information Program on Antibiotics (NIPA)

#700, 160 Bloor St. East, Toronto ON M4W 3P7
www.antibiotics-info.org
Overview: A small national organization
Mission: NIPA's objectives are to help Canadians understand the difference between viral and bacterial infections, and the importance of using antibiotics only for the treatment of bacterial infections. NIPA wants to raise awareness and understanding of the issue of antibiotic resistance and motivate behavioural changes in the prescribing and use of antibiotics.
Activities: Provides information for consumers & healthcare professionals on the issue of antibiotic resistance in Canada; *Awareness Events:* National Antibiotics Awareness Week, Feb.

National Initiative for the Care of the Elderly (NICE) / Initiative nationale pour le soin des personnes âgées

#328, 263 McCaul St., Toronto ON M5T 1W7
Tel: 416-978-0545; *Fax:* 416-978-4771
nicenetadmin@utoronto.ca
www.nicenet.ca
facebook.com/NICElderly
twitter.com/NICElderly
Overview: A small national organization
Mission: National network of researchers & practitioners involved in the care of older adults through medicine, nursing & social work
Member of: Network of Centres of Excellence
Chief Officer(s):
Anthony Lombardo, Network Manager
Meetings/Conferences: • National Initiative for the Care of the Elderly Annual Nice Knowledge Exchange 2015, May, 2015, Hart House, University of Toronto, Toronto, ON
Scope: National

National Institute of Broadcasting

1498 Yonge St., Toronto ON M4T 1Z6
Tel: 416-922-2556; *Fax:* 416-922-5470
Overview: A small national organization founded in 1962

National Institute of Disability Management & Research (NIDMAR) / Institut national de recherche et de gestion de l'incapacité au travail

c/o Pacific Coast University for Workplace Health Sciences, 4755 Cherry Creek Rd., Port Alberni BC V9Y 0A7
Tel: 778-421-0821; *Fax:* 778-421-0823
nidmar@nidmar.ca
www.nidmar.ca
Overview: A medium-sized national charitable organization
Mission: Committed to reducing the human, social, & economic cost of disability to workers, employers, & society by providing education, research, policy development, & implementation resources to promote workplace-based integration programs
Chief Officer(s):
Wolfgang Zimmermann, Executive Director
wolfgang@nidmar.ca
Finances: *Funding Sources:* Disabled Workers Foundation of Canada; Endowment fund
Staff Member(s): 8
Activities: Training; Education; Research; Disability management resources; Collection of databases
Meetings/Conferences: • International Forum on Disability Management, November, 2016, Kuala Lumpur Convention Centre, Kuala Lumpur
Scope: International
Contact Information: enquiries@ifdm2016.com.my; Phone: +603 4264 5053

Eastern Canada Office
PO Box 512, Stn. B, Ottawa ON K1P 5P6
Tel: 613-260-2951; *Fax:* 613-260-2954
Chief Officer(s):
Joyce Gravelle, Contact
joyce.gravelle@nidmar.ca

National Insulation & Energy Conservation Contractors Association *See* National Energy Conservation Association Inc.

National Inuit Youth Council (NIYC)

#1101, 75 Albert St., Ottawa ON K1P 5E7
Tel: 613-238-8181; *Fax:* 613-234-4482
Toll-Free: 866-262-8181
www.niyc.ca
www.facebook.com/332933250073292
twitter.com/inuityouth
Overview: A small national organization founded in 1994
Mission: To provide information on political & environmental issues, Inuit rights & opportunities, legal assistance; to improve communications & assist Inuit youth achieve full participation in

Davin MacIntosh, Executive Director
dmacintosh@cccski.com
Lisa Patterson, Contact, NWSA
lpatterson@cccski.com

National Youth Bowling Council *See* Youth Bowling Canada

National Youth in Care Network *See* Youth in Care Canada

National Youth Orchestra Canada (NYOC) / Orchestre national des jeunes Canada (ONJC)
#500, 59 Adelaide St. East, Toronto ON M5C 1K6
Tel: 416-532-4470; *Fax:* 416-532-6879
Toll-Free: 888-532-4470
info@nyoc.org
www.nyoc.org
www.facebook.com/nyoconjc
twitter.com/nyoc_onjc
www.youtube.com/nyoconjc
Overview: A medium-sized national charitable organization founded in 1961 overseen by Orchestras Canada
Chief Officer(s):
Barbara Smith, Executive Director
bsmith@nyoc.org
Finances: *Funding Sources:* Ontario Arts Council; Grants; Donations
Staff Member(s): 6
Activities: Orchestral training program for youth ages 16-28; *Library*

Native Addictions Council of Manitoba (NACM)
160 Salter St., Winnipeg MB R2W 4K1
Tel: 204-586-8395; *Fax:* 204-589-3921
info@nacm.ca
www.mts.net/~nacm/
Also Known As: Pritchard House
Overview: A small provincial charitable organization founded in 1972
Mission: To provide traditional holistic healing services to First Peoples through treatment of addictions; each member of First Peoples has the right to wellness.
Activities: Woman's program, youth program, gambling program, and an outreach program.; *Library*

Native Alliance of Québec Inc. *Voir* Alliance autochtone du Québec inc.

Native Brotherhood of British Columbia (NBBC) / Fraternité des Indiens de la Colombie-Britannique
#110, 100 Park Royal South, West Vancouver BC V7T 1A2
Tel: 604-913-3372
nativebrotherhood.ca
Overview: A medium-sized provincial organization founded in 1931
Mission: To advance the social, spiritual, economic & physical conditions of its members, including higher standards of education, health & living conditions; to cooperate with other organizations which concern themselves with the advancement of Indian welfare; focus is on capacity building, including fisheries, marine resources, tourism & eco-tourism, forestry & other resources with economic potential & opportunities
Membership: 450 current individual members; 6,000 charter community members; *Fees:* Schedule available

Native Canadian Centre of Toronto (NCCT)
16 Spadina Rd., Toronto ON M5R 2S7
Tel: 416-964-9087; *Fax:* 416-964-2111
reception@ncct.on.ca
www.ncct.on.ca
www.facebook.com/nativecentre
twitter.com/NativeCentre
Overview: A medium-sized local charitable organization
Mission: To provides a gathering place to deliver programs & services for Native people while striving to reflect the traditional
Member of: National Association of Friendship Centres
Chief Officer(s):
Larry Frost, Executive Director
larry.frost@ncct.on.ca
Gene Jamieson, President
J'net Cavanagh, Officer, Communications & Referrals
Jnet.Cavanagh@ncct.on.ca
Staff Member(s): 30
Membership: *Fees:* Schedule available
Activities: Traditional Awareness Gathering; *Speaker Service:* Yes; *Library:* Community History Project; by appointment

Native Child & Family Services of Toronto (NCFST)
30 College St., Toronto ON M5G 1K2
Tel: 416-969-8510; *Fax:* 416-928-0706
info@nativechild.org
www.nativechild.org
Overview: A medium-sized local charitable organization founded in 1986
Mission: To provide caring, well-being, quality of life, & healing to children in need in Toronto's Native community
Chief Officer(s):
Joe Elkerton, President
Kenn Richard, Executive Director
Finances: *Annual Operating Budget:* Greater than $5 Million; *Funding Sources:* Government; Organizations
Staff Member(s): 180
Activities: *Internships:* Yes

Native Clan Organization Inc. (NCO)
94 McGregor St., Winnipeg MB R2W 4V5
Tel: 204-943-7357
ednco@nativeclan.org
www.nativeclan.org
Overview: A small local organization founded in 1972
Mission: To supply social services to male & female inmates of Native origin incarcerated in southern Manitoba
Affliation(s): Canadian Criminal Justice Association
Chief Officer(s):
Ken Fleury, Executive Director
Finances: *Funding Sources:* Services fees

Native Communications Society of the Northwest Territories (NCS)
PO Box 2193, Yellowknife NT X1A 2P6
Tel: 320-295-7700
Toll-Free: 888-627-6208
www.ncsnwt.com
Overview: A small provincial organization
Mission: To promote & develop improved communications between aboriginal & non-aboriginal people & communities in the NWT, as well as between northerners & southern Canadians; to help educate aboriginal people through the communications media in order for them to readily understand the implications of the European way of living & the developments taking place in the NWT
Chief Officer(s):
Les L. Carpenter, CEO
lcarpenter@ncsnwt.com

Native Coordinating Council
2010 - 1st Ave. East, Prince Albert SK S6V 2B7
Tel: 306-764-6690; *Fax:* 306-764-8072
sundance.staff@sasktel.net
Also Known As: Sundance Haven
Overview: A medium-sized local organization founded in 1978
Mission: To develop programs that support Native culture; to provide needed services to Prince Albert community; to provide employment opportunities to Native People
Affliation(s): Indian Metis Friendship Center; Local 269; Local 109
Finances: *Funding Sources:* Provincial government
Membership: *Member Profile:* Aboriginal - Métis descent
Activities: Family counselling; crisis centre; parent aid program

Native Council of Canada *See* Congress of Aboriginal Peoples

Native Council of Nova Scotia (NCNS)
129 Truro Heights Rd., Truro NS B6L 1X2
Tel: 902-895-1523; *Fax:* 902-895-0024
Toll-Free: 800-565-4372
www.ncns.ca
Overview: A medium-sized provincial organization founded in 1975 overseen by Congress of Aboriginal Peoples
Mission: To aid & assist people of Aboriginal ancestry in Nova Scotia; to work with all levels of government, public & private agencies, & industry to improve social, educational & employment opportunities for Aboriginal people; to foster & strengthen cultural identity & pride; to inform the public of the special needs of Native People; to cooperate with other Native organizations
Chief Officer(s):
Grace Conrad, Chief & President
core1@eastlink.ca
Theresa Hare, Finance
theresahare@eastlink.ca
Membership: 1,000-4,999; *Member Profile:* Full - 16 years of age & over, resident of Nova Scotia, of Aboriginal ancestry & non-resident band member; Honorary - at discretion of Executive Committee, Board of Directors & General Assembly
Activities: APTEC & SARSET Programs - employment & training assistance for off-reserve Mi'kmaq/Aboriginal people in NS; Education Program - educational assistance through awards, scholarships & loans for off-reserve Mi'kmaq/Aboriginal people in NS; CHIP Program - community action program for Mi'kmaq/Aboriginal parents with young children ages 0-6 yrs.; Prenatal Program - support program for first-time Mi'kmaq/Aboriginal expectant mothers & babies; RNH Program: assists off-reserve Mi'kmaq/Aboriginal homeowners with CMHC, RRAP & ERP; *Library* Open to public

Dartmouth Regional Office
#5, 121 Isley Ave., Burnside NS
Tel: 902-354-2751; *Fax:* 902-354-2757
Chief Officer(s):
Lynn Johnston, Facilitator, APTEC
johnstonl@eastlink.ca

Liverpool Regional Office
PO Box 2028, 29 Market St., Liverpool NS B0T 1K0
Tel: 902-354-2751; *Fax:* 902-354-2757
Chief Officer(s):
Jim Wolfe, Facilitator, APTEC
wolfej@eastlink.ca

Sydney Regional Office
PO Box 813, Stn. A, 14 Wentworth St., Sydney NS B1P 6J1
Tel: 902-567-1240; *Fax:* 902-564-1123
Chief Officer(s):
Melissa Burns-Reid, Facilitator, APTEC
cbncns2@eastlink.ca

Native Council of Prince Edward Island
6 F.J. McAuley Ct., Charlottetown PE C1A 9M7
Tel: 902-892-5314; *Fax:* 902-368-7464
Toll-Free: 877-591-3003
admin@ncpei.com
www.ncpei.com
Overview: A small provincial organization overseen by Congress of Aboriginal Peoples
Mission: The Native Council of Prince Edward Island is a Community of Aboriginal People residing off reserve in traditional Mi'kmaq territory. NCPEI is the self governing authority for all off reserve Aboriginal people living on Epekwitk (PEI).
Member of: Prince Edward Island Literacy Alliance Inc.
Chief Officer(s):
Jamie Thomas, President & Chief
jamie@ncpei.com
Rikki Schock, Vice-President
Lisa Cooper, Director, Operations
Staff Member(s): 13

Native Counselling Services of Alberta (NCSA)
10975 - 124 St., Edmonton AB T5M 0H9
Tel: 780-451-4002; *Fax:* 780-428-0187
www.ncsa.ca
Overview: A medium-sized provincial organization founded in 1970
Mission: To promote wellness for Aboriginal individuals, families and communities.
Chief Officer(s):
Allen Benson, CEO
allen-benson@ncsa.ca
Finances: *Funding Sources:* Federal & provincial governments; private foundations
Staff Member(s): 9
Activities: *Library*

Native Courtworker & Counselling Association of BC (NCCABC)
#207, 1999 Marine Dr., North Vancouver BC V7P 3J3
Tel: 604-985-5355; *Fax:* 604-985-8933
Toll-Free: 877-811-1190
nccabc@nccabc.net
www.nccabc.ca
Also Known As: NCCA of BC
Overview: A small provincial charitable organization founded in 1973
Mission: To provide culturally appropriate services to aboriginal people & communities consistent with their needs; To provide access to counselling & referral services to clients with substance abuse & detox support issues; To provide advocacy service for aboriginal family & youth; To facilitate & enhance access to justice by assisting clients involved in the criminal justice system
Finances: *Annual Operating Budget:* $1.5 Million-$3 Million
Staff Member(s): 50
Membership: *Committees:* Executive; Finance; Planning

Native Earth Performing Arts Inc. (NEPA)
#250, 585 Dundas St. East, Toronto ON M5A 2B7
Tel: 416-531-1402; *Fax:* 416-531-6377
Toll-Free: 877-854-9708
office@nativeearth.ca
www.nativeearth.ca
www.facebook.com/NativeEarthPerformingArts
twitter.com/NativeEarth
Overview: A medium-sized local charitable organization founded in 1983
Mission: To enable Native actors, writers, designers, directors & technicians to work together to produce quality theatre that is vital to their development as artists & their identity as Native people; to encourage the use of theatre as form of communication within the Native community, including the use of the Native languages
Member of: Theatre Ontario
Affliation(s): Professional Association of Canadian Theatres; Toronto Theatre Alliance
Chief Officer(s):
Ryan Cunningham, Artistic Director
ryan@nativeearth.ca
Isaac Thomas, General Manager
isaac@nativeearth.ca
Finances: *Funding Sources:* Government; corporate; private donations; special events; membership dues; merchandise sales
Staff Member(s): 11
Activities: *Internships:* Yes; *Speaker Service:* Yes

Native Fishing Association (NFA)
#110, 100 Park Royal South, West Vancouver BC V7T 1A2
Tel: 604-913-2997; *Fax:* 604-913-2995
reception@shoal.ca
www.shoal.ca
www.facebook.com/native.fishing
twitter.com/nativefishing
Overview: A small local organization founded in 1985
Mission: To enhance, stabilize, & support Native participation in British Columbia's commercial fishing industry.
Chief Officer(s):
Mark Recalma, Co-Chair
Bill Wilson, Co-Chair
Violet Hill, Executive Director
vhill@shoal.ca

Native Friendship Centre of Montréal Inc. (NFCM) / Centre d'amitié autochtone de Montréal Inc.
2001 St. Laurent Blvd., Montréal QC H2X 2T3
Tel: 514-499-1854; *Fax:* 514-499-9436
Toll-Free: 855-499-1854
info@nfcm.org
www.nfcm.org
www.facebook.com/nfcm.montreal
Overview: A medium-sized local charitable organization founded in 1974
Mission: To promote, develop & enhance the quality of life of the urban Aboriginal community of Montréal
Member of: National Association of Friendship Centres
Chief Officer(s):
Brett W. Pineau, Executive Director
Finances: *Funding Sources:* Heritage Canada
Membership: *Fees:* $5; *Member Profile:* Status & non-status Indian, Inuit, Métis, & non-native
Activities: Cultural activities; Training & Employment; AIDS/HIV Workshops; Substance Abuse Therapy;

Native Investment & Trade Association (NITA)
6520 Salish Dr., Vancouver BC V6N 2C7
Tel: 604-275-6670; *Fax:* 604-275-0307
Toll-Free: 800-337-7743
nita@express.ca
www.native-invest-trade.com
Overview: A small national licensing organization founded in 1989
Mission: To promote, establish & maintain trade/investment opportunities in Native communities; encourages free enterprise solutions to economic & social problems confronting Native communities, but remains sensitive to their special cultural heritage, needs, requirements; views non-governmental business involvement with First Nations as a vital step towards greater self-reliance; fosters business ventures with high employment potential; promotes projects with potential for sustainable economic growth; conducts research into innovative approaches to economic development of Native communities
Chief Officer(s):
Calvin Helin, CEO & President
ch@native-invest-trade.com
Finances: *Annual Operating Budget:* $250,000-$500,000; *Funding Sources:* Registration fees
Staff Member(s): 10; 2 volunteer(s)
Activities: Online business directory; conferences; scholarships; business products and services; *Library:* NITA Resource Library

Native North American Traveling College
1 Ronathahon:ni Lane, Ahkwesahsne ON K6H 5R7
Tel: 613-932-9452; *Fax:* 613-932-0092
info@nnatc.org
www.nnatc.org
Overview: A small national organization founded in 1974
Mission: The cultural centre has been and continues today to be instrumental in preserving and maintaining the Mohawk cultural, history and language.
Chief Officer(s):
Russell Roundpoint, Executive Director
Finances: *Annual Operating Budget:* $100,000-$250,000
Staff Member(s): 10
Activities: *Awareness Events:* Friendship Days, July; *Speaker Service:* Yes

Native Orchid Conservation Inc.
45 Skowron Cres., Winnipeg MB R3W 1N6
Tel: 204-223-8209
www.nativeorchid.org
Overview: A small local organization
Mission: To protect unique mini-ecosystems & their plant communities
Chief Officer(s):
Doris Ames, President
adames@mts.net
Membership: *Fees:* $10 individual; $25 group

Native Women's Association of Canada (NWAC) / L'Association des femmes autochtones du Canada (AFAC)
1 Nicholas St., 9th Fl., Ottawa ON K1N 7B7
Fax: 613-722-7687
Toll-Free: 800-461-4043
www.nwac.ca
www.facebook.com/283649502474
Overview: A medium-sized national organization founded in 1974
Mission: To enhance, promote & foster the social, economic, cultural & political well-being of First Nations & Métis women with First Nations & Canadian societies; to help empower women by being involved in developing & changing legislation which affects them, & by involving them in the development & delivery of programs promoting equal opportunity for Aboriginal women. Satellite office located at 1292 Wellington St. West, Ottawa, 613-722-3033.
Member of: Indigenous Survival International
Chief Officer(s):
Michéle Audette, President
Finances: *Funding Sources:* Canadian Heritage; Corrections Service Canada
Staff Member(s): 8
Activities: The Indian Act; The Constitution; Family Violence; AIDS; Justice; Health Issues; Child Welfare; Aboriginal Rights; *Library:* Resource Centre; Open to public

Native Women's Association of the Northwest Territories
Post Office Building, 2nd Fl., PO Box 2321, Yellowknife NT X1A 2P7
Tel: 867-873-5509; *Fax:* 867-873-3152
Toll-Free: 866-459-1114
nativewomensnwt.com
www.facebook.com/NativeWomensAssociationOfTheNwt
Overview: A medium-sized provincial organization founded in 1978
Mission: Provides training & education programs for native women in the Western Arctic
Member of: Native Women's Association of Canada
Affiliation(s): Yellowknife Victim Services
Chief Officer(s):
Marilyn Napier, Executive Director
marilyn_napier@hotmail.com
Activities: Adult education; pre-employment programme; workshops

Native Women's Resource Centre of Toronto (NWRCT)
191 Gerrard St. East, Toronto ON M5A 2E5
Tel: 416-963-9963; *Fax:* 416-963-5062
info@nwrct.ca
www.nwrct.ca
www.facebook.com/292090724136835
twitter.com/NWRCT
Overview: A small local charitable organization founded in 1985
Mission: To provide ongoing support for native women in the GTA through a variety of programs; To incorporate spiritual, physical, social, economic & intellectual components into all programs
Affiliation(s): Toronto Aboriginal Social Services Association
Finances: *Funding Sources:* Government & fundraising
Membership: *Fees:* Free
Activities: Client information & referral; food bank; clothing give-away; youth activities; circles; craft classes; Pimaatisiwin developmental programs for children 0-6; Student Advancement program; Adult Literacy; Adult Education; workshops; native language class; summer day camps; Annual Winter Solstice Celebration; Women's Full Moon Ceremonies; *Library* Open to public

Native Women's Transition Centre Inc.
105 Aikins St., Winnipeg MB R2W 4E6
Tel: 204-989-8240; *Fax:* 204-586-1101
rswnwt1@nwtc.cc
www.nativewomens.mb.ca
Overview: A small local organization founded in 1979
Mission: To provide shelter to Native women & children; to provide social services to woman in need
Chief Officer(s):
Phil Lancaster, Acting-Chair
Activities: Programs: Crisis/Addiction; Learning; Parenting; Compulsive coping behavior; Women's healing/Play circle; Breaking the Silence; Practical skillsFamily violence prevention

Natural Family Planning Association
c/o #205, 3050 Yonge St., Toronto ON M4N 2K4
Tel: 416-481-5465
www.naturalfamilyplanning.ca
Also Known As: The Billings Group
Overview: A small national charitable organization
Mission: To promote the Billings Ovulation Method of natural family planning which is based on an awareness of a woman's physical systems to gauge optimum fertility state.
Member of: WOOMB International
Chief Officer(s):
Christian Elia, Executive Director
Finances: *Funding Sources:* Government
Activities: *Internships:* Yes; *Speaker Service:* Yes; *Library* by appointment

Natural Gas Employees' Association (NGEA)
#316, 9426 - 51 Ave., Edmonton AB T6E 5A6
Tel: 780-483-9330; *Fax:* 780-469-2504
Toll-Free: 877-912-9330
ngea@telus.net
www.ngea.ca
Overview: A small national organization
Mission: To represent the employees of ATCO Gas & Pipelines Limited-Gas Division & ATCO Gas & Pipelines Limited-Pipelines Division
Chief Officer(s):
Sandy Plummer, President, 587-297-1769

Natural Health Practitioners of Canada (NHP)
#600, 10339 - 124 St., Edmonton AB T5N 3W1
Tel: 780-484-2010; *Fax:* 780-484-3605
Toll-Free: 888-711-7701
www.nhpcanada.org
www.facebook.com/nhpcanada
twitter.com/NHPCANADA
Previous Name: Association of Massage Therapists & Wholistic Practitioners
Overview: A medium-sized national organization founded in 1988
Mission: To maintain professional standards of practitioners practising in massage therapy & wholistic practice in order to benefit services to clients
Chief Officer(s):
Colleen MacDougall, Executive Director
Membership: *Member Profile:* Canadian massage therapists & wholistic practitioners
Activities: Providing information to members; Promoting wellness

Natural Health Practitioners of Canada Association (NHPCA) / Association des Praticiens de la santé naturelle du Canada (PSNC)

#600, 10339 - 124 St., Edmonton AB T5N 3W1
Tel: 780-484-2010; *Fax:* 780-484-3605
Toll-Free: 888-711-7701
growingtogether@nhpcanada.org
www.nhpcanada.org
www.facebook.com/group.php?gid=142729347410
Overview: A medium-sized national organization
Mission: To provide programs, services and products for members in the service of public wellness and to serve the public by promoting and advocating the wellness professions.
Chief Officer(s):
Colleen MacDougall, Executive Director & Registrar
Publications:
• Connections [a publication of the Natural Health Practitioners of Canada]
Type: Magazine; *Frequency:* Quarterly

Natural History Society of Manitoba; Manitoba Naturalists Society *See* Nature Manitoba

Natural History Society of Newfoundland & Labrador

PO Box 1013, St. John's NL A1C 5M3
e-mail: naturenl@naturenl.ca
naturenl.ca
www.facebook.com/128262310581874
Overview: A small provincial charitable organization founded in 1963
Mission: To promote the enjoyment & protection of all wildlife and natural history resources in the Province of Newfoundland & Labrador & surrounding waters.
Member of: Canadian Nature Federation
Chief Officer(s):
Dave Innes, Secretary
Finances: *Annual Operating Budget:* Less than $50,000; *Funding Sources:* Membership fees; donations
Membership: *Fees:* $25
Activities: Field trips; monthly meetings;
Awards:
• Wild Things Scholarship (Scholarship)

Natural Products Marketing Council

PO Box 890, Truro NS B2N 5G6
Tel: 902-893-6511; *Fax:* 902-893-6573
www.novascotia.ca
Overview: A small provincial organization founded in 1946
Mission: To assure the orderly marketing of natural products
Chief Officer(s):
Elizabeth Crouse, General Manager
crouseea@gov.ns.ca
Ken Peacock, Chair
Staff Member(s): 3; 6 volunteer(s)

Natural Resources Union (NRU)

#600, 233 Gilmour St., Ottawa ON K2P 0P2
Tel: 613-560-4378; *Fax:* 613-233-7012
www.nru-srn.com
Previous Name: Union of Energy, Mines & Resources Employees
Overview: A medium-sized national organization founded in 1978 overseen by Public Service Alliance of Canada (CLC)
Chief Officer(s):
Mike Sargent, National President
sargentm@nru-srn.com
Finances: *Annual Operating Budget:* $250,000-$500,000
Staff Member(s): 2
Membership: 1,600 + 20 locals; *Member Profile:* Government employees, Natural Resources Canada, Canadian Space Agency & various other agencies & boards; *Committees:* Occupational Safety & Health; Equal Opportunities; Labour Management Consultation
Activities: *Library*

Natural Sciences & Engineering Research Council of Canada (NSERC) / Conseil de recherches en sciences naturelles et en génie du Canada (CRSNG)

350 Albert St., 16th Fl., Ottawa ON K1A 1H5
Tel: 613-995-4273; *Fax:* 613-992-5337
Toll-Free: 855-275-2861
Other Communication: President's Office e-mail: exec@nserc-crsng.gc.ca
comm@nserc-crsng.gc.ca
www.nserc-crsng.gc.ca
www.facebook.com/NSERC.CRSNG
twitter.com/nserc_crsng
www.youtube.com/user/NSERCTube
Overview: A large national organization
Mission: To support university students in advanced studies; to promote discovery research; to foster innovation through Canadian investment in postsecondary research projects
Chief Officer(s):
Suzanne Fortier, President
suzanne.fortier@nserc-crsng.gc.ca
Edwards James S., Vice-President & Chair
Finances: *Annual Operating Budget:* Greater than $5 Million
Membership: *Committees:* Standing & Advisory; Selection; Prizes; Membership

Natural Step Canada

#203, 4 Florence St., Ottawa ON K2P 0W7
Tel: 613-748-3001; *Fax:* 613-748-1649
info@naturalstep.ca
www.naturalstep.ca
www.linkedin.com/groups?mostPopular=&gid=1169257
www.facebook.com/TheNaturalStepCanada
twitter.com/thenaturalstep
www.youtube.com/user/naturalsteponline
Overview: A large national charitable organization
Mission: The Natural Step Canada is a non-profit organization that helps organizations and individuals understand and make meaningful progress toward sustainability.
Chief Officer(s):
Chad Park, Executive Director
Meetings/Conferences: • Natural Step Canada Accelerate: Collaborating for Sustainability Conference 2015, 2015
Scope: National

Nature Alberta

Percy Page Centre, 11759 Groat Rd., 3rd Fl., Edmonton AB T5M 3K6
Tel: 780-427-8124; *Fax:* 780-422-2663
info@naturealberta.ca
naturealberta.ca
www.facebook.com/NatureAB
twitter.com/naturealberta
www.youtube.com/user/naturealberta
Overview: A medium-sized provincial charitable organization founded in 1970
Mission: To encourage Albertans to increase knowledge & understanding of natural history & ecological processes; to provide a unified voice for naturalists on conservation issues; to organize field meetings, conferences, nature camps, research symposia, & other activities.
Member of: Canadian Nature Federation
Chief Officer(s):
Petra Rowell, Executive Director
petrar@naturealberta.ca
Finances: *Funding Sources:* Donations; grants; projects
Staff Member(s): 6
Membership: 5,000 individual + 40 clubs; *Fees:* Schedule available
Awards:
• Loran L. Goulden Memorial Award (Award)

Nature Canada / Canada Nature

#300, 75 Albert St., Ottawa ON K1P 5E7
Tel: 613-562-3447; *Fax:* 613-562-3371
Toll-Free: 800-267-4088
info@naturecanada.ca
www.naturecanada.ca
www.facebook.com/NatureCanada
twitter.com/NatureCanada
www.youtube.com/user/NatureCanada1
Previous Name: Canadian Nature Federation
Overview: A large national charitable organization founded in 1971
Mission: To protect & conserve wildlife & habitats throughout Canada
Chief Officer(s):
Ian Davidson, Executive Director
idavidson@naturecanada.ca
Ruth Catana, Chief Operating Officer
rcatana@naturecanada.ca
Dave Spooner, Director, Finance & Administration
dspooner@naturecanada.ca
Chris Sutton, Director, Communications
csutton@naturecanada.ca
Ted Cheskey, Manager, Bird Conservation Programs
tcheskey@naturecanada.ca
Jodi Joy, Manager, Major & Planned Giving
jjoy@naturecanada.ca
Katherine Lim, Manager, Outreach & Engagement
klim@naturecanada.ca
Alex MacDonald, Manager, Protected Areas Campaigns
amacdonald@naturecanada.ca
Carla Sbert, Manager, Conservation Programs
csbert@naturecanada.ca
Andrew Van Iterson, Manager, Green Budget Coalition
avaniterson@naturecanada.ca
Finances: *Funding Sources:* Donations
Membership: 350+ organizations + 40,000 supporters; *Member Profile:* Natualist organizations across Canada; Individual supporters
Activities: Offering outreach & educational programs; Organizing action campaigns for nature
Awards:
• Affiliate Award (Award)
To recognize conservation efforts of a partner organization that support Nature Canada's conservation initiatives or mission
• Charles Labatiuk Volunteer Award (Award)
To recognize individuals who have made outstanding contributions to Canadian conservation*Deadline:* March 31
• Volunteer Award (Award)
To honour individuals who contribute to a Nature Canada project
• Charles Labatiuk Scholarship (Scholarship)
Eligibility: Any student enrolled in an entrance level course or program at an accredited college or university in Canada, in the interdisciplinary study of natural environmental systems *Amount:* $2000
• Douglas H. Pimlott Award (Award)
Eligibility: An individual with outstanding contributions to Canadian conservation
Meetings/Conferences: • Nature Canada 2015 Annual General Meeting, 2015
Scope: National
Description: The annual meeting usually features the election of the Board of Directors, the presentation of Nature Canada awards, & the adoption of resolutions
Contact Information: Nature Canada Executive Assistant & Office Manager: Sue Robertson, E-mail: srobertson@naturecanada.ca
Publications:
• The Nature Nation
Type: Newsletter; *Frequency:* Monthly
Profile: Action alerts, reports, polls, reading suggestions, & upcoming events

The Nature Conservancy of Canada (NCC) / Société canadienne pour la conservation de la nature

#400, 36 Eglinton Ave. West, Toronto ON M4R 1A1
Tel: 416-932-3202; *Fax:* 416-932-3208
Toll-Free: 800-465-0029
nature@natureconservancy.ca
www.natureconservancy.ca
www.linkedin.com/company/the-nature-conservancy-of-canada
www.facebook.com/natureconservancy.ca
twitter.com/NatureConsCDA
www.youtube.com/user/NatureConsCDA
Overview: A large national charitable organization founded in 1962
Mission: To protect Canada's biodiversity through long-term stewardship & property securement
Chief Officer(s):
John Lounds, President & Chief Executive Officer
Jane Gilbert, Chief Communications Officer
Lynn Gran, Chief Development Officer & Vice-President, Strategic Philanthropy
Kamal Rajani, Chief Financial Officer
John Riley, Chief Science Officer & National Director, Strategies
Ian Barnett, Vice-President, Regional Operations
Michael Bradstreet, Vice-President, Conservation
Julie Wood, Vice-President, Corporate
Finances: *Funding Sources:* Donations
Membership: *Committees:* Executive; Governance & Nominating; Audit; Investment; Conservation
Activities: Partnering with landowners & corporations to protect Canada's natural areas
Publications:
• The Ark [a publication of The Nature Conservancy of Canada]
Type: Newsletter; *Frequency:* 3 pa; *Price:* A donation of $20+
Profile: A national newsletter, with updates on featured projects & properties, stewardship work, & threatened or vulnerable species

• The Nature Conservancy of Canada Annual Report to our Donors
Type: Yearbook; *Frequency:* Annually
Profile: The year in review for each region of Canada

Alberta
#830, 105 - 12 Ave. SE, Calgary AB T2G 1A1
Tel: 403-262-1253; *Fax:* 403-515-6987
Toll-Free: 877-262-1253
alberta@natureconservancy.ca
Chief Officer(s):
Bob Demulder, Regional Vice President

Atlantic
#180, 924 Prospect St., Fredericton NB E3B 2T9
Tel: 506-450-6010; *Fax:* 506-450-6013
Toll-Free: 877-231-4400
atlantic@natureconservancy.ca
Chief Officer(s):
Linda M. Stephenson, Regional Vice President

British Columbia
#200, 825 Broughton St., Victoria BC V8W 1E5
Tel: 250-479-3191; *Fax:* 250-479-0546
Toll-Free: 888-404-8428
bcoffice@natureconservancy.ca
Chief Officer(s):
Jan Garnett, Regional Vice President

Manitoba
#200, 611 Corydon Ave., Winnipeg MB R3L 0P3
Tel: 204-942-6156; *Fax:* 204-942-1016
Toll-Free: 866-683-6934
manitoba@natureconservancy.ca
Chief Officer(s):
Jeff Polakoff, Regional Vice President

Ontario
PO Box 443, London ON N6A 4W1
Toll-Free: 866-281-5331
ontario@natureconservancy.ca
Chief Officer(s):
James Duncan, Regional Vice President

Québec
#1000, 55 av Mont-Royal Ouest, Montréal QC H2T 2S6
Tél: 514-876-1606; *Téléc:* 514-876-7901
Ligne sans frais: 877-876-5444
quebec@conservationdelanature.ca
Chief Officer(s):
Nathalie Zinger, Regional Vice President

Saskatchewan
#100, 1777 Victoria Ave., Regina SK S4P 4K5
Tel: 306-347-0447; *Fax:* 306-347-2345
Toll-Free: 866-622-7275
saskatchewan@natureconservancy.ca
www.natureconservancy.ca/en/where-we-work/saskatchewan
Chief Officer(s):
Carmen Leibel, Regional Vice President

Nature Council of British Columbia *See* British Columbia Nature (Federation of British Columbia Naturalists)

Nature Manitoba (MNS)
Hammond Building, #401, 63 Albert St., Winnipeg MB R3B 1G4
Tel: 204-943-9029; *Fax:* 204-943-9029
Other Communication: editor@naturemanitoba.ca (Newsletter)
info@naturemanitoba.ca
www.naturemanitoba.ca
www.facebook.com/pages/Nature-Manitoba/67945358869
Previous Name: Natural History Society of Manitoba; Manitoba Naturalists Society
Overview: A medium-sized provincial charitable organization founded in 1920
Mission: To foster the popular & scientific study of nature; To preserve the natural environment; To act as a voice for people interested in the outdoors & natural history
Chief Officer(s):
Roger Turenne, President
Donald Himbeault, Executive Vice-President
Alain Louer, Secretary
Sean Worden, Treasurer
Susan McLarty, Office Administrator
Finances: *Funding Sources:* Donations; Nature Manitoba Store
Membership: *Fees:* $20 students; $35 seniors; $40 individuals; $55 families; *Member Profile:* Manitobans who share a passion for nature
Activities: Conducting research; Engaging in advocacy activities; Offering educational & recreational programs & field trips to observe botany, butterflies, & birds; *Library:* Nature Manitoba Library
Meetings/Conferences: • Nature Manitoba 2015 Annual General Meeting, 2015, Franco-Manitoban Cultural Centre, Winnipeg, MB
Scope: Provincial
Description: An opportunity for Nature Manitoba members to discuss & advance policy positions about nature in Manitoba
Contact Information: E-mail: info@naturemanitoba.ca
Publications:
• The Birds of Manitoba
Type: Book; *Price:* $63.95
Profile: Information about & illustrations & photographs of the 382 species of birds known in Manitoba
• Checklist of the Birds of Manitoba
Price: $1
Profile: A checklist of 391 confirmed species in Manitoba
• Finding Birds in Southern Manitoba
Type: Guide; *Price:* $20
Profile: A birding guide for southern Manitoba, featuring photographs & maps
• Nature Manitoba News
Type: Newsletter; *Frequency:* Bimonthly; *Accepts Advertising*; *Editor:* Tommy Allen; *Price:* Free with membership in Nature Manitoba
Profile: Information about Nature Manitoba's meetings & workshops, activities, members, & nature in the news
• Naturescape Manitoba
Type: Book; *Number of Pages:* 200; *Price:* $24.95
Profile: A source book about native planting & water conservation for the Prairies Ecozone of Manitoba

Nature NB
#110, 924 Prospect St., Fredericton NB E3B 2T9
Tel: 506-459-4209; *Fax:* 506-459-4209
nbfn@nb.aibn.com
www.naturenb.ca
www.facebook.com/naturenb
twitter.com/NatureNB
Previous Name: New Brunswick Federation of Naturalists
Overview: A medium-sized provincial charitable organization founded in 1979
Mission: To preserve wildlife & protect its natural habitat; to promote a public interest in & a knowledge of natural history; to promote, encourage & cooperate with organizations & individuals who have similar interests & objectives; to consider matters of environmental concern.
Member of: Nature Canada
Chief Officer(s):
Danielle Smith, Executive Director
Staff Member(s): 4
Membership: *Fees:* $25 individual; $30 family membership; *Member Profile:* Nature clubs

Nature Nova Scotia (Federation of Nova Scotia Naturalists)
c/o Nova Scotia Museum of Natural History, 1747 Summer St., Halifax NS B3H 3A6
Tel: 902-582-7176
doug@fundymud.com
www.naturens.ca
Previous Name: Federation of Nova Scotia Naturalists
Overview: A medium-sized provincial charitable organization founded in 1990
Mission: To support the interests of naturalists clubs; To represent naturalists clubs throughout Nova Scotia
Member of: Nature Conservancy of Canada (NCC); Canadian Parks & Wilderness Society (CPAWS)
Affiliation(s): Nature Canada
Chief Officer(s):
Bob Bancroft, President, 902-386-2501
Sue Abbot, Vice-President, 902-453-0435
Doug Linzey, Secretary, 902-582-7176
Jean Gibson, Treasurer, 902-678-4725
Finances: *Funding Sources:* Donations
Membership: *Fees:* $5 students & seniors; $20 single adults & families; *Member Profile:* Naturalists clubs & organizations within Nova Scotia; Members-at-large
Activities: Providing educational opportunities; Hosting field trips; Conducting research; Serving on committees & advisory boards involving issues that affect the health of the natural environment
Meetings/Conferences: • Nature Nova Scotia 2015 Annual General Meeting & Conference, 2015, NS
Scope: Provincial
Description: A weekend event, with an annual meeting featuring reports on the past year's activities to the membership, plus educational talks & field trips
Contact Information: Treasurer: Jean Gibson Collins, Phone: 902-678-4725, E-mail: ejgibson@ns.sympatico.ca
Publications:
• Nature Nova Scotia Annual Report
Type: Yearbook; *Frequency:* Annually
Profile: A summary of Nature Nova Scotia's yearly activities

Nature Québec
#207, 870, av de Salaberry, Québec QC G1R 2T9
Tél: 418-648-2104; *Téléc:* 418-648-0991
conservons@naturequebec.org
www.naturequebec.org
www.linkedin.com/company/nature-qu-bec?trx=hb_tab_compy_id_2794658
www.facebook.com/naturequebec
twitter.com/NatureQuebec
Nom précédent: Union québécoise pour la conservation de la nature
Aperçu: *Dimension:* moyenne; *Envergure:* provinciale; Organisme sans but lucratif; fondée en 1981
Mission: Regrouper les individus et les sociétés oeuvrant en sciences naturelles et en environnement; maintenir des processus écologiques essentiels; préserver la diversité génétique; utiliser soutenablement des espèces et des écosystèmes
Membre de: Union internationale pour la conservation de la nature
Membre(s) du bureau directeur:
Christian Simard, Directeur général, 418-648-2104 Ext. 2071
christian.simard@naturequebec.org
Finances: *Budget de fonctionnement annuel:* $500,000-$1.5 Million
Membre(s) du personnel: 8
Membre: 120 institutionnel; 5 000 individu; *Montant de la cotisation:* 25$
Activités: *Stagiaires:* Oui; *Service de conférenciers:* Oui

Nature Saskatchewan
#206, 1860 Lorne St., Regina SK S4P 2L7
Tel: 306-780-9273; *Fax:* 306-780-9263
Toll-Free: 800-667-4668
info@naturesask.ca
www.naturesask.ca
www.linkedin.com/pub/nature-sask-gary-seib/38/7b6/39a
www.facebook.com/NatureSask
twitter.com/naturesask
Also Known As: Saskatchewan Natural History Society
Overview: A medium-sized provincial charitable organization founded in 1949
Mission: To foster appreciation & understanding for the natural environment; To document & protect the biological diversity of Saskatchewan; To preserve the natural eco-systems of the province
Chief Officer(s):
Gary Seib, General Manager
gseib@naturesask.ca
Deanna Trowsdale-Mutafov, Manager, Conservation & Education
dtmutafov@naturesask.ca
Melissa Ranalli, Manager, Species at Risk
mranalli@naturesask.ca
Ellen Bouvier, Office Coordinator
rpr@naturesask.ca
Finances: *Annual Operating Budget:* $500,000-$1.5 Million; *Funding Sources:* Membership fees; Donations; Sponsorships
Staff Member(s): 7; 900 volunteer(s)
Membership: 1,000; *Fees:* $15 students; $20 seniors; $25 individuals; $30 families, institutions, & foreign members; $600 lifetime members; *Member Profile:* Naturalists in Saskatchewan
Activities: Conducting research; Providing education; Producing special publications, such as: Ferns & Fern Allies; Lilies, Irises & Orchids; Dragonflies & Damselflies in the Hand; Getting to know Saskatchewan Lichens; *Speaker Service:* Yes; *Library:* Nature Saskatchewan Resource Centre
Awards:
• Volunteer of the Year Award (Award)
• Cliff Shaw Award (Award)
• Fellows Award (Award)
• Larry Morgotch Memorial Award (Award)
• Conservation Award (Award)
Publications:
• Blue Jay
Type: Journal; *Accepts Advertising*; *Editor:* Chris Somers; Vicky Kjoss; *Price:* $25 / year
Profile: Conservation, nature, & scientific research news, plus artwork & poetry

• Nature Views
Type: Newsletter; *Frequency:* Quarterly; *Accepts Advertising*; *Editor:* Robert Warnock; Angela Dohms; *Price:* Free with Nature Saskatchewan membership
Profile: Discussions of environmental issues, contributions from well known naturalists, & forthcoming events

Fort Qu'Appelle Branch
PO Box 294, Balcarres SK S0G 0C0
Tel: 306-334-2862
Chief Officer(s):
Keith Stephens, President

Indian Head Nature Society
PO Box 995, Indian Head SK S0G 2K0
Chief Officer(s):
Lorne Scott, President, 306-695-3524

Kelsey Ecological Society
PO Box 549, Preeceville SK S0A 3B0
Tel: 306-547-2008
Chief Officer(s):
Kathleen Pitt, President
kathleentpitt@icloud.com

Nature Moose Jaw
PO Box 2042, Moose Jaw SK S6H 3G7
Chief Officer(s):
Rod Moran, President, 306-692-4464
moran@sasktel.net

Nature Prince Albert
PO Box 235, Prince Albert SK S6V 5R5
Tel: 306-764-2347
www.natureprincealbert.ca
Chief Officer(s):
Carman Dodge, President
carman.dodge@sasktel.net

Nature Regina
PO Box 291, Regina SK S4P 3A1
Chief Officer(s):
Dale Hjertaas, President
beathiaume@sasktel.net

Saskatoon Nature Society
PO Box 448, RPO University, Saskatoon SK S7N 4J8
Tel: 306-665-1915
www.saskatoonnaturesociety.sk.ca
www.facebook.com/pages/Saskatoon-Nature-Society/323390671033231
Chief Officer(s):
Joan Feather, President, 306-653-3160
jfeather@sasktel.net

Southwest Naturalists
370 - 4th Ave. SE, Swift Current SK S9H 3L8
Tel: 306-778-2775
info@swnaturalists.org
www.swnaturalists.org
Chief Officer(s):
Gerald Handley, President

Weyburn Nature Society
PO Box 131, McTaggart SK S0G 3G0
Chief Officer(s):
Val Thomas, Secretary, 306-842-5005
van_doyle_thomas@hotmail.com

Yellowhead Flyway Birding Trail Association
PO Box 460, Saltcoats SK S0A 4R0
yfbta.com
Chief Officer(s):
Rob Wilson, Secretary

Yorkton Natural History Society
45 Darlinton St. East, Yorkton SK S3N 0C3
Chief Officer(s):
Geoffrey Rushowick, President, 306-783-5898
rushg@sasktel.net

Nature Trust of New Brunswick (NTNB) / Fondation pour la protection des sites naturels du Nouveau-Brunswick
PO Box 603, Stn. A, 404 Queen St., 3rd Fl., Fredericton NB E3B 5A6
Tel: 506-457-2398; *Fax:* 506-450-2137
naturetrust@ntnb.org
www.naturetrust.nb.ca
www.linkedin.com/company/the-nature-trust-of-new-brunswick
www.facebook.com/NatureTrustNB
twitter.com/naturetrustNB
www.youtube.com/user/NatureTrustNB
Overview: A small provincial charitable organization founded in 1987
Mission: To identify, classify & preserve natural areas which are outstanding for their biological, geological or aesthetic value; to foster in the people of New Brunswick an awareness of their natural heritage & to educate persons in connection therewith
Chief Officer(s):
Renata Woodward, Executive Director
Lynn MacKinnon, President
Mike Bonga, Vice-President
Andy Hardie, Treasurer
Finances: *Annual Operating Budget:* $500,000-$1.5 Million; *Funding Sources:* Donations; Government grants; Membership dues
Staff Member(s): 7
Membership: *Fees:* $25 individual; $35 family/group; $75 supporting; $150 sponsoring; $250 donor; $500 benefactor; $10 student; $1000+ corporate; $5000 lifetime; *Committees:* Partnership; Membership; Communications; Nomination

Nature Vancouver
PO Box 3021, Vancouver BC V6B 3X5
Tel: 604-737-3074
info@naturevancouver.ca
www.naturevancouver.ca
Previous Name: Vancouver Natural History Society
Overview: A small local charitable organization founded in 1918
Mission: To promote the enjoyment of nature; to foster public interest & education in appreciation & study of nature; To encourage wise use & conservation of natural resources; To work for complete protection of endangered species & ecosystems; To promote access to & maintenance of natural areas in vicinity of Vancouver
Member of: The Federation of BC Naturalists
Affliation(s): Nature Canada
Finances: *Annual Operating Budget:* $50,000-$100,000; *Funding Sources:* Membership fees
100 volunteer(s)
Membership: 700; *Fees:* $40 individual; $50 family; $20 student; *Committees:* Conservation; Birding; Botany; Marine Biology
Activities: Marsh & bog restoration; bird & plant survey; conservation - briefs, forums & public information meetings; monthly speakers; annual summer camp to allow participants to learn about a special wilderness area in the province
Awards:
• Nature Vancouver Annual Scholarship (Scholarship)
Eligibility: Members or members' families

Naut'sa mawt Resource Group (NRG)
1921 Tsawwassen Dr., Tsawwassen BC V4M 4G2
Tel: 604-943-6712; *Fax:* 604-943-5367
Toll-Free: 888-382-7711
info@nautsamawt.com
www.nautsamawt.com
Previous Name: Naut'sa mawt Tribal Council, The Alliance Tribal Council
Overview: A medium-sized local organization founded in 1975
Mission: To advance the Aboriginal rights, & the concept of Indian self-government; To provide services in the fields of oil & gas, construction, manufacturing, & project management

Naut'sa mawt Tribal Council, The Alliance Tribal Council *See* Naut'sa mawt Resource Group

Naval Club of Toronto
1910 Gerrard St. East, Toronto ON M4L 2C1
Tel: 416-924-2811
info@navalcluboftoronto.com
www.navalcluboftoronto.com
Previous Name: Naval Veterans Association
Overview: A small local organization
Chief Officer(s):
Joeann Coulson, Chief Steward
Michael A. Roger, President
Staff Member(s): 4; 3 volunteer(s)
Membership: *Committees:* Budget & Finance
Publications:
• Telegraph
Type: Newsletter; *Frequency:* Monthly

Naval Museum of Alberta Society (NMAS)
4520 Crowchild Trail SW, Calgary AB T2T 5J4
Tel: 403-974-2807
Previous Name: Tecumseh Historical Society
Overview: A small local charitable organization founded in 1984
Mission: To promote an awareness & understanding of the role played by the Royal Canadian Navy to our country, province & community, with emphasis on naval establishments in Alberta & those HMC ships that were named for cities, towns & communities in the province of Alberta
Member of: Alberta Museums Association; Calgary Convention & Visitors Bureau
Affliation(s): Museum Association of Canada
Chief Officer(s):
Glenn Hardie, President
Terry Thompson, Vice-President
Murray Bialek, General Manager, Naval Museum of Alberta
Finances: *Annual Operating Budget:* $50,000-$100,000; *Funding Sources:* Donations
Staff Member(s): 1; 75 volunteer(s)
Membership: 300; *Fees:* $20; *Member Profile:* Retired military; students & scholars of military history
Activities: Naval Museum of Alberta; *Awareness Events:* Battle of Atlantic Day, May 2; Remembrance Day Service, Nov. 11; *Library:* John Burgess Library; by appointment

The Naval Officers' Association of Canada (NOAC) / L'Association des officiers de la marine du Canada
c/o Ottawa Branch, PO Box 505, Stn. B, Ottawa ON K1P 5P6
Tel: 613-841-4358
noacexdir@msn.com
www.navalassoc.ca
Overview: A medium-sized national organization founded in 1946
Mission: To maintain active interest in the Maritime affairs of Canada; To oversee 15 member branches in major cities from coast to coast & a member branch in Brussels, Belgium
Chief Officer(s):
Jim Carruthers, President
jimc@rruthers.com
Ken Lait, Executive Director
Finances: *Funding Sources:* Membership dues; Grants; Donations
Membership: *Member Profile:* Former career officers & reserve officers who have served in the several components of the Royal Canadian Navy or the Maritime Command of the Canadian Forces
Activities: *Library* by appointment

Naval Veterans Association *See* Naval Club of Toronto

Navy League of Canada / Ligue navale du Canada
66 Lisgar St., Ottawa ON K2P 0C1
Fax: 613-990-8701
Toll-Free: 800-375-6289
Other Communication: national@navyleague.ca
info@navyleague.ca
www.navyleague.ca
twitter.com/NavyLeagueCA
Overview: A large national organization founded in 1895
Mission: To promote an interest in maritime affairs generally throughout Canada; To prepare, publish & disseminate information & encourage debate relating to the role & importance of maritime matters in the interests of Canada; To promote, organize, sponsor, support & encourage the education & training of the youth of the country through Cadet movements & other youth groups with a maritime orientation; To hold conferences, symposia & meetings for the discussion & exchange of views in matters relating to the objects of The League; To raise funds as may be deemed necessary, for the welfare & benefit of seamen, for their dependents & for Seamen's Homes, Hostels & other institutions in Canada, including the establishment, operation & maintenance thereof; To co-operate with any kindred society having either in whole or in part comparable objects to The League
Member of: National Cadet Council
Affliation(s): Conference of Defence Associates; Department of National Defence; The Army Cadet League of Canada; The Air Cadet League of Canada
Chief Officer(s):
Douglas J. Thomas, National Executive Director
dthomas@navyleague.ca
Finances: *Funding Sources:* Donations; government grant
Staff Member(s): 3
Activities: *Library* by appointment
Awards:
• Navy League/RCNBF Scholarships (Scholarship)
Awarded to serving & former Royal Canadian Sea Cadets entering their first year in university or college
• Lockheed Martin Centennial Award (Award)
Awarded to serving & former Royal Canadian Sea Cadets entering their first year in university or college

Meetings/Conferences: • The Navy League of Canada 2015 Annual General Meeting, 2015
Scope: National

Cape Breton
821 Donkin Hwy., Donkin NS B1A 6N9
Tel: 902-737-2257
Chief Officer(s):
Jack Griffin, President
jgriffin@navyleague.ca

Manitoba
c/o HMCS Chippawa, 1 Navy Way, Winnipeg MB R3C 4J7
www.mb.navyleague.ca
Chief Officer(s):
Debra Barrett, President
dbarrett@navyleague.ca

Newfoundland & Labrador
5 Davis Pl., Mount Pearl NL A1N 3W8
Tel: 709-368-5620; *Fax:* 709-758-9709
Chief Officer(s):
Clayton Bailey, President
cbailey@navyleague.ca

Nova Scotia Mainland
c/o Earle Corn, 65 Grennan Dr., Lower Sackville NS B4C 2C4
Tel: 902-864-8156
www.nsmainlanddivision.ca
Chief Officer(s):
Earle Corn, President
ecorn@navyleague.ca

Ontario
#600, 4900 Yonge St., Toronto ON M2N 6B7
Tel: 416-635-2791; *Fax:* 416-635-2794
Toll-Free: 877-635-2791
navyleag@bellnet.ca
www.navyleagueont.ca
www.facebook.com/NLOntDiv
Chief Officer(s):
Gordon King, President
gking@navyleague.ca

Prince Edward Island
c/o Lise Munger, 2474 Fort Augustus, RR#21, Glenfinnan PE C1B 0Z9
Tel: 902-892-4642
Chief Officer(s):
Reg Shields, President
rshields@navyleague.ca
Lise Munger-Perry, Sec.-Treasurer
lmunger@ymail.com

Québec
a/s Jean-Claude Poirier, Unité régionale de soutien aux cadets (est), CP 1000, Succ. Forces, Courcelette QC G0A 4Z0
Tél: 800-681-8180
division@liguenavaleducanada.qc.ca
www.liguenavaleducanada.qc.ca
Chief Officer(s):
Germain Poitras, Président
president@liguenavaleducanada.qc.ca
Jacques Aubrey, Secrétaire
secretaire@liguenavaleducanada.qc.ca

Saskatchewan
1860 Lorne St., Regina SK S4P 2L7
Tel: 306-780-9294
Toll-Free: 877-335-7245
nlcsd@sasktel.net
www.nlcsd.ca
Chief Officer(s):
Marty Mollison, President

Vancouver Island
PO Box 28143, Stn. Canwest, Victoria BC V9B 6K8
www.vidcadets.ca
Chief Officer(s):
Peter Betcher, President
vid.pres@vidcadets.ca
Alex Gelinas, Administration Officer
Island.Admin2@shaw.ca

Nawican Friendship Centre
1320 - 102 Ave., Dawson Creek BC V1G 2C6
Tel: 250-782-5202; *Fax:* 250-782-8411
community@nawican.ca
Overview: A small local organization founded in 1971

Ne'Chee Friendship Centre
PO Box 241, Kenora ON P9N 3X3
Tel: 807-468-5440; *Fax:* 807-468-5340
reception@nechee.org
www.nechee.org
www.facebook.com/nechee.centre
Overview: A small local charitable organization founded in 1976
Member of: Ontario Federation of Indian Friendship Centres; National Association of Friendship Centres
Chief Officer(s):
Patti Fairfield, Executive Director
Staff Member(s): 24
Membership: *Member Profile:* All persons of aboriginal descent

NEC Native Education College Society
Native Education Centre, #220, 285 - 5 Ave. East, Vancouver BC V5T 1H2
Tel: 604-873-3772; *Fax:* 604-873-9152
info@necvancouver.org
www.necvancouver.org
Previous Name: Urban Native Indian Education Society
Overview: A small local organization founded in 1967
Mission: To provide adult Aboriginal students with developmental, vocational, & applied academic programs.
Affliation(s): Vancouver Community College
Chief Officer(s):
Keith Henry, Chair
Finances: *Annual Operating Budget:* $3 Million-$5 Million
Staff Member(s): 40
Membership: 1-99; *Fees:* $2
Activities: *Library:* NEC Library
Awards:
• First Nations Health Careers Bursary Program (Scholarship)
Amount: A limited number of bursaries up to $2,500

Nechi Training, Research & Health Promotions Institute
PO Box 2039, Stn. Main, St. Albert AB T8N 2G3
Tel: 780-459-1884; *Fax:* 780-458-1883
Toll-Free: 800-459-1884
www.nechi.com
Also Known As: Nechi Institute
Overview: A small international charitable organization founded in 1974
Mission: To promote holistic healing & healthy, addictions-free lifestyles
Member of: Canadian Society of Association Executives
Affliation(s): First Nations Adult & Higher Education Consortium
Chief Officer(s):
Geraldine Potts, Director, Operations
Staff Member(s): 7
Activities: Training; Aboriginal population health research; health promotions; *Internships:* Yes; *Library:* Aboriginal Resource Centre; Open to public

Neepawa & District Chamber of Commerce
PO Box 726, 282 Hamilton St., Neepawa MB R0J 1H0
Tel: 204-476-5292; *Fax:* 204-476-5231
info@neepawachamber.com
www.neepawachamber.com
Overview: A small local organization founded in 1900
Mission: To promote Neepawa Manitoba & the surrounding area
Member of: Yellowhead Highway Association; Manitoba Chamber of Commerce; Canadian Chamber of Commerce
Chief Officer(s):
Dean Dietrich Vice, President
Michelle Gerrard, President
Finances: *Funding Sources:* Membership dues; Projects; Grants
Staff Member(s): 1; 30 volunteer(s)
Membership: 115; *Fees:* $40 - $250; *Member Profile:* Business owners; *Committees:* Business & Membership Services; Events & Promotions; Tourism; Lobbying

Neepawa & District United Way
PO Box 1545, Neepawa MB R0J 1H0
Tel: 204-476-3410
unitedwayneepawa@mymts.net
www.neepawaunitedway.org
Overview: A small local organization overseen by United Way of Canada - Centraide Canada
Mission: Local United Way Chapter raising funds to help community organization.

Neginuk Friendship Centre *See* Kikinahk Friendship Centre

Neighbourhood Centre
c/o Secord Community Centre, 91 Barrington Ave., Toronto ON M4C 4Y9
Tel: 416-698-1626; *Fax:* 416-698-6718
info@neighbourhoodcentre.org
neighbourhoodcentre.org
Overview: A small local organization overseen by InformOntario
Mission: The Neighbourhood Centre is a community place for inquiry and dialogue as well as the Taylor-Massey's community information and referral centre.
Chief Officer(s):
Lorna Schwartzentruber, Executive Director

Neighbourhood Information Post (NIP)
269 Gerrard St. East, 2nd Fl., Toronto ON M5A 2G3
Tel: 416-924-2543; *Fax:* 416-924-4748
nipost@nipost.org
www.nipost.org
twitter.com/nip_toronto
Overview: A small local organization founded in 1970
Mission: Non-profit community help centre established to provide information, assistance & support to all persons in order to improve the quality of individual & community life; serves the eastern area of the City of Toronto
Member of: Association of Community Information Centres in Ontario
Affiliation(s): Advocacy Centre for Tenants Ontario; African Women
Finances: *Funding Sources:* Municipal, provincial & federal government; United Way
Activities: Toronto Rent Bank program; Energy Assistance programs; Community outreach & education; Crisis intervention; Housing Trusteeship program; Immigrant women's support group; Income tax clinic; Self-help drop in; Senior activities

Neighbourhood Pharmacy Association of Canada
#301, 45 Sheppard Ave. East, Toronto ON M2N 5W9
Tel: 416-226-9100; *Fax:* 416-226-9185
info@neighbourhoodpharmacies.ca
www.cacds.com
Overview: A small national organization founded in 1995
Mission: Neighbourhood Pharmacy Association of Canada strives to ensure a strong chain drug store sector access to high quality products & health care services to Canadians.
Chief Officer(s):
Denise Carpenter, President/CEO
Vivek Sood, Chair
Finances: *Funding Sources:* Membership dues; programs
Membership: *Member Profile:* Retail members include chain drug stores, grocery chains, & mass merchandisers with pharmacies. Associate members include suppliers & service providers to the retail pharmacy industry.
Activities: Promoting the role & value of chain pharmacies & their pharmacists; Communicating issues to governments & regulators; Working with suppliers to increase consumer satisfaction; Providing information to members about industry issues; *Library:* Neighbourhood Pharmacy Association of Canada Documentation Centre
Publications:
• CACDS [Canadian Association of Chain Drug Stores] News Bulletin
Type: Newsletter; *Frequency:* Weekly
Profile: CACDS achievements, member news, & national industry issues
• State of the Industry Report [a publication of the Canadian Association of Chain Drug Stores]
Type: Yearbook; *Frequency:* Annually; *Price:* $80.25 members; $215 non-members
Profile: Report on community pharmacy trends in Canada

The Neighbouring Rights Collective of Canada *See* Re:Sound

The Neil Squire Foundation (NSF)
#220, 2250 Boundary Rd., Burnaby BC V5M 4L9
Tel: 604-473-9363; *Fax:* 604-473-9364
Toll-Free: 877-673-4636
info@neilsquire.ca
www.neilsquire.ca
twitter.com/NeilSquireSoc
Overview: A medium-sized national organization founded in 1984
Mission: To respond to the needs of individuals who have significant physical disabilities; to research & develop appropriate innovative technology & services; to create opportunities for greater independence in all aspects of life
Chief Officer(s):

Greg Pyc, Western Regional Manager
gregp@neilsquire.ca
Gary Birch, Executive Director
garyb@neilsquire.ca
Finances: *Annual Operating Budget:* $3 Million-$5 Million; *Funding Sources:* National government; provincial government
Staff Member(s): 38; 125 volunteer(s)
Membership: 45 individual; *Fees:* $5

Atlantic Regional Office
#104, 440 Wilsey Rd., Fredericton NB E3B 7G5
Tel: 506-450-7999; *Fax:* 506-453-9681
Toll-Free: 866-446-7999
nb.info@neilsquire.ca
Chief Officer(s):
Diana Hall, Regional Manager
dianah@neilsquire.ca

Central Regional Office
#150, 34 Colonnade Rd., Ottawa ON K2E 7J6
Tel: 613-723-3575; *Fax:* 613-723-3579
on.info@neilsquire.ca
Chief Officer(s):
Cheryl Comer, Regional Manager
cherylc@neilsquire.ca

Prairie Regional Office
#100, 2445 - 13th Ave., Regina SK S4P 0W1
Tel: 306-781-6023; *Fax:* 306-522-9474
sk.info@neilsquire.ca
Chief Officer(s):
Nikki Langdon, Regional Manager
nikkil@neilsquire.ca

Nellie's Shelter
PO Box 98118, 970 Queen St. East, Toronto ON M4M 1J0
Tel: 416-461-8903; *Fax:* 416-461-0970; *Crisis Hot-Line:* 416-461-1084
community@nellies.org
www.nellies.org
www.facebook.com/nelliesshelter
twitter.com/nelliesshelter
www.youtube.com/nelliesshelter
Overview: A small local charitable organization founded in 1974
Mission: To advocate for social justice for all women & children.
Chief Officer(s):
Zahra Mohamed, President
Margarita Mendez, Executive Director, 416-461-9849, Fax: 416-461-0970
margarita@nellies.org
Finances: *Annual Operating Budget:* $500,000-$1.5 Million; *Funding Sources:* Ministry of Community and Social Services; City of Toronto; Canada Mortgage & Housing Corporation; United Way; Donations
Membership: *Member Profile:* Women over age 16 & community organizations

Outreach Office
754 Queen St. East, Toronto ON M4M 1H4
Tel: 416-461-3404
Chief Officer(s):
Margarita Mendez, Executive Director

Nelson & District Arts Council (NDAC)
PO Box 422, Nelson BC V1L 5R2
Tel: 250-352-2402; *Fax:* 250-352-2405
ndac@direct.ca
ndac.ca
www.facebook.com/NelsonDistrictArtsCouncil
Overview: A small local organization founded in 1969
Mission: To stimulate & encourage the development of cultural pride & activities; to render service to all participatory groups; to foster interest & pride in the cultural heritage of the district; to bring to the attention of governments the cultural needs of the district
Member of: Assembly of BC Arts Councils; BC Arts Council
Affliation(s): West Kootenay Regional Arts Council; Columbia Kootenay Cultural Alliance
Chief Officer(s):
Pat Henman, Executive Director
Ron Robinson, President
Finances: *Annual Operating Budget:* Less than $50,000
Staff Member(s): 1; 20 volunteer(s)
Membership: 20 groups + 3 individual + 3 associate; *Fees:* $25 group; $10 individual; *Member Profile:* Community art, cultural, heritage groups; *Committees:* Artwalk; Nelson Public Art Gallery Committee; Museum
Activities: Artwalk & Community Arts of all Disciplines Event

Nelson & District Chamber of Commerce
255 Hall St., Nelson BC V1L 5X4
Tel: 250-352-3433; *Fax:* 250-352-6355
Toll-Free: 877-663-5706
info@discovernelson.com
www.discovernelson.com
Overview: A small local organization founded in 1893
Mission: To promote & improve trade & commerce & the economic, civic & social welfare of the City of Nelson & the surrounding districts; to support & advance the interests of its members in local, provincial & national issues
Affliation(s): British Columbia Chamber of Commerce; Canadian Chamber of Commerce
Chief Officer(s):
Cal Renwick, President
Finances: *Annual Operating Budget:* $100,000-$250,000
Staff Member(s): 3
Membership: 460; *Fees:* $130 regular; $82 associate/non-profit; $56 private citizen; $36 senior/student; *Committees:* Tourism; Resource; Economic Development; Education; Health
Activities: Canada Day at Lakeside Park; *Library* Open to public

Nelson & District Hospice Society
PO Box 194, Nelson BC V1L 5P9
Tel: 250-352-2337; *Fax:* 250-227-9017
nelsonhospice@netidea.com
www.nelsonhospice.org
Overview: A small local charitable organization
Mission: To offer hospice & palliative care in the Nelson & District region
Chief Officer(s):
Jane DiGiacomo, Executive Director

Nelson & District Museum, Archives, Art Gallery & Historical Society
502 Vernon St., Nelson BC V1L 4E7
Tel: 250-352-9813; *Fax:* 250-352-9810
info@touchstonesnelson.ca
www.touchstonesnelson.ca
www.facebook.com/62908084663
www.flickr.com/photos/touchstonesnelson
Also Known As: Nelson Museum
Previous Name: Kootenay Museum Association & Historical Society
Overview: A small local charitable organization founded in 1955
Mission: To operate a community museum, archives, & public art gallery for Nelson & area
Member of: BC Museums Association; BC Historical Federation; Nelson & District Arts Council; Archives Association of BC; Heritage Federation of South Eastern BC
Affliation(s): Canadian Museum Association; Nelson & District Chamber of Commerce
Chief Officer(s):
R. Donald Lyon, President
Finances: *Funding Sources:* Municipal & provincial government; donations; fundraising
Staff Member(s): 6
Membership: *Fees:* Schedule available
Activities: Art Gallery exhibitions; Historical exhibits; Public programs; *Library:* Nelson Museum Archives; Open to public

Nelson & District United Way
PO Box 89, Nelson BC V1L 5P7
Tel: 250-352-6012
united_way@netidea.com
www.uw.kics.bc.ca
Overview: A small local organization overseen by United Way of Canada - Centraide Canada
Mission: Local chapter of the United Way raising funds for community organizations.
Chief Officer(s):
Carol-Joy Kaill, President

The Neocatechumenal Way
Tel: 905-951-2155
neocatechumenalcanada@gmail.com
www.camminoneocatecumenale.it
Overview: A small international charitable organization founded in 1964
Mission: To assist the church to renew herself in response to Vatican II, The Neocatechumenal Way started during the Second Vatican Council; To send missionaries from all parts of the world to evanglize & to be a Christian presence; To gift the Church with Redemptoris Mater Seminaries
Chief Officer(s):
Mario De Marchi, Contact
Finances: *Funding Sources:* Donations
Membership: *Member Profile:* Members are Christian baptized adults; The charism of the Neocatechumenal Way is the rediscovery of the gift of Christian baptism through an itinerary of Christian formation; Everyone may freely participate in the catecheses, especially the following groups: Those who have drifted away from the Church; Persons who have not been sufficiently evangelized; Individuals who wish to deepen & mature their faith; & Those who come from Christian denoninations not in full communion with the Catholic Church; The Neocatechumenal Way is represented in more than 100 countries around the world
Activities: Implementing The Neocatechumenal Way in Dioceses at request of the local Ordinary; Operating under the direction of the local Ordinary with the help & guidance of an international team, a national team, the parish priest, & the community Responsibles; Counselling; Offering programs for couples, seniors, singles, & youth; Providing faith instruction; Offering prayer groups; Presenting catecheses in parishes at the request of pastors; Giving a series of catecheses in parishes during Advent & Lent

Nepisiguit Salmon Association (NSA) / L'Association du saumon Nepisiguit
789 Riverside Dr., Bathurst NB E2A 2M8
Tel: 506-546-5279
nsa@nbnet.nb.ca
Overview: A small local organization founded in 1976
Mission: To enhance & preserve Atlantic Salmon in general & in the Nepisiguit river in particular; to educate the public as to the value of this unique, renewable, natural resource
Member of: Atlantic Salmon Federation
Affliation(s): New Brunswick Salmon Council; Nepisiguit Watershed Management Committee
Chief Officer(s):
Bob Baker, President
Finances: *Funding Sources:* Donations; Grants; Programs; Fundraising
Membership: *Member Profile:* Anglers & those interested in salmon conservation
Activities: Salmon enchancement program

Neptune Theatre Foundation
1593 Argyle St., Halifax NS B3J 2B2
Tel: 902-429-7300; *Fax:* 902-429-1211
Toll-Free: 800-565-7345
info@neptunetheatre.com
www.neptunetheatre.com
www.facebook.com/neptunetheatre
twitter.com/NeptuneTheatre
www.youtube.com/user/NeptuneHFX
Overview: A small local charitable organization founded in 1962
Mission: To pursue theatrical excellence with artistic vision; to develop local & Canadian artistic talent; to encourage the youth of our community to develop a life-long interest in live theatre
Chief Officer(s):
Amy Melmock, General Manager
George Pothitos, Artistic Director
Finances: *Funding Sources:* Box office revenue; fundraising; government
Staff Member(s): 19

Netball Alberta
PO Box 270, 7620 Elbow Dr. SW, Calgary AB T2V 1K2
Tel: 403-238-8041; *Fax:* 888-213-9218
contact@netballalberta.com
www.netballalberta.com
www.facebook.com/groups/2223869141
Previous Name: Alberta Netball Association
Overview: A small provincial charitable organization founded in 1992 overseen by Netball Canada
Mission: To promote & encourage the sport of netball in Alberta; to facilitate exchange of information & ideas; to promote education & development; to sponsor clinics & classes; to collect & distribute information; to raise funds for the Association; to organize & conduct competitions
Member of: Netball Canada
Affliation(s): International Federation of Netball Associations
Chief Officer(s):
Lucy Spence, President
president@netballalberta.com
Finances: *Annual Operating Budget:* Less than $50,000; *Funding Sources:* Fundraising
10 volunteer(s)
Membership: 350

Netball Canada
AB

e-mail: netballcanada@gmail.com
netballcanada.ca
www.facebook.com/netballcanada
Overview: A small national organization founded in 1976
Mission: To be the national governing body for netball throughout Canada
Affliation(s): International Federation of Netball Associations
Membership: 4 provincial associations

Netball Ontario
PO Box 172, 3 Concorde Gate, Toronto ON M3C 3N7
Tel: 416-765-2040
info@netballontario.com
www.netballontario.com
Previous Name: Ontario Amateur Netball Association
Overview: A small provincial organization founded in 1974 overseen by Netball Canada
Mission: To promote & develop the sport of netball in Ontario.
Member of: Netball Canada
Affliation(s): International Federation of Netball Associations

Netherlands Business & Professional Association *See* Canadian Netherlands Business & Professional Association Inc.

Network of French Speaking Women of South Ontario *Voir* Réseau des femmes du sud de l'Ontario

The Network: Interaction for Conflict Resolution *See* Conflict Resolution Network Canada

Neurofibromatosis Association of Saskatchewan
450 Kirkpatrick Ct., Saskatoon SK S7L 6Z3
Tel: 306-384-3540
Also Known As: NF Association of Saskatchewan
Overview: A small provincial charitable organization founded in 1985
Affliation(s): National NF Foundation
Finances: *Funding Sources:* Membership fees; Donations

Neurofibromatosis Society of Ontario (NFSO)
2004 Underhill Ct., Pickering ON L1X 2M6
Tel: 905-683-0811
Toll-Free: 866-843-6376
info@nfon.ca
www.nfon.ca
www.facebook.com/NFOntario
Also Known As: NF Society of Ontario
Overview: A small provincial charitable organization founded in 1985
Mission: To be a source of information; develop a participating membership; increase public awareness
Affliation(s): National NF Foundation
Chief Officer(s):
Angela Bobbett, President
a.bobbett@nfon.ca
Membership: *Fees:* $25
Activities: Support of NF research; educate members, professionals & public; support affected people

Neurolodical Centre & Children's Centre for Ability; Vancouver Neurological Association *See* British Columbia Centre for Ability

Neurological Health Charities Canada (NHCC)
#316, 4211 Yonge St., Toronto ON M2P 2A9
Tel: 416-227-9700; *Fax:* 416-227-9600
Toll-Free: 800-565-3000
info@mybrainmatters.ca
www.mybrainmatters.ca
www.facebook.com/MyBrainMatters
twitter.com/MyBrainMatters
www.youtube.com/MyBrainMatters
Overview: A large national charitable organization
Mission: To improve quality of life for persons with chronic brain conditions & their caregivers; To increase awareness in the government about neurological issues; To support research
Membership: *Member Profile:* Organizations that relate to neurological conditions
Publications:
• Brain Matters
Type: Newsletter; *Frequency:* s-a.; *Editor:* Stacey Thompson, contact

New Apostolic Church Canada
319 Bridgeport Rd. East, Waterloo ON N2J 2K9
Tel: 519-884-2862
Toll-Free: 866-622-7828
info@naccanada.org
www.newapostolicchurch.com
Overview: A medium-sized international organization
Mission: The New Apostolic Church comprises a world-wide community of Christian worshippers that are growing into the future together. We take a balanced approach to our bible-based faith and enjoy life and the many benefits that come from faith, family and friendship.
Member of: New Apostolic Church (International)
Chief Officer(s):
E. Wagner, President
T. Witt, Treasurer
Membership: 4,283,287 internationally

New Beginnings Association of Southern Alberta
2006 - 37 St. South, Lethbridge AB T1K 3T9
Tel: 403-328-6530; *Fax:* 403-394-0788
newbeginleth@shaw.ca
Overview: A small local organization
Mission: Social isolation prevention program for handicapped adults
Finances: *Funding Sources:* Provincial government

New Beginnings for Youth (NBFY)
93 O'Connor St., Ottawa ON K1P 5M8
Tel: 613-236-1656
mail@nbfy.com
www.nbfy.com
Overview: A small local organization founded in 1986
Finances: *Funding Sources:* Donations
Activities: Variety of programs that encourage life-long learning outside of the traditional classroom, including: The Roasted Cherry, Java Journey, The Can, & Passport

New Boundaries
79 Centennial Dr., Windsor NS B0N 2T0
Tel: 902-798-5160; *Fax:* 902-798-5036
new.boundaries@live.ca
newboundaries.org
Overview: A small local organization
Mission: To provide programs & work experience for mentally challenged adults
Chief Officer(s):
Doug Fraser, Chair
Cindy Carruthers, Executive Director
Activities: General contracts; cleaning; sorting; woodworking; community employment; Amigos second-hand clothing store
Publications:
• New Boundaries E-newsletter
Type: Newsletter

New Brunswick & Prince Edward Island Independent Adjusters' Association
c/o Luc Aucoin, Plant Hope Adjusters Ltd., 85 Englehart St., Dieppe NB E1A 8K2
www.ciaa-adjusters.ca
Overview: A small provincial organization overseen by Canadian Independent Adjusters' Association
Member of: Canadian Independent Adjusters' Association
Chief Officer(s):
Luc Aucoin, President, 506-853-8500, Fax: 506-853-8501
laucoin@planthope.com

New Brunswick Aboriginal Peoples Council (NBAPC)
320 St. Mary's St., Fredericton NB E3A 2S4
Tel: 506-458-8422; *Fax:* 506-451-6130
Toll-Free: 800-442-9789
www.nbapc.org
Overview: A medium-sized provincial organization founded in 1972 overseen by Congress of Aboriginal Peoples
Mission: To represent Status & Non-status First Nations who reside in New Brunswick
Chief Officer(s):
Wendy Wetteland, Chief & President
chief@nbapc.org
Carol LaBillios-Slocum, Executive Director
executivedirector@nbapc.org
Finances: *Funding Sources:* Secretary of State; federal & provincial government
Staff Member(s): 15
Membership: *Member Profile:* Aboriginal ancestry
Activities: Aboriginal & Treat Rights; Aboriginal Human Resources Development Strategy; Aboriginal Fishery Strategy; Aboriginal Seafood Network; Community Diabetes Education & Prevention; Skigin-Elnoog Housing Corp.; Educational Assistance Program; Environmental & Health programs; youth; Wabanaki; employment; Aboriginal Sport Authority;

New Brunswick Aboriginal Women's Council
29 Big Cove Rd., Elsipogtog NB E4W 2S5
Tel: 506-523-9518; *Fax:* 506-523-8350
Previous Name: New Brunswick Native Indian Women's Council
Overview: A medium-sized provincial organization overseen by Native Women's Association of Canada
Chief Officer(s):
Mary Jane Peters, President
Membership: *Fees:* $5

New Brunswick Aerospace & Defence Association (NBADA)
1630 Rte. 940, Centre Village NB E4L 1Y6
Tel: 506-878-3348
www.nbada.ca
Overview: A small provincial organization
Mission: To raise customer awareness of the services, products, & expertise provided by the New Brunswick aerospace, defence, & security sector; To develop the aerospace, defence, & security industry
Chief Officer(s):
Terry Malley, Chair & President
Kelly Ashfield, Treasurer
Peter Hess, Managing Director
peter.hess@nbada.ca
Membership: *Fees:* Schedule available based on number of employees; *Member Profile:* Organizations in New Brunswick which supply technology & components to the aerospace, defence, & security sectors

New Brunswick African Association Inc.
NB
nbaa.ca
Overview: A small provincial organization
Mission: To support the African community in New Brunswick
Chief Officer(s):
Andrew Gbongbor, President
sagyfly@yahoo.ca

New Brunswick Amateur Hockey Association *See* Hockey New Brunswick

New Brunswick Arts Council Inc. *See* Performing Arts NB, Inc.

New Brunswick Association for Community Living (NBACL) / Association du Nouveau-Brunswick pour l'intégration communautaire
800 Hanwell Rd., Fredericton NB E3B 2R7
Tel: 506-453-4400; *Fax:* 506-453-4422
Toll-Free: 866-622-2548
nbacl@nbnet.nb.ca
www.nbacl.nb.ca
www.facebook.com/nbacl
twitter.com/nbacl
www.youtube.com/communitylivingnb
Overview: A medium-sized provincial organization founded in 1957 overseen by Canadian Association for Community Living
Mission: To promote the welfare of people with handicaps & their families; To lobby for developmentally disabled people in New Brunswick; To ensure that every person in New Brunswick has access to supports to live with dignity & participate in the community of his/her choice
Member of: Canadian Association for Community Living
Chief Officer(s):
Krista Carr, Executive Director
execdirector@nbacl.nb.ca
Jason Carr, Director, Strategic Initiatives
jcarr@nbacl.nb.ca
Tammy Gallant, Director, Finance, Human Resources, & Administration
tammy@nbacl.nb.ca
Christy McLean, Manager, Communications
cmclean@nbacl.nb.ca
Shana Soucy, Manager, Inclusive Education
ssoucy@nbacl.nb.ca
Finances: *Funding Sources:* Fundraising
800 volunteer(s)
Membership: 26 branches + 2 associate
Activities: *Speaker Service:* Yes

New Brunswick Association of Community Business Development Corporations / L'Association des CBDC du Nouveau-Brunswick
Place Harbourview, PO Box 5, #212-R, 275 Main St., Bathurst NB E2A 1A9
Tel: 506-548-2406; *Fax:* 506-546-2661
Toll-Free: 888-303-2232
www.cbdc.ca/nb
www.facebook.com/AACBDC
twitter.com/CBDCatlantic
www.youtube.com/user/AtlanticCBDCs
Also Known As: New Brunswick Association of CBDCs
Overview: A medium-sized provincial organization
Mission: To assist entrepreneurs in New Brunswick's rural communities to access capital & other business resources
Chief Officer(s):
Line Doiron, Executive Director
line.doiron@cbdc.ca
Membership: *Member Profile:* Not-for-profit organizations from local business communities which strive to improve the economic viability of their areas
Activities: Reviewing business plans; Working with entrepreneurs who experience difficulty securing capital from traditional sources; Providing term loans to businesses; Monitoring progress of clients; Counselling clients; Offering training opportunities
Publications:
• New Brunswick Association of Community Business Development Corporations Annual Report
Type: Yearbook; *Frequency:* Annually

New Brunswick Association of Dietitians (NBAD) / Association des diététistes du Nouveau-Brunswick (ADNB)
530 Main St., Woodstock NB E7M 2C3
Tel: 506-324-9396; *Fax:* 506-328-2686
registrar@adnb-nbad.com
www.adnb-nbad.com
Overview: A medium-sized provincial licensing organization overseen by Dietitians of Canada
Mission: To regulate the practice of dietitians within New Brunswick
Chief Officer(s):
Jensen Thomas, President
Finances: *Annual Operating Budget:* Less than $50,000
Membership: 225; *Fees:* $250
Activities: *Awareness Events:* Nutrition Month, March

New Brunswick Association of Family Resource Centres (NBAFRC)
c/o Fredericton Regional Family Resource Centre, 60 Veteran's Dr., Fredericton NB E3A 4C3
Tel: 506-474-0252
info@frc-crf.com
www.frc-crf.com/
Overview: A medium-sized provincial organization
Mission: To promote child development & parent-child communication & bonding in New Brunswick's families; To increase awareness of issues encountered by New Brunswick families with children in the range of 0 to 6 years of age; To support family resource centres throughout New Brunswick; To sustain high standards for family resource centre employees
Chief Officer(s):
Anna Marie Hayes, Chair
Josée Arsenault, Vice-Chair
Susan Eblemton, Treasurer
Linda Floyd-Sadler, Secretary
Finances: *Funding Sources:* Community Action Program for Children (CAPC)
Membership: 13; *Member Profile:* Family resource centres operating in New Brunswick
Activities: Developing & coordinating policies for family resource centres in New Brunswick; Engaging in advocacy activities at the municipal, provincial, & federal levels of government; Offering programs & activities for parents & children, such as support groups & parent education; Promoting family literacy; Increasing public awareness of child development & safety; Partnering with other education & health organizations in New Brunswick, such as Healthy Baby & Me; Enabling networking opportunities for family resource centres; *Library:* Toy & Resource Lending Libraries; Open to public

New Brunswick Association of Food Banks (NBAFB) / Association des banques alimentaires du Nouveau-Brunswick (ABANB)
4270, Rte. 102, Lower Kingsclear NB E3E 1L3
Tel: 506-363-4217; *Fax:* 506-473-6883
www.foodbanksnb.com
Previous Name: Association of Food Banks & CVAs for New Brunswick
Overview: A medium-sized provincial charitable organization founded in 1989
Mission: To support member agencies in their efforts to alleviate hunger; to serve as a provincial voice for same
Member of: Canadian Association of Food Banks
Chief Officer(s):
George Piers, President
Stéphane Bourgoin, Vice-President
Finances: *Annual Operating Budget:* Less than $50,000
15 volunteer(s)
Membership: 47; *Fees:* $35
Activities: *Speaker Service:* Yes

New Brunswick Association of Insolvency & Restructuring Professionals (NBAIRP)
c/o Grant Thornton Poirier Limited, #401, 133 Prince William St., Saint John NB E2L 2B5
Tel: 506-643-1727
Overview: A small provincial organization overseen by Canadian Association of Insolvency & Restructuring Professionals
Member of: Canadian Association of Insolvency & Restructuring Professionals
Chief Officer(s):
Matthew Munro, President
matthew.munro@ca.gt.com

New Brunswick Association of Medical Radiation Technologists (NBAMRT)
Memramcook Institute, #129, 488, rue Centrale, Memramcook NB E4K 3S6
Tel: 506-758-9673
www.nbamrt.ca
Previous Name: New Brunswick Association of Radiation Technologists; Canadian Association of Medical Radiation Technologists - New Brunswick
Overview: A small provincial organization founded in 1957 overseen by Canadian Association of Medical Radiation Technologists
Mission: To register medical radiation techologists in New Brunswick
Chief Officer(s):
Melanie Roybedy, Registrar
Membership: *Member Profile:* Technologists from New Brunswick who operate radiographic & radiation therapy equipment to administer radiation treatment & to produce images of the body for diagnosis & treatment of injury & disease
Activities: Offering educational opportunities

New Brunswick Association of Naturopathic Doctors (NBAND)
c/o Crystal Charest, 2278 King George Hwy., Miramichi NB E1V 6N6
Tel: 506-773-3700; *Fax:* 506-773-3704
www.nband.ca
twitter.com/NewBrunswickNDs
Overview: A small provincial organization overseen by The Canadian Association of Naturopathic Doctors
Mission: To educate the public on the philosophies and values of Naturopathic Medicine and to promote the profession within the province.
Chief Officer(s):
Martin Gleixner, President
monctonnaturopathic@gmail.com
Membership: 15; *Fees:* $100 Associated Practitioner; $250 First Year Member; $500 Active Full Member; *Member Profile:* Naturopathic doctors

New Brunswick Association of Nursing Homes, Inc. (NBANH) / Association des foyers de soins du Nouveau-Brunswick, inc. (AFSNB)
#206, 1113 Regent St., Fredericton NB E3B 3Z2
Tel: 506-460-6262; *Fax:* 506-460-6253
www.nbanh.com
www.facebook.com/group.php?gid=157312207644040
twitter.com/NBANH_AFSNB
Overview: A medium-sized provincial organization founded in 1972 overseen by Canadian Alliance for Long Term Care
Mission: To assist members in the provision of quality & efficient care to their residents
Member of: Canadian Alliance for Long Term Care
Chief Officer(s):
Brian Harris, President
Michael Keating, Executive Director
mkeating@nbanh.com
Ken McGeorge, Treasurer
Finances: *Funding Sources:* Membership dues
Membership: 1-99; *Member Profile:* Licensed nursing homes in New Brunswick; *Committees:* Executive; By-Laws; Resolution; Annual Conference Planning; Personnel; Awards; Employee Benefits Advisory; Negotiating Team; Provincial Labour Management; Education; RIM User; Clinical Care; Scheduling System; Cost Efficiency; Joint Steering Planning; Association New Premise; Association Name & Mission
Activities: *Awareness Events:* Nursing Home Week, June; *Library:* Resource Centre

New Brunswick Association of Occupational Therapists (NBAOT) / Association des ergothérapeutes du Nouveau-Brunswick
PO Box 184, Stn. A, Fredericton NB E3B 4Y9
Tel: 506-458-1001; *Fax:* 506-364-8464
info@nbaot.org
nbaot.org
Overview: A small provincial licensing organization founded in 1967
Mission: To license & to provide professional support to occupational therapists in New Brunswick
Member of: Canadian Association of Occupational Therapists
Chief Officer(s):
Catherine Pente, Registrar, 506-536-4394, Fax: 888-896-2299
registrar@nbaot.org
Ellen Snider, Executive Director
executivedirector@nbaot.org
Finances: *Funding Sources:* Membership fees
Staff Member(s): 3
Membership: 367; *Fees:* $350; *Committees:* Awards; Archives; Public Relations; Clinical Practice; ErgOTour; Professioal Development; Registration; Complaints; Discipline/Appeals
Activities: *Awareness Events:* OT Week, Oct.; *Internships:* Yes; *Rents Mailing List:* Yes
Awards:
• Evelyn Fleiger Award (Award)

New Brunswick Association of Optometrists (NBAO) / Association des optométristes du Nouveau-Brunswick
#1, 490 Gibson St., Fredericton NB E3A 4E9
Tel: 506-458-8759; *Fax:* 506-450-1271
nbao@nbnet.nb.ca
www.nbao.ca
Overview: A medium-sized provincial organization overseen by Canadian Association of Optometrists
Mission: To represent Doctors of Optometry in New Brunswick
Chief Officer(s):
Krista McDevitt, President
Membership: *Member Profile:* Passed provincial board exams; graduate of recognized school of optometry; *Committees:* Complaints; Discipline; Professional Enhancement; Negotiating; Political Action
Activities: *Speaker Service:* Yes

New Brunswick Association of Radiation Technologists; Canadian Association of Medical Radiation Technologists - New Brunswick *See* New Brunswick Association of Medical Radiation Technologists

New Brunswick Association of Real Estate Appraisers (NBAREA) / Association des évaluateurs immobiliers du Nouveau-Brunswick (AEIN-B)
#204, 403 Regent St., Fredericton NB E3B 3X6
Tel: 506-450-2016; *Fax:* 506-450-3010
nbarea@nb.aibn.com
www.nbarea.org
Overview: A medium-sized provincial licensing organization founded in 1995 overseen by Appraisal Institute of Canada
Mission: To enhance the profession & to protect the public
Chief Officer(s):
Andrew Leech, President
Finances: *Funding Sources:* Membership dues
Membership: 188; *Committees:* Exxaminers; Education; Discipline; Complaints; Nominations Election & Special Awards; Political Action; Standards; Membership & Public Relations
Activities: Education; government lobbying; *Internships:* Yes; *Speaker Service:* Yes

The New Brunswick Association of Respiratory Therapists Inc. (NBART) / L'Association des thérapeutes respiratoires du Nouveau-Brunswick inc. (ATRNB)
500 St. George St., Moncton NB E1C 1Y3
Tel: 506-389-7813; *Fax:* 506-389-7814
Toll-Free: 877-334-1851
info@nbart.ca
www.nbart.ca
Overview: A medium-sized provincial organization founded in 1984 overseen by Canadian Society of Respiratory Therapists
Mission: To protect the public by ensuring that the respiratory therapists practicing in the province of New Brunswick deliver safe & ethical care
Chief Officer(s):
Seana Martin, President
president@nbart.ca
Troy Denton, Registrar & Executive Director
registrar@nbart.ca
Finances: *Annual Operating Budget:* Less than $50,000; *Funding Sources:* Membership dues
Staff Member(s): 1; 7 volunteer(s)
Membership: 400; *Fees:* $450; *Committees:* Complaints; Discipline; Fitness to Practice
Meetings/Conferences: • Atlantic Respirology & Critical Care 2015 27th Annual Conference, 2015
Scope: Provincial
Description: A meeting of respiratory therapists, respirologists, intensivists, nurses, & educators from the Atlantic provinces, who are interested in the advancements in respirology & critical care
Contact Information: E-mail: info@nbart.ca
Publications:
• New Brunswick Association of Respiratory Therapists Membership Registry
Type: Directory
Profile: A listing of active, associate, & student members

New Brunswick Association of Social Workers (NBASW) / Association des travailleurs sociaux du Nouveau-Brunswick
PO Box 1533, Stn. A, Fredericton NB E3B 5G2
Tel: 506-459-5595; *Fax:* 506-457-1421
Toll-Free: 877-495-5595
nbasw@nbasw-atsnb.ca
www.nbasw-atsnb.ca
Overview: A medium-sized provincial licensing organization founded in 1965
Mission: To regulate the profession of social work; to protect the public; To set standards; To promote the profession
Member of: Canadian Association of Social Workers; Association of Social Work Boards
Chief Officer(s):
Miguel LeBlanc, Executive Director, 506-472-6148
mleblanc@nbasw-atsnb.ca
Finances: *Funding Sources:* Membership dues
Staff Member(s): 4
Membership: 1,600; *Fees:* $60 regular; $30 student; *Committees:* Examiners; Complaints; Discipline; Educaton; Social Action; By-Laws; Practice Issues, Ethics & Professional Standards; Scope of Practice

New Brunswick Association of Speech-Language Pathologists & Audiologists (NBASLPA) / Association des orthophonistes et des audiologistes du Nouveau-Brunswick
147 Ellerdale Ave., Moncton NB E1A 3M8
Tel: 506-858-1788; *Fax:* 506-854-0343
Toll-Free: 877-751-5511
nbaslpa@nb.aibn.com
www.communicationnb.ca
Previous Name: New Brunswick Speech & Hearing Association
Overview: A small provincial licensing organization founded in 1976
Mission: To represent the professions of speech language pathology & audiology including registration of members which outlines requirements for working in New Brunswick
Member of: Canadian Association of Speech-Language Pathologists & Audiologists
Chief Officer(s):
Darrelyn Snider, President
Finances: *Annual Operating Budget:* Less than $50,000
6 volunteer(s)
Membership: 19 student + 220 individual + 9 non-practicing; *Fees:* Schedule available; *Member Profile:* Individuals qualified for practice of speech-language pathology &/or audiology according specific standards; *Committees:* Legislation; Quality Assurance; Public Relations; Schools; Discipline; Translation; Audiology; Membership; Budget
Activities: *Awareness Events:* Speech & Hearing Month, May; *Rents Mailing List:* Yes
Awards:
• NBASLPA Clinical Supervision Award (Award)
• Margaret Christie Lifetime Achievement Award (Award)
• Award for Clinical Excellence (Award)

New Brunswick Ball Hockey Association
NB
Overview: A small provincial organization
Member of: Canadian Ball Hockey Association
Chief Officer(s):
Sheila Elliott, President
sheila@committedtoyourgoals.com
Membership: *Member Profile:* Ball hockey leagues throughout New Brunswick; *Committees:* Disciplinary
Activities: Establishing rules for ball hockey in New Brunswick; Maintaining high standards of officiating; Offering the Rookie Officiating Program
Publications:
• New Brunswick Ball Hockey Association Team Handbook
Type: Handbook

New Brunswick Beekeepers Association
488 Cape Breton Rd., Sainte Philippe NB E1H 1W2
Tel: 506-388-5127
www.nbba.ca
Overview: A small provincial organization
Chief Officer(s):
Calvin Hicks, President
cfhicks18@gmail.com
Brian M. Pond, Secretary-Treasurer
beehivePond@gmail.com
Finances: *Funding Sources:* Membership dues
Membership: 250; *Fees:* Schedule available based on number of colonies

New Brunswick Block Parent Association (NBBPAI)
#47, 100 Howe Crt., Oromocto NB E2V 2R3
Tel: 506-446-5992; *Fax:* 506-446-5992
nbbpai@nbnet.nb.ca
www.blockparent.ca
Overview: A small provincial charitable organization founded in 1968 overseen by Block Parent Program of Canada Inc.
Mission: To provide immediate assistance to community members, especially children & seniors, through a safety network; To serve 35 communities & 500 homes throughout New Brunswick
Member of: Block Parent Program of Canada Inc.
Activities: Providing community education programs; Collaborating with police, educators, & community groups

New Brunswick Branch of the Royal Caledonian Curling Club of Scotland *See* New Brunswick Curling Association

New Brunswick Broomball Association
NB
Overview: A small provincial organization overseen by Ballon sur glace Broomball Canada
Member of: Ballon sur glace Broomball Canada
Chief Officer(s):
Daniel Savoie, Contact
poker-bum@hotmail.com

New Brunswick Building Officials Association (NBBOA) / L'Association des officiels de la construction du Nouveau-Brunswick
PO Box 3193, Stn. B, Fredericton NB E3A 5G9
Tel: 506-470-3375; *Fax:* 506-450-4924
admin@nbboa.ca
www.nbboa.ca
www.facebook.com/NBBOA
twitter.com/THENBBOA
Overview: A small provincial organization founded in 1976
Mission: To achieve & maintain the highest levels of professionalism in membership, education & qualifications; legislative interpretation; building inspection service; building & construction safety.
Chief Officer(s):
Sherry Sparks, President
sherry.sparks@moncton.ca
Robert Pero, Secretary
rob.pero@vonm.ca
Lucas Roze, Executive Director
lucas.roze@nbboa.ca
Staff Member(s): 3
Membership: 125; *Fees:* $250 regular; $500 corporate; *Member Profile:* Professionals; technicians; technologists; carpenters; tradesmen; *Committees:* Education; Publicity; Membership; Website; Certification
Activities: Certification courses; annual meetings; training; *Speaker Service:* Yes; *Rents Mailing List:* Yes

New Brunswick Camping Association (NBCA)
c/o Stephane Richard, 960 St. George Blvd., Moncton NB E1E 3Y3
Tel: 506-451-1623; *Fax:* 506-878-0396
nbcamping.ca
Overview: A small provincial organization overseen by Canadian Camping Association
Mission: To advance outdoor recreation in residential camps & day-camps in New Brunswick
Chief Officer(s):
Stephane Richard, President
stephane.richard@diabetes.ca
Finances: *Funding Sources:* Sponsorships
Membership: *Member Profile:* Camps in New Brunswick that have met the association's standard for accreditation
Activities: Advocating the benefits of outdoor recreation; Developing an accreditation program; Providing educational opportunities, such as the annual directors' workshop & the annual counsellor conference; Distributing information; Creating networking opportunities

New Brunswick Candlepin Bowlers Association
7 Lilac Cres., Fredericton NB E3A 2G7
Tel: 516-472-7592
Overview: A medium-sized provincial organization
Mission: To promote candlepin bowling, a sport unique to the Maritimes & New England
Member of: Sport NB
Chief Officer(s):
Don Leger, President
Finances: *Funding Sources:* Provincial government

New Brunswick Cattle Marketing Agency *See* New Brunswick Cattle Producers

New Brunswick Cattle Producers (NBCP)
PO Box 1567, #302, 259 Brunswick St., Fredericton NB E3B 5G2
Tel: 506-458-8534; *Fax:* 506-453-1985
nbcattle@nb.aibn.com
www.bovinsnbcattle.ca
Previous Name: New Brunswick Cattle Marketing Agency
Overview: A small provincial organization founded in 1982
Mission: To promote, control, & regulate the production & marketing of cattle in New Brunswick; To advocate on behalf of cattle producers in New Brunswick; To develop competitive & efficient practices in the cattle producing industry
Affliation(s): Canadian Cattlemen's Association (CCA); Maritime Beef Council (MBC)
Chief Officer(s):
Cedric MacLeod, Chair, 506-472-8033
cedric@localvalleybeef.ca
Finances: *Funding Sources:* The collection of a mandatory $3.00 levy per head of cattle sold each year.
Membership: *Member Profile:* Beef cattle producers in New Brunswick
Activities: Undertaking research activities; Providing educational opportunities; Promoting the consumption & use of beef; Liaising with government, other sectors of the beef cattle industry, consumers, & the public

New Brunswick Chamber of Commerce (NBCC)
1 ch Canada, Edmunston NB E3V 1T6
Tel: 506-737-1868; *Fax:* 506-737-1862
info@nbchamber.ca
www.nbchamber.ca
Overview: A medium-sized provincial organization founded in 1985
Chief Officer(s):
Judith Murray, Chair
Staff Member(s): 2

New Brunswick Chiropractors' Association (NBCA) / Association des chiropraticiens du Nouveau-Brunswick
#206, 944 Prospect St., Fredericton NB E3B 9M6

Tel: 506-445-6800; *Fax:* 506-455-4430
comments@nbchiropractic.ca
www.nbchiropractic.ca
Overview: A medium-sized provincial licensing organization founded in 1958 overseen by Canadian Chiropractic Association
Mission: To regulate the practice of chiropractic & govern its members in accordance with the Act & the by-laws, in order to serve & protect the public interests; to establish, maintain, develop & enforce standards of qualification for the practice of chiropractic, including the required knowledge, skill & efficiency; to establish, maintain, develop & enforce standards of professional ethics; to promote public awareness of the role of the Association & the work of chiropractic, & to communicate & cooperate with other professional organizations for the advancement of the best interests of the Association, including the publication of books, papers & journals; & to encourage studies in chiropractic & provide assistance & facilities for special studies & research
Chief Officer(s):
Mohamed El-Bayoumi, Executive Director
Finances: *Funding Sources:* Membership fees
Membership: 65 active; *Member Profile:* Graduate of accredited chiropractic college & successful completion of Canadian Chiropractic Board Examinations & Jurisprudence exam

New Brunswick Choral Federation (NBCF) / Fédération des chorales du Nouveau-Brunswick (FCNB)

Charlotte Street Arts Centre, #203, 732 Charlotte St., Fredericton NB E3B 1M5
Tel: 506-453-3731
nbcf@nbnet.nb.ca
nbchoral.blogspot.ca
Overview: A small provincial charitable organization founded in 1979
Mission: To promote & encourage the art of choral singing in New Brunswick at all levels
Chief Officer(s):
Dianne Roxborough Brown, Executive Director
Staff Member(s): 1
Membership: 1,000; *Fees:* Schedule available; *Member Profile:* Individual singers & choirs/organizations
Activities: *Awareness Events:* Spring Choral Fest, April; New Brunswick Youth Choir, Oct.; *Library:* Music Library

New Brunswick Christmas Tree Growers Co-op Ltd. (NBCTGC) / Coop des Producteurs d'arbres de Noël du N.-B. (CPANNB)

226 Montgomery St., Fredericton NB E3B 2X1
Tel: 506-454-8252
Also Known As: The Christmas Tree Growers Association
Overview: A small provincial organization founded in 1976
Mission: To represent producers of natural christmas trees & related products in all matters pertaining to the viability of the industry
Member of: Canadian Christmas Tree Growers Association; National Christmas Tree Association (USA)
Affliation(s): New Brunswick Agri-Environmental Council; The Tree House
Finances: *Funding Sources:* Membership fees; Ad revenue from newsletter
Membership: *Member Profile:* New Brunswick producer of two or more acres of Christmas trees
Activities: Field Day on the first Saturday in August
Awards:
• Annual Provincial Tree Competition (Award)

New Brunswick Coalition for Literacy *See* Literacy Coalition of New Brunswick

New Brunswick Coalition of Transition Houses/Centres for Abused Women

c/o Lynne Matheson, Secretary, PO Box 73, St Stephen NB E3L 2W9
Tel: 506-466-4590; *Fax:* 506-466-4487
frth@nb.aibn.com
Overview: A medium-sized provincial organization
Mission: To act as a provincial voice in advocating for abused women & their children
Chief Officer(s):
Lynn Matheson, Secretary
Membership: *Member Profile:* Made up of approximately 35 representatives from 12 shelters throughout the province

New Brunswick Competitive Canoe Association

c/o Sport New Brunswick, 181 Kennebecasis River Rd., Hampton NB E5N 6L1
e-mail: nbcca_m@hotmail.com
www.sportnb.com/marathoncanoe
Overview: A small provincial organization overseen by CanoeKayak Canada
Member of: Sport New Brunswick; CanoeKayak Canada
Chief Officer(s):
J. Timothy Flood, President
Activities: Offering a sprint division & a marathon division

New Brunswick Competitive Festival of Music Inc.

PO Box 2022, Saint John NB E2L 3T5
Tel: 506-635-4128
www.nbfestivalofmusic.ca
Overview: A small provincial charitable organization founded in 1936
Mission: To hold a competitive & non-competitive music festival where students of all ages & music disciplines, including piano, vocal, strings, & band may meet, compete on a friendly basis & learn from expert adjudication
Affliation(s): New Brunswick Federation of Music Festivals; Canadian Federation of Music Festivals
Chief Officer(s):
Nadine Lane, Festival Administrator
Chris Titus, President
Staff Member(s): 1
Membership: *Member Profile:* Willingness to work as volunteer for music festival; *Committees:* Adjudicators; Awards; Syllabus; Advertising/Sponsors; Concerts; Program/Scheduling; Volunteers

New Brunswick Continuing Legal Education / Formation juridique permanente du Nouveau-Brunswick

c/o CBA - New Brunswick, 422 York St., Fredericton NB E3B 3P7
Tel: 506-452-7818; *Fax:* 506-459-7959
Toll-Free: 866-452-7818
cle@cbanb.com
www.nb-cba.org
Overview: A small provincial organization
Member of: Canadian Bar Association, New Brunswick
Chief Officer(s):
Ginette Little, CLE Program Coordinator
Activities: *Library* by appointment

New Brunswick Council for Fitness & Active Living (NBCFAL); New Brunswick Fitness Council *See* Fitness New Brunswick

New Brunswick Crafts Council / Conseil d'artisanat du Nouveau-Brunswick

PO Box 1231, Stn. A, Fredericton NB E3B 5C8
Tel: 506-450-8989; *Fax:* 506-457-6010
Toll-Free: 866-622-7238
info@nbcraftscouncil.ca
www.nbcraftscouncil.ca
www.facebook.com/2411474486
Overview: A small provincial organization
Mission: To provide opportunities & support to members by developing, promoting & fostering an appreciation of excellence in craft.
Chief Officer(s):
Natalie Landry, Executive Director
ed@nbcraftscouncil.ca
Kim Bent, President
kim.bent@unb.ca
Finances: *Annual Operating Budget:* $100,000-$250,000; *Funding Sources:* Provincial government
Staff Member(s): 4
Membership: *Fees:* $25 student; $55 individual; $65 associate; $85 juried craft individual; $125 friend
Awards:
• Alfred J. Pringle Award for Ingenuity in Crafts (Award)
Awarded for devices, techniques &/or processes invented by the craftperson which will improve the quality of the item, lower the cost of production or extend the creative range of the craft; not awarded to the product but to the process*Eligibility:* All craftspeople who have resided in New Brunswick for the last three years*Deadline:* June 30 *Amount:* Two prizes of $250 each
• Strathbutler Award (Award)
Awarded in recognition of excellence in the crafts &/or visual arts in New Brunswick as wll as a substantail contribution to their respective fields ove a significant peiod of time (at least 10 years)*Eligibility:* Must be born in New Brunswick or have resided in New Brunswick for at least 10 full years & be actively pursuing a career in the fields of visual arts or fine crafts in New Brunswick*Deadline:* March *Amount:* $10,000 *Contact:* Administered by Sheila Hugh Mackay
• Susan Vida Judah Travel Award (Award)
Created to help defray transportation expenses to help attend craft related conferences, seminars, workshops, courses ect., trade shows & exhibitions excluded unless applicant visiting with the plan to survey them for the purpose of participating at a later date*Eligibility:* Open to all craftspeople who have resided in New Brunswick for three years*Deadline:* March *Amount:* Amount of regular return airfare to the event, to a maximum of $1,000
• Duffie-Crowell Award for Ecclesiastical Craft (Award)
Create to encourage craftspeople to work in the field of ecclesiastical craft & to ecourage religious insitituions to consider the talent withing the provinces when commissioning properties*Eligibility:* Open to anyone who has resided in New Brunswick for the last three years*Deadline:* April *Amount:* $1,000

New Brunswick Cricket Association *See* Cricket New Brunswick

New Brunswick Curling Association (NBCA) / Association de Curling du Nouveau-Brunswick (ACNB)

c/o Marg Maranda, 65 Newcastle Centre Rd., Newcastle Centre NB E4B 2L2
Tel: 506-327-3445; *Fax:* 506-388-5708
Toll-Free: 800-592-2875
nbca@nb.sympatico.ca
www.nbcurling.com
Also Known As: Curling NB
Previous Name: New Brunswick Branch of the Royal Caledonian Curling Club of Scotland
Overview: A medium-sized provincial organization founded in 1971 overseen by Canadian Curling Association
Mission: To promote curling in New Brunswick; To establish & govern rules for curling competitions in New Brunswick
Member of: Canadian Curling Association / Association canadienne de curling
Affliation(s): Curl Atlantic
Chief Officer(s):
Marg Maranda, Executive Director
Damien Lahiton, President
damilahi@gmail.com
Finances: *Funding Sources:* Canadian Curling Association; Curling Development Fund; Sponsorships
Membership: *Member Profile:* Members of affiliated curling clubs in New Brunswick
Activities: Organizing curling competitions; Offering learn-to-curl clinics, courses for coaching & instruction, & ice making; Supporting "Business of Curling Clinics"; Lending training equipment & resources

New Brunswick Dart Association (NBDA)

c/o William White, 526 Rte. 845, Kingston NB E3N 1P5
Tel: 506-832-7293
www.nbdarts.bravehost.com
www.facebook.com/groups/21891717440
Overview: A small provincial organization overseen by National Darts Federation of Canada
Mission: To promote the sport of darts in New Brunswick.
Member of: National Darts Federation of Canada
Chief Officer(s):
William White, President
Cathy Ross, Secretary-Treasurer, 506-433-3057
cathyross460@hotmail.com

New Brunswick Dental Assistants Association (NBDAA) / Association des Assistantes Dentaires du Nouveau-Brunswick

PO Box 8997, Shediac NB E4P 8W5
Tel: 506-532-9189; *Fax:* 506-532-3635
Toll-Free: 866-530-9189
nbdaa.ca
www.facebook.com/pages/NBDAA/309506835839025
Overview: A small provincial organization founded in 1975 overseen by Canadian Dental Assistants Association
Mission: To provide opportunities Dental Assistants in New Brunswick.
Member of: Canadian Dental Assitants' Association
Chief Officer(s):
Amber Caissie, President
Bernice Léger, Office Coordinator
bernioff@nb.sympatico.ca
Membership: 550+; *Fees:* $45 inactive/student; $100 regular

New Brunswick Dental Society / Société dentaire du Nouveau-Brunswick
HSBC Place, PO Box 488, Stn. A, #820, 520 King St., Fredericton NB E3B 4Z9
Tel: 506-452-8575; *Fax:* 506-452-1872
nbds@nb.aibn.com
www.nbdental.com
www.facebook.com/NBDentalSociety
twitter.com/NBDentalNB
Overview: A small provincial licensing organization founded in 1890 overseen by Canadian Dental Association
Mission: To regulate & promote the dentistry profession in New Brunswick. To promote professional growth, high ethical standards and quality care giving through communication, education, and regulation of denistry in New Brunswick.
Chief Officer(s):
Lia A. Daborn, Executive Director
Membership: *Member Profile:* Licensed dentists
Activities: *Rents Mailing List:* Yes; *Library* Open to public by appointment

New Brunswick Denturists Society / Société des denturologistes du Nouveau-Brunswick
PO Box 5566, 288 West St. Pierre Blvd., Caraquet NB E1W 1B7
Tel: 506-727-7411; *Fax:* 506-727-6728
www.nbdenturistsociety.ca
Overview: A small provincial licensing organization founded in 1973 overseen by Denturist Association of Canada
Member of: Denturist Association of Canada
Chief Officer(s):
Daniel J. Robichaud, President
dentureguy@nb.aibn.com
Claudette Boudreau, Administrative Assistnat
ClaudetteBoudreau@nb.aibn.com

New Brunswick Egg Marketing Board (NBEMB) / L'Office de commercialisation des oeufs de Nouveau Brunswick
#101, 275 Main St., Fredericton NB E3A 1E1
www.nbegg.ca
Overview: A small provincial organization founded in 1970
Affliation(s): Canadian Egg Marketing Agency
Membership: 17

New Brunswick Environmental Network (NBEN) / Réseau environnemental du Nouveau-Brunswick (RENB)
167 Creek Rd., Waterford NB E4E 4L7
Tel: 506-433-6101; *Fax:* 506-433-6111
nben@nben.ca
www.nben.ca
www.facebook.com/pages/NBEN-RENB/134259049952351
Overview: A medium-sized provincial organization founded in 1991 overseen by Canadian Environmental Network
Mission: To strengthen the environmental movement throughout New Brunswick; To promote ecologically sound ways of life
Affliation(s): Canadian Environmental Network
Chief Officer(s):
Mary Ann Coleman, Executive Director
Joanna Brown, Coordinator, Youth Outreach & Events
Raissa Marks, Coordinator, Education & Outreach Programs
Finances: *Funding Sources:* Environment Canada; Health Canada; NB Dept. of Environment; NB Dept. of Health; NB Dept. of Intergovernmental Affairs; NB Dept. of Natural Resources
Membership: *Member Profile:* Non-profit environmental organizations
Activities: Providing educational opportunities
Meetings/Conferences: • New Brunswick Environmental Network 2015 Annual General Meeting, 2015, NB
Scope: Provincial
Description: Featuring the election of a Steering Committee by member groups
Contact Information: E-mail: nben@nben.ca
Publications:
• Greenprint: Towards a Sustainable New Brunswick
Type: Report; *Number of Pages:* 16
Profile: Lead organizations include the New Brunswick Environmental Network, Canadian Parks & Wilderness Society - New Brunswick Chapter, Conservation Council of New Brunswick,Falls Brook Centre, Meduxnekeag River Association Inc., & Petitcodiac Riverkeeper
• Legal Information for Environmental Groups
Type: Guide; *Number of Pages:* 20
Profile: Topics include civil disobedience, property law, endangered species, & international law

New Brunswick Equestrian Association (NBEA)
#13, 900 Hanwell Rd., Fredericton NB E3B 6A3
Tel: 506-454-2353; *Fax:* 506-454-2363
horses@nbnet.nb.ca
www.nbea.ca
www.facebook.com/equinenb
twitter.com/equinenb
Overview: A small provincial organization
Mission: To promote equestrian & provide education in New Brunswick.
Member of: Equine Canada
Affliation(s): Equine Canada; New Brunswick SPCA; Maritime Saddle & Tack Ltd.; Government of New Brunswick; P'tit Trot; Greenhawk; Sport New Brunswick
Chief Officer(s):
Deanna Phelan, President
deannaphelan@gmail.com
Bonnie Robertson, Secretary
equinenb@gmail.com
Membership: *Fees:* $43 junior; $50 senior; $85 family
Activities: Recreation; Sport; Dressage; Hunter/jumper; Distance riding; Eventing; Racing; Driving; Coaching

New Brunswick Federation of Agriculture *See* Agricultural Alliance of New Brunswick

New Brunswick Federation of Dance Clubs *See* Federation of Dance Clubs of New Brunswick

New Brunswick Federation of Home & School Associations, Inc. (NBFHSA)
921 College Hill Rd., Fredericton NB E3B 6Z9
Tel: 506-451-6247
www.nbfhsa.org
Overview: A medium-sized provincial organization founded in 1937 overseen by Canadian Home & School Federation
Mission: To ensure a quality education, enhanced by parental involvement, & a safe environment for all children.
Chief Officer(s):
Cynthia Richards, Interim President
shore_bird@hotmail.com
Lynne Roy, 1st Vice President
slynroy@hotmail.com
Finances: *Annual Operating Budget:* Less than $50,000; *Funding Sources:* Membership fees; government grant
Membership: 5,000 members + 152 provincial affiliates; *Fees:* $3; *Committees:* Health Issues; Literacy; Media Violence; Membership; Resolutions
Activities: Workshops for parents & teachers; *Speaker Service:* Yes

New Brunswick Federation of Labour (NBFL) / Fédération des travailleurs et travailleuses du Nouveau-Brunswick
#314, 96 Norwood Ave., Moncton NB E1C 6L9
Tel: 506-857-2125; *Fax:* 506-383-1597
Other Communication: fttnb@nbnet.nb.ca
nbfl@nbnet.nb.ca
www.nbfl-fttnb.ca
Overview: A medium-sized provincial organization founded in 1914 overseen by Canadian Labour Congress
Mission: To act as the central voice of labour in New Brunswick; To build solidarity & support between unions; To advance the economic & social welfare of New Brunswick's workers
Chief Officer(s):
Michel Boudreau, President
Ron Oldfield, First Vice-President
Thérèse Tremblay, Second Vice-President
Alex Bailey, Vice-President, Youth
Sandy Harding, Vice-President, Women's Issues
Danny King, Secretary-Treasurer
Finances: *Funding Sources:* Membership dues
Membership: 46,000; *Member Profile:* Individual members of 375 local union affiliates & 8 local labour councils; *Committees:* Political Education; Occupational Health, Safety, & Environment; Youth; Women's; Education
Activities: Assisting in organizing the unorganized into affiliated unions; Educating members, by hosting seminars & conferences; Liaising with government to discuss concerns of members; Influencing provincial legislation which will promote free collective bargaining & the rights of workers
Awards:
• James A. Whitebone Memorial Scholarships (Scholarship)
• Tim McCarthy Environment Prize (Award)
• NBFL Solidarity Bursaries (Grant)
• J. Harold Stafford Humanitarian Award (Award)
• Dermot Kingston Life Long Learning Award (Award)
Meetings/Conferences: • New Brunswick Federation of Labour Education Conference, 2015, NB
Scope: Provincial
Contact Information: New Brunswick Federation of Labour, E-mail: nbfl_fttnb@bellaliant.com
• New Brunswick Federation of Labour 53rd Convention, May, 2015, Delta Brunswick, Saint John, NB
Scope: Provincial
Description: A biennial gathering where approximately sixty resolutions are normally submitted & handled
Contact Information: New Brunswick Federation of Labour, E-mail: nbfl_fttnb@bellaliant.com

New Brunswick Federation of Music Festivals Inc. (NBFMF) / La Fédération des festivals de musique du Nouveau-Brunswick inc. (FFMNB)
NB
e-mail: info@nbfmf.org
nbfmf.org
Overview: A medium-sized provincial organization founded in 1973 overseen by Federation of Canadian Music Festivals
Chief Officer(s):
Barbara Long, Executive Director/President
Finances: *Annual Operating Budget:* Less than $50,000
Activities: Provincial Music Festival, 1st weekend in June

New Brunswick Federation of Naturalists *See* Nature NB

New Brunswick Federation of Woodlot Owners Inc. / Fédération des propriétaires de lots boisés du Nouveau-Brunswick inc.
819 Royal Rd., Fredericton NB E3G 6M1
Tel: 506-459-2990; *Fax:* 506-459-3515
www.nbwoodlotowners.ca
Overview: A small provincial organization founded in 1965
Mission: To advocate for woodlot owners; To direct government policy as it affects private woodlots
Chief Officer(s):
Andrew Clark, President
Ken Hardie, Manager
Staff Member(s): 4

New Brunswick Fencing Association *See* Fencing - Escrime New Brunswick

New Brunswick Filmmakers' Co-op
PO Box 1537, 732 Charlotte St., Fredericton NB E3B 4Y1
Tel: 506-455-1632; *Fax:* 506-457-2006
info@nbfilmcoop.com
www.nbfilmcoop.com
Overview: A small provincial charitable organization founded in 1979
Mission: To operate a 16mm/digital video training centre for individuals interested in filmmaking
Affliation(s): Independent Media Arts Alliance
Chief Officer(s):
Tony Merzetti, Executive Director
Finances: *Annual Operating Budget:* Less than $50,000; *Funding Sources:* Federal, provincial & municipal government; corporate sponsors; memberships; equipment rental
Staff Member(s): 2
Membership: 150 individual; *Fees:* $30; *Member Profile:* Interest in film production; *Committees:* Production; Public Relations; Equipment & Materials; Workshops; Training
Activities: Screenings; workshops; committees; film productions; Tidal Wave Film Festival, Nov.; *Library:* Film Co-op Resource Centre; Open to public

New Brunswick Forest Products Association Inc. (NBFPA) / L'Association des produits forestiers du Nouveau-Brunswick (APFNB)
Hugh John Flemming Forestry Centre, 1350 Regent St., Fredericton NB E3C 2G6
Tel: 506-452-6930; *Fax:* 506-450-3128
info@nbforestry.com
www.nbforestry.com
Overview: A small provincial organization founded in 1959
Mission: To represent forest industry members by serving as a common voice in relations with the government and the public, promoting a healthy New Brunswick forest, raise public awareness of sustainable forest management practices & provide a forum for the exchange of information, ideas & concerns.
Chief Officer(s):
Jacques Cormier, Chair
Staff Member(s): 1
Membership: 31 organizations

New Brunswick Fruit Growers Association Inc.
c/o NBFGA Scholarship Committee, #206, 1115 Regent St., Fredericton NB E3B 3Z2
e-mail: nbapple@nbnet.nb.ca
Overview: A small provincial organization founded in 1904
Chief Officer(s):
Euclide Bourgeois, President
Staff Member(s): 1
Membership: *Committees:* Scholarship

New Brunswick Funeral Directors & Embalmers Association (NBFDEA)
515 Everard H. Daigle Blvd., Grand Falls NB E3Z 2R5
Tel: 506-473-3063; *Fax:* 506-473-3494
nbfdandea@nb.aibn.com
www.nbfuneraldirectors.ca
Overview: A small provincial organization
Mission: To promote quality Funeral Homes in the province of New Brunswick.

New Brunswick Genealogical Society Inc. (NBGS, Inc.) / Société Généalogique du Nouveau-Brunswick Inc.
PO Box 3235, Stn. B, Fredericton NB E3A 5G9
e-mail: webmanager@nbgs.ca
www.nbgs.ca
Overview: A medium-sized provincial charitable organization founded in 1978
Mission: To promote & facilitate family historical research in New Brunswick
Chief Officer(s):
Stephanie Heenan-Orr, President
Ron Green, Treasurer
Shirley Graves, Secretary
Finances: *Funding Sources:* Donations
Membership: *Fees:* $35; *Member Profile:* Individuals, families, & institutions interested in family historical research in New Brunswick
Publications:
• Generations
Type: Journal; *Frequency:* Quarterly; *Number of Pages:* 68; *Editor:* George Hayward; *Price:* Free withNew Brunswick Genealogical Society Inc. membership
Profile: Genealogical related material associated with New Brunswick, such as rare documents, census information, passenger lists, cemeteries, book reviews, & upcoming genealogical seminars
• New Brunswick Genealogical Society Inc. Membership Directory
Type: Directory
• New Brunswick Genealogical Society Inc. Members' Surname Interests
Editor: Frank Morehouse & Stan Balch
Profile: Listing of family surnames being researched by NBGS members
• The New Brunswick Militia Commissioned Officers' List 1787-1867

Charlotte Branch
c/o Marguerite Garnett, 3701 Rte. 127 Bayside, St. Andrew NB E5B 2T1
Chief Officer(s):
Marguerite Garnett, President
• 1861 Census of Charlotte County
Type: Book; *Price:* $35

Miramichi Branch
PO Box 403, Miramichi NB E1N 3A8
e-mail: info@nbgsmiramichi.org
www.nbgsmiramichi.org
Mission: To promote the collection, preservation, & accessibility of genealogical materials in the Miramichi area
• Anglican Church Records of Northumberland County
Type: Book
Profile: Anglican Church marriage & baptism registers
• Cemetery Records of Northumberland County
Type: Book
Profile: Transcriptions of headstones from cemeteries in New Brunswick's Northumberland County
• Census Books of Northumberland County
Type: Book
Profile: Transcriptions of indexed census returns for Northumberland County in New Brunswick
• First Families of Northumberland County
Type: Book
Profile: Two volumes about the New Brunswick county's early families
• Marriage Stats from Northumberland County Newspapers
Type: Book
Profile: Three volumes of wedding announcements from the county's local newspapers
• NBGS Miramichi Newsletter
Type: Newsletter; *Frequency:* Quarterly; *Price:* Free with New Brunswick Genealogical Society Inc., Miramichi Branch, membership
Profile: Branch updates, current events, & genalogical information
• Obituary Books
Type: Book
Profile: Seven volumes of obituaries & funeral notices for New Brunswick's Northumberland County

Restigouche Branch
PO Box 5453, Dalhousie NB E8C 3C2
Chief Officer(s):
Suzanne Blaquière, President

Saint John Branch
PO Box 2423, 125 Rothesay Ave., Saint John NB E2L 3V9
e-mail: info@nbgssj.ca
www.nbgssj.ca
Mission: To encourage the study of genealogy & family history in the Saint John area; To develop the preservation & research of family history; To promote the accessibility of heritage records
Chief Officer(s):
Carol Lee Elliot, President
Beverlee Gregg, Secretary
David Laskey, Treasurer
• Burial Records for Church of England Cemetery, Thorne Avenue
Editor: Lennox Bagnell; *Price:* $20
Profile: 6,766 recorded burials from 1837 to 1923
• New Brunswick Genealogical Society Inc. Saint John Branch Newsletter
Type: Newsletter; *Price:* Free with New Brunswick Genealogical Society Inc. Saint John Branch membership
Profile: Information for members, including upcoming meetings
• Records of Rev. James Gray
Price: $15

Southeastern Branch
PO Box 7102, Riverview NB E1B 4T8
Mission: To promote genealogy & genealogical research in New Brunswick's Westmorland, Albert, & Kent counties
• Cemeteries of Westmorland County: Dorchester Parish
Number of Pages: 335; *ISBN:* 978-0-9782223-2-1; *Price:* $42
Profile: An indexed list from twenty-three cemeteries situated in Dorchester Parish
• Cemeteries of Westmorland County: Moncton Parish
Number of Pages: 371; *ISBN:* 978-0-9782223-1-4; *Price:* $42
Profile: Listings of thiry-five cemeteries across Moncton Parish
• Cemeteries of Westmorland County: Sackville Parish
Number of Pages: 421; *ISBN:* 978-0-9782223-3-8; *Price:* $42
Profile: Listings of thirteen cemeteries located in Sackville Parish
• Cemeteries of Westmorland County: Salisbury Parish
Number of Pages: 197; *ISBN:* 0-9782223-0-X; *Price:* $22
Profile: Listings of twenty-six cemeteries located in Salisbury Parish
• Cemeteries of Westmorland County: Westmorland Parish
Number of Pages: 132; *ISBN:* 978-0-9782223-4-5; *Price:* $18
Profile: Listings of eleven cemeteries situated in Westmorland Parish
• News & Notes [a publication of the New Brunswick Genealogical Society Inc.]
Type: Newsletter

New Brunswick Golf Association (NBGA) / Association de golf du nouveau brunswick
PO Box 1555, Stn. A, Fredericton NB E3B 5G2
Tel: 506-451-1324; *Fax:* 888-307-2963
Toll-Free: 877-833-4662
info@golfnb.ca
www.golfnb.ca
Overview: A medium-sized provincial organization founded in 1934 overseen by Royal Canadian Golf Association
Mission: To determine policies & standards relating to the development & promotion of amateur golf in New Brunswick
Chief Officer(s):
Tyson Flinn, Executive Director
tflinn@golfnb.ca
Staff Member(s): 3
Membership: *Member Profile:* Amateur golfers at member clubs; *Committees:* Executive
Activities: Provincial amateur tournaments; programs & services for members clubs

New Brunswick Ground Search & Rescue Association (NBGSARA)
#247, 527 Beaverbrook Ct., Fredericton NB E3E 1X6
e-mail: media@nbgsara.nb.ca
www.nbgsara.nb.ca
Overview: A small provincial organization
Mission: To represent the Province of New Brunswick's 11 regional ground search and rescue teams.
Chief Officer(s):
Matt Cameron, President
Membership: *Member Profile:* Ground search and rescue teams

New Brunswick Ground Water Association
1278 Route 260, St-Martin de Restigouche NB E8A 2M8
Tel: 506-235-5002
nbgwa@nb.sympatico.ca
www.nbgwa.ca
Overview: A small provincial organization overseen by Canadian Ground Water Association
Mission: To preserve & protect New Brunswick's water; To promote education of members & the public; To encourage the development of ground water guidelines & strategies
Chief Officer(s):
Danny Constantine, President
Terry Burpee, Sec.-Treas.
Finances: *Annual Operating Budget:* Less than $50,000; *Funding Sources:* Membership dues
Membership: 42; *Fees:* $300

New Brunswick Guild of Dispensing Opticians *See* Opticians Association of New Brunswick

New Brunswick Gymnastics Association (NBGA) / Association gymnastique du Nouveau-Brunswick (AGNB)
1991 Route 112, Upper Cloverdale NB E1J 1Z1
Tel: 506-215-0085
nbga@gym.nb.ca
gym.nb.ca
www.facebook.com/NBGym
twitter.com/gymnasticsnb
www.youtube.com/user/GymnasticsNB
Overview: A small provincial organization founded in 1967
Mission: To promote gymnastics in New Brunswick
Member of: Gymnastics Canada Gymnastique
Chief Officer(s):
Nathalie Colpitts-Waddell, Executive Director
director@gym.nb.ca
Diane Kirk, President
president@gym.nb.ca
Staff Member(s): 1
Membership: 2500; *Committees:* Executive; Technical

New Brunswick Health Information Management Association (NBHIMA) / L'Association de gestion d'information de la santé du nouveau-brunswick (AGISNB)
NB
Tel: 506-623-3127
www.nbhima.ca
Previous Name: New Brunswick Health Record Association
Overview: A small provincial organization founded in 1967
Mission: To promote members as leaders in health information management
Affliation(s): Canadian Health Information Management Association (CHIMA); National Health Information Alliance (NHIMA)
Chief Officer(s):
Lee Vickers, President
Lee.Vickers@HorizonNB.ca
Esther Keating, Secretary
Esther.Keating@HorizonNB.ca
Finances: *Funding Sources:* Fundraising
Membership: *Member Profile:* Health information management professionals in New Brunswick
Activities: Providing financial assistance to members who take continuing education courses; Hosting educational teleconferences; Facilitating the exchange of ideas within the profession; Revising the New Brunswick Association of Medical Record Librarians Act; *Awareness Events:* Health Information Management Week, Nov.

Publications:
• New Brunswick Health Information Management Association New Brunswick
Type: Newsletter; *Frequency:* Semiannually; *Editor:* Emily Rogers

New Brunswick Health Record Association *See* New Brunswick Health Information Management Association

New Brunswick Heart Foundation *See* Heart & Stroke Foundation of New Brunswick

New Brunswick Historical Society
Loyalist House, 120 Union St., Saint John NB E2L 1A3
Tel: 506-652-3590
info@LoyalistHouse.com
www.loyalisthouse.com
Overview: A medium-sized provincial charitable organization founded in 1874
Mission: To promote the study, research & discussion of New Brunswick history; to collect & preserve New Brunswick history; to publish & educate. The Society owns & operates Loyalist House.
Membership: *Fees:* $20 individual; $100 life
Activities: *Speaker Service:* Yes; *Library:* The Loyalist Library; Open to public by appointment

New Brunswick Hog Marketing Board *See* Porc NB Pork

New Brunswick Hospice Palliative Care Association
1305 Rte. 101, Nasonworth NB E3C 2C7
e-mail: info@nbhpca-aspnb.ca
www.nbhpca-aspnb.ca
Previous Name: New Brunswick Palliative Care Association
Overview: A small provincial organization
Mission: To promote principles & standards for hospice palliative care in New Brunswick
Member of: Canadian Palliative Care Association
Chief Officer(s):
Ann Nickerson, President
president@nbhpca-aspnb.ca
Finances: *Funding Sources:* Membership dues; Donations
Membership: *Fees:* $35 individual; $20 nurses group; $70 organization; *Member Profile:* Health care professionals, volunteers, & other individuals dedicated to ensuring access to quality end-of-life care for patients in New Brunswick

New Brunswick Institute of Agrologists (NBIA) / L'Institut des agronomes du Nouveau-Brunswick (IANB)
PO Box 3479, Stn. B, Fredericton NB E3B 5H2
Tel: 506-459-5536; *Fax:* 506-454-7837
www.ianbia.com
Overview: A small provincial organization founded in 1960 overseen by Agricultural Institute of Canada
Mission: To maintain high competency & professional standards for those practicing agrology in New Brunswick; To uphold the NBIA Code of Ethics; to offer advice to the public about agriculture & related areas; To formulate policies & improve the agriculture & food industry
Chief Officer(s):
Pat Toner, President
pat.toner@gnb.ca
Duncan Fraser, Secretary
duncan.fraser@gnb.ca
Rita Rattray, Office Administrator
nbia@nbagrologists.nb.ca
Membership: 200; *Fees:* $25; *Member Profile:* Professional agrologists in New Brunswick, with a degree in agriculture from a recognized university, plus three or more years of training or experience in the field; Individuals with a degree accepted by the Council; Articling agrologists; *Committees:* Admissions; Act / Bylaws; Scholarship; Professional Development; NBIA Strategy; Communication; Discipline; Complaints; Nominating; Executive
Activities: Participating in programs to benefit the agriculture & food industry; Analyzing issues & making recommendations to organizations; Improving standards of research; Providing professional development & networking opportunities; Offering information for members, the farming industry, & the public; Promoting the profession of agrology to famers
Meetings/Conferences: • New Brunswick Institute of Agrologists 2015 Annual General Meeting, 2015, NB
Scope: Provincial

New Brunswick Institute of Chartered Accountants (NBICA) / Institut des comptables agréés du Nouveau-Brunswick
Mercantile Centre, #250, 55 Union St., Saint John NB E2L 2B2
Tel: 506-634-1588; *Fax:* 506-634-1015
nbica@nb.aibn.com
www.nbica.org
Overview: A medium-sized provincial organization founded in 1916 overseen by Chartered Professional Accountants of New Brunswick
Mission: To serve members, students & the interests of the public with integrity, objectivity & a commitment to excellence; to promote & increase the knowledge, skills & proficiency of members & students; to regulate the discipline & professional conduct of members & students; to require public practitioners to carry minimum levels of professional liability insurance; to have lay representatives sit on Council; to conduct practice inspection of its public practitioners
Chief Officer(s):
Kathy Wills, Executive Assistant, 506-634-3195
kathywills@nb.aibn.com
Membership: 1,129
Activities: Professional development opportunities (note that NBICA will integrate under the CPA banner); *Speaker Service:* Yes

New Brunswick Interscholastic Athletic Association (NBIAA)
PO Box 6000, 125 Hilton Rd., Fredericton NB E3B 5H1
Tel: 506-457-4843; *Fax:* 506-453-5311
nbiaa@gnb.ca
www.nbiaa-asinb.org
Overview: A medium-sized provincial organization overseen by School Sport Canada
Member of: School Sport Canada
Chief Officer(s):
Yvan Arseneault, President, 506-684-7610
Allyson Ouellette, Executive Director
Staff Member(s): 2
Membership: 75 schools; *Fees:* $300 per school; *Committees:* Executive
Awards:
• Sportsmanship Awards (Award)
• NBIAA Appreciation Award (Award)
• Emery Johnson Memorial Award (Award)

New Brunswick Karate Association *See* Karate New Brunswick

New Brunswick Latino Association
c/o Fredericton Multicultural Assn., 28 Saunders St., Fredericton NB E3B 1N1
Tel: 506-454-8292; *Fax:* 506-450-9033
www.nblatino.ca
Also Known As: NB Latino Association
Overview: A small provincial organization
Mission: To welcome Spanish and Portuguese-speaking newcomers to NB, to offer relevant information that will help them settle in the province, to celebrate and share our unique cultures and to provide the sense of belonging and encouragement for those aspiring to become established in the province of New Brunswick

New Brunswick Law Foundation / La Fondation pour l'avancement du droit au Nouveau-Brunswick
66, rue Avonlea Court, Fredericton NB E3C 1N8
Tel: 506-453-7776; *Fax:* 506-451-1421
amartin@lawsociety-barreau.nb.ca
www.lawsociety.nb.ca
Overview: A small provincial organization founded in 1975
Mission: To receive the interest earned on lawyers' mixed trust accounts & to use these funds to support law-related projects to benefit residents of New Brunswick
Chief Officer(s):
Alban Martin, Executive Director
Staff Member(s): 1

New Brunswick Liberal Association
715 Brunswick St., Fredericton NB E3B 1H8
Tel: 506-453-3950; *Fax:* 506-453-2476
Toll-Free: 800-442-4902
www.nbliberal.ca
www.facebook.com/nbla.alnb
twitter.com/NB_Liberals
www.youtube.com/user/NBLiberalTV
Overview: A medium-sized provincial organization overseen by The Liberal Party of Canada
Chief Officer(s):
Brian Gallant, Leader
briangallant@nbliberal.ca
Britt Dysart, President
vivianne.martin@nbliberal.ca
Ellen Creighton, Executive Director
execdirgen@nbliberal.ca

New Brunswick Library Trustees' Association (NBLTA) / Association des commissaires de bibliothèque du Nouveau-Brunswick, Inc.
PO Box 34, St. Antoine NB E0A 2X0
Overview: A small provincial organization founded in 1979
Mission: To train effective library trustees in New Brunswick
Finances: *Funding Sources:* New Brunswick Public Library System
Membership: *Member Profile:* Any member of a public library board in New Brunswick
Activities: Promoting public library services
Awards:
• NBLTA Merit Award (Award)

New Brunswick Lung Association / Association pulmonaire du Nouveau-Brunswick
65 Brunswick St., Fredericton NB E3B 1G5
Tel: 506-455-8961; *Fax:* 506-462-0939
Toll-Free: 800-565-5864
Info@nb.lung.ca
www.nb.lung.ca
Overview: A small provincial charitable organization overseen by Canadian Lung Association
Mission: To promote wellness throughout New Brunswick & prevent lung disease
Chief Officer(s):
Barbara MacKinnon, President & Chief Executive Officer
Ted Allingham, Director, Finance & Administration
Arthur Thomson, Vice President
Barbara Walls, Director, Health Initiatives
Finances: *Funding Sources:* Donations; Sponsorships; Fundraising
Staff Member(s): 10
Activities: Engaging in advocacy activities; Offering education about respiratory health; Providing resources such as fact sheets, booklets, & audio-visual & program resources; Supporting respiratory research; Organizing fundraising events to support children & adults with lung disease; *Library:* NB Lung Associations' Environment & Health Public Resource Svs.; Open to public

New Brunswick Maple Syrup Association (NBMSA)
#223, 1350 Regent St., Fredericton NB E3C 2G6
Tel: 506-458-8889; *Fax:* 506-454-0652
yrp@nb.aibn.com
www.maple.infor.ca
Overview: A medium-sized provincial organization
Mission: The New Brunswick Maple Syrup Association (NBMSA) is a non-profit organization, dedicated to representing the interests of its members, and facilitating the industry through advertisement and the constant improvement of quality and standards by collaborating with various organizations towards the enrichment of the ever-growing maple industry.
Chief Officer(s):
Yvon Poitras, General Manager
Membership: 124

New Brunswick Massotherapy Association (NBMA) / Association des massothérapeutes du Nouveau-Brunswick (AMNB)
PO Box 353, Stn. A, Fredericton NB E3B 4Z9
Toll-Free: 866-923-6262
info@nbma-amnb.ca
www.nbma-amnb.ca
Overview: A small provincial organization

New Brunswick Medical Society (NBMS) / Société médicale du Nouveau-Brunswick
176 York St., Fredericton NB E3B 3N7
Tel: 506-458-8860; *Fax:* 506-458-9853
nbms@nb.aibn.com
www.nbms.nb.ca
Overview: A medium-sized provincial organization founded in 1867 overseen by Canadian Medical Association
Mission: To advance medical science in all its branches; to promote improvement of medical services; to prevent disease in cooperation with health officers & all others engaged in such work; to maintain high scientific & professional status for its members; to promote medical science & related arts & sciences
Chief Officer(s):
Robert Rae, President
Finances: *Annual Operating Budget:* $250,000-$500,000

Staff Member(s): 8
Membership: 20 student + 40 senior/lifetime + 1,100 individual; *Fees:* Schedule available; *Member Profile:* Licensed physician by College of Physicians & Surgeons of NB; *Committees:* Economics; Health Care; Medical Education; Communications
Activities: *Internships:* Yes; *Speaker Service:* Yes; *Rents Mailing List:* Yes

New Brunswick Merit Contractors Association
NB
Tel: 506-333-8845
info@meritnb.ca
www.meritnb.ca
Overview: A small provincial organization overseen by Merit Canada
Mission: To represent and support the growth of open shop construction in New Brunswick.
Chief Officer(s):
Graeme Scaplen, Executive Director
graeme@meritnb.com
Membership: *Member Profile:* Construction contractors

New Brunswick Multicultural Council (NBMC) / Conseil multiculturel du Nouveau-Brunswick (CMNB)
#200, 361 Victoria St., Fredericton NB E3B 1W5
Tel: 506-453-1091; *Fax:* 866-644-1956
nbmc@nb-mc.ca
www.nb-mc.ca
Overview: A medium-sized provincial charitable organization founded in 1983
Mission: To represent multicultural & multi-racial interests of all member associations; to encourage development & formation of new associations; to encourage member associations in their multicultural, inter-cultural & inter-racial prograams & activities
Affliation(s): Canadian Federation of Multicultural Councils
Chief Officer(s):
Dexter Noel, President
Finances: *Annual Operating Budget:* Less than $50,000; *Funding Sources:* Dept. of Canadian Heritage; NB Dept. of Advanced Education & Labour
Staff Member(s): 1; 46 volunteer(s)
Membership: 1-99; *Fees:* $100; *Committees:* Public Policy; Race Relations; Education; Newsletter; Constitution; Finance
Activities: *Speaker Service:* Yes

New Brunswick Musicians' Association, Local 815 of the American Federation of Musicians
82 Germain St., Saint John NB E2L 2E7
Tel: 506-652-6620; *Fax:* 506-652-6624
local815@afm.org
www.sjfn.nb.ca/local815
Overview: A small provincial organization founded in 1964
Mission: To represent professional musicians in New Brunswick
Member of: American Federation of Musicians of the United States & Canada
Chief Officer(s):
Norman G. Weyman, President
Bernadette Hedar, Vice-President
Brandon Weyman, Secretary-Treasurer
Membership: *Fees:* $30 local intiation fee; $65 federation initiation fee; $152 annual dues; *Member Profile:* Professional musicians in New Brunswick; Youth members are 20 years or younger
Activities: Administering the Music Performance Funds throughout New Brunswick

New Brunswick Native Indian Women's Council *See* New Brunswick Aboriginal Women's Council

New Brunswick Nurses Union (NBNU) / Syndicat des infirmières et infirmiers du Nouveau-Brunswick (SIINB)
103 Woodside Lane, Fredericton NB E3C 2R9
Tel: 506-453-0820; *Fax:* 506-453-0828
Toll-Free: 800-442-4914
nbnu1@nbnu.ca
www.nbnu.ca
www.facebook.com/212365802133370
twitter.com/NBNU_SIINB
Previous Name: Provincial Collective Bargaining Council
Overview: A medium-sized provincial organization
Mission: To enhance the social, economic, and general worklife of nurses and their vision is NBNU as a professional, credible, and respected voice advocating for nurses and quality health care.
Member of: National Federation of Nurses' Unions
Chief Officer(s):
David Brown, Executive Director
dbrown@nbnu.ca
Marilyn Quinn, President
marilunquinn@nbnu.ca
Staff Member(s): 16
Membership: 6,200
Activities: *Speaker Service:* Yes

New Brunswick Operating Room Nurses (NBORN)
NB
Overview: A medium-sized provincial organization founded in 1974 overseen by Operating Room Nurses Association of Canada
Chief Officer(s):
Charlotte Roach, President, 506-273-7109
Charlotte.Roach@horizonnb.ca
Membership: *Member Profile:* Registered Nurses in New Brunswick who are engaged in operating room nursing or involved in the Perioperative setting.
Activities: *Awareness Events:* Perioperative Nurses Week, November

New Brunswick Outfitters Association Inc. (NBOA Inc.)
c/o Mike Roy, PO Box 451, Bathurst NB E2A 3Z4
Tel: 506-548-5157
www.nboa.nb.ca
Overview: A small provincial organization
Mission: To act as the voice of the outfitting industry in New Brunswick; to maintain high standards in New Brunswick's outfitting industry; To uphold the association's Code of Ethics; To ensure safety & satisfaction of guests
Chief Officer(s):
Mike Roy, President
mikeroy@nb.aibn.com
Membership: *Member Profile:* Hunting & fishing outfitters or guides in New Brunswick who contract with private parties to host outdoor excursions
Activities: Establishing rating standards & licensing roofed accommodations

New Brunswick Palliative Care Association *See* New Brunswick Hospice Palliative Care Association

New Brunswick Pharmaceutical Society (NBPhS) / Ordre des pharmaciens du N.-B.
#8, 1224 Mountain Rd., Moncton NB E1C 2T6
Tel: 506-857-8957; *Fax:* 506-857-8838
Toll-Free: 800-463-4434
info@nbpharmacists.ca
www.nbpharmacists.ca
Overview: A small provincial licensing organization overseen by National Association of Pharmacy Regulatory Authorities
Mission: To protect the public by regulating the profession of pharmacy in New Brunswick.
Member of: Canadian Council on Continuing Education in Pharmacy
Chief Officer(s):
Sam Lanctin, Registrar
sam.lanctin@nbpharmacists.ca
Karen DeGrace, Communications Manager
karen.degrace@nbpharmacists.ca
Staff Member(s): 7
Membership: *Member Profile:* Pharmacists - certified dispensers; pharmacies; hospitals
Activities: *Internships:* Yes

New Brunswick Pharmacists' Association (NBPA) / Association des pharmaciens du Nouveau-Brunswick (APNB)
#410, 212 Queen St., Fredericton NB E3B 1A8
Tel: 506-459-6008; *Fax:* 506-453-0736
Toll-Free: 888-358-2345
nbpa@nbnet.nb.ca
www.nbpharma.ca
twitter.com/PharmacistsNB
Overview: A small provincial organization founded in 1981
Mission: To advance the profession of pharmacy in New Brunswick; To represent the interests of members & the profession of pharmacy
Chief Officer(s):
Paul Blanchard, Executive Director
Staff Member(s): 3
Membership: *Member Profile:* New Brunswick pharmacists or certified dispensers; Corporate members; Hospital members; Persons who have a business association with pharmacists in New Brunswick; Students
Activities: Implementing programs to help members provide quality pharmacy services; Disseminating information to members

New Brunswick Physiotherapy Association (NBPA)
PO Box 28117, St. John's NL A1B 4J8
Tel: 709-765-1096
atlanticbranches@physiotherapy.ca
Overview: A small provincial organization overseen by Canadian Physiotherapy Association
Mission: To provide leadership & direction to the physiotherapy profession; To foster excellence in practice, education & research
Member of: Canadian Physiotherapy Association
Chief Officer(s):
Lisa Pike, Executive Director
Colin Hood, President
Finances: *Funding Sources:* Membership dues; Educational activities

New Brunswick Physique & Figure Association (NBPFA)
NB
www.nbpfa.com
www.facebook.com/191517260859626
Overview: A small provincial organization overseen by Canadian Bodybuilding Federation
Mission: To govern the sport of amateur bodybuilding, fitness & figure in New Brunswick.
Member of: Canadian Bodybuilding Federation; International Federation of Bodybuilding
Chief Officer(s):
Garry Bartlett, President, 506-459-0135
grbartlett@yahoo.com
Duncan Lombard, Vice-President & Chief Judge
dlombard@nbnet.nb.ca

New Brunswick Potato Agency *See* Potatoes New Brunswick

New Brunswick Purchasing Management Institute *See* Supply Chain Management Association - New Brunswick

New Brunswick Racquetball Association (NBRA)
24 Baxter St., Lower Coverdale NB E1J 1B4
Tel: 506-387-4196; *Fax:* 506-387-4196
info@nbracquetball.ca
www.sportnb.com/racquetball
Overview: A small provincial organization founded in 1977 overseen by Racquetball Canada
Mission: To promote the sport of racquetball throughout New Brunswick
Member of: Racquetball Canada
Chief Officer(s):
Barry Moore, Ranking Coordinator
moorbar@rogers.com
Activities: Providing racquetball classes; Offering racquetball coaching

New Brunswick Real Estate Association (NBREA) / Association des agents des immeubles du Nouveau-Brunswick
#1, 22 Durelle St., Fredericton NB E3C 1N8
Tel: 506-459-8055; *Fax:* 506-459-8057
Toll-Free: 800-762-1677
info@nbrea.ca
nbrea.ca
www.facebook.com/NBREALTORS
twitter.com/NBREALTORS
Overview: A medium-sized provincial organization founded in 1958
Mission: To strengthen & promote standards of professionalism in the real estate industry
Member of: The Canadian Real Estate Association
Chief Officer(s):
Jamie Ryan, CEO
jryan@nbrea.ca
Finances: *Funding Sources:* Membership dues
Staff Member(s): 7
Membership: *Member Profile:* Realtors

New Brunswick Road Builders & Heavy Construction Associatoin (NBRBHCA)
#5, 59 Avonlea Ct., Fredericton NB E3C 1N8
Tel: 506-454-5079; *Fax:* 506-452-7646
rbanb@nb.aibn.com
www.rbanb.com

Overview: A medium-sized provincial organization founded in 1958 overseen by Canadian Construction Association
Mission: To foster & enhance relations between the members, & between the members of other associations in construction; to acquire & disseminate information of value to the industry & to its membership; to improve & extend standards, conditions, methods & practices within the industry
Member of: Transportation Association of Canada
Chief Officer(s):
Marc Losier, President
Tom McGinn, Executive Director
tmcginn.rbanb@nb.aibn.com
Finances: *Funding Sources:* Membership fees
Staff Member(s): 2
Membership: *Fees:* Schedule available; *Member Profile:* Contractors, Support Service Firms, Suppliers & Engineers; *Committees:* Annual Meeting, Advertising & Membership; Construction Safety; Construction Training; Finance; Structures; Grading; Paving; Equipment Rental Rates; Environmental; Municipal Infrastructure; C.C.A./TRIP
Awards:
• Two Civil Engineering Scholarships (Scholarship)
Amount: $3,000 each
Publications:
• New Brunswick Road Builder
Type: Magazine; *Frequency:* Annually
• Road Builders Association of New Brunswick Newsletter
Type: Newsletter; *Frequency:* Monthly
• Road Builders Association of New Brunswick Membership Directory
Type: Directory; *Frequency:* Annually

New Brunswick Roofing Contractors Association, Inc. (NBRCA) / Association des entrepreneurs en couverture du Nouveau-Brunswick

PO Box 7242, 24 Coborg St., Saint John NB E2L 4S6
Tel: 506-652-7003; *Fax:* 506-696-0380
info@nbrca.ca
www.nbrca.ca
Overview: A small provincial licensing organization founded in 1969 overseen by Canadian Roofing Contractors' Association
Mission: To protect the public's interest in relation to roofing; To act as the voice of New Brunswick's roofing industry; To facilitate a competent & profitable roofing & sealed membrane system industry in the province; To foster excellence in roofing related activities; to ensure that members uphold the code of ethics
Member of: Canadian Roofing Contractors Association (CRCA)
Chief Officer(s):
Ron Hutton, Executive Director, 506-652-7003, Fax: 506-696-0380
rhutton@nbrca.ca
Gilles Boudreau, President
Andrew Lunn, Vice-President
Guy LeBlanc, Secretary
Jean Claude Vienneau, Treasurer
Membership: 40; *Member Profile:* Professional roofing contractors, sheet metal contractors, manufacturers, suppliers, roof inspectors, & building consultants in New Brunswick
Activities: Promoting the roofing industry in New Brunswick; Providing safety training; Offering information about the industry, such as materials, practices, & advances; Ensuring that members meet workmanship standards
Publications:
• NBRCA CRCA 2 Year Standard Form of Warranty
Price: $25
• NBRCA CRCA Preventative Maintenance Manual / NBRCA CRCA Manual d'Entretien Preventif
Type: Manual; *Price:* $25
• NBRCA Membership Guide
Price: $25
Profile: A guide to the responsibilities of members of the New Brunswick Roofing Contractors Association

New Brunswick Rugby Union (NBRU)

#13, 900 Hanwell Rd., Fredericton NB E3B 6A2
Tel: 506-261-2176
www.nbru.ca
Overview: A medium-sized provincial organization overseen by Rugby Canada
Mission: To govern rugby in New Brunswick & organize games between teams
Member of: Rugby Canada
Chief Officer(s):
Sherry Doiron, President
sherrydoiron@gmail.com

Finances: *Funding Sources:* Membership fees; donations; fund raising
Membership: *Committees:* Selection; Discipline; Executive

New Brunswick Safety Council Inc. *See* Safety Services New Brunswick

New Brunswick Sailing Association (NBSA)

c/o Executive Director, 105 Bird Ave., Fredericton NB E2A 2H8
Tel: 506-472-2117
www.nbsailing.nb.ca
www.facebook.com/groups/204821582997273
Overview: A small provincial organization overseen by Sail Canada
Mission: The New Brunswick Sailing Association is the provincial governing body for boating & the sport of sailing. It is the Canadian Yachting Association's representative in New Brunswick.
Member of: Sail Canada
Chief Officer(s):
Sharon Mills, Executive Director
smills@nbsailing.nb.ca

New Brunswick Salmon Council (NBSC)

PO Box 533, Stn. A, Fredericton NB E3B 5A6
Tel: 506-452-1875; *Fax:* 506-454-0336
thenbsc@nbnet.nb.ca
www.nbsalmoncouncil.com
Overview: A small provincial organization overseen by Atlantic Salmon Federation
Affliation(s): Atlantic Salmon Federation

New Brunswick Salmon Growers Association *See* Atlantic Canada Fish Farmers Association

New Brunswick Scottish Cultural Association Inc. (NBSCA)

PO Box 781, Fredericton NB E3B 5B4
Fax: 506-454-9936
Toll-Free: 877-627-2234
info@nbscots.com
www.nbscots.com
www.facebook.com/nbscots
twitter.com/nbsca
Overview: A medium-sized provincial organization founded in 1980
Mission: To promote & protect the Scottish culture in New Brunswick; to bring together people of Scottish descent & people interested in the culture; to educate children of the importance of the Scottish people & their contribution to New Brunswick & Canada. Chapters in Bathurst, & Moncton.
Chief Officer(s):
Llewellyn Smith, President
Finances: *Funding Sources:* Fundraising; sponsorships; membership dues; donations; government
Membership: *Fees:* $22 individual; $35 group/club; $38 family; $250 life; $500 sustaining; *Committees:* Fundraising; Membership; Nominating; Communications
Activities: *Speaker Service:* Yes; *Library:* NBSCA Kubrart;

New Brunswick Securities Commission *See* Financial & Consumer Services Commission

New Brunswick Senior Citizens Federation Inc. (NBSCF) / Fédération des citoyens aînés du Nouveau-Brunswick inc. (FCANB)

#214, 23 - 451 Paul St., Dieppe NB E1A 6W8
Tel: 506-857-8242; *Fax:* 506-857-0315
Toll-Free: 800-453-4333
horizons@nbnet.nb.ca
www.nbscf.ca
Overview: A medium-sized provincial organization founded in 1968
Mission: To promote the general welfare & leadership of NB's senior citizens regardless of language, race, colour, sex, or creed; to elevate the social, moral, & intellectual standing of NB's senior citizens; to provide information, coordination, communication, & advocating services to members
Chief Officer(s):
Isabelle Thériault-Arseneault, Director, Operations
Finances: *Annual Operating Budget:* $250,000-$500,000; *Funding Sources:* Special projects; membership dues
Staff Member(s): 4
Membership: 25,000; *Fees:* $9.50-15 in clubs; $20 individual; $30 couple; *Member Profile:* NB resident 50 years+
Activities: *Awareness Events:* Seniors Products & Services Expo

New Brunswick Shorthorn Breeders Association

138 Salem Rd., Havelock NB E4Z 5R5
Tel: 506-534-2492
Overview: A small provincial organization founded in 1931
Member of: Canadian Shorthorn Association
Chief Officer(s):
Arthur Carson, President
Finances: *Funding Sources:* Membership dues; harvest auctions
Membership: *Member Profile:* Owners of shorthorn cattle

New Brunswick Signallers Association (NB Sigs)

c/o 3 ASG Signal Squadron, CFB Gagetown, PO Box 17000, Stn. Forces, Oromocto NB E2V 4J5
Tel: 506-357-7314
admin@nbsigs.net
www.nbsigs.net
Overview: A small provincial organization founded in 2003
Chief Officer(s):
Al Lustig, President
Membership: *Fees:* $25

New Brunswick Snowboard Association

45, av Des Ormes, Edmunston NB E3V 4J8
Tel: 506-739-9843
Overview: A small provincial organization overseen by Canadian Snowboard Federation
Mission: To be the provincial governing body of competitive snowboarding in New Brunswick.
Member of: Canadian Snowboard Federation
Chief Officer(s):
Raymond Turgeon, Contact
rturgeon@nbnet.nb.ca

New Brunswick Society for the Prevention of Cruelty to Animals / Société protectrice des animaux du Nouveau-Brunswick

PO Box 1412, Stn. A, Fredericton NB E3B 5E3
Tel: 506-458-8208; *Fax:* 506-458-8209
www.spca-nb.ca
Also Known As: New Brunswick SPCA
Overview: A medium-sized provincial organization founded in 1881 overseen by Canadian Federation of Humane Societies
Mission: To prevent cruelty to & encourage consideration for all animals; to pursue program of humane education.
Member of: Canadian Federation of Humane Societies
Membership: *Fees:* $10

New Brunswick Society of Cardiology Techologists (NBSCT)

c/o Isabelle Desjardins, 29 Nicolas St., Dieppe NB E1A 8N3
www.nbsct.ca
Overview: A small provincial organization founded in 1968
Mission: To operate in accordance with An Act Respecting the New Brunswick Society of Cardiology Technologists; To maintain high standards for the practice of cardiology technology in New Brunswick
Member of: Canadian Society of Cardiology Technologists
Affliation(s): Canadian Medical Association
Chief Officer(s):
Lynn Douglas, President
president@nbsct.ca
Isabelle Desjardins, Registrar & Treasurer
registrar@nbsct.ca
Lisa Johnson, Director, Education
education@nbsct.ca
Andrea Neufeld, Coordinator, Continuing Education Unit
ceu_coordinator@nbsct.ca
Membership: *Fees:* $125 active members; $75 other memberships; *Member Profile:* Cardiology technologists in New Brunswick educated to test, monitor, & evaluate the human heart & its functions; Students enrolled in a a cardiology program approved by the society; *Committees:* Complaints; Discipline; Legislation / Bylaw; Membership; Public Relations; Translation; CEU
Activities: Upholding the Canon of Ethics of the Canadian Society of Cardiology Technologists as the rules of conduct of society members

New Brunswick Society of Certified Engineering Technicians & Technologists (NBSCETT) / Société des techniciens et des technologues agréés du génie du Nouveau-Brunswick (STTAGN-B)

#12B 102 Main St., Fredericton NB E3A 9N6
Tel: 506-454-6124; *Fax:* 506-452-7076
Toll-Free: 800-665-8324
nbscett@nbscett.nb.ca

www.nbscett.nb.ca
www.facebook.com/groups/376729745776586
Overview: A medium-sized provincial organization founded in 1968 overseen by Canadian Council of Technicians & Technologists
Mission: To grant certification to applied science & engineering technology technicians & technologists; to protect titles & powers of discipline for its members
Chief Officer(s):
Jean-Luc Michaud, PTech, President
Edward F. Leslie, Executive Director & CEO
Finances: *Annual Operating Budget:* $100,000-$250,000; *Funding Sources:* Membership dues
Staff Member(s): 3
Membership: 1,600; *Fees:* Schedule available; *Member Profile:* Certified - in field of engineering, applied science, technology & meets requirements for certification; Technology graduate in training - meet all of academic requirements for certification; Associate - employed in engineering technology field; *Committees:* Accreditation; Certification & Review; Finance; Human Resources
Activities: Awards; Scholarships; *Awareness Events:* Annual Awards; *Internships:* Yes; *Speaker Service:* Yes; *Library* Open to public

New Brunswick Society of Laboratory Technology ***See*** New Brunswick Society of Medical Laboratory Technologists

New Brunswick Society of Medical Laboratory Technologists (NBSMLT) / Association des technologistes de laboratoire médical du Nouveau-Brunswick (ATMLNB)

PO Box 1812, Moncton NB E1C 9X6
Tel: 506-758-9956; *Fax:* 506-758-9963
office@nbsmlt.nb.ca
www.nbsmlt.nb.ca
Previous Name: New Brunswick Society of Laboratory Technology
Overview: A medium-sized provincial licensing organization founded in 1948 overseen by Canadian Society for Medical Laboratory Science
Mission: To regulate the practice of medical laboratory technology in New Brunswick; To protect the public in matters related to medical laboratory technology; To establish & maintain high standards of practice & regulation in the profession
Chief Officer(s):
Jim Sloan, President
president@nbsmlt.nb.ca
Janelle Bourgeois, Executive Director
janelle.bourgeois@nbsmlt.nb.ca
William Allen, Registrar
registrar@nbsmlt.nb.ca
Membership: 650+; *Member Profile:* Medical laboratory technologists (MLTs) in the province of New Brunswick; *Committees:* Continuing Education; Publications; Public Relations; Admissions; Complaints; Legislation; Discipline; Nominating; Awards; Education of MLT; Training Programs; Regulation & Professional Practice; Professional Development Program; Point of Care; MLT Re-Entry
Activities: Licensing medical laboratory technologists practising in New Brunswick; Supporting partnerships; Promoting continuing education (ce@nbsmlt.nb.ca); *Awareness Events:* National Medical Laboratory Week, April
Awards:
• NBSMLT Anita Lindsay Award (Award)
To recognize the technologist who exemplifies exceptional professional service
Publications:
• MLT Analyzer: Bulletin of the New Brunswick Society of Medicatl Laboratory Technologists
Type: Newsletter; *Editor:* Janelle B. Whitlock
Profile: Society reports, conferences, & professional development activities
• New Brunswick Society of Medical Laboratory Technologist Annual Report
Type: Yearbook; *Frequency:* Annually

New Brunswick Soil & Crop Improvement Association (NBSCIA) / Association pour l'amélioration du sol et des cultures du Nouveau-Brunswick

#302, 259 Brunswick St., Fredericton NB E3B 1G8
Tel: 506-454-1736; *Fax:* 506-453-1985
nbscia@nbnet.nb.ca
www.nbscia.ca
Overview: A small provincial organization founded in 1978
Mission: To improve soil & crop sustainability in New Brunswick; To encourage research & innovation to advance the agricultural industry throughout the province
Affliation(s): Agricultural Alliance of New Brunswick; Eastern Soil & Water Conservation Centre; Soil Conservation Council of Canada
Chief Officer(s):
Susannah Banks, General Manager
John Robinson, President, 506-432-6473
Membership: *Fees:* $20 provincial membership
Activities: Promoting environmental & economical agricultural practices in New Brunswick; Organizing field days & tours; Distributing educational information to New Brunswick farmers; Conducting research projects; Sponsoring research projects & new farming techniques; Liaising with government
Publications:
• New Brunswick Soil & Crop Improvement Association Newsletter
Type: Newsletter; *Frequency:* Quarterly; *Price:* Free with New Brunswick Soil & Crop Improvement Association membership

New Brunswick Solid Waste Association (NBSWA) / l'Association des déchets solides du Nouveau-Brunswick (ADSNB)

32 Wedgewood Dr., Rothesay NB E2E 3P7
Tel: 506-849-4218; *Fax:* 506-847-1369
Toll-Free: 877-777-4218
nbswa@nbnet.nb.ca
Overview: A small provincial organization
Mission: To promote environmentally friendly solid waste management practices in New Brunswick.

New Brunswick Special Care Home Association Inc.

c/o Seely Lodge Inc., 2081 Route 845, Bayswater NB E5S 1J7
Tel: 506-738-8514; *Fax:* 506-738-0892
www.nbscha.com
Overview: A medium-sized provincial organization
Mission: To assist licensed members of the New Brunswick Special Care Home Association Inc. in providing quality, cost effective long term care for seniors and special needs adults in cooperation with the Department of Social Development.
Chief Officer(s):
Jan Seely, President
Membership: 42 homes; *Member Profile:* Long-term care and special care homes in New Brunswick

New Brunswick Special Olympics ***See*** Special Olympics New Brunswick

New Brunswick Speech & Hearing Association ***See*** New Brunswick Association of Speech-Language Pathologists & Audiologists

New Brunswick Speed Skating Association ***See*** Speed Skate New Brunswick

New Brunswick Sportfishing Association (NBSFA)

c/o Bert Beek, 758 Rte. 670, Ripples NB E4B 1E9
Tel: 506-385-2335
www.nbsportfishing.ca
www.facebook.com/550441211657133
Overview: A small provincial organization
Mission: To elevate the sport of bass fishing in New Brunswick
Finances: *Funding Sources:* Membership fees; Sponsorships
Membership: *Fees:* $50; *Member Profile:* Persons, 19 years of age or older, who are eligible to purchase a fishing license in New Brunswick; Persons, under age 19, who are recommended by a member; Organizations which provide finanial support to the association
Activities: Hosting tournaments; Promoting catch & release programs; Liaising with the government for new regulations for tournament bass fishing; Improving fish handling methods; Helping to fund studies on smallmouth bass in New Brunswick

New Brunswick Sports Hall of Fame (NBSHF) / Temple de la renommée sportive du N.-B.

503 Queen St., Fredericton NB E3B 5H1
Tel: 506-453-3747
nbsportshalloffame@gnb.ca
www.nbsportshalloffame.com
www.facebook.com/150319378347024
twitter.com/NBSHF
Overview: A small provincial charitable organization founded in 1970
Mission: N.B. Sports Hall of Fame recognizes & honours achievement in competitive sport & its development; with honour comes distinction & a rich sport legacy for the youth of the future; such achievement & legacy are kept alive for inductees, the sport community & generations of New Brunswickers through celebration, public exhibition & preservation of our sport heritage
Member of: Canadian Association for Sport Heritage; Canadian Museums Association
Affliation(s): International Sports Heritage Association
Chief Officer(s):
Jamie Wolverton, Executive Director, 506-453-8930
jamie.wolverton@gnb.ca
Finances: *Funding Sources:* Provincial government; fundraising; sponsorships; donations
Activities: Annual dinner & Induction Ceremony; exhibits; receptions; lectures; tours; *Library:* Sports Heritage Resource Centre; Open to public by appointment

New Brunswick Teachers' Association (NBTA) / Fédération des enseignants du Nouveau-Brunswick (FENB)

PO Box 752, 650 Montgomery St., Fredericton NB E3B 5G2
Tel: 506-452-8921; *Fax:* 506-453-9795
www.nbta.ca
www.facebook.com/219814221400600
Previous Name: New Brunswick Teachers' Federation (Ind.)
Overview: A medium-sized provincial organization founded in 1970 overseen by Canadian Teachers' Federation
Chief Officer(s):
Larry Jamieson, Executive Director
larry.jamieson@nbta.ca
Finances: *Funding Sources:* Membership dues
Staff Member(s): 17
Membership: 8,170 + 47 branches
Activities: *Library:* NBTF Resource Centre

New Brunswick Teachers' Federation (Ind.) ***See*** New Brunswick Teachers' Association

New Brunswick Team Handball Federation

NB
info.handballnb@gmail.com
www.handballnb.org
www.facebook.com/pages/Handball-NB/195293907261100
Également appelé: Handball NB
Aperçu: *Dimension:* petite; *Envergure:* locale; Organisme sans but lucratif
Membre de: Canadian Team Handball Federation
Membre(s) du bureau directeur:
Jason A. Ferguson, President

New Brunswick Turkey Marketing Board ***See*** Turkey Farmers of New Brunswick

New Brunswick Union (NBU) / Syndicat du Nouveau-Brunswick (SNB)

217 Brunswick St., Fredericton NB E3B 1G8
Tel: 506-458-8440; *Fax:* 506-450-8481
Toll-Free: 800-442-4420
local333@telus.net
www.nbu.ca
twitter.com/NBUSNB
Also Known As: New Brunswick Union of Public and Private Employees
Overview: A small provincial organization
Member of: National Union of Public and General Employees
Chief Officer(s):
Susie Proulx-Daigle, President
susie@nbu.ca
Membership: *Committees:* Code of Solidarity; Constitution and By-Laws; Executive; Finance; Harassment; Nominations/Elections Credentials; Occupational Health & Safety; Para Medical Educational Assistance; Pension Working Group; Resolutions; Scholarship Bursary; Staff Relations; Union Education Selection; Unison for Retired Members; Women's

New Brunswick Veterinary Medical Association (NBVMA) / Association des médecins vétérinaires du Nouveau-Brunswick (AMVNB)

c/o Dr. George Whittle, 1700 Manawagonish Rd., Saint John NB E2M 3Y5
Tel: 506-635-8100
registrar@nbvma-amvnb.ca
www.nbvma-amvnb.ca
Overview: A small provincial licensing organization founded in 1919 overseen by Canadian Veterinary Medical Association
Mission: To act as the regulatory body for the practice of veterinary medicine in New Brunswick; To establish standards of practice in the profession; To promote animal health & welfare;

To prevent public health problems related to animal disease
Member of: Canadian Veterinary Medical Association
Chief Officer(s):
George Whittle, Registrar
Membership: *Member Profile:* Veterinarians in New Brunswick
Activities: Offering continuing education programs

New Brunswick Wildlife Federation (NBWF) / Fédération de la faune du Nouveau-Brunswick

PO Box 549, Moncton NB E1C 8L9
nbwildlifefederation.org
Overview: A medium-sized provincial organization founded in 1924 overseen by Canadian Wildlife Federation
Mission: To foster sound management & wise use of the renewable & non-renewable natural resources of New Brunswick; to assist & encourage the enforcement of those game laws which are in keeping with the objectives of the Federation & to strive for better management & game laws where & when necessary; to educate membership & the public, with particular emphasis upon conservation & safety; to represent the interests & concerns of New Brunswick sportsmen; to cooperate with government departments & all related groups, where interests are mutual.
Member of: New Brunswick Salmon Council; Fur Institute of Canada
Chief Officer(s):
Charlie Leblanc, President, 506-866-4345
cleblan618@rogers.com
Rod Currie, Secretary, 506-458-5643, Fax: 506-458-9183
racurrie@nb.sympatico.ca
Membership: 30 clubs + 4,000 individual; *Fees:* $40 individual; $400 max. per club; *Committees:* Adopt-a-Stream; Constitution & By-Laws; Environment; Fisheries; Forestry; Master Angler; Membership; Memorial Cards, Merchandise & Prints; Resolutions; Wildlife & Hunter Education; Fundraising; Becoming an Outdoors-Woman
Activities: *Speaker Service:* Yes

New Brunswick Women's Institute (NBWI)

681 Union St., Fredericton NB E3A 3N8
Tel: 506-454-0798; *Fax:* 506-451-8949
nbwi@nb.aibn.com
www.nbwi.ca
Overview: A medium-sized provincial charitable organization founded in 1911 overseen by Federated Women's Institutes of Canada
Mission: To help discover, stimulate & develop leadership among women; to assist, encourage & support women to become knowledgeable & responsible citizens; to ensure basic human rights for women & work towards their equality; to network with other organizations sharing similar objectives; to promote the improvement of agricultural & other rural communities & to safeguard the environment
Member of: Federated Women's Institutes of Canada
Affliation(s): Associated Country Women of the World
Chief Officer(s):
Rose D'Amour, Administrative Officer
Holly Hersey, President
Finances: *Funding Sources:* Grants; membership dues
Membership: 1,000 members in 100 branches; *Member Profile:* New Brunswick Women 18 or older

New Canadian Centre Immigrant Service *See* New Canadians Centre Peterborough Immigrant Services

New Canadians Centre Peterborough Immigrant Services (NCC)

221 Romaine St., Peterborough ON K9J 2C3
Tel: 705-743-0882; *Fax:* 705-743-6219
info@nccpeterborough.ca
www.nccpeterborough.ca
www.facebook.com/newcanadianscentre
twitter.com/ncc_ptbo
www.youtube.com/user/newcanadianscentre
Previous Name: New Canadian Centre Immigrant Service
Overview: A small local organization founded in 1979 overseen by Ontario Council of Agencies Serving Immigrants
Mission: To provide direct assistance to New Canadians through resettlement services in Peterborough; to promote cultural bridging through public awareness & community activities
Member of: United Way; Council of Immigrant Services of Eastern Ontario
Chief Officer(s):
Hajni Hos, Executive Director
hajni@nccpeterborough.ca

Finances: *Funding Sources:* Federal; provincial; municipal; United Way; fundraising
Membership: *Fees:* $20 single; $30 organization
Activities: *Speaker Service:* Yes; *Library* Open to public

New Circles Community Services

161 Bartley Dr., Toronto ON M4A 1E6
Tel: 416-422-2591; *Fax:* 416-422-5946
info@newcircles.ca
newcircles.ca
www.facebook.com/130999970339869
twitter.com/newcircles
Overview: A small local charitable organization
Mission: To provide clothing & social services to families in need living in the Thorncliffe Park, Flemingdon Park & Victoria Village areas of Toronto
Chief Officer(s):
Alykhan Suleman, Executive Director
alykhan@newcircles.ca
Staff Member(s): 7; 200 volunteer(s)

New Clarence-Rockland Chamber of Commerce

#201, 8710 County Road 17, Rockland ON K4K 1T2
Tel: 613-761-1954; *Fax:* 866-648-2769
info@ccclarencerockland.com
ccclarencerockland.com
www.facebook.com/formationsncccr
Overview: A small local organization
Mission: To be the voice for its members & promote commerce in Clarence-Rockland
Member of: Canadian Chamber of Commerce
Chief Officer(s):
Martine Nolin-Simard, President
Membership: *Fees:* $150 self employed; $200 non-profit; $250 2-14 employees; $450 15-39 employees; $850 40+ employees

New College Alumni Association (NCAA)

#118, 300 Huron St., Toronto ON M5S 3J6
Tel: 416-978-8273; *Fax:* 416-978-0554
alumni.newcollege@utoronto.ca
www.utoronto.ca/ncaa
Overview: A medium-sized local organization
Mission: To develop a visible and mutually supportive communication network that connects New College Alumni with the other stake holders of New College and the University of Toronto. The other stake holders include the students, their parents, New College and U of T, the city of Toronto and the community as a whole.
Chief Officer(s):
Lesley Reidstra, President

New Democratic Party (NDP) / Nouveau Parti Démocratique

Federal Office, #300, 279 Laurier West, Ottawa ON K1P 5J9
Tel: 613-236-3613; *Fax:* 613-230-9950
Toll-Free: 866-525-2555; *TTY:* 866-776-7742
www.ndp.ca
www.facebook.com/group.php?gid=190502667652613
twitter.com/NDP_HQ
www.youtube.com/user/NDPCanada
Also Known As: Canada's NDP
Overview: A medium-sized national organization founded in 1961
Mission: To offer Canadians an alternative political vision based on the principles of democratic socialism; To protect & expand programs such as Medicare & the Old Age Pension through prudent & effective government, & through a truly fair tax system
Chief Officer(s):
Tom Mulcair, Leader
Rebecca Blaikie, President
Membership: 200,000+
Activities: *Library* by appointment

Alberta NDP
#201, 10544 - 114 St. NW, Edmonton AB T5H 3J7
Tel: 780-474-2415; *Fax:* 780-669-9617
Toll-Free: 800-465-6587
info@albertandp.ca
www.albertandp.ca
www.facebook.com/albertandp
twitter.com/AlbertaNDP
www.youtube.com/user/AlbertaNDP
Chief Officer(s):
Rachel Notley, Leader
edmonton.strathcona@assembly.ab.ca

British Columbia NDP
5367 Kingsway, Burnaby BC V5H 2G1
Tel: 604-430-8600; *Fax:* 604-432-9517
Toll-Free: 888-868-3637
bcndp@bcndp.ca
www.bcndp.ca
www.facebook.com/bcndp
twitter.com/bcndp
Chief Officer(s):
John Horgan, Leader
Jan O'Brien, Provincial Secretary
jan.obrien@bcndp.ca

Manitoba NDP
#803, 294 Portage Ave., Winnipeg MB R3C 0B9
Tel: 204-987-4857; *Fax:* 204-786-2443
Toll-Free: 877-863-2976
todaysndp.mb.ca
www.facebook.com/pages/Manitoba-NDP/127882984614
twitter.com/mbndp
www.youtube.com/ndpmanitoba
Chief Officer(s):
Greg Selinger, Leader
premier@leg.gov.mb.ca

New Brunswick NDP
#2, 924 Prospect St., Fredericton NB E3B 2T9
Tel: 506-458-5828
Toll-Free: 844-637-6731
www.nbndp.ca
www.facebook.com/nbndp.npdnb
twitter.com/NB_NDP
www.youtube.com/user/NBNDP
Chief Officer(s):
Dominic Cardy, Party Leader

Newfoundland & Labrador NDP
PO Box 5275, St. John's NL A1C 5W1
Tel: 709-739-6387
info@nl.ndp.ca
nlndp.ca
www.facebook.com/NLNDP
twitter.com/nlndp
Chief Officer(s):
Lorraine Michael, Leader, 709-729-0270
lorrainemichael@gov.nl.ca

Nova Scotia NDP
#603, 5151 George St., Halifax NS B3J 1M5
Tel: 902-423-9217; *Fax:* 902-423-9618
Toll-Free: 800-753-7696
www.ns.ndp.ca
www.facebook.com/nsndp
twitter.com/NSNDP
www.youtube.com/nsndp
Chief Officer(s):
Maureen MacDonald, Party Leader, 902-455-2926
mmacdonald@navnet.net

Ontario NDP
101 Richmond St. East, Toronto ON M5C 1N9
Tel: 416-591-8637; *Fax:* 416-599-4820
Toll-Free: 866-390-6637
www.ontariondp.com
www.facebook.com/OntarioNDP
twitter.com/ontariondp
www.youtube.com/user/OntarioNewDemocrat
Chief Officer(s):
Andrea Horwath, Leader
Darlene Lawson, Provincial Secretary, 416-591-5455 Ext. 2245
dlawson@on.ndp.ca

PEI NDP
81 Prince St., Charlottetown PE C1A 4R3
Tel: 902-892-1930; *Fax:* 902-368-7180
ndppei@pei.aibn.com
ndppei.ca
www.facebook.com/112650842089951
twitter.com/peindp
Chief Officer(s):
Mike Redmond, Party Leader

Québec NDP
#202, 4689, av Papineau, Montréal QC H2H 1V4
Tel: 514-590-0036; *Fax:* 514-590-0555
Toll-Free: 866-525-2555
qc.npd.ca
twitter.com/NPDQuebec
www.flickr.com/photos/npdndpqc

Saskatchewan NDP
Tommy Douglas House, 1122 Saskatchewan Dr., Regina SK S4P 0C4

Tel: 306-525-1322; *Fax:* 306-569-1363
info@saskndp.ca
saskndp.ca
www.facebook.com/SaskNDP
twitter.com/Sask_NDP
www.youtube.com/SaskNDP
Chief Officer(s):
Cam Broten, Leader
Yukon NDP
PO Box 31516, Whitehorse YT Y1A 6K8
Tel: 867-668-2203
www.yukonndp.ca
www.facebook.com/YukonNDP
twitter.com/yukonndp
Chief Officer(s):
Liz Hanson, Leader

New Denmark Historical Society
c/o New Denmark Memorial Museum, 444 Hwy. 380, New Denmark NB E7G 2Y9
Tel: 506-553-6464
Overview: A small local organization founded in 1972
Mission: To operate a museum; To preserve cultural heritage
Member of: Federation of Danish Association in Canada; NB Museum
Chief Officer(s):
Sarah Ouellette, President
Finances: *Annual Operating Budget:* Less than $50,000
12 volunteer(s)
Membership: 30 corporate; *Fees:* Schedule available

The New Directions Group (NDG)
PO Box 8105, Canmore AB T1W 2T8
Tel: 403-678-9956
info@newdirectionsgroup.org
www.newdirectionsgroup.org
Overview: A small national organization founded in 1990
Mission: To provide a forum for leaders from Canadian businesses & NGO communities to debate sustainability issues
Chief Officer(s):
Paul Griss, Coordinator
Finances: *Funding Sources:* Corporate participants; Project support from governments
Activities: Advancing policy; Releasing reports on projects;

New Experiences for Refugee Women ***See*** Newcomer Women's Services Toronto

New Hamburg Board of Trade
121 Huron St., New Hamburg ON N3A 1K1
Tel: 519-662-6628
www.nhbot.ca
twitter.com/NewHamburgBoT
Overview: A small local organization
Mission: The New Hamburg Board of Trade represents and serves local business interests in this Wilmot-based township.
Chief Officer(s):
Tim Bender, President, 519-662-1221
timbender@nhbot.ca
Steve Wagler, Vice-President, 519-662-1644
Membership: 90; *Fees:* $145 basic; $205 full + GST

New Hamilton Orchestra ***See*** Hamilton Philharmonic Orchestra

The New Homeland ***See*** Masaryk Memorial Institute Inc.

New Leaf Enterprises
3670 Kempt Rd., Halifax NS B3K 4X8
Tel: 902-455-9044; *Fax:* 902-454-6121
www.easterseals.ns.ca
Overview: A small local organization founded in 1960 overseen by Easter Seals Nova Scotia
Mission: To create a collaborative social setting in order to help adults with physical disabilities develop job skills
Member of: Easter Seals Nova Scotia; DIRECTIONS Council for Vocational Services Society
Chief Officer(s):
Veronica Dale, Executive Director/Manager
v.dale@easterseals.ns.ca
Bonnie Harrison, Contact, Client Services
b.harrison@easterseals.ns.ca
Activities: Catering services; café; business services; job skills training

New Life League ***See*** Adventive Cross Cultural Initiatives

New Media Business Alliance ***See*** Interactive Ontario

New Wave Party of BC
3040 Westwood St., Port Coquitlam BC V3C 3L7
Tel: 604-636-6004
newwaveparty@gmail.com
www.newwaveofbc.ca
Also Known As: New Wave
Overview: A small provincial organization
Chief Officer(s):
Ranjit Ahluwalia, Contact

New West Theatre Society
#111, 210A - 12A St. North, Lethbridge AB T1H 2J1
Tel: 403-381-9378
info@newwesttheatre.com
www.newwesttheatre.com
www.facebook.com/NewWestTheatreLethbridge
twitter.com/newwesttheatre
Overview: A small local charitable organization
Mission: To provide Lethbridge & surrounding region with a broad-based & diverse program of professional quality theatrical, musical & dramatic performances
Chief Officer(s):
Jeremy Mason, Artistic Director
mason@newwesttheatre.com
Natascha Hainsworth, General Manager
hainsworth@newwesttheatre.com
Finances: *Funding Sources:* Alberta Foundation for the Arts
Staff Member(s): 2
Activities: Hires 180 contract actors, directors, designers, technicians per year

New Westminster & District Labour Council (NWDLC)
#105, 3920 Norland Ave., Burnaby BC V5G 4K7
Tel: 604-291-9306; *Fax:* 604-291-0996
nwdlc@shawcable.com
www.nwdlc.ca
Overview: A large local organization founded in 1966 overseen by British Columbia Federation of Labour
Mission: To represent 123 affiliated unions in New Westminster, British Columbia & the surrounding area; To support community activism for workers & their families; To speak out on issues affecting workplaces & communities; To build a community that supports the needs of working families
Affliation(s): Canadian Labour Congress (CLC)
Chief Officer(s):
Lori Mayhew, President
Carolyn Rice, Secretary-Treasurer
Membership: 55,000+; *Member Profile:* Trade union members from New Westminster, British Columbia, & the surrounding area, including Burnaby, Delta, Surrey, Port Moody, White Rock, Pitt Meadows, Port Coquitlam, Langley City, & Langley Township
Activities: Advocating for issues, such as an increase to British Columbia's minimum wage & changes to Workers Compensation regulations to protect employees who work alone; Lobbying all levels of government about social & economic issues: Offering educational seminars & conferences; Providing networking opportunities among local union members; Supporting local community organizations, such as the Protein for People Project & the United Way Days of Caring project
Awards:
- Gerry Stoney CLC Harrison Winter School Scholarship (Scholarship)
- Bob Fortin CLC Harrison Winter School Scholarship (Scholarship)
- Joy Langan CLC Harrison Winter School Scholarship (Scholarship)

Meetings/Conferences: • New Westminster & District Labour Council 2015 Annual General Meeting, 2015, BC
Scope: Local

The New Westminster Board of Trade ***See*** New Westminster Chamber of Commerce

New Westminster Chamber of Commerce
601 Queens Ave., New Westminster BC V3M 1L1
Tel: 604-521-7781; *Fax:* 604-521-0057
nwcc@newwestchamber.com
www.newwestchamber.com
Also Known As: New Westminster Visitor Info Centre
Previous Name: The New Westminster Board of Trade
Overview: A small local organization founded in 1883
Mission: To encourage a business climate which enables our membership & community to prosper
Member of: BC Chamber of Commerce
Chief Officer(s):
Andrew Hopkins, President
Cori Lynn Germiquet, Executive Director
Finances: *Annual Operating Budget:* $250,000-$500,000
Staff Member(s): 2; 2 volunteer(s)
Membership: 327; *Fees:* $177-$1,378; *Committees:* Community Policing; Heritage Advisory
Activities: Golf tournament; awards; auction; workshops

New Westminster Historical Society (NWHS)
#309, 2559 Parkview Lane, Port Coquitlam BC V3C 6M1
Tel: 604-526-6113
www.nwheritage.org/heritagesite/orgs/nwhs/nwhs.htm
Overview: A small local organization founded in 1976
Mission: To provide monthly programs, free & open to everyone, about the history of New Westminster & other related history topics; to organize speakers
Finances: *Funding Sources:* Membership fees
Membership: *Fees:* $10
Activities: Monthly meetings

New Westminster Hyack Festival Association
204 - 6th St., New Westminster BC V3L 3A1
Tel: 604-522-6894; *Fax:* 604-522-6094
events@hyack.bc.ca
www.hyack.bc.ca
www.facebook.com/HyackFestivalAssn
twitter.com/HyackFestival
Overview: A small local organization founded in 1971
Mission: To organize & facilitate events in the City of New Westminster while preserving history and tradition, in order to promote the City, stimulate the local economy & entertain and involve people in a fun-filled atmosphere.
Chief Officer(s):
Cathie Gibson, Interim Executive Director
execdirector@hyack.bc.ca
Membership: *Fees:* $25 youth/senior; $35 single; $55 couple/family

Newcastle & District Chamber of Commerce
PO Box 11, 20 King Ave. West, Newcastle ON L1B 1H7
www.newcastle.on.ca
www.facebook.com/NewcastleAndDistrictChamber
Overview: A small local organization
Member of: Canadian Chamber of Commerce
Chief Officer(s):
Tom Ujfalussy, President
Membership: 72; *Fees:* $120

Newcastle Village & District Historical Society
#3, 20 King Ave. West, Newcastle ON L1B 1H7
Tel: 905-987-5180
newcastle.historic@gmail.com
Overview: A small local organization
Mission: To collect local historical documents & photographs
Member of: Ontario Historical Society
Chief Officer(s):
Beverly Jeeves, Director
Finances: *Funding Sources:* Membership dues
Activities: *Library:* Massey Memorial Library

Newcomer Women's Services Toronto (NEW)
#401, 745 Danforth Ave., Toronto ON M4J 1L4
Tel: 416-469-0196; *Fax:* 416-469-3307
pa@newcomerwomen.org
www.newcomerwomen.org
twitter.com/NEW_Employment
www.youtube.com/user/NewcomerWomenService
Also Known As: New Experiences for Newcomer Women
Previous Name: New Experiences for Refugee Women
Overview: A small local charitable organization founded in 1983
Mission: To promote the social, cultural & economic integration of newcomer women into Canada's multicultural society
Member of: Advocates for Community Based Training & Education for Women; Ontario Council of Agencies Serving Immigrants; Women's Centres Association Ontario
Chief Officer(s):
Maya Roy, Executive Director
maya@newcomerwomen.org
Finances: *Funding Sources:* Federal, provincial, municipal & city governments; United Way; Trillium Foundation
Staff Member(s): 22
Membership: *Member Profile:* Clients & community supporters
Activities: *Internships:* Yes
Newcomer Employment Services Toronto (NEST)
705 Danforth Ave., Toronto ON M4J 1L2

Tel: 416-751-8888; *Fax:* 416-751-8890
www.facebook.com/groups/newcomerwomen/
twitter.com/NEW_Employment
Chief Officer(s):
Grace Son, Manager, Employment Programs
grace@newcomerwomen.org

Newfoundland & Labrador AIDS Committee *See* AIDS Committee of Newfoundland & Labrador

Newfoundland & Labrador Amateur Bodybuilding Association (NLABBA)

12 Walsh's Rd., Logy Bay NL A1K 3G8
www.nlabba.ca
Overview: A small provincial organization overseen by Canadian Bodybuilding Federation
Mission: To govern the sport of amateur bodybuilding, fitness & figure in Newfoundland & Labrador.
Member of: Canadian Bodybuilding Federation; International Federation of Bodybuilding
Chief Officer(s):
Mike Newhook, President
nlabba.exec@gmail.com
Zack Howard, Vice-President
vpnlabba@gmail.com
Pam Slaney, Secretary
pslaney387@gmail.com
Ken French, Treasurer
kenfrenc@gmail.com

Newfoundland & Labrador Amateur Sports Federation *See* Sport Newfoundland & Labrador

Newfoundland & Labrador Amateur Wrestling Association (NLAWA)

NL
nlawa.wordpress.com
Overview: A small provincial organization overseen by Canadian Amateur Wrestling Association
Mission: The NLAWA is a small organization comprised of coaches, officials, parents and athletes who are dedicated to advancing the sport of wrestling in Newfoundland and Labrador
Chief Officer(s):
Randy Ralph, President
randolphralph@esdnl.ca

Newfoundland & Labrador Arts Council (NLAC)

PO Box 98, 1 Springdale St., St. John's NL A1C 5H5
Tel: 709-726-2212; *Fax:* 709-726-0619
Toll-Free: 866-726-2212
nlacmail@nlac.ca
www.nlac.ca
Overview: A medium-sized provincial charitable organization founded in 1980
Mission: To foster & promote the arts of the province; to carry on financial assistance programs for individual artists & arts groups; to work with the government & the community for development in the arts
Member of: Canadian Conference of the Arts
Chief Officer(s):
Reg Winsor, Executive Director
rwinsor@nlac.ca
Tom Gordon, Chair
Finances: *Annual Operating Budget:* $500,000-$1.5 Million; *Funding Sources:* Provincial government
Staff Member(s): 4; 12 volunteer(s)
Activities: *Library* Open to public

Newfoundland & Labrador Association for Community Living (NLACL)

PO Box 8414, 74 O'Leary Ave., St. John's NL A1B 3N7
Tel: 709-722-0790
Toll-Free: 800-701-8511
Other Communication: Alt. Phone: 709-722-1825
www.nlacl.ca
www.facebook.com/nlacl
twitter.com/nlacl1
Overview: A small provincial charitable organization founded in 1956 overseen by Canadian Association for Community Living
Mission: To develop communities in Newfoundland & Labrador that welcome individuals with developmental disabilities
Member of: Canadian Association for Community Living
Chief Officer(s):
Dennis Gill, President
dennis.gill@eastlink.ca
Gail St. Croix, Vice-President
frisky@nl.rogers.com
Una Tucker, Secretary
harvey.tucker@eastlink.ca
Helen O'Rourke, Treasurer
helenorourke_497@hotmail.com
Sherry Gambin-Walsh, Executive Director
sherrygw@nlacl.ca
Finances: *Funding Sources:* Donations; Sponsorships; Fundraising; Special events; Bequeaths
Activities: Engaging in advocacy activities; Liaising with government & service agencies; Supporting individuals, families, & local associations; Facilitating research; Providing educational opportunities about issues encountered by persons with developmental disabilities; Sponsoring a community inclusion project; *Library:* NL Association for Community Living Resource Centre
Publications:
• Gateway
Type: Newsletter; *Frequency:* Quarterly

Newfoundland & Labrador Association for Community Living (NLACL)

PO Box 8414, 74 O'Leary Ave., St. John's NL A1B 3N7
Tel: 709-722-0790; *Fax:* 709-722-1325
nlacl@nlacl.ca
www.facebook.com/nlacl
twitter.com/nlacl1
Previous Name: Labrador West Association for Community Living
Overview: A small local organization founded in 1979
Member of: Newfoundland & Labrador Association for Community Living
Chief Officer(s):
Sherry Gambin-Walsh, Executive Director, 709-722-0790 Ext. 223, Fax: 709-722-1325
sherrygw@nlacl.ca
30 volunteer(s)
Membership: *Fees:* $10 individual; $25 family; *Committees:* Education; Individual & Family Support; Public Relations; Fundraising

Newfoundland & Labrador Association of Insolvency & Restructuring Professionals

c/o Deloitte & Touche Inc., Fort William Buidling, 10 Factory Lane, St. John's NL A1C 6H5
Tel: 709-576-8480
Previous Name: Newfoundland & Labrador Insolvency Association
Overview: A small provincial organization overseen by Canadian Association of Insolvency & Restructuring Professionals
Member of: Canadian Association of Insolvency & Restructuring Professionals
Chief Officer(s):
Nancy Snedden, President
nsnedden@deloitte.ca
Membership: *Member Profile:* Persons in Newfoundland & Labrador who act as trustees in bankruptcy, agents, receivers, monitors, & consultants in insolvency matters

Newfoundland & Labrador Association of Landscape Architects (NLALA)

77 Gower St., St. John's NL A1C 1N6
Tel: 709-579-7744
www.nlala.com
Overview: A medium-sized provincial organization
Chief Officer(s):
Jim Floyd, President
jfloyd@nnet.net
Membership: 12; *Member Profile:* Landscape architects & firms

Newfoundland & Labrador Association of Medical Radiation Technologists (NLAMRT)

PO Box 29141, Stn. Torbay Rd. Post Office, St. John's NL A1A 5B5
Tel: 709-777-6036
association@nlamrt.ca
www.nlamrt.ca
Overview: A small provincial organization founded in 1951 overseen by Canadian Association of Medical Radiation Technologists
Mission: To represent all working medical radiation technologists in Newfoundland & Labrador
Chief Officer(s):
Dorothy Bennett, President
Membership: *Member Profile:* Full practice membership is available to those in Newfoundland & Labrador who have passed the Canadian Association of Medical Radiation Technologists; Medical radiation technology students
Activities: Advocating for the profession of medical radiation technology; Upholding the ethical standards of the profession; Providing continuing education
Meetings/Conferences: • Newfoundland & Labrador Association of Medical Radiation Technologists 2015 64th Annual Provincial Conference, 2015, NL
Scope: Provincial
Publications:
• NLAMRT News
Type: Newsletter; *Frequency:* Semiannually
Profile: Association reports, regional updates, awards, upcoming meetings, & continuing education information

Newfoundland & Labrador Association of Occupational Therapists (NLAOT)

PO Box 5423, St. John's NL A1C 5W2
Tel: 709-738-2434
info@nlaot.ca
www.nlaot.ca
Overview: A small provincial organization
Mission: To advocate for the profession of occupational therapy in Newfoundland & Labrador
Chief Officer(s):
Sandy Delaney, President
president@nlaot.ca
Finances: *Funding Sources:* Membership fees; Subscriptions; Bequests; Donations; Grants
Membership: 100-499; *Member Profile:* Occupational therapists who practise or reside in Newfoundland & Labrador
Activities: Developing public awareness & understanding of occupational therapy; Supporting continuing professional education; Encouraging research in occupational therapy; Facilitating communication among occupational therapists

Newfoundland & Labrador Association of Optometrists (NLAO)

PO Box 8042, St. John's NL A1B 3M7
Tel: 709-739-8284; *Fax:* 709-739-8378
nlao@nl.rogers.com
www.nao.opto.ca
Previous Name: Newfoundland Association of Optometrists
Overview: A medium-sized provincial organization overseen by Canadian Association of Optometrists
Mission: To provide an online resource for Doctors of Optometry & other healthcare providers in Newfoundland & Labrador
Chief Officer(s):
Ed Breen, Executive Director
Finances: *Funding Sources:* Membership dues

Newfoundland & Labrador Association of Public & Private Employees (NAPE)

PO Box 8100, 330 Portugal Cove Pl., St. John's NL A1B 3M9
Tel: 709-754-0700; *Fax:* 709-754-0726
Toll-Free: 800-563-4442
www.nape.nf.ca
Overview: A medium-sized provincial organization founded in 1936
Mission: The largest union in Newfoundland & Labrador
Member of: Canadian Labour Congress; National Union of Public and General Employees
Affliation(s): Newfoundland & Labrador Federation of Labour; National Union of Public and General Employees; Canadain Labour Congress
Chief Officer(s):
Bert Blundon, Secretary-Treasurer
bblundon@nape.nf.ca
Carol Furlong, President
cfurlong@nape.nf.ca
Arlene Sedlickas, General Vice-President
asedlickas@nape.nf.ca
Finances: *Funding Sources:* Membership dues
Staff Member(s): 35
Membership: 25,000; *Member Profile:* Public & private workers in government, health care, education, corrections, food processing, hospitality & financial sectors
Activities: *Library* Open to public by appointment

Central Office
PO Box 160, 15 Hardy Ave., Grand Falls-Windsor NL A2A 2J4
Tel: 709-489-6619; *Fax:* 709-489-6657
Toll-Free: 800-563-1050
inquiries@nape.nf.ca
Chief Officer(s):

Robert Cater, Vice-President
rcater@nape.nf.ca
Western Office
PO Box 884, 10 Main St., Corner Brook NL A2H 6H6
Tel: 709-639-8483; *Fax:* 709-639-1079
Toll-Free: 800-563-9343
inquiries@nape.nf.ca
Chief Officer(s):
Helen Blackwood

Newfoundland & Labrador Association of Realtors
28 Logy Bay Rd., St. John's NL A1A 1J4
Tel: 709-726-5110
boards.mls.ca/nl/index.htm
Previous Name: Newfoundland Real Estate Association
Overview: A medium-sized provincial organization
Member of: The Canadian Real Estate Association
Finances: *Funding Sources:* Membership fees
Membership: 560 individual

Newfoundland & Labrador Association of Respiratory Therapists (NLART)
Unit 50, Suite 133, Hamlyn Rd. Plaza, St. John's NL A1A 5X7
Tel: 709-777-5707; *Fax:* 709-368-8830
nlarrt@gmail.com
www.nlart.ca
Overview: A medium-sized provincial organization overseen by Canadian Society of Respiratory Therapists
Mission: To improve & maintain the standards of respiratory care in Newfoundland & Labrador
Affliation(s): Canadian Society of Respiratory Therapists (CSRT)
Chief Officer(s):
Jessie Cox, President
Dave Squires, Vice-President
Bonnie O'Leary, Secretary
Wanda Dollard, Treasurer
Membership: *Member Profile:* Registered respiratory therapists in Newfoundland & Labrador, who evaluate, treat, & care for persons with heart & breathing disorders

Newfoundland & Labrador Association of Social Workers (NLASW) / Association des travailleurs sociaux de Terre-Neuve et Labrador
PO Box 39039, 177 Hamlyn Rd., St. John's NL A1E 5Y7
Tel: 709-753-0200; *Fax:* 709-753-0120
info@nlasw.ca
www.nlasw.ca
Overview: A medium-sized provincial organization founded in 1993
Mission: To ensure excellence in social work in Newfoundland & Labrador; To speak out & take appropriate action on issues of social concern; To disseminate information & provide opportunities for continuing education; To provide consultation to agencies involved in training for or delivering human services; To promote the development & the enhancement of social service delivery system suited to the needs of Newfoundlanders
Member of: Canadian Association of Social Workers
Chief Officer(s):
Lisa Crockwell, Executive Director
lcrockwell.nlasw.ca
Finances: *Funding Sources:* Membership fees
Staff Member(s): 5
Membership: 1,507; *Fees:* $400; *Member Profile:* Social workers employed in a wide variety of settings including child welfare, youth & adult corrections, health care, senior citizens homes, hospitals & community health centres, psychiatric institutions, addictions services & social work education; also self-employed in private practice & consulting businesses; *Committees:* Registration; Dosciplinary; Editorial; Professional Issues; Promotion of the Profession; Communitt development network
Activities: *Awareness Events:* National Social Work Week, 1st week of March; *Internships:* Yes; *Speaker Service:* Yes

Newfoundland & Labrador Association of Speech-Language Pathologists & Audiologists (NLASLPA)
PO Box 21212, St. John's NL A1A 5B2
e-mail: info@nlaslpa.ca
www.nlaslpa.ca
Previous Name: Newfoundland Speech & Hearing Association
Overview: A medium-sized provincial organization founded in 1979
Mission: To foster highest quality of service to the communicatively handicapped; to advance knowledge of speech-language pathology & audiology in the region
Member of: Canadian Association of Speech-Language Pathologists & Audiologists
Chief Officer(s):
Ashley Rossiter, Contact
Finances: *Funding Sources:* Membership dues
Membership: 100+; *Fees:* $98 full-time; $72.50 reduced hours; $49 new grads; *Member Profile:* Speech-Language Pathologists & Audiologists
Activities: *Awareness Events:* Speech Hearing Awareness Month, May; *Library:* NLASLPA Library; by appointment

Newfoundland & Labrador Association of Technology Companies (NLATC)
#5, 391 Empire Ave., St. John's NL A1E 1W6
Tel: 709-772-8324; *Fax:* 709-757-6284
info@nati.net
www.nati.net
twitter.com/NATI_NL
Previous Name: Newfoundland Alliance of Technical Industries
Overview: A medium-sized provincial organization
Mission: To act collectively for technical organizations in Newfoundland industry in cooperation with educational & public sectors to promote the growth of innovative technical industries in Newfoundland & Labrador & the rest of Canada
Affliation(s): Canadian Advanced Technology Association; Information Technology Association of Canada
Chief Officer(s):
Ron Taylor, Chief Executive Officer, 709-757-3252
ron@nati.net
Finances: *Annual Operating Budget:* $500,000-$1.5 Million; *Funding Sources:* Membership dues; government
Staff Member(s): 10; 30 volunteer(s)
Membership: 200; *Fees:* $130-$695
Activities: Leadership; corporate development; market development; networking & communications; *Library:* NATI Library; Open to public

Newfoundland & Labrador Association of the Appraisal Institute of Canada
PO Box 1571, Stn. C, St. John's NL A1C 5P3
Tel: 709-753-7644; *Fax:* 709-753-7627
naaic@nf.aibn.com
Overview: A small provincial organization overseen by Appraisal Institute of Canada
Mission: To promote the appraisal profession throughout Newfoundland & Labrador.
Chief Officer(s):
Susan Chipman, Executive Director
Bill Balsom, President
Activities: Administering the designation process; Providing workshops & seminars;

Newfoundland & Labrador Association of the Deaf (NLAD)
21 Merrymeeting Rd., 3rd Fl., St. John's NL A1C 2V6
Tel: 709-726-6672; *Fax:* 709-726-6650; *TTY:* 709-726-6672
nlad@nlad.org
www.nlad.org
Overview: A small provincial organization founded in 1947
Mission: To protect & promote the rights, needs & concerns of people who have severe hearing disabilities & are profoundly deaf within the Province of Newfoundland & Labrador
Affliation(s): Canadian Association of the Deaf
Chief Officer(s):
Jodie Burke, Chair
jodie.burke@bellaliant.net

Newfoundland & Labrador Athletics Association (NLAA)
PO Box 3202, Paradise NL A1L 3W4
Tel: 709-576-1303; *Fax:* 709-576-7493
athletics@nlaa.ca
www.nlaa.ca
www.facebook.com/NLAthletics
twitter.com/nlathletics
Previous Name: Newfoundland & Labrador Track & Field Association
Overview: A small provincial organization overseen by Athletics Canada
Member of: Athletics Canada
Affliation(s): Athletics North-East; Mariners Athletics Club; Nautilus Running Club; New World Running Club; Pearlgate T&F Club; Trappers Running Club; Trinity-Conception Athletics Club; Westerland Track Club
Chief Officer(s):
Bob Walsh, President
bob@atlantichome.net
Alison Walsh, Treasurer
alisonwalsh3@hotmail.com
George Stanoev, Technical Director
Membership: *Fees:* Schedule available; *Member Profile:* Competitive membership (road running, cross country running, & track & field); Non-competitive membership (coaches & officials); *Committees:* Road Race; Coaches; Officials
Activities: Offering courses & clinics for athletes, officials, & coaches; Supervising events; Ensuring that rules are followed & criteria maintained throughout Newfoundland & Labrador

Newfoundland & Labrador Ball Hockey Association (NLBHA)
PO Box 2579, Stn. C, St. John's NL A1C 6K1
Tel: 709-726-4576
contactus@nlbha.com
www.nlbha.com
Overview: A small provincial organization
Mission: To promote the sport of ball hockey in Newfoundland & Labrador; To maintain rules & regulations of the sport
Member of: Canadian Ball Hockey Association; Sport Newfoundland & Labrador
Chief Officer(s):
Diane Kennedy, President
Activities: Organizing championships

Newfoundland & Labrador Basketball Association
1296A Kenmount Rd., Paradise NL A1L 1N3
Tel: 709-576-0247; *Fax:* 709-576-8787
nlba@sportnf.com
www.nlba.nf.ca
www.facebook.com/nlbasketball
twitter.com/nlbasketball
Previous Name: Basketball Newfoundland
Overview: A medium-sized provincial charitable organization founded in 1988 overseen by Canada Basketball
Mission: To develop & promote the sport of basketball across Newfoundland; to assest in the establishment of basketball clubs throughout Newfoundland & Labrador.
Chief Officer(s):
Bill Murphy, Executive Director
nlba@sportnf.com
David Constantine, President
Finances: *Annual Operating Budget:* $250,000-$500,000
Staff Member(s): 3
Membership: *Fees:* Schedule available; *Member Profile:* Clubs, coaches, volunteers, teams, players; *Committees:* Executive; Minor; Coaching; Awards; Halff of Fame; Policy; Hall of Fame Cup; Nominating
Activities: *Internships:* Yes; *Rents Mailing List:* Yes

Newfoundland & Labrador Brain Injury Association (NLBIA)
PO Box 21063, St. John's NL A1A 5B8
Tel: 709-579-3070
nlbia2011@gmail.com
www.nlbia.ca
www.facebook.com/119669344782709
Overview: A small provincial organization founded in 1987 overseen by Brain Injury Association of Canada
Mission: To meet the needs of acquired brain injury survivors & their families in Newfoundland & Labrador; To improve access to care & services
Chief Officer(s):
Chava Finkler, Coordinator, Programs & Services
Michelle Ploughman, President
Marina White, Vice-President
Glen Russell, Treasurer
Finances: *Funding Sources:* Donations; Fundraising
Staff Member(s): 2
Membership: *Fees:* Free; *Member Profile:* Anyone in Newfoundland & Labrador who has been affected by or is interested in acquired brain injury
Activities: Offering support groups & social activities across Newfoundland & Labrador; Raising public awareness of acquired brain injury throughout the province; Providing education about acquired brain injury; Engaging in advocacy activities

Newfoundland & Labrador Camping Association
27 Earle Dr., Pasadena NL A0L 1K0
Tel: 709-686-2363; *Fax:* 709-639-1636
Overview: A medium-sized provincial organization overseen by Canadian Camping Association
Mission: To facilitate the development of organized camping in order to provide educational, character-building & constructive

recreational experiences for all people; to develop awareness & appreciation of the natural environment

Newfoundland & Labrador Cheerleading Athletics (NLCA)

NL
e-mail: nlcasocialmedia@gmail.com
nlcheerleading.ca
www.facebook.com/groups/10418436853
twitter.com/NLCAnews
Overview: A small provincial organization overseen by Cheer Canada
Mission: To be the governing body of cheerleading in Newfoundland & Labrador.
Member of: Cheer Canada
Membre(s) du bureau directeur:
Ashley Wright, President
Julia Kavanagh, Registrar
Amanda Collins, Director, Communications
Membership: 600

Newfoundland & Labrador Chiropractic Association

#285W, 120 Torbay Rd., St. John's NL A1A 2G8
Tel: 709-739-7762; *Fax:* 709-739-7703
nlca@nl.rogers.com
www.nlchiropractic.ca
Overview: A medium-sized provincial organization overseen by Canadian Chiropractic Association
Chief Officer(s):
Carl Eustace, President
Michelle Batterson, Executive Director
Linda Slaney, Secretary
Mike Witherall, Treasurer

Newfoundland & Labrador College for Medical Laboratory Science (NLCMLS)

PO Box 39057, 453 Topsail Rd., St. John's NL A1E 5Y7
Tel: 709-754-8324
www.nlsmls.ca
Previous Name: Newfoundland & Labrador Society of Laboratory Technologists
Overview: A medium-sized provincial organization overseen by Canadian Society for Medical Laboratory Science
Mission: To serve & protect the public
Chief Officer(s):
Colin Power, President
colin.power@nf.sympatico.ca
Membership: *Member Profile:* Laboratory technicians in Newfoundland & Labrador

Newfoundland & Labrador College of Dietitians (NLCD)

PO Box 1756, Stn. C, St. John's NL A1C 5P5
Tel: 709-753-4040; *Fax:* 709-781-1044
Toll-Free: 877-753-4040
registrar@nlcd.ca
www.nlcd.ca
Overview: A medium-sized provincial licensing organization overseen by Dietitians of Canada
Mission: To regulate Registered Dietitians & to ensure competency in the dietetic profession, in the interest of the people in Newfoundland
Member of: Alliance of Canadian Regulatory Boards
Finances: *Annual Operating Budget:* Less than $50,000; *Funding Sources:* Membership fees
6 volunteer(s)
Membership: 150; *Fees:* $450 registration fee; *Member Profile:* Registered dietitians; *Committees:* Continuing Education; Nominations & Awards; Legislation Review; Professional Standards
Activities: *Internships:* Yes
Awards:
• Dr. Patricia Giovannetti Memorial Bursary (Scholarship)

Newfoundland & Labrador College of Physiotherapists (NLCP)

PO Box 21351, #80, 82 Elizabeth Ave., St. John's NL A1A 5G6
Tel: 709-753-6527; *Fax:* 709-753-6526
collegept@nf.aibn.com
nlcpt.com
Overview: A small provincial licensing organization founded in 1972 overseen by Canadian Alliance of Physiotherapy Regulators
Mission: To regulate the profession of physiotherapy in Newfoundland & Labrador
Member of: Canadian Alliance of Physiotherapy Regulators
Affliation(s): Canadian Physiotherapy Association
Chief Officer(s):
Judy Kay, Chair
Josephine Crossan, Executive Director/Registrar
Membership: *Member Profile:* Individuals who have completed the following requirements: an undergraduate or master's degree in physiotherapy at a university recognized by College; the national Physiotherapy Competency Examination; & a course of clinical practice; Registrants with the College must also carry current malpractice insurance; *Committees:* Policy Review; CNA Advisory; Membership; Continuing Competency; PTA Advisory; Complaints Authorization
Activities: Licensing physiotherapists in Newfoundland & Labrador; Liaising with the provincial Ministry of Health to ensure all physiotherapists are registered and meet standards
Publications:
• Newfoundland & Labrador College of Physiotherapists Newsletter
Type: Newsletter

Newfoundland & Labrador Construction Association (NLCA)

#201, 333 Pippy Pl., St. John's NL A1B 3X2
Tel: 709-753-8920; *Fax:* 709-754-3968
info@nfld.com
www.nlca.ca
Overview: A small provincial organization founded in 1968 overseen by Canadian Construction Association
Mission: To act as the voice of the construction industry in Newfoundland & Labrador; To enhance the professionalism & productivity of members through the development of policies
Member of: Canadian Construction Association
Chief Officer(s):
Keith McCarthy, Chair, 709-834-7473, Fax: 709-834-7310
keithmccarthy@nf.aibn.com
Rhonda Neary, President & Chief Operating Officer
rneary@nlca.ca
Frank Collins, Secretary-Treasurer, 709-726-8453, Fax: 709-726-8488
f.collins@nl.rogers.com
Susan Casey, Coordinator, Events
scasey@nlca.ca
Adelle Connors, Coordinator, Member Services
aconnors@nlca.ca
Membership: *Fees:* Schedule available, based upon volume of construction related business; *Member Profile:* Contractors, builders, & suppliers in Newfoundland & Labrador's construction industry; *Committees:* Standard Practices; Safety; Membership; Education & Training; Conference Planning; Golf
Activities: Promoting safety practices in the workplace; Facilitating networking opportunities; Offering the Electronic Plans Room for members; Providing the Gold Seal Certification program; Selling CCA / CCDC construction documents & guides; Providing educational programs & seminars; Developing standard tendering & contractual practices & procedures; Awarding scholarships & bursaries; *Speaker Service:* Yes
Meetings/Conferences: • Newfoundland & Labrador Construction Association 2015 47th Annual Conference & Annual General Meeting, March, 2015, Delta St. John's Hotel & Conference Centre, St. John's, NL
Scope: Provincial
Description: Sessions & keynote addresses of interest to persons such as general, electrical, & mechanical contractors, manufacturers, suppliers, safety professionals, engineers, training providers, LEED accredited professionals, & municipalities
Contact Information: Chair, Conference 2015 Committee: Steve Hayward, Phone: 709-747-1159, Fax: 709-747-1169, E-mail: steve@extrememetals.ca; Executive Assistant/Events Coordinator: Adelle Connors, E-mail: aconnors@nlca.ca
• Newfoundland & Labrador Construction Association 2015 Annual Awards Gala, 2015
Scope: Provincial
Description: An awards presentation to honour industry professionals, featuring a keynote address to delegates
Contact Information: Coordinator, Events Coordinator: Adelle Connors, Phone: 709-753-8920, E-mail: aconnors@nlca.ca
Publications:
• Newfoundland & Labrador Construction Association Weekly Bulletin
Type: Newsletter; *Frequency:* Weekly
Profile: Updates for NLCA members
• Newfoundland & Labrador Construction Association Membership Directory
Type: Directory
Profile: Featuring a Trade Classification Section

Newfoundland & Labrador Construction Safety Association (NLCSA)

Donovan's Industrial Park, 80 Glencoe Dr., Mount Pearl NL A1N 4S9
Tel: 709-739-7000; *Fax:* 709-739-7001
Toll-Free: 888-681-7233
info@nlcsa.com
www.nlcsa.com
Overview: A small provincial organization founded in 1996
Mission: To be the industry leaders in the creation & maintenance of a positive cultural shift within the construction industry that assists members in achieving reductions in human, social & economic loss as a result of work related accidents, injuries & death
Chief Officer(s):
Jackie Manuel, CEO
jmanuel@nlcsa.com
Staff Member(s): 23
Membership: *Fees:* Schedule available; *Member Profile:* Construction companies
Activities: Health & safety training; auditing & other services; employer certification

Newfoundland & Labrador Crafts Development Association

See Craft Council of Newfoundland & Labrador

Newfoundland & Labrador Credit Union

Corporate Office, 240 Water St., St. John's NL A1C 1B7
Tel: 709-754-2630; *Fax:* 709-576-8771
Toll-Free: 800-563-3300
www.nlcu.com
www.facebook.com/NLCUHOME
twitter.com/NLCU
Previous Name: Credit Union Central of Newfoundland & Labrador
Overview: A medium-sized provincial organization founded in 1977
Mission: To assist each owner to achieve personal financial success
Chief Officer(s):
Michael W. Boland, President
Allison Chaytor-Loveys, CEO & Treasurer
Glenn Bolger, Chief Operating Officer & Secretary
Elizabeth Duff, Chief Financial Officer
Activities: Offering access to financial & related services; Providing personalized financial solutions

Newfoundland & Labrador Cricket Association

NL
e-mail: cricketnewfoundland@gmail.com
www.canadacricket.com
www.facebook.com/185095814896295
Also Known As: Cricket NL
Overview: A small provincial organization founded in 2010 overseen by Cricket Canada
Mission: To be the provincial governing body of cricket in Newfoundland & Labrador.
Member of: Cricket Canada
Chief Officer(s):
Senthill Selvamani, President
presidentnlca@gmail.com
David Liverman, Secretary
liverman@mun.ca

Newfoundland & Labrador Criminology & Corrections Association

c/o West Coast Correctional Centre, PO Box 660, Stephenville NL A2N 3B5
Overview: A small provincial organization

Newfoundland & Labrador Curling Association

c/o Gary Oke, PO Box 2352, RR#1, Humber Valley Resort NL A2H 0E1
Tel: 709-686-6388
presidentnlca13@gmail.com
www.curlingnl.ca
Overview: A small provincial organization overseen by Canadian Curling Association
Member of: Canadian Curling Association
Chief Officer(s):
Gary Oke, President
Susan Curtis, Vice-President
scurtis@nl.rogers.com
Baxter House, Secretary, 709-695-9826
baxterhouse@gov.nl.ca
Carl Loughlin, Treasurer, 709-634-4201
carl.loughlin@nf.sympatico.ca

Jean Blackie, Coordinator, Technical
jeanblackie@gmail.com
Steve Routledge, Coordinator, Tournament
tournamentsnlca@gmail.com
Finances: *Funding Sources:* Membership fees; Sponsorships
Activities: Organizing clinics; Coordinating torunaments

Newfoundland & Labrador Darts Association
NL
nldarts.webs.com
www.facebook.com/NewfoundlandAndLabradorDartsAssociation
Overview: A medium-sized provincial organization founded in 1977 overseen by National Darts Federation of Canada
Member of: National Darts Federation of Canada
Chief Officer(s):
Cavelle Taylor, President, 709-582-2952
cavtaylor@yahoo.ca

Newfoundland & Labrador Deaf Sports Association (NLDSA)
98 Penney Cres., St. John's NL A1A 5L8
Overview: A small provincial organization overseen by Canadian Deaf Sports Association
Mission: To govern fitness, amateur sports & recreation for deaf people in Newfoundland & Labrador.
Member of: Canadian Deaf Sports Association
Chief Officer(s):
Bryan Johnson, President
bryan.johnson@nf.sympatico.ca

Newfoundland & Labrador Dental Association
#102, 1 Centennial St., Mount Pearl NL A1N 0C9
Tel: 709-579-2362; *Fax:* 709-579-1250
nfdental@nfld.net
www.nlda.net
Overview: A medium-sized provincial licensing organization overseen by Canadian Dental Association
Mission: To promote & advance dentistry or dental surgery & related arts & sciences in all their branches; to increase the knowledge, skill, standard & proficiency of its members in the practice of dentistry or dental surgery; to maintain the honour & integrity of the dental profession; to aid in the furtherance of measures designed to improve dental health & prevent disease & disability; to cooperate with & to assist public & private dental associations, agencies & commissions in the task of providing or financing dental care; to promote measures designed to improve standards of dental care & the practice of dentistry or dental surgery; to improve the welfare & social standards of its members & encourage the cooperation of its members in the protection of their rights.
Chief Officer(s):
Anthony Patey, Executive Director
anthony.patey.nlda@nfld.net
Staff Member(s): 3
Activities: Continuing Education; job opportunities listing; *Speaker Service:* Yes

Newfoundland & Labrador Dental Board
#204, 49-55 Elizabeth Ave., St. John's NL A1A 1W9
Tel: 709-579-2391; *Fax:* 709-579-2392
nldb@nf.aibn.com
nldb.ca
Overview: A small provincial licensing organization
Mission: To establish qualifying conditions for a national standard of dental competence for general practitioners; to establish & maintain an examination facility to test for this national standard of dental competence & to issue certificates to dentists who successfully meet this national standard.
Member of: Canadian Dental Regulatory Authorities
Affliation(s): National Dental Hygiene Exam Board; National Dental Assistant Exam Board
Chief Officer(s):
Paul O'Brien, Secretary-Registrar
Membership: *Member Profile:* Dentists; hygienists; associations; technicians
Activities: Licensing & discipline

Newfoundland & Labrador Drama Society (NLDS)
39 Airport Blvd., Gander NL A1V 2P8
Tel: 709-256-3796
info@nldrama.ca
nldrama.ca
Overview: A small provincial charitable organization founded in 1950
Chief Officer(s):
Brian Dove, Chair
chair@nldrama.ca
Finances: *Funding Sources:* Donations; Grants
Activities: Providing theatre workshops; Presenting a competitive festival for drama groups from across the province; Presenting awards; *Awareness Events:* Newfoundland & Labrador Provincial Drama Festival

Newfoundland & Labrador Environment Network (NLEN)
Environmental Gathering Place, PO Box 5125, Stn. C, 172 Military Rd., St. John's NL A1A 5V5
Tel: 709-753-7898; *Fax:* 709-726-2764
nlen.ed@gmail.com
www.nlen.ca
www.facebook.com/166529556721191
twitter.com/nl_environet
www.youtube.com/user/NLenvironet
Overview: A small provincial organization founded in 1990 overseen by Canadian Environmental Network
Mission: To take an active role in protecting, restoring & enhancing the environment; committed to taking an advocacy & activist role in our community; to educate the public on environmental issues
Chief Officer(s):
Chris Hogan, Executive Director
Finances: *Funding Sources:* Membership dues
Membership: *Fees:* $30-$90; *Member Profile:* Organizations interested in environmental issues

Newfoundland & Labrador Environmental Industry Association (NEIA)
#207, 90 O'Leary Ave., St. John's NL A1B 2C7
Tel: 709-237-8090
info@neia.org
neia.org
www.linkedin.com/company/3194901
www.facebook.com/NEIAssoc
twitter.com/NEIAssoc
Overview: A medium-sized provincial organization founded in 1992
Mission: To promote the growth & development of the environmental industry of Newfoundland & Labrador; to promote ethical behavior & high standards for environmental products & services; to provide a strong, unified voice toward all private sector, government & non-profit entities involved in the Newfoundland environmental industry.
Chief Officer(s):
Ted Lomond, Executive Director
ted@neia.org
Frank Ricketts, Chair
Finances: *Annual Operating Budget:* $250,000-$500,000; *Funding Sources:* Government; luncheons; seminars
Staff Member(s): 4
Membership: 124; *Member Profile:* Full - commercial enterprises that provide environmental products & services in Newfoundland & Labrador; associate - individuals & organizations supportive of the aims & objectives of NEIA

Newfoundland & Labrador Farm Direct Marketing Association
PO Box 317, 1 Goose Pond Rd., Shearstown NL A0A 3V0
Tel: 709-786-2943
bamhaadmin@hotmail.com
Overview: A small provincial organization overseen by Farmers' Markets Canada
Mission: Committed to development, promotion, leadership and representation.
Chief Officer(s):
Perry A. Mercer, President

Newfoundland & Labrador Federation of Agriculture
PO Box 1045, 308 Brookfield Rd., Bldg. 4, Mount Pearl NL A1N 3C9
Tel: 709-747-4874; *Fax:* 709-747-8827
info@nlfa.ca
www.nlfa.ca
Overview: A medium-sized provincial organization overseen by Canadian Federation of Agriculture
Mission: To act as the united voice of farmers in Newfoundland & Labrador; To improve the agricultural industry in Newfoundland & Labrador; To advance the economic & social conditions of those in the agricultural industry
Chief Officer(s):
Paul Connors, Executive Director
paul@nlfa.ca
Matthew Carlson, Officer, Communications
mcarlson@nlfa.ca
Kim O'Rourke, Administrative Assistant
kimorourke@nlfa.ca
Jamie Warren, Officer, Industry Development
jamie@nlfa.ca
Gerry Sullivan, Coordinator, Agriculture Awareness & Agri-Tourism
gerry@nlfa.ca
Christa Wright, Coordinator, Agriculture in the Classroom
christa@nlfa.ca
Finances: *Funding Sources:* Membership fees; Federal or provincial government programs
Membership: *Fees:* Schedule available, based upon farm gate revenue; *Member Profile:* Farmers & farmer groups in Newfoundland & Labrador
Activities: Assisting in the formulation of agricultural policies; Providing information about the state of the industry;
Meetings/Conferences: • Newfoundland & Labrador Federation of Agriculture 2015 Annual General Meeting, February, 2015, Hotel Gander, Gander, NL
Scope: Provincial
Description: An opportunity for members in good standing to vote & hold office
Contact Information: Phone: 709-747-4874; E-mail: info@nlfa.ca
Publications:
• AgriView [a publication of Newfoundland & Labrador Federation of Agriculture]
Type: Newsletter; *Frequency:* Semiannually; *Accepts Advertising*; *Editor:* Matthew Carlson *ISSN:* 1911-2297; *Price:* Free with Newfoundland & LabradorFederation of Agriculture membership
Profile: Feature articles, news, forthcoming events, & safety information

Newfoundland & Labrador Federation of Labour (NLFL) / Fédération du travail de Terre-Neuve et du Labrador
NAPE Bldg., PO Box 8597, Stn. A, 330 Portugal Cove Pl., 2nd Fl., St. John's NL A1B 3P2
Tel: 709-754-1660; *Fax:* 709-754-1220
fed@nlfl.nf.ca
www.nlfl.nf.ca
www.facebook.com/189773034381902
twitter.com/nlfl_labour
www.youtube.com/user/NLLABOUR
Overview: A medium-sized provincial organization founded in 1936 overseen by Canadian Labour Congress
Mission: To represent the interests of its members
Chief Officer(s):
Mary Shortall, President
president@nlfl.nf.ca
Linda Rideout, Executive Secretary
lrideout@nlfl.nf.ca
Membership: 65,000; *Committees:* Education; Occupational Health & Safety; Political Action & Legislative Review; Trustee; Women's; Workers' Compensation; Youth

Newfoundland & Labrador Federation of Municipalities *See* Municipalities Newfoundland & Labrador

Newfoundland & Labrador Federation of School Councils (NLFSC)
PO Box 23140, St. John's NL A1B 4J9
Tel: 709-834-7300; *Fax:* 709-834-7301
Toll-Free: 877-739-4830
nlfsci@gmail.com
www.nlta.nl.ca/files/nlfsc/default.html
Overview: A medium-sized provincial organization founded in 1979
Mission: Advocacy for school-age children
Affliation(s): Canadian Home & School Federation
Chief Officer(s):
Denise Pike, Executive Director
Peter Whittle, President
Finances: *Funding Sources:* Provincial government
Membership: 231 institutional; *Fees:* Schedule available based on student membership; *Member Profile:* School councils; parent groups
Activities: Providing a forum for school councils, parent associations & other groups; advocating parental participation in education; fostering cooperation; fostering the development of policies, practices & activities that enhance the quality of school programs

Newfoundland & Labrador Fencing Association (N&LFA)
#168, Unit 50 Hamlyn Road Plaza, St. John's NL A1E 5X7

Tel: 709-368-8830
nlfencing@gmail.com
sites.google.com/site/nlfencing
Overview: A small provincial organization overseen by Canadian Fencing Federation
Mission: To promote & develop the sport of fencing in Newfoundland
Member of: Canadian Fencing Federation
Chief Officer(s):
Justin So, President
Membership: 70;

Newfoundland & Labrador Folk Arts Society (NLFAS)

#206, 223 Duckworth St., St. John's NL A1C 6N1
Tel: 709-576-8508; *Fax:* 709-757-8500
Toll-Free: 866-576-8508
office@nlfolk.com
www.nlfolk.com
www.facebook.com/nlfolk
twitter.com/nlfolkfestival
Overview: A small local organization founded in 1966
Mission: To promote & preserve the folk arts of Newfoundland & Labrador
Chief Officer(s):
Erin Whitney, Office Manager
Finances: *Funding Sources:* Corporate sponsors; Canadian Heritage; CEDA; City of St. John's
Staff Member(s): 4
Membership: *Fees:* $10
Activities: Annual Newfoundland & Labrador Folk Festival; weekly folk music club; educational workshops; *Speaker Service:* Yes

Newfoundland & Labrador Funeral Services Association (NLFSA)

PO Box 138, Winterton NL A0G 3M0
Tel: 709-586-2721; *Fax:* 709-586-2888
Overview: A small provincial organization
Mission: To offer funeral service support for the province.
Affliation(s): Funeral Service Association of Canada

Newfoundland & Labrador Genealogical Society Inc. *See* Family History Society of Newfoundland & Labrador

Newfoundland & Labrador Golf Association *See* Golf Newfoundland & Labrador

Newfoundland & Labrador Handball Federation

c/o School of Human Kinetics, Memorial Univ., St. John's NL A1C 5S7
Tel: 709-737-8684
rwheeler@mun.ca
Overview: A small provincial organization
Member of: Canadian Team Handball Federation
Chief Officer(s):
Ralph Wheeler, Contact

Newfoundland & Labrador Health Information Management Association (NLHIMA)

PO Box 39029, St. John's NL A1E 5Y7
Tel: 709-777-6199
www.nlhima.ca
Previous Name: Newfoundland & Labrador Health Record Association
Overview: A small provincial organization founded in 1987
Mission: To participate in the development of government policies related to health records; To promote the profession of health information management
Affliation(s): Canadian Health Information Management Association
Chief Officer(s):
Karen Squires, President, 709-777-4298
karen.squires@easternhealth.ca
Finances: *Funding Sources:* Fundraising
Membership: *Fees:* $25 associate memberships; $30 active memberships; *Member Profile:* Health information professionals in Newfoundland & Labrador who are trained in the collection, analysis, & management of health information; *Committees:* Communications; Education & Professional Development; Executive; Fundraising
Activities: Encouraging & supporting continuing education; Liaising wtih government; *Awareness Events:* Health Information Awareness Day; Health Information & Technology Week, Nov.
Publications:
• For the Record
Type: Newsletter; *Frequency:* 3 pa
Profile: Association reports & regional information

Newfoundland & Labrador Health Libraries Association (NLHLA)

c/o Health Sciences Library, Memorial University of Newfoundland, St. John's NL A1B 3V6
e-mail: nlhla@chla-absc.ca
www.nlhla.ca
Overview: A medium-sized provincial organization founded in 1979 overseen by Canadian Health Libraries Association
Mission: To promote the provision of a high quality library service to the health community in Newfoundland & Labrador through mutual assistance & communication; to provide professional support to the membership by offering continuing education opportunities
Affliation(s): Canadian Health Libraries Association
Chief Officer(s):
Kristen Romme, President
Finances: *Annual Operating Budget:* Less than $50,000
Membership: 1-99; *Fees:* $20; *Member Profile:* People who work in hospital & other health-related libraries & resource centres throughout Newfoundland & Labrador
Activities: NLHLA Lifeline (internet newsletter); initiate & coordinate projects to improve library services & information access in the health care field in Newfoundland

Newfoundland & Labrador Health Record Association *See* Newfoundland & Labrador Health Information Management Association

Newfoundland & Labrador High School Athletic Federation *See* School Sports Newfoundland & Labrador

Newfoundland & Labrador Independent Adjusters' Association

c/o Crawford & Company (Canada) Inc., #100, 96 Clyde Ave., Mount Pearl NL A1N 4S2
Tel: 709-753-6351; *Fax:* 709-753-6129
www.ciaa-adjusters.ca
Overview: A small local organization overseen by Canadian Independent Adjusters' Association
Member of: Canadian Independent Adjusters' Association
Chief Officer(s):
Marcel Pitcher, Regional President
Marcel.Pitcher@crawco.ca

Newfoundland & Labrador Insolvency Association *See* Newfoundland & Labrador Association of Insolvency & Restructuring Professionals

Newfoundland & Labrador Institute of Agrologists (NLIA)

PO Box 978, Mount Pearl NL A1N 3C9
Tel: 709-772-4170
www.aic.ca/agrology/nlia.cfm
Overview: A small provincial licensing organization founded in 1988 overseen by Agricultural Institute of Canada
Mission: Dedicated to the professional aspects of Canadian agriculture.
Chief Officer(s):
Gary Bishop, President/Treasurer
gary.bishop@agr.gc.ca
Samir Debnath, Registrar
Finances: *Annual Operating Budget:* Less than $50,000
Membership: 40; *Fees:* $110

Newfoundland & Labrador Interpreting Service *See* Interpreting Services of Newfoundland & Labrador Inc.

Newfoundland & Labrador Judo Association

#112, Hamlyn Rd. Plaza, Unit 50, St. John's NL A1E 5X7
Fax: 709-368-8830
judo@nfld.com
www.judonl.ca
Also Known As: Judo Newfoundland & Labrador
Overview: A small provincial organization overseen by Judo Canada
Mission: To govern & promote the sport of Judo in Newfoundland & Labrador.
Member of: Judo Canada
Chief Officer(s):
George Beckett, President
georger@mun.ca
15 volunteer(s)
Membership: *Committees:* Provincial Grading Board; Medical; NCCP; Refereeing; Hall of Fame

Newfoundland & Labrador Lacrosse Association (NLLA)

PO Box 26037, 250 Lemarchant Rd., St. John's NL A1E 0A5
e-mail: general@nllacrosse.ca
nllacrosse.ca
Overview: A small provincial organization founded in 2009 overseen by Canadian Lacrosse Association
Mission: To manage & operate the sport of lacrosse in Newfoundland & Labrador.
Member of: Canadian Lacrosse Association
Chief Officer(s):
Mike Lilly, President
president@nllacrosse.ca
Jim Swyer, Executive Director
director@nllacrosse.ca

Newfoundland & Labrador Laubach Literacy Council (NLLLC)

c/o Margie Lewis, PO Box 822, 141 O'Connell Dr., Corner Brook NL A2H 6H6
Tel: 709-634-5081; *Fax:* 709-634-2126
Toll-Free: 800-863-0373
laubach@nf.aibn.com
www.nlllc.ca
www.facebook.com/102784339799297
Overview: A medium-sized provincial charitable organization
Chief Officer(s):
Lewis Margie, Executive Director

Newfoundland & Labrador Library Association (NLLA)

PO Box 23192, RPO Churchill Sq., St. John's NL A1B 4J9
Other Communication: bulletin@nlla.ca
secretary@nlla.ca
www.nlla.ca
www.facebook.com/group.php?gid=32530083934
Previous Name: Newfoundland Library Association
Overview: A medium-sized provincial organization founded in 1969
Mission: To ensure the excellence of Newfoundland & Labrador's public, special, academic, & school libraries; To foster interest in libraries
Chief Officer(s):
Erin Alcock, President
ekalcock@mun.ca
Crystal Rose, Vice-President
crose@swgc.mun.ca
Amanda Tiller, Secretary
atiller@mun.ca
Dianne Keeping, Treasurer
dckeep@mun.ca
Membership: *Fees:* $10 students, retired librarians, & library supporters; $15 library technicians, assistants & clerks; $20 librarians & teacher librarians; *Member Profile:* Librarians & library support staff in Newfoundland & Labrador; *Committees:* Communications; Web Team; Canadian Library Month; The Partnership; Happenings; Library Technician & Assistant Interest Group
Activities: Recommending policies; Facilitating networking opportunities; Providing workshops; Offering professional advice & assistance; *Awareness Events:* Canadian Library Month, October; Newfoundland & Labrador Library Week
Meetings/Conferences: • Newfoundland & Labrador Library Association Annual Conference & Annual General Meeting 2015, 2015, NL
Scope: Provincial
Description: An annual spring meeting, presenting opportunities to learn about new services, current issues, & research in Newfoundland & Labrabor libraries
• Newfoundland & Labrador Library Association Annual Conference & Annual General Meeting 2016, 2016, NL
Scope: Provincial
Description: An annual spring meeting, presenting opportunities to learn about new services, current issues, & research in Newfoundland & Labrabor libraries
Publications:
• Directory of Libraries in Newfoundland & Labrador
Type: Directory; *Price:* Free with Newfoundland & Labrador Library Association membership
Profile: Listings of public, academic, school, & special libraries across the province
• NLLA Bulletin
Type: Newsletter; *Frequency:* Semiannually
Profile: Local & national library updates, services, research, & events

Newfoundland & Labrador Lung Association (NLLA)
PO Box 13457, Stn. A, St. John's NL A1B 4B8
Tel: 709-726-4664; *Fax:* 709-726-2550
Toll-Free: 888-566-5864
info@nf.lung.ca
www.nf.lung.ca
Overview: A small provincial charitable organization founded in 1944 overseen by Canadian Lung Association
Mission: To achieve healthy breathing for the people of Newfoundland & Labrador
Chief Officer(s):
Greg Noel, Executive Director
greg.noel@nf.lung.ca
Finances: *Funding Sources:* Donations; Fundraising; Sponsorships
Activities: Organizing fundraisers; Supporting research; Providing education; Offering support groups in areas such asthma, COPD, & smoking cessation; Engaging in advocacy activities
Publications:
• Newfoundland & Labrador Lung Association Newsletter
Type: Newsletter

Newfoundland & Labrador Massage Therapists' Association (NLMTA)
PO Box 23212, Stn. Churchill Sq., St. John's NL A1B 4J9
Tel: 709-726-4006; *Fax:* 709-895-7767
Toll-Free: 877-744-2468
nlmta@nlmta.ca
www.nlmta.ca
Overview: A small provincial organization founded in 1990
Member of: Canadian Massage Therapy Alliance
Activities: *Library*

Newfoundland & Labrador Medical Association (NLMA)
164 MacDonald Dr., St. John's NL A1A 4B3
Tel: 709-726-7424; *Fax:* 709-726-7525
Toll-Free: 800-563-2003
nlma@nlma.nl.ca
www.nlma.nl.ca
Overview: A medium-sized provincial organization founded in 1924 overseen by Canadian Medical Association
Mission: To represent & support physicians in Newfoundland & Labrador; provide leadership in the promotion of good health & the provision of quality health care to the people of the province
Chief Officer(s):
Sandra Luscombe, President
president@nlma.nl.ca
Robert Ritter, Executive Director, 709-726-7424 Ext. 302
rritter@nlma.nl.ca
Finances: *Annual Operating Budget:* $500,000-$1.5 Million; *Funding Sources:* Membership dues
Staff Member(s): 11; 60 volunteer(s)
Membership: 1,600; *Fees:* $1,394; *Member Profile:* Physicians; medical students; residents; retired physicians

Newfoundland & Labrador Multicultural and Folk Arts Council *See* Newfoundland & Labrador Multicultural Council Inc.

Newfoundland & Labrador Multicultural Council Inc. (NLMC)
PO Box 2544, Stn. C, St. John's NL A1C 6K1
Tel: 709-753-2917; *Fax:* 709-726-8201
secretary@nlmfac.ca
www.nlmfac.ca
Previous Name: Newfoundland & Labrador Multicultural and Folk Arts Council
Overview: A small provincial organization founded in 1979
Mission: To advance multiculturalism in Newfoundland & Labrador
Membership: 9; *Fees:* $5 individuals; $50 organizations
Activities: Promoting multiculturalism & folk-arts; Presenting scholarships

Newfoundland & Labrador Nurse Practitioner Associatio (NLNPA)
NL
www.nlnpa.ca
Overview: A small provincial organization
Mission: Represents the professional interests of Nurse Practitioners (NPs) in NL.
Member of: Association of Registered Nurses of Newfoundland & Labrador
Chief Officer(s):
Penney Ralph, Communications Director
pennyjralph@gmail.com
Valda Duke, Treasurer
vjaw1@hotmail.com
Membership: *Member Profile:* Nurse practitioners from Newfoundland & Labrador
Activities: Providing professional support to nurse practitioners in Newfoundland & Labrador; Offering educational opportunities; Advocating for accessible, high quality health care throughout the province; Creating networking opportunities

Newfoundland & Labrador Nurses' Union (NLNU) / Syndicat des infirmières de Terre-Neuve et du Labrador
PO Box 416, Stn. C, 229 Major's Path, St. John's NL A1C 5J9
Tel: 709-753-9961; *Fax:* 709-753-1210
Toll-Free: 800-563-5100
info@nlnu.ca
www.nlnu.ca
Overview: A medium-sized provincial organization founded in 1974
Member of: Canadian Federation of Nurses Unions; Canadian Labour Congress
Chief Officer(s):
John Vivian, Executive Director
jvivian@nlnu.ca
Karyn Murphy, Communications Specialist
kmurphy@nlnu.ca
Staff Member(s): 15; 400 volunteer(s)
Membership: 5,000; *Member Profile:* Unionized nurses

Newfoundland & Labrador Occupational Therapy Board (NLOTB)
RPO Churchill Square, PO Box 23076, St. John's NL A1B 4J9
Tel: 709-697-4920; *Fax:* 709-383-0135
registrar@nlotb.ca
www.nlaot.ca/board/index.asp
Overview: A small provincial licensing organization founded in 1988
Mission: Protection of the public through implementation of legislation on occupational therapy practice
Affliation(s): Canadian Association of Occupational Therapists; Newfoundland & Labrador Association of Occupational Therapists; Association of Canadian Occupational Therapists Registering Organizations
Chief Officer(s):
Kim Doyle, Registrar
registrar@nlotb.ca
Finances: *Annual Operating Budget:* Less than $50,000; *Funding Sources:* Membership dues
Staff Member(s): 5; 5 volunteer(s)
Membership: 125; *Fees:* $100 full-time; $75 part-time; *Member Profile:* Graduation from WFOT-approved school; CAOT exam completion; *Committees:* Practice Support

Newfoundland & Labrador Organization of Women Entrepreneurs (NLOWE)
Regatta Plaza II, 84-86 Elizabeth Ave., 2nd Fl., St. John's NL A1A 1W7
Tel: 709-754-5555; *Fax:* 709-754-0079
Toll-Free: 888-656-9311
www.nlowe.org
www.linkedin.com/company/newfoundland-and-labrador-organization-of-wom
www.facebook.com/nlowe.org
twitter.com/nlowe_org
www.youtube.com/user/NLOWEVideo
Overview: A medium-sized provincial organization founded in 1997
Mission: To support women's contribution to growth in business & community economic development
Affliation(s): Atlantic Canada Opportunities Agency; Human Resources Development Canada
Chief Officer(s):
Paula Sheppard, Chief Executive Officer
psheppard@nlowe.org
Alison Stoodley, President, 709-740-4910
Finances: *Funding Sources:* Membership dues; government funding
Staff Member(s): 15
Membership: *Fees:* $100 individual; $175 non-profit; $350 corporate; *Member Profile:* Women business owners in Newfoundland & Labrador
Activities: Annual conference for women entrepreneurs; programs; online training sessions; business advice

Newfoundland & Labrador Outfitters Association (NLOA)
Goodhouse Building, 93 West St., 2nd Fl., Corner Brook NL A2H 2Y5
Tel: 709-639-5926
Toll-Free: 866-420-6562
info@nloa.ca
www.nloa.ca
Overview: A small provincial organization
Mission: To assist hunting & fishing outfitters throughout Newfoundland & Labrador; To work with government departments & other organizations that impact the outfitting industry
Chief Officer(s):
Keith Payne, Executive Director, 709-634-9962
keithpayne@nloa.ca
Melissa Byrne, Coordinator, Project Support
melissa@nloa.ca
Membership: *Member Profile:* Licensed hunting & fishing outfitter operations in Newfoundland & Labrador that uphold the ethics & goals of the association
Activities: Providing information to hunting & fishing outfitters

Newfoundland & Labrador Palliative Care Association (NLPCA)
PO Box 39023, 390 Topsail Rd., St. John's NL A1E 5Y7
e-mail: exec@nlpalliativecareassociation.com
www.nlpalliativecareassociation.com
Overview: A medium-sized provincial charitable organization founded in 1993
Mission: To strive for excellence in the care of persons near death; To lessen the suffering & loneliness of people approaching the end of life
Member of: Canadian Hospice Palliative Care Association (CHPCA)
Chief Officer(s):
Linda Abbott, President, 709-945-5026, Fax: 709-945-5158
linda.abbott@easternhealth.ca
Jennifer Forward, President Elect, 709-945-5162, Fax: 709-945-3051
jennifer.forward@easternhealth.ca
Finances: *Funding Sources:* Fundraising
Membership: *Fees:* $30; *Member Profile:* Individuals & organizations in Newfoundland & Labrador engaged in palliative care education, counselling, & services
Activities: Engaging in advocacy activities; Educating professionals & the public about palliative care; Promoting principles & standards of end of life care; Encouraging research;

Newfoundland & Labrador Parks & Recreation Association *See* Recreation Newfoundland & Labrador

Newfoundland & Labrador Pharmacy Board (NLPB)
Apothecary Hall, 488 Water St., St. John's NL A1E 1B3
Tel: 709-753-5877; *Fax:* 709-753-8615
Toll-Free: 877-453-5877
inforx@nlpb.ca
www.nlpb.ca
www.facebook.com/139887479372029
twitter.com/nlpharmacyboard
Previous Name: Newfoundland Pharmacy Association
Overview: A small provincial organization
Mission: To set, govern and advance the standards and scope of pharmacy practice and pharmacy service for the people of Newfoundland and Labrador.
Member of: Canadian Council on Continuing Education in Pharmacy
Chief Officer(s):
Margot Priddle, Registrar
mpriddle@nlpb.ca
Publications:
• The Apothecary
Type: Newsletter; *Frequency:* 3 pa

Newfoundland & Labrador Physiotherapy Association (NLPA)
St. John's NL
www.physiotherapy.ca/Atlantic-Branches/Newfoundland
www.facebook.com/NLPhysioAssoc
twitter.com/nlphysioassoc
Overview: A medium-sized provincial organization overseen by Canadian Physiotherapy Association
Mission: To provide leadership & direction to the physiotherapy profession; To foster excellence in practice, education & research
Member of: Canadian Physiotherapy Association
Chief Officer(s):

Canadian Associations

Lisa Pike, Executive Director
Sherry Lythgoe, President
Finances: *Funding Sources:* Membership dues; Educational activities

Newfoundland & Labrador Powerlifting Association
c/o Jason Fancey, 101 Branscombe St., St. John's NL A1A 5R2
Tel: 709-579-1623
www.nlpowerlifting.ca
Overview: A small provincial organization overseen by Canadian Powerlifting Union
Member of: Canadian Powerlifting Union
Chief Officer(s):
Jason Fancey, President
jasonfancey@gmail.com
Membership: *Fees:* $50 regular; $30 special olympian

Newfoundland & Labrador Prospectors Association (NLPA)
17 Nelder Dr., Mount Pearl NL A1N 4M2
Tel: 709-740-6000
www.nlprospectors.org
Overview: A small provincial organization founded in 2012
Mission: To act as a voice for all member prospectors in the provice; to raise awareness about prospecting in Newfoundland & Labrador
Chief Officer(s):
Norm Mercer, President
nmercer@nlprospectors.org

Newfoundland & Labrador Provincial Association of Family Resource Centres
c/o Kilbride to Ferryland Family Resource Centre, PO Box 1039, Goulds NL A1S 1H2
Tel: 709-747-8530; *Fax:* 709-745-2727
kffrc@avinet.net
Overview: A medium-sized provincial organization
Mission: To promote the well-being of families
Affliation(s): Canadian Association of Family Resource Programs (FRP Canada)
Chief Officer(s):
Rhonda Thomas, Contact
Activities: Providing resources to those who support families & care for children

Newfoundland & Labrador Public Health Association (NLPHA)
PO Box 8172, St. John's NL A1B 3M9
Tel: 709-364-1589
info@nlpha.ca
www.nlpha.ca
Overview: A small provincial organization founded in 1978 overseen by Canadian Public Health Association
Mission: To advocate for the physical, emotional, social, & environmental well-being of Newfoundland & Labrador's people & communities
Member of: Canadian Public Health Association (CPHA)
Chief Officer(s):
Lynn Vivian-Book, President
Elizabeth Wright, Secretary
Pat Murray, Treasurer
Finances: *Funding Sources:* Donations
Membership: *Fees:* $30 individual/affiliate; *Member Profile:* Individuals in Newfoundland & Labrador who are interested in public health & community activities, such as health & community service workers, researchers, & educators
Activities: Raising awareness of public health issues; Addressing public health issues, such as school nutrition, food security, mental health services, family life education, fetal alcohol syndrome, primary health care, & low level flying; Providing education; Offering prevention programming; Liaising with partners & community organizations to strengthen community health; Offering monthly business & educational teleconferences
Publications:
• Newfoundland & Labrador Public Health Association Newsletter
Type: Newsletter; *Editor:* Douglas Howse

Newfoundland & Labrador Right to Life Association
PO Box 5427, 195 Freshwater Rd., St. John's NL A1C 5W2
Tel: 709-579-1500; *Fax:* 709-579-1600
centreforlife@centreforlife.ca
www.centreforlife.ca
Also Known As: Centre for Life
Previous Name: Right to Life Association of Newfoundland & Labrador
Overview: A small provincial organization founded in 1977
Mission: The Association upholds the sacredness & inviolability of human life from conception to natural death. It disseminates information on such to authorities & the public, supporting mothers during & after pregnancy. It networks with similar organizations, & promotes medical research to support its beliefs.
Member of: Alliance for Life
Chief Officer(s):
Linda Holden, President

Newfoundland & Labrador Rugby Union
PO Box 9, Mount Pearl NL A1N 2C1
www.rockrugby.ca
Also Known As: The Rock Rugby
Overview: A small provincial organization overseen by Rugby Canada
Member of: Rugby Canada
Chief Officer(s):
John Cowan, President
jcowan@mun.ca

Newfoundland & Labrador Safety Council *See* Safety Services Newfoundland & Labrador

Newfoundland & Labrador Sailing Association (NLSA)
Churchill Square, PO Box 23102, St. John's NL A1B 4J9
Tel: 902-425-5450
sailing.nl@gmail.com
www.nlsailing.ca
Overview: A small provincial organization founded in 1966 overseen by Sail Canada
Mission: To regulate the sport of sailing in Newfoundland & Labrador
Member of: Sail Canada; Sport NL
Chief Officer(s):
Colin Taylor, President

Newfoundland & Labrador School Boards' Association (NLSBA)
40 Strawberry Marsh Rd., St. John's NL A1B 2V5
Tel: 709-722-7171; *Fax:* 709-722-8214
www.schoolboardsnl.ca
Overview: A medium-sized provincial organization founded in 1969 overseen by Canadian School Boards Association
Mission: To promote the interests of education in Newfoundland & Labrador
Chief Officer(s):
Brian Shortall, Executive Director
brianshortall@schoolboardsnl.ca
Brenda Pinto, Executive Assistant
brendapinto@schoolboardsnl.ca
Wayne Noseworthy, Director, Labour Relations
waynenoseworthy@schoolboardsnl.ca
Finances: *Annual Operating Budget:* $250,000-$500,000; *Funding Sources:* Member board fees; government grants
Staff Member(s): 5; 150 volunteer(s)
Membership: 11 school boards + 180 trustees; *Fees:* Based on school population; *Member Profile:* Elected school board member; *Committees:* Finance; Resolution; Legislative; Certification; Communication; Nominating
Activities: *Speaker Service:* Yes

Newfoundland & Labrador School Milk Foundation *See* School Milk Foundation of Newfoundland & Labrador

Newfoundland & Labrador Sexual Assault Crisis & Prevention Centre Inc. (NLSACPC)
#101, 360 Topsoil Rd., St. John's NL A1E 2B6
Tel: 709-747-7757; *Fax:* 709-747-7758
coordinator@sexualassaultcentre.nf.net
www.nlsacpc.com
www.facebook.com/EndSV
Previous Name: St. John's Rape Crisis & Information Centre
Overview: A small local organization overseen by Canadian Association of Sexual Assault Centres
Mission: To provide services & support to persons affected by sexual violence; To work towards prevention of sexual violence through education
Chief Officer(s):
Barbara Wadman, Centre Coordinator
Finances: *Annual Operating Budget:* $100,000-$250,000; *Funding Sources:* Donations; Fundraising; Government of Newfoundland
10-2 volunteer(s)
Membership: *Member Profile:* Persons who work towards the prevention of sexual assault
Activities: Offering educational presentations for schools, community centres, & workplaces; Providing written information; Raising awareness about matters of sexual violence by participating in community events; Providing support groups & phone support; Offering referrals; Accompanying victims, when requested, to medical & legal procedures

Newfoundland & Labrador Snowboard Association
PO Box 259, Steady Brook NL A2H 2N2
Tel: 709-634-4664
newfoundland@canadasnowboard.ca
nlsnowboard.com
Also Known As: NL Snowboard
Overview: A small provincial organization overseen by Canadian Snowboard Federation
Mission: To be the provincial governing body of competitive snowboarding in Newfoundland & Labrador.
Member of: Canadian Snowboard Federation
Chief Officer(s):
Emily Pittman, Contact

Newfoundland & Labrador Soccer Association
39 Churchill Ave., St. John's NL A1A 0H7
Tel: 709-576-0601; *Fax:* 709-576-0588
info@nlsa.ca
www.nlsa.ca
Previous Name: Newfoundland Soccer Association
Overview: A large provincial organization overseen by Canadian Soccer Association
Mission: To provide opportunities for the general public to engage in the game of soccer while having fun & competition
Member of: Canadian Soccer Association
Chief Officer(s):
Doug Redmond, President
Dragan Mirkovic, Director, Technical, 709-576-2262
dragan@nlsa.ca
Mike Power, Director & Staff Coach, Player Development, 709-576-7310
mike@nlsa.ca
Rob Comerford, Manager, Business, 709-576-0601
rob@nlsa.ca

Newfoundland & Labrador Society for the Prevention of Cruelty to Animals
PO Box 29053, St. John's NL A1A 5B5
Tel: 709-726-0301; *Fax:* 709-579-8089
spcastjohns@gmail.com
www.spcastjohns.org
Also Known As: Newfoundland & Labrador SPCA
Overview: A medium-sized provincial charitable organization founded in 1954 overseen by Canadian Federation of Humane Societies
Mission: To act as the voice for animal welfare in Newfoundland & Labrador; To promote humane treatment toward all animals
Member of: Canadian Federation of Humane Societies
Chief Officer(s):
Lynn Cadigan, President & Contact, Media, 709-233-0118
Simone Browne, Vice-President
Carolyn Hickey, Secretary
Bob Noseworthy, Treasurer
Finances: *Funding Sources:* Provincial government; Donations
Activities: Offering animal protection, shelter, & care; Increasing understanding of animal welfare

Newfoundland & Labrador Society of Laboratory Technologists *See* Newfoundland & Labrador College for Medical Laboratory Science

Newfoundland & Labrador Speed Skating Association (NLSSA)
81 Birchy Cove Dr., Corner Brook NL A2H 6W8
Tel: 709-785-1403
rzrenos@gmail.com
Overview: A small provincial organization overseen by Speed Skating Canada
Member of: Speed Skating Canada

Newfoundland & Labrador Table Tennis Association (NLTTA)
NL
Tel: 709-834-8402
www.freewebs.com/nltta
Overview: A small provincial organization overseen by Table Tennis Canada

Mission: To promote the sport of Table Tennis in Newfoundland & Labrador.
Member of: Table Tennis Canada
Affiliation(s): International Table Tennis Federation
Chief Officer(s):
Brian Ash, President
qeash@yahoo.ca
Rick Fisher, Treasurer, 709-834-0015
topsail369@gmail.com
Denise Simms, Manager, 709-673-2537
jd.taylor@nf.sympatico.ca

Newfoundland & Labrador Teachers' Association (NLTA) / Association des enseignants de Terre-Neuve

3 Kenmount Rd., St. John's NL A1B 1W1
Tel: 709-726-3223; *Fax:* 709-726-4302
Toll-Free: 800-563-3599
mail@nlta.nl.ca
www.nlta.nl.ca
twitter.com/NLTeachersAssoc
Overview: A medium-sized provincial organization founded in 1890 overseen by Canadian Teachers' Federation
Mission: To strive towards the professional excellence & personal well-being of teachers
Chief Officer(s):
Hancock Hancock, Executive Director
ehancock@nlta.nl.ca
Lily Cole, President
lcole@nlta.nl.ca
James Dinn, Vice-President
jamesdinn@nf.sympatico.ca
Jim Fox, Treasurer
jfox@nlta.nl.ca
Membership: 6,400; *Member Profile:* Teachers in Newfoundland & Labrador; *Committees:* Communications / Political Action; Curriculum; Equity Issues in Education; Electoral; Finance & Property; Group Insurance; Internal Review (Ad Hoc); Membership Benefits & Services; Professional Issues; Teacher Health & Wellness
Activities: Publishing numerous guides & brochures for teachers; Engaging in advocacy activities; Delivering supportive programs & services, such as the employee assistance program & the health & wellness promotion program; Offering professional development opportunities;
Awards:
• Alan Bishop Award (Award)
To recognize outstanding service at the provincial level of the NLTA
• Bancroft Award (Award)
To recognize outstanding service at the branch level of the NLTA
• Barnes Award (Award)
To recognize outstanding service to the NLTA in the field of professional development by teachers
• Patricia Cowan Award (Award)
To recognize individuals or groups outside the school system for outstanding support & promotion of education
• President's Award (Award)
To recognize a strong supporter of the NLTA
• Special Recognition Award (Award)
To recognize a major contribution by an NLTA member to the cultural, social, or community life of the province
• Royal C. Hill Award (Scholarship)
Formerly Hilroy Fellowship

Newfoundland & Labrador Tennis Association *See* Tennis Newfoundland & Labrador

Newfoundland & Labrador Track & Field Association *See* Newfoundland & Labrador Athletics Association

Newfoundland & Labrador Veterinary Medical Association (NALVMA)

PO Box 818, Mount Pearl NL A1N 3C8
e-mail: nalvmacouncil@gmail.com
www.nalvma.ca
Overview: A small provincial organization founded in 1971 overseen by Canadian Veterinary Medical Association
Mission: To promote better animal health care; to educate the general public & strive towards continued excellence in veterinary medicine.
Chief Officer(s):
Heather Hillier, President
Activities: *Speaker Service:* Yes; *Rents Mailing List:* Yes

Newfoundland & Labrador Volleyball Association (NLVA)

1296A Kenmount Rd., Paradise NL A1L 1N3
Tel: 709-576-0817; *Fax:* 709-576-7493
nlvaruss@sportnl.ca
www.nlva.net
www.facebook.com/259281656023
Overview: A small provincial organization founded in 1986 overseen by Volleyball Canada
Mission: To promote volleyball in Newfoundland & Labrador; to provide competitive opportunities for its members
Chief Officer(s):
Eric Hiscock, President
ehiscock@nf.sympatico.ca
Russell Jackson, Executive Director
Chad Richards, Elite Development Chair
chadrichards@nl.rogers.com

Newfoundland & Labrador Water Well Corporation *See* Newfoundland/Labrador Ground Water Association

Newfoundland & Labrador Wildlife Federation (NWLF)

15 Conran St., St. John's NL A1E 5L8
Tel: 709-364-8415
www.nlwf.ca
Overview: A medium-sized provincial organization founded in 1962 overseen by Canadian Wildlife Federation
Mission: To foster awareness & enjoyment of the natural world; To promote the sustainable use of natural resources; To protect wildlife & its habitat through conservation & effective wildlife management
Affiliation(s): Over 15 affiliated conservation groups, including the Canadian Wildlife Federation (CWF), Rod & Gun Clubs from St. John's, Bay Of Islands, Green Bay, Baie d'Espoir, Marystown, South East Placentia & Grand Falls
Chief Officer(s):
Rick Bouzan, President
Membership: *Member Profile:* Clubs or organizations; Individuals; Associate members; Honorary members
Activities: Liaising with government agencies & organizations with similar goals; Conducting educational programs in conservation

Newfoundland & Labrador Women's Institutes

c/o Arts & Culture Centre, PO Box 1854, St. John's NL A1C 5P9
Tel: 709-753-8780; *Fax:* 709-753-8708
nlwi@nfld.com
www.nlwi.ca
Overview: A small provincial organization overseen by Federated Women's Institutes of Canada
Mission: The present day Newfoundland and Labrador Women's Institutes is an informal, educational organization for women to work together to expand their skills, broaden their interests, plan meetings, workshops and conferences, and strengthen the quality of life for themselves, their families and their communities. The NLWI is a non-partisan, non-sectarian, non-racial organization
Chief Officer(s):
Jane Laite, President
Dolores Jones, President-Elect
Membership: *Fees:* $20
Activities: Scholarships; Health; Crafts; Culture; Agriculture
Awards:
• Newfoundland Women's Insitutes Scholarship (Scholarship)
Students must submit grades, a short essay & letters of reference in the application package*Eligibility:* Male & female students who have completed grade 12*Deadline:* Oct 31

Newfoundland & Labradour Institute of the Purchasing Management Association of Canada *See* Supply Chain Management Association - Newfoundland & Labrador

Newfoundland Alliance of Technical Industries *See* Newfoundland & Labrador Association of Technology Companies

Newfoundland Amateur Baseball Association *See* Newfoundland Baseball

Newfoundland and Labrador Operating Room Nurses Association (N&LORNA)

NL
Overview: A medium-sized provincial organization overseen by Operating Room Nurses Association of Canada
Chief Officer(s):
Margot Walsh, President
mwalsh@nl.rogers.com
Membership: *Member Profile:* Registered Nurses in Newfoundland & Labrador who are engaged in operating room nursing or involved in the Perioperative setting.
Activities: *Awareness Events:* Perioperative Nurses Week, November

Newfoundland Aquaculture Industry Association (NAIA)

#209, 11 Austin St., St. John's NL A1B 4C1
Tel: 709-754-2854; *Fax:* 709-754-2981
www.naia.ca
www.facebook.com/207556199255955
www.twitter.com/naia_nl
Overview: A small provincial organization
Mission: To facilitate the commercial development of aquaculture in Newfoundland; To strive towards excellence in quality, safety, environmental sustainability, & profitability; To act as the voice of the industry in the province
Member of: Canadian Aquaculture Industry Alliance (CAIA); National Seafood Sector Council (NSSC)
Chief Officer(s):
Miranda Pryor, Executive Director, 709-754-2854 Ext. 2
miranda@naia.ca
Cyr Couturier, President
Robert Barry, Secretary, 709-576-7292
Jennifer Caines, Treasurer, 709-665-3168
Membership: *Fees:* $400 regular members; $200 associate members; *Member Profile:* Finfish & shellfish farmers in Newfoundland; Primary & secondary processors; Hatcheries producers; Supply & service companies; Academic institutions
Activities: Liaising with government; Offering training & advice; Providing business intelligence; *Awareness Events:* Aquaculture Week, June
Publications:
• Cold Harvester [a publication of the Newfoundland Aquaculture Industry Association]
Type: Magazine; *Frequency:* Quarterly
Profile: Information about the successes & challenges of the aquaculture industry for Newfoundland Aquaculture Industry Association members
• Newfoundland Aquaculture Industry Association Member Directory
Type: Directory

St. Alban's Office
PO Box 27, 88 Main St., St. Alban's NL A0H 2E0

Newfoundland Association of Architects

PO Box 5204, 7 Downing St., St. John's NL A1C 5V5
Tel: 709-726-8550; *Fax:* 709-726-1549
nlaa@newfoundlandarchitects.com
www.newfoundlandarchitects.com
Overview: A small provincial organization
Mission: To support architecture & architects in Newfoundland and Labrador.
Membership: *Fees:* Schedule available

Newfoundland Association of Optometrists *See* Newfoundland & Labrador Association of Optometrists

Newfoundland Association of Visual Language Interpreters (NAVLI)

36 Ursula Cres., St. Philips NL A1M 1G6
e-mail: skinterpreter@nf.sympatico.ca
Overview: A small provincial organization overseen by Association of Visual Language Interpreters of Canada
Member of: Association of Visual Language Interpreters of Canada (AVLIC)
Membership: *Member Profile:* Professional sign language interpreters

Newfoundland Baseball

NL
Tel: 709-368-2819; *Fax:* 709-368-6080
nlbaseball@nl.rogers.com
www.sport.ca/nlbaseball
twitter.com/BaseballNL
Also Known As: Baseball NL
Previous Name: Newfoundland Amateur Baseball Association
Overview: A small provincial organization founded in 1947 overseen by Baseball Canada
Mission: Supports amatuer baseball in Newfoundland.
Member of: Baseball Canada
Chief Officer(s):
Kevin Legge, President
kevlegge@gmail.com

Finances: *Annual Operating Budget:* $50,000-$100,000; *Funding Sources:* Membership dues; fundraising; corporate; government
10 volunteer(s)
Membership: 20; *Fees:* $150; *Committees:* Hall of Fame
Activities: Amateur baseball development; *Rents Mailing List:* Yes

Newfoundland Cancer Treatment & Research Foundation (NCTRF)
#1345, Health Sciences Centre, St. John's NL A1B 3V6
Tel: 709-777-1339
zelda.burt@easternhealth.ca
www.easternhealth.ca
Overview: A medium-sized provincial charitable organization founded in 1971
Mission: To provide excellence in cancer care, including research, cancer prevention, treatment, & support, in Newfoundland & Labrador
Affliation(s): Canadian Council on Health Services Accreditation
Activities: Conducting & fostering research; Participating in the education of health care professionals & providers; Operating cancer registries; *Library:* Elaine Deluney Patient & Family Resource Library

Newfoundland Cerebral Palsy Association Inc. ***See*** Cerebral Palsy Association of Newfoundland & Labrador

Newfoundland Chicken Marketing Board ***See*** Chicken Farmers of Newfoundland & Labrador

Newfoundland Co-operative Union; Newfoundland Co-operative Services ***See*** Newfoundland-Labrador Federation of Cooperatives

Newfoundland Council for Nursing Assistants ***See*** College of Licensed Practical Nurses of Newfoundland & Labrador

Newfoundland Dental Assistants Association (NLDAA)
#274, 38 Pearson St., St. John's NL A1A 3R1
Tel: 709-579-2391
nldaa@yahoo.ca
www.nldaa.ca
Overview: A small provincial organization overseen by Canadian Dental Assistants Association
Mission: To advance the career of dental assisting in Newfoundland
Chief Officer(s):
Vera Walsh, President
Membership: *Fees:* $75 regular; $40 NLDAA membership only; $17 student; *Member Profile:* Individuals employed in the dentristry field in Newfoundland; Persons who have graduated from a dental assisting program; Students enrolled in a school of dental assisting
Activities: Providing educational opportunities
Publications:
• Newfoundland Dental Assistants Association Newsletter
Type: Newsletter; *Frequency:* Semiannually
Profile: Updates for members

Newfoundland Equestrian Association (NEA)
PO Box 372, Stn. C, St. John's NL A1C 5J9
equestriannl.ca
Overview: A small provincial organization
Member of: Equine Canada
Chief Officer(s):
Kathie Lane, President
kathielane@gmail.com
Sheila Anstey, Secretary
danstey@nf.sympatico.ca
Membership: *Member Profile:* Equestrians in Newfoundland; Equestrian associations or clubs
Activities: Offering the Learn to Ride program; Providing coaching programs; *Library:* NEA Library

Newfoundland Federation of Music Festivals
1 Marigold Place, St. John's NL A1A 3T1
Tel: 709-722-9376
Overview: A medium-sized provincial organization founded in 1969 overseen by Federation of Canadian Music Festivals
Mission: To coordinate activities of local music festivals & conduct a provincial music festival annually; to participate in the CIBC National Music Festival.
Chief Officer(s):
Joan Woodrow, Provincial Administrator
jwoodrow@bellaliant.net

Newfoundland Historical Society (NHS)
PO Box 23154, Stn. Churchill Square, St. John's NL A1B 4J9
Tel: 709-722-3191; *Fax:* 709-722-9035
nhs@nf.aibn.com
www.nlhistory.ca
Overview: A small provincial charitable organization founded in 1905
Mission: To promote study, research & public discussion of Newfoundland & Labrador's history; to record the history of the province; to promote preservation of historic sites
Chief Officer(s):
Fred Smith, President
Finances: *Funding Sources:* Membership fees; government grants; private
Membership: 526; *Fees:* $40 individual/institutional; $400 life; *Committees:* Office; Finance; Membership; Programme; Publications; Newfoundland Quarterly; AHI; Nominating
Activities: Fall/winter public lecture series; compilation of database of historical/heritage societies in the province; compilation of database of pre-1949 churches; pamphlets & monographs on Newfoundland history; symposia; *Rents Mailing List:* Yes; *Library* Open to public

Newfoundland Horticultural Society
PO Box 28086, Stn. Avalon Mall, St. John's NL A1B 4J8
e-mail: NHSweb@nl.rogers.com
nfldhort.dhs.org/page2.htm
Overview: A small provincial organization founded in 1963
Mission: To encourage an interest in all aspects of gardening as related to Newfoundland conditions
Affliation(s): Royal Horticultural Society
Chief Officer(s):
Shirley Rooney, President
Finances: *Annual Operating Budget:* Less than $50,000; *Funding Sources:* Membership fees
Membership: 104; *Fees:* $20
Activities: Monthly meetings; garden visits in summer; *Awareness Events:* Garden Show, August

Newfoundland Library Association ***See*** Newfoundland & Labrador Library Association

Newfoundland Medical Board ***See*** College of Physicians & Surgeons of Newfoundland & Labrador

Newfoundland Native Women's Association
PO Box 22, Benoits Cove NL A0L 1A0
Tel: 709-789-3430; *Fax:* 709-789-2207
nf.nativewomen@nf.aibn.com
Overview: A small provincial organization overseen by Native Women's Association of Canada
Mission: To enhance, promote & foster the social, economic, cultural and political well-being of First Nations and Métis women within First Nation, Métis and Canadian societies.
Membership: *Member Profile:* Aboriginal women residing off-reserve living in the region may particiapte if they are unemployed, under-employed or employed and seeking assistance with employment maintenance.

Newfoundland Paddling Club
PO Box 63, Cornerbrook NL A2H 6C3
Overview: A small provincial organization overseen by CanoeKayak Canada
Member of: CanoeKayak Canada
Chief Officer(s):
Joe Dicks, President
joe@explorenewfoundland.com

Newfoundland Pharmacy Association ***See*** Newfoundland & Labrador Pharmacy Board

Newfoundland Racquetball Association
16 Fairhaven Pl., St. John's NL A1E 4S1
Tel: 709-364-9151
Overview: A small provincial organization overseen by Racquetball Canada
Member of: Racquetball Canada; Sport Newfoundland & Labrador
Chief Officer(s):
Eric Easton, Vice-President, 709-364-4281
measton@roadrunner.nf.net

Newfoundland Real Estate Association ***See*** Newfoundland & Labrador Association of Realtors

Newfoundland Rock Garden Society
St. John's NL
Overview: A small provincial organization founded in 1986
Member of: North American Rock Garden Society
Chief Officer(s):
Todd Boland, Chair
Activities: Monthly meetings; Garden visits; Annual guest speaker

Newfoundland Rowing Association ***See*** Rowing Newfoundland

Newfoundland Soccer Association ***See*** Newfoundland & Labrador Soccer Association

Newfoundland Society for the Physically Disabled Inc. ***See*** Easter Seals Newfoundland & Labrador

Newfoundland Speech & Hearing Association ***See*** Newfoundland & Labrador Association of Speech-Language Pathologists & Audiologists

Newfoundland Symphony Orchestra Association (NSO)
Arts & Culture Centre, PO Box 1854, St. John's NL A1C 5P9
Tel: 709-722-4441; *Fax:* 709-753-0561
nso@nso-music.com
www.nso-music.com
twitter.com/NSOonline
Overview: A small provincial charitable organization founded in 1979 overseen by Orchestras Canada
Mission: To foster & promote in all age groups of the general public of the province an interest in & an appreciation of music; to provide the province with a symphony orchestra of the highest possible standard; to provide professional musicians, highly skilled amateur players & talented students with the opportunity of performing
Chief Officer(s):
Paul Antle, Chair
chair@nso-music.com
Mark David, Music Director
m.david@nso-music.com
Neil Edwards, CEO
n.edwards@nso-music.com
Sean Conway, Director of Operations
s.conway@nso-music.com
Finances: *Annual Operating Budget:* $500,000-$1.5 Million; *Funding Sources:* Canada Council; Arts Council; municipal government
Staff Member(s): 4; 30 volunteer(s)
Membership: 50; *Committees:* Big Ticket Gala; NSO Ball; NSO Golf Tournament
Activities: Symphony goes to the schools; *Library*

Newfoundland Symphony Youth Orchestra (NSYO)
18 Hazelwood Cres., St. John's NL A1E 6B3
Tel: 709-687-0195
info@nsyo.ca
www.nsyo.ca
www.facebook.com/NSYOmusic
www.youtube.com/user/NSYOstjohnsnl
Overview: A small local organization overseen by Orchestras Canada
Chief Officer(s):
Grant Etchegary, Artistic Director
Staff Member(s): 10

Newfoundland/Labrador Ground Water Association
PO Box 160, Doyles NL A0N 1J0
Tel: 709-955-2561; *Fax:* 709-955-3402
gwater@nf.sympatico.ca
Previous Name: Newfoundland & Labrador Water Well Corporation
Overview: A small provincial organization overseen by Canadian Ground Water Association
Mission: To promote the protection & management of ground water in Newfoundland & Labrador
Chief Officer(s):
Francis Gale, Contact
Activities: Increasing public awareness about ground water protection;

Newfoundland-Labrador Federation of Cooperatives (NLFC)
Cooperators Bldg., PO Box 13369, Stn. A, #203, 19 Crosbie Pl., St. John's NL A1B 4B7
Fax: 709-726-9433
Toll-Free: 877-726-9431
www.nlfc.coop

Previous Name: Newfoundland Co-operative Union; Newfoundland Co-operative Services
Overview: A medium-sized provincial organization founded in 1981
Mission: To represent the interests of co-operative businesses in Newfoundland & Labrador; To promote the development & growth of the co-operative business sector in the province
Member of: Canadian Co-operative Association
Chief Officer(s):
Glen Fitzpatrick, Managing Director
gfitz@nlfc.nf.ca
Membership: 40+ local co-ops; *Fees:* $100 - $2000; *Member Profile:* Co-operatives & credit unions in Newfoundland & Labrador
Activities: Liaising with the provincial government, industry associations, & community development agencies; Providing information & advice about the formation of co-operatives; Assisting existing co-operatives; Researching; Training; Offering co-op programs for young people; *Awareness Events:* Co-op Week, Oct.; Credit Union Day, Oct.

Newfoundland-Labrador Special Olympics *See* Special Olympics Newfoundland & Labrador

Newman Foundation of Toronto
89 St. George St., Toronto ON M5S 2E8
Tel: 416-979-2468; *Fax:* 416-596-6920
secretary@newmantoronto.com
www.newmantoronto.com
Overview: A small local charitable organization
Mission: To maintain & support Roman Catholic chaplaincy on University of Toronto campus
Chief Officer(s):
W.F. Morneau, President
Patrick O'Dea, Director

Newmarket & District Association for Community Living *See* Community Living Newmarket/Aurora District

Newmarket Chamber of Commerce
470 Davis Dr., Newmarket ON L3Y 2P3
Tel: 905-898-5900; *Fax:* 905-853-7271
info@newmarketchamber.com
www.newmarketchamber.ca
www.linkedin.com/groups?home=&gid=2454665
www.facebook.com/NewmarketChamberofCommerce
twitter.com/NMKTChamber
Overview: A small local organization founded in 1983
Mission: The voice of business in Newmarket since 1857. It's a major contributer to the economic and social well being of the community, representing the interests of its members - including member programs, government representation, and development of public policy.
Member of: Ontario Chamber of Commerce; Canadian Chamber of Commerce
Chief Officer(s):
Steve Hinder, Chair
steve_hinder@magna.on.ca
Debra Scott, President & CEO
debra@newmarketchamber.ca
Finances: *Annual Operating Budget:* $100,000-$250,000; *Funding Sources:* Membership dues; advertising fees; events
Staff Member(s): 3; 50 volunteer(s)
Membership: 600; *Fees:* $216-$624
Activities: *Library*

Newmarket Office *See* Heart & Stroke Foundation of Ontario

Newmarket Parents of Multiple Births Association
Newmarket ON
Other Communication: newmarketpomba@gmail.com
newmarket@multiplebirthscanada.org
yorkregionmultiples.ca
www.facebook.com/NPOMBA?v=wall&ref=ts
twitter.com/NewmarketPOMBA
Also Known As: Newmarket POMBA
Overview: A small local organization founded in 1983 overseen by Multiple Births Canada
Mission: A support network for parents of twins, triplets or more. Serving York region.
Membership: *Fees:* $30-$35

Newspapers Atlantic
#216, 7075 Bayers Rd., Halifax NS B3L 2C2
Tel: 902-832-4480; *Fax:* 902-832-4484
Toll-Free: 877-842-4480
info@newspapersatlantic.ca
newspapersatlantic.ca
Previous Name: Atlantic Community Newspapers Association
Overview: A small local organization founded in 1972 overseen by Canadian Community Newspapers Association
Mission: To promote excellence, credibility, & the economic well-being of member community newspapers throughout Atlantic Canada
Affliation(s): Canadian Community Newspapers Association; Quebec Community Newspapers Association; Hebdos Québec; Ontario Community Newspapers Association; Manitoba Community Newspapers Association; Saskatchewan Weekly Newspapers Association; Alberta Weekly Newspapers Association; British Columbia & Yukon Community Newspapers Association
Chief Officer(s):
Inez Forbes, President
Mike Kierstead, Executive Director
mike@newspapersatlantic.ca
Membership: 70 newspapers; *Member Profile:* Community newspapers from Nova Scotia, New Brunswick, Prince Edward Island, & Newfoundland & Labrador which meet certain criteria; Non-publishing members, such as suppliers to the newspaper industry
Activities: Fostering freedom of the press; Offering professional training, through the online training center; Marketing newspapers to corporations & agencies; Providing access to online marketing programs
Meetings/Conferences: • Atlantic Community Newspapers Association 2015 43rd Annual Conference, April, 2015, Hilton Hotel, Halifax, NS
Scope: Provincial
Description: A Maritime meeting with speakers, educational seminars, an awards banquet, networking opportunities with colleagues, & social events
Publications:
• Atlantic Community Newspapers Association Newsletter
Type: Newsletter
Profile: Information about the association & the industry

Niagara Association of REALTORS (NAR)
116 Niagara St., St Catharines ON L2R 4L4
Tel: 905-684-9459; *Fax:* 905-684-4778
www.mls-niagarafalls.com
Merged from: St. Catharines District Real Estate Board; Welland District Real Estate Board
Overview: A medium-sized local organization founded in 2002 overseen by Ontario Real Estate Association
Mission: To provide members with the structure & services to facilitate the marketing of real estate; to ensure a high standard of business practices & ethics; to effectively serve the real estate needs of the members
Member of: Canadian Real Estate Association
Chief Officer(s):
Brad Johnstone, President
brad@royallepage.ca
Finances: *Annual Operating Budget:* $500,000-$1.5 Million; *Funding Sources:* Membership dues
Staff Member(s): 8; 80 volunteer(s)
Membership: 975; *Member Profile:* licenced real estate agents/brokers; *Committees:* Professional Standards; Public Relations; Professional Development; Finance
Activities: charity golf tournament; charity auction;

Niagara Cattlemen's Association
4593 Brookfield Rd., Welland ON L3B 5N7
Tel: 289-214-7321
niagaracattlemen@hotmail.com
Previous Name: Niagara County Cattlemen's Association
Overview: A small local organization
Chief Officer(s):
Donna Rauscher, Secretary

Niagara Construction Association
34 Scott St. West, St Catharines ON L2R 1C9
Tel: 905-682-6661; *Fax:* 905-688-5029
office@niagaraconstruction.org
niagaraconstruction.org
www.facebook.com/330037918505
twitter.com/construct_nca
Previous Name: St. Catharines and District Builders Exchange
Overview: A small local organization founded in 1950
Mission: To represent the interests of its members who work in the construction industry
Member of: Canadian Construction Association
Chief Officer(s):
Karin Sheldrick, General Manager/Chief Operating Officer
karin@niagaraconstruction.org
Staff Member(s): 3
Membership: 275; *Member Profile:* Businesses involved with the commercial & industrial construction industry; *Committees:* Finance & Lease; Programs & Services; Personnel & Property Maintenance; Membership By-Law & Nomonations; Public Relations; Standards & Safety

Niagara County Cattlemen's Association *See* Niagara Cattlemen's Association

Niagara Economic Development (NED)
PO Box 1042, 2201 St. David's Rd., 3rd Fl., Thorold ON L2V 4T7
Tel: 905-685-4225; *Fax:* 905-688-5907
info@niagaracanada.com
www.niagaracanada.com
www.linkedin.com/company/952834
www.facebook.com/NEDCanada
twitter.com/NEDCanada
www.youtube.com/nedcanada
Previous Name: Niagara Economic Development Corporation
Overview: A medium-sized local organization founded in 1971
Mission: To attract investment & visitation to the Niagara region; to deliver economic & tourism information to customers; to facilitate decision making among partners
Affliation(s): Club 2000; Grimsby Chamber of Commerce; Niagara Falls Small Business Enterprise Centre; Niagara Immigrant Employment Council; Niagara Workforce Planning Board; Niagara-on-the-Lake Chamber of Commerce; Southern Ontario Gateway Council; St. Catharines Enterprise Centre; Venture Niagara; World Trade Centre Buffalo Niagara
Chief Officer(s):
Bob Seguin, Director
bob.seguin@niagararegion.ca
Finances: *Funding Sources:* Regional government; private & public sectors
Staff Member(s): 6
Activities: Business relocation & expansion information support; information for potential investors; economic development research; business registration, financial programs, & marketing; *Rents Mailing List:* Yes; *Library* by appointment

Niagara Economic Development Corporation *See* Niagara Economic Development

Niagara Falls Chamber of Commerce *See* Chamber of Commerce Niagara Falls, Canada

Niagara Falls Coin Club
c/o Todd Hume, 41 Radfird Ave., Fort Erie ON L2A 5H6
Overview: A small local organization
Member of: Royal Canadian Numismatic Association
Affliation(s): Ontario Numismatic Association
Chief Officer(s):
Todd Hume, Contact, 905-871-2451
humebl@aol.com
Membership: *Member Profile:* Coin collectors in the Niagara Falls area
Activities: Conducting monthly meetings at Stamford Lions Hall; Hosting coin shows

Niagara Falls Nature Club (NFNC)
PO Box 901, Niagara Falls ON L2E 6V8
e-mail: winkal@sympatico.ca
niagaranatureclub.tripod.com
Overview: A small local charitable organization founded in 1967
Mission: To promote awareness, understanding, preservation, & protection of the natural habitat of the Niagara area
Chief Officer(s):
Win Laar, President, 905-262-5057
Membership: *Fees:* $15 students; $25 single members; $35 families
Activities: Arranging programs & field trips; Conducting regular meetings at the Niagara Falls Public Library
Awards:
• R.W. Sheppard Award (Award)
To honour an individual or organization for their contribution, through education, conservation or research, in the field of nature
Publications:
• Nature Niagara News
Type: Newsletter; *Editor:* Margaret Pickles *ISSN:* 0829-1241
Profile: Articles about local nature

Niagara Falls Tourism (NFT)
5400 Robinson St, Niagara Falls ON L2G 2A6
Tel: 905-356-6061; *Fax:* 905-356-5567
Toll-Free: 800-563-2557

www.niagarafallstourism.com
www.facebook.com/nfallstourismcanada
twitter.com/nfallstourism
www.youtube.com/user/niagarafallstourism
Previous Name: Niagara Falls, Canada Visitor & Convention Bureau
Overview: A medium-sized local organization
Mission: Niagara Falls Tourism (Visitor and Convention Bureau) is the official tourism marketing organization of the Community, responsible for developing public and private sector programs that produce incremental visitor business and resulting economic development returns for the City, its residents and the business community
Member of: Tourism Industry Association of Canada
Affliation(s): 180 Marketing; AVW-TELAV Audio Visual Solutions; Bain Printing; Beatties Stationary; Brock University; Crawford Smith & Swallow Chartered Accountants; CTM Media Group; Downtown Niagara Falls; Fallsview BIA; Flexo Products; Meridian Reservation Systems; Niagara College; Niagara Falls Review; Niagara Peninsula Engery Inc.; Olsen-Sottile Insurance; Peninsula Press; Residence & Conference Centres; Robinson Show Services Inc; RVW Printing; Sightseeing & Receptive; St. Joseph's Printing; Stagevision; Stronco Group of Companies; Sullivan Mahoney; Victoria Centre BIA; Waters Meredith & Tchang, LLP
Chief Officer(s):
Toni Williams, Director, Operations
twilliams@niagarafallstourism.com
Finances: *Funding Sources:* City funding; membership fees
Staff Member(s): 15
Membership: 400; *Fees:* Schedule available

Niagara Falls, Canada Visitor & Convention Bureau *See* Niagara Falls Tourism

Niagara on the Lake Chamber of Commerce
PO Box 1043, 26 Queen St., Niagara-on-the-Lake ON L0S 1J0
Tel: 905-468-1950; *Fax:* 905-468-4930
tourism@niagaraonthelake.com
www.niagaraonthelake.com
twitter.com/niagaraonlake
Overview: A small local organization founded in 1949
Mission: To nurture the growth & prosperity of the agricultural, cultural, hospitality, retail, heritage, historical & other sectors Chamber represents; To set a strategic critical path of planning/organization/establishing objectives & goals/judgement/decision-making/implementations of actions with direct responsibility to its members
Member of: Ontario Chamber of Commerce
Chief Officer(s):
Ray Guy, President
Janice Thomson, Executive Director
manager@niagaraonthelake.com
Finances: *Annual Operating Budget:* $100,000-$250,000; *Funding Sources:* Membership fees; grants; service fees
Staff Member(s): 5
Membership: 360; *Fees:* Schedule available; *Committees:* Economic Development; Industrial; Retail; Tourism
Activities: Artistry by the Lake; Polo NOTL; Candlelight Stroll; Days of Wine & Roses; *Rents Mailing List:* Yes

Niagara Peninsula Conservation Authority (NPCA)
250 Thorold Rd. West, 3rd Fl., Welland ON L3C 3W2
Tel: 905-788-3135; *Fax:* 905-788-1121
info@npca.ca
www.npca.ca
www.facebook.com/NPCAOntario
twitter.com/NPCA_Ontario
Also Known As: Conservation Niagara Foundation
Overview: A small local charitable organization founded in 1969
Mission: To raise funds in support of the Niagara Peninsula Conservation Authority in order to undertake programs designed to further the conservation, restoration, development and management of natural resources within the Niagara Watershe.
Member of: Canadian Centre for Philanthropy
Chief Officer(s):
Carmen D'Angelo, Chief Administrative Officer, 905-788-3135 Ext. 251
cdangelo@npca.ca
Finances: *Annual Operating Budget:* $100,000-$250,000; *Funding Sources:* Donations; bequests; grants
10 volunteer(s)
Membership: 15; *Member Profile:* Member must be approved by conservation authority
Activities: Grants; Donations; Bequests and Special Events; *Awareness Events:* Golf Tournament, June; Elimination Draw & Dinner, Nov.

Niagara Peninsula Electrical Contractors Association (NPECA)
34 Scott St. West, St Catharines ON L2R 1C9
Tel: 905-688-0376; *Fax:* 905-688-5723
ecaniagara@bellnet.ca
www.ecaniagara.ca
Overview: A small local organization founded in 1974
Mission: A not-for-profit organization that represents local electrical contractors working in the Niagara Region.
Member of: Electrical Contractors Association of Ontario
Chief Officer(s):
Sue Phillips, Executive Director
Membership: *Fees:* $30; *Member Profile:* Professional contractors

Niagara Peninsula Funeral Advisory Society (NPFAS)
133 Lea Cres., Welland ON L3C 7J7
Tel: 905-732-7114
npfas@yahoo.ca
www.myfuneralplan.org/niag.htm
Overview: A small local organization founded in 1973
Mission: To provide information for informed choice in funeral planning
Member of: Federation of Ontario Memorial Societies - Funeral Consumers Alliance
Affliation(s): Funeral & Memorial Societies of America
Chief Officer(s):
Janet Dixon, Contact
Finances: *Annual Operating Budget:* Less than $50,000; *Funding Sources:* Membership dues; donations
10 volunteer(s)
Membership: 400+; *Fees:* $30

Niagara Peninsula Geological Society (NPGS)
c/o Barry Douglas, 17 Lochinvar Dr., St Catharines ON L2T 2B5
www.ccfms.ca/Clubs/NPGS
Overview: A small local organization founded in 1962
Mission: To share knowledge in geology, mineralogy, petrology, palaeontology, & lapidary
Member of: Central Canadian Federation of Mineralogical Societies (CCFMS)
Chief Officer(s):
Patti Anderson, President
meriton@cogeco.ca
Darlene Sloggett, Vice-President
desleo2056@cogeco.ca
Dave Baker, Secretary
bbaker160@cogeco.ca
Barry Douglas, Treasurer
barry.douglas@cogeco.ca
Membership: *Fees:* $15 individuals; $20 families; *Member Profile:* Individuals interested in collecting rocks, minerals, & fossils & in jewellery making
Activities: Hosting monthly meetings from September to June; Arranging collecting field trips; Teaching lapidary techniques; Lending equipment, such as a rock splitter, & microscope; *Awareness Events:* Gem, Mineral, & Fossil Show & Sale, June; *Library:* Niagara Peninsula Geological Society Lending Library
Publications:
• The Pink Dolomite Saddle Bulletin
Type: Newsletter; *Frequency:* 10 pa; *Editor:* John Tordiff; *Price:* Free with NPGS membership; $10 non-members
Profile: Upcoming regional events, club activities, & general interest articles

Niagara Philatelic Society
57 Melrose Dr., RR#1, Niagara-on-the-Lake ON L0S 1J0
Tel: 905-262-5127
Overview: A small local organization overseen by The Royal Philatelic Society of Canada
Chief Officer(s):
Ed Yonelinas, Contact
Membership: *Member Profile:* Stamp collectors

Niagara Region Orchid Society
c/o Lydia Stewart, 5831 Murray St., Niagara Falls ON L2G 2J9
e-mail: nrossociety@gmail.com
www.facebook.com/135801719803197
Overview: A small local organization
Chief Officer(s):
Rick Rempel, President
Finances: *Funding Sources:* Membership
Membership: *Fees:* $20
Activities: *Library*

Niagara Region Police Association (NRPA) / Association de la police de la région de Niagara
1706 Merrittville Hwy., RR#2, Welland ON L3B 5N5
Tel: 905-384-9800; *Fax:* 905-384-4082
Toll-Free: 866-443-8066
nrpa@nrpa.on.ca
www.nrpa.on.ca
Overview: A small local organization founded in 1971
Mission: To uphold honour of police profession; to elevate standards of police services; To encourage cooperative intercourse among police officers; to provide financial assistance in accordance with by-laws of Association
Affliation(s): Association Nationale de la Police Professionnelle/National Association of Professional Police
Finances: *Annual Operating Budget:* $500,000-$1.5 Million
Staff Member(s): 4
Membership: 849 individual + 20 temporary members + 240 lifetime; *Fees:* 1.25% of base salary; *Member Profile:* Civilian & uniform members of the Niagara Region Regional Police Service; *Committees:* Member Assistance; Business Plan; Compressed Work Week; Constitution & By-Laws; Equipment & OH&S; Job Evaluation; Legal Assistance Plan; Management Association; Member Athletics; Polical Activity; Shared Services; Special Finance; Special Functions; Strategic Planning; Technology; Uniform Job Posting; Civilian Job Reclassification; Community Policing
Activities: Negotiates two separate collective agreements; handles Police Act Discipline matters; WSIB appeals; grievanace disputes; Human Rights disputes; administers member owned long term disability plan; administers charitable organization & general membership assistance; *Library*

Niagara Region Sexual Assault Centre
#503, 43 Church St., St Catharines ON L2R 7E1
Tel: 905-682-7258; *Fax:* 905-682-2114; *Crisis Hot-Line:* 905-682-4584
carsa@sexualassaultniagara.org
www.sexualassaultniagara.org
www.facebook.com/CARSAniagara
www.youtube.com/user/SexualAssaultNiagara
Also Known As: CARSA - Committee Against Rape & Sexual Assault
Overview: A small local charitable organization founded in 1976 overseen by Canadian Association of Sexual Assault Centres
Mission: To provide counselling & support programs to survivors of sexual assault, incest & sexual child abuse; emergency services; public education & advocacy
Member of: Ontario Coalition of Rape Crisis Centres; Canadian Association of Sexual Assault Centres
Chief Officer(s):
Sharon Pazzaglia, Coordinator, Project Development, 905-682-7258
sharon@nrsac.org
Finances: *Funding Sources:* Ministry of Attorney General; fundraising
Membership: *Fees:* Yearly donations of $1000+
Activities: *Awareness Events:* Take Back the Night, Sept; *Speaker Service:* Yes

Niagara Regional Native Centre (NRNC)
382 Airport Rd., RR#4, Niagara-on-the-Lake ON L0S 1J0
Tel: 905-688-6484; *Fax:* 905-688-4033
Previous Name: St. Catharines Indian Centre
Overview: A medium-sized local charitable organization founded in 1972
Mission: To promote the development of the Native community; working in unity, to identify & address the needs of the community; to develop competent leadership; to act as an advocate within the larger community; to maintain a positive image of the Native community; to promote a better understanding between Natives & Non-Natives
Affliation(s): Ontario Federation of Indian Friendship Centres
Chief Officer(s):
Samuel Thomas, President
Jaynane Burning-Fields, Executive Director
burning-fields@hotmail.com
Staff Member(s): 20
Activities: Programs include healing & wellness, health outreach, prenatal nutrition, programs for children & youth, employment counselling, programs for seniors, literacy & basic skills; emphasis on culturally sensitive approaches

Niagara Support Services (NSS)
PO Box 190, 120 Canby St., Port Robinson ON L0S 1K0

Tel: 905-384-1172; *Fax:* 905-384-2691
nssinfo@ntec-nss.com
www.ntec-nss.com
Overview: A medium-sized local charitable organization founded in 1953
Mission: To support the abilities & contributions of persons with special needs through a professional, caring & inspired team
Member of: Ontario Agencies Supporting Individuals with Special Needs (OASIS)
Chief Officer(s):
Carolynne Canham, President
Finances: *Annual Operating Budget:* $3 Million-$5 Million; *Funding Sources:* Provincial government; fundraising; donations
Staff Member(s): 150; 20 volunteer(s)
Membership: 350; *Fees:* $8 single; $10 family; $5 associate; $15 corporate; $50 patron; *Committees:* Health & Safety; Admissions

Niagara West Employment & Learning Resource Centres (NWELRC)

PO Box 460, 4271 Queen St., Beamsville ON L0R 1B0
Tel: 905-563-1515; *Fax:* 905-563-5612
info@nwelrc.ca
www.nwelrc.ca
www.facebook.com/556944574324383
twitter.com/LCNiagaraWest
Also Known As: Literacy Council of Niagara West
Previous Name: Literacy Council of Lincoln
Overview: A small local charitable organization founded in 1985
Mission: To provide lifelong literacy & basic skills training for sustained employability
Member of: Ont. Alliance of Career Develop Practitioners; Ont. Soc. for Training & Develop.; ONESTEP; Community Based Trainers of Niagara; Lincoln C of C; Ont Literacy Coalition; Movement for Cdn Literacy; Community Literacy Ont; Literacy Link Niagara; Laubach Literacy Ont/Canada
Finances: *Funding Sources:* Provincial government; municipal government; public & private donations
Activities: Upgrading of basic, essential & literacy skills; support services for un/underemployed; specialists in employment services for the 40+ worker; transitional programs towards employability or higher education; one-to-one tutoring & small groups in reading, writing, math, computers; GED prep.; open learning computer lab; professional academic & vocational assessments; Job Finding Clubs; career counseling; résumés & cover letters; internet job search; outreach; customized workshops; research; *Speaker Service:* Yes; *Library:* Lending Library; Open to public

Niagara Youth Orchestra Association

#148, 12 - 111 Fourth Ave., St Catharines ON L2S 3P5
Tel: 905-323-5892
music@niagarayouthorchestra.ca
www.niagarayouthorchestra.ca
www.facebook.com/12038278189
Overview: A small local charitable organization founded in 1965 overseen by Orchestras Canada
Mission: To foster among youth of Niagara Region an interest in & understanding of orchestral music of high quality
Affiliation(s): Niagara Suzuki
Chief Officer(s):
Laura Thomas, Music Director
Desiree Chan, General Manager
Finances: *Funding Sources:* Membership fees; fundraising
Membership: *Fees:* $635 Jr. Orchestra; $725 Sr. Orchestra; *Member Profile:* Acceptance into orchestra - audition only; acceptance into junior orchestra - informal audition
Activities: 5-7 concerts yearly; *Library*

Niagara/Hamilton Association of Baptist Churches

ON
Overview: A small local organization overseen by Canadian Baptists of Ontario and Quebec
Member of: Canadian Baptists of Ontario & Quebec
Chief Officer(s):
Peter Dempsey, Moderator
podempsey@yahoo.ca
Membership: *Member Profile:* Baptist churches in the Niagara Falls & Hamilton area

Niagara-on-the-Lake Bed & Breakfast Association Inc.

PO Box 1228, Niagara-on-the-Lake ON L0S 1J0
Tel: 905-468-0123
Toll-Free: 866-855-0123
info@bbaboard.com
www.niagarabedandbreakfasts.com
www.facebook.com/niagarabedandbreakfasts
twitter.com/OntarioBnBs
www.youtube.com/user/niagarabnb
Overview: A small local organization
Mission: To maintain a standard of bed & breakfasts in Niagara-on-the-Lake; to allow for collaboration amongst bed & breakfast owners
Membership: *Fees:* $170 with Guestbook system; $95 without Guestbook system; *Member Profile:* Licencees of bed & breakfasts or inns

Nickel Belt Coin Club (NBCC)

c/o Larry Seguin, 4349 Chateau Cres., Hanmer ON P3P 1Y6
Tel: 705-969-5023
www.nickelbeltcoinclub.com
www.facebook.com/pages/Nickel-Belt-Coin-Club/301511356564760
Overview: A small local organization founded in 1956
Mission: To provide a meeting place, as well as a discussion forum for those interested in coin collection
Chief Officer(s):
Larry Seguin, Secretary
Slarryd@hotmail.com
Membership: 60+;

Nickel Development Institute ***See*** Nickel Institute

Nickel Institute

Brookfield Place, #2700, 161 Bay St., Toronto ON M5J 2S1
Tel: 416-591-7999; *Fax:* 416-591-7987
ni_toronto@nickelinstitute.org
www.nickelinstitute.org
Previous Name: Nickel Development Institute
Overview: A large national organization founded in 1984
Mission: Market development & applications oriented non-profit research organization of international nickel industry; to provide information for nickel users, designers, specifiers, educators & others interested in nickel-containing materials & their applications
Chief Officer(s):
Tim Aiken, Chairman
Kevin Bradley, President
Finances: *Annual Operating Budget:* Greater than $5 Million
Staff Member(s): 9
Membership: 24 corporate; *Member Profile:* Nickel miner, smelter, refiner; *Committees:* Technical Program; Advisory
Activities: *Library*

Nicola Valley & District Food Bank

PO Box 2719, 2026 Quilchena Ave., Merritt BC V1K 1B8
Tel: 250-378-2282; *Fax:* 250-378-2982
foodbank@mail.ocis.net
Overview: A small local organization overseen by Food Banks British Columbia
Member of: Food Banks British Columbia
Chief Officer(s):
Linda Monkman, Contact

Nicola Valley Community Arts Council

PO Box 2762, Merritt BC V0K 2B0
Tel: 250-378-6515
nicolavalleyartscouncil@gmail.com
www.nvartscouncil.com
Overview: A small local charitable organization founded in 1982
Mission: To increase & broaden the opportunities for residents of Nicola Valley to participate in cultural activities
Affiliation(s): Okanagan Mainline Regional Arts Council; BC Touring Council
Chief Officer(s):
Deanna Gage, President
Finances: *Annual Operating Budget:* Less than $50,000; *Funding Sources:* Municipal & provincial government
6 volunteer(s)
Membership: 38 individual & family + 7 group + 2 lifetime; *Fees:* $10 individual; $20 family; $25 groups

Nicola Valley Museum Archives Association

PO Box 1262, 1675 Tutill Crt., Merritt BC V1K 1B8
Tel: 250-378-4145; *Fax:* 250-378-4145
nvma@uniserve.com
www.nicolavalleymuseum.org/association.html
www.facebook.com/NVMuseum
Overview: A small local charitable organization founded in 1976
Mission: To collect & preserve archival & museum artifacts pertinent to the Nicola Valley area & its history; to display museum articles
Member of: BC Museums Association; Archives Association of BC; BC Historical Federation
Affliation(s): Canadian Museums Association
Chief Officer(s):
Barb Watson, Staff
Finances: *Annual Operating Budget:* Less than $50,000; *Funding Sources:* Provincial government; municipal government; regional government
Staff Member(s): 2; 12 volunteer(s)
Membership: 138; *Fees:* $20 senior/student; $30 individual; $45 family; $100 commercial; $1000 life; $1500 patron; $2000 benefactor
Activities: *Library* Open to public

Nigerian Students Association ***See*** Association of Nigerians in Nova Scotia

Niijkiwenhwag - Friends of Lake Superior Park

c/o Lake Superior Provincial Park, PO Box 267, Wawa ON P0S 1K0
Tel: 705-856-2284
info@lakesuperiorpark.ca
www.lakesuperiorpark.ca
Overview: A small local organization founded in 1993
Mission: To achieve public awareness, knowledge & appreciation of the park's natural & cultural heritage; To coordinate special events & projects related to the park's theme; To support the development of park interpretive programs; To provide supplementary funds to complement park educational & scientific research projects
Chief Officer(s):
Christina Speer, Chair
Membership: *Fees:* $10 individual; $15 family

The Nile Association of Ontario (NAO)

81 Primrose Crescent, Brampton ON L6Z 1E1
Tel: 905-840-5375
info@nileclub.org
www.nileclub.org
Overview: A small provincial organization founded in 1988
Mission: To promote the social coherence of the Egyptian community & to provide assistance, help, & guidance to new immigrants
Chief Officer(s):
Mohamed Elhalwagy, President
Membership: *Fees:* $20 student/senior; $25 adult; $50 family; *Committees:* Social; Culture; Sports; Membership; Business; Youth
Activities: Promotes & teaches Egyptian culture; promotes our heritage; organizes sports activities; promotes business within the Egyptian community; social functions

Nipawin & District Chamber of Commerce

PO Box 177, Nipawin SK S0E 1E0
Tel: 306-862-5252; *Fax:* 306-862-5350
info@nipawinchamber.ca
www.nipawinchamber.ca
twitter.com/NipawinChamber
Overview: A small local organization founded in 1923
Mission: The Chamber of Commerce encourages and aids in promotion of commercial, industrial, agricultural, and civic interests of the community and district
Chief Officer(s):
Linda Swehla, President, 306-862-4810
Finances: *Annual Operating Budget:* Less than $50,000
Staff Member(s): 2
Membership: 180; *Fees:* Schedule available

Nipawin Exhibition Association Inc.

PO Box 105, Nipawin SK S0E 1E0
Tel: 306-862-3411; *Fax:* 306-862-9669
nipawinexhibition@yahoo.ca
www.nipawinex.com
Also Known As: Nipawin AG Society
Overview: A small local licensing organization founded in 1928
Mission: To help promote light horse, heavy horse & beef cattle through exhibitions
Member of: Saskatchewan Association of Agricultural Societies & Exhibitions
Chief Officer(s):
Nathalie Hipkins, Secretary
George Belchamber, President
Finances: *Annual Operating Budget:* $50,000-$100,000
150 volunteer(s)
Membership: 44; *Fees:* $10; *Committees:* Indoor; Light Horse; Heavy Horse; Beef
Activities: *Awareness Events:* Nipawin Exhibition, July

Nipigon, Red Rock & District Association for Community Living *See* Superior Greenstone Association for Community Living

Nipissing Children's Aid Society for the District of Nipissing & Parry Sound *See* Children's Aid Society of the District of Nipissing & Parry Sound

Nipissing Coin Club
c/o W.R. Caesar, 895 Clarence St., North Bay ON P1B 3W1
Overview: A small local organization

Nipissing Environmental Watch (NEW)
PO Box 1543, North Bay ON P1B 8K6
Tel: 705-494-8935
new@bell.net
www.nipissingenvironmentalwatch.org
Overview: A small local organization
Mission: To help make positive steps towards environment conservation in Nipissing District

Nipissing Law Association
360 Plouffe St., North Bay ON P1B 9L5
Tel: 705-495-3271; *Fax:* 705-495-3487
Toll-Free: 866-899-6439
nipilaws@onlink.net
nipissinglawassociation.wordpress.com
Overview: A small local organization founded in 1981
Chief Officer(s):
Amanda Adams, Law Librarian
Membership: 98
Activities: *Library:* George C. Wallace Q.C. Law Library

Nisga'a Lisims Government
PO Box 231, 2000 Lisims Dr., Aiyansh BC V0J 1A0
Tel: 250-633-3000; *Fax:* 250-633-2367
Toll-Free: 866-633-0888
maxine.azak@nisgaa.net
www.nisgaalisims.ca
Also Known As: Nisga'a Tribal Council
Previous Name: Nishga Tribal Council
Overview: A medium-sized local organization founded in 1956
Finances: *Annual Operating Budget:* $3 Million-$5 Million
Staff Member(s): 30
Membership: 6,000; *Member Profile:* People of Nisga'a origin; *Committees:* Planning & Priorities; Ayuukhl Nisga'a; Economic Finance; Personnel Finance; Education; Joint Venture; Working groups - Fisheries; Forest, Lands, Environment; Nisga'a government; Nisga'a highways
Activities: Wilp Wilx'osk Nisga'a (Nisga'a House of Learning); Justice Department (Family Law Program, Access to Justice Program, Victim Assistance Program); Educational training programs; *Library:* Resource Centre; Open to public

Nishga Tribal Council *See* Nisga'a Lisims Government

Nishnawbe - Gamik Friendship Centre
PO Box 1299, 52 King St., Sioux Lookout ON P8T 1B8
Tel: 807-737-1909
Toll-Free: 800-619-9519
Other Communication: finance_ngfc@knet.ca
president_ngfc@knet.ca
www.ngfcreceptionslkt.myknet.org
Overview: A small local organization
Mission: To provide a meeting place for people of Aboriginal ancestry & others in the Sioux Lookout, Ontario region to exchange ideas & to develop mutual understanding & appreciation; To advance native language & culture
Member of: Ontario Federation of Indian Friendship Centres
Chief Officer(s):
Liza Angeconeb, Contact, Hall Rentals
l_angeconeb_ngfc@knet.ca
Sheila Beardy, Program Coordinator, Life Long Care Program
s_beardy_ngfc@knet.ca
Candice Goretzki, Program Coordinator, Aboriginal Family Support
c_goretzki_ngfc@knet.ca
Ramona Hill-Carter, Program Coordinator, Anokeewin Wiichiiwaawin Employment Program
r_hillcarter_ngfc@knet.ca
Brian Logan, Program Coordinator, Addictions Program
b_logan_ngfc@knet.ca
Geneva Sainnawap, Program Coordinator, Combined Courtworker Program
g_sainnawap_ngfc@knet.ca
Activities: Hosting weekly cultural nights; Offering educational & recreational activities; Providing programs such as the Akwe:go High-Risk Urban Aboriginal Children's Program; Wasa-Nabin Urban Aboriginal Youth Program; the Addictions Program, Anokeewin Wiichiiwaawin Employment Program, & the Life Long Care Program

Nistawoyou Association Friendship Centre
8310 Manning Ave., Fort McMurray AB T9H 1W1
Tel: 780-743-8555; *Fax:* 780-750-0527
executivedirector@shawcable.com
Overview: A small local organization founded in 1964 overseen by Alberta Native Friendship Centres Association
Mission: To develop social & recreational activities in the aboriginal communities in and around Fort McMurray
Member of: Alberta Native Friendship Centres Association
Affliation(s): Fort McMurray United Way
Chief Officer(s):
Flordeliza Hachac Connors, Executive Director
executivedirector@shawcable.com
Finances: *Funding Sources:* Federal government; provincial government
Staff Member(s): 3
Membership: 100
Activities: Feed the hungary program; Life enhancement & empowerment; Community Assistance; Youth summer camp; Homelessness initiatives; Employment programs

Niverville Chamber of Commerce
PO Box 157, Niverville MB R0A 1E0
Tel: 204-388-4600
chamber@niverville.com
www.niverville.com
Overview: A small local organization
Mission: Promoting business in the area.
Chief Officer(s):
Leighton Reimer, President

NL West SPCA
PO Box 7, 10 Connors Lane, Corner Brook NL A2H 3G4
Tel: 709-785-2747
nlwestspca@gmail.com
www.nlwestspca.com
www.facebook.com/NLWestSPCA
Previous Name: Bay of Islands SPCA; Bay of Islands Society for the Prevention of Cruelty to Animals
Overview: A small local organization founded in 1979
Mission: To assist animals in need, keep them healthy, & aid in their adoption
Member of: Canadian Federation of Humane Societies
Finances: *Funding Sources:* Donations

NOIA
Atlantic Place, #602, 215 Water St., St. John's NL A1C 6C9
Tel: 709-758-6610; *Fax:* 709-758-6611
noia@noia.ca
www.noia.ca
Also Known As: Newfoundland & Labrador Oil & Gas Industries Association
Overview: A medium-sized provincial organization founded in 1977
Mission: To assist, promote & facilitate the participation of members in ocean industries, with particular emphasis on oil & gas, to enhance their growth & development; to promote the growth of ocean industry; to act as a focal point for representations to government bodies & agencies; to act as a source of information & education for members
Chief Officer(s):
Robert Cadigan, President & CEO
Finances: *Annual Operating Budget:* $500,000-$1.5 Million; *Funding Sources:* Membership fees; conferences, seminars & special events
Staff Member(s): 10; 100 volunteer(s)
Membership: 600; *Fees:* $603 small company; $833 medium company; $1145 large company; *Member Profile:* Those who develop, manufacture & market products & services in the oil & gas industry, both offshore & onshore; *Committees:* Board of Directors; Conference; Executive; Arctic Greenland Committee; Exploration; Diversity; Petroleum Industry Human Resources Committee (PIHRC)
Activities: Promotes development of East Coast Canada's hydrocarbon resources & facilitates its membership's participation in oil & gas industries; *Library* by appointment
Awards:
• NOIA Hibernia Commemorative Scholarship (Award)
Eligibility: Newfoundland & Labrador post-secondary students planning to pursue a career in a petroleum-related field
Meetings/Conferences: • NOIA Conference 2015, June, 2015, Delta St. John's, St. John's, NL
Scope: National
Description: The Annual Noia Conference is a key service that provides members and the general public with information on trends and business opportunities in the East Coast Canada oil & gas industry.

Non-Academic Staff Association for the University of Alberta
College Plaza, #507, 8215 - 112 St., Edmonton AB T6G 2E1
Tel: 780-439-3181; *Fax:* 780-433-5056
Toll-Free: 877-439-3111
nasa@ualberta.ca
www.nasa.ualberta.ca
Previous Name: University of Alberta Non-Academic Staff Association
Overview: A medium-sized local organization
Chief Officer(s):
Russell Eccles, President
russell.eccles@ualberta.ca
Heather Green, Vice-President
heather.green@ualberta.ca
Donna Coombs-Montrose, Chair, Membership
Gerrie Rajotte, Director, Operations
gerrie.rajotte@ualberta.ca
Jeffrey Belore, Administrator, Accounts & Payroll
financial@nasa.ualberta.ca
Deborah Stewart, Officer, Communications
deborah.stewart@ualberta.ca
100 volunteer(s)
Membership: 6,000+; *Fees:* Schedule available; *Member Profile:* Support staff of the University of Alberta

Nonprescription Drug Manufacturers Association of Canada; NDMAC, Advancing Canadian Self-Care *See* Consumer Health Products Canada

Non-Smokers' Rights Association (NSRA) / Association pour les droits des non-fumeurs
#221, 720 Spadina Ave., Toronto ON M5S 2T9
Tel: 416-928-2900; *Fax:* 416-928-1860
toronto@nsra-adnf.ca
www.nsra-adnf.ca
Overview: A medium-sized national organization founded in 1974
Mission: To promote public health by stopping illness & death due to tobacco, including second-hand smoke
Affliation(s): Smoking & Health Action Foundation (SHAF)
Chief Officer(s):
Lorraine Fry, Executive Director
Peter Holt, Coordinator, Membership
Finances: *Funding Sources:* Membership fees
Membership: *Fees:* $29 individual; $36 family; $18 student or person over age 65; $47 institution
Activities: Advocating for tobacco-control efforts in Canada & throughout the world; Liaising with national, provincial, & local health organizatons & community groups

Montréal
833, rue Roy est, Montréal QC H2L 1E4
Tel: 514-843-3250
montreal@nsra-adnf.ca
Chief Officer(s):
François Damphousse, Director

Ottawa
#1903, 130 Albert St., Ottawa ON K1P 5G4
Tel: 613-230-4211; *Fax:* 613-230-9454
ottawa@nsra-adnf.ca
Chief Officer(s):
Melodie Tilson, Director, Policy

Norfolk Association for Community Living (NACL)
644 Ireland Rd., Simcoe ON N3Y 4K2
Tel: 519-426-5000; *Fax:* 519-426-5744
naclinfo@nacl.ca
www.nacl.ca
Overview: A medium-sized local charitable organization founded in 1953
Mission: To promote & support the inclusion of people with disabilities in all aspects of community life
Member of: Ontario Association Supporting Individuals with Special Needs (OASIS)
Chief Officer(s):
Stella Galloway, Executive Director
Al Winger, President
Finances: *Annual Operating Budget:* $3 Million-$5 Million; *Funding Sources:* M.C.S.S.; United Way; donations
Staff Member(s): 180; 90 volunteer(s)
Membership: 112; *Fees:* $10 individual; $25 family

Activities: *Internships:* Yes; *Library:* NACL Resource Library; Open to public

Norfolk Community Chest *See* United Way of Haldimand-Norfolk

Norfolk County Agricultural Society
172 South Dr., Simcoe ON N3Y 1G6
Tel: 519-426-7280; *Fax:* 519-426-7286
www.norfolkcountyfair.com
Overview: A small local organization
Chief Officer(s):
George Araujo, General Manager

Norfolk Field Naturalists (NFN)
PO Box 995, Simcoe ON N3Y 5B3
Tel: 519-586-2603
info@norfolkfieldnaturalists.org
www.norfolkfieldnaturalists.org
Overview: A small local organization founded in 1962
Mission: Dedicated to the acquisition & extension of knowledge of natural history & appreciation, enjoyment & stewardship of natural environment, especially within the region of Haldimand-Norfolk
Member of: Federation of Ontario Naturalists; Long Point Bird Observatory; Carolinian Canada
Chief Officer(s):
Bernie Solymar, President
solymar@nornet.on.ca
Finances: *Annual Operating Budget:* Less than $50,000; *Funding Sources:* Membership dues; donations; LPBO Birdathon
10 volunteer(s)
Membership: 150; *Fees:* $20 single; $30 family; *Committees:* Local Environmental Protection; Waste Management
Activities: Field trips for birding; free identification; nature appreciation; local natural heritage sites; *Speaker Service:* Yes

Norfolk Historical Society (NHC)
109 Norfolk St. South, Simcoe ON N3Y 2W3
Tel: 519-426-1583; *Fax:* 519-426-1584
office@norfolklore.com
www.norfolklore.com
www.facebook.com/evabrookdonly
twitter.com/museumnorfolk
Also Known As: Eva Brook Donly Museum & Archives
Overview: A small local charitable organization founded in 1900
Mission: Collects, preserves & provides evidence of the history of old Norfolk county in the operation of the Eva Brook Donly Museum, holding its collections in trust for the public & their descendants; Extensive material culture collection, thousands of photographs, archival documents and printed material, reference books; Loyalist Library and Genealogical Resources
Affliation(s): Ontario Genealogical Society; Ontario Museum Association; Ontario Historical Society; Simcoe Chamber of Commerce
Chief Officer(s):
Keitha Davis, President
Finances: *Funding Sources:* Membership dues; fundraising; donations; grants
Membership: *Fees:* $5 youth; $40 regular; $50 non-profit; $60 family; $200 commercial
Activities: Operates Eva Brook Donly Museum & Archives; *Speaker Service:* Yes; *Library* Open to public

Norman Wells & District Chamber of Commerce
PO Box 400, Norman Wells NT X0E 0V0
Tel: 867-587-6609; *Fax:* 867-587-2865
info@normanwellschamber.com
www.normanwellschamber.com
Overview: A small local organization
Chief Officer(s):
Chris Buist, President
president@normanwellschamber.com
Membership: 43;

Norman Wells Historical Society (NWHS)
PO Box 145, 23 Mackenzie Dr., Norman Wells NT X0E 0V0
Tel: 867-587-2415; *Fax:* 867-587-2469
canol.trail@theedgenw.ca
www.normanwellsmuseum.com
www.facebook.com/NormanWellsHistoricalSociety
Overview: A small local organization founded in 1977
Member of: Canadian Museums Association
Affliation(s): Canadian Booksellers Association; Prince of Wales Northern Heritage Centre
Chief Officer(s):
Sarah Colbeck, Curator/Manager
Staff Member(s): 2; 10 volunteer(s)
Activities: Museum, art gallery, gift shop; annual art show; travelling exhibits

Les normes canadiennes de la publicité *See* Advertising Standards Canada

Les normes canadiennes de la publicité (NCP) / Advertising Standards Canada (ASC)
#915, 2015, rue Peel, Montréal QC H3A 1T8
Tél: 514-931-8060; *Téléc:* 514-931-2797
www.adstandards.com/fr/
Nom précédent: Conseil des normes de la publicité
Aperçu: *Dimension:* petite; *Envergure:* nationale; Organisme sans but lucratif; fondée en 1957
Mission: Assurer l'autoréglementation de l'industrie canadienne de la publicité à l'aide de codes d'éthique publicitaire
Membre(s) du bureau directeur:
Linda J. Nagel, Présidente et chef de la direction
Finances: *Budget de fonctionnement annuel:* $1.5 Million-$3 Million
Membre(s) du personnel: 2; 36 bénévole(s)
Membre: 200; *Comités:* Conseil des normes
Activités: *Service de conférenciers:* Oui; *Bibliothèque:* NCP Bibliothèque

Nornet-Yukon *See* Yukon Territory Environmental Network

Norquay & District Chamber of Commerce
PO Box 457, Norquay SK S0A 2V0
Tel: 306-594-2248; *Fax:* 306-594-2347
Other Communication: Alternate Phone: 306-594-2809
Previous Name: Norquay Chamber of Commerce
Overview: A small local organization
Membership: *Fees:* $10 individual; $25 business

Norquay Chamber of Commerce *See* Norquay & District Chamber of Commerce

North Algoma Literacy Coalition (NALC)
50B Broadway Ave., Wawa ON P0S 1K0
Tel: 705-856-4394; *Fax:* 705-856-4394
wawa-adultlearningcentre.com
Also Known As: Adult Learning Centre for Wawa and Surrounding Area
Overview: A small local charitable organization
Mission: Works with the community to promote & improve life-long learning for adults & families
Chief Officer(s):
Lisa Houston, Program Director
director@wawa-nalc.com
Staff Member(s): 5
Activities: Deliver literacy & basic skills program; support family literacy activities; *Speaker Service:* Yes

North America Railway Hall of Fame (NARHF)
750 Tabot St., St Thomas ON N5P 4H4
Tel: 519-633-2535; *Fax:* 519-633-3087
info@narhf.org
www.narhf.org
Overview: A small national charitable organization founded in 1996
Mission: To establish a tribute to those who have made significant contributions relating to the railway industry in North America; To honour railway organizations, related innovations & technical accomplishments; To preserve & display a collection of library materials & railway heritage artifacts related to the Hall of Fame inductees; To educate the public about the impact of railway transportation on history & the development of communities, nations & international relations
Chief Officer(s):
Matt Janes, President

North American Association of Asian Professionals Vancouver (NAAAP)
PO Box 18518, 710 Granville St., Vancouver BC V6Z 0B3
Other Communication: communications@naaap.bc.ca
naaap@naaap.bc.ca
www.naaap.bc.ca
twitter.com/naaap
Overview: A small local organization founded in 1982
Mission: To promote the career advancement of Asian professionals in Vancouver; To support multiculturalism
Chief Officer(s):
Rudy Chung, President
Walt Woo, Vice-President
Linton Chokie, Secretary
Holman Lai, Treasurer
Tammy Tsang, Director, Communications
Finances: *Funding Sources:* Membership fees
Membership: *Fees:* $50; *Member Profile:* Asian Canadian professionals in the Vancouver area
Activities: Encouraging the leadership development of Asian professionals in all areas; Facilitating professional networking opportunities; Presenting professional development workshops & seminars; Providing resources to Asian professionals & university students; Sponsoring community activities to increase cultural awareness of Asians
Publications:
• NAAAP Insight
Type: Newsletter; *Frequency:* Quarterly; *Price:* Free with membership in North American Association of Asian Professionals Vancouver
Profile: Association activities & upcoming events

North American Bird Conservation Initiative Canada (NABCI)
c/o Canadian Wildlife Service-Environment Canada, 351, boul. St-Joseph, 3e étage, Gatineau QC K1A 0H3
Tel: 819-994-0512; *Fax:* 819-994-4445
nabci@ec.gc.ca
www.nabci.net
Mission: The NABCI is a coordinated effort among Canada, the United States & Mexico to maintain the diversity & abundance of all North American birds. National coordination of this effort in Canada occurs through the NABCI Canada Council, chaired by the Asst. Deputy Minister of Environment Canada's Environmental Conservation Service. Council members include representatives from provincial governments, non-government organizations, four bird plans (waterfowl, landbirds, shorebirds, waterbirds), & habitat joint ventures. In Canada, the joint venture conservation projects has three habitat joint ventures (Pacific Coast, Prairie Habitat, Eastern Habitat) & three species (Arctic Goose, Black Duck, Sea Duck.)

North American Broadcasters Association (NABA)
PO Box 500, Stn. A, #6C300, 25 John St., Toronto ON M5W 1E6
Tel: 416-598-9877; *Fax:* 416-598-9774
contact@nabanet.com
www.nabanet.com
Previous Name: North American National Broadcasters Association
Overview: A large international organization founded in 1972
Mission: To provide a framework for the identification, study & active solution of international questions affecting broadcasting
Member of: World Broadcasting Union
Chief Officer(s):
Robert Briskman, President
Michael McEwen, Director General
Anh Ngo, Director, Administration
Finances: *Funding Sources:* Membership fees
Staff Member(s): 5
Membership: 10 full + 3 associate + 10 affiliate; *Fees:* US$40,000 full; US$20,000 associate; *Member Profile:* Broadcasters; *Committees:* Technical; Radio; Legal; Safety & Security
Activities: NABA is a member of & houses the Secretariat of the World Broadcasting Unions (WBU) & its subcommittees - the International Satellite Operations Group & Technical Committee; NABA is also a member of the Coordinating Committee - a group of international media organizations concerned with freedom of the press

North American Chronic Pain Association of Canada *See* Chronic Pain Association of Canada

North American National Broadcasters Association *See* North American Broadcasters Association

North American Native Plant Society (NANPS)
PO Box 84, Stn. D, Toronto ON M9A 4X1
Tel: 416-631-4438
Other Communication: plantsale@nanps.org; rescues@nanps.org; land@nanps.org
nanps@nanps.org
www.nanps.org
www.facebook.com/nativeplant
Previous Name: Canadian Wildflower Society
Overview: A medium-sized provincial charitable organization founded in 1984
Mission: Dedicated to the study, conservation & cultivation of North America's wild flora.
Member of: Federation of Ontario Naturalists

Chief Officer(s):
Ruth Zaugg, Secretary
Membership: *Fees:* $20/year
Activities: Members-only seed exchange; Native Garden Award; Native Plant Sale
Publications:
• Blazing Star [a publication of the North American Native Plant Society]
Type: Journal; *Frequency:* Quarterly

North American Recycled Rubber Association (NARRA)

#24, 1621 McEwen Dr., Whitby ON L1N 9A5
Tel: 905-433-7769; *Fax:* 905-433-0905
narra@oix.com
www.recycle.net/recycle/assn/narra
Overview: A small national organization founded in 1994
Mission: The Association provides a unified voice, as well as a communication network & research facility, for issues of concern to those involved in rubber recycling across North America.
Chief Officer(s):
Diane Sarracini, Office Manager
Finances: *Funding Sources:* Membership dues; research
Activities: Provides specialized training & feasibility studies; annual convention (March) & newsletter;

North American Waterfowl Management Plan (NAWMP) / Le plan nord-américain de gestion de la sauvagine

c/o Canadian Wildlife Service, Place Vincent Massey, 351, boul St. Joseph, 7th Fl., Gatineau QC K1A 0H3
Tel: 819-934-6036; *Fax:* 819-934-6017
nawmp@ec.gc.ca
www.nawmp.ca
Mission: The North American Waterfowl Management Plan is an international action plan to conserve migratory birds throughout the continent. The Plan's goal is toreturn waterfowl populations to their 1970's levels by conserving wetland and upland habitat. Canada & the United States signed the Plan in 1986 in reaction to critically low numbers of waterfowl. Mexico joined in 1994 making it a truly continental effort. The Plan is a partnership of federal, provincial/state & municipal governments, non-governmental organizations, private companies & many individuals, all working towards achieving better wetland habitat for the benefit of migratory birds, other wetland-associated species & people. The Plan's unique combination of biology, landscape conservation & partnerships comprise its exemplary conservation legacy. Plan projects are international in scope, but implemented at regional levels. These projects contribute to the protection of habitat & wildlife species across the North American landscape. In fact, the North American Waterfowl Management Plan is considered one of the most successful conservation initiatives in the world.
Chief Officer(s):
Tasha Sargent, Coordinator, Canadian Wildlife Service
tasha_sargent@pcjv.org
Awards:
• Great Blue Heron Award (Award)
Recognizes primary participants in the Plan who have made major, long-term national contributions that result in benefits to waterfowl & other bird populations of North America; for US nominations - Executive Director, N. American Waterfowl & Wetlands Office, US Fish & Wildlife Service, Rm.110, 4401 N. Fairfax Dr., Arlington VA 22203, ph. 703/358-1784; for Mexican nominations - Humberto Berlanga, Instituto Nacional de Ecolgis, Avenida Revoluclon 1425-19, Colonia Tlacopoc San Angel, Mexico D.F.01040, ph.(52-56)24-33-09-09; for Canadian nomination contact above address*Eligibility:* Nominees must demonstrate protection, maintenance, restoration or improvement of habitat for waterfowl & migratory bird populations; or initiation of legislation or major corporate or public policy that helped attain goals of the plan, & benefit waterfowl & migratory bird populations; or donation of a gift valued at $10,000 or more to any plan partner; or fostering of cooperation & coordination that contributes to plan goals*Deadline:* February *Amount:* A carving of a Great Blue Heron & a certificate
• International Canvasback Award (Award)
For individuals, corporations, & organizations who have made substantial, long-term international contributions to the implementation & continuation of the plan throughout North America*Deadline:* February *Amount:* An original decoy carving of a Canvasback & a certificate

Arctic Goose Joint Venture
e-mail: agvj@ec.gc.ca
www.agjv.ca
Chief Officer(s):
Deanna Dixon, Coordinator
deanna.dixon@ec.gc.ca

Black Duck Joint Venture
www.blackduckjv.org
Chief Officer(s):
Brigitte Collins, Coordinator
brigitte.collins@ec.gc.ca

Eastern Habitat Joint Venture
www.ehjv.ca
Chief Officer(s):
Patricia Edwards, Coordinator
patricia.edwards@ec.gc.ca

Pacific Coast Joint Venture
www.pcjv.org
Chief Officer(s):
Tasha Sargent, Coordinator
tasha_sargent@pcjv.org

Prairie Habitat Joint Venture
e-mail: phjv@ec.gc.ca
www.phjv.ca
Chief Officer(s):
Deanna Dixon
deanna.dixon@ec.gc.ca

North Battleford & District Labour Council

PO Box 1719, North Battleford SK S9A 3W2
Tel: 306-445-0660
Overview: A small local organization overseen by Saskatchewan Federation of Labour
Mission: To support union members & workers in North Battleford, Saskatchewan & the surrounding region; To advance the economic & social welfare of workers
Affliation(s): Canadian Labour Congress (CLC)
Chief Officer(s):
Colin Lemauviel, President
coconb@sasktel.net
Activities: Promoting the interests of affiliates; Liasing with local elected officials to ensure labour's message is heard; Presenting educational opportunities; Raising awareness of occupational health & safety; Organizing ceremonies surrounding the International Day of Mourning for Workers Killed & Injured on the Job

North Battleford Chamber of Commerce *See* Battlefords Chamber of Commerce

North Bay & District Chamber of Commerce

1375 Seymour St., North Bay ON P1B 9V6
Tel: 705-472-8480; *Fax:* 705-472-8027
Toll-Free: 888-249-8998
nbcc@northbaychamber.com
www.northbaychamber.com
www.linkedin.com/company/north-bay-&-district-chamber-of-commerce
www.facebook.com/NBDCC
twitter.com/nbdcc
Overview: A small local organization founded in 1894
Member of: Ontario Chamber of Commerce; Canadian Chamber of Commerce
Chief Officer(s):
Patti Carr, Executive Director
patricia@northbaychamber.com
Staff Member(s): 5; 85 volunteer(s)
Membership: 900+; *Fees:* $149-$819

North Bay & District Society for the Prevention of Cruelty to Animals

PO Box 1383, 2060 Main St. West, North Bay ON P1B 8K5
Tel: 705-474-1251; *Fax:* 705-474-1259
nbhs@thot.net
northbayhumanesociety.ca
www.facebook.com/nbHumaneSociety
twitter.com/nbhumanesociety
Overview: A small local charitable organization founded in 1954
Member of: Canadian Federation of Humane Societies
Affliation(s): Ontario Society for the Prevention of Cruelty to Animals
Chief Officer(s):
Daryl Vallancourt, General Manager
manager@northbayhumanesociety.ca
Finances: *Annual Operating Budget:* $250,000-$500,000
Staff Member(s): 7; 50 volunteer(s)
Membership: *Fees:* $10 senior; $15 individual; $25 family; $50 corporate
Activities: Animal control & cruelty prevention; *Awareness Events:* Pawsathon, June; *Speaker Service:* Yes

North Bay & District Stamp Club

425 Fraser St., North Bay ON P1B 3X1
Tel: 705-472-6918
teron@sympatico.ca
Overview: A small local organization
Mission: To encourage & promote stamp collecting in & around North Bay; To provide a social medium for the exchange of stamps & philatelic information
Member of: Royal Philatelic Society of Canada
Chief Officer(s):
Terry Turner, Contact
Finances: *Annual Operating Budget:* $100,000-$250,000; *Funding Sources:* Membership fees
Membership: 25; *Fees:* $12

North Bay Food Bank

1356 Hammond St., North Bay ON P1B 2J3
Tel: 705-495-3290; *Fax:* 705-474-5491
www.facebook.com/pages/North-Bay-Food-Bank/120625457997222
Also Known As: North Bay Soup Kitchen Inc.
Overview: A small local charitable organization founded in 1986
Mission: To see that no child or persons go hungry in our community
Member of: Ontario Association of Food Banks; Canadian Food Bank Association
Chief Officer(s):
Donna Gauthier, Contact
Finances: *Annual Operating Budget:* $100,000-$250,000; *Funding Sources:* Food & financial donations
Staff Member(s): 2; 12 volunteer(s)
Membership: *Fees:* $100

North Bay Indian Friendship Centre (NBIFC)

980 Cassells St., North Bay ON P1B 4A6
Tel: 705-472-2811
www.nbifc.org
Overview: A small local organization founded in 1974
Mission: To improve the quality of life for First Nation, Metis, & Inuit people in North Bay, Ontario
Member of: Ontario Federation of Indian Friendship Centres
Chief Officer(s):
Peter Ferris, Executive Director
Activities: Offering services & programs to support Aboriginal people of all ages, such as the the Aboriginal Prenatal Nutrition Program, the Best Start Program, the Aboriginal Healthy Babies Healthy Children Program, Cultural Connections for Aboriginal Youth, the Apatisiwin Employment Unit, the Native Inmate Liaison Program, the Aboriginal Drug & Alcohol Program, the Aboriginal Family Support Program, & the Aboriginal Healing & Wellness Program

North Bay Police Association (NBPA)

135 Princess St. West, North Bay ON P1B 8J8
Tel: 705-197-5555
nbpa@northbaypoliceassociation.ca
www.northbaypoliceassociation.ca
Overview: A small local organization founded in 1882
Mission: To advance the interests of members
Affliation(s): Police Association of Ontario; Canadian Police Association
Chief Officer(s):
Mike Tarini, President
Ken Rice, 1st Vice-President
Denis Levasseur, 2nd Vice-President
Karen Pendergast, Secretary
Sally O'Halloran, Treasurer
Membership: 152; *Member Profile:* Sworn & civilian members of the North Bay Police
Activities: Sponsoring & supporting local organizations, such as One Kids Place

North Bay Real Estate Board

926 Cassells St., North Bay ON P1B 4A8
Tel: 705-472-6812; *Fax:* 705-472-0529
admin@nbreb.com
www.nbreb.com
Overview: A small local organization founded in 1957 overseen by Ontario Real Estate Association
Mission: To represent real estate agents and member offices in North Bay.
Member of: The Canadian Real Estate Association
Chief Officer(s):
Brad Minogue, President, 705-474-3500

Membership: 167 real estate agents and 17 member offices

North Central Labour Council of British Columbia
PO Box 1449, Prince George BC V2L 4V4
Tel: 604-430-6766
nclcboard@gmail.com
www.facebook.com/116669825022245
Overview: A small local organization founded in 1956 overseen by British Columbia Federation of Labour
Mission: To act as the voice of workers from the northern interior of British Columbia
Affliation(s): Canadian Labour Congress (CLC)
Chief Officer(s):
Troy Zohner, President
Don Iwaskow, Vice-President
Terry Archibald, Secretary-Treasurer
Membership: *Member Profile:* Unions from north central British Columbia, such as Prince George, Fort St. James, Vanderhoof, Valemount, & McBride
Activities: Liaising with locally elected officials; Advocating for political change to benefit workers; Providing local labour news; Participating in ceremonies to mark the annual Day of Mourning to remember workers injured or killed on the job

North Central Library Federation (NCLF)
PO Box 499, Burns Lake BC V0J 1E0
Tel: 250-692-3192
zope.bclibrary.ca/nclf
Overview: A small local organization
Member of: BC Libraries Cooperative
Chief Officer(s):
Bonny Remple, Coordinator
bremple@northcentral.bclibrary.ca
Membership: 10 member libraries

North Central Local Government Association (NCLGA)
c/o Maxine Koppe, #206, 155 George St., Prince George BC V2L 1P8
Tel: 250-564-6585; *Fax:* 250-564-6514
www.nclga.ca
twitter.com/NCLGA
Overview: A small local organization
Mission: To address the issues of local governments; To mobilize initiatives to benefit member governments
Chief Officer(s):
Mitch Campsall, President
president@nclga.ca
Bruce D. Christensen, First Vice-President
Brian Frenkel, Second Vice-President
Maxine Koppe, Executive Director
mkoppe@nclga.ca
Membership: 40 municipalities; *Member Profile:* Elected officials from member regional municipalities, districts, cities, towns, & villages in the north area of British Columbia
Meetings/Conferences: • North Central Local Government Association 2015 60th Annual General Meeting & Convention, May, 2015, Prince George Civic Centre, Prince George, BC
Scope: Local
Publications:
• Issues in Focus [a publication of the North Central Local Government Association]
Type: Newsletter; *Frequency:* 8 pa

North Coast Library Federation
c/o Katherine Anderson, 4153 Hawkes Ave., Victoria BC V8Z 3Y9
Fax: 866-901-8509
Toll-Free: 877-952-2112
www.nclf.ca
Overview: A small local charitable organization
Chief Officer(s):
Katherine Anderson, Manager
Finances: *Annual Operating Budget:* Less than $50,000

The North Cumberland Historical Society (NCHS)
PO Box 353, Pugwash NS B0K 1L0
Tel: 902-243-3348
nchs_2@yahoo.ca
nchsociety.wikifoundry.com
www.facebook.com/228243580590378
Overview: A small local charitable organization
Mission: To collect, preserve & make available historical data, including genealogy, pertaining to North Cumberland County
Member of: Council of Nova Scotia Archives
Chief Officer(s):
Betty Brown, Co-President, 902-243-2263
Carol Hyslop, Co-President, 902-548-2381
Activities: *Library:* Small Archives; Open to public

North Durham Social Development Council
#305, 2 Campbell Dr., Uxbridge ON L9P 1H6
Tel: 705-357-3811
info@northdurhamsdc.com
www.northdurhamsdc.com
Overview: A small local organization founded in 1991
Mission: To identify social needs in the townships of Brock, Scugog & Uxbridge; to initiate & encourage the provision of services to meet the needs identified
Chief Officer(s):
Danielle McIntyre, President
danielle.mcintyre@durhamcollege.ca
Nancy Parliament, Treasurer
nancy.parliament@region.durham.on.ca
Finances: *Annual Operating Budget:* Less than $50,000
12 volunteer(s)
Membership: 100; *Fees:* $10; *Committees:* Transportation; Interagency

North Eastern Ontario Family & Children's Services / Services à la famille et à l'enfance du Nord Est de l'Ontario
707 Ross Ave. East, Timmins ON P4N 8R1
Tel: 705-360-7100; *Fax:* 705-360-7200
www.neofacs.org
Previous Name: Child & Family Services of Timmins & District
Overview: A medium-sized local organization
Chief Officer(s):
Garry Dent, President
Staff Member(s): 160

North Grenville Chamber of Commerce
PO Box 1047, 5 Clothier St. East, Kemptville ON K0G 1J0
Tel: 613-258-4838; *Fax:* 613-258-3801
info@northgrenvillechamber.com
www.northgrenvillechamber.com
Previous Name: Kemptville & District Chamber of Commerce
Overview: A medium-sized local organization
Mission: To promote business community & quality of life
Member of: Ontario Chamber of Commerce
Chief Officer(s):
Pierre Blackburn, Chair
Finances: *Annual Operating Budget:* Less than $50,000; *Funding Sources:* Fundraising; membership dues
Staff Member(s): 1; 17 volunteer(s)
Membership: 160; *Fees:* $64.95-$405.96

North Grenville Historical Society (NGHS)
PO Box 48, Oxford Mills ON K0G 1S0
www.historynorthgrenville.ca
Overview: A small local organization founded in 2001
Chief Officer(s):
David Shanahan, President
david@historynorthgrenville.ca
Beth Nicol, Secretary
bethnicol@yahoo.com
Doug Hendry, Director, Archives
doug@mascol.ca
Finances: *Annual Operating Budget:* Less than $50,000
Membership: *Fees:* $15 household
Activities: Archives; publications; speakers
Publications:
• NGHS [North Grenville Historical Society] Quarterly
Type: Newsletter

North Hastings Community Integration Association (NHCIA)
PO Box 1508, 2 Alice St., Bancroft ON K0L 1C0
Tel: 613-332-2090; *Fax:* 613-332-4762
communityliving@nhcia.ca
www.nhcia.ca
Overview: A small local charitable organization founded in 1965
Mission: To support people with an intellectual disability & their families; To facilitate opportunities for all people to live, work & learn together
Member of: Community Living Ontario
Chief Officer(s):
Aaron Hill, Executive Director, 613-334-7929
Joanne Prentice, President
Finances: *Annual Operating Budget:* $500,000-$1.5 Million; *Funding Sources:* Ministry of Community & Social Services; fundraising; foundations; corporations; donations
Staff Member(s): 40; 30 volunteer(s)
Membership: 55; *Fees:* $5 self-advocate; $15 individual; $20 family; $25 business
Activities: *Library* Open to public
Awards:
• John & Evelyn Lock Bursary Award (Award)

North Island College Faculty Association (NICFA)
2300 Ryan Rd., Courtenay BC V9N 8N6
Tel: 250-949-2867
www.nicfa.ca
Overview: A small local organization
Member of: College Institute Educators Association of BC
Chief Officer(s):
Shirley Ackland, President
sackland@nic.bc.ca

North Island Laurentian Teachers' Union *See* Laurier Teachers Union

North Lanark Historical Society
647 River Rd., Mississippi Mills ON K0A 1A0
Tel: 613-256-2866
appletonmuseum@hotmail.com
www.northlanarkregionalmuseum.com
Also Known As: North Lanark Regional Museum
Overview: A small local charitable organization founded in 1965
Mission: To preserve & record area history
Member of: Ontario District Society
Affliation(s): Ontario Historical Society
Chief Officer(s):
Ed Wilson, President
Doreen Wilson, Manager, Museum
Finances: *Annual Operating Budget:* Less than $50,000
6 volunteer(s)
Membership: 45; *Fees:* $10
Activities: Operating the North Lanark Regional Museum; *Library:* Appletown Museum; Open to public

North of Superior Film Association (NOSFA)
#352, 1100 Memorial Ave., Thunder Bay ON P7B 4A3
Tel: 807-625-5450
info@nosfa.ca
www.nosfa.ca
Overview: A medium-sized provincial organization
Mission: To promote film and appreciation of film in the Thunder Bay area.
Chief Officer(s):
Marty Mascarin, President
Catherine Powell, Festival Coordinator
Membership: *Fees:* $10
Activities: Film screenings; *Awareness Events:* Film Festival

North of Superior Tourism Association (NOSTA)
#2, 605 Victoria Ave. East, Thunder Bay ON P7C 1B1
Tel: 807-346-1130; *Fax:* 807-346-1135
Toll-Free: 800-265-3951
info@northofsuperior.org
www.northofsuperior.org
www.facebook.com/northofsuperior
twitter.com/northosuperior
Also Known As: North of Superior Travel Association Inc.
Overview: A small local organization founded in 1974
Mission: To market the tourism opportunities for vacationing in Northwestern Ontario.
Member of: Ontario Tourism; Canadian Tourism Commission; Tourism Industry Association of Canada
Chief Officer(s):
Tim Lukinuk, President
tim@amethystmine.com
Finances: *Funding Sources:* Membership fees; government
Activities: *Speaker Service:* Yes; *Rents Mailing List:* Yes

North Okanagan Labour Council
1091 Gordon Dr., Kelowna BC V1Y 3E3
e-mail: nolc@shaw.ca
members.shaw.ca/nolc
Overview: A medium-sized local organization overseen by British Columbia federation of Labour
Mission: To represent labour unions in British Columbia's North & Central Okanagan
Affliation(s): Canadian Labour Congress (CLC)
Chief Officer(s):
Andrew Pritchard, President
Nikki Inouye, Vice-President
Ronn Dunn, Vice-President
Karen Abramsen, Vice-President

Cheryl Stone, Secretary
nolc.cstone@gmail.com
Ron Bobowski, Secretary-Treaser
Membership: 8,500; *Member Profile:* Union members in the North & Central Okanagan of British Columbia
Activities: Offering training courses, on topics such as health & safety; Marking the annual Day of Mourning, for workers injured or killed on the job; Providing labour news; Hosting monthly general meetings

North Okanagan Naturalists Club (NONC)

PO Box 473, Vernon BC V1T 6M4
Tel: 250-545-0490
www.nonc.ca
Overview: A small local charitable organization founded in 1951
Mission: To foster an interest in nature; to record data & sightings of flora & fauna; to educate young people; to hold land
Member of: The Federation of BC Naturalists; Canadian Nature Federation
Chief Officer(s):
Rod Drennan, President, 250-545-4999
Finances: *Annual Operating Budget:* Less than $50,000; *Funding Sources:* Dues; social activities; club sales
3 volunteer(s)
Membership: 180; *Fees:* $35 adults; $50 family; *Committees:* Conservation; Education; Land Stewardship; Socials; Trips; Ways & Means
Activities: *Awareness Events:* Annual Field & Dinner Day, May
Awards:
• James Grant Memorial Award (Award)

North Okanagan Neurological Association (NONA)

2802 - 34th St., Vernon BC V1T 5X1
Tel: 250-549-1281; *Fax:* 250-549-3771
administration@nona-cdc.com
www.nona-cdc.com
www.facebook.com/NONAChildDevelopmentCentre
Overview: A small local organization founded in 1975
Mission: To provide services for the treatment, education & support of special needs children & their families
Member of: B.C. Association of Child Development & Rehabilitation
Affliation(s): Cerebral Palsy Association of British Columbia
Chief Officer(s):
Helen Armstrong, Executive Director
Finances: *Annual Operating Budget:* $500,000-$1.5 Million; *Funding Sources:* Provincial Government
Staff Member(s): 42; 12 volunteer(s)
Membership: 100+ individual; *Fees:* $2

North Okanagan Organic Association (NOOA)

C76 Cedar Hill Rd., RR#1, Vernon BC V0E 1W0
Tel: 250-540-2557
northorganics@gmail.com
Overview: A small local licensing organization
Mission: To encourage the practice of soil regeneration & sustainable food production, through the use of organic methods as per the Canadian definition; To certify members' food products that are organically grown in accordance with the association's guidelines
Affliation(s): Certified Organic Associations of BC
Chief Officer(s):
Molly Thurston, President
Cara Nunn, Administrator
Finances: *Annual Operating Budget:* Less than $50,000
Membership: 101; *Fees:* $325; *Committees:* Certification; Standards
Activities: Certification of members' food products; monthly meeting for information on organic practices; *Library* by appointment

North Okanagan Social Planning Council *See* Social Planning Council for the North Okanagan

North Okanagan United Way *See* United Way of North Okanagan Columbia Shuswap

North Pacific Anadromous Fish Commission (NPAFC)

#502, 889 West Pender St., Vancouver BC V6C 3B2
Tel: 604-775-5550; *Fax:* 604-775-5577
secretariat@npafc.org
www.npafc.org
Overview: A medium-sized international organization
Mission: To promote the conservation of anadromous stocks in the North Pacific Ocean
Chief Officer(s):
Vladimir Fedorenko, Executive Director
vladf@npafc.org
Vladimir Belyaev, President
Staff Member(s): 5
Membership: *Committees:* Enforcement; Finance & Administration; Scientific Research & Statistics

North Pacific Cannery - National Historic Site

1889 Skeena Dr, Port Edward BC V0V 1G0
Tel: 250-628-3538; *Fax:* 250-628-3540
www.facebook.com/NorthPacificCannery?fref=ts
Overview: A small local organization
Chief Officer(s):
Andrew Hamilton, Chair
ahamilton@rupertport.com
Finances: *Annual Operating Budget:* $100,000-$250,000
Staff Member(s): 10

North Pacific Marine Science Organization (PICES)

c/o Institute of Ocean Sciences, PO Box 6000, Sidney BC V8L 4B2
Tel: 250-363-6366; *Fax:* 250-363-6827
secretariat@pices.int
www.pices.int
Overview: A medium-sized international organization
Mission: To promote & coordinate marine research in the northern North Pacific & adjacent seas especially northward of 30 degrees North; to advance scientific knowledge about the ocean environment, global weather & climate change, living resources & their ecosystems & the impacts of human activities; to promote the collection & rapid exchange of scientific information on these issues
Chief Officer(s):
Alexander Bychkov, Executive Secretary
bychkov@pices.int
Staff Member(s): 4
Membership: 334; *Member Profile:* Member scientists come from Canada, Japan, China, Korea, Russia & the U.S.; *Committees:* Biological Oceanography; Fishery Science; Marine Environmental Quality; Physical Oceanography & Climate; Data Exchange; Monitoring; Executive; Finance & Administration

North Peace Applied Research Association (NPARA)

PO Box 750, Manning AB T0H 2M0
Tel: 780-836-3354; *Fax:* 780-836-2670
npara1@telus.net
www.areca.ab.ca/nparahome.html
Overview: A small local organization founded in 1988 overseen by Agricultural Research & Extension Council of Alberta
Mission: To conduct agricultural research, trials, extension & research plots
Member of: Agricultural Research & Extension Council of Alberta
Chief Officer(s):
Nora Paulovich, Manager & Coordinator, Research
Tom Fromme, Specialist, Cereal & Oilseed
npara6@telus.net
Membership: *Fees:* $20
Publications:
• NPARA [North Peace Applied Research Association] Newsletter
Type: Newsletter

North Peace Cultural Society (NPCC)

10015 - 100 Ave., Fort St John BC V1J 1Y7
Tel: 250-785-1992; *Fax:* 250-785-1510
Toll-Free: 877-785-1992
reception@npcc.bc.ca
www.npcc.bc.ca
www.facebook.com/north.peace.cultural.centre
twitter.com/FSJNPCC
Also Known As: North Peace Cultural Centre
Overview: A small local charitable organization founded in 1976
Mission: To stimulate & develop cultural activities in the North Peace; to encourage individuals & groups to promote arts activities & support community events
Member of: BC Touring Council
Chief Officer(s):
Bettyanne Hampton, Executive Director
ed@npcc.bc.ca
Finances: *Annual Operating Budget:* $500,000-$1.5 Million
Staff Member(s): 14; 35 volunteer(s)
Membership: 100; *Fees:* $15

North Peace Historical Society

9323 - 100th St., Fort St John BC V1J 4N4
Tel: 250-787-0430; *Fax:* 250-787-0405
www.fsjmuseum.com
Overview: A small local charitable organization founded in 1965
Mission: To collect, preserve & house articles pertaining to the history of Fort St. John & the North Peace River area, for the education & enjoyment of local residents & tourists
Member of: BC Museum Association; Canadian Museums Association; Archives Association of BC; Northern BC Tourism Association; Fort St. John & District Chamber of Commerce
Chief Officer(s):
Evelyn Simm, President
Finances: *Annual Operating Budget:* $50,000-$100,000; *Funding Sources:* Provincial, local & regional government; fundraising
Staff Member(s): 1; 50 volunteer(s)
Membership: 150; *Fees:* $8 adult; $6 senior; $3 student
Activities: *Library:* Fort St. John North Peace Museum Archives; Open to public

North Perth Chamber of Commerce

580 Main St., Listowel ON N4W 1A8
Tel: 519-291-1551; *Fax:* 519-291-4151
npchamber.com
Previous Name: Listowel Chamber of Commerce
Overview: A small local organization
Chief Officer(s):
Dan Proctor, President
dan@keildadson.ca
Sharon DArcey, General Manager
Membership: 185; *Fees:* $125-$390

North Queens Board of Trade

PO Box 189, Caledonia NS B0T 1B0
Tel: 902-682-3116
discovercaledonia.com/board-of-trade.php
Overview: A small local organization
Mission: To support & promote commerce and trade in the North Queens area.
Member of: Nova Scotia Chamber of Commerce
Chief Officer(s):
Peter van Dyk, President
Mary Keirstead, Secretary

North Renfrew Family Services Inc. (NRFS)

PO Box 1334, 109 Banting Dr., Deep River ON K0J 1P0
Tel: 613-584-3358; *Fax:* 613-584-5520
nrfs@drdh.org
bright-ideas-software.com/NRFS
Overview: A small local charitable organization founded in 1968 overseen by Family Service Ontario
Member of: Renfrew County United Way
Affliation(s): Family Service Ontario
Chief Officer(s):
Kelly Hawley, Executive Director
Finances: *Funding Sources:* United Way; Ministry of Community & Social Services; Private donations; Town of Deep River; Town of Laurentian Hills
Staff Member(s): 3; 50 volunteer(s)

North Saskatchewan Watershed Alliance

9504 - 49 St., Edmonton AB T6B 2M9
Tel: 780-442-6363; *Fax:* 780-495-0610
water@nswa.ab.ca
www.nswa.ab.ca
www.facebook.com/NorthSaskRiver?fref=ts
twitter.com/NorthSaskRiver
www.youtube.com/user/NSaskRiverWatershed
Overview: A small local organization founded in 2000
Mission: To protect & improve water quality & ecosystem functioning in the North Saskatchewan Watershed within Alberta
Chief Officer(s):
David Trew, Executive Director, 780-496-3474
Tom Cottrell, IWMP Coordinator, 780-496-6962
tom.cottrell@edmonton.ca
Finances: *Annual Operating Budget:* $50,000-$100,000; *Funding Sources:* Industry; government; grants
Staff Member(s): 6
Membership: 140
Activities: State of watershed reporting; watershed planning; education & awareness; stewardship; *Library* by appointment

North Shore Archives Society

PO Box 402, Tatamagouche NS B0K 1V0
Tel: 902-657-3449; *Fax:* 902-657-0240
cs.archives@ns.aliantzinc.ca
Overview: A small local charitable organization founded in 1983
Member of: Federation of the Nova Scotian Heritage

Finances: *Annual Operating Budget:* Less than $50,000
6 volunteer(s)
Membership: 20; *Fees:* $5
Activities: *Library:* North Shore Archives; Open to public

North Shore Association for the Physically Handicapped
See North Shore Disability Resource Centre Association

North Shore ConneXions Society
1070 Roosevelt Cres., North Vancouver BC V7P 1M3
Tel: 604-984-9321; *Fax:* 604-984-9882
info@nsconnexions.org
nsconnexions.org
www.facebook.com/nsconnexions
twitter.com/NSConneXions
Also Known As: ConneXions
Overview: A small local organization founded in 1956
Mission: To advocate for better social & educational services for children with special needs
Chief Officer(s):
Linda Sellars, President
Finances: *Funding Sources:* Municipal, provincial & federal government; donations; membership fees
Membership: *Fees:* $2 self advocate; $10 associate; $12 individual; $15 family
Publications:
• Community ConneXions [a publication of the North Shore ConneXions Society]
Type: Newsletter; *Frequency:* 6 pa

North Shore Construction Inc. (Ind.) *Voir* Syndicat québécois de la construction

North Shore Disability Resource Centre Association (NSDRC)
3158 Mountain Hwy., North Vancouver BC V7K 2H5
Tel: 604-985-5371; *Fax:* 604-985-7594
nsdrc@nsdrc.org
www.nsdrc.org
Previous Name: North Shore Association for the Physically Handicapped
Overview: A medium-sized local charitable organization founded in 1976
Mission: To provide programs & services based on the belief that all people are important to their community; To work to ensure that people with disabilities can participate actively as members of the community; To work toward a community which is free from physical, financial, & attitudinal barriers
Member of: BC Association for Community Living; United Way of the Lower Mainland
Affliation(s): BC Federation of Private Child Care Agencies; United Way of the Lower Mainland; BC Coalition of People with Disabilities
Chief Officer(s):
Greg Travers, President
Finances: *Annual Operating Budget:* Greater than $5 Million; *Funding Sources:* Government; Fundraising; Membership fees
Staff Member(s): 330; 50 volunteer(s)
Membership: 70; *Fees:* $5
Activities: Information Services Program; Infant Development Program; Special Services to Children; Summer Program; Equipment Technicians; community-based day programs; individual life skills contracts; residential services; Pre-teen & Teen Program; Day Service Program; *Speaker Service:* Yes; *Rents Mailing List:* Yes; *Library* Open to public

North Shore Forest Products Marketing Board
PO Box 386, Bathurst NB E2A 3Z3
Tel: 506-548-8958
nsfpmb@nb.aibn.com
www.forestrysyndicate.com
Overview: A small local organization founded in 1973
Mission: To negotiate with industry & government on behalf of the private wood producers of the regulated area for fair prices for the products of the woodlots & to promote improved forest management
Affliation(s): NB Forest Products Commission
Chief Officer(s):
Alain Landry, General Manager
Patrick Doucet, Sylviculture Manager
patrick.doucet@forestrysyndicate.com
Finances: *Annual Operating Budget:* Greater than $5 Million; *Funding Sources:* Regional Government
Staff Member(s): 10; 10 volunteer(s)
Membership: 2,000 individual
Activities: *Rents Mailing List:* Yes

North Shore Hospice Society
PO Box 54019, 1562 Lonsdale Ave., North Vancouver BC V7M 3L5
Tel: 604-988-2312
www.northshorehospice.ca
Previous Name: Lions Gate Hospice Society
Overview: A small local charitable organization founded in 1982
Mission: To support hospice/palliative care for people at the end of their lives & to support their family and friends in the North Vancouver area
Chief Officer(s):
Ron Wood, President & Treasurer
Membership: *Fees:* $25; $15 seniors; $125 life

North Shore Multicultural Society (NSMS)
#207, 123 East 15th St., North Vancouver BC V7L 2P7
Tel: 604-988-2931; *Fax:* 604-988-2960
office@nsms.ca
www.nsms.ca
Overview: A small local organization founded in 1991
Mission: To assist immigrant families to settle & integrate into Canadian society; To work with community agencies & schools in making services more accessible to North Shore newcomers
Member of: Affiliation of Multicultural Societies & Service Agencies of BC
Chief Officer(s):
Mary MacDonald, President
Elizabeth Jones, Executive Director
elizabethj@nsms.ca
Finances: *Annual Operating Budget:* $500,000-$1.5 Million; *Funding Sources:* Federal & provincial governments; donations
Staff Member(s): 20; 125 volunteer(s)
Membership: 110; *Fees:* $15 individual; $25 family; $35 non-profit; $10 student/senior
Activities: Immigrant settlement orientation & orientation in formation; referral; lay counselling; workshops; short-term ESL classes; computer classes; support groups; employment programs for newcomers; youth programs; diversity & anti-racism; *Rents Mailing List:* Yes

North Shore Numismatic Society (NSNS)
3120 Fromme Rd., North Vancouver BC V7K 2C9
northshorenumismaticsociety.org
Overview: A small local organization founded in 1974 overseen by Canadian Numismatic Association
Mission: To advance numismatica
Chief Officer(s):
Lynne Balmer, President
Mike Souza, Membership Contact
Membership: *Fees:* $15 singles; $16 couples; $7.50 juniors
Activities: Conducting monthly meetings
Publications:
• The Shoreline [a publication of North Shore Numismatic Society]
Type: Newsletter; *Accepts Advertising; Editor:* Eugene Simms
ISSN: 0380-8866
Profile: Information about collecting & upcoming events

North Shore Stamp Club
135 West 15th St. North, North Vancouver BC
Tel: 604-984-3360
Overview: A small local organization
Member of: Royal Philatelic Society of Canada
Chief Officer(s):
John Thomson, Contact

North Shuswap Chamber of Commerce
3871 Squilax-Anglemont Rd., #B, Scotch Creek BC V0E 1M5
Tel: 250-955-2113
Toll-Free: 888-955-1488
requests@northshuswapbc.com
northshuswapbc.com
Overview: A small local organization
Membership: *Fees:* $100 primary; $50 secondary; $20 individual

North Shuswap Naturalists
c/o Rudy Vervoort, PO Box 24030, Scotch Creek BC V0E 3L0
Tel: 250-679-8763
Overview: A small local charitable organization overseen by Federation of BC Naturalists
Mission: To promote the enjoyment of nature through environmental appreciation & conservation; To encourage wise use & conservation of natural resources & environmental protection.
Chief Officer(s):
Rudy Vervoort, Contact
Claudette Carlsen, President
clodcarl@telus.net
Finances: *Funding Sources:* Membership fees
Membership: 21; *Fees:* $25; *Member Profile:* Mostly seniors
Activities: Monthly meetings (Sept.-June); summer field trips

North Sydney Historical Society
PO Box 163, North Sydney NS B2A 3M3
Tel: 902-794-2524
nsydmuseum@ns.sympatico.ca
northsydneymuseum.ca
Overview: A small local organization founded in 1980
Member of: Federation of the Nova Scotian Heritage
Finances: *Annual Operating Budget:* Less than $50,000; *Funding Sources:* Local & provincial government
20 volunteer(s)
Membership: 20; *Fees:* $10
Activities: Research, exhibit of artifacts reflecting past of area, histories of Western Union poiticians; *Library* Open to public

North Vancouver Chamber of Commerce (NVCC)
#102, 124 West First St., Vancouver BC V7M 3N3
Tel: 604-987-4488; *Fax:* 604-987-8272
Other Communication: events@nvchamber.ca
info@nvchamber.bc.ca
www.nvchamber.bc.ca
Overview: A medium-sized local organization founded in 1906
Mission: To ensure a healthy socio-economic base for the benefit of the North Shore region by supporting business prosperity, economic growth, & diversification
Chief Officer(s):
Anne McMullin, President & General Manager
anne@nvchamber.ca
Stephen Joyce, Chair
Misha Wilson, Manager, Visitor Centre
admin@nvchamber.ca
Membership: *Member Profile:* Businesses; Professionals; Residents; Community groups
Activities: Advocating on business issues; Providing networking opportunities; Encouraging partnerships; Liaising with municipal, provincial, & federal committees in order to encourage business; Promoting the North Vancouver city & district economy; Providing business information; Offering business seminars & expert speakers; Presenting business excellence awards; *Library:* Business Resource Centre;

North Vancouver Community Arts Council (NVCAC)
335 Lonsdale Ave., North Vancouver BC V7M 2G3
Tel: 604-988-6844; *Fax:* 604-988-2787
info@nvartscouncil.ca
www.nvartscouncil.ca
www.facebook.com/nvartscouncil
twitter.com/NVArtsCouncil
www.youtube.com/northvanartscouncil
Overview: A small local organization founded in 1969
Mission: To promote arts as a way to bridge cultures & build community
Member of: Assembly of BC Arts Councils; Vancouver Cultural Alliance; South West Regional Arts Council; Presentation House Cultural Society; Chamber of Commerce
Chief Officer(s):
Linda Feil, Executive Director
Finances: *Annual Operating Budget:* $250,000-$500,000; *Funding Sources:* Municipal & provincial government; membership dues; programmes; corporations
Staff Member(s): 5; 100 volunteer(s)
Membership: 400; *Fees:* $35 individual; $30 senior/student; $60 group; $40 family; *Committees:* Art in Public Places; Picture Rental; Newsletter; Adjudications; Craft Fair; After School Art; Art in Garden; CityScape Community Art Space; Wild Lights Festival; Mountain Mardi Gras

North West Commercial Travellers' Association (NWCTA)
39 River St., Toronto ON M5A 3P1
Fax: 877-284-8909
Toll-Free: 800-665-6928
nwcta@nwcta.com
www.nwcta.com
www.linkedin.com/NorthWestCommercialAssociation
twitter.com/NWCTAI
Also Known As: NWCTA, the Business & Travellers' Association
Overview: A medium-sized national organization founded in 1882
Mission: To protect & introduce benefits for individual business travellers

Chief Officer(s):
Peter McClure, President
pmcuct@nb.sympatico.ca
Wendy Sue Lyttle, Executive Director
wlyttle@nwcta.com
Charles Ng, Membership Coordinator
membership@nwcta.com
Finances: *Annual Operating Budget:* $250,000-$500,000
Staff Member(s): 3; 7 volunteer(s)
Membership: 900 senior/lifetime; *Fees:* $92; *Member Profile:* Business traveller representing an organization or company involved in marketing goods or providing services to business community
Activities: *Speaker Service:* Yes

North York Coin Club (NYCC)
5261 Naskapi Ct., Mississauga ON L5R 2P4
Tel: 416-897-6684
info@northyorkcoinclub.com
www.northyorkcoinclub.com
Overview: A small local organization founded in 1960
Member of: Canadian Numismatic Association; Ontario Numismatic Association
Chief Officer(s):
Bill O'Brien, President
Finances: *Annual Operating Budget:* Less than $50,000
10 volunteer(s)
Membership: 60; *Fees:* $10 individual; $15 family; $5 junior
Activities: Educational/collectible social exchange in all areas of numismatics; *Speaker Service:* Yes
Publications:
• NYCC [North York Coin Club] Bulletin
Type: Newsletter; *Frequency:* Monthly; *Editor:* Paul Petch

North York Community House
Lawrence Square Mall, #226, 700 Lawrence Ave., Toronto ON M6A 3B4
Tel: 416-784-0920
www.nych.ca
www.facebook.com/nychonline
twitter.com/nychonline
www.youtube.com/user/nychonline
Overview: A medium-sized local charitable organization founded in 1990
Mission: To assist newcomers settle, integrate and become vibrant members of our community; to help residents improve their economic conditions; and to help build strong neighbourhoods.
Chief Officer(s):
Shelley Zuckerman, Executive Director
Finances: *Annual Operating Budget:* Greater than $5 Million; *Funding Sources:* Government, United Way
Staff Member(s): 100; 347 volunteer(s)
Membership: *Fees:* $5

North York General Foundation
4001 Leslie St., Toronto ON M2K 1E1
Tel: 416-756-6944; *Fax:* 416-756-9047
foundation@nygh.on.ca
www.nyghfoundation.ca
www.linkedin.com/company/north-york-general-foundation
www.facebook.com/NYGHFoundation
twitter.com/NYGHFoundation
www.youtube.com/NYGHFoundation
Overview: A small local charitable organization
Mission: To raise money on behalf of North York General Hospital in order to fund research & improve patient care
Chief Officer(s):
Terry Pursell, President & CEO
Finances: *Annual Operating Budget:* Less than $50,000

North York Harvest Food Bank
640 Lawrence Ave. West, Toronto ON M6A 1B1
Tel: 416-635-7771; *Fax:* 416-635-5599
info@northyorkharvest.com
www.northyorkharvest.com
www.facebook.com/northyorkharvest
twitter.com/nyhfb
Overview: A small local charitable organization
Mission: To feed those in need & work to reduce hunger
Member of: Ontario Association of Food Banks
Chief Officer(s):
Anette Chawla, Executive Director
anette@northyorkharvest.com
Staff Member(s): 8; 20 volunteer(s)
Activities: Toronto second largest food bank; collects, sorts & distributes free of charge, approx. one million pounds of food per year, through more than 40 community agencies; provides direct emergency hamper service; also actively involved in anti-hunger & anti-poverty initiatives

North York Symphony Association *See* Toronto Philharmonia

North York Symphony Youth Orchestra *See* La Jeunesse Youth Orchestra

Northeast Avalon ACAP, Inc.
PO Box 8732, St. John's NL A1B 3T1
Tel: 709-726-9673; *Fax:* 709-726-2764
info@naacap.ca
www.naacap.ca
www.facebook.com/NAACAP.NL
twitter.com/naacap
Also Known As: Atlantic Coastal Action Program
Previous Name: St. John's Harbour ACAP
Overview: A small local organization
Member of: NL Environmental Industries Association; NL Environment Network
Chief Officer(s):
Myron King, Office and Outreach Coordinator
Finances: *Annual Operating Budget:* $100,000-$250,000
Staff Member(s): 2; 25 volunteer(s)
Membership: 1-99
Activities: *Library* Open to public by appointment

Northeast Highlands Chamber of Commerce
PO Box 125, Ingonish NS B0C 1L0
Tel: 902-285-2289; *Fax:* 902-285-2285
Overview: A small local organization founded in 1996
Chief Officer(s):
Walter Lauffer, President
Mary Sue Mackinnon, Staff
Ann Hussey, Secretary

Northeastern Alberta Aboriginal Business Association (NAABA)
PO Box 5993, Stn. Main, #100, 425 Gregoire Dr., Fort McMurray AB T9H 4V9
Tel: 780-791-0478; *Fax:* 780-714-6485
admin@naaba.ca
www.naaba.ca
www.facebook.com/203534376346311
twitter.com/NAABA_RMWB
Overview: A small provincial organization
Mission: To create partnerships between Aboriginal businesses & industry; to support economic development of Aboriginal people in the Wood Buffalo region
Chief Officer(s):
Boyd Madsen, President
Debbie Hahn, General Manager, 780-742-5451
debbie@naaba.ca
Membership: 236; *Fees:* Schedule available

Northeastern Ontario Building & Construction Trades Council
2413 Lasalle Blvd., Sudbury ON P3A 2A9
Tel: 705-560-0128; *Fax:* 705-560-4701
Overview: A small local organization
Mission: To act as a trade union in accordance with Ontario's Labour Relations Act

Northeastern Ontario Tourism
#401, 2009 Long Lake Rd., Sudbury ON P3E 6C3
Tel: 705-522-0104
Toll-Free: 800-465-6655
www.northeasternontario.com
www.facebook.com/northeasternontario
twitter.com/NeOntario
Overview: A small local organization founded in 1974
Member of: Tourism Federation of Ontario

The Northern AIDS Connection Society (NACS)
33 Pleasant St., Truro NS B2H 3R5
Tel: 902-895-0931; *Fax:* 902-895-3353
Toll-Free: 866-940-2437
nacsns@eastlink.ca
northernaidsconnectionsociety.ca
www.facebook.com/nacsns
Previous Name: Truro & Area Outreach Project; Pictou County AIDS Coalition
Overview: A small local organization founded in 1996 overseen by Canadian AIDS Society
Mission: Supports & promotes health, well-being of individuals living with HIV & those affected by HIV; strives to conduct prevention education within northern region of Nova Scotia
Affliation(s): Nova Scotia AIDS Coalition
Chief Officer(s):
Karen Kittilsen, Executive Director
25 volunteer(s)
Activities: Presentations in schools; support work for people living with HIV; displays; art auction; AIDS Walk; *Awareness Events:* International Day Against Homophobia, May; World Hep Day, July; World AIDS Day, Dec.
Publications:
• Extreme Reality [a publication of the Northern AIDS Connection Society]
Type: Newsletter; *Frequency:* Quarterly

Northern Air Transport Association (NATA)
PO Box 20102, Yellowknife NT X1A 3X8
Tel: 867-446-6282; *Fax:* 866-977-6282
admin@nata-yzf.ca
www.nata-yzf.ca
Overview: A small local organization founded in 1977
Mission: To promote safe & effective Northern air transportation
Chief Officer(s):
Stephen Nourse, Executive Director, 613-219-9305, Fax: 613-489-0143
exec@nata-yzf.ca
Stephen Nourse, President
snourse@firstair.ca
Teri Arychuk, Secretary-Treasurer
teri@airtindi.com
Membership: *Member Profile:* Northern air carriers
Activities: Advocating for Northern air transport; Establishing partnerships with governments & within the transportation industry; *Speaker Service:* Yes
Awards:
• Kenn Borek Memorial Scholarship (Scholarship)

Northern Alberta Brain Injury Society *See* Brain Care Centre

Northern Alberta Curling Association (NACA)
#110, 9440 - 49 St., Edmonton AB T6B 2M9
Tel: 780-440-4270; *Fax:* 780-463-4519
northernalbertacurling@shaw.ca
northernalbertacurling.com
www.facebook.com/108398119223374
Overview: A small local organization founded in 1918 overseen by Canadian Curling Association
Mission: To develop and promote the sport of curling.
Chief Officer(s):
Matt Yeo, President
Vicki Baird, Execurive Director
Staff Member(s): 2

Northern Alberta Health Libraries Association
c/o J.W. Scott Health Sciences Library, University of Alberta, 2K3.28 Walter MacKenzie Ctr., Edmonton AB T6G 2R7
e-mail: contact.nahla@gmail.com
chla-absc.ca/nahla
Overview: A small local organization founded in 1984 overseen by Canadian Health Libraries Association
Mission: This chapter of NAHLA exists to provide a forum for networking among libararians, library technicians and other interested in health libraries and health information.
Member of: Canadian Health Libraries Association
Chief Officer(s):
Linda Slater, President
linda.slater@ualberta.ca
Membership: *Fees:* $25 regular; $12 student; *Member Profile:* Librarians, library technicians and others interested in health libraries and health information.

Northern Alberta Institute of Technology Academic Staff Association (NASA)
#T110, 11762 - 106 St., Edmonton AB T5G 2R1
Tel: 780-471-8702; *Fax:* 780-474-6736
nasa@nait.ca
Also Known As: NAIT Academic Staff Association
Overview: A small local organization founded in 1982
Mission: To provide a positive work environment & to facilitate members in their delivery of high-quality instruction & their pursuit of personal & professional growth
Member of: Alberta Colleges-Institutes Faculties Association
Chief Officer(s):
Doug Short, President, 780-471-8916
dougs@nait.ca
Finances: *Annual Operating Budget:* $250,000-$500,000; *Funding Sources:* Membership dues
Staff Member(s): 3; 60 volunteer(s)

Membership: 1,000+; *Committees:* Membership Services; Bargaining; Finance

Northern British Columbia Construction Association *See* British Columbia Construction Association - North

Northern British Columbia Tourism Association (NBCTA)
1274 - 5th Ave., Prince George BC V2L 3L2
Tel: 250-561-0432
www.travelnbc.com
Overview: A small local organization founded in 1972 overseen by Council of Tourism Associations of British Columbia
Mission: To promote & develop the tourism industry of northern British Columbia
Member of: Tourism Industry Association of Canada
Chief Officer(s):
Anthony Everett, CEO
anthony@nbctourism.com
Finances: *Funding Sources:* Private tourism sector contracts; membership fees
Activities: Co-op marketing; *Library*

Northern Canada Study Group
#570, 188 Douglas St., Victoria BC V8V 2P1
Overview: A small local organization founded in 1994
Mission: To study the postal history of the northern regions of British Columbia, Ontario, & Quebec, early Manitoba, the provincial districts of Alberta, Assiniboia, Athabasca, Saskatchewan & Keewatin, plus Labrador, the Northwest Territories, & Yukon
Affiliation(s): Postal History Society of Canada
Chief Officer(s):
Gray Scrimgeour, Contact
gray@scrimgeour.ca
Publications:
• The Northerner: Newsletter of the Northern Canada Study Group
Type: Newsletter; *Frequency:* 5-6 pa; *Number of Pages:* 32; *Editor:* Gray Scrimgeour; *Price:* $15
Profile: Includes illustrations of covers or post cards, plus information about mail handling, postmarks, & life in northern Canada

Northern Film & Video Industry Association (NFVIA)
PO Box 31340, Whitehorse YT Y1A 5P7
Tel: 867-456-2978
info@nfvia.com
www.nfvia.com
Also Known As: Yukon Film Industry Association
Overview: A medium-sized provincial organization founded in 1999
Mission: To support the film & video sector in the Yukon by focussing on areas such as human resource development in the industry, development of infrastructure & production support, marketing, strategic alliances & partnerships, & membership services

Northern Finance Association (NFA)
c/o Rotman School of Management, 105 St. George St., Toronto ON M5S 3E6
www.northernfinance.org
Overview: A small local organization founded in 1989
Mission: To hear & present the latest research in all areas of finance, including asset pricing, arbitrage, behavioral finance, corporate finance, corporate governance, derivatives, emerging markets, financial development, financial institutions, finance theory, financial regulation, international finance, market efficiency, market microstructure, mathematical finance, real estate finance & others
Chief Officer(s):
Stéphane Chrétien, President
Membership: *Fees:* $50
Activities: Annual conference
Meetings/Conferences: • Northern Finance Association 2015 Conference, September, 2015, Chateau Lake Louise, Banff, AB
Scope: Local

Northern Frontier Visitors Association (NFVA)
#4, 4807 - 49 St., Yellowknife NT X1A 3T5
Tel: 867-873-4262; *Fax:* 867-873-3654
Toll-Free: 877-881-4262
info@northernfrontier.com
www.northernfrontier.com
www.facebook.com/163871037005160
Overview: A small local organization founded in 1983
Mission: To promote the Northern Frontier Region as an attractive area for tourism; to foster, encourage & assist in any way the growth of tourism into & within the Northern Frontier Region; to increase awareness within the Northern Frontier Region of the potential tourism holds as a viable, clean, labour intensive industry.
Member of: Northwest Territories Arctic Tourism; Yellowknife Chamber of Commerce
Finances: *Funding Sources:* Government of NWT; City of Yellowknife; membership fees; gift shop retail sales; rental of office
Membership: 180; *Fees:* $150 voting; $75 artist
Activities: Visitors Centre is open seven days per week, 360 days per year, to serve both residents & visitors; staff assist visitors in locating accommodation, booking tours & recommending other services provided by our members

Northern Independent Union *See* IAMAW District 78

Northern Interior Wood Workers Association *See* United Steelworkers Local 1-424

Northern Native Fishing Corporation (NNFC)
#160, 110 First Ave. West, Prince Rupert BC V8J 1A8
Tel: 250-627-8486; *Fax:* 250-624-6627
nnfc@citytel.net
nnfc.coppermoon.ca
Overview: A small local organization founded in 1982
Mission: To preserve & enhance for individual native fishermen the economic opportunity to harvest & market marine resources by creating & ensuring access to the resources
Chief Officer(s):
Corinne McKay, General Manager
Activities: Fishing licenses;

Northern Ontario Aquaculture Association
PO Box 124, 9050 Hwy. 6, #C, Little Current ON P0P 1K0
Tel: 705-368-1345; *Fax:* 705-368-0685
ontarioaquaculture@manitoulin.net
www.ontarioaquaculture.com
Overview: A small local organization
Mission: The voice of Ontario's sustainable fish farming industry
Chief Officer(s):
Mike Meeker, President
Karen Tracey, Executive Director
noaa@manitoulin.net
Membership: 30; *Fees:* Non-voting members: $100 associate. Voting members: $500 supporting; $1,000 corporate; $4,000 patron; $2,000 sustaining

Northern Ontario Curling Association
PO Box 940, #4, 214 Main St. West, Atikokan ON P0T 1C0
Tel: 807-597-8730; *Fax:* 888-622-8884
Toll-Free: 888-597-8730
info@curlnoca.ca
www.curlnoca.ca
www.facebook.com/curlnoca
twitter.com/curlnoca
Merged from: Temiskaming & Northern Ontario Curling Association; Northern Ontario Ladies Curling Association
Overview: A small local organization overseen by Canadian Curling Association
Mission: To promote curling throughout northern Ontario.
Chief Officer(s):
Leslie Kerr, Executive Director
lesliekerr@curlnoca.ca
Staff Member(s): 8
Membership: *Committees:* Executive; Finance; Communications; Development; Competitions; Sponsorship

Northern Ontario Darts Association (NODA)
#163, 159 Louis St., Sudbury ON P3B 2H4
Tel: 807-625-9373; *Fax:* 807-625-9391
nodarts.ca
www.facebook.com/groups/171446556243694
twitter.com/dartsno
Overview: A small provincial organization overseen by National Darts Federation of Canada
Mission: To promote the sport of darts on the provincial, national & world levels.
Member of: National Darts Federation of Canada
Chief Officer(s):
Christine Stark, President
czachary@tbaytel.net
Chris Arsenault, Secretary, 705-626-1030
180king@personainternet.com

Northern Ontario Hockey Association (NOHA)
110 Lakeshore Dr., North Bay ON P1A 2A8
Tel: 705-474-8851; *Fax:* 705-474-6019
noha@noha.on.ca
www.noha.on.ca
www.facebook.com/NorthernOntarioHockeyAssociation
twitter.com/nohahockey
Overview: A small local organization founded in 1919 overseen by Hockey Canada
Mission: To foster the sport of amateur hockey in northern Ontario
Member of: Hockey Canada
Affliation(s): Ontario Hockey Federation
Chief Officer(s):
Andrew Macdonald, President
amacdonald@personainternet.com
Jason Marchand, Executive Director
jmarchand@noha.on.ca
Finances: *Funding Sources:* Sponsorships; Membership fees
Staff Member(s): 6
Membership: *Member Profile:* Amateur hockey clubs in northern Ontario
Activities: Hosting tournaments; Presenting awards; Organizing specialty clinics
Publications:
• NOHA Bulletin
Type: Newsletter
Profile: Hockey Canada news, & NOHA activities, clinics, & policies
• NOHA Managers Manual
Type: Manual
Profile: A reference guide to NOHA bylaws, regulations, & policies
• Rink Report
Type: Newsletter; *Frequency:* Weekly
Profile: Information for NOHA members

Northern Ontario Native Tourism Association (NONTA)
#200, 710 Victoria Ave. East, Thunder Bay ON P7C 5P7
Tel: 807-623-0497
Overview: A small provincial organization founded in 1987
Chief Officer(s):
Tara Ingram, Contact
Finances: *Annual Operating Budget:* $500,000-$1.5 Million
Activities: *Internships:* Yes

Northern Prospectors Association (NPA)
PO Box 535, Kirkland Lake ON P2N 3J5
Tel: 705-642-1982; *Fax:* 705-567-4426
www.northernprospectors.com
Overview: A small local organization founded in 1971
Mission: To act as a strong voice for the prospecting & mining industry
Affliation(s): Ontario Prospectors Association
Chief Officer(s):
Dave Larocque, President
Membership: *Member Profile:* Members of the mining exploration community in the Kirkland Lake area, including prospectors & geologists
Activities: Offering courses on topics such as geology & geophysics; Hosting NPA gold panning events for tourists
Publications:
• The Explorationist [a publication of the Northern Prospectors Association & the Ontario Prospectors Association]
Type: Newsletter; *Frequency:* 10 pa; *Price:* Free with Northern Prospectors Association membership
Profile: Land use issues, the environment, & mining law, published in association with the Ontario Prospectors Association

Northern Quebec Inuit Association *See* Makivik Corporation

Northern Ramblers Car Club Inc. (NRCC)
C/O Tim Hendy, 85 Martin St., Bradford ON L3Z 1Z4
Tel: 905-775-2282
www.northernramblerscarclub.com
Overview: A small national organization founded in 1979
Mission: To honour the American Motors Corporation & its predecessor companies
Member of: Specialty Vehicle Association of Ontario
Chief Officer(s):
Ron Morrison, Coordinator, Membership
ronmorrison@rogers.com
Finances: *Annual Operating Budget:* Less than $50,000; *Funding Sources:* Membership fees; club events
Membership: 250 individual; *Fees:* $35-$100

Northern Rockies Alaska Highway Tourism Association (NRAHTA)
PO Box 6850, #300, 9523 - 100 St., Fort St. John BC V1J 4J3
Tel: 250-785-2544; *Fax:* 250-785-4424
Toll-Free: 888-785-2544
info@hellonorth.com
www.hellonorth.com
Also Known As: Hello North Ventures
Previous Name: Peace River Alaska Highway Tourism Association
Overview: A medium-sized provincial licensing organization founded in 1977 overseen by Council of Tourism Associations of British Columbia
Mission: To coordinate opportunites for sustainable tourism growth & development by fostering memorable year round visitor experiences; promoting social & economic benefits to members & wider community.
Member of: Tourism Industry Association of Canada
Affliation(s): Tourism BC
Finances: *Funding Sources:* Regional district
Membership: *Member Profile:* Tourism operators, accommodations, restaurants, stores, communities, chambers of commerce

Northern Territories Federation of Labour / Fédération du travail des Territoires du Nord
PO Box 2787, Yellowknife NT X1A 2R1
Tel: 867-873-3695; *Fax:* 867-873-6979
Toll-Free: 888-873-1956
ntfl@yk.com
www.ntfl.yk.com
www.facebook.com/NTFed
Previous Name: Northwest Territories Federation of Labour
Overview: A medium-sized local organization founded in 1980 overseen by Canadian Labour Congress
Mission: To promote the interests of its members
Membership: 9,000
Activities: *Library* by appointment

Northern Youth Abroad Program (NYAP)
#308, 311 Richmond Rd., Ottawa ON K1Z 6X3
Tel: 613-232-9989; *Fax:* 613-232-2121
Toll-Free: 866-212-2307
www.nya.ca
Also Known As: Nunavut Youth Abroad Program
Overview: A small provincial charitable organization founded in 1996
Mission: To send Nunavut youth to Southern Canada & Africa in a supported program where they live & volunteer in a new setting
Chief Officer(s):
Lois Philipp, Chair
Rebecca Bisson, Program Director
rebecca@nya.ca
Finances: *Annual Operating Budget:* $250,000-$500,000
Staff Member(s): 2; 100 volunteer(s)
Membership: 100-499

The North-South Institute (NSI) / L'Institut Nord-Sud
#500, 55 Murray St., Ottawa ON K1N 5M3
Tel: 613-241-3535; *Fax:* 613-241-7435
nsi@nsi-ins.ca
www.nsi-ins.ca
www.facebook.com/NSIINS
twitter.com/NSI_INS
Overview: A small international charitable organization founded in 1976
Mission: To analyze, for Canadians & others, the economic, social, & political implications of global change & to propose policy alternatives to promote global development & justice
Chief Officer(s):
Joseph K. Ingram, President & CEO
Rodney Schmidt, Vice-President & COO
Finances: *Annual Operating Budget:* $1.5 Million-$3 Million; *Funding Sources:* CIDA; research project income; donations; book sales
Staff Member(s): 20; 6 volunteer(s)
Activities: Areas of research include international finance, development cooperation, gender equality, civil society & good governance, corporate social responsibility & workers' rights, human security & conflict prevention, & international trade; *Speaker Service:* Yes; *Library* by appointment

Northumberland Central Chamber of Commerce
The Chamber Bldg., 278 George St., Cobourg NS K9A 3L8
Tel: 905-372-5831
nccofc.ca
www.facebook.com/160134906739
Previous Name: Cobourg & District Chamber of Commerce
Overview: A small local organization
Mission: To provide a voice for businesses in the Town of Cobourg, Hamilton Township, & Alnwick / Haldimand Township; to improve the commercial climate & economic growth of the area; to protect the interests of the business community
Chief Officer(s):
April Mayer-Murchison, Chair
Kevin Ward, President & CEO
Membership: 400+; *Member Profile:* Businesses in the Town of Cobourg, & the Townships of Hamilton & Alnwick/Haldimand; *Committees:* Marketing; Business Achievement Awards; Professional Development
Activities: Providing information about local products & services to consumers; Operating the Cobourg Driver & Vehicle Licensing Office; Offering networking opportunities; Providing professional development events; Presenting business awards
Publications:
- Business Directory
Type: Directory
Profile: Listings of chamber members
- Chamber Spotlight
Type: Newsletter; *Frequency:* 11 pa; *Accepts Advertising*
Profile: Business updates, events, & articles, circulated to more than 400 owners, managers, & professionals

Northumberland Hills Association of Realtors
#14, 975 Elgin St. West, Cobourg ON K9A 5J3
Tel: 905-372-8630; *Fax:* 905-372-1443
districtrealestate@bellnet.ca
boards.mls.ca/northumberland
Previous Name: Cobourg-Port Hope District Real Estate Board
Overview: A small local organization founded in 1968 overseen by Ontario Real Estate Association
Member of: The Canadian Real Estate Association

Northumberland Orchestra Society (NOC)
PO Box 1012, Cobourg ON K9A 4W4
Tel: 905-376-3021
noc@northumberlandmusic.ca
www.northumberlandmusic.ca
www.facebook.com/186929644677624
twitter.com/nocfriends
Also Known As: Northumberland Orchestra & Choir
Previous Name: Northumberland Philharmonic Choir
Overview: A small local charitable organization founded in 1978 overseen by Orchestras Canada
Member of: Orchestras Canada; Arts Council of Northumberland
Chief Officer(s):
John Kraus, Music Director & Conductor
Finances: *Funding Sources:* Fundraising; Donations; Sponsorships
Membership: *Member Profile:* Orchestra & choir members of all ages from the Northumberland County, Ontario; Orchestra members must have attained the equivalent of a grade 6 RCM music level; Choir members must have experience & the ability to read music
Activities: Hosting Northumberland orchestra & choir events; Offering professional training;
Awards:
- Foote Music Scholarship Award (Scholarship)
Presented to a promising young musician

Northumberland Philharmonic Choir *See* Northumberland Orchestra Society

Northumberland Salmon Protection Association (NSPA)
#11042, Rte 430, Trout Brook NB E9E 1R4
Tel: 506-622-8834; *Fax:* 506-622-7691
www.nbsalmoncouncil.com/northumberland.htm
Overview: A small local organization
Member of: Atlantic Salmon Federation
Affliation(s): New Brunswick Salmon Council
Chief Officer(s):
Debbie Norton, President, New Brunswick Salmon Council
adventures@upperoxbow.com
100 volunteer(s)
Membership: 200

Northumberland United Way
#700, 600 William St., Cobourg ON K9A 3A5
Tel: 905-372-6955; *Fax:* 905-372-4417
Toll-Free: 800-833-0002
office@nuw.unitedway.ca
www.northumberlandunitedway.ca
www.facebook.com/pages/Northumberland-United-Way/61851907835
www.twitter.com/nlanduw
www.youtube.com/user/NlandUnitedWay
Overview: A small local organization founded in 1969 overseen by United Way of Canada - Centraide Canada
Mission: To raise & allocate funds in an efficient manner & to promote the effective delivery of services in response to current & emerging social needs in Northumberland County.
Chief Officer(s):
Lynda Kay, CEO
lkay@nuw.unitedway.ca
Finances: *Annual Operating Budget:* $500,000-$1.5 Million; *Funding Sources:* Donations
Staff Member(s): 6; 100 volunteer(s)
Membership: 1-99
Activities: *Speaker Service:* Yes

Northwatch (NW)
PO Box 282, North Bay ON P1B 8H2
Tel: 705-497-0373; *Fax:* 705-476-7060
northwatch@northwatch.org
www.northwatch.org
www.facebook.com/pages/Northwatch/191694054468
Overview: A small local organization founded in 1988
Mission: To act as a representative body & to provide support to local citizens groups addressing environmental issues such as energy use, generation & conservation, forest conservation & wild areas protection, waste management & water quality issues, mining & militarization as well as other environmental concerns; to improve forest management, promote community involvement in mine monitoring & management & to prevent northeastern Ontario from becoming the receiving ground for foreign wastes, including Toronto's garbage, Ontario's biomedical waste, Canada's nuclear reactor fuel waste & PCBs from around the world
Member of: Great Lakes United; MiningWatch Canada; Nuclear Waste Watch; Ontario Environment Network
Chief Officer(s):
B. Lloyd, Coordinator
Finances: *Annual Operating Budget:* Less than $50,000
Staff Member(s): 2; 100 volunteer(s)
Membership: 20 organizations; *Fees:* $10 individual; $25 group/supporting; *Committees:* Forest; Mining; Energy; Waste; Water
Activities: Advocacy; public education; regional meetings; workshops; tours; *Internships:* Yes; *Speaker Service:* Yes; *Library* by appointment

Northwest Atlantic Fisheries Organization (NAFO)
PO Box 638, #100, 2 Morris Dr., Dartmouth NS B2Y 3Y9
Tel: 902-468-5590; *Fax:* 902-468-5538
info@nafo.int
www.nafo.int
Overview: A large international organization founded in 1979
Mission: To contribute through consultation & cooperation to the optimum utilization, rational management & conservation of the fishery resources of the Convention Area
Chief Officer(s):
Vladimir Shibanov, Executive Secretary
vshibanov@nafo.int
Lisa LeFort, Office Manager
Finances: *Annual Operating Budget:* $500,000-$1.5 Million; *Funding Sources:* Contracting parties
Staff Member(s): 11
Activities: Managing fisheries; *Internships:* Yes; *Library:* NAFO Library
Publications:
- Journal of Northwest Atlantic Fishery Science
Type: Journal; *Editor:* Dr. Neil Campbell
Profile: The journal features articles about ecosystems in the Atlantic Northwest, as well as articles that focus on living marine resources

Northwest Mennonite Conference
PO Box 1316, 2025 - 20 Ave., Didsbury AB T0M 0W0
Tel: 403-337-3283
www.nwmc.ca
Overview: A medium-sized local organization
Member of: Mennonite Church North America
Chief Officer(s):
Carol Gelleny, Contact

Membership: 14 congregations; *Committees:* Congregational Ministries; Congregational Leadership; Missions & Service; Stewardship

Northwest Ontario Sunset Country Travel Association
PO Box 647W, Kenora ON P9N 3X6
Tel: 807-468-5853
Toll-Free: 800-665-7567
info@ontariossunsetcountry.ca
www.ontariossunsetcountry.ca
www.facebook.com/SunsetCountry
twitter.com/Sunset_Country
sunsetcountry.tumblr.com
Overview: A medium-sized provincial organization founded in 1974
Mission: To develop, promote & advertise through cooperation, coordination & communication with clients & organizations for the betterment of tourism in Sunset Country & the province.
Member of: Tourism Industry Association of Canada
Chief Officer(s):
Gerry Cariou, Executive Director
gcariou@sunsetcountry.net
Finances: *Funding Sources:* Membership dues; provincial & federal government
Membership: *Member Profile:* Tourism-related businesses
Activities: *Rents Mailing List:* Yes

Northwest Peace Soccer Association (NWPSA)
11727 - 88A St., Grand Prairie AB T8X 1L8
Tel: 780-832-1627
www.northwestpeacesoccer.ca
Overview: A small local organization overseen by Alberta Soccer Association
Member of: Alberta Soccer Association

Northwest Territories & Nunavut Association of Professional Engineers & Geoscientists (NAPEG)
#201, 4817 - 49 St., Yellowknife NT X1A 3S7
Tel: 867-920-4055; *Fax:* 867-873-4058
www.napeg.nt.ca
Overview: A medium-sized provincial licensing organization founded in 1978 overseen by Engineers Canada
Mission: To license professional engineers & professional geoscientists in the Northwest Territories & Nunavut; To regulate the practices of professional engineering & professional geoscience; To establish & maintain standards of knowledge, skill, care, & professional ethics among registrants
Member of: Engineers Canada
Chief Officer(s):
Hendrik Falck, President
Linda Golding, Executive Director
Victoria James, Coordinator, Registration
Finances: *Funding Sources:* Membership fees; Dues
100 volunteer(s)
Membership: 397 + 781 Licensees; *Fees:* $300 registration; $220 annual dues; *Member Profile:* Accredited degree in engineering, geology or geophysics followed by 4 years of directly related experience in practice of engineering, geology & geophysics; Must pass Association's Professional Practice Examination; *Committees:* Council; Executive; Discipline; Membership/Enforcement; Professional Development; Public Relations; Newsletter; Professional Practice; Nominating; Planning; Environment; Finance
Activities: *Awareness Events:* National Engineering Week, March; National Science & Technology Week, October

Northwest Territories & Nunavut Chamber of Mines
PO Box 2818, #103, 5102-50 Ave., Yellowknife NT X1A 2R1
Tel: 867-873-5281; *Fax:* 867-920-2145
info@miningnorth.com
www.miningnorth.com
Previous Name: Northwest Territories Chamber of Mines
Overview: A medium-sized provincial organization founded in 1967
Mission: To promote & assist the development & growth of mining & mineral exploration in NWT & Nunavut
Affliation(s): Mining Association of Canada; Canadian Institute of Mining, Metallurgy & Petroleum
Chief Officer(s):
Tom Hoefer, Executive Director
executivedirector@miningnorth.com
Finances: *Annual Operating Budget:* $100,000-$250,000; *Funding Sources:* Membership fees
Staff Member(s): 2; 25 volunteer(s)
Membership: 200 corporate + 600 individual + 9 senior/lifetime; *Fees:* Schedule available; *Member Profile:* Persons & corporations interested in, or associated with, mining industry in NWT & Nunavut
Activities: *Awareness Events:* Mining Week, June; GeoScience Forum, Nov.; *Library* by appointment

Northwest Territories & Nunavut Council of the Canadian Physiotherapy Association (NWTNC)
c/o Atlantic Provinces Physiotherapy Associations, PO Box 28117, St. John's NL A1B 4J8
e-mail: lisapike02@bellaliant.net
atlanticphysiotherapyassociations.com/Northwest_Territories.html
Overview: A medium-sized provincial organization overseen by Canadian Physiotherapy Association
Member of: Canadian Physiotherapy Association
Chief Officer(s):
Sandra Mann, President
Angela Pace, President-Elect
Finances: *Funding Sources:* Membership dues; educational activities
Activities: *Awareness Events:* National Physiotherapy Month, April 20 - May 20

Northwest Territories & Nunavut Dental Association
PO Box 283, Yellowknife NT X1A 2N2
Tel: 867-873-6416; *Fax:* 877-389-6876
nwtnudentalassoc@theedge.ca
nwtnudentalassociation.ca
Overview: A small provincial organization overseen by Canadian Dental Association
Affliation(s): Canadian Dental Association
Chief Officer(s):
Roger Armstrong, President
Activities: Providing assistance in locating dentists in the Northwest Territories & Nunavut

Northwest Territories 5 Pin Bowlers' Association (NWT5PBA)
PO Box 2643, Yellowknife NT X1A 2P9
www.bowlnwt.ca
Overview: A small provincial organization
Mission: To promote 5 pin bowling in the Northwest Territories

Northwest Territories Archives Council (NWTAC)
c/o Northwest Territories Archives, Gov't of Northwest Territories, PO Box 1320, Yellowknife NT X1A 2L9
Tel: 867-873-7698; *Fax:* 867-873-0205
www.pwnhc.ca/nwtac
Overview: A small provincial organization founded in 1985 overseen by Canadian Council of Archives
Mission: To facilitate development of the archival system in the Northwest Territories; To make recommendations about the system's operation & financing; to develop & facilitate implementation & management of programs to assist the archival community; To communicate archival needs & concerns to decision-makers, researchers & the general public.
Chief Officer(s):
Erin Suliak, President
suliak.archivist@gmail.com
Membership: 7

Northwest Territories Arts Council / Conseil des arts des TNO
c/o GNWT Education, Culture & Employment, PO Box 1320, Yellowknife NT X1A 2L9
Tel: 867-920-6370; *Fax:* 867-873-0205
Toll-Free: 877-445-2787
www.nwtartscouncil.ca
Also Known As: NWT Arts Council
Overview: A small provincial organization founded in 1985
Mission: To promote and encourage the arts in the Northwest Territories.
Chief Officer(s):
Boris Atamanenko, Manager, Community Programs, 867-920-6370
boris_atamanenki@gov.nt.ca

The Northwest Territories Association for Children (& Adults) with Learning Disabilities *See* Learning Disabilities Association of The Northwest Territories

Northwest Territories Association of Architects (NWTAA)
Administrative Office, Northern Frontier Visitors Centre, PO Box 1394, Yellowknife NT X1A 2P1
Tel: 867-766-4216; *Fax:* 867-973-3654
nwtaa@yk.com
www.nwtaa.ca
Overview: A small provincial licensing organization founded in 2002
Mission: To maintain the Register of Architects, in accordance with the NWT Architects Act
Member of: Committee of Canadian Architectural Councils (CCAC)
Chief Officer(s):
Ben Russo, Executive Director
nwtaa@yk.com
Rod Kirkwood, President
Membership: *Fees:* $1000; *Member Profile:* Persons engaged in the practice of architecture in the Northwest Territories; *Committees:* Registration & Licence Review; Complaint Review; Practice Review; Continuing Education
Activities: Offering continuing education

Northwest Territories Association of Communities (NWTAC)
Finn Hansen Bldg., #200, 5105 - 50th St., Yellowknife NT X1A 1S1
Tel: 867-873-8359; *Fax:* 867-873-3042
Toll-Free: 866-973-8359
communications@nwtac.com
www.nwtac.com
twitter.com/nwtac
www.flickr.com/photos/nwtac
Overview: A medium-sized provincial organization founded in 1967
Mission: To promote the exchange of information amongst the community governments of the Northwest Territories and to provide a united front for the realization of goals.
Member of: Federation of Canadian Municipalities
Chief Officer(s):
Sara Brown, CEO
sara@nwtac.com
Staff Member(s): 6
Membership: 32 incorporated communities; *Member Profile:* Municipal corporations & community governments

Northwest Territories Association of Landscape Architects (NWTALA)
PO Box 1394, Yellowknife NT X1A 2P1
Tel: 867-920-2986; *Fax:* 867-920-2986
atborow@internorth.com
Overview: A medium-sized provincial organization founded in 1991
Mission: To represent landscape architects in the Northwest Territories
Affliation(s): Canadian Society of Landscape Architects (CSLA)
Membership: *Member Profile:* Landscape architects in the Northwest Territories

Northwest Territories Association of Provincial Court Judges
c/o Judge Garth Malakoe, Territorial Court of Northwest Territories, PO Box 550, 4093 - 49th St., Yellowknife NT X1A 2N4
Tel: 867-873-7604; *Fax:* 867-873-0203
Overview: A small provincial organization
Affliation(s): Canadian Association of Provincial Court Judges
Chief Officer(s):
Garth Malakoe, Northwest Territories Director, Canadian Association of Provincial Court Judges
Membership: *Member Profile:* Court judges in the Northwest Territories

Northwest Territories Badminton Association
PO Box 11089, Yellowknife NT X1A 3X7
Tel: 867-669-8326; *Fax:* 867-669-8327
Toll-Free: 800-661-0797
www.nwtbadminton.ca
Overview: A small provincial organization overseen by Badminton Canada
Mission: To promote badminton throughout the Northwest Territories.
Chief Officer(s):
Julie Jeffery, President, 867-446-7063
juliejeffery@me.com
Membership: *Member Profile:* Membership shall be open to any organized club in the NWT or, in the absence of an organized club, to any individual in that community, upon payment of an annual membership fee.

Northwest Territories Biathlon Association
NT

Tel: 867-874-2681
www.nwtbiathlon.com
www.facebook.com/172304639531053
Also Known As: NWT Biathlon Association
Overview: A small provincial organization overseen by Biathlon Canada
Mission: To govern the sport of biathlon in the Northwest Territories; to encourage physical activity & community through sport
Member of: Biathlon Canada
Chief Officer(s):
Pat Bobinski, President
pat@nwtbiathlon.com
Ted Kimmins, Vice-President
ted@nwtbiathlon.com
Belinda Whitford, Secretary-Treasurer
belinda@nwtbiathlon.com

Northwest Territories Broomball Association

529 Range Lake Rd., Yellowknife NT X1A 3Y1
www.nwtbroomball.com
Overview: A small provincial organization overseen by Ballon sur glace Broomball Canada
Member of: Ballon sur glace Broomball Canada
Chief Officer(s):
Jan Vallillee, President
justjan529@theedge.ca
Membership: 250; *Fees:* $20

Northwest Territories Chamber of Commerce

NWT Commerce Place, #13, 4802 - 50th Ave., Yellowknife NT X1A 1C4
Tel: 867-920-9505; *Fax:* 867-873-4174
admin@nwtchamber.com
www.nwtchamber.com
Overview: A medium-sized provincial charitable organization founded in 1973
Mission: To act as the voice for northern business; To create a business climate of profitability & competitiveness in the Northwest Territories; To foster business development; To promote business in the Northwest Territories; To involve & assist First Nations organizations; To conduct operations in an environmentally responsible manner
Chief Officer(s):
Chuck Parker, President
chuckp@discoveryair.com
Kathy Gray, First Vice-President
kathy@luluz.ca
Hughie Graham, Second Vice-President
hgraham@npreit.com
John-Eric Petersson, Secretary-Treasurer
jpetersson@nwtel.ca
Membership: 865
Activities: Liaising with territorial, national & international governments; Providing input in the development of legislation & policy

Northwest Territories Chamber of Mines ***See*** Northwest Territories & Nunavut Chamber of Mines

Northwest Territories Community Futures Association (NWTCFA)

NT
www.nwtcfa.ca
Overview: A small provincial organization founded in 1999
Mission: To improve communication between community futures organizations in the Northwest Territories; to advocate for members; to establish partnerships on behalf of members
Membership: 7 regional organizations

Northwest Territories Construction Association (NWTCA)

PO Box 2277, 4921 - 49th St., 3rd Fl., Yellowknife NT X1A 2P7
Tel: 867-873-3949; *Fax:* 867-873-8366
director@nwtca.ca
www.nwtca.ca
Overview: A medium-sized provincial organization founded in 1976 overseen by Canadian Construction Association
Mission: To act as a voice for construction-related business in the Northwest Territories & Nunavut
Chief Officer(s):
Bob Doherty, President
bdoherty@ykfireprevention.ca
Dave Brothers, Vice-President, Northwest Territories
Gary Collins, Vice-President, Nunavut
Trina Rentmeister, Secretary-Treasurer
Membership: 150+; *Fees:* Schedule available; *Member Profile:* Construction-related businesses in the Northwest Territories & Nunavut
Activities: Lobbying governments on behalf of the construction industry

Northwest Territories Council for the Disabled; NWT Council for Disabled Persons ***See*** NWT Disabilities Council

Northwest Territories Curling Association

PO Box 11089, Yellowknife NT X1A 3X7
Tel: 867-669-8339; *Fax:* 867-669-8327
Toll-Free: 800-661-0797
www.nwtcurling.com
www.facebook.com/pages/NWT-Curling/316251248400802
twitter.com/nwt_curling
Overview: A small provincial organization founded in 1990 overseen by Canadian Curling Association
Mission: To promote curling in the Northwest Territories.

Northwest Territories Federation of Labour ***See*** Northern Territories Federation of Labour

Northwest Territories Institute of the Purchasing Management Association of Canada ***See*** Supply Chain Management Association - Northwest Territories

Northwest Territories Law Foundation

PO Box 2594, 5212 - 55th St., Yellowknife NT X1A 2P9
Tel: 867-873-8275; *Fax:* 867-873-6383
www.lawsociety.nt.ca/LawFoundation
Overview: A medium-sized provincial organization
Mission: To provide funding in the Northwest Territories in the following areas: the establishment & operation of law libraries; the provision of legal education; research in law & the administration of justice; recommendations for law reform; legal aid programs & similar programs; & the Assurance Fund
Chief Officer(s):
Wendy Carter, Executive Manager
action@theedge.ca
Emerald Murphy, Chair
Finances: *Funding Sources:* Funds result from the interest which banks must pay on clients' funds held by lawyers in mixed trust accounts, according to the Legal Profession Act
Activities: Reviewing grant applications; Funding groups with projects which meet the Foundation's objectives

Northwest Territories Library Association (NWTLA)

PO Box 2276, Yellowknife NT XIA 2P7
e-mail: NWTLibraryAssociation@gmail.com
Overview: A medium-sized provincial organization
Mission: To facilitate the exchange of ideas among persons involved inlibrary services in the Northwest Territories; To recommend policies for the provision of library services; To promote intellectual freedom.
Chief Officer(s):
Eric Palmer, President

Northwest Territories Medical Association (NWTMA)

PO Box 1732, Yellowknife NT X1A 2P3
Tel: 867-920-4575; *Fax:* 867-920-4575
nwtmedassoc@ssimicro.com
www.nwtma.ca
Overview: A medium-sized provincial organization overseen by Canadian Medical Association
Mission: To advocate on behalf of its members and the citizens of the North for access to high quality health care, and provides leadership and guidance to its members.
Member of: Canadian Medical Association
Chief Officer(s):
David Pontin, President
Membership: *Fees:* Schedule available

Northwest Territories Public Service Association ***See*** Union of Northern Workers

Northwest Territories Recreation & Parks Association (NWTRPA)

PO Box 841, Yellowknife NT X1A 2N6
Tel: 867-873-5340; *Fax:* 867-669-6791
admin@nwtrpa.org
www.nwtrpa.org
www.facebook.com/260257614047483
Overview: A small provincial organization founded in 1989 overseen by Canadian Parks & Recreation Association
Mission: To increase public awareness of recreation & parks; to enhance the quality of life of residents of the NWT through fostering the development of recreation & parks services
Affliation(s): Sport North
Chief Officer(s):
Geoff Ray, Executive Director, 867-669-8380
gray@nwtrpa.org
Finances: *Annual Operating Budget:* $50,000-$100,000; *Funding Sources:* Federal, territorial government
Staff Member(s): 6
Membership: 100; *Fees:* $35 individual; $75 municipal or recreation committee; *Committees:* Executive; Corporate; Sponsorship
Activities: Recreation Code of Ethics; Recreation & Parks Resource Binder; Awards Program; Corporate Sponsorship; Active Living

Northwest Territories Registered Nurses Association ***See*** The Registered Nurses Association of the Northwest Territories & Nunavut

Northwest Territories Ski Division

PO Box 682, Yellowknife NT X1A 2N5
Tel: 867-669-8379
nwtski@gmail.com
www.nwtski.com
Previous Name: Cross Country Northwest Territories
Overview: A small provincial organization overseen by Cross Country Canada
Member of: Cross Country Canada
Chief Officer(s):
Dot Van Vliet, President

Northwest Territories Soccer Association (NWTSA)

PO Box 11089, Yellowknife NT X1A 3X7
Tel: 867-669-8396; *Fax:* 867-669-8327
Toll-Free: 800-661-0797
www.nwtkicks.ca
www.facebook.com/NWTSoccerAssociation
twitter.com/NwtSoccer
Overview: A medium-sized provincial organization overseen by Canadian Soccer Association
Mission: The NWT Soccer Association is a volunteer-run organization & the governing body for all soccer activities in the NWT; focus is on the grassroots development of the game, as well as the promotion of high performance
Member of: Canadian Soccer Association
Affliation(s): Sport North Federation
Chief Officer(s):
Ryan Fequet, President
Lyric Sandhals, Executive Director
Finances: *Funding Sources:* Operates on Sport Lottery funding
Activities: Summer camps; leagues & tournaments; developmental clinics

Northwest Territories Society for the Prevention of Cruelty to Animals (NWTSPCA)

PO Box 2278, Yellowknife NT X1A 2P7
Tel: 867-920-7722; *Fax:* 867-920-7723
nwtspcayk@gmail.com
www.nwtspca.com
www.facebook.com/nwtspca
Overview: A medium-sized provincial charitable organization
Mission: To provide animal rescue services in the north; to educate the public about the proper ways to protect & take care of animals
Chief Officer(s):
Nicole Spencer, President
Finances: *Annual Operating Budget:* $250,000-$500,000
Membership: *Fees:* $20 individual; $40 family

Northwest Territories Special Olympics ***See*** Special Olympics Northwest Territories

Northwest Territories Sport Federation ***See*** Sport North Federation

Northwest Territories Teachers' Association (NWTTA)

PO Box 2340, 5018 - 48 St., Yellowknife NT X1A 2P7
Tel: 867-873-8501; *Fax:* 867-873-2366
nwtta@nwtta.nt.ca
www.nwtta.nt.ca
Overview: A medium-sized provincial organization overseen by Canadian Teachers' Federation
Mission: The Northwest Territories Teachers' Association is the professional voice of educators as they provide quality education to Northwest Territories students. With commitment to growth, respect & security for its membership, the Association

represents all regions equally, advocates for public education & promotes the teaching profession
Chief Officer(s):
Gayla Meredith, President, 867-873-8501
president@nwtta.nt.ca
David Roebuck, Executive Director, 867-873-8501
ed@nwtta.nt.ca
Finances: *Annual Operating Budget:* $500,000-$1.5 Million
Staff Member(s): 3
Membership: 800; *Fees:* 1.4% of basic salary; *Member Profile:* Teachers; consultants; administrators; *Committees:* Aboriginal Educators & Leadership Council; Professional Relations; School Administrators; Small Communities; Teacher Welfare; Public Relations; Curriculum; Discipline; Finance; Legislation; Status of Women; other special & ad hoc committees
Activities: Awards & bursaries

Northwest Territories Tennis Association
PO Box 671, Yelloknife NT X1A 2N5
Tel: 867-444-8330
www.tennisnwt.com
Also Known As: Tennis NWT
Previous Name: Tennis Northwest Territories
Overview: A small provincial organization overseen by Tennis Canada
Member of: Tennis Canada
Chief Officer(s):
Pawan Chugh, President
Julie Coad, General Manager

Northwest Territories Tourism (NWTT)
PO Box 610, Yellowknife NT X1A 2N5
Tel: 1-867-873-7200
Toll-Free: 800-661-0788
info@spectacularnwt.com
www.spectacularnwt.com
twitter.com/spectacularnwt
Previous Name: Tourism Industry Association of the NWT
Overview: A medium-sized local organization founded in 1996
Mission: To support the development of a strong tourism sector in the Northwest Territories for the benefit of tourists, residents, & communities; To promote pan-territorial tourism; To act as a voice for the tourism industry; To preserve the integrity of the cultural & natural heritage of the Northwest Territories
Affliation(s): Canadian Tourism Commission (CTC); Yukon Travel; Nunavut Tourism; Travel Alberta; Tourism BC
Chief Officer(s):
Brian Desjardins, Executive Director
Ron Ostrom, Director, Marketing
Julie Warnock, Coordinator, Communications
Margo Thorne, Officer, Finance
Membership: 200+; *Fees:* $150; *Member Profile:* Tourism industry participants in the Northwest Territories; Aboriginal Land Claims Groups
Activities: Working with NWTT members, Aboriginal organizations, tourism associations, development corporations, communities, & territorial & federal government departments; Providing industry education; Marketing all sectors of tourism in the Northwest Territories; *Library:* NWTT Visual Library

Northwest Territories Volleyball Association (NWTVA)
4909 - 49 St., 3rd Fl., Yellowknife NT X1A 3X7
Tel: 867-669-8396
www.nwtvolleyball.ca
www.facebook.com/NWTVolleyballAssociation
twitter.com/NWTVA
Overview: A medium-sized provincial organization overseen by Volleyball Canada
Mission: To develop athletes & coaches to compete as Team NWT in the Arctic Winter Games & the Canada Games
Chief Officer(s):
Doug Rentmeister, Executive Director, Sport North

Northwest Territories/Nunavut Council of Friendship Centres
#209, 4817 - 49th St., Yellowknife NT X1A 3S7
Tel: 867-669-7064; *Fax:* 867-874-2894
Overview: A small provincial organization overseen by National Association of Friendship Centres
Mission: To assist friendship centres in the Northwest Territories

Northwest Wildlife Preservation Society (NWPS)
#720, 1190 Melville St., vancouver BC V6E 3W1
Tel: 604-568-9160; *Fax:* 604-568-6152
info@northwestwildlife.com
www.northwestwildlife.com
www.facebook.com/NorthwestWildlifePreservationSociety
twitter.com/nwpsHQ
www.facebook.com/mwpsVancouverIsland
Overview: A small local organization founded in 1987
Mission: To ensure that healthy wildlife populations are preserved for their own intrinsic value & for the appreciation of all; To develop & provide educational, research & advisory services which can advance the public's awareness & knowledge about wildlife & wildlife systems in northwest North America
Member of: BC Endangered Species Coalition; Vancouver Urban Wildlife Committee; BC Environmental Network
Chief Officer(s):
Ann Peters, Executive Director, 604-568-9160, Fax: 604-568-6152
execdirector@northwestwildlife.com
Jim Pigott, President
Michele Kvarnstrom, Vice-President
James McBeath, Sec.-Treas.
Darren Colello, Education Coordinator
edcomm@northwestwildlife.com
Finances: *Annual Operating Budget:* $100,000-$250,000; *Funding Sources:* Donations; grants; honoria
Staff Member(s): 3; 180 volunteer(s)
Membership: 100+; *Fees:* $35 family/NGO/Classroom; $25 individual; $15 senior/student; $100 corporate
Activities: *Awareness Events:* Green Ribbon Campaign, April; *Speaker Service:* Yes; *Library:* Species Reports; Open to public

Northwestern Ontario Air Search & Rescue Association (NOASARA)
411 John Paterson Dr., Thunder Bay ON P7E 6M8
Tel: 807-577-4329
Other Communication: Cell Phone: 807-627-4433
noasara@tbaytel.net
my.tbaytel.net/noasara
www.facebook.com/groups/6291689182
Overview: A small local charitable organization founded in 1986

Northwestern Ontario Associated Chambers of Commerce (NOACC)
#102, 200 Syndicate Ave. South, Thunder Bay ON P7E 1C9
Tel: 807-624-2626; *Fax:* 807-622-7752
www.noacc.ca
Overview: A medium-sized local licensing organization founded in 1931
Mission: To provide leadership to ensure quality of life & a healthy economy for member chambers, the regional business community & the citizens of Northwestern Ontario; to make representations to government; to provide a network for interaction between local chambers
Affliation(s): Ontario Chamber of Commerce
Chief Officer(s):
Lisa Sticca, Chair
Barry Streib, President
Finances: *Annual Operating Budget:* Less than $50,000; *Funding Sources:* Membership dues
Staff Member(s): 1; 60 volunteer(s)
Membership: 2,000; *Fees:* $240.62-$2,838,68, based on business size; *Committees:* Policy Development; Advocacy

Northwestern Ontario Building & Construction Trades Council
180 Clark St., Thunder Bay ON P7A 2L9
Tel: 807-344-4441; *Fax:* 807-344-4545
Overview: A small local organization
Mission: To respresent the following unions in northwestern Ontario: Construction & Allied Workers, Local 607; Greater Ontario Regional Council of Carpenters, Drywall & Allied Workers, Local 1669; International Union of Painters & Allied Trades, Local 1671; International Association of Heat & Frost Insulators & Asbestos Workers, Local 95; International Association of Bridge, Structural, Ornamental, & Reinforcing Ironworkers, Local 759; International Union of Bricklayers & Allied Craftworkers, Local 25; International Union of Operating Engineers, Local 793; International Brotherhood of Boilermakers, Iron Ship Builders, Blacksmiths, Forgers & Helpers, Local 555 & 128; International Brotherhood of Electrical Workers, Local 402; Millwrights & Machine Erectors, Local 1151; Sheetmetal Workers International Association, Local 397; Teamsters International Union, Local 938; & United Association of Plumbers & Pipefitters, Local 628
Chief Officer(s):
Terry Webb, President

Northwestern Ontario Insurance Professionals
c/o Linda Lacroix, The Standard Insurance Brokers Ltd., PO Box 2890, 319 - 2nd St. South, Kenora ON P9N 3X8
Tel: 807-468-3333; *Fax:* 807-468-4289
Overview: A small local organization
Mission: To be responsive to the requirements of the Canadian insurance industry
Member of: Canadian Association of Insurance Women
Chief Officer(s):
Linda Lacroix, President, 807-468-6678 Ext. 7006
lindal@kmts.ca
Activities: Engaging in educational programs; Providing networking opportunities;

Northwestern Ontario Municipal Association (NOMA)
PO Box 10308, Thunder Bay ON P7B 6T8
Tel: 807-683-6662
admin@noma.on.ca
www.noma.on.ca
Overview: A medium-sized local organization founded in 1946
Mission: To consider matters of interest to municipalities in northwestern Ontario; To procure enactment of legislation which may be advantageous to northwestern Ontario's municipalities
Member of: Association of Municipalities of Ontario
Chief Officer(s):
Charla Robinson, Executive Director
Dennis Brown, President
Iain Angus, Vice-President
Finances: *Funding Sources:* Operating subsidy from the Ministry of Northern Development & Mines; Membership fees
Membership: 100-499; *Fees:* $250 not-for-profit organizations; $500 businesses; *Member Profile:* Membership is attained from the Corporation of the City of Thunder Bay, the Kenora District Municipal Association, the Rainy River District Municipal Association, & the Thunder Bay District Municipal League; Associate membership is comprised of not-for-profit organizations & businesses
Activities: Advocating for northwestern Ontario's regional interests; Acting on matters where municipal rights may be affected; Promoting municipal interests; Offering opportunities for education & discussion to advance the standards of municipal government
Meetings/Conferences: • Northwestern Ontario Municipal Association 2015 Annual General Meeting & Conference, April, 2015, Victoria Inn & Conference Centre, Thunder Bay, ON
Scope: Local
Description: A meeting which is held alternatively in the association's three districts (Kenora, Rain River, or Thunder Bay), featuring informative presentations & networking opportunities
Contact Information: NOMA Executive Director, Phone: 807-683-6662, E-mail: admin@noma.on.ca
• Northwestern Ontario Municipal Association 2016 Annual Regional Conference, 2016, ON
Scope: Local
Description: A meeting, held each September or October, for both full & associate members of the Northwestern Ontario Municipal Association
Contact Information: NOMA Executive Director, Phone: 807-683-6662, E-mail: admin@noma.on.ca

Northwestern Ontario Prospectors Association (NWOPA)
PO Box 10124, Thunder Bay ON P7B 6T6
e-mail: nwopa@tbaytel.net
www.nwopa.net
Overview: A small local organization
Mission: To represent & advance the interests of northwestern Ontario's prospectors
Member of: Ontario Prospectors Association
Chief Officer(s):
Dave Hunt, President, 807-345-6258, Fax: 807-345-9546
d21hunt@shaw.ca
Ryan Weston, Vice-President, 807-631-8593
weston.rj@gmail.com
Cyndee Komar, Secretary
cyndee.komar@ontario.ca
Paul Nielsen, Treasurer
treasurer@nwopa.net
Finances: *Funding Sources:* Sponsorships; Membership fees
Membership: *Fees:* $60 individuals; $200 corporations; *Member Profile:* Prospectors in northwestern Ontario; *Committees:* Communications; Elections; Education & Events; First Nations Issues; General Meetings; Land Use; Minister Mining Act

Advisory; MNR N.W. Reg. Advisory; Ontario Prospectors Association; Policies & Procedures; Website
Activities: Engaging in lobbying activities; Planning displays about the mining industry at local events, such as the Children's Festival in Thunder Bay
Awards:
• The Lifetime Achievement Award (Award)
• The Bernie Schnieders Discovery of the Year Award (Award)
• The Developer of the Year Award (Award)
Publications:
• The Claim Post
Type: Newsletter; *Frequency:* Semiannually; *Editor:* John Halet
Profile: Current events in the mining industry

Northwestern Ontario Sports Hall of Fame & Museum
219 May St. South, Thunder Bay ON P7E 1B5
Tel: 807-622-2852; *Fax:* 807-622-2736
nwosport@tbaytel.net
www.nwosportshalloffame.com
www.facebook.com/259816551287?v=wall&ref=nf
www.youtube.com/user/nwosport
Also Known As: NWO Sports Hall of Fame
Overview: A small local charitable organization founded in 1978
Mission: To preserve & honour the sports heritage of northwestern Ontario
Member of: Canadian Association for Sport Heritage; International Association of Sports Museums & Halls of Fame; Ontario Museum Association; Archives Association of Ontario; Canadian Museums Association; Thunder Bay Chamber of Commerce
Chief Officer(s):
Kathryn Dwyer, Curator
Diane Imrie, Executive Director
Finances: *Annual Operating Budget:* $100,000-$250,000
Staff Member(s): 3; 25 volunteer(s)
Membership: 400; *Fees:* $25 individual; $40 family; $60 business/organization
Activities: A variety of structured programs are available for different grade levels; Annual Induction Dinner & Ceremony, last Sat. in Sept.; *Library*

Northwestern Ontario Technology Association (NOTA)
#213, 1294 Balmoral St., Thunder Bay ON P7B 5Z5
Tel: 807-768-6687; *Fax:* 807-768-6683
www.linkedin.com/groups/Northwestern-Ontario-Technology-Association-12
Overview: A small local organization founded in 2001
Finances: *Annual Operating Budget:* Less than $50,000
5 volunteer(s)
Membership: 40; *Fees:* $100, depends on the size of the firm; *Member Profile:* Technology industry professional, company or stakeholder in N.W.C.
Activities: Networking; marketing; seminars; training

Northwood Neighbourhood Services
Building D, #27, 2625 Weston Rd., 2nd Fl., Toronto ON M9N 3V8
Tel: 416-748-0788; *Fax:* 416-748-0525
info@northw.ca
www.northw.ca
Overview: A small local charitable organization overseen by Ontario Council of Agencies Serving Immigrants
Mission: To provide programs & services within the community that will empower individuals, families & groups to achieve, maintain & enhance a state of physical, mental & social well being
Chief Officer(s):
Jamila M. Aman, Executive Director
jaman@northw.ca
Finances: *Annual Operating Budget:* $250,000-$500,000; *Funding Sources:* Federal, provincial & municipal governments; United Way member & charitable donations
Staff Member(s): 23; 280 volunteer(s)
Membership: 365; *Fees:* Schedule available
Activities: Settlement Services; Child/Parent Programs; Language Training; *Awareness Events:* Volunteer Recognition

Norwegian Trade Council *See* Innovation Norway

Nose Creek Valley Museum Society
1701 Main St. SW, Airdrie AB T4B 1C5
Tel: 403-948-6685
ncvm@telus.net
www.nosecreekvalleymuseum.com
Overview: A small local organization founded in 1985
Mission: To operate the Nose Creek Valley Museum & Tourist Information Centre
Chief Officer(s):
Laurie Harvey, Curator
Finances: *Funding Sources:* Donations; Museum admission fees; Fundraising; Sponsorships
Activities: Providing geological, natural history, topographical, farm machinery, military, & First Nation's displays; Maintaining a settler's cabin, a blacksmith shop, & a historicl general store & barbershop

Not Far From The Tree
#365, 401 Richmond St. West, Toronto ON M5V 3A8
Tel: 647-774-7425
info@notfarfromthetree.org
www.notfarfromthetree.org
Overview: A small local organization
Mission: To harvest fruit from trees that the owners would otherwise let go to waste
Chief Officer(s):
Danielle Goldfiner, Interim Project Director
Membership: *Committees:* Steering

Notre-Dame-de-Grâce Community Council *Voir* Conseil communautaire Notre-Dame-de-Grâce

Nouveau Parti Démocratique *See* New Democratic Party

Nouveau Parti Démocratique du Canada - Section Québécoise *See* New Democratic Party

Nova Central Ringette Association
NS
e-mail: novacentralringette@live.ca
novacentralringette.ca
www.facebook.com/NovaCentralRingetteAssociation
Overview: A small local organization overseen by Ringette Nova Scotia
Member of: Ringette Nova Scotia
Affliation(s): Bedord Ringette Association; Berwick Ringette Association; Sackville Ringette Association
Chief Officer(s):
Mary Perry, President
Membership: 15 teams

Nova Forest Alliance
PO Box 208, 285 George St., Stewiacke NS B0N 2J0
Tel: 902-639-2921; *Fax:* 902-639-2981
info@novaforestalliance.com
www.novaforestalliance.com
Overview: A small provincial organization

Nova Scotia Advisory Council on the Status of Women / Conseil consultatif sur la condition féminine de la Nouvelle-Écosse
PO Box 745, Halifax NS B3J 2T3
Tel: 902-424-8662; *Fax:* 902-424-0573
Toll-Free: 800-565-8662
women@gov.ns.ca
www.women.gov.ns.ca
www.facebook.com/112218661874
Overview: A medium-sized provincial organization founded in 1977
Mission: To advise the government on matters relating to the status of women; To propose legislation & policies to promote equality of opportunity & status; To publish reports, studies & recommendations
Chief Officer(s):
Stephanie MacInnis-Langley, Executive Director
Finances: *Annual Operating Budget:* $500,000-$1.5 Million; *Funding Sources:* Provincial government
Staff Member(s): 11
Activities: *Library:* NSACSW Resource Centre; Open to public

Nova Scotia Allergy & Environmental Health Association *See* Environmental Health Association of Nova Scotia

Nova Scotia Amateur Bodybuilding Association (NSABBA)
14 White Sands Ct., Hubley NS B3Z 1A5
e-mail: nsabba@nsabba.com
www.nsabba.com
Overview: A small provincial organization founded in 1980 overseen by Canadian Bodybuilding Federation
Mission: To govern the sport of amateur bodybuilding, fitness & figure in Nova Scotia.
Member of: Canadian Bodybuilding Federation; International Federation of Bodybuilding
Chief Officer(s):
Georgina Dunnington, President
Christina Belding, Vice-President
Steve Belding, Treasurer-Secretary

Nova Scotia Archaeology Society (NSAS)
PO Box 36090, Halifax NS B3J 3S9
Tel: 902-880-3021
www.novascotiaarchaeologysociety.com
www.facebook.com/pages/Nova-Scotia-Archaeology-Society/126145457490785
twitter.com/NSArchSociety
Overview: A small provincial charitable organization founded in 1987 overseen by Canadian Archaeological Association
Mission: To promote the preservation of Nova Scotia's archaeological sites & resources
Chief Officer(s):
Brittany Houghton, President
brittany-houghton@hotmail.com
Natalie Lavoie, Vice-President
lavoien2006@gmail.com
Terry Deveau, Secretary
deveau@chebucto.ns.ca
Rob Ferguson, Treasurer
robertferguson@eastlink.ca
Membership: *Fees:* $15 students/seniors; $20 individuals; $25 families; $45 classes & institutions; *Member Profile:* Individuals interested in the study of archaeology & Nova Scotia's heritage resources
Activities: Increasing awareness of archaeology in Nova Scotia; Disseminating knowledge; Facilitating the exchange of information among both professionals & amateurs; Conducting workshops; Organizing field trips to archaeological sites;
Publications:
• Nova Scotia Archaeology Society Newsletter
Type: Newsletter
Profile: Current information for society members

Nova Scotia Arm Wrestling Association (NSAWA)
c/o Rick Pinkney, President, 192 Beaver Bank Rd., Lower Sackville NS B4E 1J7
Tel: 902-489-9008
info@novascotiaarmwrestling.com
novascotiaarmwrestling.com
www.facebook.com/groups/375248869203923
Overview: A small provincial organization overseen by Canadian Arm Wrestling Federation
Mission: To oversee & promote the sport of arm wrestling in Nova Scotia.
Member of: Canadian Arm Wrestling Federation
Chief Officer(s):
Rick Pinkney, President
Shawn Ross, Vice-President, 902-765-4656
shawnross1111@gmail.com
Chris Scott, Treasurer, 902-865-6525
chrisscottauto@hotmail.com
Mark MacPhail, Director, 902-822-1180
markmacphail3@hotmail.com

Nova Scotia Association for Community Living (NSACL)
#100, 22-24 Dundas St., Dartmouth NS B2Y 4L2
Tel: 902-469-1174; *Fax:* 902-461-0196
nsacl@accesswave.ca
nsacl.wordpress.com
facebook.com/nsacl
twitter.com/NSACL
Overview: A medium-sized provincial organization overseen by Canadian Association for Community Living
Mission: To work for the benefit of persons of all ages who have an intellectual disability in Nova Scotia; To ensure those with an intellectual disability have the same rights & access as all other persons
Member of: Canadian Association for Community Living
Chief Officer(s):
Jean Coleman, Executive Director
nsacl@eastlink.ca
Activities: Advocating for the interests of individuals with intellectual disabilities; Promoting research

Nova Scotia Association of Architects (NSAA)
1359 Barrington St., Halifax NS B3J 1Y9
Tel: 902-423-7607; *Fax:* 902-425-7024
info@nsaa.ns.ca
www.nsaa.ns.ca
Overview: A medium-sized provincial organization founded in 1932

Mission: To administer the practice of architecture in Nova Scotia
Chief Officer(s):
Mark Atwood, Registrar
mark@lydonlynch.ca
Therese LeBlanc, President
tleblanc@nycum.com
Membership: *Member Profile:* Individuals practising as architects in Nova Scotia; Associate members; Students; Architecture firms
Activities: Maintaining a register of architects licensed to practice; Administering NCARB examinations; Hosting technical meetings; Disciplining members; Liaising with governments
Publications:
• Nova Scotia Association of Architects Code of Ethics & Professional Conduct

Nova Scotia Association of Health Organizations *See* Health Association Nova Scotia

Nova Scotia Association of Insolvency & Restructuring Professionals (NSAIRP)

c/o Grant Thornton / CapServeco, Halifax Shopping Centre, Tower 1, #315, 7001 Mumford Rd., Halifax NS B3L 4N9
Tel: 902-453-6600; *Fax:* 902-453-9257
Previous Name: Nova Scotia Insolvency Association
Overview: A small provincial organization overseen by Canadian Association of Insolvency & Restructuring Professionals
Mission: To foster the provision of objective & competent insolvency & restructuring services in Nova Scotia, in order to instill public trust
Affiliation(s): Canadian Association of Insolvency & Restructuring Professionals
Chief Officer(s):
Robert Charles Hunt, President
robert.hunt@ca.gt.com
Activities: Facilitating communication among members; Providing workshops for association members

Nova Scotia Association of Medical Radiation Technologists (NSAMRT)

PO Box 9410, Stn. A, Halifax NS B3k 5S3
Tel: 902-434-6525; *Fax:* 902-425-2441
Toll-Free: 866-788-6525
info@nsamrt.ca
www.nsamrt.ca
Overview: A small provincial organization overseen by Canadian Association of Medical Radiation Technologists
Mission: To uphold standards of practice in the field of medical radiation technology in Nova Scotia, in order to ensure the public is given optimal care
Chief Officer(s):
Karren Fader, President
Vicki Sorhaindo, Vice-President
Melissa Morash, Secretary
Kelly Maloney, Treasurer
Paula Hodson, Registrar
Membership: 500+; *Member Profile:* Nova Scotia medical radiation technologists from the disciplines of nuclear medicine technology, radiological technology, magnetic resonance imaging technology, & radiation therapy; *Committees:* Continuing Education; Refresher; Historian; Public Relations; Publications; Awards; Conference
Activities: Engaging in advocacy activities; Providing professional development opportunities; Increasing public awareness of the profession of medical radiation technologists (MRTs) in Nova Scotia
Meetings/Conferences: • Nova Scotia Association of Medical Radiation Technologists 2015 75th Annual General Conference & Annual General Meeting, 2015, NS
Scope: Provincial
Description: A gathering of association members held each spring, consisting of educational presentations, exhibitor booth viewing, a business meeting, & networking events
Contact Information: E-mail: info@nsamrt.ca
• Nova Scotia Association of Medical Radiation Technologists 2015 Annual Fall Education Seminar, 2015, NS
Scope: Provincial
Description: Held the weekend before Medical Radiation Technologists Week, the annual continuing education meeting consists of talks related to the disciplines of radiation therapy, nuclear medicine, & radiological technology, as well as a keynote address related to all medical radiation technology disciplines
Contact Information: Education Committee Chair: Ryan Duggan
Publications:
• Nova Scotia Association of Medical Radiation Technologists Annual Report
Type: Yearbook; *Frequency:* Annually

Nova Scotia Association of Naturopathic Doctors (NSAND)

PO Box 245, Lower Sackville NS B4C 2S9
Tel: 902-431-8001
info@nsand.ca
www.nsand.ca
www.facebook.com/44570499509
twitter.com/NSAND_
Overview: A small provincial organization founded in 1995 overseen by The Canadian Association of Naturopathic Doctors
Mission: To be a resource for its members & to inform the public about naturopathic medicine.
Chief Officer(s):
Colin Huska, President
Membership: *Fees:* $400 full member; $50 associate; $25 student

Nova Scotia Association of Optometrists (NSAO)

PO Box 9410, Stn. A, #700, 6009 Quinpool Rd., Halifax NS B3K 5S3
Tel: 902-435-2845; *Fax:* 902-425-2441
nsao@accesswave.ca
www.nsoptometrists.ca
Previous Name: Nova Scotia Optometrical Society
Overview: A medium-sized provincial licensing organization founded in 1905 overseen by Canadian Association of Optometrists
Mission: To foster excellence in the delivery of vision & eye health services in Nova Scotia; To act as the voice of optometry in Nova Scotia
Chief Officer(s):
Sheldon Pothier, O.D., Registrar
Membership: 80+; *Member Profile:* Doctors of optometry in Nova Scotia
Activities: Promoting preventative eye health care; Providing educational resources; *Library:* Patient Education Library

Nova Scotia Association of Provincial Court Judges

c/o Judge James H. Burrill, Provincial Court of Nova Scotia, 141 High St., Bridgewater NS B4V 1W2
Tel: 902-541-5690; *Fax:* 902-543-0829
Overview: A small provincial organization
Member of: Canadian Association of Provincial Court Judges
Chief Officer(s):
James H. Burrill, Nova Scotia Director, Canadian Association of Provincial Court Judge
Activities: Providing educational opportunities; Conducting meetings

Nova Scotia Association of Quantity Surveyors (NSAQS)

PO Box 8774, Stn. A, Halifax NS B3K 5M4
e-mail: nsaqs@ciqs.org
www.nsaqs.org
Overview: A small local organization founded in 1979
Mission: To promote & advance professional status of quantity surveyors; To collaborate with other professions & organizations in the construction industry
Member of: Canadian Institute of Quantity Surveyors
Chief Officer(s):
Wanda D. Smith, President
wdvalleysmith@gmail.com
Merrill Varner, Secretary
mvarner@pcl.com
Finances: *Annual Operating Budget:* Less than $50,000; *Funding Sources:* Membership dues
10 volunteer(s)
Membership: 100+; *Fees:* $50; *Member Profile:* Examination of technical subject & work experience; *Committees:* Education; Special Events; Special Projects

Nova Scotia Association of REALTORS (NSAR)

#100, 7 Scarfe Ct., Dartmouth NS B3B 1W4
Tel: 902-468-2515; *Fax:* 902-468-2533
Toll-Free: 800-344-2001
nshomeguide.ca
www.linkedin.com/company/2406082
www.facebook.com/nsarcommunications
twitter.com/NSAR_RealEstate
Previous Name: Nova Scotia Real Estate Association
Overview: A medium-sized provincial organization founded in 2000
Mission: Provides Realtors with services & representation to enable them to best serve the public in real estate transactions
Member of: The Canadian Real Estate Association
Chief Officer(s):
Roger Boutilier, Executive Officer
rboutilier@nsar.ns.ca
Bonnie Wigg, Director, MLSr & Member Services, 902-468-5870
bwigg@nsar.ns.ca
Monica MacLean, Acting Director, Communications, 902-468-8495
mmaclean@nsar.ns.ca
Finances: *Annual Operating Budget:* $1.5 Million-$3 Million; *Funding Sources:* Membership dues
Staff Member(s): 13
Membership: 1,300; *Fees:* $168; *Member Profile:* Brokers & sales people; *Committees:* Arbitration; By-law; Professional Standards & Conduct Review; Education; Executive; Finance; MLS; Government Relations; Public Relations; Standard Forms & Practices

Nova Scotia Association of Social Workers (NSASW) / Association des travailleurs sociaux de la Nouvelle-Écosse

#700, 1888 Brunswick St., Halifax NS B3J 3J8
Tel: 902-429-7799; *Fax:* 902-429-7650
nsasw@nsasw.org
www.nsasw.org
www.facebook.com/NSASW
twitter.com/NSASWNEWS
Overview: A medium-sized provincial licensing organization founded in 1963
Mission: To promote & regulate the practice of social work so the members can provide a high standard of service that respects diversity, promotes social justice & enhances the worth, self-determination & potential of individuals, families & communities
Member of: Canadian Association of Social Workers
Chief Officer(s):
Robert R. Shepherd, Executive Director
robert.shepherd@nsasw.org
Finances: *Funding Sources:* Membership fees
Staff Member(s): 6
Membership: 1,600; *Committees:* Social Action/Social Justice; Program; Professional Development; Public Relations; Membership; Standards & Ethics; Nominating; Private Practice
Activities: Social Work Register; publishing; *Internships:* Yes; *Library* by appointment

Nova Scotia Association of the Appraisal Institute of Canada *See* Nova Scotia Real Estate Appraisers Association

Nova Scotia Automobile Dealers' Association (NSADA)

#700, 6009 Quinpool Rd., Halifax NS B3K 5S3
Tel: 902-425-2445; *Fax:* 902-425-2441
info@nsada.ca
www.nsada.ca
Overview: A medium-sized provincial organization founded in 1966
Mission: To assist & protect association members; To act as the voice of new vehicle franchised dealers in Nova Scotia
Member of: Canadian Automobile Dealer's Association (CADA)
Chief Officer(s):
John K. Sutherland, Executive Vice-President
Membership: 100+; *Member Profile:* New vehicle franchised dealers in Nova Scotia
Activities: Liaising with government, automotive manufacturers, & related industries
Meetings/Conferences: • Nova Scotia Automobile Dealers' Association 2015 Annual General Meeting, Automotive Conference, & President's Dinner, 2015, NS
Scope: National
Description: An event for association members from across Nova Scotia
Contact Information: E-mail: info@nsada.ca

Nova Scotia Badminton Association

5516 Spring Garden Rd., Halifax NS B3J 1G6
Tel: 902-425-5450; *Fax:* 902-425-5606
badmintonns@sportnovascotia.ca
www.nsba.ca
www.facebook.com/BadmintonNovaScotia
twitter.com/bdmintonNS
Overview: A small provincial organization overseen by Badminton Canada
Chief Officer(s):
Jennifer Petrie, Executive Director

Kerry Lynch, President
Membership: *Fees:* $15 individual; $75 club

Nova Scotia Ball Hockey Association (NSBHA)

Tel: 902-463-7659
nsbha@hotmail.com
nsbha.weebly.com
Overview: A small provincial organization
Mission: To promote ball hockey in Nova Scotia & to host provincial tournaments
Affliation(s): Canadian Ball Hockey Association; Sport Nova Scotia
Chief Officer(s):
Gian Scalet, Contact
Finances: *Annual Operating Budget:* Less than $50,000
20 volunteer(s)
Membership: 650 individual; *Fees:* $8 individual

Nova Scotia Band Association

884 Charles St., Kentville NS B4N 2Y7
www.novascotiabandassociation.com
Overview: A small provincial organization overseen by Canadian Band Association
Mission: To support and promote the development of bands throughout the province of Nova Scotia through communication, coordination, program development, advocacy and lobbying at the provincial level.
Chief Officer(s):
Mark Hopkins, President
presidentnsba@gmail.com
Membership: *Fees:* $30 student/retired; $50 teacher; $100 institution

Nova Scotia Barristers' Society (NSBS)

#1101, 1645 Granville St., Halifax NS B3J 1X3
Tel: 902-422-1491; *Fax:* 902-429-4869
www.nsbs.org
Overview: A medium-sized provincial licensing organization founded in 1825
Mission: To set & enforce standards of professional responsibility & ethics for lawyers; To license & discipline members of the profession, in accordance with the Legal Profession Act
Affliation(s): Canadian Lawyers' Insurance Association; Federation of Law Societies; Law Foundation of Nova Scotia; Law Reform Commission of Nova Scotia; Lawyers' Insurance Association of Nova Scotia; Nova Scotia Legal Aid Commission; Canadian Bar Association
Chief Officer(s):
Darrel I. Pink, Executive Director
dpink@nsbs.org
Jacqueline L. Mullenger, Director, Admissions & Professional Development
jmullenger@nsbs.org
Victoria Rees, Director, Professional Responsibility
vrees@nsbs.org
Membership: 2,500; *Member Profile:* Practising & non-practising lawyers in Nova Scotia; *Committees:* Administration of Justice; Complaints Investigation; Credentials; Distinguished Service Award; Ethics & Professional Responsibility; Executive; Finance; Gender Equity; Hearing; Lawyers Fund for Client Compensation; Nominating; Professional Responsibility Policies & Procedures; Professional Standards; Race Relations; Trust Accounts; Department of Justice Liaison; Service Nova Scotia & Municipal Relations Liaison; Land Registration Act Management
Activities: Providing education & guidance to members; *Library:* Nova Scotia Barristers' Society Library & Information Services

Nova Scotia Beekeepers' Association (NSBA)

c/o Barb McLaughlin, 283 McKay Siding Rd., McKay Siding NS B0N 2J0
Tel: 902-639-3064
nsbeekeepers@gmail.com
www.nsbeekeepers.ca
Overview: A small provincial organization
Mission: To help beekeepers in Nova Scotia maintain their bee farms & supply them with educational services
Chief Officer(s):
Joe Goetz, President, 902-292-8708
michelleandjoe1@me.com
Perry Brandt, Vice-President, 902-300-4171
brandt@bellaliant.net
Barb McLaughlin, Treasurer, 902-639-2064
bauld.mclau@ns.sympatico.ca
Membership: *Fees:* $46 0-10 hives; $115 11-99 hives; $230 100-500 hives; $402.50 500-1499 hives; $1150 1500+ hives; *Member Profile:* Beekeepers from Nova Scotia
Activities: Informing members about regulations regarding beekeeping; Providing updates on honey bee research; Sharing information on the code of practice for beekeepers in Nova Scotia

Nova Scotia Block Parent Advisory Board

Tel: 902-849-3525
byrnemg@hotmail.com
www.novascotiablockparent.com
Overview: A small provincial organization overseen by Block Parent Program of Canada Inc.
Member of: Block Parent Program of Canada Inc.

Nova Scotia Boxing Authority (NSBA)

c/o Amanda Noonan, PO Box 864, 5516 Spring Garden Rd., 2nd Fl., Halifax NS B3J 2V2
Tel: 902-457-0413; *Fax:* 902-484-6937
anoonan@micco.ca
Overview: A small provincial organization founded in 1975
Mission: The Nova Scotia Boxing Authority regulates professional boxing & other combat sports in the province, as well as establishes & enforces rules for the conduct of boxing, & the training of officials in accordance with national standards. The NSBA answers to the minister of health promotion & protection.
Member of: Canadian Boxing Federation
Chief Officer(s):
Michael MacDonald, Chair
mmacdonald@micco.ca
Hubert Earle, Director, Combat Sports

Nova Scotia Cattle Producers (NSCP)

60 Research Dr., Bible Hill NS B6L 2R2
Tel: 902-893-7455; *Fax:* 902-893-7063
office@nscattle.ca
www.nscattle.ca
Previous Name: Nova Scotia Cattlemen's Association
Overview: A medium-sized provincial organization founded in 2004
Mission: To assist in the sustainable development of the beef production industry in Nova Scotia
Member of: Canadian Cattlemen's Association
Affliation(s): National Check-off Agency; The Beef Cattle Research Agency; Beef Information Centre; Nappan Beef Research Committee; Maritime Beef Council; The Nova Scotia Federation of Agriculture Council of Leaders
Chief Officer(s):
Terry Prescott, Chair
Jim Fraser, Vice-Chair
Membership: *Fees:* Schedule available; *Member Profile:* Persons involved in Nova Scotia's beef & dairy production industry
Activities: Providing information about beef production & marketing; Promoting the beef industry in Nova Scotia; Monitoring & responding to issues in the industry; Advocating on behalf of producers
Publications:
• N.S.C.Action [a publication of Nova Scotia Cattle Producers]
Type: Newsletter

Nova Scotia Cattlemen's Association *See* Nova Scotia Cattle Producers

Nova Scotia Child Care Association / Association des services de garde à l'enfance de la Nouvelle-Écosse

#161, 1083 Queen St., Halifax NS B3H 0B2
Tel: 902-423-8199; *Fax:* 902-492-8106
Toll-Free: 800-565-8199
info@nschildcareassociation.org
nschildcareassociation.org
Overview: A medium-sized provincial organization
Mission: To promote high standards in service in the child care industry; to be a voice for its members
Member of: Canadian Child Care Federation
Chief Officer(s):
Kathleen Couture, Chair
Membership: *Fees:* $30; $55; *Committees:* Ethics; Membership & Standards; Advocacy

Nova Scotia Choral Federation (NSCF) / Fédération des chorales de la Nouvelle-Écosse (FCNE)

1113 Marginal Rd., Halifax NS B3H 4P7
Tel: 902-423-4688; *Fax:* 902-422-0881
Toll-Free: 888-672-3969
office@nscf.ns.ca
www.nscf.ns.ca
twitter.com/nschoralfed
Overview: A small provincial organization founded in 1976
Mission: To promote the art of choral music by encouraging high standards of artistic achievement by providing technical expertise & training; To foster an appreciation of choral music throughout Nova Scotia
Member of: Cultural Federations of Nova Scotia
Affliation(s): Association of Canadian Choral Conductors; Nova Scotia Music Educators Association; Canadian Music Educators Association; American Choral Directors Association; International Federation for Choral Music; Music Industry Association of Nova Scotia
Chief Officer(s):
Frances Farrell, President
Tim Callahan-Cross, Executive Director
tim@nscf.ns.ca
Finances: *Annual Operating Budget:* $100,000-$250,000; *Funding Sources:* Programs; provincial Dept. of Education; fundraising; membership
Staff Member(s): 2; 35 volunteer(s)
Membership: 230 individual + 140 group + 4 life; *Fees:* $35 individual; $40 student choir; $60 adult choir; *Member Profile:* Individuals engaged in choral singing; students; groups - adult & student choirs; organizations which support objectives of federation; *Committees:* Library; Workshop; Finance & Development; Policy Review; Special Projects
Activities: *Library* Open to public

Nova Scotia College Conference *See* Atlantic Collegiate Athletic Association

Nova Scotia College of Chiropractors (NSCC)

PO Box 9410, Stn. A, Halifax NS B3K 5S3
Tel: 902-407-4255; *Fax:* 902-425-2441
inquiries@chiropractors.ns.ca
www.chiropractors.ns.ca
Overview: A small provincial organization founded in 1953 overseen by Canadian Chiropractic Association
Mission: To promote & improve the proficiency of chiropractors in all matters relating to the practice of chiropractic; to protect the public from untrained & unqualified persons acting as chiropractors; to advance the chiropractic profession
Chief Officer(s):
John K. Sutherland, Executive Director
Finances: *Funding Sources:* Membership dues
Membership: *Committees:* Hearing; Peer Assessment; Continuing Education; Advertising Approval; Credentials; Nominating; Regulations & Policy Development; Registration Review

Nova Scotia College of Medical Laboratory Technologists (NSCMLT)

#202, 380 Bedford Hwy., Dartmouth NS B3M 2L4
Tel: 902-453-9605; *Fax:* 902-454-3535
Toll-Free: 888-897-4095
info@nscmlt.org
www.nscmlt.org
Overview: A medium-sized provincial licensing organization overseen by Canadian Society for Medical Laboratory Science
Mission: To provide leadership, establish partnerships & support the professional development of members so as to maintain the highest standards of practice
Chief Officer(s):
Chris Hirtle, Chair
Membership: *Member Profile:* Laboratory technologists in the province of Nova Scotia; *Committees:* Advocacy & Technology; Professional Practice

Nova Scotia College of Pharmacists (NSCP)

#200, 1559 Brunswick St., Halifax NS B3J 2G1
Tel: 902-422-8528; *Fax:* 902-422-0885
info@nspharmacists.ca
www.nspharmacists.ca
Previous Name: Nova Scotia Pharmaceutical Society
Overview: A medium-sized provincial licensing organization founded in 1876 overseen by National Association of Pharmacy Regulatory Authorities
Mission: To govern the practice of pharmacy in Nova Scotia to benefit the health & well being of the public
Member of: Canadian Council on Continuing Education in Pharmacy
Chief Officer(s):
Craig Connolly, President

Susan Wedlake, Registrar
swedlake@nspharmacists.ca
Membership: *Committees:* Executive; Continuing Competence; Registrations; Investigations; Standards of Practice; Task Force on Methadone; Task Force on Pharmacy Technicians; Task Force on Point-of-Care Testing; Hearing Panel

Nova Scotia College of Physiotherapists (NSCP)

15 Brookdale Cres., Dartmouth NS B3A 2R3
Tel: 902-454-0158; *Fax:* 902-484-6381
Toll-Free: 866-225-1060
office@nsphysio.com
www.nsphysio.com
Overview: A small provincial licensing organization founded in 1958 overseen by Canadian Alliance of Physiotherapy Regulators
Mission: To assure that the interests of the public are upheld through the regulation & promotion of safe & effective physiotherapy services; To communicate effectively with the membership & thereby affect change on issues of concern to the public
Member of: Canadian Alliance of Physiotherapy Regulators
Chief Officer(s):
Joan Ross, Registrar, 902-454-0158 Ext. 1, Fax: 902-245-3134
registrar@nsphysio.com
Patrick King, Executive Director, 902-454-0158 Ext. 2, Fax: 902-484-6381
execdir@nsphysio.com
Finances: *Annual Operating Budget:* $50,000-$100,000; *Funding Sources:* Registration fees
Staff Member(s): 2; 10 volunteer(s)
Membership: 556; *Fees:* $310; *Member Profile:* Registered physiotherapists; *Committees:* Discipline; Peer Assessment; Physiotherapy Support Worker Advisory; Post Graduate Education Fund

Nova Scotia Construction Labour Relations Association Limited (NSCLRA)

#1, 260 Brownlow Ave., Dartmouth NS B3B 1V9
Tel: 902-468-2283; *Fax:* 902-468-3705
admin@nsclra.ca
www.nsclra.ca
www.facebook.com/reseaufadoq
www.youtube.com/user/ReseauFADOQ
Previous Name: Construction Management Bureau Limited
Overview: A medium-sized provincial organization founded in 1972
Mission: To represent construction industry employers in collective bargaining with trade unions in the industrial & commercial sectors
Member of: Nova Scotia Construction Sector Council - Industrial-Commercial-Institutional
Chief Officer(s):
Allan Stapleton, President, 902-222-2036
astapleton@nsclra.ca
Nancy Canales, Administrator
ncanales@nsclra.ca
Membership: *Fees:* $500; *Committees:* Executive; Central Coordinating

Nova Scotia Construction Safety Association (NSCSA)

Burnside Industrial Park, 35 MacDonald Ave., Dartmouth NS B3B 1C6
Tel: 902-468-6696; *Fax:* 902-468-8843
Toll-Free: 800-971-3888
nscsa@nscsa.org
www.nscsa.org
www.linkedin.com/company/nova-scotia-construction-safety-association
www.facebook.com/NSCSA
www.youtube.com/user/nscsaassociation
Overview: A small provincial organization founded in 1994
Mission: To develop a positive occupational health & safety culture within the Nova Scotia construction industry through the provision of quality accessible & affordable services
Chief Officer(s):
A. Bruce Collins, General Manager
abcollins@nscsa.org
Staff Member(s): 24
Activities: Safety training; audits; member services; Certificate of Recognition; resource room; *Speaker Service:* Yes

Nova Scotia Construction Sector Council - Industrial-Commercial-Institutional (NSCSC-ICI)

#1, 10 Ragged Lake Blvd., Halifax NS B3S 1C2
Tel: 902-832-4761; *Fax:* 902-832-4763
www.nscsc.ca
Overview: A small provincial organization
Mission: To identify areas of concern related to human resource planning & skills development within Nova Scotia's construction sector
Affliation(s): Cape Breton Island Building & Construction Trades Council; Nova Scotia Construction Labour Relations Association
Chief Officer(s):
Mike Marsh, Chair
Trent Soholt, Executive Director/Project Manager
tsoholt@nscsc.ca
Activities: Better SuperVision & Leaders Being Leaders training programs; skills enhancement initiatives; *Library*

Nova Scotia Consulting Engineers Association *See* Consulting Engineers of Nova Scotia

Nova Scotia Co-operative Council

347C Willow St., Truro NS B2N 6C7
Tel: 902-893-8966; *Fax:* 902-895-0109
info@novascotia.coop
www.novascotia.coop
www.linkedin.com/company/2332853
www.facebook.com/nscoopcouncil
twitter.com/NovaScotiaCo_op
www.youtube.com/user/NSCoopCouncil
Overview: A small provincial organization
Mission: To encourage co-operatives of all types to work together to form a strong co-operative movement in Nova Scotia; to stimulate, promote & support the creation of new co-operatives across all sectors & industries in Nova Scotia; to advocate for the co-operative movement's interests to all levels of government; to enhance the profile of a "co-operative identity" among the public in Nova Scotia; to ensure innovation within the co-operative sector; to develop new ways of financing which support development opportunities. Branch offices in Sydney, & Yarmouth.
Member of: Canadian Renewable Energy Alliance
Chief Officer(s):
Dianne Kelderman, CEO
diannefk@eastlink.ca
Linda Johnson, Office Manager
linda@novascotia.coop
Staff Member(s): 8
Membership: *Fees:* Schedule available; *Member Profile:* Co-operatives in all sectors including housing co-ops, retail, agricultural, fisheries and forestry co-ops, credit unions, health co-ops, worker co-ops
Activities: Innovation Council; Renewable Energy Initiative; HealthConnex (Health Care Initiative); Youth Alliance Initiative; small business loan program; immigrant loan program; short-term equity fund; co-operative training; business planning and mentoring; conflict resolution; research; advocacy

Nova Scotia Council for the Family (NSCF)

#804, 1888 Brunswick St., Halifax NS B3J 3J8
Tel: 902-422-1316; *Fax:* 902-422-4012
Toll-Free: 877-525-0554
info@nscouncilfamily.org
www.nscouncilfamily.org
Overview: A medium-sized provincial charitable organization founded in 1967
Mission: To be devoted to the well-being of all children & families in Nova Scotia
Affliation(s): Family Service Canada; Child Welfare League of America/Canada
Chief Officer(s):
Jane Boyd Landry, Executive Director
jane@nscouncilfamily.org
100 volunteer(s)
Membership: 27; *Committees:* Adoption; Annual Meeting; Awards; Finance; Foster Care; Fundraising; Newsletter; Nominations; Personnel; Single Parent; Youth in Care
Activities: Presenting education programs for families & children & the public; Providing professional development; Engaging in advocacy activities; Reviewing research; *Speaker Service:* Yes; *Library* Open to public by appointment
Awards:
• Youth Achievement Award (Award)
• Award of Merit (Award)
• Judge Tramble Award (Award)
• Achievement of Excellence Award (Award)
• Support Staff Award (Award)
• Chuck Lake Distinguished Service Award (Award)
Amount: $500
• Honourary Life Membership (Award)
• Community Partners Award (Award)

Nova Scotia Council on Smoking & Health *See* Coalition for a Smoke-Free Nova Scotia

Nova Scotia Cricket Association (NSCA)

PO Box 31, Lunenburg NS B0J 2C0
Tel: 902-640-2448
novascotiacricket@gmail.com
www.novascotiacricket.com
www.facebook.com/296868372047
twitter.com/nscricket
Overview: A small provincial organization founded in 1965 overseen by Cricket Canada
Mission: To be the provincial governing body of cricket in Nova Scotia.
Member of: Cricket Canada; Sport Nova Scotia
Chief Officer(s):
Matt Lane, President
Yash Gugle, General Secretary
Amit Joshi, Provincial Director

Nova Scotia Criminal Justice Association (NSCJA)

PO Box 31191, Halifax NS B3K 5Y1
Tel: 902-490-5300; *Fax:* 902-490-6596
info@nscja.ca
www.nscja.ca
Previous Name: Nova Scotia Criminology & Corrections Association
Overview: A small provincial organization
Chief Officer(s):
Sebastien Decaens, President
Membership: *Fees:* $60; $35 student

Nova Scotia Criminology & Corrections Association *See* Nova Scotia Criminal Justice Association

Nova Scotia Curling Association (NSCA)

5516 Spring Garden Rd., 4th Fl., Halifax NS B3J 1G6
Tel: 902-421-2875; *Fax:* 902-425-5606
nsca@sportnovascotia.ca
www.nscurl.com
Previous Name: Nova Scotia Ladies Curling Association
Overview: A medium-sized provincial organization overseen by Canadian Curling Association
Affliation(s): Canadian Curling Association
Chief Officer(s):
Jeremiah Anderson, Executive Director
Staff Member(s): 5
Membership: 6,000; *Member Profile:* Men's, women's & juniors curlers; *Committees:* Operations; Finance; Competitions; Junior Curling; Athlete Development; Ombudsman; Disciplinary; Nominations; Awards; Curl Atlantic Reps

Nova Scotia Daylily Society

c/o Carol Harvey, Newport RR#3 999 McKay Rd., Hants County NS B0N 2A0
Tel: 902-757-2057
www.nsdaylilysociety.com
www.facebook.com/129889100496214
Overview: A small provincial organization founded in 2003
Mission: To promote the growing of Daylilies
Chief Officer(s):
Carol Harvey, Chair, Membership
cgharvey@eastlink.ca
Membership: *Fees:* $10

Nova Scotia Deaf Sports Association (NSDSA)

5516 Spring Garden Rd., 4th Fl., Halifax NS B3J 1G6
Overview: A small provincial organization overseen by Canadian Deaf Sports Association
Mission: To govern fitness, amateur sports & recreation for deaf people in Nova Scotia.
Member of: Canadian Deaf Sports Association
Chief Officer(s):
Justin DeBaie, President
justin.debaie@ns.sympatico.ca

Nova Scotia Dental Assistants' Association (NSDAA)

PO Box 9142, Stn. A, Halifax NS B3K 5M8
Tel: 902-405-1122; *Fax:* 902-405-1133
nsdaa@eastlink.ca
www.nsdaa.ca

Overview: A small provincial organization founded in 1950 overseen by Canadian Dental Assistants Association
Mission: To affiliate at local, provincial & national levels for the betterment of the dental assistant profession & patient care
Chief Officer(s):
Michelle Fowler, President
rdamdf@yahoo.ca
Lynda Foran, Executive Director
Finances: *Annual Operating Budget:* Less than $50,000; *Funding Sources:* Membership dues
Membership: 600-650; *Fees:* $85

Nova Scotia Dental Association (NSDA)
#101, 1559 Brunswick St., Halifax NS B3J 2G1
Tel: 902-420-0088; *Fax:* 902-423-6537
nsda@eastlink.ca
www.nsdental.org
Overview: A medium-sized provincial organization founded in 1891 overseen by Canadian Dental Association
Mission: To help dentists in Nova Scotia better serve their patients
Member of: Canadian Dental Association
Finances: *Funding Sources:* Membership dues
Membership: 600+ active members; *Fees:* Schedule available; *Member Profile:* Licensed to practise dentistry
Activities: *Rents Mailing List:* Yes

Nova Scotia Designer Crafts Council (NSDCC)
1113 Marginal Rd., Halifax NS B3H 4P7
Tel: 902-423-3837; *Fax:* 902-422-0881
office@nsdcc.ns.ca
www.nsdcc.ns.ca
www.facebook.com/NSDCC
twitter.com/NSDCC
www.youtube.com/user/nsdcc
Overview: A small provincial charitable organization founded in 1973
Mission: To encourage & promote the craft movement in Nova Scotia; to increase public awareness & appreciation of craft products & activities
Member of: Cultural Federations of Nova Scotia
Chief Officer(s):
Susan Hanrahan, Executive Director
susan@nsdcc.ns.ca
Finances: *Funding Sources:* Core funding from NS Dept. of Education & Culture; membership fees; fundraising endeavours
Staff Member(s): 4
Membership: *Fees:* $23 student; $28.75 associate; $34.50 senior; $69 group/general; $115 market; *Committees:* Communications; Development; Exhibitions; Standards; Jackie Mackay Library Collection; Market Advisory
Activities: Two juried craft markets annually (these markets provide marketing opportunities for members & serve as vehicle for public education & awareness of craft); exhibitions to which any Nova Scotian resident may submit work; workshops, conferences, educational programs to promote quality of craft experience & product; maintains & leads a permanent collection of Nova Scotian crafts; provides a commissions & sales portfolio service for members which may be consulted in the NSDCC office; *Awareness Events:* Summer Show, July; Christmas Show, Nov.

Nova Scotia Dietetic Association (NSDA)
#212, 1496 Bedford Hwy., Bedford NS B4A 1E5
Tel: 902-835-0253; *Fax:* 902-835-0523
info@nsdassoc.ca
www.nsdassoc.ca
Overview: A medium-sized provincial licensing organization founded in 1953 overseen by Dietitians of Canada
Mission: To regulate dietitions & nutritionists in the province, & register & discipline (when necessary) practitioners to ensure safe, ethical & competent dietetic practice
Chief Officer(s):
Patti Simpson, President
Jennifer Garus, Executive Manager (ex-officio)
Finances: *Annual Operating Budget:* Less than $50,000; *Funding Sources:* Membership dues
Membership: 450 individuals; *Fees:* $310 ($155 first time renewal); *Member Profile:* Must meet standards of Professional Dietitians Act of Nova Scotia; *Committees:* Registration; Quality Assurance
Activities: *Internships:* Yes; *Speaker Service:* Yes; *Rents Mailing List:* Yes

Nova Scotia Drama League *See* Theatre Nova Scotia

Nova Scotia Egg & Pullet Producers Marketing Board *See* Nova Scotia Egg Producers

Nova Scotia Egg Producers (NSEP)
PO Box 1096, 55 Queen St., #A, Truro NS B2N 2B2
Tel: 902-895-6341; *Fax:* 902-895-6343
www.nsegg.ca
Previous Name: Nova Scotia Egg & Pullet Producers Marketing Board
Overview: A small provincial licensing organization founded in 1972
Mission: Mandates of effective promotion, control and regulation of eggs and pullets in Nova Scotia.
Affliation(s): Canadian Egg Marketing Agency
Chief Officer(s):
Patricia Wyllie, General Manager
Finances: *Annual Operating Budget:* $250,000-$500,000
Staff Member(s): 4; 7 volunteer(s)
Membership: 28

Nova Scotia Environmental Network (NSEN)
3115 Veith St., Halifax NS B3K 3G9
Tel: 902-454-6846; *Fax:* 902-453-3633
Other Communication: board_nsen@cen-rce.org
nsen@cen-rce.org
www.nsen.ca
Overview: A medium-sized provincial organization founded in 1991 overseen by Canadian Environmental Network
Mission: To conserve & enhance the natural environment; To achieve a sustainable future for Nova Scotia; To connect environmental & health organizations
Affliation(s): Canadian Environmental Network (CEN)
Chief Officer(s):
Tamara Lorincz, Executive Director
Emma Boardman, Secretary & Agent
board_nsen@cen-rce.org
Finances: *Funding Sources:* Fundraising; Donations
Membership: *Fees:* Schedule available, based upon annual budget range; *Member Profile:* Non-profit groups, agencies, educational institutions, & individuals in Nova Scotia who share Nova Scotia Environmental Network's mission
Activities: Liaising with government at the provincial, national, & international levels; Organizing roundtables & conferences; Providing networking opportunities; Supporting members; Facilitating information exchange; Providing educational activities; *Internships:* Yes; *Library:* Nova Scotia Environmental Network Library
Publications:
• By-Laws of the Nova Scotia Environmental Network (NSEN)
• Eco-Connections [a publication of the Nova Scotia Environmental Network]
Type: Newsletter; *Frequency:* Monthly; *Price:* Free with Nova Scotia Environmental Network membership
Profile: A bulletin about Nova Scotia Environmental Network's activities & environmental actions
• General Policies of the Nova Scotia Environmental Network (NSEN)
Profile: Topics include membership, the duties of the board, delegate selection, purchasing, the newsletter, mailing lists, meeting protocol, rights & responsibilities ofgeneral members, duties of the executive director, the caucus, working groups, & duties of the member representative
• Nova Scotia Environmental Network Annual Activity Report
Type: Yearbook; *Frequency:* Annually
Profile: A report of activities plus financial statements for the Canadian Environmental Network

Nova Scotia Equestrian Federation (NSEF)
5516 Spring Garden Rd., 4th Fl., Halifax NS B3J 1G6
Tel: 902-425-5450; *Fax:* 902-425-5606
nsef@sportnovascotia.ca
www.horsenovascotia.ca
Overview: A small provincial organization
Member of: Equine Canada
Chief Officer(s):
Heather Myrer, Executive Director
Membership: 2,100; *Fees:* $35 individual; $55 family

Nova Scotia Federation of Agriculture (NSFA)
Covington Place, 332 Willow St., 2nd Fl., Truro NS B2N 5A5
Tel: 902-893-2293; *Fax:* 902-893-7063
info@nsfa-fane.ca
www.nsfa-fane.ca
Overview: A medium-sized provincial organization founded in 1895 overseen by Canadian Federation of Agriculture
Mission: To act as the voice for the agricultural community in Nova Scotia; To ensure a competitive & sustainable future for agriculture in Nova Scotia; To build financially viable, ecologically sound, & socially responsible farm businesses in the province
Member of: Canadian Federation of Agriculture
Chief Officer(s):
Beth Densmore, President
Donna Langille, Manager, Operations
dlangille@nsfa-fane.ca
Membership: 1,800+; *Member Profile:* Individual farm businesses in Nova Scotia which represent all aspects of primary agriculture; Corporations
Activities: Reviewing legislative & regulatory issues & lobbying for change; Developing & delivering programs to meet the needs of the farm community, such a environmental farm planning services

Nova Scotia Federation of Anglers & Hunters (NSFAH)
PO Box 654, Halifax NS B3J 2T3
Tel: 902-477-8898; *Fax:* 902-444-3883
tonyrodgers@eastlink.ca
www.nsfah.ca
Overview: A medium-sized provincial organization founded in 1930
Mission: The Nova Scotia Federation of Anglers and Hunters is dedicated to the conservation and propagation of the wildlife in the province for those who hunt, fish, trap or otherwise wish to enjoy the wildlife resources of Nova Scotia. This will be accomplished by education, cooperation and exchange of information will all people and by uniting provincial organizations having similar objectives.
Chief Officer(s):
Tony Rodgers, Executive Director
Membership: *Fees:* $20 individual; $50 contributing; $75 supporting; $30 family

Nova Scotia Federation of Home & School Associations (NSFHSA)
#102, 7165 Hwy. 1, Coldbrook NS B4R 1A2
Tel: 902-676-6676
Toll-Free: 800-214-8373
nsfhsa@staff.ednet.ns.ca
www.nsfhsa.org
Overview: A small provincial organization founded in 1936 overseen by Canadian Home & School Federation
Mission: To provide a forum for discussion between the home & school beyond the parent-teacher interview; to promote & secure legislation for the care & protection of & equality of educational opportunities for children; to give parents an understanding of the school & its work, assisting in interpreting the school to the public; to confer & cooperate with organizations other than the schools which concern themselves with the training & development of children & youth
Chief Officer(s):
Charla Dorrington, President
cdorrington@commissionaires.ns.ca
Membership: 5,000+ families & 400 group affiliates; *Fees:* $100 member association; $50 associate; *Member Profile:* Parents; teaching staff

Nova Scotia Federation of Labour / Fédération du travail de la Nouvelle-Écosse
#225, 3700 Kempt Rd., Halifax NS B3K 4X8
Tel: 902-454-6735; *Fax:* 902-454-7671
nsfl@ns.aliantzinc.ca
www.nsfl.ns.ca
Overview: A medium-sized provincial organization founded in 1956 overseen by Canadian Labour Congress
Mission: To speak on behalf of & represent the interests of organized & unorganized workers; to promote decent wages & working conditions, improved health & safety laws & lobbies for fair taxes & strong social programs; to work for social equality & to end racism & discrimination.
Chief Officer(s):
Rick Clarke, President
Kyle Buott, Secretary-Treasurer
Membership: 70,000 members of affiliated unions in 350+ locals; *Committees:* Anti-Racism/Human Rights; Political Action; Education; Health Care; Occupational Health & Safety/Workers' Compensation; Women's Committee; Pensions; Young Workers
Activities: Lobbying; strike support; Lighting the Way program (workplace literacy/numeracy skills)

Nova Scotia Federation of Senior Citizens & Pensioners *See* Federation of Senior Citizens & Pensioners of Nova Scotia

Nova Scotia Fish Packers Association (NSFPA)
38B John St., Yarmouth NS B5A 3H2
Tel: 902-742-6168; *Fax:* 902-742-1620
fishpackers@ns.aliantzinc.ca
www.fishpackers.com
Previous Name: Southwestern Nova Scotia Fish Packers Association
Overview: A small local organization founded in 1972
Mission: To ensure the survival of a competitive seafood processing industry in Nova Scotia; To provide leadership on industry issues, effective representation with government, R&D, project management, & volume discount purchases
Chief Officer(s):
Marc Surette, Executive Director
Finances: *Annual Operating Budget:* $50,000-$100,000
Staff Member(s): 1
Membership: 60; *Fees:* $460-$2645 plus HST; *Member Profile:* Fish processing companies dealing with a wide variety of seafood for Canadian & export sales

Nova Scotia Fishermen Draggers Association *See* Scotia Fundy Mobile Gear Fishermen's Association

Nova Scotia Forest Products Association *See* Forest Products Association of Nova Scotia

Nova Scotia Forest Technicians Association (NSFTA)
164 Forest Hills Dr., Truro NS B2N 2B7
e-mail: nsfta@nsfta.com
www.nsfta.ca
www.facebook.com/groups/129850007043042/
Overview: A small provincial organization
Chief Officer(s):
Cheryl Rudderham Cape Br, President
rudderca@gov.ns.ca
Finances: *Annual Operating Budget:* Less than $50,000
12 volunteer(s)
Membership: 200 individual; *Fees:* $35 regular; $70 certified; *Member Profile:* Forest technicians; technologists
Activities: *Library* Open to public

Nova Scotia Forestry Association (NSFA)
PO Box 696, 430 Marney Rd. (Hilden), Truro NS B2N 5E5
Tel: 902-895-1179; *Fax:* 902-893-1197
www.nsfa.ca
www.facebook.com/pages/Envirothon-Nova-Scotia/176901159022332
twitter.com/envirothonns
Overview: A medium-sized provincial charitable organization founded in 1959 overseen by Canadian Forestry Association
Mission: To conserve Nova Scotia's forests; To promote the wise use & management of forest resources
Chief Officer(s):
Debbie Waycott, Contact
Finances: *Funding Sources:* Sponsorships
Activities: Conducting programs in schools, such as Envirothon; Advocating for the full development, utilization, & protection of forests in Nova Scotia; Promoting reforestation; *Awareness Events:* Arbor Day, September

Nova Scotia Friends of Schizophrenics *See* Schizophrenia Society of Nova Scotia

Nova Scotia Fruit Growers' Association (NSFGA)
Kentville Agricultural Centre, 32 Main St., Kentville NS B4N 1J5
Tel: 902-678-1093; *Fax:* 902-679-1567
www.nsapples.com
www.facebook.com/173682379335493
Overview: A small provincial organization founded in 1863
Mission: To serve the interests of tree fruit growers in Nova Scotia
Member of: Canadian Horticulture Council
Affliation(s): Nova Scotia Federation of Agriculture
Chief Officer(s):
Dela Erith, Executive Director
derith@nsapples.com
Finances: *Annual Operating Budget:* $100,000-$250,000
Staff Member(s): 10; 16 volunteer(s)
Membership: 220; *Fees:* $225.60-$1,804.84
Meetings/Conferences: • Nova Scotia Fruit Growers' Association Annual Convention 2015, January, 2015, Old Orchard Inn, Wolfville, NS
Scope: Provincial

The Nova Scotia Genealogy Network Association (NSGNA)
e-mail: indexgans@gmail.com
nsgna.ednet.ns.ca
Overview: A small local organization founded in 1996
Finances: *Annual Operating Budget:* Less than $50,000
10 volunteer(s)
Membership: 15; *Fees:* $25

Nova Scotia Gerontological Nurses Association (NSGNA)
PO Box 33101, Stn. Quinpool, Halifax MB B3L 4T6
e-mail: ssavage@ssdha.nshealth.ca
www.nsgna.com
Overview: A medium-sized provincial organization founded in 1984 overseen by Canadian Gerontological Nursing Association
Mission: To promote a high standard of nursing care & related health services for older adults; To enhance professionalism in the practice of gerontological nursing
Chief Officer(s):
Sohani Welcher, President, 902-473-8413
Sohani.welcher@cdha.nshealth.ca
Membership: *Member Profile:* Nurses interested in gerontology
Activities: Offering professional networking opportunities; Providing professional development; Advocating for comprehensive services for older adults; Supporting research related to gerontological nursing; Promoting gerontological nursing to the public
Awards:
• NSGNA Scholarship (Scholarship)
• NSGNA Certification Bursary (Scholarship)
• Conference Bursary (Scholarship)
Publications:
• NSGNA [Nova Scotia Gerontological Nurses Association] Newsletter
Type: Newsletter

Nova Scotia Golf Association (NSGA)
#216, 30 Damascus Rd., Bedford NS B4A 0C1
Tel: 902-468-8844; *Fax:* 902-484-5327
www.nsga.ns.ca
www.facebook.com/pages/The-Nova-Scotia-Golf-Association/64019542477
twitter.com/novascotiagolf
Overview: A medium-sized provincial organization founded in 1931 overseen by Royal Canadian Golf Association
Mission: To promote, foster & develop golf at all levels in Nova Scotia; to provide a liaison between member clubs & the Royal Canadian Golf Association; to consult & assist with member clubs on turf maintenance, handicap procedures, slope ratings, rule interpretations & junior development; to organize tournaments, in cooperation with member clubs, that determine provincial champions.
Member of: Canadian Golf Foundation; International Association of Golf Administrators; Sport Nova Scotia
Affliation(s): Royal Canadian Golf Association
Chief Officer(s):
David Campbell, Executive Director
david@nsga.ns.ca
Jan Gaudette, Executive Assistant
jan@nsga.ns.ca
Finances: *Funding Sources:* Membership dues; sponsors
Membership: *Member Profile:* Must be a member club

Nova Scotia Government & General Employees Union (NSGEU) / Syndicat de la fonction publique de la Nouvelle-Écosse
255 John Savage Ave., Dartmouth NS B3B 0J3
Tel: 902-424-4063; *Fax:* 902-424-2111
Toll-Free: 877-556-7438
www.nsgeu.ns.ca
Overview: A medium-sized local organization founded in 1958
Affliation(s): Canadian Labour Congress; Nova Scotia Federation of Labour; National Union of Public & General Employees
Chief Officer(s):
Joan Jessome, President
Keiren Tompkins, Executive Director
Finances: *Funding Sources:* Membership dues
Staff Member(s): 54
Membership: 30,000 public & private sector employees; *Committees:* Constitution & By-Laws; Finance; Health, Safety & Environment; Human Rights; Political Action; Education; Women's Issues; Social/Recreation

Nova Scotia Government Libraries Council (NSGLC)
c/o Dept. of Nova Scotia Department of Health
Tel: 902-424-7214
www.nsglc.ednet.ns.ca
Overview: A small provincial organization
Mission: To provide a forum for government libraries to discuss common problems & share information
Chief Officer(s):
Ruth Hart, Chair
harte@gov.ns.ca
Natalie MacPherson, Secretary, 902-424-8474
labrlibr@gov.ns.ca
Anne Van Iderstine, Treasurer, 902-424-2078
vanideal@gov.ns.ca

Nova Scotia Ground Water Association (NSGWA)
#417, 3 - 644 Portland St., Dartmouth NS B2W 2M3
Fax: 902-435-0089
Toll-Free: 888-242-4440
nsgwa@ns.aliantzinc.ca
www.nsgwa.ca
Previous Name: Nova Scotia Well Drillers Association
Overview: A medium-sized provincial organization overseen by Canadian Ground Water Association
Mission: To act as the voice of the industry to all levels of government; To encourage the management & protection of ground water
Member of: Canadian Ground Water Association
Chief Officer(s):
Arthur Jefferson, President
Noreene McGuire, Secretary-Treasurer
Membership: *Fees:* $100 associate, non-voting, non-certifed membership; $200 drillers, diggers, pump installers, suppliers, & technical personnel; *Member Profile:* Well drillers; Well diggers; Pump installers; Manufacturers; Suppliers; Technicians
Activities: Increasing public awareness; Encouraging partnerships; Providing continuing education; Presenting awards
Meetings/Conferences: • Nova Scotia Ground Water Association 2015 Annual General Meeting, May, 2015, NS
Scope: Provincial
Description: A yearly gathering featuring divisional meetings, presentations, & association business
Contact Information: Secretary-Treasurer: Noreene McGuire, E-mail: nsgwa@ns.aliantzinc.ca
Publications:
• Water Talk [a publication of the Nova Scotia Ground Water Association]
Type: Newsletter; *Frequency:* Semiannually; *Accepts Advertising*
Profile: A publication for Nova Scotia's well drillers & diggers, pump installers, technical personnel, manufacturerer, & suppliers to the ground waterindustry, featuring association happenings & industry news

Nova Scotia Gymnastics Association *See* Gymnastics Nova Scotia

Nova Scotia Head Injury Association *See* Brain Injury Association of Nova Scotia

Nova Scotia Hearing & Speech Foundation
#5, 1350 Bedford Hwy., Bedford NS B4A 1E1
Tel: 902-423-1947; *Fax:* 902-423-3765
Toll-Free: 866-278-5678
info@hearingandspeech.ca
www.hearingandspeech.ca
Overview: A medium-sized provincial organization
Mission: To provide hearing services to all Nova Scotians & speech-language services to preschool children & adults; To work with community volunteer leaders, the families & friends of those who are hearing or speech impaired, our partners in government, & the medical & academic communities; To raise funds to support critical Centres' needs
Chief Officer(s):
Cheryl MacLeod, Office Manager
Gordon Moore, Chair

Nova Scotia Heart Foundation *See* Heart & Stroke Foundation of Nova Scotia

Nova Scotia Hereford Club
c/o Maritime Hereford Association, RR #1, New Ross NS B0J 2M0
Tel: 902-425-7427; *Fax:* 902-425-7427
Overview: A medium-sized provincial organization founded in 1940
Mission: To promote the Hereford breed of beef cattle
Affliation(s): Maritime Hereford Association
Chief Officer(s):
Pat Ward, Director, 902-675-3833

Finances: *Annual Operating Budget:* Less than $50,000
64 volunteer(s)
Membership: 115 institutional + 30 student

Nova Scotia Hockey Association *See* Hockey Nova Scotia

Nova Scotia Home Builders' Association (NSHBA)

Bayers Lake Business Park, 124 Chain Lake Drive, Unit B, Halifax NS B3S 1A2
Tel: 902-450-5554; *Fax:* 902-450-5448
Toll-Free: 800-668-2001
nshba@nshba.ns.ca
nshomebuilders.ca
www.facebook.com/nshomebuilders
Overview: A small provincial organization founded in 1959 overseen by Canadian Home Builders' Association
Chief Officer(s):
Paul Pettipas, CEO
pettipas@nshba.ns.ca
Finances: *Annual Operating Budget:* $500,000-$1.5 Million; *Funding Sources:* Membership dues; Program management; home show
Staff Member(s): 4; 18 volunteer(s)
Membership: 300; *Fees:* $552.50-$615 depending on local chapter; *Member Profile:* Builders; Renovators; Suppliers; *Committees:* Technical Research; Training & Education; Renovation; Marketing
Activities: Monthly member meetings; R 2000 Showcase of Homes; NSHBA Home Show; *Awareness Events:* Renovation Month, October; *Speaker Service:* Yes; *Rents Mailing List:* Yes; *Library* by appointment

Nova Scotia Horseshoe Players Association

NS
Tel: 902-852-3231; *Fax:* 902-852-2311
Overview: A small provincial organization overseen by Horseshoe Canada
Mission: To promote the sport of horseshoes in Canada
Member of: Horseshoe Canada
Chief Officer(s):
Cecil Mitchell, Contact
cmitchell@rainbownetrigging.com

Nova Scotia Horseshoe Players Association (NSHPA)

2085 Prospect Rd., Hatchet Lake NS B3T 1S1
Tel: 902-468-7503; *Fax:* 902-468-3939
Overview: A small provincial licensing organization founded in 1973 overseen by Horseshoe Canada
Mission: To promote the enjoyment & health benefits of the sport of horseshoe pitching throughout Nova Scotia
Member of: Sport Nova Scotia; Horseshoe Canada
Affliation(s): Maritime Horseshoe Players Association
Chief Officer(s):
Cecil Mitchell, Contact
cmitchell@rainbownetrigging.com
Finances: *Annual Operating Budget:* Less than $50,000; *Funding Sources:* Membership dues; fundraising; government grants
40 volunteer(s)
Membership: 35; *Fees:* $6; *Committees:* Club Forming; Membership; Palladian Construction; Promotion
Activities: 8 sanctioned tournaments; TV Series; conducts Special Olympics for horseshoes; *Rents Mailing List:* Yes

Nova Scotia Hospice Palliative Care Association (NSHPCA)

207 Willow St., Truro NS B2N 5A1
Tel: 902-893-7171; *Fax:* 902-893-7172
www.nshpca.ca
Overview: A medium-sized provincial charitable organization founded in 1995
Mission: To strive towards achieving comfort & peace for persons living & dying with a life-threatening illness throughout Nova Scotia; to promote the philosophy & principles of palliative care through networking, public & professional education, advocacy & research; to educate & improve public awareness of the needs of those with a life-threatening illness; thus enabling & empowering communities to recognize the values, needs & wishes of all persons across all stages of life
Member of: Canadian Palliative Care Association
Chief Officer(s):
Brenda Payne, President
Finances: *Annual Operating Budget:* Less than $50,000
Membership: 200; *Fees:* $30 individual; *Member Profile:* Interdisciplinary health professionals & volunteers; *Committees:* Administration; Education; Communications; Grief & Bereavement
Activities: *Awareness Events:* Palliative Care Week, May

Nova Scotia Independent Adjusters' Association

c/o E. Grant King, Crawford & Company (Canada) Inc., #120, 237 Brownlow Ave., Dartmouth NS B3B 2C7
www.ciaa-adjusters.ca
Overview: A small local organization overseen by Canadian Independent Adjusters' Association
Member of: Canadian Independent Adjusters' Association
Chief Officer(s):
E. Grant King, President, 902-468-7787, Fax: 902-468-5822
Grant.King@crawco.ca

Nova Scotia Insolvency Association *See* Nova Scotia Association of Insolvency & Restructuring Professionals

Nova Scotia Institute of Agrologists (NSIA)

PO Box 550, 35 Tower Rd., Truro NS B2N 5E3
Tel: 902-897-6742
nsagrologists@eastlink.ca
www.nsagrologists.ca
Overview: A medium-sized provincial licensing organization founded in 1953 overseen by Agricultural Institute of Canada
Finances: *Annual Operating Budget:* Less than $50,000; *Funding Sources:* Membership dues
15 volunteer(s)
Membership: 300; *Fees:* $110
Activities: *Internships:* Yes; *Speaker Service:* Yes
Awards:
• Outstanding Farmer (Award)
• Outstanding Young Agrologist (Award)
• Distinguished Life Member (Award)
• Distinguished Agrologist (Award)
• NSIA Scholarship (Scholarship)
Amount: $1,000
• Honourary Member (Award)
• C.A. Douglas Award (Award)
• NSIA 50th Anniversary Scholarship (Scholarship)
Amount: $1,000

Nova Scotia Institute of the Purchasing Management Association of Canada *See* Supply Chain Management Association - Nova Scotia

Nova Scotia Insurance Women's Association (NSIWA)

c/o Ann Joudrey, Marsh Adjustment Bureau Ltd., 724 King St. Plaza, Bridgewater NS B4V 1B4
Tel: 902-543-2864
info@nsiwa.com
www.nsiwa.com
Overview: A small local organization
Member of: Canadian Association of Insurance Women
Chief Officer(s):
Amber MacInnis, President

Nova Scotia Ladies Curling Association *See* Nova Scotia Curling Association

Nova Scotia League for Equal Opportunities (NSLEO)

#1211, 5251 Duke St., Halifax NS B3J 1P3
Tel: 902-455-6942; *Fax:* 902-454-4781
Toll-Free: 866-696-7536
nsleo@eastlink.ca
www.novascotialeo.org
Also Known As: LEO
Overview: A medium-sized provincial charitable organization founded in 1979
Mission: To promote a barrier-free environment; To strive for equality; To achieve recognition of the abilities of people with disabilities so that they may function as equals in society
Member of: Council of Canadians with Disabilities (CCD)
Affliation(s): Clare Organization Representing Disabilities; Community Involvement of the Disabled; Central Highlands Association of the Disabled; Disabled Consumer Society of Colchester; Richmond County Disabled
Chief Officer(s):
Earl Flynn, Chair
Staff Member(s): 2
Membership: 20; *Fees:* $50; *Member Profile:* Nova Scotians with disabilities; *Committees:* Transportation; Health Care; Nominating Constitution; Education
Activities: Challenge legislature; host regular information sessions; conduct research on accessible transportation, universal technical aids, health care/home care, attendant care provisions, building code regulations, regular contact with government officials; *Speaker Service:* Yes; *Library:* Resource Centre; by appointment
Awards:
• Recognition & Lifestyles Awards (Award)
• Certificates for Volunteers (Award)

Nova Scotia Library Association (NSLA)

c/o Kelli WooShue, Halifax Public Libraries, 60 Alderney Dr., Dartmouth NS B2Y 4P8
Tel: 902-490-5710
Other Communication: nslanewsletter@gmail.com
wooshuk@halifax.ca
www.nsla.ns.ca
Overview: A small provincial charitable organization founded in 1973
Mission: To promote the value of libraries; To facilitate the exchange of ideas & information among library workers in Nova Scotia
Chief Officer(s):
Faye MacDougall, President, 902-562-3279
fmacdoug@nssc.library.ns.ca
Denise Corey, Secretary, 902-667-2549
dcorey@nsamc.library.ns.ca
Carin Cress, Treasurer, 902-665-2995
avrbran2@nsar.library.ns.ca
Jeremy Henderson, Convenor, Newsletter, 902-490-5753
jerhender@yahoo.com
Rachel Crosby, Contact, Membership, 902-826-3330
crosbyra@halifax.ca
Debbie Kaleva, Convenor, Continuing Education, 902-755-7201
debbie.kaleva@nscc.ca
Theresa MacDonald, Convenor, Conferences, 902-562-3279
tmacdona@nssc.library.ns.ca
Lori Noseworthy, Contact, Newsletter, 902-582-2010
lori.noseworthy@staff.ednet.ns.ca
Jeff Mercer, Convenor, Membership, 902-543-9222
jmercer@southshorepubliclibraries.ca
Kelli Wooshue, Convenor, Public Relations & Promotions, 902-490-5710
wooshuk@halifax.ca
Membership: *Fees:* $10 students; $25 personal membership; $50 institutions; *Member Profile:* Library workers in Nova Scotia; *Committees:* Library Technician Interest Group; School Library Interest Group; Rural Services Interest Group
Activities: Enhancing the skills of library workers throughout Nova Scotia; Monitoring local issues at libraries in the province
Awards:
• Ann Connor Brimer Award (Award)
Awarded to writers in Atlantic Canada who have made an outstanding contribution to children's literature *Amount:* $2,000 *Contact:* Heather Mackenzie, E-mail: mackenh@halifaxpubliclibraries.ca
• Norman Horrocks Award for Library Leadership (Award)
To recognize contributions to the promotion & development of library service in Nova Scotia *Contact:* Yvette Frost, E-mail: yfrost@nsy.library.ns.ca
• Award for Library & Information Technology Student (Award)
To recognize the achievement of a graduating student *Contact:* Yvette Frost, E-mail: yfrost@nsy.library.ns.ca
• Award for School of Information Management Graduate (Award)
To recognize a graduating student with high academic achievement & a demonstrated commitment to public libraries *Contact:* Yvette Frost, E-mail: yfrost@nsy.library.ns.ca
• Emile Theriault Library & Information Technology Award (Award)
To recognize the efforts of a library support staff member who contributed to their library community *Contact:* Yvette Frost, E-mail: yfrost@nsy.library.ns.ca
• NSLA Conference Bursary (Grant)
To provide financial assistance to a library staff person who is in need of assistance to attend the NSLA annual conference *Contact:* Yvette Frost, E-mail: yfrost@nsy.library.ns.ca
Meetings/Conferences: • Nova Scotia Library Association 2015 Annual Conference, 2015, NS
Scope: Provincial
Description: Hosted by Halifax Public Libraries in the autumn
Contact Information: E-mail: conference@nsla.ns.ca
• Nova Scotia Library Association 2016 Annual Conference, 2016, NS
Scope: Provincial
Description: Hosted by Pictou Antigonish Regional Library in the autumn
Contact Information: E-mail: conference@nsla.ns.ca

• Nova Scotia Library Association 2017 Annual Conference, 2017, NS
Scope: Provincial
Description: Hosted by Annapolis Valley Regional Library in the autumn
Contact Information: E-mail: conference@nsla.ns.ca
• Nova Scotia Library Association 2018 Annual Conference, 2018
Scope: Provincial
Description: Hosted by Cumberland Regional Library in the autumn
Contact Information: E-mail: conference@nsla.ns.ca
Publications:
• NSLA [Nova Scotia Library Association] Newsletter
Type: Newsletter; *Frequency:* Quarterly; *Editor:* Jeremy Henderson *ISSN:* 1182-0209; *Price:* Free with Nova Scotia Library Association membership
Profile: Association business, regional news, & announcements

Nova Scotia Lighthouse Preservation Society (NSLPS)
c/o Maritime Museum of the Atlantic, 1675 Lower Water St., Halifax NS B3J 1S3
www.nslps.com
Overview: A medium-sized provincial charitable organization founded in 1994
Mission: To promote awareness & preservation of Nova Scotian lighthouses; to assist community groups in leasing or taking ownership of lighthouse sites; to provide access to written research & photographic documentation; to initiate oral history research, & to monitor the status of historic lighthouse sites
Member of: Federation of NS Heritage; Canadian Heritage Foundation; World Lighthouse Society
Chief Officer(s):
Barry MacDonald, President
Finances: *Annual Operating Budget:* Less than $50,000
12 volunteer(s)
Membership: 1,500; *Fees:* $20 single; $25 family; $30 group affiliates; $50 sustaining; $100 patron; US$20 foreign
Activities: *Speaker Service:* Yes

Nova Scotia Mackerel Fishermen's Association
PO Box 34, RR#2, Hubbards NS B0J 1T0
Tel: 902-857-3619; *Fax:* 902-857-2057
Overview: A small provincial organization founded in 1992
Chief Officer(s):
Robert Conrad, President
rconrad91@hotmail.com

The Nova Scotia Mineral & Gem Society (NSMGS)
N.S. Museum of Natural History, 1747 Summer St., Halifax NS B3H 3A6
e-mail: info@novascotiamineralandgemsociety.com
www.novascotiamineralandgemsociety.com
Previous Name: The Mineral & Gem Society of Nova Scotia
Overview: A small provincial organization founded in 1957
Mission: To encourage & promote mineral collecting, gem cutting & allied activities among the members & the public; to encourage & assist in the exchange of information, technical knowledge, etc., among persons interested in these activities
Member of: Gem & Mineral Federation of Canada
Chief Officer(s):
William Blinn, President
Membership: *Fees:* $20
Activities: Meetings; auctions; lectures; slide shows; field trips

Nova Scotia Mink Breeders' Association
c/o Dan Mullen, 2124 Black Rock Rd., Waterville NS B0P 1V0
Tel: 902-680-5360; *Fax:* 902-538-7799
Overview: A small provincial organization founded in 1938
Mission: To foster better mink breeding among the members; to help secure market advantage.
Chief Officer(s):
Dan Mullen, President
danmullen100@yahoo.ca
Simeon Roberts, Manager
simeonroberts@eastlink.ca
Finances: *Funding Sources:* Membership fees
Membership: *Member Profile:* Licensed mink farmers; associate members
Activities: Sponsors live mink shows; field days; information meetings; short courses

Nova Scotia Minor Hockey Council
c/o Hockey Nova Scotia, #17, 7 Mellor Ave., Dartmouth NS B3B 0E8
Tel: 902-454-9400; *Fax:* 902-454-3883
Overview: A medium-sized provincial organization founded in 1974
Mission: To provide a standard set of playing rules for minor hockey in Nova Scotia
Affliation(s): Nova Scotia Hockey Association
Chief Officer(s):
Arnie Farrell, Chair, 902-863-0221
arniefarrell@ns.sympatico.ca

Nova Scotia Music Educators' Association (NSMEA)
c/o NSMEA Membership Secretary, 1046 Church St., RR#1, Port Williams NS B0P 1T0
local.nstu.ca/web/nsmea
Overview: A small provincial organization founded in 1959
Mission: To promote & advance music education in Nova Scotia; To hold meetings, exhibitions & conferences for the discussion of problems & the exchange of views on matters relating to music education; To facilitate communication between music educators & the Department of Education through the Nova Scotia Teachers' Union
Member of: Nova Scotia Teachers Union
Chief Officer(s):
Donalda Westcott, President
djwestcott@nstu.ca
Marg Kristie, Membership Secretary
mekristie@nstu.ca
Finances: *Annual Operating Budget:* Less than $50,000
Staff Member(s): 10; 32 volunteer(s)
Membership: 31 student; 178 individual; *Fees:* $40 active; $19.50 student; $27.75 retired; *Member Profile:* Teachers of music or have an interest in music

Nova Scotia Native Women's Society
PO Box 805, Truro NS B2N 5E8
Tel: 902-893-7402; *Fax:* 902-897-7162
www.facebook.com/nsnwa
Overview: A medium-sized provincial organization overseen by Native Women's Association of Canada
Member of: Native Women's Association of Canada (NWAC)

Nova Scotia Nature Trust (NSNT)
PO Box 2202, 2085 Maitland St., Halifax NS B3J 3C4
Tel: 902-425-5263; *Fax:* 902-429-5263
Toll-Free: 877-434-5263
nature@nsnt.ca
www.nsnt.ca
www.facebook.com/novascotianaturetrust
twitter.com/nsnaturetrust
www.youtube.com/user/naturetrust/videos
Overview: A medium-sized provincial organization founded in 1994
Mission: To protect Nova Scotia's outstanding natural legacy through land conservation.
Chief Officer(s):
Corey Miller, President
Bonnie Sutherland, Executive Director
bonnie@nsnt.ca
Staff Member(s): 9

Nova Scotia Nurses' Union (NSNU)
30 Frazee Ave., Dartmouth NS B3B 1X4
Tel: 902-469-1474; *Fax:* 902-466-6935
Toll-Free: 800-469-1474
www.nsnu.ns.ca
twitter.com/TheNSNU
www.youtube.com/user/NSNursesUnion
Overview: A medium-sized provincial organization founded in 1976
Mission: To represent Registered Nurses & Licensed Practical Nurses working in acute and long term care, with the VON and Canadian Blood Services
Affliation(s): Canadian Nurses Association; Canadian Labour Congress; Canadian Federation of Nurses Unions
Chief Officer(s):
Jean Candy, Executive Director
jean.candy@nsnu.ns.ca
Janet Hazelton, President
janet.hazelton@nsnu.ns.ca
Staff Member(s): 17
Membership: 6,500; *Committees:* Executive; Personnel; AGM Operations & Nominations; Promotional Advisory; Constitution/Resolutions; Finance; Education

Nova Scotia Optometrical Society *See* Nova Scotia Association of Optometrists

Nova Scotia Pharmaceutical Society *See* Nova Scotia College of Pharmacists

Nova Scotia Physiotherapy Association (NSPA)
PO Box 31053, Halifax NS B3K 5T9
Tel: 902-405-6772
Toll-Free: 877-440-6772
info@physiotherapyns.ca
www.physiotherapyns.ca
Overview: A medium-sized provincial organization overseen by Canadian Physiotherapy Association
Mission: To provide leadership & direction to the physiotherapy profession; To foster excellence in practice, education & research
Member of: Canadian Physiotherapy Association
Chief Officer(s):
Darlene Cook, Executive Director
dcook@physiotherapyns.ca
Kate Grosweiner, President
president@physiotherapyns.ca
Finances: *Annual Operating Budget:* $100,000-$250,000; *Funding Sources:* Membership dues; Educational activities
Membership: *Fees:* Schedule available; $49.77-$512.70; *Committees:* Awards; Professional Development; Public Relations
Activities: *Awareness Events:* National Physiotherapy Month, April 20 - May 20

Nova Scotia Powerlifting Association
240 Cusack Dr., Sydney NS B1P 6A1
Tel: 902-567-0893
Overview: A small provincial licensing organization overseen by Canadian Powerlifting Union
Mission: To provide opportunities for lifters to learn the sport of powerlifting through seminars, gyms & clubs; to participate in meets locally, nationally & internationally
Member of: International Powerlifting Union
Chief Officer(s):
John Fraser, President
johnfraser56@hotmail.com
Membership: *Member Profile:* Novice; Junior; Master; Open; Special Olympian divisions; provincial, national & world calibre lifters
Activities: Lifters attend competitions on provincial, national & international levels & receive medallions or trophies according to placement; seminars given upon request

Nova Scotia Progressive Conservative Association
#603, 5151 George St., Halifax NS B3J 1M5
Tel: 902-429-9470; *Fax:* 902-423-2465
Toll-Free: 800-595-8779
www.pcparty.ns.ca
www.facebook.com/people/Jamie-Baillie/634725469
twitter.com/JamieBaillie
www.youtube.com/user/pcnovascotia
Also Known As: PC Party of Nova Scotia
Overview: A medium-sized provincial organization
Mission: The Progressive Conservative Association of Nova Scotia is one of the oldest political parties in the province, with a mission to form a fiscally responsible, socially progressive government. Jim David, Provincial Director
Chief Officer(s):
Jim David, Provincial Director
Jamie Baillie, Party Leader
JamieBaillie@gov.ns.ca
Finances: *Annual Operating Budget:* $250,000-$500,000; *Funding Sources:* Donations
Staff Member(s): 4; 25 volunteer(s)
Membership: 30,000+; *Fees:* $5-$10
Activities: *Speaker Service:* Yes; *Rents Mailing List:* Yes

Nova Scotia Prospectors Association (NSPA)
c/o 11 River Rd., Terrence Bay River ON B3T 1X2
www.prospectors.ns.ca
Overview: A medium-sized provincial organization founded in 1993
Mission: The Nova Scotia Prospectors Association was formed to foster prospecting at the professional and recreational level.
Chief Officer(s):
Lindsay Allen, President & Director
president@prospectors.ns.ca
Membership: *Fees:* $30 individual; $35 family; $10 student

Nova Scotia Provincial Literacy Coalition *See* Literacy Nova Scotia

Nova Scotia Public Interest Research Group (NSPIRG)
Student Union Building, Dalhousie University, #314, 6136 University Ave., Halifax NS B3H 4J2
Tel: 902-494-6662
Other Communication: board@nspirg.org
info@nspirg.org
www.nspirg.org
www.facebook.com/NSPIRG
twitter.com/NSPIRG_Dal
Overview: A medium-sized local organization
Mission: To link research with social justice & environmental action
Chief Officer(s):
Andrew Jantzen, Coordinator, Outreach & Administration
alia@nspirg.org
Alia Saied, Coordinator, Resources & Administration
andrew@nspirg.org
Finances: *Annual Operating Budget:* Less than $50,000
Membership: 5,000-14,999; *Fees:* $4; *Member Profile:* Dalhousie University students
Activities: *Speaker Service:* Yes; *Library:* Resource Library

Nova Scotia PWA Coalition *See* AIDS Coalition of Nova Scotia

Nova Scotia Real Estate Appraisers Association (NSREAA)
#602, 5670 Spring Garden Rd., Halifax NS B3J 1H6
Tel: 902-422-4077; *Fax:* 902-422-3717
nsreaa@nsappraisal.ns.ca
nsreaa.ca
Previous Name: Nova Scotia Association of the Appraisal Institute of Canada
Overview: A medium-sized provincial licensing organization overseen by Appraisal Institute of Canada
Mission: The Association regulates the practice of real estate appraisal in Nova Scotia, establishes & promotes the interests of appraisers, develops & maintains high standards of knowledge & best practices in the field, develops & enforces professional ethics, promotes public awareness of the profession, & encourages studies in real estate appraisal.
Chief Officer(s):
Phillip Smith, President
Carla Demsey, Vice-President
Davida Mackay, Executive Director & Registrar
Finances: *Annual Operating Budget:* $50,000-$100,000
Staff Member(s): 1; 12 volunteer(s)
Membership: 250; *Member Profile:* Appraisers; assessors; candidate members
Awards:
• Butler Education Award (Award)
• Nova Scotia Service Award (Award)

Nova Scotia Real Estate Association *See* Nova Scotia Association of REALTORS

Nova Scotia Real Estate Commission (NSREC)
7 Scarfe Ct., Dartmouth NS B3B 1W4
Tel: 902-468-3511; *Fax:* 902-468-1016
Toll-Free: 800-390-1015
info@nsrec.ns.ca
www.nsrec.ns.ca
Overview: A small provincial organization
Mission: To protect consumers by establishing standards for applicants and licensees in the real estate industry, which will promote higher standards of professionalism, competance and integrity.
Chief Officer(s):
Brad Chisholm, Registrar
bchisholm@nsrec.ns.ca

Nova Scotia Recreation Professionals in Health
c/o Alderwood Rest Home, PO Box 218, Baddeck NS B0V 1B0
Tel: 902-295-2644; *Fax:* 902-245-3000
www.nsrph.com
Overview: A small provincial organization founded in 1994
Mission: To allow for recreation professionals to communicate, network, & share concerns & ideas; To advocate for the necessity & benefits of recreation in the health care system
Chief Officer(s):
Charlotte Sabean, President
Charlottetr6@gmail.com
Wil Van Hal, Vice President, Communications
recreation@alderwoodbaddeck.ca
Finances: *Funding Sources:* Membership dues
Membership: *Fees:* $50

Nova Scotia Rifle Association (NSRA)
PO Box 482, Dartmouth NS B2Y 3Y8
Tel: 902-456-7468
nsrifle@ns.sympatico.ca
www.nsrifle.org
Overview: A small provincial organization founded in 1861
Mission: To promote & organize recreational shooting
Member of: Dominion of Canada Rifle Association
Affliation(s): Shooting Federation of Canada
Chief Officer(s):
Andy S. Webber, President
asw@tangenttheta.com
Dave G. Beaulieu, Secretary
Finances: *Annual Operating Budget:* Less than $50,000
12 volunteer(s)
Membership: 300; *Fees:* $285 senior; $20 junior under 19; *Member Profile:* Residents of the province with a valid firearm license

Nova Scotia Road Builders Association
#217, 11 Thornhill Dr., Dartmouth NS B3B 1R9
www.nsrba.ca
Overview: A medium-sized provincial organization founded in 1947 overseen by Canadian Construction Association
Mission: To speak for the heavy construction industry in Nova Scotia; to liaise with provincial Department of Transportation
Chief Officer(s):
Grant Feltmate, Executive Director, 902-499-7278, Fax: 902-876-1294
grant@nsrba.ca
Carol Ingraham, Office Manager
carol@nsrba.ca
Finances: *Annual Operating Budget:* $100,000-$250,000
Staff Member(s): 2
Membership: 140 member companies; *Fees:* $2,000-$10,000; *Committees:* Contracts & Specifications; Environment; Municipal Affairs; CCA/TRIP; Communications; TANS/Labour Relations; Rental Rates; Safety; Convention/Membership; Newsletter/Media & Website

Nova Scotia Rugby Football Union
5516 Spring Garden Rd., 4th Fl., Halifax NS B3J 1G6
Tel: 902-425-5450; *Fax:* 902-425-5606
rugby@sportnovascotia.ca
www.rugbyns.ns.ca
Also Known As: Rugby Nova Scotia
Overview: A small provincial organization founded in 1965 overseen by Rugby Canada
Mission: To promote, control, encourage & develop the game of rugby union football throughout Nova Scotia
Member of: Rugby Canada
Affliation(s): International Rugby Board
Chief Officer(s):
Geno Carew, President

Nova Scotia Safety Council; The Nova Scotia Highway Safety Council *See* Safety Services Nova Scotia

Nova Scotia Salmon Association (NSSA)
PO Box 396, Chester NS B0J 1J0
e-mail: info@nssalmon.ca
www.nssalmon.ca
Overview: A medium-sized provincial charitable organization founded in 1963 overseen by Atlantic Salmon Federation
Mission: To further the conservation & wise management of wild Atlantic salmon & trout
Member of: Atlantic Salmon Federation
Chief Officer(s):
Rene Aucoin, President
Finances: *Funding Sources:* Donations
Membership: *Fees:* $20; $5 junior; *Member Profile:* Individuals with an interest in the welfare of salmon & trout; Affiliate associations
Activities: Increasing public awareness; Offering educational activities; Conducting & supporting research; Administering programs, such as Adopt-A-Stream

Nova Scotia School Athletic Federation (NSSAF)
5516 Spring Garden Rd., Halifax NS B3J 1G6
Tel: 902-425-8662; *Fax:* 902-425-5606
nssaf.ednet.ns.ca
Overview: A small provincial organization overseen by School Sport Canada
Mission: Motto: "Education Through Sport" which thus emphasises the value of sport in relation to the multitude of benefits that participation gives to their students.
Member of: School Sport Canada
Chief Officer(s):
Darrell LeBlanc, Chair, Board of Governors
Darrell Dempster, Executive Director
Dianne Weston, Secretary
Staff Member(s): 3
Membership: 40,000 student athletes; *Member Profile:* Student atheletes and their affiliates including coaches, administrators, and officiates.

Nova Scotia School Boards Association (NSSBA) / Association des conseils scolaires de la Nouvelle-Écosse
#395, 3 Spectacle Lake Dr., Dartmouth NS B3B 1W8
Tel: 902-491-2888; *Fax:* 902-429-7405
www.nssba.ca
twitter.com/NSSchoolBoards
Overview: A medium-sized provincial organization founded in 1954 overseen by Canadian School Boards Association
Mission: To act as the voice for school boards in Nova Scotia; To strive towards excellence in public education for students in the province
Activities: Providing services to school boards such as bulk purchasing; Offering training opportunities; Advocating for school boards; Presenting awards; Providing information for school boards, parents, students, educators, journalists, & others;

Nova Scotia School Counsellor Association (NSSCA)
c/o Amherst Regional High School, 190 Willow St., Amherst NS B4H 3W5
Tel: 902-661-2540; *Fax:* 902-661-2535
local.nstu.ca/web/nssca
Overview: A small provincial organization founded in 1965
Affliation(s): Nova Scotia Teachers Union
Chief Officer(s):
Teri Cochrane, President
trcochrane@nstu.ca
Finances: *Annual Operating Budget:* Less than $50,000
Membership: 200; *Fees:* $20

Nova Scotia Securities Commission (NSSC)
Duke Tower, PO Box 458, #400, 5251 Duke St., Halifax NS B3J 2P8
Tel: 902-424-7768; *Fax:* 902-424-4625
nsscinquiries@novascotia.ca
nssc.novascotia.ca
twitter.com/NSSCommission
Overview: A medium-sized provincial organization overseen by Canadian Securities Administrators
Mission: To regulate securities trading in Nova Scotia, through the administration of the Securities Act; To report to the Legislature, through the minister responsible for the administration of the Securities Act; To foster a fair & competitive securities market; To protect investors & market integrity
Member of: Canadian Securities Administrators
Chief Officer(s):
Sarah Bradley, Chair
J. William Slattery, Executive Director
Finances: *Funding Sources:* Fees collected from market participants under the legislation
Publications:
• Annual Accountability Report
Type: Report; *Frequency:* Annually
• Nova Scotia Securities Commission Annual Report
Type: Report; *Frequency:* Annually
• Statement of Mandate
Type: Report; *Frequency:* Annually

Nova Scotia Shorthorn Association
1538 Millbrook Rd., RR#2, West River St. NS B0K 1Z0
Tel: 902-396-1937
Overview: A small provincial organization
Member of: Canadian Shorthorn Association
Chief Officer(s):
Adam Fraser, President
Kristy Fraser, Secretary

Nova Scotia Snowboard Association *See* Snowboard Nova Scotia

Nova Scotia Society for the Prevention of Cruelty to Animals (NS SPCA)
PO Box 38073, #200A - 11 Akerley Blvd., Dartmouth NS B3B 1X2
Tel: 902-835-4798; *Fax:* 902-835-7885
Toll-Free: 888-703-7722
outreach@spcans.ca

www.spcans.ca
www.facebook.com/nsspca
Also Known As: Nova Scotia SPCA
Overview: A medium-sized provincial charitable organization founded in 1877 overseen by Canadian Federation of Humane Societies
Mission: NS SPCA strives to prevent abuse & neglect of all animals in Nova Scotia. It provides leadership in humane education through outreach activities & adoption services. It also enforces laws on animal cruelty by issuing orders, warrants & laying charges. It is a registered charity, BN: 134704741RR0001.
Member of: Canadian Federation of Humane Societies
Chief Officer(s):
Sean Kelly, President
Kristan Williams, Executive Director
director@spcans.ca
Finances: *Annual Operating Budget:* $500,000-$1.5 Million; *Funding Sources:* Donations & bequests
Staff Member(s): 4; 3 volunteer(s)
Membership: 11 branches; *Fees:* $15 single; $30 family; *Committees:* Education; Finance; Fundraising; Investigations

Antigonish Branch
PO Box 1421, Antigonish NS B2G 2L2
Tel: 902-863-2111; *Fax:* 902-863-1229
antspca@eastlink.ca
www.antigonishspca.ca

Cape Breton Branch
400 East Broadway, Sydney NS B1P 6J1
Tel: 902-539-7722; *Fax:* 902-539-7391
cbspca@seasidehighspeed.com
www.capebretonspca.com

Colchester Branch
PO Box 914, Truro NS B2N 5G7
Tel: 902-893-7968; *Fax:* 902-895-6550
colchesterspca@hotmail.com
www.colchesterspca.ca

Hants Branch
PO Box 2274, Windsor NS B0N 2T0
Tel: 902-757-2000
hantsspca@gmail.com
www.hantscosp.ca

Kings Co. Branch
1285 County Home Rd., Waterville NS
Tel: 902-538-9075
kingscountyspca@yahoo.ca
www.kingsspca.com

La Baie Branch
PO Box 159, Saulnierville NS B0W 2Z0
Tel: 902-769-2589
labaiespca@hotmail.com
www.labaiespca.com

Lunenburg Branch
RR#1, Riverport NS B0J 2W0
Tel: 902-766-4787
www.purplepuppyproductions.com/spca

Metro Branch - Halifax
5 Scarfe Ct., Dartmouth NS B3B 1W4
Tel: 902-468-7877; *Fax:* 902-468-9761
info@metro.spcans.ca
www.metro.spcans.ca

Pictou Co. Branch
PO Box 786, New Glasgow NS B2H 5G2
Tel: 902-396-3595
pictoucountyspca@hotmail.com
www.pictoucountyspca.piczo.com

Queens Branch
PO Box 2012, Liverpool NS B0T 1K0
Tel: 902-350-2444
members.petfinder.org/~ns02/home.htm

Yarmouth Branch
PO Box 335, Yarmouth NS B5A 4B3
Tel: 902-742-9767
info@yarmouthspca.com
www.yarmouthspca.com

Nova Scotia Society of Occupational Therapists (NSSOT)

Halifax Shopping Centre, Box 11, #2132B, 6960 Mumford Rd., Halifax NS B3L 4P1
Toll-Free: 866-936-7768
nssot@bellaliant.com
www.nssot.ca
Overview: A small provincial organization
Mission: We strive for occupational therapy to be accessible & effective in order to maximize the independent living potential of all Nova Scotians despite disability or disadvantage; to promote development of occupational therapy practice through continuing education, support & advocacy of our members & their clients
Affliation(s): Canadian Association of Occupation Therapy
Chief Officer(s):
Anne Carswell, Executive Director
Jen Davis, President
Finances: *Annual Operating Budget:* Less than $50,000
Staff Member(s): 2; 10 volunteer(s)
Membership: 330; *Fees:* $75 practicing, $40 non-practicing; $10 student
Activities: *Awareness Events:* National Occupational Therapy Month, Oct.; *Speaker Service:* Yes

Nova Scotia Special Olympics *See* Special Olympics Nova Scotia

Nova Scotia Speed Skating Association *See* Speed Skate Nova Scotia

Nova Scotia Sport Heritage Centre *See* Novia Scotia Sports Hall of Fame

Nova Scotia Stamp Club (NSSC)

102 Birch Bear Run, Lewis Lake NS B3Z 4B8
e-mail: johneldridge@accesswave.ca
www.nsstampclub.ca
Overview: A small local organization founded in 1922
Mission: To promote awareness & enjoyment of the hobby of philately & provide a forum for discussion of topics related to philately for the advancement of members knowledge
Member of: American Philatelic Society
Affliation(s): Royal Philatelic Society of Canada
Chief Officer(s):
Keith MacKay, President
Marilyn Melanson, Treasurer
Finances: *Annual Operating Budget:* Less than $50,000
14 volunteer(s)
Membership: 120; *Fees:* $15 individual; $22.50 couple; $20 US; $25 international; *Member Profile:* Individuals 16 years of age & older; *Committees:* Executive; Membership
Activities: *Awareness Events:* NOVAPEX, Sept.; *Library:* NSSC Library
Publications:
• The Nova Scotia Post [a publication of the Nova Scotia Stamp Club]
Type: Newsletter; *Frequency:* Monthly

Nova Scotia Swordfish Association

#9, 155 Chainlake Dr., Halifax NS B3S 1B3
Tel: 902-737-4327; *Fax:* 902-457-4990
highliner@ns.sympatico.ca
Overview: A small provincial organization
Chief Officer(s):
George Rennehan, Vice-President

Nova Scotia Table Tennis Association (NSTTA)

9 Londra Ct., Dartmouth NS B2W 5A5
Tel: 902-406-6286
www.freewebs.com/nstta
Overview: A small provincial organization overseen by Table Tennis Canada
Member of: Table Tennis Canada
Affliation(s): International Table Tennis Federation
Chief Officer(s):
Erica Ans, President
eans@staff.ednet.ns.ca

Nova Scotia Teachers Association of Literacy & Learning (NSTALL)

c/o Wanda Fougere, East Antigonish Academy, 10128 Rte. #4, Monastery NS B0H 1W0
Tel: 902-232-2810
nstall.nstu.ca
Overview: A small provincial organization
Chief Officer(s):
Wanda Fougere, President
wmfougere@nstu.ca
Publications:
• NSTALL [Nova Scotia Teachers Association of Literacy & Learning] Newsletter
Editor: Tami Cox Jardine
• Salt Breezes & Fireflies [a publication of the Nova Scotia Teachers Association of Literacy & Learning]
Profile: An online publication collecting writings by Nova Scotia students.

Nova Scotia Teachers Union (NSTU) / Syndicat des enseignants de la Nouvelle-Écosse

Dr. Tom Parker Bldg., 3106 Joseph Howe Dr., Halifax NS B3L 4L7
Tel: 902-477-5621; *Fax:* 902-477-3517
Toll-Free: 800-565-6788
nstu@nstu.ca
www.nstu.ca
www.facebook.com/nsteachersunion
twitter.com/NSTeachersUnion
www.youtube.com/nstuwebcast
Overview: A medium-sized provincial organization founded in 1895 overseen by Canadian Teachers' Federation
Mission: To unify the teaching profession in Nova Scotia; To improve the quality of education
Affliation(s): Canadian Teachers' Federation
Chief Officer(s):
Alexis Allen, President
Finances: *Funding Sources:* Membership dues
Membership: 10,600; *Member Profile:* K-12 public school teachers; Atlantic Provinces Special Education Authority teachers; Nova Scotia Community College teachers; Professional support staff
Activities: Advocating on behalf of members; Promoting the teaching profession; Offering professional development opportunities; Conducting research; *Library:* Bruce Hunter Memorial Library;

Nova Scotia Tennis Association

5516 Spring Garden Rd., 4th Fl., Halifax NS B3J 1G6
Tel: 902-425-5454
tennisns@sportnovascotia.ca
www.tennisnovascotia.ca
Overview: A medium-sized provincial organization overseen by Tennis Canada
Mission: To promote & create opportunities for people to play tennis in Nova Scotia
Member of: Tennis Canada
Chief Officer(s):
Craig Bethune, President
Roger Keating, Executive Director
Kathy Russell, Contact, Communications
Staff Member(s): 2
Membership: *Member Profile:* Individuals & clubs

Nova Scotia Trails Federation (NSTF)

5516 Spring Garden Rd., 4th Fl., Halifax NS B3J 1G6
Tel: 902-425-5450; *Fax:* 902-425-5606
nstrails@sportnovascotia.ca
www.novascotiatrails.com
www.facebook.com/pages/Nova-Scotia-Trails-Federation/176318735774687
twitter.com/NSTrails
Overview: A large provincial organization
Mission: To promote the development and responsible use of recreational trails for the benefit and enjoyment of all Nova Scotians and visitors to our province.
Chief Officer(s):
Holly Woodill, President
Membership: 6000+; *Fees:* $200 group; $100 associate group; $20 individual
Publications:
• Trail Talk
Type: Newsletter

Nova Scotia Union of Public & Private Employees (CCU) (NSUPE) / Syndicat des employés du secteur public de la Nouvelle-Écosse (CCU)

#402A, 7020 Mumford Rd., Halifax NS B3L 4S9
Tel: 902-422-9495; *Fax:* 902-429-7655
www.nsupe.ca
Previous Name: Nova Scotia Union of Public Employees (CCU)
Overview: A medium-sized provincial organization founded in 1974
Mission: To better & protect the livelihood and the social and economic well-being of its members, their families and fellow citizens.
Affliation(s): Confederation of Canadian Unions; Atlantic Council of the Confederation of Canadian Unions
Chief Officer(s):
Joe Kaiser, President
Claudia MacFarlane, Vice-President
Finances: *Funding Sources:* Membership dues
Staff Member(s): 3
Membership: 2,000 + 10 locals; *Member Profile:* Professional; trade & technical; administrative; clerical

Nova Scotia Union of Public Employees (CCU) *See* Nova Scotia Union of Public & Private Employees (CCU)

Nova Scotia Veterinary Medical Association
15 Cobequid Rd., Lower Sackville NS B4C 2M9
Tel: 902-865-1876; *Fax:* 902-865-2001
info@nsvma.ca
www.nsvma.ca
Overview: A small provincial licensing organization overseen by Canadian Veterinary Medical Association
Mission: To license Nova Scotia veterinarians in small animal, large animal & mixed practice as well as those employed in government, industry or other institutions
Chief Officer(s):
Frank Richardson, Registrar
Rob Doucette, President
Finances: *Funding Sources:* Membership dues
Staff Member(s): 3
Membership: 317; *Fees:* Schedule available; *Member Profile:* Licensed to practice in Nova Scotia

Nova Scotia Water Ski Association (NSWSA)
PO Box 783, Dartmouth NS B2Y 3Z3
Other Communication: Alt. E-mail: admin@nswsa.com
nswsa@aol.com
www.nswsa.com
www.facebook.com/54546750606
Overview: A small provincial organization
Member of: Water Ski & Wakeboard Canada
Chief Officer(s):
Gary Allen, President
president@nswsa.com
12 volunteer(s)
Membership: 135; *Fees:* $15 single; $30 family

Nova Scotia Well Drillers Association *See* Nova Scotia Ground Water Association

Nova Scotia Wild Flora Society
c/o Nova Scotia Museum, 1747 Summer St., Halifax NS B3H 3A6
Tel: 902-423-7032
nswildflora@yahoo.ca
www.nswildflora.ca
Overview: A small provincial organization founded in 1990
Member of: Federation of Nova Scotia Naturalists
Affliation(s): Canadian Wildflower Society
Chief Officer(s):
Charles Cron, President
ccron72@hotmail.com
Heather Drope, Secretary-Treasurer
Finances: *Annual Operating Budget:* Less than $50,000; *Funding Sources:* Membership dues
2 volunteer(s)
Membership: 50; *Fees:* $15 individual; $20 family

Nova Scotia Wool Marketing Board
c/o Natural Products Marketing Council, NS Dept. of Agriculture, PO Box 190, Halifax NS B3J 2M4
Overview: A small provincial organization founded in 1943
Mission: To foster the production of high-quality wool in Nova Scotia, & the effective marketing of this product
3 volunteer(s)
Membership: 250 individual

Nova Scotia Yachting Association (NSYA)
5516 Spring Garden Rd., 4th Fl., Halifax NS B3J 1G6
Tel: 902-425-5450
nsya@sportnovascotia.ca
nsya.ns.ca
Overview: A small provincial organization overseen by Sail Canada
Mission: To regulate the sport of sailing in Nova Scotia
Member of: Sail Canada; Sport Nova Scotia
Affliation(s): Canadian Sport Centre
Chief Officer(s):
Frank Denis, Executive Director & Media Contact

Nova Scotia Youth Orchestra
6199 Chebucto Rd., Halifax NS B3L 1K7
Tel: 902-423-5984
nsyo@ns.sympatico.ca
www.novascotiayouthorchestra.com
www.facebook.com/novascotiayouthorchestra
Overview: A small provincial charitable organization founded in 1977 overseen by Orchestras Canada
Mission: To provide young musicians with the finest orchestral training; to provide live orchestral music to audiences in Nova Scotia
Chief Officer(s):
Dinuk Wijeratne, Music Director
Finances: *Funding Sources:* Government; private; corporate
Membership: 93; *Member Profile:* Musicians ages 12-22
Activities: Concerts; recitals; fundraising events; *Library*

Nova Scotian Institute of Science (NSIS)
Science Services, Killam Library, Dalhousie Univ., 6225 University Ave., Halifax NS B3H 4H8
Tel: 902-494-3621; *Fax:* 902-494-2062
nsis.chebucto.org
Overview: A medium-sized provincial organization founded in 1862
Mission: To provide a forum for scientists & those interested in science
Chief Officer(s):
Tom Rand, President
Patrick Ryall, Vice-President
Linda Marks, Secretary
Angelica Silva, Treasurer
Membership: *Fees:* $20 regular; $10 student; $300 life members; *Member Profile:* Individual with an amateur or professional interest in science
Activities: Conducting the NSIS Student Essay Competition; Providing a public lecture series; *Library:* Killam Library, Dalhousie University, Halifax, NS;

NovaKnowledge
Centennial Building, #201, 1660 Hollis Street, Halifax NS B3J 1V7
Tel: 902-494-1510; *Fax:* 902-494-8002
www.novaknowledge.ns.ca
www.linkedin.com/groups?gid=4451480
www.facebook.com/groups/6716604369
Overview: A small provincial organization
Chief Officer(s):
Tim Outhit, CEO
touthit@novaknowledge.ns.ca

Novia Scotia Sports Hall of Fame (NSSHF)
#446, 1800 Argyle St., Halifax NS B3J 3N8
Tel: 902-421-1266; *Fax:* 902-425-1148
sporthalloffame@eastlink.ca
www.novascotiasporthalloffame.com
www.linkedin.com/company/nova-scotia-sport-hall-of-fame
www.facebook.com/116064731766960
twitter.com/NSSHF
Previous Name: Nova Scotia Sport Heritage Centre
Overview: A small provincial organization founded in 1964
Chief Officer(s):
Don Mills, Chair
Bill Robinson, CEO
bill@nsshf.com
Staff Member(s): 5
Activities: *Awareness Events:* Golf Tournament, June; Bingo @ the Halifax Forum

NSERC Chair for Women in Science & Engineering
350 Albert St., Ottawa ON K1A 1H5
Tel: 613-944-6240; *Fax:* 613-996-2589
cwse-cfsg@nserc-crsng.gc.ca
www.nserc-crsng.gc.ca
Overview: A medium-sized national organization founded in 1996
Mission: To encourage women in Canada to enter careers in science, engineering, mathematics & computer sciences; to encourage women in Canada to attain high levels of professional achievement in these fields; to serve as an information centre for & about women in these fields; to make people aware of Canadian women scientists & engineers & of career opportunities available to them; to provide a forum for discussion of subjects of interest to members
Chief Officer(s):
Carolyn J. Emerson, Chair, Atlantic Region
Finances: *Annual Operating Budget:* Less than $50,000
Membership: 360; *Fees:* $250 corporate; $40 full; $25 associate; $10 student; $20 information (receives newsletter)
Activities: *Speaker Service:* Yes

British Columbia/Yukon
c/o Westcoast Women in Engineering, Science & Technology, #2054, 6250 Applied Science Ln., Vancouver BC V6T 1Z4
Tel: 604-822-6584; *Fax:* 604-822-2403
wwest@mech.ubc.ca
wwest.mech.ubc.ca
Chief Officer(s):
Jennifer Pelletier, Manager

Ontario
c/o Department of Mechanical Engineering, University of Ottawa, 161 Louis Pasteur, Ottawa ON K1N 6H5
e-mail: info@scieng-women-ontario.ca
scieng-women-ontario.ca
www.facebook.com/CWSE.ON
twitter.com/CWSE_ON
pinterest.com/cwseon
Chief Officer(s):
Cahterine Mavriplis, Chair

Prairie Region
c/o Fort Garry Campus of the University of Manitoba, Winnipeg MB R3T 2N2
cwse-prairies.ca
www.facebook.com/pages/CWSE-Prairies/122236287886586
Chief Officer(s):
Jackie Onagi, Chair, Prairie Region, 204-474-9556, Fax: 204-474-7644
Jacqueline.onagi@umanitoba.ca

WISE (Women in Science & Engineering) Newfoundland & Labrador
#293, 38 Pearson St., St. John's NL A1A 3R1
Tel: 709-864-2484
info@wisenl.ca
www.wisenl.ca
www.facebook.com/245047002313019
Mission: To increase female involvement in the science, technology, engineering & math fields
Chief Officer(s):
Gloria Montano, President

Nuclear Insurance Association of Canada (NIAC) / Association canadienne d'assurance nucléaire
#1600, 401 Bay St., Toronto ON M5H 2Y4
Tel: 416-646-6232; *Fax:* 905-771-5312
www.niac.biz
Overview: A small national organization founded in 1958
Mission: NIAC is a voluntary, non-profit association of insurers. Members may provide insurance protection by participation in property and liability pools; the association underwrites and accepts nuclear risks located within Canadian territorial limits for Nuclear Liability and Physical Damage (liability &/or property insurance)
Member of: Canadian Nuclear Association
Chief Officer(s):
Colleen P. DeMerchant, Manager
colleen@niac.biz
Staff Member(s): 3

Numeris
1500 Don Mills Rd., 3rd Fl., Toronto ON M3B 3L7
Tel: 416-445-9800; *Fax:* 416-445-8644
Other Communication: Human Resources e-mail: hrrecruitment@bbm.ca
en.numeris.ca
Previous Name: BBM Bureau of Measurement; Bureau of Broadcast Measurement; BBM Canada
Overview: A large national organization founded in 1944
Mission: To provide broadcast measurement & consumer behaviour data to broadcasters, advertisers, & agencies
Chief Officer(s):
Jim MacLeod, President & CEO
Glen Shipp, Executive Vice-President & CFO
Lisa Eaton, Senior Vice-President, Member Engagement
Anna Giagkou, Vice-President, Finance
Ricardo Gomez-Insausti, Vice-President, Research
Jane Hill, Vice-President, Operations
Randy Missen, Vice-President, Technical Implementation
Dorena Quinn, Vice-President, Human Resources & Corporate Services
Finances: *Funding Sources:* Membership fees
Membership: 1,600 organizations; *Member Profile:* Licensed radio/TV broadcasters; Advertisers; Agencies
Activities: Surveys, reports & guides

Moncton Office
#2000, 1222 Main St., Moncton NB E1C 1H6
Tel: 506-859-7700; *Fax:* 506-852-4445

Montréal Office
2055, rue Peel, 11ième étage, Montréal QC H3A 1V4
Tél: 514-878-9711; *Téléc:* 514-878-4210

Chief Officer(s):
Robert Langlois, Vice-President, Eastern Region
Western Office
#208, 10991 Shellbridge Way, Richmond BC V6X 3C6
Tel: 604-248-0770; *Fax:* 604-214-9648
Chief Officer(s):
Catherine Kelly, Vice-President, Western Region

Nunasi Corporation

#301, 5109 - 48th St., Yellowknife NT X1A 1N5
Tel: 867-920-4587; *Fax:* 867-920-4592
reception@nunasi.com
www.nunasi.com
www.facebook.com/404280886308303
twitter.com/nunasicorp
Overview: A small local organization founded in 1976
Mission: Nunasi Corporation is a birthright development corporation wholly-owned by its shareholders which are all Inuit enrolled as beneficiaries under the Nunavut Land Claim Agreement
Chief Officer(s):
Archie Angnakak, CEO, 867-979-2175
archie@nunasi.com

Nunavummi Disabilities Makinnasuaqtiit Society (NDMS) / Société Nunavummi Disabilities Makinnasuaqtiit

PO Box 4212, #105, 8 Storey Bldg., Iqaluit NU X0A 1H0
Tel: 867-979-2228; *Fax:* 867-979-2293
Toll-Free: 877-354-0916
ndms@qiniq.com
www.nuability.ca
Also Known As: Nunavut Disability Society
Overview: A small provincial organization overseen by Canadian Association for Community Living
Mission: To improve the quality of life for people with disabilities in Nunavut through encouragement, advocation & promotion of opportunities.
Member of: Canadian Association for Community Living

Nunavut Arts & Crafts Association (NACA)

PO Box 1539, Iqaluit NU X0A 0H0
Tel: 867-979-7808; *Fax:* 867-979-6880
Toll-Free: 866-979-7808
r.house@nacaarts.org
www.nacaarts.org
Overview: A medium-sized provincial organization
Mission: To promote the growth & appreciation of Nunavut artists & the production of arts & crafts
Chief Officer(s):
Jerry Ell, Chairman, 867-979-4483
jell@northwesttel.ca
Membership: *Fees:* free for artists, $50 organization

Nunavut Curling Association (NCA)

PO Box 413, Rankin Inlet NU X0C 0G0
Tel: 867-645-2534
Overview: A small provincial organization overseen by Canadian Curling Association

Nunavut Economic Developers Association (NEDA)

PO Box 1990, 1104B Inuksugait Plaza, Phase II, Iqaluit NU X0A 0H0
Tel: 867-979-4620; *Fax:* 867-979-4622
info@nunavuteda.com
www.nunavuteda.com
www.facebook.com/pages/NEDA/170058311362?v=wall
Overview: A small provincial organization founded in 2000
Chief Officer(s):
Mark Morrissey, Executive Director
exdir@nunavuteda.com
Finances: *Annual Operating Budget:* $50,000-$100,000
Staff Member(s): 1; 50 volunteer(s)
Membership: *Fees:* $50 individual associate; $100 institutional associate

Nunavut Employees Union (NEU)

PO Box 869, Iqaluit NU X0A 0H0
Tel: 867-979-4209; *Fax:* 867-979-4522
Toll-Free: 877-243-4424
reception@neu.ca
www.neu.ca
Overview: A small provincial organization founded in 1999 overseen by Public Service Alliance of Canada (CLC)
Mission: The Nunavut Employees Union represents the interests of the employees of the Government of Nunavut, the Northwest Territories Power Corporation who live in Nunavut, Workers Compensation Board in Nunavut, Nunavut Housing Corporation, and the unionized employees of Nunavut municipalities and Housing Associations. Most of our members work for the Government of Nunavut and live all across the territory. Others belong to Canada Labour Code bargaining units representing Housing Associations and Authorities, Hamlet and town employees, and support staff in schools. NEU members are social workers and nurses, health care professionals, power plant workers, security guards, hamlet bylaw officers, renewable resource officers, engineers, and many more.
Chief Officer(s):
Bill Fennell, President
bill@neu.ca
Brian Boutilier, Executive Director
brian@neu.ca
Staff Member(s): 5
Membership: *Member Profile:* Territorial employees

Nunavut Harvesters Association (NHA)

c/o Brian Zawadski, PO Box 249, Rankin Inlet NU X0C 0G0
Tel: 867-645-3170; *Fax:* 867-645-3755
www.harvesters.nu.ca
Overview: A small provincial organization
Mission: To develop & promote the sustainable harvesting of natural resources & wildlife in Nunavut
Chief Officer(s):
Brian Zawadski, Executive Director, 867-645-3170
brian@ndcorp.nu.ca
Activities: Promoting conservation of wildlife & natural resources in Nunavut; Administering & delivering the Agriculture & Agri-Food Canada program, entitled Advancing Canadian Agriculture & Agri-Food;

Nunavut Library Association (NLA)

PO Box 1321, Iqaluit NT X0A 0H0
e-mail: info@nunavutlibraryassociation.ca
www.nunavutlibraryassociation.ca
Overview: A small provincial organization
Mission: To support persons who work in Nunavut libraries; To advocatefor excellent library services for Nunavut; To promote library services & literacy; To provide professional development for members.
Membership: *Member Profile:* Anyone who serves residents of Nunavut and is interested in our work with library issues, regardless of geographic location.

Nunavut Securities Office

Brown Bldg., 1st Fl., PO Box 1000, Stn. 570, Iqaluit NU X0A 0H0
Other Communication: Alt. E-mail: securities@nulegalregistries.ca
securities@gov.nu.ca
nunavutlegalregistries.ca/sr_index_en.shtml
Overview: A medium-sized provincial organization overseen by Canadian Securities Administrators
Mission: To govern the sale & trading of securities in Nunavut
Member of: Canadian Securities Administrators

Nunavut Speed Skating Association

PO Box 761, 563 Suputi St., Iqaluit NU X0A 0H0
Tel: 867-979-1226; *Fax:* 867-975-3384
www.nunavutspeedskating.ca
Overview: A small provincial organization overseen by Speed Skating Canada
Member of: Speed Skating Canada
Chief Officer(s):
John Maurice, President
jtmaurice@northwestel.net

Nunavut Teachers Association (NTA)

PO Box 2458, Iqaluit NU X0A 0H0
Tel: 867-979-0750; *Fax:* 867-979-0780
piadmin@ntanu.ca
www.ntanu.ca
Previous Name: Federation of Nunavut Teachers
Overview: A small provincial organization overseen by Canadian Teachers' Federation
Mission: The Nunavut Teachers Association, or NTA, is the negotiating and representative organization for teachers, vice-principals, principals, and RSO and TLC coordinators in Nunavut.
Chief Officer(s):
Terry Young, President
Terry@ntanu.ca
Emile Hatch, Executive Director
emile@ntanu.ca
Membership: *Member Profile:* Teachers; principals; vice-principals in Nunavut

Nunavut Teachers' Association (NTA)

PO Box 2458, Iqaluit NU X0A 0H0
Tel: 867-979-0750; *Fax:* 867-979-0780
www.ntanu.ca
Overview: A small provincial organization founded in 1997
Mission: To represent & negotiate for teachers, vice-principals, & principals, as well as RSO & TLC coordinators in Nunavut; To ensure that members' rights & benefits are advocated & protected
Chief Officer(s):
Terry Young, President
Terry@ntanu.ca
Emile Hatch, Executive Director, 867-222-1275
emile@ntanu.ca
Shannon Hessian, Coordinator, Professional Improvement
Shannon@ntanu.ca
Membership: *Member Profile:* Teachers, vice-principals, & principals, as well as RSO & TLC coordinators in Nunavut; *Committees:* Inuit Educators; Collective Bargaining; Curriculum Support; Discipline; Finance; Legislation; Professional Relations; Professional Improvement; Public Relations; Status of Women; Finance; Health & Safety; Discipline
Publications:
• NunaTeach News
Type: Newsletter
Profile: Executive reports, regional news, & committee news

Nunavut Tourism

PO Box 1450, Iqaluit NU X0A 0H0
Toll-Free: 866-686-2888
info@nunavuttourism.com
www.nunavuttourism.com
www.facebook.com/nunavuttourism
twitter.com/NunavutTourism
www.youtube.com/nunavuttourism
Overview: A small provincial organization founded in 1995
Mission: To represent the tourism industry for the private sector in Nunavut; to promote & market Nunavut tourism products
Member of: Tourism Industry Association of Canada
Affliation(s): Team Canada
Finances: *Funding Sources:* Territorial government; industry partners
Membership: *Member Profile:* Outfitters; accommodation providers; tour operators
Activities: To encourage tourism development by providing knowledge & expertise in: marketing, research, industry development, training, & visitor services
Awards:
• Tourism Operator of the Year (Award)

Nuns' Island Tenants Association *Voir* Association des locataires de l'×le-des-Soeurs

Nurse Practitioners Association of Alberta (NPAA)

PO Box 9015, Stn. Aspen Glen, 2 Aspen Glen Dr., Spruce Grove AB T7X 4H5
www.albertanps.com
www.facebook.com/131524033527571
twitter.com/NPalberta
Overview: A small provincial organization
Mission: To develop an evidence based, flexible, & integrated practice for nurse practitioners in Alberta; To support the full scope of the nurse practitioner practice in Alberta, to ensure accessible, efficient, & effective health care system
Chief Officer(s):
Daris Klemmer, Interim President
president@albertanps.com
Jolene Medynski, Interim Treasurer
treasurer@albertanps.com
Membership: *Fees:* $45 students & associate & out of province members; $100 / year, regular members; *Member Profile:* Nurse practitioners who are registered with the CARNA; Registered nurses who are committed to the advancement of the nurse practitioner role; Students who are registered full time in nurse practitioner programa; *Committees:* Communication; Education; Advocacy
Activities: Engaging in advocacy activities to support nurse practitioners; Offering networking opportunities; Facilitating educational & research opportunities; Providing education to the public, other health care professionals, & the government about the role of nurse practitioners

Nurse Practitioners of Saskatchewan (NPOS)
c/o Kelly Hughes RN(NP), 69 Red River Rd., Saskatoon SK S7K 1G2
e-mail: npos@npos.ca
www.npos.ca
Overview: A small provincial organization
Mission: To raise awareness of the roles of the nurse practitioners in Saskatchewan; To develop the role & scope of practice of nurse practitioners; To promote established standards of nursing practice for nurse practitioners
Affliation(s): Saskatchewan Registered Nurses' Association; Canadian Association of Advanced Practice Nurses (CAAPN)
Chief Officer(s):
Mary Ellen Andrews, Chair
me.andrews@usask.ca
Finances: *Funding Sources:* Membership fees; Sponsorships
Membership: *Member Profile:* Nurse practitioners who are part of the Saskatchewan health care system; Registered nurses who are interested in advanced nursing practice, or who work with nurse practitioners; Students in nurse practitioner programs
Activities: Exchanging information related to the role of the nurse practitioners; Supporting research to improve nursing practice;
Meetings/Conferences: • 11th Annual Saskatchewan Nurse Practitioner Conference, 2015
Scope: Provincial
Publications:
• Nurse Practitioners of Saskatchewan Newsletter
Type: Newsletter; *Frequency:* Quarterly

Nurse Practitioners' Association of Nova Scotia (NPANS)
c/o Lynn Miller, 1440 Gulf Shore Rd., RR#4, Pugwash NS B0K 1L0
www.npans.ca
Overview: A small provincial organization
Mission: To promote the practice of nurse practitioners throughout Nova Scotia; To support nurse practitioners in various settings; To advocate for nurse practitioner integration & healthcare access
Affliation(s): College of Registered Nurses of Nova Scotia
Chief Officer(s):
Jennifer Forrest, Co-Chair
Dawn Lowe, Co-Chair
Membership: *Fees:* $50 students; $80 regular members (includes membership in the Canadian Association of Advanced Practice Nurses); *Member Profile:* Nurse practitioners throughout Nova Scotia; Students enrolled in a nurse practitioner program
Activities: Facilitating exchange of practice experiences among nurse practitioners; Offering continuing education opportunities for nurse practitioners throughout Nova Scotia; Educating the public regarding the work of nurse practitioners

Nurse Practitioners' Association of Ontario (NPAO)
#1801, 1 Yonge St., Toronto ON M5E 1W7
Tel: 416-593-9779; *Fax:* 416-369-0515
admin@npao.org
www.npao.org
www.facebook.com/NursePractitionersAssociationofOntario
twitter.com/NPAO2
Overview: A small provincial organization founded in 1973
Mission: To represent nurse practitioners in Ontario
Chief Officer(s):
Theresa Agnew, Executive Director
tagnew@npao.org
Tannice Fletcher-Stackhouse, President
tfletcher-stackhouse@npao.org
Wendy McKay, President-Elect
rmckay12@cogeco.ca
Membership: 1500+; *Fees:* Schedule available
Awards:
• Jerry Gerow Nurse Practitioner Leadership Award (Award)
Amount: $1500.00
• AstraZeneca Award for Innovation in Chronic Disease Management (Award)
Amount: $5000.00
• NPAO Member Bursary (Scholarship)
Amount: $1000.00
• NPAO President's Award (Award)
Amount: $1500.00
• Pfizer Consumer Healthcare Bursary (Scholarship)
Amount: $1500.00
• Pfizer Award for Clinical Excellence (Award)
Amount: $2500.00
• Huronia Nurse Practitioner Network Bursary (Scholarship)
Amount: $1500.00
Meetings/Conferences: • Nurse Practitioners' Association of Ontario Annual Conference 2015, 2015, ON
Scope: Provincial

Nursery School Teachers Association *See* Association of Early Childhood Educators of Quebec

Nursery Sod Growers' Association of Ontario
PO Box 25045, Guelph ON N1G 4T4
Tel: 519-265-6742; *Fax:* 519-265-8873
nsga@rogers.com
www.nsgao.com
Overview: A small provincial organization founded in 1960
Mission: The main objectives of the association are to develop and maintain high standards of turfgrass sod quality, to stimulate consumer knowledge of quality turfgrass sod, to work in close co-operation with allied professions to the benefit of consumer and trade alike, and to gather, analyse and disseminate information of general interest to the public, governmental agencies and other organizations.
Chief Officer(s):
Greg Skotnicki, President

Nurses Association of New Brunswick (NANB) / Association des infirmières et infirmiers du Nouveau-Brunswick (AIINB)
165 Regent St., Fredericton NB E3B 7B4
Tel: 506-458-8731; *Fax:* 506-459-2838
Toll-Free: 800-442-4417
www.nanb.nb.ca
Overview: A medium-sized provincial licensing organization founded in 1916
Mission: To act as the professional voice & regulatory body of nursing in New Brunswick; To protect the public by maintaining standards for nursing education & practice
Member of: Canadian Nurses Association (CNA)
Chief Officer(s):
France Marquis, President
president@nanb.nb.ca
Roxanne Tarjan, Executive Director
rtarjan@nanb.nb.ca
Finances: *Funding Sources:* Membership fees
Membership: 8,700
Activities: Registering nurses in New Brunswick in accordance with the 1984 Nurses Act; Advocating for public policy; Offering professional liability protection; Providing continuing education; Preventing undesirable practice; Intervening with unacceptable practice; Presenting awards

Nursing Home Association of Prince Edward Island
c/o Whisperwood Villa, 160 St. Peters Rd., Charlottetown PE C1A 5P8
Tel: 902-566-5556; *Fax:* 902-566-5222
Overview: A small provincial organization
Chief Officer(s):
Ray Brow, Contact
4 volunteer(s)
Membership: 9 institutional

NWT Boardsport Association
PO Box 11089, Yellowknife NT X1A 3X7
Tel: 867-669-8326; *Fax:* 867-669-8327
Toll-Free: 800-661-0797
www.nwtboardsport.ca
Overview: A small provincial organization overseen by Canadian Snowboard Federation
Mission: To be the governing body of competitive boardsports in the Northwest Territories.
Member of: Canadian Snowboard Federation; Sport North Federation
Chief Officer(s):
Louise Dundas-Mathews, President
Justin Mager, Coach & Technical Director

NWT Disabilities Council (NWTCPD)
B-321 Old Airport Rd., Yellowknife NT X1A 3T3
Tel: 867-873-8230; *Fax:* 867-873-4124
Toll-Free: 800-491-8885
admin@nwtdc.net
www.nwtability.ca
www.facebook.com/436138019806132
Previous Name: Northwest Territories Council for the Disabled; NWT Council for Disabled Persons
Overview: A medium-sized provincial charitable organization founded in 1978
Mission: To encourage & support the self-determination of people with disabilities
Affliation(s): Council of Canadians with Disabilities
Chief Officer(s):
Denise McKee, Executive Director
ed@nwtdc.net
Staff Member(s): 8
Membership: *Member Profile:* Persons with disabilities or committed to disability issues
Activities: Celebrity Auction & Ability Cup; *Speaker Service:* Yes; *Library* Open to public

NWT School Athletic Federation (NWTSAF)
PO Box 266, Fort Smith NT X0E 0P0
www.nwtsaf.com
Overview: A medium-sized provincial organization overseen by School Sport Canada
Member of: School Sport Canada
Affliation(s): Canadian School Sport Federation; Sport North
Chief Officer(s):
Fraser Oliver, President, 867-873-4888
fraser_oliver@mail.ycs.nt.ca
Kelly Webster, Vice-President, 867-874-6538
kwebster66@bdec.learnnet.nt.ca
Richard Daitch, Executive Director, 867-872-2334
rwdaitch@yahoo.com
Activities: Regional tournaments

NWT Seniors' Society (NWTSS)
#102, 4916 - 46th Ave., Yellowknife NT X1A 1L2
Tel: 867-920-7444; *Fax:* 867-920-7601
Toll-Free: 800-661-0878
seniors@yk.com
www.nwtseniorssociety.ca
www.facebook.com/nwtseniorssociety
twitter.com/NWTSeniors
Overview: A small provincial organization
Mission: To promote the independence & well-being of older citizens through the provision of programs & services in partnership with responsible government & other organizations; to serve as a consulting body & advocate for the elderly
Member of: Yukon Council on Aging; Alberta Council on Aging; Saskatchewan Council on Aging
Chief Officer(s):
Barbara Hood, Executive Director
Leon Peterson, President
Finances: *Funding Sources:* Territorial government; Federal funding; Raffle; Bingo
Membership: *Member Profile:* 50+ age group
Activities: 1-800 Seniors Information Line; Resource library; Advisory council; Workshops; *Awareness Events:* Intergenerational Day, June 1; World Elder Sbuse Awareness Day, June 15; Senior Citizens' Month, June; *Library* Open to public

NWT Softball
PO Box 11089, Yellowknife NT X1A 3X7
Tel: 867-669-8339; *Fax:* 867-669-8327
Toll-Free: 800-661-0797
www.nwtsoftball.ca
Overview: A small provincial organization overseen by Canadian Amateur Softball Association
Mission: To be responsible for fastpitch, minor ball & slo-pitch softball in the Northwest Territories.
Member of: Canadian Amateur Softball Association
Chief Officer(s):
James McCarthy, President
kingsting55@hotmail.com
Kyle Kruger, Executive Director
edcurlingsoftball@sportnorth.com

NWT Speed Skating Association
PO Box 2664, Yellowknife NT X1A 2P9
www.nwtspeedskating.ca
Overview: A small provincial organization overseen by Speed Skating Canada
Mission: To promote the sport of speed skating in the NWT
Member of: Sport North Federation; Speed Skating Canada
Chief Officer(s):
Pam Dunbar, President
Finances: *Annual Operating Budget:* Less than $50,000
40 volunteer(s)
Membership: 140

NWT Squash
NT
www.nwtsquash.com

Overview: A small provincial organization overseen by Squash Canada
Mission: To develop & provide squash programs to athletes of all ages in the Northwest Territories.
Member of: Squash Canada
Chief Officer(s):
Al Cook, President
Damien Healy, Secretary

O Vertigo Danse
175, rue Sainte-Catherine ouest, Montréal QC H2X 1Z8
Tél: 514-251-9177; *Téléc:* 514-251-7358
info@overtigo.com
www.overtigo.com
Aperçu: *Dimension:* petite; *Envergure:* locale; Organisme sans but lucratif; fondée en 1985
Mission: Se consacre à la création en nouvelle danse et la diffusion des oeuvres de la fondatrice et directrice artistique de la compagnie
Membre(s) du bureau directeur:
Diane Boucher, Directrice générale
Ginette Laurin, Directrice générale
Finances: *Budget de fonctionnement annuel:* $500,000-$1.5 Million
Membre(s) du personnel: 17
Activités: *Stagiaires:* Oui; *Listes de destinataires:* Oui

O'Keefe Ranch & Interior Heritage Society
PO Box 955, Vernon BC V1T 6M8
Tel: 250-542-7868
info@okeeferanch.ca
www.okeeferanch.ca
www.facebook.com/HistoricOkeefeRanch
twitter.com/okeeferanchca
Also Known As: Historic O'Keefe Ranch
Overview: A small local charitable organization founded in 1977
Mission: Preservation & presentation of the rural history of the North Okanagan
Affiliation(s): BC Museums Association
Finances: *Funding Sources:* Municipal government; provincial Arts Board
Activities: *Rents Mailing List:* Yes; *Library:* O'Keefe Ranch Archives; Open to public by appointment

Oak Ridges Moraine Foundation (ORMF)
120 Bayview Pkwy., Newmarket ON L3Y 4X1
Tel: 289-279-5733
support@ormf.com
www.ormf.com
twitter.com/ormoraine
Overview: A medium-sized local organization
Mission: To provide support and encouragement for activities that preserve, protect, and restore the environmental integrity of the Oak Ridges Moraine and support a trail along it.
Chief Officer(s):
Michele Donnelly, Senior Administrative Assistant
Staff Member(s): 1

Oak Ridges Trail Association (ORTA)
PO Box 28544, Aurora ON L4G 6S6
Tel: 905-833-6600; *Fax:* 905-833-8379
Toll-Free: 877-319-0285
info@oakridgestrail.org
www.oakridgestrail.org
www.facebook.com/group.php?gId=21365674512
Previous Name: Citizens for an Oak Ridges Trail
Overview: A medium-sized local organization founded in 1992
Mission: To develop a trail across the Oak Ridges moraine linking the Bruce Trail in the west to the Northumberland Forest in the east
Member of: Hike Ontario
Chief Officer(s):
Michele Donnelly, Office Manager
Finances: *Annual Operating Budget:* Less than $50,000
20 volunteer(s)
Membership: 800+; *Fees:* $30 individual/family; $20 student; $450 lifetime
Activities: *Awareness Events:* Hike Ontario Day, 1st Sunday Oct.; The Annual Moraine For Life Adventure Relay, June

Oakville & District Chamber of Commerce
PO Box 263, Oakville MB R0H 0Y0
Tel: 204-267-2730; *Fax:* 888-552-9910
oakvillechamberoffice@gmail.com
Overview: A small local organization
Chief Officer(s):
Kam Blight, President
Barb Ingram, Contact
bingram@mts.net

Oakville & District Humane Society *See* Oakville & Milton Humane Society

Oakville & Milton Humane Society
445 Cornwall Rd., Oakville ON L6J 7S8
Tel: 905-845-1551; *Fax:* 905-845-1973
shelter@omhs.ca
omhs.ca
www.facebook.com/OakvilleMiltonHumaneSociety
twitter.com/OakvilleHumane
www.youtube.com/user/oakvillehumane
Previous Name: Oakville & District Humane Society
Overview: A small local charitable organization founded in 1936
Mission: To promote the human/animal bond & relationship; to assist animals which are sick, have been injured, abused, sick, or abandoned, or are in need of rescue; to legally investigate & prosecute on the animals' behalf; to assist in finding suitable homes for unclaimed stray animals & to assist owners in finding their animals which have strayed or become lost; to construct, equip & maintain places for the reception & care of sick, injured or straying animals & for the humane destruction of unwanted animals.
Member of: Canadian Federation of Humane Societies
Affliation(s): Ontario Society for the Prevention of Cruelty to Animals
Chief Officer(s):
Jacqui Gerrard, Chair
board@omhs.ca
Kim Millan, Interim Executive Director
exec.director@omhs.ca
Finances: *Annual Operating Budget:* $500,000-$1.5 Million
Staff Member(s): 40; 140 volunteer(s)
Membership: 2,000; *Fees:* $25 single; $40 family; $150 life
Activities: *Awareness Events:* Be Kind to Animals Month, May; *Library* Open to public

Oakville Art Society
560 Bronte Rd., Oakville ON L6L 6S1
Tel: 905-827-5711; *Fax:* 905-827-3835
info@oakvilleartsociety.com
www.oakvilleartsociety.com
www.facebook.com/pages/Oakville-Art-Society/322766561303
Overview: A small local organization
Chief Officer(s):
Brenda Smith, President
Paul Musiol, Director of Facility
Membership: *Fees:* $50 adult; $65 family; $35 student/seniors

Oakville Arts Council (OAC)
120 Navy St., Oakville ON L6J 2Z4
Tel: 905-815-5977; *Fax:* 905-815-2024
artscouncil@oakville.ca
www.oakvillearts.com
Overview: A medium-sized local charitable organization founded in 1978
Mission: To promote & encourage the development of arts organizations & activities in the town of Oakville
Member of: Community Arts Ontario
Chief Officer(s):
Megan Whittington, Executive Director
mwhittington@oakville.ca
Finances: *Annual Operating Budget:* $250,000-$500,000; *Funding Sources:* 40% fundraising; 35% government grants; 25% revenue
Staff Member(s): 4; 60 volunteer(s)
Membership: 500; *Fees:* $35 individual; $15 student; $100 group; $125 business; *Committees:* Cultural Grants; Finance; Mayor's Awards; Artworks; Membership; Fundraising
Activities: Art Works; members' centre; skills training workshops; administrative support; Cultural Grants Advisory; municipal arts advisory; Mayor's Awards for Business & the Arts; Film Festival; Festival for Fibre Arts; *Internships:* Yes; *Speaker Service:* Yes; *Library:* Resource Centre; Open to public

Oakville Chamber Ensemble *See* Oakville Chamber Orchestra

Oakville Chamber of Commerce
#200, 700 Kerr St., Oakville ON L6K 3W5
Tel: 905-845-6613; *Fax:* 905-845-6475
info@oakvillechamber.com
www.oakvillechamber.com
www.linkedin.com/company/3527781
www.facebook.com/oakvillechamber
twitter.com/OakvilleChamber
instagram.com/oakvillechamber
Overview: A small local organization founded in 1953
Mission: To provide leadership for the business community in general & its members in particular by: communicating its views regarding economic development in a timely, informed & effective way; acting as a strong business advocate supporting sound government policies which promote economic development & business opportunities in the Oakville area; providing networking opportunities for its primary stakeholders to sustain & develop business; promoting partnership among its stakeholders & fostering community involvement.
Member of: Canadian Chamber of Commerce
Affliation(s): Ontario Chamber of Commerce; Burlington Chamber of Commerce; Milton Chamber of Commerce; Halton Hills Chamber of Commerce; AmCham; Bronte Village Business Improvement Area; Downtown Oakville Business Improvement Area; Kerr Village Business Improvement Area
Chief Officer(s):
John Sawyer, President
johnsawyer@oakvillechamber.com
Staff Member(s): 8
Membership: *Fees:* Schedule available based on number of employees in a company; *Committees:* Executive; Nominating; Government Relations & Advocacy; Golf; Small Business Week; Good Morning Oakville

Oakville Chamber Orchestra
PO Box 76036, 1500 Upper Middle Rd. West, Oakville ON L6M 3H5
Tel: 905-483-6787
mail@oakvillechamber.org
www.oakvillechamber.org
www.linkedin.com/company/oakville-chamber-orchestra
www.facebook.com/oakvillemusic
twitter.com/oakvillemusic
www.youtube.com/user/oakvillemusic
Previous Name: Oakville Chamber Ensemble
Overview: A small local organization founded in 1984 overseen by Orchestras Canada
Chief Officer(s):
Bob Wong, President
Charles Demuynck, Music Director

Oakville Community Centre for Peace, Ecology & Human Rights
PO Box 52007, Oakville ON L6J 7N5
Tel: 905-849-5501
info@oakvillepeacecentre.org
www.oakvillepeacecentre.org
Overview: A small local organization
Chief Officer(s):
Stephen Dankowich, Executive Director

Oakville Distress Centre
PO Box 776, Oakville ON L6J 5C1
Tel: 905-849-4559; *Crisis Hot-Line:* 905-849-4541
info@distresscentreoakville.com
www.distresscentreoakville.com
www.linkedin.com/company/distress-centre-oakville
www.facebook.com/DistressCentreOakville
twitter.com/DCOakville
Overview: A small local charitable organization founded in 1974 overseen by Distress Centres Ontario
Mission: To provide a confidential listening, befriending & crisis intervention telephone service for people in Oakville, Milton & surrounding areas; to provide outreach programmes to serve the changing needs of the community, includes suicide prevention & programs for youth; the training & experience given to our volunteers provides them with valuable communication skills, personal growth & satisfaction of helping & serving others
Finances: *Funding Sources:* United Way; Donations

Oakville Historical Society
PO Box 69501, 109 Thomas St., Oakville ON L6J 7R4
Tel: 905-844-2695; *Fax:* 905-844-7380
info@oakvillehistory.org
www.oakvillehistory.org
Overview: A small local organization founded in 1953
Mission: To preserve & promote the historical heritage of the area now making up the Town of Oakville
Chief Officer(s):
George Chisholm, President
pres@oakvillehistory.org
Membership: *Fees:* $25 individual; $15 student; $20 senior; $35 family/institution; $100 corporate

Canadian Associations

Oakville Symphony Orchestra (OSO)
#310, 200 North Service Rd. West, Oakville ON L6M 2Y1
Tel: 905-338-1462; *Fax:* 905-338-7954
oakville.symphony@cogeco.ca
www.oakvillesymphony.com
www.facebook.com/oakvillesymphony
twitter.com/oaksymphony
Overview: A small local charitable organization founded in 1967 overseen by Orchestras Canada
Mission: To bring audiences a variety of music for all ages & to contribute to the cultural growth of the community
Affliation(s): Oakville Arts Council
Chief Officer(s):
Peggy Steele, General Manager
Finances: *Funding Sources:* Town of Oakville; donations; sponsors; bingo
Membership: 83; *Member Profile:* Musicians; non-playing members "Friends of OSO"
Activities: Concerts; *Library:* OSO Music Library; by appointment
Awards:
• Young Artists Awards (Award)
• Kenneth Hollier Award (Award)

The Oakville, Milton & District Real Estate Board
125 Navy St., Oakville ON L6J 2Z5
Tel: 905-844-6491; *Fax:* 905-844-6699
info@omdreb.on.ca
www.omdreb.on.ca
www.facebook.com/OMDREB
twitter.com/OMDREB_Official
Overview: A small local organization overseen by Ontario Real Estate Association
Mission: To represent its members & provide them with services to help further their career
Member of: The Canadian Real Estate Association
Chief Officer(s):
Marta Sponder, Executive Officer
msponder@omdreb.on.ca
Staff Member(s): 15
Membership: 1,500;

Oasis Centre des femmes
CP 73022, Succ. wood Street, 465 Yonge Street, Toronto ON M4Y 2W5
Tél: 416-591-6565; *Téléc:* 416-591-7525
services@oasisfemmes.org
www.oasisfemmes.org
www.facebook.com/oasisfemmes?ref=ts&fref=ts
twitter.com/OasisFemmes
Aperçu: *Dimension:* petite; *Envergure:* locale; Organisme sans but lucratif; fondée en 1995
Mission: OASIS a pour mission d'éliminer la violence et d'améliorer la situation des femmes francophones de la grande région de Toronto
Membre(s) du bureau directeur:
Odette Doumbe, Gestionnaire des programmes
Membre: 1-99
Activités: Nous offrons nos services aux femmes francophones qui sont victimes de violence, qui sont immigrantes, réfugiées ou nouvelles arrivantes, ou qui sont à la recherche d'un emploi
Brampton
CP 74089, 150 Main St., Brampton ON L6V 1M0
Tél: 905-454-3332; *Téléc:* 905-454-9437
josettes@oasisfemmes.org

Oblate Missionaries of Mary Immaculate *Voir* Les Oblates Missionnaires de Marie Immaculée

Les Oblates Missionnaires de Marie Immaculée (OMMI) / Oblate Missionaries of Mary Immaculate
7625, boul Parent, Trois-Rivières QC G9A 5E1
Tél: 819-375-7317; *Téléc:* 819-691-1769
ommi@ommi-is.org
www.ommi-is.org
Aperçu: *Dimension:* petite; *Envergure:* internationale; fondée en 1952

Occupational & Environmental Medical Association of Canada (OEMAC) / Association canadienne de la médecine du travail et de l'environnement (ACMTE)
#503, 386 Broadway, Winnipeg MB R3C 3R6
Toll-Free: 888-223-3808
info@oemac.org
oemac.org
Overview: A medium-sized national organization founded in 1983
Mission: To act as the voice of the Canadian occupational & environmental medicine sector
Affliation(s): Canadian Medical Association; Canadian Board of Occupational Medicine; Royal College of Physicians & Surgeons of Canada
Chief Officer(s):
Maureen Cividino, President
Finances: *Funding Sources:* Membership fees
Membership: 264; *Fees:* $334.75 active; $51.50 non-resident; *Member Profile:* Licensed physicians with an interest in occupational medicine
Activities: Exchanging scientific & professional information
Publications:
• Liaison [a publication of the Occupational & Environmental Medical Association of Canada]
Type: Newsletter; *Frequency:* Quarterly

Occupational First Aid Attendants Association of British Columbia (OFAAA)
#108, 2323 Boundary Rd., Vancouver BC V5M 4V8
Tel: 604-294-0244; *Fax:* 604-294-0289
Toll-Free: 800-667-4566
ofaaa@ofaaa.bc.ca
www.ofaaa.bc.ca
www.facebook.com/119440864766772
twitter.com/OFAAABC
Previous Name: Industrial First Aid Attendants Association of British Columbia
Overview: A small provincial organization founded in 1931
Mission: To enhance the professional status of first aid attendants & to promote accessibility to high standards of first aid for the workers of the province of British Columbia
Chief Officer(s):
Russ Brown, Vice-President
rbrown@ofaaa.bc.ca
Adrian Metcalf, Treasurer
ametcalf@ofaaa.bc.ca
Allan Zdunic, President
azdunich@ofaaa.bc.ca
Membership: *Fees:* $70; $30 associate; *Member Profile:* First aid attendants

Occupational Health Clinics for Ontario Workers (OHCOW)
#601, 15 Gervais Dr., Toronto ON M3C 1Y8
Tel: 416-510-8713; *Fax:* 416-443-9132
Toll-Free: 877-817-0336
info@ohcow.on.ca
www.ohcow.on.ca
Overview: A medium-sized provincial organization
Mission: To prevent work-related illnesses & injuries; To improve workers' physical, mental & social well-being
Chief Officer(s):
Lyle Hargrove, President

Occupational Hygiene Association of Ontario (OHAO)
6519B Mississauga Rd., Mississauga ON L5N 1A6
Tel: 905-567-7196; *Fax:* 905-567-7191
office@ohao.org
www.ohao.org
Overview: A medium-sized provincial organization founded in 1984
Mission: To protect people's health from hazards arising in or from the workplace; to develop & promote the profession of occupational hygiene; to sponsor professional development, training & research; to provide public education
Chief Officer(s):
Elizabeth A. Walpac, President
Richard Quenneville, Sec.-Treas.
Jason Boyer, Executive Manager
office@ohao.org
Finances: *Annual Operating Budget:* $50,000-$100,000; *Funding Sources:* Membership dues; seminars
10 volunteer(s)
Membership: 300; *Fees:* $84 individual; $26.25 student; *Committees:* Education; Program; Membership; Public Affairs
Activities: Regional meetings; *Awareness Events:* Technical Symposia; *Speaker Service:* Yes; *Rents Mailing List:* Yes
Awards:
• Hugh Nelson Award (Award)
Presented to an individual who has made a significant long-term contribution to the advancement of occupational hygiene in Ontario

Occupational Nurses' Specialty Association of British Columbia (ONSA BC)
onsabc.shawwebspace.ca
Previous Name: British Columbia Occupational Health Nurses Professional Practice Group
Overview: A small provincial organization founded in 2010
Chief Officer(s):
Tine Lathouwers, Acting President
tinelath@uvic.ca
Doreen Yanick, Treasurer
Doreen.Yanick@catalystpaper.com
Janet Morrison, Webmaster & General Contact
janetm123@shaw.ca
Membership: *Fees:* $60 regular; $40 associate; *Member Profile:* Occupational health nurses in British Columbia, who are responsible for safe & healthy work environments, work practices, & workers
Activities: Providing information about occupational issues encountered by British Columbia's occupational health nurses

Ocean Renewable Energy Group *See* Marine Renewables Canada

Oceanside Community Arts Council (OCAC)
c/o McMillan Arts Centre, PO Box 1662, 133 McMillan St., Parksville BC V9P 2H5
Tel: 250-248-8185; *Fax:* 250-248-8185
mcmillanartscentre.com
www.youtube.com/channel/UCnMExnRHlsZjWlNNnOXi2Q
Previous Name: District 69 Community Arts Council
Overview: A small local charitable organization
Mission: To promote & facilitate the production & appreciation of all creative cultural activities
Member of: Assembly of BC Arts Councils
Chief Officer(s):
Chris Raines, President
Finances: *Funding Sources:* Municipal, provincial grants
Membership: *Fees:* $26

Odawa Native Friendship Centre
12 Stirling Ave., Ottawa ON K1Y 1P8
Tel: 613-722-3811; *Fax:* 613-722-4667
info@odawa.on.ca
www.odawa.on.ca
Overview: A small local charitable organization
Affliation(s): Ontario Federation of Indian Friendship Centres
Chief Officer(s):
John Henri Commanda, President
onfc-board@odawa.on.ca
Morgan Hare, Executive Director, 613-722-3811 Ext. 246
executive.director@odawa.on.ca
Staff Member(s): 22
Activities: Administers the following programs: Community Justice; Family Support; Healthy Babies, Healthy Children; Akwe:go; Healing & Wellness; Life Long Care; Healthy Living; Homeless Partnering Strategy; Wasa-Nabin; Recreation; Cultural Awareness; Support/Information Referral. The Centre also runs a drop-in centre, child care agency, & alternative high school

Odre des enseignantes et des enseignants de l'Ontario *See* Ontario College of Teachers

Oeuvres pour enfants Ronald McDonald du Canada *See* Ronald McDonald House Charities of Canada

Office canadien de commercialisation des oeufs d'incubation de poulet à chair *See* Canadian Broiler Hatching Egg Marketing Agency

Office canadien de vérification de la diffusion *See* Canadian Circulations Audit Board Inc.

L'Office de Certification Commerciale du Québec Inc. (OCCQ) / Québec Commercial Certification Office Inc. (QCCO)
#206, 1565, boul de l'Avenir, Laval QC H7S 2N5
Tél: 514-905-3893; *Téléc:* 450-663-6316
info@occq-qcco.com
www.occq-qcco.com
Aperçu: *Dimension:* moyenne; *Envergure:* provinciale

L'Office de commercialisation des oeufs de Nouveau Brunswick *See* New Brunswick Egg Marketing Board

Office de Tourisme de Percé *Voir* Office de Tourisme du Rocher-Percé

Office de Tourisme du Rocher-Percé (OTRP)
CP 243, 9, rue du Quai, Percé QC G0C 2L0
Tél: 418-782-2258; *Téléc:* 418-782-2285
services@rocherperce.qc.ca
www.rocherperce.qc.ca
Nom précédent: Office de Tourisme de Percé
Aperçu: *Dimension:* petite; *Envergure:* locale; Organisme sans but lucratif; fondée en 1998
Mission: Améliorer l'offre touristique de la MRC du Rocher-Percé, sa commercialisation et l'éthique professionnelle, soutenir les événements
Membre de: Association touristique de la Gaspésie
Affiliation(s): Québec Maritime
Finances: *Budget de fonctionnement annuel:* $100,000-$250,000; *Fonds:* Emploi-Québec; Association des centres locaux de développement; Société d'assurance-dépôts du Canada
Membre(s) du personnel: 8; 5 bénévole(s)
Membre: 142; *Montant de la cotisation:* 100$; *Critères d'admissibilite:* Commerçants; villes; organismes de développement; *Comités:* Éthique; Formation
Activités: Billetterie, animation publique

Office de vente des produits forestiers du Madawaska *See* Madawaska Forest Products Marketing Board

Office des normes générales du Canada *See* Canadian General Standards Board

Office des producteurs de tabac jaune du Québec
110, rue Beaudry Nord, Joliette QC J6E 6A5
Aperçu: *Dimension:* moyenne; *Envergure:* provinciale
Membre(s) du personnel: 1
Membre: 95 institutionnel; 83 individu

Office du tourisme et des congrès de la communauté urbaine de Québec *Voir* Office du tourisme et des congrès de Québec

Office du tourisme et des congrès de Québec (OTCQ) / Québec City & Area Tourism & Convention Board
399, rue St-Joseph est, Québec QC G1K 8E2
Tél: 418-641-6654; *Téléc:* 418-641-6578
Ligne sans frais: 877-783-1608
www.quebecregion.com
www.facebook.com/QuebecRegion
Nom précédent: Office du tourisme et des congrès de la communauté urbaine de Québec
Aperçu: *Dimension:* moyenne; *Envergure:* locale; fondée en 1985 surveillé par Associations touristiques régionales associées du Québec
Mission: Organisme responsable de la mise en marché de la région touristique de Québec
Membre de: Tourism Industry Association of Canada
Membre(s) du bureau directeur:
Gabriel Savard, Directeur général
Daniel Gagnon, Directeur, Communication et publicité
Finances: *Budget de fonctionnement annuel:* $3 Million-$5 Million
Membre(s) du personnel: 44
Membre: 1,050; *Montant de la cotisation:* Barème
Activités: *Stagiaires:* Oui; *Listes de destinataires:* Oui

Office municipal d'habitation de Longueuil (OMHL)
445, rue Labonté, Longueuil QC J4H 2P8
Tél: 450-670-2733; *Téléc:* 450-670-7757
omhl@omhl.org
www.omhl.org
Aperçu: *Dimension:* petite; *Envergure:* locale
Mission: Pour fournir la qualité, le logement à faible revenu pour les personnes défavorisées
Membre(s) du bureau directeur:
Sylvain Boily, Directeur général
Monique Brisson, Présidente, Conseil d'administration

Office of Greening Government Operations (OGGO)
Tel: 416-241-4000
www.greeninggovernment.ca
Mission: Greening Government is an electronic information system developed by the Government of Canada for the internet. It is designed to provide a one-window access to sustainable development in government operations knowledge in the Government of Canada. This website was developed to support the Sustainable Development in Government Operations (SDGO) initiative, whose purpose is to coordinate the federal effort to green government operations & encourage the report of concrete results among the departments & agencies that prepare Sustainable Development Strategies (SDSs). There are seven priority areas of operations: Energy Efficiency/Buildings, Human Resources Management, Land Use Management, Procurement, Vehicle Fleet Management, Waste Management & Water Conservation & Wastewater Management
Chief Officer(s):
Nigel Marsh, President & Conference Director, 416-241-4000 Ext. 221
nigel.marsh@govpages.ca

Office of the Superintendent of Securities of Newfoundland & Labrador
Confederation Bldg., West Block, PO Box 8700, St. John's NL A1B 4J6
Tel: 709-729-4189; *Fax:* 709-729-6187
www.servicenl.gov.nl.ca/securities/index.html
Overview: A medium-sized provincial organization overseen by Canadian Securities Administrators
Member of: Canadian Securities Administrators
Activities: Administering the securities laws of Newfoundland & Labrador

Office of the Superintendent of Securities of the Northwest Territories
Stuart M. Hodgson Bldg., PO Box 1320, 5009 - 49th St., 1st Fl., Yellowknife NT X1A 2L9
Tel: 867-920-3318
SecuritiesRegistry@gov.nt.ca
www.justice.gov.nt.ca/SecuritiesRegistry
Also Known As: Securities Office
Overview: A medium-sized provincial organization overseen by Canadian Securities Administrators
Mission: To govern the sale & trading of securities in the Northwest Territories; to administer the Securities Act
Member of: Canadian Securities Administrators
Chief Officer(s):
Ann Hall, Deputy Superintendent, Registration & Filings
Ann_Hall@gov.nt.ca

Office of the Yukon Superintendent of Securities
PO Box 2703, Stn. C-6, 307 Black St., Whitehorse YT Y1A 2C6
Tel: 867-667-5466; *Fax:* 867-393-6251
Toll-Free: 800-661-0408
securities@gov.yk.ca
www.community.gov.yk.ca/corp/securities_about.html
Overview: A medium-sized provincial organization overseen by Canadian Securities Administrators
Mission: To foster fair & efficient capital markets; to protect investors
Member of: Canadian Securities Administrators
Chief Officer(s):
Rhonda Horte, Securities Officer, 867-667-5466
Activities: Administering Yukon's securities laws;

Offshore / Onshore Technologies Association of Nova Scotia (OTANS) *See* The Maritimes Energy Association

Offshore Energy Research Association of Nova Scotia (OERA)
Bank of Montreal Building, #602, 5151 George St., Halifax NS B3J 1M5
Tel: 902-406-7010; *Fax:* 902-406-7019
Toll-Free: 888-257-8688
www.oera.ca
Merged from: Offshore Energy Environmental Research (OEER); Offshore Energy Technical Research (OETR)
Overview: A medium-sized provincial organization founded in 2012
Mission: To foster offshore energy & environmental research & development; To develop offshore petroleum exploration & development for Nova Scotia
Chief Officer(s):
Stephen Dempsey, Executive Director, 902-406-7011, Fax: 902-406-7019
Wanda Barrett, Manager, Operations, 902-406-7010, Fax: 902-406-7019
Jennifer Pinks, Manager, Research, 902-406-7013, Fax: 902-406-7019

Ogemawahj Tribal Council (OTC)
5984 Rama Rd., Rama ON L3V 6H6
Tel: 705-329-2511; *Fax:* 705-329-2509
admin@ogemawahj.on.ca
www.ogemawahj.on.ca
www.facebook.com/140117852674787
Overview: A small local organization founded in 1990
Mission: To provide professional & technical services to its members; to promote self-sufficiency for First Nations
Chief Officer(s):
Joanne Smoke, Executive Director
jsmoke@ogemawahj.on.ca
Membership: 6 First Nations
Activities: Economic development; education; employment & training; financial management; technical services; policy, planning & intergovernmental relations

Oil & Gas Services Association of Québec *Voir* L'association québécoise des fournisseurs de services pétroliers et gaziers du Québec

Ojibway & Cree Cultural Centre
#204, 273 Third Ave., Timmins ON P4N 1E2
Tel: 705-267-7911; *Fax:* 705-267-4988
info@occc.ca
www.occc.ca
Overview: A medium-sized local charitable organization founded in 1975
Mission: To uphold the strength, integrity & growth of the Native culture within the Nishnawbe-Aski Nation; To support the Nisnawbe-Aski Nation in nurturing a sense of pride, independence & self-determination through the development & provision of culturally oriented materials & resources; To assist in the recognition & acceptance of Native culture within mainstream society
Member of: Ontario Library Association
Affliation(s): First Nations Confederacy of Cultural & Education Centres
Chief Officer(s):
Dianne Riopel, Executive Director
Finances: *Annual Operating Budget:* $250,000-$500,000
Staff Member(s): 7
Membership: 1-99
Activities: Provides curriculum & resource materials for use in Nishnawbe-Aski schools; preserves Cree & Ojibway through the creation of such materials as well as developing vocabularies & archives of Elders' stories; translation services; *Library:* Resource Centre;

Ojibway Power Toboggan Association (OPTA)
PO Box 1466, Sioux Lookout ON P8T 1B9
Tel: 807-737-1976; *Fax:* 807-737-1722
www.opta.ca
Overview: A medium-sized provincial organization
Mission: To keep snowmobile trails in the Sioux Lookout area in good condition and promote safe snowmobiling
Member of: North West Ontario Snowmobile Trails Association; Ontario Federation of Snowmobile Clubs; Sunset Country; Patricia Region Tourist Bureau
Chief Officer(s):
Gail Sayers, President
president@opta.ca
Membership: *Committees:* Trails; Membership; Grooming; Safety; Building; Equipment; Signage; Risk Management; STOP
Activities: Training courses; *Awareness Events:* Poker Derby; Snowmobile Raffle; Snowarama

Okanagan Historical Society (OHS)
PO Box 313, Vernon BC V1T 6M3
Tel: 250-838-9341
okheritagehistory@gmail.com
www.okanaganhistoricalsociety.org
Overview: A small local charitable organization founded in 1925
Mission: To promote the history & geography of the Okanagan & Shuswap areas of British Columbia
Affliation(s): BC Historical Federation
Chief Officer(s):
Tracy Satin, President, 250-718-5928
Rosemary Wilson, Vice-President, 250-835-4359
jrw4359@gmail.com
Bob Cowan, Treasurer, 250-838-9641
robertscowan@gmail.com
Finances: *Funding Sources:* Report sales

Okanagan Mainline Municipal Association; Okanagan Valley Municipal Association; Okanagan Valley Mayors & Reeves Association *See* Southern Interior Local Government Association

Okanagan Mainline Real Estate Board (OMREB)
#112, 140 Commercial Dr., Kelowna BC V1X 7X6
Tel: 250-491-4560; *Fax:* 250-491-4580
admin@omreb.com
www.omreb.com

www.facebook.com/okanaganmainlineREB
twitter.com/OMREB1
Overview: A small local organization founded in 1959 overseen by British Columbia Real Estate Association
Mission: To provide a forum for the exchange of property-related information between members so that they may provide the public with outstanding service; to establish & maintain optimum standards of business practices; to provide continuing education for the betterment of the members' knowledge; to monitor proposed & legislated laws which inhibit or restrict the right of Canadians or British Columbians to own or use real property
Member of: The Canadian Real Estate Association
Finances: *Funding Sources:* Membership fees
Membership: 90; *Member Profile:* Real estate licensees in Kelowna, Vernon & Salmon Arm areas
Activities: *Library*

Okanagan Miniature Horse Club (OMHC)

c/o Judy Aschenmeier, 4240 Noble Rd., Armstrong BC V0E 1B4
Tel: 250-546-9345
aschjudy@hotmail.com
www.miniaturehorsesbc.com/okclubinfo.htm
Overview: A small local organization founded in 2004
Mission: To provide education & information about the miniature horse breed in the Okanagan region of British Columbia
Chief Officer(s):
Barb Aschemeier, President, 250-379-2513
bentfir@telus.net
Joan Cunningham, Vice-President & Member, Show Committee, 250-545-9566
vistavalleyminis@shaw.ca
Anna DeWolff, Secretary, 250-832-9832
adewolff@telus.net
Ann Iceton, Treasurer, 250-832-9832
ann@paragonbc.com
Finances: *Funding Sources:* Membership fees; Fundraising; Sponsorships
Membership: *Fees:* $10 youth members; $15 single members; $25 families; *Member Profile:* Miniature horse owners, breeders, & enthusiasts who are involved in the industry in the central interior of British Columbia & Alberta
Activities: Hosting annual American Miniature Horse Association & American Miniature Horse Registry sanctioned shows in Armstrong, British Columbia; Participating in shows for miniature horses in the Okanagan region; Offering demonstrations of miniature horses at various events; Organizing educational clinics about the miniature horse breed; Providing networking opportunities for members to exchange information
Publications:
• Okanagan Miniature Horse Club Newsletter
Type: Newsletter; *Accepts Advertising*
Profile: Club information, member profiles, informative articles about miniature horses, events, & fun activities for members of the Okanagan Miniature Horse Club

Okanagan Neurological Association *See* Central Okanagan Child Development Association

Okanagan Orchid Society

Okanagan BC
www.members.shaw.ca/oos
Overview: A small local organization founded in 1993
Membership: 30; *Fees:* $25

Okanagan Similkameen Parks Society (OSPS)

PO Box 787, Summerland BC V0H 1Z0
Tel: 250-494-8996
okanagansimilkameenparkssociety.ca
Overview: A small local charitable organization founded in 1965
Member of: West Coast Environmental Law; Sierra Club
Affliation(s): Friends of Stikine; Friends of Strathcona Park; Creston Wildlife; Okanagan Naturalists
Chief Officer(s):
Jeremy McCall, Executive Director
Finances: *Annual Operating Budget:* Less than $50,000; *Funding Sources:* Donations; membership fees; bequests; Penticton Foundation
Membership: 273; *Fees:* $10 single; $15 couple/family; $20 organization; *Member Profile:* Interest in parks; land & wildlife stewardship/conservation; historic trails; forestry practices; watershed protection; urban green spaces
Activities: Monthly meetings; special events; seminars; workshops; film; brochures & booklets; *Awareness Events:* Meadowlark Festival, Penticton - May

Okanagan Similkameen Tourism Association *See* Thompson Okanagan Tourism Association

Okanagan Symphony Society

PO Box 20238, Kelowna BC V1Y 9H2
Tel: 250-763-7544; *Fax:* 250-763-3553
Toll-Free: 855-763-7544
admin@okanagansymphony.com
okanagansymphony.com
www.facebook.com/OkanaganSymphonyOrchestra
twitter.com/oksymphonyorch
www.youtube.com/user/OkSymphonyOrchestra
Overview: A small provincial charitable organization founded in 1967 overseen by Orchestras Canada
Mission: To provide the communities of the Okanagan Valley with an orchestra that is committed to excellence in the performance of classical music
Chief Officer(s):
Rosemary Thomson, Music Director
Staff Member(s): 5
Membership: 54
Activities: *Internships:* Yes; *Speaker Service:* Yes; *Library* by appointment

Okotoks & District Chamber of Commerce

PO Box 1053, 14 McRae St., Okotoks AB T1S 1B1
Tel: 403-938-2848; *Fax:* 403-938-6649
info@okotokschamber.ca
www.okotokschamber.ca
Overview: A small local organization
Chief Officer(s):
Cheryl Actemichuk, President
Finances: *Funding Sources:* Membership dues
Membership: 265; *Fees:* $175 business; $150 individual/home-based; $50 non-profit
Activities: Lite-up Okotoks; Okotoks Rocks - Sports Day; Okotoks Pro-Rodeo; Tailgate Sale & Parade

Okotoks Arts Council

PO Box 149, Okotoks AB T1S 2A2
Tel: 403-938-3204; *Fax:* 403-938-8963
okotoksartscouncil.ca
www.facebook.com/pages/Okotoks-Culture/111124055619045
twitter.com/okotoksarts
Overview: A small local organization
Mission: Developing and promoting cultural activities in the community.
Chief Officer(s):
Stephen Pope, President
Activities: *Awareness Events:* Alberta Culture Days, September

Old Chrysler Corporation Auto Club

57 Pinehurst Cr., Kitchener ON N2N 1E3
Tel: 519-342-1284; *Fax:* 519-342-1285
moparfest@rogers.com
www.moparfest.com
Also Known As: OCC Auto Club
Overview: A small local organization founded in 1979
Mission: A non-profit organization with a common interest of Chrysler/AMC vehicles with the purpose of enjoyment, maintenance and restoration.
Chief Officer(s):
Phil Hahn, President
Finances: *Annual Operating Budget:* $50,000-$100,000
Staff Member(s): 10; 100 volunteer(s)
Membership: 125; *Fees:* $30; *Member Profile:* Interest in old Chrysler automobiles
Activities: *Awareness Events:* Mopar Fest, Aug.

Old Strathcona Foundation (OSF)

Queen Alexandra School, 7730 - 106 St., 3rd Fl., Edmonton AB T6E 4W3
Tel: 780-433-5866; *Fax:* 780-431-1938
info@oldstrathconafoundation.ca
www.oldstrathconafoundation.ca
Overview: A small national charitable organization founded in 1974
Chief Officer(s):
Karen Tabor, Executive Director
Wayne Moen, President/Treasurer
Staff Member(s): 1; 100 volunteer(s)
Membership: 170; *Fees:* $20; *Committees:* Murals; Planning; Historical
Activities: *Awareness Events:* Silly Summer Parade, July 1; Art Walk, end of July

Old Sydney Society

225 George St., Sydney NS B1P 1J5
Tel: 902-539-1572; *Fax:* 902-539-1572
oldsydneysociety@ns.aliantzinc.ca
www.oldsydney.com
www.facebook.com/OldSydneySociety
twitter.com/OldSydney
Overview: A small local charitable organization founded in 1966
Mission: To preserve & promote interest in local heritage; To mark historic sites in Sydney & area; To operate museums under its jurisdiction
Member of: Federation of the Nova Scotian Heritage
Finances: *Funding Sources:* NS Museum Assistance; municipal; membership fees; shop; special events
Membership: *Fees:* $10 individual; $15 family; $100 sustaining
Activities: Operates St. Patrick's Church Museum, Cossit House & Jost House, heritage houses (seasonal), & C.B. Centre for Heritage & Science (year-round); works with local school boards to provide educational experiences for students; hosts travelling exhibits & walking tours; *Speaker Service:* Yes; *Library* Open to public

The Olde Forge Community Resource Centre (OFCRC) / Centre de ressources communautaires Olde Forge

2730 Carling Ave., Ottawa ON K2B 7J1
Tel: 613-829-9777; *Fax:* 613-829-9318
oldeforge.ca
Overview: A small local charitable organization founded in 1970
Mission: To provide an information & referral service; To operate a support service to enable senior citizens to remain in their own homes as long as possible
Member of: Ontario Community Support Association
Chief Officer(s):
Anita Bloom, Executive Director
a.bloom@oldeforge.ca
Finances: *Annual Operating Budget:* $100,000-$250,000; *Funding Sources:* Municipal & provincial government; community donations; fundraising
Staff Member(s): 6; 107 volunteer(s)
Membership: 50

Older Adult Centres' Association of Ontario (OACAO) / Association des centres pour aînés de l'Ontario

PO Box 65, Caledon East ON L7C 3L8
Tel: 905-584-8125; *Fax:* 905-584-8126
Toll-Free: 866-835-7693
sue@oacao.org
www.oacao.org
Overview: A large provincial charitable organization founded in 1973
Mission: To ensure that seniors in Ontario have opportunities & choices that lead to healthy, active lifestyles
Member of: Federation of Provincial Non-Profit Organizations Working with Seniors; Ontario Community Support Association; Ontario Coalition of Senior Citizens Organizations; United Generations Ontario
Chief Officer(s):
Sue Hesjedahl, Executive Director
sue@oacao.org
Ellen Hope, President
ehope@centresforseniors.org
Marilyn Latham, Treasurer
marilyn@oacao.org
Debra Prescott, Secretary
dprescott@.oshawa.ca
Finances: *Annual Operating Budget:* $100,000-$250,000; *Funding Sources:* Membership fees; business; grants; events
Staff Member(s): 300; 30 volunteer(s)
Membership: 121 centres representing over 300 staff & 150,000 seniors; *Fees:* Schedule available; *Member Profile:* Older adult centres in Ontario; *Committees:* Advocacy; Budget & Finance; Business Partnerships; Conference; Nomination; Seniors Development; Standards & Accreditation; Marketing
Activities: *Library:* Resource Centre; by appointment
Awards:
• Award of Merit (Award)
• Person of Distinction Award (Award)
• Past President's Award (Award)
• Life Membership Award (Award)
• Print Media Award of Merit (Award)
• Electronic Media Award of Merit (Award)
• Community Spirit Award (Award)

Meetings/Conferences: • Older Adult Centres' Association of Ontario Annual Conference 2015, 2015, ON
Scope: Provincial

The Older Women's Network (OWN) / Réseau des femmes aînées
115 The Esplanade, Toronto ON M5E 1Y7
Tel: 416-214-1518
info@olderwomensnetwork.org
olderwomensnetwork.org
Overview: A small provincial charitable organization founded in 1988
Mission: To initiate & support discussion on issues relevant to the well-being of older women; To develop & support legislation to expand opportunities for housing, economic security, & optimum health; To monitor the media in order to encourage a more realistic & positive portrayal of older women; To support the efforts of young women to achieve equal opportunity, freedom from discrimination, abuse & exploitation, & the right to reproductive choice; To support the needs of children; To liaise with movements for social justice in Canada & abroad
Member of: National Action Committee on the Status of Women; Ontario Coalition of Senior Citizens Associations
Affiliation(s): One Voice; National Association of Women & the Law; Women's Legal Education & Action Fund
Finances: *Funding Sources:* Membership fees; individual donors
Membership: *Fees:* $35 individuals; *Member Profile:* Older women who support OWN's objectives; *Committees:* Finance; Anam Cara; Special Interest Groups & Outreach; Housing; Alfreda Mordas Reading Room; Nominating & Bylaws; Membership; Communications
Activities: Engaging in advocacy activities; Providing presentations to all levels of government; *Speaker Service:* Yes

Oldman River Antique Equipment & Threshing Club
PO Box 2496, Pincher Creek AB T0K 1W0
Tel: 403-628-2764
Overview: A small local charitable organization founded in 1987
Mission: To collect, preserve, & demonstrate antique farm equipment from southern Alberta
Chief Officer(s):
Rick Bell, Contact
Finances: *Funding Sources:* Donations; Fundraising
Activities: Operating a museum

Olds & District Chamber of Commerce
PO Box 4210, Olds AB T4H 1P8
Tel: 403-556-7070; *Fax:* 403-556-1515
chamber@oldsalberta.com
www.oldsalberta.com
www.facebook.com/oldschamber?ref=stream
Overview: A small local organization
Mission: The Chamber of Commerce serves the business, economic, and social communities of our town and area.
Chief Officer(s):
Doug Rieberger, President
doug.r@ultimatesafety.ca
Barb Babiak, Executive Director
Melanie Hepp, Vice-President

Olds Agricultural Society (OAS)
PO Box 3751, 5116 - 54 St., Olds AB T4H 1P5
e-mail: office@oldsagsociety.com
www.oldsagsociety.com
www.facebook.com/oldsagsociety
Overview: A small local organization founded in 1899
Mission: To promote awareness of agriculture's role in the community through events
Member of: Canadian Beef Breeds Council
Chief Officer(s):
Curtis Flewelling, President
Tami Gardner, General Manager
tami@oldsagsociety.com
Membership: *Fees:* $10; *Member Profile:* Individuals over 18 who reside in Alberta; *Committees:* Finance
Activities: Festivals; agricultural shows & events; conferences
Awards:
• RBC Dominion Securities Youth Ambassador Scholarship Program (Scholarship)
Eligibility: Youth who participate in the yearly Fair & Rodeo
Amount: $1,000

Olds College Faculty Association (OCFA) / Association des professeurs du Collège Olds
Olds College, 4500 - 50 St., Olds AB T4H 1R6
Tel: 403-556-4636; *Fax:* 403-556-4637
ocfaea@oldscollege.ca
www.oldscollege.ca/OCFA
Overview: A small local organization founded in 1968
Member of: Alberta Colleges & Institutes Faculties Association (ACIFA)
Chief Officer(s):
Sandi Hallett, Executive Assistant
Carmel Maloney, President, 403-556-4648
cmaloney@oldscollege.ca
Finances: *Annual Operating Budget:* Less than $50,000
Staff Member(s): 1
Membership: 93; *Committees:* Professional Practices; Faculty Professional Development; Academic Council; Safety; Graduation; Education & Training; Community Learning Campus Governance Team; Student Development; Nominations; Negotitations; Ethics; Legislative Grievance; Faculty Centre; Social; Professional Affairs; Student Award
Awards:
• OCFA Outstanding Student Award (Award)

Oliver & District Chamber of Commerce ***See*** South Okanagan Chamber Of Commerce

Oliver Community Arts Council (OCAC)
PO Box 1711, Oliver BC V0H 1T0
Tel: 250-498-0183; *Fax:* 250-498-0183
olivercac@gmail.com
www.oliverartscouncil.org
Overview: A small local charitable organization founded in 1976
Mission: To increase & broaden the opportunities of Oliver residents to enjoy & participate in cultural activities
Member of: Assembly of BC Arts Councils
Chief Officer(s):
Jo Ann Turner
Terry Irvine
Penelope Johnson
Finances: *Annual Operating Budget:* Less than $50,000
60 volunteer(s)
Membership: 12 member groups; 60 individual/family; *Fees:* $10 individual; $15 family; $25 group; $35 business; *Committees:* Executive; Board of Directors; Development & Design; Fall Art Show; Summer Studio; Public Relations; Building Operations; Finance; Entertainment
Activities: Summer Studio; Music in the Park; Fall Arts Show; Showcase of Talent; Arts & Culture Week

Oliver Food Bank
PO Box 405, Oliver BC V0H 1T0
Tel: 250-498-4555
Overview: A small local organization overseen by Food Banks British Columbia
Member of: Food Banks British Columbia
Chief Officer(s):
Jim Ouellette, Contact
jimo@persona.ca

Oliver-Osoyoos Naturalists
PO Box 1181, Osoyoos BC V0H 1V0
Tel: 250-485-0263
Overview: A small local organization founded in 1973
Mission: To cooperate and communicate with other naturalists. To foster an awareness, appreciation and understanding of our natural environment so that it may be wisely used and maintained for future generations.
Member of: The Federation of BC Naturalists
Chief Officer(s):
Jackie Castellarin, Contact
ivocastellarin@gmail.com
Finances: *Annual Operating Budget:* Less than $50,000
Membership: 60; *Fees:* $25 individual; $30 family; *Member Profile:* People interested in nature & the environment
Activities: Walks; hiking; bird watching; outdoor education; caretaking of two ecological reserves; environmental restoration; "clean-up" projects.

Olympic Aid ***See*** Right to Play

Olympiques spéciaux Canada ***See*** Special Olympics Canada

OmbudService for Life & Health Insurance (OLHI) / Ombudsman des assurances de personnes (OAP)
PO Box 7, 401 Bay St., Toronto ON M5H 2Y4
Tel: 416-777-9002
Toll-Free: 888-295-8112
Other Communication: Bell Relay Service: 1-800-855-0511
www.olhi.ca
Previous Name: Canadian Life & Health Insurance OmbudService
Overview: A medium-sized national organization
Mission: An independent service that assists consumers with concerns & complaints about life & health insurance products & services.
Member of: Financial Services OmbudsNetwork (FSON)
Chief Officer(s):
Janice MacKinnon, Chair

Montréal Office
2001, rue University, 17e étage, Montréal QC H3A 2A6
Tel: 514-282-2088
Toll-Free: 866-582-2088
www.olhi.ca

Ombudsman des assurances de personnes ***See*** OmbudService for Life & Health Insurance

Ombudsman des services bancaires et d'investissement ***See*** Ombudsman for Banking Services & Investments

Ombudsman for Banking Services & Investments (OBSI) / Ombudsman des services bancaires et d'investissement (OSBI)
PO Box 5, #1505, 401 Bay St., Toronto ON M5H 2Y4
Tel: 416-287-2877; *Fax:* 416-225-4722
Toll-Free: 888-451-4519; *TTY:* 855-889-6274
Other Communication: Toll-Free Fax: 1-888-422-2865
ombudsman@obsi.ca
www.obsi.ca
Previous Name: Canadian Banking Ombudsman
Overview: A medium-sized national organization founded in 1996
Mission: To investigate complaints from individuals & small businesses about banking services; To provide impartial & prompt resolution of complaints, based on fairness & good business & banking practices
Member of: Financial Services OmbudsNetwork (FSON)
Chief Officer(s):
Fernand Bélisle, Chair
Douglas Melville, Ombudsman & CEO
Membership: 500-999; *Member Profile:* Retail & commercial banks; Investment dealers; Mutual fund dealers; Fund companies; *Committees:* Finance & Audit; Governance, Human Resources & Compensation; Policy & Standards
Activities: *Speaker Service:* Yes

OMF International - Canada (OMF)
5155 Spectrum Way, Bldg. 21, Mississauga ON L4W 5A1
Tel: 905-568-9971; *Fax:* 905-568-9974
Toll-Free: 888-657-8010
omfcanada@omf.ca
www.omf.ca
Also Known As: Overseas Missionary Fellowship
Previous Name: China Inland Mission
Overview: A medium-sized international organization founded in 1865
Member of: Interdenominational Foreign Mission Association
Affiliation(s): Evangelical Fellowship of Canada
Chief Officer(s):
Ron Adams, Director, Administration & Finance
Jon Fuller, National Director
Staff Member(s): 120
Membership: 1,300 missionaries worldwide; *Member Profile:* Four years post-secondary education

Alberta Region
Tel: 780-483-8025
george.jakeway@gmail.com
Chief Officer(s):
George Jakeway, Regional Ministry Coordinator

Atlantic Region
152 Douglas Crescent, Halifax NS E9B 1R8
Tel: 902-454-9665
ca.atl.rmc@omfmail.com
Chief Officer(s):
Hasell Kerr, Regional Ministry Coordinator

Manitoba Region
MB

Ontario Region
ON
Tel: 905-568-9971
ca.ont.rd@omfmail.com
Chief Officer(s):
CY Yan, Region Director

Pacific Region
BC

Tel: 604-278-1208; *Fax:* 604-278-1208
CA.BC.RD@omfmail.com
Chief Officer(s):
Gary Roosma, Regional Director
Québec Region
QC
Tel: 514-488-9383
Chief Officer(s):
Brian Ludgate, Regional Ministry Coordinator
Saskatchewan Region
SK
Tel: 306-975-1298
Chief Officer(s):
David Ginther, Regional Ministry Coordinator

On Screen Manitoba
#003, 100 Albert St., Winnipeg MB R3B 1H3
Tel: 204-927-5898; *Fax:* 204-272-8792
info@onscreenmanitoba.com
www.onscreenmanitoba.com
www.facebook.com/onscreenmanitoba
twitter.com/OnScreenMB
www.youtube.com/user/OnScreenManitoba
Previous Name: Manitoba Motion Picture Industries Association
Overview: A medium-sized provincial organization founded in 1987
Mission: To build & represent the motion picture industry in Manitoba; To foster excellence & innovation in the industry
Chief Officer(s):
Nicole Matiation, Executive Director, 204-927-5893
nicole@onscreenmanitoba.com
Trevor Suffield, Coordinator, Communications, 204-927-5896
trevor@onscreenmanitoba.com
Finances: *Funding Sources:* Sponsorships; Department of Culture, Heritage & Tourism; Western Economic Diversification; Telefilm Canada; MB Film & Sound Recording Development Corp
Membership: *Fees:* $25 students & corporate & production company employees; $50 voting individuals; $100 production company producers; $200 procduction companies
Activities: Engaging in advocacy activities; Offering networking opportunities; Providing information about industry statistics, training programs, funding, & festivals; Raising public awareness of the benefits of the industry in the province
Awards:
• Blizzard Awards (Award)
To recognize excellence in Manitoba film & video production
Publications:
• The Manitoba Film & Television Production Guide
Type: Directory; *Frequency:* Annually
Profile: Published by On Screen Manitoba, in partnership with Manitoba Film & Sound
• On Screen Manitoba Newsletter
Type: Newsletter

On to Ottawa Historical Society
c/o Joey Hartman, Vancouver BC
Tel: 604-254-0703
webmaster@ontoottawa.ca
www.ontoottawa.ca
Overview: A small local organization founded in 1988
Mission: To preserve labour's heritage, specifically the history of the On to Ottawa trek
Chief Officer(s):
Joey Harman, Contact

One Full Circle (OFC)
882, boul Décarie, Saint-Laurent QC H4L 3L9
Tel: 514-651-4545
onefullcircleofc@gmail.com
theofc.org
www.facebook.com/theofc
twitter.com/1fullcircle
www.youtube.com/channel/UCHz2HhkluaA112A3g_RNd_Q
Overview: A small local organization founded in 2011
Mission: To provide social & community services to members of the black community in Montréal
Chief Officer(s):
Shiata Lewis, Co-Founder
Pharaoh Freeman, Co-Founder & Head Coordinator
Membership: *Fees:* $54 supporting; $108 core; $162 business
Meetings/Conferences: • One Full Circle Annual General Meeting & Gala 2015, March, 2015

1000 Islands Gananoque Chamber of Commerce
10 King St. East, Gananoque ON K7G 1E6
Tel: 613-382-7744; *Fax:* 613-382-1585
Toll-Free: 800-561-1595
info@1000islandsganchamber.com
www.1000islandsganchamber.com
www.linkedin.com/company/1000-islands-gananoque-chamber-of-commerce
www.facebook.com/1000IslandsGananoqueChamber
twitter.com/gananoquechamb
Overview: A small local organization
Mission: To improve commerce in Ganonoque
Member of: Canadian Chamber of Commerce
Chief Officer(s):
Joe Baptista, President
Membership: 200; *Fees:* $60 non-profit/service club; $120 1-5 employees; $170 6-10 employees; $220 11-15 employees; $270 16+ employees

One Parent Families Association of Canada / Association des familles uniparentales du Canada
PO Box 628, Pickering ON L1V 3T3
Tel: 905-831-7098
Toll-Free: 877-773-7714
oneparentfamilies@gmx.com
oneparentfamilies.net
Overview: A small national charitable organization founded in 1973
Mission: To develop & provide a broad comprehensive program for the enlightenment & guidance of single parents & their children on the special problems they encounter & for assistance on the various readjustments involved.
Chief Officer(s):
Greg Mercer, President
Membership: *Member Profile:* Separated, divorced, widowed or never married parents; custodial & non-custodial parents

One Sky
PO Box 3352, 3768 - 2 Ave., Smithers BC V0J 1N0
Tel: 250-877-6030
www.onesky.ca
Overview: A medium-sized national organization founded in 2000
Mission: To promote sustainable living globally; To inspire and promote solutions, provide practical solutions, and network across sectors with like-minded organizations.
Chief Officer(s):
Michael Simpson, Executive Director
Finances: *Funding Sources:* Donations
Membership: *Fees:* $10
Activities: *Internships:* Yes

One World Arts (OWA)
323 Chapel St., 3rd Fl., Ottawa ON K1N 7Z2
Tel: 613-238-4659; *Fax:* 613-238-1888
inquiries@oneworldarts.ca
oneworldarts.ca
www.facebook.com/214778781880093
twitter.com/OneWorldArts
Previous Name: World Inter-Action Mondiale; Ottawa-Hull Learner Centre
Overview: A medium-sized local charitable organization founded in 1972
Mission: To raise awareness about global issues, using different types of media & performing arts projects
Member of: Global Education Centres of Ontario; Ontario Council for International Cooperation; Canadian Council for International Cooperation
Chief Officer(s):
Pixie Cam, Manager, Film Festival Program
pixie.cram@oneworldarts.ca
Micheline Shoebridge, Manager, Arts Program & Festival
micheline.shoebridge@oneworldarts.ca
Staff Member(s): 3
Activities: *Awareness Events:* One World Film Festival, September

100 Mile & District Arts Council
PO Box 2262, 100 Mile House BC V0K 2E0
Tel: 250-395-2697; *Fax:* 250-791-6420
administration@100milearts.com
www.100milearts.com
Overview: A small local organization founded in 1975
Mission: To develop opportunities for area residents to experience &/or participate in creative & cultural endeavours
Member of: Assembly of BC Arts Councils; Central Interior Regional Arts Council
Finances: *Annual Operating Budget:* Less than $50,000
10 volunteer(s)
Membership: 40; *Fees:* $30 group; $15 individual
Activities: *Awareness Events:* Winter Arts & Crafts Fair, November; Festival of the Arts Recitals & Presentations

100 Mile House Food Bank Society
199 - 7 St., 100 Mile House BC V0K 2E3
Tel: 250-395-3923; *Fax:* 250-397-2579
Overview: A small local organization overseen by Food Banks British Columbia
Member of: Food Banks British Columbia

Online Party of Canada
#411, 637 Lake Shore Blvd. West, Toronto ON M5V 3J6
Tel: 416-567-6913
Contact@OnlineParty.ca
www.onlineparty.ca
www.facebook.com/onlinepartyca
Overview: A small national organization
Chief Officer(s):
Michael Nicula, Leader

Onoway & District Chamber of Commerce
PO Box 723, Onoway AB T0E 1V0
Tel: 780-967-2550
info@onowaychamber.ca
business.onowaychamber.ca
Overview: A small local organization
Chief Officer(s):
Ed Gallagher, President

Ontaria Esperanto-Asocio (OEA) / Association ontarienne d'espéranto
Tel: 613-996-8216
esperanto.ca/ottawa
Also Known As: Ontario Esperanto Association
Overview: A medium-sized local organization founded in 1989
Mission: To provide a forum where Ontario speakers of Esperanto may find & become acquainted with each other, practise the language, exchange expertise about the Esperanto movement & language, & generally enjoy themselves together; To inform & educate Ontarians about the Esperanto language, movement & the community, & how these can provide the most efficient communication channel between speakers of different mother tongues; To establish relations with the Ontario government & provincial-level enterprises & other Ontario associations potentially showing some common goal or interest with the association, & linking the association with other organizations at the local, provincial, national, & international levels in the worldwide Esperanto movement
Chief Officer(s):
Yves Bellefeuille, Contact
yan@storm.ca
Finances: *Annual Operating Budget:* Less than $50,000;
Funding Sources: Membership fees; donations
Membership: 1-99; *Committees:* Local Conference & Get-together Committees
Activities: *Speaker Service:* Yes

Ontario 5 Pin Bowlers' Association (O5PBA)
#302, 3 Concorde Gate, Toronto ON M3C 3N7
Tel: 416-426-7167; *Fax:* 416-426-7364
o5pba@o5pba.ca
www.o5pba.ca
Overview: A medium-sized provincial organization founded in 1963
Mission: To act as the governing body for 5 pin bowling in Ontario
Member of: Canadian 5 Pin Bowlers' Association
Chief Officer(s):
John Cresswell, President
Rhonda Gifford, Coordinator, Program
Jackie Henriques, Coordinator, Finances
Al Hong, Coordinator, Events
Staff Member(s): 3
Membership: 10,000
Publications:
• Pinboard
Type: Newsletter; *Frequency:* Monthly
Profile: Event highlights

Ontario Aboriginal Lands Association (OALA)
c/o Wanda McGonigle, Hiawatha First Nation, 123 Paudash St., RR #2, Keene ON K0L 2G0
Tel: 705-295-4421
Overview: A small provincial organization founded in 1995 overseen by National Aboriginal Lands Managers Association

Mission: To network towards the enhancement of professional development & expertise in Lands Management issues; To achieve a recognized role within the federal & provincial governments, & provincial & territorial organizations
Chief Officer(s):
Wanda McGonigle, Chair
wmcgonig@hiawathafn.ca
Staff Member(s): 1
Membership: 22; *Fees:* $250; *Member Profile:* First Nations in Ontario

Ontario Aerospace Council (OAC)
549 Mill Park Dr., Kitchener ON N2P 1V4
Tel: 519-895-2442; *Fax:* 519-895-2452
www.ontaero.org
Overview: A medium-sized provincial organization
Mission: To enhance Ontario's aerospace industry in the global market; to ensure growth & prosperity
Chief Officer(s):
Todd Young, Chair
Rod Jones, Executive Director, 416-399-2648
rod.jones@theOAC.ca
Membership: *Fees:* Schedule available; *Member Profile:* Companies in the Ontario aerospace industry

Ontario Agencies Supporting Individuals with Special Needs (OASIS)
c/o Lambton County Developmental Services, PO Box 1210, 339 Centre St., Petrolia ON N0N 1R0
Tel: 519-882-0933; *Fax:* 519-882-0933
www.oasisonline.ca
Overview: A medium-sized provincial organization
Mission: To facilitate the sharing of ideas, resources, systems & information; to liaise with government on behalf of member organizations with the goal of improving the development of cost effective quality supports for individuals with developmental disabilities
Chief Officer(s):
Judy Reid, President
jreid@becon.org
Lu-Ann Cowell, Treasurer
lcowell@clc-k.ca

Ontario Agri Business Association (OABA)
#104, 160 Research Lane, Guelph ON N1G 5B2
Tel: 519-822-3004; *Fax:* 519-822-8862
info@oaba.on.ca
www.oaba.on.ca
Merged from: Ontario Grain & Feed Association; Fertilizer Institute of Ontario
Overview: A medium-sized provincial organization founded in 1965
Mission: To serve & represent firms engaged in the crop inputs, country grain elevator, & feed & farm supply industy, plus related agricultural businesses operating within Ontario
Member of: Canadian Fertilizer Institute; Animal Nutrition Association of Canada
Chief Officer(s):
D.O. Buttenham, CEO
dave@oaba.on.ca
Gwen Paddock, President
Cory McDonald, Vice-President
Dale Cowan, Treasurer
Finances: *Funding Sources:* Annual membership dues from regular, branch, &c associate members
Membership: *Member Profile:* Country grain elevators in Ontario; Ontario crop input supply businesses; Feed manufacturing facilities in the province; Associated businesses that provide products & services to the crop input, grain, & feed industry
Activities: Delivering products, programs, & services to members; Promoting the crop input, grain, & feed industry; Coordinating services of member sectors in areas such as food safety & environmental stewardship; Providing educational opportunities; Liaising with stakeholders, consumers, & government; Studying legislation affecting members; Disseminating information to members; Engaging in & sponsoring research

Ontario Agri-Food Education Inc. (OAFE)
PO Box 460, 8560 Tremaine Rd., Milton ON L9T 4Z1
Tel: 905-878-1510; *Fax:* 905-878-0342
info@oafe.org
www.oafe.org
www.linkedin.com/company/ontario-agri-food-education-inc-?trk=fc_badge
www.facebook.com/OAFEInc
twitter.com/OntAgriFoodEd
Overview: A small provincial organization founded in 1991
Mission: To build awareness & understanding of the importance of an agriculture & food system; To provide high quality, objective & relevant agriculture & food related learning materials & services for Ontario educators to enhance the learning experiences of students in Ontario classrooms
Chief Officer(s):
Colleen Smith, Executive Director, 905-878-151 Ext. 22
director@oafe.org
Membership: *Fees:* $50 individual

Ontario Agri-Food Technologies (OAFT)
#200, 120 Research Lane, Guelph ON N1G 0B4
Tel: 519-826-4195; *Fax:* 519-821-7361
info@oaft.org
www.oaft.org
Overview: A medium-sized provincial organization founded in 1997
Mission: To generate wealth & sustainability for the Ontario agriculture & food industries by utilizing current technologies
Affliation(s): Agriculture and Agri-Food Canada; Ontario Ministry of Agriculture and Food/Ministry of Rural Affairs; Ontario Ministry of Economic Development, Trade and Employment
Chief Officer(s):
Gord Surgeoner, President
Kathy Derksen, Office Manager
Membership: *Member Profile:* Grower organizations; industry; universities; government; affiliates

Ontario Allergy Society *See* Allergy, Asthma & Immunology Society of Ontario

Ontario Alliance of Christian Schools (OACS)
790 Shaver Rd., Ancaster ON L9G 3K9
Tel: 905-648-2100; *Fax:* 905-648-2110
oacs@oacs.org
www.oacs.org
www.twitter.com/oacsnews
Overview: A medium-sized provincial organization founded in 1952 overseen by Federation of Independent Schools in Canada
Mission: To promote independent schools in Ontario; to promote Christian education in Canada; to provide educational services for member schools; to lobby government for educational choice. Canada's largest & oldest independent school organization, representing 79 schools with approximately 14,000 students.
Affliation(s): Christian Schools International; Christian Schools Canada
Chief Officer(s):
Julius de Jager, Executive Director
julesdj@oacs.org
Finances: *Annual Operating Budget:* $500,000-$1.5 Million; *Funding Sources:* Membership dues
Staff Member(s): 15; 200 volunteer(s)
Membership: 1-99; *Fees:* Schedule available; *Committees:* Finance; Education; PR; Planning; Government Relations; Personnel
Activities: *Speaker Service:* Yes; *Rents Mailing List:* Yes

Ontario Amateur Netball Association *See* Netball Ontario

Ontario Amateur Softball Association (OASA)
c/o Registrar, RR#1, 44 Hilltop Blvd., Gormley ON L0H 1G0
Tel: 905-727-5139
www.oasa.ca
Overview: A medium-sized provincial organization founded in 1923 overseen by Softball Ontario
Mission: To coordinate the game of softball for players of all ages throughout Ontario
Member of: Canadian Amateur Softball Association; Softball Ontario
Chief Officer(s):
Roy Patenaude, President, 705-549-2485
rpatenaude@hotmail.ca
Mary Myers, Registrar
mjnm@sympatico.ca
Finances: *Funding Sources:* Sponsors; Partners; Government grants; Player/team fees

Ontario Amateur Wrestling Association (OAWA)
#213, 3 Concorde Gate, Toronto ON M3C 3N7
Tel: 416-426-7274; *Fax:* 416-426-7343
admin@oawa.ca
www.oawa.ca
Also Known As: Ontario Wrestling
Overview: A medium-sized provincial organization founded in 1980 overseen by Canadian Amateur Wrestling Association
Mission: To provide essential services & programs dedicated to developing amateur wrestling at all age levels within Ontario
Affliation(s): International Amateur Wrestling Association; Canadian Amateur Wrestling Association
Chief Officer(s):
Tim MaGarrey, Provincial Director
Finances: *Annual Operating Budget:* $100,000-$250,000; *Funding Sources:* Government; private donors; sponsors; fundraising; user fees
Membership: 1,800; *Fees:* $15-50 depending on age & level of involvement
Activities: Competitons; demonstrations;

Ontario Amputee & Les Autres Sports Association (OALASA)
#104, 3 Concorde Gate, Toronto ON M3C 3N7
oalasa.webs.com
Previous Name: Ontario Amputee Sports Association
Overview: A small provincial organization founded in 1976
Member of: Sport for Disabled Ontario; Canadian Amputee Sports Association
Chief Officer(s):
Rodney Reimer, President, 519-659-7452
rodreimer@rogers.com
Dan Oettinger, Secretary
deckhart-oettinger@cogeco.ca
Douglas Walker, Treasurer
walker1499@yahoo.ca
Finances: *Annual Operating Budget:* Less than $50,000; *Funding Sources:* Bingos
15 volunteer(s)
Membership: 100 individual; *Fees:* $20; $15 associate; *Member Profile:* Anyone interested in amputee & les autres sports
Activities: Golf clinics & tournaments; speakers; lawn bowls tournament; boccia tournament; *Speaker Service:* Yes

Ontario Amputee Sports Association *See* Ontario Amputee & Les Autres Sports Association

Ontario Angus Association (OAA)
PO Box 331, Fergus ON N1M 3E2
Tel: 519-787-2397; *Fax:* 519-928-9972
secretary@ontarioangus.com
www.ontarioangus.com
Overview: A small provincial organization
Mission: To encourage the breeding of quality livestock
Member of: Canadian Angus Association
Chief Officer(s):
Julie Smith, Secretary-Treasurer
Membership: 100-499

The Ontario Archaeological Society Inc.
PO Box 62066, Stn. Victoria Terrace, #102, 1444 Queen St. East, Toronto ON M4A 2W1
Tel: 416-406-5959
Toll-Free: 888-733-0042
oasociety@ontarioarchaeology.on.ca
www.ontarioarchaeology.on.ca
www.facebook.com/groups/2241248392
www.youtube.com/user/OntarioArchaeology
Overview: A medium-sized provincial charitable organization founded in 1950 overseen by Canadian Archaeological Association
Mission: To preserve, promote, investigate, record & publish an archaeological record of the province of Ontario
Chief Officer(s):
Rob MacDonald, President-Elect
presidentelect@ontarioarchaeology.on.ca
Neal Ferris, President
president@ontarioarchaeology.on.ca
Jim Keron, Treasurer
treasurer@ontarioarchaeology.on.ca
Lorie Harris, Executive Director
executive-director@ontarioarchaeology.on.ca
Finances: *Funding Sources:* Membership dues; government; programs
Membership: 600 individual + 25 senior/lifetime + 75 family; *Fees:* Schedule available
Activities: Public archaeology programs; trips; lecture series; *Speaker Service:* Yes; *Library* by appointment
Awards:
- Ian Kenyon Memorial Award (Award)
- J. Norman Emerson Silver Medal (Award)
- Heritage Conservation Award (Award)
- J.V. Wright Lifetime Achievement Award (Award)

• Tim Kenyon Memorial Award (Award)
• Peggi Armstrong Public Archaeology Award (Award)
• Killarney Award for Outstanding Service (Award)
• Award for Excellence in Cultural Resource Management (Award)
• Award for Excellence in Publishing (Award)
• OAS Student Paper-Poster Award (Award)
• Valerie Sonstenes Student Research Fund (Award)
Publications:
• Arch Notes [a publication of the Ontario Archaeology Society]
Type: Newsletter; *Frequency:* bi-m.; *Editor:* Sheryl A. Smith
• Monographs in Ontario Archaeology
Type: Monograph
• Ontario Archaeology
Type: Journal; *Editor:* Chris Ellis

Hamilton Chapter
c/o Dr. Gary Warrick, Laurier Brantford, 73 George St., Brantford ON N3T 2Y3
Tel: 866-243-7028
oashamilton@gmail.com
hamilton.ontarioarchaeology.on.ca
Chief Officer(s):
Gary Warwick, President

Huronia Chapter
c/o Huronia Museum, PO Box 638, 549 Little Lake Park, Midland ON L4R 4P4
huronia.ontarioarchaeology.on.ca
Chief Officer(s):
John Raynor, President

London Chapter
Museum of Ontario Archaeology, 1600 Attawandaron Rd., London ON N6G 3M6
Tel: 519-473-1360; *Fax:* 519-473-1363
www.ssc.uwo.ca/assoc/oas
twitter.com/londonchapOAS
Chief Officer(s):
Nancy Van Sas, President

Ottawa Chapter
PO Box 4939, Stn. E, Ottawa ON K1S 5J1
e-mail: contact@ottawaoas.ca
www.ottawaoas.ca
Chief Officer(s):
Glenna Roberts, President
glennaroberts@sympatico.ca

Peterborough
c/o Harry Johnson, #205, 2 Testa Rd., Uxbridge ON L9P 1L9
Tel: 905-852-5097
peterborough.ontarioarchaeology.on.ca
Chief Officer(s):
Tom Mohr, President
mohr@utsc.utoronto.ca
Harry Johnson, Treasurer
hjohnson@powergate.ca

Thunder Bay Chapter
c/o Lakehead University, 955 Oliver Rd., Thunder Bay ON P7B 5E1
Chief Officer(s):
Clarence Surette, President
clsurett@lakeheadu.ca

Toronto Chapter
Toronto's First Post Office, PO Box 48, 260 Adelaide St. East, Toronto ON M5A 1N1
toronto.ontarioarchaeology.on.ca
Chief Officer(s):
Janice Teichroeb, President

Windsor Chapter
#409, 3461 Peter St., Windsor ON N9C 3Z6
e-mail: oaswindsor@gmail.com
sites.google.com/site/windsoroas
www.facebook.com/WindsorOAS
Chief Officer(s):
Amanda Black, President

Ontario Archery Association *See* Ontario Association of Archers Inc.

Ontario Arenas Association Inc. *See* Ontario Recreation Facilities Association Inc.

Ontario Arms Collectors' Association (OACA)
PO Box 477, Richmond Hill ON L4C 4Y8
Tel: 705-792-2538
oaca4579@hotmail.com
www.hockings.net/rso/oaca.html
Overview: A small provincial organization
Mission: To promote interest in the collection, possession, & lawful use of all types of arms by holding matches, competitions, meetings & exhibitions

Ontario Art Education Association (OAEA)
e-mail: membership@OAEA.ca
www.oaea.ca
www.facebook.com/291406104216483
Overview: A small provincial organization founded in 1942
Mission: Promotes and advocates for learning through visual and media arts.
Member of: Donations; member fees
Affliation(s): Ontario Teachers' Federation
Chief Officer(s):
Patricia Rocco, President
president@oaea.ca
Staff Member(s): 1
Membership: 100-499; *Committees:* Web; outreach; regional representation; advocacy resources; membership
Meetings/Conferences: • Ontario Art Education Association 2015 Annual Conference, 2015
Scope: Provincial

Ontario Art Therapy Association (OATA)
#103, 611 Wonderland Rd. N, London ON N6H 5N7
e-mail: president@oata.ca
www.oata.ca
Overview: A small provincial licensing organization founded in 1978
Mission: To provide for the development, the promotion & the maintenance of the field of art therapy in Ontario; to grant registration to its professional members upon successful completion of a rigorous process & documentation of training & experience
Chief Officer(s):
Susan Richardson, President
president@oata.ca
Finances: *Annual Operating Budget:* Less than $50,000
Membership: 150-175; *Fees:* $40-$125; *Committees:* Registration; Membership; Newsletter; Education
Activities: *Speaker Service:* Yes

Ontario Arts Council (OAC) / Conseil des arts de l'Ontario
151 Bloor St. West, 5th Fl., Toronto ON M5S 1T6
Tel: 416-961-1660; *Fax:* 416-961-7796
Toll-Free: 800-387-0058
info@arts.on.ca
www.arts.on.ca
www.facebook.com/118143304897633
twitter.com/oac_cao
Overview: A large provincial organization founded in 1963
Mission: Ontario's primary funding body for professional arts activity; promotes & assists the development of the arts & artists; offers 50+ funding programs
Chief Officer(s):
John Brotman, Executive Director
Finances: *Annual Operating Budget:* Greater than $5 Million
Staff Member(s): 55
Membership: *Committees:* Governance; Finance & Audit; Compensation/Management/Resources; Public Affairs
Activities: *Library* Open to public
Awards:
• John Hirsch Director's Award (Award)
Established by a bequest to the Ontario Arts Council from the late John Hirsch; presented every three years to a promising theatre director in Ontario
• Pauline McGibbon Award (Award)
Annual award alternates between designers, directors & production craftspersons *Amount:* $7,000
• The Venture Fund (Grant)
Assists in artistic projects that embody a sense of challenge, experimentation or risk
• The Vida Peene Fund (Grant)
Provides assistance to projects which benefit the orchestra community as a whole
• John Adaskin Memorial Fund (Award)
Established in memorial of the Canadian Music Centre's first executive secretary; supports a project that encourages the promotion & development of Canadian music in the school system
• Tim Sims Encouragement Fund Award (Award)
Established in 1995; to be awarded annually to a promising young comedic performer or troupe *Amount:* $1,000
• K.M. Hunter Artists Awards (Award)
Designed to support & encourage artists who have completed their professional training & have begun to establish themselves & make an impact in their chosen field; 1 award in each field of dance, literature, music, theatre & visual arts *Amount:* $8,000
• Lieutenant-Governor's Awards for the Arts (Award)
Approximately $300,000 to be awarded annually for the visual & performing arts that recognize institutional achievements rather than celebrating particular productions or artists; established in 1995 & co-sponsored by the J.P. Bickell Foundation
• Heinz Unger Award for Conducting (Award)
Awarded every two years; Established 1968 & awarded biennially to honour the memory of the York Concert Society music director; administered by the Music Office of the Ontario Arts Council in cooperation with the Association of Canadian Orchestras
• Leslie Bell Scholarship for Choral Conducting (Award)
Established 1973; awarded biennially in competition; the purpose of the award is to help young emerging choral conductors in Ontario further their studies in the choral music field either in Canada or abroad; competition organized by the Ontario Choral Federation *Amount:* Up to $2,000
• Ruth Schwartz Children's Book Award (Award)
Two awards presented annually; $3,000 for best picture book & $2,000 for best young adult/middle reader book; in conjunction with the Canadian Booksellers Association
• William & Mary Corcoran Craft Award (Award)
Established to encourage excellence in crafts in the disciplines of glass, textiles, wood & ceramics; for college students
• Paul de Hueck & Norman Walford Career Achievement Award in the Performing Arts and in Visual Arts (Award)
Recognizes the acheivement of outstanding Canadian artists in keyboard artistry, art photography & singing
• Diana Crawford Prize (Award)
Established in 1998 in honor of Diana Crawford; awarded annually; recognizes exceptional young professionals employed by Tarragon Theatre for outstanding work in theatrical production
• Fabian Lemieux Award (Award)
Established in memory of educator Fabian Lemieux; Recognizes arts educators who have encouraged arts education in schools, colleges and universities in Ontario
• Linda Zwicker Fund (Award)
Established in memory of writer/playwright & former Arts Education Officer at the Ontario Arts Council, is designed to encourage women writers
• Hugh D. McKellar Fund (Award)
Established by Hugh McKellar to support the Lambton Country Music Festival & St. Michael's Cathedral Choir School.
• Louis Applebaum Composers Award (Award)
Established in 1998 by Canadian composer & champion of the arts, Louis Applebaum, the income generated funds an annual award recognizing excellence in composition
• Orford String Quartet Scholarship (Award)
Established by the members of the renowned Orford String Quartet; awarded every 2 years; Assists a Canadian string musician with studies, commissions or performances related to work in chamber music *Amount:* $2,000

Ontario Asbestos Removal Contractors Association *See* Environmental Abatement Council of Ontario

Ontario Asparagus Growers' Marketing Board *See* Asparagus Farmers of Ontario

Ontario Association for Behaviour Analysis (ONTABA)
#413, 283 Danforth Ave., Toronto ON M4K 1N2
e-mail: contact@ontaba.org
www.ontaba.org
twitter.com/ONTABA1
Overview: A small provincial organization
Affliation(s): Association for Behaviour Analysis International
Chief Officer(s):
Albert Malkin, President
Membership: *Committees:* Conference; Elections; Membership; Recruitment; Professional Regulation; Newsletter; Webpage; Public and Community Relations; Awards; Satellite Conference
Meetings/Conferences: • Ontario Association for Behaviour Analysis Annual Conference 2015, 2015, ON
Scope: Provincial

Ontario Association for Family Mediation (OAFM)
PO Box 102, Almonte ON K0A 1A0
Tel: 416-740-6236; *Fax:* 866-352-1579
Toll-Free: 800-989-3025
www.oafm.on.ca
Overview: A small provincial organization founded in 1982

Mission: OAFM is a not for profit association promoting family mediation as a dispute resolution process for separating couples & for families in conflict. OAFM also promotes professionalism within the family mediation community. It is run by a volunteer Board Directors comprised of members from across Ontario, Canada.
Member of: Family Mediation Canada
Affliation(s): Family Mediation Canada
Chief Officer(s):
Nancy Huntley, President
compassmediation@rogers.com
Membership: *Fees:* $35 student; $95 supporting; $150 associate; $250 accredited; *Member Profile:* Individuals working in the field of mediation in Ontario
Meetings/Conferences: • Ontario Association for Family Mediation Annual AGM & Conference 2015, 2015, ON
Scope: Provincial
Contact Information: Phone: 416-740-6236

Ontario Association for Geographic & Environmental Education (OAGEE) / Association pour l'enseignement de la géographie et de l'environnement en Ontario (AEGEO)

#202, 10 Morrow Ave., Toronto ON M6R 2J1
Tel: 416-538-1650; *Fax:* 416-489-1713
www.oagee.org
www.facebook.com/pages/Oagee/152607121453776
Overview: A small provincial organization founded in 1949
Chief Officer(s):
Shawn Hughes, President
Ewan Geddes, Vice-President, Membership Services
Jonathan Fletcher, Vice-President, Communications
Ivan Ius, Vice-President, Curriculum
Brenda Scarlett, Secretary
Lew French, Treasurer
Membership: *Fees:* $25 university students & faculty; $30 retired members; $50 individuals; *Member Profile:* Teachers of geography from across Ontario
Activities: Providing information & resources to elementary & secondary school teachers of geography & environmental education
Meetings/Conferences: • Ontario Association for Geographic & Environmental Education Spring Conference 2015, 2015
Scope: Provincial
• Ontario Association for Geographic & Environmental Education Fall Conference 2015, 2015
Scope: Provincial
Publications:
• The Monograph Editor
Type: Journal; *Frequency:* Quarterly; *Editor:* Gary Birchall; *Price:* Free with Ontario Association of Geographic & Environmental Education membership
Profile: Lesson plans & activities, for geography courses, designed by teachers

Ontario Association for Impact Assessment (OAIA)

87 Irondale Dr., 2nd Fl., Toronto ON M9L 2S6
e-mail: info@oaia.on.ca
www.oaia.on.ca
Overview: A medium-sized provincial organization
Chief Officer(s):
Steven Rowe, President
Membership: *Fees:* $40 regular; $10 student

Ontario Association for Marriage & Family Therapy (OAMFT)

PO Box 693, Tottenham ON L0G 1W0
Tel: 905-936-3338; *Fax:* 905-936-9192
Toll-Free: 800-267-2638
admin@oamft.com
www.oamft.com
Overview: A small provincial organization founded in 1974
Mission: To serve members of the association, the profession of marriage & family therapy, & the public; To uphold the Code of Ethics of the American Association for Marriage & Family Therapy
Affliation(s): Canadian Registry of Marriage & Family Therapy; American Association for Marriage & Family Therapy (AAMFT)
Chief Officer(s):
Brenda Spitzer, President
President@OAMFT.com
Donna Chamberlain, Administrator
Membership: *Member Profile:* Registered marriage & family therapists; Approved supervisors; Associate members who have completed graduate training; Students; Affiliate members who are professionals in other disciplines such as medicine & religious leadership
Activities: Engaging in advocacy activities; Collaborating with other agencies to provide seminars & workshops; Organizing networking opportunities; Providing public education & awareness programs

Ontario Association for the Application of Personality Type (OAAPT)

#B1, 116 Viceroy Rd., Concord ON L4K 2M2
Tel: 905-760-1339; *Fax:* 905-760-0113
info@oaapt.ca
www.oaapt.ca
Overview: A small provincial organization founded in 1985
Mission: To promote direction, mechanisms & resources to a broad-based community, an understanding of psychological type & the most effective applications of the MBTI & other related instruments in Ontario
Affliation(s): Association of Psychological Type
Chief Officer(s):
Ken MacDonald, President
Denise Hughes, Treasurer
Finances: *Annual Operating Budget:* Less than $50,000; *Funding Sources:* Memberships; Program Activities; Conference
11 volunteer(s)
Membership: 170; *Fees:* $52.50 individual; $40 student/senior; $150 organization; *Member Profile:* Persons interested in personality-type instruments focusing on the Myers-Briggs type indicator
Activities: *Rents Mailing List:* Yes
Awards:
• Founders Award (Award)

Ontario Association for University Lifelong Learning *See* Ontario Council for University Lifelong Learning

Ontario Association of Acupuncture & Traditional Chinese Medicine (OAATCM)

370B Dupont St., Toronto ON M5R 3G3
Tel: 416-944-2265
oaatcm@gmail.com
www.oaatcm.ca
Overview: A small provincial organization
Mission: To encourage the standardization of educational requirements for all practitioners of traditional Chinese medicine (TCM); To support high standards of professional training, competency & qualifications of TCM practitioners
Staff Member(s): 8

Ontario Association of Agricultural Societies (OAAS)

PO Box 189, Glencoe ON N0L 1M0
Tel: 519-287-3553; *Fax:* 519-287-2000
oaas@bellnet.ca
www.ontariofairs.com
Overview: A medium-sized provincial organization founded in 1900
Mission: To provide education, information & leadership to members & to act as a single voice when dealing with members, media, public & government
Member of: Canadian Association of Fairs & Exhibitions; International Association of Fairs & Expositions
Chief Officer(s):
Harry Emmott, President
Finances: *Annual Operating Budget:* $50,000-$100,000
Staff Member(s): 3
Membership: 234; *Fees:* Depends on size of fair; *Member Profile:* Open to agricultural fair or service manager

Ontario Association of Alternative & Independent Schools *See* Ontario Federation of Independent Schools

Ontario Association of Archers Inc. (OAA)

PO Box 45, Stn. Caledon Village, Caledon ON L7K 3L3
Tel: 519-927-3256; *Fax:* 519-927-9137
info@oaa-archery.on.ca
www.oaa-archery.on.ca
www.facebook.com/groups/385376888165218
Previous Name: Ontario Archery Association
Overview: A medium-sized provincial organization founded in 1927 overseen by Archery Canada Tir à l'Arc
Member of: Archery Canada Tir à l'Arc
Chief Officer(s):
Adam Thomas, President
president@oaa-archery.on.ca
Cathy Fischer, Secretary-Treasurer
secretary@oaa-archery.on.ca
Membership: 800; *Fees:* $25-35 Individual; $70 Family; $60 Club

Ontario Association of Architects (OAA)

111 Moatfield Dr., Toronto ON M3B 3L6
Tel: 416-449-6898; *Fax:* 416-449-5756
Toll-Free: 800-565-2724
Other Communication: practiceadvisor@oaa.on.ca (oaamail@oaa.on.ca
www.oaa.on.ca
Overview: A medium-sized provincial licensing organization founded in 1889
Mission: To operate in accordance with the Government of Ontario's Architects Act; To serve & protect the public interest by promoting & increasing the knowledge, skill, & proficiency of members
Chief Officer(s):
I. Hillel Roebuck, Registrar
hillelr@oaa.on.ca
Gordon Masters, Director, Operations
gordonm@oaa.on.ca
Kristi Doyle, Director, Policy
kristid@oaa.on.ca
Andrew Fuller, Administrator, Accounting & Information Technology
andrewf@oaa.on.ca
Gail Hanselman, Administrator, Certificate of Practice
gailh@oaa.on.ca
Tamara La Pierre King, Administrator, Web site & Communications
tamarak@oaa.on.ca
Jessica O'Rafferty, Administrator, Admission
jessicao@oaa.on.ca
Ellen Savitsky, Administrator, Continuing Education
ellens@oaa.on.ca
Kim Sumi, Administrator, Licence
kims@oaa.on.ca
Finances: *Funding Sources:* Membership dues; Rental of meeting facilities; Document sales; Sponsorships
Membership: 2,500 licensed architects + 1,200 intern architects + 750 associates (honorary, life, retired, & student associates); *Committees:* Practice; Complaints; Discipline; Experience Requirements; Public Interest Review; Registration; Audit; Perspectives Editorial
Activities: Regulating the profession in the interest of all Ontarians; Presenting the OAA Continuing Education Program; *Internships:* Yes; *Speaker Service:* Yes
Awards:
• G. Randy Roberts Service Award (Award)
To honour an OAA member for extraordinary service to the membership
• Honour Roll (Award)
For prominent members of the architectural profession who are now deceased (a record of achievement is given to a relative)
• Lifetime Design Achievement Award (Award)
To honour an individual for career-long achievement in architectural design excellence
• Order of Da Vinci (Award)
To reconize architects who have demonstrated exceptional leadership in education, the profession, or in the community
Meetings/Conferences: • Ontario Association of Architects 2015 Annual Conference: Urban Renewal, May, 2015, Hamilton, ON
Scope: Provincial
Description: Continuing education sessions by speakers who excel in their field of expertise
Contact Information: Continuing Education Coordinator: Ellen Savitsky, E-mail: ellens@oaa.on.ca
Publications:
• Ontario Association of Architects Annual Report
Type: Yearbook; *Frequency:* Annually
Profile: A review of the year, with Ontario Association of Architects programs & services
• Perspectives [a publication of the Ontario Association of Architects]
Type: Journal; *Frequency:* Quarterly

Ontario Association of Art Galleries (OAAG)

#125, 111 Peter St., Toronto ON M5V 2H1
Tel: 416-598-0714; *Fax:* 416-598-4128
oaag@oaag.org
oaag.org
Overview: A medium-sized provincial organization founded in 1968
Mission: To encourage the highest standards for the exhibition, interpretation, & conservation of the visual arts; to develop tools

to assist gallery professionals in achieving institutional goals; to advance positive, responsive relations with government, its agencies & the citizens of Ontario
Chief Officer(s):
Demetra Christakos, Executive Director
Veronica Quach, Assistant Director
Finances: *Funding Sources:* Ontario Ministry of Citizenship, Culture, Tourism & Recreation; Ontario Arts Council; memberships
Staff Member(s): 2; 9 volunteer(s)
Membership: 200+ art organizations + individuals involved in the visual arts; *Fees:* $30 student; $75 individual; $200-$900 organization; *Member Profile:* Non-profit organization which shares aims of OAAG; individuals are encouraged to join as 'Friends/Colleagues of OAAG'; *Committees:* Awards; Membership; Policy; New Technology; Cultural Equity
Activities: Seminars, workshops, annual meetings; awards; publications; job file; member directory; advisory service; *Speaker Service:* Yes

Ontario Association of Bovine Practitioners
RR#1, Alma ON N0B 1A0
Tel: 519-846-2290; *Fax:* 519-846-8165
info@oabp.ca
www.oabp.ca
Overview: A medium-sized provincial organization
Chief Officer(s):
Ruth Cudmore, Executive Assistant & Membership
David Douglas, President

Ontario Association of Broadcasters (OAB)
PO Box 54040, 5762 Hwy. 7 East, Markham ON L3P 7Y4
Tel: 905-554-2730; *Fax:* 905-554-2731
www.oab.ca
Previous Name: Central Canada Broadcasters Association
Overview: A small provincial organization founded in 1950 overseen by Canadian Association of Broadcasters
Chief Officer(s):
Doug Kirk, President
president@oab.ca
Dave Hughes, Vice-President
dave.hughes@star933.com
Ross Davies, Treasurer
rdavies@bbm.ca
Membership: 100-499
Meetings/Conferences: • Ontario Association of Broadcasters 2015 Annual General Meeting, 2015, ON
Scope: Provincial

Ontario Association of Cemeteries *See* Ontario Association of Cemetery & Funeral Professionals

Ontario Association of Cemetery & Funeral Professionals (OACFP)
PO Box 10173, 27 Legend Ct., Ancaster ON L9K 1P3
Tel: 905-383-6528; *Fax:* 905-383-2771
Toll-Free: 888-558-3335
info@oacfp.com
www.oacfp.com
Previous Name: Ontario Association of Cemeteries
Overview: A medium-sized provincial organization founded in 1913
Mission: To promote high standards of service & the professional operation of cemeteries, funeral homes, crematoria, & related bereavement services
Chief Officer(s):
Anita Mazzara, President
Terry Eccles, First Vice-President
Tim Vreman, Sec.-Treas.
Jo-Anne Rogerson, Executive Director
Membership: *Member Profile:* All professional sectors of the death care industry including cemeteries, funeral homes, crematoria, monument retailers, casket retailers, funeral transfer services, & industry suppliers & consultants
Activities: Offering educational seminars & conferences; Emcouraging legislation for the betterment of the death care industry; Advising & cooperating with government in the implementation of legislation

Ontario Association of Certified Engineering Technicians & Technologists (OACETT)
#404, 10 Four Seasons Pl., Toronto ON M9B 6H7
Tel: 416-621-9621; *Fax:* 416-621-8694
info@oacett.org
www.oacett.org
www.linkedin.com/groups/official-oacett-group-149199
www.facebook.com/OACETT
twitter.com/OACETT
Overview: A small provincial organization founded in 1962
Mission: To advance the profession of applied science & engineering technology through standards for society's benefit.
Member of: Canadian Council of Technicians & Technologists
Chief Officer(s):
David J. Thomson, CEO
dthomson@oacett.org
Stephen Morley, President
Staff Member(s): 28
Membership: 24,000+; *Fees:* Schedule available; *Member Profile:* Applied science technicians & technologists
Activities: *Internships:* Yes; *Speaker Service:* Yes
Publications:
• Ontario Technologist
Frequency: Bi-Monthly; *Price:* $24 (Canada), $48 (U.S.A.), $96(International)
Profile: Includes technical features written by experts, cover stories on interesting topics and consistent coverage of major disciplines by knowledgeable columnists.

Ontario Association of Chiefs of Police (OACP)
#605, 40 College St., Toronto ON M5G 2J3
Tel: 416-926-0424; *Fax:* 416-926-0436
Toll-Free: 800-816-1767
oacpadmin@oacp.ca
www.oacp.on.ca
www.facebook.com/OACPOfficial
twitter.com/OACPOfficial
www.youtube.com/OACPOfficial
Overview: A medium-sized provincial organization founded in 1952
Mission: The Association coordinates police training & education. It advocates on behalf of its membership, expressing concerns & priorities to the government, public & to any other bodies.
Chief Officer(s):
Ron Bain, Executive Director Ext. 25
rbain@oacp.ca
Joe Couto, Director, Government Relations & Communications Ext. 22
jcouto@oacp.ca
Sharon Seepersad, Manager, Administration/Member Services Ext. 22
sharons@oacp.ca
Jennifer Evans, President
Finances: *Funding Sources:* Membership dues & programs
Staff Member(s): 4
Membership: 1,500+; *Member Profile:* Police leaders in Ontario
Activities: Conferences; seminars & workshops; zone meetings; communications & networking; advocacy
Meetings/Conferences: • Ontario Association of Chiefs of Police 2015 Annual Meeting, June, 2015, ON
Scope: Provincial

Ontario Association of Child & Youth Counsellors (OACYC) / L'Association ontarienne des conseilliers à l'enfance et à la jeunesse
#111, 290 North Queen St., Toronto ON M9C 5L2
e-mail: office@oacyc.org
www.oacyc.org
Overview: A medium-sized provincial organization founded in 1969
Member of: Council of Canadian Child & Youth Care Associations
Chief Officer(s):
Jennifer Foster, Executive Director
Finances: *Funding Sources:* Membership fees; Donations; Revenue from conferences & workshops; Sale of advertising & print materials
25 volunteer(s)
Membership: 2,200; *Fees:* $63-$210
Activities: Offering professional liability insurance for members
Meetings/Conferences: • Ontario Association of Child & Youth Counsellors 2015 Conference, 2015, ON
Scope: Provincial

Ontario Association of Children's Aid Societies (OACAS) / Association ontarienne des sociétés de l'aide à l'enfance
#308, 75 Front St. East, Toronto ON M5E 1V9
Tel: 416-987-7725; *Fax:* 416-366-8317
Toll-Free: 800-718-7725
reception@oacas.org
www.oacas.org
twitter.com/our_children
www.youtube.com/YourChildrensAid
Overview: A medium-sized provincial organization founded in 1912
Mission: To provide leadership for the achievement of excellence in the protection of children & in the promotion of their well-being within their families & communities
Chief Officer(s):
Mary Ballantyne, Executive Director
Finances: *Funding Sources:* Membership fees; government grants; other revenue producing activities

Ontario Association of Children's Rehabilitation Services (OACRS) / Association ontarienne des services de réhabilitation pour enfants (AOSRE)
150 Kilgour Rd., Toronto ON M4G 1R8
Tel: 416-424-3864; *Fax:* 416-467-7083
info@oacrs.com
www.oacrs.com
Previous Name: Association of Treatment Centres of Ontario
Overview: A medium-sized provincial charitable organization founded in 1973
Mission: To promote a province-wide, coordinated, community-based service system for children & youth with multiple disabilities & their families; To support members centres to achieve responsive, family-centred care
Affliation(s): Kid's Coalition
Chief Officer(s):
Linda Kenny, Chief Executive Officer
lkenny@oacrs.com
Jennifer Inkpen, Director, Member Services
jinkpen@oacrs.com
Carol Moore, Policy Analyst & Coordinator, Stakeholder Relations
cmoore@oacrs.com
Finances: *Funding Sources:* Membership fees; Donations
Membership: 20 centres; *Fees:* Schedule available; *Member Profile:* Treatment centres for children & youth with physical disabilities &/or communication disorders; *Committees:* Administrators; Finance; Nominating; Conference; Consumers Advisory Group; Board of Directors; Best Practices; Strategic Relations & Communications

Ontario Association of Committees of Adjustment & Consent Authorities (OACA)
PO Box 568, Cayuga ON N0A 1E0
e-mail: oaca@primus.ca
www.oaca.info
Overview: A small provincial organization founded in 1973
Mission: To promote laws that benefit its members & set a standard for their practices
Chief Officer(s):
Linda Gavey, Secretary-Treasurer
Andreas Peterson, President
Membership: 500-999; *Fees:* $110 active; $120 associate; *Committees:* Finance; Site Selection; Accreditation; Publicity & Website; Conference; Seminar; Education Monitoring; Legislation; Resolutions; Nominations
Activities: March seminar; annual meeting; *Rents Mailing List:* Yes

Ontario Association of Community Care Access Centres (OACCAC)
#200, 130 Bloor St. West, Toronto ON M5S 1N5
Tel: 416-750-1720
frontdeskservices@ccac-ont.ca
www.ccac-ont.ca
Overview: A medium-sized provincial organization
Mission: To serve as a collective voice for the contributions made by CCACs to & an integrated health care system, & to provide leadership, inspiration & evidence-based outcomes in support of innovative & cost-effective community health care services
Affliation(s): Ontario Hospital Association
Chief Officer(s):
Margaret Mottershead, CEO
Finances: *Annual Operating Budget:* Greater than $5 Million
Staff Member(s): 20
Membership: 42 community care access centres in Ontario; *Fees:* varies based on CCAC budget

Ontario Association of Community Futures Development Corporations (OACFDC) / Association des Sociétés d'aide au développement des collectivités de l'Ontario (ASADCO)
300 South Edgeware Rd., St Thomas ON N5P 4L1

Tel: 519-633-2326; *Fax:* 519-633-3563
Toll-Free: 888-633-2326
info@oacfdc.com
www.ontcfdc.com
twitter.com/OACFDC
Overview: A medium-sized provincial organization founded in 1994
Mission: To support members as leaders for rural community economic development in Ontario; To support members to deliver quality services in their communities and to provide the voice for the Community Futures Program in Ontario
Affliation(s): Community Futures Network of Canada
Chief Officer(s):
Diana Jedig, Executive Director
Finances: *Annual Operating Budget:* $250,000-$500,000
Staff Member(s): 3
Membership: 61 Community Futures Development Corporations (CFDCs)

Ontario Association of Consultants, Counsellors, Psychometrists & Psychotherapists (OACCPP) / Association des consultants et conseillers en santé mentale, psychométriciens, et psychothérapeutes de l'Ontario

#410, 586 Eglinton Ave. East, Toronto ON M4P 1P2
Tel: 416-298-7333; *Fax:* 416-298-9593
Toll-Free: 888-622-2779
oaccpp@oaccpp.ca
www.oaccpp.ca
www.linkedin.com/company/2202979?trk=tyah
twitter.com/OACCPP
Overview: A small provincial organization founded in 1978
Mission: The OACCPP is a provincial body of mental health service providers that provides for the professional needs of its members, and meets the needs of the community in identifying and certifying practitioners.
Chief Officer(s):
James Whetstone, President
Carol Cox, Administrative Director
admin-director@oaccpp.ca
Membership: *Fees:* $115-$200
Meetings/Conferences: • Ontario Association of Consultants, Counsellors, Psychometrists & Psychotherapists 2015 Conference, September, 2015, Toronto, ON
Scope: Provincial
Publications:
• Psychologica Magazine
Type: Magazine; *Frequency:* 2 pa

Ontario Association of Credit Counselling Services (OACCS)

ON
e-mail: info@oaccs.ca
www.indebt.org
Overview: A medium-sized provincial charitable organization founded in 1968
Mission: To represent member agencies & provide them with a forum for the pursuit of common interests in order to support, strengthen & enhance not-for-profit credit counselling services; to enhance the quality & availability of not-for-profit credit counselling
Chief Officer(s):
Henrietta Ross, Executive Director
hross@indebt.org
Finances: *Annual Operating Budget:* $100,000-$250,000; *Funding Sources:* Member agency fees
Membership: 1-99; *Fees:* % of operating budget
Activities: *Speaker Service:* Yes

Ontario Association of Deans of Education (OADE)

c/o Council of Ontario Universities, #1100, 180 Dundas St. West, Toronto ON M5G 1Z8
Tel: 416-979-2165; *Fax:* 416-979-8635
cou.on.ca
Overview: A small provincial organization
Affiliation(s): Council of Ontario Universities
Chief Officer(s):
Peter Gooch, Contact
Finances: *Funding Sources:* 13 participating faculties
Membership: 21 (15 Deans, 6 associate);

Ontario Association of Dental Specialists (OADS)

4261 Hwy. 7, Unionville ON L3R 9W6
Tel: 905-513-7722; *Fax:* 905-513-7833
Overview: A medium-sized provincial organization founded in 1992
Mission: Organization representing all dental specialties in Ontario
Chief Officer(s):
Neil Applebaum, President
neilapplebaum@rogers.com
Membership: *Member Profile:* Dental specialist societies

Ontario Association of Distress Centres *See* Distress Centres Ontario

Ontario Association of Equine Practitioners (OAEP)

c/o Heather Ferguson, 12027 Guelph Line, Milton ON L0P 1B0
e-mail: info@equinedevelopment.ca
oaep.ca
Overview: A small provincial organization founded in 1980
Mission: To facilitate communication & collegiality among equine practitioners in Ontario; To support continuing education, & provide a link between equine clinical practice, academia, industry, media, government & the community
Chief Officer(s):
John Baird, President
Greg Worley, Treasurer
Heather Ferguson, Executive Assistant
Membership: *Fees:* $80; $20 student; *Member Profile:* Equine veterinarians

Ontario Association of Fire Chiefs (OAFC)

#14, 530 Westney Rd. South, Ajax ON L1S 6M3
Tel: 905-426-9865; *Fax:* 905-426-3032
Toll-Free: 800-774-6651
www.oafc.on.ca
Overview: A medium-sized provincial organization founded in 1973
Mission: To ensure that Ontario has a well trained & well equipped fire service
Chief Officer(s):
Tim Beckett, President
Frank Lamie, Treasurer
Barry Malmsten, Executive Director
barry.malmsten@oafc.on.ca
Membership: *Member Profile:* Assistant Chiefs; Deputy Chiefs; Platoon Chiefs; Battalion Chiefs; District Chiefs; Division Chiefs; Directors of fire departments in Ontario
Activities: Organizing annual conventions; Reviewing government regulations & legislation; Providing networking opportunities
Meetings/Conferences: • Ontario Association of Fire Chiefs 2015 Conference, May, 2015, Toronto Congress Centre, Toronto, ON
Scope: Provincial
Attendance: 600+
Contact Information: Mercedes Sturges, Conference and Event Manager; Phone: 905-426-9865 x224; mercedes.sturges@oafc.on.ca

Ontario Association of Food Banks (OAFB)

555 Bloor St. West, 2nd Fl., Toronto ON M5S 1Y6
Tel: 416-656-4100; *Fax:* 416-656-4104
Toll-Free: 866-220-4022
info@oafb.ca
www.oafb.ca
www.facebook.com/pages/Ontario-Association-of-Food-Banks/8982327261
twitter.com/OAFB
www.youtube.com/foodbanks
Overview: A small provincial charitable organization
Mission: To support the work of individual member food banks in Ontario which aim to achieve an immediate response to hunger while supporting & initiating long-term solutions to the problems which bring about hunger
Affliation(s): Canadian Association of Food Banks
Chief Officer(s):
Bill Laidlaw, Executive Director, 416-656-4100 Ext. 2931
bill@oafb.ca
Finances: *Annual Operating Budget:* $100,000-$250,000
Staff Member(s): 4
Membership: 105; *Fees:* $50; *Member Profile:* Small, medium & large food banks across Ontario; *Committees:* Reclaim Ontario; Membership & Development
Activities: *Internships:* Yes

Ontario Association of Former Parliamentarians / Association ontarienne des ex-parlementaires

Whitney Block, #1612, 99 Wellesley St. West, Toronto ON M7A 1A2
Tel: 416-325-4647; *Fax:* 416-326-4650
oafp@ontla.org
www.oafp.ca
Overview: A small provincial organization
Mission: To protect former parliamentarians & to put their skills to use in other sectors of Ontario
Chief Officer(s):
Canon Derwyn Shea, Rev., Chair, 416-787-7911
dshea@sthildastowers.com
Membership: *Fees:* $50; *Member Profile:* Former sitting members of the Legislative Assembly

Ontario Association of Gastroenterology (OAG)

#210, 2800 - 14 Ave., Markham ON L3R 0E4
Tel: 416-494-7233; *Fax:* 416-491-1670
Toll-Free: 866-560-7585
info@gastro.on.ca
www.gastro.on.ca
twitter.com/ontario_gastros
Overview: A small provincial organization
Mission: Serves the practice of gastroenterology in Ontario, promoting, maintaining & improving its knowledge & standards; Represents Ontario gastroenterologists in discussions, meetings & communications with other organizations
Chief Officer(s):
Melonie Hart, Director, Operations
Finances: *Funding Sources:* Membership fees
Staff Member(s): 3
Membership: *Fees:* $250 active; $0 residents

Ontario Association of Homes for the Aged *See* Ontario Association of Non-Profit Homes & Services for Seniors

Ontario Association of Insolvency & Restructuring Professionals (OAIRP)

c/o A. Farber & Partners Inc., #1600, 150 York St., Toronto ON M5H 3S5
Tel: 416-496-3732; *Fax:* 416-496-9651
www.oairp.com
Previous Name: Ontario Insolvency Practitioners Association
Overview: A small provincial organization overseen by Canadian Association of Insolvency & Restructuring Professionals
Member of: Canadian Association of Insolvency & Restructuring Professionals
Chief Officer(s):
Allan Nackan, President
anackan@farberfinancial.com
Activities: *Rents Mailing List:* Yes

Ontario Association of Interval & Transition Houses (OAITH)

#1404, 2 Carleton St., Toronto ON M5B 1J3
Tel: 416-977-6619
info@oaith.ca
www.oaith.ca
www.facebook.com/OAITH
www.youtube.com/user/OAITH
Overview: A small provincial organization founded in 1977
Mission: To work towards social change by ensuring that the voices of abused women are heard; To remove barriers to equality for women & children
Chief Officer(s):
Charlene Catchpole, Chair, Board of Directors
Susan H. Young, Director
susan@oaith.ca
Finances: *Funding Sources:* Donations
Membership: *Member Profile:* First stage emergency shelters for abused women & their children; Second stages housing programs; Community-based women's service organizations; *Committees:* Membership; Social Justice & Action/Anti-Racism Anti-Oppression; Member Education & Training; Personnel; Finance
Activities: Engaging in advocacy activities; Raising public awareness; Offering public education

Ontario Association of Jewish Dayschools; Ontario Jewish Association for Equity in Education *See* Centre for Jewish Education

Ontario Association of Landscape Architects (OALA)

#407, 3 Church St., Toronto ON M5E 1M2
Tel: 416-231-4181; *Fax:* 416-231-2679
oala@oala.ca
www.oala.ca

Overview: A medium-sized provincial licensing organization founded in 1968
Mission: To promote, improve & advance the profession; to maintain standards of professional practice & conduct consistent with the need to serve & to protect the public interest; to support improvement &/or conservation of the natural, cultural, social & built environment
Member of: Canadian Society of Landscape Architects; Council of Landscape Architectural Registration Boards
Affliation(s): American Society of Landscape Architects
Chief Officer(s):
Linda MacLeod, Registrar
Glenn O'Connor, President
Finances: *Annual Operating Budget:* $3 Million-$5 Million; *Funding Sources:* Membership dues
Staff Member(s): 2; 100 volunteer(s)
Membership: 690 full + 250 associate + 20 affiliate; *Fees:* $696.25 full; $150 associate; $141.75 affiliate; *Member Profile:* Professional landscape architects; *Committees:* Ethics; Honours, Awards & Protocol; Discipline; Continuing Education; Marketing
Activities: *Internships:* Yes
Awards:
• Emeritus & Honorary Award (Award)
Honorary members being non-landscape architects appointed by Council, nominated by another member
• Public Practice Award (Award)
Recognizes the outstanding leadership of a member of the profession in public practice who promotes & enhances landscape architecture by working for improved understanding & appreciation of the work of landscape architects in both public & private practice
• Carl Borgstrom Award for Service to the Environment (Award)
Given to an individual landscape architect or landscape architectural group, organization or agency to recognize & encourage a special or unusual contribution to the sensitive, sustainable design for human use of the environment
• OALA Award for Service to the Environment (Award)
Given to a non-landscape architectural individual, group, organization or agency to recognize & encourage a special or unusual contribution to the sensitive, sustainable design for human use of the environment
• Pinnacle Award for Landscape Architectural Excellence (Award)
Recognizes an OALA member and their professional work
• David Erb Memorial Award (Award)
Recognizes an OALA member who has made an exemplary vountary contribution to the work of the association

Ontario Association of Library Technicians (OALT) / Association des bibliotechniciens de l'Ontario (ABO)

Abbey Market, PO Box 76010, 1500 Upper Middle Rd. West, Oakville ON L6M 3H5
e-mail: info@oaltabo.on.ca
oaltabo.on.ca
Overview: A medium-sized provincial organization founded in 1973
Mission: To promote the interests of library & information technician graduates & students throughout Ontario; To advance library & information technician graduates & students
Chief Officer(s):
Michael David Reansbury, President
Daisy Collins, Treasurer
Donna Brown, Coordinator, External Communications
Lisa Eschli, Coordinator, Internal Communications
Amna Hussain, Coordinator, Internal Communications
Amy Dwyer, Coordinator, Membership
Maria Ripley, Coordinator, Chapters
Millie Yip, Coordinator, Chapters
Kathi Vandenheuvel, Archivist
Membership: *Member Profile:* Library & information technician graduates in Ontario; Retired or unemployed individuals; Library & information technician students; Associate members; Institutional members
Activities: Instituting recognized standards; Promoting the value of library information technicians; Liaising with related professions & institutions; Disseminating information; Offering educational & professional development opportunities; Advocating for library information technicians; Providing networking events
Meetings/Conferences: • Ontario Association of Library Technicians / Association des bibliotechniciens de l'Ontario 2015 42nd Annual Conference, 2015, ON
Scope: Provincial
Description: Featuring educational sessions, speeches, the annual business meeting, & award presentations
Contact Information: Ontario Association of Library Technicians External Communications Coordinator: Dana Schwarz; Internal Communications Coordinator: Serena McGovern, E-mail: info@oaltabo.on.ca
• Ontario Association of Library Technicians / Association des bibliotechniciens de l'Ontario 2016 43rd Annual Conference, 2016
Scope: Provincial
Description: Featuring educational sessions, speeches, the annual business meeting, & award presentations
Contact Information: Ontario Association of Library Technicians External Communications Coordinator: Dana Schwarz; Internal Communications Coordinator: Serena McGovern; E-mail: info@oaltabo.on.ca
Publications:
• Ontario Association of Library Technicians Newsletter
Type: Newsletter; *Editor:* Julie Cristinzo; Jessica Goodman
• Ontario Association of Library Technicians Membership Directory
Type: Directory

Ontario Association of Medical Laboratories (OAML)

#1802, 5000 Yonge St., Toronto ON M2N 7E9
Tel: 416-250-8555; *Fax:* 416-250-8464
oaml@oaml.com
www.oaml.com
Overview: A medium-sized provincial organization founded in 1978
Mission: To act as the voice of Ontario's community laboratory sector; To promote professionalism, technical excellence, & accountability in the delivery of laboratory services throughout Ontario
Membership: 9; *Member Profile:* Independently owned laboratories in Ontario that perform diagnostic testing for patients outside hospitals
Activities: Speaking to government on behalf of the industry; Liaising with other health service professional associations & colleges to bring about positive changes in health care services in Ontario; Administering the OAML quality assurance program
Awards:
• OAML Scholarships (Scholarship)
Eligibility: Ontario students enrolled in programs in medical laboratory sciences *Amount:* $1,000
• OAML Research Trust Small Grants (Grant)
To recognize innovation & excellence in the clinical laboratory sciences & the delivery of laboratory services in Ontario

Ontario Association of Medical Radiation Sciences (OAMRS)

PO Box 1054, Stn. Main, #101, 233 Colborne St., Brantford ON N3T 5S7
Tel: 519-753-6037; *Fax:* 519-753-6408
Toll-Free: 800-387-4674
mbrshpcoord@oamrs.org
www.oamrs.org
www.linkedin.com/company/oamrs---ontario-association-of-medical-radiati
www.facebook.com/401916469893394
twitter.com/OAMRS1
Merged from: Ont. Assn. of Medical Radiation Technologists; Ont. Society of Diagnostic Medical Sonographers
Overview: A medium-sized provincial organization founded in 2012 overseen by Canadian Association of Medical Radiation Technologists
Mission: To advocate on behalf of the profession of medical radiation science practitioners to government bodies
Chief Officer(s):
Greg Toffner, President & CEO
toffnerg@oamrs.org
Cathy Baxter, Manager, Professional Services
baxterc@oamrs.org
Marg Torelli, Finance Officer
finoffr@oamrs.org
Finances: *Funding Sources:* Membership fees; Sponsorships
Staff Member(s): 8
Membership: *Member Profile:* Medical radiation technologists, therapists, & students from across Ontario; *Committees:* Executive & By-Laws; Nominating; Strategic Planning & Advisory Council (SPAC); Marketing & Communications; Professional Recognition; M.E. (Beth) Wastle Research Bursary; Practice Evolution & Extended Learning
Activities: Presenting education programs; Conducing research; Promoting the profession of medical radiation technology
Meetings/Conferences: • Ontario Association of Medical Radiation Sciences 2015 Annual General Conference, 2015
Scope: Provincial
Contact Information: Contact, Professional Services: Dana Steane, steaned@oamrs.org
Publications:
• Filter: The Journal of The Ontario Association of Medical Radiation Sciences
Type: E-Newsletter; *Frequency:* Bimonthly; *Accepts Advertising*
Profile: Information for technologists who specialize in radiography, C.T., P.E.T., M.R.I, radiation therapy, ultrasound, & nuclear medicine

Ontario Association of Midwives *See* Association of Ontario Midwives

Ontario Association of Naturopathic Doctors (OAND)

#603, 789 Don Mills Rd., Toronto ON M3C 1T5
Tel: 416-233-2001; *Fax:* 416-233-2924
Toll-Free: 877-628-7284
info@oand.org
www.oand.org
Previous Name: Ontario Naturopathic Association
Overview: A medium-sized provincial organization founded in 1950 overseen by The Canadian Association of Naturopathic Doctors
Mission: To act as a voice for naturopathic doctors in Ontario
Affliation(s): Canadian Association of Naturopathic Doctors
Chief Officer(s):
Alison Dantas, CEO
adantas@oand.org
Elias Markou, Chair
Alfred Hauk, Secretary
Meghan Walker, Treasurer
Membership: 1,100+; *Member Profile:* Registered / licensed naturopathic doctors in Ontario; Students of accredited colleges of naturopathic medicine; Corporate members
Activities: Advocating for naturopathic doctors; Conducting public awareness campaigns; Providing resources for the profession & the public; Setting standards of practice for clinical excellence; Promoting research in naturopathic medicine; *Awareness Events:* Naturopathic Medicine Week, May
Meetings/Conferences: • Ontario Association of Naturopathic Doctors 2015 Convention & Tradeshow, 2015, ON
Scope: Provincial

Ontario Association of Non-Profit Homes & Services for Seniors (OANHSS)

#700, 7050 Weston Rd., Woodbridge ON L4L 8G7
Tel: 905-851-8821; *Fax:* 905-851-0744
www.oanhss.org
Previous Name: Ontario Association of Homes for the Aged
Overview: A medium-sized provincial organization founded in 1919 overseen by Canadian Alliance for Long Term Care
Mission: To support members in the provision of quality non-profit long term care, seniors' community services, & housing
Chief Officer(s):
Kevin Queen, Board Chair
Donna A. Rubin, Chief Executive Officer
Finances: *Funding Sources:* Membership fees; Revenue from programs & services
Membership: 585+; *Member Profile:* Non-profit providers of long term care, services, & housing for seniors; Commercial suppliers; Associate & personal members
Activities: Engaging in political advocacy activities; Providing educational opportunities & certification programs
Awards:
• OANHSS Leadership Award (Award)
To recognize a senior executive who has demonstrated exemplary leadership
• The Norma Rudy Award (Award)
To recognize voluntary contributions to OANHSS
• Innovation & Excellence Awards (Award)
To recognize innovative programs in the provision of care & services for seniors
Meetings/Conferences: • Ontario Association of Non-Profit Homes & Services for Seniors 2015 Annual Meeting & Convention: Great Places to Live & Work, April, 2015, Sheraton Centre, Toronto, ON
Scope: Provincial
Description: A professional development event & trade show, featuring expert speakers, for senior staff from the long term care, seniors' housing, & community services sectors
Contact Information: Contact, Sponsorship Information: Ellen

Maracle-Benton, Phone: 905-404-9545, E-mail: ellen@eventsinsync.com

Ontario Association of Nurses in Independent Practice *See* Independent Practice Nurses Interest Group

Ontario Association of Optometrists (OAO)

Plaza 3, #300, 2000 Argentia Rd., Mississauga ON L5N 1V9
Tel: 905-826-3522; *Fax:* 905-826-0625
Toll-Free: 800-540-3837
wbishop@optom.on.ca
www.optom.on.ca
www.facebook.com/pages/Ontario-Association-of-Optometrists/28166312427
www.youtube.com/user/OntarioOptometrists
Overview: A medium-sized provincial organization founded in 1909 overseen by Canadian Association of Optometrists
Mission: To advance the profession of optometry at the government, regulatory, & public levels
Chief Officer(s):
Cam Jackson, Chief Executive Officer, 905-826-3522 Ext. 221
Bethany Carey, Controller & Director, Member Services, 905-826-3522 Ext. 227
Melissa Secord, Director, Continuing Education, 905-826-3522 Ext. 243
Sandra Ng, Manager, Policy & Government Relations, 905-826-3522 Ext. 225
Membership: 1,200+; *Member Profile:* Licensed optometrists in Ontario
Activities: Monitoring provincial legislation; Providing education credits; Organizing an annual symposium; Disseminating public information material; Providing the Ethical Guide for OAO Members

Ontario Association of Orthodontists (OAO)

ON
e-mail: str8smiles@sympatico.ca
www.oao.on.ca
Overview: A small provincial organization
Mission: Official voice of orthodontists to organized dental associations, recognized educational institutions, licensing bodies, the public & government
Chief Officer(s):
Drew Smith, President
Gayle Fielding, Executive Secretary
Finances: *Funding Sources:* Membership dues
Membership: *Member Profile:* Orthodontists

Ontario Association of Pathologists (OAP)

c/o Mt. Sinai Hospital, Pathology & Laboratory Medicine, #600, 600 University Ave., Toronto ON M5G 1X5
Tel: 416-586-1575; *Fax:* 416-586-8628
www.ontariopathologists.org
Overview: A small provincial organization founded in 1937
Mission: To advance pathology & its allied sciences; To maintain a high standard of proficiency & ethics among its members; To promote research in pathology; To promote the scientific interests of its members
Chief Officer(s):
Katherine A. Chorneyko, President, 519-751-5544 Ext. 2446, Fax: 519-752-7809
choka@bchsys.org
Brendan Mullen, Secretary-Treasurer
cmacmillan@mtsinai.on.ca
Finances: *Annual Operating Budget:* Less than $50,000
8 volunteer(s)
Membership: 250 individual; *Fees:* $100 individual
Meetings/Conferences: • Ontario Association of Pathologists 2015 Annual Meeting, September, 2015, Niagara Falls, ON
Scope: Provincial

Ontario Association of Physics Teachers (OAPT)

Contact us via email
e-mail: president_8@oapt.ca
www.oapt.ca
Overview: A small provincial organization founded in 1979
Mission: To improve physics teaching in Ontario through the interaction & cooperation of high school teachers & university & college faculty
Affliation(s): American Association of Physics Teachers
Chief Officer(s):
Roberta Tevlin, President/Chair
president_8@oapt.ca
Olga Michalopoulos, Secretary
20 volunteer(s)
Membership: 300; *Fees:* $20 individual
Activities: Annual conference; province-wide high school physics contest

Ontario Association of Police Services Boards (OAPSB)

Suite A, 10 Peel Centre Dr., Brampton ON L6T 4B9
Tel: 905-458-1488; *Fax:* 905-458-2260
Toll-Free: 800-831-7727
admin@oapsb.ca
www.oapsb.ca
Previous Name: Municipal Police Authorities
Overview: A medium-sized provincial organization founded in 1962
Mission: To act as the voice of police services boards to government; To provide services to assist police services boards in Ontario
Chief Officer(s):
Alok Mukherjee, President
Fred Kaustinen, Executive Director
Finances: *Funding Sources:* Membership dues
Activities: Providing educational opportunities; Offering networking opportunities; Advocating on issues & concerns of police services boards
Meetings/Conferences: • Ontario Association of Police Services Boards Annual General Meeting & Spring Conference 2015, May, 2015, Marriot Eaton Centre, Toronto, ON
Scope: Provincial

Ontario Association of Property Standards Officers Inc.

PO Box 43209, 3980 Grand Park Dr., Mississauga ON L5B 4A7
www.oapso.org
Overview: A small provincial organization founded in 1974
Mission: To provide training for professionals involved in the governing of property & the environment
Chief Officer(s):
Warwick Perrin, President, 416-392-8096
wrp47@hotmail.com
Membership: *Fees:* $69 individual; $26 associate/venerable; $69/$128+ municipality; *Member Profile:* Municipal government employees
Activities: *Speaker Service:* Yes

Ontario Association of Prosthetists & Orthotists (OAPO)

#316, 3200 Deziel Dr., Windsor ON N8W 5K8
e-mail: info@oapo.org
oapo.org
Overview: A small provincial organization overseen by Canadian Association for Prosthetics & Orthotics
Mission: To promote professionalism & high standards of care in the prosthetic & orthotic field in Ontario
Chief Officer(s):
W. Alan Rigby, President
president@oapo.org
Adrienne Cuch, Secretary
secretary@oapo.org
Derek Kozar, Treasurer
Membership: *Member Profile:* Persons involved in the prosthetic & orthotic field in Ontario
Activities: Reviewing patients' questions about fees; Promoting continuing education

Ontario Association of Quick Printers (OAQP)

PO Box 182, 44 Fox Lane, Foxboro ON K0K 2B0
Tel: 613-966-3081
rutandrut@aol.com
Overview: A small provincial organization founded in 1985
Affiliation(s): Association of Graphic Solutions Providers
Chief Officer(s):
Dean Baxendale, President, 416-921-2111
Finances: *Annual Operating Budget:* Less than $50,000
Staff Member(s): 1; 11 volunteer(s)
Membership: 100-499; *Fees:* $210 printers; $380 suppliers; *Member Profile:* Copy shops; off set & in-plant printers; trade shops; manufacturers; *Committees:* Nominating; Programs; Conference; Golf Tournament
Activities: Educational events; networking; support; communications; public relations; public affairs; Print Ontario Trade Show; Graphics Canada Trade Show

Ontario Association of Radiology Managers (OARM)

26 Gateway Crt., Whitby ON L1R 3M9
Tel: 905-655-5645
headoffice@oarm.org
www.oarm.org
Overview: A medium-sized provincial organization founded in 1983
Mission: The Ontario Association of Radiology Managers provides an education and communication forum for Managers in Imaging Departments throughout the province of Ontario.
Chief Officer(s):
Mike Mukesh Sharma, President
Membership: 160
Meetings/Conferences: • Ontario Association of Radiology Managers 2015 Annual Fall Conference, 2015, ON
Scope: Provincial

Ontario Association of Residences Treating Youth (OARTY)

#210, 550 Alden Rd., Markham ON L3R 6A8
Tel: 905-475-5437; *Fax:* 905-475-5430
info@oarty.net
www.oarty.net
Overview: A medium-sized provincial charitable organization founded in 1990
Mission: To promote the provision of high quality care for vulnerable children, youth, adults, & their families
Chief Officer(s):
Rebecca Harris, Executive Director
rharris@oarty.net
Kim Donaldson, Consultant, Government Relations
kdonaldson@capitalhill.ca
Robert Fulton, Consultant, Research
r.fulton@rogers.com
Membership: 1-99

Ontario Association of Residents' Councils (OARC)

#207-208, 10155 Yonge St., Toronto ON L4T 1T5
Tel: 905-770-3710; *Fax:* 905-770-2755
Toll-Free: 800-532-0201
info@ontarc.com
www.residentscouncils.ca
Overview: A small provincial organization founded in 1981
Mission: To represent the views of residents on issues that affect the quality of their lives in long term care facilities & to promote & support the role & development of Residents' Councils
Chief Officer(s):
Sharron Cooke, President
Milly Radford, 1st Vice-President
Finances: *Annual Operating Budget:* $100,000-$250,000
Staff Member(s): 2
Membership: 250; *Fees:* $50-$150; *Member Profile:* Residents' councils in long term care facilities
Activities: *Speaker Service:* Yes

Ontario Association of School Business Officials (OASBO)

#207, 144 Main St., Markham ON L3P 5T3
Tel: 905-209-9704; *Fax:* 905-209-9705
office@oasbo.org
www.oasbo.org
Overview: A medium-sized provincial organization founded in 1945
Mission: Dedicated to the pursuit & support of quality education for all students. OASBO is the professional organization for school business officials in Ontario, Our purpose is to improve the quality of school business management and the status, competency, leadership qualities and ethical standards of school business officials at all levels; focus is on information sharing, the promotion of learning at all opportunities, the optimization of operational processes, & the development of partnerships to promote & recognize business practices excellence.
Chief Officer(s):
Bill Blackie, Executive Director
Finances: *Annual Operating Budget:* $250,000-$500,000; *Funding Sources:* PD events; membership fees
Staff Member(s): 2
Membership: 700; *Fees:* $210 active member; $420 business; *Member Profile:* School business officials employed by Ontario school boards; *Committees:* Finance; Health & Safety; Human Resources; Operations, Maintenance & Construction; Payroll & Benefits; Planning; Purchasing; Senior Business Officials; Transportation; Information Technology; Disability Management; Information Management/Privacy & Access; Admissions/Enrolment
Awards:
• McCordic Award (Award)
Awarded in recognition of the contribution made to the field of school business by an OASBO member

Meetings/Conferences: • Ontario Association of School Business Officials 72nd Annual Conference & Education Industry Show, May, 2015, Blue Mountain Resort, Collingwood, ON
Scope: Provincial

Ontario Association of Sign Language Interpreters (OASLI)

233 - 6 St., Toronto ON M8V 3A8
e-mail: contactus@oasli.on.ca
www.oasli.on.ca
Overview: A small provincial organization founded in 1985 overseen by Association of Visual Language Interpreters of Canada
Mission: To provide support & professional development, & to promote ethical & professional behaviour among our membership; To advocate for professional recognition & to provide public education about the role of sign language interpreters
Member of: Association of Visual Language Interpreters of Canada (AVLIC)
Chief Officer(s):
Jennifer Best, President
pres_ident@oasli.on.ca
Membership: *Member Profile:* ASL - English Interpreters; LSQ - French Interpreters; Deaf Interpreters; students of interpretation
Activities: Advocacy; Professional development; Public education; Interpreter certification

Ontario Association of Social Workers (OASW) / Association des travailleuses et travailleurs sociaux de l'Ontario (ATTSO)

410 Jarvis St., Toronto ON M4Y 2G6
Tel: 416-923-4848; *Fax:* 416-923-5279
info@oasw.org
www.oasw.org
Overview: A medium-sized provincial organization founded in 1964
Mission: To act as the voice of social workers in Ontario
Member of: Canadian Association of Social Workers
Chief Officer(s):
Kate Power, President
katepower@familyserviceguelph.on.ca
Finances: *Funding Sources:* Membership fees
Membership: 4,400; *Member Profile:* Individuals with a university degree in social work at the bachelor's, master's or doctoral level; Students in an accredited university-based program in social work
Activities: Offering a wide variety of publications & educational materials; Developing professional practice guidelines; Advocating for improvement of social policies & programs; Increasing public awareness on the role of the profession; Workshops; Webinars; *Awareness Events:* Social Work Week, March
Meetings/Conferences: • 2015 Social Work Provincial Conference, 2015, ON
Scope: Provincial

Ontario Association of Speech-Language Pathologists & Audiologists (OSLA)

410 Jarvis St., Toronto ON M4Y 2G6
Tel: 416-920-3676; *Fax:* 416-920-6214
Toll-Free: 877-740-6009
mail@osla.on.ca
www.osla.on.ca
www.facebook.com/162240417157549
twitter.com/osla_ontario
Overview: A medium-sized provincial organization founded in 1958
Mission: Represents & promotes the professional interests of its members; provides a comprehensive range of services that support its professional members in their work on behalf of people with communication disorders
Chief Officer(s):
Mary Cook, Executive Director
mcook@osla.on.ca
Finances: *Funding Sources:* Membership dues
Staff Member(s): 4
Membership: 1,600; *Fees:* $257.25; *Member Profile:* Speech language pathologists; audiologists; students of both
Activities: Private practice referrals; career information; advocacy on behalf of profession, membership benefits; *Awareness Events:* Speech & Hearing Month (May)

Ontario Association of Student Financial Aid Administrators (OASFAA)

c/o Student Awards & Financial Aid, University of Waterloo, 200 University Ave. West, 2nd Fl., Waterloo ON N2L 3G1
www.uwindsor.ca/oasfaa
Overview: A medium-sized provincial organization
Mission: To concern itself with the scholastic & need-based assistance programs available to the students of its member institutions, & their effect upon the financial well being of students; To conduct studies & workshops for the exchange of information & professional development; to cooperate & maintain effective liaison with other agencies, councils & committees, as appropriate; To act as a lobby group on issues related to scholastic or need-based assistance programs for students
Affliation(s): Canadian Association of Student Financial Aid Administrators
Chief Officer(s):
Maureen Jones, Treasurer, 519-888-4567 Ext. 36039
maureen@uwaterloo.ca
Finances: *Annual Operating Budget:* Less than $50,000
10 volunteer(s)
Membership: 60 institutional; 1 associate; *Fees:* $30

Ontario Association of the Appraisal Institute of Canada (OA-AIC)

#108, 16 Four Seasons Place, Toronto ON M9B 6E5
Tel: 416-695-9333; *Fax:* 877-413-4081
info@oaaic.on.ca
www.aicanada.ca/ontario
Overview: A medium-sized provincial organization overseen by Appraisal Institute of Canada
Mission: To serve the public interest by advancing high standards in the analysis & valuation of real property matters by enhancing the professional competence of its members.
Chapters: Credit Valley, Hamilton-Niagara, Huronia, Kingston, London, North Bay, Oshawa/Durham, Ottawa, Peterborough/Lindsay, Sudbury & Sault Ste. Marie, Thunder Bay, Toronto, Waterloo/Wellington, Windsor.
Chief Officer(s):
Robin Jones, President
Bonnie Prior, Executive Director
aicontario.ca
Finances: *Annual Operating Budget:* $250,000-$500,000; *Funding Sources:* Membership fees
Staff Member(s): 3
Membership: 2,100 in 14 chapters; *Fees:* $265; *Committees:* Finance; Leadership Development & Nominations; Public & Government Relations; Professional Development; Paralegal Working Group; By-Law Task Force
Activities: *Internships:* Yes

Ontario Association of Trading Houses (OATH)

PO Box 43086, Toronto ON M2N 6N1
Tel: 416-223-2028; *Fax:* 416-223-5707
info@oath.on.ca
www.oath.on.ca
www.linkedin.com/company/ontario-association-of-trading-houses
Overview: A small provincial organization founded in 1996
Mission: To develop & expand international trade; To help Canadian companies to increase their international trade & investment
Member of: Federation of International Trade Associations
Membership: *Fees:* $500 international; $250 associate; $100 Ontario Trade & Investment Professionals

Ontario Association of Triathletes (OAT)

#205, 3 Concorde Gate, Toronto ON M3C 3N7
Tel: 416-426-7025; *Fax:* 416-426-7303
info@triathlonontario.com
www.triathlonontario.com
www.facebook.com/239733609379054
Also Known As: Triathlon Ontario
Overview: A small provincial organization overseen by Triathlon Canada
Mission: To encourage participation in multi-sport events & to ensure safety & fair competition; to assist, support & promote Ontario athletes
Member of: Triathlon Canada
Chief Officer(s):
Phil Dale, Executive Director
ed@triathlonontario.com
Jonathan Hutchinson, Manager, Program & Technical
technical@triathlonontario.com
Finances: *Funding Sources:* Fees; sponsorship; government

Membership: 1,000-4,999; *Fees:* $25 youth; $50 juniors, adults & coaches; $50 elite; $10 official

Ontario Association of Veterinary Technicians (OAVT)

#104, 100 Stone Rd. West, Guelph ON N1G 5L3
Tel: 519-836-4910; *Fax:* 519-836-3638
Toll-Free: 800-675-1859
oavt@oavt.org
www.oavt.org
www.facebook.com/OntarioAssociationOfVeterinaryTechnicians
twitter.com/The_OAVT
Overview: A small provincial licensing organization founded in 1972
Mission: To promote registered veterinary technicians & advocate on behalf of its members
Member of: Canadian Association of Animal Health Technologists & Technicians
Chief Officer(s):
Rory Demetrioff, Executive Director & Registrar
rory@oavt.org
Staff Member(s): 9
Membership: *Fees:* $257.64
Meetings/Conferences: • Ontario Association of Veterinary Technicians 2015 Conference, February, 2015, Scotiabank Convention Centre, Niagara Falls, ON
Scope: Provincial

Ontario Association on Developmental Disabilities (OADD)

2 Surrey Pl., Toronto ON M5S 2C2
Tel: 416-657-2267; *Fax:* 416-925-6508
oadd@oadd.org
www.oadd.org
Overview: A medium-sized provincial organization
Mission: To support professionals & students in the field of developmental disabilities through the promotion of the highest standards of research, education, & practice
Affliation(s): Great Lakes Society for Developmental Services of Ontario (GLS); Research Special Interest Group (RSIG)
Chief Officer(s):
Michelle Palmer, Chair
Finances: *Funding Sources:* Membership dues
Membership: 100-499; *Fees:* $0 general; $25 sustaining student; $50 sustaining; $200 organizational; $250-$500 patron (bronze, silver, gold); *Member Profile:* Professionals & students working in the field of developmental disabilities; Organizations dealing with developmental disabilities
Meetings/Conferences: • Ontario Association on Developmental Disabilities 2015 Annual Conference, April, 2015, Four Points by Sheraton, Thorold, ON
Scope: Provincial
Description: Participants include front-line staff such as clinicians, therapists, & case-workers, as well as management, including program managers, supervisors, & human resources personnel
Contact Information: Ontario Association on Developmental Disabilities Conference Committee, E-mail: oadd@oadd.org
Publications:
• BrOADDcast
Type: Newsletter
Profile: Brief articles submitted by families, service providers, students, & researchers
• Journal on Developmental Disabilities
Editor: Maire Percy et al.; *Price:* oadd@oadd.org
Profile: A peer-reviewed journal, featuring research on issues relevant to developmental disabilities for both a Canadian & international audience

Ontario Athletic Therapists Association (OATA)

#302, 140 Allstate Pkwy., Markham ON L3R 5Y8
Tel: 905-946-8080; *Fax:* 905-946-1517
oatamembers@cggroup.com
www.ontarioathletictherapists.org
www.linkedin.com/groups?gid=4044330&trk=myg_ugrp_ovr
www.facebook.com/187942491304864
twitter.com/ontherapists
www.youtube.com/watch?v=FnbJdWyZD6Y&feature=plcp
Overview: A small provincial organization
Member of: Canadian Athletic Therapists Association
Chief Officer(s):
Andrew Laskoski, President
drew.laskoski@bellnet.ca
6 volunteer(s)
Membership: 400; *Fees:* $50-$200; *Member Profile:* Must be enrolled or graduate of an accredited institution - Sheridan

College, Oakville Athletic Therapy Program or York University, Sport Therapy Program

Ontario Automotive Recyclers Association (OARA)
#1, 1447 Upper Ottawa St., Hamilton ON L8W 3J6
Tel: 905-383-9788; *Fax:* 905-383-1904
Toll-Free: 800-390-8743
admin@oara.com
www.oara.com
www.facebook.com/211714578841191
twitter.com/autorecyclersCA
Overview: A small provincial organization founded in 1992
Mission: The association is the voice of the automotive recycling industry in Ontario. OARA works to improve recycling industry practices, and to promote the benefits of responsbile auto recycling to the general public, to stakeholders, and to local and provincial governments.
Member of: Automotive Recyclers of Canada
Chief Officer(s):
Steve Fletcher, Executive Director
Finances: *Funding Sources:* Membership fees
Staff Member(s): 3
Membership: *Fees:* $150 Private vehical recycling businesses; $750 associate member; $500 direct membership; *Member Profile:* Automotove recyclers; Direct Members must demonstrate compliance with the Ontario Certified Auto Recylcers Program; *Committees:* Government Affairs; Health & Safety; Meetings; Membership; Transportation; Budget & Audit; Nominations; Parts Procurement; Certification; Member Benefits
Activities: *Rents Mailing List:* Yes
Meetings/Conferences: • Ontario Automotive Recyclers Association 2015 Convention & Trade Show, March, 2015, Hilton Toronto/Markham Suites Conference Centre, Markham, ON
Scope: Provincial

Ontario Badminton Association ***See*** Badminton Ontario

Ontario Bailiff Association (OBA)
#203, 262 Queen St. East, Sault Ste. Marie ON P6A 1Y7
Toll-Free: 888-622-9909
ontariobailiff.org
Overview: A small provincial organization
Mission: Association of recovery and liquidation experts located throughout Ontario
Chief Officer(s):
Kevin Richards, President
Craig Danford, Treasurer

Ontario Ball Hockey Association (OBHA)
#5, 56 Pennsylvania Ave., Concord ON L4K 3V9
Tel: 905-738-3320; *Fax:* 905-738-3321
www.ontarioballhockey.ca
Overview: A medium-sized provincial organization founded in 1974
Mission: To promote & increase participation in the sport of ball hockey in Ontario; to improve opportunities for competition at all levels of participation; to create & implement leadership opportunities for officials, coaches & administrators; to establish standards of play & for quality of equipment to ensure good sport & safety for all participants
Affliation(s): Canadian Ball Hockey Association; International Street & Ball Hockey Association; Sport Canada; Canadian Hockey Association
Chief Officer(s):
Mauro Cugini, Executive Director
Finances: *Funding Sources:* Self-generated revenue
Staff Member(s): 2; 12 volunteer(s)
Membership: 18,000
Activities: *Awareness Events:* Provincial Championships; Regional & National Champions

Ontario Ballet Theatre
1133 St. Clair Ave. West, Toronto ON M6E 1B1
Tel: 416-656-9568; *Fax:* 416-651-4803
www.ontarioballettheatre.com
Overview: A small provincial charitable organization
Mission: To nurture & develop an appreciation of contemporary & classical ballet by reaching new audiences through artistic excellence
Member of: Dance Ontario

Ontario Band Association
c/o Membership Co-ordinator, 459 Concord Ave., Toronto ON M6H 2P9
e-mail: membership@onband.ca
www.onband.ca
Previous Name: Canadian Band Directors Association (Ontario) Inc.
Overview: A small provincial charitable organization founded in 1934 overseen by Canadian Band Association
Mission: To promote & develop musical, educational & cultural values of bands in Ontario by sponsoring annual band & solo instrument competition, composition competition, original works
Chief Officer(s):
Andria Kilbride, President
president@onband.ca
Steffan Brunette, Secretary
secretary@onband.ca
Finances: *Funding Sources:* Membership fees
Membership: *Fees:* $50; $35 student
Activities: *Rents Mailing List:* Yes

Ontario Basketball
Abilities Centre, #2A, 55 Gordon St., Whitby ON L1N 0J2
Tel: 416-477-8075; *Fax:* 416-477-8120
basketball.on.ca
www.facebook.com/OBAonFB
twitter.com/OBANews
www.youtube.com/user/OntarioBasketballOBA
Overview: A medium-sized provincial organization founded in 1977 overseen by Canada Basketball
Mission: To promote & develop basketball on an amateur basis in the province of Ontario.
Affliation(s): Provincial Sports Organizations Council; Canada Basketball; Toronto Raptors Basketball Club; NBA Canada; Coaches Association of Ontario; Canadian Sports Centre; and other provincial basketball organizations
Chief Officer(s):
Michael Cvitkovic, Executive Director
mcvitkovic@basketball.on.ca
Jason Jansson, Director, Business Development
jjansson@basketball.on.ca
Finances: *Annual Operating Budget:* $1.5 Million-$3 Million; *Funding Sources:* Sponsorship; fundraising; grants
Staff Member(s): 6
Membership: 9,000; *Fees:* $25; *Member Profile:* Players & coaches
Activities: *Internships:* Yes; *Speaker Service:* Yes; *Library* Open to public by appointment

Ontario Baton Twirling Association (OBTA)
c/o Susan Palmer, Registrar, #263, 55 Collinsgrove Rd., Toronto ON M1E 4Z2
www.obta.ca
Overview: A small provincial organization overseen by Canadian Baton Twirling Federation
Mission: To be the largest governing body of the sport of baton twirling in Ontario.
Member of: Canadian Baton Twirling Federation
Chief Officer(s):
LeeAnn Wilson, President
president@obta.ca
Susan Palmer, Membership Registrar
membership@obta.ca

Ontario Bean Growers Association (OBG)
#D, 59 Lorne Ave. East, Stratford ON N5A 6S4
Tel: 519-271-8641
info@ontariobeans.on.ca
ontariobeans.on.ca
Merged from: Ontario Bean Producers' Marketing Board; Ontario Coloured Bean Growers Association
Overview: A small provincial licensing organization founded in 2013
Member of: Ontario Agricultural Commodity Council; Canadian Special Crops Association; Pulse Canada; National Edible Bean Committee
Membership: *Member Profile:* Farmers of dry beans

Ontario Beef Improvement Association; Ontario Cattlemen's Association ***See*** Beef Farmers of Ontario

Ontario Beekeepers' Association (OBA)
#476, 8560 Tremaine Rd., Milton ON L9T 4Z1
Tel: 905-636-0661; *Fax:* 905-636-0662
info@ontariobee.com
www.ontariobee.com
Overview: A small provincial organization founded in 1881
Mission: To coordinate & advance the beekeeping industry in Ontario
Member of: Canadian Honey Council; Ontario Federation of Agriculture; Eastern Apicultural Society; Ontario Agricultural Commodity Council; Canadian Agricultural Hall of Fame; AGCare; Agricultural Adaptation Council; Ont. Agricultural Research Coalition
Chief Officer(s):
Maureen Vandermarel, Business Administrator
Dan Davidson, President
sddavidson@brktel.ca
Finances: *Annual Operating Budget:* $50,000-$100,000
Staff Member(s): 1
Membership: 450; *Fees:* $85 associate; $100 voting plus $0.50 per hive up to $700; *Member Profile:* Voting - reside in Ontario; associate (non-voting) - interested in beekeeping; 49 hives or less
Activities: Resources; courses; workshops; information meetings; *Speaker Service:* Yes; *Rents Mailing List:* Yes

Ontario Berry Growers' Association (OBGA)
30 Harmony Way, Kemptville ON K0G 1J0
Tel: 613-258-4587; *Fax:* 613-258-9129
info@ontarioberries.com
ontarioberries.com
www.facebook.com/ontarioberries
twitter.com/OntarioBerries
www.youtube.com/user/ontarioberries
Overview: A small provincial organization founded in 1973
Chief Officer(s):
Kevin Schooley, Contact
Staff Member(s): 2; 17 volunteer(s)
Membership: 200; *Fees:* $150 + GST; *Member Profile:* Berry growers & agribusiness; *Committees:* Research; Annual Conference; Finance; Promotion; Education & Membership

Ontario Bison Association
c/o Secretary, RR#6, Line 45679, St. Marys ON N4X 1C8
Tel: 519-229-6316
www.canadianbison.ca/producer/The_CBA/OntarioBisonAssociation.htm
www.facebook.com/OntarioBisonAssociation
Overview: A small provincial organization
Member of: Canadian Bison Association
Chief Officer(s):
Shirley Mills, Secretary
Membership: *Fees:* $175

Ontario Black History Society (OBHS) / Société historique des Noirs de l'Ontario
#402, 10 Adelaide St. East, Toronto ON M5C 1J3
Tel: 416-867-9420; *Fax:* 416-867-8691
admin@blackhistorysociety.ca
www.blackhistorysociety.ca
www.facebook.com/109773629168
twitter.com/tweetOBHS
www.youtube.com/user/OntarioBlackHistory
Overview: A medium-sized provincial charitable organization founded in 1978
Mission: To study Black history in Canada; to recognize, preserve & promote the contribution of Black peoples & their collective histories through education, research & cooperation; to promote the inclusion of material on Black history in school curricula; to sponsor & support educational conferences & exhibits in this field.
Affliation(s): Ontario Historical Society
Finances: *Funding Sources:* Membership fees; provincial government
Membership: *Fees:* $15 senior/student; $35 individual; $50 family; $100 organization
Activities: Discover Black History Bus Tour; Black History presentations; travelling exhibits; *Awareness Events:* Black History Month, Feb.; *Speaker Service:* Yes; *Library* Open to public by appointment

Ontario Blind Sports Association (OBSA)
#104, 3 Concorde Gate, Toronto ON M3C 3N6
Tel: 416-426-7191; *Fax:* 416-426-7361
Toll-Free: 888-711-1112
info@blindsports.on.ca
www.blindsports.on.ca
www.facebook.com/OntarioBlindSports
twitter.com/BlindSports
Overview: A small provincial charitable organization founded in 1984 overseen by Canadian Blind Sports Association Inc.
Mission: To organize sporting events & activities for blind & visually impaired athletes in Ontario
Chief Officer(s):
Kyle Pelly, Executive Director, 416-426-7244
Greg Theriault, Office Coordinator
Finances: *Annual Operating Budget:* $100,000-$250,000; *Funding Sources:* Membership fees; government

Staff Member(s): 2; 20 volunteer(s)
Membership: 200; *Fees:* $20; *Member Profile:* Sport association
Activities: *Speaker Service:* Yes

Ontario Block Parent Program Inc. (OBPPI)

902 Maitland St., London ON N5Y 2X1
Tel: 519-438-2016
Toll-Free: 800-563-2771
obppi@live.com
www.blockparent.on.ca
Overview: A medium-sized provincial charitable organization founded in 1977 overseen by Block Parent Program of Canada Inc.
Mission: To provide immediate assistance through a safety network & to offer supportive community education programs; to provide a network of police screened, easily recognizable safe homes for members of the community, especially children, to turn to in times of distress; to educate children about the program, safety on the streets & safety within the home; to develop promotions & materials to educate the community about the program, latch key children & streetproofing; to work together with the police, educators & other community groups toward safer communities
Member of: Block Parent Program of Canada Inc.
Chief Officer(s):
Marg Rooke, Acting Chair
mrooke@blockparent.on.ca
Finances: *Annual Operating Budget:* Less than $50,000
9 volunteer(s)
Activities: Promotional displays; safety presentations to students; *Awareness Events:* Block Parent Week, Oct.; *Speaker Service:* Yes

Ontario Blonde d'Aquitaine Association

40 Gazley Rd., RR#1, Wooler ON K0K 3M0
Tel: 613-397-1890
www.ontarioblondes.com
Overview: A small provincial organization
Member of: Canadian Blonde d'Aquitaine Association
Chief Officer(s):
Ilse Vink, President
jiv@rogers.com
Activities: Fairs; exhibitions
Publications:
• The Blonde Banner [a publication of Ontario Blonde d'Aquitaine Association]
Type: Newsletter

Ontario Board of Directors, Drugless Therapy/Naturopathy
See Board of Directors of Drugless Therapy, Naturopathy (Ontario)

Ontario Bobsleigh Skeleton Association (OBSA)

22 Lynwood Ave., Ottawa ON K1Y 2B3
Tel: 613-864-0702
www.ontariobobsleighskeleton.ca
www.facebook.com/OntarioBobsleighSkeleton
Overview: A medium-sized provincial organization founded in 1960
Mission: To promote bobsleigh & skeleton in Ontario
Affliation(s): Bobsleigh Canada Skeleton; International Bobsleigh & Skeleton Federation
Chief Officer(s):
Esther Dalle, Director, High Performance
edalle@hotmail.com

Ontario Brain Injury Association (OBIA)

3550 Schmon Parkway, 2nd floor, St. Catharines ON L2R 7R9
Tel: 905-641-8877; *Fax:* 905-641-0323
Toll-Free: 800-263-5404
obia@obia.on.ca
www.obia.ca
www.facebook.com/OntarioBIA?fref=ts
twitter.com/OntarioBIA
Overview: A medium-sized provincial organization founded in 1987 overseen by Brain Injury Association of Canada
Mission: To provide on-going support to persons in Ontario whose lives have been affected by acquired brain injury
Chief Officer(s):
Barbara Claiman, President
Brad Borkwood, Treasurer
Finances: *Funding Sources:* Donations; Directory revenues
Membership: *Fees:* $5 subsidized membership in OBIA & one other local association; $30 individual membership in OBIA & one other local association; $50 families
Activities: Providing education & information about acquired brain injury; Offering a Peer Support Mentoring Program for people Living with acquired brain injury; Increasing public awareness; Liaising with community associations;; *Library:* Ontario Brain Injury Association Library
Publications:
• Directory of ABI Services [a publication of the Ontario Brain Injury Association]
Type: Directory
Profile: Company listings with program descriptions
• OBIA [Ontario Brain Injury Association] Review
Type: Newsletter; *Frequency:* Quarterly; *Accepts Advertising*; *Editor:* Jennifer Norquay
Profile: Feature articles, survivor stories, upcoming events, & training information

Belleville
281 Front St., Belleville ON K8N 2Z6
Tel: 613-967-2756; *Fax:* 613-967-1108
Toll-Free: 866-894-8884
biaqd@bellnet.ca
www.biaqd.ca
Mission: To support persons affected by acquired brain injury in Quinte Distric
Member of: United Way of Quinte
Affliation(s): Ontario Brain Injury Association
Chief Officer(s):
Brad Conboy, President
Tim Hammell, Vice-President
Pam Ferrill, Office Administrator, 613-967-2756, Fax: 613-967-1108
Carole Vincent, Coordinator, Peer Support
• On the Sunnier Side
Type: Newsletter; *Frequency:* Monthly; *Accepts Advertising*
Profile: Notices of upcoming events, information about programs & services, plus prevention updates

Chatham
9 Maple Leaf Dr., Chatham ON N7M 6H2
Tel: 519-351-0297; *Fax:* 519-351-7600
lgall@newbeginnings-cksl.com
newbeginnings-cksl.com
www.facebook.com/370648369630107
Mission: To reduce the occurrence of acquired brain injury; To enhance the quality of life for survivors of acquired brain injury & their family members in Chatham-Kent
Chief Officer(s):
Lori Gall, Executive Director
Sean St.Amand, Community Integration Director
sean@newbeginnings-cksl.com
Greg Davenport, Vice-President
Cathy Weir, Vice-President
Kevin Deacon, Treasurer

Fort Erie
649 Niagara Blvd., Fort Erie ON L2A 3H7
Tel: 905-871-7789; *Fax:* 905-871-7832
hiafeadmin@bellnet.ca
Mission: To support persons with acquired brain injury & their families in Fort Erie & area
Chief Officer(s):
Donna Summerville, Coordinator, Programs
Julie Anthony, President
hiafepresident@bellnet.ca
Shirley Athoe, Treasurer
hiafetreasure@bellnet.ca

Hamilton-Wentworth
822 Main St. East, Hamilton ON L8M 1L6
Tel: 905-521-2100; *Fax:* 905-521-7927
info@hbia.ca
www.hbia.ca
Mission: To support persons with acquired brain injury in Hamilton; To improve treatment opportunites in Hamilton for persons affected by acquired brain injury; To advocate on behalf of survivors of acquired brain injury
Chief Officer(s):
Jane Grech, President
Ted Newbigging, Vice-President
Diana Velikonja, Secretary
Shannon Moffat, Treasurer
• Headstrong
Type: Newsletter; *Frequency:* Quarterly; *Accepts Advertising*; *Editor:* Sandra Best; Celeste Gallant
Profile: Updates on association events & groups, plus new developments related to acquired brain injuries

Kingston
c/o Epilepsy Kingston, 100 Stuart St., Kingston ON K7L 2V6
Tel: 613-547-6969; *Fax:* 613-548-4162
BIASEO@epilepsykingston.org
braininjuryhelp.ca
www.facebook.com/407323819294054
twitter.com/abi_help
Mission: To enhance the quality of life for people affected by acquired brain injury in southeastern Ontario
Chief Officer(s):
Kim Smith, Contact, 613-536-1555

London
560 Wellington St., Lower Level, London ON N6A 3R4
Tel: 519-642-4539; *Fax:* 519-642-4124
support@braininjurylondon.on.ca
www.braininjurylondon.on.ca
www.facebook.com/49465350232
Mission: To maximize the quality of life of persons with acquired brain injury in London & area; To advocate on behalf of those affected by acquired brain injury
Chief Officer(s):
Donna Thomson, Executive Director
Mary Carter, President
Chris Collins, Vice-President
Margo Clinker, Secretary
Gary Phelps, Treasurer
• The Monarch
Type: Newsletter; *Frequency:* Quarterly

Mississauga
#204, 2155 Leanne Blvd., Mississauga ON L5K 2K8
Tel: 905-823-2221; *Fax:* 905-823-9960
Toll-Free: 800-565-8594
biaph@biaph.com
www.biaph.com
facebook.com/biaph
twitter.com/BrainAwareBIAPH
Mission: To meet the needs of survivors of acquired brain injury & their families in the Peel & Halton region; To improve the quality of care for persons with acquired brain injury
Chief Officer(s):
Alexis Moskal, Contact

North Bay
280 Oakwood Ave., North Bay ON P1B 9G2
Tel: 705-840-8882
contact@bianba.ca
www.bianba.ca
Mission: To support & assist persons living with acquired brain injury in North Bay & the surrounding area
Chief Officer(s):
Katy Snoddon, Chair
Robert McKay, Secretary
Michael Cairns, Treasurer

Oshawa
#24, 850 King St. West, Oshawa ON L1J 8N5
Tel: 905-723-2732; *Fax:* 905-723-4936
Toll-Free: 866-354-4464
headinjassoc@rogers.com
Mission: To enrich the lives of people in Durham Region who are affected by acquired brain injury
Chief Officer(s):
Frank Murphy, Executive Director
fmurphy@biad.ca
Frank Welling, President
• The Front Page
Type: Newsletter; *Frequency:* Monthly
Profile: Association activities & forthcoming events

Ottawa
#300A, 211 Bronson Ave., Ottawa ON K1R 6H5
Tel: 613-233-8303; *Fax:* 613-233-8422
braininjuryottawavalley@bellnet.ca
www.biaov.org
Mission: To support persons with acquired brain injury, their families, caregivers, & friends in the Ottawa Valley
Chief Officer(s):
Wendy Charbonneau, President
Lise Marcoux, Vice-President
Robert Allen, Secretary-Treasurer

Peterborough
#100, 160 Charlotte St., Peterborough ON K9J 2T8
Tel: 705-741-1172; *Fax:* 705-741-5129
Toll-Free: 800-854-9738
biapr@nexicom.net
biapr.ca
twitter.com/biapeterboro
Mission: To provide services to persons living with the effects of acquired brain injury in the four counties of

Haliburton, Northumberland, Peterborough, & the City of Kawartha Lakes
Chief Officer(s):
Cheryl-Ann Hassan, Executive Director
Jeff Lanctot, President
• Heads & Tales
Type: Newsletter; *Frequency:* Monthly; *Accepts Advertising*
Profile: Information about the association & acquired brain injuries for members

Richmond Hill
11181 Yonge St., 3rd Fl., Richmond Hill ON L4S 1L2
Tel: 905-780-1236; *Fax:* 905-780-1524
Toll-Free: 800-263-5404
daveblakemore@rogers.com
Mission: To support acquired brain injury survivors & their families in York Region
Chief Officer(s):
Dave Blakemore, President
• The Headway
Type: Newsletter
Profile: Current information related to acquired brain injury in York Region

St. Catharines
c/o Stokes Community Village, PO Box 2338, 4-36 Page Street, St. Catharines ON L2R 4A7
Tel: 905-984-5058; *Fax:* 905-984-5354
Mission: To maximize the quality of life for persons with acquired brain injury & their families in the Niagara region
Chief Officer(s):
Pat Dracup, Program Director
• Brain Injury Association of Niagara Newsletter
Type: Newsletter; *Frequency:* Quarterly
Profile: Association activities for members

Sarnia-Lambton
#1032, 1705 London Line, Sarnia ON N7S 1B2
Tel: 519-337-5657; *Fax:* 519-337-1024
info@sarniabiasl.ca
www.sarniabiasl.ca
Mission: To support individuals with acquired brain injury & their families in the Sarnia & Lambton region
Chief Officer(s):
Roy Marshall, Contact, 519-542-2151

Sault Ste Marie
#127, 31 Old Garden River Rd., Sault Ste Marie ON P6B 5Y7
Tel: 705-946-0172; *Fax:* 705-946-0594
biassmd@shaw.ca
www.braininjuryssm.ca/bia.htm
Mission: To assist persons living with acquired brain injury in Sault Ste Marie & area; To reduce the incidents of brain injury
Chief Officer(s):
Frank Halford, President
Jennifer Trepasso, Secretary
Karen McKinley, Treasurer
Dawn Kuhlenbaumer, Coordinator, Peer Support
• Brain Injury Association of Sault Ste Marie & District Newsletter
Type: Newsletter

Sudbury & District
2750 Bancroft Dr., Sudbury ON P3B 1T9
Tel: 705-670-0200; *Fax:* 705-670-1462
info@biasd.com
www.biasd.com
Mission: To support survivors of acquired brain injury in Sudbury & the surrounding district
Chief Officer(s):
Sean Parsons, President, Chair-Executive

Thunder Bay
#217, 1100 Memorial Ave., Thunder Bay ON P7B 4A3
Tel: 807-621-4164
info@biatba.org
www.biatba.org
Mission: To support individuals of all ages who are affected by acquired brain injury in the Thunder Bay area

Timmins
733 Ross Ave. E., Timmins ON P4N 8S8
Tel: 705-264-2933; *Fax:* 705-264-0350
www.seizurebraininjurycentre.com
www.facebook.com/seizurebraininjurycentre
twitter.com/letstalkbrain
Mission: To ensure that brain injuries or epilepsy are not deciding factors in an individual's opportunities
Affliation(s): Canadian Epilepsy Alliance; Epilepsy Canada; Epilepsy Ontario
Chief Officer(s):
Rhonda Latendresse, Executive Director
rhondal@seizurebraininjurycentre.com
Stacey DeLaurier, Communications Officer
staceyd@seizurebraininjurycentre.com
Samantha Saley, Client Services Coodinator
sams@seizurebraininjurycentre.com

Toronto
#205, 40 St. Clair Ave. East, Toronto ON M4T 1M9
Tel: 416-830-1485
info@bist.ca
www.bist.ca
Mission: To support survivors of acquired brain injury & their family members in the City of Toronto
Chief Officer(s):
Judy Moir, Chair
Paul McCormack, Vice-Chair & Treasurer
Gary Gerber, Secretary
Todd Gotlieb, Treasurer
• BIST Beacon
Type: Newsletter; *Frequency:* Irregular
Profile: Information about the Brain Injury Society of Toronto, available to members & donors to the society

Waterloo-Wellington
#1, 871 Victoria St. North, Kitchener ON N2B 3S4
Tel: 519-579-5300; *Fax:* 519-579-0118
biaww@bellnet.ca
www.biaww.com
www.linkedin.com/groups/Brain-Injury-Association-WaterlooWellington-38
www.facebook.com/biaww
Mission: To support persons suffering from acquired brain injury & their families in the Waterloo-Wellington region
Chief Officer(s):
Patti Lehman, Executive Director

Windsor-Essex
#201, 200 West Grand Blvd., Windsor ON N9E 3W7
Tel: 519-981-1329
info@biawe.com
www.biawe.com
www.facebook.com/BIAWE
www.youtube.com/channel/UC-VWaZbdUVoC4zw-_9jrKFA
Mission: To enhance the lives of residents of Windsor & Essex County who are affected by acquired brain injury
Chief Officer(s):
Melanie Gardin, President
Lois Caldwell, Vice-President
Cheryl Henshaw, Secretary
Nancy Nicholson, Treasurer
• Step Ahead!
Type: Newsletter; *Accepts Advertising*
Profile: Review of association activites & announcements of future events

Ontario Broiler Hatching Egg & Chick Commission (OBHECCA)
#213, 251 Woodlawn Rd. West, Guelph ON N1H 8J1
Tel: 519-837-0005; *Fax:* 519-837-0464
info@obhecc.com
www.obhecc.com
Overview: A medium-sized provincial organization
Mission: To administer the supply management system for broiler hatching eggs & chicks in Ontario
Chief Officer(s):
Bob Guy, General Manager

Ontario Brown Swiss Association (OBSA)
RR#1, Bognor ON N0H 1E0
Tel: 519-372-1803
Overview: A small provincial organization
Mission: To promote Brown Swiss cow as dairy animal in Canada
Member of: Canadian Brown Swiss Association
Chief Officer(s):
Tracy Reid, Sec.-Treas.
Membership: *Member Profile:* Ownership of or interest in Brown Swiss breed of cattle
Activities: *Rents Mailing List:* Yes

Ontario Building Envelope Council (OBEC)
#310, 2175 Sheppard Ave. East, Toronto ON M2J 1W8
Tel: 647-317-5754; *Fax:* 416-491-1670
info@obec.on.ca
www.obec.on.ca
www.facebook.com/147901538606379
Overview: A medium-sized provincial organization founded in 1987
Mission: To promote the pursuit of excellence in the design, construction & performance of the building envelope
Member of: National Building Envelope Council
Chief Officer(s):
Paul J. Pushman, President
paul.pushman@exp.com
Sherry Denesha, Operations Manager
sherryd@taylorenterprises.com
Finances: *Funding Sources:* Membership fees; seminars
Staff Member(s): 2
Membership: *Fees:* $660 corporate; $165 individual; $240 professional; $25 student

Ontario Building Officials Association Inc. (OBOA) / Association de l'Ontario des officers en bâtiment inc.
#8, 200 Marycroft Ave., Woodbridge ON L4L 5X4
Tel: 905-264-1662; *Fax:* 905-264-8696
admin@oboa.on.ca
www.oboa.on.ca
Overview: A medium-sized provincial organization founded in 1956
Mission: To foster & cooperate in the establishment of uniform regulations relating to the fire protection & structural adequacy of buildings & the safety & health of the occupants; to promote the understanding & uniform interpretation & enforcement of these regulations & their companion documents; to provide assistance in the development & improvement of these regulations & their companion documents; to promote a close liaison & interchange of ideas on these regulations with related associations, the building industry, government & the consumer public
Chief Officer(s):
Ronald M. Kolbe, CAO
cao@oboa.on.ca
Leo Cusumano, President
Finances: *Annual Operating Budget:* $500,000-$1.5 Million
Staff Member(s): 2; 24 volunteer(s)
Membership: 2,184 individual; 200 institutions; *Fees:* $100; *Member Profile:* Open to individuals, firms, corporations, associations, governments & government agencies interested or engaged in the administration & enforcement of regulations related to buildings & structures & their planning, construction, demolition, alteration, renovation, maintenance, operation & renewal insofar as such matters relate to fire prevention & protection, structural adequacy, safety, health, durability & the environment; *Committees:* Certification; Education; HRDC; Journal; Nominations; Objective Base Codes; PUblic Relations; Rural Affairs; Training; Website
Activities: Single-day symposiums & information sessions; seven courses, covering individual & specialized parts of the Building Code; Code & Administrative training seminars; a one-year post diploma community college course; certification program; *Awareness Events:* International Building Safety Week; *Speaker Service:* Yes

Ontario Business Education Partnership (OBEP)
Tel: 519-208-5966; *Fax:* 519-208-5919
info@obep.on.ca
www.obep.on.ca
www.facebook.com/148570541846133?v=info
twitter.com/ontbep
Previous Name: Ontario Learning Partnership Group
Overview: A medium-sized provincial organization
Mission: To promote & facilitate mutually beneficial alliances between education, business, community organizations & government that enhance education & employment opportunities for the students of Ontario
Chief Officer(s):
Sherryl Petricevic, Executive Director
sherryl@obep.on.ca
Finances: *Annual Operating Budget:* $50,000-$100,000
Staff Member(s): 5
Membership: 25 organizations

Ontario Camelids Association (OCA)
RR#3, Harrowsmith ON K0H 1V0
Tel: 613-372-0290
info@ontariocamelids.org
www.ontariocamelids.org
Overview: A small provincial organization founded in 1991
Mission: To promote llamas & alpacas in Ontario; to enhance the visibility & versatility of camelids
Finances: *Funding Sources:* Membership fees
Membership: 50; *Fees:* $50; *Member Profile:* Llama & alpaca enthusiasts

Activities: Educational displays at fairs; information pamphlets; library containing books & videos; *Speaker Service:* Yes
Publications:
• Update [a publication of the Ontario Camelids Association]
Type: Newsletter

The Ontario Campaign for Action on Tobacco
c/o Ontario Medical Association, #900, 150 Bloor St. West, Toronto ON M5S 3C1
Tel: 416-340-2992; *Fax:* 416-340-2995
ocat@oma.org
www.ocat.org
Overview: A small provincial organization founded in 1992
Mission: To secure the passage of Ontario's Tobacco Control Act (TCA)
Chief Officer(s):
Michael Perley, Director
michael_perley@oma.org

Ontario Camping Association ***See*** Ontario Camps Association

Ontario Camps Association (OCA)
70 Martin Ross Ave., Toronto ON M3J 2L4
Tel: 416-485-0425; *Fax:* 416-485-0422
info@ontariocamps.ca
www.ontariocamps.ca
www.facebook.com/OntarioCampsAssociation
twitter.com/OCACamps
Previous Name: Ontario Camping Association
Overview: A medium-sized provincial organization founded in 1937 overseen by Canadian Camping Association
Mission: To promote youth camping throughout Ontario; To maintain high standards for organized camping; To advocate on issues which impact members
Chief Officer(s):
Adam Kronick, President
Heather Heagle, Executive Director
Staff Member(s): 4
Membership: 600; *Fees:* $300 provisional camp; $100 regular; $60 senior/student; $350 commercial; $250 affiliate; *Member Profile:* Ontario camps which meet the association's standards; Individuals; Like-minded organizations & agencies; *Committees:* Archives; Awards; Educational Events; Finance; Health Care; Human Resources; Legislative; Membership; Nominations; Special Needs; Standards; Standards Review
Activities: Enforcing camp standards, through inspections, in order to ensure sound camp operation & administration & safe camping experiences; Sharing information & ideas; Supporting training seminars & workshops; Informing the public about the benefits of camping & the role of the association; Conducting research, through the OCA Educational Research Task Force;
Meetings/Conferences: • Ontario Camps Association 2015 Annual General Meeting, January, 2015, Vaughan Estates, Toronto, ON
Scope: Provincial
Publications:
• Camp Health Issues
Price: $20
Profile: Articles about health & safety issues at camps
• How to be a Camp Counsellor . . . The Best Job in the World!
Author: Catherine Ross; *Price:* $19.95
Profile: Tips & tools to become a summer camp counsellor, such as leadership styles, teaching techniques, & behaviour management
• OCA [Ontario Camps Association] Bulletin
Type: Newsletter
• OCA [Ontario Camps Association] Camps Guide
Type: Directory; *Frequency:* Annually; *Accepts Advertising*
Profile: Listings & descriptions of accredited camps in Ontario
• OCA [Ontario Camps Association] Crisis Response & Management Plan
Price: $10.50
Profile: Information about managing a crisis, plus forms for camps to use, such as a crisis response log, & a parent / guardian call form
• Ontario Camps Association's Guidelines for Accreditation
Price: $15
Profile: Addressing aspects of a day or residential camp's operations, such as health & safety, facilities, & leadership

Ontario Campus Radio Organization
c/o CFRU-FM, Radio Gryphon, University of Guelph, Level 2 UC, Guelph ON N1G 2W1
Tel: 519-824-4120; *Fax:* 519-763-9603
cfru-fm@uoguelph.ca
www.uoguelph.ca/~cfru-fm/
Overview: A small provincial organization founded in 1980
Member of: National Campus Community Radio Association
Chief Officer(s):
Peter Bradley, Station Manager
Staff Member(s): 4; 200 volunteer(s)
Activities: "Raise Your Voice" fundraising campaign

Ontario Canoe Kayak Sprint Racing Affiliation (OCSRA)
c/o Joanne Bryant, 610 Sunset Beach Rd., Richmond Hill ON L4E 3J6
Tel: 905-773-3509
www.ocsra.ca
Overview: A small provincial organization founded in 1985 overseen by CanoeKayak Canada
Mission: To represent the sport of Olympic Sprint Canoe Kayak racing in Ontario.
Member of: CanoeKayak Canada
Chief Officer(s):
Joanne Bryant, Chair
joanne.i.bryant@gmail.com

Ontario Catholic School Trustees' Association (OCSTA)
PO Box 2064, #1804, 20 Eglinton Ave. West, Toronto ON M4R 1K8
Tel: 416-932-9460; *Fax:* 416-932-9459
ocsta@ocsta.on.ca
www.ocsta.on.ca
www.facebook.com/CatholicEducationInOntario
twitter.com/catholicedu
www.youtube.com/user/OCSTAVideo1
Overview: A medium-sized provincial organization founded in 1930
Affliation(s): Canadian Catholic School Trustees Association
Chief Officer(s):
Kevin Kobus, Executive Director
kkobus@ocsta.on.ca
Staff Member(s): 9
Membership: 39 Catholic School Boards

Ontario Catholic Supervisory Officers' Association (OCSOA)
730 Courtneypark Dr. West, Mississauga ON L5W 1L9
Tel: 905-564-8206; *Fax:* 905-564-8210
office@ocsoa.ca
www.ocsoa.ca
www.facebook.com/CatholicEducationInOntario
twitter.com/catholicedu
www.youtube.com/watch?v=T3PYrlpouqU
Overview: A medium-sized provincial organization founded in 1967
Mission: To represent supervisory officers employed in Catholic school boards
Chief Officer(s):
Theresa Harris, Executive Director
theresaharris@ocsoa.ca
Marie Osborne, Executive Assistant
marieosborne@ocsoa.ca
Membership: 150 individual; 18 associate

Ontario Cavy Club (OCC)
c/o Kelly Roth, PO Box 217, 2003 Nelson St., Gorrie ON N0G 1X0
www.ontariocavyclub.net
Overview: A small local organization founded in 1973
Mission: To unite all persons interested in the study, breeding & showing of guinea pigs (cavies); To promote interest in the study & breeding of cavies; To establish & recognize breeds & varieties of cavies & standards with respect thereto; To encourage, hold & sponsor showings & exhibitions, conferences, meetings & discussions; To cooperate, collaborate & affiliate with & to assist other clubs & organizations having objectives in whole or in part similar to those of the club
Chief Officer(s):
Kelly Roth, Sec.-Treas.
kjroth@wightman.ca
Finances: *Annual Operating Budget:* Less than $50,000; *Funding Sources:* Membership dues; shows; donations; ads
Membership: 1-99; *Fees:* $16 adult; $20 family; $12 youth

Ontario Centres of Excellence (OCE)
#200, 156 Front St. West, Toronto ON M5J 2L6
Tel: 416-861-1092; *Fax:* 416-971-7164
Toll-Free: 866-759-6014
Other Communication: www.flickr.com/photos/40288081@N07
anne.wettlaufer@oce-ontario.org
www.oce-ontario.org
www.linkedin.com/groups/Ontario-Centres-Excellence-1811772
www.facebook.com/OCEInnovation
twitter.com/oceinnovation
www.youtube.com/ocediscovery
Previous Name: Ontario Centres of Excellence - Centre for Earth & Environmental Technologies
Overview: A large provincial organization founded in 1987
Mission: To create new jobs, products, services, technologies & businesses by creating partnerships between industry & academia
Affliation(s): Accelerator Centre for Commercialization Excellence (ACE)
Chief Officer(s):
Michael J. Nobrega, Chair
Tom Corr, President & CEO
Tanya Dunn, Executive Assistant, Office of President
tanya.dunn@oce-ontario.org
Membership: *Committees:* Social Innovation Steering; Centre for Commercialization of Research Advisory Board; Advanced Health Technologies Sector Advisory Board; Advanced Manufacturing Sector Advisory Board; Energy & Environment Sector Advisory Board; Information, Communications & Digital Media Sector Advisory Board
Activities: Ontario Network of Excellence (ONE); Industry-Academic Collaboration Program (IACP); Centre for Commercialization of Research (CCR); Networks of Centres of Excellence (NCE);
Awards:
• Martin Walmsley Fellowship for Technological Entrepreneurship (Award)
• Annual Media Award (Award)
Publications:
• OCE [Ontario Centres of Excellence] Newsletter
Type: Newsletter

Ontario Centres of Excellence - Centre for Earth & Environmental Technologies ***See*** Ontario Centres of Excellence

Ontario Cerebral Palsy Sports Association (OCPSA)
#7, 46 Antares Dr., Nepean ON K2E 7Z1
Tel: 613-723-1806; *Fax:* 613-723-6742
ocpsa.com
Overview: A small provincial organization overseen by Canadian Cerebral Palsy Sports Association
Mission: To provide, promote & coordinate competitive opportunities for persons with with cerebral palsy & other neuromuscular disorders in Ontario.
Member of: Canadian Cerebral Palsy Sports Association
Affliation(s): Canadian Sport Institute - Ontario; Coaches Association of Ontario; ParaSport Ontario
Chief Officer(s):
Don Sinclair, President
president@ocpsa.com
Activities: Athletics; Boccia; other sports

Ontario CGIT Association
PO Box 371, Norwich ON N0J 1P0
Tel: 519-863-6760; *Fax:* 519-863-6760
ontario@cgit.ca
www.cgit.ca
Also Known As: Canadian Girls in Training - Ontario
Previous Name: National CGIT Association - Ontario
Overview: A small provincial charitable organization founded in 1915
Affliation(s): The United Church of Canada; The Presbyterian Church in Canada
Finances: *Annual Operating Budget:* Less than $50,000
Staff Member(s): 1; 150 volunteer(s)
Membership: 350; *Member Profile:* Teen girls & adult women; *Committees:* Leadership Training; Camps; Publicity & Promotion
Activities: Leadership training weekend; camp council leadership training for senior girls; Red Maple Leaf Program

Ontario Chamber of Commerce (OCC)
#505, 180 Dundas St. West, Toronto ON M5G 1Z8
Tel: 416-482-5222; *Fax:* 416-482-5879
info@occ.on.ca
www.occ.on.ca
www.linkedin.com/company/876425
twitter.com/OntarioCofC
www.youtube.com/user/OntarioChamber
Previous Name: Associated Boards of Trade of Ontario
Overview: A large provincial organization founded in 1911
Mission: As "Ontario's Business Advocate", the Ontario Chamber of Commerce is a ISO certified organization providing leadership to the province's business community. The focus is

on the development of soundly research policy positions, representing the business community to government, & providing consultation, information & programs to the membership
Chief Officer(s):
Allan O'Dette, President & CEO
allanodette@occ.on.ca
Scott McCammon, Vice-President & General Manager
scottmccammon@occ.on.ca
Finances: *Annual Operating Budget:* $500,000-$1.5 Million; *Funding Sources:* Membership dues
Staff Member(s): 29; 600 volunteer(s)
Membership: 160 local chambers of commerce & boards; *Member Profile:* Business organizations of all sizes, from all economic sectors & from all parts of Ontario; *Committees:* Borders & Transportation Infrastructure; Finance & Taxation; Education; Energy; Health Policy
Activities: Knowledge is Power Program; Public Awareness; Support to women living with ovarian cancer; Online knowledge centre at www.ovarianknowledge.ca; *Awareness Events:* Ovarian Cancer Walk of Hope
Awards:
• Chair's Awards (Award)
• International Trade Contest (Award)
For senior high school students
• Membership Marketing Award (Award)
• Outstanding Business Achievement Award (Award)

Ontario Charterboat Association *See* Ontario Sportfishing Guides' Association

Ontario Cheerleading Federation (OCF)
c/o Adrianna Cesarano, 21 Oceanpearl Cres., Whitby ON L1N 0C5
www.ocfcheer.com
Overview: A small provincial organization overseen by Cheer Canada
Mission: To provide training & certification courses for coaches across Ontario.
Member of: Cheer Canada
Chief Officer(s):
Amanda Maronese, President
president@ocfcheer.com
Adrianna Cesarano, Registrar
registrar@ocfcheer.com

Ontario Chiropractic Association (OCA) / Association chiropratique de l'Ontario
#200, 20 Victoria St., Toronto ON M5C 2N8
Tel: 416-860-0070; *Fax:* 416-860-0857
Toll-Free: 877-327-2273
oca@chiropractic.on.ca
www.chiropractic.on.ca
Overview: A medium-sized provincial organization founded in 1929 overseen by Canadian Chiropractic Association
Mission: To serve its members by promoting the philosophy, art, & science of chiropractic & thereby enhance the health & well-being of the citizens of Ontario
Chief Officer(s):
Robert Haig, Chief Executive Officer, 416-860-0070 Ext. 4155
Valerie Carter, Director, External Relations, 416-860-0070 Ext. 4157
Kimbalin Kelly, Director, Operations, 416-860-0070 Ext. 4156
Joyce Chow Ng, Manager, Finance, 416-860-0070 Ext. 7185
Nathalie Plourde, Manager, Member Services, 416-860-0070 Ext. 7184
12 volunteer(s)
Membership: 2,500; *Member Profile:* Licensed Doctor of Chiropractic
Activities: Providing public education & professional development; *Speaker Service:* Yes
Awards:
• Chiropractor of the Year (Award)

Ontario Christian Music Assembly
90 Topcliff Ave., Downsview ON M3N 1L8
Tel: 416-636-9779; *Fax:* 905-775-2230
landmkooy@rogers.com
Overview: A small provincial organization founded in 1961
10 volunteer(s)
Membership: 130 individual
Activities: Spring & Christmas concerts series; annual Christian festival concert

Ontario Clean Air Alliance (OCAA)
#300, 160 John St., Toronto ON M5V 2E5
Tel: 416-260-2080; *Fax:* 416-598-9520
contact@cleanairalliance.org
www.cleanairalliance.org
www.facebook.com/groups/ontariocleanairalliance/
twitter.com/NoNukeBailouts
Overview: A medium-sized provincial organization founded in 1997
Mission: To ensure that Ontario's electricity needs are met by ecologically sustainable renewable sources
Chief Officer(s):
Jack Gibbons, Chair, 416-260-2080 Ext. 2
jack@cleanairalliance.org
Angela Bischoff, Director, Outreach, 416-260-2080 Ext. 1
Angela@cleanairalliance.org
Finances: *Funding Sources:* Donations
Membership: *Member Profile:* Organizations & individuals who work for cleaner air through a coal phase-out & a move to a renewable electricity future
Publications:
• Finishing the Coal Phase Out: An Historic Opportunity for Climate Leadership
Type: Report
Profile: A review of the Government of Ontario's coal phase-out to reduce greenhouse gas emission
• Increasing Productivity & Moving Towards a Renewable Future: A New Electricity Strategy for Ontario
Type: Report; *Number of Pages:* 60; *Author:* Jack Gibbons
• Ontario Clean Air Alliance E-Bulletin
Type: Newsletter; *Frequency:* Semimonthly
Profile: The most recent news & reports about energy issues & air quality
• The Ontario Power Authority's Coal Phase-Out Strategy: A Critical Review
Type: Report; *Number of Pages:* 13
• Ontario's Coal Phase-Out: A Major Climate Accomplishment Within Our Grasp
Type: Report; *Number of Pages:* 10
Profile: A review of the coal phase-out's progress
• Ontario's Green Future: How We Can Build a 100% Renewable Electricity Grid by 2027
Type: Report; *Number of Pages:* 32; *Author:* Jack Gibbons
Profile: An Ontario Clean Air Alliance report with recommendations
• Powerful Options: A Review of Ontario's Options for Replacing Aging Nuclear Plants
Type: Report; *Number of Pages:* 18
Profile: A presentation of options for replacing nuclear plants that are less expensive than building new nuclear reactors

Ontario Coalition Against Poverty (OCAP)
#206, 157 Carlton St., Toronto ON M5A 2K3
Tel: 416-925-6939; *Fax:* 416-925-6995
ocap@tao.ca
www.ocap.ca
twitter.com/OCAPtoronto
Overview: A small provincial organization
Mission: To organize campaigns against regressive policies that affect poor & working people
Finances: *Funding Sources:* Donations
Activities: Engaging in advocacy activities; *Rents Mailing List:* Yes

Ontario Coalition for Abortion Clinics (OCAC)
PO Box 495, Stn. P, 427 Bloor St. West, Toronto ON M5S 2Z1
Tel: 416-969-8463; *Fax:* 416-789-0762
ocac88@gmail.com
ocac-choice.com
www.facebook.com/OCAC88
twitter.com/OCAC25
Overview: A medium-sized provincial organization founded in 1982
Mission: To work for reproductive rights & access to abortions
Activities: Presenting workshops & speakers; Lobbying; Organizing demonstration & community action

Ontario Coalition for Better Child Care (OCBCC)
#206, 489 College St., Toronto ON M6G 1A5
Tel: 416-538-0628; *Fax:* 416-538-6737
Toll-Free: 800-594-7514
info@childcareontario.org
www.childcareontario.org
www.facebook.com/OCBCC
twitter.com/ChildCareON
Also Known As: Better Child Care Ontario, Inc.
Overview: A medium-sized provincial organization founded in 1981
Mission: Advocates on behalf of Ontario's non-profit, licensed child care programs
Affliation(s): Canadian Child Care Advocacy Association
Chief Officer(s):
Tracy Saarikoski, President
Carrol Anne Sceviour, Vice-President
Finances: *Annual Operating Budget:* $250,000-$500,000; *Funding Sources:* Government research grants; foundations; membership
Staff Member(s): 3; 39 volunteer(s)
Membership: 456; *Fees:* $44 individuals; $16.50 unwaged; $27.50 child care workers; $90-$1,000 organizations; *Member Profile:* Child care programs, individuals, trade unions, students, rural, native & francophone groups
Activities: *Library* Open to public by appointment

Ontario Coalition for Social Justice (OCSJ) / La coalition ontarienne pour la justice sociale
#305, 15 Gervais Dr., Toronto ON M3C 1Y8
Tel: 416-441-3714
info@ocsj.ca
www.ocsj.ca
Overview: A medium-sized provincial organization founded in 1985 overseen by Solidarity Network
Mission: To foster the growth of community coalitions & networks working for a people-oriented society & for social justice
Chief Officer(s):
John Argue, Coordinator
Finances: *Annual Operating Budget:* Less than $50,000; *Funding Sources:* Donations
Membership: 70 groups; 33 local community coalitions
Activities: *Speaker Service:* Yes

Ontario Coalition of Aboriginal Peoples (OCAP)
PO Box 189, Wabigoon ON P0V 2W0
Tel: 807-938-1321
www.o-cap.ca
Overview: A large provincial organization founded in 2007 overseen by Congress of Aboriginal Peoples
Mission: A not-for-profit advocacy organization representing the rights & interests of Métis, Status & Non-Status Aboriginal peoples living off-reserve in urban, rural or remote areas. Focus is on training programs & employment services
Affiliation(s): 23 organizations
Chief Officer(s):
Brad Maggrah, President, 807-938-1321, Fax: 807-938-1275
Finances: *Annual Operating Budget:* $1.5 Million-$3 Million
Membership: 15,000-49,999; *Fees:* $5-$25; *Member Profile:* Métis, Status, Non-Status, Inuit people living off-reserve in Ontario

Ontario Coalition of Rape Crisis Centres (OCRCC) / Coalition des centres anti-viol de l'Ontario
PO Box 6597, Stn. A, Toronto ON M5S 1A8
Tel: 416-597-1171; *Crisis Hot-Line:* 416-597-8808
www.ocrcc.ca
Overview: A medium-sized provincial charitable organization founded in 1977
Mission: To work for prevention & eradication of sexual assault; to implement legal, social & attitudinal changes regarding sexual assault; to provide mechanism for communication, education & mobilization to alleviate political & geographical isolation of rape crisis centres in Ontario; to encourage, direct & generate research into sexual violence; to work with Canadian Association of Sexual Assault Centres (see listing) on developing national policies; to liaise with other provincial organizations addressing similar issues
Member of: Canadian Association of Sexual Assault Centres; National Action Committee on the Status of Women; National Coalition of Sexual Assault (US)
Chief Officer(s):
Jacqueline Benn-John, President
Finances: *Annual Operating Budget:* Less than $50,000; *Funding Sources:* Provincial government
Staff Member(s): 1
Membership: 24; *Fees:* $2; *Member Profile:* Member centres that work for social change & prevention of sexual assault through education & crisis intervention; *Committees:* Executive; Finance; Personnel; Lobby; Policy
Activities: Information Exchange Centre Referrals; *Awareness Events:* Take Back the Night

Ontario Coalition of Senior Citizens' Organizations (OCSCO) / Coalition des organismes d'aînés et d'aînées de l'Ontario (COAAO)
#406, 333 Wilson Ave., Toronto ON M3H 1T2

Tel: 416-785-8570; *Fax:* 416-785-7361
Toll-Free: 800-265-0779
ocsco@web.net
www.ocsco.ca
Also Known As: Ontario Society of Senior Citizens' Organizations
Overview: A large provincial charitable organization founded in 1986
Mission: To improve the quality of life for Ontario's seniors by encouraging seniors' involvement in all aspects of society, by keeping them informed of current issues, & by focusing on programs to benefit an aging population
Chief Officer(s):
Morris Jesion, Executive Director
Deborah Spencer, Program Coordinator
Finances: *Annual Operating Budget:* $250,000-$500,000; *Funding Sources:* Membership dues; grants; fundraising
Staff Member(s): 6; 150 volunteer(s)
Membership: 160 groups (500,000 individuals); *Fees:* $10-$100; *Member Profile:* Open to adults over 55 years of age; *Committees:* Personnel; Bylaws; Finance; PR; Health; Housing
Activities: Education; alliances; information; referral & counselling; policy; outreach; special programs; drop-in; research; joint programs; self-help; volunteerism; speakers' bureau; *Speaker Service:* Yes; *Library:* Resource Centre; Open to public

Ontario College & University Library Association (OCULA)

c/o Ontario Library Association, 2 Toronto St., 3rd Fl., Toronto ON M5C 2B6
Tel: 416-363-3388; *Fax:* 416-941-9581
info@accessola.com
www.accessola.com/ocula/
Overview: A medium-sized provincial charitable organization founded in 1969
Mission: To support librarians & to improve Library Science in Ontario's college & university libraries
Affliation(s): Ontario Library Association
Chief Officer(s):
Sophia Apostol, President
Shanna Pearson, Vice-President/President Elect
shanna.pearson@senecacollege.ca
Finances: *Annual Operating Budget:* Less than $50,000
Activities: *Rents Mailing List:* Yes
Meetings/Conferences: • Ontario College & University Library Association 2015 Annual General Meeting, 2015
Scope: Provincial
Description: OCULA's Annual General Meetings are held during the Ontario Library Association Superconference, usually in January or February of each year.

Ontario College Administrative Staff Associations (OCASA)

PO Box 263, #201-202, 120 Centre St. North, Napanee ON K7R 3M4
Fax: 866-742-5430
Toll-Free: 866-742-5429
info@ocasa.on.ca
www.ocpinfo.com
www.linkedin.com/groups?mostPopular=&gid=3274946
twitter.com/#!/OCASA_APACO
www.flickr.com/photos/ocasa
Overview: A medium-sized provincial licensing organization
Mission: OCASA is a voluntary, professional association which supports and advocates for Ontario's community college administrators, while building and promoting administrative excellence for the betterment of the college system.
Chief Officer(s):
Diane Posterski, Executive Director, 866-742-5429 Ext. 102
diane.posterski@ocasa.on.ca
Meetings/Conferences: • 2015 Leaders & Innovators Conference, June, 2015, Kingbridge Conference Centre & Institute, King City, ON
Scope: Provincial

Ontario College of Certified Social Workers *See* Ontario College of Social Workers & Social Service Workers

Ontario College of Pharmacists (OCP)

483 Huron St., Toronto ON M5R 2R4
Tel: 416-962-4861; *Fax:* 416-847-8200
Toll-Free: 800-220-1921
ocpclientservices@ocpinfo.com
www.ocpinfo.com
twitter.com/ocpinfo
Overview: A medium-sized provincial licensing organization founded in 1871 overseen by National Association of Pharmacy Regulatory Authorities
Mission: To administer the Regulated Health Professions Act; To regulate the practice of pharmacy, in accordance with standards of practice; To ensure that members provide quality pharmaceutical service & care to the public
Member of: Canadian Council on Continuing Education in Pharmacy
Activities: Developing & maintaining qualification standards for individuals to be issued certificates of accreditation; Regulating drugs & pharmacies, under the Drug & Pharmacies Regulation Act; Ensuring adherence to professional & operational standards by pharmacists & pharmacies; Collaborating with other health profession colleges; Establishing & maintaining programs to assist members with their response to changes in practice environments, advances in technology, & other emerging issues; Educating the public
Publications:
• Pharmacy Connection
Type: Journal; *Frequency:* Bimonthly
Profile: College activities & policies for Ontario's 12,000 pharmacists

Ontario College of Reflexology (OCR)

PO Box 220, 1232 Twin Lakes Rd. A, New Liskeard ON P0J 1P0
Tel: 705-647-5354; *Fax:* 705-648-6247
Toll-Free: 888-627-3338
ocr@ocr.edu
www.ocr.edu
www.facebook.com/ontarioreflexology
twitter.com/profbisson
plus.google.com/117621303948681834740
Overview: A small provincial organization
Mission: To provide accreditation for reflexologists in the province of Ontario, where required & as permitted by applicable statues of Ontario; To improve & maintain the qualifications & standards of the reflexology profession; To promote reflexology in the province
Finances: *Funding Sources:* Membership dues
Membership: *Fees:* $50; *Member Profile:* Certified practitioners; Persons interested in reflexology
Activities: Offering a referral system
Publications:
• OCR [Ontario College of Reflexology] Foot Notes
Type: Newsletter; *Frequency:* Quarterly

Ontario College of Social Workers & Social Service Workers (OCSWSSW) / Ordre des travailleurs sociaux et des techniciens en travail social de l'Ontario

#1000, 250 Bloor St. East, Toronto ON M4W 1E6
Tel: 416-972-9882; *Fax:* 416-972-1512
Toll-Free: 877-828-9380
info@ocswssw.org
www.ocswssw.org
Previous Name: Ontario College of Certified Social Workers
Overview: A medium-sized provincial organization founded in 1982
Mission: To establish & maintain qualification for College membership; To regulate the practice of social work & the practice of social service work in order to protect the public; To investigate complaints agaains members of the College
Chief Officer(s):
Mukesh Kowlessar, President
Glenda McDonald, Registrar
registrar@ocswssw.org
Marlene Zagdanski, Director, Complaints & Discipline
mzagdanski@ocswssw.org
Anne Vezina, Administrator, Membership
avezina@ocswssw.org
Yvonne Armstrong, Manager, Communications
yarmstrong@ocswssw.org
Membership: *Member Profile:* Persons in Ontario who wish to use the titles social worker, social service worker, registered social worker, or registered social service worker; *Committees:* Executive; Complaints; Registration Appeals; Discipline Decisions; Fitness to Practise; Elections; Corporations; Standards of Practice; Finance; Nominating; Governance
Activities: Issuing certificates of registration to members; Approving continuing education programs for members of the College; Dealing wtih issues of discipline or incompetence; Communicating with the public on behalf of members
Publications:
• Ontario College of Social Workers & Social Service Workers Annual Report
Type: Yearbook; *Frequency:* Annually; *Editor:* Yvonne Armstrong
• Perspective
Type: Newsletter; *Frequency:* Semiannually; *Editor:* Yvonne Armstrong
Profile: College activites, practice notes, council highlights, discipline decision summaries, information sessions, questions & answers, & a bulletin board

Ontario College of Teachers (OCT) / Odre des enseignantes et des enseignants de l'Ontario

101 Bloor St. East, Toronto ON M5S 0A1
Tel: 416-961-8800; *Fax:* 416-961-8822
Toll-Free: 888-534-2222; *TTY:* 416-961-6331
info@oct.ca
www.oct.ca
www.facebook.com/OntarioTeachers
www.youtube.com/user/OCTvideoOEEO
Overview: A large provincial licensing organization founded in 1997
Mission: To ensure Ontario students are taught by skilled teachers who adhere to clear standards of practice & conduct; To establish standards of practice & conduct; To issue teaching certificates & may also suspend or revoke them; To accredit teacher education programs; To provide for ongoing professional learning opportunities for members
Chief Officer(s):
Michael Salvatori, Registrar & CEO
Linda Zaks-Walker, Director, Membership Services
Richard Lewko, Director, Corporate & Council Services
Finances: *Annual Operating Budget:* Greater than $5 Million; *Funding Sources:* Membership fees
Staff Member(s): 170
Membership: 213,000+; *Fees:* $138 annual; $130 reinstatement or renewal; $140 registration, teachers educated in Ontario; *Member Profile:* Accredited teachers in Ontario; Vice-principals; Principals; Supervisory officers; Directors of education; *Committees:* Executive; Accreditation; Accreditation Appeal; Discipline; Editorial Board; Election; Finance; Fitness to Practise; Human Resources; Investigation; Nomination; Quality Assurance; Registration appeals; Standards of Practice & Education
Activities: *Library:* Margaret Wilson Library
Awards:
• Joseph W. Atkinson Scholarship For Excellence In Teacher Education (Scholarship)
Eligibility: Studying in the faculty of education in Ontario; must be in a consecutive program or going into their final year in a concurrent program; outstanding academic achievement while demonstrating a high level of preparedness for teacher education.*Deadline:* July *Amount:* $2,000
Meetings/Conferences: • Ontario College of Teachers 2015 Annual Meeting of Members, June, 2015
Scope: Provincial
Description: Presentations of interest to teachers
• Ontario College of Teachers 2016 Annual Meeting of Members, 2016
Scope: Provincial
Description: Presentations of interest to teachers
Publications:
• Professionally Speaking: The Magazine of The Ontario College of Teachers
Type: Magazine; *Frequency:* Quarterly; *Accepts Advertising*; *Price:* $10 in Canada; $20 outside Canada
Profile: Features, resources & reviews, teacher profiles, & governance reports

Ontario Colleges Athletic Association (OCAA)

#201, 3 Concorde Gate, Toronto ON M3C 3N7
Tel: 416-426-7043; *Fax:* 416-426-7308
www.ocaa.com
Overview: A small provincial charitable organization founded in 1967
Mission: To govern intercollegiate sports in Ontario; To promote student athlete & sport development as well as academic success; To ensure a safe environment; To provide a forum for personal development; To enhance student life
Member of: Canadian Collegiate Athletic Association
Affliation(s): Pacific Western Athletic Association; Alberta Colleges Athletic Conference; Fédération Québécoise du Sport Étudiant; Atlantic Colleges Athletic Association; Ontario Federation of School Athletic Associations; Ontario University Athletics; Athletics Ontario; Ontario Badminton Association; Basketball Ontario; Ontario Curling Council; Golf Association of

Ontario; Rugby Ontario; Ontario Soccer Association; Softball Ontario; Ontario Volleyball Association
Chief Officer(s):
Fred Batley, President
Blair Webster, Executive Director, 416-426-7043
webster@ocaa.com
Josh Bell-Webster, Coordinator, Marketing & Communications, 416-426-7041
bell-webster@ocaa.com
Mark Couch, Coordinator, Sport Services, 416-426-7043
couch@ocaa.com
Membership: *Committees:* Executive; OCCCR; Academic / Athletic Awards; Awards; Constitution; Eligibility; Finance; Marketing & Sport Development; Policies & Procedures; Safety & Risk Management; Ways & Means

Ontario Commercial Fisheries' Association (OCFA)
PO Box 2129, 45 James St., Blenheim ON N0P 1A0
Tel: 519-676-0488; *Fax:* 519-676-0944
Toll-Free: 800-461-7890
www.myfishquota.com
Overview: A medium-sized provincial organization founded in 1945
Mission: To be dedicated to the growth & continued strength of a responsible, competitive, & sustainable licensed commercial fishery in Ontario; To represent the industry's interests & its view to government, the media, & consumers
Chief Officer(s):
Peter Meisenheimer, Executive Director
Finances: *Annual Operating Budget:* $500,000-$1.5 Million; *Funding Sources:* Membership dues; Contractual programs
Staff Member(s): 22; 19 volunteer(s)
Membership: 267; *Fees:* $150; *Member Profile:* Licensed Ontario commercial fishing license holders; Federal registered processing plants
Activities: Maintaining a code of conduct for responsible fishing practices; Hosting an annual convention

Ontario Commercial Rabbit Growers' Association
#12, 449 Laird Rd., Guelph ON N1G 4W1
Tel: 519-638-3349
info@livestockalliance.ca
www.ontariorabbit.ca
Also Known As: Ontario Rabbit
Overview: A small provincial organization founded in 1964
Mission: To enhance the profitability of meat rabbit production through activities such as lobbying, education, research & market development
Chief Officer(s):
Steve Bowier, President

Ontario Community Newspapers Association (OCNA)
#116, 3228 South Service Rd., Burlington ON L7N 3H8
Tel: 905-639-8720; *Fax:* 905-639-6962
www.ocna.org
www.facebook.com/171125688577
Overview: A large provincial organization founded in 1950 overseen by Canadian Community Newspapers Association
Mission: To support members with information about the Ontario community newspaper industry & market; to improve the competitive position of the industry
Affliation(s): Newspapers Canada; Atlantic Community Newspapers Association; Québec Community Newspapers Association; Hebdos Québec; Manitoba Community Newspapers Association; Saskatchewan Weekly Newspapers Association; Alberta Weekly Newspapers Association; British Columbia & Yukon Community Newspapers Association
Chief Officer(s):
Mike Mount, President
David Harvey, Secretary-Treasurer
Anne Lannan, Executive Director
a.lannan@ocna.org
Todd Frees, Controller
t.frees@ocna.org
Kelly Gorven, Coordinator, Member Services
k.gorven@ocna.org
Karen Shardlow, Coordinator, Member Services
k.shardlow@ocna.org
Lucia Shepherd, Coordinator, Accounting/Newsprint
l.shepherd@ocna.org
Finances: *Funding Sources:* Membership fees; Grants; Sponsorships
Staff Member(s): 12
Membership: 800+ newspapers; *Fees:* Schedule available, based upon circulation for active members; $250 associate members; *Member Profile:* Newspapers throughout Ontario which serve a specific geographical or ethnic community, publish less frequently than a daily newspaper, but at least once a month, & meet other criteria; Other organizations that support community newspapers
Activities: Engaging in advocacy activities for favourable government policies; Promoting the Ontario community newspaper industry; working with advertisers, agencies, & government to place advertising in member newspapers, through Ad*Reach; posting industry-related positions; providing educational opportunities through the online training center
Awards:
• General Excellence Awards (Award), Better Newspapers Competition
To honour achievement by circulation class in editorial, layout, & advertising
• Premier Awards (Award), Better Newspapers Competition
Examples of awards include Best Editorial, Best Front Page, Best Feature Photo, & Best Original Advertising
• College & University Awards (Award), Better Newspapers Competition
To recognize college & university member newspapers
• The Molson Coors Community Award in Memory of Mary Knowles (Award)
An award created by the Community Newspapers Foundation, the charitable division of the Ontario Community Newspapers Association
• Ontario Junior Citizen of the Year Awards (Award)
Awards to recognize the best of Ontario's youth, coordinated by the the Ontario Community Newspapers Association
• Quill Awards (Award)
Awarded to community newspaper owners & employees for long time service to the industry
Meetings/Conferences: • Ontario Community Newspapers Association 2015 Annual Spring Convention, 2015, ON
Scope: Provincial
Description: A gathering of newspaper professionals & youth from throughout Ontario, featuring the Ontario Community Newspapers Association's Supplier Showcase
Publications:
• E-clips [a publication of the Ontario Community Newspapers Association]
Type: Newsletter; *Frequency:* Weekly; *Price:* Free with membership in the Ontario Community Newspapers Association
Profile: A news bulletin for Ontario Community Newspapers Association members, with information about the association's services & events, plus industryrelated job postings
• NewsClips [a publication of the Ontario Community Newspapers Association]
Type: Newsletter; *Frequency:* Monthly; *Price:* Free with membership in the Ontario Community NewspapersAssociation
Profile: Industry information & details about upcoming association services & events

Ontario Community Support Association (OCSA) / Association ontarienne de soutien communautaire
#104, 970 Lawrence Ave. West, Toronto ON M6A 3B6
Tel: 416-256-3010; *Fax:* 416-256-3021
Toll-Free: 800-267-6272
reception@ocsa.on.ca
www.ocsa.on.ca
Previous Name: Meals on Wheels Ontario Inc.
Overview: A medium-sized provincial charitable organization founded in 1992
Mission: To support & represent the common goals of community-based, not-for-profit health & social service organizations which assist individuals to live at home in their own community
Member of: Canadian Centre for Philanthropy
Chief Officer(s):
Deborah Simon, Chief Executive Officer
deborah.simon@ocsa.on.ca
Finances: *Annual Operating Budget:* $500,000-$1.5 Million; *Funding Sources:* Membership fees; donations
Staff Member(s): 11; 15 volunteer(s)
Membership: 350; *Fees:* Based on budget; *Member Profile:* A not-for-profit community based agency delivering home support & or Meals on Wheels & or homemaking services
Activities: *Awareness Events:* Community Support Month, Oct.; *Rents Mailing List:* Yes; *Library:* OCSA Resource Collection; Open to public by appointment
Meetings/Conferences: • 2015 Ontario Community Support Association Annual Conference, 2015, ON
Scope: Provincial

Ontario Community Transit Association *See* Ontario Public Transit Association

Ontario Competitive Trail Riding Association Inc. (OCTRA)
c/o Doug Price, 457102 Conc. 3A, RR#4, Chatsworth ON N0H 1G0
Tel: 519-377-0652
www.octra.on.ca
Overview: A small provincial organization founded in 1967 overseen by Canadian Long Distance Riding Association
Mission: To encourage the growth & popularity of competitive trail, endurance riding & Ride'n'Tie; to establish a set of rules & quality for managing & judging same; to encourage & maintain a high standard of horsemanship & sportsmanship amongst competitors; to encourage the selection, care, training & conditioning of horses for long distance riding; to provide guidance & help to clubs & groups in establishing & running competitive rides; to ensure that all rides are run humanely so as to avoid cruelty & suffering to competing animals; to formulate promotional & educational programs; to foster goodwill & understanding between horse owners, land owners & conservation authorities with a view to opening up more land for riding trails
Member of: Canadian Long Distance Riding Association
Affliation(s): Horse Ontario; Ontario Equestrian Federation
Chief Officer(s):
Doug Price, President
khofire@gmail.com
Nancy Beacon, Vice-President
rabbitrun1@me.com
Jackie Redmond, Secretary
jackieredmond@sympatico.ca
Michelle Bignell, Treasurer
arabians@cayusecreekranch.com
Membership: *Fees:* $60 family; $45 individual; $35 associate non-voting; $25 junior; *Committees:* Awards; Competitive; Education; Endurance; Fundraising; Mileage Programs; Newsletter; Publicity & Promotions; Ride 'n' Tie; Ride Management/Sanctioning; Set Speed; Veterinary; Website; Worker Credit; Youth
Activities: *Speaker Service:* Yes; *Rents Mailing List:* Yes; *Library:* Archives; by appointment

Ontario Concrete Block Association *See* Canadian Concrete Masonry Producers Association

Ontario Concrete Pipe Association (OCPA)
447 Frederick St., 2nd Fl, Kitchener ON N2H 2P4
Tel: 519-489-4488; *Fax:* 519-578-6060
admin@ocpa.com
www.ocpa.com
Overview: A medium-sized provincial organization founded in 1957
Mission: To represent the concrete pipe & maintenance hole industry throughout Ontario; to promote engineered concrete products of permanence
Member of: Canadian Standards Association
Affliation(s): Municipal Engineers Association; Canadian Concrete Pipe Association; Tubecon; American Concrete Pipe Association; Canadian Portland Cement Association; Water Environment Association of Ontario; Canadian Public Works Association; Ontario Sewer & Watermain Construction Association; Consulting Engineers of Ontario
Chief Officer(s):
Brian Wood, President, 800-668-7473, Fax: 519-763-1982
brwood@concastpipe.com
Mike Leathers, Vice President, 888-888-3222
mike.leathers.hanson.com
John Munro, Sec.-tres., 705-734-2892, Fax: 705-734-2920
jmunro@munroltd.com
Finances: *Annual Operating Budget:* $250,000-$500,000; *Funding Sources:* Membership dues
Staff Member(s): 2; 30 volunteer(s)
Membership: 40; *Member Profile:* Manufacturers of precast concrete pipe & associated products; *Committees:* Prequalification; Public Relations & Communications; Technical
Activities: *Awareness Events:* Construct Canada; Ontario Good Roads; *Speaker Service:* Yes; *Library* by appointment

Ontario Confederation of University Faculty Associations (OCUFA) / Union des associations des professeurs des universités de l'Ontario
17 Isabella St., Toronto ON M4Y 1M7
Tel: 416-979-2117; *Fax:* 416-593-5607
ocufa@ocufa.on.ca
www.ocufa.on.ca

www.facebook.com/OCUFA
twitter.com/ocufa
Overview: A small provincial organization founded in 1964 overseen by Canadian Association of University Teachers
Mission: To act as the voice of Ontario's approximately 15,000 university faculty & academic librarians; To advance the professional & economic interests of university faculty & academic librarians; To enhance the quality of Ontario's higher education system
Chief Officer(s):
Kate Lawson, President, 519-888-4567 Ext. 33965
klawson@uwaterloo.ca
Judy Bates, Vice-President, 519-884-1970 Ext. 2387
Mark Rosenfeld, Executive Director, 416-979-2117 Ext. 229
mrosenfeld@ocufa.on.ca
Mark Rosenfeld, Associate Executive Director, Research & Communications, 416-979-2117 Ext. 233
Glen Copplestone, Treasurer, 519-433-3491 Ext. 4432
Staff Member(s): 11
Membership: 27 associations; *Member Profile:* Member faculty associations throughout Ontario
Activities: Providing on-campus support to faculty associations; Engaging in advocacy activities; Liaising with government, the media, & higher education stakeholders; Providing research to support collective bargaining & grievance management
Awards:
• Teaching & Academic Librarianship Awards (Award)
• Lorimer Award (Bargaining Award) (Award)
• Status of Women Award of Distinction (Award)
• The Henry Mandelbaum Graduate Fellowship (Award)
Eligibility: A full-time graduate student at a publicly-assisted Ontario University who has demonstrated academic excellence, shows exceptional academic promise, and has provided significant community service in his/her university career.
Publications:
• The Academic Matters
Profile: Highlights of current trends in postsecondary education, of interest to faculty in Ontario
• Ontario University Report
Type: Newsletter; *Frequency:* Semimonthly
Profile: News about postsecondary education & the association's activities
• Trends in Higher Education
Profile: A research series, featuring in-depth analysis

Ontario Conference, Church of the United Brethren in Christ
See The United Brethren Church in Canada

Ontario Construction Secretariat (OCS)
#120, 940 The East Mall, Toronto ON M9B 6J7
Tel: 416-620-5210; *Fax:* 416-620-5310
Toll-Free: 888-878-8868
info@iciconstruction.com
www.iciconstruction.com
Overview: A large provincial organization
Mission: Represents the 25 Employee & the 25 Employer Bargaining Agencies of the unionized industrial, commercial, & institutional (ICI) sector of Ontario's construction industry
Chief Officer(s):
Sean Strickland, CEO
seans@iciconstruction.com
Katherine Jacobs, Director, Research & Analysis
kjacobs@iciconstruction.com
Staff Member(s): 7
Activities: *Speaker Service:* Yes

Ontario Consultants on Religious Tolerance (OCRT)
PO Box 27026, Stn. Frontenac, Kingston ON K7M 8W5
Fax: 613-547-9015
ocrt4@religioustolerance.org
www.religioustolerance.org
www.facebook.com/group.php?gid=115060631838983
www.twitter.com/ReligiousTol
Overview: A small provincial organization founded in 1995
Mission: To promote religious tolerance & expose religious hatred & misinformation
Chief Officer(s):
B.A. Robinson, Coordinator
Finances: *Annual Operating Budget:* Less than $50,000; *Funding Sources:* Lecture fees; donations; banner ads
Staff Member(s): 1; 5 volunteer(s)
Membership: 1-99
Activities: *Speaker Service:* Yes

Ontario Convenience Store Association (OCSA)
#217, 466 Speers Rd., Oakville ON L6K 3W9
Tel: 905-845-9152; *Fax:* 905-849-9947
www.conveniencestores.ca
twitter.com/ontariocstores
Overview: A medium-sized provincial organization overseen by Canadian Convenience Store Association
Mission: To represent convenience store retailers in Ontario
Affiliation(s): Canadian Convenience Stores Association; Western Convenience Stores Association; Association Québécoise des dépanneurs en alimentation; Atlantic Convenience Stores Association
Chief Officer(s):
Dave Bryans, Chief Executive Officer
bryans@conveniencestores.ca
Finances: *Funding Sources:* Membership fees
Membership: *Member Profile:* Major convenience store companies; independent owners; food retailers; suppliers & wholesalers; oil companies; gasoline & automotive product vendors

Ontario Co-operative Association
#101, 450 Speedvale Ave. West, Guelph ON N1H 7Y6
Tel: 519-763-8271; *Fax:* 519-763-7239
Toll-Free: 888-745-5521
info@ontario.coop
www.ontario.coop
www.facebook.com/oncoop/
twitter.com/ontariocoops/
www.youtube.com/user/OntarioCoopAssoc/
Also Known As: On Co-op
Overview: A small provincial organization founded in 1979
Mission: The Ontario Co-operative Association (On Co-op) develops, unites and promotes co-operatives throughout the province of Ontario
Member of: The Ontario Rural Council; Foundation for Rural Living; Agricultural Adaptation Council; Association of Co-operative Education
Chief Officer(s):
Mark Ventry, Executive Director, 519-763-8271 Ext. 30
mventry@ontario.coop
Membership: *Fees:* $750-$10,000; *Member Profile:* Agriculture, finance, insurance, consumer, supply & services cooperatives

Ontario Cooperative Education Association (OCEA) / Association de l'éducation coopérative de l'Ontario
35 Reynar Dr., Quispamsis NB E2G 1J9
Fax: 506-849-8375
ocea@rogers.com
www.ocea.on.ca
Overview: A medium-sized provincial organization founded in 1976
Mission: To support excellence in the education of Ontario students by providing leadership for the professional development of its members
Affiliation(s): Career, Cooperative Work Education Association of Canada
Chief Officer(s):
Susanna Scocchia, Executive Secretary, 416-395-3330 Ext. 20140, Fax: 416-395-4453
susanna.scocchia@tdsb.on.ca
Donna Flasza, President
donna_flasza@Lakeheadschools.ca
Mona Safarian, Treasurer
safarmo@ecolecatholique.ca
Finances: *Funding Sources:* Membership fees; conference fees; donations
Membership: *Fees:* $80.75 statutory & non-statutory; $21.55 associate; $37.70 retired; *Member Profile:* Ontario cooperative education & experiential learning professionals; *Committees:* Communications; Finance; Membership; Teacher Professional Learning
Activities: Facilitating access to information, resources, & supports for its members; Providing a forum for the exchange of ideas & experiences among educators, employers, students, & others; Responding to issues; Researching future directions
Awards:
• The George King Award of Excellence (Award)
• The S.J. "Jack" Ulan Professional Contribution Award (Award)
• The Honorary Member Award (Award)
• The Career / LifeSkills Resources Award of Excellence in Cooperative Education (Award)
Meetings/Conferences: • 2015 Annual Ontario Cooperative Education Association Spring Conference, April, 2015, Delta Meadowvale Hotel & Conference Centre, Mississauga, ON
Scope: Provincial
Publications:
• OCEA [Ontario Cooperative Education Association] News
Type: Newsletter; *Frequency:* Semiannually
Profile: Distributed to members

Ontario Council for International Cooperation (OCIC) / Conseil de l'Ontario pour la coopération internationale
#209, 344 Bloor St. West, Toronto ON M5S 3A7
Tel: 416-972-6303; *Fax:* 416-972-6996
info@ocic.on.ca
www.ocic.on.ca
Overview: A medium-sized international organization founded in 1988
Mission: Community of Ontario-based international development and global education organizations and individual associate members working globally for social justice
Member of: Canadian Council for International Cooperation
Chief Officer(s):
Kimberly Gibbons, Executive Director
Staff Member(s): 2; 10 volunteer(s)
Membership: 70; *Fees:* Depends on the budget; *Committees:* Anti-Racism & Equity; Personnel; Policy; Global Citizenship
Activities: Weekly radio show; international development; public engagement; *Library:* Resource Centre; Open to public by appointment

Ontario Council for University Lifelong Learning
c/o Lakehead University, Thunder Bay ON P7B 5E1
Tel: 807-343-8210; *Fax:* 807-343-8008
www.ocull.ca
Previous Name: Ontario Association for University Lifelong Learning
Overview: A small provincial organization
Mission: To advocate for adult learners at Ontario universities, a collegial network, and a vehicle for professional development for its members.
Affliation(s): Council of Ontario Universities
Chief Officer(s):
Lisa Fanjoy, President
lfanjoy@wlu.ca
Membership: 20; *Fees:* $250 institution; $60 subscriber

Ontario Council of Agencies Serving Immigrants (OCASI)
#200, 110 Eglinton Ave. West, Toronto ON M4R 1A3
Tel: 416-322-4950; *Fax:* 416-322-8084
generalmail@ocasi.org
www.ocasi.org
Overview: A medium-sized provincial charitable organization founded in 1978
Mission: To act as a collective voice for immigrant services; to provide access for immigrants & refugees to settlement services; to provide social organizational development with community groups, policy analysis & government relations, professional development of member agency staff & research into issues facing immigrant service agencies
Member of: Canadian Council for Refugees; United Way; Canadian Council on Social Development; Toronto Refugee Affairs Council
Chief Officer(s):
Josie Di Zio, President, 416-658-1600 Ext. 38
dizio@costi.org
Debbie Douglas, Executive Director, 416-322-4950 Ext. 229
ddouglas@ocasi.org
Finances: *Annual Operating Budget:* $1.5 Million-$3 Million; *Funding Sources:* Government; United Way; Foundations
Staff Member(s): 19; 4 volunteer(s)
Membership: 175 agencies; *Fees:* $80-$1,000; *Member Profile:* Non-profit community-based agencies in Ontario whose primary objectives include the provision of social & community services to immigrants; *Committees:* Board Development; Executive; Finance; Management; Personnel; Policy & Research; Membership
Activities: Regional training workshop; technical liaison training; refugee rights week events; *Speaker Service:* Yes; *Rents Mailing List:* Yes; *Library:* Resource Centre; by appointment

Ontario Council of Alternative Businesses (OCAB)
#203, 1499 Queen St. West, Toronto ON M6R 1A3
Tel: 416-504-1693; *Fax:* 416-504-8063
Toll-Free: 866-504-1693
ocab@on.aibn.com
www.ocab.ca
Overview: A small provincial organization founded in 1994
Mission: To increase economic opportunities for psychiatric survivors by developing community businesses; To reduce discrimination & ignorance of general public in regards to psychiatric survivors

Chief Officer(s):
Joyce Brown, Co-Director
jmbrown@on.aibn.com
Becky McFarlane, Co-Director
becky@on.aibn.com
Finances: *Annual Operating Budget:* $100,000-$250,000
Staff Member(s): 9
Activities: Operating a variety of community businesses, including the Raging Spoon, OTWCafe, & Parkdale Green Thumb; *Rents Mailing List:* Yes

Ontario Council of University Libraries (OCUL)

Robarts Library, 130 St. George St., 7th Fl., Toronto ON M5S 1A5
Tel: 416-978-4211; *Fax:* 416-978-6755
www.ocul.on.ca
Overview: A small provincial organization
Member of: Council of Ontario Universities
Chief Officer(s):
Kathy Scardellato, Executive Director
kathy.scardellato@ocul.on.ca
Staff Member(s): 5
Membership: 20; *Member Profile:* Chief Librarian at Ontario university library

Ontario Council on Graduate Studies (OCGS) / Conseil ontarien des études supérieures

#1100, 180 Dundas St. West, Toronto ON M5G 1Z8
Tel: 416-979-2165; *Fax:* 416-979-8635
cou.on.ca/ocgs-1
Overview: A small provincial organization founded in 1965
Mission: To ensure quality graduate education & research across Ontario
Member of: Council of Ontario Universities
Chief Officer(s):
Peter Gooch, Secretariat, COU
pgooch@cou.on.ca
Clarke Anthony, Chair
aclarke@registrar.uoguelph.ca
Staff Member(s): 1
Membership: 20; *Member Profile:* Deans of Graduate Studies (or equivalent officer) of each provincially assisted universities in Ontario; *Committees:* Executive; Nominating
Activities: Conducts quality reviews of graduate (Master's & Ph.D.) programs that have been proposed for implementation in Ontario's universities, as well as quality reviews of existing programs on a seven-year cycle;
Awards:
• Women's Health Scholar Award (Award)
• Autism Scholars Award (Award)
• John Charles Polanyi Prizes (Award)
In honour of the achievement of John Charles Polanyi, co-recipient of the 1986 Nobel Prize in Chemistry, the Government of Ontario has established a fund to provide annually up to five prizes to persons continuing to post-doctoral studies at an Ontario university; prizes available in the areas of Physics, Chemistry, Physiology or Medicine, Literature & Economic Science *Amount:* $15,000

Ontario Craft Brewers (OCB)

#1, 75 Horner Ave., Toronto ON M8Z 4X5
Tel: 416-494-2766
Other Communication: pr@ontariocraftbrewers.com
info@ontariocraftbrewers.com
www.ontariocraftbrewers.com
www.facebook.com/pages/Ontario-Craft-Brewers/196804020357258
twitter.com/OntCraftBrewers
www.youtube.com/OntarioCraftBrewers
Overview: A small provincial organization
Mission: To promote craft brewers in the province on Ontario.
Membership: 35+

Ontario Crafts Council (OCC)

990 Queen St. West, Toronto ON M6J 1H1
Tel: 416-925-4222; *Fax:* 416-925-4223
info@craft.on.ca
www.craft.on.ca
www.facebook.com/OntarioCraftsCouncil
twitter.com/OntarioCrafts
Previous Name: Canadian Guild of Crafts (Ontario); Ontario Craft Foundation
Overview: A medium-sized provincial charitable organization founded in 1976
Mission: To have craft recognized as a valuable part of life and the excellence of Ontario craft and craftspeople acknowledged across Canada and around the world.
Chief Officer(s):
Emma Quin, Executive Director
equin@craft.on.ca
Finances: *Funding Sources:* Membership dues; donations; corporate; foundations; government
Staff Member(s): 7
Membership: 1,500; *Fees:* $150 business; $125 affiliate; $130 craft professional; $45 student; $70 standard
Activities: Operates the Craft Gallery & the Guild Shop, Yorkville; *Rents Mailing List:* Yes; *Library* Open to public
Awards:
• James H. McPherson Scholarship in Wood (Scholarship)
Provides assistance for an individual to pursue further educationin woodworking, especially in lathe or inlay work *Amount:* $225
• Hey Frey Memorial Award (Award)
Awarded to an established or emerging artist working in any craft medium whose work demonstrates excellence & a commitment to expand the horizons in their field *Amount:* $100
• Tommia Vaughan-Jones Award for Excellence in Metal Arts (Award)
Award in metal arts *Amount:* $400
• Don McKinley Award for Excellence in Wood (Award)
Awarded to a woodworking student studying at one of the Crafts Councils affiliated educational institutions to recognize excelolene in woodworking design *Amount:* $150
• Diana Crawford Craft Careet Development Grant (Grant)
For the development of emerging craftspeople in their first five years of professional practice, to be applied towards the development of business skills *Amount:* $250
• Hildreth G. Holden Wood Scholarship (Scholarship)
For a person intending to pursue further education in wood, including joinery, carving, musical instruments & inlay *Amount:* $250
• Volunteer Committee Emerging Professional Grant (Grant)
Intended to enable crafts people who are in their first five years of professional practice to establish or expand their studio or facilities *Amount:* $1,000 maximum
• RBC-Lakatos Craft Career Award (Award)
To enable emerging craftspeople in their first five years of professional practice to participate in an exhibition, craft or trade show in Ontario *Amount:* Maximum of $450
• Critical Craft Writing Award (Award)
Celebrates & recognizes the importance of documenting the work of craftspeople; offered to raise the profile of critical writing about contemporary Canadian craft *Amount:* $400 & article published in Ontario Crafts magazine
• Helen Frances Gregor Scholarship (Scholarship)
Awarded to provide funds for a fibre artist to pursue further study *Amount:* $550
• Ontario Crafts Council Scholarships (Scholarship)
Awarded to craftspeople to further their study *Amount:* 3 awards of $1,000
• Volunteer Committee Scholarship (Scholarship)
For further study in volunteer work *Amount:* $1,500
• Kingcrafts/Lady Flavelle Award (Award)
Granted to a person intending to pursue further education *Amount:* $1,000
• Mary Diamond Butts Award in Embroidery (Award)
Eligibility: Provides assistance to pursue self-directed study or participate in an established couse of study *Amount:* $250
• Mary Robertson Textile Award (Award)
Eligibility: To assist a person intending to pursue further education in textiles, including textile printing, surface embellishments, weaving, basketry & embroidery *Amount:* $500

Ontario Creamerymen's Association

26 Dominion St., Alliston ON L9R 1L5
Tel: 705-435-6751; *Fax:* 705-435-6797
Overview: A small provincial organization founded in 1935
Chief Officer(s):
Lloyd Kennedy, President
Finances: *Funding Sources:* Membership dues

Ontario Cricket Association Inc. *See* Cricket Council of Ontario

Ontario Criminal Justice Association (CJAO)

PO Box 949, Stn. K, Toronto ON M4P 2V3
cjao.info
Overview: A small local organization
Mission: To encourage co-operation among individuals, groups & governmental organizations interested & active in the field of criminal justice; to further the study of criminal justice issues.
Affliation(s): Canadian Criminal Justice Association
Membership: 200; *Committees:* Policy Review; Social Issues; Public Awareness & Visibility

Ontario Crown Attorneys Association (OCAA) / Association des procureurs de la couronne de l'Ontario (APCO)

PO Box 30, #1905, 180 Dundas St. West, Toronto ON M5G 1Z8
Tel: 416-977-4517; *Fax:* 416-977-1460
reception@ocaa.ca
www.ocaa.ca
Overview: A medium-sized provincial organization founded in 1946
Mission: To promote & protect the professional interests of crown counsels, assistant crown attorneys, & articling students
Chief Officer(s):
Scott Childs, President
scott.rogers@ocaa.ca
Membership: 850; *Member Profile:* Crown counsel, assistant crown attorneys, & articling students employed by the criminal law division of the Ontario Ministry of the Attorney General
Activities: Engaging in collective bargaining on behalf of the association's members; Ensuring the continuing legal education of members

Ontario Curling Association (OCA)

Office Mall 2, #2B, 1400 Bayly St., Pickering ON L1W 3R2
Tel: 905-831-1757; *Fax:* 905-831-1083
Toll-Free: 877-668-2875
www.ontcurl.com
Overview: A large provincial organization founded in 1875 overseen by Canadian Curling Association
Mission: To promote & facilitate the growth & development of curling
Member of: Canadian Curling Association
Affliation(s): Ontario Curling Council; Northern Ontario Curling Association; Ontario Special Olympics
Chief Officer(s):
Ian McGillis, President, 613-657-4597
ianmcgillis@hotmail.com
Steve Chenier, Executive Director
steve@ontcurl.com
Finances: *Funding Sources:* Membership dues; competition fees; sponsorships
Staff Member(s): 7
Membership: 55,000 people in 200 clubs; *Committees:* Executive; Credentials; Rules; Nominating
Activities: Competitions; seminars; workshops; Marketing & Development Programme
Awards:
• OCA Achievement Award (Award)
Deadline: March 31
• Pat "O" Reid Coaching Award (Award)
Deadline: April 15
• John McCrae Scholarship Award (Award)
Deadline: May 31
• OCA Honorary Life Membership (Award)
Deadline: May 31
• Sportsmanship Awards (Award)
• Coaching Awards (Award)
• OCA Media Awards (Award)
• Honorary Life Members (Award)
Publications:
• OCA [Ontario Curling Association] Annual
Type: Yearbook; *Frequency:* Annually

Ontario Cycling Association (OCA) / Association cycliste ontarienne

#212, 3 Concorde Gate, Toronto ON M3C 3N7
Tel: 416-426-7416; *Fax:* 416-426-7349
info@ontariocycling.org
www.ontariocycling.org
www.facebook.com/129640691224
twitter.com/ontariocycling
Overview: A medium-sized provincial licensing organization founded in 1882 overseen by Cycling Canada Cyclisme
Mission: To act as the provincial governing body for road, track & cyclocross, mountain biking, & BMX racing in Ontario; To develop & deliver quality programs & services for the sport of cycling in Ontario
Member of: Cycling Canada Cyclisme
Chief Officer(s):
Chris Chambers, President
Malcolm Eade, Vice-President, Administration & Finance
Glenn Meeuwisse, Vice-President, High Performance
Matthias Schmidt, Vice-President, Development

Jim Crosscombe, Executive Director
execdir@ontariocycling.org
Denise Kelly, Director, Provincial Coaching
Chris Baskys, Coordinator, Membership
Greg Rawson, Coordinator, Sport
events@ontariocycling.org
Finances: *Funding Sources:* Membership fees; Sponsorships
Membership: *Member Profile:* OCA affiliated club members; Riders who wish to compete only in Ontario; Riders who wish to compete out of the province or at national & international events held within Ontario; Non-racers; Certified Can-Bike & OMBI instructors
Activities: Promoting the benefits of cycling, as well as cycling programs & services in Ontario; Advocating for cyclists in Ontario; Sharing resources & expertise; Promoting safe cycling, through the CanBike safe cycling program; Coordinating mountain bike, road, & track race competitions;
Publications:
• Cycle Ontario
Type: Magazine; *Frequency:* Semiannually; *Accepts Advertising*
Profile: Information for Ontario cyclists in road, MTB, MBX, cyclo-cross, 4X, & track, as well as certified cycling coaches & commissaries
• Ontario Cycling Association Handbook
Type: Handbook; *Price:* Free with membership in the Ontario Cycling Association
• Young Cyclist's Guide
Type: Guide; *Price:* Free
Profile: Produced by the Ministry of Transportation in cooperation with the Ontario Cycling Association

Ontario Dairy Council (ODC)
6533D Mississauga Rd., Mississauga ON L5N 1A6
Tel: 905-542-3620; *Fax:* 905-542-3624
Toll-Free: 866-542-3620
info@ontariodairies.ca
www.ontariodairies.ca
Overview: A medium-sized provincial organization founded in 1971
Mission: To represent interests of dairy product processors, marketers & distributors in Ontario
Affiliation(s): International Dairy Federation
Chief Officer(s):
Tom Kane, President
tomkane@ontariodairies.ca
Christina Lewis, Vice-President
clewis@ontariodairies.ca
Finances: *Annual Operating Budget:* $500,000-$1.5 Million;
Funding Sources: Membership fees
Staff Member(s): 3
Membership: 40 corporate + 50 associate; *Fees:* Schedule available; *Member Profile:* Licensed processor, marketer or distributor; *Committees:* Technical; Advisory; Environment; Policy & Technical
Activities: *Library* by appointment

Ontario DanceSport (ODS)
ON
Tel: 905-831-2426
publicity@ontariodancesport.com
www.ontariodancesport.com
Overview: A medium-sized provincial organization overseen by Canada DanceSport
Chief Officer(s):
Gord Brittain, President

Ontario Daylily Society (ODS)
6798 9th Line, R R#2, Beeton ON L0G 1A0
Tel: 905-729-2718
www.ontariodaylily.on.ca
Overview: A small provincial organization founded in 1997
Chief Officer(s):
Faye Collins, President
president@ontariodaylily.on.ca
Membership: *Fees:* $8 youth; $20 individual; $25 family

Ontario Deaf Sports Association (ODSA)
#303, 3 Concorde Gate, Toronto ON M3C 3N7
e-mail: info@ontariodeafsports.on.ca
www.ontariodeafsports.on.ca
Overview: A small provincial organization founded in 1964 overseen by Canadian Deaf Sports Association
Member of: Canadian Deaf Sports Association
Chief Officer(s):
Rohan Smith, President

Ontario Delphinium Club
c/o Christine Gill, 4691 Hwy. 7A, RR#1, Nestleton Station ON L0B 1L0
Tel: 905-986-0310
www.ondelphiniums.com
Overview: A small provincial organization
Chief Officer(s):
Don Wick, President
Membership: *Fees:* $10 family

Ontario Dental Assistants Association (ODAA)
869 Dundas St., London ON N5W 2Z8
Tel: 519-679-2566; *Fax:* 519-679-8494
info@odaa.org
www.odaa.org
www.facebook.com/yourODAA
Previous Name: Ontario Dental Nurses & Assistants Association
Overview: A medium-sized provincial licensing organization founded in 1927 overseen by Canadian Dental Assistants Association
Mission: To act as the certifying body for dental assistants in Ontario
Chief Officer(s):
Jennifer Gill, President
Nancy Niely, Vice-President
Judy Melville, Executive Director
jmelville@odaa.org
Staff Member(s): 6
Membership: *Fees:* $45.20 students; $135.60 regular members; *Member Profile:* Dental assistants in Ontario; Students training to become dental assistants
Activities: Working with the Ontario government to have dental assisting become a regulated profession; Producing brochures for students & brochures about certification; Organizing networking opportunities
Publications:
• The Journal
Type: Journal; *Frequency:* 3 pa
Profile: Educational articles, profiles of ODAA members, regulation efforts, & meetings

Ontario Dental Association (ODA)
4 New St., Toronto ON M5R 1P6
Tel: 416-922-3900; *Fax:* 416-922-9005
Toll-Free: 800-387-1393
info@oda.ca
www.oda.ca
www.facebook.com/203452689666842
www.youtube.com/user/OntarioDentalAssoc
Overview: A medium-sized provincial organization overseen by Canadian Dental Association
Mission: To represent the dentists of Ontario; to provide exemplary oral health care & promote the attainment of optimal health for the people of Ontario
Chief Officer(s):
Rick Caldwell, President
Gerald Smith, President-Elect
Victor Kutcher, Vice-President
Tom Magyarody, Executive Director
Membership: 6,500;
Meetings/Conferences: • Ontario Dental Association Annual Spring Meeting 2015, May, 2015, Metro Toronto Convention Centre, Toronto, ON
Scope: Provincial
Attendance: 11,700
• Ontario Dental Association Annual Spring Meeting 2016, May, 2016, Metro Toronto Convention Centre, Toronto, ON
Scope: Provincial
Attendance: 11,700
• Ontario Dental Association Annual Spring Meeting 2017, May, 2017, Metro Toronto Convention Centre, Toronto, ON
Scope: Provincial
Attendance: 11,700

Ontario Dental Hygienists' Association (ODHA)
201, 3425 Harvester Rd., Burlington ON L7N 3N1
Tel: 905-681-8883; *Fax:* 905-681-3922
Toll-Free: 888-895-6044
info@odha.on.ca
www.odha.on.ca
Overview: A medium-sized provincial organization
Mission: To provide a program of services & benefits to members
Affiliation(s): Canadian Dental Hygienists' Association
Chief Officer(s):
Shelly Newton, President
Finances: *Annual Operating Budget:* $500,000-$1.5 Million
Staff Member(s): 5; 60 volunteer(s)
Membership: *Fees:* $199.50; *Member Profile:* Registered Dental Hygienists

Ontario Dental Nurses & Assistants Association *See* Ontario Dental Assistants Association

Ontario Disc Sports Association (ODSA)
3 Concorde Gate, Toronto ON M3C 3N7
Fax: 855-847-6948
Toll-Free: 855-847-6942
www.ondisc.org
www.facebook.com/196714475958
twitter.com/ondisc
Overview: A small provincial organization
Mission: To be the provincial governing body for disc sports in Ontario.
Chief Officer(s):
Ryan Briggs, Executive Director
Activities: Beach ultimate; discathon; disc golf; double disc court; field events; freestyle; Goaltimate; guts; Catch & Fetch; ultimate

Ontario DX Association (OXDA)
#23, 3211 Centennial D., Vernon BC V1T 2T8
e-mail: odxa@rogers.com
www.odxa.on.ca
Overview: A medium-sized provincial organization founded in 1974
Chief Officer(s):
Joe Robinson, General Manager
Harold Sellers, Managing Editor
Finances: *Annual Operating Budget:* $50,000-$100,000;
Funding Sources: Membership fees
20 volunteer(s)
Membership: 500; *Fees:* $40
Activities: Radiofest Convention, Sept.;

Ontario East Tourism Association (OETA)
PO Box 730, #200, 104 St. Lawrence St., Merrickville ON K0G 1N0
Tel: 613-269-4113; *Fax:* 613-659-4306
Toll-Free: 800-567-3278
support@realontario.ca
www.realontario.ca
Also Known As: Real Ontario
Previous Name: Eastern Ontario Travel Association
Overview: A small local organization founded in 1974
Mission: To encourage visitation to Eastern Ontario by means of cooperative tourism marketing
Chief Officer(s):
Rose Bertoia, Executive Director
John Bonser, President
Finances: *Annual Operating Budget:* $500,000-$1.5 Million
Staff Member(s): 3
Membership: 110 tourist associations & operators; *Fees:* Schedule available; *Member Profile:* Tourist associations, businesses & municipalities; *Committees:* Marketing; Membership; Motorcoach; Finance; Government Relations; Constitution; Tourism Liaison; Special Projects
Activities: *Speaker Service:* Yes

Ontario Electric Railway Historical Association
PO Box 578, Milton ON L9T 5A2
Tel: 519-856-9802; *Fax:* 519-856-1399
streetcar@hcry.org
www.hcry.org
twitter.com/streetcarmuseum
Also Known As: Halton County Radial Railway
Overview: A small provincial charitable organization founded in 1953
Mission: To collect & return to operating capacity, electric railway equipment representing North American city & interurban systems
Affiliation(s): Association of Railway Museums; Ontario Museum Association; Canadian Museums Association
Finances: *Funding Sources:* Operations; membership fees; donations
Membership: *Member Profile:* Persons interested in restoration/operation of Canadian streetcars
Activities: Operates a museum for the pleasure & education of the public; *Speaker Service:* Yes; *Library:* Archives; by appointment

Ontario Electrical League (OEL)
#300, 180 Attwell Dr., Toronto ON M9W 6A9
Tel: 905-238-1382; *Fax:* 905-238-1420
communications@oel.org
www.oel.org
www.linkedin.com/oeleague
www.facebook.com/132812900129239?fref=ts
twitter.com/OEL3
Overview: A medium-sized provincial organization founded in 1966
Mission: To represent & strengthen the electrical industry in Ontario
Chief Officer(s):
Stephen Sell, President
stephen.sell@oel.org
Sheila Sage, Manager, Operations
sheila.sage@oel.org
Cynthia Kenth, Editor, Dialogue
dialogue@oel.org
Staff Member(s): 3
Membership: 21 chapters, with 2,500+ members; *Member Profile:* Educators; Electricians; Electrical contractors; Electrical inspectors; Manufacturers; Consulting engineers; Distributors
Activities: Promoting Ontario's electrical industry; Providing educational opportunities
Awards:
• EFC / OEL Scholarship (Scholarship)
A post-secondary school scholarship, for enrollment in an electrical or related program, for members of the Ontario Electrical League & their families
Publications:
• Contractor News [a publication of the Ontario Electrical League]
Type: Newsletter; *Frequency:* Monthly
Profile: Update on industry news, plus issues that affect contractors & their businesses
• Contractor Newsbrief [a publication of the Ontario Electrical League]
Type: Newsletter
Profile: Contractor Committee activities, for Ontario Electrical League contractor members
• Dialogue [a publication of the Ontario Electrical League]
Type: Magazine; *Frequency:* Quarterly; *Accepts Advertising; Price:* Free with membership in the Ontario Electrical League
Profile: League activities, member news, plus updates about industry & government issues
• Ontario Electrical League Chapter Newsletter
Type: Newsletter
Profile: Chapter committee update

Ontario Energy Association (OEA)
#202, 121 Richmond St. West, Toronto ON M5H 2K1
Tel: 416-961-2339; *Fax:* 416-961-1173
Other Communication: committees@energyontario.ca
oea@energyontario.ca
www.energyontario.ca
www.linkedin.com/company/ontario-energy-association
twitter.com/ontarioenergy
Overview: A small provincial organization
Mission: To represent the energy industry of Ontario
Chief Officer(s):
Elise Herzig, President & Chief Executive Officer
Tina Arvanitis, Vice-President, Government Relations & Communications, 647-920-3269
tarvanitis@energyontario.ca
Finances: *Funding Sources:* Sponsorships
Membership: 150+ corporate members; *Member Profile:* Members of Ontario's energy industry, such as power producers, manufacturers, contractors, service providers, energy retailers, marketers, energy distributors, & energy consultants; *Committees:* Energy Markets Joint Sector; Environment Joint Sector; Government Relations Joint Sector; Green Energy & Conservation Joint Sector; Marketers & Retailers Sector; Utility Sector
Activities: Providing education & resources about the energy sector; Engaging in advocacy activities for members; Conducting research into energy matters; *Speaker Service:* Yes
Meetings/Conferences: • Ontario Energy Association 2015 Annual Conference & Annual General Meeting, 2015, ON
Scope: Provincial
Description: Examples of programming includes panel sessions, the presentation of awards, information sharing opportunities, & social events
Contact Information: Phone: 416-961-2339; E-mail: events@energyontario.ca

Ontario English Catholic Teachers' Association (CLC) (OECTA)
#400, 65 St. Clair Ave. East, Toronto ON M4T 2Y8
Tel: 416-925-2493; *Fax:* 416-925-7764
Toll-Free: 800-268-7230
Other Communication: AQ Courses e-mail: registrar@oecta.on.ca
membership@oecta.on.ca
www.oecta.on.ca
www.facebook.com/OECTA
twitter.com/OECTAProvincial
Overview: A large provincial organization founded in 1944
Mission: To advance Catholic education; To provide professional services, support, protection, & leadership
Member of: Canadian Teachers' Federation; Canadian Labour Congress; Ontario Federation of Labour
Affliation(s): Ontario Teachers' Federation
Chief Officer(s):
Kevin O'Dwyer, President
k.odwyer@oecta.on.ca
Marshall Jarvis, General Secretary
m.jarvis@oecta.on.ca
David Church, Deputy General Secretary
d.church@oecta.on.ca
Staff Member(s): 61
Membership: 45,000; *Fees:* $950; *Committees:* Audit; Awards; Beginning Teachers; Catholic Education; Collective Bargaining; Communications & Public Relations; Educational Aid; Elementary Schools; Finance; Health & Safety; Human Rights; Legislation; Occasional Teachers; Personnel; Political Advisory; Program & Structures; Professional Development Steering; Secondary Schools; Status of Women; Teacher Education Network
Activities: *Library:* Resource Library;
Awards:
• Annual General Meeting Awards (Award)
• 25-Year Annual General Meeting Recognition Service Award (Award)
• Excellence in Communication Awards (Award)
• Fintan Kilbride Memorial Social Justice Recognition Award (Award)
• Young Authors Awards/Prix Jeunes Écrivains (Award)
Meetings/Conferences: • Ontario English Catholic Teachers' Association 2015 Beginning Teachers Conference, 2015, ON
Scope: Provincial
Description: A conference for all Ontario English Catholic Teachers' Association members in their first five years of teaching
Contact Information: Ontario English Catholic Teachers' Association Office, Phone: 416-925-2493
• Ontario English Catholic Teachers' Association 2015 Annual General Meeting, March, 2015, Westin Harbour Castle, Toronto, ON
Scope: Provincial
Attendance: 600+
Description: Delegates attend to the business of the association, elect Provincial Executive members, & listen to presentations by guest speakers
Contact Information: Ontario English Catholic Teachers' Association Office, Phone: 416-925-2493
• Ontario English Catholic Teachers' Association 2015 Leadership Training Program, 2015, ON
Scope: Provincial
Description: A workshop for association members
Contact Information: Ontario English Catholic Teachers' Association Office, Phone: 416-925-2493
• Ontario English Catholic Teachers' Association 2015 GSN Seminar, 2015, ON
Scope: Provincial
Contact Information: Ontario English Catholic Teachers' Association Office, Phone: 416-925-2493
Publications:
• Agenda [a publication of the Ontario English Catholic Teachers' Association (CLC)]
Type: Newsletter
• e-agenda [a publication of the Ontario English Catholic Teachers' Association (CLC)]
Type: Newsletter

Ontario Environment Industry Association (ONEIA)
#410, 215 Spadina Ave., Toronto ON M5T 2C7
Tel: 416-531-7884
info@oneia.ca
www.oneia.ca
Overview: A large provincial organization founded in 1991
Mission: To represent the interests of the environmental industry in Ontario; To promote environmental business to industry & government in Ontario
Membership: 175 corporate; *Fees:* $395-$1375; *Committees:* Finance; Nominations; EID; Advocacy; Water; Air; Waste; Brownfields; Communications & Programming; Membership & Business Development

Ontario Environment Industry Association (ONEIA)
#401, 215 Spadina Ave., Toronto ON M5T 2C7
Tel: 416-531-7884; *Fax:* 416-644-0116
info@oneia.ca
www.oneia.ca
Previous Name: Canadian Environment Industry Association - Ontario Chapter
Overview: A medium-sized provincial organization founded in 1991
Mission: To promote the growth of environment business in Ontario
Member of: Canadian Environmental Auditing Association; CRESTech; Retail Council of Canada
Affliation(s): Canadian Standards Association; Cements Association of Canada; Ontario Concrete Pipe Association; Ontario Sewer & Watermain Construtions Association; Ontario Environmental Training Consortium; Ontario Centre for Environmental Technology Advancement
Chief Officer(s):
Marjan Lahuis, Operations Manager, Membership Recruitment and Sponsor Relations
Alex Gill, Executive Director
Finances: *Annual Operating Budget:* $100,000-$250,000; *Funding Sources:* Membership dues; projects
Staff Member(s): 1; 12 volunteer(s)
Membership: 167; *Fees:* $395-$1,375; *Member Profile:* Ontario-based companies, business associations & organizations which actively provide environmental technologies & services that help protect or improve the environment & that help achieve sustainable development; *Committees:* Advocacy; Business Development; Member Services
Activities: Has been an active participant in a number of initiatives - the Green Industry Strategy for Ontario led by the Ministry of Energy in collaboration with MOE & MITT; the 3R's Municipal Infrastructure Task Force to implement the MOE's Waste Management Initiative; the CCME Task Force for a National Waste Management Strategy; the Canadian-American Environmental Marketing Council to establish a facilitation office in Washington DC for Canadian companies pursuing the USA environmental market; *Library* by appointment

Ontario Environmental Network (OEN)
PO Box 1412, Stn. Main, North Bay ON P1B 8K6
Tel: 705-840-2888
oen@oen.ca
www.oen.ca
www.facebook.com/180386751992826
www.youtube.com/ontarioenvironment
Overview: A large provincial organization founded in 1981 overseen by Canadian Environmental Network
Mission: To encourage discussions of ways to protect the environment; To increase environmental awareness throughout Ontario; To serve the environmental non-profit, non-governmental community in Ontario
Affliation(s): Canadian Environmental Network
Chief Officer(s):
Phillip Penna, Coordinator, 705-840-2888
Membership: 500+ environmental groups; *Fees:* $15 individuals; $30 government agencies & businesses; $40 organizations; *Member Profile:* Non-government, not-for-profit organizations in Ontario concerned with the preservation of the environment; Government agencies; Businesses; Individuals
Activities: Facilitating communication among environmental organizations; Maintaining a database of Ontario's environmental groups; Increasing awareness of environmental organizations; Operating the First Ontario TimeBank (firstontario.timebanks.org)
Meetings/Conferences: • Ontario Environment Network Conference & AGM 2015, 2015
Scope: Provincial
Publications:
• OEN [Ontario Environmental Network] News
Type: Newsletter; *Frequency:* Semimonthly; *Accepts Advertising; Price:* Free with Ontario Environmental Network membership
Profile: Ontario Environment Network updates, events, & action alerts sent to member groups & subscribers

• Ontario Environmental Directory [a publication of the Ontario Environmental Directory]
Type: Directory; *Editor:* Peter Blanchard; *Price:* Free with Ontario EnvironmentalNetwork membership
Profile: Comprehensive information about Ontario environmental organizations & agencies

Ontario Equestrian Federation (OEF)

#201, 1 West Pearce St., Richmond Hill ON L4B 3K3
Tel: 905-709-6545; *Fax:* 905-709-1867
Toll-Free: 877-441-7112
horse@horse.on.ca
www.horse.on.ca
www.facebook.com/OEF.Horse
twitter.com/OEF_Horse
Overview: A medium-sized provincial organization founded in 1977
Mission: Committed to equine welfare & to providing leadership & support to the individuals, associations & industries in Ontario's horse community
Member of: Equine Canada
Affliation(s): Equine Guelph; Ontario Trails Council; Ontario Federation of Agriculture; Ontario Minitry of Tourism, Culture & Sport
Chief Officer(s):
Allan Ehrlick, President
aoc@milestoneac.ca
Dianne Graham, Executive Director
d.graham@horse.on.ca
Finances: *Annual Operating Budget:* $250,000-$500,000; *Funding Sources:* Membership dues; government grant; merchandise sales
Staff Member(s): 14; 100 volunteer(s)
Membership: 22,000 individuals; *Fees:* Schedule available; *Member Profile:* Individuals, associations & corporations with interests in equine sport & industry; *Committees:* Associations; Competitions; Horse Facilities; Industry; Recreation
Activities: Education; equine welfare; member services; competitions administration; coaching certification; industry promotion; *Awareness Events:* Horse Day, June; Royal Agricultural Winter Fair, Nov.; Can-Am Equine Emporium, March; *Rents Mailing List:* Yes; *Library* Open to public
Awards:
• Media, Volunteer, Sponsor, Coach, Official of the Year Awards (Award)
• OEF Senior & Junior Equestrian of the Year (Award)
• OEF Recognition Award (Award)

Ontario Farm & Country Accommodations Association (OFCA)

8724 Wellington Rd. 18, RR#5, Belwood ON N0J 1J0
www.countryhosts.com
Overview: A small provincial organization founded in 1967
Mission: To be a self-supporting, accredited association whose members provide warm hospitality, country accommodations & farm tours, for guests seeking a unique getaway with the opportunity to experience rural culture, farming & the environment
Chief Officer(s):
Paul Faires, Secretary
paul.faires@sympatico.ca
Activities: *Speaker Service:* Yes; *Rents Mailing List:* Yes

Ontario Farm Fresh Marketing Association (OFFMA)

2002 Vandorf Sideroad, Aurora ON L4G 7B9
Tel: 905-841-9278; *Fax:* 905-726-3369
info@ontariofarmfresh.com
ontariofarmfresh.com
www.facebook.com/OntarioFarmFresh
twitter.com/OFFMA
www.youtube.com/user/OntarioFarmFresh
Overview: A medium-sized provincial organization founded in 1973
Mission: To assist members in marketing skills; To liaise with other farm-oriented organizations such as Ontario Fruit & Vegetable Growers Association
Chief Officer(s):
Cathy Bartolic, Executive Director
Finances: *Annual Operating Budget:* Less than $50,000
Staff Member(s): 1; 9 volunteer(s)
Membership: 193 individual; 27 associate; *Fees:* $129

Ontario Farmland Trust (OFT)

c/o University of Guelph, Johnston Hall, #017, Guelph ON N1G 2W1
Tel: 519-824-4120; *Fax:* 519-767-1686
info@ontariofarmlandtrust.ca
www.ontariofarmlandtrust.ca
Overview: A medium-sized provincial organization founded in 2004
Mission: To protect & preserve farmland in Ontario
Chief Officer(s):
Matt Setzkorn, Acting Executive Director
Staff Member(s): 3

Ontario Fashion Exhibitors (OFE)

PO Box 218, #2219, 160 Tycos Dr., Toronto ON M6B 1W8
Tel: 416-596-2401; *Fax:* 416-596-1808
Toll-Free: 800-765-7508
info@profileshow.ca
www.profileshow.ca
Overview: A medium-sized provincial organization founded in 1955
Mission: To produce fashion marketplace events
Affliation(s): Canadian Association of Wholesale Sales Representatives (CAWS)
Chief Officer(s):
Serge Micheli, Executive Director
sm@profileshow.ca
Michael Dargavel, Show Manager
md@profileshow.ca
Membership: *Member Profile:* Wholesale sales representatives in the apparel industry who are not part of ownership or management of design, manufacturing, or importing businesses
Activities: Organizing shows & seminars for the ladies wear industry
Meetings/Conferences: • The Profile Show 2015, March, 2015, Toronto Congress Centre, North Building, Toronto, ON
Scope: Provincial
• The Profile Show 2015, September, 2015, Toronto Congress Centre, North Building, Toronto, ON
Scope: Provincial

Ontario Federation for Cerebral Palsy (OFCP)

#104, 1630 Lawrence Ave. West, Toronto ON M6L 1C5
Tel: 416-244-9686; *Fax:* 416-244-6543
Toll-Free: 877-244-9686
info@ofcp.ca
www.ofcp.ca
www.facebook.com/OntarioFederationforCerebralPalsy
twitter.com/OntarioFCP
Overview: A medium-sized provincial organization founded in 1947
Mission: To address the changing needs of people in Ontario with cerebral palsy
Chief Officer(s):
Cathy Samuelson, Executive Director, 416-244-9626 Ext. 228
ed@ofcp.ca
Activities: Programs: Planning Services; Long Term Planning and Support; Assistive Devices Funding; Vacation Funding Assistance; Day Activities Funding Assistance; Membership Services; Educational and Recreational Services; Children and Families Program; Ontario Services Information Database; Household Pickup Service (used clothing and household goods); *Awareness Events:* OFCP Annual Conference, Oct.; Annual Conference for people who provide support for people with disabilities, May
Publications:
• InformAction
Type: Newsletter; *Frequency:* 3 pa

Ontario Federation for Cerebral Palsy (OFCP)

#104, 1630 Lawrence Ave. West, Toronto ON M6L 1C5
Tel: 416-244-9686; *Fax:* 416-244-6543
Toll-Free: 877-244-9686; *TTY:* 866-740-9501
info@ofcp.ca
www.ofcp.ca
www.facebook.com/OntarioFederationforCerebralPalsy
twitter.com/OntarioFCP
Overview: A medium-sized provincial charitable organization founded in 1947
Mission: To improve the quality of life of persons with cerebral palsy through a broad range of programs, education, support of research & the delivery of needed services to people with cerebral palsy & other physical disabilities & their families.
Affliation(s): Neurological Health Charities Canada; Ontario Association of Non-Profit Homes & Services for Seniors
Chief Officer(s):
Cathy Samuelson, Executive Director
cathys@ofcp.ca
Activities: Financial assistance for purchase of equipment; home visits; activities funding; child care; *Speaker Service:* Yes

Ontario Federation of Agriculture (OFA)

Ontario AgriCentre, #206, 100 Stone Rd. West, London ON N1G 5L3
Tel: 519-821-8883; *Fax:* 519-821-8810
Toll-Free: 800-668-3276
info@ofa.on.ca
www.ofa.on.ca
www.facebook.com/ontariofarms
twitter.com/ontariofarms
www.youtube.com/user/ontariofarms
Overview: A large provincial organization founded in 1936 overseen by Canadian Federation of Agriculture
Mission: To represent farm families throughout Ontario; to champion the interests of Ontario farmers; to work towards a sustainable future for farmers
Member of: Agricultural Credit Corporation; AgEnergy Co-operative Ltd.; Agricultural Adaptation Council; Biosolids Utilization Committee; Canadian Federation of Agriculture; Cooperators Insurance; Drains Action Working Group; Farm & Food Care Ontario; Guelph Chamber of Commerce; and more...
Affliation(s): SHARE Agriculture Foundation
Chief Officer(s):
Mark Wales, President
Don McCabe, Vice-President
Debra Pretty-Straathof, Vice-President
Finances: *Funding Sources:* Membership fees; Sponsorships
Staff Member(s): 21
Membership: 38,000 individual + 31 organizations; *Fees:* $220.35
Activities: Engaging in advocacy activities; providing networking opportunities
Meetings/Conferences: • Ontario Federation of Agriculture 2015 79th Annual Convention, 2015
Scope: Provincial
Contact Information: Ag Business Centre, Phone: 519-674-1500 ext. 63596, Toll-Free: 1-866-222-9682
Publications:
• Ag Buyer's Guide [a publication of the Ontario Federation of Agriculture]
Type: Guide
Profile: Information to assist Ontario farmers purchase equipment
• Better Farming
Type: Magazine; *Frequency:* Monthly; *Price:* Free with Ontario Federation of Agriculture membership
Profile: A business magazine about Ontario agriculture
• Country Guide
Type: Magazine
Profile: Suggestions to improve farm profitability plus innovative technologies
• Ontario Federation of Agriculture Policy Handbook
Type: Handbook; *Number of Pages:* 42; *Price:* Free with Ontario Federation of Agriculture membership
Profile: Topics addressed include animal welfare & control; education, schools, & training; energy; environment; farm implements; finance; labour, employment, & human resources;land use planning; marketing & production; rural affairs; science & technology; telecommunications; & transportation

Ontario Federation of Anglers & Hunters (OFAH)

PO Box 2800, 4601 Guthrie Dr., Peterborough ON K9J 8L5
Tel: 705-748-6324; *Fax:* 705-748-9577
ofah@ofah.org
www.ofah.org
www.facebook.com/127166042780
twitter.com/ofah
www.youtube.com/ofahcommunications
Overview: A medium-sized provincial charitable organization founded in 1928 overseen by Canadian Wildlife Federation
Mission: To save & defend from waste the natural resources of Ontario, its soils, minerals, air, water, forests & wildlife
Chief Officer(s):
Rob Hare, President
Mike Reader, Executive Director
Finances: *Funding Sources:* Membership fees; Donations
Membership: 83,000 individuals + 655 affiliated clubs; *Fees:* $45.50 adult; $57.50 family; $33.00 youth; $1,000 life; *Member Profile:* Interest in fish & wildlife conservation; *Committees:* Land Access; Forestry; Fisheries; Hunter Education
Activities: Ontario Family Fishing Weekend, July; Project Purple Week, Aug.

Meetings/Conferences: • Ontario Federation of Anglers & Hunters 2015 Annual Get Outdoors Youth Leadership Conference, 2015, ON
Scope: Provincial
Description: An opportunity for young people to participate in activities to promote interest in outdoor activities, hunting, & fishing
Contact Information: Communications Manager: Lezlie Goodwin, Phone: 705-748-6324, ext. 270
• Ontario Federation of Anglers & Hunters 2015 87th Annual General Meeting & Fish & Wildlife Conference, 2015, ON
Scope: Provincial
Description: Presentations for anglers & hunters in Ontario
Contact Information: Communications Manager: Lezlie Goodwin, Phone: 705-748-6324, ext. 270

Ontario Federation of Home & School Associations Inc. (OFHSA)

51 Stuart St., Hamilton ON L8L 1B5
Tel: 905-308-9563
info@ofhsa.on.ca
www.ofhsa.on.ca
www.facebook.com/159974104078740
Overview: A medium-sized provincial charitable organization founded in 1916 overseen by Canadian Home & School Federation
Mission: To provide facilities for the bringing together of members of Home & School Associations for discussion of matters of general interest & to stimulate cooperative effort; to assist in forming public opinion favorable to reform & advancement of the education of the child; to develop between educators & the general public such united effort as shall secure for every child the highest advantage in physical, mental, moral & spiritual education; to raise the standard of home & national life; to maintain a non-partisan, non-commercial, non-racial & non-sectarian organization
Chief Officer(s):
Teresa Blum, President
Sandra Binns, 1st Executive Vice-President
Michelle Ercolini, 2nd Executive Vice-President
Membership: *Fees:* $15; *Member Profile:* Parents & others interested in advocating for children in public education
Activities: Annual conference; leadership camps; regional education workshops; *Speaker Service:* Yes

Ontario Federation of Independent Schools (OFIS)

PO Box 27011, 101 Holiday Inn Dr., Cambridge ON N3C 0E6
Tel: 519-249-1665
info@ofis.ca
www.ofis.ca
www.facebook.com/OFISOntario
twitter.com/OFIS_Ontario
www.youtube.com/user/subtlevox
Previous Name: Ontario Association of Alternative & Independent Schools
Overview: A medium-sized provincial charitable organization founded in 1974 overseen by Federation of Independent Schools in Canada
Mission: To secure guarantees from Ontario government for independent schools' right to exist, curricular freedom, self-governance & acceptance by government of its responsibility to let education grants follow a child to any bona fide school that meets acceptable social & educational criteria
Chief Officer(s):
Barbara Bierman, Executive Director
barbara.bierman@ofis.ca
Barbara Brown, President
barbarakec@bellnet.ca
Finances: *Funding Sources:* Membership fees
Staff Member(s): 2
Membership: 140 schools; *Fees:* Schedule available; *Committees:* Finance; Professional Developmen; Governance
Activities: *Speaker Service:* Yes

Ontario Federation of Indian Friendship Centres (OFIFC)

219 Front St. East, Toronto ON M5A 1E8
Tel: 416-956-7575; *Fax:* 416-956-7577
Toll-Free: 800-772-9291
ofifc@ofifc.org
www.ofifc.org
www.facebook.com/TheOFIFC
Also Known As: Ontario Federation of Friendship Centres
Overview: A medium-sized provincial organization founded in 1971 overseen by National Association of Friendship Centres
Mission: To represent the collective interests of Ontario's friendship centres; To administer programs delivered by friendship centres, such as justice, health, employment, & family support; To improve the quality of life for Aboriginal people for equal access & participation in Canadian society
Chief Officer(s):
Sylvia Maracle, Executive Director
smaracle@ofifc.org
Celeste Hayward, Director, Program
chayward@ofifc.org
Juliette Nicolet, Director, Policy
jnicolet@ofifc.org
Meri Saunders, Director, Finance
msaunders@ofifc.org
Membership: 27 friendship centres; *Member Profile:* Friendship centres located across Ontario
Activities: Managing provincial programs, such as Aboriginal Healing & Wellness Strategy, Ontario Aboriginal Health Advocacy Initiative, & O-GI Employment Services

Ontario Federation of Labour (OFL) / Fédération du travail de l'Ontario

#202, 15 Gervais Dr., Toronto ON M3C 1Y8
Tel: 416-441-2731; *Fax:* 416-441-0722
Toll-Free: 800-668-9138; *TTY:* 416-443-6305
info@ofl.ca
www.ofl.ca
www.facebook.com/OFLabour
twitter.com/OFLabour
Overview: A large provincial organization founded in 1957 overseen by Canadian Labour Congress
Mission: To represent the interests of organized workers in Ontario; To provide support services to its affiliated local unions & labour councils
Chief Officer(s):
Sid Ryan, President
SRyan@ofl.ca
Nancy Hutchinson, Sec.-Treas.
NHutchison@ofl.ca
Finances: *Annual Operating Budget:* $3 Million-$5 Million; *Funding Sources:* Per capita revenue; literature & videos sales
Staff Member(s): 35
Membership: 700,000; *Fees:* $0.63 member/month; *Member Profile:* Trade unions; *Committees:* Education; Energy & Environment; Health & Safety; Women's; Human Rights; Social Services; Health Care; Labour Relations; Peace & Disarmament; Political Education; Youth; Visible Minority; Gay, Lesbian & Bisexual; Aboriginal Persons; Persons with Disabilities
Activities: *Speaker Service:* Yes; *Library* by appointment

Ontario Federation of School Athletic Associations (OFSAA) / Fédération des associations du sport scolaire de l'Ontario

#204, 3 Concorde Gate, Toronto ON M3C 3N7
Tel: 416-426-7391; *Fax:* 416-426-7317
www.ofsaa.on.ca
www.facebook.com/OFSAA
twitter.com/ofsaa
Overview: A medium-sized provincial charitable organization founded in 1948 overseen by School Sport Canada
Mission: To enhance school sport in Ontario; To handle issues that affect students, coaches, schools, & communities; To work with volunteer teacher-coaches to offer provincial championships & festivals for student-athletes across Ontario
Member of: School Sport Canada
Chief Officer(s):
Jim Wolley, President
jim_woolley@wrdsb.on.ca
Ian Press, Vice-President
ipress@hpedsb.on.ca
Doug Gellatly, Executive Director
doug@ofsaa.on.ca
Devin Gray, Coordinator, Communications
devin@ofsaa.on.ca
Finances: *Funding Sources:* Sponsorships
Staff Member(s): 9
Membership: 19 associations; *Member Profile:* Regional school athletic associations throughout Ontario, such as the Central Ontario Secondary Schools Association, Northern Ontario Secondary Schools Association, Southern Ontario Secondary Schools Association, & the Toronto District College Athletic Association; *Committees:* Alpine Skiing; Badminton; Baseball; Basketball; Cross Country; Curling; Field Hockey; Field Lacrosse; Football; Golf; Gymnastics; Hockey; Nordic Skiing; Rugby; Snowboard Racing; Soccer; Swimming; Tennis; Track & Field; Volleyball; Wrestling; Championship Review Ad Hoc; Classifications Ad Hoc; Coaching Ad Hoc; Constitutional Review Ad Hoc; Future Directions Ad Hoc; Gender Equity Ad Hoc; Sanctions Ad Hoc; Transfers Ad Hoc
Activities: Organizing programs, such as student leadership & coach development programs; Sanctioning tournaments; Preparing & distributing resources; Providing professional development opportunities; *Awareness Events:* Canadian School Sport Week
Awards:
• Pete Beach Award (Award)
• OFSAA Leadership in School Sport Award (Award)
• Colin Hood OFSAA School Sport Award (Award)
• Roger Neilson / Toronto Maple Leafs Alumni Scholarship Award (Scholarship)
• Ministry Long Service Award (Award)
• Syl Apps Special Achievement Award (Award)
• Brian Maxwell Memorial Scholarship (Scholarship)
• OFSAA Alumni Scholarship (Scholarship)
Publications:
• Baseball Coaching Manual
Type: Manual; *Price:* $15
• Curling Coaching Manual
Type: Manual; *Price:* $18
• Football Coaching Manual: Teacher's Instruction Manual
Type: Manual; *Price:* $25
Profile: Featuring rules, lesson plans, & practices
• In the Zone
Type: Newsletter
Profile: Articles on current issues, plus upcoming events
• Rugby Coaching Manual
Type: Manual
• Volleyball Coaching Manual
Type: Manual; *Price:* $28

Ontario Federation of Snowmobile Clubs (OFSC)

#9, 501 Welham Rd., Barrie ON L4N 8Z6
Tel: 705-739-7669; *Fax:* 705-739-5005
www.ofsc.on.ca
Overview: A medium-sized provincial organization founded in 1966
Mission: To support member snowmobile clubs & volunteers; To establish & maintain quality snowmobile trails; To further the enjoyment of organized snowmobiling
Member of: Canadian Council of Snowmobile Organizations
Finances: *Funding Sources:* Sale of trail permits; Donations; Sponsorships
6 volunteer(s)
Membership: 231 clubs in 17 districts, consisting of 200,000 families; *Member Profile:* Ontario local snowmobile clubs
Activities: Setting policies & procedures; Providing advice to member clubs; Handling trail plans & issues; Promoting concern for the environment & safety; Campaigning to attract new participants
Awards:
• President's Award (Award)
Club of the year
• Ron Jones Memorial Award (Award)
• Volunteer of the Year (Award)
• Lois Beckett Memorial Award (Award)
Publications:
• How to Make Smart Choices: Take It Easy
Type: Kit; *Price:* $19.95
Profile: A snowmobile safety kit, which includes a 32 page Smart Choices booklet & a Smart Choices DVD
• Ontario Federation of Snowmobile Clubs District Trail Guides
Profile: Ontario snowmobilers using trails should also consult "Assumptions for OFSC Trail Use"
• The Right Way: Snowmobile Driver Training Safety Course - Adult Training Kit
Type: Kit; *Price:* $37
Profile: Kit consists of a 52 page manual, DVD, CD, online test, & certificate

Ontario Federation of Teaching Parents (OFTP)

PO Box 66551, Stn. McCowan, Toronto ON M1J 3N8
Tel: 416-410-5218
Toll-Free: 800-704-0448
enquiries@ontariohomeschool.org
www.ontariohomeschool.org
www.facebook.com/182154071937198
Overview: A small provincial organization founded in 1987
Mission: To support parental choice in education as stated in the UN Declaration of Human Rights; to act as link between home educators & institutions such as the provincial government & school boards

Member of: Ontario Federation of Independent Schools
Affiliation(s): Association of Canadian Home-based Educators
Chief Officer(s):
Glenda Willemsma, Administrator
Membership: *Fees:* $30/year; $75/3 years; *Member Profile:* Home educators
Activities: Provides information & support on home education

Ontario Fencing Association (OFA) / Association d'escrime de l'Ontario

984 Main St. West, Hamilton ON L8S 1B2
Tel: 905-525-6693
info@fencingontario.ca
fencingontario.ca/cms
Overview: A medium-sized provincial organization overseen by Canadian Fencing Federation
Mission: To promote & develop the sport of fencing in Ontario
Member of: Canadian Fencing Federation
Chief Officer(s):
Lucie Hamelin, Interim President
president@fencingontario.ca
June McGuire, Executive Director
info@fencingontario.ca
Staff Member(s): 4
Membership: *Fees:* $5 associate; $20 recreation; $80 competitive; $35 coaches & officials

Ontario Field Ornithologists (OFO)

PO Box 116, Stn. F, Toronto ON M4Y 2L4
e-mail: membership@ofo.ca
www.ofo.ca
Overview: A medium-sized international charitable organization founded in 1982
Mission: To study bird life in Ontario
Chief Officer(s):
Robert Maciver, President, 519-260-0729
robert.maciver@gmail.com
Lynne Freeman, Vice-President, 416-463-9540
lynnef.to@gmail.com
Brian Gibbon, Treasurer, 705-726-8969
bwg@backland.net
Claire Nelson, Director, Advertising
advertising@ofo.ca
David Milsom, Director, Publicity & Field Trips
fieldtrips@ofo.ca
Doug Woods, Director, Website, 416-466-4660
doug.woods@rogers.com
Finances: *Funding Sources:* Membership fees; Donations
Membership: *Fees:* $35 Canada; $40US USA; $45US international; $700 Canadian life membership; $800US USA life membership; $900US international life membership; *Member Profile:* Field ornithologists from Ontario & abroad; *Committees:* Convention; Certificates; Field Trips; Website; Membership; Birdathon; Advertising; Ontario Bird Records; ONTBIRDS Listserv; Nomination
Activities: Offering field trips to birding spots in Ontario; Publishing site guides to birding areas of Ontario; Facilitating the exchange of information
Awards:
• Distinguished Ornithologist Award; Certificates of Appreciation (Award)
Meetings/Conferences: • Ontario Field Ornithologists 2015 Annual Convention, October, 2015, Point Pelee, ON
Scope: Provincial
Description: Activities include guest speakers, birding displays, field trips, & a social event
Contact Information: Lynne Freeman; Phone: 416-463-9540; lynnef.to@gmail.com
Publications:
• Field Checklist of Ontario Birds
Type: Booklet; *Price:* $2
• OFO [Ontario Field Ornithologists] News
Type: Newsletter; *Frequency:* 3 pa; *Editor:* Seabrooke Leckie; *Price:* Free with Ontario Field Ornithologists membership
Profile: Announcements, field trip reports, site guides, & Ontario Bird Records Committe reports
• Ontario Birds
Type: Journal; *Frequency:* 3 pa; *Editor:* R. James; G. Coady; D.V. Weseloh; *Price:* Free with Ontario Field Ornithologists membership
Profile: New information about the status, distribution, identification, & behaviour of birds in Ontario
• Ornithology in Ontario
Type: Book; *Number of Pages:* 400; *Editor:* Martin McNicholl; John Cranmer-Byng
Profile: Historical overview, archaeology, early naturalists, biographies, zoology, museums, bird banding, species accounts, & studies

Ontario Fire Buff Associates (OFBA)

PO Box 56, Stn. Don Mills Station, Toronto ON M3C 2R6
e-mail: ontariofirebuffs@yahoo.ca
www.ofba.ca
Overview: A small provincial organization founded in 1971
Mission: To bring together people who share a common interest - the fire service of Ontario
Member of: International Fire Buff Associates
Chief Officer(s):
Bob Rupert, President
Finances: *Annual Operating Budget:* Less than $50,000
170 volunteer(s)
Membership: 100-499; *Fees:* $15-$28; *Member Profile:* Open to any eligible individual or organization upon required recommendation, payment of fees & approval of the Board of Directors

Ontario Flue-Cured Tobacco Growers' Marketing Board (OFCTGMB)

4B Elm St., Tillsonburg ON N4G 0C4
Tel: 519-842-3661; *Fax:* 519-842-7813
otb@ontarioflue-cured.com
www.ontarioflue-cured.com
Also Known As: Ontario Tobacco Board
Overview: A medium-sized provincial organization founded in 1957
Mission: To administer & enforce the provisions of Regulation 207/09 (Tobacco - Plan) & Regulation 208/09 (Tobacco - Powers of Local Board), made under the Farm Products Marketing Act; To control & regulate the production & marketing of tobacco, within the limits imposed by the Farm Products Marketing Act
Activities: Engaging in a continuing monitoring process, during which Board inspectors, accompanied by Excise Duty Officers from the Canada Revenue Agency, visit tobacco farms

Ontario Folk Dance Association (OFDA)

Toronto ON
e-mail: ontariofolkdancers@gmail.com
www.ofda.ca
Overview: A small provincial organization founded in 1969
Mission: To promote the practice of international folk arts & dance; to prepare, collect & disseminate information & material relating to folk arts & dance
Finances: *Funding Sources:* Membership fees; events
Membership: *Fees:* $24 single; $30 family
Activities: Recreational folk dancing

Ontario Food Protection Association (OFPA)

PO Box 51575, 2140A Queen St. East, Toronto ON M4E 1C0
Tel: 519-265-4119; *Fax:* 416-981-3368
info@ofpa.on.ca
www.ofpa.on.ca
Overview: A small provincial organization
Mission: Provides a common forum for those associated with food safety in the food industry and enables those interested in food safety to exchange ideas, experiences and information.
Chief Officer(s):
Jeff Hall, President
Membership: *Fees:* Professional - $59; Sustaining Corporate Member - $188; Student - $16; Retired - $26; *Member Profile:* Food safety professionals
Meetings/Conferences: • Ontario Food Protection Association (OFPA) Spring Meeting 2015, 2015, ON
Scope: Provincial
• Ontario Food Protection Association (OFPA) Fall Meeting 2015, 2015, ON
Scope: Provincial

Ontario Football Alliance

7384 Wellington Rd. 30, #B, Guelph ON N1H 6J2
Tel: 519-780-0200; *Fax:* 519-780-0705
Toll-Free: 888-313-9419
admin@ontariofootballalliance.ca
www.ontariofootballalliance.ca
www.facebook.com/35986040778
Previous Name: Football Ontario
Overview: A medium-sized provincial organization founded in 1971
Mission: To develop football in Ontario by providing programs to improve the game through participation & mandates developed by its membership
Member of: Football Canada
Chief Officer(s):
Tina Turner, Executive Director
director@ontariofootballalliance.ca
Smith Ian, President
president@ontariofootballalliance.ca
Staff Member(s): 4
Membership: *Fees:* $20
Activities: *Rents Mailing List:* Yes; *Library* by appointment

Ontario Forest Industries Association (OFIA) / l'Industrie forestière de l'Ontario

#1704, 8 King St. East, Toronto ON M5C 1B5
Tel: 416-368-6188; *Fax:* 416-368-5445
info@ofia.com
www.ofia.com
Overview: A medium-sized provincial organization founded in 1943
Mission: To act as a unified voice on behalf of member companies to ensure industry positions are considered; To respond to industry issues, such as economic, environmental, & technological developments
Membership: 10 member companies + 10 affiliate members + 4 associate members; *Member Profile:* Companies, ranging from large multinational corporations to small businesses, that produce materials such as pulp, paper, paperboard, plywood, panelboard, veneer & lumber
Activities: Liaising with government & other business sectors; Developinig partnerships, such as the Ontario Forestry Coalition; Raising awareness of the forest industry in Ontario; Providing opportunities for members to discuss industry issues
Publications:
• Canadian Forests: A Primer
Number of Pages: 50; *Author:* Dr. Ken Armson; *ISBN:* 1-895540-17-8
Profile: Part of the Environmental Literacy Series, the contents address the ownership & governance of forests, forest management, the economy

Ontario Formwork Association (OFA)

#7, 951 Wilson Ave., Toronto ON M3K 1Z7
Tel: 416-630-7912; *Fax:* 416-630-7181
info@ontarioformworkassociation.com
www.ontarioformworkassociation.com
Overview: A medium-sized provincial organization founded in 1968
Mission: To discuss issues related to the formwork sector of the construction industry in Ontario.
Member of: Council of Ontario Construction Associations
Finances: *Annual Operating Budget:* $250,000-$500,000
Membership: 50 member companies; *Fees:* Schedule available

Ontario Foundation for Visually Impaired Children Inc. (OFVIC)

PO Box 1116, Stn. D, Toronto ON M6P 3K2
Tel: 416-767-5977; *Fax:* 416-767-5530
ofvic@look.ca
Overview: A small provincial organization
Chief Officer(s):
April Cornell, Executive Director

Ontario Friends of Schizophrenics *See* Schizophrenia Society of Ontario

Ontario Fruit & Vegetable Growers' Association (OFVGA) / L'Association des fruiticulteurs et des maraîchers de l'Ontario

#105, 355 Elmira Rd. North, Guelph ON N1K 1S5
Tel: 519-763-6160; *Fax:* 519-763-6604
info@ofvga.org
www.ofvga.org
Overview: A medium-sized provincial organization founded in 1859
Mission: Dedicated to the advancement of horticulture, working proactively through effective lobbying for the betterment of the industry & producers as a whole through advocacy, research, education, communication & marketing
Member of: Canadian Horticultural Council
Chief Officer(s):
Art Smith, CEO Ext. 115
artsmith@ofvga.org
Finances: *Annual Operating Budget:* $500,000-$1.5 Million; *Funding Sources:* Membership fees; advertising revenue
Staff Member(s): 7
Membership: 7,500; *Fees:* $30
Activities: *Speaker Service:* Yes
Meetings/Conferences: • Ontario Fruit and Vegetable Growers' Association Annual Meeting & Convention 2015, January, 2015,

Crowne Plaza Hotel, Niagara Falls, ON
Scope: Provincial

Ontario Funeral Service Association (OFSA)
#103, 3228 South Service Rd., Burlington ON L7N 3N1
Tel: 905-637-3371; *Fax:* 905-637-3583
Toll-Free: 800-268-2727
info@ofsa.org
www.ofsa.org
www.facebook.com/ofsa.socialmedia
twitter.com/OFSAsocialmedia
Previous Name: Embalmers' Association
Overview: A medium-sized provincial organization founded in 1883
Mission: To maintain high standards of services & ethical business practices among Ontario's funeral homes for the welfare of the public; To represent & support Ontario's independently owned funeral establishments
Chief Officer(s):
Lesley Bingley, President, 416-241-6356
Kerri Douglas, Executive Director
kerri@ofsa.org
Membership: *Member Profile:* Independent & family owned funeral homes in Ontario
Activities: Advocating on behalf of funeral homes in Ontario; Liaising with various levels of government; Offering professional development activities & resources; Creating networking opportunities; Raising public awareness of the funeral profession
Awards:
• Cornerstone Award (Award)
To recognize members who have made an outstanding contribution to the betterment of the funeral profession
• Humanitarian Award (Award)
To recognize excellence in community service
• Association Activist Award (Award)
To recognize outstanding contributions to the Ontario Funeral Service Association by volunteers
Publications:
• Your Family Matters: Official Monthly Newsletter of OFSA
Type: Newsletter; *Frequency:* Monthly
Profile: Featuring the president's message, association activities, member news, & legislation information

Ontario Gang Investigators Association (ONGIA)
PO Box 57085, Stn. Jackson Square, Hamilton ON L8P 4W9
ongia.org
Overview: A medium-sized provincial organization
Mission: ONGIA is a non-profit organization that is committed to addressing the street gang phenomenon.
Chief Officer(s):
Jim Aspiotis, President
president@ongia.org
Membership: *Member Profile:* Law enforcement professionals and members of the criminal justice community throughout Ontario.
Meetings/Conferences: • Ontario Gang Investigators Association 2015 Conference, 2015, ON
Scope: Provincial

Ontario Gay & Lesbian Chamber of Commerce
39 River St., Toronto ON M5A 3P1
Tel: 416-646-1600; *Fax:* 416-646-9460
info@oglcc.com
www.oglcc.com
Overview: A medium-sized provincial organization
Mission: To create an environment in which the Ontario gay & lesbian business & professional communities can thrive through the sharing of knowledge, resources, & communications
Chief Officer(s):
Ryan Tollofson, President
Membership: *Fees:* Members: $10.00; Non-members: $20

Ontario Genealogical Society (OGS)
#102, 40 Orchard View Blvd., Toronto ON M4R 1B9
Tel: 416-489-0734; *Fax:* 416-489-9803
provoffice@ogs.on.ca
www.ogs.on.ca
www.facebook.com/OntarioGenealogicalSociety
www.ogs.on.ca/ogsblog
Overview: A medium-sized provincial charitable organization founded in 1961
Mission: To encourage, bring together & assist all those interested in the pursuit of family history; to promote genealogical research; to set standards for genealogical excellence; to make available the knowledge, availability, diversity & comprehensiveness of the genealogical resources of Ontario; to share expertise in other geographic areas
Chief Officer(s):
Sarah Newitt, Executive Director
Ruthann LaBlance, Manager, Digitization Division
Finances: *Annual Operating Budget:* $250,000-$500,000; *Funding Sources:* Membership dues; grants; donations
Staff Member(s): 8; 500 volunteer(s)
Membership: 3,500; *Fees:* Schedule available
Activities: *Library:* OGS Library holdings are housed at North York Central Library; Open to public
Meetings/Conferences: • Ontario Genealogical Society 2015 Annual Conference, May, 2015, Georgian College, Barrie, ON
Scope: Provincial
Description: Theme: Tracks through Time

Brant County Branch
#114, 118 Powerline Rd., Brantford ON N3T 5L8
Tel: 519-753-4140; *Fax:* 519-753-9866
brantogs@bellnet.ca
www.ogs.on.ca/brant

Bruce & Grey Branch
PO Box 66, Owen Sound ON N4K 5P1
e-mail: bgogs@bmts.com
www.bruceandgreygenealogy.com

Durham Region Branch
PO Box 174, Whitby ON L1N 5S1
Tel: 905-720-0985
durham@ogs.on.ca
www.ogs.on.ca/durham
Chief Officer(s):
Anne Delong, Co-Chair
Stephen Wood, Co-Chair, 905-668-1362
• Kindred Spirits [a publication of the Ontario Genealogical Society, Durham Region Branch]
Type: Newsletter; *Frequency:* Quarterly

Elgin County Branch
PO Box 20060, St Thomas ON N5P 4H4
e-mail: info@elginogs.ca
www.elginogs.ca

Essex County Branch
c/o Ontario Genealogical Society, PO Box 2, Stn. A, Windsor ON N9A 6J5
Tel: 519-255-6770
essexogs@gmail.com
www.ogs.on.ca/essex
linkedin.com/groups/Essex-County-branch-Ontario-Genealogical-4483476
www.facebook.com/EssexCountyOGS
twitter.com/EssexOGS
Vacant, Chair
• Trails [a publication of the Ontario Genealogical Society, Essex County Branch]
Type: Newsletter; *Frequency:* Quarterly

Haldimand Branch
PO Box 11, Dunnville ON N1A 2X1
www.ogs.on.ca/haldimand
Mission: Assisting people whose ancestors resided in Dunn, Canborough, Moulton, North Cayuga, South Cayuga, Oneida, Sherbrooke, Rainham, Seneca, & Walpole Townships

Halton-Peel Branch
PO Box 24, Streetsville ON L5M 2B7
e-mail: jwatt@ica.net
www.halinet.on.ca/sigs/ogshp
Chief Officer(s):
Fran Murphy, Chair
fmurphy2@rogers.com
• Halton-Peel KINnections [a publication of the Ontario Genealogical Society, Halton-Peel Branch]
Type: Newsletter; *Frequency:* Quarterly

Hamilton Branch
Lincoln Alexander Elementary School, 50 Ravenbury Dr., Hamilton ON L8W 2B5
Tel: 905-318-8086
hbogsadmin@bellnet.ca
www.ogs.on.ca/hamilton
Chief Officer(s):
Catherine Niemi, Chair

Huron County Branch
PO Box 469, Goderich ON N7A 4C7
www.hurontel.on.ca/~ogshuron
Chief Officer(s):
Arlyn Montgomery, Chair, 519-357-1279

Kawartha Branch
PO Box 861, Peterborough ON K9J 7A2
www.rootsweb.ancestry.com/~onkbogs
Chief Officer(s):
Alvina Seawright, Acting Chair

Kent County Branch
PO Box 964, 120 Queen St., Chatham ON N7M 5L3
e-mail: kent@ogs.on.ca
ogs.on.ca/kent
• Roots, Branches & Twigs [a publication of the Ontario Genealogical Society, Kent County Branch]
Type: Newsletter; *Frequency:* Quarterly

Kingston Branch
PO Box 1394, Kingston ON K7L 5C6
e-mail: kingston@ogs.on.ca
www.ogs.on.ca/kingston
Chief Officer(s):
Joyce Morrison, Chair
• Kingston Relations [a publication of the Ontario Genealogical Society, Kingston Branch]
Type: Newsletter; *Frequency:* 5 pa

Lambton County Branch
PO Box 2857, Sarnia ON N7T 7W1
Tel: 519-786-4677
lambton@ogs.on.ca
www.ogs.on.ca/lambton
Chief Officer(s):
Noreen Croxford, Chair
• Lambton Lifeline [a publication of the Ontario Genealogical Society, Lambton County Branch]
Type: Newsletter; *Frequency:* Quarterly

Leeds & Grenville Branch
Brockville Museum, 5 Henry St., Brockville ON K6V 6M4
Tel: 613-342-7773
leedsgrenvillegenealogical@bellnet.ca
www.leedsandgrenvillegenealogy.com
Chief Officer(s):
Patti Mordasewicz, Chair, 613-925-1437
pattim@magma.ca

London-Middlesex County Branch
Grosvenor Lodge, Coach House, 1017 Western Rd., London ON N6G 1G5
www.ogs.on.ca/londonmiddlesex
Chief Officer(s):
David Elliott, Acting Chair
dr.david.r.elliott@sympatico.ca

Niagara Peninsula Branch
PO Box 2224, St Catharines ON L2R 7R8
e-mail: niagara@ogs.on.ca
www.ogs.on.ca/niagara
Chief Officer(s):
Steve Fulton, Chair
smfulton@gmail.com

Nipissing Branch
PO Box 93, North Bay ON P1B 8G8
e-mail: nipissing@ogs.on.ca
www.nipissing.ogs.on.ca

Norfolk County Branch
PO Box 145, Delhi ON N4B 2W9
e-mail: norfolk@ogs.on.ca
www.norfolkcountybranchogs.ca

Ottawa Branch
PO Box 8346, Stn. t, Ottawa ON K1G 3H8
www.ogsottawa.on.ca
Chief Officer(s):
Norah Cousins-La Rocque, Chair

Oxford County Branch
PO Box 20091, Woodstock ON N4S 8X8
Tel: 519-421-1700
oxford@ogs.on.ca
www.oxford.ogs.on.ca
• The Tracer [a publication of the Ontario Genealogical Society, Oxford Country Branch]
Type: Newsletter; *Frequency:* Quarterly

Perth County Branch
24 St Andrew St., Stratford ON N5A 1A3
Tel: 519-271-0531
perthcountyogs@gmail.com
www.ogs.on.ca/perth/Front%20page.htm

Quinte Branch
PO Box 1371, Trenton ON K8V 5R9
Tel: 613-394-3381
quintebranch@ogs.on.ca
www.rootsweb.ancestry.com/~canqbogs
Chief Officer(s):
Peter Johnson, Chair

• The Quinte Searchlight [a publication of the Ontario Genealogical Society, Quinte Branch]
Type: Newsletter; *Frequency:* Quarterly
Sault Ste. Marie District Branch
PO Box 20007, 150 Churchill Rd., Sault Ste Marie ON P6A 6W3
Tel: 705-946-3170
www.rootsweb.ancestry.com/~onogsssm
Chief Officer(s):
Mary Anne MacDonald, Chair, 705-842-2722
• Sault Channels [a publication of the Ontario Genealogical Society, Sault Ste. Marie District Branch]
Type: Newsletter; *Frequency:* Quarterly *ISSN:* 11836628
Simcoe County Branch
PO Box 892, Barrie ON L4M 4Y6
www.simcoebogs.com
Chief Officer(s):
Tamsin Walker, Chair
chair@simcoebogs.com
• Simcoe County Ancestor News (SCAN) [a publication of the Ontario Genealogical Society, Simcoe County Branch]
Type: Newsletter; *Frequency:* Quarterly
Sudbury District Branch
c/o Greater Sudbury Public Library, 74 Mackenzie St., Sudbury ON P3C 4X8
Tel: 705-675-1743
www.rootsweb.ancestry.com/~onogs/ogs.htm
Chief Officer(s):
Lynn Gainer, Chair
lynn.gainer@personainternet.com
Thunder Bay District Branch
PO Box 10373, Thunder Bay ON P7C 6T8
e-mail: thunderbay@ogs.on.ca
www.ogs.on.ca/thunderbay
Chief Officer(s):
Christine Hettrick, Chair
chrisehet@yahoo.ca
• Past Tents [a publication of the Ontario Genealogical Society, Thunder Bay District Branch]
Type: Newsletter; *Frequency:* Quarterly
• Pick & Shovel [a publication of the Ontario Genealogical Society, Thunder Bay District Branch]
Type: Book
Profile: Northwestern Ontario genealogical resources.
Toronto Branch
PO Box 518, Stn. K, Toronto ON M4P 2G9
Tel: 416-733-2608
info@torontofamilyhistory.org
www.torontofamilyhistory.org
www.facebook.com/TOFamilyHistory
twitter.com/TOFamilyHistory
Chief Officer(s):
Diana Thomson, Chair
chair@torontofamilyhistory.org
• Toronto Tree [a publication of the Ontario Genealogical Society, Toronto Branch]
Type: Newsletter; *Frequency:* 6 pa
Waterloo Region Branch
#104, 525 Highland Rd. West, Kitchener ON N2M 5P4
e-mail: watogs@yahoo.com
www.waterlooogs.ca
• Our Waterloo Kin [a publication of the Ontario Genealogical Society, Waterloo Region Branch]
Type: Newsletter; *Frequency:* Quarterly
Wellington County Branch
PO Box 1211, Guelph ON N1H 6N6
e-mail: wellington@ogs.on.ca
www.ogs.on.ca/wellington
Chief Officer(s):
Catherine Pacey, Chair
• Traces & Tracks [a publication of the Ontario Genealogical Society, Wellington County Branch]
Type: Newsletter; *Frequency:* Quarterly
York Region Branch
PO Box 32215, Stn. Harding, Richmond Hill ON L4C 9S3
e-mail: york@ogs.on.ca
www.rootsweb.ancestry.com/~onyrbogs
Chief Officer(s):
Susan Smart, Chair
smarts27@rogers.com
• York Region Ancestors [a publication of the Ontario Genealogical Society, York Region Branch]
Type: Journal; *Frequency:* Quarterly

Ontario General Contractors Association (OGCA)
#703, 6299 Airport Rd., Mississauga ON L4V 1N3
Tel: 905-671-3969; *Fax:* 905-671-8212
www.ogca.ca
Overview: A medium-sized provincial organization founded in 1939 overseen by Canadian Construction Association
Mission: To offer experience & expertise dealing with contracts, architects, engineers and owners
Affiliation(s): Ontario Association of Architects; Consulting Engineers of Ontario; Ontario Realty Corporation; Canadian Construction Association
Chief Officer(s):
Clive Thurston, President
clive@ogca.ca
Finances: *Funding Sources:* Membership dues
Staff Member(s): 5
Membership: 217 corporate; *Fees:* Schedule available; *Member Profile:* General Contractors, industrial, commercial & institutional; *Committees:* Education; Executive; Marketing; Safety; Best Practices

Ontario Geothermal Association (OGA)
#201, 2800 Skymark Ave., Mississauga ON L4W 5A6
Tel: 905-602-4700; *Fax:* 905-602-1197
Toll-Free: 800-267-2231
www.ontariogeothermal.ca
Overview: A large provincial organization founded in 2009
Affliation(s): Heating, Refrigeration & Air Conditioning Institute of Canada
Chief Officer(s):
John Bosman, President
john.bosman@ontariogeothermal.ca
Meetings/Conferences: • Ontario Geothermal Association's 2015 Conference, 2015, ON
Scope: Provincial
Contact Information: Heather Grimoldby-Campbell; hgrimoldby@hrai.ca

Ontario Gerontology Association (OGA) / Association ontarienne de gérontologie
#216C, 351 Christie St., Toronto ON M6G 3C3
Tel: 416-535-6034; *Fax:* 416-535-6907
info@gerontario.org
www.gerontario.org
Overview: A small provincial organization founded in 1981
Affliation(s): Canadian Association on Gerontology
Chief Officer(s):
Norm Schulman, Executive Director
Staff Member(s): 2; 50 volunteer(s)
Membership: 500
Activities: Publishing newsletters; Organizing regional events
Meetings/Conferences: • Ontario Gerontology Association's 34th Annual Conference, April, 2015, Toronto, ON
Scope: Provincial
Description: Theme - Aging 2015: Innovation in Care, Networks and Communities

Ontario Ginseng Growers Association
PO Box 587, 1283 Blueline Rd., Simcoe ON N3Y 4N5
Tel: 519-426-7046; *Fax:* 519-426-9087
info@ginsengontario.com
www.ginsengontario.com
Overview: A medium-sized provincial organization
Mission: To conduct research on how to improve ginseng growing, as well as new varieties of ginseng; to help market North American ginseng
Chief Officer(s):
Rebecca Coates, Executive Director
rebecca.coates@ginsengontario.com
Staff Member(s): 2
Membership: 140; *Committees:* Research; Marketing/Buyer Relations; Government/Liason; Social/Public Relations

Ontario Goat Breeders Association (OGBA)
#12, 449 Laird Rd., Guelph ON N1G 4W1
Tel: 519-824-2942
Toll-Free: 866-311-6422
info@livestockalliance.ca
www.ogba.ca
Also Known As: Ontario Goat
Overview: A medium-sized provincial organization founded in 1951
Mission: To provide & circulate sound information about goats in Ontario; to improve & develop the goat breeds in Ontario; to encourage & promote the expansion of the goat industry in Ontario; to assist the development of chevon, fibre & dairy industries
Finances: *Annual Operating Budget:* Less than $50,000; *Funding Sources:* Membership dues; sales; advertising; fundraising; sponsorship donations
8 volunteer(s)
Membership: 300; *Fees:* $25; *Member Profile:* Goat owners, breeders; industry partners; *Committees:* Milk; Chevon; Fibre
Activities: *Library*

Ontario Golf Superintendents' Association (OGSA)
328 Victoria Rd. South, Guelph ON N1L 0H2
Tel: 519-767-3341; *Fax:* 519-766-1704
Toll-Free: 877-824-6472
admin@ogsa.ca
www.ogsa.ca
Overview: A small provincial organization
Chief Officer(s):
Sally E. Ross, Executive Manager, 519-767-3341 Ext. 202
manager@ogsa.ca
Membership: *Committees:* Member Services; Research; Education; Communications; Governance; Gov't Industry Relations; Golf & Events
Meetings/Conferences: • 2015 Ontario Golf Course Management Conference and Trade Show, January, 2015, Scotiabank Convention Centre, Niagara, ON
Scope: Provincial

Ontario Good Roads Association (OGRA)
#22, 1525 Cornwall Rd., Oakville ON L6J 0B2
Tel: 289-291-6472; *Fax:* 289-291-6477
info@ogra.org
www.ogra.org
ca.linkedin.com/pub/ontario-good-roads-association/43/b08/829
twitter.com/Ont_Good_Roads
Overview: A medium-sized provincial organization founded in 1894
Mission: To represent the transportation & public works-related interests of Ontario's municipalities & First Nation communities; To deliver programs & services that meet the needs of members; To support municipalities in the provision of effective & efficient transportation systems throughout Ontario
Chief Officer(s):
Joseph W. Tiernay, Executive Director
Brian Anderson, Manager, MEmber & Technical Services
Scott Butler, Manager, Policy & Research
Heather Crewe, Manager, Education & Training
Rayna Gillis, Manager, Finance & Administration
Colette Caruso, Coordinator, Communications & Marketing
Roni Kean, Coordinator, Curriculum
Cherry-Lyn Sales, Coordinator, Training Services
Fahad Shuja, Coordinator, Member Services & OPS
James Smith, Coordinator, Member Services & Infrastructure
Finances: *Funding Sources:* Membership fees; Sponsorships
Membership: 400+ municipalities; *Member Profile:* Ontario municipalities; First Nations communities; Corporations; Life & honourary members; *Committees:* Executive; Policy; Member Services; Nominating; Combined Conference; Companions Program
Activities: Advocating for the collective interests of municipal transportation & works departments; Analyzing policies; Reviewing legislation; Consulting with stakeholders & partners; Offering education & training opportunities
Meetings/Conferences: • Ontario Good Roads Association / Rural Ontario Municipal Association 2015 Combined Conference, February, 2015, Fairmount Royal York, Toronto, ON
Scope: Provincial
Attendance: 1,500+
Description: Workshops, information about current municipal issues, a trade show, & social events
Contact Information: Ontario Good Roads Association, Phone: 905-795-2555; Fax: 905-795-2660
Publications:
• Milestones [a publication of the Ontario Good Roads Association]
Type: Magazine; *Frequency:* 4 pa; *Accepts Advertising*; *Editor:* Colette Caruso; Scott Butler
Profile: Articles of interest to the municipal services sector, including a conference issue & a wintermaintenance issue
• Ontario Good Roads Association Annual Report
Type: Yearbook; *Frequency:* Annually

Ontario Grape Growers' Marketing Board *See* Grape Growers of Ontario

The Ontario Greenhouse Alliance (TOGA)
PO Box 175, #6, 76 Main St., Grimsby ON L3M 1S5

Tel: 905-945-9773; *Fax:* 905-945-5767
Toll-Free: 888-480-0659
info@theontariogreenhousealliance.com
www.theontariogreenhousealliance.com
Overview: A small provincial organization founded in 2003
Mission: To provide an infrastructure & approach that will integrate all the current resources & future potential of the Ontario greenhouse stakeholders into a community & international marketplace presence, with the synergy & standards to be a world leader in greenhouse operations
Chief Officer(s):
Rejean Picard, Chair
Membership: *Member Profile:* Ontario's greenhouse vegetable, pepper & flower growers

Ontario Greenhouse Vegetable Growers (OGVG)
32 Seneca Rd., Leamington ON N8H 5H7
Tel: 519-326-2604; *Fax:* 519-326-7842
Toll-Free: 800-265-6926
www.ontariogreenhouse.com
Overview: A large provincial organization founded in 1967
Mission: To represent growers' interests & ensure that they have the necessary resources to continue to prosper
Affliation(s): Ontario Greenhouse Marketers' Association; Ontario Greenhouse Alliance
Chief Officer(s):
George Gilvesy, General Manager
gilvesy@ontariogreenhouse.com
Staff Member(s): 9
Membership: 200; *Committees:* Energy & Environment; Finance; Food Safety; Human Resources; Marketing; Research; Trade

The Ontario Greens *See* The Green Party of Ontario

Ontario Ground Water Association (OGWA)
48 Front St. East, Strathroy ON N7G 1Y6
Tel: 519-245-7194; *Fax:* 519-245-7196
www.ogwa.ca
Previous Name: Ontario Water Well Association
Overview: A medium-sized provincial organization founded in 1952 overseen by Canadian Ground Water Association
Mission: To protect & promote Ontario's ground water; To provide guidance to members, government representatives, & the public
Chief Officer(s):
Greg Bullock, President
Rob MacKinnon, Secretary-Treasurer
Anne Gammage, Office Manager, 519-245-7194, Fax: 519-245-7196
Finances: *Funding Sources:* Membership dues
Membership: *Member Profile:* Ground water professionals
Activities: Disseminating information & providing education about ground water; Promoting technical skills of ground water professional
Meetings/Conferences: • Ontario Ground Water Association 62nd Annual Convention & Trade Show 2015, 2015
Scope: Provincial
Description: Meetings, seminars, networking opportunities, & a social program
Publications:
• The Source [a publication of the Ontario Ground Water Association]
Type: Newsletter; *Accepts Advertising*; *Editor:* Shannon Savory
Profile: Ontario Ground Water Association information, plus feature articles & industry news

Ontario Gymnastic Federation (OGF)
#214, 3 Concorde Gate, Toronto ON M3C 3N7
Tel: 416-426-7100; *Fax:* 416-426-7377
Toll-Free: 866-565-0650
info@ogf.com
www.ogf.com
Also Known As: Gymnastics Ontario
Overview: A small provincial organization founded in 1968
Mission: To lead the sport of gymnastics throughout Ontario; To provide services & programs which encourage lifelong involvement in gymnastics
Affiliation(s): Gymnastics Canada
Chief Officer(s):
Dave Sandford, Chief Executive Officer, 416-426-7095
ceo@gymnasticsontario.ca
Linda Clifford, President
Angel Crossman, Director, Policies & Procedures
Michelle Pothier, Coordinator, Recreation
recreation@gymnasticsontario.ca
Yuliana Korolyova, Coordinator, Education, 416-426-7096
education@gymnasticsontario.ca
Kristina Galloway, Coordinator, Membership Services, 416-426-7096
membership@gymnasticsontario.ca
Siobhan Covington, Manager, Finance, 416-426-7094
scovington@gymnasticsontario.ca
Finances: *Funding Sources:* Fundraising
Activities: Providing professional development & training activities; Offering resources such as technical manuals, workbooks, & videos; Providing a development award program; *Awareness Events:* I Love Gymnastic Week; *Library:* Gymnastics Ontario Resource Centre
Meetings/Conferences: • Gymnastics Ontario Coaches Congress, 2015, ON
Scope: Provincial

Ontario Halfway House Association (OHHA)
224 Cornwallis Ct., Oshawa ON L1H 8E8
Tel: 905-571-1999; *Fax:* 877-772-9695
Toll-Free: 800-698-7689
ohha@rogers.com
halfwayhouses.ca/en/region/ohha
Overview: A small provincial organization overseen by Regional Halfway House Assocation
Mission: To help offenders reintegrate themselves into society
Member of: Regional Halfway House Association
Chief Officer(s):
Darrell Rowe, President, Executive Commitee

Ontario Handball Association (OHA)
ON
www.ontariohandball.ca
Overview: A small provincial organization
Mission: To promote & develop the sport of handball in Ontario
Chief Officer(s):
Jenine Wilson, President
president@ontariohandball.ca
Activities: Tournaments; junior programs

Ontario Harness Horse Association *See* Central Ontario Standardbred Association

Ontario Hatcheries Association
7660 Mill Rd., RR#4, Guelph ON N1H 6J1
Tel: 519-763-6360; *Fax:* 519-837-0729
stevens@sentex.net
Overview: A small provincial organization
Chief Officer(s):
Deborah Carroll, Secretary
Membership: 58 corporate

Ontario Health Care Housekeepers Association Inc. *See* Ontario Healthcare Housekeepers' Association Inc.

Ontario Health Information Management Association (OHIMA)
#500, 4243C Dundas St. West, Toronto ON M8X 1Y3
www.ohima.ca
Also Known As: Ontario Health Record Association
Overview: A small provincial organization founded in 1935
Mission: To be recognized leaders in Health Information Management; To provide members with education opportunities; to maintain strong partnerships with other allied groups; To provide direction & make recommendations in the management of health information issues at the provincial & national levels
Chief Officer(s):
Andrew Quayle, President & Newsletter Development
aquayle@stjoes.ca
Finances: *Annual Operating Budget:* Less than $50,000
6 volunteer(s)
Membership: 225; *Fees:* $50-$75; $20 student

Ontario Health Libraries Association (OHLA)
c/o Karen Gagnon, Staff Library, Providence Care, Mental Health Servic, 752 King St. West, Bag 603, Kingston ON K7L 4X3
e-mail: askohla@accessola.com
www.ohla.on.ca
www.linkedin.com/groups/Ontario-Health-Libraries-Association-2670522
www.facebook.com/303797462978073
Overview: A medium-sized provincial organization
Mission: To represent views of members; To advocate for the value of health libraries & specialists; To provide a forum for leadership, education, & communications; To build & strengthen relationships with members & other organizations.
Chief Officer(s):
Toni Janik, President
janik@hdgh.org
Meetings/Conferences: • Ontario Health Libraries Association Annual General Meeting and Awards Presentations, January, 2015, Metro Toronto Convetion Centre, Toronto, ON
Scope: Provincial

Ontario Healthcare Housekeepers' Association Inc. (OHHA)
2053 County Road 22, Bath ON K0H 1G0
Tel: 613-352-5696; *Fax:* 613-352-5840
secretary@ontariohealthcarehousekeepers.com
www.ohha.org
www.facebook.com/ontariohealthcarehousekeepersassociation/info
twitter.com/healthcarehskpr
Previous Name: Ontario Health Care Housekeepers' Association Inc.
Overview: A small provincial organization founded in 1957
Affliation(s): Ontario Hospital Association, CSSA, OLTCA, ISSA
Chief Officer(s):
Wendy Boone-Watt, Executive Director
boonewatt@kos.net
Staff Member(s): 1; 15 volunteer(s)
Membership: 240 individual; *Fees:* $95; *Member Profile:* Supervisors, managers, directors of housekeeping/environmental services in health care facilities
Activities: *Awareness Events:* Pack Your Backpack Conference & Trade Show, May; *Speaker Service:* Yes

Ontario Healthy Communities Coalition (OHCC) / Coalition des communautés en santé de l'Ontario
#1810, 2 Carlton St., Toronto ON M5B 1J3
Tel: 416-408-4841; *Fax:* 416-408-4843
Toll-Free: 800-766-3418
www.ohcc-ccso.ca
Overview: A medium-sized provincial charitable organization
Mission: To achieve social, environmental, economic & physical well-being for individuals, communities & local governments throughout Ontario
Chief Officer(s):
Anderson Rouse, Coordinator, Finance & Administration
Lorna Heidenheim, Executive Director
lorna@healthycommunities.on.ca
Finances: *Annual Operating Budget:* $250,000-$500,000; *Funding Sources:* Trillium Foundation; Ministry of Health & Long Term Care; Ministry of Environment
Staff Member(s): 10; 2 volunteer(s)
Membership: 94 organizations; *Member Profile:* Provincial associations; community; individuals; *Committees:* Diversity; Communication; Resource Develoment; Food Security
Activities: *Speaker Service:* Yes; *Library* Open to public by appointment

Ontario Heart Foundation *See* Heart & Stroke Foundation of Ontario

Ontario Herbalists Association (OHA)
PO Box 123, Stn. D, Toronto ON M9A 4X2
Tel: 416-236-0090
Toll-Free: 877-642-4372
info@herbalists.on.ca
www.herbalists.on.ca
Overview: A medium-sized provincial organization founded in 1979
Mission: To bring together people with interest in & knowledge about herbs; To facilitate a sharing of information & research; To promote advancement of understanding of medicinal plants; To serve as liaison between herbalists & other healing professionals & to work actively for recognition & promotion of herbal therapy
Member of: British Herbal Medicine Association
Chief Officer(s):
Diane Kent, President
Finances: *Annual Operating Budget:* Less than $50,000; *Funding Sources:* Membership fees; events
Staff Member(s): 1; 20 volunteer(s)
Membership: 736; 2,400 distributors; *Fees:* $45 general; $225 professional; $45 student; $55US; *Member Profile:* Professional herbalists, gardeners, herbal product manufacturers & retailers, organic herb growers, wildcrafters, etc.; *Committees:* Professional Wing; Herb Fair; Journal; Promotions; Website
Activities: Herb fair; professional conference; herb walks; seminars; lectures; *Awareness Events:* "A Celebration of Herbs" at Harbourfront

Ontario Hereford Association
2253 Concession 14 Greenock Twp., RR#2, Cargill ON N0G 1J0
Tel: 519-366-1260; *Fax:* 519-366-1261
ont.herefords@sympatico.ca
www.ontarioherefords.ca
Overview: A small provincial organization
Mission: To promote & regulate Hereford cattle breeding in Ontario
Member of: Canadian Hereford Association
Chief Officer(s):
Robert Thurston, President
bob@thurstonlivestock.com
Ron Wells, Secretary-Manager
Staff Member(s): 1
Activities: *Speaker Service:* Yes

Ontario Heritage Trust (OHT) / Fiducie du patrimoine ontarien
10 Adelaide St. East, Toronto ON M5C 1J3
Tel: 416-325-5000; *Fax:* 416-325-5071
marketing@heritagefdn.on.ca
www.heritagetrust.on.ca
Overview: A medium-sized provincial charitable organization founded in 1967
Mission: Dedicated to the preservation, protection & promotion of Ontario's built, natural & cultural heritage for all of us to enjoy now & for others to experience in the future
Chief Officer(s):
Richard Moorhouse, Executive Director
Activities: Enters into conservation easement agreements with the owners of heritage properties to ensure that the significant heritage features of these properties are protected; holds provincially significant heritage properties & collections "in trust" on behalf of the people of Ontario; provides technical assistance to individuals & groups involved in heritage preservation; protects significant natural areas & geological land formations through Natural Heritage & Niagara Escarpment Programs

Ontario High School Chess Association
c/o Stephen Leacock Collegiate Institute, 2450 Birchmount Rd., Toronto ON M1T 2M5
Tel: 416-396-8000; *Fax:* 416-396-8042
high.school.chess@gmail.com
www.ohscc.on.ca
Overview: A small provincial organization founded in 1970
Affliation(s): Chess Federation of Canada; Ontario Chess Association; Chess 'n Math
Chief Officer(s):
Chris Field, President
3 volunteer(s)
Activities: Supprting the Ontario High School Chess Championships

Ontario Historical Society (OHS) / La Société historique de l'Ontario
34 Parkview Ave., Willowdale ON M2N 3Y2
Tel: 416-226-9011; *Fax:* 416-226-2740
ohs@ontariohistoricalsociety.ca
www.ontariohistoricalsociety.ca
Previous Name: The Pioneer Association of Ontario
Overview: A medium-sized provincial charitable organization founded in 1888
Mission: To bring people together who are interested in preserving some aspect of Ontario's history; to encourage & assist museums, historical societies & other heritage groups to research, preserve & interpret artifacts, architecture, archaeological sites & archival resources of local communities; to provide a forum to exchange ideas, research & experiences related to the history of Ontario; to sponsor programs & projects with a wide general appeal that help discover Ontario history
Member of: Heritage Canada
Chief Officer(s):
Robert Leverty, Executive Director
Finances: *Annual Operating Budget:* $500,000-$1.5 Million; *Funding Sources:* Membership fees; donations; program fees; book sales; grants
Staff Member(s): 4; 30 volunteer(s)
Membership: 2,000 individuals + 900 organizations; *Fees:* Schedule available; *Committees:* Museums; Fundraising
Activities: Workshops; Young Ontario Program; participation program; *Speaker Service:* Yes; *Library* by appointment
Awards:
• Alison Prentice Award (Award)
• Scadding Award for Excellence (Award)
• Museum Award of Excellence (Award)
• Dorothy Duncan Award (Award)
• B. Napier Simpson Jr. Award of Merit (Award)
• Riddell Award (Award)
• Joseph Brant Award (Award)
• Fred Landon Award (Award)
• J.J. Talman Award (Award)
• President's Award (Award)
• Cruikshank Gold Medal (Award)
• Carnochan Award (Award)

Ontario HIV Treatment Network
#600, 1300 Yonge St., Toronto ON M4T 1X3
Tel: 416-642-6486; *Fax:* 416-640-4245
Toll-Free: 877-743-6486
info@ohtn.on.ca
www.ohtn.on.ca
www.facebook.com/theOHTN
twitter.com/theOHTN
www.youtube.com/user/OntarioHIVTreatment
Overview: A small provincial organization
Mission: To optimize the quality of life of people living with HIV in Ontario & to promote excellence & innovation in treatment, research, education & prevention through a collaborative network of excellence representing consumers, providers, researchers & other stakeholders
Chief Officer(s):
Sean Rourke, Scientific & Executive Diretor
srourke@ohtn.on.ca
Staff Member(s): 55

Ontario Hockey Federation (OHF)
#9, 400 Sheridon Dr., Cambridge ON N1T 2H9
Tel: 226-533-9070; *Fax:* 519-620-7476
info@ohf.on.ca
www.ohf.on.ca
www.facebook.com/OHFHockey
twitter.com/ohfhockey
Overview: A medium-sized provincial organization founded in 1989 overseen by Hockey Canada
Member of: Hockey Canada; Hockey Development Centre for Ontario (HDCO)
Affliation(s): Minor Hockey Alliance of Ontario; Greater Toronto Hockey League; Northern Ontario Hockey Association; Ontario Minor Hockey Association; Ontario Hockey Association; Ontario Hockey League; Ontario Women's Hockey Association
Chief Officer(s):
Phillip McKee, Executive Director, 226-533-9075
pmckee@ohf.on.ca
Bill Bowman, President
wjbow@sympatico.ca
Membership: 228,251 registered players; 33,500 coaches; 7,300 officials; *Committees:* Constitution; Finance; Rules; Risk Management; Registration; Minor Council; Junior Council; Hockey Development Council; Senior / Adult Recreational Council; Female Hockey (operates under the auspices of the Ontario Women's Hockey Association)
Awards:
• Bill Richmond Memorial Award (Award)
To recognize outstanding achievement in the area of hockey development within the Ontario Hockey Federation
• Past Referee-in-Chief Recognition (Award)
• Past President's Recognition (Award)
• Dr. Allan Morris Honour Award (Award)
To recognize an individual who has exemplified dedication to amateur hockey
• President's Award (Award)
To recognize an individual who has provided service & leadership to amateur hockey
• Ontario Hockey Federation Volunteer of the Year Award (Award)
To recognize significant contribution to the game & the hockey community
• Ontario Hockey Federation Order of Merit (Award)
To honour individuals who have served amateur hockey for many years
• Ontario Hockey Federation Minor Hockey Award (Award)
To recognize an individual who has made a significant contribution to minor hockey in an administrative role
• Ontario Hockey Federation Junior Hockey Award (Award)
To recognize an individual who has made a significant contribution to junior hockey in an administrative role
• Ontario Hockey Federation Senior Hockey Award (Award)
To recognize an individual who has made a significant contribution to senior hockey in an administrative role
• Ontario Hockey Federation Officiating Program Award (Award)
To recognize individuals involved in the officiating program
• Ontario Hockey Federation Staff Award (Award)
To honour a staff person who exemplifies commitment to the values & objectives of the Ontario Hockey Federation
• Ontario Hockey Federation Life Membership (Award)
To recognize distinctive services & contributions to the Ontario Hockey Federation
Publications:
• OHF Handbook
Type: Handbook; *Frequency:* Annually
Profile: Featuring the Ontario Hockey Federation constitution, by-laws, regulations, policies, & directory

Ontario Home Builders Association (OHBA)
#101, 20 Upjohn Rd., Toronto ON M3B 2V9
Tel: 416-443-1545; *Fax:* 416-443-9982
Toll-Free: 800-387-0109
www.ohba.ca
www.linkedin.com/company/2233011?trk=tyah
www.facebook.com/group.php?gid=203305789711914
twitter.com/OntarioHBA
Overview: A medium-sized provincial organization overseen by Canadian Home Builders' Association
Mission: To represent the interests of members involved in Ontario's residential construction industry in legislation, regulation & policy issues; To promote association activities to the public, other groups & non-members
Chief Officer(s):
Doug Tarry, President
Bridget Sneddon, Secretary
Diane Murray, Treasurer
Meetings/Conferences: • Ontario Home Builders' Association Conference 2015, 2015, ON
Scope: Provincial

Ontario Home Care Association (OHCA)
PO Box 68018, Stn. Blakely, Hamilton ON L8M 3M7
Tel: 905-543-9474; *Fax:* 905-545-1568
info@homecareontario.ca
www.homecareontario.ca
Previous Name: Ontario Home Health Care Providers' Association
Overview: A medium-sized provincial organization founded in 1986
Mission: To service excellence & client satisfaction in the provision of home health & support services in Ontario
Member of: Canadian Home Care Association; Ontario Health Providers' Alliance; Ontario Home & Community Care Council
Chief Officer(s):
Susan D. VanderBent, Executive Director
Finances: *Annual Operating Budget:* $250,000-$500,000; *Funding Sources:* Membership fees
Staff Member(s): 1
Membership: 66; *Fees:* $450 & up; *Member Profile:* Home care agencies

Ontario Home Economics Association (OHEA)
c/o Registrar/Office Administrator, 1225 Meadowview Rd., RR#2, Omemee ON K0L 2W0
Tel: 705-799-2081; *Fax:* 705-799-0605
info@ohea.on.ca
www.ohea.on.ca
www.facebook.com/OntarioHomeEconomicsAssociation
twitter.com/OntarioHEA
Overview: A small provincial organization founded in 1979
Mission: To further the field of home economics; Establish standards of professional conduct, ethics & standards of practice
Affliation(s): Ontario Family Studies/Home Economics Educators' Association; Ontario Family Studies Leadership Council; Ontario Home Economists in Business; International Federation for Home Economics
Chief Officer(s):
Nancy Greiter, Registrar & Office Administrator
nancyohea@rogers.com
Membership: 300+; *Fees:* $209.05 registered/provisional/assoc.; $30.79 student; $104.54 new grad; $96.05 ret.; $129.95 active ret.; $45.20 corresp.; $45.20 affiliate; *Member Profile:* Home economists
Awards:
• Engberg-Fewster International Development Grant (Grant)
• Edith Rowles Simpson Family Finance Award (Award)
• OHEA President's Distinguished Service Award (Award)
• OHEA Founder's Honour Award (Award)
• Volunteer Recognition Awards (Award)
• OHEA Incentive Award (Award)
• Federated Women's Institutes of Ontario International Scholarship (Scholarship)

Meetings/Conferences: • Ontario Home Economics Association Annual General Meeting & Conference, March, 2015, ON
Scope: Provincial
Publications:
• The Vegetarian's Complete Quinoa Cookbook
Type: Book
Profile: Cookbook featuring over 125 recipes for quinoa-based meals.

Ontario Home Health Care Providers' Association ***See*** Ontario Home Care Association

Ontario Home Respiratory Services Association (OHRSA)
#600, 55 University Ave., Toronto ON M5J 2H7
Tel: 416-961-8001; *Fax:* 416-961-9935
info@ohrsa.ca
www.ohrsa.ca
Overview: A small provincial organization founded in 1985
Mission: To foster & promote an innovative & viable home respiratory services industry; to provide opportunities for future growth & to offer, through its members, quality products & services that are both cost-effective & provide value
Member of: Ontario Health Providers Alliance
Chief Officer(s):
Joseph Millage, President
Finances: *Annual Operating Budget:* $100,000-$250,000
Staff Member(s): 1; 8 volunteer(s)
Membership: 28 corporate; *Member Profile:* Home oxygen suppliers
Activities: Promotes Ontario home respiratory services; address industry issues;

Ontario Homeopathic Association (OHA)
#801, 60 Pleasant Bldv., Toronto ON M4T 1K1
Tel: 416-516-6109; *Fax:* 416-516-7725
info@ontariohomeopath.com
www.ontariohomeopath.com
Overview: A medium-sized provincial organization founded in 1992
Chief Officer(s):
Wendy Walker, President
wwalker@ontariohomeopath.com
Finances: *Annual Operating Budget:* Less than $50,000
Staff Member(s): 1
Membership: 150; *Fees:* $275 professional; $120 associate; $50 student

Ontario Horse Racing Industry Association (OHRIA)
PO Box 456, Stn. B, Toronto ON M9W 5L4
Tel: 416-679-0741; *Fax:* 416-679-9114
ohria@ohria.com
www.ohria.com
twitter.com/value4money_ca
Overview: A small provincial organization founded in 1994
Mission: Promote the horse racing industry as a vital part of Ontario's lifestyle, heritage & agricultural economy
Chief Officer(s):
Sue Leslies, President and Chair
Membership: 21 associations; *Member Profile:* Industry organization/associations

Ontario Horse Trials Association (OHTA)
#186, 3-304 Stone Rd. West, Guelph ON N1G 4W4
e-mail: ohtainfo@gmail.com
www.horsetrials.on.ca
Previous Name: Ontario Horse Trials Canada
Overview: A small provincial charitable organization founded in 1965
Mission: OHTA is a volunteer, not-for-profit organization whose main functions are to support, develop & promote events in Ontario.
Member of: Canadian Equestrian Federation
Chief Officer(s):
Peggy Hambly, President
peggy@glenardenfarms.com
Lisa Thompson, Secretary
lisat26@sympatico.ca
Finances: *Annual Operating Budget:* Less than $50,000
Staff Member(s): 1
Membership: 1,257; *Fees:* Schedule available; *Committees:* Championship Selection; Competitions; Young Riders; Event Evaluations; Event Schedule; Funding Programs; Officials; Omnibus; Omnibus Ad Sales; Organizer Meeting; Volunteer Incentive Program; Communications; Memberships; Points/Leaderboard; AGM/Banquet/Royal Winter Fair; Strategic Planning; Coach Outreach Program; Rules; Safety; Budget/Financial Statements
Activities: Overall program development, implementation & monitoring programs regarding the sport

Ontario Horse Trials Canada ***See*** Ontario Horse Trials Association

Ontario Horticultural Association (OHA)
448 Paterson Ave., London ON N5W 5C7
e-mail: secretary@gardenontario.org
www.gardenontario.org
www.facebook.com/home.php?sk=group_167342733299811
twitter.com/gardenontario
Overview: A medium-sized provincial charitable organization founded in 1906
Mission: To promote civic beautification, preservation of the environment, youth work & education of many aspects of horticulture
Chief Officer(s):
Carol Dunk, President
president@gardenontario.org
Finances: *Annual Operating Budget:* Less than $50,000; *Funding Sources:* Membership dues; grants; fundraising
Staff Member(s): 1
Membership: 278 societies; 40,000 members; *Fees:* $1; *Member Profile:* Gardener
Meetings/Conferences: • Ontario Horticultural Association 109th Convention in District 6, July, 2015, Redeemer University College, Ancaster, ON
Scope: Provincial

Ontario Hospital Association (OHA)
#2800, 200 Front St. West, Toronto ON M5V 3L1
Tel: 416-205-1300; *Fax:* 416-205-1301
Toll-Free: 800-598-8002
info@oha.com
www.oha.com
www.linkedin.com/company/ontario-hospital-association
www.facebook.com/onthospitalassn
twitter.com/OntHospitalAssn
www.youtube.com/onthospitalassn
Overview: A medium-sized provincial organization founded in 1924 overseen by Canadian Healthcare Association
Mission: To build a strong, innovative, & sustainable health care system that meets patient care needs throughout Ontario; To promote an efficent & effective health care system
Chief Officer(s):
Marcia Visser, Chair
Anthony Dale, Interim President & CEO
Warren DiClemente, Chief Operating Officer & VP, Educational Services
Julie Giraldi, Chief Human Resources Officer
Doug Miller, Chief Financial Officer
Colin Goodfellow, Treasurer
Membership: 150 public hospitals; *Member Profile:* Public hospitals throughout Ontario; Affiliated associations & organizations; *Committees:* Audit; Finance; Governance; Nominating
Activities: Engaging in advocacy activities to help shape health care policy in Ontario; Building partnerships; Providing opportunities for professional development
Publications:
• Healthcare Governance Update
Type: Newsletter
Profile: Information from the Governance Centre of Excellence to maintain & increase trustees' knowledge of health care governance issues
• Hospital Perspectives
Type: Newsletter; *Editor:* Tamarah Harel *ISSN:* 1198-0192
Profile: Articles about innovations in health care
• OHA [Ontario Hospital Association] Executive Report
Type: Newsletter; *Frequency:* Weekly; *Editor:* Alessandra Nigro; *Price:* Free with membership in the Ontario Hospital Association
Profile: Current health care news
• Ontario Hospital Association Annual Report
Type: Yearbook; *Frequency:* Annually

Ontario Hot Mix Producers Association (OHMPA)
#4, 365 Brunel Rd., Mississauga ON L4Z 1Z5
Tel: 905-507-3707; *Fax:* 905-507-3709
info@ohmpa.org
www.ohmpa.org
Overview: A medium-sized provincial organization
Mission: To provide a voice for hot mix asphalt producers on all subjects affecting our industry or our member's businesses
Chief Officer(s):
Mike O'Connor, Executive Director
oconnor@ohmpa.org
Finances: *Annual Operating Budget:* $500,000-$1.5 Million
Membership: *Member Profile:* Major producers across Ontario; supportive manufacturer/supplier members
Activities: *Speaker Service:* Yes; *Library* by appointment

Ontario Hotel & Motel Association ***See*** Ontario Restaurant, Hotel & Motel Association

The Ontario Imported Wine-Spirit-Beer Association (OIWSBA) ***See*** Drinks Ontario

Ontario Independent Insurance Adjusters' Association
c/o Dorothy Lowry, Crawford & Company (Canada) Inc., #15, 431 Bayview Dr., Barrie ON L4N 8Y2
www.ciaa-adjusters.ca
Overview: A small provincial organization overseen by Canadian Independent Adjusters' Association
Member of: Canadian Independent Adjusters' Association
Chief Officer(s):
Dorothy Lowry, President, 705-728-5597, Fax: 705-728-2167
Dorothy.Lowry@crawco.ca

Ontario Independent Meat Packers & Processors Society ***See*** Ontario Independent Meat Processors

Ontario Independent Meat Processors (OIMP)
7660 Mill Rd., RR#4, Guelph ON N1H 6J1
Tel: 519-763-4558; *Fax:* 519-763-4164
info@oimp.ca
www.oimp.ca
Previous Name: Ontario Independent Meat Packers & Processors Society
Overview: A medium-sized provincial organization founded in 1979
Staff Member(s): 6; 11 volunteer(s)
Membership: *Member Profile:* Meat & poultry industry
Meetings/Conferences: • Ontario Independent Meat Processors Meat Industry Expo 2015, October, 2015, Niagara Falls, ON
Scope: Provincial

Ontario Industrial Development Council Inc. ***See*** Economic Developers Council of Ontario Inc.

Ontario Industrial Fire Protection Association (OIFPA)
193 James St. South, Hamilton ON L8P 3A8
Tel: 905-527-0700; *Fax:* 905-527-6254
oifpa@interlynx.net
www.oifpa.org
Overview: A medium-sized provincial organization founded in 1981
Mission: To unite individuals with a concern for fire protection within Ontario's industrial community
Finances: *Funding Sources:* Membership fees
Membership: *Member Profile:* Individuals from the chemical industry & the oil & gas industry; Consulting engineers; Emergency response personnel; Municipal fire departments & fire protection consultants; Government agencies; Industrial underwriters
Activities: Creating networking opportunities with members from organizations such as municipal fire departments & government agencies; Providing educational seminars, on topics such as Ontario Fire Code updates, explosion protection, & fire pump installation
Publications:
• Firewatch
Type: Newsletter
Profile: Information updates from the association

Ontario Industrial Roofing Contractors' Association (OIRCA)
#301, 940 The East Mall, Toronto ON M9B 6J7
Tel: 416-695-4114; *Fax:* 416-695-9920
Toll-Free: 888-336-4722
oirca@ontarioroofing.com
www.ontarioroofing.com
Overview: A medium-sized provincial organization founded in 1964 overseen by Canadian Roofing Contractors' Association
Mission: To act as the voice of the industrial-commercial roofing industry in Ontario; To promote excellence in roofing construction
Affiliation(s): Construction Safety Association of Ontario
Chief Officer(s):
Rob Kucher, President, Board of Directors

Peter Serino, Treasurer
Membership: *Member Profile:* Roofing & sheet metal contractors from Ontario; Engineers; Manufacturers; Product suppliers; Industry members who are interested in roofing activities; *Committees:* 50th Anniversary; Labour Relations; Membership; Strategic Planning; Technical; IHSA Roofer Safety
Activities: Promoting good business ethics; Encouraging compliance with standards of occupational health & safety; Providing continuing education & training
Awards:
• Ontario Industrial Roofing Contractors' Association Annual Zero Frequency Category Awards (Award)
To recognize companies in Ontario that worked without a lost time injury during the year
Publications:
• Health & Safety Guidelines for Low-Sloped Roofing
Number of Pages: 136; *Price:* Free
Profile: Information about roofing safety, published in conjuction with the Construction Safety Association of Ontario
• Ontario Roofing News
Type: Newsletter
Profile: Articles about current trends in roofing, plus association news, & upcoming events

Ontario Insolvency Practitioners Association *See* Ontario Association of Insolvency & Restructuring Professionals

Ontario Institute of Agrologists (OIA)

Ontario AgriCentre, #108, 100 Stone Rd. West, Guelph ON N1G 5L3
Tel: 519-826-4226; *Fax:* 519-826-4228
Toll-Free: 866-339-7619
www.oia.on.ca
Overview: A medium-sized provincial organization founded in 1960 overseen by Agricultural Institute of Canada
Mission: To regulate Ontario's Professional Agrologists & ensure that competencies meet a Standard of Practice within a specific scope of agrology
Affliation(s): Certified Crop Advisor Program; Ontario Agricultural Hall of Fame Association; Ontario Agricultural Training Institute; Ontario Farm Animal Council; Western Fair Association
Chief Officer(s):
Drew Orosz, President
Terry Kingsmill, Registrar
Staff Member(s): 2
Membership: *Fees:* Schedule available; *Member Profile:* B.Sc (Agriculture) from Canadian university or equivalent
Activities: *Internships:* Yes
Awards:
• Public Relations Award (Award)
Presented to a member who has made an outstanding contribution to promoting OIA
• Branch Newsletter Award (Award)
Presented to the branch newsletter editor deemed by the Membership Committee to produce the most effective branch newsletter for their members
• Cheryl Somerville Memorial Distinguished Young Agrologist Award (Award)
Presented annually to an individual under 40 years of age who has made significant contributions to the agriculture & food industry in this province, the profession of agrology &/or the OIA
• Distinguished Agrologist (Award)
Member individuals who have rendered signal service to the agricultural industry of Ontario &/or the affairs of the OIA
• Honourary Life Member (Award)
Individuals who have rendered signal service to the agricultural industry of Ontario
• President's Honour Roll (Award)
Member individuals who have contributed greatly to branch effectiveness during the year
Meetings/Conferences: • The Canadian Greenhouse Conference (CGC) 2015, October, 2015, ON
Scope: National
Description: Held annually since 1979 the CGC is committed to providing a high quality conference experience for the extension of information through speakers, workshops, demonstration and exhibits.
Contact Information: Website: www.canadiangreenhouseconference.com
• The Canadian Greenhouse Conference (CGC) 2016, 2016, ON
Scope: National
Description: Held annually since 1979 the CGC is committed to providing a high quality conference experience for the extension of information through speakers, workshops, demonstration and exhibits.

Central Branch
Toronto ON
Chief Officer(s):
Paul Klosler, Contact, 519-824-4120 Ext. 53768
pklosler@uoguelph.ca
Guelph Branch
Guelph ON
Chief Officer(s):
Adalat Khan, Secretary
kan57@hotmail.com
Hamilton Branch
Hamilton ON
Chief Officer(s):
Doug Walters, Contact, 905-637-8843
dwalters@iprimus.ca
Huronia Branch
Midland ON
Chief Officer(s):
Terry Sullivan, Contact, 519-941-4813
tjsullivan@sympatico.ca
Long Point Branch
RR#4, Hagersville ON N0E 1W0
Chief Officer(s):
D. Brian Snyder, President, 519-426-2952
Niagara Branch
St. Catharines ON
Chief Officer(s):
Neil Miles, Contact, 905-687-6964
miles.neil@sympatico.ca
Northern Branch
PO Box 555, Emo ON P0W 1E0
Tel: 807-482-2420
puritysl@jam21.net
Chief Officer(s):
Larry Lamb, President
Ottawa-St. Lawrence Branch
Ottawa ON
Chief Officer(s):
Kalima Nkoma Mwange, Contact, 613-694-2547
mwangekn@gmail.com
Quinte Branch
RR#1, 4727 County Rd. 2, Port Hope ON L1A 3V5
Tel: 905-475-4908; *Fax:* 905-475-3835
pcoughler@cogeco.ca
Chief Officer(s):
Peter Coughler, President
Southwestern Branch
PO Box 5147, 4045 Charlie St., Petrolia ON N0N 1R0
Tel: 519-882-4209; *Fax:* 519-882-1180
woolaver@mnsi.net
Chief Officer(s):
Earle Woolaver, President
Western Branch
London ON
e-mail: oaa.westernbranch@gmail.com
Chief Officer(s):
Ross Wilson, Communications Coordinator

Ontario Institute of the Purchasing Management Association of Canada *See* Supply Chain Management Association - Ontario

Ontario Insurance Adjusters Association (OIAA)

29 De Jong Dr., Mississauga ON L5M 1B9
Tel: 905-542-0576; *Fax:* 905-542-1301
Toll-Free: 888-259-1555
manager@oiaa.com
www.oiaa.com
www.facebook.com/OntarioInsuranceAdjustersAssociation
twitter.com/PresidentOIAA
Overview: A medium-sized provincial organization founded in 1930
Mission: To promote & maintain a high standard of ethics in the business of insurance claims adjusting
Chief Officer(s):
Tammie Norn, President
tnorn@proadjusting.ca
Membership: *Fees:* $45.20; *Member Profile:* Insurance adjusters actively adjusting claims; *Committees:* Communications; Education; Benevolent & Community; Conferences; Industry; Association Operations; Entertainment
Meetings/Conferences: • 2015 Claims Conference, February, 2015, Metro Toronto Convention Centre, Toronto, ON
Scope: Provincial

Ontario Jaguar Owners Association (OJOA)

ON
www.ojoa.org
Overview: A small provincial organization founded in 1959
Affliation(s): Jaguar Clubs of North America (JCNA)
Chief Officer(s):
Duane Grady, Secretary
durielly@yahoo.com
John Taglione, President, 416-494-4551
taglione@sympatico.ca
Membership: 260; *Fees:* $60 annually

Ontario Jiu-Jitsu Association (OJA)

#7, 40 Bell Farm Rd., Barrie ON L4M 5L3
Tel: 705-725-9186; *Fax:* 705-725-8562
Toll-Free: 800-352-1338
www.ontariojiujitsu.com
www.facebook.com/jiujitsuontario
Overview: A medium-sized provincial organization founded in 1963
Mission: To promote Jiu Jitsu among amateurs in Ontario
Chief Officer(s):
Doug Knispel, President
dknispel@rci.rogers.com
Membership: *Fees:* $150 club; $20 club; $35 black belt; $25 adult; $190 private training centre; *Committees:* Finance; Membership & Promotion; Safety & Insurance; Technical; Tournament; Volunteer; Canadian Jiu Jitsu Grading Board

Ontario Katahdin Sheep Association Inc. (OKSA)

c/o Kim Henzie, Sweetwater Farms, RR#2, Norwood ON K0L 2V0
Tel: 705-696-3193
www.katahdin.ca
Overview: A small provincial organization overseen by Canadian Katahdin Sheep Association Inc.
Mission: To develop & expand the Katahdin sheep industry in Ontario
Chief Officer(s):
Donna Aziz, President, 905-852-9252
rolypolyfarms@yahoo.com
Brian Harris, Vice-President, 705-526-7509
brianrobertharris@gmail.com
Kim Henzie, Secretary-Treasurer
kim@sweetwaterfarms.com
Membership: 20; *Member Profile:* Katahdin sheep breeders in Ontario
Activities: Promoting Katahdin sheep; Educating association members & the public about the breeding, raising, uses, & heritage of Katahdin sheep; Hosting inspection clinics for members; Collecting & preserving data; Increasing efficiency in animal husbandry

Ontario Kinesiology Association (OKA)

6519B Mississauga Rd., Mississauga ON L5N 1A6
Tel: 905-567-7194; *Fax:* 905-567-7191
info@oka.on.ca
www.oka.on.ca
www.oka.on.ca/index.php?page=facebook
Overview: A medium-sized provincial organization founded in 1982
Mission: To promote the application of the science of human movement to other professionals & to the community; to uphold the standards of the profession of kinesiology; to assist kinesiologists in the performance of their duties & responsibilities
Member of: Canadian Kinesiology Alliance
Chief Officer(s):
Janice Ray, President
Finances: *Funding Sources:* Membership fees; sponsorship; advertising
Staff Member(s): 3; 50 volunteer(s)
Membership: 2,000; *Fees:* $78.75
Activities: *Awareness Events:* Kin Week; *Speaker Service:* Yes; *Rents Mailing List:* Yes
Meetings/Conferences: • 2015 Ontario Kinesiology Association Conference & AGM, 2015, ON
Scope: Provincial

Ontario Labour-Management Arbitrators Association (OLMAA)

#701, 100 Adelaide St. West, Toronto ON M5H 1S3
Tel: 416-366-3091; *Fax:* 416-366-0879
info@labourarbitrators.org
www.labourarbitrators.org
Overview: A small provincial organization
Mission: To promote practices that mediate labour relations
Membership: 123; *Member Profile:* Labour arbitrators

Ontario Lacrosse Association
#306, 3 Concorde Gate, Toronto ON M3C 3N7
Tel: 416-426-7066; *Fax:* 416-426-7382
www.ontariolacrosse.com
twitter.com/OntarioLacrosse
Overview: A small provincial organization founded in 1897 overseen by Canadian Lacrosse Association
Member of: Canadian Lacrosse Association
Chief Officer(s):
Stan Cockerton, Executive Director
stan@ontariolacrosse.com
Meetings/Conferences: • Ontario Lacrosse Association 2015 Annual General Meeting, 2015, ON
Scope: Provincial

Ontario Lawn Bowls Association
c/o Edith Pedden, 471 Silvery Lane, RR#3, Maberly ON K0H 2B0
e-mail: olba@olba.ca
www.olba.ca
www.facebook.com/groups/138144062931120
Overview: A medium-sized provincial organization overseen by Bowls Canada Boulingrin
Chief Officer(s):
Alan Dean, President, 905-726-9501
dean@olba.ca
Bob O'Neil, Executive Director, 905-468-7796
oneil@olba.ca
Edith Pedden, Secretary, 613-273-2958
pedden@olba.ca
Finances: *Funding Sources:* Membership fees; Sponsorships
Membership: *Member Profile:* Ontario lawn bowls clubs; *Committees:* Annual General Meetings; Achievement Awards; Annual; Bowls Canada Delegates; By-Laws; Championships, Indoors/Short-Mat & Championship Awards; Coaching; Database; Distribution, Sales, New Bowler Kits; E-Banter; Finance; Funding/Grants; Greens; Juniors; Marketing/Go Lawn Bowl; Memorial Fund; Nominating; Officiating; Planning & Development; Player Development; Promotion & Sponsorship; Safety & Risk Management; Visually Impaired/Physically Disabled Bowlers; Website
Activities: Providing programs, information & resources to member clubs; Campaigning for member recruitment; Assisting clubs that want to host provincial or national championships; Presenting awards, plaques, & certificates
Publications:
• E-Banter
Type: Newsletter; *Editor:* Bob Machan
Profile: Reports on championships & forthcoming events
• Ontario Lawn Bowls Association Tournament Listings
Type: Book; *Frequency:* Y; *Editor:* Bob Machan
Profile: Reports on championships & forthcoming events

Ontario Lawn Tennis Association ***See*** Ontario Tennis Association

Ontario Learning Partnership Group ***See*** Ontario Business Education Partnership

Ontario Liberal Party (OLP)
#210, 10 St. Mary St., Toronto ON M4Y 1P9
Fax: 416-323-9425
Toll-Free: 800-268-7250
info@ontarioliberal.ca
www.ontarioliberal.ca
www.linkedin.com/groups/Ontario-Liberal-Party-3410725
www.facebook.com/OntarioLiberalParty
twitter.com/OntLiberal
www.youtube.com/OntarioLiberalTV
Overview: A medium-sized provincial organization
Chief Officer(s):
Kathleen Wynne, Leader
Siloni Waraich, President
Finances: *Funding Sources:* Donations
Membership: *Fees:* $10 regular; $5 youth and seniors

Ontario Library & Information Technology Association (OLITA)
c/o Ontario Library Association, 2 Toronto St., 3rd Fl., Toronto ON M5C 2BS
Tel: 416-363-3388; *Fax:* 416-941-9581
www.accessola.com/olita/
Overview: A medium-sized provincial organization founded in 1992
Mission: Planning, development, design, application & integration of technology in the library & information environment with the impact of emerging technologies on library service, & with the effect of automated technologies on people
Chief Officer(s):
May Yan, President
may.yan@ryerson.ca
Activities: *Rents Mailing List:* Yes

Ontario Library Association (OLA)
#201, 50 Wellington St. East, Toronto ON M5E 1C8
Tel: 416-363-3388; *Fax:* 416-941-9581
Toll-Free: 866-873-9867
Other Communication: olaprograms@accessola.com
info@accessola.com
www.accessola.com
www.linkedin.com/groups/Ontario-Library-Association
www.facebook.com/group.php?gid=2233680329
twitter.com/ollibraryassoc
Overview: A medium-sized provincial charitable organization founded in 1900
Mission: To provide opportunities for people in the library & information field to share experience & expertise, & to create innovative solutions
Affliation(s): Ontario College & University Library Association; Ontario Library & Information Technology Association; Ontario Library Boards' Association; Ontario Public Library Association; Ontario School Library Association; L'Association des bibliothécaires francophones de l'Ontario
Chief Officer(s):
Shelagh Paterson, Executive Director, 416-363-3388 Ext. 224
spaterson@accessola.com
Karen McGrath, President
kmcgrath@niagaracollege.ca
Paul Takala, Treasurer
ptakala@hpl.ca
Helios He, Manager, Operations, 416-363-3388 Ext. 225
hhe@accessola.com
Beckie MacDonald, Manager, Member Services, 416-363-3388 Ext. 226
bmacdonald@accessola.com
Michelle Arbuckle, Coordinator, Education, 416-363-3388 Ext. 230
marbuckle@accessola.com
Liz Kerr, Coordinator, Conferences, 416-363-3388 Ext. 232
lkerr@accessola.com
Meredith Tutching, Coordinator, Programs, 416-363-3388 Ext. 222
mtutching@accessola.com
Carla Wintersgill, Coordinator, Marketing & Communications, 416-363-3388 Ext. 231
cwintersgill@accessola.com
Finances: *Funding Sources:* Sponsorships; Education programs; Publication sales; Membership fees; Donations; Funding from the Ministry of Citizenship, Culture & Recreation
Membership: 5,000+; *Member Profile:* Librarians, library technicians, library suppliers, library staff, systems specialists, publishers, authors, producers, school administrators, teacher librarians, financial officers, directors, trustees, & friends of libraries; *Committees:* OLA Special Libraries
Activities: Providing education & information, through seminars & virtual programs; Lobbying & political action; Coordinating mutual interests & needs; Offering services & products; Researching & developing programs & services; Defending free & equitable access to information; Providing networking opportunities through listservs & chat groups; *Awareness Events:* "A Forest of Reading": The Ontario Library Association's Literacy Initiative, April (voting day) & May (ceremony)
Awards:
• OLA's Larry Moore Distinguished Service Award (Award)
• OLA President's Award for Exceptional Achievement (Award)
• OLA's Les Fowlie Intellectual Freedom Award (Award)
• OLA's Media & Communications Award (Award)
• OLA's Library Building Award (Award)
• Brodart / OLA Technical Services Award (Award)
• OLA Archival & Preservation Achievement Award (Award)
Meetings/Conferences: • Ontario Library Association 2015 Super Conference, January, 2015, Metro Toronto Convention Centre, Toronto, ON
Scope: Provincial
Attendance: 4,500+
Description: An annual gathering of delegates, speakers, & exhibitors for a continuing education event in librarianship. Theme: "Think it. Do it!"
Contact Information: Conference Coordinator: Liz Kerr, Phone: 416-363-3388, ext. 232, E-mail: lkerr@accessola.com; Education Coordinator: Michelle Arbuckle, Phone: 416-363-3388, ext. 230, E-mail: marbuckle@accessola.com; Manager, Member Services: Beckie MacDonald, Phone: 416-363-3388, ext. 226, E-mail: bmacdonald@accessola.com
Publications:
• Access
Type: Magazine; *Frequency:* Quarterly; *Accepts Advertising*; *Editor:* Wayne Jones
Profile: Association activities plus trends & issues affecting libraries
• Teaching Librarian
Type: Magazine; *Frequency:* 3 times a year; *Editor:* Diana Maliszewski *ISSN:* 1188-679X
Profile: Official magazine of the Ontario School Library Association supports teacher-librarians in providing library programs & services in Ontario schools; Promotes librarycurriculum development; Provides a forum for sharing of experience & expertise; Subscription available with OSLA membership

Ontario Library Boards' Association (OLBA)
c/o Ontario Library Association, #201, 50 Wellington St. East, Toronto ON M5E 1C8
Tel: 416-363-3388; *Fax:* 416-941-9581
Toll-Free: 866-873-9867
info@accessola.com
www.accessola.com/olba
Previous Name: Ontario Library Trustees Association
Overview: A medium-sized provincial charitable organization
Mission: To represent Ontario public library board members on issues that affect library board leadership; To advance public library board development & improve the management & services of libraries throughout Ontario; To enhance the visibility of library boards
Affliation(s): Ontario Library Association
Chief Officer(s):
Joyce Cunningham, President
joycec@jam21.net
Frances Ryan, Vice-President
fryan@shaw.ca
Membership: *Fees:* Schedule available, based on populations served by libraries; *Member Profile:* Ontario public library board members (trustees)
Activities: Building a professional development program & ensuring continuing education of Ontario public library trustees; Providing information materials about public library governance, board roles, & the legislation on public libraries; Promoting Ontario Public Library Guidelines; Collaborating with related agencies; Promoting government support; Providing the listserv to connect members across the province
Meetings/Conferences: • Ontario Library Boards' Association 2015 Annual General Meeting, January, 2015, Metro Toronto Convention Centre, Toronto, ON
Scope: Provincial
Description: AGM reports from executive members, the business of the association, statement of expenses, & the introduction of the new council
• Ontario Library Boards' Association 2016 Annual General Meeting, 2016, ON
Scope: Provincial
Description: AGM reports from executive members, the business of the association, statement of expenses, & the introduction of the new council
Publications:
• Inside OLBA [Ontario Library Boards' Association]
Type: Newsletter; *Frequency:* Quarterly
Profile: Articles about current library issues, OLBA activities, & profiles of trustees
• Ontario Library Boards' Association Annual Report
Type: Yearbook; *Frequency:* Annually

Ontario Library Trustees Association ***See*** Ontario Library Boards' Association

Ontario Limousine Owners Association (OLOA)
10 Sunbeam Ave, Toronto ON M3H 1W7
Tel: 416-233-3029; *Fax:* 416-638-1699
info@oloa.ca
www.oloa.ca
Overview: A small provincial organization founded in 1996
Mission: OLOA is a nonprofit organization responsible for & dedicated to representing limousine operators in Ontario. It was formed to provide members with a unified voice to approach regulatory agencies, politicians & lawmakers with information regarding the problems faced by the limousine industry. It represents 175 companies who employ approximately 4,000 people.

Canadian Associations

Membership: 175

Ontario Literacy Coalition (OLC)

#503, 65 Wellesley St. East, Toronto ON M4Y 1G7
Tel: 416-963-5787; *Fax:* 416-963-8102
olc@on.literacy.ca
www.on.literacy.ca
www.facebook.com/270794520054
twitter.com/ontarioliteracy
Overview: A medium-sized provincial organization founded in 1986
Mission: To ensure that all people in Ontario can successfully meet the everyday reading & writing demands they encounter at home, work & in the community
Chief Officer(s):
Lesley Brown, Executive Director, 416-963-5787 Ext. 27
lesley@on.literacy.ca
Patricia Brady, Learner Coordinator
Finances: *Annual Operating Budget:* $250,000-$500,000
Staff Member(s): 5
Membership: 250+; *Fees:* Sliding scale
Activities: Researches & raises public awareness concerning literacy issues; supports policies & practices associated with accessible, appropriate & high quality literacy education; supports policies & practices that make it easier for people with low literacy skills to access information; encourages literacy promotion; *Speaker Service:* Yes
Awards:
• Frances Lever Memorial Award (Award)

Ontario Long Term Care Association (OLTCA)

345 Renfrew Dr., 3rd Fl., Markham ON L3R 9S9
Tel: 905-470-8995; *Fax:* 905-470-9595
info@oltca.com
www.oltca.com
twitter.com/oltcanews
Previous Name: Ontario Nursing Home Association
Overview: A medium-sized provincial licensing organization founded in 1959 overseen by Canadian Alliance for Long Term Care
Mission: Provides professional leadership to the long-term care sector; to empower long-term care facilities to provide high quality & cost-effective health care & accommodation services
Member of: Canadian Alliance for Long Term Care
Chief Officer(s):
Candace Chartier, CEO, 905-470-8995 Ext. 24
cchartier@oltca.com
Lesley Atkinson, Interim Director, Communications & Public Affairs, 904-470-8995 Ext. 25
latkinson@oltca.com
Brian Baillie, Director, Corporate Affairs & Member Services, 904-470-8995 Ext. 23
Finances: *Annual Operating Budget:* $1.5 Million-$3 Million; *Funding Sources:* Membership dues
Staff Member(s): 15
Membership: 427 long term care homes; *Fees:* $160 + $30.23 per bed
Activities: *Awareness Events:* Long Term Care Facility Month, June; Occupational Health & Safety Week, Oct.; *Rents Mailing List:* Yes

Ontario Luge Association (OLA)

3073 Victoria Heights Cres., Ottawa ON K1T 3M7
Tel: 613-262-5513
ontarioluge@gmail.com
ontarioluge.ca
www.facebook.com/OntarioLugeAssociation
twitter.com/OntarioLuge
Overview: A medium-sized provincial organization
Mission: To promote luge in Ontario
Affliation(s): Canadian Luge Association
Membership: *Fees:* $5 indiviual; $10 under 16

Ontario Lumber Manufacturers' Association (OLMA) / Association des manufacturiers de bois de sciage de l'Ontario

244 Viau Rd., Noelville ON P0M 2N0
Tel: 705-618-3403; *Fax:* 705-898-3403
info@olma.ca
olma.ca
Overview: A medium-sized provincial organization founded in 1966
Mission: To ensure a sound & renewable forest economy; To oversee lumber grading licenses & quality control at member sawmills in Ontario; To ensure market access within Northern America, Europe, & Japan
Affliation(s): Canadian Lumber Standards Accreditation Board; American Lumber Standards Committee, Inc.
Chief Officer(s):
André G. Boucher, President/Chief Lumber Grading Inspector
aboucher@olma.ca
Membership: *Member Profile:* Ontario sawmills, planing mills, lumber remanufacturers, & MSR & Fj manufacturers; Ontario companies engaged in equipment manufacturing, & lumber sales & distribution
Activities: Training persons to classify lumber; Supervising the grading of lumber; Authorizing manufacturing facilities to mark pieces of lumber with the OLMA facsimile stamp; Mediating disputes between sellers & buyers of lumber with the OLMA stamp; Promoting trade & diversification; Improving access to markets for Canadian softwood lumber; Reviewing forestry issues & policies; Liaising with government;
Awards:
• Ontario Lumber Manufacturers' Association Lumberjack Award (Award)
To recognize the outstanding lumberjack of the year

Ontario Lung Association (OLA)

573 King St. East, Toronto ON M5A 4L3
Tel: 416-864-9911; *Fax:* 416-864-9916
Toll-Free: 888-344-5864
Other Communication: donors@on.lung.ca; airquality@on.lung.ca
olalung@on.lung.ca
www.on.lung.ca
www.facebook.com/OntarioLungAssociation?ref=ts
twitter.com/OntarioLung
www.youtube.com/user/ONLungAssociation
Overview: A large provincial charitable organization founded in 1945 overseen by Canadian Lung Association
Mission: To provide lung health information & support to people affected by lung disease; To prevent & control chronic lung disease
Chief Officer(s):
Hélène Michaud, Chair
George Habib, President & Chief Executive Officer
Eric Bentzen, Treasurer
Finances: *Funding Sources:* Donations; Fundraising; Sponsorships
Activities: Supporting lung health research; Providing education about asthma (Asthma Action Helpline) & chronic obstructive pulmonary disease (BreathWorks Program); Offering smoking cessation information; *Awareness Events:* Lungs Are For Life Program; The Amazing Pace; Tulip Day
Publications:
• Asthma Action
Type: Newsletter
• Breathworks
Type: Newsletter
• Oxygen
Type: Newsletter
Profile: Lung health information, donor & research profiles, & forthcoming events

Belleville Office (Hastings & Prince Edward Counties)
c/o Century Place, #107, 199 Front St., Belleville ON K8N 5H5
Tel: 613-969-0323; *Fax:* 613-969-0359
www.on.lung.ca
Mission: To provide lung health resources in the Ontario counties of Hastings & Prince Edward
Chief Officer(s):
Kerry McCloy, Area Manager
KMcCloy@on.lung.ca

Brantford Office (Brant County)
410 Colborne St., Lower Level, Brantford ON N3S 3N6
Tel: 519-753-4682; *Fax:* 519-753-4667
brant@on.lung.ca
www.on.lung.ca
Mission: To provide lung health resources in Brant County, Ontario

Hamilton Office (Hamilton, Niagara, & Waterloo & Wellington Regions)
#4, 1447 Upper Ottawa St., Hamilton ON L8W 3J6
Tel: 905-383-1616; *Fax:* 905-383-1213
hamilton@on.lung.ca
www.on.lung.ca
Mission: To provide resources about lung health to persons in Hamilton, Ontario & the surrounding regions

Kingston Office (Kingston & the Thousand Islands)
c/o The Woolen Mill, #18, 6 Cataraqui St., Kingston ON K7L 1Z7
Tel: 613-545-3462; *Fax:* 613-545-1007
www.on.lung.ca
Mission: To serve the Ontario counties of Frontenac, Lennox, Addington, Leeds & Grenville
Chief Officer(s):
Kerry McCloy, Area Manager
kmccloy@on.lung.ca

London Office (Bluewater-Thames Valley)
480 Egerton St., London ON N5W 3Z6
Tel: 519-453-9086; *Fax:* 519-453-9184
london@on.lung.ca
www.on.lung.ca
Mission: To serve Lambton, Elgin, London, Middlesex, & Oxford Counties

Ottawa Office (Ottawa, Renfrew County, & Cornwall Area)
#500, 2319 St. Laurent Blvd., Ottawa ON K1G 4J8
Tel: 613-230-4200; *Fax:* 613-230-5210
www.on.lung.ca
Mission: To provide service & support in Renfrew, Ottawa, Lanark, Prescott, Russell, Stormont, & Dundas & Glengarry Counties

Sault Ste Marie Office (Algoma Area)
516 Queen St. East, Sault Ste Marie ON P6A 2A1
Tel: 705-256-2335; *Fax:* 705-256-1210
www.on.lung.ca
Mission: To serve the Algoma District

Simcoe Office (Haldimand-Norfolk)
203 John St., Simcoe ON N3Y 2Y6
Tel: 519-426-4973; *Fax:* 519-426-2729
haldimand@on.lung.ca
www.on.lung.ca
Mission: To provide resources about lung health to persons in the Haldimand-Norfolk region

Stratford Office (Huron-Perth)
c/o Jenny Trout Centre, #121, 342 Erie St., Stratford ON N5A 2N4
Tel: 519-271-7500; *Fax:* 519-271-7503
www.on.lung.ca
Mission: To serve Huron & Perth Counties

Toronto Office (Greater Toronto Area West)
#401, 18 Wynford Dr., Toronto ON M3C 0K8
Fax: 416-864-9916
Toll-Free: 800-972-2636
olalung@on.lung.ca
www.on.lung.ca
Mission: To serve the Halton, Dufferin, Peel, & Mississauga areas of Ontario
Chief Officer(s):
Stephanie Lear, Contact
slear@on.lung.ca

Windsor Office (Windsor-Essex & Chatham-Kent Area)
#104, 647 Ouellette Ave., Windsor ON N9A 4J4
Tel: 519-256-3433; *Fax:* 519-256-8179
www.on.lung.ca
Mission: To provide services to the Chatham-Kent & Windsor-Essex region
• Windsor-Essex & Chatham-Kent Area Breathworks Support Group Newsletter
Type: Newsletter; *Frequency:* Monthly
Profile: Support & advice for patients with COPD & their caregivers

Ontario Maple Syrup Producers' Association (OMSPA)

275 Country Rd. 44, RR#4, Kemptville ON K0G 1J0
Tel: 613-258-2294; *Fax:* 613-258-0207
Toll-Free: 866-566-2753
admin@ontariomaple.com
www.ontariomaple.com
Overview: A small provincial organization founded in 1966
Mission: To promote Ontario maple products through research & education
Chief Officer(s):
Rhonda Roantree, Office Administrator
Membership: 400+; *Fees:* $80 prducer under 250 taps; $110 producer 250 or more taps; $110 associate; $30 affiliate; *Committees:* Finance; Promotion; Research; Membership; Quality Assurance; Web Site Development

Ontario Marathon Canoe & Kayak Racing Association (OMCKRA)

2725 Baylie Ave., Ottawa ON K2H 6Y7
e-mail: info@omckra.com
www.omcra.ca

Overview: A small provincial organization overseen by CanoeKayak Canada
Mission: To represent, promote & develop the sport of marathon canoe & kayak racing in Ontario.
Member of: CanoeKayak Canada
Chief Officer(s):
Mike Devine, President
omckrapres@gmail.com

Ontario March of Dimes (OMOD) / Marche des dix sous de l'Ontario

10 Overlea Blvd., Toronto ON M4H 1A4
Tel: 416-425-3463; *Fax:* 416-425-1920
Toll-Free: 800-263-3463
info@marchofdimes.ca
www.marchofdimes.ca
Also Known As: Rehabilitation Foundation for the Disabled
Overview: A large provincial charitable organization founded in 1951
Mission: To maximize the independence, personal empowerment & community participation of people with physical disabilities
Affliation(s): March of Dimes Canada; Ontario March of Dimes Non-Profit Housing Corporation (NPHC); OMOD Independence Non-Profit Corporation; Rehabilitation Foundatation for Disabled Persons Inc., U.S.; Polio Canada; Stroke Recovery Canada
Chief Officer(s):
Andria Spindel, President & CEO
Jerry Lucas, Vice-President, Programs
Mary Lynne Stewart, Director, Communications & Fund Development
Finances: *Annual Operating Budget:* Greater than $5 Million; *Funding Sources:* Government grants; fundraising; fee for services
Staff Member(s): 1551; 2200 volunteer(s)
Membership: 155; *Member Profile:* Consumers, Donors, Sustaining & Volunteers
Activities: Service provider; advocacy; government relations; research; information services; fundraising includes Door to Door Campaign, direct mail, events & on-line divisions employment services; Independent Living Services; AccessAbility Services; Community Relations; Conductive Education; Recreation/Integration; Peer Support (Post-Polio & Stroke Recovery); Northern Clinics; *Awareness Events:* Door to Door Campaign, Jan.; Post-Polio Awareness, March; Stroke Awareness, May; *Internships:* Yes
Awards:
• Public Services Awards (Award)
• Jeannette Shannon Leadership Award (Award)
• The Right Honourable Paul Martin Sr. Award (Award)
• The Reverend Roy Essex Award (Award)
• Community Partnership Award (Award)
• Richard Kall Employee Award of Excellence (Award)
• Wade Hampton Employment Training Bursary (Award)
Meetings/Conferences: • Living & Thriving with a Disability Conferences 2015, 2015
Scope: Provincial
• 2015 Annual Breaking the ICE Conference, 2015
Scope: Provincial
Description: A consumer-centered conference aimed at helping people who use Alternative and Augmentative Communication (AAC) systems to develop their lives to the best of their abilities
• 2015 Annual Breaking the ICE West Conference, October, 2015, Nikkei Centre, Burnaby, BC
Scope: Provincial
Description: A consumer-centered conference aimed at helping people who use Alternative and Augmentative Communication (AAC) systems to develop their lives to the best of their abilities
Contact Information: Phone: 800-263-3463
• The Leadership in Volunteer Education (L.I.V.E) Conference 2015, 2015
Scope: Provincial
Description: Peer Support's annual 3-day training and networking event for active members, current and future volunteer leaders in stroke, polio and caregiver support groups across Canada
Contact Information: Phone: 800-263-3463

Ontario Marine Operators Association *See* Boating Ontario

Ontario Masonry Contractors' Association (OMCA)

360 Superior Blvd., Mississauga ON L5T 2N7
Tel: 905-564-6622; *Fax:* 905-564-5744
info@canadamasonrycentre.com
www.canadamasonrycentre.com/cmca
Overview: A medium-sized provincial organization founded in 1971
Mission: To actively promote masonry in Ontario by providing technical & design assistance to professionals & help in the training of the labour force
Member of: Canadian Masonry Contractors' Association
Chief Officer(s):
John Blair, Executive Director
Finances: *Funding Sources:* Membership dues
Staff Member(s): 7
Membership: 11 professional; 38 associate; 35 contractor; *Fees:* $460
Activities: *Library* by appointment

Ontario Massage Therapist Association (OMTA)

2943B Bloor St. West, Toronto ON M8X 1B3
Tel: 416-979-2010; *Fax:* 416-979-1144
Toll-Free: 800-668-2022
info@omta.com
www.omta.com
twitter.com/OMTA
www.youtube.com/user/TheRMTAO
Overview: A medium-sized provincial organization founded in 1936
Mission: To advocate on behalf of all masssage therapists in Ontario; To ensure public access to the services of massage therapists; To encourage high standards for massage therapists
Chief Officer(s):
Krystin Bokalo, Chair
Board_Chair@rmtao.com
Jill Haig, Planner, Education & Administration
jill@rmtao.com
Rachel Chuffart, Planner, Communication & Member Services
jill@rmtao.com
Finances: *Funding Sources:* Membership fees; Advertising; Sponsorships
Staff Member(s): 3
Membership: *Fees:* Schedule available; *Member Profile:* Registered massage therapists in Ontario; Students of massage therapy
Activities: Creating networking opportunities with professional colleagues; Providing access to technical & clinical information about massage therapy; Offering learning opportunities; Liaising with the government & the College of Massage Therapists of Ontario; Increasing awareness of massage therapy & massage therapists as health professionals
Publications:
• The Friday File
Type: Newsletter; *Frequency:* Weekly; *Accepts Advertising*
Profile: A news digest for members of the Ontario Massage Therapist Association

Ontario Masters Track & Field Association (OMTFA)

1185 Eglinton Ave. East, Toronto ON M3C 3C6
Tel: 416-426-4427; *Fax:* 416-426-7358
douglasj.smith@sympatico.ca
www.ontariomasters.ca
www.facebook.com/group.php?gid=10266993781&ref=mf
twitter.com/OntarioMasters
www.youtube.com/OntarioMasters
Overview: A small provincial organization founded in 1978
Member of: Canadian Masters Athletic Association
Chief Officer(s):
Doug Smith, President
douglasj.smith@sympatico.ca
Karla Del Grande, Vice-President
karla.delgrande@bell.net
Membership: *Fees:* $40 individual; $60 family

Ontario Medical Association (OMA)

#900, 150 Bloor St. West, Toronto ON M5S 3C1
Tel: 416-599-2580; *Fax:* 416-340-2944
Toll-Free: 800-268-7215
Other Communication: membership@oma.org
info@oma.org
www.oma.org
Overview: A large provincial organization founded in 1880 overseen by Canadian Medical Association
Mission: To represent the clinical, political, & economic interests of Ontario physicians; To promote an accessible, quality health-care system
Chief Officer(s):
Mark MacLeod, President
Catherine Flaman, Contact, Member Relations, Public Affairs & Communications, 416-340-2915, Fax: 416-340-2950
mentor@oma.org
Membership: 30,000+; *Member Profile:* Practicing physicians, residents, & students who are enrolled in one of Ontario's faculties of medicine
Activities: Advocating for the health of Ontarians; Promoting health care services throughout Ontario; Providing a continuing medical education program; Offering tools to manage an effective practice, such as legal advice & incorporation services
Awards:
• Ontario Medical Student Bursary Fund (Scholarship)
• Ontario Medical Foundation Elective Bursaries (Scholarship)
• Student Leadership Development Subsidy Program (Scholarship)
• OMA Medical Student Achievement Award (Award)
Meetings/Conferences: • 60th Annual Ontario Anesthesia Meeting, 2015, ON
Scope: Provincial
Contact Information: OMA Public Affairs & Communications Department Contact: Catherine Flaman, Phone: 416-340-2915
• 38th Day in Primary Eye Care Conference, 2015, ON
Scope: Provincial
Contact Information: OMA Public Affairs & Communications Department Contact: Catherine Flaman, Phone: 416-340-2915
Publications:
• Ontario Medical Review
Type: Journal

Ontario Medical Student Association (OMSA)

c/o Ontario Medical Association, #900, 150 Bloor St. West, Toronto ON M5S 3C1
Tel: 416-599-2580; *Fax:* 416-340-2232
Toll-Free: 800-268-7215
omsa.squarespace.com
www.facebook.com/OntarioMedicalStudents
twitter.com/OMSA_Executive
www.flickr.com/people/ontariomedicalstudents/
Overview: A medium-sized provincial organization founded in 1974 overseen by Ontario Medical Association
Mission: To represent the concerns & views of medical students in Ontario
Member of: Ontario Medical Association
Affliation(s): Canadian Medical Association
Chief Officer(s):
Nahid Punjani, Co-Chair
chair@omsa.ca
Rahul Sharma, Co-Chair
co-chair@omsa.ca
Membership: 3,000; *Fees:* $22; *Member Profile:* Ontario medical students
Activities: Lobbying the provincial government on issues such as tuition & government assistance to lower income students; Working to ensure adequate postgraduate training positions in Ontario; Offering seminars & a mentorship program, through the Ontario Medical Association (mentor@oma.org).
Awards:
• Ontario Medical Student Bursary Fund (Grant)
Publications:
• Scrub-In
Type: Magazine; *Frequency:* 3 pa; *Editor:* Nancy Dale; Matthew Radford
Profile: Articles of interest to Ontario's medical students

Ontario Mental Health Foundation

441 Jarvis St., 2nd Fl., Toronto ON M4Y 2G8
Tel: 416-920-7721; *Fax:* 416-920-0026
grants@omhf.on.ca
www.omhf.on.ca
Overview: A small provincial charitable organization
Mission: To promote the mental health of people in Ontario; To improve the diagnosis & treatment of mental illness
Chief Officer(s):
Alexander Greer, Executive Director
agreer@omhf.on.ca
Emmanuelle Fontaine, Officer, Grants
grants@omhf.on.ca
Activities: Providing research grants, fellowships, & studentships; Supporting the professional development of researchers; Disseminating the results of funded research
Publications:
• Ontario Mental Health Foundation Annual Report
Type: Yearbook; *Frequency:* Annually

Ontario Military Vehicle Association (OMVA)

c/o Peter Simundson, 6929 Estoril Rd., Mississauga ON L5N 1N2
www.omva.ca
Overview: A small provincial organization founded in 1986

Mission: To promote the place in history of Canadian military vehicles
Affliation(s): Military Preservation Association
Chief Officer(s):
Peter Simundson, President, 905-826-6136
psimundson@rogers.com
Syd Schatzker, Treasurer, 905-881-1929
pschatzker@rogers.com
Finances: *Funding Sources:* Membership fees
Membership: 230+; *Fees:* $25 Canadian members; $30 international members; *Member Profile:* Military vehicle enthusiasts
Activities: Preserving Canadian military vehicles; Participating in parades, shows, & festivals;
Publications:
• CMP Magazine
Type: Magazine; *Frequency:* Quarterly; *Accepts Advertising*; *Editor:* Eric Booth; *Price:* Free with Ontario Military Vehicle Association membership

Ontario Milk Transport Association (OMTA)
#301, 660 Speedvale Ave. West, Guelph ON N1K 1E5
www.milk.org/Corporate/View.aspx?Content=Students/Transportation
Overview: A medium-sized provincial organization founded in 1967
Chief Officer(s):
John Johnston, General Manager, 519-766-1133
Membership: 60 companies; *Member Profile:* Transporters of milk, such as producer-owned co-operatives, which collect raw milk from Ontario farms & take it to processing plants in Ontario, Quebec, & Manitoba

Ontario Mineral Exploration Federation (OMEF) *See* Ontario Prospectors Association

Ontario Mining Association (OMA)
#520, 5775 Yonge St., Toronto ON M2M 4J1
Tel: 416-364-9301; *Fax:* 416-364-5986
info@oma.on.ca
www.oma.on.ca
Overview: A medium-sized provincial organization founded in 1920 overseen by Mining Association of Canada
Mission: To help improve the competitiveness of the Ontario mineral industry
Chief Officer(s):
Chris Hodgson, President
Finances: *Funding Sources:* Membership fees
Staff Member(s): 7
Membership: 88; *Member Profile:* Companies involved in the mining industry; *Committees:* Aboringal Relations; Energy; Education & Outreach; Environment; Hoist Plant; Mining Rules; Safety & Training; Workers' Compensation & Occupational Health
Activities: *Awareness Events:* Ontario Mining Week, 1st week of May

Ontario Minor Hockey Association (OMHA)
#3, 25 Brodie Dr., Richmond Hill ON L4B 3K7
Tel: 905-780-6642; *Fax:* 905-780-0344
omha@omha.net
www.omha.net
twitter.com/HometownHockey
Overview: A medium-sized provincial organization founded in 1935
Mission: To provide community-based minor hockey programming for men, women, & children; To monitor the safety of the game, from equipment to rules
Affliation(s): Ontario Hockey Federation
Chief Officer(s):
Marg Ensoll, President
Richard Ropchan, Executive Director, 905-780-2150
rropchan@omha.net
Kevin Boston, Director, Marketing & Events, 905-780-2174
kboston@omha.net
Ian Taylor, Director, Development, 905-780-2172
ian.taylor@omha.net
Bill Rowney, Treasurer
Mark Dickie, Manager, Communications & IT, 905-780-2155
Mark.dickie@omha.net
Finances: *Funding Sources:* Membership fees; Sponsorships
Membership: *Committees:* AAA Zone; Annual General Meeting; Appeals; Competition with Overseas Teams; By-law & Regulations; Development & Playing Rules; Finance; Group Structure; Maintenance Trust; Manual & Forms; Nominations; Select & Local League; Tournaments
Activities: Providing development programs; Conducting seminars, coaches clinics, skills camps, & festivals; Initiating safety measures, such as the concussion awareness program, a mouthguard policy, & helmets for all on-ice personnel
Meetings/Conferences: • Ontario Minor Hockey Association 2015 Annual General Meeting & Hometown Hockey Consumer Show, 2015, ON
Scope: Provincial
Description: Addressing the business of the association, plus revisions to regulations, policies, & procedures for the upcoming season
Contact Information: Contact: Daniel Clement, Phone: 905-780-6642, ext. 247
Publications:
• Hometown Hockey
Type: Magazine; *Frequency:* Quarterly
• OHF & OMHA [Ontario Minor Hockey Association]: Your Memberhip Opportunities & Benefits
• OMHA [Ontario Minor Hockey Association] Insider
Type: Newsletter; *Frequency:* Weekly; *Editor:* Mark Dickie
• OMHA [Ontario Minor Hockey Association] Manual of Operations: By-law, Regulations, & Policies
Type: Manual
• OMHA [Ontario Minor Hockey Association] Participant Guide
Type: Guide; *Frequency:* Annually
Profile: Detailed information of interest to OMHA parents & players

Ontario Mission of the Deaf *See* Bob Rumball Foundation for the Deaf

Ontario Modern Language Teachers Association (OMLTA)
#246, 55 Northfield Dr. East, Waterloo ON N2K 3T6
Tel: 519-763-2099
omlta@omlta.org
www.omlta.org
Overview: A small provincial organization founded in 1886
Mission: The OMLTA/AOPLV, in existence since 1886, is a non-profit organization which represents the interests of over 1200 French and International Languages teachers in the province of Ontario.
Chief Officer(s):
Jayne Evans, President
Meetings/Conferences: • Ontario Modern Language Teachers Association Spring Conference 2015, March, 2015, Sheraton On The Falls Hotel & Conference Centre, Niagara Falls
Scope: Provincial

Ontario Modern Pentathalon Association
c/o Shaun LaGrange, 513428 - 2 Line Amaranth, RR#4, Orangeville ON L9W 2Z1
Tel: 519-940-3721
www.ompa.ca
Overview: A medium-sized provincial organization
Mission: To promote modern pentathalon
Chief Officer(s):
Shaun LaGrange, President
salagrange@sympatico.ca
Membership: *Fees:* $65 competitive; $20 supporting; $15 coach

Ontario Monument Builders Association (OMBA)
Tel: 905-262-1359; *Fax:* 905-262-5666
inquire@omba.com
www.omba.com
Overview: A medium-sized provincial organization
Mission: To further the interests of the monument industry; To maintain high standards of business ethics for association members
Chief Officer(s):
Doug King, Executive Director
Membership: *Member Profile:* Monument manufacturers & builders in Ontario, who subscribe to a code of ethics, & who comply with all legislation & regulations
Activities: Promoting the monument industry; Liaising with government & similar organizations
Publications:
• Ontario Monument Builders Association Members Directory
Type: Directory

Ontario Motor Coach Association (OMCA)
#505, 555 Burnhamthorpe Rd., Toronto ON M9C 2Y3
Tel: 416-229-6622; *Fax:* 416-229-6281
info@omca.com
www.omca.com
www.facebook.com/72333053744
Overview: A medium-sized provincial organization founded in 1929
Mission: To further the interests of member bus companies by all possible & available means; To promote & further the interest of the inter-city bus & motor coach tour industry
Chief Officer(s):
Doug Switzer, President/CEO, 416-229-6622 Ext. 222
doug@omca.com
Ann Fairley, Executive Vice-President, 416-229-6622 Ext. 223
ann@omca.com
Finances: *Funding Sources:* Membership dues; services
Staff Member(s): 5
Membership: *Fees:* Schedule available; *Member Profile:* Bus operators, tour operators, tour service providers & bus products & services manufacturers; *Committees:* Tour Operator; Supplier; Bus Operator; Executive; Conference; Golf; Membership
Activities: *Library*

Ontario Motor Vehicle Industry Council (OMVIC) / Conseil ontarien de commerce des véhicules automobiles
#800, 789 Don Mills Rd., Toronto ON M3C 1T5
Tel: 416-226-4500; *Fax:* 416-226-3208
Toll-Free: 800-943-6002
www.omvic.on.ca
Overview: A medium-sized provincial licensing organization founded in 1997
Mission: To enforce the Motor Vehicle Dealers Act (MVDA); To act as the self-management body of the motor vehicle dealer industry in Ontario, in order to protect the rights of consumers; to maintain a fair & safe marketplace in Ontario; To advance professionalism within the motor vehicle industry
Chief Officer(s):
Matt Rispin, President & Chair
Jeff Gray, Vice-President
Kevin Bavelaar, Secretary-Treasurer
Carl Compton, Executive Director
Staff Member(s): 55
Membership: 8,800 registered dealers + 22,000 registered salespersons; *Member Profile:* Registered motor vehicle salespersons & registered dealers in Ontario, who must abide by the rules & regulations established in Ontario's Motor Vehicle Dealers Act (MVDA)
Activities: Providing services to motor vehicle dealers & salespersons in Ontario, the provincial government, consumers, & stakeholders in the industry; Informing consumers;
Publications:
• Consumer Line
Type: Guide; *Frequency:* Monthly; *Price:* Free
Profile: A guide for consumers to the motor vehicle dealer industry in Ontario, featuring timely information about the industry & practical tips
• The Dealer Standard (formerly The Registrar's Report)
Author: Brenda McIntryre & Rob Kirsic
Profile: Information for registered dealers & salespersons throughout Ontario
• OMVIC Annual Report & Business Plan
Type: Yearbook; *Frequency:* Annually
Profile: Summary of Council activities, accomplishments, finances, & goals, submitted to the Minister of Government Services for review & approval

Ontario Municipal Human Resources Association (OMHRA)
#307, 1235 Fairview St., Burlington ON L7S 2K9
Tel: 905-631-7171; *Fax:* 905-631-2376
customerservice@omhra.on.ca
www.omhra.ca
Previous Name: Ontario Municipal Personnel Association
Overview: A medium-sized provincial organization founded in 1963
Mission: To provide direction on issues of human resources management; To represent the interests of the association, related to legislation & policies
Chief Officer(s):
Elizabeth Bourns, President
Louise Ann Riddell, Vice-President
Christine A. Ball, Executive Officer
christine.ball@omhra.ca
Finances: *Funding Sources:* Membership fees; Sponsorships
Staff Member(s): 2
Membership: 300; *Fees:* $325 populations less than 50,000; $425 populations more than 50,000; *Member Profile:* Ontario human resources professionals who are employed by municipalities, commissions, & local public sector boards

Activities: Facilitating the exchange of information from the field of human resources; Promoting education
Meetings/Conferences: • Ontario Municipal Human Resources Association Spring Workshop 2015, April, 2015, Delta Hotel & Conference Centre, Guelph, ON
Scope: Provincial
• Ontario Municipal Human Resources Association Fall Conference 2015, September, 2015, Fern Resort, Orillia, ON
Scope: Provincial

Ontario Municipal Management Development Board ***See*** Ontario Municipal Management Institute

Ontario Municipal Management Institute (OMMI)

618 Balmoral Dr., Oshawa ON L1J 3A7
Tel: 905-434-8885; *Fax:* 905-434-7381
www.ommi.on.ca
Previous Name: Ontario Municipal Management Development Board
Overview: A small provincial organization founded in 1979
Mission: To enhance management skills, in order to strengthen local government administration
Chief Officer(s):
Bill McKim, Executive Director
Shea-Lea Latchford, Administrative Assistant
Membership: 350; *Member Profile:* Local governments, including cities, towns, regions, & municipalities
Activities: Providing educational workshops & seminars; Conducting training opportunities; Certifying qualified candidates with the Certified Municipal Manager designation (CMM); Liaising with other professional local government associations
Awards:
• Excellence in Training (Award)
• Distinguished Service Award (Award)
Publications:
• Councillor Development Resource Manual
Type: Manual
• You & Your Local Government
Type: Handbook

Ontario Municipal Personnel Association ***See*** Ontario Municipal Human Resources Association

Ontario Municipal Social Services Association (OMSSA) / Association des services sociaux des municipalités de l'Ontario

#2500, 1 Dundas St West, Toronto ON M5G 1Z3
Tel: 416-642-1659; *Fax:* 416-979-4627
info@omssa.com
www.omssa.com
Overview: A large provincial organization founded in 1950
Mission: To promote high standards of competency within the profession to ensure quality delivery of human services in communities; To improve social policies & programs in the areas of affordable housing, homelessness prevention, children's services, & social assistance; To act as the voice for Consolidated Municipal Service Managers in Ontario
Chief Officer(s):
Kira Heineck, Executive Director, 416-646-0518, Fax: 416-979-4627
kheineck@omssa.com
David Landers, President
Janet Menard, Vice-President
Catherine Matheson, Secretary-Treasurer
Membership: *Member Profile:* Individuals who plan, manage, deliver, & fund social & community services in Ontario at the municipal level; *Committees:* Policy & Advocacy; Professional Development; Human Services Integration Steering
Activities: Offering professional development opportunities; Providing networking activities; Presenting awards; Engaging in advocacy activities; Disseminating information; Raising awareness of the importance of human services
Meetings/Conferences: • Ontario Municipal Social Services Association 2015 Policy and Research Conference, 2015, ON
Scope: Provincial
Publications:
• Connection [a publication of the Ontario Municipal Social Services Association]
Type: Newsletter; *Frequency:* 8 pa
Profile: OMSSA activities & initiatives
• Ontario Municipal Social Services Association Annual Report
Type: Yearbook; *Frequency:* Annually
Profile: Association acheivements & financial information

Ontario Municipal Tax & Revenue Association (OMTRA)

#119, 14845 - 6 Yonge St., Aurora ON L4G 6H8
e-mail: webmaster@omtra.ca
www.omtra.ca
www.facebook.com/278364522173943
twitter.com/omtra1
Previous Name: Association of Municipal Tax Collectors of Ontario
Overview: A medium-sized provincial organization founded in 1967
Mission: To bring those persons in the municipal field of tax collecting into helpful association with each other; To promote improved standards of ethics & efficiency in tax collection methods & procedures: To consider, resolve, & recommend amendments to Provincial Acts which may improve the tax billing & collection administration; To encourage submissions & disseminate information of interest to its members; To encourage & assist in the development of educational training programs for collection personnel; To cooperate with other municipal associations; To foster good public relations
Chief Officer(s):
Connie Mesih, President
connie.mesih@mississauga.ca
Membership: 277 Municipalities + 22 Associate
Meetings/Conferences: • Ontario Municipal Tax & Revenue Association 2015 Fall Conference, September, 2015, JW Marriott The Rosseau Muskoka Resort & Spa, Minett, ON
Scope: Provincial

Ontario Municipal Water Association (OMWA)

c/o Doug Parker, 43 Chelsea Cres., Belleville ON K8N 4Z5
Tel: 613-966-1100; *Fax:* 613-966-3024
Toll-Free: 888-231-1115
www.omwa.org
Overview: A medium-sized provincial organization
Mission: To act as the voice of municipal water supply in Ontario; To ensure the safety, quality, reliability, & sustainability of drinking water in Ontario
Affliation(s): Ontario Water Works Association (a section of the American Water Works Association)
Chief Officer(s):
Andrew J. Henry, President, 519-930-3505 Ext. 3505
ahenry@london.ca
Ed Houghton, Executive Director, 705-445-1800, Fax: 705-445-0791
ehoughton@collus.com
Membership: 200+ public drinking water authorities in Ontario; *Fees:* Schedule available, based upon population; *Member Profile:* Ontario's public water supply authorities; *Committees:* Resolutions; Communications & Website; Annual Conference; Awards/Service Recognition/Bursary; Nominations; Government Affairs; Finance
Activities: Reviewing policy, & legislative, & regulatory issues; Liaising with government, agencies, & associations to maintain safe & sustainable water sources; Lobbying to improve conditions; Promoting high standards of treatment, infrastructure, & operations; Offering technical training for operating authorities, operators, & owners of drinking water systems; Encouraging dissemination of information for public education
Awards:
• Award of Exceptional Merit (Award)
• Don Black Award (Award)
• OMWA Industry Leadership Award (Award)
• OMWA Student Bursary (Scholarship)
Deadline: November 15 *Amount:* $500 (4)
Meetings/Conferences: • Ontario Water Works Association / Ontario Municipal Water Association 2015 Annual Joint Conference & Trade Show, April, 2015, Toronto, ON
Scope: Provincial
Description: A conference featuring a plenary session, technical sessions, a trade show, & networking opportunities
• Ontario Water Works Association / Ontario Municipal Water Association 2016 Annual Joint Conference & Trade Show, May, 2016, Windsor, ON
Scope: Provincial
Description: A conference featuring a plenary session, technical sessions, a trade show, & networking opportunities
Publications:
• Councillors Handbook: Stewardship Responsibilities Under the Safe Drinking Water Act
Type: Handbook
• Ontario Municipal Water Association Members' Handbook
Type: Handbook

Ontario Museum Association (OMA) / Association des musées de l'Ontario

George Brown House, 50 Baldwin St., Toronto ON M5T 1L4
Tel: 416-348-8672; *Fax:* 416-348-0438
Toll-Free: 866-662-8672
www.museumsontario.com
Overview: A medium-sized provincial charitable organization founded in 1972
Mission: To enhance the mission of museums as significant cultural resources in the service of Ontario society & its development
Member of: Canadian Museums Association
Affliation(s): Ontario Heritage Alliance
Chief Officer(s):
Marie Lalonde, Executive Director
Finances: *Annual Operating Budget:* $250,000-$500,000; *Funding Sources:* Ontario Ministry of Citizenship, Culture & Recreation; Dept. of Canadian Heritage; membership fees
Staff Member(s): 6
Membership: 650 individual + 225 institutional; *Fees:* Schedule available; *Committees:* Advocacy; Award of Merit; Computer Advisory; Conference; Finance; Human Resources; Membership & Public Affairs; Publications
Activities: Serves as an information resource on Ontario's museums; advocates on behalf of museums & their supporters; fosters professional standards through seminars & courses; promotes public understanding of museums;; *Library* by appointment
Meetings/Conferences: • 2015 Ontario Museum Association Annual Conference, 2015, ON
Scope: National

Ontario Music Educators' Association (OMEA)

ON
www.omea.on.ca
www.facebook.com/OMEAOntario
twitter.com/OMEAOntario
Overview: A small provincial organization founded in 1949
Mission: The Ontario Music Educators' Association (OMEA), a non-profit organization that represents music educators in Ontario.
Chief Officer(s):
David Gueulette, President
Membership: *Member Profile:* Music educators in Ontario
Meetings/Conferences: • OMEA/CMIEC Soundscapes 2015, 2015, ON
Scope: Provincial
Publications:
• The Recorder
Type: Journal; *Frequency:* Quarterly

Ontario Music Festivals Association (OMFA)

c/o Pam Allen, 1422 Bayview Ave., #A, Toronto ON M4G 3A7
Toll-Free: 888-307-6632
mail@omfa.info
www.omfa.info
www.facebook.com/ONTMUSFEST
Overview: A medium-sized provincial organization overseen by Federation of Canadian Music Festivals
Mission: To promote the performance of classical music by Ontario's youth; To encourage knowledge of classical music
Member of: Federation of Canadian Music Festivals (FCMF)
Chief Officer(s):
Martha Gregory, President
pgtamf@gmail.com
Meghan Hila, 1st Vice-President
kiwanisinfo@bellnet.ca
Sue Belleperche, 2nd Vice President
suebelleperche@gmail.com
Pam Allen, Festival Administrator
Finances: *Funding Sources:* Membership fees; Sponsorships
Membership: 40 music festivals; *Member Profile:* Music festivals across Ontario
Activities: Providing educational opportunities for music students & teachers; Creating networking opportunities with people from other music festivals; Facilitating the exchange of information

Ontario Mutual Insurance Association (OMIA)

350 Pinebush Rd., Cambridge ON N1T 1Z6
Tel: 519-622-9220; *Fax:* 519-622-9227
info@omia.com
www.omia.com
Previous Name: Purely Mutual Underwriters Association; Mutual Fire Underwriters Association
Overview: A small provincial organization founded in 1882
Mission: To assist mutual insurance companies to achieve excellence in service provision

Affliation(s): Canadian Association of Mutual Insurance Companies
Membership: *Member Profile:* Mutual insurance companies in Ontario that provide home, business, farm, & automobile insurance; Associate members in other provinces
Activities: Providing educational & training opportunities; Offering support services to member companies

Ontario Muzzle Loading Association (OMLA)

433 Queen St., Chatham ON N7M 5K5
Tel: 519-352-0924; *Fax:* 519-352-4380
Overview: A small provincial organization founded in 1973
Activities: Posting rsults from provincial matches & the Soper event

Ontario Native Education Counselling Association (ONECA)

PO Box 220, 37A Reserve Rd., Naughton ON P0M 2M0
Tel: 705-692-2999; *Fax:* 705-692-9988
oneca@oneca.com
www.oneca.com
Overview: A small provincial organization founded in 1985
Mission: To promote Native People to aspire to meet their potential through the ongoing development and improvement of Native Counselling and Education services.
Chief Officer(s):
Cindy Fisher, President
cfisher@picriver.com
Awards:
• Colin Wasacase Scholarship (Scholarship)
• Four Directions Scholarship (Scholarship)
Meetings/Conferences: • 31st Annual Ontario Native Education Counselling Association Conference, 2015, ON
Scope: Provincial

Ontario Native Women's Association (ONWA)

380 Ray Blvd., Thunder Bay ON P7B 4E6
Tel: 807-623-3442; *Fax:* 807-623-1104
Toll-Free: 800-667-0816
www.onwa-tbay.ca
www.facebook.com/onwa7
twitter.com/_onwa_
Overview: A medium-sized provincial organization founded in 1972 overseen by Native Women's Association of Canada
Mission: To foster & promote the economic, social, cultural, & political well-being of First Nations & Métis women in Ontario; To represent Native women on issues that affect their lives
Chief Officer(s):
Dawn Harvard, President
Finances: *Funding Sources:* Government of Ontario, Aboriginal Healing & Wellness Strategy
Membership: *Member Profile:* Aboriginal women in Ontario from more than 80 organizations
Activities: Providing programs & services to improve the lives of Native women, such as recreational activities, workshops, & referrals

Ontario Nature

#612, 214 King St West, Toronto ON M5H 3S6
Tel: 416-444-8419; *Fax:* 416-444-9866
Toll-Free: 800-440-2366
info@ontarionature.org
www.ontarionature.org
www.facebook.com/OntarioNature?ref=ts
twitter.com/ontarionature
www.youtube.com/user/ONNature
Previous Name: Federation of Ontario Naturalists
Overview: A large provincial charitable organization founded in 1931
Mission: To promote knowledge, understanding & respect for Ontario's natural heritage & commitment to its conservation & protection on the part of the FON membership, landowners, decision makers & the general public; To seek legislation, policies, practices & institutions which permanently protect Ontario's natural ecosystem & indigenous biodiversity, including the establishment of a comprehensive natural heritage system for Ontario with an enlarged system of parks & other protected areas linked by a network of existing & rehabilitated natural corridors
Affiliation(s): Coalition on the Niagara Escarpment; Conservation Council of Ontario; Great Lakes United; International Union for Conservation of Nature & Natural Resources; International Committee for Bird Preservation
Chief Officer(s):
Nidhi Tandon, President
Caroline Schultz, Executive Director
Finances: *Annual Operating Budget:* $1.5 Million-$3 Million; *Funding Sources:* Private donations; membership dues; foundations
Staff Member(s): 24; 100 volunteer(s)
Membership: 30,000 individuals + 140 member groups; *Fees:* $50
Activities: *Library* by appointment

Ontario Naturopathic Association *See* Ontario Association of Naturopathic Doctors

Ontario Network for the Prevention of Elder Abuse (ONPEA)

#500, 234 Eglinton Ave. East, Toronto ON M4P 1K5
Tel: 416-916-6728; *Fax:* 416-916-6742; *Crisis Hot-Line:* 866-299-1011
info@onpea.org
www.onpea.org
www.facebook.com/ONPEA
twitter.com/ONPEA
Overview: A small provincial charitable organization founded in 1989
Mission: To stop abuse & restore respect of seniors in Ontario
Chief Officer(s):
Anadel Hastie, Chair
Teri Kay, Executive Director
ed@onpea.org
Mary Mead, Administrative Coordinator
admin@onpea.org
Monita Persaud, Regional Elder Abuse Consultant, Greater Toronto Area Office
multicultural@onpea.org
Finances: *Funding Sources:* Ontario Trillium Foundation
Staff Member(s): 9
Membership: *Fees:* $25 individuals & organizations; $15 students & seniors; *Member Profile:* Individuals interested in, or working in, the field of elder abuse
Activities: Raising awareness about the neglect & abuse of older adults in Ontario; Engaging in advocacy activities; Providing educational & training opportunities; Disseminating information; Collaborating with other organizations; Implementing Ontario's Strategy to Combat Elder Abuse; Supporting research in elder abuse; Establishing the Vibrancy campaign, featuring a touring exhibition & spokesperson; Providing networking opportunities; *Awareness Events:* Elder Abuse Awareness Day; *Speaker Service:* Yes
Publications:
• Elder Abuse Newsletter
Type: Newsletter; *Price:* Free with membership in the Ontario Network for the Prevention of Elder Abuse
• Ontario Network for the Prevention of Elder Abuse Annual Report
Type: Yearbook; *Frequency:* Annually

Barrie - Central East Regional Office
c/o Royal Victoria Hospital, 201 Georgina Dr., Barrie ON L4M 6M2
Tel: 705-817-3111
centraleast2@onpea.org
Chief Officer(s):
Inga Thompson, Regional Elder Abuse Consultant

Mississauga - Central West Regional Office
831 North Service Rd., Mississauga ON L4Y 1A2
Tel: 905-276-3282; *Fax:* 905-276-0005
centralwest@onpea.org
Chief Officer(s):
Maureen Etkin, Regional Elder Abuse Consultant

Ottawa - East Regional Office
c/o Council on Aging in Ottawa, #101, 1247 Kilborn Pl., Ottawa ON K1H 6K9
Tel: 613-789-3577; *Fax:* 613-789-4406
east@onpea.org
Chief Officer(s):
Manon Thompson, Regional Elder Abuse Consultant

Peterborough - Central East Regional Office
c/o Sexual Assault Ctr., #102, 411 Water St., Peterborough ON K9H 3L9
Tel: 705-745-4100
centraleast@onpea.org
Chief Officer(s):
Raeanne Rideout, Regional Elder Abuse Consultant

Sudbury - North East Regional Office
960 Notre Dame Ave., Sudbury ON P3A 2T4
Tel: 705-525-0077; *Fax:* 705-525-2598
northeast@onpea.org
Chief Officer(s):
Josée Miljours, Regional Elder Abuse Consultant

Thunder Bay - North West Regional Office
c/o The Pottery House, Lakehead University, 955 Oliver Rd., Thunder Bay ON P7B 5E1
Tel: 807-343-8563
northwest@onpea.org
Chief Officer(s):
Lee Stones, Regional Elder Abuse Consultant

Windsor - West Regional Office
c/o Centres for Seniors Windsor, 635 McEwan Ave., Windsor ON N9B 2E9
Tel: 519-254-9342; *Fax:* 519-254-1869
east@onpea.org
Chief Officer(s):
Deana Johnson, Regional Elder Abuse Consultant

Ontario Network of Employment Skills Training Projects / Réseau ontarien des organismes pour le développement de l'employabilité (ROODE)

#207, 517 Wellington St. West, Toronto ON M5V 1G1
Tel: 416-591-7151; *Fax:* 416-591-9126
info@onestep.on.ca
www.onestep.on.ca
Also Known As: ONESTEP
Overview: A medium-sized provincial charitable organization founded in 1982
Member of: Canadian Centre for Philanthropy
Affliation(s): Canadian Association of Educators & Trainers Organization
Chief Officer(s):
Lorraine Katanik, Resource Solutions
Finances: *Annual Operating Budget:* $500,000-$1.5 Million
Staff Member(s): 4; 15 volunteer(s)
Membership: 95; *Fees:* $80-$1,500 full membership; $160 auxiliary; *Member Profile:* Organization must be non-profit in operation for at least 2 years & provide employment-related supports &/or services using the community-based training model
Activities: Advocacy; professional development; researcy; policy development; systems change; *Speaker Service:* Yes; *Library:* Onestep Resource Centre; Open to public

Ontario Neurotrauma Foundation (ONF)

#601, 90 Eglinton Ave. East, Toronto ON M4P 2Y3
Tel: 416-422-2228; *Fax:* 416-422-1240
info@onf.org
www.onf.org
Overview: A medium-sized provincial organization founded in 1998
Mission: Dedicated to reducing the impact, incidence & prevalence of neurotrauma injuries, through knowledge creation, Research Capacity Building, & knowledge mobilization
Chief Officer(s):
Kent Bassett-Spiers, CEO
kent@onf.org
Barry Munro, Chair
chairperson@onf.org
Finances: *Annual Operating Budget:* $1.5 Million-$3 Million; *Funding Sources:* Ontario Ministry of Health; Partnerships
Staff Member(s): 10
Membership: *Committees:* Finance
Activities: Offers grants to those researching neurotrauma

Ontario Non-Profit Housing Association (ONPHA)

#400, 489 College St., Toronto ON M6G 1A5
Tel: 416-927-9144; *Fax:* 416-927-8401
Toll-Free: 800-297-6660
Other Communication: communications@onpha.org
mail@onpha.org
www.onpha.on.ca
Overview: A medium-sized provincial organization founded in 1988
Mission: To build a strong non-profit housing sector in Ontario; To strive for excellence in non-profit housing management; To represent non-profit housing
Chief Officer(s):
Keith Ward, President
Sharad Kerur, Executive Director, 416-927-9144 Ext. 102
sharad.kerur@onpha.org
Jo Ferris-Davies, Director, Member Development & Education, 416-927-9144 Ext. 105
jo.ferris-davies@onpha.org
Alice Radley, Treasurer
Diana Summers, Manager, Policy, Research, & Government Relations, 416-927-9144 Ext. 115
diana.summers@onpha.org

Rhona Duncan, Coordinator, Communications & Marketing, 416-927-9144 Ext. 126
rhona.duncan@onpha.org
Finances: *Funding Sources:* Membership dues; Sponsorships
Membership: 760+ organizations (housing more than 400,000 people); *Member Profile:* Non-profit organizations throughout Ontario which house persons in rental units; Individuals & organizations that support non-profit housing
Activities: Promoting new, affordable, & supportive housing for people in need in Ontario; Liaising with government & other organizations; Preparing position papers; Developing policy alternatives; Providing training; Offering management advice
Meetings/Conferences: • Ontario Non-Profit Housing Association 2015 Annual Conference, General Meeting & Trade Show, October, 2015, Toronto Sheraton Centre, Toronto, ON
Scope: Provincial
Attendance: 1,400
Description: Featuring speakers, workshops, & company exhibitors
Contact Information: Phone: 1-800-297-6660, ext. 110; E-mail: conference@onpha.org; Manager, Conference & IT: Patsy Duffy, Phone: 416-927-9144, ext. 110, E-mail: patsy.duffy@onpha.org
• Ontario Non-Profit Housing Association 2016 Annual Conference, General Meeting & Trade Show, November, 2016, Toronto Sheraton Centre, Toronto, ON
Scope: Provincial
Attendance: 1,400
Description: Featuring speakers, workshops, & company exhibitors
Contact Information: Phone: 1-800-297-6660, ext. 110; E-mail: conference@onpha.org; Manager, Conference & IT: Patsy Duffy, Phone: 416-927-9144, ext. 110, E-mail: patsy.duffy@onpha.org
Publications:
• Ontario Non-Profit Housing Association Annual Report
Type: Yearbook; *Frequency:* Annually
• Ontario Non-Profit Housing Association Member Directory
Type: Directory
• Ontario Non-Profit Housing Association Administrative Policy Handbook
Type: Handbook; *Price:* $90
• Ontario Non-Profit Housing Association Asbestos Management Plan
Type: Handbook; *Price:* $70
• Ontario Non-Profit Housing Association Financial Policies & Procedures Handbook
Type: Handbook; *Price:* $120
• Ontario Non-Profit Housing Association Governance & Corporate Practices Handbook
Type: Handbook; *Price:* $120
• Ontario Non-Profit Housing Association Human Resources Handbook
Type: Handbook; *Price:* $100
• Ontario Non-Profit Housing Association Maintenance Planning Handbook
Type: Handbook; *Price:* $120
• Ontario Non-Profit Housing Association Tenant Handbook & Disk
Type: Handbook; *Price:* $70
• Ontario Non-Profit Housing Association Integrated Pest Management in Housing
Type: Handbook; *Price:* $79
• Ontario Non-Profit Housing Association Residential Tenancies Act Handbook
Type: Handbook; *Price:* $75
• Quick Connections
Type: Newsletter; *Frequency:* Bimonthly; *Accepts Advertising*; *Editor:* Sharad Kerur
Profile: Management advice & news for non-profit housing staff

Ontario Numismatic Association (ONA)

c/o Bruce Raszmann, PO Box 40033, Stn. Waterloo Square, 75 King St. South, Waterloo ON N2J 4V1
the-ona.ca
Overview: A small local organization founded in 1962
Member of: Royal Canadian Numismatic Association
Chief Officer(s):
Paul Petch, President, 416-745-3067
president@ontario-numismatic.org
Len Trakalo, Secretary
secretary@ontario-numismatic.org
Bruce Raszmann, Treasurer & Chair, Membership, 519-745-3104
Membership: 320+; *Fees:* $5 juniors; $15 regular members; $17 spouses; $20 clubs or associations; $450 individual life membership; *Member Profile:* Numismatic clubs or associations; Individuals, such as professional numismatists & collectors; Families; Juniors up to age 18
Activities: Conducting research; Disseminating information; *Library:* Ontario Numismatic Association Education Library
Meetings/Conferences: • Ontario Numismatic Association 2015 53rd Annual Convention, April, 2015, Crowne Plaza Niagara Falls-Fallsview, Niagara Falls, ON
Scope: Provincial
Description: Education program, dealer participation, business meetings, & networking events
Publications:
• The ONA Numismatist
Type: Newsletter; *Frequency:* Bimonthly; *Number of Pages:* 36
Profile: Educational articles & information about Ontario coin club activities, plus a special annual convention issue

Ontario Nurses' Association (ONA) / Association des infirmières et infirmiers de l'Ontario

#400, 85 Grenville St., Toronto ON M5S 3A2
Tel: 416-964-8833; *Fax:* 416-964-8864
Toll-Free: 800-387-5580
onamail@ona.org
www.ona.org
www.facebook.com/OntarioNurses
twitter.com/ontarionurses
www.youtube.com/OntarioNurses
Overview: A large provincial organization founded in 1973
Mission: To improve the socio-economic welfare of members
Member of: Canadian Federation of Nurses Unions; Canadian Labour Congress
Chief Officer(s):
Linda Haslam-Stroud, President/Interim CEO, 416-964-1979 Ext. 2254
lindahs@ona.org
Finances: *Annual Operating Budget:* $1.5 Million-$3 Million; *Funding Sources:* Membership dues
Staff Member(s): 150
Membership: 54,000 + 234 locals
Activities: *Speaker Service:* Yes; *Library* by appointment

Hamilton Office
#2R, 2 King St. West, Dundas ON L9H 6Z1
Tel: 905-628-0850; *Fax:* 905-628-2557
Toll-Free: 866-928-3496

Kingston Office
#201, 4 Cataraqui St., Kingston ON K7K 1Z7
Tel: 613-545-1110; *Fax:* 613-531-9043

London Office
#109, 1069 Wellington Rd. South, London ON N6E 2H6
Tel: 519-438-2153; *Fax:* 519-433-2050
Toll-Free: 866-933-2050

Orillia Office
#126A, 210 Memorial Ave., Orillia ON L3V 7V1
Tel: 705-327-0404; *Fax:* 705-327-0511
Toll-Free: 866-927-0511

Ottawa Office
#211, 1400 Clyde Ave., Nepean ON K2G 3J2
Tel: 613-226-3733; *Fax:* 613-723-0947
Toll-Free: 866-523-0947

Sudbury Office
#203, 40 Larch St., Sudbury ON P5E 5M7
Tel: 705-560-2610; *Fax:* 705-560-1411
Toll-Free: 866-460-1411

Thunder Bay Office
#200, 1139 Alloy Dr., Thunder Bay ON P7B 6M8
Tel: 807-344-9115; *Fax:* 807-344-8850
Toll-Free: 866-744-8850

Timmins Office
Canadian Mental Health Association Bldg., #203, 330 - 2nd Ave., Timmins ON P4N 8A4
Tel: 705-264-2294; *Fax:* 705-268-4355
Toll-Free: 866-568-4355

Windsor Office
#220, 3155 Howard Ave., Windsor ON N8X 3Y9
Tel: 519-966-6350; *Fax:* 519-972-0814
Toll-Free: 866-972-0814

Ontario Nursing Home Association *See* Ontario Long Term Care Association

Ontario Occupational Health Nurses Association (OOHNA)

#605, 302 The East Mall, Toronto ON M9B 6C7
Tel: 416-239-6462; *Fax:* 416-239-5462
Toll-Free: 866-664-6276
administration@oohna.on.ca
www.oohna.on.ca
Overview: A medium-sized provincial organization founded in 1973
Mission: To foster a climate of excellence, innovation & partnership enabling Ontario Occupational Health Nurses to achieve positive workplace health & safety objectives
Member of: Canadian Occupational Health Nurses Association
Chief Officer(s):
Karen Watson, President, 519-254-5577 Ext. 52802
board@oohna.on.ca
Brian Verrall, Executive Director
Finances: *Annual Operating Budget:* $250,000-$500,000; *Funding Sources:* Membership fees
Staff Member(s): 3; 7 volunteer(s)
Membership: 1,200; *Fees:* $384 regular; $168 associate; *Member Profile:* RN's practising occupational health & safety
Activities: *Speaker Service:* Yes
Awards:
• Award of Excellence (Award)
• Pat Ewen Bursary Award (Award)
• Lifetime Achievement Award (Award)
Meetings/Conferences: • Ontario Occupational Health Nurses Association 44th Annual Conference, June, 2015, Niagara Falls Mariott Gateway on the Falls, Niagara Falls, ON
Scope: Provincial

Ontario Opticians Association (OOA)

PO Box 23518, Stn. Dexter, 5899 Leslie St., Toronto ON M2H 3R9
Tel: 905-709-4141; *Fax:* 416-226-6879
Toll-Free: 877-709-4141
info@ontario-opticians.com
www.ontario-opticians.com
www.facebook.com/ontarioopticiansassociation
Overview: A small provincial organization founded in 1946
Mission: To advance & protect the profession of opticianry
Member of: Opticians Association of Canada (OAC)
Membership: 1,200; *Fees:* $150 + $7.50 GST; Free students (first year); $25 students (second year & beyond); *Member Profile:* Dispensing opticians in Ontario; Students; New graduates; Intern opticians; Optical industry affiliates
Activities: Engaging in lobbying activities; Liaising with government; Presenting awards; Providing educational opportunities for Ontario opticians; Promoting the profession of opticianry; *Library:* Ontario Opticians Association Distance Module Library; Open to public
Awards:
• Optician of the Year (Award)
• Student Achievement Awards (Award)
• Annual Industry Award (Award)
Publications:
• Focus
Type: Newsletter; *Price:* Free with Ontario Opticians Association membership
Profile: Local & national issues, business advice, member benefits, & upcoming events

Ontario Painting Contractors Association (OPCA)

#10, 7611 Pine Valley Dr., Woodbridge ON L4L 0A2
Tel: 416-498-1897; *Fax:* 416-498-6757
Toll-Free: 800-461-3630
info@opca.org
www.ontpca.org
Overview: A medium-sized provincial organization founded in 1976
Mission: To foster, develop & maintain unity & stability among members by acting as a bargaining agent; providing services & educational opportunities; acting as a liaison between industry groups; upholding & improving the standards of the industry; promoting the use of modern specifications; advancing an attitude of ethical responsibility & pride
Member of: Construction Employers Coordinating Council of Ontario; Council of Ontario Construction Associations; Ontario Construction Secretariat
Affliation(s): Federation of Painting & Decorating Contractors of Toronto; Architectural Painting Specifications Services Ltd.
Chief Officer(s):
Thomas Corbett, President
Andrew Sefton, Executive Director
andrew.sefton@ontpca.org
Finances: *Annual Operating Budget:* $250,000-$500,000; *Funding Sources:* Membership dues
Staff Member(s): 2; 14 volunteer(s)

Membership: 57; *Fees:* Schedule available; *Member Profile:* Unionized, commercial, industrial & institutional painting contractors
Activities: *Speaker Service:* Yes

Ontario Paramedic Association (OPA)

PO Box 21016, Stn. Mapleridge, 1875 Landsowne St. West, Peterborough ON K9J 8M7
Toll-Free: 888-672-5463
www.ontarioparamedic.ca
www.facebook.com/sendaparamedic
twitter.com/OntParamedic
Overview: A small provincial organization founded in 1996
Mission: To act as a voice for both professional & patient care issues; To advocate for improvements in patient care
Member of: Paramedic Association of Canada (PAC)
Finances: *Funding Sources:* Membership dues
Membership: 1,900; *Fees:* $84 full; $70 associate; $40 student; $400 corporate; *Member Profile:* Paramedics certified under the Ontario Ministry of Health; Individuals interested in the field of paramedicine; Paramedic students; Corporations & organizations involved in emergency medical services
Activities: Raising public awareness of the role of paramedics; Providing seminars & workshops; Offering networking opportunities; *Awareness Events:* EMS Week, May; National Paramedic Competition
Publications:
• OPA [Ontario Paramedic Association] News
Type: Newsletter; *Accepts Advertising*; *Editor:* Elizabeth Anderson; *Price:* Free with Ontario Paramedic Association membership
Profile: Association newsletter contained in Canadian Emergency News

Ontario Parks Association (OPA)

7856 - 5th Line South, RR#4, Milton ON L9T 2X8
Tel: 905-864-6182; *Fax:* 905-864-6184
Toll-Free: 866-560-7783
opa@ontarioparksassociation.ca
www.ontarioparksassociation.ca
Overview: A medium-sized provincial charitable organization founded in 1936
Mission: To develop & protect parks & green spaces in Ontario
Chief Officer(s):
Paul Ronan, Executive Director, 905-864-6182 Ext. 6730
paul@ontarioparksassociation.ca
Eric Trogdon, Executive Director
eric@opassoc.on.ca
Shelley May, Coordinator, Operations & Administration, 905-864-6182 Ext. 6710
opa@ontarioparksassociation.ca
Maureen Sinclair, President
msinclair@brantford.ca
Bill Harding, Vice-President
bhardin@toronto.ca
Finances: *Funding Sources:* Donations
Membership: *Fees:* $70 students & seniors; $130 individuals; $500 associates
Activities: Offering education to park professionals
Meetings/Conferences: • Ontario Parks Association 2015 59th Annual Educational Forum, February, 2015, Holiday Inn Burlington Hotel and Conference Centre, Burlington, ON
Scope: Provincial
Description: Educational presentations of interest to park & green space managers & operational staff. This year's theme is "Parks for Life: Making the Connections."
• 6th Annual Ontario Parks Association 2015 Equipment Education & Golf Forum, 2015, ON
Scope: Provincial
Publications:
• OPA [Ontario Parks Association] Playability Tool Kit: Building Accessible Playspaces
Type: Kit
Profile: Creating playspaces that are accessible to persons with disabilities
• Urban Parks in Ontario
Type: Book; *Author:* Dr. J.R. Wright
Profile: The evolution of parks & open space development

Ontario Percheron Horse Association Inc.

c/o Michelle Campbell, 2321 Cockshutt Rd., Waterford ON N0E 1Y0
Tel: 519-443-6399
Secretary@ontariopercherons.ca
www.ontariopercherons.ca
Also Known As: opha
Overview: A small provincial organization overseen by Canadian Percheron Association
Mission: To promote the Percheron draft horse breed in Ontario
Chief Officer(s):
Kim Davidson, President, 519-454-8734
Regina Baezner, 1st Vice-President
Dan Barron, 2nd Vice-President
Michelle Campbell, Secretary-Treasurer, 519-443-6399
Secretary@ontariopercherons.ca
Finances: *Funding Sources:* Membership fees; Sponsorships
Membership: *Fees:* $10 juniors, 18 years & under as of January 1; $20 adults, with a Canadian address; $30 adults, with non-Canadian addresses; *Member Profile:* Percheron horse owners & enthusiasts from Canada & elsewhere; *Committees:* Annual Dinner; Futurity & Extravaganza Day; Percheron Newsletter; Website; Juniors
Activities: Offering programs, such as the junior showmanship program & a futurity program; Sponsoring shows, such as the Regional Percheron Show & the Provincial Percheron Show
Meetings/Conferences: • Ontario Percheron Horse Association 2015 Annual Meeting, February, 2015, Holiday Inn Express, Newmarket, ON
Scope: Provincial
Contact Information: Meeting Contact: Hedy Edwards, Phone: 905-887-5485
Publications:
• Ontario Percheron Horse Association Inc. Ontario Breeders Directory
Type: Directory
• Percheron Newsletter
Type: Newsletter; *Frequency:* Quarterly; *Editor:* Susan Davidson

Ontario Personal Support Worker Association (OPSWA)

PO Box 1056, Stn. Main, Brantford ON N3T 5S7
Tel: 519-654-9317
www.opswa.com
Overview: A small provincial organization
Mission: To continuously strive to improve the professional status of the Personal Support Workers of Ontario through advocacy for excellence & consistency in training, services, working conditions & value to those they serve.
Chief Officer(s):
Miranda Ferrier, President
mferrier@opswa.ca

Ontario Pest Control Association *See* Structural Pest Management Association of Ontario

Ontario Petroleum Institute Inc. (OPI)

#104, 555 Southdale Rd. East, London ON N6E 1A2
Tel: 519-680-1620; *Fax:* 519-680-1621
opi@ontariopetroleuminstitute.com
ontariopetroleuminstitute.com
www.facebook.com/700315586681356
twitter.com/opi1963
Overview: A medium-sized provincial organization founded in 1963
Mission: To promote responsible exploration & development by Ontario's oil, gas, hydrocarbon storage, & solution-mining industries
Chief Officer(s):
Hugh Moran, Executive Director
hughmoran@ontariopetroleuminstitute.com
Finances: *Funding Sources:* Sponsorships
Membership: *Member Profile:* Geologists in Ontario; Geophysicists; Explorationists; Producers; Contractors; Petroleum engineers; Companies involved in the oil & gas, hydrocarbon storage, & solution mining industries
Activities: Liaising with government agencies; Disseminating information to members; Increasing public awareness of the importance of the industry in Ontario; *Library:* Ontario Oil, Gas, & Salt Resources Library
Meetings/Conferences: • Ontario Petroleum Institute 2015 54th Conference & Trade Show, May, 2015, Oakwood Resort, Grand Bend, ON
Scope: Provincial
Description: Presentation of papers about oil & natural gas exploration, production, & storage
Contact Information: E-mail: opi@ontpet.com
Publications:
• Ontario Oil & Gas
Type: Magazine; *Accepts Advertising*; *Editor:* Carly Peters
Profile: Articles about the oil & gas industry & technical features
• Ontario Petroleum Institute Conference Proceedings
Frequency: Annually; *Price:* $50
Profile: Topics presented by guest speakers from around the world at the Institute's annual conference & trade show
• Ontario Petroleum Institute Membership Directory
Type: Directory; *Frequency:* Annually; *Accepts Advertising*
Profile: Listings & advertising are available to members of the Ontario Petroleum Institute only
• OPI [Ontario Petroleum Institute Inc.] Newsletter
Type: Newsletter; *Frequency:* Bimonthly; *Accepts Advertising*; *ISSN:* 14802201
Profile: Membership updates, reports, conferences, & legislation information

Ontario Pharmacists' Association (OPA)

#800, 375 University Ave., Toronto ON M5G 2J5
Tel: 416-441-0788; *Fax:* 416-441-0791
mail@opatoday.com
www.opatoday.com
Overview: A medium-sized provincial organization
Mission: To promote excellence in the practice of pharmacy & the wellness of patients; To act as the voice of pharmacists throughout Ontario
Chief Officer(s):
Dennis Darby, Chief Executive Officer
ddarby@opatoday.com
Amedeo Zottola, CFO & COO
azottola@opatoday.com
Allan H. Malek, Vice-President, Professional Affairs
amalek@opatoday.com
Lisa Mayeski, Director, Corporate Development & Partnerships
lmayeski@opatoday.com
Deborah McNorgan, Director, Communications
dmcnorgan@opatoday.com
Eija Kanniainen, Manager, Insurance Services
ekanniainen@opatoday.com
Eric Li, Manager, Pharmacy Policy
eli@opatoday.com
Wendy Furtenbacher, Coordinator, Membership
wfurtenbacher@opatoday.com
Finances: *Funding Sources:* Membership fees; Sponsorships
Membership: 7,200; *Member Profile:* Pharmacists throughout Ontario, who work in settings such as hospitals, long-term care facilities, community pharmacies, universities, & government; Pharmacists in training
Activities: Operating the Drug Information & Research Centre in Toronto; Providing continuing education; Advocating for pharmacists & their patients; Offering networking opportunities; *Speaker Service:* Yes
Meetings/Conferences: • Ontario Pharmacists' Association 2015 Conference, May, 2015, Ottawa, ON
Scope: Provincial
Attendance: 600
Description: An annual event for Ontario's pharmacists, featuring the annual general meeting of the association, an educational program, keynote speaker presentations, a showcase of new products & services, an awards presentation, networking opportunities, & social events
Contact Information: Events & Development Specialist: Kristen Stamper, Phone: 416-441-0788, ext. 4247; kstamper@opatoday.com
Publications:
• The Ontario Pharmacist
Type: Magazine; *Frequency:* Quarterly; *Accepts Advertising*; *Price:* Free with Ontario Pharmacists' Association membership
Profile: Current issues of interest to Ontario's pharmacists & pharmacists in training

Ontario Philharmonic (OP)

PO Box 444, Oshawa ON L1H 7L5
Tel: 905-579-6711
contact@ontariophil.ca
www.ontariophil.ca
www.facebook.com/176411532317
Previous Name: Oshawa-Durham Symphony Orchestra
Overview: A small local charitable organization founded in 1957 overseen by Orchestras Canada
Mission: To bring fine orchestral music to residents of the area by operating a high-quality orchestra
Chief Officer(s):
Monica Anguiano, Executive Director
executive@ontariophil.ca
Charles S. Morison, Chair
Finances: *Funding Sources:* Municipal & provincial grants; fundraising; ticket sales; donations; sponsorship
Activities: *Library*

Ontario Physical & Health Education Association (OPHEA)

#608, 1 Concorde Gate, Toronto ON M3C 3N6
Tel: 416-426-7120; *Fax:* 416-426-7373
Toll-Free: 888-446-7432
www.ophea.org
www.facebook.com/OpheaCanada
twitter.com/opheacanada
www.youtube.com/opheacanada
Overview: A medium-sized provincial organization
Mission: To support communities & schools to encourage healthy active living
Chief Officer(s):
Heather Sears, President
Chris Markham, Executive Director & CEO, 416-426-7126
Activities: Promoting physical activity, & health & physical literacy; Providing program supports to schools & communities; Forming partnerships; Engaging in advocacy activities
Awards:
• Ophea Award of Distinction (Award)
To recognize a leader in the advancement of active, healthy living opportunities for children & youth
• Ophea Award for Outstanding Contribution (Award)
To recognize a person or organization for contributions to the lives of children & youth in areas of health & physical education, promotion, advocacy, or community development
• Ophea School Community Award (Award)
To recognize a school community that has demonstrated excellence in successfully bringing together all members of the community
• Ophea Award for Outstanding New Professional (Award)
To recognize an individual who has been working in the health & education sector for five years or less
Publications:
• e-Connection [a publication of the Ontario Physical & Health Education Association]
Type: Newsletter
• OPHEA [Ontario Physical & Health Education Association] Annual Report
Type: Yearbook; *Frequency:* Annually

Ontario Physiotherapy Association (OPA)

#210, 55 Eglinton Ave. East, Toronto ON M4P 1G8
Tel: 416-322-6866; *Fax:* 416-322-6705
Toll-Free: 800-672-9668
physiomail@opa.on.ca
www.opa.on.ca
www.linkedin.com/company/2385075
www.facebook.com/OntarioPT
twitter.com/OntarioPT
www.youtube.com/user/OntarioPhysiotherapy
Overview: A medium-sized provincial organization founded in 1964 overseen by Canadian Physiotherapy Association
Mission: To act as a voice for the physiotherapy profession in Ontario; To ensure the provision of quality physiotherapy services to residents of Ontario
Member of: Canadian Physiotherapy Association
Chief Officer(s):
Dorianne Sauvé, Chief Executive Officer
dsauve@opa.on.ca
Stephen Pattpn, President
president@opa.on.ca
Sara Pulins, Manager, Marketing & Communications
spulins@opa.on.ca
Finances: *Funding Sources:* Membership dues; Educational activities
Staff Member(s): 8
Membership: *Member Profile:* Physiotherapists registered with the College of Physiotherapists of Ontario; Support workers; Students
Activities: Liaising with provincial government ministries, such as the Ministry of Health & Long Term Care & the Ministry of Finance, as well as other professional & health care associations; Engaging in advocacy activities; Providing professional development opportunities; Developing resources for members; Increasing public awareness of the profession; *Speaker Service:* Yes
Meetings/Conferences: • Ontario Physiotherapy Association 2015 Annual Conference: InterACTION 2015, March, 2015, Ottawa Marriott, Ottawa, ON
Scope: Provincial
Publications:
• i-Blast
Type: Newsletter; *Price:* Free with Ontario Physiotherapy Association membership
• Physiotherapy Today
Type: Newsletter; *Frequency:* Bimonthly; *Price:* Free with Ontario Physiotherapy Association membership

Ontario Physique Association (OPA)

ON
e-mail: info@physiqueassociation.ca
www.bao.on.ca
www.facebook.com/ontario.physique
twitter.com/AroundtheOPA
Overview: A small provincial organization overseen by Canadian Bodybuilding Federation
Mission: To govern the sport of amateur bodybuilding, fitness & figure in Ontario.
Member of: Canadian Bodybuilding Federation; International Federation of Bodybuilding
Chief Officer(s):
Ron Hache, President
president@physiqueassociation.ca
Al Cook, Vice-President
vicepresident@physiqueassociation.ca
Membership: *Fees:* $100

Ontario Pinzgauer Breeders Association (OPBA)

c/o Terrylynn Scott, RR#1, Orton ON L0N 1N0
Tel: 519-855-4964; *Fax:* 519-855-4964
Overview: A small provincial organization
Mission: To facilitate the exhibition & sale of Pinzgauer cattle in Ontario; To develop interest in the breed
Chief Officer(s):
Terrylynn Scott, Secretary
david.scott1@sympatico.ca
Membership: 1-99; *Member Profile:* Pinzgauer cattle breeders across Ontario

Ontario Pioneers

21 Meadowland Dr., Brampton ON L6W 2R5
Tel: 905-451-5607; *Fax:* 905-453-3996
Overview: A small provincial organization overseen by TelecomPioneers of Canada
Chief Officer(s):
Sheila O'Donoghue, Manager
she.rob@sympatico.ca

Ontario Pipe Trades Council

#206, 400 Dundas St. East, Whitby ON L1N 3X2
Tel: 905-665-3500; *Fax:* 905-665-3400
info@optc.org
www.optc.org
www.facebook.com/pipetradescouncil
twitter.com/Pipe_Trades
Overview: A medium-sized provincial organization
Mission: To promote the many technical, commercial & environmental benefits of the Pipe Trades & maximize their use in the construction industry; to promote the interest of the plumbing, pipe fitting, sprinkler fitting & HVAC industry in the province of Ontario
Chief Officer(s):
Neil McCormack, Business Manager
Membership: 16 local unions

Ontario Plowmen's Association (OPA)

188 Nicklin Rd., Guelph ON N1H 7L5
Tel: 519-767-2928; *Fax:* 519-767-2101
Toll-Free: 800-661-7569
eventadmin@plowingmatch.org
www.plowingmatch.org
Overview: A medium-sized provincial organization founded in 1913
Mission: Provides ledership to local plowing associations; oversees the International Plowing Match; mission is to advance interest & involvement in agriculture by promoting new technologies, environmental & safety issues; preserving the history of soil cultivation
Member of: North American Farm Show Council
Chief Officer(s):
Ray Dedman, 1st Vice-President
Robert MacLean, 2nd Vice-President
Cathy Lasby, Executive Director
Bob Hammell, President
Finances: *Annual Operating Budget:* $250,000-$500,000; *Funding Sources:* Sale of space; gate admissions; sponsorships
Staff Member(s): 5; 200 volunteer(s)
Membership: 1,800 individual + 48 organizations; *Fees:* $1; *Member Profile:* Farmers; agricultural community members; *Committees:* Executive; Jr. Plowing; Management; Queen of the Furrows
Activities: Branch meetings throughout the province

Ontario Plumbing Inspectors Association (OPIA)

129 Dumble Ave., Peterborough ON K9H 5A9
Tel: 705-748-0120
opia@opia.info
www.opia.info/members
Overview: A medium-sized provincial organization founded in 1920
Mission: To promote uniform enforcement of plumbing regulations; close liaison & interchange of ideas & knowledge between members of the OPIA & members of other associations; provide education & training to members & the industry
Member of: World Plumbing Council
Affliation(s): Ontario Ministry of Municipal Affairs, Building Branch
Chief Officer(s):
Doug Flucker, President
Rainier Blundel, Vice President
Finances: *Annual Operating Budget:* $50,000-$100,000; *Funding Sources:* Membership fees
14 volunteer(s)
Membership: 800; *Fees:* $60; *Committees:* Advisory; Auditors; Awards; Bulletin; Certification Review; Code Technical; Conference; Education; Election; Executive; Finance; Future Conference; Membership; Memorial; Nominations; Public Relations; Reciprocal Licensing; Resolutions; Special; Zone Meetings
Activities: CMX Show; CIPH Ex; Annual conference; *Library*

Ontario Podiatric Medical Association (OPMA)

#900, 45 Sheppard Ave. East, Toronto ON M2N 5W9
Tel: 416-927-9111; *Fax:* 416-927-9111
Toll-Free: 866-424-6762
contact@opma.ca
www.opma.ca
www.facebook.com/756620137694740
Overview: A small provincial organization
Mission: To act as the voice of podiatry & podiatrists in Ontario; To advance the profession of podiatry in Ontario; To ensure timely access to high quality foot care services in Ontario in order to serve & protect the public
Member of: American Podriatric Medical Association, Inc., Region 5
Chief Officer(s):
Bruce Ramsden, President
Kevin Orvitz, Vice-President
Martin Brain, Secretary
Peter Higenell, Treasurer
Membership: *Member Profile:* Podiatrists (Doctors of Podiatric Medicine) in Ontario
Activities: Promoting the profession of podiatry in Ontario; Advocating on behalf of the profession; Liaising with government & stakeholders
Meetings/Conferences: • 2015 Annual Ontario Podiatric Medical Association Conference, 2015, ON
Scope: Provincial

The Ontario Poetry Society (TOPS)

#710, 65 Spring Garden Ave., Toronto ON M2N 6H9
www.theontariopoetrysociety.ca
Overview: A small provincial charitable organization founded in 2000
Mission: To establish a democratic organization for members to unite in friendship for emotional support & encouragement in all aspects of poetry, including writing, editing, performing & publishing
Chief Officer(s):
Fran Figge, President
Mel Sarnese, Vice-President
Bunny Iskov, Treasurer
Joan Sutcliffe, Secretary
Finances: *Funding Sources:* Membership fees; contest fees
Membership: *Fees:* $30; *Member Profile:* Poets or fans of poetry
Activities: Events held every other month in different cities throughout the province, including Ottawa, Sarnia & Toronto
Awards:
• Annual Chapbook Contests Awards (Award)
• "No Matter What Shape Your Poem Is" Contest Award (Award)
• Ted Plantos Memorial Award (Award)
• The Second Time Around Poetry Contest Awards (Award)

Ontario Pollution Control Equipment Association (OPCEA)

PO Box 137, Midhurst ON L0L 1X0

Tel: 705-725-0917; *Fax:* 705-725-1068
opcea@opcea.com
www.opcea.com
Previous Name: Ontario Sanitation Equipment Association
Overview: A small provincial organization founded in 1970
Mission: To assist members in the promotion of their services & equipment in Ontario
Affliation(s): Water Environment Association of Ontario
Chief Officer(s):
Kelly Manden, Executive Administrator
Brian Allen, President, 416-743-3751, Fax: 416-743-2038
Wayne Harrison, Vice-President, 905-944-2777, Fax: 905-474-1660
Heinz Held, Treasurer, 905-791-1553, Fax: 905-791-2999
Finances: *Funding Sources:* Membership fees
Membership: 160+; *Fees:* $339 initiation fee; $282 / year; *Member Profile:* Ontario firms that manufacture or distribute environmental & related equipment for the air & water pollution control marketplace
Publications:
• Influents [a publication of the Ontario Pollution Control Equipment Association]
Type: Magazine; *Accepts Advertising*; *Editor:* Cole Kelman
Profile: A combined publication of the Ontario Pollution Control Equipment Association & the Water Environment Association of Ontario,featuring information about forthcoming trade shows & events
• OPCEA [Ontario Pollution Control Equipment Association] Membership Directory & Buyers Guide
Type: Directory; *Frequency:* Annually; *Accepts Advertising*; *Editor:* Steve Davey
Profile: Listings of member companies, with their products & services, distributed to the Ontario marketplace

Ontario Pork Producers' Marketing Board

655 Southgate Dr., Guelph ON N1G 5G6
Tel: 519-767-4600; *Fax:* 519-829-1769
Toll-Free: 877-668-7675
www.ontariopork.on.ca
Overview: A medium-sized provincial organization
Chief Officer(s):
Tess Raay, Director, Strategic Management
teresa.vanraay@ontariopork.on.ca

Ontario Potato Board (OPB)

485 Washington St., Elora ON N0B 1S0
Tel: 519-846-5553; *Fax:* 519-846-8803
info@ontariopotatoes.ca
www.ontariopotatoes.ca
Merged from: Ontario Potato Growers Marketing Board; Fresh Potato Growers of Ontario
Overview: A medium-sized provincial organization founded in 1999
Mission: To provide consumers with high-quality potatoes
Chief Officer(s):
Don Brubacher, General Manager
Activities: Providing information about potatoes, potato processing, storage, preparation, & nutrition;

Ontario Potters Association *See* Fusion; The Ontario Clay & Glass Association

Ontario Poultry Council *See* Poultry Industry Council

Ontario Powerlifting Association

c/o Golden Triangle Powerlifting, 278 Thaler Ave., Kitchener ON N2A 1R6
Tel: 519-894-5913
info@ontariopowerlifting.org
www.ontariopowerlifting.org
Overview: A small provincial organization overseen by Canadian Powerlifting Union
Chief Officer(s):
Dave Hoffman, President
dave.hoffman@ontariopowerlifting.org
Membership: *Fees:* $65; $45 junior/special athlete; $30 associate

Ontario Prader-Willi Syndrome Association (OPWSA)

PO Box 73514, Toronto ON M6C 4A7
Tel: 416-481-8657; *Fax:* 416-981-7788
opwsa@rogers.com
www.opwsa.com
www.facebook.com/106828009519275
Overview: A small provincial charitable organization founded in 1982
Mission: To enhance the quality of life for individuals with Prader-Willi Syndrome
Affliation(s): International Prader-Willi Syndrome Association
Chief Officer(s):
Jessie Phillips, Family Services Coordinator
jessie.opwsa@gmail.com
Dan Yashinsky, Co-chair
dan_yashinsky@hotmail.com
Cathy Mallove, Co-chair
cmallove@sympatico.ca
Finances: *Funding Sources:* Provincial Government
Membership: *Member Profile:* Individuals with PWS, their families, friends & concerned professionals
Activities: Counselling; referral & support services; medical information & resource linkage; province-wide parent groups; teaching seminars; on-site case consultation; client advocacy; *Library* Open to public by appointment

Ontario Prepress Association *See* Digital Imaging Association

Ontario Press Council / Conseil de presse de l'Ontario

#1706, 2 Carlton St., Toronto ON M5B 1J3
Tel: 416-340-1981; *Fax:* 416-340-8724
info@ontpress.com
www.ontpress.com
Overview: A medium-sized provincial organization founded in 1972
Mission: To receive & adjudicate complaints from the public against Ontario newspapers; to defend freedom of expression on behalf of the public & press
Chief Officer(s):
Don McCurdy, Executive Secretary
Finances: *Annual Operating Budget:* $100,000-$250,000; *Funding Sources:* Newspapers
Staff Member(s): 2; 21 volunteer(s)
Membership: 21 individual + 220 daily & community newspapers; 11 public members + 10 journalists; *Committees:* Executive; Finance; Inquiry
Activities: *Speaker Service:* Yes

Ontario Principals' Council (OPC)

180 Dundas St. West, 25th Fl., Toronto ON M5G 1Z8
Tel: 416-322-6600; *Fax:* 416-322-6618
Toll-Free: 800-701-2362
admin@principals.ca
www.principals.ca
www.facebook.com/pages/Ontario-Principals-Council
twitter.com/OPCouncil
Overview: A medium-sized provincial organization founded in 1998
Mission: To support the work of Ontario's principals & vice-principals to provide excellent leadership in the public education system
Chief Officer(s):
Ian McFarlane, Executive Director, 416-322-6600
imcfarlane@principals.ca
Bob Pratt, President, 416-322-6600
president@principals.ca
Peggy Sweeney, Senior Communications Consultant
psweeney@principals.ca
Finances: *Annual Operating Budget:* $3 Million-$5 Million; *Funding Sources:* Membership dues
Staff Member(s): 20
Membership: 5,500; *Fees:* $1133; *Member Profile:* Practising principals & vice-principals from publicly funded elementary & secondary schools across Ontario
Activities: Liaising with government & district school boards; Advocating for public education; Influencing education decision-making; Promoting the professional interests of members; Providing professional educational opportunities for principlas & vice-principals; Offering networking opportunities; *Speaker Service:* Yes
Awards:
• Honorary Life Membership (Award)
• Outstanding Contribution to Education Award (Award)
• Principals Award for Student Leadership (Award)
Publications:
• The Register
Type: Magazine; *Frequency:* 3 times yearly; *Accepts Advertising*; *Editor:* Peggy Sweeney; *Price:* Free with membership in the Ontario Principals' Council
Profile: Articles to build the professional capacity of principals & vice-principals

Ontario Printing & Imaging Association (OPIA)

#135, 3-1750 The Queensway, Toronto ON M9C 5H5
Tel: 905-602-4441; *Fax:* 905-602-9798
www.opia.on.ca
Overview: A medium-sized provincial organization
Mission: To provide leadership for a successful printing & imaging industry in Ontario
Affliation(s): Canadian Printing Industries Association (CPIA); Printing Industries of America (PIA); Graphic Arts Technical Foundation (GATF)
Chief Officer(s):
Kim Stewart, Chair
Membership: *Committees:* Events; Government Affairs; Environment, Health & Safety; Human Resource Services; Membership; Communications; Strategic Planning
Activities: Providing technical advice; Facilitating the exchange of ideas; Offering print referral services
Awards:
• Excellence in Print Awards (Award)

Ontario Processing Vegetable Growers

435 Consortium Ct., Longon ON N6E 2S8
Tel: 519-681-1875; *Fax:* 519-685-5719
www.opvg.org
Overview: A large provincial organization
Mission: To negotiate prices of crops on behalf of growers
Chief Officer(s):
Jim Poel, Vice-Chairman, 519-851-8267
Membership: 600
Meetings/Conferences: • Ontario Processing Vegetable Industry Conference 2015, January, 2015, Four Points by Sheraton, London, ON
Scope: Provincial

Ontario Professional Fire Fighters Association (OPFFA) / Association des pompiers professionnels de l'Ontario (ind.)

292 Plains Rd. East, Burlington ON L7T 2C6
Tel: 905-681-7111; *Fax:* 905-681-1489
www.opffa.org
Previous Name: Provincial Federation of Ontario Fire Fighters
Overview: A medium-sized provincial organization founded in 1997
Affliation(s): International Association of Fire Fighters
Chief Officer(s):
Fred LeBlanc, President
Mark McKinnon, Executive Vice-President
Barry Quinn, Secretary-Treasurer
Jeff Braun-Jackson, Office Manager & Researcher
Membership: *Member Profile:* Full-time professional fire fighters throughout Ontario; *Committees:* Education; Health & Safety & Section 21; Finance; Workplace Safety & Insurance Board; Occupational Disease; Pension; Legislative; Human Relations
Activities: Educating members to negotiate & administer collective agreements
Awards:
• The Ed Hothersall Award (Award)
To recognize an individual who has displayed a dedication for service to their association & the community
• The Patrick J DeFazio Award (Award)
To recognize an individual who has contributed in the area of improving fire fighter health & safety
• The Joe Adamkowski Award (Award)
To recognize an individual who has demonstrated dedication & diligence within their own Local, the OPFFA, or the IAFF
Meetings/Conferences: • Ontario Professional Fire Fighters Association 2015 Annual Legislative Conference, 2015, ON
Scope: Provincial
Description: An opportunity for representatives from across Ontario to meet with Members of Provincial Parliament to advocate issues of concern
• Ontario Professional Fire Fighters Association 2015 18th Annual Convention, 2015
Scope: Provincial

Ontario Professional Foresters Association (OPFA)

#201, 5 Wesleyan St., Georgetown ON L7G 2E2
Tel: 905-877-3679; *Fax:* 905-877-6766
opfa@opfa.ca
www.opfa.ca
Overview: A medium-sized provincial organization founded in 1957
Mission: To operate as a regulatory body for the practice of professional forestry in Ontario; To govern members in accordance with the Ontairo Professional Foresters Act 2000
Chief Officer(s):
Tony Jennings, R.P.F, Executive Director; Registrar

Finances: *Annual Operating Budget:* $100,000-$250,000; *Funding Sources:* Membership fees
Staff Member(s): 7
Membership: 850; *Fees:* Schedule available; *Member Profile:* Registered professional foresters who are committed to services in relation to the development, management, conservation, & sustainability of forest & urban forests; *Committees:* Statutory Committees: Executive; Complaints, Discipline; Registration. Standing Committees: Annual General Meeting; Blue Ribbon Panel; By-Laws; Competency; Communications Working Group; Editorial Board; Finance; Membership Standards; Private Land Forestry Network; Recognition & Awards Website
Activities: *Speaker Service:* Yes
Meetings/Conferences: • Ontario Professional Foresters Association 2015 58th Annual Meeting, April, 2015, ON
Scope: National

Ontario Professional Planners Institute (OPPI) / Institut des planificateurs professionnels de l'Ontario

#201, 234 Eglinton Ave. East, Toronto ON M4P 1K5
Tel: 416-483-1873; *Fax:* 416-483-7830
Toll-Free: 800-668-1448
info@ontarioplanners.on.ca
www.ontarioplanners.on.ca
www.linkedin.com/company/3068747
www.facebook.com/OntarioProfessionalPlannersInstitute
twitter.com/OntarioPlanners
www.youtube.com/user/OntarioPlanners
Overview: A medium-sized provincial organization founded in 1986 overseen by Canadian Institute of Planners
Mission: To act as the voice of Ontario's planning profession; To provide leadership on policies related to planning & development
Affliation(s): Canadian Institute of Planners (CIP)
Chief Officer(s):
Paul J. Stagl, President
pstagl@sympatico.ca
Mary Ann Rangam, Executive Director
executivedirector@ontarioplanners.ca
Robert Fraser, Director, Finance & Administration
finance@ontarioplanners.ca
Loretta Ryan, Director, Public Affairs
policy@ontarioplanners.ca
Brian Brophey, Registrar & Director, Professional Standards
standards@ontarioplanners.ca
Finances: *Funding Sources:* Membership fees; Program & activity revenue
Staff Member(s): 7
Membership: 3,500 planners + 500 students; *Fees:* Schedule available; *Member Profile:* Practising planners throughout Ontario; Students; *Committees:* Discipline; Executive; Governance & Nominating; Professional Standards & Registration
Activities: Offering professional development courses; Preparing position statements, policy papers, & other documents of interest to planners; Presenting awards for excellence in planning
Meetings/Conferences: • Ontario Professional Planners Institute 2015 Conference, 2015
Scope: Provincial
Publications:
• Consultants' Directory [a publication of the Ontario Professional Planners Institute]
Type: Directory
Profile: A source used by OPPI members & potential clients
• Ontario Planning Journal
Type: Journal; *Frequency:* Bimonthly; *Accepts Advertising*; *Editor:* Glenn Miller; *Price:* $55 / year Canada; $65 / year International
Profile: Ontario Professional Planners Institute activities & planning issues
• OPPI [Ontario Professional Planners Institute] Members Update
Type: Newsletter; *Frequency:* Monthly; *Price:* Free with membership in the Ontario Professional Planners Institute
Profile: Recent news from the institute for members only
• Planning by Design: A Healthy Communities Handbook
Type: Handbook
Profile: Produced by the Ontario Professional Planners Institute in partnership with the Ministry of Municipal Affairs & Housing

Ontario Progressive Conservative Party

59 Adelaide St. East, 4th Fl., Toronto ON M5C 1K6
Tel: 416-861-0020; *Fax:* 416-861-9593
Toll-Free: 800-903-6453
www.ontariopc.com
www.facebook.com/ProgressiveConservativePartyofOntario
twitter.com/OntarioPCParty
www.youtube.com/user/ontariopcparty
Also Known As: Ontario PC
Overview: A small provincial organization
Chief Officer(s):
Jim Wilson, Party Leader
Richard Ciano, President

Ontario Prospectors Association (OPA)

c/o Garry Clark, 1000 Alloy Dr., Thunder Bay ON P7B 6A5
Tel: 807-622-3284; *Fax:* 807-622-4156
Toll-Free: 866-259-3727
www.ontarioprospectors.com
Previous Name: Ontario Mineral Exploration Federation (OMEF)
Overview: A small provincial organization founded in 1987
Mission: To advance the interests of prospectors & the mineral exploration industry; To promote ethical standards among prospectors in Ontario; To ensure adherence by members to the code of conduct
Chief Officer(s):
Garry Clark, Executive Director
gjclark@ontarioprospectors.com
Wally Rayner, President
Roger Poulin, Vice-President
John McCance, Secretary:
Membership: 3,000; *Committees:* Audit; Membership; Symposium; Education; Land Use / Access; Issue Resolution; Communications; Policy; Finance
Activities: Engaging in lobbying activities; Designing prospector development initiatives; Providing information; Developing awareness of the industry; Offering networking opportunities; Presenting awards
Publications:
• Building a Dialogue with Aboriginal Communities: A Guide for Junior Exploration Companies & Prospectors
Type: Guide
• The Explorationist [a publication of the Northern Prospectors Association & the Ontario Prospectors Association]
Type: Newsletter; *Frequency:* 10 pa
Profile: Information distributed to OPA members, associates, & government personnel about Ontario's mineralexploration scene
• Ontario Mining & Exploration Directory
Type: Directory
• The Ontario Prospector
Type: Magazine; *Frequency:* Semiannually; *Accepts Advertising*; *Editor:* Cadence Hays
Profile: Conference reports, feature articles, & buyers' guide

Ontario Provincial Police Association (OPPA)

119 Ferris Lane, Barrie ON L4M 2Y1
Fax: 705-721-4867
www.oppa.ca
Overview: A medium-sized provincial organization founded in 1954
Mission: To represent members in negotiations with the Ontario government; to promote safe & healthy work environments
Chief Officer(s):
Jim Christie, President
Martin Bain, Vice-President
Membership: 13,000; *Member Profile:* Civilian & uniform members of the Ontario Provincial Police; retirees; surviving family members

Ontario Provincial Trapshooting Association (OPTA)

c/o 273 Bousfield Cres., Milton ON L9T 3N5
Tel: 905-878-5669
info@trapshooting.on.ca
www.ontariotrap.com
Overview: A small provincial organization
Chief Officer(s):
Neville Henderson, President
neville.s.henderson@cogeco.ca
Pam Muma, Secretary-Treasurer
ppmuma@rogers.com
Finances: *Annual Operating Budget:* Less than $50,000
Membership: 500-999

Ontario Psychiatric Association (OPA)

#100, 2233 Argentia Rd., Mississauga ON L5N 2X7
Tel: 905-813-0105; *Fax:* 905-826-4873
opa@eopa.ca
www.eopa.ca
www.linkedin.com/groups?gid=4618836
www.facebook.com/pages/Ontario-Psychiatric-Association/146883128706932
twitter.com/OntPsychAssoc
Overview: A medium-sized provincial organization founded in 1956
Mission: To represent Ontario psychiatrists in relationships with governments at all levels, universities & other associations
Chief Officer(s):
Gary Chaimowitz, President
Finances: *Funding Sources:* Membership dues
Membership: *Fees:* $50 first year memeber; $100 second year member/associate; $280 full; *Member Profile:* Psychiatrists in good standing; Students; Qualified medical practicioners in a related field; *Committees:* Advocacy; Communications; Continuing Education; Finance/Audit; Member Services; Nominations

Ontario Psychological Association (OPA)

#403, 21 St. Clair Ave. East, Toronto ON M4T 1L8
Tel: 416-961-5552
opa@psych.on.ca
www.psych.on.ca
www.facebook.com/114986531859137
Overview: A medium-sized provincial organization founded in 1947
Mission: To advance the practice & science of psychology in Ontario communities; To promote the highest ethical standards in the profession
Chief Officer(s):
Connie Kushnir, President
Janet Kasperski, Chief Executive Officer
Membership: *Fees:* $499; $195 first time member; $450 affiliate; $338 first time affiliate; $225 new graduate affiliate; $25 graduate student; $15 undergrad student; *Member Profile:* Psychologists who reside in Ontario; *Committees:* Audit and Finance; Auto Insurance Taskforce; Communications; Convention; Disaster Response Network; Diversity Taskforce; Early Career Psychologists; Ethics and Policy; Governance; Membership; Mental Health Accessibility Taskforce; Ministry of Education Liaison; Nominations; ONPsych; Public Education; Referral Service Taskforce; Prescriptive Authority; Section on Psychology in Education
Activities: Engaging in advocacy activities; Providing educational opportunities; Offering information to the public
Meetings/Conferences: • 2015 Ontario Psychological Association Annual Conference, April, 2015, The King Edward Hotel, Toronto, ON
Scope: Provincial
• 2016 Ontario Psychological Association Annual Conference, April, 2016, The King Edward Hotel, Toronto, ON
Scope: Provincial
Publications:
• Psychology Ontario
Type: Magazine

Ontario Public Buyers Association, Inc. (OPBA)

Ridley Square, #361, 111 Fourth Ave., St Catharines ON L2S 3P5
Tel: 905-682-2644
info@opba.ca
www.opba.ca
Overview: A medium-sized provincial organization founded in 1952
Mission: To promote the ethical & effective expenditure of public funds through the principles of professional procurement
Affliation(s): National Institute of Governmental Purchasing, Inc.; Institute of Purchasing & Supply of Great Britain; International Federation of Purchasing & Materials Management
Chief Officer(s):
Lisa Buitenhuis, President
James Macintyre, Vice President
Bart Menage, Secretary
Barbara Cosby, Treasurer
bcosby@stcatherines.ca
Finances: *Annual Operating Budget:* $100,000-$250,000; *Funding Sources:* Membership dues
Staff Member(s): 3; 20 volunteer(s)
Membership: 400 individual + 25 senior/lifetime; *Fees:* $225; discount for multiple members; *Committees:* Professional Development; Communications; Legal; Newsletter; Technology; Professional Relations; Management Issues; Symposium; Benchmarking
Activities: *Rents Mailing List:* Yes; *Library:* OPBA Specification Library

Ontario Public Health Association (OPHA) / Association pour la santé publique de l'Ontario

#1850, 439 University Ave., Toronto ON M5G 1Y8
Tel: 416-367-3313; *Fax:* 416-367-2844
Toll-Free: 800-267-6817
info@opha.on.ca
www.opha.on.ca
www.linkedin.com/company/ontario-public-health-association
www.facebook.com/195756817126713
twitter.com/OPHA_Ontario
twitter.com/nutritionrc
Overview: A medium-sized provincial charitable organization founded in 1949 overseen by Canadian Public Health Association
Mission: To provide leadership on issues affecting public health in Ontario, such as preserving the environment, promoting disease prevention, narrowing health disparities & reducing poverty; To strengthen the influence of persons involved in public & community health across Ontario
Chief Officer(s):
Sue Makin, President
Barb Prud'homme, Knowledge Management Coordinator, 416-367-3313 Ext. 256
barbp@opha.on.ca
Finances: *Funding Sources:* Membership fees; Sponsorships
Membership: 350; *Fees:* $85 students, retired persons; $150 individuals; $1,750 organizational member; *Member Profile:* Individuals & constituent societies interested in advancing public health
Activities: Providing education opportunities; Analyzing policy; Advocating for public health policies to improve the health of Ontarians; Liaising with governments; Partnering with other organizations to address broader elements of public health issues
Meetings/Conferences: • Ontario Public Health Association 2015 Annual Conference & General Meeting, 2015
Scope: Provincial
Description: A review of association bylaws, presentation of the annual report, & the appointment of the Board of Directors
Publications:
• Ontario Public Health Association E-Bulletin
Type: Newsletter; *Frequency:* Monthly
Profile: Current topics in public health & information about the association's workgroups & partnerships
• Public Health Today
Type: Magazine; *Price:* Free with membership in the Ontario Public Health Association

Ontario Public Interest Research Group (OPIRG) / Groupe de recherche d'intérêt public de l'Ontario

North Borden Building, #101, 563 Spadina Ave., Toronto ON M5S 2J7
Tel: 416-978-7770; *Fax:* 416-971-2292
opirg.toronto@utoronto.ca
www.opirg.org
Overview: A medium-sized provincial organization founded in 1973
Mission: To make information available to the general public that enables them to make informed decisions on issues & understand & possibly influence decisions made by others on their behalf; to provide an alternative to the information provided by the academic community, government & business; to offer an analysis of environmental & social issues aimed at motivating change & placing issues in the broader social, economic & political perspective in which they need to be understood
Chief Officer(s):
, Chief Returning Officer
cro.opirgtoronto@gmail.com
Finances: *Annual Operating Budget:* $50,000-$100,000; *Funding Sources:* Student & community membership fees
Staff Member(s): 2; 50 volunteer(s)
Membership: 30,000; *Fees:* $1-$5; *Member Profile:* U of T students mostly; *Committees:* Environment; Anti-Racism; Education; Global
Activities: Activism; education; research; action; social & environmental justice; *Speaker Service:* Yes; *Library* by appointment

OPIRG Brock
Brock University, Almuni Student Centre, #204, 500 Glenridge Ave., St Catharines ON L2S 3A1
Tel: 905-688-5555; *Fax:* 905-378-5701
info@opirgbrock.org
www.opirgbrock.org
www.facebook.com/opirgbrock
twitter.com/opirgbrock/
plus.google.com/115989504119091960180
Chief Officer(s):
Em (Matthew) Heppler, Coordinator, Promotions & Public Relations

OPIRG Carleton
Carleton University, 326 Unicentre, 1125 Colonel By Dr., Ottawa ON K1S 5B6
Tel: 613-520-2757; *Fax:* 613-520-3989
opirgadmin@gmail.com
www.opirg-carleton.org

OPIRG Guelph
University of Guelph, 1 Trent Lane, Guelph ON N1G 2W1
Tel: 519-824-2091; *Fax:* 519-824-8990
opirg@uoguelph.ca
www.opirgguelph.org
Chief Officer(s):
Mandy Hiscocks, Coordinator, Volunteer & Programming

OPIRG Kingston
Queens University, The Grey House, 51 Bader Lane, Kingston ON K7L 3N6
Tel: 613-533-3189
info@opirgkingston.org
www.opirgkingston.org
twitter.com/opirgkingston

OPIRG McMaster
McMaster University, MUSC 229, 1280 Main St. West, Hamilton ON L8S 4S4
Tel: 905-525-9140
opirg@mcmaster.ca
www.opirg.ca

OPIRG Peterborough
751 George St. North, 1st Fl., Peterborough ON K9H ET2
Tel: 705-741-1208
opirg@trentu.ca
www.opirgpeterborough.ca
Chief Officer(s):
Yolanda Jones, Coordinator

OPIRG Windsor
University Of Windsor, 252 Dillon Hall, Windsor ON N9B 3P4
Tel: 519-253-3000
opirg@uwindsor.ca
opirg.uwindsor.ca
Chief Officer(s):
Samina Yousuf Esha, President

OPIRG York
York University, C449 Student Centre, 4700 Keele St., Toronto ON M3J 1P3
Tel: 416-736-5724; *Fax:* 416-650-8014
opirgyork@gmail.com
www.opirgyork.ca
www.facebook.com/opirg.yorku
twitter.com/opirgyork
Chief Officer(s):
Imran, Coordinator of Administration and Informatio
imran@opirgyork.ca

Waterloo PIRG
Univ. of Waterloo, Student Life Centre, #2139, 200 University Ave. West, Waterloo ON N2L 3G1
Tel: 519-888-4882; *Fax:* 519-725-3093
info@wpirg.org
www.wpirg.org
Chief Officer(s):
Tammy Kovich, Coordinator, Programming & Volunteer Support
tammy@wpirg.org

Ontario Public Library Association (OPLA)

#201, 50 Wellington St. East, Toronto ON M5E 1C8
Tel: 416-363-3388; *Fax:* 416-941-9581
Toll-Free: 866-873-9867
info@accessola.com
www.accessola.com/opla
Overview: A medium-sized provincial organization founded in 1900
Mission: To foster the expansion & improvement of public library service in Ontario; To support public librarians throughout Ontario; To encourage standards & certification for public library workers
Member of: Ontario Library Association
Chief Officer(s):
Tammy Robinson, President
trobinson@oshawalibrary.on.ca
Lila Saab, Vice-President
lsaab@oakville.ca
Joanna Aegard, Secretary
jaegard@tbpl.ca
Laura Carter, Treasurer
lcarter@kfpl.ca
Rudi Denham, Editor, HoOPLA
rdenham@st-thomas.library.on.ca
Membership: 1,300+; *Member Profile:* Individuals & organizations interested in librarianship & in library & information service; *Committees:* Child & Youth Services; Readers' Advisory
Activities: Organizing professional development activities for public librarians in Ontario; Facilitating networking opportunities; Liaising with government
Meetings/Conferences: • Ontario Public Library Association 2015 36th Annual General Meeting, January, 2015, Metro Toronto Convention Centre, Toronto, ON
Scope: Provincial
Description: Featuring the introduction of the new council, as well as reports from the association's president, treasurer, & committees
• Ontario Public Library Association 2016 37th Annual General Meeting, 2016, ON
Scope: Provincial
Description: Featuring the introduction of the new council, as well as reports from the association's president, treasurer, & committees
Publications:
• HoOPLA
Type: Newsletter; *Frequency:* Quarterly; *Editor:* Rudi Denham
ISSN: 1192 5175
Profile: Association activities, public library news from around the province, & upcoming events

Ontario Public School Boards Association (OPSBA)

#1850, 439 University Ave., Toronto ON M5G 1Y8
Tel: 416-340-2540; *Fax:* 416-340-7571
webmaster@opsba.org
www.opsba.org
twitter.com/OPSBA_Official
Previous Name: Association of Large School Boards of Ontario
Overview: A medium-sized provincial organization founded in 1988 overseen by Canadian School Boards Association
Mission: To represent Ontario's public school authorities & public district school boards; To advocate on behalf of the public school system in Ontario; To promote & enhance public education
Member of: Canadian School Boards Association
Chief Officer(s):
Michael Barrett, President
Gail Anderson, Executive Director
Florenda Tingle, Executive Coordinator
Finances: *Funding Sources:* Sponsorships
Membership: *Member Profile:* Representatives of public district school boards & public school authorities in Ontario
Activities: Developing policy positions & responses to government legislation & regulations; Providing input on legislation; Establishing partnerships with other organizations
Awards:
• Bernardine Yackman Award (Award)
• Jack A. MacDonald (Award)
• Fred L. Bartlet Award (Award)
Meetings/Conferences: • Ontario Public School Boards' Association 2015 AGM, June, 2015, Westin Trillium House, Blue Mountain, ON
Scope: Provincial
• 2015 Public Education Symposium, January, 2015, Sheraton Centre Hotel, Toronto, ON
Scope: Provincial
Publications:
• Ontario Public School Boards Association Annual Report
Type: Yearbook; *Frequency:* Annually

Ontario Public Service Employees Union (OPSEU) / Syndicat des employées et employés de la fonction publique de l'Ontario

100 Lesmill Rd., Toronto ON M3B 3P8
Tel: 416-443-8888; *Fax:* 416-443-9670
Toll-Free: 800-268-7376
Other Communication: organizing@opseu.org
opseu@opseu.org
www.opseu.org
www.facebook.com/OPSEU?v=app_4949752878
twitter.com/OPSEU
www.youtube.com/user/OPSEUSEFPO
Previous Name: Civil Service Association of Ontario

Overview: A large provincial organization founded in 1911
Mission: To negotiate collective agreements; to conduct membership education; to lobby governments to maintain & improve public services; to defend the principle of social unionism by speaking out on public policy issues such as taxes, free trade, privatization, health care, social services, occupational health & safety, & employment equity.
Member of: National Union of Public and General Employees
Affliation(s): Canadian Labour Council; Ontario Federation of Labour
Chief Officer(s):
Warren (Smokey) Thomas, President
Staff Member(s): 250
Membership: 125,000 + 450 bargaining units; *Member Profile:* Public sector workers; *Committees:* Audit; Women's; Race Relations
Activities: *Awareness Events:* Injured Workers Day, June; *Library:* OPSEU Resource Centre; by appointment
Publications:
• Autumn View
Type: Newsletter; *Frequency:* Quarterly
• In Solidarity
Type: Newsletter; *Frequency:* Quarterly

Ontario Public Supervisory Officials' Association (OPSOA)

1123 Glenashton Dr., Oakville ON L6H 5M1
Tel: 905-845-7003; *Fax:* 905-845-2044
frank_kelly@opsoa.org
www.opsoa.org
Overview: A medium-sized provincial licensing organization founded in 1989
Mission: To achieve excellence in public education for the students of Ontario; To advance the cause of public education; To provide a distinctive voice for public supervisory officials in the province of Ontario; To further common interests in the cause of education in Ontario, by working collaboratively with other organizations & associations; To promote effective leadership through professional growth; To promote ethical practices among the members; To maintain a liaison with &, where appropriate, to advise the Ministry of Education & other partners on matters pertaining to education; To provide welfare, counselling, & advice for members
Chief Officer(s):
Frank Kelly, Executive Director
Finances: *Annual Operating Budget:* $250,000-$500,000
Staff Member(s): 4
Membership: 286; *Fees:* .85 of 1% of annual salary; *Member Profile:* Community of senior educational leaders of school districts

Ontario Public Transit Association (OPTA)

#400, 1235 Bay St., Toronto ON M5R 3K4
Tel: 416-229-6222; *Fax:* 416-969-8916
www.ontariopublictransit.ca
Previous Name: Ontario Community Transit Association
Overview: A medium-sized provincial organization founded in 1997
Mission: To strengthen & improve public transit services in Ontario; To ensure excellence & sustainability in public transit
Chief Officer(s):
Dave Sherlock, Chair
Alex Milojevic, Vice-Chair
Norman Cheesman, Chief Executive Officer
Mike Spicer, Secretary
Pat Delmore, Treasurer
Membership: *Fees:* Annual fees for transportation service providers sales based on operating budget or net sales; $560 for affiliates; *Member Profile:* Representatives of public transit systems; Health & social service agency transportation providers; Government representatives; Suppliers to the industry; Consultants
Activities: Engaging in advocacy activities; Sharing information; *Awareness Events:* OTE, annual conference & trade show
Meetings/Conferences: • Ontario Transportation Exposition 2015, April, 2015, Sheraton Toronto Airport Hotel and the International Centre, Toronto, ON
Scope: Provincial
Publications:
• OPTA [Ontario Public Transit Association] News
Type: Newsletter; *Frequency:* Quarterly
Profile: Association activities & upcoming events

Ontario Public Works Association (OPWA)

#22, 1525 Cornwall Rd., Oakville ON L6J 0B2
Tel: 647-726-0167; *Fax:* 289-291-6477
info@opwa.ca
opwa.ca
www.facebook.com/149305988463789
www.youtube.com/user/apwatv?feature=watch
Overview: A medium-sized provincial organization overseen by Canadian Public Works Association
Mission: The Ontario Public Works Association (OPWA) promotes professional excellence and public awareness through education, advocacy and the exchange of knowledge regarding public works in Ontario.
Member of: American Public Works Association
Chief Officer(s):
Terry Hardy, Executive Director, 647-726-0167, Fax: 289-291-6477
Membership: 630; *Committees:* Adovacy; Young Professionals; Awards; Historical; IT Symposium; APWA Congress Networking; Nominating; Membership; National Public Works Week; Communications; Annual Conference & Awards Luncheon; Education; Special Functions

Ontario Puppetry Association

c/o Mike Harding, 160 Baronwood Ct., Brampton ON L6V 3H8
Tel: 416-895-3492
www.onpuppet.ca
Overview: A small provincial charitable organization founded in 1956
Mission: To promote recognition of puppetry as art; to distribute information on all aspects; to assist in eventual formation of national puppet theatre
Member of: Toronto Theatre Alliance
Affiliation(s): UNIMA International
Chief Officer(s):
Mike Harding, President
mike@applefun.ca
Jamie Ashby, Vice-President
jamesashby@me.com
Membership: 53; *Fees:* $15 student; $30 individual; $60 group; $350 lifetime; *Member Profile:* Puppeteers of different styles & at all levels of expertise
Activities: Professional development for artists

Ontario Real Estate Association (OREA)

99 Duncan Mill Rd., Toronto ON M3B 1Z2
Tel: 416-445-9910; *Fax:* 416-445-2644
Toll-Free: 800-265-6732
info@orea.com
www.orea.com
www.facebook.com/OREAinfo
twitter.com/oreainfo
www.youtube.com/OREAinfo
Overview: A large provincial organization founded in 1922
Mission: To represent the vocational interests of members; To advocate for a better working environment; To communicate with members & the public; To develop educational opportunities for the betterment of the real estate profession; To develop programs to assist members in providing quality services to the public; To develop & administer the educational courses required for registration to trade in real estate on behalf of The Real Estate Council of Ontario
Member of: The Canadian Real Estate Association; International Real Estate Association
Chief Officer(s):
Ron Abraham, President, 905-833-5316
Finances: *Funding Sources:* Membership dues; Education course fees
Staff Member(s): 100; 200 volunteer(s)
Membership: 55,000 individuals; *Fees:* Schedule available; *Member Profile:* Registered real estate brokers or salespeople belonging to local real estate boards; *Committees:* Arbitration & Ethics; Communication; Data Sharing; Education; Finance/Audit; Government Relations; Instructor Review Panel; Leadership; Legal Resource; Ontario Commercial Council; Standard Forms
Meetings/Conferences: • Ontario Real Estate Association 2015 Leadership Conference: Rock Solid Leadership, March, 2015, Westin Harbour Castle, Toronto, ON
Scope: Provincial
Description: Educational & networking opportunities for current & future leaders in the real estate industry, plus the Ontario Real Estate Association Annaul Assembly Meeting & elections
Contact Information: Event Coordinator: Christine Gruber, christineg@orea.com

Ontario Recovery Group Inc. (ORG)

#1, 15 Keith Rd., Bracebridge ON P1L 0A1
Tel: 705-645-0033; *Fax:* 705-645-0017
Toll-Free: 866-356-0033
info@ontariorecoverygroup.com
www.ontariorecoverygroup.com
Also Known As: ORG Inc.
Overview: A small provincial organization founded in 1981
Mission: To promote harmony among members & competitors; to provide members with a means of exchanging information with respect to the towing & recovery industry; to encourage development of a professional approach; to sponsor, sanction & promote training courses; to develop & promote acceptable standards of equipment, facilities & drivers; to develop methods of regulation of standards for the industry; to provide all levels of government & law enforcement with a means of communication to the industry
Chief Officer(s):
Doug Nelson, Executive Director
doug@ptao.org
Finances: *Annual Operating Budget:* Less than $50,000; *Funding Sources:* Membership dues
Staff Member(s): 2; 6 volunteer(s)
Membership: 38; *Fees:* $350; *Member Profile:* Heavy duty tow operators; *Committees:* Executive; Training
Activities: Heavy duty towing & recovery in Ontario; *Speaker Service:* Yes

Ontario Recreation Facilities Association Inc. (ORFA)

#102, 1 Concorde Gate, Toronto ON M3C 3N6
Tel: 416-426-7062; *Fax:* 416-426-7385
Toll-Free: 800-661-6732
Other Communication: admin@orfa.com
info@orfa.com
www.orfa.com
Previous Name: Ontario Arenas Association Inc.
Overview: A medium-sized provincial organization founded in 1947
Mission: To provide leadership for the recreation facility profession in Ontario; To promote the professional operation of recreation facilities throughout the province
Chief Officer(s):
Steve Hardie, RRFA, CIT, CPT, President & Chair
shardie@northperth.ca
John Milton, Chief Administrative Officer
jmilton@orfa.com
Remo Petrongolo, Director, Business Development
rpetrongolo@orfa.com
Terry Piche, RRFA, CIT, Director, Technical
tpiche@orfa.com
Hubie Basilio, Coordinator, Public Relations & Communications
hbasilio@orfa.com
Rebecca Russell, Facilities Librarian
library@orfa.com
Membership: 4,000+; *Member Profile:* Persons who operate & manage recreation facilities in municipalities, First Nations communities, government agencies, educational institutions, & in the private recreation sector; Businesses that support the recreation sector; *Committees:* Aquatics Technical Advisory; Arena Technical Advisory; Grounds Technical Advisory; EXPO Tradeshow; Refrigeration Technical Advisory
Activities: Promoting safe & accessible recreation facilities; Providing training & education programs, such as a program with the Canadian Red Cross - Ontario Zone which leads to the professional designation, Certified Aquatic Professional (CAP); Presenting awards to recognize commitment to the recreation facility industry; *Awareness Events:* Parks & Recreation Month, Ontario; *Library:* Facilities Library
Publications:
• Facility Forum [a publication of the Ontario Recreation Facilities Association Inc.]
Type: Newsletter; *Frequency:* Quarterly; *Accepts Advertising*
Profile: Information for government representatives, municipal chief building officials, municipal supervisors, facility managers, recreationdirectors, libraries, educational institutions, conservation authorities, & museum boards
• Ontario Recreation Facilities Association Inc. Members & Products / Services Directory
Type: Directory; *Frequency:* Annually
• ORFA [Ontario Recreation Facilities Association Inc.] E-News
Type: Newsletter
Profile: Issues & trends that affect the recreation facilities sector

Ontario Recreational Canoeing & Kayaking Association (ORCKA)

#209, 3 Concorde Gate, Toronto ON M3C 3N7

Tel: 416-426-7016; *Fax:* 416-426-7363
info@orcka.ca
www.orcka.ca
www.facebook.com/228950560506530
Previous Name: Canoe Ontario; Ontario Recreational Canoeing Association
Overview: A medium-sized provincial organization founded in 1975
Mission: To promote development of safe, competent & knowledgeable recreational paddlers
Chief Officer(s):
Bruce Hawkins, President, 613-623-9950
bhawkins@orcka.on.ca
Finances: *Annual Operating Budget:* $100,000-$250,000; *Funding Sources:* Trillium Grant
Staff Member(s): 2
Membership: *Fees:* $42.20 - $141.25; *Member Profile:* Canoe, kayak instructors & recreational paddlers in Ontario; *Committees:* Safety; Promotion; Environment; Instructor Service; Membership
Activities: Canoeing in Ontario

Ontario Refrigeration & Air Conditioning Contractors Association (ORAC)
#43, 6770 Davand Dr., Mississauga ON L5T 2G3
Tel: 905-670-0010; *Fax:* 905-670-0474
contact@oraca.ca
www.oraca.ca
Overview: A medium-sized provincial organization
Mission: To represent Ontario's contractor practitioners in the refrigeration & air conditioning trade; To enhance quality & efficiency in the industry to benefit customers
Chief Officer(s):
Dino Russo, President, 905-474-4449
dino@readair.com
David Sinclair, Vice-President, 416-465-7581
dsinclair@toromont.com
Mike Verge, Interim Managing Director, 905-670-0010 Ext. 102
mike.verge@orac.ca
Gregg Little, Treasurer, 905-569-8990
gregg@springbank.com
Membership: *Fees:* $1,500 initiation fee & $500 membership dues for provincial members; $1,500 initiation fee & $1,500 membership dues for associate members; *Member Profile:* Individuals, partnerships, & corporations in Ontario, who are engaged in selling, installing, repairing, & maintaining refrigeration & air conditioning equipment; Individuals, partnerships or corporations in Ontario, who provide materials, equipment, or training to the heating, ventilation, refrigeration & air conditioning industry
Activities: Liaising with government & other organizations that represent trade local, provincial, & national bodies; Managing a state of the art training centre; Educating the public about the profession
Meetings/Conferences: • Ontario Refrigeration & Air Conditioning Contractors Association 2015 AGM & Cruise, April, 2015, Fort Lauderdale, FL
Scope: Provincial

Ontario Regional Poison Information Centre (ORPIC)
The Hospital for Sick Children, 555 University Ave., Toronto ON M5G 1X8
Tel: 416-813-5900
Toll-Free: 800-268-9017; *TTY:* 416-597-0215
www.ontariopoisoncentre.com
Overview: A small provincial organization founded in 1978
Mission: To provide telephone information & advice about exposures to poisonous substances; operates 24 hour, 7 day a week through local & toll free numbers
Member of: Canadian Association of Poison Control Centres
Chief Officer(s):
Lutfi Haj-Assaad, Director, Child Health Services
Activities: *Internships:* Yes

Ontario Registered Music Teachers' Association (ORMTA) / Association des professeurs de musique enregistrés de l'Ontario (APMEO)
PO Box 635, Timmins ON P4N 7G2
Tel: 705-267-1224; *Fax:* 705-264-0978
ormta@ntl.sympatico.ca
www.ormta.org
www.linkedin.com/groups/Ontario-Registered-Music-Teachers-Association-
www.facebook.com/223312484348113
twitter.com/ORMTA
Overview: A medium-sized provincial organization founded in 1885
Member of: Canadian Federation of Music Teachers
Chief Officer(s):
Ron Spadafore, Secretary-Registrar
Membership: 1300; *Fees:* $33.29 auxiliary; $50 regular; *Member Profile:* Music teachers
Activities: Music Writing Competition, March; *Awareness Events:* Canada Music Week, November; *Internships:* Yes

Ontario Research Council on Leisure (ORCOL) / Conseil Ontarien de Recherche en Loisir
c/o Recreation & Leisure Studies, Faculty of Applied Health Sciences, University of Waterloo, Waterloo ON N2L 3G1
e-mail: ahsweb@healthy.uwaterloo.ca
www.orcol.uwaterloo.ca
Overview: A small provincial organization founded in 1975
Mission: To disseminate research about leisure & recreation, including culture, tourism, fitness, & sports
Chief Officer(s):
Bryan Smale, President
Don Reid, Treasurer
Membership: *Member Profile:* Researchers in the field of leisure from academe, government, & consultancies
Publications:
• Leisure / Loisir
Type: Journal; *Frequency:* Semiannually *ISSN:* 1492-7713; *Price:* $40 students; $75 individuals; $100 institutions
Profile: Prepared in cooperation with the Canadian Association for Leisure Studies
• ORCOL [Ontario Research Council on Leisure] Symposium Proceedings
Profile: Abstracts of presentations made at the symposium

Ontario Residential Care Association ***See*** Ontario Retirement Communities Association

Ontario Respiratory Care Society (ORCS)
#401, 18 Wynford Dr., Toronto ON M3C 0K8
Tel: 416-864-9911; *Fax:* 416-864-9916
orcs@on.lung.ca
www.on.lung.ca
Overview: A medium-sized provincial charitable organization
Mission: To improve lung health through the provision of excellent interdisciplinary respiratory care
Chief Officer(s):
Sheila Gordon-Dillane, Director, 416-864-9911 Ext. 236
Libby Groff, Chair, Volunteers
Finances: *Funding Sources:* Sponsorships
Membership: *Member Profile:* Persons involved in respiratory care, such as pulmonary function technologists, nurses, occupational therapists & physiotherapists, dietitians, & social workers; *Committees:* Provincial; Research & Fellowship; Editorial Board; Education; Membership & Program Promotion
Activities: Funding graduate education & research in respiratory care; Providing education & disseminating information for health care professionals; Offering professional expertise to the Ontario Lung Association & other interested groups
Awards:
• ORCS Research Grants (Grant)
• ORCS Fellowship Awards (Award)
• Education Awards for Advanced Respiratory Practice (Award)
Meetings/Conferences: • Ontario Respiratory Care Society 2015 Annual Better Breathing Conference: Global Threats, Local Responses, January, 2015, Toronto Marriott Downtown Eaton Centre, Toronto, ON
Scope: Provincial
Description: A forum for professional education to implement strategies for optimal respiratory health in Ontario
Contact Information: E-mail: orcs@on.lung.ca
Publications:
• ORCS [Ontario Respiratory Care Society] Update
Type: Newsletter; *Frequency:* 3 pa; *Price:* Free with membership in the Ontario Respiratory Care Society
Profile: ORCS activities & respiratory articles
• Research Review [a joint publication of the Ontario Respiratory Care Society & the Ontario Thoracic Society]
Frequency: Annually; *Price:* Free with membership in the Ontario Respiratory Care Society
Profile: Highlights of researchers & their studies
• RHEIG [Respiratory Health Educators Interest Group] Connections
Frequency: 3 pa; *Price:* Free with membership in the Ontario Respiratory Care Society
Profile: Published by the Respiratory Health Educators Interest Group for members of the group

Ontario Restaurant, Hotel & Motel Association (ORHMA)
#8-201, 2600 Skymark Ave., Mississauga ON L4W 5B2
Tel: 905-361-0268; *Fax:* 905-361-0288
Toll-Free: 800-668-8906
info@orhma.com
www.orhma.com
www.facebook.com/ORHMA
twitter.com/orhma
Previous Name: Ontario Hotel & Motel Association
Overview: A medium-sized provincial organization founded in 1999 overseen by Hotel Association of Canada Inc.
Mission: To foster a positive business climate for the hospitality industry in Ontario; To represent members before municipal & provincial governments
Chief Officer(s):
Darren Sim, Chair
Tony Elenis, President & CEO, 905-361-0268
telenis@orhma.com
Staff Member(s): 9
Membership: 4,000+; *Fees:* Schedule available, based upon volume of sales for foodservice members, & number of rooms for accommodation members; $650 associate members; $185 s; *Member Profile:* Foodservice & accommodation establishments; Industry suppliers; Instructors & students
Activities: Liaising with government; Providing educational services

Ontario Retail Farm Equipment Dealers' Association ***See*** Canada East Equipment Dealers' Association

Ontario Retail Lumber Dealers Association ***See*** Lumber & Building Materials Association of Ontario

Ontario Retirement Communities Association (ORCA)
#202, 2401 Bristol Circle, Oakville ON L6H 6P1
Tel: 905-403-0500; *Fax:* 905-829-1594
Toll-Free: 888-263-5559
info@orcaretirement.com
www.orcaretirement.com
twitter.com/ORCAhomes
www.youtube.com/user/ORCAhomes
Previous Name: Ontario Residential Care Association
Overview: A small provincial organization founded in 1977
Mission: To support high quality retirement communities throughout Ontario; To act as the voice of retirement communities in Ontario
Chief Officer(s):
Laurie Johnston, Chief Executive Officer
Membership: 534 retirement residences; *Member Profile:* Retirement residences across Ontario
Activities: Setting operating standards; Conducting inspections; Accrediting Ontario-based retirement residences; Influencing public policy; Educating members; Enhancing public awareness
Awards:
• Rick Winchell Resident of the Year Award (Award)
• The Award of Excellence (Award)
To honour leader in service excellence, quality, & innovation
Meetings/Conferences: • Ontario Retirement Communities Association "Together We Care" Convention 2015, March, 2015, Metro Toronto Convention Centre, Toronto, ON
Scope: Provincial
Description: Canada's largest gathering of retirement and long term care professionals.
Contact Information: maureen@orcaretirement.com; Phone: 905-403-0500 Ext. 231

Ontario Rett Syndrome Association (ORSA)
PO Box 50030, London ON N6A 6H8
Tel: 519-474-6877; *Fax:* 519-850-1272
www.rett.ca
www.facebook.com/OntarioRettSyndromeAssociation
twitter.com/OntarioRettSA
Overview: A small provincial charitable organization founded in 1991
Mission: To ensure that girls & women with Rett Syndrome are enabled to achieve their full potential & enjoy the highest quality of life within their community
Chief Officer(s):
Terry Boyd, President
Cynthia Martineau, Contact, Eastern Ontario Chapter
Joseph Moriceau, Contact, Central Ontario Chapter, 416-651-3143
jmoriceau@deloitte.ca

Shari Hamelin, Contact, Western Ontario Chapter, 519-429-3136
jhamelin1@sympatico.ca
Finances: *Annual Operating Budget:* $50,000-$100,000; *Funding Sources:* Donations; Nevada tickets; fundraising events
Staff Member(s): 11
Membership: 125; *Fees:* $30; *Member Profile:* Families & friends of women/girls with Rett Syndrome
Activities: Workshops; information; support; *Library:* Rett Syndrome Resource Centre Canada; by appointment
Meetings/Conferences: • Ontario Rett Syndrome Association 2015 Conference, 2015, ON
Scope: Provincial

Ontario Rheumatology Association (ORA)

#244, 12 - 16715 Yonge St., Newmarket ON L3X 1X4
Tel: 905-952-0698; *Fax:* 905-952-0708
admin@ontariorheum.ca
ontariorheum.ca
Overview: A small provincial organization founded in 2001
Mission: To represent Ontario Rheumatologists and promote their pursuit of excellence in Arthritis care in Ontario.
Affliation(s): Canadian Rheumatology Association
Chief Officer(s):
Arthur Karasik, President
president@ontariorheum.ca
Meetings/Conferences: • Ontario Rheumatology Association 2015 Annual Meeting, May, 2015, JW Marriott, Minett, ON
Scope: Provincial

Ontario Rifle Association (ORA)

c/o ORA Membership Secretary, PO Box 22019, Stn. Elmwood Square, St. Thomas ON H5R 6A1
e-mail: oraatt@yahoo.ca
www.ontariorifleassociation.org
Overview: A medium-sized provincial organization founded in 1868
Affliation(s): Dominion of Canada Rifle Association
Chief Officer(s):
Fazal Mohideen, Secretary
orafazal@bell.net
Membership: *Fees:* $157 Probationary Basic; $182 Probationary ORA Membership with Associate DCRA; $257 Probationary ORA Membership with Full DCRA

Ontario Ringette Association (ORA) / Association de ringuette de l'Ontario

#207, 3 Concorde Gate, Toronto ON M3C 3N7
Tel: 416-426-7204; *Fax:* 416-426-7359
admin@ontario-ringette.com
www.ontario-ringette.com
twitter.com/OntRingette
www.youtube.com/channel/UCWGddPSY6p6_X8wQqe1csPw
Overview: A medium-sized provincial organization founded in 1963 overseen by Ringette Canada
Mission: To promote fun, fitness, & friendship in a safe play environment; To be dedicated to quality performance & fair play opportunity for all ages
Member of: Ringette Canada
Chief Officer(s):
Keith Kaiser, President
president@ontario-ringette.com
Michael Beaton, Executive Director, 416-426-7205
ed@ontario-ringette.com
Karla Romphf, Director, Technical, 416-426-7206
tech@ontario-ringette.com
Rose Snagg, Coordinator, Administration, 416-426-7204
admin@ontario-ringette.com
Membership: *Committees:* Officiating Development; Games & Tournament; Adult Development; Elite Development; Membership Services; Coaching Development; Sport Development; Rules Development

Ontario Road Builders' Association (ORBA)

#1, 365 Brunel Rd., Mississauga ON L4Z 1Z5
Tel: 905-507-1107; *Fax:* 905-890-8122
www.orba.org
www.facebook.com/OntarioRoadBuildersAssociation
twitter.com/onroadbuilders
Overview: A medium-sized provincial organization founded in 1926 overseen by Canadian Construction Association
Mission: To act as the voice of the Ontario road building industry; To maintain high standards in the road building industry; To promote worker health & safety
Chief Officer(s):
Geoff Wilkinson, Executive Director
Geoff@orba.org
Karen Renkema, Director, Government Relations
karen@orba.org
Kathryn Thomas, Director, Member Services
kathryn@orba.org
Kim Le Fort, Office Manager & Coordinator, Events
kim@orba.org
Patrick McManus, Policy Analyst
patrick@orba.org
Membership: 75+ road building contractors; 85+ associate members; *Fees:* Schedule available based upon annual civil contracting volume; *Member Profile:* Road building contractors across Ontario; Organizations that manufacture or supply products & services to the road building industry; *Committees:* Area Maintenance Contractor Council; Associate Members; Contacts & Documents; Education, Training, & Industry Promotion; Structures & Concrete Technical; Transportation & Equipment; Environment; Hot Mix Technical; Occupational Health & Safety; CCA Civil Infrastructure Council
Activities: Advocating for road building contractors throughout Ontario; Promoting the benefits of infrastructure investment; Providing education & training; Offering information & research
Meetings/Conferences: • 88th Ontario Road Builders' Association 2015 Annual General Meeting & Convention - "The Road Ahead", February, 2015, The Fairmont Royal York, Toronto, ON
Scope: Provincial
Description: Informative sessions of interest to members of the road building industry
Contact Information: Office Manager & Coordinator, Events: Kim Le Fort, E-mail: kim@orba.org
Publications:
• ORBA [Ontario Road Builders' Association] Directory
Type: Directory; *Frequency:* Annually; *Price:* Free with Ontario Road Builders' membership
Profile: Member contact information, plus product & services information
• Road Builder Magazine
Type: Magazine; *Frequency:* Semiannually
Profile: Industry issues, new technology, & articles about member companies for Ontario Road Builders' Association members, Ministry of Transporation staff, as well as consulting engineers

Ontario Roadrunners Association

#211, 3 Concorde Gate, Toronto ON M4E 3N7
Tel: 416-691-9556
info@ontarioroadrunners.com
www.ontarioroadrunners.com
Overview: A small provincial organization
Mission: Promotes roadrunning & provides runners of all ages & abilities the opportunity to achieve personal excellence through programs & services founded on the principles of safety & fair play
Membership: *Fees:* $35, $30 student/senior

Ontario Rock Garden Society

c/o Carol Clark, 88 Cottonwood Dr., Toronto ON M3C 2B4
e-mail: info@onrockgarden.com
www.onrockgarden.com
Overview: A small provincial organization founded in 1984
Mission: To promote the study & cultivation of alpine & related garden plants & the creation of rock gardens
Member of: North American Rock Garden Society
Chief Officer(s):
Donna McMaster, Chair
Finances: *Annual Operating Budget:* Less than $50,000; *Funding Sources:* Membership fees; plant sales
Membership: 450; *Fees:* $25 individual; $30 family or overseas; $10 student
Activities: 10 meetings per year; spring & fall plant sales; seed exchange in Dec.; handbook listing members, gardens to visit, mail order & non-mail order services; *Speaker Service:* Yes

Ontario Rodeo Association (ORA)

#3, 62 Gruhn St., Kitchener ON N2G 1S6
Tel: 519-954-4635
www.orarodeo.com
www.facebook.com/orarodeo
www.twitter.com/orarodeo
Overview: A small provincial organization founded in 1957
Mission: To promote rodeo in Ontario & produce a standard set of rules to be followed by the rodeo cowboys & rodeo producers & also, a set of rules to protect the stock used in rodeos from inhumane treatment
Chief Officer(s):
Joe Scully, President
Earl Foster, Vice-President
Membership: 375; *Fees:* $125 contestant, $93.75 contract; $31.25 associate
Activities: Seven standard events: Saddle Bronc Riding; Bareback Bronc Riding; Bull Riding; Calf Roping; Steer Wrestling; Team Roping & Ladies Barrel Racing; three optional events: Jr. Steer Riding & Ladies Breakaway Roping & Jr. Barrel Racing

Ontario Rowing Association (ORA)

#206, 19 Waterman Ave., Toronto ON M4B 1Y2
Tel: 416-759-8405
rowontarioadmin@rowontario.ca
www.rowontario.ca
www.facebook.com/pages/ROWONTARIO/84916401948
twitter.com/ROWONTARIO
Overview: A medium-sized provincial organization founded in 1970 overseen by Rowing Canada Aviron
Mission: To promote the sport of rowing at all levels in Ontario; to provide assistance to member clubs in the encouragement of competitive & recreational rowing; to maintain the principles of amateurism; to develop provincial rowing teams to represent Ontario at the Canada Games; to host an annual provincial rowing championship
Member of: Rowing Canada Aviron
Affliation(s): Ontario Sport Council
Chief Officer(s):
Derek Ventor, Executive Director
derek@rowontario.ca
Finances: *Funding Sources:* Membership dues; services; government grants; donations
Membership: 6,000 individuals; *Fees:* $1 non-rower; $3 highschool; $10 sport rower; $44 competitive rower; $275 club; *Member Profile:* Organized amateur rowing clubs in Ontario; *Committees:* Adaptive; Umpire

Ontario Rural Softball Association (ORSA)

c/o Secretary-Treasurer, 716029 - 18th Line, RR#1, Innerkip ON N0J 1M0
Tel: 519-469-3593
www.ontarioruralsoftball.ca
Overview: A medium-sized provincial organization founded in 1931 overseen by Softball Ontario
Mission: To promote softball in rural districts, communities & small villages
Member of: Canadian Amateur Softball Association; Softball Ontario
Chief Officer(s):
Earl Hall, President, 519-882-1599
Carl Littlejohns, Secretary-Treasurer
clittlejohnsorsa@live.ca
Finances: *Funding Sources:* Sponsors; Partners; Government grants; Player/team fees

Ontario Rural Softball Association (ORSA)

716029 - 18th Line, RR#1, Innerkip ON N0J 1M0
Tel: 519-469-3593; *Fax:* 519-469-8439
www.ontarioruralsoftball.ca
Overview: A small provincial organization founded in 1931
Mission: To supply softball to small communities with a population of less than 12,000
Member of: Softball Ontario
Chief Officer(s):
Don McConnell, President
don.mcconnell@conservationhamilton.ca
Carl Littlejohns, Secretary-Treasurer
clittlejohnsorsa@live.ca
Finances: *Annual Operating Budget:* Less than $50,000; *Funding Sources:* Provincial government
18 volunteer(s)
Membership: 100-499

Ontario Safety League (OSL) / Ligue de sécurité de l'Ontario

#212, 2595 Skymark Ave., Mississauga ON L4W 4L5
Tel: 905-625-0556; *Fax:* 905-625-0677
www.ontariosafetyleague.com
Overview: A medium-sized provincial licensing charitable organization founded in 1913
Mission: Safety through education with an emphasis on traffic & child safety
Affliation(s): Canada Safety Council; Provincial Safety Leagues/Councils
Chief Officer(s):
Brian J. Patterson, President & General Manager
Finances: *Annual Operating Budget:* $1.5 Million-$3 Million
Staff Member(s): 10

Membership: 300; *Fees:* $30-$300
Activities: Video production sales; courses for instructors of all vehicle types & road safety professionals; safety services for commercial fleets; *Speaker Service:* Yes; *Library:* OSL Film & Video Library

Ontario Sailing / Association de voile de l'Ontario
65 Guise St. East, Hamilton ON L8L 8B4
Tel: 905-572-7245; *Fax:* 905-572-6056
Toll-Free: 888-672-7245
info@ontariosailing.ca
www.ontariosailing.ca
www.facebook.com/OntarioSailing
twitter.com/ontariosailing
Also Known As: Sail Ontario
Previous Name: Ontario Sailing Association
Overview: A medium-sized provincial organization founded in 1970 overseen by Sail Canada
Mission: To foster interest in sailing & to promote & encourage proficiency in the sport, particularly among young people in the province of Ontario; to promote sailboat racing events & to encourage the development of skills in sailboat handling & seamanship
Member of: Sail Canada
Affliation(s): International Sailing Federation; Canadian Safe Boating Council
Chief Officer(s):
Glenn Lethbridge, Executive Director
execdir@ontariosailing.ca
Finances: *Annual Operating Budget:* $500,000-$1.5 Million; *Funding Sources:* Membership fees; provincial government; corporate sponsorship; grants
Staff Member(s): 6; 25 volunteer(s)
Membership: 180 clubs/schools/associations; 10,000 families; 100,000 boaters;

Ontario Sailing Association *See* Ontario Sailing

Ontario Sanitation Equipment Association *See* Ontario Pollution Control Equipment Association

Ontario School Bus Association (OSBA)
#304, 1 Eva Rd., Toronto ON M9C 4Z5
Tel: 416-695-9965; *Fax:* 416-695-9977
Toll-Free: 888-675-6722
info@osba.on.ca
www.osba.on.ca
Overview: A medium-sized provincial organization
Chief Officer(s):
Richard Donaldson, Executive Director
Gord Taylor, President
Staff Member(s): 3
Membership: 100-499

Ontario School Counsellors' Association (OSCA)
1 Mountainview Cres., Erin ON N0B 1T0
Tel: 519-800-0872; *Fax:* 519-800-0874
www.osca.ca
Overview: A medium-sized provincial organization founded in 1964
Mission: To provide progressive leadership & to support the work of school teacher-counsellors; committed to shaping a vision of the future through the development of specific initiatives which will influence the direction of change in programs & policies in Ontario
Chief Officer(s):
Marie-Josée Pouliotte, President, 613-742-8960 Ext. 2207, Fax: 613-742-3816
Marie-Josee.Pouliotte@cepeo.on.ca
Staff Member(s): 6; 13 volunteer(s)
Membership: 1,500; *Fees:* $65 statutory/associate; $40 retired
Awards:
• Olive Diefenbaker Award of Merit (Award)
• Russ Seltzer Award for Contribution to Counsellor Education in Ontario (Award)
Deadline: September 15
• Twenty-Fifth Anniversary Award (Award)
Deadline: September 15
• Certificate of Appreciation (Award)
Deadline: September 15
• Marion Axford Award for Elementary Guidance (Award)
Deadline: September 15
• Daryl L. Cook Peer Helping Award (Award)
Deadline: September 15
• The Morgan D. Parmenter Memorial Award (Award)
Deadline: September 15
• Career Education Citation (Award)
Deadline: September 15
• Elmer Huff Award for Media Resources (Award)
Deadline: September 15
• Frank Clute Award for Professional Research (Award)
Deadline: September 15
• Howard R. Beattie Award for Professional Contribution (Award)
Deadline: September 15

Ontario School Library Association (OSLA)
c/o Ontario Library Association, 2 Toronto St., 3rd Fl., Toronto ON M5C 2B6
Tel: 416-363-3388; *Fax:* 416-941-9581
Toll-Free: 866-873-9867
www.accessola.com/osla
Overview: A medium-sized provincial organization founded in 1972
Mission: To act as the voice of elementary & secondary school teacher-librarians in Ontario; To promote teacher-librarians as curriculum leaders; To support student success
Member of: Ontario Library Association
Chief Officer(s):
Isabelle Hobbs, President
President@oslacouncil.org
Membership: *Member Profile:* Teacher-librarians in Ontario; School board consultants
Activities: Advocating for the interests of teacher-librarians; Developing school libraries & school library programs; Providing continuing education; Promoting research related to school libraries
Awards:
• Teacher-Librarian of the Year (Award)
To recognize a teacher-librarian who has demonstrated leadership in the implementation of school library program
• Administrator of the Year (Award)
To recognize a school administrator who has influenced the development of school library information centres & school library programs
• Award for Special Achievement (Award)
To recognize individuals or organizations outside schools & school boards who have supported teacher-librarians & school library information centre development
Publications:
• The Teaching Librarian
Type: Newsletter; *Frequency:* 3 pa; *Editor:* Diana Maliszewski

Ontario Secondary School Teachers' Federation (OSSTF) / Fédération des enseignants des écoles secondaires de l'Ontario (FEESO)
60 Mobile Dr., Toronto ON M4A 2P3
Tel: 416-751-8300; *Fax:* 416-751-3394
Toll-Free: 800-267-7867
www.osstf.on.ca
www.facebook.com/osstfnews
twitter.com/osstf
www.youtube.com/user/OSSTF
Overview: A large provincial organization founded in 1919
Mission: To protect & enhance Ontario's public education system; to establish working conditions for members
Chief Officer(s):
Ken Coran, President & CEO
Harvey Bischof, Vice-President
Paul Elliott, Vice-President
Pierre Côté, General Secretary
Earl Burt, Treasurer
Staff Member(s): 110
Membership: 60,000+; *Member Profile:* Ontario's English & French public high school teachers, occasional teachers, continuing education instructors, educational assistants, speech-language pathologists, psychologists, social workers, secretaries, & plant support personnel
Activities: Working with goverments, school boards, & parents to improve the public education system; Lobbying; Communicating with the media; Preventing the commercialization & privatization of educational institutions; Engaging in negotiations; Sponsoring professional conferences, workshops, & union training; *Library:* Ontario Secondary School Teachers' Federation Research Library;
Awards:
• OSSTF/FEESO Awards of Recognition for Members (Award)
• OSSTF/FEESO Awards for Non-Members (Award)
• OSSTF/FEESO Financial Assistance Awards for Further Education (Award)
• OSSTF/FEESO Grants in Support of Staff Development (Award)
Meetings/Conferences: • Annual Meeting of the Provincial Assembly (AMPA) 2015, March, 2015, The Sheraton Centre Toronto Hotel, Toronto, ON
Scope: Provincial
Attendance: 500+
Publications:
• Education Forum [a publication of the Ontario Secondary School Teachers' Federation]
Type: Magazine; *Frequency:* 3 pa; *Editor:* Wendy Anes Hirschegger
• The Education Team: Education Watch [a publication of the Ontario Secondary School Teachers' Federation]
• Ontario Secondary School Teachers' Federation Update
Type: Newsletter; *Frequency:* Monthly
Profile: News for all Ontario Secondary School Teachers' Federation members

Ontario Securities Commission (OSC)
20 Queen St. West, 20th Fl., Toronto ON M5H 3S8
Tel: 416-593-8314; *Fax:* 416-593-8122
Toll-Free: 877-785-1555; *TTY:* 866-827-1295
inquiries@osc.gov.on.ca
www.osc.gov.on.ca
www.facebook.com/OntarioSecuritiesCommission
twitter.com/OSC_News
www.youtube.com/user/OntarioSecurities
Overview: A medium-sized provincial organization founded in 1928 overseen by Canadian Securities Administrators
Mission: To regulate securities trading in Ontario, through the administration of the Securities Act (Ontario) & the Commodity Futures Act (Ontario); To report to the Legislature, through the minister responsible for the administration of the Acts; To foster a fair & competitive securities market; To protect investors & market integrity
Member of: Canadian Securities Administrators
Chief Officer(s):
Howard Wetston, Q.C., Chair & CEO
Maureen Jensen, Executive Director & CAO
Finances: *Funding Sources:* Fees collected from market participants under the legislation
Publications:
• Ontario Securities Commission Annual Report
Type: Report; *Frequency:* Annually
• OSC [Ontario Securities Commission] Investor News
Type: Newsletter; *Frequency:* Annually
• Statement of Priorities
Type: Report; *Frequency:* Annually

Ontario Seed Corn Growers' Marketing Board *See* Seed Corn Growers of Ontario

Ontario Seed Growers Association (OSGA)
1 Stone Rd. West, Guelph ON N1G 4Y2
Tel: 519-826-4214; *Fax:* 519-826-4224
Toll-Free: 800-265-9751
Overview: A medium-sized provincial organization founded in 1953 overseen by Canadian Seed Growers' Association
Mission: To ensure the supply of genetically pure seed crop
Member of: Canadian Seed Growers Association
Affliation(s): Ontario Soil & Crop Improvement Association
Chief Officer(s):
Harold Rudy, Secretary
Harold.Rudy@ontariosoilcrop.org
Finances: *Funding Sources:* Grower fees; Government
11 volunteer(s)
Membership: 1,200

Ontario Senior Games Association (OSGA)
#310, 3 Concorde Gate, Toronto ON M3C 3N7
Tel: 416-426-7031; *Fax:* 416-426-7226
Toll-Free: 800-320-6423
info@ontarioseniorgames.ca
www.ontarioseniorgames.ca
www.facebook.com/Ontario55plus
Overview: A medium-sized provincial organization
Mission: To provide physical & social activities to senior citizens
Chief Officer(s):
Gail Prior, President
president@ontarioseniorgames.ca
Geoffrey Johnson, Program Coordinator
geoff@ontarioseniorgames.ca
Membership: *Committees:* Rules

Ontario Sewer & Watermain Construction Association (OSWCA)
#300, 5045 Orbitor Dr., Unit 12, Mississauga ON L4W 4Y4

Tel: 905-629-7766; *Fax:* 905-629-0587
info@oswca.org
www.oswca.org
Overview: A small provincial organization
Mission: To represent sewer & watermain construction contractors throughout Ontario; To increase business opportunities for members
Chief Officer(s):
Giovanni Cautillo, Executive Director, 905-629-8658
giovanni.cautillo@oswca.org
Patrick McManus, Manager, Stakeholder Relations and Services, 905-629-8819
patrick.mcmanus@oswca.org
Daniela Di Ilio, Office Coordinator, 905-629-8638
daniela.diilio@oswca.org
Membership: 700+ companies; *Committees:* Young Executives; Government Relations; Members Services; Marketing Initiatives; Education Program; Administration
Activities: Liaising with the Government of Ontario & its agencies; Increasing public awareness about the maintenance of water & wastewater systems in Ontario; Providing apprenticeship training & upgrading training; Informing members of industry developments
Publications:
• Ontario Sewer & Watermain Construction Association Membership Directory
Type: Directory; *Frequency:* Annually; *Accepts Advertising*
Profile: A buyers' guide for products & services used by sewer & watermain construction contractors, municipalities, utilities, & engineers
• Undergrounder [a publication of the Ontario Sewer & Watermain Construction Association]
Type: Magazine; *Frequency:* 3 pa; *Accepts Advertising*
Profile: Association business, industry issues, & regulatory updates available in print or digital editions

Ontario Shade Tree Council ***See*** Ontario Urban Forest Council

Ontario Sheep Association ***See*** Ontario Sheep Marketing Agency

Ontario Sheep Marketing Agency (OSMA)
130 Malcolm Rd., Guelph ON N1K 1B1
Tel: 519-836-0043; *Fax:* 519-836-2531
www.ontariosheep.org
Previous Name: Ontario Sheep Association
Overview: A medium-sized provincial organization founded in 1985
Mission: To represent all aspects of the sheep, lamb, & wool industry in Ontario; To improve the marketing of sheep & enhance producers' returns; To provide the public with safe, quality lamb & related products
Chief Officer(s):
Jennifer MacTavish, General Manager, 519-836-0043 Ext. 23
jmactavish@ontariosheep.org
Membership: *Member Profile:* All producers of sheep & wool in Ontario must register with the Ontario Sheep Marketing Agency
Activities: Advocating on behalf of sheep producers; Educating producers; Providing consumer education; Increasing public awareness of the industry; Developing promotional campaigns; Supporting research in the industry
Awards:
• Ontario Sheep Marketing Agency Scholorship (Scholarship)
Publications:
• The Messenger
Type: Newsletter
Profile: Agency activities, industry news, & upcoming events

Ontario Sheet Metal & Air Handling Group ***See*** Ontario Sheet Metal Contractors Association

Ontario Sheet Metal Contractors Association (OSM)
#26, 30 Wertheim Ct., Richmond Hill ON L4B 1B9
Tel: 905-886-9627; *Fax:* 905-886-9959
shtmetal@bellnet.ca
www.osmca.org
Previous Name: Ontario Sheet Metal & Air Handling Group
Overview: A small provincial organization founded in 1967
Mission: To negotiate & administer all provincial collective agreements between OSM, the Ontario Sheet Metal Workers' & Roofers' Conference & the Sheet Metal Workers International Association.
Chief Officer(s):
Kim Crossman, President, 416-663-4300, Fax: 416-663-4305
kimcrossman@dmcmechanical.com
Wayne Peterson, Executive Director
Membership: *Member Profile:* Contractors engaged in manufacturing, installing, servicing & maintaining of all sheet metal work associated with air handling systems & directly related processes

Ontario Shorthorn Club (OSA)
c/o Dale Asser, PO Box 83, Duntroon ON L0M 1H0
Tel: 705-444-0386
hillhavenshorthorns@sympatico.ca
www.ontarioshorthorns.com
Overview: A small provincial organization
Member of: Canadian Shorthorn Association
Chief Officer(s):
Brigit Martin, Secretary
Finances: *Annual Operating Budget:* Less than $50,000
Membership: 100; *Fees:* $20; *Member Profile:* Shorthorn cattle owners
Activities: *Speaker Service:* Yes

Ontario Shuffleboard Association (OSA)
PO Box 1690, Guelph ON N1H 6Z9
ontarioshuffleboard.com
Overview: A medium-sized provincial organization founded in 1964
Member of: Canadian Shuffleboard Congress
Chief Officer(s):
Rico Beaulieu, President
rick@ritewayaluminum.com

Ontario Sikh & Gurudwara Council (OSGC)
PO Box 38636, 545 Steeles Ave. West, Brampton ON L6Y 4W5
e-mail: OntarioSikh.GurdwaraCouncil@gmail.com
osgc.ca
Overview: A small provincial organization
Mission: To provide leadership to the Sikh community & to arrange social gatherings for its members
Chief Officer(s):
Ranjit S. Dulay, Chair, 647-290-4704
ranjitsinghdulay@hotmail.com
Membership: 62; *Fees:* $51 individual; $251 Gurdwaras

Ontario Simmental Association (OSA)
c/o Debbie Elliot, Line 26 #7062, RR#2, Staffa ON N0K 1Y0
Tel: 519-345-2785; *Fax:* 519-345-2779
ircc@nexicom.net
www.ontariosimmentalassociation.com
Overview: A small provincial organization founded in 1979
Mission: To represent & assist the breeders of Ontario in the development & marketing of Simmental
Member of: Canadian Simmental Association
Chief Officer(s):
Grace Oesch, Secretary
gravandale@netflash.net
Debbie Elliot, Treasurer
dje@djfarmscattle.com
Dan O'Brien, President
dan.obrien@sympatico.ca
Membership: *Fees:* $30 annual; $85 three-year; *Member Profile:* Breeder of Simmental cattle in Ontario
Activities: Shows & sales

Ontario Skeet Shooting Association (OSSA)
PO Box 96, Hampton ON L0B 1J0
Tel: 905-263-8174; *Fax:* 905-263-4870
info@ontarioskeet.com
www.ontarioskeet.com
Overview: A small provincial organization
Mission: To educate persons in the safe & efficient handling of shotguns; to encourage competition in shotgun target shooting; to promote the sport of skeet shooting in the province of Ontario
Member of: Shooting Federation of Canada; National Skeet Shooting Association
Chief Officer(s):
Bill Marsh, Secretary
Brad McRae, President
Finances: *Annual Operating Budget:* Less than $50,000
8 volunteer(s)
Membership: 165; *Fees:* $15

Ontario Sledge Hockey Association (OSHA)
ON
www.alpineontario.ca
www.facebook.com/467967866581968
twitter.com/OSHASledge
Overview: A medium-sized provincial organization
Mission: To oversee three regular season sledge hockey leagues
Member of: Ontario Hockey Federation; Hockey Canada
Chief Officer(s):
Dave Kisel, President, 905-560-8287
dkisel@bell.net
Membership: 20 clubs + 400 players; *Committees:* Rules

Ontario Small Urban Municipalities (OSUM)
c/o Association of Municipalities of Ontario, #801, 200 University Ave., Toronto ON M5H 3C6
Tel: 416-971-9856; *Fax:* 416-971-6191
Toll-Free: 877-426-6527
amo@amo.on.ca
www.osum.ca
Overview: A medium-sized provincial organization
Mission: To take matters which affect Ontario's small urban communities to the attention of the provincial & federal governments
Member of: Association of Municipalities of Ontario
Chief Officer(s):
Paul Grenier, Chair, 905-788-2624
Jim Collard, Vice-Chair & Conference Chair, 905-658-1977
Larry McCabe, Administrative Member, OSUM Executive Committee, 519-524-8344, Fax: 519-524-7209
lmccabe@goderich.ca
Finances: *Funding Sources:* Sponsorships
Membership: 100-499; *Member Profile:* Small urban municipalities in Ontario
Activities: Providing a forum for both elected & appointed municipal officials of Ontario's small urban municipalities to exchange information
Meetings/Conferences: • Ontario Small Urban Municipalities 2015 62nd Annual Conference & Trade Show, April, 2015, Belleville, ON
Scope: Provincial
Attendance: 200+
Contact Information: OSUM Annual Conference & Trade Show Coordinator: Ted Blowes, Phone: 519-271-0250, ext. 241, E-mail: ted.b@quadro.net
• Ontario Small Urban Municipalities 2016 63rd Annual Conference & Trade Show, May, 2016, Stratford, ON
Scope: Provincial
Attendance: 200+
Contact Information: OSUM Annual Conference & Trade Show Coordinator: Ted Blowes, Phone: 519-271-0250, ext. 241, E-mail: ted.b@quadro.net
• Ontario Small Urban Municipalities 2017 64th Annual Conference & Trade Show, May, 2017, Niagara Falls, ON
Scope: Provincial
Attendance: 200+
Contact Information: OSUM Annual Conference & Trade Show Coordinator: Ted Blowes, Phone: 519-271-0250, ext. 241, E-mail: ted.b@quadro.net

Ontario Soccer Association (OSA)
7601 Martin Grove Rd., Vaughan ON L4L 9E4
Tel: 905-264-9390; *Fax:* 905-264-9445
www.soccer.on.ca
www.facebook.com/TheOntarioSoccerAssociation
twitter.com/OSA_Tweeter
www.youtube.com/OSAVideoMaster
Overview: A medium-sized provincial organization founded in 1901 overseen by Canadian Soccer Association
Mission: To provide leadership & support for the advancement of soccer; To provide programs & services
Member of: Canadian Soccer Association
Chief Officer(s):
Ron Smale, President
Lisa Beatty, Executive Director
lbeatty@soccer.on.ca
Staff Member(s): 39
Membership: 500,000 players; 70,000 coaches; 10,000 referees; *Committees:* Discipline & Appeals; Competitions; Information Management System Oversight; League Management; Referee Development; Technical Advisory; Women in Soccer; Rules Review; Audit; Executive; Finance; Governance; Human Resources; Nominations; Risk Management; Strategic Planning

Ontario Society for Autistic Citizens ***See*** Autism Ontario

Ontario Society for Environmental Education (OSEE)
PO Box 587, Lakefield ON K0L 2H0

Tel: 705-652-0923
home.osee.ca
www.facebook.com/OS4EE
Overview: A small provincial organization
Mission: To develop a population that is aware of, & concerned about, the environment & its associated problems, & which has the knowledge, skills, attitudes, motivations & commitment to work individually & collectively toward solutions of current problems & the prevention of new ones (from UNESCO)
Chief Officer(s):
Sherri Owen, President
sherri.owen@osee.ca
Finances: *Annual Operating Budget:* Less than $50,000
Staff Member(s): 2; 10 volunteer(s)
Membership: *Fees:* $40 individual; $20 student; $57 overseas; $300 corporate; *Member Profile:* Teachers & outdoor education leaders
Meetings/Conferences: • EcoLinks 2015
Scope: Provincial

Ontario Society for Environmental Management (OSEM)

85 Irondale Dr., Toronto ON M9L 2S6
Tel: 416-746-9076; *Fax:* 416-745-6761
Overview: A small provincial organization founded in 1976
Mission: To encourage the exchange of information on matters of environmental management through seminars, meetings, position papers, newsletter, etc.; to develop an interdisciplinary forum for information exchange with other professions; to help persons & institutions responsible for decisions affecting the environment to make & implement policy consistent with the Society's environmental management ethic; to encourage high standards of competence & ethics among environmental management practitioners; to encourage education in the field of environmental management; to encourage individuals to become environmental management practitioners
Chief Officer(s):
Sue Ruggero, Administrator
Membership: *Member Profile:* Open to those professionally involved in environmental management; potential members must have appropriate academic &/or professional credentials
Activities: Seminars; conferences

Ontario Society for the History of Nursing *See* Margaret M. Allemang Centre for the History of Nursing

Ontario Society for the Prevention of Cruelty to Animals (OSPCA)

16586 Woodbine Ave., RR#3, Newmarket ON L3Y 4W1
Tel: 905-898-7122
Other Communication: donate@ospca.on.ca
info@ospca.on.ca
www.ontariospca.ca
www.facebook.com/OntarioSPCA?v=wall&viewas=0
twitter.com/ontariospca
www.youtube.com/user/OntarioSPCA
Also Known As: Ontario Humane Society
Overview: A large provincial charitable organization founded in 1873 overseen by Canadian Federation of Humane Societies
Mission: To provide care & shelter for animals, especially pets; To enforce animal cruelty laws in the province; To investigate cruelty complaints; To carry out rescues & bring perpetrators to court; To advocates for humane laws; To promote humane education & public awareness of the humane treatment of animals; To operate a Wildlife Rehabilitation Centre in Midland, ON
Member of: World Society for the Protection of Animals; Canadian Federation of Humane Societies
Chief Officer(s):
Kate MacDonald, Chief Executive Officer
abuonaiuto@ospca.on.ca
Tanya Firmage, Director, Operations, Animal Welfare, 888-668-7722 Ext. 336
tfirmage@ospca.on.ca
Connie Mallory, Chief Inspector, 888-668-7722
Alison Cross, Senior Manager, Marketing & Communications, 888-668-7722 Ext. 305
across@ospca.on.ca
Finances: *Funding Sources:* Fundraising; Public donations; Legacies
850 volunteer(s)
Membership: 60,000; *Fees:* $10
Activities: *Awareness Events:* Spay/Neuter Month, March; Adopt-a-Cat Month, June; Adopt-a-Dog Month, October; *Speaker Service:* Yes; *Library* Open to public
Publications:
• Animals' Voice
Type: Magazine; *Frequency:* Quarterly

Alliston Branch (Affiliate)
Alliston & District Humane Society, PO Box 378, Beeton ON L0G 1A0
Tel: 705-458-9038; *Fax:* 705-435-2851
wendyh@idirect.com
www.allistonhumane.com

Arnprior Branch (Affiliate)
Arnprior & District Humane Society, PO Box 45, 490 Didak Dr., Arnprior ON K7S 3H2
Tel: 613-623-0916
district.spca@bellnet.ca
www.arnpriorhumanesociety.ca

Barrie Branch
91 Patterson Rd., Barrie ON L4N 3V9
Tel: 705-728-7311; *Fax:* 705-728-7243
barrie@ospca.on.ca
www.barrie.ontariospca.ca
Chief Officer(s):
Melissa Bainbridge, Branch Manager

Brant County Branch (Affiliate)
PO Box 163, 539 Mohawk Rd., Brantford ON N3T 5M8
Tel: 519-756-6620; *Fax:* 519-756-6910
www.brantfordspca.com
Chief Officer(s):
Robin Kuchma, Branch Manager

Bruce Grey Branch
#8, 427 - 10th Street, Hanover ON N4N 1P8
Tel: 519-364-0400; *Fax:* 519-364-0401
brucegrey@ospca.on.ca
www.brucegrey.ontariospca.ca

Cambridge Branch (Affiliate)
Cambridge & District Humane Society, 1650 Dunbar Rd., Cambridge ON N1R 8J5
Tel: 519-623-7722; *Fax:* 519-623-9442
spca@cambridgeweb.net
spca.cambridgeweb.net

Durham Region Branch (Affiliate)
Humane Society of Durham Region, #1, 79 Taunton Rd. West, Oshawa ON L1G 7B4
e-mail: humanedurham@auracom.com
www.humanedurham.com

Etobicoke Branch (Affiliate)
Etobicoke Humane Society, #B, 1500 Royal York Rd., 2nd Fl., Toronto ON M9P 3B6
Tel: 416-249-6100
www.etobicokehumanesociety.com

Fort Erie Branch (Affiliate)
Fort Erie SPCA, 410 Jarvis St., Fort Erie ON L2A 2T1
Tel: 905-871-2461; *Fax:* 905-871-9746
forteriespca@bellnet.ca
www.forteriespca.org

Gananoque Branch (Affiliate)
Gananoque & District Humane Society, 85 Hwy. 32, RR#1, Gananoque ON K7G 2V3
Tel: 613-382-1512; *Fax:* 613-382-0333
humanesociety@bellnet.ca
www.ganhumanesociety.ca

Guelph Branch (Affiliate)
Guelph Humane Society, PO Box 684, 500 Wellington St. West, Guelph ON N1H 6L3
Tel: 519-824-3091; *Fax:* 519-824-3075
ghs-shelter@bellnet.ca
www.guelph-humane.on.ca

Hamilton Branch (Affiliate)
Hamilton/Burlington SPCA, 245 Dartnall Rd., Hamilton ON L8W 3V9
Tel: 905-574-7722; *Fax:* 905-574-9087
info@hamiltonspca.com
www.hbspca.com

Huron County Branch
48 East St., Goderich ON N7A 1N3
Tel: 519-440-0250
huroncounty@ospca.on.ca
www.huroncounty.ontariospca.ca

Kawartha Lakes Branch (Affiliate)
c/o Humane Society of Kawartha Lakes, 107 McLaughlin Rd., Lindsay ON K9V 6K5
Tel: 705-878-4618; *Fax:* 705-878-5141
shelter.hskl@cogeco.net
www.hskl.ca
www.facebook.com/HumaneSocietyKawarthaLakes
Chief Officer(s):
Lynne Florence, Manager
manager.hskl@cogeco.net

Kenora/Dryden Branch
PO Box 1148, Keewatin ON P0X 1C0
Toll-Free: 877-548-2194
www.kenoradryden.ontariospca.ca

Kent Branch
405 Park Ave. East, Chatham ON N7M 3W4
Tel: 519-354-1713; *Fax:* 519-354-1716
kent@ospca.on.ca
www.kent.ontariospca.ca

Kingston Branch (Affiliate)
Kingston Humane Society, 1 Binnington Ct., Kingston ON K7M 8M9
Tel: 613-546-1291; *Fax:* 613-546-3398; *TTY:* s - -
inspector@kingstonhumanesociety.ca
www.kingstonhumanesociety.ca

Kitchener-Waterloo Branch (Affiliate)
Kitchener-Waterloo Humane Society, 250 Riverbend Dr., Kitchener ON N2B 2E9
Tel: 519-745-5619; *Fax:* 519-745-3224
info@kwhumane.com
www.kwhumane.com

Lanark Branch (Affiliate)
Lanark Animal Welfare Society, PO Box 156, Smith Falls ON K7A 4T1
Tel: 613-283-9308; *Fax:* 613-283-0982
shelter@lanarkanimals.ca
www.lanarkanimals.ca

Leeds & Grenville Branch
RR#4, 800 Centennial Rd., Brockville ON K6V 5T4
Tel: 613-345-5520; *Fax:* 613-345-2169
leedsgrenville@ospca.on.ca
www.leedsgrenville.ontariospca.ca

Lennox & Addington Branch
156 Richmond Blvd. East, Napanee ON K7R 3Z7
Tel: 613-354-2492; *Fax:* 613-354-4802
lennoxaddington@ospca.on.ca
www.lennoxaddington.ontariospca.ca

Lincoln Branch (Affiliate)
Lincoln County Humane Society, 160 Fourth Ave., St. Catharines ON L2R 6P9
Tel: 905-682-0767; *Fax:* 905-682-8133
myconnect@lchs.ca
www.lchs.ca
www.facebook.com/lincolncountyhumanesociety
twitter.com/lincolncountyhs
Chief Officer(s):
Ann Davidson, President
director@lchs.ca

London Branch (Affiliate)
London Humane Society, 624 Clarke Rd., London ON N5V 3K5
Tel: 519-451-0630; *Fax:* 519-451-8995
administration@londonhumane.ca
www.londonhumanesociety.ca

Midland & District Branch
15979 Highway 12 East, RR#1, Midland ON L0K 1R0
Tel: 705-534-4459; *Fax:* 705-534-4745
midland@ospca.org
www.midland.ontariospca.ca
Chief Officer(s):
Maureen Dool, Branch Manager

Muskoka Branch
PO Box 2804, 4 Ferrier Rd., Bracebridge ON P1L 1W5
Tel: 705-645-6225; *Fax:* 705-645-3382
muskoka@ospca.on.ca
www.muskoka.ontariospca.ca
Chief Officer(s):
Judith Aubin, Branch Manager

Niagara Falls Branch (Affiliate)
Niagara Falls Humane Society, 6025 Chippawa Pkwy., Niagara Falls ON L2E 6X8
Tel: 905-356-4404; *Fax:* 905-356-7652
manager@nfhs.ca
www.nfhs.ca

North Bay Branch (Affiliate)
North Bay & District Humane Society, PO Box 1383, 2060 Main St. West, North Bay ON P1B 8K5

Tel: 705-474-1251; *Fax:* 705-474-1259
info@northbayhumanesociety.ca
www.northbayhumanesociety.ca

Northumberland Branch (Affiliate)
Northumberland Humane Society, 371 Ward St., Port Hope ON L1A 4A4
Tel: 905-885-4131; *Fax:* 905-885-8027
north1@eagle.ca
www.northumberlandhumanesociety.com

Oakville Branch (Affiliate)
Oakville & Milton Humane Society, 445 Cornwall Rd., Oakville ON L6J 7S8
Tel: 905-845-1551; *Fax:* 905-845-1973
www.oakvillemiltonhumane.ca

Ontario SPCA Centre Veterinary Hospital
91A Patterson Rd., Barrie ON L4N 3V9
Tel: 705-734-9883; *Fax:* 705-720-7321
spayneuter@ospca.on.ca
www.spayneuter.ontariospca.ca

Orangeville & District Branch
650 Riddell Rd., Orangeville ON L9W 5G5
Tel: 519-942-3140; *Fax:* 519-942-3678
orangeville@ospca.on.ca
www.orangeville.ontariospca.ca

Orillia Branch
467 West St. North, Orillia ON L3V 5G1
Tel: 705-325-1304; *Fax:* 705-325-1027
orillia@ospca.on.ca
www.orillia.ontariospca.ca
Chief Officer(s):
Carol Beard, Branch Manager

Ottawa Branch (Affiliate)
Ottawa Humane Society, 101 Champagne Ave., Ottawa ON K1S 4P3
Tel: 613-725-3166; *Fax:* 613-725-5674
ohs@ottawahumane.ca
www.ottawahumane.ca

Oxford-Elgin Branch
485023 Sweaburg Rd., RR#1, Woodstock ON N4S 7V6
Tel: 519-456-5988; *Fax:* 519-456-5989
Toll-Free: 888-668-7722
oxfordspca@hotmail.com
www.oxfordelgin.ontariospca.ca

Parry Sound Branch
Bracebridge ON
Tel: 705-645-6225
Toll-Free: 888-668-7722
kwilliams@ospca.on.ca
www.parrysound.ontariospca.ca

Perth County Branch
345 Douro St., Stratford ON N5A 3S8
Tel: 519-273-6600; *Fax:* 519-273-7319
perthcounty@ospca.on.ca
www.perthcounty.ontariospca.ca
Chief Officer(s):
Sue Porter, Branch Manager

Peterborough Branch (Affiliate)
Peterborough Humane Society, 385 Landsdowne St. East, Peterborough ON K9L 2A3
Tel: 705-745-4722; *Fax:* 705-745-9770
ptbospca@nexicom.net
www.peterboroughhumanesociety.ca

Quinte Branch (Affiliate)
Quinte Humane Society, 527 Avonlough Rd., Belleville ON K8N 4Z2
Tel: 613-968-4673
qhs@quintehumanesociety.com
www.quintehumanesociety.com

Renfrew Branch
PO Box 322, 387 Paquette Rd., Petawawa ON K8H 3J1
Tel: 613-588-4508; *Fax:* 613-588-4882
renfrewcounty@ospca.on.ca
www.renfrewcounty.ontariospca.ca

Sarnia Branch (Affiliate)
Sarnia & District SPCA, 131 Exmouth St., Sarnia ON N7T 7W8
Tel: 519-344-7064; *Fax:* 519-344-2145
sarniahumane@ebtech.net
www.sarniahumanesociety.com

Sault Ste. Marie Branch (Affiliate)
Sault Ste. Marie Humane Society, 962 Second Line East, Sault Ste Marie ON P6B 4K4
Tel: 705-949-3573; *Fax:* 705-949-0169
ssmhs@soonet.ca
hosting.soonet.ca/humanesociety

Scarborough Branch
Toronto ON
Toll-Free: 888-668-7722
www.sny.ontariospca.ca

Simcoe Branch (Affiliate)
Simcoe & District Humane Society, PO Box 193, 24 Grigg Dr., Simcoe ON N3Y 4L1
Tel: 519-428-9161
info@s-dhs.ca
www.s-dhs.ca

Stormont, Dundas & Glengarry Branch
PO Box 52, 550 Boundary Rd., Cornwall ON K6H 5S3
Tel: 613-936-0072; *Fax:* 613-936-0137
sdg@ospca.on.ca
www.sdg.ontariospca.ca
Chief Officer(s):
Carol Link, Branch Manager

Sudbury & District Branch
760 Notre Dame Ave., Sudbury ON P3A 2T4
Tel: 705-566-9582; *Fax:* 705-566-6625
sudbury@ospca.on.ca
www.sudbury.ontariospca.ca
Chief Officer(s):
Peggy Byers

Temiskaming Branch
PO Box 2474, 280 Armstrong St., New Liskeard ON P0J 1P0
Tel: 705-647-5288
ospcatem@onlink.net
www.temiskaming.ontariospca.ca

Thunder Bay Branch (Affiliate)
Thunder Bay & District Humane Society, 1535 Rosslyn Rd., Thunder Bay ON P7E 6W2
Tel: 807-475-8803; *Fax:* 807-475-8803
tbayhumane@gmail.com
www.tbayhumane.ca

Timmins Branch (Affiliate)
Timmins & District Humane Society, 620 Mahoney Dr., Timmins ON P4N 7C3
Tel: 705-264-1816; *Fax:* 705-264-3870
adoptions@ntl.sympatico.ca
www.timminshumanesociety.ca

Toronto Branch (Affiliate)
Toronto Humane Society, 11 River St., Toronto ON M5A 4C2
Tel: 416-392-2273; *Fax:* 416-392-9978
info@torontohumanesociety.com
www.torontohumanesociety.com

Upper Credit Branch (Affiliate)
Upper Credit Humane Society, #24, 5383 Wellington Rd., RR#2, Erin ON N0B 1T0
Tel: 519-833-2287; *Fax:* 519-833-2247
adoptions@uppercredit.com
www.uppercredit.com

Welland Branch (Affiliate)
Welland & District Humane Society, 60 Provincial St., Welland ON L3B 5W7
Tel: 905-735-1552; *Fax:* 905-735-7414
info@wellandhumanesociety.org
www.wellandhumanesociety.org
Chief Officer(s):
Georges L'Esperance, Président

Wildlife Rehabilitation Centre
15979 Hwy. 12 East, RR#1, Port McNicoll ON L0K 1R0
Tel: 705-534-4350; *Fax:* 705-534-3751
Toll-Free: 888-668-7722
wildlifecentre@ospca.on.ca
www.wildlifecentre.ontariospca.ca

Windsor-Essex Branch (Affiliate)
Windsor-Essex County Humane Society, 1375 Provincial Rd., Windsor ON N8W 5V8
Tel: 519-966-5751; *Fax:* 519-966-1848
info@windsorhumane.org
www.windsorhumane.org

York Branch
16586 Woodbine Ave., RR#3, Newmarket ON L3Y 4W1
Tel: 905-898-7122; *Fax:* 905-853-8643
yorkregion@ospca.on.ca
www.yorkregion.ontariospca.ca

Ontario Society of Artists (OSA)

#101, 1444 Queen St. East, Toronto ON M4L 1E1
Tel: 416-867-9448
info@ontariosocietyofartists.org
ontariosocietyofartists.org
Overview: A small provincial charitable organization founded in 1872
Mission: To preserve Ontario's artistic heritage & to enrich Canada's cultural life
Chief Officer(s):
Tony Vander Voet, President
Mary Ng, Treasurer
Membership: *Fees:* $125; *Member Profile:* Professional visual artists
Activities: Members' shows; Open-juried shows; Educational programs

Ontario Society of Chiropodists (OSC)

#100, 6700 Century Ave., Mississauga ON L5N 6A4
Tel: 905-567-3094; *Fax:* 905-567-7191
Toll-Free: 877-823-1508
info@ontariochiropodist.com
www.ontariochiropodist.com
Overview: A small provincial organization founded in 1985
Mission: To provide extensive & regular postgraduate education programs to ensure that the chiropodist remains a first rate foot care specialist
Chief Officer(s):
Sarah Robinson, President
Membership: *Fees:* $452 full; $339 second year grad; $226 first year grad
Activities: *Awareness Events:* Foot Health Month, May; *Speaker Service:* Yes

Ontario Society of Medical Technologists (OSMT)

#402, 234 Eglinton Ave. East, Toronto ON M4P 1K5
Tel: 416-485-6768; *Fax:* 416-485-7660
Toll-Free: 800-461-6768
osmt@osmt.org
www.osmt.org
www.facebook.com/217098608317170
twitter.com/osmt2011
Overview: A medium-sized provincial organization founded in 1963 overseen by Canadian Society For Medical Laboratory Science
Mission: To represent the professional interests of medical technologists & medical laboratory assistants/technicians in relations with government & the public; to provide continuing education & technical consulting services
Affiliation(s): Canadian Society for Medical Laboratory Science
Chief Officer(s):
Blanca McArthur, Executive Director
bmcarthur@osmt.org
Debbie Brooks, Executive Assistant
dbrooks@osmt.org
Finances: *Annual Operating Budget:* $250,000-$500,000; *Funding Sources:* Membership dues & certification fees
Staff Member(s): 5; 50 volunteer(s)
Membership: 2,500; *Fees:* $135.60 active & subscriber; $108.48 inactive & affiliate; $27.12 student & retired; *Member Profile:* Medical laboratory technologists & medical laboratory assistants & technicians
Activities: Annual conference & trade show; *Awareness Events:* National Medical Laboratory Week, April
Publications:
• Advocate
Type: Magazine; *Accepts Advertising*; *Editor:* Blanca McArthur
Profile: The magazine features articles that pertain to medical technologists, including case studies & educational reports

Ontario Society of Nutrition Professionals in Public Health (OSNPPH) / La société ontarienne des professionelles et professionnels de la nutrition en santé publique

c/o Ontario Public Health Association, #1850, 439 University Ave., Toronto ON M5G 1Y8
e-mail: info@osnpph.on.ca
www.osnpph.on.ca
twitter.com/RDsPubHealthON
Overview: A small provincial organization founded in 1977
Mission: To provide an official organization that will give nutrition personnel in public health a strong voice within public health & for commenting on public health issues
Member of: Ontario Public Health Association
Chief Officer(s):
Rebecca Davids, Co-Chair
Heather Thomas, Co-Chair
Rachel Morgan, Coordinator, Communications

Membership: *Member Profile:* Dietitians/nutritionists in public health departments/units
Activities: Annual Nutrition Exchange, 2-day conference

Ontario Society of Occupational Therapists (OSOT)
#210, 55 Eglinton Ave. East, Toronto ON M4P 1G8
Tel: 416-322-3011; *Fax:* 416-322-6705
Toll-Free: 877-676-6768
osot@osot.on.ca
www.osot.on.ca
Overview: A medium-sized provincial organization founded in 1920
Mission: To promote & represent the profession of occupational therapy in the areas of government affairs, education, professional issues & public relations in Ontario
Affliation(s): Canadian Association of Occupational Therapists
Chief Officer(s):
Christie Benchley, Executive Director
cbrenchley@osot.on.ca
Rob Linkiewicz, Office Manager & Bookkeeper
rlinkiewicz@osot.on.ca
Seema Sindwani, Manager, Professional Development & Practice Support
ssindwani@osot.on.ca
Melissa Macks, Manager, Membership Services
mmacks@osot.on.ca
Finances: *Annual Operating Budget:* $250,000-$500,000
Staff Member(s): 5; 100 volunteer(s)
Membership: 3,800 individual; *Fees:* $195 full time; $132 part time; $100 non-practising; $99 associate; $32-$50 new graduate
Activities: *Awareness Events:* Occupational Therapy Month, Oct.; *Rents Mailing List:* Yes
Awards:
• OT Research Fund Awards (Award)
• Honorary Life Membership (Award)
• Student Achievement Awards (Award)
Meetings/Conferences: • Ontario Society of Occupational Therapists Conference 2015, 2015
Scope: Provincial

Ontario Society of Periodontists (OSP)
#300, 1370 Don Mills Rd., Toronto ON M3B 3N7
Tel: 416-424-6632; *Fax:* 416-441-0591
Toll-Free: 855-336-8556
info@osp.on.ca
www.osp.on.ca
Overview: A medium-sized provincial organization
Mission: To be the official voice of Ontario periodontists; to serve the providers and recipients of periodontal care
Member of: Ontario Dental Association
Chief Officer(s):
Shari Bricks, Managing Director
shari@osp.on.ca
Stephen Gangbar, President
president@osp.on.ca
Finances: *Funding Sources:* Membership dues
Membership: *Fees:* $150 active; $75 student to active; $0 student; *Member Profile:* Certified periodontal specialists in Ontario

Ontario Society of Professional Engineers (OSPE)
#502, 4950 Yonge St., Toronto ON M2N 6K1
Tel: 416-223-9961; *Fax:* 416-223-9963
Toll-Free: 866-763-1654
info@ospe.on.ca
www.ospe.on.ca
www.linkedin.com/e/vgh/1968967
www.facebook.com/140328494064
twitter.com/O_S_P_E
www.youtube.com/OSPETV
Overview: A large provincial organization
Mission: To advance the interests of professional engineers in Ontario by advocating on behalf of engineers & the profession; to provide members with a sense of belonging & mutual support; to supply valued & innovative services; to offer quality professional training
Chief Officer(s):
Nadine Miller, M.Eng., P.Eng., President & Chair
Mark Dietrich, CEO
mdietrich@ospe.on.ca
Staff Member(s): 17
Membership: *Fees:* $165 professional; $83 professional (65+); $132 associate; $90 intern; $26 student; *Committees:* Advocacy; Environment; Women in Engineering Advisory; Ontario Professional Engineers Awards; PEO Chapter Liaison; Social; Membership Advisory; mployer Salary Survey Advisory; Fee Schedule; Audit & Investments; Executive; Finance; Human Resources; Nominations; PEO/OSPE Joint Relations
Activities: *Library:* Reports Library
Publications:
• Employer Salary Survey [a publication of the Ontario Society of Professional Engineers]
Type: Report; *Frequency:* Annually
• The OSPE [Ontario Society of Professional Engineers] Advocate
Type: Newsletter; *Frequency:* Weekly
Profile: Electronic newsletter
• OSPE [Ontario Society of Professional Engineers] Annual Report
Type: Yearbook; *Frequency:* Annually
• Society Notes [a publication of the Ontario Society of Professional Engineers]
Type: Newsletter; *Frequency:* Bi-weekly
Profile: Electronic newsletter
• The Voice [a publication of the Ontario Society of Professional Engineers]
Type: Magazine; *Frequency:* q.
Profile: Formerly a print newsletter, The Voice is now a full-colour magazine

Ontario Society of Psychotherapists (OSP)
#1, 189 Queen St. East, Toronto ON M5A 1S2
Tel: 416-923-4050; *Fax:* 416-968-6818
mail@psychotherapyontario.org
psychotherapyontario.com
Overview: A small provincial organization
Mission: The Ontario Society of Psychotherapists is committed to the continuing development of ethically responsible and self-reflective psychotherapists
Chief Officer(s):
Pat Rayman, President
Membership: 300; *Fees:* $183.75 Clinical Membership; $157.50 Qualifying Membership; $78.75 Student, Supporting, Retired and Friend of the Society membership; *Committees:* Ethics; membership; PR

Ontario Society of Safety Engineering *See* Canadian Society of Safety Engineering, Inc.

Ontario Soil & Crop Improvement Association (OSCIA) / Association pour l'amélioration des sols et des récoltes de l'Ontario
1 Stone Rd. West, Guelph ON N1G 4Y2
Tel: 519-826-4214; *Fax:* 519-826-4224
Toll-Free: 800-265-9751
oscia@ontariosoilcrop.org
www.ontariosoilcrop.org
Overview: A medium-sized provincial organization founded in 1939
Mission: To communicate & facilitate the responsible management of soil, water, air, & crops
Chief Officer(s):
Harold Rudy, Executive Director, 519-826-4217
Julie Henderson, Administrator, Finance, 519-826-4221
Steven Nadeau, Administrator, Information Technology, 519-826-6059
Andrew Graham, Manager, Programs, 519-826-4216
John Laidlaw, Program Manager, Farm Business Management, 519-826-4218
Membership: *Member Profile:* Farmers & persons involved in agriculture in Ontario; *Committees:* Nomination; Resolutions; Finance; Research; Membership; Constitution & Bylaws; Annual Meeting; Ontario Soil Management Research; Soil & Water Quality Sub-Committee; Waste Utilization Sub-Committee; Field Crops Sub-Committee; Ontario Corn; Ontario Weed; Ontario Cereal Crop; Ontario Forage Crops; Ontario Oil & Protein; Biosolids Utilization; Ontario Forage Council; Ontario Agri-Food Education; AGCare; Ontario Field Crops Research Coalition; Canada's Outdoor Farm Show; Ontario Agri-Food Technologies; Soil Conservation Council of Canada
Activities: Offering information about agricultural management practices; Networking with farmers
Meetings/Conferences: • Ontario Soil & Crop Improvement Association 2015 Provincial Annual Meeting, 2015, ON
Scope: Provincial
Description: An opportunity for farmers & persons involved in agriculture in Ontario to bring local views to give direction to the association
Contact Information: & Conference Centre Improvement Association, E-mail: oscia@ontariosoilcrop.org
Publications:
• New Crops, Old Challenges: Tips & Tricks for Managing New Crops!
Number of Pages: 76
Profile: Crop profiles
• Ontario Soil & Crop Improvement Association Newsletter
Type: Newsletter; *Frequency:* Quarterly; *Price:* Free with Ontario Soil & Crop Improvement Association membership
• Rotational Grazing in Extensive Pastures
Type: Report
Profile: Discusses using rotational grazing to increase health of pastures, cattle & the environment.

Ontario Special Olympics *See* Special Olympics Ontario

Ontario Speed Skating Association (OSSA)
PO Box 1179, Lakefield ON K0L 2H0
Tel: 705-652-9490; *Fax:* 705-652-1227
ossa@ontariospeedskating.ca
ontariospeedskating.ca
www.facebook.com/OntarioSpeedSkating
twitter.com/OSSA
www.flickr.com/photos/ontariospeedskating
Previous Name: Ice Skating Association of Ontario
Overview: A medium-sized provincial organization founded in 1981 overseen by Speed Skating Canada
Mission: To promote & develop the sport of speed skating in Ontario.
Member of: Speed Skating Canada
Chief Officer(s):
Jacqueline Deschenes, Executive Director
executivedirector@ontariospeedskating.ca
Sarah Leslie, Manager, Sport Programs, 613-422-5210
sportmanager@ontariospeedskating.ca
Finances: *Funding Sources:* Membership fee
Membership: *Committees:* Coaching; Marketing; Officials Development; Technical; Club & Membership Development; Fundraising; Personnel; Finance; Nominating
Activities: *Speaker Service:* Yes

Ontario Spondylitis Association (OSA)
18 Long Crescent, Toronto ON M4E 1N6
Tel: 416-694-5493
info@spondylitis.ca
spondylitis.ca
www.facebook.com/6562917242
Overview: A small provincial organization
Mission: To provide support, education & public awareness of the disease called Ankylosing Spondylitis
Member of: The Arthritis Society, Canadian Spondylitis Association
Chief Officer(s):
Michael Mallinson, President
Finances: *Funding Sources:* Membership fees; donations
30 volunteer(s)
Membership: 300; *Committees:* Membership; Communications; Fundraising
Activities: Seminars; social events

Ontario Sportfishing Guides' Association (OSGA)
4504 Trent Trail, Washago ON L0K 2B0
Tel: 705-689-3332; *Fax:* 705-689-1085
info@ontariofishcharters.ca
www.ontariofishcharters.ca
Previous Name: Ontario Charterboat Association
Overview: A small provincial organization founded in 1980
Mission: To monitor & participate in any regulation reform regarding sportfishing in the province; to lobby as a unified voice on behalf of its members, & serve as a network where members can promote & learn from each other.
Chief Officer(s):
George Watkins, Secretary
Finances: *Funding Sources:* Membership fees
Membership: *Fees:* $100; *Member Profile:* Professional fishing charter boat operators & guides

Ontario Sports & Recreation Centre Inc. *See* Sport Alliance Ontario

Ontario Square & Round Dance Federation (OSRDF)
c/o President, 8 Seven Oaks Circle, St Catharines ON L2P 3N6
Tel: 905-641-1872
Toll-Free: 866-206-6696
info@squaredance.on.ca
www.squaredance.on.ca
Overview: A medium-sized provincial organization overseen by Canadian Square & Round Dance Society
Chief Officer(s):

Wayne Hall, President
whall3@cogeco.ca
Membership: *Fees:* $1 plus $2 society fee per individual; $1 plus $5 society fee per organization
Activities: *Library*

Ontario Standardbred Adoption Society (OSAS)
PO Box 297, 36 Main St. South, Campbellville ON L0P 1B0
Tel: 905-854-6099; *Fax:* 905-854-6100
osasadmin@bellnet.ca
www.osas.ca
Overview: A small provincial charitable organization founded in 1996
Mission: To aid in the adoption & relocation of retired Standardbred horses, as well as those no longer able to race, within Ontario.
Chief Officer(s):
Jim Evans, President
Anita TenBruggencate, Coordinator, Adoptions
anitaosas@bellnet.ca
Finances: *Funding Sources:* Fundraising; industry associations; donations
Staff Member(s): 1

Ontario Standardbred Improvement Association *See* Standardbred Breeders of Ontario Association

Ontario Steam & Antique Preservers Association (OSAPA)
PO Box 133, Stn. Main, Milton ON L9T 2Y3
Tel: 905-878-3114
www.steam-era.com
www.facebook.com/46132187050
Also Known As: Steam-Era
Overview: A small provincial organization founded in 1960
Mission: To promote interest in antiques & local history.
Chief Officer(s):
Brian Walsh, President
brian@realprocess.net
Membership: *Fees:* $25; $5 junior; *Member Profile:* Anyone interested in antique farm equipment; *Committees:* Antique cars/trucks; Antiques under grandstand; Antique Lawn tractors; Camping; Concessions; Gas Engines; Gas tractors; Membership; Souvenirs; Stationary steam; Steam engines; Trading post; Steam-Era Compound
Activities: Steam-era show

Ontario Steelheaders
PO Box 604, Brantford ON N3T 5T3
e-mail: president@ontariosteelheaders.ca
www.ontariosteelheaders.ca
www.facebook.com/pages/Ontario-Steelheaders/117486061781254
twitter.com/ONSteelheaders
Overview: A small provincial organization
Mission: To improve access and habitat for migratory rainbow trout, provide young rainbow trout with suitable nursery habitat, provide relevent and appropriate input to government, agencies and other organizations, and to educate members and the public on relevent issues, conservation practices and proper angling techniques.
Chief Officer(s):
Karl Redin, President, 519-756-3640
Membership: *Fees:* $30 individual; $35 family

Ontario Stone, Sand & Gravel Association (OSSGA)
#103, 5720 Timberlea Blvd., Mississauga ON L4W 4W2
Tel: 905-507-0711; *Fax:* 905-507-0717
www.ossga.com
twitter.com/_OSSGA
Previous Name: Aggregate Producers' Association of Ontario
Overview: A medium-sized provincial organization founded in 1956
Chief Officer(s):
Moreen Miller, CEO
mmiller@ossga.com
Finances: *Annual Operating Budget:* $250,000-$500,000; *Funding Sources:* Membership dues
Staff Member(s): 7
Membership: 200+ corporate
Meetings/Conferences: • Ontario Stone, Sand & Gravel Association 2015 Annual General Meeting, February, 2015, Hilton Toronto Hotel, Toronto, ON
Scope: Provincial

Ontario Streams
50 Bloomington Rd. West, Aurora ON L4G 3G8
Tel: 905-713-7399; *Fax:* 905-713-7361
www.ontariostreams.on.ca
Overview: A medium-sized provincial organization founded in 1995
Mission: To promote the conservation & rehabilitation of streams & wetlands, through education & community involvement
Chief Officer(s):
Doug Forder, General Manager
doug.forder@ontariostreams.on.ca

Ontario Students Against Impaired Driving / Élèves ontariens contre l'ivresse au volant
PO Box 3, #2B, 1015 Lakeshore Blvd. East, Toronto ON M4M 1B4
Toll-Free: 877-706-7243
www.osaid.org
www.facebook.com/OntarioStudentsAgainstImpairedDriving
twitter.com/OSAIDInc
Overview: A small provincial organization
Mission: To eliminate impaired driving through practical & positive peer education
Chief Officer(s):
Robin MacDonald, President
Matt John Evans, Executive Director

Ontario Sustainable Energy Association (OSEA)
#400, 215 Spadina Ave., Toronto ON M5T 2C7
Tel: 416-977-4441; *Fax:* 416-644-0116
Other Communication: employment@ontario-sea.org
info@ontario-sea.org
www.ontario-sea.org
www.linkedin.com/company/ontario-sustainable-energy-association
www.facebook.com/ontariosea
twitter.com/ontariosea
www.youtube.com/ontariosea2009
Overview: A small provincial organization founded in 2002
Mission: To represent & serve municipalities, First Nations, institutions, businesses, cooperatives, farms, & households; To support the work of local sustainable energy organizations
Chief Officer(s):
Kristopher Stevens, Executive Director
Kristopher@ontario-sea.org
Nicole Risse, Manager, Business Development & Outreach
nicole@ontario-sea.org
Lori Steuart, Office Administrator
admin@ontario-sea.org
Nik Spohr, Lead, Green Energy Doors Open Project
nik@ontario-sea.org
Ian Jackson, Coordinator, Web
ian@ontario-sea.org
Michel Fortin, Director, Strategy & Member Services
michel@ontario-sea.org
Finances: *Funding Sources:* Sponsorships
Staff Member(s): 6
Membership: *Fees:* $100 Friend; $1,000 Community; $2,000 Supporter; $5,000 Champion
Activities: Engaging in advocacy activities, capacity building, & non-partisan policy work; Providing public outreach services
Meetings/Conferences: • Ontario Sustainable Energy Association 2015 Annual All-Energy Canada Exhibition & Conference, 2015
Scope: Provincial
Contact Information: Executive Director: Kristopher Stevens, E-mail: kristopher@ontario-sea.org
Publications:
• Arts Revision Report: Renewables Without Limits [a publication of the Ontario Sustainable Energy Association]
Type: Report; *Price:* $1 + $13.50 shipping & handling, members; $10 +$13.50 S&H, non-members
Profile: A review of Ontario's Renewable Energy Standard Offer Program
• Community Power Financing Guidebook
Type: Manual; *Price:* $40 + $13.50 shipping & handling,members; $65 + $13.40 S&H, non-members
Profile: Contents include pre-development financing, land acquisition, legal contracting, permits & approvals, resource assessment, & community engagement
• The Community Power Guidebook
Type: Guide
Profile: A guide to the development of a community power project, from conception to commissioning
• Green Energy ACTion Kit
Type: Kit; *Price:* $10 + $13.50 shipping & handling, members; $20 + $13.40 S&H, non-members
Profile: Suggestions to help citizens advocate for green energy in Ontario
• Ontario Landowner's Guide to Wind Energy
Type: Guide; *Author:* Paul Gipe; James Murphy; *Price:* $10 + $13.50 shipping & handling, members; $20 + $13.50 S&H,non-members
Profile: A comprehensive manual for rural landowners & farmers who are interested in wind power
• Ontario Sustainable Energy Association E-Bulletin
Type: Newsletter; *Price:* Free with Ontario Sustainable Energy Association membership
Profile: Updates about the association & upcoming events
• OSEA [Ontario Sustainable Energy Association] Member Directory
Type: Directory
Profile: Contact information for members
• Permitting & Approvals Processes for CP Projects [a publication of the Ontario Sustainable Energy Association]
Type: Guide; *Price:* $40 + $13.50 shipping & handling, members; $65 + $13.50 S&H, non-members
Profile: An overview of the policy environment for biogas & wind projects in Ontario, of interest to municipal planners,project proponents, & the general public
• Powering Ontario Communities: Proposed Policy for Projects up to 10mw
Type: Study
Profile: Options to encourage small or community-owned renewable energy generation in Ontario
• Proposal for a Green Energy Act for Ontario
Profile: A proposal for renewable energy sources to protect the environment & to manage climate change
• Recommendations for Procuring Sustainable Energy: An Addendum to Renewables Without Limits
Profile: An update to recommendations from the Arts Revision Report: Renewable Without Limits
• Solar PV Community Action Manual
Type: Manual
Profile: Information for Canadian residents about residential-scale or small-scale commercial Solar PV installations, as well as related topics such as financing & home assessment
• Solar Thermal Community Action Manual
Type: Manual
Profile: Information for Canadians about residential-scale or small-scale commercial solar thermal installations, as well as the establishment of a community based organization

Ontario Table Soccer Association & Tour
ON
Tel: 905-812-9994
Toll-Free: 866-247-7702
info@ontariotablesoccer.com
www.ontariotablesoccer.com
Overview: A small provincial organization founded in 2002
Mission: To promote the sport of table soccer through hosting, sanctioning, & coordinating tournaments, events & clinics for players based in Ontario & to assist them in competing in national & international sanctioned events
Chief Officer(s):
Mario Recupero, Executive Director
director@ontariotablesoccer.com

Ontario Table Tennis Association (OTTA)
19 Wax Myrtle Way, Toronto ON M3B 3K6
Tel: 416-441-1929
otta.visualclubweb.nl
Overview: A small provincial organization founded in 1934 overseen by Table Tennis Canada
Member of: Table Tennis Canada
Affliation(s): International Table Tennis Federation
Chief Officer(s):
Attila Mosonyi, President
attila.mosonyi@gmail.com
Dejan Papic, Executive Director
dejan_papic@yahoo.com
Membership: 500+; *Fees:* $30 adult; $15 junior (under 17); $10 single tournament

Ontario Taekwondo Association
#500, 4560 Hwy 7 East, Markham ON L3R 1M5
Tel: 416-245-8582; *Fax:* 416-245-8582
otatkdinfo@gmail.com
www.taekwondo.on.ca
Overview: A medium-sized provincial organization
Chief Officer(s):

Hwa Sun Myung, President
otapresident@gmail.com
Hwan Yong Seong, Secretary General
masterseong@gmail.com

Ontario Teachers' Federation (OTF) / Fédération des enseignantes et des enseignants de l'Ontario (FEO)
#200, 1300 Yonge St., Toronto ON M4T 1X3
Tel: 416-966-3424; *Fax:* 416-966-5450
Toll-Free: 800-268-7061
www.otffeo.on.ca
Overview: A large provincial organization founded in 1944 overseen by Canadian Teachers' Federation
Mission: To represent the interests of all registered teachers in Ontario's publicly funded schools
Affliation(s): Association des enseignantes et des enseignants franco-ontariens; Elementary Teachers' Federation of Ontario; Ontario English Catholic Teachers' Association; Ontario Secondary School Teachers' Federation
Chief Officer(s):
Terry Hamilton, President
Rhonda Kimberley-Young, Sec.-Treas.
Finances: *Annual Operating Budget:* $1.5 Million-$3 Million
Membership: 155,000; *Member Profile:* Teachers in publicly-funded schools in Ontario
Activities: *Speaker Service:* Yes; *Library* by appointment

Ontario Telecommunications Association *See* Independent Telecommunications Providers Association

Ontario Tender Fruit Producers Marketing Board
PO Box 100, Stn. Vineland Station, ON L0R 2E0
Tel: 905-688-0990; *Fax:* 905-688-5915
info@ontariotenderfruit.ca
www.ontariotenderfruit.ca
www.facebook.com/OntarioTenderFruit
twitter.com/OntTenderFruit
Overview: A small provincial organization founded in 1979
Chief Officer(s):
Sarah Marshall, Manager
Staff Member(s): 8
Membership: 500 grower members

Ontario Tennis Association (OTA)
#200, 1 Shoreham Dr., Toronto ON M3N 3A7
Tel: 416-514-1100; *Fax:* 416-514-1112
Toll-Free: 800-387-5066
ota@tennisontario.com
www.tennisontario.com
Previous Name: Ontario Lawn Tennis Association
Overview: A medium-sized provincial organization founded in 1918 overseen by Tennis Canada
Mission: To act as the provincial governing body for tennis in Ontario; To promote participation in tennis in Ontario; To create tennis opportunities for players of every level, from grassroots to national calibre athlete; To encourage the quest for excellence for all players
Member of: Tennis Canada
Chief Officer(s):
Scott Fraser, President
James N. Boyce, Executive Director
jboyce@tennisontario.com
Andrew Chappell, Interim Manager, Events
achappell@tennisontario.com
Peter Malcomson, Manager, Marketing
pmalcomson@tennisontario.com
Jay Neill, Manager, Membership
jneill@tennisontario.com
Finances: *Funding Sources:* Membership fees; Sponsorships; The Ontario Trillium Foundation
Membership: 220 clubs (55,000 youth & adult tennis players) + 2,200 individuals; *Member Profile:* Tennis clubs across Ontario, including private & commercial clubs, recreation departments, municipal parks, community clubs, & resorts
Activities: Offering professional development activities, such as clinics & tennis instructor courses; Coordinating the OTA Tennis Fair for clubs; Sanctioning tournaments; Providing guidance to clubs in the area of club management
Publications:
• Ontario Tennis
Type: Magazine; *Frequency:* Quarterly; *Accepts Advertising*
Profile: Junior development information, trade news, tournament reports, equipment information, health & lifestyle, tennis travel, & regional reports
• OTA Club Manual
Type: Directory
Profile: Sections on programming, facilities, & administration
• OTA News
Type: Newsletter; *Frequency:* Weekly
• OTA Yearbook
Frequency: Annually; *Accepts Advertising*
Profile: An overview of the association's activities from the past year, plus recognition of provincial champions

Ontario Tenpin Bowling Association
3064 Tecumseh Dr., Burlington ON L7N 3M4
e-mail: am@otba.ca
www.otba.ca
Overview: A small provincial organization overseen by Canadian Tenpin Federation, Inc.
Mission: To oversee the sport of tenpin bowling in Ontario.
Member of: Canadian Tenpin Federation, Inc.
Chief Officer(s):
Charlotte Konkle, President
president@otba.ca
Della Trude, 1st Vice-President
1stVicePresident@otba.ca
Wayne Dubs, 2nd Vice-President
2ndVicePresident@otba.ca
Membership: 16 associations

Ontario Therapeutic Riding Association (OnTRA) / Association ontarienne d'équitation thérapeutique
47 Fairlane Rd., London ON N6K 3E3
e-mail: info@ontra.ca
www.ontra.ca
www.facebook.com/group.php?gid=158261594210016
Overview: A small provincial charitable organization founded in 1983
Mission: The Ontario Therapeutic Riding Association (OnTRA) promotes horseback riding as a form of therapy and sport for children and adults living with physical, cognitive, emotional, and/or behavioural challenges. OnTRA provides volunteers and therapeutic riding professionals with on-going information and training to ensure riders with disabilities receive the best possible therapy.
Member of: Canadian Therapeutic Riding Association; Ontario Equestrian Federation
Chief Officer(s):
Megan Watson, Acting President
Virginia Pohler, Treasurer
Finances: *Annual Operating Budget:* Less than $50,000
2500 volunteer(s)
Membership: 250; *Fees:* $20 individual; $30 family; $12 junior; $300 lifetime; *Committees:* Fundraising; Education; Competition; Public Relations; Physiotherapy
Activities: Competitions; promotion; educational clinic; grants; Used Equipment Program; *Speaker Service:* Yes
Awards:
• OnTRA Show Your Stuff! Grant (Grant)
Eligibility: Current members of OnTRA*Deadline:* June *Amount:* $2,500

Ontario Thoracic Society (OTS)
#201, 573 King St. East, Toronto ON M5A 4L3
Tel: 416-864-9911; *Fax:* 416-864-9916
olalung@on.lung.ca
www.on.lung.ca
Overview: A medium-sized provincial charitable organization founded in 1961
Mission: To promote respiratory health through medical research & education
Member of: Ontario Lung Association
Affliation(s): Canadian Thoracic Society
Chief Officer(s):
Kelly Mu¤oz, Chair
Finances: *Annual Operating Budget:* Less than $50,000; *Funding Sources:* Lung Association
Staff Member(s): 2; 100 volunteer(s)
Membership: 250; *Fees:* $75; *Member Profile:* Open to MD, Ph.D., or medical resident (student); *Committees:* Executive; Education; Research
Activities: Research & education; *Speaker Service:* Yes
Awards:
• Cameron C. Gray Fellowship in Respiratory Medicine (Award)

Ontario Tire Dealers Association
PO Box 516, 34 Edward St., Drayton ON N0G 1P0
Tel: 888-207-9059; *Fax:* 866-375-6832
www.otda.com
Overview: A medium-sized provincial organization
Mission: To represent & promote members
Affliation(s): Tire Dealers Association of Canada; Tire Industry Association
Chief Officer(s):
Robert Bignell, Executive Director
bbignell@otda.com
Glenn Warnica, President
gwarnica@sympatico.ca
Ron Spiewak, Secretary-Treasurer
rons@bellnet.ca
Eric Gilbert, Chair, Ontario Tire Dealers Associaton Committee
ericwaytire@primus.ca
Finances: *Funding Sources:* Membership fees; Fundraising
Activities: Educating members; Promoting standards of ethics; Engaging in lobbying activities
Meetings/Conferences: • Ontario Tire Dealers Association 2015 National Trade Show & Conference, January, 2015, RIU Aruba Palace
Scope: Provincial
Publications:
• Ontario Tire Dealers Association Membership Directory
Type: Directory
Profile: Contact information about Ontario's tire professionals
• Trends [a publication of the Ontario Tire Dealers Association]
Type: Newsletter; *Frequency:* Quarterly; *Accepts Advertising*
Profile: Information for members about industry issues

Ontario Track & Field Association *See* Athletics Ontario

Ontario Track 3 Ski Association for the Disabled
PO Box 67, Stn. D, Toronto ON M9A 4X1
Tel: 416-233-3872; *Fax:* 416-233-7862
Toll-Free: 877-308-7225
track3@track3.org
www.track3.org
www.facebook.com/OntarioTrack3
twitter.com/OntarioTrack3
Also Known As: Track 3
Overview: A small provincial charitable organization founded in 1972
Mission: To discover ability through the magic of snow sports.
Chief Officer(s):
Steve Jones, President
Darrell Jarvic, Secretary
Tracy Johnston, Treasurer
450 volunteer(s)
Activities: *Speaker Service:* Yes
Publications:
• On Track
Type: Newsletter; *Frequency:* Quarterly; *Accepts Advertising*

Ontario Traffic Council (OTC)
#2068, 170 The Donway West, Toronto ON M3C 2C3
Tel: 647-346-4050; *Fax:* 647-346-4060
info@otc.org
www.otc.org
twitter.com/ontariotraffic
Overview: A medium-sized provincial organization founded in 1950
Mission: To improve traffic conditions & traffic safety in municipalities of Ontario
Chief Officer(s):
Marco D'Angelo, Executive Director
Jeffrey Smart, President
Nelson Cadete, Vice-President
Kimberly Rossi, Treasurer
Heide Schlegl, Director Engineering
John Crass, Director of Training & Education
Scott Godwin, Operations Manager
Staff Member(s): 4

Ontario Trail Riders Association (OTRA)
PO Box 3038, Elmvale ON L0L 1P0
www.otra.ca
Overview: A small provincial organization founded in 1970
Mission: To identify, develop, & preserve multi-use trails throughout Ontario
Affliation(s): Ontario Trails Council; Ontario Equestrian Federation
Chief Officer(s):
Janice Clegg, President
pineriverranch@gmail.com
Membership: 100-499; *Fees:* $25 single; $35 family; $50 club; *Committees:* Trail Development; Government Relations; Public Relations; Trail Rides; Education

Ontario Trails Council
PO Box 500, Deseronto ON K0K 1X0
e-mail: ontrails@ontrails.on.ca
www.ontariotrails.on.ca

www.facebook.com/OntarioTrails?ref=mf
twitter.com/ontrails
www.youtube.com/user/ontrails
Overview: A medium-sized provincial organization founded in 1988
Mission: To promote the creation, development, preservation, management & use of an integrated, recreational, multi-seasonal trail network in Ontario; To show interest in all types of trails for non-motorized & motorized (where applicable) use in all seasons; To acquire & convert Ontario's abandoned railway rights-of-way to linear greenways for year-round recreational activities for the people of Ontario
Affliation(s): Bruce Trail Association; Canadian Motorcycling Association; Guelph Trail Club; Hike Ontario; Kawartha Rail-Trail; Ontario Federation of Snowmobile Clubs; Ontario Cycling Association; Ontario Competitive Trail Riders Association; Ontario Working Dog Association; Parry Sound Rail Line Task Force; Rideau Trail Association; Northland Associates; Ontario Trail Riders Association; Rails to Trails Conservancy - USA; Credit Valley Conservation Authority; Georgian Cycle & Ski Trail Association; Grand Valley Trail Association; Southeastern Ontario Rails to Tracks
Chief Officer(s):
Chris Laforest, President, 519-534-2092
claforest@brucecounty.on.ca
Forbes Symon, Vice-President, 613-258-9569
fsymon@northgrenville.on.ca
Patrick Connor, CAE, Executive Director, 613-396-3226, Fax: 613-396-2144
execdir@ontariotrails.on.ca
Damian Braley, Secretary, 705-559-6705
damian.bradley@gmail.com
Finances: *Annual Operating Budget:* Less than $50,000; *Funding Sources:* Membership fees; Corporate donations
Membership: 500,000 individuals + 21 groups; *Fees:* $26.50 individual; $106-$795 club/association + GST; *Member Profile:* Association or club with interest in recreational trail acquisition, maintenance & use; individuals concerned with environment & trail recreation; *Committees:* Government Relations; Public Affairs; Trails Development
Activities: *Library*
Meetings/Conferences: • Ontario Trails Council 2015 Trailhead Ontario, 2015, ON
Scope: Provincial
Description: An event in Oxford County, Ontario for participants to discuss Ontario's trails, development, policy, & tourism, & to view displays
Contact Information: Web Site: trailheadontario.com; Facebook: www.facebook.com/TrailheadOntario; Twitter: twitter.com/trailheadon; E-mail: ontrails@gmail.com
Publications:
• OTC [Ontario Trails Council] Newsletter
Type: Newsletter; *Frequency:* Monthly; *Price:* Free with membership in the Ontario Trails Council
Profile: Information about events, activities, & news from trails

Ontario Trial Lawyers Association (OTLA)
1190 Blair Rd., Burlington ON L7M 1K9
Tel: 905-639-6852; *Fax:* 905-639-3100
www.otla.com
Overview: A medium-sized provincial organization founded in 1990
Affliation(s): Association of Trial Lawyers of America
Chief Officer(s):
Linda Langston, Executive Director
llangston@otla.com
Julia De Faria, Director, Finance & Administration
jdefaria@otla.com
Dianne Halcovitch, Director, Education & Events
dhalcovitch@otla.com
John Karapita, Director, Public Affairs
jkarapita@otla.com
Janie Hames, Coordinator, Membership Services
jhames@otla.com
Susanne Hasulo, Coordinator, Communications
shasulo@otla.com
Finances: *Funding Sources:* Membership dues; Conference fees; Advertising
Membership: 1,190; *Fees:* $125-$495
Activities: Providing a continuing legal education program; *Library*
Meetings/Conferences: • Ontario Trial Lawyers Association 2015 Long Term Disability Conference: Good Practices and Bad Faith From Coast to Coast, January, 2015, Twenty Toronto Street Conferences and Events, Toronto, ON
Scope: Provincial
Contact Information: Conference Chairs: Najma Rashid, Jason Singer & Brad Moscato
• Ontario Trial Lawyers Association 2015 Medical Malpractice Conference - Medical Malpractice: Strategies for Success, February, 2015, Atlantis Paradise Island, Nassau
Scope: Provincial
Contact Information: Conference Chairs: Richard Halpern and Maria Damiano
• Ontario Trial Lawyers Association 2015 Products Liability Conference: Products Liability Litigation, April, 2015, Twenty Toronto Street Conferences and Events, Toronto, ON
Scope: Provincial
Contact Information: Conference Chairs: Gary Will and Matt Lalande

The Ontario Trillium Foundation / La Fondation Trillium de l'Ontario
800 Bay St., 5th Fl., Toronto ON M5S 3A9
Tel: 416-963-4927; *Fax:* 416-963-8781
Toll-Free: 800-263-2887; *TTY:* 416-963-7905
otf@otf.ca
www.otf.ca
www.facebook.com/213404512034051
twitter.com/ONTrillium
www.youtube.com/user/trilliumfoundation1
Overview: A medium-sized provincial organization founded in 1982
Mission: To work with others to make strategic investments to build healthy, sustainable & caring communities in Ontario
Chief Officer(s):
Andrea Cohen Barrack, CEO
corpoffice@otf.ca
Finances: *Funding Sources:* Ontario government
330 volunteer(s)
Activities: *Library:* Resource Centre; Open to public by appointment

Ontario Trucking Association (OTA)
555 Dixon Rd., Toronto ON M9W 1H8
Tel: 416-249-7401; *Fax:* 866-713-4188
Other Communication: membership@ontruck.org
publicaffairs@ontruck.org
www.ontruck.org
twitter.com/ontruck
Overview: A large provincial organization founded in 1926 overseen by Canadian Trucking Alliance
Mission: To represent companies & industry suppliers; To provide political advocacy, education, & information services to North American freight transport companies
Chief Officer(s):
Brian Taylor, Chair
David H. Bradley, President
Jeff Bryan, Secretary
Scott Tilley, Treasurer
Barrie Montague, Senior Policy Advisor
Doug Switzer, Manager Government Relations
Rebecka Torn, Manager Communications
Rolf VanderZwaag, Manager Maintenance/Tech. Issues
Finances: *Funding Sources:* Membership fees
Membership: 1,700 member companies; *Committees:* Axle Weight; Credit; Education; Executive; Social/Labour; Tech./Ops; Convention; Dues; Membership; Insurance; Finance; Environmental Issues
Activities: Offering training courses & seminars; *Speaker Service:* Yes
Meetings/Conferences: • 89th Annual Ontario Trucking Association Convention, 2015, ON
Scope: Provincial

Ontario Trucking Association Education Foundation
555 Dixon Rd., Toronto ON M9W 1H8
Tel: 416-249-7401; *Fax:* 866-713-4188
info@otaef.com
www.otaef.com
Overview: A small provincial charitable organization founded in 1958
Mission: To further education for post-secondary students in Ontario who have links to the Ontario trucking industry
Chief Officer(s):
Betsy Sharples, Executive Director
Finances: *Funding Sources:* Donations
Activities: Providing scholarships for Ontario post-secondary students with a parent empolyed by an Ontario trucking company or trucking service
Awards:
• J.O. Goodman & C.V. Hoar Awards
Scholarship for first-year student enrolled in full-time studies at an accredited University (J.O. Goodman Award) or an accredited Community College (C.V. Hoar Award).

Ontario Umpires Association
ON
Tel: 905-791-0280
Other Communication: Alt. Phone: 905-338-9829
ontario_umpires@sympatico.ca
www.ontarioumpires.com
Overview: A small provincial organization
Mission: To provide officials for the games of baseball, softball, volleyball, flag football, hockey, basketball & soccer.
Affliation(s): Ontario Sports Administration; Ontario Academy of Sports Officials; Sports Events International
Chief Officer(s):
Jim Cottrell, President

Ontario Undergraduate Student Alliance (OUSA)
#345, 26 Soho St., Toronto ON M5T 1Z7
Tel: 416-341-9948
info@ousa.ca
www.ousa.ca
www.facebook.com/98136969146
twitter.com/ousa
www.youtube.com/user/EducatedSolutions
Overview: A medium-sized provincial organization founded in 1992
Mission: The represent the interests of undergraduate students who attend Brock University, McMaster University, Queen's University, Trent University, Wilfrid Laurier University, the University of Waterloo & the University of Western Ontario
Chief Officer(s):
Jen Carter, President
president@ousa.ca
Sean Madden, Executive Director
sean@ousa.ca
Staff Member(s): 5
Membership: 7 associations representing 140,000 students; *Committees:* Steering

Alma Mater Society at Queen's University
John Deutsch University Centre, Queen's University, Kingston ON K7L 3N6
Tel: 613-533-2729; *Fax:* 613-533-3002
vpua@ams.queensu.ca
www.myams.org
Chief Officer(s):
Philip Lloyd, Vice-President, University Affairs

Brock University Students' Union
Student-Alumni Centre, 500 Glendridge Ave., St Catharines ON L2S 3A1
Tel: 905-688-5550
vpea@busu.net
www.busu.net
Drew Ursacki, Vice-President, External Affairs

Federation of Students, University of Waterloo
Student Life Centre, 200 University Ave. West, Waterloo ON N2L 3G1
Tel: 519-888-4567
vped@feds.uwaterloo.ca
www.feds.uwaterloo.ca
Chief Officer(s):
Stéphane Hamade, Vice President, Education

McMaster University Students Union
1280 Main St. West, Hamilton ON L8S 4S4
Tel: 905-525-9140
vped@msu.mcmaster.ca
www.msu.mcmaster.ca
Chief Officer(s):
Rodrigo Narro-Perez, Vice President, Education

Trent in Oshawa Students Association
Trent University, #122, 55 Thornton Rd. South, Oshawa ON L1J 5Y1
Tel: 905-435-5102; *Fax:* 905-435-5101
vpua@tosa.ca
www.tosa.ca
Chief Officer(s):
Shawn Murphy, Vice President, University Affairs

University Students' Council at the University of Western Ontario
University of Western Ontario, London ON N6A 3K7

Tel: 519-661-3574; *Fax:* 519-661-2094
uscvpext@uwo.ca
www.usc.uwo.ca
Chief Officer(s):
Jen Carter, Vice President, External
Wilfrid Laurier University Students' Union
75 University Ave. West, Waterloo ON N2L 3C5
Tel: 519-884-0710
rcamman@wlu.ca
www.wlusu.com
Chief Officer(s):
Rick Camman, Vice President, University Affairs
rcamman@wlu.ca

Ontario Underwater Council (OUC)

#109, 1 Concorde Gat, Toronto ON M3C 3C6
Tel: 416-426-7033; *Fax:* 416-426-7280
ouc@underwatercouncil.com
www.underwatercouncil.com
www.facebook.com/groups/39720054237
Overview: A small provincial organization
Mission: To represent all divers in Ontario; to promote the sport of scuba diving
Chief Officer(s):
Rick Le Blanc, President
ouc.president@underwatercouncil.com
Staff Member(s): 1; 100 volunteer(s)
Membership: 2,600+; *Fees:* $15 blue; $37 gold; $130 commercial

Ontario Universities Athletics *See* Ontario University Athletics

Ontario University Athletics (OUA) / Sports universitaires de l'Ontario

#230, 1119 Fennell Ave. East, Hamilton ON L8T 1S2
Tel: 905-540-1966; *Fax:* 905-574-2840
info@oua.ca
www.oua.ca
www.facebook.com/OntarioUniversityAthletics
twitter.com/ouasport
www.youtube.com/ouachampionsforlife
Previous Name: Ontario Universities Athletics
Overview: A small provincial organization founded in 1898
Mission: To provide leadership, stewardship & policy direction for university sport; to govern interuniversity sport competition in Ontario on behalf of member institutions
Member of: Canadian Interuniversity Sport
Chief Officer(s):
Jennifer Myers, President, 416-736-5968
jmyers@yorku.ca
Ward Disle, Executive Director, 905-540-5151
ward.dilse@oua.ca
Finances: *Annual Operating Budget:* $250,000-$500,000
Staff Member(s): 4
Membership: 19 schools; 9,000 student athletes
Activities: *Awareness Events:* Women of Influence Luncheon, Nov.; *Internships:* Yes

Ontario University Registrars' Association (OUSA)

900 McGill Rd., Kamloops BC V2C 0C8
Tel: 250-828-5019
www.oura.ca
Overview: A medium-sized provincial organization founded in 1964 overseen by Association of Registrars of Universities and Colleges of Canada
Chief Officer(s):
Lucy Bellissimo, President
Membership: *Member Profile:* Ontario university registrars, admissions, records, computer systems, recruitment, financial aid, graduate studies and other university personnel involved in registrarial work.
Meetings/Conferences: • Ontario University Registrars' Association 2015 Conference, February, 2015, Toronto Marriott Downtown Eaton Centre Hotel, Toronto, ON
Scope: Provincial

Ontario Urban Forest Council (OUFC)

Mount Pleasant Group of Cemeteries, #23/25, 1523 Warden Ave., Toronto ON M1R 4Z8
Tel: 416-936-6735; *Fax:* 416-291-5709
info@oufc.org
www.oufc.org
Previous Name: Ontario Shade Tree Council
Overview: A medium-sized provincial organization founded in 1964
Mission: To promote & assist in the protection & preservation of shade trees; to cooperate with all associations, government agencies, industry & individuals with a mutual interest in preserving & developing Ontario's shade tree heritage & landscape; to promote management of urban forest in Ontario
Affiliation(s): Urban Forest Network
Chief Officer(s):
Jack Radecki, Executive Director
Finances: *Annual Operating Budget:* Less than $50,000
11 volunteer(s)
Membership: 189 corporate + 9 senior/lifetime + 55 individual; *Fees:* Student: $25; Individual: $75; Group/Corporate: $150
Activities: *Speaker Service:* Yes

Ontario Veal Association

449 Laird Rd., Guelph ON N1G 4W1
Tel: 519-824-2942; *Fax:* 519-824-2534
info@ontarioveal.on.ca
www.ontarioveal.on.ca
twitter.com/OntarioVeal
Overview: A small provincial organization founded in 1990
Mission: To promote & enhance a viable & competitive Ontario veal industry through innovation, marketing, advocacy & education; to represent Ontario's veal producers as a progressive & dynamic organization that is dedicated to strategically & effectively addressing the needs of the industry through a responsible regulatory marketing system

Ontario Vegetation Management Association (OVMA)

4 Spruce Blvd., Acton ON L7J 2Y2
Tel: 905-805-2294; *Fax:* 519-853-0352
info@ovma.ca
www.ovma.ca
Overview: A small provincial organization founded in 1984
Chief Officer(s):
Geoff Gordon, President
Membership: *Fees:* $90 individual; $300 corporate gold; $450 Corporate Platinum; *Member Profile:* Promotes environmentally safe vegetation management

Ontario Veterinary Medical Association (OVMA)

#205, 420 Bronte St. South, Milton ON L9T 0H9
Tel: 905-875-0756; *Fax:* 905-875-0958
Toll-Free: 800-670-1702
info@ovma.org
www.ovma.org
www.facebook.com/onvetmedassoc
twitter.com/OnVetMedAssoc
www.youtube.com/user/TheOVMA
Overview: A medium-sized provincial organization founded in 1874 overseen by Canadian Veterinary Medical Association
Mission: To represent Ontario veterinarians in small animal, large animal & mixed practice as well as those employed in government, industry or other institutions; programs include government & public relations, humane veterinary practice, continuing education in veterinary science & practice management & direct services to members.
Chief Officer(s):
Doug Raven, CEO
draven@ovma.org
Melissa Carlaw, Manager, Communications & Public Relations
mcarlaw@ovma.org
Finances: *Funding Sources:* Membership fees; events; advertising
Staff Member(s): 15
Membership: 4,400+; *Fees:* Schedule available; *Member Profile:* Veterinarians, Ontario

Ontario Vintage Radio Association (OVRA)

ON
www.ovra.ca
Overview: A small provincial organization founded in 1970
Mission: To preserve Canada's radio history, literature & equipment; to serve as a forum for members to exchange information & continue the legacy of the original club.
Finances: *Funding Sources:* Membership fees
Activities: Auctions; flea markets of radio & related material; guest speakers; *Speaker Service:* Yes; *Library:* OVRA Library; by appointment

Ontario Volleyball Association (OVA)

#304, 3 Concorde Gate, Toronto ON M3C 3N7
Tel: 416-426-7316; *Fax:* 416-426-7109
Toll-Free: 800-563-5938
info@ontariovolleyball.org
www.ontariovolleyball.org
www.facebook.com/OntarioVolleyball
twitter.com/ova_updates
www.youtube.com/user/ontariovolley
Overview: A large provincial organization founded in 1929 overseen by Volleyball Canada
Mission: To lead in the promotion & development of volleyball in Ontario
Chief Officer(s):
Linda Melnick, President
OVAPresident@ontariovolleyball.org
Janet Cairns, Secretary & Vice-President, Administration
VPSecretary@ontariovolleyball.org
John Nguyen, Treasurer & Vice-President, Finance
VPTreasurer@ontariovolleyball.org
Jo-Anne Ljubicic, Executive Director
jljubicic@ontariovolleyball.org
Staff Member(s): 13
Membership: *Fees:* Schedule available; *Committees:* Train to Compete; Beach; Executive
Activities: Championships for indorr & beach volleyball; *Internships:* Yes
Awards:
• Scarborough Solars Award (Award)
• Quarter Century Club (Award), Volunteer Awards
• Doug Robbie Volunteer of the Year Award (Award), Volunteer Awards
• Special Achievement Award (Award), Volunteer Awards
• Achievement Award (Award), Volunteer Awards
• Recognition Award (Award), Volunteer Awards
• Corporate & Partner Awards (Award), Volunteer Awards
• Club Recognition Awards (Award), Volunteer Awards
• Ken Davies Memorial Award (Award), Athlete/Coach/Officials Awards
• Evelyn Holick Award (Award), Athlete/Coach/Officials Awards
• Mike Bugarski Coach of the Year Award (Award), Athlete/Coach/Officials Awards
• Developmental Coach of the Year Award (Award), Athlete/Coach/Officials Awards
• Officials' Committee Award of Merit (Award), Athlete/Coach/Officials Awards
• Child & Heese Trophy (Award), Athlete/Coach/Officials Awards

Ontario Waste Management Association (OWMA) / Société ontarienne de gestion des déchets

#3, 2005 Clark Blvd., Brampton ON L6T 5P8
Tel: 905-791-9500; *Fax:* 905-791-9514
info@owma.org
www.owma.org
www.linkedin.com/company/ontario-waste-management-association
twitter.com/OWMA1
Overview: A medium-sized provincial organization founded in 1977
Mission: To act as the voice of the private sector waste industry in Ontario; To protect the enviroment by properly managing waste & recyclable materials
Membership: *Member Profile:* Private sector independent companies in Ontario which provide waste & recycling services; Associate members include equipment manufacturers, suppliers, legal firms, & consultants; *Committees:* Safety & Transportation; Waste Diversion & Recycling; Waste Transfer & Disposal; Organics Diversion; Resource Recovery
Activities: Monitoring & assessing regulatory & policy initiatives; Promoting new standards & regulatory policies to improve waste management services; Providing information to members about government initiatives, waste management, & business issues
Meetings/Conferences: • Ontario Waste Management Association Canadian Waste to Resource Confernece 2015, November, 2015, Palais des congrès de Montréal, Montréal, QC
Scope: Provincial

Ontario Water Garden Society *See* Greater Toronto Water Garden & Horticultural Society

Ontario Water Polo Association Incorporated (OWP) / L'Association de water polo d'Ontario

#206, 3 Concorde Gate, Toronto ON M3C 3N7
Tel: 416-426-7028; *Fax:* 416-426-7356
www.ontariowaterpolo.ca
Also Known As: Ontario Water Polo
Overview: A medium-sized provincial organization founded in 1967 overseen by Water Polo Canada
Member of: Water Polo Canada
Chief Officer(s):
Meighan Colterjohn, President
Kathy Torrens, Secretary
kathy.torrens@ontariowaterpolo.ca

Finances: *Annual Operating Budget:* $100,000-$250,000
Staff Member(s): 2; 100 volunteer(s)
Membership: 1,200 individual; *Fees:* $12-$56 individual; $30-$460 club
Activities: *Speaker Service:* Yes

Ontario Water Ski Association (OWSA)

#209, 3 Concorde Gate, Toronto ON M3C 3N7
Tel: 416-426-7092; *Fax:* 416-426-7378
office@wswo.ca
www.wswo.ca
www.facebook.com/waterskiwakeboardontario
twitter.com/wswo
Also Known As: Water Ski Wakeboard Ontario
Overview: A medium-sized provincial organization founded in 1976
Mission: To promote & develop the sport of water skiing through safety & instructional tournaments, courses & demonstrations
Member of: Water Ski & Wakeboard Canada
Chief Officer(s):
Paul Roberts, President
pwroberts@sympatico.ca
Finances: *Funding Sources:* Private; provincial grant
Staff Member(s): 1
Membership: *Fees:* $10 associate; $40 active; $100 family; $80 camp; $100 club/school; *Member Profile:* Individual & families involved in recreational &/or competitive water skiing, also water ski schools, camps & clubs
Activities: Watersport/waterski/wakeboard events & tournaments in Ontario; *Library* by appointment
Awards:
• Water Ski Skill Awards (Award)

Ontario Water Well Association *See* Ontario Ground Water Association

Ontario Water Works Association (OWWA)

#100, 922 The East Mall Dr., Toronto ON M9B 6K1
Tel: 416-231-1555; *Fax:* 416-231-1556
Toll-Free: 866-975-0575
waterinfo@owwa.ca
www.owwa.com
www.linkedin.com/company/ontario-water-works-association
Overview: A medium-sized provincial organization
Mission: To protect public health through the delivery of safe, sufficient, & sustainable drinking water in Ontario
Member of: American Water Works Association
Affliation(s): Ontario Municipal Water Association; Ontario Water Works Equipment Association
Chief Officer(s):
Saad Jasim, President
jasims@windsor.ijc.org
Lee Anne E. Jones, Vice-President
ljones@toronto.ca
Bill Balfour, Executive Director, 905-642-5283
bbalfour@owwa.ca
Lesia Lachmaniuk, Manager, Marketing & Membership, 416-231-1555, Fax: 416-231-1556
llachmaniuk@owwa.ca
Glenn Powell, Director, Communications, 905-827-4508, Fax: 905-827-6483
gpowell@owwa.ca
Ray Miller, Secretary-Treasurer
rmiller@clowcanada.com
Membership: 1,100+; *Member Profile:* Drinking water professionals in Ontario, such as hydrogeologists, scientists, engineers, chemists, & managers & technicians employed by Ontario's municipal water systems; *Committees:* Climate Change; C-PAC; Conference Management; Continuing Education; Cross Connection Control; Distribution; Government Affairs; Groundwater; Joint OWWA / OMWA; Management; Membership; OWWA / WEAO Joint Asset Management; Publications; Small Systems; Source Water Protection; Training, Certification, & Safety; Treatment; University Forum; Water Efficiency; Water for People - Canada; Young Professionals; Youth Education
Activities: Improving technology, science & management; Influencing government policy; Providing education for members; *Library:* Ontario Water Works Association Library
Awards:
• The George Warren Fuller Award (Award)
Presented to a Section member for their distinguished service to the water supply field in commemoration of the sound engineering skill, brilliant diplomatic talent, and constructive leadership which characterized the life of George Warren Fuller.
Meetings/Conferences: • 2015 OWWA/OMWA Joint Annual Conference and OWWEA Trade Show, April, 2015, Toronto, ON
Scope: Provincial
Description: This annual industry highlight features a full slate of plenary and technical sessions focusing on the latest in technology and research affecting drinking water from source to tap. The Trade Show consistently has more than 100 exhibitors representing the manufacturers and suppliers of products and services for the water industry.
• 2016 OWWA/OMWA Joint Annual Conference and OWWEA Trade Show, May, 2016, Windsor, ON
Scope: Provincial
Description: This annual industry highlight features a full slate of plenary and technical sessions focusing on the latest in technology and research affecting drinking water from source to tap. The Trade Show consistently has more than 100 exhibitors representing the manufacturers and suppliers of products and services for the water industry.
• 2017 OWWA/OMWA Joint Annual Conference and OWWEA Trade Show, May, 2017, Niagara Falls, ON
Scope: Provincial
Description: This annual industry highlight features a full slate of plenary and technical sessions focusing on the latest in technology and research affecting drinking water from source to tap. The Trade Show consistently has more than 100 exhibitors representing the manufacturers and suppliers of products and services for the water industry.
Publications:
• Consultants' Listing [a publication of the Ontario Water Works Association]
Frequency: 3 pa; *Accepts Advertising*
• Ontario Pipeline
Type: Magazine; *Frequency:* 3 pa; *Accepts Advertising*
Profile: A joint publication of the Ontario Water Works Association, the Ontario Municipal Water Association, & the Ontario Water Works Equipment Association

Ontario Waterpower Association (OWA)

#264, 380 Armour Rd., Peterborough ON K9H 7L7
Fax: 705-743-1570
Toll-Free: 866-743-1500
info@owa.ca
www.owa.ca
Overview: A medium-sized provincial organization
Mission: Promotes the achievement of sustainable development, provides a source for quality information about waterpower & grows & enhances the competitiveness of the Ontario waterpower industry.
Chief Officer(s):
Paul Norris, President, 866-743-1500 Ext. 22
Meetings/Conferences: • 15th Annual Power of Water Caanada Conference 2015, October, 2015, White Oaks Conference Resort, Niagara-on-the-Lake, ON
Scope: Provincial
Description: The largest gathering of the hydroelectric sector in Canada and will feature a tradeshow with more than 50 exhibitors.
Contact Information: Website: conference.owa.ca; Twitter: twitter.com/PowerofWaterCan

Ontario Weightlifting Association (OWA)

PO Box 14012, Stn. Glebe, Ottawa ON K1S 3T2
e-mail: owamembership@gmail.com
www.onweightlifting.ca
www.facebook.com/OntarioWeightlifting
twitter.com/ONWeightlifting
www.youtube.com/user/ontarioweightlifting
Overview: A medium-sized provincial organization founded in 1968
Mission: To govern weightlifting in Ontario
Member of: Ontario Hockey Federation; Hockey Canada
Affliation(s): Canadian Weightlifting Federation; Sport Alliance of Ontario; Sport4Ontario
Chief Officer(s):
Moira Lassen, President
owapresident1@gmail.com
Staff Member(s): 6
Membership: 36 clubs; *Fees:* $80 competitive; $50 introductory; $35 participation/coach/official; $2 volunteer

Ontario Wheelchair Sports Association (OWSA)

#104, 3 Concordia Gate, Toronto ON M3C 3N7
Tel: 416-426-7189
info@ontwheelchairsports.org
ontwheelchairsports.org
Overview: A medium-sized provincial organization founded in 1972
Mission: To provide sporting & recreational opportunities for athletes who compete in wheelchairs
Member of: Canadian Wheelchair Sports Association
Affliation(s): Canadian Wheelchair Sports Association
Chief Officer(s):
Ken Thom, President
kenthom@rogers.com
Bonnie Hartley, Interim Executive Director
Finances: *Funding Sources:* Provincial Government
Staff Member(s): 3

Ontario Women's Health Network (OWHN)

#301, 180 Dundas St. West, Toronto ON M5G 1Z8
Tel: 416-408-4840
Toll-Free: 877-860-4545
owhn@owhn.on.ca
www.owhn.on.ca
twitter.com/The_OWHN
Overview: A medium-sized local organization founded in 1997
Mission: To act as a network of individuals & organizations that promote women's health in Ontario

Ontario Women's Hockey Association (OWHA) / Association de hockey féminin de l'Ontario

#3, 5155 Spectrum Way, Mississauga ON L4W 5A1
Tel: 905-282-9980; *Fax:* 905-282-9982
info@owha.on.ca
www.owha.on.ca
twitter.com/OWHAhockey
Overview: A medium-sized provincial organization founded in 1975
Mission: To provide & develop opportunities for girls & women to play female hockey in all aspects of female hockey; To foster & encourage leadership programs in all areas related to the development of female hockey in Ontario; To promote hockey as a game played primarily for enjoyment while also fostering sportsmanship
Member of: Hockey Canada
Chief Officer(s):
Suzanne Essex, Chair
sessex@owha.on.ca
Fran Rider, President
fran@owha.on.ca
Michelle Smith, Secretary
msmith@owha.on.ca
Darrell Burt, Treasurer
dburt@owha.on.ca

Ontario Women's Justice Network (OWJN)

METRAC, 158 Spadina Rd., Toronto ON M5R 2T8
Tel: 416-392-3135; *TTY:* 877-558-5570
info@metrac.org
www.owjn.org
www.facebook.com/owjn.org
twitter.com/owjn
Overview: A medium-sized provincial organization founded in 1996
Mission: To demystify the legal system; to examine various justice issues; to provide legal information
Member of: National Association of Women & the Law
Membership: *Member Profile:* Violence against women organizations; community activists; researchers; students
Activities: Online legal resource for women's organizations & individuals working on issues related to justice & violence against women & children

Ontario Woodlot Association

RR#4, 275 County Rd. 44, Kemptville ON K0G 1J0
Tel: 613-258-0110; *Fax:* 613-258-0207
info@ont-woodlot-assoc.org
www.ont-woodlot-assoc.org
www.facebook.com/pages/Ontario-Woodlot-Association/237050606357425
Overview: A small provincial organization founded in 1992
Mission: To promote the wise & profitable use of Ontario's private land forest resource
Chief Officer(s):
Wade Knight, Executive Director
Pieter Leenhouts, President
David Sexsmith, Vice-President
Membership: 1,700; *Fees:* $40

Ontario Workers' Compensation Institute *See* Institute for Work & Health

Ontario Zoroastrian Community Foundation (OZCF)
Zoroastrian Religious and Cultural Centre (OZCF Centre), 1187 Burnhamthorpe Road East, Oakville ON L6H 7B3
Tel: 905-271-0366
www.ozcf.com
Overview: A small provincial charitable organization
Chief Officer(s):
Percy Dastur, President
percydastur@gmail.com
Membership: *Fees:* $100 family; $30 seniors; $65 single; $25 student; *Member Profile:* Zoroastrians living in Ontario; *Committees:* Communication/IT, Social & Entertainment, Facility Management, Finance, Lectures & Learning, Membership, Newsletter, Religious, Seniors, Sports, Youth
Activities: Religious education program for children; Zoroastrian Scouts; Seniors program; Cultural Kanoun for Farsi speakers; Lecture group; Library; Youth group; Committees for newly landed immigrants & others in need;

Ontario's Finest Inns & Spas
PO Box 9, 435 Turnberry St., Brussels ON N0G 1H0
Tel: 519-887-8383; *Fax:* 519-887-8192
Toll-Free: 800-340-4667
info@ontariosfinestinns.com
www.ontariosfinest.ca
Previous Name: Innkeepers of Ontario
Overview: A small provincial organization
Membership: *Member Profile:* Innkeepers, spa proprietors

Open Door Group
#300, 30 East 6 Ave., Vancouver BC V5T 1J4
Tel: 604-876-0773; *Fax:* 604-873-1758
Toll-Free: 866-377-3670
info@opendoorgroup.org
www.opendoorgroup.org
www.facebook.com/OpenDoorGroup
Previous Name: Arbutus Vocational Society; THEO BC
Overview: A medium-sized provincial organization founded in 1976
Mission: To assist psychiatrically, emotionally, & socially disadvantaged people to develop the necessary skills to lead to more satisfying lives
Chief Officer(s):
Tom Burnell, CEO
tom.burnell@opendoorgroup.org
Alona Puehse, Director, Public Relations & Corporate Development
alona.puehse@opendoorgroup.org
Finances: *Funding Sources:* Provincial Government

Burnaby Office
210-5066 Kingsway, Burnaby BC V5H 2E7
Tel: 604-434-0770; *Fax:* 604-434-0778

Coquitlam Office
#204, 504 Cottonwood Ave., Coquitlam BC V3J 2R5
Tel: 604-937-0775; *Fax:* 604-937-0776

Gardengate Office
915 Southill St., Kamloops BC V2B 7Z9
Tel: 250-554-9453; *Fax:* 250-554-9402

Kamloops North Shore Office
795 Tranquille Rd., Kamloops BC V2B 3J3
Tel: 250-377-3670; *Fax:* 250-377-3695

Kamloops South Shore Office
#100, 275 Lansdowne St., Kamloops BC V2C 1X8
Tel: 250-434-9441; *Fax:* 250-434-9442

Kelowna Office
#101, 591 Bernard Ave., Kelowna BC V1Y 6N9
Tel: 250-763-9002; *Fax:* 250-763-9088

Merritt Office
PO Box 1389, #117, 1700 Garcia St., Merritt BC V1K 1B8
Tel: 250-378-2045; *Fax:* 250-378-5830

Penticton Office
#203, 3115 Skaha Lake Rd., Penticton BC V2A 6G5
Tel: 250-493-4010; *Fax:* 250-493-4011

Richmond Office
#415, 5900 No. 3 Rd., Richmond BC V6X 3P7
Tel: 604-247-0770; *Fax:* 604-247-1758

Surrey Office
#266, 8128 - 128th St., Surrey BC V3W 1R1
Tel: 604-495-1775; *Fax:* 604-572-3008

Vernon Office
#301, 3605 - 31st St., Vernon BC V1T 5J4
Tel: 250-260-4974; *Fax:* 250-260-3724

Open Learning Agency *See* Open Learning at Thompson Rivers University

Open Learning at Thompson Rivers University (TRU-OL)
BC Centre for Open Learning, 900 McGill Rd., 4th Fl., Kamloops BC V2C 0C8
Tel: 250-852-7000
Toll-Free: 800-663-9711
student@tru.ca
www.tru.ca/distance.html
Previous Name: Open Learning Agency
Overview: A small provincial organization founded in 1988
Mission: To enhance the personal growth of individuals & their performance in society & in the workplace through the provision of high quality, flexible learning products, services & systems
Member of: Association of Community Colleges of Canada; Association of Universities & Colleges of Canada; Canadian Virtual University
Chief Officer(s):
Katherine Sutherland, Vice-Provost
Finances: *Funding Sources:* Provincial government
Activities: Open School; Open College; BC Open University; Knowledge Network; OLA Skills Centres; Learning Systems Institute; Canadian Learning Bank; International Credential Evaluation Service

Open Space Arts Society (OS)
510 Fort St., Victoria BC V8W 1E6
Tel: 250-383-8833; *Fax:* 250-383-8841
openspace@openspace.ca
www.openspace.ca
www.facebook.com/openspacevic
twitter.com/OpenSpaceVic
Overview: A small local organization founded in 1972
Mission: Open Space supports experimental artistic practices in all contemporary arts disciplines, acting as a laboratory for engaging art, artists, and communities.
Member of: Pacific Association of Artist-Run Centres; Canadian Museums Association; Canadian Conference for the Arts; Professional Arts Organizations of Greater Victoria
Chief Officer(s):
Helen Marzolf, Executive Director, 250-383-8833
director@openspace.ca
Ted Hiebert, Chair
Finances: *Annual Operating Budget:* $100,000-$250,000; *Funding Sources:* Federal, provincial & regional government
Staff Member(s): 3; 5 volunteer(s)
Membership: 150; *Fees:* $15-$75; *Committees:* Community Relations Committee; Facility Committee; Human Resources Committee; Program Committee
Activities: Visual Arts; New Media; Interarts; New Music; Literary; *Internships:* Yes; *Library:* Open Space Resource Centre;

Opéra Atelier (OA)
St. Lawrence Hall, 157 King St. East, 4th Fl., Toronto ON M5C 1G9
Tel: 416-703-3767; *Fax:* 416-703-4895
opera.atelier@operaatelier.com
www.operaatelier.com
www.facebook.com/466529060483
twitter.com/OperaAtelier
Also Known As: Atelier Theatre Society
Overview: A small local organization founded in 1986
Mission: To produce opera, ballet, & drama from the 17th & 18th centuries
Chief Officer(s):
Bryan Graham, Chair
Patricia Barretto, Executive Director
patricia.barretto@operaatelier.com
Jeannette Lajeunesse Zingg, Co-Artistic Director/Choreographer
Marshall Pynkoski, Co-Artistic Director
David Fallis, Music Director
david.fallis@operaatelier.com
Finances: *Annual Operating Budget:* $500,000-$1.5 Million; *Funding Sources:* Government; Corporations; Individual donations; Ticket sales
Staff Member(s): 12; 50 volunteer(s)
Membership: 35; *Fees:* $50+; *Member Profile:* Arts patrons
Awards:
• Marshall Pynkoski Lieutenant Governor Award for the Arts (Award)

L'Opéra de Montréal (ODM) / Montréal Opera
260, boul de Maisonneuve ouest, Montréal QC H2X 1Y9
Tél: 514-985-2222; *Téléc:* 514-985-2219
Ligne sans frais: 877-385-2222
info@operademontreal.com
www.operademontreal.com
www.facebook.com/23275515418
twitter.com/operademontreal
www.youtube.com/user/OperadeMtl
Aperçu: *Dimension:* petite; *Envergure:* locale; fondée en 1980
Mission: Afin de présenter des productions d'opéra de comparable qualité et originalité à ceux observés dans les plus grands opéras du monde; cherche la contribution du personnel de création de niveaux local et national; ainsi que d'inviter les meilleurs artistes de l'étranger; soutient l'émergence de nouveaux talents opéra canadienne
Affliation(s): Professional Opera Companies of Canada; Opera America
Membre(s) du bureau directeur:
Pierre Dufour, Directeur général
pdufour@operademontreal.com
Christine Krebs, Directrice, Services financiers et administratifs
ckrebs@operademontreal.com
Michel Beulac, Directeur Artistique
mbeaulac@operademontreal.com
Monique Denis, Responsable, Dons et commandites
mdenis@operademontreal.com
Pierre Vachon, Directeur, Communications, communauté et éducation
pvachon@operademontreal.com
Bernard Stotland, Président
Chantal Lambert, Directrice, Atelier Lyrique
Membre(s) du personnel: 33
Activités: Six productions d'opéra pour la saison; atelier lyrique; programme d'apprentissage; gala-bénéfice annuel; Signature concert-bénéfice de l'événement; *Stagiaires:* Oui; *Service de conférenciers:* Oui

Opéra de Québec
1220, av Taché, Québec QC G1R 3B4
Tél: 418-529-4142; *Téléc:* 418-529-3735
operaqc@mediom.qc.ca
www.operadequebec.qc.ca
fr-fr.facebook.com/operadequebec
Aperçu: *Dimension:* petite; *Envergure:* locale; fondée en 1983
Mission: Produire des spectacles d'opéra professionnels à Québec
Membre(s) du bureau directeur:
Gaston Déry, Président
Grégoire Legendre, Directeur général et artistique
Membre(s) du personnel: 7

Opera Lyra
#110, 2 Daly Ave., Ottawa ON K1N 6E2
Tel: 613-233-9200; *Fax:* 613-233-5431
Toll-Free: 877-233-5972
frontdesk@operalyra.ca
www.operalyra.ca
www.facebook.com/operalyraottawa
twitter.com/OperaLyraOttawa
www.flickr.com/photos/operalyraottawa/
Also Known As: Opera Lyra Ottawa
Overview: A small local organization founded in 1984
Mission: Opera Lyra's mandate is to produce and present opera productions in the National Capital Region of the highest quality; to promote opera as an art form and make it as accessible to as large a segment of the population as possible through community outreach and education; and, wherever possible, to encourage, nurture and support Canadian artists.
Chief Officer(s):
Elizabeth Howarth, General Director
Finances: *Funding Sources:* Ticket Sales, Sponsorships, Grants, and Private Donations
Staff Member(s): 8; 3 volunteer(s)
Membership: *Fees:* $250; *Committees:* Opera Lyra Guild; Young Opera Lovers; Board of Directors: Finance Committee, Fundraising Committee, Special Events Committee, Marketing Committee
Activities: Two main stage opera productions a year, studio program with accompanying school production, fundraising galas, community concerts; *Internships:* Yes; *Library:* Opera Lyra Library

Opera.ca
#6286, 3200 Bloor St. West, Toronto ON M6S 5A5
Tel: 416-591-7222
www.opera.ca
www.facebook.com/pages/Operaca/142045112454
twitter.com/opera_ca
Overview: A medium-sized national organization

Mission: Opera.ca works with members across the country to advance the interests of Canada's opera community and create greater opportunity for opera audiences and professionals alike.
Affiliation(s): Canadian Children's Opera Chorus; International Resource Centre for Performing Artists; National Arts Centre; Opera Canada; Opera in Concert; Saskatoon Opera; Théâtre Lyrichorégra 20; Toronto Operetta Theatre; Toronto Summer Music
Chief Officer(s):
Christina Loewen, Executive Director
Krista Wodelet, Coordinator, Membership & Communications
Staff Member(s): 2
Membership: 13 opera companies; *Fees:* $75 individual; $175 career services subscription; $350 educational producing affiliate; $300 business; $250 affiliate

Operating Room Nurses Association of Canada (ORNAC) / Association des infirmières et infirmiers de salles d'opération du Canada

Tel: 604-466-7965
info@ornac.ca
www.ornac.ca
Overview: A large national organization founded in 1983
Mission: To promote operating nursing for the betterment of surgical patient care
Member of: Canadian Nurses Association; International Federation of Perioperative Nurses (IFPN)
Chief Officer(s):
Rupinder Khotar, President
president@ornac.ca
Liz Beck, RN, CPN(C), Treasurer
treasurer@ornac.ca
Catherine Harley, Executive Director
executivedirector@ornac.ca
Finances: *Annual Operating Budget:* Less than $50,000
25 volunteer(s)
Membership: 3,500; *Fees:* $25-50; *Member Profile:* Perioperative RN; *Committees:* Standards; Research; By-Laws; National Conference; Awards; Editorial Advisory; Finance; Nominations; Public Awareness; Scope of Practice; Translation
Activities: Professional & personal enhancement of operating room nurses; *Awareness Events:* OR Nurse Day, Nov.; *Speaker Service:* Yes
Awards:
• Gloria Stephens Award for Excellence as an Educator of Perioperative Nursing (Award)
• RMAC Patient Safety Award (Award)
• ORNAC - Muriel Shewchuk Leadership Award (Award)
• Isabelle Adams Award for Excellence in Perioperative Nursing (Award)
• ORNAC / Johnson & Johnson Drake Thompson Writing Award (Award)
• Lorne Flower Memorial Award (Award)
• 3M Canadian Infection Prevention Champion Award (Award)
• Cardinal Health Research Grant (Grant)
Deadline: March 15 *Amount:* $5,000
• Bursary for OR Nurse (Scholarship)
Deadline: January 5
Meetings/Conferences: • Operating Room Nurses Association of Canada National Conference 2015, May, 2015, Shaw Conference Centre, Edmonton, AB
Scope: National
Description: Theme: "Bridging Excellence in Perioperative Practice"
Contact Information: Margot Walsh, Chair, National Conference; nationalconference@ornac.ca
Publications:
• ORNAC Journal
Type: Journal
Profile: Journal promotes professional perioperative nursing practice and provides its membership with relevant, practice-based information to apply in today's OR environment.

Operating Room Nurses Association of Nova Scotia (ORNANS)

NS
www.ornans.ca
Overview: A medium-sized provincial organization overseen by Operating Room Nurses Association of Canada
Chief Officer(s):
Ida Berry, President, 902-479-3330
idaberryornans@gmail.com
Membership: *Member Profile:* Registered Nurses in Nova Scotia who are engaged in operating room nursing or involved in the Perioperative setting.
Activities: *Awareness Events:* Perioperative Nurses Week, November
Meetings/Conferences: • Operating Room Nurses Association of Nova Scotia Annual General Meeting 2015, June, 2015, Old Orchard Inn Resort & Spa, Annapolis Valley, NS
Scope: Provincial

Operating Room Nurses Association of Ontario (ORNAO)

ON
e-mail: info@ornao.org
www.ornao.org
Overview: A medium-sized provincial organization overseen by Operating Room Nurses Association of Canada
Chief Officer(s):
Debra Bastone, President, 807-468-9861 Ext. 2223
president@ornao.org
Membership: *Member Profile:* Registered Nurses in Ontario who are engaged in operating room nursing or involved in the Perioperative setting.
Activities: *Awareness Events:* Perioperative Nurses Week, November

Operating Room Nurses of Alberta Association (ORNAA)

AB
e-mail: info@ornaa.org
www.ornaa.org
Overview: A medium-sized provincial organization overseen by Operating Room Nurses Association of Canada
Chief Officer(s):
Lucia Pfeuti, President
president@ornaa.org
Charlotte Parker, Secretary
secretary@ornaa.org
Membership: *Member Profile:* Registered Nurses in Alberta who are engaged in operating room nursing or a member of CARNA who are involved in the Perioperative setting.
Activities: *Awareness Events:* Perioperative Nurses Week, November
Awards:
• Muriel Shewchuk Excellence in Leadership Award for Alberta (Award)
• The ORNAA Promising Star Award (Award)
Meetings/Conferences: • 2015 Operating Room Nurses of Alberta Association Provincial Conference, 2015, AB

Operation Come Home

PO Box 53157, Ottawa ON K1N 1C5
Tel: 613-230-4663; *Fax:* 613-230-8223
Toll-Free: 800-668-4663
info@operationcomehome.ca
www.operationcomehome.ca
Previous Name: Operation Go Home
Overview: A medium-sized national charitable organization founded in 1971
Mission: To reunite runaway youth (aged 16-19) with their families or to connect them with a safe environment off the streets
Chief Officer(s):
Elspeth McKay, Executive Director
Finances: *Annual Operating Budget:* $250,000-$500,000; *Funding Sources:* Private; fundraising; corporate; service clubs
Staff Member(s): 8; 50 volunteer(s)
Activities: Spring Gala; Raceway; Steam Train; *Speaker Service:* Yes

Operation Eyesight Universal

4 Parkdale Cres. NW, Calgary AB T2N 3T8
Tel: 403-283-6323; *Fax:* 403-270-1899
Toll-Free: 800-585-8265
info@operationeyesight.ca
www.operationeyesight.ca
www.linkedin.com/company/operation-eyesight
www.facebook.com/OperationEyesightUniversal
twitter.com/OpEyesight
www.youtube.com/user/OpEyesightUniversal
Overview: A large international charitable organization founded in 1963
Mission: To eliminate avoidable blindness through the development & support of permanent, self-sustaining, quality blindness prevention & sight restoration programs for those people in greatest need
Member of: International Agency for the Prevention of Blindness
Affiliation(s): International Agency for the Prevention of Blindness; L.V. Prasad Eye Institute; Vision 2020
Chief Officer(s):
Brian Foster, Acting President & CEO
Finances: *Annual Operating Budget:* $3 Million-$5 Million; *Funding Sources:* Government of Canada provided through the Canadian International Development Agency
Staff Member(s): 20; 28 volunteer(s)
Activities: Gift of Sight Tour; *Speaker Service:* Yes
Publications:
• SightLines
Type: Newsletter

Vancouver Regional Office
#200, 4 Parkdale Crescent NW, Calgary AB T2N 3T8
Tel: 403-283-6323; *Fax:* 403-270-1899
Toll-Free: 800-585-8265
vancouver@operationeyesight.ca
www.linkedin.com/company/operation-eyesight
www.facebook.com/OperationEyesightUniversal
twitter.com/OpEyesight
www.youtube.com/user/OpEyesightUniversal
Affliation(s): Vision 2020; IAPB; L.V. Prasad Eye Institute; Optometry Givign Sight; Eyesight International; Seeing is Believing
Chief Officer(s):
Brian Foster, Executive Director
Rob Ohlson, Chair

Opération Gareautrain ***See*** Operation Lifesaver

Operation Go Home ***See*** Operation Come Home

Operation Go Home - Winnipeg Office ***See*** Resource Assistance for Youth

Operation Harvest Sharing

PO Box 522, 58 Buell St., Brockville ON K6V 5V7
Tel: 613-342-0605; *Fax:* 613-342-1713
info@oafb.ca
operationharvestsharing.ca
Also Known As: Brockville & Area Food Bank
Overview: A small local organization
Member of: Ontario Association of Food Banks
Chief Officer(s):
Myra Garvin, President

Operation Lifesaver (OL) / Opération Gareautrain

#1401, 99 Bank St., Ottawa ON K1P 6B9
Tel: 613-564-8100; *Fax:* 613-567-6726
admin@operationlifesaver.ca
www.operationlifesaver.ca
www.facebook.com/oplifesaver
twitter.com/oplifesaver
www.youtube.com/user/OperationLifesaverCA
Overview: A small national organization founded in 1981
Mission: To create an awareness by the general public of the potential hazards of rail/highway crossings; to improve drivers' & pedestrians' behaviour at these intersections; to inform the public of the dangers associated with trespassing on railway property; & to reduce the number of accidents resulting in fatalities, injuries & monetary losses
Chief Officer(s):
Dan Di Tota, National Director
Finances: *Annual Operating Budget:* $250,000-$500,000; *Funding Sources:* Transport Canada; Railway Association of Canada
Staff Member(s): 2; 150 volunteer(s)
Activities: *Awareness Events:* OL Rail Safety Week, April

Operation Mobilization Canada (OM)

84 West St., Port Colborne ON L3K 4C8
Tel: 905-835-2546; *Fax:* 905-835-2533
Toll-Free: 877-487-7777
info.ca@om.org
www.omcanada.org
www.facebook.com/omcanada
twitter.com/om_canada
Overview: A small international charitable organization founded in 1966
Mission: Missionary training movement operating in 80 countries with 6,000 people in program every year; mobilizes & trains young Protestant believers for mission fields.
Member of: Evangelical Fellowship of Canada; Canadian Council of Christian Charities
Chief Officer(s):
Harvey Thiessen, Executive Director
Finances: *Annual Operating Budget:* $1.5 Million-$3 Million
Staff Member(s): 25
Activities: *Speaker Service:* Yes

Opération Nez rouge / Operation Red Nose
Maison Couillard, Université Laval, 2539, rue Marie-Fitzbach, Québec QC G1V 0A6
Tél: 418-653-1492; *Téléc:* 418-653-3315
Ligne sans frais: 800-463-7222
info@operationnezrouge.com
www.operationnezrouge.com
www.facebook.com/OperationNezrouge
twitter.com/ORNose
www.youtube.com/user/OperationNezrouge
Aperçu: *Dimension:* grande; *Envergure:* nationale; fondée en 1984
Mission: Service de chauffeur privé gratuit & bénévole offert pendant la période des Fêtes à tout automobiliste qui a consommé de l'alcool, our qui ne se sent pas en état de conduire son véhicule.
Membre(s) du bureau directeur:
Stéphane Thériault, Directeur général
stheriault@operationnezrouge.com

Operation Red Nose *Voir* Opération Nez rouge

Operation Springboard
#800, 2 Carlton St., Toronto ON M5B 1J3
Tel: 416-977-0089; *Fax:* 416-977-2840
info@operationspringboard.on.ca
www.operationspringboard.on.ca
www.linkedin.com/company/springboard-services
www.facebook.com/OperationSpringboard
twitter.com/OpSpringboard
www.youtube.com/user/OperationSpringbord
Also Known As: Springboard
Overview: A large provincial charitable organization founded in 1969
Mission: To design & provide services & programs that effectively reintegrate offenders into the community as responsible individuals; to develop crime prevention strategies; To promote community involvement in design & provision of services along with continuous effort to encourage understanding & support; To bring forward recommendations that will improve effectiveness of the criminal justice system.
Member of: Canadian Criminal Justice Association; American Corrections Association
Chief Officer(s):
Brad Lambert, President & Chair
Margaret Stanowski, Executive Director
Alain Mootoo, Chief Administrative Officer
Finances: *Annual Operating Budget:* Less than $50,000; *Funding Sources:* General public; corporations; foundations; government
Membership: *Committees:* Human Resources; Finance; Communication; Program; Executive; Nominating; Fundraising; Advisory Board; Audit; Innovation

Aris Kaplanis Centre for Youth, Resource Room & Attendance Program
2568 Lawrence Ave. East, Toronto ON M1P 2R7
Tel: 416-615-0788
Chief Officer(s):
Mark Schuler, Supervisor

Blue Jays Lodge
51 Dawes Rd., Toronto ON M4C 5B1
Tel: 416-698-0047; *Fax:* 416-698-0051

Diversion Office - Old City Hall
60 Queen St. West, Toronto ON M5H 2M4
Tel: 416-214-2469
Chief Officer(s):
Liz Igoe, Supervisor

Diversion Office - Scarborough Ct.
1911 Eglinton Ave. East, Toronto ON M1L 4P4
Tel: 416-755-1168
Chief Officer(s):
Nicole Howes, Diversion Counsellor

Employment Services
3195 Sheppard Avenue East, Fl. 1A, Toronto ON M1T 3K1
Tel: 416-849-4421

North Beaches Residence
2305 Gerrard St. East, Toronto ON M4E 2E4
Tel: 416-690-8001; *Fax:* 416-690-9646

Terry Fox House
230 Beverley St., Toronto ON M5T 1Z3
Tel: 416-588-7706; *Fax:* 416-536-6676

Operative Plasterers' & Cement Masons' International Association of the US & Canada (AFL-CIO/CFL) - Canadian Office
Varette Bldg., #1902, 130 Albert St., Ottawa ON K1P 5G4
Tel: 613-236-0653; *Fax:* 613-230-5138
www.buildingtrades.ca
twitter.com/CDNTrades
www.youtube.com/user/Buildingtrades12
Also Known As: Building & Construction Trades Dept.
Overview: A medium-sized national organization
Mission: To represent the interests of those employed in the building, construction, fabrication & maintenance industry in Canada ensuring safe working conditions
Chief Officer(s):
Robert Blakely, Canadian Operating Officer, 613-236-0653 Ext. 22
rblakely@buildingtrades.ca
Staff Member(s): 6
Membership: 500,000+
Activities: *Library* by appointment

Opimian Society / La Société Opimian
#420, 5165, rue Sherbrooke ouest, Montréal QC H4A 1T6
Tel: 514-483-5551; *Fax:* 514-481-9699
Toll-Free: 800-361-9421
opim@opim.ca
www.opim.ca
www.facebook.com/home.php?#!/group.php?gid=151105651580630
twitter.com/OpimianSociety
Also Known As: Wine Society of Canada
Overview: A large national organization founded in 1973
Mission: To work as Canada's only national non-profit wine ordering co-operative
Member of: International Wine Clubs Association
Chief Officer(s):
Phil Grewar, President
Phil Grewar, Vice-President
Finances: *Funding Sources:* Membership fees
25 volunteer(s)
Membership: 20,000; *Fees:* $69 annual + $40 registration + applicable taxes

Opportunity For Advancement (OFA)
54 Wolseley St., 2nd Fl., Toronto ON M5T 1A5
Tel: 416-787-1481; *Fax:* 416-787-1500
info@ofacan.com
www.ofacan.com
Overview: A small local organization founded in 1974
Mission: To work with women in disadvantaged life situations; to promote women's economic self sufficiency; to build self-esteem, reduce social isolation, explore the roots of problem situations, learn & share information & skills, set new goals
Finances: *Funding Sources:* Regional government
Activities: Program delivery; social advocacy; *Internships:* Yes; *Speaker Service:* Yes

Opticians Association of Canada (OAC)
#2706, 83 Garry St., Winnipeg MB R3C 4J9
Tel: 204-982-6060; *Fax:* 204-947-2519
Toll-Free: 800-842-3155
canada@opticians.ca
www.opticians.ca
www.facebook.com/215512795151373
Overview: A medium-sized national organization
Chief Officer(s):
Robert Dalton, Executive Director
rdalton@opticians.ca
Finances: *Annual Operating Budget:* $100,000-$250,000; *Funding Sources:* Sponsorship
Staff Member(s): 7
Membership: 1,500

Opticians Association of New Brunswick / Association des otpiciens du Nouveau-Brunswick
PO Box 6743, Stn. Brunswick Square, Saint John NB E2L 4S2
Tel: 506-642-2878; *Fax:* 506-642-7984
nbgdo@nbnet.nb.ca
www.opticiansnb.com
Previous Name: New Brunswick Guild of Dispensing Opticians
Overview: A small provincial licensing organization founded in 1976
Mission: To regulate the practice of opticianry in New Brunswick; To oversee education of candidates for licensing

Opticians of Manitoba (OOM)
#2706, 83 Garry St., Winnipeg MB R3C 4J9
Tel: 204-982-6060; *Fax:* 204-947-2519
Toll-Free: 800-847-3155
oom@opticians.ca
www.opticiansofmanitoba.ca
Overview: A small provincial organization founded in 1953
Mission: To protect the public through the self-regulation of the practice of Opticianry; To set standards of practice for the profession; To ensure that opticians practice safely & competently; To investigate concerns raised about registrants' practice
Chief Officer(s):
Carol Ellerbeck, Registrar
cellerbeck@opticians.ca
Membership: *Fees:* $75
Publications:
• Opticians of Manitoba Newsletter
Type: Newsletter

Optimist International Canada (OIC)
#200, 5205, boul Metropolitain est, Saint-Léonard QC H1R 1Z7
Tel: 514-593-4401; *Fax:* 514-721-1104
Toll-Free: 800-363-7151
canadianservice@optimist.org
www.optimist.org
Overview: A medium-sized national organization founded in 1919
Chief Officer(s):
Jacques Pelland, Senior Director
Staff Member(s): 4
Membership: 20000

Option consommateurs
#440, 50, rue Ste-Catherine Ouest, Montréal QC H2X 3V4
Tél: 514-598-7288; *Téléc:* 514-598-8511
Ligne sans frais: 888-412-1313
info@option-consommateurs.org
www.option-consommateurs.org
www.facebook.com/option.consommateurs.fbp
twitter.com/OptionConso
Également appelé: ACEF - Centre
Nom précédent: Association coopérative d'économie familiale - Montréal (Centre)
Aperçu: *Dimension:* petite; *Envergure:* provinciale; Organisme sans but lucratif; fondée en 1983
Mission: Travailler à la défense et la promotion des droits des consommateurs
Membre de: Consumers International; Agence de la consommation en matière financière du Canada
Membre(s) du bureau directeur:
Caroline Arel, Directrice générale par intérim
arel@option-consommateurs.org
Membre(s) du personnel: 31
Membre: *Montant de la cotisation:* 22$
Activités: Cours sur le budget, consultation budgétaire; service juridique; défense des droits aux consommateurs; information des consommateurs; recours collectifs; *Stagiaires:* Oui; *Service de conférenciers:* Oui

Options for Sexual Health (OPT)
3550 East Hastings St., Vancouver BC V5K 2A7
Tel: 604-731-4252; *Fax:* 604-731-4698
info@optbc.org
www.optionsforsexualhealth.org
Previous Name: Planned Parenthood Association of British Columbia
Overview: A medium-sized provincial charitable organization founded in 1963 overseen by Canadian Federation for Sexual Health
Mission: To promote optimal sexual health for all British Columbians by supporting reproductive choice, reducing unplanned pregnancy, & providing quality education, information & clinical services
Member of: United Way
Affliation(s): International Planned Parenthood Federation
Chief Officer(s):
Siobhan Aspinall, President
Finances: *Annual Operating Budget:* $1.5 Million-$3 Million; *Funding Sources:* Donations; memberships; grants; fees for service
Staff Member(s): 100; 400 volunteer(s)
Membership: 440
Activities: Clinic & sexual health education services throughout British Columbia; pamphlets, manuals & publications, videos, teaching kits, fact sheets; *Library* by appointment

OPTIONS Sexual Health Association
#50, 9912 - 106 St., Edmonton AB T5K 1C5

Tel: 780-423-3737; *Fax:* 780-425-1782
options@optionssexualhealth.ca
www.optionssexualhealth.ca
www.facebook.com/64347076574
Previous Name: Planned Parenthood Association of Edmonton
Overview: A small local charitable organization founded in 1964
Mission: To promote healthy sexuality for all, through education, counselling, advocacy, in partnership with the community
Member of: Canadian Federation for Sexual Health; International Planned Parenthood
Affiliation(s): Planned Parenthood Alberta
Finances: *Annual Operating Budget:* $500,000-$1.5 Million; *Funding Sources:* Municipal government; United Way; foundations; fundraising; donors
Staff Member(s): 10; 50 volunteer(s)
Membership: 60; *Fees:* $15
Activities: Educational presentations of accurate, comprehensive & holistic information on all aspects of sexuality; counselling services with regard to sexuality, pregnancy options & contraception; advocacy; annual auction; community events; summer programs for teens; *Awareness Events:* Edmonton's Pride Parade, June

Options: Services to Communities Society
9815 - 140 St., Surrey BC V3T 4M4
Tel: 604-584-5811; *Fax:* 604-584-7628
info@options.bc.ca
www.options.bc.ca
www.facebook.com/OptionsCommunityServices
Overview: A small local organization founded in 1973
Mission: To empower individuals, support families & promote community health
Chief Officer(s):
Christine Mohr, Executive Director
Staff Member(s): 310; 200 volunteer(s)
Membership: 1-99
Activities: Family & child services; youth; women's services; housing & shelter; mental health; multicultural services; child care;

Newton Office
13520 - 78 Ave., Surrey BC V3W 8J6
Tel: 604-596-4321; *Fax:* 604-572-7413

Optometric Institute of Toronto *See* Vision Institute of Canada

Oral History Committee, Canadian Historical Association *See* Canadian Oral History Association

Orangeville & District Chamber of Commerce *See* Greater Dufferin Area Chamber of Commerce

Orangeville & District Real Estate Board (ODREB)
228 Broadway Ave., Orangeville ON L9W 1K5
Tel: 519-941-4547; *Fax:* 519-941-8482
www.odreb.com
twitter.com/odrebrealtors
Overview: A small local organization founded in 1965 overseen by Ontario Real Estate Association
Member of: The Canadian Real Estate Association; Ontario Real Estate Association; Toronto Real Estate Board
Chief Officer(s):
David Grime, President

Oraynu Community for Secular Humanistic Judaism; Secular Jewish Association *See* Oraynu Congregation for Humanistic Judaism

Oraynu Congregation for Humanistic Judaism
#14, 156 Duncan Mill Rd., Toronto ON M3B 3N2
Tel: 416-385-3910
info@oraynu.org
www.oraynu.org
Previous Name: Oraynu Community for Secular Humanistic Judaism; Secular Jewish Association
Overview: A small local charitable organization founded in 1969
Mission: To integrate secular, humanistic Jewish ethics into members' daily lives
Affliation(s): Society for Humanistic Judaism; Jewish Federation of Greater Toronto; Centre for Enhancement of Jewish Education; International Federation of Secular Humanistic Jews; International Institute for Secular Humanistic Jews; Leadership Conference of Secular Humanistic Jews
Chief Officer(s):
Louise Sherman, President
Les Kelman, Secretary
Robert Horwitz, Treasurer
Roby Sadler, Manager, Office
Finances: *Funding Sources:* Donations; Rasch Foundation; UJA Federation; Centre for Enhancement of Jewish Education
Activities: Providing information about Oraynu & Humanistic Judaism; Offering programs for youth; Providing cultural & social activities
Publications:
• The Shofar
Type: Newsletter; *Frequency:* Bimonthly; *Editor:* Sandi Horwitz
Profile: Upcoming events, board news, committee reports, & member information

Orchestra London Canada Inc.
609 Wellington St., London ON N6A 3R6
Tel: 519-679-8558; *Fax:* 519-679-8914
boxoffice@orchestralondon.ca
www.orchestralondon.ca
www.facebook.com/OrchestraLondon
twitter.com/OrchestraLondon
www.youtube.com/orchestralondon1
Overview: A small local charitable organization founded in 1937 overseen by Orchestras Canada
Mission: To enrich the quality of life in the London area by maintaining a professional orchestra, serving the community through a wide variety of musical activities
Member of: Orchestras Ontario
Chief Officer(s):
Ailene Wittstein, Chair
Joe Swan, Executive Director, 519-679-8558 Ext. 227
jswan@orchestralondon.ca
Eadie Micks, Chief Operating Officer, 519-679-8558 Ext. 230
emicks@orchestralondon.ca
Finances: *Annual Operating Budget:* $3 Million-$5 Million; *Funding Sources:* Government; private & corporate donations; membership fees
Staff Member(s): 12; 1000 volunteer(s)
Membership: 500-999; *Fees:* $100 membership
Activities: *Library*

Orchestra Toronto (OT)
5040 Yonge St., Toronto ON M2N 6R8
Tel: 416-467-7142
info@orchestratoronto.ca
orchestratoronto.ca
www.facebook.com/pages/Orchestra-Toronto/172229189138
twitter.com/OrchToronto
www.youtube.com/user/orchestratoronto
Previous Name: Bennington Heights Community Orchestra; East York Symphony Orchestra
Overview: A small local charitable organization founded in 1954
Mission: To provide affordable family entertainment, music education, & full repertoire in all its programs
Member of: Orchestras Canada
Chief Officer(s):
Samantha Little, Executive Director
Kevin Mallon, Music Director
Finances: *Funding Sources:* Municipal & Provincial Arts Councils; Corporate & Individual Donations
Staff Member(s): 5
Membership: 66 musicians; *Committees:* Musician's
Activities: Providing a community volunteer symphony orchestra; Offering resources for motivated, dedicated musicians of all ages to rehearse & perform the complete orchestral repertoire; *Library:* Orchestra Toronto Library

Orchestras Canada (OC) / Orchestres Canada
#700, 425 Adelaide St. West, Toronto ON M5V 3C1
Tel: 416-366-8834; *Fax:* 416-504-0437
info@oc.ca
www.orchestrascanada.org
www.facebook.com/orchestrascanada
twitter.com/OrchCanada
www.youtube.com/user/orchestrascanada
Merged from: Association of Canadian Orchestras; Orchestras Ontario
Overview: A large national organization founded in 1998
Mission: To strengthen Canada's orchestral community through leadership in advocacy, education, & professional development
Member of: Canadian Conference of the Arts
Affliation(s): American Symphony Orchestra League; International Alliance of Orchestra Associations
Chief Officer(s):
Katherine Carleton, Executive Director, 416-366-8834 Ext. 226
katherine@oc.ca
Finances: *Annual Operating Budget:* $500,000-$1.5 Million; *Funding Sources:* Membership dues; conference; workshops; publication sales
Staff Member(s): 6
Membership: 500-999; *Fees:* Schedule available; *Committees:* Government Communications; Marketing; Professional Development; Volunteer
Activities: *Internships:* Yes; *Library:* Resource Centre; Music Library; by appointment
Awards:
• Betty Webster Award (Award)
Awarded to an individual or organization that has made a sustained and significant contribution over a number of years to the Canadian orchestral community, with an emphasis on leadership, education and volunteerism.*Deadline:* May 1
Meetings/Conferences: • 2015 National Orchestras Meeting, June, 2015, Sheraton Vancouver Wall Centre Hotel, Vancouver, BC
Scope: National

Orchestras Mississauga
Living Arts Centre, 4141 Living Arts Dr., 2nd Fl., Mississauga ON L5B 4B8
Tel: 905-615-4405; *Fax:* 905-615-4402
info@mississaugasymphony.ca
www.mississaugasymphony.ca
www.linkedin.com/company/mississauga-symphony-orchestra
www.facebook.com/207803209261897
twitter.com/MSymph
www.youtube.com/user/MississaugaSymph
Also Known As: Sinfonia Mississauga; Mississauga Philharmonic; Mississauga Symphony
Overview: A medium-sized local charitable organization founded in 1972 overseen by Orchestras Canada
Mission: To provide & promote orchestral music; to ensure its accessibility to all segments of the community
Affliation(s): Mississauga Board of Trade; Orchestras Canada; Mississauga Arts Council
Chief Officer(s):
Denis Mastromonaco, Music Director
Eileen Keown, General Manager
Finances: *Funding Sources:* Ontario Arts Council; Mississauga Arts Council
Staff Member(s): 7
Activities: *Rents Mailing List:* Yes; *Library* by appointment

Orchestre civique des jeunes de Montréal *Voir* Orchestre symphonique des jeunes de Montréal

Orchestre de chambre de Montréal (OCM) / Montréal Chamber Orchestra (MCO)
#2001, 1, Place Ville Marie, Montréal QC H3B 2C4
Tél: 514-871-1224
info@mco-ocm.qc.ca
www.mco-ocm.qc.ca
www.facebook.com/Orchestredechambredemontreal
twitter.com/mcoocm
Aperçu: *Dimension:* petite; *Envergure:* locale; Organisme sans but lucratif; fondée en 1974 surveillé par Orchestras Canada
Mission: Se consacrer au répertoire pour ensemble de chambre & oeuvres canadiennes
Membre(s) du bureau directeur:
Wanda Kaluzny, Music Director
Membre: 31
Activités: *Evénements de sensibilisation:* Banquet Chinois de l'Orchestre de Chambre de Montréal; Tournoi annuel de golf

Orchestre de chambre McGill *See* McGill Chamber Orchestra

L'Orchestre des jeunes d'Ottawa *See* Ottawa Youth Orchestra Academy

Orchestre du Centre national des Arts *See* National Arts Centre Orchestra of Canada

Orchestre métropolitain du Grand Montréal
#401, 486, rue Sainte-Catherine, Montréal QC H3B 1A6
Tel: 514-598-0870; *Fax:* 514-840-9195
info@orchestremetropolitain.com
www.orchestremetropolitain.com
www.facebook.com/orchestremetropolitain
twitter.com/lemetropolitain
www.youtube.com/LeMetropolitain1
Overview: A small local organization founded in 1981 overseen by Orchestras Canada
Chief Officer(s):
Jean R. Dupré, Directeur général
jrdupre@orchestremetropolitain.com
Kim Lajeunesse, Directeur artistique
klajeunesse@orchestremetropolitain.com
Staff Member(s): 15

Membership: 60+;

Orchestre national des jeunes Canada ***See*** National Youth Orchestra Canada

Orchestre symphonique d'Ottawa ***See*** Ottawa Symphony Orchestra Inc.

Orchestre symphonique de Laval

#203, 3235 boul Saint-Martin Est, Laval QC H7E 5G8
Tél: 450-978-3666; *Téléc:* 450-661-6741
osl@osl.qc.ca
www.osl.qc.ca
www.facebook.com/OSLaval
twitter.com/OSLaval
Aperçu: *Dimension:* petite; *Envergure:* locale; fondée en 1984 surveillé par Orchestras Canada
Mission: Diffuser la musique classique et symphonique
Membre(s) du bureau directeur:
Marcel Lemay, Président
Alain Trudel, Directeur artistique
Membre(s) du personnel: 10

Orchestre symphonique de Longueuil

156, boul Churchill, Greenfield Park QC J4V 2M3
Tél: 450-466-6661; *Téléc:* 450-466-3331
info@osdl.ca
www.osdl.ca
www.linkedin.com/groups/Fondation-Orchestre-symphonique-Longueuil-4110
www.facebook.com/OSDL.ca
twitter.com/Votre_OSDL
Aperçu: *Dimension:* petite; *Envergure:* locale surveillé par Orchestras Canada
Mission: Assurer la diffusion du grand répertoire classique et la promotion de l'excellence musicale en Montérégie
Membre(s) du bureau directeur:
Gilles Choquet, Directeur général
Marc David, Directeur artistique
mdavid@osdl.ca
Membre(s) du personnel: 8

Orchestre symphonique de Montréal

260, boul de Maisonneuve Ouest, 2e étage, Montréal QC H2X 1Y9
Tél: 514-842-3402; *Téléc:* 514-842-0728
www.osm.ca
www.facebook.com/OSMconcerts
twitter.com/OSM_official
www.youtube.com/user/OSMofficial
Aperçu: *Dimension:* petite; *Envergure:* locale; fondée en 1934 surveillé par Orchestras Canada
Mission: De diffuser, au plus large public possible, le répertoire mondial de la musique symphonique, & les artistes de niveau international; assumer son rôle social & institutionnel
Membre(s) du bureau directeur:
Madeleine Careau, Chef de la direction
Kent Nagano, Directeur musical
Membre(s) du personnel: 47
Activités: *Stagiaires:* Oui; *Bibliothèque* rendez-vous

Orchestre symphonique de Québec

401, av Grande Allée Est, Québec QC G1R 2J5
Tél: 418-643-5598
www.osq.qc.ca
www.facebook.com/orchestresymphoniquedequebec
Aperçu: *Dimension:* moyenne; *Envergure:* locale; Organisme sans but lucratif; fondée en 1903 surveillé par Orchestras Canada
Mission: Interpréter le répertoire symphonique; être le principal moteur de l'activité musicale de la région. L'OSM est reconnu comme un organisme de grande qualité, dynamique, accessible, et financièrement sain
Membre(s) du bureau directeur:
Emmanuelle Peguin, Administratrice Artistique
epequin@osq.ca
Membre(s) du personnel: 19
Membre: 63

Orchestre symphonique de Sault Ste-Marie ***See*** Sault Symphony Association

Orchestre symphonique de Sherbrooke (OSS) / Sherbrooke Symphony Orchestra

Domain Howard, Pavillon 3, CP 610, 1304, boul de Portland, Sherbrooke QC J1H 5H9
Tél: 819-821-0227; *Téléc:* 819-821-1959
info@ossherbrooke.com
www.ossherbrooke.com
Aperçu: *Dimension:* petite; *Envergure:* locale; Organisme sans but lucratif; fondée en 1939 surveillé par Orchestras Canada
Mission: Faire connaître la musique symphonique dans la région et permettre aux musiciens de la région de jouer dans un orchestre professionnel
Membre de: Chambre de Commerce; Society of Compsers, Authors and Music Publishers of Canada
Affliation(s): Conseil Québecois de la Musique
Membre(s) du bureau directeur:
Vincent Cloutier, Président
Stéphane Laforest, Directeur artistique
stephanelaforest@ossherbrooke.com
Finances: *Fonds:* Conseil des arts et des lettres du Québec; Canadian Council for the Arts; Ville de Sherbrooke
Membre(s) du personnel: 6
Activités: Concerts symphoniques; orchestre de chambre; vente à cachet; musique de chambre; gestion de projets

Orchestre symphonique de Sudbury inc ***See*** Sudbury Symphony Orchestra Association Inc.

Orchestre symphonique de Trois-Rivières (OSTR)

CP 1281, Trois-Rivières QC G9A 5K8
Tél: 819-373-5340; *Téléc:* 819-373-6693
administration@ostr.ca
www.ostr.ca
www.facebook.com/127291994012065
www.youtube.com/user/OSTRofficiel
Aperçu: *Dimension:* petite; *Envergure:* locale; Organisme sans but lucratif; fondée en 1978 surveillé par Orchestras Canada
Mission: Poursuivre l'atteinte des objectifs inhérents à ses axes de développement: éducation, implication dans son milieu, diffusion de musique symphonique, création musicale et diffusion de nouveaux produits
Membre de: Conseil québécois de la musique; Orchestres Canada
Affiliation(s): Guilde des musiciens (AFM)
Membre(s) du bureau directeur:
Natalie Rousseau, Directrice générale
direction@ostr.ca
Jacques Lacombe, Directeur artistique
directionartistique@ostr.ca
Jean-Marc Vanasse, Président
Finances: *Fonds:* Conseil des arts Canada; Conseil des arts et des lettres du Québec; Ville de Trois-Rivières
Membre(s) du personnel: 6
Activités: *Stagiaires:* Oui; *Service de conférenciers:* Oui; *Bibliothèque*

Orchestre symphonique des jeunes de Montréal (OSJM)

CP 83566, Succ. Garnier, Montréal QC H2J 4E9
Tél: 514-645-0311; *Téléc:* 514-524-9894
osjmontreal@gmail.com
www.osjm.org
Nom précédent: Orchestre civique des jeunes de Montréal
Aperçu: *Dimension:* petite; *Envergure:* locale; Organisme sans but lucratif; fondée en 1986 surveillé par Orchestras Canada
Mission: Présenter le jeune musicien de talent à un auditoire et lui fournir une expérience formative sous la supervision d'artistes reconnus; encourager et soutenir le choix d'une carrière musicale qui peut mener à un grand orchestre; promouvoir un intérêt dans les concerts et développer un soutien plus diversifié dans les activités de l'orchestre; fournir à l'entreprise privée l'occasion de participer plus activement dans une activité culturelle d'envergure et l'aider à faire apprécier son rôle dans la communauté
Membre de: Association des orchestres de jeunes du Québec (AOJQ)
Membre(s) du bureau directeur:
Vincent Heir, Président
Anne-Marie Desbiens, Directrice générale
Finances: *Fonds:* Ministère de la Culture et des communications du Québec
Membre: *Montant de la cotisation:* 250$; *Critères d'admissibilité:* Passer une audition annuelle; payer sa cotisation; s'engager à satisfaire les exigences des programmes
Activités: 3 concerts réguliers par saison; *Stagiaires:* Oui

Orchestre symphonique des jeunes de Sherbrooke

CP 1536, Succ. Place de la Cité, Sherbrooke QC J1H 5M4
Tél: 819-566-1888
www.osjs.ca
www.facebook.com/153626511336448
Aperçu: *Dimension:* petite; *Envergure:* locale surveillé par Orchestras Canada
Mission: Fournir aux jeunes musiciennes et musiciens de Sherbrooke et de la région un milieu où ils pourront apprendre à faire de la musique d'ensemble, développer la maîtrise de leur instrument et perfectionner leur art dans un contexte de vie collective particulièrement enrichissante
Membre(s) du bureau directeur:
Julien Prolux, Directeur musical

Orchestre symphonique des jeunes du West Island (OSJWI) / West Island Youth Symphony Orchestra (WIYSO)

CP 1028, Succ. Pointe-Claire, Pointe-Claire QC H9S 4H9
Tél: 514-428-9643
info@osjwi.qc.ca
www.osjwi.qc.ca
Aperçu: *Dimension:* petite; *Envergure:* locale; Organisme sans but lucratif; fondée en 1986 surveillé par Orchestras Canada
Mission: Permettre aux jeunes de 8-25 ans de jouer dans un orchestre regroupant tous les instruments sous la direction d'un chef professionel
Affliation(s): Association des orchestres de jeunes du Québec
Membre(s) du bureau directeur:
Jackie Landry-Bigelow, Présidente
Stewart Grant, Directeur artistique
Membre: 78; *Montant de la cotisation:* 300$ l'orchestre sénior; 200$ l'orchestre de la Relève; *Critères d'admissibilite:* Musiciens qui ont 8 à 25 ans

Orchestre symphonique des jeunes Philippe-Filion

2100, boul des Hêtres, Shawinigan QC G9N 8R8
Tél: 819-539-6000
info@aosjpf.ca
www.aosjpf.ca
www.facebook.com/121002454597454
Aperçu: *Dimension:* petite; *Envergure:* locale; fondée en 1978 surveillé par Orchestras Canada
Membre(s) du bureau directeur:
Michel Kozlovsky, Chef d'orchestre

Orchestre symphonique du Saguenay-Lac-St-Jean (OSSLSJ)

202, rue Jacques-Cartier Est, Chicoutimi QC G7H 6R8
Tél: 418-545-3409; *Téléc:* 418-545-8287
info@lorchestre.org
www.lorchestre.org
www.facebook.com/151993804859233
twitter.com/orchestreSLSJ
www.youtube.com/channel/UCTPHtHRjL3-VnMomYcCRVNQ
Aperçu: *Dimension:* petite; *Envergure:* locale; Organisme sans but lucratif; fondée en 1979 surveillé par Orchestras Canada
Mission: Produire et diffuser des concerts professionnels à travers tout le Saguenay-Lac-Saint-Jean en regard des enjeux financiers et des structures d'accueil existantes. Ses qualités artistiques et administratives en constante évolution lui permettent d'exercer un leadership au sein des organismes musicaux régionaux, basé sur un partenariat serré avec le milieu, au service du développement de sa discipline et de sa communauté
Membre(s) du bureau directeur:
Jacques Clément, Directeur artisique
Finances: *Fonds:* Conseil des Arts du Canada; Conseil des arts et lettres du Québec; Ville de Saguenay
Membre(s) du personnel: 7
Activités: La corporation gère sous une même administration les activités de l'Orchestre symphonique; l'Orchestre de chambre; le Quatuor Alcan; le Quintette à vent; le Choeur symphonique; l'Orchestre des jeunes;; *Bibliothèque:* Musicothèque; rendez-vous

Orchestre symphonique régional Abitibi-Témiscamingue

CP 2305, Rouyn-Noranda QC J9X 5A9
Tél: 819-762-0043
info@osrat.ca
www.osrat.ca
www.facebook.com/125183814205328
Également appelé: Société des Mélomanes
Aperçu: *Dimension:* petite; *Envergure:* locale; Organisme sans but lucratif; fondée en 1985 surveillé par Orchestras Canada
Mission: Diffusion de la musique classique et integration de la relève
Membre(s) du bureau directeur:
Jacques Marchand, Directeur artistique
Membre(s) du personnel: 6

Membre: *Montant de la cotisation:* Un don de 25$ ou plus; *Critères d'admissibilité:* Mélomane amateur

Orchestres Canada ***See*** Orchestras Canada

Orchid Socety of Alberta

PO Box 31117, Stn. Namao Centre, Edmonton AB T5Z 3P3
e-mail: info@orchidsalberta.com
www.orchidsalberta.com
Overview: A small provincial organization founded in 1976
Mission: To promote orchid gardening & share knowledge
Member of: Canadian Orchid Congress
Affliation(s): American Orchid Society
Chief Officer(s):
Darrell Albert, President
president@orchidsalberta.com
Membership: *Fees:* $15 senior; $20 senior family; $25 single; $30 family

Orchid Society of Nova Scotia

c/o Ruth Ann Moger, 20 Christies Rd., Boutiliers Point NS B3Z 1S1
www.nsorchidsociety.com
www.facebook.com/101539916572332
Overview: A small local organization founded in 2010
Membership: *Fees:* $20 household; $10 student

Orchid Society of Royal Botanical Gardens

680 Plains Rd. West, Burlington ON L7T 1J1
e-mail: osrbgorchidinfo@gmail.com
www.osrbg.ca
Overview: A small local organization founded in 1981
Mission: To provide education & information for its members & to help conserve orchid species
Membership: 100;

Orchidophiles de Québec

Pavillon Envirotron, FSAA, Université Laval, #1246, 2480, boul. Hochelaga, Québec QC G1V 0A6
www.orchidophilesdequebec.ca
www.facebook.com/Orchidophiles.de.Quebec
Aperçu: *Dimension:* petite; *Envergure:* locale; fondée en 1981
Membre(s) du bureau directeur:
Patricia Caris, Présidente
president@orchidophilesdequebec.ca
Membre: *Montant de la cotisation:* $35 individuel; $55 famille
Activités: *Bibliothèque*

Order of Certified Pastoral Counsellors of America ***See*** The Evangelical Order of Certified Pastoral Counsellors of America

The Order of St. Lazarus

#100, 1435 Sanford Fleming Ave., Ottawa ON K1G 3H3
Tel: 613-746-5280; *Fax:* 613-746-3982
chancery@stlazarus.ca
www.stlazarus.ca
twitter.com/mhoslj
Overview: A small local organization
Chief Officer(s):
Peter A. S. Milliken, Grand Prior
Staff Member(s): 2; 30 volunteer(s)
Membership: 400 individual

Order of Sons of Italy in Canada

1375 Main St., Cambridge ON N1R 5S7
Tel: 905-388-9328; *Fax:* 905-383-9926
www.ordersonsofitalycanada.com
Overview: A small national organization founded in 1919
Mission: To assist the needy, the ill, and disabled through financial support, the provision of housing, and other support programs; To encourage the active participation of our members in the political, social and economic life of our community; to participate in programs combating discrimination, racism, and social injustice; To promote and preserve the Italian language, culture, and traditions in our country.
Chief Officer(s):
Josie Cumbo, National President, 519-623-9993
Patsy Giammarco, National Administative Secretary, 905-892-3352
Finances: *Funding Sources:* Membership fees; sponsorships
Activities: Golden Lion Award; Ethnic Festival

The Order of United Commercial Travelers of America (UCT)

Canadian Office, #300, 901 Centre St. North, Calgary AB T2E 2P6
Tel: 403-277-0745; *Fax:* 403-277-6662
Toll-Free: 800-267-2371
Other Communication: www.flickr.com/photos/uctinaction
www.uct.org
www.linkedin.com/company/united-commercial-travelers
www.facebook.com/UCTinAction
www.youtube.com/UCTinaction
Overview: A large international charitable organization founded in 1888
Mission: To provide members with affordable insurance & support through fraternal benefit & discount programs
Affliation(s): American Special Hockey Association
Chief Officer(s):
Larry Pilon, President
Joseph Hoffman, CEO
Finances: *Annual Operating Budget:* $250,000-$500,000
Staff Member(s): 2
Membership: 70,000
Activities: Aid to physically & mentally challenged individuals; fraternal benefits to members; *Awareness Events:* Join Hands Day, 1st Saturday in May
Publications:
• The Sample Case [a publication of The Order of United Commercial Travelers of America]
Type: Magazine

Ordre des Acupuncteurs de Québec (OAQ)

#1106, 505, boul René-Lévesque ouest, Montréal QC H2Z 1Y7
Tél: 514-523-2882; *Téléc:* 514-523-9669
Ligne sans frais: 800-474-5914
info@ordredesacupuncteurs.qc.ca
www.ordredesacupuncteurs.qc.ca
Aperçu: *Dimension:* petite; *Envergure:* provinciale
Mission: Réglementer et de surveiller des activités professionnelles qui comportent des risques de préjudices pour le public. Ils sont les intervenants de première ligne du système professionnel.
Membre(s) du bureau directeur:
Raymond Bourret, President
president@o-a-q.org

Ordre des administrateurs agréés du Québec (OAAQ)

#100, 910, rue Sherbrooke ouest, Montréal QC H3A 1G3
Tél: 514-499-0880; *Téléc:* 514-499-0892
Ligne sans frais: 800-465-0880
info@adma.qc.ca
www.adma.qc.ca
www.linkedin.com/groups/Ordre-administrateurs-agréés-Québec-OAAQ-43624
www.facebook.com/OrdreAdmA
twitter.com/OrdreAdmA
Aperçu: *Dimension:* grande; *Envergure:* provinciale; Organisme sans but lucratif; Organisme de réglementation; fondée en 1973
Mission: Favorise auprès des professionnels de l'administration, l'innovation et l'atteinte d'un niveau de compétence supérieur pour qu'ils contribuent de façon proactive et dynamique au développement des entreprises et des organisations; assure la protection du public en garantissant le respect des normes et standards professionnels en administration, en conformité avec le code de déontologie et par le biais des mécanismes prévus au code des professions; contribue à l'avancement de l'administration, discipline essentielle au développement social et économique du Québec.
Affliation(s): Institut des Auditeurs internes - Section Montréal (IAIM)
Membre(s) du bureau directeur:
Chantal Dalpé, Présidente
presidente@adma.qc.ca
Denise Brosseau, Directrice générale et Secrétaire
dbrosseau@adma.qc.ca
Finances: *Budget de fonctionnement annuel:* $1.5 Million-$3 Million
Membre(s) du personnel: 9; 125 bénévole(s)
Membre: 3 000; *Montant de la cotisation:* 500$; *Critères d'admissibilite:* Gestionnaires; *Comités:* Inspection professionnelle; révision des demandes d'equivalence; discipline; révision; arbitrage; vérification; formation
Activités: Petit-déjeuner; activités de formation et de développement professionnels; remise des permis; activités régionales
Prix, Bouses:
• Fellow Adm.A. (Prix)
• Fellow C.M.C. (Prix)
• Prix Reconnaissance (Prix)
• Prix Robert P. Morin (Prix)
• Médaille des gouverneurs (Prix)
• Mérite du CIQ (Prix)
Publications:
• Info Adm.A. [a publication of the Ordre des administrateurs agréés du Québec]
Type: Bulletin

Ordre des agronomes du Québec (OAQ)

#810, 1001, rue Sherbrooke Est, Montréal QC H2L 1L3
Tél: 514-596-3833; *Téléc:* 514-596-2974
agronome@oaq.qc.ca
www.oaq.qc.ca
Nom précédent: Corporation des agronomes du Québec
Aperçu: *Dimension:* moyenne; *Envergure:* provinciale; Organisme sans but lucratif; fondée en 1937
Mission: Assurer les utilisateurs de services agronomiques et les consommateurs de la compétence, du professionnalisme et de l'engagement des agronomes et ainsi favoriser le mieux-être de la société
Membre(s) du bureau directeur:
René Mongeau, Président
rene.mongeau@oaq.qc.ca
Guillaume LaBarre, Directeur général
guillaume.labarre@oaq.qc.ca
Membre(s) du personnel: 14
Membre: 3,372; *Critères d'admissibilité:* Agronomes; *Comités:* Équivalences; Formation des agronomes; Inspection Professionnelle; Révision des décisions d'équivalences; Révision des décisions du bureau du syndic; Arbitrage des comptes; Admission; Formation Continue; Consultatif des prix de L'OAQ; Résolutions; Consultatif sur les pesticides; Consultatif sur la gestion des matières fertilisantes; Formation continue des agronomes; Consultatif sur les actes agronomiques en aménagement des sols
Prix, Bouses:
• Prix Henri-C.Bois (Prix)
Souligne la valeur inestimable du travail bénévole d'un agronome au sein de différents comités de l'OAQ
• Médaille de distinction agronomique (Prix)
Décernée à un agronomes pour souligner ses réalisations professionnelles exceptionnelles et son rayonnement au sein de la profession et de la collectivité
• Ordre du Mérite agronomique (Prix)
Décerné à un agronome qui a rendu des services exceptionnels dans le domaine de l'agriculture ou pour la cause agronomique
• Mérite Spécial Adélard-Godbout (Prix)
Reconnaît l'apport exceptionnel d'une entreprise, d'un organisme, d'un individu ou d'un groupe d'individus au développement de l'agriculture, de l'agronomie et/ou du secteur agroalimentaire québecois

Ordre des architectes du Québec (OAQ)

#200, 420 rue McGill, Montréal QC H2Y 2G1
Tél: 514-937-6168; *Téléc:* 514-933-0242
Ligne sans frais: 800-599-6168
info@oaq.com
www.oaq.com
www.facebook.com/133353596740232
twitter.com/OAQenbref
vimeo.com/user2657182
Aperçu: *Dimension:* moyenne; *Envergure:* provinciale; Organisme de réglementation; fondée en 1890
Mission: D'assurer la protection du public en régissant l'exercice de la profession d'architecte au Québec.
Affliation(s): Institut royal d'architecture du Canada
Membre(s) du bureau directeur:
Jean-Pierre Dumont, Directeur général
jpdumont@oaq.com
Membre(s) du personnel: 21
Membre: 3,500; *Critères d'admissibilite:* Architectes; *Comités:* Admission; Formation continue; Inspection professionnelle; Discipline; Révision des plaintes; Concours; Techniques et bâtiments durables; Orientation des Prix d'excellence en architecture
Activités: *Stagiaires:* Oui
Prix, Bouses:
• Prix d'excellence en Architecture (Prix)

Ordre des arpenteurs-géomètres du Québec (OAGQ) / Québec Land Surveyors Association

Iberville Quatre, #350, 2954, boul Laurier, Québec QC G1V 4T2
Tél: 418-656-0730; *Téléc:* 418-656-6352
oagq@oagq.qc.ca
www.oagq.qc.ca
Aperçu: *Dimension:* moyenne; *Envergure:* provinciale; fondée en 1882 surveillé par Professional Surveyors Canada

Mission: La protection du public et le contrôle de la profession
Membre de: Association de géomatique municipale
Affiliation(s): Fédération des arpenteurs-géomètres du Québec
40 bénévole(s)
Membre: 1 000; *Montant de la cotisation:* 830$; *Critères d'admissibilité:* BAC en géomatique; Stage d'un an; Examens de l'Ordre; *Comités:* Arbitrage; Assurances et sinistres; Discipline; Examinateurs; Formation; Inspection; Réglementation; Révision; Stages; Syndic
Activités: Ateliers divers; *Stagiaires:* Oui; *Listes de destinataires:* Oui
Meetings/Conferences: • Ordre des arpenteurs-géomètres du Québec 47e Congrès, D'autres conférences en 2015, 2015, QC
Scope: Provincial

Ordre des audiologistes et des orthophonistes de l'Ontario *See* College of Audiologists & Speech-Language Pathologists of Ontario

Ordre des audioprothésistes du Québec (OAQ)

#202-A, 11370, rue Notre-Dame est, Montréal QC H1B 2W6
Tél: 514-640-5117; *Téléc:* 514-640-5291
Ligne sans frais: 866-676-5117
oaq@ordreaudio.qc.ca
www.ordreaudio.qc.ca
Nom précédent: Corporation professionnelle des audioprothésistes du Québec
Aperçu: *Dimension:* petite; *Envergure:* provinciale
Membre(s) du bureau directeur:
Sophie Gagnon, Président
sophie.gagnon@bellnet.ca
Membre: *Comités:* Administratif; inspection professionnelle; discipline; formation; formation continue; règlements; équivalence de diplôme; information; révision

Ordre des chimistes du Québec (OCQ)

Place du Parc, #2199, 300 rue Léo-Pariseau, Montréal QC H2X 4B3
Tél: 514-844-3644; *Téléc:* 514-844-9601
information@ocq.qc.ca
www.ocq.qc.ca
Aperçu: *Dimension:* moyenne; *Envergure:* provinciale; Organisme de réglementation; fondée en 1926
Mission: L'Ordre est une corporation professionnelle dont la raison d'être est la protection du public
Membre(s) du bureau directeur:
Guy Collin, Président du Conseil d'administration
Finances: *Budget de fonctionnement annuel:* $500,000-$1.5 Million
Membre(s) du personnel: 5; 120 bénévole(s)
Membre: 2 500; *Critères d'admissibilité:* Chimistes, biochimistes; *Comités:* Réglementaires prévus par le code des professions (L.R.Q., chapitre C-26)

Ordre des chiropraticiens du Québec

7950, boul Métropolitain est, Montréal QC H1K 1A1
Tél: 514-355-8540; *Téléc:* 514-355-2290
Ligne sans frais: 888-655-8540
info@ordredeschiropraticiens.qc.ca
www.ordredeschiropraticiens.qc.ca
Aperçu: *Dimension:* petite; *Envergure:* provinciale; Organisme sans but lucratif; fondée en 1973
Mission: Organisme paragouvernemental qui assure la protection du public & octroie les permis de pratique; fondation de recherche chiropratique
Membre: 925; *Montant de la cotisation:* 1 660$; *Critères d'admissibilité:* Docteur en chiropratique

L'Ordre des comptables professionels agréés du Québec

#800, 5, Place Ville Marie, Montréal QC H3B 2G2
Tél: 514-288-3256; *Téléc:* 514-843-8375
Ligne sans frais: 800-363-4688
info@cpaquebec.com
cpaquebec.com
www.linkedin.com/groups/Ordre-CPA-Quebec-3996221
www.facebook.com/CPAquebec
twitter.com/CPAquebec
www.youtube.com/cpaquebec; instagram.com/#cpaquebec
Également appelé: Ordre des CPA
Merged from: l'Ordre des CGA du Québec; l'Ordre des CMA du Québec
Aperçu: *Dimension:* grande; *Envergure:* provinciale; fondée en 2012 surveillé par Chartered Professional Accountants Canada
Mission: Tous les comptables professionnels du Québec sont regroupés au sein de l'Ordre des comptables professionnels agréés depuis le 2012.
Membre de: Conseil interprofessionel du Québec
Membre(s) du bureau directeur:
Alain Dugal, Président
André Dugal, Premier vice-président
Nathalie Houle, Deuxième vice-présidente
Membre: 36 000 membres & 7 000 candidats; *Critères d'admissibilite:* Détenir DESS, réussir examen final uniforme et completer un stage de 2 ans dans un cabinet d'expert-comptables; *Comités:* Audit; Évaluation des candidatures au titre de FCPA; Évaluation des demandes d'équivalence; Évaluation de la formation continue; Inspection professionnelle; Développement professionnel; Formation des CPA du Québec; Comptabilité publique; Évaluation de l'examen national; Révision; Vigie en certification, comptabilité financière et fiscalité; Vigie en management et en comptabilité de management; Assurances; CPA en cabinet; CPA en entreprise; CPA dans la secteur public et parapublic; Examens CGA; Programmes affinités; Programmes de formation professionnelle; Regroupements régionaux
Activités: Formation professionnelle; formation continue; inspection professionnelle; *Stagiaires:* Oui

Ordre des conseillers en ressources humaines agréés (CRHA)

#1400, 1200, av McGill College, Montréal QC H3B 4G7
Tél: 514-879-1636
Ligne sans frais: 800-214-1609
info@portailrh.org
www.portailrh.org
www.linkedin.com/groups?mostPopular=&gid=3233907
www.facebook.com/OrdreCRHACRIA
twitter.com/crha_quebec
Nom précédent: Association des professionnels en ressources humaines du Québec
Aperçu: *Dimension:* moyenne; *Envergure:* provinciale; fondée en 1934
Mission: De promouvoir l'importance stratégique de la gestion des ressources humaines dans la gestion des organisations ainsi que la promotion des nouveaux concepts et champs de développement qui caractérisent son évolution
Membre de: Conseil canadien des associations en ressources humaines/Canadian Council of Human Resources Associations
Membre(s) du bureau directeur:
Florent Francoeur, Président-directeur général
Membre: 9,000; *Critères d'admissibilite:* Gens qui sont dans les sectuers industriel et commercial, services et oublique et parapublique; *Comités:* Admissions; Révision; Inspection professionnelle; Conseil de discipline
Activités: Développement professionnel: colloques et compétences (40 par année); *Listes de destinataires:* Oui
Prix, Bouses:
• Concours Iris (Prix)
• EXCALIBUR: Le tournoi universitaire canadien en ressources humaines (Prix)
Promouvoir un enseignement de la gestion des ressources humaines dans les universités canadiennes préparant les étudiants au marché du travail*Amount:* 3 000$; 2 250$; 1 500$

Ordre des conseillers et conseillères d'orientation du Québec (OCCOQ)

#520, 1600, boul Henri-Bourassa Ouest, Montréal QC H3M 3E2
Tél: 514-737-4717; *Téléc:* 514-737-2172
Ligne sans frais: 800-363-2643
ordre@orientation.qc.ca
www.orientation.qc.ca
Nom précédent: Corporation professionnelle des conseillers et conseillères d'orientation du Québec
Aperçu: *Dimension:* moyenne; *Envergure:* provinciale; fondée en 1944
Mission: De veiller à ce que les services offerts par leurs membres sont de la plus haute qualité.
Membre(s) du bureau directeur:
Laurent Matte, Président
lmatte@orientation.qc.ca
Membre(s) du personnel: 20
Membre: 2,458; *Montant de la cotisation:* 560$; *Comités:* Admissions par équivalence; Inspection professionnelle; Formation; Révision des plaintes; Arbitrage des comptes; Discipline

Ordre des dentistes du Québec (ODQ)

625, boul René-Lévesque ouest, 15e étage, Montréal QC H3B 1R2
Tél: 514-875-8511; *Téléc:* 514-393-9248
Ligne sans frais: 800-361-4887
www.odq.qc.ca
www.facebook.com/102225303175310
twitter.com/ordredentistes
www.youtube.com/webmestreodq
Aperçu: *Dimension:* grande; *Envergure:* provinciale; Organisme sans but lucratif; Organisme de réglementation; fondée en 1974
Mission: Assurer la qualité des services en médecine dentaire par le respect de normes élevées de pratique et d'éthique et de promouvoir la santé bucco-dentaire auprès de la population du Québec
Membre de: Conseil interprofessionnel du Québec
Affiliation(s): Association dentaire canadienne
Membre(s) du bureau directeur:
Caroline Daoust, Directrice générale et secrétaire
dirgen@odq.gc.ca
Finances: *Budget de fonctionnement annuel:* $3 Million-$5 Million
Membre(s) du personnel: 45
Membre: 4 720
Activités: *Evénements de sensibilisation:* Mois de la santé bucco dentaire, avril; Journées dentaires internationales du Québec, mai; *Stagiaires:* Oui; *Listes de destinataires:* Oui
Meetings/Conferences: • Journées dentaires internationales du Québec (JDIQ) 2015, May, 2015, Palais des congrès de Montréal, Montréal, QC
Scope: Provincial
Contact Information: Directeur, Dr Denis Forest, téléphone: 514-875-8511, poste 2222; adresse denis.forest@odq.qc.ca
• Journées dentaires internationales du Québec (JDIQ) 2016, May, 2016, QC
Scope: Provincial
Contact Information: Directeur, Dr Denis Forest, téléphone: 514-875-8511, poste 2222; adresse denis.forest@odq.qc.ca
• Journées dentaires internationales du Québec (JDIQ) 2017, May, 2017, QC
Scope: Provincial
Contact Information: Directeur, Dr Denis Forest, téléphone: 514-875-8511, poste 2222; adresse denis.forest@odq.qc.ca
• Journées dentaires internationales du Québec (JDIQ) 2018, May, 2018, QC
Scope: Provincial
Contact Information: Directeur, Dr Denis Forest, téléphone: 514-875-8511, poste 2222; adresse denis.forest@odq.qc.ca
• Journées dentaires internationales du Québec (JDIQ) 2019, May, 2019, QC
Scope: Provincial
Contact Information: Directeur, Dr Denis Forest, téléphone: 514-875-8511, poste 2222; adresse denis.forest@odq.qc.ca
• Journées dentaires internationales du Québec (JDIQ) 2020, May, 2020, QC
Scope: Provincial
Contact Information: Directeur, Dr Denis Forest, téléphone: 514-875-8511, poste 2222; adresse denis.forest@odq.qc.ca
• Journées dentaires internationales du Québec (JDIQ) 2021, D'autres conférences en 2021, 2021, QC
Scope: Provincial
Contact Information: Directeur, Dr Denis Forest, téléphone: 514-875-8511, poste 2222; adresse denis.forest@odq.qc.ca

Ordre des denturologistes du Québec (ODQ)

395, rue du Parc-Industriel, Longueuil QC J4H 3V7
Tél: 450-646-7922; *Téléc:* 450-646-2509
Ligne sans frais: 800-567-2251
info@odq.com
www.odq.com
Aperçu: *Dimension:* moyenne; *Envergure:* provinciale; fondée en 1974
Membre(s) du bureau directeur:
Monique Bouchard, Directrice générale et secrétaire
Robert Cabana, Président
Finances: *Budget de fonctionnement annuel:* $500,000-$1.5 Million
Membre(s) du personnel: 6
Membre: 966; *Comités:* Discipline; Formation continue; Inspection professionnelle; Pratique illégale
Activités: Protection du public; réception des plaintes par le syndic; *Stagiaires:* Oui

L'Ordre des diététistes de l'Ontario *See* College of Dietitians of Ontario

Ordre des ergothérapeutes de l'Ontario *See* College of Occupational Therapists of Ontario

L'Ordre des ergothérapeutes du Manitoba *See* College of Occupational Therapists of Manitoba

Ordre des ergothérapeutes du Québec (OEQ)

#920, 2021, av Union, Montréal QC H3A 2S9
Tél: 514-844-5778; *Téléc:* 514-844-0478
Ligne sans frais: 800-265-5778
ergo@oeq.org
www.oeq.org
Aperçu: *Dimension:* moyenne; *Envergure:* provinciale; Organisme sans but lucratif; Organisme de réglementation; fondée en 1974
Mission: Protéger le public; assurer la qualité d'ergothérapie; promouvoir l'accessibilité aux services d'ergothérapie; soutenir la pratique professionnelle et son évolution; favoriser le rayonnement de la profession
Membre(s) du bureau directeur:
Alain Bibeau, Président-directeur général
bibeaua@oeq.org
Louise Tremblay, Secrétaire générale
tremblayl@oeq.org
Finances: *Budget de fonctionnement annuel:* $500,000-$1.5 Million
Membre(s) du personnel: 19; 50 bénévole(s)
Membre: 4,100; *Montant de la cotisation:* 435$
Activités: Remise de prix et bourses annuels; *Événements de sensibilisation:* Mois de l'ergothérapie en octobre
Prix, Bouses:
• Mention d'excellence (Prix)
• Bourse de recherche Anne-Lang-Étienne (Brouse)
Projet de maîtise
• Bourse de recherche Anne-Étienne (Brouse)
Projet de doctorat
• Prix Nicole-Ébacher (Prix)
• Prix Ginette-Théorêt (Prix)
• Prix de l'OEQ (Prix)

Ordre des évaluateurs agréés du Québec (OEAQ)

#450, 415, rue St-Antoine Ouest, Montréal QC H2Z 2B9
Tél: 514-281-9888; *Téléc:* 514-281-0120
Ligne sans frais: 800-982-5387
oeaq@oeaq.qc.ca
www.oeaq.qc.ca
Aperçu: *Dimension:* moyenne; *Envergure:* provinciale; fondée en 1969
Mission: De réglementer la profession d'évaluation afin de s'assurer que le public reçoit le meilleur servicee réglementer la profession d'évaluation afin de s'assurer que le public reçoit le meilleur service
Membre(s) du bureau directeur:
Celine Viau, Secrétaire générale
cviau@oeaq.qc.ca
Membre(s) du personnel: 8
Membre: *Critères d'admissibilite:* Évaluateur immobilier; *Comités:* Révision; Inspection professionnelle; Admission; Formation continue; Formation

Ordre des Géologues du Québec

#900, 500, rue Sherbrooke Ouest, Montréal QC H3A 3C6
Tél: 514-278-6220; *Téléc:* 514-844-7556
info@ogq.qc.ca
www.ogq.qc.ca
Aperçu: *Dimension:* moyenne; *Envergure:* provinciale; Organisme de réglementation
Mission: Pour régir la profession de géologue
Membre(s) du bureau directeur:
Alain Liard, Directeur général et secrétaire
Membre(s) du personnel: 3
Membre: *Comités:* Révision; Inspection professionnelle; Normes d'admission

Ordre des hygiénistes dentaires du Québec (OHDQ)

#1212, 1155 rue University, Montréal QC H3B 3A7
Tél: 514-284-7639; *Téléc:* 514-284-3147
Ligne sans frais: 800-361-2996
jcote@ohdq.com
www.ohdq.com
Aperçu: *Dimension:* moyenne; *Envergure:* provinciale; fondée en 1975
Membre(s) du bureau directeur:
Johanne Côté, Présidente
jcote@ohdq.com
Dominique Derome, Directrice générale
Finances: *Budget de fonctionnement annuel:* $500,000-$1.5 Million
Membre(s) du personnel: 8; 20 bénévole(s)
Membre: 3 106; *Comités:* Administratif; inspection professionnelle; discipline; formation; équivalences; syndic; révision; publications; bourses; vérification
Prix, Bouses:
• Prix Sylvie de Grandmont (Prix)
• Prix du Lecteur (Prix)
• Bourse de Perfectionnement (Bourse d études)

Ordre des infirmières et infirmiers auxiliaires du Québec (OIIAQ)

531, rue Sherbrooke Est, Montréal QC H2L 1K2
Tél: 514-282-9511; *Téléc:* 514-282-0631
Ligne sans frais: 800-283-9511
oiiaq@oiiaq.org
www.oiiaq.org
Nom précédent: Corporation professionnelle des infirmières et infirmiers auxiliaires du Québec
Aperçu: *Dimension:* moyenne; *Envergure:* provinciale; fondée en 1974 surveillé par Canadian Council of Practical Nurse Regulators
Mission: Favoriser le développement professionnel des infirmières et infirmiers auxiliaires du Québec pour viser l'excellence dans l'exercice professionnel et tendre à une plus grande humanisation des soins
Membre de: Conseil interprofessionnel du Québec
Membre(s) du bureau directeur:
Régis Paradis, Président et directeur général
Membre(s) du personnel: 24
Membre: 26 000+
Activités: *Bibliothèque*

Ordre des infirmières et infirmiers de l'Ontario *See* College of Nurses of Ontario

Ordre des infirmières et infirmiers du Québec (OIIQ)

4200, boul Dorchester ouest, Westmount QC H3Z 1V4
Tél: 514-935-2501; *Téléc:* 514-935-1799
Ligne sans frais: 800-363-6048
inf@oiiq.org
www.oiiq.org
www.facebook.com/Ordre.infirmieres.infirmiers.Quebec
twitter.com/OIIQ
www.flickr.com/photos/ordreinf/sets/
Également appelé: Corporation professionnelle des infirmières et infirmiers du Québec
Aperçu: *Dimension:* grande; *Envergure:* provinciale; Organisme de réglementation; fondée en 1920
Mission: Assurer la protection du public; contrôler l'exercice de la profession par ses membres
Membre de: Conseil interprofessionnel du Québec (CIQ)
Membre(s) du bureau directeur:
Lucie Tremblay, Présidente-directrice générale
presidente@oiiq.org
Claudia Gallant, Vice-présidente
claudia.gallant@ssss.gouv.qc.ca
François-Régis Fréchette, Administratrice
outaouais.president@gmail.com
Finances: *Budget de fonctionnement annuel:* Plus de $5 Million*Fonds:* Fondation de recherche en sciences infirmières du Québec (FRESIQ)
Membre(s) du personnel: 125
Membre: 65 000; *Montant de la cotisation:* 262.31$; *Critères d'admissibilite:* Détenir un permis d'exercice d'infirmière et être inscrit au Tableau des membres; *Comités:* Révision; Inspection professionnelle; Sélection de la récipiendaire de l'Insigne du mérite; Formation (2); Finances et Vérification; Jeunesse
Activités: *Événements de sensibilisation:* Congrès; Semaine de l'infirmière; Tournoi de golf; *Bibliothèque:* Centre de documentation; Bibliothèque publique
Prix, Bouses:
• Prix Innovation clinique (Prix)
• Prix Insigne du mérite de l'Ordre (Prix)
• Bourses de baccalauréat, maîtrise, doctorat (Brouse)
• Prix Florence (Prix)
Publications:
• Le Journal
Type: Journal; *Frequency:* cinq fois par a

Ordre régional des infirmières et infirmiers du Bas-Saint-Laurent/Gaspésie-Iles-de-la-Madeleine
49, rue Saint-Jean-Baptiste Ouest, Rimouski QC G5L 4J2
Tél: 418-725-3353; *Téléc:* 418-725-3350
oriibslg@cgocable.ca
www.oiiq.org/ordres/basStLaurent/
Membre(s) du bureau directeur:
Renée Rivière, Présidente

Ordre régional des infirmières et infirmiers de Québec
#102, 915, boul René-Lévesque ouest, Sillery QC G1S 1T8
Tél: 418-527-2507; *Téléc:* 418-527-8621
oriiq03@globetrotter.net
www.oiiq.org/ordres/quebec/
Membre(s) du bureau directeur:
Colombe Harvey, Présidente
harveycolombe@hotmail.com

Ordre régional des infirmières et infirmiers de Chaudière-Appalaches
69, rue Champagnat ouest, Lévis QC G6V 2B2
Tél: 418-835-1475; *Téléc:* 418-835-3587
oriica@videotron.ca
www.oiiq.org/ordres/chaudiere/
Membre(s) du bureau directeur:
Ginette Bernier, Présidente
ginette_bernier@ssss.gouv.qc.ca

Ordre régional des infirmières et infirmiers de Mauricie/Centre-du-Québec
CP 955, #208, 188, rue Radisson, Trois-Rivières QC G9A 5K2
Tél: 819-374-1512; *Téléc:* 819-374-4150
oriimcq@cgocable.ca
www.oriimcq.qc.ca
Membre de: OIIQ
Membre(s) du bureau directeur:
Marie-Andrée Gauthier, Présidente
magauthier@oriimcq.qc.ca
Francine Boulé, Vice-Présidente
Yvon Charland, Trésorier

Ordre régional des infirmières et infirmiers de l'Estrie
375, rue Argyll, Sherbrooke QC J1H 3H5
Tél: 819-346-6890; *Téléc:* 819-346-2077
oriie.csss-iugs@ssss.gouv.qc.ca
www.oiiq.org/ordres/estrie/
Membre(s) du bureau directeur:
Yvan Parenteau, Président
yparenteau@videotron.ca

Ordre régional des infirmières et infirmiers de la Montérégie
Complexe Cousineau, #2300, 5245, boul Cousineau, Saint-Hubert QC J3Y 6J8
Tél: 450-462-4868; *Téléc:* 450-462-3654
oriim@videotron.ca
www.oiiq.org/ordres/monteregie/
Membre(s) du bureau directeur:
Denise Gaudreau, Présidente

Ordre régional des infirmières et infirmiers de Laurentides/Lanaudière
#100, 30, rue de Martigny, Saint-Jérôme QC J7Y 2E9
Tél: 450-436-6217; *Téléc:* 450-436-6610
Ligne sans frais: 877-436-6217
oriill@qc.aira.com
www.oiiq.org/ordres/laurentides/
Membre(s) du bureau directeur:
Lise Racette, Présidente

Ordre régional des infirmières et infirmiers de l'Outaouais
#160, 221, ch Freeman, Gatineau QC J8Z 1L3
Tél: 819-770-4121; *Téléc:* 819-770-3606
oriio@qc.aira.com
www.oiiq.org/ordres/Outaouais/
Membre(s) du bureau directeur:
François-Régis Fréchette, Président
francois_regis_frechette@ssss.gouv.qc.ca

Ordre régional des infirmières et infirmiers de Montréal/Laval
#120, 2120, rue Sherbrooke est, Montréal QC H2K 1C3
Tél: 514-343-3707; *Téléc:* 514-343-9070
oriiml@bellnet.ca
www.oriiml.org
Membre(s) du bureau directeur:
Linda Ward, Présidente
linda.ward@muhc.mcgill.ca

Ordre régional des infirmières et infirmiers de la Côte-Nord
#222B, 690, boul Laure, Sept-Iles QC G4R 4K7
Tél: 418-968-1500
Ligne sans frais: 866-968-1500
www.oiiq.org/ordres/cote_nord/
Membre(s) du bureau directeur:
Marie-Blanchet Legendre, Présidente
marie.legendre@si.cgocable.ca

Ordre régional des infirmières et infirmiers de Saguenay—Lac-Saint-Jean/Nord-du-Québec
Plaza II, CP 282, 540, rue Sacré-Coeur ouest, 2e étage, Alma QC G8B 1M4
Tél: 418-662-5051; *Téléc:* 418-622-5052
Ligne sans frais: 866-662-5051
oriislsjnq@cgocable.ca
www.oiiq.org/ordres/saguenay/
Membre(s) du bureau directeur:
Pierre Boulianne, Président
pierre.boulianne@chs02.qc.ca

Ordre régional des infirmières et infirmiers de l'Abitibi-Témiscamingue
210, av du Lac, Rouyn-Noranda QC J9X 4N7
Tél: 819-762-3768; *Téléc:* 819-762-3760
oriat@tlb.sympatico.ca
www.oiiq.org/ordres/abitibi/
Membre(s) du bureau directeur:
Lorraine Lamontagne, Présidente
lorraine.lamontagne@cablevision.qc.ca

Ordre des ingénieurs du Québec (OIQ)
Gare Windsor, #350, 1100, av des Canadiens-de-Montréal, Montréal QC H3B 2S2
Tél: 514-845-6141; *Téléc:* 514-845-1833
Ligne sans frais: 800-461-6141
info@oiq.qc.ca
www.oiq.qc.ca
Aperçu: *Dimension:* grande; *Envergure:* provinciale; fondée en 1920 surveillé par Engineers Canada
Mission: Faire de la promotion et s'assurer de la qualité des services rendus à la société par les ingénieurs, individuellement et collectivement, en tant que membres d'un corps professionnel; Favoriser leur épanouissement professionnel et personnel; Contribuer au développement socio-économique de la société
Membre de: Engineers Canada
Affliation(s): Conseil Interprofessionnel du Québec
Membre(s) du bureau directeur:
Daniel Lebel, PMP, Président
Martin Lapointe, ing., Vice-président, Finances
Stéphane Bilodeau, ing., Vice-président, Affaires publiques
Éric Potvin, ing., Vice-président, Affaires professionnelles
600 bénévole(s)
Membre: 60 000; *Montant de la cotisation:* 180$; *Comités:* Discipline; Inspection professionnelle; Révision; Examinateurs; Surveillance des élections; Finances et de vérification; Gouvernance; Orientation des affaires publiques; Promotion et la valorisation de la profession et des femmes en génie; Surveillance de la pratique illégale; Assurance-responsabilité professionnelle; Liaison CODIQ-OIQ-CRÉIQ; Liaison des regroupements d'ingénieurs
Activités: Préparation d'avis, mémoires et de documents professionnels; Organisation ou préparation à des conférences; Groupes de travail sur: la gestion des déchets solides, l'eau de consommation, le bilan technologique, l'analyse technologique des secteurs d'activité économique du Québec, le transfert de technologie, le génie-conseil; *Evénements de sensibilisation:* Journée de l'ingénieur(e); *Stagiaires:* Oui; *Service de conférenciers:* Oui; *Bibliothèque*
Prix, Bouses:
- Bourse Krashinsky (Prix)
- Grand prix d'excellence (Prix)
- Prix du Président au bénévolat (Prix)
- Prix d'encouragement aux études supérieures (Prix)

Meetings/Conferences: • Ordre des ingénieurs du Québec Assemblée générale annuelle 2015, June, 2015, Palais des congrès des Montréal, Montréal, QC
Scope: Provincial
Publications:
- Bulletins aux membres [a publication of the Ordre des ingénieurs du Québec]
Type: Bulletin
- PLAN [a publication of the Ordre des ingénieurs du Québec]
Type: Revue

Ordre des ingénieurs forestiers du Québec (OIFQ)
#110, 2750, rue Einstein, Québec QC G1P 4R1
Tél: 418-650-2411; *Téléc:* 418-650-2168
oifq@oifq.com
www.oifq.com
Aperçu: *Dimension:* moyenne; *Envergure:* provinciale; Organisme sans but lucratif; Organisme de réglementation; fondée en 1921
Mission: Assurer la protection du public; assurer la qualité des services rendus au public québécois; favoriser l'amélioration continue de l'expertise et de la compétence des ingénieurs forestiers; mettre en place des actions favorisant la durabilité de l'aménagement forestier pour le bénéfice de l'ensemble de la société
Membre de: Conseil interprofessionnel du Québec
Affliation(s): Fédération canadienne des associations d'ingénieurs forestiers
Membre(s) du bureau directeur:
Denis Villeneuve, Président
Finances: *Budget de fonctionnement annuel:* $500,000-$1.5 Million
Membre: 2 260; *Montant de la cotisation:* 435$; *Critères d'admissibilite:* Diplôme universitaire de premier cycle en foresterie
Activités: *Service de conférenciers:* Oui

L'Ordre des massothérapeutes de l'Ontario *See* College of Massage Therapists of Ontario

Ordre des médecins vétérinaires du Québec (OMVQ)
#200, 800, av Ste-Anne, Saint-Hyacinthe QC J2S 5G7
Tél: 450-774-1427; *Téléc:* 450-774-7635
Ligne sans frais: 800-267-1427
omvq@omvq.qc.ca
www.omvq.qc.ca
Aperçu: *Dimension:* moyenne; *Envergure:* provinciale; Organisme sans but lucratif; Organisme de réglementation; fondée en 1902
Mission: Protection du public; contribuer à l'amélioration de la santé et du bien-être des animaux; formation des membres; maintien de la qualité des services vétérinaires
Membre(s) du bureau directeur:
Joël Bergeron, Président
Suzie Prince, Directrice générale/Secrétaire
suzie.prince@omvq.qc.ca
Finances: *Budget de fonctionnement annuel:* $500,000-$1.5 Million; *Fonds:* Cotisation annuelle
Membre(s) du personnel: 15
Membre: 1 940 actifs; *Montant de la cotisation:* 650$; *Critères d'admissibilite:* Ötre médecin vétérinaire; *Comités:* Administratif; Inspection professionnelle; Discipline; Communications; Médicaments
Activités: *Evénements de sensibilisation:* Semaine de la vie animale, oct.

Ordre des opticiens d'ordonnances du Québec (OOOQ)
#601, 630, rue Sherbrooke ouest, Montréal QC H3A 1E4
Tél: 514-288-7542; *Téléc:* 514-288-5982
Ligne sans frais: 800-563-6345
ordre@opticien.qc.ca
www.oodq.qc.ca
Aperçu: *Dimension:* moyenne; *Envergure:* provinciale; Organisme de réglementation; fondée en 1940 surveillé par Office des professions du Québec
Mission: Assurer la protection du public; contrôler l'exercice de la profession par ses membres
Membre de: National Accreditation Committee of Opticians
Affliation(s): Conseil interprofessionnel du Québec (CIQ)
Membre(s) du bureau directeur:
Linda Samson, Présidente
Finances: *Budget de fonctionnement annuel:* $500,000-$1.5 Million
Membre(s) du personnel: 5; 30 bénévole(s)
Membre: 1140; *Montant de la cotisation:* 695$
Activités: *Stagiaires:* Oui; *Listes de destinataires:* Oui

Ordre des optométristes de l'Ontario *See* College of Optometrists of Ontario

Ordre des optométristes du Québec
#700, 1265, rue Berri, Montréal QC H2L 4X4
Tél: 514-499-0524; *Téléc:* 514-499-1051
Ligne sans frais: 888-499-0524
www.ooq.org
Aperçu: *Dimension:* moyenne; *Envergure:* provinciale; Organisme de réglementation
Mission: De réglementer la profession d'optométriste afin de s'assurer que le public reçoit la plus haute qualité de service
Membre(s) du bureau directeur:
Marco Laverdière, Secrétaire et directeur général
Membre(s) du personnel: 5
Membre: *Montant de la cotisation:* 194,91$ inactif; 1346,55$ actif; *Comités:* Exécutif; Gouvernance; Admission à l'exercice; Formation; Législation et réglementation; Enquête relatif aux affaires pénales; Exercice; Communications; Révision

Ordre des orthophonistes et audiologistes du Québec (OOAQ)
#601, 235, boul René-Levesque Est, Montréal QC H2X 1N8
Tél: 514-282-9123; *Téléc:* 514-282-9541
Ligne sans frais: 888-232-9123
info@ooaq.qc.ca
www.ooaq.qc.ca
Aperçu: *Dimension:* moyenne; *Envergure:* provinciale; Organisme de réglementation; fondée en 1973
Mission: D'assurer la protection du public en regard du domaine d'exercice de ses membres, soit les troubles de la communication humaine; surveiller l'exercice professionnel des orthophonistes et des audiologistes et voir à favoriser l'accessibilité du public à des services de qualité; contribuer à l'intégration sociale des individus et à l'amélioration de la qualité de vie de la population québécoise
Membre(s) du bureau directeur:
Marie-Pierre Caouette, Présidente et directrice générale
presidence@ooaq.qc.ca
Membre(s) du personnel: 15
Membre: 2,518; *Critères d'admissibilite:* Maîtrise en orthophonie-audiologie; *Comités:* Admission; Inspection professionnelle; Discipline; Révision des plaintes; Révision des équivalences; Formation; Prix
Activités: Surveillance de l'exercice professionnel; favoriser l'accès aux services; amélioration de la qualité de vie; intégration sociale; *Bibliothèque* Bibliothèque publique rendez-vous

Ordre des pharmaciens du N.-B. *See* New Brunswick Pharmaceutical Society

Ordre des pharmaciens du Québec (OPQ)
#301, 266, rue Notre Dame Ouest, Montréal QC H2Y 1T6
Tél: 514-284-9588; *Téléc:* 514-284-3420
Ligne sans frais: 800-363-0324
ordrepharm@opq.org
www.opq.org
www.facebook.com/OrdredespharmaciensduQuebec
twitter.com/ordrepharmaQc
www.youtube.com/user/ordrepharmaciensqc
Aperçu: *Dimension:* moyenne; *Envergure:* provinciale; Organisme de réglementation; fondée en 1871 surveillé par National Association of Pharmacy Regulatory Authorities
Mission: Protection du public en matières de services pharmaceutiques.
Membre de: Conseil canadien de l'Éducation permanente en pharmacie; Conseil interprofessionnel du Québec
Membre(s) du bureau directeur:
Bertrand Bolduc, Président
Manon Lambert, Directrice générale et secrétaire
Membre(s) du personnel: 50
Membre: *Montant de la cotisation:* Barème; *Critères d'admissibilite:* Détenteur d'un permis d'exercice de la pharmacie valide pour le Québec; *Comités:* Discipline; Révision; Arbitrage des compte; Enquête sur le contrôle de l'utilisation des médicaments; Admission à la pratique; Formation des pharmaciens; Réviseur de l'admission à la pratique; Inspection professionnelle; Veille sur les nouvelles pratiques liées aux développements technologiques; Attribution des prix; Gouvernance et d'éthique; Règlement sur l'exercice de la pharmacie en société; Déontologie; Étude des demandes de dispense des formations obligatoires; Vigie interordres; Ordre des pharmaciens du Québec / Collège des médecins du Québec
Activités: *Service de conférenciers:* Oui
Prix, Bouses:
- Prix Louis-Hébert (Prix)

Ordre des physiothérapeutes de l'Ontario *See* College of Physiotherapists of Ontario

Ordre des Podiatres du Québec
#900, 500, rue Sherbrooke ouest, Montréal QC H3A 3C6
Tél: 514-288-0019; *Téléc:* 514-288-5463
Ligne sans frais: 888-514-7433
podiatres@ordredespodiatres.qc.ca
www.ordredespodiatres.qc.ca
Aperçu: *Dimension:* petite; *Envergure:* provinciale
Membre(s) du bureau directeur:
Charles Faucher, Président

Ordre des psychoéducateurs et psychoéducatrices du Québec (OPP)
#510, 1600, boul Henri-Bourassa Ouest, Montréal QC H3M 3E2
Tél: 514-333-6601; *Téléc:* 514-333-7502
Ligne sans frais: 877-913-6601
info@ordrepsed.qc.ca
www.ordrepsed.qc.ca

Aperçu: *Dimension:* moyenne; *Envergure:* provinciale; Organisme de réglementation
Mission: De réglementer la profession de psychoéducateurs afin de protéger le public et d'assurer la meilleure qualité de service possible est fournie
Membre(s) du bureau directeur:
Renée Verville, Directrice générale
Membre(s) du personnel: 19
Membre: *Montant de la cotisation:* Barème; *Comités:* Exécutif; Admission par équivalence; Inspection professionnelle; Formation; Révision des plaintes; Discipline; Arbitrage des comptes; Affaires professionnelles

L'Ordre des psychologues du Québec (OPQ)

#510, 1100, av Beaumont, Montréal QC H3P 3H5
Tél: 514-738-1881; *Téléc:* 514-738-8838
Ligne sans frais: 800-363-2644
www.ordrepsy.qc.ca
Aperçu: *Dimension:* moyenne; *Envergure:* provinciale; fondée en 1962
Mission: Assurer la protection du public; contrôler l'exercice de la profession par ses membres; veiller à la qualité des services dispensés par ses membres; favoriser le développement de la compétence professionnelle, le respect des normes déontologiques et l'accessibilité aux services psychologiques
Affiliation(s): American Psychological Association
Membre(s) du bureau directeur:
Rose-Marie Charest, Présidente
presidence@ordrepsy.qc.ca
Finances: *Budget de fonctionnement annuel:* $1.5 Million-$3 Million
Membre(s) du personnel: 22
Membre: 7 000; *Montant de la cotisation:* 381$; *Critères d'admissibilite:* Maîtrise en psychologie
Activités: *Service de conférenciers:* Oui; *Listes de destinataires:* Oui

Ordre des Sages-Femmes de l'Ontario ***See*** College of Midwives of Ontario

Ordre des sages-femmes du Québec

#300, 4126, rue Saint-Denis, Montréal QC H2W 2M5
Tél: 514-286-1313
Ligne sans frais: 877-711-1313
info@osfq.org
www.osfq.org
Aperçu: *Dimension:* petite; *Envergure:* provinciale
Mission: Pour surveiller les pratiques des sages-femmes au Québec
Membre(s) du bureau directeur:
Lorena Garrido, Directrice générale
lorena.garrido@osfq.org
Membre(s) du personnel: 4
Membre: *Comités:* Finances; Gouvernance; Lignes directrices; Inspection professionnelle; Syndique; Révision; Discipline; Surveillance de la pratique illégale; Formation continue; Formation; Étude pour la pratique en régions rurales et éloignées; Admission par équivalence; Médicaments, examens et analyses; Statistiques; Étude et d'enquête sur la mortalité et la morbidité périnatales

Ordre des techniciens et techniciennes dentaires du Québec (OTTDQ)

#900, 500, rue Sherbrooke Ouest, Montréal QC H3A 3C6
Tél: 514-282-3837; *Téléc:* 514-844-7556
www.ottdq.com
www.facebook.com/OTTDQ
Aperçu: *Dimension:* petite; *Envergure:* provinciale; Organisme de réglementation
Mission: De réglementer la profession des techniciens dentaires afin de protéger le public et d'assurer la meilleure qualité de service possible est fournie
Membre(s) du bureau directeur:
Linda Carbone, Secrétaire
Membre(s) du personnel: 3
Membre: *Comités:* Formation continue; Formation; Normes d'équivalences; Inspection professionnelle; Conciliation et arbitrage des comptes; Exercice illégal et usurpation de titre réservé; Conseil de discipline; Révisions des plaintes; Finances et régie interne

Ordre des technologues en imagerie médicale, en radio-oncologie et en élétrophysiologie médicale du Québec

#401, 6455, rue Jean-Talon, Saint-Léonard QC H1S 3E8
Tél: 514-351-0052; *Téléc:* 514-355-2396
Ligne sans frais: 800-361-8759
info@otimroepmq.ca
www.otimroepmq.ca
Nom précédent: Ordre des technologues en radiologie du Québec
Aperçu: *Dimension:* moyenne; *Envergure:* provinciale; Organisme de réglementation; fondée en 1941
Mission: De surveiller l'exercice de la profession par ses membres, contribuer à leur développement professionnel & assurer au public des services de qualité en matière d'imagerie médicale & de radio-oncologies
Membre de: Canadian Association of Medical Radiation Technologists
Membre(s) du bureau directeur:
Alain Cromp, Directeur général
Danielle Boué, Présidente
Finances: *Fonds:* Les frais d'adhésion
Membre(s) du personnel: 22
Membre: 5,800; *Montant de la cotisation:* Barème; *Critères d'admissibilite:* Technologues qui travaillent dans le radiodiagnostic, la médecine nucléaire, la radio-oncologie et l'électrophysiologie médicale; *Comités:* Exécutif; Inspection professionnelle; Équivalences de diplôme et de formation; Discipline; Révision des plaintes; Formation; Développement professionnel; Relève; Magazine; Vérification; Examens; Révision des notes
Activités: *Stagiaires:* Oui; *Listes de destinataires:* Oui; *Bibliothèque:* Centre de doc;

Ordre des technologues en radiation médicale de l'Ontario ***See*** College of Medical Radiation Technologists of Ontario

Ordre des technologues en radiologie du Québec ***Voir*** Ordre des technologues en imagerie médicale, en radio-oncologie et en élétrophysiologie médicale du Québec

Ordre des technologues professionnels du Québec (OTPQ)

#720, 1265, rue Berri, Montréal QC H2L 4X4
Tél: 514-845-3247; *Téléc:* 514-845-3643
Ligne sans frais: 800-561-3459
info@otpq.qc.ca
www.otpq.qc.ca
www.linkedin.com/groups?home=&gid=4134994
www.facebook.com/TechnologuesProfessionnels
twitter.com/otpq
Nom précédent: Corporation professionnelle des technologues professionnelles du Québec
Aperçu: *Dimension:* moyenne; *Envergure:* provinciale; fondée en 1927 surveillé par Canadian Council of Technicians & Technologists
Mission: Promouvoir et assurer la compétence des technologues professionnels dans l'intérêt public
Membre de: Conseil canadiens des techniciens et technologues
Membre(s) du bureau directeur:
Denis Beauchamp, Directeur général et secrétaire, 514-845-3247 Ext. 107
dbeauchamp@otpq.qc.ca
Finances: *Budget de fonctionnement annuel:* $500,000-$1.5 Million
Membre(s) du personnel: 9
Membre: 5 000; *Comités:* Admission; Discipline; Inspection professionnelle; Prix
Activités: *Stagiaires:* Oui; *Listes de destinataires:* Oui
Prix, Bouses:
- Technologue de l'année (Prix)
- Prix Robert Daigneault (Bénévole de l'année) (Prix)
- Bourse méritas (Brouse)

Ordre des traducteurs et interprètes agréés du Québec ***Voir*** Ordre des traducteurs, terminologues et interprètes agréés du Québec

Ordre des traducteurs, terminologues et interprètes agréés du Québec (OTTIAQ)

#1108, 2021, rue Union, Montréal QC H3A 2S9
Tél: 514-845-4411; *Téléc:* 514-845-9903
Ligne sans frais: 800-265-4815
info@ottiaq.org
www.ottiaq.org
Nom précédent: Ordre des traducteurs et interprètes agréés du Québec
Aperçu: *Dimension:* moyenne; *Envergure:* provinciale; Organisme sans but lucratif; fondée en 1992 surveillé par Canadian Translators, Terminologists & Interpreters Council
Mission: L'OTTIAQ assure la protection du public en octroyant les titres de traducteur agréé, de terminologue agréé et d'interprète agréé, en veillant au respect de son code de déontologie et des normes professionnelles et en mettant en ouvre les mécanismes prévus au Code des professions.
Membre de: Fédération internationale des traducteurs
Membre(s) du bureau directeur:
Johanne Boucher, Directrice générale
direction@ottiaq.org
Finances: *Budget de fonctionnement annuel:* $500,000-$1.5 Million
Membre(s) du personnel: 7; 100 bénévole(s)
Membre: 2150 société + 14 d'honneur + 447 adhérents + 1376 agréés; *Montant de la cotisation:* 150$ adhérents; 430$ agréés; *Critères d'admissibilite:* Traducteur; terminologue; interprète
Activités: Congrès annuel; *Evénements de sensibilisation:* Journée mondiale de la traduction, 30 sept.

Ordre des travailleurs sociaux et des techniciens en travail social de l'Ontario ***See*** Ontario College of Social Workers & Social Service Workers

Ordre des urbanistes du Québec (OUQ)

#410, 85, rue St-Paul ouest, Montréal QC H2Y 3V4
Tél: 514-849-1177; *Téléc:* 514-849-7176
info@ouq.qc.ca
www.ouq.qc.ca
Nom précédent: Ordre professionnel des urbanistes du Québec
Aperçu: *Dimension:* moyenne; *Envergure:* provinciale; fondée en 1963 surveillé par Canadian Institute of Planners
Mission: Assurer la protection du public dans l'exercice de la profession par ses membres et la promotion de la pratique de l'urbanisme au Québec
Membre(s) du bureau directeur:
Claude Beaulac, Directeur général
cbeaulac@ouq.qc.ca
Odette Michaud, Secrétaire de l'Ordre
omichaud@ouq.qc.ca
Nathalie Corso, Coordonnatrice, Admission et qualité
ncorso@ouq.qc.ca
Membre: 700; *Montant de la cotisation:* 360$; *Comités:* Admission; Déontologie; Discipline; Formation Continue; Inspection Professionnelle

Ordre professionnel de la physiothérapie du Québec (OPPQ)

#1000, 7151, Jean Talon est, Anjou QC H1M 3N8
Tél: 514-351-2770; *Téléc:* 514-351-2658
Ligne sans frais: 800-361-2001
physio@oppq.qc.ca
www.oppq.qc.ca
Nom précédent: Ordre professionnel des physiothérapeutes du Québec; Corporation professionnelle des physiothérapeutes du Québec
Aperçu: *Dimension:* moyenne; *Envergure:* provinciale; fondée en 1973 surveillé par Canadian Alliance of Physiotherapy Regulators
Mission: Assurer la protection du public en surveillant l'exercice de la physiothérapie par ses membres et en contribuant à leur développement professionnel
Membre de: Alliance canadienne des organismes de réglementation de la physiothérapie; Association canadienne de physiothérapie
Membre(s) du bureau directeur:
Lucie Forget, Présidente
lforget@oppq.qc.ca
Claude Laurent, Directeur général et Secrétaire
claurent@oppq.qc.ca
Finances: *Budget de fonctionnement annuel:* $500,000-$1.5 Million
Membre(s) du personnel: 27
Membre: 7 145; *Critères d'admissibilite:* Physiothérapeutes

Ordre professionnel des diététistes du Québec (OPDQ)

#1220, 2155, rue Guy, Montréal QC H3H 2R9
Tél: 514-393-3733; *Téléc:* 514-393-3582
Ligne sans frais: 888-393-8528
opdq@opdq.org
www.opdq.org
Aperçu: *Dimension:* moyenne; *Envergure:* provinciale; Organisme de réglementation; fondée en 1956 surveillé par Dietitians of Canada
Mission: Assurer la protection du public en contrôlant notamment l'exercice de la profession par ses membres.
Membre(s) du bureau directeur:
Annie Chapados, Directrice générale et secrétaire
achapados@opdq.org
Membre(s) du personnel: 10

Membre: *Montant de la cotisation:* Barème; *Critères d'admissibilité:* Bac. en Diététique/Nutrition; *Comités:* Conseil de discipline; Comité de révision; Comité d'inspection professionnelle; Comité sur l'exercice illégal; Comité de la formation des diététistes
Activités: *Listes de destinataires:* Oui

Ordre professionnel des inhalothérapeutes du Québec (OPIQ)

#320, 1440, rue Sainte-Catherine ouest, Montréal QC H3G 1R8
Tél: 514-931-2900; *Téléc:* 514-931-3621
Ligne sans frais: 800-561-0029
info@opiq.qc.ca
www.opiq.qc.ca
Aperçu: *Dimension:* moyenne; *Envergure:* provinciale; Organisme sans but lucratif; fondée en 1969
Mission: Protection du public; surveillance de l'exercice professionnel de l'inhalothérapie
Affiliation(s): Alliance nationale des organismes de réglementation de la thérapie respiratoire
Membre(s) du bureau directeur:
Céline Beaulieu, Présidente
Josée Prud'Homme, Directrice générale et secrétaire
Finances: *Budget de fonctionnement annuel:* $500,000-$1.5 Million
Membre(s) du personnel: 8; 20 bénévole(s)
Membre: 3 300; *Montant de la cotisation:* 290$; *Critères d'admissibilité:* Professionnel en santé cardio-respiratoire
Activités: Congrès annuel et Assemblée générale en automne; *Stagiaires:* Oui; *Service de conférenciers:* Oui

Ordre professionnel des physiothérapeutes du Québec; Corporation professionnelle des physiothérapeutes du Québec *Voir* Ordre professionnel de la physiothérapie du Québec

Ordre professionnel des sexologues du Québec (OPSQ)

#300, 4126, rue St-Denis, Montréal QC H2W 2M5
Tél: 438-386-6777
Ligne sans frais: 855-386-6777
info@opsq.org
opsq.org
Aperçu: *Dimension:* petite; *Envergure:* provinciale; Organisme de réglementation
Mission: De réglementer la profession des sexologues afin de protéger le public et d'assurer la meilleure qualité de service possible est fournie
Membre(s) du bureau directeur:
Isabelle Beaulieu, Directrice générale et secrétaire de l'Ordre
isabelle.beaulieu@opsq.org
Membre(s) du personnel: 5
Membre: *Montant de la cotisation:* Barème

Ordre professionnel des technologistes médicaux du Québec (OPTMQ)

281, av Laurier Est, Montréal QC H2T 1G2
Tél: 514-527-9811; *Téléc:* 514-527-7314
Ligne sans frais: 800-567-7763
info@optmq.org
www.optmq.org
Nom précédent: Corporation professionnelle des technologistes médicaux du Québec
Aperçu: *Dimension:* moyenne; *Envergure:* provinciale; Organisme sans but lucratif; Organisme de réglementation; fondée en 1973 surveillé par Canadian Society for Medical Laboratory Science
Mission: Protection du public en vérifiant la pratique des membres, en effectuant un contrôle lors de l'émission du permis, par la discipline et l'inspection professionnelle
Membre de: Conseil Interprofessionnel du Québec
Membre(s) du bureau directeur:
Nathalie Rodrigue, Présidente
Alain Collette, Avocat Secrétaire et Directeur général
Membre: *Montant de la cotisation:* 355,99$; *Comités:* Congrès; Développement professionnel; Normes; Communications; Admission; Jeunesse

Ordre professionnel des travailleurs sociaux du Québec (OPTSQ)

#520, 255, boul. Crémazie Est, Montréal QC H2M 1M2
Tél: 514-731-3925; *Téléc:* 514-731-6785
Ligne sans frais: 888-731-9420
info.general@optsq.org
www.optsq.org
www.facebook.com/OTSTCFQ
twitter.com/OTSTCFQ1
Aperçu: *Dimension:* moyenne; *Envergure:* provinciale; Organisme de réglementation; fondée en 1960
Mission: Assurer la protection du public par le contrôle de l'exercice de la profession, par la formation continue, et le développement professionnel.
Membre de: Canadian Association of Social Workers
Affliation(s): Conseil interprofessionnel du Québec
Membre(s) du bureau directeur:
Ghislaine Brosseau, Directrice générale
Membre(s) du personnel: 44
Membre: *Critères d'admissibilite:* Diplôme universitaire en travail social; *Comités:* Exécutif; Révision; Révision en matière d'équivalences; Admissions et des équivalences; Inspection professionnelle; Formation; Formation Continue; Pratique Autonome; Médiation Familiale; Pratique de 'a thérapie conjugale et familiale; Enquête sur l'utilisation illégale des titres et l'exercice illégal de la profession; Éthique; Pratique en protection de la jeunesse; Jeunesse - secteur T.S.
Activités: *Service de conférenciers:* Oui

Ordre professionnel des urbanistes du Québec *Voir* Ordre des urbanistes du Québec

Ordre souverain militaire hospitalier de St-Jean de Jérusalem, de Rhodes et de Malte - Association canadienne *See* Sovereign Military Hospitaller Order of St-John of Jerusalem of Rhodes & of Malta - Canadian Association

Ordres de réglementation des professionnels de la santé de l'Ontario *See* Federation of Health Regulatory Colleges of Ontario

Organ Donors Canada / Donneurs d'organes du Canada

5326 Ada Blvd. NW, Edmonton AB T5W 4N7
Tel: 780-474-9363
Previous Name: Human Parts Banks of Canada
Overview: A medium-sized national organization founded in 1974
Mission: Information service dedicated to assisting the process of anatomical gift giving in Canada & increasing public awareness of the need for, & the human & economic advantages of all types of human organ & tissue donations for transplant, teaching & research.
Chief Officer(s):
Mae Cox, Executive Director
Finances: *Annual Operating Budget:* Less than $50,000; *Funding Sources:* Voluntary donations
Membership: 1-99
Activities: *Speaker Service:* Yes

Organic Crop Improvement Association - Alberta Chapter #1 *See* Alberta Organic Producers Association

Organic Crop Improvement Association - New Brunswick (OCIA-NB)

2002 Cedar Camp Rd., South Beach Kings NB E4E 5E7
Tel: 506-433-3935
ocianb@nbnet.nb.ca
Overview: A small provincial organization founded in 1987
Mission: To provide organic certification & crop improvement for New Brunswick farmers
Member of: OCIA International
Affiliation(s): New Brunswick Federation of Agriculture
Chief Officer(s):
Susan Tyler, Administrator
Staff Member(s): 1; 12 volunteer(s)
Membership: *Fees:* $30; *Member Profile:* Growers both in New Brunswick & northern Maine

Organic Producers Association of Manitoba Co-operative Inc. (OPAM)

PO Box 279, Miniota MB R0M 1M0
Tel: 204-567-3745; *Fax:* 204-567-3749
www.opam-mb.com
Overview: A medium-sized provincial organization founded in 1988
Mission: To provide organic certification inspection service to farmers & processors; to teach & promote standards, methods & techniques for growing, producing & processing organically grown products
Staff Member(s): 1; 20 volunteer(s)
Membership: 881; *Fees:* $25 individual
Activities: Marketing seminars; farm tours; production seminars; AGM;

L'Organisation canadienne des physiciens médicaux *See* Canadian Organization of Medical Physicists

L'Organisation des musées militaires du Canada inc. *See* Organization of Military Museums of Canada, Inc.

Organisation mondiale des personnes handicapées *See* Disabled Peoples' International

Organisation montréalaise des personnes atteintes de cancer inc. *Voir* Organisation multiressources pour les personnes atteintes de cancer

Organisation multiressources pour les personnes atteintes de cancer (OMPAC)

3849, rue Sherbrooke est, Montréal QC H1X 2A3
Tél: 514-729-8833; *Téléc:* 514-729-5390
Ligne sans frais: 866-248-6444
Nom précédent: Organisation montréalaise des personnes atteintes de cancer inc.
Aperçu: *Dimension:* petite; *Envergure:* locale; Organisme sans but lucratif; fondée en 1981
Mission: Apporter aide et assistance aux personnes atteintes de cancer et à leurs proches en offrant des services d'écoute téléphonique, de rencontres individuelles et de groupe, de documentation et de référence, et des activités diverses
Membre(s) du bureau directeur:
Colette Coudé, Directrice générale
Finances: *Budget de fonctionnement annuel:* $250,000-$500,000; *Fonds:* Gouvernement; Centraide
Membre(s) du personnel: 6; 41 bénévole(s)
Membre: 130; *Montant de la cotisation:* $10 individu; *Critères d'admissibilité:* Personnes atteintes de cancer et leurs proches

Organisation nationale des femmes immigrantes et des femmes appartenant à une minorité visible du Canada *See* National Organization of Immigrant & Visible Minority Women of Canada

Organisation ontarienne pour la cybernétique en éducation *See* Educational Computing Organization of Ontario

Organisation pour le tourisme étudiant au Québec et Fédération québécoise d'ajisme *Voir* Fondation Tourisme Jeunesse

L'Organisation pour les carrières en environnement du Canada *See* Environmental Careers Organization of Canada

Organisation québécoise des personnes atteintes de cancer (OQPAC)

#401, 363, de la Couronne, Québec QC G1K 6E9
Tél: 418-529-1425
coordination@oqpac.com
www.oqpac.com
www.facebook.com/99211283481
Aperçu: *Dimension:* petite; *Envergure:* provinciale; Organisme sans but lucratif; fondée en 1984
Membre: *Montant de la cotisation:* 10$

Organisme canadien de réglementation du commerce des valeurs mobilières *See* Investment Industry Regulatory Organization of Canada

Organisme catholique pour la vie et la famille *See* Catholic Organization for Life & Family (COLF)

Organisme communautaire des services aux immigrants d'Ottawa *See* Ottawa Community Immigrant Services Organization

Organisme d'autoréglementation du courtage immobilier du Québec (OACIQ) / Québec Real Estate Association

#2200, 4905, boul Lapinière, Brossard QC J4Z 0G2
Tél: 450-676-4800; *Téléc:* 450-676-7801
Ligne sans frais: 800-440-5110
www.oaciq.com
Aperçu: *Dimension:* grande; *Envergure:* provinciale
Mission: Protéger le public par l'encadrement des activités professionnelles de tous les courtiers et agents immobiliers exerçant au Québec
Membre(s) du bureau directeur:
Serge Brousseau, Président du conseil
Serge Brousseau, Chef de la direction
Claude Barsalou, Vice-président & direction générale
Membre: *Comités:* Éthique; évaluation du président et chef de la direction et du syndic; inspection; discipline; liaison; vérification et des finances; nominations; étude des infractions criminelles; congrès; formulaires; pratiques professionnelles
Activités: Séances de formation; examens de certification

The Organization for Bipolar Affective Disorder (OBAD)
1019 - 7th Ave. SW, Calgary AB T2P 1A8
Tel: 403-263-7408
Toll-Free: 866-263-7408
obad@obad.ca
www.obad.ca
www.facebook.com/groups/35640153998/
Overview: A medium-sized national charitable organization
Mission: To assist people affected directly or indirectly by bipolar disorder, depression, & anxiety
Chief Officer(s):
Kaj Korvela, Executive Director

Organization for Quality Education *See* Society for Quality Education

Organization of Book Publishers of Ontario (OBPO)
#401, 20 Maud St., Toronto ON M5V 2M5
Tel: 416-536-7584; *Fax:* 416-536-7692
marganne@obpo.ca
www.openbooktoronto.com
Overview: A medium-sized provincial organization founded in 1990
Mission: To act as a centralized representative of Ontario book publishers in lobbying the provincial government & arts organizations about issues directly of concern to members; to share information & education opportunities that relate to the provincial, national & international book publishing industries; to provide the opportunities for group marketing projects
Member of: ACP
Chief Officer(s):
Marg Anne Morrison, Director, 416-536-7584
marganne@obpa.ca
Amy Holmes, Executive Director- Toronto/Ontario, 416-592-6444
amy@obpa.ca
Staff Member(s): 2
Membership: 40; *Member Profile:* Book Publishers based in Ontario

Organization of CANDU Industries (OCI) / Association des industries CANDU
#2, 1730 McPherson Ct., Pickering ON L1W 3E6
Tel: 905-839-0073; *Fax:* 905-839-7085
www.oci-aic.org
Overview: A medium-sized national organization founded in 1979
Mission: To represent companies in the Canadian private sector engaged in the supply of goods & services for CANDU power plants in export markets; to provide a focal point for industrial collaboration between the private sector of Canada's nuclear industry & foreign purchasers of a CANDU plant; functions separately from AECL, but participates with it in the design, manufacture, construction & commissioning of CANDU facilities in foreign countries
Affliation(s): Atomic Energy of Canada
Chief Officer(s):
Ron Oberth, President
ron.oberth@oci-aic.org
Marina Oeyangen, Manager, Member Services
marina.oeyangen@oci-aic.org
Finances: *Annual Operating Budget:* Less than $50,000; *Funding Sources:* Membership dues
Staff Member(s): 3
Membership: 105; *Fees:* Schedule available; *Member Profile:* Manufacturing & engineering companies engaged in supply of goods & services for CANDU nuclear steam plants

Organization of Military Museums of Canada, Inc. (OMMC) / L'Organisation des musées militaires du Canada inc.
PO Box 60042, Stn. Unicity, Winnipeg MB R3K 2E7
e-mail: ommcinc@gmail.com
www.ommcinc.ca
Overview: A medium-sized national charitable organization founded in 1967
Mission: To preserve the military heritage of Canada by encouraging the establishment & operation of military museums; to educate museum staffs through lectures, discussions, workshops, visits, publications & exhibits; to cooperate with others having the same or similar purposes.
Member of: Canadian Museums Association
Affliation(s): Department of National Defence/Director of History & Heritage; Friends of the Canadian War Museum; Military Collectors Club of Canada
Chief Officer(s):
Marilyn Gurney, President
Stuart Beaton, Vice President
Finances: *Annual Operating Budget:* $100,000-$250,000; *Funding Sources:* Membership dues; DND support
Staff Member(s): 3; 10 volunteer(s)
Membership: 200+ individuals; 100+ museums; *Fees:* $40; *Member Profile:* Interest in military museums & artifacts & military history; *Committees:* Long-Range Planning; Bursary
Activities: Millennium project "An Inventory of Canadian Military Memorials"; *Speaker Service:* Yes; *Library:* Canadian War Museum Library

Organization of Saskatchewan Applied Economic Research *See* Saskatchewan Economics Association

Organization of Saskatchewan Arts Councils (OSAC)
1102 - 8th Ave., Regina SK S4R 1C9
Tel: 306-586-1250; *Fax:* 306-586-1550
Other Communication: www.flickr.com/photos/osac
info@osac.ca
www.osac.ca
www.facebook.com/OSACsask
twitter.com/OSACsask
www.youtube.com/user/OSACSask
Overview: A medium-sized provincial charitable organization founded in 1968
Mission: To assist the membership in their endeavors to develop, promote & present the visual arts &/or performing arts
Member of: SaskCulture Inc.
Affliation(s): CAPACOA; Saskatchewan Tourism; SPRA
Chief Officer(s):
Kevin Korchinski, Executive Director, 306-586-1220
kevin@osac.ca
Finances: *Annual Operating Budget:* $500,000-$1.5 Million; *Funding Sources:* Saskatchewan Lotteries; sponsorship; fundraising; Sask Arts Board; donations; Canadian Heritage
Staff Member(s): 6
Membership: 50 full + 75 associate; *Fees:* $185 full; $25 associate
Activities: Saskatchewan..Art on the Move (Touring Exhibitions); Stars for Saskatchewan (Member Arts Councils' performance series); Koncerts for Kids; Junior Concerts (school-based performing arts series); *Library*

Orienteering Association of British Columbia (OABC)
1428 Edinburgh St., New Westminter BC V3M 2W4
www.orienteeringbc.ca
Overview: A small provincial organization
Member of: Sport BC; Orienteering Canada
Affliation(s): Canadian Orienteering Federation (COF); Coaching Association of Canada
Chief Officer(s):
John Rance, President
rance1@shaw.ca
Activities: Offering technical coaching courses in orienteering; *Awareness Events:* National Orienteering Week

Orienteering Association of Nova Scotia (OANS)
5516 Spring Garden Rd., 4th Fl., Halifax NS B3J 1G6
Tel: 902-446-2295
info@orienteeringns.ca
www.orienteeringns.ca
Overview: A small provincial organization founded in 1971
Mission: To operate as the governing body for orienteering in Nova Scotia; To train & certify orienteering coaches, officials, & mapmakers
Member of: Canadian Orienteering Federation; Sport Nova Scotia
Chief Officer(s):
Ashley Harding, President
ashleyaharding@hotmail.com
Ian Clark, Vice-President
clark@eastlink.ca
Dale Ellis, Treasurer
dale.ellis@ns.sympatico.ca
Membership: *Committees:* Mapping; Technical & Competition; Education; Promotion; Finance; Junior Development
Activities: Coordinating local club activities; Publishing event results; Promoting orienteering; Providing programs in map, compass, & wilderness navigation skills, introductory skills, & junior development; Preparing orienteering maps

Orienteering New Brunswick (ONB)
34 Fairview Dr., Moncton NB E1E 3C7
Tel: 506-389-8091
www.orienteering.nb.ca
www.facebook.com/OrienteeringNB
Overview: A small provincial organization founded in 1975
Mission: To promote, develop & encourage the sport & recreation of orienteering in New Brunswick
Member of: Canadian Orienteering Federation
Affliation(s): International Orienteering Federation
Chief Officer(s):
David Ross, President
president@orienteering.nb.ca
Paul Looker, Secretary
Finances: *Annual Operating Budget:* Less than $50,000
Membership: *Fees:* $15-$40; *Member Profile:* Family groups; individuals; cadets & scouts
Activities: Competitive & recreational orienteering

Orienteering Ontario Inc.
ON
e-mail: info@orienteeringontario.ca
www.orienteeringontario.ca
Also Known As: Ontario Orienteering Association, Inc.
Overview: A small provincial licensing organization founded in 1975
Mission: To encourage, promote & give leadership in all aspects of the sport of orienteering & associated activities at local, provincial & national levels
Member of: Canadian Orienteering Federation
Chief Officer(s):
Michael Johnston, Co-President
Ian Sidders, Co-President
Membership: *Fees:* $35 adults; $20 juniors; $60 family

Orienteering Québec (OQ) / Fédération québécoise de course d'orientation
QC
e-mail: orientering_quebec@orienteringquebec.ca
www.orienteringquebec.ca
Overview: A small provincial charitable organization founded in 1967
Member of: Canadian Orienteering Federation (COF); International Orienteering Federation (IOF)
Affliation(s): Ramblers Orienteering Club; Lou Garou Orienteering Club; Ottawa Orienteering Club
Chief Officer(s):
Isabelle Robert, President
liriel@sympatico.ca
Paul Dubois, Vice-President
dubpaul@gmail.com
Bill Meldrum, Treasurer
bill.meldrum@videotron.ca
Finances: *Funding Sources:* Members
Activities: Organizing events; Posting event results; Coordinating club activities; mapping
Publications:
• OQ Newsletter
Type: Newsletter; *Frequency:* Quarterly; *Price:* Free with memship in Orienteering Québec

Original Hockey Hall of Fame & Museum
PO Box 82, 1350 Gardiners Rd., 2nd Fl., Kingston ON K7L 4V6
Tel: 613-583-1718
info@originalhockeyhalloffame.com
www.originalhockeyhalloffame.com
www.facebook.com/207141552735961
Previous Name: International Hockey Hall of Fame & Museum; International Ice Hockey Federation Museum Inc.
Overview: A small local organization founded in 1943
Mission: The first sports hall of fame in Canada, the Hall features exhibits on the original six NHL teams, Kingston native Don Cherry & historic hockey artifacts
Chief Officer(s):
Mark Potter, President
mpotter1@cogeco.ca
Finances: *Funding Sources:* Provincial government grants; special events; museum
Activities: *Awareness Events:* Historic Hockey Series, 1st Sat. in Feb.

Orillia & District Chamber of Commerce
150 Front St. South, Orillia ON L3V 4S7
Tel: 705-326-4424; *Fax:* 705-327-7841
www.orillia.com
Overview: A small local organization founded in 1890
Mission: To operate as a cohesive force for business interests; To represent & promote Orillia & district businesses to government, community interest groups, businesses, & other

Chambers of Commerce; To provide membership services
Affliation(s): Canadian Chamber of Commerce
Chief Officer(s):
Susan Lang, Managing Director
Finances: *Annual Operating Budget:* $500,000-$1.5 Million
Staff Member(s): 10
Membership: 600; *Fees:* $165
Awards:
• Business Achievement Awards (Award)

Orillia & District Construction Association
PO Box 235, Orillia ON L3V 6J3
Tel: 705-326-1844
www.orilliaconstruction.ca
www.linkedin.com/company/2814901?trk=tyah&trkInfo=tas%3Aorillia%20cons
www.facebook.com/101221763341770?ref=ts&fref=ts
twitter.com/OrilliaConstruc
Overview: A small local organization founded in 1959
Chief Officer(s):
Wayne Rowbotham, President
Finances: *Annual Operating Budget:* Less than $50,000; *Funding Sources:* Membership dues
Staff Member(s): 1; 11 volunteer(s)
Membership: 74 corporate; *Fees:* $295; $225 affiliate
Activities: Golf tournament; night at the Georgian Downs Raceway; boat cruise; family Xmas party; *Rents Mailing List:* Yes

Orillia Youth Symphony Orchestra (OYSO)
168 Parkview Ave., Orillia ON L3V 4M3
Tel: 705-326-7548
oysotuba@sympatico.ca
www.oyso.ca
Overview: A small local charitable organization founded in 1982 overseen by Orchestras Canada
Mission: To offer opportunity to participate in symphonic orchestra for young people 8-18 years of age
Chief Officer(s):
Mayumi Kumagai, Music Director
mayumikuba@hotmail.com
Finances: *Funding Sources:* Donations
Membership: *Fees:* $200 individual; *Member Profile:* 8-18 years of age; play musical instrument needed in symphonic orchestra
Activities: Performances at community events

Orléans Chamber of Commerce / Chambre de commerce d'Orléans
880 Taylor Creek Dr., Orleans ON K1C 1T1
Tel: 613-824-9137; *Fax:* 613-824-0090
contact@orleanschamber.ca
www.orleanschamber.ca
Previous Name: Cumberland Chamber of Commerce
Overview: A small local organization founded in 1990
Mission: To act as a focal point for the business community on behalf of members with regard to business, social & political issues; to promote economic, environmental & social well-being of business community; to provide information & education on a variety of subjects of interest to members & community.
Member of: Canadian Chamber of Commerce
Affliation(s): National Capital Business Alliance
Chief Officer(s):
Jamie Kwong McDonald, Executive Director
jmcdonald@orleanschamber.ca
Finances: *Annual Operating Budget:* Less than $50,000; *Funding Sources:* Membership dues; luncheons/breakfasts
Staff Member(s): 1; 9 volunteer(s)
Membership: 226; *Fees:* $175; *Committees:* Social; Membership; Economic Development; Communication; Political; Science & Technology
Activities: Networking luncheons/breakfasts; monthly luncheons with quest speakers; awards gala; golf tournament

Oro-Medonte Chamber of Commerce (OMCC)
PO Box 100, 148 Line 7 South, Oro ON L0L 2X0
Tel: 705-487-7337; *Fax:* 705-487-0133
info@oromedontecc.com
www.oromedontecc.com
www.facebook.com/142718922412363
twitter.com/OroMedonteCC
Overview: A small local organization
Mission: To advocate for business in the Oro-Medonte area; To improve the local economy
Member of: Ontario Chamber of Commerce
Chief Officer(s):
Nadia Fitzgerald, Executive Director
Dave Dahinten, President
Lisa Groves, Secretary-Treasurer
Membership: 200; *Fees:* $120
Activities: Providing networking & trade show opportunities; Providing business promotional items, such as flyers & business cards
Publications:
• Business / Membership Directory
Type: Directory; *Frequency:* Annually; *Accepts Advertising*
Profile: Contact information & description of services for members of Oro-Medonte Chamber of Commerce
• Chamber Newsletter
Type: Newsletter; *Frequency:* Monthly; *Accepts Advertising*; *Price:* Free for Oro-Medonte Chamber of Commerce members
Profile: Chamber activities, events, & updates from the Ontario Chamber of Commerce
• North Simcoe Community News
Frequency: Bimonthly; *Accepts Advertising*; *Editor:* Anna Proctor
Profile: Information & business opportunities for persons in Oro-Medonte & Severn townships
• Oro-Medonte Guide Map
Accepts Advertising

Oromocto & Area Chamber of Commerce
Oromocto Mall, PO Box 20124, Oromocto NB E2V 2R6
Tel: 506-446-6043; *Fax:* 506-446-6925
oromoctochamber@nb.aibn.com
www.facebook.com/oromoctochamber
Overview: A small local organization
Membership: *Fees:* $100

Oromocto & Area Food & Clothing Bank
74 Iroquois Ave., Oromocto NB E2V 2A1
Tel: 506-357-3461; *Fax:* 506-446-6168
ofb@nb.aibn.com
www.facebook.com/oromoctofoodbank
Also Known As: Helpline Inc.
Previous Name: Oromocto Food & Clothing Bank
Overview: A small local charitable organization founded in 1987
Mission: To provide services to those in need in Oromocto & the surrounding area
Chief Officer(s):
Greg Doucet, Director
Finances: *Funding Sources:* Donations
Activities: Accepting & distributing donations of food, clothing, & household items; Offering information about local support groups; Maintaining a job bank

Oromocto & Area SPCA
111 D'Amours St., Oromocto NB E2V 0G5
Tel: 506-446-4107
orphans@oromoctospca.ca
www.oromoctospca.ca
Overview: A small local charitable organization founded in 1973
Mission: To improve the welfare of animals through protection & advocacy
Affliation(s): New Brunswick SPCA (NBSPCA)
Chief Officer(s):
Vicky Ring, President
Tracy Marcotullio, Manager
Finances: *Funding Sources:* Membership fees; Donations; Fundraising
Staff Member(s): 4
Membership: *Fees:* $5 student; $10 adult; $25 family; $100 life members; *Member Profile:* Individuals who support the work of the SPCA
Activities: Providing shelter to animals; Finding homes for adoptable animals; Offering educational programs to promote responsible pet ownership & humane attitudes; *Awareness Events:* Pet Photos With Santa, Nov.; Christmas Tree Sale, Dec.
Publications:
• Paws For Thought
Type: Newsletter; *Editor:* Susan Sears; *Price:* Free for members
Profile: SPCA activities, information, profiles

Oromocto Food & Clothing Bank ***See*** **Oromocto & Area Food & Clothing Bank**

ORT Canada
c/o ORT Toronto, #604, 3101 Bathurst St., Toronto ON M6A 2A6
Tel: 416-787-0339; *Fax:* 416-787-9420
Toll-Free: 866-991-3045
info@ort-toronto.org
www.ortcanada.com
www.facebook.com/pages/ORT-Toronto/299243785455
Also Known As: Organization for Educational Resources & Technological Training
Overview: A medium-sized national organization founded in 1942
Mission: To fundraise in support of the worldwide vocational-training-school network of ORT.
Member of: World ORT
Chief Officer(s):
Janis Finkelstein, President
Lindy Meshwork, Executive Director
Finances: *Annual Operating Budget:* $250,000-$500,000
Staff Member(s): 3
Membership: 10,000+; *Fees:* $36

Montréal Office
#250, 5165, ch Queen Mary, Montréal QC H3W 1X7
Tel: 514-481-2787; *Fax:* 514-481-4119
info@ortmontreal.org
www.ortmontreal.org

Orthodox Church in America Archdiocese of Canada (OCA ADOC)
31 Lebreton St. North, Ottawa ON K1R 7H1
Tel: 613-233-7780; *Fax:* 613-233-1931
office@archdiocese.ca
www.archdiocese.ca
Also Known As: Orthodox Church in Canada
Previous Name: Russian Orthodox Greek Catholic Church (Metropolia)
Overview: A medium-sized international organization founded in 1902
Mission: A component of the Orthodox Church in America, an autocephalous (self-governing) church with territorial jurisdiction in Canada, the USA & Mexico; its doctrine & worship are those of the world-wide One Holy Catholic & Apostolic Church
Member of: Canadian Council of Churches; Churches of Manitoba; Orthodox Clergy Association of Québec
Chief Officer(s):
Irénée Rochon, Administrator & Bishop of Quebec City, 450-834-2870
bishopirenee@archdiocese.ca
Anatoliy Melnyk, Chancellor, 514-522-2801
montreal.sobor@gmail.com
Membership: 10,000+

Orthodox Rabbinical Council of British Columbia (BCK)
#401, 1037 West Broadway, Vancouver BC V6H 1E3
Tel: 604-731-1803; *Fax:* 604-731-1804
info@bckosher.org
www.bckosher.org
www.facebook.com/pages/BC-Kosher/103372337180
www.youtube.com/watch?v=ujujK_r3xAc
Also Known As: BC Kosher
Overview: A small provincial charitable organization founded in 1983
Finances: *Annual Operating Budget:* $100,000-$250,000
Staff Member(s): 4; 6 volunteer(s)
Membership: 1-99
Activities: Providing information about Kashruth (kosher food - kashruth symbol BCK); *Speaker Service:* Yes

Orthophonie et Audiologie Canada ***See*** **Speech-Language & Audiology Canada**

Osgoode Twp. Historical Society
PO Box 74, 7814 Lawrence St., Vernon ON K0A 3J0
Tel: 613-821-4062; *Fax:* 613-821-3140
manager@osgoodemuseum.ca
www.osgoodemuseum.ca
www.facebook.com/125725207465630
twitter.com/OsgoodeMuseum
Overview: A small local charitable organization founded in 1972
Mission: To promote, preserve & publicize history in the Township of Osgoode & to foster genealogical research
Member of: Ontario Historical Society
Affliation(s): Ontario Geneology Society; Ontario Museum Association; Archives Association of Ontario
Chief Officer(s):
Gary Briggs, President
Ann Robinson, Administrator
Finances: *Funding Sources:* Provincial, municipal grants; Heritage Ontario; Ontario Lotteries Corp.; City of Ottawa
Staff Member(s): 3
Membership: *Fees:* $15; *Member Profile:* Interest in local history
Activities: Open House; Heritage Day; Pioneer Day/Genorama/Outreach Community; *Library:* Museum Archives; Open to public

Oshawa & District Coin Club
Tel: 905-436-7164
papman@ibell.net
oshawaanddistrictcoinclub.wordpress.com
Overview: A small local organization founded in 1960
Affliation(s): Ontario Numismatic Association; Canadian Numismatic Association
Chief Officer(s):
Bruce Watt, President
Membership: *Fees:* $8
Activities: Providing education about coin & stamp collecting through monthly meetings
Publications:
• The Numismatic Reporter [a publication of the Oshawa & District Coin Club]
Type: Newsletter; *Editor:* David Goreski

Oshawa & District Labour Council *See* Durham Regional Labour Council

Oshawa & District Real Estate Board *See* Durham Region Association of REALTORS

Oshawa / Clarington Association for Community Living *See* Community Living Oshawa / Clarington

Oshawa Historical Society
1450 Simcoe St. South, Oshawa ON L1H 8S8
Tel: 905-436-7624; *Fax:* 905-436-7625
Other Communication: membership@oshawamuseum.org
info@oshawamuseum.org
www.oshawamuseum.org
www.facebook.com/OshawaMuseum
twitter.com/oshawamuseum
Overview: A small local organization founded in 1957
Mission: To research, record, retain, & preserve historical information about Oshawa, Ontario; To provide historical research material, such as newspapers on microfilm, a photograph collection, & local history books
Chief Officer(s):
Laura Suchan, Director
Finances: *Funding Sources:* Donations; Membership fees; City of Oshawa
Membership: *Fees:* $5 students; $20 individuals; $25 families & community organizations; $30 corporations; $300 life memberships
Activities: Administering the Oshawa Community Museum & Archives; Disseminating information about the history of the area through publications & presentations; Providing curriculum linked educational programs; *Speaker Service:* Yes; *Library:* Oshawa Community Museum & Archives Reference Library; Open to public
Publications:
• Historical Happenings
Type: Newsletter; *Frequency:* Quarterly; *Price:* Free e-newsletter for members of the Oshawa Historical Society; $5 hard copy format

Oshawa/Clarington Chamber of Commerce *See* Greater Oshawa Chamber of Commerce

Oshawa-Durham Rape Crisis Centre (ODRCC)
PO Box 567, Stn. Main, Whitby ON L1N 5V3
Tel: 905-444-9672; *Fax:* 905-444-9277; *Crisis Hot-Line:* 905-668-9200
info@drcc.ca
www.drcc.ca
Overview: A small local charitable organization overseen by Canadian Association of Sexual Assault Centres
Mission: To provide counselling to those who are survivors of incest, sexual assault/sexual harassment
Affliation(s): Ontario Coalition of Rape Crisis Centres
Finances: *Annual Operating Budget:* $250,000-$500,000
Staff Member(s): 6; 22 volunteer(s)
Activities: Counselling; crisis intervention; public education; volunteer training; children's program for sexual assault/abuse victims; *Awareness Events:* Take Back the Night; *Library* Open to public by appointment

Oshawa-Durham Symphony Orchestra *See* Ontario Philharmonic

Oshawa-Whitby Kiwanis Music & Theatre Festival
PO Box 10017, 910 Dundas St. West, Whitby ON L1P 1P7
Tel: 905-430-1455
info@oshawawhitbykifest.ca
www.oshawawhitbykifest.ca
Also Known As: Kifest
Overview: A small local charitable organization founded in 1972
Mission: To organize an adjudicated event for youth to present their musical & theatrical talents; to encourage youth creativity
Member of: Ontario Music Festivals' Association
Chief Officer(s):
John Chave, Chair
Tina-Marie Schaaf, Festival Coordinator
Finances: *Funding Sources:* Admissions; Donations; Sponsorships
Activities: Presenting an annual festival; Awarding scholarships

Oshki Anishnawbeg Student Association
Confederation College, Student Union, PO Box 398, Thunder Bay ON P7C 4W1
Tel: 807-475-6314; *Fax:* 807-473-5160
succi.com/oasa
Previous Name: Confederation College Aboriginal Student Association
Overview: A small local organization
Mission: To provide a supportive environment that facilitates Indigenous inclusion in post-secondary education, fosters personal growth and furthers Indigenous contributions to Canadian society.
Chief Officer(s):
Mariah Wigwas, President
mwigwas@confederationc.on.ca
9 volunteer(s)

Osoyoos & District Arts Council
PO Box 256, 8713 Main St., Osoyoos BC V0H 1V0
Tel: 250-495-7968
jwhit@persona.ca
www.osoyoosarts.com
www.facebook.com/OsoyoosArtsCouncil
Overview: A small local charitable organization founded in 1981
Mission: To increase & broaden the opportunities for residents of Osoyoos & area to enjoy & participate in cultural activities
Member of: BC Arts Councils; BC Touring Council; Art Gallery of South Okanagan; Thompson/Okanagan Network of Arts Councils; Assembly of BC Arts Council
Chief Officer(s):
Sue Whittaker, President
swhit@persona.ca
Finances: *Annual Operating Budget:* $50,000-$100,000; *Funding Sources:* Fundraising; government grants; donations; membership fees
70 volunteer(s)
Membership: 60; *Fees:* $10 individual; $15 non-profit group; $25 business; *Committees:* Art Gallery; Membership; Fundraising; Street Banner Project; Christmas Light-Up; Osoy Concerts
Activities: Operate art gallery; concert series; help coordinate community arts & cultural events; fundraising; provide street banners to town; *Awareness Events:* Arts & Culture Week
Awards:
• Dorothy Fraser Award for Piano (Award)
Given to a student who obtains the highest marks in any Canadian Board Examination for the current year
• Christmas Light-Up Awards (Award)
Best Business; Best Residence; 2nd & 3rd for Best Residence
• Music Scholarships for Highest Marks (Scholarship)
Grades I-III; Grades IV-VI; Grades VII & up
• Fine Arts Scholarships (Scholarship)
Given to a graduating student who plans to continue his/her education in Fine Arts

Osoyoos Desert Society (ODS)
PO Box 123, Osoyoos BC V0H 1V0
Tel: 250-495-2470
Toll-Free: 877-899-0897
mail@desert.org
www.desert.org
www.facebook.com/OsoyoosDesert
Also Known As: Desert Centre, Osoyoos
Overview: A small local charitable organization founded in 1991
Mission: To conserve the endangered desert environment, featuring unique plants &animals, located in the south of British Columbia's Okanagan Valley
Chief Officer(s):
Mat Hassen, President
Vaughan Denis, Treasurer
Denise Eastlick, Executive Director
Finances: *Funding Sources:* Western Diversification Canada; McLean's Foundation; BC Gaming Commission; Citizen's Bank of Canada; Town of Osoyoos; Osoyoos Golf & Country Club
Membership: *Fees:* $20
Activities: Conducting research; Restoring the Antelope-brush ecosystem; Increasing public awareness; Providing education; Operating the Desert Centre; *Speaker Service:* Yes
Publications:
• Desert Society News
Type: Newsletter; *Frequency:* Quarterly; *Price:* Free for members
Profile: Society reports, upcoming events, species profiles, conservation updates, & volunteer news
• Native Plant Landscaping for The South Okanagan Similkameen
Type: Booklet; *Number of Pages:* 32; *Author:* Tamara Bonnemaison

Osoyoos Food Bank
6210 - 97th St., Osoyoos BC V0H 1V4
Tel: 250-495-6581; *Fax:* 250-495-8011
Overview: A small local organization overseen by Food Banks British Columbia
Member of: Food Banks British Columbia
Chief Officer(s):
Lu Ahrendt, Contact
rlahrendt@live.ca

Ostéoporose Canada *See* Osteoporosis Canada

Osteoporosis Canada / Ostéoporose Canada
#301, 1090 Don Mills Rd., Toronto ON M3C 3R6
Tel: 416-696-2663; *Fax:* 416-696-2673
Toll-Free: 800-463-6842
info@osteoporosis.ca
www.osteoporosis.ca
www.facebook.com/osteoporosiscanada
twitter.com/OsteoporosisCA
Previous Name: Osteoporosis Society of Canada
Overview: A large national charitable organization founded in 1982
Mission: To encourage research into the prevention, diagnosis, & treatment of osteoporosis; To improve access to osteoporosis care & support
Chief Officer(s):
Famida Jiwa, President & CEO
Cheryl Baldwin, Chair
Finances: *Funding Sources:* Donations; Fundraising
Membership: *Fees:* $25; $20 outside Camnada
Activities: Promoting awareness; Engaging in advocacy activities; Providing educational materials related to osteoporosis; Offering support groups; *Speaker Service:* Yes
Publications:
• Osteoblast
Type: Newsletter; *Frequency:* 3 pa; *Price:* Free for members
Profile: Scientifically based information on osteoporosis & Osteoporosis Canada activities, for members & donors

Calgary - Alberta Chapter
Bldg. B8, Currie Barracks, #104, 2526 Battleford Dr., Calgary AB T3E 7J4
Tel: 403-237-7022; *Fax:* 403-220-1727
alberta@osteoporosis.ca
Chief Officer(s):
Loretta Brown, Chair

Charlottetown - Prince Edward Island Chapter
76 MacRae Dr., Charlottetown PE C1C 0S3
Tel: 902-367-3933
pei@osteoporosis.ca
Chief Officer(s):
Michelle Lafford, Chair

Dartmouth - Nova Scotia Chapter
#206, 44 - 46 Portland St., Dartmouth NS B2Y 1H4
Tel: 902-407-4053
novascotia@osteoporosis.ca
Chief Officer(s):
Charmaine Hollett, Chair

Garson - Sudbury Chapter
68 Eva St., Garson ON P3L 1J5
Tel: 705-522-2908
sudbury@osteoporosis.ca
Chief Officer(s):
Betty Parcher, Chair

Hamilton - Hamilton-Burlington Chapter
75 MacNab St. South, Hamilton ON L8P 3C1
Tel: 905-525-5398; *Fax:* 905-577-0396
hamilton@osteoporosis.ca
Chief Officer(s):
Kim Thompson, Chair
Vacant, Chair, Volunteer Development

• Osteoporosis Canada, Hamilton-Burlington Chapter Newsletter
Type: Newsletter; *Frequency:* Semiannually

Kelowna Chapter
PO Box 21072, Stn. Orchard Park, Kelowna BC V1Y 9N8
Tel: 250-861-6880
kelowna@osteoporosis.ca
Chief Officer(s):
Trish Gunning, Chair

Laval - Greater Montreal Chapter
274 Antoine Forestier, Laval QC H7M 6B9
Tel: 514-212-5549
Toll-Free: 800-977-1778
montreal@osteoporosis.ca
Chief Officer(s):
Lucille Dumont, Chair

London - London & Thames Valley Chapter
PO Box 32017, London ON N5Y 5K4
Tel: 519-457-0624; *Fax:* 519-659-0694
london-thamesvalley@osteoporosis.ca
Chief Officer(s):
Joanne Legros-Kelly, Chair

Mississauga Chapter
#76, 6797 Formentera Ave., Mississauga ON L5N 2L6
Tel: 416-696-2663
mississauga@osteoporosis.ca
Chief Officer(s):
Vacant, Chair

Moncton - Greater Moncton Chapter
960 St. George Blvd., Moncton NB E1E 3Y3
Tel: 506-386-0007
greatermoncton@osteoporosis.ca
Chief Officer(s):
Sharron Steeves, Chair

New Brunswick Chapter
Tel: 506-389-2214
greatermoncton@osteoporosis.ca
Chief Officer(s):
Sharron Steeves, Chair

North Vancouver - North Shore Chapter
1691 Davenport Pl., North Vancouver BC V1J 1N4
Tel: 604-985-5430
northshore@osteoporosis.ca

Ottawa Chapter
#301, 1090 Don Mills Rd., Toronto ON M3C 3R6
Tel: 416-696-2663; *Fax:* 416-696-2673
osteoporosis@live.ca

Parksville - Mid-Island Chapter
PO Box 1967, Parksville BC V9P 2H7
Tel: 250-228-8840; *Fax:* 250-951-0343
mid-island@osteoporosis.ca
Chief Officer(s):
Lisa Leger, Chair

Peterborough Chapter
#29, 360 George St. North, Peterborough ON K9H 7E7
Tel: 705-740-2776; *Fax:* 705-740-2107
Toll-Free: 866-376-2776
peterborough@osteoporosis.ca
Chief Officer(s):
Heather Drysdale, Chair

Québec - Québec City Chapter
#100, 1200, av Germain-des-Prés, Québec QC G1V 3M7
Tél: 418-651-8661; *Téléc:* 418-650-3916
Ligne sans frais: 800-977-1778
sectiondequebec@osteoporosecanada.ca
Chief Officer(s):
Lucille Dumont, Chair

Regina Chapter
90C Cavendish St., Regina SK S4N 5G7
Tel: 306-757-2663; *Fax:* 306-789-2663
regina@osteoporosis.ca
Chief Officer(s):
Sylvia Fisk, Chair

St. Catharines - Niagara Chapter
#406, 36 Page St., St Catharines ON L2R 4A7
Tel: 905-227-9646
niagara@osteoporosis.ca
Chief Officer(s):
Judy Cline, Chair

Saskatoon Chapter
#1, #24 Packham Ave., Saskatoon SK S4N 2T1
Tel: 306-931-2663; *Fax:* 306-249-9065
saskatoon@osteoporosis.ca
Chief Officer(s):
Carole Young, Chair

Surrey / White Rock Chapter
13845 - 18th Ave., Surrey BC V4A 1W6
Tel: 778-588-3362
surrey-whiterock@osteoporosis.ca
Chief Officer(s):
Rycarda Smith, Chair

Waterloo - Waterloo-Wellington Chapter
510 Erbsville Rd., Waterloo ON N2J 3Z4
Tel: 416-696-2663
Toll-Free: 800-463-6842
waterloowellington@osteoporosis.ca
Chief Officer(s):
Mairi McLean, Acting Chair

Winnipeg - Manitoba Chapter
123 St. Anne's Rd., Winnipeg MB R2M 2Z1
Tel: 204-772-3498; *Fax:* 204-772-4200
manitoba@osteoporosis.ca
Chief Officer(s):
Cherylle Unryn, Chair

Osteoporosis Society of Canada *See* Osteoporosis Canada

Ostomy Canada Society

#501, 344 Bloor St. West, Toronto ON M5S 3A7
Tel: 416-595-5452; *Fax:* 416-595-9924
Toll-Free: 888-969-9698
info1@ostomycanada.ca
www.ostomycanada.ca
www.linkedin.com/company/united-ostomy-association-of-canada-inc-?trk=
www.facebook.com/OstomyCanada
www.twitter.com/UOACweb
www.youtube.com/channel/UCjHdm7WOJokLkXgKS9Gnjng
Previous Name: United Ostomy Association of Canada
Overview: A medium-sized national charitable organization founded in 1997
Mission: To assist all persons with gastrointestinal or urinary diversions, & their families & caregivers, by providing emotional & practical support & help, information & instruction
Affliation(s): United Ostomy Association - USA
Chief Officer(s):
Peter Folk, President
peter.folk@ostomycanada.ca
Ann Ivol, Vice-President
Finances: *Funding Sources:* Annual fundraising drive
Membership: *Fees:* $39 national; $42 international; $50 health care professional; $150 corporate; *Member Profile:* Member chapters; *Committees:* Outreach; Governance; Advocacy; Finance & Fundraising; Marketing & Communications
Activities: Operates 46 chapters across Canada; *Awareness Events:* World Ostomy Day; *Library* by appointment
Meetings/Conferences: • 15th Ostomy Canada Society National Conference, 2016
Scope: National

Ottawa & District Foster Parent Association *See* Foster Parents Association of Ottawa

Ottawa & District Labour Council (ODLC) / Conseil du travail d'Ottawa et du district

#500, 280 Metcalfe St., Ottawa ON K2P 1R7
Tel: 613-233-7820; *Fax:* 613-230-8404
Other Communication: ottawalabour.blogspot.com
odlc@ottawalabour.org
www.ottawalabour.org
twitter.com/ottawalabour
Overview: A small local organization founded in 1872 overseen by Ontario Federation of Labour
Mission: To act as the voice of workers in the Ottawa area; To carry out the policies of the Canadian Labour Congress & the Ontario Federation of Labour in Ottawa
Affliation(s): Ontario Federation of Labour (OFL); Amalgamated Transit Union; AFM; CAW; CUPE; CUPW; CUASA; CEP; Hospitality & Service Trades Union; IATSE; IBEW; OECTA; OPSEU; OSSTF; OCETF; ONG; PSAC; Service Employees Interntational Union; Ottawa Steel Plate Feeders and Examiners; UBCJA; United Steelworkers
Membership: 55,000 workers from 90 unions; *Committees:* Political Municipal Affairs; Women's; Human Rights; Health, Safety & the Environment; International Solidarity; Education
Activities: Liaising with municipal governments; *Awareness Events:* Labour Day March; Day of Mourning, April 28

Ottawa Baptist Association (OBA)

249 Bronson Ave., Ottawa ON K1R 6H6
www.ottawabaptist.org
Overview: A small local organization founded in 1836 overseen by Canadian Baptists of Ontario and Quebec
Member of: Canadian Baptists of Ontario & Quebec
Affliation(s): Canadian Baptist Ministries; Baptist World Alliance
Chief Officer(s):
Hugh Willet, Moderator
hwillett@sympatico.ca
Membership: 20 churches; *Member Profile:* Baptist churches in Ottawa

Ottawa Builder's Exchange *See* Ottawa Construction Association

Ottawa Carleton Ultimate Association (OCUA)

#1, 875 Banks St., Ottawa ON K1S 3W4
Tel: 613-860-6282
info@ocua.ca
www.ocua.ca
www.facebook.com/ocua.ca
twitter.com/ocua
Overview: A medium-sized local organization founded in 1993
Mission: To promote ultimate & disc sports in the Ottawa-Carleton region
Chief Officer(s):
Christiane Marceau, Executive Director
ed@ocua.ca
Christopher Castonguay, Program Officer
christopher@ocua.ca
Nevan Sullivan, Program Officer, Youth & Junior
nevan@ocua.ca
Staff Member(s): 3
Activities: Organizing & conducting the operations of leagues & tournaments; Operating a multi-field sports facility designed for ultimate
Publications:
• Ultimate Happenings
Type: Newsletter; *Editor:* Catharina Israel
Profile: News about ultimate in Ottawa & league events & issues

Ottawa Centre for Research & Innovation; Ottawa Carleton Research Institute *See* Invest Ottawa

Ottawa Chamber of Commerce (OCC)

328 Somerset St. West, Ottawa ON K2P 0J9
Tel: 613-236-3631; *Fax:* 613-236-7498
info@ottawachamber.ca
www.ottawachamber.ca
www.facebook.com/ottawachamberofcommerce
twitter.com/ottawachamber
Previous Name: Ottawa-Carleton Board of Trade
Overview: A medium-sized local organization founded in 1857
Mission: To provide leadership in the community to enhance economic prosperity & quality of life
Member of: Ontario Chamber of Commerce; Canadian Chamber of Commerce
Chief Officer(s):
Alexa Ryan, Interim Executive Director
alexa.ryan@ottawachamber.ca
Laura Haber, Director, Events & Partnerships, 613-236-3631 Ext. 124
laura.haber@ottawachamber.ca
Scott Williams, Director, Member Services, 613-236-3631 Ext. 127
scott.williams@ottawachamber.ca
Kenny Leon, Manager, Communications, 613-236-3631 Ext. 130
kenny.leon@ottawachamber.ca
Finances: *Funding Sources:* Membership fees; Programs; Events; Services
50 volunteer(s)
Membership: 750; *Fees:* Schedule available; *Committees:* Municipal Action; Education; Transportation; Ambassador Program; Business Achievement; Awards Gala/Nominations
Awards:
• Annual Business Achievement Award (Award)
Meetings/Conferences: • Ottawa Chamber of Commerce Ottawa Business Summit 2015, 2015, Ottawa, ON
Scope: Provincial
Description: Featuring a guest speaker, take-away learning materials, & facilitated networking to help improve one's business
Contact Information: E-mail: info@ottawachamber.ca
• Ottawa Chamber of Commerce 2015 Annual General Meeting, 2015, Ottawa, ON
Scope: Provincial
Contact Information: E-mail: info@ottawachamber.ca

Ottawa Chamber Orchestra (OCO)
Ottawa ON
www.ottawachamberorchestra.ca
www.facebook.com/OttawaChamberOrchestra
twitter.com/OttChamberOrch
Overview: A small local organization founded in 1992 overseen by Orchestras Canada
Chief Officer(s):
Donnie Deacon, Musical Director
Activities: *Awareness Events:* Concerto Competition

Ottawa Chinese Community Services Centre (OCCSC)
#4004, 381 Kent St., Ottawa ON K2P 2A8
Tel: 613-232-4875; *Fax:* 613-235-5466
occsc@occsc.org
www.occsc.org
www.facebook.com/ottawachinese
twitter.com/chineseottawa
Overview: A small local charitable organization founded in 1975 overseen by Ontario Council of Agencies Serving Immigrants
Mission: To advance the full social & economic integration of newcomers into the mainsteam society in the Ottawa-Carleton region
Chief Officer(s):
Sharon Kan, Executive Director
sharon.kan@occsc.org
Finances: *Funding Sources:* Citizenship & Immigration Canada; Ontario Ministry of Citizenship; City of Ottawa
Staff Member(s): 37
Membership: *Fees:* $10 regular; $5 senior; *Committees:* Personnel; Governance; Executive; Finance; Fundraising
Activities: Settlement & integration of newcomers; orientation workshops; counselling services; ESL classes; special needs groups; income tax filing services; job search workshop; mental health support

Ottawa Coin Club *See* Ottawa Numismatic Society

Ottawa Community Immigrant Services Organization (OCISO) / Organisme communautaire des services aux immigrants d'Ottawa
959 Wellington St. West, Ottawa ON K1Y 2X5
Tel: 613-725-0202; *Fax:* 613-725-9054
info@ociso.org
www.ociso.org
Overview: A medium-sized local charitable organization founded in 1976
Mission: To enable newcomers & their families to fully participate in an open & welcoming Ottawa, through innovative services, community building & public engagement
Member of: Ontario Council of Agencies Serving Immigrants; Canadian Council for Refugees; Association of United Way Agencies; Local Agencies Serving Immigrants
Chief Officer(s):
Hamdi Mohamed, Executive Director, 613-725-0202 Ext. 307
Finances: *Annual Operating Budget:* $1.5 Million-$3 Million; *Funding Sources:* Government; United Way
Staff Member(s): 72; 278 volunteer(s)
Membership: 291; *Fees:* $25 individual; $30 not-for-profit; $65 other organization; $10 seniors/unwaged; *Member Profile:* Over 18 years ald & supports our mission; *Committees:* Programs; Finance; Resource Development
Activities: Provides assistance to newcomers, agencies & institutions serving immigrants; Resettlement Service offers immigrants assistance with orientation to life in Canada, access to housing, education, employment & health services; individual advocacy; in-depth information sessions to groups on various themes; Counselling Service offers personal, family & crisis counselling; English language training in two locations; immigrant women's program; public education & communication program; vocational training program;OCISO Gala; *Internships:* Yes; *Speaker Service:* Yes

Ottawa Construction Association (OCA) / L'Association de la construction d'Ottawa
196 Bronson Ave., Ottawa ON K1R 6H4
Tel: 613-236-0488; *Fax:* 613-238-6124
oca@oca.ca
www.oca.ca
Previous Name: Ottawa Builder's Exchange
Overview: A small local organization founded in 1889 overseen by Canadian Construction Association
Mission: To act as the voice of the non-residential construction industry in Ottawa; To promote & maintain industry best practices & high ethical standards
Affliation(s): Canadian Construction Association; Council of Ontario Construction Associations
Chief Officer(s):
John DeVries, President & General Manager
jdv@oca.ca
Mike Sharp, Chair
Michael Caletti, Treasurer
Membership: 1000+
Activities: Promoting suitable legislation that affects the construction industry; Providing networking opportunities; Offering education & training
Publications:
• Who's Who - Buyers Guide
Type: Directory; *Frequency:* Annually; *Price:* Free for OCA members
Profile: Alphabetical & classified listings of members

Ottawa Council of Social Agencies *See* Social Planning Council of Ottawa-Carleton

Ottawa District Minor Hockey Association (ODMHA)
#300, 1247 Kilborn Pl., Ottawa ON K1H 6K9
Tel: 613-224-3589; *Fax:* 613-224-4625
odmha@odmha.on.ca
www.odmha.on.ca
Overview: A medium-sized local organization founded in 1972
Mission: To promote minor hockey throughout the region
Member of: Hockey Canada
Chief Officer(s):
Denis Dumais, President
denisdumais@sympatico.ca
Membership: *Committees:* Development; Discipline & Appeals; Risk & Safety; Rules & Officials; Zoning & Constitution
Activities: *Speaker Service:* Yes; *Library:* Resource Centre; Open to public

Ottawa Duck Club (ODC)
841 Kingsmere Ave., Ottawa ON K2A 3J8
www.ottawaduckclub.com
Overview: A small local organization founded in 1966
Mission: To actively improve the nesting habitat for waterfowl and other birds along the Ottawa River.
Chief Officer(s):
Bill Bower, President, 613-824-9104
bigbuckbill@hotmail.com
Membership: *Fees:* $20 individual; $25 family

Ottawa Economics Association (OEA)
PO Box 264, Stn. B, Ottawa ON K1P 6C4
Tel: 613-837-9415
oea@cabe.ca
www.cabe.ca/jmv3/index.php/cabe-chapters/oea
Overview: A small local organization founded in 1975 overseen by Canadian Association for Business Economics
Mission: To organize programs of interest to members
Member of: Canadian Association for Business Economics
Chief Officer(s):
Joe Macaluso, Contact, 613-745-8916
Emile Franco, Treasurer
Finances: *Annual Operating Budget:* Less than $50,000
8 volunteer(s)
Membership: 300; *Fees:* $57.14-$71.43 regular; $47.62 retired; $4.76 students; *Member Profile:* Economists & others with an interest in economics & economic policy
Activities: Luncheons with a public policy theme; technical workshops; annual conference

Ottawa Environmental Law Clinic *See* Ecojustice Canada Society

Ottawa Field-Naturalists' Club (OFNC)
PO Box 35069, Stn. Westgate, Ottawa ON K1Z 1A2
Tel: 613-722-3050
ofnc@ofnc.ca
www.ofnc.ca
Overview: A small local charitable organization founded in 1879
Mission: To promote the preservation & conservation of Canada's natural heritage
Chief Officer(s):
Ann Mackenzie, President
Ken Young, Treasurer
Membership: *Fees:* $40 individuals; $45 families; *Member Profile:* Individuals who share an interest in nature; *Committees:* Birds; Education & Publicity; Excursions & Lectures; Nominations; Finance; Fletcher Wildlife Garden; Membership; Publications; Awards; Macoun Club for Young Naturalists
Activities: Encouraging research in all fields of natural history
Awards:
• George McGee Service Award (Award)
• Conservation Award - Member (Award)
• Conservation Award - Non-Member (Award)
• Anne Hanes Natural History Award (Award)
• Mary Stuart Education Award (Award)
• President's Prize (Award)
• Honorary Member (Award)
Publications:
• Autobiography of John Macoun, Canadian Explorer & Naturalist, 1831-1920
Price: $20
• A Birder's Checklist of Ottawa
Price: $2
• The Canadian Field-Naturalist
Type: Journal; *Editor:* Carolyn Callaghan *ISSN:* 0008-3550
• Checklist of the Butterflies of the Ottawa District
Price: $2
• A Guide to the Geology of the Gatineau-Lièvre District
Price: $5
• A Guide to the Geology of the Ottawa District
Price: $5
• Lichens of the Ottawa Region
Price: $10
• Nature & Natural Areas in Canada's Capital
Price: $5
• Trail & Landscape [a publication of the Ottawa Field-Naturalists' Club]
Type: Newsletter; *Frequency:* Quarterly; *Editor:* Karen McLachlan-Hamilton; *Price:* Free for OFNC members
Profile: Club activities & articles on the natural history of the Ottawa Valley

Ottawa Flute Association (OFA) / Association des flûtistes d'Ottawa
Ottawa ON
Tel: 613-421-1601
www.ottawafluteassociation.com
Overview: A small local organization
Mission: To promote flute playing in Ottawa & the surrounding area
Chief Officer(s):
Diana Lam, President
Paula Rolfe, Treasurer
Membership: *Fees:* $20 youth; $40 adults; $100 corporate members; *Member Profile:* Professional & amateur flutists in the Ottawa region
Activities: Organizing classes & workshops; Arranging concerts & events; Providing flute choirs, flute fairs, & flute camps; *Library:* The OFA Library
Publications:
• Ottawa Flute Association Newsletter
Type: Newsletter
Profile: OFA activities & upcoming events

Ottawa Food Bank / La banque d'alimentation d'Ottawa
1317B Michael St., Ottawa ON K1B 3M9
Tel: 613-745-7001; *Fax:* 613-745-7377
foodbank@theottawafoodbank.ca
www.theottawafoodbank.ca
www.facebook.com/OttawaFoodBank
twitter.com/OttawaFoodBank
www.youtube.com/ottawafoodbank
Overview: A small local charitable organization founded in 1984
Mission: To arrange for, collect, process, store, & distribute food to service agencies in the National Capital Region for delivery to the needy
Chief Officer(s):
Peter Tilley, Executive Director
peter@theottawafoodbank.ca
Michael Adams, President
Diane Morrison, Vice-President
Barbara Carroll, Treasurer
Finances: *Funding Sources:* Donations
Activities: Food Sort Challenge; BBQ; *Awareness Events:* Holiday Food Drive, December; Lunch Money Day
Publications:
• Ottawa Food Bank Annual Report
Type: Yearbook; *Frequency:* Annually

Ottawa Fundraising Executives *See* Association of Fundraising Professionals

Ottawa Humane Society (OHS) / La Société protectrice des animaux d'Ottawa
245 West Hunt Club Rd, Ottawa ON K2E 1A6

Tel: 613-725-3166; *Fax:* 613-725-5674
ohs@ottawahumane.ca
ottawahumane.ca
www.facebook.com/OttawaHumane
twitter.com/ottawahumane
Previous Name: Humane Society of Ottawa-Carleton
Overview: A small local charitable organization founded in 1888
Mission: To provide leadership in the humane treatment of all animals; To give care to neglected, abused, exploited, stray, or homeless animals
Chief Officer(s):
Bruce Roney, Executive Director
Natalie Pona, Manager, Communications, 613-725-3166 Ext. 261
Finances: *Annual Operating Budget:* Greater than $5 Million; *Funding Sources:* Donations
Membership: *Fees:* $15 juniors; $25 individuals; $35 schools; $40 families; $500 life memberships
Activities: Encouraging people to take responsibility for their animals, through humane education; Offering programs such as companion animals pet visiting & dog walking; Conducting cruelty investigations; *Awareness Events:* Summer Garden Harvest Party, August; Wiggle Waggle Walkathon, September
Publications:
• A Legacy for the Animals
Type: Newsletter
Profile: Discussion of legacy giving options
• The OHS Volunteer Connection
Type: Newsletter; *Frequency:* Monthly; *Editor:* Christine Wheeler
Profile: Information for OHS volunteers
• The Ottawa Animal Advocate
Type: Newsletter; *Frequency:* Bimonthly
Profile: Updates on animal welfare in the Ottawa area
• Ottawa Humane Society Annual Report
Type: Yearbook; *Frequency:* Annually
• Our Best Friends
Type: Newsletter; *Frequency:* Quarterly; *Accepts Advertising*; *Editor:* Tara Jackson; *Price:* Free for OHS members

Ottawa Independent Writers (OIW) / Les écrivains indépendants d'Ottawa
PO Box 23137, Ottawa ON K2A 4E2
Tel: 613-841-0572
communications@oiw.ca
www.oiw.ca
www.linkedin.com/groups?gid=4680889
Overview: A small local organization founded in 1984
Mission: To promote writing & writers in Ottawa; To act as the voice of Ottawa writers in areas of legislation, municipal activities, & grants
Chief Officer(s):
Susan Jennings, President
sajennings@sympatico.ca
Bill Horne, Vice-President & Corporate Secretary
wghorne@rogers.com
Darren Jerome, Treasurer
djerome11@gmail.com
Membership: *Fees:* $30 students; $50 seniors; $75 adults; $135 families; *Member Profile:* All types of writers
Activities: Providing networking & learning opportunities; Offering advice regarding the business of writing, such as finding a publisher & marketing; *Awareness Events:* Annual Fall Book Fair; *Speaker Service:* Yes
Publications:
• Capital Letter
Frequency: 4-5 pa; *Editor:* Rosaleen Dickson; *Price:* Free with OIW membership
Profile: Compilation of OIW members' work
• Gems
Type: Anthology; *Frequency:* Annually
Profile: Writing contributions from members
• Jewels
Type: Anthology
Profile: Writing contributions from members
• OIW Book Catalogue
Profile: Showcase of books written by OIW members
• OIW Digest
Type: Newsletter; *Frequency:* Weekly; *Editor:* Roy Acres; *Price:* Free with OIW membership
Profile: Information about writing

Ottawa Japanese Community Association Inc. (OJCA)
#B16, 2285 St. Laurent Blvd., Ottawa ON K1G 4Z4
Tel: 613-731-7939; *Fax:* 613-731-1367
ojca_ojcc@yahoo.ca
www.ottawajapanesecommunity.ca
www.facebook.com/ojcaojcc
Overview: A small local organization founded in 1976
Mission: To promote & maintain Japanese heritage in Ottawa
Member of: National Association of Japanese Canadians
Membership: *Fees:* $15 single; $20 family; $10 student/senior
Activities: Arts & Crafts; Cooking Class; Fundraisers

Ottawa Light Car Club *See* Motorsport Club of Ottawa

Ottawa Muslim Association (OMA)
251 Northwestern Ave., Ottawa ON K1Y 0M1
Tel: 613-722-8763
oma@ottawamosque.ca
www.ottawamosque.ca
Overview: A small local charitable organization
Mission: To foster unity among various Muslims; to promote better understanding of Muslims & Islam among Canadians of other faiths; to maintain cultural identity
Chief Officer(s):
Mahmood Rasheed, President
Activities: Social services; seminars & conferences; *Library* Open to public

Ottawa New Car Dealers Association
400 Slater St., Ottawa ON K1R 7S7
Tel: 613-241-7557
info@oncda.com
www.oncda.com
Overview: A small local organization

Ottawa Numismatic Society / Société numismatique d'Ottawa
PO Box 42004, RPO St. Laurent, Ottawa ON K1K 4L8
e-mail: Info@ons-sno.ca
www.ons-sno.ca
Previous Name: Ottawa Coin Club
Overview: A small local organization founded in 1891
Member of: Royal Canadian Numismatic Association

Ottawa Orchid Society
13 Sandringham Crt., Ottawa ON K2C 2H9
www.ottawaorchidsociety.com
www.facebook.com/pages/Ottawa-Orchid-Society/196485693713178
Overview: A small local organization founded in 1978
Mission: To promote knowledge, development, improvement, & conservation of orchids
Chief Officer(s):
Jean Hollebone, President
jhollebone@sympatico.ca
Janet Johns, Treasurer
Membership: *Fees:* $25
Activities: Offering programs about the care of orchids; *Awareness Events:* Annual Orchid Show; *Library:* Ottawa Orchid Society Library
Publications:
• Spike [a publication of the Ottawa Orchid Society]
Type: Newsletter; *Frequency:* Monthly; *Editor:* Rick Sobkowicz

Ottawa Philatelic Society (OPS)
586 David Manchester Rd., Carp ON K0A 1L0
www.ottawaphilatelicsociety.org
Overview: A small local organization founded in 1891
Mission: To promote the study & history of stamps
Member of: Royal Philatelic Society of Canada; American Philatelic Society; American Topical Association
Chief Officer(s):
Tom Toomey, Contact
ttoomey@tiplimo.com
Membership: *Fees:* $40 full; $20 youth
Activities: *Library:* Ottawa Philatelic Society Library; Open to public

Ottawa Police Association (OPA)
#200, 141 Catherine St., Ottawa ON K2P 1C3
Tel: 613-232-9434; *Fax:* 613-232-1044
ottawapa@ottawapa.ca
www.ottawapa.ca
www.facebook.com/OttawaPoliceAssoc
twitter.com/OPA_President
Previous Name: Ottawa-Carleton Regional Police Association
Merged from: Ottawa Police Association; Nepean Police Association; Gloucester Police Association
Overview: A small local organization founded in 1948
Mission: To act as the voice for members at both the provincial & federal levels; To bargain collectively; To raise the standards of police services
Affliation(s): Police Association of Ontario; Canadian Police Association
Chief Officer(s):
Steve Boucher, President
Membership: 1900; *Member Profile:* Police officers; Civilian & Special Constable personnel
Activities: Providing moral support & financial assistance to members in accordance with the association's constitution

Ottawa Rape Crisis Centre (ORCC)
PO Box 20206, Ottawa ON K1N 9P4
Tel: 613-562-2334; *Fax:* 613-562-2291; *TTY:* 613-562-3860; *Crisis Hot-Line:* 613-562-2333
Other Communication: orccnewsletter@magma.ca
orcc@magma.ca
www.orcc.net
www.facebook.com/pages/Ottawa-Rape-Crisis-Centre/409070515814808?ref=h
twitter.com/ORCC8964
Overview: A small local charitable organization founded in 1974
Mission: To end all forms of sexual violence to create a safe community; To provide education about sexual violence; To counsel & support those who have experienced sexual violence
Chief Officer(s):
Ikram Jama, Coordinator, Public Education Program
Josephine Basudde, Coordinator, Crisis Line
Finances: *Funding Sources:* Donations
Membership: *Fees:* $25 annual; $250 lifetime; $50 annual organization; *Member Profile:* All members of the general public, regardless of gender identity, over the age of 18 are eligible for membership.
Activities: Providing public education; Offering Girls Chat Groups in Ottawa high schools; Educating youth & children throught the project, Kids on the Block Teach About Sexual Abuse & Sexuality; Providing volunteer training
Publications:
• ORCC [Ottawa Rape Crisis Centre] Newsletter
Type: Newsletter; *Editor:* Nicole Bedard
Profile: Reports from Centre coordinators & current events affecting the Centre

Ottawa Real Estate Board (OREB) / Chambre d'immeuble d'Ottawa
1826 Woodward Dr., Ottawa ON K2C 0P7
Tel: 613-225-2240; *Fax:* 613-225-6420
orebadmin@oreb.ca
www.ottawarealestate.org
twitter.com/OREB1
Overview: A small local organization founded in 1921 overseen by Ontario Real Estate Association
Member of: The Canadian Real Estate Association; Ontario Real Estate Association
Finances: *Funding Sources:* Membership dues
Membership: 2,800; *Member Profile:* Registered brokers & salespeople

Ottawa Riverkeeper / Sentinelle Outaouais
#301, 1960 Scott St., Ottawa ON K1Z 8L8
Tel: 613-321-1120; *Fax:* 613-822-5258
Toll-Free: 888-953-3737
info@ottawariverkeeper.ca
www.ottawariverkeeper.ca
Overview: A medium-sized local organization founded in 2001
Mission: To protect and promote the ecological health and diversity of the Ottawa River and its tributaries; To ensure swimmable, fishable, drinkable waterways
Chief Officer(s):
Meredith Brown, Executive Director
Finances: *Annual Operating Budget:* $250,000-$500,000
300 volunteer(s)
Activities: *Speaker Service:* Yes

Ottawa Safety Council (OCSC) / Conseil de sécurité d'Ottawa
#105, 68 Robertson Rd., Nepean ON K2H 5Y8
Tel: 613-238-1513; *Fax:* 613-238-8744
info@ottawasafetycouncil.ca
www.ottawasafetycouncil.ca
www.facebook.com/OttawaSafetyCouncil
twitter.com/SafetyOttawa
Previous Name: Ottawa-Carleton Safety Council
Overview: A small local charitable organization founded in 1957
Mission: To assist the citizens of Ottawa to protect themselves & others from injury, property destruction due to accidents, & accidental death
Chief Officer(s):

Sophia Hanafi, Executive Director
sophia.hanafi@ottawasafetycouncil.ca
Claude Blain, President
president@ottawasafetycouncil.ca
Activities: Providing safety programs, such as the school guard crossing program, the motorcycle training program, the Children's Safety Village, & a safety education outreach program; Offering a children's summer camp
Publications:
• Ottawa Safety Council Newsletter
Type: Newsletter
Profile: Council reports & program updates

Ottawa South Community Association (OSCA)

Old Firehall, 260 Sunnyside Ave., Ottawa ON K1S 0R7
Tel: 613-247-4872
osca@oldottawasouth.ca
www.oldottawasouth.ca
www.facebook.com/oldottsouth
twitter.com/OldOttSouth
Overview: A small local organization
Mission: To improve the living conditions of Old Ottawa South
Chief Officer(s):
Christy Savage, Executive Director
Membership: *Member Profile:* Residents of Old Ottawa South; *Committees:* Traffic; Planning & Zoning; Special Events; Program

Ottawa Sports Hall of Fame Inc. (OSHOF) / Temple de la renommée des sports d'Ottawa

Heritage Bldg., Ottawa City Hall, 110 Laurier St. East, Ottawa ON K0A 1B0
e-mail: ottawasportshalloffame@gmail.com
www.ottawasportshalloffame.com
www.facebook.com/195672987173454
twitter.com/OttawaSportsHoF
Overview: A small local organization founded in 1968
Mission: To preserve the history & development of sports in Ottawa
Chief Officer(s):
Dave Best, Chair
Finances: *Funding Sources:* Sponsorships
Membership: 200+ inductees
Activities: Recognizing individuals & teams who, through their achievements in or contributions to sport, have brought fame to Ottawa; *Awareness Events:* Inducation Ceremony, May

Ottawa Symphony Orchestra Inc. (OSO) / Orchestre symphonique d'Ottawa

#250, 2 Daly Ave., Ottawa ON K1N 6E2
Tel: 613-231-7802; *Fax:* 613-231-3610
marketing@ottawasymphony.com
www.ottawasymphony.com
www.facebook.com/ottawasymphony
Overview: A small local organization founded in 1965 overseen by Orchestras Canada
Mission: To develop the highest possible artistic level of performance of symphonic repertoire among local musicians, local & Canadian soloists, Canadian music, partnership opportunities for performance with other local performing arts organizations, educational outreach opportunities for young audiences & young performers
Chief Officer(s):
Peter L. Feldman, General Manager
gm@ottawasymphony.com
Finances: *Annual Operating Budget:* $500,000-$1.5 Million; *Funding Sources:* City of Ottawa; Ontario Arts Council; Trillium Foundation; donations
Staff Member(s): 2; 50 volunteer(s)
Membership: 500-999
Activities: *Internships:* Yes

Ottawa Tourism / Tourisme Ottawa

#1800, 130 Albert St., Ottawa ON K1P 5G4
Tel: 613-237-5150; *Fax:* 613-237-7339
Toll-Free: 800-363-4465
info@ottawatourism.ca
www.ottawatourism.ca
www.facebook.com/visitottawa
twitter.com/Ottawa_Tourism
www.youtube.com/OttawaTourism
Previous Name: Ottawa Tourism & Convention Authority
Overview: A small local organization founded in 1972
Mission: To maximize the number of visits to Ottawa & Canada's Capital Region through effective marketing & communication programs; to help develop & promote awareness of the contribution of tourism in the community; to facilitate the development & promotion of the products, services & needs of members
Member of: Tourism Industry Association of Canada
Chief Officer(s):
Noel Buckley, President & CEO
Finances: *Annual Operating Budget:* Greater than $5 Million; *Funding Sources:* Membership fees; city government & 3% destination marketing fee
Staff Member(s): 28
Membership: 350; *Member Profile:* Hotels; attractions; festivals; restaurants; suppliers; *Committees:* Convention; Marketing; Convention; Rural Tourism; Membership; Travel Trade
Activities: Industry leadership, strategic direction & destination marketing of Ottawa

Ottawa Tourism & Convention Authority *See* Ottawa Tourism

Ottawa Twins' Parents Association *See* Multiple Birth Families Association

Ottawa Valley Curling Association (OVCA)

27 Veermeer Way, Ottawa ON K2K 2L9
e-mail: webmaster@ovca.com
ottawavalleycurling.ca
www.facebook.com/ovcacurling
Overview: A small local organization founded in 1959 overseen by Canadian Curling Association
Mission: To foster curling in the Ottawa & St. Lawrence Valleys & Outaouais
Affliation(s): Ladies Curling Association; Curling Quebec
Chief Officer(s):
Elaine Brimicombe, President
elaine@ovca.com
Peter Smith, Coordinator, Events
ovca.eventscoordinator@hotmail.com
Finances: *Annual Operating Budget:* Less than $50,000
Membership: 45 clubs; *Committees:* OVCA Ottawa Men's Bonspiel; OVCA Mixed Bonspiel; The Royal LePage OVCA Women's Fall Classic; JSI OVCA Junior SuperSpiel
Activities: Overseeing intermediate competitions between Eastern Ontario & Quebec; Offering instruction to new curlers
Awards:
• Ken Thain Award (Award)
Publications:
• OVCA [Ottawa Valley Curling Association] Newsletter
Type: Newsletter

Ottawa Valley Health Libraries Association (OVHLA) / Association des bibliothèques de santé de la Vallée d'Outaouais

c/o Canadian Agency for Drugs and Technology in Health, #600, 865 Carling Ave., Ottawa ON K1S 5S8
Tel: 613-226-2553
www.chla-absc.ca/ovhla
Merged from: Ottawa-Hull Health Libraries Association; OHA Region 9 chapter of the Ontario Health Libraries Assoc
Overview: A small local organization founded in 1994 overseen by Canadian Health Libraries Association
Mission: The Ottawa Valley Health Libraries Association / l'Association des Bibliothèques de la Santé de la Vallée de l'Outaouais is an association of over twenty health-related libraries whose purpose is to promote the provision of quality library services in the health sciences throughout the Ottawa Valley and the Outaouais. It was formed in 1994 through the amalgamation of the Ottawa-Hull Health Libraries Association and the OHA Region 9 chapter of the Ontario Health Libraries Association and is a chapter of the Ontario Health Libraries Association (OHLA) and the Canadian Health Libraries Association (CHLA).
Member of: Ontario Health Libraries Association (OHLA) and the Canadian Health Libraries Association (CHLA).
Chief Officer(s):
Melissa Severn, President
melissas@cadth.ca
Michelle Purcell, Secretary, 613-884-8206
michelle.purcell@sympatico.ca
Finances: *Funding Sources:* Membership fees; Grants
Membership: *Fees:* $20 regular; $5 student; $30 institutional; *Member Profile:* Librarians; Library Technicians

Ottawa Valley Historical Society (OVHS)

c/o Champlain Trail Museum, 1032 Pembroke St. East, Pembroke ON K8A 6Z2
Tel: 613-735-0517; *Fax:* 613-629-5067
pembrokemuseum@nrtco.net
champlaintrailmuseum.com/Ottawa_Valley_Historical_Society.html
Also Known As: Champlain Trail Museum & Pioneer Village
Overview: A small local charitable organization founded in 1958
Mission: To store & preserve historical artifacts from the Ottawa Valley area & to research & provide knowledge of these artifacts to the public
Chief Officer(s):
Stephen Handke, President
Membership: *Fees:* Schedule available
Activities: Operating the Champlain Trail Museum, including a school house, pioneer log home, church, train station, sawmill, & agricultural work sheds; Collecting & displaying historic artifacts of the Ottawa Valley; Organizing & maintaining research archives of the local area

Ottawa Valley Rock Garden & Horticultural Society

PO Box 9123, Stn. T, Ottawa ON K1G 3T8
e-mail: info@ovrghs.ca
www.ovrghs.ca
Overview: A small local organization founded in 1992
Affliation(s): North American Rock Garden Society, Ontario Horticultural Association
Chief Officer(s):
Zandra Bainas, Co-President
president@ovrghs.ca
Margaret Don, Membership Secretary
membership@ovrghs.ca
Membership: *Fees:* $20 individual, $25 family
Activities: Meetings held second Saturday of each month from Sept.-May at Woodroffe Campus of Algonquin College

Ottawa Valley Tourist Association (OVTA)

9 International Dr., Pembroke ON K8A 6W5
Tel: 613-732-4364; *Fax:* 613-735-2492
Toll-Free: 800-757-6580
info@ottawavalley.travel
www.ottawavalley.travel
www.facebook.com/ottawavalleytravel
twitter.com/theottawavalley
www.youtube.com/ottawavalleytravel
Overview: A medium-sized local organization
Mission: To promote Renfrew County as a prime tourist destination
Chief Officer(s):
Alastair Baird, Manager
Chris Hinsperger, President, 613-628-2283
Staff Member(s): 4
Membership: *Fees:* $60 artist/artisan; $95 allied; $125 event/festival; $200 regular; *Committees:* Membership
Activities: Tourism marketing;

Ottawa West Office *See* Heart & Stroke Foundation of Ontario

Ottawa Youth Orchestra Academy (OYO) / L'Orchestre des jeunes d'Ottawa

#38, 2450 Lancaster Rd., Ottawa ON K1B 5N3
Tel: 613-233-9318; *Fax:* 613-233-5038
info@oyoa-aojo.ca
www.oyoa-aojo.ca
Also Known As: The Ottawa Youth Orchestra Academy
Overview: A small local organization overseen by Orchestras Canada
Finances: *Funding Sources:* Tuition fees & grants
Membership: *Fees:* Schedule available

Ottawa-Carleton Board of Trade *See* Ottawa Chamber of Commerce

Ottawa-Carleton Children's Aid Society *See* Children's Aid Society of Ottawa

Ottawa-Carleton Council on Aging *See* The Council on Aging of Ottawa

Ottawa-Carleton Regional Police Association *See* Ottawa Police Association

Ottawa-Carleton Safety Council *See* Ottawa Safety Council

Ottawa-Hull Ice Carvers' Society *See* Canadian Ice Carvers' Society

Otter Valley Chamber of Commerce

PO Box 36, Port Burwell ON N0J 1T0
Tel: 519-550-0088
ottervalleychamber.com
www.facebook.com/OtterValleyChamberOfCommerce
Overview: A small local organization
Member of: Canadian Chamber of Commerce
Chief Officer(s):

Val Donnell, President
c1v2donnell@msn.com
Membership: 41; *Fees:* $70

Our Harbour / Le Havre

95, av Lorne, Saint-Lambert QC J4P 2G7
Tel: 450-671-9160; *Fax:* 450-671-9171
info@ourharbour.org
ourharbour.org
Overview: A small local charitable organization
Mission: To provide supportive, long-term housing; to provide life management support; to assist each resident's integration into society; to decrease risk of re-hospitalization; to educate the wider community about mental illness
Chief Officer(s):
Perveen Khokhar, Coordinator

Our Lady of The Prairies Foundation

PO Box 22076, Saskatoon SK S7J 5P1
e-mail: info@ourladyfoundation.org
www.ourladyfoundation.org
Overview: A small national charitable organization founded in 1957
Mission: To nurture love & compassion; to achieve peace & freedom, through prayers, words, & actions
Activities: Working with charitable organizations in the community; Distributing grants to registered Canadian charities with missions in Saskatchewan; Supporting spiritual, social, healing, educational, & environmental programs;
Awards:
• Grant (Grant)
Supports spiritual, healing, educational, social or environmental programs. Eligibility: A registered Canadian chairty that carries on at 75% of their business in Saskatchewan.

Our Lady of the Rosary of Manaoag Evangelization Group

25 Mahoney Ave., Toronto ON M6M 2H5
Tel: 416-240-9249
franteo_lamadrid@rogers.com
Overview: A small local organization founded in 1989
Affliation(s): Archdiocese of Toronto
Chief Officer(s):
Teodora S. La Madrid, Contact
Activities: Providing evangelization, faith formation & instruction, prayer, retreats, & pilgrimages

Our Place (Peel)

3579 Dixie Rd., Mississauga ON L4Y 2B3
Tel: 905-238-6916
info@ourplacepeel.org
www.ourplacepeel.org
Overview: A small local charitable organization founded in 1985
Mission: To develop & operate emergency shelter & residential services for disadvantaged & homeless youth, from ages 16 to 21, in Peel Region
Chief Officer(s):
Christy Upshall, Executive Director
cupshall@ourplacepeel.org
Finances: *Funding Sources:* Donations; Province of Ontario; Region of Peel; United Way
Staff Member(s): 10

Outdoor Marketing Association of Canada *See* Out-of-Home Marketing Association of Canada

Outdoor Recreation Council of British Columbia (ORC)

47 West Broadway, Vancouver BC V5Y 1P1
Tel: 604-873-5546
outdoorrec@orcbc.ca
www.orcbc.ca
Overview: A medium-sized provincial charitable organization founded in 1976
Mission: To advise industry & government in the development & implementation of outdoor recreation & conservation plans for BC; to contribute to the coordination of regional outdoor recreation by assisting in the establishment of a provincial network of outdoor recreationists to address recreational use conflicts & to advise government & industry on local & regional needs for noncompetitive outdoor recreation; to encourage active participation by the residents of BC in outdoor recreation activities; to promote the quality & diversity of outdoor recreation opportunities in BC by working cooperatively with government, industry, business & the public.
Member of: Volunteer Vancouver; BC Environmental Network
Affliation(s): Environmental Fund of BC
Chief Officer(s):
Dennis Webb, Chair
Jeremy McCall, Executive Director
Finances: *Funding Sources:* Membership dues; fundraising; grants; foundations; donations
Staff Member(s): 1
Membership: 42 organizations; *Fees:* $84 non-voting; $156 voting; *Member Profile:* Voting - provincial outdoor non-profit recreation organization; non-voting organizations are not provincial in scope
Activities: *Library* by appointment

Outdoor Writers of Canada

PO Box 934, Cochrane AB T4C 1B1
Tel: 403-932-3585; *Fax:* 403-851-0618
outdoorwritersofcanada@shaw.ca
www.outdoorwritersofcanada.com
Overview: A small national organization founded in 1957
Mission: To promote high standards of craftsmanship in the portrayal of outdoor life
Chief Officer(s):
T.J. Schwanky, Executive Director
Membership: *Fees:* $40 student; $90 active & associate membership; $280 corporate; *Member Profile:* Professional communicators who specialize in the outdoor field, such as writers, photographers, artists, cinematographers, broadcasters, & government information officers; Corporate members that share the organization's goals; Students
Activities: Increasing appreciation of the outdoors
Meetings/Conferences: • Outdoor Writers of Canada 2015 National Conference & Annual General Meeting, 2015
Scope: National
Description: Craft improvement sessions for communicators with expertise in the outdoor field
Contact Information: Executive Director: T.J. Schwanky, E-mail: outdoorwritersofcanada@shaw.ca
Publications:
• Inside Outdoors
Type: Newsletter; *Frequency:* 6 pa
Profile: Happenings of Outdoor Writers of Canada, corporate news, craft improvement articles, & new markets

Outdoors Unlittered *See* Pitch-In Canada

Outdoors Unlittered (Alberta) *See* Pitch-In Alberta

Outlook & District Chamber of Commerce

PO Box 431, Outlook SK S0L 2N0
Tel: 306-867-9580; *Fax:* 306-867-9559
outlookchamber@gmail.com
outlookchamber.webs.com
Overview: A small local organization
Chief Officer(s):
Justin Turton, Executive President
jturton@sasktel.net
Ken Fehr, Executive Treasurer
ken.h.fehr@ca.pwc.com
Finances: *Funding Sources:* Membership fees
Membership: 69; *Fees:* $50

Out-of-Home Marketing Association of Canada (OMAC) / Association marketing canadienne de l'affichage (AMCA)

#500, 111 Peter St., Toronto ON M5V 2H1
Tel: 416-968-3435; *Fax:* 416-968-6538
rcaron@omaccanada.ca
www.omaccanada.ca
Previous Name: Outdoor Marketing Association of Canada
Overview: A small national organization
Mission: To increase out-of-home's share of ad dollars by promoting the benefits & effectiveness of out-of-home media to agencies & advertisers; to develop & implement new initiatives that serve as a resource to the industry & increase understanding of out-of-home media; to foster development of standards & guidelines that make out-of-home easier to plan & buy; to serve as the united voice of the industry through involvement in issues that represent the interests of its members
Chief Officer(s):
Rosanne Caron, President
Finances: *Funding Sources:* Membership fees
Staff Member(s): 4
Membership: 8
Activities: *Library*

Outreach Literacy Program of the John Howard Society of Victoria / Haliburton / Simcoe & Muskoka *See* John Howard Society of Kawartha Lakes & Haliburton Outreach Literacy Program

Outremangeurs Anonymes

312, rue Beaubien Est, Montréal QC H2S 1R8
Tél: 514-490-1939
Ligne sans frais: 877-509-1939
reunions@outremangeurs.org
outremangeurs.org
Aperçu: *Dimension:* grande; *Envergure:* internationale; fondée en 1960
Mission: Aide les hommes et les femmes de maîtriser les problèmes ils ont avec la suralimentation

Outward Bound Canada

Centre for Green Cities, #404, 550 Bayview Ave., Toronto ON M4W 3X8
Fax: 705-382-5959
Toll-Free: 888-688-9273
info@outwardbound.ca
www.outwardbound.ca
www.linkedin.com/company/outward-bound-canada
www.facebook.com/pages/Outward-Bound-Canada/8376438193?ref=ts
twitter.com/OutwardBoundCan
www.youtube.com/user/OutwardBoundCanada
Also Known As: Canadian Outward Bound Wilderness School
Overview: A small provincial charitable organization founded in 1976
Mission: To promote self-reliance, care & respect for others, responsibility to community & concern for the environment
Member of: Ontario Camping Association; Ontario Society for Training & Development; Association for Experiential Education; Council of Outdoor Educators of Ontario
Chief Officer(s):
Sarah Wiley, Executive Director
sarah_wiley@outwardbound.ca
Finances: *Annual Operating Budget:* $1.5 Million-$3 Million
Staff Member(s): 11; 20 volunteer(s)
Activities: Youth - 21-day Adventure courses available for 15-16 yrs. old & 22-day Voyageur programs for 17+ yrs.; Adults - courses vary from 7 - 24 days, including canoeing, sea-kayaking, hiking or dog-sledding & skiing; special courses for 50+ yrs., for women only & courses for managers & educators; leadership courses; *Internships:* Yes; *Speaker Service:* Yes

Ovarian Cancer Canada (OCC) / Cancer de l'ovaire Canada (COC)

#205, 145 Front St. East, Toronto ON M5A 1E3
Tel: 416-962-2700; *Fax:* 416-962-2701
Toll-Free: 877-413-7970
info@ovariancanada.org
www.ovariancanada.org
www.linkedin.com/company/728166
www.facebook.com/pages/Ovarian-Cancer-Canada/102394063730
twitter.com/OvarianCanada
www.youtube.com/ovariancancercanada
Previous Name: National Ovarian Cancer Association
Overview: A medium-sized national charitable organization founded in 1997
Mission: To support women & their families living with the disease; to raise awareness in the general public & with health care professionals; to fund research to develop reliable early detection techniques, improved treatments & ultimately, a cure.
Chief Officer(s):
Tammy Brown, Chair
Elisabeth Baugh, CEO
ebaugh@ovariancanada.org
Karen Cinq Mars, Vice-President, Marketing & Business Innovation
kcinqmars@ovariancanada.org
Hoda Brooke, Finance Director
hbrooke@ovariancanada.org
Finances: *Funding Sources:* Donations
Activities: Listen to the Whispers public education sessions; *Speaker Service:* Yes

Atlantic Regional Office
#100, 2085 Maitland St., Halifax NS B3K 2Z8
Tel: 902-404-7070; *Fax:* 902-404-7071
Toll-Free: 866-825-0788
Chief Officer(s):
Emilie Chiasson, Regional Manager
echiasson@ovariancanada.org

Ontario Regional Office
#205, 145 Front St. East, Toronto ON M5A 1E3
Tel: 416-962-2700; *Fax:* 416-962-2701
Toll-Free: 877-413-7970
Chief Officer(s):
Marilyn Sapsford, Regional Manager
msapsfor@ovariancanada.org

Pacific-Yukon Regional Office
#330, 470 Granville St., Vancouver BC V6C 1V5
Tel: 604-676-3431; *Fax:* 604-676-3435
Toll-Free: 800-749-9310
Chief Officer(s):
Tracy Kolwich, Regional Manager
tkolwich@ovariancanada.org

Quebec Regional Office
#260, 4950 rue Queen-Mary, Montreal QC H3W 1X3
Tel: 514-369-2972; *Fax:* 514-940-0158
Toll-Free: 888-369-2972
Chief Officer(s):
Monique Beaupré-Lazure, Regional Manager
mbeauprelazure@ovariancanada.org

Western Regional Office
#105B, 1409 Edmonton Trail Northweast, Calgary AB T2E 3K8
Tel: 403-277-9444; *Fax:* 403-277-9919
Toll-Free: 866-591-6622
Chief Officer(s):
Michelle Pilon
mpilon@ovariancanada.org

Overseas Book Centre *See* Canadian Organization for Development through Education

Owen Sound & District Association for the Mentally Retarded *See* Community Living Owen Sound & District

Owen Sound & District Chamber of Commerce
PO Box 1028, 704 - 6th St. East, Owen Sound ON N4K 6K6
Tel: 519-376-6261; *Fax:* 519-376-5647
www.oschamber.com
Overview: A small local organization founded in 1864
Mission: To be the voice of business committed to the enhancement of economic prosperity in Owen Sound & surrounding area.
Member of: Ontario Chamber of Commerce; Canadian Chamber of Commerce
Chief Officer(s):
Bert Loopstra, Manager
bert@oschamber.com
Finances: *Funding Sources:* Membership dues; fundraising
Staff Member(s): 2; 12 volunteer(s)
Membership: 450
Activities: Business After Hours events, monthly; AGM, March; Golf Tournament, Sept.; Outstanding Business Achievement Awards, Oct.; Business Women's Monthly Network;

Oxfam Canada
39 McArthur Ave., Ottawa ON K1L 8L7
Tel: 613-237-5236; *Fax:* 613-237-0524
Toll-Free: 800-466-9326
info@oxfam.ca
www.oxfam.ca
www.facebook.com/OxfamCanada
twitter.com/oxfamcanada
www.youtube.com/user/OxfamCanada
Overview: A medium-sized international charitable organization founded in 1963
Mission: To build solutions for the creation of a fair world, without poverty & injustice
Affiliation(s): Oxfam International
Chief Officer(s):
Margaret Hancock, Chair
Don MacMillan, Treasurer
Finances: *Funding Sources:* Individual & institutional donations; Fundraising
Activities: Raising public awareness; Offering workshops & educational resources; Supporting organizations in oversees communities; Engaging in advocacy activities for just policies
Publications:
• Oxfam Canada Annual Report
Type: Yearbook; *Frequency:* Annually

St. John's Regional Office
382 Duckworth St., St. John's NL A1C 1H8
Tel: 709-753-2202; *Fax:* 709-753-4110
bill.hynd@oxfam.ca

Saskatoon - Prairies Regional Office
#200, 416 - 21st St. East, Saskatoon SK S7K 0C2
Tél: 306-242-4097; *Téléc:* 306-665-2128

Toronto Regional Office & National Fundraising Office
#210, 410 Adelaide St. West, Toronto ON M5V 1S8
Tel: 416-535-2335; *Fax:* 416-537-6435
Toll-Free: 800-466-9326
toronto@oxfam.ca

Vancouver BC & Yukon Regional Office
#201, 343 Railway St., Vancouver BC V6A 1A4
Tel: 604-736-7678; *Fax:* 604-736-9646
miriamp@oxfam.ca

Oxford Child & Youth Centre (OCYC)
912 Dundas St., Woodstock ON N4S 1H1
Tel: 519-539-0463; *Fax:* 519-539-7058
Toll-Free: 877-539-0463
info@ocyc.on.ca
www.ocyc.on.ca
Overview: A small local charitable organization founded in 1987
Mission: To provide a wide range of recreational & support services for children under 18
Chief Officer(s):
Marc Roberts, Executive Director
mroberts@ocyc.on.ca
Finances: *Funding Sources:* Ministry of Community & Social Services; Ministry of Child & Youth Services

Oxford County Geological Society
PO Box 20091, Woodstock ON N4S 8X8
Tel: 519-421-1700
oxford@ogs.on.ca
oxford.ogs.on.ca
Overview: A small local organization founded in 1977 overseen by Central Canadian Federation of Mineralogical Societies
Mission: To arouse interest & knowledge in all fields of earth sciences; to ensure that all age-group needs are considered
Member of: Canadian Central Federation Minerals Society
Finances: *Funding Sources:* Membership dues
Membership: *Fees:* $73.20
Activities: Workshops; seminars; monthly meetings meetings 2nd Friday of the month; guest speakers; *Speaker Service:* Yes; *Library* by appointment

Oxford County Law Association
415 Hunter St., 3rd Fl., Woodstock ON N4S 4G6
Tel: 519-539-7711; *Fax:* 519-539-7962
Overview: A small provincial organization founded in 1893
Chief Officer(s):
Shabira Tamachi, Contact
stamachi@ocl.net
Finances: *Annual Operating Budget:* $50,000-$100,000; *Funding Sources:* Law Society of Upper Canada; membership dues
Membership: 60; *Member Profile:* Lawyers
Activities: *Library*

Oxford Family & Child Services *See* Children's Aid Society of Oxford County

Oxford Philatelic Society
PO Box 20113, Woodstock ON N4S 8X8
Tel: 519-537-7840
ward2221@rogers.com
www.oxfordphilsoc.com
Overview: A small local organization founded in 1949
Chief Officer(s):
Ron Wilton, President
John Hunt, Contact, Public Relations
Betty Thomas, Membership Officer
Membership: 60+; *Fees:* $2 juniors; $10 adults
Activities: Conducting monthly meetings, featuring stamp news & views & guest speakers

Oxford Regional Labour Council
PO Box 663, Woodstock ON N4S 7Z5
Tel: 519-485-1083
Overview: A small local organization founded in 1955
Mission: To promote & defend the interests of workers in the Oxford area
Affiliation(s): Canadian Labour Congress
Chief Officer(s):
Broderick Carey, President
Membership: 28 affiliates, representing 8,500 members
Activities: Liaising with all levels of government; Assisting individuals with their concerns; Supporting groups; Contributing to charities in the community; *Awareness Events:* Day of Mourning Ceremony, April 28

Oxford-Brant Association of Baptist Churches
ON
www.oxfordbrant.com
Overview: A small local organization founded in 1896 overseen by Canadian Baptists of Ontario and Quebec
Member of: Canadian Baptists of Ontario & Quebec
Chief Officer(s):
Chris Crocker, Moderator
nbcpastor@execulink.com
Membership: 17 churches; *Member Profile:* Baptist churches in Oxford & Brant counties; *Committees:* Area ministry; Association Educational

Oxygène
CP 85087, Gatineau QC J8P 7V2
Tél: 819-770-9794
cluboxygene@live.ca
www.cluboxygene.qc.ca
Aperçu: *Dimension:* petite; *Envergure:* locale
Mission: Pour fournir aux membres des activités de randonnée en plein air
Affiliation(s): La Fédération québécoise de la marche
Membre(s) du bureau directeur:
Suzanne Bisson-Girard, Présidente, Conseil d'administration

Oxy-jeunes
2020, rue de la Visitation, Montréal QC H2L 3C7
Tél: 514-728-6146
direction@oxy-jeunes.com
oxy-jeunes.com
www.facebook.com/page.oxyjeunes
www.youtube.com/user/oxyjeunes
Aperçu: *Dimension:* petite; *Envergure:* locale; fondée en 1981
Mission: Pour orienter les adolescents loin de décrochage scolaire, le suicide et la toxicomanie en utilisant diverses activités artistiques et ainsi renforcer l'estime de soi
Membre(s) du bureau directeur:
Jovette Demers, Présidente, Conseil d'administration
Membre: *Critères d'admissibilite:* Jeunes de 12 à 17 ans
Activités: Spectacles; Concernts; Expositions; Ateliers de perfectionnement; Mentorat; Sorties

Oyen & District Chamber of Commerce
PO Box 420, Oyen AB T0J 2J0
Tel: 403-664-3622; *Fax:* 403-664-3622
oyenecho@telusplanet.net
Overview: A small local organization
Member of: Alberta Chamber of Commerce

Pacific Association of First Nations' Women
2017 Dundas St., Vancouver BC V5L 1J5
Tel: 604-872-1849; *Fax:* 604-872-1845
pafnwl@telus.com
pafnw.ca
Also Known As: Pacific Association of First Nations' Women
Previous Name: Association of First Nations' Women; West Coast Professional Native Women's Association
Overview: A small local organization founded in 1981
Mission: To assist Aboriginal women & their families with health, education & social services issues
Member of: Council of Aboriginal Women of BC
Affiliation(s): Vancouver Aboriginal Council
Chief Officer(s):
Joy Chalmers, Contact, Community Homecare Services Program
joy_bc@hotmail.com
Finances: *Funding Sources:* Canadian Heritage; Aboriginal Healing Foundation; Ministry of Health
Staff Member(s): 5; 3 volunteer(s)
Membership: 60; *Fees:* $5; *Member Profile:* Aboriginal women; *Committees:* Finance; Fundraising; Personnel
Activities: Monthly meetings; participation in cultural events; Christmas party; AGM; support & direct client services; Aboriginal Community Health Advocate; Aboriginal Women's Family Violence Prevention Training; Button Blanket Sharing Circles; Aboriginal Elder Women's Support Program; First Nations Advocate for GF Strong & Pearson Hospitals; *Library:* Small Resource Library;

Pacific Bluegrass Heritage Society (PBHS)
c/o The Anza Club, 3 West 8th Ave., Vancouver BC V5Y 1M8
e-mail: pacificbluegrass@yahoo.ca
www.pacificbluegrass.ca
Overview: A small provincial licensing organization

Mission: To encourage education & participation in bluegrass music by the effective use of resources & volunteers
Affiliation(s): Canadian Music Centre
Chief Officer(s):
David Zaruba, President
davidzaruba@hotmail.com
Membership: 200 individual; *Fees:* $20 individual; $30 family; *Member Profile:* Individual musicians, bands, families, supporters
Activities: Workshops, band showcase, picking sessions, summer festivals, Band of the Year Award

Pacific Cinémathèque Pacifique (PCP)
#200, 1131 Howe St., Vancouver BC V6Z 2L7
Tel: 604-688-8202; *Fax:* 604-688-8204
info@cinematheque.bc.ca
www.cinematheque.bc.ca
Overview: A medium-sized provincial charitable organization founded in 1972
Mission: To promote the understanding of film & moving images in Canadian & international contexts; To foster critical media literacy through screenings, film tours, & educational services & resources
Member of: Alliance for Arts & Culture
Chief Officer(s):
Jim Sinclair, Executive Director
Finances: *Annual Operating Budget:* $500,000-$1.5 Million; *Funding Sources:* Canada Council; City of Vancouver; provincial government
Staff Member(s): 14; 75 volunteer(s)
Membership: 13,000; *Fees:* $3
Activities: *Library:* Film Reference Library

Pacific Corridor Enterprise Council (PACE)
PO Box 3032, Vancouver BC V6B 3X5
Tel: 604-688-0222; *Fax:* 604-608-2818
pace@pacebordertrade.org
www.pacebordertrade.org
Overview: A medium-sized international organization founded in 1990
Mission: To build relationships through the production & dissemination of new information, the communication of information relevant to cross border business; To promote public policy that removes barriers to the free flow of capital, people goods & services across borders & the facilitation of networking among members & the public/private sector
Chief Officer(s):
K. David Andersson, Chair
Greg Boos, President
Finances: *Annual Operating Budget:* $50,000-$100,000
Staff Member(s): 2; 30 volunteer(s)
Membership: 150; *Fees:* $300 - $700; *Committees:* Border Crossing; Transportation; Venture Capital
Activities: Seminars & conferences organized around specific & timely topics & featuring case studies from members & dialogue with professionals through panel discussions & roundtables; industry-specific working sessions & other events designed to bring together business people with common interests & problems; advises government of private sector perspective

Pacific Immigrant Resources Society (PIRS)
#210, 3680 East Hastings St., Vancouver BC V5K 2A9
Tel: 604-298-5888; *Fax:* 604-289-7115
info@pirs.bc.ca
www.pirs.bc.ca
www.linkedin.com/company/pacific-immigrant-resources-society
www.facebook.com/163220843762811
twitter.com/PIRSVancouver
Overview: A small local charitable organization founded in 1975
Mission: To ensure that immigrant women & preschool children can participate actively in Canadian community life
Member of: Multicultural Societies & Service Agencies of BC
Chief Officer(s):
Gyda Chud, Chair
Jennifer McCarthy-Flynn, Executive Director
Membership: *Fees:* $5 student/senior; $10 individual; $25 non-profit organization; $50 business; $150 individual lifetime; *Committees:* Board Development; Fund Development; Personnel
Activities: ESL & ELSA; women's development; children's programs; volunteer programs

Pacific Independent Insurance Adjusters' Association
c/o Dave Portier, Granite Claims Solutions, #400, 4370 Dominion St., Burnaby BC V5G 4L7
www.ciaa-adjusters.ca
Overview: A small provincial organization overseen by Canadian Independent Adjusters' Association
Member of: Canadian Independent Adjusters' Association
Chief Officer(s):
David Porter, President, 604-659-6559, Fax: 604-659-6570
david.porter@graniteclaims.com

Pacific Institute for Sport Excellence (PISE)
4371 Interurban Rd., Victoria BC V9E 2C5
Tel: 250-220-2512
piseworld.com
www.facebook.com/PacificInstituteforSportExcellence
twitter.com/PISEworld
www.youtube.com/user/piseworld
Overview: A small provincial organization
Mission: To be a leader in high performance sport development; community programs; sport & exercise education; & applied research & innovation.
Chief Officer(s):
Robert Bettauer, CEO
rbettauer@piseworld.com
Andrea Carey, Director, Operations & Community Engagement, 250-220-2511
rbettauer@piseworld.com

Pacific Institute for the Mathematical Sciences (PIMS)
University Of British Columbia, #4176, 22017 Main Mall, Vancouver BC V6T 1Z4
Tel: 604-822-3922; *Fax:* 604-822-0883
reception@pims.math.ca
www.pims.math.ca
twitter.com/pimsmath
Overview: A medium-sized local organization founded in 1998
Mission: To promote research in mathematics; To strengthen ties & collaboration between the mathematical scientists in the academic community, in the industrial & business sector, & in government; To enhance education & training in mathematical sciences; To broaden communication of mathematical ideas; To create strong mathematical partnerships & links within Canada & with organizations in other countries, focusing on the nations of the Pacific Rim
Affiliation(s): Mathematical Sciences Research Institute; University of Lethbridge; University of Regina; University of British Columbia
Chief Officer(s):
Alejandro Adem, Director
adem@pims.math.ca
Finances: *Funding Sources:* Fundraising; Donations
Publications:
- Pacific Institute for the Mathematical Sciences Newsletter
Type: Newsletter
- Pi in the Sky [a publication of the Pacific Institute for the Mathematical Sciences]
Type: Magazine; *Frequency:* Annually
- PIMS [Pacific Institute for the Mathematical Sciences] Magazine
Type: Magazine

Pacific Legal Education Association ***See*** PLEA Community Services Society of BC

Pacific Life Bible College
15030 - 66A Ave., Surrey BC V3S 2A5
Tel: 604-597-9082; *Fax:* 604-597-9090
Toll-Free: 877-597-7522
info@christcollege.ca
www.christcollege.ca
www.facebook.com/pacificlifebiblecollege
twitter.com/plbc
vimeo.com/channels/plbc
Merged from: Pacific Life Bible College; Christ College
Overview: A small national charitable organization founded in 1997
Member of: International Church of the Foursquare Gospel
Chief Officer(s):
Dennis Hixson, President, 604-597-9082 Ext. 254
dhixson@pacificlife.edu
Staff Member(s): 10
Membership: *Member Profile:* Applicants to the college must be born-again Christians actively involved in a church for a minimum of a full year prior to application.
Activities: *Library:* Wolf Memorial Library

Pacific Music Industry Association ***See*** Music BC Industry Association

Pacific National Exhibition
2901 East Hastings St., Vancouver BC V5K 5J1
Tel: 604-253-2311; *Fax:* 604-251-7753
info@pne.ca
www.pne.ca
www.facebook.com/pages/Vancouver-BC/PNEPlayland/113568129034
twitter.com/pne_playland
www.youtube.com/user/pneclips
Also Known As: PNE
Overview: A small local organization
Chief Officer(s):
Michael McDaniel, President & CEO

Pacific Northwest Library Association (PNLA)
c/o Michael Burris, Public Library InterLINK, 7252 Kingsway, Burnaby BC V5E 1G3
Tel: 604-517-8441; *Fax:* 604-517-8410
www.pnla.org
Overview: A medium-sized international organization
Chief Officer(s):
Michael Burris, President, 604-517-8441, Fax: 604-517-8410
michael.burris@interlinklibraries.ca
Heidi Chittim, First Vice-President
Jason Openo, Second Vice President & Chair, Membership, 780-496-8348
jopeno@epl.ca
Katie Cargill, Treasurer, 509-999-6714
kcargill@ewu.edu
Darlene Hert, Secretary
dhert@msubillings.edu
Membership: *Member Profile:* Persons who work in, with, & for libraries in British Columbia, Alberta, Alaska, Idaho, Montana, Oregon, & Washington
Activities: Providing educational opportunities; Offering the cultivation of leadership skills through the Pacific Northwest Library Association Leadership Institute; Providing forums for networking
Awards:
- Young Reader's Choice Award (Award)

Meetings/Conferences:
- Pacific Northwest Library Association 2015 Conference, August, 2015, Hilton Vancouver, Vancouver, BC
Scope: Provincial
- Pacific Northwest Library Association 2016 Conference, 2016
Scope: Provincial

Publications:
- PNLA Quarterly
Type: Newsletter; *Frequency:* Quarterly; *Editor:* Mary Bolin

Pacific Opera Victoria (POV)
#500, 1815 Blanshard St., Victoria BC V8T 5A4
Tel: 250-382-1641; *Fax:* 250-382-4944
www.pov.bc.ca
Overview: A medium-sized local organization founded in 1975
Mission: To create a dynamic operatic experience, & to inspire audiences, artists & community
Member of: Opera America Inc.; Opera.ca
Chief Officer(s):
Timothy Vernon, Artistic Director
Patrick Corrigan, Director, Markting & Development
Finances: *Annual Operating Budget:* $100,000-$250,000
Staff Member(s): 10
Membership: 1-99
Activities: *Internships:* Yes

Pacific Peoples Partnership (PPP)
#407, 620 View St., Victoria BC V8W 1J6
Tel: 250-381-4131; *Fax:* 250-388-5258
info@pacificpeoplespartnership.org
www.pacificpeoplespartnership.org
Previous Name: South Pacific Peoples Foundation
Overview: A small international organization founded in 1975
Mission: To promote increased understanding of social justice, environment, development, health & other issues of importance to the people of the Pacific Islands; To support equitable, environmentally sustainable development & social justice in the region
Member of: Canadian Council for International Cooperation; British Columbia Council for International Cooperation
Affiliation(s): Nuclear Free & Independent Pacific Movement
Chief Officer(s):
April Ingham, Executive Director
director@pacificpeoplespartnership.org

Finances: *Annual Operating Budget:* $100,000-$250,000; *Funding Sources:* Membership dues; donors; sales; Canadian International Development Agency; professional service fees
Staff Member(s): 5; 15 volunteer(s)
Membership: 160; *Fees:* $35 regular; $45 family; $20 student; *Member Profile:* Supporter of SPPF's aims & objectives, Canadian citizen or a current resident of Canada, annual donation required; *Committees:* Program; Finance; Fundraising; Journal; Public Relations
Activities: Pacific Networking Conference, every two years; *Awareness Events:* One Wave Festival, September; *Speaker Service:* Yes; *Library:* Resource Centre; Open to public

Pacific Post Partum Support Society (PPPSS)

#200, 7342 Winston St., Burnaby BC V5A 2H1
Tel: 604-255-7955; *Fax:* 604-255-7588
Other Communication: Volunteer e-mail: volunteer@postpartum.org
admin@postpartum.org
www.postpartum.org
Overview: A small local charitable organization founded in 1984
Mission: To end the isolation & distress experienced by many women & their families with the profound life change that accompanies the birth or adoption of a child
Affliation(s): United Way of the Lower Mainland
Chief Officer(s):
Joanna Joniec, Chair
Finances: *Annual Operating Budget:* $100,000-$250,000; *Funding Sources:* City of Vancouver, Social Planning-Ministry of Children & Families; Simon Fraser Health Board
Staff Member(s): 9; 20 volunteer(s)
Membership: 105 individual; *Fees:* $10; *Committees:* Fundraising; Visibility; Outreach & Education; Personal
Activities: Weekly support groups for postpartum, depressed or anxious mothers; public education about PPD & its treatment; telephone helpline for families; community training for support people; presentations, booths, conferences, fairs & shows;

Pacific Riding for Developing Abilities (PRDA)

1088 - 208 St., Langley BC V2Z 1T4
Tel: 604-530-8717; *Fax:* 604-530-8617
www.prda.ca
www.facebook.com/PRDALangley
Previous Name: Pacific Riding for Disabled Association
Overview: A small local charitable organization founded in 1973
Mission: To enhance the quality of life for people with a range of disabilities, providing therapeutic equestrian activities & educational opportunities.
Member of: Canadian Therapeutic Riding Association; Langley Chamber of Commerce; North American Riding for the Handicapped Association
Affliation(s): Ishtar Transition Housing Society; Burnaby Association for Community Inclusion
Chief Officer(s):
Michelle Meacher, Executive Director
Finances: *Funding Sources:* Donations; fundraising; United Way of the Lower Mainland
Staff Member(s): 8
Activities: Day camp; summer camp; horse shows; *Speaker Service:* Yes; *Rents Mailing List:* Yes; *Library* Open to public
Awards:
• Volunteer of the Year (Award)
• Spirit of PRDA (Award)

Chilliwack Branch
47240 Greenhill Rd., Chilliwack BC V2R 4T2
Tel: 604-858-2149

Vancouver Branch
Southlands Riding Club, C/O 1088 - 208th St., Langley BC V6Z 1T4
Tel: 604-263-4817

Pacific Riding for Disabled Association *See* Pacific Riding for Developing Abilities

Pacific Rim Institute of Tourism *See* Pacific Rim Tourism Association

Pacific Rim Tourism Association (PRTA)

The Train Station, 3100 Kingsway, Port Alberni BC V9Y 3B1
Tel: 604-723-7529; *Fax:* 604-724-6328
cottages@millslanding.com
Previous Name: Pacific Rim Institute of Tourism
Overview: A medium-sized provincial organization founded in 1989
Mission: To coordinate human resource development activities designed to attract, develop, & sustain a professional workforce in British Columbia's tourism industry
Finances: *Funding Sources:* Government; Industry; Public & private sector
Activities: *Library:* Tourism Resource Centre; Open to public by appointment

Pacific Salmon Commission

#600, 1155 Robson St., Vancouver BC V6E 1B5
Tel: 604-684-8081; *Fax:* 604-666-8707
info@psc.org
www.psc.org
Overview: A medium-sized international organization
Mission: The Pacific Salmon Commission is the body formed by the governments of Canada and the United States to implement the Pacific Salmon Treaty.
Chief Officer(s):
John Field, Executive Secretary
Susan Falinger, Canadian Commissioner
John McCulloch, Canadian Commissioner
Murray Ned, Canadian Commissioner
Bob Rezansoff, Canadian Commissioner
Staff Member(s): 27
Membership: *Committees:* Chinook; Chum; Coho; Data Sharing; Fraser River; Habitat & Restoration; Northern Boundary; Selective Fishery Evaluation; Transboundary; Finance & Administration; Scientific Cooperation

Pacific Salmon Foundation (PSF)

#300, 1682 West 7th Ave., Vancouver BC V6J 4S6
Tel: 604-664-7664; *Fax:* 604-664-7665
salmon@psf.ca
www.psf.ca
www.linkedin.com/company/pacific-salmon-foundation
www.facebook.com/pages/Pacific-Salmon-Foundation/193973967301391
twitter.com/PSF
www.youtube.com/user/SalmonFoundation
Overview: A small national organization founded in 1987
Chief Officer(s):
Paul Kariya, Executive Director
Dianne Ramage, Director, Salmon Recovery
Chad Brealey, Director, Communications
Finances: *Funding Sources:* Fundraising; Endowment income; Revenue from salmon conservation stamps
Staff Member(s): 10
Activities: Fund community salmon projects; manage comprehensive salmon recovery programs for priority watersheds; fund public awareness & educational programs pertaining to pacific salmon; fund critical research

Pacific Society of Nutrition Management (PSNM)

#3, 7488 Mulberry Pl., Burnaby BC V3N 5B4
e-mail: info@psnm.net
www.psnm.net
Overview: A small local organization
Affliation(s): Canadian Society of Nutrition Management
17 volunteer(s)
Membership: *Fees:* $55

Pacific Space Centre Society *See* H.R. MacMillan Space Centre Society

Pacific States/British Columbia Oil Spill Task Force

Environmental Emergencies Branch, BC Ministry of Environment, PO Box 9377, Stn. Prov Govt, 2975 Jutland Rd., 3rd Fl., Victoria BC V8W 9M6
Tel: 250-356-8383; *Fax:* 250-387-9935
www.oilspilltaskforce.org
Mission: The Pacific States/British Columbia Oil Spill Task Force was authorized by a Memorandum of Cooperation signed in 1989 by the Governors of Alaska, Washington, Oregon, and California and the Premier of British Columbia following the Nestucca and Exxon Valdez oil spills. These events highlighted their common concerns regarding oil spill risks and the need for cooperation across shared borders. In June 2001 a revised Memorandum of Cooperation was adopted to include the State of Hawaii and expand the focus to spill preparedness and prevention needs of the 21st century. Now in the second decade, the Task Force provides a forum where Members can work with stakeholders from the Western US and Canada to implement regional initiatives that protect 56,660 miles of coastline from Alaska to California and the Hawaiian archipelago. The Task Force Members are senior executives from the environmental agencies with oil spill regulatory authority in the states of Alaska, Washington, Oregon, California and Hawaii and the Province of British Columbia. Oil spill program managers from each member agency comprise the Task Force's Coordinating Committee, which oversees activities and projects as authorized by the Members when they adopt a Five Year Strategic Plan and Annual Work Plans. The Coordinating Committee convenes four times a year. The Task Force Members hold their Annual Meetings each summer, rotating locations among member jurisdictions.
Chief Officer(s):
Sarah Brace, Executive Coordinator, 206-409-3253
sarah@vedaenv.com

Pacific Urchin Harvesters Association (PUHA)

902 - 4th Street, New Westminster BC V3L 2W6
Tel: 604-524-0322; *Fax:* 604-524-1023
info@puha.org
www.puha.org
www.facebook.com/153381171388169
twitter.com/puhaorg
Overview: A small local organization founded in 1994
Mission: To examine issues around the commercial dive fishery for Red Sea Urchins; to enhance the urchins' market profile & that of the Canadian seafood production industry in general
Chief Officer(s):
Mike Featherstone, President, 604-230-1686
president@puha.org
Ross Morris, Secretary-Treasurer, 604-524-0322
secretary@puha.org
Publications:
• Pacific Urchin Harvesters Association Newsletter
Type: Newsletter

Pacific Western Athletic Association (PACWEST)

BC
Tel: 250-740-6402; *Fax:* 250-740-6487
www.pacwestbc.ca
www.facebook.com/pacwestbc
twitter.com/pacwestbc
Previous Name: British Columbia Colleges Athletics Association
Overview: A small provincial organization
Mission: To govern intercollegiate sports in British Columbia
Member of: Canadian Collegiate Athletic Association
Affliation(s): Atlantic Collegiate Athletic Association; Alberta Colleges Athletic Conference; Réseau du sport étudiant du Québec; Ontario Colleges Athletic Association
Chief Officer(s):
Bruce Hunter, President
Jake McCallum, Vice-President, Administration, 604-323-5421
Activities: Soccer; volleyball; badminton; basketball; golf

Packaging Association of Canada (PAC) / Association canadienne de l'emballage

#607, 1 Concorde Gate, Toronto ON M3C 3N6
Tel: 416-490-7860; *Fax:* 416-490-7844
pacinfo@pac.ca
www.pac.ca
www.linkedin.com/company/the-packaging-association
www.facebook.com/ThePackagingAssociation
twitter.com/PackagingAssoc
Overview: A large national organization founded in 1950
Mission: To represent both users & suppliers on the strength of environmental & economic policy
Chief Officer(s):
James D. Downham, President & CEO, 416-646-4637
jdd@leaderlinx.com
Jan McCallum, Communications Director, 416-646-4642
janmccallum@pac.ca
Finances: *Funding Sources:* Membership dues; Activities
Staff Member(s): 11
Membership: 1,700+; *Fees:* Schedule available; *Member Profile:* Canadian packaging industry
Awards:
• The PAC Leadership Awards (Award)
• PAC Sustainable Packaging Award (Award)
Meetings/Conferences: • Packaging Association of Canada PACKEX Toronto - Canada's Packaging Marketplace, June, 2015, Toronto Congress Centre, Toronto, ON
Scope: National
Contact Information: URL: www.canontradeshows.com/expo/packex13

Québec Office
CP 43010, Succ. Vilamont, 1859, boul René-Laënnec, Laval QC H7M 6A1
Tél: 514-990-0134
quebec@pac.ca
Chief Officer(s):
Mary Ann Gryn, Coordinatrice, Chapitre du Québec, 514-990-0134

Paddle Alberta
PO Box 71039, Stn. Silversprings, Calgary AB T3B 5K2
Tel: 403-247-0083; *Fax:* 866-477-8791
Toll-Free: 877-388-2722
info@paddlealberta.org
www.paddlealberta.org
www.facebook.com/PaddleAlbertaSociety
twitter.com/PaddleAlberta
Overview: A small provincial organization
Mission: To promote safety & sustainability in recreational canoeing & kayaking in Alberta.
Member of: Paddle Canada
Chief Officer(s):
Karla Handy, Coordinator, Program Services
Membership: *Committees:* Safety & Touring; Education; Environment

Paddle Canada (PC) / Pagaie Canada
PO Box 126, Stn. Main, Kingston ON K7L 4V6
Tel: 613-547-3196; *Fax:* 613-547-4880
Toll-Free: 888-252-6292
info@paddlecanada.com
www.paddlingcanada.com
www.facebook.com/pages/Paddle-Canada/111266462242503
twitter.com/paddlecanada
www.youtube.com/user/PaddleCanada
Previous Name: Canadian Recreational Canoeing Association
Overview: A large national licensing charitable organization founded in 1971
Mission: To promote all forms of recreational paddling to Canadians of diverse abilities, culture or age; to advocate for a healthy natural environment; To develop an appreciation for the canoe & the kayak in our Canadian heritage
Affliation(s): Active Living Alliance for Canadians with a Disability; Girl Guides of Canada
Chief Officer(s):
Graham Ketcheson, Executive Director
Finances: *Funding Sources:* Membership fees; Donations; Program delivery; Sponsorships
80 volunteer(s)
Membership: 1,700; *Fees:* $42 individual; *Committees:* Canoeing Program Development; River Kayaking Program Development; Sea Kayaking Program Development; SUP Board Program Development; Finance; Instruction & Safety; Communications (Marketing & Promotions); Member Services; Environment
Activities: Reviewing park management plans, hydroelectric developments & timber management plans; Promoting waterway conservation through the Waterwalker Film Festival; Providing educational programs; Increasing environmental awareness; *Awareness Events:* National Paddling Week, June 6-15
Awards:
• Bill Mason Memorial Scholarship Fund (Scholarship)
Scholarship to a Canadian student enrolled in outdoor recreational or environmental studies at a Canadian college or university *Amount:* $1,000 awarded annually
Publications:
• Current Strokes [a publication of Paddle Canada]
Type: Newsletter

Paddle Manitoba
PO Box 2663, Winnipeg MB R3C 4B3
e-mail: info@paddle.mb.ca
www.paddle.mb.ca
www.facebook.com/373524412660987
twitter.com/paddlemanitoba
Previous Name: Manitoba Recreational Canoeing Association
Overview: A small provincial charitable organization founded in 1988
Mission: To promote safe canoeing & kayaking in the province.
Member of: Paddle Canada
Affliation(s): Manitoba Paddling Association
Chief Officer(s):
Chris Randall, President
president@paddle.mb.ca
Finances: *Funding Sources:* Membership fees; tuition fees; fundraising
Membership: *Fees:* $30 individual; $40 family/affliate; $50 instructor
Activities: Canoe & kayak instruction (flatwater & moving water); information presentations; resource pamphlets; *Speaker Service:* Yes; *Library:* Resource Centre
Publications:
• The Ripple
Type: Newsletter; *Frequency:* Quarterly

Paddle Newfounfdland & Labrador
PO Box 23072, Stn. Churchill Sq., St. John's NL A1B 4J9
Tel: 709-364-1601; *Fax:* 709-368-8357
www.paddlenl.ca
Previous Name: Canoe Newfoundland & Labrador
Overview: A small provincial organization
Mission: A local club that welcomes members from all parts of the province. It is a non-profit group of canoeing enthusiasts who get together regularly to enjoy the sport of canoeing and socialize with other canoeing lovers.
Member of: Paddle Canada
Chief Officer(s):
Hazen Scarth, President
Membership: *Fees:* Individual $20; Associate $50; Family $25

Pagaie Canada *See* Paddle Canada

Pagan Federation International - Canada (PFI)
PO Box 986, Tavistock ON N0B 2R0
e-mail: Nuhyn@paganfederation.org
www.paganfederation.org
Overview: A small national organization founded in 1998
Publications:
• Pagan Dawn
Type: Magazine

Pain Society of Alberta (PSA)
132 Warwick Rd., Edmonton AB T5X 4P8
Tel: 780-457-5225; *Fax:* 780-475-7968
info@painsocietyofalberta.org
painsocietyofalberta.org
Overview: A medium-sized provincial organization
Chief Officer(s):
Gaylord Wardell, President
Meetings/Conferences: • Pain Society of Alberta 9th Annual Conference, October, 2015, Banff Conference Centre, Banff, AB
Scope: Provincial

Pakistan Canada Association of Calgary
PO Box 6909, Stn. D, Calgary AB T2P 2G1
Tel: 403-239-7311
pcacalgary.ca
Overview: A small local organization founded in 1975
Member of: National Federation of Pakistani Canadians Inc.
Chief Officer(s):
Athar Zaidi, President
Finances: *Annual Operating Budget:* Less than $50,000
Membership: 100-499; *Fees:* $20 single; $25 family; $10 student/senior
Activities: Socio-cultural association; *Awareness Events:* National Days of Pakistan & Canada

Pakistan Canada Association of Edmonton (PCAE)
9226 - 39 Ave. NW, Edmonton AB T6E 5T9
Tel: 780-463-7233; *Fax:* 780-469-8346
contactus@pcaedmonton.ca
www.pcaedmonton.ca
Overview: A small local organization founded in 1973
Mission: To generate goodwill & understanding among ethnic & mainstream communities; To provide support to new immigrants through language courses & cultural programs open to all
Chief Officer(s):
Habib Fatmi, Chair
president@pcaedmonton.com
Finances: *Funding Sources:* Community
Membership: *Fees:* $5; *Member Profile:* Pakistani Canadian or any sympathiser of association objectives
Activities: *Speaker Service:* Yes; *Rents Mailing List:* Yes

Pakistan Canada Cultural Association (PCCA)
3030 Franze Dr., Mississauga ON L5A 2R7
Tel: 416-597-0002
Toll-Free: 877-401-7222
info@pccabc.ca
pccabc.ca
www.facebook.com/PCCA.BC?ref=ts
twitter.com/PCCAinBC
www.youtube.com/user/Nav32?feature=mhum
Overview: A small local charitable organization founded in 1972
Mission: To promote harmony & friendship among Pakistanis & other Canadians; to assist new immigrants for housing, employment & rehabilitation; To offer translation services; To arrange cultural programs
Member of: National Federation of Pakistani Canadians Inc.
Chief Officer(s):
Nasar Khan, President
Membership: *Committees:* Sports; Immigration; Education; Cultural Programs
Activities: *Awareness Events:* Heritage Day, May; Independence Day of Pakistan, Aug. 14; *Speaker Service:* Yes

Palais Montcalm
Bureau des arts et de la culture, 995, place D'Youville, Québec QC G1R 3P1
Tél: 418-641-6220; *Téléc:* 418-691-5171
Ligne sans frais: 877-641-6040
info@palaismontcalm.ca
www.palaismontcalm.ca
www.facebook.com/palaismontcalm
twitter.com/PalaisMontcalm
www.youtube.com/user/PalaisMontcalmQuebec
Aperçu: *Dimension:* petite; *Envergure:* locale
Mission: Pour faire fonctionner un centre de culture et de promouvoir les arts
Membre(s) du bureau directeur:
Sylvie Roberge, Directrice générale
sylvie.roberge@palaismontcalm.ca
Membre(s) du personnel: 16
Membre: *Comités:* Programmation; Gouvernance et nomination; Financement; Ressources humaines; Budget et d'audit

Palliative Care Association of Alberta *See* Alberta Hospice Palliative Care Association

Palliser Wheat Growers Association *See* Western Canadian Wheat Growers

The Palyul Foundation of Canada
c/o Orgyan Osal Cho Dzong, Buddhist Monastery & Retreat Centre, 1755 Lingham Lake Rd., RR#3, Box 68, Madoc ON K0K 2K0
Tel: 613-967-7432; *Fax:* 416-604-8101
palyul@ca.inter.net
www.palyulcanada.org
Overview: A small local charitable organization founded in 1981
Mission: Dedicated to the preservation & advancement of the teachings of the Nyingma lineage of Vajrayana Buddhism
Activities: Classes on Buddhism, meditation, ritual practices; retreats; empowerments; celebration of Buddhist holy days & festivals

Pamiqsaiji Association for Community Living
PO Box 708, Rankin Inlet NU X0C 0G0
Tel: 867-645-2542; *Fax:* 867-645-2543
pamiqad@qiniq.com
Overview: A small provincial charitable organization overseen by Nunavummi Disabilities Makinnasuaqtiit Society
Member of: Canadian Association for Community Living
Chief Officer(s):
Yvonne Cooper, Manager

Pan American Hockey Federation (PAHF)
c/o Mary Cicinelli, Field Hockey Canada, #240, 1101 Prince of Wales Dr., Ottawa ON K2C 3W7
Tel: 613-521-8776; *Fax:* 613-521-0261
info@panamhockey.org
www.panamhockey.org
www.facebook.com/174792322573292
twitter.com/PanAmHockey
www.youtube.com/user/PAHFvideo
Overview: A large international organization founded in 1955
Mission: To be the governing continental federation for all field hockey in the Pan American region
Member of: International Hockey Federation
Chief Officer(s):
Alberto Budeisky, President
president@panamhockey.org
Aaron Sher, Honorary General Secretary
secretary@panamhockey.org
Derek Sandison, Honorary Treasurer
derek.sandison@rogers.com
Finances: *Annual Operating Budget:* $100,000-$250,000; *Funding Sources:* Grants; Membership dues; Tournament fees; International Hockey Federation; Sponsorship
Membership: 26 national associations; *Member Profile:* National association recognized by national olympic committees & the International Hockey Federation; *Committees:* Appointments; Competitions; Development & Coaching; Media & Communications; Medical; Umpiring
Activities: Organizing international hockey tournaments; organizing instructional courses

Awards:
• Honorary Life Member (Award)
To honour long-time contribution by a member of the Board
• Order of Merit (Award)
To recognize Pan American Hockey Federation board or committee members who have served for ten years or more & made a significant contribution
• President's Award (Award)
To recognize a shorter-term contribution to the development of hockey

Paper & Paperboard Packaging Environmental Council (PPEC)
#3, 1995 Clark Blvd., Brampton ON L6T 4W1
Tel: 905-458-0087; *Fax:* 905-458-2052
ppec@ppec-paper.com
www.ppec-paper.com
www.linkedin.com/company/2516029
Overview: A medium-sized national organization founded in 1990
Mission: To represent member companies to various levels of government, as well as to environmental and consumer interest groups
Affliation(s): American Forest & Paper Association; Fibre Box Association; Association of Independent Corrugated Converters (AICC)
Membership: *Member Profile:* Packaging mills, and packaging converters

Paper Packaging Canada *See* Canadian Corrugated Containerboard Association

Parachute
#300, 150 Eglinton Ave. East, Toronto ON M4P 1E8
Tel: 647-776-5100
Toll-Free: 888-537-7777
info@parachutecanada.org
www.parachutecanada.org
www.linkedin.com/company/parachute---leaders-in-injury-prevention
www.facebook.com/parachutecanada
twitter.com/parachutecanada
Merged from: Safe Kids Canada; Safe Communities Canada; SMARTRISK; ThinkFirst Canada
Overview: A medium-sized national charitable organization founded in 2012
Mission: To promote effective strategies to prevent unintentional injuries; to build partnerships & uses a comprehensive approach to advance safety & reduce the burden of injuries to Canada's children & youth
Affliation(s): The Hospital for Sick Children
Chief Officer(s):
Louise Logan, President & CEO
Finances: *Annual Operating Budget:* Greater than $5 Million; *Funding Sources:* Corporate donations
Staff Member(s): 35
Membership: 4,000+; *Committees:* Parachute Expert Advisory
Activities: *Library*

Paradise Hill Chamber of Commerce
PO Box 118, Paradise Hill SK S0M 2G0
Tel: 306-344-2123
Overview: A small local organization
Member of: Saskatchewan Chamber of Commerce
Chief Officer(s):
George H Palen, President
Sheila M Phillips, Secretary
phfarmsupply@sasktel.net

Paralegal Society of Ontario (PSO)
#3262, 2255B Queen St. East, Toronto ON M4E 1G3
e-mail: contact@paralegalsociety.on.ca
www.paralegalsociety.on.ca
www.facebook.com/groups/191017120953391
twitter.com/PSO_Paralegal
Overview: A medium-sized provincial organization founded in 1990
Mission: To act as the self-regulating body for all paralegals who provide legal services to the public in Ontario
Chief Officer(s):
John Tzanis, President
Crystal Sankey, Administrator
Janet Wigle-Vence, Treasurer
7 volunteer(s)
Membership: 296 individual + 18 corporate; *Committees:* Membership; Finance; Education; Policy; Standards; Communications; Nominating

Paralympic Sports Association (Alberta) (PSA)
10024 - 79 Ave., Edmonton AB T6E 1R5
Tel: 780-439-8687; *Fax:* 780-432-0486
info@parasports.net
www.parasports.net
Overview: A medium-sized provincial charitable organization founded in 1965
Mission: To provide sports & recreation programs for people with a physical disability
Affliation(s): Wheelchair Sports Alberta
Chief Officer(s):
Kim McDonald, Executive Director
kim@parasports.net
Suzanne Harrison, Coordinator, Programs
suzanne@parasports.net
Staff Member(s): 2
Membership: *Fees:* $20 individual; $40 family; *Member Profile:* Persons with physical disabilities
Activities: *Speaker Service:* Yes

Paralympics PEI Inc. *See* ParaSport & Recreation PEI

Paramedic Association of Canada
#201, 4 Florence St, Ottawa ON K2P 0W7
Tel: 613-836-6581; *Fax:* 613-836-2914
info@paramedic.ca
www.paramedic.ca
Overview: A medium-sized national organization founded in 1988
Mission: To represent the public & practitioner nationally on health related paramedic issues; To lobby government & to speak to the media; To establish national communications network for all practitioners
Affliation(s): Ambulance Paramedics of British Columbia; Alberta College of Paramedics; Saskatchewan College of Paramedics; Paramedic Association of Manitoba; Ontario Paramedic Association; Association Professionnelle des Paramédics du Québec; Paramedic Association of New Brunswick; Paramedic Association of Newfoundland & Labrador
Chief Officer(s):
Chris Hood, President
Dwayne Forsman, Sec.-Treas.
Pierre Poirier, Executive Director
Membership: 14,000
Activities: Developed the National Occupational Competency Profiles, Canadian Paramedic Standards; established the Canadian EHS Research Consortium

Paramedic Association of Manitoba (PAM)
201 Portage Ave., 18th Fl., Winnipeg MB R3B 3K6
Tel: 204-775-8482; *Fax:* 866-222-6471
Toll-Free: 866-726-1210
info@paramedicsofmanitoba.ca
www.paramedicsofmanitoba.ca
www.facebook.com/262118083807029
www.twitter.com/PAM_manitoba
Overview: A small provincial organization founded in 2001
Mission: To promote excellence in pre-hospital emergency health care & excellence in the profession of paramedicine
Member of: Paramedic Association of Canada
Chief Officer(s):
Jodi Possia, Chair
chairman@paramedicsofmanitoba.ca
Christy Beazley, Director, Public Relations
cbeazley@paramedicsofmanitoba.ca
Membership: 500-999; *Fees:* $80 active; $30 associate; $200 corporate

Paramedic Association of New Brunswick (PANB) / L'Association des paramédics du Nouveau-Brunswick
298 Main St., Fredericton NB E3A 1C9
Tel: 506-459-2638; *Fax:* 506-459-6728
Toll-Free: 888-887-7262
info@panb.ca
www.panb.ca
twitter.com/PANB_Paramedic
Overview: A small provincial organization
Mission: To develop & promote the highest ethical, educational, & clinical standards for all levels of Prehospital Care Professionals in New Brunswick
Member of: Paramedic Association of Canada
Chief Officer(s):
Chris Hood, Executive Director/Registrar
chris.hood@panb.ca
Chantale Hayes, Assistant Registrar/Office Manager
chantale.hayes@panb.ca

Membership: *Committees:* Executive; Complaints; Disipline & Fitness to Practice; Admin & Finance; Legislation; Policy Review; Public Relations; Honours & Awards

Paramedic Association of Newfoundland & Labrador (PANL)
PO Box 8533, St. John's NL A1B 3N9
e-mail: info@panl.ca
www.panl.ca
Overview: A small provincial organization founded in 2005
Mission: To improve prehospital patient care in Newfoundland & Labrador
Member of: Paramedic Association of Canada
Chief Officer(s):
Chris Harris, President
Membership: *Fees:* $20 full/associate; $15 student

ParaSport & Recreation PEI
Royalty Center House Of Sport, PO Box 841, Charlottetown PE C1A 7L9
Tel: 902-368-4540; *Fax:* 902-368-4548
info@parasportpei.ca
www.parasportpei.ca
Previous Name: Paralympics PEI Inc.
Overview: A small provincial charitable organization founded in 1974
Mission: To ensure the ample provision of sport & recreation opportunities for persons who are physically challenged
Member of: Canadian Blind Sport Association; Canadian Association for Disabled Skiing; Canadian Wheelchair Sports Association
Affliation(s): The JoyRiders Therapeutic Riding Association of PEI Inc.; The Canadian Council of the Blind - Prince County and Queensland Chapters; The Abegweit Club of Summerside; G.E.A.R. (Getting Everyone Accessibly Riding)
Chief Officer(s):
Tracy Stevenson, Executive Director, 902-368-4540
tracy@parasportpei.ca
Finances: *Funding Sources:* Province of PEI; City of Charlottetown; business sector; community & service clubs; fundraising
Staff Member(s): 2
Activities: Demonstrations; presentations; sport/recreation events; *Speaker Service:* Yes; *Library* Open to public
Awards:
• ParaSport & Recreation PEI School Award (Award), ParaSport & Recreation PEI
Eligibility: Must be enrolled in the PEI School System, have a physical disability, and is active in sport/recreation programs at the community or school lovel.*Deadline:* June *Amount:* $25 for elementary students; $50 for intermediate students; $75 for high school students
• ParaSport & Recreation PEI Scholarships (Scholarship), ParaSport & Recreation PEI
Eligibility: Applicants with a physical disability that are entering university/college in the ensuing year.*Deadline:* June*Amount:* 2 scholarships for $500

ParaSport Ontario
#104, 3 Concorde Gate, Toronto ON M3C 3N7
Tel: 416-426-7187; *Fax:* 416-426-7361
Toll-Free: 800-265-1539
info@parasportontario.ca
www.parasportontario.ca
twitter.com/parasport_ont
Previous Name: Sport for Disabled - Ontario; Paralympics Ontario
Overview: A medium-sized provincial charitable organization founded in 1981
Mission: To provide leadership, resources, & opportunities to ensure a strong community for persons with a disability in the Ontario sport & recreation community
Affliation(s): Ontario Amputee & Les Autres Sports Association; Ontario Blind Sports Association; Ontario Cerebral Palsy Sports Association; Ontario Wheelchair Sports Association
Chief Officer(s):
Brian McLean, Interim Executive Director, 416-426-7186
brian@parasportontario.ca
Staff Member(s): 3
Membership: 1800+
Activities: *Speaker Service:* Yes

Parasports Québec
4545, av Pierre-de Coubertin, Montréal QC H1V 0B2
Tél: 514-252-3108; *Téléc:* 514-254-9793
info@parasportsquebec.com

www.aqsfr.qc.ca
www.facebook.com/367668269915613
Nom précédent: Association québécoise des sports en fauteuil roulants
Aperçu: *Dimension:* moyenne; *Envergure:* provinciale; Organisme sans but lucratif; fondée en 1983
Mission: Favoriser un accès à la pratique sportive en fauteuil roulant à tous les niveaux de performance pour le bénéfice des personnes ayant une limitation physique
Membre de: Canadian Wheelchair Sports Association
Membre(s) du bureau directeur:
Antoine Ducharme, Directeur général
maducharme@parasportsquebec.com
Finances: *Budget de fonctionnement annuel:* $250,000-$500,000
Membre(s) du personnel: 5; 25 bénévole(s)
Membre: 350; *Montant de la cotisation:* 30$ ou 15$
Activités: *Service de conférenciers:* Oui

Parcelles de tendresse
CP 582, Chibougamau QC G8P 2Y8
Tél: 418-748-3753
Aperçu: *Dimension:* petite; *Envergure:* locale
Membre(s) du bureau directeur:
Lisa Fradette Caron, Présidente

Parcs et loisirs de l'Ontario *See* Parks & Recreation Ontario

PARD Therapeutic Riding (PARD)
PO Box 1654, Peterborough ON K9J 5S4
Tel: 705-742-6441
info@pard.ca
www.pard.ca
www.facebook.com/137292022962475
Previous Name: Peterborough Association for Riding for the Disabled
Overview: A small local charitable organization
Mission: Provides the benefits of riding to people with disabilities.
Member of: Canadian Therapeutic Riding Association; Ontario Therapeutic Riding Association
Chief Officer(s):
Angie Muir, Co-Chair
Activities: Horseback riding instruction as a form of therapeutic & social recreation for physically, emotionally, developmentally challenged individuals;

Parent Action on Drugs (PAD)
7 Hawksdale Rd., Rm. 121, Toronto ON M3K 1W3
Tel: 416-395-4970; *Fax:* 866-591-7685
pad@parentactionondrugs.org
www.parentactionondrugs.org
www.facebook.com/pages/Parent-Action-on-Drugs-PAD/390301531674
Overview: A small provincial charitable organization founded in 1983
Mission: To address issues of substance use among youth through outreach, prevention, education & parent support; enhances the capacity of parents, youth & communities to promote an environment that encourages youth to make informed choices
Member of: HC Link
Chief Officer(s):
Diane Buhler, Executive Director, 416-395-4970, Fax: 866-591-7685
pad@sympatico.ca
Finances: *Annual Operating Budget:* $250,000-$500,000
Staff Member(s): 4; 20 volunteer(s)
Membership: 30 corporate + 10 institutional + 500 individual; *Committees:* Governance, finance/audit, nominating, HR/compensation
Activities: Peer education programs for youth (CBC: Challenges, Beliefs & Changes; WWW: What's With Weed); Resources for parents & professionals
Publications:
• PAD Parent & COmmunity Handbook
Profile: Facts on tobacco, alcohol, cannabis and other drugs

Parent Cooperative Preschools International (PCPI)
8725 Westport Dr., Niagara Falls ON L2H 0A2
Tel: 905-374-6605
www.preschools.coop
www.facebook.com/parentcooperatives
plus.google.com/118022490917296587831
Previous Name: American Council of Co-operative Preschools
Overview: A medium-sized international organization founded in 1962
Mission: To promote the family & community; to strengthen & expand the parent cooperative movement & community appreciation of parent education for adults & preschool education for children; to promote desirable standards for program, practices & conditions in parent cooperative preschools & encourage continuing education for parents, teachers & directors; to promote interchange of information among parent cooperative nursery schools, kindergartens & other parent-sponsored preschool programs; to cooperate with family living, adult education & early childhood educational organizations in the interest of more effective service relationships with parents of young children; to study & promote legislation designed to further the health & well-being of children & families
Chief Officer(s):
Lesley Romanoff, President
lesley@romanoffstudio.com
Maria Campbell, Canadian Secretary
mcampbell16@cogeco.ca
Finances: *Annual Operating Budget:* Less than $50,000; *Funding Sources:* Membership fees; fundraising
Membership: 50,000+; *Fees:* $40 individual; $50 school/group; $200 council; $40 library; $100 sponsor; $500 individual life; *Committees:* Advisotrs; Awards; Katharine Whiteside Taylor Bursary; Becky Allen Fund; Marika Townshend Travel Grants; Digital Communications

Parent Finders of Canada
PO Box 21025, Stn. Ottawa South, Ottawa ON K1S 5N1
Tel: 613-730-8305; *Fax:* 613-730-0345
pfncr@yahoo.com
www.parentfindersottawa.ca
Also Known As: Canadian Adoption Reunion Register
Overview: A small national organization founded in 1974
Mission: To assist adult adoptees/foster persons & birth relatives to obtain background information from adoption files kept in social services departments; To assist in search & reunion; To promote a feeling of openness about the adoption experience & a better understanding about the longing for a reunion between adult adoptees & birth relatives
Affliation(s): American Adoption Congress; International Soundex Reunion Register
Chief Officer(s):
Patricia McCarron, President
Finances: *Annual Operating Budget:* Less than $50,000; *Funding Sources:* Registration fees
Staff Member(s): 4; 4 volunteer(s)
Membership: 59,101; *Fees:* $25; *Member Profile:* Must be of legal age - 18 or 19 as applies in each province; *Committees:* Legislative; Freedom of Information
Activities: Canadian Adoption Reunion Register; lobbying; government social services; *Library* Open to public by appointment

Parent Support Services Society of BC (PSSS)
#204, 5623 Imperial St., Burnaby BC V5J 1G1
Tel: 604-669-1616; *Fax:* 604-669-1636
Toll-Free: 877-345-9777
office@parentsupportbc.ca
www.parentsupportbc.ca
www.facebook.com/ParentSupportBC
Previous Name: BC Parents in Crisis Society
Overview: A medium-sized provincial charitable organization founded in 1974
Mission: To promote parent support circles to help parents & guardians learn positive parenting skills & receive emotional support
Member of: Federation of Child & Family Services of BC
Chief Officer(s):
Cyrus Sy, President
Carol Ross, Executive Director
carol.ross@parentsupportbc.ca
Finances: *Funding Sources:* Ministry for Children & Families; United Way; private donations; membership dues; gaming
Staff Member(s): 11
Membership: *Fees:* $5-$35 volunteer; $35 individual; $100 agency
Activities: Parent support circles across BC; *Internships:* Yes
Awards:
• Bill McFarland Award (Award)

Central Island Office
PO Box 86, Nanoose Bay BC V9P 9J9
Tel: 250-468-9658; *Fax:* 250-468-9668
Toll-Free: 877-345-9777
parent@telus.net
www.parentsupportbc.ca/central-island
Chief Officer(s):
Sandi Halvorson, Program Manager

Prince George Office
PO Box 21106, RPO Spruceland, Prince George BC V2M 2A5
Tel: 250-962-0600
Toll-Free: 877-345-9777
parentnorth@shaw.ca
www.parentsupportbc.ca/prince-george
Chief Officer(s):
Jessica Turner, Program Coordinator

Victoria Office
PO Box 31075, RPO University Heights, Victoria BC V8N 6J3
Tel: 250-384-8042; *Fax:* 250-384-8043
psscoordinator@shaw.ca
www.parentsupportbc.ca/victoria
Chief Officer(s):
Annie Lavack, Program Coordinator

Parenting Education Saskatchewan
#306, 506 - 25th St. East, Saskatoon SK S7K 4A7
Tel: 306-934-2095; *Fax:* 306-934-2087
parent.educ@sasktel.net
www.parenteducationsask.ca
Overview: A medium-sized provincial organization founded in 1992
Mission: To link parenting services across the province & provide support & information to those facilitating or organizing parent support/education services
Member of: Canadian Association of Family Resource Programs (FRP Canada)
Chief Officer(s):
Bev Digout, Coordinator

Parents & Friends of Lesbians & Gays (Parents FLAG) *See* PFLAG Canada Inc.

Parents as First Educators (PAFE)
PO Box 84556, Toronto ON M6S 4Z7
Tel: 416-763-7233
pafe4you@gmail.com
www.p-first.com
www.facebook.com/pafe4
twitter.com/PAFE4
Overview: A medium-sized provincial organization
Mission: To ensure Ontario Catholic school board trustees are promoting Catholic teachings & to make parents aware of the work trustees are doing
Membership: 15,000

Parents for Children's Mental Health (PCMH)
PO Box 20004, St. Catharines ON L2M 7W7
Tel: 416-220-0742
Toll-Free: 855-254-7264
admin@pcmh.ca
www.pcmh.ca
www.facebook.com/PCMHOntario
twitter.com/PCMHontario
Overview: A small provincial organization founded in 1994
Mission: To provide voice for children & their families who face the challenges of mental health problems in Ontario
Chief Officer(s):
Janice Matthews, President
Sarah Cannon, Executive Director

Parents of Multiple Births Association of Canada Inc. *See* Multiple Births Canada

Parents of the Handicapped of Southeastern Alberta *See* Bridges Family Programs Association

Parents partenaires en éducation (PPE)
#B-150, 2445, boul St-Laurent, Ottawa ON K1G 6C3
Tél: 613-741-8846; *Téléc:* 613-741-7322
Ligne sans frais: 800-342-0663
info@reseauppe.ca
www.reseauppe.ca
www.facebook.com/reseauppe
twitter.com/info_ppe
Nom précédent: Fédération des associations de parents francophones de l'Ontario
Aperçu: *Dimension:* grande; *Envergure:* provinciale; Organisme sans but lucratif; fondée en 1954
Mission: Travailler en étroite collaboration avec ses partenaires en éducation, outiller les parents dans leur rôle de partenaires en éducation et agir comme porte-parole provincial des parents; promouvoir l'excellence de l'éducation de langue française et

l'épanouissement global des enfants francophones
Membre de: Association canadienne d'éducation de langue française; Commission nationale des parents francophones; Regroupement des organismes francophones en éducation
Membre(s) du bureau directeur:
Geneviève Folliet, Présidente
Finances: *Budget de fonctionnement annuel:* $100,000-$250,000
Membre(s) du personnel: 2; 13 bénévole(s)
Membre: 100-499; *Montant de la cotisation:* 60$; *Critères d'admissibilite:* Parents qui ont choisi d'offrir à leurs enfants une éducation de langue française publique ou catholique en Ontario
Activités: Programme de formation: Parents en forme; congrès annuel

Parents-secours du Québec inc. (PSQI)
#203, 17, rue Fusey, Trois-Rivières QC G8T 2T3
Ligne sans frais: 800-588-8173
info@parentssecours.ca
www.parentssecours.ca
www.facebook.com/262687173759603
twitter.com/ParentsSecours
www.youtube.com/user/ParentsSecours
Aperçu: *Dimension:* moyenne; *Envergure:* provinciale surveillé par Block Parent Program of Canada Inc.
Mission: Parents-Secours du Québec inc. (PSQI) est un organisme à but non lucratif qui assure la sécurité et la protection des enfants et des aînés-es en offrant un réseau de foyers-refuges sécuritaires tout en contribuant à promouvoir la prévention par l'information et l'éducation.
Membre de: Block Parent Program of Canada Inc.
Publications:
• Infolettre [a publication of Parents-secours du Québec inc.]
Type: Newsletter

Parents-Unis Repentigny (Lanaudière) (PURL)
260, rue Lavaltrie sud, Joliette QC J6E 5X7
Tél: 450-755-6755; *Téléc:* 450-755-1773
Ligne sans frais: 800-229-1152
purl@parentsunisrepentigny.qc.ca
www.parentsunisrepentigny.qc.ca
Aperçu: *Dimension:* petite; *Envergure:* locale; Organisme sans but lucratif; fondée en 1985
Mission: Entraide à toute personne impliquée dans une situation incestueuse ou sexuellement abusive; contrer l'inceste et l'agression sexuelle à l'égard des enfants; aider les victimes et les parents touchés par ce problème
Membre(s) du bureau directeur:
Hélène Chartand, Présidente
Monique Fortin, Directrice générale
Finances: *Budget de fonctionnement annuel:* $100,000-$250,000; *Fonds:* Gouvernement
Membre(s) du personnel: 3; 30 bénévole(s)
Membre: 50; *Montant de la cotisation:* $1; *Critères d'admissibilite:* Toute personne de plus 18 ans ayant un intérêt pour la problématique de l'agression sexuelle envers les enfants
Activités: *Stagiaires:* Oui; *Service de conférenciers:* Oui

Paris & District Chamber of Commerce
PO Box 130, Paris ON N3L 3E1
Tel: 519-758-5095
www.pariscoc.ca
Overview: A small local organization
Chief Officer(s):
Leigha Oakes, President
Sue Swinton, Secretary
sue@pariscoc.ca
Membership: 105; *Fees:* $125

Parkdale Community Information Centre (PCIC)
1303 Queen St. West, Toronto ON M6K 1L6
Tel: 416-393-7689; *Fax:* 416-532-6531
info@pcic.ca
www.pcic.ca
Overview: A small local charitable organization founded in 1976
Mission: To establish & maintain in Parkdale a central, comprehensive, up-to-date & indexed collection of information about services & resources; To provide such information to anyone requiring it & to assist residents of Parkdale to find services or resources appropriate to their needs; To be active in identifying duplication & gaps or deficiencies in services or resources, to bring these to attention of appropriate organizations & assist community to fill gaps in services or resources whenever possible
Affliation(s): Association of Community Information Centres in Ontario; Federation of Community Information Centres in the Greater Toronto Area; Ontario Council of Agencies Serving Immigrants
Chief Officer(s):
Loreen Barbour, Executive Director
Finances: *Annual Operating Budget:* $100,000-$250,000; *Funding Sources:* United Way; City of Toronto
Staff Member(s): 3
Membership: 1-99; *Fees:* $5 regular; $3 seniors; $25 agency; *Member Profile:* Individuals who live or work in Parkdale
Activities: Youth outreach, community outreach

Parkdale Community Legal Services
1266 Queen St. West, Toronto ON M6K 1L3
Tel: 416-531-2411; *Fax:* 416-531-0885
mailbox@parkdalelegal.org
www.parkdalelegal.org
twitter.com/parkdalelegal
www.flickr.com/photos/59309375@N05/
Overview: A small local charitable organization founded in 1971
Member of: Association of Community Legal Clinics of Ontario
Affliation(s): Legal Aid Ontario; Osgoode Hall Law School
Finances: *Annual Operating Budget:* $500,000-$1.5 Million
Staff Member(s): 20; 14 volunteer(s)
Membership: 1-99
Activities: Free legal advice & representation to Parkdale residents; *Internships:* Yes

Parkdale Focus Community Project
#103, 1497 Queen St. West, Toronto ON M6R 1A3
Tel: 416-536-1234
www.stchrishouse.org/adults/alcohol-drug-pre-pro
Overview: A small local organization founded in 1991
Member of: St. Christopher House
Activities: Family & youth programs; drug, alcohol & injury prevention programs; early intervention programs; educational workshops; outreach to high-risk groups; *Awareness Events:* Drug Awareness Week

Parkdale Intercultural Association (PIA)
1257 Queen St. West, Toronto ON M6K 1L5
Tel: 416-536-4420; *Fax:* 416-538-3931
pia@piaparkdale.com
www.piaparkdale.com
www.facebook.com/media/set/?set=a.10150126675512836.299301.44834302835
Overview: A small local charitable organization founded in 1977
Mission: To provide settlement programs & services to refugees & new immigrants; To engage in the community development process to nurture a healthy, equitable & sustainable community that builds on the diversity of Parkdale
Member of: Ontario Council of Agencies Serving Immigrants
Finances: *Annual Operating Budget:* $500,000-$1.5 Million
Staff Member(s): 16; 16 volunteer(s)
Membership: 57; *Fees:* $5-25
Activities: Language Instruction for Newcomers to Canada (LINC); programs & activities celebrating diversity, multiculturalism & anti-racism; community development projects; partnerships & collaborations

Parkinson Alberta Society (PAS)
Westech Building, #102, 5636 Burbank Cres. SE, Calgary AB T2H 1Z6
Tel: 403-243-9901; *Fax:* 403-243-8283
Toll-Free: 800-561-1911
info@parkinsonalberta.ca
www.parkinsonalberta.ca
www.facebook.com/281448621909497?sk=wall
Overview: A small provincial charitable organization founded in 1981 overseen by Parkinson Society Canada
Mission: PAS is dedicated to helping people and families of Southern Alberta who live with Parkinson's and related disorders
Chief Officer(s):
John Petryshen, CEO
jpetryshen@parkinsonalberta.ca
Finances: *Annual Operating Budget:* $500,000-$1.5 Million
Staff Member(s): 10; 150 volunteer(s)
Membership: 350; *Fees:* $25 individual/family; $30 organization/health facility; *Member Profile:* Anyone with interest in learning about Parkinson's
Activities: Golf Tournament, July; *Awareness Events:* SuperWalk for Parkinsons, Sept.; *Internships:* Yes; *Speaker Service:* Yes
Publications:
• Parkinson Pulse
Type: Newsletter

Edmonton Office
Stanley Building, #102, 11748 Kingsway Ave., Edmonton AB T2G 0X5
Tel: 780-425-6400; *Fax:* 780-425-6425
Chief Officer(s):
Barb Foxall, Director, Client Services
bfoxall@parkinsonalberta.ca

Grande Prairie Office
#103, 10901 - 100 St., Grande Prairie AB T8V 2M9
Tel: 780-882-6640; *Fax:* 780-882-7674
Chief Officer(s):
Sherry Theuerkauf, Coordinator, Client Services
stheuerkauf@parkinsonalberta.ca

Lethbridge Office
St. John's Ambulance Building, 1254 - 3 Ave. South, Lethbridge AB T1J 0J9
Tel: 403-317-7710
Chief Officer(s):
Brian Treadwell, Coordinator, Client Services
btreadwell@parkinsonalberta.ca

Medicine Hat Office
United Way of South Eastern Alberta, #101, 928 Allowance Ave. SE, Medicine Hat AB T1A 3G7
Tel: 403-526-5521
Chief Officer(s):
Beth Metcalf, Coordinator, Client Services
bmetcalf@parkinsonalberta.ca

Red Deer Office
The Lending Cupboard Society, 5406D - 43 St., Red Deer AB T4P 1C9
Tel: 403-346-4463
Chief Officer(s):
Marilynne Herron, Coordinator, Client Services
mherron@parkinsonalberta.ca

Parkinson Foundation of Canada *See* Parkinson Society Canada

Parkinson Society British Columbia (PSBC)
#600, 890 West Pender St., Vancouver BC V6C 1J9
Tel: 604-662-3240; *Fax:* 604-687-1327
Toll-Free: 800-668-3330
info@parkinson.bc.ca
www.parkinson.bc.ca
www.facebook.com/191326604220827
twitter.com/ParkinsonsBC
www.youtube.com/user/ParkinsonSocietyBC
Overview: A medium-sized provincial organization founded in 1969 overseen by Parkinson Society Canada
Chief Officer(s):
Diane Robinson, CEO
drobinson@parkinson.bc.ca
Staff Member(s): 7
Membership: *Fees:* $25 individual

Parkinson Society Canada (PSC) / Société Parkinson Canada
#316, 4211 Yonge St., Toronto ON M2P 2A9
Tel: 416-227-9700; *Fax:* 416-227-9600
Toll-Free: 800-565-3000
general.info@parkinson.ca
www.parkinson.ca
Previous Name: Parkinson Foundation of Canada
Overview: A small national organization founded in 1965
Mission: To raise funds for research into the causes & treatment of Parkinsons; to provide services which support Parkinsonians & their families; to disseminate information about the condition to individuals & organizations across Canada
Member of: Neurological Health Charities Canada; Health Partners
Chief Officer(s):
Joyce Gordon, President & CEO
Marina Joseph, Director, Marketing & Communication
communications@parkinson.ca
Finances: *Annual Operating Budget:* Greater than $5 Million; *Funding Sources:* Individual giving, Corporate and Foundation support, Events, Government, support from regional partners, investment income
Staff Member(s): 26
Membership: 15,000; *Fees:* $25; *Committees:* National Advocacy; Research Policy; Scientific Advisory; Finance; Audit
Activities: Programs, services, support and education about Parkinson's disease and related conditions (MSA, PSP) for public and health professionals.; *Awareness Events:* Parkinson's Awareness Month, April; Parkinson's Canadian Open

Championships, Oct.; *Internships:* Yes; *Library* Open to public by appointment
Meetings/Conferences: • Parkinson Society Canada Annual General Meeting, 2015
Scope: National
Publications:
• ParkinsonPost
Type: Newsletter; *Frequency:* 5 pa; *Editor:* Marina Joseph
Profile: An online subscription for Canada's Parkinson's community, distributed 5 times per year.

Parkinson Society Canada - Central & Northern Ontario Region *See* Parkinson Society Central & Northern Ontario

Parkinson Society Canada - Manitoba Region *See* Parkinson Society Manitoba

Parkinson Society Canada - Southwestern Ontario Region *See* Parkinson Society Southwestern Ontario

Parkinson Society Central & Northern Ontario
#321, 4211 Yonge St., Toronto ON M2P 2A9
Tel: 416-227-1200; *Fax:* 416-227-1520
Toll-Free: 800-565-3000
info.cno@parkinson.ca
www.cno.parkinson.ca
www.facebook.com//101248525517?ref=ts
twitter.com/ParkinsonCNO
Previous Name: Parkinson Society Canada - Central & Northern Ontario Region
Overview: A small local organization overseen by Parkinson Society Canada
Chief Officer(s):
Debbie Davis, CEO
debbie.davis@parkinson.ca

Parkinson Society Manitoba
7 - 414 Westmount Dr., Winnipeg MB R2J 1P2
Tel: 204-786-2637; *Fax:* 204-786-2327
Toll-Free: 866-999-5558
www.parkinsonmanitoba.ca
Previous Name: Parkinson Society Canada - Manitoba Region
Overview: A medium-sized provincial organization overseen by Parkinson Society Canada
Chief Officer(s):
Howard Koks, CEO
howard.koks@parkinson.ca

Brandon/Westman Office
Scotia Towers, #228, 101 Rosser Ave., Brandon MB R7A 0L5
Tel: 204-726-1702

Parkinson Society Maritime Region (PSMR) / Société Parkinson - Region Maritime (SPRM)
#150, 7071 Bayers Rd., Halifax NS B3L 2C2
Tel: 902-422-3656; *Fax:* 902-422-3797
Toll-Free: 800-663-2468
psmr@parkinsonmaritimes.ca
www.parkinsonmaritimes.ca
www.facebook.com/parkinsonmaritimes
twitter.com/psmr
Overview: A small provincial charitable organization overseen by Parkinson Society Canada
Mission: To give information to people with Parkinson & their family, children & caregivers
Chief Officer(s):
John McCarthy, Chair
Finances: *Annual Operating Budget:* $250,000-$500,000; *Funding Sources:* Private donations, events, SuperWalk
Staff Member(s): 5; 600 volunteer(s)
Membership: 1,500
Activities: Support groups; Physiotherapy Clinic; Speaker series; *Awareness Events:* Parkinson SuperWalk; *Internships:* Yes; *Speaker Service:* Yes; *Library* Open to public

Parkinson Society Newfoundland & Labrador
The Viking Bldg., #305, 136 Crosbie Rd., St. John's NL A1B 3K3
Tel: 709-574-4428; *Fax:* 709-754-5868
Toll-Free: 800-567-7020
parkinson@nf.aibn.com
Overview: A medium-sized provincial organization overseen by Parkinson Society Canada
Chief Officer(s):
Patricia Morrissey, Executive Director

Parkinson Society of Eastern Ontario / Société Parkinson de l'est de l'Ontario
#1, 200 Colonnade Rd., Ottawa ON K2E 7M1
Tel: 613-722-9238; *Fax:* 613-722-3241
psoc@toh.on.ca
www.parkinsons.ca
twitter.com/ParkinsonEastOn
Previous Name: Parkinson Society Ottawa
Overview: A small local organization founded in 1978 overseen by Parkinson Society Canada
Affliation(s): Parkinson Society of Canada
Chief Officer(s):
Dennise Taylor-Gilhen, CEO
dtaylorgilhen@toh.on.ca
Hilary Evans, Director, Resource Development
hievans@toh.on.ca
Staff Member(s): 4
Membership: 700 individual; *Fees:* $30 individual; $375 lifetime
Activities: *Speaker Service:* Yes; *Library* Open to public
Publications:
• The Parkinson Paper
Type: Newsletter; *Frequency:* Quarterly

Parkinson Society Ottawa *See* Parkinson Society of Eastern Ontario

Parkinson Society Québec *Voir* Société Parkinson du Québec

Parkinson Society Saskatchewan (PSS)
610 Duchess St., Saskatoon SK S7K 0R1
Fax: 306-933-4455
Toll-Free: 888-685-0059
saskatchewan@parkinson.ca
www.parkinsonsaskatchewan.ca
Overview: A medium-sized provincial charitable organization founded in 1972 overseen by Parkinson Society Canada
Mission: To provide education & support services in Saskatchewan to ease the burdens of people living with Parkinson's disease & their families; To support research to find a cure for Parkinson's disease
Member of: Parkinson Society Canada / Société Parkinson Canada
Chief Officer(s):
Travis Low, Executive Director
traivs.low@parkinson.ca
Finances: *Funding Sources:* Donations
Activities: Providing informative resources; Hosting special educational events; Increasing public awareness through displays; Collaborating with movement disorder clinics; Offering clinical & peer counselling services; Providing support, information, & referral by phone; *Awareness Events:* Annual Fall Lecture by Movement Disorder Specialist; *Speaker Service:* Yes; *Library:* SPDF Resource Lending Library

Parkinson Society Southwestern Ontario
Meadowbrook Business Park, #117, 4500 Blakie Rd., London ON N6L 1G5
Tel: 519-652-9437; *Fax:* 519-652-9267
Toll-Free: 888-851-7376
info@parkinsonsociety.ca
www.parkinsonsociety.ca
Previous Name: Parkinson Society Canada - Southwestern Ontario Region
Overview: A small local organization overseen by Parkinson Society Canada
Chief Officer(s):
Marilyn Matheson, Chief Executive Officer
marilyn.matheson@parkinsonsociety.ca
Joanne Bernard, Manager, Administration
joanne.bernard@parkinsonsociety.ca
Tracey Jones, Manager, Programs & Services
tracey.jones@parkinsonsociety.ca
Shelley Ralf, Manager, Special Events
shelley.ralf@parkinsonsociety.ca
Beverly Trist-Stewart, Senior Fund Development Officer
beverly.triststewart@parkinsonsociety.ca
Finances: *Funding Sources:* Charity
Staff Member(s): 7; 200+ volunteer(s)
Activities: Support services; Education & awareness; Advocacy; *Awareness Events:* Parkinson Awareness Month, April; Parkinson Superwalk; Parkinson Cut-A-Thon

Parkland Community Living & Supports Society
6010 - 45 Ave., Red Deer AB T4N 3M4
Tel: 403-347-3333; *Fax:* 403-342-2677
www.parklandclass.org
Also Known As: Parkland CLASS
Overview: A small local charitable organization founded in 1960
Mission: To improve the quality of life of disabled children & adults through individual choice, rights, & dignity
Member of: Alberta Association for Community Living
Affliation(s): Alberta Association of Rehabilitation Centres
Chief Officer(s):
Phil Stephan, CEO
pstephan@shaw.ca
Staff Member(s): 600
Membership: 400; *Member Profile:* Adult with disabilities, their parents &/or adult siblings

Parkland Crisis Centre & Women's Shelter
PO Box 651, Dauphin MB R7N 2V4
Tel: 204-622-4620; *Fax:* 204-622-4625; *Crisis Hot-Line:* 877-977-0007
pkndcris@mts.net
www.mts.net/~pkndcris
Overview: A small local organization founded in 1982
Mission: To provide short & long-term counselling for women & children, support & parenting groups, resource & referral information, advocacy & education; To provide shelter to women & their children who are fleeing abusive relationships
Member of: Manitoba Association of Women's Shelters, Inc.
Chief Officer(s):
Kari Prawdzik, Executive Director
Staff Member(s): 18; 20 volunteer(s)
Membership: 1-99
Activities: Emergency shelter for women & their children; support groups; child & youth program; referrals to other agencies; follow-up services; *Awareness Events:* Domestic Violence Awareness Month, Nov.; *Speaker Service:* Yes; *Library* by appointment

Parkland Food Bank
PO Box 5213, 105 Madison Cres., Spruce Grove AB T7X 3A3
Tel: 780-962-4565
parklandfoodbank.org/wordpress
www.facebook.com/PrklndFoodBank
Overview: A small local charitable organization founded in 1985
Mission: Addresses the needs of hunger by providing food to those in need.
Member of: Canadian Food Bank Association; Alberta Food Bank Network Association
Chief Officer(s):
Angela Fawn Lindberg, Executive Director
angela@parklandfoodbank.org
Finances: *Annual Operating Budget:* Less than $50,000; *Funding Sources:* Donations

Parkland Humane Society *See* Red Deer & District SPCA

Parkland Music Festival
Stony Plain AB
www.parklandmusicfestival.org
Overview: A small local organization
Affliation(s): Canadian Federation of Music Festivals; Alberta Music Festival Association
Chief Officer(s):
RJ Chambers, Chair, Syllabus, 780-919-9132
rj@parklandmusicfestival.org
Gillian Brinston-Kurschat, Adjudicator Contact, 780-237-0248
gillian@parklandmusicfestival.org

Parks & Recreation Ontario (PRO) / Parcs et loisirs de l'Ontario
#302, 1 Concorde Gate, Toronto ON M3C 3N6
Tel: 416-426-7142; *Fax:* 416-426-7371
pro@prontario.org
www.prontario.org
Overview: A large provincial organization founded in 1984 overseen by Canadian Parks & Recreation Association
Mission: To enhance the quality of life, health & well-being of people, their communities & their environments; To advocate provincially for parks & recreation issues; To provide networking as well as multi-discipline professional development opportunities
Chief Officer(s):
Larry Ketcheson, CEO, 416-426-7143
lketcheson@prontario.org
Finances: *Annual Operating Budget:* $500,000-$1.5 Million; *Funding Sources:* Self-funding through programs; provincial grants for special projects; membership dues
Staff Member(s): 14; 100 volunteer(s)
Membership: 1,000; *Fees:* Schedule available; *Member Profile:* Individual; student; corporate; *Committees:* Anti-Harassment Policies; Day Care Reform; Government Relations; Benefits of Recreation; Violence in Recreation Activities
Activities: Recreation - An Essential Service; *Library*

Awards:
• ProAwards Program (Award)
Recognizes individuals & organizations who have contributed to the advancement of parks & recreation in Ontario, in 3 sections: member, community & special awards
• Hugh Clydesdale Bursary (Award)
Awarded to promising female parks & recreation students or practitioners in Ontario to further their education *Amount:* up to $2000
• Student Paper Competition (Award)
To recognize the capabilities of students in writing a research paper on parks & recreation *Amount:* $100
• President's Award of Distinction (Award)
To recognize the capabilities of students in writing a research paper on parks & recreation *Amount:* $100
• Excellence in Design Award (Award)
To recognize the capabilities of students in writing a research paper on parks & recreation *Amount:* $100
• Innovation Award (Award)
To recognize the capabilities of students in writing a research paper on parks & recreation *Amount:* $100
• Emerging Leader Award (Award)
To recognize the capabilities of students in writing a research paper on parks & recreation *Amount:* $100
Meetings/Conferences: • Parks & Recreation Ontario / Parcs et loisirs de l'Ontario 2015 Educational Forum & Trade Show, March, 2015, Blue Mountain Resort, Collingwood, ON
Scope: Provincial
• Parks & Recreation Ontario / Parcs et loisirs de l'Ontario 2015 Aquatics Conference and Exhibitors' Expo, 2015, ON
Scope: Provincial

Parksville & District Association for Community Living (PDACL)
PO Box 578, 118 McMillan St., Parksville BC V9P 2G6
Tel: 250-248-2933; *Fax:* 250-248-4774
execassistant@pdacl.ca
www.pdacl.ca
Previous Name: District 69 Association for the Disabled
Overview: A medium-sized local organization founded in 1959
Member of: British Columbia Association for Community Living
Chief Officer(s):
Rebecca Ryane, Contact
Finances: *Funding Sources:* Provincial government
Staff Member(s): 24; 15 volunteer(s)
Activities: Providing support services to adults with developmental disabilities

Parksville & District Chamber of Commerce
PO Box 99, 1275 East Island Hwy., Parksville BC V9P 2G3
Tel: 250-248-3613; *Fax:* 250-248-5210
info@parksvillechamber.com
www.parksvillechamber.com
www.facebook.com/parksvillechamber
twitter.com/parksvillechmbr
Overview: A small local organization founded in 1978
Member of: BC Chamber of Commerce; Canadian Chamber of Commerce
Chief Officer(s):
Kim Burden, Executive Director
Linda Tchorz, Manager, Member Services
linda@parksvillechamber.com
Lynda Schneider, Bookkeeper
Patti Lee, Manager, Visitor Centre
Finances: *Annual Operating Budget:* $250,000-$500,000
Staff Member(s): 4; 6 volunteer(s)
Membership: 475; *Committees:* Advocacy; Communication; Economic Health; Membership; Business Initiatives
Activities: *Speaker Service:* Yes; *Rents Mailing List:* Yes

Parksville & District Rock & Gem Club
PO Box 812, Parksville BC V9P 2V1
Tel: 250-248-6177
pdrockngem@shaw.ca
www.pdrockngem.org
Previous Name: 69'ers Club of Coombs
Overview: A small local organization
Member of: British Columbia Lapidary Society (BCLS); Gem & Mineral Federation of Canada (GMFC)
Chief Officer(s):
Doug Shewan, President
Karen Anderson, Co-Secretary
Ruthie Shewan, Co-Secretary
Jim Dixon, Co-Treasurer
Cathy Sovereign, Co-Treasurer
Membership: *Member Profile:* Persons in the Parksville area of British Columbia who have an interest in rocks, minerals, gems, & lapidary
Activities: Hosting meetings; Organizing field trips; Offering information about geology, rockhounding, & lapidary to members; *Library:* Parksville & District Rock & Gem Club Library

Parksville Golden Oldies Sports Association (PGOSA)
PO Box 957, Parksville BC V9P 2G9
e-mail: mail@pgosa.org
www.pgosa.org
Overview: A small local organization founded in 1993
Mission: To provide physical activities to citizens of Parksville over 55.
Chief Officer(s):
Bruan Ball, President, 250-240-0007
parksville.pgosa.executive@gmail.com
Membership: *Fees:* $15; *Member Profile:* People over 55

Parliamentary Centre / Le Centre parlementaire
#1000, 66 Slater St., Ottawa ON K1P 5H1
Tel: 613-237-0143; *Fax:* 613-235-8237
parlcent@parl.gc.ca
www.parlcent.org
www.linkedin.com/company/parliamentarycentre
www.facebook.com/parliamentarycentre
twitter.com/parlcent
Previous Name: Parliamentary Centre for Foreign Affairs & Foreign Trade
Overview: A medium-sized national charitable organization founded in 1968
Mission: To strengthen legislatures through continuous learning & innovation in parliamentary development, mutual sharing & practical parliamentary experience, & the provision of advisory services
Chief Officer(s):
Jean-Paul Ruszkowski, President/CEO, 613-237-0143 Ext. 303
jean-paul.ruszkowski@parl.gc.ca
Finances: *Annual Operating Budget:* $500,000-$1.5 Million; *Funding Sources:* Contracts with House of Commons & Senate; CIDA; World Bank
Staff Member(s): 15
Membership: 1-99
Activities: *Internships:* Yes

Parliamentary Centre (CLE) / Le Centre parlementaire
#1000, 66 Slater St., Ottawa ON K1P 5H1
Tel: 613-237-0143; *Fax:* 613-235-8237
parlcent@parl.gc.ca
www.parlcent.org
www.linkedin.com/company/parliamentarycentre
www.facebook.com/parliamentarycentre
twitter.com/parlcent
Previous Name: Centre for Legislative Exchange
Overview: A small international charitable organization founded in 1971
Mission: To provide small groups of members of parliament & senators from Canada or senators & representatives & their staff from the United States with an opportunity to broaden their understanding of a policy issue of interest to them through specially planned visits to the other country
Chief Officer(s):
Michael Murphy, Chair
Carole Chouinard, Secretary
David Schijns, Treasurer
Jean-Paul Ruszkowski, President/Chief Executive Officer, 613-237-0143 Ext. 303
jean-paul.ruszkowski@parl.gc.ca
Angela Hamill, Chief Financial Officer, 613-237-0143 Ext. 314
angela.hamill@parl.gc.ca
Finances: *Funding Sources:* National government
Staff Member(s): 6
Activities: Study tours, seminars & policy discussions, annual general meeting; *Speaker Service:* Yes

Parliamentary Centre for Foreign Affairs & Foreign Trade
See Parliamentary Centre

Parlimage CCF
561, rue Canning, Montréal QC H3J 2R1
Tél: 514-288-1400; *Téléc:* 514-288-1400
comm@parlimageccf.qc.ca
www.parlimageccf.qc.ca
Nom précédent: Parlimage Inc.
Aperçu: *Dimension:* petite; *Envergure:* nationale; Organisme sans but lucratif; fondée en 1978
Mission: Centre de formation et de consultation en communications, cinéma, vidéo, télévision; offrir des formations professionnelles spécifiques à tous les aspects de la communication et de la production audio-visuelle, par des professionnelles pratiquants les métiers
Membre de: Association de recherche en communication du Québec
Finances: *Budget de fonctionnement annuel:* $250,000-$500,000
Membre(s) du personnel: 11
Membre: 1-99; *Montant de la cotisation:* 75$
Activités: Cours et formation en: Comptabilité de production; Assistance à la réalisation film; Tournage et montage vidéo; Prise de son; Étapes de la post-production; Recherchiste radio; Montage AVID; Régie ciné-vidéo-pub; Doublage-postsynchronisation; Direction de production vidéo; Scripte au cinéma, etc.; *Stagiaires:* Oui; *Service de conférenciers:* Oui
Prix, Bouses:
• Prix du leadership chambre de commerce Montréal métropolitain (Prix)

Parlimage Inc. *Voir* Parlimage CCF

PARN Your Community AIDS Resource Network (PARN)
#302, 159 King St., Peterborough ON K9J 2R8
Tel: 705-749-9110; *Fax:* 705-749-6310
Toll-Free: 800-361-2895
getinfo@parn.ca
www.parn.ca
www.facebook.com/PARNStaff
twitter.com/PARN4Counties
Previous Name: Peterborough AIDS Resource Network
Overview: A small local charitable organization founded in 1990 overseen by Canadian AIDS Society
Mission: To support people HIV-infected & HIV-affected
Member of: Canadian AIDS Society; Ontario AIDS Network.
Chief Officer(s):
Kim Dolan, Executive Director
John Lyons, Chair
Mark Phillips, Treasurer
Finances: *Funding Sources:* Donations; Ontario Ministry of Health & Long Term Care; Public Health Agency of Canada; United Way of Peterborough & District; City of Peterborough
Activities: Promoting health; Engaging in advocacy activities; Providing education; Organizing support groups; Raising awarenss of AIDS issues; *Library:* PARN Resource Centre
Publications:
• PARN News
Type: Newsletter; *Frequency:* Quarterly; *Accepts Advertising Profile:* Thematic issues, such as Hepatitis C, testing, harm reduction, & disclosure

Parrainage civique Montréal / Citizen Advocacy Montreal
#282, 3740, rue Berri, Montréal QC H2L 4G9
Tél: 514-843-8813; *Téléc:* 514-843-6028
info@parrainagemontreal.org
www.parrainagemontreal.org
www.facebook.com/parrainagemontreal
www.youtube.com/channel/UC_1lD2tsWNKvrH4_16AAdxg
Aperçu: *Dimension:* petite; *Envergure:* locale; Organisme sans but lucratif; fondée en 1979
Mission: Vise l'intégration des personnes ayant une déficience intellectuelle
Affliation(s): Regroupement des Parrainages Civique du Québec
Membre(s) du bureau directeur:
Cynthia Marinelli, Présidente
Johanne Téodori, Directrice générale
direction@parrainagemontreal.org
Finances: *Budget de fonctionnement annuel:* $100,000-$250,000; *Fonds:* Gouvernement; Centraide
Membre(s) du personnel: 4; 150 bénévole(s)
Membre: 100-499
Activités: *Stagiaires:* Oui

Parrot Association of Canada (PAC)
PO Box 637316, RR#1, St. Vincent Township ON N4L 1W5
www.parrotscanada.org
Overview: A small national organization founded in 1994
Mission: To promote high standards in the keeping of parrots by educating the public & the media; To monitor, report on & influence the actions of government at all levels as they pertain

to parrots; To promote professionalism in psittacine aviculture by establishing an aviary certification program & by providing services that will encourage cooperation in parrot breeding; to support parrot related research & conservation projects
Member of: Avicultural Advancement Council of Canada
Affliation(s): Golden Triange Parrot Club; Parrot Club of Manitoba; PIJAC
Chief Officer(s):
Mark Koenig, President, 519-699-5656
Chris Holoboff, Vice-President, 416-868-0878
Finances: *Annual Operating Budget:* Less than $50,000; *Funding Sources:* Membership dues; donations
15 volunteer(s)
Membership: 130; *Fees:* Schedule available; *Member Profile:* People who have a pet parrot; parrot breeders; avian veterinarians; bird curators of zoos; hobbyists
Activities: MAP - Model Aviary Program, a service provided to members to show that their aviary meets a high set of standards set to ensure the well-being, health & protection of the parrots in their care; *Speaker Service:* Yes
Publications:
• The PAC [Parrot Association of Canada] Journal
Type: Journal; *Frequency:* Quarterly

Parrsboro & District Board of Trade
PO Box 297, Parrsboro NS B0M 1S0
Tel: 902-254-3266
Overview: A small local organization
Member of: Atlantic Canada Chamber of Commerce
Chief Officer(s):
Frank Hartman, President
Karen Dickinson, Secretary
Finances: *Funding Sources:* Membership fees; fund raising; town grant
20 volunteer(s)
Membership: *Fees:* $57-$142.50 business; $20 individual

Parrsborough Shore Historical Society
PO Box 98, 1155 Whitehall Rd., Parrsboro NS B0M 1S0
Tel: 902-254-2376
ottawa.house@ns.sympatico.ca
www.ottawahousemuseum.ca
Overview: A small local charitable organization founded in 1977
Mission: To collect, preserve & celebrate the social & cultural history of the Parrsboro Shore; To operate the historic Ottawa House by-the-Sea Museum
Chief Officer(s):
Colin Curleigh, Chair
Susan Clarke, Facility Manager
Finances: *Annual Operating Budget:* Less than $50,000; *Funding Sources:* Provincial government; Donations; Fundraising
Staff Member(s): 1; 15 volunteer(s)
Membership: 150 individual; *Fees:* $12 individual
Activities: *Library:* Ottawa House Genealogy Room; Open to public

Parry Sound Area Chamber of Commerce
70 Church St., Parry Sound ON P2A 1Y9
Tel: 705-746-4213
Toll-Free: 800-461-4261
www.parrysoundchamber.ca
Overview: A small local organization founded in 1897
Mission: To support its members by providing them with networking opportunities, government services, education & marketing services
Member of: Canadian Chamber of Commerce; Ontario Chamber of Commerce
Chief Officer(s):
Andrew Ryeland, President
Perry S. Harris, CEO
perry@parrysoundchamber.ca
Membership: 375; *Fees:* $187.85 1-3 employees; $280.99 4-10 employees; $375.25 11+ employees; *Committees:* Waterfront; Events; Social Media-Ecommerce; Advocacy; Membership

Parry Sound Friendship Centre
13 Bowes St., Parry Sound ON P2A 2K7
Tel: 705-746-5970; *Fax:* 705-746-2612
postmaster@parrysoundfriendshipcentre.com
www.parrysoundfriendshipcentre.com
Overview: A medium-sized local organization founded in 1966
Member of: National Association of Friendship Centres; Ontario Federation of Indian Friendship Centres
Chief Officer(s):
Ann Pamajewon, Executive Director
ann_pamajewon@parrysoundfriendshipcentre.com
Finances: *Funding Sources:* Secretary of State; National Association of Friendship Centres; Ministry of Health; Casino Rama
40 volunteer(s)
Membership: 500+; *Committees:* Personnel; Finance; Property; Programs; Annual Meeting; Fundraising; Membership
Activities: *Speaker Service:* Yes; *Library:* Marion Rice Memorial Library;

Parry Sound Real Estate Board
47A James St., Parry Sound ON P2A 1T6
Tel: 705-746-4020; *Fax:* 705-746-2955
psreb@vianet.on.ca
www.parrysoundrealestateboard.ca
Overview: A small local organization founded in 1969 overseen by Ontario Real Estate Association
Mission: To set a high standard of practice & ethics for its members so that they may better serve the public
Member of: Canadian Real Estate Association; Ontario Real Estate Association
Membership: 100

Partage de Noël *See* Christmas Exchange

Partage Humanitaire
#219, 435, boul Curé-Labelle, Laval QC H7V 2S8
Tél: 450-681-1536; *Téléc:* 450-681-3484
info@partagehumanitaire.ca
www.partagehumanitaire.ca
Aperçu: *Dimension:* petite; *Envergure:* locale; Organisme sans but lucratif; fondée en 1971
Mission: A pour but de meubler la solitude et valoriser les aînés vivant en établissement et c'est par le biais de loisirs spécialement adaptés à leurs besoins, que sont rejoints ces gens trop souvent oubliés
Membre(s) du bureau directeur:
Gilles Leduc, Président
Julie Perrotte, Agente de communication
jperrotte@partagehumanitaire.ca
Finances: *Budget de fonctionnement annuel:* $500,000-$1.5 Million
Membre(s) du personnel: 23; 200 bénévole(s)
Membre: 100-499

Partenaires des parcs canadiens *See* Canadian Parks Partnership

Les Partenaires en alphabétisation du Manitoba *See* Literacy Partners of Manitoba

Partenaires en recherche *See* Partners in Research

Le Partenariat canadien pour la santé des enfants et l'environnement *See* Canadian Partnership for Children's Health & Environment

Partenariat communauté en santé (PCS)
#328, 302, rue Strickland, Whitehorse YU Y1A 2K1
Tél: 867-268-2663
pcsyukon@francosante.ca
www.francosante.org
Aperçu: *Dimension:* petite; *Envergure:* provinciale; fondée en 2003 surveillé par Société santé en français
Membre(s) du bureau directeur:
Sandra St-Laurent, Directrice

Partenariat pour des environnements intérieurs sains *See* Healthy Indoors Partnership

Parti Communiste du Canada *See* Communist Party of Canada

Parti communiste du Canada (marxiste-léniniste) *See* Communist Party of Canada (Marxist-Leninist)

Parti communiste du Québec (PCQ)
CP 482, Succ. Place d'Armes, Montréal QC H2Y 3H3
Tél: 514-528-6142
info@pcq.qc.ca
www.pcq.qc.ca
Aperçu: *Dimension:* petite; *Envergure:* provinciale; fondée en 1965
Mission: Unifier avec la classe ouvrière et les couches populaires pour que s'installe le pouvoir populaire dans le but de construire le socialisme
Affiliation(s): Solidarité populaire Québec; Ligue des droits et libertés
Membre(s) du bureau directeur:
André Parizeau, Party Leader
Membre: *Critères d'admissibilite:* Adhérer au programme et aux statuts du PCQ
Activités: *Stagiaires:* Oui

Parti communiste révolutionnaire (PCR) / Revolutionary Communist Party (RCP)
1918, rue Frontenac, Montréal QC H1V 3T8
Tél: 514-563-1487
info@pcr-rcp.ca
www.pcr-rcp.ca
www.facebook.com/maison.normanbethune
Aperçu: *Dimension:* petite; *Envergure:* provinciale; fondée en 2009
Mission: Créer un nouveau parti communiste révolutionnaire qui dirigera la lutte pour renverser le système capitaliste pourri dans lequel nous vivons, mettre fin à toute forme d'exploitation et d'oppression et conduire la société vers le socialisme et le communisme
Finances: *Budget de fonctionnement annuel:* Moins de $50,000
Activités: *Service de conférenciers:* Oui; *Bibliothèque*

Parti conservateur du Canada *See* Conservative Party of Canada

Parti de l'héritage du Canada *See* Christian Heritage Party of Canada

Parti libéral de l'Ile du Prince Édouard *See* Liberal Party of Prince Edward Island

Parti libéral de Terre-Neuve et du Labrador *See* Liberal Party of Newfoundland & Labrador

Le Parti Libéral du Canada *See* The Liberal Party of Canada

Parti libéral du Canada (Colombie-Britannique) *See* The Liberal Party of Canada (British Columbia)

Parti libéral du Canada (Ontario) *See* Liberal Party of Canada (Ontario)

Parti libéral du Québec (PLQ) / Québec Liberal Party (QLP)
7240, rue Waverly, Montréal QC H2R 2Y8
Tél: 514-288-4364; *Téléc:* 514-288-9455
Ligne sans frais: 800-361-1047
info@plq.org
www.plq.org
www.facebook.com/liberalquebec
twitter.com/LiberalQuebec
www.youtube.com/PartiLiberalduQuebec
Aperçu: *Dimension:* moyenne; *Envergure:* provinciale surveillé par The Liberal Party of Canada
Membre(s) du bureau directeur:
Philippe Couillard, Chef du Parti
Gilbert Grimard, Président
Membre: *Montant de la cotisation:* 5$

Parti marxiste-léniniste du Québec (PMLQ)
1867, rue Amherst, Montréal QC H2L 3L7
Tél: 514-522-5872
bureau@pmlq.qc.ca
www.pmlq.qc.ca
Aperçu: *Dimension:* petite; *Envergure:* provinciale
Membre(s) du bureau directeur:
Pierre Chénier, Chef du Parti, 514-970-1867
Membre: *Montant de la cotisation:* Schedule available

Le Parti Progressiste-Conservateur de Nouveau-Brunswick *See* Progressive Conservative Party of New Brunswick

Parti Progressiste Canadien *See* Progressive Canadian Party

Parti québécois (PQ)
#150, 1200 ave. Papineau, Montréal QC H2K 4R5
Tél: 514-526-0020; *Téléc:* 514-526-0272
Ligne sans frais: 800-363-9531
info@pq.org
www.pq.org
www.facebook.com/lepartiquebecois
twitter.com/PartiQuebecois
www.youtube.com/user/Lepartiquebecois
Aperçu: *Dimension:* grande; *Envergure:* provinciale; fondée en 1968
Mission: Réaliser démocratiquement la souveraineté du Québec pour s'épanouir comme peuple francophone, pour ne plus être minoritaire, pour mettre fin au gaspillage, pour se doter d'une politique économique qui répond aux intérêts du Québec; donner au Québec une place dans le monde
Membre(s) du bureau directeur:

Stéphane Bédard, Chef par intérim
Raymond Archambault, Président
Membre(s) du personnel: 15; 5000 bénévole(s)
Membre: 90 000; *Montant de la cotisation:* Jusqu'à 3000$; *Comités:* Action politique des femmes; Jeunes; Écologie et environnement; Relations internationales et ethnoculturelles

Parti Socialiste du Canada *See* Socialist Party of Canada

Parti Vert d'Ontario *See* The Green Party of Ontario

Parti vert du Canada *See* Green Party of Canada

Parti Vert du Nouveau Brunswick *See* Green Party of New Brunswick

Parti Vert du Québec (PVQ) / Green Party of Québec
#220, 10000 rue Lajeunesse, Montréal QC H3L 2E1
Tél: 514-303-7750
Ligne sans frais: 888-998-8378
info@partivertquebec.org
www.partivertquebec.org
www.facebook.com/partivert
twitter.com/claudesabourin_
Aperçu: *Dimension:* moyenne; *Envergure:* provinciale surveillé par Green Party of Canada
Membre(s) du bureau directeur:
Alex Tyrrell, Chef

Partners FOR the Saskatchewan River Basin (PFSRB)
402 - 3rd Ave. South, Saskatoon SK S7K 3G5
Tel: 306-665-6887; *Fax:* 306-665-6117
Toll-Free: 800-567-8007
partners@saskriverbasin.ca
www.saskriverbasin.ca
Overview: A small local charitable organization founded in 1993
Mission: To promote watershed sustainability through awareness, linkages & stewardship
Chief Officer(s):
Ray Fast, Chair
Susan Lamb, Managing Partner
Lis Mack, Manager
Finances: *Annual Operating Budget:* $250,000-$500,000
Staff Member(s): 2; 50 volunteer(s)
Membership: 110; *Fees:* $25 individual/family; $50-$10,000 corporations/organizations based on budget; *Member Profile:* Individuals & organizations from all sectors of society & all the geographic areas of the basin - Alberta, Saskatchewan & Manitoba
Activities: Watershed monitoring; low water landscaping; storm drain marking; basin-wide stewardship program; aquatic restoration projects; integrated research; ecotourism development & marketing; watershed stewardship program for children
Awards:
• Fred Heal Conservation Award (Award)
• Fred Heal Scholarship (Scholarship)
Publications:
• The River Current [a publication of Partners FOR the Saskatchewan River Basin]
Type: Newsletter; *Frequency:* Quarterly

Partners for Youth Inc.
#B-10, 535 Beaverbrook Ct., Fredericton NB E3B 1X6
Tel: 506-462-0323; *Fax:* 506-462-0328
Toll-Free: 888-739-1555
info@partnersforyouth.ca
partnersforyouth.ca
www.facebook.com/partnersforyouthNB
twitter.com/pfyouthnb
Overview: A small provincial organization
Mission: To help underprivileged youth through programs that encourage learning & help to foster self-esteem.
Chief Officer(s):
John Sharpe, CEO
Staff Member(s): 9

Partners in Research (PIR) / Partenaires en recherche
700 York St., London ON N5W 2S8
Tel: 519-433-7866; *Fax:* 519-645-8899
info@pirweb.org
www.pirweb.org
twitter.com/vroccanada
Also Known As: London Citizens for Medical Research
Overview: A medium-sized national charitable organization founded in 1988
Mission: To promote the value of all aspects of health research, including the wise & humane use of animals when necessary; To educate the public about means to achieve the control & cure of disease processes (including the history & potential of health research), providing literature & audio-visual information at no cost
Chief Officer(s):
Kevin Cougler, Executive Director, 519-433-7866 Ext. 24
kcougler@pirweb.org
Nicole Tate-Hill, Manager, VROC National Program, 519-433-7866 Ext. 23
ntate@pirweb.org
Finances: *Annual Operating Budget:* $100,000-$250,000
Staff Member(s): 3; 100 volunteer(s)
Membership: 4,000; *Committees:* Education; Speakers Bureau; Fundraising
Activities: Education about the history, promise & potential of health research for humans & animals; Virtual Researcher On Call (VROC) program; *Library*
Awards:
• Biomedical Science Ambassador Award (Award)

The Pas & District Chamber of Commerce
PO Box 996, The Pas MB R9A 1L1
Tel: 204-623-7256; *Fax:* 204-623-2589
tpchamber@mailme.ca
www.thepaschamber.com
Overview: A small local charitable organization founded in 1913
Mission: To promote local businesses & help them grow
Member of: Manitoba Chambers of Commerce; Canadian Chamber of Commerce
Chief Officer(s):
James Berscheid, President
Finances: *Funding Sources:* Membership fees; Tradeshow; Sales
Staff Member(s): 1
Membership: 133

The Pas Arts Council Inc.
PO Box 1409, The Pas MB R9A 1L2
Tel: 204-623-7035
thepasartscouncil@gmail.com
thepasarts.blogspot.ca
Overview: A small local charitable organization
Mission: To promote arts & culture in our community through education & live performance
Member of: Manitoba Arts Network
Chief Officer(s):
Barb, Contact
Finances: *Annual Operating Budget:* Less than $50,000; *Funding Sources:* Local & provincial government grants
12 volunteer(s)
Membership: 1-99; *Fees:* $10 individual; $15 group

Pas de la rue
CP 284, Succ. C, 1575, boul. René-Lévesque Est, Montréal QC H2K 4K1
Tél: 514-526-1699; *Téléc:* 514-526-1411
www.pasdelarue.org
www.facebook.com/366730670033857
www.youtube.com/user/lepasdelarue
Aperçu: *Dimension:* petite; *Envergure:* locale
Mission: Pour apporter soutien et assistance aux personnes sans-abri, âgé de 55 ans et plus
Membre(s) du bureau directeur:
Sebastien Payeur, Directeur
direction@pasdelarue.org
Jean Paul Pratte, Président, Conseil d'administration
Membre(s) du personnel: 7
Activités: Tables ronde; Soirées cinéma; Sorties; Dîners mensuels;

The Pas Friendship Centre Inc.
PO Box 2638, 81 Edwards Ave., The Pas MB R9A 1M3
Tel: 204-627-7500; *Fax:* 204-623-4268
tpfc@mts.net
www.mac.mb.ca
Overview: A small local organization
Chief Officer(s):
Ron Chief, Executive Director
tpfc@cancom.net

Pasadena Chamber of Commerce
c/o Town of Pasadena, 18 Tenth Ave., Pasadena NL A0L 1K0
Tel: 709-686-2075; *Fax:* 709-686-2507
info@pasadena.ca
www.pasadena.ca/chamber.html
Overview: A small local organization

Passons à l'action Canada *See* Pitch-In Canada

Pastel Artists Canada
995 Southcote Rd., RR#2, Ancaster ON L9G 3L1
e-mail: info@pastelartists.ca
pastelartists.ca
Also Known As: Pastel Artists.Ca
Overview: A small national organization founded in 1989
Mission: To represent Canadian artists who use pastels in the creation of works of fine art
Member of: International Association of Pastel Societies
Affliation(s): Pastel Artists of Eastern Canada
Chief Officer(s):
Ruth Rodgers, President
rodgers.ruth@gmail.com
Membership: *Member Profile:* Pastel painters

Patent & Trademark Institute of Canada *See* Intellectual Property Institute of Canada

The Paterson Foundation
1918 Yonge St., Thunder Bay ON P7E 6T9
www.patersonfoundation.ca
Overview: A small national charitable organization founded in 1970
Mission: To assist educational, religious & cultural, charitable, non-profit registered organizations with particular interest in health care & relief work
Chief Officer(s):
Donald C. Paterson, President

PATH Canada *See* HealthBridge Foundation of Canada

Pathways to Education Canada
439 University Ave., 16th Fl., Toronto ON M5G 1Y8
Tel: 416-646-0123; *Fax:* 416-646-0122
Toll-Free: 877-516-0123
info@pathwayscanada.ca
www.pathwaystoeducation.ca
www.facebook.com/pathwaystoeducationcanada
twitter.com/PathwaysCanada
Overview: A large national charitable organization founded in 2001
Mission: Help youth in low-income communities to stay in school and attain post-secondary training by providing tutoring, mentoring & scholarships.
Chief Officer(s):
David Hughes, President & CEO
Membership: Over 10,000 students & alumni

Pathways to Education - Halifax-Spryfield
Chebucto Connections, #52, 16 Dentith Rd., spryfield NS B3R 2H9
Tel: 902-477-0964
www.pathwaysspryfield.ca
Chief Officer(s):
Marjorie Willison, Contact
ccda.willison@ns.sympatico.ca

Pathways to Education - Hamilton
North Hamilton Community Health Centre, 438 Hughson St. North, Hamilton ON L8L 4N5
Tel: 905-523-6719
pathways@nhchc.ca
www.nhchc.ca

Pathways to Education - Kingston
Kingston Community Health Centres, #6, 263 Weller Ave., Kingston ON K7K 2V4
Tel: 613-507-7107
www.kchc.ca
Chief Officer(s):
Wendy Vuyk, Program Director
wendyv@kchc.ca
Lisa Lund, Contact
lisal@kchc.ca
Petra Hanson, Contact
petrah@kchc.ca

Pathways to Education - Kitchener
Mosaic Counselling & Family Services, 400 Queen St. South, Kitchener ON N2G 1W7
Tel: 519-743-6333
www.mosaiconline.ca
Chief Officer(s):
Sanjida Khan, Contact
skhan@mosaiconline.ca

Pathways to Education - Montréal-Verdun
Toujours Ensemble, 601, 2nd Ave., Montréal QC H4G 2W7

Tel: 514-761-7867
www.toujoursensemble.org
Chief Officer(s):
Luc Mantha, Acting Program Director
lmantha.passeport@gmail.com

Pathways to Education - Ottawa
Pinecrest-Queensway Community Health Centre, 1365 Richmond Rd., Ottawa ON K2B 6R7
Tel: 613-820-4922
www.pqchc.com/youth/pathways-to-education
Chief Officer(s):
Dawn Lyons, Program Manager
d.lyons@pqchc.com

Patients Canada

3560 Bathurst St., Toronto ON M6A 2E1
Tel: 416-785-2500
communications@patientsassociation.ca
patientsassociation.ca
www.facebook.com/113395605361806
twitter.com/PatientsAssocCa
Previous Name: Patients' Association of Canada
Overview: A medium-sized national charitable organization
Mission: To highlight instances where the health care system worked & where it needs improvement, from the perspective of patients.
Chief Officer(s):
Sholom Glouberman, President
Finances: *Funding Sources:* Donations; grants
Activities: Meetings; forums; research; resources for patients
Awards:
• The Patients' Choice Awards (Award)
Patients can nominate their physicians for this award.

Patients' Association of Canada ***See*** Patients Canada

Patinage Canada ***See*** Skate Canada

Patinage de vitesse Canada ***See*** Speed Skating Canada

Patrimoine et Culture du Portage

655, rte du Fleuve, Notre-Dame-du-Portage QC G0L 1Y0
Tél: 418-862-7333
www.notredameduportage.org
Aperçu: *Dimension:* petite; *Envergure:* locale; fondée en 2007
Mission: Patrimoine et Culture du Portage est un organisme sans but lucratif dont la mission consiste à promouvoir la protection et la mise en valeur du patrimoine naturel et culturel de Notre-Dame-du-Portage, soutenir les activités culturelles et aider les enfants ayant des besoins spéciaux.
Membre(s) du bureau directeur:
Aubert Ouellet, Président

Patrimoine Huntingville

150 McKay St., North Hatley QC J0B 2C0
Tel: 819-842-3102
huntingville@gmail.com
Overview: A small local organization founded in 1995
Chief Officer(s):
Terry Skeats, President

Patronato INAS (Canada)

PO Box 201, #205, 1263 Wilson Ave., Toronto ON M3M 3G2
Tel: 416-240-1844; *Fax:* 416-240-1785
inascanadatoronto@bellnet.ca
www.canada.inas.it
Also Known As: Instituto Nazionale di Assistenza Sociale
Previous Name: INAS (Canada)
Overview: A medium-sized international organization founded in 1972
Mission: To assist people in matters related to pensions, both nationally & internationally
Affiliation(s): Labour Council of Metropolitan Toronto
Finances: *Annual Operating Budget:* $250,000-$500,000; *Funding Sources:* Italian government
Membership: 15,000; *Member Profile:* Pensioners
Activities: Pension services; *Speaker Service:* Yes

Calgary Office
201-A, 4th St. NE, Calgary AB TZE 3S1
Tel: 403-277-2772

Edmonton Office
9111 - 110 Ave., Edmonton AB T5H 4J9
Tel: 780-421-9559; *Fax:* 780-429-1984

Guelph Office
PO Box 872, 127 Feguson St., Guelph ON N1H 6M6
Tel: 519-837-2822
inascanadaguelph@bellnet.ca

Hamilton Office
#500, 105 Main St. East, Hamilton ON L8N 1G6
Tel: 905-529-8989; *Fax:* 905-529-2776
inascanadahamilton@bellnet.ca

La Salle Office
#303, 8190, boul Newman, La Salle QC H8N 1X9
Tél: 514-903-5004

London Office
120 Clarke Side Rd., London ON N5W 5E1
Tel: 519-455-7950

Mississauga Office
#101, 195 Forum Dr., Mississauga ON L4Z 3M9
Tel: 905-507-3189; *Fax:* 905-507-4826
inascanadamississauga@bellnet.ca

Montréal Office
505, rue Jean Talon est, Montréal QC H2R 1T6
Tel: 514-844-0010; *Fax:* 514-844-5174
inasquebec@qc.aira.com

Saint Leonard Office
#305, 8370, boul Lacordaire, Saint Leonard QC H1R 3Y6
Tél: 514-326-7262; *Téléc:* 514-326-1882
c.daniello@inas.it

Sarnia Office
#601-B, 546 North Christina St., Sarnia ON N7T 5W6
Tel: 519-542-8890; *Fax:* 519-542-5599

Winnipeg Office
88 Sherbrooke St., Winnipeg MB R3C 2B3
Tel: 204-284-0663

Woodbridge Office
#204, 7700 Pine Valley Dr., Woodbridge ON L4L 2X4
Tel: 905-856-9926; *Fax:* 905-856-4310
inascanadawoodbridge@bellnet.ca

Patrouille canadienne de ski ***See*** Canadian Ski Patrol

Patrouille de ski St-Jean

651, 6e rue ouest, Chibougamau QC G8P 2T8
Tél: 418-748-7162
Aperçu: *Dimension:* petite; *Envergure:* locale
Membre(s) du bureau directeur:
Patrice Bolduc, Président, 418-748-6914
p.bol.duc@hotmail.com

Pauktuutit Inuit Women of Canada

#520, 1 Nicholas St, Ottawa ON K1N 7B7
Tel: 613-238-3977; *Fax:* 613-238-1787
Toll-Free: 800-667-0749
info@pauktuutit.ca
www.pauktuutit.ca
Also Known As: Inuit Women Association of Canada
Overview: A medium-sized national charitable organization founded in 1984
Mission: To foster a greater awareness of the needs of Inuit women & to encourage their participation in community, regional & national concerns in relation to social, cultural & economic development
Affliation(s): Inuit Tapirisat of Canada; Nunavut Implementation Commission
Chief Officer(s):
Elisapee Sheutiapik, President
Finances: *Annual Operating Budget:* $500,000-$1.5 Million; *Funding Sources:* Government
Staff Member(s): 8
Membership: *Member Profile:* Inuit women resident in Canada
Activities: *Speaker Service:* Yes; *Library* by appointment

Paved Arts New Media Inc.

424 - 20th St. West, Saskatoon SK S7M 0X4
Tel: 306-652-5502
www.pavedarts.ca
Previous Name: Photographers Gallery Society Inc.
Overview: A small provincial charitable organization founded in 1971
Mission: To develop photography & photo-based art
Chief Officer(s):
Biliana Velkova, Executive Director
executive@pavedarts.ca
David LaRiviere, Artistic Director
artistic@pavedarts.ca
Finances: *Annual Operating Budget:* $250,000-$500,000; *Funding Sources:* Saskatchewan Arts Board; Canada Council for the Arts; City of Saskatchewan; SaskCulture
Staff Member(s): 5; 40 volunteer(s)
Membership: 100-499; *Fees:* $25 Associate/Student Producing; $50 Producing; $100 Institutional; *Committees:* Archive/Resource Centre; Exhibitions; Programming; Fundraising
Activities: Exhibitions, workshops, special events, creative residencies for media artists, permanent collection of contemporary Canadian photography; collection of media works produced by members; *Library* Open to public by appointment

Pavillion Marguerite de Champlain

PO Box 51535, Stn. Taschereau, Greenfield Park QC J4V 3N8
Tel: 450-656-1946; *Fax:* 450-656-6548
info@pavillonmarguerite.com
pavillonmarguerite.com
Overview: A small local organization
Mission: Pour aider les femmes et leurs enfants échapper à des relations abusives et pour les aider à rester loin de l'abus
Activities: Interventions; Sensbilisation; Groupes mères; Activités pour les enfants

Pax Natura Society for Rehabilitation of the Deaf

11460 - 60th Ave. NW, Edmonton AB T6H 1J5
Tel: 780-434-1671; *Fax:* 780-435-7788; *TTY:* 780-434-1671
Overview: A small local charitable organization founded in 1975
Mission: To administer & employ its property, assets & rights for the purpose of promoting or aiding in the promotion of programs to benefit the deaf community
Chief Officer(s):
R.A. Bauer, Executive Director
Finances: *Funding Sources:* Provincial government; Private & government grants; Donations
Membership: *Member Profile:* Voting - deaf community; associate - family members, supporters, professionals from hearing community
Activities: Camp; Retreat; Counselling; Work events/work experience; Education; Outdoor/conservation; Recreation; *Library*
Awards:
• G.W. Sutherland Memorial Scholarship (Scholarship)
Eligibility: Deaf student, any age
• E.L. Palate Memorial Scholarship (Scholarship)
Eligibility: Deaf student in post-secondary education

Peace & Environment Resource Centre

PO Box 4075, Stn. E, 174 First Ave., Ottawa ON K1S 5B1
Tel: 613-230-4590
info@perc.ca
www.perc.ca
Overview: A small local charitable organization
Mission: To ensure peaceful, equitable, healthy, & sustainable local & global communities
Finances: *Funding Sources:* Donations; Fundraising
Activities: Developing community projects; Organizing workshops & events; *Library:* Peace & Environment Resource Centre Library; Open to public
Publications:
• The Peace & Environment News
Type: Newsletter; *Price:* Free
Profile: Information about critical issues for Canada & the world

Peace Agricultural Research & Demonstration Association (PARDA)

PO Box 1551, Fairview AB T0H 1L0
Tel: 780-835-9158
peaceagrd@gmail.com
www.areca.ab.ca/pardahome.html
www.facebook.com/pages/PARDA/105160659548217
Previous Name: Fairview Applied Research Association
Overview: A small local organization overseen by Agricultural Research & Extension Council of Alberta
Mission: To increase the profitability of grain producers in Northern Alberta through developing new technology & improving management practices
Member of: Agricultural Research & Extension Council of Alberta
Chief Officer(s):
Janette McDonald, Executive Director
Membership: *Fees:* $20
Publications:
• PARDA [Peace Agricultural Research & Demonstration Association] Newsletter
Type: Newsletter

Peace Arch Community Services ***See*** Sources Foundation

Peace Area Riding for the Disabled (PARDS)

8202 - 84 St., Grande Prairie AB T8X 0L6
Tel: 780-538-3211; *Fax:* 780-538-3683
www.pards.ca

Overview: A small local charitable organization founded in 1984
Mission: To enhance the lives of individuals with disabilities through "equine assisted therapy"; To promoten physical, emotional, intellectual & social growth for individuals with disabilities through therapeutic riding services; To build a community that embraces differences & supports growth & success for all of its members
Member of: Canadian Therapeutic Riding Association
Chief Officer(s):
Raymond Binks, Chair
Jennifer Douglas, Executive Director
Staff Member(s): 8
Activities: Summer camp;

Peace Brigades International (Canada) (PBI)
323 Chapel St., Ottawa ON K1N 7Z2
Tel: 613-237-6968
info@pbicanada.org
www.pbicanada.org
www.facebook.com/pbicanada
twitter.com/pbicanada
Overview: A small international charitable organization founded in 1981
Mission: To explore & implement non-violent approaches to peacekeeping & support for basic human rights; to provide protective accompaniment & peace education training in Colombia, Indonesia, & Mexico
Affliation(s): Canadian Peace Alliance
Chief Officer(s):
Meaghen Simms, Executive Director
Finances: *Funding Sources:* Donations
Staff Member(s): 3
Activities: Non-violence & peace education workshops; *Speaker Service:* Yes; *Library:* Peace Brigades International (Canada) Library; Open to public

Peace Country Beef & Forage Association (PCGFA)
PO Box 3000, Fairview AB T0H 1L0
Tel: 780-835-6799; *Fax:* 780-835-6626
www.areca.ab.ca/pcbfahome.html
Overview: A small local organization founded in 1982 overseen by Agricultural Research & Extension Council of Alberta
Mission: To demontrate new forage varieties & technology
Member of: Agricultural Research & Extension Council of Alberta
Chief Officer(s):
Ryan Leiske, President
Morgan Hobin, Acting Manager
mhobin@gprc.ab.ca
Akim Omokanye, Coordinator, Program
aomokanye@gprc.ab.ca
Staff Member(s): 3
Membership: 175; *Fees:* $25
Publications:
• Forage Facts [a publication of the Peace Country Beef & Forage Association]
Type: Newsletter

High Prairie Office
PO Box 2803, 5226 - 53 Ave., High Prairie AB T0G 1E0
Tel: 780-523-4033; *Fax:* 780-523-6569
Member of: Agricultural Research & Extension Council of Alberta
Chief Officer(s):
Karlah Rudolph, Coordinator, Extension/ASB
krudolph@gprc.ab.ca

Peace Curling Association (PCA)
PO Box 265, Grande Prairie AB T8V 3A4
Tel: 780-532-4782; *Fax:* 780-538-2485
peacecurl@telusplanet.net
www.peacecurl.org
Overview: A small local organization
Member of: Alberta Curling Federation; Canadian Curling Association
Chief Officer(s):
Bob Cooper, President
bcooper@png.ca
Dan Kleinschroth, Technical Director
dklein@telusplanet.net
Finances: *Annual Operating Budget:* Less than $50,000; *Funding Sources:* Casino
Staff Member(s): 1

Peace Parkland Naturalists
PO Box 1451, Grande Prairie AB T8V 4Z2
Tel: 780-539-6102
www.peacenaturalists.fanweb.ca
Overview: A small local organization founded in 1990
Mission: To promote awareness & appreciation of the natural history of the Peace Region of northwestern Alberta
Member of: Federation of Alberta Naturalists
Chief Officer(s):
Margot Hervieux, Contact
hervieux@telusplanet.net
Finances: *Annual Operating Budget:* Less than $50,000
Membership: 40; *Fees:* $10 individual; $15 family
Activities: Field trips; meetings
Publications:
• The Hooter [a publication of the Peace Parkland Naturalists]
Type: Newsletter
• Kleksun Hill: A Discovery Guide [a publication of the Peace Parkland Naturalists]
Type: Book; *Author:* Margot Hervieux; *Price:* $6

Peace Region Internet Society (PRIS)
929 - 106th Ave., Dawson Creek BC V1G 2N8
Tel: 250-782-5128; *Fax:* 250-782-2459
Toll-Free: 800-768-3311
Other Communication: Fort St. John Phone: 250-785-8877
pris@pris.ca
portal.pris.ca
Overview: A small local organization founded in 1994
Mission: To provide affordable Internet access for individuals, businesses, & organizations in the Peace Region of British Columbia
Chief Officer(s):
Travous Quibell, President
Anne Mah, Office Manager
acct@pris.ca

Peace River & District Chamber of Commerce
PO Box 6599, 9309 - 100 St., Peace River AB T8S 1S4
Tel: 780-624-4166; *Fax:* 780-624-4663
www.peaceriverchamber.com
Previous Name: Peace River Board of Trade
Overview: A small local organization founded in 1920
Mission: To promote & enhance the private enterprise in Peace River
Chief Officer(s):
Tony Nickonchuk, President
Michelle Snyder, General Manager
michelle@peaceriverchamber.com
Finances: *Funding Sources:* Municipal government; membership fees
Staff Member(s): 2; 40 volunteer(s)
Membership: 130; *Fees:* $125

Peace River Alaska Highway Tourism Association *See* Northern Rockies Alaska Highway Tourism Association

Peace River Board of Trade *See* Peace River & District Chamber of Commerce

Peace Valley Environment Association (PVEA)
PO Box 6062, Fort St John BC V1J 4H6
e-mail: pvea@shaw.ca
www.peacevalley.ca
twitter.com/SavePeaceValley
Overview: A small local organization
Mission: To protect and defend the natural environment of the Peace Valley area of British Columbia
Membership: *Fees:* $10

Peacebuild: The Canadian Peacebuilding Network
c/o Peggy Mason, Chair, #406, 575 Byron Ave., Ottawa ON K2A 1R7
Tel: 613-241-3446; *Fax:* 613-241-4846
info@peacebuild.ca
www.peacebuild.ca
www.facebook.com/Peacebuild1
twitter.com/Peacebuild1
www.youtube.com/user/peacebuild
Previous Name: Canadian Peacebuilding Coordinating Committee
Overview: A small national organization
Mission: To engender greater coherence & effectiveness in building peace through fostering collaboration & coordination amond diverse stakeholders in Canada, & partners overseas
Chief Officer(s):
Silke Reichrath, Coordinator
Finances: *Funding Sources:* The Canadian Partnerships Program, International Development Research Centre (IDRC)
Membership: *Fees:* $10 student; $50 individual; $100 coalition; $200 organization
Activities: Working Groups: Small Arms; Children & Conflict; Gender & Peacebuilding; Conflict Prevention; Peace Operations

Peace-Laird Regional Arts Council (PLRAC)
PO Box 337, Hudson's Hope BC V0C 1V0
Tel: 250-783-9351
tacsote@pris.ca
www.peaceliardarts.org
Overview: A small local charitable organization founded in 1989
Mission: To assist with the promotional growth of the arts community in the Peace-Laird; involved in promoting, encouraging, offering help & guidance, & coordinating all the communities in the region
Member of: Assembly of BC Arts Councils; Canadian Conference of the Arts; BC Touring Council
Chief Officer(s):
Patricia Markin, Chair
Finances: *Annual Operating Budget:* $50,000-$100,000; *Funding Sources:* Regional & provincial government
Staff Member(s): 1; 10 volunteer(s)
Membership: 20; *Fees:* $35 or $15 every member group; *Member Profile:* Made up of members from Arts Councils within each community
Activities: Grants include activity & special events; arts collection, training & assistance; arts development
Awards:
• HRT Collection Award (Award)

Peachland Chamber of Commerce
5684 Beach Ave., Peachland BC V0H 1X6
Tel: 250-767-2422; *Fax:* 250-767-2420
peachlandchamber@gmail.com
www.peachlandchamber.bc.ca
www.facebook.com/chamberpeachland
twitter.com/PeachlandChambe
Overview: A small local organization founded in 1999
Mission: To encourage & strengthen business activity through the collective actions of its members for the benefit of the community at large
Member of: BC Chamber of Commerce; Canadian Chamber of Commerce
Chief Officer(s):
Patrick Van Minsel, Executive Director
Finances: *Funding Sources:* Membership dues; municipal
Membership: *Fees:* Schedule available

Peachland Food Bank
6490 Keyes Ave., Peachland BC V0H 1X0
Tel: 250-767-3312
Overview: A small local organization overseen by Food Banks British Columbia
Member of: Food Banks British Columbia
Chief Officer(s):
Judy Bedford, Contact

PEDVAC Foundation (PEDVAC)
12 Church St., Port Elgin NB E4M 2C9
Tel: 506-538-7638; *Fax:* 506-538-7638
pedvacfoundation@nb.aibn.com
www.pedvac.com
www.facebook.com/pages/Pedvac-Foundation
Previous Name: Port Elgin District Voluntary Action Group Inc.
Overview: A small local organization founded in 1988
Mission: To enable individuals & groups to create, maintain & extend throughout the community an improved quality of life
Member of: Association of Food Banks & C.V.A.'s for New Brunswick; Canadian Association of Food Banks; Laubach Literacy Canada & New Brunswick
Chief Officer(s):
Val MacDermid, Executive Director
Finances: *Annual Operating Budget:* $100,000-$250,000; *Funding Sources:* Government grants; fundraising; donations
Staff Member(s): 5; 200 volunteer(s)
Activities: After School Homework Assistance Program; Hot School Lunch Program; Food Bank; Tax Return Preparation for Seniors & Low Income Individuals; Used clothing & household goods boutique
Awards:
• Milton F. Gregg Conservation Award (Award)
• New Brunswick Family Award (Award)

Peel Committee Against Woman Abuse (PCAWA)
PO Box 45070, Mississauga ON L5G 1C9
Tel: 905-823-3441; *Fax:* 905-823-9695
pcawa@pcawa.org

www.pcawa.org
www.linkedin.com/company/2882034
www.facebook.com/321162981322389
twitter.com/PCAWA1
www.youtube.com/user/PCAWA
Overview: A small local organization founded in 1984
Mission: To promote a comprehensive & effective response to woman abuse in the region of Peel
Finances: *Funding Sources:* United Way; Region of Peel; Government of Ontario; Neighbours, Friends and Families

Peel Dufferin Catholic Services ***See*** Catholic Family Services of Peel Dufferin

Peel Family Services

#501, 151 City Centre Dr., Mississauga ON L5B 1M7
Tel: 905-270-2250; *Fax:* 905-270-2869
fsp@fspeel.org
www.fspeel.org
Also Known As: Family Services of Peel
Overview: A medium-sized local organization overseen by Family Service Ontario
Member of: Family Service Canada; Ontario Association of Credit CounsellingServices
Chief Officer(s):
Chuck MacLean, Executive Director
cmaclean@fspeel.org

Peel HIV/AIDS Network

#1, 160 Traders Blvd., Mississauga ON L4Z 3K7
Tel: 905-361-0523; *Fax:* 905-361-1004
Toll-Free: 866-896-8700
info@phan.ca
www.phan.ca
www.facebook.com/group.php?gid=52615398400
www.flickr.com/photos/31432883@N05/
Overview: A small local organization
Chief Officer(s):
Keith Wong, Executive Director
keithw@phan.ca
Membership: *Fees:* $20 contributing; $50 corporate; $50 bronze; $100 silver; $250 gold; $500 hero

Peel Law Association (PLA)

#160, 7755 Hurontario St., Brampton ON L6W 4T1
Tel: 905-451-2924; *Fax:* 905-451-3137
Toll-Free: 866-228-0235
info@plalawyers.ca
www.peellawassn.ca
Overview: A small local organization founded in 1947
Mission: To promote, protect & advance the interests of its members by providing resources to enhance the practice of law
Chief Officer(s):
Rajneesh K. Sharda, President
Staff Member(s): 2; 15 volunteer(s)
Membership: 500-999; *Fees:* $70-$170; $50 student; *Member Profile:* Lawyers in good standing with the Law Society of Upper Canada with offices in Peel; *Committees:* Executive; financial; personnel; membership; strategic planning; governence; key objectives; social activities
Activities: *Speaker Service:* Yes

Peel Multicultural Council (PMC)

6630 Turner Valley Rd., Mississauga ON L5N 2P1
Tel: 905-819-1144; *Fax:* 905-542-3950
pmcgeneral@peelmc.com
www.peelmc.com
www.facebook.com/profile.php?id=15988712827
www.youtube.com/peelpmc
Overview: A small local charitable organization founded in 1977 overseen by Ontario Council of Agencies Serving Immigrants
Mission: To promote a harmonious multicultural society by increasing communication & by building bridges of understanding between ethocultural groups, institutions, & the community; To facilitate the settlement & integration of newcomers to Canada
Affliation(s): Parks & Recreation Mississauga; Parks & Recreation Brampton
Chief Officer(s):
Joyce Rodriguez, President
Naveed Chaudhdry, Executive Director
Finances: *Annual Operating Budget:* $250,000-$500,000
Staff Member(s): 9; 98 volunteer(s)
Membership: 150 groups + 350 individuals; *Fees:* $10 individual; $20 group; *Committees:* Housing; Membership; Advocacy; Public Relations; Cultural & Social; Personnel
Activities: Public education on race relations, equity, settlement of immigrants; ESL classes; community development; *Library* Open to public

Peel Music Festival

PO Box 70083, Stn. Fletcher's Creek, Brampton ON L7A 0N6
Tel: 647-282-7335
admin@peelmusicfestival.ca
www.peelmusicfestival.ca
Overview: A small local organization founded in 1927
Mission: A music competition for young performers, the festival is a not-for-profit organization run by volunteer music teachers.
Member of: Ontario Music Festivals Association Inc.
Finances: *Funding Sources:* Ontario Trillium Foundation

Peel Regional Police Association (PRPA) / Association des policiers de la région de Peel

10675 Mississauga Rd., Brampton ON L7A 0B6
Tel: 905-846-0615; *Fax:* 905-846-0649
admin@peelpa.on.ca
www.peelpa.on.ca
Overview: A medium-sized local organization founded in 1974
Mission: To represent the uniform & civilian members of Ontario's Peel Regional Police; To promote the mutual interests of members; To elevate the standards of police services
Chief Officer(s):
Bruce Chapman, Chair
bchapman@peelpa.on.ca
Wayne Omardeen, President
womardeen@peelpa.on.ca
Lynn Dobson, Chief Administrative Officer
ldobson@peelpa.on.ca
Finances: *Funding Sources:* Banquet hall rental fees; Store sales
Staff Member(s): 2
Membership: 2,700; *Member Profile:* Uniform & civilian members of the Peel Regional Police
Activities: Supporting charities

PeerNetBC

#408, 602 West Hastings, Vancouver BC V6B 1P2
Tel: 604-733-6186
info@peernetbc.com
www.peernetbc.com
www.linkedin.com/company/peernetbc
www.facebook.com/PeerNetBC
twitter.com/PeerNetBC
Previous Name: Self-Help Resource Association of British Columbia
Overview: A medium-sized provincial charitable organization founded in 1986
Mission: To promote peer support approaches that build the capacity of individuals, & therefore communities, to become healthy, responsive & self-determining
Chief Officer(s):
Romi Chandra Herbert, Co-Executive Director
Iris Yong Pearson, Co-Executive Director
Finances: *Funding Sources:* Provincial government; Foundations; Membership dues
Staff Member(s): 5
Membership: *Member Profile:* Individuals interested in & supportive of self-help/mutual aid
Activities: Central resource centre & self-help library; Group development & facilitator training; Public education & outreach; Production of annual directory of self-help groups; Self-help/community development; Information & referral service; Youth outreach & facilitator training; *Library:* SHRA Resource Centre; Open to public

PEERS Victoria Resource Society

#1, 744 Fairview Rd., Victoria BC V9A 4V1
Tel: 250-388-5325; *Fax:* 250-388-5324
info@peers.bc.ca
peers.bc.ca
www.facebook.com/pages/Peers-Victoria/168869749809046
twitter.com/#peersvictoria
Overview: A small local organization
Mission: PEERS is a non-profit society established by former sex workers and community supporters and is dedicated to the empowerment, education and support of sex workers, by working to improve their safety and working conditions, assisting those who desire to leave the sex industry, increasing public understanding and awareness of these issues, and promoting the experiential voice.
Chief Officer(s):
Marion Little, Executive Director
ed@peers.bc.ca
Activities: Education; outreach programs;

P.E.I. Cattlemen's Association ***See*** Prince Edward Island Cattle Producers

PEI Cricket Association (PEI-CA)

Stratford PE
cricketpei.org
www.facebook.com/375538377835
Overview: A small provincial organization founded in 2010 overseen by Cricket Canada
Mission: To promote the development of cricket in Prince Edward Island.
Member of: Cricket Canada
Chief Officer(s):
Chandrasekere Sarath, President
Richard Raiswell, Director, Communications
Membership: 100; *Fees:* $20

PEI Field Hockey Association

40 Enman Cres., Charlottetown PE C1A 1E6
Tél: 902-368-4110; *Téléc:* 902-368-4548
Ligne sans frais: 800-247-6712
sports@sportpei.pe.ca
Aperçu: *Dimension:* moyenne; *Envergure:* provinciale surveillé par Field Hockey Canada
Membre(s) du bureau directeur:
Barb Carmichael, President, 902-566-4056
bcarmichael@eastlink.ca

PEI Music Festival Association ***See*** Prince Edward Island Kiwanis Music Festival Association

PEI Powerlifting Association (PEIPLA)

PE
www.peipowerlifting.ca
Overview: A small provincial organization founded in 1996 overseen by Canadian Powerlifting Union
Member of: Canadian Powerlifting Union
Affliation(s): Canadian Powerlifting Union; International Powerlifting Federation
Chief Officer(s):
John MacDonald, President
john@peipowerlifting.ca
Membership: *Fees:* $70 regular; $40 high school; *Committees:* Fundraising; Competition & Promotion; Selection & Grant

PEI Roadbuilders Association ***See*** Prince Edward Island Roadbuilders & Heavy Construction Association

PEI Sailing Association (PEISA)

c/o Ellen MacPhail, PO Box 6708, York Point PE C0A 1H0
www.peisailing.com
Overview: A medium-sized provincial organization overseen by Sail Canada
Mission: The PEI Sailing Association is a volunteer organization that promotes sailing in the province of Prince Edward Island, Canada. As the provincial chapter of the Canadian Sailing Association the PEI Sailing Association provides support and training to anybody interested in learning to sail or expanding their sailing.
Member of: Sail Canada
Chief Officer(s):
Ellen McPhail, Executive Director

PEI Special Olympics ***See*** Special Olympics Prince Edward Island

PEI Tuberculosis League ***See*** Prince Edward Island Lung Association

Pelham Historical Society

PO Box 903, Fonthill ON L0S 1E0
Overview: A small local organization founded in 1975
Affliation(s): Ontario Historical Society
Chief Officer(s):
Robert Young, President
Mary Lamb, Collections Coordinator
mblamb@sympatico.ca

Pemberton & District Chamber of Commerce

PO Box 370, Pemberton BC V0N 2L0
Tel: 604-894-6477; *Fax:* 604-894-5571
info@pembertonchamber.com
www.pembertonchamber.com
www.facebook.com/PembertonCofC
twitter.com/pemchamber
Overview: A small local organization founded in 1932

Mission: To promote the commercial, industrial, agricultural & welfare of Pemberton & the surrounding area
Member of: Vancouver Coast & Mountains Tourism Region; B.C. Chamber of Commerce; Tourism Pemberton
Affliation(s): Vancouver Board of Trade
Chief Officer(s):
Karen Ross, President
Shirley Henry, Secretary-Treasurer
Finances: *Annual Operating Budget:* Less than $50,000; *Funding Sources:* Membership dues; fundraising; grants
Staff Member(s): 2; 2 volunteer(s)
Membership: 149; *Fees:* $150-$200 business; $55 individual/non-profit; *Committees:* Visitor Centre; Design Review; Business Development; Events; Tourism Pemberton; Fundraising
Activities: Visitor Centre; barn dance; golf tournament; dinners; workshops; events

The Pembina Institute

219 - 19 St. NW, Calgary AB T2N 2H9
Tel: 403-269-3344; *Fax:* 403-269-3377
www.pembina.org
Overview: A medium-sized provincial charitable organization founded in 1985
Mission: To develop & promote public policy & educational programs which protect the environment & encourage environmentally sound resource management strategies; to implement a conserver society
Member of: Canadian Renewable Energy Alliance
Chief Officer(s):
Ed Whittingham, Executive Director, 403-537-0579
Staff Member(s): 16
Membership: 32
Activities: Major program areas include Environmental Education & Publishing (teacher professional development; national environmental education resource cataloguing service; curricular materials for schools; classroom presentations & student workshops; community adult environmental education courses); Research, Development & Promotion of Environmental Policy (analyzing & developing municipal, provincial & federal energy-related environmental policy, as well as policy related to other conservation & recycling issues; *Speaker Service:* Yes; *Library* Open to public by appointment

Pembroke & Area Chamber of Commerce *See* Upper Ottawa Valley Chamber of Commerce

Pembroke & District Association for Community Living *See* Community Living Upper Ottawa Valley

Pembroke Area Field Naturalists (PAFN)

PO Box 1242, Pembroke ON K8A 6Y6
www.pafn.on.ca
Overview: A small local charitable organization founded in 1983
Member of: Federation of Ontario Naturalists
Chief Officer(s):
Leo Boland, President
leoboland@pafn.on.ca
Finances: *Annual Operating Budget:* Less than $50,000; *Funding Sources:* Donations; fundraising
Membership: 50; *Fees:* $15 individual; $20 family; $10 student/senior
Activities: Nature walks; bird & insect counts; fundraisers

Pembroke District Construction Association (PDCA)

1145 Pembroke St. West, Pembroke ON K8A 7R4
Tel: 613-732-7311
Overview: A small local organization founded in 1960
Chief Officer(s):
Ken Day, Contact

Pembroke Kiwanis Music Festival

PO Box 1093, Pembroke ON K8A 6Y6
Tel: 613-735-7773
www.pembrokekiwanis.org
Overview: A small local organization founded in 1948
Affliation(s): Kiwanis Club of Pembroke
Chief Officer(s):
Lloyd Koch, President, Kiwanis Pembroke
Susan Fisher, Secretary
fisher@nrtco.net
Finances: *Annual Operating Budget:* Less than $50,000
80 volunteer(s)
Membership: 20
Activities: Kiwanis Music Festival

Pembroke Symphony Orchestra

PO Box 374, Pembroke ON K8A 6X6
Tel: 613-587-4826
pembrokesymphony.org
Overview: A small local organization overseen by Orchestras Canada
Chief Officer(s):
Angus Armstrong, Music Director
Gail Marion, President
bluroom@nrtco.net
Membership: *Fees:* $75; $30 student

Pender Harbour & Egmont Chamber of Commerce

Madeira Park, PO Box 265, Madeira Park BC V0N 2H0
Tel: 604-883-2561; *Fax:* 604-883-2561
Toll-Free: 877-873-6337
chamber@penderharbour.ca
www.penderharbour.ca
Overview: A small local organization founded in 1928
Member of: BC Chamber of Commerce
Chief Officer(s):
Kerry Milligan, Secretary
Dave Milligan, President
Finances: *Annual Operating Budget:* Less than $50,000; *Funding Sources:* Membership dues
Staff Member(s): 1; 5 volunteer(s)
Membership: 87; *Fees:* $40-$135
Activities: Operates the Pender Harbour Information Centre, Information & Tourist Sign Boards

Pender Island Chamber of Commerce

PO Box 123, Pender Island BC V0N 2M0
Tel: 250-629-3988
Toll-Free: 866-468-7924
travel@penderislandchamber.com
www.penderislandchamber.com
www.facebook.com/155758237803188
twitter.com/penderchamber
Overview: A small local organization

Pender Island Field Naturalists (PIFN)

1105 Ogden Rd., Pender Island BC V0N 2M1
Overview: A small local organization
Membership: 1-99; *Fees:* $18/year; *Member Profile:* Birding & botany enthusiasts

Peninsula Field Naturalists (PFN)

PO Box 23031, Stn. Carlton, St Catharines ON L2R 7P6
Tel: 905-892-2566
info@peninsulafieldnats.com
peninsulafieldnats.com
Overview: A small local charitable organization founded in 1954
Mission: To promote the enjoyment of nature through environmental appreciation & conservation; to encourage wise use & conservation of natural resources; to promote environmental protection
Member of: Ontario Nature
Chief Officer(s):
Bob Highcock, President
Finances: *Funding Sources:* Membership fees
Membership: *Fees:* $10 student; $25 adult; $35 family; *Member Profile:* Interest in natural history
Activities: Outdoor natural history walks; annual park clean-up; annual bird & plant inventories

The Pennsylvania German Folklore Society of Ontario

c/o York Chapter, 10292 McCowan Rd., Markham ON L3P 3J3
Tel: 905-640-3906; *Fax:* 905-640-9394
www.pennsylvania-german-folklore-society.com
Overview: A small provincial organization founded in 1951
Mission: To research, record, interpret history of the Town of Markham
Chief Officer(s):
Ralph Shantz, President
Finances: *Annual Operating Budget:* Less than $50,000
Membership: 250; *Fees:* $13 single; $20 family

Pension Investment Association of Canada (PIAC) / Association canadienne des gestionnaires de fonds de retraite

#123, 20 Carlton St., Toronto ON M5B 2H5
Tel: 416-640-0264
www.piacweb.org
Overview: A medium-sized national organization founded in 1977
Mission: To promote the financial security of pension fund beneficiaries through sound investment policy & practices
Chief Officer(s):
Peter Waite, Executive Director
Finances: *Annual Operating Budget:* $250,000-$500,000; *Funding Sources:* Membership fees
Membership: 130 pension funds; *Fees:* Schedule available; *Member Profile:* Pension fund employees who have investment responsibilities at their respective pension funds/organizations
Awards:
• Chuck Harvie Award (Award)
• Terry Staples Award (Award)

Pentathlon Alberta

AB
e-mail: info@pentathlonalberta.com
www.pentathlonalberta.com
Previous Name: Alberta Modern Pentathlon Association
Overview: A small provincial organization
Mission: To develop world-class athletes while promoting & developing the sport in Alberta.
Member of: Canadian Modern Pentathlon Association
Chief Officer(s):
Deb Langvand, President
Membership: 4 local clubs/groups

Pentathlon Canada

70 Como Gardens, Hudson QC J0P 1H0
Tel: 450-458-7974; *Fax:* 450-458-1746
www.pentathloncanada.ca
www.facebook.com/PentathlonCanada
Previous Name: Canadian Modern Pentathlon Association
Overview: A medium-sized national charitable organization
Mission: To promote Modern Pentathlon in Canada
Affliation(s): Union internationale de pentathlon moderne et biathlon
Chief Officer(s):
Angela Ives, President
president@pentathloncanada.ca
Mike Davis, Vice-President
Media & Communications
Bob Noble, Vice-President & Director, High Performance
Colin Peace, Vice-President & Chair, Technical Committee
Membership: 2,000;

Pentecostal Assemblies of Canada (PAOC) / Assemblées de la Pentecôte du Canada

2450 Milltower Ct., Mississauga ON L5N 5Z6
Tel: 905-542-7400; *Fax:* 905-542-7313
info@paoc.org
www.paoc.org
www.facebook.com/ThePAOC
twitter.com/thepaoc
www.youtube.com/paoctube
Overview: A large national charitable organization founded in 1919
Mission: PAOC makes disciples everywhere by the proclamation & practice of the gospel of Christ in the power of the Holy Spirit with the goal to establish local congregations & to train spiritual leaders.
Affliation(s): World Pentecost; Pentecostal/Charismatic Churches of North America; Pentecostal World Fellowship; World Assemblies of God Fellowship; Focus on the Family; Canadian Foodgrains Bank; Pentecostal European Mission; Seeds International; VisionLEDD; Canadian Council of Christian Charities; Every Home for Christ; Evangelical Missiological Society; Evangelical Fellowship of Canada; Canadian Children's Ministries Network; Canadian Bible Society; Family Life Ministries; Society of Pentecostal Studies
Chief Officer(s):
David Wells, General Superintendent
David Hazzard, Asst. Superintendent, Fellowship Services
Murray Cornelius, Asst. Superintendent, International Missions
Finances: *Annual Operating Budget:* Greater than $5 Million; *Funding Sources:* Local churches; individuals
Staff Member(s): 50
Membership: 1,100 churches, 3,500 pastors representing 236,000 parishoners; *Committees:* General Executive; Administrative; International Missions; Audit; Credentials
Activities: Task Force; Work Force; Volunteers in Mission; Short-Term Missions; Volunteers in Special Assignment; ERDO (Emergency Relief & Development Overseas); Child Care Plus; *Library:* The PAOC Archives; Open to public by appointment
Meetings/Conferences: • 2016 Bienniel Conference of the Pentecostal Assemblies of Canada, May, 2016, Palais des congrès de Montréal, Montréal, QC
Scope: National
Publications:
• Testimony [a publication of Pentecostal Assemblies of Canada]

Type: Magazine; *Frequency:* Bimonthly; *Editor:* Stephen Kennedy; *Price:* $2.50

Alberta & Northwest Territories Office
Vanguard College, 12140 - 103 St. NW, 2nd Fl., West Wing, Edmonton AB T5G 2J9
Tel: 780-426-0018; *Fax:* 780-420-1318
abnwt.com
Chief Officer(s):
Ken Solbrekken, District Superintendent

British Columbia & Yukon District Office
20411 Douglas Cres., Langley BC V3A 4B6
Tel: 604-533-2232; *Fax:* 604-533-5405
info@bc.paoc.org
www.bc.paoc.org
www.facebook.com/pages/BC-Yukon-PAOC-District/1187659 74838094
twitter.com/bcydist
www.flickr.com/photos/bcydnet
Chief Officer(s):
Ken Russell, District Superintendent

Eastern Ontario District Office
PO Box 337, Cobourg ON K9A 4K8
Tel: 905-373-7374; *Fax:* 905-373-1911
info@eod.paoc.org
www.eod.paoc.org
Chief Officer(s):
Craig Burton, District Superintendent

Manitoba & Northwest Ontario District Office
187 Henlow Bay, Winnipeg MB R3Y 1G4
Tel: 204-940-1000; *Fax:* 204-940-1009
paoc.net
Chief Officer(s):
Jim S. Poirier, District Superintendent

Maritime District Office
PO Box 1184, Truro NS B2N 5H1
Tel: 902-895-4212; *Fax:* 902-897-0705
maritimepaoc.org
twitter.com/MaritimePAOC
Chief Officer(s):
Kevin Johnson, District Superintendent

Québec District Office
839, rue La Salle, Longueuil QC J4K 3G6
Tel: 450-442-2732; *Fax:* 450-442-3818
info@dq.paoc.org
www.dqpaoc.org
Chief Officer(s):
Michel Bisaillon, District Superintendent

Saskatchewan District Office
1303 Jackson Ave., Saskatoon SK S7H 2M9
Tel: 306-683-4646; *Fax:* 306-683-3699
www.skpaoc.com
www.youtube.com/channel/UCFXk7ls11W2p0NNYarBwBkQ
Chief Officer(s):
John Drisner, District Superintendent

Western Ontario District Office
3214 South Service Rd., Burlington ON L7N 3J2
Tel: 905-637-5566; *Fax:* 905-637-7558
reception@wodistrict.org
www.wodistrict.org
Chief Officer(s):
Lorrie Gibbons, District Superintendent

The Pentecostal Assemblies of Newfoundland & Labrador (PAONL)

PO Box 8895, Stn. A, 57 Thorburn Rd., St. John's NL A1B 3T2
Tel: 709-753-6314; *Fax:* 709-753-4945
info@paonl.ca
www.paonl.ca
www.facebook.com/252330011920
twitter.com/paonl
Overview: A medium-sized provincial charitable organization founded in 1911
Mission: To promote evangelism, world missions, famine relief, & education
Affliation(s): Pentecostal Fellowship of North America
Chief Officer(s):
Calvin T. Andrews, General Superintendent
Finances: *Annual Operating Budget:* $1.5 Million-$3 Million
Membership: 40,000
Activities: *Internships:* Yes; *Speaker Service:* Yes; *Library* by appointment

Penticton & District Community Arts Council

220 Manor Park Ave., Penticton BC V2A 2R2
Tel: 250-492-7997; *Fax:* 250-492-7969
arts_council@shawcable.com
www.pentictonartscouncil.com
www.facebook.com/Penticton.council
twitter.com/PentictonArtCou
Also Known As: Leir House Cultural Centre
Overview: A medium-sized local organization founded in 1960
Mission: To increase & broaden the opportunities for public enjoyment of & participation in cultural activities; to help co-ordinate the work & programmes of cultural groups; to act as a clearing house for information on cultural projects & activities
Member of: Assembly of BC Arts Councils
Chief Officer(s):
George Traicheff, President
Jane Shaak, Vice-President
Finances: *Funding Sources:* Rentals; grants; fundraising
Staff Member(s): 2
Membership: 240; *Fees:* $15 individual; $25 family; $35 group; $45 business; $100 corporate; *Member Profile:* Local arts groups & societies; individuals & families; businesses

Penticton & District Community Resources Society (PDCRS)

330 Ellis St., Penticton BC V2A 4L7
Tel: 250-492-5814; *Fax:* 250-492-7572
pdcrs@vip.net
www.pdcrs.com
Overview: A small local organization founded in 1966
Mission: To help people achieve their maximum independence & potential through effective & efficient delivery of services
Member of: BC Association for Community Living; Child Welfare League; Federation of Child & Family Services; United Community Services Coop.
Chief Officer(s):
Craig Cunningham, Executive Director
Finances: *Annual Operating Budget:* $3 Million-$5 Million
Staff Member(s): 70; 20 volunteer(s)
Membership: 25; *Fees:* $2
Activities: After-School Program; child care resource & referral; community services office; family enhancement programs; FAS/FAE Project; Hand In Hand Infant/Toddler Centre; handyDART service; Little Trimphs Pre-School; parenting after separation; Penticton Alternate School; Penticton Family Centre; Penticton Paper Shuffle; Reconnect; residential services; sexual abuse treatment program; special services to children; supported child care; The Club; Lazy Lizard Fair; *Awareness Events:* Community Living Month

Penticton & District Multicultural Society *See* South Okanagan Immigrant & Community Services

Penticton & District Society for Community Living (PDSCL)

180 Industrial Ave. West, Penticton BC V2A 6X9
Tel: 250-493-0312; *Fax:* 250-493-9113
admin@pdscl.org
www.pdscl.org
Overview: A small local charitable organization founded in 1958
Mission: Serves vulnerable persons & families with physical or developmental disabilites &/or economic disadvantages; provides community based day & residential supports, affordable housing, outreach services & education
Member of: British Columbia Association for Commmunity Living
Chief Officer(s):
Tony Laing, Executive Director
Finances: *Annual Operating Budget:* $3 Million-$5 Million
Staff Member(s): 50; 25 volunteer(s)
Membership: 22; *Fees:* $5

Penticton & Wine Country Chamber of Commerce

#8, 273 Power St., Penticton BC V2A 7K9
Tel: 250-492-4103; *Fax:* 250-492-6119
Toll-Free: 800-663-5052
admin@penticton.org
www.penticton.org
www.facebook.com/200338503334345
twitter.com/PentChamber
Overview: A medium-sized local organization founded in 1907
Member of: BC Chamber of Commerce; Canadian Chamber of Commerce
Chief Officer(s):
Judy Poole, Manager
Joe Morelli, President
Finances: *Annual Operating Budget:* $250,000-$500,000; *Funding Sources:* Membership dues; publishing; sponsorship; provincial & municipal government
Staff Member(s): 9; 10 volunteer(s)
Membership: 700; *Fees:* $187.25
Activities: *Rents Mailing List:* Yes

Penticton Geology & Lapidary Club

426 Woodruff Ave., Penticton BC V2A 2H5
Tel: 250-493-1027
Overview: A small local organization founded in 1959
Affliation(s): British Columbia Lapidary Society
Chief Officer(s):
Gloria Bordass, Contact
Activities: Hosting monthly meetings; *Awareness Events:* Penticton Geology & Lapidary Club Gem Show

People First of Canada (PFC) / Personnes d'abord du Canada

#5, 120 Maryland St., Winnipeg MB R3G 1L1
Tel: 204-784-7362; *Fax:* 204-784-7364
info@peoplefirstofcanada.ca
www.peoplefirstofcanada.ca
www.facebook.com/10150117531825354
Previous Name: National People First
Overview: A small national organization founded in 1981
Mission: To educate the public on issues faced by persons with intellectual disabilities; To promote equality; To work toward the deinstitutionalization of persons with intellectual disabilities
Chief Officer(s):
Shelley Rattai, Executive Director
srattai@peoplefirstofcanada.ca
Richard Ruston, President
Catherine Rodgers, Coordinator, Community Inclusion & Resources
crodgers@peoplefirstofcanada.ca
Heather Tracey, Treasurer
Activities: Increasing awareness of issues encountered by people with intellectual disabilities, such as discrimination, segregation, unemployment, & poverty; Providing information, education, training; Advocating for persons labelled with intellectual disabilities
Meetings/Conferences: • People First of Canada 2015 24th Annual General Meeting & Conference, 2015
Scope: National
Description: A meeting for People First representatives from across Canada, featuring the presentation of awards

People with AIDS Foundation *See* Toronto PWA Foundation

People's Alliance of New Brunswick

76 Creek Rd., Dow Settlement NB E6H 2G9
Tel: 506-279-2255
kaustin@rogers.com
www.peoplesalliancenb.com
Overview: A small provincial organization
Chief Officer(s):
Kris Austin, Party Leader
Membership: *Fees:* $10

People's Front

#18, 3370, Dewdney Trunk Rd., Port Moody BC V3H 2E3
Tel: 604-949-0777; *Fax:* 604-949-0777
Overview: A small provincial organization overseen by Marxist-Leninist Party Of Canada
Chief Officer(s):
Charles Boylan, Party Leader

People's Law School

#150, 900 Howe St., Vancouver BC V6Z 2M4
Tel: 604-331-5400; *Fax:* 604-331-5401
info@publiclegaled.bc.ca
www.publiclegaled.bc.ca
www.linkedin.com/company/2024453?trk=tyah
www.facebook.com/pages/Peoples-Law-School-BC/1813663719 05105
twitter.com/PLSBC
www.youtube.com/user/plsbc
Overview: A small provincial organization founded in 1972
Mission: To make law & the legal system understandable & accessible to residents of British Columbia
Member of: Public Legal Education Association of Canada
Affliation(s): Battered Women's Support Center; BC Center for Elder Advocacy and Support; Bully Free BC; Clicklaw; BC Chamber of Commerce; CourtHouse Libraries; Immigrant Public Legal Education and Information Consortium (IPC); Justice Education Society; The Law Foundation of British Columbia; British Columbia Ministry of Justice; Notary Foundation; PovNet; Public Legal Education Association of Canada (PLEAC); Public Legal Education and Information Working Group (PLEIWG);

Tenant Resource and Advisory Centre (TRAC); Vancouver Community Network (VCN)
Chief Officer(s):
Terresa Augustine, Executive Director
Staff Member(s): 6
Activities: Publishing & distributing plain language legal information in multiple formats such as print, online books, fact sheets & video; Offering public legal education through hands-on workshops, lectures & Justice Theatre; Providing referral services as well as a reading & resource room for the public; *Awareness Events:* Legal@Lunch; Public Legal Aid in the Community

People's Memorial Society *See* People's Memorial Society of BC & Vancouver Island Memorial Society

People's Memorial Society of BC & Vancouver Island Memorial Society
PO Box 505, Stn. Main, Vernon BC V1T 9Z9
Fax: 250-558-3552
Toll-Free: 800-661-3358
info@peoplesmemorialsocietybc.com
www.peoplesmemorialsocietybc.com
Previous Name: People's Memorial Society
Overview: A small local organization founded in 1991
Membership: 15,000; *Fees:* $10 lifetime

People's Senate Party *See* Unparty: The Consensus-Building Party

People, Words & Change (PWC) / Monde des mots
Heartwood House, 153 Chapel St., Ottawa ON K1N 1H5
Tel: 613-234-2494; *Fax:* 613-234-4223
dee@pwc-ottawa.ca
www.nald.ca/pwc
Overview: A small local charitable organization founded in 1979
Mission: To teach adults to read & write in English
Member of: Ottawa-Carleton Coalition for Literacy
Chief Officer(s):
Dee Sullivan, Coordinator
Finances: *Annual Operating Budget:* $100,000-$250,000; *Funding Sources:* Provincial government; donations
130 volunteer(s)
Membership: 275; *Member Profile:* Interest in literacy
Activities: *Library*

Peretz Centre for Secular Jewish Culture
6184 Ash St., Vancouver BC V5Z 3G9
Tel: 604-325-1812; *Fax:* 604-325-2470
info@peretz-centre.org
www.peretz-centre.org
Previous Name: Vancouver Peretz Institute; Vancouver Peretz Shule
Overview: A small local organization founded in 1945
Mission: To preserve Jewish secular humanistic culture & thought; To provide a broad range of educational & cultural programs for all ages, with secular humanist Yidishkayt at the core
Affliation(s): International Federation of Secular Humanistic Jews; Congress of Secular Jewish Organizations; Jewish Federation of Greater Vancouver
Chief Officer(s):
Gene Homel, President
Finances: *Funding Sources:* Membership fees; Donations; Banquet hall, auditorium, & meeting room rentals
Membership: *Fees:* $65 students & seniors; $120 individuals; $160 single parent families; $230 families; *Member Profile:* Persons with Jewish family ties in the Greater Vancouver area
Activities: Offering classes for children, in Jewish heritage, tradition, & culture, to help them develop their Jewish identity; Providing B'nai (Bar / Bas) Mitzvah classes & Yiddish classes; Organizing an Yiddish Reading Circle; Coordinating a seniors' group; Offering bursaries; Administrating the Vancouver Jewish Folk Choir; Operating a Kirman English & Yiddish Library; *Library:* The Kirman Library at the Peretz Centre
Publications:
- Peretz Papers

Type: Newsletter; *Frequency:* Bimonthly
Profile: Executive reports & notices of upcoming events

Performing Arts BC
PO Box 22042, Penticton BC V2A 8L1
Tel: 250-493-7279; *Fax:* 250-493-7279
festival@bcprovincials.com
www.bcprovincials.com
Previous Name: BC Association of Performing Arts Festivals
Overview: A medium-sized provincial organization founded in 1964 overseen by Federation of Canadian Music Festivals
Chief Officer(s):
Antonia Mahon, Executive Director
Membership: 34 performing arts festivals
Activities: Provincial level performing arts festival

Performing Arts NB, Inc. (PANB)
Brunswick Sq., 3rd Level, 39 King St., Saint John NB E2L 4W3
Tel: 506-635-8019; *Fax:* 506-657-7832
www.nbinfo.ca
WWW.FACEBOOK.COM/PAGES/pERFORMING-aRTS-nb-panb/127945243882172
Previous Name: New Brunswick Arts Council Inc.
Overview: A medium-sized provincial charitable organization founded in 1979
Mission: To achieve the vision of New Brunswick as a place where all residents attend a diversity of quality, live performances in their own community; all students attend performances in their own school by performing artists; artists residing in New Brunswick find a supportive arts community & the resources necessary to establish a career in the performing arts in New Brunswick & beyond; maintain a resource centre; assume an advocacy for the performing arts in the community
Member of: Canadian Conference of the Arts
Chief Officer(s):
Nancy Schell, Executive Director
Nicole L. Gallant, President
Finances: *Annual Operating Budget:* Less than $50,000; *Funding Sources:* Government grants; membership dues; blockbooking fees
Staff Member(s): 1; 20 volunteer(s)
Membership: 50 organizations; *Fees:* Schedule available; *Member Profile:* NB presenters, performers, musicians' unions, NB schools, arts councils, arts organizations, towns & municipalites, marketing & promotions firms; *Committees:* Executive; Membership; Nominations; Booking Services; Sponsorship & Fundraising
Activities: Coordination of provincial performing arts tours; coordination of NB school performances, young audience community performing arts series, promotion of the performing arts in NB; speakers series; booking services;

Periodical Marketers of Canada (PMC)
South Tower, #1007, 175 Bloor St. East, Toronto ON M4W 3R8
Tel: 416-968-7547; *Fax:* 416-968-6281
info@periodical.ca
www.periodical.ca
Overview: A medium-sized national organization founded in 1942 overseen by Book & Periodical Council
Mission: To represent Canadian wholesalers; To promote Canadian magazines
Member of: Book & Periodical Council
Chief Officer(s):
Ray Argyle, Executive Director
rargyle@periodical.ca
Finances: *Funding Sources:* Grants
Membership: *Member Profile:* Canadian wholesalers of periodicals
Activities: Sponsoring National Magazine Awards
Awards:
- Authors Award (Award)
- Book of the Year Award (Award)
- Authors Award for Leadership (Award)
- Canadian Letters Award (Award)

Periodical Writers Association of Canada *See* Professional Writers Association of Canada

Perioperative Registered Nurses Association of British Columbia (PRNABC)
BC
www.prnabc.ca
Overview: A medium-sized provincial organization overseen by Operating Room Nurses Association of Canada
Chief Officer(s):
Marlene Skucas, President
president@prnabc.ca
Coleen Newland, Treasurer
treasurer@prnabc.ca
Membership: *Member Profile:* Registered Nurses in British Columbia who are engaged in operating room nursing or a member of the College of Registered Nurses (CRNBC) who are involved in the Perioperative setting and are interested in promoting the purpose of PRNABC.
Activities: *Awareness Events:* Perioperative Nurses Week, November

Personal Computer Club of Toronto
34 Ravenal St., Toronto ON M6N 3Y7
e-mail: membership@pcct.org
www.pcct.org
Overview: A small local organization
Chief Officer(s):
Cristina Enretti-Zoppo, President, 416-925-8570
president@pcct.org
Finances: *Annual Operating Budget:* Less than $50,000
50 volunteer(s)
Membership: 300; *Fees:* $65
Activities: General & S.I.G. meetints

Personnel Association of Ontario *See* Human Resources Professionals Association

Personnel professionnel des services aux étudiants *See* Professional Student Services Personnel

Personnes d'abord du Canada *See* People First of Canada

Persons Living with AIDS Network of Saskatchewan Inc.
PO Box 7123, Saskatoon SK S7K 4J1
Tel: 306-373-7766; *Fax:* 306-374-7746
Toll-Free: 800-226-0944
plwa@sasktel.net
www.aidsnetworksaskatoon.ca
Also Known As: PLWA Network of Saskatchewan
Overview: A small provincial charitable organization founded in 1987 overseen by Canadian AIDS Society
Mission: To provide & operate support & social activities for persons diagnosed with HIV disease, as well as their families, friends & partners
Member of: Saskatoon Interagency Council on STD's & AIDS; Canadian Centre for Philanthropy
Chief Officer(s):
Lynn Crapper, Vice-President
Lorraine Stewart, President
Brenda Andreas, Vice-President
Finances: *Annual Operating Budget:* $100,000-$250,000; *Funding Sources:* Donations; fundraising; Saskatchewan Dept. of Health
Staff Member(s): 2; 9 volunteer(s)
Membership: 170; *Fees:* $10; *Member Profile:* Persons infected/affected by HIV/AIDS
Activities: *Awareness Events:* World AIDS Day, Dec.; Red Ribbon Campaign, Nov; Jump for AIDS, Aug; *Speaker Service:* Yes; *Library:* The Tracie Wood Memorial Library
Awards:
- Gordon Tater Merit Award (Award)

To be awarded to HIV+ individuals in Saskatchewan who have distinguished themselves in working with their peers
- Sr. Emilie Bandet Award (Award)

To those individuals who have made outstanding contributions to help people with HIV/AIDS

Perth & District Chamber of Commerce
34 Herriott St., Perth ON K7H 1T2
Tel: 613-267-3200; *Fax:* 613-267-6797
Toll-Free: 888-319-3204
welcome@perthchamber.com
perthchamber.com
www.facebook.com/perthchamber
twitter.com/perthchamber
Previous Name: Perth Chamber of Commerce
Overview: A small local organization founded in 1889
Mission: To promote economic development & prosperity for the enrichment of the community
Affliation(s): Canadian Chamber of Commerce; Ontario Chamber of Commerce
Chief Officer(s):
Pauline Fitchett, General Manager
Finances: *Annual Operating Budget:* $50,000-$100,000
Staff Member(s): 2; 2 volunteer(s)
Membership: 350; *Fees:* $85-$356

Perth Chamber of Commerce *See* Perth & District Chamber of Commerce

Peruvian Horse Association of Canada (PHAC)
Lyalta AB T0J 1Y0
Tel: 403-935-4435; *Fax:* 403-935-4774
www.phac.ca
Overview: A medium-sized national charitable organization founded in 1974
Mission: To assure registration of Pure Peruvian Paso Horses & to keep members informed of changes

Chief Officer(s):
Gus McCollister, Executive Secretary
gusmccollister@efirehose.net
Membership: *Fees:* $15 aficionado; $45 owner-breeder
Activities: *Rents Mailing List:* Yes

Ontario Peruvian Horse Association
4723 Sixteen Rd., St. Anns ON L0R 1X0
Tel: 905-957-9676
rembab@talkwireless.ca
Chief Officer(s):
Betty Bassett, President

Peruvian Horse Club of Alberta
PO Box 31, Millarville AB T0L 1K0
Tel: 403-931-7773
Chief Officer(s):
Chantelle Sawatzky, President

Peruvian Horse Club of BC
PO Box 207, Armstrong BC V0E 1B0
Tel: 250-832-1188
4beat@telus.net
Chief Officer(s):
Rob Sjodin, President

Saskatchewan Peruvian Horse Club Inc.
147 Rao Cres., Saskatoon SK S7K 6V7
Tel: 306-929-2350
foxcreek@inet2000.com
Chief Officer(s):
Phoebe Soles, President

Pest Management Association of Alberta (PMAA)
c/o John Patton, #1550, 246 Stewart Green SW, Calgary AB T3H 3C8
Tel: 403-242-2467
pmaa@telus.net
www.pmaapestworld.com
Previous Name: Structural Pest Management Association of Alberta
Overview: A small provincial organization
Mission: To improve & maintain standards of pest management services in the province
Member of: Canadian Pest Management Association; National Pest Management Association Inc.
Chief Officer(s):
John Patton, President
jpatton@japco.ca
Tom Schultz, Treasurer, 780-466-8535
edexterm@telusplanet.net
Susan Baker, Secretary, 780-446-7428
sbaker@telus.net
Membership: *Fees:* $385

Pesticide Education Network
web.ncf.ca/bf250/pen.html
Overview: A small local organization
Chief Officer(s):
John Sankey, Contact
johnsankey@ncf.ca
Finances: *Annual Operating Budget:* Less than $50,000
20 volunteer(s)
Membership: 1-99
Activities: Reduction of pesticide use within urban areas; *Speaker Service:* Yes

Pet Food Association of Canada (PFAC) / Association des fabricants d'aliments pour animaux familiers du Canada
PO Box 35570, 2528 Bayview Ave., Toronto ON M2L 2Y4
Tel: 416-447-9970; *Fax:* 416-443-9137
www.pfac.com
Overview: A medium-sized national organization founded in 1970
Mission: To provide association members with a unified voice on issues that affect the pet food industry in Canada
Membership: *Member Profile:* Representatives from all areas of the Canadian pet food industry, including ingredient suppliers, manufacturers, packagers, & companies that market pet food sold in Canada; *Committees:* Regulatory affairs; Public relations
Activities: Providing recommendations about the Canadian pet food industry & shaping policies; Liaising with government, media, industry, & consumers; Offering networking opportunities; Providing information about the pet food industry

Pet Therapy Society of Northern Alberta
14620 - 111 Ave., Edmonton AB T5M 2P4
Tel: 780-413-4682; *Fax:* 780-440-3341
info@pettherapysociety.com
www.pettherapysociety.com
www.facebook.com/PetTherapySociety
Overview: A small local organization founded in 1994
Mission: To provide animal assisted therapy & pet visitation programs; To provide competent & compassionate support/services to grieving pet owners; To initiate or participate in new programs involving the human animal bond in response to proven needs in the community
Activities: Pet Loss Support Line: 780-418-1949

Peterborough & District Labour Council
PO Box 1928, 246 Romaine St., Peterborough ON K9J 7X7
Tel: 705-742-9286; *Fax:* 705-742-6102
info@ptbolabour.ca
www.ptbolabour.ca
twitter.com/ptbolabour
Overview: A small local organization overseen by Ontario Federation of Labour
Chief Officer(s):
Marion Burton, President
president@ptbolabour.ca
Membership: 38 locals; 6,000 members;

Peterborough & the Kawarthas Association of Realtors Inc. (PKAR)
PO Box 1330, 273 Charlotte St., Peterborough ON K9J 7H5
Tel: 705-745-5724; *Fax:* 705-745-9377
info@peterbororealestate.com
www.peterbororealestate.com
www.facebook.com/PtboAssocRealtors
twitter.com/pkarrealestate
Previous Name: Peterborough Real Estate Board Inc.
Overview: A small local organization overseen by Ontario Real Estate Association
Member of: The Canadian Real Estate Association
Finances: *Funding Sources:* Membership dues; services; programs
Membership: 470

Peterborough & the Kawarthas Tourism
1400 Crawford Dr., Peterborough ON K9J 6X6
Tel: 705-742-2201; *Fax:* 705-742-2494
Toll-Free: 800-461-6424
info@thekawarthas.net
www.thekawarthas.net
www.facebook.com/TheKawarthas
twitter.com/pktourism
www.pinterest.com/pktourism
Previous Name: Peterborough Kawartha Tourism & Convention Bureau
Overview: A small local organization founded in 1982
Mission: To help market the Peterborough area to visitors
Member of: Tourism Industry Association of Canada
Membership: 400
Activities: *Speaker Service:* Yes

Peterborough AIDS Resource Network *See* PARN Your Community AIDS Resource Network

Peterborough Association for Riding for the Disabled *See* PARD Therapeutic Riding

Peterborough Chamber of Commerce *See* Greater Peterborough Chamber of Commerce

Peterborough Field Naturalists (PFN)
PO Box 1532, Peterborough ON K9J 7H7
Tel: 705-742-1524
www.peterboroughnature.org
Overview: A small local organization founded in 1940 overseen by Ontario Nature
Mission: To promote the enjoyment of nature through environmental appreciation & conservation; To encourage wise use & conservation of natural resources & environmental protection
Chief Officer(s):
Martin Parker, President
mparker19@cogeco.ca
Jim Young, Head, Memberships
12 volunteer(s)
Membership: 200; *Fees:* $25 single; $30 family/couple; $15 student; *Committees:* Program, Project
Activities: Monthly meetings with guest speakers, nature walks, birding excursions
Publications:
• The Orchid
Type: Newsletter; *Editor:* Rebecca Zeran

Peterborough Historical Society (PHS)
270 Brock St., Peterborough ON K9H 2P9
Tel: 705-740-2600
info@peterboroughhistoricalsociety.ca
www.peterboroughhistoricalsociety.ca
Overview: A small local organization founded in 1897
Mission: To preserve & promote the cultural & architectural history of Peterborough, Ontario
Chief Officer(s):
Dennis Carter-Edwards, President
Barbara McIntosh, Vice-President
Don Willcock, Secretary
Peter Darling, Treasurer
Finances: *Funding Sources:* Peterborough Community Futures Development Corporation; Federal Economic Development Agency for Southern Ontario; Donations; Fundraising
Membership: *Fees:* $35 individuals; $45 families; $500 lifetime memberships
Activities: Operating the Hutchison House Living History Museum; Hosting public meetings with presentation on local history; Erecting historical plaques
Awards:
• Heritage Awards (Award)
Presented annually to a member of the community
• History Awards (Award)
Presented annually to deserving high school students
Publications:
• Peterborough Historical Society Bulletin
Type: Newsletter; *Frequency:* Monthly; *Price:* Free with membership in the Peterborough Historical Society
Profile: Articles of historical interest & upcoming events

Peterborough Kawartha Tourism & Convention Bureau *See* Peterborough & the Kawarthas Tourism

Peterborough Law Association
470 Water St., Peterborough ON K9H 3M3
Tel: 705-742-9341; *Fax:* 705-742-6173
library@peterboroughlaw.org
www.peterboroughlaw.org
Overview: A small local organization founded in 1879
Member of: Law Society of Upper Canada
Chief Officer(s):
Allison Killin, Librarian
Staff Member(s): 1
Membership: 120
Activities: *Library* by appointment

Peterborough Numismatic Society
c/o Don C. Hurl, 1331 Buckhorn Rd., RR#1, Lakefield ON K0L 2H0
Tel: 705-652-0072
Overview: A small local organization
Chief Officer(s):
Don. C Hurl, Treasurer
donhurl@yahoo.ca

Peterborough Police Association (PPA) / Association de la police de Peterborough
c/o Headquarters, Peterborough Lakefield Community Police, PO Box 2050, 500 Water Street, Peterborough ON K9J 7Y4
Tel: 705-876-1122; *Fax:* 705-743-1540
Toll-Free: 888-876-1122
www.facebook.com/149692195114005
Overview: A small local organization

Peterborough Real Estate Board Inc. *See* Peterborough & the Kawarthas Association of Realtors Inc.

Peterborough Social Planning Council (PSPC)
Peterborough Square, 360 George St. North, Lower Level, Peterborough ON K9H 7E7
Tel: 705-743-5915; *Fax:* 705-748-6174
pspc@pspc.on.ca
www.pspc.on.ca
Overview: A small local organization founded in 1977
Mission: To facilitate citizen participation in forming strong, healthy, & just communities in the City & County of Peterborough, Ontario; To act as a catalyst for positive social change; To promote social justice
Chief Officer(s):
Brenda Dales, Executive Director
Dawm Berry Merriam, Research & Policy Analyst
Finances: *Funding Sources:* Donations; Fundraising
Activities: Conducting social research; Analyzing social policy; Providing information & public education about social issues &

trends; Partnering with other organizations; Implementing community plans

Peterborough Symphony Orchestra (PSO)

PO Box 1135, Peterborough ON K9J 7H4
Tel: 705-742-1992
info@thepso.org
www.thepso.org
www.facebook.com/Peterborough.Symphony.Orchestra
twitter.com/thepso
Overview: A small local charitable organization founded in 1967 overseen by Orchestras Canada
Mission: To perform & develop excellence in symphonic music that will enrich, stimulate & attract the widest possible audience by presenting & perpetuating quality orchestral music to the people of Peterborough & beyond
Member of: Kawartha Tourism
Affliation(s): Peterborough Chamber of Commerce
Chief Officer(s):
Michael Newnham, Music Director
Finances: *Funding Sources:* Earned revenue; Ontario Arts Council; City of Peterborough; Lloyd Carr-Harris Foundation
Staff Member(s): 3
Membership: 44
Activities: Concert series; Children's Concert; partnership concerts; Beat Beethoven Run; Family Matinee Concert; *Internships:* Yes; *Speaker Service:* Yes; *Library:* PSO Music Library

Petite ligue Canada *See* Little League Canada

Petites-Mains

7595, boul St-Laurent, Montréal QC H2R 1W9
Tél: 514-738-8989; *Téléc:* 514-738-6193
info@petitesmains.com
www.petitesmains.com
www.facebook.com/pages/Petites-Mains/376743143539
twitter.com/PetitesMains
Aperçu: *Dimension:* petite; *Envergure:* locale; fondée en 1994
Mission: Petites-Mains a pour mission de venir en aide aux gens, surtout les femmes immigrantes, monoparentales, sans revenu et prestataires de l'Assistance-Emploi. Il aide ces femmes à sortir de leur isolement, à échanger avec d'autres, à apprendre un métier, à intégrer le marché du travail et à vivre en dignité dans la société.
Membre(s) du bureau directeur:
Nahid Aboumansour, Directrice générale
Membre(s) du personnel: 14

Petits frères des pauvres

4624. rue Garnier, Montréal QC H2L 3S7
Tél: 514-527-8653; *Téléc:* 514-527-7162
Ligne sans frais: 866-627-8653
info@petitsfreres.ca
www.petitsfreres.ca
www.facebook.com/LesPetitsFreres
Aperçu: *Dimension:* moyenne; *Envergure:* internationale; fondée en 1962
Mission: Pour connecter les seniors avec les jeunes afin de les faire sortir de l'isolement et d'avoir la compagnie
Membre(s) du bureau directeur:
Luc Villeneuve, Président, Conseil d'administration
Activités: Activité de collecte de fonds

Petits Frères du Bon-Pasteur *See* Little Brothers of the Good Shepherd

Petroleum Accountants Society of Canada (PASC)

PO Box 4520, Stn. C, #400, 1040 - 7 Ave. SW, Calgary AB T2T 5N3
Tel: 403-262-4744; *Fax:* 403-244-2340
info@petroleumaccountants.com
www.petroleumaccountants.com
www.linkedin.com/groups/Petroleum-Accountants-Society-Canada-3814298
Overview: A medium-sized national organization founded in 1950
Mission: To contribute to the long term success of the Canadian petroleum industry by staying abreast of the constantly changing needs of the industry & striving to satisfy those needs
Member of: Council of Petroleum Societies of North America
Chief Officer(s):
Josh Molcak, President
josh.molcak@paramountres.com
Tracy Kozak, Treasurer
tracy.kozak@baytex.ab.ca
Finances: *Annual Operating Budget:* $50,000-$100,000; *Funding Sources:* Membership dues
Staff Member(s): 1; 70 volunteer(s)
Membership: 260+ from more than 160 energy companies; *Fees:* $100 regular; $20 student; *Member Profile:* Accounting, auditing, finance or economics employees with organizations associated with the petroleum or natural gas industry; *Committees:* Education; Emerging Issues; Joint Venture Audit; Joint Interest Research; Material Inventory; Member Services
Activities: Professional development, continuing education, standards & information; *Library* Open to public by appointment

Petroleum Human Resources Council of Canada (PHRCC)

5055 - 11 St. NE, Calgary AB T2E 8N4
Tel: 403-516-8100; *Fax:* 403-516-8171
info@petrohrsc.ca
www.petrohrsc.ca
twitter.com/PetroHRCouncil
Overview: A medium-sized national organization
Mission: Collaborative forum that addresses human resources issues within the petroleum industry
Membership: 11; *Member Profile:* Oil and gas national and regional industry organizations

Petroleum Industry Training Service *See* Enform: The Safety Association for the Upstream Oil & Gas Industry

Petroleum Research Atlantic Canada (PRAC) *See* Petroleum Research Newfoundland & Labrador

Petroleum Research Newfoundland & Labrador

Baine Johnston Centre, #802, 10 Fort William Pl., St. John's NL A1C 1K4
Tel: 709-738-7916; *Fax:* 709-738-7922
www.pr-ac.ca
Previous Name: Petroleum Research Atlantic Canada (PRAC)
Overview: A small local organization founded in 1999
Mission: To fund & facilitate research & development on behalf of the offshore oil & gas industry of Newfoundland & Labrador
Chief Officer(s):
Doug Cook, Chief Executive Officer, 709-738-7920
doug.cook@petroleumresearch.ca
David Finn, Chief Operating Officer, 709-738-7917
dave.finn@petroleumresearch.ca
Susan Hunt, Program Manager, HSE, 709-738-7904
susan.hunt@petroleumresearch.ca
Lisa A. Hutchens, Manager, Business Services, 709-738-7921
lisa.hutchens@petroleumresearch.ca
Matilda Maddigan, Manager, Office, 709-738-7916
matilda.maddigan@petroleumresearch.ca
Metzi Prince, Manager, Project Delivery, 709-738-7919
metzi.prince@petroleumresearch.ca
Charles E. Smith, Senior Technical Advisor, 709-738-7918
charles.smith@petroleumresearch.ca
Robert Trask, Coordinator, Research Grants, 709-738-7974
robert.trask@petroleumresearch.ca
Membership: *Member Profile:* Representatives from the oil & gas industry

Petroleum Services Association of Canada (PSAC)

#1150, 800 - 6 Ave. SW, Calgary AB T2P 3G3
Tel: 403-264-4195; *Fax:* 403-263-7174
www.psac.ca
www.linkedin.com/groups/PSAC-Working-Energy-4706150
Overview: A large national organization founded in 1981
Mission: To represent the supply, manufacturing, & service sectors of the upstream petroleum industry
Chief Officer(s):
Lucas Mezzano, Chair
Mark Salkeld, MBA, President & CEO
msalkeld@psac.ca
Elizabeth Aquin, CAE, Senior Vice-President
eaquin@psac.ca
Patrick J. Delaney, CRSP, Vice-President, Health & Safety
pdelaney@psac.ca
Kelly Morrison, Vice-President, Communications
kmorrison@psac.ca
Heather Doyle, Manager, Meetings & Events
hdoyle@psac.ca
Membership: 250+ companies; *Fees:* Schedule available; *Member Profile:* Petroleum services industry companies; *Committees:* Corporate Finance; Education Fund; Health & Safety; Human Resources; Special Events; Transportation Issues; Cathodic Protection; Drilling Fluids; Oilwell Perforators' Safety Training & Advisory; Snubbing Services; Well Testing
Activities: Engaging in lobbying activities; Providing educational opportunities
Meetings/Conferences: • Petroleum Services Association of Canada 2015 Annual Spring Conference, 2015
Scope: National
Description: A gathering of petroleum service industry workers
Contact Information: Manager, Meetings & Events: Heather Doyle, Phone: 403-213-2796, E-mail: hdoyle@psac.ca
• Petroleum Services Association of Canada 2015 Annual Mid-Year Update, 2015
Scope: National
Description: A respected petroleum industry event to update the Canadian Drilling Activity Forecast
Contact Information: Manager, Meetings & Events: Heather Doyle, Phone: 403-213-2796, E-mail: hdoyle@psac.ca
• Petroleum Services Association of Canada 2015 Annual General Meeting, Canadian Drilling Activity Forecast Session, & Industry Dinner, 2015
Scope: National
Description: At the end of October each year, the Petroleum Services Association of Canada Annual Report is released, in conjunction with the Annual General Meeting & the Canadian Drilling Activity Forecast
Contact Information: Manager, Meetings & Events: Heather Doyle, Phone: 403-213-2796, E-mail: hdoyle@psac.ca
Publications:
• Canadian Drilling Activity Forecast
Type: Yearbook; *Frequency:* Annually
Profile: Five years of historical data, plus forecasts for the coming year across Canada
• FAST-Line [a publication of the Petroleum Services Association of Canada]
Type: Newsletter; *Frequency:* Biweekly
Profile: Association news & upcoming events
• Petroleum Services Association of Canada Membership Directory
Type: Directory
Profile: Contact information for association members
• Petroleum Services Association of Canada Annual Report
Type: Yearbook; *Frequency:* Annually
Profile: A review of the association's activities, released at the end of each October in conjunction with the Canadian Drilling Activity Forecast & the Annual GeneralMeeting
• Petroleum Services News [a publication of the Petroleum Services Association of Canada]
Type: Magazine; *Frequency:* Quarterly; *Accepts Advertising*
Profile: Covering issues of importance to the upstream oil & gas industry
• Total Compensation Survey [a publication of the Petroleum Services Association of Canada]
Type: Yearbook; *Frequency:* Annually
Profile: An analysis of current salary & benefits practices in the petroleum service, supply, & manufacturing industry
• Well Cost Study
Type: Study
Profile: Geological, technical, & financial data on wells drilled across Canada

Petroleum Tank Management Association of Alberta (PTMAA)

#980, 10303 Jasper Ave., Edmonton AB T5J 3N6
Tel: 780-425-8265; *Fax:* 780-425-4722
Toll-Free: 866-222-8265
ptmaa@ptmaa.ab.ca
www.ptmaa.ab.ca
Overview: A medium-sized provincial licensing charitable organization founded in 1994
Mission: To offer programs to enhance the management of petroleum storage tank systems in Alberta
Chief Officer(s):
Don Edgecombe, Operations Manager
Mark Tse, Chair
Randy Hall, Secretary
Sim Koopmans, Treasurer
Activities: Monitoring new storage tank installations; Inspecting existing storage tank installations; Investigating accidents & incidents

Petroleum Technology Alliance Canada (PTAC)

Chevron Plaza, #400, 500 - 5th Ave. SW, Calgary AB T2P 3L5
Tel: 403-218-7700; *Fax:* 403-920-0054
info@ptac.org
www.ptac.org
Overview: A medium-sized national organization
Mission: To facilitate innovation, technology transfer & research & development in the upstream oil & gas industry

Chief Officer(s):
Soheil Asgarpour, President, 403-218-7701
sasgarpour@ptac.org
Tannis Such, Director, Environmental Research Initiatives, 403-218-7703
tsuch@ptac.org
Activities: *Library:* PTAC Knowledge Centre;

Petrolia Discovery

PO Box 1480, 4381 Discovery Line, Petrolia ON N0N 1R0
Tel: 519-381-5979; *Fax:* 519-882-4209
petdisc@xcelco.on.ca
www.petroliadiscovery.com
Overview: A small national charitable organization founded in 1980
Mission: To provide information about Petrolia's oil heritage
Activities: Maintaining historical displays; Organizing programs for schools

PFLAG Canada Inc.

265 Montreal Rd., Ottawa ON K1L 6C4
Fax: 888-959-4128
Toll-Free: 888-530-6777
inquiries@pflagcanada.ca
www.pflagcanada.ca
www.facebook.com/PFLAGCA
twitter.com/pflagcanada
Also Known As: Parents, Families & Friends of Lesbians & Gays
Previous Name: Parents & Friends of Lesbians & Gays (Parents FLAG)
Overview: A medium-sized national charitable organization founded in 2003
Mission: To support individuals with questions & concerns about sexual orientation or gender identity; to make Canada a more accepting place for persons of all gender identities & sexual orientations
Chief Officer(s):
Stephen Hartley, President & Director
president@pflagcanada.ca
Dino Benganovic, Vice-President
vp@pflagcanada.ca
Tim Mt. Pleasant, Treasurer
treasurer@pflagcanada.ca
Finances: *Funding Sources:* Donations
Membership: *Fees:* Free
Activities: Providing education & resources about gender identity & sexual orientation; Offering peer support; *Internships:* Yes; *Speaker Service:* Yes

Abbotsford Chapter
Abbotsford BC
Tel: 604-217-4616
abbotsfordbc@pflagcanada.ca
Chief Officer(s):
Kristie Johnson, Contact

Alberni Chapter
4345 Glenside Rd., Port Alberni BC V9Y 5W9
Tel: 250-723-3540
Chief Officer(s):
Pat Messenger, Contact

Barrie Chapter
Barrie ON
Tel: 705-725-9748
barrieon@pflagcanada.ca
Chief Officer(s):
Deborah Batt, Contact

Belleville - Quinte Chapter
1600 Thorpe Rd. RR#2, Odessa ON K0H 2H0
Tel: 613-386-1922
region3a@plfagcanada.ca
Chief Officer(s):
Eric Hargreaves, Contact

Brandon - Brandon / Westman Chapter
c/o Sexuality Education Resource Centre, 719 Rosser Ave., Brandon MB R7A 0K8
Tel: 204-727-0417
Chief Officer(s):
Laura Crookshanks, Contact

Bridgewater Chapter
107 Pleasant St., Bridgewater NS B4V 1N3
Toll-Free: 888-530-6777
bridgewtrns@pflagcanada.ca
Chief Officer(s):
Philip Lauren, Regional Director

Brockville Chapter
PO Box 194, 34 Buell St., Brockville ON K6V 5V2
Tel: 613-640-2273
brockvilleon@pflagcanada.ca
sites.google.com/site/pflagcanadabrockville/
www.facebook.com/PFLAGBrockville
Chief Officer(s):
Lori Taylor, Contact

Calgary Chapter
439 Tuscany Ridge Height NW, Calgary AB T3L 3B6
Tel: 403-695-5791
calgaryab@pflagcanada.ca
Chief Officer(s):
Sean Alley, Contact

Campbell River Chapter
Campbell River BC
e-mail: crpflag@hotmail.com
Chief Officer(s):
Yvonne Buxton, Contact

Carleton Place/Lanark Chapter
11358 Hwy. 15, RR#3, Smith Falls ON K7A 4S4
Tel: 613-283-2055
grandpa@magma.ca
Chief Officer(s):
Jim MacGregor, Contact

Cornwall Chapter
3523 Besner Rd., St. Isidore ON K0C 2B0
Tel: 613-524-4085
Toll-Free: 877-874-4424
Chief Officer(s):
Lorna Cunningham, Regional Director
Lornacr@gmail.com

Cranbrook Chapter
2617 - 3rd St. South, Cranbrook BC V1C 4W4
Tel: 250-426-6558
cranbrookbc@pflagcanada.ca
Chief Officer(s):
Earl Waugh, Contact

Edmonton Chapter
c/o Institute for Sexual Minority Studies & Services, Univ. of Alberta, #7, 104 Education North, Edmonton AB T6G 2G5
Tel: 780-248-1971
Chief Officer(s):
Tamara Gartner, Contact
gartner1@ualberta.ca

Fenelon Falls Chapter
67 Fells Point Rd., RR#1, Fenelon Falls ON K0M 1N0
Tel: 705-887-6830
Chief Officer(s):
Carol Milroy, Contact
carol_milroy@hotmail.com

Fredericton Chapter
Fredericton NB
Toll-Free: 888-530-6777
Chief Officer(s):
Philip Lauren, Regional Director

Halifax Chapter
PO Box 223, Shearwater NS B0J 3A0
Toll-Free: 888-530-6777
halifaxns@pflagcanada.ca
Chief Officer(s):
Philip Lauren, Regional Director

Halton Region Chapter
87 - 5th Concession Rd. East, Waterdown ON L0R 2H1
Tel: 289-895-8933
Chief Officer(s):
Joanne Stacey, Contact

Kamloops Chapter
#17, 481 Monarch Ct., Kamloops BC V2E 2P1
Tel: 250-851-9385
kamloopsbc@pflagcanada.ca
Chief Officer(s):
Judy Lusk, Contact

Kimberley Chapter
2617 - 3rd St. South, Cranbrook BC V1C 4W4
Tel: 780-427-1087
kimberleybc@pflagcanada.ca
Chief Officer(s):
Melanie Wilson, Contact

Kindersley Chapter
PO Box 754, Kindersley SK S0L 1S0
Tel: 306-463-4381
dewhyley@sasktel.net

Kingston Chapter
#202, 298 Guthrie Dr., Kingston ON K7K 7B9
Tel: 613-766-1444
KingstonON@pflagcanada.ca
www.facebook.com/pflagkingston
ww.facebook.com/pflagkingston
Chief Officer(s):
Stephen Hartley, Contact

Kitchener - Guelph & Kitchener / Waterloo Chapter
ON
Tel: 888-530-6777

Lethbridge & Area Chapter
Lethbridge AB
e-mail: lethbridgeab@pflagcanada.ca
Chief Officer(s):
Dino H. Beganovic, Regional Director
vp@pflagcanada.ca

London Chapter
170 Tarbart Terrace, London ON N6H 3B2
Tel: 519-319-6934
Chief Officer(s):
Joanne King, Contact

Medicine Hat & Area Chapter
Medicine Hat AB
Tel: 403-581-4923
www.facebook.com/pflagcanadamedicinehat

Middleton Chapter
Middleton NS
Tel: 888-530-6777
middletonns@pflagcanada.ca
www.pflagcanada.ca/middleton.html
Chief Officer(s):
Philip Lauren, Regional Director

Miramichi Chapter
#2, 117 Dolan Ave., Miramichi NB E1V 1C3
Toll-Free: 888-530-6777
Chief Officer(s):
Philip Lauren, Regional Director

Moncton Chapter
Moncton NB
Tel: 506-875-1220
monctonnb@pflagcanada.ca
www.pflagcanada.ca/moncton
Chief Officer(s):
Steven Brown, Contact

Montréal Chapter
Montréal QC
Tel: 514-561-0462
region5b@pflagcanada.ca
Chief Officer(s):
Karan Singh, Contact

Moose Jaw Chapter
Moose Jaw SK
Toll-Free: 888-530-6777
Chief Officer(s):
Dino Beganovic, Regional Director
vp@pflagcanada.ca

Muskoka Chapter
178 Dill St., Bracebridge ON P1L 1E6
Tel: 877-721-7520
Chief Officer(s):
Karla Stewart, Contact, 705-645-9731
karlastewart@hotmail.com

Niagara Chapter
417 Bunting Rd., St Catharines ON L2M 3Z1
Tel: 905-937-0202
www.pflagcanada.ca/niagara
Chief Officer(s):
Cathy Mackenzie, Contact

Oshawa - Durham Region / Oshawa Chapter
PO Box 30555, 438 King St. West, Oshawa ON L1J 8L8
Tel: 905-231-0533
Inquiries@pflagdurhamregion.com
Chief Officer(s):
Tanya Shaw-White, President
President@PFLAGDurhamRegion.com

Ottawa Chapter
PO Box 71028, 174 Bank St., Ottawa ON K2P 2L9
Toll-Free: 888-530-6777
contact@pflagottawa.ca
www.pflagottawa.ca
Chief Officer(s):
Darrell Comeau, Contact

Peel Region Chapter
ON
Tel: 905-602-4082
Toll-Free: 888-530-6777
peelon@pflagcanada.ca
Mission: To support persons with concerns about gender identity or sexual orientation in Brampton, Caledon, & Mississauga
Chief Officer(s):
Stephen Hartley, Contact
President@pflagcanada.ca

Peterborough Chapter
PO Box 115, Warsaw ON K0L 3A0
Tel: 705-749-9723
pflagpeterborough@hotmail.com
pflagpeterborough.com
Chief Officer(s):
Dianne McKay, Volunteer Co-ordinator

Prince Albert Chapter
Comp. 42, Site 28, RR#5, Prince Albert SK S6V 5R3
Tel: 306-764-5150
pralbertsk@pflagcanada.ca
Chief Officer(s):
Lynne Delorme, Contact

Prince George Chapter
#12, 1475 Queensway St., Prince George BC V2L 1L4
Tel: 250-640-1874
prgeorgebc@pflagcanada.ca
www.pflagcanada.ca/princegeorge.html
Chief Officer(s):
Rory Allen, Contact

Regina Chapter
3720 Queens Gate, Regina SK S4S 7J1
Tel: 306-533-3965
reginask@pflagcanada.ca
Chief Officer(s):
Francine Proulx-Kenzle, Contact
fproulxkenzle@yahoo.ca

Richmond Hill - York Region Chapter
333 Crosby Ave., Richmond Hill ON L4C 2R5
Tel: 888-905-5428
pflagyork@yahoo.ca
www.pflagyork.ca

Sackville - Sackville NB / Amherst NS Chapter
14 Devon Ave., Sackville NB E4L 3W2
Tel: 506-536-4245
sacknb-amns@pflagcanada.ca
Chief Officer(s):
Janet Hammock, Contact

Saint John Chapter
27 Wasson Ct., Saint John NB E2K 2K6
Tel: 506-648-9227
www.pflagcanada.ca/saintjohn.html
Chief Officer(s):
Mack MacKenzie, Contact

St. John's Chapter
St. John's NL
Tel: 709-722-5791
stjohnsnl@pflagcanada.ca
Affliation(s): AIDS Committee of Newfoundland & Labrador; Planned Parenthood Newfoundland & Labrador; Egale Canada; Canadians for Equal Marriage
Chief Officer(s):
Tony Braithwaite, Contact

Salt Spring Island Chapter
Salt Spring Island BC
Tel: 250-537-7773
Chief Officer(s):
Jill Simpson, Contact

Sarnia - Sarnia / Bluewater Chapter
1059 Willa Dr., Sarnia ON N7S 1T1
Tel: 519-344-8246
sarnia-bwon@pflagcanada.ca
Chief Officer(s):
Ruth Lambert, Contact, 519-337-2992

Saskatoon Chapter
2209 McKinnon Ave. South, Saskatoon SK S7J 1N5
Tel: 306-491-3484
saskatoonsk@pflagcanada.ca
Chief Officer(s):
Fran Forsberg, Contact

Sault Ste Marie Chapter
Sault Ste Marie ON
Tel: 705-777-0496
Chief Officer(s):
Susan Meades, Contact
ssmarieon@pflagcanada.ca

Stoney Creek - Hamilton Chapter
45 Glen Cannon Dr., Stoney Creek ON L8G 2Z6
e-mail: hamiltonon@pflagcanada.ca

Sussex Chapter
Sussex NB
Tel: 506-672-6072
sussexnb@pflagcanada.ca
Chief Officer(s):
Joanne Jones, Contact

Sydney Chapter
c/o PLAG Contact, Family Place Resource Centre, 714 Alexandra St., Sydney NS B1S 2H4
Toll-Free: 888-530-6777
sydneyns@pflagcanada.ca
Chief Officer(s):
JoAnne Fitzgerald, Contact

Thunder Bay Chapter
Thunder Bay ON
Tel: 807-767-2447
thunderbayon@pflagcanada.ca

Timmins Chapter
Timmins ON
Tel: 705-268-0706
timminson@pflagcanada.ca
Chief Officer(s):
Julie DeMarchi, Contact

Toronto Chapter
200 Wolverleigh Blvd., Toronto ON M4C 1S2
Tel: 416-406-1727
office@pflagtoronto.org
www.torontopflag.org
www.facebook.com/TorontoPFLAG
twitter.com/torontopflag
Chief Officer(s):
Anne Creighton, President

Vancouver Chapter
Vancouver BC
Tel: 604-626-5667
info@pflagvancouver.com
www.pflagvancouver.com
www.linkedin.com/groups/PFLAG-Canada-1443017
www.facebook.com/PFLAGVancouver
twitter.com/PFLAGCanada

Victoria Chapter
1834 Newton St., Victoria BC V8R 2R4
Tel: 250-385-9462
victoriabc@pflagcanada.ca
Chief Officer(s):
Dino Beganovic, Regional Director
vp@pflagcanada.ca

Windsor Chapter
Windsor ON
Tel: 519-978-2777
windsoron@pflagcanada.ca
Chief Officer(s):
Karen McMahon, Contact

Windsor, Nova Scotia Chapter
Windsor NS
Tel: 888-530-6777
windsorns@pflagcanada.ca
Chief Officer(s):
Philip Lauren, Regional Director

Winnipeg Chapter
PO Box 66, Victoria Beach MB R0E 2C0
Tel: 204-981-9342
winnipegmb@pflagcanada.ca
Chief Officer(s):
Dino Beganovic, Regional Director
vp@pflagcanada.ca

Woodstock Chapter
119 Jules Dr., Woodstock NB E7M 1Z2
Toll-Free: 888-530-6777
Chief Officer(s):
Philip Lauren, Regional Director

Yarmouth Chapter
60 Vancouver St., Yarmouth NS B5A 2P5
Tel: 902-742-3542
Chief Officer(s):
Jaqi Sutherland-Allan, Contact
jsutherland-allan@swndha.nshealth.ca

Yorkton - East Central Chapter
72 Newfield Pl., Yorkton SK S3N 2M9
Tel: 306-782-0113
axios@sasktel.net
Chief Officer(s):
Andy Piasta, Contact

Pharmaceutical & Personal Care Logistics Association (PPCLA) / Association de logistique des soins personnels et pharmaceutiques

PO Box 40568, Stn. Six Points Plaza, Toronto ON M9B 6K8
Tel: 416-232-6817; *Fax:* 416-232-6818
Toll-Free: 866-293-1238
ppcla@ppcla.org
www.ppcla.org
Previous Name: Pharmaceutical & Toilet Preparations Traffic Association
Overview: A medium-sized national organization founded in 1958
Mission: To develop & promote the interchange of ideas & information concerning traffic & transportation matters of the pharmaceutical & toilet preparations industry; To foster fair dealings & cordial relationships among members & between representatives of the various modes of transportation employed by members
Chief Officer(s):
Doris Hamel, President
dhamel@shire.com
Finances: *Annual Operating Budget:* Less than $50,000
1 volunteer(s)
Membership: 47 institutional; *Fees:* $350; *Member Profile:* Logistics managers in the pharmaceutical & personal care industries
Awards:
• The PPCLA Agnes French Scholarship (Scholarship)
Awarded annual to a first year or continuing under graduate university student *Amount:* $1,000

Pharmaceutical & Toilet Preparations Traffic Association
See Pharmaceutical & Personal Care Logistics Association

Pharmaceutical Advertising Advisory Board

#300, 1305 Pickering Pkwy., Pickering ON L1V 3P2
Tel: 905-509-2275; *Fax:* 905-509-2486
info@paab.ca
www.paab.ca
www.linkedin.com/groups?gid=2104835
www.youtube.com/watch?v=MVAQB2QsbMw&feature=relmfu
Overview: A small national organization
Chief Officer(s):
Ray Chepesiuk, Commissioner

Pharmaceutical Manufacturers Association of Canada *See* Canada's Research-Based Pharmaceutical Companies (Rx&D)

Pharmacists' Association of Newfoundland & Labrador (PANL)

#203, 85 Thorburn Rd., St. John's NL A1B 3M2
Tel: 709-753-7881; *Fax:* 709-753-8882
Toll-Free: 866-753-7881
email@panl.net
www.panl.net
Overview: A small provincial organization founded in 2003
Mission: To improve the profession of pharmacy throughout Newfoundland & Labrador; To support members in the the provision of quality services to the people of Newfoundland & Labrador; To advance the professional, economic, & social well-being of pharmacists
Chief Officer(s):
Mary Ann Butt, Executive Director, 709-753-5881
mbutt@panl.net
Jim Organ, Manager, Professional Services, 709-753-3771
jorgan@panl.net
Finances: *Funding Sources:* Membership fees; Sponsorships
Membership: *Member Profile:* Pharmacists licensed to practice in Newfoundland & Labrador; Pharmacies in Newfoundland & Labrador; Non-practicing pharmacists (retired persons & those taking a leave of absence); Persons employed directly or indirectly in the profession of pharmacy; Students
Activities: Promoting the profession of pharmacy in Newfoundland & Labrador; Advocating for pharmacists; Presenting continuing education programs; Providing industry information to members; Offering a new pharmacist mentorship program; Organizing networking opportunities; *Awareness Events:* Pharmacist Awareness Week
Meetings/Conferences: • Pharmacists' Association of Newfoundland & Labrador 2015 Annual Conference, 2015

Scope: Provincial
Description: Educational sessions & networking opportunities
Contact Information: E-mail: email@panl.net
Publications:
• Newfoundland & Labrador Pharmacist Directory
Type: Directory
Profile: Pharmacists, their practice sites, & contact information
• Newfoundland & Labrador Pharmacy Directory
Type: Directory
Profile: Listings of pharmacies in the province & contact information
• Pharmacists' Association of Newfoundland & Labrador Newsletter
Type: Newsletter; *Frequency:* 7 pa; *Accepts Advertising; Price:* Free with membership in the Pharmacists' Association of Newfoundland & Labrador

Pharmacists' Association of Saskatchewan, Inc. (PAS)

#202, 2629 - 29th Ave., Regina SK S4S 2N9
Tel: 306-359-7277; *Fax:* 306-352-6770
info@skpharmacists.ca
www.skpharmacists.ca
www.facebook.com/saskatchewanpharmacists
twitter.com/PAS_SK
Overview: A small provincial organization
Mission: To advance the profession of pharmacy in Saskatchewan; To act as the voice of pharmacists throughout Saskatchewan; To protect the interests of pharmacists
Chief Officer(s):
Christine Hrudka, Chair
chris@pharmacyfirst.ca
Dawn Martin, Executive Director
dawn.martin@skpharmacists.ca
Myla Wollbaum, Director, Professional Practice
myla.wollbaum@skpharmacists.ca
Staff Member(s): 5
Membership: *Fees:* Schedule available; *Member Profile:* Practicing pharmacists across Saskatchewan; Students; Retired members; *Committees:* Governance; Audit & Finance; Compensation; Economics; Professional Practice; Conference; Members Services; Awards
Activities: Engaging in advocacy activities on behalf of the profession; Presenting professional development sessions; Offering assistance & advice on professional issues; Providing access to malpractice insurance
Publications:
• PAS It On
Type: Bulletin; *Price:* Free with memberships in the Pharmacists' Association of Saskatchewan, Inc.
Profile: Vital issues for Saskatchewan pharmacists

Pharmacological Society of Canada; Canadian Society for Clinical Pharmacology ***See*** Canadian Society of Pharmacology & Therapeutics

Pharmacy Association of Nova Scotia (PANS)

#225, 170 Cromarty Dr., Dartmouth NS B3B 0G1
Tel: 902-422-9583; *Fax:* 902-422-2619
pans@pans.ns.ca
pans.ns.ca
www.facebook.com/152014618179908
twitter.com/pharmacyns
www.youtube.com/pharmacyassocns
Overview: A small provincial organization founded in 1979
Mission: To advance the professional, academic, & commercial aspects of pharmacy & pharmacists throughout Nova Scotia; To represent the interests of Nova Scotia's pharmacists; To improve public health in Nova Scotia
Chief Officer(s):
Allison Bodnar, CEO
abodnar@pans.ns.ca
Finances: *Funding Sources:* Membership fees; Sponsorships
Membership: *Member Profile:* Pharmaceutical chemists & certified dispensers in Nova Scotia; Students enrolled in the School of Pharmacy at Dalhousie University; International pharmacy graduates; Corporate members
Activities: Engaging in advocacy activities; Liaising with governments; Disseminating information to assist members in pharmacy management; Offering educational opportunities; *Awareness Events:* Pharmacy Awareness Week
Meetings/Conferences: • Pharmacy Association of Nova Scotia 2015 Annual Conference, 2015, NS
Scope: Provincial
Description: Educational sessions on topics of interest to pharmacists in Nova Scotia
Contact Information: Pharmacy Association of Nova Scotia CEO: Allison Bodnar, E-mail: abodnar@pans.ns.ca
Publications:
• The Pharmacist
Type: Newsletter; *Frequency:* Quarterly
Profile: Updates distributed to all pharmacists in Nova Scotia
• Pharmacy Association of Nova Scotia Annual Report
Type: Yearbook; *Frequency:* Annually

The Pharmacy Examining Board of Canada (PEBC) / Le Bureau des examinateurs en pharmacie du Canada (BEPC)

717 Chursh St., Toronto ON M4W 2M4
Tel: 416-979-2431; *Fax:* 416-599-9244
pebcinfo@pebc.ca
www.pebc.ca
Overview: A large national organization founded in 1963
Mission: To establish qualifications for pharmacists; To provide for examinations of those qualifications
Chief Officer(s):
Jeff Whissell, President
Anne Marie Whelan, Vice-President
Membership: *Member Profile:* Registration by examination

Pharmacy Technician Society of Alberta (PTSA)

PO Box 52134, Edmonton AB T6G 2T5
e-mail: info@pharmacytechnicians.ab.ca
www.pharmacytechnicians.ab.ca
www.facebook.com/146233402078217
twitter.com/ThePTSA
Overview: A small provincial organization founded in 2008
Mission: To represent pharmacy technicians in Alberta; To optimize pharmacy services; To promote professionalism among pharmacy technicians
Chief Officer(s):
Peggy Pischke, President
peggy.pischke@pharmacytechnicians.ab.ca
Diane Reeder, Treasurer
diane.reeder@pharmacytechnicians.ab.ca
Dena Boxma, Coordinator, Membership
dena.boxma@pharmacytechnicians.ab.ca
Teresa Hennessey, Coordinator, Promotions & Communications
teresa.hennessey@pharmacytechnicians.ab.ca
Diana Somer, Coordinator, Education
diana.somer@pharmacytechnicians.ab.ca
Finances: *Funding Sources:* Membership fees; Sponsorships
Membership: *Fees:* $31.50 students & pharmacy assistants; $42 associate members; $52.50 full members; *Member Profile:* Pharmacy technicians, who live in Alberta; Associate members are pharmacy technicians who do not live in Alberta & pharmacy industry representatives; Support personnel in pharmacies, who are not pharmacy technicians; Students, enrolled in a pharmacy technician training program; *Committees:* Newsletter; Web Page; Conference Planning; Continuing Education Events - Calgary Area; Continuing Education Events - Edmonton Area; Continuing Education Events - Grande Prairie Area; Certification
Activities: Upholding a Code of Ethics; Providing continuing education; Communicating through social media (www.twitter.com/ThePTSA)
Publications:
• Techs In Touch
Type: Newsletter
Profile: Current issues & regulation information for members

Philanthropic Foundations Canada (PFC) / Fondations philanthropiques Canada (FPC)

#1220, 615 René-Lévesque Blvd. West, Montréal QC H3B 1P5
Tel: 514-866-5446; *Fax:* 514-866-5846
info@pfc.ca
pfc.ca
Overview: A medium-sized national charitable organization founded in 1999
Mission: To encourage public policies that promote philanthropy; to increase awareness of philanthropy & provide opportunities for foundations to learn from one another
Chief Officer(s):
Hilary Pearson, President & CEO
hpearson@pfc.ca
Liza Goulet, Director, Research & Member Services
lgoulet@pfc.ca
Membership: 112 (foundations); *Member Profile:* Canadian grantmakers, including private & public foundations, charities & corporations

Philharmonique Portugais de Montréal ***Voir*** Filarmónica Portuguesa de Montreal

Philippine Association of Manitoba, Inc. (PAM)

88 Juno St., Winnipeg MB R3A 1J1
Tel: 204-772-7210
Overview: A small provincial organization
Mission: To serve the needs of Filipino newcomers & the established Filipino community in Manitoba
Member of: Asian Heritage Society of Manitoba
Membership: *Member Profile:* Members of the Filipino community in Manitoba
Activities: Sponsoring English as a Second Language programs;

Phobies-Zéro

CP 83, Sainte-Julie QC J3E 1X5
Tél: 450-922-5964; *Téléc:* 450-388-5935
admin@phobies-zero.qc.ca
phobies-zero.qc.ca
Aperçu: *Dimension:* petite; *Envergure:* provinciale; fondée en 1991
Mission: Aider les gens avec leurs troubles anxieux en leur faisant comprendre leurs problèmes et en leur montrant les moyens de faire face à leur anxiété
Membre(s) du bureau directeur:
Ginette Gonthier, Directrice
ggonthier@phobies-zero.qc.ca
Membre(s) du personnel: 6
Membre: *Montant de la cotisation:* 20$ par membre; *Critères d'admissibilite:* Toute personne qui souffre d'un trouble anxieux

Phoenix Community Works Foundation (PCWF)

#505, 344 Bloor St. West, Toronto ON M5S 3A7
Tel: 416-964-3388; *Fax:* 416-964-8516
www.pcwf.ca
Overview: A medium-sized national charitable organization founded in 1973
Mission: To assist in the development of a healthy community by encouraging creativity; To promote educational programs relating to the emotional, intellectual & physical well-being of individuals & society; To foster studies & experimental projects related to the physical & social environments; To promote studies & programs in area of emotional health
Chief Officer(s):
Larry Rooney, Executive Director
Edmund O'Sullivan, Director
Finances: *Annual Operating Budget:* Greater than $5 Million
Staff Member(s): 4; 10 volunteer(s)
Membership: 50; *Fees:* $30 (suggested)
Activities: Community development in the areas of arts, education, environment, mental health; *Speaker Service:* Yes
Awards:
• The Chap-Book Award (Award)
Awarded for the best poetry chap-book in English, published in Canada; entries must be from 10-48 pages in length *Amount:* $1,000

Photo Marketing Association International - Canada (PMAI)

PO Box 81191, Ancaster ON L9G 4X2
Tel: 905-304-8800; *Fax:* 905-304-7700
Toll-Free: 800-461-4350
www.pmai.org/content.aspx?id=21982
Overview: A medium-sized national organization founded in 1924
Mission: To disseminate timely information while providing market research & business improvement products & services that contribute to increased profitability & business growth for its membership
Chief Officer(s):
Bob Moggach, Director of Canadian Activities
bmoggach@pmai.org
Staff Member(s): 1
Membership: 1,200; *Fees:* Schedule available; *Member Profile:* Voting - must be in photo & imaging retailing or processing; non-voting - manufacturing, distributing & supply side of the photo & imaging industry
Activities: Professional development seminars; Certification programs; trade shows; *Library:* Resource Centre; Open to public

Photographers Gallery Society Inc. ***See*** Paved Arts New Media Inc.

Photographes Professionnels du Canada ***See*** Professional Photographers of Canada 1970 Incorporated

Photographes professionnels du Québec (PPDQ) / Professional Photographers of Québec
23, rue Frère André Daoust, Rigaud QC J0P 1P0
Tél: 438-397-8182
web@ppdq.ca
www.ppdq.ca
www.facebook.com/PhotographesProfessionnelsduQuebec
twitter.com/PhotographesQc
www.youtube.com/user/cmpqadmin
Aperçu: *Dimension:* moyenne; *Envergure:* provinciale; fondée en 1950 surveillé par Professional Photographers of Canada
Mission: Pour faire avancer la photographie professionnelle tout en assurant aux consommateurs la protection et un haut niveau de qualité.
Membre(s) du bureau directeur:
Nathalie Mathieu, Présidente
nathaliemathieu@ppdq.ca

Photographic Historical Society of Canada (PHSC)
PO Box 239, 6021 Yonge St., Toronto ON M2M 3W2
Tel: 416-691-1555; *Fax:* 416-693-0018
info@phsc.ca
www.phsc.ca
Overview: A small national charitable organization founded in 1974
Mission: To facilitate the sharing of photographic knowledge; To help research & preserve Canada's photographic heritage
Chief Officer(s):
Clint Hyrorijiw, President
Finances: *Annual Operating Budget:* $50,000-$100,000; *Funding Sources:* Membership fees; fairs; auction; donations
20 volunteer(s)
Membership: 300; *Fees:* $32; *Member Profile:* Individuals; collectors; researchers; libraries; archives; museums; companies in the photographic industry; *Committees:* Executive
Activities: Spring & fall photo fairs; spring photo auction; public displays & presentations; monthly meetings; *Library* by appointment
Awards:
• Research Grant (Scholarship)
Presented annually to a current PHSC member for original research into Canada's photographic history *Amount:* $500
• Publication Grant (Scholarship)
Awarded to aid the publication, in book or monograph form, of original research into Canada's photographic history *Amount:* Up to $1,000
• Kodak Canada Student Award (Scholarship)
Presented annually for the best student paper on original research into any aspect of Canadian photographic history *Amount:* $500 first prize, $250 second prize
Publications:
• Photographic Canadiana
Type: Journal; *Frequency:* Quarterly; *Editor:* Robert Lansdale

Physical & Health Education Canada / Éducation physique et santé Canada
#301, 2197 Riverside Dr., Ottawa ON K1H 7X3
Tel: 613-523-1348; *Fax:* 613-523-1206
Toll-Free: 800-663-8708
info@phecanada.ca
www.phecanada.ca
www.facebook.com/PHECanada
twitter.com/PHECanada
Also Known As: PHE Canada
Previous Name: Canadian Physical Education Association; Canadian Association for Health, Physical Education, Recreation, & Dance
Overview: A large national charitable organization founded in 1933
Mission: To promote quality school health programs & the healthy development of Canadian children & youth
Chief Officer(s):
Jacki Nylen, President
Chris Jones, Executive Director & CEO, 613-523-1348 Ext. 224
chris@phecanada.ca
Sarah E. Jackson, Manager, Programs, 613-523-1348 Ext. 222
Sarah@phecanada.ca
Membership: *Member Profile:* Principals, teachers, public health professionals, & recreation leaders from across Canada; *Committees:* Quality Daily Physical Education; Health Promoting Schools; Quality School Intramural Recreation; Dance Education
Activities: Advocating for quality, school-based physical & health education; Offering professional learning experiences; Creating networking opportunities
Awards:
• R. Tait McKenzie Award of Honour (Award)
To recognize Canadians who have made a significant impact on physical education, health promotion, recreation, & dance
• North American Society Fellowship Award (Award)
To recognize outstanding professionals within the professions of health education, physical education, recreation, sport, & dance
• PHE Canada Student Award (Award)
To recognize outstanding undergraduate student leadership in the field of physical & health education
• Physical Education Teaching Excellence (PETE) Award (Award)
To recognize excellence in teaching physical education
• Dr. Andy Anderson Young Professional Award (Award)
To recognize one person in each province for exemplary work in the profession
• Recognition Award Program (RAP) (Award)
Encouraging excellence in school physical education programs
• Health Promoting School Champion Award (Award)
Recognizing an individual, group or organization for their work with the Health Promoting School approach
• Health Educator Award (Award)
Recognizing an individual for his or her work in promoting the importance of health education
• Health Promoting Schools Grants (Grant)
For elementary & secondary, & post-secondary schools
• Legacy Fund Grants (Grant)
Meetings/Conferences: • Physical & Health Education Canada National Conference 2015, April, 2015, Banff, AB
Scope: National
Description: The conference is in partnership with the Manitoba Physical Education Teacher's Association (MPETA).
Publications:
• In Touch Newsletter [a publication of the Physical & Health Education Canada]
Type: Newsletter
• phénEPS-PHEnex Journal [a publication of the Physical & Health Education Canada]
Type: Journal
Profile: Research, position papers, reviews & critical essays
• Physical & Health Education Journal
Type: Journal; *Frequency:* Quarterly
Profile: School physical education programs, quality school health programs, ready-to-use activities, resource reviews, & teaching strategies

Physical Culture Association of Alberta
Percy Page Centre, 11759 Groat Rd., Edmonton AB T5M 3K6
Tel: 780-415-1744
physicalculturealberta@gmail.com
www.physicalculture.ca
Overview: A small provincial organization
Mission: To promote mental & physical well-being for all, using Physical Culture methods
Chief Officer(s):
Lesley McEwan, Executive Director
Staff Member(s): 1
Membership: 7,000; *Fees:* $10; *Member Profile:* Children, teens, adults, older adults, seniors, pre/post-natal, post-cardiac, diabetics, & the physically & mentally challenged
Activities: Exercise to music; training programs; fitness classes

Physical Education in British Columbia (PE-BC)
c/o British Columbia Teachers' Federation, #100, 550 West 6th Ave., Vancouver BC V5Z 4P2
Tel: 604-871-2283; *Fax:* 604-871-2286
www.bctf.ca/pebc
www.facebook.com/PhysicalEducationBC
Previous Name: British Columbia Physical Education Provincial Specialist Association
Overview: A medium-sized provincial organization overseen by British Columbia Teachers' Federation
Mission: To provide leadership, advocacy, & resources for teachers of physical education
Member of: British Columbia Teachers' Federation
Chief Officer(s):
Sue MacDonald, President
smacdonald@sd57.bc.ca

Physical Medicine Research Foundation *See* Canadian Institute for the Relief of Pain & Disability

Physicians for a Smoke-Free Canada / Médecins pour un Canada sans fumée
134 Caroline Ave., Ottawa ON K1Y 0S9
Tel: 613-600-5794; *Fax:* 613-728-9049
psc@NOSPAMsmoke-free.ca
www.smoke-free.ca
Overview: A medium-sized national organization founded in 1985
Chief Officer(s):
Atul Kapur, President
James Walker, Sec.-Treas.
Finances: *Funding Sources:* Health Canada; Membership dues
Staff Member(s): 1
Membership: 1,500

Physicians for Global Survival (Canada) (PGS) / Médecins pour la survie mondiale (Canada)
#208, 145 Spruce St., Ottawa ON K1R 6P1
Tel: 613-233-1982; *Fax:* 613-233-9028
pgsadmin@web.ca
www.pgs.ca
www.facebook.com/pages/Physicians-For-Global-Survival/134022454568
www.youtube.com/user/pgsottawa
Previous Name: Canadian Physicians for the Prevention of Nuclear War
Overview: A small international charitable organization founded in 1980
Mission: Committed to the abolition of nuclear weapons, the prevention of war, the promotion of non-violent means of conflict resolution & social justice in a sustainable world
Affliation(s): International Physicians for the Prevention of Nuclear War (IPPNW)
Chief Officer(s):
Richard Denten, President
Finances: *Annual Operating Budget:* $250,000-$500,000; *Funding Sources:* Contributions
Staff Member(s): 2; 20 volunteer(s)
Membership: 1,000-4,999; *Fees:* Annually - $120 physicians; $60 supporters; $25 student; *Member Profile:* Open to members of the medical profession & the general public
Activities: Education for the abolition of nuclear war; recommendations of measures, both national & international, which will help to prevent war; campaigning for limits on the free trade in arms; discussion of the impact of militarism on human health & environment; works toward the elimination of land mines; Greening of Hospitals & Health Care Facilities project; *Awareness Events:* Abolition of Nuclear Weapons Day, Aug. 6; *Speaker Service:* Yes; *Library* Open to public by appointment

Physicians Services Inc. Foundation
#1006, 5160 Yonge St., Toronto ON M2N 6L9
Tel: 416-226-6323; *Fax:* 416-226-6080
psif@psifoundation.org
www.psifoundation.org
Also Known As: P.S.I. Foundation
Overview: A small provincial charitable organization founded in 1970
Mission: To promote charitable & educational purposes related to health, science & practice of medicine & healing arts
Chief Officer(s):
Kathryn McGuire, Executive Director
Finances: *Annual Operating Budget:* $3 Million-$5 Million
Staff Member(s): 4
Membership: 1-99; *Member Profile:* Composed of physicians representing each of the 75 medical societies in Ontario, the Ontario Medical Association, & six other persons appointed by the Board for their interest in the foundation's activities
Awards:
• Health Research Grant (Grant)
• Resident Research Grant (Grant)

Physiotherapy Alberta - College + Association
Dorchester Bldg., #300, 10357 - 109 St., Edmonton AB T5J 1N3
Tel: 780-438-0338; *Fax:* 780-436-1908
Toll-Free: 800-291-2782
info@physiotherapyalberta.ca
www.physiotherapyalberta.ca
twitter.com/PTAlberta
Previous Name: College of Physical Therapists of Alberta
Overview: A medium-sized provincial licensing organization founded in 1985 overseen by Canadian Alliance of Physiotherapy Regulators
Mission: To protect the public by the regulation of the practice of physical therapy
Member of: Canadian Alliance of Physiotherapy Regulators; Canadian Physiotherapy Association
Affliation(s): Alberta Federation of Regulated Health Professions
Chief Officer(s):
Dianne Millette, Registrar, 780-702-5353
registrar@physiotherapyalberta.ca

Canadian Associations

Finances: *Annual Operating Budget:* $250,000-$500,000;
Funding Sources: Membership dues
Staff Member(s): 4; 35 volunteer(s)
Membership: 2,117; *Fees:* $555 active; $40 student; *Member Profile:* Members must have completed an approved program of physical therapy
Activities: Registration; Practice Standard; Complaint Resolution; Manpower Utilization; Communication; Government Relations; Governance
Publications:
• PT Alberta [a publication of Physiotherapy Alberta - College + Association]
Type: Newsletter

Physiotherapy Association of British Columbia (PABC)

#402, 1755 West Broadway, Vancouver BC V6J 4S5
Tel: 604-736-5130; *Fax:* 604-736-5606
Toll-Free: 888-330-3999
info@bcphysio.org
www.bcphysio.org
www.facebook.com/bcphysio
twitter.com/PABCInfo
www.youtube.com/user/BCPhysio
Overview: A medium-sized provincial organization founded in 1927 overseen by Canadian Physiotherapy Association
Mission: To provide leadership & direction to the physiotherapy profession; To foster excellence in practice, education & research
Member of: Canadian Physiotherapy Association
Chief Officer(s):
Rebecca Bing Tunnacliffe, Chief Executive Officer
rbt@bcphysio.org
Finances: *Funding Sources:* Membership dues; Educational activities
Staff Member(s): 3
Membership: 2,100; *Fees:* Schedule available

Physiotherapy Education Accreditation Canada (PEAC) / Agrément de l'enseignement de la physiothérapie au Canada (EPAC)

#26, 509 Commissioners Rd. West, London ON N6J 1Y5
Tel: 250-494-0677; *Fax:* 778-724-0669
info@peac-aepc.ca
www.peac-aepc.ca
Previous Name: Accreditation Council for Canadian Physiotherapy Academic Programs
Overview: A medium-sized national licensing organization founded in 2000
Mission: To provide leadership in assuring the quality of physiotherapy education in Canada through a comprehensive program of accreditation.
Member of: Association of Accrediting Agencies of Canada (AAAC); The Canadian Council of Physiotherapy University Programs
Affliation(s): Accreditation of Interprofessional Health Education (AIPHE)
Chief Officer(s):
Sharon Switzer-McIntyre, President
Kathy Davidson, Executive Director
kathy.davidson@peac-aepc.ca
Membership: *Member Profile:* Conducts accreditation reviews of Canada's physiotherapist education programs.
Publications:
• Accreditation Manual: Education Programs
Type: Manual; *Number of Pages:* 40
Profile: Information about the accreditation of physiotherapy education programs in Canada, for physiotherapy education program faculty & staff who are preparing for accreditation review,members of the accreditation Peer Review Team teams, university administrators, & members of the public
• Peer Review Team Manual
Type: Manual; *Number of Pages:* 23
Profile: Includes the responsibilities of the peer review team members, a detailed schedule for the on-site accreditation review, & information about the final meeting & the written report

Pickering & Ajax Citizens Together for the Environment (PACT)

e-mail: dj.steele@sympatico.ca
Overview: A small local organization founded in 1987
Mission: To protect the environment in the Pickering/Ajax area, especially with reference to waste management issues
Member of: Ontario Environmental Network
Finances: *Funding Sources:* Fundraising
Activities: *Speaker Service:* Yes
Awards:
• High School Awards (Award)
Eligibility: Eight top students moving on to environmental subjects

Pickering Naturalists

PO Box 304, Pickering ON L1V 2R6
Tel: 905-831-1639
pnclub@pickeringnaturalists.org
www.pickeringnaturalists.org
Overview: A small local organization founded in 1977
Member of: Federation of Ontario Naturalists
Finances: *Funding Sources:* Membership dues
Membership: *Fees:* $21 individual; $25 family; $250 life
Publications:
• Pickering Naturalist [a publication of Pickering Naturalists]
Type: Newsletter; *Frequency:* Quarterly
Profile: Nature articles & information on upcoming events.

Picton United Church County Food Bank

PO Box 96, 12 Chapel St., Picton ON K0K 2T0
Tel: 613-476-8516
pictonunitedchurch@bellnet.ca
pictonunitedchurch.ca/fbank.html
Previous Name: Picton United Church Food Bank
Overview: A small local charitable organization founded in 1984
Member of: Ontario Association of Food Banks
Finances: *Annual Operating Budget:* Less than $50,000;
Funding Sources: Donations
20 volunteer(s)

Picton United Church Food Bank *See* Picton United Church County Food Bank

Pictou County Chamber of Commerce

East River Plaza, 980 East River Rd., New Glasgow NS B2H 3S5
Tel: 902-755-3463; *Fax:* 902-755-2848
info@pictouchamber.com
www.pictouchamber.com
www.facebook.com/173337132712998
Overview: A medium-sized local organization founded in 1983
Mission: To distinguish itself as the pre-eminent voice of business in our region
Member of: Atlantic Provinces Chamber of Commerce; Nova Scotia Chamber of Commerce; Canadian Chamber of Commerce
Chief Officer(s):
Faus Johnson, Executive Director
faus.johnson@pictouchamber.com
Gerald Green, President
Finances: *Annual Operating Budget:* $50,000-$100,000
Staff Member(s): 2
Membership: 295; *Fees:* Schedule available
Activities: *Internships:* Yes; *Speaker Service:* Yes; *Library:* Business Service Centre; Open to public

Pictou County Historical Society

86 Temperance St., New Glasgow NS B2H 3A7
Tel: 902-752-5583
pictoucounty@ns.sympatico.ca
www.parl.ns.ca/csmuseum/historicalsociety.htm
Overview: A small local organization founded in 1964
Mission: To operate & manage Carmichael Stewart House Museum, property owned by the Town of New Glasgow
Affliation(s): NS Museums
Chief Officer(s):
Fergie MacKay, President
Membership: 200 individual; *Fees:* $10 individual

Pictou County Tourist Association

980 East River Rd., New Glasgow NS B2H 3S8
Tel: 902-752-6383
Toll-Free: 877-816-2326
admin@visitdeans.ca
Overview: A small local organization founded in 1978 overseen by Tourism Industry Association of Nova Scotia
Mission: To promote the county to residents & visitors
Member of: Pictou County Chamber of Commerce
Membership: *Member Profile:* Accommodation operators; restaurants; service stations; retail stores

Picture Butte & District Chamber of Commerce

PO Box 540, Picture Butte AB T0K 1V0
Tel: 403-732-4302; *Fax:* 403-732-4703
chamber@picturebutte.ca
Overview: A small local organization
Chief Officer(s):
Wes Brouwer, President
Corrine McInnis, Office Manager

Pier 21 Society

1055 Marginal Rd., Halifax NS B3H 4P6
Tel: 902-425-7770; *Fax:* 902-423-4045
Toll-Free: 855-526-4721
info@pier21.ca
www.pier21.ca
www.facebook.com/210412625764977
twitter.com/pier21
www.youtube.com/Pier21Museum
Overview: A small national charitable organization
Mission: To preserve & share information about the Canadian immigration experience through history
Chief Officer(s):
Tung Chan, Chair
Marie Chapman, Chief Executive Officer
Monica MacDonald, Manager, Research, 902-425-7770 Ext. 278
mmacdonald@pier21.ca
Cailin MacDonald, Manager, Communication
cmacdonald@pier21.ca
Finances: *Funding Sources:* Donations; Gift shop sales; Sponsorships; Rental services
Staff Member(s): 49
Activities: Operating the national museum of immigration at Pier 21; Offering reference services on topics such as immigration, nautical history, World War II, & genealogy at the Soctiabank Research Centre; *Library:* Scotiabank Research Centre; Open to public

Pigeon Lake Regional Chamber of Commerce (PLRCC)

#6B Village Dr., RR#2, Westerose AB T0C 2V0
Tel: 780-586-6263; *Fax:* 780-586-3667
info@pigeonlakechamber.ca
www.pigeonlakechamber.ca
Overview: A small local charitable organization founded in 1988
Mission: To build an economic base for permanent & seasonal residence that will provide services for tourists, while maintaining environmental characteristics & quality of life; To promote the commercial, industrial, social, & civic interests of the community
Affliation(s): Alberta Chambers of Commerce
Chief Officer(s):
Doug McKenzie, President
dhmfin@telus.net
Sereda Bernadette, Manager
Finances: *Annual Operating Budget:* Less than $50,000;
Funding Sources: Fundraising; Membership fees
Staff Member(s): 1; 70 volunteer(s)
Membership: 106; *Fees:* $60 + GST
Activities: Organizing dinner meetings & forums; *Library:* Tourist Booth; Open to public
Awards:
• Business Awards (Award)

PIJAC Canada / Conseil consultatif mixte de l'industrie des animaux de compagnie

#14, 1010 Polytek, Ottawa ON K1J 9H9
Tel: 613-730-8111; *Fax:* 613-730-9111
Toll-Free: 800-667-7452
information@pijaccanada.com
www.pijaccanada.com
www.linkedin.com/company/pijac-canada
Also Known As: Pet Industry Joint Advisory Council of Canada
Overview: A medium-sized national organization founded in 1988
Mission: To ensure the highest level of pet care attainable & a guarantee of a fair & equitable representation for all facets of the Canadian pet industry.
Member of: International Pet Advisory Council
Affliation(s): PIJAC International
Chief Officer(s):
Louis McCann, President & CEO, 613-730-8111 Ext. 112
executiveoffice@pijaccanada.com
Rénald Sabourin, Assistant Executive Director, 613-730-8111 Ext. 116
operations@pijaccanada.com
Finances: *Annual Operating Budget:* $500,000-$1.5 Million;
Funding Sources: Membership fees; trade show revenues
Staff Member(s): 7; 20 volunteer(s)
Membership: 350 corporate; *Fees:* Schedule available; *Member Profile:* Working in the Pet Industry
Activities: Certified Companion Animal Specialist Program; Safe Handling of Pets Information Campaign; National Pet

Industry Trade Shows; *Speaker Service:* Yes; *Library* Open to public by appointment

Pillar Nonprofit Network
251 Dundas St., 2nd Fl., London ON N6A 6H9
Tel: 519-433-7876; *Fax:* 519-435-0227
www.pillarv.com
www.facebook.com/pages/Pillar-Nonprofit-Network/2566003931 0
twitter.com/PillarNN
www.youtube.com/user/pillarnonprofit
Also Known As: Pillar - Voluntary Sector Network
Overview: A small local charitable organization founded in 2001
Mission: To strengthen & leverage the impact of the nonprofit sector for a civic & just society
Chief Officer(s):
Michelle Baldwin, Executive Director
mbaldwin@pillarnonprofit.ca
Finances: *Annual Operating Budget:* $50,000-$100,000
Staff Member(s): 2; 50 volunteer(s)
Membership: 125; *Fees:* $50 individual; $50-$300 corporate; *Committees:* Training; Technology; Research; Marketing; Policy; Special Events
Activities: Volunteer referral; policy input; training; networking; raising awareness of the voluntary sector; *Library* Open to public

Pilot Mound & District Chamber of Commerce
Tel: 204-825-2587
chamberofcommerce@pilotmound.com
www.pilotmound.com
Overview: A small local organization
Member of: Manitoba Chamber of Commerce
Finances: *Annual Operating Budget:* Less than $50,000; *Funding Sources:* Fundraising
Staff Member(s): 1
Membership: 69; *Fees:* $15 individual; $30 business; *Committees:* Housing; Promotion; Development; Smorg

Pilot Parents
c/o Community Living Toronto, 8 Spadina Ave., Toronto ON M5R 2S7
Tel: 416-968-0650
Overview: A small local charitable organization founded in 1982
Mission: To provide emotional support & understanding to parents of children with developmental handicaps; to provide information about developmental handicaps & the services available for parents & children
Affliation(s): Toronto Association for Community Living
Finances: *Annual Operating Budget:* $50,000-$100,000; *Funding Sources:* United Way
Staff Member(s): 1; 40 volunteer(s)
Membership: 90 individual
Activities: Individual parent-to-parent partnerships; workshops; support groups; social events to connect parents with other parents;

Pin Collectors' Club *Voir* Club des collectionneurs d'épinglettes Inc.

Pinawa Chamber of Commerce
PO Box 544, Pinawa MB R0E 1L0
www.pinawachamber.com
Overview: A small local organization
Mission: To represent local businesses
Chief Officer(s):
Jeff Simpson, President
president@pinawachamber.com
Membership: 44; *Fees:* $60

Pincher Creek & District Chamber of Commerce
Ranchland Mall, PO Box 2287, #4, 1300 Hewetson Ave., Pincher Creek AB T0K 1W0
Tel: 403-627-5199
www.pincher-creek.com
www.facebook.com/219210741437000
twitter.com/PC_Chamber
Previous Name: Pincher Creek & District Chamber of Economic Development
Overview: A small local organization founded in 1972
Mission: To enhance the economic & social well-being of the area
Member of: Alberta Chamber of Commerce
Chief Officer(s):
James Van Leeuwen, President
Finances: *Annual Operating Budget:* $50,000-$100,000; *Funding Sources:* Membership fees; Town; Municipal District
Staff Member(s): 2; 12 volunteer(s)
Membership: 139

Pincher Creek & District Chamber of Economic Development *See* Pincher Creek & District Chamber of Commerce

Pincher Creek Allied Arts Council
696 Kettles St., Pincher Creek AB T0K 1W0
Tel: 403-627-5272; *Fax:* 403-627-1559
lebelpc@gmail.com
www.pinchercreekarts.com
Overview: A small local charitable organization
Mission: To promote & advance arts education in Pincher Creek & to restore & preserve the Lebel Mansion Historic Site
Member of: Alberta Municipal Association for Culture
Affliation(s): Heritage Canada
Chief Officer(s):
Sharon Polski, Administrator
Finances: *Annual Operating Budget:* $50,000-$100,000; *Funding Sources:* Donations
Staff Member(s): 1
Membership: 130; *Fees:* $15 single; $20 family

Pincher Creek Humane Society (PC SPCA)
PO Box 2647, 1068 Kettles St., Pincher Creek AB T0K 1W0
Tel: 403-627-5191; *Fax:* 403-627-1406
pchs@toughcountry.net
www.pinchercreekhumanesociety.org
www.facebook.com/142406202447008
Previous Name: Pincher Creek Society for the Prevention of Cruelty to Animals
Overview: A small local charitable organization founded in 1998
Mission: To educate the public about responsible pet ownership; To foster a sense of community in caring fo & dealing with lost or unwanted animals; To ensure a safe environment for lost or unwanted animals; To advocate for & ensoure animals are spayed or neutered; To return animals to their owners & to find caring homes for unwanted animals; to promote positive public awareness & acceptance of the Society; To ensure kind, efficient, cost-effective & humane euthanasia; To seek public & corporate sponsorship to ensure financial support & viability of the Society; To develop & encourage volunteers to participate in self-growth, self-expression & a positive volunteer experience
Affliation(s): Alberta SPCA
Finances: *Annual Operating Budget:* Less than $50,000; *Funding Sources:* Municipal government; fundraising
Staff Member(s): 1; 5 volunteer(s)
Membership: 1-99;

Pincher Creek Society for the Prevention of Cruelty to Animals *See* Pincher Creek Humane Society

Pine Tree Potters Guild
PO Box 28586, Aurora ON L4G 6S6
Tel: 905-727-1278
www.pinetreepotters.ca
www.facebook.com/pinetreepottersguild
Overview: A small local organization founded in 1979
Mission: To preserve & advance ceramic arts.
Chief Officer(s):
Sara Stevens, President

Pink Triangle Services (PTS) / Les services du Triangle Rose
#200, 331 Cooper St., Ottawa ON K2P 0G5
Tel: 613-563-4818; *Fax:* 613-563-1967
communications@ptsottawa.org
www.pinktriangle.org
Previous Name: Association of Lesbians, Gays & Bisexuals of Ottawa
Overview: A small local charitable organization founded in 1984
Mission: To foster the wellness of all lesbian, gay & bisexual persons in the National Capital Region; To provide leadership to identify & address the needs of diverse groups, through communtiy development, delivery of & advocacy for, respectful & inclusive services & programs, provided in a safe environment; To build partnerships with other groups that share cultural & sociopolitical history, in order to work on common goals, issues, needs, & services
Chief Officer(s):
Claudia Van den Heuvel, Executive Director
executive.director@ptsottawa.org
Michael Henschel, President
Finances: *Annual Operating Budget:* $100,000-$250,000; *Funding Sources:* Donations; Grants
Staff Member(s): 2; 82 volunteer(s)
Activities: Discussion groups; peer support; Gayline/Télégai; library; *Library:* Dr. Kelly McGinnis Library

The Pioneer Association of Ontario *See* Ontario Historical Society

Pioneer Clubs Canada Inc.
Toll-Free: 800-465-5437
www.pioneerclubs.org
www.facebook.com/pioneerclubs
Also Known As: Pioneer Girls/Pioneer Boys
Overview: A large national licensing charitable organization founded in 1974
Mission: To serve God by assisting churches & other ministries in helping children & youth make Christ Lord in every aspect of life
Affliation(s): Canadian Council of Christian Charities
Finances: *Annual Operating Budget:* $250,000-$500,000
Staff Member(s): 9
Membership: 216 institutional; 16,000 individual; *Fees:* $12 child
Activities: *Speaker Service:* Yes
Publications:
• Pioneer Clubs Canada Inc. Leadership eNewsletter
Type: Newsletter

Pioneer Women Organization of Canada Inc. *See* Na'amat Canada Inc.

Pipe Line Contractors Association of Canada (PLCAC)
#201, 1075 North Service Rd. West, Oakville ON L6M 2G2
Tel: 905-847-9383; *Fax:* 905-847-7824
plcac@pipeline.ca
www.pipeline.ca
Overview: A small national organization founded in 1954
Mission: To represent contractors in labour relations
Chief Officer(s):
O.J. Kavanaugh, President
Neil G. Lane, Executive Director
Michael J. Gallardo, Assistant Executive Director
Membership: 35 regular members; 66 associate members; 18 honorary members; *Member Profile:* Employers engaged in contacting for the construction, installation, & maintenance of piplines; Corporations or individuals engages in manufacturing, supplying, & transporting material for the construction & maintenance of piplines; *Committees:* Convention Planning; Education & Training; Equipment Rental; Executive; Membership & Promotion; National Labour Relations; Negotiating - Distribution; Negotiating - Mainline; Pipeline Standards; Safety
Activities: Establishing training courses; Reviewing legislation
Meetings/Conferences: • Pipe Line Contractors Association of Canada 2015 61st Annual Convention, April, 2015, Hyatt Regency Maui Resort & Spa, Maui, HI
Scope: National
Description: A program about the special pipeline construction industry, including various speakers & the association's annual general meeting
Contact Information: E-mail: plcac@pipeline.ca
Publications:
• Canadian Pipeliner
Type: Newsletter; *Frequency:* 4 pa
Profile: News, industry information, & upcoming events
• PLCAC [Pipe Line Contractors Association of Canada] Membership Directory
Type: Directory; *Frequency:* Annually
Profile: Featuring membership profiles & contact information

Pirate Party of Canada
#155, 3-212 Henderson Hwy., Winnipeg MB R2L 1L8
Tel: 778-800-2744
Toll-Free: 877-978-2023
Other Communication: press@pirateparty.ca
info@pirateparty.ca
www.pirateparty.ca
facebook.com/piratepartyca
twitter.com/piratepartyca
Overview: A small national organization founded in 2010
Chief Officer(s):
James Wilson, Leader

Pitch-In Alberta (PIA)
PO Box 45011, RPO Ocean Park, White Rock BC V4A 9L1
Fax: 604-535-4653
Toll-Free: 877-474-8244
www.pitch-in.ca

Previous Name: Outdoors Unlittered (Alberta)
Overview: A medium-sized provincial charitable organization founded in 1974
Mission: To carry out promotional, educational & action programs aimed at reducing, reusing, recycling & properly managing & disposing of waste & solid wastes in particular; To initiate cleanup & beautification programs; To secure support of all levels of government, industry, media, other public sector organizations & the public for these objectives
Member of: Pitch-In Canada
Affliation(s): Clean World International
Chief Officer(s):
Misha van Veen, Program Manager
Allard W. van Veen, Founder
Finances: *Annual Operating Budget:* $50,000-$100,000; *Funding Sources:* Local governments; foundations; industry; individuals
Staff Member(s): 2
Activities: *Awareness Events:* Pitch-In Canada Week, May; Coastal Clean Up Campaign, Sept.; *Speaker Service:* Yes

Pitch-In Canada (PIC) / Passons à l'action Canada
PO Box 45011, RPO Ocean Park, White Rock BC V4A 9L1
Tel: 604-536-4726; *Fax:* 604-535-4653
Toll-Free: 877-474-8244
pitch-in@pitch-in.ca
www.pitch-in.ca
www.facebook.com/pitchin.canada
www.twitter.com/@pitch_in_canada
Previous Name: Outdoors Unlittered
Overview: A medium-sized national charitable organization founded in 1967
Mission: To improve communities & the envionment by providing programs to reduce, re-use, recycle, & properly manage & dispose waste
Affliation(s): Clean World International; Clean up the World
Chief Officer(s):
Misha Cook, Executive Director, 877-474-8244 Ext. 1
misha@pitch-in.ca
Erika Tibbe, Marketing & Program Coordinator
erika@pitch-in.ca
Finances: *Funding Sources:* Donations; Sponsorships; Grants; Fees for service; Merchandising of materials
Activities: Working with all levels of government & other organizations; *Awareness Events:* National Pitch-In Week; *Library:* Pitch-In Canada Resource Centre

Pittsburgh Historical Society
PO Box 61, Kingston ON K7L 4V6
Tel: 613-546-4421
www.facebook.com/220786231304185
Overview: A small local organization founded in 1976
Mission: To create & maintain community awareness & interest in the heritage of Pittsburgh Township; To meet regularly for the presentation & discussion of papers; To encourage research & documentation; To encourage the establishment of a historical museum; To encourage the identification & conservation of historic sites within the township
Member of: Ontario Historical Society
Finances: *Annual Operating Budget:* Less than $50,000; *Funding Sources:* Membership fees
Activities: Meetings; publications; exhibitions; plaques; presentations

Pius X Secular Institute *Voir* Institut Séculier Pie X

Place Benoît Bon Courage Community Centre *Voir* Centre Communautaire Bon Courage De Place Benoît

Place Vermeil
#206, 2600 rue Ontario Est, Montréal QC H2K 4K4
Tél: 514-251-7822
info@placevermeil.org
placevermeil.org
Aperçu: *Dimension:* petite; *Envergure:* locale; fondée en 1974
Mission: Pour aider les personnes âgées lutte contre l'isolement et de devenir indépendant
Membre(s) du bureau directeur:
Annie Boilon, Directrice générale
Membre: *Montant de la cotisation:* 6$
Activités: Art plastique; chant choral; cours de langue Italienne; atelier photo; éveil musical; clinique d'impôts

Placentia Area Chamber of Commerce (PACC)
PO Box 109, 1 O'Reilly St., Placentia NL A0B 2Y0
Tel: 709-227-0003; *Fax:* 709-227-0016
www.placentiachamber.org
Previous Name: Argentia Area Chamber of Commerce
Overview: A small local organization
Member of: Canadian Chamber of Commerce
Chief Officer(s):
Gerry Hynes, President, 709-227-1700, Fax: 709-227-1701
ghynes@persona.ca
Eugene Collins, Executive Director
eugene.collins@placentiachamber.ca
Staff Member(s): 1
Membership: 120; *Fees:* $100

Plan Canada
#1001, 95 St. Clair Ave. West, Toronto ON M4V 3B5
Tel: 416-920-1654; *Fax:* 416-920-9942
Toll-Free: 800-387-1418
info@plancanada.ca
plancanada.ca
www.linkedin.com/company/plan-canada
www.facebook.com/PlanCanada
twitter.com/PlanCanada
www.youtube.com/user/plancanadavideos
Previous Name: Foster Parents Plan Canada
Overview: A large international charitable organization founded in 1968
Mission: To help children, their families, & communities in developing countries; To raise funds through sponsorship program & implement programs in health, education, & community development overseas
Member of: Canadian Council for International Cooperation
Chief Officer(s):
Rosemary McCarney, President & CEO
Staff Member(s): 53
Membership: 90,000 foster parents; *Fees:* $348; *Member Profile:* Sponsorship fee; *Committees:* Finance; Legal
Activities: *Internships:* Yes

Le plan nord-américain de gestion de la sauvagine *See* North American Waterfowl Management Plan

Planetary Association for Clean Energy, Inc. (PACE) / Société planétaire pour l'assainissement de l'énergie
#1001, 100 Bronson Ave., Ottawa ON K1R 6G8
Tel: 613-236-6265; *Fax:* 613-235-5876
paceincnet@gmail.com
pacenet.homestead.com
Overview: A medium-sized international charitable organization founded in 1975
Mission: To steward & facilitate the implementation of clean energy systems worldwide
Chief Officer(s):
Andrew Michrowski, President
Finances: *Annual Operating Budget:* $100,000-$250,000; *Funding Sources:* Membership fees; donations
Staff Member(s): 2; 10 volunteer(s)
Membership: 3,600 in 60 countries; *Fees:* $50
Activities: Electromagnetic bioaffect, analyses & abatement; monitors unclean developments; peer review of new technologies; books, databases & technical reports; *Internships:* Yes; *Speaker Service:* Yes; *Library* by appointment

Planned Lifetimie Advocacy Network (PLAN)
#260, 3665 Kingsway, Vancouver BC V5R 5W2
Tel: 604-439-9566; *Fax:* 604-439-7001
inquiries@plan.ca
plan.ca
www.facebook.com/JoinPLAN
twitter.com/plannedlifetime
www.youtube.com/user/PLANvids
Overview: A small local organization
Mission: To help families with disabled relatives plan for their future
Affliation(s): PLAN Toronto; Thunderbay Family Network; PLAN Edmonton; Lethbridge Association for Community Living; PLAN Calgary; Lifetime Networks Ottawa; Planned Lifetime Networks; LifeSPAN; PLAN Okanagan; Regina RDACL PLAN; Family Link; PLAN of Arizona
Chief Officer(s):
Tim Ames, Executive Director
tames@plan.ca
Membership: *Member Profile:* Families with disabled relatives

Planned Parenthood - Newfoundland & Labrador Sexual Health Centre (NLSHC)
203 Merrymeeting Rd., St. John's NL A1C 2W6
Tel: 709-579-1009
Toll-Free: 877-666-9847
info@nlsexualhealthcentre.org
www.nlsexualhealthcentre.org
Overview: A medium-sized provincial organization founded in 1972 overseen by Canadian Federation for Sexual Health
Mission: To promote positive sexual health attitudes & practices throughout Newfoundland & Labrador; To support & respect individual choice
Member of: Coalition Against the Sexual Exploitation of Youth
Chief Officer(s):
Rolanda Ryan, President
Costa Kasimos, Executive Director
Andrea Murphy, Secretary
Terri Hancock, Treasurer
Finances: *Funding Sources:* Fundraising; Donations
Membership: *Fees:* $25 regular members; $10 students
Activities: Providing information & education to assist people to make informed sexual health choices; Offering workshops for schools, youth, & community groups, & agencies; Partnering with other community organizations; Promoting preventive health care & responsible sexual practices; Offering support groups; Counselling; Providing medical clinics & exams for women & men; *Awareness Events:* National Day Against Homophobia, May; Annual 5 km Run For Respect, August; Take Back The Night, September; *Speaker Service:* Yes; *Library:* Newfoundland & Labrador Sexual Health Centre Resource Library
Publications:
• The Messenger
Type: Newsletter; *Frequency:* Semiannually; *Price:* Free with NLSHC membership
Profile: Centre reports, informative articles. & upcoming activities

Planned Parenthood Association of British Columbia *See* Options for Sexual Health

Planned Parenthood Association of Edmonton *See* OPTIONS Sexual Health Association

Planned Parenthood Banff; Banff YWCA Community Resource Centre *See* YWCA of Banff Programs & Services

Planned Parenthood Bridgewater *See* Sexual Health Centre Lunenburg County

Planned Parenthood Cape Breton *See* Cape Breton Centre for Sexual Health

Planned Parenthood Centre (Regina) *See* Planned Parenthood Regina

Planned Parenthood Fredericton (PPF)
PO Box 20181, #210, 390 King St., Fredericton NB E3B 7A2
Tel: 506-454-6333; *Fax:* 506-450-4899
ppf@nbnet.nb.ca
Overview: A small local organization founded in 1971
Member of: Planned Parenthood Federation of Canada
Chief Officer(s):
Kim Howland, Interim Executive Director
JoAnn Majerovich, President
Staff Member(s): 2; 15 volunteer(s)
Activities: "Let's Talk: A Sexual Health";

Planned Parenthood Manitoba *See* Sexuality Education Resource Centre Manitoba

Planned Parenthood Metro Clinic *See* Halifax Sexual Health Centre

Planned Parenthood Montréal *See* Sexual Health Network of Québec Inc.

Planned Parenthood of Toronto (PPT)
36B Prince Arthur Ave., Toronto ON M5R 1A9
Tel: 416-961-0113; *Fax:* 416-961-2512
ppt@ppt.on.ca
www.ppt.on.ca
www.facebook.com/PPToronto
twitter.com/PPofTO
Overview: A small local charitable organization founded in 1961
Mission: Committed to the principles of equity & to providing accessbile & inclusive services which promote healthy sexuality & informed decision-making to the people of the city of Toronto
Member of: Canadian Federation for Sexual Health; United Way Toronto
Chief Officer(s):
Sarah Hobbs, Executive Director
Finances: *Annual Operating Budget:* $1.5 Million-$3 Million; *Funding Sources:* Membership fees; donations; United Way Toronto
Staff Member(s): 30; 140 volunteer(s)

Membership: *Fees:* $10 general; $20 organization; $5 student; *Member Profile:* Individuals living in Toronto who are 18 and over; corporations
Activities: Programming for women, teens, young men, & young parents; anti-homophobia education; community based research

Planned Parenthood Ottawa (PPOC) / Planning des naissances d'Ottawa
#403, 2197 Riverside Dr., Ottawa ON K1H 7X3
Tel: 613-226-3234; *Fax:* 613-226-8955
ppottawa@ppottawa.ca
www.ppottawa.ca
www.facebook.com/285360338462
twitter.com/knowppo
Overview: A small local charitable organization founded in 1964
Mission: To offer education, couselling, & referral services to assist & support people making informed sexual & reproductive health choices
Member of: Planned Parenthood Federation of Canada
Affliation(s): Planned Parenthood Ontario
Chief Officer(s):
Rachel Horsley, Interim Executive Director, 613-226-3234 Ext. 301
director@ppottawa.ca
Finances: *Annual Operating Budget:* $100,000-$250,000; *Funding Sources:* Government; United Way; City of Ottawa: Peoples Services; Program fees; Sponsorship
Staff Member(s): 3; 100 volunteer(s)
Membership: 100-499; *Fees:* $30
Activities: Providing sexual health information & support; Offering teen outreach support; Providing community education; *Speaker Service:* Yes; *Library:* Dorothea Palmer Ferguson Resource Library; Open to public

Planned Parenthood Pictou County (PPPC)
Pictou County Women's Centre, PO Box 964, 35 Riverside St., New Glasgow NS B2H 5K7
Tel: 902-755-4647; *Fax:* 902-752-2233
pppc@ns.sympatico.ca
www.pictoucounty.cfsh.info
Also Known As: Pictou County Centre for Sexual Health
Overview: A small local organization founded in 1979
Mission: To provide comprehensive & accessible sexual & reproductive health services to men & women of all ages in Pictou County
Member of: Planned Parenthood Nova Scotia
Finances: *Annual Operating Budget:* Less than $50,000
Staff Member(s): 1
Membership: 1-99
Activities: *Library* Open to public

Planned Parenthood Regina
1431 Victoria Ave., Regina SK S4P 0P4
Tel: 306-522-0902; *Fax:* 306-522-8860
admin.ppr@accesscomm.ca
www.plannedparenthoodregina.com
Previous Name: Planned Parenthood Centre (Regina)
Overview: A small local organization founded in 1986
Mission: To provide education, counselling & medical services in the areas of sexuality, birth control & family planning
Finances: *Funding Sources:* Regina Health District; community grants; corporate & individual donations
Staff Member(s): 5; 8 volunteer(s)
Membership: 100-499
Activities: Birth Control Centre

Planned Parenthood Saskatoon Centre (PPSC)
210 - 2 Ave. North, Saskatoon SK S7K 2B5
Tel: 306-244-7989; *Fax:* 306-652-4034
info@shcsaskatoon.ca
sexualhealthcentresaskatoon.ca
Overview: A medium-sized local charitable organization founded in 1971 overseen by Canadian Federation for Sexual Health
Mission: To ensure that information, resources & support services of the highest quality regarding sexuality, contraception & reproduction are available & accessible to all in our community who need them; to encourage responsible decision-making & behaviour which is respectful of the needs & of the choices available to each individual
Chief Officer(s):
Linzi Williamson, Interim Executive Director
admin@shcsaskatoon.ca
Patrick LaPointe, Interim Executive Director
admin@shcsaskatoon.ca
Finances: *Funding Sources:* Donations; fundraising

Membership: *Fees:* $5 student/unemployed; $10 individual; $15 family; $25 organization
Activities: *Library* Open to public by appointment

Planned Parenthood Society of Hamilton
#611, 20 Hughson St. South, Hamilton ON L8N 2A1
Tel: 905-528-3009; *Fax:* 905-528-4702
ppsh@canada.com
ppsh.tripod.com
Also Known As: Sexual Health Awareness Centre
Overview: A small local charitable organization founded in 1932
Mission: To advance healthy sexuality & reproductive wellness for all individuals in Hamilton, by acting as a resource for services, education, advocacy & community partnerships
Member of: Canadian Federation for Sexual Health
Finances: *Annual Operating Budget:* $250,000-$500,000; *Funding Sources:* City of Hamilton; Hamilton Community Foundation; donations; memberships; special events
Staff Member(s): 7; 20 volunteer(s)
Membership: 125; *Fees:* $15
Activities: Clinical services; community outreach education; *Speaker Service:* Yes; *Library:* Thelma Will Resource Centre; Open to public

Planned Parenthood Waterloo Region (PPWR)
#500, 151 Frederick St., Kitchener ON N2H 2M2
Tel: 519-743-9360; *Fax:* 519-743-6710
director@ppwr.on.ca
www.ppwr.on.ca
www.facebook.com/ppwaterloo
Overview: A small local charitable organization founded in 1971
Mission: To promote healthy & responsible sexuality throughout the human life cycle
Member of: Planned Parenthood Federation of Canada
Finances: *Annual Operating Budget:* $100,000-$250,000; *Funding Sources:* Private donations; foundation grants
Staff Member(s): 5; 40 volunteer(s)
Activities: *Speaker Service:* Yes; *Library:* Sexuality Resource Centre; Open to public

Planning & Land Administrators of Nunavut (PLAN)
NU
Tel: 867-360-7705; *Fax:* 867-360-7142
Overview: A small provincial organization founded in 2004 overseen by National Aboriginal Lands Managers Association
Chief Officer(s):
TRoy Beaulieu, Chair
gjoalands@qiniq.com
Staff Member(s): 1

Planning des naissances d'Ottawa *See* Planned Parenthood Ottawa

The Planning Forum *See* Strategic Leadership Forum

Planning Institute of British Columbia (PIBC)
#1750, 355 Burrard St., Vancouver BC V6C 2G8
Tel: 604-696-5031; *Fax:* 604-696-5032
Toll-Free: 866-696-5031
info@pibc.bc.ca
www.pibc.bc.ca
Overview: A medium-sized provincial organization founded in 1958 overseen by Canadian Institute of Planners
Mission: To promote orderly use of land, buildings & natural resources; to maintain high standard of professional competence; to protect rights & interests of those engaged in planning profession
Chief Officer(s):
Andrew Young, President
andrew.young@pibc.bc.ca
Dave Crossley, Executive Director
dave.crossley@pibc.bc.ca
Staff Member(s): 2
Membership: 1,500; *Fees:* Schedule available; *Member Profile:* Professional working in the planning industry & planning students; *Committees:* Executive; Membership; Education; Communications; Mentorship; Awards; Professional Practice Review
Meetings/Conferences: • Planning Institute of British Columbia 2015 Annual Conference, April, 2015, Washington State Convention Center, Seattle, WA
Scope: Provincial

Plant Biology Research Institute *Voir* Institut de recherche en biologie végétale

Plant Engineering & Maintenance Association of Canada (PEMAC)
#402, 6 - 2400 Dundas St. West, Mississauga ON L5K 2R8
Fax: 905-823-8001
Toll-Free: 877-532-7255
admin@pemac.org
www.pemac.org
Overview: A medium-sized national licensing organization founded in 1989
Mission: To be recognized as a nationwide centre of excellence in plant engineering & maintenance; To form positive & constructive links with industry & service sectors, in support of local & nationwide developments & productivity; To deliver strongly identifiable services & commitments across the range of disciplines embraced by the association; to educate & introduce new concepts; To provide representation at all government levels; To provide career enhancement & networking opportunities; To promote research in the field of plant engineering & maintenance
Affliation(s): Annex Business Media; Canadian Institute for Nondestructive Evaluation; Canadian Network of Asset Managers; Canadian Association for University Continuing Education; Global Forum on Maintenance & Asset Management
Chief Officer(s):
Rob Lash, President
Finances: *Funding Sources:* Membership fees; website; colleges
Membership: *Member Profile:* Maintenance professionals & practitioners
Activities: Certification Program, MMP - Maintenance Management Professional; *Speaker Service:* Yes; *Library* by appointment
Awards:
• Annual Sergio Guy Memorial Award (Award)

Plast Ukrainian Youth Association of Canada
516 The Kingsway, Toronto ON M9A 3W6
Tel: 416-769-9998; *Fax:* 416-767-5278
toronto@plastcanada.ca
www.plast.ca/toronto
www.facebook.com/pages/Plast-Toronto/135071499928751
Also Known As: PLAST
Overview: A small national charitable organization

The Platinum Party of Employers Who Think & Act to Increase Awareness
PO Box 8068, Stn. Main, Victoria BC V8W 3R7
Tel: 250-483-7717
www.platinumparty.org
Also Known As: Platinum Party
Overview: A small provincial organization
Mission: The party's aim is to ensure that the Government of British Columbia has in place the procedures necessary to maintain a legitimate position of authority over the commercial sector in BC.
Chief Officer(s):
Espavo Sozo, Party Leader
treasurer@platinumparty.org

Playwrights Guild of Canada (PGC)
#350, 401 Richmond St. West, Toronto ON M5V 3A8
Tel: 416-703-0201; *Fax:* 416-703-0059
Toll-Free: 800-561-3318
info@playwrightsguild.ca
www.playwrightsguild.ca
twitter.com/PGuildCanada
Previous Name: Playwrights Union of Canada
Overview: A medium-sized national organization founded in 1972
Mission: To encourage Canadian playwriting; to publish, promote & distribute Canadian plays; to provide current information of Canadian plays & their authors; to offer copyright protection; to promote the study & appreciation of Canadian plays; to safeguard freedom of expression on the stage
Member of: Association of Canadian Publishers; Literary Press Group; Canadian Conference of the Arts
Chief Officer(s):
Robin Sokoloski, Executive Director
robin@playwrightsguild.ca
Finances: *Annual Operating Budget:* $250,000-$500,000; *Funding Sources:* Canada Council; provincial, municipal & city government; 45% earned revenue
Staff Member(s): 3; 23 volunteer(s)
Membership: 500; *Fees:* $155 full; $75 associate; $35 individual supporting; $100 institutional; $65 senior; *Member Profile:* Canadian citizens or landed immigrants with one play produced

or revived within the past ten years, either as an Equity production or an equivalent production; *Committees:* Contracts; Copyright; Women's Caucus
Activities: PUC's imprint - Playwrights Canada Press - releases several plays each year in high-quality trade paperbacks (Canada's largest publisher of Canadian drama with annual season of six titles & special projects, a scene book, a high school play anthology & a book of theatre for young audiences); special cultural events such as playwrights' cabarets; touring programs; manages reading rooms in more than 10 countries; administration of amateur performance rights; forwarding of royalties from scripts; *Rents Mailing List:* Yes; *Library:* Drama Reading Room; Open to public

Playwrights Theatre Centre
#202, 739 Gore Ave., Vancouver BC V6A 2Z9
Tel: 604-685-6228
plays@playwrightstheatre.com
www.playwrightstheatre.com
www.facebook.com/playwrightstheatre
Overview: A small local organization
Mission: To develop new Canadian plays; to provide support to experienced, emerging, & aspiring playwrights from across the country through dramaturgy, workshops, writers' groups and other programs
Chief Officer(s):
Stephen Heatley, President
Heidi Taylor, Artistic & Executive Director
Staff Member(s): 5
Membership: 192; *Fees:* $25

Playwrights Union of Canada ***See*** Playwrights Guild of Canada

Playwrights' Workshop Montréal (PWM)
#240, 5337, boul St. Laurent, Montréal QC H2T 1S5
Tel: 514-843-3685; *Fax:* 514-843-9384
info@playwrights.ca
www.playwrights.ca
Overview: A small local charitable organization founded in 1963
Chief Officer(s):
Delphine Hervot, President, 514-843-4894
delphine.hervot@bydeluxe.com
Chris Gobeil, Secretary, 450-458-0644
cegobeil@videotron.ca
Paul Garellek, Treasurer, 514-487-1788
paul.garellek@ca.ey.com
Ned Cox, Director, 514-483-4523
nedcox3@aol.com
Gabriel Di Genova, Director, 514-284-2322 Ext. 210
gdigenova@mitchellgattuso.com
An-Luiza Georgescu, Director, 514-840-2538
algeorgescu@kpmg.ca
Lizbeth Lopez, Director
lopliz@yahoo.com
Sandra Patino, Director, 514-939-6944
Sandra_Patino@mckinsey.com

PLEA Community Services Society of BC (PLEA)
3894 Commercial St., Vancouver BC V5N 4G2
Tel: 604-871-0450; *Fax:* 604-871-0408
info@plea.bc.ca
www.plea.ca
Previous Name: Pacific Legal Education Association
Overview: A medium-sized local charitable organization founded in 1979
Mission: Provision of justice services, with a particular emphasis on young offenders & on at-risk children & youth
Member of: Community Legal Services Employers Association; United Community Services Group
Chief Officer(s):
David S. Duncan, President
Timothy Agg, Executive Director
tagg@plea.bc.ca
Finances: *Annual Operating Budget:* Greater than $5 Million; *Funding Sources:* Provincial government; charitable donations
Staff Member(s): 346; 250 volunteer(s)
Membership: 25

Plum Coulee & District Chamber of Commerce
www.townofplumcoulee.com/chamber.html
Overview: A small local organization
Chief Officer(s):
Moira Porte, Contact, 204-362-4195
Finances: *Annual Operating Budget:* Less than $50,000
8 volunteer(s)
Membership: 34; *Fees:* $75; *Committees:* Heritage; Millennium; Centennial; Foundation; Sports
Activities: *Awareness Events:* Plum Fest, every 3rd week-end in August

Plumbing & Mechanical Contractors Association of New Brunswick ***See*** Mechanical Contractors Association of New Brunswick

Plumbing Officials' Association of British Columbia (POABC)
2328 Hollyhill Pl., Victoria BC V8N 1T9
Tel: 250-361-0342; *Fax:* 250-385-1128
bhusband@victoria.ca
www.bcplumbingofficials.com
Overview: A medium-sized provincial organization
Chief Officer(s):
Brian Husband, President
Meetings/Conferences: • Plumbing Officials' Association of British Columbia 2015 Conference, 2015, BC
Scope: Provincial

Point d'appui, centre d'aide et de prévention des agressions à caractère sexuel de Rouyn-Noranda (CAPACS)
CP 1274, Rouyn-Noranda QC J9X 6E4
Tél: 819-797-0101; *Téléc:* 819-797-0102
info@pointdappui.org
www.pointdappui.org
Aperçu: *Dimension:* petite; *Envergure:* locale; fondée en 1983
Mission: Service d'urgence, aide, support et écoute auprès des femmes agressées sexuellement; sensibilisation et prévention dans la communauté; relation d'aide individuelle et de groupe; collaboration avec les organismes du milieu (policiers, hôpitaux, etc)
Affiliation(s): Regroupement québécois des Calacs; Association canadienne des centres contre le viol
Membre(s) du bureau directeur:
Carmen Dion, Bénévole-militante
Finances: *Budget de fonctionnement annuel:* $50,000-$100,000; *Fonds:* Gouvernement provincial
Membre(s) du personnel: 2; 16 bénévole(s)
Membre: 30
Activités: *Evénements de sensibilisation:* Journée d'action contre la violence sexuelle, 3e vendredi de sept.

Pointe-au-Baril Chamber of Commerce
PO Box 67, Pointe-au-Baril-Station ON P0G 1K0
Tel: 705-366-2331; *Fax:* 705-366-2331
info@pointeaubarilchamber.com
www.pointeaubarilchamber.com
Also Known As: Information Booth
Overview: A small local licensing organization
Mission: To offer the travelling public the best accomodations in the area
Member of: Ontario Chamber of Commerce
Affliation(s): Rainbow County Travel Association
Chief Officer(s):
Matt French, President
Finances: *Annual Operating Budget:* $50,000-$100,000; *Funding Sources:* Membership fees
Staff Member(s): 6; 1 volunteer(s)
Membership: 110; *Fees:* $150 business; $50 associate; $40 family; $500 corporate; *Committees:* Canada Day Committee

Poison & Drug Information Service
Foothills Medical Centre, North Tower, 1402 - 29th St. NW, Calgary AB T2N 2T9
Tel: 403-944-6900
Toll-Free: 800-332-1414
padis.secretary@albertahealthservices.ca
www.albertahealthservices.ca/5423.asp
Also Known As: PADIS
Previous Name: Alberta Poison Centre
Overview: A small provincial organization
Member of: Canadian Association of Poison Control Centres
Chief Officer(s):
Thomas McMillan, Manager, Strategic Communications & Outcome Evaluation
thomas.mcmillan@calgaryhealthregion.ca

Polanie-Polish Song & Dance Association
3015 - 15 St. NE, Calgary AB T2E 7L8
Tel: 403-287-7336
info@polanie.ca
www.polanie.ca
Overview: A small local organization founded in 1977
Mission: To present the richness of Polish folklore in a stylized artistic adaptation
Chief Officer(s):
Sandro Barbosa, Artistic Director
artisticdirector@polanie.ca
Membership: 45

Polarettes Gymnastics Club
4061 - 4th Ave., Whitehorse YT Y1A 1H1
Tel: 867-668-4794
polarettesgymnastics@yahoo.com
www.polarettes.org
Overview: A small provincial organization
Mission: To promote recreational & competitive gymnastics programs to Yukon residtents.
Chief Officer(s):
Seamus Venasse, President
svenasse@gmail.com
Activities: Toddler Movement program (18 months); competitive programs start from 6-8 years old

Police Association of Nova Scotia (PANS) / Association des policiers de la Nouvelle-Écosse
#2, 1000 Windmill Rd., Dartmouth NS B3B 1L7
Tel: 902-468-7555; *Fax:* 902-468-2202
Toll-Free: 888-468-2798
www.pansguide.com
Overview: A medium-sized provincial organization
Chief Officer(s):
David W. Fisher, CEO
dfisher@accesscable.net

Police Association of Ontario (PAO) / Association des policiers de l'Ontario
#1-3, 6730 Davand Dr., Mississauga ON L5T 2K8
Tel: 905-670-9770; *Fax:* 905-670-9755
pao@pao.ca
www.pao.ca
Overview: A large provincial organization founded in 1944
Mission: To preserve safe communities
Member of: Canadian Police Association
Chief Officer(s):
Ronald Middel, CAO
David McFadden, President
Edward Parent, Chair
Finances: *Annual Operating Budget:* $500,000-$1.5 Million; *Funding Sources:* Membership dues; assessment
Staff Member(s): 4
Membership: 33,000 individual + 57 organizations
Activities: *Library*
Meetings/Conferences: • 24th Annual Police Employment Conference, March, 2015, Delta Meadowvale, Mississauga, ON
Scope: Provincial
Description: Labour relations
Publications:
• PAO Magazine
Type: Magazine; *Frequency:* Quarterly

Police Brotherhood of the Royal Newfoundland Constabulary Association (Ind.) ***See*** Royal Newfoundland Constabulary Association

Police Martial Arts Association Inc. (PMAA)
PO Box 7303, Sub. #12, 162 Trites Rd., Top Fl., Riverview NB E1B 4T9
Tel: 506-387-5126; *Fax:* 506-387-5126
www.policemartialarts.org
Also Known As: Riverview Karate Studio
Overview: A small international organization founded in 1993
Mission: To provide a forum for members from 34 nations for instructional technical development, information resources, officer safety & public concerns
Member of: World Head of Family Sokeship Council; Kam Lung Kempo Karate
Chief Officer(s):
Rannie MacDonald, Grand Master
Grand_Master_Rannie_MacDonald@policemartialarts.org
Foster MacLeod, Grand Master
Grand_Master_Foster_MacLeod@policemartialarts.org
Finances: *Annual Operating Budget:* Less than $50,000
Staff Member(s): 2; 20 volunteer(s)
Membership: 2,306; *Fees:* US$40 North America; US$50 International; *Member Profile:* Law enforcement officers - martial arts participants; *Committees:* Global Use of Force Research Committee
Activities: *Awareness Events:* Youth Intervention Initiative

Police Sector Council (PSC) / Conseil sectoriel de la police (CSP)
#303, 1545 Carling Ave., Ottawa ON K1Z 8P9
Tel: 613-729-2789
info@policecouncil.ca
www.policecouncil.ca
twitter.com/PoliceCouncil
Overview: A medium-sized national organization founded in 2004
Mission: Improving the ways in which human resource planning & management support police operations & enhance police service in communities across Canada
Chief Officer(s):
Geoff Gruson, Executive Director, 613-729-2789, Fax: 613-729-9691
ggruson@policecouncil.ca
Finances: *Funding Sources:* Federal government
Membership: *Committees:* Competency Based Management (CBM) Framework Steering; Leadership Framework; Recruit Training Comparative Analysis; E-Learning; HR Diagnostic; Sector Scanning

Polio Québec
#263, 3500 boul. Décarie, Montréal QC H4A 3J5
Tél: 514-489-1143
Ligne sans frais: 877-765-4672
association@polioquebec.org
www.polioquebec.org
Également appelé: Polio Quebec Association
Aperçu: *Dimension:* moyenne; *Envergure:* provinciale; fondée en 1985
Mission: La mission de Polio Québec est d'aider toutes les personnes atteintes par la polio et de sensibiliser la population en général sur tous les aspects de la polio, incluant la prévention
Affliation(s): L'Institut et Hôpital Neurologiques de Montréal; Le centre de réadaptation MAB-Mackay; Confédération des organismes de personnes handicapées du Québec (COPHAN); L'Association multi-ethnique pour l'intégration des personnes handicapées (AMEIPH); Le Carrefour familial des personnes handicapées (Québec)
Membre(s) du bureau directeur:
Gilles Besner, Président
Steward Valin, Vice-président
Finances: *Budget de fonctionnement annuel:* $50,000-$100,000
Membre: 640; *Montant de la cotisation:* $20
Activités: *Evénements de sensibilisation:* World Polio Awareness Month, October; *Stagiaires:* Oui

Polio Regina
825 McDonald St., Regina SK S4N 2X5
e-mail: polio@accesscomm.ca
nonprofits.accesscomm.ca/polio
Overview: A small local organization
Mission: To provide support & information to those who suffer & have suffered from polio.
Chief Officer(s):
Wilf Tiefenbach, President
Membership: *Fees:* $10 single; $15 family

Polish Alliance of Canada (PAC)
c/o Mississauga Branch, 3060 Eden Oak Cres., Mississauga ON L5L 5V2
Tel: 905-569-7139
www.polishalliance.ca
Merged from: Society of Mutual Aid "Sons of Poland"; Society of St. Stanislaus; Progressuve Polish Union
Overview: A small national organization founded in 1907
Mission: To promote Polish history, culture & interests
Affliation(s): Polish Women Circle, Youth Groups, PAC-Mutual Aid Societ; Canadian Polish Congress; Canadian Polish Millennium Fund; Polish Canadian Womens Federation; Polish Combatants Association of Canada; Association of Polish Engineers in Canada; Polish National Union of Canada; Polish Scouting Association in Canada; Polish Teachers Association of Canada
Chief Officer(s):
Robert Zawierucha, President
president@polishalliance.ca
Membership: *Committees:* Litigation; Audit

Polish Army Veterans Association of America
PO Box 68064, Stn. Blakely, Hamilton ON L8M 3M7
Tel: 905-544-4901
Overview: A small local organization
Affliation(s): Polish Army Veterans Association of America
Chief Officer(s):
George Obminski, Secretary
Membership: 1-99; *Member Profile:* Polish veterans

Polish Canadian Women's Federation
ON
e-mail: info@federacjapolek.ca
www.federacjapolek.ca
Overview: A medium-sized national organization founded in 1956
Mission: To preserve Polish culture in Canada & bring women of Polish heritage together
Member of: Canadian Polish Congress Head Executive Board; Canadian National Council of Women; World Polish Women's Federation
Chief Officer(s):
Ewa L. Zadarnowski, President
ewazadar@hotmail.com

Polish Combatants Association (SPK)
206 Beverley St., Toronto ON M5T 1Z3
Tel: 416-591-6584; *Fax:* 905-881-9039
spkzg.tripod.com
Overview: A small local charitable organization founded in 1950
Member of: National Council of Veteran Associations
Chief Officer(s):
Andrzej M. Garlicki, CM, President
Monika Wyrzykowska, Contact, Media Relations
Membership: 3,000; *Member Profile:* WWII veterans
Activities: *Speaker Service:* Yes

Polish Combatants Association - Winnipeg
1364 Main St., Winnipeg MB R2X 0P2
Tel: 204-589-7638; *Fax:* 204-589-7638
Other Communication: Pub Phone: 204-586-6223
www.pcaclub13.com
Also Known As: Polish Combatants Association Club #13
Overview: A small local organization
Chief Officer(s):
Elizabeth Pazerniuk, Club Manager
club13@mts.net
Krysia (Christine) Kovach, Contact
ckovach@pembinatrails.ca
Activities: *Library:* SPK Library

Polish Home Army Ex-Servicemen Association
8681 Joseph Quintal, Montréal QC H2H 2M9
e-mail: ak@citinet.net
www.citinet.net/ak
Overview: A small national organization founded in 1948
Chief Officer(s):
Wanda de Roussan, President
Staff Member(s): 6
Membership: 105; *Fees:* $20; *Member Profile:* Former World War II resistance fighters

Polish National Catholic Church of Canada *See* St. John's Cathedral Polish Catholic Church

Polish National Union of Canada
2316 Fairview St., Burlington ON L7R 2E4
Tel: 905-639-3236
Overview: A small local organization
Chief Officer(s):
Barbara Sawala, Contact, 905-335-8119

Polish Society in Canada *See* Canadian Polish Society

Polish Teachers Association in Canada / Zwiazek Nauczycielstwa Polskiego w Kanadzie
3055 Lakeshore Blvd. West, Toronto ON M8V 1K6
Tel: 416-532-2876
zg@znp.ca
www.znp.ca
Overview: A small national organization
Chief Officer(s):
Maria Walicka, President
rwalicki@cogeco.ca

Polish-Canadian Coin & Stamp Club "Troyak"
Toronto ON
Tel: 416-258-1651
info@troyakclub.com
www.troyakclub.com
Overview: A small local organization
Mission: To promote the collection of Polish coins, paper money & stamps.
Member of: Ontario Numismatic Association; Greater Toronto Area Philatelic Alliance
Chief Officer(s):
Wieslaw Grzesicki, Vice-President

Polish-Jewish Heritage Foundation of Canada
#61, 396 Woodsworth Rd., Toronto ON M2L 2T9
e-mail: contact@pjhftoronto.ca
www.pjhftoronto.ca
Overview: A small local organization founded in 1988
Mission: To preserve the unique heritage of Polish Jews & to actively foster better understanding & cooperation between Polish & Jewish communities in Canada

Pollution Control Association of Ontario *See* Water Environment Association of Ontario

The Pollution Probe Foundation (PPF)
#200, 150 Ferrand Dr., Toronto ON M3C 3E5
Tel: 416-926-1907; *Fax:* 416-926-1601
pprobe@pollutionprobe.org
www.pollutionprobe.org
www.linkedin.com/company/989805
www.facebook.com/PollutionProbe
twitter.com/PollutionProbe
Also Known As: Pollution Probe
Overview: A medium-sized national charitable organization founded in 1969
Mission: A registered Canadian charity which seeks to define environmental problems through research; to promote understanding through education & to press for practical solutions through advocacy. The organization is non-partison & works collaboratively with government agencies, other non-profit organizations, & private business to engage key issues & find solutions. Offices in Toronto & Ottawa
Member of: Canadian Environmental Network; Canadian Renewable Energy Alliance
Affliation(s): Clean Air Network; Ontario Clean Air Alliance
Chief Officer(s):
Bob Oliver, CEO
boliver@pollutionprobe.org
Husam Mansour, COO
hmansour@pollutionprobe.org
Finances: *Annual Operating Budget:* $250,000-$500,000; *Funding Sources:* Individual & corporate charitable donations; foundation grants; publication sales; government grants
Staff Member(s): 16; 20 volunteer(s)
Membership: 100 corporate donors + 50 institutional
Activities: Programme areas include: Air, Water, Energy, Climate Change, Environment & Child Health, Mercury, Environmental Policy Development; *Awareness Events:* Clean Air Campaign & Commute

Ottawa
#101, 63 Sparks St., Ottawa ON K1P 5A6
Tel: 613-237-3786; *Fax:* 613-237-6111
rfindlay@pollutionprobe.org
Chief Officer(s):
Rick Findlay, Director, Ottawa Office

Pommes de terre Nouveau-Brunswick *See* Potatoes New Brunswick

Ponoka & District Chamber of Commerce
PO Box 4188, 4900 Highway 2A, Ponoka AB T4J 1R6
Tel: 403-783-3888; *Fax:* 403-783-3888
info@ponokaLive.ca
www.ponokalive.ca
twitter.com/ponokaChamber
Overview: A small local charitable organization
Member of: Alberta Chamber of Commerce; Canadian Chamber of Commerce
Chief Officer(s):
Greg Braat, President
Jim Hamilton, Vice-President
Finances: *Annual Operating Budget:* $50,000-$100,000; *Funding Sources:* Membership dues; events
Staff Member(s): 2; 15 volunteer(s)
Membership: 185; *Fees:* $100; *Member Profile:* Business professionals
Activities: Tourist Information Booth; *Library* Open to public

Ponoka Food Bank
Bay 6B, 4612 - 50th St., Ponoka AB T4J 1S7
Tel: 403-783-5910; *Fax:* 403-782-2546
Overview: A small local organization founded in 1984 overseen by Alberta Food Bank Network Association
Chief Officer(s):
Violet Smith, Contact
15 volunteer(s)

Pontiac Chamber of Commerce
PO Box 119, Campbell's Bay QC J0X 1K0
Tel: 819-647-2312
Toll-Free: 855-647-2312
info@pontiacchamberofcommerce.ca
www.pontiacchamberofcommerce.ca
www.facebook.com/CommercePontiac
Overview: A small local organization
Member of: Canadian Chamber of Commerce
Chief Officer(s):
Jean-Claude Rivest, President, 819-648-2990
jc@jericom.biz
Membership: *Fees:* $100-$500

Pool & Hot Tub Council of Canada (PHTCC) / Conseil canadien des piscines et spas
5 MacDougall Dr., Brampton ON L6S 3P3
Tel: 905-458-7242; *Fax:* 905-458-7037
Toll-Free: 800-879-7066
info@poolcouncil.ca
www.poolcouncil.ca
www.facebook.com/273144795787
Previous Name: National Spa & Pool Institute of Canada
Overview: A medium-sized national organization founded in 1959
Mission: To promote the image & sales of the pool, spa & hot tub industry throughout Canada; to promote & enhance consumer awareness of the industry's products; to encourage & promote increased health & safety standards within the industry; to support efforts to improve pool, hot tub & spa equipment facilities, services & products; &, generally, to promote & advance the common interests of members
Member of: Canadian Association of Exposition Managers; Canadian Society of Association Executives
Chief Officer(s):
Robert Wood, National Executive Director
rwood@poolcouncil.ca
Finances: *Annual Operating Budget:* $500,000-$1.5 Million; *Funding Sources:* Membership dues; trade show
Staff Member(s): 2
Membership: 360; *Fees:* Schedule available; *Member Profile:* In pool & spa trade or related trade; *Committees:* Manufacturers' Council; Education; Industry Growth; Trade Show; Membership
Activities: Industry training & education; Advocacy; Safety Promotion; Networking; Conferences; *Library*
Awards:
• Awards of Design Excellence (Award)
Meetings/Conferences: • 2015 Canadian Pool & Spa Conference & Expo, November, 2015, Scotiabank Convention Centre, Niagara Falls, ON
Description: The conference features seminars & courses, as well as the expo
Contact Information: URL: www.poolandspaexpo.ca

Alberta Chapter
6349 - 76 Ave. NW, Edmonton AB T6B 0A7
Tel: 780-466-4428; *Fax:* 780-466-4091
Chief Officer(s):
Rodney Taylor, President
pools@telusplanet.net

Atlantic Chapter
c/o R&R Pools, 1949 St Margaret's Bay Rd., Timberlea NS B3T 1C3
Tel: 902-876-2773; *Fax:* 902-876-1167
Chief Officer(s):
Kara Redden, President
info@rrpools.ca

British Columbia Central Chapter
1920 Kent Rd., Kelowna BC V1Y 7S1
Tel: 250-868-4831
ipools@telus.net
poolcouncil.ca
Chief Officer(s):
Brian Pavia, President

British Columbia Chapter

Central Ontario Chapter
7541 Wellington Rd., 34 Comp 152, Guelph ON N1H 8H9
Tel: 519-821-1495
Chief Officer(s):
Ted Eaton, President
eatonemarketing@bellnet.ca

Eastern Ontario Chapter
100 Augusta North, Brockville ON K6V 2X9
Tel: 613-345-2977; *Fax:* 613-345-2984
Chief Officer(s):
Peter Kelly, President
peter@carefreepoolsltd.com

Niagara Chapter
4 Nihan Dr., St Catharines ON L2N 1L1
Tel: 905-934-9019; *Fax:* 905-934-9033
Chief Officer(s):
Don Martens, President
aquadon@sympatico.ca

Prairies Chapter
MB
Chief Officer(s):
Rob Pyrz, President
rob@aqua-tech.ca

Toronto Chapter
c/o TayFam Enterprises Inc., #55059, 1800 Sheppard Ave. East, Toronto ON M2J 1L5
Tel: 416-596-6555
Chief Officer(s):
Steven Taylor, President
steven@mattspoolcare.com

Western Ontario Chapter
RR#3, Ilderton ON N0M 2A0
Tel: 519-659-3356; *Fax:* 519-559-0256
Chief Officer(s):
Josh Randall, President
woc.pahtcc@live.com

POPIR-Comité logement (St-Henri, Petite Bourgogne, Ville Émard, Côte St-Paul)
4017, rue Notre-Dame Ouest, Montréal QC H4C 1R3
Tél: 514-935-4649; *Téléc:* 514-935-4067
info@popir.org
popir.org
twitter.com/lepopir
Aperçu: *Dimension:* petite; *Envergure:* locale
Membre(s) du bureau directeur:
Antoine Morneau-Sénéchal, Organisateur Communautaire
antoine.ms@popir.org
Membre(s) du personnel: 7

Poplar Council of Canada (PCC) / Conseil du peuplier du Canada
c/o Canadian Forest Service, 5320 - 122 St., Edmonton AB T6H 3S5
Tel: 780-430-3843; *Fax:* 780-435-7356
poplar@poplar.ca
www.poplar.ca
www.facebook.com/163419440417089
Overview: A medium-sized national organization founded in 1977
Mission: Committed to the wise use, conservation & sustainable management of Canada's poplar resources
Affliation(s): Canadian Forest Service
Chief Officer(s):
Raju Soolanayakanahally, Chair
raju.soolanayakanahally@agr.gc.ca
Finances: *Funding Sources:* Government
Membership: *Fees:* $550 corporate; $15 student; $35 individual; *Member Profile:* Forest industry, universities, government
Activities: Workshops, projects

Populomix Cancer Research Institute / Institut de recherche sur le cancer Populomix
#324, 46 Dineen Dr., Fredericton NB E3B 9W4
Tel: 506-444-0546; *Fax:* 506-473-3794
info@populomix.org
www.populomix.org
Overview: A small local organization
Mission: To identify & manage resources to support research initiatives; to identify opportunities & facilitate interactions among researchers in the region; to develop programs to support collaborative initiatives that draw on our strengths, & to facilitate interactions & exchanges with the Fred Hutchinson Cancer Research Center to build productive collaborations
Chief Officer(s):
Warren McKenzie, Chair
Activities: Research on the prevention & early detection of cancer

Porc NB Pork
#302, 259 Brunswick St., Fredericton NB E3B 1G8
Tel: 506-458-8051; *Fax:* 506-453-1985
info@porcnbpork.nb.ca
www.porcnbpork.nb.ca
Previous Name: New Brunswick Hog Marketing Board
Overview: A small provincial organization founded in 1951
Affliation(s): Canadian Pork Council
Chief Officer(s):
Linda Volpé, Chair
Staff Member(s): 3
Membership: 75 individual

Porcupine Prospectors & Developers Association
PO Box 234, Timmins ON P4N 7H9
e-mail: ppda@ntl.sympatico.ca
www.porcupineprospectors.com
Overview: A small local organization
Mission: To represent the interests of mineral explorationists in the Porcupine District of Northeastern Ontario
Chief Officer(s):
Dean Rogers, President
Robert Calhoune, Secretary
Membership: *Fees:* $60 individual; $50-$1000 corporate

Porcupine United Way
PO Box 984, #312, 60 Wilson Ave., Timmins ON P4N 7H6
Tel: 705-268-9696; *Fax:* 705-268-9700
puw@ntl.sympatico.ca
porcupineunitedway.com
www.facebook.com/pages/Porcupine-United-Way/85026973282
Overview: A small local charitable organization founded in 1967 overseen by United Way of Canada - Centraide Canada
Mission: To promote the organized capacity of people to care for one another
Chief Officer(s):
Jean Warren, Executive Director
Finances: *Annual Operating Budget:* $250,000-$500,000; *Funding Sources:* Donations
Staff Member(s): 2; 460 volunteer(s)
Membership: 100-499; *Committees:* Campaign; Citizen Review; Finance; Special Events
Activities: *Speaker Service:* Yes

Pork Nova Scotia
Perennia Innovation Park, 60 Research Dr., Bible Hill NS B6L 2R2
Tel: 902-895-0581; *Fax:* 902-893-7063
info@porknovascotia.ca
porknovascotia.ca
Overview: A small provincial organization founded in 1952
Mission: To provide the most economical allocation & sale of live hogs & to represent the special needs & concerns of the pork industry in Nova Scotia
Affliation(s): Canadian Pork Council
Chief Officer(s):
Terry Beck, Chair, 902-765-2018
Finances: *Annual Operating Budget:* $250,000-$500,000
Staff Member(s): 125
Membership: 250 individual; *Member Profile:* To create the most favorable environment possible for the production & marketing of pork in Nova Scotia & to assist in maximizing returns for N.S. producers

Port Alberni & District Labour Council (PADLC)
3940 Johnson Rd., Port Alberni BC V9Y 5N5
Tel: 250-724-7966; *Fax:* 250-724-7966
www.portalberni.ca/node/293
Overview: A small local organization overseen by British Columbia Federation of Labour
Mission: To promote the interests of affiliates in Port Alberni, British Columbia & the surrounding area; To advance the economic & social welfare of workers
Affliation(s): Canadian Labour Congress (CLC)
Chief Officer(s):
Kelly Drybrough, President, 250-723-6352
Dave Warrender, First Vice-President
mdwarrender@shaw.ca
Nancy Czigany, Secretary, 250-724-1139
czigany@shaw.ca
Leslie Walerius, Treasurer
lwalerius@shaw.ca
Activities: Presenting educational opportunities; Recognizing the annual Day of Mourning, for workers who have suffered workplace illness, injury, or death; Organizing public forums surrounding local labour issues
Meetings/Conferences: • Port Alberni & District Labour Council 2015 Annual General Meeting, 2015, Port Alberni, BC
Scope: Local

Port Alberni Association for Community Living
3008 - 2nd Ave., Port Alberni BC V9Y 1Y9

Tel: 250-724-7155; *Fax:* 250-723-0404
admin@paacl.ca
www.paacl.ca
Overview: A small local organization
Chief Officer(s):
Dominic Rockall, Executive Director
drockall@paacl.ca
Cathie Waddington, President

Port Alberni Friendship Center
3555 - 4 Ave., Port Alberni BC V9Y 4H3
Tel: 250-723-8281; *Fax:* 250-723-1877
www.pafriendshipcenter.com
Overview: A small local organization
Chief Officer(s):
Cindi Stevens, Executive Director
cstevens@pafriendshipcenter.com
Staff Member(s): 18; 50 volunteer(s)
Membership: 100; *Fees:* $2 person; $5 family
Activities: Counselling; parenting programs; childhood development; family support; literacy programs; legal advocates; early intervention program

Port Clements Historical Society
PO Box 417, Port Clements BC V0T 1R0
Tel: 250-557-4576; *Fax:* 250-557-4576
pcmuseum@island.net
www.portclementsmuseum.org
Also Known As: Port Clements Museum
Overview: A small local charitable organization founded in 1985
Mission: To collect, catalogue, preserve & display marine history items & artifacts of Queen Charlotte Islands history relating to logging, mining, homesteading
Chief Officer(s):
Kathleen E. Dalzell, Historical Coordinator
Finances: *Annual Operating Budget:* Less than $50,000; *Funding Sources:* Grant; BC Heritage Trust; Skeena-Queen Charlotte Regional District; Village of Port Clements
Staff Member(s): 1; 7 volunteer(s)
Membership: 16; *Fees:* $10 voting; $1 non-voting; $5 senior
Activities: *Library:* Documentation Centre & Archives; by appointment

Port Colborne Community Association for Research Extension
PO Box 21, 92 Charlotte St., Port Colborne ON L3K 5V7
Tel: 905-834-3629; *Fax:* 905-835-6600
Toll-Free: 888-370-8738
portcares@portcares.on.ca
www.portcares.on.ca
Also Known As: PORT CARES
Overview: A small local charitable organization founded in 1986
Mission: To facilitate efforts to improve the quality of life for the residents of Port Colborne & region by undertaking initiatives & by responding to identified community needs
Member of: Port Colborne/Wainfleet Chamber of Commerce
Chief Officer(s):
Lynda Reinhart, Executive Director, 905-834-3629 Ext. 248
lreinhart@portcares.on.ca
Finances: *Annual Operating Budget:* $500,000-$1.5 Million
Staff Member(s): 35; 60 volunteer(s)
Membership: 90; *Fees:* $25 individual; $20 senior; $50 charity; $100 corporate; *Member Profile:* Residents of Port Colborne & district who subscribe to the principles & objectives of Port Cares; *Committees:* Board of Directors; Fundraising; Advisory; Youth Justice; Auction
Activities: *Library* Open to public

Port Colborne District Association for Community Living, Inc. *See* Community Living Port Colborne-Wainfleet

Port Colborne-Wainfleet Chamber of Commerce
76 Main St. West, Port Colborne ON L3K 3V2
Tel: 905-834-9765; *Fax:* 905-834-1542
office@pcwchamber.com
www.pcwchamber.com
www.facebook.com/118999308131584
Overview: A small local organization founded in 1902
Mission: To promote the commercial, industrial, agricultural, educational & civic interests of Port Colborne & Wainfleet; To work for sound legislation & efficient administration of municipal, regional, provincial & federal governments
Member of: Niagara Regional Chambers of Commerce; Ontario Chamber of Commerce
Finances: *Annual Operating Budget:* Less than $50,000; *Funding Sources:* Membership dues; fundraising
Staff Member(s): 1; 1 volunteer(s)

Membership: 200+; *Fees:* Schedule available; *Member Profile:* Businesses & members of community
Activities: Golf Tournament, Meet the Reps Barbecue, Information Seminars; Training Sessions; Networking Events; Annual General Meeting; *Speaker Service:* Yes; *Library* Open to public

Port Dover Board of Trade
PO Box 239, 19 Market St. West, Port Dover ON N0A 1N0
Tel: 519-583-1314; *Fax:* 519-583-3275
info@portdover.ca
www.portdover.ca
Overview: A small local organization founded in 1912
Mission: To improve the social & economic welfare of community
Chief Officer(s):
Andrew Schneider, President
Finances: *Annual Operating Budget:* $100,000-$250,000; *Funding Sources:* Membership dues; festivals
Staff Member(s): 1
Membership: 235; *Fees:* $100-150; *Member Profile:* Business owners & community residents
Activities: Perch Derby; Norfolk Dragonboat Challenge; Fish Fest; Summer Festival; Christmas Fest; free Sunday concerts in the park

Port Elgin & District Chamber of Commerce *See* Saugeen Shores Chamber Office

Port Elgin District Voluntary Action Group Inc. *See* PEDVAC Foundation

Port Hardy & District Chamber of Commerce
PO Box 249, 7250 Market St., Port Hardy BC V0N 2P0
Tel: 250-949-7622; *Fax:* 250-949-6653
Toll-Free: 866-427-3901
phcc@cablerocket.com
www.ph-chamber.bc.ca
Also Known As: Port Hardy Chamber of Commerce & Visitor Centre
Overview: A small local organization founded in 1975
Member of: BC Chamber of Commerce
Chief Officer(s):
James Emerson, President
emersonj@telus.net
Yana Hrdy, Executive Director
phccmgr@cablerocket.com
Kari Watkins, Office Administrator
phccadm@cablerocket.com
Finances: *Annual Operating Budget:* $100,000-$250,000; *Funding Sources:* Membership fees
Staff Member(s): 2; 1 volunteer(s)
Membership: 200; *Fees:* $20-$150
Activities: *Library* Open to public

Port Hardy Harvest Food Bank
PO Box 849, 7135 Market St., Port Hardy BC V0N 2P0
Tel: 250-902-0332; *Fax:* 250-902-0613
harvest9@telus.net
Overview: A small local charitable organization overseen by Food Banks British Columbia
Mission: The agency provides food to the needy in the local area.
Member of: Food Banks British Columbia
Chief Officer(s):
Suzanne Talitzaine, Contact

Port Hastings Historical Society
24 Hwy. 19, Port Hastings NS B9A 1M1
Tel: 902-625-1295
porthastingsmuseum@gmail.com
porthastingsmuseum.ca
Overview: A small local charitable organization founded in 1978
Mission: To collect, preserve, study, exhibit & interpret those objects that will best serve to illustrate the founding, settlement & development of the Strait area
Member of: Federation of the Nova Scotian Heritage; Council of Nova Scotia Archives; Iona Connection; Canadian Museums Association
Finances: *Funding Sources:* Nova Scotia Museum; fundraising; donations
Activities: *Library:* Genealogy Records; Open to public by appointment

Port Hawkesbury Chamber of Commerce *See* Strait Area Chamber of Commerce

Port Hope & District Chamber of Commerce
58 Queen St., Port Hope ON L1A 3Z9
Tel: 905-885-5519; *Fax:* 905-885-1142
thechamber@porthope.ca
www.porthopechamber.com
Overview: A small local organization
Mission: To be dedicated to Port Hope's economic development & prosperity
Chief Officer(s):
Cathy Moore, President, 905-885-6367, Fax: 905-885-6368
Bree Nixon, Manager
bnixon@porthope.ca
Staff Member(s): 4; 20 volunteer(s)
Membership: 160; *Fees:* Schedule available
Activities: *Awareness Events:* Golf Tournament, Sept.
Awards:
• Business Excellence Awards (Award)
Publications:
• Port Hope & District Chamber of Commerce Newsletter
Type: Newsletter

Port Hope/Cobourg & District Association for Community Living *See* Community Living West Northumberland

Port McNeill & District Chamber of Commerce
PO Box 129, 1594 Beach Dr., Port McNeill BC V0N 2R0
Tel: 250-956-3131; *Fax:* 250-956-3132
Toll-Free: 888-956-3131
pmccc@island.net
www.portmcneill.net
Overview: A small local organization
Mission: To promote & improve trade & commerce & the economic, civic, & social welfare of the district
Member of: Tourism BC; BC Chamber of Commerce; Canadian Chamber of Commerce
Chief Officer(s):
David Mitchell, President, 250-956-2220
Cheryl Jorgenson, Executive Director, 250-956-3131
Finances: *Annual Operating Budget:* Less than $50,000
Staff Member(s): 1
Membership: 100; *Fees:* $50-200; *Committees:* Tourism; Primary Resources; Education; Retail/Services Sector; Membership; Website
Activities: Operates the Port McNeill Info Centre

Port Moody Heritage Society
2734 Murray St., Port Moody BC V3H 1X2
Tel: 604-939-1648; *Fax:* 604-939-1647
info@portmoodymuseum.org
portmoodymuseum.org
www.facebook.com/169200448399
twitter.com/pmmuseum
www.flickr.com/photos/55316408@N00/
Also Known As: Port Moody Station Museum
Previous Name: Port Moody Historical Society
Overview: A small local charitable organization founded in 1969
Mission: To collect, preserve display, research & educate regarding local artifacts
Chief Officer(s):
Jim Millar, Curator/Manager
jim@portmoodymuseum.org
Richard Simons, President
Finances: *Annual Operating Budget:* $50,000-$100,000
Staff Member(s): 3; 60 volunteer(s)
Membership: 150; *Fees:* $5 basic; $25 corporate; $500 life
Activities: Operate Port Moody Station Museum, archive; *Library*
Publications:
• Tracks of time: Port Moody's First 100 Years
Type: Book; *Accepts Advertising*; *Number of Pages:* 192; *Price:* $40 plus tax

Port Moody Historical Society *See* Port Moody Heritage Society

Port Moody Rock & Gem Club
c/o The Kyle Centre, 125 Kyle St., Port Moody BC V3H 2N6
e-mail: info@portmoodyrockclub.com
www.portmoodyrockclub.com
Overview: A small local organization founded in 1978
Member of: Port Moody Arts Centre Society; ArtsConnect; British Columbia Lapidary Society; Gem & Mineral Federation of Canada
Chief Officer(s):
Lisa Elser, Co-Chair, 778-996-5620
Rose Kapp, Show Chair; Historian; Librarian, 604-941-3023
rock.show@portmoodyrockclub.com

Lynne Johnston, Contact, Field Trips, 604-945-6695
field.trips@portmoodyrockclub.com
Membership: *Fees:* $25 individuals; $45 families; *Member Profile:* Persons in the Port Moody British Columbia area who are interested in geology & the earth sciences as well as the hobbies of rock hunting, faceting, & lapidary
Activities: Offering weekly lapidary & faceting workshops; Hosting monthly meetings, except in July, August, & December; Arranging field trips; *Awareness Events:* Annual Rock & Gem Show, October

Port Renfrew Chamber of Commerce
PO Box 39, Port Renfrew BC V0S 1K0
Tel: 250-858-7665
renfrewchamber@gmail.com
www.portrenfrewcommunity.com
www.facebook.com/groups/2365371947
Overview: A small local organization
Chief Officer(s):
Dan Hager, President, 250-858-7665
tworabbits@shaw.ca
Finances: *Annual Operating Budget:* $100,000-$250,000
9 volunteer(s)
Membership: 75; *Fees:* $80-$135

Port Sydney/Utterson & Area Chamber of Commerce
#4, 15 South Mary Lake Rd., Port Sydney ON P0B 1L0
Tel: 705-385-1117; *Fax:* 705-385-9753
info@portsydneycoc.com
www.portsydneycofc.com
www.facebook.com/182339001818525
Overview: A small local organization
Member of: Canadian Chamber of Commerce; Ontario Chamber of Commerce
Chief Officer(s):
Gordon Haig, President, 705-787-8962
ghaig@vianet.ca
Membership: 100-499; *Fees:* $124.80 self-employed; $142.48 2-10 employees; $186.16 11-40 employees; $75 clubs/associations; $60 individual

Portage & District Arts Council (PDAC)
11 - 2nd St. NE, Portage la Prairie MB R1N 1R8
Tel: 204-239-6029; *Fax:* 204-239-1472
pdac@mts.net
www.portageartscentre.ca
Previous Name: Portage La Prairie & District Arts Council
Overview: A small local charitable organization founded in 1977
Mission: To provide the opportunity for exposure & education in the arts; to stimulate & develop cultural projects & activities; to act as a clearinghouse for information on cultural projects & activities; to foster an interest & pride in the cultural heritage of the community; to interpret work of cultural groups to the community; to bring to the attention of the civic, provincial & federal authorities the cultural needs of the community
Member of: Manitoba Association of Community Arts Councils Inc.
Chief Officer(s):
Jazz de Montigny, Executive Director
Staff Member(s): 2; 130 volunteer(s)
Membership: 400 individual + 23 group/corporate + 2 lifetime; *Fees:* $20 student; $25 adult; $45 family; $55 group; *Committees:* Exhibition; Art Rental; Touring
Activities: Art classes; workshops; dance classes; art studios; monthly art exhibits & receptions; gallery events; members meetings; *Awareness Events:* Celebration of the Arts, May 9; Dance Recital, April 12; Art Craft Market, Nov. 2

Portage & District Chamber of Commerce *See* Portage la Prairie & District Chamber of Commerce

Portage Friendship Centre Inc. (PFC)
20 - 3rd St. NE, Portage la Prairie MB R1N 1N4
Tel: 204-239-6333; *Fax:* 204-856-2470
info@ptgfc.org
www.ptgfc.org
Previous Name: Portage La Prairie Friendship Centre
Overview: A small local organization
Chief Officer(s):
Sheila James, President
Dennis Meeches, Executive Director
d_meeches@ptgfc.org

Portage Industrial Exhibition Association
PO Box 278, Portage la Prairie MB R1N 3B5
Tel: 204-857-3231; *Fax:* 204-239-1701
portagex@mts.net
www.portageex.com
Also Known As: Portage X
Overview: A small local organization founded in 1872
Mission: To assist in providing educational & social activities related to the agricultural industry in the community
Member of: Western Canada Fairs Association
Affliation(s): Canadian Association of Exhibitions; Manitoba Association of Agricultural Societies
Finances: *Annual Operating Budget:* $50,000-$100,000; *Funding Sources:* Provincial government; fundraising activities; donations
Staff Member(s): 2; 60 volunteer(s)
Membership: 156 institutional

Portage La Prairie & District Arts Council *See* Portage & District Arts Council

Portage la Prairie & District Chamber of Commerce
11 - 2nd St. NE, Portage la Prairie MB R1N 1R8
Tel: 204-857-7778; *Fax:* 204-239-0176
info@portagechamber.com
www.portagechamber.com
Previous Name: Portage & District Chamber of Commerce
Overview: A medium-sized local charitable organization founded in 1889
Mission: To foster an environment which will enhance the commercial development of the district
Member of: Manitoba Chamber of Commerce
Affiliation(s): Canadian Chamber of Commerce
Chief Officer(s):
Jerry Lupkowski, President, 204-239-6117, Fax: 204-857-3972
Cindy McDonald, Executive Director
Finances: *Annual Operating Budget:* $50,000-$100,000; *Funding Sources:* Membership dues; events
Staff Member(s): 2
Membership: 245; *Fees:* $141.75-$787.50 based on number of employees
Activities: Central Manitoba Trade Fair; Santa's Parade of Lights; Best Business Awards; Agriculture Appreciation Evening; *Library:* Resource Centre; Open to public

Portage La Prairie Friendship Centre *See* Portage Friendship Centre Inc.

Portage La Prairie Real Estate Board
PO Box 1288, Portage la Prairie MB R1N 3L5
Tel: 204-857-4111
Overview: A small local organization overseen by Manitoba Real Estate Association
Member of: The Canadian Real Estate Association

Portage Plains United Way
PO Box 953, 224 Saskatchewan Ave. East, Portage la Prairie MB R1N 3C4
Tel: 204-857-4440; *Fax:* 204-239-1740
info@portageplainsuw.ca
www.portageplainsuw.ca
www.facebook.com/pages/Portage-Plains-United-Way
Overview: A small local charitable organization founded in 1968 overseen by United Way of Canada - Centraide Canada
Mission: To unite our community to enhance the quality of life for those in need
Chief Officer(s):
Kathee Thurston, President
Finances: *Annual Operating Budget:* Less than $50,000; *Funding Sources:* Manitoba Lotteries
Staff Member(s): 2; 200 volunteer(s)
Membership: 15 agencies; *Committees:* Executive; Finance; Allocations; Special Events; Campaign
Activities: *Speaker Service:* Yes

Portage Women's Shelter *See* Manitoba Association of Women's Shelters

Portfolio Management Association of Canada (PMAC)
#1210, 155 University Ave., Toronto ON M5H 3B7
Tel: 416-504-1118; *Fax:* 416-504-1117
info@portfoliomanagement.org
www.portfoliomanagement.org
Overview: A medium-sized national organization founded in 1952
Mission: To provide a way for investment management firms to share best practices& industry knowledge
Chief Officer(s):
John McCutcheon, Chair
Staff Member(s): 6
Membership: 170 investment management firms; *Member Profile:* Investment Managers

Portfolio Management Association of Canada (PMAC)
#1210, 155 University Ave., Toronto ON M5H 3B7
Tel: 416-504-1118; *Fax:* 416-504-1117
info@portfoliomanagement.org
www.portfoliomanagement.org
www.linkedin.com/company/portfolio-management-association-of-canada
twitter.com/PMACnews
Previous Name: Investment Counsel Association of Canada
Overview: A medium-sized provincial organization founded in 1952
Mission: To represent the Investment Counsel and portfolio managers in Canada; To advocate high standards of unbiased portfolio management in the interest of investors
Chief Officer(s):
Paul Harris, Chair
Katie Walmsley, President
kwalmsley@portfoliomanagement.org
Membership: *Committees:* Practices & Standards; AGM; Industry, Regulation & Tax; Member Services; Operation Heads' Network; Compliance Officers' Network
Activities: Offering member networking services; Increasing public awareness of investment counselling & its benefits; Liaising with securities regulators & other government agencies

Portuguese Assocation of Canada *See* Associaça Portuguesa Do Canada

Portuguese Canadian National Congress / Congrès national canadien-portugais
358 Danforth Ave, Toronto ON M4K 3Z2
Tel: 416-532-3233; *Fax:* 416-532-8703
congressonacional@yahoo.ca
www.congresso.ca
Overview: A medium-sized national organization founded in 1993
Mission: To provide members with a national forum & voice in all social & economic matters; To assist in the promotion, development, maintenance & enhancement of Portuguese-Canadian culture & communities
Member of: Canadian Ethnocultural Council; Portuguese Canadian Coalition for Better Education
Chief Officer(s):
Emanuel Linhares, President
Finances: *Annual Operating Budget:* $100,000-$250,000
Staff Member(s): 1; 60 volunteer(s)
Membership: 1,500; *Committees:* Management; Executive; Advisory
Awards:
• COPA Awards (Award)
Celebrating outstanding Portuguese Canadian achievement in the areas of Arts & Culture, Athletics, Education & Academia, Vision and Leadership

Portuguese Canadian Seniors Foundation
5455 Imperial St., Burnaby BC V5J 1E5
Tel: 604-873-2979; *Fax:* 604-873-2974
www.pcsf.piczo.com
Overview: A small local organization founded in 1988

Portuguese Club of London
134 Falcon St., London ON N5W 4Z1
Tel: 519-453-4330; *Fax:* 519-453-3599
info@portugueseclubofiondon.com
www.portugueseclubofiondon.com
Overview: A small local organization founded in 1976 overseen by Ontario Council of Agencies Serving Immigrants
Mission: To provide assistance, information & orientation to the Portuguese-speaking communities to ensure full participation in Canadian society & equal access to service respecting uniqueness of their culture & tradition; To assist the Portuguese community in integration with new social, cultural & political environment
Chief Officer(s):
Domingos Mendes, President
Finances: *Annual Operating Budget:* $50,000-$100,000
Staff Member(s): 3; 30 volunteer(s)
Membership: *Committees:* Personnel; Social
Activities: Counselling; educational workshops

Portuguese Interagency Network (PIN)
e-mail: pin002000@yahoo.com
portugueseintnetwork.tripod.com
Overview: A small provincial charitable organization founded in 1978
Finances: *Annual Operating Budget:* Less than $50,000
Staff Member(s): 1; 42 volunteer(s)
Membership: 40; *Fees:* $10 individual; $20 agency; *Member Profile:* Individuals & agencies who are concerned with the provision of services to Portuguese speaking Canadians in Ontario; *Committees:* Elderly; Youth; Health; Fundraising
Activities: Community development; needs assessment; public education; consulting body; information & referral centre

posAbilities Association of BC
#240, 4664 Lougheed Hwy., Burnaby BC V5C 5T5
Tel: 604-299-4001; *Fax:* 604-299-0329
info@posAbilities.ca
www.posabilities.ca
www.facebook.com/posAbilitiesCA
www.twitter.com/posAbilitiesCA
Previous Name: Mainstream Association for Proactive Community Living
Overview: A small local organization founded in 1968
Chief Officer(s):
Fernando Coelho, CEO
Celso A. A. Boscariol, President
Finances: *Annual Operating Budget:* Greater than $5 Million
Staff Member(s): 700; 60 volunteer(s)
Membership: 100; *Fees:* $5; *Member Profile:* Parents; selfadvocates; professionals
Activities: Accredited housing; day programs; recreation; socialization; *Awareness Events:* Annual Art Show, Oct.

A Post Psychiatric Leisure Experince (APPLE)
Bronson Center, 211 Bronson Ave., Ottawa ON K1R 6H5
Tel: 613-238-1209; *Fax:* 613-238-5806
contact_apple@hotmail.com
www.appledropin.com
www.facebook.com/appledropin
Overview: A small local organization founded in 1981
Mission: To enhance the quality of life for their members by offering support & activities; to prevent hospitalization of their members
Membership: 350; *Fees:* Free; *Member Profile:* Former & current mental health patients

Post Traumatic Stress Disorder Association
93 Dufferin Ave., Toronto ON N6A 1K3
Tel: 604-525-7566; *Fax:* 604-525-7586
info@ptsdassociation.com
ptsdassociation.com
Overview: A small provincial charitable organization
Mission: To empower individuals suffering from Post Traumatic Stress Disorder through education, linkages with appropriate services, facilitation of research and discovery into the causation.
Chief Officer(s):
Roméo A. Dallaire, O.C., C.M.M., G, Honorary Chair
Ute Lawrence-Fisher, President & Founder

Positive Living BC
1107 Seymour St., 2nd Fl., Vancouver BC V6B 5S8
Tel: 604-893-2200; *Fax:* 604-893-2251
Toll-Free: 800-994-2437
info@positivelivingbc.org
www.positivelivingbc.org
www.facebook.com/positivelivingbc
twitter.com/pozlivingbc
Previous Name: British Columbia Persons with AIDS Society
Overview: A small provincial charitable organization founded in 1986
Mission: To empower persons in British Columbia who live with AIDS & HIV disease
Member of: CAS; CAAN; Red Road HIV/AIDS Society; BC Health Coalition; Canadian HIV/AIDS Legal Network
Chief Officer(s):
John Bishop, Chair, 604-646-5348
johnb@positivelivingbc.org
Wayne Campbell, Vice-Chair, 604-646-5326
waynec@positivelivingbc.org
Finances: *Annual Operating Budget:* $3 Million-$5 Million; *Funding Sources:* Donations; Fundraising
Staff Member(s): 32; 238 volunteer(s)
Membership: 5,000+; *Fees:* Free; *Member Profile:* Persons in British Columbia living with AIDS & HIV disease; *Committees:* Board & Volunteer Development; Community Representation & Engagement; Communications & Education; Health Promotion; Membership Development; Support Services
Activities: Engaging in advocacy activities (E-mail: advdesk@positivelivingbc.org); Providing support services (E-mail: support@positivelivingbc.org); Offering information about treatment (E-mail: treatment@positivelivingbc.org); Conducting prison outreach services (E-mail: pop@positivelivingbc.org); Providing educational opportunities; Organizing awareness campaigns; health promotion & wellness; *Awareness Events:* AccodAIDS, Apr.; AIDS Walk for Life, Sept.; Red Ribbon Breakfast, Nov.; *Internships:* Yes; *Speaker Service:* Yes
Awards:
• AccolAIDS Awards (Award)
Categories include science, research, & technology, the hero award, philanthropy, innovative programs & services, social, political, & community action, the media award, & health promotion & harm reduction
Publications:
• British Columbia Persons with AIDS Society Annual Report
Type: Yearbook; *Frequency:* Annually
• British Columbia Persons with AIDS Society HIV/AIDS eNewslist
Type: Newsletter; *Frequency:* Weekly
• eScoop
Type: Newsletter; *Frequency:* Bimonthly
• Living+
Type: Magazine
Profile: Current issues encountered by those infected & affected by HIV/AIDS
• Positive Living Manual
Type: Manual
Profile: Information for BCPWA members, interested individuals, PWAs, AIDS service organizations, & health care workers

Positive Living North: No kheyoh t'sih'en t'sehena Society (PLN)
1563 - 2nd Ave., Prince George BC V2L 3B8
Tel: 250-562-1172; *Fax:* 250-562-3317
Toll-Free: 888-438-2437
info@positivelivingnorth.ca
www.positivelivingnorth.ca
www.facebook.com/103410213083441
Previous Name: Prince George AIDS Prevention Program; AIDS Prince George; Prince George AIDS Society
Overview: A small local organization founded in 1992 overseen by Canadian AIDS Society
Mission: To provide services to people live with HIV & their families; 75 per cent of PLN's clients are of Aboriginal descent
Chief Officer(s):
Vanessa West, Executive Director
Membership: 120
Activities: Fire Pit Cultural Centre; social support; advocacy; crisis intervention; personal & group support; support for substance abuse issues; support team services; health information; grief & loss support; education & prevention services; *Awareness Events:* AIDS Walk for Life, Sept.; Smithers Camera Project
Publications:
• Common Threads [a publication of Positive Living North]
Type: Newsletter; *Frequency:* Quarterly

Positive Women's Network (PWN)
#614, 1033 Davie St., Vancouver BC V6E 1M7
Tel: 604-692-3000; *Fax:* 604-684-3126
Toll-Free: 866-692-3001
pwn@pwn.bc.ca
www.pwn.bc.ca
www.facebook.com/Positivewomensnetwork
twitter.com/pwn_bc
Overview: A small local charitable organization founded in 1989 overseen by Canadian AIDS Society
Mission: Challenging HIV, Changing Women's Lives
Member of: Pacific AIDS Network; Canadian HIV/AIDS Legal Network
Chief Officer(s):
Marcie Summers, Executive Director
marcies@pwn.bc.ca
Finances: *Annual Operating Budget:* $250,000-$500,000; *Funding Sources:* ACAP; Provincial Health Services Authority; donations
Staff Member(s): 11
Membership: *Fees:* Free; *Member Profile:* Women living with HIV/AIDS
Activities: Support programs; drop-in centre; food bank; retreats; lunch program; support groups; education; health promotion resources; *Awareness Events:* AIDS Walk, Sept.

Positive Youth Outreach (PYO)
399 Church St., 4th Fl., Toronto ON M5B 2J6
Tel: 416-340-8484
pyo@actoronto.org
www.actoronto.org/home.nsf/pages/positiveyouthoutreach
Overview: A small local organization founded in 1990 overseen by Canadian AIDS Society
Mission: To provide education, support, advocacy & referral to all youth living with HIV/AIDS regardless of the mode of transmission
Member of: AIDS Committee of Toronto; Ontario AIDS Network
Chief Officer(s):
Alex McClelland, Program Coordinator
Finances: *Annual Operating Budget:* Less than $50,000; *Funding Sources:* Ontario Ministry of Health
Membership: 50
Activities: Support & discussion groups; workshop; peer support; community outreach; leadership development; *Speaker Service:* Yes

Postal History Society of Canada (PHSC)
PO Box 562, Stn. B, Ottawa ON K1P 5P7
e-mail: secretary@postalhistorycanada.net
www.postalhistorycanada.net
Previous Name: Postal History Society of Ontario
Overview: A medium-sized national organization founded in 1972
Mission: To promote the study of postal history of Canada
Affliation(s): American Philatelic Society; British North America Philatelic Society
Chief Officer(s):
Chris Green, Contact
Finances: *Annual Operating Budget:* Less than $50,000
Membership: 700 institutional
Activities: *Library* by appointment

Postal History Society of Ontario *See* Postal History Society of Canada

Postpartum Depression Association of Manitoba (PPDAM)
MB
e-mail: info@ppdmanitoba.ca
www.ppdmanitoba.ca
Overview: A small provincial organization
Mission: PPDAM is committed to helping Manitoba families get connected with the help dealing with postpartum depression or related illnesses through education, awareness and resources.

Post-Polio Awareness & Support Society of BC (PPASS/BC)
102 - 9775 - 4th St., Sidney BC V8L 2Z8
Tel: 250-655-8849; *Fax:* 250-655-8859
ppass@ppassbc.com
www.ppassbc.com
Overview: A medium-sized provincial charitable organization founded in 1986
Mission: To develop awareness, communication & education between society & community; to disseminate information concerning research & treatment about Post-Polio Syndrome; to support polio survivors other than through direct financial aid
Chief Officer(s):
Joan Toone, President
Finances: *Annual Operating Budget:* $50,000-$100,000; *Funding Sources:* Membership fees; donations; bingo
Membership: 1,950; *Fees:* $20 BC resident; $25 others; *Member Profile:* Polio survivors & their friends; *Committees:* Public Relations
Activities: Special Water Exercise Program; *Speaker Service:* Yes; *Library* Open to public

Post-Polio Network Manitoba Inc. (PPN-MB)
#204, 825 Sherbrook St., Winnipeg MB R3A 1M5
Tel: 204-975-3037; *Fax:* 204-975-3027
postpolionetwork@gmail.com
www.postpolionetwork.ca
Overview: A small provincial charitable organization founded in 1986
Mission: To serve as a support group & information centre for polio survivors throughout Manitoba, especially those suffering from post-polio syndrome; To acquaint the medical community & those responsible for government services as to the nature & extent of the problems associated with the late effects of polio

Member of: Society of Manitobans with Disabilities
Affliation(s): Polio Canada; SMD - Fostering Growth & Clearinghouse of Self-Help Organizations
Chief Officer(s):
Cheryl Currie, President
Donna Remillard, Treasurer
Estelle Boissonneault, Secretary
Finances: *Annual Operating Budget:* Less than $50,000; *Funding Sources:* Membership fees; bequests; Grey Cup tickets
11 volunteer(s)
Membership: 300; *Fees:* $30; *Member Profile:* Polio survivors; their families; health care professionals; *Committees:* Newsletter; Funding; Programming
Activities: *Library:* SMD Library

Potato Growers of Alberta (PGA)
6008 - 46 Ave., Taber AB T1G 2B1
Tel: 403-223-2262; *Fax:* 403-223-2268
pga@albertapotatoes.ca
www.albertapotatoes.ca
www.facebook.com/pages/Potato-Growers-of-Alberta/174598775914665
www.youtube.com/user/albertapotatoes
Previous Name: Alberta Potato Marketing Board
Overview: A small provincial licensing organization founded in 1968
Mission: To create success in Alberta's potato industry by supporting sustainable production, marketing, development & cooperation
Member of: Canadian Horticultural Council; Alberta Food Processors Association; Canadian Produce Marketing Association
Affliation(s): Calgary Produce Marketing Association; Canadian Snack Foods Association
Chief Officer(s):
Helmut Leili, Executive Director
helmut@albertapotatoes.ca
Finances: *Annual Operating Budget:* $500,000-$1.5 Million
Staff Member(s): 6; 27 volunteer(s)
Membership: 150; *Fees:* $50; *Member Profile:* Commercial/seed/table growers; *Committees:* Negotiating; Alberta Crop Insurance; Alberta Seed Potato Grower; Research
Activities: Promotion & research of potatoes & potato products; policy development for potato farmers; *Awareness Events:* Potato Month, Feb.; *Speaker Service:* Yes

Potatoes New Brunswick / Pommes de terre Nouveau-Brunswick
PO Box 7878, Grand Falls NB E3Z 3E8
Tel: 506-473-3036; *Fax:* 506-473-4647
gfpotato@potatoesnb.com
www.potatoesnb.com
www.facebook.com/pages/Potatoes-New-Brunswick/223361891051973
Previous Name: New Brunswick Potato Agency
Overview: A medium-sized provincial organization founded in 1979
Mission: To work in close collaboration with industry partners in advocating, coordinating, promoting, negotiating, & leading growth & development of New Brunswick potato producers
Member of: Canadian Horticultural Council
Chief Officer(s):
Joe Brennan, Chair
Matt Hemphill, Executive Director
Robert Corriveau, Director, Finance
Gisele Beardsley, Bookkeeper & Translator
Membership: 400 individual
Meetings/Conferences: • Potatoes New Brunswick 2015 Conference & Trade Show, February, 2015, E.P. Senechal Center, Grand Falls, NB
Scope: Provincial
Attendance: 200+
Description: An event for New Brunswick potato growers & interested stakeholders to present happening in the industry
Contact Information: E-mail: gfpotato@potatoesnb.com

Grand Falls
PO Box 7878, Grand Falls NB E3Z 3E8
Tel: 506-473-3036; *Fax:* 506-473-4647
gfpotato@potatoesnb.com
www.potatoesnb.com
www.facebook.com/pages/Potatoes-New-Brunswick/223361891051973
twitter.com/POTATOESNB
Chief Officer(s):
Matt Hemphill, Executive Director

Pouce Coupe & District Museum & Historical Society
PO Box 83, 5006 - 49 St., Pouce Coupe BC V0C 2C0
Tel: 250-786-5555; *Fax:* 250-786-5794
Overview: A small local charitable organization founded in 1972
Mission: To collect artifacts, pioneer histories & displays in order to preserve heritage of Pouce Coupe & district
Member of: BC Museums Association
Chief Officer(s):
Ellen DeWetter, Contact
Finances: *Annual Operating Budget:* Less than $50,000; *Funding Sources:* Government grants; museum fundraising
12 volunteer(s)
Membership: 20; *Fees:* $5
Activities: Monthly meetings; fundraising; community events

Poultry Industry Council (PIC)
483 Arkell Rd., Guelph ON N1H 6H8
Tel: 519-837-0284; *Fax:* 519-837-3584
pic@poultryindustrycouncil.ca
www.poultryindustrycouncil.ca
Previous Name: Ontario Poultry Council
Overview: A medium-sized provincial organization
Mission: To foster life-long learning programmes for members of the poultry industry; To foster research initiatives
Chief Officer(s):
Ed McKinlay, Chair
Staff Member(s): 3
Membership: 250; *Fees:* $100 individual; $300 corporate; *Committees:* Fundraising; Research; Special Events; Communications
Activities: Poultry Health Conference; London Poultry Show

Powell River & District Labour Council
6239 Walnut St., Powell River BC V8A 4K4
Tel: 604-483-9800; *Fax:* 604-483-3369
Overview: A small local organization
Chief Officer(s):
Ron Van't Schip, President
skippies@shaw.ca

Powell River & District United Way
PO Box 370, #205, 4750 Joyce Ave., Powell River BC V8A 5C2
Tel: 604-485-2791
admin@unitedwayofpowellriver.ca
www.unitedwayofpowellriver.ca
www.facebook.com/pages/Powell-River-District-United-Way/322827261966
Overview: A small local charitable organization founded in 1976 overseen by United Way of Canada - Centraide Canada
Chief Officer(s):
Ashley Hull, President
hullashley@gmail.com
Finances: *Annual Operating Budget:* $100,000-$250,000; *Funding Sources:* Donations
29 volunteer(s)
Membership: 11;

Powell River Association for Community Living (PRACL)
#201, 4675 Marine Ave., Powell River BC V8A 2L2
Tel: 604-485-6411; *Fax:* 604-485-6419
info@pracl.ca
www.pracl.ca
www.facebook.com/241189675918848
Overview: A small local charitable organization founded in 1954
Mission: Supports people with disabilities, children who are at risk for, or who have a developmental delay, & their families; offers respectful, lifelong supports with the goal that each individual will have a change to have the life they want; advocates with & for individuals & families; strengthens the community by offering education that celebrates differences by valuing contributions of all citizens
Member of: British Columbia Association for Community Living
Affliation(s): Association for the Severely Handicapped; Council for Exceptional Children; Family Support Institute; Cerebral Palsy Association; Learning Disabilities Association
Chief Officer(s):
Lilla Tipton, Executive Director, 604-485-6411 Ext. 227
ltipton@pracl.ca
Finances: *Annual Operating Budget:* Greater than $5 Million; *Funding Sources:* Provincial government; fundraising
Staff Member(s): 3; 20 volunteer(s)
Membership: 48; *Fees:* $5; *Member Profile:* Attendance at 3 meetings to have voting privilege at annual general meeting; *Committees:* Buildings; Finances; Monitoring
Activities: Powell River Infant Development Program; early childhood community therapy service; employment support service; Cranberry Children's Centre; family support service; Community Living Place (multi purpose facility); Free Spirit Leisure Club; residential service; supported child care; day programs for adults; *Awareness Events:* Community Living Day; *Library* Open to public

Powell River Chamber of Commerce
6807 Wharf St., Powell River BC V8A 2T9
Tel: 604-485-4051; *Fax:* 604-485-4272
office@powellriverchamber.com
www.powellriverchamber.com
Overview: A medium-sized local licensing organization founded in 1933
Member of: British Columbia Chamber of Commerce; Canadian Chamber
Chief Officer(s):
Jack Barr, President
Finances: *Annual Operating Budget:* Less than $50,000
Staff Member(s): 2
Membership: 230; *Committees:* Youth; Membership; Government; Technology
Activities: To promote & enhance trade, commerce & the civil well-being of the Powell River communities; *Library* Open to public
Awards:
• Horizon Business Awards (Award)

Powell River Lapidary Club
2544 Dixon Rd., Powell River BC V8A 5C1
Tel: 604-487-0444
Overview: A small local organization
Affliation(s): British Columbia Lapidary Society; Gem & Mineral Federation of Canada
Chief Officer(s):
Belinda Fogarty, Contact, 604-485-2141
udemuth@shaw.ca
Membership: *Member Profile:* Persons in the Powell River region of British Columbia who are interested in the hobbies of lapidary & wire wrapping
Activities: Hosting monthly meetings

Powell River Sunshine Coast Real Estate Board
PO Box 307, Powell River BC V8A 5C2
Tel: 604-485-6944; *Fax:* 604-485-6944
prscreb@shaw.ca
www.thesunshinecoast.com
Overview: A small local organization overseen by British Columbia Real Estate Association
Chief Officer(s):
Geri Powell, Board Administrator

Power Workers' Union (PWU)
244 Eglinton Ave. East, Toronto ON M4P 1K2
Fax: 416-481-7115
pwu@pwu.ca
www.pwu.ca
Overview: A large provincial organization founded in 1944
Affliation(s): Canadian Union of Public Employees; Canadian Labour Congress; Ontario Federation of Labour; Labourers International Union of North America; Canadian Union of Skilled Workers
Chief Officer(s):
Don MacKinnon, President
dmackinnon@pwu.ca
Brad Carnduff, Vice-President, Sector 2
bcarnduff@pwu.ca
Mel Hyatt, Vice-President, Sector 3
hyattm@pwu.ca
Bob Walker, Vice-President, Sector 1
bwalker@pwu.ca
Staff Member(s): 31
Membership: 15,000-49,999; *Member Profile:* Individuals who work in the power production industry in Ontario.

Prader-Willi Syndrome Association of Alberta
9006 - 120 St., Edmonton AB TG6 1X7
Tel: 780-459-1959
Other Communication: 403-256-0612 (Calgary); 403-340-1057 (Red Deer)
www.pwsaa.ca
Also Known As: PWSA of AB
Overview: A small provincial charitable organization founded in 1986

Mission: To advocate for individuals affected by Prader-Willi Syndrome; To improve the quality of life for affected individuals
Affliation(s): Canadian Prader-Willi Syndrome Association
Chief Officer(s):
Trudi Jamesen, President
trudi@lundeen.ca
Doris Chura, Vice-President
chura_d@hotmail.com
Tamara Linklater, Treasurer
Finances: *Funding Sources:* Donations; Fundraising; Membership fees
Membership: *Fees:* $20 families; *Member Profile:* Parents, relatives, & support workers of individuals affected by Prader-Willi Syndrome
Activities: Raising awareness & knowledge of Prader-Willi Syndrome; *Awareness Events:* Prader-Willi Syndrome Association of Alberta Walk-a-thon, June
Publications:
• PWSA of AB Newsletter
Type: Newsletter; *Editor:* Holly McGhan
Profile: Association reports, stories, & events

Prairie Agricultural Machinery Institute (PAMI)
PO Box 1150, 2215 - 8th Ave., Humboldt SK S0K 2A0
Tel: 306-682-2555; *Fax:* 306-682-5080
Toll-Free: 800-567-7264
humboldt@pami.ca
www.pami.ca
Overview: A medium-sized local charitable organization founded in 1974
Mission: To serve manufacturers & farmers in Manitoba & Saskatchewan's agricultural sector through applied research, development, & testing
Affliation(s): Manitoba Ministry of Agriculture, Food, & Rural Initiatives; Saskatchewan Ministry of Agricultue
Finances: *Funding Sources:* Fee-for-service work; Government
Staff Member(s): 45
Activities: *Library:* Prairie Agricultural Machinery Institute Research Library;
Publications:
• Direct Seeding Manual: A Farming System for the New Millennium
Price: $50 Manitoba, Saskatchewan, & Alberta; $55 elsewhere
• The Rancher's Guide to Elk & Bison Handling Facilities
Type: Book; *Number of Pages:* 35; *Price:* $20 Canada; $25 international
• The Stockman's Guide to Range Livestock Watering from Surface Sources
Type: Book; *Number of Pages:* 36; *Price:* $10 Canada; $12 international
Profile: Includes a workbook

Portage la Prairie
PO Box 1060, 390 River Rd., Portage la Prairie MB R1N 3C5
Tel: 204-857-4811; *Fax:* 204-239-7124
portage@pami.ca
Chief Officer(s):
Harvey Chorney, Vice-President, Manitoba Operations

Prairie Conservation Forum
c/o Southern Region, Alberta Environment, 200 - 5th Ave. South, 2nd Fl., Lethbridge AB T1J 4L1
Tel: 403-381-5562; *Fax:* 403-382-4428
info@albertapcf.org
www.albertapcf.org
Overview: A small local organization
Mission: Conservation of native prairie & parkland environments in Alberta
Chief Officer(s):
Bill Dolan, Chair
bill.dolan@gov.ab.ca
Activities: Alberta Prairie Conservation Action Plan

Prairie Fruit Growers Association (PFGA)
PO Box 2430, Altona MB R0G 0B0
Tel: 204-324-5058; *Fax:* 204-324-5058
pfga@xplornet.com
www.pfga.com
Overview: A small local organization founded in 1974
Mission: To educate members, access quality planting stock, direct research & develop markets
Member of: North American Berry Association
Finances: *Annual Operating Budget:* $100,000-$250,000
Staff Member(s): 1
Membership: 115; *Fees:* $195

Prairie Implement Manufacturers Association; PIMA - Agricultural Manufacturers of Canada *See* Agricultural Manufacturers of Canada

Prairie Music Alliance *See* Western Canadian Music Alliance

Prairie Osteopathic Association
1603 - 20 Ave NW, Calgary AB T2M 1G9
Tel: 403-282-7165; *Fax:* 403-289-8269
Overview: A small local organization
Affliation(s): Canadian Osteopathic Association
Chief Officer(s):
C.E. (Ted) Findlay, President

Prairie Provinces Forestry Association *See* Manitoba Forestry Association Inc.

Prairie Ready Mixed Concrete Association *See* Saskatchewan Ready Mixed Concrete Association Inc.

Prairie Region Halfway House Association (PRHHA)
PO Box 45007, Stn. Inglewood, Calgary AB T2G 5H7
prhha.net
Overview: A small provincial organization overseen by Regional Halfway House Association
Mission: To help offenders reintegrate themselves into society
Member of: Region Halfway House Association
Chief Officer(s):
Pamela Gaudette, Executive Director, 403-969-4967
pam@prhha.net

Prairie Rock & Gem Society (PRGS)
c/o Regina Senior Citizens Centre, 2134 Winnipeg St., Regina SK S4P 3X6
www.prairierockandgem.info
Overview: A small provincial organization founded in 1955
Mission: To promote rockhounding & lapidary
Member of: Gem & Mineral Federation of Canada
Chief Officer(s):
Joan Riemer, Contact, 306-545-7111
jriemer@myaccess.ca
Membership: *Member Profile:* Persons of all ages who like rocks & the hobby of lapidary
Activities: Hosting monthly meeting from September to June; Offering a fully equipped workshop; Organizing field trips; Providing educational programs; *Awareness Events:* Prairie Rock & Gem Society Annual Show & Sale; *Library:* Prairie Rock & Gem Society Resource Library

Prairie Saengerbund Choir Association
4823 Claret St. NW, Calgary AB T2L 1B9
Tel: 403-284-3731; *Fax:* 403-284-1470
Overview: A medium-sized local charitable organization founded in 1977
Mission: To share, enhance, encourage & celebrate our wonderful German musical heritage
Chief Officer(s):
Ellen Rossi, Contact
domelen@telus.net
Finances: *Funding Sources:* Grants; self support
Membership: *Member Profile:* 13 German choirs in three prairie provinces in Canada
Activities: Biennial song festival of Prairie choirs (German)
Awards:
• 25 Year Member of the Choir (Award)
• Singer of the Year (Award)

Prairie Theatre Exchange (PTE)
Portage Place, #Y300, 393 Portage Ave., 3rd Fl., Winnipeg MB R3B 3H6
Tel: 204-942-7291; *Fax:* 204-942-1774
pte@pte.mb.ca
www.pte.mb.ca
www.facebook.com/423687680006
twitter.com/PrairieTheatre
Overview: A medium-sized provincial charitable organization founded in 1972
Mission: To operate a professional theatre of high calibre for the entertainment & edification of a broad spectrum of people; to operate a school to encourage appreciation of theatre & to provide accessible, high quality, innovative drama education; to support the development of new plays; to foster theatre arts-related endeavours of others through use of our facilities & expertise; to manage one or more community theatre arts centres
Member of: Professional Association of Canadian Theatres; Canadian Actors' Equity Association; Canadian Conference of the Arts; Cultural Human Resources Council
Affliation(s): Canadian Institute of Theatre Technology
Chief Officer(s):
Greg Doyle, President
Cherry Karpyshin, General Manager, 204-925-5251
generalmgr@pte.mb.ca
Finances: *Annual Operating Budget:* $500,000-$1.5 Million; *Funding Sources:* Earned revenue; Canada Council; Manitoba Arts Council; fundraising; City of Winnipeg; The Winnipeg Foundation; individual & corporate donations
Staff Member(s): 17; 180 volunteer(s)
Membership: 3,800; *Member Profile:* Subscribers; donors; volunteers; students (or parents) of our school; *Committees:* Executive; Finance; Special Events; Fundraising
Activities: Conducts a theatre school for ages 6 & up; offers outreach services; produces 5 adult plays & 1 play for youths

Prairie West Historical Society Inc.
PO Box 910, 946 - 2nd St. SE, Eston SK S0L 1A0
Tel: 306-962-3772
Overview: A small local charitable organization founded in 1981
Mission: To educate & entertain visitors with the history of the Eston area; To collect, preserve, organize, & exhibit artifacts
Finances: *Funding Sources:* Donations; Grants
Activities: Operating a museum, consisting of a restored farmhouse, the Lovedale Schoolhouse, the Acadia school barn, & a Homesteader's shack, with artifacts, photographs, & documentation from the local area; Providing heritage programs for students; Offering research services; *Library:* Prairie West Historical Society Archives; Open to public by appointment

Prairie/Saskatoon Apparel Market
PO Box 55065, Stn. Dakota Crossing, Winnipeg MB R2N 0A8
Tel: 204-793-3256; *Fax:* 204-947-0561
prairieapparelmarkets.com
Overview: A small local organization overseen by Canadian Association of Wholesale Sales Representatives
Chief Officer(s):
Leo Kelsch, Director, Market
leo@prairieapparelmarkets.com

Presbyterian Church in Canada (PCC) / Église presbytérienne au Canada
50 Wynford Dr., Toronto ON M3C 1J7
Tel: 416-441-1111; *Fax:* 416-441-2825
Toll-Free: 800-619-7301
presbyterian.ca
www.facebook.com/pcconnect
twitter.com/pcconnect
youtube.com/presvideo
Overview: A large national organization founded in 1875
Member of: The Canadian Council of Churches; World Alliance of Reformed Churches; World Council of Churches; Action By Churches Together; Ecumenical Advocacy Alliance
Chief Officer(s):
Stephen Kendall, Principal Clerk, General Assembly Office
skendall@presbyterian.ca
Tony Plomp, Deputy Clerk, General Assembly Office
tony_plomp@telus.net
Frances Hogg, Secretary, General Assembly Office
fhogg@presbyterian.ca
Donald Muir, Associate Secretary & Deputy Clerk, General Assembly Office
dmuir@presbyterian.ca
Stephen Roche, CFO & Treasurer, Support Services
sroche@presbyterian.ca
Richard Fee, General Secretary, Life & Mission Agency
rfee@presbyterian.ca
Dorcas J. Gordon, Principal, Knox College, Toronto
jd.gordon@utoronto.ca
John Vissers, Principal, Presbyterian College
jvissers@presbyteriancollege.ca
Finances: *Funding Sources:* Congregations
Membership: 125,509; *Member Profile:* Presbyteries; congregations; communicants on roll; ministers; *Committees:* Assembly Council; Committee to Advise with the Moderator
Activities: *Library:* Knox College & Presbyterian College Libraries; Open to public
Awards:
• Presbyterian Woman of Faith Award (Award)
To recognize the courageous and faithful work of women within the church. Eligibility: Any woman who is or has been part of The Presbyterian Church in Canada; Lay, elders, diaconal ministers or ordained clergy
Publications:
• Presbyterian Record [a publication of Presbyterian Church in

Canada]
Type: Magazine; *Editor:* Andrew Faiz

Prescott & District Chamber of Commerce
950 Edward St. North, Prescott ON K0E 1T0
Tel: 613-925-2171; *Fax:* 613-925-4381
prescottchamberofcommerce@gmail.com
www.prescottanddistrictchamber.com
Overview: A small local organization founded in 1893
Mission: To continue to lead & direct the municipalities of Prescott & District through focused preservation of the community's past & the continued & relentless promotion of the district's future
Member of: Ontario Chamber of Commerce; Canadian Chamber of Commerce
Chief Officer(s):
Dan Roddick, President
Finances: *Annual Operating Budget:* Less than $50,000; *Funding Sources:* Membership; fundraising
Staff Member(s): 1; 50 volunteer(s)
Membership: 150; *Fees:* $35-$215

Prescott & Russell Association for Community Living ***See*** Valoris for Children & Adults of Prescott-Russell

Prescott Board of Trade; Prescott Chamber of Commerce; Prescott and District Chamber of Commerce ***See*** South Grenville Chamber of Commerce

Prescott Group
3430 Prescott St., Halifax NS B3K 4Y4
Tel: 902-454-7387; *Fax:* 902-453-0275
Other Communication: Human Resources e-mail: prescotthr@eastlink.ca
prescottgroup@eastlink.ca
prescottgroup.ca
www.facebook.com/337804192957428
Overview: A small local organization
Mission: To provide work skills & employment opportunities to adults with intellectual disabilities, in order to build independence
Member of: Halifax Adult Services Society; DIRECTIONS Council for Vocational Services Society
Chief Officer(s):
Mona Reeves, Chair
Susan Slaunwhite, Executive Director
susanslaunwhite@eastlink.ca
Finances: *Funding Sources:* Donations; sponsors; government
Membership: *Committees:* Human Resources; Finance; Futures; Program
Activities: Operates the Atlantic Bag, Fireside Kitchen & Prescott Mailing Services businesses

Préservation du bois Canada ***See*** Wood Preservation Canada

Préservation du bois Canada ***See*** Canadian Wood Preservers Bureau

La presse canadienne ***See*** The Canadian Press

La Presse spécialisée du Canada ***See*** Canadian Business Press

Presse universitaire canadienne ***See*** Canadian University Press

Preventative Social Services Association ***See*** Family & Community Support Services Association of Alberta

Préventex - Association paritaire du textile
1936, rue Rossignol, Brossard QC J4X 2C6
Tél: 450-671-6925; *Téléc:* 450-671-9267
www.preventex.qc.ca
Nom précédent: Association paritaire pour la santé et la sécurité du travail - Textiles primaires
Aperçu: *Dimension:* moyenne; *Envergure:* provinciale; fondée en 1983
Mission: Amener les employeurs et les travailleurs du secteur à prendre charge activement de la prévention des accidents du travail et des maladies professionnelles
Membre(s) du bureau directeur:
François Lauzon, Co-président
Daniel Vallée, Co-président
Membre(s) du personnel: 8
Activités: Formation; information; conseil et assistance technique; hygiène industrielle; ergonomie; *Service de conférenciers:* Oui

Prevention CDN/NDG
5319, av Notre-Dame-de-Grâce, Montréal QC H4A 1L2
info@preventionndg.org
www.preventionndg.org
Aperçu: *Dimension:* petite; *Envergure:* locale; fondée en 1988
Mission: To offer human resources as well as tools to increase their quality of life, at home, in the borough as well as in the community in general, focusing on crime prevention & environmental issues.

PRIDE - People to Reduce Impaired Driving Everywhere (Ontario) ***See*** MADD Canada

Pride Centre of Edmonton
10608 - 105 Ave., Edmonton AB T5H 0L2
Tel: 780-488-3234; *Fax:* 780-482-2855
exec@pridecentreofedmonton.org
www.pridecentreofedmonton.org
www.facebook.com/34126834504
twitter.com/yegpridecentre
Previous Name: Gay & Lesbian Community Centre of Edmonton
Overview: A small local organization founded in 2004
Mission: To provide a place where gay men, lesbians, bisexuals & transgendered may meet together in peace & harmony; to provide peer support to individuals in need in a lesbian, gay, bisexual & transgendered community; to act when requested as education & information resource for any person; to foster sense of community among gay men, lesbians, bisexual women & men & transgendered
Chief Officer(s):
Mickey Wilson, Executive Director
Finances: *Funding Sources:* Fundraising; membership dues
Staff Member(s): 3
Activities: Edmonton Gay & Lesbian Archives; *Speaker Service:* Yes

Pride of Israel
59 Lissom Cres., Toronto ON M2R 2P2
Tel: 416-226-0111; *Fax:* 416-226-0128
office@prideofisraelsynagogue.com
www.prideofisraelsynagogue.com
Overview: A small local organization founded in 1905
Chief Officer(s):
Steven Bloom, Chair
Wilfred Lindo, President
Sean Gorman, Rabbi
rav_sean@ prideofisraelsynagogue.com
Larry Spring, Ritual Director
ritualdirector@ prideofisraelsynagogue.com
Bonnie Moatti, Chair, Membership
bonnie.moatti@rogers.com
Finances: *Funding Sources:* Donations
Activities: Offering a Kosher Food Bank; Providing Jewish educational programming
Publications:
• Pages of Pride
Type: Newsletter; *Accepts Advertising*; *Editor:* Jeffrey Sherman
Profile: Articles & forthcoming activities

The Primate's World Relief & Development Fund (PWRDF) / Le fonds du Primat pour le secours et le développement mondial
Anglican Church of Canada, 80 Hayden St., Toronto ON M4Y 3G2
Tel: 416-924-9192; *Fax:* 416-924-3483
Toll-Free: 866-308-7973
Other Communication: www.flickr.com/photos/45005153@N07
pwrdf@pwrdf.org
www.pwrdf.org
www.facebook.com/111501932203731
twitter.com/PWRDF
www.youtube.com/user/PWRDF
Overview: A small international charitable organization founded in 1959
Mission: PWRDF connects Anglicans in Canada to communities around the world in dynamic partnerships to advance development, to respond to emergencies, to assist refugees, and to act for positive change.
Member of: Canadian Council for International Cooperation; Action by Churches Together (ACT)
Affliation(s): Canadian Council of Churches
Chief Officer(s):
Fred Hiltz, Primate & President
Adele Finney, Executive Director
afinney@pwrdf.org
Finances: *Annual Operating Budget:* Greater than $5 Million; *Funding Sources:* Anglican Church contributions; Canadian International Development Agency
Staff Member(s): 16; 2000 volunteer(s)
Activities: *Library:* Resource Centre - Anglican Church of Canada; Open to public

Prince Albert & District Association of Realtors
615 Branion Dr., Prince Albert SK S6V 2R9
Tel: 306-764-8755; *Fax:* 306-763-0555
pareb@sasktel.net
www.princealbertrealtors.ca
Previous Name: Prince Albert Real Estate Board
Overview: A small local organization founded in 1959 overseen by Saskatchewan Real Estate Association
Mission: To support realtors in the Prince Albert Real Estate community.
Member of: The Canadian Real Estate Association
Chief Officer(s):
Candy Marshall, Executive Officer
Staff Member(s): 1
Membership: 11
Activities: *Internships:* Yes

Prince Albert & District Labour Council
107 - 8th St. East, Prince Albert SK S6V 0V8
Tel: 306-763-2303
Overview: A small local organization overseen by Saskatchewan Federation of Labour
Mission: To promote the interests of affiliates in Prince Albert, Saskatchewan, & the surrounding district; To advance the economic & social welfare of workers
Affliation(s): Canadian Labour Congress (CLC)
Chief Officer(s):
Craig Thebaud, President, 306-764-0194
craigthebaud@gmail.com
Activities: Organizing rallies to voice concerns of local workers; Liaising with local elected officials to present workers' issues; Presenting educational opportunities; Raising awareness about occupational health & safety; Organizing events, such as a ceremony on the International Day of Mourning for Workers Killed and Injured on the Job

Prince Albert Chamber of Commerce
3700 - 2nd Ave. West, Prince Albert SK S6W 1A2
Tel: 306-764-6222; *Fax:* 306-922-4727
pachamber@sasktel.net
www.princealbertchamber.com
www.facebook.com/PrinceAlbertandDistrictChamberOfCommerce
twitter.com/ChamberPA
Overview: A small local organization founded in 1887
Mission: Umbrella organization & voice of the business community whose role is to enhance the economic & social conditions of Prince Albert & area
Member of: Regional Economic Development Alliance; Tourism & Convention Bureau; Saskatchewan Outfitters Association
Affliation(s): Canadian Chamber of Commerce; Saskatchewan Chamber of Commerce
Chief Officer(s):
Mike Mitchell, Chair
Merle Lacert, CEO
Finances: *Annual Operating Budget:* $100,000-$250,000; *Funding Sources:* Membership dues; fundraising
Staff Member(s): 3
Membership: 489; *Fees:* $174.71-$1347.87; *Committees:* Agriculture; Forestry; Economic Development; Finance; Membership; Public Relations; Retail

Prince Albert Construction Association Inc. (PACA)
70 - 17th St. West, Prince Albert SK S6V 3X3
Tel: 306-764-2789; *Fax:* 306-764-3443
pacon@sasktel.net
www.pacaonline.ca
Overview: A small local organization overseen by Canadian Construction Association
Member of: Saskatchewan Construction Association (SCA); Canadian Construction Association (CCA)
Chief Officer(s):
David Thorpe, President, 306-763-8454
Kelly Miller, 1st Vice-President
Brent Mills, 2nd Vice-President
Membership: *Fees:* $575 associate; $585 affiliate; $975 full; *Member Profile:* Professional contractors; Commercial & industrial suppliers; Manufacturers; *Committees:* Bid Depository; Finance; Membership; Golf; Social; Liaison with City of Prince Albert; Nominating; Technology
Activities: Providing industry information; Offering networking opportunities; Presenting educational seminars & workshops; *Library:* PACA Lending Library;

Publications:
• PACA Newsletter
Type: Newsletter; *Frequency:* Weekly
Profile: Up-to-date information for members

Prince Albert Exhibition Association (PAEX)
PO Box 1538, 815 Exhibition Dr., Prince Albert SK S6V 5T1
Tel: 306-764-1711; *Fax:* 306-764-5246
paex@sasktel.net
www.paexhibition.com
Previous Name: Lorne Agricultural & Industrial Society
Overview: A small local charitable organization founded in 1883
Mission: To engage in activities which reflect the non-profit organization's motto, "Where Town & Country Meet"
Affliation(s): Saskatchewan Association of Agricultural Societies & Exhibitions (SAASE)
Chief Officer(s):
Brian Schlosser, President
Dave Young, General Manager
Sandy Ackerman, Manager, Finance
Finances: *Funding Sources:* Sponsorships
Activities: Hosting a summer fair; *Awareness Events:* Summer Fair

Prince Albert Gliding & Soaring Club (PAG&SC)
219 Scissons Ct., Saskatoon SK S7S 1B7
Tel: 306-789-1535; *Fax:* 306-792-2532
soar@soar.sk.ca
www.soar.sk.ca/pagsc
Overview: A small local organization founded in 1986
Mission: To foster the sport of soaring
Affliation(s): Soaring Association of Saskatchewan; Soaring Association of Canada
Chief Officer(s):
Keith Andrews, President, 306-249-1859
k.andrews@sk.sympatico.ca
Rob Lohmaier, Treasurer, 306-764-7381
ka7@shaw.ca
Finances: *Funding Sources:* Annual membership dues; Launch fees; Glider rental fees
Membership: 15; *Fees:* $85 youth; $170 regular
Activities: Promoting the sport of soaring; Providing flying activities; Offering flight instruction

Prince Albert Indian & Métis Friendship Centre *See* Indian & Metis Friendship Centre of Prince Albert

Prince Albert Model Forest Association Inc. (PAMF)
PO Box 2406, Prince Albert SK S6V 7G3
Tel: 306-953-8921; *Fax:* 306-763-6456
www.pamodelforest.sk.ca
Overview: A small provincial organization founded in 1992
Mission: To work towards sustainable forest management through development & testing of new forest management tools, sharing our successes, developing linkages & expanding the PAMF partnership
Member of: Saskatchewan Forestry Association; Canadian Model Forest Network; International Model Forest Network
Affliation(s): University of Saskatchewan; University of Regina
Chief Officer(s):
Susan Carr, General Manager
susan.carr@sasktel.net
Finances: *Annual Operating Budget:* $250,000-$500,000; *Funding Sources:* Canadian Forest Service; partners; grants
Staff Member(s): 2
Membership: *Committees:* Science & Technology; Communications & Outreach; Beyond our Boundaries; Planning & Operations
Activities: Applied research in sustainable forestry; technology transfer of research findings; *Library:* PAMF Reference Library; Open to public

Prince Albert Real Estate Board *See* Prince Albert & District Association of Realtors

Prince Albert Tourism & Convention Bureau Inc. *See* Tourism Prince Albert

Prince County Hospital Foundation (PCHF)
PO Box 3000, 65 Roy Boates Ave., Summerside PE C1N 2A9
Tel: 902-432-2547; *Fax:* 902-432-2551
info@pchcare.com
www.pchcare.com
www.facebook.com/PCHFoundation
Overview: A medium-sized local charitable organization
Mission: To raise money for Prince County Hospital in order to keep up with medical equipment needs
Chief Officer(s):
Heather Matheson, Managing Director
hematheson@ihis.org
Gord Coffin, President
Finances: *Funding Sources:* Donations; Fundraising
Staff Member(s): 4
Activities: *Awareness Events:* Grassroots & Cowboys Fundraiser, September; Women's Golf Classic Fundraiser, September; Lights for Life Fundraiser, December

Prince Edward Association for Community Living *See* Community Living Prince Edward (County)

Prince Edward County Arts Council (PECAC)
PO Box 6180, Picton ON K0K 2T0
Tel: 613-476-8767
info@pecartscouncil.org
www.pecartscouncil.org
Overview: A small local charitable organization founded in 1979
Mission: To enrich the life of the community by encouraging artists & artisans & their work & by promoting our arts community both as an important part of the fabric of life in the county & beyond its shores
Membership: *Fees:* Schedule available
Activities: Maker's Hand, Nov.; Art in the County, June/July; Jazz Festival, Aug.; Music Festival, Sept.; *Awareness Events:* Art in the County, June; Clic Photo Show, July; The Maker's Hand, October

Prince Edward County Chamber of Tourism & Commerce (PECCTAC)
116 Main St., Picton ON K0K 2T0
Tel: 613-476-2421; *Fax:* 613-476-7461
Toll-Free: 800-640-4717
contactus@pecchamber.com
www.pecchamber.com
www.facebook.com/PECChamber
Overview: A small local organization
Chief Officer(s):
Mike McLeod, General Manager
manager@pecchamber.com
Membership: 300; *Fees:* $185; $75 associate; $125 non-profit

Prince Edward Historical Society
c/o Prince Edward County Archives, 261 Main St., Wellington ON K0K 3L0
pehistsoc.wordpress.com
www.facebook.com/PrinceEdwardHistoricalSociety
twitter.com/PEHistSoc
Overview: A small local organization founded in 1899
Mission: To promote & preserve the history of the county
Member of: Archives Association of Ontario
Chief Officer(s):
Steve Ferguson, President
Membership: *Fees:* $20 individual; $30 family

Prince Edward Island Alpine Ski Association
PO Box 2026, Charlottetown PE C1A 7N7
Tel: 902-368-4110; *Fax:* 902-368-4548
Toll-Free: 800-247-6712
sports@sportpei.pe.ca
www.sportpei.pe.ca
Overview: A medium-sized provincial organization overseen by Sport PEI

Prince Edward Island Amateur Baseball Association *See* Baseball PEI

Prince Edward Island Amateur Boxing Association
2595 Horne Cross Rd., Wilsloe PE C1E 1Z3
Tel: 902-394-1574; *Fax:* 902-628-3865
Overview: A medium-sized provincial organization overseen by Canadian Amateur Boxing Association
Member of: Canadian Amateur Boxing Association
Chief Officer(s):
Holly Morrison, President
hollymorrison@pei.sympatico.ca

Prince Edward Island Aquaculture Alliance (PEIAA)
101 Longworth Ave., 1st Fl., Charlottetown PE C1A 5A9
Tel: 902-368-2757; *Fax:* 902-626-3954
peiaqua@aquaculturepei.com
www.aquaculturepei.com
Overview: A small provincial organization founded in 1998
Mission: To provide focus for the Prince Edward Island aquaculture industry; to enhance industry prosperity through its development as an effective world competitor
Member of: Canadian Aquaculture Industry Alliance
Chief Officer(s):
Gary Rogers, President
Ann Worth, Executive Director
ed@aquaculturepei.com
Finances: *Annual Operating Budget:* $100,000-$250,000; *Funding Sources:* Government; industry
Staff Member(s): 3
Membership: 130+; *Fees:* $1,070 supporting; $267.50 supplier; $53.50 associate; *Member Profile:* Mussel, Oyster, Clam & Finfish culturists in PEI & companies which supply goods & services to them
Activities: Co-Host of International PEI Shellfish Festival; Co-Host of Great Atlantic Shellfish Exchange
Publications:
• Soundings [a publication of the Prince Edward Island Aquaculture Alliance]
Type: Newsletter; *Frequency:* Quarterly

Prince Edward Island Association for Community Living (PEIACL)
161 St. Peters Rd., Charlottetown PE C1A 5P7
Tel: 902-566-4844; *Fax:* 902-368-8057
Toll-Free: 888-360-8681
info@peiacl.ca
www.peiacl.ca
Overview: A medium-sized provincial charitable organization founded in 1956 overseen by Canadian Association for Community Living
Mission: To work on behalf of individuals with an intellectual disability & their families; To empower families to increase options available to Islanders with an intellectual disability
Member of: Canadian Association for Community Living; Prince Edward Island Literacy Alliance
Chief Officer(s):
Bridget Cairns, Executive Director
bridget@peiacl.ca
Trudi Barry, Provincial Coordinator
65 volunteer(s)
Membership: 500-999; *Fees:* $10 families; $75 schools/professionals
Activities: *Speaker Service:* Yes; *Library:* PEI ACL Resource Library; Open to public

Prince Edward Island Association for Newcomers to Canada (PEI ANC)
49 Water St., Charlottetown PE C1A 1A3
Tel: 902-628-6009; *Fax:* 902-894-4928
www.peianc.com
Overview: A medium-sized provincial organization founded in 1993
Mission: To provide immigrants to Prince Edward Island with short-term settlement services & community integration programs
Member of: Prince Edward Island Literacy Alliance Inc.
Chief Officer(s):
Craig Mackie, Executive Director
Myra Thorkelson, President
Dan Doran, Secretary-Treasurer
Finances: *Funding Sources:* Citizenship & Immigration Canada; Service Canada; Government of Prince Edward Island; Health Canada
Activities: Increasing cross-cultural awareness; Providing public education programs; Offering training & resources to service providers & government departments; Conducting life skills training for immigrants; Engaging in advocacy activities; *Speaker Service:* Yes; *Library:* PEI ANC Resource Library
Publications:
• PEI ANC [Prince Edward Island Association for Newcomers to Canada] Annual Report
Type: Yearbook; *Frequency:* Annually

Prince Edward Island Association of Exhibitions (PEIAE)
Royalty Centre, PO Box 2000, #237, 40 Enman Cres., Charlottetown PE C1E 1E6
Tel: 902-368-4848; *Fax:* 902-368-5651
peiexhibitions@gov.pe.ca
peiae.ca
www.facebook.com/PEIAE
www.twitter.com/peiexhibitions
Overview: A small provincial licensing organization founded in 1973
Member of: Canadian Association of Fairs & Exhibitions; Intl. Association of Fairs & Exhibitions
Chief Officer(s):
Adele Moore, Executive Director
Finances: *Annual Operating Budget:* $250,000-$500,000

Staff Member(s): 2
Membership: 1-99

Prince Edward Island Association of Family Resource Programs
c/o Family Place, 75 Central St., Summerside PE C1N 3L2
Tel: 902-436-1348; *Fax:* 902-888-3954
familyplace@eastlink.ca
Overview: A medium-sized provincial organization
Chief Officer(s):
Laura Quinn Graham, Contact

Prince Edward Island Association of Medical Radiation Technologists (PEIAMRT)
61 Queen Elizabeth St., Charlottetown PE C1A 3A8
www.peiamrt.com
Overview: A small provincial organization founded in 1982 overseen by Canadian Association of Medical Radiation Technologists
Mission: To act in accordance with the Public Health Act, "Radiation Safety Regulations"; To promote excellence in health care
Chief Officer(s):
Cathy Clarke, President
cathyEClarke@Eastlink.ca
Lisa Pyke, Vice-President
lmpyke@ihis.org
Chelsea Smith, Secretary
chasmith@ihis.org
Tanya MacKay, Treasurer
tdmackay@ihis.org
Karen MacDonald, Registrar
peiamrtregistrar@bellaliant.net
Membership: *Member Profile:* Persons from Prince Edward Island who are involved in the following professions: nuclear medicine, magnetic resonance, radiation therapy, & radiological technology (including bone mineral densitometry, computed tomography, & mammography)
Activities: Offering continuing professional development; Providing public education; Partnering with allied health professionals to meet goals
Meetings/Conferences: • Prince Edward Island Association of Medical Radiation Technologists 2015 Annual Meeting, 2015, PE
Scope: Provincial

Prince Edward Island Association of Optometrists (PEIAO)
PO Box 1812, Charlottetown PE C1A 7N5
e-mail: visionpei@gmail.com
www.peioptometrists.ca
Previous Name: Prince Edward Island Optometrical Association
Overview: A medium-sized provincial organization founded in 1922 overseen by Canadian Association of Optometrists
Mission: To promote the professional interests of optometrists in Prince Edward Island Association; To improve optometrists' proficiency
Chief Officer(s):
Jayne Toombs, President
David McKenna, Vice-President
Carolyn Acorn, Secretary
J.E. Hickey, Treasurer
Membership: *Member Profile:* Optometrists in Prince Edward Island
Activities: Encouraging continuing education for optometrists in Prince Edward Island; Disseminating information about optometry; Collaborating with other optometry associations & professional bodies

Prince Edward Island Association of Social Workers (PEIASW) / Association des travailleurs sociaux de l'Île-du-Prince-Édouard
81 Prince St., Charlottetown PE C1A 4R3
Tel: 902-368-7337; *Fax:* 902-368-7180
contact@peiasw.ca
peiasw.ca
Overview: A small provincial organization overseen by Canadian Association of Social Workers
Mission: To acknowledge & promote the work of social workers in Prince Edward Island; To advance the social work profession throughout the province, to ensure well-being for residents
Member of: Canadian Association of Social Workers
Chief Officer(s):
Kelly MacWilliams, President
Membership: *Member Profile:* Social workers in Prince Edward Island
Activities: *Awareness Events:* Social Work Month, March

Prince Edward Island Association of the Appraisal Institute of Canada
PO Box 1796, Charlottetown PE C1A 7N4
Tel: 902-368-3355; *Fax:* 902-368-3582
peiaic@bellaliant.net
Overview: A small provincial organization overseen by Appraisal Institute of Canada
Chief Officer(s):
Boyce Costello, President
bdcostello@gov.pe.ca
Suzanne Pater, Executive Director

Prince Edward Island Automobile Dealers Association
PO Box 22004, Charlottetown PE C1A 9J2
Tel: 902-566-3639; *Fax:* 902-368-7116
peiada@eastlink.ca
Overview: A small provincial organization
Member of: Canadian Automobile Dealers Association
Chief Officer(s):
Lisa Doyle-MacBain, Manager

Prince Edward Island Badminton Association
c/o Sport PEI, PO Box 302, 40 Enman Cres., Charlottetown PE C1N 7K7
Tel: 902-368-4262; *Fax:* 902-368-4548
Also Known As: Badminton PEI
Overview: A small provincial organization founded in 1987 overseen by Badminton Canada
Member of: Badminton Canada
Chief Officer(s):
Nancy MacKinnon, President
nandn.mackinnon@route2.net
Activities: Organizing tournaments

Prince Edward Island Baseball Umpires Association (PEIBUA)
PE
Tel: 902-367-0564
peibua@gmail.com
www.peibua.com
Overview: A small provincial organization
Mission: To represent certified amateur baseball umpires in the province of PEI.
Chief Officer(s):
Kent Walker, Supervisor of Officials
kentwalker019@gmail.com
Activities: *Library* Open to public

Prince Edward Island Beekeepers' Cooperative Association
4686 Rte. 17, Montague PE C0A 1R0
Tel: 902-651-8405
Overview: A small provincial organization
Mission: To promote beekeeping throughout Prince Edward Island; To provide education & information to members
Chief Officer(s):
John Burhoe, President
Membership: *Member Profile:* Beekeepers from Prince Edward Island
Activities: Undertaking regional studies related to bees, beeswax, honey, & pollen

Prince Edward Island Building & Construction Trades Council
326 Patterson Dr., Charlottetown PE C1A 8K4
Tel: 902-894-4269
Overview: A small provincial organization
Member of: AFL-CIO
Chief Officer(s):
Blair MacKinnon, President

Prince Edward Island Business Women's Association (PEIBWA)
161 St. Peter's Rd., Charlottetown PE C1A 5P7
Tel: 902-892-6040; *Fax:* 902-892-6050
Toll-Free: 866-892-6040
office@peibwa.org
www.peibwa.org
www.facebook.com/PEIBWA
twitter.com/peibwa
Overview: A medium-sized provincial organization
Mission: To assist women in business to succeed by providing services and programs to meet their objectives.
Member of: Prince Edward Island Literacy Alliance Inc.
Chief Officer(s):
Michelle Ryder-MacEwen, President
Membership: 313; *Fees:* $50 individual; $95 business

Prince Edward Island Canoe Kayak Association
RR#4, Alliston, Montague PE C0A 1R0
Tel: 902-962-3883; *Fax:* 902-962-3883
www.facebook.com/235534456533194
Overview: A small provincial organization overseen by CanoeKayak Canada
Member of: CanoeKayak Canada
Chief Officer(s):
Justin Richard Batten, President
justin.heidi@windsinc.com

Prince Edward Island Cattle Producers (PEICP)
420 University Ave., Charlottetown PE C1A 7Z5
Tel: 902-368-2229; *Fax:* 902-367-3082
cattlemen@eastlink.ca
www.peicattleproducers.com
Previous Name: P.E.I. Cattlemen's Association
Overview: A medium-sized provincial organization founded in 1976
Mission: To support the beef industry in Prince Edward Island; To ensure a responsible production of safe, quality beef; To foster a profitable industry
Member of: Canadian Cattlemen's Association (CCA)
Chief Officer(s):
Peter Verleun, Chair
Rinnie Bradley, Executive Director
Justin Lawless, Coordinator, Atlantic Verified Beef Program
Brian Morrison, Secretary-Treasurer
Finances: *Funding Sources:* Mandatory levies; Membership fees
Membership: 550+; *Fees:* Levies collected by processing facilities or a $5 membership fee; *Member Profile:* Prince Edward Island beef producers
Activities: Representing the beef industry in Prince Edward Island; Providing education
Publications:
• Beef Newsletter
Type: Newsletter
Profile: Timely information for Prince Edward Island's beef producers
• PEI Cattle Producers Annual Report with Financial Statements
Type: Yearbook; *Frequency:* Annually

Prince Edward Island Cerebral Palsy Association Inc.
PO Box 22034, Charlottetown PE C1A 9J2
Tel: 902-892-9694; *Fax:* 902-628-8751
info@peicpa.com
www.peicpa.com
Also Known As: Cerebral Palsy Association of PEI
Overview: A small provincial charitable organization founded in 1953
Mission: To improve the quality of life of persons with cerebral palsy through a broad range of programs, education, support of research, & the delivery of needed services to people with cerebral palsy & their families
Member of: United Way of PEI; Atlantic Cerebral Palsy Association
Activities: *Speaker Service:* Yes; *Library* by appointment

Prince Edward Island Certified Organic Producers Co-op
PO Box 1776, #110, 420 University Ave., Charlottetown PE C1A 7Z5
Tel: 902-894-9999
Toll-Free: 866-850-9799
www.organicpei.com
www.facebook.com/organicpei
Overview: A medium-sized provincial organization founded in 2002
Mission: To increase organic production, research and market development; invite growers into the organic industry and promote and educate Islanders about organic food.
Chief Officer(s):
Fred Dollar, President
Membership: 34; *Fees:* $25; *Member Profile:* Certified organic agriculture producers
Activities: Farmers Market

Prince Edward Island Chiropractic Association (PEICA)
228 Grafton St., Charlottetown PE C1A 1L5
Tel: 902-894-4400; *Fax:* 902-894-3762
dtownchiro@pei.aibn.com

Overview: A small provincial organization overseen by Canadian Chiropractic Association
Mission: To represent the chiropractic profession in Prince Edward Island; To advance the chiropractic profession in the province; To encourage high standards of service; To protect the residents of Prince Edward Island from unqualified individuals acting as chiropractors
Chief Officer(s):
Christopher MacCarthy, Chair
Membership: *Member Profile:* Chiropractors in Prince Edward Island
Activities: Raising public awareness of the chiropractic profession in Prince Edward Island; Encouraging continuing education;

Prince Edward Island College of Physiotherapists (PEICP)

PO Box 20078, Charlottetown PE C1A 9E3
Tel: 902-894-2063; *Fax:* 902-894-2490
www.peicpt.com
Overview: A small provincial licensing organization overseen by Canadian Alliance of Physiotherapy Regulators
Mission: To regulate the practice of physiotherapy on Prince Edward Island, in accordance with the provincial legislation, "Physiotherapy Act"; To protect the public by ensuring competent & ethical practice
Member of: Canadian Alliance of Physiotherapy Regulators
Chief Officer(s):
Joyce Ling, Registrar
Membership: *Fees:* $225
Activities: Setting standards of care for physiotherapists; Registering physiotherapists

Prince Edward Island Colt Stakes Association

c/o PEI Harness Racing Industry Association, #204A, 420 University Ave., Charlottetown PE CIA 7L1
Tel: 902-569-1682; *Fax:* 902-569-1827
peracing@eastlink.ca
Previous Name: Prince Edward Island Harness Racing Club
Overview: A small provincial organization founded in 1934
Member of: Prince Edward Island Harness Racing Industry Association
Chief Officer(s):
Wayne Pike, Executive Director, PEI Harness Racing Industry Association
Finances: *Funding Sources:* Prince Edward Island governments
Activities: Sponsoring the Prince Edward Island Colt Stakes, the oldest standardbred stakes races in Canada; Sponsoring a summer camp for children; Forming a history committee to document the history of the association & to arrange a permanenet historical exhibit

Prince Edward Island Convention Partnership; Meetings Prince Edward Island; Prince Edward Island Convention Bureau *See* Meetings & Conventions Prince Edward Island

Prince Edward Island Council of People with Disabilities (PEICOD)

Landmark Plaza, #2, 5 Lower Malpeque Rd., Charlottetown PE C1E 1R4
Tel: 902-892-9149; *Fax:* 902-566-1919
Toll-Free: 888-473-4263
peicod@peicod.pe.ca
www.peicod.pe.ca
www.facebook.com/PEICOD
Overview: A small provincial charitable organization founded in 1974
Mission: To improve the quality of life of people with disabilities on PEI
Member of: Prince Edward Island Literacy Alliance Inc.
Chief Officer(s):
Marcia Carroll, Executive Director
Finances: *Annual Operating Budget:* $500,000-$1.5 Million; *Funding Sources:* Provincial & federal governments; United Way
Staff Member(s): 9; 60 volunteer(s)
Membership: 1,000-4,999; *Fees:* $2
Activities: Accessibility guides; Sourcebook; Employment Counselling & Services Program; information & referral; advocacy; Computer Recycle Program; Snoezelen Room - recreational environment for children with disabilities; *Speaker Service:* Yes; *Library* Open to public

Prince Edward Island Council of the Arts (PEICA)

115 Richmond St., Charlottetown PE C1A 1A7
Tel: 902-368-4410
Toll-Free: 888-734-2784
www.peiartscouncil.com
www.facebook.com/peiartscouncil
twitter.com/peiartscouncil
Overview: A medium-sized provincial charitable organization founded in 1974
Mission: To make the Arts integral to the lives of all Prince Edward Islanders; Through advocacy, education, distribution of funds, management of the Arts Guild & program of prizes & awards.
Member of: Canadian Conference of the Arts.
Affliation(s): West Prince Arts Council; East Kings Arts Council; Conseil des arts Evangeline; Southern Kings Arts Council; South Shore Arts Council; Malpak Arts Council
Chief Officer(s):
Darrin White, Executive Director
dwhite@peica.ca
Finances: *Funding Sources:* PEI Government
Staff Member(s): 2
Membership: *Fees:* $5
Activities: Arts Calendar - promotional listing of arts events & activities sent to media; Artists' Network - contact with local artists; Free Promotion - coordination of provincial events offers artists & organizations free promotion of their events; Funding Assistance - access to addresses, information & applications for grant funding; Special Activities - speakers & seminars arranged by the Council; Funding program operates to assist artistic endeavours; *Library*
Awards:
• Senior Arts Award (Award)
Awarded every two years to a PEI professional artist with an accumulated body of work who has contributed in general to art in PEI *Amount:* $5,000
• Island Literary Awards (Award)
Established in 1987 in recognition of Island writers in six categories: Short Story, Poetry, Children's Literature, Feature Article, Creative Writing for Children, Playwriting; an additional award is made "for distinguished contribution to the literary arts" *Amount:* $500, $200 & $100

Prince Edward Island Crafts Council (PEICC)

PO Box 20071, Stn. Sherwood, Charlottetown PE C1A PE3
Tel: 902-892-5152; *Fax:* 902-628-8740
info@peicraftscouncil.com
peicraftscouncil.com
www.facebook.com/peicraftscouncil
twitter.com/PECraftsCouncil
Overview: A small provincial organization founded in 1965
Mission: To promote the making & acceptance of quality handcrafted items through the provision of programs & services
Member of: Canadian Crafts Federation; Canadian Conference of the Arts
Chief Officer(s):
Suzanne Scott, President
Laura Cole, Executive Director
Finances: *Funding Sources:* Provincial government; projects; The Island Craft Shop
Membership: *Fees:* Schedule available
Activities: The Islands Crafts Shop; scholarships; workshops; Craft Fair; Loan Program; equipment rental; handcraft bags

Prince Edward Island Cultured Mussel Growers Association (PEICMGA)

c/o PEI Aquaculture Alliance, 101 Longworth Ave., 1st Fl., Charlottetown PE C1A 5A9
Tel: 902-386-2757; *Fax:* 902-626-3954
www.aquaculturepei.com/pei_cultured_mussels.php
Also Known As: PEI Mussel Growers
Overview: A small local organization founded in 1981
Mission: To advance the well-being of the cultured mussel industry in Prince Edward Island; to provide a forum for mussel growers to discuss concerns
Member of: PEI Aquaculture Alliance
Chief Officer(s):
Martin MacDonald, President
Membership: 1-99
Activities: Promoting the cultured mussel industry in PEI; Liaising with the provincial government

Prince Edward Island Curling Association (PEICA)

40 Enman Cres., Charlottetown PE C1E 1E6
Tel: 902-368-4208; *Fax:* 902-368-4548
info@peicurling.com
www.peicurling.com
www.facebook.com/peicurling
twitter.com/peicurling
Overview: A medium-sized provincial organization overseen by Canadian Curling Association
Mission: To advance & promote curling as a competitive & recreational sport in Prince Edward Island
Affliation(s): Sports PEI, Curl Atlantic
Chief Officer(s):
Amy Duncan, Executive Director
aduncan@sportpei.pe.ca

Prince Edward Island Dietetic Association (PEIDA)

c/o Prince Edward Island Dietitians Registration Board, PO Box 152, Summerside PE C1N 4Y8
Tel: 902-436-2438
peidietitians@gmail.com
www.peidietitians.ca
www.facebook.com/peidieteticassociation
Overview: A small provincial organization founded in 1965 overseen by Dietitians of Canada
Mission: To promote, encourage & improve the status of dietitians & nutritionists in the province of PEI; to promote & increase the knowledge & proficiency of its members in all matters relating to nutrition & dietetics; to promote public awareness
Chief Officer(s):
Mary Laura Coady, President
Finances: *Annual Operating Budget:* Less than $50,000
Activities: *Rents Mailing List:* Yes

Prince Edward Island Draft Horse Association (PEIDHA)

PE
e-mail: info@peidrafthorse.com
peidrafthorse.com
Overview: A small provincial organization
Mission: To promote draft horses in Prince Edward Island
Chief Officer(s):
Chris MacGillivray, President
president@peidrafthorse.com
Ron Newcombe, Vice-President
vice.president@peidrafthorse.com
Dianne Delaney, Secretary
secretary@peidrafthorse.com
Membership: 1-99
Activities: Participating in shows; Providing information about draft horses

Prince Edward Island Eco-Net (PEIEN)

#216, 40 Enman Cres., Charlottetown PE C1E 1E6
Tel: 902-566-4170; *Fax:* 902-566-4037
network@eastlink.ca
www.facebook.com/peieconet?ref=ts
Also Known As: Prince Edward Island Environmental Network
Overview: A medium-sized provincial organization founded in 1990 overseen by Canadian Environmental Network
Mission: To promote communication & cooperation among ENGO's (Environmental NGO's) & between ENGO's & governments; to provide referral services; to coordinate workshops & conferences; to provide consultations; to publish & distribute information
Chief Officer(s):
Matthew McCarville, Executive Director
Finances: *Annual Operating Budget:* Less than $50,000
Membership: 29; *Fees:* $25
Activities: *Speaker Service:* Yes

Prince Edward Island Federation of Agriculture (PEIFA)

420 University Ave., Charlottetown PE C1A 7Z5
Tel: 902-368-7289; *Fax:* 902-368-7204
www.peifa.ca
Overview: A medium-sized provincial organization founded in 1941 overseen by Canadian Federation of Agriculture
Mission: To provide a united voice for Island farmers
Chief Officer(s):
John Jaimeson, Executive Director
Finances: *Annual Operating Budget:* $100,000-$250,000
Staff Member(s): 4
Membership: 500-999

Prince Edward Island Federation of Foster Families

32 Doc Blanchard Cres., Charlottetown PE C1A 9K3
Tel: 902-963-3888; *Fax:* 902-963-3888
Overview: A small provincial organization
Mission: To provide support & information to families in West Prince region involved in providing foster care.
Chief Officer(s):
Wayne MacFarlane, Director
waynemacfarlane@pei.sympatico.ca

Prince Edward Island Federation of Labour / Fédération du travail de l'Ile-du-Prince-Édouard
326 Patterson Dr., Charlottetown PE C1A 8K4
Tel: 902-368-3068
peifed@pei.aibn.com
www.peifl.ca
Overview: A medium-sized provincial organization founded in 1964 overseen by Canadian Labour Congress
Member of: Prince Edward Island Literacy Alliance Inc.
Chief Officer(s):
Carl Pursey, President

Prince Edward Island Fencing Association (PEIFA)
c/o Sport PEI, PO Box 302, 40 Enman Cres., Charlottetown PE C1A 7K7
Tel: 902-368-4110; *Fax:* 902-386-4548
Toll-Free: 800-247-6712
sports@sportpei.pe.ca
Overview: A small provincial organization overseen by Canadian Fencing Federation
Mission: To promote & develop the sport of fencing in PEI
Member of: Sport PEI; Canadian Fencing Federation
Chief Officer(s):
Phil Stewart, Contact, 902-566-1073
pstewart@pei.sympatico.ca
Membership: *Fees:* $25 student; $200 regular

Prince Edward Island Finfish Association
c/o Dover Fish Hatchery, RR#2, Murray River PE C0A 1W0
Tel: 902-962-3446
Overview: A small provincial organization founded in 2000
Mission: To represent the interests of the finfish aquaculture sector in Prince Edward Island
Affliation(s): Prince Edward Island Aquaculture Alliance (PEIAA)
Chief Officer(s):
Leon Moyaert, President
Dawn Runighan, Vice-President
Mike Murray, Secretary-Treasurer
Membership: 1-99; *Member Profile:* Prince Edward Island individuals & companies occupied in finfish farming, including the production of Rainbow Trout, Halibut, & Atlantic Salmon, plus eggs, fry, & smolt

Prince Edward Island Fishermen's Association (PEIFA)
#102, 420 University Ave., Charlottetown PE C1A 7Z5
Tel: 902-566-4050; *Fax:* 902-368-3748
Other Communication: researchpeifa@pei.eastlink.ca
adminpeifa@pei.eastlink.ca
www.peifa.org
Overview: A small provincial organization
Mission: To represent fishermen across Prince Edward Island; To act as a single, united voice on behalf of Island fishers on industry issues
Chief Officer(s):
Ian MacPherson, Manager
managerpeifa@pei.eastlink.ca
Membership: *Fees:* $105; *Member Profile:* Prince Edward Island fishers from the following Locals: Central Northumberland Strait Fishermen's Association (CNSFA), Eastern Kings Fishermen's Association (EKFA), North Shore Fishermen's Association (NSFA), Prince County Fishermen's Association (PCFA), Southern Kings & Queens Fishermen's Association (SKQFA), & Western Gulf Fishermen's Association (WGFA)
Activities: Liaising with government; Facilitating networking opportunities; Collaborating with fisher organizations in other provinces

Prince Edward Island Five Pin Bowlers Association Inc.
c/o Sport PEI, PO Box 302, Charlottetown PE C1A 7K7
Tel: 902-368-4110; *Fax:* 902-368-4548
Toll-Free: 800-247-6712
sports@sportpei.pe.ca
www.sportpei.pe.ca
Overview: A medium-sized provincial organization founded in 1981

Prince Edward Island Flying Association
250 Brackley Point Rd., Charlottetown PE C1A 6Y9
Tel: 902-368-3008
bmartin@Islandtelecom.com
www.peiflying.com
Overview: A small provincial organization founded in 1983
Membership: *Fees:* $48.15 single; $58.85 family
Publications:
• PEI Flying Association Newsletter
Type: Newsletter

Prince Edward Island Forest Improvement Association (PEIFIA)
RR#1, York PE C9A 1P0
Tel: 902-672-2114; *Fax:* 902-672-2620
Previous Name: Prince Edward Island Silvicultural Contractors Association
Overview: A medium-sized provincial organization overseen by Canadian Forestry Association
Chief Officer(s):
Wanson Hemphill, Contact
wm.hemphill@pei.sympatico.ca
Finances: *Annual Operating Budget:* Less than $50,000
Staff Member(s): 1; 17 volunteer(s)
Membership: *Fees:* $40 individual; $30 associate
Activities: Umbrella organization of PEI forest-related groups

Prince Edward Island Forestry Training Corp.
Covehead Rd., RR#1, York PE C0A 1P0
Tel: 902-672-2114
Overview: A small provincial organization
Chief Officer(s):
Wanson Hemphill, General Manager

Prince Edward Island Funeral Directors & Embalmers Association
PO Box 540, Kensington PE C0B 1M0
Tel: 902-836-3313; *Fax:* 902-836-4461
Overview: A small provincial organization founded in 1958
Mission: To ensure professional services of the highest standards
Affliation(s): Funeral Service Association of Canada
Membership: *Member Profile:* Funeral directors & embalmers in Prince Edward Island

Prince Edward Island Genealogical Society Inc. (PEIGS)
PO Box 2744, Charlottetown PE C1A 8C4
e-mail: peigs_queries@yahoo.ca
www.peigs.ca
Overview: A small provincial charitable organization founded in 1976
Mission: To encourage & promote the study of family history in PEI; to collect & preserve local genealogical & historical records & materials; to foster education in genealogical research
Member of: Canadian Federation of Genealogical & Family History Societies
Affliation(s): Genealogy Institute of the Maritimes
Membership: *Fees:* $25

Prince Edward Island Gerontological Nurses Association (PEIGNA)
www.cgna.net/PEIGNA.html
Overview: A medium-sized provincial organization founded in 2004 overseen by Canadian Gerontological Nursing Association
Mission: To promote a high standard of nursing care & related health services for older adults; To enhance professionalism in the practice of gerontological nursing
Chief Officer(s):
Elaine E. Campbell, President
eecampbell@ihis.org
Activities: Offering professional networking opportunities; Providing professional development; Advocating for comprehensive services for older adults; Supporting research related to gerontological nursing; Promoting gerontological nursing to the public

Prince Edward Island Golf Association (PEIGA)
PO Box 51, Charlottetown PE C1A 7K2
Tel: 902-393-3293
peiga@peiga.ca
www.peiga.ca
twitter.com/PEIGolfAssoc
Overview: A small provincial organization founded in 1971 overseen by Royal Canadian Golf Association
Mission: To be the governing body of amateur golf in the province
Chief Officer(s):
Wayne Levy, President
Ron MacNeil, Executive Director
Staff Member(s): 1; 32 volunteer(s)

Prince Edward Island Ground Water Association
PO Box 857, RR#2, Cornwall PE C0A 1H0
Tel: 902-675-2360; *Fax:* 902-675-2360
Overview: A small provincial organization overseen by Canadian Ground Water Association
Mission: To promote the protection of ground water in Prince Edward Island
Affliation(s): Canadian Ground Water Association
Chief Officer(s):
Watson MacDonald, Contact
Activities: Encouraging education about ground water resources;

Prince Edward Island Harness Racing Club *See* Prince Edward Island Colt Stakes Association

Prince Edward Island Harness Racing Industry Association (PEIHRIA)
#204A, 420 University Ave., Charlottetown PE C1A 7Z5
Tel: 902-569-1682; *Fax:* 902-569-1827
peracing@isn.net
www.peiharnessracing.com/hria.html
Overview: A small provincial organization founded in 1999
Mission: To establish the financial stability & future viability of Prince Edward Island's harness racing industry; To provide a unified approach to the industry & sport of harness racing; To advance the interests of the industry to contribute to the social & economic well-being of Prince Edward Island
Affliation(s): Maritime Development Council
Chief Officer(s):
Wayne Pike, Executive Director
Earl Smith, President
Tom Clark, Vice-President
Eldred Nicholson, Secretary
Blair Campbell, Treasurer
Staff Member(s): 1
Membership: *Member Profile:* Organizations within the harness racing industry in Prince Edward Island & the Maritimes, such as the Atlantic Standardbred Breeders Association, the Maritime Breeders Association, the Prince Edward Island Standardbred Horseowners Association, & the Prince Edward Island Colt Stakes Association; *Committees:* Finance; Purse Pool; Stakes; Atlantic Classic Sale; Classification
Activities: Advocating on behalf of the harness racing industry on Prince Edward Island; Providing a forum for the exchange of information for the industry; Monitoring practices on the part of owners, trainers, drivers, grooms, & officials; Liaising with the Maritime Provinces Harness Racing Commission; Proposing changes to harness racing in order to attract new supporters

Prince Edward Island Hockey Association *See* Hockey PEI

Prince Edward Island Hockey Referees Association
c/o Hockey PEI, 40 Enman Cres., Charlottetown PE C1A 7K7
Tel: 902-367-8373
Overview: A medium-sized provincial organization
Member of: Hockey PEI; Hockey Canada
Chief Officer(s):
Troy Howatt, Chair

Prince Edward Island Hog Commodity Marketing Board
#209, 420 University Ave., Charlottetown PE C1A 7Z5
Tel: 902-892-4201; *Fax:* 902-892-4203
peipork@hotmail.com
www.peipork.pe.ca
twitter.com/porkisyummy
www.youtube.com/user/SwineTV
Overview: A small provincial organization
Mission: To provide information to the pork production industry of Prince Edward Island; To voice the concerns of hog farmers
Chief Officer(s):
Tim Seeber, Executive Director
Paul Larsen, Chair
Membership: *Member Profile:* Hog farmers on Prince Edward Island
Activities: Pursuing off-Island markets for hogs; Liaising with the provincial government

Prince Edward Island Home & School Federation Inc. (PEIHSF)
PO Box 1012, 40 Enman Cres., Charlottetown PE C1A 7M4
Tel: 902-620-3186; *Fax:* 902-620-3187
Toll-Free: 800-916-0664
peihsf@edu.pe.ca
peihsf.ca
www.facebook.com/peihsf
twitter.com/peihsf
Overview: A medium-sized provincial organization founded in 1953 overseen by Canadian Home & School Federation

Member of: Prince Edward Island Literacy Alliance Inc.
Chief Officer(s):
Wendy MacDonald, President
Shirley Jay, Executive Director
Staff Member(s): 1
Activities: Annual meeting

Prince Edward Island Humane Society (PEIHS)
PO Box 20022, 309 Sherwood Rd., Charlottetown PE C1A 9E3
Tel: 902-892-1190; *Fax:* 902-892-3617
info@peihumanesociety.com
www.peihumanesociety.com
www.facebook.com/peihumanesociety
twitter.com/peihs
Overview: A medium-sized provincial organization founded in 1974 overseen by Canadian Federation of Humane Societies
Mission: To promote & provide the humane treatment of animals recognizing that each is deserving of moral concern
Member of: Canadian Federation of Humane Societies (CFHS)
Chief Officer(s):
Kelly Mullaly, Executive Director
kmullaly@peihumanesociety.com
Leanne Cail, Manager, Marketing & Development
lcail@peihumanesociety.com
Beckie MacLean, Manager, Shelter
bmaclean@peihumanesociety.com
Finances: *Annual Operating Budget:* $250,000-$500,000; *Funding Sources:* Donations; fundraising
Staff Member(s): 13; 100 volunteer(s)
Membership: 11; *Fees:* $10; *Member Profile:* Interest in & love for animals, concern for animal welfare issues
Activities: Animal control; animal adoption & rescue; humane investigations; public education; pet therapy; *Speaker Service:* Yes

Prince Edward Island Institute of Agrologists (PEIIA)
PO Box 2712, Charlottetown PE C1A 8C3
Tel: 902-892-1943
info@peiia.ca
www.peiia.ca
Overview: A small provincial organization overseen by Agricultural Institute of Canada
Mission: To safeguard the public by ensuring its members are qualified & competent to provide knowledge & advice on agriculture & related areas
Chief Officer(s):
Allison Weeks, Registrar
aaweeks@gov.pe.ca
Finances: *Funding Sources:* Membership fees
Membership: *Fees:* $115 P.Ag.; $70 AIT; $75 Permit to Practice; *Committees:* Policy/Long Term Planning; Agrologist in Training/Membership; Honours & Awards; Publicity; Program; Nominations
Activities: Professional development; *Internships:* Yes
Awards:
- Recognition Award (Award)
- Outstanding Agrologist Award (Award)
- NSAC Scholarship Awards (Award)
- Science Fair & Heritage Awards (Award)

Prince Edward Island Karate Association (PEIKA)
c/o Dawn Brown, 131 Blue Heron Lane, Cornwall PE C0A 1H0
www.karatepei.ca
Also Known As: Prince Edward Island Karate Association
Overview: A small provincial organization founded in 1971 overseen by Karate Canada
Mission: To teach, train & coach karate & allied physical arts; to teach physical culture generally; to promote the principles & teaching of the sport of karate & to work toward the advancement of the sport in conjunction with all other groups throughout Canada; to arrange matches, contests & competitions of every nature relating to karate & to offer or grant & contribute towards judges, awards & distinctions; to provide conditional assistance on the approval of the Executive of the Association
Member of: Karate Canada; Sport PEI
Chief Officer(s):
Dawn Brown, President
dawn.brown@pei.sympatico.ca
Finances: *Annual Operating Budget:* Less than $50,000

Prince Edward Island Kiwanis Music Festival Association
c/o 227 Keppoch Rd., Stratford PE C1B 2J5
Tel: 902-569-2885; *Fax:* 902-569-2885
peikmfa@gmail.com
www.peikiwanismusicfestival.ca
Previous Name: PEI Music Festival Association
Overview: A medium-sized provincial charitable organization founded in 1946 overseen by Federation of Canadian Music Festivals
Mission: To make possible performances of young & older musicians in a semi-professional atmosphere; to adjudicate using professionals; & to encourage performance & study in music
Affliation(s): West Prince Music Festival; East Prince Music Festival; Queens County Music Festival; Kings County Music Festival
Chief Officer(s):
Diane Campbell, Provincial Administrator
ddcampbell@eastlink.ca
Finances: *Annual Operating Budget:* $50,000-$100,000; *Funding Sources:* Community; service clubs
10 volunteer(s)
Membership: 50

Prince Edward Island Lawn Bowling Association
Sport PEI, PO Box 302, Charlottetown PE C1A 7K7
Tel: 902-368-4110; *Fax:* 902-368-4548
Toll-Free: 800-247-6712
sports@sportpei.pe.ca
Overview: A small provincial organization overseen by Bowls Canada Boulingrin
Mission: To provide guidance to bowlers and all people interested in the sport. They wish to assit in the growth and development of Lawn Bowling on PEI Island, they wish to promote and encourage fair play in the sport at club level and at National lvel, they wish to develop leadership and to provide oppourtunities for development in the field of coaching, umpiring, and administration. They also provide interesting tournaments and events throughout the playing season.

Prince Edward Island Literacy Alliance *See* Prince Edward Island Literacy Alliance Inc.

Prince Edward Island Literacy Alliance Inc.
Sherwood Business Centre, PO Box 20107, 161 St. Peters Rd., Charlottetown PE C1A 9E3
Tel: 902-368-3620; *Fax:* 902-368-3269
Toll-Free: 866-827-3620
www.pei.literacy.ca
www.facebook.com/116524735097357
twitter.com/PEILiteracy
www.youtube.com/user/LiteracyPEI
Previous Name: Prince Edward Island Literacy Alliance
Overview: A small provincial charitable organization founded in 1990
Mission: To improve literacy levels on Prince Edward Island
Chief Officer(s):
Lori Johnston, Chair
lajohnston@edu.pe.ca
Catherine O'Bryan, Executive Director
catherine@peiliteracy.ca
Finances: *Funding Sources:* Donations; Sponsorships; Office of Literacy & Essential Skills of HRSDC; PEI Department of Education; PGI Golf Tournament for Literacy
Membership: *Member Profile:* Provincial & national organizations with an interest in literacy
Activities: Raising public awareness about literacy; Providing information & referrals; Presenting workshops on topics such as study skills; Offering tutoring programs for youth; Liaising with other organizations to create partnerships; Advising government & educational institutions about programs & services; Conducting research; Producing fact sheets; Awarding bursaries & scholarships; *Awareness Events:* PGI Golf Tournament for Literacy; Family Literacy Day, Jan.; International Adult Learners' Week, April
Publications:
- Family Literacy Things to Do
- A Guide to Social Assistance in PEI
Type: Book; *Author:* Norman Finlayson
- Instructor's Manual
Type: Book; *Author:* Karen Chandler & Ruth Rogerson
- Live & Learn
Type: Newsletter; *Frequency:* Quarterly
Profile: Alliance project news, events, announcements, & awards
- The New Adventures of Word Monster - Volumes 1 & 2
Author: Erin Casey & Brian Stevens
- PEI Literacy Alliance Annual Report
Type: Yearbook; *Frequency:* Annually
- Promoting Family Literacy in PEI: A Strategic Plan for Family Literacy in PEI

Prince Edward Island Lung Association
#2, 1 Rochford St., Charlottetown PE C1A 9L2
Tel: 902-892-5957; *Fax:* 902-566-9901
Toll-Free: 888-566-5864
info@pei.lung.ca
www.pei.lung.ca
Previous Name: PEI Tuberculosis League
Overview: A small provincial charitable organization founded in 1936 overseen by Canadian Lung Association
Mission: To improve the respiratory health of Islanders through education, advocacy & research; To raise funds to support medical research
Chief Officer(s):
Margaret Munro, President
Judy Hansen, Vice-President
Joanne Ings, Executive Director
Bev McCormick, Treasurer
Finances: *Funding Sources:* Donations; Fundraising; Sponsorships
Staff Member(s): 3
Activities: Promoting lung health in Prince Edward Island; Helping people to stop smoking through the Provincial Cessation Program (QuitCare);

Prince Edward Island Marketing Council
PO Box 1600, Charlottetown PE C1A 7N3
Tel: 902-569-7575; *Fax:* 902-569-7745
Overview: A small provincial organization
Mission: To administer the Natural Products Marketing Act under which commodity boards & groups
Chief Officer(s):
Ian MacIssac, Secretary & General Manager
ijmacissac@gov.pe.ca
Finances: *Annual Operating Budget:* $50,000-$100,000
Staff Member(s): 2
Membership: 8 individual

Prince Edward Island Massage Therapy Association
PO Box 1882, Charlottetown PE C1A 7N5
Fax: 902-368-7281
Toll-Free: 866-566-1955
www.peimta.com
Overview: A medium-sized provincial organization
Mission: To raise the awareness of all Islanders on the benefits of therapeutic massage.
Chief Officer(s):
Jennifer White, President
president@peimta.com
Membership: 39; *Fees:* $25; *Member Profile:* Registerd Massage Therapists

Prince Edward Island Museum & Heritage Foundation (PEIMHF) / Le Musée et la fondation du patrimoine de l'Ile-du-Prince-Édouard
2 Kent St., Charlottetown PE C1A 1M6
Tel: 902-368-6600
mhpei@gov.pe.ca
www.gov.pe.ca/peimhf
www.facebook.com/124989037532122
twitter.com/PEIMUSEUM
Overview: A medium-sized provincial charitable organization founded in 1983
Mission: To study, preserve, interpret & protect the human & natural heritage of PEI
Member of: Canadian Museums Association
Chief Officer(s):
Nora J. Young, Contact
Finances: *Annual Operating Budget:* $500,000-$1.5 Million; *Funding Sources:* Federal & provincial government; endowment; book sales; admissions
Staff Member(s): 30; 40 volunteer(s)
Membership: 1,000; *Fees:* $20 senior; $25 regular; $40 family
Activities: *Library*
Awards:
- PEI Museums Heritage Annual Heritage Awards (Award)

Prince Edward Island Numismatic Association
c/o Colonel Gray Senior High School, 175 Spring Park Rd., Charlottetown PE C1A 3Y8
Tel: 902-566-5837
Also Known As: PEI Coin Club
Overview: A small provincial organization founded in 1964
Affliation(s): The Royal Canadian Numismatic Association
Chief Officer(s):
Corey Bryan, President
peina@live.ca
Membership: *Fees:* $15

Activities: Hosting regular meetingsat Colonel Gray Senior High School

Prince Edward Island Nurses' Union (PEINU) / Syndicat des infirmières de l'Ile-du-Prince-Édouard
10 Paramount Dr., Charlottetown PE C1E 0C7
Tel: 902-892-7152; *Fax:* 902-892-9324
Toll-Free: 866-892-7152
office@peinu.com
www.peinu.com
Overview: A medium-sized provincial organization founded in 1987
Mission: To regulate employment relations between nurses & employers through collective bargaining & negotiation of written contracts with employers implementing progressively better conditions of employment
Affliation(s): Canadian Federation of Nurses Unions; Canadian Labour Congress
Chief Officer(s):
Mona O'Shea, President
mona@peinu.com
Finances: *Annual Operating Budget:* $500,000-$1.5 Million; *Funding Sources:* Membership dues
Staff Member(s): 2; 25 volunteer(s)
Membership: 925 individuals in 8 locals; *Fees:* Schedule available; *Member Profile:* Employment in job classification covered by collective agreement; *Committees:* Constitution & Resolutions; Finance; Grievance; Negotiating; Nominations; Public Relations
Activities: *Library*

Prince Edward Island Occupational Therapy Society (PEIOTS)
PO Box 2248, Stn. Central, Charlottetown PE C1A 8B9
Tel: 902-892-1266
www.peiot.org
Overview: A small provincial organization
Mission: To represent occupational therapists in Prince Edward Island
Member of: Canadian Association of Occupational Therapists
Chief Officer(s):
Heather Cutcliffe, Spokesperson
Yvonne Thompson, Secretary
ycthompson@ihis.org
Grant MacLeod, Treasurer
Membership: 1-99
Activities: Promoting the profession; Supporting professional development; Providing networking opportunities

Prince Edward Island Office of the Superintendent of Securities
Shaw Bldg., PO Box 2000, 95 Rochford St., 4th Fl., Charlottetown PE C1A 7N8
www.gov.pe.ca/securities
Overview: A medium-sized provincial organization overseen by Canadian Securities Administrators
Mission: To foster fair & efficient capital markets; to protect investors
Member of: Canadian Securities Administrators
Chief Officer(s):
Katherine Tummon, Superintendent of Securities
kptummon@gov.pe.ca

Prince Edward Island Optometrical Association *See* Prince Edward Island Association of Optometrists

Prince Edward Island Pharmacists Association
PO Box 24042, Stratford ON C1B 2V5
Tel: 902-367-7080
peipharm@gmail.com
www.peipharm.info
www.facebook.com/193958177311345
Overview: A small provincial organization
Mission: To support & advance the role of the pharmacist in Prince Edward Island
Chief Officer(s):
Erin MacKenzie, Executive Director
Finances: *Funding Sources:* Membership fees; Sponsorships
Activities: Promoting the profession of pharmacy in Prince Edward Island; Negotiating with government
Publications:
• Prince Edward Island Pharmacists Association Newsletter
Type: Newsletter
Profile: Information for members, supporters, & friends of the association

Prince Edward Island Pharmacy Board (PEIPB)
PO Box 89, 20454 Trans Canada Hwy., Crapaud PE C0A 1J0
Tel: 902-658-2780; *Fax:* 902-658-2528
info@pepharmacists.ca
www.pepharmacists.ca
Overview: A small provincial licensing organization founded in 1983 overseen by National Association of Pharmacy Regulatory Authorities
Mission: To prescribe qualifications, grant authorization & monitor adherence to established standards, so as to promote high standards & safeguard the public with regard to pharmaceutical service
Member of: Canadian Council on Continuing Education in Pharmacy
Affliation(s): National Association of Pharmacy Regulatory Authorities
Chief Officer(s):
Kenneth Crawford, Chair
asdm100@shoppersdrugmart.ca
Neila I. Auld, Registrar
nauld@pepharmacists.ca
Michelle Wyand, Assistant Registrar
mwyand@pepharmacists.ca
Rachel Lowther-Doiron, Administrative Assistant
rlowtherdoiron@pepharmacists.ca
Finances: *Annual Operating Budget:* $100,000-$250,000; *Funding Sources:* Licensing fees
Staff Member(s): 3; 9+ volunteer(s)
Membership: 188; *Fees:* $775; *Member Profile:* Successful completion of degree program for pharmacists from recognized college of pharmacy; current competency, as demonstrated by such examination as Board may administer upon applicant's payment of prescribed fee; *Committees:* Investigations/Complaints; CE/Competence Assessment; Pharmacy Endowment Board - Dalhousie; Practice Experience - Dalhousie; Examinations; Standards for Long Term Care Facilities; National Advisory Committee on Licensing; NAPRA Voting Delegate; Council of Pharmacy Registrars of Canada; PEI Health Sector Council; PhIP Advisory; Methadone Maintenance; Communication of Medication Prescriptions
Activities: *Internships:* Yes

Prince Edward Island Physiotherapy Association (PEI CPA)
PE
www.physiotherapy.ca/Atlantic-Branches/Prince-Edward-Island
Overview: A medium-sized provincial organization overseen by Canadian Physiotherapy Association
Mission: To provide leadership & direction to the physiotherapy profession; To foster excellence in practice, education & research
Member of: Canadian Physiotherapy Association
Chief Officer(s):
Trish Helm Neima, Contact
Finances: *Funding Sources:* Membership dues; Educational activities

Prince Edward Island Police Association (PEIPA)
PE
www.peipolice.com
Overview: A medium-sized provincial organization
Mission: To help members of the community become more familiar with the Prince Edward Island Police force; To promote the public's role in crime prevention; To support Youth Development; To speak for Prince Edward Island's municipal police officers
Chief Officer(s):
Ron MacLean, Corporal, President
Jason Blacquiere, Vice-President West
John Flood, Vice-President East
Membership: *Member Profile:* Members of the Prince Edward Island Municipal Police
Publications:
• Annual Crime Prevention Guide
Type: Magazine; *Frequency:* Annual; *Editor:* Fenety Marketing Services; *Price:* Free
Profile: Distributed to schools, libraries & public facilities in order to educated public on potential hazards & risks.

Prince Edward Island Poultry Meat Commodity Marketing Board
RR#6, Cardigan PE C0A 1G0
Tel: 902-838-4108; *Fax:* 902-838-4108
mmyles@dfpei.pe.ca
Overview: A medium-sized provincial organization founded in 1973

Chief Officer(s):
Janet Murphy Hilliard, Secretary-Manager

Prince Edward Island Professional Librarians Association (PEIPLA)
c/o Julie Cole, QEH Frank J. MacDonald Library, PO Box 6600, Charlottetown PE C1A 8T5
Tel: 902-894-2371
peipla.wordpress.com
Overview: A small provincial organization founded in 1982
Mission: To advocate for librarians & library services in the province
Member of: Prince Edward Island Literacy Alliance Inc.
Chief Officer(s):
Louise Mould, President
lmould@hollandcollege.com
Roseanne Gauthier, Secretary/Treasurer
rmgauthier@upei.ca
Finances: *Funding Sources:* Membership fees
Membership: *Fees:* $15; *Member Profile:* Professional library degree
Activities: Continuing education;

Prince Edward Island Rape & Sexual Assault Centre (PEIRSAC)
PO Box 1522, 1 Rochford St., Charlottetown PE C1A 7N3
Tel: 902-566-1864; *Fax:* 902-368-2957
Toll-Free: 866-566-1864
admin@peirsac.org
www.peirsac.org
Overview: A small provincial charitable organization founded in 1981
Mission: To ensure that the people of Prince Edward Island are safe from sexual violence; To support abuse & sexual assault survivors
Chief Officer(s):
Sigrid Rolfe, Organizational Coordinator
Shanna Farrell, Chair
Finances: *Funding Sources:* Donations; Fundraising; PEI Provincial Government
Activities: Offering support, information (902-566-8999), & therapy (902-368-8055) telephone service; Providing individual & group therapy; Accompanying persons to police stations & hospitals; Liasing with other community groups; Engaging in advocacy activities, such as representation on the Premier's Family Violence Prevention Action Committee & the PEI Child Sexual Abuse Prevention Advisory Committee; Offering public education; *Awareness Events:* Golf Against Assault Tournament

Prince Edward Island Real Estate Association
75 St. Peter's Rd., Charlottetown PE C1A 5N7
Tel: 902-368-8451; *Fax:* 902-894-9487
office@peirea.com
www.peirea.com
Overview: A small provincial organization founded in 1963
Member of: The Canadian Real Estate Association
Chief Officer(s):
Jim "Benson" Carragher, President
Jane Brewster, First Vice-President, Education
Greg Lipton, Second Vice-President, Finance
Finances: *Annual Operating Budget:* $250,000-$500,000
Staff Member(s): 3
Membership: 230

Prince Edward Island Recreation & Facilities Association *See* Recreation Prince Edward Island

Prince Edward Island Rifle Association (PEIPRA)
PO Box 160, Charlottetown PE C1A 7K4
Tel: 902-672-2773
peipra.ca/PEIPRA
Overview: A small provincial organization founded in 1861
Member of: Dominion of Canada Rifle Association
Chief Officer(s):
Ian Hogg, Director, Finance & Public Relations
irhogg@edu.pe.ca
Finances: *Annual Operating Budget:* Less than $50,000; *Funding Sources:* Macdonald Stewart Foundation; local business; investment interest
Membership: 10; *Fees:* Adult: $130-$230; Under 25: $80-$100; *Committees:* Ammunition; Match; Publicity; Social
Activities: Annual prize matches;

Prince Edward Island Right to Life Association
PO Box 1988, Charlottetown PE C1A 7N7

Tel: 902-894-5473; *Fax:* 902-892-2424
info@lifesanctuarypei.ca
www.peirighttolife.ca
Overview: A small provincial charitable organization founded in 1974
Mission: To value & promote respect for human life, from conception to natural death; To act as a unified voice for life issues
Finances: *Funding Sources:* Donations
Activities: Increasing awareness of respect for life in all its stages; Providing educational projects
Publications:
• PEI Right to Life News: "Life Sanctuary"
Type: Newsletter; *Frequency:* Semiannually; *Editor:* B. Connolly; A. Annema; M. Dykeman
Profile: Organizational reports, conferences, & related news

Prince Edward Island Roadbuilders & Heavy Construction Association

PO Box 1901, Charlottetown PE C1A 7N5
Tel: 902-894-9514; *Fax:* 902-894-9512
pei.roadbuilders@pei.sympatico.ca
www3.pei.sympatico.ca/pei.roadbuilders/
Previous Name: PEI Roadbuilders Association
Overview: A medium-sized provincial organization founded in 1962 overseen by Canadian Construction Association
Mission: To be a strong, effective voice in the Heavy Construction industry.
Member of: Atlantic Roadbuilders Association; Transportation Association of Canada
Chief Officer(s):
Joe Murphy, Manager
JoeMurphy10@hotmail.com
Finances: *Annual Operating Budget:* $50,000-$100,000
Membership: 90; *Member Profile:* Contractor, road & or heavy construction supplier of goods & services; *Committees:* Specifications; Asphalt Producers Group; CCA; Negotiated Prices & Rental Rates; Environment; FW Curtis Scholarship; WCB Employers' Council Representative; Education & Training; TRIP; Bursary; Public Relations; Membership; Principals' Committee

Prince Edward Island Roadrunners Club

c/o Sport PEI, PO Box 302, 40 Enman Cres., Charlottetown PE C1A 7K7
e-mail: peirunners@gmail.com
peiroadrunners.pbworks.com
www.facebook.com/groups/2248364862
Overview: A small provincial organization founded in 1977
Mission: The PEI RoadRunners Club is an organization whose objective is to promote & encourage running as a sport & healthful exercise. The Club welcomes all runners, regardless of ability & attempts to meet the needs of competitive & recreational runners.
Chief Officer(s):
Kent Mill, President
Membership: *Fees:* $15 individual; $10 student; $20 family

Prince Edward Island Rugby Union (PEIRU)

10 Kenwood Circle, Charlottetown PE C1E 1Z8
e-mail: peirugbyunion@gmail.com
peirugbyunion.com
twitter.com/PEIRugbyUnion
Also Known As: PEI Rugby Union
Overview: A medium-sized provincial organization overseen by Rugby Canada
Mission: To promote rugby in Prince Edward Island
Member of: Rugby Canada
Chief Officer(s):
Alex Field, President
Finances: *Funding Sources:* Membership fees; Gate receipts; Government; Sponsorship
Membership: *Committees:* Provincial team coordination; Youth Development; Women's Development; Official's Development; Newsletter; Summer League; Host Event

Prince Edward Island Salmon Association (PEISA)

PO Box 3315, Charlottetown PE C1A 8W5
Tel: 902-892-3635
david.olafson@pei.sympatico.ca
Overview: A small provincial organization
Affiliation(s): Atlantic Salmon Federation
Chief Officer(s):
David Olafson, Contact

Prince Edward Island School Athletic Association (PEISAA)

#101, 250 Water St., Summerside PE C1N 1B6
Tel: 902-438-4846; *Fax:* 902-438-4884
www.peisaa.pe.ca
Overview: A medium-sized provincial organization overseen by School Sport Canada
Mission: Supporting sports including but not exclusive to, badminton, softball, wrestling, golf, cross country, curling, and volleyball, in PEI.
Member of: School Sport Canada
Chief Officer(s):
Trevor Bridges, Chair
Rick MacKinnon, Coordinator
Gerald MacCormack, Secretary-Treasurer

Prince Edward Island School Trustees Association (PEISTA)

e-mail: trusteespei@yahoo.ca
trusteespei.blogspot.com
Overview: A medium-sized provincial organization founded in 1985 overseen by Canadian School Boards Association
Mission: To act as umbrella organization in coordinating & supporting efforts of school trustees in furthering education & education needs for all children in PEI
Chief Officer(s):
Ron Lee, President
Finances: *Annual Operating Budget:* $100,000-$250,000
Staff Member(s): 2
Membership: 29 trustees; *Member Profile:* Elected school boards; elected school trustees; *Committees:* Negotiations; Education & Curriculum; Finances; Resolutions
Activities: *Rents Mailing List:* Yes

Prince Edward Island Senior Citizens Federation Inc. (PEISCF)

#214, 40 Enman Cres., Charlottetown PE C1E 1E6
Tel: 902-368-9008; *Fax:* 902-368-9006
Toll-Free: 877-368-9008
peiscf@pei.aibn.com
www.peiscf.com
Overview: A small provincial organization founded in 1972
Mission: To advance the education opportunities for seniors on PEI; to improve the quality of life for seniors by advising government & other decision making bodies regarding seniors' concerns; to improve the quality of life for seniors; to increase societal understanding of seniors & the aging process through positive role modelling
Chief Officer(s):
Linda Jean Nicholson, Executive Director
Finances: *Annual Operating Budget:* Less than $50,000; *Funding Sources:* Membership fees; fundraising
Staff Member(s): 3
Membership: 2,500; *Member Profile:* 50 years & over
Activities: *Speaker Service:* Yes

Prince Edward Island Sharpshooters Association

PE
www.sharpshooterspei.com
Also Known As: The Sharpshooters
Overview: A small provincial organization overseen by National Darts Federation of Canada
Mission: To promote the game of darts in Prince Edward Island.
Member of: National Darts Federation of Canada
Chief Officer(s):
Malcolm Buchanan, President
drywall56@hotmail.com
Terri Affleck, Provincial Director
taffleck11@hotmail.com

Prince Edward Island Sheep Breeders Association

RR#1, Charlottetown PE C1A 7J6
Tel: 902-569-3002
peisheepbreeders.weebly.com
Overview: A small provincial organization
Affliations(s): Canadian Sheep Federation; Canadian Sheep Breeders' Association
Chief Officer(s):
Arthur Jones, Director, 902-569-3002
thornleighfarm@yahoo.ca

Prince Edward Island Shorthorn Association

General Delivery, Cornwall PE C0A 1H0
Tel: 902-628-8476
Overview: A small provincial organization
Member of: Canadian Shorthorn Association
Chief Officer(s):
David Livingston, President
Stella Boswall, Secretary, 902-892-4201

Prince Edward Island Silvicultural Contractors Association
See Prince Edward Island Forest Improvement Association

Prince Edward Island Snowboard Association

Charlottetown PE
Also Known As: Snowboard PEI
Overview: A small provincial organization overseen by Canadian Snowboard Federation
Mission: To be the provincial governing body of competitive snowboarding in Prince Edward Island.
Member of: Canadian Snowboard Federation
Chief Officer(s):
Zak Likely, Contact
zak.likely@gmail.com

Prince Edward Island Soccer Association (PEISA)

40 Enman Cres., Charlottetown PE C1A 7N5
Tel: 902-368-6251
referee@peisoccer.com
www.peisoccer.com
www.facebook.com/197098723677560
Overview: A medium-sized provincial organization founded in 1979 overseen by Canadian Soccer Association
Mission: To promote & regulate soccer in PEI; to provide competitive opportunities for members.
Member of: Canadian Soccer Association; Sport PEI
Chief Officer(s):
John Diamond, President
jrdiamond@gov.pe.ca
Tammy Wall, Secretary/Registrar
tammy.wall@gmail.com
Kirk McAleer, Treasurer
kirkjmcaleer@gmail.com
Finances: *Annual Operating Budget:* $250,000-$500,000
Staff Member(s): 1
Membership: 6,000 individual + 14 club; *Fees:* $350

Prince Edward Island Society for Medical Laboratory Science (PEIMLS)

PO Box 20061, Stn. Sherwood, 161 St. Peters Rd., Charlottetown PE C1A 9E3
peismls.com
www.facebook.com/320495861437823
twitter.com/peismls
Overview: A medium-sized provincial organization founded in 1953 overseen by Canadian Society for Medical Laboratory Science
Mission: To promote, maintain & protect professional identity & interests of medical laboratory technologist & of the profession; to promote development of continuing education; to provide information on current developments in medical laboratory technology
Chief Officer(s):
Carolyn McCarville, President
Andrea Dowling, Vice-President
Gerard Fernando, Treasurer
Activities: Career expos; education days; *Awareness Events:* National Medical Laboratory Week, April
Awards:
• Dr. John Craig Award of Merit (Award)
Recipient represents importance of education & professionalism*Eligibility:* Registered technologist, member of association but not part of executive
Meetings/Conferences: • Maritech 2015, 2015
Scope: Provincial

Prince Edward Island Society of Certified Engineering Technologists *See* Association of Certified Engineering Technicians & Technologists of Prince Edward Island

Prince Edward Island Speech & Hearing Association (PEISHA)

PO Box 20076, Charlottetown PE C1A 9E3
Tel: 902-884-5559
info@peispeechhearing.ca
www.peispeechhearing.ca
Overview: A small provincial organization
Mission: To promote the study, research, discussion & dissemination of information concerning the process of human communication in speech & hearing; To encourage the development & improvement of skills in the diagnosis & treatment of human communication disorders
Member of: Canadian Association of Speech-Language Pathologists & Audiologists

Chief Officer(s):
Nicole Leger, President
Finances: *Annual Operating Budget:* Less than $50,000; *Funding Sources:* Professional dues; workshops
Membership: 20; *Fees:* $100; *Committees:* Public Relations; Membership; Workshop; Legislation
Activities: *Awareness Events:* Speech & Hearing Month, May; *Internships:* Yes

Prince Edward Island Speed Skating Association *See* Speed Skate PEI

Prince Edward Island Sports Hall of Fame *See* Prince Edward Island Sports Hall of Fame & Museum Inc.

Prince Edward Island Sports Hall of Fame & Museum Inc.
40 Enman Cres., Charlottetown PE C1E 1E6
Tel: 902-368-4547
publicrelations@sportpei.pe.ca
www.peisportshalloffame.ca
www.facebook.com/210800825622110
Previous Name: Prince Edward Island Sports Hall of Fame
Overview: A small provincial charitable organization founded in 1968
Chief Officer(s):
Nick Murray, Executive Director
Finances: *Funding Sources:* Fees; events; admissions; fundraising events; government grants; sponsorships
Membership: 150+ inductees
Activities: *Library*

Prince Edward Island Square & Round Dance Clubs
32 Centennial Dr., Charlottetown PE C1A 6C5
Tel: 902-964-2414
www.csrds.ca/pei
Overview: A small provincial organization
Member of: Canadian Square & Round Dance Society
Chief Officer(s):
Ken MacLeod, Contact, 902-629-1672

Prince Edward Island Standardbred Horseowners' Association
c/o PEI Harness Racing Industry Association, #204A, 420 University Ave., Charlottetown PE C1A 7Z5
Tel: 902-569-1682; *Fax:* 902-569-1827
peracing@eastlink.ca
Overview: A small provincial organization
Mission: To support & recognize standardbred horseowners on Prince Edward Island
Member of: Prince Edward Island Harness Racing Industry Association
Chief Officer(s):
Wayne Pike, Executive Director, PEI Harness Racing Industry Association
Membership: *Member Profile:* Standardbred horseowners on Prince Edward Island
Activities: Presenting harness racing awards annually, such as Horse of the Year & Horseman of the Year

Prince Edward Island Swine Breeders' Association
General Delivery, North Wiltshire PE C0A 1Y0
Tel: 902-621-0470; *Fax:* 902-368-5561
Overview: A small provincial organization
Affliation(s): Canadian Swine Breeders Association
Chief Officer(s):
Jane Palmer, Contact
Awards:
• PEI Swine Breeders' Association Award (Award)
Eligibility: Second or third year student in veterinary medicine, who graduated from a PEI high school, who is interested in food animal veterinary medicine

Prince Edward Island Symphony Society (PEISO)
PO Box 185, Charlottetown PE C1A 7K4
Tel: 902-892-4333
admin@peisymphony.com
www.peisymphony.com
www.facebook.com/PEISymphony
twitter.com/PEISymphony
Also Known As: PEI Symphony Orchestra
Overview: A small provincial charitable organization founded in 1968 overseen by Orchestras Canada
Mission: To establish & promote symphonic music; to further & foster appreciation of musical education; to promote the welfare of musicians; to give & arrange performances, entertainments & concerts; to employ teachers & instructors to inform the public & awaken interest
Member of: Volunteers Canada
Chief Officer(s):
Mark Shapiro, Music Director
Finances: *Funding Sources:* Corporate sponsorship; corporate, business & individual donations; fundraising; Canada Council
Staff Member(s): 3
Membership: *Member Profile:* Subscriber; musician
Activities: *Library*

Prince Edward Island Table Tennis Association (PEITTA)
c/o Sport PEI Inc., PO Box 302, Charlottetown PE C1A 7K7
Tel: 902-368-4110; *Fax:* 902-368-4548
Toll-Free: 800-247-6712
sports@sportpei.pe.ca
www.freewebs.com/peitta
Overview: A small provincial organization founded in 1965 overseen by Table Tennis Canada
Mission: To promote table tennis in PEI; to provide competitive opportunities for its members
Member of: Table Tennis Canada; Sport PEI Inc.
Affliation(s): International Table Tennis Federation
Chief Officer(s):
Najam Chishti, President
nchishti@biovectra.com
Wade Gregory, Treasurer
gregory@islandtelecom.com
Finances: *Annual Operating Budget:* Less than $50,000; *Funding Sources:* Provincial government; fundraising
10 volunteer(s)
Membership: 55-75; *Fees:* $100 family; $50 single; *Member Profile:* Table tennis players; *Committees:* Fundraising; Coaching
Activities: Hosts provincial championships, local tournaments & recreational games; *Internships:* Yes

Prince Edward Island Teachers' Federation (PEITF) / Fédération des enseignants de l'Île-du-Prince-Édouard
PO Box 6000, Charlottetown PE C1A 8B4
Tel: 902-569-4157; *Fax:* 902-569-3682
Toll-Free: 800-903-4157
www.peitf.com
www.facebook.com/413184622069166
twitter.com/PEITF
Overview: A medium-sized provincial organization founded in 1880 overseen by Canadian Teachers' Federation
Mission: To promote & support education as well as the professional & economic well-being of PEI teachers
Member of: Prince Edward Island Literacy Alliance Inc.
Chief Officer(s):
Gilles Arsenault, President
garsenault@peitf.com
Shaun MacCormac, General Secretary
smaccormac@peitf.com
Finances: *Funding Sources:* Membership dues
Staff Member(s): 7
Membership: *Member Profile:* Employed as teacher (administrator) by school board in PEI; *Committees:* Annual Convention Planning; Awards, Grants & Projects; Constitution & By-laws; Curriculum, Professional Development & Teacher Education; Diversity/Equity; Economic Welfare; Ethics; Finance & Property; General Secretary Evaluation; Nomination; Pension; Personnel; Provinicial Public Relations; Student Services; Technology
Activities: *Library* by appointment

Prince Edward Island Tennis Association
PO Box 302, 40 Enman Cres., Charlottetown PE C1A 7K7
Tel: 902-368-4985; *Fax:* 902-368-4548
tennispei@gmail.com
www.tennispei.ca
www.facebook.com/286640596313
twitter.com/TennisPEI
Also Known As: Tennis PEI
Overview: A medium-sized provincial organization overseen by Tennis Canada
Mission: To promote the sport of tennis on PEI.
Member of: Tennis Canada
Chief Officer(s):
Brian Hall, Technical Director
Finances: *Funding Sources:* Government; sponsors; participants
Staff Member(s): 2; 20 volunteer(s)
Membership: 600; *Fees:* $5 junior; $8 adult; $12 family
Activities: Clinics; tournaments; programs

Prince Edward Island Track & Field Association
c/o Sport PEI, 3 Queen St., Charlottetown PE C1A 7K7
Tel: 902-368-4110
Overview: A small provincial organization

Prince Edward Island Trucking Sector Council (PEITSC)
#211, 420 University Ave., Charlottetown PE C1A 7Z5
Tel: 902-566-5563; *Fax:* 902-566-4506
info@peitsc.ca
www.peitsc.ca
www.facebook.com/peitsc
twitter.com/peitsc
www.youtube.com/user/peitruckingsc
Overview: A medium-sized provincial organization
Mission: To addressing human resources issues and opportunities in the Trucking Industry on Prince Edward Island and provide a vehicle for effective industry participation in identifying and addressing issues related to workforce attraction and retention, career awareness, skills upgrading and training.
Member of: Prince Edward Island Literacy Alliance Inc.
Chief Officer(s):
Scott Annear, Chair
Brian Oulton, Executive Director

Prince Edward Island Underwater Council
c/o Sport PEI, 3 Queen St., Charlottetown PE C1A 7K7
Tel: 902-368-4110
Overview: A small provincial organization
Mission: The PEI Underwater Council's mission is to help support & promote the sport of scuba diving in Prince Edward Island through safety, advocacy, cultural & environmental awareness, self-governance & education.

Prince Edward Island Union of Public Sector Employees / Syndicat de la fonction publique de l'Île-du-Prince-Édouard
4 Enman Cres., Charlottetown PE C1E 1E6
Tel: 902-892-5335; *Fax:* 902-569-8186
Toll-Free: 800-897-8773
peiupse@peiupse.ca
www.peiupse.ca
Overview: A medium-sized provincial organization
Mission: To represent & advocate on behalf of its members in order to ensure safe & fair working conditions
Chief Officer(s):
Debbie Bovyer, President
dbovyer@peiupse.ca
Staff Member(s): 9
Membership: *Committees:* Constitution & Structure; Education; Finance; Membership Services & Communications; Occupational Health & Safety; Pension & Insurance; Public Relations & Recreation/Convention; Staff Relations

Prince Edward Island Vegetable Growers Co-op Association
PO Box 1494, 280 Sherwood Rd., Charlottetown PE C1A 7J7
Tel: 902-892-5361; *Fax:* 902-566-2383
Overview: A small provincial organization founded in 1969
Chief Officer(s):
Don Read, Manager
Finances: *Annual Operating Budget:* Greater than $5 Million
Staff Member(s): 25
Membership: 95; *Fees:* $1,000

Prince Edward Island Veterinary Medical Association (PEIVMA)
PO Box 21097, Stn. 465 University Ave., Charlottetown PE C1A 9h6
Tel: 902-367-3757; *Fax:* 902-367-3176
admin.peivma@gmail.com
www.peivma.com
Overview: A small provincial licensing organization founded in 1920 overseen by Canadian Veterinary Medical Association
Mission: To represent PEI veterinarians in small animal, large animal & mixed practice as well as those employed in government, industry or other institutions; to licence & regulate veterinarians in PEI
Chief Officer(s):
Wade Sweet, President
Jenn Reid, Vice-President
Membership: 160 individual; *Fees:* $625 regular; $312.50 short-term
Meetings/Conferences: • 2015 Prince Edward Island Veterinary Medical Association Annual General Meeting, November, 2015,

Rodd Charlottetown Hotel, Charlottetown, PE
Scope: Provincial

Prince Edward Island Wildlife Federation

#103B, 420 University Ave., Charlottetown PE C1A 7Z5
Tel: 902-626-9699
www.facebook.com/145488672186392
Overview: A small provincial organization founded in 1906 overseen by Canadian Wildlife Federation
Mission: To foster sound management & wise use of the renewable resources of PEI; to assist & encourage the enforcement of those game laws which are in keeping with the objectives of the Federation & to strive for better management & game laws where & when necessary; to cooperate with government departments & related groups where interests are mutual; to educate membership & the public, with particular emphasis upon conservation & safety; to represent the interests & concerns of PEI sportsmen
Chief Officer(s):
Duncan Crawford, Contact
Activities: Assists with the Central Queens, O'Leary Wildlife & Souris Wildlife Federations

Prince Edward Island Women's Institute (PEIWI)

#105, 40 Enman Cres., Charlottetown PE C1E 1E6
Tel: 902-368-4860; *Fax:* 902-368-4439
wi@gov.pe.ca
www.peiwi.ca
Overview: A small provincial organization overseen by Federated Women's Institutes of Canada
Mission: To help discover, stimulate & develop leadership among women; to assist, encourage & support women to become knowledgeable & responsible citizens; to ensure basic human rights for women & to work towards their equality; to be a strong voice through which matters of utmost concern can reach the decision makers; to network with organizations sharing similar objectives; to promote the improvement of agricultural & other rural communities & to safeguard the environment
Chief Officer(s):
Cynthia Mitchell, President
Membership: 1,300

Prince George & District Truck Loggers Association *See* Central Interior Logging Association

Prince George AIDS Prevention Program; AIDS Prince George; Prince George AIDS Society *See* Positive Living North: No kheyoh t'sih'en t'sehena Society

Prince George Alzheimer's Society

#202, 575 Quebec St., Prince George BC V2L 1W6
Tel: 250-564-7533; *Fax:* 250-564-1642
Toll-Free: 866-564-7533
Overview: A small local charitable organization founded in 1985
Mission: To provide information about Alzheimer's Disease in the Prince George, British Columbia area; To help people concerned with or facing dementia
Member of: Alzheimer Society British Columbia
Chief Officer(s):
Leanne Jones, Coordinator, Support & Education
ljones@alzheimerbc.org
Laurie De Croos, Coordinator, First Link
ldecroos@alzheimerbc.org
Finances: *Funding Sources:* Donations
Activities: Offering early stage & family cargiver support groups; Providing education for people impacted by dementia; *Library:* Alzheimer Resource Centre; Open to public by appointment

Prince George Backcountry Recreation Society (PGBRS)

PO Box 26, Stn. A, Prince George BC V2L 4R9
e-mail: info@pgbrs.com
www.pgbrs.com
Overview: A small local organization founded in 1998
Mission: To promote and encourage safe non-motorized backcountry recreation in the Prince George region.
Member of: Federation of BC Naturalists
Chief Officer(s):
Duncan McColl, President

Prince George Brain Injured Group (PGBIG)

1237 - 4 Ave., Prince George BC V2L 3J7
Tel: 250-564-2447; *Fax:* 250-564-6928
Toll-Free: 866-564-2447
info@pgbig.ca
pgbig.ca
Overview: A small local organization founded in 1987
Mission: To provide assistance to adults whose lives have changed as a result of an acquired brain injury
Member of: Prince George United Way
Chief Officer(s):
Alison Hagreen, Executive Director
Staff Member(s): 30

Prince George Chamber of Commerce (PGCOC)

890 Vancouver St., Prince George BC V2L 2P5
Tel: 250-562-2454; *Fax:* 250-562-6510
chamber@pgchamber.bc.ca
www.pgchamber.bc.ca
www.linkedin.com/company/prince-george-chamber-of-commerce
www.facebook.com/124651797620486
twitter.com/PGChamber1
Overview: A medium-sized local organization founded in 1911
Mission: The PG Chamber of Commerce strives to connect, engage and enhance the quality of life in our community by providing opportunities for businesses to succeed.
Member of: BC Chamber of Commerce; Canadian Chamber of Commerce
Chief Officer(s):
Jennifer Brandle-McCall, CEO
Finances: *Annual Operating Budget:* $250,000-$500,000
Staff Member(s): 7; 35 volunteer(s)
Membership: 827; *Fees:* $153.75 - $1,101.75
Activities: *Speaker Service:* Yes; *Library* Open to public

Prince George Construction Association (PGCA)

3851 - 18th Ave., Prince George BC V2N 1B1
Tel: 250-563-1744; *Fax:* 250-563-1107
www.pgca.bc.ca
Overview: A small local organization founded in 1958
Mission: To establish & improve industry standards; to further fellowship & cooperation within the industry; To increase public awareness; To improve & standardize tendering & award practices; To disseminate information among members; To cooperate with other industry groups
Member of: BC Construction Association; Canadian Construction Association; Northern British Columbia Construction Association
Chief Officer(s):
Brad Popoff, Chair
bpequity@shaw.ca
Rosalind Thorn, President
Staff Member(s): 3; 500 volunteer(s)
Membership: 127 institutional; 25 associate; *Member Profile:* General & trade contractors, manufacturers, suppliers, allied service, professional associations
Activities: Chairman's Ball, Feb.

Prince George Native Friendship Centre

1600 - 3rd Ave., Prince George BC V2L 3G6
Tel: 250-564-3568; *Fax:* 250-563-0924
info@pgnfc.com
www.pgnfc.com
Overview: A small local organization founded in 1969
Mission: To serve the needs of Aboriginal people residing in the urban area; To improve the quality of life in the community as a whole
Chief Officer(s):
Emma Palmantier, President
Lyle Lloyd, Treasurer
Staff Member(s): 120
Activities: Off-site services: Friendship Home, Ketso Yoh Men's Hostel, Reconnect Youth Services Drop-in/Downtown Youth Shelter; Prince George Aboriginal Head Start; Power of Friendship Aboriginal Head Start; Aboriginal Infant & Family Development Program; Native Art Gallery; Annual Pow Wow

Prince George Naturalists Club (PGNC) / Club de naturalistes de Prince George

PO Box 1092, Prince George BC V2L 4V2
e-mail: pgnc@shaw.ca
pgnc.wordpress.com
www.facebook.com/pgnc
Overview: A small local organization founded in 1969
Mission: To promote the enjoyment of nature through environmental appreciation & conservation; To encourage wise use & conservation of natural resources & environmental protection.
Member of: Federation of BC Naturalists
Membership: *Fees:* $25 individual; $40 family
Activities: Monthly guest speakers; weekly field trips; birding; annual bird counts;

Prince George Parents of Twins & Triplets Association (PGPOTTA)

7138 Harvard Cres., Prince George BC V2N 2V7
Tel: 250-640-6405
Other Communication: princegeorge@multiplebirthscanada.org
pgpotta@hotmail.com
www.multiplebirthscanada.org/~princegeorge
Overview: A small local organization founded in 1976 overseen by Multiple Births Canada
Mission: A support group for parents of multiple births.
Membership: *Fees:* $50

Prince George Recycling & Environmental Action Planning Society (REAPS)

PO Box 444, 1950 Gorse Street, Prince George BC V2L 4S6
Tel: 250-561-7324; *Fax:* 250-561-7324
garden@reaps.org
www.reaps.org
www.facebook.com/group.php?gid=115633161790444
Overview: A small local organization founded in 1989
Mission: To educate the public on where & what can be recycled, how to compost & vermicompost, organic gardening, environmentally friendly alternatives & promotion of the 5 R's (Rethink, Refuse, Reduce, Recycle & Reuse); To provide educational programs to schools, daycares & committee groups
Member of: Recycling Council of British Columbia; Volunteer PG; Downtown Community Gardens
Chief Officer(s):
Terri McClaymont, Executive Director, 250-561-7327, Fax: 250-561-7324
terri@reaps.org
Finances: *Annual Operating Budget:* $100,000-$250,000; *Funding Sources:* Regional District Fraser Fort George; Dept. Fisheries & Oceans; City of Prince George
Staff Member(s): 2; 20 volunteer(s)
Membership: 61; *Fees:* $25 institutional; $8 student; $8 individual; $15 family; *Committees:* EnhancePG, Recycling Council of BC; Civic Pride
Activities: Adopt-a-Worm Program; Dump the Overfed Landfill; Workshops on gardening, composting, recycling; Earth Day Celebration; Pitch-In Canada; Buy Nothing Day; *Awareness Events:* Earth Day, April 22; Composting Week, May 5; Buy Nothing Day, November 3; *Internships:* Yes; *Speaker Service:* Yes; *Library* Open to public by appointment

Prince George Symphony Orchestra Society (PGSO)

2880 - 15 Ave., Prince George BC V2M 1T1
Tel: 250-562-0800; *Fax:* 250-562-0844
www.pgso.com
www.facebook.com/pgsymphony
twitter.com/pgsymphony
www.youtube.com/pgsymphony
Overview: A small local charitable organization founded in 1971 overseen by Orchestras Canada
Mission: To provide symphonic music for Prince George & region consistent with Prince George Symphony Orchestra artistic policy that facilitates artistic development of its players; to foster & facilitate positive community image & financial responsiblity so that a wide spectrum of musical experiences is offered to players & audiences alike
Chief Officer(s):
Marnie Hamagami, General Manager
Finances: *Funding Sources:* Box office; sponsors; donations (personal & corporate); program advertising; government grants
Staff Member(s): 5
Membership: 48
Activities: *Library*

Prince George United Way

1600 - 3rd Ave., Prince George BC V2L 3G6
Tel: 250-561-1040; *Fax:* 250-562-8102
info@unitedwaynbc.ca
www.pguw.bc.ca
www.facebook.com/unitedwaynorthernbc
Overview: A small local charitable organization founded in 1969 overseen by United Way of Canada - Centraide Canada
Mission: To promote the organized capacity of persons to care for one another through voluntarism, leadership & education; To ensure the effective raising & allocation of charitable funds for community-based social services; To foster the effective provision of services that are in the best interest of the community
Chief Officer(s):
Trevor Williams, Executive Director
trevorw@unitedwaynbc.ca
Scotty Raitt, President

Finances: *Annual Operating Budget:* $500,000-$1.5 Million
Staff Member(s): 8; 300 volunteer(s)
Activities: Volunteer Leadership Development to provide training & support to develop effective leadership of not-for-profit voluntary agencies;

Prince of Wales Northern Heritage Centre (PWNHC)
PO Box 1320, 4750 - 4th St., Yellowknife NT X1A 2L9
Tel: 867-873-7551; *Fax:* 867-873-0205
pwnhcweb@ece.learnnet.nt.ca
www.pwnhc.ca
Overview: A small provincial organization founded in 1979
Mission: To house the Central Museum operation of the Government of the Northwest Territories & the Northwest Territories Archives; To provide a broad range of heritage services; To preserve, promote, & portray the natural & human history of the Northwest Territories
Member of: Canadian Museums Association; Council of Canadian Archives
Chief Officer(s):
Barb Cameron, Director
Finances: *Annual Operating Budget:* $3 Million-$5 Million
Staff Member(s): 18; 5 volunteer(s)
Membership: *Committees:* Acquisitions; Exhibits
Activities: Collections management; archives; exhibits; website; public programs; *Library:* NWT Archives Library; Open to public

Prince Rupert & District Chamber of Commerce (PRDCC)
#170, 110 - 1st Ave., Prince Rupert BC V8J 1A8
Tel: 250-624-2296; *Fax:* 250-624-6105
www.princerupertchamber.ca
www.youtube.com/user/princerupertchamber
Overview: A small local organization founded in 1908
Mission: To promote & improve trade & commerce, economic, civil & social welfare of the City of Prince Rupert & District
Member of: BC Chamber of Commerce, Canadian Chamber of Commerce
Chief Officer(s):
Jason Scherr, President
John Farrell, 1st Vice-President
Carol Bulford, Chamber Manager
manager@princerupertchamber.ca
Finances: *Annual Operating Budget:* $100,000-$250,000;
Funding Sources: Membership dues; Christmas dinner; auction
Staff Member(s): 2; 200 volunteer(s)
Membership: 290; *Fees:* Based on number of employees; *Committees:* Membership; Technology; Communications & Liaison; Tourism
Activities: Membership meeting, speaker program 3rd Wednesday of each month; *Library:* Visitor Information Centre; Open to public

Prince Rupert Association for Community Living
PO Box 442, Prince Rupert BC V8J 3R2
Tel: 250-624-5256; *Fax:* 250-627-7182
Overview: A small local organization
Member of: British Columbia Association for Community Living
Chief Officer(s):
Shirley Duchscherer, President
duchsher@citytel.net
Pat Marshall, Manager

Prince Rupert Fire Museum Society
200 - 1st Ave. West, Prince Rupert BC V8J 1A8
Tel: 250-624-2211; *Fax:* 250-624-3407
shirts@citytel.net
www.princerupertlibrary.ca/fire
Overview: A small local charitable organization founded in 1986
Finances: *Annual Operating Budget:* Less than $50,000
Activities: *Library*

Prince Rupert Labour Council
867 Fraser St., Prince Rupert BC V8J 1R1
Tel: 250-627-8833; *Fax:* 250-627-8833
prlc@citytel.net
Overview: A small local organization overseen by British Columbia Federation of Labour
Mission: To advance the economic & social welfare of workers in the Prince Rupert area of British Columbia
Affliation(s): Canadian Labour Congress (CLC)
Chief Officer(s):
Dave Smith, President
Ken Lippet, Vice-President
kenl@citytel.net
Eszter Rusznyak, Secretary
Yvonne Ramsey, Treasurer
Activities: Advocating for workers in the Prince Rupert area; Liaising with locally elected officials; Preparing presentations for Prince Rupert City Council, on workers' issues, such as pensions; Presenting educational opportunities for members; Marking the annual Day of Mourning for workers injured or killed on the job

Princess Margaret Hospital Foundation
700 University Ave., 10th Fl., Toronto ON M5G 1Z5
Tel: 416-946-6560; *Fax:* 416-946-6563
Toll-Free: 866-224-6560
info@thepmcf.ca
thepmcf.ca
www.facebook.com/thePMCF
twitter.com/thePMCF
www.youtube.com/user/PrincessMargaretHF
Overview: A small local charitable organization
Chief Officer(s):
Paul Alofs, President & CEO

Princess Patricia's Canadian Light Infantry Association
PO Box 210, Denwood AB T0B 1B0
Tel: 780-842-1363; *Fax:* 780-842-4106
www.army.gc.ca/ppclic
Overview: A medium-sized national charitable organization
Chief Officer(s):
Bud Hawkins, President, Manitoba/Northwest Ontario Branch
Finances: *Annual Operating Budget:* Less than $50,000
Membership: 950; *Fees:* $20

Princeton & District Chamber of Commerce
PO Box 540, 105 Hwy. 3 East, Princeton BC V0X 1W0
Tel: 250-295-3103; *Fax:* 250-295-3255
chamber@nethop.net
www.princeton.ca
Overview: A small local organization founded in 1913
Member of: BC Chamber of Commerce; Canadian Chamber of Commerce
Chief Officer(s):
Lori Thomas, Manager
Finances: *Annual Operating Budget:* $50,000-$100,000;
Funding Sources: Membership dues
Staff Member(s): 1
Membership: 119; *Fees:* Schedule available
Activities: Trade Show in May; *Speaker Service:* Yes; *Library* Open to public

Princeton Community Arts Council
PO Box 281, Princeton BC V0X 1W0
Tel: 250-295-7588
princetonartscouncilbc@gmail.com
princetonarts.ca/Princeton_Arts.html
Overview: A small local organization founded in 1992
Mission: To promote & support community culture
Chief Officer(s):
Marjorie Holland, President

Print Measurement Bureau (PMB)
#1101, 77 Bloor St. West, Toronto ON M5S 1M2
Tel: 416-961-3205; *Fax:* 416-961-5052
Toll-Free: 800-762-0899
www.pmb.ca
Overview: A medium-sized national organization founded in 1971
Mission: To conduct research on the topics of print readership, non-print media exposure, product usage & lifestyles.
Chief Officer(s):
Steve Ferley, President
steve@pmb.ca
Hastings Withers, Executive Vice President/Research Director
hastings@pmb.ca
Lina Di Santo, Client Services Manager
Membership: *Committees:* Research

Printing & Graphics Industries Association of Alberta (PGIA)
PO Box 61229, RPO Kensington, Calgary AB T2N 4S6
Tel: 403-281-1421; *Fax:* 403-225-1421
info@pgia.ca
www.pgia.ca
Overview: A small provincial organization founded in 1987
Mission: Committed to the advancement of a healthy, effective & ethical graphic arts industry by providing leadership in the development of imaged communications; by enabling members to work to strengthen the industry
Member of: Canadian Printing Industries Association
Chief Officer(s):
Caron Evans, Association Manager
Dean McElhinney, President
Finances: *Annual Operating Budget:* $50,000-$100,000;
Funding Sources: Membership fees; Programs
8 volunteer(s)
Membership: 50 corporate; *Fees:* Schedule available; *Member Profile:* Printing company or supplier
Activities: *Internships:* Yes

Printing Equipment & Supply Dealers' Association of Canada (PESDA)
11 Alderbrook Place, Bolton ON L7E 1V3
Tel: 416-524-1954; *Fax:* 905-951-6374
www.pesda.com
Overview: A medium-sized national organization founded in 1975
Mission: To promote & advance the interests of the printing equipment, consumables & related services industries in Canada
Chief Officer(s):
Richard Armstrong, President
Bob Kirk, General Manager
bkirk@pesda.com
Finances: *Annual Operating Budget:* $50,000-$100,000;
Funding Sources: Trade show; membership dues
Staff Member(s): 2
Membership: 25 organizations

Prison Fellowship Canada / Fraternite des prisons du Canada
#144, 5945 Airport Road, Mississauga ON L4V 1R9
Tel: 905-673-5867; *Fax:* 905-673-6955
Toll-Free: 844-618-5867
info@prisonfellowship.ca
www.prisonfellowship.ca
twitter.com/ServingLifePFC
Overview: A small national organization founded in 1980
Mission: To challenge, equip, & serve the body of Christ in its ministry to prisoners, ex-prisoners, their families, & victims; To promote the advancement of restorative justice
Member of: Prison Fellowship International
Chief Officer(s):
Stacey Campbell, Executive Director/CEO
Michael Van Dusen, Chair, Advocacy Committee

Prisoners' HIV/AIDS Support Action Network (PASAN)
#100, 314 Jarvis Street, Toronto ON M5B 2C5
Tel: 416-920-9567; *Fax:* 416-920-4314
Toll-Free: 866-224-9978
info@pasan.org
www.pasan.org
Overview: A small national organization founded in 1991
Mission: Prisoners, ex-prisoners, organizations, activists & individuals working together to provide advocacy, education, & support to prisoners on HIV/AIDS, HCV & related issues
Chief Officer(s):
Anne Marie, Executive Director
annemarie@pasan.org

Private Capital Markets Association of Canada (PCMA)
First Canadian Place, #5700, 100 King St. West, Toronto ON M5X 1C7
Toll-Free: 877-363-3632
info@pcmacanada.com
www.pcmacanada.com
www.linkedin.com/groups/Exempt-Market-Dealers-Association-Canada-34316
www.facebook.com/PCMACanada
twitter.com/PCMACanada
www.youtube.com/user/EMDACanada
Previous Name: Exempt Market Dealers Association of Canada; Limited Markets Dealers Association of Canada
Overview: A medium-sized national organization founded in 2002
Mission: The PCMA is focused on strengthening and growing the private capital markets to ensure robust capital raising opportunities across Canada.
Chief Officer(s):
Geoffrey Ritchie, Executive Director
geoffrey.ritchie@pcmacanada.com

Private Career Educational Council; Ontario Association of Career Colleges *See* Career Colleges Ontario

Private Forest Landowners Association (PFLA)
PO Box 48092, Victoria BC V8Z 7H5
Tel: 250-381-7565; *Fax:* 250-381-7409
Toll-Free: 888-634-7352
info@pfla.bc.ca
www.pfla.bc.ca
www.facebook.com/PFLABC?ref=ts
twitter.com/PFLABC
Overview: A medium-sized provincial organization founded in 1995
Mission: The Private Forest Landowners Association (PFLA) represents owners of private Managed Forest land in BC.
Chief Officer(s):
Rod Bealing, Executive Director
rod.bealing@pfla.bc.ca

Private Home Day Care Association of Ontario *See* Home Child Care Association of Ontario

Private Motor Truck Council of Canada (PMTC) / Association canadienne du camionnage d'entreprise (ACCE)
#115, 1660 North Service Rd. East, Oakville ON L6H 7G3
Tel: 905-827-0587; *Fax:* 905-827-8212
Toll-Free: 877-501-7682
info@pmtc.ca
www.pmtc.ca
Overview: A medium-sized national organization founded in 1977
Mission: Recognized as the leader of the private trucking community in Canada; represents the varied interests of private fleet operators with integrity & sound business practices.
Member of: North American Private Truck Council
Affliation(s): National Private Truck Council
Chief Officer(s):
Bruce J. Richards, President
trucks@pmtc.ca
Richard Lalonde, Québec Director
richard_lalonde@praxair.com
Finances: *Annual Operating Budget:* $250,000-$500,000; *Funding Sources:* Seminars; social events; membership fees
Staff Member(s): 4
Membership: 400; *Member Profile:* Private truck fleets or suppliers to same; private truck fleets operated by companies whose principal business is other than transportation, but use their own truck fleets to further their business
Activities: Seminars; annual conference; benchmarking and best practices survey;National Vehicle Graphics Design Competition
Awards:
• Vehicle Graphics Awards (Award)
• Driver Hall of Fame (Award)
• Fleet Safety Awards (Award)
Meetings/Conferences: • Private Motor Truck Council of Canada Annual Conference 2015, 2015
Scope: National
Publications:
• The Counsellor [a publication of the Private Motor Truck Council of Canada]
Type: Magazine; *Frequency:* Quarterly
• NewsBriefs [a publication of the Private Motor Truck Council of Canada]
Type: Newsletter

Les Prix du Gouverneur Général pour les arts de la scène *See* Governor General's Performing Arts Awards Foundation

Pro Bono Law Ontario (PBLO)
PO Box 102, 260 Adelaide St. East, Toronto ON M5A 1N1
Tel: 416-977-4448; *Fax:* 416-977-6668
Toll-Free: 866-466-7256
info@pblo.org
www.pblo.org
Overview: A small provincial organization founded in 2002
Mission: To broker partnerships & provide strategic guidance, training & tailored technical assistance to groups, law firms, & law associations that are dedicated to addressing the legal needs of low-income & disadvantaged individuals as well as the communities & charitable organizations that serve them
Chief Officer(s):
Lynnd Burns, Executive Director
Activities: Volunteer Lawyers Service; South Asian Legal Clinic of Ontario; Child Advocacy Project; Lawyers for Aboriginal Arts Project; Wills & Powers of Attorney Project; Community Economic Development Project

Pro Bono Québec
CP 55043, Succ. Notre-Dame, 11, rue Notre-Dame Ouest, Montréal QC H2Y 4A7
Tél: 514-954-3434; *Téléc:* 514-954-3427
Ligne sans frais: 800-361-8495
info@probonoquebec.ca
www.probonoquebec.ca
www.facebook.com/150444894975367
twitter.com/probonoquebec
Aperçu: *Dimension:* moyenne; *Envergure:* provinciale; fondée en 2008
Mission: Pour fournir le coût des conseils juridiques gratuits ou faible pour la population déshérités du Québec
Affiliation(s): Barreau du Québec; Justice Québec; Barreau de Montréal; Centre d'accès à l'information juridique; SOQUIJ
Membre(s) du bureau directeur:
Nancy Leggett-Bachand, Directrice générale
Alexander De Zordo, President, Conseil d'administraion

Pro Coro Canada
Birks Building, #309, 10113 - 104 St., Edmonton AB T5J 1A1
Tel: 780-420-1247
thechoir@procoro.ab.ca
www.procoro.ab.ca
www.facebook.com/procorocanada
twitter.com/ProCoroCanada
Previous Name: Pro Coro Society-Edmonton
Overview: A small local charitable organization founded in 1981
Member of: Alberta Choral Federation; Association of Canadian Choral Directors; Chorus America
Chief Officer(s):
Michael Zaugg, Artistic Director & Conductor
Finances: *Annual Operating Budget:* $250,000-$500,000; *Funding Sources:* Federal, provincial & municipal government; private foundations; business & individuals production
Staff Member(s): 5; 100 volunteer(s)
Membership: 210 individual
Activities: Annual subscription concert series; regional performances; tours; caberet; *Library:* Pro Coro Music Library; by appointment

Pro Coro Society-Edmonton *See* Pro Coro Canada

Pro Musica Society Inc. *Voir* Société Pro Musica Inc.

Probation Officers Association of Ontario (POAO)
#6245, 2100 Bloor St. West, Toronto ON M6S 5A5
www.poao.org
www.facebook.com/POAOntario
twitter.com/POAOntario
Overview: A small provincial organization founded in 1952
Mission: To represent the professional interests of the probation & parole Officers across the province; to provide representation on legislative issues to policy makers; to act as a forum for exchange of experience & information.
Chief Officer(s):
Elana Lamese, President
president@poao.org
Membership: *Fees:* $197.75 full membership; $84.75 associate; $339 affliate
Activities: Symposiums with workshops & speakers
Publications:
• The Monitor
Type: Newsletter; *Frequency:* Quarterly

Central Branch
Brampton ON
Tel: 905-456-4700
www.poao.org
Chief Officer(s):
Kerry Gray, Contact

Eastern Branch
Ottawa West Probation & Parole Services, 10A Hearst Way, Ottawa ON K2L 2P4
Tel: 613-270-8260; *Fax:* 613-270-8422
www.poao.org
Chief Officer(s):
Jamie Pearson, Chair

Midwest Branch
Stratford ON
Tel: 519-271-5220
www.poao.org
Chief Officer(s):
Anna Brenneman, Chair

Northeast Branch
Minden ON
Tel: 705-286-1489
www.poao.org
Chief Officer(s):
Terry Goodwin, Chair

Northwest Branch
Kenora Probation & Parole Office, 810 Robertson St., Kenora ON P9N 1S9
Tel: 807-468-2857
www.poao.org
Chief Officer(s):
Jane Van Toen, Chair

Southwest Branch
Chatham ON
Tel: 519-352-1243
www.poao.org
Chief Officer(s):
Jill Johns, Chair

Probe International (PI)
225 Brunswick Ave., Toronto ON M5S 2M6
Tel: 416-964-9223; *Fax:* 416-964-8239
probeinternational@nextcity.com
journal.probeinternational.org
www.facebook.com/ProbeInternational
twitter.com/probeintl
Overview: A medium-sized international charitable organization founded in 1980
Mission: To educate Canadians about the environmental, social, & economic effects of Canada's aid & trade abroad; To monitor & expose the effects of projects financed by Canadian tax dollars (through international financial institutions, such as the World Bank & the Asian Development Bank, & through agencies such as CIDA & the Export Development Corp.) & by Canadian corporations
Member of: Energy Probe Research Foundation; Canadian Environmental Network
Affliation(s): Environment Liaison Centre (International); International Organization of Consumers Unions; Energy Probe; Environment Probe; Consumer Policy Institute; Environmental Bureau of Investigation
Chief Officer(s):
Patricia Adams, Executive Director
Finances: *Annual Operating Budget:* $50,000-$100,000; *Funding Sources:* Private donations
Staff Member(s): 2
Activities: *Speaker Service:* Yes; *Library* by appointment

Product Care Association
12337 - 82A Ave., Surrey BC V3W 0L5
Tel: 604-592-2972; *Fax:* 604-592-2982
contact@productcare.org
www.productcare.org
www.facebook.com/ProductCare
twitter.com/Product_Care
Overview: A medium-sized national organization
Mission: To manage product stewardship programs for household hazardous and special waste
Chief Officer(s):
Mark Kruschner, President
Membership: 173
Publications:
• The Circular
Type: Newsletter

Producteurs d'oufs du Canada *See* Egg Farmers of Canada

Producteurs de pommes du Nouveau-Brunswick *See* Apple Growers of New Brunswick

Les Producteurs de poulet du Canada *See* Chicken Farmers of Canada

Les Producteurs laitiers du Canada *See* Dairy Farmers of Canada

Producteurs Laitiers du Manitoba *See* Dairy Farmers of Manitoba

Producteurs laitiers du Nouveau-Brunswick *See* Dairy Farmers of New Brunswick

Les Productions DansEncorps Inc.
Centre Culturel Aberdeen, #14A, 140, rue Botsford, Moncton NB E1C 4X5
Tél: 506-855-0998; *Téléc:* 506-852-3401
dansencorps@bellaliant.com
www.dansencorps.ca
www.facebook.com/dansencorps

Aperçu: *Dimension:* moyenne; *Envergure:* provinciale; Organisme sans but lucratif; fondée en 1979
Mission: De contribuer au développement des arts au Nouveau-Brunswick
Finances: *Fonds:* Provinciaux et fédéraux
Activités: *Stagiaires:* Oui

Produits alimentaires et de consommation du Canada *See* Food & Consumer Products of Canada

Professional Administrators of Volunteer Resources - Ontario (PAVR-O)

#5, 22 Millwood Rd., Toronto ON M4S 1J7
Tel: 705-654-3261; *Fax:* 519-836-0588
Toll-Free: 877-297-2876
pavro@pavro.on.ca
www.pavro.on.ca
Overview: A medium-sized provincial organization founded in 1998
Mission: To build individual, organizational, & community capacity to effectively engage volunteers through the professional management of volunteer resources
Member of: Canadian Administrators of Volunteer Resources
Chief Officer(s):
Erin Spink, President
Membership: *Fees:* $143.46 individual; $306.99 corporate; $91.80 affiliate/associate

Professional Association of Canadian Theatres (PACT)

#555, 215 Spadina Ave., Toronto ON M5T 2C7
Tel: 416-595-6455; *Fax:* 416-595-6450
Toll-Free: 800-263-7228
marlaf@pact.ca
www.pact.ca
www.facebook.com/group.php?gid=189415132023
Also Known As: PACT Communications Centre
Previous Name: The League of Canadian Theatres
Overview: A large national charitable organization founded in 1976
Mission: To gain recognition & support for professional theatre in Canada; To support the development of Canadian theatre companies by sharing resources & knowledge; to develop working standards & relationships with theatre professionals through their associations; To inform & connect theatres across Canada through a communications network; To act as a major force in influencing cultural policy at all levels of government
Affiliation(s): PACT Communications Centre; Canadian Conference of the Arts
Chief Officer(s):
Lucy White, Executive Director
lucyw@pact.ca
Eric Coates, President
ecoates@blythfestival.com
Linda Gorrie, Treasurer
linda@playwrightstheatre.com
Finances: *Funding Sources:* Membership fees; government grants; donations
Staff Member(s): 6; 36 volunteer(s)
Membership: 140 professional theatres; *Fees:* Schedule available; *Member Profile:* Canadian professional theatres; *Committees:* Cultural Diversity; Labour Relations; Membership; Negotiating Teams; Professional Development; Fundraising; Caucus Advisory; Distinct Artistic Practices; Finance; Regional Advisory
Activities: Regional meetings
Awards:
• Mallory Gilbert Leadership Award (Award)
An individual who has demonstrated outstanding leadership within the Canadian theatre community. *Amount:* $5,000
Publications:
• Artsboard
Type: Newsletter
• impact!
Type: Newsletter; *Frequency:* Monthly

Professional Association of Foreign Service Officers (Ind.) (PAFSO) / L'Association professionnelle des agents du service extérieur (ind.) (APASE)

#412, 47 Clarence St., Ottawa ON K1N 9K1
Tel: 613-241-1391; *Fax:* 613-241-5911
info@pafso.com
www.pafso.com
Overview: A medium-sized national organization founded in 1965
Chief Officer(s):
Ron Cochrane, Executive Director
ron.cochrane@pafso-apase.com
Staff Member(s): 6
Membership: 1,544
Awards:
• Canadian Foreign Service Officer Award (Award)

Professional Association of Inhalation Therapists of Québec (Ind.) *Voir* Association professionnelle des inhalothérapeutes du Québec (ind.)

Professional Association of Internes & Residents of Newfoundland (PAIRN) / Association professionnelle des internes et résidents de Terre-Neuve

c/o Student Affairs, Health Sciences Complex, Memorial University, #2713, 300 Prince Philip Dr., St. John's NL A1B 3V6
Tel: 709-777-7118; *Fax:* 709-777-6968
pairn@mun.ca
www.pairn.ca
Overview: A small provincial organization overseen by Canadian Association of Internes & Residents
Mission: To collaborate with local & national health care organizations to advocate on behalf of internes, resident physicians, & fellows of Newfoundland & Labrador; To advocate for the acknowledgement of the resident's role in medical education
Affliation(s): Canadian Association of Internes & Residents; Newfoundland & Labrador Medical Association; Canadian Medical Association
Chief Officer(s):
Sarah Kean, President
Robert Mercer, Vice-President
Heather O'Reilly, Secretary
Erika Hansford, Treasurer
Finances: *Funding Sources:* Membership fees
Membership: *Fees:* 1% of members' salary; *Member Profile:* Internes, residents, or fellows in any Newfoundland or Labrador hospital or its affiliate
Activities: Ensuring that resident physicians in Newfoundland & Labrador have input into health policy decisions that affect them; Helping members with situations during their residencies; Advising members on issues, such as contracts, benefits, education, & wellness; Participating in the community & donating to community organizations throughout Newfoundland & Labrador
Awards:
• Dr. John G. Williams Clinical Teaching Award (Award)
To recognize the best clinical teacher of the year
• Lorimer Scholarship (Scholarship)
To recognize non-academic qualities, such as patient support *Amount:* $1,000

Professional Association of Internes & Residents of Ontario (PAIRO)

#1901, 400 University Ave., Toronto ON M5G 1S5
Tel: 416-979-1182; *Fax:* 416-595-9778
Toll-Free: 877-979-1183
pairo@pairo.org
www.pairo.org
Overview: A small provincial organization overseen by Canadian Association of Internes & Residents
Mission: To improve the quality of life for young doctors training in Ontario; To advocate for acknowledgment of the resident's role in medical education; To ensure that patients receive excellent care
Affiliation(s): Canadian Association of Internes & Residents
Chief Officer(s):
Robert Conn, CEO
Jonathan DellaVedova, President
Membership: *Member Profile:* Residents & internes who train in Ontario
Activities: Working to achieve optimal training & working conditons for residents throughout Ontario; Administering funds from the PAIRO Trust Fund for the welfare of internes & residents
Awards:
• PAIRO Excellence in Clinical Teaching Awards (Award)
To recognize excellent clinical teachers who train new physicians
• Lois H. Ross Resident Advocate Award (Award)
To recognize an individual who has advocated on behalf of residents & resident issues
• Residency Program Excellence Award (Award)
To recognize programs that create a positive environment to produce excellent clinicians
• Citizenship Awards for Medical Students (Award)
To recognize a medical student who has maintained an adquate academic standing & who has contributed to the general welfare of fellow medical students
• Resident Teaching Awards (Award)
To recognize a resident at each university centre who provides outstanding clinical teaching experiences *Amount:* $1,000
• Canadian Research Awards for Family Medicine Residents (Award)
Sponsored jointly by the PAIRO Trust Fund & The Royal College of Physicians & Surgeons of Canada, the award recognizes family medicine residents for original research
• Canadian Research Awards for Specialty Residents in the Divisions of Medicine & Surgery (Award)
Sponsored by the PAIRO Trust Fund, The Royal College of Physicians & Surgeons of Canada, & The Canadian Society for Clinical Investigation, the awards recognize original work by postgraduate trainees
• Travel Award for Clinical Educators (Award)
Eligibility: Faculty members who wish to visit another centre to improve his or her clinical teaching ability *Amount:* $4,000

Professional Association of Interns & Residents of Saskatchewan (PAIRS) / Association professionnelle des internes et résidents de la Saskatchewan (ind.)

C Wing, Royal University Hospital, PO Box 23, #5687, 103 Hospital Dr., 5th Fl., Saskatoon SK S7N 0W8
Tel: 306-655-2134; *Fax:* 306-655-2134
pairs.sk@usask.ca
www.saskresidents.ca
Overview: A small provincial organization founded in 1996 overseen by Canadian Association of Internes & Residents
Mission: To represent resident physicians of Saskatchewan at the university & hospital levels, as well as provincially & nationally; To improve education, salaries, & other benefits for resident physicians
Affliation(s): Canadian Association of Internes & Residents
Chief Officer(s):
Paul Dhillon, President
Dilip Gill, Vice-President
Laura Weins, Secretary-Treasurer
Kristin Johnson, Executive Director
Membership: *Member Profile:* All resident physicians of Saskatchewan
Activities: Negotiating with the provincial goverment for contracts; Arranging social activities;
Awards:
• PAIRS Teaching Excellence Award (Award)
To recognize an individual who has demonstrated outstanding attributes in teaching residents

Professional Association of Residents & Internes of the Maritime Provinces *See* Professional Association of Residents in the Maritime Provinces

Professional Association of Residents & Interns of Manitoba (PARIM) / Association professionnelle des résidents et internes du Manitoba

#AD107, 720 McDermot Ave., Winnipeg MB R3E 0T3
Tel: 204-787-3673; *Fax:* 204-787-2692
parim.office@gmail.com
www.parim.org
Also Known As: PARI Manitoba
Overview: A small provincial organization founded in 1975 overseen by Canadian Association of Internes & Residents
Mission: To represent the concerns of all residents & interns in Manitoba; To advocate for the well-being of residents & interns; To promote quality medical education & excellent patient care
Affliation(s): Canadian Association of Internes & Residents
Chief Officer(s):
Elizabeth Berg, Co-President
Markus Ziesmann, Co-President
Debarsi Das, Vice-President, Communications
Membership: 400; *Member Profile:* Manitoba residents & interns who are receiving education & training at hospitals
Activities: Working to achieve optimal working conditions for physicians in training in Manitoba; Maintaining liaisons with other health care organizations in Manitoba; Raising public awareness about the roles of residents

Professional Association of Residents in the Maritime Provinces (PARI-MP) / Association professionnelle des résidents des provinces maritimes

Halifax Professional Centre, #460, 5991 Spring Garden Rd., Halifax NS B3H 1Y6

Tel: 902-404-3597
Toll-Free: 877-972-7467
www.parimp.ca
Previous Name: Professional Association of Residents & Internes of the Maritime Provinces
Overview: A small local organization founded in 1969 overseen by Canadian Association of Internes & Residents
Mission: To represent the interests of resident physicians who train at Dalhousie University; To improve the well-being & working conditions of residents in the Maritimes; To advocate on the behalf of residents
Affliation(s): Canadian Association of Internes & Residents
Chief Officer(s):
Philip Davis, President
Sandi Carew Flemming, Executive Director
sandi@parimp.ca
Staff Member(s): 5
Membership: 540; *Member Profile:* Maritime residents who train at Dalhousie University & who are based in Halifax, Nova Scotia, Sydney, Nova Scotia, Moncton, New Brunswick, Fredericton, New Brunswick, & Saint John, New Brunswick
Activities: Organizing information seminars for Maritime resident physicians; Negotiating & enforcing the collective agreement; Arranging social events for residents; Adminstering an annual bursary program; Collaborating with other organizations for advocacy purposes
Publications:
• PARIscope
Type: Newsletter; *Frequency:* Quarterly
Profile: Association updates & information, plus upcoming events for members

Professional Association of Residents of Alberta (PARA) / Association professionnelle des résidents de l'Alberta

Garneau Professional Center, #340, 11044 - 82 Ave., Edmonton AB T6G OJ2
Tel: 780-432-1749; *Fax:* 780-432-1778
Toll-Free: 877-375-7272
para@para-ab.ca
www.para-ab.ca
Overview: A medium-sized provincial organization founded in 1975 overseen by Canadian Association of Internes & Residents
Mission: To represent physicians completing further training in residency programs; To promote excellence in education & patient care; To advocate for health care issues & for improvement in working conditions, salary, & benefits for resident physicians of Alberta
Affliation(s): Canadian Association of Internes & Residents
Chief Officer(s):
David Weatherby, President
djweathe@ucalgary.ca
Tana Findlay, Interim Chief Executive Officer
tana.findlay@para-ab.ca
Aimee Kozun, Coordinator, Communications
aimee.kozun@para-ab.ca
Finances: *Funding Sources:* Membership dues
Staff Member(s): 5
Membership: *Member Profile:* Resident physicians of Alberta
Activities: Organizing information seminars & social events for residents in Alberts; Assisting residents who experience academic or professional difficulties or personal problems; Liaising with all levels of administration & government; Advocating for issues which affect residents; Preparing for & conducting contract negotiations on behalf of residents in Alberta; Enforcing the terms of contracts; Arranging payment for member life insurance & long term disability insurance

Professional Association of Residents of British Columbia (PAR-BC) / Association professionnelle des résidents de la Colombie-Britannique

#2010, 401 West Georgia St., Vancouver BC V6B 5A1
Tel: 604-876-7636
Toll-Free: 888-877-2722
par@par-bc.org
www.par-bc.org
www.facebook.com/PARBC
twitter.com/PAR_BC
Overview: A medium-sized provincial organization overseen by Canadian Association of Internes & Residents
Mission: To bargain collectively on behalf of residents in British Columbia; To foster the personal well-being of members
Affliation(s): Canadian Association of Internes & Residents
Chief Officer(s):
Arun Jagdeo, President
Paul Hentz, Vice-President
Mary Masotti, Director, Communications
Michael Suen, Director, Finance
Finances: *Funding Sources:* Union dues
Membership: *Member Profile:* All residents of British Columbia become members of PAR-BC upon commencement of employment; *Committees:* Advocacy; Communications; Distributed Medical Education; Finance; Governance; Resident Physician Health & Wellness
Activities: Promoting the educational concerns of residents in British Columbia; Advocating for members' interests; Liaising with government; Preparing position papers
Awards:
• Dr. Patricia Clugston Memorial Award For Excellence in Teaching (Award)
To recognize clinical faculty for their contributions to the continuing medical education of residents
• Residents' Advocate Award (Award)
To recognize an individual who advocates on behalf of residents to improve their well-being
• Award of Merit (Award)
To recognize a resident physician whose achievements reflect the aims of the Professional Association of Residents of British Columbia

Professional Convention Management Association - Canada West Chapter (PCMA)

BC
Tel: 604-647-7346
canadawest@pcma.org
www.pcma.org
Overview: A medium-sized international organization founded in 1957
Mission: To promote the convention management industry & provide education to its memebers
Chief Officer(s):
Diana Reid, President
dreid@vancouverconventioncentre.com
Membership: 233; *Member Profile:* Meetings industry professionals; suppliers; faculty members; students; *Committees:* Membership; Program
Activities: Educational seminars; networking opportunities with peers
Publications:
• Western News
Type: Newsletter; *Frequency:* Quarterly

Professional Council of Licensed Practical Nurses *See* College of Licensed Practical Nurses of Alberta

Professional Employees Association (Ind.) (PEA) / Association des employés professionnels (ind.)

#505, 1207 Douglas St., Victoria BC V8W 2E7
Tel: 250-385-8791; *Fax:* 250-385-6629
Toll-Free: 800-779-7736
www.pea.org
www.facebook.com/peaonline
twitter.com/pea_online
www.youtube.com/user/PEAblogger
Overview: A medium-sized provincial organization founded in 1974
Mission: To provide collective bargaining representation to professionals employed in the provincial public service & elsewhere in the BC public sector
Chief Officer(s):
Scott McCannell, Executive Director
smccannell@pea.org
Ben Harper, Communications Officer
bharper@pea.org
Finances: *Annual Operating Budget:* $500,000-$1.5 Million; *Funding Sources:* Fees, grants, donations
Staff Member(s): 9
Membership: 2,500 (9 units)
Activities: *Library*

Professional Engineers & Architects of the Ontario Public Service *See* Professional Engineers Government of Ontario

Professional Engineers & Geoscientists Newfoundland & Labrador (PEG-NL)

PO Box 21207, #203, 10 Fort William Pl., St. John's NL A1A 5B2
Tel: 709-753-7714; *Fax:* 709-753-6131
main@pegnl.ca
www.pegnl.ca
Previous Name: Association of Professional Engineers & Geoscientists of Newfoundland
Overview: A medium-sized provincial licensing organization founded in 1952 overseen by Engineers Canada
Mission: To provide competent & ethical practice of engineering & geoscience in Newfoundland & Labrador; To ensure public confidence, sustainability, & stewardship of the professions; To provide leadership to enhance quality of life through the application & management of engineering & geoscience
Member of: Engineers Canada; Canadian Council of Professional Geoscientists
Chief Officer(s):
Geoff Emberley, P. Eng., FEC, Chief Executive Officer & Registrar
Mark Fewer, B. Comm., Chief Operating Officer & Deputy Registrar
Leo White, P. Eng., Director, Professional Standards
Carl King, Councilor, Western District
Steve McLean, Executive Director
Finances: *Funding Sources:* Membership dues
200 volunteer(s)
Membership: 2,500 individual + 286 student + 31 licensee + 296 corporate; *Fees:* $224 individual; $564-1,031 corporate; $530 licensee; *Member Profile:* Bachelor's degree in engineering or geoscience; *Committees:* Discipline; Board of Examiners; Awards; Professional Development & Education; Code of Ethics; Complaints; Conference; Environmental; Geoscience Issues; National Engineering Week; Endowment Fund
Activities: Administering The Engineers & Geoscientists Act in Newfoundland; *Awareness Events:* National Engineering Week; Science & Technology Week
Awards:
• Award for Merit (Award)
To recognize members who have made outstanding contributions to the profession &/or to the community
• Award for Service (Award)
Awarded to members who have served their profession diligently for many years & who have made substantial contributions to the Association & to the advancement of the professions
• Environmental Award (Award)
Recognizes the application of science, technology & engineering to human & resource environmental management in Newfoundland & Labrador
• Early Accomplishment Award (Award)
Given to members in recognition of exceptional achievement in the early years of an engineer's or geoscientist's professional career
• Community Service Award (Award)
Given to members in recognition of outstanding service & dedication to society
• Teaching Award (Award)

Professional Engineers for Public Safety (PEPSA)

4559.cupe.ca
Previous Name: The Professional Engineers Group of the Canadian Standards Association
Overview: A small national organization
Chief Officer(s):
Martin Buchanan, President
Pres4559@members.cupe.ca

Professional Engineers Government of Ontario

4711 Yonge St., 10th Fl., Toronto ON M2N 6K8
Tel: 416-784-1284; *Fax:* 416-784-1366
pego@pego.on.ca
www.pego.on.ca
Previous Name: Professional Engineers & Architects of the Ontario Public Service
Overview: A small provincial organization
Mission: The Professional Engineers Government of Ontario (PEGO) is a certified bargaining association representing Professional Engineers and Ontario Land Surveyors working directly for the Government of the Province of Ontario.

The Professional Engineers Group of the Canadian Standards Association *See* Professional Engineers for Public Safety

Professional Engineers Ontario (PEO)

#101, 40 Sheppard Ave. West, Toronto ON M2N 6K9
Tel: 416-224-1100; *Fax:* 416-224-9527
Toll-Free: 800-339-3716
financialservices@peo.on.ca
www.peo.on.ca
Previous Name: Association of Professional Engineers of Ontario
Overview: A large provincial licensing organization founded in 1922 overseen by Engineers Canada

Mission: To meet the needs of Ontario society by licensing & regulating the entire practice of professional engineering in an open, transparent, inclusive manner. There are 36 chapters across the province
Member of: Engineers Canada
Chief Officer(s):
Denis Dixon, P.Eng., FEC, President
Michael Price, P.Eng., MBA, Acting CEO & Registrar, 416-840-1060
mprice@peo.on.ca
Scott Clark, LL.B., CAO, 416-840-1126
sclark@peo.on.ca
Eric Brown, P.Eng., ISP, PM, Director, IT & Facilities Management, 416-840-1110
ebrown@peo.on.ca
Connie Mucklestone, Director, Communications, 416-840-1061
cmucklestone@peo.on.ca
Moody Samuel Farag, M.Eng., P.Eng., Manager, Admissions, 416-840-1055
mfarag@peo.on.ca
Brian MacEwen, P.Eng., Manager, Registration, 416-840-1056
bmacewen@peo.on.ca
Finances: *Funding Sources:* Membership fees
700 volunteer(s)
Membership: 70,000; *Fees:* Schedule available; *Committees:* Executive; Audit; Finance; Human Resources; Legislation; Regional Councillors; Academic Requirements; Advisory Committee on Volunteers; Awards; Central Election & Search; Complaints; Complaints Review Councillor; Consulting Engineer Designation; Discipline; Education; Enforcement; Equity & Diversity; Experience Requirements; Fees Mediation; Government Liaison; Ontario Centre for Engineering & Public Policy Advisory Bd.; OSPE-PEO Joint Relations; Overlapping Practices; PEO-OAA Joint Liaison; Professional Standards; Registration; Regional
Activities: *Speaker Service:* Yes
Awards:
• The Engineering Medal (Award)
Established 1964; silver medal awarded to members of PEO who have made a substantial contribution to the technical side of the profession in any of its branches; awarded in the following categories: engineering, management, research & development; there is no limit to the number of medals that may be awarded each year
• V.G. Smith Award (Award)
Established 1962; awarded annually to a member of PEO who has achieved registration during the year by examination, with the highest standing of the candidates who have completed their examinations in that year
• S.E. Wolfe Thesis Award (Award)
Established 1965; awarded to a member who has passed at least one of the association examinations, & whose thesis has been awarded the highest mark of all those presented during the year
• The Professional Engineers Gold Medal (Award)
Established 1947; awarded to a member of PEO who has spent some years working in the profession & has subsequently given outstanding public service to the country in the federal, provincial, educational, charitable, or other fields; winner receives a gold medal & a citation
• The Professional Engineers Citizenship Award (Award)
Established 1970; awarded to members of PEO who have made a substantial contribution in such fields as education, the arts, medicine, law, & social service while maintaining their identity as professional engineers; there is no limit to the number of these awards made each year
• Order of Honour Service Awards (Award)
An honorary society of PEO, the purpose of which is to recognize & honour those professional engineers & others who have rendered conspicuous service to the engineering profession in varying degrees & normally through the association; awards are made in three classes: Member, Officer, & Companion
• Fellow of Engineers Canada (Award)
• G. Gordon M. Sterling Engineering Intern Award (Award)
• The President's Award (Award)
Publications:
• Employer Salary Survey [a publication of the Professional Engineers Ontario]
Type: Report
• Engineering Dimensions [a publication of the Professional Engineers Ontario]
Type: Magazine; *Editor:* Jennifer Coombes
• Membership Salary Survey [a publication of the Professional Engineers Ontario]
Type: Report
• PEO [Professional Engineers Ontario] Practice Bulletins
Type: Bulletin
• Professional Engineers Ontario Annual Report
Type: Yearbook; *Frequency:* Annual

Algoma
ON
e-mail: algoma@peo.on.ca
www.peo.on.ca
Chief Officer(s):
Jeanette Biemann, P. Eng, Chair, 705-949-5291

Algonquin
Algonquin ON
e-mail: algonquin@peo.on.ca
www.peo.on.ca
Member of: Engineers Canada
Chief Officer(s):
Lawrence Lupton, P. Eng, Chair

Brampton
Brampton ON
e-mail: info@peobrampton.ca
www.peobrampton.ca
www.facebook.com/190569797256
twitter.com/PEO_Brampton
Chief Officer(s):
Satyendra Bhavsar, P. Eng, Chair
satyendra.bhavsa@peobrampton.ca

Brantford
ON
e-mail: brantford@peo.on.ca
www.peo.on.ca
Chief Officer(s):
Mike Crutchley, P. Eng, Chair
mikec@ciaccess.com

Chatham-Kent
ON
www.peo.on.ca
Chief Officer(s):
Angela Scott, P. Eng, Chair, 519-436-4600 Ext. 5002049
AScott@uniongas.com

East Toronto
ON
www.peo.on.ca
Chief Officer(s):
Hugo Maureira, P. Eng, Chair, 416-368-3139
hmaureira@rogers.com

Etobicoke
ON
www.etobicoke.peo.on.ca
Chief Officer(s):
Roy Fernandes, P. Eng, Chair

Georgian Bay
ON
e-mail: georgianbay@peo.on.ca
www.peo.on.ca
Chief Officer(s):
Vaj Banday, P. Eng, Chair

Grand River
ON
grandriverpeo.ca
ca.linkedin.com/in/grandriverpeo
www.facebook.com/GrandRiverChapterPEO
twitter.com/grandriverpeo
Chief Officer(s):
Kaoru Yajima, P. Eng, Chair, 519-575-4757 Ext. 3349, Fax: 519-575-4452
YKaoru@region.waterloo.on.ca

Hamilton
ON
www.hamilton.peo.on.ca
Chief Officer(s):
Bozena Bednarska, P. Eng, Chair
bbednarska@ajclarke.com

Kingston
Kingston ON
e-mail: kingston@peo.on.ca
www.peo.on.ca
Chief Officer(s):
Doug Hamilton, P. Eng, Chair
douglas.hamilton@gmail.com

Kingsway
ON
e-mail: kingsway@peo.on.ca
www.kingsway.peo.on.ca
Chief Officer(s):
Steve Favell, P. Eng, Chair
sfavell@alumni.uwaterloo.ca

Lake of the Woods
ON
www.peo.on.ca
Chief Officer(s):
Ian A. Finke, P. Eng, Chair

Lake Ontario
ON
www.peolakeontario.ca
Chief Officer(s):
Raymond Chokelal, P. Eng, Chair
rchokelal@rogers.com

Lakehead
ON
e-mail: lakehead@peo.on.ca
www.peo.on.ca
Chief Officer(s):
Philip Riegle, P. Eng, Chair

Lambton
ON
e-mail: lambton@peo.on.ca
www.peo.on.ca
Chief Officer(s):
Phil Lasek, P. Eng, Chair

London
ON
e-mail: london@peo.on.ca
www.peo.on.ca
Chief Officer(s):
Diego Cardenas, P. Eng, Chair

Mississauga
ON
e-mail: support@peo-mc.ca
peo-mc.ca
www.linkedin.com/groups/PEO-Mississauga-Chapter-3838507
twitter.com/peomc
Chief Officer(s):
Art Kirnichansky, E. Eng, Chair, 416-897-1069
art.kirnichansky@peo-mc.ca

Niagara
PO Box 30023, Stn. Ridley Square, 275 - 4 Ave., St. Catharines ON L2S 4A1
e-mail: niagara@peo.on.ca
www.peo.on.ca
Chief Officer(s):
Jonathan Atkinson, P. Eng, Chair

North Bay
ON
www.peo.on.ca
Chief Officer(s):
Luc Roberge, P. Eng, Chair, 705-474-2364 Ext. 2013
luc.roberge@opg.com

Northern Regional Office
ON
Tel: 807-343-8345
peonro@lakeheadu.ca
www.northernregionaloffice.peo.on.ca
Chief Officer(s):
Meilan Liu, P. Eng, Contact

Oakville
PO Box 60017, 300 North Service Rd. West, Oakville ON L6M 3H2
www.peo-oakvillechapter.ca
Chief Officer(s):
Warren Turnbull, Chair
chair@peo-oakvillechapter.ca

Ottawa
#208, 1568 Merivale Rd., Nepean ON K2G 5Y7
e-mail: ottawa@peo.on.ca
www.peo.on.ca
Chief Officer(s):
Pierre Legault, P. Eng, Chair
Pierre.legault2@forces.gc.ca

Peterborough
Peterborough ON
e-mail: peterborough@peo.on.ca
www.peo.on.ca
Chief Officer(s):
Clarence Klassen, P. Eng, Chair

Porcupine/Kapuskasing
ON
e-mail: porcupine-kapuskasing@peo.on.ca
www.peo.on.ca
Chief Officer(s):
Serge Robert, P. Eng, Chair
srobert@jlrichards.ca
Quinte
ON
e-mail: quinte@peo.on.ca
www.peo.on.ca
twitter.com/PEOQuinte
Chief Officer(s):
Randy Walker, P. Eng, Chair
Scarborough
ON
e-mail: scarborough@peo.on.ca
www.scarborough.peo.on.ca
Chief Officer(s):
Madu Sutheranan, P. Eng, Chair
Simcoe Muskoka
ON
e-mail: simcoe-muskoka@peo.on.ca
www.peo.on.ca
Chief Officer(s):
Ted Ratajczak, P. Eng, Chair, 705-380-0456
ted.ratajczak@gmail.com
Sudbury
ON
e-mail: sudbury@peo.on.ca
www.peo.on.ca
Chief Officer(s):
Elise Idnani, Chair
Termiskaming
ON
www.peo.on.ca
Thousand Islands
Unit P/Q, #132, 163 Ormond St., Brockville ON K6V 7E6
e-mail: thousandislands@peo.on.ca
www.peo.on.ca
Chief Officer(s):
Ray Linseman, P. Eng, Chair, 613-342-0017
Toronto Humber
PO Box 12526, Stn. Martinway Plaza, 415 The Westway, Toronto ON M9R 4C7
e-mail: toronto-Humber@peo.on.ca
www.peo.on.ca
Chief Officer(s):
Harneet Pansesar, P. Eng, Chair
Upper Canada
ON
e-mail: uppercanada@peo.on.ca
www.peo.on.ca
Chief Officer(s):
Ivan Rodriguez, P. Eng, Chair
sergioiv@yahoo.com
West Toronto
ON
e-mail: westtoronto@peo.on.ca
www.peo.on.ca
www.linkedin.com/groups/West-Toronto-PEO-Chapter-4196637
www.facebook.com/148953528500919
twitter.com/WestTorontoPEO
Chief Officer(s):
Jim Chisholm, Chair
Western Regional Office
Spencer Engineering Building, University of Western Ontario, #2084, London ON N6A 5B8
Tel: 519-661-3764
wro@peo.on.ca
www.peo.on.ca
Chief Officer(s):
Alex Hockin, Contact
Shahram Amirnia, Contact
Willowdale/Thornhill
ON
e-mail: willowdale-thornhill@peo.on.ca
www.willowdalethornhill.peo.on.ca
www.linkedin.com/in/peowillowdalethonhill
www.facebook.com/peo.willowdalethornhillchapter
twitter.com/peowillowdale
Chief Officer(s):
Maziyar Bolour, P. Eng, Chair
maziyar.bolour@wtpeo.org
Windor-Essex
ON
e-mail: windsor-essex@peo.on.ca
www.windsoressex.peo.on.ca
www.linkedin.com/groups/PEO-WindsorEssex-5092970
www.facebook.com/PeoWindsorEssex
twitter.com/PEOWindsorEssex
www.flickr.com/photos/85475524@N02/
Chief Officer(s):
Andrew Dowie, P. Eng, Chair, 519-819-4433
York
PO Box 186, 7305 Woodbine Ave., Markham ON L3R 3V7
www.peoyork.com
Chief Officer(s):
Dennis Woo, P. Eng, PhD, Chair
chair@peoyork.com

Professional Golfers' Association of British Columbia (PGA of BC)
#3280, 21331 Gordon Way, Richmond BC V6W 1J9
Tel: 604-303-6766; *Fax:* 604-303-6765
Toll-Free: 800-667-4653
info@pgabc.org
www.pgabc.org
www.facebook.com/pgabc
twitter.com/pgaofbc
www.youtube.com/user/pgaofbc
Previous Name: British Columbia Professional Golfers Association
Overview: A medium-sized provincial organization
Mission: To promote the game of golf and enhance all players' enjoyment of the sport.
Member of: Professional Golf Association
Chief Officer(s):
Donald Miyazaki, Executive Director
donald@pgabc.org
Brian McDonald, President
Finances: *Funding Sources:* Corporate sponsorship
Staff Member(s): 5
Membership: 650+; *Member Profile:* Individuals employed in the golf industry; *Committees:* Membership & Employment; Captain's; Education & Events; Long Range Planning & Grow the Game; Buying Show; Awards
Activities: PGA tournaments;

Professional Golfers' Association of Canada / Association des golfeurs professionnels du Canada
13450 Dublin Line, RR#1, Acton ON L7J 2W7
Tel: 519-853-5450; *Fax:* 519-853-5449
Toll-Free: 800-782-5764
info@pgaofcanada.com
www.pgaofcanada.com
www.facebook.com/PGAofCanada
twitter.com/pgaofcanada
www.youtube.com/user/thepgaofcanada
Also Known As: PGA of Canada
Previous Name: Canadian Professional Golfers' Association
Overview: A medium-sized national organization founded in 1911
Mission: The Canadian Professional Golfer's Association is a member based non-profit organization representing golf professionals across Canada.
Chief Officer(s):
Gary Bernard, Chief Executive Officer
gary@pgaofcanada.com
Heather Bodden, Manager & Member Liaison, Operations
heather@pgaofcanada.com
Finances: *Annual Operating Budget:* $500,000-$1.5 Million
Staff Member(s): 10
Membership: 3,500
Activities: *Rents Mailing List:* Yes

Professional Hockey Players' Association (PHPA)
3964 Portage Rd., Niagara Falls ON L2J 2K9
Tel: 289-296-5561; *Fax:* 289-296-4567
www.phpa.com
Overview: A small national organization founded in 1967
Staff Member(s): 12
Membership: 1,600+; *Member Profile:* All professional hockey players in the AHL & ECHL; *Committees:* Alumni Association; Workers' Compensation; Panel of Attorneys; Registered Agents Program; Career Enhancement Program; Membership Assistance Program

The Professional Institute of the Public Service of Canada (PIPSC) / Institut professionnel de la fonction publique du Canada
250 Tremblay Rd., Ottawa ON K1G 3J8
Tel: 613-228-6310; *Fax:* 613-228-9048
Toll-Free: 800-267-0446
www.pipsc.ca
www.facebook.com/pages/PIPSC-IPFPC/396834117052072
twitter.com/PIPSC_IPFPC
www.youtube.com/user/4PublicGood
Overview: A large national organization founded in 1920
Mission: To serve members by serving as their collective bargaining agent & by providing representational services
Chief Officer(s):
Gary Corbett, President
gcorbett@pipsc.ca
Edward Gillis, COO/Executive Secretary
egillis@pipsc.ca
Staff Member(s): 100
Membership: 57,000; *Fees:* $38; *Committees:* By-Laws & Policies; Elections; Executive Compensation; Finance; Human Rights in the Workplace; Member Services; Professional Recognition & Qualifications; Science Advisory
Activities: *Library*
Awards:
• Life Membership Award (Award)
• Institute Service Awards (Award)
Established 1970; not more than five awards (brass plaques) may be made annually to members of the Institute in any classification, or to persons ineligible for membership, for outstanding service to the Institute
• Professional Institute Gold Medals (Award)
Established 1937; two gold medals are presented biennially. Those eligible are scientific, professional, or technical workers or groups of workers employed by the federal, provincial, or municipal government services of Canada who have made a contribution of outstanding importance to national or world well-being in either pure or applied science or in some field outside pure or applied science
Publications:
• Communications
Type: Magazine; *Frequency:* Biannually
Alberta & Northwest Territories Regional Office
#1700, 10020 - 101A Ave., Edmonton AB T5J 3G2
Tel: 780-428-1347; *Fax:* 780-426-5962
Toll-Free: 800-661-3939
Chief Officer(s):
Grace Chychul, Regional Representative
gchychul@pipsc.ca
British Columbia & Yukon Regional Office
#2015, 401 West Georgia St., Vancouver BC V6B 5A1
Tel: 604-688-8238; *Fax:* 604-688-8290
Toll-Free: 800-663-0485
Chief Officer(s):
Ernie McLean, Regional Representative
emclean@pipsc.ca
Manitoba/Saskatchewan Regional Office
#700, 125 Garry St., Winnipeg MB R3C 3P2
Tel: 204-942-1304; *Fax:* 204-942-4348
Toll-Free: 800-665-0094
Chief Officer(s):
Grace Chychul, Regional Representative
gchychul@pipsc.ca
National Capital Region
250 Tremblay Rd., Ottawa ON K1G 3J8
Tel: 613-228-6310; *Fax:* 613-228-9048
Toll-Free: 800-267-0446
Chief Officer(s):
Nancy Lamarche, Regional Representative
Nova Scotia/New Brunswick/Newfoundland/Prince Edward Island Regional Office
#610, 1718 Argyle St., Halifax NS B3J 3N6
Tel: 902-420-1519; *Fax:* 902-422-8516
Toll-Free: 800-565-0727
Chief Officer(s):
Karyn Ladurantaye, Regional Representative
kladurantaye@pipsc.ca
Ontario Regional Office
#701, 110 Yonge St., Toronto ON M5C 1T4
Tel: 416-487-1114; *Fax:* 416-487-7268
Toll-Free: 800-668-3943
Chief Officer(s):
Marcia Kredentser, Regional Representative
mkredentser@pipsc.ca

Québec Regional Office
#2330, 1000, rue Sherbrooke ouest, Montréal QC H3A 3G4
Tél: 514-288-3545; *Téléc:* 514-288-0494
Ligne sans frais: 800-363-0622
Chief Officer(s):
Pierrette Gosselin, Regional Representative
gosselin@pipsc.ca

Professional Interior Designers Institute of Manitoba

137 Bannatyne Ave. East, 2nd Fl., Winnipeg MB R3B 0R3
Tel: 204-925-4625
pidim@shaw.ca
www.pidim.ca
Overview: A small provincial organization overseen by Interior Designers of Canada
Mission: To practice interior design in order to improve the lives of the public
Membership: 132; *Fees:* $26.25 student; $171.15 associate; $341.25 provisional; $622.91 professional; *Member Profile:* Interior designers & those interested in interior design

Professional Locksmith Association of Alberta (PLAA)

36 Sunridge Close, Airdrie AB T4B 2G6
Tel: 403-948-9997; *Fax:* 403-948-9997
Toll-Free: 877-765-7522
www.plaa.org
Overview: A small provincial organization founded in 1976
Mission: To promote public awareness of security matters; To promote training of members; To promote proper legislation for the security industry
Chief Officer(s):
Dave Kennedy, Executive Director
Finances: *Annual Operating Budget:* $50,000-$100,000; *Funding Sources:* Membership fees; annual convention & trade show; newsletter ads
Membership: 296; *Fees:* $100 individual; $200 corporate
Activities: *Internships:* Yes
Meetings/Conferences: • Professional Locksmiths Association of Alberta Annual General Meeting, 2015, AB
Scope: Provincial

Professional Organizers in Canada (POC)

39 River St., Toronto ON M5A 3P1
e-mail: inquiries-poc@organizersincanada.com
www.organizersincanada.com
www.facebook.com/132020106822948
twitter.com/poc_canada
Overview: A small national organization founded in 1999
Mission: To provide a supportive environment for professional organizers, promote networking, share ideas, encourage referrals, & increase public awareness of the field of professional organizing in Canada
Chief Officer(s):
Jacki Brown, President
POC-president@organizersincanada.com
20 volunteer(s)
Membership: 310; *Fees:* $180 + one time admin fee $50; *Member Profile:* Individuals who create customized solutions to increase the efficiency of any home, office or individual

Professional Outfitters Association of Alberta *See* Alberta Professional Outfitters Society

Professional Petroleum Data Management Association (PPDM)

PO Box 22155, Stn. Bankers Hall, #860, 736 - 8th Ave. SW, Calgary AB T2P 4J5
Tel: 403-660-7817; *Fax:* 403-660-0540
info@ppdm.org
www.ppdm.org
www.linkedin.com/groups?home=&gid=146440
www.facebook.com/group.php?gid=108325212519325
twitter.com/PPDMAssociation
Previous Name: Public Petroleum Data Model Association
Overview: A small national organization founded in 1991
Mission: To develop data management standards for the collection & exchange of data in the petroleum industry; To promote information standards
Chief Officer(s):
Trevor Hicks, Chair
trevor.hicks@noah-consulting.com
Janet Hicks, Secretary
jhicks@lgc.com
Peter MacDougall, Treasurer
peter.macdougall@ihs.com
Trudy Curtis, CEO
curtist@ppdm.org
Membership: *Committees:* Global Framework; Well Identification - US; Well Identification - Western Canada; Business Rules; Education Task Force
Activities: Increasing awareness of the value of data management; Providing training

Professional Photographers Association of British Columbia (PPABC) *See* Professional Photographers of Canada - British Columbia

Professional Photographers Association of Canada - Atlantic / Atlantique (PPAC Atlantic)

c/o Cindi-Lee Campbell, 9195 Rte. 102, Morrisdale NB E5K 4N3
Tel: 506-757-1198
www.mppaphoto.com
Previous Name: Maritime Professional Photographers Association (MPPA)
Overview: A small local organization founded in 1933 overseen by Professional Photographers of Canada
Mission: To uphold the association's code of ethics
Affliation(s): The Professional Photographers of Canada
Chief Officer(s):
Berni Wood, President
bwood@reelmedia.ca
Cindi-Lee Campbell, Secretary-Treasurer
moonmagc@nbnet.nb.ca
Membership: 45; *Member Profile:* Professional photographers throughout the Maritimes; *Committees:* Branch Events; Ethics; Audit; Newsletter & Advertising
Activities: Providing educational opportunities
Publications:
• Developments
Type: Newsletter; *Accepts Advertising*; *Editor:* Susanne Hovey
Profile: Member profiles, articles, continuing education & upcoming events

Professional Photographers of Canada - British Columbia (PPOC-BC)

PO Box 1329, 4543 - 201 St., Langley BC V3A 6M5
Tel: 604-857-1569; *Fax:* 604-857-1570
Toll-Free: 877-857-1569
contact@ppoc-bc.ca
www.ppoc-bc.ca
twitter.com/PPOC_BC
Previous Name: Professional Photographers Association of British Columbia (PPABC)
Overview: A medium-sized provincial organization founded in 1945 overseen by Professional Photographers of Canada
Mission: To promote & foster the personal ethics & professional development of the working photographer &/or specialist through education, fellowship & public awareness
Affliation(s): Professional Photographers of America
Chief Officer(s):
Jillian Chateauneuf, PPOC Director, British Columbia
ppocdelegate@ppoc-bc.ca
Melissa Walsh, President
president@ppoc-bc.ca
Finances: *Annual Operating Budget:* $50,000-$100,000; *Funding Sources:* Membership fees
Staff Member(s): 1; 20 volunteer(s)
Membership: 300; *Fees:* $205
Activities: Education; seminars; exhibitions; rental library

Professional Photographers of Canada - Ontario Branch

209 Light St., Woodstock ON N4S 6H6
Tel: 519-537-2555; *Fax:* 888-831-4036
Toll-Free: 888-643-7762
bureauduppoc@ppoc.ca
www.ppocontario.com
www.facebook.com/PPOC.ONTARIO
twitter.com/PPOC_Ontario
www.youtube.com/ppocontario
Also Known As: PPOC-Ontario
Overview: A medium-sized provincial licensing organization founded in 1884 overseen by Professional Photographers of Canada
Mission: To provide an educational, business & creative environment for professional photographers & with the purpose of promoting the highest standard of personal & creative excellence within the craft
Member of: Professional Photographers of America
Chief Officer(s):
Robert Nowell, President
robertnowell@cogeco.ca
Tanya Thompson, Executive Director
exec.director@ppoc.ca
Finances: *Funding Sources:* Membership fees; advertising; donations
Membership: *Member Profile:* Professional photographer
Activities: *Speaker Service:* Yes; *Library:* PPO Library

Professional Photographers of Canada 1970 Incorporated (PPOC) / Photographes Professionnels du Canada

209 Light St., Woodstock ON N4S 6H6
Tel: 519-537-2555; *Fax:* 519-537-5573
Toll-Free: 888-643-7762
www.ppoc.ca
Previous Name: Commercial & Press Photographers Association of Canada (CAPPAC)
Overview: A medium-sized national organization founded in 1946
Mission: To promote excellence in professional imaging; To elevate professional standards & ethics; To act as a voice for the photographic profession on legal matters & legislative issues
Affliation(s): Professional Photographers Association of British Columbia (PPABC); Professional Photographers of Canada Alberta (PPOC-AB); Professional Photographers of Saskatchewan (PPOC-SK); Professional Photographers of Canada Manitoba (PPOC-MB); Professional Photographers of Ontario (PPO); Corporation des Maîtres Photographes du Québec (CMPQ); Professional Photographers of Canada Atlantic (PPOC-Atlantic); Professional Government Military Photographers of Canada (PGMPC)
Chief Officer(s):
Tanya Thompson, Executive Director, 888-643-7762, Fax: 519-537-5573
exec.director@ppoc.ca
Chris Stambaugh, President, 780-452-0293, Fax: 780-452-0293
president@ppoc.ca
Brian Boyle, Vice-President
vicepresident@ppoc.ca
John Beesley, Corporate Secretary
secretary@ppoc.ca
Cam Colclough, Corporate Treasurer
treasurer@ppoc.ca
Membership: *Committees:* Accreditation; Archives; Bylaws; Convention Procedures Manual; Copyright; eContact; Education Project; Estimating Manual; Exhibition; Image Salon; Social Media; Speaker Registry; Student Program; Public Awareness; National Convention; Trade Liaison
Activities: Liaising with government agencies; Offering educational opportunities, such as seminars & practical workshops; Providing an accreditation program for members to earn an accreditation in a specific field; Facilitating networking opportunities; Offering annual print competitions; Providing a help line for photographers' questions in areas such as technical information; *Speaker Service:* Yes
Meetings/Conferences: • Professional Photographers of Canada 2015 46th Canadian Imaging Conference & Trade Show, April, 2015, Sheraton Inn on the Falls, Niagara Falls, ON
Scope: National
Description: An opportunity for the exchange of professional ideas
Contact Information: URL: conference.ppoc.ca
Publications:
• Convention Procedures Manual
Type: Manual; *Editor:* Carmen Matthews, MPA, F.
• Professional Photographers of Canada Magazine
Type: Magazine; *Frequency:* Bimonthly
Profile: Educational information & changing trends in photography

Professional Photographers of Québec *Voir* Photographes professionnels du Québec

Professional Property Managers Association Inc. (PPMA)

PO Box 2279, Stn. Main, Winnipeg MB R3C 4A6
Tel: 204-957-1224; *Fax:* 204-957-1239
info@ppmamanitoba.com
www.ppmamanitoba.com
Overview: A small provincial organization founded in 1984
Mission: To improve & advance the standards of the professional property management industry in Manitoba
Affliation(s): Canadian Federation of Apartment Associations
Chief Officer(s):
Shirley Tillett, Executive Director
Mario Lopes, President
Finances: *Funding Sources:* Membership dies

13 volunteer(s)
Membership: 74 principal; 134 associates; *Fees:* $400 associate; maximum $1200 principal; *Committees:* Awards; Education; Energy & Environmental; Ethics; Golf; Membership; Political Action; Program; Public Relations; Robert L. Simpson Memorial Scholarship; Safety & Security; Social; Trade Show & Conference
Activities: Monthly membership meetings; annual conference & trade show; annual golf tournament
Awards:
- Member of the Year (Award)
- Associate Member of the Year (Award)
- Caretaker of the Year (Award)
- Community Service Lifetime Achievement (Award)
- Robert L. Simpson Memorial Scholarship Fund (Scholarship)

Deadline: June *Amount:* $1,000

Professional Student Services Personnel (PSSP) / Personnel professionnel des services aux étudiants
PSSP Bargaining Unit Office, 1501 Danforth Ave., Toronto ON M4J 5C3
Tel: 647-348-3351; *Fax:* 647-348-3352
pssp.on.ca
Overview: A small local organization
Chief Officer(s):
Olga DeMelo, President
president@pssp.on.ca

Professional Surveyors Canada / Géomètres professionnels du Canada
#303, 1390 Prince of Wales Dr., Ottawa ON K2C 3N6
Tel: 613-695-8333
www.psc-gpc.ca/surveyors
Overview: A medium-sized national organization
Mission: To foster cooperation amongst surveyors in Canada; To advocate for an integrated Canadian surveying profession
Chief Officer(s):
Sarah Cornett, BSc, OLS, Executive Director

Professional Union of Government of Québec Physicians (Ind.) ***Voir*** Syndicat professionnel des médecins du gouvernement du Québec (ind.)

Professional Writers Association of Canada (PWAC)
#130, 215 Spadina Ave., Toronto ON M5T 2C7
Tel: 416-504-1645
info@pwac.ca
www.pwac.ca
Previous Name: Periodical Writers Association of Canada
Overview: A small national organization founded in 1976
Mission: To protect & promote interests of periodical writers in Canada; to develop & maintain professional standards in editor/writer relationships by instituting use of standard publication agreement in all freelance assignments; to improve quality of periodical writing in Canada; to work actively for survival of periodical writing in a highly competitive communications market; to lobby for higher standard fees for freelance magazine & newspaper writing; to mediate grievances between writers & editors; to provide professional development workshops; to lobby for freedom of press & expression; to offset isolation of freelance writers by circulating news, information on market
Chief Officer(s):
Michelle Greysen, President
michellegreysen@gmail.com
Sandy Crawley, Executive Director
Staff Member(s): 2
Membership: *Fees:* Scale; *Committees:* Communications; Finance & Fundraising; Government Action; Industry Relations; Membership Services & Development; National Conferences; Nominations & Awards; Professional Development Task Force
Activities: *Library*

Professionnels en produits promotionnels du Canada ***See*** Promotional Product Professionals of Canada Inc.

Programme Action Réfugiés Montréal (ARM) / Refugee Action Montreal
#2, 1439 rue Sainte-Catherine ouest, Montréal QC H3H 2L7
Tel: 514-935-7799; *Fax:* 514-935-9848
info@actionr.org
www.actionr.org
Overview: A small international charitable organization founded in 1994
Mission: Nous offrons des services qui permettent aux réfugiés de faire valoir leur droit d'asile et de refaire leur vie dans un nouveau milieu.
Member of: Canadian Council for Refugees; Table de Concertation des organismes de refugiés de Montréal
Chief Officer(s):
Glynis Williams, Director
Finances: *Annual Operating Budget:* $100,000-$250,000; *Funding Sources:* Anglican Diocese of Montreal; Presbyterian Church in Canada
Staff Member(s): 3; 40 volunteer(s)
Membership: 1-99
Activities: Parrainage; accompagnement; amitié-jumelage; intervention auprès des personnes détenues; *Library*

Programme d'aide aux membres du barreau (PAMBA)
#003, 315, boul. René-Lévesque Est, Montréal QC H2X 3P3
Tél: 514-286-0931
Ligne sans frais: 800-747-2622
aide@pamba.info
www.barreau.qc.ca
Aperçu: *Dimension:* petite; *Envergure:* provinciale; fondée en 1996
Mission: Pour aider les membres du Barreau du Québec qui souffrent de toxicomanie et de problèmes de santé mentale
Membre(s) du bureau directeur:
François Lajoie, Président, Conseil d'administraion
Membre: *Critères d'admissibilite:* Membres du Barreau du Québec; Les conjoints des membres du Barreau; Étudiants d l'École du Barreau

Programme Parents-Secours du Canada inc. ***See*** Block Parent Program of Canada Inc.

Progressive Canadian Party / Parti Progressiste Canadien
#200, 730 Davis Dr., Newmarket ON L3Y 2R4
Tel: 905-853-8949; *Fax:* 905-853-7214
info@pcparty.org
progressivecanadian.ca
Overview: A small national organization
Chief Officer(s):
Sinclair M. Stevens, Leader
Staff Member(s): 5
Membership: *Fees:* $10

Progressive Conservative Association of Alberta
PC Alberta Edmonton Office, #120 12420 - 104 Ave. NW, Edmonton AB T5N 3Z9
Tel: 780-423-1624; *Fax:* 780-423-1634
Toll-Free: 800-461-4443
Other Communication: www.flickr.com/photos/pc_alberta
pcalta@albertapc.ab.ca
www.albertapc.ab.ca
www.facebook.com/pc.alberta
twitter.com/pc_alberta
www.youtube.com/user/PCAlberta
Also Known As: PC Alberta
Overview: A large provincial organization
Mission: To assist in nominating & supporting Progressive Conservative canadidates in Alberta provincial elections; To promote the Progressive Conservative Association of Alberta
Chief Officer(s):
Jim Prentice, Party Leader
Terri Beaupre, President
Courtney Day, Secretary
Ron Renaud, Treasurer
Finances: *Funding Sources:* Membership purchases; Donations
Membership: *Member Profile:* Members in good standing of Provincial Progressive Conservative Constituency Associations in Alberta; Members in good standing of the Progressive Conservative Youth of Alberta

Calgary Office
#340, 999 - 8th St. SW, Calgary AB T2K 1E2
Tel: 403-244-8528; *Fax:* 403-228-1915
Toll-Free: 800-263-3408

Progressive Conservative Association of Prince Edward Island
PO Box 578, 30 Pond St., #B, Charlottetown PE C1A 7L1
Tel: 902-628-8679; *Fax:* 902-628-6428
Toll-Free: 800-859-4221
info@peipcparty.ca
peipcparty.ca
www.facebook.com/peipcparty
twitter.com/PEIPCParty
Also Known As: PEI PC Party
Overview: A small provincial organization
Mission: To form a government that is socially progressive
Chief Officer(s):
Steven Myers, Party Leader
Membership: *Fees:* $5 senior/youth; $10 individual; $25 family; *Member Profile:* Citizens of Prince Edward Island age 14 and older

Progressive Conservative Party of Canada, Canadian Alliance Party; Canadian Conservative Reform Alliance ***See*** Conservative Party of Canada

Progressive Conservative Party of Manitoba
23 Kennedy St., Winnipeg MB R3C 1S5
Tel: 204-942-8283; *Fax:* 204-943-1706
Toll-Free: 800-663-8679
pcmanitoba@pcmanitoba.com
www.pcmanitoba.com
www.facebook.com/BrianPallister
twitter.com/PC_Party_Of_MB
Also Known As: PC Manitoba
Overview: A small provincial organization
Chief Officer(s):
Brian Pallister, Party Leader
Staff Member(s): 5

Progressive Conservative Party of New Brunswick / Le Parti Progressiste-Conservateur de Nouveau-Brunswick
336 Regent St., Fredericton NB E3B 3X4
Tel: 506-453-3456; *Fax:* 506-444-4713
Other Communication: www.scribd.com/PCNBCA
info@pcng.org
www.pcnb.ca
www.facebook.com/PremierAlward
twitter.com/pcnbca
www.youtube.com/pcnbtv
Overview: A large provincial organization
Chief Officer(s):
Bruce Fitch, Interim Leader
J.P. Soucy, Executive Director, 506-453-3456
jp.soucy@pcnb.org
Staff Member(s): 15
Membership: 55 institutional; 20,000 individual; *Fees:* $5

Progressive Conservative Party of Saskatchewan
72 High St. East, Moose Jaw SK S6H 0B8
Tel: 306-693-7572; *Fax:* 306-693-7580
www.pcsask.ca
Also Known As: PC Saskatchewan
Overview: A small provincial organization
Chief Officer(s):
Rick Swenson, Party Leader
Staff Member(s): 5

Progressive Housing Society
7836 - 6th St., Burnaby BC V3N 3N2
Tel: 604-522-9669; *Fax:* 604-522-4081
info@progressivehousing.net
www.progressivehousing.net
www.facebook.com/pages/Progressive-Housing-Society/219395788150763
twitter.com/PHS604
Overview: A small local organization
Chief Officer(s):
Jaye Robertson, Executive Director
jrobertson@progressivehousing.net

Progressive Nationalist Party of British Columbia
PO Box 2577, Vanderhoof BC V0J 3A0
Tel: 250-567-4875
Also Known As: Progressive Nationalist
Previous Name: Bloc British Columbia Party
Overview: A small provincial organization founded in 2004
Mission: A platform of independence for British Columbia.
Chief Officer(s):
Brian Taylor, Party Leader
Patrick Roberts, Contact
tyroberts@omineca.com

Project 10 ***Voir*** Projet 10

Project Adult Literacy Society (PALS)
#41, 9912 - 106 St., Edmonton AB T5K 1C5
Tel: 780-424-5514; *Fax:* 780-425-5176
www.facebook.com/pages/Project-Adult-Literacy-Society-PALS/13151384635
Also Known As: PALS
Overview: A small local charitable organization founded in 1979

Mission: To offer literacy programs for adults in Edmonton
Affliation(s): Laubach Literacy of Canada
Chief Officer(s):
Shirley Sandul, Executive Director
Activities: Offering ESL, literacy, & math tutoring & classes

Project Chance
3950, boul Cavendish, Montréal QC H4B 2N3
Tel: 514-934-6199
Overview: A small local organization
Mission: To offer social housing for single mothers, from ages 18 to 30, who are pursuing full-time post-secondary education
Activities: Providing parenting workshops, a food bank, & after-school programs

Project Genesis
4735 Côte-Ste-Catherine Rd., Montréal QC H3W 1M1
Tel: 514-738-2036; *Fax:* 514-738-6385
genese.qc.ca
Overview: A small local organization
Mission: Community group that provides community organization, advocacy, and education, as well as legal advice involving tenant rights, debt & bankruptcy, family law, and immigration
Chief Officer(s):
Michael Chervin, Executive Director
Staff Member(s): 16

Project Peacemakers
745 Westminster Ave., Winnipeg MB R3G 1A5
Tel: 204-775-8178; *Fax:* 204-784-1339
info@projectpeacemakers.org
www.projectpeacemakers.org
www.facebook.com/pages/project-peacemakers/108617822532248
twitter.com/ProjectPeacmkrs
www.youtube.com/user/peacemakers
Overview: A small international charitable organization founded in 1983 overseen by Project Ploughshares
Mission: Project Peacemakers is a group of people working for peace from a faith perspective. Its activities are varied, from peace delegations in war zones to educational forums on such issues as child soldiers & violent video games.
Member of: Project Ploughshares
Affiliation(s): Canadian Centre for Arms Control & Disarmament; Manitoba Environmental Network; Mennonite Central Committee; Peace Alliance Winnipeg; Manitoba Japanese-Canadian Citizens Association
Chief Officer(s):
Dianne Cooper, Chair
Finances: *Annual Operating Budget:* Less than $50,000; *Funding Sources:* Member donations; church grants
Staff Member(s): 2; 30 volunteer(s)
Membership: 200; *Fees:* $25 one year; $40 two years; $8 low income
Activities: Concerts; film festivals; protests; witness-for-peace delegations; forums; *Speaker Service:* Yes; *Library* Open to public
Publications:
- Peace Projections

Type: Newsletter; *Frequency:* Quarterly

Project Ploughshares
57 Erb St. West, Waterloo ON N2L 6C2
Tel: 519-888-6541; *Fax:* 519-888-0018
plough@ploughshares.ca
www.ploughshares.ca
Overview: A medium-sized international organization founded in 1976
Mission: Ecumenical peace agency of the Canadian Council of Churches that identifies, develops & advances approaches that build peace & prevent war
Member of: Canadian Council for International Cooperation; Canadian Centre for Philanthropy
Affiliation(s): Canadian Council of Churches; Conrad Grebel College
Chief Officer(s):
John Siebert, Executive Director, 519-888-6541 Ext. 702
jsiebert@ploughshares.ca
Finances: *Annual Operating Budget:* $1.5 Million-$3 Million; *Funding Sources:* Donations 46%; grants 44%; other 10%
Staff Member(s): 10; 10 volunteer(s)
Membership: 8 sponsor + 10,000 donor + 10 affiliated; *Member Profile:* Representatives from sponsoring churches
Activities: Research (collects & analyzes information on a wide range of issues related to militarism, security & development); publications; policy development & education (staff often serve as public speakers or media commentators & testify at parliamentary hearings) public conferences, workshops, works in Canada & internationally; *Internships:* Yes; *Speaker Service:* Yes; *Library* Open to public

Project READ Literacy Network Waterloo-Wellington (PRLN)
298 Frederick St., Kitchener ON N2H 2N6
Tel: 519-570-3054; *Fax:* 519-570-9510
info@projectread.ca
www.projectread.ca
www.facebook.com/ProjectREADLitNetwork?v=wall&ref=sgm
twitter.com/ProjectREADWW
Overview: A small local charitable organization founded in 1988
Mission: To provide coordination, advocacy, referrals & support to & for literacy, literacy providers & students; to enhance the effective & efficient provision of literacy services to meet the needs in Waterloo-Wellington
Member of: Kitchener-Waterloo Chamber of Commerce; Ontario Literacy Coalition; Movement for Canadian Literacy
Affliation(s): Ontario Literacy Coalition
Chief Officer(s):
Anne Ramsay, Executive Network Director
Finances: *Annual Operating Budget:* $100,000-$250,000; *Funding Sources:* National government; provincial government; donations
Staff Member(s): 4; 14 volunteer(s)
Membership: 35; *Fees:* $60 institutional; $15 individual; *Member Profile:* Organizations & individuals concerned with literacy in the community; *Committees:* Waterloo Literacy Services Planning Committee; Wellington Literacy Services Planning Committee
Activities: Public awareness; information & referral to literacy programs; literacy assessments; professional development of literacy workers; literacy service planning; *Awareness Events:* International Literacy Day, Sept. 8; Family Literacy Day, Jan. 27; *Speaker Service:* Yes; *Library:* PRLN Literacy Resources Library; Open to public

Project Share
#2, 4129 Stanley Ave., Niagara Falls ON L2E 7H3
Tel: 905-357-5121; *Fax:* 905-357-0143
info@projectshare.ca
www.projectshare.ca
www.facebook.com/pages/Project-S-H-A-R-E/136606766416948
twitter.com/P_SHARE
www.youtube.com/user/PSHAREofNiagara?feature=mhee
Overview: A small local charitable organization founded in 1991
Mission: To assist these residents of Niagara Falls who live below the poverty line with basic needs in a proactive manner
Member of: Ontario Association of Food Banks
Affiliation(s): Canadian Association of Food Banks
Chief Officer(s):
Elaine Harvey, Executive Director
Finances: *Annual Operating Budget:* $250,000-$500,000; *Funding Sources:* City of Niagara Falls; United Way; provincial government; donations
Staff Member(s): 12; 240 volunteer(s)
Activities: Subsidy programs; food bank; clothing; community garden; transportation; workshops

Projet 10 / Project 10
1575, rue Amherst, Montréal QC H2L 3L4
Tél: 514-989-0001
questions@p10.qc.ca
www.p10.qc.ca
www.facebook.com/P10montreal
Aperçu: *Dimension:* petite; *Envergure:* locale
Mission: Ligne d'entraide anonyme et confidentielle; services pour les jeunes lesbiennes, gais, bisexuel(le)s, intersexuel(le)s, allosexuel(le)s, trans, et bispirituel(le)s
Membre(s) du bureau directeur:
Remy Attig, Co-coordinatrice
remy@p10.qc.ca
Sarah Butler, Co-coordinatrice
sarah@p10.qc.ca
Membre(s) du personnel: 2

Le Projet Faim ***See*** **The Hunger Project Canada**

Projet Prométhée / Prometheus Project Inc.
Grands Frères Grandes Sours du Grand Montré, #300, 3740, rue de Berri, Montréal QC H2L 4G9
Tél: 514-842-9715; *Téléc:* 514-842-2454
info@gfgsmtl.qc.ca
www.gfgsmtl.qc.ca
www.facebook.com/108357135855036
Également appelé: Les Jeunes Associés; Fondation québécoise des jeunes associés en éducation
Aperçu: *Dimension:* petite; *Envergure:* provinciale; Organisme sans but lucratif; fondée en 1992
Mission: Notre mandat est d'utiliser le temps et les efforts de jeunes bénévoles, professionnels, entrepreneurs et universitaires, afin d'appuyer et de motiver des élèves du secondaire à risque de décrocher
Finances: *Budget de fonctionnement annuel:* $50,000-$100,000
Membre(s) du personnel: 1; 70 bénévole(s)
Membre: *Critères d'admissibilite:* Etre un professionnel ou étudiant universitaire; *Comités:* Exécutif
Activités: *Stagiaires:* Oui; *Service de conférenciers:* Oui

Projet T.R.I.P.
#2520, 2000, rue Pathenais, Montréal QC H2K 3S9
Tél: 514-596-5711; *Téléc:* 514-596-7722
projet_trip@yahoo.ca
projet-trip.org
Aperçu: *Dimension:* petite; *Envergure:* locale
Mission: Pour éviter les problèmes de toxicomanie entre les 12 à 20 ans dans le centre-sud de Montréal et de promouvoir une meilleure qualité de vie

Projets pour une agriculture écologique ***See*** **Ecological Agriculture Projects**

Prologue aux arts de la scène ***See*** **Prologue to the Performing Arts**

Prologue to the Performing Arts / Prologue aux arts de la scène
#201, 15 Case Goods Lane, Toronto ON M5A 3C4
Tel: 416-591-9092; *Fax:* 416-591-2023
Toll-Free: 888-591-9092
info@prologue.org
www.prologue.org
www.facebook.com/PrologueToThePerformingArts
Also Known As: Prologue
Overview: A small local charitable organization founded in 1966
Mission: To bring diverse performing art experiences into schools & communities
Affiliation(s): BC Touring Council; Festival Events Ontario; CAPACOA
Chief Officer(s):
Patty Jarvis, Executive Director
Sue Daniel, Chair
Finances: *Annual Operating Budget:* $1.5 Million-$3 Million; *Funding Sources:* Ontario Arts Council; City of Toronto; Canada Council
Staff Member(s): 6; 16 volunteer(s)
Membership: 1-99; *Fees:* $25 institutional; *Committees:* Program; Fundraising; Marketing
Activities: Prologue showcases
Awards:
- Lieutenant Governor's Award (Award)
- Paula Award (Award)

To enable a work for young audiences by one or more Prologue artists and companies to be brought to completion.

Prometheus Project Inc. ***Voir*** **Projet Prométhée**

Promoting Awareness of RSD & CRPS in Canada (PARC)
PO Box 21026, St Catharines ON L2M 7X2
Tel: 905-934-0261
www.rsdcanada.org/parc
Also Known As: PARC
Overview: A small national charitable organization
Mission: To support persons with CRPS, type 1 & 2 (Reflex Sympathetic Dystrophy & Causalgia), their families, & medical professionals who treat CRPS
Finances: *Funding Sources:* Donations
Membership: *Fees:* $35 deluxe memberships; $25 regular memberships
Activities: Providing education & information for persons with CRPS, the public, & the health care community; Funding research; Organizing support groups
Publications:
- PARC Pearl

Type: Newsletter; *Frequency:* Quarterly
Profile: Articles by professionals, latest research, coping techniques, resources, & upcoming conferences

ProMOTION Plus
#301, 470 Granville St., Vancouver BC V6C 1V5

Tel: 604-333-3475; *Fax:* 604-629-2651
info@promotionplus.org
www.promotionplus.org
Overview: A small provincial organization founded in 1990
Mission: To promote equity & opportunity for British Columbian women in sport.
Affliation(s): Sport BC
Chief Officer(s):
Bryna Kopelow, Chair
Stephanie Marshall-White, Coordinator
Communications & Events
Finances: *Funding Sources:* BC Ministry of Community; Sport & Cultural Development; 2010 Legacies Now; BC Gaming Commission; Government of Canada
Membership: *Fees:* $20 students; $35 adults; $75 organizations

Promotional Product Professionals of Canada Inc. / Professionnels en produits promotionnels du Canada

#100, 6700, Côte-de-Liesse, Saint-Laurent QC H4T 2B5
Tel: 514-489-5359; *Fax:* 514-489-7760
Toll-Free: 866-450-7722
info@pppc.ca
www.pppc.ca
twitter.com/PPPCInc
Also Known As: PPPC
Previous Name: Promotional Products Association of Canada; Specialty Advertising Association of Canada; Specialty Advertising Counselors of Canada
Overview: A medium-sized national organization founded in 1956
Mission: To advance the promotional products industry; To act as the voice of the predominant advertising medium in Canada
Affliation(s): Canadian Professional Sales Association (CPSA); Incentive Marketing Association (IMA); National Advertising Benevolent Society (NABS)
Chief Officer(s):
Edward Ahad, President & Chief Executive Officer
ed@pppc.ca
Chantal Fontaine, Director, Professional Development & Certification
chantal@pppc.ca
Carol Phillips, Director, Publications
carol@pppc.ca
Marc C. Phillips, Director, Information Technology
marc@pppc.ca
Debbie Pinkerton, Director, Member Services
debbie@pppc.ca
Linda Sloan, Manager, Events
linda@pppc.ca
Staff Member(s): 12
Membership: 1,700+; *Member Profile:* Suppliers; Distributors; *Committees:* Publications & Advertising; Marketing & Industry Awareness; Awards; Education & Certification; Events; Premium & Incentives: Member Relations; Information Technology; Finance & Administration; Governance
Activities: Providing seminars & workshops for members, which lead to industry professional certifications; Offering online education towards Certified Advertising Specialist (CAS) & Master Advertising Specialist (MAS) certification; *Speaker Service:* Yes
Awards:
• Promotional Product Professionals of Canada Image Award (Award)
To recognize the most creative campaigns using promotional products & programs by distributor & supplier member companies *Contact:* Gladys Kasp, Director, Awards Committee, E-mail: gladys@pppc.ca
• Promotional Product Professionals of Canada Distributor of the Year (Award)
• Promotional Product Professionals of Canada Supplier of the Year (Award)
• Promotional Product Professionals of Canada Supplier Customer Service Representative of the Year (Award)
• Promotional Product Professionals of Canada Supplier Sales Representative of the Year (Award)
• Promotional Product Professionals of Canada Distributor Sales Representative of the Year (Award)
• Promotional Product Professionals of Canada Multi-Line Agency of the Year (Award)
• Promotional Product Professionals of Canada Best Catalogue of the Year (Award)
• Promotional Product Professionals of Canada Best Website of the Year (Award)
• Promotional Product Professionals of Canada Scholarship / Bursary (Scholarship)
Eligibility: A member's employees or family members *Contact:* Gladys Kasp, Director, Awards Committee, E-mail: gladys@pppc.ca
Meetings/Conferences: • Promotional Product Professionals of Canada 2015 National Convention, January, 2015, Metro Toronto Convention Centre, South Building, Toronto, ON
Scope: National
Description: Educational seminars, business meetings, roundtable discussions, networking events, plus a trade show with over 600 exhibitors
Contact Information: Events Coordinator: Mara Welch, E-mail: shows@pppc.ca
• Promotional Product Professionals of Canada 2016 National Convention, 2016
Scope: National
Description: Educational seminars, business meetings, roundtable discussions, networking events, plus a trade show with over 600 exhibitors
Contact Information: Events Coordinator: Mara Welch, E-mail: shows@pppc.ca
Publications:
• Idea Book
Type: Yearbook; *Frequency:* Annually; *Editor:* Carol Phillips
Profile: Promotional product ideas from suppliers, for distributors
• PPPC Weekly
Type: Newsletter; *Frequency:* Weekly; *Editor:* Carol Phillips;
Price: Free with Promotioanl Product Professionals of Canada membership
Profile: News & updates for more than 5,000 recipients
• Promotional Product Professionals of Canada Membership Directory
Type: Directory; *Frequency:* Annually; *Editor:* Carol Phillips;
Price: Free with Promotioanl Product Professionals of Canada membership
Profile: A roster of current members in Canada & the United States, with contact information, product listings, sales policies, supplieradvertisements & associaiton information
• promoVantage
Type: Magazine; *Frequency:* Quarterly; *Editor:* Carol Phillips
Profile: Promotion of the industry, targeting 10,000+ potential buyers
• promoXpert
Type: Magazine; *Accepts Advertising*; *Editor:* Carol Phillips;
Price: Free with Promotioanl Product Professionals of Canada membership
Profile: Articles & sales aids for members' sales forces

Promotional Products Association of Canada; Specialty Advertising Association of Canada; Specialty Advertising Counselors of Canada *See* Promotional Product Professionals of Canada Inc.

Property Owners League of Montréal *Voir* Ligue des propriétaires de Montréal

Prospect Human Services

915 - 33 St. NE, Calgary AB T2A 6T2
Tel: 403-273-2822; *Fax:* 403-273-0090
info@prospectnow.ca
www.prospectnow.ca
Previous Name: Rehabilitation Society of Calgary
Overview: A small local organization
Mission: To identify situations where groups face challenges with full participation; To develop services & supports for individuals & employers
Chief Officer(s):
Melanie Mitra, Chief Executive Officer
Activities: Providing work search resources & strategies; Offering employment placement supports for persons having difficulty finding a job due to mental health illness or issues; Providing support to individuals with disabilities to obtain & maintain paid employment;

Prospectors & Developers Association of Canada (PDAC) / Association canadienne des prospecteurs & entrepreneurs

135 King St. East, Toronto ON M5C 1G6
Tel: 416-362-1969; *Fax:* 416-362-0101
info@pdac.ca
www.pdac.ca
Overview: A medium-sized national organization founded in 1932
Mission: To protect & promote the interests of the Canadian mineral exploration & development sector
Chief Officer(s):
Ross Gallinger, Executive Director
rgallinger@pdac.ca
Lisa J. McDonald, Chief Operations Officer
lmcdonald@pdac.ca
Philip Bousquet, Senior Program Director, Finance & Taxation & Securities
pbousquet@pdac.ca
Sheriden Barnett, Program Director, Land Use Planning & Resource Development
sbarnett@pdac.ca
Scott Cavan, Program Director, Aboriginal Affairs
scavan@pdac.ca
Nicole Sampson, Director, Convention
nsampson@pdac.ca
Steve Virtue, Director, Communications
svirtue@pdac.ca
Lesley Williams, Program Manager, Advvocacy & Issues Management
lwilliams@pdac.ca
Florence MacLeod, Coordinator, Membership
fmacleod@pdac.ca
Finances: *Funding Sources:* Membership fees
Membership: 6,000 individuals + 950 corporate members; *Member Profile:* Individuals, such as professional geoscientists, mining executives, prospectors, developers; geological consultants, & those working in the drilling, financial, investment, legal, & other related fields; Students; Corporate members, such as producing companies, junior non-producing exploration companies, & non-mining companies; *Committees:* Aboriginal Affairs; Audit; Awards; Convention Planning; Corporate Social Responsibility; Education; Environment; Executive; Finance & Taxation; Geosciences; Health & Safety; Human Resources Development; International; Lands & Regulations; Membership; Nomination; Public Affairs, Securities
Activities: Compiling statistics; Providing information; Offering continuing education; Engaging in advocacy activities; Providing networking opportunities; *Speaker Service:* Yes
Meetings/Conferences: • Prospectors & Developers Association of Canada (PDAC) 2015 83rd International Convention, Trade Show, & Investors Exchange Mining Investment Show, March, 2015, Metro Toronto Convention Centre, Toronto, ON
Scope: International
Attendance: 30,300+
Description: A four day event that attracts more than 1,000 exhibitors & attendees from 125 countries to participate in short courses, technical sessions, & networking opportunities
Contact Information: Director, Convention: Nicole Sampson, Phone: 416-362-1969, ext. 226, E-mail: nsampson@pdac.ca
Publications:
• Communiqué [a publication of the Prospectors & Developers Association of Canada]
Frequency: Irregular
Profile: Each occasional publication deals with a particular topic related to exploration & development
• Exploration & Development Highlights
Type: Yearbook; *Frequency:* Annually
Profile: Articles about exploration & development activities in each Canadian province & territory distributed to all members
• News & Activities [a publication of the Prospectors & Developers Association of Canada]
Type: Newsletter; *Frequency:* Monthly
Profile: Association activities & events of interest to members
• PDAC [Prospectors & Developers Association of Canada] Activities
Type: Yearbook; *Frequency:* Annually
Profile: Summary of the association's work distributed to all members
• PDAC [Prospectors & Developers Association of Canada] in Brief
Type: Newsletter; *Frequency:* Quarterly; *Editor:* Cameron Ainsworth-Vincze
Profile: Information about the association's activities for members

Prosserman Jewish Community Centre

4588 Bathurst St., Toronto ON M2R 1W6
Tel: 416-638-1881; *Fax:* 416-636-5813
www.prossermanjcc.com
www.facebook.com/theprossermanjcc
twitter.com/prossermanjcc
Previous Name: Bathurst Jewish Community Centre
Overview: A small local organization
Mission: To provide social, educational, cultural, health and wellness programs rooted in Jewish values, and offers a variety

of facilities & courses, including: fitness centre, culinary arts studio, media studio, courses in visual arts, dance, music, Jewish learning program, day camps, daycare.
Chief Officer(s):
Jennifer Appleby-Goosen, Program Director
jennifer@srcentre.ca
Staff Member(s): 27
Membership: *Fees:* $45 senior; $50 single; $100 family

Prostate Cancer Research Foundation of Canada (PCRFC) / Fondation canadienne de recherche sur le cancer de la prostate
#306, 145 Front St. East, Toronto ON M5A 1E3
Tel: 416-441-2131; *Fax:* 416-441-2325
Toll-Free: 888-255-0333
info@prostatecancer.ca
www.prostatecancer.ca
www.facebook.com/prostatecancercanada
twitter.com/ProstateCancerC
www.youtube.com/ProstateCancerCanada
Overview: A small national organization founded in 1997
Mission: To raise funds for research into the causes, cure & prevention of prostate cancer by engaging Canadians through awareness, education, & advocacy
Member of: Prostate Cancer Alliance of Canada
Affliation(s): Canadian Urological Association
Chief Officer(s):
Donald McInnes, Chair
Helene Vassos, Interim President & CEO
Finances: *Annual Operating Budget:* $1.5 Million-$3 Million
Staff Member(s): 15; 100 volunteer(s)
Membership: 1-99
Activities: Green & White Gala; Fathers' Day Run & Family Picnic; Business breakfast; Movember; *Awareness Events:* National Prostate Cancer Awareness Week, 3rd. week in Sept.
Awards:
• Research Grants (Grant)

Prosthetics & Orthotics Association of British Columbia (POABC)
c/o Canadian Association for Prosthetics & Orthotics, #605, 294 Portage Ave., Winnipeg MB R3C 0B9
www.poabc.ca
Overview: A small provincial organization founded in 1974 overseen by Canadian Association for Prosthetics & Orthotics
Mission: To promote quality patient care & professionalism in the field of prosthetics & orthotics in British Columbia
Chief Officer(s):
James Tarrant, President
Lisa Bennett, Vice-President
Corey Kennedy, Treasurer
Membership: *Member Profile:* Individuals in British Columbia involved in the prosthetic & orthotic field
Activities: Representing members throughout British Columbia; Encouraging continuring education for members

Protected Areas Association of Newfoundland & Labrador (PAA)
PO Box 1027, Stn. C, St. John's NL A1C 5M5
Tel: 709-726-2603; *Fax:* 709-726-2764
www.paanl.org
Overview: A small provincial charitable organization founded in 1989
Mission: To promote the establishment of a provincial network of reserves that preserve representative portions of all eco-regions & protect biodiversity; To promote sound ecological practices that support sustainable development
Member of: Newfoundland & Labrador Environment Network
Affliation(s): World Wildlife Fund Canada; Canadian Parks & Wilderness Society
Chief Officer(s):
Ruth French, Development & Outreach Coordinator
rfrench@nf.aibn.com
Finances: *Annual Operating Budget:* $100,000-$250,000
Staff Member(s): 4; 45 volunteer(s)
Membership: 500; *Fees:* $20 individual; *Member Profile:* People interested in conservation of nature, wilderness; *Committees:* Lac Joseph-Atikonak; Main River
Activities: Issue-related public meetings; *Awareness Events:* Benefit Concert, Nov.

Protestant Children's Home *See* Family Day Care Services (Toronto)

Provancher Society of Natural History of Canada *Voir* Société Provancher d'histoire naturelle du Canada

Province of Québec Rifle Association (PQRA) / Association de tir de la province de Québec (ATPQ)
973, rue Turcotte Est, Thetford Mines QC G1J 5K3
e-mail: info@pqra.org
www.pqra.org
twitter.com/atpq
Overview: A small provincial organization founded in 1869
Mission: To promote marksmanship training & competition especially at long range; To provide extensive cadet program; To organize & run cadet provincial championships
Member of: Dominion of Canada Rifle Association; Shooting Federation of Canada
Chief Officer(s):
Robert Fortier, President
Finances: *Funding Sources:* Membership fees
Activities: Long Range Target Shooting; Black Powder Long Range; Service Rifle Matches; Cadet Shooting Programs

Provincial Administrators of Volunteer Resources Ontario (PAVR-O)
#5, 22 Millwood Rd., Toronto ON M4S 1J7
Tel: 705-654-3261
pavro@pavro.on.ca
www.pavro.on.ca
Merged from: Ontario Association for Volunteer Administration; Ontario Directors of Volunteers in Healthcare
Overview: A small provincial organization founded in 1988
Affliation(s): Ontario Directors of Volunteers in Hospitals
Chief Officer(s):
Erin Spink, President
Judy Amyotte, Administrative Assistant
Finances: *Annual Operating Budget:* $50,000-$100,000; *Funding Sources:* Membership dues; fundraising; conference
20 volunteer(s)
Membership: 276; *Fees:* $84.75 student; $115.26 supporter & organization; $172.89 individual; *Member Profile:* Must be an administrator of volunteers
Activities: *Speaker Service:* Yes
Publications:
• PAVR-O [Professional Administrators of Volunteer Resources] Powerline
Type: Newsletter; *Frequency:* Monthly; *Price:* Free with membership in PAVR-O

The Provincial Agricultural Fairs Association *See* British Columbia Association of Agricultural Fairs & Exhibitions

Provincial Association of CBDCs *See* Atlantic Association of CBDCs

Provincial Association of Home Builders of Québec *Voir* Association provinciale des constructeurs d'habitations du Québec inc.

Provincial Association of Resort Communities of Saskatchewan (PARCS)
PO Box 52, Elbow SK S0H 1J0
Tel: 306-545-6253; *Fax:* 306-854-4412
parcs@sasktel.com
www.parcs-sk.com
Overview: A medium-sized provincial organization founded in 1986
Mission: To promote the interests of resort communities in Saskatchewan; To promote fair & equitable policies & procedures for all resort communities
Chief Officer(s):
Shirley Gange, President, 306-982-3311
hgange@sasktel.net
Lynne Saas, Contact, Member Servivces, 306-854-4658
parcs@sasktel.net
Finances: *Annual Operating Budget:* Less than $50,000; *Funding Sources:* Membership dues; grants
Staff Member(s): 2; 30 volunteer(s)
Membership: 200; *Fees:* $50-$550 active member; $200 associate; $100 affiliate; $25 individual
Activities: *Library* by appointment

The Provincial Autism Centre *See* Autism Nova Scotia

Provincial Black Basketball Association (PBBA)
PO Box 2702, Halifax NS B3J 3P7
Tel: 902-452-0682
pbba.blackbasketball@gmail.com
www.blackbasketball.ca
Overview: A medium-sized provincial organization founded in 1972
Mission: To promote basketball within the African Canadian community in Nova Scotia & across the country.
Membre(s) du bureau directeur:
Carl Gannon, President
gannoncs@eastlink.ca

Provincial Building & Construction Trades Council of Ontario
35 International Blvd., Toronto ON M9W 6H3
Tel: 416-679-8887; *Fax:* 416-679-8882
info@ontariobuildingtrades.com
www.ontariobuildingtrades.com
Also Known As: Provincial Building Trades Council
Overview: A medium-sized provincial organization founded in 1959
Affliation(s): International Foundation of Employee Benefit Plans - Building Trades Department
Chief Officer(s):
Patrick J. Dillon, Business Manager
Finances: *Annual Operating Budget:* $250,000-$500,000
Staff Member(s): 2
Membership: 100,000 union

Provincial CGIT Board of BC
c/o Janice Grinnell, 13780 Hill Rd., Ladysmith BC V9G 1G7
Tel: 250-245-4016
grinncon@nanaimo.ark.com
www.cgit.ca/index.htm
Also Known As: Canadian Girls in Training - BC
Previous Name: National CGIT Association - BC Provincial Board
Overview: A small provincial organization

Provincial Collective Bargaining Council *See* New Brunswick Nurses Union

Provincial Council of Women of Manitoba Inc. (PCWM)
#204, 825 Sherbrook Ave., Winnipeg MB R3A 1M5
Tel: 204-992-2751
pcwm@mts.net
pcwmanitoba.ca
Overview: A medium-sized provincial organization founded in 1949
Mission: To empower all women to work towards improving the quality of life for women, families & society through a forum of member organizations & individuals
Affliation(s): National Council of Women of Canada
Chief Officer(s):
Sharon Taylor, President
Finances: *Annual Operating Budget:* Less than $50,000
30 volunteer(s)
Membership: 28 institutional; 50 individual; *Fees:* $40 federate; $20 individual
Activities: Resolutions & briefs to the provincial government

Provincial Dental Board of Nova Scotia
#102, 1559 Brunswick St., Halifax NS B3J 2G1
Tel: 902-420-0083; *Fax:* 902-492-0301
admin@pdbns.ca
www.pdbns.ca
Overview: A small provincial licensing organization
Mission: To protect the public in the delivery of dental care by licensure & regulation
Chief Officer(s):
Martin Gillis, Registrar
Membership: *Committees:* Complaints; Discicpline; Mandatory Continuing Dental Education; Dental Practice Review

Provincial Exhibition of Manitoba
115 - 10th St., Brandon MB R7A 4E7
Tel: 204-726-3590; *Fax:* 204-725-0202
Toll-Free: 877-729-0001
info@brandonfairs.com
www.brandonfairs.com
www.facebook.com/provincial.exhibition
twitter.com/ProvincialEx
www.flickr.com/photos/provex/
Overview: A medium-sized provincial organization founded in 1882
Mission: To showcase agriculture; to link urban & rural regions through education & awareness while providing entertainment, community pride & economic enhancement to the region
Member of: Canadian Association of Fairs & Exhibitions
Chief Officer(s):
Ron Kristjansson, General Manager
ronkristjansson@brandonfairs.com

Darrell Hack, President
Staff Member(s): 8
Membership: *Fees:* $10; *Member Profile:* Shareholder
Awards:
• Royal Manitoba Winter Fair Awards (Award)
Prizes given in various categories for best of show for agricultural products, animals & crops; several equestrian events offer prizes for best in competition

Provincial Federation of Ontario Fire Fighters ***See*** Ontario Professional Fire Fighters Association

Provincial French Immersion & Francophone Programme Teachers' Association ***Voir*** Association Provinciale des Professeurs d'Immersion et du Programme Francophone

Provincial Health Ethics Network

Guardian Bldg., #507, 10240 - 124 St., Edmonton AB T5N 3W6
Tel: 780-447-1180; *Fax:* 780-447-1181
Toll-Free: 800-472-4066
middleton@phen.ab.ca
www.phen.ca
Overview: A small provincial organization
Mission: To provide resources on addressing ethical issues related to health; To facilitate informed & reasoned ethical decision-making
Chief Officer(s):
Amy Middleton, Programming Director
middleton@phen.ab.ca
Al-Noor Nenshi Nathoo, Executive Director
nathoo@phen.ab.ca
Staff Member(s): 5
Membership: 500; *Fees:* $0; *Member Profile:* Anyone interested in bioethics
Publications:
• Health Ethics Today
Type: Magazine; *Frequency:* Semiannually
Profile: Periodical covering bioethics topics
• PHEN Communiqué
Type: Newsletter; *Frequency:* Monthly
Profile: Regarding bioethics events & programs

Provincial Intermediate Teachers' Association

c/o South Slope Elementary School, 4446 Watling St., Burnaby BC V5J 5H3
Tel: 604-664-8300; *Fax:* 604-664-8308
rmyrtle@shaw.ca
www.pita.ca
www.facebook.com/108078755947920
Overview: A small provincial organization
Member of: BC Teachers' Federation
Chief Officer(s):
Elaine Jaltema, President
President@pita.ca
Membership: 1000; *Fees:* $15 TOC and Student Teacher; $35 BCTF Active Members; $57.50 Subscriber
Meetings/Conferences: • Provincial Intermediate Teachers' Association Annual Fall Conference, 2015
Scope: Provincial
• Provincial Intermediate Teachers' Association Annual Whistler Conference, 2015, Whistler, BC
Scope: Provincial

Provincial Medical Board of Nova Scotia ***See*** College of Physicians & Surgeons of Nova Scotia

Provincial Staff Nurses Committee ***See*** United Nurses of Alberta

Provincial Towing Association (Ontario) (PTAO)

65 Keith Rd., Bracebridge ON P1L 0A1
Tel: 705-646-0536; *Fax:* 705-645-0017
Toll-Free: 866-582-0855
www.ptao.org
www.facebook.com/234988159852788
Also Known As: Provincial Towing Association
Overview: A medium-sized provincial organization founded in 1998
Mission: To inform its members of revelant news regarding the industry; To set standards for its members; To represent its members at all levels of government
Chief Officer(s):
Doug Nelson, Executive Director
doug@ptao.org
Finances: *Annual Operating Budget:* $50,000-$100,000; *Funding Sources:* Membership dues
Staff Member(s): 2; 9 volunteer(s)
Membership: *Fees:* $350; *Member Profile:* Towing companies within Ontario
Activities: *Speaker Service:* Yes
Meetings/Conferences: • The Provincial Towing Association Annual Trade & Tow Show, 2015
Description: The Trade & Tow Show features training sessions, the PTAO general meeting, competitions & the awards banquet

Provincial Water Polo Association ***See*** Water Polo Nova Scotia

Provincial Women's Softball Association of Ontario (PWSAO)

c/o Registrar, 50 Capri St., Thorold ON L2V 4S8
Tel: 905-227-7574; *Fax:* 905-227-3574
info@ontariopwsa.com
www.ontariopwsa.ca
www.facebook.com/OntarioPWSA
twitter.com/OntarioPWSA
Overview: A medium-sized provincial organization founded in 1931 overseen by Softball Ontario
Mission: To support & advance women softball players in Ontario
Member of: Canadian Amateur Softball Association; Softball Ontario
Chief Officer(s):
Debbie Malisani, Chair & President, 905-564-3533
littlehands1@rogers.com
Debbie DeMoel, Registrar
jondeb50@cogeco.ca
Finances: *Funding Sources:* Sponsors; Partners; Government grants; Player/team fees
Membership: *Committees:* Annual General Meeting; Awards Banquet; Bids (Provincial/National); Canada Games/Talent ID; Draw Book; Eastern Canadian Liaison; Fundraising; Insurance (Associated Teams, Third Party & PWSA Teams); Rules & Constitution; Scholarship; Skills Camp; Travel Permits; House League Select; LTPD - Colour Your Dream

Provincial Youth Council ***Voir*** Conseil jeunesse provincial (Manitoba)

Provost & District Chamber of Commerce

PO Box 637, Provost AB T0B 3S0
Tel: 780-753-6643
provostchamberofcommerce@gmail.com
www.provost.ca/chamberofcommerce.html
Overview: A small local organization
Chief Officer(s):
Anne Fraser, Contact
Membership: *Fees:* $100

Psoriasis Society of Canada / Société psoriasis du Canada

National Office, PO Box 25015, Halifax NS B3M 4H4
Tel: 902-443-8680; *Fax:* 902-443-2073
Toll-Free: 800-656-4494
www.psoriasissociety.org
Overview: A medium-sized national charitable organization founded in 1983
Mission: To provide programs & services to people who suffer from psoriasis in Canada; to encourage formation of support groups where individual sufferers may share experiences & exchange information; to provide facts about psoriasis to medical community, general public & teaching profession; to promote & encourage research directed towards treatment & cure for psoriasis
Affiliation(s): International Federation of Psoriasis Associations
Chief Officer(s):
Judy Misner, President
judymisner@eastlink.ca
Finances: *Annual Operating Budget:* $50,000-$100,000; *Funding Sources:* Membership fees; donations
125 volunteer(s)
Membership: 12,000; *Fees:* $25, $35 outside of Canada; *Committees:* Fundraising; Volunteer
Activities: *Awareness Events:* National Psoriasis Awareness Month & Walk, Oct.

Psychological Association of Manitoba (PAM) / Association des psychologues du Manitoba

#253, 162-2025 Corydon Ave., Winnipeg MB R3P 0N5
Tel: 204-487-0784; *Fax:* 204-489-8688
pam@mymts.net
www.cpmb.ca
Overview: A small provincial licensing organization founded in 1966
Mission: To provide screening & examination of candidates &, if eligible, registration as a psychologist; to protect the public from fraudulent services & provide referral to & liaison with psychologists
Chief Officer(s):
John Arnett, President
Alan Slusky, Registrar
Finances: *Annual Operating Budget:* $50,000-$100,000
Membership: *Fees:* $985 psychologist; $605 associate; $180 candidate; $250 associate candidate; $425 out of province psychologists; $215 out of province associates; *Member Profile:* Psychologists practicing in Manitoba; *Committees:* Registration & Membership; Complaints; Inquiry; Examinations; Publications; Standards; Legislative Review

Psychological Association of Prince Edward Island (PAPEI)

www.peipsychology.org/papei
Overview: A small provincial organization
Chief Officer(s):
Nadine DeWolfe, Ph.D., President
Finances: *Funding Sources:* Membership fees; workshops
Membership: 20; *Fees:* $60
Awards:
• Elizabeth Fox Percival Papei Professional Award (Award)
• Papei Humanitarian Award (Award)

Psychologists Association of Alberta (PAA)

#103, 1207 - 91 St. SW, Edmonton AB T6X 1E9
Tel: 780-424-0294; *Fax:* 780-423-4048
Toll-Free: 888-424-0297
paa@psychologistsassociation.ab.ca
www.psychologistsassociation.ab.ca
www.facebook.com/169589246436220
Overview: A medium-sized provincial licensing organization founded in 1960
Mission: To enhance & promote the profession of psychology
Chief Officer(s):
David Piercy, President
Pierre Berube, Executive Director
pberube@psychologistsassociation.ab.ca
Staff Member(s): 5
Membership: *Fees:* $310 full; $95 provisional; $190 affiliate/out-of-province; $40 student; *Member Profile:* Registered psychologists & psychology students; *Committees:* Awards Adjudicating; Awards Nominating; Fees; Public Education; Psychologically Healthy Workplace; School Psychology; Continuing Education; Executive Director Evalution
Activities: *Rents Mailing List:* Yes
Meetings/Conferences: • Psychologists Association of Alberta Connect 2015, May, 2015, Cochrane, AB
Scope: Provincial

Psychology Association of Saskatchewan

PO Box 4528, Regina SK S4P 3W7
e-mail: info@psychsask.ca
psychsask.ca
twitter.com/PsychSask
Overview: A small provincial organization
Mission: To represent the interests of its members & to further & promote interest in psychology
Member of: Council of Provincial Associations of Psychologists
Chief Officer(s):
Kristi Wright, President
11 volunteer(s)
Membership: *Fees:* $95 full; $50 affiliate; $35 student; *Member Profile:* Registered psychologists & psychology students
Activities: Spring Institute & AGM
Awards:
• Jillings Award (Award)
• Student Research Award (Award)

Psychosocial Rehabilitation Canada / Réadaptation Psychosociale Canada (RPS)

PO Box 13060, 140 Holland St. West, Bradford ON L3Z 2Y5
Fax: 705-456-9786
Toll-Free: 866-655-8548
phoenixsociety@accesscomm.ca
www.psrrpscanada.ca
Also Known As: PSR Canada/RPS Canada
Overview: A small national organization founded in 2002
Mission: To achieve full community participation of persons with mental health issues; To promote the principles & practice of psychosocial rehabilitation through practice standards, education, quality, outcome measures, advocacy & public policy
Affiliation(s): International Association of Psychosocial Rehabilitation Services; Ontario Federation of Community

Mental Health & Addictions Programs; Association québécoise pour la readaptation psychosociale; Psychosocial Rehabilitation Manitoba, BC, Atlantic Region, Ont.
Chief Officer(s):
Vicky Huehn, President
Sue Carr, Vice-President
John Higenbottam, Treasurer
Finances: *Annual Operating Budget:* Less than $50,000; *Funding Sources:* Membership fees; conference revenue
11 volunteer(s)
Membership: 300; *Fees:* $120 individual; $200-$2000 organizations; *Member Profile:* Adherance to principles of PSR in service delivery; *Committees:* Membership; Certification; Affiliation; Publicity; Website; Newsletter
Activities: Conferences; chapter building; membership development; public awareness; advocacy; certification of PSR Practitioners;

Public Accountants Council for the Province of Ontario / Conseil des experts-comptables de la province de l'Ontario

#901, 1200 Bay St., Toronto ON M5R 2A5
Tel: 416-920-1444; *Fax:* 416-920-1917
Toll-Free: 800-387-2154
generalinquiries@pacont.org
www.pacont.org
Also Known As: Public Accountants Council
Overview: A medium-sized provincial licensing organization founded in 1950
Chief Officer(s):
Michael Bryant, Chair
Shoba Khetrapal, Vice-Chair
Finances: *Annual Operating Budget:* $1.5 Million-$3 Million; *Funding Sources:* Licence fees
Membership: 1-99; *Member Profile:* Institute of Chartered Accountants of Ontario; Certified General Accountants of Ontario; Society of Management Accountants of Ontario; *Committees:* Audit; Governance

The Public Affairs Association of Canada (PAAC) / Association des affaires publiques du Canada

c/o John Capobianco, Fleishman-Hillard Canada Inc., #1500, 33 Bloor St. East, Toronto ON M4W 3H1
Tel: 416-645-8182; *Fax:* 416-361-2447
info@publicaffairs.ca
www.publicaffairs.ca
www.linkedin.com/groups/Public-Affairs-Association-Canada-PAAC-4790500
twitter.com/PAAC84
Overview: A medium-sized national organization founded in 1984
Mission: To improve the professionalism of members to enhance the relations of members' organizations with their publics
Chief Officer(s):
John Capobianco, President
john.capobianco@fleishman.ca
Jennifer Dent, Events Chair
jennifer.e.dent@gsk.com
Stephen Andrews, Secretary-Treasurer
sandrews@blg.com
Rick Hall, Vice-President
rickhall@rickhallpr.com
Finances: *Funding Sources:* Membership fees
Membership: *Fees:* $56.50 student; $282.50 indvidual; $1130 corporate
Activities: Seminars; conferences; workshops; *Rents Mailing List:* Yes

Public Dreams Society (PDS)

#141, 2050 Scotia St., Vancouver BC V5T 4T1
Tel: 604-879-8611; *Fax:* 604-879-8614
ed@publicdreams.org
www.publicdreams.org
www.facebook.com/publicdreams
twitter.com/publicdreams
www.flickr.com/photos/publicdreams/sets/
Also Known As: Imaginate
Overview: A small local charitable organization founded in 1985
Mission: To revive & redefine community arts & the artist's role in the community by developing community-based celebration events
Member of: Alliance of Arts & Culture; Greater Vancouver Professional Theatre Alliance; Public Health Association of BC; Vancouver Community Arts Council; Vancouver Board of Trade
Affiliation(s): Spirit of Vancouver
Chief Officer(s):
Azfir, Artistic Director
azfir@publicdreams.org
Finances: *Annual Operating Budget:* $250,000-$500,000; *Funding Sources:* Municipal & provincial government; foundations; donations; Canada Council; special events
Staff Member(s): 5; 400 volunteer(s)
Membership: 75; *Fees:* $15; *Member Profile:* Community supporters
Activities: Produces participatory public art events & community celebrations - Illuminares; Parade of Lost Souls; Mountain Mardi Gras; *Awareness Events:* Illuminares, July; Parade of the Lost Souls, Oct.; *Internships:* Yes

Public Health Association of British Columbia (PHABC)

#210, 1027 Pandora Ave., Victoria BC V8V 3P6
Tel: 250-595-8422; *Fax:* 250-595-8622
staff@phabc.org
www.phabc.org
Overview: A medium-sized provincial organization overseen by Canadian Public Health Association
Mission: To constitute a special resource in BC for the betterment & maintenance of the population's health at the community & personal level
Chief Officer(s):
Ted Bruce, President
Finances: *Annual Operating Budget:* $100,000-$250,000; *Funding Sources:* Membership dues; project grants
Staff Member(s): 2; 25 volunteer(s)
Membership: 300; *Fees:* $25 individual; $15 student; $50 organization
Activities: BC Healthy Communities Network
Meetings/Conferences: • Public Health Association of British Columbia Conference and AGM 2015, 2015, BC
Scope: Provincial

Public Health Association of Nova Scotia (PHANS)

PO Box 33074, Halifax NS B3L 4T6
e-mail: info@phans.ca
www.phans.ca
Overview: A small provincial charitable organization overseen by Canadian Public Health Association
Mission: To build public health capacity & to make progress on the determinants of health in Nova Scotia
Affliation(s): Canadian Public Health Association
Membership: *Fees:* $20 students & retired persons; $40 regular members; *Member Profile:* Persons interested in health & health issues in Nova Scotia
Activities: Advocating for policy change on issues that affect health; Liaising with government departments & voluntary agencies; Increasing professional & public awareness of health issues; Providing education; Offering networking opportunities; Delivering updates on health policy issues

The Public Interest Advocacy Centre (PIAC) / Centre pour la défense de l'intérêt public

#1204, 1 Nicholas St., Ottawa ON K1N 7B7
Tel: 613-562-4002
piac@piac.ca
www.piac.ca
Overview: A medium-sized national charitable organization founded in 1976
Mission: To provide legal services on a non-profit basis to groups & individuals addressing public interest issues of broad concern who would not otherwise have access to such services; the centre's special interests are telecommunications, energy, transportation, broadcasting, privacy, technical services & consumer protection
Member of: National Association of State Utility Consumer Advocates; Consumers International
Chief Officer(s):
John Lawford, Executive Director & General Counsel
Staff Member(s): 6
Membership: 900 individuals; 7 organizations

Public Legal Education Association of Canada (PLEAC)

First Enterprise Pl., #100, 5520 - 48A Ave., Red Deer AB T4N 3V6
Tel: 403-343-3712
contact@pleac.ca
www.pleac.ca
www.facebook.com/110888695617465
twitter.com/pleac
Overview: A small national organization founded in 1987
Finances: *Funding Sources:* Membership dues
Membership: 26; *Fees:* $25 non-voting; $50 individual; $300 organization; $301-$500 sustaining; $500 patron; *Member Profile:* Agencies carrying out public legal education activities

Public Legal Education Association of Saskatchewan, Inc. (PLEA Sask.)

#500, 333 - 25th St. East, Saskatoon SK S7K 0L4
Tel: 306-653-1868; *Fax:* 306-653-1869
plea@plea.org
www.plea.org
Overview: A medium-sized provincial organization founded in 1980
Mission: To provide the public with information regarding the law
Member of: Public Legal Education Association of Canada
Chief Officer(s):
Heather Jensen, President
Joel Janow, Executive Director
Staff Member(s): 8
Membership: *Fees:* $20
Activities: *Speaker Service:* Yes; *Library:* Public Legal Education Association of Saskatchewan Library; Open to public

Public Legal Education Society of Nova Scotia *See* Legal Information Society of Nova Scotia

Public Legal Information Association of Newfoundland (PLIAN)

Tara Place, #227, 31 Peet St., St. John's NL A1B 3W8
Tel: 709-722-2643; *Fax:* 709-722-0054
Toll-Free: 888-660-7788
info@publiclegalinfo.com
www.publiclegalinfo.com
twitter.com/PLIAN_NL
Overview: A small provincial organization founded in 1984
Mission: To provide plain language legal information to the general public of Newfoundland, in both official languages, through a telephone enquiry line, public speaking engagements, publications, & a lawyer referral service
Member of: Public Legal Information Association of Canada
Chief Officer(s):
Kevin O'Shea, Executive Director
Finances: *Annual Operating Budget:* $100,000-$250,000; *Funding Sources:* Justice Canada; Newfoundland Dept. of Justice; Law Foundation of Newfoundland
Staff Member(s): 4; 3 volunteer(s)
Membership: 30
Activities: *Speaker Service:* Yes

Public Petroleum Data Model Association *See* Professional Petroleum Data Management Association

Public School Boards' Association of Alberta (PSBAA)

#12, 10227 - 118 St., Edmonton AB T5K 2V4
Tel: 780-479-8080; *Fax:* 780-477-1892
Toll-Free: 800-661-4605
gensec@public-schools.ab.ca
www.public-schools.ab.ca
twitter.com/PublicSchoolsAB
Overview: A medium-sized provincial organization founded in 1989
Mission: To ensure the continuation & constant improvement of a universally accessible system of public education which is locally governed, student centred & challenging; to provide constructive leadership, represented by effective strategies, advocacy & communication, & to work with others, wherever possible, for the good of public education
Member of: Canadian Education Association
Chief Officer(s):
Mary Campbell, Executive Director
execdir@public-schools.ab.ca
Finances: *Annual Operating Budget:* $250,000-$500,000; *Funding Sources:* Membership fees
Staff Member(s): 5
Membership: 34; *Fees:* $2,000 + component determined by student enrollment; *Member Profile:* Public school boards in Alberta
Activities: Political advocacy on behalf of public school education; data gathering & analysis; leadership & community development; Spring assembly; AGM; *Speaker Service:* Yes

Public Service Alliance of Canada (PSAC) / Alliance de la Fonction publique du Canada (AFPC)

233 Gilmour St., Ottawa ON K2P 0P1
Tel: 613-560-4200; *Fax:* 613-567-0385
Toll-Free: 888-604-7722

www.psacunion.ca
www.facebook.com/psac.national
twitter.com/psacnat
www.youtube.com/psacafpc
Overview: A large national organization founded in 1966
Mission: To unite all workers in a single democratic organization; To obtain for all public service employees the best standards of compensation & other conditions of employment & to protect the rights & interests of all public service employees; To maintain & defend the right to strike
Member of: Canadian Labour Congress
Affliation(s): Public Services International
Chief Officer(s):
Robyn Benson, National President
Jeannie Baldwin, Regional Executive Vice-President, Atlantic
Bob Jackson, Regional Executive Vice-President, B.C.
Marianne Hladun, Regional Executive Vice-President, Prairies
Chris Aylwarde, National Executive Vice-President
Sharon DeSousa, Regional Executive Vice-President, Ontario
Magali Picard, Vice-président exécutif régional, Québec
Julie Docherty, Regional Executive Vice-President, North
Larry Rousseau, Regional Executive Vice-President, National Capital Region
Finances: *Annual Operating Budget:* Greater than $5 Million
Staff Member(s): 300
Membership: 17 components + 1,219 locals + 180,000 individual; *Member Profile:* The majority of members work for the federal government & its agencies.
Activities: *Library:* PSAC Library

Atlantic Branch
#301, 287 Lacewood Dr., Halifax NS B3M 3Y7
Tel: 902-445-0925; *Fax:* 902-443-8291
revp-atl@psac-afpc.com
www.psacatlantic.ca
Chief Officer(s):
Jeannie Baldwin, Regional Executive Vice-President, Atlantic

British Columbia Branch
#302, 5238 Joyce St., Vancouver BC V5R 6C9
Tel: 604-760-0191; *Fax:* 604-430-0194
Toll-Free: 866-811-7700
revp-bc@psac-afpc.com
www.psacbc.com
Chief Officer(s):
Bob Jackson, Regional Executive Vice-President, BC

Calgary Branch
Hillhurst Professional Building, #302, 301 - 14 St. NW, Calgary AB T2N 2A1
Tel: 403-270-6555; *Fax:* 403-270-6591
Toll-Free: 800-641-8914

Charlottetown Branch
614 North River Rd., #D, Charlottetown PE C1E 1K2
Tel: 902-892-5481; *Fax:* 902-892-6407

Edmonton Branch
First Edmonton Place, #670, 10665 Jasper Ave., Edmonton AB T5J 3S9
Tel: 780-423-1290; *Fax:* 780-429-2278

Halifax Branch
Park West Centre, #301, 287 Lacewood Dr., Halifax NS B2M 3Y7
Tel: 902-443-3541; *Fax:* 902-443-8291

Kingston Branch
City Place 1, #412, 1471 John Counter Blvd., Kingston ON K7M 8S8
Tel: 613-542-7322; *Fax:* 613-542-7387

London Branch
#U-11, 480 Sovereign Rd., London ON N6M 1A4
Tel: 519-659-1124; *Fax:* 519-659-1132

Moncton Branch
30 Englehart St., #G, Dieppe NB E1A 8H3
Tel: 506-857-4220; *Fax:* 506-857-9792

National Capital Region Branch
15 Holland Ave., Main Fl., Ottawa ON K1Y 4T2
Tel: 613-256-0438; *Fax:* 613-234-6209
revp-national-capital@psac-afpc.com
www.psac-ncr.com
Chief Officer(s):
Larry Rousseau, Regional Executive Vice-President, National Capital Region

Northern Branch
Building 1412, Sikituuq Court, PO Box 220, Iqaluit NU X0A 0H0
Tel: 867-979-7430; *Fax:* 867-979-5517
Toll-Free: 866-268-7097
revp-north@psac-afpc.com
psacnorth.com
Chief Officer(s):
Jack Bourassa, Regional Executive Vice-President, North

Ontario Branch
#608, 90 Eglinton Ave. East, Toronto ON M4P 2Y3
Tel: 416-485-3558; *Fax:* 416-485-8607
Toll-Free: 800-354-9086
revp-ont@psac-afpc.com
ontario.psac.com
Chief Officer(s):
Sharon DeSousa, Regional Executive Vice-President, Ontario

Ottawa Branch
15 Holland Ave., Main Fl., Ottawa ON K1Y 4T2
Tel: 613-560-2560; *Fax:* 613-234-6209

Prairies Branch
#460, 175 Hargrave St., Winnipeg MB R3C 3R8
Tel: 204-956-4625; *Fax:* 204-943-0652
revp-prairies@psac-afpc.com
prairies.psac.com
Chief Officer(s):
Marianne Hladun, Regional Executive Vice-President, Prairies

Regina Branch
#200, 2445 - 13 Ave., Regina SK S4P 0W1
Tel: 306-757-3575; *Fax:* 306-569-8425

St. John's Branch
#105, 33 Pippy Pl., St. John's NL A1B 2X3
Tel: 709-726-6453; *Fax:* 709-726-1821

Saskatoon Branch
#5, 511 - 1st Ave. North, Saskatoon SK S7K 1X5
Tel: 306-244-3033; *Fax:* 306-664-2016

Section de Gatineau
Place du Centre, #310, 200 Promenade du Portage, Gatineau QC J8X 4B7
Tel: 819-777-4647; *Fax:* 819-777-9407

Section de Montréal
#1104, 5800, rue Saint-Denis, Montréal QC H2S 3L5
Tél: 514-875-7100; *Téléc:* 514-875-8399
Ligne sans frais: 800-642-8020

Section de Québec
#130, 5050, boul des Gradins, Québec QC G2J 1P8
Tél: 418-666-6500; *Téléc:* 418-666-6999
Ligne sans frais: 800-566-6530

Section provinciale du Québec
#1104, 5800, rue Saint-Denis, Montréal QC H2S 3L5
Tél: 514-875-2690; *Téléc:* 514-868-1678
vper-que@psac-afpc.com
www.afpcquebec.com
Chief Officer(s):
Magali Picard, Regional Executive Vice-President, Québec

Sudbury Branch
#500A, 10 Elm St., Sudbury ON P3C 5N3
Tel: 705-674-6907; *Fax:* 705-674-8652
Toll-Free: 800-354-9134

Thunder Bay Branch
#109, 1205 Amber Dr., Thunder Bay ON P7M 6M4
Tel: 807-345-8442; *Fax:* 807-344-0704

Toronto Branch
#608, 90 Eglinton Ave. East, London ON M4P 2Y3
Tel: 416-485-3558; *Fax:* 416-485-8607
Toll-Free: 800-354-9086
PSAC_Toronto_Mail@psac-afpc.com

Vancouver Branch
#200, 5238 Joyce St., Vancouver BC V5R 6C9
Tel: 604-430-5631; *Fax:* 604-430-0451
Toll-Free: 800-663-1655

Vancouver Satellite Office
#300, 5238 Joyce St., Vancouver BC V5R 6C9
Tel: 604-430-5761; *Fax:* 604-431-6727

Victoria Branch
#210, 1497 Admirals Rd., Victoria BC V9A 2P8
Tel: 250-953-1050; *Fax:* 250-953-1066
Toll-Free: 866-953-1050

Whitehorse Branch
#100, 2285 - 2 Ave., Whitehorse YT Y1A 1C9
Tel: 867-667-2331; *Fax:* 867-633-5347

Winnipeg Branch
#460, 175 Hargrave St., Winnipeg MB R3C 3R8
Tel: 204-947-1601; *Fax:* 204-943-0652

Yellowknife Branch
PO Box 637, 4916 - 49 St., Yellowknife NT X1A 2N4
Tel: 867-873-5670; *Fax:* 867-873-4295
Toll-Free: 800-661-0870

Public Services Health & Safety Association (PSHSA)

#902, 4950 Yonge St., Toronto ON M2N 6K1
Tel: 416-250-2131; *Fax:* 416-250-7484
Toll-Free: 877-250-7444
www.healthandsafetyontario.ca/PSHSA
twitter.com/PSHSA1
Previous Name: Education Safety Association of Ontario; Municipal Health & Safety Assn; Ontario Safety Assn. for Community & Healthcare
Overview: A small provincial organization founded in 2010
Mission: PSHSA is a not-for profit association that works with Ontario public service sector employers & workers to reduce workplace risks & prevent occupational injuries & illness. Its consultants come from a range of disciplines & can serve municipalities, universities & colleges, hospitals, long-term care homes, school boards, police & emergency services, & community care providers.
Affiliation(s): Health & Safety Ontario
Chief Officer(s):
Donald MacLeod, Chair
Louise Logan, President & CEO
Finances: *Annual Operating Budget:* $1.5 Million-$3 Million
Membership: 9,000+ organizations; 1.2 million individuals; *Member Profile:* Public service sector organizations; *Committees:* Municipal & Community Affairs; Community & Healthcare; Education & Culture
Activities: Access to sector-specific advisory councils; onsite courses; safety audit services; safety resource materials; statistical data; interactive electronic communications; *Library* by appointment

Public Works Association of British Columbia (PWABC)

#102, 211 Columbia St., Vancouver BC V6A 2R5
Toll-Free: 877-356-0699
info@pwabc.ca
www.pwabc.ca
www.linkedin.com/groups?gid=5156461&trk=my_groups-b-grp-v
www.facebook.com/pages/Public-Works-Association-of-BC/248964305172358
www.twitter.com/PWABCExecDir
Overview: A medium-sized provincial organization overseen by Canadian Public Works Association
Mission: PWABC is a non-profit society registered in B.C. that exists to serve its members by providing opportunities for mutual support, education and professional development. It does this through workshops, newsletters, teleconferences and an annual technical conference.
Member of: American Public Works Association
Chief Officer(s):
Deryk Lee, President, 250-361-0467
Membership: *Fees:* $164 individual; $403.00 for Heritage, $1683 for Prestige, $7991 for Crown corporations
Awards:
• Dedicated Service Awards (Award), Awards to Individuals
• PWABC Manager of the Year Award (Award), Awards to Individuals
• PWABC Professional - Dedicated Service Award (Award), Awards to Individuals
• Project of the Year Award (Award), Awards to Municipalities
• Public Works Week - Community Celebration Award (Award), Awards to Municipalities
• Innovations Award (Award), Awards to Municipalities
• PWABC Scholarship for Further Training (Scholarship)
Eligibility: Members only
• $1000 Education Scholarship (Scholarship)
Meetings/Conferences: • Public Works Association of British Columbia 2015 Technical Conference & Trade Show, September, 2015, Penticton Trade & Conference Centre, Penticton, BC
Scope: Provincial

Pueblito Canada Incorporated

215 Spadina Ave., 4th Fl., Toronto ON M5T 2C7
Tel: 416-642-5781; *Fax:* 416-644-0116
pueblito@pueblito.org
www.pueblito.org
www.linkedin.com/company/449752
www.facebook.com/263268173703693
twitter.com/PueblitoCanada
Overview: A small international charitable organization founded in 1974
Mission: To work in partnership with Latin American organizations; To support the development of local programs for children in health care, childcare & education

Chief Officer(s):
Miriam Buttu, Program Director
Staff Member(s): 3; 28 volunteer(s)
Awards:
• Making Children a Priority Award (Award)

Pugwash & Area Chamber of Commerce
PO Box 239, Pugwash NS B0K 1L0
Tel: 902-243-2606
Overview: A small local organization founded in 2007
Member of: Canadian Chamber of Commerce; Atlantic Chamber of Commerce

Pulaarvik Kablu Friendship Centre
PO Box 429, Rankin Inlet NU X0C 0G0
Tel: 867-645-2600; *Fax:* 867-645-2538
recept_pkfcmain@qiniq.com
www.pulaarvik.ca
Previous Name: Sappujjijit Friendship Centre
Overview: A small local organization founded in 1973
Member of: National Association of Friendship Centres
Chief Officer(s):
Marianne Taparti, Chair
George Dunkerley, Executive Director
Finances: *Annual Operating Budget:* $1.5 Million-$3 Million
Activities: Workshops, programs & projects aimed at education, health & well-being of people of the community

Pulp & Paper Centre
University of British Columbia, 2385 East Mall, Vancouver BC V6T 1Z4
Tel: 604-822-8560
ppc-info@ubc.ca
www.ppc.ubc.ca
Previous Name: Canadian Pulp & Paper Network for Innovation in Education & Research; Mechanical Wood-Pulps Network
Overview: A medium-sized provincial organization
Mission: To act as a university-industry partnership for innovation & education; to house inter-disciplinary, cross-faculty post-graduate research programs
Affliation(s): FPInnovations; PAPIER
Chief Officer(s):
James Olson, Ph.D., P.Eng., Director & Professor, Mechanical Engineering, 604-822-5705
James.Olson@ubc.ca
George Soong, Safety & Operations Officer, Building/Technical Inquiries, 604-822-2530
gsoong@mail.ubc.ca
Richard Kerekes, Director
kerekes@chml.ubc.ca
Membership: *Member Profile:* UBC faculty & students involved in teaching & research for the pulp & paper industry; members of the manufacturing, utilities & supplier industries, as well as consultants & government agencies
Publications:
• Canadian Pulp & Paper Network for Innovation in Education & Research Newsletter
Type: Newsletter; *Frequency:* Semiannually
Profile: Papier's recent activities, such as meetings & award presentations

Pulp & Paper Employee Relations Forum
c/o Westcott Consulting, 6627 Westcott Rd., Duncan BC V9L 6A4
Tel: 250-748-9445; *Fax:* 888-273-7148
westcot@telus.net
paperforum.com
Overview: A medium-sized national organization
Mission: To act primarily as a research & information service for the industry; to service the pulp & paper industry in job evaluation, benefit & pension plan administration & trusteeship, contract interpretation & any other matters relating to labour relations
Chief Officer(s):
Fred Oud, Executive Director

Pulp & Paper Products Council (PPPC)
#1000, 1200, av McGill College, Montréal QC H3B 4G7
Tel: 514-861-8828; *Fax:* 514-866-4863
general@pppc.org
www.pppc.org
Overview: A medium-sized international organization
Mission: To collect & provide market data & intelligence on the pulp, newsprint, printing, & writing papers sectors; the PPPC operates out of Montréal, Brussels, Beijing, & Delhi
Staff Member(s): 25
Membership: 72 corporate
Activities: *Awareness Events:* International Pulp Week, May
Publications:
• Monthly Flash Reports [a publication of the Pulp & Paper Products Council]
Type: Newsletter; *Frequency:* Monthly

Pulp & Paper Technical Association of Canada (PAPTAC) / Association technique des pâtes et papiers du Canada
#1070, 740, rue Notre-Dame ouest, Montréal QC H3C 3X6
Tel: 514-392-0265; *Fax:* 514-392-0369
tech@paptac.ca
www.paptac.ca
Previous Name: Canadian Pulp & Paper Association - Technical Section
Overview: A medium-sized national organization founded in 1915
Mission: To provide means for the interchange of knowledge & expertise among its members; to improve the skill levels & effectiveness of present & future employees through training & education; to provide technical & practical information on pulp & paper manufacture & use
Chief Officer(s):
Greg Hay, Executive Director, 514-392-6964
ghay@paptac.ca
Finances: *Funding Sources:* Membership fees; Events
Publications:
• Journal of Pulp and Paper Science (JPPS)
Type: Journal; *Frequency:* Quarterly

Pulp, Paper & Woodworkers of Canada (PPWC)
#201, 1184 - West 6 Ave., Vancouver BC V6H 1A4
Tel: 604-731-1909; *Fax:* 604-731-6448
Toll-Free: 888-992-7792
www.ppwc.ca
www.facebook.com/PulpPaperandWoodworkersofCanada
www.youtube.com/user/PPWCUnion
Overview: A medium-sized national organization founded in 1963
Mission: To ensure fair working conditions for its members
Affliation(s): Confederation of Canadian Unions
Chief Officer(s):
Arnold Bercov, President
abercov@ppwc.ca
Staff Member(s): 1

Pumphouse Theatres Society
2140 Pumphouse Ave. SW, Calgary AB T3C 3P5
Tel: 403-263-0079; *Fax:* 403-237-5357
www.pumphousetheatres.ca
www.facebook.com/154210604615247
twitter.com/PumphouseTS
Also Known As: Pumphouse Theatre
Overview: A small local charitable organization founded in 1972
Mission: To provide a theatrical performance facility that is consistent with the heritage character of the site & to encourage, develop & maintain community theatre in Calgary
Member of: Professional Association of Canadian Theatres; Canadian Institute for Theatre Technology
Affliation(s): Theatre Alberta; Calgary Professional Arts Alliance
Chief Officer(s):
Karen Almadi, President & Secretary
Scott McTavish, Executive Director
exec@pumphousetheatre.ca
Finances: *Annual Operating Budget:* $250,000-$500,000; *Funding Sources:* Municipal government; corporate sponsorship; individual donations
Staff Member(s): 11; 100 volunteer(s)
Membership: 40 individual; *Fees:* $20
Activities: One Act Play Festival; drama day camps; fall & winter drama classes; *Speaker Service:* Yes

Purchasing Management Association of Canada - Québec Institute *Voir* Corporation des approvisionneurs du Québec

Purebred Sheep Breeders Association of Nova Scotia
RR#1, Maitland NS B0N 1T0
Tel: 902-369-2969
www.sheepnovascotia.ns.ca
Overview: A small provincial organization founded in 1980
Mission: To improve the quality of purebred sheep in Nova Scotia; To advance breeders' interests & speak on their behalf when necessary
Member of: Canadian Sheep Breeders Association
Chief Officer(s):
Andrew Hebda, President, 902-369-2969
nantymor9982@ns.sympatico.ca
Finances: *Funding Sources:* Membership fees; commission on annual breeding stock sale
Membership: 40 individual; *Fees:* $20

Purebred Swine Breeders' Association of Canada *See* Canadian Swine Breeders' Association

Purely Mutual Underwriters Association; Mutual Fire Underwriters Association *See* Ontario Mutual Insurance Association

Qalipu Mi'kmaq First Nations Band
3 Church St., Corner Brook NL A2H 6J3
Tel: 709-634-0996; *Fax:* 709-639-3997
Toll-Free: 800-561-2266
qalipu.ca
Overview: A small provincial organization overseen by Congress of Aboriginal Peoples
Chief Officer(s):
Annie Randell, Chief Executive Officer
arandell@qalipu.ca

Qikiqtani Inuit Association (QIA)
Igluvut Building, 2nd Fl., PO Box 1340, Iqaluit NU X0A 0H0
Tel: 867-975-8400; *Fax:* 867-979-3238
Toll-Free: 800-667-2742
info@qia.ca
www.qia.ca
twitter.com/Qikiqtani_Inuit
Overview: A small local organization founded in 1975
Chief Officer(s):
Okalik Eegeesiak, President
Terry Audla, Executive Director
Staff Member(s): 37

QMI *See* QMI - SAI Global

QMI - SAI Global
#200, 20 Carlson Ct., Toronto ON M9W 7K6
Tel: 416-401-8700; *Fax:* 416-401-8650
Toll-Free: 800-465-3717
www.qmi.com
Also Known As: Quality Management Institute
Previous Name: QMI
Overview: A small provincial organization founded in 1984
Mission: The management systems registrar evaluates business processes against ISO or industry standards
Member of: CSA Group
Affliation(s): Accredited by the American National Standards Institute - Registrar Accreditation Board of the USA (ANSI-RAB), the Standards Council of Canada (SCC), entidada mexicana de acreditacion a.c. (EMA), & the International Automotive Oversight Bureau (IAOB)
Chief Officer(s):
Peter Mullins, CEO
Andrew Dutton, Chair
Activities: Registering manufacturing & service organizations to a wide range of ISO & industry standards for quality & environmental systems; Increasing knowledge & understanding of standards by offering a variety of training courses; *Library:* Standards Library
Publications:
• QMI Brief
Type: Newsletter; *Frequency:* 3 pa
Profile: News about management systems & registration, plus information on the automotive, aerospace, forestry, & environment sectors

Montréal
#605, 1, av Holiday, Pointe-Claire QC H9R 5N3
Tel: 514-426-3432
Toll-Free: 888-723-7755

Vancouver
PO Box 36002, 10991 No. One Rd., Richmond BC V7E 1S0
Tel: 778-297-5524; *Fax:* 778-297-1694
Toll-Free: 800-268-7321

Western Canada
Toll-Free: 800-268-7321

Qu'Appelle Valley Friendship Centre (QVFC)
PO Box 240, Fort Qu'appelle SK S0G 1S0
Tel: 306-332-5616; *Fax:* 306-332-5091
www.qvfc.ca
Overview: A small local charitable organization founded in 1980
Mission: To provide support & direct services to the Aboriginal community; To strive to bridge the gap between Aboriginial

people & society at large, through assisting in the process of social interaction, sharing of cultures & the educating of harmonious working relationships between all communities & cultures
Affliation(s): Friendship Centres of Saskatachewant; National Friendship Centre
Chief Officer(s):
Rob Donison, Executive Director
rdonison@qvfc.ca
Finances: *Annual Operating Budget:* $250,000-$500,000
Staff Member(s): 6
Membership: 1-99; *Fees:* $3
Activities: Personal services; housing & employment services; sustenance, maintenance & basic services; referral services; legal services; youth programs

Quad County Support Services (QCSS)
PO Box 65, 195 Wellington St., Wardsville ON N0L 2N0
Tel: 519-693-4812; *Fax:* 519-693-7055
qcss01@golden.net
Overview: A small local charitable organization founded in 1963
Mission: To encourage the acceptance of all people by fostering a lifestyle that lends itself to the betterment of everyone in the community, safeguarding the rights & responsibilities of all individuals
Member of: Community Living Ontario
Chief Officer(s):
William Shurish, Executive Director
Bonnie Campbell, President
Finances: *Annual Operating Budget:* $500,000-$1.5 Million; *Funding Sources:* Ministry of Community & Social Services; municipal grants
Staff Member(s): 32; 14 volunteer(s)
Membership: 20; *Fees:* $5; *Member Profile:* Parents; advocates; family

Quadra Island Food Bank
PO Box 242, Heriot Bay BC V0P 1H0
Tel: 250-285-3888
Overview: A small local organization overseen by Food Banks British Columbia
Member of: Food Banks British Columbia
Chief Officer(s):
Teresa Tate, Contact
teresa_tate@yahoo.com

Quaker Aboriginal Affairs Committee (QAAC)
c/o Canadian Friends Service Committee, 60 Lowther Ave., Toronto ON M5R 1C7
Tel: 416-920-5213; *Fax:* 416-920-5214
quakerservice.ca
Also Known As: Quaker Committee for Native Concerns
Overview: A small national charitable organization founded in 1976
Mission: Support for Aboriginal fights & justice, public education & campaigns
Member of: Canadian Friends Service Committee
Affliation(s): Aboriginal Rights Coalition
Chief Officer(s):
Jennifer Preston, Program Coordinator
jennifer@quakerservice.ca
Activities: *Internships:* Yes

Quakers Fostering Justice (QFJ)
c/o Canadian Friends Service Committee, 60 Lowether Ave., Toronto ON M5R 1C7
Tel: 416-920-5213; *Fax:* 416-920-5214
qfj@quakerservice.ca
quakerservice.ca/our-work/justice
Overview: A small national organization founded in 1975
Mission: To build caring community without need for prisons; to explore alternatives to prison based on economic, social justice & fulfillment of human needs; to foster awareness within & outside Quaker community of roots of crime & violence in society; to reach & support prisoners, guards, victims & families
Member of: Church Council on Justice & Corrections; Coalition for Gun Control; Canadian Friends Service Committee; Canadian Criminal Justice Association; Victim Offender Mediation Association
Affliation(s): Alternatives to Violence Project - Canada
Chief Officer(s):
Tasmin Rajotte, Program Coordinator
Finances: *Funding Sources:* Private donations
Activities: Workshops; seminars; conferences

Qualicum Beach Chamber of Commerce
PO Box 159, 124 West 2nd Ave., Qualicum Beach BC V9K 1S7
Tel: 250-752-0960; *Fax:* 250-752-2923
chamber@qualicum.bc.ca
www.qualicum.bc.ca
www.facebook.com/QBChamber
twitter.com/qbchamber
Overview: A small local organization founded in 1927
Mission: To promote local trade & commerce; To enhance to economic, civic & social well-being of the community; To represent a unified voice through which businesses & professional people can work together to build a strong & vibrant business climate
Member of: BC Chamber of Commerce; Tourism Vancouver Island
Affliation(s): Oceanside Tourism Association
Chief Officer(s):
Moira Hauk, Chair
Peter Doukakis, President & CEO
Finances: *Annual Operating Budget:* $100,000-$250,000; *Funding Sources:* Town of Qualicum Beach; membership fees; fundraising events
Staff Member(s): 35; 5 volunteer(s)
Membership: 500; *Fees:* $75-650
Activities: *Library:* Business Information Centre; Open to public
Awards:
• Three $750 scholarships each year to students from Kwalikum Secondary (Scholarship)
Publications:
• Qualicum Beach Chamber of Commerce Eflash
Type: Newsletter

Qualifications Evaluation Council of Ontario / Le Conseil ontarien d'évaluation des qualifications
#308, 1300 Yonge St., Toronto ON M4T 1X3
Tel: 416-323-1969
Toll-Free: 800-385-1030
www.qeco.on.ca
Overview: A medium-sized provincial organization founded in 1969
Mission: To provide & to objectively administer the evaluation of teacher qualifications for salary purposes.
Affliation(s): AEFO; ETFO; OECTA
Chief Officer(s):
Sam Hammond, President
Ken Collins, Executive Director
Membership: *Member Profile:* Teachers

Quality Council of Alberta
#2517 - 20th St. SW, Calgary AB T2T 4Z4
Tel: 403-802-6877
info@qualityalberta.ca
www.qca.org
Overview: A small provincial organization founded in 1991
Member of: National Quality Institute
Affliation(s): American Society for Quality
Chief Officer(s):
Rodger Cole, General Manager
Drew Thomson, Sec.-Treas.
Chris Tsaros, Chair
Staff Member(s): 1; 12 volunteer(s)
Membership: 250; *Fees:* $75 individual; $250 corporate
Activities: Alberta Quality Awards Program; workshops; luncheons with speakers; brown bag sessions; resource centre; implementation assistance; mentors; speakers

Quality in Lifelong Learning Network (QUILL)
PO Box 1148, #202, 200 McNabb St., Walkerton ON N0G 2V0
Tel: 519-881-4655; *Fax:* 519-881-4638
Toll-Free: 800-530-6852
execdir.quill@gmail.com
www.quillnetwork.ca
www.facebook.com/QUILLNetwork
Also Known As: QUILL Learning Network
Previous Name: Queensbush Initiatives for Literacy & Learning Inc.
Overview: A small local charitable organization founded in 1995
Mission: To support & promote learning activities in Bruce, Grey, Perth & the Georgian Triangle
Member of: Essential Skills Ontario; Community Literacy of Ontario; Learning Networks of Ontario
Chief Officer(s):
Debera Flynn, Executive Director
execdir@quillnetwork.ca
Finances: *Annual Operating Budget:* $50,000-$100,000; *Funding Sources:* Ministry of Training, Colleges & Universities
Staff Member(s): 2
Membership: 45; *Fees:* $15 individual; $30 associate; $35 organization; *Member Profile:* Literacy programs & interested community members; *Committees:* Nominating
Activities: Ensures quality literacy programs for learners; provides training for literacy & upgrading providers; raises public awareness & promotes action on literacy issues; provides referral service; *Speaker Service:* Yes; *Library:* QUILL Network Resources;
Awards:
• QUILL Network Recognition Awards (Award)

Quantity Surveyors Society of British Columbia (QSSBC)
#102, 211 Columbia St., Vancouver BC V6A 2R5
Tel: 604-662-3671; *Fax:* 604-681-4545
info@qsbc.ca
www.qsbc.ca
Overview: A small provincial organization
Member of: Canadian Institute of Quantity Surveyors
Chief Officer(s):
Donna Denham, Administrator
Finances: *Annual Operating Budget:* Less than $50,000
Staff Member(s): 1
Membership: 350 individual

Québec 4-H
6500, boulevard Arthur-Sauvé, bur. 202, Laval QC H7R 3X7
Tel: 450-314-1942; *Fax:* 450-314-1952
info@clubs4h.qc.ca
www.clubs4h.qc.ca
Previous Name: Québec Young Farmers
Overview: A medium-sized provincial organization founded in 1969
Mission: To develop life skills, such as leadership, cooperation, responsibility, & independence, for the English speaking rural youth of Québec, through achievement & skill-development
Member of: Canadian 4-H Council; Québec Community Groups Network
Chief Officer(s):
Tammy Oswick-Kearney, Provincial Coordinator
Finances: *Annual Operating Budget:* $50,000-$100,000
Staff Member(s): 1; 10 volunteer(s)
Membership: 450; *Fees:* Schedule available; *Member Profile:* Must be 6-21 years of age & member of Québec 4-H; *Committees:* Lifestock Management Tour; Provincial Rally

Québec Aboriginal Tourism Corporation *See* Société touristique des Autochtones du Québec

Québec Amateur Netball Federation *Voir* Fédération de Netball du Québec

Québec Anglophone Heritage Network (QAHN) / Reseau du Patrimoine Anglophone du Québec
#400, 257, rue Queen, Lennoxville QC J1M 1K7
Tel: 819-564-9595; *Fax:* 819-564-6872
Toll-Free: 877-964-0409
home@qahn.org
www.qahn.org
Overview: A small provincial organization founded in 2000
Mission: To operate as a non-profit, non-partisan umbrella organization to help advance knowledge of the history & culture of English-speaking society in Québec
Member of: Quebec Community Groups Network; Fédération des societés d'histoire du Québec
Finances: *Annual Operating Budget:* $50,000-$100,000
Staff Member(s): 2; 100 volunteer(s)
Membership: 150+; *Fees:* $20-30
Activities: *Library* Open to public

Québec Angus Association
3 North Hill Rd., Gould QC J0B 2Z0
Tél: 819-877-5603; *Téléc:* 819-877-3845
quebecangus@live.ca
www.quebecangus.ca
Aperçu: *Dimension:* petite; *Envergure:* provinciale
Membre de: Canadian Angus Association
Membre(s) du bureau directeur:
Cynthia Jackson, Propagandiste, 418-784-2311
doublejranch@sympatico.ca

Québec Anxiety, Depressive & Bipolar Disorder Support Association *Voir* Revivre - Association Québécoise de soutien aux personnes souffrant de troubles anxieux, dépressifs ou bipolaires

Québec Association for Community Living / Québec Institute for Intellectual Disability *Voir* Association du Québec pour l'intégration sociale / Institut québécois de la déficience intellectuelle

Québec Association for ICT Freelancers *Voir* Association québécoise des informaticiennes et informaticiens indépendants

Quebec Association for Parents of Visually Impaired Children *Voir* Association québécoise des parents d'enfants handicapés visuels

Quebec Association of Baptist Churches

6215 Côte St. Luc Rd., Montreal QC H3X 2H3
Tel: 514-744-6918
www.quebecbaptist.org
www.facebook.com/groups/111827773155
Also Known As: Eastern Association
Overview: A small provincial organization founded in 1887
Mission: To help churches carry out their services & goals
Member of: Canadian Baptists of Ontario & Quebec
Chief Officer(s):
Carl Plett, Moderator
cpplett@gmail.com
Membership: 19 churches; *Member Profile:* Baptist churches in Quebec

Québec Association of Energy Managers *Voir* Association québécoise pour la maîtrise de l'énergie

Québec Association of Export Trading Houses *Voir* Association des maisons de commerce extérieur du Québec

Québec Association of Fire Chiefs *Voir* Association des chefs en sécurité incendie du Québec

Québec Association of Independent Journalists *Voir* Association des journalistes indépendants du Québec

Québec Association of Independent Schools (QAIS) / Association des écoles privées du Québec

PO Box 398, Stn. Snowdon, Montréal QC H3X 3T6
Tel: 514-483-6111; *Fax:* 514-483-0865
Toll-Free: 866-909-6111
qais@qc.aibn.com
www.qais.qc.ca
Overview: A medium-sized provincial organization founded in 1965
Mission: To promote collaboration, provide services that further educational leadership & advocate for independent English language education in Quebec on behalf of its member schools.
Chief Officer(s):
Sidney Benudiz, Executive Director
Membership: 24 schools
Activities: *Rents Mailing List:* Yes

Quebec Association of Insolvency & Restructuring Professionals (QAIRP) / Association québécoise des professionnels de la rèorganisation et de l'insolvabilité (AQPRI)

c/o Tremblay & Compagnie Syndices et Gestionnaires Ltée, 582, boul. Saguenay est, Chicoutimi QC G7H 1L2
Tel: 819-549-5642; *Fax:* 819-549-5829
conseilsyndic.com
Previous Name: Association québécoise des professionnels d'insolvabilité
Overview: A small provincial organization overseen by Canadian Association of Insolvency & Restructuring Professionals
Mission: Promouvoir la pratique de l'administration de l'insolvabilité et l'intérêt public en ce domaine
Member of: Canadian Association of Insolvency & Restructuring Professionals
Chief Officer(s):
Charles Tremblay, President
ctremblay@tremblaycie.com
Finances: *Funding Sources:* Cotisations; séminaires

Québec Association of International Cooperation *Voir* Association québécoise des organismes de coopération internationale

Québec Association of Marriage & Family Therapy (QAMFT) / Association québécoise pour la thérapie conjugale et familiale

#300, 360 Victoria Ave., Westmount QC H3H 2N4
e-mail: info@qamft.org
www.qamft.org
Overview: A medium-sized provincial organization
Mission: To promote understanding, research & education in the field of couple & family therapy & to ensure that public needs are met by practitioners of the highest quality
Member of: American Association for Marriage & Family Therapy
Chief Officer(s):
Andrew Sofin, President
asofin@qamft.org
Finances: *Funding Sources:* Membership dues
Staff Member(s): 1; 8 volunteer(s)
Membership: 135; *Member Profile:* M.A. or Ph.D. in psychology or social work

Québec Association of Naturopathic Medicine (QANM) / Association de medecine naturapathique du Québec

1173, boul du Mont Royal ouest, Montréal QC H2V 2H6
Tel: 514-279-6629
qanm.org
www.linkedin.com/groups/AMNQ-QANM-4267434
www.facebook.com/amnq.qanm
twitter.com/amnq_qanm
Overview: A small provincial organization founded in 1995
Affiliation(s): Canadian Association of Naturopathic Doctors
Chief Officer(s):
André Saine, DC, ND, President
Staff Member(s): 1
Membership: 6; *Fees:* $300

Québec Association of Pharmacy Owners *Voir* Association québécoise des pharmaciens propriétaires

Québec Association of Protestant School Boards *See* Québec English School Boards Association

Québec Association of Provincial Court Judges

c/o Juge Jacques A. Nadeau, Cour du Québec, #4-223, 410, rue de Bellechasse est, Montréal QC H2S 1K3
Tel: 514-490-2380; *Fax:* 514-490-2483
Overview: A small provincial organization
Member of: Canadian Association of Provincial Court Judges
Chief Officer(s):
Jacques A. Nadeau, Directeur

Québec Association of Teachers of French as a Second Language *Voir* Association québécoise des enseignants de français langue seconde

Québec Association of the Appraisal Institute of Canada *Voir* L'Association du Québec de l'Institut canadien des évaluateurs

Québec Ball Hockey Association (QBHA) / Association de Hockey-Balle du Québec (AHBQ)

2890 boul Dagenais West, Laval QC H7P 1T1
Tel: 450-963-9346; *Fax:* 450-622-4466
info@ahbq.com
www.qbha.com
www.facebook.com/AHBQ.QBHA
twitter.com/AHBQ_QBHA
Overview: A small provincial organization
Mission: To promote & organize ball hockey in Québec & across the country
Member of: Canadian Ball Hockey Association; International Street & Ball Hockey Federation; Hockey Canada

Québec Basketball Federation *Voir* Fédération de basketball du Québec

Québec Bio-Industries Business Network *Voir* BIOQuébec

Québec Black Medical Association

#101, 1832 Sherbrooke St. W, Montréal QC H3H 1C4
Tel: 514-937-8822
www.qbma.org
Overview: A medium-sized provincial organization
Mission: The Québec Black Medical Association aims to enable young people from the Black community to pursue careers as health professionals and to advance medical practice and research in Quebec.
Chief Officer(s):
E.C. Tucker, Contact

Québec Board of Black Educators (QBBE)

#310, Cavendish Blvd., Montréal QC H4B 2M5
Tel: 514-481-9400; *Fax:* 514-481-0611
qbbe@videotron.ca
www.qbbe.org
Overview: A medium-sized local organization founded in 1968
Mission: The Quebec Board of Black Educators mission is to promote the development of educational services for Black Youth and other youth between the ages of 5 to 25 who reside in the Greater Montreal area.
Chief Officer(s):
Phylicia Burke, Contact
Clarence Bayne, President

Québec Brewers Association *Voir* Association des brasseurs du Québec

Québec Building Envelope Council *Voir* Conseil de l'enveloppe du bâtiment du Québec

Québec Camping Association *Voir* Association des camps du Québec inc.

Québec Celiac Foundation *Voir* Fondation québécoise de la maladie coeliaque

Québec Centre of Hearing Impaired *Voir* Centre québécois de la déficience auditive

Québec Cerebral Palsy Association *Voir* Association de paralysie cérébrale du Québec

Québec Chess Federation *Voir* Fédération québécoise des échecs

Québec City & Area Tourism & Convention Board *Voir* Office du tourisme et des congrès de Québec

Québec City Summer Festival *Voir* Festival d'été de Québec

Québec Command *Voir* The Royal Canadian Legion

Québec Commercial Certification Office Inc. *Voir* L'Office de Certification Commerciale du Québec Inc.

Québec Community Newspaper Association (QCNA) / Association des journaux régionaux du Québec (AJRQ)

#5, 400, boul Grand, L'Ile-Perrot QC J7V 4X2
Tel: 514-453-6300; *Fax:* 514-453-6330
info@qcna.qc.ca
www.qcna.org
Previous Name: Association of Québec Regional English Media
Overview: A medium-sized provincial organization founded in 1980 overseen by Canadian Community Newspapers Association
Mission: To promote Québec community English media; To serve as clearinghouse for information; To promote good journalism among members; to enhance the role of the media as social catalysts; To represent its members to pertinent government departments; To interact with other provincial & national newspaper associations in Canada; To help members better their financial condition
Affiliation(s): Conseil du presse du Québec
Chief Officer(s):
Greg Duncan, Executive Director
Finances: *Annual Operating Budget:* $250,000-$500,000; *Funding Sources:* Federal government; advertising commissions surplus; membership fees
Staff Member(s): 3; 8 volunteer(s)
Membership: 30; *Fees:* $150; *Member Profile:* Printed medium for Québec English-speaking community; *Committees:* By-laws; Editorial; Nomination; Awards
Activities: Member Services: Quebec regional news service (QCNA Press); advertising clearing/monitoring; promotions & marketing; networking & expertise; workshops, general meetings, telephone information services; advocacy of the communities' right to information in their language; community building through media support; *Speaker Service:* Yes; *Rents Mailing List:* Yes

Québec Competitive Festival of Music / Festival de concours du Québec

136 Duke-of-Kent Ave., Pointe-Claire QC H9R 1X9
Tel: 514-398-4535; *Fax:* 514-398-8061
Previous Name: Québec Competitive Music Festival
Overview: A medium-sized provincial organization overseen by Federation of Canadian Music Festivals
Chief Officer(s):
Tom Davidson, Provincial Administrator
thomas.davidson@mcgill.ca

Québec Competitive Music Festival *See* Québec Competitive Festival of Music

Québec Council on Tobacco & Health *Voir* Conseil québécois sur le tabac et la santé

Québec Crafts Council (Ind.) *Voir* Conseil des métiers d'art du Québec (ind.)

The Quebec Cricket Federation Inc. *Voir* La Fédération Québécoise du Cricket Inc.

Québec Cycling Sports Federation *Voir* Fédération québécoise des sports cyclistes

Québec Dairy Council Inc. *Voir* Conseil des industriels laitiers du Québec inc.

Québec dans le monde
CP 8503, #404, 1001, route de l'Église, Sainte-Foy QC G1V 4N5
Tél: 418-659-5540; *Téléc:* 418-659-4143
info@quebecmonde.com
www.quebecmonde.com
www.facebook.com/pages/Qu%C3%A9bec-dans-le-monde/282129985132094
twitter.com/Quebec_Monde
Également appelé: Association Québec dans le monde
Nom précédent: Alliance Champlain
Aperçu: *Dimension:* moyenne; *Envergure:* internationale; Organisme sans but lucratif; fondée en 1983
Mission: Faire connaître le Québec et sa spécificité culturelle dans le monde; éditer des ouvrages de référence (annuaires, bottins, répertoires) sur le Québec
Finances: *Budget de fonctionnement annuel:* $250,000-$500,000; *Fonds:* Cotisations des membres; vente des produits d'édition; abonnements aux périodiques
Membre(s) du personnel: 3; 15 bénévole(s)
Membre: 1 200 membres québécois; *Montant de la cotisation:* 48$ individu; 74$ collectif
Activités: Édite 20 annuaires et répertoires sur le Québec et ses ressources; gère 30 listes informatisées sur le Québec totalisant 40,000 entreprises ou organismes parmi les plus importants du Québec; *Listes de destinataires:* Oui

Québec Dart Association Inc. *Voir* Association de Dards du Québec inc.

The Québec Drama Federation (QDF) / Fédération dramatique du Québec
#807, 460, rue Ste-Catherine ouest, Montréal QC H3B 1A7
Tel: 514-875-8698
Toll-Free: 877-875-7863
qdf@quebecdrama.org
www.quebecdrama.org
www.facebook.com/pages/Quebec-Drama-Federation/106309432727648
twitter.com/QuebecDramaFed
Overview: A small provincial charitable organization founded in 1972
Mission: To encourage & support English-language theatre in predominantly francophone Québec; to offer leadership in the promotion & development of professional theatre artists, companies & organizations; to offer consultation & advocacy services, as well as professional training & promotion
Member of: Conseil québécoise du théâtre; In Kind Canada
Affliation(s): Canadian Conference of the Arts; Association of Drama Educators of Québec; Professional Association of Canadian Theatres; Québec Community Groups Network; Academie québécoise du théâtre
Chief Officer(s):
Jane Needles, Executive Director
Anne Clark, President
Finances: *Annual Operating Budget:* $50,000-$100,000; *Funding Sources:* Provincial government; Federal government; municipal government; regional government
Staff Member(s): 4; 22 volunteer(s)
Membership: 225; *Fees:* $15-$150; *Member Profile:* Theatre companies; individuals; artists; educators; students
Activities: *Library*

Québec Employers Council *Voir* Conseil du patronat du Québec

Quebec English Literacy Alliance (QELA)
PO Box 3542, #236, 410 St. Nicholas St., Montreal QC H2Y 2P5
Tel: 450-242-2360; *Fax:* 450-242-2543
Toll-Free: 866-942-7352
info@qela.qc.ca
qela.qc.ca
Overview: A medium-sized provincial organization founded in 1997
Mission: To be the unified voice of Quebec English literacy providers nationally & provincially
Chief Officer(s):
Louise Quinn, Executive Director
lquinn@qela.qc.ca
Staff Member(s): 3
Membership: 25
Activities: Networking, training & information-sharing activities; advancement of literacy in the province

Québec English School Boards Association (QESBA) / Association des commissions scolaires anglophones du Québec (ACSAQ)
#515, 1410, rue Stanley, Montréal QC H3A 1P8
Tel: 514-849-5900; *Fax:* 514-849-9228
Toll-Free: 877-512-7522
qesba@qesba.qc.ca
www.qesba.qc.ca
www.facebook.com/122225577919
Previous Name: Québec Association of Protestant School Boards
Overview: A medium-sized provincial charitable organization founded in 1929 overseen by Canadian School Boards Association
Mission: To represent English school boards in Québec
Chief Officer(s):
David Birnbaum, Executive Director
dbirnbaum@qesba.qc.ca
Finances: *Annual Operating Budget:* $500,000-$1.5 Million; *Funding Sources:* Membership fees
Staff Member(s): 6
Membership: 9 English school boards; 178 school trustees; *Fees:* $6.90 per pupil
Activities: Advocacy; research & analysis; professional development;

Québec Environment Foundation *Voir* Fondation québécoise en environnement

Québec Environmental Law Centre *Voir* Centre québécois du droit de l'environnement

Québec Esperanto Society *Voir* Société québécoise d'espéranto

Québec Eye Bank Foundation *Voir* Fondation de la banque d'yeux du Québec inc.

Québec Family History Society (QFHS) / Société de l'histoire des familles du Québec
PO Box 1026, Pointe-Claire QC H9S 4H9
Tel: 514-695-1502; *Fax:* 514-695-3508
qfhs@bellnet.ca
www.qfhs.ca
Overview: A medium-sized provincial charitable organization founded in 1977
Mission: To promote genealogy & genealogical research in Québec (particularly English & Protestant records) to collect & preserve books, manuscripts & other related material; To conduct workshops & seminars & discuss topics of interest to members
Member of: Québec Anglophone Heritage Network
Affliation(s): International Federation of Family History Societies
Chief Officer(s):
Gary Schroder, President
Joan Benoit, Executive Secretary
Finances: *Annual Operating Budget:* Less than $50,000; *Funding Sources:* Membership dues; book sales & research
20 volunteer(s)
Membership: 130 institutional + 800 individual; *Fees:* $35 institutional; $55 individual; $55 family; *Member Profile:* Individual - regular; family - two persons at the same address; institutional - libraries & other organizations; *Committees:* Cemetery Transcription
Activities: Monthly lectures; workshops; *Library*

Québec Farmers' Association (QFA)
#255, 555, boul Roland-Therrien, Longueuil QC J4H 4E7
Tel: 450-679-0540; *Fax:* 450-463-5291
qfa@upa.qc.ca
www.quebecfarmers.org
Overview: A medium-sized provincial organization founded in 1957
Member of: Quebec Community Groups Network
Chief Officer(s):
Ivan Hale, Executive Director
Wendy Jones, Director, Operations
Membership: 3,000; *Fees:* $56.98; *Member Profile:* Québec's English-speaking farmers & rural citizens

Québec Federation for Autism & Other Pervasive Developmental Disorders *Voir* Fédération québécoise de l'autisme et des autres troubles envahissants du développement

Québec Federation of General Practitioners *Voir* Fédération des médecins omnipraticiens du Québec

Québec Federation of Home & School Associations Inc. (QFHSA) / Fédération des associations foyer-école du Québec Inc.
#560, 3285, boul Cavendish, Montréal QC H4B 2L9
Tel: 514-481-5619; *Fax:* 514-481-5610
Toll-Free: 888-808-5619
info@qfhsa.org
www.qfhsa.org
Previous Name: Québec Federation of Protestant Home & School Associations
Overview: A medium-sized provincial charitable organization founded in 1944 overseen by Canadian Home & School Federation
Mission: To provide facilities for the bringing together of members of Home & School Associations for discussion of matters of general interest & to stimulate cooperative effort; To assist in forming public opinion favorable to reform & advancement of the education of the child; to develop between educators & the general public such a united effort as shall secure for every child the highest advantage in physical, mental, moral & spiritual education; To raise the standard of home & national life; To maintain non-partisan, non-commercial, non-racial & non-sectarian organization
Affliation(s): Center for Literacy
Chief Officer(s):
Liette Chamberland, President
president@qfhsa.org
Rosalind Hoenig, Secretary
literacy@qfhsa.org
Finances: *Funding Sources:* Membership fees
Staff Member(s): 2; 20 volunteer(s)
Membership: 5,000 families; *Fees:* $60 group affiliate; $16 family (includes affiliation with national home & school federation); *Member Profile:* Mainly parents in local schools; *Committees:* Education; Safety; Literacy; Health; Advocacy; Membership; Rights
Activities: Workshops on parenting & child-related issues; provides resources to parents in schools; annual Think Tank; Fall Leadership Conference; AGM; *Speaker Service:* Yes; *Library* Open to public by appointment
Awards:
• Lewis Peace Prize (Award)
• Leslie N. Buzzell Award (Award)
Awarded to a home & school member who has given outstanding service at the provincial level
• Gordon Paterson Award (Award)
Awarded to an outstanding educator who has encouraged parent participation in the educational process
• Pat Lewis Humanitarian Award (Award)

Québec Federation of Labour *Voir* Fédération des travailleurs et travailleises du Québec

Quebec Federation of Laryngectomees *Voir* Fédération québécoise des laryngectomisés

Quebec Federation of Managers & Professional Salaried Workers (CNTU) *Voir* Fédération des professionnèles

Québec Federation of Policemen (Ind.) *Voir* Fédération des policiers et policières municipaux du Québec (ind.)

Québec Federation of Professional Employees in Education *Voir* Fédération des professionnelles et professionnels de l'éducation du Québec

Québec Federation of Professional Firefighters *Voir* Syndicat des pompiers et pompières du Québec (CTC)

Québec Federation of Protestant Home & School Associations *See* Québec Federation of Home & School Associations Inc.

Québec Federation of Residents (Ind.) *Voir* Fédération des médecins résidents du Québec inc. (ind.)

Québec Federation of Senior Citizens *Voir* Réseau FADOQ

Québec Federation of the Blind Inc. (QFB) / Fédération des aveugles du Québec inc.
7000, rue Sherbrooke ouest, Montréal QC H4B 1R3
Tel: 514-484-9232
qfb@ssss.gouv.qc.ca

Overview: A small provincial charitable organization founded in 1970
Chief Officer(s):
Anita Stewer, Contact
Finances: *Funding Sources:* Donations; Fundraising
Membership: 100-499;

Québec Federation of University Professors *Voir* Fédération québécoise des professeures et professeurs d'université

Quebec Fish and Seafood Marketing Association *Voir* Association québécoise de commercialisation de poissons et de fruits de mer

Québec Fish Processors Association *Voir* Association québécoise de l'industrie de la pêche

Québec Food Retailers' Association *Voir* Association des détaillants en alimentation du Québec

Québec Forestry Industry Council *Voir* Conseil de l'industrie forestière du Québec

Québec Furniture Manufacturers Association Inc. *Voir* Association des fabricants de meubles du Québec inc.

Québec Gardens Association *Voir* Association des jardins du Québec

The Québec Gay Chamber of Commerce *Voir* Chambre de commerce gaie du Québec

Québec Golf Federation *Voir* Fédération de golf du Québec

Québec Golf Superintendents Association *Voir* Association des surintendants de golf du Québec

Québec Government Employees' Union (Ind.) *Voir* Syndicat de la fonction publique du Québec inc. (ind.)

Québec Gymnastics Federation *Voir* Fédération de gymnastique du Québec

Québec Handball Association *Voir* Balle au mur Québec

Québec Harvest *Voir* Moisson Québec

Québec Hospital Association *Voir* Association québécoise d'établissements de santé et de services sociaux (AQESSS)

Québec Institute of Floor Covering *Voir* Fédération québécoise des revêtements de sol

Québec Interprofessional Council *Voir* Conseil interprofessionnel du Québec

Québec Jewellers' Corporation *Voir* Corporation des bijoutiers du Québec

Québec Land Surveyors Association *Voir* Ordre des arpenteurs-géomètres du Québec

Quebec Landlords Association *Voir* Association des propriétaires du Québec inc.

Québec Lawn Bowling Federation / Fédération de Boulingrin du Québec

662, av Oak, Saint-Lambert QC J4P 2R6
e-mail: pclawnbowls@hotmail.com
www.qlbf.org
Overview: A medium-sized provincial organization overseen by Bowls Canada Boulingrin

Quebec Lawyers Abroad *Voir* Avocats Hors Québec

Québec Lesbian Network *Voir* Réseau des lesbiennes du Québec

Québec Liberal Party *Voir* Parti libéral du Québec

Québec Library Association *Voir* Association des bibliothécaires du Québec

Québec Liquor Board Store & Office Employees Union (Ind.) *Voir* Syndicat des employé(e)s de magasins et de bureau de la Société des alcools du Québec (ind.)

Québec Liquor Board's Union of Technical & Professional Employees (Ind.) *Voir* Syndicat du personnel technique et professionnel de la Société des alcools du Québec (ind.)

Québec Lung Association (QLA) / Association pulmonaire du Québec (APQ)

5790, av Pierre-de Coubertin, Montréal QC H1N 1R4
Tel: 514-287-7400; *Fax:* 514-287-1978
Toll-Free: 888-768-6669
info@pq.poumon.ca
www.pq.poumon.ca
www.linkedin.com/groups?gid=2111754
www.facebook.com/poumon.qc
www.youtube.com/user/PoumonAPQ
Overview: A medium-sized provincial charitable organization founded in 1938 overseen by Canadian Lung Association
Mission: To provide resources in Québec about lung cancer, chronic obstructive pulmonary disease, sarcoidosis, tuberculosis, asthma, chronic bronchitis, sleep apnea, pneumonia, & emphysema
Member of: World Health Organization; International Union against Tuberculosis & Lung Disease; American Lung Association; European Lung Association
Chief Officer(s):
Dominique Massie, Executive Director, 514-975-5382 Ext. 224
dominique.massie@pq.poumon.ca
Raymond Jabbour, Chief Financial Officer & Director, Direct Marketing & Information Technology, 514-975-5382 Ext. 226
Carole Bouchard, Director, Development & Communications, 514-975-5382 Ext. 225
carole.bouchard@pq.poumon.ca
Lynda Monière, Coordinator, Media Relations & Major Events, 514-975-5382 Ext. 229
lynda.moniere@pq.poumon.ca
Lise Vaillancourt, Respiratory Therapist & Coordinator, Programs, 514-975-5382 Ext. 232
lise.vaillancourt@pq.poumon.ca
Finances: *Funding Sources:* Donations; Fundraising; Sponsorships
Staff Member(s): 15; 20 volunteer(s)
Activities: Supporting respiratory health research; Providing education about respiratory illness; Offering support groups for persons affected by lung disease; Organizing events to raise funds; *Awareness Events:* Provincial Ragweed Extermination Campaign
Publications:
• Le Bulletin de l'association pulmonaire du Québec
Type: Newsletter; *Editor:* Louis P. Brisson *ISSN:* 0843-381X
Profile: Respiratory health information, plus donation news
• Le Rapport annuel de l'association pulmonaire du Québec
Type: Yearbook; *Frequency:* Annually

Québec Maple Syrup Producers Federation *Voir* Fédération des producteurs acéricoles du Québec

Québec Master Roofers Association *Voir* Association des maîtres couvreurs du Québec

Québec Medical Association *Voir* Association médicale du Québec

Québec Mineral Exploration Assocation *Voir* Association de l'exploration minière de Québec

Québec Mining Association *Voir* Association minière du Québec

Québec Motorcyclist Federation *Voir* Fédération motocycliste du Québec

Québec Native Women Inc. *Voir* Femmes autochtones du Québec inc.

Quebec Oil and Gas Association *Voir* Association pétrolière et gazière du Québec

Québec Oil Heating Association *Voir* Association québécoise du chauffage au mazout

Québec Optometric Association *Voir* Association des optométristes du Québec

Québec Press Council *Voir* Conseil de presse du Québec

Québec Produce Growers Association *Voir* Association des producteurs maraîchers du Québec

Québec Produce Marketing Association *Voir* Association québécoise de la distribution de fruits et légumes

Québec Professional Association of Medical Technologists (Ind.) *Voir* Association professionnelle des technologistes médicaux du Québec (ind.)

Québec Professional Union of Dieticians (Ind.) *Voir* Syndicat professionnel des diététistes et nutritionnistes du Québec

Québec Provincial Association of Teachers *Voir* Association provinciale des enseignantes et enseignants du Québec

Québec Provincial Police Association (Ind.) *Voir* Association des policières et policiers provinciaux du Québec (ind.)

Quebec Psoriasis Alliance *See* Alliance Québécoise du Psoriasis

Québec Psychiatrists' Association *Voir* Association des médecins-psychiatres du Québec

Québec Public Health Association *Voir* Association pour la santé publique du Québec

Québec Public Interest Research Group - McGill / Groupe de recherche d'intérêt public du Québec - McGill

3647, rue Université, 3e étage, Montréal QC H3A 2B3
Tél: 514-398-7432; *Téléc:* 514-398-8976
qpirg@ssmu.mcgill.ca
qpirgmcgill.org
www.facebook.com/QPIRG.GRIP.McGill
twitter.com/qpirgmcgill
Également appelé: QPIRG-McGill
Aperçu: *Dimension:* petite; *Envergure:* nationale
Mission: To work on social justice & environmental issues
Membre: *Critères d'admissibilite:* Students; *Comités:* Conflict Resolution & Complaints

Québec Racquetball Association *Voir* Association québécoise de racquetball

Québec Raptor Rehabilitation Network *Voir* Union québécoise de réhabilitation des oiseaux de proie

Québec Real Estate Association *Voir* Organisme d'autoréglementation du courtage immobilier du Québec

Québec Regional Tourist Associations Inc. *Voir* Associations touristiques régionales associées du Québec

Quebec Rehabilitation Centres Association *Voir* Association des établissements de réadaptation en déficience physique du Québec

Québec Restaurant Association *Voir* Association des restaurateurs du Québec

Québec Road Builders & Heavy Construction Association *Voir* Association des constructeurs de routes et grands travaux du Québec

Quebec Rugby Union *Voir* Fédération de rugby du Québec

Québec Shooting Federation *Voir* Fédération québécoise de tir

Québec Shorthorn Association / Club Shorthorn du Québec

27 Wells Rd., West Brome QC J0E 2P0
Tel: 450-263-3090
Overview: A small provincial organization
Member of: Canadian Shorthorn Association
Chief Officer(s):
Kevin Dempsey, President
Raymond Dempsey, Secretary

Québec Simmental Association (QSA) / Association Simmental du Québec (ASQ)

530, rte 239, Saint-Germain QC J0C 1K0
Tel: 819-395-4453; *Fax:* 819-395-4453
info@simmentalquebec.ca
www.simmentalquebec.ca
Overview: A small provincial organization founded in 1981
Mission: To promote the Québec Simmental breeding programs to the market, purebred as well as commercial, within the province of Québec & abroad
Member of: Canadian Simmental Association
Chief Officer(s):
René Larose, Treasurer
Rosaire Côté, President, 450-796-5914
Finances: *Annual Operating Budget:* Less than $50,000; *Funding Sources:* Canadian Simmental Association; Comité Conjoint des Races de Boucherie
6 volunteer(s)
Membership: 135; *Fees:* $34.19 annual; $227.90 lifetime; *Member Profile:* Purebred Simmental cattle breeders
Publications:
• Simmental du Québec

Québec Snowboard Association *Voir* Association Québec Snowboard

Quebec Society for Disabled Children *Voir* Société pour les enfants handicapés du Québec

Québec Society for the Defense of Animals *Voir* Société québécoise pour la défense des animaux

Québec Society for the Protection of Plants *Voir* Société de protection des plantes du Québec

Quebec Society of Comparitive Law *Voir* Association québécoise de doit comparé

Québec Society of Lipidology, Nutrition & Metabolism Inc. (QSLNM) / Société québécoise de lipidologie, de nutrition et de métabolisme (SQLNM)

2705, boul Laurier, Sainte-Foy QC G1V 4G2
Tel: 418-656-4141; *Fax:* 418-654-2145
sqlnm@crchul.ulaval.ca
www.lipidologie.qc.ca
Overview: A small provincial charitable organization founded in 2000
Mission: To promote training, education & research in lipidology, nutrition, metabolism & cardiovascular health
Chief Officer(s):
Pierre Julien, PhD, President
pierre.julien@crchul.ulaval.ca
Finances: *Annual Operating Budget:* $50,000-$100,000
Membership: 632; *Fees:* Free; *Member Profile:* Scientists; physicians; lipidologists
Awards:
- Prix des fondateurs (Award)
- Prix des meilleures affiches (Award)

Québec Special Olympics *Voir* Jeux Olympiques Spéciaux du Québec Inc.

Québec Square & Round Dance Clubs *See* Border Boosters Square & Round Dance Association

Quebec Technology Association *Voir* Association québécoise des technologies

Québec Thistle Council Inc. / Le Conseil Québécois du Chardon Inc.

#703, 3495, rue de la Montagne, Montréal QC H3G 2A5
Tel: 514-982-4525; *Fax:* 514-849-4137
www.thistlecouncil.ca
Also Known As: Auld Alliance in Canada
Overview: A small provincial charitable organization founded in 1991
Mission: To promote & maintain Scottish culture & traditions in the Province of Québec & in particular, Montréal, through the organization, sponsorship & coordination of Scottish cultural activities & events
Chief Officer(s):
Mildred Benoit, Contact
mildredbenoit@sympatico.ca
Finances: *Annual Operating Budget:* Less than $50,000; *Funding Sources:* Private
10 volunteer(s)
Membership: 15
Activities: Auld Alliance Awards Dinner & Ceilidh

Québec Trotting & Pacing Society *Voir* Association Trot & Amble du Québec

Québec Trucking Association Inc. *Voir* Association du camionnage du Québec inc.

Québec Union of Firefighters (CLC) *Voir* Syndicat des pompiers et pompières du Québec (CTC)

Québec Union of Health Professionals & Technicians *Voir* Syndicat des professionnels et des techniciens de la santé du Québec

Québec Union of Nurses *Voir* Union québécoise des infirmières et infirmiers

Québec University Students' Federation *Voir* Fédération étudiante universitaire du Québec

Quebec Urban Transit Association *Voir* Association du transport urbain du Québec

Quebec Urological Association *Voir* Association des urologues du Québec

Québec Water Bottlers' Association *Voir* Association des embouteilleurs d'eau du Québec

Québec Welsh Pony & Cob Association *See* Association des Poneys Welsh & Cob au Québec

Québec Winter Carnival *Voir* Carnaval de Québec

Québec Women's Institutes (QWI)

c/o Linda Hoy, 77, rte 108, Cookshire-Eaton QC J0B 1M0
Tel: 819-566-2105; *Fax:* 819-822-3145
Overview: A medium-sized provincial organization founded in 1911 overseen by Federated Women's Institutes of Canada
Mission: To help discover, stimulate & develop leadership among women; To assist, encourage & support women to become knowledgeable & responsible citizens; To ensure basic human rights for women & to work toward their equality; To be a strong voice through which matters of utmost concern can reach the decision makers; To promote the improvement of agricultural & other rural communities & to safeguard the environment
Affliation(s): Associated Country Women of the World
Chief Officer(s):
Linda Hoy, Executive Officer
Finances: *Annual Operating Budget:* Less than $50,000; *Funding Sources:* Membership dues; fundraising
Membership: 630 individuals in 14 counties & 52 branches; *Fees:* $25; *Committees:* Agriculture; Education & Personal Development; Health & Community; Publicity & Awareness
Activities: Community work & activities
Awards:
- The Mrs. Alfred Watt Memorial Scholarship (Scholarship)
- The Frederica Campbell McFarlane Prize (Scholarship)
- The Edna L. Smith Memorial Bursary (Scholarship)
- The Frances Taylor Memorial Bursary (Scholarship)

Québec Wrestling Association *Voir* Fédération de lutte olympique du Québec

Québec Writers' Federation (QWF) / Fédération des Écrivaines et Écrivains du Québec

#3, 1200 Atwater Ave., Montréal QC H3Z 1X4
Tel: 514-933-0878
admin@qwf.org
www.qwf.org
Merged from: Québec Society for the Promotion of English Language Literature; Federation of English Writers of QC
Overview: A small provincial charitable organization founded in 1998
Mission: To encourage & support English-language writing in Québec to ensure a lasting place for English literature in the province's cultural scene.
Chief Officer(s):
David Homel, President
Lori Schubert, Executive Director
Finances: *Funding Sources:* Corporation, government & individual donations
Staff Member(s): 2
Membership: *Fees:* $25; *Member Profile:* Professional & emerging writers; anyone interested
Activities: Writing workshops; literary readings; festival; short story competition in collaboration with CBC Radio; mentorship program; *Library:* Documentation Centre; by appointment
Awards:
- QWF Prizes (Award)

Established 1988; awards five annual prizes of $2,000 each to honour literary excellence: The A.M. Klein poetry prize, The Hugh MacLennan fiction prize, Mavis Gallant prize for non-fiction, The McAuslan First Book Award & Translation award*Eligibility:* Book by Québec author; 6 categories - fiction, non-fiction, poetry, 1st book, translation, children/young adult *Amount:* 6 awards of $2000 each

Québec Young Farmers *See* Québec 4-H

Québec-Labrador Foundation (Canada) Inc. (QLF (Canada)) / Fondation Québec Labrador du (Canada) inc.

#901, 505, boul René Lévesque ouest, Montréal QC H2Z 1Y7
Tel: 514-395-6020; *Fax:* 514-395-4505
montreal@qlf.org
www.qlf.org
Overview: A small national charitable organization founded in 1969
Mission: To promote local leadership & assist in improvement of human conditions in northern New England, Eastern Québec, & Canadian Atlantic provinces; to conserve cultural heritage & natural resources of region; To conduct scientific research; To enrich educational experience of Canadian & US students
Affliation(s): Atlantic Centre for the Environment
Chief Officer(s):
Lawrence B. Morris, President
Finances: *Annual Operating Budget:* $500,000-$1.5 Million
Staff Member(s): 17
Membership: 4,000 individual; 50 institutional
Awards:
- Sounds Conservancy Grants Program (Award)
- Caring for the Earth Award (Award)

Queen Charlotte Islands Arts Council *See* Haida Gwaii Arts Council

Queen Elizabeth Hospital Foundation

PO Box 6600, Charlottetown PE C1A 8T5
Tel: 902-894-2425; *Fax:* 902-894-2433
info@qehfoundation.pe.ca
www.qehfoundation.pe.ca
www.facebook.com/289345824414870
twitter.com/QEHFoundation
Also Known As: QEH Foundation
Overview: A small local charitable organization
Mission: To receive donations on behalf of the Queen Elizabeth Hospital & utilize those funds in order to improve the quality of care at the Queen Elizabeth Hospital
Chief Officer(s):
Barb Dunphy, Chief Executive Officer
bdunphy@qehfoundation.pe.ca
Finances: *Funding Sources:* Donations
Staff Member(s): 9

The Queen of Puddings Music Theatre Company

The Case Good Warehouse, Bldg. 74, Studio 206, 55 Mill St., Toronto ON M5A 3C4
Tel: 416-203-4149; *Fax:* 416-203-8027
queenofpuddings@bellnet.ca
www.queenofpuddingsmusictheatre.com
Overview: A small local charitable organization
Mission: Queen of Puddings has consistently produced provocative, dramatic presentations that have challenged the parameters of the opera genre. The company works solely with Canadian artists.
Chief Officer(s):
Dairine Ni Mheadhra, Artistic Director
dairine@queenofpuddingsmusictheatre.com
John Hess, Artistic Director

Queen's University Faculty Association (QUFA) / Association des professeurs de l'Université Queen's

Queen's University, 9 St. Lawrence Ave., Kingston ON K7L 3N6
Tel: 613-533-2151; *Fax:* 613-533-6171
qufa2@queensu.ca
www.qufa.ca
www.facebook.com/home.php?sk=group_374595686308
twitter.com/qufatweet
Overview: A small local organization founded in 1951
Mission: To act as the certified bargaining agent for Queen's University faculty members; To promote the interests of the Queen's University academic staff
Chief Officer(s):
Paul Young, President
Paul Young, Vice-President
Monika Holzschuh Sator, Secretary
Ken Ko, Treasurer
Marvin Baer, Chief Negotiator
mgb1@post.queensu.ca
Elaine Berman, Administrative Officer, 613-533-3033
qufa@queensu.ca
Phil Goldman, Grievance Officer, 613-533-6241
goldmanp@post.queensu.ca
Membership: 1,200; *Member Profile:* Queen's University faculty, librarians, & archivists; *Committees:* Executive; Joint Committee to Administer the Agreement; Finance; Grievance; Nominations & Elections; Political Action & Communications; Staff Relations; Benefits Oversight; Anomalies Fund; Employment Systems Review; Intellectual Property; Merit & Career Development / Compensation; Budget Analysis Sub-Committee; Constitutional Review Sub-Committee; Equity Sub-committee; Fund for Scholarly Research & Creative Work & Professional Development Sub-Committee; Teaching Assessment Sub-Committee; Pension Ad hoc; Negotiators for the Employees Group Ad hoc; Past President's Ad hoc; Website Ad hoc
Activities: Promoting a positive, equitable working environment for Queen's University academic staff; Offering workshops for members
Publications:
- QUFA Voices

Type: Newsletter; *Frequency:* every 2 months; *Editor:* Robert G.

May
Profile: QUFA news, opinions, & events

Queen's University International Centre (QUIC)
Queen's University, John Deutsch University Centre, 99 University Ave., Kingston ON K7L 3N6
Tel: 613-533-2604; *Fax:* 613-533-3159
quic.queensu.ca
www.facebook.com/quic.queensu.ca
twitter.com/quic
Previous Name: International Centre
Overview: A small international organization founded in 1961
Mission: To focus primarily on the university constituency with program links into the broader Kingston community
Member of: Canadian Bureau for International Education; Canadian Association of College & University Student Services; NAFSA: Association of International Educators
Chief Officer(s):
Wayne Myles, Director
wayne.myles@queensu.ca
Finances: *Annual Operating Budget:* $250,000-$500,000; *Funding Sources:* Queen's University; Ed & Anna Churchill Foundation
Staff Member(s): 24; 300 volunteer(s)
Membership: 2,000 - 3,000; *Committees:* International Centre Council
Activities: *Library:* International Resource Library

Queens Association for Supported Living (QASL)
44 Pleasant St., Milton NS B0T 1P0
Tel: 902-354-2723; *Fax:* 902-354-2262
info@qasl.ca
www.qasl.ca
Overview: A small local organization founded in 1969
Mission: To improve the quality of life for individuals with disabilities
Member of: DIRECTIONS Council for Vocational Services Society
Chief Officer(s):
Treena Dexter, Executive Director/Manager
qasl@eastlink.ca
Activities: Residential services; integration programs; vocational programs, including Penny Lane Enterprises & Riverbank General Store

Queens County Historical Society
PO Box 1078, 109 Main St., Liverpool NS B0T 1K0
Tel: 902-354-4058; *Fax:* 902-354-2050
www.queenscountymuseum.com
www.facebook.com/QueensCountyHistoricalSociety
Overview: A small local organization founded in 1929
Mission: To collect, preserve & display the human & natural history of Queens County, Nova Scotia
Member of: Federation of the Nova Scotian Heritage
Finances: *Funding Sources:* Provincial & regional government
Membership: *Fees:* $10 single; $12 family
Activities: *Library:* Thomas Raddall Research Centre; Open to public

Queensbush Initiatives for Literacy & Learning Inc. *See* Quality in Lifelong Learning Network

Quest Centre Community Initiatives
PO Box 550, 3581 Concession Dr., Glencoe ON N0L 1M0
Tel: 519-287-2726; *Fax:* 519-287-3804
quest_centre@yahoo.com
www.quest-centre.com
Also Known As: The Quest Centre
Overview: A small local organization founded in 1999
Member of: CSAE
Chief Officer(s):
Shirley Slaats, Manager
Finances: *Annual Operating Budget:* $100,000-$250,000; *Funding Sources:* United Way; Fundraisers; Thames Valley District School Board
Staff Member(s): 1; 1 volunteer(s)
Membership: *Committees:* Government information & forms; computer courses; children's programs
Activities: Employment councilling; Correspondance courses; First Aid & CPR training; Beginner computer taining; Workshops

Quest Residential & Support Services *See* Quest Support Services Inc.

Quest Support Services Inc.
PO Box 1201, Stn. Main, 1245 - 2nd Ave. South, Lethbridge AB T1J 0E5
Tel: 403-381-9515; *Fax:* 403-320-6555
Toll-Free: 866-382-9515
www.questsupport.com
Previous Name: Quest Residential & Support Services
Overview: A small local organization founded in 1990
Mission: To provide services for people with developmental disabilities, community based agencies
Chief Officer(s):
Michele Currie, Contact, Children Services Program
m.currie@questsupport.com
Finances: *Annual Operating Budget:* Less than $50,000; *Funding Sources:* Persons with Developmental Disabilities (PDD) provincial funding program
Staff Member(s): 13; 10 volunteer(s)
Membership: 25

Quesnel & District Association for the Mentally Handicapped *See* Quesnel Community Living Association

Quesnel & District Chamber of Commerce
335 East Vaughan St., Quesnel BC V2J 2T1
Tel: 250-992-7262
qchamber@quesnelbc.com
quesnelchamber.com
www.facebook.comm/10150128152340257
Overview: A small local organization founded in 1910
Mission: To undertake those policies & programs established annually that will effectively promote Quesnel & District in a manner improving trade, commerce & the welfare of its citizens; To create & maintain a cooperative enterprise of business people helping one another
Member of: BC Chamber of Commerce; Canadian Chamber of Commerce; Better Business Bureau
Chief Officer(s):
Colin Ketchum, President
Coralee Oakes, Executive Director
Finances: *Annual Operating Budget:* $100,000-$250,000
Staff Member(s): 3
Membership: 212; *Fees:* $100-$700 based on number of full-time employees
Activities: Small Business Week; Business Excellence; Professional Assistants Luncheon; monthly guest speakers; workshops; fair; *Library* Open to public
Awards:
• Business Excellence Awards (Award)
Publications:
• Quesnel & District Chamber of Commerce Newsletter
Type: Newsletter

Quesnel & District Child Development Centre Association (QDCDCA)
488 McLean St., Quesnel BC V2J 2P2
Tel: 250-992-2481; *Fax:* 250-992-3439
www.quesnelcdc.com
Overview: A small local charitable organization founded in 1976
Mission: Children with special needs are entitled to quality programs of intervention which facilitate their physical, social, emotional, communicative & intellectual development
Affliation(s): BC Association for Child Development & Intervention
Chief Officer(s):
Kurt Pedersen, Executive Director
kurtp@quesnelcdc.com
Finances: *Annual Operating Budget:* $500,000-$1.5 Million; *Funding Sources:* Provincial Government
Staff Member(s): 23; 40 volunteer(s)
Membership: 20 individual; *Fees:* $1 individual
Activities: *Awareness Events:* Telethon, last Sun. in Oct.

Quesnel & District Labour Council (QDLC)
PO Box 4245, Quesnel BC V2J 3J3
Tel: 250-992-7725
qdlc@telus.net
Overview: A small local organization founded in 1975 overseen by British Columbia Federation of Labour
Mission: To act as the voice for working people of the Quesnel area of British Columbia
Affliation(s): Canadian Labour Congress (CLC)
Activities: Promoting the interests of local affiliated unions; Hosting monthly meeting to share information about issues affecting unions & their membership; Raising awareness of workers' issues; Organizing rallies related to local labour issues; Providing local labour news

Quesnel Community Living Association (QCLA)
658 Doherty Dr., Quesnel BC V2J 1B9
Tel: 250-992-7774
qcla.ca
Previous Name: Quesnel & District Association for the Mentally Handicapped
Overview: A small local charitable organization founded in 1959
Mission: To support all individuals with mental handicaps
Member of: British Columbia Association for Community Living
Chief Officer(s):
Ken Calihou, President
Finances: *Funding Sources:* Bingo; membership dues
Membership: *Fees:* $5

Quesnel Multicultural Society
2155 Dragon Hill Rd., Quesnel BC V2J 3J9
Tel: 250-747-1727
bheinzel@quesnelbc.com
www.quesnelarts.ca/old_site/qms.html
Overview: A small local organization founded in 1990
Mission: To promote multiculturalism through education
Member of: Affiliation of Multicultural Societies & Service Agencies of BC
Chief Officer(s):
Bernice Heinzelman, Contact
bheinzel@quesnelbc.com
Finances: *Annual Operating Budget:* Less than $50,000; *Funding Sources:* Fundraising; government
20 volunteer(s)
Membership: *Fees:* $10
Activities: *Awareness Events:* Multicultural Week

Quesnel Naturalists
c/o Lorna Schley, 128 Lindsey St., Quesnel BC V2J 3E3
www.bcnature.ca
Overview: A small local organization
Mission: To promote the enjoyment of nature through environmental appreciation & conservation; To encourage wise use & conservation of natural resources & environmental protection.
Member of: Federation of BC Naturalists
Chief Officer(s):
Lorna Schley, Contact
lschley@quesnelbc.com
Membership: 40; *Fees:* $20 single; $25 family

Quesnel Tillicum Society Friendship Centre
319 North Fraser Dr., Quesnel BC V2J 1Y9
Tel: 250-992-8347; *Fax:* 250-992-5708
www.quesnel-friendship.org
Overview: A small local charitable organization founded in 1971
Mission: To improve the quality of life & to meet the needs of First Nations & other people who are faced with adjusting to the social, economic & cultural lifestyle of the community
Member of: National Association of Friendship Centres
Chief Officer(s):
Sandy Brunton, Contact
sandy.brunton@qnfc.bc.ca
Activities: Referral; Outreach; Youth worker

Quetico Foundation
#216, 642 King St. West, Toronto ON M5V 1M7
Tel: 416-941-9388; *Fax:* 416-941-9236
office@queticofoundation.org
www.queticofoundation.org
www.facebook.com/pages/QueticoFoundation
Overview: A small provincial charitable organization founded in 1954
Mission: To preserve wilderness areas of Ontario, particularly Quetico Provincial Park, for recreation & scientific use
Chief Officer(s):
Glenda McLachlan, Executive Director
Finances: *Annual Operating Budget:* $100,000-$250,000; *Funding Sources:* Endowment & donations
Staff Member(s): 1; 20 volunteer(s)
Membership: 34 trustees & trustees Emeriti; *Fees:* $40
Activities: Scientific research, education & public awareness, liaison; *Internships:* Yes; *Library:* John B. Ridley Research Library; Open to public
Publications:
• The Quetico
Type: Newsletter; *Frequency:* Quartley

Quickdraw Animation Society (QAS)
#201, 351 - 11 Ave. SW, Calgary AB T2R 0C7
Tel: 403-261-5767; *Fax:* 403-261-5644
Other Communication: Digital Coordinator e-mail: digital@quickdrawanimation.ca
email@quickdrawanimation.ca

www.quickdrawanimation.ca
www.facebook.com/quickdrawanimation
twitter.com/GIRAFFEST
vimeo.com/quickdrawanimation
Overview: A small international charitable organization founded in 1984
Mission: To promote the study of animation & to encourage the production of independent animated films; to provide the general public with all types of animated film, particularly works that are innovative & independently produced; to establish & maintain a production facility for the discussion, study & production of independent animated film; to provide lectures, workshops & courses on all aspects of animation for the professional development of artists as well as for public education & appreciation of animation; to establish & maintain a resource centre on animation & related subjects; to facilitate the production of independent animated films & to extend this opportunity to all interested individuals
Member of: Alberta Media Arts Alliance Society; Association Internationale du Film d'Animation (ASIFA); Independent Media Arts Alliance
Chief Officer(s):
Kim Walton, President
Evangelos Diavolitsis, Executive Director
director@quickdrawanimation.ca
Finances: *Annual Operating Budget:* $100,000-$250,000; *Funding Sources:* Alberta Foundation for the Arts; The Canada Council; Calgary Region Arts Foundation
Staff Member(s): 4; 50 volunteer(s)
Membership: 172 individual; *Fees:* $50 producing; $25 associate; $30 youth; *Member Profile:* Interest in the production & appreciation of animation as an artistic medium; *Committees:* Programming; Library; Production; Promotion
Activities: *Library*
Awards:
• Members' Awards (Award)

Quidi Vidi Rennie's River Development Foundation (QVRRDF)
Nagle's Place, St. John's NL A1B 2Z2
Tel: 709-754-3474; *Fax:* 709-754-5947
info@fluvarium.ca
www.fluvarium.ca
Overview: A small local organization founded in 1985
Mission: To promote responsible environmental stewardship; To raise awareness of the nature of freshwater systems; To provide leadership in urban watershed management; To operate The Fluvarium as a public centre for environmental education
Member of: Hospitality Newfoundland & Labrador; St. John's Board of Trade; Newfoundland & Labrador Environmental Industry Association
Chief Officer(s):
Deborah Picco Garland, Executive Director
Finances: *Annual Operating Budget:* $250,000-$500,000; *Funding Sources:* Admission fees; building rentals; catering services; corporate & private donations; fundraising
Staff Member(s): 7; 100 volunteer(s)
Membership: 200; *Fees:* $30.00; *Member Profile:* Friends of Rennie's River; *Committees:* Development; Education; Facilities & Operations; Finance; Science & Exhibitions
Activities: Environmental education; tourism; restoration & habitat enhancement; *Awareness Events:* River Dance, March; Duck Race, Sept.; Fish Fry, August

Quinte - Saint Lawrence Building & Construction Trades Council
#4, 1724 Bath Rd., Kingston ON K7M 4Y2
Tel: 613-384-2269; *Fax:* 613-384-7682
Overview: A small local organization
Mission: To act as a trade union in the Quinte, Saint Lawrence region
Chief Officer(s):
Steve Cronkite, Contact
Activities: Supporting local organizations

Quinte & District Real Estate Board
PO Box 128, 51 Cannifton Rd. North, Cannifton ON K0K 1K0
Tel: 613-969-7873; *Fax:* 613-962-1851
quinte.MLS@reach.net
www.quinterealestate.ca
twitter.com/quinte_REALTORS
Overview: A small local organization founded in 1977 overseen by Ontario Real Estate Association
Member of: The Canadian Real Estate Association; Ontario Real Estate Association; Real Estate Council of Ontario
Chief Officer(s):
Edie Haslauer, President
Membership: 370;

Quinte Arts Council (QAC)
PO Box 22113, 36 Bridge St. East, Belleville ON K8N 5A2
Tel: 613-962-1232; *Fax:* 613-962-7163
qac@quinteartscouncil.org
www.quinteartscouncil.org
www.facebook.com/QuinteArtsCouncil
twitter.com/QAC1967
Overview: A small local charitable organization founded in 1967
Mission: To develop, integrate & promote a creative culture & artistic opportunities in our community; to raise awareness for the value of creativity & artistic expression within our community through programs & services that engage & nurture artists
Member of: Visual Arts Ontario; CARFAC; Canadian Association of Gift Planners; Canadian Centre for Philanthropy
Affliation(s): Ontario Arts Council
Chief Officer(s):
Carol Feeney, Executive Director
feeney@quinteartscouncil.org
Finances: *Annual Operating Budget:* $100,000-$250,000
Staff Member(s): 5; 400 volunteer(s)
Membership: 500; *Fees:* $30 community friends; $40 artists/groups; $50 business; $5 student; *Committees:* Executive; Strategic Planning; Awards & Bursaries; Fundraising & Finance; Programming
Activities: Kids' Playhouse Performing Arts Series; Desjardins Concerts; Ear Candy Music Festival; Festival of Trees; Expressions; *Internships:* Yes; *Speaker Service:* Yes; *Library:* Resource Area; Open to public
Awards:
• Eugene Lang Memorial Bursary (Award)
• Hugh P. O'Neill Bursary (Award)
• The Arts Recognition Awards (Award)
• QAC Student Bursaries (Award)
• QAC Arts & Education Fund - Performing Arts (Award)
• QAC Arts & Education Fund - Visual Arts (Award)

Quinte Beekeepers' Association (QBA)
c/o Liz Corbett, 762 Clearview Rd., RR#2, Stirling ON K0K 3E0
Tel: 613-398-8422
Overview: A small local organization
Mission: To promote the beekeeping industry in the Quinte area; To educate & assist local beekeepers
Member of: Ontario Beekeepers' Association
Chief Officer(s):
Liz Corbett, President
ebcorbett@yahoo.ca
Membership: *Member Profile:* Beekeepers of the Quinte region of Ontario
Activities: Hosting meetings for members; Offering networking opportunities for beekeepers to exchange information; Mentoring persons new to beekeeping; Educating the public about beekeeping; Presenting displays about beekeeping & honey; Establishing a cooperative beeyard; Participating in the creation of renewed sustainable communities

Quinte Construction Association (QCA)
54 Station St., Belleville ON K8N 2S5
Tel: 613-962-2877; *Fax:* 613-962-0268
qca@on.aibn.com
www.quinteconstructionassociation.ca
Overview: A small local organization founded in 1948
Chief Officer(s):
Barbara Tebworth, Office Manager
Katie Riddell, President
Staff Member(s): 1; 10 volunteer(s)
Membership: 100; *Fees:* $450-$585
Activities: Annual golf tournament; curling day; education and safety training

Quinte Labour Council
281 Albert St., Belleville ON K8N 3P1
Tel: 613-848-7190
Toll-Free: 877-968-3666
www.lcs-quinte.ca/qlc
Overview: A small local organization overseen by Ontario Federation of Labour
Mission: To meet the on-going needs of organized & unorganized workers & to improve their quality of life in the workplace, in the home & in the community
Member of: Ontario Federation of Labour
Chief Officer(s):
Donna Howes, President
sister.donna@cupe1022.ca
Membership: 4,000; *Committees:* Education; Fundraising; Political Action
Activities: *Awareness Events:* Day of Mourning, April 28; *Speaker Service:* Yes
Awards:
• Loyalist College Bursary (Scholarship)

Quinte Symphony
c/o Quinte Arts Council, PO Box 22113, Belleville ON K8N 2Z5
Tel: 613-967-3970
info@quintesymphony.com
www.quintesymphony.com
www.facebook.com/quintesymphony
twitter.com/quintesymphony
Previous Name: Eastern Ontario Concert Orchestra
Overview: A small local charitable organization founded in 1960 overseen by Orchestras Canada
Mission: Committed to enriching the Quinte community by actively promoting an appreciation of Classical & Canadian orchestral music
Member of: Quinte Arts Council, Belleville & District Chamber of Commerce, Volunteer & Information Centre
Chief Officer(s):
Gordon Craig, Music Director
Jack Evans, President
Finances: *Funding Sources:* Grants; sponsors; ticket sales; advertising; donations; fundraising
Membership: 47
Activities: Four to five concerts per season; *Speaker Service:* Yes
Awards:
• Stephen Choma Memorial Scholarship (Scholarship)

Quinte Therapeutic Riding Association (QUINTRA)
173 McGee Rd., RR#2, Stirling ON K0K 3E0
Tel: 613-395-4472
www.quintra.org
Overview: A small local charitable organization founded in 1985
Mission: To offer therapeutic horseback-riding sessions to disabled children & young adults to maximize the disabled person's physical & mental capabilities; To improve disabled young people's self-confidence & the ability to cope with everyday living
Member of: Canadian Therapeutic Riding Association; Ontario Therapeutic Riding Association
Affliation(s): United Way of Quinte
Chief Officer(s):
Barb Davis, Contact
barbara.davis@sympatico.ca
Finances: *Funding Sources:* Donations; Bingos; United Way Quinte
Activities: *Speaker Service:* Yes

Quinte United Immigrant Services (QUIS)
PO Box 22141, Belleville ON K8N 5V7
Tel: 613-968-7723; *Fax:* 613-968-2597
info@quis-immigration.org
www.quis-immigration.org
Overview: A small local organization founded in 1986 overseen by Ontario Council of Agencies Serving Immigrants
Mission: To prevent & relieve distress experienced by immigrants in Canada; To assist immigrants in locating affordable housing, furnishings & other related items; To locate agencies & services to meet needs of immigrants; To cooperate & collaborate with & assist other organizations concerned with general welfare of immigrants to Canada
Member of: United Way; Ontario Trillium Foundation
Chief Officer(s):
Orlando Ferro, Executive Director
Paul Osbourne, President
Finances: *Annual Operating Budget:* $100,000-$250,000; *Funding Sources:* Federal & provincial government; United Way; fundraising
Staff Member(s): 5; 155 volunteer(s)
Membership: 46; *Fees:* $10 individual; $15 organizational; *Committees:* Financial; Special Projects; Policies & Personnel; Recruitment
Activities: Settlement programs; language orientation; host program; community support; economic development; interpretation & translation; public education; *Awareness Events:* Stop Racism, March 21; *Internships:* Yes; *Library* by appointment

Quinte West Chamber of Commerce (QWCC)
97 Front St., Trenton ON K8V 4N6
Tel: 613-392-7635; *Fax:* 613-392-8400
Toll-Free: 800-930-3255

Canadian Associations

info@quintewestchamber.ca
www.quintewestchamber.ca
www.linkedin.com/groups?mostPopular=&gid=3774934
www.facebook.com/QWChamber
twitter.com/qwchamber
Previous Name: Trenton & District Chamber of Commerce
Overview: A small local organization founded in 1886
Mission: To promote business growth & prosperity for the local economy through effective leadership
Member of: Ontario Chamber of Commerce; Canadian Chamber of Commerce
Chief Officer(s):
Mike Cowan, President, 613-394-4837, Fax: 613-394-2897
mike@mikecowan.com
Suzanne Andrews, Manager
manager@quintewestchamber.ca
Finances: *Annual Operating Budget:* $250,000-$500,000; *Funding Sources:* Membership fees
Staff Member(s): 3; 15 volunteer(s)
Membership: 405; *Fees:* $100 individual; $190-$500 corporate; *Member Profile:* Businesses; *Committees:* Court affairs; Advocacy
Activities: Business services; tourism information; *Awareness Events:* Quinte BUsiness Week, Oct.
Publications:
• Business to Business Directory [a publication of the Quinte Chamber of Commerce]
Type: Directory; *Frequency:* Annual

RA Stamp Club

2451 Riverside Dr., Ottawa ON K1H 7X7
Tel: 613-733-5100; *Fax:* 613-736-6234
racentre@racentre.com
www.racentre.com
Overview: A small local organization
Member of: The Recreation Association
Chief Officer(s):
Gord Aitken, Acting CEO/General Manager, RA Centre, 613-736-6211
gaitken@racentre.com
Finances: *Annual Operating Budget:* Less than $50,000; *Funding Sources:* Membership fees
Membership: *Fees:* $29 RA Member; *Member Profile:* Local stamp collectors
Activities: Club meetings & shows; *Awareness Events:* MINIEX, Feb.; ORAPEX National Stamp Show, May

Racquetball Canada

145 Pacific Ave., Winnipeg MB R3B 2Z6
Tel: 613-692-5394
www.racquetball.ca
twitter.com/RBallCanada
Previous Name: Canadian Racquetball Association
Overview: A medium-sized national charitable organization founded in 1972
Mission: To promote racquetball as a sport & physical activity; To provide leadership by developing & coordinating services & programs designed to meet the needs of the racquetball community
Member of: International Racquetball Federation
Affliation(s): Canadian Sport Council; Canadian Olympic Association; Coaching Association of Canada
Chief Officer(s):
Jack McBride, President
mcbridejm@shaw.ca
Darrell Davis, Vice-President, High Performance
d.d.davis@sasktel.net
Jan Hanson, Vice-President, Marketing & Communications
jhanson@accesscomm.ca
Terry Nelson, Vice-President, Technical
ternelson3@gmail.com
Bob Papineau, Vice-President, Finance
rapapin@yahoo.com
Cheryl Adlard, Executive Director
ed.rbcanada@sportmanitoba.ca
Finances: *Annual Operating Budget:* 0; *Funding Sources:* Government; Membership dues; Sponsorships
50 volunteer(s)
Membership: 5 life + 700 individual + 350 club + 8 provincial associations (incl. 18,000 members); *Fees:* $1,500 life; $25 individual; $50 club; *Member Profile:* Individual resident in Canada or Canadian citizen involved in the sport of racquetball at any level of structured activity; *Committees:* National Team; Coaching; Sport Science; Tournament; Ranking; Officiating; Junior Development; Membership; Ways & Means; Wheelchair; Women
Activities: *Awareness Events:* National Championship Week, May; *Speaker Service:* Yes; *Rents Mailing List:* Yes
Publications:
• Canadian Racquetball
Type: Magazine; *Price:* Free with Racquetball Canada membership
• Racquetball Canada Newsletter
Type: Newsletter; *Frequency:* Monthly
Profile: Team information, administration news, coaching, awards, & events

Racquetball Manitoba Inc.

145 Pacific Ave., Winnipeg MB R3B 2Z7
Tel: 204-925-5666; *Fax:* 204-925-5703
racquetball@sportmanitoba.ca
racquetballmb.ca
Overview: A small provincial organization founded in 1974 overseen by Racquetball Canada
Mission: To promote racquetball as a sport & a physical activity throughout the Province of Manitoba; To provide leadership by developing & coordinating services & programs designed to meet the needs of the racquetball community
Member of: Racquetball Canada; Sport Manitoba
Chief Officer(s):
Gwen Smoluk, President
Staff Member(s): 1; 50 volunteer(s)
Membership: 600; *Fees:* $20 adult; $10 junior

Racquetball Ontario (RO)

5591 McAdam Rd., Mississauga ON L4Z 1N4
Tel: 519-584-0235
www.racquetballontario.ca
twitter.com/Rball_Ontario
Overview: A medium-sized provincial organization overseen by Racquetball Canada
Member of: Racquetball Canada
Chief Officer(s):
Sue Swaine, Vice-President & Director, Coaching
Peter Fisher, Director, Development
Tanya Hodgin, Director, Memberships
Bob Lickers, Director, Rankings
Membership: *Fees:* $25 individual; $50 family; $100 event coordinator

Racquetball PEI

c/o Sport PEI, PO Box 302, Charlottetown PE C1A 7K7
Tel: 902-368-4110; *Fax:* 902-368-4548
Overview: A small provincial organization overseen by Racquetball Canada
Member of: Racquetball Canada
Chief Officer(s):
Jerry Campbell, Provincial Representative, 902-363-6085, Fax: 902-368-6089
jf_campbell9@hotmail.com

Radiation Safety Institute of Canada / Institut de radioprotection du Canada

Head Office & National Education Centre, #300, 165 Avenue Rd., Toronto ON M5R 3S4
Tel: 416-650-9090; *Fax:* 416-650-9920
Toll-Free: 800-263-5803
info@radiationsafety.ca
www.radiationsafety.ca
www.facebook.com/group.php?gid=143472245714096
Previous Name: Canadian Institute for Radiation Safety
Overview: A medium-sized national charitable organization founded in 1981
Mission: To be an independent source for knowledge about radiation safety in the environment, the community, & the workplace
Chief Officer(s):
Fergal Nolan, President & Chief Executive Officer
R. Moridi, Vice-President, Chief Scientist
Bruce Sylvester, Vice-President, Finance & Administration
Mike Haynes, Scientific Director
Natalia Mozayani, Program Manager
Tara Hargreaves, Scientist & Coordinator, Training
Activities: Providing information about radiation & radiation safety

National Laboratories
#102, 110 Research Dr., Saskatoon SK S7N 3R3
Tel: 306-975-0566; *Fax:* 306-975-0494
www.radiationsafety.ca
Chief Officer(s):
Tim Armstrong, Chair

Radio Advisory Board of Canada (RABC) / Conseil consultatif canadien de la radio

#811, 116 Albert St., Ottawa ON K1P 5G3
Tel: 613-230-3261
Toll-Free: 888-902-5768
rabc.gm@on.aibn.com
www.rabc-cccr.ca
Previous Name: Canadian Radio Technical Planning Board
Overview: A medium-sized national organization founded in 1944
Mission: To consult & advise Industry Canada on behalf of industry on the development, management, & regulation of radio services in Canada
Chief Officer(s):
Roger Poirier, General Manager
Finances: *Funding Sources:* Membership fees; grant
Membership: *Fees:* Schedule available; *Member Profile:* Generally non-profit associations of commercial companies, both operating & manufacturing; technical societies; amateur users, or any group concerned with radio spectrum use; a number of federal & provincial government bodies are also members; *Committees:* Broadcasting; Electromagnetic Compatibility; Mobile & Personal Communications; Fixed Wireless Communications

Radio Amateur Québec inc. (RAQI)

CP 1000, Succ. M, 4545, av Pierre-de Coubertin, Montréal QC H1V 3R2
Tél: 514-252-3012; *Téléc:* 514-254-9971
admin@raqi.ca
www.raqi.ca
Aperçu: *Dimension:* moyenne; *Envergure:* provinciale; fondée en 1951
Membre(s) du bureau directeur:
Guy Lamoureux, Président et directeur-général
president@raqi.ca
Membre(s) du personnel: 2; 200 bénévole(s)
Membre: 4 500; *Montant de la cotisation:* 35$
Activités: *Bibliothèque* Bibliothèque publique rendez-vous

Radio Amateurs du Canada inc. *See* Radio Amateurs of Canada Inc.

Radio Amateurs of Canada Inc. (RAC) / Radio Amateurs du Canada inc.

#217, 720 Belfast Rd., Ottawa ON K1G 0Z5
Tel: 613-244-4367
Toll-Free: 877-273-8304
rachq@rac.ca
www.rac.ca
Previous Name: Canadian Amateur Radio Federation
Overview: A medium-sized national organization founded in 1993
Mission: To act as coordinating body of amateur radio organizations in Canada, liaison agency between members & other amateur organizations in Canada & other countries, coordinating & advisory agency between members & industry Canada; to promote interests of amateur radio operators through program of technical & general education in amateur matters
Chief Officer(s):
Geoff Bawden, President
ghbawden@shaw.ca
Alvin Masse, Secretary
ve3cwp@mnsi.net
Membership: *Fees:* Schedule available; *Committees:* Administration & Finance; Membership Services; Youth Education; VHF/UHF Band Planning; MF/HF Band Planning; Microwave Band Planning; Antenna Structures; ARISS Technical; ARRL Contest Advisory; ARRL DXAC

Radio Starmaker Fund

#203, 372 Bay St., Toronto ON M5H 2W9
Tel: 416-597-6622; *Fax:* 416-597-2760
Toll-Free: 888-256-2211
info@starmaker.ca
www.starmaker.ca
Overview: A medium-sized national organization
Mission: To provide funding for Canadian musicians, bands & labels that have achieved a proven "track record" with previous work
Affliation(s): Canadian Association of Broadcasters
Chief Officer(s):
Chip Sutherland, Executive Director
chipsutherland@starmaker.ca

Radio Television News Directors' Association (Canada) (RTNDA Canada) / Association canadienne des directeurs de l'information en radio-télévision
#310, 2175 Sheppard Ave. East, Toronto ON M2J 1W8
Tel: 416-756-2213; *Fax:* 416-491-1670
Toll-Free: 877-257-8632
info@rtndacanada.com
www.rtndacanada.com
www.linkedin.com/groups/RTDNA-Canada-1800955
www.facebook.com/rtdna.canada
twitter.com/RTDNA_Canada
Also Known As: Association of Electronic Journalists
Overview: A small national organization founded in 1961
Mission: RTNDA Canada is the voice of electronic journalists. It sets the standards for the field of broadcast journalism, fosters high standards of electronic news presentation, & promotes the free flow of information.
Affliation(s): Radio-Television News Directors Association International
Chief Officer(s):
Ian Koenigsfest, President
president@rtdnacanada.com
Sherry Denesha, Operations Manager
sherry@rtdnacanada.com
Finances: *Annual Operating Budget:* $100,000-$250,000
Staff Member(s): 1; 15 volunteer(s)
Membership: 400; *Fees:* schedule; *Member Profile:* Radio, television & online news directors, producers, executives, reporters, educators, & students; *Committees:* Awards; Diversity; Ethics; Membership; Sponsorship
Activities: Annual awards for industry excellence; annual national conference
Awards:
• Ron Laidlaw Award (Award)
Continuing coverage of a major developing story
• Sam Ross Award (Award)
Outstanding editorial comment
• Byron MacGregor Award (Award)
Best radio newscast
• Charlie Edwards Award (Award)
Best breaking news coverage
• Dave Rogers Award (Award)
Feature presentation
• Gord Sinclair Award (Award)
Special events coverage
• Bert Cannings Award (Award)
Best TV newscast
• Dan McArthur Award (Award)
Best investigative reporting

Radiocomm Association of Canada *See* Canadian Wireless Telecommunications Association

Radios Rurales Internationales *See* Farm Radio International

Radisson & District Chamber of Commerce
PO Box 397, Radisson SK S0K 3L0
Tel: 306-827-4801; *Fax:* 306-827-2336
www.radisson.ca/business/chamber-of-commerce
Overview: A small local organization founded in 2003
Chief Officer(s):
Tina Hamel, President, 306-827-2346

Radium Hot Springs Chamber of Commerce
PO Box 225, Radium Hot Springs BC V0A 1M0
Tel: 250-347-9331; *Fax:* 250-347-9127
Toll-Free: 888-347-9331
info@RadiumHotSprings.com
www.RadiumHotSprings.com
www.facebook.com/pages/Radium-Hot-Springs/139332756088819
twitter.com/radium_tourism
www.youtube.com/tourismradium
Previous Name: Columbia Valley Chamber of Commerce; Invermere Business Committee; Fairmont Business Association; Windermere Board of Trade
Overview: A small local organization founded in 1956
Mission: To promote & support quality, ethical business as well as facilitate growth for responsible commercial development in Radium Hot Springs & area
Member of: BC Chamber of Commerce
Finances: *Funding Sources:* Government; fund raising; corporate
Membership: *Fees:* $260 radium/associate; *Member Profile:* Business, tourism, resource membership
Activities: Internet access; washrooms; visitor information; retail store; interpretive centre; *Library* Open to public

Radville Chamber of Commerce
PO Box 799, Radville SK S0C 2G0
Tel: 306-869-2610; *Fax:* 306-869-2859
town.radville@sasktel.net
Overview: A small local organization
Chief Officer(s):
S.L. Scott, Sec.-Treas.
B.L. Loewen, President
loewenagencies@sasktel.net

Railway Association of Canada (RAC) / L'Association des chemins de fer du Canada (ACFC)
#901, 99 Bank St., Ottawa ON K1P 6B9
Tel: 613-567-8591; *Fax:* 613-567-6726
rac@railcan.ca
www.railcan.ca
twitter.com/RailCanada
www.youtube.com/user/racmain
Overview: A large national organization founded in 1917
Mission: To promote the commercial viability & the safe & efficient operation of the Canadian railway industry; to act on behalf of, or work jointly with, member companies to promote public policy & regulation that provides equitable treatment between shipping modes; to provide factual information on the railway industry for the public, government & industry, & to provide the views of the industry on public policy issues. PUBLICATIONS: Interchange; Canadian Railway Medical Rules Handbook; Canada's Railway Lead North America.
Affliation(s): Association of American Railroads
Chief Officer(s):
Michael Bourque, President & CEO, 613-564-8090
Gérald Gauthier, Vice-President, Public & Corporate Affairs, 613-564-8106
geraldg@railcan.ca
Finances: *Annual Operating Budget:* Greater than $5 Million; *Funding Sources:* Members fees
Staff Member(s): 23
Membership: 55 railways & 40 associates; *Fees:* $2,000 minimum; *Member Profile:* Railway companies operating in Canada; *Committees:* Policy; Accounting; Finance; Human Resources; Safety & Operations Management; Taxation
Activities: Operation Lifesaver;

The Rainbow Alliance
c/o OPSEU, 100 Lesmill Rd., Toronto ON M3B 3P8
Tel: 416-443-8888
Toll-Free: 800-268-7376
pride@opseu.org
www.opseu.org/committees/rainbow.htm
Overview: A small local organization overseen by Ontario Public Service Employees Union
Mission: To provide representation & support to lesbian, gay, bisexual & transgendered members of OPSEU
Chief Officer(s):
Robert Hampsey, Chair
Activities: *Awareness Events:* World AIDS Day, December 1; International Day Against Homophobia & Transphobia, May 17

Rainbow Association of Canadian Artists (Spectra Talent Contest)
#PH22, 650 Parliament St., Toronto ON M4X 1R3
Tel: 647-218-2643
www.spectrashowcase.com
Overview: A small local organization founded in 2009
Mission: A community encouraging amateur artistic expression regardless of cultural background, sexual orientation &/or gender identity
Chief Officer(s):
Paul Bellini, Chair
paul@spectrashowcase.com
Ralph Hamelmann, President & Producer
producer@spectrashowcase.com

Rainbow Resource Centre
PO Box 1661, Stn. Main, 170 Scott St., Winnipeg MB R3L 0L3
Tel: 204-474-0212; *Fax:* 204-478-1160
Toll-Free: 888-399-0005
info@rainbowresourcecentre.org
www.rainbowresourcecentre.org
www.facebook.com/groups/280300125172
twitter.com/RainbowCentreMB
Also Known As: Gays for Equality
Previous Name: Campus Gay Club (University of Manitoba)
Overview: A small local charitable organization founded in 1972
Mission: To work toward an equal & diverse society, free of homophobia & discrimination, by encouraging visibility & fostering health & self-acceptance through education, support, resources & outreach
Chief Officer(s):
Matthew Wiebe, President
Mike Tuthill, Vice-President
Finances: *Annual Operating Budget:* $100,000-$250,000; *Funding Sources:* Donations from individuals & organizations
Staff Member(s): 16; 45 volunteer(s)
Membership: 200; *Fees:* $25; *Committees:* Education; Advocacy; Law Reform; Management
Activities: Workshops; lectures; anti-homophobia training; peer support; counselling; *Library:* Rainbow Resource Centre Library; Open to public

The Rainbow Society
#303, 1 Wesley Ave., Winnipeg MB R3C 4C6
Tel: 204-989-4010; *Fax:* 204-944-9549
Toll-Free: 866-989-4010
rainbow@therainbowsociety.com
www.therainbowsociety.com
www.facebook.com/302693499755482
twitter.com/DreamFactoryMB
www.youtube.com/user/TheDreamFactoryMB
Overview: A small provincial charitable organization founded in 1983
Mission: To provide the opportunity for children (ages 3 to 18) who are suffering from life-threatening illness, to experience a special dream
Affliation(s): Rainbow Society of Alberta
Chief Officer(s):
Tom Malkiewicz, President
Grace Thomson, Executive Director
Finances: *Annual Operating Budget:* $250,000-$500,000
Staff Member(s): 3; 100 volunteer(s)
Membership: 1-99; *Fees:* $25 individual

The Rainbow Society of Alberta
6604 - 82nd Ave., Edmonton AB T6B 0E7
Tel: 780-469-3306; *Fax:* 780-469-2935
www.rainbowsociety.ab.ca
www.facebook.com/pages/Rainbow-Society-of-Alberta/317391988337
twitter.com/RainbowSociety
Overview: A small provincial charitable organization founded in 1986
Mission: To grant the wishes of Alberta children between the ages of three years & eighteen who have been diagnosed with a chronic or life-threatening illness
Member of: Volunteer Centre of Edmonton & Calgary
Affliation(s): The Rainbow Society Inc.
Chief Officer(s):
Craig Hawkins, Executive Director
craigh@rainbowsociety.ab.ca
Finances: *Annual Operating Budget:* $250,000-$500,000
Staff Member(s): 6; 200 volunteer(s)
Membership: 300 individual; *Fees:* $10 individual; $25 family; $200 corporate; *Committees:* Fundraising; Communications

Calgary
PO Box 1153, Stn. Main, Calgary AB T2P 2K9
Tel: 403-252-3891; *Fax:* 403-252-4839
debbiev@rainbowsociety.ab.ca
Chief Officer(s):
Debbie Van Camp, Regional Manager, Southern Alberta
debbiev@rainbowsociety.ab.ca

Grande Prairie Office
PO Box 21069, Grande Prairie AB T8V 6W7
Tel: 780-882-4855; *Fax:* 888-415-9474
Chief Officer(s):
Teri Clarke, Regional Manager, Northern Alberta
teric@rainbowsociety.ab.ca

Rainy Hills Historical Society
PO Box General Delivery, Iddesleigh AB T0J 1T0
Tel: 403-898-2443
Also Known As: Rainy Hills Pioneer Exhibits
Overview: A small local organization founded in 1965
Mission: To preserve history of the area
Chief Officer(s):
Chris M. Olson, President
Margaret Harahus, Sec.-Treas.
Michelle Olson, Vice-President
Finances: *Funding Sources:* Grants; donations; fundraising
Membership: 30; *Fees:* $1; *Committees:* Historical Society
Activities: *Library:* Archives; by appointment

Rainy River & District Chamber of Commerce
PO Box 458, Atwood Aee., Rainy River ON P0W 1L0
Tel: 807-852-3343
rrdcoc@gmail.com
rainyriverchamber.ca
www.facebook.com/groups/Rainyriver/?fref=ts
twitter.com/RainyRiverChamb
pinterest.com/singlepole
Overview: A small local organization
Member of: Northwestern Ontario Associated Chambers of Commerce
Chief Officer(s):
Richard Trenchard, President
Membership: 39; *Fees:* $110; $60 associate

Rainy River Beekeepers' Association
c/o Richard Neilson, RR#1, Stratton ON P0W 1N0
Tel: 807-487-2387; *Fax:* 807-483-1217
Overview: A small local organization
Mission: To educate & inform beekeepers in the Rainy River area
Member of: Ontario Beekeepers' Association
Chief Officer(s):
Richard Neilson, President, 807-487-2387
Membership: *Member Profile:* Apiarists from the Rainy River area of Ontario

Rainy River District Municipal Association (RRDMA)
Tel: 807-274-5323; *Fax:* 807-274-8479
www.noma.on.ca
Overview: A small local organization founded in 1908
Mission: To consider matters of general interest to the members & to take united action as required to promote their interests; to promote the free exchange of information; To petition for the enactment of legislation advantageous to the members
Member of: Northwestern Ontario Municipal Association
Affliation(s): Kenora District Municipal Association & Thunder Bay District Municipal League
Chief Officer(s):
Deborah Ewald, President
Glenn Treftlin, Secretary-Treasurer
gtreftlin@fort-frances.com
Finances: *Annual Operating Budget:* Less than $50,000; *Funding Sources:* Membership fees
Staff Member(s): 1
Membership: 10 incorporated municipalities; *Fees:* Per capita; *Member Profile:* Municipalities in Rainy River District

Ralliement national des Métis *See* Métis National Council

Ralph Thornton Centre
765 Queen St. East, Toronto ON M4M 1H3
Tel: 416-392-6810
info@ralphthornton.org
www.ralphthornton.org
www.youtube.com/user/ralphthorntoncentre
Overview: A medium-sized local charitable organization founded in 1980
Mission: To create a supportive environment in which the Riverdale community responds to issues and needs.
Chief Officer(s):
Paula Fletcher, President
Finances: *Annual Operating Budget:* $500,000-$1.5 Million
Staff Member(s): 4; 150 volunteer(s)

Ramara & District Chamber of Commerce
PO Box 144, 2304 Hwy. 12, Brechin ON L0K 1B0
Tel: 705-484-2141; *Fax:* 705-484-0161
info@ramarachamber.com
www.ramarachamber.com
Overview: A small local organization
Chief Officer(s):
Walt Meyers, President
Membership: 83; *Fees:* $75

Ranch Ehrlo Society
Pilot Butte Campus, PO Box 570, Pilot Butte SK S0G 3Z0
Tel: 306-781-1800; *Fax:* 306-757-0599
inquiries@ranchehrlo.ca
www.ehrlo.com
www.facebook.com/RanchEhrlo
twitter.com/RanchEhrlo
www.youtube.com/user/ranchehrlo1
Previous Name: Saskatchewan Council on Children & Youth
Overview: A medium-sized provincial charitable organization
Mission: To provide a range of quality assessment, treatment, education & support services that improves the social & emotional functioning of children & youth referred to our program
Chief Officer(s):
Marion MacIver, President & CEO

Randonnées plein air du Québec
4545, rue Pierre-de-Coubertin, Montréal QC H1V 0B2
Tél: 514-252-3330; *Téléc:* 514-253-5537
info@randopleinair.com
randopleinair.com
Aperçu: *Dimension:* petite; *Envergure:* locale
Mission: D'encourager et d'organiser des activités de conditionnement physique en plein air
Membre(s) du bureau directeur:
Nicole Beauvais, Présidente, Conseil d'administration

Randonneurs du Saguenay
CP 8116, Chicoutimi QC G7H 5B5
randonneursdusaguenay.qc.ca
Aperçu: *Dimension:* petite; *Envergure:* locale; Organisme sans but lucratif; fondée en 1982
Mission: D'organiser des activités de randonnée et la raquette pour découvrir la région du Lac-St-Jean Saguenay
Affliation(s): Fédération Québécoise de la Marche
Membre(s) du bureau directeur:
Louis Langevin, Président, Conseil d'administration
Membre: *Montant de la cotisation:* 20$ Individuelle; 30$ Famille
Activités: Randonnée pédestre; Kayak; *Événements de sensibilisation:* Assemblée générale annuelle (avril)

Ranfurly & District Recreation & Agricultural Society
PO Box 162, 5119 - 49th St., Ranfurly AB T0B 3T0
Tel: 780-658-2107
Overview: A small local organization
Activities: Hosting community events, such as the Annual Summer Fair & Horseshow;

Rape Crisis Centre Timmins *See* Timmins & Area Women in Crisis Support & Information Centre on Violence Against Women

Rare Breeds Canada (RBC)
2495 boul Perrot, N.D. de L'Ile Perrot ON J7V 8PA
Tel: 514-901-0999
rbc@rarebreedscanada.ca
www.rarebreedscanada.ca
Overview: A medium-sized national charitable organization founded in 1986
Mission: To make Canadians more aware of their agricultural heritage; through education & niche marketing involve them in conserving endangered breeds of farm livestock & poultry
Affliation(s): Canadian Coalition for Biodiversity
Chief Officer(s):
Pam Heath, Office Manager
Finances: *Annual Operating Budget:* Less than $50,000; *Funding Sources:* Membership dues
Staff Member(s): 1; 20 volunteer(s)
Membership: 600; *Fees:* $35 individual; $50 family; $100 corporate
Activities: *Speaker Service:* Yes

Island Heritage Livestock
c/o Margaret Thomson, Chair, 1432 North Beach Rd., Salt Spring Island BC V8K 1B2
Tel: 250-537-4669
www.islandsheritagelivestock.com
Chief Officer(s):
Wynnie Konkle, Contact
olderbonz@shaw.ca

Raspberry Industry Development Council (RIDC)
#265, 32160 South Fraser Way, Abbotsford BC V2T 1W5
Tel: 604-854-8010; *Fax:* 604-854-6050
Other Communication: Blog: bcraspberries.blogspot.ca
council@bcraspberries.com
bcraspberries.com
www.facebook.com/303279116431836
twitter.com/bcraspberries
www.flickr.com/photos/bcraspberries
Previous Name: British Columbia Raspberry Industry Council
Overview: A small provincial organization founded in 1999
Mission: To promote the interests of raspberry growers
Member of: British Columbia Chamber of Commerce
Finances: *Annual Operating Budget:* $100,000-$250,000; *Funding Sources:* Membership levy fee; government; private donations & membership fees
Staff Member(s): 1
Membership: 277; *Member Profile:* Produce over 1 ton of raspberries; *Committees:* Labour; Research; Environment

Rassemblement canadien pour l'alphabétisation *See* Canadian Literacy & Learning Network

Rassemblement des bibliothèques publiques du Lac-Saint-Jean et Saguenay-Lac-Saint-Jean *Voir* Réseau BIBLIO du Saguenay-Lac-Saint-Jean

Rassemblement pour l'alphabétisation de la communauté urbaine de Toronto *See* Metro Toronto Movement for Literacy

Raymond Chamber of Commerce
Raymond AB
Tel: 403-330-9057
www.facebook.com/pages/Raymond-Chamber-of-Commerce/146864378801811
Overview: A small local licensing organization
Member of: Alberta Chamber of Commerce
Chief Officer(s):
Cory Rasmussen, President
cory@nutratek.com
Finances: *Funding Sources:* Membership dues
Activities: Annual Awards Banquet, April; Free Pancake Breakfast, July; Old Fashioned Christmas, Dec.

Rayons de Soleil pour enfants *See* Sunshine Dreams for Kids

RBC Fondation *See* RBC Foundation

RBC Foundation / RBC Fondation
Royal Bank Plaza, South Tower, #950, 200 Bay St., Toronto ON M5J 2J5
Tel: 416-974-3113; *Fax:* 416-955-7800
www.rbc.com/community-sustainability/community/index.html
Previous Name: Royal Bank of Canada Charitable Foundation
Overview: A medium-sized national organization founded in 1993
Chief Officer(s):
Gayle Longley, Contact
gayle.longley@rbc.com
Finances: *Funding Sources:* RBC Financial Group
Activities: RBC After School Project; RBC Blue Water Project; RBC Children's Mental Health Project; RBC Emerging Artists Project; RBC Learn to Play Project; RBC Play Hockey; RBC Olympians Program

RCMP Civilian Search & Rescue Civilian Search Dog Program; RCMP Civilian Search Dog Association *See* Canadian Search Dog Association

Re:Sound
#900, 1235 Bay St., Toronto ON M5R 3K4
Tel: 416-968-8870; *Fax:* 416-962-7797
info@resound.ca
www.resound.ca
Previous Name: The Neighbouring Rights Collective of Canada
Overview: A medium-sized national organization
Mission: To obtain fair compensation for artists and record companies for their performance rights
Chief Officer(s):
Matthew Fortier, 416-355-8349
mfortier@resound.ca
Staff Member(s): 18

Reach Canada
400 Coventry Rd., Ottawa ON K1K 2C7
Tel: 613-236-6636; *Fax:* 613-236-6605
Toll-Free: 800-465-8898; *TTY:* 613-236-9478
reach@reach.ca
www.reach.ca
twitter.com/reachcanada1
Previous Name: Reach Equality & Justice for People with Disabilities; Resource, Education & Advocacy Centre for the Handicapped
Overview: A small local organization founded in 1981
Mission: To provide legal referral services & educational programs for people with disabilities
Chief Officer(s):
Chantelle Bowers, President
Finances: *Annual Operating Budget:* $250,000-$500,000
Staff Member(s): 5; 250 volunteer(s)
Membership: 1-99
Activities: *Awareness Events:* Reach Annual Auction, Oct.; Minto Run for Reach, April; *Speaker Service:* Yes

Reach Equality & Justice for People with Disabilities; Resource, Education & Advocacy Centre for the Handicapped *See* Reach Canada

Reach for the Rainbow
20 Torlake Cres., Toronto ON M8Z 1B3
Tel: 416-503-0088; *Fax:* 416-503-0485
info@reachfortherainbow.ca
www.reachfortherainbow.ca
www.facebook.com/ReachForTheRainbow?ref=ts
twitter.com/RFTRCharity
Overview: A small provincial charitable organization
Mission: To offer integrated recreational & respite programs for disabled children within the province of Ontario
Chief Officer(s):
David Neal, Executive Director
dneal@reachfortherainbow.ca
Paul Pellegrini, Chair

REACT Canada Inc.
32 The Queensway North, Keswick ON L4P 1E3
Tel: 905-476-5231
react@react-canada.org
www.react-canada.org
Overview: A medium-sized national charitable organization founded in 1962
Mission: To provide skilled volunteer two-way radio communications for safety; To provide volunteer emergency radio communications for travellers; To provide safety communications for walkathons & parades.; To offer speakers to community groups on correct use of radio in emergencies
Affliation(s): REACT International Inc.; Salvation Army; Red Cross; American Radio Relay League
Chief Officer(s):
Ronald W. McCracken, Director
Finances: *Annual Operating Budget:* Less than $50,000; *Funding Sources:* Donations; grants; membership dues
100 volunteer(s)
Membership: 15 teams + 100 individuals; *Fees:* Schedule available; *Member Profile:* Interest in using two-way radio for safety & for community service
Activities: Monitors CB Emergency Channel 9, GMRS 462.675, & FRS Emergency Channel 1; distributes radio safety information; provides safety communications for public events; Safety Breaks; safety displays; emergency communications; co-operates with amateur radio groups; *Awareness Events:* REACT Month, May; *Internships:* Yes; *Speaker Service:* Yes; *Rents Mailing List:* Yes

Réadaptation Psychosociale Canada *See* Psychosocial Rehabilitation Canada

Reading Council for Literacy Advance in Montréal (RECLAIM) / Conseil pour l'enseignement de la lecture aux analphabètes de Montréal
#A 2-10, 1001, rue Lenoir, Montréal QC H4C 2Z6
Tel: 514-369-7835
www.reclaimliteracy.ca
Overview: A small local charitable organization founded in 1980
Mission: To provide free, confidential, individualized literacy instruction to adults in the Greater Montréal area; to provide one-to-one tutoring & computer-assisted instruction, using trained voluteers; to raise the public's awareness of literacy issues, & carrying out literacy-related projects, including family literacy
Member of: Literacy Volunteers of Québec; Québec Literacy Alliance
Affliation(s): Laubach Literacy of Canada
Chief Officer(s):
Margaret Suttie, President
Joy Fyckes, Executive Director
joy@reclaimliteracy.ca
Finances: *Annual Operating Budget:* $250,000-$500,000
Staff Member(s): 6; 270 volunteer(s)
Membership: 300; *Fees:* $20
Activities: *Speaker Service:* Yes

Ready Mixed Concrete Association of Ontario (RMCAO)
#3, 365 Brunel Rd., Mississauga ON L4Z 1Z5
Tel: 905-507-1122; *Fax:* 905-890-8122
www.rmcao.org
www.linkedin.com/company/ready-mixed-concrete-association-of-ontario
www.facebook.com/ConcreteOntario
twitter.com/ConcreteOntario
www.youtube.com/concreteontario
Overview: A large provincial organization founded in 1959 overseen by Canadian Ready Mixed Concrete Association
Mission: To promote & further the business, technology & use of quality concrete through partnership between producers & the construction & specifying industries
Chief Officer(s):
John D. Hull, President
jdhull@rmcao.org
Bart Kanters, P.Eng., MBA, Director, Technical Services
bkanters@rmcao.org
Ross Monsour, Director, Marketing, Eastern & Northern Ontario
rmonsour@rmcao.org
Nancy Chapman, Manager, Administration & Member Services
nchapman@rmcao.org
Mick Prieur, Senior Pavement Engineer
mprieur@rmcao.org
Finances: *Funding Sources:* Membership dues; Events
Membership: 78 associate + 86 active; *Fees:* Schedule available; *Committees:* Associate Members; Education; Environment; Health & Safety; Marketing; Membership; Pavements; Promotion; Technical; Transportation
Awards:
• Ontario Concrete Awards (Award)
Meetings/Conferences: • RMCAO [Ready Mixed Concrete Association of Ontario] 56th Annual General Meeting & Convention, 2016
Scope: Provincial
Publications:
• FLASH
Type: Newsletter; *Frequency:* Bimonthly

Real Estate Board of Greater Vancouver
2433 Spruce St., Vancouver BC V6H 4C8
Tel: 604-730-3000; *Fax:* 604-730-3100
Toll-Free: 800-304-0565
www.rebgv.org
www.facebook.com/rebgv
www.twitter.com/rebgv
www.youtube.com/user/rebgv
Overview: A small local organization overseen by British Columbia Real Estate Association
Chief Officer(s):
Robert K. Wallace, CEO

Real Estate Board of the Fredericton Area Inc. (FREB)
544 Brunswick St., Fredericton NB E3B 1H5
Tel: 506-458-8163; *Fax:* 506-459-8922
freb01@rogers.com
www.frederictonrealestateboard.com
Overview: A small local organization founded in 1963 overseen by New Brunswick Real Estate Association
Mission: To address member education, motivation & appreciation
Member of: The Canadian Real Estate Association; New Brunswick Real Estate Association
Affliation(s): Mortgage Lenders Association
Chief Officer(s):
Edie Whitman, Executive Officer
Finances: *Annual Operating Budget:* $250,000-$500,000
Staff Member(s): 1
Membership: 280

Real Estate Council of Alberta (RECA)
#350, 4954 Richard Rd. SW, Calgary AB T3E 6L1
Tel: 403-228-2954; *Fax:* 403-228-3065
Toll-Free: 888-425-2754
info@reca.ca
www.reca.ca
www.facebook.com/150222881696865
twitter.com/RECA
www.youtube.com/user/RECAAdmin
Overview: A medium-sized provincial organization founded in 1995
Mission: To protect consumers; To provide services that enhance & improve the industry & the business of industry professionals
Chief Officer(s):
Bob Myroniuk, Executive Director
Finances: *Annual Operating Budget:* Greater than $5 Million
Membership: 12 council members; *Committees:* Audit & Finance; Governance; Hearings
Publications:
• Annual Report of the Real Estate Council of Alberta
Type: Yearbook; *Frequency:* Annually
Profile: Messages from the chair & executive director, education, financial statements, & officers
• The Regulator [a publication of the Real Estate Council of Alberta]
Type: Newsletter; *Frequency:* Monthly
Profile: News from the Council

Real Estate Council of British Columbia (RECBC)
#900, 750 West Pender St., Vancouver BC V6C 2T8
Tel: 604-683-9664; *Fax:* 604-683-9017
Toll-Free: 877-683-9664
info@recbc.ca
www.recbc.ca
Overview: A medium-sized provincial organization founded in 1958
Mission: Protects the public interest by assuring the competency of real estate licensees and ensuring their compliance with the Real Estate Services Act. The Council is accountable to and advises government on industry issues and encourages public confidence, by impartially setting and enforcing standards of conduct, education, competency and licensing for real estate licensees in the province.
Chief Officer(s):
Robert O. Fawcett, Executive Officer
Finances: *Annual Operating Budget:* Greater than $5 Million
Staff Member(s): 26
Membership: 16; *Committees:* Education; Real Estate Services Act; Rental Property Management; Strata Management; Trading Services

Real Estate Council of Ontario (RECO)
East Tower, #600, 3250 Bloor St. West, Toronto ON M8X 2X9
Tel: 416-207-4800; *Fax:* 416-207-4820
Toll-Free: 800-245-6910
communications@reco.on.ca
www.reco.on.ca
Overview: A medium-sized provincial organization
Mission: To administer the regulatory requirements of the real estate industry as set down by the Government of Ontario; To protect consumers & members through a fair & safe & informed marketplace
Chief Officer(s):
Thomas Wright, President/CEO
Membership: *Committees:* Appeals; Audit; By-laws; Discipline; Education; Finance; Governance; Insurance; Premium Stabilization

Real Estate Institute of British Columbia
#1750, 355 Burrard St., Vancouver BC V6C 2G8
Tel: 604-685-3702; *Fax:* 604-685-1026
Toll-Free: 800-667-2166
info@reibc.org
www.reibc.org
www.linkedin.com/groups?about=&gid=2701493
Overview: A medium-sized provincial organization founded in 1960
Mission: To advance the highest standards of education, knowledge, professional development & business practice in all sectors of the real estate industry
Chief Officer(s):
Brenda Southam, Executive Officer
Nathan Worbets, President, 604-681-9474
Finances: *Annual Operating Budget:* $250,000-$500,000
Staff Member(s): 3; 100 volunteer(s)
Membership: 1,600; *Fees:* $425.25 professional; $125.50 associate; $50 student; $60 retired; *Committees:* Public Relations; Education; Admittance & Membership; Executive & Management; Government Liaison; Professional Conduct

Real Estate Institute of Canada (REIC) / Institut canadien de l'immeuble (ICI)
#208, 5407 Eglinton Ave. West, Toronto ON M9C 5K6
Tel: 416-695-9000; *Fax:* 416-695-7230
Toll-Free: 800-542-7342
infocentral@reic.com
www.reic.ca
Previous Name: Canadian Institute of Realtors
Overview: A large national organization founded in 1955
Mission: To advance opportunities for persons involved in real estate
Chief Officer(s):
Maura McLaren, Executive Director, 416-695-9000 Ext. 30
maura.mclaren@reic.com
Kitty Mach, Manager, Education
kitty.mach@reic.com
Pam Seran-Wallace, Manager, Marketing & Communications
pam.seran-wallace@reic.com

Finances: *Annual Operating Budget:* $500,000-$1.5 Million
Staff Member(s): 9; 2000 volunteer(s)
Membership: 2,000; *Fees:* $370; *Member Profile:* REIC designations: FRI - Fellow of the Real Estate Institute; FRI(E) - Fellow of the Real Institute (Executive); FRI(A) - Fellow of the Real Estate Institute (Appraisal); CPM - Certified Property Manager; ARM - Accredited Residential Manager; CRF - Certified in Real Estate Finance; CLO - Certified Leasing Officer; CRU - Certified Residential Underwriter; CRES - Certified Real Estate Specialist; CRP - Certified Reserve Planner; ARP - Associate Reserve Planner; CMOC - Certified Manager of Condominiums; *Committees:* Professional Standards; Audit; Liaison; Awards; Chapter Review; Bylaws
Awards:
• Morguard Literary Awards (Award), Pursuit of Excellence Awards Program
• Real Estate Board or Association of the Year Award (Award)
• Most Improved Chapter of the Year (Award), Chapter Yearbook Award
• O & Y Enterprise Excellence Award (Award), Calculated Award
• J.A. Weber Award (Award), Pursuit of Excellence Awards Program
• REIC Community Service Award (Award)
• REIC Corporate Citizen of the Year Award (Award)
• Don Hill Trophies (Award), Calculated Award
• Chapter of the Year Award (Award), Chapter Yearbook Award
• Patrick J. Harvey Memorial Award (Award), Pursuit of Excellence Awards Program
Meetings/Conferences: • Real Estate Institute of Canada 2015 Annual Conference & Annual General Meeting: Opening Opportunities, May, 2015, Vancouver, BC
Scope: National
Description: A gathering of real estate professionals to participate in professional development programs, listen to guest speakers, & to network with industry experts, colleages, & suppliers

Alberta - Calgary Chapter
c/o Greg McPherson, Calgary AB
Tel: 403-541-0911; *Fax:* 403-541-0915
calgary@reic.com
www.reic.ca/chapters/calgary/index.cfm
Chief Officer(s):
Bruce Simpson, Administrator

Alberta - Edmonton Chapter
REIC & IREM Edmonton Chapters, Box 20, Site 7, RR#2, Stony Plain AB T7Z 1X2
Tel: 780-453-9368; *Fax:* 780-451-6613
www.reic.ca/chapters/REICedm/index.cfm
Chief Officer(s):
Sharon Radford, Administrator
sharondr@telusplanet.net

British Columbia - Greater Vancouver Chapter
c/o Dean Lapointe, President, 5489 Kingsway, Burnaby BC V5H 2G1
Tel: 604-437-1123
admin@reicvancouver.org
reicvancouver.org

British Columbia Chapter - The Real Estate Institute of British Columbia
#1750, 355 Burrard St., Vancouver BC V6C 2G8
Tel: 604-685-3702; *Fax:* 604-685-1026
Toll-Free: 800-667-2166
info@reibc.org
www.reibc.org
Chief Officer(s):
Nathan Worbets, President, 604-681-9474
Brenda Southam, Executive Officer
David Graham, Secretary-Treasurer, 250-427-0372
Maureen McKnight, Coordinator, Administration

Manitoba Chapter
65 Gary Street, 3rd Fl., Winnipeg MB R3C 4K4
Tel: 204-415-5711; *Fax:* 204-339-7261
admin@reim.ca
Chief Officer(s):
Shirley Tillett, Administrator

Nova Scotia Chapter
c/o Stacy C. Wentzell, Harbourside Realty Ltd., 3476 Dutch Village Rd., Halifax NS B3N 2R9
Tel: 902-444-7301; *Fax:* 902-422-0556
swentzell@stacywentzell.com
www.reic.ca/chapters/ns/index.cfm
Chief Officer(s):
Matthew Pendlebury, President, 902-420-0599
mpendlebury@montrosemortgage.com
Kelly Hamilton, Administrator, 902-422-0555
kellyh@domus.ns.ca
Alice Galpin-Nicholson, Secretary, 902-420-6005
galpinam@gov.ns.ca
Theresa Salsman, Treasurer, 902-464-7784
tdawson@citigroup.ns.ca

Ontario - Lakeshore-Niagara Chapter
c/o Colin Gage, Victoria Park Community Homes, Hamilton ON
Tel: 905-527-0221
cgage@vpch.com
Chief Officer(s):
Mary Jones, President

Ontario - Ottawa Chapter
c/o Patricia Riccio, #803, 1568 Merivale Rd., Ottawa ON K2G 5Y7
Tel: 613-565-7342
ottawa@reic.com
www.reic.ca/chapters/ottawa
Chief Officer(s):
Debbie MacEwen, Administrator

Ontario - Toronto Chapter
c/o Beth MacKenzie, Taylor Enterprises, #310, 2175 Sheppard Ave. East, Toronto ON M2J 1W8
Tel: 416-491-2886
BethM@taylorenterprises.com
www.reic.ca/chapters/toronto/index.cfm
Chief Officer(s):
Beth McKenzie, Administrator

Québec Chapter
Léo Ziadé, Invest Gain Ltée, 4180 Grande Allée, Longueuil QC J4V 3N2
Tel: 450-926-9966; *Fax:* 450-926-4155
www.reic.ca/chapters/Quebec
Chief Officer(s):
Louis Marcoux, Président
louismarcoux@royallepage.ca
Serge Rivet, Vice-Président / Secrétaire
remax@heleneetserge.com
Léo Ziadé, Administrator
investgain@videotron.ca
Antoine Gagnon, Trésorier
antoine@boulevardimmobilier.ca

Saskatchewan Chapter
c/o Carrie Weir, 3204 Winchester Rd., Regina SK S4V 2T4
Tel: 306-596-7926; *Fax:* 306-205-3501
reisk@accesscomm.ca
www.reic.com/chapters/reis/index.cfm
Chief Officer(s):
Carrie Weir, Administrator

Real Property Association of Canada
#1410, One University Ave., Toronto ON M5J 2P1
Tel: 416-642-2700; *Fax:* 416-642-2727
Toll-Free: 855-732-5722
info@realpac.ca
www.realpac.ca
www.linkedin.com/company/realpac
www.facebook.com/111245762249174
twitter.com/realpac_news
www.youtube.com/user/REALpacVideos
Also Known As: REALpac
Previous Name: Canadian Institute of Public & Private Real Estate Companies
Overview: A medium-sized national organization
Mission: To represent the real estate industries point of view to government at all levels on legislative & regulatory matters
Chief Officer(s):
Paul Morse, CEO
pmorse@realpac.ca
Deborah Prestwich, Manager, Events & Office Services
dprestwich@realpac.ca
Julia St. Michael, Manager, Research & Environmental Programs
jstmichael@realpac.ca
Finances: *Annual Operating Budget:* $500,000-$1.5 Million
Staff Member(s): 3
Membership: 45 corporate; *Member Profile:* Owners & developers of substantial real estate assets; *Committees:* Tax; Accounting; Telecommunications
Activities: *Internships:* Yes

REAL Women of Canada / Vraies femmes du Canada
PO Box 8813, Stn. T, #403, 116 Albert St., Ottawa ON K1G 3J1
Tel: 613-236-4001; *Fax:* 613-236-7203
www.realwomenofcanada.ca
www.facebook.com/REALWomenofCanada
Overview: A small national organization founded in 1983
Finances: *Annual Operating Budget:* $50,000-$100,000
Membership: 55,000; *Fees:* $25 individual/family; $30 group
Activities: *Speaker Service:* Yes

Realtors Association of Edmonton
14220 - 112 Ave., Edmonton AB T5M 2T8
Tel: 780-451-6666; *Fax:* 780-452-1135
Toll-Free: 888-674-7479
www.ereb.com
Overview: A small local organization founded in 1909 overseen by Alberta Real Estate Association
Member of: Alberta Real Estate Association; The Canadian Real Estate Association
Chief Officer(s):
Marc Perras, President
Ron Hutchinson, Executive Vice-President
Membership: *Fees:* $415; *Member Profile:* Realtors in the Edmonton area.

REALTORS Association of Grey Bruce Owen Sound (RAGBOS)
517 - 10 St., Lower Level, Hanover ON N4N 1R4
Tel: 519-364-3827
www.ragbos.ca
Previous Name: Grey Bruce Real Estate Board; Grey Bruce Owen Sound Real Estate Board
Overview: A small local organization founded in 2000 overseen by Ontario Real Estate Association
Mission: To provide a web-based multiple listing service for its members
Member of: The Canadian Real Estate Association
Chief Officer(s):
Dawn Lee McKenzie, President, 519-534-5453
Finances: *Funding Sources:* Membership fees
Membership: 360+
Activities: *Speaker Service:* Yes

Realtors Association of Lloydminster & District
#203, 5009 - 48 St., Lloydminster AB T9V 0H7
Tel: 780-875-6939; *Fax:* 780-875-5560
lloydreb@telus.net
rald.realtyserver.com
Previous Name: Lloydminster Real Estate Board
Overview: A small local organization overseen by Alberta Real Estate Association
Member of: Canadian Real Estate Assn.; Saskatchewan Real Estate Assn.; Alberta Real Estate Assn.

Realtors Association of South Central Alberta
PO Box 997, Brooks AB T1R 1B8
Tel: 403-362-4643; *Fax:* 403-362-3276
Overview: A small local organization overseen by Alberta Real Estate Association
Member of: Alberta Real Estate Association; The Canadian Real Estate Association
Chief Officer(s):
Carol Breakell, Executive Officer
Creitia Morishita, President

reBOOT Canada
#1, 2450 Lawrence Ave. East, Toronto ON M1P 2R7
Tel: 416-534-6017; *Fax:* 416-534-6083
rose@rebootcanada.ca
www.rebootcanada.ca
Overview: A small national charitable organization founded in 1995
Mission: Refurbishes old computers received from individual & corporate donors & distributes them, free of charge, to other charitable organizations
Chief Officer(s):
Nicholas Brinckman, Executive Director
nick@rebootcanada.ca

Receivables Insurance Association of Canada (RIAC) / Association canadienne de l'assurance comptes clients
122 Bagot St., Cobourg ON K9A 3G1
Tel: 613-794-6683
receivablesinsurancecanada.com
www.linkedin.com/company/3165607
www.facebook.com/ReceivablesInsuranceCanada
twitter.com/RcvblsInsCanada
www.youtube.com/user/RcvblsInsCanada

Overview: A small national organization
Mission: To promote the business opportunity for receivables insurance to Canadian insurance brokers, the banking industry & businesses engaged in domestic trade & exporting
Chief Officer(s):
Mark Attley, President
mark.attley@receivablesinsurancecanada.com
Staff Member(s): 2
Membership: 7 insurers + 5 specialist brokers + 2 industry associates + 4 regular members; *Fees:* $200 regular; $1,000 regional broker/corporate/industry member; $2,500 active specialist broker member; $5,000 licensed insurer & EDC member

Receivables Management Association of Canada Inc. / Association Canadienne de la Gestion de Créances Inc.

#440, 141 Adelaide St. West, Toronto ON M5H 3L5
Fax: 905-671-1579
Toll-Free: 855-690-7047
info@rmacanada.org
www.rmacanada.org
Overview: A medium-sized national organization
Mission: To bring the concerns of those involved in accounts receivable to those in charge, in order to improve daily operations, as well as to bring more attention and development to the industry
Chief Officer(s):
Mark Ball, President, Board of Directors
Steve Sheather, Vice President, Board of Directors
Scott Coffin, Secretary, Board of Directors
Elliot Ocopnick, Treasurer, Board of Directors
14 volunteer(s)
Membership: 52; *Fees:* Affiliate Membersip $295; Full Membership for companies with 10+ employees) $750; Full Membership for companies with under 10 employees $460
Activities: Educational sessions; Round table discussions; Annual general meeting

Recherches amérindiennes au Québec

6742, rue St-Denis, Montréal QC H2S 2S2
Tél: 514-277-6178
reamqu@globetrotter.net
www.recherches-amerindiennes.qc.ca
Aperçu: *Dimension:* moyenne; *Envergure:* provinciale; fondée en 1971
Mission: Diffuser des informations sur les populations amérindiennes
Membre(s) du bureau directeur:
Sylvie Vincent, Présidente
Brian Gettler, Vice-président
Gérald McKenzie, Vice-président
Martin Hébert, Directeur
Alexandre Lefrançois, Secrétaire
Laurent Girouard, Trésorier
10 bénévole(s)
Membre: 180 institutionnel; 270 individu

Recreation & Parks Association of New Brunswick Inc. *See* Recreation New Brunswick

Recreation & Parks Association of the Yukon (RPAY)

4061 - 4th Ave., Whitehorse YT Y1A 1H1
Tel: 867-668-3010; *Fax:* 867-668-2455
rpay@klondiker.com
www.rpay.org
facebook.com/goRPAY
twitter.com/RPAY1
Overview: A medium-sized provincial organization founded in 1993
Mission: To promote, encourage and foster the growth and development of all areas of recreation throughout the Yukon Territory.
Chief Officer(s):
Ian Spencer, President
Anne Morgan, Executive Director
Staff Member(s): 4
Membership: *Fees:* $15 individual; $50 associate/community

The Recreation Association / L'Association récréative

2451 Riverside Dr., Ottawa ON K1H 7X7
Tel: 613-733-5100; *Fax:* 613-736-6238
racentre@racentre.com
www.racentre.com
twitter.com/RACentreOttawa
Also Known As: RA Centre
Overview: A large national organization founded in 1941
Mission: To provide quality leisure & lifestyle activities to the membership
Chief Officer(s):
Diana Monnet, President
Gord Aitken, Acting CEO/General Manager
gaitken@racentre.com
Jane Proudfoot, Director, Recreation, Sports & Fitness Services, 613-736-6227
jproudfoot@racentre.com
Finances: *Annual Operating Budget:* Greater than $5 Million; *Funding Sources:* Membership dues; program revenue; special projects revenue
Staff Member(s): 70; 500 volunteer(s)
Membership: 27,000; *Fees:* $33-$57
Activities: 100+ programs & services in health, fitness, recreation & leisure
Publications:
• The Recreation Association E-News & Offers
Type: Newsletter

Recreation Facilities Association of British Columbia (RFABC)

PO Box 112, Powell River BC V8A 4Z5
Toll-Free: 877-285-3421
info@rfabc.com
www.rfabc.com
Overview: A medium-sized provincial organization founded in 1948
Mission: To promote safe & successful operating standards for community centres, swimming pools, arenas, stadiums, & parks in British Columbia; To encourage professionalism among recreation facility operators
Chief Officer(s):
Lori Blackman, Executive Director
lori@rfabc.com
Steve McLain, President
smclain@fortstjohn.ca
Karin Carlson, Secretary/Treasurer
kcarlson@fortstjohn.ca
Chante Patterson-Elden, Chair, Marketing
celden@dawsoncreek.ca
Membership: *Fees:* $42,50 retired persons; $42.86 students; $107 practitioners & interested individuals; $500 facilities or agencies; *Member Profile:* Practitioners, who work in the field of recreation & parks in British Columbia; Students, attending a full-time program in a post secondary institution; Individuals, who are interested in the purpose of the association; Associate members, who are engaged in a business related to recreation facilities; Facilities, or agencies & communities involved in the operations of parks & recreation facilities
Activities: Supporting recreation facility operators in British Columbia; Promoting education of recreation facility operators; Offering courses for members, such as pool operators & arena ice makers; Facilitating the exchange of ideas among members; Providing access to employment opportunities; *Library:* RFABC Resource Library
Awards:
• RFABC Associates' Scholarship (Scholarship)
Meetings/Conferences: • Recreation Facilities Association of British Columbia 2015 Conference, 2015, BC
Scope: Provincial
Publications:
• Facility to Facility
Frequency: Quarterly; *Price:* Free with membership in the Recreation Facilities Association of British Columbia
• RFABC Communiqué
Type: Newsletter; *Frequency:* Bimonthly; *Price:* Free with membership in the Recreation Facilities Association of British Columbia

Recreation New Brunswick

#34, 55 Whiting Rd., Fredericton NB E3B 5Y5
Tel: 506-459-1929; *Fax:* 506-450-6066
www.recreationnb.ca
www.facebook.com/RecreationNB
twitter.com/RecreationNB
Previous Name: Recreation & Parks Association of New Brunswick Inc.
Overview: A medium-sized provincial organization founded in 1987 overseen by Canadian Parks & Recreation Association
Mission: To develop a professional organization for members; To enhance the image of recreation to government & the general public; To develop liaisons with other recreation groups; To affect legislation in the field of recreation & parks; to expand the NB Skills Program for Management Volunteers; To promote the need for education for leisure
Chief Officer(s):
Sarah Wagner, Executive Director
rnb@recreationnb.ca
Finances: *Annual Operating Budget:* $100,000-$250,000
Membership: *Fees:* $87 general; $265-$565 municipal; $132 associate; $295 corporate
Activities: Annual conference; awards; resource centre; membership directory; workshops; counsellors conference; Canoe School; career videos for high schools

Recreation Newfoundland & Labrador

PO Box 8700, St. John's NL A1B 4J6
Tel: 709-729-3892; *Fax:* 709-729-3814
info@recreationnl.com
www.recreationnl.com
www.facebook.com/455370901173112
Previous Name: Newfoundland & Labrador Parks & Recreation Association
Overview: A medium-sized provincial organization founded in 1971 overseen by Canadian Parks & Recreation Association
Mission: To promote, foster & develop recreation; to provide a full range of services to enrich the concept of leisure throughout Newfoundland & Labrador; to enable individual citizens to improve their quality of life.
Affliation(s): Provincial/Territorial parks & recreation associations
Chief Officer(s):
Dawn Sharpe, President
dawnsharpe12@gmail.com
Gary Milley, Executive Director
garymilley@recreationnl.com
Finances: *Funding Sources:* Membership fees; services; government grants; corporate
Staff Member(s): 5
Membership: *Fees:* Schedule available; *Member Profile:* Municipalities, communities, individuals, non-profit groups, students or businesses interested or involved in recreation
Activities: Playground Training Workshops; *Library*
Awards:
• Bridging the Gap (Award)
Presented annually to recognize efforts of volunteers who have made a significant contribution to the development of recreational opportunities for persons with a diability in an integrated setting
• Ebert J. Broomfield Memorial Scholarship (Scholarship)
Established in 1989; presented annually on a rotation basis between Eastern, Central, Western & Northern regions to a student based on academic achievement, atheltic participation & community involvement
• Pitcher Plant Award (Award)
Presented annually to recognize outstanding efforts in the development of recreation & leisure services in Newfoundland & Labrador
• Cy Hoskins Award (Award)
Presented annually to a full-time recreation practitioner who has made significant contributions to the growth & development of parks, recreation & leisure services

Recreation Nova Scotia (RNS)

#309, 5516 Spring Garden Rd., Halifax NS B3J 1G6
Tel: 902-425-1128; *Fax:* 902-422-8201
www.recreationns.ns.ca
www.linkedin.com/company/recreation-nova-scotia
www.facebook.com/RecreationNovaScotia
twitter.com/recreationns
Overview: A medium-sized provincial charitable organization founded in 1998 overseen by Canadian Parks & Recreation Association
Mission: To build healthier futures through programs & services that promote the benefits of recreation
Member of: Volunteer Canada; Sport Nova Scotia; Active Living Alliance for Canadians with Disability; NS Council for the Family
Chief Officer(s):
Rhonda Lemire, Executive Director
rlemire@recreationns.ns.ca
Rae Gunn, President
coordinator@activepictoucounty.ca
Finances: *Annual Operating Budget:* $500,000-$1.5 Million; *Funding Sources:* Membership fees; provincial & federal government; fundraising
Staff Member(s): 6
Membership: *Fees:* Schedule available; *Member Profile:* Municipal recreation directors; community group volunteers; community development associations; individuals; students;

business; elected officials; *Committees:* Recreation Matters Campaign; HIGH FIVE; Membership Services; Inclusion; Conference; Education; Training
Activities: NS Volunteer Training Workshop; Liability Insurance Program for community groups; lottery for community groups; awards program; social marketing campaign; advocacy; conference; special events; *Library* Open to public
Awards:
• Bluenose Achievement Award (Award)
• Mayflower Community Cooperation Award (Award)
• Rick Hansen Award (Award)
• Professional Achievement Award (Award)
• Provincial Volunteer Week Awards (Award)

Recreation Prince Edward Island

40 Enman Cres., Charlottetown PE C1E 1E6
Tel: 902-892-6445; *Fax:* 902-368-4548
info@recreationpei.ca
www.recreationpei.ca
www.youtube.com/user/RecPEI
Also Known As: Recreation PEI
Previous Name: Prince Edward Island Recreation & Facilities Association
Overview: A small provincial organization
Chief Officer(s):
Kim Meunier, President
kmeunier@town.cornwall.pe.ca
Beth Grant, Executive Director
Finances: *Funding Sources:* Canadian Parks & Recreation Association (CPRA)

Recreation Vehicle Dealers Association of Alberta

10561 - 172 St. NW, Edmonton AB T5S 1P1
Tel: 780-455-8562; *Fax:* 780-453-3927
Toll-Free: 888-858-8787
rvda@rvda-alberta.org
www.rvda-alberta.org
Also Known As: RVDA of Alberta
Overview: A medium-sized provincial organization founded in 1978 overseen by Recreation Vehicle Dealers Association of Canada
Mission: To develop professionalism & customer confidence in the RV industry
Member of: Canadian Society of Association Executives; Recreation Vehicle Dealers of America
Finances: *Annual Operating Budget:* $500,000-$1.5 Million; *Funding Sources:* Membership dues; trade shows
Staff Member(s): 2; 12 volunteer(s)
Membership: 140; *Fees:* $495; *Member Profile:* Dealers of RVs; parts & service companies; financial institutions; RV parks
Activities: Production of RV consumer shows in Calgary & Edmonton

Recreation Vehicle Dealers Association of British Columbia (RVDABC)

#201, 17700 - 56th Ave., Surrey BC V3S 1C7
Tel: 604-575-3868; *Fax:* 604-575-3869
info@rvda.bc.ca
www.rvda.bc.ca
Also Known As: RVDA of BC
Overview: A small provincial organization founded in 1976 overseen by Recreation Vehicle Dealers Association of Canada
Mission: To promote, protect, educate, & enhances benefits for its members
Chief Officer(s):
Joan Jackson, Executive Officer
joan@rvda.bc.ca
Finances: *Annual Operating Budget:* $100,000-$250,000; *Funding Sources:* Membership fees
Staff Member(s): 2
Membership: 95; *Fees:* $530-$1,080 based on number of full-time staff; *Member Profile:* RV dealers; suppliers of RV services, parts & accessories
Activities: Recreation vehicles sales & shows; education & training; *Library*

Recreation Vehicle Dealers Association of Canada (RVDA) / Association des commerçants de véhicules recréatifs du Canada

#204, 6411 Buswell St., Richmond BC V6Y 2G5
Tel: 604-718-6325; *Fax:* 604-204-0154
info@rvda.ca
www.rvda.ca
www.facebook.com/RVDAofCanada
Overview: A medium-sized national licensing organization founded in 1986
Mission: To promote professionalism in the RV industry through educational programs & events; to present the views of the industry to government & the general public
Affliation(s): Recreation Vehicle Dealers Association of America
Chief Officer(s):
Eleonore Hamm, President
eleonorehamm@rvda.ca
Finances: *Annual Operating Budget:* $250,000-$500,000; *Funding Sources:* Membership dues
Staff Member(s): 3; 20 volunteer(s)
Membership: 700; *Committees:* Funding; Education; Program Development; Marketing
Activities: *Speaker Service:* Yes

Recreation Vehicle Dealers Association of Manitoba

#503, 386 Broadway, Winnipeg MB R3C 3R6
Tel: 204-975-8219; *Fax:* 204-947-9767
rvshow@mbrvda.ca
www.manitobarvda.com
Also Known As: RVDA of Manitoba
Overview: A small provincial organization overseen by Recreation Vehicle Dealers Association of Canada
Mission: To build & improve the RV industry
Affliation(s): Recreation Vehicles Dealers Association of Canada
Chief Officer(s):
Richard Willard, President, 204-338-0264, Fax: 204-339-1245
ggs@mts.net
Geoff Powell, Executive Director
Finances: *Annual Operating Budget:* Less than $50,000; *Funding Sources:* Membership fees; RV Camping & Leisure Show & Sale
Staff Member(s): 1
Membership: 12 dealer; 21 associate; *Member Profile:* RV dealers; suppliers; manufacturers & financial groups; insurance groups
Activities: Lobby government to improve safety in RVs; educate & train personnel within the industry; increase awareness of RV industry;

Recreation Vehicle Dealers Association of Saskatchewan

342 Armstrong Way, Saskatoon SK S7N 3N1
Tel: 306-955-7832; *Fax:* 306-955-7952
skrvda@sasktel.net
www.saskatchewanrvda.ca
Also Known As: RVDA of Saskatchewan
Overview: A small provincial organization founded in 1995 overseen by Recreation Vehicle Dealers Association of Canada
Affliation(s): Recreation Vehicle Dealers Association of Canada
Chief Officer(s):
Garret Porten, President
president@saskatchewanrvda.ca

Recreational Aircraft Association (RAA) / Réseau aéronefs amateur

22 - 4881 Fountain St. North, Breslau ON N0B 1M0
Tel: 519-648-3030
Toll-Free: 800-387-1028
raa@raa.ca
www.raa.ca
Previous Name: Experimental Aircraft Association of Canada
Overview: A medium-sized national organization founded in 1983
Mission: To be a national leader in the development & advancement of recreational aviation; to promote recreational flying & building of amateur built aircraft, restorations of classic & antique aircraft
Affliation(s): Recreational Aviation Foundation
Chief Officer(s):
Gary Wolf, President, 519-648-3030
garywolf@rogers.com
Wayne Hadath, Treasurer
whadath@rogers.com
Finances: *Annual Operating Budget:* $100,000-$250,000; *Funding Sources:* Membership dues
Staff Member(s): 1; 150 volunteer(s)
Membership: 2,000; *Fees:* $40; *Committees:* 12 regional
Activities: Fly-ins across Canada; *Speaker Service:* Yes

Recreational Canoeing Association BC (RCABC)

1755 East 7th Ave., Vancouver BC V5N 1S1
Tel: 250-592-4170
sec@bccanoe.com
www.bccanoe.com
Overview: A small provincial organization founded in 1984
Member of: Paddle Canada
Chief Officer(s):
Kari-Ann Thor, President, 604-253-5410
Tony Shaw, Secretary, 250-468-7955
Finances: *Annual Operating Budget:* Less than $50,000; *Funding Sources:* Membership dues; government
16 volunteer(s)
Membership: 350; *Fees:* $20; $45 instructor; *Committees:* Course Standards; Conservation & Access
Activities: Canoe instruction & standards

Recycling Council of Alberta (RCA)

PO Box 23, Bluffton AB T0C 0M0
Tel: 403-843-6563; *Fax:* 403-843-4156
info@recycle.ab.ca
www.recycle.ab.ca
www.facebook.com/RecyclingCouncilOfAlberta
twitter.com/3RsAB
Overview: A medium-sized provincial charitable organization founded in 1987
Mission: To promote & facilitate waste reduction, recycling, & resource conservation in Alberta
Chief Officer(s):
Jason London, President
Sharon Howland, Vice-President
Maegan Lukian, Secretary
Anne Auriat, Treasurer
Membership: *Fees:* Fee based upon sales for corporations & small businesses; Fee based upon population for municipalities & regional waste authorities; *Member Profile:* Corporations; Small Businesses; Institutions; Governments; Municipalities; Regional Waste Authorities; Not-for-Profit Organizations; Individuals; *Committees:* Leadership & Advocacy; Small & Rural Communities; Communications; Indstrial, Commercial, & Institutional Sector Issues
Activities: Facilitating the exchange of information between environmental groups, governments, industries, & consumers; Providing public education campaigns; Encouraging research in the recycling of waste materials; *Awareness Events:* Waste Reduction Week, October; *Speaker Service:* Yes
Meetings/Conferences: • Recycling Council of Alberta Waste Reduction 2015 Conference, September, 2015, Banff, AB
Scope: Provincial
Description: Presentations, exhibits, & networking opportunities. Held jointly with the Conference on Canadian Stewardship.
Contact Information: Phone: 403-843-6563; E-mail: info@recycle.ab.ca
Publications:
• Connector [a publication of the Recycling Council of Alberta]
Type: Newsletter
Profile: RCA activities, member profiles, & success stories
• Enviro Business Guide
Type: Directory
Profile: Contact information & descriptions of businesses

Recycling Council of British Columbia (RCBC)

#10, 119 West Pender St., Vancouver BC V6B 1S5
Tel: 604-683-6009; *Fax:* 604-683-7255
Toll-Free: 800-667-4321
Other Communication: hotline@rcbc.bc.ca
rcbc@rcbc.bc.ca
www.rcbc.bc.ca
www.facebook.com/home.php?sk=group_10340005498
twitter.com/RecyclingBC
www.youtube.com/user/RCBCTrailerTrashed
Overview: A medium-sized provincial charitable organization founded in 1974
Mission: To promote the principles of zero waste; To decrease British Columbia's environmental footprint
Chief Officer(s):
Brock Macdonald, Executive Director, 604-683-6009 Ext. 307
brock@rcbc.bc.ca
Anna Rochelle, Director, Finance, 604-683-6009 Ext. 302
anna@rcbc.bc.ca
Harvinder Gill, Manager, Information Services, 604-683-6009 Ext. 313
harv@rcbc.bc.ca
Ben Ramos, Manager, Member Services, 604-683-6009 Ext. 314
ben@rcbc.bc.ca
Finances: *Funding Sources:* Sponsorships; Donations
Membership: *Member Profile:* Individuals & corporations that support environmental sustainability
Activities: Conducting research; Providing information services; Participating in community-based events & activities;

Establishing public policy positions; *Awareness Events:* Waste Reduction Week
Meetings/Conferences: • Recycling Council of British Columbia 2015 Annual Zero Waste Conference & Annual General Meeting, 2015
Scope: Provincial
Description: An event each spring about recycling & waste reduction in British Columbia
Contact Information: E-mail: conference@rcbc.bc.ca
Publications:
• Best Practices for Multi-Family Food Scraps Collection
Type: Report; *Number of Pages:* 18; *Author:* Jordan Best
Profile: Topics include barriers in the multi-family sector, materials collected, collection details, containers & liners, education & outreach, & incentives &policies
• Examining the Waste-to-Energy Option
Type: Report; *Number of Pages:* 24; *Author:* Jordan Best
Profile: A background paper examining environmental performance & compatibility with zero waste principles
• On the Road to Zero Waste: Priorities for Local Governments
Type: Report; *Number of Pages:* 16
Profile: Guidance for municipal & regional governments across British Columbia
• Organics Working Group Report: Recommendations for Residential Collection
Type: Report; *Number of Pages:* 16
Profile: Recommendations developed by the Organics Working Group to service single family homes
• RCBC [Recycling Council of British Columbia] Backgrounder: Degradable Plastic Bags
Type: Report
• Recycling Council of British Columbia Annual Report
Type: Yearbook; *Frequency:* Annually
Profile: Featuring the executive director's report, the auditor's report, & organizational information

Recycling Council of Manitoba; Resource Conservation Manitoba Inc. ***See*** Green Action Centre

Recycling Council of Ontario (RCO) / Conseil du recyclage de l'Ontario

#225, 215 Spadina Ave., Toronto ON M5T 2C7
Tel: 416-657-2797
Toll-Free: 888-501-9637
rco@rco.on.ca
www.rco.on.ca
twitter.com/RCOntario
Overview: A medium-sized provincial charitable organization founded in 1978
Mission: To minimize impact on the environment by eliminating waste
Chief Officer(s):
Jo-Anne St. Godard, Executive Director, 416-657-2797 Ext. 3
joanne@rco.on.ca
Diane Blackburn, Manager, Events, 416-657-2797 Ext. 4
events@rco.on.ca; diane@rco.on.ca
David Hanson, Program Manager, Waste Diversion Certification Program, 416-657-2797 Ext. 8
david@rco.on.ca
Sarah Mills, Manager, Special Projects & Take Back the Light, 416-657-2797 Ext. 7
sarah@rco.on.ca
Lucy Robinson, Manager, Member Relations, 416-657-2797 Ext. 1
lucy@rco.on.ca; members@rco.on.ca
Catherine Leighton, Coordinator, Special Projects, 416-657-2797 Ext. 5
catherine@rco.on.ca
Andrew Reeves, Coordinator, Outreach & Communications, 416-657-2797 Ext. 10
andrew@rco.on.ca
Finances: *Funding Sources:* Donations; Sponsorships
Membership: *Fees:* Schedule available based upon annual gross sales for businesses & population for municipalities; *Member Profile:* Businesses; Municipalities; Communities; Educational organizations; Individuals; Students; Families; *Committees:* Executive / Finance; Membership / Communications; Policy / Advocacy; Program Development; Events
Activities: Liaising with all levels of government, environmental organizations, & industry; *Awareness Events:* Waste Reduction Week in Ontario; Waste Free Lunch Challenge
Awards:
• Visual Arts, Sculpture, & Arts Installation Award (Award)
• Business Award (Award)
• Communications Award (Award)
• Festivals & Events Award (Award)
• Municipal Awards (Award)
• Sustainable Product or Service Award (Award)
• Waste Diversion Program Operator Award (Award)
• Waste Reduction Week in Canada Participation Award (Award)
Meetings/Conferences: • Recycling Council of Ontario 2015 Annual General Meeting & Policy Forum, 2015, ON
Scope: Provincial
Description: Voting by members for the Board of Directors
Contact Information: Contact: Lucy Robinson, Phone: 416-657-2797, E-mail: lucy@rco.on.ca
Publications:
• RCO [Recycling Council of Ontario] Highlights the Headlines
Price: Free with Recycling Council of Ontario membership
Profile: Information about local, national, & international environmental, waste management, & diversion issues
• Recycling Council of Ontario Annual Report
Type: Yearbook; *Frequency:* Annually
Profile: Operational highlights of the council
• Recycling Council of Ontario e-Newsletter
Type: Newsletter; *Price:* Free with Recycling Council of Ontario membership
• Recycling Council of Ontario Member Bulletin
Type: Newsletter; *Frequency:* Irregular; *Price:* Free with Recycling Council of Ontario membership

Red Deer & District Allied Arts Council

#111, 4818 - 50 St., Red Deer AB T4N 4A3
Tel: 403-348-2787
info@reddeerartscouncil.ca
www.reddeerartscouncil.ca
www.facebook.com/reddeerartscouncil
twitter.com/RDArtsCouncil
Previous Name: Red Deer Allied Arts Council
Overview: A small local organization founded in 1964
Mission: To foster & encourage participation of young people & adults in the arts; to stimulate interest & appreciation of the arts in general
Chief Officer(s):
Diana Anderson, Coordinator
Membership: *Fees:* $15 student; $30 individual; $50 group; *Member Profile:* Interest & willingness to encourage the arts in central Alberta
Activities: Art gallery; artist and youth education; support to local artists and groups; scholarship programs; *Internships:* Yes; *Speaker Service:* Yes; *Rents Mailing List:* Yes

Red Deer & District Community Foundation (RDDCF)

Mid City Plaza, 4805 - 48 St., Red Deer AB T4N 1S6
Tel: 403-341-6911; *Fax:* 403-341-4177
info@rddcf.ca
www.rddcf.ca
twitter.com/rddcf
www.youtube.com/user/rddcf
Overview: A small local organization founded in 1989
Mission: To strengthen the quality of life in the Red Deer area by growing a legacy through the development of endowment funds, fostering collaboration & partnerships, responding to community needs & promoting innovation
Member of: Community Foundations of Canada
Chief Officer(s):
Kristine Bugayong, CEO
Joanne Packham, Chair
Rhonda Elder, Vice-Chair
Finances: *Funding Sources:* Individual & corporate contributions
Staff Member(s): 3

Red Deer & District SPCA

4505 - 77 St., Red Deer AB T4P 2J1
Tel: 403-342-7722; *Fax:* 403-341-3147
office@reddeerspca.com
www.reddeerspca.com
www.facebook.com/233609360018185
twitter.com/RedDeerSPCA
Previous Name: Parkland Humane Society
Overview: A small local charitable organization founded in 1970 overseen by Canadian Federation of Humane Societies
Mission: To care for & protect companion animals & promote humane treatment of animals & responsible pet ownership
Member of: Alberta Society for the Prevention of Cruelty to Animals; Red Deer Chamber of Commerce; Canadian Federation of Humane Societies
Chief Officer(s):
Tara Hellewell, Executive Director
Finances: *Funding Sources:* United Way; municipal grants
Staff Member(s): 20
Membership: *Fees:* $20 single; $25 family; $100 corporate; $200 individual lifetime; $250 family lifetime; $1000 corporate lifetime
Activities: Bark @ the Bend

Red Deer Action Group

#301, 4805 - 48 St., Red Deer AB T4N 1S6
Tel: 403-343-1198; *Fax:* 403-343-8945
rdag@telus.net
www.rdactiongroup.ca
Previous Name: Red Deer Action Group for the Physically Disabled
Overview: A small local charitable organization founded in 1976
Mission: To work toward providing a better quality of life for people with disabilities
Affliation(s): Alberta Committee for Citizens with Disabilities
Chief Officer(s):
Jean Stinson, President
Finances: *Annual Operating Budget:* Less than $50,000
Staff Member(s): 2; 25 volunteer(s)
Membership: 75 individual; *Fees:* $10 individual

Red Deer Action Group for the Physically Disabled ***See*** Red Deer Action Group

Red Deer Allied Arts Council ***See*** Red Deer & District Allied Arts Council

Red Deer Chamber of Commerce

3017 Gaetz Ave., Red Deer AB T4N 5Y6
Tel: 403-347-4491; *Fax:* 403-343-6188
rdchamber@reddeerchamber.com
www.reddeerchamber.com
www.facebook.com/109831038638
twitter.com/RedDeerChamber
Overview: A medium-sized local organization founded in 1894
Mission: To promote a thriving environment by advocating for Red Deer & area members on issues affecting business in the community
Member of: Alberta Chamber of Commerce; Canadian Chamber of Commerce
Chief Officer(s):
Maureen McMurtrie, President
Tim Creedon, Executive Director
Finances: *Annual Operating Budget:* $1.5 Million-$3 Million; *Funding Sources:* Membership dues; trade shows; seminars
Staff Member(s): 24; 100 volunteer(s)
Membership: 870; *Fees:* Schedule available; *Committees:* Ambassadors; Economic Development; Airport; Youth Activities
Activities: *Rents Mailing List:* Yes; *Library* by appointment

Red Deer City Soccer Association

6905 Edgar Industrial Dr., Red Deer AB T4P 3R2
Tel: 403-346-4259; *Fax:* 403-340-1044
office@rdcsa.com
www.rdcsa.com
Overview: A small local organization overseen by Alberta Soccer Association
Member of: Alberta Soccer Association
Chief Officer(s):
Joan Van Wolde, Administrator
Staff Member(s): 2

Red Deer Construction Association (RDCA)

7471 Edgar Ind. Bend, Bay #3, Red Deer AB T4P 3Z5
Tel: 403-346-4846; *Fax:* 403-343-3280
rdca@telusplanet.net
www.reddeerconstructionassociation.com
Overview: A small local organization founded in 1957
Mission: To serve its members by displaying plans & information on current projects in the industry; To act as members' collective voice on issues of concern; To promote standards, education & communication in an effort to benefit the industry & society
Member of: Alberta Construction Association; Canadian Construction Association
Chief Officer(s):
Josh Edwards, President
Mary Lu Bryson, Manager
Finances: *Annual Operating Budget:* $50,000-$100,000; *Funding Sources:* Membership fees
Staff Member(s): 1; 12 volunteer(s)
Membership: 152; *Fees:* $662.50-$1,070.60; *Member Profile:* General contractors, trade contractors, manufacturers & suppliers & associates; *Committees:* Executive; Finance; Membership; Recreation; WCB/Safety; Standard Practices; Acts;

Government Action; Electronic Communications & Technology/COOLNet; RCDA Scholarship; Marketing, Research & Technology; ACA Director
Activities: Golf tournaments; open houses; Christmas festivities; *Library:* ACSA Safety Video Library;

Red Deer Danish Canadian Club (RDDCC)
PO Box 173, Red Deer AB T4N 5E8
Tel: 403-783-4734
rddcc.com
Overview: A small local organization founded in 1959
Member of: Federation of Danish Associations in Canada
Chief Officer(s):
Pernille Nielsen, President
apernille@live.com

Red Deer Food Bank Society
#12, 7429 - 49 Ave., Red Deer AB T4P 1N2
Tel: 403-342-5355; *Fax:* 403-346-1551
rdfoodbank@hotmail.com
www.linkedin.com/ReddeerFoodbank
www.facebook.com/ReddeerFoodbank
twitter.com/ReddeerFoodBank
Overview: A small local organization founded in 1984
Mission: To feed the hungry; To promote human dignity; To help prevent the senseless waste of food; To develop community awareness of poverty issues; To intervene with policy makers on behalf of those in need
Member of: Food Banks Alberta
Chief Officer(s):
Fred R. Scaife, Executive Director
Alice Kolisnyk, Deputy Director
Finances: *Annual Operating Budget:* $100,000-$250,000; *Funding Sources:* Public donations
Staff Member(s): 8; 40 volunteer(s)
Membership: 43; *Fees:* $100; *Committees:* Advocacy; Finance
Activities: *Speaker Service:* Yes

Red Deer Landlord & Tenant Services *See* Volunteer Red Deer

Red Deer Native Friendship Society
4808-51 Ave., Red Deer AB T4N 4H3
Tel: 403-340-0020; *Fax:* 403-324-1610
anfca.com/friendship-centres/red-deer
Overview: A small local organization founded in 1984 overseen by Alberta Native Friendship Centres Association
Mission: To inform the community of the problems experiences by Aboriginal people living in urban areas, & to work with the community to resolve these problems where possible; To provide a medium for the development of Aboriginal Leadership in the community; To promote friendship & understanding between Aboriginal & Non-Aboriginal people; To preserve & promote Aboriginal Culture & Heritage within the community; To assist Aboriginal people to use & derive advantages from services & facilities & to improve generally the lives of Aboriginal people; To establish organizational leadership, management effectiveness & responsive program planning & delivery in addressing the issues facing the Native community
Member of: Alberta Native Friendship Centres Association
Chief Officer(s):
Sheralle Graystone, Executive Director

Red Deer River Naturalists (RDRN)
PO Box 785, Red Deer AB T4N 5H2
Tel: 403-347-8200; *Fax:* 403-347-8200
rd.rn@hotmail.com
www.rdrn.fanweb.ca
Previous Name: Alberta Natural History Society
Overview: A small local charitable organization founded in 1906
Mission: To foster increased knowledge, understanding & appreciation of natural history; to support conservation measures dealing with environment, wildlife & natural resources; to cooperate with other clubs & organizations having similar views & objectives
Member of: Federation of Alberta Naturalists
Affiliation(s): Canadian Nature Federation
Chief Officer(s):
Don Wales, President
Finances: *Annual Operating Budget:* Less than $50,000; *Funding Sources:* Membership fees; donations; grants
300 volunteer(s)
Membership: 300 individual; *Fees:* $15 individual; $20 family; *Committees:* Habitat Preservation
Activities: Field trips; Habitat Steward Program; educational programs; species counts

Red Deer Symphony Orchestra
Cultural Services Building, PO Box 1116, 3827 - 39th St., Red Deer AB T4N 6S5
Tel: 403-340-2948; *Fax:* 403-309-4612
reddeersymphony@telus.net
www.rdso.ca
www.facebook.com/reddeersymphony
twitter.com/RedDeerSymphony
Overview: A small local charitable organization founded in 1987 overseen by Orchestras Canada
Chief Officer(s):
Melody McKnight, Executive Director
Claude Lapalme, Music Director
Finances: *Annual Operating Budget:* $100,000-$250,000
Staff Member(s): 5
Membership: 1-99
Activities: Choir kids program; symphonic show and tell program; woodwind quintet program

Red Feather United Appeal; United Way of Greater Toronto *See* United Way Toronto

Red Lake & District Association for Community Living
PO Box 906, Red Lake ON P0V 2M0
Tel: 807-727-2828; *Fax:* 807-727-1102
Also Known As: Harmony Centre For Community Living
Previous Name: Red Lake & District Association for the Mentally Retarded
Overview: A small local charitable organization founded in 1975
Member of: Community Living Ontario
Chief Officer(s):
Margaret Kudlowsky, Executive Director
Bob Conner, President
Finances: *Annual Operating Budget:* Less than $50,000
8 volunteer(s)
Membership: 6; *Fees:* $5
Activities: Provides support to disabled individuals; *Awareness Events:* Annual Tea & Bake Sale

Red Lake & District Association for the Mentally Retarded *See* Red Lake & District Association for Community Living

Red Lake Chamber of Commerce
PO Box 430, Red Lake ON P0V 2M0
Tel: 807-727-3722; *Fax:* 807-727-3285
redlakechamber@shaw.ca
www.facebook.com/469121443150316
Overview: A small local organization
Mission: To promote & improve trade & commerce & the economy, civic & social welfare of the district
Member of: Northwestern Ontario Associated Chambers of Commerce
Chief Officer(s):
Carol McPherson, President
Colin Knudsen, Vice President
Mark Vermette, Second Vice President
Yvonne Davis, Treasurer
Membership: *Fees:* Schedule available
Activities: Trade show; community events
Awards:
• Business Program Award Bursary (Award)
Amount: $500

Red Lake Indian Friendship Centre (RLIFC)
PO Box 244, 1 Legion Rd., Red Lake ON P0V 2M0
Tel: 807-727-2847; *Fax:* 807-727-3253
rlifc@shaw.ca
Previous Name: District Indian Youth Club
Overview: A small local charitable organization founded in 1964
Mission: To provide a gathering place for the Aboriginal community in the Red Lake, Ontario region; To promote economic development for Aboriginal people
Member of: Ontario Federation of Indian Friendship Centres
Finances: *Funding Sources:* Donations
Activities: Offering counselling & referral services; Organizing social, recreational, & cultural activities; Working with government official & local service agencies; Engaging in advocacy activities; Providing programs in areas such as prenatal nutrition, fetal alcohol spectrum disorder, child nutrition, & life long care

Red River Apiarists' Association (RRAA)
231 Buxton Rd., Winnipeg MB R3T 0H4
Tel: 204-284-7064
www.beekeepingmanitoba.com
Also Known As: Beekeeping Manitoba
Overview: A small local organization founded in 1963
Mission: To provide members with continuing education in beekeeping skills & to provide a forum for the exchange of beekeeping ideas; To increase public awareness of the value of beekeeping
Chief Officer(s):
Charles Polcyn, President
Charles_Polcyn@ymail.com
Finances: *Annual Operating Budget:* Less than $50,000; *Funding Sources:* Membership fees
Membership: 1-99; *Fees:* $25
Activities: Monthly meetings; field day tours; Honey Show; Convention/Symposium; *Library*

Red River Exhibition Association
Red River Exhibition Park, 3977 Portage Ave., Winnipeg MB R3K 2E8
Tel: 204-888-6990; *Fax:* 204-888-6992
www.redriverex.com
www.facebook.com/redriverex
twitter.com/redriverex
www.youtube.com/watch?v=JUHjPfs02bM
Overview: A small national organization founded in 1951
Mission: To enhance the lives of the people of Manitoba by showcasing their talents, abilities & achievements to each other & the world
Member of: Canadian Association Fairs & Exhibitions; International Association Fairs & Exposition; Manitoba Association of Agricultural Societies
Chief Officer(s):
Darren Lewis, President
Garth Rogerson, CEO
garth.rogerson@redriverex.com
Finances: *Annual Operating Budget:* $500,000-$1.5 Million
Staff Member(s): 8; 300 volunteer(s)
Membership: 100-499
Activities: *Awareness Events:* Red River Exhibition; Heart of the Continent Fair
Awards:
• Bob Lang Memorial Scholarship (Scholarship)

Red Road HIV/AIDS Network (RRHAN)
#61-1959 Marine Dr., North Vancouver BC V7P 3G1
Tel: 778-340-3388; *Fax:* 778-340-3328
info@red-road.org
www.red-road.org
twitter.com/RRHAN
Overview: A small national organization founded in 1999
Mission: The Red Road HIV/AIDS Network works to reduce or prevent the spread of HIV/AIDS; improve the health and wellness of Aboriginal people living with HIV/AIDS; and increase awareness about HIV/AIDS and establish a network which supports the development and delivery of culturally appropriate, innovative, coordinated, accessible, inclusive and accountable HIV/AIDS programs and services
Chief Officer(s):
Kim Louie, Executive Director
klouie@red-road.org
Heidi Standeven, Provincial Coordinator
hstandeven@red-road.org
Finances: *Funding Sources:* First Nations & Inuit Health, Health Canada; Public Health Agency of Canada; First Nations Health Authority; private organizations
Membership: *Fees:* $50 full; $25 associate; $5 individual
Activities: Workshops, conferences; support groups
Publications:
• Bloodlines Magazine
Type: Magazine
Profile: a forum in which Aboriginal Persons Living with HIV/AIDS can share their personal experiences, discuss issues affecting them, offer advice and suggestions to their peers.
• Red Road Aboriginal HIV/AIDS Resource Directory
Type: Directory; *Frequency:* Semi-Annually

Redvers Chamber of Commerce
PO Box 249, Redvers SK S0C 2H0
Tel: 306-452-3155; *Fax:* 306-452-3155
rdaycare@sasktel.net
www.facebook.com/pages/Redvers-Chamber-of-Commerce/128057020575695
Overview: A small local organization
Chief Officer(s):
Tricia Martel, President
Tanis Chalmers, Director
Membership: 42
Activities: Redvers AgEx & Bull Congress, April

Redwater & District Chamber of Commerce
PO Box 322, Redwater AB T0A 2W0
Tel: 780-942-3519
Overview: A small local organization
Affliation(s): Alberta Chamber of Commerce; Canadian Chamber of Commerce

ReelWorld Film Festival
#300, 438 Parliament St., Toronto ON M5A 3A2
Tel: 416-598-7933
www.reelworld.ca
www.facebook.com/ReelWorld.Film.Festival.Toronto
twitter.com/ReelWorldFilm
www.youtube.com/ReelWorldFestival;
www.flickr.com/photos/reelworldfilm
Overview: A medium-sized local organization founded in 1999
Mission: To present a culturally & racially diverse film festival showcasing films & music videos, & to connect filmmakers with producers, acquisitions personnel & distributors through The RealWorld Foundation.
Chief Officer(s):
Moe Jiwan, Chair & Treasurer
Tonya Lee Williams, Founder, Executive Director & Head, Programming

Reena
927 Clark Ave. West, Thornhill ON L4J 8G6
Tel: 905-889-6484; *Fax:* 905-889-3827
info@reena.org
www.reena.org
Previous Name: Reena Foundation
Overview: A medium-sized local charitable organization founded in 1975
Mission: To integrate developmentally disabled people towards independent living within community, with emphasis on Judaic programming
Affliation(s): Jewish Federation of Greater Toronto
Chief Officer(s):
Bryan Keshen, President & CEO
bkeshen@reena.org
Minnie Ross, Manager, Communications
minnie.ross@reena.org
Finances: *Funding Sources:* Provincial government; community fundraising
Activities: Programs for children, adults, seniors with developmental disabilities; *Speaker Service:* Yes

Reena Foundation *See* Reena

Reflexology Association of Canada (RAC) / Association canadienne de réflexologie
#304, 414 Graham Ave., Winnipeg MB R3C 0L8
Tel: 204-477-4909; *Fax:* 204-477-4955
Toll-Free: 877-722-3338
memberservices@reflexolog.org
www.reflexologycanada.ca
Overview: A medium-sized national organization founded in 1976
Mission: To set & maintain high standards among practising reflexologists; To advance quality training; To develop an effective referral system across Canada
Chief Officer(s):
Judy Carey, Executive Director
Penny Rossiter, Administrator
penny.rossiter@reflexolog.org
Staff Member(s): 6
Membership: 2,000; *Fees:* $100
Activities: *Speaker Service:* Yes

Reform Party of British Columbia
1796 McGuire Ave., North Vancouver BC V7P 3B1
Tel: 604-980-7779; *Fax:* 604-980-8833
info@reformbc.net
www.reformbc.net
Also Known As: Reform BC
Overview: A small provincial organization
Mission: A populist right-wing political party in British Columbia.
Chief Officer(s):
Ron Gamble, President, 604-980-7779
David Hawkins, Party Leader, 604-542-0891
Membership: *Fees:* $10

The Reformed Episcopal Church of Canada - Diocese of Central & Eastern Canada (REC)
PO Box 2532, 320 Armstrong St. N., New Liskeard ON P0J 1P0
Tel: 705-647-4565
trinityfed@hotmail.com
recus.org
Overview: A medium-sized provincial charitable organization founded in 1886
Mission: We believe the Bible to be the inspired, the only infallible, inerrant, authoritative Word of God
Finances: *Annual Operating Budget:* Less than $50,000; *Funding Sources:* Donations
4 volunteer(s)
Membership: 210 + 6 churches; *Committees:* Standing; Constitution & Canons; Church Extension
Activities: Synodical Council, 3rd week of Sept.; *Library* Open to public by appointment

The Reformed Episcopal Church of Canada - Diocese of Western Canada & Alaska (RECWCAN)
2604 Quadra St., Victoria BC V8T 4E4
Tel: 250-727-3722; *Fax:* 250-727-3722
recwcan@islandnet.com
www.recwcan.ca
Overview: A small national licensing charitable organization founded in 1874
Mission: To reach out to those outside the existing congregation; establish new churches; assist congregations within the Diocese; receive congregations wishing to affiliate with the Reformed Episcopal Church; ordain candidates into the ministry
Affliation(s): Common Cause Network
Chief Officer(s):
John Boudewyn, Treasurer, 250-544-0098
Jack Cryderman, Secretary, 250-339-4014
Charles W. Dorrington, Diocesan Bishop, 250-652-8850
Finances: *Annual Operating Budget:* Less than $50,000; *Funding Sources:* Offerings; bequests; church assessments
Staff Member(s): 2
Membership: 300; *Fees:* Church offerings; *Committees:* Council; Vestry; Executive; Standing; Synod
Activities: Douglas House Retirement Home Ministry; Victoria Prayer Counselling; Healing Rooms; *Internships:* Yes; *Speaker Service:* Yes; *Library:* Diocesan Office Library; by appointment

Refreshments Canada; Canadian Bottlers of Carbonated Beverages; Canadian Soft Drink Association *See* Canadian Beverage Association

Refrigeration & Air Conditioning Contractors Association of British Columbia (RACCA-BC)
26121 Fraser Hwy., Aldergrove BC V4X 2E3
Tel: 604-856-8644
raccabc@hrai.ca
Overview: A medium-sized provincial organization
Mission: To act on behalf of the members to promote positive & effective employee development & labour relations
Chief Officer(s):
Blaire Masztalar, President
Finances: *Annual Operating Budget:* Less than $50,000
Staff Member(s): 1
Membership: 15 corporate;

Refrigeration Service Engineers Society (Canada) (RSES Canada)
PO Box 3, Stn. B, Toronto ON M9W 5K9
Tel: 905-842-9199
Toll-Free: 877-955-6255
www.rsescanada.com
Overview: A medium-sized national organization founded in 1952
Mission: To lead all segments of the HVAC industry by providing superior educational & training programs; to create an environment that encourages maximum member participation in the development & decision process of the Society
Member of: Refrigeration Service Engineers Society - International
Chief Officer(s):
Denis Hebert, President, 506-857-3233
denis.hebert@bellaliant.net
Nick Reggi, Secretary, 905-842-9199
dreggi@cogeco.ca
Finances: *Annual Operating Budget:* $50,000-$100,000; *Funding Sources:* Membership dues; educational seminars
2 volunteer(s)
Membership: 2,200; *Fees:* $125; *Committees:* Awards; Budget & Finance; Bulletin Committee; CFC Training; Commercial Membership; Conference Liaison; Education; Mary Syer Memorial Education Fund; Membership & Welfare; Past Presidents Council; Strategic Planning Committee
Activities: Education program

Refugee Action Montreal *See* Programme Action Réfugiés Montréal

Refugee Reception House
101 David St., Kitchener ON N2G 1Y1
Tel: 519-743-2113; *Fax:* 519-576-8570
mira@kwrcentre.ca
www.kwrcentre.ca
www.facebook.com/107083659365767
Also Known As: KW Reception Centre
Overview: A small local organization founded in 1988 overseen by Ontario Council of Agencies Serving Immigrants
Mission: To provide initial temporary accommodation, orientation & locate permanent accommodation for newly arrived government-sponsored refugees; To assist them with initial settlement needs
Chief Officer(s):
Agnes Kiciak
Mira Malioranovic
Barbara Lehto
Finances: *Annual Operating Budget:* $100,000-$250,000; *Funding Sources:* Federal government
Staff Member(s): 8; 5 volunteer(s)

Refugee Research Network (RRN)
4700 Keele St., 8th Fl., Toronto ON M3J 1P3
Tel: 416-736-2100
www.refugeeresearch.net
www.facebook.com/groups/30614536012
twitter.com/refugeeresearch
www.youtube.com/user/refugeeresearch
Overview: A large international organization
Mission: The Refugee Research Network (RRN) aims to contribute to the improvement of the well-being of refugees and forced migrants around the world by expanding our awareness of refugee issues and forced migration; improving communication concerning this knowledge within and between academic, policy-making and practice sectors in the Global South and North; and alliance-building and active policy involvement in the development of national and international policy frameworks and humanitarian practices affecting refugees and forced migrants.
Chief Officer(s):
Michele Millard, Project Coordinator, 416-736-2100 Ext. 30391
mmillard@yorku.ca
Susan McGrath, Principal Investigator, 416-736-2100 Ext. 66662
smcgrath@yorku.ca

Regina *See* Juvenile Diabetes Research Foundation

Regina & District Chamber of Commerce
2145 Albert St., Regina SK S4P 2V1
Tel: 306-757-4658; *Fax:* 306-757-4668
info@reginachamber.com
www.reginachamber.com
www.facebook.com/ReginaChamber
twitter.com/ReginaChamber
www.youtube.com/ReginaChamber
Overview: A small local organization founded in 1886
Mission: To enhance the business community of Regina by actively promoting economic growth & providing a collective voice for the benefit of our members
Affliation(s): Canadian Chamber of Commerce; Saskatchewan Chamber of Commerce
Chief Officer(s):
John Hopkins, CEO
jhopkins@reginachamber.com
Cory Furman, Chair
Finances: *Annual Operating Budget:* $500,000-$1.5 Million; *Funding Sources:* Membership fees; programs
Staff Member(s): 6; 150 volunteer(s)
Membership: 925; *Fees:* $291.90-$4305
Activities: Festival of Lights; programs; services; trade shows; networking; lobbying; Paragon Awards; Business to Business Expo; *Internships:* Yes; *Rents Mailing List:* Yes

Regina & District Food Bank Inc.
445 Winnipeg St., Regina SK S4R 8P2
Tel: 306-791-6533; *Fax:* 306-347-0884
Toll-Free: 800-567-8008
info@reginafoodbank.ca
www.reginafoodbank.ca
Overview: A medium-sized local charitable organization founded in 1982

Mission: To work in co-operation with others to meet the needs of the hungry in the Regina & district community; To promote an understanding of the issues of poverty & hunger; To facilitate a multi-dimensional holistic approach to those in need, including education, awareness & life skills training; To advocate on behalf of those in need
Member of: Canadian Association of Food Banks
Chief Officer(s):
Wayne Hellquist, CEO
Finances: *Annual Operating Budget:* $3 Million-$5 Million
Staff Member(s): 13; 350 volunteer(s)
Membership: *Fees:* Any taxable donation

Regina & District Labour Council (RDLC)
2709 - 12th Ave., #E, Regina SK S4T 1J3
Tel: 306-757-7076; *Fax:* 306-585-2874
rdlc@sasktel.net
www.facebook.com/reginadistrict.labourcouncil
Overview: A medium-sized local organization overseen by Saskatchewan Federation of Labour
Mission: To advance the economic & social welfare of workers in Regina & the surrounding region; To engage in political activity at the municipal level
Affliation(s): Canadian Labour Congress (CLC)
Chief Officer(s):
Janice Bernier, President, 306-775-2333
jmbernier@sasktel.net
Laurie Temple, Secretary
Carol Mullaney, Treasurer
Membership: 25,560; *Member Profile:* Nineteen unions & forty locals from Regina & the surrounding region
Activities: Increasing the council's affiliate base; Promoting the interests of affiliates; Liaising with the city council to discuss issues of importance to affiliates; Hosting an annual Day of Mourning Ceremony to recognize workers killed on the job; Ensuring that occupational health & safety laws are enforced; Supporting local causes to make the community a better place to work & live; Establishing the Janice Bernier Endowment Fund for long-term food sustainability with the United Way; Coordinating lobbies in Regina ridings;

Regina Coin Club (RCC)
PO Box 174, Regina SK S4P 2Z6
Tel: 306-352-2337
info@reginacoinclub.com
www.reginacoinclub.com
Overview: A small local organization founded in 1953
Mission: To provide numismatic knowledge & good fellowship
Affliation(s): Canadian Numismatic Association; American Numismatic Association
Finances: *Annual Operating Budget:* Less than $50,000; *Funding Sources:* Coin shows & sales
12 volunteer(s)
Membership: 140; *Fees:* $20 family; $15 regular; $5 junior; *Committees:* Social; Spring & Fall Coin Show
Activities: Meetings; coin shows; CoinHawks Club for kids

Regina Community Foundation **See** South Saskatchewan Community Foundation Inc.

Regina Construction Association Inc.
1935 Elphinstone St., Regina SK S4T 3N3
Tel: 306-791-7422; *Fax:* 306-565-2840
general@rcaonline.ca
www.rcaonline.ca
Overview: A small local organization overseen by Canadian Construction Association
Chief Officer(s):
Brenda Braaler, Executive Director

Regina Exhibition Association Ltd. (REAL)
PO Box 167, Regina SK S4P 2Z6
Tel: 306-781-9200; *Fax:* 306-565-3443
Toll-Free: 888-734-3975
info@evrazplace.com
www.evrazplace.com
Overview: A medium-sized local organization founded in 1884
Mission: To provide a forum for the pursuit of excellence in agriculture & other selected fields of endeavour through the managment & development of the facilities & grounds of Exhibition Park; To organize, promote & present agriculture, education, sports & entertainment facilities of & for the betterment of the people of the community & the province of Saskatchewan
Member of: Saskatchewan Association of Agricultural Societies & Exhibitions
Affliation(s): Canadian Association of Fairs & Exhibitions; International Association of Fairs & Exhibitions
Chief Officer(s):
Denise Wanner, Executive Assistant
Mark Allan, President & CEO
Finances: *Annual Operating Budget:* Greater than $5 Million
Staff Member(s): 150; 650 volunteer(s)
Membership: 500-999
Activities: Western Canada Farm Progress Show; Buffalo Days; "Taste of Spring" Food & Beverage Show

Regina Film & Video Students' Society Inc. (RFVSS)
3737 Wascana Pkwy., Regina SK S4A 0A2
e-mail: the.rfvss@gmail.com
www.facebook.com/RFVSS
Overview: A small local organization founded in 1986
Mission: To serve the intersts of video, film, & new media students in Regina & the province of Saskatchewan
Activities: Offering professional development; Providing technical support; *Awareness Events:* Annual National Student Film & Video Festival

Regina Gliding & Soaring Club
PO Box 4093, Regina SK S4P 3W5
Tel: 306-536-4119
fly@soar.regina.sk.ca
www.soar.regina.sk.ca
Overview: A small local organization
Member of: Soaring Association of Canada; soaring Association of Saskatchewan
Membership: *Fees:* $55-$390

Regina Humane Society Inc.
PO Box 3143, Regina SK S4P 3G7
Tel: 306-543-6363; *Fax:* 306-545-7661; *Crisis Hot-Line:* 306-543-6363
Other Communication: volunteer@reginahumane.ca
info@reginahumane.ca
www.reginahumanesociety.ca
Overview: A medium-sized local charitable organization founded in 1965 overseen by Canadian Federation of Humane Societies
Mission: To be responsible for the welfare of animals
Member of: Saskatchewan Society for the Prevention of Cruelty to Animals
Chief Officer(s):
Lisa Koch, Executive Director
Finances: *Funding Sources:* City of Regina; Fundraising
200 volunteer(s)
Membership: 8,000; *Fees:* $25 single; $35 family; $15 senior; $200 lifetime; *Committees:* Board; Promotions; Education; Management; Policy; Philosophy
Activities: Providing Animal shelters; Conducting animal cruelty investigations; Offering education; Providing lost & found services; *Library* Open to public

Regina Immigrant Women Centre (RIWC)
2248 Lorne St., Regina SK S4P 2M7
Tel: 306-359-6514; *Fax:* 306-522-9959
iwsregina@accesscomm.ca
www.reginaiwc.ca
Also Known As: Immigrant, Refugee & Visible Minority Women of Saskatchewan Inc.
Previous Name: Immigrant Women of Saskatchewan
Overview: A small provincial organization
Mission: To provide a forum for immigrant women in Saskatchewan to voice their needs & concerns; to provide support & services to immigrant women
Member of: United Way; Multicultural Council of Saskatchewan
Affliation(s): Regina Multicultural Council
Chief Officer(s):
Gabrielle Henry, President
Neelu Sachdev, Program Director
Finances: *Funding Sources:* Municipal, provincial & federal government; Saskatchewan Literacy Commission; Saskatchewan Lotteries
Staff Member(s): 4; 15 volunteer(s)
Membership: 500-999; *Fees:* $5; *Member Profile:* Any immigrant or ethno-racial woman living in Regina
Activities: Drop-in centre; research; information & referral services; educational, recreational & social services; translation services

Regina Multicultural Council (RMC)
2054 Broad St., Regina SK S4P 1Y3
Tel: 306-757-5990; *Fax:* 306-352-1977
rmc.pa@sasktel.net
reginamulticulturalcouncil.ca
www.facebook.com/RMCMosaic
twitter.com/RMCMosaic
Overview: A medium-sized provincial charitable organization founded in 1965
Mission: To promote recognition of cultural diversity in Saskatchewan; to recognize, foster & promote the development of multilingualism; to promote positive cross-cultural relations
Affliation(s): SaskCulture
Chief Officer(s):
Terry Zwarych, President
Finances: *Annual Operating Budget:* $250,000-$500,000
Membership: 50 member groups; 50,000 individuals
Activities: *Awareness Events:* Mosaic: A Festival of Cultures, June; *Library* by appointment

Regina Musicians' Association
2835B - 13 Ave., Regina SK S4T 1N6
Tel: 306-352-1337; *Fax:* 306-359-6558
rma.446@sasktel.net
www.wearethemusic.org
Also Known As: AFM Local 446
Overview: A small local organization founded in 1912
Mission: To improve welfare & working conditions for professional musicians
Member of: American Federation of Musicians of the United States & Canada
Affliation(s): Canadian Conference of Musicians; Canadian Labour Congress; Saskatchewan Federation of Labour
Chief Officer(s):
Don Young, President
Sandra Pulles, Secretary/Treasurer
Finances: *Annual Operating Budget:* $50,000-$100,000; *Funding Sources:* Membership dues; fines; assessments
Staff Member(s): 1
Membership: 300+; *Fees:* $144
Activities: Annual charity fundraiser featuring showcase of bands; *Speaker Service:* Yes

Regina Orchid Society (ROS)
Regina SK
www.reginaorchidsociety.com
Overview: A small local organization
Mission: To promote orchid gardening & help with the conservation of orchids
Member of: Canadian Orchid Congress
Membership: *Fees:* $20 single; $30 family

Regina Peace Council
97 Martin St., Regina SK S4S 3W4
Tel: 306-949-8678
Overview: A small local organization founded in 1949
Mission: To help work for world peace & disarmament; To support victims of war & injustice
Member of: Canadian Peace Congress
Affliation(s): World Peace Council; Canadian Peace Alliance; Regina Coalition for Peace & Disarmament; Saskatchewan Coalition Against Racism
Membership: 20 individual; *Committees:* Editorial Board; Solidarity
Activities: *Speaker Service:* Yes; *Library* Open to public by appointment

Regina Philatelic Club
PO Box 1891, Regina SK S4P 3E1
Overview: A small provincial organization founded in 1910

Regina Policemen Association Inc. / Association des agents de police de la ville de Regina
2168 McIntyre St., Regina SK S4P 2R7
Tel: 306-569-2991; *Fax:* 306-522-0053
association.office@reginapolice.com
www.reginapolice.com
Overview: A small local organization
Chief Officer(s):
E. Bray, President
Staff Member(s): 1
Membership: 390 officers, 145 civilians;

Regina Regional Opportunities Commission (RROC)
1925 Rose St., Regina SK S4P 3P1
Tel: 306-789-5099; *Fax:* 306-352-1630
Toll-Free: 800-661-5099
info@reginaroc.com
www.reginaroc.com
www.facebook.com/ReginaRoc
twitter.com/ReginaRoc

www.youtube.com/user/thereginaroc;
www.flickr.com/photos/54562633@N05
Merged from: Tourism Regina Convention & Visitor Bureau; Regina Regional Economic Development Authority
Overview: A medium-sized local organization founded in 2009
Mission: Providing information & services to visitors & meeting planners, the RROC is a non-profit organization dedicated to promoting tourism in Regina, & business opportunities for its members
Member of: Tourism Industry Association of Canada
Chief Officer(s):
Deborah Rush, Manager, Marketing Communications
drush@reginaroc.com
John Lee, President & CEO
jdlee@reginaroc.com
Andrea Soby, Office Manager
asoby@reginaroc.com
Finances: *Funding Sources:* Municipal government; Saskatchewan Tourism

Regina Symphony Orchestra (RSO)

2424 College Ave., Regina SK S4P 1C8
Tel: 306-791-6395; *Fax:* 306-586-2133
info@reginasymphony.com
reginasymphony.com
www.facebook.com/reginasymphony
twitter.com/ReginaSymphony
Overview: A small local charitable organization founded in 1908 overseen by Orchestras Canada
Mission: To promote & enhance the performance & enjoyment of live orchestral music in Regina & southern Saskatchewan & contribute to the cultural life of the city, province & nation
Affliation(s): Saskatchewan Arts Alliance
Chief Officer(s):
Victor Sawa, Musical Director
Maxim Antoshin, Executive Director
mantoshin@reginasymphony.com
Finances: *Funding Sources:* Canada Council; Saskatchewan Arts Board; City of Regina
Staff Member(s): 8
Activities: Mozart in the Meadow; *Library*

Regina Therapeutic Recreation Association (RTRA)

c/o Sandra Procyk, 1150 Broadway Ave., Regina SK S4P 4V3
nonprofits.accesscomm.ca/rtra
Overview: A small local organization
Mission: To provide professional development, education, & support to recreation practitioners & students in any vocational setting in Regina & surrounding area
Chief Officer(s):
Angela Strelioff, Chair
rec.mutchmor@sasktel.net
Membership: *Fees:* $20; *Committees:* Membership; Issues; Education; Bursary

Regina Therapeutic Riding Association (RTRA)

PO Box 474, Regina SK S4P 3A2
Tel: 306-530-0794
ReginaTRA@sasktel.net
rtra.ca
www.facebook.com/148825211854915
Overview: A small provincial charitable organization founded in 1992
Mission: To provide medically supervised horseback riding lessons for individuals with special needs.
Chief Officer(s):
Ed Gendall, Contact

Regina Transition Women's Society

Regina SK
Tel: 306-757-2096; *Crisis Hot-Line:* 306-569-2292
info@reginatransitionhouse.ca
www.reginatransitionhouse.ca
Also Known As: Regina Transition House
Overview: A small local organization founded in 1975
Mission: To provide shelter, education, support, counselling & advocacy for women & children fleeing any form of abuse by operating a safe temporary shelter with a supportive environment offering a range of services
Member of: Provincial Association of Transition Houses & Services of Saskatchewan
Chief Officer(s):
Maria Hendrika, Executive Director
maria@reginatransitionhouse.ca
Finances: *Funding Sources:* Provincial Government; United Way; City of Regina
Activities: Safe shelter; 24-hour counselling; 24-hour crisis line; Children's program; Referral & advocacy for clients

Regional Halfway House Association (RHHA) / Association régionale des maisons de transition

ON
halfwayhouses.ca
Overview: A medium-sized national organization
Mission: To help offenders reintegrate themselves into society

The Regional Health Authorities of Manitoba (RHAM)

#2, 203 Duffield St., Winnipeg MB R3J 0H6
Tel: 204-833-1721; *Fax:* 204-940-2042
www.rham.mb.ca
Previous Name: Manitoba Health Organizations
Overview: A medium-sized provincial organization founded in 1998 overseen by Canadian Healthcare Association
Mission: To establish programs that help to improve Manitoba health authorities
Chief Officer(s):
Monique Vielfaure Mackenzie, Executive Director
mvmackenzie@rham.mb.ca
Finances: *Funding Sources:* Membership fees; service fees
Staff Member(s): 5
Membership: *Member Profile:* Regional health authorities
Activities: *Rents Mailing List:* Yes

Regional HIV/AIDS Connection

#30, 186 King St., London ON N6A 1C7
Tel: 519-434-1601; *Fax:* 519-434-1843
Toll-Free: 866-920-1601
info@hivaidsconnection.ca
www.aidslondon.com
www.facebook.com/189146047805897
twitter.com/_RHAC
www.youtube.com/user/AIDSLondon
Previous Name: AIDS Committee of London
Overview: A small local organization founded in 1985 overseen by Canadian AIDS Society
Mission: To bring people together in partnership to provide leadership in education, support & advocacy to meet the challenge of HIV/AIDS; To create an atmosphere of trust which enables people living with & affected by HIV/AIDS to make informed choices; To serve the counties of Perth, Huron, Lambton, Elgin, Middlesex, & Oxford.
Member of: Ontario AIDS Network
Chief Officer(s):
Brian Lester, Executive Director, 519-434-1601 Ext. 243
blester@hivaidsconnection.ca
Shannon Dougherty, Director, Client Services, 519-434-1601 Ext. 237
sdougherty@hivaidsconnection.ca
Finances: *Annual Operating Budget:* $500,000-$1.5 Million; *Funding Sources:* Provincial & federal ministries of health; fundraising
175 volunteer(s)
Membership: 60; *Fees:* $10
Activities: HIV/AIDS prevention services to those at risk of infection (harm reduction materials, Counterpoint Needle Exchange, Outreach initiatives, educational resources); support services to those with HIV (counselling, practical supports, food program, volunteer assistance); awareness campaigns; *Speaker Service:* Yes

Regional Occupation Centre Foundation

Regional Occupation Centre, 3 MacQuarrie Dr. Ext., Port Hawkesbury NS B9A 3A3
Tel: 902-625-0132; *Fax:* 902-625-5344
www.rocsociety.ca/Foundation
Also Known As: ROC Foundation
Overview: A small local charitable organization founded in 2009
Mission: To raise funds to support the mission & objectives of the Regional Occupation Centre Society
Finances: *Funding Sources:* Donations; fundraisers
Activities: *Awareness Events:* Harvest Moon Craft Market; Rock for the ROC Bonspiel; Abilities in Disabilities - Bike Run

Regional Occupation Centre Society

3 MacQuarrie Dr., Port Hawkesbury NS B9A 3A3
Tel: 902-625-0132; *Fax:* 902-625-5344
www.rocsociety.ca
Also Known As: ROC Society
Overview: A small local organization founded in 1975
Mission: To support individuals with disabilities through vocational & community programs
Member of: DIRECTIONS Council for Vocational Services Society
Chief Officer(s):
Juleen MacEachern, President
Diana Poirier, Executive Director/Manager
dproc@eastlink.ca
Membership: 30 individuals
Activities: Vocational work, including woodworking, baking, recycling, mowing contracts & crafts; community activites, including swimming, dance & Special Olympics

Regional Solicitors' Association of Ontario *See* Municipal Law Departments Association of Ontario

Régionale Ringuette Rive-Sud

431, rue des Pinsons, Ste-Julie QC J3E 1C2
www.ringuetterivesud.com
Aperçu: *Dimension:* petite; *Envergure:* provinciale surveillé par Ringuette-Québec
Membre de: Ringuette-Québec
Membre(s) du bureau directeur:
Clémence Duchesneau, Présidente
clemdu@hotmail.com

Registered Deposit Brokers Association (RDBA)

#308A, 49 High St., Barrie ON L4N 5J4
Tel: 705-730-7599; *Fax:* 705-730-0477
Toll-Free: 866-261-6263
www.rdba.ca
Previous Name: Federation of Canadian Independent Deposit Brokers
Overview: A large national organization founded in 1987
Mission: To represent interests of deposit clients & independent deposit brokers
Chief Officer(s):
Brian L. Smith, President, 866-261-6263 Ext. 323, Fax: 705-730-0477
Brenda Molnar, Executive Director, 866-261-6263 Ext. 321, Fax: 519-825-3184
Finances: *Annual Operating Budget:* Less than $50,000
Staff Member(s): 1; 12 volunteer(s)
Membership: 116; *Fees:* $112 affiliate; $725 deposit broker; $4,000-$8,000 financial institution; *Member Profile:* 27 major financial institutions

Registered Insurance Brokers of Ontario (RIBO)

PO Box 45, #1200, 401 Bay St., Toronto ON M5H 2Y4
Tel: 416-365-1900; *Fax:* 416-365-7664
Toll-Free: 800-265-3097
www.ribo.com
Overview: A medium-sized provincial licensing organization founded in 1981
Mission: To regulate the licensing, professional competence, ethical conduct, & insurance related financial obligations of all independent general insurance brokers in the province
Chief Officer(s):
Doug Grahlman, President
dgrahlman@chatsworthinsurance.ca
Beth Pearson, Vice-President
bethp@apont.ca
Patty Crawford, Secretary
pattycrawford@rogers.com
Norma Hitchlock, Treasurer
norma@marshinsurance.com
Jeff Bear, Chief Executive Officer
jeff@ribo.com
Activities: Licensing & examinations; resources for brokers
Publications:
• Principal Broker Handbook
Type: Handbook
Profile: Regulatory requirements & guidelines
• RIBO [Registered Insurance Brokers of Ontario] Bulletin
Type: Newsletter

Registered Massage Therapists' Association of British Columbia (RMTBC)

#180, 1200 West 73rd Ave., Vancouver BC V6P 6G5
Tel: 604-873-4467; *Fax:* 604-873-6211
Toll-Free: 888-413-4467
info@rmtbc.ca
www.rmtbc.ca
www.facebook.com/MTABC
twitter.com/RMTBC
www.youtube.com/user/MTABCVideo
Overview: A small provincial organization founded in 1983
Mission: To develop & advance the massage therapy profession in BC through education, promotion, empowerment & representation
Chief Officer(s):

Brenda Locke, Executive Director
locke@rmtbc.ca
Joseph Lattanzio, President
joseph@rmtbc.ca
Finances: *Funding Sources:* Membership dues
Staff Member(s): 8
Membership: *Fees:* Schedule available

Registered Nurses Association of British Columbia *See* College of Registered Nurses of British Columbia

Registered Nurses Association of Nova Scotia *See* College of Registered Nurses of Nova Scotia

The Registered Nurses Association of the Northwest Territories & Nunavut (RNANT/NU)

PO Box 2757, Yellowknife NT X1A 2R1
Tel: 867-873-2745; *Fax:* 867-873-2336
info@rnantnu.ca
www.rnantnu.ca
Previous Name: Northwest Territories Registered Nurses Association
Overview: A medium-sized provincial licensing organization founded in 1974 overseen by Canadian Nurses Association
Mission: To promote & ensure competent nursing practice for the people of the NWT
Chief Officer(s):
Donna Stanley-Young, Executive Director
ed@rnantnu.ca
Finances: *Funding Sources:* Membership fees
Staff Member(s): 6
Membership: *Member Profile:* Registered nurses

Registered Nurses' Association of Ontario (RNAO) / L'Association des infirmières et infirmiers autorisés de l'Ontario

158 Pearl St., Toronto ON M5H 1L3
Tel: 416-599-1925; *Fax:* 416-599-1926
Toll-Free: 800-268-7199
www.rnao.org
www.facebook.com/RNAOHomeOffice
twitter.com/rnao
www.youtube.com/RNAOVideo
Overview: A large provincial organization founded in 1925 overseen by Canadian Nurses Association
Mission: To promote excellence in nursing practice; Ro advocate the role of nursing in empowering the people of Ontario to achieve & maintain their optimal health; To provide membership-centred services
Chief Officer(s):
Rhonda Seidman-Carlson, RN, MN, President
Doris Grinspun, RN, MSN, PhD, L, Chief Executive Officer
Finances: *Annual Operating Budget:* Greater than $5 Million; *Funding Sources:* Membership fees; conference fees; educational workshops
Staff Member(s): 30
Membership: 35,000; *Fees:* $285.19; *Member Profile:* Registered to practise in province of Ontario
Awards:
• Chapter of the Year (Award)
• Interest Group of the Year (Award)
• Leadership Award in Political Action (Award)
• Leadership Award in Nursing Administration (Award)
• Leadership Award in Nursing Education (Award)
• Award of Merit (Award)
• Leadership Award in Nursing Research (Award)
• Leadership Award in Nursing Education (Academic) (Award)
• President's Award for Leadership in Clinical Nursing Practice (Award)
Meetings/Conferences: • Registered Nurses' Association of Ontario Annual General Meeting 2015, April, 2015, Hilton Toronto, Toronto, ON
Scope: Provincial
• Registered Nurses' Association of Ontario 4th Annual Nurse Executive Leadership Academy, March, 2015, White Oaks Conference Centre, Niagara-on-the-Lake, ON
Scope: Provincial
Description: The program features expert faculty from policy, practice and academic settings, providing up-to-date insights for knowledge and competence in governance, policy formulation, evidence-based accountability and leadership.
Publications:
• Registered Nurses' Journal
Type: Journal; *Frequency:* 6 pa; *Editor:* Kimberley Kearsey

Registered Practical Nurses Association of Ontario (RPNAO)

Bldg. 4, #200, 5025 Orbitor Dr., Mississauga ON L4W 4Y5
Tel: 905-602-4664; *Fax:* 905-602-4666
Toll-Free: 877-602-4664
info@rpnao.org
www.rpnao.org
www.facebook.com/RPNAO
twitter.com/rpnao
Overview: A medium-sized provincial charitable organization founded in 1958
Mission: Dedicated to decisions that enhance professional practical nursing
Member of: Ontario Hospital Association; Ontario Association of Non-Profit Homes & Services for Seniors; Canadian Practical Nurses Association
Chief Officer(s):
Dianne Martin, RPN, RN, BScN, Executive Director, 905-602-4664 Ext. 226
dmartin@rpnao.org
Beth McCracken, Nursing Practice & Outreach Specialist, 905-602-4664 Ext. 227
bmccracken@rpnao.org
Pia Ramos-Javellana, Director, Finance, 905-602-4664 Ext. 239
pjavellana@rpnao.org
Finances: *Funding Sources:* Membership fees; education & training revenue
Staff Member(s): 17
Membership: 13,367; *Fees:* $226.89 regular; $113.45 senior, non-practising, & new graduate; $17.70 student; $573.25 corporate; *Member Profile:* RPN with current certificate of registration from College of Nurses; practical nurse student; retired RPN; *Committees:* Archives; Nominations; Legislation & By-laws; Regional Councils; Membership; Conference; Finance
Activities: *Awareness Events:* Registered Practical Nurses Day, May
Publications:
• Registered Practical Nursing Journal
Type: Journal; *Frequency:* Quarterly

Registered Practical Nurses Association of Ontario (RPNAO)

Building 4, #200, 5025 Orbitor Dr., Mississauga ON L4W 4Y5
Tel: 905-602-4664; *Fax:* 905-602-4666
info@rpnao.org
www.rpnao.org
www.facebook.com/RPNAO
twitter.com/RPNAO
Overview: A small provincial organization founded in 1958
Mission: To conduct the business of a trade union, representing registered practical nurses in Ontario; To improve the working conditions of registered practical nurses throughout the province
Chief Officer(s):
Dianne Martin, Executive Director
dmartin@rpnao.org
Staff Member(s): 13
Membership: 32,000+; *Fees:* Schedule available; *Member Profile:* Registered practical nurses in Ontario
Activities: Engaging in collective bargaining

Registered Professional Accountants Association of Canada (RPAC)

PO Box 306, Stn. Main, AB T5J 2J6
Toll-Free: 855-541-4703
advice@rpacanada.ca
rpacanada.ca
www.facebook.com/RPAofCanada
twitter.com/RPACanada
www.youtube.com/user/RPACanada
Also Known As: RPA Canada
Overview: A small national organization founded in 1980
Mission: To develop & support the professional accountant members of it provincial counterparts
Chief Officer(s):
Angel Meinecke, President
President@RPACanada.ca
Membership: 3 provincial associations; *Member Profile:* Professionals working in the areas of personal & corporate tax, GST & HST, payroll, bookkeeping & the preparation of financial statements
Activities: Professional designation; career centre

Registered Professional Foresters Association of Nova Scotia (RPFANS)

PO Box 1031, Truro NS B2N 5G9
Tel: 902-893-0099
contact@rpfans.ca
www.rpfans.ca
Overview: A medium-sized provincial organization founded in 1999
Mission: To improve the holistic management of forest resources in Nova Scotia
Chief Officer(s):
Roger Aggas, Registrar
John Ross, President
Mike Brown, Treasurer
Membership: *Member Profile:* Professional foresters in Nova Scotia; Foresters-in-training & students
Activities: Disciplining members who fail to comply with the code of ethics; Ensuring that the public receives proper forest management advice; Encouraging further education
Meetings/Conferences: • Registered Professional Foresters Association of Nova Scotia 2015 Annual General Meeting, 2015
Scope: Provincial
Description: A business meeting for Nova Scotia's professional foresters
Publications:
• Forest Steward [a publication of the Registered Professional Foresters Association of Nova Scotia]
Type: Newsletter
Profile: Contents include the message from the president & news from the association & forestry sector

Registered Psychiatric Nurses Association of Alberta *See* College of Registered Psychiatric Nurses of Alberta

Registered Psychiatric Nurses Association of British Columbia *See* College of Registered Psychiatric Nurses of British Columbia

Registered Psychiatric Nurses Association of Manitoba *See* College of Registered Psychiatric Nurses of Manitoba

Registered Psychiatric Nurses Association of Saskatchewan (RPNAS)

2055 Lorne St., Regina SK S4P 2M4
Tel: 306-586-4617; *Fax:* 306-586-6000
www.rpnas.com
Overview: A large provincial licensing organization founded in 1948
Mission: To regulate psychiatric nursing as a distinct profession
Chief Officer(s):
Shirley Bedford, President
Robert Allen, Executive Director
rallen@rpnas.com
Finances: *Annual Operating Budget:* $250,000-$500,000; *Funding Sources:* Membership licensing fees
Staff Member(s): 4; 150 volunteer(s)
Membership: 1,080; *Fees:* $602 active; $50 non-active
Awards:
• Baccalaureate Level Program Scholarship (Scholarship)
• Master's Level Program Scholarship (Scholarship)
• Doctorate Level Program Scholarship (Scholarship)
• RPN Bursary (Scholarship)
• Psychiatric Nursing Program Student Year III Bursary (Scholarship)
• Psychiatric Nursing Program Student Year III Joyce P. Long Memorial Bursary (Scholarship)
• Psychiatric Nursing Program Student Year II Terrence B. Christiansen Memorial Bursary (Scholarship)
• RPN Award - in Recognition of Performance in Nursing (Award)
Deadline: April 30

Registered Public Accountants' Association of Alberta (RPAA)

PO Box 306, Stn. Main, #206, 10544 - 106th St., Edmonton AB T5H 2X6
Tel: 780-448-9692; *Fax:* 780-448-9698
Toll-Free: 800-665-7941
Other Communication: Alt. Phone: 780-468-4889
rpaaofficemgr@shaw.ca
www.rpaa.org
Overview: A small provincial organization founded in 1980 overseen by Registered Professional Accountants Association of Canada
Mission: To promote, organize & coordinate the educational activities of members
Member of: Registered Professional Accountants Association of Canada
Chief Officer(s):
Margo Desmarais, President, 780-448-9692

Linda Johnson, Office Administrator
Staff Member(s): 1
Membership: *Member Profile:* Professional accountants in BC, Alberta, Saskatchewan, Manitoba, Northwest Territories, Yukon, & Nunavut
Activities: Professional designation; annual convention; Errors & Omissions Insurance for members

Registered Public Accountants' Association of Atlantic Canada & Québec (RPA-ATL)

#213, 30 Damascus Rd., Bedford NS B4A 0C1
Tel: 902-835-3923; *Fax:* 902-832-0239
Toll-Free: 888-772-1001
info@rpa-atl.ca
www.rpa-atl.ca
Also Known As: RPAA-Atlantic
Overview: A small provincial organization founded in 2003 overseen by Registered Professional Accountants Association of Canada
Mission: To promote, organize & coordinate the educational activities of members
Member of: Registered Professional Accountants Association of Canada
Chief Officer(s):
Art Pearce, President, 902-832-2999
apearce@ns.sympatico.com
Naomi Cook, Office Manager
admin@rpa-atl.ca
Staff Member(s): 1
Membership: *Fees:* $575 regular; $325 associate; *Member Profile:* Professional accountants
Activities: Professional designation; annual convention; Errors & Omissions Insurance for members

Registered Public Accountants' Association of Ontario

#705, 130 Spadina Ave., Toronto ON M5V 2L4
Tel: 416-362-3664
admin@RPAAOntario.org
www.rpaaontario.org
www.facebook.com/RPAAOntario
twitter.com/RPAAOntario
Also Known As: RPAA Ontario
Overview: A small provincial organization overseen by Registered Professional Accountants Association of Canada
Mission: To promote, organize & coordinate the educational activities of members
Member of: Registered Professional Accountants Association of Canada
Chief Officer(s):
Alan Doody, President
alandoody@live.ca
Membership: *Fees:* $450; *Member Profile:* Professional accountants
Activities: Professional designation; annual convention; Errors & Omissions Insurance for members

Regnum Christi Movement

c/o Legionaries of Christ, 19119 Hwy. 2, RR#1, Cornwall ON K6H 5R5
Tel: 613-931-1600
cornwallbm@arcol.org
www.regnumchristi.org
www.facebook.com/regnumchristi.english
twitter.com/RegnumChristiEn
www.youtube.com/regnumchristi
Overview: A small international charitable organization founded in 2004
Mission: To love Christ, serve others, & build the Church
Affliation(s): Archdiocese of Toronto; Legionaries of Christ
Chief Officer(s):
Alvaro Corcuera, General Director
Lisa Francis, Contact
Finances: *Funding Sources:* Donations
Membership: *Member Profile:* Catholic young people, adults, deacons, & diocesan priests who wish to experience Christ's love & spread it to others; Members are active in service to the Church
Activities: Leading Christian lives; Taking apostolic action, in cooperation with bishops & parish priests; Providing faith instruction, prayer groups, religious books, & renewal programs; Offering programs, such as Familia, for families to learn & live their Catholic faith, Challenge youth programs, for girls, Catholic Kids Net of Canada Vacation Bible Schools, Conquest Boys' youth programs, Father & Son programs, Compass programs, for university students, & missions, for young people & families;
Publications:
• Mission
Type: Newsletter
Profile: Features, news, & events for members of Regnum Christi, their families & friends, & supporters

Regroupement canadien des associations de centres communautaires de santé *See* Canadian Alliance of Community Health Centre Associations

Regroupement de Bouches à Oreilles (RBO)

#1, 317, rue Lanctôt, Chibougamau QC G8P 2P5
Tél: 418-748-2239; *Téléc:* 418-748-2761
bouchesaoreilles@yahoo.ca
www.abc02.org
Aperçu: *Dimension:* petite; *Envergure:* locale; fondée en 1983
Mission: Formation de base: compter, lire, écrire
Membre(s) du bureau directeur:
Isabelle Lamontagne, Coordonnatrice

Regroupement de parents de personnes ayant une déficience intellectuelle de Montréal

5927, rue Boyer, bureau 02, Montréal QC H2S 2H8
Tél: 514-255-3064; *Téléc:* 514-255-3635
www.rppadim.com
Aperçu: *Dimension:* petite; *Envergure:* locale; Organisme sans but lucratif
Mission: Défendre les droits des personnes ayant une déficience intellectuelle
Membre de: Parents de personne ayant déficience intellectuelle
Affliation(s): Association du Québec pour l'intégration sociale
Membre(s) du bureau directeur:
Marcel Faulkner, Directeur
marcelfaulkner@rppadim.com
Membre(s) du personnel: 14; 10 bénévole(s)
Membre: 300; *Montant de la cotisation:* Parents stimulants, 3 $ par semaine; loisirs 150 $ par 10 samedis (automne/hiver); 75 $ par semaine (été)
Activités: Parents stimulants (0 à 5 ans) et Activités loisirs (15 ans et plus)

Regroupement des Aidantes et Aidants Naturel(le)s de Montréal (RAANM)

#002, 1150, boul Saint-Joseph est, Montréal QC H2J 1L5
Tél: 514-374-1056; *Téléc:* 514-374-3040
Aperçu: *Dimension:* petite; *Envergure:* locale
Membre(s) du bureau directeur:
Josée Côté, Directrice générale
Membre: *Montant de la cotisation:* 5$ individuel; 15$ corporatif; $50 beinfaiteur

Regroupement des artistes en arts visuels du Québec (ind.) (RAAV)

460, rue Ste-Catherine ouest, Montréal QC H3B 1A7
Tél: 514-866-7101; *Téléc:* 514-866-9906
raav@raav.org
www.raav.org
www.facebook.com/RAAVQc
Aperçu: *Dimension:* petite; *Envergure:* provinciale; fondée en 1989 surveillé par Canadian Artists' Representation
Mission: Représentation collective des intérêts socio-économiques et professionnels des artistes des arts visuels
Membre(s) du bureau directeur:
Manon Pelletier, Présidente
Hélène Rochette, Vice-présidente
Christian Bédard, Directeur
Finances: *Budget de fonctionnement annuel:* $250,000-$500,000; *Fonds:* Conseil des arts et des lettres du Québec
Membre(s) du personnel: 6; 30 bénévole(s)
Membre: 1 480; *Critères d'admissibilite:* Artiste professionnel en arts visuels
Activités: Défense collective des artistes; conseils représentation officielle; *Stagiaires:* Oui

Regroupement des associations de personnes traumatisées craniocérébrales du Québec (RAPTCCQ) / Coalition of Associations of Craniocerebral Trauma in Quebec

220, av du Parc, Laval QC H7N 3X4
Tél: 514-274-7447; *Téléc:* 514-274-1717
info@raptccq.com
www.raptccq.com
www.facebook.com/RAPTCCQ
Aperçu: *Dimension:* petite; *Envergure:* provinciale; fondée en 1999 surveillé par Brain Injury Association of Canada
Mission: Pour soutenir les personnes vivant avec une lésion cérébrale au Québec
Membre(s) du bureau directeur:
Nicole Tremblay, Présidente
Denis Veilleux, Vice-Président
Pascal Brodeur, Secrétaire et trésorier
Guy Lemieux, Directeur
Membre(s) du personnel: 1
Membre: 13 associations; *Critères d'admissibilite:* Associations de traumatisme cranio-cérébral au Québec
Activités: Engaging in advocacy activities on behalf of persons who live with the consequences of brain injury in Québec; Educating the public about brain injuries; Encouraging cooperation between member associations; Facilitating the exchange of information among members; Supporting members' projects

Regroupement des associations forestières régionales du Québec

#100, 138, rue Wellington nord, Sherbrooke QC J1H 5C5
Tél: 819-562-3388
info@afce.qc.ca
www.afce.qc.ca
Aperçu: *Dimension:* moyenne; *Envergure:* provinciale surveillé par Canadian Forestry Association
Membre(s) du bureau directeur:
Daniel Archambault

Regroupement des assureurs de personnes à charte du Québec (RACQ)

#1501, 1445, rue Stanley, Montréal QC H3A 3T1
Tél: 514-282-2207; *Téléc:* 514-282-2214
Aperçu: *Dimension:* petite; *Envergure:* provinciale; fondée en 1995
Mission: Regrouper les compagnies d'assurance à charte québécoise et agir comme porte-parole pour promouvoir leurs intérêts
Membre(s) du bureau directeur:
Richard Gagnon, Président-directeur général
Membre: 9; *Critères d'admissibilite:* Compagnie d'assurance de personnes à charte québécoise

Regroupement des Auberges du Coeur

#32, 2000, boul Saint-Joseph est, Montréal QC H2H 1E4
Tél: 514-523-8559; *Téléc:* 514-523-5148
www.aubergesducoeur.com
Aperçu: *Dimension:* moyenne; *Envergure:* provinciale; fondée en 1987
Mission: Défendre l'existence & l'autonomie des ressources communautaires d'hébergement pour jeunes adolescents & jeunes adultes en difficulté ou sans abri; agir comme porte-parole des jeunes sans abri; favoriser entre les maisons, les jeunes & les partenaires des communautés d'appartenance de chacune des Auberges des échanges sur les besoins des jeunes
Membre(s) du bureau directeur:
Rémi Fraser, Directeur général
remi.fraser@aubergesducoeur.org

Regroupement des aveugles et amblyopes du Montréal métropolitain (RAAMM)

#200, 5215, rue Berri, Montréal QC H2J 2S4
Tél: 514-277-4401; *Téléc:* 514-277-8961
info@raamm.org
raamm.org
Aperçu: *Dimension:* petite; *Envergure:* locale; fondée en 1975
Mission: Faire la défense des droits pour les gens avec une déficience visuelle et fournir le service d'aide bénévole
Membre(s) du bureau directeur:
Pascale Dussault, Directeur général
Membre(s) du personnel: 8
Membre: *Montant de la cotisation:* 10$ par membre régulier; 20$ par membre associé; 50$ par membre affinitaire; *Critères d'admissibilite:* Toute personne qui est aveugle ou amblyope et qui vie dans la région de Montréal

Regroupement des cabinets de courtage d'assurance du Québec (RCCAQ) / Insurance Brokers Association of Québec - Assembly

Complexe Saint-Charles, #550, 1111 rue Saint-Charles Ouest, Tour Est, Longueuil QC J4K 8G4
Tél: 450-674-6258; *Téléc:* 450-674-3609
Ligne sans frais: 800-516-6258
info@rccaq.com
www.rccaq.com
Aperçu: *Dimension:* petite; *Envergure:* provinciale; Organisme sans but lucratif; fondée en 1973

Mission: Promouvoir les intérêts socio-économiques des membres
Membre(s) du bureau directeur:
Jean Bilodeau, Président
jean.bilodeau@bc-assur.com
Guy Parent, Directeur général
gparent@rccaq.com
Finances: *Budget de fonctionnement annuel:* $1.5 Million-$3 Million
Membre(s) du personnel: 8
Membre: 620 cabinets; 4560 courtiers; *Montant de la cotisation:* Variable, en fonction du profil du cabinet; *Critères d'admissibilité:* Courtier d'assurance de dommages, propriétaire

Regroupement des centres d'amitié autochtone du Québec (RCAAQ)
#250, 225, rue Max-Gros-Louis, Wendake QC G0A 4V0
Tél: 418-842-6354; *Téléc:* 418-842-9795
Ligne sans frais: 877-842-6354
infos@rcaaq.info
www.rcaaq.info
Aperçu: *Dimension:* moyenne; *Envergure:* nationale; Organisme sans but lucratif; fondée en 1976 surveillé par National Association of Friendship Centres
Mission: Etre la voix provinciale des centres existants ou en voie de développement et de leurs communautés; appuyer ses membres dans l'atteinte de leurs objectifs; favoriser leur concertation et les représenter collectivement pour qu'ils remplissent au mieux leur mandat
Membre(s) du bureau directeur:
Josée Goulet, Directrice générale
Membre: 1-99;

Regroupement des éditeurs canadiens-français (RECF)
265, rue St-Patrick, #B, Ottawa ON K1N 5K4
Tél: 613-562-4507; *Téléc:* 613-562-3320
Ligne sans frais: 888-320-8070
info@recf.ca
www.recf.ca
Aperçu: *Dimension:* moyenne; *Envergure:* nationale; Organisme sans but lucratif; fondée en 1989
Mission: Former une plate-forme d'échanges et un front commun pour mener des actions concertées pertinentes à l'ensemble des éditeurs canadiens-français, tant sur le plan des politiques que de la promotion, la distribution et le développement de marchés
Membre de: Fédération culturelle canadienne-française
Membre(s) du bureau directeur:
Marc Haentjens, Président
Serge Patrice Thibodeau, Vice-Président
Catherine Voyer-Léger, Directrice générale
dg@recf.ca
Safiatou Ali, Administratrice
admin@recf.ca
Anne Molgat, Secrétaire
Brigitte Bergeron, Trésorière
5 bénévole(s)
Membre: 1-99; *Montant de la cotisation:* 100$; *Critères d'admissibilite:* Éditeurs

Regroupement des femmes de la Côte-de-Gaspé
189, rue Jacques-Cartier, Gaspé QC G4X 2P8
Tél: 418-368-1929; *Téléc:* 418-368-6697
micheminggaspe@globetrotter.uil
Aperçu: *Dimension:* petite; *Envergure:* locale
Mission: Promotion de la condition féminine; défense des droits des femmes; formations sur mesure pour les femmes; démarche d'autonomie
Affliation(s): Regroupement des centres de femmes du Québec
Membre(s) du bureau directeur:
Carmen Boulay, Secrétaire
Finances: *Budget de fonctionnement annuel:* $50,000-$100,000; *Fonds:* Provincial government
Membre(s) du personnel: 3; 30 bénévole(s)
Membre: 99; *Montant de la cotisation:* $3

Regroupement des jeunes chambres de commerce du Québec (RJCCQ)
#1100, 555, rue René-Lévesque Ouest, Montréal QC H2Z 1B1
Tél: 514-933-7595
info@rjccq.com
www.rjccq.com
www.linkedin.com/groups?home=&gid=2161090
www.facebook.com/rjccq
twitter.com/RJCCQ
www.youtube.com/user/RJCCQ
Nom précédent: Regroupement des jeunes gens d'affaires du Québec
Aperçu: *Dimension:* petite; *Envergure:* locale; fondée en 1992
Mission: Défendre et promouvoir les intérêts sociaux et économiques des jeunes gens d'affaires du Québec.
Membre(s) du bureau directeur:
Virginie Leblanc, Chargée de projets
Membre(s) du personnel: 3
Membre: 8,000 individuelles + 34 chambres de commerce;

Regroupement des jeunes gens d'affaires du Québec *Voir* Regroupement des jeunes chambres de commerce du Québec

Regroupement des offices d'habitation du Québec (ROHQ)
#170, 1135 Grande Allée Ouest, Québec QC G1S 1E7
Tél: 418-527-6228; *Téléc:* 418-527-6382
Ligne sans frais: 800-463-6257
rohq@rohq.qc.ca
www.rohq.qc.ca
Nom précédent: Association des offices municipaux d'habitation du Québec
Aperçu: *Dimension:* petite; *Envergure:* provinciale; Organisme sans but lucratif; fondée en 1972
Mission: Répresenter, informer, former des offices municipaux d'habitations du Québec
Membre de: Réseau Habitat et Francophonie
Membre(s) du bureau directeur:
Denis Robitaille, Directeur général
denis.robitaille@rohq.qc.ca
Membre(s) du personnel: 8
Membre: *Comités:* Gouvernance et orientations stratégiques; Consultatif de formation; retraite; Paritaire de l'assurance collective
Activités: Congrès; rencontres régionales; *Service de conférenciers:* Oui

Regroupement des organismes de bassins versants du Québec (ROBVQ)
#106, 870, av de Salaberry, Québec QC G1R 2T9
Tél: 418-800-1144; *Téléc:* 418-780-6666
info@robvq.qc.ca
www.robvq.qc.ca
twitter.com/mcleclerc
www.youtube.com/user/lesobvduquebec
Aperçu: *Dimension:* petite; *Envergure:* provinciale; fondée en 2001
Mission: Le Regroupement des organismes de bassins versants du Québec (ROBVQ) est un organisme à but non lucratif créé et reconnu par le ministère du Développement durable, de l'Environnement et de la Lutte contre les changements climatiques du Québec comme étant son interlocuteur privilégié pour la mise en place de la gestion intégrée de l'eau par bassin versant au Québec.
Membre(s) du bureau directeur:
Marie-Claude Leclerc, Directrice générale
mcleclerc@robvq.qc.ca
Membre: 40; *Critères d'admissibilite:* Organismes de bassins versants du Québec
Publications:
• Tempo
Type: Newsletter; *Frequency:* 6 pa
Profile: Le bulletin de liaison Tempo du ROBVQ vise à diffuser l'information relative aux programmes, projets et dossiers en cours du ROBVQ. Il permet aussi de mettre en lumière certaines initiatives ou projetsd'envergure entrepris par les organisations de bassin versant membres du ROBVQ.

Regroupement des organismes du patrimoine franco-ontarien *Voir* Réseau du patrimone franco-ontarien

Regroupement des personnes vivant avec le VIH-sida de Québec et la région
#100, 190 O'Connor St., Ottawa ON K2P 2R3
Tél: 613-230-3580; *Téléc:* 613-563-4998
casinfo@cdnaids.ca
www.facebook.com/aidsida
twitter.com/CDNAIDS
Aperçu: *Dimension:* petite; *Envergure:* locale; fondée en 1990 surveillé par Canadian AIDS Society
Mission: Regrouper les personnes vivant avec le VIH/sida
Finances: *Budget de fonctionnement annuel:* Moins de $50,000
Membre(s) du personnel: 5; 11 bénévole(s)
Membre: *Montant de la cotisation:* $100-$2,000, calculated based on member organization's annual budget; *Critères d'admissibilite:* 73

Regroupement des professionnels de la construction Richelieu Yamaska *Voir* Association de la Construction Richelieu Yamaska

Regroupement des professionnels de la danse du Québec *Voir* Regroupement québécois de la danse

Regroupement des Sourds de Chaudière-Appalaches (RSCA)
1294, chemin Filteau, Saint-Nicolas QC G7A 2L7
Tél: 418-831-3723; *Téléc:* 418-831-3723; *TTY:* 418-831-3723
rsca@globetrotter.net
www.facebook.com/834524883229339
Nom précédent: Association des Sourds de Beauce
Aperçu: *Dimension:* petite; *Envergure:* locale; Organisme sans but lucratif; fondée en 1982
Mission: Travailler à l'amélioration des conditions de vie des personnes sourdes et malentendantes; les regrouper; les représenter et les supporter afin qu'elles aient accès et reçoivent tous les services auxquels elles ont droit et ce, dans leur langue respective; défense de droits
Membre de: Centre québécois de la déficience auditive; Regroupement des associations de personnes handicapées région Chaudière-Appalaches; Coallitions Sida des sourds du Québec
Membre(s) du bureau directeur:
Michel Laurent, Directeur
Finances: *Budget de fonctionnement annuel:* Moins de $50,000; *Fonds:* Agence de santé et des services sociaux
Membre(s) du personnel: 6; 15 bénévole(s)
Membre: 85; *Montant de la cotisation:* 15$ membre actif; 12$ membre associé; 10$ membre partenaire
Activités: Conférences portant sur des thèmes touchant la surdité des enfants; distribution de dépliants; cours de Langue des signes Québécoise; rencontres d'information; conférences; activités mensuelles; accueil et référence; rencontres individuelle pour aider le Sourd dans différentes sphères de la vie

Regroupement des universités de la francophonie Hors-Québec *Voir* Association des universités de la francophonie canadienne

Regroupement pour l'intégration dans la communauté de Rivière-des-Prairies
3418, Place Désy, Laval QC H7P 3J2
Tél: 450-629-0096; *Téléc:* 450-629-1726
ropphl.free.fr/ricrp.htm
Aperçu: *Dimension:* petite; *Envergure:* locale
Mission: Promouvoir et défendre les droits des personnes ayant une déficience intellectuelle et leur famille; améliorer les conditions de vie des personnes ayant une déficience intellectuelle. Soutien aux parents et aux personnes ayant une déficience intellectuelle; rédaction de dossiers et de mémoires
Affliation(s): Association du Québec pour l'intégration sociale
Membre(s) du bureau directeur:
Paulette Berthiaume, Présidente
Membre: *Critères d'admissibilite:* Personnes ayant une déficience intellectuelle et leur famille

Regroupement pour l'intégration sociale de Charlevoix (RISC)
#301, 367, St-Étienne, La Malbaie (Québec) QC G5A 1M3
Tél: 418-665-7811
rischarlevoix@hotmail.com
Aperçu: *Dimension:* petite; *Envergure:* locale; Organisme sans but lucratif; fondée en 1990
Mission: Regrouper les parents d'enfants ayant une déficience intellectuelle; offrir du support, de l'entraide, de l'info, quant aux droits et intérêts de leurs enfants; favoriser la concertation avec les organismes communautaires, les établissements du réseaux, pour mieux répondre aux familles; sensibiliser la population face à la différence; informer les familles sur l'entraide et formation, la documentation et les services existants; proposer des activités culturelles, sociales et éducatives aux membres et leurs familles
Affliation(s): Association du Québec pour l'intégration sociale
Finances: *Budget de fonctionnement annuel:* Moins de $50,000
Membre(s) du personnel: 1; 7 bénévole(s)
Membre: 26; *Montant de la cotisation:* 5$ par famille par année; *Critères d'admissibilite:* Famille avec un ou plusiers enfants handicapés, trouble d'apprentissage, retard de développement
Activités: Semaine Québécoise de la déficience intellectuelle; social pour les jeunes; sorties familiales; rencontres d'échange; sensibilisation; intégration; *Evénements de sensibilisation:* Semaine Québécoise en déficience intellectuelle, mars

Regroupement pour la surveillance du nucléaire *See*
Canadian Coalition for Nuclear Responsibility

Regroupement Pour-Valorisation
430, rue Principale Est, Farnham QC J2N 1L8
Tél: 450-293-0066
Aperçu: *Dimension:* petite; *Envergure:* locale; fondée en 2001
Mission: Promouvoir le patrimoine religieux; d'établir des liens entre les différentes églises et de créer des partenariats avec des organisations ocuméniques
Membre(s) du bureau directeur:
Michel Goudoury, Propriétaire

Regroupement provincial des maisons d'hébergement et de transition pour femmes victimes de violence conjugale
CP 55005, Succ. Notre-Dame, 11, rue Notre-Dame Ouest, Montréal QC H2Y 4A7
Tél: 514-878-9134; *Téléc:* 514-878-9136
info@maisons-femmes.qc.ca
www.maisons-femmes.qc.ca
www.facebook.com/RMFVVC
Aperçu: *Dimension:* petite; *Envergure:* locale; fondée en 1979
Mission: Venir en aide aux femmes victimes de violence conjugale et leurs enfants, par tous les moyens jugés nécessaires et appropriés; 51 maisons membres
Finances: *Budget de fonctionnement annuel:* $250,000-$500,000; *Fonds:* Gouvernement provincial
Membre(s) du personnel: 4; 1 bénévole(s)
Membre: 48 associés

Regroupement québécois de la danse (RQD)
#440, 3680 rue Jeanne-Mance, Montréal QC H2X 2K5
Tél: 514-849-4003; *Téléc:* 514-849-3288
Autres numéros: www.flickr.com/photos/rqd
info@quebecdanse.org
www.quebecdanse.org
www.facebook.com/quebecdanse
twitter.com/quebecdanse
www.youtube.com/user/quebecdanse
Nom précédent: Regroupement des professionnels de la danse du Québec
Aperçu: *Dimension:* moyenne; *Envergure:* nationale; Organisme sans but lucratif; fondée en 1984
Mission: Promouvoir, encourager et soutenir le développement artistique, social et économique des danseurs, chorégraphes et de tout intervenant professionnel de la communauté de la danse au Québec
Membre de: Conférence canadienne des arts; Coalition québécoise des arts de la scène; Les Arts et La Ville; Le mouvement pour les arts et les lettres
Affliation(s): Agora de la danse; Regroupement québécois des créateurs professionnels
Membre(s) du bureau directeur:
Anik Bissonette, Présidente
Finances: *Budget de fonctionnement annuel:* $250,000-$500,000
Membre(s) du personnel: 8
Membre: 500; *Montant de la cotisation:* Barème; *Critères d'admissibilite:* Individu - formation complétée; deux ans d'expérience; Organisme - organismes de création, production, diffusion établies au Québec; *Comités:* Formation; Interprétation; c/prd (création/production/diffusion)
Activités: *Service de conférenciers:* Oui

Regroupement québécois des organismes pour le développement de l'employabilité (RQuODE)
#202, 533, rue Ontario Est, Montréal QC H2L 1N8
Tél: 514-721-3051; *Téléc:* 514-721-9114
inforquode@rquode.com
www.savie.qc.ca/rquode2
Aperçu: *Dimension:* moyenne; *Envergure:* provinciale; fondée en 1987
Mission: Favoriser l'intégration au travail des personnes éprouvant des difficultés sur le plan de l'emploi en regroupant et soutenant les organismes communautaires spécialisés en développement de l'employabilité
Membre(s) du bureau directeur:
Nicole Galarneau, Directrice générale
Valérie St-Gelais, Agente de recherche
vstgelais@rquode.com
Finances: *Budget de fonctionnement annuel:* $100,000-$250,000; *Fonds:* Développement des ressources humaines du Canada
Membre(s) du personnel: 1
Membre: 54 membres qui sont répartis dans 11 des 17 régions du Québec; *Montant de la cotisation:* 600$
Activités: *Listes de destinataires:* Oui

Regroupement QuébecOiseaux
CP 1000, Succ. M, 4545, av Pierre-de Coubertin, Montréal QC H1V 3R2
Tél: 514-252-3190; *Téléc:* 514-251-8038
Ligne sans frais: 866-583-4846
info@quebecoiseaux.org
www.quebecoiseaux.org
Nom précédent: Association québécoise des groupes d'ornithologues
Aperçu: *Dimension:* moyenne; *Envergure:* provinciale; Organisme sans but lucratif; fondée en 1981
Mission: Favoriser le développement du loisir ornithologique; promouvoir l'étude des oiseaux; veiller à leur protection et à celle de leurs habitats
Membre(s) du bureau directeur:
Jean-Sébastien Guénette, Directeur général
Finances: *Budget de fonctionnement annuel:* $100,000-$250,000
Membre(s) du personnel: 4; 13 bénévole(s)
Membre: 6,000; *Montant de la cotisation:* 20$ non-membre d'un club; 15$ membre d'un club; 50$ Organismes sans but lucratif; 100$ autres membres associés; *Critères d'admissibilite:* Toute personne intéressée par l'observation des oiseaux
Activités: Banques de données; *Stagiaires:* Oui

Rehabilitation Society of Calgary *See* Prospect Human Services

Rehabilitation Society of Southwestern Alberta
Ability Resource Centre, 1610 - 29th St. North, Lethbridge ON T1H 5L3
Tel: 403-329-3911; *Fax:* 403-329-3581
staff@rehab.ab.ca
www.abilityresource.ca
Overview: A small local charitable organization
Mission: To support adults living with disabilities & provide them with a means of accessing opportunities; to facilitate personal growth; to promote inclusion
Chief Officer(s):
Art Tamminga, President
Ed Hinger, Executive Director
edh@rehab.ab.ac
Activities: Operates the JobLinks Employment Centre & the Ability Resource Centre

JobLinks Employment Centre
416 - 8th St. South, Lethbridge ON T1J 2J7
Tel: 403-327-1099; *Fax:* 403-317-4552
joblinks@rehab.ab.ca
www.job-links.ca

REHOBOTH Christian Ministries
3920 - 49th Ave., Stony Plain AB T7Z 2J7
Tel: 780-963-4044; *Fax:* 780-963-3075
provincial_admin@rehoboth.ab.ca
rehoboth.ab.ca
Also Known As: Christian Association for the Mentally Handicapped of Alberta
Overview: A medium-sized provincial charitable organization founded in 1976
Mission: To convey God's love to persons with disabilities through support, advocacy & public education, & by providing opportunities for personal growth & meaningful participation in society
Member of: Alberta Council of Disability Services; Canadian Centre for Philanthropy
Affliation(s): Christian Stewardship Services
Chief Officer(s):
Ron Bos, CEO & Executive Director
ron.bos@rehoboth.ab.ca
Finances: *Annual Operating Budget:* Greater than $5 Million; *Funding Sources:* Provincial government; membership fees; donations; church offerings
Staff Member(s): 535; 950 volunteer(s)
Membership: 4,600; *Fees:* $10; *Member Profile:* Everybody accepting their mission statement; *Committees:* Regional Advisory
Activities: Residential, vocational & recreational support for individuals who live with disabilities; summer camp program; fundraising golf tournament; *Internships:* Yes

Calgary Branch
#20, 3740 - 27 St. NE, Calgary AB T1Y 5E2
Tel: 403-250-7333; *Fax:* 403-250-7148
calgary_region@rehoboth.ab.ca

Coaldale Branch
PO Box 1312, Coaldale AB T1M 1N1
Tel: 403-345-5199; *Fax:* 403-345-3483
coaldale_region@rehoboth.ab.ca

Grande Prairie Branch
#1063 - 3, 9899 - 112 Ave, Grande Prairie AB T8V 7T2
Tel: 780-532-5611; *Fax:* 780-532-5642
grandeprairie@rehoboth.ab.ca

Stony Plain Branch
3920 - 49th Ave., Stony Plain AB T7Z 2J7
Tel: 780-968-4315; *Fax:* 780-968-4318
stonyplain@rehoboth.ab.ca

Three Hills Branch
117 - 4th Ave. South, Three Hills AB T0M 2A0
Tel: 403-443-2239; *Fax:* 403-443-2399
threehills_region@rehoboth.ab.ca

Rehtaeh Parsons Society
NS
rehtaehparsons.ca
www.facebook.com/angelrehtaehofficial
twitter.com/angelrehtaeh
Overview: A small national organization founded in 2014
Mission: To prevent sexual assault & cyber-harassment; to raise awareness of suicide & mental health; to support victims & engage in public education of healthy relationships
Chief Officer(s):
Glen Canning, Co-founder
Leah Parsons, Co-founder
Finances: *Funding Sources:* Donations
Activities: Outreach to schools, youth groups, assault centres, & community members; funding other non-profits with similar mandates; pursuing reforms in education, healthcare, & law enforcement.

Reinforcing Steel Institute of Ontario (RSIO)
PO Box 30104, RPO New Westminster, Thornhill ON L4J 0C6
Tel: 416-239-7746; *Fax:* 416-239-7745
rsio@rebar.org
www.rebar.org
Overview: A small provincial organization
Mission: To promote reinforced concrete as a building material
Membership: 36

Reinsurance Research Council (RRC) / Conseil de recherche en réassurance (CRR)
#1, 189 Queen St. East, Toronto ON M5A 1S2
Tel: 416-968-0183; *Fax:* 416-968-6818
mail@rrccanada.org
www.rrccanada.org
Overview: A small national organization founded in 1973
Mission: Represents the majority of professional reinsurers registered in Canada; conducts research into all lines of property/casualty reinsurance, presents the views of its members where appropriate, and provides liaison with governments, the primary insurance market, & other interested parties; promotes high standards of service and ethical business practices; develops and maintains cordial relations among members and with kindred associations and the public
Chief Officer(s):
Anthony Laycock, General Manager
Finances: *Funding Sources:* Membership dues
Staff Member(s): 1
Membership: 26 corporate; *Member Profile:* Licenced reinsurers; *Committees:* Executive; Finance; Underwriting Research

Relance jeunes et familles
2700, rue de Rouen, Montréal QC H2K 1N1
Tél: 514-525-1508
info@relance.org
www.relance.org
Aperçu: *Dimension:* petite; *Envergure:* locale
Mission: Pour aider les enfants défavorisés et leur famille aient des chances égales en offrant des ateliers éducatifs pour les familles et les activités de loisirs pour les enfants
Membre(s) du bureau directeur:
Benoit DeGuire, Directeur général
direction@relance.org
Membre(s) du personnel: 19

Religieuses du Sacré-Coeur *See* Religious of The Sacred Heart

Religious Freedom Council of Christian Minorities
PO Box 223, Stn. A, Vancouver BC V6C 2M3

Tel: 250-492-3376
www.bible-holiness-movement.com
Also Known As: Bible Holiness Movement
Overview: A small local organization founded in 1979
Mission: To act as a sponsored organization of the Bible Holiness Movement. The Bible Holiness Movement is an aggressive Christian evangelistic and missionary movement.
Chief Officer(s):
Wesley H. Wakefield, Chair
Finances: *Annual Operating Budget:* Less than $50,000
4 volunteer(s)
Activities: *Speaker Service:* Yes; *Library* by appointment
Awards:
• Religious Freedom Essay Contest Award (Award)

Religious of The Sacred Heart / Religieuses du Sacré-Coeur

#811, 325 Dalhousie St., Ottawa ON K1N 7G2
Tel: 613-241-4050; *Fax:* 613-241-3142
sshcph@on.aibn.com
rscj.org
Also Known As: Society of the Sacred Heart
Overview: A small local charitable organization founded in 1800
Mission: To make known the love of Jesus in the world, through educaton & social justice activities
Chief Officer(s):
Barbara Dawson, Provincial Superior
Staff Member(s): 35
Membership: 1-99
Activities: *Library:* Provincial Archives; by appointment

The Renascent Centres for Alcoholism & Drug Addiction

Lillian & Don Wright Family Health Centre, 38 Isabella St., Toronto ON MR7 1N1
Tel: 416-927-1202; *Fax:* 416-927-0363
Toll-Free: 866-232-1212
Other Communication: Access Centre Phone: 416-927-7649
info@renascent.ca
www.renascent.ca
twitter.com/renascentcanada
Overview: A small local charitable organization founded in 1970
Mission: To facilitate prevention, education & recovery from addiction to alcohol & other drugs through a continuum of programs & services with equitable access
Chief Officer(s):
Adam Fisher, Director, Business Development
afisher@renascent.ca
Finances: *Annual Operating Budget:* $3 Million-$5 Million
Staff Member(s): 80; 150 volunteer(s)
Membership: 1-99
Activities: Operates following treatment centres: Graham Munro Centre (Women), 416/598-2649; Graham Munro Centre (Day Program - Men & Women), 416/598-7976; Sullivan Centre (Men), 905/655-8484; Punanai Centre (Men) 416/924-3433; *Internships:* Yes; *Speaker Service:* Yes

Renfrew & Area Chamber of Commerce

161 Raglan St. South, Renfrew ON K7V 1R2
Tel: 613-432-7015; *Fax:* 613-432-8645
info@renfrewareachamber.ca
www.renfrewareachamber.ca
Overview: A small local organization
Mission: To be the recognized voice of business committed to improving the economy of Renfrew & area
Member of: Canadian Chamber of Commerce
Chief Officer(s):
Rob Campbell, President, 613-432-4448
rcampbell@tipsunltd.com
Finances: *Funding Sources:* Town grant; membership fee
Staff Member(s): 1
Membership: 120; *Committees:* Tourism; Industrial Lumber Baron Festival; Year Book
Awards:
• Citizen of the Year (Award)
• Business Achievement Award (Award)

Renfrew & District Association for the Mentally Retarded *See* Community Living Renfrew County South

Renfrew & District Food Bank

163 Argyle St. South, Renfrew ON K7V 2X9
Tel: 613-433-9216
Overview: A small local organization
Member of: Ontario Association of Food Banks

Renfrew & District Historical Society

PO Box 554, Renfrew ON K7V 4B1
Tel: 613-432-7015
museum@renfrewmuseum.ca
www.renfrewmuseum.ca
Overview: A small local charitable organization
Mission: To operate McDougall Mill Museum
Member of: Ontario Museum Association; Ontario Historical Association; Chamber of Commerce
Affliation(s): Ottawa Valley Travel Association

Renfrew County Law Association

#1211, 297 Pembroke St. East, Pembroke ON K8A 3K2
Tel: 613-732-4880; *Fax:* 613-732-2262
rcla@bellnet.ca
www.rcla.on.ca
Overview: A small local organization
Chief Officer(s):
Michael March, President
Activities: *Library:* County Courthouse Library

Renfrew County Real Estate Board (RCREB)

197 Pembroke St. East, Pembroke ON K8A 3J6
Tel: 613-735-5840; *Fax:* 613-735-0405
eo@rcreb.com
www.renfrewcountyrealestateboard.com
www.facebook.com/RCREB
Overview: A small local organization founded in 1975 overseen by Ontario Real Estate Association
Mission: To promote standard practices among its members in order to unify & strengthen their abilities
Member of: The Canadian Real Estate Association; Ontario Real Estate Association
Chief Officer(s):
Natalie Frodsham, President
Membership: 160

Renfrew County United Way

1330 Pembroke St. West, #B, Pembroke ON K8A 7A3
Tel: 613-735-0436; *Fax:* 613-735-8362
Toll-Free: 888-592-2213
unitedw@nrtco.net
www.renfrewcountyunitedway.ca
Merged from: United Way/Centraide of the Upper Ottawa Valley Inc. and The Deep River District United Way
Overview: A small local charitable organization founded in 1971 overseen by United Way of Canada - Centraide Canada
Mission: To identify & address the needs of our community by organizing the resources of community members to care for one another
Affliation(s): Arnprior Community Council; Upper Ottawa Valley Chamber of Commerce; Pembroke Downtown Development Commission
Chief Officer(s):
Etienne Lantos, Chair
Sheila Bucholtz, Executive Director
Finances: *Annual Operating Budget:* $250,000-$500,000; *Funding Sources:* Donations
Staff Member(s): 1; 300 volunteer(s)
Membership: 10 institutional; *Member Profile:* Non-profit organization, health & social services; *Committees:* Allocations; Campaign; Executive; Communications; Planning & Assessment
Activities: Star-light Night Golf; 24-hour Ball Marathon

Renfrew Family & Child Services *See* Family & Children's Services of Renfrew County

Rental Association of Canada *See* Canadian Rental Association

Rental Owners & Managers Society of British Columbia; Apartment Owners & Property Managers Association of Vancouver Island *See* LandlordBC

Reorganized Church of Jesus Christ of Latter Day Saints (Canada) *See* Community of Christ - Canada East Mission

Répertoire canadien des psychologues offrant des services de santé *See* Canadian Register of Health Service Psychologists

Research & Development Institute for the Agri-Environment (IRDA) / Institut de recherche et de développement en agroenvironnement (IRDA)

Head Office & Research Center, PO Box 480, 3300, rue Sicotte, Saint-Hyacinthe QC J2S 7B8
Tel: 450-778-6522; *Fax:* 450-778-6539
www.irda.qc.c
Overview: A medium-sized national organization founded in 1998
Mission: To contribute to the sustainable development of agriculture, through research, knowledge acquisition, & transfer activities
Chief Officer(s):
Pierre Lemieux, President, Board
Gisèle Grandbois, President & Chief Executive Officer
Robert Doré, Director, Research Services & Human Resources
Staff Member(s): 100
Activities: Publishing fact sheets, research reports, scientific papers, & technology transfer papers
Publications:
• Agro Solutions / Revue Agrosolutions [a publication of the Research & Development Institute for the Agri-Environment]
Editor: Marcel Giroux
• Research & Development Institute for the Agri-Environment Annual Report
Type: Yearbook; *Frequency:* Annually
• Research & Development Institute for the Agri-Environment Scientific Activity Report
Type: Yearbook

Research & Education Foundation of the College of Family Physicians of Canada (REF)

2630 Skymark Ave., Mississauga ON L4W 5A4
Tel: 905-629-0900; *Fax:* 905-629-0893
Toll-Free: 800-387-6197
ref@cfpc.ca
www.cfpc.ca/REF
Overview: A large national charitable organization founded in 1995
Mission: To raise funds in order to support family doctors
Finances: *Funding Sources:* Fundraisers; donations
Activities: Awarding over 200 awards, grants & scholarships; *Awareness Events:* Walk for Doctors of Tomorrow, Nov.
Awards:
• Jean-Pierre Despins Award (Award)
To recognize an individual who has been an outstanding advocate & spokesperson for family medicine and/or physicians & their patients*Eligibility:* Must be a CFPC family physician member
• Hollister King Rural Family Practice Scholarship (Scholarship)
To recognize continuing medical education/continuing professional development related to rural family practice*Eligibility:* Must be a practicing family doctor & CFPC member
• Ian McWhinney Family Medicine Education Award (Award)
To recognize an outstanding family medicine teacher
Publications:
• Partners [a publication of Research & Education Foundation of the College of Family Physicians of Canada]
Type: Newsletter

Research Council Employees' Association (Ind.) (RCEA) / Association des employés du conseil de recherches (ind.) (AECR)

PO Box 8256, Stn. Alta Vista Terminal, Ottawa ON K1G 3H7
Tel: 613-746-9341; *Fax:* 613-745-7868
office@rcea.ca
www.rcea.ca
Overview: A medium-sized local organization founded in 1966
Mission: To act as the certified bargaining agent for six groups and categories and represents the majority of NRC employees, which are: AD (Administrative Support) Group, AS (Administrative Services) Group, CS (Computer Systems Administration) Group, OP (Operational) Category, PG (Purchasing and Supply) Group, and TO(Technical) Category.
Member of: National Joint Council
Chief Officer(s):
Cathie Fraser, President
cathie@rcea.ca
Finances: *Funding Sources:* Membership dues
Staff Member(s): 6
Membership: 1,600;

Réseau ACTION TI

Tour Ouest, #355, 550, rue Sherbrooke ouest, Montréal QC H3A 1B9
Tél: 514-840-1240; *Téléc:* 514-840-1243
info@actionTI.com
www.actionti.com
www.linkedin.com/groups?home=&gid=90428
www.facebook.com/pages/Reseau-ACTION-TI/218532705051
twitter.com/ActionTI
www.youtube.com/reseauactionti

Nom précédent: Fédération de l'informatique du Québec
Aperçu: *Dimension:* moyenne; *Envergure:* provinciale
Mission: De regrouper et de mobiliser les acteurs du secteur des technologies de l'information au Québec; de créer des occasions de rassemblement et aide à l'amélioration des connaissances et des compétences; de souligner la qualité des réalisations et de contribuer à valoriser les TI au Québec.
Membre(s) du bureau directeur:
Patrice-Guy Martin, Président-directeur général, 514-840-1255
pgmartin@actionti.com
Membre(s) du personnel: 10
Membre: 2,300; *Montant de la cotisation:* Barème

Réseau aéronefs amateur *See* Recreational Aircraft Association

Reseau Biblio de l'Abitibi-Témiscamingue Nord-du-Québec
20, boul Québec, Rouyn-Noranda QC J9X 2E6
Tél: 819-762-4305; *Téléc:* 819-762-5903
info@reseaubiblioatnq.qc.ca
www.reseaubiblioduquebec.qc.ca
Aperçu: *Dimension:* petite; *Envergure:* locale; fondée en 1985
Mission: Promotion du livre et de la lecture en Abitibi-Témiscamingue; promotion des bibliothèques
Membre de: Association des bibliothèques publiques du Québec
Membre(s) du bureau directeur:
Louis Dallaire, Directeur général
louis.dallaire@reseaubiblioatnq.qc.ca
Membre(s) du personnel: 8
Membre: *Critères d'admissibilité:* Bibliothèque publique
Publications:
• L'Échange
Type: Bulletin; *Frequency:* 4 fois par ans *ISSN:* 0706-5205
Profile: Donne des informations sur les évéments qui se déroulent dans les bibliothèques de la CRSBP de l'Abitibi-Témiscamingue du nord du Québec

Réseau BIBLIO de la Côte-Nord
59, rue Napoléon, Sept-Iles QC G4R 5C5
Tél: 418-962-1020; *Téléc:* 418-962-5124
www.reseaubiblioduquebec.qc.ca
Aperçu: *Dimension:* petite; *Envergure:* locale
Mission: Promouvoir les bibliothèques publiques; concertation dans des dossiers concernant les bibliothèques publiques; faire connaître nos services
Membre(s) du bureau directeur:
Jean-Roch Gagnon, Directeur général
jrgagnon@reseaubibliocn.qc.ca
Membre(s) du personnel: 4

Réseau BIBLIO du Québec
3189, rue Albert-Demers, Charny QC G6X 3A1
Tél: 819-561-6008; *Téléc:* 819-561-6767
www.reseaubiblioduquebec.qc.ca
Aperçu: *Dimension:* grande; *Envergure:* provinciale; fondée en 1984
Mission: Le Réseau BIBLIO du Québec est un regroupement national qui vise à unir les ressources des Réseaux BIBLIO régionaux pour maintenir et développer leur réseau de bibliothèques et de les représenter auprès des diverses instances sur des dossiers d'intérêts communs.
Membre(s) du bureau directeur:
Sylvie Thibault, Secrétaire générale
sylvie.thibault@crsbpo.qc.ca
Membre: Près de 750 bibliothèques publiques membres; *Comités:* Comité de liaison / MCCCf; Comité de liaison / BAnQ; Comité de communication

Réseau BIBLIO du Saguenay-Lac-Saint-Jean (RBSLSJ)
100, rue Price ouest, Alma QC G8B 4S1
Tél: 418-662-6425; *Téléc:* 418-662-7593
Ligne sans frais: 800-563-6425
info@reseaubiblioslsj.qc.ca
www.mabibliotheque.ca/saguenay-lac-saint-jean
www.facebook.com/reseaubiblioSLSJ
twitter.com/reseaubiblio
Nom précédent: Rassemblement des bibliothèques publiques du Lac-Saint-Jean et Saguenay-Lac-Saint-Jean
Aperçu: *Dimension:* petite; *Envergure:* locale; fondée en 1981
Mission: Promouvoir les bibliothèques publiques; concertation dans des dossiers concernant les bibliothèques publiques; faire connaître nos services
Membre(s) du bureau directeur:
Sophie Bolduc, Directrice générale
Activités: Service régional d'animation

Réseau canadien contre les accidents cérébrovasculaires *See* Canadian Stroke Network

Réseau canadien d'éducation et de communication relatives à l'environnement *See* Canadian Network for Environmental Education & Communication

Réseau canadien d'information sur le patrimoine *See* Canadian Heritage Information Network

Réseau canadien d'info-traitements sida *See* Canadian AIDS Treatment Information Exchange

Le Réseau canadien de l'arthrite *See* Canadian Arthritis Network

Réseau canadien de l'eau *See* Canadian Water Network

Réseau canadien de l'environnement *See* Canadian Environmental Network

Réseau canadien des associations nationales d'organismes de réglementation *See* Canadian Network of National Associations of Regulators

Réseau canadien des centres de toxicologie *See* Canadian Network of Toxicology Centres

Réseau canadien des subventionneurs en environnement *See* Canadian Environmental Grantmakers' Network

Réseau canadien du cancer du sein *See* Canadian Breast Cancer Network

Réseau Canadien en Obésité *See* Canadian Obesity Network

Réseau canadien pour l'innovation en éducation *See* Canadian Network for Innovation in Education

Le Réseau canadien pour la conservation de la flore *See* Canadian Botanical Conservation Network

Réseau canadien pour la santé des femmes *See* Canadian Women's Health Network

Réseau canadien pour les essais VIH *See* Canadian HIV Trials Network

Réseau canadien pour les musiques nouvelles *See* Canadian New Music Network

Réseau Canadien pour les soins respiratoires *See* Canadian Network for Respiratory Care

Réseau canadien sur les maladies génétiques *See* Canadian Genetic Diseases Network

Réseau communautaire Chebucto *See* Chebucto Community Net

Réseau d'Action des Femmes Handicapées du Canada *See* DisAbled Women's Network of Canada

Réseau d'action et de communication pour le développement international / Alternatives Action & Communication Network for International Development
#300, 3720, av du Parc, Montréal QC H2X 2J1
Tél: 514-982-6606; *Téléc:* 514-982-6122
Ligne sans frais: 800-982-6646
www.alternatives.ca
www.facebook.com/pages/Alternatives/126337067392854
twitter.com/alternativesMTL
www.youtube.com/alternativesngo
Aperçu: *Dimension:* petite; *Envergure:* internationale; Organisme sans but lucratif
Mission: Pour soutenir les organisations communautaires qui travaillent à transformer leur environnement social, économique, politique et écologique au Canada et à l'étranger
Membre(s) du bureau directeur:
Ronald Cameron, Président
Michel Lambert, Directeur général
Finances: *Fonds:* Dons; revenus auto-générés
Membre(s) du personnel: 10
Membre: *Montant de la cotisation:* 120$ partisan; 60$ régulier; 36$ chômeurs/étudiants
Activités: Formation et aide financière; lutter contre l'appauvrissement et l'exclusion sociale; aider les immigrants; *Stagiaires:* Oui; *Service de conférenciers:* Oui; *Listes de destinataires:* Oui

Québec City Office
266, St-Vallier ouest, Québec QC G1K 1K2
Tel: 418-521-4000; *Fax:* 418-521-4000
quebec@alternatives.ca
www.alternatives.ca/eng
Mission: To support community-based organizations that work to transform their social, economic, political & ecological environment in Canada & abroad
Membre(s) du bureau directeur:
Luc Phaneuf, President

Réseau d'aide aux personnes seules et itinérantes de Montréal (RAPSIM)
#204, 105, rue Ontario Est, Montréal QC H2X 1G9
Tel: 514-879-1949; *Fax:* 514-879-1948
rapsim@qc.aira.com
www.rapsim.org
Overview: A small local organization
Mission: Pour aider les personnes sans-abri à avoir accès aux services de santé et les services sociaux et de réduire le niveau de pauvreté à Montréal
Chief Officer(s):
Pierre Gaudreau, Coordonnateur
pierre.gaudreau@qc.aira.com
Membership: 95; *Member Profile:* Organismes communautaires

Le Réseau d'enseignement francophone à distance du Canada (REFAD)
CP 47542, Succ. Plateau Mont-Royal, Montréal QC H2H 2S8
Tél: 514-284-9109; *Téléc:* 514-284-9363
refad@sympatico.ca
www.refad.ca
twitter.com/_refad
Aperçu: *Dimension:* moyenne; *Envergure:* nationale; Organisme sans but lucratif; fondée en 1988
Mission: Favoriser la collaboration entre les personnes et les organisations intéressées par l'enseignement à distance en français; rassembler en réseau les établissements qui ont recours à la formation à distance en français; appuyer et compléter d'autres réseaux d'enseignement à distance existant déjà à travers le Canada; promouvoir et accroître la qualité et la quantité des programmes et des cours offerts dans la francophonie canadienne.
Membre(s) du bureau directeur:
Caroll-Ann Keating, Présidente
Alain Langlois, Directeur général
Finances: *Budget de fonctionnement annuel:* $50,000-$100,000
Membre: 27 institutionnels + 16 individuels; *Montant de la cotisation:* 2 000$ institutionnel; 250$ individuel
Activités: Finance des programmes d'éducation d'envergure pancanadienne; organise un colloque annuel; publie différents ouvrages

Réseau de cellules souches *See* Stem Cell Network

Réseau de développement économique et d'employabilité Ontario
880, promenade Taylor Creek, Ottawa ON K1C 1T1
Tél: 613-590-2493; *Téléc:* 613-590-2494
communications@rdee-ont.ca
www.rdee-ont.ca
Également appelé: RDÉE Ontario
Aperçu: *Dimension:* petite; *Envergure:* provinciale
Mission: Optimise le potentiel économique des communautés francophones et acadiennes
Membre de: Réseau national de développement économique francophone
Membre(s) du bureau directeur:
Daniel Sigouin, Directeur général

Réseau de la coopération du travail du Québec
#200, 3188, ch Sainte-Foy, Québec QC G1X 1R4
Tél: 418-651-0388; *Téléc:* 418-651-3860
www.reseau.coop
Également appelé: RESEAU
Aperçu: *Dimension:* petite; *Envergure:* provinciale
Mission: De promouvoir le développement des coopératives au Québec
Membre: *Critères d'admissibilité:* Coop de tracailleurs; coop de solidarité; coop de travailleurs actionnaires

Réseau de la Santé Sexuelle du Québec inc. *See* Sexual Health Network of Québec Inc.

Réseau de Santé en Français au Nunavut (SAFRAN)
CP 1516, Iqaluit NT X0A 0H0

Tél: 867-222-2107
resefan.nu@gmail.com
www.resefan.ca
Aperçu: *Dimension:* petite; *Envergure:* provinciale; fondée en 2004 surveillé par Société santé en français
Membre(s) du bureau directeur:
Daniel Hubert, Directeur général

Réseau des aliments et des matériaux d'avant-garde ***See*** Advanced Foods & Materials Network

Réseau des archives du Québec (RAQ)

a/s Archives nationales du Québec à Montréal, 535 av Viger est, local 5.27.1, Montréal QC H2L 2P3
Tél: 514-864-9213
raq@bellnet.ca
www.raq.qc.ca
Aperçu: *Dimension:* moyenne; *Envergure:* provinciale; fondée en 1987 surveillé par Canadian Council of Archives
Mission: Promouvoir le développement et la mise en valeur des archives historiques; favoriser l'échange et la mise en commun d'information, d'expérience et de ressources; devenir un instrument de consultation et un groupe de pression reconnu des divers intervenants des milieux archivistiques
Membre(s) du bureau directeur:
Diane Baillargeon, Présidente
Bernard Savoie, Secrétaire
Finances: *Budget de fonctionnement annuel:* Moins de $50,000
6 bénévole(s)
Membre: 150; *Montant de la cotisation:* 125$ réguliers; 50$ associés; *Critères d'admissibilité:* Organismes du Québec qui conserve, traite ou rend accessible des archives historiques; *Comités:* Préservation
Activités: Programmes coopératifs de subventions pour la conservation des archives

Réseau de diffusion des archives du Québec
a/s Archives nationales du Québec à Montréal, 535 av Viger est, local 5.27.1, Montréal QC H2L 2P3
Tél: 514-864-9213
rdaq@banq.qc.ca
rdaq.banq.qc.ca
Mission: Le RDAQ permet la recherche d'archives québécoises ainsi que la mise en valeur des expositions virtuelles créées par les centres d'archives québécois.
Membre(s) du bureau directeur:
Susan Rubin, District Coordinator

Réseau des cégeps et des collèges francophones du Canada (RCCFC)

#1015, 130, rue Slater, Ottawa ON K1P 6E2
Tél: 613-241-0430; *Téléc:* 613-241-0457
Ligne sans frais: 888-253-2486
rccfc.ca
Aperçu: *Dimension:* moyenne; *Envergure:* nationale; fondée en 1995
Mission: Le Réseau des cégeps et des collèges francophones du Canada a pour mission d'établir un véritable partenariat entre les établissements d'enseignement collégial francophones du Canada. Il constitue un réseau d'entraide, de promotion et d'échanges lié au développement de l'enseignement collégial en français au Canada tout en favorisant l'utilisation des technologies de l'information et des communications.
Membre(s) du bureau directeur:
Laurier Thibault, Directeur général
dg@rccfc.ca
Finances: *Budget de fonctionnement annuel:* $1.5 Million-$3 Million
Membre(s) du personnel: 2
Membre: 61

Réseau des femmes aînées ***See*** The Older Women's Network

Réseau des femmes d'affaires du Québec inc. (RFAQ)

474, rue Jean-Neveu, Longueuil QC J4G 1N8
Tél: 514-521-2441; *Téléc:* 514-521-1410
Ligne sans frais: 800-332-2683
info@rfaq.ca
www.rfaq.ca
www.linkedin.com/groups?gid=2390552
www.facebook.com/RFAQinc
twitter.com/RFAQinc
www.youtube.com/user/RFAQinc
Aperçu: *Dimension:* moyenne; *Envergure:* provinciale; fondée en 1981
Mission: Afin d'encourager et de promouvoir les femmes à devenir des leaders dans les instances sociales, politiques et économiques
Membre(s) du bureau directeur:
Ruth Vachon, Présidente/Directrice générale
rvachon@rfaq.ca
Membre: 2,000; *Montant de la cotisation:* 100$ autres provinces/hors Canada; 125$ étudiante; 195$ OBNL; 225$ régulier

Réseau des femmes du sud de l'Ontario / Network of French Speaking Women of South Ontario

Serres #102, College Glendon, 2295, av Bayview, Toronto ON M4N 3M6
Tél: 416-487-6794; *Téléc:* 416-487-6794
Ligne sans frais: 800-387-8603
reseaudesfemmes@on.aibn.com
Également appelé: SOS-femmes; Institut de leadership social et communautaire des femmes
Aperçu: *Dimension:* petite; *Envergure:* provinciale; Organisme sans but lucratif; fondée en 1982
Mission: Améliorer les conditions de vie des femmes francophones
Membre(s) du personnel: 5; 8 bénévole(s)
Membre: 500; *Montant de la cotisation:* $10
Activités: *Stagiaires:* Oui

Réseau des femmes exécutives ***See*** Women's Executive Network

Réseau des lesbiennes du Québec (RLQ) / Québec Lesbian Network

#110, 2075, rue Plessis, Montréal QC H2L 2Y4
Tél: 438-929-6928; *Téléc:* 514-528-9708
rlqln.info@gmail.com
rlq-qln.algi.qc.ca
www.facebook.com/RLQQLN
Aperçu: *Dimension:* petite; *Envergure:* provinciale; fondée en 1996

Réseau des SADC du Québec ***Voir*** Réseau des SADC et CAE

Réseau des SADC et CAE (SADC)

#530, 979, av de Bourgogne, Québec QC G1W 2L4
Tél: 418-658-1530; *Téléc:* 418-658-9900
www.sadc-cae.ca
twitter.com/ReseauSADCCAE
Également appelé: Sociétés d'aide au développement des collectivités & Centre d'aide aux entreprises
Nom précédent: Réseau des SADC du Québec
Aperçu: *Dimension:* moyenne; *Envergure:* provinciale; Organisme sans but lucratif; fondée en 1995
Mission: Soutenir les efforts de regroupement des SADC (Sociétés d'aide au développement des collectivités) et des CAE (Centres d'aide aux entreprises) du Québec; il veille à leurs intérêts et procure des services qui facilitent le développement de ses membres; au cours des années, les SADC et CAE sont devenus de véritables experts en développement local et régional
Membre(s) du bureau directeur:
Hélène Deslauriers, Directrice générale
Finances: *Budget de fonctionnement annuel:* Moins de $50,000
Membre(s) du personnel: 400; 1350 bénévole(s)
Membre: 67; *Critères d'admissibilité:* Sociétés d'investissement (financement d'entreprises et accompagnement personnalisé)

CAE Beauce-Chaudière inc
595-J, 93 av., Beauceville QC G5X 1J3
Tél: 418-774-2022; *Téléc:* 418-774-2024
caebci@sogetel.net
www.caebeauce.com
Membre(s) du bureau directeur:
Johanne Jacques, Directrice générale
johanne.jacques@caebeauce.com

CAE Capital
#200, 270, boul Sir-Wilfrid-Laurier, Beloeil QC J3G 4G7
Tél: 450-446-3650; *Téléc:* 450-446-3806
info@caers.ca
www.caers.ca
Membre(s) du bureau directeur:
Michel Aubin, Directeur général
m.aubin@caecapital.com

CAE de Drummond
#475, 230 rue Brock, Drummondville QC J2C 1M3
Tél: 819-474-6477; *Téléc:* 819-474-5944
www.caedrummond.ca
Membre(s) du bureau directeur:
Errold Mayrand, Directeur général
errold.mayrand@caedrummond.ca

CAE Haute-Montérégie
Parc industriel E.L. Farrar, 700, rue Lucien-Beaudin, Saint-Jean-sur-Richelieu QC J2X 5M3
Tél: 450-357-9800; *Téléc:* 450-357-9583
info@caehm.com
www.caehm.com
Membre(s) du bureau directeur:
Édouard Bonaldo, Directeur général
edouard.bonaldo@caehm.com

CAE Haute-Yamaska et région inc.
#102, 90, rue Robinson sud, Granby QC J2G 7L4
Tél: 450-378-2294; *Téléc:* 450-378-7370
info@caehyr.com
www.caehyr.com
Membre(s) du bureau directeur:
Isabelle Brochu, Directeur général
i.brochu@caehyr.com

CAE LaPrade Trois-Rivière inc.
#300, 370, rue des Forges, Trois-Rivières QC G9A 2H1
Tél: 819-378-6000; *Téléc:* 819-378-2019
info@caelaprade.com
www.caelaprade.com
Membre(s) du bureau directeur:
Claude Lavergne, Directrice générale
jbouliane@caelaprade.com

CAE Memphrémagog inc
#206, 146, rue Principale ouest, Magog QC J1X 2A5
Tél: 819-843-4342; *Téléc:* 819-843-4393
www.caememphre.com
Membre(s) du bureau directeur:
Louise Paradis, Directrice générale
louisep@caememphre.com

CAE Montmagny-L'Islet
191, ch des Poirier, Montmagny QC G5V 4L2
Tél: 418-248-4815; *Téléc:* 418-248-4836
info@caeml.qc.ca
www.caeml.qc.ca
www.facebook.com/643623969022048
Membre(s) du bureau directeur:
Gilles Boulet, Directeur général
gboulet@caeml.qc.ca

CAE Rive-Nord
13035, rue Brault, Mirabel QC J7J 1P3
Tél: 450-437-0999; *Téléc:* 450-437-2080
info@caebl.ca
www.caebl.ca
www.facebook.com/256764761066491
twitter.com/CAERiveNord
Membre(s) du bureau directeur:
Renée Courchesne, Directrice générale
rcourchesne@caebl.ca

CAE Val-St-François
745, rue Gouin, Richmond QC J0B 2H0
Tél: 819-826-6571; *Téléc:* 819-826-6281
info@caevsf.com
www.caevsf.com
Membre(s) du bureau directeur:
Marc Ducharme, Directeur général

Eeyou Economic Group
CP 39, 12, rue Poplar, Waswanipi QC J0Y 3C0
Tél: 819-753-2560; *Téléc:* 819-753-2568
info@eeyoueconomicgroup.ca
www.eeyoueconomicgroup.ca
www.facebook.com/eeyoueconomicgroup
twitter.com/EEG_CFDC
Membre(s) du bureau directeur:
David Neeposh, Directeur général
dneeposh@eeyoueconomicgroup.ca

Nunavik Investment Corporation
CP 789, Kuujjuaq QC J0M 1C0
Tél: 819-964-1872; *Téléc:* 819-964-1497
Membre(s) du bureau directeur:
Martha Gordon, Directeur général
marthag@tamaani.ca

SADC Abitibi-Ouest
#202, 80, 12e av est, La Sarre QC J9Z 3K6
Tél: 819-333-3113; *Téléc:* 819-333-3132
sadc_abitibi@ciril.qc.ca
www.sadcao.com
Membre(s) du bureau directeur:
Thérèse Grenier, Directrice générale
tgrenier@sadcao.com

SADC Achigan-Montcalm inc.
104, rue St-Jacques, Saint-Jacques QC J0K 2R0
Tél: 450-839-9218; *Téléc:* 450-839-7036
info@sadc.org
www.sadc.org
Membre(s) du bureau directeur:
Claude Chartier, Directeur général
chartierc@sadc.org

SADC Arthabaska-Érable inc.
#101, 975, boul Industriel est., Victoriaville QC G6T 1T8
Tél: 819-758-1501; *Téléc:* 819-758-7971
sadc_ae@ciril.qc.ca
www.sadcae.ca
www.facebook.com/551798181594341
Membre(s) du bureau directeur:
Jean-François Girard, Directeur général
jfgirard@sadcae.ca

SADC Baie-des-Chaleurs
122, boul Perron ouest, New Richmond QC G0C 2B0
Tél: 418-392-5014; *Téléc:* 418-392-5425
sadc_chaleurs@ciril.qc.ca
www.sadcbc.ca
Membre(s) du bureau directeur:
Lyne Lebrasseur, Directrice générale
llebrasseur@sadcbc.ca

SADC Barraute-Senneterre-Quévillon inc
CP 308, 674, 11e ave., Senneterre QC J0Y 2M0
Tél: 819-737-2211; *Téléc:* 819-737-8888
sadc_bsq@ciril.qc.ca
www.sadcbsq.ca
Membre(s) du bureau directeur:
Marc Hardy, Directeur général
mhardy@ciril.qc.ca

SADC Bellechasse-Etchemins
CP 158, 494-B, rue Principale, Saint-Léon-de-Standon QC G0R 4L0
Tél: 418-642-2844; *Téléc:* 418-642-5316
info@sadcbe.qc.ca
www.sadcbe.qc.ca
Membre(s) du bureau directeur:
Marie-Claire Larose, Directrice générale
mclarose@sadcbe.qc.ca

SADC Centre-de-la-Mauricie
812, ave des Cèdres, Shawinigan QC G9N 1P2
Tél: 819-537-5107; *Téléc:* 819-537-5109
info@sadccm.ca
www.sadccm.ca
Membre(s) du bureau directeur:
Simon Charlebois, Directeur général
scharlebois@sadccm.ca

SADC Chibougamau-Chapais inc
#1, 600, 3e rue, Chibougamau QC G8P 1P1
Tél: 418-748-6477; *Téléc:* 418-748-6160
sadc.administration@lino.com
www.sadccc.ca
Membre(s) du bureau directeur:
Annie Potvin, Directrice générale
sadc.dg@lino.com

SADC Côte-Nord inc.
#205, 456, av Arnaud, Sept-Iles QC G4R 3B1
Tél: 418-962-7233; *Téléc:* 418-968-5513
Ligne sans frais: 877-962-7233
info@sadccote-nord.org
www.sadccote-nord.org
www.linkedin.com/groups/SADC-CôteNord-4316537
www.facebook.com/254939334588954
twitter.com/SADCCoteNord
Membre(s) du bureau directeur:
Soraya Zarate, Directrice générale
szarate@sadccote-nord.org

SADC d'Antoine-Labelle
#4, 636 rue de la Madone, Mont-Laurier QC J9L 1S9
Tél: 819-623-3300; *Téléc:* 819-623-7300
info@sadcal.com
www.sadcal.com
www.facebook.com/sadcal
Membre(s) du bureau directeur:
Benoit Cochet, Directeur général
bcochet@sadcal.com

SADC de Autray-Joliette
#500, 550, rue Montcalm, Berthierville QC J0K 1A0
Tél: 450-836-0990; *Téléc:* 450-836-2001
Ligne sans frais: 877-777-0990
info@masadc.ca
masadc.ca
Membre(s) du bureau directeur:
Jocelyn de Grandpré, Directeur général
jdegrandpre@MaSADC.ca

SADC de Charlevoix
#208, 11, rue Saint-Jean-Baptiste, Baie-Saint-Paul QC G3Z 1M1
Tél: 418-435-4033; *Téléc:* 418-435-4050
sadc_charlevoix@ciril.qc.ca
www.sadccharlevoix.ca
Membre(s) du bureau directeur:
Pascal Harvey, Directeur général
p.harvey@sadccharlevoix.ca

SADC de Gaspé
CP 5012, #200, 15, rue Adams, Gaspé QC G4X 1E5
Tél: 418-368-2906; *Téléc:* 418-368-3927
sadcgasp@globetrotter.net
www.sadcgaspe.ca
www.facebook.com/sadc.degaspe
Membre(s) du bureau directeur:
Mario Cotton, Directeur général
mcotton@ciril.qc.ca

SADC de l'Amiante
725, boul Frontenac ouest, Thetford Mines QC G6G 7X9
Tél: 418-338-4531; *Téléc:* 418-338-9256
sadc_amiante@ciril.qc.ca
www.sadcamiante.com
Membre(s) du bureau directeur:
Luce Dubois, Directrice générale
dg@sadcamiante.com

SADC de la Haute-Gaspésie
Édifice des Monts, 10G, boul Sainte-Anne ouest, 1er étage, Sainte-Anne-des-Monts QC G4V 1P3
Tél: 418-763-5355; *Téléc:* 418-763-2933
info@sadchautegaspesie.com
sadchautegaspesie.com
www.facebook.com/SADCdelaHauteGaspesie
Membre(s) du bureau directeur:
Richard Marin, Directeur général
rmarin@sadchautegaspesie.com

SADC de la MRC de Maskinongé
#100, 871, boul Saint-Laurent est, Louiseville QC J5V 1L3
Tél: 819-228-5921; *Téléc:* 819-228-0497
pcloutier@ciril.qc.ca
www.sadcmaskinonge.qc.ca
www.linkedin.com/company/5011533
twitter.com/SADCMaskinonge
plus.google.com/113296207301131382242
Membre(s) du bureau directeur:
Julie Lemieux, Directrice générale
jlemieux@sadcmaskinonge.qc.ca

SADC de la MRC de Rivière-du-Loup
#101, 646, rue Lafontaine, Rivière-du-Loup QC G5R 3C8
Tél: 418-867-4272; *Téléc:* 418-867-8060
info@sadcmrcriviereduloup.ca
www.riviereduloup.ca/sadc
www.facebook.com/La.Vraie.Vie.MRCRDL
Membre(s) du bureau directeur:
Gilles Goulet, Directeur général

SADC de la Neigette inc.
#101, 79, rue De l'Évêché, Rimouski QC G5L 1X7
Tél: 418-735-2514; *Téléc:* 418-723-5879
info@sadcneigette.ca
www.sadcneigette.ca
www.facebook.com/sadcneigette
Membre(s) du bureau directeur:
Yvan Collin, Directeur général
ycollin@sadcneigette.ca

SADC de la région d'Acton inc.
#101, 1545, rue Peerless, Acton Vale QC J0H 1A0
Tél: 450-546-3239; *Téléc:* 450-546-3619
sadcacton@cooptel.qc.ca
www.sadcacton.qc.ca
Membre(s) du bureau directeur:
Éric Thubodeau, Directeur général
ericthibodeau@cooptel.qc.ca

SADC de la région de Matane
#312, 235, av St-Jérôme, Matane QC G4W 3A7
Tél: 418-562-3171; *Téléc:* 418-562-1259
sadcmat@globetrotter.net
www.sadc-matane.qc.ca
www.facebook.com/SADCMatane
Membre(s) du bureau directeur:
Annie Fournier, Directrice générale
afournier@ciril.qc.ca

SADC de Lotbinière
#100, 153, boul Laurier, Laurier-Station QC G0S 1N0
Tél: 418-596-3300; *Téléc:* 418-728-3345
Ligne sans frais: 866-596-3300
sadc_lotbiniere@ciril.qc.ca
www.sadclotbiniere.qc.ca
www.facebook.com/SADClotbiniere
Membre(s) du bureau directeur:
Sylvie Drolet, Directrice générale
sdrolet@ciril.qc.ca

SADC de Papineau inc.
565, av de Buckingham, Gatineau QC J8L 2H2
Tél: 819-986-1747; *Téléc:* 819-281-0303
Ligne sans frais: 888-986-7232
info@sadcpapineau.com
www.sadcpapineau.ca
www.facebook.com/sadcpapineau
Membre(s) du bureau directeur:
Mélissa Bergeron, Directeur général
mebergeron@sadcpapineau.ca

SADC de Rouyn-Noranda
161, av Murdoch, Rouyn-Noranda QC J9X 1E3
Tél: 819-797-6068; *Téléc:* 819-797-0096
info@sadcrn.ca
www.sadcrn.ca
www.facebook.com/105328519513571
Membre(s) du bureau directeur:
Jocelyn Lévesque, Directrice générale
jocelyn.levesque@sadcrn.ca

SADC de Témiscouata
#202, 3, rue Hôtel-de-Ville, Témiscouata-Sur-le-lac QC G0L 1X0
Tél: 418-899-0808; *Téléc:* 418-899-0808
sadctemis@videotron.ca
www.sadctemiscouata.com
Membre(s) du bureau directeur:
Serge Ouellet, Directeur
sergeouellet@ciril.qc.ca

SADC des Basques inc.
400-3, rue Jean Rioux, Trois-Pistoles QC G0L 4K0
Tél: 418-851-3172; *Téléc:* 418-851-3171
sadc_basques@ciril.qc.ca
www.sadcbasques.qc.ca
www.facebook.com/223623494391230
Membre(s) du bureau directeur:
Yvanho Rioux, Directeur général
yrioux@ciril.qc.ca

SADC des Iles-de-la-Madeleine
#203, 735, ch Principal, Cap-aux-Meules QC G4T 1G8
Tél: 418-986-4601; *Téléc:* 418-986-4874
sadc_iles@ciril.qc.ca
www.sadcim.qc.ca
www.facebook.com/sadcdesiles
Membre(s) du bureau directeur:
Daniel Gaudet, Directeur général
dgaudet@ciril.qc.ca

SADC des Laurentides
#230, 1332, boul Sainte-Adéle, Sainte-Adèle QC J8B 2N5
Tél: 450-229-3001; *Téléc:* 450-229-6928
Ligne sans frais: 888-229-3001
info@sadclaurentides.org
www.sadclaurentides.org
twitter.com/SADCL_DD
Membre(s) du bureau directeur:
Sylvie Bolduc, Directrice générale
sbolduc@sadclaurentides.org

SADC des Sources
309, rue Chassé, Asbestos QC J1T 2B4
Tél: 819-879-7147; *Téléc:* 819-879-5188
info@sadcdessources.com
www.sadcdessources.com
Membre(s) du bureau directeur:
Marc Grimard, Directeur général
mgrimard@sadcdessources.com

SADC du Fjord inc.
#101, 613, rue Albert, La Baie QC G7B 3L6
Tél: 418-544-2885; *Téléc:* 418-544-0303
courrier@sadcdufjord.qc.ca
www.sadcdufjord.qc.ca
Membre(s) du bureau directeur:
André Nepton, Directeur général
anepton@sadcdufjord.qc.ca

SADC du Haut-Saguenay
328, rue Gagnon, Saint-Ambroise QC G7P 2R1
Tél: 418-672-6333; *Téléc:* 418-672-4882
sadc@videotron.ca
www.sadchs.qc.ca
www.facebook.com/212354118628
Membre(s) du bureau directeur:
André Boily, Directeur général

SADC du Haut-Saint-François
47, rue Angus nord, East Angus QC J0B 1R0
Tél: 819-832-2447; *Téléc:* 819-832-1831
Ligne sans frais: 877-473-7232
sadc_haut-saint-francois@ciril.qc.ca
www.sadchsf.qc.ca
Membre(s) du bureau directeur:
Danielle Simard, Directrice générale
dsimard@ciril.qc.ca

SADC du Haut-Saint-Maurice inc.
290, rue St. Joseph, La Tuque QC G9X 3Z8
Tél: 819-523-4227; *Téléc:* 819-523-5722
info-sadchsm@ciril.qc.ca
www.sadchsm.qc.ca
Membre(s) du bureau directeur:
Chantal Fortin, Directeur général

SADC du Rocher-Percé
#S-101, 129, boul René-Lévesque ouest, Chandler QC G0C 1K0
Tél: 418-689-5699; *Téléc:* 418-689-5556
sadc@globetrotter.qc.ca
www.sadcrp.ca
Membre(s) du bureau directeur:
Andreé Roy, Directrice générale
aroy@ciril.qc.ca

SADC du Suroît-Sud
#203, 50, rue Jacques-Cartier, Salaberry-de-Valleyfield QC J6T 4R3
Tél: 450-370-3332; *Téléc:* 450-370-4448
info@sadc-suroitsud.org
www.sadc-suroitsud.org
www.facebook.com/sadc.dusuroitsud
twitter.com/SADCSS
www.youtube.com/user/sadcdusuroitsud
Membre(s) du bureau directeur:
Robert Lafrance, Directeur Général

SADC du Témiscamingue
7B, rue des Oblats nord, Ville-Marie QC J9V 1H9
Tél: 819-629-3355; *Téléc:* 819-629-2793
sdt@temiscamingue.net
www.lasdt.com
www.facebook.com/sdt.temis
Membre(s) du bureau directeur:
Guy Trépanier, Directeur général

SADC Harricana inc.
550, 1re av ouest, Amos QC J9T 1V3
Tél: 819-732-8311; *Téléc:* 819-732-2240
sadc@sadc-harricana.qc.ca
www.sadc-harricana.qc.ca
www.facebook.com/439503636123429
Membre(s) du bureau directeur:
Éric Laliberté, Directeur générale
elaliberte@sadc-harricana.qc.ca

SADC Haute-Côte-Nord inc.
#200, 459, rte 138, Les Escoumins QC G0T 1K0
Tél: 418-233-3495; *Téléc:* 418-233-2485
sadchcn@ciril.qc.ca
www.sadchcn.com
Membre(s) du bureau directeur:
Léna St-Pierre, Directrice générale
lstpierre@ciril.qc.ca

SADC Kamouraska
#100, 901, 5e rue, La Pocatière QC G0R 1Z0
Tél: 418-856-3482; *Téléc:* 418-856-5053
sadck@sadckamouraska.com
www.sadckamouraska.com
www.facebook.com/1403247896598126
Membre(s) du bureau directeur:
Brigitte Pouliot, Directrice générale
bpouliot@sadckamouraska.com

SADC La Mitis
#101, 1534, boul Jacques-Cartier, Mont-Joli QC G5H 2V8
Tél: 418-775-4619; *Téléc:* 418-775-5504
sadc_mitis@ciril.qc.ca
www.sadcmitis.ca
Membre(s) du bureau directeur:
Benoît Thériault, Directeur général
btheriault@sadcmitis.ca

SADC Lac-Saint-Jean Ouest inc.
#203, 915, boul St-Joseph, Roberval QC G8H 2M1
Tél: 418-275-2531; *Téléc:* 418-275-5787
sadc@sadclacstjeanouest.com
www.sadclacstjeanouest.com
www.linkedin.com/company/sadc-lac-st-jean-ouest-inc.
www.facebook.com/152811554739548
twitter.com/SADCLacStJeanO
Membre(s) du bureau directeur:
Serge Desgagné, Directeur général
sdesgagne@sadclsjo.com

SADC Lac-Saint-Jean-Est inc.
#101, 65 rue Saint-Joseph Sud, 1e étage, Alma QC G8B 6V4
Tél: 418-668-3148; *Téléc:* 418-668-6977
www.sadc.lacstjean.qc.ca
Membre(s) du bureau directeur:
Daniel Deschênes, Directeur général
ddeschenes@sadc.lacstjean.qc.ca

SADC Manicouagan
#101, 810, rue Bossé, Baie-Comeau QC G5C 1L6
Tél: 418-295-7232; *Téléc:* 418-295-7233
solution@sadcmanic.ca
sadcmanic.ca
www.facebook.com/185152361597283
Membre(s) du bureau directeur:
Martin Ouellet, Directeur général
mouellet@sadcmanic.ca

SADC Maria-Chapdelaine
#107, 1500 rue des Érables, Dolbeau-Mistassini QC G8L 2W7
Tél: 418-276-0405; *Téléc:* 418-706-6061
sadc@sadcmaria.qc.ca
www.sadcmaria.qc.ca
Membre(s) du bureau directeur:
Jean-François Laliberté, Directeur général
lalibertejf@sadcmaria.qc.ca

SADC Matagami
CP 910, 180, place du Commerce, Matagami QC J0Y 2A0
Tél: 819-739-2155; *Téléc:* 819-739-4271
fcossette@ciril.qc.ca
www.sadcdematagami.qc.ca
Membre(s) du bureau directeur:
François Cossette, Directeur général
fcossette@ciril.qc.ca

SADC Matapédia inc.
#401, 123, rue Desbiens, 4e étage, Amqui QC G5J 3P9
Tél: 418-629-4474; *Téléc:* 418-629-5530
sadcmatapedia@ciril.qc.ca
www.sadcmatapedia.com
www.facebook.com/sadcdelamatapedia
twitter.com/SADCMATAPEDIA
Membre(s) du bureau directeur:
Guy Côté, Directeur général
gcote@ciril.qc.ca

SADC Matawinie inc.
1080, rte 343, Saint-Alphonse-Rodriguez QC J0K 1W0
Tél: 450-883-0717; *Téléc:* 450-883-2006
sadc@matawinie.qc.ca
www.matawinie.qc.ca
Membre(s) du bureau directeur:
Michel Clément, Directeur général
mclement@matawinie.qc.ca

SADC Nicolet-Bécancour inc.
#102, 19205, boul des Acadiens, Bécancour QC G9H 1M5
Tél: 819-233-3315; *Téléc:* 819-233-3338
sadc_nicolet@ciril.qc.ca
www.sadcnicoletbecancour.ca
www.facebook.com/137821253004427
www.youtube.com/user/sadcnicoletbecancour
Membre(s) du bureau directeur:
Steve Brunelle, Directeur général
sbrunelle@sadcnicoletbecancour.ca

SADC Pierre-De Saurel
#220, 26, place Charles-De Montmagny, Sorel-Tracy QC J3P 7E3
Tél: 450-746-5595; *Téléc:* 450-746-1803
sadc@bellnet.ca
www.soreltracyregion.net/sadc
Membre(s) du bureau directeur:
Sylvie Pouliot, Directrice générale
sadcdg@bellnet.ca

SADC Pontiac CFDC
CP 425, 1409, rte 148, Campbell's Bay QC J0X 1K0
Tél: 819-648-2186; *Téléc:* 819-648-2226
info@sadcpontiac.ca
www.sadc.commercepontiac.ca
www.facebook.com/SADCPontiac
Membre(s) du bureau directeur:
Rhonda Perry, Directrice générale
rhonda.perry@sadcpontiac.ca

SADC Portneuf
#201, 120, rue Armand-Bombardier, Donnacona QC G3M 1V3
Tél: 418-286-4422; *Téléc:* 418-285-3281
sadc_portneuf@ciril.qc.ca
www.sadcportneuf.qc.ca
Membre(s) du bureau directeur:
Guy Beaulieu, Directeur général
guybeaulieu@sadcportneuf.qc.ca

SADC région de Coaticook
#140, 38, rue Child, Coaticook QC J1A 2B1
Tél: 819-849-3053; *Téléc:* 819-849-7393
info@sadccoaticook.ca
www.sadccoaticook.ca
www.facebook.com/157109334304594
twitter.com/SADCCoaticook
Membre(s) du bureau directeur:
Joanne Beaudin, Directrice générale
direction@sadccoaticook.ca

SADC région de Mégantic
4336, rue Laval, Lac-Mégantic QC G6B 1B8
Tél: 819-583-5332; *Téléc:* 819-583-5957
sadc_megantic@ciril.qc.ca
www.sadcmegantic.ca
Membre(s) du bureau directeur:
Ginette Isabel, Directrice générale

SADC Vallée de la Batiscan
390, rue Goulet, Saint-Stanislas QC G0X 3E0
Tél: 418-328-4200; *Téléc:* 418-328-4201
sadcvb@cgocable.ca
www.sadcvb.ca
Membre(s) du bureau directeur:
Gilles Mercure, Directeur général
gmercure.sadcvb@cgocable.ca

SADC Vallée-de-l'Or
#1200, 1740, ch Sullivan, Val-d'Or QC J9P 7H1
Tél: 819-874-3676; *Téléc:* 819-874-3670
info@sadcvdo.com
www.sadcvdo.com
Membre(s) du bureau directeur:
Francis Dumais, Directeur général
fdumais@ciril.qc.ca

SADC Vallée-de-la-Gatineau
#210, 100, rue Principale sud, Maniwaki QC J9E 3L4
Tél: 819-449-1551; *Téléc:* 819-449-7431
Ligne sans frais: 866-449-1551
info@sadc-vg.ca
www.sadc-vg.ca
Membre(s) du bureau directeur:
Pierre Monette, Directeur général

Réseau des services de santé en français de l'Est de l'Ontario
#300, 1173, ch Cyrville, Ottawa ON K1J 7S6
Tél: 613-747-7431; *Téléc:* 613-747-2907
Ligne sans frais: 877-528-7565
reseau@rssfe.on.ca
www.rssfe.on.ca
Aperçu: *Dimension:* petite; *Envergure:* provinciale; fondée en 1998 surveillé par Société santé en français
Membre(s) du bureau directeur:
Jacinthe Desaulniers, Directrice générale
jdesaulniers@rssfe.on.ca
Membre(s) du personnel: 11

Réseau des soins palliatifs du Québec
CP 321, Succ. Chef, Granby QC J2G 8E5
Tél: 514-826-9400; *Téléc:* 438-238-1336
info@reseaupalliatif.org
www.aqsp.org
twitter.com/PalliatifQc
Aperçu: *Dimension:* moyenne; *Envergure:* provinciale; fondée en 1990
Mission: Offrir aux intervenants de différentes disciplines de soins et de services, un organisme de référence et d'échange en soins palliatifs; favoriser le perfectionnement par la formation, le

raffinement des soins et la recherche, pour assurer une meilleure qualité de vie aux malades atteints de maladie à issue fatale
Membre(s) du bureau directeur:
Alberte Déry, Présidente, Conseil d'administration
Marlene Side, Vice-présidente, Conseil d'administration
Jessy Savaria, Directeur général
Finances: *Budget de fonctionnement annuel:* Moins de $50,000
Membre: 1,200; *Montant de la cotisation:* 65$; *Critères d'admissibilité:* Intervenants en soins palliatifs; bénévoles
Activités: Conférences
Meetings/Conferences: • 25e congrès annuel du Réseau de Soins Palliatifs du Québec, mai, 2015, Centre des congrès de l'Hôtel Universel à Rivière-du-Loup, Rivière-du-Loup, QC
Description: La réunion accueille des médecins, des professionnels et des bénévoles qui sont intéressés par les soins palliatifs. Le but de la conférence est de partager les expériences et de connaissances entre ceux dans le milieu des soins palliatifs.
Contact Information: Courriel: congresrspq@pluricongres.com

Réseau du mieux-être francophone du Nord de l'Ontario
435, av Notre-Dame, Sudbury ON P3C 5K6
Tél: 705-674-9381; *Téléc:* 705-675-5106
Ligne sans frais: 866-489-7484
reseaudumieuxetre.ca
Aperçu: *Dimension:* petite; *Envergure:* provinciale surveillé par Société santé en français
Membre(s) du bureau directeur:
Diane Quintas, Directrice générale par intérim
dquintas@rmefno.ca

Reseau du Patrimoine Anglophone du Québec *See* Québec Anglophone Heritage Network

Réseau du patrimoine franco-ontarien (RPFO)
#B151, 2445 boul St-Laurent, Ottawa ON K1G 6C3
Tél: 613-729-5769; *Téléc:* 613-729-2209
Ligne sans frais: 866-307-9995
www.rpfo.ca
Nom précédent: Société franco-ontarienne d'histoire et de généalogie
Aperçu: *Dimension:* moyenne; *Envergure:* provinciale; fondée en 1981
Mission: Permettre à ses membres de découvrir le patrimoine franco-ontarien par l'entremise de l'histoire et de la généalogie
Membre(s) du bureau directeur:
Alexandre Ranger, Coordonnateur administratif
administration@sfohg.com
Richard St-Georges, Président
Andréanne Joly, Vice-présidente
Finances: *Fonds:* Ministère de la culture de l'Ontario; La Fondation Trillium
Membre(s) du personnel: 2
Membre: 1,000-4,999; *Critères d'admissibilité:* Professionnels retraités; *Comités:* Exécutif; Administration; Chaînon; Prix Décarie-Marier; Bourses Jean-Roch-Vachon; Restructuration
Activités: Recherches; publications; rencontres; colloques; *Stagiaires:* Oui; *Bibliothèque* rendez-vous

Jean-Nicolet
327 av Dudley, North Bay ON P1B 7A4
Tél: 705-495-2242
jeannicolet@sfohg.com
Membre(s) du bureau directeur:
André Tardif, Président

Joseph-Marie-Couture
CP 445, Longlac ON P0T 2A0
Tél: 807-876-2671
josephmariecouture@sfohg.com
Membre(s) du bureau directeur:
Monique Rousseau, Présidente

La Pionnière du Sud-Ouest (Belle Rivière)
CP 1021, Belle-Rivière ON N0R 1A0
Tél: 519-727-4273
lapionniere@sfohg.com
Membre(s) du bureau directeur:
Claire Grondin, Présidente

La Vieille Branche
CP 1344, Hearst QC P0L 1N0
Tél: 705-372-1496
lavieillebranche@sfohg.com
Membre(s) du bureau directeur:
Claire Payeur, Présidente

Niagara
50, The Boardwalk, Welland ON L3B 6J1
Tél: 905-734-7260
duniagara@sfohg.com
Membre(s) du bureau directeur:
Madeleine Boilard, Présidente

Samuel-de-Champlain
#B-181, 2445, boul. St-Laurent, Ottawa ON K1G 6C3
Tél: 613-729-5769
samueldechamplain@sfohg.com
Membre(s) du bureau directeur:
Benoit Martin, Président

Timmins
#229, 70-C rue Mountjoy Nord, Timmins ON P4N 4V7
Tél: 705-267-2148
timmins@sfohg.com
Membre(s) du bureau directeur:
Lynn Cayen, Président

Réseau du patrimone franco-ontarien (RPFO)
2445, boul. Saint-Laurent, Ottawa ON K1G 6C3
Tél: 613-729-5769
Ligne sans frais: 866-307-9995
www.rpfo.ca
Nom précédent: Regroupement des organismes du patrimoine franco-ontarien
Aperçu: *Dimension:* moyenne; *Envergure:* provinciale; fondée en 1989
Mission: Promouvoir la conservation du patrimoine franco-ontarien
Membre(s) du bureau directeur:
Alexandre Ranger, Coordonnateur administratif
administration@sfohg.com
Finances: *Budget de fonctionnement annuel:* Moins de $50,000
Membre(s) du personnel: 2
Membre: 70 institutionnel, 67 associés, 30 individu; *Montant de la cotisation:* 25$ individuel; 100$ bienfaiteurs; 15$ étudiants
Activités: Offrir des services permanents aux individus et aux groupes intéressés au patrimoine en collaboration avec tous les groupes membres du ROPFO; identification des organismes qui touchent le patrimoine; identification des ressources disponibles pour le financement d'associations, de projets collectifs et individuels; expertise dans l'élaboration d'une demande de subvention; collaboration dans les célébrations de la semaine du patrimoine (février); préparation d'un répertoire de personnes-ressources dans plusieurs domaines; *Evénements de sensibilisation:* Semaine du patrimoine (février)
Prix, Bouses:
• Prix du patrimoine Roger-Bernard (Prix)

Réseau du sport étudiant du Québec (RSEQ)
4545, av Pierre-de Coubertin, Montréal QC H1V 0B2
Tél: 514-252-3300; *Téléc:* 514-254-3292
info@rseq.ca
rseq.ca
www.facebook.com/RSEQ1
twitter.com/RSEQ1
Nom précédent: Fédération québécoise du sport étudiant
Aperçu: *Dimension:* moyenne; *Envergure:* provinciale; Organisme sans but lucratif; fondée en 1988 surveillé par School Sport Canada
Mission: Favoriser les actions éducatives dans le domaine de l'activité physique et sportive que se donne le milieu de l'éducation dans le but de contribuer, et cela dans les trois ordres d'enseignement, au développement intégral des élèves, des étudiantes et des étudiants du Québec.
Membre de: Sport Scolaire Canada; Canadian Colleges Athletic Association
Membre(s) du bureau directeur:
Gustave Roel, Président
Alain Roy, Directeur général
aroy@rseq.ca
Finances: *Budget de fonctionnement annuel:* Plus de $5 Million
Membre(s) du personnel: 28
Membre: *Critères d'admissibilité:* Établissements scolaires, collégiaux et universitaires
Activités: *Stagiaires:* Oui

Réseau du sport étudiant du Québec Abitibi-Témiscamingue (RSEQAT)
QC
Ligne sans frais: 866-626-2047
at.rseq.ca
Également appelé: RSEQ Abitibi-Témiscamingue
Nom précédent: Association régionale du sport étudiant de l'Abitibi-Témiscamingue
Aperçu: *Dimension:* petite; *Envergure:* locale; Organisme sans but lucratif; fondée en 1969
Mission: Regrouper sur le plan du sport étudiant les représentants des différentes institutions d'enseignement de la région de l'Abitibi-Témiscamingue; stimuler l'intérêt et favoriser le développement du sport étudiant dans cette région
Membre de: Réseau du sport étudiant du Québec
Membre(s) du bureau directeur:
Alain Dubois, Président
Alain Groleau, Directeur général
agroleau@ulsat.qc.ca
Finances: *Fonds:* Gouvernement provincial
Membre: 1-99

Réseau du sport étudiant du Québec Cantons-de-l'Est
5182, boul Bourque, Sherbrooke QC J1N 1H4
Tel: 819-864-0792; *Fax:* 819-864-1864
ce.rseq.ca
Also Known As: RSEQ Cantons-de-l'Est
Overview: A small local organization
Member of: Réseau du sport étudiant du Québec
Chief Officer(s):
Paul Deshaies, Président
Olivier Audet, Directeur général
oaudet@ce.rseq.ca

Réseau du sport étudiant du Québec Chaudière-Appalaches (RSEQ-QCA)
762, rue Jacques-Berthiaume, Québec QC G1V 3T1
Tél: 418-657-7678; *Téléc:* 418-657-1367
sportetudiant.qc.ca
Également appelé: RSEQ Chaudière-Appalaches
Nom précédent: Association régionale du sport étudiant de Québec et Chaudière-Appalaches
Aperçu: *Dimension:* petite; *Envergure:* locale
Mission: Organisme à but non-lucratif qui regroupe l'ensemble des institutions d'enseignement des régions de Québec et de Chaudière-Appalaches
Membre de: Réseau du sport étudiant du Québec
Membre(s) du bureau directeur:
Daniel Veilleux, Directeur général
dveilleux@qca.rseq.ca

Réseau du sport étudiant du Québec Côte-Nord
110, rue Comeau, Sept-Iles QC G4R 1J4
Tél: 418-968-3731; *Téléc:* 418-968-4033
cote-nord.rseq.ca
Également appelé: RSEQ Côte-Nord
Nom précédent: Association régionale du sport étudiant de la Côte-Nord
Aperçu: *Dimension:* petite; *Envergure:* locale
Mission: Regrouper sur le plan du sport étudiant, les différentes commissions scolaires, institutions privées et institutions collégiales de la Côte-Nord; stimuler l'intérêt et favoriser le développement du sport étudiant; définir les politiques générales du sport étudiant; promouvoir l'établissement des programmes; coordonner et sanctionner les différentes compétitions du sport étudiant; organiser des stages de perfectionnement; établir les règlements que doivent régir les différentes compétitions du sport étudiant; homologuer les records établis lors des compétitions du sport étudiant
Membre de: Réseau du sport étudiant du Québec
Membre(s) du bureau directeur:
Yvette Cyr, Directrice générale

Réseau du sport étudiant du Québec Est-du-Québec
#J-201, 60 rue de L'Evêché ouest, Rimouski QC G5L 4H6
Tél: 418-723-1880; *Téléc:* 418-722-0457
estduquebec.rseq.ca
www.facebook.com/RSEQ1
Également appelé: RSEQ Est-du-Québec
Nom précédent: Association régionale du sport étudiant de l'Est du Québec
Aperçu: *Dimension:* petite; *Envergure:* locale; fondée en 1989
Mission: Favoriser la réalisation de l'ensemble des actions éducatives par l'activité physique et particulièrement le sport en vue de contribuer au développement intégral des étudiants des niveaux primaire, secondaire et collégial dans la région Est du Québec.
Membre de: Réseau du sport étudiant du Québec
Membre(s) du bureau directeur:
Marc Boudreau, Directeur
marcboud@cegep-rimouski.qc.ca
Finances: *Budget de fonctionnement annuel:* $250,000-$500,000; *Fonds:* Unité régionale de loisir et de sport de Québec
Membre(s) du personnel: 2; 25 bénévole(s)
Membre: 28; *Critères d'admissibilité:* Institutions scolaires

Activités: *Stagiaires:* Oui

Réseau du sport étudiant du Québec Lac Saint-Louis
2900, rue Lake, Dollard-des-Ormeaux QC H9B 2P1
Tél: 514-855-4230; *Téléc:* 514-685-4643
www.arselsl.qc.ca
Également appelé: RSEQ Lac Saint-Louis
Nom précédent: Association régionale du sport étudiant Lac Saint-Louis
Aperçu: *Dimension:* petite; *Envergure:* locale
Mission: Réseau du sport étudiant du Québec Lac Saint-Louis est un organisme sans but lucratif qui regroupe l'ensemble des institutions d'enseignement affiliées de la région Lac Saint-Louis
Membre de: Réseau du sport étudiant du Québec
Membre(s) du bureau directeur:
Karine Mayrand, Directrice générale
kmayrand@lsl.rseq.ca

Réseau du sport étudiant du Québec Laurentides-Lanaudière
401, boul du Domaine, Sainte-Thérèse QC J7E 4S4
Tél: 450-419-8786; *Téléc:* 450-419-8892
ll.rseq.ca
Également appelé: RSEQ Laurentides-Lanaudière
Nom précédent: Association régionale du sport étudiant Laurentides-Lanaudière
Aperçu: *Dimension:* petite; *Envergure:* locale; Organisme sans but lucratif
Mission: Favoriser la réalisation de l'ensemble des actions éducatives par l'activité physique et particulièrement le sport en vue de contribuer au développement intégral des étudiants des niveaux primaire, secondaire et collégial dans la région Laurentides-Lanaudière
Membre de: Réseau du sport étudiant du Québec
Membre(s) du bureau directeur:
Jacinthe Lussier, Directrice générale
jacinthe.lussier@cssmi.qc.ca

Réseau du sport étudiant du Québec Montérégie
c/o École secondaire Gérard-Filion, 1330, boul Curé-Poirier ouest, Longueuil QC J4K 2G8
Tel: 450-463-4055; *Fax:* 450-463-4229
info@monteregie.rseq.ca
monteregie.rseq.ca
www.facebook.com/RseqMonteregie
Also Known As: RSEQ Montérégie
Overview: A small local organization
Member of: Réseau du sport étudiant du Québec
Chief Officer(s):
Sylvie Cornellier, Directrice Générale
scornellier@monteregie.rseq.ca

Réseau du sport étudiant du Québec Montréal
6875, rue Jarry est, Montréal QC H1P 1W7
Tél: 514-645-6923; *Téléc:* 514-354-8632
secretariat@montreal.rseq.com
www.montreal.rseq.com
www.facebook.com/RSEQMontreal
www.youtube.com/user/RSEQMontreal
Également appelé: RSEQ Montréal
Nom précédent: Association régionale du sport étudiant de Montréal
Aperçu: *Dimension:* petite; *Envergure:* locale; Organisme sans but lucratif; fondée en 1989
Mission: Regrouper les associations régionales de sport scolaire, de sport collégial et de sport universitaire de l'Ile de Montréal et les représenter; développer et soutenir des réseaux de compétition régionaux en concertation avec les autres partenaires; offrir des stages de formation et de perfectionnement de cadres en étroite collaboration avec une fédération de sport donnée; participer à la programmation développée par leur instance provinciale; déléguer des officiers auprès des instance provinciales du sport en milieu d'éducation; développer une approche du sport en milieu d'éducation pour chacun des niveaux d'enseignement et développer des programmes en conséquence; promouvoir la pratique de l'activité physique et du sport en milieu d'éducation; coopérer dans le respect des valeurs éducatives avec les organismes intéressés au développement de l'activité physique et du sport
Membre de: Réseau du sport étudiant du Québec
Membre(s) du bureau directeur:
Jacques Desrochers, Directeur général
jdesrochers@montreal.rseq.ca
Finances: *Fonds:* Gouvernement provincial
Membre(s) du personnel: 5
Membre: *Critères d'admissibilite:* Personnel du monde de l'éducation
Activités: Ligues; championnats; stages de perfectionnement pour entraOneurs, officiels et arbitres; *Stagiaires:* Oui

Réseau du sport étudiant du Québec Outaouais
#102, 394, boul Maloney ouest, Gatineau QC K8P 7Z5
www.arseo.qc.ca/ARSEO.php
Également appelé: RSEQ Outaouais
Aperçu: *Dimension:* petite; *Envergure:* locale
Membre de: Réseau du sport étudiant du Québec
Membre(s) du bureau directeur:
Hélène Boucher, Directrice générale
helene.boucher@arseo.qc.ca

Réseau du sport étudiant du Québec Saguenay-Lac St-Jean
CEGEP de Chicoutimi, 534, rue Jacques Cartier Est, Chicoutimi QC G7H 1Z6
Tél: 418-543-3532; *Téléc:* 418-693-0503
saglac.rseq.ca
Également appelé: RSEQ Saguenay-Lac St-Jean
Nom précédent: Association régionale du sport étudiant du Saguenay-Lac St-Jean
Aperçu: *Dimension:* petite; *Envergure:* locale; Organisme sans but lucratif; fondée en 1974
Mission: Favoriser la réalisation de l'ensemble des actions éducatives dans le domaine de l'activité physique et particulièrement du sport en vue de contribuer au développement intégral des élèves et étudiants de niveaux primaire, secondaire, collégial et universitaire dans la région du Saguenay-Lac St-Jean
Membre de: Réseau du sport étudiant du Québec
Membre(s) du bureau directeur:
Stéphanie Tremblay, Directrice
stremblay@saglac.rseq.ca
Finances: *Fonds:* Gouvernement provincial
Membre: 16; *Critères d'admissibilite:* Écoles privées; commissions scolaires; CÉGEPS; universités
Activités: Manifestations sportives régionales et provinciales; perfectionnement; *Stagiaires:* Oui; *Service de conférenciers:* Oui

Réseau du sport étudiant du Québec, secteur Mauricie
260, rue Dessureault, Trois-Rivières QC G8T 9T9
Tél: 819-693-5805; *Téléc:* 819-693-1189
mauricie.rseq.ca
Également appelé: RSEQ Mauricie
Nom précédent: Association régionale du sport étudiant de la Mauricie
Aperçu: *Dimension:* petite; *Envergure:* locale
Mission: Réseau du sport étudiant du Québec, secteur Mauricie, est un organisme sans but lucratif qui regroupe les institutions d'enseignement situées sur le territoire de la Mauricie et sur la rive sud du fleuve Saint-Laurent, jusqu'à l'autoroute 20
Membre de: Réseau du sport étudiant du Québec
Membre(s) du bureau directeur:
Micheline Guillemette, Directrice générale

Réseau écologique du Manitoba inc. *See* Manitoba Eco-Network Inc.

Réseau Enfants Retour Canada *Voir* Enfant-Retour Québec

Réseau environnement
#220, 911, rue Jean Talon est, Montréal QC H2R 1V5
Tél: 514-270-7110; *Téléc:* 514-270-7154
info@reseau-environnement.com
www.reseau-environnement.com
Nom précédent: Association québécoise des techniques de l'environnement
Aperçu: *Dimension:* moyenne; *Envergure:* provinciale; Organisme sans but lucratif; fondée en 1959
Mission: Regrouper des entreprises spécialisées dans la gestion des déchets commerciaux, industriels et des services municipaux reliés à l'environnement; Assurer l'avancement des technologies et de la science, la promotion des expertises et le soutien des activités en environnement
Membre(s) du bureau directeur:
Stéphanie Myre, Présidente-directrice générale
smyre@reseau-environnement.com
Mario Laplante, Directeur général adjointé
mlaplante@reseau-environnement.com
Josianne Lafantaisie, Coordonnatrice principale, Communications et relations publiques
jlafantaisie@reseau-environnement.com
Romy Regis, Coordonnatrice, Événements
rregis@reseau-environnement.com
Lyne Dubois, Merlicom, 514-935-3830 Ext. 227
ldubois@merlicom.com
Mihaela Sandor, Comptable, 514-935-3830 Ext. 237
msandor@reseau-environnement.com
Membre: 364 corpratif

Réseau environnemental du Nouveau-Brunswick *See* New Brunswick Environmental Network

Réseau FADOQ / Québec Federation of Senior Citizens
4545, av Pierre-de Coubertin, Montréal QC H1V 0B2
Tél: 514-252-3017; *Téléc:* 514-252-3154
Ligne sans frais: 800-828-3344
info@fadoq.ca
www.fadoq.ca
www.facebook.com/reseaufadoq
www.youtube.com/user/ReseauFADOQ
Également appelé: FADOQ
Nom précédent: Fédération de l'âge d'or du Québec
Aperçu: *Dimension:* grande; *Envergure:* provinciale; Organisme sans but lucratif; fondée en 1970
Mission: Promouvoir un concept positif du vieillissement; encourager le maintien et l'amélioration de la qualité de vie et de l'autonomie des aînés; initier et soutenir l'organisation d'activités physiques et de loisirs; redonner aux aînés une nouvelle fierté en les revalorisant à leurs propres yeux comme à ceux de la société; remettre entre les mains des aînés la gestion de leurs affaires
Membre de: Fédération internationale des associations des personnes âgées; Association internationale francophone des aînés; Fédération internationale du vieillissement
Affliation(s): Association québécoise de gérontologie; Conseil canadien de développement social; Réseau canadien des aînés (One Voice); l'Assemblée des aîné(e)s francophones du Canada
Membre(s) du bureau directeur:
Cécile Plourde, Présidente
Danis Prud'homme, Directeur Générale
Finances: *Budget de fonctionnement annuel:* $500,000-$1.5 Million
Membre(s) du personnel: 19; 1500 bénévole(s)
Membre: 265,000 individus; 835 clubs; 16 regroupements régionaux; *Montant de la cotisation:* 30$; *Critères d'admissibilite:* Etre âgé de 50 ans et plus
Activités: *Evénements de sensibilisation:* Jeux provinciaux des aînés, sept.; Ainé avisé; Programme qualité logi-être mentorat; *Stagiaires:* Oui; *Service de conférenciers:* Oui; *Listes de destinataires:* Oui; *Bibliothèque:* Bibliotheque

Région Abitibi-Témiscamingue
33B, rue Gable Ouest, SS#11, Rouyn-Noranda QC J9X 2R3
Tél: 819-768-2142; *Téléc:* 819-768-2144
fadoqat@tlb.sympatico.ca
www.fadoqat.ca
Membre(s) du bureau directeur:
Monic Roy, Directrice régionale

Région Bas St-Laurent
474, rue des Étudiants, Pohénégamook QC G0L 1J0
Tél: 418-893-2111; *Téléc:* 418-893-7878
fadoqbsl@bellnet.ca
www.fadoq.ca
Membre de: Tables de concertation des aînés
Membre(s) du bureau directeur:
Guy Genest, Président

Région Centre-du-Québec
#110, 59, rue Monfette, Victoriaville QC G6P 1J8
Tél: 819-752-7876; *Téléc:* 819-752-7630
Ligne sans frais: 800-828-3344
fadoq.info@cdcbf.qc.ca
www.fadoq-qdc.ca
Membre(s) du bureau directeur:
Annie Belcourt, Directrice générale

Région Côte-Nord
#107, 859, rue Bossé, Baie-Comeau QC G5C 3P8
Tél: 418-589-7870; *Téléc:* 418-589-7871
Ligne sans frais: 800-828-3344
fadoqcn@globetrotter.net
www.fadoqcote-nord.ca
Membre(s) du bureau directeur:
Marie-Bois Turcotte, Présidente

Région Estrie
#102, 288, rue Marquette, Sherbrooke QC J1H 1M2
Tél: 819-566-7748; *Téléc:* 819-566-7263
Ligne sans frais: 800-828-3344

infos@fadoqestrie.ca
www.fadoqestrie.ca
Membre(s) du bureau directeur:
Martine Grégoire, Directrice générale
Région Gaspésie Iles-de-la-Madeleine
189, rue Jacques-Cartier, Gaspé QC G4X 2P8
Tél: 418-368-4715; *Téléc:* 418-368-4310
info@fadoq.ca
www.fadoqgim.ca
Membre(s) du bureau directeur:
François Lapierre, Président
Région Ile de Montréal
#215, 7378, rue Lajeunesse, Montréal QC H2R 2H8
Tél: 514-271-1411; *Téléc:* 514-271-1640
info@fadoqmtl.org
www.montreal.fadoq.ca
www.facebook.com/fadoqmontreal
twitter.com/FadoqMontreal
Membre(s) du bureau directeur:
Ghislain Bilodeau, Président
Région Lanaudière
626, boul Manseau, Joliette QC J6E 3H6
Tél: 450-759-7422; *Téléc:* 450-759-8279
info@fadoqlanaudiere.ca
www.fadoqlanaudiere.org
Membre(s) du bureau directeur:
Danielle Perreault, Directrice général
Région Laurentides
#201, 499, rue Charbonneau, Mont-Tremblant QC J8E 3H4
Tél: 819-429-5858; *Téléc:* 819-429-6850
Ligne sans frais: 800-828-3344
info@fadoqlaurentides.org
www.fadoqlaurentides.org
Membre(s) du bureau directeur:
Micheline Chalifour, Présidente
Région Laval
#218, 1450, boul Pie X, Laval QC H7V 3C1
Tél: 450-686-2339; *Téléc:* 450-686-4845
Ligne sans frais: 800-828-3344
info@fadoqlaval.com
www.fadoqlaval.com
Membre(s) du bureau directeur:
Andrée Vallée, Directrice générale
Région Mauricie
1325, rue Brébeuf, Trois-Rivières QC G8Z 1Z9
Tél: 819-374-5774; *Téléc:* 819-374-8850
Ligne sans frais: 800-828-3344
www.fadoq-mauricie.com
Membre(s) du bureau directeur:
Ginette Lapointe, Directrice générale
Région Outaouais
CP 12009, Gatineau QC J8T 0C3
Tél: 819-777-5774; *Téléc:* 819-205-0787
Ligne sans frais: 800-828-3344
admin@fadoqoutaouais.qc.ca
www.fadoqoutaouais.qc.ca
Membre(s) du bureau directeur:
Lise Desaulniers, Présidente
Région Richelieu-Yamaska
2775, av Bourdage Nord, Saint-Hyacinthe QC J2S 5S3
Tél: 450-774-8111; *Téléc:* 450-774-6161
Ligne sans frais: 800-828-3344
info@fadoqry.ca
www.fadoqry.ca
Membre(s) du bureau directeur:
Claude Leblanc, Directeur général
Région Rive-Sud-Suroît
6A, ch du Grand-Bernier Sud, Saint-Jean-sur-Richelieu QC J3B 4P8
Tél: 450-347-0910; *Téléc:* 450-347-6385
Ligne sans frais: 800-828-3344
fadoq@fadoqrrss.org
www.fadoqrrss.org
Membre(s) du bureau directeur:
Denise Charest, Directrice générale
denise.charest@fadoqrrss.org
Région Saguenay - Lac-St-Jean - Ungava
414, rue Collard ouest, Alma QC G8B 1N2
Tél: 418-668-4795; *Téléc:* 418-668-0265
Ligne sans frais: 800-828-3344
reception@fadoqsaglac.com
www.fadoqsaglac.com
Membre(s) du bureau directeur:
Patrice St-Pierre, Directeur général
direction@fadoqsaglac.com
Régions de Québec et Chaudière-Appalaches
CP 8832, Succ. Sainte-Foy, Sainte-Foy QC G1V 3V9
Tél: 418-650-3552; *Téléc:* 418-650-1659
Ligne sans frais: 800-828-3344
info@fadoq-quebec.qc.ca
www.fadoq-quebec.qc.ca
Membre(s) du bureau directeur:
Gérald Lépine, Directeur général
glepine@fadoq-quebec.qc.ca

Réseau Femmes Québec (RFQ)
#134, 911, rue Jean-Talon est, Montréal QC H2R 1V5
Tél: 514-484-2375
reseau.femmes.quebec@gmail.com
www.reseau-femmes-quebec.qc.ca
Aperçu: *Dimension:* moyenne; *Envergure:* provinciale
Affliation(s): Réseau Hommes Québec
Membre(s) du bureau directeur:
Ruth Vachon, Présidente

Réseau franco-santé du Sud de l'Ontario (RFSSO)
CP 90057, 1000, rue Golf Links, Anacaster ON L9K 0B4
Tél: 416-413-1717
Ligne sans frais: 888-549-5775
info@francosantesud.ca
francosantesud.ca
Aperçu: *Dimension:* petite; *Envergure:* provinciale; fondée en 2004 surveillé par Société santé en français
Membre(s) du bureau directeur:
Julie Lantaigne, Directrice générale
jlantaigne@francosantesud.ca

Réseau HEC Montréal
3000, ch de la Côte Ste-Catherine, Montréal QC H3T 2A7
Tél: 514-340-6025; *Téléc:* 514-340-6508
Ligne sans frais: 888-861-222
reseauhec@hec.ca
www.hec.ca/diplome/reseau/index.html
www.facebook.com/HECMontreal
twitter.com/HEC_Montreal
www.youtube.com/HECMontreal;
www.flickr.com/photos/hecmontreal
Également appelé: Association des diplômés HEC Montréal
Nom précédent: Association des diplômés de l'École des hautes Études commerciales
Aperçu: *Dimension:* grande; *Envergure:* locale; Organisme sans but lucratif; fondée en 1921
Mission: Contribuer au développement socio professionnel de ses membres; établir des relations amicales; promouvoir les intérêts de l'école des HEC; relier les promotions et utiliser ces rapports au profit du commerce, de l'industrie et de la finance; étendre les connaissances des membres sur les recherches du commerce et de la finance dans les divers programmes
Membre(s) du bureau directeur:
Michel Lemay, Directeur, Service aux diplômés, 514-340-6712
michel.lemay@hec.ca
Finances: *Budget de fonctionnement annuel:* $1.5 Million-$3 Million
Membre(s) du personnel: 5; 150 bénévole(s)
Membre: 51 000+ diplômés; *Montant de la cotisation:* 85$ diplômés réguliers; *Critères d'admissibilite:* Diplômés de l'École des hautes études commerciales de Montréal; *Comités:* AGA; Entre-Vues du Réseau HEC; Ce qu'il me reste à vous dire; Rendez-vous annuel des diplômés; Prix Relève d'Excellence; Activités du Comité Jeunes (Rencontres d'un leader, 6@8...); Retrouvailles; Section de l'Outaouais; Section de Québec; Section de Toronto; Section de New York; International; HEC Conjuguée au féminin
Activités: Assemblée générale; tournoi de golf; Gala du commerce
Prix, Bouses:
• Prix Relève d'Excellence du Réseau HEC Montréal (Prix) Reconnaît les réalisations exceptionnelles des diplômés HEC Montréal de 35 ans ou moins

Réseau Hommes Québec (RHQ)
#134, 911, rue Jean-Talon est, Montréal QC H2R 1V5
Tél: 514-276-4545
Ligne sans frais: 877-908-4545
Autres numéros: communications@rhquebec.org
info@rhquebec.org
www.rhquebec.org
www.facebook.com/pages/Réseau-Hommes-Québec-RHQ/114381705296554
Aperçu: *Dimension:* grande; *Envergure:* provinciale; fondée en 1992
Mission: Organisme sans but lucratif; a pour mission d'entretenir un réseau de groupes autogérés d'écoute, de parole & d'entraide aux hommes
Affliation(s): Réseau Hommes Belgique; Réseau Hommes France; Réseau Hommes Romandie; Réseau Femmes Québec
Membre(s) du bureau directeur:
Guy Corneau, Fondateur
François Guindon, Directeur général
Publications:
• Vivre
Type: Magazine

Réseau indépendant des diffuseurs d'événements artistiques unis (RIDEAU)
1550, boul Saint-Joseph est, Montréal QC H2J 1M7
Tél: 514-598-8024; *Téléc:* 514-598-8353
admin@rideau-inc.qc.ca
www.rideau-inc.qc.ca
Aperçu: *Dimension:* moyenne; *Envergure:* provinciale; fondée en 1978
Mission: Favoriser la diffusion des arts de la scène
Membre de: Chambre de Commerce du Québec
Membre(s) du bureau directeur:
Colette Brouillé, Directrice générale
direction@rideau-inc.qc.ca
Marie-Christine Coulombe, Directrice générale adjointe
mccoulombe@rideau-inc.qc.ca
Christiane Verroeulst, Contrôleure
cverroeulst@rideau-inc.qc.ca
Marlène Morin, Responsable, Communication et marketing
mmorin@rideau-inc.qc.ca
Marie-Pier Pilote, Responsable, Services aux membres et projets
projets@rideau-inc.qc.ca
Membre: 145; *Montant de la cotisation:* $150-$900; *Critères d'admissibilite:* Diffuseurs de spectacles

Réseau Info Style de Vie *See* Lifestyle Information Network

Réseau international pour la diversité culturelle *See* International Network for Cultural Diversity

Réseau juridique canadien VIH/sida *See* Canadian HIV/AIDS Legal Network

Réseau national d'action EM/FM encéphalomyélite myalgique/fibromyalgie *See* National ME/FM Action Network

Réseau ontarien des organismes pour le développement de l'employabilité *See* Ontario Network of Employment Skills Training Projects

Réseau pour la résolution de conflits Canada *See* Conflict Resolution Network Canada

Réseau pour le développement de l'alphabétisme et des compétences (RESDAC)
#205, 235 ch Montréal, Ottawa ON K1L 6C7
Tél: 613-749-5333; *Téléc:* 613-749-2252
Ligne sans frais: 888-906-5666
info@resdac.net
www.resdac.net
www.facebook.com/128384640568102
Aperçu: *Dimension:* petite; *Envergure:* nationale; fondée en 1991
Mission: Promouvoir l'alphabétisation en français au Canada; assurer une concertation des intervenantes en alphabétisation en français au Canada.
Membre(s) du bureau directeur:
Normand Lévesque, Directeur général
directiongenerale@resdac.net
Isabelle Salesse, Présidente
presidence@resdac.net
Donald Desroches, Vice-président
Membre(s) du personnel: 6
Membre: 13
Activités: *Stagiaires:* Oui; *Service de conférenciers:* Oui; *Bibliothèque* Bibliothèque publique rendez-vous

Réseau québécois de l'asthme et de la MPOC (RQAM)
Institut universitaire de cardiologie et de pneumologie de Québec, #U-3771, 2723, ch Sainte-Foy, Québec QC G1V 4G5
Tél: 418-650-9500; *Téléc:* 418-650-9391
Ligne sans frais: 877-441-5072

info@rqam.ca
qww.rqam.ca
Aperçu: *Dimension:* petite; *Envergure:* provinciale
Mission: De fournir un soutien aux professionnels travaillant dans l'asthme dans le secteur de la santé et de leurs patients
Membre(s) du bureau directeur:
Jean Bourbeau, Président
Membre: *Montant de la cotisation:* 30$; *Comités:* Scientifique

Réseau québécois des groupes écologistes (RQGE)
454, av Laurier Est, Montréal QC H2J 1E7
Tél: 514-587-8194
info@rqge.qc.ca
www.rqge.qc.ca
www.facebook.com/Reseau.quebecois.des.groupes.ecologistes
twitter.com/InfoRQGE
www.youtube.com/user/RQgroupesecologistes
Aperçu: *Dimension:* petite; *Envergure:* provinciale; Organisme sans but lucratif; fondée en 1982 surveillé par Canadian Environmental Network
Mission: Pour recueillir de services et d'information pour les groupes écologiques du Québec; aider les groupes à communiquer entre eux
Membre(s) du bureau directeur:
Stéphane Gingras, Président
presidence@rqge.qc.ca
Bruno Massé, Coordonnateur général
coordo@rqge.qc.ca
Membre(s) du personnel: 3
Membre: 80
Activités: *Service de conférenciers:* Oui

Réseau québécois pour contrer les abus envers les aînés (RQCAA)
7484, rue St-Denis, Montréal QC H2R 2E4
Tél: 514-270-2777; *Téléc:* 514-270-2787
Aperçu: *Dimension:* moyenne; *Envergure:* provinciale; fondée en 2003
Mission: Rassembler les personnes et les regroupements de personnes qui se préoccupent de la prévention, du dépistage ou de l'intervention en matière d'abus envers les aînés
Membre de: Canadian Network for the Prevention of Elder Abuse
Membre: 459; *Montant de la cotisation:* $10
Activités: *Evénements de sensibilisation:* World Elder Abuse Awareness Day, June 15

Réseau régional de l'industrie biologique du Canada atlantique *See* Atlantic Canadian Organic Regional Network

Réseau Santé - Nouvelle-Écosse
#227, 1589, rue Walnut, Halifax NS B3H 3S1
Tél: 902-222-5871
reseau@reseausantene.ca
www.reseausantene.ca
Aperçu: *Dimension:* petite; *Envergure:* provinciale surveillé par Société santé en français
Membre(s) du bureau directeur:
Jeanne-Françoise Caillaud, Directrice générale

Réseau santé albertain
8627, rue Marie-Anne-Gaboury, Edmonton AB T6C 4S8
Tél: 780-466-9816
info@reseausantealbertain.ca
www.reseausantealbertain.ca
www.facebook.com/162905357095396
twitter.com/inforsab
www.youtube.com/user/reseausantealbertain
Aperçu: *Dimension:* petite; *Envergure:* provinciale surveillé par Société santé en français
Membre(s) du bureau directeur:
Luc Therrien, Directeur général
luc.therrien@reseausantealbertain.ca

Réseau Santé en français de la Saskatchewan (RSFS)
#103, 308, 4 av Nord, Saskatoon SK S7K 2L7
Tél: 306-653-7445; *Téléc:* 306-664-6447
rsfs@shaw.ca
www.rsfs.ca
Aperçu: *Dimension:* petite; *Envergure:* provinciale; fondée en 2003 surveillé par Société santé en français
Membre(s) du bureau directeur:
Roger Gauthier, Directeur
rsfs@shaw.ca

Réseau Santé en français I.-P.-É
CP 58, 48, ch Mill, Wellington PE C0B 2E0
Tél: 902-854-7440; *Téléc:* 902-854-7255
info@santeipe.ca
www.santeipe.ca
www.facebook.com/RSFIPE
Aperçu: *Dimension:* petite; *Envergure:* provinciale surveillé par Société santé en français
Membre(s) du bureau directeur:
Élise Arsenault, Directrice
elisearsenault@gov.pe.ca
Membre: 19

Réseau santé en français Terre-Neuve-et-Labrador
Centre scolaire et communautaire des Grads-Vants, #233, 65 ch Ridge, St. John's NL A1B 4P5
Tél: 709-575-2862; *Téléc:* 709-722-9904
reseauSante@fftnl.ca
www.francotnl.ca
Aperçu: *Dimension:* petite; *Envergure:* provinciale surveillé par Société santé en français
Membre(s) du bureau directeur:
Jean-Marc Bélanger, Coordonnateur

Réseau Tara Canada (Québec)
CP 156, Succ. Ahuntsic, Montréal QC H3L 3N7
Ligne sans frais: 888-886-8272
medias@taraquebec.org
www.taraquebec.org
Également appelé: Réseau Tara; Tara Québec
Aperçu: *Dimension:* petite; *Envergure:* locale; Organisme sans but lucratif; fondée en 1985
Mission: Répandre le message de l'Enseignant universel Maitreya, le Christ, dirigeant de la Hiérarchie spirituelle de la planète
Membre de: Tara Canada
Finances: *Budget de fonctionnement annuel:* Moins de $50,000
6 bénévole(s)
Membre: 400
Activités: Meditation; Conférence; *Service de conférenciers:* Oui; *Bibliothèque* rendez-vous

Réseau TNO Santé en français
CP 1325, 5016, 48 rue, Yelloknife NT X1A 2N9
Tél: 867-920-2919; *Téléc:* 867-873-2158
santetno@franco-nord.com
reseautnosante.ca
Aperçu: *Dimension:* petite; *Envergure:* provinciale surveillé par Société santé en français
Membre(s) du bureau directeur:
Jean de Dieu Tuyishime, Coordonnateur

Le réseau Toucher Thérapeutique de l'Atlantique *See* Atlantic Therapeutic Touch Network

Residential Construction Council of Ontario (RESCON)
#13, 25 North Rivermede Rd., Vaughan ON L4K 5V4
Tel: 905-760-7777; *Fax:* 905-760-7718
Toll-Free: 866-531-1608
www.rescon.ws
Overview: A small local organization
Mission: To represent the Ontario Residential Contractors Construction Association during labour reltations negotiations, as well as in matters regarding health & safety, WSIB, training & education
Membership: *Committees:* Technical; Marketing & Membership; Training & Education; Health & Safety

Resilient Flooring Contractors Association of Ontario (RFCAO)
70 Leek Cres., Richmond Hill ON L4B 1H1
Tel: 416-499-4000; *Fax:* 416-499-8752
info@resilientflooring.ca
www.resilientflooring.ca
Overview: A medium-sized provincial organization founded in 1954
Mission: Engaged in the supply & installation of flooring materials, including tiles, marble, carpet in the residential & institutional, commercial & industrial sectors of the construction industry
Chief Officer(s):
Eric Babiak, President
ebabiak@live.ca
Armando Pompeo, Secretary-Treasurer
armando@calligarotile.com
Finances: *Annual Operating Budget:* Less than $50,000
10 volunteer(s)
Membership: 44

Réso Santé Colombie Britannique (RSCB)
#201, 2929, rue Commercial, Vancouver BC V5N 4C8
Tél: 604-629-1000
www.resosante.ca
Aperçu: *Dimension:* petite; *Envergure:* provinciale; fondée en 2003 surveillé par Société santé en français
Membre(s) du bureau directeur:
Louis Giguère, Directeur générale

RESOLVE: Research & Education for Solutions to Violence & Abuse
#108, Isbister Building, University of Manitoba, Winnipeg MB R3T 2N2
Tel: 204-474-8965; *Fax:* 204-474-7686
resolve@umanitoba.ca
www.umanitoba.ca/resolve
Overview: A small provincial organization
Chief Officer(s):
Jane Ursel, O.M., Contact

Resorts Ontario
29 Albert St. North, Orillia ON L3V 5J9
Tel: 705-325-9115; *Fax:* 705-325-7999
Toll-Free: 800-363-7227
escapes@resorts-ontario.com
ww.resortsofontario.com
www.facebook.com/ResortsofOntario
twitter.com/ResortsOntario
www.youtube.com/user/ResortsofOntario
Also Known As: Association of Tourist Resorts of Ontario
Overview: A medium-sized provincial organization founded in 1942
Mission: To serve & promote the collective interests of resorts, lodges & inns of Ontario
Chief Officer(s):
Grace Sammut, Executive Director
grace@resortsofontario.com
Finances: *Funding Sources:* Membership fees
Membership: 100+

Resource and Intervention Center for Men Sexually Abused during their Childhood *Voir* Centre de ressources et d'intervention pour hommes abusés sexuellement dans leur enfance

Resource Assistance for Youth (RAY)
125 Sherbrooke St., Winnipeg MB R3C 2B5
Tel: 204-783-5617; *Fax:* 204-775-4988
info@rayinc.ca
www.rayinc.ca
www.linkedin.com/company/3040355
www.facebook.com/raywinnipeg
twitter.com/raywinnipeg
www.youtube.com/user/RaYWinnipeg
Previous Name: Operation Go Home - Winnipeg Office
Overview: A small local organization overseen by Operation Come Home
Mission: To improve the lives of homeless youth & help them reintegrate into society.
Chief Officer(s):
Kelly Holmes, Executive Director
kelly@rayinc.ca
Staff Member(s): 17

Resource Centre on Non-Violence *Voir* Centre des ressources sur la non-violence inc

Resource Efficient Agricultural Production (REAP Canada)
PO Box 125, Stn. Centennial Centre CCB13, #21, 111 Lakeshore Rd., Sainte-Anne-de-Bellevue QC H9X 3V9
Tel: 514-398-7743; *Fax:* 514-398-7972
info@reap-canada.com
www.reap-canada.com
Also Known As: Sustainable Farming
Overview: A medium-sized national charitable organization founded in 1988
Mission: To improve farm profits & productivity while minimizing adverse health & environmental effects
Affliation(s): Canadian Organic Growers; Ecological Farmers Association of Ontario
Chief Officer(s):
Roger Samson, Executive Director
Staff Member(s): 5
Membership: *Fees:* $25 individual; $100 organization

Activities: Sustainable farming research into biomass energy on farm sustainable agriculture research for carbon dioxide reduction; *Speaker Service:* Yes; *Library* by appointment

Resource Industry Suppliers Association (RISA)
#104, 14020 - 128th Ave., Edmonton AB T5L 4M8
Tel: 780-489-5900; *Fax:* 780-489-6262
risa@resourcesuppliers.com
www.resourcesuppliers.com
www.linkedin.com/company/2369860
www.facebook.com/RISA.012
twitter.com/risa_allan
Overview: A medium-sized national organization
Mission: To source project information & contracts from members of the energy, mining, forest & bio-products industries
Chief Officer(s):
Allan Bartolcic, Executive Director
allan@resourcesuppliers.com

Respiratory Therapists Society of Nova Scotia (RTSNS)
#700, 6009 Quinpool Rd., Halifax NS B3K 5J7
Tel: 902-425-2445; *Fax:* 902-425-2441
www.rtsns.com
Overview: A small provincial organization founded in 1964
Mission: Dedicated to excellence in cardiorespiratory care.
Chief Officer(s):
Shannon McDonald, Registrar
registrar@nscrt.com
Membership: *Fees:* $150 Registered Member; Students, Corporate, Associate, Honourar and Inactive member fees are under review.

Respiratory Therapy Society of Ontario (RTSO) / Société de la thérapie respiratoire de l'Ontario
440 - 2 Country Crt Blvd., Brampton ON L6W 4V1
Tel: 647-729-2717; *Fax:* 647-729-2715
Toll-Free: 855-297-3089
office@rtso.ca
www.rtso.ca
Overview: A medium-sized provincial organization founded in 1972 overseen by Canadian Society of Respiratory Therapists
Mission: To represent & advance the professional interests of Ontario's respiratory therapists; To develop & maintain standards of practice for respiratory therapy
Chief Officer(s):
David McKay, President
Mike Keim, Treasurer
Membership: *Fees:* $105 practicing members; $40 associate members; $20 students; *Member Profile:* Respiratory therapists in Ontario
Activities: Engaging in advocacy activities; Promoting respiratory therapy in Ontario; Supporting educational opportunities; Providing public education on respiratory health; Supporting research
Publications:
• Airwaves
Type: Newsletter; *Price:* Free with RTSO membership
Profile: Society reports, events, & information plus articles

Responsible Dog Owners of Canada (RDOC)
9 Liette Crt., RR1, Kemptville ON K0G 1J0
Tel: 613-206-6885
inquiries@responsibledogowners.ca
www.responsibledogowners.ca
Overview: A medium-sized national organization founded in 1999
Mission: To promote responsible dog ownership and public safety through education and support, cultivate respect for the rights and privileges of all members of society, both dog-owning and non-dog owning, encourage and foster recognition of the contribution that canines make in society through companionship, service/assistance and therapy and assemble a strong network of responsible dog owners to ensure the restoration and preservation of a dog-friendly society.
Chief Officer(s):
Candice O'Connell, Chair
coconnell@responsibledogowners.ca
Membership: *Fees:* $20 single/family; $10 student/senior; $35 non-profit; $50 corporate

Responsible Gambling Council (Ontario) (RGC(O)) / Le Conseil ontarien pour le jeu responsable
#205, 411 Richmond St. East, Toronto ON M5A 3S5
Tel: 416-499-9800; *Fax:* 416-499-8260
www.responsiblegambling.org
Previous Name: Canadian Foundation on Compulsive Gambling (Ontario)
Overview: A small provincial charitable organization founded in 1983
Mission: To increase awareness of compulsive gambling among families, community & service club leaders & supports research into the causes & treatment.
Affliation(s): Responsible Gambling Council of Canada
Chief Officer(s):
Robin Boychuk, Chair
Jon E. Kelly, Executive Director, 416-499-9800 Ext. 224
jonk@rgco.org
Finances: *Funding Sources:* Ministry of Health; Ontario Lottery & Gaming Corporation
Staff Member(s): 35
Membership: *Committees:* Governance & Nominating; Strategic Directions; Audit
Activities: *Speaker Service:* Yes; *Library* Open to public

Responsible Investment Association (RIA)
#300, 215 Spadina Ave., Toronto ON M5T 2C7
Tel: 416-461-6042
staff@riacanada.ca
riacanada.ca
www.linkedin.com/company/responsible-investment-association
www.facebook.com/ResponsibleInvestmentAssociation
twitter.com/riacanada
Previous Name: Social Investment Organization
Overview: A medium-sized national organization founded in 1989
Mission: To take a leadership role in coordinating the responsible investing (RI) agenda in Canada; to raise public awareness of RI in Canada; to reach out to other groups interested in RI; to provide information on RI to members & the public
Chief Officer(s):
Deb Abbey, Chief Executive Officer
deb@riacanada.ca
Wendy Mitchell, Financial Coordinator
wendy@riacanada.ca
Dustyn Lanz, Director, Research & Communications
dustyn@riacanada.ca
Staff Member(s): 4
Membership: 100-499; *Fees:* $15,000 sustaining; $5,500 associate; $1,000 pension fund; $350 financial advisor & consultant; $300 organizational; *Member Profile:* Asset management companies; investment fund companies; financial advisors; investors
Activities: *Internships:* Yes; *Speaker Service:* Yes; *Rents Mailing List:* Yes
Meetings/Conferences: • Responsible Investment Association 2015 Conference, May, 2015, Banff Centre, Banff, AB
Scope: National

Ressources Saint-Jean-Vianney
CP 21036, Succ. Jacques Cartier, Longueuil QC J4J 5J4
Tél: 450-646-8690
direction@rsjv.org
rsjv.org
Aperçu: *Dimension:* petite; *Envergure:* locale
Mission: Pour aider les personnes défavorisées en leur offrant des activités sociales ainsi que des activités éducatives
Membre(s) du bureau directeur:
Benjamin Sirois-Caouette, Directeur
Annelies Van Laer, Présidente, Conseil d'administration
Activités: Magasin-partage; Clinique d'impôts; Activités familiales; Activités pour les enfants

Restaurants Canada
1155 Queen St. West, Toronto ON M6J 1J4
Tel: 416-923-8416; *Fax:* 416-923-1450
Toll-Free: 800-387-5649
info@restaurantscanada.org
www.restaurantscanada.org
www.facebook.com/RestaurantsCanada?sk=wall
twitter.com/RestaurantsCA
Previous Name: Canadian Restaurant & Foodservices Association
Overview: A large national organization founded in 1944
Mission: To create a favourable business environment & deliver tangible value to members in all sectors of Canada's foodservice industry
Chief Officer(s):
Garth Whyte, President & Chief Executive Officer
gwhite@cfra.ca
Joyce Reynolds, Executive Vice-President, Government Affairs
jreynolds@cfra.ca
Jill Holroyd, Senior Vice-President, Marketing & Communications
jholroyd@cfra.ca
Stephanie Jones, Vice-President, Membership
sjones@cfra.ca
Tamara Kapel, Vice-President, Finance
tkapel@cfra.ca
Justin Taylor, Vice-President, Labour & Supply
jtaylor@cfra.ca
Natalie Angeja, Coordinator, Member Services, 416-649-4245 Ext. 4245
membership@crfa.ca
Prasanthi Vasanthakumar, Specialist, Communications, 416-649-4254 Ext. 4254
pvasanthakumar@crfa.ca
Finances: *Funding Sources:* Membership dues; Trade shows; Sale of materials
Membership: 30,000; *Fees:* Staggered to correspond with the sales volume; *Member Profile:* Foodservice or restaurant establishment or supplier to industry
Activities: Engaging in government affairs; *Library:* Resource Centre; by appointment
Meetings/Conferences: • Restaurants Canada Show 2015, March, 2015, Direct Energy Centre, Toronto, ON
Scope: National
Attendance: 13,000+
Description: A trend-setting event, featuring culinary demonstrations, seminars, workshops, presentations, more than 700 exhibitors, & numerous networking opportunities for members of Canada's foodservice sector
Contact Information: Toll-Free Phone: 1-800-387-5649; E-mail: info@crfa.ca
• Restaurants Canada Annual Event: CONNECT 2015, 2015, BC
Scope: Provincial
Attendance: 5,000+
Description: A trade show to highlight British Columbia's culinary excellence, with workshops, seminars, cooking competitions, & celebrity chef demonstrations
Contact Information: Canadian Restaurant & Foodservices Association Toll-Free Phone: 1-8800-387-5649; E-mail: bcexpo@crfa.ca, info@crfa.ca
• Restaurants Canada Annual Event: Atlantic Canada's Foodservice & Hospitality Trade Show 2015 (ApEx), March, 2015, Cunard Centre, Halifax, NS
Scope: Provincial
Attendance: 2,000+
Description: A showcase of the latest products, services, & trends for maritime foodservice operators
Contact Information: Toll-Free Phone: 1-877-755-1938; Canadian Restaurant & Foodservices Association, E-mail: info@crfa.ca
• Restaurants Canada Annual Event: Alberta Foodservice Expo 2015, 2015, AB
Scope: Provincial
Attendance: 2,000+
Description: An opportunity for Alberta's foodservice executives, restaurateurs, chefs, & qualified buyers to learn the latest trends from more than 200 food distributors & foodservice equipment manufacturers, suppliers, & dealers
Contact Information: MediaEdge Communications Inc. Contact: Chris Torry, Phone: 416-512-8186, ext. 280, E-mail: christ@mediaedge.ca

Atlantic Canada Office
#201, 5121 Sackville St., Halifax NS B3J 1K1
Tel: 902-425-0061; *Fax:* 902-422-1161
Toll-Free: 877-755-1938
Chief Officer(s):
Luc Erjavec, Vice-President, Atlantic Canada
lerjavec@restaurantscanada.org

Manitoba-Saskatchewan Office
201 Portage Ave., 18th Fl., Winnipeg MB R3B 3K6
Tel: 204-926-8557; *Fax:* 204-926-8687
Toll-Free: 877-926-8557
Chief Officer(s):
Dwayne Marling, Vice-President, Manitoba-Saskatchewan
dmarling@restaurantscanada.org

Québec Office
#2400, 1000 de la Gauchetière ouest, Montréal QC H3B 4W5
Tel: 514-448-2154; *Fax:* 514-448-5154
Chief Officer(s):
Jean Lefebvre, Vice-President, Quebec
jlefebvre@restaurantscanada.org

Western Canada Office
PO Box 12125, #2410, 555 West Hastings St., Vancouver BC V6B 4N6
Tel: 604-685-9655; *Fax:* 604-685-9633
Toll-Free: 866-300-7675
Chief Officer(s):
Mark von Schellwitz, Vice-President, Western Canada
mvonschellwitz@restaurantscanada.org

Restigouche County Society for the Prevention of Cruelty to Animals
165 Baybreeze Dr., Dalhousie NB E8C 1E4
Tel: 506-684-4396
restspca@nb.aibn.com
restigouchecountyspca.7p.com
www.facebook.com/RestigoucheCountySpca
Also Known As: Restigouche County SPCA
Overview: A small local organization
Member of: Canadian Federation of Humane Societies
Chief Officer(s):
Kathy Vautour, Manager
Staff Member(s): 5
Membership: *Fees:* $5 student/senior; $10 individual; $25 family; $100 life

Restigouche County Volunteer Action Association Inc. (RCVAA) / L'Association d'Action Communautaire Bénévole du Restigouche
PO Box 1007, 13 Aberdeen St., Campbellton NB E3N 3H4
Tel: 506-753-2252; *Fax:* 506-753-6403
rcvaa@nb.aibn.com
Overview: A small local organization founded in 1983
Chief Officer(s):
Brenda Renouf, Executive Director
Activities: Providing a food, clothing, & furniture bank for residents of Restigouche County

Retail Advertising & Marketing Club of Canada (RAC)
#800, 1255 Bay St., Toronto ON M5R 2A9
Tel: 416-495-6826; *Fax:* 416-922-8011
info@raccanada.ca
www.raccanada.ca
Overview: A medium-sized local organization founded in 1987
Mission: To provide a forum for retail advertising & marketing professionals to meet, discuss vital issues, explore trends, exchange ideas & experience dynamic presentations featuring renowned retailing experts
Affliation(s): RAMA Chicago
Chief Officer(s):
Lisa Tompkins, Chair
Finances: *Annual Operating Budget:* $100,000-$250,000; *Funding Sources:* Membership fees; dinner fees
Staff Member(s): 3; 29 volunteer(s)
Membership: 115; *Fees:* $97 individual; $184-$383 corporate; *Member Profile:* Advertising executives & their suppliers; *Committees:* Program; Promotion; Membership
Activities: Dinner events focusing on who is who of retail with topical issues of the day; speaker events; Flyer Symposium
Awards:
• Scholarships (Scholarship)
Six scholarships going to students from Humber, Centennial, Seneca, George Brown, Ryerson & Sheridan *Amount:* $300

Retail Council of Canada (RCC) / Conseil canadien du commerce de détail
#800, 1881 Yonge St., Toronto ON M4S 3C4
Tel: 416-922-6678; *Fax:* 416-922-8011
Toll-Free: 888-373-8245
info@retailcouncil.org
www.retailcouncil.org
www.linkedin.com/company/retail-council-of-canada
www.facebook.com/retailcouncil
twitter.com/RetailCouncil
www.youtube.com/user/RetailCouncil
Overview: A large national organization founded in 1963
Mission: To be the best at delivering the services our retail members value most; To serve, promote & represent the diverse needs of Canada's retailing industry to the highest standards of quality
Affliation(s): Canadian Health Food Association; Footwear Council of Canada; Le Conseil quebeçois du commerce de rétail; Retail Merchants' Association of Alberta; Retail Merchants' Association of Manitoba
Chief Officer(s):
Anna Martini, Chair
Diane J. Brisebois, CAE, President & CEO
David Wilkes, Senior Vice-President, Grocery Division & Government Relations
Andrew Siegwart, Vice-President, Membership Services
Membership: 45,000 companies; *Fees:* Schedule available; *Member Profile:* Retailers of all sizes across Canada; *Committees:* CFO Network; Commitment to Parents; Environment; Ontario Business Sector Working Group; Payments; Privacy; Public Affairs Forum; Regional Advisory Networks; Responsible Trade; Retail General Counsel Roundtable; Alberta Labour Supply Task Force; Human Resources; Independent Retailer Task Force; Loss Prevention; Safety Group; Senior Retail Marketing Network; Executive; Audit; Governance; Public Affairs
Activities: *Speaker Service:* Yes; *Library* by appointment

Western Office
#209, 1730 West 2nd Ave., Vancouver BC V6J 1H6
Tel: 604-736-0368
Toll-Free: 800-663-5135
Chief Officer(s):
Mark Startup, Vice-President, 604-730-5252
mstartup@retailcouncil.org

Retail Council of Québec *Voir* Conseil québécois du commerce de détail

Rethink Breast Cancer
#570, 215 Spadina Ave., Toronto ON M5T 2C7
Tel: 416-920-0980; *Fax:* 416-920-5798
Toll-Free: 866-738-4465
hello@rethinkbreastcancer.com
www.rethinkbreastcancer.com
Overview: A medium-sized national charitable organization
Mission: To help young people concerned about & affected by breast cancer
Chief Officer(s):
Mary-Jo DeCoteau, Executive Director
Alison Gordon, Vice-President, Strategy, Marketing, & Communications
Finances: *Funding Sources:* Donations; Fundraising; Corporate support
Activities: Providing support groups & breast cancer education; Supporting medical research; Increasing awareness of breast cancer; *Awareness Events:* Annual Little Sweetheart Ball; Urban Après Ski; Rethink Romp
Publications:
• Upfront
Type: Newsletter; *Frequency:* Quarterly
Profile: Information about upcoming events

The Retired Teachers of Ontario (RTO) / Les Enseignants et enseignantes retraités de l'Ontario (ERO)
#300, 18 Spadina Rd., Toronto ON M5R 2S7
Tel: 416-962-9463; *Fax:* 416-962-1061
Toll-Free: 800-361-9888
info@rto-ero.org
www.rto-ero.org
www.facebook.com/rto.ero
twitter.com/rto_ero
www.youtube.com/erorto
Previous Name: Superannuated Teachers of Ontario
Overview: A medium-sized provincial organization founded in 1968
Mission: To promote the interests of persons in receipt of a pension under the Ontario Teachers' Pension Act
Member of: Canadian Association of Retired Teachers
Chief Officer(s):
Howard Braithwaite, Executive Director
hbrathwaite@rto-ero.org
Finances: *Funding Sources:* Membership fees
Staff Member(s): 17
Membership: 69,000+; *Fees:* $53; *Member Profile:* Persons in receipt of a pension under the Ontario Teachers' Pension Act; *Committees:* Audit; Communications; Health Services & Insurance; Member Services; Nominating; Political Advocacy; Pension Retirement & Concerns; Project - Service to Others
Activities: Services available to members only;

Retirement Planning Association of Canada (RPAC) / Association des planificateurs de retraite du Canada (APRC)
RPAC National Office, #600, 3660 Hurontario St., Mississauga ON L5B 3C4
Fax: 647-723-6457
Toll-Free: 866-933-0233
info@retirementplanners.ca
www.retirementplanners.ca
Overview: A small national organization founded in 1980
Chief Officer(s):
Robert Jeffrey, Administrator
Finances: *Funding Sources:* Sponsorships
Membership: *Fees:* $173.25 individuals; $467.25 corporations; *Member Profile:* Financial planners; Lifestyle advisors; Retirement planners; Human resources personnel; Counsellors; Educators
Activities: Offering educational programs & networking opportunities; Providing information on retirement planning in Canada to the general public
Publications:
• RPAC Newsletter
Type: Newsletter; *Frequency:* Semiannually; *Price:* Free for RPAC members

Retraités canadiens en action ***See*** Canadian Pensioners Concerned Inc.

Revelstoke Arts Council (RAC)
PO Box 1931, 320 Wilson St., Revelstoke BC V0E 2S0
Tel: 250-814-9325
info@revelstokeartscouncil.com
revelstokeartscouncil.com
Overview: A small local organization
Mission: To promote the visual & performing arts in Revelstoke
Affliation(s): Assembly of British Columbia Arts Councils
Chief Officer(s):
Carol Palladino, President
Meghann Hutton, Vice-President
Activities: Overseeing the local art group, art gallery, concert series, community band, theatre company, women's writing group; Supporting community arts festivals, such as the Summer Street Festival & the Mountain Arts Festival

Revelstoke Chamber of Commerce
PO Box 490, 204 Campbell Ave., Revelstoke BC V0E 2S0
Tel: 250-837-5345; *Fax:* 250-837-4223
revelstokeinfo@telus.net
revelstokechamber.com
Overview: A small local organization founded in 1895
Mission: To promote the progress & development of Revelstoke & region in order to make it a better place to live & work
Member of: BC Rockies Tourism Association; BC Chamber of Commerce; Kootenay Rockies Tourism
Chief Officer(s):
Judy Goodman, Executive Director
Finances: *Annual Operating Budget:* $250,000-$500,000; *Funding Sources:* Membership dues; municipal; Ministry of Small Business, Tourism & Culture; gift shop
Staff Member(s): 2; 11 volunteer(s)
Membership: 335; *Fees:* $125-$565 business; $85 non-profit; $75 individual; *Committees:* Retail; Government; Transportation & Communications; Tourism
Activities: *Internships:* Yes; *Library:* Business Information Center; Open to public

Revelstoke Community Connections Food Bank
c/o Community Connections, PO Box 2880, 314 - 2nd St. East, Revelstoke BC V0E 2S0
Tel: 250-837-2920; *Fax:* 250-837-2909
plarson@community-connections.ca
Overview: A small local organization
Mission: To meet the immediate food needs of people in the community of Revelstoke; To work towards long term solutions to hunger & poverty
Chief Officer(s):
Patti Larson, Contact
Finances: *Funding Sources:* Donations
Activities: Coordinating free food distribution

Revelstoke Women's Shelter Society
PO Box 1150, Revelstoke BC V0E 2S0
Tel: 250-837-4382; *Fax:* 250-837-4386; *Crisis Hot-Line:* 250-837-1111
revelstokewomensshelter.com
Overview: A small local organization founded in 1985
Mission: To offer support, assistance, information & referrals in a courteous & compassionate manner that respects the dignity, privacy, cultural & diversity of women (& their children) who are victims of abuse
Chief Officer(s):
Nelli Richardson, Executive Director
Finances: *Funding Sources:* Provincial government; private donations; fundraising

Membership: *Member Profile:* Women & children suffering from abuse
Activities: Advocacy; Outreach; Transporation; Accompaniment; Referrals; Awareness; Promotion of prevention strategies

Revivre
5140, rue St-Hubert, Montréal QC H2J 2Y3
Tél: 514-783-4873; *Téléc:* 514-529-3081
Ligne sans frais: 866-738-4873
revivre@revivre.org
revivre.org
www.facebook.com/173729222663452
twitter.com/revivre_org
Aperçu: *Dimension:* petite; *Envergure:* locale
Mission: Pour offrir aux personnes souffrant de maladies mentales et de leurs familles avec l'appui
Membre(s) du bureau directeur:
Jean-Rémy Provost, Directeur général
Guy Latraverse, Président, Conseil d'administration
Membre: *Montant de la cotisation:* 30$ Individuelle; 50$ Famille; 100$Assoié
Activités: Ateliers; Conférences

Revivre - Association Québécoise de soutien aux personnes souffrant de troubles anxieux, dépressifs ou bipolaires / Québec Anxiety, Depressive & Bipolar Disorder Support Association
5140, rue Saint-Hubert, Montréal QC H2J 2Y3
Tél: 514-529-3081; *Téléc:* 514-529-3081
Ligne sans frais: 866-738-4873
revivre@revivre.org
www.revivre.org
Également appelé: Association des dépressifs et maniaco-dépressifs
Nom précédent: Association québécoise des cyclothymiques
Aperçu: *Dimension:* petite; *Envergure:* provinciale; Organisme sans but lucratif; fondée en 1983
Mission: Diffuser de l'information sur les troubles anxieux, dépressifs et bipolaires; favoriser le diagnostic et la prise en charge des personnes atteintes de ces maladies; supporter les personnes atteintes et leurs proches; briser l'isolement de ces personnes; partager notre expertise avec les professionnels et autres intervenants du milieu de la santé
Membre de: Association des professionnels en gestion philantropique
Affliation(s): Réseau alternatif et communautaire des organismes en santé mentale
Membre(s) du bureau directeur:
Jean-Rémy Provost, Directeur général
jean-remy.provost@revivre.org
Finances: *Budget de fonctionnement annuel:* $250,000-$500,000
Membre: 850; *Montant de la cotisation:* 30$ individus; 50$ famille; 100$ professionnels; *Critères d'admissibilite:* Personnes atteintes; proches; professionnels de la santé
Activités: Ligne d'écoute, d'information et de références; groupes d'entraide; conférences relation d'aide individuelle; internet; centre de documentation; *Evénements de sensibilisation:* Journée Dépistage de la Dépression, oct.; *Bibliothèque* rendez-vous

Revolutionary Communist Party *Voir* Parti communiste révolutionnaire

Rexdale Community Legal Services (RCLC)
Woodbine Centre, #24, 21 Panorama Ct., Toronto ON M9V 4E3
Tel: 416-741-5201; *Fax:* 416-741-6540
www.rexdalecommunitylegalclinic.ca
Overview: A small local charitable organization founded in 1971
Mission: To provide legal advice & referrals to all Northern Etobicoke residents; to provide legal representation to low-income community residents in certain areas of law
Chief Officer(s):
Jayne Mallin, Director, Legal Services
Italica Battiston, Director, Administration
Finances: *Annual Operating Budget:* $500,000-$1.5 Million
Activities: *Library*

Rexdale Community Microskills Development Centre *See* Community Microskills Development Centre

Rexdale Women's Centre (RWC)
#400, 23 Westmore Dr., Toronto ON M9V 3Y7
Tel: 416-745-0062; *Fax:* 416-745-3995
admin@rexdalewomen.org
www.rexdalewomen.org
Overview: A small local charitable organization founded in 1982 overseen by Ontario Council of Agencies Serving Immigrants
Mission: To serve high-need women & their families in the Greater Toronto Area; To assist women to become self-sufficient, financially secure, safe, healthy, & socially active
Chief Officer(s):
Fatima Filippi, Executive Director
Rebecca Rabinovitch, Chair & President
Finances: *Funding Sources:* Donations
Membership: *Fees:* $2 client; $5 unemployed individuals & students; $10 employed individuals; $20 organizations
Activities: Facilitating access to resources & community services; Providing programs, such as violence prevention services, settlement services, English language classes, & family support services; Collaborating with other organizations; *Awareness Events:* Walk 4 Change

REZO
#207, 2075, rue Plessis, Montréal QC H2L 2Y4
Tel: 514-521-7778; *Fax:* 514-521-7665
info@rezosante.org
www.rezosante.org
twitter.com/rezosante
www.youtube.com/REZOsante
Overview: A small local organization
Mission: Pour empêcher la propagation du VIH-Sida chez les hommes gais et bisexuels et fournir une éducation sur la santé sexuelle
Member of: Association pour la santé publique du Québec; Centre communautaire des gais et lesbiennes de Montréal; Coalition santé Arc-en-ciel du Canada; Coalition des organismes communautaires québécois de lutte contre le sida; Égale Canada; La chambre de commerce gaie de Montréal; Société canadienne du sida
Activities: Cliniques de dépistage; consultations

RÉZO
CP 246, Succ. C, Montréal QC H2L 4K1
Tél: 514-521-7778; *Téléc:* 514-521-7665
www.rezosante.org
www.facebook.com/REZOsante
twitter.com/rezosante
www.youtube.com/REZOsante
Nom précédent: Action Séro Zéro
Aperçu: *Dimension:* petite; *Envergure:* locale; fondée en 1991
Mission: Développer et coordonner des activités d'éducation et de prévention du VIH-sida et des autres ITSS dans un contexte de promotion de la santé sexuelle auprès des hommes gais, bisexuels et hommes ayant des relations sexuelles avec d'autres hommes de Montréal.
Membre(s) du bureau directeur:
Robert Rousseau, Directeur général, 514-521-7778 Ext. 227
robertrousseau@rezosante.org

Rhinoceros Party
4540, av de l'Hôtel-de-Ville, Montréal QC H2T 2B1
Tel: 514-903-9450
www.neorhino.ca
Overview: A small national organization
Chief Officer(s):
François Yo Gourd, Leader

Rhythmic Gymnastics Alberta (RGA)
c/o Percy Page Centre, 11759 Groat Rd., 3rd Fl., Edmonton AB T5M 3K6
Tel: 780-427-8152; *Fax:* 780-427-8153
Toll-Free: 800-881-2504
rga@rgalberta.com
www.rgalberta.com
www.facebook.com/298160665303
Previous Name: Alberta Rhythmic Sportive Gymnastics Federation
Overview: A medium-sized provincial organization founded in 1979
Mission: To foster & encourage participation & the development of excellence in rhythmic gymnastics
Member of: Gymnastics Canada Gymnastique
Finances: *Annual Operating Budget:* $100,000-$250,000
Staff Member(s): 2; 100 volunteer(s)
Membership: 800; *Fees:* $10; *Member Profile:* Children 5-18; Active adults/coaches 16-80
Activities: Provincial Gymnastrada; National & international competitions & events; *Speaker Service:* Yes

Rhythmic Gymnastics Manitoba Inc. (RGM)
145 Pacific Ave., Winnipeg MB R3B 2Z6
Tel: 201-492-5573
rhythmic@sportmanitoba.ca
www.rgmanitoba.com
Previous Name: Manitoba Rhythmic Sportive Gymnastics Association
Overview: A medium-sized provincial organization founded in 1985
Mission: To support & promote rhythmic gymnastic programs
Affliation(s): Sport Manitoba; Rhythmic Gymnastics Canada; Gymnastics Canada; International Gymnastics Federation; Canadian Sport Centre - Manitoba; Coaching Manitoba; Gymnastics Manitoba
Chief Officer(s):
Katherine Kwiecien, Executive Director, 204-925-5739
rgm.ed@sportmanitoba.ca
Raymond Chu, President
Zdravka Tchonkova, Vice-President, Marketing Finance
Susan Yurkiw, Vice-President, Finance
John Matthews, Director, Events
Membership: 8 clubs in the Winnipeg & Eastman regions
Activities: Hosting performing & competitive events; Posting event results; Providing programs to the rhythmic gymnastics community in Manitoba, such as the long term athlete development program & training for gymnastics coaches, & judges; Promoting standards for programs
Meetings/Conferences: • Rhythmic Gymnastics Manitoba Inc. 2015 Annual General Meeting & Awards Presentation, 2015, MB
Scope: Provincial
Contact Information: Phone: 204-925-5738; E-mail: rhythmic@sportmanitoba.ca

Richard Eaton Singers (RES)
c/o Stanley Milner Library, #6-06, 7 Sir Winston Churchill Sq., Edmonton AB T5J 2V4
Tel: 780-428-3737; *Fax:* 780-428-3736
info@richardeatonsingers.com
www.richardeatonsingers.com
Previous Name: University Singers
Overview: A small local charitable organization founded in 1951
Chief Officer(s):
Leonard Ratzlaff, Music Director & Conductor
Finances: *Funding Sources:* Donations; Sponsorships
Membership: *Committees:* The RES Educational Outreach Committee
Activities: Presenting performances; Offering the RES Education Program to high school students; *Library:* The Richard Eaton Singers Music Library

Richard III Society of Canada
c/o 156 Drayton Ave., Toronto ON M4C 3M2
e-mail: richardiii@cogeco.ca
home.cogeco.ca/~richardiii/
twitter.com/RichardIIICA
Overview: A small local organization founded in 1966
Mission: To promote research into the life & times of Richard III to secure a re-assessment of the material relating to this period & this monarch's role in English history.
Member of: Richard III Society (UK)
Finances: *Funding Sources:* Membership fees
Membership: *Fees:* $65 regular; $55 senior/student
Activities: Medieval Banquet in Oct.; *Library:* Buyers' Library; by appointment

Richard Ivey Foundation
#400, 11 Church St., Toronto ON M5E 1W1
Tel: 416-867-9229; *Fax:* 416-601-1689
info@ivey.org
www.ivey.org
Overview: A medium-sized provincial charitable organization founded in 1947
Mission: To pursue & support excellence by making grants that will improve the well-being of Canadians. Today, the Conserving Canada's Forests Program provides critical support for environmental sustainability across the country.
Chief Officer(s):
Rosamond Ivey, Chair
Richard W. Ivey, Secretary-Treasurer
Bruce Lourie, President
Activities: Participating in the Conserving Canada's Forests program, by providing support to national or provincial charitable environmental organizations

Richelieu International (RI)
#25, 1010 rue Polytek, Ottawa ON K1J 9J1
Tél: 613-742-6911; *Téléc:* 613-742-6916
Ligne sans frais: 800-267-6525

international@richelieu.org
www.richelieu.org
www.linkedin.com/company/richelieu-international?trk=company_name
www.facebook.com/277906642896
twitter.com/Le_Richelieu
www.youtube.com/watch?v=7pqgbohjM6A
Aperçu: *Dimension:* petite; *Envergure:* internationale; fondée en 1944
Mission: A pour mission l'épanouissement de la personalité de ses membres & au développement de leurs aptitudes personnelles & collectives; la promotion de la langue française; aider la jeunesse
Membre(s) du bureau directeur:
Laurier Thériault, Directeur général
lauriertheriault@hotmail.com
Denis Daigle, Directeur administratif
denis@richelieu.org
Finances: *Budget de fonctionnement annuel:* $250,000-$500,000; *Fonds:* Cotisation des membres
Membre(s) du personnel: 4; 20 bénévole(s)
Membre: 4 000 individus; *Montant de la cotisation:* 60$ individu

Richibouctou chambre de commerce ***See*** Kent Centre Chamber of Commerce

Richmond Agricultural Society
PO Box 1210, 6121 Perth St., Richmond ON K0A 2Z0
Tel: 613-838-3420; *Fax:* 613-838-3933
richmondfair@sympatico.ca
www.richmondfair.ca
www.facebook.com/pages/Richmond-Fair/273996526030979?fref=ts
Overview: A small local charitable organization founded in 1841 overseen by Ontario Association of Agricultural Societies
Mission: To promote agricultural awareness to the community by hosting a Fall Agricultural Fair
Member of: Society of Composers, Authors & Music Publishers of Canada
Affliation(s): Canadian Association of Fairs & Exhibitions; Ontario Association of Agricultural Societies
Chief Officer(s):
Dale Greene, General Manager/Secretary
Finances: *Annual Operating Budget:* $250,000-$500,000; *Funding Sources:* Federal, provincial & regional government; local businesses, individuals
Staff Member(s): 2; 450 volunteer(s)
Membership: 400 individual; *Fees:* $10 individual; *Member Profile:* To promote agricultural awareness to the community; *Committees:* Over 30, Livestock, Homecraft, Kiddyland, Entertainment, 4-H, Advertising, Consessions
Activities: Richmond Fair, Sept.; livestock shows; fundraising events

Richmond Board of Trade ***See*** Richmond Chamber of Commerce

Richmond Caring Place Society (RCPS)
#140, 7000 Minoru Blvd., Richmond BC V6Y 3Z5
Tel: 604-279-7000; *Fax:* 604-279-7008
admin.caringplace@shaw.ca
www.richmondcaringplace.ca
Overview: A small local organization founded in 1994
Mission: RCPS operates Richmond Caring Place, a facility that serves as one convenient location housing several, non-profit, community service agencies. The agencies have common access to meeting rooms & can collaborate on programs with ease due to proximity. Agencies include: Alzheimer Society of BC; Canadian Cancer Society; Canadian Hemochromatosis Society; BC Centre for Ability; Richmond Hospice Association; & more. RCPS is a registered charity, BN: 130560139RR0001.
Chief Officer(s):
Gary M. Hagel, Chair
Finances: *Funding Sources:* Government, corporate, private donations
Membership: 13 agencies; *Member Profile:* Non-profit, social service agencies

Richmond Chamber of Commerce
South Tower, #101, 5811 Cooney Rd., Richmond BC V6X 3M1
Tel: 604-278-2822; *Fax:* 604-278-2972
rcc@richmondchamber.ca
www.richmondchamber.ca
Previous Name: Richmond Board of Trade
Overview: A medium-sized local organization founded in 1910
Mission: To support & represent the interests of business in the city on behalf of its membership; to promote, enhance & improve trade & commerce, & the economic, civic & social well-being of Richmond; to support & communicate to all levels of government the informed opinion & positions of policy of its members on key local, provincial & national issues
Member of: BC Chamber of Commerce; Canadian Chamber of Commerce
Affliation(s): Tourism Richmond; Sister Chamber - Kent, Washington
Chief Officer(s):
Carol Young, Manager, Administration & Events
caroly@richmondchamber.ca
Finances: *Annual Operating Budget:* $250,000-$500,000
Staff Member(s): 6
Membership: 1,200; *Fees:* $290.85-$1094.10 business; $168 associations
Activities: *Speaker Service:* Yes; *Library:* Business Resource Centre Library;

Richmond Club of Toronto
655 Chiswick Line, Powassan ON P0H 1Z0
Tel: 416-640-1002
www.richmondclub.com
Overview: A small local organization
Affliation(s): Chapters in New York & London
Chief Officer(s):
Scott Barber, President
sbarber@richmondclub.com
Greg Beckett, Director
greg.beckett@richmondclub.com
Activities: Every two months 50 fund managers, stock brokers & analysts attend a complementary lunch, held at various private clubs; 2-3 undervalued, high growth companies are showcased at each event

Richmond Community Orchestra & Chorus
#130, 10691 Shellbridge Way, Richmond BC V6X 2W8
Tel: 604-276-2747; *Fax:* 604-270-3644
roca@roca.ca
www.roca.ca
Overview: A small local organization founded in 1986 overseen by Orchestras Canada
Chief Officer(s):
Paul Dufour, Administrator
Membership: 100; *Member Profile:* Orchestra & chorus members

Richmond County Disabled Association (RCD)
PO Box 379, Petit de Grat NS B0E 2L0
Tel: 902-226-1353
petitdeg@nsme.library.ns.ca
Overview: A small local organization
Affliation(s): Nova Scotia League For Equal Opportunities
Chief Officer(s):
Kenneth L. David, Contact
Finances: *Funding Sources:* Grants

Richmond County Historical Society (RCHS) / Société historique du comté de Richmond
1296, rte. 243, RR#7, Melbourne QC J0B 2B0
Tel: 819-826-1332
www.richmondcountyhistoricalsociety.com
Overview: A small local charitable organization founded in 1962
Mission: To preserve & organize historical documents of the County of Richmond & adjacent areas
Finances: *Funding Sources:* Donations; Fundraising; Museum admission fees
Membership: 200+
Activities: Operating a museum, with guided tours to visitors, schools, & other organizations; Maintaining archives, such as cemetery indexes, original newspapers, photographs, & maps, for use by researchers; *Library:* Archives o Richmond County Historical Society; Open to public by appointment

Richmond Delta Youth Orchestra
PO Box 26064, Stn. Central, Richmond BC V6Y 3V3
Tel: 604-365-3584
admin@rdyo.ca
www.rdyo.ca
www.facebook.com/deltayouthorchestra
twitter.com/rdyorchestra
Previous Name: Delta Symphony Society
Overview: A small local charitable organization founded in 1971 overseen by Orchestras Canada
Mission: To provide an educationally oriented experience for young musicians from the lower mainland of British Columbia
Chief Officer(s):
Stephen Robb, Music Director
Activities: *Library* by appointment
Awards:
• Harry Gomez - Fred Preuss Memorial Award
Used to support various musical endeavours, and as a scholarship
• Wallace Leung Memorial Award
Awarded to string players who have made excellent contributions to the Orchestra

Richmond Food Bank Society (RFB)
#100, 5800 Cedarbridge Way, Richmond BC V6X 2A7
Tel: 604-271-5609
info@richmondfoodbank.org
www.richmondfoodbank.org
www.facebook.com/pages/Richmond-Food-Bank-Society/256182874445999
Overview: A small local charitable organization founded in 1993 overseen by Food Banks British Columbia
Mission: To distribute free food to low-income Richmond residents; to assist food bank clients to break from the despair of poverty; to encourage responsibility & to maximize participation in the community
Member of: Food Banks British Columbia; Food Banks Canada; Richmond Chamber of Commerce; Richmond Community Services Advisory Council; Volunteer Richmond
Chief Officer(s):
Margaret Hewlett, Coordinator
margaret@richmondfoodbank.org
Finances: *Annual Operating Budget:* $100,000-$250,000; *Funding Sources:* Donations
Staff Member(s): 3; 120 volunteer(s)
Membership: 1-99; *Member Profile:* Past & present board members
Activities: Nutrition demonstrations; distribute food & books (food for the body & for the mind); *Awareness Events:* Richmond Rotary Walk for the Richmond Food Bank; *Speaker Service:* Yes

Richmond Gem & Mineral Club
c/o Richmond Cultural Centre, 7700 Minoru Gate, Richmond BC V6Y 1R9
Tel: 604-278-5141
Overview: A small local organization
Affliation(s): British Columbia Lapidary Society; Gem & Mineral Federation of Canada
Chief Officer(s):
George Howe, Contact, 604-274-4893
geohowe@telus.net
Finances: *Funding Sources:* Donations to attend the Gem Show
Activities: Hosting monthly meetings; Arranging workshops; *Awareness Events:* Annual Gem Show

Richmond Hill Arts Council ***See*** Arts Richmond Hill

Richmond Hill Chamber of Commerce (RHCOC)
376 Church St. South, Richmond Hill ON L4C 9V8
Tel: 905-884-1961; *Fax:* 905-884-1962
info@rhcoc.com
www.rhcoc.com
Overview: A medium-sized local organization founded in 1970
Mission: To foster a business enviornment that enhances the success of our members & improves the quality of life in Richmond Hill
Member of: Canadian Chamber of Commerce; Ontario Chamber of Commerce
Affliation(s): Toronto Board of Trade
Chief Officer(s):
George Simpson, Chair
Leslie Walker, CEO
Finances: *Annual Operating Budget:* $250,000-$500,000; *Funding Sources:* Membership fees; events
Staff Member(s): 3
Membership: 571; *Fees:* $315-$1102.50 business; $262.50 non-profit; *Committees:* Advocacy; Membership Services; Home Show
Activities: *Rents Mailing List:* Yes

Richmond Hill Naturalists (RHN)
PO Box 33217, Stn. Harding Post Outlet, Richmond Hill ON L4C 9S3
Tel: 905-883-3047
Other Communication: trips@rhnaturalists.ca
membership@rhnaturalists.ca
www.rhnaturalists.ca
twitter.com/RHNaturalists
Overview: A small local organization founded in 1955
Mission: To encourage interest in natural history; To preserve natural areas; To discover & appreciate the natural world

Chief Officer(s):
Marianne Yake, President, 905-883-3047
president@rhnaturalists.ca
Gene Denzel, Treasurer
treasurer@rhnaturalists.ca
Membership: *Fees:* $25 students; $30 individuals; $35 families
Activities: Offering field trips; Arranging programs on nature topics
Publications:
• The RHN [Richmond Hill Naturalists] Bulletin
Type: Newsletter; *Frequency:* 9 pa; *Accepts Advertising*; *Editor:* Denise Potter; *Price:* Free with Richmond Hill Naturalists membership
Profile: Organization activities, nature news, & forthcoming events

Richmond Hill Symphony *See* York Symphony Orchestra Inc.

Richmond Multicultural Community Services (RMCS)
#210, 7000 Minoru Blvd., Richmond BC V6Y 3Z5
Tel: 604-279-7160; *Fax:* 604-279-7168
www.rmcs.bc.ca
www.facebook.com/285164472034
Previous Name: Richmond Multicultural Concerns Society
Overview: A small local charitable organization founded in 1986
Mission: To achieve inter-cultural harmony in the Richmond area; To identify & meet the needs of Richmond's ethno-cultural community
Chief Officer(s):
Kanwarjit Sandhu, President
Parm Grewal, Executive Director, 604-279-7160 Ext. 7161
parm@rmcs.bc.ca
Activities: Assisting newcomers to the Richmond area; Providing information & referrals to citizens, immigrants, & refugees; Increasing awareness of multiculturalism, through activities such as cross cultural understanding workshops; Liaising with government & other organizations; Offering group programs, such as the senior group & the women self-help group; Providing ESL conversation classes
Publications:
• Richmond Multicultural Concerns Society Newsletter
Type: Newsletter; *Price:* Free with RMCS membership
Profile: Information for RMCS members

Richmond Multicultural Concerns Society *See* Richmond Multicultural Community Services

Richmond Orchid Club
Richmond Public Library, #100, 7700 Minoru Gate, Richmond BC V6Y 1R8
www.richmondorchidclub.com
www.facebook.com/richmond.orchid.club
Overview: A small local organization founded in 2007
Mission: To provide information to orchid enthusiasts
Member of: Canadian Orchid Congress
Chief Officer(s):
Elizabeth Markus, President

Richmond Society for Community Living (RSCL)
#170, 7000 Minoru Blvd., Richmond BC V6Y 3Z5
Tel: 604-279-7040; *Fax:* 604-279-7048
info@rscl.org
www.rscl.org
www.facebook.com/125201840847163
Overview: A small local organization founded in 1982
Member of: Inclusion BC
Chief Officer(s):
Janice Barr, Executive Director, 604-279-7043, Fax: 604-279-7058
jbarr@rscl.org
Finances: *Funding Sources:* Donations; Ministry for Children & Family Development; Community Living BC
Membership: *Fees:* $10 individual; $15 family; $100 individual (lifetime); $150 family (lifetime); *Member Profile:* Infants & children with special needs; Adults with developmental disabilities
Activities: Offering workshops on topics such as positive parenting & autism; Producing brochures on subjects such as infant development & support child development; Increasing public understanding of the rights of people with disabilities; *Awareness Events:* RSCL Annual Family Picnic, August; Benefit of Possibilities, November; Annual Children's Christmas Party, December
Publications:
• Respite Caregiver Guide
Type: Guide
• RSCL General Family Handbook
Type: Handbook
Profile: Available in the following languages: English, Chinese, & Punjabi
• RSCL Infant Development Family Handbook
Type: Handbook
Profile: Available in the following languages: English, Chinese, & Punjabi
• RSCL Program Family Handbooks
Type: Handbook
Profile: Subjects include children's respite, adult respite, residential services, day programs, youth connections, & treehouse early learning centre
• RSCL Supported Child Development Family Handbook
Type: Handbook
Profile: Available in the following languages: English, Chinese, & Punjabi
• RSCL Views: Richmond Society for Community Living Bi-annual Newsletter
Type: Newsletter; *Frequency:* Semiannually
Profile: Society activities
• Supported Child Development Caregiver Guide
Type: Guide
• Supported Living Caregiver Guide
Type: Guide
• Volunteer Handbook
Type: Handbook

Rick Hansen Foundation
#300, 3820 Cessna Dr., Richmond BC V7B 0A2
Tel: 604-295-8149; *Fax:* 604-295-8159
Toll-Free: 800-213-2131
info@rickhansen.com
www.rickhansen.com
Overview: A medium-sized national charitable organization founded in 1988
Mission: To improve the quality of life of people with spinal cord injury; To create more accessible & inclusive communities; to advance research
Chief Officer(s):
Rick Hansen, Co-Chair
Art Reitmayer, Chief Executive Officer
Lyall Knott, Co-Chair
George Gaffney, Treasurer
Finances: *Funding Sources:* Donations; Fundraising; Corporate partnerships
Activities: Offering programs such as the ambassador program (mrsmith@rickhansen.com) & the school program (nearley@rickhansen.com); Liaising with government; Increasing awareness of spinal cord injury; Creating inclusive play spaces for children with physical disabilities; *Awareness Events:* Rick Hansen Wheels In Motion, June; Annual Rick Hansen Fishing Challenge, June; Rick Hansen Sturgeon Classic, October
Publications:
• In Motion: The Rick Hansen Foundation Newsletter
Type: Newsletter; *Frequency:* Quarterly
Profile: Donation information, related news stories, possibilities, & solutions

Rideau Chamber of Commerce
PO Box 247, Manotick ON K4M 1A3
Tel: 613-692-6262
rideauchamber.com
Overview: A small local organization
Affliation(s): Ontario Chamber of Commerce
Chief Officer(s):
Salima Ismail, President
drsalima@doctor.com
Finances: *Funding Sources:* Membership fees
10 volunteer(s)
Membership: 105; *Fees:* $85
Activities: Student job bank; business referral service; trade show

Rideau Environmental Action League (REAL)
PO Box 1061, Smiths Falls ON K7A 5A5
Tel: 613-283-9500
info@realaction.ca
www.realaction.ca
twitter.com/RideauEnvActL
Overview: A medium-sized local organization founded in 1989
Mission: To conduct community-wide environmental projects and promote environmental improvements within the Town of Smiths Falls and Lanark, Leeds and Grenville Counties.
Chief Officer(s):
Larry Manson, President
Membership: *Fees:* $15 individual/schools; $20 family; $5 student; $25 associate; $50 corporate

Rideau Trail Association (RTA)
PO Box 15, Kingston ON K7L 4V6
Tel: 613-545-0823
info@rideautrail.org
www.rideautrail.org
www.facebook.com/343658645521
Overview: A small local charitable organization founded in 1971
Mission: To preserve & maintain a hiking trail from Kingston to Ottawa
Member of: Hike Ontario
Finances: *Funding Sources:* Donations
Activities: Hiking, cross-country skiing, & snowshoeing
Awards:
• End-to-End (Award)
Amount: Certificate & badge for those completing the trail
• Outstanding Service Award (Award)
Annually for each club
• Winter End-to-End (Award)
Amount: Certificate & badge for those completing the trail
Publications:
• Rideau Trail Association E-Letter
Type: Newsletter; *Frequency:* Biweekly; *Price:* Free with RTA membership
• Rideau Trail Association Newsletter
Type: Newsletter; *Frequency:* Quarterly; *Price:* Free with RTA membership
Profile: Hiking articles & club activities
• The Rideau Trail Guidebook
Number of Pages: 109; *Editor:* Ernie Trischuk; *ISBN:* 0-9693759-7-2; *Price:* $25.50 members; $39.95 non-members
Profile: Maps & trail directions & descriptions

Central Rideau Trail Club
PO Box 213, Perth ON K7H 3E4
Tel: 613-264-8338

Ottawa Rideau Trail Club
PO Box 4616, Stn. E, Ottawa ON K1S 5H8
Tel: 613-860-2225

Rideau Valley Conservation Authority (RVCA)
PO Box 599, 3889 Rideau Valley Dr., Manotick ON K4M 1A5
Tel: 613-692-3571; *Fax:* 613-692-0831
Toll-Free: 800-267-3504
info@rvcf.ca
www.rvca.ca
www.facebook.com/108941882522595
twitter.com/RideauValleyCA
www.flickr.com/photos/64684563@N08
Overview: A large local organization
Mission: To advocate for clean water, natural shorelines and sustainable land use throughout the Rideau Valley watershed.
Chief Officer(s):
Ken Graham, Chair
Charles Billington, Executive Director
charles.billington@rvca.ca
Finances: *Annual Operating Budget:* Greater than $5 Million; *Funding Sources:* Province; Fundraising; Municipalities
Staff Member(s): 65
Membership: 30 municipalities
Publications:
• Watershed Briefs
Type: Newsletter
Profile: Newsletter for municipal councillors

Rideau Valley Field Naturalists (RVFN)
PO Box 474, Perth ON K7H 3G1
rvfn.colmar176.ca
Overview: A small local organization founded in 1983
Mission: To promote the enjoyment of nature through environmental appreciation & conservation; To encourage the wise use & conservation of natural resources; to promote environmental protection
Member of: Federation of Ontario Naturalists; World Wildlife Federation; Canadian Nature Federation
Chief Officer(s):
Murray Hunt, Treasurer, 613-264-9273
mkhunt@ripnet.com
Finances: *Annual Operating Budget:* Less than $50,000; *Funding Sources:* Membership fees
12 volunteer(s)
Membership: 96; *Fees:* $5 student; $20 individual; $30 family/institution; *Committees:* Flora & Fauna; Outings

Activities: Monthly meetings except July & August; mall displays; educational outings; bird identification; clinics; bird, mammal & amphibian monitoring; *Library*

Rideau Valley Soaring
PO Box 1164, Manotick ON K4M 1A9
Tel: 613-366-8208
Other Communication: Alt. phone: 613-489-2691
club.pres@rvss.ca
rvss.ca
www.facebook.com/200156480081876
twitter.com/rvssca
Overview: A small local organization
Member of: Soaring Association of Canada
Affliation(s): Gatineau Gliding Club; Montreal Soaring Club
Chief Officer(s):
George Domaradzki, President
club.pres@rvss.ca
Membership: *Fees:* $345 youth; $395 junior; $516 spouse; $566 self launch/tow pilot; $735 adult

Rideau-St. Lawrence Real Estate Board
#12, 1275 Kensington Pkwy., Brockville ON K6V 6C3
Tel: 613-342-3103; *Fax:* 613-342-1637
rideau@bellnet.ca
boards.mls.ca/rideau
Previous Name: Central St. Lawrence Real Estate Board
Overview: A small local organization founded in 1954 overseen by Ontario Real Estate Association
Member of: The Canadian Real Estate Association
Finances: *Funding Sources:* Membership dues
Membership: 216

Ridge Meadows Association of Community Living (RMACL)
11641 - 224th St., Maple Ridge BC V2X 6A1
Tel: 604-467-8700; *Fax:* 604-467-8767
www.rmacl.org
www.facebook.com/RMACL.ORG
Overview: A small local organization
Mission: To assist children & adults with developmental disabilities in the Maple Ridge & Pitt Meadows area to live & work in their home & community
Member of: British Columbia Association for Community Living
Chief Officer(s):
Danette Kugler, Executive Director
danette.kugler@rmacl.org
Kelly Meier, Contact
kelly.meier@rmacl.org
Finances: *Annual Operating Budget:* $1.5 Million-$3 Million; *Funding Sources:* Donations; United Way of the Lower Mainland
Staff Member(s): 250; 10 volunteer(s)
Activities: Providing children's services, community support services, residential services, & vocational programs

Ridgetown & South East Kent Chamber of Commerce
PO Box 522, Ridgetown ON N0P 2C0
Tel: 519-359-6597
ridgetownchamber@gmail.com
www.ridgetown.com
Overview: A small local charitable organization
Mission: Promoting business and tourism in Ridgetown, the "friendliest town in Ontario".
Chief Officer(s):
Charlie Mitton, President
Finances: *Funding Sources:* Membership fees
Membership: 60; *Fees:* Schedule available

The Right to Die Network of Canada *See* The Right to Die Society of Canada

The Right to Die Society of Canada (RTDSC) / Société Canadienne pour le Droit de Mourir (SCDM)
145 Macdonell Ave., Toronto ON M6R 2A4
Tel: 416-535-0690
Toll-Free: 866-535-0690
info@righttodie.ca
www.righttodie.ca
Previous Name: The Right to Die Network of Canada
Overview: A small national organization founded in 1991
Mission: To work with legislators, policy makers & the public to expand the range of humane options for people who are suffering intolerably from incurable conditions & who want a self-directed dying; to work with sufferers to expand their awareness of the options that are legal & may be appropriate for them
Chief Officer(s):
Ruth von Fuchs, President & Secretary
Finances: *Funding Sources:* Membership fees; donations
Membership: 400; *Fees:* $30 single; $40 family/couple; *Member Profile:* Must be over 18 years of age
Activities: *Speaker Service:* Yes

Right to Life Association of Newfoundland & Labrador *See* Newfoundland & Labrador Right to Life Association

The Right to Life Association of Toronto & Area
#302, 120 Eglinton Ave., Toronto ON M4P 1E2
Tel: 416-483-7869; *Fax:* 416-483-7052
office@righttolife.to
www.righttolife.to
www.facebook.com/righttolifeto
Also Known As: Toronto Right to Life Association
Overview: A small local charitable organization founded in 1971
Mission: To uphold the right to life as the basic human right on which all others depend; to provide information & services to that end
Affiliation(s): Life Canada
Finances: *Funding Sources:* Donations
Staff Member(s): 3; 4 volunteer(s)
Membership: 2,000; *Fees:* $10 student/senior; $20 adult; $25 family
Activities: *Speaker Service:* Yes; *Library:* Resource Centre; Open to public
Publications:
- The Right to Life Association of Toronto Newsletter
Type: Newsletter; *Frequency:* Quarterly

Right to Play
65 Queen St. West, Toronto ON M5H 2M5
Tel: 416-203-0190
canada@righttoplay.com
www.righttoplay.com/canada
www.linkedin.com/company/right-to-play?trk=fc_badge
www.facebook.com/RightToPlayCAN
twitter.com/RighttoPlayCAN
www.youtube.com/user/RightToPlayCan
Previous Name: Olympic Aid
Overview: A medium-sized international charitable organization founded in 2002
Mission: Educating and empowering children and youth to use sport and play to overcome the effects of poverty, conflict and disease in disadvantaged communities.
Chief Officer(s):
Robert Witchel, National Director
Finances: *Funding Sources:* Donations
Activities: PLAY program, resource development, training; *Internships:* Yes

Right to Quiet Society
#359, 1985 Wallace St., Vancouver BC V6R 4H4
Tel: 604-222-0207
info@quiet.org
www.quiet.org
Also Known As: Society for Soundscape Awareness & Protection
Overview: A small national organization founded in 1982
Mission: To promote awareness of the increasing problem of noise pollution & the dangers of noise to our physical, emotional & spiritual well-being; to work for noise abatement through regulation & enforcement & by encouraging responsible behaviour; to foster recognition of the right to quiet as a basic human right
Chief Officer(s):
Hans Schmid, President
Finances: *Annual Operating Budget:* Less than $50,000
6 volunteer(s)
Membership: 280; *Fees:* $12 individual; $18 family; $6 low income; $25 non-profit; $50 business
Activities: *Awareness Events:* International Noise Awareness Day, April

Rimbey Chamber of Commerce
PO Box 87, Rimbey AB T0C 2J0
Tel: 403-843-2020; *Fax:* 403-843-2027
rimbeychamber@rimbey.com
www.rimbeylive.ca
Overview: A small local organization
Member of: Alberta Chamber of Commerce; Canadian Chamber of Commerce
Chief Officer(s):
Audreyann Bresnahan, President
Finances: *Funding Sources:* Local government; membership fees
Membership: 63
Activities: Winterfest; Main Street Beautification Program; tourism

Rimbey Fish & Game Association
PO Box 634, Rimbey AB T0C 2J0
Tel: 403-843-3858
Other Communication: Campground Reservation Phone: 403-843-6931
www.rimbeyfishandgame.com
Overview: A small local organization
Member of: Alberta Fish & Game Association
Chief Officer(s):
Daryl Hunt, President, 403-843-6466
Finances: *Annual Operating Budget:* Less than $50,000
Membership: 104; *Fees:* $29 family; $19 regular; $18 associate; $12 youth under 18
Activities: Fish & Game annual awards & trophies

Rimbey Historical Society
PO Box 813, 5620 - 51 St., Rimbey AB T0C 2J0
Tel: 403-843-2004
paskapoo@telus.net
www.paskapoopark.com
Overview: A small local charitable organization founded in 1963
Mission: To preserve the heritage of the Rimbey region of Alberta
Finances: *Funding Sources:* Alberta Museums Association
Membership: *Fees:* $10
Activities: Maintaining the Pas-Ka-Poo Historical Park museums & historic buildings & the Smithson International Truck Museum
Publications:
- Over the Years: A History of the Rimbey Area
Type: Book; *Editor:* Rimbey History Book Committee

Ringette Alberta
Percy Page Centre, 11759 Groat Rd., 2nd Fl., Edmonton AB T5M 3K6
Tel: 780-451-1750; *Fax:* 780-415-1749
www.ringettealberta.com
www.facebook.com/ringettealberta
twitter.com/ringettealberta
www.youtube.com/channel/UCx0Yyv-lwy-mZJPFUPf8xZQ
Overview: A medium-sized provincial organization overseen by Ringette Canada
Mission: To provide ringette services to its members
Member of: Ringette Canada
Chief Officer(s):
David Myers, Executive Director
david@ringettealberta.com
Staff Member(s): 4

Ringette Association of Saskatchewan (RAS) / Association de ringuette de Saskatchewan
1860 Lorne St., Regina SK S4P 2L7
Tel: 306-780-9432; *Fax:* 306-780-9460
www.ringettesask.com
twitter.com/RingetteSask
Overview: A medium-sized provincial organization founded in 1976 overseen by Ringette Canada
Mission: To develop, promote, communicate, & administer programs, policies & procedures which will enhance the development & participation of coaches, players, officals, volunteers, & administrators from all levels throughout Saskatchewan
Member of: Sask Sport
Chief Officer(s):
Jodi Lorenz, President
Crystal Gellner, Executive Director
executivedirector@ringettesask.com
Keith Doering, Director, Technical
technicaldirector@ringettesask.com
Finances: *Funding Sources:* Saskatchewan Lotteries; Corporate sponsorships; Membership fees
Staff Member(s): 2
Activities: Coaching & officiating clinics; Providing player development camps; Organizing provincial championships

Ringette Canada (RC) / Ringuette Canada
#201, 5510 Canotek Rd., Ottawa ON K1J 9J4
Tel: 613-748-5655; *Fax:* 613-748-5860
Other Communication: www.flickr.com/photos/7738799@N02
ringette@ringette.ca
www.ringette.ca

twitter.com/ringettecanada
www.youtube.com/ringettecanada
Overview: A large national organization founded in 1975
Mission: To formulate, publish & administer national policies beneficial to the sport; To enforce laws & regulations governing ringette; To encourage ringette participants to strive for excellence in teamwork, team spirit & team discipline
Member of: International Ringette Federation
Chief Officer(s):
Jane Casson, President
president@ringette.ca
Natasha Johnston, Executive Director
natasha@ringette.ca
Frances Losier, Director, High Performance & Events, 613-748-5655 Ext. 221
frances@ringette.ca
Nathalie Muller, Director, Technical, 613-748-5655 Ext. 224
nathalie@ringette.ca
Alayne Martel, Contact, Media & Public Relations, 902-839-2532
alayne@ringette.ca
Finances: *Annual Operating Budget:* $1.5 Million-$3 Million; *Funding Sources:* Membership fees; Federal government; Corporate sponsorships
Staff Member(s): 7
Membership: *Member Profile:* Provincial or territorial ringette associations; *Committees:* Coach Development; Officials Development; High Performance; National Ringette League
Activities: Organizing the Canadian Ringette Championships; *Library:* Resource Centre;
Awards:
• Cara Brown Scholarship Award (Award)
• Agnes Jacks Scholarship Award (Award)

Ringette New Brunswick (RNB) / Ringuette Nouveau-Brunswick
487 rte La Vallée, Memramcook NB E4K 3C7
Tel: 506-851-5641
www.ringette-nb.com
twitter.com/RingetteNB
Also Known As: New Brunswick Ringette Association
Overview: A small provincial organization overseen by Ringette Canada
Mission: To ensure the well-being & development of ringette athletes in New Brunswick
Chief Officer(s):
Chantal Poirier, Manager, Program
cpoirierRNB@hotmail.com
Activities: Consulting with the Province of New Brunswick Wellness, Culture, & Sport; Providing direction in areas such as athlete development, officiating, coaching, & technical issues; Organizing coaching & officiating clinics; Establishing standards for bench staff

Ringette Nova Scotia
5516 Spring Garden Rd., 4th Fl., Halifax NS B3J 1G6
Tel: 902-425-5454; *Fax:* 902-425-5606
ringette@sportnovascotia.ca
www.ringette.ns.ca
Overview: A small provincial organization founded in 1973 overseen by Ringette Canada
Mission: To promote, develop & administer the sport of ringette within Nova Scotia
Member of: International Ringette Federation
Chief Officer(s):
Brian Rawding, President
ringettenspresident@gmail.com
Lindsay Bennett, Executive Director
lbennett@sportnovascotia.ca
Finances: *Annual Operating Budget:* Less than $50,000; *Funding Sources:* Provincial Sport & Recreation Commission
20 volunteer(s)
Membership: 800; *Fees:* $24.75; *Committees:* Canada Winter Games; Fundraising; Provincial Teams; Strategic Plan
Activities: *Awareness Events:* Ringette Week, Feb.; *Library:* Resource Library; by appointment

Ringette PEI (RPEI)
40 Enman Cres., Charlottetown PE C1A 7K7
Tel: 902-368-6570
ringettepei.ca
www.facebook.com/ringettepei
twitter.com/RingettePEI
Also Known As: Prince Edward Island Ringette Association
Overview: A small provincial organization founded in 1982 overseen by Ringette Canada
Mission: To promote ringette throughout PEI
Chief Officer(s):
Valerie Vuillemot, Executive Director
vvuillemot@sportpei.pe.ca
Michael James, President
mjames@islandtelecom.com
Steve Campbell, Vice-President
steve@curranandbriggs.com
Breanne MacInnis, Treasurer
bemacinnis@gmail.com
Activities: Offering officiating clinics, coaching courses & related resources; Providing tournament & championship information

Ringuette 96 Montréal-Nord-Est
a/s Sylvie Horth, 3512, rue Charles-Goulet, Montréal QC H1A 5L7
Tél: 514-644-0153
ringuette96mn@hotmail.com
ringuette96s.brinkster.net
Aperçu: *Dimension:* petite; *Envergure:* provinciale surveillé par Ringuette-Québec
Membre de: Ringuette-Québec
Membre(s) du bureau directeur:
Sylvie Horth, Président
Membre: *Montant de la cotisation:* Barème

Ringuette Boucherville
490, ch du Lac, Boucherville QC J4B 6X3
www.ringuetteboucherville.com
Aperçu: *Dimension:* petite; *Envergure:* provinciale surveillé par Ringuette-Québec
Membre de: Ringuette-Québec
Membre(s) du bureau directeur:
Lynda Pouliot, Présidente, 450-645-0276
eric.lynda@sympatico.ca
Membre: *Critères d'admissibilite:* Filles de 4 ans et plus

Ringuette Bourrassa-Laval-Lanaudière
QC
www.ringuettebll.com
Aperçu: *Dimension:* petite; *Envergure:* provinciale surveillé par Ringuette-Québec
Membre de: Ringuette-Québec
Membre(s) du bureau directeur:
Michel Latendresse, Président
michel.lat@hotmail.com

Ringuette Canada ***See*** Ringette Canada

Ringuette de la Capitale
QC
ca@ringuettedelacapitale.com
www.ringuettedelacapitale.com
www.facebook.com/ringuettedelacapitale
Aperçu: *Dimension:* petite; *Envergure:* provinciale surveillé par Ringuette-Québec
Membre de: Ringuette-Québec
Membre(s) du bureau directeur:
Manon Audet, Présidente, 418-843-9652
manon-audet@hotmail.com
Membre: 4 équipes;

Ringuette Nouveau-Brunswick ***See*** Ringette New Brunswick

Ringuette St-Hubert
CP 29542, 5950, boul. Cousineau, St-Hubert QC J3Y 9A9
ringuette@ringuette-st-hubert.com
www.ringuette-st-hubert.com
Aperçu: *Dimension:* petite; *Envergure:* provinciale surveillé par Ringuette-Québec
Membre de: Ringuette-Québec
Membre(s) du bureau directeur:
David Létouneau, Président
Davidletourneau.cma@gmail.com

Ringuette St-Hyacinthe
2288, rue Denis, Ste-Marie-Madeleine QC J0H 1S0
info@ringuettesth.com
www.ringuettesth.com
Aperçu: *Dimension:* petite; *Envergure:* provinciale surveillé par Ringuette-Québec
Membre de: Ringuette-Québec
Membre(s) du bureau directeur:
Luc Babineau, Président, 450-321-0543
nbabineau@ringuettesth.com
Membre: *Montant de la cotisation:* Barème

Ringuette-Québec
4545, av. Pierre-de-Coubertin, Montréal QC H1V 0B2
Tél: 514-252-3085; *Téléc:* 514-254-1069
ringuette@ringuette-quebec.qc.ca
www.ringuette-quebec.qc.ca
Aperçu: *Dimension:* petite; *Envergure:* provinciale surveillé par Ringette Canada
Membre de: Ringuette-Canada
Membre(s) du bureau directeur:
Florent Gravel, Président
florent.gravel@ringuette-quebec.qc.ca

Ripple Rock Gem & Mineral Club
PO Box 6, Campbell River BC V9W 4Z9
e-mail: info@ripplerockgemandmineralclub.com
www.ripplerockgemandmineralclub.com
Overview: A small local organization founded in 1989
Mission: To increase knowledge of rocks & minerals; To promote lapidary arts
Member of: British Columbia Lapidary Society; Gem & Mineral Federation of Canada
Chief Officer(s):
Janet Burkholder, Show Chair
Membership: *Fees:* $15 individuals; $25 families; *Member Profile:* People from Campbell River & the surrounding area of British Columbia who are interested in gems & minerals
Activities: Hosting monthly meetings, except July & August; Organizing field trips & camps; Providing workshops for people to learn lapidary arts; *Awareness Events:* Ripple Rock Gem & Mineral Show; *Library:* Ripple Rock Gem & Mineral Club Library
Publications:
• The Bugle [a publication of The Ripple Rock Gem & Mineral Club]
Type: Newsletter; *Frequency:* Monthly
Profile: Information about club activities, upcoming events, & member profiles

Risk & Insurance Management Society Inc. (RIMS)
c/o Thomas Oystrick, RIMS Canada Council, Mount Royal University, 4825 Mount Royal Gate SW, Calgary AB T3E 6K6
Other Communication: membership@rims.org
canada@rims.org
www.rimscanada.ca
www.facebook.com/groups/258125305110
twitter.com/rimsorg
Also Known As: RIMS Canada (A Standing Committee of RIMS)
Previous Name: American Society of Insurance Management
Overview: A large international organization founded in 1950
Mission: To advance the practice of risk management in Canada
Chief Officer(s):
Bonnie Wasser, Canadian Consultant, 416-636-9745
bwasser@sympatico.ca
Tino Brambilla, Chair, RIMS Canada Council
Thomas Oystrick, Treasurer, RIMS Canada Council, 403-440-6196, Fax: 403-440-8927
TOystrick@mtroyal.ca
Bruce Tainsh, Membership Coordinator, RIMS Canada Council
Phil Corbeil, Chair, Communications & External Affairs Committee
Marley Drainville, Chair, National Conference Committee
Dave Jackson, Chair, National Education Committee
Finances: *Funding Sources:* Membership fees; Conferences
Membership: 950+ individual members + 380+ corporate members; *Fees:* No charge for students & affiliate members; US$100 educational & retired members; US$490 corporations; *Member Profile:* Risk managers; Vendors or service providers; Risk management or insurance related professors; Students; Retired persons; *Committees:* RIMS Canada Council Subcommittees: National Conference; National Education; Communications & External Affairs
Activities: Providing professional educational courses & workshops; Offering career services; *Speaker Service:* Yes
Awards:
• William H. McGannon Foundation Scholarships (Scholarship)
• RIMS Membership Growth Award (Award)
Meetings/Conferences: • RIMS (Risk & Insurance Management Society Inc.) 2015 Annual Conference & Exhibition, April, 2015, New Orleans Ernest N. Morial Convention Center, New Orleans, LA
Scope: International
Description: An international conference & exhibition presenting professional development & networking opportunities for risk professionals

• RIMS (Risk & Insurance Management Society Inc.) Canada 2015 Conference, 2015
Scope: National
Attendance: 1,000+
Description: A risk management conference & exhibition, held each autumn, of interest to Canadian risk professionals
• RIMS (Risk & Insurance Management Society Inc.) 2016 Annual Conference & Exhibition, 2016
Scope: International
Description: A gathering of risk professionals from around the world to share experiences
• RIMS (Risk & Insurance Management Society Inc.) Canada 2016 Conference, 2016
Scope: National
Description: An annual risk management conference & exhibition held in the autumn for risk managers & the vendor community
Publications:
• RIMS Canada Newsletter
Type: Newsletter; *Frequency:* Irregular; *Editor:* M. Ferreira; E. Henley; P. Corbeil
Profile: Activities & news from RIMS Canada Council & its subcommittees
• Risk Management Magazine
Type: Magazine; *Frequency:* 10 pa; *Accepts Advertising*; *Editor:* Morgan O'Rourke; *Price:* $115 / year
Profile: Analysis, insight, & news for corporate risk managers
• Risk Professionals Directory
Type: Directory
• RiskWire
Type: Newsletter; *Frequency:* Daily
Profile: A daily news service, presenting the most important risk management stories, exclusively for RIMS members

British Columbia Chapter
Vancouver BC
britishcolumbia.rims.org
Mission: To improve & promote risk management in British Columbia; To encourage the development of members
Chief Officer(s):
Vilma Zanchettin, President
Jeff Schaafsma, Vice-President & RCC Liaison
Janiece Brown, Secretary
Dan Heaman, Treasurer & RIMS Delegate
Gloria Gao, Director

Canadian Capital Region Chapter
Ottawa ON
canadiancapital.rims.org
Mission: To promote the discipline of risk management throughout eastern Ontario
Chief Officer(s):
Rachel Steen, Vice-President
Brigitte Cayer, Secretary
John Lammey, Treasurer

Manitoba Chapter
Winnipeg MB
manitoba.rims.org
Mission: To promote all aspects of risk management in Manitoba
Chief Officer(s):
Tim Lucko, President
Cindy Bauer, Vice-President
Stacie Dheilly, Secretary
Beverley Duthoit, Treasurer
Valerie Barber, Assistant Secretary & Director, Membership
• MaRIMS Newsletter
Type: Newsletter; *Editor:* John Rislahti
Profile: Manitoba chapter activities & forthcoming programs

Maritime (New Brunswick, Nova Scotia, & Prince Edward Island) Chapter
Stellarton NB
maritime.rims.org
Chief Officer(s):
Stephen Trueman, President
Andrea Cameron, Vice-President
Dee Vipond, Secretary
Trevor Gonnason, Treasurer
Vanessa MacLean, Contact, Membership

Newfoundland & Labrador Chapter
St. John's NL
newfoundlandlabrador.rims.org
Chief Officer(s):
Gail Cullen, President
Gordon Payne, Vice-President & RIMS Delegate
Patrick Ryan, Secretary, Treasurer & Webmaster

Northern Alberta Chapter
Sherwood Park AB
Tel: 780-400-2025
northernalberta.rims.org
Leatherland Angela, President

Ontario Chapter
PO Box 1021, 66 Wellington St. West, Toronto ON M5K 1P2
ontario.rims.org
Chief Officer(s):
Paul Provis, Vice-President, 416-865-8411, Fax: 416-868-0701
pprovis@oxforproperties.com
Agata Jamroz, Secretary, 416-955-7681, Fax: 416-955-7621
agata.jamroz@rbc.com
Mark Cosgrove, Treasurer, 416-592-4487, Fax: 416-592-4775
mark.cosgrove@opg.com
Sandra Alwazani, Contact, Public Relations & External Affairs, 416-736-2100 Ext. 22922, Fax: 416-736-5815
alwazani@yorku.ca
Joseph Costello, Contact, Membership, 416-345-5019, Fax: 416-345-6266
joe.costello@hydroone.com
• PULSE
Type: Newsletter; *Frequency:* Irregular; *Accepts Advertising*; *Editor:* Suzanne M. Barrett
Profile: Activities of the Ontario chapter, including educational workshops & seminars & social functions, as well as industry news

Québec Chapter
CP 1102, Succ. B, Montréal QC H3B 3K9
agraq.qrima@gmail.com
www.agraq.org
Chief Officer(s):
Michel Pontbriand, Président
Stephane Cossette, 1er Vice-président & Trésorier
• InfoRisque
Type: Newsletter; *Editor:* Ginette Demers
Profile: Updates on chapter activities & announcements of upcoming programs

Saskatchewan Chapter
c/o David Jackson, Saskatchewan School Boards Association, #400, 2222 - 13th Ave., Regina SK S4P 3M7
Tel: 306-569-0750
saskatchewan.rims.org
Mission: To promote the discipline of risk management; To encourage a competitive insurance marketplace
Chief Officer(s):
David Jackson, President
djackson@saskschoolboards.ca
Randy Besse, Vice-President, Program, 306-775-6757
rbesse@sgi.sk.ca
David Boehm, Vice-President & Secretary, South, 306-787-0835
david.boehm@gov.sk.ca
Merv Dahl, Vice-President, North, 306-966-8753
merv.dahl@usask.ca
Marnie McCallum, Treasurer, 306-787-1440
marnie.maccallum@gov.sk.ca

Southern Alberta Chapter
c/o Darius Delon, Mount Royal University, 4825 Mount Royal Gate SW, Calgary AB T3E 6K6
Tel: 403-440-6196
southernalberta.rims.org
Mission: To promote awareness & understanding of risk management
Chief Officer(s):
Darius Delon, President
ddelon@mtroyal.ca
Rob Groves, Vice-President & Treasurer, 403-500-2455, Fax: 403-298-1483
rob.groves@cssd.ab.ca
Lynne Kulchitsky, Secretary, 403-220-5719, Fax: 403-282-2765
lynne.kulchitsky@ucalgary.ca
Curtis Desiatnyk, Director, Membership, 403-440-5574, Fax: 403-440-8927
cdesiatnyk@mtroyal.ca

River Valley Chamber of Commerce (RVCC)
PO Box 3123, Grand Bay-Westfield NB E5K 4V4
Tel: 506-738-8666; *Fax:* 506-738-3697
Other Communication: www.flickr.com/photos/65004067@N06
www.rvchamber.ca
www.facebook.com/104532436309510
twitter.com/rvcc
www.youtube.com/rvchamberofcommerce
Overview: A small local organization
Chief Officer(s):
Danny Harrigan, President
Jim Balcomb, Vice-President/Treasurer
Finances: *Annual Operating Budget:* Less than $50,000; *Funding Sources:* Membership; insurance
Membership: 50; *Fees:* $50

Riverdale Immigrant Women's Centre (RIWC)
1326 Gerrard St. East, Toronto ON M4L 1Z1
Tel: 416-465-6021; *Fax:* 416-465-4785
reception.riwc@gmail.com
www.riwc.ca
Overview: A small local organization founded in 1982 overseen by Ontario Council of Agencies Serving Immigrants
Mission: To support Chinese speaking & South Asian women & their families; To empower immigrant women
Membership: *Fees:* $10 new members & renewals; $25 organizations
Activities: Providing workshops on topics such as settlement issues, violence against women, legal issues, ESL, & health issues; Offering counselling support services; Assisting newcomers to Canada with employment services
Publications:
• Background & Model for Parent-Child Resource Centre
Author: Laura Jones
• Celebrating Women, Aging, & Cultural Diversity
• Child Family Resources
Author: Laura Jones
• ELT Community Based Mode for Language Training
Type: Report; *Author:* Baktygul Ismailova
• Mawan Thandian Chawan: A Parenting Manual for Community Workers & Activists Working with South Asian Survivors of Wife Abuse
Type: Manual
• A Tribute to Grassroots Organizing For Women's Health: Cases From Around the World
Author: S. Torres, P. Khosla, N. Leedham
• Violence Against Women Training Manual
Type: Manual; *Author:* Anna Willats & Jaswant Kaur
• Ward 30: Broadview-Greenwood Environmental Scan
Author: Laura Jones

Rivers & District Chamber of Commerce
PO Box 795, Rivers MB R0K 1X0
Tel: 204-328-7316; *Fax:* 204-328-5212
riverschamber@gmail.com
riversdaly.ca/chamber-of-commerce/
Overview: A small local organization founded in 1908
Mission: To encourage growth in Rivers and district by supporting their existing businesses and to encourage new businesses.
Member of: Manitoba Chamber of Commerce
Chief Officer(s):
Melissa MacMillan, President
Jean Young, Sec./Tres.
Finances: *Annual Operating Budget:* Less than $50,000; *Funding Sources:* Craft sale; Town of Rivers; Fundraisers
Staff Member(s): 1; 10 volunteer(s)
Membership: 28; *Fees:* $10-$100, based on # of employees; *Committees:* Crafty, Christmas, Downtown promo
Activities: Home and craft sale, Santa parade

Riverton & District Chamber of Commerce
PO Box 258, Riverton MB R0C 2R0
Tel: 204-378-2084; *Fax:* 204-378-2085
berniced@mts.net
www.rivertoncanada.com
Overview: A small local organization
Chief Officer(s):
Susie Eyolfson, Vice-Chair

Riverton & District Friendship Centre
PO Box 359, 53 Laura Ave., Riverton MB R0C 2R0
Tel: 204-378-2800; *Fax:* 204-378-5705
rdfc@mts.net
www.rivertonfc.com
Overview: A small local charitable organization founded in 1981
Mission: To provide a meeting place for individuals & community groups of different cultures; To create fellowship between the native members of the Riverton area
Member of: Manitoba Association of Friendship Centres
Affliation(s): National Association of Friendship Centres; National Aboriginal Health Organization

Activities: Delivering a youth drop-in program; Promoting health & prevention; Providing resources; Offering a social network; Providing regular community & family activities; Assisting Aboriginals with employment placements, in a program entitled, Partners for Careers; Helping native people to settle in Riverton; Providing a referral service to governments & agencies; Liaising with other community organizations; *Library:* Riverton & District Friendship Centre Seniors Resource Centre

The Road & Infrastructure Program Canada (TRIP Canada)
#1900, 275 Slater St., Ottawa ON K1P 5H9
Tel: 613-236-9455; *Fax:* 613-236-9526
cca@cca-acc.com
careersincivilconstruction.ca
www.twitter.com/CareersInCivil
www.youtube.com/user/CareersInCivil
Overview: A small national organization
Mission: To articulate the need for increased investment in Canada's municipal infrastructure & national highway system
Member of: Canadian Construction Association
Chief Officer(s):
Bill Ferreira, Executive Director
Finances: *Annual Operating Budget:* $50,000-$100,000
Staff Member(s): 1; 35 volunteer(s)
Membership: 11 associations
Activities: *Speaker Service:* Yes

Robert Sauvé Occupational Health & Safety Research Institute *Voir* Institut de recherche Robert-Sauvé en santé et en sécurité du travail

Robin Hood Association for the Handicapped
141 Broadway Blvd., Sherwood Park AB T8H 2A4
Tel: 780-467-7140; *Fax:* 780-449-2028
info@robinhoodassoc.com
www.robinhoodassoc.com
www.facebook.com/135479853139658
Overview: A medium-sized local charitable organization founded in 1963
Mission: To assist individuals with disabilities to achieve their personal best
Member of: Alberta Council of Disability Services (ACDS)
Chief Officer(s):
Ed Riediger, CEO
riediger@robinhoodassoc.com
Finances: *Funding Sources:* Donations
Staff Member(s): 400
Activities: Offering programs for children, such as early childhood development, early intervention, family support services, & a summer program; Providing services to adults, such as the Centre for Learning day program, community access, residential services, resources, & transportation
Publications:
• Arrow
Type: Newsletter; *Frequency:* Quarterly
Profile: Current information about the association, including upcoming events

Roblin & District Chamber of Commerce
PO Box 160, 147 Main St., Roblin MB R0L 1P0
Tel: 204-937-3194
rdcoc@mts.net
www.roblinmanitoba.com/index.php?pageid=BUSCOC
Overview: A small local organization
Member of: Manitoba Chambers of Commerce
Chief Officer(s):
Norma Gaber, President, 204-937-4473
Finances: *Annual Operating Budget:* Less than $50,000; *Funding Sources:* Membership dues
Staff Member(s): 1; 15 volunteer(s)
Membership: 85; *Fees:* Based on number of employees; *Committees:* Event Committees
Activities: Trade show; Christmas promotion; craft show; parade; *Library* Open to public

Robson Street Business Association (RSBA)
#412, 1155 Robson St., Vancouver BC V6E 1B5
Tel: 604-669-8132; *Fax:* 604-669-0181
info@robsonstreet.ca
www.robsonstreet.ca
www.facebook.com/RobsonStreet
twitter.com/RobsonStreet
instagram.com/robsonstreet
Overview: A small local charitable organization founded in 1991
Mission: To promote the businesses on Robson St.
Member of: Business Improvement Association British Columbia; Tourism Vancouver
Finances: *Annual Operating Budget:* $100,000-$250,000; *Funding Sources:* Property tax levies
Staff Member(s): 2; 20 volunteer(s)
Membership: 200; *Member Profile:* Merchants & property owners

Rocanville & District Museum Society Inc.
PO Box 490, Rocanville SK S0A 3L0
Tel: 306-645-2113
rocanvillemuseum@gmail.com
rocanvillemuseum.wix.com
Overview: A small local charitable organization founded in 1964
Mission: To gather & display artifacts from the area so as to preserve for all time the historical beginnings & progress of this & surrounding communities
Member of: Saskatchewan Museums Association
Affliation(s): Rocanville Recreation Board
Chief Officer(s):
Ray Behrns, President
Finances: *Funding Sources:* Museum gallery grant; fundraising
Activities: Displays; demonstrations of threshing, oat rolling, wheat gristing on Museum Day; guided tours available on request; *Library:* Documentation Centre; by appointment

Rocky Mountain House & District Chamber of Commerce
PO Box 1374, 5406 - 48 St., Rocky Mountain House AB T4T 1B1
Tel: 403-845-5450; *Fax:* 403-845-7764
Toll-Free: 800-565-3793
rmhcofc@rockychamber.org
www.rockychamber.org
Overview: A small local charitable organization
Mission: To develop strategic initiatives to promote & enhance the growth of economic development
Affliation(s): AB Chamber of Commerce; Canadian Chamber of Commerce
Chief Officer(s):
Patrick Danis, President
Cindy Taschuk, Executive Director
Finances: *Annual Operating Budget:* $100,000-$250,000; *Funding Sources:* Memberships; projects
Staff Member(s): 3; 18 volunteer(s)
Membership: 350; *Fees:* Schedule available; *Committees:* Administration & Finance; Membership; Development; Communication & Promotion; Municipal Partnering; Downtown Enhancement
Activities: Annual banquet; trade show; *Speaker Service:* Yes; *Library:* Business Resource Centre; Open to public by appointment

Rocky Mountain Naturalists
PO Box 791, Cranbrook BC V1C 4J5
www.kootenaynaturalists.org/rocky
Overview: A small local charitable organization founded in 1985
Mission: To promote the enjoyment of nature through environmental appreciation & conservation; to encourage the wise use & conservation of natural resources & environmental protection
Member of: Federation of BC Naturalists
Chief Officer(s):
Greg Ross, Contact
gsross@shaw.ca
Membership: 40; *Fees:* $20 individual; $25 family
Activities: Field trips; study nights; conservation projects

Rocky Native Friendship Society
PO Box 1927, 4917 - 52 St., Rocky Mountain House AB T4T 1B4
Tel: 403-845-2788; *Fax:* 403-845-3093
www.friendshipcentre.shawbiz.ca
www.facebook.com/147332261987888
Overview: A small local organization founded in 1975 overseen by Alberta Native Friendship Centres Association
Mission: To create a healthy & supportive community to empower Aboriginal people in the Rocky Mountain House area; To strengthen Aboriginal cultural awareness
Member of: Alberta Native Friendship Centres Association
Affliation(s): Alberta Native Friendship Centres Association
Chief Officer(s):
Merle White, Executive Director
Helge Nome, President
Douglas Bonaise, Vice-President
Tani Amarook, Treasurer
Activities: Offering services in early intervention, addictions, & for youth; Providing programs, such as Aboriginal Neighborhood Place & the Family Literacy Program; Advocating on behalf of clients for respectful & appropriate treatment;

Rogersville Chamber of Commerce *Voir* Chambre de commerce de Rogersville

Roller Sports Canada / Sports à roulettes du Canada
1 Bancroft Cres., Whitby ON L1R 2E6
Tel: 905-666-9343
rollersports@hotmail.com
rollersports.ca
Previous Name: Canadian Federation of Amateur Roller Skaters
Overview: A small national organization
Chief Officer(s):
Wayne Burret, President
wayneburrett@rogers.com

Romanian Children's Relief
12 Homedale Dr., Toronto ON M1V 1M2
Tel: 416-292-3688
romanianchildrensrelief@rogers.com
www.rcr.org
Previous Name: Association for Democracy in Romania
Overview: A small international charitable organization founded in 1990
Mission: To provide relief supplies to selected orphanages, asylums & hospitals in Romania
Chief Officer(s):
Flavia Cosma, Chair
Finances: *Annual Operating Budget:* Less than $50,000
45 volunteer(s)
Membership: 1-99
Activities: Collecting & sending goods to selected orphanages (1-2 times a year)

Romanian Orthodox Deanery of Canada
PO Box 4023, Regina SK S4P 3R9
romanianorthodoxdeanery.org
Overview: A small national organization
Mission: The Romanian Orthodox Episcopate of America is grouped geographically into 7 deaneries & the Deanery of Canada is one of them, with 30 parishes across the country. It is non-profit, registered charity, BN: 888289642RR0001.
Member of: Romanian Orthodox Episcopate of America; Orthodox Church in America
Chief Officer(s):
Nathaniel Popp, Archbishop, 517-522-4800
nathaniel@roea.org
Ionel Cudritescu, Dean, Eastern Canada, 416-614-1942
icudritescu5303@rogers.com
Michael Lupu, Dean, Western Canada, 403-203-7033
fatherlupu@shaw.ca

Ronald McDonald Children's Charities of Canada *See* Ronald McDonald House Charities of Canada

Ronald McDonald House Charities of Canada (RMHC) / Oeuvres pour enfants Ronald McDonald du Canada
1 McDonald's Place, Toronto ON M3C 3L4
Tel: 416-446-3493; *Fax:* 416-446-3588
Toll-Free: 800-387-8808
rmhc@ca.mcd.com
www.rmhc.ca
www.facebook.com/RMHCCanada
Previous Name: Ronald McDonald Children's Charities of Canada
Overview: A medium-sized national charitable organization founded in 1982
Mission: To help children in need by improving the physical & emotional quality of life for children with serious illnesses, disabilities &/or chronic conditions, allowing them to lead happier, healthier & more productive lives
Chief Officer(s):
Cathy Loblaw, President & CEO
cathy.loblaw@ca.mcd.com
Richard Ellis, Chair
Roxanna Kassam Kara, Manager, Communications & Marketing
roxanna.kassamkara@ca.mcd.com
Staff Member(s): 7
Membership: 14; *Member Profile:* Ronald McDonald Houses

Ronald McDonald House Toronto
240 McCaul St., Toronto ON M5T 1W5

Tel: 416-977-0458; *Fax:* 416-977-8807
info@rmhtoronto.org
www.rmhtoronto.org
Also Known As: Toronto Children's Care Inc.
Previous Name: Children's Oncology Care of Ontario Inc.
Overview: A small local charitable organization founded in 1981
Mission: To provide a home away from home for out-of-town families whose children are receiving treatment in Toronto hospitals for serious illness; we strongly believe that when a child is seriously ill, the love & support of family can be as important as any course of treatment
Chief Officer(s):
Jane Marco, Executive Director
G. Keith Graham, President
Finances: *Annual Operating Budget:* $500,000-$1.5 Million; *Funding Sources:* Public
Staff Member(s): 10; 105 volunteer(s)
Membership: 30 board; *Fees:* $10
Activities: Child Life Program; Play Program; Summer Fun; Support and Courtesy Services; Family Room Program; *Speaker Service:* Yes

Roncesvalles Macdonell Residents' Association (RMRA)

c/o 49 Fermanagh Ave., Toronto ON M6R 1M1
e-mail: info@rmra-to.org
www.rmra-to.org
Overview: A small local organization founded in 1973
Mission: To preserve & promote the community
Chief Officer(s):
Brian Torry, Co-Chair
Norman Kolasky, Co-Chair
Membership: *Fees:* $10 waged; $5 unwaged

La Ronge & District Chamber of Commerce

PO Box 1046, La Ronge SK S0J 1L0
e-mail: chamber@laclarongechamber.ca
www.laclarongechamber.ca
Overview: A small local organization
Member of: Saskatchewan Chamber of Commerce; Canadian Chamber of Commerce
Chief Officer(s):
Clarence Neault, President
Victoria Magee, Secretary
Finances: *Annual Operating Budget:* Less than $50,000; *Funding Sources:* Membership dues
Membership: 79; *Fees:* Schedule available

Roofing Contractors Association of British Columbia (RCABC)

9734 - 201st St., Langley BC V1M 3E8
Tel: 604-882-9734; *Fax:* 604-882-1744
bporth@rcabc.org
www.rcabc.org
Also Known As: RCABC Educational Foundation
Overview: A medium-sized provincial organization founded in 1958 overseen by Canadian Roofing Contractors' Association
Mission: To provide continuing education for roofing contractors, their workers & interested others; to represent the roofing contracting industry in its relationships with legislative & regulating bodies; to work closely with affiliate organizations & liaison groups in advancing the professionalism of roofing contracting; to provide a forum for the interaction of members; to encourage high standards of professional conduct among roofing contractors; to develop a comprehensive body of knowledge about roofing management & technology; to disseminate ideas & knowledge to members & others; to monitor new products & systems; to work for cooperation & greater understanding between contracting, inspection, manufacturing & supply segments of the roofing industry
Member of: National Roofing Contractors' Association (USA); Western States Roofing Contractors Association
Affliation(s): International Federation of Roofing Contractors
Chief Officer(s):
Ivan van Spronsen, Executive Vice-President, 604-882-9734
ivan@rcabc.org
Finances: *Annual Operating Budget:* $1.5 Million-$3 Million; *Funding Sources:* Membership dues; government funding; administration fees
Staff Member(s): 15
Membership: 119 corporate; *Member Profile:* Professional roofers, suppliers, manufacturers; *Committees:* Entertainment; Ethics; Membership; Technical; Education & Training
Activities: Third party labour & material guarantees; training; professional development; *Library* Open to public by appointment
Awards:
• Klaus Thiel Educational Endowment Fund (Award)

Roofing Contractors Association of Manitoba Inc. (RCAM)

1447 Waverley St., Winnipeg MB R3T 0P7
Tel: 204-783-6365; *Fax:* 204-783-6446
www.rcam.ca
Overview: A small provincial organization founded in 1966 overseen by Canadian Roofing Contractors' Association
Chief Officer(s):
Marian Boles, Contact
marianboles@rcam.ca
Finances: *Funding Sources:* Membership fees
Membership: 27

Roofing Contractors Association of Nova Scotia (RCANS)

7 Frederick Ave., Mount Uniacke NS B0N 1Z0
Tel: 902-866-0505; *Fax:* 902-866-0506
Toll-Free: 888-278-0133
contact@rcans.ca
www.rcans.ca
Overview: A small provincial organization founded in 1965 overseen by Canadian Roofing Contractors' Association
Mission: To promote quality workmanship in the commerical, industrial & institutional roofing industry; to encourage training for roofers
Member of: Canadian Roofing Contractor's Association
Affliation(s): Construction Association of Nova Scotia
Chief Officer(s):
Mike Croft, President, 902-758-1364, Fax: 902-758-1219
Marg Woodworth, Office Manager
Membership: 32; *Member Profile:* Roofing companies; suppliers; manufacturers

Rosaries for Canadian Forces Abroad

e-mail: rosarymaker@canada.com
oparcher.blogspot.com
Overview: A small national organization
Mission: Providing military support by making & donating Rosaries to members of the Canadian Forces serving abroad
Affliation(s): Archdiocese of Toronto
Membership: *Member Profile:* Any person who wishes to assist in the making or distribution of Rosaries for Canadian Forces deployed abroad may join the private Catholic lay apostolate
Activities: Making Rosaries in parish guilds, led by a guild leader

The Rosary Apostolate, Inc.

1208 Warden Ave., Toronto ON M1R 2R3
e-mail: info@rosaryapostolate.com
www.rosaryapostolate.com
Overview: A small local charitable organization founded in 1997
Mission: To lead children, youth, & families to Jesus through Mary
Chief Officer(s):
Michael D'Cruz, Spiritual Director
Marilina Cinelli, Spiritual Director
Finances: *Funding Sources:* Donations
Membership: *Member Profile:* Individuals, who are practising Catholics, are devoted to Mary & her rosary, & who respect & love children; Volunteers, who cater to the schools in their parishes as rosary visitors; Rosary visitors teach children by praying the Rosary & the Act of Consecration
Activities: Forming parish prayer groups for evangelization through prayer; Conducting school visits to pray the rosary with children in Catholic schools; Providing director workshops & regional meetings; Recruiting, screening, & training rosary visitors; Outlining themes & meditations for rosary visitors; Offering annual retreats
Publications:
• The Rosary Apostolate Newsletter
Type: Newsletter

Rose & Max Rady Jewish Community Centre (RJCC)

123 Doncaster St., Winnipeg MB R3M 0S3
Tel: 204-477-7510; *Fax:* 204-477-7530
inquiry@radyjcc.com
radyjcc.com
Also Known As: RADY Centre
Previous Name: Jewish Community Centre of Winnipeg
Overview: A small local charitable organization founded in 1919
Mission: Multi-service agency created by & primarily for, but not only for the benefit of the Jewish community of Winnipeg
Member of: Jewish Community Centers Association of North America
Affliation(s): Canadian Council of Jewish Community Centres; Association of Jewish Center Professionals; Manitoba Camping Association; Folk Arts Council of Winnipeg
Chief Officer(s):
Jeff Lieberman, President
Gayle Waxman, Executive Director
Finances: *Annual Operating Budget:* $1.5 Million-$3 Million; *Funding Sources:* Program & membership generated; United Way; Jewish Federation of Winnipeg/Combined Jewish Appeal
Staff Member(s): 36; 200 volunteer(s)
Membership: 6,500; *Fees:* $250-1,800
Activities: Fitness; aerobics & water fitness; aquatics; recreation & sport; health & wellness programs; children & youth; preschool programs; birthday parties; teen drop-in; adult & judaic program; Stay Young Centre; cultural & performing arts & special events; special needs services; resident & day camping; *Internships:* Yes; *Library:* Kaufman-Silverberg Resource Centre
Meetings/Conferences: • 43rd Annual Rady JCC Sports Dinner 2015, May, 2015, RBC Convention Centre, Winnipeg, MB
Scope: Provincial

North End Branch
123 Matheson Ave. East, Winnipeg MB R2W 0C3
Tel: 204-589-6305; *Fax:* 204-582-0246
Chief Officer(s):
Syva Lee Wildenmann, Director

Pearl & Max Herman Branch JCC
4715 McTavish St., Regina SK S4S 6H2
Tel: 306-757-8643; *Fax:* 306-352-3499
Chief Officer(s):
Mary Jane Katz, Director

Rose Society of Ontario *See* Canadian Rose Society

Rosetown & District Chamber of Commerce

PO Box 744, Rosetown SK S0L 2V0
Tel: 306-882-1300; *Fax:* 306-882-1310
www.rosetown.ca
Overview: A small local organization
Chief Officer(s):
Gerry Clark, Chair
Shirley Helgason, Executive Director
Finances: *Annual Operating Budget:* Less than $50,000
Membership: 100-499

Ross Township Historical Society of Whitewater Region; Ross Township Historical Society *See* Whitewater Historical Society

Rossburn & District Chamber of Commerce

PO Box 579, Rossburn MB R0J 1V0
Tel: 204-859-3334; *Fax:* 204-859-3313
rossburn.chamber@live.ca
Overview: A small local organization
Mission: To enhance & promote established businesses & encourage new businesses to come to Rossburn
Member of: Manitoba Chamber of Commerce
Chief Officer(s):
Tony White, President
Myra Drul, Secretary
Finances: *Annual Operating Budget:* Less than $50,000
20 volunteer(s)
Membership: 49; *Fees:* $50; *Committees:* Membership; Events; Promotions; Welcome to Rossburn & Area
Activities: Annual Summer Festival Parade; Christmas Lighting Contest; Welcome Baskets; *Awareness Events:* Welcome to Rossburn

Rossland Chamber of Commerce

PO Box 1385, #204, 2012 Washington St., Rossland BC V0G 1Y0
Tel: 250-362-5666; *Fax:* 250-362-5399
commerce@rossland.com
www.rossland.com/about
Also Known As: Rossland Red Mountain Resort Association
Overview: A small local organization
Mission: To market Rossland & Red Mountain as a four season destination resort community
Member of: Canadian Chamber of Commerce
Chief Officer(s):
Paul Gluska, President
Renee Clark, Executive Director
Finances: *Annual Operating Budget:* $100,000-$250,000; *Funding Sources:* Municipal & provincial contracts; membership dues
Staff Member(s): 2

Membership: 160; *Fees:* $100.07 bronze; $153.70 silver; $286.20 gold; *Committees:* Education; Marketing; Membership; Policies
Activities: *Library:* Business Info Centre; Open to public

Rotary Club of Stratford Charitable Foundation

PO Box 21135, Stratford ON N5A 7V4
Tel: 519-273-6297
request@rotarystratford.com
www.rotarystratford.com
Overview: A small local charitable organization founded in 1922
Member of: Rotary International
Chief Officer(s):
James Corkery, Contact
Membership: 100-499

The Rotary Club of Toronto

Fairmont Royal York Hotel, 100 Front St. West, Toronto ON M5J 1E3
Tel: 416-363-0604; *Fax:* 416-363-0686
office@rotarytoronto.com
www.rotarytoronto.com
Overview: A medium-sized local charitable organization founded in 1913
Mission: To encourage & foster the ideal of service as a basis of worthy enterprise through fellowship among members, ethical behavior in business & the professions, service to the community & the advancement of international understanding, goodwill & peace; dedicated to improving lives of those most vulnerable in the Toronto community
Affliation(s): Rotary of International
Chief Officer(s):
William N. Morari, President
Finances: *Annual Operating Budget:* $250,000-$500,000
Staff Member(s): 2; 240 volunteer(s)
Membership: 240; *Fees:* $2,280
Activities: Fundraising; granting activities; funding local projects; *Speaker Service:* Yes

Rotman Institute for International Business (RIIB)

University of Toronto, 105 St. George St., Toronto ON M5S 3E6
Tel: 416-978-5781
riib@utoronto.ca
www.rotman.utoronto.ca
Previous Name: Institute for Policy Analysis
Merged from: Institute for Policy Analysis; Institute for International Business
Overview: A medium-sized national organization founded in 2008
Mission: RIIB merges the former Institute for Policy Analysis & the Institute for International Business, & focusses on research on the global business environment, enterprise decision making in the global economy, & the urban service economy.
Affliation(s): University of Toronto
Chief Officer(s):
Wendy Dobson, Co-Director
dobson@rotman.utoronto.ca
Ig Horstman, Co-Director, Prof. of Economics
Ihorstmann@rotman.utoronto.ca
Finances: *Annual Operating Budget:* $100,000-$250,000; *Funding Sources:* Grants; contracts; donations
Staff Member(s): 3
Membership: 1-99
Activities: *Library*

La Route Celtique *See* The Celtic Way

Routes to Learning Canada (RLC)

4 Cataraqui St., Kingston ON K7K 1Z7
Fax: 613-530-2096
Toll-Free: 866-745-1690
information@routestolearning.ca
www.routestolearning.ca
Previous Name: Elderhostel Canada
Overview: A large national charitable organization founded in 1980
Mission: To develop, manage & facilitate educational experiences for older adults through cooperative partnership with educational agents; to balance education & travel in an environment of comradeship & respect; to continue to experiment with pilot projects to reach broader populations of older adults; to be a "learner-centered" organization that responds to the learning needs of older adults; to work towards a better understanding of our relationship with our current populations; to use new methods of reaching out to an ever more diverse multicultural Canada; to promote cost-effective educational opportunities to an ever widening group of older adults
Chief Officer(s):
Victoria Pearson, President/CEO
Finances: *Annual Operating Budget:* $500,000-$1.5 Million
Staff Member(s): 15; 175 volunteer(s)
Membership: 300,000; *Member Profile:* Open to people in their retirement years, 55 & over
Activities: Offers residential, educational programs to interested adults (55+) through a variety of educational institutions; *Speaker Service:* Yes

Row Nova Scotia

#400, 5516 Spring Garden Rd., Halifax NS B3J 1G6
Tel: 902-425-5450
rowing@rowns.ca
www.rowns.ca
www.facebook.com/RowNovaScotia
twitter.com/RowNovaScotia
Overview: A medium-sized provincial organization overseen by Rowing Canada Aviron
Mission: To govern the sport of rowing in Nova Scotia.
Member of: Rowing Canada Aviron
Chief Officer(s):
Peter Webster, President
president@rowns.ca
Janessa Green, PSO Administrative Coordinator

Rowing British Columbia

#155, 3820 Cessna Dr., Richmond BC V7B 0A2
Tel: 604-273-4769; *Fax:* 604-333-3450
Toll-Free: 877-330-3638
info@rowingbc.ca
www.rowingbc.ca
www.facebook.com/176456622408863
Also Known As: Rowing BC
Overview: A medium-sized provincial organization founded in 1987 overseen by Rowing Canada Aviron
Mission: To govern the sport of rowing in British Columbia.
Member of: Rowing Canada Aviron
Chief Officer(s):
Jennifer Fitzpatrick, Executive Director
exdirector@rowingbc.ca
Ben Rutledge, Provincial Coach
coach@rowingbc.ca
Membership: *Member Profile:* Community, secondary & post-secondary educational rowing clubs

Rowing Canada Aviron (RCA) / Association canadienne d'aviron amateur

#321, 4371 Interurban Rd., Victoria BC V9E 2C5
Fax: 250-220-2503
Toll-Free: 877-722-4769
rca@rowingcanada.org
www.rowingcanada.org
www.facebook.com/81982893039
twitter.com/rowingcanada
www.youtube.com/user/RowingCan
Also Known As: Canadian Amateur Rowing Association
Previous Name: The Canadian Association of Amateur Oarsmen
Overview: A large national organization founded in 1880
Mission: To encourage the formation of rowing clubs & provincial associations; To encourage the organization of national regattas; To define & to maintain the principles of amateurism in all competitions; To organize, develop, & select national rowing teams to represent Canada internationally
Affiliation(s): Fédération Internationale des Sociétés d'Aviron; Canadian Olympic Association
Chief Officer(s):
Michael Walker, President
Donna Atkinson, Chief Executive Officer
datkinson@rowingcanada.org
Finances: *Funding Sources:* Sport Canada; Sponsors
Staff Member(s): 12
Membership: *Fees:* $650 rowing association; $500 associate organization & special association; $350 rowing club; *Committees:* Governance Review; Executive
Awards:
• Recognition of National Champions / Reconnaissance des champions nationaux (Award)
• Recognition of International Medal Winners / Reconnaissance des gagnants de médailles internationales (Award)
• Long Service Recognition / Reconnaissance de long service (Award)
• Recognition of Those Retiring / Reconnaissance des membres qui prennent leur retraite cette année (Award)
• Club Level Awards / Récompenses au niveau des clubs (Award)
• Petro-Canada Excellece Awards / Prix d'excellence Petro-Canada aux entraîneurs (Award)
• RCA International Achievement Award / Récompense d'accomplissement international (Award)
• RCA National Level Awards / Récompense au niveau national (Award)
• Centennial Medal (Award)
• Award of Merit / Prix du mérite (Award)
• The President's Award / Le Prix Du Président (Award)

Rowing New Brunswick Aviron

10 Fallow Lane, McLeod Hill NB E3G 6A8
e-mail: info@rowingnb.ca
www.rowingnb.ca
www.facebook.com/248560025170763
Also Known As: Rowing NB Aviron
Overview: A medium-sized provincial organization overseen by Rowing Canada Aviron
Mission: To govern the sport of rowing in New Brunswick.
Member of: Rowing Canada Aviron
Chief Officer(s):
John Oxley, Acting President
Alan Oldham, High Performance Coach

Rowing Newfoundland

331 Thorburn Rd., St. John's NL A1B 4R1
freeteams.net/rowingnl
Previous Name: Newfoundland Rowing Association
Overview: A small provincial organization overseen by Rowing Canada Aviron
Mission: To govern the sport of rowing in Newfoundland.
Member of: Rowing Canada Aviron
Chief Officer(s):
Doreen Hamlyn, President
doreenhamlyn@nl.rogers.com

Rowing PEI

PO Box 965, Charlottetown PE C1A 7M4
e-mail: rowingpei@gmail.com
rowingpei.ca
Overview: A medium-sized provincial organization founded in 2010 overseen by Rowing Canada Aviron
Mission: To govern the sport of rowing in Prince Edward Island.
Member of: Rowing Canada Aviron
Chief Officer(s):
Stephen Murray, President

Royal Academy of Dance Canada

#500, 1200 Sheppard Ave. East, Toronto ON M2K 2S5
Tel: 416-489-2813; *Fax:* 416-489-3222
Toll-Free: 888-709-0895
info@radcanada.org
www.radcanada.org
Also Known As: RAD Canada
Overview: A small national organization founded in 1920
Mission: To provide dance education & training
Affliation(s): Royal Academy of Dance
Chief Officer(s):
Clarke MacIntosh, National Director, Canada
cmacintosh@radcanada.org
Joyce McGuire, Contact, Sales & Mambership
jmcguire@radcanada.org
Finances: *Annual Operating Budget:* $500,000-$1.5 Million; *Funding Sources:* Membership dues
Staff Member(s): 8
Membership: 15,500+; *Fees:* $67-$232
Activities: Offering professional development courses;

Royal Agricultural Winter Fair Association (RAWF) / Foire agricole royale d'hiver

The Ricoh Coliseum, 100 Prince's Blvd., Toronto ON M6K 3C3
Tel: 416-263-3400
info@royalfair.org
www.royalfair.org
www.facebook.com/royalfair
twitter.com/THERAWF
theroyalagriculturalwinterfair.tumblr.com
Also Known As: Royal Winter Fair
Overview: A medium-sized national charitable organization founded in 1922
Mission: To promote excellence in agricultural & equestrian activities through world class competition, exhibitions &

Canadian Associations

education
Member of: Canadian Association of Fairs & Exhibitions
Chief Officer(s):
Sandra G. Banks, Chief Executive Officer
Finances: *Funding Sources:* Sponsors; government; gate admissions; advertising
Activities: *Internships:* Yes
Awards:
• Performance Horse Awards (Award)
35 divisions & classes offer prizes; Leading International Rider is the highest honour in the horse show
• Breeding Horse Awards (Award)
17 sections award prizes in this category
• Agricultural Awards (Award)
Grand Champion is the highest honour in the following categories: dairy, beef, sheep, goats, swine, market livestock, field crops, vegetables, honey & maple, poultry, jams/jellies/pickles, dairy products, square dancing, fiddling, fleece wool, rabbits, & eight youth activities
Meetings/Conferences: • 2015 Royal Winter Agricultural Fair, November, 2015, Ricoh Coluseum & Direct Energy Centre, Toronto, ON
Scope: International
Description: The Royal is the largest combined indoor agricultural fair and international equestrian competition in the world.

Royal Alberta United Services Institute (RAUSI)

c/o Mewata Armouries, 801 - 11 St., Calgary AB T2P 2C4
Tel: 403-265-6628; *Fax:* 403-265-8347
rausi@telus.net
www.rausi.ca
Overview: A small provincial organization founded in 1920
Mission: To support H.M. forces, regular, reserve & cadet
Member of: The Federation of Military & United Services Institutes of Canada
Chief Officer(s):
Gord Leek, CD, President
Finances: *Annual Operating Budget:* Less than $50,000
Staff Member(s): 1; 16 volunteer(s)
Membership: 200; *Fees:* $20-$85
Activities: *Library* Open to public

Royal Arch Masons of Canada

361 King St. West. 2nd Fl., Hamilton ON L8P 1B4
Tel: 905-522-5775; *Fax:* 905-522-5099
office@royalarchmasons.on.ca
www.royalarchmasons.on.ca
Overview: A small national organization
Chief Officer(s):
Melvyn J. Duke, Grand Scribe E.

Royal Architectural Institute of Canada (RAIC) / Institut royal d'architecture du Canada

#330, 55 Murray St., Ottawa ON K1N 5M3
Tel: 613-241-3600; *Fax:* 613-241-5750
info@raic.org
www.raic.org
Overview: A medium-sized national organization founded in 1907
Mission: To represent Canadian architects nationally & internationally; to foster public awareness & appreciation of architecture; to engage in architectural research & education; to lobby government on architectural issues
Chief Officer(s):
Jim McKee, Executive Director Ext. 206
Paule Boutin, President
Staff Member(s): 9
Membership: 3,735; *Fees:* $332.25; *Member Profile:* Registered architect
Activities: *Internships:* Yes
Awards:
• RAIC Student Medal (Award)
Available to a student in each Canadian University School of Architecture in the graduating class for the degree of Bachelor of Architecture*Eligibility:* Awarded only to a student who, in the opinion of the School, has attained a high proficiency in the course & shows those qualities of character & ability which promise outstanding achievement in the profession
• RAIC Gold Medal (Award)
Established 1930; gold medals awarded annually in recognition of a person of science or letters related to architecture & the arts, in addition to an architect, for great achievement & contribution to the architectural profession

RAIC Syllabus National Office
#210, 318 Homer St., Vancouver BC V6B 2V2
Tel: 604-669-9830; *Fax:* 604-669-5513
info@raic-syllabus.ca
www.raic-syllabus.ca
Chief Officer(s):
Ian Macdonald, Chair, Interim Program Advisory Committee
macdona@cc.umanitoba.ca

Royal Astronomical Society of Canada (RASC) / Société royale d'astronomie du Canada

#203, 4920 Dundas St. West, Toronto ON M9A 1B7
Tel: 416-924-7973; *Fax:* 416-924-2911
Toll-Free: 888-924-7272
www.rasc.ca
www.facebook.com/theRoyalAstronomicalSocietyofCanada
twitter.com/rasc
Overview: A medium-sized national licensing charitable organization founded in 1868
Mission: To promote the advancement of astronomy across Canada
Chief Officer(s):
James Edgar, President
Randy Attwood, Executive Director
Finances: *Funding Sources:* Membership dues; publication sales
Membership: 4,500; *Fees:* Schedule available; *Committees:* Awards; Constituttion; Education & Public Outreach; Finance; History; Information Technology; Light-Pollution; Membership & Development; Nominating; Observing; Publications
Activities: Telescope viewings; workshops; speakers; mall displays; *Awareness Events:* International Astronomy Week, April; *Library* Open to public by appointment
Awards:
• The Plaskett Medal (Award)
Presented jointly with CASCA for an outstanding doctoral thesis
• Simon Newcomb Award (Award)
Established 1978; trophy awarded annually for the best article on astronomy, astrophysics or space sciences submitted by a member of the society during the year
• Chant Medal (Award)
Established 1940 in appreciation of the great work of the late Prof. C.A. Chant in furthering the interests of astronomy in Canada; silver medal is awarded no more than once a year to an amateur astronomer resident in Canada on the basis of the value of the work which he/she has carried out in astronomy & closely allied fields of original investigation
• Service Award Medal (Award)
Established 1959; bronze medal presented to members who have performed outstanding service to a Centre or to the National Society
• Ken Chilton Prize (Award)
Established 1977; plaque awarded annually to an amateur astronomer resident in Canada, in recognition of a significant piece of work carried out or published during the year
Publications:
• Journal
Frequency: Bimonthly; *Editor:* Jay Anderson
Profile: Welcomes articles on Canadian astronomers and current activities of the RASC and its Centres, research and review papers by professional and amateur astronomers, and articles of a historical, biographical,or educational nature of general interest to the astronomical community
• Obersver's Handbook
Frequency: Annually *ISSN:* 0080-4193
Profile: The material in the Handbook is of interest to professional and amateur astronomers, scientists, teachers at all levels, students, science writers, campers, Scout and Guide leaders, as well asinterested general readers

Belleville Centre
c/o Greg Lisk, 11 Robert Dr., Trenton ON K8V 6P2
e-mail: info@rascbelleville.ca
rascbelleville.ca

Calgary Centre
PO Box 20282, #250, 300 - 5th Ave. SW, Calgary AB T2P 4J3
Tel: 403-237-7827
calrascsec@telus.net
calgary.rasc.ca
www.facebook.com/#!/pages/RASC-Calgary-Centre/1647533 50226370
Chief Officer(s):
Jason Nishiyama, President

Centre de Québec
2000, boul Montmorency, Québec QC G1J 5E7
Tel: 418-660-2815
sracquebec@gmail.com
www.srac-quebec.org
Chief Officer(s):
Guy Campeau, Président
president@astro-caaq.org

Charlottetown Centre
PO Box 1734, Charlottetown PE C1A 7N4
e-mail: PE_Centre@rasc.ca
www.rasccharlottetown.ca
twitter.com/peiastronomy
Chief Officer(s):
Clair Perry, President
Brian Gorveatt, Vice-President

Edmonton Centre
c/o Telus World of Science, 11211 - 142 St., Edmonton AB T5M 4A1
Chief Officer(s):
Sherry Campbell, President
edm.president@edmontonrasc.com
Peter Hall, Vice-President
edm.vicepresident@edmontonrasc.com

Halifax Centre
PO Box 31011, Halifax NS B3K 5T9
Tel: 902-252-9453
www.halifax.rasc.ca
Chief Officer(s):
Paul Heath, President
pheath@eastlink.ca
Wes Howie, 1st Vice-President
firstvp@lightimages.org
Karl Penney, 2nd Vice-President

Hamilton Centre
2266 Lakeshore Rd. West, Oakville ON L6L 1G8
Tel: 905-689-0266
astronomers@hamiltonrasc.ca
www.hamiltonrasc.ca
www.facebook.com/271133892909573?fref=ts
Chief Officer(s):
Gary Colwell, President
president@hamiltonrasc.ca

Kingston Centre
c/o 76 Colebrook Rd., RR#1, Kingston ON K0K 3N0
Tel: 613-377-6029
kingston@rasc.ca
kingston.rasc.ca
www.facebook.com/pages/RASC-Kingston-Centre/16172129 0520084
Chief Officer(s):
Kim Hay, President
Kevin Kell, Treasurer

Kitchener/Waterloo Centre
#3-127, 133 Weber St. North, Waterloo ON N2J 3G9
Tel: 519-576-5301
kw-rasc-sec@sympatico.ca
kw.rasc.ca
www.facebook.com/AstronomyinKitchenerWaterloo
Chief Officer(s):
Gerald Bissett, President, 519-747-1275
president@kw.rasc.ca
Ognian Kabranov, 1st Vice-President
kabranov@hotmail.com
Marvin Warkentin, 2nd Vice-President
mwarkentin@rogers.com

London Centre
PO Box 842, Stn. B, London ON N6A 4Z3
e-mail: info@rasclondon.ca
www.rasclondon.ca
Chief Officer(s):
Rick Saunders, President
prez@rasclondon.ca

Mississauga Centre
PO Box 98011, 2126 Burnhamthorpe Rd., Mississauga ON L5L 5V4
Tel: 416-894-4629
inquiries@mississauga.rasc.ca
www.mississauga.rasc.ca
Chief Officer(s):
Leslie Strike, President
pres@mississauga.rasc.ca
Andrew Opala, Vice-President
vpres@mississauga.rasc.ca

Montréal Centre - Centre francophone de Montréal
7110, 8ième av, Montréal QC H2A 3C4

Tél: 514-808-6219
info@lasam.org
www.lasam.ca
www.facebook.com/group.php?gid=116443358369383
twitter.com/lasamontreal
www.youtube.com/profile?user=lasamontreal
Montréal Centre - English
PO Box 39061, Montréal QC H3B 0B2
e-mail: info@rascmontreal.org
www.rascmontreal.org
www.facebook.com/pages/RASC-Montreal-Centre/120104748051743
Chief Officer(s):
Morrie Portnoff, President
New Brunswick Centre
70 Ian St., Saint John NB E2J 3K7
Tel: 506-696-6071
president@nb.rasc.ca
www.nb.rasc.ca
www.facebook.com/pages/RASC-New-Brunswick/101959113210475
www.twitter.com/RASCNB
Chief Officer(s):
Curt Nason, President
president@nb.rasc.ca
Niagara Centre
c/o Dr. Brian Pihack, 4245 Portage Rd., Niagara Falls ON L2E 6A2
www.astronomyniagara.com
www.facebook.com/rascniagara
Chief Officer(s):
Brian Pihack, President
drbgpdc@on.aibn.com
Brian Pihack, Vice-President
drbgpdc@on.aibn.com
Okanagan Centre
Kelowna BC
www.ocrasc.ca
Chief Officer(s):
Colleen O'Hare, President, 250-763-3573
chohare@shaw.ca
Ottawa Centre
PO Box 33012, 1363 Woodroffe Ave., Nepean ON K2C 3Y9
Tel: 613-830-3381
codale0806@rogers.com
www.ottawa-rasc.ca
www.facebook.com/group.php?gid=119345671462428
Prince George Centre
7365 Tedford Rd., Prince George BC V2N 6S2
Tel: 250-964-3600
rascpg@telus.net
www.vts.bc.ca/pgrasc/
Chief Officer(s):
Blair Stunder, President, 250-962-2334
blair.s@shaw.ca
Bob Nelson, Vice-President
bob.nelson@shaw.ca
Regina Centre
PO Box 20014, Stn. Cornwall Centre, Regina SK S4P 4J7
Tel: 306-751-0128
regina.rasc.ca
Chief Officer(s):
Chris Beckett, President
Mike O'Brien, Vice-President
St. John's Centre
206 Frecker Dr., St. John's NL A1E 5H9
Tel: 709-745-2903
info@stjohnsrasc.ca
www.stjohnsrasc.ca
Randy Dodge, Secretary
randy@mun.ca
Sarnia Centre
Sarnia ON
e-mail: mr_scope2@hotmail.com
sites.google.com/site/rascsarnia/home
www.facebook.com/group.php?gid=286531205397
Saskatoon Centre
PO Box 317, RPO University, Saskatoon SK S7N 4J8
Tel: 306-373-3902
skstars@shaw.ca
homepage.usask.ca/~ges125/rasc/
www.facebook.com/#!/pages/RASC-Saskatoon-Centre/166503696724479
Chief Officer(s):
Jim Gorkoff, President
jgorkoff@yahoo.ca
Sunshine Coast Centre
PO Box 577, Sechelt BC V0N 3A0
Tel: 778-458-2666
cuhulain@telus.net
sunshinecoastastronomy.wordpress.com
www.facebook.com/pages/Sunshine-Coast-Astronomy-Club/215347841270
twitter.com/CoastRASC
Chief Officer(s):
Michael Bradley, President
Adrian Payne, Vice-President
Thunder Bay Centre
286 Trinity Cres., Thunder Bay ON P7C 5V6
Tel: 807-475-3406
www.tbrasc.org
Chief Officer(s):
Brendon Roy, President
Toronto Centre
c/o Ontario Science Centre, 770 Don Mills Rd., Toronto ON M3C 1T3
Tel: 416-724-7827
secretary@toronto.rasc.ca
rascto.ca
www.facebook.com/rascto
www.twitter.com/rasctc
Chief Officer(s):
Charles Darrow, President
Vancouver Centre
PO Box 19115, 2302 West Fourth Ave., Vancouver BC V6K 4R8
rasc-vancouver.com
www.facebook.com/#!/group.php?gid=18968091904
Chief Officer(s):
Mark Eburne, President
president@rasc-vancouver.com
Suzanna Nagy, Vice-President
vp@rasc-vancouver.com
Victoria Centre
c/o Nelson Walker, 3836 Pitcombe Pl., Victoria BC V8N 4B9
Tel: 250-477-4820
secretary@victoria.rasc.ca
victoria.rasc.ca
Chief Officer(s):
Nelson Walker, President, 250-477-4820
president@victoria.rasc.ca
Windsor Centre
1508 Greenwood Rd., Kingsville ON N9Y 2V7
Tel: 519-969-8552
www.rascwindsor.com
Chief Officer(s):
Rick Marion, President
rmarion@mdirect.net
Matt McCall, Education Director, 519-984-3572
edu_director@outlook.com
Winnipeg Centre
PO Box 2694, Winnipeg MB R3C 4B3
Tel: 204-956-2830
www.winnipeg.rasc.ca
www.facebook.com/#!/group.php?gid=155824851116076
twitter.com/WinnipegRASC

Royal Bank of Canada Charitable Foundation *See* RBC Foundation

Royal Botanical Gardens (RBG) / Les jardins botaniques royaux

680 Plains Rd. West, Hamilton ON L7T 4H4
Tel: 905-527-1158; *Fax:* 905-577-0375
Toll-Free: 800-694-4769
info@rbg.ca
www.rbg.ca
www.facebook.com/pages/Royal-Botanical-Gardens/140038459379746
twitter.com/RBGCanada
www.youtube.com/user/royalbotanicalgarden
Overview: A medium-sized local organization founded in 1932
Mission: To be recognized in Canada & throughout the world for its unique contribution to the collection, research, exhibition, & interpretation of the plant world & for the development of public understanding & appreciation of the relationship between the plant world, humanity, & the rest of nature
Member of: American Association of Botanical Gardens; Archives Association of Ontario; Canadian Museum Association; Museum Trustee Association
Chief Officer(s):
Mark C. Runciman, CEO
mrunciman@rbg.ca
Finances: *Annual Operating Budget:* Greater than $5 Million; *Funding Sources:* Ministry of Citizenship, Culture & Recreation
Staff Member(s): 37; 400 volunteer(s)
Membership: 7,500; *Fees:* $50 single; $70 dual; $25 youth; $750+ corporate
Activities: Over 150 programs a year for all ages including gardening, plant care, art, cooking, environmental awareness & wildlife; over 30 public festivals/events; RBG is open year-round & receives approx. 500,000 visitors annually; 5 garden areas: Arboretum, Laking Garden, Rock Garden, Hendrie Park, Mediterannean Greenhouse; *Speaker Service:* Yes

Royal Canadian Academy of Arts (RCA) / Académie royale des arts du Canada

#375, 401 Richmond St. West, Toronto ON M5V 3A8
Tel: 416-408-2718; *Fax:* 416-408-2286
rcaarts@interlog.com
www.rca-arc.ca
Overview: A medium-sized national charitable organization founded in 1880
Mission: To celebrate the achievement of excellence & innovation by visual artists across Canada; to encourage the new generation of artists; to facilitate the exchange of ideas about visual culture for the benefit of all Canadians
Member of: Canadian Conference of the Arts
Affliation(s): National Gallery of Canada (founded by RCA in 1880); Royal Academy, England
Chief Officer(s):
Ann McCall, President
Finances: *Annual Operating Budget:* $100,000-$250,000; *Funding Sources:* Membership dues; Friends & corporate donations
Staff Member(s): 2
Membership: 700; *Fees:* $200; *Member Profile:* Canadian visual artists in all disciplines; *Committees:* Management Committee; Council; Finance Committee; Exhibition Committee; National Nominations Committee; Trust Fund Committee; Friends' Events Committee
Activities: President's Reception, Nov.; Scholarships; Symposium; *Speaker Service:* Yes; *Library* Open to public by appointment

Royal Canadian Air Force Association *See* Air Force Association of Canada

Royal Canadian Armoured Corps Association

17 Mandel Crescent, Toronto ON M2H 1B8
www.rcaca.org
Overview: A small national organization
Chief Officer(s):
David Stones, President

Royal Canadian Army Service Corps Association-(Atlantic Region) (RCASC Atlantic)

PO Box 435, 175 Main Street East, Stewaicke NS B0N 2J0
www.rcasc-atlantic.org
Overview: A small local organization
Chief Officer(s):
Doug Horsman, President
Membership: 224; *Fees:* $10; *Member Profile:* Maritimers who served in the RCASC

Royal Canadian Artillery Association (RCAA)

1346 Mitchell Dr., Victoria BC V8S 4P8
Tel: 250-385-7922
www.rcaa-aarc.ca
Overview: A small national charitable organization founded in 1876
Mission: Promotion of the efficiency & welfare of the RRCA & all matters pertaining to the defence of Canada
Member of: Conference of Defense Associations
Chief Officer(s):
James L. Brazill, President
Finances: *Annual Operating Budget:* Less than $50,000
22 volunteer(s)
Membership: 350; *Fees:* $30; *Member Profile:* Serving & retired members
Activities: *Speaker Service:* Yes
Awards:
• The Lieutenant-Colonel Jack de Hart, MC CD Bursary (Award)
Eligibility: For junior officers; Successful completion of Phase 2 of the Reserve Entry Scheme Officers

• The Master Gunner E.M. Evoy, MM & Bar Bursary (Award)
Eligibility: For NCMs
Meetings/Conferences: • Royal Canadian Artillery Association 14th Annual Seminar & 129th Annual General Meeting, 2015
Scope: National

Royal Canadian College of Organists (RCCO) / Collège royal canadien des organistes (CRCO)

#202, 204 St. George St., Toronto ON M5R 2N5
Tel: 416-929-6400; *Fax:* 416-929-2265
manager@rcco.ca
www.rcco.ca
www.facebook.com/RCCO.ca
twitter.com/RCCO_CRCO
Overview: A medium-sized national licensing charitable organization founded in 1909
Mission: To promote a high standard of organ playing, choral directing, church music & composition; to hold examinations in organ playing, choir directing, theory & general knowledge of music; to encourage recitals; to increase the understanding among church musicisans, authorities & the public of matters relating to church music
Member of: Canadian Conference of the Arts
Chief Officer(s):
Nicholas Fairbank, President
president@rcco.ca
Sharon Adamson, General Manager
manager@rcco.ca
Finances: *Funding Sources:* Membership fees
Staff Member(s): 4
Membership: *Fees:* Schedule available; *Member Profile:* Professional & non-professional organists, choirmasters, students & all who support the aims & objectives; *Committees:* Competitions; Conventions; Professional Development; Examinations; Historic Organs; Honorary Awards; Membership; Music Publications; Religious Denominations Liaison; Professional Support; Scholarships & Bursaries; Finance & Administration; Development; By-Laws
Activities: *Library* by appointment

The Royal Canadian Geographical Society (RCGS) / La Société géographique royale du Canada

#200, 1155 Lola St., Ottawa ON K1K 4C1
Tel: 613-745-4629; *Fax:* 613-744-0947
Toll-Free: 800-267-0824
rcgs@rcgs.org
www.rcgs.org
www.facebook.com/theRCGS
Overview: A large national organization founded in 1929
Mission: To impart a broader knowledge of Canada, including its environmental, economic, & social challenges, as well as it natural & cultural heritage
Chief Officer(s):
John Geiger, President
Beth Dye, Secretary
André Préfontaine, Executive Director
Finances: *Funding Sources:* Membership fees; Donations
Activities: Presenting education programs through the education committee, The Canadian Council for Geographic Education; Conducting research; *Speaker Service:* Yes
Awards:
• Camsell Medal (Award)
To recognize individuals who have given outstanding service to The Royal Canadian Geographical Society
• Canadian Award for Environmental Innovation (Award)
Presented by The Royal Canadian Geographical Society & 3M Canada to recognize individuals who contribute to the restoration & protection of the environment*Deadline:* August 31
• The Massey Medal (Award)
Awarded annually for outstanding achievement in the exploration, development, or description of the geography of Canada
• The Gold Medal (Award)
To recognize an achievement of one or more individuals in the field of geography, or a significant national or international event
• Geographic Literacy Award (Award)
To honour the contributions of a Canadian geography educator
• Research Grants (Grant)
Amount: Up to $3000 for individuals; Up to $5000 for groups
• The Martin Bergmann Medal (Award)
To recognizes achievement for "excellence in Arctic leadership and science."
Meetings/Conferences: • The Royal Canadian Geographical Society 2015 Annual General Meeting & Annual Dinner of the College of Fellows, 2015
Scope: National
Description: A gathering of Society members, featuring the approval of the audited financial statement, a guest speaker, & the presentation of awards
Publications:
• Canadian Geographic
Type: Magazine; *Frequency:* Bimonthly *ISSN:* 1182-3895
Profile: Subscription includes 4 issues of Canadian Geographic Travel
• géographica
Type: Magazine
Profile: The Royal Canadian Geographical Society's French publication
• Royal Canadian Geoographical Society Annual Report
Type: Yearbook; *Frequency:* Annually
Profile: Featuring the Society's audited financial statements

Royal Canadian Golf Association (RCGA) / Association royale de golf du Canada

#1, 1333 Dorval Dr., Oakville ON L6M 4X7
Tel: 905-849-9700; *Fax:* 905-845-7040
Toll-Free: 800-263-0009
Other Communication: Member Services e-mail: members@golfcanada.ca
info@golfcanada.ca
www.golfcanada.ca
www.facebook.com/TheGolfCanada
twitter.com/TheGolfCanada
www.youtube.com/user/TheGolfCanada
Also Known As: Golf Canada
Overview: A large national organization founded in 1895
Mission: To work with the provincial golf associations & member clubs to foster the growth & development of golf
Affliation(s): Canadian Golf Superintendent Association; PGA of Canada; Canadian Society of Club Managers; National Golf Course Owners Association Canada; Canadian Golf Industry Association
Chief Officer(s):
Doug Alexander, President
Scott Simmons, Chief Executive Officer
ssimmons@golfcanada.ca
Dave Lafleur, CFO, 905-849-9700 Ext. 367
dlafleur@golfcanada.ca
Jeff Thompson, Chief Sport Officer, 905-849-9700 Ext. 436
jthompson@golfcanada.ca
Rick Desrochers, Senior Director, Sponsorships/Professional Championships, 905-849-9700 Ext. 260
rdesrochers@golfcanada.ca
Bill Paul, Chief Championship Officer & Director, RBC Canadian Open, 905-849-9700 Ext. 203
bpaul@golfcanada.ca
Milaina Wright, Manager, Professional Championships, 905-849-9700
mwright@golfcanada.ca
Brent McLaughlin, Director, Rules, Competitions & Amateur Status, 905-849-9700 Ext. 325
bmclaughlin@golfcanada.ca
Finances: *Funding Sources:* Membership dues; Sponsorships
Membership: 322,000+ at 1,500 clubs; *Fees:* Schedule available; *Member Profile:* Member of a member golf club
Activities: *Awareness Events:* RBC Canadian Open; Canadian Pacific Women's Open; *Speaker Service:* Yes; *Library:* RCGA Library; by appointment
Publications:
• Golf Canada [a publication of the Royal Canadian Golf Association]
Type: Magazine; *Editor:* Christopher Reynolds

Royal Canadian Institute (RCI)

#H7D, 700 University Ave., Toronto ON M5G 1X6
Tel: 416-977-2983; *Fax:* 416-962-7314
royalcanadianinstitute@sympatico.ca
www.royalcanadianinstitute.org
www.facebook.com/481071185037
twitter.com/RCI_Canada
www.youtube.com/RCIonline
Overview: A medium-sized national charitable organization founded in 1849
Mission: To increase public understanding of science; to create an environment in which science can flourish & be appreciated
Chief Officer(s):
Helle Tosine, President
John W. Johnston, Treasurer
Membership: *Fees:* $20 senior/student; $30 individual; $500 lifetime
Activities: Sunday afternoon public science lectures

The Royal Canadian Legion (RCL) / La Légion royale canadienne

Dominion Command, 86 Aird Place, Ottawa ON K2L 0A1
Tel: 613-591-3335; *Fax:* 613-591-9335
info@legion.ca
www.legion.ca
Overview: A large national organization founded in 1925
Mission: To serve veterans, ex-military & military members, their families, communities & Canada
Affliation(s): Royal Commonwealth Ex-Services League
Chief Officer(s):
Larry Murray, Grand President
Gordon Moore, Dominion President
Michael Cook, Dominion Treasurer
Bradley Kenneth White, Dominion Secretary
Finances: *Annual Operating Budget:* Greater than $5 Million; *Funding Sources:* Membership dues
Staff Member(s): 48
Membership: 360,000, including 40,000 Ladies' Auxiliary members; *Fees:* Schedule available; *Committees:* Veterans' Services; Legion Seniors; Membership; Sports; Remembrance & Poppy; Ceremonies; Financial Advisory; Investment; Staff Pension; Dominion Convention; National Defence; Appeals; Planning & Administration; Canadian Unity; Canvet Publications; Public Relations; Youth
Activities: Veterans & ex-service member assistance; veterans disability pension plan application processing; youth programs; seniors program; National Track & Field Championships & Clinic; Canadian Unity Program; Member Sports Program; Community Sports Program; Pilgrimages; *Awareness Events:* Remembrance & Poppy Campaign, Nov. 11; *Speaker Service:* Yes
Awards:
• Meritorious Service Medal (Award)
• Meritorious Service Award (Award)
• Palm Leaf (Award)
• Friendship Award (Award)
• Media Award (Award)
Publications:
• Legion Magazine
Type: Magazine; *Frequency:* Bimonthly

Alberta & NWT Command
2020 - 15th St. NW, Calgary AB T2M 3N8
Tel: 403-284-1161; *Fax:* 403-284-9899
office@abnwtlegion.com
www.abnwtlegion.com

British Columbia/Yukon Command
#101, 17618 - 58 Ave., Surrey BC V3S 1L3
Tel: 604-575-8840; *Fax:* 604-575-8820
Toll-Free: 888-261-2211
info@legionbcyukon.ca
www.legionbcyukon.ca
www.facebook.com/LegionBCYukon
twitter.com/LegionBCYukon
www.youtube.com/user/BCYukonCommandRCL
Chief Officer(s):
Inga Kruse, Executive Director
inga.kruse@legionbcyukon.ca
Angus Stanfield, President

Manitoba & Northwest Ontario Command
563 St. Mary's Rd., Winnipeg MB R2M 3L6
Tel: 204-233-3405; *Fax:* 204-237-1775
mblegion@mbnwo.ca
www.mbnwo.ca
Chief Officer(s):
Dawn Golding, Executive Director
dgolding@mbnwo.ca

New Brunswick Command
490 Douglas Ave., Saint John NB E2K 1E7
Tel: 506-634-8850; *Fax:* 506-633-4836
Toll-Free: 866-320-8387
legion@nbnet.nb.ca
www.nb.legion.ca
Chief Officer(s):
Rick Love, President

Newfoundland & Labrador Command
PO Box 5745, St. John's NL A10 5X3
Tel: 709-753-6666; *Fax:* 709-753-5514
Toll-Free: 888-335-6666
www.legionnl.ca
twitter.com/legionnlca
Chief Officer(s):
Brenda Slaney, Contact
bslaney@nfld.net

Nova Scotia/Nunavut Command
Burnside Business Park, 61 Gloria McCluskey Ave., Dartmouth NS B3B 2Z3
Tel: 902-429-4090; *Fax:* 902-429-7481
Toll-Free: 877-809-1145
info@ns.legion.ca
www.ns.legion.ca
Chief Officer(s):
Ronald T. Trowsdale, Command President

Ontario Command
89 Industrial Pkwy. North, Aurora ON L4G 4C4
Tel: 905-841-7999; *Fax:* 905-841-9992
Toll-Free: 888-207-0939
info@on.legion.ca
www.on.legion.ca
Chief Officer(s):
Bruce Julian, President

Prince Edward Island Command
161 St. Peters' Rd., Charlottetown PE C1A 5P6
Tel: 902-892-2161; *Fax:* 902-368-8853
royalcanadianlegion@pei.aibn.com
www.peilegion.com
Chief Officer(s):
Wayne Pike, Provincial Service Officer

Direction du Québec
#410, 1000, rue Saint-Antoine ouest, Montréal QC H3C 3R7
Tél: 514-866-7491; *Téléc:* 514-866-6303
Ligne sans frais: 877-401-7111
info@qc.legion.ca
www.qc.legion.ca
Chief Officer(s):
Norman Shelton, Président

Saskatchewan Command
3079 - 5th Ave., Regina SK S4T 0L6
Tel: 306-525-8739; *Fax:* 306-525-5023
sasklegion@sasktel.net
www.sasklegion.ca
Chief Officer(s):
Cherilyn Cooke, Executive Director

Royal Canadian Military Institute (RCMI)
426 University Ave., Toronto ON M5G 1S9
Tel: 416-597-0286; *Fax:* 416-597-6919
Toll-Free: 800-585-1072
info@rcmi.org
www.rcmi.org
Overview: A medium-sized national organization founded in 1890
Mission: To promote the navy, army & air force art, science, literature & interests; promotion of good fellowship & esprit de corps amongst the officers of the various branches of the services; to maintain of a clubhouse for the accommodation, recreation, enlightenment, convenience & entertainment of its members.
Chief Officer(s):
Chris Corrigan, Executive Director
ccorrigan1@cogeco.ca
Membership: *Member Profile:* 60% military & former service personnel who have been or were commissioned officers; 40% associates of professional status
Activities: *Library* by appointment

Royal Canadian Mounted Police Veterans' Association / Association des anciens de la Gendarmerie royale du Canada
1200 Vanier Pkwy., Ottawa ON K1A 0R2
Tel: 613-993-8633; *Fax:* 613-993-4353
Toll-Free: 877-251-1771
rcmp.vets@rcmp-grc.gc.ca
www.rcmpvetsnational.ca
Previous Name: Royal Northwest Mounted Police Veterans Association
Overview: A medium-sized national charitable organization founded in 1924
Finances: *Annual Operating Budget:* $50,000-$100,000; *Funding Sources:* Membership dues; grants
Membership: 6,000; 30 divisions across Canada; *Member Profile:* One year service in RCMP or associated services
Meetings/Conferences: • Royal Canadian Mounted Police Veterans Association 2015 Annual General Meeting, May, 2015, Québec, QC
Scope: National
Contact Information: URL: www.grc-rcmp-vets.qc.ca/en/agm-2015
• Royal Canadian Mounted Police Veterans Association 2016 Annual General Meeting, 2016, NS
Scope: National
• Royal Canadian Mounted Police Veterans Association 2017 Annual General Meeting, 2017, PE
Scope: National
• Royal Canadian Mounted Police Veterans Association 2018 Annual General Meeting, 2018, NB
Scope: National
• Royal Canadian Mounted Police Veterans Association 2019 Annual General Meeting, 2019
Scope: National

Royal Canadian Naval Benevolent Fund (RCNBF)
PO Box 505, Stn. B, Ottawa ON K1P 5P6
Tel: 613-996-5087; *Fax:* 613-236-8830
Toll-Free: 888-557-8777
rcnbf@rcnbf.com
www.rcnbf.ca
Overview: A medium-sized national organization founded in 1945
Mission: To relieve distress & promote the well-being of members & former members of the naval forces of Canada & Canadian merchant navy war veterans & of their dependants
Chief Officer(s):
L.F. Harrison, Secretary-Treasurer
Finances: *Funding Sources:* Donations & investments
Staff Member(s): 2
Membership: 46

Western Committee
CFB Esquimalt, PO Box 17000, Stn. Forces, Victoria BC V9A 7N2
Tel: 250-383-6264

Royal Canadian Numismatic Association (RCNA)
#432, 5694 Hwy. 7 East, Markham ON L3P 1B4
Tel: 647-401-4014; *Fax:* 905-472-9645
info@rcna.ca
www.rcna.ca
Previous Name: Canadian Numismatic Association
Overview: A medium-sized national organization founded in 1950
Mission: To encourage & promote education in the science of numismatics, through the study of coins, paper money, medals, tokens, & all other numismatic items, with special emphasis on material pertaining to Canada
Chief Officer(s):
Kevin McCann, Chair, Membership
canadian@coinoisseur.com
Membership: *Fees:* $16.50 juniors; $35 regular & corporate members; $44 families; $50 international members; $595 life membership; *Member Profile:* Persons interested in coin collecting / numismatics; Clubs, societies, libraries, & other non-profit organizations
Activities: Providing advocacy for the hobby; Offering educational seminars & RCNA junior programs; *Library:* Royal Canadian Numismatic Association Lending Library
Meetings/Conferences: • Royal Canadian Numismatic Association 2015 Convention, July, 2015, Westin Nova Scotian, Halifax, NS
Scope: National
Description: An annual event, presenting an education symposium, a bourse & display, business meetings, award presentations, plus social & networking activities
Contact Information: E-mail: 2015convention@rcna.ca
• Royal Canadian Numismatic Association 2016 Convention, 2016, Ottawa, ON
Scope: National
Description: An annual event, presenting an education symposium, a bourse & display, business meetings, award presentations, plus social & networking activities
Contact Information: E-mail: info@rcna.ca
• Royal Canadian Numismatic Association 2017 Convention, 2017, Boucherville, QC
Scope: National
Description: An annual event, presenting an education symposium, a bourse & display, business meetings, award presentations, plus social & networking activities
Contact Information: E-mail: info@rcna.ca; URL: www.boucherville2017.com
Publications:
• Canadian Numismatic Association E-Bulletin
Type: Newsletter; *Price:* Free
Profile: Numismatic personalities, coin club activities, sources of information, upcoming events, Canadian numismatic issues, tips for collectors, & RCNA news
• The CN Journal
Type: Journal; *Frequency:* 10 pa; *Accepts Advertising*; *Editor:* Dan Gosling (dan@gosling.ca); *Price:* Free with membership in the The Royal Canadian Numismatic Association
Profile: Papers written by accomplished Canadian numismatists
• A Half Century of Advancement in Numismatics
Type: Book; *Number of Pages:* 148; *Editor:* Stan Clute

The Royal Canadian Regiment Association (RCR)
c/o 1st Battalion, Victoria Barracks, PO Box 9999, Stn. Main, Petawawa ON K8H 2X3
Tel: 613-687-5511; *Fax:* 613-588-5932
thercr.ca
Overview: A medium-sized national organization
Mission: To perpetuate the close bonds of comradeship and esprit de corps created by members of The Royal Candian Regiment; To preserve the memory of those who have died in service; To assist the sick, wounded and needy who have served in the Regiment; To assist widows and children of deceased members; To maintain the Regiments's memorials and develop its history.
Chief Officer(s):
Bob McBride, Chair
bobmcbride@royalcanadianregiment.ca
Randy Kemp, President
rjkemp11@gmail.com
Membership: *Fees:* $25
Awards:
• Bursaries (Grant)
Three bursaries given to eligible family members *Amount:* $1,000

Royal City Field Naturalists
#903, 1219 Harwood St., Vancouver BC V6E 1S5
Tel: 604-609-0679
Overview: A small local organization
Mission: To promote the enjoyment of nature through environmental appreciation & conservation; to encourage wise use & conservation of natural resources & environmental protection
Member of: Federation of BC Naturalists
Chief Officer(s):
Gareth Llewellyn, Contact
gllew@telus.net
Membership: 12; *Fees:* $25

Royal College of Dental Surgeons of Ontario
6 Crescent Rd., 5th Fl., Toronto ON M4W 1T1
Tel: 416-961-6555; *Fax:* 416-961-5814
Toll-Free: 800-565-4591
info@rcdso.org
www.rcdso.org
Also Known As: RCDS of Ontario
Overview: A large provincial licensing organization founded in 1868
Mission: To operate as the governing body for dentists in Ontario; To protect the public's right to quality dental services by providing leadership to the dental profession in self-regulation
Chief Officer(s):
Ted Schipper, Chair
Peter Trainor, President
Finances: *Annual Operating Budget:* Greater than $5 Million; *Funding Sources:* Membership fees
Staff Member(s): 35
Membership: 8,100 individual; *Fees:* $1,075; *Member Profile:* Mandatory membership under Regulated Health Professional Act of government of Ontario; *Committees:* Audit; Complaints; Discipline; Executive; Finance & Property; Fitness to Practise; Legal & Legislation; Professional Liability Program; Quality Assurance; Registration
Activities: Registration of Dentists/Specialists in Ontario; handling complaints; discipline; *Rents Mailing List:* Yes
Publications:
• Dispatch
Type: Magazine; *Frequency:* Quarterly

Royal College of Dentists of Canada (RCDC) / Collège Royal des Chirurgiens Dentistes du Canada
#2404, 180 Dundas St. West, Toronto ON M3G 1Z8
Tel: 416-512-6571; *Fax:* 416-512-6468
office@rcdc.ca
www.rcdc.ca
Overview: A medium-sized national organization founded in 1965
Mission: To provide examinations for dental sciences & for nationally recognized dental specialties in Canada
Chief Officer(s):

Hugh Lamont, President
Christopher Robinson, Vice-President
Peter McCutcheon, Secretary
Garnet Packota, Acting Registrar
Paul Jackson, Examiner-in-Chief
Staff Member(s): 9
Membership: *Member Profile:* A Fellow in the Royal College of Dentists of Canada is a dentist who has achieved the following: graduation from a post-graduate program; completion of the National Dental Specialty Examination; a Fellowship diploma; association with a specialty recognized by the Canadian Dental Association; payment of fees; & good ethical standing in the profession; *Committees:* Examinations; Credentials; Nomination
Meetings/Conferences: • Royal College of Dentists of Canada 2015 Annual General Meeting, 2015
Scope: National
Publications:
• Royal College of Dentists of Canada Bulletin
Type: Yearbook; *Frequency:* Annually
Profile: Produced each year following Convocation
• Royal College of Dentists of Canada Communiqué
Type: Newsletter; *Frequency:* every six weeks

The Royal College of Physicians & Surgeons of Canada (RCPSC) / Le Collège royal des médecins et chirurgiens du Canada (CRMCC)

774 Echo Dr., Ottawa ON K1S 5N8
Tel: 613-730-8177; *Fax:* 613-730-8830
Toll-Free: 800-668-3740
info@royalcollege.ca
rcpsc.medical.org
www.facebook.com/TheRoyalCollege
twitter.com/Royal_College
Overview: A large national charitable organization founded in 1929
Mission: To oversee the medical education of specialists in Canada; To set the highest standards in postgraduate medical education, through national certification examinations & lifelong learning programs; To promote sound health policy
Affiliation(s): Canadian Medical Association; College of Family Physicians of Canada; Association of Canadian Medical Colleges; National Specialty Societies; Federation of Medical Licensing Authorities of Canada
Chief Officer(s):
Andrew Padmos, CEO, 613-730-6205, Fax: 613-730-8250
ceo@royalcollege.ca
Danielle Fréchette, Director, Communications & Health Policy, 613-730-6205, Fax: 613-730-8250
dfrechette@rcpsc.edu
Ken Harris, Director, Education
Craig Campbell, Director, Professional Affairs
Finances: *Funding Sources:* Membership dues; credentials & examination fees; donations
Staff Member(s): 142; 3000 volunteer(s)
Membership: 42,983 fellows & residents; *Fees:* $350-$695 active; $175 senior; *Member Profile:* Certification in medical specialty with application for admission to fellowship; *Committees:* Executive; Council; Education; Professional Development; Fellowship Affairs; Corporate Affairs; Health & Public Policy
Activities: Certification of specialists; continuing professional development; health policy; professional association; *Internships:* Yes; *Library:* Roddick Room; by appointment
Awards:
• Medical Education Research Grant (Grant)
To support research in the field of postgraduate medical education or continuing professional development *Amount:* $25,000/year, up to three years
• Detweiler Travelling Fellowships (Scholarship)
To enable six Fellows to visit medical centres in Canada or abroad to study or gain experience in the use or application of new knowledge or techniques, or to further the pursuit of a project relevant to clinical practice or research *Amount:* $1,750/month, up to $21,000
• Walter C. MacKenzie-Scotiabank Fellowship in Surgery (Scholarship)
To allow Fellows to visit one or more centres to acquire surgical research or clinical surgical expertise *Amount:* $1,750/month, up to $21,000
• Regional Clinical Traineeships (Scholarship)
Amount: $3,000
• National Specialty Society Annual Meeting Grants (Grant)
Amount: Up to $1,200
• Regional CME Grants (Grant)
Amount: Up to $1,200
• International Travelling Fellowship (Scholarship)
To enable Fellows residing outside of Canada to study in a medical centre in Canada; or to enable Fellows residing in Canada to practice & teach in a less developed country*Amount:* $1,750/month, up to $21,000
• Royal College Fellowship for Studies in Medical Education (Scholarship)
To increase the number & quality of professionally trained medical educators in Canada by providing training in the science of medical education *Amount:* $45,000 per year of study to a maximum of three years
• Medical Education Travelling Fellowship (Scholarship)
For the recipient to acquire knowledge & expertise in the field of medical education *Amount:* $1,750/month, up to $21,000
• The Royal College of Physicians & Surgeons of Canada Annual Medal (Award)
The purpose of the awards is to provide national recognition for original work by young clinicians & investigators *Amount:* $5,000 & a bronze medal
• RCPSC-AMS CanMEDS Research & Development Grant (Grant)
Amount: Up to $25,000
• Royal College Faculty Development Grants (Grant)
Applicable to projects of a maximum of 12 months duration
Amount: $5,000
• KJR Wightman Award for Research in Ethics (Award)
Amount: $1,000
• Canadian Research Awards for Specialty Residents, Medicine & Surgery (Award)
Amount: $2,000
• RSPSC/AMS Donald Richards Wilson Award (Award)
Amount: $2,000
• Duncan Graham Award (Award)
• James H. Graham Award of Merit (Award)
• Mentor of the Year Award (Award)
• Program Director of the Year Award (Award)
• Royal College Teasdale-Corti Humanitarian Award (Award)
• Kristin Sivertz Resident Leadership Award (Award)
• Prix d'excellence / Specialist of the Year (Award)
Meetings/Conferences: • Royal College of Physicians & Surgeons of Canada 2015 Annual General Meeting, 2015
Scope: National

The Royal Commonwealth Society of Canada (RCS) / La Société royale du Commonwealth du Canada

c/o RCS Ottawa, PO Box 8023, Stn. T, Ottawa ON K1G 3H6
www.rcs.ca
www.facebook.com/RCSCanada
twitter.com
Overview: A medium-sized national organization founded in 1868
Mission: A charitable, non-partisan organization which promotes knowledge of the Commonwealth & its member countries; fosters unity in diversity in matters of common concern; promotes international understanding, cooperation & peace; upholds the best traditions of the Commonwealth
Chief Officer(s):
Norman Macfie, Chair
Activities: National Student Commonwealth Conference; Canadian Regional Student Commonwealth Conference; libraries & reading rooms; publications; professorships, fellowships; information services

British Columbia Mainland Branch
#816, 402 West Pender St., Vancouver BC V6B 1T6
Tel: 604-683-3201; *Fax:* 604-681-3589
Chief Officer(s):
Shawn M. Wade, President
shawnmwade@hotmail.com

Montréal Branch
235 Sherbrooke St. West, Montréal QC H2X 1X8
Tel: 514-281-6718; *Fax:* 450-656-7621
Chief Officer(s):
Judith Elson, President
jelson@rsb.qc.ca

Newfoundland Branch
16 Osbourne St., St. John's NL A1B 1X8
Tel: 709-753-6472; *Fax:* 709-738-5679
newfoundland@rcs.ca
Chief Officer(s):
Norman Macfie, Chair
nmacfie@nl.rogers.com

Nova Scotia Branch
PO Box 153, Chester NS B0J 1J0
Tel: 902-275-2358
chesteragu@eastlink.ca
Chief Officer(s):
Heather Mackinnon, President

Ottawa Branch
PO Box 8023, Stn. T, Ottawa ON K1G 3H6
e-mail: rcs.bytown@gmail.com
rcs-ottawa.ca
Chief Officer(s):
Peter Meincke, President
peter.meincke@bell.net

Prince Edward Island Branch
6 Sunset Dr., Charlottetown PE C1A 7S9
e-mail: rcs.pei@gmail.com
Chief Officer(s):
David Ashby, Chair
dashby@islandtelecom.com

Toronto Branch
1849 Lincoln Green Close, Mississauga ON L5K 1C4
Tel: 905-823-2819
rcstoronto1@gmail.com
www.facebook.com/theroyalcommonwealthsocietycanada
Chief Officer(s):
Andrew McMurtry, President
Andrew_McMurtry@alumni.unwo.ca

Vancouver Island
8191 Lochside Dr., Saanichton BC V8M 1T9
Tel: 250-544-1120
Chief Officer(s):
Wendy Halliday, President
wendyandjockhalliday@shaw.ca

Winnipeg Branch
#1602, 277 Wellington Cres., Winnipeg MB R3M 3V7
Tel: 204-488-0167
Chief Officer(s):
Murray Burt, President
burt@mts.net

Royal Conservatory Orchestra

273 Bloor St. West, Toronto ON M5S 1W2
Tel: 416-408-2824; *Fax:* 416-408-5025
glenngouldschool@rcmusic.ca
www.rcmusic.ca
Overview: A small local charitable organization overseen by Orchestras Canada
Member of: The Royal Conservatory of Music
Affliation(s): The Glenn Gould School
Membership: *Member Profile:* Students
Activities: Four concert season featuring world-class guest conductors; *Library*

Royal Danish Guards Association of Western Canada

c/o Svend Aage Storm, General Delivery, James River Bridge AB T0M 1C0
Tel: 403-638-4345
www.garderforening.dk/wcgf.html
Overview: A small local organization founded in 1944
Chief Officer(s):
Svend Aage Storm, Vice-President
xxsstorm.p@gmail.com
Jens Lind, President
xxjenslind@telus.net
Kurt Nielsen, Secretary & Treasurer
Membership: *Member Profile:* Individuals who have served in the Danish Royal Guards Regiment
Activities: Hosting regular meetings
Publications:
• Garderbladet
Type: Newsletter; *Frequency:* 11 pa; *Price:* Free with Royal Danish Guards Association of Western Canada membership
Profile: Information for association members

Royal Heraldry Society of Canada / Société royale héraldique du Canada

PO Box 8128, Stn. T, Ottawa ON K1G 3H9
e-mail: secretary@heraldry.ca
www.heraldry.ca
Previous Name: Heraldry Society of Canada
Overview: A small national charitable organization founded in 1966
Mission: To maintain, foster & develop the heraldic traditions of Canadians by: increasing public awareness of heraldry & the society; advocating with governments for the protection & proper use of heraldry in Canada; advising the Canadian Heraldic Authority on matters of mutual concern
Affliation(s): Commonwealth Heraldry Board
Chief Officer(s):

David E. Rumball, President
president@heraldry.ca
Edward McNabb, 1st Vice-President
first_vice@heraldry.ca
Vicken Koundakjian, 2nd Vice-President
second_vice@heraldry.ca
Membership: *Fees:* $25 student; $60 institution; $75 regular; *Committees:* Bylaws; Editorial Board; Education; Heraldic Arts; Honours & Awards; Investment; Library & Archives; Marketing; Membership; Periodicals; Special Publications; Special Projects; Roll of Arms; Gift Planning & Donations
Activities: *Internships:* Yes; *Library* by appointment

Royal Life Saving Society Canada *See* Lifesaving Society

Royal New Brunswick Rifle Association Inc. (RNBRA)

PO Box 181, Stn. A, Fredericton NB E3B 4Y9
Tel: 506-363-5927
Bullsi_2000@yahoo.com
www.rnbra.ca
Overview: A small provincial organization founded in 1866
Mission: Promoting marksmenship in New Brunswick
Affliation(s): National Firearms Association; Dominion of Canada Rifle Association; Firearms Canada; 30 New Brunswick clubs
Chief Officer(s):
Bob Kierstead, President

Royal Newfoundland Constabulary Association (RNCA) / Association de la gendarmerie royale de Terre-Neuve

125 East White Hills Rd., St. John's NL A1A 5R7
Tel: 709-739-5946; *Fax:* 709-739-6276
office@rnca.ca
www.rnca.ca
Previous Name: Police Brotherhood of the Royal Newfoundland Constabulary Association (Ind.)
Overview: A small provincial organization founded in 1970
Mission: To improve benefits & working conditions for police officers; to improve public safety & strive to create a positive relationship between the police & the community they protect
Chief Officer(s):
Tim Buckle, President
Warren Sullivan, 1st Vice-President
Albert Gibbons, 2nd Vice-President
Finances: *Annual Operating Budget:* $250,000-$500,000
Staff Member(s): 1
Membership: 380 non-commussioned ranks; *Fees:* $783.07

Royal Northwest Mounted Police Veterans Association *See* Royal Canadian Mounted Police Veterans' Association

The Royal Nova Scotia Historical Society (RNSHS)

PO Box 2622, Halifax NS B3J 3P7
e-mail: RoyalNSHS@gmail.com
www.rnshs.ca
Overview: A small provincial charitable organization founded in 1878
Mission: To promote an understanding & appreciation of Nova Scotia's history & cultural development; to encourage the preservation of published & archival materials & artifacts; to read papers pertaining to Nova Scotia's history at meetings of the society; to publish selected papers in the society's periodical
Member of: Heritage Canada; Federation of Nova Scotian Heritage
Affliation(s): Genealogical Association of Nova Scotia
Chief Officer(s):
David Sutherland, President
Finances: *Annual Operating Budget:* Less than $50,000; *Funding Sources:* Membership fees & subscription sales
14 volunteer(s)
Membership: 280; *Fees:* $25; *Member Profile:* Amateur & professional historians
Activities: Lecture series; *Internships:* Yes
Publications:
• Journal of the Royal Nova Scotia Historical Society
Type: Journal; *Accepts Advertising; Editor:* Brian Cuthbertson
ISSN: 1193-9451; *Price:* Included with membership
Profile: Articles on Nova Scotia history; book reviews on publications pertaining to Nova Scotia history

The Royal Philatelic Society of Canada (RPSC) / La Société royale de philatélie du Canada (SRPC)

PO Box 929, Stn. Q, Toronto ON M4T 2P1
Tel: 416-921-2077; *Fax:* 416-921-1282
Toll-Free: 888-285-4143
info@rpsc.org
www.rpsc.org
Previous Name: Canadian Philatelic Society
Overview: A small national organization founded in 1887
Mission: To promote the hobby of stamp collecting; to use stamps & postal history in education for youths & adults
Member of: Fédération internationale de philatélie
Chief Officer(s):
George Pepall, President
president@rpsc.org
Peter Butler, Executive Director
director@rpsc.org
Finances: *Annual Operating Budget:* $50,000-$100,000
Staff Member(s): 2; 24 volunteer(s)
Membership: 2,200; *Fees:* Schedule available; *Committees:* Finance; Ethics; Nominating
Activities: *Speaker Service:* Yes; *Library:* Harry Sutherland Philatelic Library
Publications:
• The Canadian Philatelist [a publication of The Royal Philatelic Society of Canada]
Type: Journal; *Frequency:* 6 pa.; *Editor:* Tony Shaman

The Royal Society of Canada (RSC) / La Société royale du Canada

Walter House, 282 Somerset West, Ottawa ON K2P 0J6
Tel: 613-991-6990; *Fax:* 613-991-6996
www.rsc.ca
www.linkedin.com/pub/the-royal-society-of-canada-rsc/23/592/418
www.facebook.com/RSC.SRC
twitter.com/rsctheacademies
www.youtube.com/user/RSCSRC1
Also Known As: Canadian Academy of the Sciences & Humanities
Overview: A medium-sized national charitable organization founded in 1882
Mission: To promote learning & research in the arts, humanities & sciences in Canada; in its role as a National Academy, to draw on the breadth of knowledge & expertise of its members to recognize & honour distinguished accomplishments; to advise on the state of scholarship & culture across Canada; to inform the public on noteworthy social, scientific & ethical questions of the day; it is organized into three academies covering the arts & humanities, the social sciences, & the natural & applied sciences
Chief Officer(s):
Darren Gilmour, Executive Director
dgilmour@rsc-src.ca
Finances: *Funding Sources:* Membership dues; endowments; government; corporate
Staff Member(s): 5
Membership: 2000 fellows; *Member Profile:* Fellows are elected by their peers on the basis of distinction in their field; *Committees:* Promotion of Women in Scholarship; Freedom of Scholarship
Activities: *Library* Open to public
Awards:
• Award in Gender Studies (Scholarship)
• Miroslaw Romanowski Medal (Award)
Established in 1994; awarded every year in recognition of significant contributions to the resolution of scientific aspects of environmental problems or for important improvements to the quality of an eco-system in all aspects, terrestrial, atmospheric & aqueous brought about by scientific means. *Amount:* $3,000 & a medal *Contact:* Geneviève Gouin, Coordinator, 613/991-5760
• Ecology Award (Scholarship)
• John L. Synge Award (Award)
Established 1986; awarded at irregular intervals for outstanding research in any of the branches of mathematics *Amount:* $2,500 & a diploma
• Alice Wilson Award (Award)
Awarded annually to a woman of outstanding academic qualifications who is entering a career in scholarship or research at the post-doctoral level *Amount:* $1,000 & a diploma
• Eadie Medal (Award)
Established 1975; awarded annually in recognition of major contributions to any field in engineering or applied science with preference given to those having an impact on communications. *Amount:* $3,000 & a bronze medal *Contact:* Geneviève Gouin, Coordinator, 613/991-5760
• Jason A. Hannah Medal (Award)
Established 1976; awarded annually for an important publication in the history of medicine *Amount:* $1,500 & a bronze medal
• Centenary Medal (Award)
Established 1982; awarded at irregular intervals in recognition of outstanding contributions to the object of the society & to recognize links to international organizations
• The McNeil Medal (Award)
Awarded to encourage communication of science to students & the public *Amount:* $1,500 bursary & a medal
• The Henry Marshall Tory Medal (Award)
Established 1941; awarded every two years (since 1947) for outstanding research in a branch of astronomy, chemistry, mathematics, physics, or an allied science
• The J.B. Tyrrell Historical Medal (Award)
Established 1927; awarded at least every two years for outstanding work in the history of Canada
• Bancroft Award (Award)
Established 1968; awarded every two years for publication, instruction & research in the earth sciences that have conspicuously contributed to public understanding & appreciation of the subject *Amount:* $2,500 & a presentation scroll *Contact:* Geneviève Gouin, Coordinator, 613/991-5760
• Rutherford Memorial Medals: Chemistry & Physics (Award)
Established 1980; awarded annually for outstanding research, one in chemistry, one in physics *Amount:* Two medals & $2,500 each
• Innis-Gérin Medal (Award)
Established 1966; awarded every two years for a distinguished & sustained contribution to the literature of the social sciences including human geography & social psychology
• The McLaughlin Medal (Award)
Awarded annually for important research of sustained excellence in any branch of medical science *Amount:* $2,500 & a medal
• Lorne Pierce Medal (Award)
Established 1926; awarded every two years for an achievement of special significance & conspicuous merit in imaginative or critical literature written in either English or French, preferably dealing with a Canadian subject
• Willet G. Miller Medal (Award)
Established 1943; awarded every two years for outstanding research in any branch of the earth sciences *Contact:* Geneviève Gouin, Coordinator, 613/991-5760
• Sir John William Dawson Medal (Award)
Established 1985; awarded for important & sustained contributions by one individual in at least two different fields in the general areas of interest of the Society or in a broad domain that transcends the usual disciplinary boundaries *Amount:* $2,500 & a silver medal
• Pierre Chauveau Medal (Award)
Established 1951; awarded every two years (since 1966) for a distinguished contribution to knowledge in the humanities other than Canadian literature & Canadian history
• The Flavelle Medal (Award)
Established 1924; awarded every two years (since 1966) for an outstanding contribution to biological science during the preceding 10 years or for significant additions to a previous outstanding contribution to biological science

Royal United Services Institute of New Brunswick (RUSINB)

PO Box 7373, Stn. A, Saint John NB E2L 4S7
Tel: 506-696-3014
Previous Name: United Services Institute of New Brunswick
Overview: A small provincial charitable organization
Mission: To foster a link between the public & the Armed Forces; To support youth in their interest in the Canadian Forces
Member of: The Federation of Military & United Services Institutes of Canada (FMUSIC); Conference of Defence Associations
Affliation(s): The Crow's Nest
Chief Officer(s):
Ronald J. Brown, President, 519-696-3014
randjbrown@rogers.com
Membership: *Member Profile:* Serving & retired officers from the Canadian & Commonwealth Forces, the Royal Canadian Mounted Police (RCMP), & allied nations

Royal United Services Institute of Regina (RUSIR)

1660 Elphinstone St., Regina SK S4T 3N1
Tel: 306-757-8405; *Fax:* 306-522-2556
rusirom@accesscomm.ca
www.rusiregina.ca
Overview: A small provincial charitable organization
Mission: To support the enhancement of national security & national defence policies by the government, & a capable Canadian Armed Forces
Member of: The Federation of Military & United Services Institutes of Canada (FMUSIC); Conference of Defence Associations
Affliation(s): The Crow's Nest

Chief Officer(s):
Eddie Matthews, Managing Director
Membership: *Fees:* $200 yearly; $70 yearly, out of town/province/country; $120 yearly, members of the Canadian Forces; *Member Profile:* Serving & retired officers from the Canadian & Commonwealth Forces, the Royal Canadian Mounted Police (RCMP), & allied nations
Activities: *Library:* The Royal United Services Institute of Regina Library; by appointment

Royal United Services Institute of Vancouver (RUSI)
2025 West 11th Ave., Vancouver BC V6J 2C7
e-mail: secretary@rusivancouver.ca
www.rusivancouver.ca
Overview: A small local organization founded in 1921
Member of: The Federation of Military & United Services Institutes of Canada
Chief Officer(s):
Jim Stanton, President
Finances: *Funding Sources:* Membership fees
20 volunteer(s)
Membership: 150; *Fees:* $20; *Member Profile:* Army, Naval, Airforce, RCMP officers; *Committees:* Defence Research; Program; Membership/Welfare
Activities: *Speaker Service:* Yes

Royal United Services Institute of Vancouver Island (RUSI-VI)
Bay Street Armoury, #414, 715 Bay St., Victoria BC V8T 1R1
e-mail: usiviccda@yahoo.ca
www.rusiviccda.org
Overview: A small local organization founded in 1927
Mission: To support the enhancement & maintenance of the Canadian Armed Forces, with adequate troops, training, & equipment, & of effective national defence policies by the government
Chief Officer(s):
WD (Don) Macnamara, OMM, CD, PhD, President
WC (Bill) Weston, CD, Vice-President
G. Del Villano, OMM, CD, Secretary
Membership: 200+; *Fees:* $30 individuals; $40 families; *Member Profile:* Serving & retired officers from the Canadian & Commonwealth Forces, the Royal Canadian Mounted Police (RCMP), & allied nations
Activities: Hosting regular meetings; Presenting awards;
Publications:
• RUSI: Newsletter of the Royal United Services Institute of Vancouver Island
Type: Newsletter; *Frequency:* Quarterly; *Editor:* Capt (Ret.) LE (Skip) Triplett
Profile: Information for members of the Royal United Services Institute of Vancouver Island

Royal University Hospital Foundation (RUHF)
103 Hospital Dr., Saskatoon SK S7N 0W8
Tel: 306-655-1984; *Fax:* 306-655-1979
ruhfoundation@saskatoonhealthregion.ca
www.ruhf.org
www.twitter.com/RUHFoundation
Overview: A small local charitable organization founded in 1983
Mission: To help provide additional funds for the Royal University Hospital, a university teaching hospital
Chief Officer(s):
Bill Johnson, Chair
Finances: *Funding Sources:* Donations; Corporations
Staff Member(s): 6

Royal Winnipeg Ballet (RWB)
380 Graham Ave., Winnipeg MB R3C 4K2
Tel: 204-956-0183; *Fax:* 204-943-1994
customerservice@rwb.org
www.rwb.org
www.facebook.com/RWBallet
twitter.com/RWBallet
instagram.com/rwballet
Also Known As: Canada's Royal Winnipeg Ballet
Overview: A medium-sized local charitable organization founded in 1939
Mission: To enrich the human experience by teaching, creating & performing outstanding dance
Affliation(s): Association of Cultural Executives; Canadian Conference of the Arts; Canadian Arts Presenting Association; Council for Business & the Arts in Canada; Dance USA; International Society for the Performing Arts
Chief Officer(s):
Jeff Herd, Executive Director
David Reid, Chair
André Lewis, Artistic Director
Finances: *Funding Sources:* Government, corporate & private
Staff Member(s): 178
Membership: *Committees:* Audit; Governance; Evaluation & Compensation; Nominations
Meetings/Conferences: • Royal Winnipeg Ballet Diamond Gala, April, 2015, RBC Convention Centre, Winnipeg, MB
Scope: Local

RP Research Foundation - Fighting Blindness *See* The Foundation Fighting Blindness

The Rubber Association of Canada *See* Tire and Rubber Association of Canada

Rug Hooking Guild of Nova Scotia (RHGNS)
c/o Gail Feetham, 52 Greendale Ct., Timberlea NS B3T 1J6
Tel: 902-576-2894
www.rhgns.com
Overview: A small provincial organization
Mission: To promote excellence & participation in the craft; to preserve its history; to promote public awareness through exhibits & publicity
Chief Officer(s):
Joyce LeMoine, President
lemoinejoyce@yahoo.ca
Membership: *Fees:* $35; $50 outside Canada; *Committees:* Awards; Heritage; Magazine; Nominating; Publicity; School

Rugby Canada
#110, 30 East Beaver Creek Rd., Richmond Hill ON L4B 1J2
Tel: 905-707-8998
info@rugbycanada.ca
www.rugbycanada.ca
www.facebook.com/RugbyCanada
twitter.com/rugbycanada
Previous Name: Canadian Rugby Union
Overview: A medium-sized national organization founded in 1974
Mission: To be the national governing body for the sport of rugby in Canada.
Chief Officer(s):
Pat Aldous, Chair
paldous@rugbycanada.ca
Graham Brown, Chief Executive Officer
gbrown@rugbycanada.ca
Myles Spencer, Chief Operating Officer
mspencer@rugbycanada.ca
Membership: *Member Profile:* Official rugby teams in Canada
Activities: Player development; youth clinics

Rugby Manitoba
145 Pacific Ave., Winnipeg MB R3B 2Z6
Tel: 204-925-5664
www.rugbymanitoba.com
Overview: A medium-sized provincial organization overseen by Rugby Canada
Mission: To govern rugby in Manitoba
Member of: Rugby Canada
Chief Officer(s):
Brad Hirst, Executive Director
executivedirector@rugbymanitoba.com
Staff Member(s): 1

Rugby Ontario
#307, 3 Concorde Gate, Toronto ON M3C 3N7
Tel: 416-426-7050; *Fax:* 416-426-7369
www.rugbyontario.com
www.facebook.com/RugbyOntario
twitter.com/rugbyontario
Overview: A medium-sized provincial organization founded in 1949 overseen by Rugby Canada
Member of: Rugby Canada
Affliation(s): Canadian Rugby Union
Chief Officer(s):
Andrew Backer, Executive Director, 416-426-7146
abacker@rugbyontario.com
David Nelson, President
president@rugbyontario.com
Fran Mason, Coordinator, Coaching & Events, 416-426-7050
fmason@rugbyontario.com
Finances: *Annual Operating Budget:* $1.5 Million-$3 Million
Staff Member(s): 6
Membership: 10827; *Member Profile:* Athletes, coaches, officials, administrators; *Committees:* Coaching; Executive

Ruiter Valley Land Trust (RVLT) / Fiducie foncière Vallée de Ruiter
PO Box 462, Mansonville QC J0E 1X0
e-mail: info@valleeruiter.org
valleeruiter.org
Overview: A small local charitable organization founded in 1987
Mission: To acquire & protect forest land
Affliation(s): Nature Conservancy of Canada
Chief Officer(s):
Marie-Claire Planet, President
Membership: *Fees:* $25 individual; $40 family; $100 patron; $250 corporation; $450 steward; $1000 benefactor
Activities: *Speaker Service:* Yes

Rumble Productions Society
1422 William St., Vancouver BC V5L 2P7
Tel: 604-662-3395; *Fax:* 604-630-7294
info@rumble.org
rumble.org
www.facebook.com/rumbleproductions
twitter.com/RumbleTheatre
Overview: A small local charitable organization founded in 1990
Mission: To research, develop & produce new & found works for the theatre & other media; to create work through a spirit of community & interdisciplinary collaboration; to initiate & produce events that foster communication, cooperation & exchange between artists of various disciplines locally, nationally & internationally
Member of: Vancouver Cultural Alliance; Vancouver Professional Theatre Alliance; Vancouver Dance Centre
Chief Officer(s):
Becky Low, Managing Producer
Finances: *Funding Sources:* Province; Progress Lab 1422; British Columbia Arts Council; Canada Council for the Arts; City of Vancouver; Private donors
Staff Member(s): 4
Activities: *Internships:* Yes

Rural Advancement Foundation International *See* ETC Group

Rural Education & Development Association *See* Alberta Community & Co-operative Association

Rural Municipal Administrators' Association of Saskatchewan (RMAA)
PO Box 130, Wilcox SK S0G 5E0
Tel: 306-732-2030; *Fax:* 306-732-4495
rmaa@sasktel.net
www.rmaa.ca
Previous Name: Rural Municipal Secretary-Treasurers' Association of Saskatchewan
Overview: A medium-sized provincial organization founded in 1955
Mission: To address the needs of rural administrators in Saskatchewan
Affliation(s): Saskatchewan Association of Rural Municipalities
Chief Officer(s):
Kevin Ritchie, Executive Director
Tim Leurer, President
rm366@sasktel.net
Finances: *Funding Sources:* Membership fees; Sponsorships
Membership: *Member Profile:* Practising rural municipal administrators, assistant administrators, secretary-treasurers & assistant secretary-treasurers in Saskatchewan; Associate members include non-practising rural municipal administrators & secretary-treasurers; Honorary life members; *Committees:* Forms & Computer Programs; Curling; Salary Negotiations; Local Government Administration Program; Seminars / Workshops / Guest Speakers; Board of Examiners; Disciplinary; Municipal Employees' Pension Plan; Golfing; Executive & Finance; Wine & Cheese Reception; Convention Sponsors / Door Prizes; Rural Advisory to SAMA; Professional Development; Enhanced Benefits; Resolutions; Humanitarian Services; Board of Reference; Council Mediation; Career Promotion; RMAA Home Page; Workshop; Ex-Officio to S.A.R.M.
Activities: Coordinating the certification of rural municipal administrator in Saskatchewan; Providing professional development activities; Carrying out disciplinary measures regarding professional practice;

Rural Municipal Secretary-Treasurers' Association of Saskatchewan *See* Rural Municipal Administrators' Association of Saskatchewan

Rural Ontario Municipal Association (ROMA)
#801, 200 University Ave., Toronto ON M5H 3C6
Tel: 416-971-9856; *Fax:* 416-971-6191
Toll-Free: 877-426-6527
www.roma.on.ca
twitter.com/share
Overview: A medium-sized provincial organization
Mission: The Rural Ontario Municipal Association (ROMA) is the rural arm of the Association of Municipalities of Ontario (AMO).
Member of: Association of Municipalities of Ontario
Chief Officer(s):
Ron Eddy, Chair
ron.eddy@brant.ca
Finances: *Funding Sources:* Membership fees; Sales of services & products; Sponsorships
Membership: 100-499; *Member Profile:* Ontario rural municipalities; Related non-profit organizations & private corporations
Activities: Developing policy positions; Reporting on issues; Liaising with the Ontario provincial government; Informing & educating the media & the public; Marketing services to the municipal sector
Meetings/Conferences: • 2015 ROMA/OGRA Combined Conference, February, 2015, Fairmont Royal York, Toronto, ON
Scope: Provincial
Description: Theme: CTRL+ALT+DEL

Rushnychok Ukrainian Folk Dancing Association (RUFDA)
PO Box 85529, Stn. Main, Saskatoon SK S7L 6K6
e-mail: rushnychok@gmail.com
www.rushnychokukrainiandance.com
Overview: A small local organization
Mission: To provide an opportunity to learn & develop the art of Ukrainian dance in a safe & friendly environment
Affliation(s): AUDA Alberta Ukrainian Dance; SUDA Saskatchewan Ukrainian Dance
Finances: *Annual Operating Budget:* Less than $50,000
Staff Member(s): 10; 60 volunteer(s)
Membership: 70 student; *Fees:* $205 student

Russell & District Chamber of Commerce
PO Box 155, Russell MB R0J 1W0
Tel: 204-773-2456
chamber@russellmb.com
www.russellmb.com/chamber.html
Overview: A small local organization
Mission: To promote the economics of trade & commerce, & improve the quality of community life
Chief Officer(s):
Dale Wray, President
Finances: *Annual Operating Budget:* Less than $50,000; *Funding Sources:* Grants
Staff Member(s): 1
Membership: 111; *Committees:* Russell & Area Promotions; Asessippi Parkland Tourism

Russian Orthodox Church in Canada
10812 - 108 St., Edmonton AB T5H 3A6
Tel: 780-420-9945
www.orthodox-canada.com
Overview: A medium-sized national organization
Chief Officer(s):
Iov Job, Bishop of Kashira
bishjob@telus.net
Membership: 25 parishes;

Russian Orthodox Greek Catholic Church (Metropolia) *See* Orthodox Church in America Archdiocese of Canada

Ruth Cansfield Dance
525 Beresford Ave., Winnipeg MB R3L 1J4
Tel: 204-284-5810; *Fax:* 204-284-1131
Toll-Free: 866-405-5810
info@ruthcansfield.com
Previous Name: Dance Collective
Overview: A small local charitable organization founded in 1995
Mission: To create & perform the choreography of Ruth Cansfield; to create an educational experience that will benefit dancers & non-dancers alike; to take dance to provincial, national, & international audiences
Member of: CAPACOA; Dance USA; Association of Performing Arts Presenters; The Canadian Club of Winnipeg; CADA Ontario; Manitoba Arts Network; Gas Station Theatre
Chief Officer(s):
Ruth Cansfield, Artistic Director
Finances: *Annual Operating Budget:* $100,000-$250,000; *Funding Sources:* Municipal, provincial, federal arts councils; private & corporate donations; box office receipts
Activities: Creation, production, touring & training in the discipline of contemporary dance; *Internships:* Yes

RVDA of Québec *Voir* Association des commerçants de véhicules récréatifs du Québec

RX-7 Club of Toronto *See* Mazda Sportscar Owners Club

Ryerson Faculty Association (RFA) / Association des professeurs de Ryerson
Kerr Hall South, #KHS-46, 40 Gould St., Toronto ON M5B 2K3
Tel: 416-979-5186
rfa@ryerson.ca
www.rfa.ryerson.ca
Overview: A small local organization founded in 1969
Mission: To act as the certified bargaining agent for Ryerson University's full-time faculty; To advance post-secondary education in Canada
Member of: Canadian Association of University Teachers; Ontario Confederation of University Faculty Associations
Chief Officer(s):
Anver Saloojee, President
Membership: 550; *Member Profile:* Full-time faculty of Ontario's Ryerson University; *Committees:* Representatives' Council; Executive; Grievance; Health & Safety; Equity Issues; Negotiating; Professional Affairs; Services
Awards:
• RFA Scholarship Award (Scholarship)
To recognize full time students, part-time students, & Aboriginal students *Amount:* $2,500 each
Publications:
• Ryerson Faculty Association News Link
Type: Newsletter
Profile: Previously known as the Forum & the Bulletin, the periodic publication covers the association's activities & features reports from committees

S'affirmer Ensemble *See* Affirm United

Saanich Historical Artifacts Society (SHAS)
7321 Lochside Dr., Saanichton BC V8M 1W4
Tel: 250-652-5522
shas@shas.ca
www.shas.ca
Overview: A small local charitable organization founded in 1963
Mission: To collect, restore, display & demonstrate artifacts
Member of: Saanich Peninsula Chamber of Commerce; Victoria Tourist Bureau
Chief Officer(s):
Hopkins Dave, President
Membership: *Fees:* $20 single; $30 family
Activities: Summer Fair; Fall Threshing; *Library:* Michell Building Library;

Saanich Native Heritage Society
PO Box 28, 7449 West Saanich Rd., Brentwood Bay BC V8M 1R3
Tel: 250-652-5980; *Fax:* 250-652-5957
saanichnativeheritage@hotmail.com
Overview: A small local organization
Chief Officer(s):
Adelynne Claxton, Contact
Publications:
• Sencoten: Legends & Stories
Type: Booklet; *Number of Pages:* 126; *ISBN:* 1-4251-0456-8; *Price:* $15
Profile: For use in the LAU, WELNEW Tribal School primary & intermediate levels

Saanich Peninsula Chamber of Commerce (SPCOC)
#209, 2453 Beacon Ave., Sidney BC V8L 1X7
Tel: 250-656-3616; *Fax:* 250-656-7111
info@peninsulachamber.ca
www.peninsulachamber.ca
www.linkedin.com/groups/Saanich-Peninsula-Chamber-Commerce-2470553
www.facebook.com/Peninsula.Chamber
twitter.com/penchamber
www.youtube.com/sanpenchamber
Also Known As: Peninsula Chamber
Previous Name: Sidney & North Saanich Board of Trade
Overview: A small local organization founded in 1947
Mission: To represent business interests in a responsible manner & to provide services to our members
Member of: BC Chamber of Commerce
Chief Officer(s):
Chris Fudge, Executive Director
Wendy Everson, President
Finances: *Funding Sources:* Membership dues
Staff Member(s): 3
Membership: 400+; *Fees:* $288 1-4 employees; $333 5-19 employees; $456 20+ employees
Activities: *Speaker Service:* Yes; *Rents Mailing List:* Yes; *Library:* Business Information Centre; Open to public

Sackville Rivers Association (SRA)
PO Box 45071, Sackville NS B4E 2Z6
Tel: 902-865-9238; *Fax:* 902-864-3564
sackvillerivers@ns.sympatico.ca
www.sackvillerivers.ns.ca
Overview: A medium-sized local organization founded in 1988
Mission: To promote the preservation, restoration and enhancement of the Sackville River Watershed.
Chief Officer(s):
Damon Conrad, Contact
Membership: 200+; *Fees:* $10; $5 student

SADC région d'Asbestos *Voir* Réseau des SADC et CAE

Safe Workplace Promotion Services Ontario *See* Workplace Safety & Prevention Services

Safety Services Manitoba (SSM)
#3, 1680 Notre Dame Ave., Winnipeg MB R3H 1H6
Tel: 204-949-1085; *Fax:* 204-949-2897
Toll-Free: 800-661-3321
registrar@safetyservicesmanitoba.ca
www.safetyservicesmanitoba.ca
ca.linkedin.com/in/gotosafetyservicesmanitoba
www.facebook.com/SafetyServicesManitoba
twitter.com/SafetyServMB
Previous Name: Manitoba Safety Council
Overview: A medium-sized provincial licensing charitable organization founded in 1920
Mission: To prevent accidental injury or occupational illness in Manitoba by providing effective safety & health programs.
Chief Officer(s):
Judy Murphy, President & CEO
Finances: *Funding Sources:* Membership & course fees; fundraising
Staff Member(s): 10
Membership: *Fees:* $500 partner; $750 leader; *Committees:* Executive; Motorcycle; Seat Belt; Operation Lifesaver; Road Safety Conference; OHS Conference
Activities: *Awareness Events:* Conference & AGM; Annual Golf Classic; Operation Red Nose
Meetings/Conferences: • Safety Services Manitoba SAFE Work Conference 2015, January, 2015, Victoria Inn & Conference Centre, Winnipeg, MB
Scope: Provincial
Description: Theme: "A Safety Odyssey"

Safety Services New Brunswick (SSNB) / Services de Sécurité Nouveau-Brunswick
#204, 440 Wilsey Rd., Fredericton NB E3B 7G5
Tel: 506-458-8034; *Fax:* 506-444-0177
Toll-Free: 877-762-7233
info@safetyservicesnb.ca
www.safetyservicesnb.ca
www.facebook.com/motorcyclecourse
twitter.com/safetynb
Previous Name: New Brunswick Safety Council Inc.
Overview: A small provincial charitable organization founded in 1967
Mission: To promote traffic, occupational & public safety issues & practices through safety training courses & programs, educational material, public information, safety campaigns & conferences.
Member of: National Safety Council
Affliation(s): Canada Safety Council
Chief Officer(s):
Bill Walker, President & CEO, 506-444-0171
bill@ssnb.ca
Jim Arsenault, Director of OSH & Traffic Training, 506-444-0178
jim@ssnb.ca
Finances: *Annual Operating Budget:* $250,000-$500,000; *Funding Sources:* Safety training & workshop fees; membership fees; donations; grants
Staff Member(s): 8; 50 volunteer(s)
Membership: 200; *Fees:* Schedule available; *Committees:* Financial; Operation Lifesaver
Activities: *Speaker Service:* Yes

Meetings/Conferences: • Safety Services New Brunswick Health & Safety Conference 2015, April, 2015, Deltra Brunswick, Saint John, NB
Scope: Provincial

Safety Services Newfoundland & Labrador
1076 Topsail Rd., Mount Pearl NL A1N 5E7
Tel: 709-754-0210; *Fax:* 709-754-0010
info@safetyservicesnl.ca
safetyservicesnl.ca
www.facebook.com/303428916390762
twitter.com/SafetyNL
Previous Name: Newfoundland & Labrador Safety Council
Overview: A medium-sized provincial organization
Mission: Safety Services Newfoundland Labrador is dedicated to the prevention of injuries and fatalities; represents all the major sectors of the province's industry, business, government departments, volunteer organizations and many individuals who have a personal interest in safety, both on and off the job.
Affliation(s): Canada Safety Council

Safety Services Nova Scotia (SSNS)
#1, 201 Brownlow Ave., Dartmouth NS B3B 1W2
Tel: 902-454-9621; *Fax:* 902-454-6027
Toll-Free: 866-511-2211
www.safetyservicesns.com
www.facebook.com/SafetyNS
twitter.com/SafetyNS
Previous Name: Nova Scotia Safety Council; The Nova Scotia Highway Safety Council
Overview: A small provincial organization founded in 1958
Mission: To develop & provide quality safety & health services, education & training programs to improve the quality of life of Nova Scotians.
Affliation(s): Canada Safety Council
Chief Officer(s):
Jackie Norman, Executive Director, 902-454-9621 Ext. 223
norman@safetyservicesns.ca
Finances: *Funding Sources:* Membership; Courses; Provincial government
Staff Member(s): 9
Membership: *Fees:* $270 associate; $525 corporate; *Member Profile:* Members include Nova Scotian businesses, government departments, charitable agencies, families, & hospital & police services.
Activities: Informing members of injury trends, new legislation, or anything that may affect the health & safety of members, their coworkers, family, & friends; *Library*
Publications:
• Safety Lines
Type: Newsletter; *Frequency:* Quarterly

Sagitawa Friendship Centre / Where the Rivers Meet
PO Box 5083, 10108 - 100 Ave., Peace River AB T8S 1R7
Tel: 780-624-2443; *Fax:* 780-624-2728
tracy-sagitawa@telus.net
anfca.com/friendship-centres/peace-river
Overview: A small local organization founded in 1964 overseen by Alberta Native Friendship Centres Association
Mission: To encourage respect & acceptance of all people; To enhance the quality of life of Aboriginal people in the Peace River area
Member of: Alberta Native Friendship Centres Association
Chief Officer(s):
Tracy Sagitawa, Contact
Activities: Increasing awareness & understanding of Aboriginal people in the local community; Partnering with other community agencies, & providing community referrals; Providing culturally based programs, as guided by elders, to assist indigenous people to meet their full potential; Offering social development programming; Providing employment & health related services; Conducting language & literacy classes; Revitalizing Aboriginal culture

The Saidye Bronfman Centre for the Arts *See* Segal Centre for the Performing Arts at the Saidye

Sail Canada / Voile Canada
Portsmith Olympic Harbour, 53 Yonge St., Kingston ON K7M 6G4
Tel: 613-545-3044; *Fax:* 613-545-3045
Toll-Free: 877-416-4720
sailcanada@sailing.ca
www.sailing.ca
www.facebook.com/196992790349209
Previous Name: Canadian Yachting Association
Overview: A medium-sized national charitable organization founded in 1931
Mission: To promote the sport of sailing in Canada
Affliation(s): International Sailing Federation; International Sailing Schools Association
Chief Officer(s):
Paddy Boyd, Executive Director
paddy@sailing.ca
Ken Dool, Head Coach & Director, High Performance
ken@sailing.ca
Finances: *Annual Operating Budget:* $1.5 Million-$3 Million
Staff Member(s): 12
Membership: 10 provincial associations; 255 clubs; 175 sailing schools; 30 class associations; 80,000 active members; over 1 million Canadian sailors; *Member Profile:* Member of member yacht club or person with interest in sailing; *Committees:* Provincial; Nominating; Standing Board; Governance; Human Resources; Audit; Finance; Racing Appeals; Olympic Policy; Athlete Appeals; Operational; Athlete Development; Business Development; Training & Certification
Activities: *Library*

Sail Manitoba
#409, 145 Pacific Ave., Winnipeg MB R3B 2Z6
Tel: 204-925-5650
sailing@sportmanitoba.ca
sailmanitoba.com
www.facebook.com/200107080070072
twitter.com/SailManitoba
Previous Name: Manitoba Sailing Association Inc.
Overview: A small provincial organization founded in 1965 overseen by Sail Canada
Mission: To be the sport's provincial regulator
Member of: Sail Canada
Chief Officer(s):
Nancy Folliott, President
folliott@mymts.net
Brigitte Smutny, Executive Director/Head Coach
Staff Member(s): 1
Membership: 1,000; *Committees:* Finance; Operations; Recreation; Training; Racing; Team

Saint Elizabeth Health Care (SEHC) / Les soins de santé Sainte-Elizabeth
#300, 90 Allstate Pkwy., Markham ON L3R 6H3
Tel: 905-940-9655; *Fax:* 905-940-9934
Toll-Free: 800-463-1763
communications@saintelizabeth.com
www.saintelizabeth.com
www.linkedin.com/company/saint-elizabeth-health-care
www.facebook.com/SaintElizabethSEHC
twitter.com/stelizabethSEHC
www.youtube.com/user/SaintElizabethSEHC
Previous Name: Saint Elizabeth Visiting Nurses' Association of Ontario
Overview: A medium-sized provincial charitable organization founded in 1908
Mission: To serve the physical, emotional, & spiritual needs of people in their homes & communities
Member of: Nursing Best Practice Research Unit, through the RNAO & the University of Ottawa
Affliation(s): Canadian Council on Health Services Accreditation
Chief Officer(s):
Shirlee M. Sharkey, President & CEO
Noreen Taylor, Chair
Heather McClure, Treasurer
Janet Holder, Secretary
Finances: *Funding Sources:* Donations; Grants
Staff Member(s): 7000
Activities: Providing nursing, supportive care, rehabilitation, & specialty services, such as long-term care, mental health & addictions, & palliative care; Offering customized consulting services; Investing in research, education, & best practices; Presenting a driver assessment & training program, including DriveABLE & Driver Rehabilitation Services
Publications:
• Saint Elizabeth Health Care e-Newsletter
Type: Newsletter
• Saint Elizabeth Health Care Foundation Newsletter
Type: Newsletter
• SEHC Research Activity Report
Type: Report
Profile: Highlights of research achievements

Barrie - North Simcoe Muskoka Service Delivery Centre
#104, 85 Ferris Lane, Barrie ON L4M 6B9
Tel: 888-737-5055; *Fax:* 877-619-4033
NorthSimcoeSDC@saintelizabeth.com

Cornwall - Eastern Counties Service Delivery Centre
#5, 1916 Pitt St., Cornwall ON K6H 5H3
Tel: 613-936-8668; *Fax:* 866-619-4059
ChamplainSDC@saintelizabeth.com

Hamilton - Hamilton, Niagara, Haldimand & Brant Service Delivery Centre
1525 Stone Church Rd. East, Hamilton ON L8K 5W9
Tel: 888-275-2299; *Fax:* 905-704-4578
HamiltonSDC@saintelizabeth.com

Kingston - South East Service Delivery Centre
#410, 1471 John Counter Blvd., Kingston ON K7M 8S8
Tel: 613-530-3400; *Fax:* 866-619-4063
SouthEastSDC@saintelizabeth.com

London - South West Service Delivery Centre
#15, 1100 Dearness Dr., London ON N6E 1N9
Tel: 519-668-2997; *Fax:* 866-619-4065
SouthWestSDC@saintelizabeth.com
Chief Officer(s):
Eileen Cunningham, Regional Director
ecunningham@saintelizabeth.com

Markham - Central Service Delivery Centre
#201, 90 Allstate Pkwy., Markham ON L3R GH3
Tel: 905-944-1743; *Fax:* 866-619-4074
CentralSDC@saintelizabeth.com

Mississauga - Peel Service Delivery Centre
#5, 6745 Century Ave., Mississauga ON L5N 7K2
Tel: 905-826-0854; *Fax:* 905-826-0854; *Crisis Hot-Line:* 905-278-9036
PeelSDC@saintelizabeth.com

Nepean - Champlain Service Delivery Centre
#225, 30 Colonnade Rd., Nepean ON K2E 7J6
Tel: 613-738-9661; *Fax:* 877-619-4038
ChamplainSDC@saintelizabeth.com

Seaforth - Huron Service Delivery Centre
87 Main St. South, Seaforth ON
Fax: 519-600-0105
Toll-Free: 888-823-1626
SouthWestSDC@saintelizabeth.com

Thunder Bay - North West Service Delivery Centre
#103, 920 Tungsten St., Thunder Bay ON P7B 5Z6
Tel: 807-344-2002; *Fax:* 807-344-1999
ThunderBaySDC@saintelizabeth.com
Chief Officer(s):
Mary Anne Fish, Manager
mafish@saintelizabeth.com

Toronto - Toronto Central Service Delivery Centre
#600, 2 Lansing Sq., Toronto ON M2J 4P8
Tel: 416-498-8600; *Fax:* 416-498-0213; *Crisis Hot-Line:* 416-498-0043
TorontoCentralSDC@saintelizabeth.com

Whitby - Central East Service Delivery Centre
1549 Victoria St. East, Whitby ON L1N 8R1
Tel: 905-430-6997; *Fax:* 905-430-2921
CentralEastSDC@saintelizabeth.com
Chief Officer(s):
Gale Coburn, Manager
gcoburn@saintelizabeth.com

Windsor - Erie St. Clair Service Delivery Centre
2473 Ouellette Ave., Windsor ON N8X 1L5
Tel: 519-972-3895; *Fax:* 866-619-4073
ErieStClairSDC@saintelizabeth.com

Woodstock - Oxford County Service Delivery Centre
65 Springbank Ave., Woodstock ON N4S 7P6
Tel: 519-539-9807; *Fax:* 866-619-4070
SouthWestSDC@saintelizabeth.com

Saint Elizabeth Visiting Nurses' Association of Ontario *See* Saint Elizabeth Health Care

Saint Francis Xavier Association of University Teachers / Association des professeurs de l'Université Saint-François-Xavier
St. Francis Xavier University, Old Municipal Bldg., PO Box 5000, #219, 42 West St., Antigonish NS B2G 2W5
Tel: 902-867-3368; *Fax:* 902-867-3747
stfxaut@stfx.ca
stfxaut.ca
Also Known As: St. FXAUT
Overview: A small local organization
Member of: Canadian Association of University Teachers
Chief Officer(s):
Peter McInnis, President

Finances: *Annual Operating Budget:* $100,000-$250,000
Membership: 300 individual

Saint John & District Labour Council (SJDLC)
#30, 1216 Sand Cove Rd., Saint John NB E2M 5V8
Tel: 506-635-1541
Overview: A small local organization overseen by New Brunswick Federation of Labour
Chief Officer(s):
Ron Oldfield, President, 506-658-1212
ron.unitedway@nb.aibn.com
Activities: *Awareness Events:* Labour Day Parade, Sept.

Saint John Alzheimer Society
152 Westmorland Rd., Saint John NB E2J 2E7
Tel: 506-634-8722; *Fax:* 506-648-9404
saintjohn@alzheimernb.ca
www.alzheimernb.ca
Overview: A small local charitable organization founded in 1983
Mission: To alleviate the personal & social consequences of Alzheimer disease & related dementia; to promote the search for a cause & cure
Member of: Alzheimer Society of New Brunswick
Activities: Caregiver Support Group; Early Stage Support Group; *Speaker Service:* Yes; *Library:* Resource Centre; Open to public

Saint John Board of Trade
PO Box 6037, 40 King St., Saint John NB E2L 4R5
Tel: 506-634-8111; *Fax:* 506-632-2008
info@sjboardoftrade.com
www.sjboardoftrade.com
Overview: A medium-sized local organization
Chief Officer(s):
Imelda Gilman, President, 506-634-4157
igilman@sjboardoftrade.com

Saint John Coin Club (SJCC)
c/o 37 Valley View Dr., Grand Bay NB E5X 1X1
www.sjcoinclub.com
Overview: A small local organization founded in 1959
Chief Officer(s):
S. McCullough, Contact
Membership: 15;

Saint John Community Food Basket
215 Charlotte St., Saint John NB E2L 2K1
Tel: 506-652-2707; *Fax:* 506-658-9441
www.saintjohnfoodbasket.org
twitter.com/SJCFB
Overview: A small local charitable organization founded in 1984
Mission: The food bank serves the needs of the people of the inner city & South End of St. John.
Member of: New Brunswick Association of Food Banks; Food Banks Canada
Affliation(s): Hestia House; Coverdale Center; Inner City Youth Ministry
Chief Officer(s):
Carolyn Danells, Chair
cmdanells@rogers.com
Finances: *Funding Sources:* Donations; Churches

Saint John Construction Association
263 Germain St., Saint John NB E2L 2G7
Tel: 506-633-1101; *Fax:* 506-633-1265
sjcic@nb.aibn.com
www.sjcic.ca
www.facebook.com/CANBSJ
twitter.com/CANBSJ
Overview: A small local organization founded in 1883 overseen by Canadian Construction Association
Mission: To provide a wide variety of benefits & services to the construction communtiy
Chief Officer(s):
Krista Collins, Association Coordinator
Staff Member(s): 2
Membership: 149; *Fees:* $1395.55 General & Trade Contractors; $1254.30 Supplier & Manufacturer Representatives; $1000.05 Professional Services Providers; $689.30 associate

Saint John Deaf & Hard of Hearing Services, Inc (SJDHHS)
324 Duke St. West, Saint John NB E2M 1V2
Tel: 506-633-0599; *Fax:* 506-652-3382; *TTY:* 506-634-8037
sjdhhs@nb.sympatico.ca
www.sjdhhs.com
www.facebook.com/sj.dhhs
Overview: A small local charitable organization founded in 1979
Mission: To empower deaf, hard of hearing & late deafened people to live independent, productive lives with the same full access to services & opportunites as the hearing population
Member of: United Way
Chief Officer(s):
Lynn LeBlanc, Executive Director
Finances: *Funding Sources:* Donations; United Way
Staff Member(s): 16
Membership: *Member Profile:* Deaf & hard of hearing
Activities: Mentorship Program; HARP, recycling program for hearing aids; interpreter services; speech reading courses; community education; deaf culture courses; Community Academic Services Program; life skills program; employability skills program; *Library*

Saint John East Food Bank Inc.
105 Wilton St., Saint John NB E2J 1H6
Tel: 506-633-8298
Overview: A small local organization
Mission: To serve the community through our local churches by supplying food to the needy.
Chief Officer(s):
Valerie McNeil, President

Saint John Gallery Association
Saint John Arts Centre, 20 Hazen Ave., Saint John NB E2L 5A5
Tel: 506-633-4870; *Fax:* 506-674-1040
sjac@saintjohnartscentre.com
www.saintjohnartscentre.com
www.facebook.com/pages/Saint-John-Arts-Centre/11437540857 5288?ref=ts
twitter.com/SJArtsCentre
Overview: A small local organization
Mission: To promote fine art in uptown Saint John
Chief Officer(s):
A. Kierstead, Contact
a.kierstead@saintjohnartscentre.com
Staff Member(s): 5
Membership: 11; *Fees:* $1; *Member Profile:* Galleries located in Saint John that sell and promote fine art and have scheduled exhibitions

Saint John Jeux Canada Games Foundation Inc. / La Fondation Jeux Canada Games Saint John, Inc.
206 King St. West, Saint John NB E2M 1S6
Tel: 506-634-1985
info@sjcanadagamesfoundation.ca
www.sjcanadagamesfoundation.ca
Overview: A small national charitable organization founded in 1986
Mission: To promote amateur athletics not only in New Brunswick, but across Canada, by providing funding for athletes, amateur athletic organizations, governing bodies, universities & others involved in the training & development of amateur athletes.
Chief Officer(s):
Patrick Darrah, Chair

Saint John Jewish Historical Society
91 Leinster St., Saint John NB E2L 1J2
Tel: 506-633-1833; *Fax:* 506-642-9926
sjjhm@nbnet.nb.ca
personal.nbnet.nb.ca/sjjhm/
Overview: A small local charitable organization founded in 1986
Mission: To preserve the heritage of the Saint John Jewish community
Affliation(s): Association for Canadian Jewish Studies; New Brunswick Historical Society; Association Museums New Brunswick; Canadian Heritage Information Network; Council of New Brunswick Archives
Finances: *Funding Sources:* Membership dues; government grant; private individuals; donations
Membership: *Member Profile:* Former Saint John residents; other interested individuals/groups
Activities: Jewish education outreach kits - Sabbath; Rosh Hashanah; Yom Kippur; Chanukah; Purim; Passover; Succot & Lifecycles (from the Cradle to the Grave); Chanukah Menoral Lighting; annual art exhibition; *Library:* Dr. Moses I. Polowin Memorial Library; Open to public by appointment

Saint John Law Society
Library, PO Box 5001, 110 Charlotte St., Saint John NB E2L 4Y9
Tel: 506-658-2542; *Fax:* 506-634-7556
sjlaw@nbnet.nb.ca
Overview: A small local organization
Activities: *Library*

Saint John Naturalists' Club
PO Box 2071, Saint John NB E2L 3T5
saintjohnnaturalistsclub.org
Also Known As: sjnc
Overview: A small local organization founded in 1962
Affliation(s): NatureNB (The New Brunswick Federation of Naturalists)
Chief Officer(s):
Charles Graves, President
president_at_saintjohnnaturalistsclub.org
Jan Riddell, Vice-President
Jeanne Finn-Allen, Secretary
Don MacPhail, Treasurer
Membership: *Fees:* $20 individuals; $25 families; *Member Profile:* Individuals interested in the conservation, study, & enjoyment of nature in New Brunswick; *Committees:* Program; Social; Greenlaw Mountain Hawk Watch (GMHW); Point Lepreau Bird Observatory (PLBO)
Activities: Hosting monthly meeting at the New Brunswick Museum; Planning field trips; Administering the Point Lepreau Bird Observatory project
Publications:
- Saint John Naturalists' Club Bulletin
Type: Newsletter
Profile: Information assembled by a different editor for each issue

Saint John Real Estate Board Inc.
#100, 55 Drury Cove Rd., Saint John NB E2K 2Z8
Tel: 506-634-8772; *Fax:* 506-634-8775
www.sjrealestateboard.ca
twitter.com/SJ_REALTORS
Overview: A medium-sized local organization founded in 1959 overseen by New Brunswick Real Estate Association
Mission: To provide services to & set standards for members; to preserve & promote the MLS marketing system to benefit buyers & sellers of real property
Member of: The Canadian Real Estate Association
Chief Officer(s):
Jason Stephen, President
Finances: *Funding Sources:* Membership fees
Membership: 300; *Member Profile:* Realtors
Activities: *Library*

Saint John SPCA Animal Rescue
295 Bayside Dr., Saint John NB E2J 1B1
Tel: 506-642-0920; *Fax:* 506-634-6101
www.spcaanimalrescue.com
www.facebook.com/Saint.John.SPCA.Animal.Rescue
twitter.com/SPCAAR
Overview: A small local charitable organization founded in 1913
Mission: To provide rescue, care, & temporary shelter to stray & unwanted animals in the Saint John area
Chief Officer(s):
Janet Foster, Executive Director
arlexec@nb.aibn.com
Melody McElman, President
Meredith Herny, Vice-President
Kevin Hoyt, Treasurer
Finances: *Funding Sources:* Donations; Fundraising; Sponsorships; Membership fees; Services
Membership: *Fees:* $25
Activities: Finding homes for animals; Educating residents of Saint John about humane treatment of animals, including information sessions at local schools; Providing humane euthanasia at owners' request; Conducting a seniors' program; Offering public tours; *Awareness Events:* Pets in the Park, including the Annual Dog Jog, July; "No Fleas" Flea Market; Be Kind To Animals Week, May
Publications:
- ARL [Animal Rescue League] Shelter Speak
Type: Newsletter; *Frequency:* 3-4 pa; *Price:* Free with League membership
Profile: Fundraising & donation updates & League information

Saint John Symphony *See* Symphony New Brunswick

Saint John Visitor & Convention Bureau *See* Tourism Saint John

Saint Mary's University Faculty Union (SMUFU) / Syndicat des professeurs de l'Université Saint Mary
Saint Mary's University, McNally Main 221, 923 Robie St., Halifax NS B3H 3C3
Tel: 902-496-8190; *Fax:* 902-496-8102
unionoffice@smufu.org
www.smufu.org

Overview: A small local organization founded in 1974
Mission: To promote & maintain harmonious relations between the university administration & its faculty & professional librarians
Member of: Canadian Association of University Teachers
Affliation(s): Canadian Labour Congress; NS Federation of Labour
Chief Officer(s):
Marc Lamoureux, President
marc.lamoureux@smu.ca
Ron Russell, Vice-President
ron.russell@smu.ca
Finances: *Annual Operating Budget:* $50,000-$100,000
Staff Member(s): 1
Membership: 269 individuals; *Fees:* Schedule available; *Member Profile:* Faculty, full-time, teaching at least two courses & professional librarians

Saint Swithun's Society
427 Lynett Cres., Richmond Hill ON L4C 2V6
Tel: 905-883-0984
www.stswithunssociety.ca
Overview: A small local organization founded in 1974
Mission: To promote feelings of goodwill; to encourage the celebration of Saint Swithun's Day (July 15) & to pattern members' lives after the example of our Patron
Affliation(s): Friends of Winchester Cathedral (England)
Chief Officer(s):
Norman McMullen, President
norman@stswithunssociety.ca
Kevin Dark, Vice-President
Elisabeth Stenson, Sec.-Treas.
Finances: *Annual Operating Budget:* Less than $50,000
Staff Member(s): 3
Membership: 300; *Member Profile:* Non-denominational, non-political/sectarian & inclusive
Activities: Annual Celebration; *Library*
Awards:
• Honourary Memberships (Award)
Awarded annually to those individuals who best represent the aims of the Society
• Gonzo Award (Award)
Awarded to member who has given special service to the Society
• Raging Bull (Award)
Awarded to member who has given special service to the Society
• Umbrage Award (Award)
For annoying behaviour by an individual or group found to have offended the greatest number of people

St. Albert & District Chamber of Commerce
71 St. Albert Trail, St. Albert AB T8N 6L5
Tel: 780-458-2833; *Fax:* 780-458-6515
chamber@stalbertchamber.com
www.stalbertchamber.com
www.facebook.com/stalbertchamber
twitter.com/StAlbertchamber
Previous Name: St Albert Chamber of Commerce
Overview: A small local organization founded in 1984
Mission: To be the voice of business in St. Albert
Member of: Alberta Chamber of Commerce; Canadian Chamber of Commerce
Chief Officer(s):
Darel Baker, Chair
Lynda Moffat, President & CEO
lynda@stalbertchamber.com
Finances: *Annual Operating Budget:* $50,000-$100,000; *Funding Sources:* Membership dues; farmers' market; trade show
Staff Member(s): 1; 17 volunteer(s)
Membership: 780; *Fees:* Schedule available; *Committees:* Farmers' Market; Gala; Golf; Government Relations; Healthy Business Challenge; Member Services; Perron District; Small Business; St. Albert Lifestyle Expo & Sale

St Albert Chamber of Commerce *See* St. Albert & District Chamber of Commerce

St. Albert Family Resource Centre
#10A, 215 Carnegie Dr., St. Albert AB T8N 5B1
Tel: 780-459-7377; *Fax:* 780-459-7399
recpt@stalbertfrc.ca
www.stalbertfrc.ca
Also Known As: St. Albert FRC
Previous Name: St. Albert Parents' Place
Overview: A small local organization founded in 1982
Mission: To provide informational resources, support & educational services to families in St. Albert, Alberta, & its surrounding communities; To advocate for policies & systems that support families' abilities to raise healthy children
Chief Officer(s):
Heather McKinnon, Operations Manager
opsmgr@stalbertfrc.ca
Finances: *Funding Sources:* Membership fees
Activities: Courses & workshops in Family Life Education & Family Support Program
Publications:
• Parenting Resource Guide
Profile: Articles & advice for parents of children from birth to preschool

St. Albert Fire Fighters Union
PO Box 127, St Albert AB T8N 1N2
Tel: 780-458-0588
info@syncopatemedia.com
www.stalbertfirefighters.com
Overview: A small local organization
Chief Officer(s):
Scott Wilde, President

St. Albert Fish & Game Association
St. Albert Community Hall, PO Box 158, 17 Perron St., St Albert AB T8N 1N3
Tel: 780-458-2015
Other Communication: Alternate Phone: 780-459-9581
phil123@telus.net
Overview: A small local organization
Mission: To encourage the wise use of the environment & wild life resources in the St. Albert area
Member of: Alberta Fish & Game Association

St. Albert Heritage Society
PO Box 77012, St Albert AB T8N 6C1
Tel: 780-459-7663; *Fax:* 780-427-0808
rpinco@interbaun.com
Previous Name: St. Albert Historical Society
Overview: A small local charitable organization founded in 1971
Mission: To provide public awareness of the history of St. Albert & district
Chief Officer(s):
Raymond Pinco, Chair
rpinco@interbaun.com
75 volunteer(s)
Membership: 119 individual; *Fees:* $15 family; $10 individual; $5 senior/youth

St. Albert Historical Society *See* St. Albert Heritage Society

St. Albert Parents' Place *See* St. Albert Family Resource Centre

St. Albert Soccer Association (SASA)
61 Riel Dr., St. Albert AB T8N 3Z3
Tel: 780-458-8973; *Fax:* 780-458-8994
www.stalbertsoccer.com
Overview: A small local organization overseen by Alberta Soccer Association
Member of: Alberta Soccer Association
Chief Officer(s):
Melody Martyn, Executive Director
melodym@stalbertsoccer.com
Staff Member(s): 5

St. Albert Stop Abuse Families Society (SAIF)
#402, 22 Sir Winston Churchill Ave., St. Albert AB T8N 1B4
Tel: 780-460-2195; *Fax:* 780-460-2190
info@stopabuse.ca
www.stopabuse.ca
twitter.com/SAIFSociety
Overview: A small local charitable organization founded in 1989
Mission: To provide services to adults in the St. Albert area of Alberta who are experiencing domestic abuse
Chief Officer(s):
Craig Pilgrim, President
Doreen Slessor, Executive Director
Finances: *Funding Sources:* Membership fees; Donations; Grants; Fundraising
Staff Member(s): 10
Activities: Offering support groups & confidential counselling services to persons affected by family violence; Partnering with St. Albert Parents' Place Association & Merchant Consulting Services to offer New Directions, a program for children, youth, & mothers who have experienced or witnessed spousal abuse; Providing educational prevention programs to schools & community groups; Offering informational ressources to clients & the public; Engaging in advocacy activities on behalf of persons in abusive relationships; *Library:* St. Albert Stop Abuse Families Society Resource Center; Open to public
Publications:
• SAIF Notes
Type: Newsletter
Profile: Society news & upcoming events

St. Andrew's Charitable Foundation *See* St. Andrew's Society of Toronto

St. Andrew's Society of Montréal (SASM)
1195B Sherbrooke St. West, Montréal QC H3A 1H9
Tel: 514-842-2030; *Fax:* 514-842-9848
info@standrews.qc.ca
standrews.qc.ca
www.facebook.com/214046318618928
Overview: A small local organization founded in 1835
Mission: To assist those less fortunate of Scottish birth or descent; to provide youth of Scottish ancestry in Québec with opportunities to advance their education through grants, scholarships & loans; to maintain & preserve Scottish traditions in the community by promoting historical, cultural, patriotic, social & sporting activities
Chief Officer(s):
G. Scot Diamond, President
Membership: *Fees:* $40 regular; $500 lifetime; *Committees:* Welfare; Scottish Culture; St. Andrew's Ball; Communications; Activities
Activities: *Library*

St. Andrew's Society of Toronto
75 Simcoe St., Toronto ON M5J 1W9
Tel: 416-348-0083
information@standrews-society.ca
www.standrews-society.ca
Previous Name: St. Andrew's Charitable Foundation
Overview: A small local charitable organization
Mission: to assist immigrant Scots in Canada, address aspects of Scottish heritage, and hold functions for the community
Affliation(s): St. Andrew's Society of Toronto
Finances: *Annual Operating Budget:* Less than $50,000
40 volunteer(s)
Membership: 350
Activities: *Awareness Events:* Society Spring Dinner, May; Society Church Parade, November; St Andrew's Charity Ball, November

St. Andrews Chamber of Commerce
PO Box 3936, St Andrews NB E5B 3S7
e-mail: stachamb@nbnet.nb.ca
www.standrewsbythesea.ca
www.facebook.com/standrewsbythesea
Overview: A small local organization founded in 1968
Mission: To promote & improve trade & commerce & the economic, civic & social welfare of the district
Member of: Canadian Chamber of Commerce
Chief Officer(s):
Dave Bennett, President
Julie Crichton, Executive Director
Finances: *Annual Operating Budget:* $50,000-$100,000
Staff Member(s): 1
Membership: 120; *Fees:* $280

St Anthony & Area Chamber of Commerce
PO Box 650, St Anthony NL A0K 4S0
Tel: 709-454-6667
Other Communication: President's Alternate Phone: 709-454-7055
stanthonyandareachamber@yahoo.ca
www.town.stanthony.nf.ca/chamber.php
Overview: A small local organization founded in 1978
Mission: To promote & improve trade & commerce & the economic, civic & social welfare of the district
Member of: Atlantic Provinces Chambers of Commerce
Chief Officer(s):
Maurice Simmonds, President, 709-454-3434
Agnes Patey, Coordinator, 709-454-3465
Finances: *Annual Operating Budget:* Less than $50,000
Staff Member(s): 1
Membership: 70; *Fees:* $100/year
Activities: Involved in many local committees

St Catharines & District Labour Council
124 Bunting Rd., St Catharines ON L2P 3G5

Tel: 905-641-1646
labourcouncil@gmail.com
www.labourcouncil.blogspot.com
Overview: A small local organization overseen by Ontario Federation of Labour
Member of: Ontario Federation of Labour
Chief Officer(s):
Larry Savage, President

St. Catharines and District Builders Exchange ***See*** Niagara Construction Association

St Catharines Association for Community Living
#200, 82 Lake St., St Catharines ON L2R 5X4
Tel: 905-688-5222; *Fax:* 905-688-9926
administration@clstcatharines.ca
www.clstcatharines.ca
Overview: A medium-sized local charitable organization
Mission: To help people with a developmental disability live in a state of dignity & have the opportunity to participate effectively
Member of: Community Living Ontario
Chief Officer(s):
Al Moreland, Executive Director
amoreland@clstcatharines.ca
Finances: *Funding Sources:* Ministry of Community & Social Services, Ministry of Housing, United Way
Membership: *Fees:* Donation
Activities: *Library:* Resource Centre; Open to public by appointment

St. Catharines Coin Club
PO Box 511, Thorold ON L2V 4W1
Overview: A small local organization

St. Catharines Indian Centre ***See*** Niagara Regional Native Centre

St Catharines Stamp Club
c/o David Hillier, 6 Northridge Ave., St Catharines ON L2T 2G5
Tel: 905-641-2318
www.stcatharinesstampclub.ca
Overview: A small local organization
Chief Officer(s):
David Hillier, President
Jim Glen, Treasurer
Membership: *Fees:* $15 youth & seniors; $20 adults & families; *Member Profile:* Individuals interested in stamp collecting
Activities: Conducting meetings at Holy Cross School; *Library:* St Catharines Stamp Club Library;

St Catharines-Thorold Chamber of Commerce; St Catharines Chamber of Commerce ***See*** Greater Niagara Chamber of Commerce

St. Christopher House
588 Queen St. West, Toronto ON M6J 1E3
Tel: 416-504-3535; *Fax:* 416-504-3047
info@stchrishouse.org
www.stchrishouse.org
Overview: A small local charitable organization founded in 1912 overseen by Ontario Council of Agencies Serving Immigrants
Mission: To enable less advantaged individuals, families & groups in the community to gain greater control over their lives & within their community
Member of: United Way of Greater Toronto
Affliation(s): Toronto Neighbourhood Centres; Canadian Association of Neighbourhood Services
Membership: *Fees:* Schedule available; *Member Profile:* Donors; volunteers; staff; program participants
Activities: *Speaker Service:* Yes

St. Christopher House Adult Literacy Program ***See*** West Neighbourhood House

St. Elias Chamber of Commerce
PO Box 5419, Haines Junction YT Y0B 1L0
Tel: 867-634-2916; *Fax:* 867-634-2034
kluaneridin@yknet.ca
Previous Name: Haines Junction Chamber of Commerce
Overview: A small local organization
Chief Officer(s):
Wade Istchenko, President

The St. George's Society of Toronto
#306, 50 Baldwin St., Toronto ON M5T 1L4
Tel: 416-597-0220
admin@stgeorgesto.com
stgeorgesto.com
www.linkedin.com/company/3235027
www.facebook.com/89559883760
Overview: A medium-sized local organization founded in 1834
Mission: To provide a focal point for people of English sympathies; to hold up English institutions & traditions; to host functions, the financial proceeds of which fund a range of educational & benevolent traditions
Chief Officer(s):
Michele McCarthy, President
Samuel Minniti, Executive Director
Danny Ramgobin, Treasurer
Finances: *Funding Sources:* Charitable trust; Membership fees; Donations
Membership: *Fees:* $5 student; $25 under 30 & family member; $85 senior; $125 member; *Member Profile:* British roots or heritage; *Committees:* Investment; Charitable Trust; Education; Red Rose Ball; Membership; Events; Heritage
Activities: Raising money for charities through the society's annual Red Rose Ball, as well as other events; *Awareness Events:* Red Rose Ball to Celebrate St. George's Day, April

St. James Community Service Society
331 Powell St., Vancouver BC V6A 1G5
Tel: 604-606-0300; *Fax:* 604-606-0309
www.sjcss.com
twitter.com/StJamesCSS
www.youtube.com/user/StJamesSociety
Overview: A small local organization founded in 1961
Mission: Offers aid & assistance to those who are in need, especially to those bypassed by the normal channels of charitable assistance
Chief Officer(s):
Jonathan Oldman, Executive Director, 604-646-0307
Finances: *Annual Operating Budget:* Greater than $5 Million; *Funding Sources:* Regional & federal government
Staff Member(s): 332; 50 volunteer(s)
Membership: 1-99; *Fees:* $5 individual

St. John Ambulance / Ambulance Saint-Jean
#400, 1900 City Park Dr., Ottawa ON K1J 1A3
Tel: 613-236-7461; *Fax:* 613-236-2425
Toll-Free: 888-840-5646
info@nhq.sja.ca
www.sja.ca
www.facebook.com/St.John.Ambulance.TO
twitter.com/sja_canada
Also Known As: The Priory of Canada of the Most Venerable Order of the Hospital of St. John of Jerusalem
Overview: A medium-sized international charitable organization founded in 1883
Mission: To enable Canadians to improve their health, safety & quality of life by providing training & community service. Courses in CPR, emergency first aid, & safety training are offered, as well as community service programs (medical first response, therapy dog services, emergency preparedness, youth programs), & first aid kits
Chief Officer(s):
F. Richard Bruce, Chancellor
Louis Barré, Executive Director
Staff Member(s): 300; 2113 volunteer(s)
Membership: 6,000
Activities: Range of safety-oriented first aid courses; 4 levels of CPR training; specialized training for people working in high-risk occupations & remote areas; health promotion courses; community service; emergencies & disaster relief; 2 schools of paramedicine in Eastern Canada; *Library* by appointment
Awards:
• Life-saving Awards of the Order of St. John (Award) Instituted in 1874, recognizes those who risk their lives in unselfish acts of bravery & heroism when saving or attempting to save a life

Alberta Council
12304 - 118 Ave., Edmonton AB T5L 5G8
Tel: 780-452-6565; *Fax:* 780-452-2835
Toll-Free: 800-665-7114
phq@stjohn.ab.ca
ab.sjatraining.ca
Chief Officer(s):
Sol Rolingher, Chair

British Columbia & Yukon Council
6111 Cambie St., 2nd Fl., Vancouver BC V5Z 3B2
Tel: 604-321-2652; *Fax:* 604-321-5316
Toll-Free: 866-321-2651
info@bc.sja.ca
bc.sjatraining.ca
Chief Officer(s):
Larry Odegard, CEO

Federal District Council (Ottawa Area)
5 Corvus Ct., Ottawa ON K2E 7Z4
Tel: 613-722-2002; *Fax:* 613-722-7024
fdgd@fd.sja.ca
Chief Officer(s):
Ann Ralph, CEO

Manitoba Council
1 St John Ambulance Way, Winnipeg MB R3G 3H5
Tel: 204-784-7000; *Fax:* 204-786-2295
Toll-Free: 800-471-7771
info@mb.sja.ca
mb.sjatraining.ca
Chief Officer(s):
Steven D. Gaetz, Executive Director/CEO

New Brunswick Council
PO Box 3599, Stn. B, 200 Miles St., Fredericton NB E3A 5J8
Fax: 506-452-8699
Toll-Free: 800-563-9998
stjohnnb@nbnet.nb.ca
nb.sjatraining.ca
Chief Officer(s):
Larry Broad, Executive Director
lbroad@nb.sja.ca

Newfoundland Council
8 Thomas Byrne Dr., Mt. Pearl NL A1N 0E1
Tel: 709-726-4200; *Fax:* 709-726-4117
Toll-Free: 800-801-0181
sja@nl.sja.ca
nl.sjatraining.ca
Chief Officer(s):
Glenda Janes, CEO, 709-757-3374

Nova Scotia/PEI Council
72 Highfield Park Dr., Dartmouth NS B3A 4X2
Fax: 902-469-9609
Toll-Free: 800-565-5056
info@ns.sja.ca
ns.sjatraining.ca
Chief Officer(s):
Paul Millen, CEO
paul.millen@ns.sja.ca

NWT & Nunavut Council
5023 - 51st St., Yellowknife NT X1A 1S5
Tel: 867-873-5658; *Fax:* 867-920-4458
info.yellowknife@nt.sja.ca
ntnu.sjatraining.ca
Chief Officer(s):
Steven D. Gaetz, CEO
steven.gaetz@mb.sja.ca

Ontario Council
#800, 15 Toronto St., Toronto ON M5C 2E3
Tel: 416-923-8411; *Fax:* 416-923-4856
Toll-Free: 800-268-7581
info@on.sja.ca
Chief Officer(s):
William Laidlaw, Executive Director

Québec Council
#40, 529, rue Jarry, Montréal QC H2P 1V4
Tél: 514-842-4801; *Téléc:* 514-842-4807
Ligne sans frais: 877-272-7607
info@qc.sja.ca
Chief Officer(s):
Ian Bennett, CEO

Saskatchewan Council
2625 - 3rd Ave., Regina SK S4T 0C8
Tel: 306-522-7226; *Fax:* 306-525-4177
Toll-Free: 888-273-0003
inquiries@sk.sja.ca
sk.sjatraining.ca
Chief Officer(s):
Kevin Moore, CEO

Yukon Branch
128 Copper Rd., #C, Whitehorse YT Y1W 2Z6
Tel: 867-668-5001; *Fax:* 867-668-5050
Toll-Free: 866-321-2651
yukon@yt.sja.ca

St. John River Valley Tribal Council (SJRVTC)
7 Wulastook Ct., Woodstock NB E7M 4K6
Tel: 506-328-0400; *Fax:* 506-328-0987
tribalsecretary@gmail.com
www.sjrvtribalcouncil.com
Overview: A small local organization

Mission: To provide advisory services & assistance to the member First Nations
Chief Officer(s):
Eric Paul, Executive Director
Membership: 4 First Nations; *Member Profile:* Madawaska Maliseet First Nation; Woodstock First Nation; St. Mary's First Nation; The Oromocto First Nation
Activities: Aboriginal Skills & Employment & Training Strategy (ASETS) program

St. John's Board of Trade
PO Box 5127, 34 Harvey Rd., 3rd Floor, St. John's NL A1C 5V5
Tel: 709-726-2961; *Fax:* 709-726-2003
mail@bot.nf.ca
www.bot.nf.ca
Overview: A medium-sized local organization founded in 1971
Mission: To act as St. John's voice of business; To enhance economic prosperity & quality of life
Chief Officer(s):
Nancy Healey, CEO Ext. 1
pthomey@bot.nf.ca
Finances: *Funding Sources:* Membership fees; programs & projects
Staff Member(s): 6
Membership: 1,000; *Fees:* Based on number of employees
Activities: *Awareness Events:* Annual Business Development Summit, January; Business Excellence Awards, December; *Speaker Service:* Yes

St. John's Cathedral Polish Catholic Church
186 Cowan Ave., Toronto ON M6K 2N6
Tel: 416-532-8249; *Fax:* 416-532-4653
stjohnscathedralcc@sympatico.com
Previous Name: Polish National Catholic Church of Canada
Overview: A small national organization
Member of: The Canadian Council of Churches
Chief Officer(s):
Joris Vercammen, Bishop Administrator
Finances: *Annual Operating Budget:* $100,000-$250,000
Membership: 300

St. John's Clean & Beautiful (SJCAB)
PO Box 908, 10 New Gower St., St. John's NL A1C 5M2
Tel: 709-570-0350; *Fax:* 709-754-3100
sjcab@cleanandbeautiful.nf.ca
www.cleanandbeautiful.nf.ca
Overview: A small local organization founded in 1992
Mission: To inspire community pride & action in St. John's to lead to a clean community
Affliation(s): Keep America Beautiful, Inc. (KAB)
Chief Officer(s):
Michelle Eagles, Chair
Activities: Increasing public awareness in the city's cleanliness; Encouraging community involvment; Promoting partnerships; Coordinating efforts for litter reduction; Planning beautification projects; Publishing brochures, such as the Litter Free Event Guide, the Graffiti Removal Guide, Are You Running a Dirty Business? & Beautiful Gardens & A Healthy Environment

St. John's Francophone Community Association ***Voir*** L'Association communautaire francophone de St-Jean

St. John's Harbour ACAP ***See*** Northeast Avalon ACAP, Inc.

St. John's International Women's Film Festival (SJIWFF)
PO Box 984, Stn. C, St John's NL A1C 5M3
Tel: 709-754-3141; *Fax:* 709-754-0049
info@womensfilmfestival.com
www.womensfilmfestival.com
www.linkedin.com/company/st-john%27s-international-women%27s-film-fest
www.facebook.com/womensfilmfestival
twitter.com/sjiwff
www.youtube.com/user/womensfilmfest
Overview: A medium-sized local organization founded in 1989
Mission: To promote international women filmmakers through the annual film festival
Chief Officer(s):
Noreen Golfman, Chair
Kelly Davis, Executive Director
kelly@womensfilmfestival.com
Finances: *Funding Sources:* Canadian Heritage; Canada Council for the Arts; CBC; Telefilm Canada; Gov't of Newfoundland & Labrador; Atlantic Canada Opportunities Agency
Membership: 4,000 participants
Activities: *Awareness Events:* Film Festival, Oct.
Awards:
• RBC Michelle Jackson Emerging Filmmaker Award (Award)

St. John's Kiwanis Music Festival
210-90 O'Leary Ave, St. John's NL A1B 2C7
Tel: 709-579-1523; *Fax:* 709-579-2007
kiwanismusicfest@nf.aibn.com
www.kiwanismusicfestivalsj.org
Overview: A small local organization
Mission: To stimulate in the citizens of Newfoundland a greater appreciation and understanding of good music; and to discover and encourage musical talents in young and old.
Chief Officer(s):
Charlie Pope jr, President
Activities: *Awareness Events:* Major festival, February-March

St. John's Native Friendship Centre
716 Water St., St. John's NL A1E 1C1
Tel: 709-726-5902; *Fax:* 709-722-0874
www.sjnfc.com
www.facebook.com/168614253196399?fref=ts
twitter.com/St_Johns_NFC
Overview: A small local organization
Member of: National Association of Friendship Centres
Chief Officer(s):
David Penner, Executive Director
Staff Member(s): 8
Membership: 200+; *Fees:* $1

St. John's Philatelic Society
c/o 107 Springdale Rd., St. John's NL A1C 5B7
Tel: 709-754-2807
mdeal@mun.ca
Overview: A small local organization
Mission: To encourage & promote all aspects of philately
Affliation(s): British North America Philatelic Society
Chief Officer(s):
Michael Deal, Contact
mdeal@mun.ca
Finances: *Annual Operating Budget:* Less than $50,000
Membership: 62; *Fees:* $20 year; $12 subscription; *Member Profile:* Stamp collector
Activities: *Library* by appointment

St. John's Rape Crisis & Information Centre ***See*** Newfoundland & Labrador Sexual Assault Crisis & Prevention Centre Inc.

St. Joseph's Healthcare Foundation
224 James St. South, Hamilton ON L8P 3A9
Tel: 905-521-6036; *Fax:* 905-577-0860
Toll-Free: 866-478-5037
info@stjoesfoundation.ca
www.stjoesfoundation.ca
Overview: A small local charitable organization founded in 1970
Mission: Raises money for St. Joseph's Hospital in Hamilton
Chief Officer(s):
Bob Beckerson, Director & Head
Finances: *Annual Operating Budget:* Greater than $5 Million; *Funding Sources:* Donations; Fundraising
Activities: Around the Bay Road Race; Golf Tournament; Holiday Gala

St. Josephine Bakhita Black Heritage
6 Dewberry Dr., Markham ON L3S 2R7
Tel: 905-472-3337
Overview: A small national organization
Mission: To promote new evangelization in black heritage communities through devotion to St. Josephine Bakhita
Affliation(s): Archdiocese of Toronto
Chief Officer(s):
Audrey Johnson, Contact
atjohnson@sympatico.ca

St. Lambert Choral Society ***Voir*** Société chorale de Saint-Lambert

St. Lambert Choral Society / Société chorale de Saint-Lambert
PO Box 36546, St. Lambert QC J4P 3S8
Tel: 450-878-0200
info.choeur.scsl@gmail.com
www.chorale-stlambert.qc.ca
www.facebook.com/239010928525
Overview: A small local organization founded in 1919
Mission: To promote the performance & appreciation of vocal music
Chief Officer(s):
David Christiani, Director, Music
Finances: *Funding Sources:* Membership fees; Donations; Sponsorships; Ticket sales
Membership: *Member Profile:* Individuals with choral experience & musical knowledge who are prepared to audition for the choir
Activities: Performing season concerts;

St. Lambert Council for Seniors ***Voir*** Conseil du troisième âge de Saint-Lambert

St. Lawrence Economic Development Council ***Voir*** Société de développement économique du Saint-Laurent

St. Lawrence Shipoperators ***Voir*** Armateurs du Saint-Laurent

St. Lawrence Valley Natural History Society (SLVNHS) / Société d'histoire naturelle de la vallée du St-Laurent (SHNVSL)
21125, ch Ste-Marie, Sainte-Anne-de-Bellevue QC H9X 3Y7
Tel: 514-457-9449; *Fax:* 514-457-0769
info@ecomuseum.ca
www.zooenville.ca
Also Known As: Ecomuseum
Overview: A small local charitable organization founded in 1981
Mission: To foster an appreciation & understanding of the physical & biotic characters of the St. Lawrence Valley; to awaken public interest in the conservation of natural resources of the Valley; to stimulate interest in research on & development of renewable resources for the betterment of society
Member of: Canadian Association of Zoos & Aquariums
Affliation(s): Canadian Nature Federation; Union québécoise pour la conservation de la nature
Chief Officer(s):
David Rodrigue, Director, 514-457-9449 Ext. 105
david.rodrigue@ecomuseum.ca
Caroline Bourque, Assistant Director, 514-457-9449 Ext. 104
caroline.bourque@ecomuseum.ca
Isabelle Mayer, Communications Director, 514-457-9449 Ext. 103
isabelle.mayer@ecomuseum.ca
Finances: *Annual Operating Budget:* $500,000-$1.5 Million
Staff Member(s): 27; 100 volunteer(s)
Membership: 500-999; *Fees:* $50 individual; $120 family
Activities: *Speaker Service:* Yes

St. Leonard's Society of Canada (SLSC) / Société St-Léonard du Canada
Bronson Centre, #208, 211 Bronson Ave., Ottawa ON K1R 6H5
Tel: 613-233-5170; *Fax:* 613-233-5122
Toll-Free: 888-560-9760
slsc@on.aibn.com
www.stleonards.ca
www.facebook.com/SLSCanada
twitter.com/st.leonards_Can
Overview: A medium-sized national charitable organization founded in 1967
Mission: Committed to the prevention of crime through programs which promote responsible community living & safer communities
Member of: National Associations Active in Criminal Justice; Canadian Criminal Justice Association
Affliation(s): Volunteer Ottawa; Imagine Canada; Canada Helps.org
Chief Officer(s):
Elizabeth White, Executive Director
Finances: *Annual Operating Budget:* $100,000-$250,000; *Funding Sources:* Donations; membership; grants
Staff Member(s): 5; 18 volunteer(s)
Membership: 12 affiliate agencies; *Fees:* Schedule available; *Committees:* Research & Development; Operations; Executive; External Relations; Executive Directors
Awards:
• The Cody Award (Award)
• The Luxton Award (Award)
• The Libby Fund Award (Award)
• The Gallagher Award (Award)

Larch Halfway House of Sudbury
238 Larch St., Sudbury ON P3B 1M1
Tel: 705-674-2887; *Fax:* 705-674-4312
v-mack@hotmail.com
Chief Officer(s):
Vince Marconato, Executive Director

Maison "Crossroads" de la Société St-Léonard de Montréal
5262, rue Notre Dame ouest, Montréal QC H4C 1T5

Tél: 514-932-7188; *Téléc:* 514-932-6668
maisoncrossroads@qc.aibn.com
maisoncrossroads.qc.ca
Chief Officer(s):
Michel Gagnon, Directeur executif

St. Leonard's Home Trenton
RR#5, Trenton ON K8V 5P7
Tel: 613-392-7149; *Fax:* 613-392-3507
slh@xplornet.com
Chief Officer(s):
Dennis Acquafreddo, Executive Director
slh@xplornet.com

St. Leonard's House Peel
PO Box 2607, 1105 Queen St. East, Brampton ON L6T 5M6
Tel: 905-457-2670; *Fax:* 905-457-2294
richardb@stleonardshouse.com
www.stleonardshouse.com
Chief Officer(s):
Richard Brown, Executive Director
richardb@stleonardshouse.com

St. Leonard's House Windsor
491 Victoria Ave., Windsor ON N9A 4N1
Tel: 519-256-1878; *Fax:* 519-256-4142
stleonardshouse1@cogeco.net
www.stleonardswindsor.com
Chief Officer(s):
Skip Graham, Executive Director

St. Leonard's Society of Hamilton
73 Robert St., Hamilton ON L8L 2P2
Tel: 905-572-1150; *Fax:* 905-572-9152
jtclinton@slsh.ca
www.slsh.ca/
Chief Officer(s):
Doug Caldwell, Executive Director

St. Leonard's Society of London
405 Dundas St., London ON N6B 1V9
Tel: 519-850-3777; *Fax:* 519-850-1396
paharan@slcs.ca
slcs.ca
Chief Officer(s):
Peter Aharan, Executive Director

St. Leonard's Society of North Vancouver
312 Benwick Ave., North Vancouver BC V7M 3B7
Tel: 604-980-3684; *Fax:* 604-980-5339
mkhorne@shaw.ca
Chief Officer(s):
Wilma Douglas-Dungey, Executive Director

St. Leonard's Society of Nova Scotia
#900, 45 Alderney Dr., Dartmouth NS B2Y 2N6
Tel: 902-463-6077; *Fax:* 902-461-2619
saintlen99@hotmail.com
www.saintleonards.com/
Chief Officer(s):
Bill Pratt, Executive Director, 902-463-2574
billpratt@shelternovascotia.com

St. Leonard's Society of Peterborough
458 Rubidge St., Peterborough ON K9J 7S4
Tel: 705-743-9351; *Fax:* 705-743-9975
edmisonhouse@on.aibn.com
Chief Officer(s):
Darrell Rowe, Executive Director

St. Leonard's Society of Toronto
50 Euston Ave., Toronto ON M4J 3N2
Tel: 416-462-3684; *Fax:* 416-462-3894
slstoronto@rogers.com
www.stleonardstoronto.com
Chief Officer(s):
Sonya Spencer, Executive Director
sspencer.slst@rogers.com

St. Leonard's Youth & Family Services Society
7181 Arcola Way, Burnaby BC V5E 0A6
Tel: 604-524-1511; *Fax:* 604-524-1510
www.stleo.ca
Overview: A medium-sized local charitable organization founded in 1967
Mission: To provide innovative high quality social services to the community; to be the most responsive forward moving agency in our field; to promote the development of skills & values which embrace the ideals of a healthy community
Member of: Federation of Child & Family Services
Chief Officer(s):
Renata Aebi, Executive Director
Finances: *Funding Sources:* Provincial government
Membership: *Member Profile:* People interested in well being of others
Activities: Child & family services, both residential & non-residential
Awards:
• Annual Scholarship (Scholarship)
Eligibility: Available to University of British Columbia School of Social Work entering 4th year of studies *Amount:* $1,000
Contact: UBC School of Social Work

St. Martins & District Chamber of Commerce
229 Main St., St Martins NB E5R 1B7
Tel: 506-833-2019; *Fax:* 506-833-2028
info@stmartinscanada.com
stmartinscanada.com
Overview: A small local organization
Chief Officer(s):
Kathy Miller-Zinn, President
Eric Bartlett, Secretary

St. Mary's Prayer Group
St. Mary's Roman Catholic Parish, 66A Main St. South, Brampton ON L6W 2C6
Tel: 905-451-2300
info@stmarysbrampton.com
www.stmarysbrampton.com
Overview: A small local organization
Affliation(s): Archdiocese of Toronto
Chief Officer(s):
Kathy Butcher, Contact
kathy-b@rogers.com
Membership: *Member Profile:* Open to everyone; Core members plan meetings & activities & gather for prayer
Activities: Offering healing masses, intercessory prayer, & Life in the Spirit seminars

St Mary's River Association (SMRA)
PO Box 179, 8404 #7 Hwy., Sherbrooke NS B0J 3C0
Tel: 902-522-2099; *Fax:* 902-522-2241
stmarysriver@ns.sympatico.ca
stmarysriverassociation.com
Overview: A small local charitable organization founded in 1979
Mission: To further in all ways possible the conservation, protection, propagation & perpetuation of the fishery in the St Mary's River & its tributaries in eastern Nova Scotia; to support & assist the efforts of the federal Department of Fisheries, the provincial Department of Fisheries, other government bodies & voluntary associations in any program to conserve & improve the fishery; to impress upon all concerned that the fresh & salt water fishery must be developed, harvested & protected in a spirit of cooperation, with each being dependent on the other for survival & each recognizing the need for conservation measures in this area; to work with the federal, provincial & municipal governments & the private sector in undertaking capital works programs which will enhance the fishery in the St Mary's River & tributaries
Member of: Atlantic Salmon Federation; Nova Scotia Salmon Association
Finances: *Annual Operating Budget:* $50,000-$100,000; *Funding Sources:* Private donations; Industry donations; fundraising activities
Staff Member(s): 1
Membership: 273; *Fees:* $20 regular; $50 contributing; $200 corporate; $5 junior; $500 gold; $300 silver; $100 bronze; *Member Profile:* Anglers; conservationists; business; *Committees:* Newsletter; Membership; River Projects; Fundraising; Interpretive Centre
Activities: River habitat improvement; operation of interpretive centre; fundraising; newsletter; community events; *Library*

St. Patrick's Society of Richmond & Vicinity
Richmond QC
www.richmondstpats.org
Overview: A small local organization founded in 1877
Mission: To promote & celebrate the Irish culture in the Richmond area, the oldest Irish society in mainland Québec
Chief Officer(s):
Érika Lockwood, President, 819-826-3322
Membership: *Fees:* $5 single; $10 family

St Paul & District Chamber of Commerce
PO Box 887, 4802 - 50 Ave., St Paul AB T0A 3A0
Tel: 780-645-5820; *Fax:* 780-645-5820
admin@stpaulchamber.ca
www.stpaulchamber.ca
Overview: A small local organization founded in 1929
Mission: To represent & speak for the business, agricultural & professional community; translate into action the thinking of our members; to render specific services of a type that can be most effectively provided by an organization of people with business experience
Affliation(s): Alberta Chambers of Commerce
Chief Officer(s):
Alice Herperger, President
aliceatthejungle@live.com
Penny Fox, Executive Director
Finances: *Annual Operating Budget:* $50,000-$100,000; *Funding Sources:* Membership & grants
Staff Member(s): 1
Membership: 160; *Fees:* $68.51-$241.76; *Member Profile:* Businesses; individuals; non-profit organizations

St. Paul Abilities Network (SPAN)
4637 - 45 Ave., St Paul AB T0A 3A3
Tel: 780-645-3441; *Fax:* 780-645-1885
Toll-Free: 866-645-3900
mail@spanet.ab.ca
stpaulabilitiesnetwork.ca
Overview: A small local organization founded in 1964
Mission: To lead through empowerment & excellence; believes that all individuals have the right to full participation in society, enjoying benefits, respect for preferences & individuality
Member of: Alberta Association for Community Living
Affliation(s): Alberta Association of Rehabilitaion Centres; Elk Point Abilities Network
Chief Officer(s):
Tim Bear, Executive Director
tbear@spanet.ab.ca
Activities: Many supports to families; *Library:* SPAN Library; Open to public

St. Pierre Chamber of Commerce
PO Box 71, St-Pierre-Jolys MB R0A 1V0
Tel: 204-377-4384
sundowng@mts.net
www.stpierrejolys.com
Overview: A small local organization overseen by The Manitoba Chambers of Commerce
Mission: To organize & facilitate the economic development of the St. Pierre area
Chief Officer(s):
Robert Bruneau, President
Finances: *Funding Sources:* Membership fees; advertising
Membership: 83; *Member Profile:* Businesses
Activities: *Library:* Centre bilingue

St. Stephen Area Chamber of Commerce
73 Milltown Blvd., St Stephen NB E3L 1G5
Tel: 506-466-7703; *Fax:* 506-466-7753
chamber.ststephen@nb.aibn.com
www.ststephenchamber.com
Overview: A small local organization
Affliation(s): Atlantic Chamber of Commerce; Canadian Chamber of Commerce
Chief Officer(s):
Dale Weeks, President
Finances: *Annual Operating Budget:* Less than $50,000; *Funding Sources:* Membership dues
Staff Member(s): 1; 30 volunteer(s)
Membership: 100+; *Fees:* $25-155; *Committees:* Awareness; Education; Membership; Policy; Promotion
Activities: Annual business recognition dinner

St. Stephen's Community House
91 Bellevue Ave., Toronto ON M5T 2N8
Tel: 416-925-2103
execassistant@sschto.ca
www.sschto.ca
www.facebook.com/St.StephensHouse
twitter.com/StStephensHouse
www.youtube.com/channel/UCZhnIUtPv8BSKAUxZFVI5Tw
Overview: A small local charitable organization founded in 1962 overseen by Ontario Council of Agencies Serving Immigrants
Mission: To help eliviate social problems through their programming
Chief Officer(s):
Liane Regendanz, Executive Director
Staff Member(s): 200; 400 volunteer(s)
Activities: Provides professional mediation, coaching & consulting services; training in mediation communication & conflict management; *Internships:* Yes

St Thomas & District Chamber of Commerce
#115, 300 South Edgeware Rd., St Thomas ON N5P 4L1
Tel: 519-631-1981; *Fax:* 519-631-0466
mail@stthomaschamber.on.ca
www.stthomaschamber.on.ca
Previous Name: St. Thomas Board of Trade
Overview: A medium-sized local organization founded in 1869
Mission: To serve as the voice of the business community & to work to ensure economic success in central Elgin county
Affliation(s): Ontario Chamber of Commerce; Canadian Chamber of Commerce
Chief Officer(s):
Bob Hammersley, President & CEO Ext. 524
bob@stthomaschamber.on.ca
Finances: *Annual Operating Budget:* $250,000-$500,000; *Funding Sources:* Membership dues; projects & activities
Staff Member(s): 6; 100 volunteer(s)
Membership: 720 corporate + 1,220 individual; *Fees:* Schedule available
Activities: Free Enterprise Dinner & Awards; *Awareness Events:* Annual Best Ball Open Golf Tournament, August; *Speaker Service:* Yes; *Rents Mailing List:* Yes
Awards:
• Chair's Award (Award)
• Bell Canada Communication Innovation Award (Award)
• Free Enterprise Award of Merit (Award)
• The Free Enterprise Master Award (Award)

St. Thomas Board of Trade ***See*** St Thomas & District Chamber of Commerce

St. Vincent & the Grenadines Association of Montreal Inc. (SVGAM) / L'Association St.Vincent et Grenadines de Montrèal Inc.
PO Box 396, Stn. Snowdon Station, Montréal QC H3X 3T3
Tel: 514-344-9924
www.svgamontreal.com
Overview: A small local organization
Chief Officer(s):
Alfred Dear, President, 514-364-3299

St. Walburg Chamber of Commerce
PO Box 501, St Walburg SK S0M 2T0
Tel: 306-248-3269
townofstwalburg@sasktel.net
www.stwalburg.com
Overview: A small local organization
Member of: Saskatchewan Chamber of Commerce
Chief Officer(s):
Ali Schmidt, Contact, 206-248-4681
Finances: *Annual Operating Budget:* Less than $50,000
Membership: 45; *Fees:* $25; *Member Profile:* Business owners

SAIT Academic Faculty Association (SAFA) / Association des professeurs du SAIT
Senator Patrick Burns Bldg., SAIT Campus, #N201, 1301 - 16 Ave. NW, Calgary AB T2M 0L4
Tel: 403-284-8321; *Fax:* 403-284-0005
safa@sait.ca
www.safacalgary.com
Previous Name: SAIT Instructors Association
Overview: A small local organization founded in 1983
Mission: To foster standards of excellence in instruction; to carry on liaison with external organizations; to foster good relations between the Institute & the community; to promote & establish appropriate renumeration, fringe benefits & good working conditions
Member of: Alberta College-Institute Faculty Association
Affliation(s): Canadian Association of College-Institute Faculty
Chief Officer(s):
James McWilliams, President, 403-210-4056
james.mcWilliams@sait.ca
Kathie Dann, Administrator
kathie.dann@sait.ca
Staff Member(s): 4
Membership: *Fees:* 1.2% of salary; *Member Profile:* Full-time & part-time instructors at SAIT; *Committees:* Negotiations; Dispute Resolution/Grievance

SAIT Instructors Association ***See*** SAIT Academic Faculty Association

Sakatchewan Party
PO Box 545, Regina SK S4P 3A2
Tel: 306-359-1638; *Fax:* 306-359-9832
saskparty.com
www.facebook.com/SaskParty
twitter.com/SaskParty
www.youtube.com/SaskatchewanParty
Overview: A small provincial organization founded in 1997
Chief Officer(s):
Brad Wall, Party Leader
Membership: *Fees:* $5 youth; $10 regular

Salers Association of Canada (SAC) / Association salers du Canada
5160 Skyline Way NE, Calgary AB T2E 6V1
Tel: 403-264-5850; *Fax:* 403-264-5895
info@salerscanada.com
www.salerscanada.com
Also Known As: Canadian Salers
Overview: A small national organization founded in 1974
Mission: To develop & register Salers cattle
Member of: Canadian Beef Breeds Council
Chief Officer(s):
Gar Williams, President
gmwilliams@sasktel.net
Ray Depalme, Treasurer
raymondj@xplornet.com
Lois Chivilo, Registrar
Staff Member(s): 4
Membership: 62; *Member Profile:* Canadian Salers breeders
Activities: Promoting the Salers breed; Disseminating information about the breed at promotional booths at fairs & expositions, auction markets, bull test stations, & international trade events; Coordinating Salers sales & shows; Supporting young cattlemen & women;
Publications:
• Salers
Type: Magazine; *Frequency:* Semiannually; *Accepts Advertising*; *Price:* $17 / year Canada; $21 / year foreign
Profile: Articles about the breed & industry, executive & provincial reports, show & sale news, plus association announcements

Sales & Marketing Executives of Vancouver (SMEV)
PO Box 8000-191, Abbotsford BC V2S 6H1
Tel: 604-266-0090; *Fax:* 604-264-8543
vancouver@smei.org
www.smeivancouver.org
www.linkedin.com/groups?home=&gid=45880
www.facebook.com/smeivancouver
twitter.com/smei_org
www.youtube.com/smeiorg
Also Known As: SMEI Vancouver
Overview: A small local organization founded in 1946
Member of: Sales & Marketing Executives International
Chief Officer(s):
Craig Lovell, President
Bonnie Turner, Executive Director
Finances: *Funding Sources:* Membership fees; fundraising
Staff Member(s): 1; 18 volunteer(s)
Membership: 152; *Fees:* $275 + GST; *Member Profile:* CEO; marketing & sales executives; *Committees:* Membership; Breakfast; Advisory Council
Activities: Monthly meetings; keynote speakers; workshops & breakfasts

Salesian Cooperators, Association of St. Benedict Centre
c/o St. Benedict Parish, 2194 Kipling Ave., Etobicoke ON M9W 4K9
Tel: 416-743-3830; *Fax:* 416-743-8884
connect@stbenedicts.ca
stbenedicts.ca/salesiancooperators.html
Also Known As: Don Bosco's Cooperators
Overview: A small local organization founded in 1876
Mission: To bring a priviledged attention to young people, especially those who are poorest, or victims of marginalization, exploitation, & violence
Affliation(s): Archdiocese of Toronto
Chief Officer(s):
Marilena Berardinelli, Contact
marilena.berardinelli@tcdsb.org
Finances: *Funding Sources:* Fundraising
Membership: *Member Profile:* Lay, mature adults & priest members, accompanied by SDB or FMA religious, form the lay apostolic association; Members must be accepted by the provincial council & make personal, public promises

La Salle & District Chamber of Commerce
PO Box 172, La Salle MB R0G 1B0
Fax: 866-234-6272
Toll-Free: 855-273-3278
info@lasalleonline.ca
lasalleonline.ca
www.facebook.com/254436004642699
Overview: A small local organization founded in 1990
Mission: To promote local businesses & help them grow
Member of: Manitoba Chambers of Commerce
Chief Officer(s):
Drew Howard, President
Jared Cormier, Treasurer
Staff Member(s): 1
Membership: 62; *Fees:* $60 individual/organization; $125 business; *Member Profile:* Local businesses

Salmo & District Chamber of Commerce
PO Box 400, 100 - 4th St., Salmo BC V0G 1Z0
Tel: 250-357-2596
salmoch@telus.net
discoversalmo.ca/Chamber.aspx
Overview: A small local organization
Chief Officer(s):
Dave Reid, President
Membership: *Fees:* $70 business; $25 association; $20 individual; $10 student/senior

Salmo Community Resource Society (SCRS)
PO Box 39, Salmo BC V0G 1Z0
Tel: 250-357-2277; *Fax:* 250-357-2385
www.scrs.ca
Overview: A small local organization
Mission: Provides support for underpriviledged families & children
Chief Officer(s):
Maureen Berk, Executive Director
maureen@scrs.ca
2 volunteer(s)

Salmon Arm - Salvation Army Food Bank
PO Box 505, 191 - 2nd Ave., Salmon Arm BC V1E 4N6
Tel: 250-832-9194; *Fax:* 250-832-9148
Overview: A small local organization overseen by Food Banks British Columbia
Mission: To provide food and services to the needy in the Salmon Arm area.
Member of: Food Banks British Columbia
Chief Officer(s):
Matthew Juhasz, Contact

Salmon Arm & District Chamber of Commerce (SACC)
PO Box 999, #101, 20 Hudson Ave. NE, Salmon Arm BC V1E 4P2
Tel: 250-832-6247; *Fax:* 250-832-8382
Other Communication: Visitor Centre e-mail: info@visitsalmonarm.com
admin@sachamber.bc.ca
www.sachamber.bc.ca
www.facebook.com/102087637078
Overview: A small local organization founded in 1909
Mission: To provide a business perspective within the Salmon Arm region; to stimulate prosperity by promoting tourism, identifying business opportunities, & encouraging new & existing businesses
Member of: BC Chamber of Commerce
Chief Officer(s):
Jim Kimmerly, President
Corryn Grayston, General Manager
Finances: *Annual Operating Budget:* $100,000-$250,000; *Funding Sources:* Membership dues; service fees
Staff Member(s): 2
Membership: 600; *Fees:* Based on number of employees; *Committees:* Forestry; Tourism; Manufacturing; Retail; Centennial; Events; Education; Membership; Scholarship

Salmon Arm Bay Nature Enhancement Society (SABNES)
PO Box 27, Salmon Arm BC V1E 4N2
Tel: 250-833-9717
sabnes.org@gmail.com
www.sabnes.org
Overview: A small local organization founded in 1986
Mission: To assist the Wildlife Branch of the provincial government with the development & operation of their management plan for the Salmon Arm foreshore as a Nature Conservancy & viewing area; To develop, operate & promote a system of walkways, viewing areas & interpretive facilities for scientific, educational, environmental protection & public viewing

purposes; & to promote environmental awareness & assist in projects meeting that goal in the Salmon Arm area.
Chief Officer(s):
Mike Saul, Treasurer
Finances: *Funding Sources:* Corporate sponsorship; Membership dues
Membership: *Fees:* $10 individual; $20 family; $50 sustaining individual; $100 sustaining family; $500 life membership; $50-2500 corporate membership

Salmon Preservation Association for the Waters of Newfoundland (SPAWN)

93 West St., Corner Brook NL A2H 2Y6
Tel: 709-634-3012; *Fax:* 709-634-4091
Toll-Free: 866-634-3012
spawn@nl.rogers.com
www.spawn1.ca
Overview: A small local charitable organization founded in 1979
Mission: Works with Government to help improve the migrating numbers of salmon.
Member of: Salmonid Council of Newfoundland & Labrador
Affliation(s): Atlantic Salmon Federation
Chief Officer(s):
Keith Cormier, President
Finances: *Annual Operating Budget:* $50,000-$100,000; *Funding Sources:* Auctions
Staff Member(s): 1; 300 volunteer(s)
Membership: 300; *Fees:* $25 Canadian member; US$30 American member; US$35 outside North America; *Member Profile:* Conservationists; *Committees:* Enhancement; Enforcement; Habitat; Dinner/Auction; Magazine
Activities: Conservation projects; data collection; *Library* by appointment

Salmonid Association of Eastern Newfoundland (SAEN)

PO Box 29122, #8, 50 Pippy Pl., St. John's NL A1A 5B5
Tel: 709-722-9300; *Fax:* 709-722-9320
saen@nfld.com
www.saen.org
twitter.com/SAEN_NL
Overview: A small provincial organization founded in 1979
Mission: Dedicated to the preservation of Newfoundland's freshwater resources
Chief Officer(s):
Don Hutchens, Office Manager
Scott Nightingale, President
scottn@nl.rogers.com
Staff Member(s): 1
Membership: *Fees:* $20 individual; $50 corporate
Activities: Fly-tying; Moose stew; Rod building club; River talks

Salon du livre de Toronto et Festival des écrivains / Toronto French Book Fair

789, rue Yonge, Toronto ON M4W 2G8
Tél: 416-670-9847
info@salondulivredetoronto.ca
www.salondulivredetoronto.ca
www.facebook.com/SalonDuLivreDeToronto
twitter.com/SDLTO
Aperçu: *Dimension:* petite; *Envergure:* internationale; Organisme sans but lucratif; fondée en 1993
Mission: Promouvoir le livre d'expression française et les écrivains francophones, pour le bénéfice des francophones et francophiles de Toronto et d'ailleurs
Membre(s) du bureau directeur:
Jacques Charette, Chargé de la logistique
Jacques.Charette@salondulivredetoronto.ca
Vlad Valéry, Président
Finances: *Fonds:* Subventions gouvernementales (50%)
Membre(s) du personnel: 1
Membre: *Critères d'admissibilite:* Écrivain, professeur, critique littéraire, libraire, bibliothécaire, éditeur, journaliste, etc.
Activités: Exposition de livres avec ventes; soirées littéraires; tables rondes; conférences, ateliers; animation jeunesse; spectacles; lancements et signatures de livres; *Evénements de sensibilisation:* Le Festival des écrivains
Prix, Bouses:
• Prix Christine-Dumitriu-Van-Saanen (Prix)
Amount: 5 000$
• Prix du Consulat Général de France (Prix)
Un voyage au Salon du livre de Paris

Salt Spring Community Centre Food Bank

268 Fulford Ganges Rd., Salt Spring Island BC V8K 2K6
Tel: 250-537-9971; *Fax:* 250-537-9974
connect@ssics.ca
www.saltspringcommunityservices.ca/foodbank
Overview: A small local organization founded in 1975
Mission: To provide food & services to the needy in the Salt Spring Island area
Chief Officer(s):
Annika Lund, Contact
alund@ssics.ca
Finances: *Funding Sources:* Donations; Grants; United Way; Public Health Agency
Activities: Resources & referrals; Adult counselling; Child & youth; Community housing; Outreach; Community living; Early childhood; Food security; Seniors services; Psychiatric services

Salt Spring Island Chamber of Commerce (SSI Chamber)

121 Lower Ganges Rd., Salt Spring Island BC V8K 2T1
Tel: 250-537-4223; *Fax:* 250-537-4276
Toll-Free: 866-216-2936
chamber@saltspringchamber.com
www.saltspringchamber.com
www.facebook.com/116793475083257?fref=ts
twitter.com/saltspringchamb
Also Known As: Salt Spring Island Chamber of Commerce & Visitor Centre
Overview: A small local organization founded in 1948
Member of: Destination BC; Canadian Chamber of Commerce; Tourism Vancouver Island
Chief Officer(s):
Janet Clouston, General Manager
Finances: *Annual Operating Budget:* $100,000-$250,000; *Funding Sources:* BC Ministry of Tourism; Tourism Vancouver Island
Staff Member(s): 1; 100 volunteer(s)
Membership: 300; *Fees:* $50-$315; *Committees:* Events; Membership; Tourism; Economic Development
Activities: *Awareness Events:* Sip & Savour Salt Spring; Salt Spring Blooms, April; Christmas on Salt Spring

S.A.L.T.S. Sail & Life Training Society (SALTS)

451 Herald St., Victoria BC V8W 3N8
Tel: 250-383-6811; *Fax:* 250-383-7781
Toll-Free: 888-383-6811
info@salts.ca
www.salts.ca
www.facebook.com/saltsvictoria
twitter.com/saltsvictoria
Overview: A small provincial charitable organization founded in 1974
Mission: Christian organization that believes through the medium of sail training both spiritual & physical development is encouraged in each individual
Member of: Canadian Council of Christian Charities
Chief Officer(s):
Loren Hagerty, Executive Director
Finances: *Annual Operating Budget:* $500,000-$1.5 Million; *Funding Sources:* Trainee fees; donations; membership fees; fundraising
Staff Member(s): 7; 40 volunteer(s)
Membership: 450 single & family; *Fees:* $50 single; $100 family; $200 corporate

SalvAide

#411, 219 Argyle Ave., Ottawa ON K2P 2H4
Tel: 613-233-6215; *Fax:* 613-233-7375
info@salvaide.ca
www.salvaide.ca
www.facebook.com/pages/SalvAide/163091010412408
twitter.com/salvaide
www.youtube.com/user/SalvAide
Overview: A small national organization founded in 1985
Mission: To foster economic & democratic development in El Salvador
Member of: Canadian Council for International Cooperation
Chief Officer(s):
René Guerra Salazar, Executive Director
director@salvaide.ca
Finances: *Annual Operating Budget:* $250,000-$500,000
Staff Member(s): 3
Membership: 1-99

The Salvation Army in Canada

Territorial Headquarters, Canada & Bermuda, 2 Overlea Blvd., Toronto ON M4H 1P4
Toll-Free: 800-725-2769
Other Communication: www.flickr.com/photos/salvationarmy
www.salvationarmy.ca
www.facebook.com/salvationarmy
twitter.com/salvationarmy
www.youtube.com/user/salvationarmy
Overview: A large international charitable organization founded in 1882
Mission: To preach the Gospel of Jesus Christ; To supply basic human needs; To provide personal counselling & undertake the spiritual & moral regeneration & physical rehabilitation of all persons in need who come within its sphere of influence regardless of race, colour, creed, sex or age
Member of: Evangelical Fellowship of Canada
Chief Officer(s):
Brian Peddle, Territorial Commander
Andrew B. Lennox, Chair, Advisory Board
Mark Tillsley, Chief Secretary
Finances: *Annual Operating Budget:* $3 Million-$5 Million
Staff Member(s): 152
Membership: 311 Corps (congregations); 330+ social-service institutes across Canada
Activities: *Speaker Service:* Yes
Publications:
• Salvationist
Type: Magazine; *Frequency:* Monthly; *Editor:* Geoff Moulton; *Price:* $30/yr.
Profile: Magazine informing readers about the mission and ministry of the Salvation Army in Canada and Bermuda.

Burnaby - British Columbia Division
#103, 3833 Henning Dr., Burnaby BC V5V 6N5
Tel: 604-299-3908; *Fax:* 604-291-0345
www.salvationarmy.ca/britishcolumbia
twitter.com/SalArmyBC

Edmonton - Alberta & Northern Territories Division
9618 - 101A Ave. NW, Edmonton AB T5H 0C7
Tel: 780-423-2111; *Fax:* 780-425-9081
www.salvationarmy.ca/alberta
www.facebook.com/SalvationArmyAB
twitter.com/tsaedmonton
www.youtube.com/user/TSAAlberta
Chief Officer(s):
Pam Goodyear, Divisional Secretary, Public Relations & Development
pam_goodyear@can.salvationarmy.org

Halifax - Maritime Division
330 Herring Cove Road, Halifax NS B3R 1V4
Tel: 902-455-1201; *Fax:* 902-455-0055
www.salvationarmy.ca/maritime
www.facebook.com/SAmaritime
twitter.com/SAmaritime
www.youtube.com/SAmaritime
Chief Officer(s):
Rhonda Harrington, Divisional Secretary
Rhonda_Harrington@can.salvationarmy.org

London - Ontario Great Lakes Division
371 King St., London ON N6B 1S4
Tel: 519-433-6106; *Fax:* 519-433-0250
www.salvationarmy.ca/ontariogreatlakes
Chief Officer(s):
Patricia Phinney, Divisional Secretary, Public Relations & Development
pat_phinney@can.salvationarmy.org

Montréal
1655, rue Richardson, Montréal QC H3K 3J7
Toll-Free: 877-288-7441
www.armeedusalut-quebec.ca
www.linkedin.com/company/166406
www.facebook.com/armeedusalut
www.youtube.com/user/salvationarmy
Chief Officer(s):
Brian Venables, PR Contact
brian_venables@can.salvationarmy.org

Regina Office
T.B. Coombs Centre, 2240 - 13th Ave., Regina SK S4P 3M7
Tel: 306-757-1631; *Fax:* 306-955-1378
www.salvationarmy.ca/prairie
Chief Officer(s):
Chad Jeremy, Contact, Media Inquiries, 306-757-3111 Ext. 222

St. John's - Newfoundland & Labrador Division
21 Adams Ave., St. John's NL A1C 4Z1
Tel: 709-579-2022; *Fax:* 709-576-7034
www.salvationarmy.ca/newfoundland
Chief Officer(s):

Ken Ritston, Contact
ken_ritson@can.salvationarmy.org

Saskatoon Office
Public Relations & Development, 1027 - 8th St. East, Saskatoon SK S7H 0S2
Tel: 306-244-9111; *Fax:* 306-244-9115
www.salvationarmy.ca/prairie
Chief Officer(s):
Heather Hedstrom, Contact, Media Inquiries, 306-244-9144

Toronto - Ontario Central East Division
1645 Warden Ave., Toronto ON M1R 5B3
Tel: 416-321-2654; *Fax:* 416-321-8005
www.salvationarmy.ca/ontariocentraleast
twitter.com/tsatoronto
Chief Officer(s):
Sandra Rice, Divisional Commander & Director
sandra_rice@can.salvationarmy.org

Winnipeg - Prairie Division
#204, 290 Vaughan St., Winnipeg MB R3B 2N8
Tel: 204-946-9101; *Fax:* 204-946-9498
www.salvationarmy.ca/prairie
Chief Officer(s):
Brenden Roemich, Contact, Media Inquiries, 204-946-9177

Salvation Army Mt. Arrowsmith Community Ministries - Food Bank
PO Box 1874, 886 Wembley Rd., Parksville BC V9P 2H6
Tel: 250-248-8793; *Fax:* 250-248-8601
Also Known As: Parksville Food Bank
Overview: A small local organization overseen by Food Banks British Columbia
Member of: Food Banks British Columbia

The Salvation Army START Program
9919 MacDonald Ave., Fort McMurray AB T9H 1S7
Tel: 780-743-4135; *Fax:* 780-791-2909
sastart@shawcable.com
Also Known As: Support Today Achieves Results Tomorrow Program
Overview: A small local organization founded in 1983
Member of: ACDS
Affliation(s): Alberta Association of Rehab Centres
Chief Officer(s):
Alyson McAlister, Program Director
alyson.mcalister@shawcable.com
Hibbs Stephen, Corporal Officers
Elaine Hibbs, Corporal Officer
Finances: *Annual Operating Budget:* $1.5 Million-$3 Million; *Funding Sources:* N.E. Regional Persons with Developmental Disabilities Board
Staff Member(s): 49
Membership: 49; *Fees:* $10

Sam Sorbara Charitable Foundation
#800, 3700 Steeles Ave. West, Woodbridge ON L4L 8M9
Tel: 905-850-6154; *Fax:* 905-850-6166
info@sorbaragroup.com
www.sorbaragroup.com/sorbara-group-charitable-foundation.php
Overview: A small local organization
Chief Officer(s):
Joseph Sorbara, Contact

Samaritan House Ministries Inc.
630 Rosser Ave., Brandon MB R7A 0K7
Tel: 204-726-0758; *Fax:* 204-729-9951
samaritanhouse.net
Overview: A small local charitable organization founded in 1987
Mission: To provide support & services to at-risk populations - the homeless, those living in poverty, people with literacy challenges or persons leaving abusive relationships
Chief Officer(s):
Marla Somersall, Executive Director
exec@samaritanhouse.net
Staff Member(s): 10; 50 volunteer(s)
Activities: *Internships:* Yes; *Speaker Service:* Yes

Samaritan's Purse Canada (SPC)
20 Hopewell Way NE, Calgary AB T3J 5H5
Tel: 403-250-6565; *Fax:* 403-250-6567
Toll-Free: 800-663-6500
info@samaritan.ca
www.samaritanspurse.ca
www.facebook.com/samaritanspurse.ca
twitter.com/spcanada
pinterest.com/spcanada
Also Known As: Operation Christmas Child
Overview: A large international charitable organization founded in 1973
Mission: To meet both physical & spiritual needs of people who are victims of war, poverty, natural disasters, disease & famine. Focus is on emergency relief & development programs, medical projects. International offices in Canada, Australia, Germany, Ireland, the Netherlands, the U.S. & the U.K.
Member of: Canadian Council of Christian Charities
Affliation(s): Samaritan's Purse USA
Chief Officer(s):
Franklin Graham, President & CEO
Fred Weiss, Executive Director
fweiss@samaritan.ca
Ken Forbes, Senior Director, Ministry Support
kforbes@samaritan.ca
Jeff Adams, Communications Director
jadams@samaritan.ca
Finances: *Annual Operating Budget:* Greater than $5 Million; *Funding Sources:* Donations
Staff Member(s): 100; 1500 volunteer(s)
Activities: Operation Christmas Child packages; Turn on the Tap access to safe water program; *Internships:* Yes; *Speaker Service:* Yes

Samuel & Saidye Bronfman Family Foundation (SSBFF) / Fondation de la famille Samuel et Saidye Bronfman
#800, 1170, rue Peel, Montréal QC H3B 4P2
Tel: 514-878-5270; *Fax:* 514-878-5299
Overview: A large national charitable organization founded in 1952
Mission: To support non-profit organizations in Canada that deal with challenging social, cultural & education issues
Chief Officer(s):
Nancy Rosenfeld, Executive Director
Stephen R. Bronfman, President
Carol-Ann Bray, Executive Assistant
Finances: *Annual Operating Budget:* $3 Million-$5 Million
Staff Member(s): 3

Samuel Lunenfeld Research Institute (SLRI)
Mount Sinai Hospital, Joseph & Wolf Lebovic Health Complex, #982, 600 University Ave., Toronto ON M5G 1X5
Tel: 416-586-4800
www.lunenfeld.ca
www.facebook.com/MountSinaiHospital
twitter.com/mountSinai
www.youtube.com/SamuelLunenfeld
Overview: A large international organization founded in 1985
Mission: To advance scientific knowledge; To ensure the application of such knowledge to the promotion of human health; To assist Mount Sinai Hospital in meeting its mission as a leading health care facility
Affliation(s): Mount Sinai Hospital; University of Toronto Faculty of Medicine; Ontario Health Study
Chief Officer(s):
Keith Peters, Chair, Scientific Advisory Board
Jim Woodgett, Director, Research, 416-586-4800 Ext. 8811
Stephen Lye, Associate Director, Research, 416-586-4800 Ext. 8640
Finances: *Annual Operating Budget:* Greater than $5 Million; *Funding Sources:* Mount Sinai Hospital Foundation; medical research granting agencies; pharmaceutical companies
Staff Member(s): 475
Membership: 100-499; *Committees:* Research
Activities: Conducting medical & scientific research; Publishing papers in scientific journals; *Speaker Service:* Yes

Sanctuary
25 Charles St. East, Toronto ON M4Y 1R9
Tel: 416-922-0628; *Fax:* 416-922-4961
info@sanctuarytoronto.ca
www.sanctuarytoronto.ca
Overview: A small local organization
Mission: To establish & develop a holistic, inclusive & healthy community for people who are homeless, people who run their own businesses, middle-aged, middle-class people, squeegee kids, university students & hardened street people
Chief Officer(s):
Alan Beattie, Executive Director
alanb@sanctuarytoronto.ca
Finances: *Funding Sources:* Donations from churches, agencies & organizations
Staff Member(s): 15
Activities: Arts; Church; Drop-ins; Health clinic; Street outreach

Sandbox Project
#1600, 30 Adelaide St. East, Toronto ON M5C 3H1
Tel: 416-554-2610
sandboxproject.ca
www.facebook.com/SandboxProject
twitter.com/sandboxcanada
Overview: A small local charitable organization
Mission: To make Canada a place that emphasizes healthy living, for the benefit of Canadian children
Chief Officer(s):
Paul J. Brown, Chair
Membership: *Committees:* Governance; Finance; Injury Prevention; Building Healthy Bodies; Mental Health; Environment

Sandford Fleming Foundation
University of Waterloo, #E2 3336, 200 University Ave. West, Waterloo ON N2L 3G1
Tel: 519-888-4008; *Fax:* 519-746-1457
sff@uwaterloo.ca
www.eng.uwaterloo.ca/~sff/
Overview: A small national organization
Mission: To encourage cooperation between industry & university in engineering education
Chief Officer(s):
Bettina Wahl, Office Manager

Santé Mentale pour Enfants Ontario *See* Children's Mental Health Ontario

Sappujjijit Friendship Centre *See* Pulaarvik Kablu Friendship Centre

Sar-El Canada
#315, 788 Marlee Ave., Toronto ON M6B 3K1
Tel: 416-781-6089; *Fax:* 416-785-7687
toronto@sarelcanada.org
www.sarelcanada.org
Also Known As: Canadian Volunteers for Israel
Overview: A small international organization founded in 1986
Mission: Facilitates volunteering in Israel
Chief Officer(s):
Len Berk, President
Finances: *Annual Operating Budget:* Less than $50,000
10 volunteer(s)
Membership: 1-99
Activities: 1,200 clients; *Speaker Service:* Yes

Montréal
1 Cummings Sq., 5th Fl., Montréal QC H3W 1M6
Tel: 514-735-0272
montreal@sarelcanada.org
Chief Officer(s):
Jack Bordan, Vice-President

Sargeant Bay Society (SBS)
PO Box 1486, Sechelt BC V0N 3A0
Tel: 604-885-5539
sargbay@dccnet.com
www.sargbay.ca
Also Known As: Society for the Protection of Sargeant Bay
Overview: A small local charitable organization founded in 1978
Mission: To protect the natural habitat of Sargeant Bay & its watershed
Chief Officer(s):
Tony Greenfield, President, 604-885-5539
tony@whiskeyjacknaturetours.com
Maggie Marsh, Treasurer, 604-885-4532
maggiem@dccnet.com
Membership: *Fees:* $10; $25 for 3 years
Publications:
- Sargeant Bay Society Newsletter
Type: Newsletter; *Editor:* Joop Burgerjon

SARI Riding for Disabled *See* SARI Therapeutic Riding

SARI Therapeutic Riding
12659 Medway Rd., RR#1, Arva ON N0M 1C0
Tel: 519-666-1123; *Fax:* 519-666-1971
office@sari.ca
www.sari.ca
www.facebook.com/pages/SARI-Therapeutic-Riding/144808638863962
Also Known As: Special Ability Riding Institute
Previous Name: SARI Riding for Disabled
Overview: A medium-sized local charitable organization founded in 1978
Mission: To provide opportunities for people with special needs to move towards greater independence & freedom, through their

connection with horses, by providing therapeutic riding & driving programs which meet individual needs; To balance safety & challenge to maximize opportunities for growth; To support contributions of participants, parents, volunteers & staff
Member of: Canadian Therapeutic Riding Association
Affliation(s): Ontario Therapeutic Riding Association
Chief Officer(s):
Diane Blackall, Executive Director
Finances: *Funding Sources:* Individual & service club donations; fundraising events
200 volunteer(s)
Membership: 150; *Committees:* Fund Development; Human Resources; Program; Marketing & Communications
Activities: Summer equestrian program

Sarnia & District Humane Society
131 Exmouth St., Sarnia ON N7T 7W8
Tel: 519-344-7064; *Fax:* 519-344-2145
humanesocietyfd@ebtech.net
www.sarniahumanesociety.com
www.facebook.com/group.php?gid=279102513444
Also Known As: Sarnia & District SPCA
Overview: A small local charitable organization founded in 1953
Affliation(s): Ontario SPCA
Chief Officer(s):
Tami Holmes, Manager
tholmes@ebtech.net
Finances: *Annual Operating Budget:* $250,000-$500,000; *Funding Sources:* Municipal poundage fees; adoption fees; fundraising events; donations; bequests
Staff Member(s): 15; 50 volunteer(s)
Membership: 1,000; *Fees:* $15; *Committees:* Education; Fundraising
Activities: Provides animal pound service to local municipalities; performs cruelty investigations; educates public regarding humane treatment of animals through news media & classes for children; *Awareness Events:* People-Pet Walkathon; Tag Days; Bazaar; Garage Sale; Lottery

Sarnia & District Labour Council (SDLC)
900 Devine St., Sarnia ON N7T 1X5
Tel: 519-542-2375; *Fax:* 519-542-0178
rivaitro@cogeco.ca
sarniaanddistrictlabourcouncil.com
Overview: A small local organization founded in 1956 overseen by Ontario Federation of Labour
Mission: To promote the interests of its union local affiliates; To advance the economic & social welfare of workers; To aid the sale of union made goods & services
Affliation(s): Chatham-Kent Labour Council; Ontario Federation of Labour; Canadian Labour Congress
Chief Officer(s):
Raymond Fillion, President
Membership: 6,800; *Fees:* Schedule available; *Committees:* Political Action; Good & Welfare; Health & Safety; Environmental; Education
Activities: *Awareness Events:* Day of Mourning, April 28; Labour Day Parade, first Monday of September

Sarnia Building Trades Council
1151 Confederation St., Sarnia ON N7S 3Y5
Tel: 519-344-4680; *Fax:* 519-344-4680
smwia539@cogeco.net
Overview: A small local organization
Member of: AFL-CIO
Chief Officer(s):
Jim Bradshaw, Contact

Sarnia Concert Association (SCA)
PO Box 2777, Sarnia ON N7T 7W1
Tel: 519-862-2401
sarniaconcertassociation.ca
Overview: A small local charitable organization founded in 1936
Mission: To bring musical entertainment to the Sarnia area through annual concert series
Chief Officer(s):
Grace White, President
Finances: *Funding Sources:* Department of Canadian Heritage
20 volunteer(s)

Sarnia Construction Association
PO Box 545, 954 Upper Canada Dr., Sarnia ON N7T 7J4
Tel: 519-344-7441; *Fax:* 519-344-7501
sarniaconstructionassociation.ca
Overview: A small local organization founded in 1948 overseen by Canadian Construction Association
Chief Officer(s):
Andrew J. Pilat, General Manager

Sarnia Lambton Chamber of Commerce
556 North Christina St., Sarnia ON N7T 5W6
Tel: 519-336-2400; *Fax:* 519-336-2085
info@sarnialambtonchamber.com
www.sarnialambtonchamber.com
www.facebook.com/137164216300545
twitter.com/SarLamChamber
www.youtube.com/user/SarniaLambtonChamber
Overview: A small local organization
Mission: Voice of business committed to serving the needs of our members & community
Chief Officer(s):
Mike Elliot, Chair, 519-481-2913
Rory Ring, President
rring@sarnialambtonchamber.com
Staff Member(s): 6
Membership: 890; *Fees:* $304.29-$1,600.20 business; $267.54 non-profit; *Member Profile:* Business in good standing
Activities: *Rents Mailing List:* Yes

Sarnia Minor Athletic Association (SMAA)
Chaytor Building - Germain Park, PO Box 524, Sarnia ON N7T 7J4
Tel: 519-332-1896; *Fax:* 519-332-1569
smaa@ebtech.net
www.sarniaminorathletic.com
Overview: A small local organization founded in 1947
Mission: To instill the knowledge that accompanies minor sports participation in the athletes
Chief Officer(s):
Murray Rempel, President

Sarnia Rock & Fossil Club
www.sarnia.com/groups/srfc
Overview: A small local organization founded in 1966
Chief Officer(s):
Ivan McKay, Contact, 519-287-2506
i.mckay@sympatico.ca
Mary Rastall, Contact, 519-542-6830
rastalls@gmail.com
Wayne Wilcocks, Contact, 519-786-6072
dotw@eastlink.ca
Membership: *Member Profile:* Individuals interested in rocks, minerals, fossils, & lapidary
Activities: Hosting monthly meetings, including children's programs, at the Kinsmen Oakwood Club; Organizing field trips
Publications:
- The Narrow News
Type: Newsletter
Profile: Upcoming events & general interest articles

Sarnia-Lambton Chinese-Canadian Association *See* Chinese Canadian National Council

Sarnia-Lambton Environmental Association (SLEA)
1489 London Rd., Sarnia ON N7S 1P6
Tel: 519-332-2010; *Fax:* 519-332-2015
www.sarniaenvironment.com
Overview: A small local organization founded in 1952
Mission: To monitor ambient environmental conditions to assess the impact of its members on the local environment's air, water and soil.
Chief Officer(s):
Dean Edwardson, General Manager
Membership: 20
Activities: *Library:* Lending Library

Sarnia-Lambton Environmental Association (SLEA)
1489 London Rd., Sarnia ON N7S 1P6
Tel: 519-332-2010; *Fax:* 519-332-2015
www.sarniaenvironment.com
Previous Name: Lambton Industrial Society: An Environmental Co-operative
Overview: A small local organization founded in 1952
Mission: To be recognized by members, regulatory agencies & the community for excellence in promoting & fostering a healthy environment consistent with sustainable development
Membership: 19 corporations; *Member Profile:* Industrial facilities operating in Lambton County
Activities: Environmental research; monitoring regional air & water quality; *Speaker Service:* Yes; *Library* Open to public

Sarnia-Lambton Real Estate Board (SLREB)
555 Exmouth St., Sarnia ON N7T 5P6
Tel: 519-336-6871; *Fax:* 519-344-1928
slreb@fonenet.ca
www.mls-sarnia.com
www.facebook.com/152351484834475
Overview: A small local organization founded in 1944 overseen by Ontario Real Estate Association
Mission: To help its members succeed
Member of: The Canadian Real Estate Association
Chief Officer(s):
Dearl Hill, President
dearlhil@ebtech.net
David Burke, Executive Officer
dburke@fonenet.ca
Membership: 229; *Member Profile:* Licensed to sell real estate in Ontario; employed by member office; completion of board orientation course; committed to leadership, optimism & services that are valued by its membership; *Committees:* Arbitration; Nominating; Education & Membership; Government Relations; Professional Standards; Communications & Public Relations; Social Media
Activities: *Library*

Sartre Society of Canada *See* Society for Existential & Phenomenological Theory & Culture

Sasha's Legacy Equine Rescue
RR#1, Northbrook ON K0H 2G0
Tel: 613-336-1804
sler@mazinaw.on.ca
Overview: A small local organization
Mission: To take in abused, neglected & unwanted horses & ponies; To rehabilitate these animals & place them in loving adoptive homes
Finances: *Funding Sources:* Donations; Sponsorship

Sask Pork
#2, 502 - 45th St. West, Saskatoon SK S7L 6H2
Tel: 306-244-7752; *Fax:* 306-244-1712
info@saskpork.com
www.saskpork.com
Overview: A small provincial organization founded in 1998
Mission: To position the Saskatchewan pork industry as a preferred supplier of high quality, competitively priced pork products for the global market.
Chief Officer(s):
Neil Ketilson, General Manager
nketilson@saskpork.com
Staff Member(s): 5
Membership: *Committees:* Audit

Sask Sport Inc.
1870 Lorne St., Regina SK S4P 2L7
Tel: 306-780-9300; *Fax:* 306-781-6021
sasksport@sasksport.sk.ca
www.sasksport.sk.ca
Overview: A medium-sized provincial organization founded in 1972
Mission: To ensure the total development of amateur sport through the provincial sport governing bodies; to promote extensive participation towards excellence
Chief Officer(s):
Jim Burnett, General Manager
Finances: *Annual Operating Budget:* $500,000-$1.5 Million; *Funding Sources:* Lotteries
Staff Member(s): 50; 13 volunteer(s)
Membership: 70 active & affiliate; *Fees:* $50
Activities: *Library:* Resource Centre for Sport, Culture & Recreation

Sask Taekwondo
106 Franklin Ave., Yorkton SK S3N 2G4
Tel: 306-782-1272; *Fax:* 306-782-0171
www.saskwtf.ca
Also Known As: Sask. WTF
Overview: A small provincial organization founded in 1981
Mission: To govern the sport of Tae Kwon Do in Saskatchewan.
Member of: World Taekwondo Federation
Chief Officer(s):
Dale Halewich, President
dahalewich@hotmail.com
Audrey Ashcroft, Treasurer & Membership Chair
a.cmi@sasktel.net

Saskatchewan 5 Pin Bowlers' Association (S5PBA)
#100, 1805 - 8th Ave., Regina SK S4R 1E8
Tel: 306-780-9412; *Fax:* 306-780-9455
bowling@sasktel.net
www.saskbowl.com/s5pba

Overview: A small provincial organization founded in 1980 overseen by Bowling Federation of Saskatchewan
Mission: To develop trust & harmony among member organizations; to assist in the development & promotion of the sport of bowling through the provision of stable funding
Member of: Canadian 5 Pin Bowlers' Association; Bowling Federation of Saskatchewan
Chief Officer(s):
Rhonda Sereda, Executive Director
Finances: *Annual Operating Budget:* $100,000-$250,000
Staff Member(s): 1; 1000 volunteer(s)
Membership: 6,500; *Fees:* $3.21

Saskatchewan Abilities Council

2310 Louise Ave., Saskatoon SK S7J 2C7
Tel: 306-374-4448; *Fax:* 306-373-2665
provincialservices@abilitiescouncil.sk.ca
www.abilitiescouncil.sk.ca
www.facebook.com/saskatchewanabilitiescouncil
Also Known As: Easter Seals Saskatchewan
Previous Name: Saskatchewan Council for Crippled Children & Adults
Overview: A medium-sized provincial charitable organization founded in 1950 overseen by Easter Seals Canada
Mission: To enhance the independence & community participation of people of varying abilities in Saskatchewan
Chief Officer(s):
Ian Wilkinson, Executive Director
Membership: *Fees:* $10 minimum annual membership donation; *Member Profile:* Individuals who wish to support the services offered by the Saskatchewan Abilities Council
Activities: Providing vocational, rehabilitation, & recreational services; Operating Camp Easter Seal (campeasterseal@abilitiescouncil.sk.ca); Offering training & employment opportunities; Providing adaptive technology & special needs equipment; Offering special needs transportation; Operating the Farmers with Disabilities Program (farmerswithdisabilities@abilitiescouncil.sk.ca)

Regina Branch
825 McDonald St., Regina SK S4N 2X5
Tel: 306-569-9048; *Fax:* 306-352-3717
regina@abilitiescouncil.sk.ca
www.abilitiescouncil.sk.ca

Saskatoon Branch
1410 Kilburn Ave., Saskatoon SK S7M 0J8
Tel: 306-653-1694; *Fax:* 306-652-8886
saskatoon@abilitiescouncil.sk.ca
www.abilitiescouncil.sk.ca

Swift Current Branch
1551 North Railway St. West, Swift Current SK S9H 5G3
Tel: 306-773-2076; *Fax:* 306-778-9188
swiftcurrent@abilitiescouncil.sk.ca
www.abilitiescouncil.sk.ca
Chief Officer(s):
Jason Loewer, Regional Director
Sandra Brong, Senior Supervisor, Programs
sbrong@abilitiescouncil.sk.ca

Yorkton Branch
PO Box 5011, 162 Ball Rd., Yorkton SK S3N 3Z4
Tel: 306-782-2463; *Fax:* 306-782-7844
yorkton@abilitiescouncil.sk.ca
www.abilitiescouncil.sk.ca

Saskatchewan Aboriginal Land Technicians (SALT)

c/o Cowessess First Nation Lands & Resources Dept., PO Box 100, Cowessess SK S0G 5L0
Tel: 306-696-3121; *Fax:* 306-696-3121
Overview: A small provincial organization overseen by National Aboriginal Lands Managers Association
Chief Officer(s):
Denise Pelletier, Director
denise.pelletier@cowessessfn.com
Staff Member(s): 1

Saskatchewan Aboriginal Women's Circle Corporation

PO Box 1174, Yorkton SK S3N 2X3
Tel: 306-783-1228; *Fax:* 306-783-1771
communications@sawcc.sk.ca
www.sawcc.sk.ca
Previous Name: Saskatchewan Native Women's Association
Overview: A small provincial organization founded in 1972 overseen by Native Women's Association of Canada
Mission: To walk in balance with guidance by the creator; to unite people together as healthy nations to ensure a better life for future generations
Chief Officer(s):
Judy Hughes, President
Staff Member(s): 7
Membership: *Fees:* $5; *Member Profile:* Council & member locals

Saskatchewan Advanced Technology Association (SATA)

#207, 120 Sonnenschen Way, Saskatoon SK S7M 1M8
Tel: 306-244-3889; *Fax:* 306-244-6449
info@sata.ca
www.sata.ca
Overview: A small provincial organization
Mission: To develop Saskatchewan's advanced technology sector by bringing together small to medium sized Saskatchewan-based technology organizations
Chief Officer(s):
Don Prokopetz, Executive Director
dprokopetz@sata.ca
Dave Schroeder, Chair
Membership: 300; *Committees:* Membership & Sponsorship; Events; Advanced Technology Strategy
Publications:
• SATA Newsletter
Type: Newsletter

Saskatchewan Agricultural Graduates' Association Inc. (SAGA)

College of Agriculture, University of Saskatchewan, Rm 2D27, 51 Campus Dr., Saskatoon SK S7N 5A8
e-mail: saga.uofs@usask.ca
www.saskaggrads.com
Overview: A small provincial licensing organization founded in 1935
Mission: To promote the social well-being of graduates of the School & College of Agriculture; to ensure close relationships among graduates & between the College & School, including faculty & students; to keep graduates informed of some of the most recent developments in various fields of agriculture; to cooperate with University of Saskatchewan Alumni Association in promoting interests of the University as a whole
Chief Officer(s):
Jill Turner, President
Finances: *Annual Operating Budget:* Less than $50,000; *Funding Sources:* Membership fees
20 volunteer(s)
Membership: 2,000; *Fees:* $10 annually; $100 life
Activities: Annual reunion weekend;

Saskatchewan Agricultural Hall of Fame (SAHF)

2610 Lorne Ave. South, Saskatoon SK S7J 0S6
Tel: 306-931-4057
www.sahf.ca
Overview: A small provincial charitable organization founded in 1972
Mission: To honour Saskatchewan people who have contributed to the field of agriculture
Member of: Museums Association of Saskatchewan
Chief Officer(s):
Jack Hay, Chair
netherdale@sasktel.net
Valerie Pearson, Secretary
Finances: *Annual Operating Budget:* Less than $50,000; *Funding Sources:* Agricultural companies & associations; SK Agriculture & Food grant
Staff Member(s): 1; 5 volunteer(s)
Membership: 23; *Fees:* $25; *Member Profile:* Interest in agriculture; *Committees:* Marketing & Publicity; Executive; Finance; Induction
Activities: *Awareness Events:* Annual Induction Ceremony, Aug.

Saskatchewan Alzheimer & Related Diseases Association *See* Alzheimer Society Of Saskatchewan Inc.

Saskatchewan Amateur Speed Skating Association (SASSA)

2205 Victoria Ave., Regina SK S4P 0S4
Tel: 306-780-9400; *Fax:* 306-525-4009
sassa@sasktel.net
www.saskspeedskating.ca
www.facebook.com/SaskatchewanSpeedSkating
Previous Name: Saskatchewan Speed Skating Association
Overview: A medium-sized provincial organization overseen by Speed Skating Canada
Mission: Working together to develop & promote the sport of speed skating at all levels as a fun, competitive, healthy, family activity
Member of: Speed Skating Canada
Affliation(s): Sask Sport Inc.
Chief Officer(s):
Shawn MacLennan, Executive Director
Finances: *Annual Operating Budget:* $100,000-$250,000; *Funding Sources:* Provincial government
Staff Member(s): 2; 650 volunteer(s)
Membership: 10 institutional; 200 student; 600 individual

Saskatchewan Amateur Wrestling Association (SAWA)

510 Cynthia St., Saskatoon SK S7L 7K7
Tel: 306-975-0822; *Fax:* 306-242-8007
sk.wrestling@shaw.ca
www.saskwrestling.com
www.facebook.com/groups/253817611302960
twitter.com/SaskWrestling
Overview: A small provincial organization founded in 1972 overseen by Canadian Amateur Wrestling Association
Mission: To govern & promote the sport of wrestling in Saskatchewan
Chief Officer(s):
Anna-Beth Zulkoskey, Executive Director
Finances: *Annual Operating Budget:* $250,000-$500,000; *Funding Sources:* Sasksport; lotteries
Staff Member(s): 1; 12 volunteer(s)
Membership: 700; *Fees:* $40 elementary; $60 senior; *Committees:* High Performance; Development; Administration; Finance
Activities: Athlete assistance grants

Saskatchewan Anti-Tuberculosis League *See* Saskatchewan Lung Association

Saskatchewan Applied Science Technologists & Technicians (SASTT)

363 Park St., Regina SK S4N 5B2
Tel: 306-721-6633; *Fax:* 306-721-0112
info@sastt.ca
www.sastt.ca
Previous Name: Society of Engineering Technicians & Technologists of Saskatchewan (SETTS)
Overview: A medium-sized provincial licensing organization founded in 1965 overseen by Canadian Council of Technicians & Technologists
Mission: To regulate the professional conduct of applied science technologists & certified technicians in Saskatchewan, in order to protect the public
Affliation(s): Applied Science Technologists & Technicians of British Columbia; Association of Science & Engineering Technology Professionals of Alberta; Saskatchewan Applied Science Technologists and Technicians; Certified Technicians & Technologists Association of Manitoba; Ontario Association of Certified Engineering Technicians & Technologists; Ordre des technologues preofessionels du Quebec; New Brunswick Society of Certified Engineering Technicians & Technologists; Society of Certified Engineering Technicians & Technologists of Nova Scotia; Island Technology Professionals (PEI)
Finances: *Funding Sources:* Membership fees
Membership: *Fees:* $125 technician/technologist; $90 association; $0 student; *Member Profile:* Individuals who have a recognized level of post-secondary academic & practical training in a specialized applied science or engineering technology field in Saskatchewan
Activities: Increasing the knowledge of applied science technologists & certified technicians; Raising awareness & understanding of applied science technologists & certified technicians
Awards:
• ASET / SASTT Lloydminster Scholarship (Scholarship)
To recognize a graduating student from a high school in the attendance area of The Lloydminster Bi-Provincial Chapter of ASET / SASTT, who plans to continue his or her education in applied science technology, information technology, or engineering technology*Deadline:* August 20 *Amount:* $500
• Outstanding Technical Achievement Award (Award)
To recognize excellence in professional life
• Outstanding Employer Award (Award)
To recognize outstanding technical achievement by employers of applied science & engineering technologists & technicians in Saskatchewan
• Merit Award (Award)
To recognize persons who have distinguished themselves in the service of the association

• Applied Research Project Award (Award)
To recognize the outstanding achievement of a graduating student*Deadline:* June 30
• SASTT Student Awards (Award)
To recognize students from recognized programs at Saskatoon's Kelsey Campus, Moose Jaw's Palliser Campus, & Regina's Wascana Campus *Amount:* $250
Publications:
• Saskatchewan Applied Science Technologists & Technicians Salary Survey
Type: Survey; *Frequency:* Annually
Profile: Information distributed to all Saskatchewan Applied Science Technologists & Technicians members
• SASTT [Saskatchewan Applied Science Technologists & Technicians] Journal
Type: Journal; *Frequency:* Quarterly; *Accepts Advertising*
Profile: Technical articles, association news, & upcoming events

Saskatchewan Archaeological Society (SAS)

#1, 1730 Quebec Ave., Saskatoon SK S7K 1V9
Tel: 306-664-4124; *Fax:* 306-665-1928
saskarchsoc@sasktel.net
www.saskarchsoc.ca
ca.linkedin.com/pub/saskatchewan-archaeological-society/77/37 2/436
www.facebook.com/137032406371156
twitter.com/saskarchsoc
Overview: A medium-sized provincial charitable organization founded in 1963 overseen by Canadian Archaeological Association
Mission: To promote & conserve archaeology
Member of: Council of Affiliated Societies; Plains Anthropological Society; SaskCulture Inc.; Multicultural Council of Saskatchewan; Architectural Heritage Society of Saskatchewan
Affliation(s): Society for American Archaeology; Plains Anthropological Society
Chief Officer(s):
Tomasin Playford, Executive Director
saskarchsoc@sasktel.net
Belinda Riehl-Fitzsimmons, Business Administrator
Finances: *Annual Operating Budget:* $250,000-$500,000; *Funding Sources:* Saskatchewan Lotteries; Self-generated funds
Staff Member(s): 3; 20 volunteer(s)
Membership: 350; *Fees:* $20 student or senior; $25 active membership; $35 family, institutional, school, or chapter; $350 lifetime membership; $450 couple life membership; *Committees:* Advocacy; Archaeological Conservation; Awards; Education; Festivals & Special Events; Finance & Fundraising; Management; Member Funding; Membership / Publicity
Activities: Promoting & carrying out edutational programs such as a field school, workshops, & tours; *Library:* Saskatchewan Archaeological Society Resource Centre; Open to public by appointment
Awards:
• William A. Marjerrison Award (Award)
• Honourary Life Membership (Award)
• Certificate of Appreciation (Award)
Publications:
•
• Saskatchewan Archaeological Society Newsletter
Type: Newsletter; *Frequency:* Quarterly; *Editor:* Belinda Riehl-Fitzsimmons
Profile: The newsletter publishes articles on archeology, history & geology

Archaeological & Historical Society of West Central Saskatchewan
Eatonia SK
Tel: 306-967-2266
Chief Officer(s):
Ted Douglas, Contact
ted.al.douglas@sasktel.net

Eagle Creek Historical Society
Rosetown SK
Chief Officer(s):
Sharon Farrell, Contact
sharon.farrell@sasktel.net

Northwest Archaeological Society
North Battleford SK
Tel: 306-445-2549
Chief Officer(s):
Jeff Baldwin, Contact
jefflaw@sasktel.net

Regina Archaeological Society
Regina SK
reginaarchaeological.zzl.org

Saskatchewan Association of Professional Archaeologists
PO Box 8954, Saskatoon SK S7K 6S7
e-mail: sapaexec@gmail.com
www.saskarchaeologist.org
Chief Officer(s):
Mike Markowski, President

Saskatoon Archaeological Society
PO Box 328, RPO University, Saskatoon SK S7N 4J8
Tel: 306-244-4650; *Fax:* 306-966-5640
saskatoon.archaeology@gmail.com
saskatoonarchaeologicalsociety.zzl.org
Chief Officer(s):
David Meyer, President

South West Saskatchewan Archaeological Society
Swift Current SK
Chief Officer(s):
Jim Worrell, Contact, 306-774-5255
jamesworrell@sasktel.net

Saskatchewan Archery Association (SAA)

PO Box 36, RR#7, Site 708, Saskatoon SK S7K 1N2
Tel: 306-241-0814
www.saskarchery.com
www.facebook.com/SaskatchewanArcheryAssociation
Overview: A small provincial organization overseen by Archery Canada Tir à l'Arc
Mission: To foster, to perpetuate & direct the practice of Archery in a spirit of good fellowship & sportsmanship.
Member of: Archery Canada Tir à l'Arc
Chief Officer(s):
Randy Rathy, President
coldbuck@hotmail.com
Finances: *Annual Operating Budget:* $50,000-$100,000
20 volunteer(s)
Membership: 850; *Fees:* $25 adult; $13 under 18

Saskatchewan Arts Board (SAB)

1355 Broad St., Regina SK S4P 1Y6
Tel: 306-787-4056; *Fax:* 306-787-4199
Toll-Free: 800-667-7526
info@artsboard.sk.ca
www.artsboard.sk.ca
www.facebook.com/saskatchewanartsboard
twitter.com/saskartsboard
Overview: A medium-sized provincial organization founded in 1948
Mission: To cultivate an environment in which the arts thrive for the benefit of everyone in Saskatchewan
Chief Officer(s):
David Kyle, Executive Director
dkyle@artsboard.sk.ca
Byrna Barclay, Chair
Finances: *Annual Operating Budget:* $3 Million-$5 Million; *Funding Sources:* Provincial government
Staff Member(s): 13
Membership: 1-99; *Committees:* Aboriginal Advisor; Governance
Activities: *Library* by appointment

Saskatchewan Association for Community Living (SACL)

3031 Louise St., Saskatoon SK S7J 3L1
Tel: 306-955-3344; *Fax:* 306-373-3070
sacl@sacl.org
www.sacl.org
www.facebook.com/SaskACL
twitter.com/thesacl
www.youtube.com/SACL3031
Overview: A medium-sized provincial charitable organization founded in 1955 overseen by Canadian Association for Community Living
Mission: To enhance the lives of individuals with intellectual disabilities throughout Saskatchewan; To develop programs & services to meet the needs of people with intellectual disabilities
Member of: Canadian Association for Community Living
Chief Officer(s):
Kevin McTavish, Executive Director, 306-955-3344 Ext. 129
Andrea Young, Coordinator, Youth Programs, 306-955-3344 Ext. 119
Bonnie Cherewyk, Advocate, Communications & Research, 306-955-3344 Ext. 111
Finances: *Funding Sources:* Donations; Fundraising
Activities: Engaging in advocacy activities to support persons with disabilities & their families; Creating networking opportunities, through the SACL Family Network; Connecting people to community resources; *Awareness Events:* International Day of Persons with Disabilities, December; *Library:* John Dolan Resource Centre; Open to public
Publications:
• Dialect
Type: Magazine; *Frequency:* Semiannually
Profile: Stories, informative articles, & branch news
• School to Life Transition Handbook
Type: Handbook
Profile: Stories of successful transitions, & steps for transition from school to adult life

Saskatchewan Association for Multicultural Education (SAME)

2454 Atkinson St., Regina SK S4N 3X5
Tel: 306-780-9428
same@sk.sympatico.ca
Overview: A medium-sized provincial organization founded in 1984
Mission: To promote multicultual & anti-racist education throughout Saskatchewan; To raise awareness & acceptance of cultural diversity in the province; To respond to changes in multicultural policies & demographics; To address social justice issues
Finances: *Funding Sources:* Canadian Heritage; Saskatchewan Lotteries; SaskCulture; Multicultural Council of Saskatchewan
Activities: Collaborating with other organizations to further educational opportunities to learn more about other cultures; Supporting formal & informal multicultural & intercultural education; Organizing workshops & conferences to explore issues of racism; Fostering research & projects to increase recognition of cultural identity & equity; Providing resources & advice to assist teachers
Publications:
• Saskatchewan Cultural Profiles
Profile: A set of profiles identifying holidays & celebrations

Saskatchewan Association of Agricultural Societies & Exhibitions (SAASE)

PO Box 31025, Regina SK S4R 8R6
Tel: 306-565-2121; *Fax:* 306-565-2079
www.saase.ca
Overview: A medium-sized provincial organization founded in 1987
Mission: To provide the forum for exchange of ideas among Association members; to provide educational opportunities for members; to address relevant issues affecting members; to provide for district, board & provincial meetings of members; to promote fair & agricultural industry; to help promote & form new societies; to provide a liaison with the extension program of University of Saskatchewan; to assist governments & universities to reach their agricultural & educational objectives
Member of: Foundation for Animal Care Saskatchewan; International Association of Fairs & Exhibitions; Agriculture in the Classroom
Affliation(s): Canadian Association of Fairs & Exhibitions
Chief Officer(s):
Glen Duck, Executive Director
gduck.saase@sasktel.net
Membership: 76 organizations; *Fees:* $200 associate

Saskatchewan Association of Architects (SAA)

#200, 642 Broadway Ave., Saskatoon SK S7N 1A9
Tel: 306-242-0733; *Fax:* 306-664-2598
www.saskarchitects.com
Overview: A medium-sized provincial licensing organization founded in 1906
Mission: To regulate the profession of architecture in Saskatchewan, in order to ensure the protection of the public interest; To advance the profession of architecture in the province; To ensure that high standards for practice & conduct are followed
Chief Officer(s):
Robert Croft, President
Paul Blaser, 1st Vice-President
Bob Burnyeat, 2nd Vice-President
Jeff Howlett, Secretary-Treasurer
Janelle Unrau, Executive Director
Membership: *Fees:* $50 intern architects & retired members; $85 associate members; $670 individuals; *Member Profile:* Registered architects; Students of architecture; Retired architects; Corporations & firms; *Committees:* Executive; Practice Affairs; Registration; Communications
Activities: Providing continuing education programs

Saskatchewan Association of Certified Nursing Assistants
See Saskatchewan Association of Licensed Practical Nurses

Saskatchewan Association of Chiropodists (SAC)
100 - 2nd Ave. NE, Moose Jaw SK S6H 1B8
Tel: 306-691-6405; *Fax:* 306-691-3608
asta@fhhr.ca
Also Known As: Podiatry Association of Saskatchewan
Overview: A small provincial organization founded in 1943
Mission: To participate in the improvement of podiatry; To increase the scope & availability of practitioners in Saskatchewan; To encourage continuing post-graduate education in order to keep up with current trends
Activities: Legislative changes to podiatry; Promote public awareness; Diabetes foot health; Regulation of the profession in Saskatchewan

Saskatchewan Association of Health Organizations (SAHO)
#500, 2002 Victoria Ave., Regina SK S4P 0R7
Tel: 306-347-1740; *Fax:* 306-347-1043
www.saho.ca
Overview: A small provincial charitable organization founded in 1993 overseen by Canadian Healthcare Association
Mission: To serve members through services, support, & programs
Finances: *Funding Sources:* Membership fees; Government grants; Fee-for-service revenue; Interest revenue
Membership: *Member Profile:* Saskatchewan health agencies
Activities: Providing education for boards & administrators; Assisting with collective bargaining & employee relations; Offering payroll services, group purchasing, benefits administration
Publications:
• Health Matters
Type: Magazine; *Frequency:* Quarterly
Profile: Issues in the health care system

Saskatoon Office
Saskatoon SK
e-mail: info@saho.org
www.saho.org

Saskatchewan Association of Historical High Schools (SAHHS)
c/o Luther College High School, 1500 Royal St., Regina SK S4T 6G3
Tel: 306-791-9150; *Fax:* 306-359-6962
lutherhs@luthercollege.edu
www.luthercollege.edu
Overview: A medium-sized provincial organization overseen by Federation of Independent Schools in Canada
Chief Officer(s):
Mark Anderson, Principal
principal@luthercollege.edu
Finances: *Funding Sources:* Membership fees; Saskatchewan Department of Education
8 volunteer(s)
Membership: 8 schools; *Fees:* $250; *Member Profile:* Recognized historical high school in Saskatchewan

Saskatchewan Association of Human Resource Professionals (SAHRP)
2106 Lorne St., Regina SK S4P 2M5
Tel: 306-522-0184; *Fax:* 306-522-1783
communications@sahrp.ca
www.sahrp.ca
www.linkedin.com/company/saskatchewan-association-of-human-resource-pr
www.facebook.com/443863815729899
twitter.com/SAHRP1
Previous Name: Saskatchewan Council of Human Resource Associations
Overview: A small provincial organization
Mission: To promote & encourage leadership & expertise within human resource practitioners in all functional areas of human resource management through provincial networks & developmental opportunities while supporting professional standards to influence organizational excellence
Member of: Canadian Council of Human Resources Associations
Chief Officer(s):
Nicole Norton Scott, Executive Director & Registrar, 306-522-0184
Nicole.nortonscott@sahrp.ca
Greg Honey, President
Finances: *Funding Sources:* Membership dues
Staff Member(s): 4; 75 volunteer(s)
Membership: 1,500; *Fees:* $0 student members; $160 regular & associate members; *Member Profile:* Human resources students & professionals living in Saskatchewan; *Committees:* Recertification; Communications; Conference; Mentorship; Programming; Investigation & Discipline
Meetings/Conferences: • 9th Annual Saskatchewan Association of Human Resource Professionals Conference, October, 2015, Saskatoon, SK
Contact Information: communications@sahrp.ca
Publications:
•
• HR Saskatchewan
Type: Magazine; *Frequency:* Twice annually; *Accepts Advertising*; *Price:* Included with membership

Saskatchewan Association of Insolvency & Restructuring Professionals (SAIRP)
c/o Deloitte & Touche Inc., #400, 122 - 1st Ave. South, Saskatoon SK S7K 7E5
Tel: 306-343-4205; *Fax:* 306-343-4240
Previous Name: Saskatchewan Insolvency Practitioners Association
Overview: A small provincial organization overseen by Canadian Association of Insolvency & Restructuring Professionals
Member of: Canadian Association of Insolvency & Restructuring Professionals
Chief Officer(s):
Marla Lee Adams, President
madams@deloitte.ca

Saskatchewan Association of Landscape Architects (SALA)
#200, 642 Broadway Ave., Saskatoon SK S7N 1A9
www.sala.sk.ca
Overview: A small provincial organization founded in 1980
Mission: To promote, improve, & advance the profession of landscape architecture; To maintain standards of professional practice & conduct
Member of: Canadian Society of Landscape Architects
Chief Officer(s):
Trevor Tumach, President
trevor.tumach@aecom.ca
Membership: *Fees:* $430 full; $259.90 out-of-province; $100 associate and allied; $20 student; *Member Profile:* Landscape architects in Saskatchewan
Awards:
• SALA Academic Award (Award)
Based on academic standing and qualities of character, leadership skills and participation in student and community activities. Eligibility: Resident of Saskatchewan; enrolled in relevant academic program *Amount:* $1000
• Design Excellence Awards (Award)

Saskatchewan Association of Library Technicians, Inc. (SALT)
PO Box 24019, Saskatoon SK S7K 8B4
Fax: 306-543-4487
sasksalt@gmail.com
www.libraries.gov.sk.ca/salt
www.facebook.com/groups/172347699530506
Overview: A small provincial organization founded in 1976
Mission: To promote the value of library technicians in Saskatchewan
Chief Officer(s):
Dorothy Richard, President
Carole-Anne Wilson-Hough, Secretary
Finances: *Funding Sources:* Membership fees; Donations Fundraising
Membership: *Fees:* $10 students, unemployed persons, & retired people; $20 regular members; $30 institutions; *Member Profile:* Institutions throughout Saskatchewan; Graduate library technicians; Librarians; Library clerks & assistants; Students; Persons interested in the development of libraries & library technology
Activities: Supporting library technicians throughout Saskatchewan; Fostering the exchange of information between library technicians; Providing continuing education in library technology; Liaising with other library associations
Awards:
• Dorothy Roberts Scholarship (Scholarship)
Meetings/Conferences: • Saskatchewan Association of Library Technicians 2015 Annual General Meeting & Fall Workshops, 2015, SK
Scope: Provincial
Description: A business meeting, speakers, & networking opportunities for library technicians from Saskatchewan
Contact Information: E-mail: sasksalt@gmail.com
Publications:
• SALT [Saskatchewan Association of Library Technicians] Newsletter
Type: Newsletter; *Frequency:* Quarterly
Profile: Association activities & news of upcoming events

Saskatchewan Association of Licensed Practical Nurses (SALPN)
#700A, 4400 - 4th Ave., Regina SK S4T 0H8
Tel: 306-525-1436; *Fax:* 306-347-7784
Toll-Free: 888-257-2576
www.salpn.com
Previous Name: Saskatchewan Association of Certified Nursing Assistants
Overview: A medium-sized provincial licensing organization founded in 1957 overseen by Canadian Council of Practical Nurse Regulators
Mission: To regulate Licensed Practical Nurses (LPNs) in Saskatchewan, in order to ensure public safety; To ensure that Saskatchewan's Licensed Practical Nurses provide professional nursing care; To maintain an efficient investigation & disciplinary process
Chief Officer(s):
Lynsay Donald, Executive Director
ldonald@salpn.com
Kari Pruden, President
Cara Brewster, Registrar
registrar@salpn.com
Staff Member(s): 7
Membership: *Member Profile:* Graduates; Practising licensed practical nurses; Non-practising licensed practical nurses; Honourary members; *Committees:* Education; Event Planning; Nominations; Counselling & Investigation; Discipline; Awards & Recognition; Policy Development; Finance
Activities: Registering & issuing licenses to Licensed Practical Nurses; Ensuring ethical practice; Providing continuing education program
Awards:
• LPN of Distinction Award (Award)
To recognize exemplary service to the public
• Mentorship Award (Award)
• Lifetime Achievement Award (Award)

Saskatchewan Association of Medical Radiation Technologists (SAMRT)
#218, 408 Broad St., Regina SK S4R 1X3
Tel: 306-525-9678; *Fax:* 306-525-9680
info@samrt.org
samrt.org
Previous Name: Saskatchewan Society of X-Ray Technicians
Overview: A small provincial organization founded in 1940 overseen by Canadian Association of Medical Radiation Technologists
Mission: To serve & protect the public by regulating the practice of the profession of medical radiation technology
Chief Officer(s):
Peter Derrick, President
Bashir Jalloh, Vice-President
Chelsea Wilker, Executive Director
chelseawilker@samrt.org
Finances: *Annual Operating Budget:* $250,000-$500,000
Membership: 633; *Fees:* $100 students; $130 associate members; $150 restricted license; $355 active members (SAMRT license); $200 non-practicing members (SAMRT); *Member Profile:* Persons involved in the technological disciplines of nuclear medicine, radiology, radiation therapy, & magnetic resonance imaging; *Committees:* Discipline; Professional Conduct; Audit; Ownership Linkage; Awards; Nominations; Credentials; Professional Development; Professional Practice
Activities: Offering continuing educational opportunities to members; Providing public education about the profession
Publications:
• SAMRT Newsletter
Type: Newsletter; *Frequency:* Quarterly
Profile: Reports from the Saskatchewan Association of Medical Radiation Technologists, upcoming seminars, plus updates on legislation & bylaws, health & safety, & professional practice

Saskatchewan Association of Naturopathic Practitioners (SANP)
2146 Robinson St., #2A, Regina SK S4T 2P7
Tel: 306-757-4325; *Fax:* 306-522-0745
info@sanp.ca

www.sanp.ca
www.facebook.com/169544933105033
Overview: A small provincial licensing organization overseen by The Canadian Association of Naturopathic Doctors
Mission: To act as the governing body for naturopathic doctors in Saskatchewan; To license & regulate naturopathic physicians in the province; To ensure members are educated & trained according to strict standards
Chief Officer(s):
Julie Zepp Rutledge, President, 306-757-4325
president@sanp.ca
Tim Mrazek, Vice-President, 306-525-5027
vicepresident@sanp.ca
Amy Velichka, Secretary, 306-373-5209
secretary@sanp.ca
Jacqui Fleury, Treasurer, 306-373-5209
treasurer@sanp.ca
Allison Ziegler, Registrar, 306-757-4325
registrar@sanp.ca
Membership: *Member Profile:* Licensed naturopathic doctors in Saskatchewan
Activities: Encouraging continuing medical education; Providing information about naturopathic medicine, from regulation to health topics; Resolving complaints about concerns with naturopathic physicians;

Saskatchewan Association of Optometrists (SAO)

#108, 2366 Ave. C North, Saskatoon SK S7L 5X5
Tel: 306-652-2069; *Fax:* 306-652-2642
Toll-Free: 877-660-3937
saskop@sasktel.net
optometrists.sk.ca
Previous Name: Saskatchewan Optometric Association
Overview: A medium-sized provincial licensing organization founded in 1909 overseen by Canadian Association of Optometrists
Mission: To license the delivery of optometric care in Saskatchewan; To regulate doctors of optometry throughout the province; To ensure excellence in the delivery of vision & eye health services across Saskatchewan; To enforce high standards of optometric eye care, in order to protect the public; To act as the voice of optometry in Saskatchewan
Chief Officer(s):
Leland Kolbenson, Registrar
l.kolbenson@gmail.com
Membership: *Member Profile:* Licensed doctors of optometry; Students
Activities: Providing information about vision & eye health to the government, other health organizations, the public, & the media; Coordinating an occupational vision care program; Offering programs & services to promote optometry; *Speaker Service:* Yes; *Library:* Patient Education Library
Publications:
• Eye on SAO
Type: Newsletter; *Frequency:* Monthly; *Price:* Free with membership in the Saskatchewan Association of Optometrists

Saskatchewan Association of Prosthetists & Orthotists (SAPO)

c/o Canadian Association for Prosthetics & Orthotics, #605, 294 Portage Ave., Winnipeg MB R3C 0B9
Overview: A small provincial organization founded in 1999 overseen by Canadian Association for Prosthetics & Orthotics
Mission: To represent the prosthetic & orthotic field in Saskatchewan
Chief Officer(s):
Vacant, President
Vacant, Vice-President
Lyle Cassidy, Secretary-Treasurer
Membership: *Member Profile:* Individuals involved in the prosthetic & orthotic field throughout Saskatchewan
Activities: Promoting high standards of care & professionalism; Encouraging continuing education

Saskatchewan Association of Recreation Professionals (SARP)

2205 Victoria Ave., Regina SK S4P 0S4
Tel: 306-780-9267; *Fax:* 306-525-4009
Toll-Free: 800-667-7780
sarp.sk@sasktel.net
www.sarp-online.ca
Also Known As: Saskatchewan Recreation Society
Overview: A medium-sized provincial organization founded in 1970
Mission: To represent & support present & future recreation professionals; To promote the pursuit of excellence in the profession; To advocate for the profession
Chief Officer(s):
Nicole Goldsworthy, Chair
Finances: *Funding Sources:* Saskatchewan Lotteries
Membership: *Member Profile:* Professionals; Affiliates; Associates; Students; Alumni; Honorary life members
Activities: Offering professional development activities & networking; Developing professional standards
Awards:
• Education Assistance Grant (Grant)
• Professional Development Grant (Grant)
• The Roy Ellis Bursary (Grant)
• Employer Professional Development Award (Award)
• Annual Achievement Award (Award)
Publications:
• Saskatchewan Association of Recreation Professionals Update Newsletter
Type: Newsletter; *Frequency:* 3 pa

Saskatchewan Association of Rehabilitation Centres (SARC)

111 Cardinal Cres., Saskatoon SK S7L 6H5
Tel: 306-933-0616; *Fax:* 306-653-3932
contact@sarcan.sk.ca
www.sarcsarcan.ca
www.facebook.com/487285284623365
twitter.com/sarc_sk
Overview: A medium-sized provincial charitable organization founded in 1968
Mission: To provide vision, leadership & support to agencies through advocacy, education, provision & development of employment opportunities
Member of: Saskatchewan Association of Rehabilitation Centres
Membership: 81
Activities: Network of organizations which provide vocational & residential services to persons with disabilites

Saskatchewan Association of Rural Municipalities (SARM)

2075 Hamilton St., Regina SK S4P 2E1
Tel: 306-757-3577; *Fax:* 306-565-2141
Toll-Free: 800-667-3604
sarm@sarm.ca
www.sarm.ca
Overview: A medium-sized provincial organization founded in 1905
Mission: To represent & advocate for rural municipal government in Saskatchewan
Chief Officer(s):
Dale Harvey, Executive Director, 306-761-3721
dharvey@sarm.ca
David Marit, President
dmarit@sasktel.net
Membership: 296; *Member Profile:* Rural municipalities in Saskatchewan
Activities: Researching policies; Reviewing legislation; Providing employee benefits, municipal insurance, & fuel supply programs
Meetings/Conferences: • Saskatchewan Association of Rural Municipalities 2015 Annual Convention, March, 2015, Prairieland Park, SK
Scope: Provincial
• Saskatchewan Association of Rural Municipalities 2015 Midterm Convention, November, 2015, Regina, SK
Scope: Provincial
• Saskatchewan Association of Rural Municipalities 2016 Annual Convention, 2016
Scope: Provincial
Publications:
• Rural Councillor
Type: Magazine; *Frequency:* Bimonthly; *Accepts Advertising*
Profile: Issues facing rural Saskatchewan

Saskatchewan Association of School Councils (SASC)

c/o Regina Literacy Network, 1909 Ottawa St., Regina SK S4P 1P7
Tel: 306-569-1368; *Fax:* 306-569-1360
sasc@literacyhub.ca
Previous Name: Saskatchewan Federation of Home & School Associations
Overview: A medium-sized provincial charitable organization founded in 1938 overseen by Canadian Home & School Federation
Mission: To enhance the education & general well-being of children & youth; to promote the involvement of parents, students, educators & the community at large in the advancement of learning & to act as a voice for parents; to promote effective communication between the home & the school; to encourage parents to participate in educational activities & decision making
Chief Officer(s):
Hilary Dahnke, Contact
rln.executivedirector@literacyhub.ca
Finances: *Funding Sources:* Government grant; membership fees; donations
Membership: *Member Profile:* Parents of school children
Activities: Teacher/Staff Appreciation Week; PALS Program - Parents Assist Learning & Schooling; leadership workshops; resources; speakers
Awards:
• Principal Appreciation Award (Award)

Saskatchewan Association of Social Workers (SASW) / Association des travailleurs sociaux de la Saskatchewan

Edna Osborne House, 2110 Lorne St., Regina SK S4P 2M5
Tel: 306-545-1922; *Fax:* 306-545-1895
Toll-Free: 877-517-7279
sasw@accesscomm.ca
www.sasw.ca
Overview: A medium-sized provincial licensing organization founded in 1962
Mission: To conduct the work of a professional regulator; To act as the voice of social workers in Saskatchewan; To develop & maintain standards of knowledge, skill, conduct, & competence among members to serve & protect the public interest
Member of: Canadian Association of Social Workers (CASW); Association of Social Work Boards (ASWB)
Chief Officer(s):
Carole Bryant, President
Richard Hazel, Executive Director
rhazel-sasw@accesscomm.ca
Bill Tingley, Registrar
Diane Lauritzen, Secretary
Leann Keach, Treasurer
Finances: *Funding Sources:* Membership fees
Membership: *Fees:* Schedule available; *Member Profile:* Individuals with a certificate, bachelor, master, or doctorate in social work; Students; *Committees:* Professional Conduct; Discipline; Standards of Practice; Public Relations; Student Award; Health Services; Social Justice; Practice Ethics; Education; Newsletter; Psychologists Act Task Team; Aboriginal Social Workers Task Team
Activities: Lobbying the Saskatchewan provincial government & others for improvement in the status & recognition of social workers; Offering continuing education opportunities; Providing a means for members to take action on social policy issues; *Awareness Events:* Social Work Week, March; *Library:* Saskatchewan Association of Social Workers Library
Awards:
• SASW Student Award (Award)
Presented to a Saskatchewan social work student in recognition of contributions to the community, beyond the immediate requirements of education & employment
• SASW Distinguished Service Award (Award)
To honour outstanding contributions in any area of social work practice *Contact:* SASW Selection Committee, Address: 2110 Lorne St., Regina, SK, S4P 2M5; Fax: 306-545-1895
Meetings/Conferences: • Saskatchewan Association of Social Workers 2015 Annual General Meeting & Provincial Conference, May, 2015, Executive Royal Hotel, Regina, SK
Scope: Provincial
Description: A conference usually held each April at one of the association's branch locations
Contact Information: E-mail: sasw@accesscomm.ca
Publications:
• Saskatchewan Association of Social Workers Annual Report
Type: Yearbook; *Frequency:* Annually
• Saskatchewan Social Worker
Type: Newsletter; *Frequency:* 3 pa; *Accepts Advertising*; *Editor:* R. Yachiw (ryachiw@cr.gov.sk.ca); *Price:* Free with membership in the Saskatchewan Association of Social Workers
Profile: Current events & reports of the Saskatchewan Association of Social Workers, plus articles, the CASW section, & the University of Regina Faculty of Social Worksection

Saskatchewan Association of Speech-Language Pathologists & Audiologists (SASLPA)
#11, 2010 - 7th Ave., Regina SK S4R 1C2
Tel: 306-757-3990; *Fax:* 306-757-3986
Toll-Free: 800-757-3990
saslpa@sasktel.net
www.saslpa.ca
twitter.com/SASLPA
Overview: A small provincial licensing organization founded in 1957
Mission: To encourage public awareness, professional development & quality service in the fields of speech-language pathology & audiology in the province
Member of: Canadian Association of Speech-Language Pathologists & Audiologists
Chief Officer(s):
Stacey Harpell, President
Louise Watley, Registrar
Finances: *Funding Sources:* Membership fees
Membership: *Fees:* $480 non-practicing; $750 practicing; *Member Profile:* Practicing & non-practicing speech therapists; *Committees:* Registration & Membership; Legislation & Bylaws; Professional Conduct; Discipline; Professional Development; Audiology; Private Practice; Website
Activities: Provides information about communication disorders & appropriate treatment resources; identifies issues & concerns through discussions with consumer groups, governments departments & other associations; establishes minimum standards for practice; investigates concerns regarding members & services; assists consumers in advocating for speech, language & hearing services; sponsors workshops & seminars; *Awareness Events:* Speech & Hearing Month, May

Saskatchewan Association of the Appraisal Institute of Canada
2424 College Ave., Regina SK S4P 1C8
Tel: 306-352-4195
skaic@sasktel.net
Overview: A small provincial organization overseen by Appraisal Institute of Canada
Mission: To assist members, those hoping to become appraisers & the public
Chief Officer(s):
Kimberly Maber, President
Marilyn Sterdnica, Executive Director
Membership: *Fees:* $150 associate

Saskatchewan Association of Veterinary Technologists, Inc. (SAVT)
PO Box 346, Stn. University, Saskatoon SK S7N 4J8
Tel: 306-931-2957; *Fax:* 855-861-6255
Toll-Free: 866-811-7288
www.savt.ca
www.facebook.com/SaskVetTech
twitter.com/SaskVetTech
Overview: A small provincial licensing organization founded in 1984
Mission: To promote recognition of the profession, offer opportunities for educational advancement, improve animal health & welfare & support its members
Member of: Canadian Association of Animal Health Technologists & Technicians
Chief Officer(s):
Nadine Schuelle, Executive Director
Nicole Wood, President
president@savt.ca
Finances: *Funding Sources:* Membership dues
Membership: *Fees:* $0 student; $100 non practicing; $185 active; *Member Profile:* Graduate of a formal, approved course in animal health technology/veterinary technology; Student in an approved animal health technology/veterinary technology program; Associate member is an individual out of the province of Saskatchewan
Activities: Registering veterinary technologists in Saskatchewan; Promoting the profession through public relations; Communicating for the profession regarding legislation; Developing & maintaining a Code of Ethics
Awards:
• Award of Appreciation (Award)
• Award of Merit (Award)
• SAVT Bursary (Scholarship)
Publications:
• SAVT Newsletter
Type: Newsletter; *Editor:* Nadine Schueller RVT

Saskatchewan Athletic Therapists Association (SATA)
309B Durham Dr., Regina SK S4S 4Z4
Tel: 306-291-6069
info@saskathletictherapy.ca
www.saskathletictherapy.ca
twitter.com/therapySK
Overview: A small provincial organization
Mission: To certify, regulate, & discipline athletic therapists in Saskatchewan in order to protect the public
Member of: Canadian Athletic Therapists Association; Athletic Therapists in Canada
Chief Officer(s):
Nicole Renneberg, President
president@saskathletictherapy.ca
Membership: *Member Profile:* Athletic therapists in Saskatchewan; *Committees:* Ethics; Insurance Billing

Saskatchewan Athletics
2020 College Dr., Saskatoon SK S7N 2W4
Tel: 306-664-6744; *Fax:* 306-664-6761
athletics@sasktel.net
www.saskathletics.ca
twitter.com/SaskAthletics
Overview: A small provincial organization overseen by Athletics Canada
Mission: Promotes the sport of athletics by facilitating the development & maintenance of effective programs which assists athletes, coaches, officials, & volunteers in a fair & positive environment
Member of: Athletics Canada
Chief Officer(s):
Alan Sharp, President
asharp@mail.gssd.ca
Bob Reindl, Executive Director
Janine Platana, Administrative Assistant
Finances: *Funding Sources:* Saskatchewan Lotteries; Athletics Canada; Sask Sport Inc.; Corporate sponsorships
Staff Member(s): 3

Saskatchewan Automobile Dealers Association (SADA)
610 Broad St., Regina SK S4R8H81
Tel: 306-721-2208; *Fax:* 306-721-1009
Overview: A medium-sized provincial organization
Affliation(s): Canadian Automobile Dealers Association
Chief Officer(s):
Susan Buckle, Executive Director
Membership: *Member Profile:* Franchised new automobile & truck dealer in Saskatchewan
Activities: Providing advocacy on behalf of members;

Saskatchewan Badminton Association (SBA)
55 Dunsmore Dr., Regina SK S4R 7G1
Tel: 306-780-9368
saskbadminton@sasktel.net
www.saskbadminton.ca
www.facebook.com/SaskatchewanBadminton
Overview: A small provincial organization overseen by Badminton Canada
Mission: Dedicated to the development of badminton in Saskatchewan.
Chief Officer(s):
Grant McDonald, President
Frank Gaudet, Executive Director

Saskatchewan Band Association (SBA)
34 Sunset Dr. North, Yorkton SK S3N 3K9
Fax: 306-783-2060
Toll-Free: 877-475-2263
sask.band@sasktel.net
www.saskband.org
Overview: A medium-sized provincial charitable organization founded in 1983 overseen by Canadian Band Association
Mission: To promote & support instrumental music in Saskatchewan; To act as a voice on issues that affect bands in Saskatchewan
Member of: Canadian Band Association
Chief Officer(s):
Darren Oehlerking, President
darrin.oehlerking@usask.ca
Tim Linsley, Executive Director
sask.band@sasktel.net
Finances: *Funding Sources:* Donations; Sponsorships; Saskatchewan Lotteries Trust Fund for Sport, Culture & Recreation; SaskCulture; Saskatchewan Arts Board
Membership: *Fees:* $10 students; $25 retired individuals; $50 regular individuals & organizations; $200 corporate members; *Member Profile:* Individuals in Saskatchewan who wish to further the development of bands; Students; Retired individuals; Organizations, such as school bands & community bands; Corporations
Activities: Supporting bands & band students in Saskatchewan; Providing learning & performance opportunities for performers; Engaging in advocacy activities for bands in schools & communities; Sponsoring band camps & festivals & mentorship programs; Facilitating networking opportunities; Liaising with similar organizations
Awards:
• Saskatchewan Band Association Scholarships (Scholarship)
To fund attendance at summer band camps & the national youth band *Amount:* $10,000
• Saskatchewan Band Distinguished Band Director Award (Award)
To recognize a band director in Saskatchewan who has made an outstanding contribution to band*Deadline:* September 20
• Distinguished Saskatchewan Music Volunteer Award (Award)
To recognize a volunteer who has made an outstanding contribution to band in Saskatchewan
Publications:
• Saskatchewan Band Association eNews
Type: Newsletter; *Frequency:* Weekly; *Accepts Advertising Profile:* Information about association programs & serives, members, scholarships, plus forthcoming band festivals, camps, & seminars
• Saskatchewan Band Association Membership Directory
Type: Directory; *Price:* Free with membership in the Saskatchewan Band Association

Saskatchewan Baseball Association (SBA)
1870 Lorne St., Regina SK S4P 2L7
Tel: 306-780-9237; *Fax:* 306-352-3669
www.saskbaseball.ca
www.facebook.com/10150095674130384
Overview: A medium-sized provincial organization founded in 1959 overseen by Baseball Canada
Mission: To provide quality baseball programs to interested participants at whatever level they may choose
Member of: Baseball Canada; International Baseball Association; Sask Sport; Western Canada Baseball Association
Chief Officer(s):
Mike Ramage, Executive Director
Finances: *Annual Operating Budget:* $250,000-$500,000; *Funding Sources:* Lottery proceeds
Staff Member(s): 3
Membership: 14,000; *Fees:* $3.25

Saskatchewan Basketball *See* Basketball Saskatchewan

Saskatchewan Baton Twirling Association (SBTA)
510 Cynthia St., Saskatoon SK S7L 7K4
Tel: 306-975-0847; *Fax:* 306-242-8007
skbaton@shaw.ca
www.saskbaton.com
Also Known As: Sask Baton
Overview: A small provincial organization overseen by Canadian Baton Twirling Federation
Mission: To coordinate the sport of baton twirling in Saskatchewan.
Member of: Canadian Baton Twirling Federation
Chief Officer(s):
Alison Pickrell, Chair
Brenda O'Connor, Sport Coordinator
Finances: *Funding Sources:* Sask Sport Inc.; SaskTel

Saskatchewan Bed & Breakfast Association (SBBA)
PO Box 694, 172 Cambridge Ave., Regina SK S4N 0L2
Tel: 306-789-3259; *Fax:* 306-789-3250
bbsask@gmail.com
www.bbsask.ca
Previous Name: Saskatchewan Country Vacations Association
Overview: A small provincial organization founded in 1972
Mission: To provide marketing, information & networking programs to increase members' growth & success
Member of: Tourism Saskatchewan
Chief Officer(s):
Cathy Currey, Director
Finances: *Annual Operating Budget:* $50,000-$100,000; *Funding Sources:* Membership fees
Staff Member(s): 1; 6 volunteer(s)
Membership: 80; *Fees:* $135; *Member Profile:* Accredited bed & breakfast & country vacation operators in Saskatchewan

Saskatchewan Beekeepers Association (SBA)
PO Box 55, RR#3, Yorkton SK S3N 2X5
Tel: 306-743-5469; *Fax:* 306-743-5528
whowland@accesscomm.ca
www.saskatchewanbeekeepers.ca
Overview: A small provincial organization founded in 1923
Mission: To support Saskatchewan's beekeeping industry; To represent the province's beekeeping industry at both the provincial & national levels
Affliation(s): Canadian Honey Council (CHC)
Chief Officer(s):
Calvin Parsons, President, 306-864-2632
Corey Bacon, Vice-President, 306-864-3774, Fax: 306-864-3260
Wink Howland, Secetary-Treasurer, 306-783-7046, Fax: 306-786-6001
Dennis Glennie, Coordinator, SBA Bear Fence Program
Finances: *Funding Sources:* Donations; Sponsorships; Agriculture Council of Saskatchewan's (ACS) Canadian Agriculture Adaptation Program (CAAP)
Membership: 250+; *Fees:* $30 / year (minimum) or $0.35 / hive; $30 / year associates; *Member Profile:* Commercial & hobby beekeepers in Saskatchewan
Activities: Providing information & education to Saskatchewan beekeepers, on topics such as wildlife damage compensation; Offering an annual field day to focus on beekeeping issues & to showcase a local producer; Conducting research, on subjects such as pollination needs, mite control, & nectar production; Providing a bear fence subsidy program & a crop advance program; *Awareness Events:* Day of the Honey Bee, May; Honey Month, October
Meetings/Conferences: • Saskatchewan Beekeepers Association 2015 93rd Annual Convention & Meeting, 2015, SK
Scope: Provincial
Description: Featuring speakers & research results
Publications:
• Saskatchewan Beekeepers Association Newsletter
Type: Newsletter; *Frequency:* Quarterly; *Accepts Advertising*; *Editor:* Rhonda Baker
Profile: Association activities & executive reports

Saskatchewan Bison Association (SBA)
PO Box 31, Regina SK S4P 2Z5
Tel: 306-585-6304; *Fax:* 306-522-4768
saskbison@sasktel.net
Overview: A small provincial organization
Mission: To promote the bison industry; To encourage market development for bison products
Member of: Canadian Bison Association; Saskatchewan Food Processors Association
Chief Officer(s):
Les Kroeger, President, 306-544-2869
leskro@sasktel.net
Activities: Administering research projects; *Awareness Events:* Annual Fall Production Sale; Annual Spring Premium Stock Show & Sale
Publications:
• Saskatchewan Bison Association Newsletter
Type: Newsletter; *Frequency:* Quarterly

Saskatchewan Black Powder Association (SBPA)
PO Box 643, Saskatoon SK S7K 3L7
www.sbpa.ca
Overview: A small provincial organization founded in 1980
Mission: To provide a common voice for all Black Powder Shooters in the province; To encourage development of the old skills & trades related to Black Powder; & to co-ordinate activities of the Black Powder Shooters in the province
Member of: Shooting Federation of Canada
Finances: *Funding Sources:* Membership dues; Donations
Membership: *Fees:* $6 individual; $10 family; $25 associate member
Activities: *Library*

Saskatchewan Blind Sports Association Inc. (SBSA)
510 Cynthia St., Saskatoon SK S7L 7K7
Tel: 306-975-0888
Toll-Free: 877-772-7798
sbsa.sk@shaw.ca
www.saskblindsports.ca
Overview: A small provincial organization founded in 1978 overseen by Canadian Blind Sports Association Inc.
Mission: To assist persons who are blind or with visual impairment to achieve excellence in sport, satisfaction in recreation, independence, self-reliance & full community participation
Chief Officer(s):
Jerry Johnson, President
Glenn Hunks, Executive Director
Finances: *Annual Operating Budget:* $100,000-$250,000
Staff Member(s): 1; 250 volunteer(s)
Membership: 100-499; *Fees:* $5
Activities: *Awareness Events:* Run for Light

Saskatchewan Bodybuilding Association (SABBA)
#308, 615 Lynd Cres., Saskatoon SK S7T 0G8
Fax: 306-382-3948
www.sabba.net
twitter.com/Sk_Bodybuilding
Overview: A small provincial organization overseen by Canadian Bodybuilding Federation
Mission: To govern the sport of amateur bodybuilding, fitness & figure in Saskatchewan.
Member of: Canadian Bodybuilding Federation; International Federation of Bodybuilding
Chief Officer(s):
Colin Keess, President, 306-382-2997
ckeezer@hotmail.com
Vince Wawryk, Vice-President, 306-978-2614
vinneez@sasktel.net
Leigh Keess, Secretary-Treasurer, 306-382-2997
fitnmom2@yahoo.ca

Saskatchewan Brain Injury Association (SBIA)
PO Box 3843, Saskatoon SK S4P 3Y3
Tel: 306-373-1555; *Fax:* 306-373-5655
Toll-Free: 888-373-1555
info_sbia@sasktel.net
www.sbia.ca
www.facebook.com/SaskBrainInjury
twitter.com/SKBrainInjury
www.youtube.com/user/sbiaPrograms?feature=mhee
Previous Name: Saskatchewan Head Injury Association
Overview: A small provincial charitable organization founded in 1985 overseen by Brain Injury Association of Canada
Mission: To improve the quality of life for person living with an acquired brain injury, their families, & service providers throughout Saskatchewan; To provide support, information, & services to persons living with the effects of acquired brain injury
Chief Officer(s):
Gordon MacFadden, President
Glenda James, Executive Director
Finances: *Funding Sources:* Donations; Fundraising; Sponsorships
Membership: *Member Profile:* Persons with an acquired brain injury, their families, & service providers in Saskatchewan
Activities: Advocating on behalf of persons in Saskatchewan with traumatic or acquired brain injury; Organizing survivor support groups; Offering information & educational programs; Increasing awareness of the effects & causes of acquired brain injury; Promoting prevention of brain injury, through educational seminars & materials; Referring persons to other organizations in the area when appropriate; *Awareness Events:* Brain Awareness Week; Positive Steps Walkathon; *Library:* SBIA Provincial Information / Resource Centre; Open to public
Publications:
• Connections [a publication of the Saskatchewan Brain Injury Association]
Type: Newsletter
Profile: Association activities & event reviews & announcements

Saskatchewan Broomball Association (SBA)
2205 Victoria Ave., Regina SK S4P 0S4
Tel: 306-780-9215; *Fax:* 306-525-4009
www.saskbroomball.ca
www.facebook.com/307730589864
Overview: A medium-sized provincial organization overseen by Ballon sur glace Broomball Canada
Mission: To promote multi-level programs to members & non-member groups in both competitive & recreational settings; to promote broomball within the province of Saskatchewan
Member of: Ballon sur glace Broomball Canada
Membership: *Fees:* Schedule available

Saskatchewan Building Officials Association Inc. (SBOA)
PO Box 1671, Prince Albert SK S6V 5T2
Tel: 306-445-1733; *Fax:* 306-445-1739
membership@sboa.sk.ca
www.sboa.sk.ca
Overview: A small provincial organization founded in 1960
Member of: Alliance of Canadian Building Officials' Associations
Chief Officer(s):
Dan Knutson, President
Todd Russell, Secretary-Treasurer
Finances: *Funding Sources:* Membership dues; Conference registration
Membership: 500+; *Fees:* $40 active member; $400 government agency or corporation; $100 associate member; *Member Profile:* Persons engaged in the administration & enforcement of building statutes & regulations; Employees of municipal, provincial, or federal agencies or non-profit agencies concerned with building regulations; Persons, companies, or association with knowledge of any phase of building construction or materials
Publications:
• SBOA Newsletter
Type: Newsletter; *Editor:* Dale Wagner

Saskatchewan Camping Association (SCA)
3950 Castle Rd., Regina SK S4S 6A4
Tel: 306-586-4026; *Fax:* 306-790-8634
info@saskcamping.ca
www.saskcamping.ca
Overview: A medium-sized provincial organization founded in 1974 overseen by Canadian Camping Association
Mission: To promote the development of quality organized camping in Saskatchewan; To act as the voice for leaders of organized camps throughout Saskatchewan
Chief Officer(s):
Donna Wilkinson, Executive Director, 306-586-4026
donnaw@sasktel.net
Finances: *Funding Sources:* Sask Lotteries Trust Fund
Membership: *Member Profile:* Camps in Saskatchewan
Activities: Engaging in advocacy activities; Facilitating the sharing of ideas among camp leaders; Providing education for camp leaders
Meetings/Conferences: • Saskatchewan Camping Association 2015 Annual General Meeting, 2015, SK
Scope: Provincial
Description: Featuring the election of the board of directors of the association
Contact Information: Executive Director: Donna Wilkinson, Phone: 306-586-4026, E-mail: donnaw@sasktel.net
Publications:
• Saskatchewan Directory of Camps
Type: Directory
Profile: Listings of camps that are members of the Saskatchewan Camping Association
• SCAN: The Saskatchewan Camping Association Newsletter
Type: Newsletter; *Accepts Advertising*; *Price:* Free with Saskatchewan Camping Association membership
Profile: News, issues, & articles of interest to the camping community of Saskatchewan

Saskatchewan Cancer Agency
#400, 2631 - 28th Ave., Regina SK S4S 6X3
Tel: 306-791-2775; *Fax:* 306-584-2733
www.saskcancer.ca
Also Known As: Saskatchewan Cancer Foundation
Overview: A large provincial charitable organization
Mission: To deliver effective & sustainable research, education, prevention, early detection, treatment & supportive care programs for the control of cancer in Saskatchewan
Chief Officer(s):
Stewart McMillan, Chair
Scott Livingstone, Chief Executive Officer, 306-791-2775, Fax: 306-791-2781
Finances: *Annual Operating Budget:* Greater than $5 Million; *Funding Sources:* Provincial government; Grants
Staff Member(s): 600
Activities: Operating two cancer treatment facilities: the Allan Blair Cancer Centre in Regina, & the Saskatoon Cancer Centre, as well as two residences that house out-of-town patients
Publications:
• A Call to Action for a Cancer Prevention Plan for Saskatchewan
Type: Report
Profile: Prepared by the Prevention Department of the Saskatchewan Cancer Agency (SCA), in consultation with the SCA Prevention Advisory Committee & the Departments ofEpidemiology, Cancer Registry, & Public Affairs
• Saskatchewan Cancer Agency Annual Report
Type: Yearbook; *Frequency:* Annually
Profile: A review of the year, including a financial summary
• Saskatchewan Cancer Control Report
Type: Report
Profile: Information for health providers, organizations, & the public about the status of cancer control aspects in Saskatchewan

Canadian Associations

Saskatchewan Canoe Association *See* Canoe Kayak Saskatchewan

Saskatchewan Canola Development Commission
#212, 111 Research Dr., Saskatoon SK S7N 3R2
Tel: 306-975-0262; *Fax:* 306-975-0136
Toll-Free: 877-241-7044
info@saskcanola.com
www.saskcanola.com
Also Known As: SaskCanola
Overview: A medium-sized provincial organization founded in 1991
Mission: SaskCanola enhances canola producers' competitiveness and profitability through research, market development, extension, and policy development.
Affliation(s): Canola Council of Canada
Chief Officer(s):
Catherine Folkersen, Executive Director, 306-975-6620, Fax: 306-975-0136
cfolkersen@saskcanola.com
Franck Groeneweg, Chair
franck@greenatlantic.com
Ellen Grueter, Manager
Market Development & Communications
Finances: *Funding Sources:* Membership fees
Membership: *Member Profile:* Canola producers in Saskatchewan
Activities: Monitoring all areas of the canola growing industry; Liaising with governments & industry stakeholders on policy related issues; Developing policies in areas such as safety nets, transportation, biofuels, & biotechnology; Providing agronomic information & market trends to canola growers in Saskatchewan; Publishing statements on issues that affect canola growers throughout Saskatchewan

Saskatchewan Cattle Breeders Association
PO Box 3771, Regina SK S4P 3N8
Tel: 306-757-6133; *Fax:* 306-525-5852
Overview: A small provincial organization
Mission: To encourage a general & constant improvement of cattle quality through cooperation with the federal & provincial Departments of Agriculture, the University of Saskatchewan & various fair associations
Affliation(s): Saskatchewan Stock Growers Association; Canadian Western Agribition Association
Chief Officer(s):
Belinda Wagner, Sec.-Treas.
Staff Member(s): 3; 25 volunteer(s)
Membership: 250; *Fees:* $10

Saskatchewan Cerebral Palsy Association (SCPA)
2310 Louise Ave., Saskatoon SK S7J 2C7
Tel: 306-955-7272; *Fax:* 306-373-2665
Toll-Free: 800-925-4524
saskcpa@shaw.ca
www.saskcp.ca
www.facebook.com/7281979481
Overview: A medium-sized provincial charitable organization founded in 1985
Mission: To improve the quality of life of persons with cerebral palsy through a broad range of programs, education, support of research & the delivery of needed services to people with cerebral palsy & their families
Membership: 400; *Fees:* $15 association; $10 individual
Activities: Great Canadian Stationary Bike Race; *Speaker Service:* Yes
Awards:
• Grant Program (Grant)
• Scholarship Program (Scholarship)

Saskatchewan CGIT Committee
3624 - 28th Ave., Regina SK S4S 2N6
e-mail: saskcgit@accesscomm.ca
www.cgit.ca/saskatchewan
Also Known As: Canadian Girls in Training - Saskatchewan
Previous Name: National CGIT Association - Saskatchewan Committee
Overview: A small provincial organization
Chief Officer(s):
Alice Monks, Chair

Saskatchewan Chamber of Commerce
The Saskatchewan Chamber of Commerce, #1630, 1920 Broad St., Regina SK S4P 3V2
Tel: 306-352-2671; *Fax:* 306-781-7084
info@saskchamber.com
www.saskchamber.com
www.facebook.com/saskchamber
Overview: A medium-sized provincial organization
Mission: To act as the voice of business in Saskatchewan; To make Saskatchewan a better place for living, working, & investing; To promote commercial & industrial progress in Saskatchewan; To improve the competitiveness of Saskatchewan's economy
Chief Officer(s):
Steve McLellan, CEO
Membership: *Member Profile:* Business & professional individuals in Saskatchewan
Activities: Lobbying for business in Saskatchewan; Meeting with foreign delegations to create importing & exporting opportunities; Providing timely educational & informational programs; Offering economic analysis & market research services to members; Hosting conferences; Conducting surveys of businesses; Promoting sustainable economic development & social responsibility; *Library:* Research Library

Saskatchewan Charolais Association
PO Box 256, Hudson Bay SK S0E 0Y0
Tel: 306-865-3953; *Fax:* 306-865-3953
www.charolaisbanner.com/sca/
Overview: A small provincial organization
Mission: To educate and infrom those about the Charolais breed of cattle.
Affliation(s): Saskatchewan Stock Growers Association
Chief Officer(s):
Orland Walker, President
diamondw@sasktel.net

Saskatchewan Cheerleading Association (SCA)
PO Box 31090, Regina BC S4R 8R6
Tel: 306-343-7221; *Fax:* 306-343-7229
sca.ca
www.facebook.com/SaskCheer
twitter.com/SaskCheer
Overview: A small provincial organization overseen by Cheer Canada
Mission: To promote & develop cheerleading in Saskatchewan.
Member of: Cheer Canada
Chief Officer(s):
Ana Kuzenko, President
president@sca.ca
Shanda Leftley, Director, Communications
communicationsdirector@sca.ca

Saskatchewan Child Care Association *See* Saskatchewan Early Childhood Association

Saskatchewan Choral Federation (SCF)
#201, 1870 Lorne St., Regina SK S4P 2L7
Tel: 306-780-9230
Toll-Free: 877-524-6725
www.saskchoral.ca
Overview: A small provincial organization founded in 1978
Mission: To promote the choral arts in Saskatchewan
Member of: Association of Canadian Choral Conductors; SaskCulture
Chief Officer(s):
Marcia McLean, President
mmclean@chinooksd.ca
Denise Gress, Executive Director
gress@saskchoral.ca
Finances: *Annual Operating Budget:* $100,000-$250,000
Staff Member(s): 1
Membership: 5,280 associate + 160 individual + 148 choirs; *Fees:* $50 individual; $15 choir; *Member Profile:* Singer; conductor; *Committees:* Program; Finance; Personnel; Communications
Activities: Youth & adult choir camps; *Library* by appointment
Awards:
• Golden Note Award (Award)
• ProMusica Award (Award)
• Community Service Award (Award)

Saskatchewan Coalition for Tobacco Reduction (SCTR)
1080 Winnipeg St., Regina SK S4R 8P8
Tel: 306-766-6327; *Fax:* 306-766-6945
Previous Name: Saskatchewan Interagency Council on Smoking & Health
Overview: A small provincial organization founded in 1975
Mission: To advocate, coordinate & educate to ensure a tobacco-free Saskatchewan for all its residents
Member of: Canadian Centre for Tobacco Control
Chief Officer(s):
Lynn Greaves, Contact
sctr@rqhealth.ca
Finances: *Funding Sources:* Grants

Saskatchewan College of Paramedics (SCoP)
851 Argyle St. North, Regina SK S4R 8H1
Tel: 306-585-0145; *Fax:* 306-543-6161
Toll-Free: 877-725-4202
office@collegeofparamedics.sk.ca
www.collegeofparamedics.sk.ca
Overview: A small provincial organization
Member of: Paramedic Association of Canada
Chief Officer(s):
Sheri Hupp, Executive Director & Registrar
sheri.hupp@collegeofparamedics.sk.ca
Derek Dagenais, President
derek.dagenais@collegeofparamedics.sk.ca
Daniel Lewis, Vice-President
ddagenais.hems@sasktel.net
Membership: *Committees:* Professional Conduct; Disciplinary Committee; Legislation & Bylaws; Education; Audit; Nominations; Registration; Executive
Activities: Licensing Emergency Medical Responders, Emergency Medical Technicians, Emergency Medical Technicians - Advanced, & Emergency Medical Technicians - Paramedics in Saskatchewan

Saskatchewan College of Pharmacists (SCP)
#700, 4010 Pasqua St., Regina SK S4S 7B9
Tel: 306-584-2292; *Fax:* 306-584-9695
info@saskpharm.ca
www.napra.ca/pages/Saskatchewan
Overview: A small provincial licensing organization founded in 1911 overseen by National Association of Pharmacy Regulatory Authorities
Mission: To regulate pharmacists, pharmacies, & drugs in Saskatchewan; To register pharmacists who meet the education & training qualifications specified in "The Pharmacy Act, 1996"; To issue permits to operate pharmacies
Member of: Canadian Council on Continuing Education in Pharmacy
Affliation(s): Canadian Council on Continuing Education; Council of Pharmacy Registrars of Canada; National Association of Pharmacy Regulatory Authorities; PEBC; University of Saskatchewan; University of Regina
Chief Officer(s):
Spiro Kolitsas, President
Justin Kosar, Vice-President
Ray Joubert, Registrar
Membership: *Committees:* Audit; Complaints; Discipline; Finance: Professional Practice; Registration & Licensing Policies; Awards & Honours
Activities: Liaising with government; Publishing research reports, concept papers, & discussion papers
Awards:
• SCP Award of Merit (Award)
Deadline: January 31 *Contact:* SCP Awards Committee, Fax: 306-584-9695; E-mail: info@saskpharm.ca
• SCP Presidential Citation (Award)
Deadline: January 31 *Contact:* SCP Awards Committee, Fax: 306-584-9695; E-mail: info@saskpharm.ca
Publications:
• Reference Manual
Type: Manual; *Frequency:*
Profile: Standards, guidelines, & policy statements
• Saskatchewan College of Pharmacists Newsletter
Type: Newsletter
Profile: College information, executive reports, & upcoming training programs
• Saskatchewan College of Pharmacists Annual Report
Type: Yearbook; *Frequency:* Annually

Saskatchewan College of Physical Therapists (SCPT)
#102, 320 - 21st St. West, Saskatoon SK S7M 4E6
Tel: 306-931-6661; *Fax:* 306-931-7333
www.scpt.org
Previous Name: Saskatchewan College of Physical Therapy
Overview: A small provincial licensing organization overseen by Canadian Alliance of Physiotherapy Regulators
Member of: Canadian Alliance of Physiotherapy Regulators
Membership: *Fees:* $75 - $150 administration; $95 - $375 licensure

Saskatchewan College of Physical Therapy *See* Saskatchewan College of Physical Therapists

Saskatchewan College of Podiatrists (SCOP)
2105 Retallack St., Regina SK S4T 2K5
Tel: 306-352-9091; *Fax:* 306-352-9124
registrar@scop.ca
www.scop.ca
Overview: A small provincial licensing organization founded in 2003
Mission: To regulate the practice of podiatry; Establish standards of practice; Establish educational requirements; Establish continuing education; Educate the public on the practice of podiatry
Chief Officer(s):
Ata Stationwala, President
Axel Rohrmann, Registrar
Membership: 26; *Member Profile:* Podiatrists; *Committees:* Executive; Legislation; Professional Conduct; Quality Assurance; NIRO; Website

Saskatchewan College of Psychologists (SCP)
348 Albert St., Regina SK S4R 2N7
Tel: 306-352-1699; *Fax:* 306-352-1697
skcp@sasktel.net
www.skcp.ca
Previous Name: Saskatchewan Psychological Association
Overview: A small provincial licensing organization
Mission: To protect the public by guiding & regulating the professional conduct of Saskatchewan psychologists
Chief Officer(s):
Gary Halbert, M.Ed., President
Karen Messer-Engel, M.A., R.Psych., Executive Director & Registrar
Membership: *Fees:* $250; *Committees:* Discipline; Nominations; Professional Conduct; Professional Practice & Ethics; Finance & Personnel; Oral Examination; Registration; Privacy Issues

Saskatchewan Commercial Egg Producers Marketing Board *See* Saskatchewan Egg Producers

Saskatchewan Community Theatre Inc. *See* Theatre Saskatchewan

Saskatchewan Construction Safety Association Inc. (SCSA)
498 Henderson Dr., Regina SK S4N 6E3
Tel: 306-525-0175; *Fax:* 306-525-1542
Toll-Free: 800-817-2079
www.scsaonline.ca
Overview: A medium-sized provincial organization founded in 1995
Mission: To provide safety programs & servies to construction employers & employees in order to reduce human & financial loss associated with injuries in the construction industry
Chief Officer(s):
Bill Johnson, Executive Director
billj@scsaonline.ca
Dan Sherven, Manager, Operations
dans@scsaonline.ca
Kellie Lefebvre, Coordinator, Human Resources & Finance
kelliel@scsaonline.ca
Linda Rea-Rosseker, Coordinator, Publications & Communications
lindar@scsaonline.ca
Membership: *Fees:* $750 Supporter member; *Member Profile:* Saskatchewan companies with an active Workers' Compensation Board account within the construction rate group; Supporter members with accounts outside the construction rate group
Publications:
• Safety Advocate Newsletter
Type: Newsletter

Saskatchewan Co-operative Association (SCA)
1515 - 20th St. West, Saskatoon SK S7M 0Z5
Tel: 306-244-3702; *Fax:* 306-244-2165
sca@sask.coop
www.sask.coop
www.facebook.com/SaskCoopAssociation
twitter.com/coopnewssk
Overview: A medium-sized provincial organization
Mission: Provincial coalition of co-operatives, including credit unions, that collaborates to support & promote the co-operative model for community & economic development
Affliation(s): Canadian Co-operative Association
Chief Officer(s):
Victoria Morris, Executive Director
victoria.morris@sask.coop
Membership: *Member Profile:* Co-operatives & credit unions; *Committees:* Co-op Merit Awards Program; Co-op Classic; Co-operative Development; CMAP Nominations
Activities: Training; educational resources; youth seminars; advisory services; *Awareness Events:* Co-op Classic charity golf fundraiser; Annual Awards
Publications:
• The Co-operative Spotlight
Type: Newsletter; *Frequency:* 8-10 pa

Saskatchewan Council for Archives & Archivists (SCAA)
#202, 1275 Broad St., Regina SK S4R 1Y2
Tel: 306-780-9414; *Fax:* 306-585-1765
www.scaa.sk.ca
www.facebook.com/145242068843146
Overview: A small provincial organization founded in 1987 overseen by Canadian Council of Archives
Mission: To facilitate the development of the archival system in Saskatchewan; To develop standard archival policies & practices; To promote public awareness of the use of archives
Chief Officer(s):
Lovella Jones, Executive Director
Cheryl Avery, President
Cameron Hart, Archives Advisor
Membership: 66; *Fees:* $100 staffed archives; $50 volunteer run archives; $45 development institution; $25 individual; $10 general; *Member Profile:* Institutions & individuals that are involved with the maintenance of archival records
Activities: Offering workshops, educational programs, & networking opportunities; Providing an Archival Advisory Service to assist archives; Maintaining the Saskatchewan Archival Information Network, with information about holdings in the province; *Awareness Events:* Archives Week, Feb.
Awards:
• SCAA Institutional Grants (Grant)
Eligibility: For "stand alone" projects that are not connected to any other grant program; or as matching funding for eligible grant opportunities offered by other agencies; institutional members in good standing with the Saskatchewan Council for Archives and Archivists. *Amount:* $2000 *Contact:* Lenora Toth, ltoth@archives.gov.sk.ca
Publications:
• SCAA Newsletter
Type: Newsletter
Profile: Information for SCAA members

Saskatchewan Council for Crippled Children & Adults *See* Saskatchewan Abilities Council

Saskatchewan Council for Educators of Non-English Speakers (SCENES)
PO Box 486 Delaronde Rd., Saskatoon SK S7J 4A6
e-mail: scenes@sasktel.net
Overview: A small provincial organization
Mission: To represent and express the professional concerns of those involved in English as a Second Language/Dialect (ESL/D) in Saskatchewan.
Finances: *Funding Sources:* government, corporate sponsors
Membership: *Fees:* $40 individual; $70 couples; $15 students; $100 institutional
Activities: Learning conferences

Saskatchewan Council for International Co-operation (SCIC) / Conseil de la Saskatchewan pour la co-opération internationale
2138 McIntyre St., Regina SK S4P 2R7
Tel: 306-757-4669; *Fax:* 306-757-3226
scic@earthbeat.sk.ca
www.earthbeat.sk.ca
Overview: A medium-sized international charitable organization founded in 1974
Mission: To act as the umbrella organization for international development agencies in Saskatchewan; To distribute international development funds provided by the Government of Saskatchewan; To facilitate communications among member agencies in Saskatchewan and across Canada; To support cooperative government relations, public education, & fundraising
Member of: Canadian Council for International Cooperation
Staff Member(s): 6
Membership: 29; *Member Profile:* Local committees of churches, educational organizations, & international development agencies
Activities: Advocating on international issues; *Awareness Events:* International Development Week, Feb.

Saskatchewan Council of Cultural Organizations *See* SaskCulture Inc.

Saskatchewan Council of Human Resource Associations *See* Saskatchewan Association of Human Resource Professionals

Saskatchewan Council on Children & Youth *See* Ranch Ehrlo Society

Saskatchewan Country Vacations Association *See* Saskatchewan Bed & Breakfast Association

Saskatchewan Craft Council (SCC)
813 Broadway Ave., Saskatoon SK S7N 1B5
Tel: 306-653-3616; *Fax:* 306-244-2711
Toll-Free: 866-653-3616
saskcraftcouncil@sasktel.net
www.saskcraftcouncil.org
www.facebook.com/SaskatchewanCraftCouncil
twitter.com/skcraftcouncil
Overview: A medium-sized provincial charitable organization founded in 1975
Member of: SaskCulture Inc.; Saskatchewan Tourism
Affliation(s): Canadian Crafts Federation
Finances: *Funding Sources:* Government
Staff Member(s): 9; 50 volunteer(s)
Membership: 414; *Fees:* $50 students or patrons; $100 organizations, professional craftspeople, or affiliated marketers; *Committees:* Exhibition; Markets; Publications; Curatorial
Activities: Operating Affinity Gallery & SCC Fine Craft Boutique; Organizing craft markets & exhibitions; Offering workshops & conferences; *Library:* Saskatchewan Craft Council Library

Saskatchewan Cricket Association (SCA)
Regina SK
www.saskcricket.com
www.facebook.com/SaskatchewanCricketAssociation
Overview: A small provincial organization founded in 1977 overseen by Cricket Canada
Mission: To be the provincial governing body of cricket in Saskatchewan.
Member of: Cricket Canada
Affliation(s): Regina Cricket Association; Saskatoon Cricket Association
Membership: 2 associations;

Saskatchewan Cultural Exchange Society (SCES)
2431 - 8 Ave., Regina SK S4R 5J7
Tel: 306-780-9494; *Fax:* 306-780-9487
sces@sasktel.net
www.sces.ca
www.facebook.com/groups/5599472389
twitter.com/TheExchangeClub
www.youtube.com/user/theexchangeclub;
www.myspace.com/the_exchange
Overview: A medium-sized provincial charitable organization founded in 1979
Mission: To support & facilitate cultural exchange & communication by providing a base for sharing community cultural experiences; to attract & involve practising artists in a cultural exchange in Saskatchewan; to enhance the opportunities for residents of smaller communities in Saskatchewan to experience & learn about contemporary cultural production; to provide an alternative for artists to interact with the public
Member of: SaskCulture Inc.
Affliation(s): Tourism Saskatchewan; Canadian Tourism Human Resource Council; Saskatchewan Fiddle Association
Chief Officer(s):
Margaret Fry, CEO
mfry@sasktel.net
Carol Morin, Chair
Finances: *Annual Operating Budget:* $250,000-$500,000; *Funding Sources:* Saskatchewan Trust; Provincial & federal governments; self-generated revenue
Staff Member(s): 6; 50 volunteer(s)
Membership: 425; *Fees:* $10; $50 organization; *Committees:* Club; Festival; Performing Arts
Activities: Workshop tour; Fiddle Camp; live performances

Saskatchewan Cultural Society of the Deaf
511 Main St. East, Saskatoon SK S7N 0C2
Overview: A small provincial organization
Chief Officer(s):
Laurie Eva-Miller, Acting President
le-miller1@shaw.ca

Saskatchewan Curling Association (SCA)

613 Park St., Regina SK S4N 5N1
Tel: 306-780-9202; *Fax:* 306-780-9404
Toll-Free: 877-722-2875
Other Communication: Alt. URL: curlsask.ca
saskcurling@sasktel.net
www.saskcurl.com/sca
Also Known As: CurlSask
Overview: A small provincial organization overseen by Canadian Curling Association
Mission: To govern and promote the sport of curling in Saskatchewan.
Chief Officer(s):
Amber Holland, Executive Director, 306-780-9403
aholland.sca@sasktel.net
Membership: *Committees:* Executive; Finance & Audit; Governance & Policy; Strategic Planning; Competition; Participation & Development

Saskatchewan Cycling Association

2205 Victoria Ave., Regina SK S4P 0S4
Tel: 306-780-9299; *Fax:* 306-525-4009
cycling@accesscomm.ca
www.saskcycling.ca
www.facebook.com/327882317318669
Overview: A small provincial organization overseen by Cycling Canada Cyclisme
Mission: To promote & enhance the Saskatchewan cycling experience while recognizing its benefits to the individual & society.
Member of: Cycling Canada Cyclisme
Chief Officer(s):
Barret Kropf, President
Finances: *Funding Sources:* Saskatchewan Lotteries
Staff Member(s): 2
Activities: *Speaker Service:* Yes; *Rents Mailing List:* Yes

Saskatchewan Darts Association (SDA)

c/o Pat Copeman, 17 Eden Ave., Regina SK S7R 5M2
Tel: 306-949-5180
www.saskdarts.com
Overview: A small provincial organization overseen by National Darts Federation of Canada
Mission: To promote the sport of darts for players of all ages & abilities in Saskatchewan.
Member of: National Darts Federation of Canada
Chief Officer(s):
Pat Copeman, President
pac.mom@accesscomm.ca
Frank Zimmer, Secretary, 306-545-5192
frank.zimmer@sasktel.net

Saskatchewan Deaf & Hard of Hearing Services Inc. (SDHHS)

2341 Broad St., Regina SK S4P 1Y9
Tel: 306-352-3323; *Fax:* 306-757-3252
Toll-Free: 800-565-3323
Other Communication: Video Phone: 306-352-3322
regina@sdhhs.com
www.sdhhs.com
Overview: A small provincial charitable organization founded in 1981
Mission: To promote independence of deaf, late deafened, & hard of hearing persons; To provide services for persons with a hearing loss in order to enhance their quality of life
Affliation(s): Canadian Hard of Hearing Association; Canadian Association of the Deaf; Regina Association of the Deaf; Saskatchewan Institute of Applied Science & Technology; United Way; United Way of Regina; United Way of Saskatoon
Chief Officer(s):
Crystal Montoya, Office Administrator
Dale Birley, President
Finances: *Funding Sources:* Donations; Sponsorships
Membership: *Member Profile:* People who are deaf, late deafened, hard of hearing, or deaf blind; Professionals who work with these groups; Families & friends of those with hearing loss
Activities: Youth camp; Cmmunity service workers; Voational counselling; Discount Hearing Aid Battery Program; Computerized note taking; Interpreting services; *Awareness Events:* Annual Silent Walk

Saskatoon Office
#3, 511 - 1st Ave. North, Saskatoon SK S7K 1X5
Tel: 306-665-6575; *Fax:* 306-665-7746
Toll-Free: 800-667-6575
saskatoon@sdhhs.com
Chief Officer(s):
Roger Carver, Executive Director

Saskatchewan Deaf Sports Association (SDSA)

#3, 511 - 1st Ave North, Saskatoon SK S7K 1X5
www.saskdeafsports.ca
Overview: A small provincial charitable organization overseen by Canadian Deaf Sports Association
Mission: SDSA is a provincial organization that fosters sporting opportunities to members of the deaf & hard-of-hearing communities. With the aid of local clubs, it selects & trains deaf & hard-of-hearing athletes for international competitions.
Member of: Canadian Deaf Sports Association
Affliation(s): Regina Deaf Athletic Club; Saskatoon Deaf Athletic Club; Saskatchewan Sport Inc.
Chief Officer(s):
Kenneth Hoffman, President
khoffman99@sasktel.net
Pamela Rustoen, Provincial Director
parkmb@sasktel.net
Finances: *Annual Operating Budget:* Less than $50,000; *Funding Sources:* Provincial subsidy; Sask. Lotteries; tickets sales; special events
10 volunteer(s)
Membership: 300-400; *Fees:* $25 adult; $5 adult (no championships); $75 organization
Activities: Annual general meetings; outdoor social; indoor social;

Saskatchewan Dental Assistants' Association (SDAA)

PO Box 294, 603 - 3rd St., Kenaston SK S0G 2N0
Tel: 306-252-2769; *Fax:* 306-252-2089
sdaa@sasktel.net
www.sdaa.sk.ca
Overview: A small provincial organization overseen by Canadian Dental Assistants Association
Mission: To promote excellence in dental health care; To advance public protection through enforcement of regulations, education, ethical practice, & standardization
Chief Officer(s):
Susan Anholt, Executive Director
Calla Effa, President
Robin McKay Ganshorn, Coordinator, Professional Development
rmckay@sasktel.net
Activities: Advocating for the health & safety of dental assistants
Awards:
- Past President's Plaque (Award)
- Honorary Life Membership (Award)
- Penny Waite Achievement Award (Award)
- The Marg Steckler Award of Excellence (Award)
- The Susan Anholt Mentorship Award (Award)
- SDAA General Merit Award (Award)
- SDAA Outstanding Academic Achievement (Award)
- Twenty-Five Year Service Awards (Award)

Publications:
- Accent on Assisting

Type: Newsletter

Saskatchewan Dental Hygienists' Association (SDHA)

#114, 3502 Taylor St. East, Saskatoon SK S7H 5H9
Tel: 306-931-7342; *Fax:* 306-931-7334
sdha@sasktel.net
www.sdha.ca
Overview: A small provincial organization
Chief Officer(s):
Kellie Watson, Executive Director
Staff Member(s): 1
Membership: 500+; *Committees:* Professional Conduct; Discipline; Continuing Competency

Saskatchewan Dental Therapists Association (SDTA)

PO Box 360, 2364 Proton Ave., Gull Lake SK S0N 1A0
Tel: 306-672-3699; *Fax:* 306-672-3619
sdta@sasktel.net
www.sdta.ca
Overview: A small provincial organization founded in 1974
Mission: Dedicated to improving & promoting oral health excellence for all, respecting diversity & individuality
Chief Officer(s):
Cindy G. Reed, Executive Director/Registrar/Sec.-Tres.
Loretta Singh, President
Membership: *Fees:* $30 affiliate; $100 non-practicing; $377 public health preventative practice; $495 clinical restorative practice; *Committees:* Professional Conduct; Discipline; Executive; Credentials; Continuing Education/Bursary/Scholarship; Editorial; Community Oral Health; Conventions

Saskatchewan Dietitians Association (SDA)

#17, 2010 - 7th Ave., Regina SK S4R 1C2
Tel: 306-359-3040; *Fax:* 306-359-3046
registrar@saskdietitians.org
www.saskdietitians.org
Overview: A small provincial licensing organization founded in 1958 overseen by Dietitians of Canada
Mission: To protect the public by registering competent dietitians; To set standards of practice; To uphold codes of conduct; To provide a framework for continuing competence, consisting of a self-assessment tool, a learning plan, & a quality assurance audit
Affliation(s): Network of Interprofessional Regulatory Organizations; Alliance of Dietetic Regulatory Bodies
Chief Officer(s):
Charlotte Pilat Burns, President
Lana Moore, Registrar
Membership: 300; *Member Profile:* A graduate from an accredited baccalaureate program, or a graduate from an accredited practical training program which may or may not be included in a degree; Graduates must have completed the Canadian Dietetic Registration Examination; *Committees:* Finance; Communication; Registration; Legislation; Professional Standards; Professional Conduct; Discipline
Activities: Investigating complaints; Recommending alternate dispute resolutions; Determining discipline

Saskatchewan Diving

1870 Lorne St., Regina SK S4P 2L7
Tel: 306-780-9405; *Fax:* 306-781-6021
info@divesask.ca
www.saskdiving.ca
www.facebook.com/DIVESASK
twitter.com/divesask
Also Known As: Sask Diving Inc.
Overview: A small provincial organization
Mission: To develop & promote safe diving; To ensure that diving clubs operate with safety & integrity; To provide opportunities for self fulfillment & the pursuit of excellence
Member of: Diving Plongeon Canada
Chief Officer(s):
Karen Swanson, Executive Director
kswanson@divesask.ca
Finances: *Funding Sources:* Sask Lotteries
Staff Member(s): 3
Membership: *Member Profile:* Diving clubs; Individuals, such as coaches, athletes, officials, parents, & executive members
Activities: Ensuring coaches are trained through the National Coaching Certification Program

Saskatchewan Early Childhood Association (SECA)

#5, 3041 Sherman Dr., Prince Albert SK S6V 7B7
Tel: 306-975-0875; *Fax:* 306-975-0877
Toll-Free: 888-658-4408
saskcare@sasktel.net
www.skearlychildhoodassociation.ca
Previous Name: Saskatchewan Child Care Association
Overview: A medium-sized provincial organization founded in 1988
Mission: To support high quality early childhood care, development, & education throughout Saskatchewan; To advance professional development in the early learning & child care community
Affliation(s): Canadian Child Care Federation
Chief Officer(s):
Lyn Brown, Contact
Finances: *Funding Sources:* Membership fees; Saskatchewan Ministry of Education; Sponsorships; Merchandise
Membership: *Fees:* $50 students & parents; $89 professionals & corporate members; $105 child care centres; *Member Profile:* Professional early childhood educators; Full-time students; Parents; Child care centres; Corporate members involved in or interested in the field of early childhood education
Activities: Providing education, resources, research, services, & networking opportunities to early childhood educators across Saskatchewan; Promoting awareness of the early learning & child care community
Awards:
- SECA Student Award (Award)

Meetings/Conferences: • Saskatchewan Early Childhood Association 2015 Annual General Meeting, 2015, SK
Scope: Provincial

• Saskatchewan Early Childhood Association 2015 Excellence in Early Learning Conference, 2015, SK
Scope: Provincial
Description: A conference offering demonstration classrooms, peer to peer learning, & hands-on activities
Publications:
• Child Care Connections
Type: Magazine; *Frequency:* 3 pa; *Price:* Free with Saskatchewan Early Childhood Association membership

Saskatchewan Eco-Network (SEN)
535 - 8 St. East, Saskatoon SK S7K 0P9
Tel: 306-652-1275
info@econet.sk.ca
www.econet.sk.ca
Overview: A small provincial organization founded in 1980 overseen by Canadian Environmental Network
Mission: To provide educational activities to develop an awareness of conservation & enhancement of the environment
Affiliation(s): Canadian Environmental Network
Chief Officer(s):
Rick Morrell, Executive Director
Staff Member(s): 2
Membership: 55; *Fees:* Schedule available; *Member Profile:* Non-profit, non-governmental organizations in Saskatchewan concerned with environmental issues
Activities: Promoting networking opportunities for members; Providing referrals for members, media, government personnel, & the public
Publications:
• Saskatchewan's Green Directory
Type: Directory
Profile: A project of the Saskatchewan Eco-Network, with assistance from the Saskatchewan Research Council & the Ministry of Environment, the directory presents information about green products forconsumers.
• SEN [Saskatchewan Eco-Network] Bulletin
Type: Newsletter; *Frequency:* Biweekly; *Price:* Free
Profile: News & events from across Saskatchewan

Saskatchewan Economic Development Association (SEDA)
PO Box 113, #202, 120 Sonnenschein Way, Saskatoon SK S7K 3K1
Tel: 306-384-5817; *Fax:* 306-384-5818
Toll-Free: 877-551-7332
seda@seda.sk.ca
www.seda.sk.ca
www.linkedin.com/in/saskecdevassoc
www.facebook.com/148408781882152
twitter.com/saskecdevassoc
Overview: A small provincial organization
Mission: To secure the economic future of Saskatchewan by helping communities to grow
Chief Officer(s):
Russ McPherson, President, 306-867-9557, Fax: 306-867-9559
russmcpherson@midsask.ca
Verona Thibault, Executive Director
verona.thibault@seda.sk.ca
Finances: *Funding Sources:* Membership fees
Membership: 100-499; *Fees:* Schedule available
Activities: Business Counts Saskatchewan program; online resources; education & training
Awards:
• SEDA Economic Development Awards of Excellence (Award)
Publications:
• SEDA [Saskatchewan Economic Development Association] Directory
Type: Directory

Saskatchewan Economics Association (SEA)
826 Ave. K south, Saskatoon SK S7M 2E8
e-mail: sea@cabe.ca
www.cabe.ca/jmv3/index.php/cabe-chapters/oskaer
Previous Name: Organization of Saskatchewan Applied Economic Research
Overview: A small provincial organization founded in 2013 overseen by Canadian Association for Business Economics
Mission: To provide a forum for individuals & agencies interested in economics, including the following: economic policy analysts; certified financial, management and accounting officials; economic development consultants; statisticians; banking officials; university officials; & students of economics.
Member of: Canadian Association for Business Economics
Chief Officer(s):
Aaron Murray, President
aamurray@accesscomm.ca
Rahatjan Judge, Treasurer
Finances: *Funding Sources:* Membership
Membership: *Fees:* $25

Saskatchewan Egg Producers
PO Box 1263, 496 Hoffer Dr., Regina SK S4P 3B8
Tel: 306-924-1505; *Fax:* 306-924-1515
sep@saskegg.ca
www.saskegg.ca
Previous Name: Saskatchewan Commercial Egg Producers Marketing Board
Overview: A small provincial licensing organization founded in 1969
Affiliation(s): Egg Farmers of Canada
Activities: Providing educational information about egg production, nutrition, handling & storage, & safety
Publications:
• Saskatchewan Egg Producers Egg-Zine
Type: Newsletter
Profile: Nutritional information, facts, & recipes for eggs

Saskatchewan Elocution & Debate Association (SEDA) / Association d'élocution et des débats de la Saskatchewan
1860 Lorne St., Regina SK S4P 2L7
Tel: 306-780-9243; *Fax:* 306-781-6021
info@saskdebate.com
www.saskdebate.com
www.facebook.com/sask.debate
twitter.com/SaskDebate
Overview: A medium-sized provincial charitable organization founded in 1974
Mission: To foster debate & public speaking
Affiliation(s): Canadian Student Debating Federation; SaskCulture Inc.
Chief Officer(s):
Lorelie DeRoose, Executive Director
Finances: *Funding Sources:* Saskatchewan Lotteries Trust Fund for Sport, Culture & Recreation
Staff Member(s): 2
Membership: *Member Profile:* Schools in Saskatchewan
Activities: *Library* by appointment

Saskatchewan Emergency Medical Services Association (SEMSA)
#105, 111 Research Dr., Saskatoon SK S7N 3R2
Tel: 306-382-2147; *Fax:* 306-955-5353
semsa@semsa.org
www.semsa.org
Overview: A medium-sized provincial organization founded in 1959
Mission: To strengthen & advance EMS in Saskatchewan by ensuring high-quality, accountable patient care
Chief Officer(s):
Larise Skoretz, Administrator, 306-382-2147
l.skoretz@semsa.org
Steven Skoworodko, President, 306-233-4308
Staff Member(s): 1; 23 volunteer(s)
Membership: *Member Profile:* EMS employees in Saskatchewan; *Committees:* Executive; Member Services
Meetings/Conferences: • Saskatchewan Emergency Medical Services Association 2015 Annual Convention & Trade Show, May, 2015, SHeraton Cavalier, Saskatoon, SK
Scope: Provincial
Description: An informative convention with a trade show that provides the opportunitiy for those working in emergency medicl services to meet with suppliers to discuss products & services
Contact Information: SEMSA Office, Phone: 306-382-2147, E-mail: semsa@semsa.org

Saskatchewan Environmental Industry & Managers' Association (SEIMA)
2341 McIntyre St., Regina SK S4P 2S3
Tel: 306-543-1567; *Fax:* 306-543-1568
info@seima.sk.ca
www.seima.sk.ca
www.facebook.com/146987992039835
Previous Name: Saskatchewan Environmental Managers Association
Overview: A medium-sized provincial organization founded in 1994
Mission: To act as the voice of practitioners in Saskatchewan's environmental industry on environmental matters; To promote responsible environmental management in the province; To develop the environmental industry in Saskatchewan
Chief Officer(s):
Kathleen Livingston, Executive Director & COO
klivingston@seima.sk.ca
Al Shpyth, President
ashpyth@ecometrix.ca
Lenore Swystun, Vice-President
prairiewildconsulting@sasktel.net
Lois Miller, Treasurer
lmiller@traceassociates.ca
Cheryl Hender, Secretary
chender@innovationplace.com
Membership: *Fees:* $15 undergrad students; $50 graduate students; Schedule, based upon number of employees for corporate & associate members; *Member Profile:* Environmental managers from various industries in Saskatchewan, such as agriculture, mining, & forestry; Companies in Saskatchewan's environmental industry; Suppliers to Saskatchewan's environmental industry; Students; Researchers; Consultants; Public policy developers; *Committees:* Government Relations; Governance; Finance; Program; First Nations & Metis Relations; Membership
Activities: Engaging in advocacy activities; Liaising with governments; Providing access to current industry intelligence, such as environmental legislation & regulations, & potential opportunities; Offering professional development activities for Saskatchewan's environmental businesses & managers, such as seminars & conferences; Facilitating networking opportunities with industry colleagues, for the exchange of information & ideas; Presenting an Aboriginal Youth Career Fair; Conferences & trade shows; *Speaker Service:* Yes
Publications:
• Saskatchewan Environmental Industry & Managers' Association Member Directory & Buyer's Guide
Type: Directory; *Frequency:* Annually; *Price:* Free with membership in Saskatchewan Environmental Industry & Managers' Association
Profile: Information about Saskatchewan Environmental Industry & Managers' Association member businesses & their areas ofspecialization, to provide marketing support for its users throughout North America & Europe
• Saskatchewan Environmental Industry & Managers' Association Newsletter
Type: Nesletter

Saskatchewan Environmental Managers Association *See* Saskatchewan Environmental Industry & Managers' Association

Saskatchewan Environmental Society (SES)
PO Box 1372, 220 - 20 St. West, Saskatoon SK S7K 3N9
Tel: 306-665-1915; *Fax:* 306-665-2128
info@environmentalsociety.ca
www.environmentalsociety.ca
www.facebook.com/environmentalsociety
twitter.com/skenvsociety
Overview: A medium-sized provincial charitable organization founded in 1970
Mission: The Society works to maintain the integrity of Saskatchewan's forests, farmlands and natural prairie landscapes; protect the atmosphere, and promote energy conservation and the development of renewable energy resources; and build sustainable communities, responsible waste management, and enhanced water quality in the province's lakes and rivers.
Member of: Canadian Renewable Energy Alliance
Chief Officer(s):
Allyson Brady, Executive Director
allysonb@environmentalsociety.ca
Peter Prebble, Director, Environmental Policy
prebble@sasktel.net
Angie Bugg, Coordinator, Energy Conservation Coordinator
angieb@environmentalsociety.ca
Angie Bugg, Coordinator, Energy Conservation
angieb@environmentalsociety.ca
Greg Rooke, Coordinator, Pesticide Reduction
pesticidefree@environmentalsociety.ca
Alina Siegfried, Coordinator, Water Issues
water@environmentalsociety.ca
Finances: *Funding Sources:* Membership fees; Donations; Fundraising; Sponsorships
Membership: *Fees:* $20 / year; *Member Profile:* Persons concerned about the environment
Activities: Advocacy; policy development; educational projects; reports & fact sheets; *Speaker Service:* Yes; *Library:* Saskatchewan Environmental Society Resource Centre
Publications:
• Saskatchewan Environmental Society Newsletter

Type: Newsletter; *Frequency:* Bimonthly
Profile: Information about the society's involvement in environmental issues, plus upcoming events, for society members

Saskatchewan Families for Effective Autism Treatment (SASKFEAT)
PO Box 2150, Tisdale SK S0E 1T0
Tel: 306-862-4768
saskfeat@hotmail.com
www.saskfeat.com
Previous Name: Saskatchewan Society for the Autistic Inc.
Overview: A small provincial organization founded in 1976 overseen by Autism Society Canada
Mission: To act as a voice for the concerns & needs of parents & families of autistic children & individuals in Saskatchewan; To find the most effective treatment for autistic children & individuals
Affliation(s): Autism Society Canada
Chief Officer(s):
Tim Verklan, President
Carolyn Forsey, Vice-President
Ron Luciw, Secretary
Brad Hayes, Treasurer
Finances: *Funding Sources:* Donations; Sponsorships
Membership: *Fees:* No membership fee; *Member Profile:* Individuals interested in the objectives of the association, such as families & friends of individuals with autism, plus professionals who are concerned with the well-being of persons with autism
Activities: Supporting Saskatchewan individuals with autism spectrum disorders & their families

Saskatchewan Federation of Home & School Associations
See Saskatchewan Association of School Councils

Saskatchewan Federation of Labour (SFL) / Fédération du travail de la Saskatchewan
#220, 2445 - 13th Ave., Regina SK S4P 0W1
Tel: 306-525-0197; *Fax:* 306-525-8960
sfl@sfl.sk.ca
www.sfl.sk.ca
www.facebook.com/SkFedLabour
twitter.com/SFLLabourIssues
www.youtube.com/user/SaskFedLabour
Overview: A large provincial organization overseen by Canadian Labour Congress
Mission: To act as Saskatchewan's voice of labour; Supporting Saskatchewan's union members & workers
Affliation(s): 700+ locals throughout Saskatchewan
Chief Officer(s):
Larry Hubich, President
l.hubich@sfl.sk.ca
Jennifer Britton, Secretary
jenbritton@sasktel.net
Lori Johb, Treasurer
lejohb@saskatel.net
Stacy Durning, Coordinator, Ready for Work
s.durning@sfl.sk.ca
Membership: 95,000+ unionized workers; *Member Profile:* Members from thirty-seven national & international unions; *Committees:* Aboriginal; Ad Hoc Committee on Trade; Apprentice; Balancing Work & Family; Collective Bargaining; Education; Enviroment; Health Care; Human Rights; Office & Administration Workers; Occupational Health & Safety; Pension & Benefits; Political Education; Shiftwork; Solidarity & Pride; Women's; Workers' Compensation; Youth
Activities: Speaking out on local, provincial, national, & international issues to support social & economic justice; Offering scholarships
Meetings/Conferences: • Saskatchewan Federation of Labour 2015 Pension Conference, 2015, SK
Scope: Provincial
Contact Information: Office Administration Contact: Debbie Lussier, E-mail: d.lussier@sfl.sk.ca
• Saskatchewan Federation of Labour 2015 59th Annual Convention, 2015, SK
Scope: Provincial
Contact Information: Office Administration Contact: Debbie Lussier, E-mail: d.lussier@sfl.sk.ca
Publications:
• Labour Reporter
Type: Newsletter

Saskatchewan Federation of Police Officers (SFPO)
SK
Tel: 306-539-0960
www.saskpolice.com
Overview: A medium-sized provincial organization
Mission: To advance police work as a profession; To support members in their police careers
Chief Officer(s):
Bernie Eiswirth, Executive Officer
beiswirth@saskpolice.com
Evan Bray, President
ebray@saskpolice.com
Jason Stonechild, Executive Vice-President
ebray@saskpolice.com
Membership: 1,000+; *Member Profile:* Police personnel from six municipalities in Saskatchewan; Police associations from Regina, Saskatoon, Prince Albert, Moose Jaw, Weyburn, & Estevan
Activities: Supporting public relations programs; Instituting charitable programs; Maintaining philanthropic programs; Presenting recommendations to the Saskatchewan Police Commission; Liaising with government about police issues
Meetings/Conferences: • Saskatchewan Federation of Police Officers 2015 Annual Meeting, 2015, SK
Scope: Provincial
Description: The Executive Board reports on matters dealt with for & on behalf of members of the Federation at a meeting held each year between April 1st & May 31st

Saskatchewan Fencing Association (SFA)
510 Cynthia St., Saskatoon SK S7L 7K7
Tel: 306-975-0823; *Fax:* 306-242-8007
saskfencing@shaw.ca
saskfencing.com
www.facebook.com/groups/SASKFA
twitter.com/SKFencingAssoc
Overview: A small provincial charitable organization overseen by Canadian Fencing Federation
Mission: To promote & develop the sport of fencing in Saskatchewan
Member of: Canadian Fencing Federation
Affliation(s): Saskatchewan Sport
Chief Officer(s):
Brian Guillemin, President
bj.guillemin@sasktel.net
Marcia Coulic-Salahub, Office Manager
saskfencing@shaw.ca
Finances: *Annual Operating Budget:* $100,000-$250,000; *Funding Sources:* Saskatchewan Sport; fundraising
Staff Member(s): 2; 20 volunteer(s)
Membership: 300; *Fees:* $10-$110
Activities: Competitions; athlete training camps

Saskatchewan Field Hockey Association
1860 Lorne St., Regina SK S4P 2L7
Tel: 306-780-9256; *Fax:* 306-781-6021
sfha@sasktel.net
www.facebook.com/saskatchewan.fieldhockey
twitter.com/SaskFieldHockey
Overview: A small provincial organization overseen by Field Hockey Canada
Mission: To promote the sport of field hockey in Saskatchewan.
Member of: Field Hockey Canada
Chief Officer(s):
Michelle Soika, President
msoika@accesscomm.ca
Vacant, Technical Director

Saskatchewan Film & Video Development Corporation
1831 College Ave., Regina AB S4P 4V5
Tel: 306-798-9800; *Fax:* 306-798-7768
Toll-Free: 800-561-9933
www.saskfilm.com
www.facebook.com/pages/SaskFilm/148650991834609
twitter.com/saskfilm
www.flickr.com/photos/62302815@N05
Also Known As: SaskFilm
Overview: A medium-sized provincial organization
Mission: To be the film commission & funding agency for the province of Saskatchewan
Chief Officer(s):
Chris A. Woodland, Chair
Susanne Bell, CEO & Film Commissioner
bell@saskfilm.com

Saskatchewan Filmpool Co-operative
#301, 1822 Scarth St., Regina SK S4P 2G3
Tel: 306-757-8818; *Fax:* 306-757-3622
Other Communication: plus.google.com/111287203811213570676
info@filmpool.ca
www.filmpool.ca
www.facebook.com/27856059701
www.youtube.com/user/FilmpoolProduction
Also Known As: Filmpool
Overview: A small provincial charitable organization founded in 1977
Mission: To support & encourage independent visionary filmmaking; to develop an awareness & appreciation of independent & indigenous film
Member of: Independent Media Arts Alliance; Saskatchewan Motion Picture Assoc.; SaskCulture; Sask Arts Alliance
Chief Officer(s):
Gordon Pepper, Executive Director
gm@filmpool.ca
Finances: *Annual Operating Budget:* $100,000-$250,000; *Funding Sources:* Saskatchewan Lotteries; Saskatchewan Arts Board; Canada Council; City of Regina; National Film Board
Staff Member(s): 3
Membership: 168; *Fees:* $70 full; $55 basic; $15 subscriber; *Committees:* Production; Workshops; Communications; Exhibitions; Membership; Fundraising
Activities: Film production equipment; production assistance funding; filmmaking workshops; screening; *Library*

Saskatchewan Food Processors Association (SFPA) / Association des manufacturiers de produits alimentaires de Saskatchewan
#389, 8B-3110 - 8th St. East, Saskatoon SK S7H 0W2
e-mail: info@sfpa.sk.ca
www.sfpa.sk.ca
www.facebook.com/SaskFoodProcessors
Overview: A small provincial organization founded in 1990
Mission: To encourage the growth of the Saskatchewan food & beverage industry by assisting our members in meeting the needs of the consumer through the promotion of Saskatchewan-made products in & beyond our province
Chief Officer(s):
Kim Hill, Executive Director
kimhill@sfpa.sk.ca
Membership: 200; *Fees:* $220: 1-24 employees; $440: 25-29 employees; $660: 50+ employees; 325 associate; *Member Profile:* Food & beverage companies located in Saskatchewan; companies that provide services to the food industry
Activities: "Premier" & "Taste of Spring" wine & food festivals; market development, export development, business development activities that assist the growth of companies within the Saskatchewan food industry

Saskatchewan Forestry Association (SFA)
#139, 1061 Central Ave., Prince Albert SK S6V 4V4
Tel: 306-763-2189; *Fax:* 306-763-6456
info@whitebirch.ca
www.whitebirch.ca
Overview: A medium-sized provincial charitable organization founded in 1972 overseen by Canadian Forestry Association
Mission: To promote the wise use, protection, & management of forests, water, & wildlife in Saskatchewan
Affliation(s): Canadian Forestry Association
Chief Officer(s):
Sindy Nicholson, President
Finances: *Funding Sources:* Membership fees; Donations; Sponsorships; Fundraising
Membership: *Fees:* Schedule available for corporations, based upon size; $15 students; $25 individuals; $35 families; *Member Profile:* Individuals, families, groups, & corporations who care about the future of Saskatchewan's forest resources
Activities: Delivering forest education materials & programming to schools & the public; Managing interpretive trails
Publications:
• TreeLines [a publication of the Saskatchewan Forestry Association]
Type: Newsletter; *Frequency:* Quarterly; *Editor:* Andrea Atkinson; *Price:* Free with membershipin the Saskatchewan Forestry Association
Profile: Information about association activities & forestry industry issues, as well as a "Teacher's Corner" for educators

Saskatchewan Francophone Youth Association
Voir Association jeunesse fransaskoise

Saskatchewan Freestyle Ski Incorporated
SK
saskfreestyle.ca

Also Known As: Sask Freestyle Ski Incorporated
Overview: A small provincial organization overseen by Canadian Freestyle Ski Association
Mission: To run programs developed by the Canadian Freestyle Ski Association.
Member of: Canadian Freestyle Ski Association
Chief Officer(s):
Julie Brandt, President
jebrandt@gmail.com
Cathie Ornawka, Secretary
cathie.ornawka@canadianseedcoaters.com
Leon Botham, Treasurer
Botham.sfsc@sasktel.net

Saskatchewan Friends of Schizophrenics *See* Schizophrenia Society of Saskatchewan

Saskatchewan Funeral Service Association *See* Funeral & Cremation Services Council of Saskatchewan

Saskatchewan Genealogical Society (SGS)

#110, 1514 - 11th Ave., Regina SK S4P 0H2
Tel: 306-780-9207
saskgenealogy@sasktel.net
www.saskgenealogy.com
www.facebook.com/216892188363312
Overview: A medium-sized international charitable organization founded in 1969
Mission: To provide assistance in researching family history throughout the world; to preserve heritage documents; to collect materials for study
Chief Officer(s):
Linda Dunsmore-Porter, Executive Director
Finances: *Annual Operating Budget:* $250,000-$500,000; *Funding Sources:* Sask Lotteries; Membership fees; Fundraising; Donations; Sponsorships
Staff Member(s): 4
Membership: 569; *Fees:* $50 individual; $25 student; $55 organization; $250 corporate; $1000 lifetime; *Committees:* Conference; Newspaper Publication; Summer Camp
Activities: Locating & recording burial sites in Saskatchewan through the Saskatchewan Cemetery Program; Maintaining the Saskatchewan Obituary File & the Saskatchewan Residents Index; Offering workshops & cerification courses;; *Library:* Saskatchewan Genealogical Society Library; Open to public
Awards:
• Heritage Volunteer of the Year Award (Award)
Publications:
• Births, Deaths, Marriages from Regina Newspapers
• Change of Name - The Saskatchewan Gazette - 1917 to 1950
• R.C.M.P. Obituary Index 1933-1989
• Saskatchewan Genealogical Society Bulletin
Type: Journal; *Frequency:* Quarterly; *Price:* Free with SGS membership
Profile: Information about genealogical resources in Saskatchewan & across the world
• Saskatchewan Heritage Resources Directory
Type: Directory
Profile: Location & identification of heritage resources in Saskatchewan
• Tracing Your Aboriginal Ancestors in the Prairie Provinces
• Tracing Your Saskatchewan Ancestors

Battlefords Branch
RR#3, North Battleford SK S9A 2X4
Tel: 306-445-5425
Chief Officer(s):
Janice Walker, Contact

Biggar Branch
PO Box 1103, Biggar SK S0K 0M0
Tel: 306-948-3638
rwcambe@sasktel.net
biggargenealogy.wetpaint.com
Chief Officer(s):
Rae Chamberlain, Contact
rwcambe@sasktel.net

Central Butte Branch
PO Box 298, Central Butte SK S0H 0T0
Tel: 306-796-2148
barry.berg@sasktel.net
Chief Officer(s):
Joanne Berg, Contact

Craik Branch
PO Box 386, Craik SK S0G 0V0
Tel: 306-734-2751
webmaster@craik.ca
www.craik.ca/genealog.html
Chief Officer(s):
Doug Dale, Contact

Grasslands Branch
PO Box 272, Mankota SK S0H 2W0
Tel: 306-478-2314
jsanders@xplornet.com
Chief Officer(s):
Linda Calvin, Contact

Grenfell Branch
PO Box 537, Grenfell SK S0G 2B0
Tel: 306-697-3234
Chief Officer(s):
Sandra Karlunchuk, Contact

Moose Jaw Branch
PO Box 154, Briercrest SK S0H 0K0
Tel: 306-799-2004
grcleave@sasktel.net
www.rootsweb.ancestry.com/~skmjbsgs/index.htm
Chief Officer(s):
Marge Cleave, Contact

North-East Branch
PO Box 1988, Melfort SK S0E 1A0
Tel: 306-752-4080
r.a.unger@sasktel.net
Chief Officer(s):
Ron Unger, Contact

Pangman Branch
PO Box 23, Pangman SK S0C 2C0
Tel: 306-267-4450
emerritt@sasktel.net
Chief Officer(s):
Edith Merritt, Contact

Pipestone Branch
PO Box 331, Maryfield SK S0G 3K0
Tel: 306-646-4952
gerry.pat@sasktel.net
Chief Officer(s):
Gerald Adair, Contact

Prince Albert Branch
RR#2, Site 3, Box 91, Prince Albert SK S6V 5P9
Tel: 306-763-8262
barbbeck@sasktel.net
Chief Officer(s):
Barbara Beck, Contact

Quill Plains Branch
PO Box 68, Kelvington SK S0A 1W0
Tel: 306-327-5379
gdgradin@sasktel.net
Chief Officer(s):
Dianne Gradin, Contact

Regina Branch
PO Box 1894, Regina SK S4P 3E1
Tel: 306-586-2301
sgsregina@gmail.com
www.rootsweb.ancestry.com/~canrbsgs
Chief Officer(s):
Shelley Kloczko, Contact

Saskatoon Branch
PO Box 32004, #3, 402 Ludlow St., Saskatoon SK S7S 1M7
Tel: 306-653-1285
eritchie@sasktel.net
www.rootsweb.ancestry.com/~sksgs/
Chief Officer(s):
Eleanor Richie, Contact

Southeast Branch
PO Box 795, Carnduff SK S0C 0S0
Tel: 306-483-2865
medreher@sasktel.net
Chief Officer(s):
Evelyn Dreher, Contact
Lynette Lang, Contact, 306-482-3378
cl.lang@sasktel.net

Swift Current Branch
819 - 9th Ave. NE, Swift Current SK S9H 2S7
Tel: 306-773-0280
jensen@sasktel.net
Chief Officer(s):
Bob Jensen, Contact

West Central Branch
PO Box 472, Eston SK S0L 1A0
Tel: 306-962-3382
Chief Officer(s):
Gail Milton, Contact

Weyburn Branch
PO Box 66, Griffin SK S0C 1G0
Tel: 306-842-6217
bossenberry@sasktel.net
www.weyburnbrsgs.com
Chief Officer(s):
Lorna Bossenberry, Contact
Ilene Johnston, Contact, 306-848-0941
ilenel@accesscomm.ca

Yorkton Branch
30 Pinkerton Bay, Yorkton SK S3N 3C9
Tel: 306-783-0182
ammadawn@sasktel.net
www.parkland.lib.sk.ca/search.htm
Chief Officer(s):
Dawn Peturson, Contact
Glenn Wiseman, Contact, 306-782-7969
gwiseman@accesscomm.ca

Saskatchewan German Council Inc. (SGC)

John V. Remai Centre, 510 Cynthia St., Saskatoon SK S7L 7K7
Tel: 306-975-0845; *Fax:* 306-242-8007
office@saskgermancouncil.org
www.saskgermancouncil.org
www.facebook.com/pages/Saskatchewan-German-Council-Inc/234355995253
twitter.com/saskgerman
Overview: A medium-sized provincial organization founded in 1984
Mission: To promote & preserve the culture, language, customs, traditions & interests of Saskatchewan people of German-speaking backgrounds
Member of: German-Canadian Congress
Chief Officer(s):
Sabine Doebel-Atchison, Executive Director
sabine@saskgermancouncil.org
Josephin Dick, President
Staff Member(s): 3
Membership: 38 organizations; *Fees:* $15 individual/associate; $30 organization; $45 supporting
Activities: *Speaker Service:* Yes
Awards:
• Special Volunteer Awards (Award)

Saskatchewan Golf Association Inc.

510 Cynthia St., Saskatoon SK S7L 7K7
Tel: 306-975-0850; *Fax:* 306-975-0840
info@golfsaskatchewan.org
www.saskgolf.ca
www.facebook.com/GolfSaskatchewan
twitter.com/GolfSK
Also Known As: Golf Saskatchewan
Merged from: Saskatchewan Golf Association; Canadian Ladies Golf Association of Saskatchewan
Overview: A large provincial organization founded in 1999 overseen by Royal Canadian Golf Association
Mission: To promote & maintain amateur golf in Saskatchewan by providing access to information & clinics on golf skills development, rules, handicapping, & etiquette
Chief Officer(s):
Richard Smith, President
Brian Lee, Executive Director, 306-975-0841
Darren Dupont, Manager, Tournaments & Player Services, 306-975-0834
Candace Dunham, Manager, Programs & Member Services, 306-975-0850
Staff Member(s): 3
Membership: *Fees:* $42 adult public players club; $31.50 junior public players club; $28.35 adult club member; $22.05 junior club member
Activities: Providing provincial championships, scholarships, player clinics, & rules workshops, & handicap clinics; *Internships:* Yes

Saskatchewan Government & General Employees' Union (SGEU) / Syndicat de la fonction publique de la Saskatchewan

1440 Broadway Ave., Regina SK S4P 1E2
Tel: 306-522-8571; *Fax:* 306-352-1969
Toll-Free: 800-667-5221
general@sgeu.org
www.sgeu.org
www.facebook.com/SGEU.SK
twitter.com/sgeu
www.youtube.com/user/SGEUtube
Overview: A medium-sized provincial organization

Mission: To represent & protect the interests of its members who work in the public sector in Saskatchewan
Member of: National Union of Public and General Employees
Chief Officer(s):
Bob Bymoen, President
bbymoen@sgeu.org
Finances: *Annual Operating Budget:* Greater than $5 Million; *Funding Sources:* Membership dues
Membership: 20,000+
Activities: *Library:* Resource Centre

Saskatchewan Graphic Arts Industries Association (SGAIA)
PO Box 7152, Saskatoon SK S7K 4J1
Tel: 306-373-3202; *Fax:* 306-373-3246
info@sgaia.ca
sgaia.ca
Merged from: Saskatoon Employing Printers Association; Employing Printers Association of Regina
Overview: A medium-sized provincial organization founded in 1960
Mission: To promote the interests of Saskatchewan's printing & allied industries; To increase the influence of graphic arts industry to the government & the general business community; To promote programs for the graphic arts industry at universities & technical institutions
Affliation(s): Canadian Printing Industries Association; Printing Industries of America; Graphic Arts Technical Foundation
Chief Officer(s):
Blair J. Baron, President, 306-359-7500, Fax: 306-359-3480
president@sgaia.ca
Don Breher, Executive Director, 306-373-3202, Fax: 306-373-3246
execdir@sgaia.ca
Darren Schaffer, Secretary-Treasurer, 306-525-8796, Fax: 306-565-2525
secretarytreasurer@sgaia.ca
Membership: 28; *Fees:* Schedule available, based on sales ranges; *Member Profile:* Companies engaged in the production of printed materials for sale; Firms in the pre-press, binding & finishing sectors; Associate members are firms that sell equipment & operating supplies; *Committees:* Annual General Meeting; Environment, Publicity & Promotion; Government Affairs; Membership
Activities: Providing information about the graphic arts industry; Improving members' management skills; Developing programs & seminars on topics such as production, sales, & marketing; Assisting suppliers to serve the needs of the industry; Facilitating networking opportunities for the exchange of business ideas; Upholding a code of ethics to maintain a high standard of service & products offered

Saskatchewan Ground Water Association (SGWA)
PO Box 9434, Saskatoon SK S7K 7E9
Tel: 306-244-7551; *Fax:* 306-343-0001
teksmarts.com/skgwa/home.html
Previous Name: Saskatchewan Water Well Association
Overview: A small provincial organization overseen by Canadian Ground Water Association
Mission: To act as the voice of the ground water industry throughout Saskatchewan; To promote the management of ground water throughout the province
Chief Officer(s):
Kathleen Watson, Contact
Activities: Providing education about ground water

Saskatchewan Gymnastics Association *See* Gymnastics Saskatchewan

Saskatchewan Handball Association (SHA)
SK
Tel: 306-584-8035
dkazymyra@cableregina.com
nonprofits.accesscomm.ca/sha
Overview: A small provincial organization
Mission: To promote & develop the sport of handball in Saskatchewan

Saskatchewan Head Injury Association *See* Saskatchewan Brain Injury Association

Saskatchewan Health Libraries Association (SHLA)
c/o Regina-Qu'Appelle Health Region, Health Sciences Library, 1440 - 14th Ave., Regina SK S4P 0W5
Tel: 306-766-3832
chla-absc.ca/shla
twitter.com/chlaabsc
Overview: A medium-sized provincial organization founded in 1988 overseen by Canadian Health Libraries Association
Mission: To promote access to health care literature for physicians & allied health care staff
Chief Officer(s):
Caitlin Carter, President
caitlin.carter@rqhealth.ca
Membership: *Fees:* $30 individuals; $75 institutions

Saskatchewan Heavy Construction Association
1939 Elphinstone St., Regina SK S4T 3N3
Tel: 306-586-1805; *Fax:* 306-585-3750
slipp@saskheavy.ca
www.saskheavy.com
www.facebook.com/SaskHeavy
twitter.com/saskheavy
www.youtube.com/saskheavy
Overview: A medium-sized provincial organization founded in 1919 overseen by Canadian Construction Association
Mission: The Saskatchewan Heavy Construction Association is committed to the heavy construction industry by actively promoting quality, cost-effective, socially responsible services for the public & its members.
Member of: Saskatchewan Construction Association
Affliation(s): Western Canada Roadbuilders & Heavy Construction Association
Chief Officer(s):
Dave Paslawski, Chair
dpaslawski@aslpaving.ca
Shantel Lipp, President
slipp@saskheavy.ca
Ellie Weare, Financial Officer
eweare@saskheavy.ca
Finances: *Annual Operating Budget:* $500,000-$1.5 Million
Staff Member(s): 3; 15 volunteer(s)
Membership: 200+

Saskatchewan Herb & Spice Association (SHSA)
PO Box 7568, Stn. Main, Saskatoon SK S7K 4L4
Tel: 306-694-4622
shsa@sasktel.net
www.saskherbspice.org
Overview: A small provincial organization
Mission: To support research, development & promotion of crops & products from yesterday & tomorrow for producers to processors to retails today
Chief Officer(s):
Connie Kehler, Executive Director
Membership: 300; *Fees:* $65 regular; $220 corporate; $540 corporate sponsorship
Activities: Member networking; annual member directory; public awareness; ongoing research of production & market promotion

Saskatchewan Hereford Association (SHA)
PO Box 713, Weyburn SK S4H 2K8
Tel: 306-842-6149; *Fax:* 306-842-0296
skhereford@sasktel.net
www.saskhereford.com
Overview: A small provincial organization founded in 1919
Mission: To promote Saskatchewan Herefords provincially, nationally & internationally
Member of: Canadian Hereford Association
Chief Officer(s):
Doug Mann, President
w_mann@xplornet.ca
Marilyn Charlton, General Manager
Membership: 300

Saskatchewan High Schools Athletic Association (SHSAA)
#1, 575 Park St., Regina SK S4N 5B2
Tel: 306-721-2151; *Fax:* 306-721-2659
shsaa@shsaa.ca
www.shsaa.ca
www.facebook.com/264860913591330
twitter.com/shsaasport
Overview: A medium-sized provincial organization founded in 1948 overseen by School Sport Canada
Mission: To use interschool athletics as a means for fostering positive opportunities for students
Member of: School Sport Canada
Chief Officer(s):
Roger Morgan, President
morgan.roger@prairiesouth.ca
Kevin Vollet, Executive Director
k.vollet@shsaa.ca
Staff Member(s): 4
Awards:
• Merit Award (Award)
• Service Awards (Award)

Saskatchewan History & Folklore Society Inc. (SHFS)
1860 Lorne St., Regina SK S4P 2L7
Tel: 306-780-9204; *Fax:* 306-780-9489
Toll-Free: 800-919-9437
shfs.fa@sasktel.net
www.shfs.ca
Overview: A medium-sized provincial organization founded in 1957
Mission: To encourage & promote the gathering, preservation & sharing of the history & folklore of Saskatchewan
Member of: Heritage Canada; Sask Culture
Affliation(s): American Association for State & Local History
Chief Officer(s):
Finn Andersen, Executive Director
Finances: *Annual Operating Budget:* $100,000-$250,000
Staff Member(s): 2; 25 volunteer(s)
Membership: 500 individuals + 30 organizations; *Fees:* $30
Activities: Summer Motorcoach Tours; provides funding for permanent recognition of local historical events; Saskatchewan Historical Recognition Registry; Local History Marker Program; oral history training; Publish quarterly magazine "Folklore"; *Library* Open to public
Publications:
• Folklore
Type: Magazine; *Frequency:* Quarterly; *Price:* Included with membership, or annual subscription for $21
Profile: Original manuscripts that contain Saskatechwan history. The magazine publishes stories about folklore & history, as well as poetry

Saskatchewan Hockey Association (SHA) / Association de hockey de la Saskatchewan
#2, 575 Park St., Regina SK S4N 5B2
Tel: 306-789-5101; *Fax:* 306-789-6112
www.sha.sk.ca
www.facebook.com/324377598563
twitter.com/sask_hockey
Overview: A medium-sized provincial organization founded in 1912 overseen by Hockey Canada
Mission: To administer the operation of amateur hockey in the Province of Saskatchewan; To foster & promote amateur hockey within the province & to assist in the promotion of amateur hockey outside the province; To promote, supervise & administer all competitions for amateur hockey within the jurisdiction of the SAHA
Member of: Hockey Canada
Chief Officer(s):
Kelly McClintock, General Manager
kellym@sha.sk.ca
Finances: *Annual Operating Budget:* $1.5 Million-$3 Million
Staff Member(s): 10
Membership: 46,000

Saskatchewan Home Based Educators (SHBE)
PO Box 8541, Saskatoon SK S7K 6K6
e-mail: help_desk@shbe.info
www.shbe.info
Overview: A small provincial licensing charitable organization
Mission: Assist in creating a positive social network and a positive political environment for all those who choose home-based education.
Membership: *Committees:* Home Schooling; Special Needs Advisory Council; High School & Post-Secondary Advisory Council; Unschooling Advisory Council
Activities: Annual provincial information meetings
Meetings/Conferences: • 24th Annual Saskatchewan Home Based Educators (SHBE) Home Based Educators Convention, February, 2015, Evraz Place (Queensbury Centre), Regina, SK
Scope: Provincial

Saskatchewan Home Builders' Association *See* Canadian Home Builders' Association - Saskatchewan

Saskatchewan Home Economics Teachers Association (SHETA)
Saskatoon SK
www.sheta.ca
Overview: A small provincial organization founded in 1969
Mission: To allow Home Economics teachers from across Saskatchewan to network & share ideas
Affliation(s): Saskatchewan Teachers Federation
Chief Officer(s):

Michelle Hardy, President
shetapresident@gmail.com
Membership: *Fees:* $30
Awards:
• SHETA Undergraduate Award (Award)
Meetings/Conferences: • Saskatchewan Home Economics Teachers Association Conference 2015, October, 2015, Regina, SK
Scope: Provincial

Saskatchewan Horse Breeders Association
PO Box 3771, Regina SK S4P 3N8
Tel: 306-757-6133; *Fax:* 306-525-5852
sla@accesscomm.ca
Overview: A small provincial organization
Member of: Saskatchewan Livestock Association
Affliation(s): Canadian Western Agribition Association

Saskatchewan Horse Federation (SHF)
2205 Victoria Ave., Regina SK S4P 0S4
Tel: 306-780-9449; *Fax:* 306-525-4041
shfadmin@sasktel.net
www.saskhorse.ca
www.facebook.com/SaskHorse
Overview: A medium-sized provincial organization founded in 1976
Mission: To work with other equestrian organizations in order to bring educational & recreational programs to the public.
Member of: Equine Canada
Affliation(s): Sask Sport; Western College Veterinary Medicine; SK Agriculture & Food (SAF)
Chief Officer(s):
Pam Duckworth, Senior Administrator
pamduckworth@saskhorse.ca
Finances: *Funding Sources:* Self-help; Saskatchewan Lotteries
Staff Member(s): 2
Membership: *Fees:* $50 adults; $35 junior; $120 family; $85-$225 clubs; *Member Profile:* Individuals; family; corporate; clubs; sustaining
Activities: Coaching certification; competition circuit; clinics; grants; rider certification; officials development; horse industry; member insurance; Horsin' Around raffle; Agribition; Youth Equestrian Games; Sask Horse Week;

Saskatchewan Hotel & Hospitality Association (SHHA)
#302, 2080 Broad St., Regina SK S4P 1Y3
Tel: 306-522-1664; *Fax:* 306-525-1944
Toll-Free: 800-667-1118
www.shha.co
Previous Name: Hotels Association of Saskatchewan
Overview: A medium-sized provincial organization overseen by Hotel Association of Canada Inc.
Chief Officer(s):
Michael Billard, Chair
Meetings/Conferences: • The Saskatchewan Hotel & Hospitality Association (SHHA) Hotel & Hospitality Conference, April, 2015, DoubleTree by Hilton Hotel, Regina, SK
Scope: Provincial

Saskatchewan Independent Insurance Adjusters' Association
c/o Cheryl Hanson, Crawford & Company (Canada) Inc., #210, 227 Primrose Dr., Saskatoon SK S7K 5E4
www.ciaa-adjusters.ca
Overview: A small provincial organization overseen by Canadian Independent Adjusters' Association
Member of: Canadian Independent Adjusters' Association
Chief Officer(s):
Cheryl Hanson, President, 306-931-1999, Fax: 306-931-2212
cheryl.hanson@crawco.ca

Saskatchewan Insolvency Practitioners Association *See* Saskatchewan Association of Insolvency & Restructuring Professionals

Saskatchewan Institute of Agrologists (SIA)
#29, 1501 - 8th St. East, Saskatoon SK S7H 5J6
Tel: 306-242-2606; *Fax:* 306-955-5561
info@sia.sk.ca
www.sia.sk.ca
www.linkedin.com/company/saskatchewan-institute-of-agrologists
www.facebook.com/sia.sk.ca
twitter.com/SKAgrologists
Overview: A small provincial organization founded in 1946
Mission: To promote and increase the knowledge, skill & proficiency of its members in the practice of agrology; Do all things that may be necessary, incidental or conducive to the usefulness of agrologists to the public; Protect the public in all matters relating to the gathering, analyzing and distributing of information respecting agrology; Ensure the proficiency and competency of agrologists
Member of: Agrology/Agronomes Canada
Chief Officer(s):
Al Schola, Executive Director & Registrar
Finances: *Annual Operating Budget:* $500,000-$1.5 Million; *Funding Sources:* Membership dues
Staff Member(s): 4; 75 volunteer(s)
Membership: 1,300; *Fees:* $385; *Member Profile:* Agrologists; *Committees:* Act & Bylaw; Admissions & Registration; Executive; Professional Conduct; Discipline; Honours & Awards; Articling Program; Education; Issues; Nominations; Professional Development & Standards; Public Awareness & Communications; Student Relations

Saskatchewan Institute of the Purchasing Management Association of Canada *See* Supply Chain Management Association - Saskatchewan

Saskatchewan Institute on Prevention of Handicaps *See* Saskatchewan Prevention Institute

Saskatchewan Interagency Council on Smoking & Health *See* Saskatchewan Coalition for Tobacco Reduction

Saskatchewan Intercultural Association Inc. (SIA)
#405, 1702 - 20th St. West, Saskatoon SK S7M 0Z9
Tel: 306-978-1818; *Fax:* 306-978-1411
info@saskintercultural.org
saskintercultural.org
www.facebook.com/saskintercultural
twitter.com/skintercultural
Previous Name: Saskatoon Multicultural Council
Overview: A small provincial charitable organization founded in 1964
Mission: To promote equal opportunity & fair treatment for everyone
Chief Officer(s):
Bob Cram, Executive Director
bcram@saskintercultural.org
Finances: *Funding Sources:* Sponsorships
Staff Member(s): 15
Membership: *Fees:* $20 individual; $50 group
Activities: Employment programs; Education programs; Equity & anti-racism programs; Performing arts programs; *Speaker Service:* Yes; *Library:* SIA Resource Centre; Open to public

Saskatchewan Joint Board, Retail, Wholesale & Department Store Union (CLC) / Conseil mixte du syndicat des employés de gros, de détail et de magasins à rayons de la Saskatchewan (CTC)
1233 Winnipeg St., Regina SK S4R 1K1
Tel: 306-569-9311; *Fax:* 306-569-9521
Toll-Free: 877-747-9378
rwdsu.regina@sasktel.net
www.rwdsu.sk.ca
Also Known As: RWDSU-Sask
Overview: A medium-sized provincial organization
Chief Officer(s):
Chris Banting, Secretary-Treasurer
Staff Member(s): 11
Membership: 6,000+

Saskatchewan Karate Association (SKA)
510 Cynthia St., Saskatoon SK S7L 7K7
Tel: 306-374-7333; *Fax:* 306-374-7334
sk.karate@shaw.ca
www.saskarate.com
Overview: A small provincial organization founded in 1977 overseen by Karate Canada
Mission: To promote & develop karate as a sport throughout the province of Saskatchewan.
Member of: Karate Canada
Chief Officer(s):
Owen Hartman, President
Linda Crosson, Executive Director

Saskatchewan Katahdin Sheep Association Inc. (SKSA)
PO Box 548, Quill Lake SK S0A 3E0
Tel: 306-383-2861
www.saskkatahdinsheep.com
www.facebook.com/570204566350748
twitter.com/SaskKatahdin
Overview: A small provincial organization founded in 1993 overseen by Canadian Katahdin Sheep Association Inc.
Mission: To develop & advance the Katahdin sheep breed in Saskatchewan
Chief Officer(s):
Jean L'Arrivee, President, 306-769-8981, Fax: 306-769-8916
cccranch@sasktel.net
Janette Mish, Vice-President, 306-429-2221, Fax: 306-429-2221
jmish@sasktel.net
Donna Schryver, Secretary, 306-383-2861
schryvers@sasktel.net
Donna Bruynooghe, Treasurer, 306-937-2041
dbruynooghe@highways.gov.sk.ca
Membership: 1-99; *Fees:* $10 junior members, age 15 & under; $25 senior members; *Member Profile:* Owners of Canadian registered Katahdin sheep in Saskatchewan; *Committees:* Show & Sale; New Producer Liaison
Activities: Distributing breed information; Preparing displays for various shows throughout the province; Creating networking opportunities with other sheep producers; Providing education, such as on-farm seminars & hands-on-training sessions; Showing sheep at events such as the Canadian Western Agribition
Publications:
• News for Ewes
Type: Newsletter; *Frequency:* Quarterly; *Accepts Advertising*; *Editor:* Janette Mish
• Saskatchewan Katahdin Sheep Association Membership Directory
Type: Directory; *Price:* Free

Saskatchewan Lacrosse Association
2205 Victoria Ave., Regina SK S4P 0S4
Tel: 306-780-9216; *Fax:* 306-525-4009
lacrosse@sasktel.net
www.sasklacrosse.net
www.facebook.com/SaskLacrosse
twitter.com/SaskLacrosse
Also Known As: Sask Lacrosse
Overview: A medium-sized provincial organization overseen by Canadian Lacrosse Association
Mission: To promote & deliver lacrosse programs to the residents of Saskatchewan
Member of: Canadian Lacrosse Association; Sask Sport Inc.
Chief Officer(s):
Shawn Williams, President
s.williams@sasktel.net
Bridget Pottle, Executive Director
Finances: *Annual Operating Budget:* $250,000-$500,000
Staff Member(s): 1; 10 volunteer(s)
Membership: 3,000; *Fees:* $25

Saskatchewan Land Surveyors' Association (SLSA)
#230, 408 Broad St., Regina SK S4R 1X3
Tel: 306-352-8999; *Fax:* 306-352-8366
info@slsa.sk.ca
www.slsa.sk.ca
Overview: A small provincial licensing organization founded in 1910 overseen by Professional Surveyors Canada
Mission: To uphold the stewardship & standards of the legal survey profession in Saskatchewan; To regulate & govern members in the practice of professional land surveying & professional surveying; To ensure the competency of members; To administer the profession to protect the public
Chief Officer(s):
Mike Waschuk, President
Carla Stadnick, Executive Director
Membership: 95; *Member Profile:* Registered members of the association, who are licensed to practice as Saskatchewan land surveyors in Saskatchewan, in accordance with the provisions of the Land Surveyors & Professional Surveyors Act of Saskatchewan
Activities: Providing continuing education to licensed members; Investigating complaints from the public
Awards:
• I.W. Tweddell Memorial Award (Scholarship)
Eligibility: A student land surveyor from Saskatchewan enrolled in a program that will result in a Certificate of Completion from The Canadian Board of Examiners for Professional Surveyors*Deadline:* May 31 *Amount:* $1,250
Publications:
• SLSA [Saskatchewan Land Surveyors' Association] Corner Post
Type: Newsletter; *Frequency:* Quarterly; *Accepts Advertising*;

Editor: Doug A. Bouck, SLS
Profile: Articles about surveying, in addition to regular features, such as the president's message & council highlights

Saskatchewan Landlords Association *See* Saskatchewan Rental Housing Industry Association

Saskatchewan Liberal Association

845A McDonald St., Regina SK S4N 2X5
Tel: 306-522-5202; *Fax:* 306-569-9271
info@lpcsask.ca
saskatchewan.liberal.ca
www.facebook.com/group.php?gid=2399956913
Also Known As: Saskatchewan Liberal Party
Overview: A medium-sized provincial organization overseen by The Liberal Party of Canada
Chief Officer(s):
Evatt Merchant, President
president@saskliberals.ca

Saskatchewan Library Association (SLA)

#15, 2010 - 7th Ave., Regina SK S4R 1C2
Tel: 306-780-9413; *Fax:* 306-780-9447
Other Communication: slaprograms@sasktel.net
slaexdir@sasktel.net
www.saskla.ca
www.facebook.com/group.php?gid=106445391816
Overview: A small provincial charitable organization founded in 1914
Mission: To further the development of library services in Saskatchewan
Chief Officer(s):
Jeff Mason, President, 306-766-3833, Fax: 306-766-3839
Caroline Selinger, Executive Director
Kirsten Hansen, Program Administrator
Brett Waytuck, Treasurer, 306-787-8020, Fax: 306-787-2029
brett.waytuck@gov.sk.ca
Finances: *Funding Sources:* Membership fees; Donations; Sponsorships
Membership: *Fees:* Schedule available, based upon salary; *Member Profile:* Individuals, organizations, & institutions interested in library service & cultural activities in Saskatchewan
Activities: Supporting Saskatchewan library staff & libraries; Advocating for Saskatchewan libraries; Supporting continuing education; Providing information; Raising awareness of libraries; Coordinating programs; Promoting cooperation among libraries throughout the province; *Awareness Events:* Saskatchewan Library Week, October
Awards:
• Saskatchewan Libraries Education Bursary (Grant)
Awarded annually towards completion of a graduate degree program in Master of Library & Information Science*Eligibility:* Master of Library & Information Sciences students
• SLA Frances Morrison Award (Award)
Awarded for outstanding service to libraries
• Mary Donaldson Award (Award)
To recognize a graduating library technician enrolled at a library education institution in Saskatchewan
• SLA Continuing Education Workshop Grant (Grant)
To support continuing education activities
Meetings/Conferences: • Saskatchewan Library Association 2015 Annual Conference & Annual General Meeting, May, 2015, Doubletree Inn by Hilton, Regina, SK
Scope: Provincial
Description: Featuring discussions of issues affecting library service in Saskatchewan, the Mary Donaldson Memorial Lecture, & networking occasions, held during a two or three day period
Contact Information: Saskatchewan Library Association, Phone: 306-780-9409, Fax: 306-780-9447, E-mail: slaprograms@sasktel.net
• Saskatchewan Library Association 2016 Annual Conference & Annual General Meeting, 2016
Scope: Provincial
Description: Featuring discussions of issues affecting library service in Saskatchewan, the Mary Donaldson Memorial Lecture, & networking occasions, held during a two or three day period
Contact Information: Saskatchewan Library Association, Phone: 306-780-9413, Fax: 306-780-9447, E-mail: slaprograms@sasktel.net
Publications:
• Forum: The Journal of the Saskatchewan Library Association
Type: Journal; *Accepts Advertising*; *Editor:* Phil Jeffreys *ISSN:* 1918-6746
Profile: Report of association programs & library issues in the province
• Saskatchewan Library Association Annual Report
Type: Yearbook; *Frequency:* Annually
• Saskatchewan Library Association Conference Handbook
Type: Handbook
Profile: Featuring conference planning information, such as finances, facilities, registration, programs, public relations, volunteers, & social events
• SLA [Saskatchewan Library Association] Governance Handbook
Type: Handbook
Profile: Featuring constitutions, by-laws, & policies

Saskatchewan Library Trustees Association (SLTA)

79 Mayfair Cres., Regina SK S4S 5T9
Tel: 306-584-2495; *Fax:* 306-585-1473
slta.ca
www.facebook.com/sasklibrarytrusteesassoc
Overview: A small provincial organization founded in 1942
Mission: To foster the development of libraries & library services throughout Saskatchewan
Chief Officer(s):
Nancy Kennedy, Executive Director, 306-584-2495
njk@sasktel.net
Gerald Kleisinger, President
kleisingerg@reginalibrary.ca
Maureen McGirr, Vice-President
lmcgirr@sasktel.net
Donna Hartley, Treasurer
dhartley@sasktel.net
Finances: *Annual Operating Budget:* Less than $50,000
Membership: 756; *Member Profile:* Library trustees from across Saskatchewan; Residents of Saskatchewan who support libraries; Administrative bodies responsible for public libraries
Activities: Facilitating the exchange of ideas & experiences among library board members; Cooperating with other associations of library trustees; Seeking improvements to legislation affecting libraries in Saskatchewan
Meetings/Conferences: • Saskatchewan Library Trustees Association 2015 Annual General Meeting, May, 2015, Doubletree Inn, Regina, SK
Scope: Provincial
Description: Featuring the president's report, auditor's report, library system reports, & elections
Contact Information: Saskatchewan Library Trustees Association Executive Director: Nancy Kennedy, E-mail: njk@sasktel.net
• Saskatchewan Library Trustees Association 2016 Annual General Meeting, 2016, SK
Scope: Provincial
Description: Featuring the president's report, auditor's report, library system reports, & elections
Contact Information: Saskatchewan Library Trustees Association Executive Director: Nancy Kennedy, E-mail: njk@sasktel.net
Publications:
• The Trustee
Type: Newsletter; *Frequency:* 3 pa
Profile: Association updates, library news from around the province, & upcoming events
• Trustees' Manual
Type: Manual; *Frequency:* 3 pa
Profile: Contents include the role of a trustee, responsibilites, the provincial public library system & legislation, library technology, copyright, & funding & budgets

Saskatchewan Lions Eye Bank

Eye Dept., Saskatoon City Hospital, PO Box 447, Kipling SK S0G 2S0
www.eyebank.sklions.ca
Overview: A small provincial charitable organization founded in 1982
Mission: To promote corneal/eye donations after death to be used for transplantation to restore vision to people who have been rendered blind due to corneal injury, disease or degeneration
Member of: Eye Bank Association of America
Affliation(s): CNIB
Chief Officer(s):
Lorne Olver, President
lolver@sasktel.net
Finances: *Annual Operating Budget:* $50,000-$100,000; *Funding Sources:* Lions Clubs of Saskatchewan; provincial government
Staff Member(s): 3
Membership: 1-99
Activities: *Awareness Events:* National Donor Awareness Week, April

Saskatchewan Literacy Network

#11, 2155 Airport Dr., Saskatoon SK S7L 6M5
Tel: 306-653-7388; *Fax:* 306-653-1704
Toll-Free: 888-511-2111
saskliteracy@sasktel.net
www.sk.literacy.ca
www.facebook.com/SaskatchewanLiteracyNetwork
twitter.com/SkLitNet
www.youtube.com/user/SkLitNet
Overview: A small provincial charitable organization
Mission: To promote literacy in Saskatchewan
Member of: Movement for Canadian Literacy
Chief Officer(s):
Karen Rosser, Executive Director, 306-651-7283
karen.rosser@sk.literacy.ca
Staff Member(s): 6
Membership: *Fees:* $70 organization; $25 individual; $5 learner
Activities: Fall & Spring Mini-Conference; workshops; Train the Trainer courses; *Speaker Service:* Yes; *Library:* SLN Resource Centre; by appointment

Saskatchewan Livestock Association (SLA)

Canada Center Building, Evraz Place, PO Box 3771, Regina SK S4P 3N8
Tel: 306-757-6133; *Fax:* 306-525-5852
sla@accesscomm.ca
www.sasklivestock.com
Overview: A medium-sized provincial organization founded in 1075
Mission: To promote cooperation among the livestock organizations in Saskatchewan; To communicate opinions of livestock producers to government & other agencies; To encourage improvement in the production of livestock
Chief Officer(s):
Murray Andrew, Executive Director
Belinda Wagner, General Manager
Meetings/Conferences: • Saskatchewan Beef Industry 2015 6th Annual Conference: Harvesting the Future, January, 2015, Evraz Place, Regina, SK
Scope: Provincial
Description: An event organized by the Saskatchewan Livestock Association, Saskatchewan Cattlemen's Association, Saskatchewan Cattle Feeders Association, Saskatchewan Beef & Forage Symposium Committee, & the Saskatchewan Stock Growers Association
Contact Information: E-mail: sla@accesscomm.ca

Saskatchewan Lung Association

Saskatoon Office, 1231 - 8 St. East, Saskatoon SK S7H 0S5
Tel: 306-343-9511; *Fax:* 306-343-7007
Toll-Free: 888-566-5864
info@sk.lung.ca
www.sk.lung.ca
www.facebook.com/LungSask
twitter.com/lungsk
www.youtube.com/user/LungAssociationSK
Previous Name: Saskatchewan Anti-Tuberculosis League
Overview: A medium-sized provincial charitable organization founded in 1911 overseen by Canadian Lung Association
Mission: To improve respiratory health & overall quality of life; To advocate for support of education & research
Chief Officer(s):
Helen Cotton, Chair
Pat Smith, Vice-Chair
Brian Graham, President & CEO
Jennifer Miller, Vice-President, Health Promotion
Sharon Kremeniuk, Vice-President, Development
Leah Sullivan, Vice-President, Finance & Operations
Karen Davis, Treasurer
Finances: *Funding Sources:* Donations; Sponsorships; Fundraising
Staff Member(s): 16
Membership: *Fees:* $25
Activities: Supporting & conducting research into respiratory health & disease; Providing educational programs; Offering the most current lung health information; Organizing sleep apnea support groups; Promoting the prevention of lung disease; Raising public awareness of the impact of respiratory diseases; Collaborating with other organizations to work toward lung health
Publications:
• Breathworks: COPD Newsletter
Type: Newsletter

Profile: Educational articles plus notices of forthcoming support group meetings
• Lung Association of Saskatchewan Annual Report
Type: Yearbook; *Frequency:* Annually
• Nightly Nezzz Newsletter
Type: Newsletter; *Frequency:* Quarterly
Profile: Information for persons with sleep apnea & their families

Saskatchewan Manitoba Galloway Association
PO Box 178, Petersfield MB R0C 2L0
Tel: 204-886-7851
Overview: A small provincial organization founded in 1969
Mission: To inform about and promote the breeding of the Galloway breed of cattle.
Member of: Canadian Galloway Association
Chief Officer(s):
Doug Noakes, Secretary
doogie992011@hotmail.com
Finances: *Funding Sources:* Membership dues
Membership: *Member Profile:* Farmer/rancher

Saskatchewan Martial Arts Association (SMAA)
1210 Lorne St., Regina SK S4R 2J8
Tel: 306-565-2266
smaa@sasktel.net
www.saskmaa.com
Overview: A small provincial organization
Mission: To be a provincial sport governing body for a variety of martial arts styles practiced in Saskatchewan.
Member of: Sask Sport Inc.

Saskatchewan Meat Processors' Association (SMPA)
RR#1, Wymark SK S0N 2Y0
Tel: 306-741-9886; *Fax:* 306-773-9067
smpa@sasktel.net
www.smpa.ca
Overview: A medium-sized provincial organization founded in 1945
Mission: To act as the spokesman for Saskatchewan meat processors, to represent the industry in Saskatchewan & to be responsive to the needs of its members
Chief Officer(s):
David Mumm, President
Membership: *Fees:* $150; *Member Profile:* Small industry, manufacturers & processors
Activities: *Rents Mailing List:* Yes

Saskatchewan Medical Association (SMA)
#402, 321A - 21st St. East, Saskatoon SK S7K 0C1
Tel: 306-244-2196; *Fax:* 306-653-1631
Toll-Free: 800-667-3781
sma@sma.sk.ca
www.sma.sk.ca
www.facebook.com/SMAdocs
twitter.com/SMA_docs
Overview: A medium-sized provincial organization founded in 1906 overseen by Canadian Medical Association
Mission: To represent physicians in Saskatchewan; To advance the professional, educational, & economic welfare of physicians in the province
Chief Officer(s):
Vino Padayachee, CEO
Maria Derzko, Coordinator, Communications
Ed Hobday, Administrative Director
Clare Kozroski, President
Staff Member(s): 28
Membership: *Member Profile:* Saskatchewan physicians; *Committees:* Appointments & Awards; Rural & Regional Practice; Finance; Medical Compensation Review; Economics; Legislation & Policy; Payment Schedule Review; Intersectional Council; Primary Care; Council on Education & Quality Care; Physician Health Program; Specialist Recruitment & Retention; eHealth; Insurance
Activities: Engaging in advocacy activities; Promoting quality health care in Saskatchewan; Acting as the bargaining agent for fee-for-service physicians; Providing information about health care issues in Saskatchewan; Supporting continuing professional learning; Managing funds to offer programs such as bursaries & educational grants; Supporting physician health, through programs such as the Saskatchewan Physician Support Program
Publications:
• SMA [Saskatchewan Medical Association] News
Type: Newsletter
Profile: Association issues & events

Saskatchewan Mining Association (SMA)
#1500, 2002 Victoria Ave., Regina SK S4P 0R7
Tel: 306-757-9505; *Fax:* 306-569-1085
saskmining@sasktel.net
www.saskmining.ca
twitter.com/SaskMiningAssoc
Overview: A small provincial organization founded in 1965 overseen by Mining Association of Canada
Mission: To ensure the safe & profitable development of mineral resources in Saskatchewan; To act as the voice of the mining industry throughout the province; To promote understanding of the development of mineral resources in Saskatchewan
Chief Officer(s):
Steve Fortney, President, 306-933-8500, Fax: 306-933-8510
Pamela Schwann, Executive Director, 306-757-9505, Fax: 306-569-1085
Tracey Irwin, Manager, Communications & Membership, 306-757-9505, Fax: 306-569-1085
Finances: *Funding Sources:* Membership fees
Membership: 50; *Member Profile:* Individuals & enterprises involved with mining & metallurgical industries; *Committees:* Safety; Public Awareness; Human Resources; Taxation; Environmental; Geotechnical
Activities: Liaising with both provincial & federal governments; Organizing research into matters such as industrial relations; Cooperating with similar organizations

Saskatchewan Motion Picture Industry Association (SMPIA)
PO Box 31088, Regina SK S4R 6R8
Tel: 306-529-1832
office@smpia.sk.ca
www.smpia.sk.ca
www.facebook.com/SaskatchewanMediaProductionIndustryAssociation
twitter.com/smpiaoffice
Overview: A medium-sized provincial organization founded in 1985
Mission: Committed to the intrinsic cultural & economic value of motion pictures;to work toward the creation & advancement of opportunities for the production, promotion & appreciation of motion pictures in Saskatchewan
Chief Officer(s):
Holly Baird, President
Vanessa Bonk, Executive Director
vanessa@smpia.sk.ca
Finances: *Annual Operating Budget:* $250,000-$500,000
Staff Member(s): 4; 50 volunteer(s)
Membership: 75 corporate; 15 institutional; 20 student; 2 senior; 300 individual; *Fees:* Schedule available; *Member Profile:* Individual, corporation or organization interested in Saskatchewan film, video & multimedia; *Committees:* Communications; Issues & Advocacy; Professional Development
Activities: *Library*

Saskatchewan Municipal Hail Insurance Association (SMHI)
2100 Cornwall St., Regina SK S4P 2K7
Tel: 306-569-1852; *Fax:* 306-522-3717
Toll-Free: 877-414-7644
smhi@smhi.ca
www.smhi.ca
twitter.com/MunicipalHail
Overview: A medium-sized provincial organization founded in 1917
Mission: To provide spot-loss hail insurance coverage to Saskatchewan grain farmers at cost
Chief Officer(s):
Rodney Schoettler, Chief Executive Officer
rschoettler@municipalhail.ca
Mark Holfeld, Chief Operating Officer
mholfeld@municipalhail.ca
Finances: *Annual Operating Budget:* Greater than $5 Million

Saskatchewan Museums Association *See* Museums Association of Saskatchewan

Saskatchewan Music Educators Association (SMEA)
PO Box 632, Cudworth SK S0K 1B0
Tel: 306-256-7187
smea@sasktel.net
www.musiceducationonline.org/smea/smea.html
Overview: A small provincial organization founded in 1957
Mission: To promote the development of high standards of music & music education; To exchange information & ideas with those interested in music; To sponsor conventions, workshops, clinics & other means of musical development, information & education
Affliation(s): Saskatchewan Teachers Federation; ISME; Canadian Music Educators Association; SaskCulture Inc.; Saskatchewan Arts Board; The Canadian Coalition for Music Education; Canadian Conference of the Arts; The National Symposium on Arts Educations; The Canada Council; The British Columbia MEA; The Alberta Music Association; The Manitoba MEA; The Ontario MEA; The New Brunswick MEA; The University of Sask. Music Department; The University of Regina Music Department; Brandon School of Music; The International Music Camp (North Dakota); The Conservatory of Music.; Saskatchewan Choral Federation
Chief Officer(s):
Val Kuemper, Executive Director
smea@sasktel.net

Saskatchewan Music Festival Association Inc.
PO Box 37005, Regina SK S4S 7K3
Tel: 306-757-1722; *Fax:* 306-347-7789
Toll-Free: 888-892-9929
sask.music.festival@sasktel.net
www.smfa.ca
twitter.com/SKMusicFestival
Overview: A medium-sized provincial charitable organization founded in 1908 overseen by Federation of Canadian Music Festivals
Mission: To provide a classical competitive music festival system of the highest standard at the local, provincial & national levels
Member of: Saskatchewan Council of Cultural Organizations
Chief Officer(s):
Carol Donhauser, Executive Director
carol.smfa@sasktel.net
Staff Member(s): 2
Activities: *Library*

Saskatchewan Native Women's Association *See* Saskatchewan Aboriginal Women's Circle Corporation

Saskatchewan Nursery Landscape Association (SNLA)
c/o Landscape Alberta Nursery Trades Association, #200, 10331 - 178 St., Edmonton AB T5S 1R5
Toll-Free: 888-446-3499
www.snla.ca
Previous Name: Saskatchewan Nursery Trades Association
Overview: A medium-sized provincial organization overseen by Canadian Nursery Landscape Association
Mission: To encourage people in the landscaping industry to network in order to spread their wealth of knowledge among each other
Chief Officer(s):
Leslie Cornell, President
Membership: 40; *Fees:* Schedule available

Saskatchewan Nursery Trades Association *See* Saskatchewan Nursery Landscape Association

Saskatchewan Opthalmic Dispensers Association (SODA)
A4 116, 103 St. East, Saskatoon SK S7N 1Y7
Tel: 306-652-0769; *Fax:* 306-652-0784
office@scoptic.ca
www.scoptic.ca
Overview: A small provincial organization
Mission: To improve the practice of opticians in the public interest by ensuring that Saskatchewan Opticians provide quality professional care to help people achieve better vision.
Chief Officer(s):
Paul Johnson, President

Saskatchewan Optometric Association *See* Saskatchewan Association of Optometrists

Saskatchewan Orchestral Association, Inc. (SOA)
1-3504 - 13 Ave., Regina SK S4T 1P9
Tel: 306-546-3050
info@saskorchestras.com
www.saskorchestras.com
Overview: A medium-sized provincial organization founded in 1985 overseen by Orchestras Canada
Mission: To serve as resource base & coordinating body for orchestral & string programs in Saskatchewan; To procure funds to make achievement of goals & objectives of SOA possible
Member of: Orchestras Canada; SK Music; SK Music Alliance
Affliation(s): SaskCulture
Chief Officer(s):
Tara Solheim, Executive Director

Finances: *Funding Sources:* Membership fees; Saskatchewan Lotteries Trust Fund for Sport, Culture & Recreation
Membership: *Fees:* $25; *Member Profile:* Interest in strings, orchestra, music
Activities: Summer String Workshop, Regina; Chamber Orchestra Workshop, Saskatoon; Conducting Workshop, Saskatoon; Honour Orchestra;

Saskatchewan Orchid Society (SOS)
PO Box 411, Saskatoon SK S7K 3L3
e-mail: info@saskorchids.com
www.saskorchids.com
Overview: A small provincial organization founded in 1983
Mission: To promote orchid habitats & to provide a place for members to share knowledge amongst each other
Chief Officer(s):
Cal Carter, President
Membership: 65; *Fees:* $25 single; $30 family

Saskatchewan Organization for Heritage Languages Inc. (SOHL)
2144 Cornwall St., Regina SK S4P 2K7
Tel: 306-780-9275; *Fax:* 306-780-9407
sohl@sasktel.net
www.heritagelanguages.sk.ca
ca.linkedin.com/pub/sohl-sk/51/541/aa5
www.facebook.com/sohl.sask
twitter.com/sohl_sk
Overview: A medium-sized provincial charitable organization founded in 1985
Mission: To promote & develop teaching of heritage languages in Saskatchewan; to act in advocacy capacity to make representation to government, institutions & boards regarding matters pertaining to heritage languages; to promote cooperation with & mutual support of provincial organizations with similar aims & objectives; to encourage inter-provincial & national liaison
Affiliation(s): SaskCulture
Chief Officer(s):
Tamara Ruzic, Executive Director
sohl@sasktel.net
Finances: *Annual Operating Budget:* $100,000-$250,000; *Funding Sources:* Saskatchewan Lotteries
Staff Member(s): 2; 11 volunteer(s)
Membership: 80 institutional + 5 associate; *Fees:* $25 regular; $10 associate
Activities: *Awareness Events:* Heritage Language Recognition Day

Saskatchewan Outdoor & Environmental Education Association (SOEEA)
26 Corkery Bay, Regina SK S4T 7K6
e-mail: soeea.sk@gmail.com
www.soeea.sk.ca
www.facebook.com/271057812846?ref=ts
twitter.com/SOEEA
Overview: A small provincial organization founded in 1972
Mission: To encourage educators & people who participate in outdoor education to teach & practise environmental responsibility
Affiliation(s): North American Association for Environmental Education
Chief Officer(s):
Dennie Fornwald, President
denniefornwald@gmail.com
Leah Japp, Outreach Coordinator
soeeaoutreach@gmail.com
Alexandra Fourlas, Treasurer
Fourlasfamily@gmail.com
Membership: *Committees:* Communications Working Goup; Decision Makers Working Group; Education Working Group; Partners Working Group; Public & Families Working Group
Activities: Developing & evaluating education activities; Providing professional development workshops; Partnering with related organizations; Facilitating networking opportunities
Awards:
• B.M. Melanson Award (Award)
To be presented periodically to an individual who has made an outstanding contribution to outdoor & environmental education in Saskatchewan; candidates shall be active participants in outdoor & environmental education in Saskatchewan; candidates need not be a member of SOEEA *Contact:* Yvette Crane
Meetings/Conferences: • SaskOutdoors' Annual General Meeting 2015, January, 2015, Saskatoon, SK
Scope: Provincial
Publications:
• Envisage [a publication of the Saskatchewan Outdoor & Environmental Education Association]
Type: Newsletter; *Frequency:* Quarterly
Profile: Articles on topics such as educational strategies & instructional methods
• Green Teacher

Saskatchewan Outfitters Association (SOA)
PO Box 572, Stn. Main, Saskatoon SK S7K 3L6
Tel: 306-668-1388; *Fax:* 306-668-1353
soa@sasktel.net
www.soa.ca
Overview: A small provincial organization founded in 1967
Mission: Working together to promote & foster excellence in outfitting
Chief Officer(s):
Brian Hoffart, President
baitmaster@sasktel.net
Membership: 109

Saskatchewan Palliative Care Association
PO Box 37053, Regina SK S4S 7K3
Tel: 306-773-6523; *Fax:* 306-637-2494
info@saskpalliativecare.ca
www.saskpalliativecare.ca
Overview: A medium-sized provincial charitable organization founded in 1991
Mission: To promote the philosophy & principles of palliative care through networking, education, advocacy & research; to improve quality of life for the dying
Member of: Canadian Palliative Care Association
Chief Officer(s):
Carla Carlson, President
cmcarlson@sasktel.net
Finances: *Annual Operating Budget:* Less than $50,000
Staff Member(s): 1
Membership: 75-100; *Fees:* $40 regular; $50 CHPA nurses group
Activities: Educational programs; grant disbursement; *Library:* Resource Library; Open to public

Saskatchewan Parks & Recreation Association (SPRA)
#100, 1445 Park St., Regina SK S4N 4C5
Tel: 306-780-9231; *Fax:* 306-780-9257
Toll-Free: 800-563-2555
Other Communication: resourcecentre@spra.sk.ca
office@spra.sk.ca
www.spra.sk.ca
Overview: A medium-sized provincial charitable organization founded in 1962 overseen by Canadian Parks & Recreation Association
Mission: To stimulate & advance parks, recreation & leisure activities, facilities, & programs in Saskatchewan
Finances: *Funding Sources:* Lottery ticket sales
Membership: 600 organizations; *Fees:* Schedule available
Activities: *Speaker Service:* Yes; *Library:* Resource Centre for Sport, Culture & Recreation; Open to public
Meetings/Conferences: • Saskatchewan Parks & Recreation Association 2015 Spring Education & Training Symposium, 2015, SK
Scope: Provincial
Contact Information: SPRA Consultant: Kelly Skotnitsky, E-mail: kskotnitsky@spra.sk.ca
• Saskatchewan Parks & Recreation Association 2015 Conference & Annual General Meeting, October, 2015
Scope: Provincial
Description: Presentations on the themes of technology, issues affecting small town Saskatchewan, & current issues
Contact Information: SPRA Consultant: Kelly Skotnitsky, E-mail: kskotnitsky@spra.sk.ca
Publications:
• DIRECTION [a publication of the Saskatchewan Parks & Recreation Association]
Type: Newsletter; *Accepts Advertising*; *Price:* Free with membership in the Saskatchewan Parks &Recreation Association
Profile: A newsmagazine with news, articles, stories, & funding opportunities

Saskatchewan Pattern Dance Association
SK
Tel: 306-374-9383
webmaster@patterndance-sk.ca
www.patterndance-sk.ca
Overview: A small provincial organization founded in 1989
Chief Officer(s):
Armand Bourassa, President
ab.bourassa@shaw.ca
Activities: *Library:* Instructional Video Library

Saskatchewan PeriOperative Registered Nurses' Group (SORNG)
SK
Overview: A medium-sized provincial organization overseen by Operating Room Nurses Association of Canada
Chief Officer(s):
Candace Franke, President
cfranke@yourlink.ca
Membership: *Fees:* $40 active; $25 associate; *Member Profile:* Registered Nurses in Saskatchewan who are engaged in operating room nursing or involved in the Perioperative setting.
Activities: *Awareness Events:* Perioperative Nurses Week, November

Saskatchewan Physical Education Association (SPEA)
PO Box 193, Harris SK S0L 1K0
Tel: 306-656-4423; *Fax:* 306-656-4405
spea@xplornet.com
www.speaonline.ca
www.facebook.com/speaonline
twitter.com/SPEA4
Overview: A small provincial organization founded in 1951
Mission: The Saskatchewan Physical Education Association is a provincial nonprofit incorporated organization that provides quality leadership, advocacy and resources for professionals in physical education and wellness in order to positively influence the lifestyles of Saskatchewan's children and youth.
Member of: PHE Canada, SPRA, STF, SHSAA, U of S, U of R,SHEA, In Motion
Affliation(s): Physical Health Education Canada; Saskatchewan Parks & Recreation Association; Saskatchewan Teachers Federal PHE Canada; Saskatchewan Teachers' Federation
Chief Officer(s):
Holly Stevens, Executive Director
Cole Wilson, President
Finances: *Annual Operating Budget:* $100,000-$250,000; *Funding Sources:* Membership fees; Sask Lotteries Trust; Sponsorships
Staff Member(s): 1; 15 volunteer(s)
Membership: 485; *Fees:* $25 regular; $10 student; $15 retired teacher; *Member Profile:* Individuals with a professional interest in the teaching of physical education; *Committees:* Social Media, Journal Editor/Website, New Resources/Wellness, Curriculum, Advocacy/Mentorship, Membership Services, Regional Directors
Activities: *Library*
Awards:
• Paul Renwick Award (Award)
For an individual who has made an outstanding contribution to physical education in Saskatchewan *Amount:* $200 (gift), $250 (honorarium)
• Local Initiative Award (Award)
For individuals, schools or school divisions for their contributions to physical education in their region*Eligibility:* Recipients do not have to be members of the SPEA*Deadline:* February *Amount:* 5 awards of $25 *Contact:* Daunean Dash-Rewcastle, dauneandash@gmail.com
• SPEA Book Prizes (Award)
Presented to post-secondary students of kinesiology, health or education *Amount:* $150
• SPEA Scholarships (Scholarship)
Eligibility: Student must have at least 2 physical education credits and be enrolleged in first year studies in physical education, kinesiology, education, health studies, applied science & technology in Saskatchewan*Deadline:* June 30, annually *Amount:* 2 awards of $700
• QDPE (Quality Daily Physical Education) Professional of the Year Award (Award)
Eligibility: Employee of QDPE school and involved in promoting QDPE *Amount:* $25 *Contact:* Daunean Dash-Rewcastle, dauneandash@gmail.com
• SPEA Classroom QDPE Award (Award)
• SPEA Elementary School QDPE Award (Award)
• SPEA Secondary & Combined Elementary / Secondary School QDPE Award (Award)
Meetings/Conferences: • Saskatchewan Physical Education Association Conference 2015: Moving With Synergy, May, 2015, University of Regina and Ramada Plaza Hotel, Regina, SK
Scope: Provincial
Publications:
• On the Move

Type: Journal; *Frequency:* Semiannually; *Editor:* Jennifer Foley; *Price:* Free for members

Saskatchewan Physiotherapy Association (SPA)
#118, 1121 College Dr., Saskatoon SK S7N 0W3
Tel: 306-955-7265; *Fax:* 306-955-7260
www.saskphysio.org
www.facebook.com/saskphysio
twitter.com/saskphysio
Overview: A medium-sized provincial organization overseen by Canadian Physiotherapy Association
Mission: To provide leadership to the physiotherapy profession; To foster excellence in practice, education & research; To promotes high standards of health in Saskatchewan
Member of: Canadian Physiotherapy Association
Chief Officer(s):
Lorna MacMillan, Executive Director
Allison Stene, President
Finances: *Funding Sources:* Membership dues; Educational activities
Staff Member(s): 3
Membership: 400+

Saskatchewan Playwrights Centre (SPC)
#700, 601 Spadina Cres. East, Saskatoon SK S7K 3G8
Tel: 306-665-7707; *Fax:* 306-244-0255
sk.playwrights@sasktel.net
www.saskplaywrights.ca
www.facebook.com/pages/Saskatchewan-Playwrights-Centre/114748828547948
twitter.com/SaskPlaywrights
Overview: A small provincial organization founded in 1982
Mission: To develop playwrights.
Chief Officer(s):
Charlie Peters, President
Staff Member(s): 1
Membership: *Fees:* $20 associate; $55 playwright
Activities: Spring Festival of New Plays;

The Saskatchewan Poetry Society
3809 Regina Ave., Regina SK S4S 0H8
Tel: 306-586-5898
Overview: A small provincial organization founded in 1935
Mission: To further the writing of poetry in Saskatchewan
Membership: *Member Profile:* All members must live in Saskatchewan at the time of joining, but may retain membership if they later move to some other province; members agree to buy 6 books
Activities: Monthly meetings

Saskatchewan Powerlifting Association (SPA)
PO Box 42, North Weyburn SK S0C 1X0
Tel: 306-842-4299; *Fax:* 306-842-2682
saskpowerlifting@gmail.com
www.saskpowerlifting.ca
www.facebook.com/saskpowerlifting
Overview: A small provincial organization overseen by Canadian Powerlifting Union
Mission: To promote fitness & provide opportunities to weightlifting athletes.
Chief Officer(s):
Ryan Fowler, President
Membership: 100+; *Fees:* $60 regular; $35 new/special; $10 referee; $2 associate

Saskatchewan Prevention Institute (SPI)
1319 Colony St., Saskatoon SK S7N 2Z1
Tel: 306-651-4300; *Fax:* 306-651-4301
Other Communication: www.healthyparenting.sk.ca
info@skprevention.ca
www.skprevention.ca
ca.linkedin.com/pub/communication-department/33/276/594
www.facebook.com/SaskatchewanPreventionInstitute
www.youtube.com/user/PreventionInstitute1
Previous Name: Saskatchewan Institute on Prevention of Handicaps
Overview: A small provincial charitable organization founded in 1980
Mission: To reduce the occurrence of disabling conditions in children
Member of: Saskatchewan Health Care Association; Canadian College of Health Service Executives
Chief Officer(s):
Noreen Agrey, Executive Director, 306-651-4302
nagrey@skprevention.ca
Finances: *Annual Operating Budget:* $250,000-$500,000
Staff Member(s): 22; 1 volunteer(s)
Activities: *Awareness Events:* FASD (Fetal Alcohol Spectrum Disorder) Awareness Day, Sept. 9; *Speaker Service:* Yes; *Library* Open to public
Meetings/Conferences: • Prevention Matters Conference 2015, September, 2015, TCU Place, Saskatoon, SK
Scope: Provincial
Contact Information: Contact: Lee Hinton, Education & Promotions Coordinator, Phone: 306-651-4318, lhinton@skprevention.ca
Publications:
• Prevention Post
Type: Newsletter

Saskatchewan Pro Life Association (SPLA)
Box 27093, RPO Avonhurst, Regina SK S4R 8R8
Tel: 306-352-3480; *Fax:* 306-352-3481
Toll-Free: 888-842-7752
spla@sasktel.net
www.saskprolife.com
Overview: A small provincial charitable organization founded in 1974
Mission: To work for the protection & respect for all human life from conception to natural death
Chief Officer(s):
Daniel Thomas, President
Finances: *Annual Operating Budget:* $100,000-$250,000
Staff Member(s): 1; 2 volunteer(s)
Membership: 5,000-14,999; *Fees:* $25
Activities: *Library* Open to public

Saskatchewan Professional Fire Fighters Burn Unit Fund
c/o Brian Belitsky, 62 Milne Bay, Yorkton SK S3N 3Z8
Tel: 306-782-4290; *Fax:* 306-783-0109
burnfund@burnfund.ca
www.burnfund.ca
Overview: A small provincial organization founded in 1974
Mission: To raise and distribute funds to help Saskatchewan families of burn patients with treatment, care, and rehabilitations.
Affiliation(s): British Columbia Professional Fire Fighters Burn Fund
Chief Officer(s):
Kirby Benning, President
Finances: *Funding Sources:* private donations; corporate sponsorship

Saskatchewan Professional Photographers Association Inc.
c/o Professional Photographers Association of Canada, 209 Light St., Woodstock ON N4S 6H6
Tel: 519-537-2555; *Fax:* 888-831-4036
Toll-Free: 888-643-7762
admin@sppa.org
ppoc-sk.com
Overview: A small provincial organization overseen by Professional Photographers of Canada
Mission: To advance professional photography through educational seminars, fellowship & competitions
Affiliation(s): Professional Photographers of Canada
Chief Officer(s):
Wayne Inverarity, President, 306-530-8888
winverar@sasktel.net
Tanya Thompson, Administrative Coordinator
Membership: 110; *Fees:* $391.65 active; $294 observer

Saskatchewan Professional Planners Institute (SPPI)
2424 College Ave., Regina SK S4P 1C8
Tel: 306-584-3879; *Fax:* 306-352-6913
msteranka@sasktel.net
sppi.ca
www.facebook.com/SaskPlanning
twitter.com/SaskPlanning
Previous Name: Association of Professional Community Planners of Saskatchewan
Overview: A medium-sized provincial organization founded in 1963 overseen by Canadian Institute of Planners
Mission: To promote & maintain professionalism in planning field
Affiliation(s): Canadian Institute of Planners
Chief Officer(s):
Marilyn Steranka, Executive Director, 306-584-3879, Fax: 306-352-6913
msteranka@sasktel.net
Bill Delainey, Secretary, 306-975-1663, Fax: 306-242-6965
Ryan Walker, Treasurer, 306-966-5664, Fax: 306-966-5680
8 volunteer(s)
Membership: 24 student + 78 individual + 11 non-resident; *Committees:* Program; Education; Membership
Activities: *Speaker Service:* Yes; *Rents Mailing List:* Yes
Meetings/Conferences: • Association of Professional Community Planners of Saskatchewan 2015 Conference, June, 2015, Saskatoon, SK
Scope: Provincial
Description: A meeting of planners & related professionals to share new ideas, enhance professional practice, network & socialize
Contact Information: URL: www.thrive2015fleurir.ca
• Association of Professional Community Planners of Saskatchewan 2016 Conference, 2016
Scope: Provincial
Description: A meeting of planners & related professionals to share new ideas, enhance professional practice, network & socialize

Saskatchewan Provincial Mediation Board
#120, 2151 Scarth St., Regina SK S4P 2H8
Tel: 306-787-5408; *Fax:* 306-787-5574
Toll-Free: 877-787-5408
pmb@gov.sk.ca
www.justice.gov.sk.ca/pmb
Overview: A small provincial organization overseen by Credit Counselling Canada
Mission: To offer counselling & budget advice to persons who are experiencing personal debt difficulties
Affliation(s): Government of Saskatchewan, Justice & Attorney General; Credit Counselling Canada
Chief Officer(s):
Dale Beck, Chair, 306-787-2695
dale.beck@gov.sk.ca
Staff Member(s): 3
Activities: Assisting debtors with problems such as property tax arrears & residential mortgage foreclosures; Arranging mediated debt repayment with creditors; Using legal rememdies for debt repayment, through the Bankruptcy & Insolvency Act; *Speaker Service:* Yes

Saskatchewan Provincial Rifle Association Inc. (SPRA)
PO Box 40, Mazenod SK S0H 2Y0
Tel: 306-354-7493
www.saskrifle.ca
Overview: A small provincial organization founded in 1885
Mission: The governing body for fullbore target rifle shooting in Saskatchewan & promotes the pursuit of excellence in marksmanship & the safe & responsible handling of firearms
Chief Officer(s):
Keith Skjerdal, Match Director, 306-652-2065
Finances: *Funding Sources:* Membership dues; SaskSport Inc.
Membership: *Fees:* Schedule available

Saskatchewan Psychiatric Association
Saskatoon SK
www.cpa-apc.org/browse/documents/276
Overview: A small provincial organization
Mission: To increase psychiatric knowledge in Saskatchewan
Affliation(s): Canadian Psychiatric Association
Chief Officer(s):
Declan Quinn, President
Keriem, Secretary
Finances: *Funding Sources:* Membership fees; Donations; Grants
Membership: *Member Profile:* Psychiatrists in Saskatchewan
Activities: Fostering research into the cause, treatment, & prevention of mental disorders; Engaging in advocacy activities; Liaising with government, universities & other medical associations

Saskatchewan Psychological Association *See* Saskatchewan College of Psychologists

Saskatchewan Public Health Association Inc.
PO Box 845, Regina SK S4P 3B1
e-mail: saskpha@gmail.com
Overview: A small provincial organization overseen by Canadian Public Health Association
Mission: To constitute a resource in Saskatchewan for the improvement & maintenance of health
Chief Officer(s):
Greg Riehl, President

Saskatchewan Publishers Group (SPG)
2405 - 11th Ave., Regina SK S4P 0K4

Tel: 306-780-9808; Fax: 306-780-9810
info@saskbooks.com
www.skbooks.com
twitter.com/SaskBooks
Also Known As: SaskBooks
Overview: A medium-sized provincial organization founded in 1989
Mission: To promote the Saskatchewan book publishing industry; to provide a forum for sharing information & ideas; to speak for the common interests of its members; to undertake specific projects, programs & studies; to work closely with other publishing & cultural organizations across Canada
Member of: SaskCulture
Affliation(s): Association of Canadian Publishers
Chief Officer(s):
Brenda Niskala, Co-Executive Director
bniskala@saskbooks.com
Jillian Bell, Co-Executive Director
Staff Member(s): 3
Membership: 46; *Fees:* $300 full/non publisher; $150 associate; $100 supporting; *Member Profile:* Full - individuals & companies who publish original Canadian books as the primary function of their business & who have in print no fewer than 4 original Canadian titles & an ongoing publishing program of at least 1 title each year; no more than 25% of the publishing program may be authored by owners or employees of the company
Activities: *Internships:* Yes; *Speaker Service:* Yes; *Library* by appointment

Saskatchewan Pulse Growers (SPG)
#207, 116 Research Dr., Saskatoon SK S7N 3R3
Tel: 306-668-5556; *Fax:* 306-668-5557
pulse@saskpulse.com
www.saskpulse.com
www.facebook.com/SaskPulse
twitter.com/SaskPulse
www.youtube.com/SaskPulse
Also Known As: Saskatchewan Pulse Crop Development Board
Overview: A medium-sized provincial organization founded in 1976
Mission: To develop the pulse crop industry in Saskatchewan
Member of: Pulse Canada
Chief Officer(s):
Carl Potts, Executive Director, 306-668-6676
cpotts@saskpulse.com
Rachel Kehrig, Director, Communications
rkehrig@saskpulse.com
Finances: *Annual Operating Budget:* Greater than $5 Million; *Funding Sources:* Provincial government; Producer levy
Staff Member(s): 14
Membership: 18,000+; *Fees:* 1% levy of the value of the gross sale is deducted at the first point of sale or distribution; *Member Profile:* Growers of peas, lentils, chickpeas, beans

Saskatchewan Racquetball Association (SRA)
SK
racquetballsask.com
www.facebook.com/SaskatchewanRacquetballAssociation
twitter.com/saskracquetball
Overview: A small provincial organization overseen by Racquetball Canada
Mission: To To promote the sport of racquetball throughout Saskatchewan.
Chief Officer(s):
Karla Drury, President
k.drury@sasktel.net
Tim Landeryou, Executive Director
ed.rballsask@gmail.com

Saskatchewan Reading Council
c/o Good Spirit School Div., Fairview Education Centre, 63 King St. East, Yorkton SK S3N OT7
Tel: 306-786-5500; *Fax:* 306-783-0355
Toll-Free: 866-390-0773
saskreading.com
Also Known As: Council No: CR150
Overview: A small provincial organization overseen by International Reading Association
Chief Officer(s):
Karen Koroluk, President
k.koroluk@rcsd.ca
Activities: *Library:* Professional Library
Meetings/Conferences: • 46th Annual Saskatchewan Reading Conference 2015, April, 2015, Delta Hotel, Regina, SK
Scope: Provincial

Saskatchewan Ready Mixed Concrete Association Inc. (SRMCA)
#203, 1801 McKay St., Regina SK S4N 6E7
Tel: 306-757-2788; *Fax:* 306-569-9144
srmca@sasktel.net
www.concreteworksharder.com
Previous Name: Prairie Ready Mixed Concrete Association
Overview: A small provincial organization founded in 1963 overseen by Canadian Ready Mixed Concrete Association
Mission: To maintain the highest quality of concrete produced by its members; To improve the industry in all aspects & represents its members in relation to governments, environmental agencies & other industry-related associations
Chief Officer(s):
Rod Smith, President, 306-545-3200
Garth Sanders, Executive Director, Finance
gsanders@accesscomm.ca
Membership: 60 concrete plants; *Member Profile:* Concrete producers & those with a direct interest in the industry

Saskatchewan Real Estate Association *See* Association of Saskatchewan Realtors

Saskatchewan Recording Industry Association (SRIA)
#210, 2300 Dewdney Ave., Regina SK S4R 1H5
Tel: 306-347-0676; *Fax:* 306-347-7735
Toll-Free: 800-347-0676
info@saskmusic.org
www.saskmusic.org
www.facebook.com/SaskMusic1
twitter.com/SaskMusic
www.myspace.com/saskmusic
Also Known As: SaskMusic
Overview: A medium-sized provincial organization founded in 1987
Mission: To develop & promote the music & sound recording industry of Saskatchewan
Member of: SaskCulture
Affliation(s): Foundation to Assist Canadian Talent on Records; Canadian Recording Industry Association; Canadian Independent Record Production Association; Society of Composers, Authors & Music Publishers of Canada; Canadian Academy of Recording Arts & Sciences; Western Canadian Music Awards
Chief Officer(s):
Derek Bachman, Executive Director
derek@saskmusic.org
Finances: *Funding Sources:* Sask Lotteries; Dept. of Culture, Youth & Recreation; Canadian Heritage; SOCAN; FACTOR; Astral Media
Staff Member(s): 6
Membership: *Fees:* $30 youth $50 individual; $75 band; $100 corporate/affiliate; *Member Profile:* Anyone related to the Saskatchewan music industry: musicians, studios, radio stations, graphic artists, etc.
Activities: Conference, festivals, workshops & other training, advocacy; *Awareness Events:* Beer Bacon Bands Festival, Jan.; StirCrazy Blues Festival, Feb.; *Internships:* Yes; *Speaker Service:* Yes; *Library:* SRIA Resource Library; by appointment
Awards:
• Western Canadian Music Awards (Award)

Saskatchewan Registered Music Teachers' Association (SRMTA)
45 Martin St., Regina SK S4S 3W4
e-mail: srmta@sasktel.net
www.srmta.com
Overview: A medium-sized provincial organization founded in 1938
Mission: To promote progressive ideas & methods in the teaching of music; to encourage systematic preparation in the art of teaching; to seek agreement among members about a high standard of musicianship
Member of: Canadian Federation of Music Teachers' Association
Affliation(s): Saskatchewan Music Educators Association
Chief Officer(s):
Laureen Kells, President
lkells@sasktel.net
Lynn Ewing, Vice President
lewing@sasktel.net
Membership: *Fees:* $25 application fee; $138.40 individual

Battleford Branch
PO Box 241, Battleford SK S0M 0E0
Tel: 306-937-2305
Chief Officer(s):
Cathy Swerid, President
cathysw@sasktel.net
Diane Neil, Secretary
jdneil228@sasktel.net

East Central Branch
c/o Angel Liebrecht, PO Box 148, Lanigan SK S0K 2M0
Tel: 306-365-9989
Chief Officer(s):
Angel Liebrecht, Secretary
liebrecht.a@sasktel.net
Maureen Loeffelholz, President

Lloydminster Branch
PO Box 3012, Lloydminster AB S9V 1P4
Tel: 306-825-4168
dan2@telusplanet.net
Pamela Rollheiser, President
nprollheiser@bellevista.ca

Prince Albert Branch
303 - 25 Ave., Prince Albert SK S6V 4P5
Tel: 306-763-7382
Marilyn Lohrenz, President
wmlz@shaw.ca

Regina Branch
335 Orchard Cres. South, Regina SK S4S 5B8
Tel: 306-585-7810
Kimberly Engen, President
engenk@gmail.com
Marina Wensley, Secretary
wensleytm@sasktel.net

Saskatoon Branch
519 Steiger Way, Saskatoon SK S7N 4K2
Tel: 306-373-9739
Chief Officer(s):
Bonnie Nicholson, President
stephen.nicholson@shaw.ca
Michelle Aalders, Secretary
m.aalders@sasktel.net

Swift Current Branch
427 - 15 Ave. NE, Swift Current SK S9H 2X5
Tel: 306-773-1468
Chief Officer(s):
Lois Noble, Secretary
noble.one@sasktel.net

West Central Branch
PO Box 2024, Rosetown SK S0L 2V0
Tel: 306-882-3591
Chief Officer(s):
Claire Seibold, President
rcseibold@sasktel.net
Helen Barclay, Secretary
helen.barclay2@gmail.com

Yorkton Branch
385 Circlebrooke Dr., Yorkton SK S3N 3C5
Tel: 306-783-6858
Laurel Teichroeb, President
lteichroab@accesscomm.ca

Saskatchewan Registered Nurses' Association (SRNA)
2066 Retallack St., Regina SK S4T 7X5
Tel: 306-359-4200; *Fax:* 306-359-0257
Toll-Free: 800-667-9945
info@srna.org
www.srna.org
twitter.com/SRNAdialogue
Overview: A medium-sized provincial licensing organization founded in 1917 overseen by Canadian Nurses Association
Mission: To ensure competent, knowledge-based, & ethical nursing in Saskatchewan, for the protection of the public; To establish registration & licensure requirements
Chief Officer(s):
Signy Klebeck, President
Karen Eisler, Executive Director
Finances: *Funding Sources:* Membership fees; Sponsorships
Staff Member(s): 15
Membership: *Committees:* Discipline; Education Approval; Legislation & Bylaws; Membership Advisory; Registration and Membership; Advisory; Investigations; General Information; Awards
Activities: Setting standards of practice of RNs & RN(NP)s; Approving nursing education programs & offering continuing education opportunities; Responding to complaints of

professional incompetence or misconduct against nurses; Providing liability protection for nurses;
Awards:
• Life Membership (Award)
To honour members of the association who are retiring from registered nursing employment*Deadline:* February 1 *Contact:* Barb Fitz-Gerald, RN, Fax: 306-359-0183; E-mail: bfitz-gerald@srna.org
• Honorary Membership (Award)
Eligibility: A non-nurse, or a nurse registered outside of Saskatchewan*Deadline:* February 1 *Contact:* Barb Fitz-Gerald, RN, Fax: 306-359-0183; E-mail: bfitz-gerald@srna.org
• Memorial Book (Award)
Eligibility: Nominees must have held an SRNA practicing membership during their careers*Deadline:* February 1 *Contact:* Barb Fitz-Gerald, RN, Fax: 306-359-0183; E-mail: bfitz-gerald@srna.org
• Millennium Award: Jean Browne Award for Leadership in Nursing Practice (Award)
To recognize a registered nurse or group whose leadership has made an outstanding contribution to the profession
• Millennium Award: Nora Armstrong Award for Health Advocacy (Award)
To recognize a registered nurse or group who promote & advocate quality care or health policy
• Millennium Award: Jean Wilson Award for Employer of the Year (Award)
To recognize an individual or group who have demonstrated leadership in the provision of a positive work environment for registered nurses
• Millennium Award: Granger Campbell Award for Clinical Excellence (Award)
To recognize a registered nurse or group who has demonstrated clinical excellence in any practice setting
• Millennium Award: Effie Feeny Award for Nursing Research (Award)
To recognize a registered nurse or group who has made an outstanding contribution in nursing or health related research
• Millennium Award: Helen Walker Award for Innovation in Nursing (Award)
To recognize a registered nurse or group who developed & implemented methods to meet health care challenges
• Millennium Award: Elizabeth Van Valkenburg Award for Leadership in Nursing Education (Award)
To recognize a registered nurse or group who has made an outstanding contribution in the field of nursing education
• Millennium Award: Ruth Hicks Award for Student Leadership (Award)
To recognize a nursing student or group who made a significant contribution as a student leader or group
• Mentorship Award (Award)
To recognize an SRNA practicing member who exhibits exceptional mentoring abilities*Deadline:* February 1 *Contact:* Barb Fitz-Gerald, RN, Fax: 306-359-0183; E-mail: bfitz-gerald@srna.org
Publications:
• Employer Newsbulletin [a publication of the Saskatchewan Registered Nurses' Association]
Type: Newsletter; *Frequency:* Semiannually
Profile: Information about registration, licences, examination dates, bylaws, & resolutions
• RN Connections
Type: Newsletter
Profile: Information for workplace representatives, professional practice groups, special interest groups, & chapters
• Saskatchewan Registered Nurses' Association Annual Report
Type: Yearbook; *Frequency:* Annually
• SRNA [Saskatchewan Registered Nurses' Association] Newsbulletin
Type: Magazine; *Frequency:* Quarterly; *Accepts Advertising*; *Editor:* Shelley Svedahl *ISSN:* 1494-76668; *Price:* $21.40 Canada; $30 international
Profile: Information for RNs about the association's activities, plus topical articles

Saskatchewan Rental Housing Industry Association (SRHIA)

#2, 333 - 4th Ave. North, Saskatoon SK S7K 2L8
Tel: 306-653-7149; *Fax:* 306-665-7548
srhia@shaw.ca
www.srhia.ca
Previous Name: Saskatchewan Landlords Association
Overview: A small provincial organization founded in 1994
Mission: To advocate on behalf of landlords & property managers
Member of: Canadian Federation of Apartment Associations
Chief Officer(s):
Della Thomas, President
Activities: *Speaker Service:* Yes

Saskatchewan Rowing Association (SRA)

510 Cynthia St., Saskatoon SK S7L 7K7
Tel: 306-975-0842; *Fax:* 306-242-8007
saskrowing@sasktel.net
www.saskrowing.ca
Overview: A medium-sized provincial organization founded in 1977 overseen by Rowing Canada Aviron
Mission: To promote & develop the sport of rowing for all individuals in addition to the development of competitive excellence
Member of: Sask Sport; Rowing Canada Aviron
Affliation(s): Rowing Aviron Canada, Saskatchewan Sports Hall of Fame & Museum, Saskatchewan Coaches Association
Chief Officer(s):
John Haver, Provincial Head Coach North
haver_john@hotmail.com
Raymond Blake, President
Raymond.blake@uregina.ca
Finances: *Funding Sources:* Sponsors; Merchandise
Activities: *Internships:* Yes
Awards:
• Member (Award)
• Athlete of the Year Awards (Award)
• Senior (Award)
• Masters (Award)
• Coach (Award)
• Youth (Award)

Saskatchewan Rugby Union (SRU)

#213, 1870 Lorne St., Regina SK S4P 2L7
Tel: 306-975-0895; *Fax:* 306-781-6021
sru@sasktel.net
www.saskrugby.com
www.facebook.com/SaskRugby
Overview: A small provincial charitable organization overseen by Rugby Canada
Mission: To encourage, promote, organize, administer & otherwise regulate the sport of Rugby Union Football in the province of Saskatchewan in accordance with the laws of the game in a safe & proper manner
Member of: Rugby Canada; Sask Sport
Chief Officer(s):
David Kot, President
Finances: *Annual Operating Budget:* $100,000-$250,000
Staff Member(s): 1; 200 volunteer(s)
Membership: 2,500; *Fees:* $1,300/club

Saskatchewan Safety Council

445 Hoffer Dr., Regina SK S4N 6E2
Tel: 306-757-3197; *Fax:* 306-569-1907
sasksafety.org
www.facebook.com/sasksafetycouncil
twitter.com/SkSafetyCouncil
www.flickr.com/sasksafetycouncil
Overview: A small provincial organization founded in 1955
Mission: To inform the public in order that they are able to make sound decisions regarding their safety
Chief Officer(s):
Harley P. Toupin, Chief Executive Officer
Dianne Wolbaum, Director, Operations
Staff Member(s): 21
Membership: *Fees:* Schedule available

Saskatchewan Sailing Clubs Association (SSCA)

510 Cynthia St., Saskatoon SK S7L 7K7
Tel: 306-975-0833
sasksail@sasktel.net
www.sasksail.com
Overview: A small provincial organization overseen by Sail Canada
Mission: To regulate the sport of sailing in Saskatchewan
Member of: Sail Canada
Chief Officer(s):
Mike Ritchie, President, 306-445-5775
mike@mrwebsites.ca
Mark Lammens, Technical Director & Coach

Saskatchewan School Boards Association (SSBA)

#400, 2222 - 13th Ave., Regina SK S4P 3M7
Tel: 306-569-0750; *Fax:* 306-352-9633
admin@saskschoolboards.ca
www.saskschoolboards.ca
Previous Name: Saskatchewan School Trustees Association
Overview: A medium-sized provincial organization founded in 1915 overseen by Canadian School Boards Association
Mission: Represents boards of education, including school division boards, conseils scolaires, & local or district boards; ensures advocacy, leadership & support for member boards of education by speaking as the voice for quality public education for all children; offers opportunities for trustee development; provides information & services
Chief Officer(s):
Darren McKee, Executive Director, 306-569-0750 Ext. 140
dmckee@saskschoolboards.ca
Lori Mann, Director, Corporate Services, 306-569-0750 Ext. 112
lmann@saskschoolboards.ca
Leslie Anderson, Director, Communications Services, 306-569-0750 Ext. 142
landerson@saskschoolboards.ca
Finances: *Annual Operating Budget:* Greater than $5 Million; *Funding Sources:* Membership fees; fees for service
Staff Member(s): 23
Membership: 28; *Fees:* Schedule available
Activities: *Library*

Saskatchewan School Library Association (SSLA)

c/o Saskatchewan Teachers' Federation, 2317 Arlington Ave., Saskatoon SK S7J 2H8
e-mail: sasksla@gmail.com
www.ssla.ca
www.facebook.com/SaskatchewanSchoolLibraryAssociation
twitter.com/SaskSLA
www.pinterest.com/sasksla
Overview: A medium-sized provincial organization founded in 1959
Mission: To develop, improve, & promote school libraries in Saskatchewan in order to enhance student learning
Affliation(s): Saskatchewan Teachers' Federation
Chief Officer(s):
Carlene Walter, President
carlenewalter@gmail.com
Charlotte Raine, Secretary & Archivist
craine@mail.gssd.ca
Dawn Morgan, Treasurer/Membership
dawnmorgan20@gmail.com
Membership: *Fees:* $30 Regular; $35 Associate; $41 Institutional
Activities: Providing information about school library issues; Hosting learning events
Awards:
• Dr. Alixie Hambleton Bursary (Grant)
• Art Forgay Award of Recognition of Administrators (Award)
• Connie Acton Award of Merit (Award)
• John G. Wright Distinguished Service Award (Award)
Meetings/Conferences: • Saskatchewan School Library Association Conference 2015, 2015, SK
Scope: Provincial
Publications:
• The Medium
Type: Journal; *Editor:* Jennifer Climenhaga & C. Walter
Profile: Professional development information, library programs, literacy articles, technolgy & resources for SSLA members
• The SSLA Newsletter
Type: Newsletter; *Frequency:* 3 pa; *Editor:* Hélène Préfontaine
Profile: Information for school library personnel in Saskatchewan

Saskatchewan School Trustees Association *See* Saskatchewan School Boards Association

Saskatchewan Sheep Breeders' Association

c/o Saskatchewan Sheep Development Board, 2213C Hanselman Ct., Saskatoon SK S7L 6A8
e-mail: info@sksheepbreeders.ca
sksheepbreeders.ca
Also Known As: SaskCanada Sheep Industry Development Inc.
Overview: A small provincial organization founded in 1978
Mission: To promote the sheep industry, deal with significant issues & support each other in the raising of high caliber breeding sheep.
Member of: Canadian Sheep Breeders Association
Chief Officer(s):
Clint Wiens, President
Finances: *Funding Sources:* Donations; membership dues
Membership: *Fees:* $21

Saskatchewan Shorthorn Association
c/o Betty Wyatt, PO Box 1528, Carlyle SK S0C 0R0
Tel: 306-557-4664; *Fax:* 306-577-2106
www.sasksshorthorns.com
Overview: A small provincial organization
Mission: To promote the breeding of shorthorn cattle in Saskatchewan.
Member of: Canadian Shorthorn Association
Affiliation(s): Saskatchewan Livestock Association; Saskatchewan Cattle Breeders; Saskatchewan Stockgrowers Association; Canadian Western Agribition
Chief Officer(s):
Betty Wyatt, Secretary
gerrybetty@gmail.com
Arron Huber, President
huberdale@sasktel.net
Membership: 32; *Member Profile:* Purebred shorthorn breeders in Saskatchewan
Activities: Canadian Western Agribition; National Shorthorn Show, Elite Shorthorn Sale; Autumn Alliance Sale; Sponsorship: involved in all 4H youth shows within Saskatchewan

Saskatchewan Ski Association - Skiing for Disabled (SASKI)
1860 Lorne St., Saskatoon SK S4P 2L7
Tel: 306-780-9236; *Fax:* 306-781-6021
sask.ski@sasktel.net
www.saski.ca
Also Known As: SASKI - Skiing for Disabled
Overview: A medium-sized provincial organization founded in 1982 overseen by Canadian Association for Disabled Skiing
Mission: To promote all aspects of winter skiing in Saskatchewan, including alpine, biathlon, cross country & skiing for disabled, & to provide assistance to clubs & individual athletes, instruction & training, adaptive equipment, & a resource library
Member of: Canadian Association for Disabled Skiing
Chief Officer(s):
Alana Ottenbreit, Executive Director
Finances: *Funding Sources:* Provincial lotteries; occasional grants; bingos
Membership: 1,000-4,999
Activities: Alpine/cross country/biathlon/freestyle skiing; skiing for disabled; snowboarding

Saskatchewan Snow Vehicles Association *See*
Saskatchewan Snowmobile Association

Saskatchewan Snowboard Association (SSA)
PO Box 844, Outlook SK S0L 2N0
Tel: 306-867-8489
contact@sasksnowboard.ca
sasksnowboard.ca
www.facebook.com/238209089572128
twitter.com/sasksnowboard
Overview: A small provincial organization overseen by Canadian Snowboard Federation
Mission: To be the provincial governing body of competitive snowboarding in Saskatchewan.
Member of: Canadian Snowboard Federation
Chief Officer(s):
Brent Larwood, President
brent@sasksnowboard.ca
Dave Woods, Coordinator, Sport Development
dave@sasksnowboard.ca

Saskatchewan Snowmobile Association (SSA)
PO Box 533, 221 Centre St., Regina Beach SK S0G 4C0
Tel: 306-729-3500; *Fax:* 306-729-3505
Toll-Free: 800-499-7533
sasksnow@sasktel.net
www.sasksnowmobiling.sk.ca
www.facebook.com/people/Sask-Snow/100001758383580
twitter.com/sasksnow
Previous Name: Saskatchewan Snow Vehicles Association
Overview: A medium-sized provincial organization founded in 1971
Mission: To promote the benefits of snowmobiling & increase access & participation; To provide leadership & support to members; To establish & maintain safe, high quality trails; To provide support to club development
Member of: International Snowmobile Council; Canadian Council of Snowmobile Organizations
Chief Officer(s):
Chris Brewer, President & Chief Executive Officer, 306-729-3506, Fax: 306-729-3505
cb2@sasktel.net
Chelsie Stuermer, Club Coordinator, 306-729-3507, Fax: 306-729-3505
ssa.admin@sasktel.net
Jeannie Brewer, Comptroller, 306-729-3504, Fax: 306-729-3505
jbrewer@sasktel.net
Finances: *Funding Sources:* Membership dues; Saskatchewan Lotteries
20 volunteer(s)
Membership: 5,000; *Fees:* $25 single/family; $50 clubs; $50 dealers/business; *Committees:* Membership; Raffles; Rallies; Grants; Equipment; Safety; Trails
Meetings/Conferences: • Saskatchewan Snowmobile Association 2015 Annual General Meeting & The Diamond in the Snow Awards Banquet, 2015, SK
Scope: Provincial
Description: Reports from the chairman, president & chief executive officer, & discussions about finances & association issues

Saskatchewan Soccer Association Inc. (SSA)
SaskSport Administration Bldg., 1870 Lorne St., Regina SK S4P 2L7
Tel: 306-780-9225; *Fax:* 306-780-9480
adminasst@sasksoccer.com
www.sasksoccer.com
www.facebook.com/SaskatchewanSoccer
twitter.com/SaskSoccerAssoc
www.youtube.com/SaskatchewanSoccer
Overview: A medium-sized provincial organization founded in 1906 overseen by Canadian Soccer Association
Member of: Canadian Soccer Association
Chief Officer(s):
Doug Pederson, Executive Director
d.pederson@sasksoccer.com
Staff Member(s): 10; 12 volunteer(s)
Membership: 33,000
Activities: *Internships:* Yes

Saskatchewan Society for Education through Art (SSEA)
205A Pacific Ave., Saskatoon SK S7K 1N9
Tel: 306-975-0222
Overview: A small provincial organization
Mission: To promote the need for art education in Saskatchewan schools
Member of: Saskatchewan Council of Cultural Organizations

Saskatchewan Society for the Autistic Inc. *See*
Saskatchewan Families for Effective Autism Treatment

Saskatchewan Society for the Prevention of Cruelty to Animals
PO Box 37, Saskatoon SK S7K 3K1
Tel: 306-382-7722; *Fax:* 306-384-3425
Toll-Free: 877-382-7722
info@sspca.ca
www.sspca.ca
www.facebook.com/SaskSPCA
twitter.com/SaskSPCA
www.pinterest.com/saskspca
Also Known As: Saskatchewan SPCA
Overview: A medium-sized provincial organization overseen by Canadian Federation of Humane Societies
Mission: To promote humane treatment of animals
Member of: Canadian Federation of Humane Societies
Chief Officer(s):
Frances Wach, Executive Director, 306-382-4471
Staff Member(s): 10
Membership: *Fees:* $15 junior/senior; $25 single; $35 family; $50 individual/SPCA/humane society; $200 life; $250 business

Saskatchewan Society of Medical Laboratory Technologists (SSMLT)
PO Box 3837, Regina SK S4P 3R8
Tel: 306-352-6791; *Fax:* 306-352-6791
Toll-Free: 877-334-3301
exec.dir@ssmlt.ca
www.ssmlt.ca
Overview: A medium-sized provincial licensing organization founded in 1983 overseen by Canadian Society for Medical Laboratory Science
Mission: To ensure the professional competence of its members, thus contributing to excellence in health care; to promote the nationally accepted standard of medical laboratory technology; to promote, maintain & protect the professional identity & interests of the medical laboratory technologist & of the profession; to support a national system of certification which meets the changing needs of medical laboratory services & which has credibility with employers, governments & academic institutions; to encourage eligible laboratory personnel to seek & maintain membership in the CSMLS & SSMLT & participate in society activities; to encourage & assist members to improve their knowledge & qualifications
Affiliation(s): Canadian Society for Medical Laboratory Science; International Association of Medical Laboratory Technologists
Chief Officer(s):
Del Windrum, Executive Director
Finances: *Funding Sources:* Membership fees
Staff Member(s): 2
Membership: *Member Profile:* Practicing - working as a medical laboratory technologist; Non-practicing - not working; *Committees:* Counselling & Investigation; Education Marketing & Development; Discipline; Regulatory Affairs
Activities: *Library:* SSMLT Loan Library
Awards:
• MDS-Raymond LePage Scholarship (Scholarship)
• Honorary Membership (Award)
• Special Recognition Award (Award)
• Wheatland Bounty Professional Development Grant (Grant)
• Wheatland Bounty Professional Development Scholarship (Scholarship)

Saskatchewan Society of Occupational Therapists (SSOT)
PO Box 9089, Saskatoon SK S7K 7E7
Tel: 306-956-7768; *Fax:* 306-242-7941
admin@ssot.sk.ca
www.ssot.sk.ca
Overview: A small provincial licensing organization founded in 1971
Mission: To register & maintain a current listing of individuals whom SSOT has approved to practise occupational therapy in Saskatchewan; to develop & enforce standards of practice; to facilitate the development & strengthening of the profession & of individual members by providing a network for formal & informal communication, by encouraging & providing opportunities for continuing education & research; to promote awareness of the profession & the society by representing the occupational therapy point of view during interactions with other health care professions, employers, educational institutions, government, the media, & special interest groups
Member of: Canadian Association of Occupational Therapists
Chief Officer(s):
Coralie Lennea, Executive Director
ed@ssot.sk.ca
Finances: *Annual Operating Budget:* $50,000-$100,000; *Funding Sources:* Membership fees
Staff Member(s): 2; 8 volunteer(s)
Membership: 230; *Fees:* $398 full-time member; *Member Profile:* Degree or equivalent in OT & completion of approved exams; *Committees:* Public Relations; Education; Professional Development Fund; Professional Conduct; Discipline; Credentials; Finance; Nominations; Awards; Legislative; AGM; Professional Practice; Government Affairs
Activities: *Rents Mailing List:* Yes
Awards:
• Outstanding Contributions to the Community (Award)
• Outstanding Contributions to Society (Award)
• Outstanding Contributions to the Profession (Award)
• Clinical Teaching Award (Award)
• Clinical Fieldwork Award (Award)

Saskatchewan Society of X-Ray Technicians *See*
Saskatchewan Association of Medical Radiation Technologists

Saskatchewan Soil Conservation Association (SSCA)
PO Box 1360, Indian Head SK S0G 2K0
Tel: 306-695-4233; *Fax:* 306-695-4236
Toll-Free: 800-213-4287
info@ssca.ca
www.ssca.ca
Overview: A small provincial charitable organization founded in 1987
Mission: To improve the land & environment; To increase public awareness of soil conservation; To promote conservation production systems to Saskatchewan producers
Chief Officer(s):
Tim Nerbas, President
tnerbas@ssca.ca
Marilyn Martens, Office Manager, 306-695-4233
Finances: *Funding Sources:* Donations; Federal-Provincial sustainable agriculture programs

Membership: 800; *Member Profile:* Farmers in Saskatchewan
Activities: Sharing soil conservation information
Meetings/Conferences: • Saskatchewan Soil Conservation Association 2015 27th Annual Conservation Agriculture Conference, 2015, SK
Scope: Provincial
Description: A meeting during Crop Production Week
Contact Information: Office Manager: Marilyn Martens, Phone: 306-695-4233
Publications:
• Direct Seeding Manual
Type: Manual
Profile: Developed & published with the Prairie Agricultural Machinery Institute for Saskatchewan growers
• Prairie Soils & Crops eJournal
Type: Journal
Profile: Peer-reviewed information from the Saskatchewan Soil Conservation Association, Agriculture & Agri-Food Canada, & the University of Saskatchewan for prairie producers & agrologists
• Prairie Steward
Type: Newsletter; *Frequency:* 3 pa
Profile: Association news & technical articles for Saskatchewan Soil Conservation Association members

Saskatchewan Special Olympics Society *See* Special Olympics Saskatchewan

Saskatchewan Speed Skating Association *See* Saskatchewan Amateur Speed Skating Association

Saskatchewan Sports Hall of Fame & Museum (SSFHM)
2205 Victoria Ave., Regina SK S4P 0S4
Tel: 306-780-9232; *Fax:* 306-780-9427
sshfm@sasktel.net
www.sshfm.com
www.facebook.com/SaskSportsHF
twitter.com/SaskSportsHF
Overview: A small provincial charitable organization founded in 1966 overseen by Sask Sport Inc.
Mission: To recognize sport excellence, preserve sport history & educate the public on the contribution of sport to Saskatchewan's cultural fabric
Member of: Canadian Museums Association; Museums Association of Saskatchewan; Canadian Association for Sports Heritage; International Association of Sport Museums & Halls of Fame
Chief Officer(s):
Sheila Kelly, Executive Director
skelly@sshfm.com
Finances: *Annual Operating Budget:* $250,000-$500,000; *Funding Sources:* Lotteries & self-help
Staff Member(s): 4; 95 volunteer(s)
Membership: 1,450; *Fees:* $25 individuals; $40 family; $50 associations; $75 corporate
Activities: Museum galleries, archives, research facilities; Induction dinner; Annual Hall of Fame Game (Football); *Speaker Service:* Yes; *Library* by appointment

Saskatchewan Square & Round Dance Federation
SK
Tel: 306-463-3620
www.sksquaredance.ca
Overview: A medium-sized provincial organization founded in 1979 overseen by Canadian Square & Round Dance Society
Mission: To guide & promote Square & Round Dancing & Clogging throughout the province as a recreation for people of all ages & in all walks of life to enjoy
Member of: Canadian Square & Round Dance Society
Chief Officer(s):
Pat Campbell, Co-President
Earl Campbell, Co-President
Finances: *Funding Sources:* National conventions; membership dues; Saskatchewan Lotteries

Saskatchewan Squash
214 Wickenden Cres., Saskatoon SK S7N 3X7
Tel: 306-280-4320
sasksquash@gmail.com
www.sasksquash.com
www.facebook.com/SaskSquash
Overview: A medium-sized provincial organization overseen by Squash Canada
Member of: Squash Canada
Chief Officer(s):
Brad Birnie, Executive Director
Membership: *Fees:* $10

Saskatchewan Stock Growers Association (SSGA)
Main Floor, Canada Centre Building, Evraz Place, PO Box 4752, Regina SK S4P 3Y4
Tel: 306-757-8523; *Fax:* 306-569-8799
skstockgrowers.com
Overview: A medium-sized provincial organization founded in 1913
Mission: To serve, protect, & advance the interests of the beef industry in Saskatchewan; To represent the cattle industry in Saskatchewan on the legislative front
Member of: Canadian Cattlemen's Association
Affliation(s): Saskatchewan Prairie Conservation Action Plan (SK PCAP) Partnership
Chief Officer(s):
Chad MacPherson, General Manager
Harold Martens, President
mranchltd@shaw.ca
Finances: *Funding Sources:* Membership fees
Membership: *Fees:* $105 active/associate; $262.50-$525 affiliate; *Member Profile:* Active members are individuals engaged in livestock production in Saskatchewan; Affiliate members are groups that are engaged in livestock marketing; Associate members have an interest in the industry; *Committees:* Beef; Policy/Trade; Land Use; Promotional
Activities: Providing education; Engaging in research; Advocating on behalf of the beef industry
Awards:
• Stewardship Award (Award)
To recognize excellence & environmental stewardship in the ranching industry
Publications:
• Beef Business
Type: Magazine; *Frequency:* Bimonthly; *Accepts Advertising*; *Editor:* Jim Warren; *Price:* Included with SSGA membership
Profile: Industry news, markets & trade, features, analysis & opinion, science & productions, association news & reports, & stewardship

Saskatchewan Swine Breeders' Association
c/o Saskatechwan Livestock Association, PO Box 3771, Regina SK S4P 3N8
Tel: 306-757-6133; *Fax:* 306-525-5852
sla@accesscomm.ca
Overview: A small provincial organization
Mission: To support improved swine breeding practices; to establish & maintain a recognized organization to represent & voice the concerns & interests of swine breeders in Saskatchewan; to foster better swine health & management practices
Member of: Purebred Swine Breeders' Association of Canada
Membership: *Member Profile:* Swine producers

Saskatchewan Table Tennis Association Inc. (STTA)
John V. Remai Centre, 510 Cynthia St., Saskatoon SK S7N 7K7
Tel: 306-975-0835
sktta@shaw.ca
www.sktta.ca
www.facebook.com/422614287776110
twitter.com/SKTableTennis
Overview: A small provincial organization overseen by Table Tennis Canada
Mission: To promote & govern the sport of table tennis in saskatchewan.
Member of: Table Tennis Canada; Sask Sport
Affiliation(s): International Table Tennis Federation
Chief Officer(s):
Robert Chan, President
Dwayne Yachiw, Executive Director
Membership: 2,200; *Fees:* $125 school club, communtiy club; $75 junior & senior development; $20 individual junior; $30 individual senior
Activities: *Rents Mailing List:* Yes

Saskatchewan Teachers' Federation (STF) / Fédération des enseignants et des enseignantes de la Saskatchewan
2317 Arlington Ave., Saskatoon SK S7J 2H8
Tel: 306-373-1660; *Fax:* 306-374-1122
Toll-Free: 800-667-7762
stf@stf.sk.ca
www.stf.sk.ca
Overview: A medium-sized provincial organization overseen by Canadian Teachers' Federation
Mission: To help provide the best possible education to children
Chief Officer(s):
Colin Keess, President
provincial.executive@stf.sk.ca
Gwen Dueck, Executive Director
administrative.staff@stf.sk.ca
Membership: 12,000; *Member Profile:* Teachers & students enrolled in teachers' college; *Committees:* Economic Services; Social & Political Advocacy; Professional Stewardship & Responsibility; Ethics; Collective Interests; Professional Competency
Activities: *Library:* Stewart Resource Centre; Open to public

Saskatchewan Tennis Association *See* Tennis Saskatchewan

Saskatchewan Trade & Export Partnership Inc. (STEP)
PO Box 1787, #320, 1801 Hamilton St., Regina SK S4P 3C6
Tel: 306-933-6551; *Fax:* 306-933-6556
Toll-Free: 888-976-7875
inquire@sasktrade.com
www.sasktrade.com
Overview: A medium-sized provincial organization founded in 1996
Mission: To work in partnership with Saskatchewan exporters & emerging exporters to maximize commercial success in global ventures; To deliver custom export solutions & market intelligence to member companies; To coordinate international development projects
Chief Officer(s):
Lionel LaBelle, President & Chief Executive Officer, 306-787-1550
Angela Krauss, Executive Director, Export Services, 306-787-3972
Brad Michnik, Executive Director, Trade Development, 306-933-6555
Pam Bartoshewski, Controller, 306-787-7946
Finances: *Funding Sources:* Private & public funding
Membership: 426; *Member Profile:* Saskatchewan exporters & companies providing services to exporters
Activities: Providing market intelligence, international finance solutions, export education, & marketing services; *Library*
Publications:
• STEP Global Newsletter
Type: Newsletter; *Frequency:* Quarterly

Saskatchewan Triathlon Association Corporation (STAC)
PO Box 21008, Saskatoon SK S7H 5N9
Tel: 306-292-8270; *Fax:* 306-477-0495
info@triathlonsaskatchewan.org
www.triathlonsaskatchewan.org
www.facebook.com/287275596696
twitter.com/SaskTriathlon
Overview: A small provincial organization overseen by Triathlon Canada
Mission: To be the provincial governing body of triathlon in Saskatchewan.
Member of: Triathlon Canada
Chief Officer(s):
Mark Gibson, President
Fred Dyck, Executive Director

Saskatchewan Trucking Association (STA)
1335 Wallace St., Regina SK S4N 3Z5
Tel: 306-569-9696; *Fax:* 306-569-1008
Toll-Free: 800-563-7623
www.sasktrucking.com
Overview: A medium-sized provincial licensing organization founded in 1937 overseen by Canadian Trucking Alliance
Mission: To help the industry fight its battles in everything from deregulation to weights and measures; to represent the industry in discussions with government
Chief Officer(s):
Al Rosseker, Executive Director
arosseker@sasktrucking.com
Finances: *Funding Sources:* Membership fees; sponsorship of programs
Staff Member(s): 3
Membership: *Fees:* Schedule available
Activities: Truck Driver Roadeos
Awards:
• Safe Driver Award Program (Award)

Saskatchewan Turkey Producers' Marketing Board (STPMB)
1438 Fletcher Rd., Saskatoon SK S7M 5T2
Tel: 306-931-1050; *Fax:* 306-931-2825
saskaturkey@sasktel.net

Overview: A small provincial organization
Mission: To manage the supply managed system in Saskatchewan, which includes negotiating the province's quota levels with the CTMA, negotiating price levels with local processors and developing a long-term strategic focus for Saskatchewan's turkey industry
Member of: Turkey Farmers of Canada
Chief Officer(s):
Rose Olson, Executive Director
Finances: *Annual Operating Budget:* $250,000-$500,000; *Funding Sources:* Levy on production
Staff Member(s): 1
Membership: 12; *Fees:* $5

The Saskatchewan Underwater Council Inc.
PO Box 7651, Saskatoon SK S7K 4R4
Tel: 306-374-8341; *Fax:* 306-374-8341
executive@saskuc.com
www.saskuc.com
Overview: A small provincial organization
Mission: To represent those interested in underwater activities in Saskatchewan.
Chief Officer(s):
Cliff Lange, Contact
Membership: *Fees:* $30 single; $35 family

Saskatchewan Union of Nurses (SUN) / Syndicat des infirmières de la Saskatchewan
2330 - 2nd Ave., Regina SK S4R 1A6
Tel: 306-525-1666; *Fax:* 306-522-4612
Toll-Free: 800-667-7060
regina@sun-nurses.sk.ca
www.sun-nurses.sk.ca
www.facebook.com/SUNnurses
twitter.com/sunnurses
Overview: A medium-sized provincial organization founded in 1974
Mission: To advocate to protect the rights of members; to enhance the socio-economic & general welfare of members through collective bargaining, research, & education
Affliation(s): Saskatchewan Federation of Labour; Canadian Labour Congress; Canadian Federation of Nurses Unions; Saskatchewan Registered Nurses' Association; Registered Psychiatric Nurses Association of Saskatchewan; Canadian Nurses Association
Chief Officer(s):
Tracy Zambory, President
tracy.zambory@sun-nurses.sk.ca
Donna Trainor, Executive Director
donna.trainor@sun-nurses.sk.ca
Finances: *Funding Sources:* Membership dues
Membership: 9,000

Saskatchewan Urban Municipalities Association (SUMA)
#200, 2222 - 13th Ave., Regina SK S4P 3M7
Tel: 306-525-3727; *Fax:* 306-525-4373
suma@suma.org
www.suma.org
Overview: A medium-sized provincial organization founded in 1906
Mission: To work to enhance urban life in Saskatchewan, by providing administrative & consultative services to members, a forum for the discussion & resolution of current issues, & a negotiating vehicle for improvements in legislation, financing & programs. SUMA provides information & training for aldermen & mayors, and group benefits for its members
Member of: Federation of Canadian Municipalities
Chief Officer(s):
Laurent Mougeot, CEO
lmougeot@suma.org
Sean McEachern, Director, Policy & Communication
smceachern@suma.org
Finances: *Funding Sources:* Membership fees
Staff Member(s): 14
Membership: 450 municipalities
Activities: Group Benefits; Group Purchasing; *Rents Mailing List:* Yes
Awards:
• Honourary, Meritorius, Life Awards (Award)
Meetings/Conferences: • Saskatchewan Urban Municipalities Association (SUMA) 110th Annual Convention and Tradeshow 2015, February, 2015, TCU Place, Saskatoon, SK
Scope: Provincial
Contact Information: registration@suma.org
• Saskatchewan Urban Municipalities Association (SUMA) 111th Annual Convention and Tradeshow 2016, 2016
Scope: Provincial

Saskatchewan Veterinary Medical Association (SVMA)
#202, 224 Pacific Ave., Saskatoon SK S7K 1N9
Tel: 306-955-7862; *Fax:* 306-975-0623
svma@svma.sk.ca
www.svma.sk.ca
Overview: A small provincial licensing organization overseen by Canadian Veterinary Medical Association
Mission: To protect the public by ensuring the proficiency, competency & ethical behaviour of its members in the practice of veterinary medicine; to license veterinarians; to approve practices; to discipline members as required; to promote veterinary medicine by supporting the physical, personal & financial well-being of members through continuing education & professional interaction
Chief Officer(s):
Judy Currie, Registrar & Secretary-Treasurer
jacurrie@svma.sk.ca
Sue Gauthier, Co-ordinator, Communications & Member Services
sgauthier@svma.sk.ca
Staff Member(s): 3
Membership: *Fees:* Schedule available
Publications:
• SVMA News
Type: Newsletter; *Frequency:* Quarterly; *Accepts Advertising*; *Number of Pages:* 35

Saskatchewan Voice of People with Disabilities, Inc. (SVOPD)
984 Albert St., Regina SK S4R 2P7
Tel: 306-569-3111; *Fax:* 306-569-1889
Toll-Free: 877-569-3111; *TTY:* 306-569-3111
Other Communication: pinterest.com/SVOPD
voice@saskvoice.com
www.saskvoice.com
www.facebook.com/SaskVoice
twitter.com/SVOPD
www.youtube.com/user/SaskVoice
Also Known As: Sask Voice
Previous Name: Saskatchewan Voice of the Handicapped
Overview: A medium-sized provincial charitable organization founded in 1973
Mission: To act as a voice for people with disabilities throughout Saskatchewan; To participate in the life of society without discrimination; To increase employment opportunities, accessible housing & tranportation, & family support services
Member of: Council of Canadians with Disabilities
Chief Officer(s):
Mauride Bourassa, Chair
Bev Duncan, Executive Director
Bev@saskvoice.com
George Thomas, Treasurer
Doron Giroux, Administrative Assistant
doron@saskvoice.com
Finances: *Annual Operating Budget:* $100,000-$250,000; *Funding Sources:* Donations; Fundraising; Grants; Social Services; CCD
Staff Member(s): 3; 5 volunteer(s)
Membership: *Fees:* $10; *Committees:* DISC, PIND, PIAT, DESK, SKF, IF
Activities: Advocating for services to assist people with disabilities in Saskatchewan; Raising awareness of the needs of people with disabilities & the Independent Living Model; Liaising with Disabled First Nation People & other groups with similar interests; Developing local chapters; *Awareness Events:* The United Nations International Day for Person with Disabilities, December 3; *Library:* Saskatchewan Voice of People with Disabilities Resource Library
Meetings/Conferences: • End Exclusion, 2015
Scope: Provincial
Publications:
• Prairie Voice
Type: Newsletter; *Frequency:* Quarterly; *Accepts Advertising*; *Editor:* Amber-Jay Boyd; *Price:* $10/year
Profile: Information for persons with disabilities in Saskatchewan

Saskatchewan Voice of the Handicapped ***See*** Saskatchewan Voice of People with Disabilities, Inc.

Saskatchewan Volleyball Association
1750 McAra St., Regina SK S4N 6L4
Tel: 306-780-9250; *Fax:* 306-780-9288
meta@saskvolleyball.ca
www.saskvolleyball.ca
www.facebook.com/groups/121947301797
Overview: A small provincial organization overseen by Volleyball Canada
Mission: To develop interest, participation & excellence in volleyball through the promotion & provision of quality services for all
Chief Officer(s):
Charlene Callander, President
Aaron Demyen, Executive Director, 306-780-9801
aaron@saskvolleyball.ca
Tammy Schneider, Office Manager
officemanager@saskvolleyball.ca
Finances: *Annual Operating Budget:* $500,000-$1.5 Million; *Funding Sources:* Lotteries
Staff Member(s): 5; 2200 volunteer(s)
Membership: 5,000-14,999

Saskatchewan Wall & Ceiling Bureau Inc.
532 - 2 Ave. North, Saskatoon SK S7K 2C5
Tel: 306-359-3282; *Fax:* 306-569-0260
Overview: A small provincial organization overseen by Northwest Wall & Ceiling Bureau
Mission: To promote quality workmanship in Saskatchewan's wall & ceiling industry
Chief Officer(s):
Eric Donnelly, President
edonnelly@westcor.ca
Membership: *Member Profile:* Manufacturers, suppliers, & contractors involved in Saskatchewan's wall & ceiling industry
Activities: Offering networking opportunities for the exchange of information & experience

Saskatchewan Waste Reduction Council (SWRC)
The Two-Twenty, #208, 220 - 20th St. West, Saskatoon SK S7M 0W9
Tel: 306-931-3242; *Fax:* 306-955-5852
info@saskwastereduction.ca
www.saskwastereduction.ca
Overview: A medium-sized provincial charitable organization founded in 1991
Mission: To lead in addressing the underlying causes of waste by identifying opportunities, creating connections & promoting solutions.
Chief Officer(s):
Joanne Fedyk, Executive Director
joanne@saskwastereduction.ca
Martha Hollinger, Contact, Member Services & Administration
martha@saskwastereduction.ca
Staff Member(s): 3
Membership: 150; *Fees:* Schedule available
Activities: *Awareness Events:* Waste Reduction Week; *Speaker Service:* Yes
Awards:
• Waste Minimization Awards (Award)
Eligibility: Categories: Individual Adult, Youth/School, Corporate Leadership, Non-profit Organization, Municipality, Partnerships*Deadline:* Feb.
Meetings/Conferences: • Saskatchewan Waste Reduction Council Waste ReForum 2015, April, 2015, Sheraton Cavalier, Saskatoon, SK
Scope: Provincial
Description: Workshops & sessions on environmental issues
Publications:
• SWRC Report
Frequency: a.

Saskatchewan Water & Wastewater Association (SWWA)
PO Box 7831, Saskatoon SK S7K 4R5
Tel: 306-761-1278; *Fax:* 306-761-1279
Toll-Free: 888-668-1278
office@swwa.ca
www.swwa.sk.ca
www.facebook.com/SaskatchewanWaterAndWastewaterAssociation
twitter.com/SWWA_2012
Overview: A medium-sized provincial organization
Mission: Dedicated to the professional operation and maintenance of water & wastewater facilities
Chief Officer(s):
Randy Antoniuk, President
rantoniuk@citypa.com

Membership: *Fees:* $42; *Member Profile:* People involved in the operation, maintenance & troubleshooting of water & wastewater systems
Activities: Hosting workshops & training sessions; Providing access to job opportunities; Publishing a newsletter; Providing certification through the Operator Certification Board
Meetings/Conferences: • Saskatchewan Water and Wastewater Association 2015 Conference & Trade Show, November, 2015, TCU Place Saskatoon, Saskatoon, SK
Scope: National
Publications:
• The Pipeline
Type: Newsletter; *Frequency:* Quarterly
Profile: Latest association news; events in the province & elsewhere

Saskatchewan Water Polo Association *See* Water Polo Saskatchewan Inc.

Saskatchewan Water Ski Association *See* Water Ski & Wakeboard Saskatchewan

Saskatchewan Water Well Association *See* Saskatchewan Ground Water Association

Saskatchewan Weekly Newspapers Association (SWNA)

#14, 401 - 45th St. West, Saskatoon SK S7L 5Z9
Tel: 306-382-9683; *Fax:* 306-382-9421
Toll-Free: 800-661-7962
www.swna.com
www.facebook.com/sask.newspaper
twitter.com/swnainfo
Overview: A medium-sized provincial organization founded in 1913 overseen by Canadian Community Newspapers Association
Mission: To assist persons to issue press releases, buy advertising, & place classifieds in member newspapers in central Saskatchewan & the Northwest Territories
Chief Officer(s):
Steven Nixon, Executive Director, 306-382-9683 Ext. 301
Rob Clark, President
Louise Simpson, Treasurer & Office Manager, 306-382-9683 Ext. 308
Staff Member(s): 8
Membership: 86; *Member Profile:* Weekly newspapers in the central part of Saskatchewan & the Northwest Territories
Activities: Offering a press monitor & clipping service
Awards:
• Junior Citizen of the Week (Award)
• Better Newspapers Competition (Award)

Saskatchewan Wheelchair Sports Association (SWSA)

510 Cynthia St., Saskatoon SK S7L 7K7
Tel: 306-975-0824; *Fax:* 306-975-0825
info@swsa.ca
www.swsa.ca
www.facebook.com/182080694193
twitter.com/skwcsports
www.youtube.com/user/SKWheelchairSports
Overview: A small provincial organization founded in 1977
Mission: Dedicated to developing & supporting opportunities for children, teens & adults with disabilities to participate in the Association's sport, recreation & leisure time activities to the best of their abilities.
Member of: Canadian Wheelchair Sports Association

Saskatchewan Wildlife Federation (SWF)

9 Lancaster Rd., Moose Jaw SK S6J 1M8
Tel: 306-692-8812; *Fax:* 306-692-4370
Toll-Free: 877-793-9453
sask.wildlife@sasktel.net
www.swf.sk.ca
www.facebook.com/pages/Saskatchewan-Wildlife-Federation/178255362147
Overview: A medium-sized provincial charitable organization founded in 1929 overseen by Canadian Wildlife Federation
Mission: To promote the wise use & management of natural resources in Saskatchewan
Chief Officer(s):
Darrell Crabbe, Executive Director
dcrabbe.swf@sasktel.net
Ray Wild, President, 306-731-2718
Marilee Herone, Manager, Office
mheron.swf@sasktel.net
Maureen Horrocks, Coordinator, Communications
maureenhorrocks@gmail.com
Jim Kroshus, Coordinator, Habitat Trust Land
jkroshus.swf@sasktel.net
Adam Matichuk, Coordinator, Fisheries Project
amatichuk.swf@sasktel.net
JeanAnne Prysliak, Coordinator, Education Program
jprysliak.swf@sasktel.net
Finances: *Funding Sources:* Membership fees; Donations; Fundraising
Membership: 30,000+
Activities: Advocating on behalf of members; *Awareness Events:* Great Canadian Shoreline Cleanup, September
Meetings/Conferences: • Saskatchewan Wildlife Federation 2015 86th Annual Convention, February, 2015, Weyburn, SK
Scope: Provincial
Description: A yearly gathering of members, featuring the presentation of awards
Contact Information: Receptionist/Clerk: Dianne Bloski
Publications:
• Outdoor Edge [a publication of the Saskatchewan Wildlife Federation]
Type: Magazine; *Price:* Free with Saskatchewan Wildlife Federation membership

Elbow & District Wildlife Federation
c/o Village of Elbow, PO Box 8, 201 Saskatchewan St., Elbow SK S0H 1J0
Tel: 306-854-2277; *Fax:* 306-854-2229
recdirector@elbowsask.com
elbowsask.com
Member of: Saskatchewan Wildlife Federation

Moose Jaw Wildlife Federation
1396 - 3rd Ave. NE, Moose Jaw SK S6H 0A1
Tel: 306-693-4047
MJWildlife.Federation@gmail.com
sites.google.com/site/moosejawwildlife
Member of: Saskatchewan Wildlife Federation
Chief Officer(s):
Doreen Dodd, Contact, 306-692-4148
doreendodd@sasktel.net

Regina Wildlife Federation
PO Box 594, Regina SK S4P 3A3
Tel: 306-359-7733
rwf1@accesscomm.ca
nonprofits.accesscomm.ca/rwf
Mission: The RWF is a non-profit wildlife conservation organization.
Member of: Saskatchewan Wildlife Federation
Chief Officer(s):
Gil White, President
gilwhite@sasktel.net

Saskatoon Wildlife Federation
PO Box 32041, Saskatoon SK S7S 1N8
Tel: 306-242-1666; *Fax:* 306-933-0617
www.saskatoonwildlifefederation.com
Mission: Saskatoon Wildlife Federation is a non-profit organization committed to providing a clean welcoming enviroment for individuals who enjoy hunting, fishing and various other outdoor sports. The organization works closely with Ducks Unlimited and other groups to preserve wetlands and other wildspaces for habitat.
Member of: Saskatchewan Wildlife Federation

Weyburn Wildlife Federation
415 - 3 Ave. NW, Weyburn SK S4H 1R2
Tel: 306-842-7658
Member of: Saskatchewan Wildlife Federation

Saskatchewan Women's Institute (SWI)

103 Ross Dr., Yorkton SK S3N 3Z9
Tel: 306-782-3570
Overview: A medium-sized provincial organization founded in 1911 overseen by Federated Women's Institutes of Canada
Mission: To help discover, stimulate & develop leadership among women; to assist, encourage & support women to become knowledgeable & responsible citizens; to ensure basic human rights for women & to work towards their equality; to be a strong voice through which matters of the utmost concern can reach the decision makers; to promote the improvement of agricultural & other rural communities & to safeguard the environment
Member of: Associated Country Women of the World
Finances: *Funding Sources:* Membership fees; fundraising

Saskatchewan Writers Guild (SWG)

PO Box 3986, Regina SK S4P 3R9
Tel: 306-757-6310; *Fax:* 306-565-8554
info@skwriter.com
www.skwriter.com
www.facebook.com/groups/5067566475
twitter.com/SKWritersGuild
Overview: A medium-sized provincial charitable organization founded in 1969
Mission: To promote excellence in writing by Saskatchewan writers; to advocate for Saskatchewan writers; to promote the teaching of Saskatchewan & Canadian literature & instruction in the art of writing at all levels of education; to improve public access to writers & their work; to develop professionalism in the business of writing; to improve the economic status of Saskatchewan writers
Member of: Saskatchewan Council of Cultural Organizations
Chief Officer(s):
Judith Silverthorne, Executive Director, 306-791-7742
edswg@skwriter.com
Milena Dzordeski, Administrative Assistant, 306-791-7740
Finances: *Annual Operating Budget:* $500,000-$1.5 Million; *Funding Sources:* Government grants & membership fees
Staff Member(s): 5; 10 volunteer(s)
Membership: 550 individuals; *Fees:* $65 regular; $45 students/seniors; *Member Profile:* Represents writers in all disciplines & at all levels of development
Activities: Readings & school visits; workshops; Provincial reading series; The Caroline Heath Memorial Lecture; Mentorship Program; Manuscript Evaluation Service; Award Program; administers the Resident Writer Program; Saskatchewan Writers/Artists Colonies & Retreats; The Writers' Assistance Fund (WAF); *Speaker Service:* Yes
Awards:
• Writing Scholarships (Scholarship)
John V. Hicks Scholarship, The Jerry Rush Scholarship & the Saskatchewan Playwrights Centre Scholarship; also the $200 Saskatchewan Story Scholarship is administered by SWC & funded by the Story family
• City of Regina Writing Award (Award)
To a Regina writer to reward merit & enable a writer to work on a specific writing project; funded by the City of Regina Arts Commission & administered by the SWG *Amount:* $4,000
• Hicks Award (Award)
Amount: $1,000

Saskatchewan/Manitoba Gelbvieh Association

PO Box 379, Hudson Bay SK S0E 0Y0
Tel: 306-865-2929; *Fax:* 306-865-2860
firriver@xolornet.com
Previous Name: Manitoba/Saskatchewan Gelbvieh Association
Overview: A small local organization
Member of: Canadian Gelbvieh Association
Chief Officer(s):
Darcy Hrebeniuk, Contact
Membership: 39

Saskatoon & District Chamber of Commerce *See* Greater Saskatoon Chamber of Commerce

Saskatoon & District Labour Council (SDLC)

#110B, 2103 Airport Rd., Saskatoon SK S7L 6W2
Tel: 306-384-0303; *Fax:* 306-382-3642
sdlc@sasktel.net
www.saskatoondlc.ca
Overview: A medium-sized local organization overseen by Saskatchewan Federation of Labour
Mission: To support local unions in Saskatoon & the surrounding area; To advance the economic & social welfare of workers
Chief Officer(s):
Kelly Harrington, President, 306-652-1011 Ext. 225
kelly.harrington@seiu333.org
Craig Thebaud, First Vice-President
Dana Hough, Second Vice-President
Tracy Goodheart, Recording Secretary
Andrea Howe, Treasurer
Tom Howe, Registrar
Lily Olson, Coordinator, Labour Programs & Services
Activities: Hosting council meetings & activities to share information on issues that affect unions; Promoting interests of affiliates; Engaging in municipal political action; Presenting educational opportunities; Raising awareness of workplace injuries & deaths, & advocating for the strengthening & enforcing of health & safety rules; Organizing a commemorative service to mark the annual National Day of Mourning For Workers Killed or Injured On The Job; Networking with community organizations;

Meetings/Conferences: • Saskatoon & District Labour Council 2015 Annual General Meeting, 2015, SK
Scope: Local
Contact Information: Registrar: Donna Rederburg

Saskatoon City Police Association (SCPA) / Association de la police de la ville de Saskatoon

PO Box 170, Saskatoon SK S7K 3K4
Tel: 306-652-5662
scpa@sasktel.net
www.spassoc.ca
Overview: A small local organization founded in 1926
Mission: To establish friendly relationship between all members of police department; To encourage & strengthen cooperation between Chief of Police, Board of Police Commissioners, members of police department, Saskatoon, & those charged with enforcement of law & order
Member of: Canadian Police Association; Saskatchewan Federation of Police Officers
Affliation(s): Canadian Professional Police Association
Chief Officer(s):
Wally Romanuck, Treasurer
Stan Goertzen, President
Membership: 100-499

Saskatoon Civic Middle Management Association (SCMMA)

PO Box 151, Saskatoon SK S7K 3K4
scmma.org
Overview: A small local organization founded in 1996
Chief Officer(s):
Roger Bradley, President
Membership: 220+

Saskatoon Coin Club

PO Box 1674, Saskatoon SK S7K 3R8
e-mail: info@saskatooncoinclub.ca
www.saskatooncoinclub.ca
Overview: A small local organization founded in 1960
Membership: *Fees:* Free

Saskatoon Community Foundation

#101, 308 - Fourth Ave. North, Saskatoon SK S7K 2L7
Tel: 306-665-1766; *Fax:* 306-665-1777
office@saskatooncommunityfoundation.ca
www.saskatooncommunityfoundation.ca
Previous Name: The Saskatoon Foundation
Overview: A small local organization founded in 1970
Mission: To provide a significant & sustaining contribution to the quality of life in Saskatoon & area through stewardship, strategic grant making, & community leadership
Member of: Community Foundations of Canada
Chief Officer(s):
Trevor Forrest, Executive Director
Trevor.Forrest@saskatooncommunityfoundation.ca
Don Ewles, Manager, Grants & Communications
Don.Ewles@saskatooncommunityfoundation.ca
Susan Skrypnyk, Manager, Administration
susan.skrypnyk@saskatooncommunityfoundation.ca
Kristy Rempel, Manager, Donor Services
kristy.rempel@saskatooncommunityfoundation.ca
Finances: *Funding Sources:* Donations
Membership: *Committees:* Asset Development; Grants; Investment
Activities: *Speaker Service:* Yes

Saskatoon Construction Association

532 - 2 Ave. North, Saskatoon SK S7K 2C5
Tel: 306-653-1771; *Fax:* 306-653-3515
www.saskatooncaonline.ca
www.facebook.com/buildyxe
twitter.com/buildyxe
www.youtube.com/channel/UCxP5C9E2GeA4A9rul-Fpn6g
Overview: A small provincial organization overseen by Canadian Construction Association
Mission: To provide current information on construction procurement opportunities, networking opportunities, educational events and industry activities for its members
Chief Officer(s):
Deb Labersweiler, Executive Director
deb@saskatooncaonline.ca
Membership: *Fees:* $825 associate; $1030 affiliate; $1350 full; *Committees:* Finance/Governance; Government & Industry Relations; Nominations; Membership & Promotion; Bid Depository; Social; Bonspiel; Gala; Golf; Education; Young Executives; Safety & Environment

Saskatoon Crisis Intervention Service

#103, 506 - 25th St. East, Saskatoon SK S7K 4A7
Tel: 306-664-4525; *Fax:* 306-664-1974; *Crisis Hot-Line:* 306-933-6200
info@saskatooncrisis.ca
www.saskatooncrisis.ca
Also Known As: Mobile Crisis
Overview: A small provincial organization founded in 1980
Mission: To respond to crisis situations: suicide intervention, child abuse & neglect, marriage & family problems, mental health crisis intervention, drug & alcohol abuse, seniors in distress & individual crisis counselling; response may be on the telephone, in the office or in the community
Finances: *Funding Sources:* United Way

Saskatoon Farmers' Markets (SFM)

414 Avenue B South, Saskatoon SK S7M 1M8
Tel: 306-384-6262; *Fax:* 306-384-4850
skfarm@sasktel.net
www.saskatoonfarmersmarket.com
Overview: A small provincial organization founded in 1975 overseen by Farmers' Markets Canada
Mission: Providing residents and visitors the best in local agricultural products, baking, prepared foods and crafts.

Saskatoon Food Bank & Learning Centre

202 Ave. C South, Saskatoon SK S7M 1N2
Tel: 306-664-6565; *Fax:* 306-664-6563
office.admin@saskatoonfoodbank.org
www.saskatoonfoodbank.org
www.facebook.com/saskatoonfoodbank
twitter.com/yxeFoodBank
www.youtube.com/user/SaskatoonFoodBank
Also Known As: Grassroots Resource & Learning Centre
Overview: A small local charitable organization founded in 1984
Mission: To distribute emergency food hampers (through a referral system) to those who require them
Member of: Canadian Association of Food Banks
Chief Officer(s):
Laurie O'Connor, Executive Director
Finances: *Annual Operating Budget:* $250,000-$500,000; *Funding Sources:* donations
Staff Member(s): 7; 20 volunteer(s)
Membership: 60; *Fees:* $5 organization; $1 individual
Activities: Annual general meeting; open house; food hamper program; adult literacy classes; community kitchen; personal development workshops; *Library* Open to public

The Saskatoon Foundation ***See*** Saskatoon Community Foundation

Saskatoon Heritage Society

PO Box 7051, Saskatoon SK S7K 4J1
e-mail: saskatoonheritagesociety@gmail.com
www.saskatoonheritage.ca
Overview: A small local charitable organization founded in 1976
Mission: To promote awareness of the history & heritage of Saskatoon
Member of: Heritage Canada; SaskCulture; Saskatchewan Architectural Heritage Society
Chief Officer(s):
Adam Pollock, President
Finances: *Annual Operating Budget:* Less than $50,000
20 volunteer(s)
Activities: Heritage tours & visits; advocacy; historical research; President's New Year's Levee in Jan.; annual fundraising dinner in Feb.; AGM in May.

Saskatoon Indian & Métis Friendship Centre

168 Wall St., Saskatoon SK S7K 1N4
Tel: 306-244-0174; *Fax:* 306-664-2536
reception_SIMFC@shaw.ca
www.simfc.ca
Overview: A small local organization
Mission: To improve the quality of life for Aboriginal people in the City of Saskatoon.
Member of: Charities; donations; corporate sponsorship; government
Chief Officer(s):
Bill Mintram, Executive Director
Activities: Youth Programs; Family Programs; Urban Aboriginal Strategy Project; Community Access Program; Muisc Lessons; Sports; Cultural Classes

Saskatoon Lapidary & Mineral Club

210 Braeshire Lane, Saskatoon SK S7B 1B2
Tel: 306-382-1871
Overview: A small local organization founded in 1961
Mission: To promote interest in minerals & lapidary in the Saskatoon Saskatchewan area
Activities: Hosting regular meetings

Saskatoon Multicultural Council ***See*** Saskatchewan Intercultural Association Inc.

Saskatoon Musicians' Association (SMA)

#304, 416 - 21st St. East, Saskatoon SK S7K 0C2
Tel: 306-477-2506; *Fax:* 306-665-5694
afm553@sasktel.net
www.facebook.com/SaskatoonMusiciansAssociation
Also Known As: Local 553 AFM
Overview: A small local organization founded in 1910
Mission: To promote the quality & standard of live music in the community
Member of: American Federation of Musicians
Affliation(s): AFL - CIO/CLC
Chief Officer(s):
Ross Nykiforuk, President
Vesti Hanson, Secretary/Treasurer
Finances: *Annual Operating Budget:* Less than $50,000; *Funding Sources:* Membership dues
Staff Member(s): 1
Membership: 230; *Fees:* $65 half year; $120 full year

Saskatoon Open Door Society Inc. (SODS)

#100, 129 - 3 Ave. North, Saskatoon SK S7K 2H4
Tel: 306-653-4464; *Fax:* 306-653-7159
skopendoor@sods.sk.ca
www.sods.sk.ca
Overview: A small local charitable organization founded in 1980
Mission: To welcome & assist refugees & immigrants to become informed & effective participants in Canadian society; to involve the Saskatoon community in their hospitable reception & just acceptance
Affliation(s): Saskatchewan Association of Immigrant Settlement & Integration Agencies; Association of Western Canada Immigrant Serving Agencies
Chief Officer(s):
Beulah Gana, Executive Director
Haidah Amirzadeh, President
Finances: *Annual Operating Budget:* Greater than $5 Million; *Funding Sources:* Federal & provincial governments; United Way; Foundations
Staff Member(s): 150; 300 volunteer(s)
Membership: 70; *Fees:* $10
Activities: Settlement Support; Family Support; Language Education; Daycare; Employment Services; Translatoin Services; *Speaker Service:* Yes

Saskatoon Parents of Twins & Triplets Organization (SPOTTO)

PO Box 25093, RPO River Heights, Saskatoon SK S7K 8B7
Tel: 306-384-4234
saskatoon@multiplebirthscanada.org
spotto.ca
Overview: A small local organization overseen by Multiple Births Canada
Mission: Supports the multiple birth community in and around the Saskatoon area.
Membership: *Fees:* $35

Saskatoon Real Estate Board ***See*** Saskatoon Region Association of REALTORS

Saskatoon Region Association of REALTORS (SRAR)

1149 - 8 St. East., Saskatoon SK S7H 0S3
Tel: 306-244-4453; *Fax:* 306-343-1420
info@srar.ca
www.srar.ca
Previous Name: Saskatoon Real Estate Board
Overview: A medium-sized local organization founded in 1911 overseen by Saskatchewan Real Estate Association
Mission: To represent the real estate interests of its members & the public; to provide services & programs to enhance the professionalism, competency & effectiveness of its members; to advocate public policy towards improving the real estate market environment
Member of: The Canadian Real Estate Association
Chief Officer(s):
Jason Yochim, Executive Officer
Darrin Sych, Director, Advertising
Finances: *Annual Operating Budget:* $500,000-$1.5 Million; *Funding Sources:* Membership dues

Staff Member(s): 8
Membership: 610; *Committees:* Arbitration; Education; Finance; Discipline; Professional Standards; Public Relations; Newspaper; Legislation; Political Action

Saskatoon Senior Citizens Action Now Inc.
310 F Ave. South, Saskatoon SK S7M 1T2
Tel: 306-244-6408
Previous Name: Saskatoon Seniors Action Now Inc.
Overview: A small local charitable organization founded in 1972
Mission: To help develop positive quality of life for seniors & improve community environment for all
Affliation(s): National Pensioners & Senior Citizens Federation

Saskatoon Seniors Action Now Inc. *See* Saskatoon Senior Citizens Action Now Inc.

Saskatoon Soaring Club
510 Cynthia St., Saskatoon SK S7L 7K7
e-mail: saskatoonsoaringclub@gmail.com
www.soar.sk.ca/ssc
Overview: A small local organization
Mission: To promote the sport of gliding and soaring in Saskatoon.
Member of: Soaring Association of Canada
Chief Officer(s):
Ian Barrett, President
John Toles, Vice-President

Saskatoon Society for the Prevention of Cruelty to Animals Inc.
5028 Clarence Ave. South, Grasswood SK S7T 1A7
Tel: 306-374-7387; *Fax:* 306-373-7912
info@saskatoonspca.com
www.saskatoonspca.com
www.facebook.com/group.php?gid=47300934606
Also Known As: Saskatoon SPCA
Overview: A small local organization founded in 1968
Mission: To work for the protection of all animals & to develop in the public at large a humane attitude toward all animal life; to promote the enactment of laws for the prevention of cruelty to & neglect of animals; to promote quality of life for companion animals through responsible stewardship, successful adoptions, education and enforcement of the Animal Protection Act.
Member of: Canadian Federation of Humane Societies; Volunteer Saskatoon; Saskatchewan Society for Fundraising Executives; Association of Fundraising Professionals
Chief Officer(s):
Tiffiny Koback, Shelter Director
director@saskatoonspca.com
Marv Le Nahat, Human Resources Manager
humanresources@saskatoonspca.com
Tricia McAuley, Donor/Public Relations
fundraising@saskatoonspca.com
Dealon McAuley, Volunteer/Public Relations
volunteers@saskatoonspca.com
Finances: *Annual Operating Budget:* $500,000-$1.5 Million; *Funding Sources:* Fundraising; donations; city pound contract; shelter services
Staff Member(s): 25; 200 volunteer(s)
Membership: 400 individual; *Fees:* $25 individual; $40 family; $10 junior/senior; $100 corporate; $200 life
Activities: Humane Education; adoptions; lost & found; cruelty investigations; special events; *Internships:* Yes

Saskatoon Symphony Society (SSO)
408 - 20 St. West, Saskatoon SK S7M 0X4
Tel: 306-665-6414; *Fax:* 306-652-3364
marketing@saskatoonsymphony.org
saskatoonsymphony.org
www.facebook.com/18975919587
twitter.com/SSO_Stoon
www.youtube.com/user/SaskatoonSymphonyMM
Also Known As: Saskatoon Symphony Orchestra
Overview: A small local charitable organization founded in 1931 overseen by Orchestras Canada
Mission: To promote, encourage & support symphonic & classical music in Saskatoon & elsewhere in Saskatchewan
Member of: Saskatchewan Chamber of Commerce; Saskatchewan Arts Alliance
Chief Officer(s):
Victor Sawa, Music Director
Finances: *Funding Sources:* Box office; donations; sponsorships; grants
Staff Member(s): 11
Membership: *Member Profile:* Donation over $100; subscription
Activities: *Speaker Service:* Yes

Saskatoon Youth Orchestra
PO Box 21108, Saskatoon SK S7H 5N9
Tel: 306-373-6408
info@syo.ca
syo.ca
www.facebook.com/SaskatoonYouthOrchestra
Overview: A small local charitable organization founded in 1958 overseen by Orchestras Canada
Mission: A full orchestra whose players are 12-25 years old, run by volunteers
Chief Officer(s):
Richard Carnegie, Director
Finances: *Funding Sources:* Grants
Membership: *Member Profile:* Musicians 12-25 years old living in the Saskatoon area

SaskCentral
PO Box 3030, 2055 Albert St., Regina SK S4P 3G8
Tel: 306-566-1200; *Fax:* 306-566-1372
Toll-Free: 866-403-7499
info@saskcentral.com
www.saskcentral.com
Overview: A small provincial organization founded in 1938 overseen by Credit Union Central of Canada
Mission: To provide leadership, services, & support to Saskatchewan's sixty-five credit unions
Member of: Credit Union Central of Canada
Chief Officer(s):
Ken Anderson, Chief Executive Officer
Darlene Osborne, Contact, Media, 306-566-1314
Saskcentral-MediaRelations@saskcentral.com
Membership: *Member Profile:* Credit unions in Saskatchewan
Activities: Offering services to credit unions in Saskatchewan, such as financial liquidity management, consulting, research, & development support; Working with government & regulators to create a business environment where credit unions will succeed; Promoting credit unions by presenting a positive public image
Meetings/Conferences: • SaskCentral 2015 Annual General Meeting, April, 2015, SK
Scope: Provincial
Publications:
• SaskCentral Annual Report
Type: Yearbook; *Frequency:* Annually

SaskCulture Inc.
#404, 2125 - 11th Ave., Regina SK S4P 3X3
Tel: 306-780-9284
saskculture.info@saskculture.sk.ca
www.saskculture.sk.ca
www.facebook.com/SaskCulture
twitter.com/SaskCulture
www.youtube.com/user/SaskCult
Previous Name: Saskatchewan Council of Cultural Organizations
Overview: A medium-sized provincial organization founded in 1997
Mission: To bring together organizations which work to further the course of culture
Member of: Canadian Centre of Philanthropy; Tourism Saskatchewan; Regina Chamber of Commerce; Saskatoon Chamber of Commerce; Saskatchewan Association of Rural Municipalities; Saskatchewan Urban Municipalities
Affliation(s): Canadian Society of Association Executives
Chief Officer(s):
Rose Gilks, General Manager, 306-780-9282
rgilks@saskculture.sk.ca
Diane Ell, Communications Manager, 306-780-9453
dell@saskculture.sk.ca
Finances: *Annual Operating Budget:* Greater than $5 Million; *Funding Sources:* Saskatchewan Lotteries Trust Fund for Sport, Culture & Recreation
Staff Member(s): 17
Membership: 137; *Fees:* $15 individual; $75 non-voting; $150 voting; *Member Profile:* Non-profit, cultural organizations, province-wide, local-based, mandated to provide cultural programs, services & information

SaskTel Pioneers
2121 Saskatchewan Dr., 2nd Fl., Regina SK S4P 3Y2
Tel: 306-777-2515; *Fax:* 306-777-2831
Toll-Free: 866-944-4442
sasktel.pioneers@sasktel.sk.ca
www.sasktelpioneers.com
twitter.com/sasktelpioneers
Also Known As: Chapter 59
Overview: A small provincial organization founded in 1995 overseen by TelecomPioneers of Canada
Chief Officer(s):
Darrell Liebrecht, Manager
Darrell.Liebrecht@sasktel.sk.ca
Membership: *Committees:* Advisory

Sauble Beach Chamber of Commerce
672 Main St., Sauble Beach ON N0H 2G0
Tel: 519-422-1262; *Fax:* 519-422-3198
www.saublebeach.com
www.facebook.com/186918464685326
Overview: A small local organization founded in 1947
Mission: To promote Sauble Beach as the vacation destination of choice throughout the world
Member of: Canadian Chamber of Commerce; Ontario Chamber of Commerce
Finances: *Annual Operating Budget:* Less than $50,000; *Funding Sources:* Membership fees; sponsorship
20 volunteer(s)
Membership: 130; *Fees:* $250 + GST
Activities: Sauble Sandfest; Oktoberfest; Winterfest; Business Achievement Awards; Canada Day Fireworks

Saugeen Shores Chamber Office
559 Goderich St., Port Elgin ON N0H 2C4
Tel: 519-832-2332; *Fax:* 519-389-3725
Toll-Free: 800-387-3456
portelginfo@saugeenshores.ca
www.saugeenshores.ca/chamber/index.php
www.facebook.com/353177708063160
Previous Name: Port Elgin & District Chamber of Commerce
Overview: A small local organization
Chief Officer(s):
John Kirkham, President
kirkham@bmts.com
Membership: 413; *Fees:* $202.50

Sault Naturalists
PO Box 21035, 306 Northern Ave. East, Sault Ste Marie ON P6B 6H3
e-mail: carrie@ginou.ca
soonats.pbworks.com
Overview: A small local organization
Mission: To promote the enjoyment of nature through environmental appreciation & conservation; to encourage wise use & conservation of natural resources
Member of: Federation of Ontario Naturalists
Affliation(s): Canadian Nature Federation
Chief Officer(s):
Don Hall, President, 705-248-1834
Finances: *Annual Operating Budget:* Less than $50,000
30 volunteer(s)
Membership: *Fees:* $20 individual; $25 family; $10 student

Sault Ste. Marie Music Festival
c/o Algoma Conservatory of Music, 1520 Queen St. East, Sault Ste Marie ON P6A 2G4
Tel: 705-253-4373
algomaconservatory@algomau.ca
Previous Name: Kiwanis Music Festival
Overview: A small local organization founded in 1937

Sault Ste Marie & 49th Field Regt. RCA Historical Society
690 Queen St. East, Sault Ste Marie ON P6A 2A4
Tel: 705-759-7278; *Fax:* 705-759-3058
heritage@saultmuseum.com
www.saultmuseum.com
www.facebook.com/pages/Sault-Ste-Marie-Museum/143320129039949?ref=sgm
www.youtube.com/user/saultmuseum?feature=mhum
Also Known As: Sault Ste Marie Museum
Overview: A small local charitable organization founded in 1920
Mission: To preserve, interpret & exhibit the heritage of Sault Ste Marie
Member of: Ontario Historical Society; Ontario Musuem Association; Ontario Archive Association; Attractions Ontario; Canadian Heritage Information Network
Chief Officer(s):
Kim Forbes, Curator, 705-759-7278
Finances: *Annual Operating Budget:* $100,000-$250,000; *Funding Sources:* Provincial, municipal government
Staff Member(s): 4; 50 volunteer(s)
Membership: 200; *Fees:* $25 individual; $35 family; $12 seniors; $60 group/business
Activities: Sault Ste Marie Museum; *Library* by appointment

Sault Ste Marie Chamber of Commerce (SSMCOC)
489 Bay St., Sault Ste Marie ON P6A 1X6
Tel: 705-949-7152; *Fax:* 705-759-8166
info@ssmcoc.com
www.ssmcoc.com
www.facebook.com/ssmcoc
Overview: A small local organization founded in 1889
Mission: To be the recognized voice of business committed to the enhancement of economic prosperity in Sault Ste Marie
Member of: Canadian Chamber of Commerce; Ontario Chamber of Commerce
Chief Officer(s):
Robert W. Reid, President
Shelley Barich, General Manager
Finances: *Annual Operating Budget:* $100,000-$250,000; *Funding Sources:* Membership dues; fundraising
Staff Member(s): 5; 150 volunteer(s)
Membership: 680; *Fees:* $181 & up
Activities: *Speaker Service:* Yes

Sault Ste Marie Economic Development Corporation (SSMEDC)
99 Foster Dr., Sault Ste Marie ON P6A 5X6
Tel: 705-759-5432; *Fax:* 705-759-2185
Toll-Free: 866-558-5144
info@ssmedc.ca
www.sault-canada.com
www.facebook.com/76704661918
twitter.com/SaultEDC
www.youtube.com/user/SSMEDC
Overview: A small local organization founded in 1982
Mission: To create jobs in the municipality & business attraction to the city
Affliation(s): Economic Developers Council of Ontario
Chief Officer(s):
Don Mitchell, President
Tom Dodds, Chief Executive Officer
Finances: *Annual Operating Budget:* Greater than $5 Million; *Funding Sources:* Municipal, provincial & federal government; Partnership contributions
Staff Member(s): 18
Membership: 1-99; *Committees:* Executive; Finance & Audit; Business Sault Ste. Marie Advisory; Tourism Sault Ste. Marie Management; Meetings, Conventions & Sports Tourism Product Team; Festivals & Events Product Team

Sault Ste Marie Musicians' Association
#216, 451 Queen St. East, Sault Ste Marie ON P6A 5N2
Tel: 705-254-2210; *Fax:* 705-253-2140
afm276@soonet.ca
saultmusicians.org
Also Known As: AFM Local 276
Overview: A small local organization founded in 1918 overseen by American Federation of Musicians of the United States & Canada (AFL-CIO/CLC)
Mission: Committed to raising industry standards and placing the professional musician in the foreground of the cultural landscape by negotiating fair agreements, protecting ownership of recorded music, securing benefits such as health care and pension, or lobbying legislators.
Affliation(s): Fédération internationale des musiciens
Chief Officer(s):
Paul Leclair, Sec.-Treas.
Finances: *Annual Operating Budget:* Less than $50,000; *Funding Sources:* Membership dues; work dues; fines
Staff Member(s): 1; 6 volunteer(s)
Membership: 130; *Fees:* $115
Activities: *Rents Mailing List:* Yes

Sault Ste Marie Police Association / Association de la police de Sault-Ste-Marie
262 Queen St. East, Sault Ste Marie ON P6A 5M6
Tel: 705-949-7632
Overview: A small local organization

Sault Ste Marie Real Estate Board (SSMREB)
372 Albert St. East, Sault Ste Marie ON P6A 2J6
Tel: 705-949-4560; *Fax:* 705-949-5935
info@ssmreb.ca
www.saultstemarierealestate.ca
www.facebook.com/SaultSteMarieRealEstateBoard
Overview: A small local organization overseen by Ontario Real Estate Association
Member of: The Canadian Real Estate Association; Ontario Real Estate Association
Chief Officer(s):
Derek Crowell, President
Membership: 176; *Member Profile:* Realtors

Sault Symphony Association / Orchestre symphonique de Sault Ste-Marie
#2, 121 Brock St., Sault Ste Marie ON P6A 3B6
Tel: 705-945-5337; *Fax:* 705-945-8865
info@saultsymphony.com
www.saultsymphony.com
www.facebook.com/saultsymphony
twitter.com/SaultSymphony
Overview: A small local charitable organization founded in 1972 overseen by Orchestras Canada
Mission: To promote symphonic music in Sault Ste Marie, Ontario & the surrounding region
Chief Officer(s):
Patti Gardi, General Manager
Finances: *Funding Sources:* Grants; Corporate sponsors; Individual donations; Fundraising
Staff Member(s): 4; 50 volunteer(s)
Membership: 360; *Committees:* Executive; Financial; Fundraising; Program
Activities: *Awareness Events:* Bratwurst, Beer, & Beethoven Music Festival, June; *Library:* Sault Symphony Association Music Library;

SauveTerre ***See*** Earthsave Canada

Save a Family Plan (SAFP)
PO Box 3622, London ON N6A 4L4
Tel: 519-672-1115; *Fax:* 519-672-6379
safpinfo@safp.org
www.safp.org
twitter.com/SaveaFamilyPlan
Overview: A large international charitable organization founded in 1965
Mission: Implements sustainable family & community development programs in 5 states in India, with 41 social service societies, 26 homes of health, approximately 10,550 grass roots community organiziations & 15,000 poor families; programs are developed through needs assessments; within all aspects of programming, environmental & gender impact assessments are undertaken. Offices in Canada, the U.S. & India
Member of: Coalition for the Right of Children
Chief Officer(s):
Lesley Porter, Executive Director
Lois Côté, President
Finances: *Annual Operating Budget:* $3 Million-$5 Million; *Funding Sources:* Canadian International Development Agency (CIDA); businesses; groups; individual benefactors
Staff Member(s): 6; 70 volunteer(s)
Membership: 16,000
Activities: Public engagement program including presentations, displays guest speakers
Publications:
• Ektha (Unity)
Type: Newsletter

Save Ontario Shipwrecks (SOS)
PO Box 2389, Blenheim ON N0P 1A0
Tel: 519-676-4110; *Fax:* 519-676-7058
www.saveontarioshipwrecks.on.ca
www.facebook.com/groups/68638569592
Overview: A small provincial organization founded in 1981
Mission: To promote & preserve Ontario's marine heritage
Member of: Canadian Maritime Heritage Federation
Affliation(s): Underwater Council
Chief Officer(s):
Chris Phinney, President
cphinney@SaveOntarioShipwrecks.ca
Nicole AuCoin, Secretary
naucoin@rogers.com
Finances: *Annual Operating Budget:* Less than $50,000
Membership: 350-400; *Fees:* $25 individual; $40 family/institution; $250 corporate; *Committees:* Data Base; Forum; Education; Membership; Promotion

Save Our Heritage Organization (SOHO)
PO Box 578, 96 Young St., Brighton ON K0K 1H0
Tel: 613-475-2144
info@proctorhousemuseum.ca
www.proctorhousemuseum.ca
Also Known As: Proctor House Museum
Overview: A small local charitable organization founded in 1970
Mission: To discover, protect & preserve any material which may help to establish or illustrate the history of the Brighton area
Member of: Ontario Museum Association
Affliation(s): Ontario Heritage Association
Finances: *Funding Sources:* Grants; admissions; special events; membership fees; donations
Activities: Restores & maintains the Proctor House Museum, reconstruction & restoration of 19th century barn on original site of Proctor House barn, 2-4 theatre productions a year; *Awareness Events:* Applefest Celebrations, last weekend in Sept.; *Library* Open to public by appointment

Save the Children - Canada (SCC) / Aide à l'enfance - Canada
#300, 4141 Yonge St., Toronto ON M2P 2A8
Tel: 416-221-5501; *Fax:* 416-221-8214
Toll-Free: 800-668-5036
info@savethechildren.ca
www.savethechildren.ca
www.facebook.com/savethechildren.ca
twitter.com/SaveChildrenCan
www.youtube.com/savethechildrenCA
Overview: A large national charitable organization founded in 1919
Mission: To fight for children's rights; To deliver immediate & lasting improvements to children's lives worldwide in Canada & 10 countries overseas
Member of: Canadian Council for International Cooperation
Affliation(s): International Save the Children Alliance
Chief Officer(s):
Patricia Erb, President/CEO
Finances: *Annual Operating Budget:* Greater than $5 Million; *Funding Sources:* Individual; corporate donations; CIDA
Staff Member(s): 30
Membership: 1-99; *Fees:* $25; *Member Profile:* Volunteers
Activities: Child participation; children & education; children & violence; child labour; children & health; children & emergencies; child poverty; juvenile justice; children's rights; rural children; street kids; rural development; child prostitution; *Internships:* Yes

Save Your Skin Foundation
#319, 3600 Windcrest Dr., North Vancouver BC V7G 2S5
Tel: 604-734-4223
kfm@saveyourskin.ca
www.saveyourskin.ca
www.facebook.com/SaveYourSkinFoundation
twitter.com/saveyourskinfdn
Overview: A small provincial organization
Mission: To provide help & support to patients with skin cancer; To raise awareness about melanoma; To raise funds for research
Chief Officer(s):
Kathy Barnard, President
kathy@saveyourskin.ca
Membership: *Committees:* Editing & Strategic Development; Strategic Development; Corporate Governance; Fundraising; Patient Advocacy; Medical Advisory

Savoy Foundation Inc. / Fondation Savoy inc.
230, rue Foch, Saint-Jean-sur-Richelieu QC J3B 2B2
Tél: 450-358-9779; *Téléc:* 450-346-1045
epilepsy@savoy-foundation.ca
www.savoy-foundation.ca
Aperçu: *Dimension:* petite; *Envergure:* internationale; Organisme sans but lucratif; fondée en 1971
Mission: Recherche en épilepsie
Membre(s) du bureau directeur:
George Savoy, Président
Finances: *Budget de fonctionnement annuel:* $250,000-$500,000
Membre: *Comités:* Scientifique

Scadding Court Community Centre (SCCC)
707 Dundas St. West, Toronto ON M5T 2W6
Tel: 416-392-0335; *Fax:* 416-392-0340
www.scaddingcourt.org
www.facebook.com/people/Scadding-Court/100001939237499
twitter.com/scadding_court
Overview: A medium-sized local charitable organization founded in 1978
Mission: To support and foster the well being of individuals, families, and community groups by providing and encouraging both local and international opportunities for recreation, education, athletics, community participation and inclusive social interaction.
Chief Officer(s):
Kevin Lee, Executive Director
Finances: *Funding Sources:* Government
Staff Member(s): 16
Membership: *Fees:* Schedule available

Scandinavian Home Society of Northwestern Ontario
147 Algoma St. South, Thunder Bay ON P7B 3B7
Tel: 807-345-7442
www.scandihs.com
Overview: A small local organization founded in 1923
Mission: To preserve & promote Scandinavian culture & heritage in Northwestern Ontario
Affliation(s): Lutheran Community Care of Thunder Bay; Swedish Council of America
Finances: *Funding Sources:* Restaurant (The Scandinavian Home Café) operated by the society; Membership dues; Contributions
Membership: *Fees:* $15; *Committees:* Social; Fundraising; Membership; Personnel; Property Membership
Activities: *Library* by appointment

Scandinavian Society of Nova Scotia
Box 31241, Gladstone RPO, Halifax NS B3K 5Y1
e-mail: scansons@gmail.com
www.scandinaviansociety.ca
Overview: A small provincial organization founded in 1976
Mission: To foster interest in the culture & traditions of Scandinavian countries
Chief Officer(s):
Eric Nobbe, President
enobbe@nsbi.ca
Birgit Ballantyne, Chair, Social Affairs Committee
gudnib39@eastlink.ca
Anna-Lisa Jones, Chair, Cultural Affairs Committee
realteam@ns.sympatico.ca
Riina Vahertimo, Chair, Membership
r.vahertimo@gmail.com
Elisabeth Lindboe, Secretary
elisabethlindboe@hotmail.com
Lisbeth Jolley, Treasurer
Lisbeth.Jolley@forces.gc.ca
Activities: Assisting Scandinavians who are new to Nova Scotia; Teaching about Scandinavian life; Organizing cultural activities
Meetings/Conferences: • Scandinavian Society of Nova Scotia 2015 Annual General Meeting, 2015, NS
Scope: Provincial
Attendance: 45
Description: The presentation of society reports, a summary of events from the previous year, & an award ceremony
Publications:
• Scandinavian Society of Nova Scotia Newsletter
Type: Newsletter; *Frequency:* Quarterly; *Editor:* J. Marshall Burgess, Q.C.; *Price:* marshallburgess@ns.sympatico.ca
Profile: Information for members about upcoming events & articles about Scandinavia

Scarboro Foreign Mission Society (SFM)
2685 Kingston Rd., Toronto ON M1M 1M4
Tel: 416-261-7135; *Fax:* 416-261-0820
Toll-Free: 800-260-4815
info@scarboromissions.ca
www.scarboromissions.ca
Also Known As: Scarboro Missions
Overview: A small international charitable organization founded in 1918
Mission: To promote evangelization & human development in a cross-cultural context
Member of: Canadian Council for International Cooperation
Chief Officer(s):
Brian Swords, Moderator
bswords@scarboromissions.ca
Staff Member(s): 11
Membership: *Member Profile:* Priests & lay missionaries
Activities: Overseas missions; *Library:* Archives; by appointment

Scarborough Arts Council (SAC)
1859 Kingston Rd., Toronto ON M1N 1T3
Tel: 416-698-7322; *Fax:* 416-698-7972
office@scarborougharts.com
www.scarborougharts.com
facebook.com/scarborougharts
twitter.com/scararts
youtube.com/scarborougharts
Previous Name: Arts Scarborough
Overview: A small local charitable organization founded in 1979
Mission: To develop all arts disciplines in Scarborough, Ontario; To link artists & the community
Chief Officer(s):
Tim Whalley, Executive Director
ed@scarborougharts.com
Finances: *Funding Sources:* Donations; Sponsorships; Toronto Culture; Ontario Arts Council; The Ontario Trillium Foundation
Membership: *Fees:* $25 subscription (newspaper); $30 students & seniors; $35 individuals; $45 families & groups with 10 members or less; $60 groups of more than 10
Activities: Serving artists, from young & emerging artists to senior & professional artists; Hosting exhibitions, such as the SAC Annual Juried Art Exhibition & Art in the Park; Arranging exhibition space for members at The Bluffs Gallery, Agincourt Public Library, & Cliffcrest Public Library; Providing sales opportunities for members; Offering an after-school program for young people, known as Scarborough C.A.R.E.S. (Community, Art, Recreation, & Education Services); Arranging workshops; Providing networking opportunities
Awards:
• Youth Scholarship Awards for Art (Scholarship)
To help talented youth in Scarborough & east Toronto develop their skills, expose their work, & receive recognition for their accomplishments
Publications:
• Surface & Symbol
Type: Newspaper; *Frequency:* Bimonthly
Profile: Informative articles about local arts

Scarborough Centre for Healthy Communities (SCHC)
#2, 629 Markham Rd., Toronto ON M1H 2A4
Tel: 416-642-9445
www.schcontario.ca
ca.linkedin.com/company/scarborough-centre-for-healthy-communities?trk
www.facebook.com/168437703270987
twitter.com/schcont
www.youtube.com/schcont
Overview: A medium-sized local charitable organization
Mission: SCHC operates 38 distinct and integrated programs across 10 sites. They provide programming for individuals and families, focusing on priority populations such as seniors, the homeless, single parent-led families, refugees and youth.
Chief Officer(s):
Jeanie Joaquin, CEO
Finances: *Funding Sources:* United Way

Scarborough Coin Club
c/o Dick Dunn, PO Box 562, Pickering ON L1V 2R7
Tel: 905-509-1146
cpms@idirect.com
Overview: A small local organization
Member of: Ontario Numismatic Association; Canadian Numismatic Association
Chief Officer(s):
Dick Dunn, Program Director
Finances: *Funding Sources:* Membership fees
Membership: *Member Profile:* Coin & paper money collectors
Activities: Monthly meetings & annual show

Scarborough Cricket Association (SCA)
44 Huddleston Crt., Toronto ON M1L 4L2
www.cricketstar.net
Overview: A small local organization founded in 1981
Mission: To oversee the game of cricket in Scarborough, Ontario.
Member of: West Indies Cricket Umpires Association
Chief Officer(s):
Deo Samaroo, President, 905-470-2849
deosamaroo@gmail.com
Shiv Persaud, Registrar & Statistician, 647-291-4792
shiv_persaud@hotmail.com

Scarborough Historical Society
6282 Kingston Rd., Toronto ON M1C 1K9
Tel: 416-282-2710; *Fax:* 416-282-9482
info@scarboroughhistorical.ca
www.scarboroughhistorical.ca
www.facebook.com/scarborough.lookingback
Overview: A small local charitable organization founded in 1956
Mission: To preserve, study & stimulate an interest in the history of Scarborough
Affliation(s): Ontario Historical Society
Chief Officer(s):
Richard Schofield, Executive Secretary/Treasurer
Finances: *Annual Operating Budget:* Less than $50,000
Staff Member(s): 1; 10 volunteer(s)
Membership: 400; *Fees:* $10; *Committees:* Archives & Research; Programme; Communications; Museum; Editorial; St. Andrew's; Finance
Activities: *Speaker Service:* Yes; *Library:* Scarborough Archives; Open to public by appointment

Scarborough Muslim Association (SMA)
2665 Lawrence Ave. East, Toronto ON M1P 2S2
Tel: 416-750-2253; *Fax:* 416-750-1616
info@smacanada.ca
www.smacanada.ca
Overview: A small local charitable organization founded in 1984
Chief Officer(s):
Yakub Hatia, President

Scarborough Philharmonic Orchestra
#209, 3007 Kingston Rd., Toronto ON M1M 1P1
Tel: 416-429-0007
spo@spo.ca
www.spo.ca
www.linkedin.com/company/scarborough-philharmonic-orchestra
www.facebook.com/ScarboroughPhilharmonicOrchestra
twitter.com/SPOGreatMusic
www.youtube.com/user/SPOGreatMusic
Overview: A small local organization founded in 1980 overseen by Orchestras Canada
Mission: To enrich the cultural life of Scarborough, through the promotion & presentation of high calibre musical performances; To develop a strong & financially viable organization
Member of: Orchestras Ontario, Scarborough Arts Council
Chief Officer(s):
Ronald Royer, Music Director
Finances: *Funding Sources:* Bingo; OAC; Metro Toronto; sponsors
Activities: *Library* by appointment
Awards:
• Scarborough Philharmonic Music Camp Scholarship (Scholarship)
• Rotary Club of North Scarborough Scholarship (Scholarship)
• Youth Concerto Scholarship (Scholarship)

Scarborough Women's Centre (SWC)
#245, 2100 Ellesmere Rd., Toronto ON M1H 3B7
Tel: 416-439-7111; *Fax:* 416-439-6999
ed@scarboroughwomenscentre.ca
www.scarboroughwomenscentre.ca
www.linkedin.com/company/scarborough-women's-centre?trk=fc_badge
www.facebook.com/scarboroughwomenscentre
twitter.com/scarbwomensctr
Overview: A small local organization founded in 1982
Mission: To provide information, education & support to women & girls
Member of: Toronto Board of Trade; Volunteer Toronto
Affliation(s): Ontario Association of Women's Centres; Woman Abuse Council
Chief Officer(s):
Lynda Kosowan, Executive Director
ed@scarboroughwomenscentre.ca
Finances: *Annual Operating Budget:* $250,000-$500,000; *Funding Sources:* Provincial & regional government; fundraising
Staff Member(s): 8; 100 volunteer(s)
Membership: 300; *Fees:* $10 general; $5 student/senior; *Member Profile:* Women
Activities: Information, education, support for women in transition; Young women's outreach; Outreach to women with disabilities; *Internships:* Yes
Awards:
• Mayor's Community Safety Award (Award)

Scented Products Education & Information Association of Canada (SPEIAC)
e-mail: scents@scentedproducts.ca
www.scentedproducts.ca
Overview: A medium-sized national organization
Mission: To disseminate information & provide education about scented products including fine fragrances, cosmetics, toiletries & scented household products
Affliation(s): Allied Beauty Association; Canadian Association of Chain Drug Stores; Canadian Cosmetic, Toiletry & Fragrance Association; Canadian Fragrance Materials Association; Canadian Consumer Specialty Products Association; Direct Sellers Association; Advancing Canadian Self-Care; The Soap & Detergent Association of Canada

Schizophrenia Society of Alberta (SSA)
4809 - 48 Ave., Red Deer AB T4N 3T2

Tel: 403-986-9440; *Fax:* 403-986-9442
info@schizophrenia.ab.ca
www.schizophrenia.ab.ca
www.linkedin.com/groups/Schizophrenia-Society-Alberta-SSA-2604548/abou
www.facebook.com/SchizophreniaSocietyofAlberta
twitter.com/SchizophreniaAB
Previous Name: Alberta Friends of Schizophrenics
Overview: A small provincial charitable organization founded in 1980 overseen by Schizophrenia Society of Canada
Mission: To alleviate the suffering caused by schizophrenia & related illnesses
Affliation(s): Schizophrenia Society of Canada
Chief Officer(s):
Douglas Holmes, President
Len O'Connor, Vice-President
Sandor Sajnovics, Secretary
Finances: *Funding Sources:* Membership fees; Donations; Fundraising; Sponsorships
Membership: 586+; *Fees:* $20 - $25; *Member Profile:* People in Alberta with schizophrenia; Family members impacted by schizophrenia; Professionals whose focus is mental illness; *Committees:* Advocacy; Finance; Nominating; Bylaw
Activities: Offering information about schizophrenia & services in Alberta; Raising public awareness & understanding of schizophrenia; Providing education; Researching; Advocating for better services to persons who suffer from schizophrenia; Collaborating with other organizations; *Awareness Events:* Schizophrenia Society of Alberta Annual Open Minds Walk & Run; *Library:* Schizophrenia Society of Alberta Library
Publications:
• The Summary
Type: Newsletter; *Price:* Free with membership in the Schizophrenia Society of Alberta

Calgary & Area Chapter
#309, 8989 Macleod Trail South, Calgary AB T2H 0M2
Tel: 403-264-5161; *Fax:* 403-269-1727
fhaynes@schizophrenia.ab.ca
Mission: To support persons with the illness of schizophrenia & family members in the Calgary area

Camrose & Area Chapter
#206, 5010 - 50 Ave., Camrose AB T4V 3P7
Tel: 780-679-4280
aholler@schizophrenia.ab.ca
Mission: To provide support for persons affected by schizophrenia & other related illnesses in the Camrose region

Edmonton & Area Chapter
5215 - 87 St., Edmonton AB T6E 5L5
Tel: 780-452-4661; *Fax:* 780-482-3027
nnicholson@schizophrenia.ab.ca
Mission: To provide support & information to people affected by schizophrenia & related illnesses in the Capital Health Region & in communities in northern Alberta
• Grey Matters
Type: Newsletter; *Frequency:* Monthly; *Price:* Free with membership in the Schizophrenia Society of Alberta, Edmonton & Area Chapter
Profile: Information about local activities & groups involved with mental illness

Lethbridge & Area Chapter
234C - 12th St. B North, Lethbridge AB T1H 2K7
Tel: 403-327-4305; *Fax:* 403-328-0124
jhansen@schizophrenia.ab.ca

Medicine Hat & Area Chapter
526B - 3 St. SE, Medicine Hat AB T1A 0H3
Tel: 403-526-8515
wbonertz@schizophrenia.ab.ca
Mission: To provide support & information for family members & persons living with schizophrenia in the Medicine Hat region

Red Deer & Area Chapter
4811 - 48 St., Red Deer AB T4N 3T2
Tel: 403-342-5760; *Fax:* 403-342-4866
JLund@schizophrenia.ab.ca
Mission: To offer support & information to family members, & persons living with schizoprenia & other mental illness in Red Deer & area
Chief Officer(s):
Lyle McKellar, Chair
Don Simpson, Vice-Chair
Gary Lathan, Executive Director
Marion Weidner, Secretary
Roger Goodwin, Treasurer
Lana King Kottman, Coordinator, Education
lana@ssard.com
Chris Thomas, Coordinator, Programs & Services
chris@ssard.com
• Courage
Type: Newsletter; *Frequency:* Quarterly; *Price:* Free with Schizophrenia Society of Alberta, Red Deer Chapter, membership
Profile: Information about Red Deer area & provincial events

Schizophrenia Society of Canada (SSC) / Société canadienne de schizophrénie

#100, 4 Fort St., Winnipeg MB R3C 1C4
Tel: 204-786-1616; *Fax:* 204-783-4898
Toll-Free: 800-263-5545
info@schizophrenia.ca
www.schizophrenia.ca
www.facebook.com/pages/Schizophrenia-Society-of-Canada/197088263635191
Previous Name: Canadian Friends of Schizophrenics
Overview: A medium-sized national charitable organization founded in 1979
Mission: To improve the quality of life for those affected by schizophrenia & psychosis; To advocate on behalf of individuals & families affected by schizophrenia for improved treatment & services
Chief Officer(s):
Chris Summerville, D. Min, CPRP, Chief Executive Officer
chris@schizophrenia.ca
Catherine Willinsky, Manager, National Programs & Projects
willinskyc@schizophrenia.ca
Finances: *Funding Sources:* Donations; Sponsorships; Public Health Agency of Canada
Activities: Contributing to public policy; Supporting & conducting research; Providing education about schizophrenia & psychosis; Offering support programs to individuals & families; Raising public awareness about schizophrenia & psychosis to reduce stigma & discrimination
Awards:
• Bill Jefferies Family Member Award (Award)
To recognize family members of persons with schizophrenia who have made outstanding voluntary contributions towards the mission of the Schizophrenia Society of Canada*Deadline:* June 15 *Contact:* Viola MacKay, E-mail: info@schizophrenia.ca
• Flag of Hope Award for Schizophrenia (Award)
To recognize people with schizophrenia who have shown self-determination in their recovery process*Deadline:* June 15 *Contact:* Viola MacKay, E-mail: info@schizophrenia.ca
• Initiatives / Programs of Excellence Award (Award)
To recognize initiatives or programs implemented at the local or provincial levels that have made significant impacts on the quality of life of individuals & family members affected by schizophrenia*Deadline:* June 15 *Contact:* Viola MacKay, E-mail: info@schizophrenia.ca
• Media Award (Award)
To recognize individuals or organizations in the media who have have advanced the cause of schizophrenia*Deadline:* June 15 *Contact:* Viola MacKay, E-mail: info@schizophrenia.ca
• Michael Smith Award for Schizophrenia (Award)
To recognize researchers & clinicians who have supported people with schizophrenia & psychosis & their families*Deadline:* June 15 *Contact:* Viola MacKay, E-mail: info@schizophrenia.ca
• Outstanding Achievement Award (Award)
To recognize individuals or groups who have made an exceptional contribution to the cause & cure of schizophrenia*Deadline:* June 15 *Contact:* Viola MacKay, E-mail: info@schizophrenia.ca
• Outstanding Staff Award (Award)
To recognize a staff member who has made an outstanding contribution toward the mission of the Schizophrenia society of Canada*Deadline:* June 15 *Contact:* Viola MacKay, E-mail: info@schizophrenia.ca
Publications:
• A Future With Hope
Type: Newsletter; *Frequency:* 3 pa; *Price:* Free with membership in the Schizophrenia Society of Canada
Profile: Society activities, executive reports, & current issues
• Psychosis & Substance Use: A Booklet for Youth
Type: Booklet; *Number of Pages:* 6
• Rays of Hope
Type: Manual; *Number of Pages:* 268; *ISBN:* 0-9733913-0-8
Profile: A reference publication for families & caregivers of individuals with schizophrenia
• Reaching Out
Type: Kit
Profile: An awareness & learning resource for students in grades seven to twelve, including a video
• Respite Needs of People Living with Schizophrenia
Number of Pages: 80; *Editor:* Michelle Bergin; Heather Stuart
Profile: Results of a national survey of Schizophrenia Society of Canada members
• Schizophrenia & Substance Use: Information for Families
Type: Booklet; *Number of Pages:* 9
• Schizophrenia & Substance Use: Information for Consumers
Type: Booklet; *Number of Pages:* 7
• Schizophrenia & Substance Use: Information for Service Providers
Type: Booklet; *Number of Pages:* 7
• Schizophrenia in Canada: A National Report
Type: Report
Profile: Sections include understanding schizophrenia, stigma & discrination, & solutions
• Schizophrenia Society of Canada Annual Report
Type: Yearbook; *Frequency:* Annually
• Schizophrenia: The Journey to Recovery, A Consumer & Family Guide to Assessment & Treatment
Type: Booklet; *Number of Pages:* 48; *Author:* Mary Metcalfe, M.S.; *Editor:* Deborah Kelly; Francine Knoops
Profile: A guide produced by the Schizophrenia Society of Canada & the CanadianPsychiatric Association
• Strengthening Families Together: Helping Canadians Live with Mental Illness
Type: Handbook; *Number of Pages:* 146; *Editor:* Edna Barker
Profile: A book for facilitators of the Stenghtening Families Together program

Schizophrenia Society of New Brunswick (SSNB)

PO Box 562, 130 Duke St., Miramichi NB E1V 3T7
Tel: 506-622-1595; *Fax:* 506-622-8927
ssnbmiramichi@nb.aibn.com
www.schizophreniasociety.nb.ca
Overview: A small provincial charitable organization founded in 1986 overseen by Schizophrenia Society of Canada
Member of: Schizophrenia Society of Canada
Chief Officer(s):
Barb Johnson, President
ssbj@rogers.com

Fredericton Chapter
#25, 91 Angel Ct., Fredericton NB E3B 7B9
Tel: 506-451-7770
www.schizophreniasociety.nb.ca/chapters/fredericton.htm
Chief Officer(s):
Mary Louise Luck, President
mluck@nb.sympatico.ca

Moncton Chapter
178 Summer Ave., Moncton NB E1C 8A5
Tel: 506-384-8668; *Fax:* 506-854-7524
cormiergc@rogers.com
www.schizophreniasociety.nb.ca/chapters/moncton.htm

Saint John Chapter
Open Door Club, 157 Duke St., Saint John NB E2L 1N7
schizophreniasocietysj.wordpress.com

Schizophrenia Society of Newfoundland & Labrador

UB Waterford Hospital, PO Box 28029, 48 Kenmount Rd., St. John's NL A1B 1X0
Tel: 709-777-3335; *Fax:* 709-777-3224
info@ssnl.org
ssnl.org
www.facebook.com/171941232764
twitter.com/schizophreniaNL
Overview: A small provincial charitable organization overseen by Schizophrenia Society of Canada
Mission: To alleviate the suffering caused by schizophrenia
Member of: Schizophrenia Society of Canada
Activities: Partnership Education Program; Strengthening Families Together; Schizophrenia Awareness Days

Schizophrenia Society of Nova Scotia (SSNS)

#B-23, E.C. Purdy Building, PO Box 1004, Stn. Main, 300 Pleasant St., Dartmouth NS B2Y 3Z9
Tel: 902-465-2601; *Fax:* 902-465-5479
Toll-Free: 800-465-2601
ssns@bellaliant.com
www.ssns.ca
www.facebook.com/schizophrenia.society.ns
twitter.com/ssnsc
Previous Name: Nova Scotia Friends of Schizophrenics
Overview: A small provincial charitable organization founded in 1982 overseen by Schizophrenia Society of Canada

Mission: To alleviate the suffering caused by schizophrenia
Member of: Schizophrenia Society of Canada
Chief Officer(s):
Stephen Ayer, Executive Director
stephenayer@bellaliant.com
Finances: *Annual Operating Budget:* $100,000-$250,000
Staff Member(s): 2; 20 volunteer(s)
Membership: 200; *Fees:* $15; *Committees:* Education; Advocacy; Fundraising; Public Awareness
Activities: *Awareness Events:* Walk the World for Schizophrenia, May & Sept.; *Speaker Service:* Yes; *Library* Open to public

Schizophrenia Society of Ontario (SSO) / Société de schizophrénie de l'Ontario

#302, 130 Spadina Ave., Toronto ON M5V 2L4
Fax: 416-449-8434
Toll-Free: 800-449-6367
info@schizophrenia.on.ca
www.schizophrenia.on.ca
www.facebook.com/SchizophreniaSocietyON
twitter.com/peace_of_minds
www.youtube.com/user/SSOOntario
Previous Name: Ontario Friends of Schizophrenics
Overview: A medium-sized provincial charitable organization founded in 1979 overseen by Schizophrenia Society of Canada
Mission: To improve the quality of life for families affected by schizophrenia, by offering support to them, & by promoting community awareness of the disease.
Chief Officer(s):
Norm Tasevski, President
Mary Alberti, CEO
malberti@schizophrenia.on.ca
Finances: *Funding Sources:* Fundraising; provincial government
Membership: *Fees:* $35 family; $50 associate; *Member Profile:* Friends & family of people suffering from schizophrenia; health professionals
Activities: Family support; public awareness & education; advocacy; fundraising for research; *Awareness Events:* Peace of Minds Yogathon, Feb.; National Schizophrenia & Psychosis Awareness Day, May; Hole Out for Hope Golf Tournament, June

Halton / Peel Region
136 Cross Ave., Main Fl., Oakville ON L6J 2W6
Tel: 905-338-2112; *Fax:* 905-338-2113
Chief Officer(s):
Marina Sue-Ping, Family & Community Coordinator
msue-ping@schizophrenia.on.ca

Hamilton/Niagara Region
193 James St. South, Hamilton ON L8P E8A
Tel: 905-523-7413; *Fax:* 905-523-8345
Chief Officer(s):
Jill Dennison, Regional Coordinator
jdennison@schizophrenia.on.ca

Ottawa Region
c/o ROH, 1145 Carling Ave., Ottawa ON K1Z 7K4
Tel: 613-722-6521; *Fax:* 613-729-8980
Chief Officer(s):
Sheila Deighton, Regional Coordinator Ext. 7775
sdeighton@schizophrenia.on.ca

Peterborough/Durham Region
#3, 421 Water St., Peterborough ON K9H 3L9
Tel: 705-749-1753; *Fax:* 705-749-6175
Chief Officer(s):
Allyson Susko, Regional Coordinator
asusko@schizophrenia.on.ca

Schizophrenia Society of Prince Edward Island (SSPEI)

PO Box 25020, Charlottetown PE C1A 9N4
Tel: 902-368-5850; *Fax:* 902-368-5467
schizophreniapei@pei.aibn.com
Overview: A small provincial charitable organization founded in 1984 overseen by Schizophrenia Society of Canada
Mission: To alleviate the suffering caused by schizophrenia
Member of: Schizophrenia Society of Canada
Activities: *Library* Open to public

Schizophrenia Society of Saskatchewan (SSS)

PO Box 305, Stn. Main, 2123 Broad St., Regina SK S4P 3A1
Tel: 306-584-2620; *Fax:* 306-584-0525
sssprov@sasktel.net
www.schizophrenia.sk.ca
www.facebook.com/201415453215067
Previous Name: Saskatchewan Friends of Schizophrenics
Overview: A small provincial charitable organization founded in 1982 overseen by Schizophrenia Society of Canada
Mission: The Society provides easily understood information on schizophrenia for concerned families. It works to increase public awareness of the illness with initiatives aimed at all age groups, & speaks on behalf of affected families. It is a registered charity, BN :894249861RR0001.
Member of: Schizophrenia Society of Canada
Chief Officer(s):
Chris Summerville, Interim CEO
Anita Hopfauf, Contact
ahopfauf@sasktel.net
Finances: *Annual Operating Budget:* $100,000-$250,000; *Funding Sources:* Government & foundation grants; donations; bequests; United Way
Staff Member(s): 3; 5 volunteer(s)
Membership: 205; *Fees:* $20; *Committees:* Advocacy; Public Awareness & Education; Fundraising; Research; Human Resource Development
Activities: Raises funds for research; counselling; public education; family support groups; advocacy; *Speaker Service:* Yes; *Library* Open to public

Saskatoon Chapter
#219, 230 Ave. R South, Saskatoon SK S7M 2Z1
Tel: 306-374-2224; *Fax:* 306-477-5649
ssssaskatoon@sasktel.net
www.schizophrenia-saskatoon.com
www.facebook.com/pages/Sasktoon-Schizophrenia-Society/217889741572764
www.youtube.com/user/SkSchizophrenia

Schneider Employees' Association (Ind.) / Association des employés de Schneider (ind.)

321 Courtland Ave. East, Kitchener ON N2G 3X8
Tel: 519-741-5000; *Fax:* 519-744-5099
schneider@cwa-scacanada.ca
Overview: A medium-sized national organization
Chief Officer(s):
Sandy Russell, National President
Membership: 2,000 + 2 locals

Schneider Office Employees' Association (SOEA) / Association des employés de bureau de Schneider (FCNSI)

PO Box 130, 321 Courtland Ave. East, Kitchener ON N2G 3X8
Tel: 519-741-5000; *Fax:* 519-749-7465
Toll-Free: 800-567-3212
schneider@cwa-scacanada.ca
Overview: A small local organization founded in 1983
Member of: Local 30009 TNG Canada/CWA
Chief Officer(s):
Sandy Russell, President
Finances: *Annual Operating Budget:* $50,000-$100,000
Membership: 150 + 1 local

School Counsellors' Association of Manitoba *See* Manitoba School Counsellors' Association

School Lunch Association

Macpherson School, 40 Newton Rd., St. John's NL A1C 4E1
Tel: 709-754-5323; *Fax:* 709-754-4520
sla@schoollunch.ca
www.schoollunch.ca
www.facebook.com/schoollunch.ca
Previous Name: School Lunch Association, Inc.
Overview: A small local charitable organization founded in 1989
Mission: To operate a non-stigmatizing meal program for primary & elementary school children regardless of their ability to pay
Chief Officer(s):
Ken Hopkins, Executive Director
khopkins@schoollunch.ca
Finances: *Funding Sources:* Provincial government; donations; meal revenue
Staff Member(s): 5

School Lunch Association, Inc. *See* School Lunch Association

School Milk Foundation of Newfoundland & Labrador (SMFNL)

27 Sagona Ave., Mount Pearl NL A1N 4P8
Tel: 709-364-2776; *Fax:* 709-364-8364
info@schoolmilkfdn.nf.net
www.schoolmilk.nf.ca
Previous Name: Newfoundland & Labrador School Milk Foundation
Overview: A medium-sized provincial organization founded in 1991
Mission: To increase the availability of milk throughout Newfoundland & Labrador schools; to increase the affordability of milk in all schools, so that cost does not become the reason for not drinking milk; to educate students, teachers, parents & the general public about the nutritional value of milk & the importance of it for a healthy lifestyle; to develop & implement interesting & educational campaigns to promote milk consumption in all schools; to create a lifelong milk drinking habit amongst children in the province
Affliation(s): Canadian Public Health Association; Coalition for School Nutrition
Finances: *Annual Operating Budget:* $500,000-$1.5 Million; *Funding Sources:* Dairy producers; processors; provincial government
Staff Member(s): 3
Membership: 288 Schools + 80,0000 students; *Member Profile:* Schools & K-12 students
Activities: *Speaker Service:* Yes

School Sport Canada (SSC) / Sport Scolaire Canada

c/o Alberta Schools' Athletic Association, 11759 Groat Rd., Edmonton AB T5M 3K6
Tel: 780-860-4200
schoolsportcanada@gmail.com
www.schoolsport.ca
Overview: A large national organization
Mission: To be the national body for school sport in Canada
Chief Officer(s):
Karen Richard, President, 709-729-2795
karen@sportnl.ca
John Paton, President-Elect
Tyler Callaghan, Executive Director
tyler.callaghan@schoolsport.ca
Membership: 12 member associations

School Sports Newfoundland & Labrador (SSNL)

1296A Kenmount Rd., St. John's NL A1B 3W8
Tel: 709-729-2795; *Fax:* 709-729-2705
ssnl@sportnl.ca
www.schoolsportsnl.ca
www.facebook.com/141101766485
Previous Name: Newfoundland & Labrador High School Athletic Federation
Overview: A medium-sized provincial charitable organization founded in 1969 overseen by School Sport Canada
Mission: To organize, promote & govern all high school sports within the province; to assist student athletes in reaching their full physical, educational & social potential through participation & sportsmanship in interscholastic sports
Member of: School Sport Canada; National Federation of High Schools
Chief Officer(s):
Karen Richard, Executive Director
karen@sportnl.ca
Dennis Lush, President
dennislush@ncsd.ca
Finances: *Annual Operating Budget:* $500,000-$1.5 Million; *Funding Sources:* Provincial government; Federal govnerment; corporate sponsors; membership dues
Staff Member(s): 3; 700 volunteer(s)
Membership: 150 schools; *Fees:* $75-$325
Activities: School sports tournaments; *Internships:* Yes
Awards:
• Br. G. I. Moore Student-Athlete of the Year (Scholarship)
Amount: $250 - $750
Meetings/Conferences: • School Sports Newfoundland & Labrador Annual General Meeting, 2015

Science Alberta Foundation

#260, 3512 - 33 St. NW, Calgary AB T2L 2A6
Tel: 403-220-0077; *Fax:* 403-284-4132
info@sciencealberta.org
www.sciencealberta.org
twitter.com/sciencealberta
Overview: A medium-sized provincial organization founded in 1990
Mission: To increase science literacy by creating innovative programs for all Albertans
Chief Officer(s):
Arlene Ponting, CEO
Jill Maryniuk, Manager, Marketing & Communications
Finances: *Funding Sources:* Provincial government; private donations
Activities: Science-in-a-Crate; science festivals

Science Atlantic / Science Atlantique

PO Box 15000, 1390 Le Marchant St., Halifax NS B3H 4R2

Tel: 902-494-3421
admin@scienceatlantic.ca
www.scienceatlantic.ca
twitter.com/scienceatlantic
Previous Name: Atlantic Provinces Council on the Sciences; Atlantic Provinces Inter-University Committee on the Sciences
Overview: A medium-sized local organization founded in 1962
Mission: To advance science & technology through education & public awareness & the promotion of scientific literacy education & research throughout the region
Chief Officer(s):
Rob Raeside, Chair
rob.raeside@acadiau.ca
Lois Whitehead, Executive Director
lois.whitehead@scienceatlantic.ca
Finances: *Annual Operating Budget:* $100,000-$250,000; *Funding Sources:* Membership dues
Staff Member(s): 2; 150 volunteer(s)
Membership: 18; *Committees:* Aquaculture & Fisheries; Biology; Chemistry; Computer Science; Earth Science; Environment; Mathematics & Statistics; Physics & Astronomy; Psychology; Animal Care; Research Working Group
Activities: Student conferences in nine disciplines; speaker tours by notable scientists; awards for outstanding undergraduate research
Meetings/Conferences: • 2015 Atlantic Universities Physics & Astronomy Conference (AUPAC), February, 2015, Mount Allison University, Sackville, NB
Scope: Provincial

Science Atlantique *See* Science Atlantic

Science et paix *See* Science for Peace

Science for Peace (SfP) / Science et paix

c/o University College, #045, 15 King's College Circle, Toronto ON M5S 3H7
Tel: 416-978-3606; *Fax:* 416-978-3606
sfp@physics.utoronto.ca
www.scienceforpeace.ca
Overview: A small national charitable organization founded in 1981
Mission: To understand & act against forces of militarism, social injustice, & environmental destruction
Chief Officer(s):
Metta Spencer, President
president@scienceforpeace.ca
Margrit Eichler, Secretary
secrectary@scienceforpeace.ca
Pieter Basedow, Treasurer
treasurer@scienceforpeace.ca
Finances: *Funding Sources:* Membership fees; Donations
Membership: *Fees:* $20 students; $40 retired members; $60 regular members; Pay what you can for underwaged persons; *Member Profile:* Natural & social scientists; Scholars in the humanities; *Committees:* Carbon Tax; Peace in Outer Space; Violence in the Media; Peace & Sustainability Education
Activities: Conducting research; Providing education services, such as public lectures & panel discussions; Publishing statements, essays, & books
Publications:
• The Bulletin
Type: Newsletter; *Frequency:* Quarterly; *Price:* Free with membership in Science for Peace
Profile: Association activities & articles about issues of interest to members

---

Science Teachers' Association of Ontario (STAO) / Association des professeurs de sciences de l'Ontario (APSO)

PO Box 771, Dresden ON N0P 1M0
Fax: 800-754-1654
Toll-Free: 800-461-2264
info@stao.org
www.stao.org
twitter.com/staoapso
plus.google.com/u/0/communities/105551248505159738951
Overview: A small provincial organization founded in 1890
Mission: To promote excellence in the teaching of science throughout Ontario; To act as the voice of science educators in the province
Chief Officer(s):
Gerrie Storr, President
gerrie_storr@stao.org
Jocelyn Paas, Vice-President
jocelyn_paas@stao.org
Stephen Houlden, Treasurer
stephen_houlden@stao.org
Finances: *Funding Sources:* Membership fees; Corporate sponsors
Membership: *Fees:* $28.25 students/retired; $56.50 regular; *Member Profile:* Science educators in Ontario, from elementary & secondary schools, as well as colleges & universities; Students in a full time program at a faculty of education; Corporations; Exhibitors at the STAO/APSO annual conference; *Committees:* Elementary; Secondary; Website; Editorial Sub-Committee; Promotions; STAO Program
Activities: Advocating for excellence in science education throughout Ontario; Supporting new teachers; Providing the ScienceWorks workshop series; Operating The Science Store; *Library:* STAO Virtual Library
Awards:
• STAO / APSO Merit Award (Award)
To recognize excellence & leadership in science teaching*Deadline:* September 1 *Contact:* Chair of the STAO / APSO Awards Committee, Fax: 1-800-754-1654; E-mail: awards@stao.org
• STAO / APSO Service Award (Award)
To honour outstanding contributions to the association*Deadline:* September 1 *Contact:* Chair of the STAO / APSO Awards Committee, Fax: 1-800-754-1654; E-mail: awards@stao.org
• Irwin Talesnick Award for Excellence in the Teaching of Science (Award)
To recognize excellence in the teaching of science in Ontario*Deadline:* September 1 *Contact:* Chair of the STAO / APSO Awards Committee, Fax: 1-800-754-1654; E-mail: awards@stao.org
• Jack Bell Award for Leadership in Science Education (Award)
To honour outstanding & sustained leadership in science education in Ontario*Deadline:* September 1 *Contact:* Chair of the STAO / APSO Awards Committee, Fax: 1-800-754-1654; E-mail: awards@stao.org
• STAO / APSO Emeritus Award (Award)
To recognize leadership & excellence in the teaching of science during a career*Deadline:* September 1 *Contact:* Chair of the STAO / APSO Awards Committee, Fax: 1-800-754-1654; E-mail: awards@stao.org
• STAO / APSO Life Member Award (Award)
Deadline: September 1 *Contact:* Chair of the STAO / APSO Awards Committee, Fax: 1-800-754-1654; E-mail: awards@stao.org
Meetings/Conferences: • Science Teachers' Association of Ontario 2015 Conference, November, 2015, Toronto, ON
Scope: Provincial
Publications:
• Crucible
Type: Magazine; *Frequency:* 5 pa; *Editor:* Brenda Kosky; *Price:* Free with membership in the Science Teachers' Association of Ontario
Profile: Innovative approaches to science education, including a section entitled "Elements" about elementary science education
• Science Teachers' Association of Ontario Newsletter
Type: Newsletter; *Frequency:* Monthly
Profile: Science ideas, plus information about upcoming events & workshops
• Tips & Strategies for the Novice Science Teacher
Profile: Advice to assist beginning teachers

Sciences jeunesse Canada *See* Youth Science Canada

Scleroderma Association of British Columbia

PO Box 218, Stn. Delta Main, Delta BC V4K 3N7
Tel: 604-940-9343; *Fax:* 604-940-9346
Toll-Free: 888-940-9343
www.sclerodermabc.ca
www.facebook.com/scleroderma.bc
Overview: A small provincial charitable organization founded in 1984
Mission: To support, educate & keep informed those diagnosed with scleroderma (in skin form - localized, or in systemic form - systemic sclerosis); To raise research funds
Member of: Scleroderma Society of Canada
Chief Officer(s):
Rosanne Queen, President
rq.sabc@telus.net
Membership: 450 patients; *Fees:* $20; *Member Profile:* Ages 9-89 all nationalities
Activities: Community support meetings; *Library*

Scleroderma Society of Canada (SSC)

#206, 41 King William St., Hamilton ON L8R 1A2
Toll-Free: 866-279-0632
info@scleroderma.ca
www.scleroderma.ca
Overview: A small national organization founded in 2000
Mission: To promote awareness of scleroderma, to support research toward finding a cure and to provide support and information to those affected by the disease.
Chief Officer(s):
Maureen Sauvé, President
Meetings/Conferences: • Scleroderma Society of Canada 16th Annual Conference, September, 2015, Hamilton Sheraton Hotel, Hamilton, ON
Contact Information: Anna McCusker, anna@sclerodermaontario.ca, URL: www.sclerodermaconference.ca

---

The Scleroderma Society of Ontario (SSO)

#206, 41 King William St., Hamilton ON L8R 1A2
Tel: 905-544-0343
info@sclerodermaontario.ca
www.sclerodermaontario.ca
Overview: A small provincial charitable organization
Mission: To promote public awareness; To advance patient wellness; To support research in Scleroderma
Member of: The Arthritis Society
Chief Officer(s):
Maureen Sauvé, President
Norma Augustine, Executive Assistant
norma.augustine@sclerodermaontario.ca
Finances: *Annual Operating Budget:* $50,000-$100,000
50 volunteer(s)
Membership: 300; *Fees:* $25; *Committees:* Board of Directors

---

Scotia Chamber Players

6181 Lady Hammond Rd., Halifax NS B3K 2R9
Tel: 902-429-9467; *Fax:* 902-425-6785
admin@scotiafestival.ns.ca
www.scotiafestival.ns.ca
www.facebook.com/scotiafestivalofmusic
twitter.com/scotiafestival
www.youtube.com/user/scotiafestival
Also Known As: Scotia Festival of Music
Overview: A small local charitable organization founded in 1976 overseen by Orchestras Canada
Mission: To enhance the quality of music by producing an annual festival of world-class chamber music in study & performance for the benefit of musicians, students & audiences
Chief Officer(s):
Christopher Wilcox, Managing Director
Finances: *Funding Sources:* Halifax Regional Municipality; NS Government; Canada Council; Dept. of Canadian Heritage; NS Tourism
Staff Member(s): 4
Activities: Two-week chamber music festival annually
Awards:
• Maxie Grant Scholarship (Award)

Scotia Fundy Mobile Gear Fishermen's Association

355 Main St., Yarmouth NS B5A 1E7
Tel: 902-742-6732; *Fax:* 902-742-6732
sfmobile@ns.sympatico.ca
Previous Name: Nova Scotia Fishermen Draggers Association
Overview: A small local organization
Chief Officer(s):
Brian Giroux, Executive Director
Staff Member(s): 1
Membership: *Member Profile:* Vessel owners in NS fishery

The Scots

PO Box 9410, Stn. A, Halifax NS B3K 5S3
Tel: 902-425-2445; *Fax:* 902-425-2441
info@thescots.ca
www.thescots.ca
Also Known As: The North British Society
Overview: A small provincial organization founded in 1768
Chief Officer(s):
J. William MacLeod, President
Membership: 330; *Fees:* $32.50; *Member Profile:* Scottish descent, marriage, affiliation

---

The Scott Mission

502 Spadina Ave., Toronto ON M5S 2H1
Tel: 416-923-8872; *Fax:* 416-923-1067
info@scottmission.com
www.scottmission.com
www.facebook.com/scottmission

twitter.com/TheScottMission
www.flickr.com/photos/thescottmission
Overview: A small local charitable organization founded in 1941
Mission: To serve Jesus Christ, as Lord & Master, in faith & through effective stewardship, putting His spirit into concrete, positive action, through well-rounded spiritual & social services to men, women & children where there is a defined need & as means are provided
Member of: Canadian Council of Christian Charities; Evangelical Fellowship of Canada
Chief Officer(s):
Joe Nemni, Chair
Peter Duraisami, CEO
Finances: *Annual Operating Budget:* Greater than $5 Million
Staff Member(s): 95; 5000 volunteer(s)
Activities: *Internships:* Yes; *Speaker Service:* Yes

Scottish Rite Charitable Foundation of Canada
4 Queen St. South, Hamilton ON L8P 3R3
Tel: 905-522-0033; *Fax:* 905-522-3716
info@srcf.ca
www.srcf.ca
Overview: A medium-sized national charitable organization founded in 1964
Mission: To provide assistance through major grants in the physical/biological & socio/economic areas; student grants for research into the causes of intellectual impairment as opposed to active treatment or palliative care
Chief Officer(s):
Allard B. Loopstra, President
James E. Ford, Secretary
Finances: *Annual Operating Budget:* $250,000-$500,000
Staff Member(s): 29
Membership: 26,000
Activities: *Speaker Service:* Yes; *Library:* Learning Centres for Children; Open to public
Awards:
• Research Grants (Grant)
To support biomedical research into intellectual impairment; to support research into the causes & cure of Alzheimer's Disease *Amount:* $35,000
• Graduate Student Awards (Award)
To support research by Doctoral candidates into the causes, cure & treatment of intellectual impairment *Amount:* $10,000
Publications:
• Annual Report [a publication of The Scottish Rite Charitable Foundation of Canada]
Type: Report
• Clarion [a publication of The Scottish Rite Charitable Foundation of Canada]
Type: Magazine
• The Foundation Newsletter [a publication of The Scottish Rite Charitable Foundation of Canada]
Type: Newsletter

Scottish Settlers Historical Society (SSHS)
201 Kensington Rd., Charlottetown PE C1A 5K9
Tel: 902-894-9885
Also Known As: PEI Scottish Settlers Historical Society
Overview: A small local organization founded in 1968
Mission: To restore & maintain Scottish historical sites such as cemeteries & to promote Scottish music, dancing & culture
Affliation(s): Prince Edward Island Multicultural Council
Chief Officer(s):
Etta Anderson, President

Scottish Studies Foundation Inc.
PO Box 45069, 2482 Yonge St., Toronto ON M4P 3E3
Tel: 416-699-9942
scottishstudies@yahoo.com
www.scottishstudies.com
twitter.com/ssfcanada
Overview: A small national charitable organization founded in 1984
Mission: To fund in perpetuity a Chair in Scottish Studies at the University of Guelph; to provide funding towards the Scottish Library Collection at the University of Guelph; to provide funds for graduate scholarships in Scottish Studies
Chief Officer(s):
Catherine McKenzie Jansen, Membership Secretary
Graeme Morton, Chair
Finances: *Annual Operating Budget:* $50,000-$100,000
Staff Member(s): 1; 20 volunteer(s)
Membership: 450; *Fees:* $20; $100 patron; $500 sponsor; *Committees:* Board of Directors; Finance
Activities: Sail-Past, Toronto Harbour in Sept.; colloquia twice a year at University of Guelph
Publications:
• International Review of Scottish Studies
Editor: G. Morton *ISSN:* 0703-1580
Profile: Annual journal

Scouts Canada / Scouts du Canada
National Office, 1345 Baseline Rd., Ottawa ON K2C 0A7
Toll-Free: 888-855-3336
helpcentre@scouts.ca
www.scouts.ca
www.linkedin.com/company/scouts-canada
www.facebook.com/scoutscanada
twitter.com/scoutscanada
www.youtube.com/scoutscanada
Also Known As: Boy Scouts of Canada
Previous Name: The Boy Scouts Association - Canadian General Council
Overview: A large national charitable organization founded in 1907
Mission: To contribute to the education of young people through a value system based on the Scout Promise & Law; To emphasize learning by doing, particularly in small groups, with outdoor activities as a learning resource
Member of: World Organization of the Scout Movement
Chief Officer(s):
Michael McKay, Executive Commissioner & CEO
mmckay@scouts.ca
Valarie Dillon, Executive Director, Human Resources & Volunteer Services
vdillon@scouts.ca
John Petitti, Executive Director, Marketing & Communications
jpetitti@scouts.ca
Bethany Tory, Executive Director, Membership Services
btory@scouts.ca
Danielle McNeil Taylor, Director, Public Relations
dtaylor@scouts.ca
Alan Mimeault, Director, Retail Services
amimeault@scouts.ca
Ilan Yampolsky, Director, Child & Youth Safety
iyampolsky@scouts.ca
Finances: *Funding Sources:* Membership fees; Donations; Fundraising
Membership: 100,000+; *Member Profile:* Boys, girls, & youths, age 5-26
Activities: Offering programs such as Beaver Scouts (ages 5-7), SCOUTSabout (ages 5-10), Cub Scouts (ages 8-10), Scouts (ages 11-14), Venturer Scouts (ages 14-17), Extreme Adventure (ages 14-17), & Rover Scout (ages 18-26)

British Columbia - Yukon Operations Centre
664 West Broadway, Vancouver BC V5Z 1G1
Tel: 604-879-5721; *Fax:* 604-879-5725
Toll-Free: 888-726-8876
bcy@scouts.ca
www.scouts.ca/dnn/cas
www.facebook.com/pages/pacific-coast-council/182524060844
Chief Officer(s):
Alamin Pirani, Centre Exec. Director

Central Canada Administrative Centre
395 Stafford St., Winnipeg MB R3E 2X4
Tel: 204-786-6661; *Fax:* 204-722-5248
Toll-Free: 888-726-8876
manitoba@scouts.ca
www.scouts.ca/dnn/man
Chief Officer(s):
Don MacDonald, Centre Exec. Director

Central Ontario Administrative Centre
265 Yorkland Blvd., Toronto ON M2J 5C7
Tel: 416-490-6364; *Fax:* 416-490-6911
gtc@scouts.ca
www.gtc.scouts.ca
Chief Officer(s):
Danny Anckle, Centre Exec. Director

Chinook Council
2140 Brownsea Dr. NW, Calgary AB T2N 3G9
Tel: 403-283-4993
chinook@scouts.ca
www.scouts.ca/dnn/chin
Chief Officer(s):
Doug MacDonald, Council Exec. Director

Eastern Ontario Administrative Centre
#200, 1345 Baseline Rd., Ottawa ON K2C 0A7
Tel: 613-225-2770; *Fax:* 613-225-2802
Toll-Free: 888-726-8876
easternontario@scouts.ca
www.whitepine.scouts.ca
Chief Officer(s):
Barry Hardaker, Centre Exec. Director

New Brunswick Council
PO Box 21042, Quispamsis NB E2E 4Z4
Tel: 506-847-9593; *Fax:* 506-847-9579
www.scoutsnb.ca
Chief Officer(s):
Tom Heath, Council Exec. Director

Newfoundland & Labrador Council
55 Karwood Dr., Paradise NL A1L 0L3
Tel: 709-722-0931
nlcouncil@scouts.ca
nfldlabrador.scouts.ca
www.linkedin.com/company/scouts-canada
www.facebook.com/NLScouts
twitter.com/NLScouts
www.youtube.com/scoutscanada
Chief Officer(s):
Jennifer Neary, Council Exec. Director

Northern Lights Council
14205 - 109 Ave., Edmonton AB T5N 1H5
Tel: 780-454-8561; *Fax:* 780-451-5333
Toll-Free: 800-480-2054
northernlights@scouts.ca
www.scouts.ca/dnn/nlc
Chief Officer(s):
D.J. Gough, Council Exec. Director

Northern Ontario Council
c/o 395 Stafford St., Winnipeg MB R3M 2X4
Tel: 204-786-6661; *Fax:* 204-772-5248
Toll-Free: 888-992-4499
northernontario@scouts.ca
www.scouts.ca/dnn/noc
Chief Officer(s):
Barry Hardaker, Council Exec. Director

Nova Scotia Council
84 Thorne Ave., Dartmouth NS B3B 1Y5
Tel: 902-423-9227; *Fax:* 902-423-7989
Toll-Free: 800-557-7268
nsoffice@scouts.ca
www.scouts.ca/dnn/nsc
Chief Officer(s):
Jimmy Khatri, Council Exec. Director

Prince Edward Island Council
PO Box 533, 100 Upper Prince St., Charlottetown PE C1A 7L1
Tel: 902-566-9153; *Fax:* 902-628-6396
office@pei.scouts.ca
www.scouts.ca/dnn/pei
Chief Officer(s):
Rob Stewart, Interim Council Exec. Dir.

Québec Council
#200, 265 Dorval Ave., Dorval QC H9S 3H5
Tel: 514-334-3004; *Fax:* 514-636-8773
info@qc.scouts.ca
www.qc.scouts.ca
Chief Officer(s):
Jon Wiersma, Council Exec. Director

Saskatchewan Council
1313 Broadway Ave., Regina SK S4P 1E2
Tel: 306-757-3701; *Fax:* 306-584-3366
saskatchewan@scouts.ca
www.scouts.ca/dnn/sask
Chief Officer(s):
Don MacDonald, Council Exec. Director

Southwestern Ontario Administrative Centre
531 Windermere Rd., London ON N5X 2T1
Tel: 519-432-2646; *Fax:* 519-432-1677
Toll-Free: 866-568-7472
trishores@scouts.ca
www.scouts.ca/dnn/tri
Chief Officer(s):
Grant Ferron, Centre Exec. Director

Scouts du Canada *See* Scouts Canada

Screen Composers Guild of Canada (SCGC)
2A Wheeler Ave., Toronto ON M4L 3V2
Tel: 416-410-5076; *Fax:* 416-410-4516
Toll-Free: 866-657-1117

www.screencomposers.ca
twitter.com/ScreenComposers
Overview: A small national organization
Mission: To improve the status & quality of music as it applies to film/tv/new media through education & the professional development of its members & the producing community; to represent & communicate the interests of its members to the music & film/tv/new media industries as well as other institutions; to collaborate with trade & industry associations with common interests; to represent all Canadian composers within the certified territories & producer entities detailed in our certification under the Canadian Status of the Artist Act, as the exclusive organization for collective negotiations
Chief Officer(s):
Maria Topalovich, Executive Director
maria@screencomposers.ca
Staff Member(s): 4
Membership: *Fees:* $75 associate; $150 professional; $250 gold; *Member Profile:* One film or TV credit
Activities: Member meetings, seminars, workshops, representing film/tv composers' interests to government & industry; *Internships:* Yes

ScreenScene-Film & Television for Young People *See* The Atlantic Film Festival Association

Scugog Chamber of Commerce
PO Box 1282, #G1, 181 Perry St., Port Perry ON L9L 1A7
Tel: 905-985-4971; *Fax:* 905-985-7698
Toll-Free: 877-820-3595
scugogchamber.ca
Overview: A small local organization founded in 1956
Mission: To promote the commercial, industrial, agricultural & civic interest of the Township of Scugog
Member of: Ontario Chamber of Commerce
Affliation(s): Joint Chambers of Durham Region; Durham Network for Excellence; Tourism Durham; Tourist Association of Durham Region; Durham Home & Small Business Association
Chief Officer(s):
Julie Curran, President
Finances: *Annual Operating Budget:* Less than $50,000; *Funding Sources:* Membership fees; sponsored events
Membership: 227; *Fees:* $135; *Member Profile:* Commercial, entrepreneurial, industrial, agricultural, business & professional people
Activities: Canada Day; Festival Days; Countryside Adventure; Santa Parade; Business for Breakfast (monthly); *Rents Mailing List:* Yes

Sculptors Society of Canada (SSC) / Société des sculpteurs du Canada
c/o Canadian Sculpture Centre, 500 Church St., Toronto ON M4Y 2C8
Tel: 647-435-5858
gallery@cansculpt.org
www.cansculpt.org
Also Known As: Canadian Sculpture Centre
Overview: A small national charitable organization founded in 1928
Mission: To promote Canadian sculpture; to provide encouragement to sculptors through public exhibitions & discussions in Canada & other countries
Affliation(s): Canadian Museum Association; International Sculpture Centre; Ontario Museum Association; Carfac ON; Toronto Arts Council
Chief Officer(s):
Judi Michelle Young, President
Finances: *Funding Sources:* Membership fees; Private donations
Membership: 157; *Fees:* $150
Activities: *Rents Mailing List:* Yes; *Library:* SSC Resource/Documentation Centre; by appointment

Sculptors' Association of Alberta (SAA)
PO Box 11212, Stn. Main, Edmonton AB T5J 3K5
Tel: 780-718-0486
info@sculptorsassociation.ca
www.sculptorsassociation.ca
Overview: A small provincial organization founded in 1988
Mission: To encourage & to promote the creation & exhibition of sculpture; to provide means of communication & information exchange among sculptors; to promote public awareness & appreciation of sculpture & activities of sculptors in Alberta
Member of: Canada Craft Council
Chief Officer(s):
Robert Woodbury, President
Erin DiLoreto, Administrator
Finances: *Funding Sources:* Membership dues; ice carving
Membership: *Fees:* $30
Activities: *Speaker Service:* Yes

Sea Shepherd Conservation Society (SSCS)
PO Box 48446, Vancouver BC V7X 1A2
Tel: 604-688-7325
canada@seashepherd.org
www.seashepherd.org
www.facebook.com/SeaShepherdVancouver
Overview: A medium-sized national organization founded in 1977
Mission: To investigate & document violations of international laws, regulations & treaties protecting marine wildlife species
Chief Officer(s):
Farley Mowat, International Chair
Activities: Volunteers work as crew members aboard our ships to investigate & document any violations of international laws, treaties or regulations against marine wildlife & then enforce those laws; *Speaker Service:* Yes

Sea to Sky Free-Net Association
Hotspot Community Resource Centre, PO Box 2676, Squamish BC V0N 3G0
Tel: 604-815-4142
hotspot@seatoskycommunity.org
www.seatoskycommunity.org
Overview: A small local organization
Mission: To build a local community information system for the Sea to Sky corridor; To work to ensure universal participation in the system & the internet through free public access & education

Seacoast Trail Arts Association
PO Box 235, Sheet Harbour NS B0J 3B0
Tel: 902-654-2696
Toll-Free: 877-654-2696
seasideinn@ns.sympatico.ca
seacoasttrailart.com
Overview: A small local organization founded in 2006
Mission: To celebrate, foster & promote the talent from the Eastern Shore of Nova Scotia.
Chief Officer(s):
Pat Bennett, Contact
Membership: 25; *Fees:* $10 associate/student; $20 regular

Seafarers' International Union of Canada (AFL-CIO/CLC) / Syndicat international des marins canadiens (FAT-COI/CTC)
#200, 1333, rue Saint-Jacques, Montréal QC H3C 4K2
Tel: 514-931-7859; *Fax:* 514-931-3667
siuofcanada@seafarers.ca
www.seafarers.ca
www.facebook.com/pages/SIU-of-Canada/221924054504351
twitter.com/SIUCanada
Overview: A medium-sized international organization
Mission: To ensure its members safe & fair working conditions
Affliation(s): Seafarers' International Union of North America (AFL-CIO); International Transport Workers' Federation
Chief Officer(s):
James Given, President
Staff Member(s): 9

Seafood Producers Association of Nova Scotia
#900, 45 Alderney Dr., Dartmouth NS B2Y 3Z6
Tel: 902-463-7790; *Fax:* 902-469-8294
spans@ns.sympatico.ca
Overview: A medium-sized provincial organization overseen by Fisheries Council of Canada
Chief Officer(s):
Roger C. Stirling, President

Seagull Foundation
PO Box 108, Pugwash NS B0K 1L0
Tel: 902-243-2416
Overview: A small local charitable organization
Mission: To protect significant wilderness areas; to support environmental education & conservation; to support Third World development projects; to support programs that create environmental awareness
Chief Officer(s):
Bonnie Bond, Chair
Finances: *Annual Operating Budget:* Less than $50,000
Staff Member(s): 1; 2 volunteer(s)

Sealant & Waterproofing Association (SWA)
70 Leek Cres., Richmond Hill ON L4B 1H1
Tel: 416-499-4000; *Fax:* 416-499-8752
info@swao.com
www.swao.com
Also Known As: Sealant & Waterproofing Association of Ontario
Merged from: Waterproofing & Caulking Contractors Association
Overview: A medium-sized national organization founded in 1989
Mission: To promote the exchange of ideas for the development of the highest standards & operating efficiency within the sealant & waterproofing industry
Member of: Toronto Construction Association
Chief Officer(s):
Robert J. Montpetit, President
robert@aquacontracting.ca
Andrew Porciello, Vice President
andrewporciello@maximgroup.on.ca
Finances: *Annual Operating Budget:* Less than $50,000; *Funding Sources:* Membership dues; industry funds
Staff Member(s): 2; 30 volunteer(s)
Membership: 25 contractors, 30 associate members, 19 allied professionals

Search & Rescue Volunteer Association of Canada (SARVAC)
24 McNamara Dr., Paradise NL A1L 0A6
Tel: 709-368-5533; *Fax:* 709-368-1298
Toll-Free: 866-972-7822
info@sarvac.ca
www.sarvac.ca
Overview: A small national charitable organization founded in 1996
Mission: A national voice for ground search and rescue volunteers in Canada to address issues of common concern, to develop consistency and promote standardization or portability of programs and volunteers and deliver initiatives that benefit and support all ground search and rescue volunteers in Canada as well as the general public.
Finances: *Funding Sources:* Donations
Membership: 13 associations

Seasons Centre for Grieving Children *See* Grieving Children at Seasons Centre

SeCan Association / Association SeCan
#400, 300 Terry Fox Dr., Kanata ON K2K 0E3
Tel: 613-592-8600; *Fax:* 613-592-9497
Toll-Free: 800-764-5487
seed@secan.com
www.secan.com
Overview: A small national organization founded in 1976
Mission: As Canada's Seed Partner, SeCan actively seeks partnerships which promote profitability in Canadian agriculture. SeCan is the largest supplier of certified seed to Canadian farmers with more than 1,000 members from coast to coast engaged in seed production, processing and marketing. They are a private, not-for-profit, member corporation with the primary goal of accessing and promoting leading genetics.
Chief Officer(s):
Jeff Reid, General Manager
jreid@secan.com
Finances: *Annual Operating Budget:* $1.5 Million-$3 Million
Staff Member(s): 10
Membership: 1,000; *Fees:* $525; *Committees:* Cereals, Oilseeds & Special Crops; Forage; Promotion; Liaison
Activities: *Library*

Sechelt & District Chamber of Commerce
PO Box 360, #102 - 5700 Cowrie St., Sechelt BC V0N 3A0
Tel: 604-885-0662; *Fax:* 604-885-0691
Toll-Free: 877-633-2963
sdcoc9@telus.net
www.secheltchamber.bc.ca
Overview: A medium-sized local organization founded in 1947
Mission: To provide resources & services to members, including business information, community profiles, discounts & benefits plans, payroll services & networking opportunities
Member of: BC Chamber of Commerce
Chief Officer(s):
Jim Cleghorn, President
sunshinekids@dccnet.com
Colleen Clark, Executive Director
Finances: *Annual Operating Budget:* $50,000-$100,000; *Funding Sources:* Provincial & municipal governments; membership dues
Staff Member(s): 1; 16 volunteer(s)

Membership: 268; *Fees:* $75+; *Committees:* Portfolios: Governance; Operations; Communications; Events; Programs & Services; Membership
Activities: *Speaker Service:* Yes; *Library:* Resource Library; Open to public
Awards:
• Good Citizen Award (Award)

Sechelt Marsh Protective Society *See* Sunshine Coast Natural History Society

Second Harvest Food Support Committee *See* Second Harvest

Second Harvest
#18, 1450 Lodestar Rd., Toronto ON M3J 3C1
Tel: 416-408-2594; *Fax:* 416-408-2598
email@secondharvest.ca
www.secondharvest.ca
www.facebook.com/SecondHarvestTO
twitter.com/2ndharvestto
www.youtube.com/user/SecondHarvestToronto?feature=mhee
Previous Name: Second Harvest Food Support Committee
Overview: A small local organization founded in 1985
Mission: Helps feed hungry people by picking up & preparing excess fresh food & delivering it daily to social services in Toronto
Member of: Ontario Association of Food Banks
Chief Officer(s):
Jo-Anne Sobie, Executive Director
Joannes@secondharvest.ca
Activities: *Awareness Events:* Lunch Money Day, Feb.; Toronto Taste, June

Second Story Women's Centre
PO Box 821, 18 Dufferin St., Lunenburg NS B0J 2C0
Tel: 902-543-1315; *Fax:* 902-640-3044
info@secstory.com
www.secstory.com
www.facebook.com/secstory?ref_type=bookmark
twitter.com/Sec_Story
Overview: A small local organization
Chief Officer(s):
Jeanne Fay, Executive Co-ordinator
exec@secstory.com
Membership: *Fees:* $10 (waged); $2 (unwaged)

Secours aux lépreux (Canada) inc. (SLC) / Leprosy Relief (Canada) Inc. (LR)
#305, 1805, rue Sauvé ouest, Montréal QC H4N 3H4
Tél: 514-744-3199; *Téléc:* 514-744-9095
Ligne sans frais: 866-744-3199
info@slc-lr.ca
www.slc-lr.ca
Aperçu: *Dimension:* petite; *Envergure:* internationale; Organisme sans but lucratif; fondée en 1961
Mission: Venir en aide médicalement et socialement aux personnes affectées par la lèpre.
Membre de: Federation internationale des associations de lutte contre la lèpre
Membre(s) du bureau directeur:
Paul E. Legault, Prèsident
Maryse Legault, Director
maryse.legault@slc-lr.ca
Marie Gilbert, Secretaire
Christiane Beauvois, Trèsorière
Finances: *Budget de fonctionnement annuel:* $500,000-$1.5 Million
Membre(s) du personnel: 3; 4 bénévole(s)
Membre: 10; *Montant de la cotisation:* 10$

Secours Quaker Canadien *See* Canadian Friends Service Committee

Secrétariat des conférences intergouvernementales canadiennes *See* Canadian Intergovernmental Conference Secretariat

Secrétariat nationale du MFC - Mouvement des femmes Chrétiennes (MFC)
Att: Mme Louisette Gingras, 625 - 1300, chemin Sainte-Foy, québec QC G1S 0A6
Tél: 581-742-7176
sec.mfcnational@videotron.ca
www.mfcnational.net
Nom précédent: Fédération nationale du MFC - Mouvement des Femmes Chrétiennes
Aperçu: *Dimension:* grande; *Envergure:* nationale; Organisme sans but lucratif; fondée en 1962
Mission: Un mouvement d'action catholique générale, il forme des femmes efficaces et dynamiques sur le plan familial, paroissial, social, et chrétien afin de transformer le milieu de vie par des projects concrets et en utilisant la méthode de l'action catholique
Membre de: Regroupement des Organismes Volontaires d'Éducation Populaire
Membre(s) du bureau directeur:
Pierrette Vachon, Présidente
Finances: *Budget de fonctionnement annuel:* Moins de $50,000
Membre(s) du personnel: 1; 700 bénévole(s)
Membre: 3 000; *Montant de la cotisation:* 15$; *Critères d'admissibilite:* Femmes de tout âge, condition et culture
Activités: Rencontre mensuelle sur le programme d'action; formation
Publications:
• La Famille Chrétienne [a publication of the Fédération nationale du MFC - Mouvement des Femmes Chrétiennes]
Type: Revue; *Frequency:* Quarterly

Sectorial Association - Transportation Equipment & Machinery Manufacturing *Voir* Association sectorielle - Fabrication d'équipement de transport et de machines

Seed Corn Growers of Ontario
825 Park Ave. West, Chatham ON N7M 5J6
Tel: 519-352-6710; *Fax:* 519-352-0526
scgo.ca
twitter.com/SeedCornOntario
Previous Name: Ontario Seed Corn Growers' Marketing Board
Overview: A medium-sized provincial organization founded in 1942
Mission: To work with the individual seed corn companies to negotiate production contracts that not only make growers competitive, but also provide incentives to produce excellent seed. Also works to ensure that growers are provided with the best information and programs to maintain and broaden their seed corn production skills.
Chief Officer(s):
Chris Nanni, Contact
cnanni@scgo.ca
Staff Member(s): 1
Membership: *Member Profile:* Seed corn producers

SEEDS Foundation
#400, 144 - 4th Ave. SW., Calgary AB T2P 3N4
Tel: 403-221-0884; *Fax:* 403-221-0876
Toll-Free: 800-661-8751
seeds@telusplanet.net
www.seedsfoundation.ca
ca.linkedin.com/pub/seeds-foundation/3a/909/44
www.facebook.com/pages/SEEDS-Foundation/117021191648133
Also Known As: Society, Environment & Energy Development Studies Foundation
Overview: A medium-sized national charitable organization founded in 1976
Mission: To provide educational support materials & professional assistance to teachers in the area of energy, environment & sustainable development; To work toward the development of a society which understands & is committed to actions leading to wise stewardship of resources, resource use & the environment
Affliation(s): Connections Education Society
Chief Officer(s):
Corinne Craig, Executive Director, 403-663-2575
ccraig@seedsfoundation.ca
Finances: *Annual Operating Budget:* $250,000-$500,000; *Funding Sources:* Donations (industry, business); government (federal/provincial, less than 5%); sponsorships
Staff Member(s): 6; 19 volunteer(s)
Membership: 19; *Committees:* Education; Environment; Industry
Activities: Providing educational resources on the environment for high school students, such as the Energy Literacy Series, Habitat in the Balance & the Climate of Change Program; Creating the Connections & Green School leadership programs for elementary, junior high & high school students; Creating challenge programs & projects for students such as the Canadian Bird Challenge, the Canadian Water Conservation Challenge & the Environmental Writing Challenge; *Awareness Events:* Green School Celebrations; Annual Bird Challenge; *Speaker Service:* Yes

Seeds of Diversity Canada (SoDC) / Semences du patrimoine Canada
PO Box 36, Stn. Q, Toronto ON M4T 2L7
Toll-Free: 866-509-7333
mail@seeds.ca
www.seeds.ca
Also Known As: Heritage Seed Program
Overview: A medium-sized national organization founded in 1984
Mission: To search out & preserve rare & endangered varieties of vegetables, fruits, flowers, herbs & grains
Affliation(s): Rare Breeds Canada; Canadian Organic Growers
Chief Officer(s):
Bob Wildfong, Executive Director
Finances: *Funding Sources:* Membership fees; grants
Staff Member(s): 2
Membership: 1,700; *Fees:* $30 regular; $50 overseas; $25 fixed income
Activities: Canadian Tomato Project; Great Canadian Garlic Collection; Pollination Canada; *Awareness Events:* Seedy Saturdays & Seedy Sundays

Canadian Associations

Segal Centre for the Performing Arts at the Saidye / Centre des arts Saidye Bronfman
5170, ch Côte Sainte-Catherine, Montréal QC H3W 1M7
Tel: 514-739-2301; *Fax:* 514-739-9340
www.segalcentre.org
www.facebook.com/segalcentre
twitter.com/segalcentre
www.youtube.com/user/segalcentre
Previous Name: The Saidye Bronfman Centre for the Arts
Overview: A small local charitable organization founded in 1967
Mission: To provide cultural activities to all Montréal communities
Affliation(s): YM-YWHA Montreal Jewish Community Centres
Chief Officer(s):
Lisa Rubin, Artistic & Executive Director, 514-739-2301 Ext. 8310
lrubin@segalcentre.org
Jon Rondeau, General Manager, 514-739-2301 Ext. 8347
jrondeau@segalcentre.org
Activities: Cultural activities

Seguin Arts Council
535 Tally-Ho Rd., RR#1, Rosseau ON P0C 1J0
Tel: 705-732-1985
info@seguinartscouncil.com
www.seguinartscouncil.com
Previous Name: Seguin Township Arts Council
Overview: A small local charitable organization founded in 1988
Mission: To represent & develop the arts in Seguin Township
Member of: Community Arts Ontario
Chief Officer(s):
Barb Harding, President
Finances: *Funding Sources:* Donations; Grants; Membership dues
Membership: *Fees:* $25
Activities: Annual Art Tour & Crafts Sale; Comedy Night; Concerts; Artisan's Market & antiques
Awards:
• Wendy Marsh Memorial Award (Award)

Seguin Township Arts Council *See* Seguin Arts Council

Seicho-No-Ie Toronto Centre
662 Victoria Park Ave., Toronto ON M4C 5H4
Tel: 416-690-8686; *Fax:* 416-690-3917
www.seicho-no-ie.org
Also Known As: Home of Infinite Growth
Previous Name: Seicho-No-Ie Canada Truth of Life Centre
Overview: A small national organization founded in 1963
Mission: Provides a place of worship for those who believe in the Seicho-No-Ie Humanity Enlightenment Movement, which says that all religions emanate from one universal god
Member of: Seicho-No-Ie (Canada)

Seicho-No-Ie Vancouver Centre
305 East 16th Ave., Vancouver BC V5T 2T7
Tel: 604-879-8116; *Fax:* 604-876-8083
snivancouver.blogspot.ca

Seicho-No-Ie Canada Truth of Life Centre *See* Seicho-No-Ie Toronto Centre

Self-Help Connection Clearinghouse Association
63 King St., Dartmouth NS B2Y 2R7
Tel: 902-466-2011; *Fax:* 902-404-3205
Toll-Free: 866-765-6639

selfhelp@eastlink.ca
www.selfhelpconnection.ca
www.facebook.com/113299068696700
Overview: A small local charitable organization founded in 1987
Mission: To enable Nova Scotians to improve control over their health by increasing their knowledge, skills & resources for individual & collective action
Member of: Canadian Network of Self-Help Centres; International Network of Mutual Help Centres
Affliation(s): National Network for Mental Health; Canadian Coalition of Mental Health Resources
Chief Officer(s):
Linda Bayers, Director
linda.bayers@eastlink.ca
Finances: *Annual Operating Budget:* $100,000-$250,000
Staff Member(s): 6
Activities: Workshops; conferences; displays; *Library* Open to public

Self-Help Resource Association of British Columbia *See* PeerNetBC

Self-Help Resource Centre (SHRC)

#307, 40 St. Clair Ave. East, Toronto ON M4T 1M9
Tel: 416-487-4355; *Fax:* 416-487-0344
Toll-Free: 888-283-8806
shrc@selfhelp.on.ca
www.selfhelp.on.ca
twitter.com/selfhelprc
Overview: A small local charitable organization founded in 1987
Mission: To promote self-help/mutual aid; to increase awareness about self-help/mutual aid in the community & among helping professionals; to facilitate the growth & development of self-help groups, networks & resources
Affliation(s): Centre of Health Promotion; Canadian Health Network
Chief Officer(s):
Jennifer Poole, President
Mark Freeman, Executive Director
Staff Member(s): 5
Activities: Information/referral service for over 500 self-help groups in the Greater Toronto area; coordination of self-help networks & organizations across the province; *Speaker Service:* Yes; *Library* Open to public

Selkirk & District Chamber of Commerce

City of Selkirk Bldg., 100 Eaton Ave., Selkirk MB R1A 0W6
Tel: 204-482-7176; *Fax:* 204-482-5448
info@selkirkanddistrictchamber.ca
www.selkirkanddistrictchamber.ca
Overview: A small local organization founded in 1901
Mission: To promote the economic, civic, educational & cultural interests of the citizens of Selkirk & district & the furtherance of the development of resources
Member of: Manitoba Chamber of Commerce
Finances: *Annual Operating Budget:* Less than $50,000; *Funding Sources:* Membership dues
15 volunteer(s)
Membership: 155 institutional; 4 individual; *Fees:* $85 individual; $150-$500 business

Selkirk Friendship Centre (SFC)

425 Eveline St., Selkirk MB R1A 2J5
Tel: 204-482-7525; *Fax:* 204-785-8124
sfc@mts.net
www.selkirkfriendshipcentre.ca
Overview: A small local organization founded in 1968
Mission: Promotes the progress in the educational, social, ecmonic, social, athletic & cultural life of both Aboriginal & Non-Aboriginal peoples
Chief Officer(s):
Mark Mostoway, Executive Director, 204-485-1337
edsfc@mts.net
Activities: Provides assistance in employment, housing, daycare, youth activities; Fosters cultural awareness

Semences du patrimoine Canada *See* Seeds of Diversity Canada

Semiahmoo Foundation

15306 - 24th Ave., Surrey BC V4A 2J1
Tel: 604-536-1242; *Fax:* 604-536-9507
shs@shsbc.ca
www.semi-house-society.com/foundation.html
Overview: A medium-sized national charitable organization
Mission: To fund, support & enhance the programs & services offered by the Semiahmoo House Society
Chief Officer(s):
Ron Jones, President
Christine Scott, Executive Director
cscott@sfscl.org
Finances: *Funding Sources:* Donations; memberships; fundraising
Activities: *Awareness Events:* Purdy's Campaign, Dec.

Semiahmoo House Society (SHS)

15306 - 24th Ave., Surrey BC V4A 2J1
Tel: 604-536-1242; *Fax:* 604-536-9507
shs@shsbc.ca
www.semi-house-society.com
www.facebook.com/SemiahmooHouseSociety
twitter.com/SemiahmooHouse
Overview: A small local organization founded in 1976
Mission: To provide vocational, residential life skills support services to adults with a mental handicap; community integration, advocacy & housing
Member of: Inclusion BC
Affliation(s): American Association on Mental Retardation; National Association for the Dually Diagnosed; The Association for the Severely Handicapped
Chief Officer(s):
Matt Houghton, Chair
Paul Wheeler, Executive Director
Doug Tennant, Co-Executive Director
d.tennant@shsbc.ca
Finances: *Annual Operating Budget:* Greater than $5 Million; *Funding Sources:* Provincial government
Staff Member(s): 250; 50 volunteer(s)
Membership: 160; *Member Profile:* Community individuals; *Committees:* Performance & Quality Improvement (PQI); Occupational Health & Safety; Labour Management
Activities: Programs & services include: Acquired Brain Injury; advocacy; adult day & work programs; programs for children & youth; recreation & leisure; family servies; respite support; Snoezelen room for relaxation; supported living options; *Awareness Events:* Community Awareness Month, Oct.; *Speaker Service:* Yes

Senate Protective Service Employees Association (SPSEA) / Association des employés du Service de sécurité du Sénate (AESSS)

c/o Senate of Canada, 140 Wellington St., Ottawa ON K1A 0A4
Tel: 613-992-9265; *Fax:* 613-943-0032
Overview: A small local organization founded in 1978
Membership: 87

Seneca Centennial Committee *See* York-Grand River Historical Society

Senior Citizens' Central Council of Calgary *See* Calgary Seniors' Resource Society

Senior Link

3036 Danforth Ave., Toronto ON M4C 1N2
Tel: 416-691-7407; *Fax:* 416-691-8466
info@neighbourhoodlink.org
www.neighbourhoodlink.org/seniors
Overview: A small local charitable organization founded in 1975
Mission: To promote the independence & dignity of seniors in their own community
Member of: Ontario Non-Profit Housing Association; Ontario Association of Non-Profit Homes & Services for Seniors; Ontario Community Support Association
Chief Officer(s):
Judith Leon, Contact
Finances: *Annual Operating Budget:* Greater than $5 Million
Staff Member(s): 60; 300 volunteer(s)
Membership: 165; *Member Profile:* 50 hours of volunteering
Activities: Home support, supportive housing, advocacy & counselling services all designed to help older adults keep their independence for as long as possible; *Internships:* Yes; *Speaker Service:* Yes

Seniors Association of Greater Edmonton (SAGE)

15 Sir Winston Churchill Sq., Edmonton AB T5J 2E5
Tel: 780-423-5510; *Fax:* 780-426-5175
info@mysage.ca
www.mysage.ca
www.facebook.com/438132792913806
twitter.com/sageYEG
Previous Name: Society for the Retired & Semi-Retired
Overview: A medium-sized local charitable organization founded in 1970
Mission: To enhance the quality of life of older persons through service, innovation, advocacy & voluntarism
Affliation(s): United Way; Imagine Canada
Chief Officer(s):
D. Lynn Skillen, President
Roger E. Laing, Executive Director
Finances: *Annual Operating Budget:* $1.5 Million-$3 Million; *Funding Sources:* City of Edmonton; Community Services; Alberta Seniors; United Way; Donations; Memberships; Casino
112 volunteer(s)
Membership: *Fees:* $26.25 individual; $131.25 non-profit; $262.50 for-profit
Activities: *Awareness Events:* SAGE Awards; *Library:* Heritage Library

Seniors for Nature Canoe Club (SFNCC)

PO Box 94051, Stn. Bedford Park, Toronto ON M4N 3R1
e-mail: info@sfncc.org
www.sfncc.org
Overview: A small local organization founded in 1985
Mission: To offer seniors the opportunity to canoe, camp, hike, ski & cycle
Member of: Federation of Ontario Naturalists
Chief Officer(s):
Paul Short, President
Finances: *Annual Operating Budget:* Less than $50,000; *Funding Sources:* Membership fees
12 volunteer(s)
Membership: 135 senior; *Fees:* $35; *Member Profile:* Over 55 years of age; able to help transport & steer canoes & to swim; *Committees:* Program & Training; Purchasing & Inventory; Membership; Social; Publicity & Newsletter
Activities: Canoeing, hiking, skiing, biking, camping trips

Seniors in Need

#102, 40 St. Clair West, Toronto ON M4V 1M2
Tel: 416-481-2733
www.seniorsinneed.ca
www.facebook.com/SeniorsInNeed
twitter.com/seniorsinneed
Overview: A medium-sized local charitable organization founded in 2011
Mission: A grassroots organization that connects concerns Canadians to impoverished seniors; Registered nonprofit sponsors submit the details of a senior in need to a database and donors can find and help a senior of their choosing.
Chief Officer(s):
Peter D. Cook, Founder
Finances: *Funding Sources:* Seniors for Seniors

Seniors Peer Helping Program

80 Lothian Ave., Toronto ON M8Z 4K5
Tel: 416-239-7252
Also Known As: Peer Helping Centre
Overview: A small local organization founded in 1981
Mission: To provide growth experience for older adults in group setting; to train seniors to help other seniors
Chief Officer(s):
Mary Neale, Chair
Finances: *Funding Sources:* Fundraising
Membership: *Member Profile:* Individuals 55 years of age & over
Activities: Personal growth courses; "Time for Me" course; Growing Further; Peer helping training; monthly time grads get together

Seniors Resource Centre *See* Seniors Resource Centre Association of Newfoundland & Labrador Inc.

Seniors Resource Centre Association of Newfoundland & Labrador Inc. (SRC NL)

#W100, 370 Torbay Rd., St. John's NL A1A 3W8
Tel: 709-737-2333; *Fax:* 709-737-3717
Toll-Free: 800-563-5599
info@seniorsresource.ca
www.seniorsresource.ca
Previous Name: Seniors Resource Centre
Overview: A small provincial organization founded in 1990
Mission: Dedicated to promoting the independence & well being of older adults in Newfoundland & Labrador through the provision of information as well as various programs & services.
Chief Officer(s):
Kelly Heisz, Executive Director
Finances: *Annual Operating Budget:* $500,000-$1.5 Million; *Funding Sources:* Donations; Will bequests; Memorial gifts; Grants; Fundraising; Foundations; Sponsorships
Staff Member(s): 9; 425 volunteer(s)

Activities: Provincial Peer Support Volunteer Program; Friendly Visiting Program; Mall-Walkers Club; NL Network for the Prevention of Elder Abuse (NLNPEA); Information Referral Line; *Internships:* Yes; *Speaker Service:* Yes

Sensibilisation au cancer du sein ***See*** Breast Cancer Action

Sentier Urbain
#310, 1710, rue Beaudry, Montréal QC H2L 3E7
Tél: 514-521-9292; *Téléc:* 514-596-7093
info@sentierurbain.org
www.sentierurbain.org
www.facebook.com/115278308497487
twitter.com/sentierurbain
Aperçu: *Dimension:* petite; *Envergure:* locale; fondée en 1993
Mission: De mettre en ouvre des programmes respectueux de l'environnement dans la communauté
Membre(s) du bureau directeur:
Pierre Dénommé, Directeur général
direction@sentierurbain.org

Sentiers de l'estrie
5182, boul. Bourque, Sherbrooke QC J1N 1H4
Tél: 819-864-6314; *Téléc:* 819-864-1864
marche@lessentiersdelestrie.qc.ca
www.lessentiersdelestrie.qc.ca
www.facebook.com/202589809771641
Aperçu: *Dimension:* petite; *Envergure:* locale
Mission: Pour promouvoir la marche en faisant les repérages en Estrie plus accessible

Sentinelle Outaouais ***See*** Ottawa Riverkeeper

Separation Party of Alberta (SPA)
PO Box 266, Hussar AB T0J 1S0
Tel: 403-787-2837
albertanswill@gmail.com
www.separationalberta.com
Overview: A large provincial organization
Chief Officer(s):
Bart Hampton, Party Leader
Glen Dundas, President

Serbian National Shield Society of Canada
#303, 1900 Sheppard Ave. East, Toronto ON M2J 4T4
Tel: 416-496-7881; *Fax:* 416-493-0335
Also Known As: Voice of Canadian Serbs
Overview: A small national organization
Mission: To promote & inform about interests & heritage of Canadian Serbs
Member of: Canadian Ethnocultural Council
Chief Officer(s):
Diane Dragasevich, Contact

Serbian Orthodox Church in the United States of America & Canada - Diocese of Canada
7470 McNiven Rd., RR#3, Campbellville ON L0P 1B0
Tel: 905-878-0043; *Fax:* 905-878-1909
vladika@istocnik.com
www.istocnik.com
Overview: A medium-sized national charitable organization founded in 1983
Mission: To serve the Serbian Orthodox community & teach the Orthodox faith & culture
Chief Officer(s):
Georgije, Bishop, 905-878-3438, Fax: 905-878-1909
vladika@istocnik.com
Stavrophor Vasilije Tomic, Episcopal Deputy, 416-450-4555
o.bajo@rogers.com
Finances: *Annual Operating Budget:* $500,000-$1.5 Million; *Funding Sources:* Donations; parish taxes; dispensations
Staff Member(s): 23
Membership: 150,000; *Committees:* Diocesan Executive Board; Diocesan Assembly
Activities: *Library:* Holy Transfiguration; Open to public by appointment

Serena Canada
151 Holland Ave., Ottawa ON K1Y 0Y2
Tel: 613-728-6536
Toll-Free: 888-373-7362
sc@serena.ca
www.serena.ca
Overview: A small national charitable organization founded in 1955
Mission: To promote natural family planning methods based on information from a woman's body
Affiliation(s): International Federation for Family Life Promotion; Roman Catholic Church
Finances: *Funding Sources:* Provincial corporations; revenue from publication sales; donations
Activities: *Speaker Service:* Yes

Alberta Branch
131 Twin Brooks Cove NW, Edmonton AB T6J 6T1
Tel: 780-488-5221
Toll-Free: 866-488-5221
serena-a@telus.net

British Columbia Branch
2540 Tulip Cres., Abbotsford BC V2T 1R6
Tel: 604-677-4132
bc@serena.ca
www.vcn.bc.ca/serenabc
www.facebook.com/pages/Serena-BC/198824256810301
twitter.com/Serena_BC

Manitoba Branch
Ed. & Res. Centre, #317, 99 Cornish, Winnipeg MB R3C 1A2
Tel: 204-783-0091; *Fax:* 204-774-7834
Toll-Free: 866-317-5362
mbserena@gmail.com
serenamb.com
www.facebook.com/serenamanitoba
Chief Officer(s):
Linda Kuehn, Executive Director

New Brunswick Branch
30 Saint Coeur Ct., St. John NB E2M 5R3
Tel: 506-759-9557
nb@serena.ca

Nova Scotia Branch
344 Main St., Antigonish NS B2G 2R6
Tel: 902-863-5061
ns@serena.ca

Ontario Branch
151 Holland Ave., Ottawa ON K1Y 0Y2
Tel: 613-728-6536
ontario@serena.ca

Québec Branch
6646, rue Saint-Denis, Montréal QC H2S 2R9
Tél: 514-273-7531
Ligne sans frais: 866-273-7362
communication@serena.ca
serena.ca
www.facebook.com/serenaqc
twitter.com/SerenaQuebec

Saskatchewan Branch
PO Box 7375, Saskatoon SK S7K 4J3
Tel: 306-934-8223
Toll-Free: 800-667-1637
sask@serena.ca

Service à la famille chinoise du Grand Montréal / Chinese Family Service of Greater Montréal
987, rue Côté, 4e étage, Montréal QC H2Z 1L1
Tél: 514-861-5244; *Téléc:* 514-861-9008
famillechinoise@hotmail.com
www.famillechinoise.qc.ca
Aperçu: *Dimension:* petite; *Envergure:* locale; Organisme sans but lucratif; fondée en 1976
Membre de: Chinese Canadian National Council
Affiliation(s): Centre Sino-Québec de la Rive-Sud
Membre(s) du bureau directeur:
Xixi Li, Directrice générale
Membre(s) du personnel: 13; 150 bénévole(s)
Activités: Club des femmes; Services aux personnes âgées et Centre Man Sau; Camp pour les enfants; Projet jeu problématique; *Stagiaires:* Oui; *Service de conférenciers:* Oui

Service budgétaire et communautaire d'Alma inc. ***Voir*** Service budgétaire Lac-Saint-Jean-Est

Service budgétaire et communautaire de Chicoutimi inc (SBC)
2422, rue Roussel, Chicoutimi QC G7G 1X6
Tél: 418-549-7597; *Téléc:* 418-549-1325
sbc@vl.videotron.ca
servicebudgetaire.org
Aperçu: *Dimension:* petite; *Envergure:* locale; Organisme sans but lucratif; fondée en 1980
Mission: Aider les personnes dans leurs difficultés financières et aux prises avec les problèmes sociaux qui en découlent
Membre(s) du bureau directeur:
Dominique Langevin-Proulx, Directrice
directionsbc@videotron.ca
Membre(s) du personnel: 6; 54 bénévole(s)

Service budgétaire Lac-Saint-Jean-Est
CP 594, 415, rue Collard ouest, Alma QC G8B 5W1
Tél: 418-668-2148; *Téléc:* 418-668-2048
info@servicebudgetaire.com
www.servicebudgetaire.com
Nom précédent: Service budgétaire et communautaire d'Alma inc.
Aperçu: *Dimension:* petite; *Envergure:* locale; Organisme sans but lucratif; fondée en 1977
Mission: Aider les individus et les familles à faibles et moyens revenus, à résoudre leur difficultés financières et les problèmes qui en découlent; prévenir l'endettement; informer les consommateurs et les consommatrices sur les lois et sur leurs droits; travailler sur différentes problématiques au niveau des habitudes de consommation et de leurs conséquences sur le budget, la santé, l'organisation familiale, etc.
Membre(s) du bureau directeur:
Thérèse Gagnon, Coordonnatrice
Finances: *Budget de fonctionnement annuel:* Moins de $50,000
Membre(s) du personnel: 2; 40 bénévole(s)
Membre: 100-499; *Comités:* Prêts; Promotion; Recherche
Activités: Cours de budget et consommation; consultation budgétaire individuelle; fonds d'épargne et de prêt populaire; *Bibliothèque:* Centre de documentation au service budgétaire; Bibliothèque publique

Service canadien d'évaluation de documents scolaires internationaux ***See*** International Credential Assessment Service of Canada

Service d'aide au consommateur ***Voir*** Service de protection et d'information du consommateur

Service d'assistance canadienne aux organismes ***See*** Canadian Executive Service Organization

Service de conciliation en assurance de dommages ***See*** General Insurance OmbudService

Service de protection et d'information du consommateur (SPIC)
1852, av St-Marc, Shawinigan QC G9N 2H7
Tél: 819-537-1414; *Téléc:* 819-537-5259
Ligne sans frais: 800-567-8552
info@serviceconsommateur.org
www.serviceconsommateur.org
Nom précédent: Service d'aide au consommateur
Aperçu: *Dimension:* petite; *Envergure:* locale; fondée en 1974
Mission: Le Service d'aide au consommateur (SAC) est un organisme privé sans but lucratif voué à la promotion et à la défense des droits et intérêts des consommateurs.
Membre: *Montant de la cotisation:* 24$

Service des programmes d'études Canada ***See*** Curriculum Services Canada

Service familial catholique d'Ottawa ***See*** Catholic Family Service of Ottawa

Service familial de Sudbury (SFS) / Sudbury Family Service
c/o Sudbury Counselling Centre, 260, rue Cedar, Sudbury ON P3B 1M7
Tél: 705-524-9629; *Téléc:* 705-524-1530
Ligne sans frais: 800-833-0822
info@counsellingccs.com
www.counsellingccs.com
Aperçu: *Dimension:* petite; *Envergure:* locale; Organisme sans but lucratif; fondée en 1971 surveillé par Family Service Ontario
Mission: Amélioration de la qualité de vie et la résolution des problèmes psychosociaux des individus, des familles, des groupes & de la communauté
Affiliation(s): Conseil de Développement social
Membre(s) du bureau directeur:
Gaetanne Lacourciere, Secrétaire de direction
Denis Constantineau, Directeur général
Linda Menard, Présidente
Finances: *Budget de fonctionnement annuel:* $500,000-$1.5 Million
Membre(s) du personnel: 16; 8 bénévole(s)
Membre: 32; *Montant de la cotisation:* 2$
Activités: Counselling général; intervention contre la violence faite aux femmes; aide aux employés; *Evénements de sensibilisation:* Semaine nationale de la famille, oct.; *Bibliothèque:* Centre de ressources du SFS; rendez-vous

Service Intégration Travail Outaouais (SITO)
#400, 4, rue Taschereau, Gatineau QC J8Y 2V5
Tél: 819-776-2260; *Téléc:* 819-776-2988
info@sito.qc.ca
sito.qc.ca
Aperçu: *Dimension:* petite; *Envergure:* locale
Mission: Pour aider les immigrants à trouver un emploi
Membre(s) du bureau directeur:
Robert Mayrand, Directeur
Membre(s) du personnel: 11
Membre: *Montant de la cotisation:* 5$

Le Service juif d'information et de référence *See* Jewish Information Referral Service Montréal

Service Social International Canada *See* International Social Service Canada

Service universitaire canadien outre-mer (SUCO)
#210, 1453 rue Beaubien Est, Montréal QC H2G 3C6
Tél: 514-272-3019; *Téléc:* 514-272-3097
Ligne sans frais: 866-357-0475
montreal@suco.org
www.suco.org
www.facebook.com/SUCO.solidarite.union.cooperation
twitter.com/SUCOInc
www.youtube.com/user/SUCOMontreal
Aperçu: *Dimension:* petite; *Envergure:* internationale; fondée en 1961
Mission: Promouvoir la solidarité directe entre les peuples en vue d'un développement durable pris en charge démocratiquement par les populations concernées
Affiliation(s): AQCI-Association québécoise des organismes de coopération internationale
Membre(s) du bureau directeur:
Richard Veenstra, Directeur général
richardveenstra@suco.org
Finances: *Fonds:* International Government
Membre(s) du personnel: 17

Services à la famille - Canada *See* Family Service Canada

Services à la Famille - Kent *See* Family Service Kent

Services à la famille - Moncton, Inc *See* Family Service Moncton Inc.

Services à la famille - Ontario *See* Family Service Ontario

Services à la famille et à l'enfance du Nord Est de l'Ontario *See* North Eastern Ontario Family & Children's Services

Services canadiens d'assistance aux immigrants juifs *See* Jewish Immigrant Aid Services of Canada

Services communautaires catholiques inc. *See* Catholic Community Services Inc.

Services d'évaluation pédagogique *See* Canadian Test Centre Inc.

Services de Sécurité Nouveau-Brunswick *See* Safety Services New Brunswick

Les services du Triangle Rose *See* Pink Triangle Services

Services familiaux catholiques de Toronto *See* Catholic Family Services of Toronto

Services pour femmes immigrantes d'Ottawa *See* Immigrant Women Services Ottawa

Seton Portage/Shalalth District Chamber of Commerce
PO Box 2067, Seton Portage BC V0N 3B0
Tel: 250-259-8268
Overview: A small local organization
Chief Officer(s):
Ray Klassen, Vice-President

Settlement Assistance & Family Support Services
#214, 1200 Markham Rd., Toronto ON M1H 3C3
Tel: 416-431-4847; *Fax:* 416-431-7283
reception@safss.org
www.safss.com
www.youtube.com/channel/UCElY8hHUthem2DooDwhj73A
Previous Name: South Asian Family Support Services
Overview: A small local organization
Mission: To offer linguistically & culturally appropriate services to newcomers
Chief Officer(s):
Kazi Hoque, Executive Director
Staff Member(s): 21
Membership: *Fees:* $5 clients/volunteers; $10 individual; $50 organization; $100 corporation

Seva Canada Society
#100, 2000 West 12th Ave., Vancouver BC V6J 2G2
Tel: 604-713-6622; *Fax:* 604-733-4292
Toll-Free: 877-460-6622
admin@seva.ca
www.seva.ca
www.facebook.com/134455149912301
twitter.com/sevacanada
www.youtube.com/user/SevaCanada
Previous Name: Seva Service Society
Overview: A small international charitable organization founded in 1982
Mission: To prevent & relieve suffering & generate meaningful change through compassionate action
Member of: British Columbia Council for International Cooperation
Chief Officer(s):
Penny Lyons, Executive Director
Finances: *Annual Operating Budget:* $500,000-$1.5 Million
Staff Member(s): 5; 35 volunteer(s)
Membership: 4,000; *Committees:* Fundraising; Management; P.R. Events; International Opthalmology
Activities: Works in partnerships in Nepal, Tibet, India & Tanzania, to build eye care programs to eliminate avoidable blindness; *Awareness Events:* World Sight Day, 2nd Thu. of Oct.; *Speaker Service:* Yes; *Library* by appointment
Awards:
• MPB Achievement Award (Award)
• Lewis Perinbaum Award for International Development (Award)

Seva Service Society *See* Seva Canada Society

Seventh Step Society of Canada
#2017, 246 Stewart Green SW, Calgary AB T3H 3C8
Tel: 403-650-1902
seventh@7thstep.ca
www.7thstep.ca
Overview: A small national organization founded in 1967
Mission: Self-help organization dedicated to help adult & young offenders to become useful & productive members of society; to provide follow-up to those who wish to use organization as means to maintain freedom
Chief Officer(s):
Patrick Graham, Executive Director
Membership: *Fees:* $5

Seventh-day Adventist Church in Canada (SDACC) / Église adventiste du septième jour au Canada
1148 King St. East, Oshawa ON L1H 1H8
Tel: 905-433-0011; *Fax:* 905-433-0982
communication@adventist.ca
www.adventist.ca
Overview: A large national charitable organization founded in 1901
Mission: To be a significant Christian movement that recognizes the unique role to which Christ has called it & the urgency of the message of salvation & judgment; To lead people to salvation in Jesus; To teach them the biblical faith & discipline of the Christian life; To equip them to serve with their God-given abilities through the leadership of our various administrative & ministry teams; To proclaim Christ; To nurture believers; To serve humanity
Chief Officer(s):
Mark Johnson, President, 905-433-0011 Ext. 2086
johnson.mark@adventist.ca
Dennis Marshall, Vice-President, 905-433-0011 Ext. 2073
marshall.dennis@adventist.ca
Daniel Dragan Stojanovic, Secretary/Vice-President, Administration, 905-433-0011 Ext. 2083
stojanovic.dragan@adventist.ca
John Ramsay, Treasurer/Vice-President, Finance, 905-433-0011 Ext. 2088
ramsay.john@adventist.ca
Finances: *Annual Operating Budget:* $3 Million-$5 Million; *Funding Sources:* Donations
Staff Member(s): 23
Membership: 375 churches + 66,907 individual members
Activities: Adventist Development & Relief Agency (ADRA); Native Ministries; It Is Written Canada; Christian Record Services; Canadian University College; Kingsway College
Publications:
• Canadian Adventist Messenger
Type: Magazine; *Frequency:* Monthly; *Accepts Advertising*; *Editor:* Stan Jensen
Profile: Church news & feature articles on spiritual topics.

Severn Sound Environmental Association (SSEA)
67 Fourth St., Midland ON L4R 3S9
Tel: 705-527-5166; *Fax:* 705-527-5167
sseainfo@midland.ca
www.severnsound.ca
Overview: A small local organization
Mission: To forge cooperative initiatives to address environmental issues by planning, designing, arranging funding and implementing environmental projects and promoting a sustainable Severn Sound community.
Chief Officer(s):
Keith Sherman, Executive Director, 705-527-5166 Ext. 206
ksherman@midland.ca
Membership: 9 municipalities

Sex Information & Education Council of Canada (SIECCAN) / Conseil d'information et éducation sexuelles du Canada
850 Coxwell Ave., Toronto ON M4C 5R1
Tel: 416-466-5304; *Fax:* 416-778-0785
sieccan@web.ca
www.sieccan.org
Overview: A large national charitable organization founded in 1964
Mission: To inform & educate public & professionals about all aspects of human sexuality in order to support the positive integration of sexuality into people's lives
Chief Officer(s):
Michael Barrett, Executive Director
Stephen Holzapfel, Chair
Alexander McKay, Research Coordinator
Finances: *Annual Operating Budget:* $50,000-$100,000
Staff Member(s): 2; 13 volunteer(s)
Membership: 325 institutional + 30 student/senior/retiree + 550 individual; *Fees:* $40 individual; $60 organization; $25 student/senior/retiree
Activities: *Speaker Service:* Yes; *Library* Open to public by appointment
Publications:
• Canadian Journal of Human Sexuality (CJHS)
Type: Journal; *Frequency:* Quarterly

Sexsmith & District Chamber of Commerce
PO Box 146, Sexsmith AB T0H 3C0
e-mail: info@sexsmithchamber.com
www.sexsmithchamber.com
Overview: A small local organization
Chief Officer(s):
Freda King, President
Membership: 44

Sexual Assault Centre Kingston Inc. (SACCK)
PO Box 1461, Kingston ON K7L 5C7
Tel: 613-545-0762; *Fax:* 613-545-9744; *Crisis Hot-Line:* 877-544-6424
sack@sackingston.com
www.sackingston.com
www.facebook.com/100698016685171
twitter.com/sackingston
Overview: A small local charitable organization founded in 1978 overseen by Canadian Association of Sexual Assault Centres
Mission: To provide non-judgmental support & counselling to people who have been sexually assaulted
Member of: Ontario Coalition of Rape Crisis Centres
Chief Officer(s):
Kim Allen, Executive Director
Finances: *Annual Operating Budget:* $500,000-$1.5 Million; *Funding Sources:* Ministry of the Attorney General; Ministry of Health; Queen's University; United Way; fundraising; United Way; Membership fees; Donations
Activities: 24-hour crisis line; counselling (individual & group); information & referral; public education; *Awareness Events:* Take Back the Night, Sept.; National Day of Remembrance & Action on Violence Against Women, Dec 6; *Internships:* Yes; *Speaker Service:* Yes; *Library* Open to public

Sexual Assault Centre London (SACL)
#5, 255 Horton St., 3rd Fl., London ON N6B 1L1
Tel: 519-439-0844; *Fax:* 519-439-9931
Toll-Free: 877-529-2272; *TTY:* 519-439-0690; *Crisis Hot-Line:* 519-438-2272
sacl@sacl.ca
www.sacl.ca
www.facebook.com/SACLondon

twitter.com/SACLondon
www.youtube.com/user/SACLondon
Overview: A small local charitable organization founded in 1975
Mission: To promote social & attitudinal changes toward sexual violence through public education, outreach & cooperative effort with other community groups; to provide services in a safe environment to survivors of sexual violence through peer support, counselling, advocacy & information
Affliation(s): Ontario Coalition of Rape Crisis Centres; London Coordinating Committee to End Woman Abuse
Chief Officer(s):
Louise Pitre, Executive Director
Finances: *Funding Sources:* Ministry of the Attorney General; United Way; Ontario Trillium Foundation; City of London; Status of Women Canada; Sisters of St. Joseph
Activities: 24-hour crisis & support line; peer support services; accompaniment; public education; training programs for volunteers & staff; crisis intervention & stabilization; support groups for survivors; young women's support groups; therapy groups for adult survivors of child sexual abuse; *Speaker Service:* Yes

Sexual Assault Centre of Edmonton (SACE)
#205, 14964 - 121A Ave., Edmonton AB T5V 1A3
Tel: 780-423-4102; *Fax:* 780-421-8734; *TTY:* 780-421-1482;
Crisis Hot-Line: 780-423-4121
info@sace.ab.ca
www.sace.ab.ca
www.facebook.com/pages/Sexual-Assault-Centre-of-Edmonton/285801329326
twitter.com/sacetalks
Overview: A small local charitable organization founded in 1976
Mission: To assist individuals affected by sexual abuse & assault; To encourage the community of Edmonton to take action against sexual violence
Finances: *Funding Sources:* United Way; Family & Community Support Services; Alberta Justice; Alberta Children's Services; Edmonton Community Foundation; Fundraising
Activities: Providing crisis intervention & counselling; Offering public education & information; Delivering a diversity outreach program; *Awareness Events:* National Day of Remembrance & Action on Violence Against Women, December 6

Sexual Assault Centre of Guelph *See* Guelph-Wellington Women in Crisis

Sexual Assault Crisis Centre of Essex County Inc. (SACC)
1407 Ottawa St., #G, Windsor ON N8X 2G1
Tel: 519-253-3100; *Fax:* 519-253-0175
sacc@cogeco.net
www.wincom.net/~sacc/
Previous Name: Windsor Sexual Assault Crisis Centre
Overview: A small local charitable organization founded in 1978 overseen by Canadian Association of Sexual Assault Centres
Member of: United Way of Windsor & Essex County
Finances: *Funding Sources:* Provincial government; Donations
Staff Member(s): 13; 15 volunteer(s)
Activities: Providing crisis intervention services; Counselling; Offering education; Engaging in advocacy activities

Sexual Assault Support Centre Ottawa (SASC)
PO Box 4441, Stn. E, Ottawa ON K1S 5B4
Tel: 613-725-2160; *Fax:* 613-725-9259; *TTY:* 613-725-1657;
Crisis Hot-Line: 613-234-2266
info@sascottawa.com
sascottawa.com
www.facebook.com/SASCOttawa
twitter.com/SascOttawa
Overview: A small local charitable organization founded in 1983
Mission: To offer accessible, confidential support to female survivors of sexual violence; to offer a non-directive service; to encourage self-confidence & self-esteem; to increase public awareness; to offer training on the politics & effects of violence against women; to engage in political action to pressure for change in the structures & systems that contribute to the practice, maintenance, & tolerance of violence, oppression, discrimination & exploitation
Member of: Ontario Coalition of Rape Crisis Centres; Regional Coordinating Committee to End Violence Against Women
Chief Officer(s):
Elizabeth Aldrich, Coordinator, Finance & Administration
admin@sascottawa.com
Staff Member(s): 9
Activities: Survivors of sexual violence groups; individual support; accompaniments (to hospital & police); public education; volunteer trainings; work with survivors of war & torture; Young Women at Risk Program; drop-in information sessions; 24-hour support line; fundraising; *Speaker Service:* Yes; *Library* by appointment

Sexual Assault Survivors' Centre - Sarnia-Lambton
#3, 189 Wellington St., Sarnia ON N7T 1G6
Tel: 519-337-3154; *Fax:* 519-337-0819
Toll-Free: 888-231-0536; *Crisis Hot-Line:* 519-337-3320
www.sexualassaultsarnia.on.ca
Overview: A small local organization founded in 1982 overseen by Canadian Association of Sexual Assault Centres
Member of: Ontario Coalition of Rape Crisis Centres
Finances: *Funding Sources:* Ministry of the Attorney General; Donations
Activities: 24-hour crisis line; Counselling; Public education; Information & referral; Advocacy; Rural & First Nation outreach; *Library* Open to public

Sexual Health Centre for Cumberland County
PO Box 661, Amherst NS B4H 4B8
Tel: 902-667-7500; *Fax:* 902-667-0585
shccc@ns.aliantzinc.ca
www.amherstsexualhealth.ca
www.facebook.com/25778277501746
Previous Name: Cumberland County Family Planning Association
Overview: A small local organization founded in 1981
Mission: To promote informed, responsible attitudes toward healthy sexuality, & strives to reduce unwanted pregnancy & sexually transmitted diseases; to encourage parents' involvement in their children's sexuality education
Member of: Nova Scotia Association for Sexual Health; Canadian Federation for Sexual Health; United Way of Cumberland County
Affliation(s): Planned Parenthood Federation of Canada
Finances: *Funding Sources:* Health Canada
Activities: Girl Power program; Go Girl website, www.forgirls.ca; *Speaker Service:* Yes; *Library* Open to public

Sexual Health Centre Lunenburg County
#8, 4 Hillcrest St., Bridgewater NS B4V 1S9
Tel: 902-527-2868
lunco@nssexualhealth.ca
www.lunco.cfsh.info
www.facebook.com/shclc
twitter.com/shclc
Previous Name: Planned Parenthood Bridgewater
Overview: A small local charitable organization founded in 1988
Mission: To ensure that information & services concerning human sexuality & fertility are available; to encourage informed, responsible attitudes toward sexuality from childhood to old age
Chief Officer(s):
Katie Boudreau, Executive Director
Finances: *Funding Sources:* Nova Scotia Department of Health; fundraising
Membership: *Fees:* $10
Activities: Sex-positive; youth-positive; offers free condoms, pregnancy tests, counselling & information on sexuality issues; educational services; *Awareness Events:* Sexual & Reproductive Health Week, Feb.; Aids Awareness Week, Nov.

Sexual Health Network of Québec Inc. / Réseau de la Santé Sexuelle du Québec inc.
PO Box 22516, 5683 Monkland Ave., Montréal QC H4A 3T4
e-mail: info@shnq.ca
www.shnq.ca
www.facebook.com/shnq.rssq
Previous Name: Planned Parenthood Montréal
Overview: A small local charitable organization founded in 1964
Mission: To advance sexual health
Chief Officer(s):
Laurie Betito, President
Membership: *Fees:* $35 full; $20 student

Sexual Violence Support & Information Centre of the Kawarthas *See* Kawartha Sexual Assault Centre

Sexuality Education Resource Centre Manitoba (SERC)
#200, 226 Osborne St. North, Winnipeg MB R3C 1V4
Tel: 204-982-7800; *Fax:* 204-982-7819
info@serc.mb.ca
www.serc.mb.ca
Previous Name: Planned Parenthood Manitoba
Overview: A medium-sized provincial organization founded in 1966 overseen by Canadian Federation for Sexual Health
Mission: To promote universal access to comprehensive, reliable information & services on sexuality & related health issues by fostering awareness, understanding, & support through education
Affliation(s): Canadian Federation for Sexual Health; International Planned Parenthood Federation
Chief Officer(s):
Lori S. Johnson, Executive Director
Gina Sylvestre, President
Finances: *Annual Operating Budget:* $250,000-$500,000; *Funding Sources:* Government; United Way; Donations; Fee for service
Staff Member(s): 14; 75 volunteer(s)
Membership: 100-499; *Committees:* Aboriginal Community Initiatives; Immigrant/Refugee Services
Activities: Facts of Life Program; Translation services; Pamphlets & fact sheets; Education & training; *Awareness Events:* Sexual & Reproductive Health Awareness Day, Feb.; *Speaker Service:* Yes; *Library:* SERC Lending Library

Brandon Office
161 - 8th St., Brandon MB R7A 3W9
Tel: 204-727-0417; *Fax:* 204-729-8364
brandon@serc.mb.ca

SF Canada
7433 East River Rd., Washago ON L0K 2B0
www.sfcanada.org
Overview: A small national organization founded in 1989
Mission: To foster growth of quality writing in the genre of speculative fiction
Chief Officer(s):
Steve Stanton, President
Susan Forest, Vice-President
Sherry Ramsey, Secretary-Treasurer
Membership: *Fees:* $30; *Member Profile:* Canadian writers of speculative fiction who have published for payment at least two short stories or three poems, or received a royalty advance for a novel; Editors who have been contracted for payment for a least one book or three issues of a magazine; Canadians with a professional interest in speculative fiction, such as publishers, librarians, & academics
Activities: Lobbying on behalf of Canadian writers; Promoting translation of Canadian speculative fiction; Arranging critique groups for members

Shaare Zion Congregation
5575 Côte St. Luc Rd., Montréal QC H3X 2C9
Tel: 514-481-7727; *Fax:* 514-481-1219
info@shaarezion.org
www.shaarezion.org
www.youtube.com/channel/UCoBzdW0f-6q68vM9P941EXw/videos
Overview: A small local charitable organization founded in 1924
Affliation(s): United Synagogue of Conservative Judaism
Chief Officer(s):
David Moscovitch, Executive Director
david.moscovitch@shaarezion.org
Lionel E. Moses, Rabbi
Staff Member(s): 10

Shad Valley International
8 Young St. East, Waterloo ON N2J 2L3
Tel: 519-884-8844; *Fax:* 519-884-8191
info@shad.ca
www.shad.ca
www.linkedin.com/groups?mostPopular=&gid=2101
www.facebook.com/ShadValley
twitter.com/shadvalley
www.youtube.com/ShadValleyOfficial
Also Known As: Shad Valley
Previous Name: Canadian Centre for Creative Technology
Overview: A medium-sized national charitable organization founded in 1981
Mission: To advance the scientific & technological capabilities of youth, integrated with the development of their entrepreneurial spirit; To collaborate with education, business & other communities, both domestic & international, to provide exceptional development opportunities
Chief Officer(s):
Barry Bisson, President
president@shad.ca
Wendy Zufelt-Baxter, Executive Director, Advancement
wendy@shad.ca
Mary Hamoodi, Director, Finance & Operations
maryh@shad.ca
Finances: *Annual Operating Budget:* $500,000-$1.5 Million

Staff Member(s): 8; 100 volunteer(s)
Membership: 13,000; *Fees:* $3,950
Activities: Shad Valley program involves 600+ outstanding senior high school students, some 200 corporate partners, & 12 Canadian universities each summer in an academic/co-op experience; *Speaker Service:* Yes

Shamattawa Crisis Centre

PO Box 126, Shamattawa MB R0B 1K0
Tel: 204-565-2551; *Fax:* 204-565-2544; *Crisis Hot-Line:* 204-565-2548
Previous Name: Shamattawa Shelter
Overview: A small local organization
Mission: To provide an emergency shelter for battered women & their children

Shamattawa Shelter *See* Shamattawa Crisis Centre

SHARE Agriculture Foundation

14110 Kennedy Rd., Caledon ON L7C 2G3
Tel: 905-838-0897; *Fax:* 905-838-0794
Toll-Free: 888- 33-7427
info@shareagfoundation.org
www.shareagfoundation.org
www.facebook.com/119869878092172
Overview: A medium-sized international organization founded in 1976
Mission: To help improve the quality of life for agriculturally impoverished communities worldwide; SHARE stands for "Sending Help & Resources Everywhere."
Chief Officer(s):
Murray Brownridge, Chair
Les Frayne, Project Manager, Central America
Bob Thomas, Project Manager, South America
Finances: *Annual Operating Budget:* $500,000-$1.5 Million; *Funding Sources:* Canadian International Development Agency; donations
Membership: *Committees:* Communications; Fundraising; Finance; Human Resources
Publications:
• SHARE News [a publication of SHARE Agriculture Foundation]
Type: Newsletter

Share Family & Community Services Society

#200, 25 King Edward St., Coquitlam BC V3K 4S8
Tel: 604-540-9161; *Fax:* 604-540-2290
www.sharesociety.ca
www.facebook.com/sharefcs
twitter.com/SHAREFamily
instagram.com/sharesociety
Overview: A small local organization founded in 1972 overseen by Food Banks British Columbia
Mission: To act as a multi-service, non-profit agency providing a range of programs & social services to residents of Coquitlam, Port Coquitlam, Port Moody & surrounding communities
Member of: Food Banks British Columbia
Affliation(s): Federation of Child & Family Services of BC
Chief Officer(s):
Martin Wyant, Chief Executive Officer
martin.wyant@sharesociety.ca
Finances: *Annual Operating Budget:* Greater than $5 Million; *Funding Sources:* Government; Grants; Fundraising; Program Fees
Staff Member(s): 126; 1695 volunteer(s)
Activities: Food bank; youth counselling; addiction counselling; settlement support services; ESL groups

ShareLife

1155 Yonge St., Toronto ON M4T 1W2
Tel: 416-934-3411; *Fax:* 416-934-3412
Toll-Free: 800-263-2595
slife@archtoronto.org
www.sharelife.org
www.facebook.com/ShareLifeCan
twitter.com/ShareLifeCan
Overview: A large international charitable organization founded in 1976
Mission: ShareLife is the Catholic Community's response to helping the whole community through Catholic agencies by effectively raising & allocating funds
Member of: International Catholic Stewardship Council
Affliation(s): Canadian Centre for Philanthropy
Chief Officer(s):
Arthur Peters, Executive Director, 416-934-3411 Ext. 559
arthurpeters@archtoronto.org
David Clubine, Communications Officer, 416-934-3411 Ext. 348
dclubine@archtoronto.org
Finances: *Annual Operating Budget:* $500,000-$1.5 Million
Membership: 34 organizations
Activities: Golf tournament; *Awareness Events:* Kickoffs; *Speaker Service:* Yes
Awards:
• Bishop Michael Power Award (Award)
Eligibility: Individual or couple who have shown leadership, selflessness & financial generosity in supporting the mission of ShareLife
• Mother Delphine Award (Award)
Eligibility: Individual or couple who have actively volunteered with ShareLife

ShareOwner Education Inc.

#806, 4 King St. West, Toronto ON M5H 1B6
Tel: 416-595-9600; *Fax:* 416-595-0400
Toll-Free: 800-268-6881
customercare@shareowner.com
www.shareowner.com
Overview: A medium-sized national organization founded in 1987
Mission: To offer practical education & portfolio training to individual investors & investment clubs, so that they may invest successfully in quality growth stocks; To increase stock market literacy
Chief Officer(s):
John Bart, Founder & Chief Mentor
Activities: Providing the ShareOwner's Stock Market Mentorship program
Publications:
• Discover the Great Stocks to Buy
Type: Manual; *Price:* $49.95
Profile: Topics include developing judgments about a stock's prospects for future growth, methods for studying cyclical stocks, & tests to determine if a company's stock price is currently on sale
• Investing in Growth Stocks
Type: Manual; *Number of Pages:* 65
• Investment Club Starter Kit
Type: Kit; *Price:* $129.95
Profile: Kit includes the manual entitled, "Use a Club to Beat the Market", the current issue of "Top Stock Case Studies", & a set of record-keeping forms for the club
• Mentorship Manual
Type: Manual; *Price:* $49.95
Profile: Practical information for students about investing successfully in growth stocks over the longer term
• Stock Market Starter Kit
Type: Kit; *Price:* $195.95
Profile: Kit includes the "Investing in Growth Stocks" manual, a "Stock Study Guide" software licence for two months, a two month subscription to "Top Stock Case Studies", & a two month subscription to afinancial database of companies
• Top Stock Case Studies
Type: Magazine; *Frequency:* Bimonthly; *Price:* $169.95
Profile: Use of research resources to identify top stocks, updates on the growth & valuation images for companies, & case studies featuring exchange-traded funds
• Use a Club to Beat the Market
Type: Manual; *Number of Pages:* 93
Profile: A sample club constitution, duties of officers, examples of record-keeping forms, & a model education program

The Sharing Place - Orillia & District Food Bank

PO Box 743, 22 West St. South, Orillia ON L3V 6K7
Tel: 705-327-4273; *Fax:* 705-327-4273
sharingplacefoodbank@rogers.com
www.sharingplaceorillia.org
www.facebook.com/212183205492276
twitter.com/ChristineHager4
Overview: A small local charitable organization founded in 1988
Mission: To provided needed, nutritious food to people of all ages
Member of: Ontario Association of Food Banks
Chief Officer(s):
Don Evans, Executive Director, 306-326-0307
Michael Hefferon, President
Michael Craig, Treasurer
Finances: *Funding Sources:* Donations from individuals, organizations, & corporations

Shaunavon Arts Council

PO Box 358, Shaunavon SK S0N 2M0
Tel: 306-297-3882
Overview: A small local organization founded in 1977
Mission: To promote cultural & artistic opportunities for the community of Shaunavon & district
Member of: Organization of Saskatchewan Arts Council
Finances: *Annual Operating Budget:* Less than $50,000
35 volunteer(s)
Membership: *Fees:* $5

Shaunavon Chamber of Commerce

PO Box 1048, 410 Centre St., Shaunavon SK S0N 2M0
Tel: 306-297-2671; *Fax:* 306-297-3051
shaunavonchamber@hotmail.com
www.shaunavon.com/?p=980
Overview: A small local organization
Member of: Saskatchewan Chamber of Commerce
Chief Officer(s):
Joanne Gregoire, President, 306-297-7383
Debbie Widmer, Secretary, 306-297-2669
Finances: *Annual Operating Budget:* Less than $50,000; *Funding Sources:* Membership dues; grants
Staff Member(s): 1
Membership: 75; *Fees:* $110

Shaunawan Ability Centre *See* Cypress Hills Ability Centres, Inc.

Shaw Festival

PO Box 774, Niagara-on-the-Lake ON L0S 1J0
Tel: 905-468-2153; *Fax:* 905-468-5438
Toll-Free: 800-657-1106
dlg@shawfest.com
www.shawfest.com
www.facebook.com/shawfestival
twitter.com/shawtheatre
www.youtube.com/theshawfestival
Also Known As: Shaw Festival Theatre Foundation
Overview: A medium-sized local charitable organization founded in 1963
Mission: To create intellectually challenging & entertaining theatre at an affordable price
Member of: Canadian Conference for the Arts; Professional Association of Canadian Theatres (PACT); Theatre Ontario
Affliation(s): Canadian Institute for Theatre Technology
Chief Officer(s):
Jackie Maxwell, Artistic Director
Elaine Calder, Executive Director
Finances: *Funding Sources:* Box Office; corporate & individual fundraising programs; federal & provincial funding
400 volunteer(s)
Membership: *Fees:* Schedule available; *Committees:* Shaw Boxing Evening; Shaw Shivaree; Festival Film Series; ShawFest!
Activities: Professional workshops, seminars, classes & costume rental, in addition to theatre productions; *Internships:* Yes; *Speaker Service:* Yes; *Library:* Sonja J. Korrner Library; Open to public by appointment

Shaw Rocket Fund

#210, 2421 - 37th Ave., Calgary AB T2E 6Y7
www.rocketfund.ca
www.facebook.com/rocketfund
twitter.com/RocketFund
Overview: A medium-sized national organization
Mission: To provide funding for children's programming
Chief Officer(s):
Annabel Slaight, Chair
Agnes Augustin, President & Treasurer
Finances: *Funding Sources:* Shaw Communications Inc., Shaw Pay Per View Ltd. & Shaw Direct

Sheena's Place

87 Spadina Rd., Toronto ON M5R 2T1
Tel: 416-927-8900; *Fax:* 416-927-8844
info@sheenasplace.org
www.sheenasplace.org
www.facebook.com/pages/Sheenas-Place/118354831586196
twitter.com/sheenasplace
www.youtube.com/user/SheenasPlace
Overview: A small local organization
Mission: To offer hope & support for people with eating disorders
Chief Officer(s):
Deborah Berlin-Romalis, Executive Director
dberlin-romalis@sheenasplace.org
Staff Member(s): 7

Sheep Creek Arts Council (SCAC)

PO Box 277, 133 Sunset Blvd., Turner Valley AB T0L 2A0

Tel: 403-933-4020
info@sheepcreekarts.ca
www.sheepcreekarts.ca
Overview: A small local organization founded in 1958
Mission: To donate funds to local groups; To provide bursaries to secondary students in the arts
Affliation(s): Camera Club; Sheep Creek Creative Writers; Sheep Creek Sketch Group
Finances: *Funding Sources:* Membership dues; Events
Membership: *Fees:* $10

Sheet Harbour & Area Chamber of Commerce & Civic Affairs
PO Box 239, Sheet Harbour NS B0J 3B0
sheetharbourchamber.com
Previous Name: Sheet Harbour & Area Chamber of Commerce; Sheet Harbour Board of Trade
Overview: A small local organization founded in 1935
Chief Officer(s):
Kent Smith, Acting President
Janice Christie, Secretary
Finances: *Annual Operating Budget:* Less than $50,000; *Funding Sources:* Membership fees
Membership: 84; *Fees:* $20 individual; $50 business; *Committees:* Waterfront development

Sheet Harbour & Area Chamber of Commerce; Sheet Harbour Board of Trade *See* Sheet Harbour & Area Chamber of Commerce & Civic Affairs

Sheet Metal Contractors Association of Alberta (SMCAA)
#203, 2725 - 12th St. NE, Calgary AB T2E 7J2
Tel: 403-250-7040; *Fax:* 403-735-5910
Toll-Free: 888-265-6665
wilma@smcaa.ca
www.smcaa.ca
twitter.com/smcaa1
Merged from: Edmonton Association of Sheet Metal Contractors; Calgary Air Conditioning & Sheet Metal Association
Overview: A small local organization founded in 2000
Mission: To collaborate with the municipal, provincial & federal governments in order to promote positive changes for the members of the Heating, Ventilation & Air Conditioning industry in Alberta
Member of: Sheet Metal & Air Conditioning Contractors' National Association
Chief Officer(s):
Ken Fulmer, Provincial President, 780-469-7791
Darcy Spicer, Treasurer
darcy@asmindustries.com
Wilma Agnew, Executive Director
Finances: *Funding Sources:* Membership
Staff Member(s): 1; 10+ volunteer(s)
Membership: 150+; *Fees:* Schedule available; *Member Profile:* Contractors, suppliers & manufacturers in Alberta; *Committees:* Bylaw & Code of Ethics Review; Golf; Old-Timers; Programming
Activities: Working with local & provincial governments to modify codes, permits & standards of practice; Providing educational programs; Preparing information about the profession for participation in career fairs; Assisting employers with employee benefit programs & volume discounts; Organizing a variety of annual events including dinner meetings, golf tournaments, Christmas parties & conferences; *Library:* SMACNA Manuals
Awards:
• Alberta Apprenticeship & Industry Training Scholarship (Scholarship)
Eligibility: Alberta residents that are registered as an apprentice in a trade & have passed their first or subsequent period apprenticeship & industry training exam*Location:* Alberta*Deadline:* June *Amount:* $1,000 *Contact:* Alberta Scholarship Programs, Phone: 780-427-8640; E-mail: scholarships@gov.ab.ca

Shelburne & Area Chamber of Commerce
PO Box 1150, Shelburne NS B0T 1W0
Tel: 902-875-0224; *Fax:* 902-875-3214
www.shelburnechamber.ca
Overview: A small local organization
Chief Officer(s):
Elizabeth Rhuland, President
Raymond Davis, Secretary

Shelburne Arts Council *See* Dufferin Arts Council

Shelburne Association Supporting Inclusion (SASI)
PO Box 59, 151 Water St., Shelburne NS B0T 1W0
Tel: 902-875-1083; *Fax:* 902-875-1056
sasi@eastlink.ca
www.supportinginclusion.ca
Overview: A small local charitable organization founded in 1985
Mission: To improve the quality of life for individuals with disabilities & mental health difficulties through person-centred programs
Member of: DIRECTIONS Council for Vocational Services Society
Chief Officer(s):
Heath Spencer, Executive Director/Manager
Staff Member(s): 13
Membership 68 individuals
Activities: Products & services include: Shelburne Café, catering, tropies & engraving, baking & crafts/textiles;
Publications:
• Shelburne Association Supporting Inclusion Newsletter
Type: Newsletter

Shelburne County Genealogical Society
PO Box 248, Shelburne NS B0T 1W0
Tel: 902-875-4299
gencentre@ns.sympatico.ca
nsgna.ednet.ns.ca/shelburne/index.php
Overview: A small local charitable organization founded in 1987
Mission: To promote and encourage the study of family history in Shelburne County; to assist with research of Shelburne County Genealogy; to promote standards of accuracy, responsibility, and scholarly excellence among genealogists; to contribute to the Society's holdings through volunteer activities and donations in a manner compatible with the aims and purposes of the Society; and to encourage and assist in the publication of genealogical source material
Member of: Council of Nova Scotia Archives
Membership: *Fees:* $25 single; $30 family; $225 single (life); $300 family (life); $3 student; $15 institution
Activities: *Library:* Genealogy Centre; Open to public

Shelburne Historical Society
PO Box 39, Shelburne NS B0T 1W0
Tel: 902-875-3219; *Fax:* 902-875-4141
shelburne.museum@ns.sympatico.ca
www.historicshelburne.com
www.facebook.com/364893103570881
Overview: A small local charitable organization founded in 1948
Mission: To promote & encourage interest in the history of our town & county; to gather, preserve & disseminate data relating to the early history of the town & county; to operate museums; to build & sell traditional wooden boats
Member of: Federation of Nova Scotian Heritage
Affliation(s): Nova Scotia Museum
Finances: *Annual Operating Budget:* $100,000-$250,000
Staff Member(s): 4; 60 volunteer(s)
Membership: 60; *Fees:* $10; *Committees:* Museums
Activities: Shelburne County Museum; Ross-Thomson House & Store Museum; Dory Shop Museum; Muir-Cox Shipbuilding Interpretive Centre; *Library* Open to public

Shelter for Helpless Animals in Distress (SHAID)
#138, 450 LaHave St., Unit 17, Bridgewater NS B4V 4A3
Tel: 902-543-4849
shiadshelter@gmail.com
www.shaid.ca
www.facebook.com/ShaidTreeAnimalShelter
Overview: A small local organization founded in 1986
Mission: To provide shelter for animals & to help find them a permanent home
Member of: Canadian Federation of Humane Societies
Chief Officer(s):
Harold Rowsell, Manager
Staff Member(s): 6
Membership: 136; *Fees:* $10
Activities: Yard sale & auction; cat show; dog walk; penny auction; open house; craft sale

The Shepherds' Trust
Catholic Pastoral Centre, #603, 1155 Yonge St. Dr., Toronto ON MRT 1W2
Tel: 416-934-3400; *Fax:* 416-934-3444
retiredpriests@archtoronto.org
www.shepherdstrust.org
Overview: A medium-sized local charitable organization founded in 1996
Mission: To assist elderly & disabled priests by raising awareness & funds; to provide retired priests with the financial resources to allow them to live a dignified life
Affliation(s): Archdiocese of Toronto
Chief Officer(s):
Brian Clough, Elected Representative, Board of Trustees
Timothy K. Hanley, Elected Representative, Board of Trustees
Marisa Rogucki, Coordinator, Retired Diocesan Priests
Finances: *Annual Operating Budget:* $1.5 Million-$3 Million; *Funding Sources:* Donations
Membership: *Member Profile:* Retired Catholic priests; *Committees:* Collection
Publications:
• The Sheperds' Trust Newsletter
Type: Newsletter; *Frequency:* Annual

Sherbrooke Snow Shoe Club
1900, rue Prospect, Sherbrooke QC J1J 1K7
Tel: 819-565-0355
Overview: A small local organization founded in 1877
Mission: To promote the grand old Canadian tradition of snow shoeing & to provide an environment for socializing among the members of the community

Sherbrooke Symphony Orchestra *Voir* Orchestre symphonique de Sherbrooke

Sheridan Park Association (SPA)
PO Box 811, Mississauga ON L5J 2Z1
Tel: 905-823-7091; *Fax:* 905-823-4403
contact@sheridanpark.ca
www.sheridanpark.ca
Overview: A small local organization founded in 1965
Mission: To maintain the Sheridan Science & Technology Park
Chief Officer(s):
Richard Perrier, President
rperrier@suncor.com
Membership: *Member Profile:* Companies located in the Sheridan Science & Technology Park

Sherwood Park & District Chamber of Commerce
100 Ordze Ave., Sherwood Park AB T8B 1M6
Tel: 780-464-0801; *Fax:* 780-449-3581
Toll-Free: 866-464-0801
www.sherwoodparkchamber.com
Overview: A small local organization founded in 1978
Member of: Alberta Chamber of Commerce; Canadian Chamber of Commerce
Chief Officer(s):
Todd Banks, Executive Director
tbanks@sherwoodparkchamber.com
Finances: *Annual Operating Budget:* $250,000-$500,000; *Funding Sources:* Membership dues
Staff Member(s): 3
Membership: 1225; *Fees:* $120-$600
Activities: Strathcona County Trade Fair & Sale, March

Sherwood Park District Soccer Association
#102, 241 Kaska Rd., Sherwood Park AB T8A 4E8
Tel: 780-449-1343; *Fax:* 780-464-5821
www.spdsa.net
Overview: A small local organization founded in 1976 overseen by Alberta Soccer Association
Member of: Alberta Soccer Association; Federation Internationale de Football Association; Canada Soccer Association
Affliation(s): Breton Soccer Association; Calmar Soccer Association; Devon Soccer Association; Leduc Soccer Association; Millet Soccer Association; New Sarepta Soccer Association; Pigeon Lake Soccer Association; Thorsby Soccer Association; Warburg Soccer Association; Wetaskiwin Soccer Association
Chief Officer(s):
Debbie Ballam, General Manager
d.ballam@spdsa.net
Membership: 3,000 players in 10 associations; *Committees:* Human Resources; Bylaw Reviewl Financial Policy; IT

Sherwood Park Fish & Game Association
PO Box 3098, Stn. Main, Sherwood Park AB T8A 2A6
Tel: 780-467-0085
info@spfga.org
www.spfga.org
Overview: A small local organization founded in 1962
Mission: To promote through education, lobbying and programs, the conservation and utilization of fish and wildlife and to protect and enhance the habitat they depend on.
Member of: Alberta Fish & Game Association
Affliation(s): Canadian Wildlife Federation

Chief Officer(s):
Pat Harris, Contact

Shiatsu Therapy Association of Ontario (STAO)
#1056, 7B Pleasant Blvd., Toronto ON M4T 1K2
Tel: 416-923-7826
Toll-Free: 877-923-7826
info@shiatsuassociation.com
www.shiatsuassociation.com
Overview: A small provincial organization founded in 1983
Mission: To promote awareness of Shiatsu to the public, health care professionals, government agencies & insurance companies; to protect the integrity of the profession with high educational standards & dedication to safeguarding the welfare of the public through strict adherence by its members to the STAO code of conduct
Chief Officer(s):
Chris Thompson, President, 647-894-8489
Finances: *Annual Operating Budget:* Less than $50,000; *Funding Sources:* Membership fees
20 volunteer(s)
Membership: 170; *Fees:* $638; *Member Profile:* Graduates of the 2,200 hr. Shiatsu course who have passed the STAO exams & paid the membership fee; *Committees:* Membership; Examinations; Complaints; Disciplines; Marketing; CST Violations; Telephone
Activities: Promotes awareness & educates the public, health care providers, government agencies & insurance companies about Shiatsu Therapy; provides referral service for Certified Shiatsu Therapists (CST); provides speakers, presentations & demonstrations on Shiatsu Therapy; pursues government regulation of Shiatsu Therapy; *Library:* Resource Centre

Shibogama First Nations Council (SFNC)
PO Box 449, 81 King St., Sioux Lookout ON P0V 2T0
Tel: 807-737-2662; *Fax:* 807-737-1583
Toll-Free: 866-877-6057
www.shibogama.on.ca
Overview: A small local organization
Mission: To promote the economic and community development of the Aboriginal people of the Shibogama area; to initiate, support and manage projects and programs which improve the social, cultural, economic, educational, recreational, or spiritual life of members of the Shibogama First Nations; and to provide assistance to the First Nations of the Shibogama area with regard to program development and administration.
Chief Officer(s):
Margaret Kenequanash, Executive Director
margaretk@shibogama.on.ca

Shipbuilding Association of Canada / Association de la construction navale du Canada
#1502, 222 Queen St., Ottawa ON K1P 5V9
Tel: 613-232-7127; *Fax:* 613-238-5519
Previous Name: Canadian Maritime Industries Association
Overview: A medium-sized national organization founded in 1995
Mission: Represents the interests of the Canadian shipbuilding, ship repair & associated marine equipment & services industries
Chief Officer(s):
Peter Cairns, President
David Reid, Chair
Finances: *Funding Sources:* Membership dues
Membership: 1-99; *Fees:* Schedule available; *Member Profile:* Canadian organizations engaged in provision of services, products &/or facilities related to ship design, shipbuilding & ship repair, must be 65% Canadian content/owned; *Committees:* Technical; Finance; Personnel; International Marketing; Procurement Outlook; SAC/Government Working Groups
Activities: *Rents Mailing List:* Yes

Shipping Federation of Canada / Fédération maritime du Canada
#326, 300, rue St-Sacrement, Montréal QC H2Y 1X4
Tel: 514-849-2325; *Fax:* 514-849-8774
Toll-Free: 877-534-7367
info@shipfed.ca
www.shipfed.ca
Overview: A medium-sized national organization founded in 1903
Mission: The association that represents and promotes the interests of the owners, operators and agents of ships involved in Canada's world trade.
Chief Officer(s):
Michael H. Broad, President
Anne Legars, Vice President
David Cardin, Chairman
Jean-François Belzile, Director of Marine Operations
James Moram, Director Marine Administration
Caroline Gravel, Director Environmental Affairs
Mario Minotti, Director Finance/Administration
Karen Kancens, Director of Customs and Immigration
Finances: *Funding Sources:* International shipping
Staff Member(s): 8
Membership: 83; *Member Profile:* Direct involvement in steamship business; *Committees:* Customs; Dangerous Goods; EDI; Immigration; Pilotage; Railways; Tanker Safety
Activities: To protect members in all matters affecting the operation of shipping from & to Eastern Canada, the St. Lawrence River, the Great Lakes & Arctic ports; areas of concern include pilotage, pollution, navigation aids, port operations, port charges, & federal government legislation & regulation

Shipyard General Workers' Federation of British Columbia (CLC) / Fédération des ouvriers des chantiers navals de la Colombie-Britannique (CTC)
#130, 111 Victoria Dr., Vancouver BC V5L 4C4
Tel: 604-254-8204; *Fax:* 604-254-7447
office@bcshipyardworkers.com
www.bcshipyardworkers.com
Overview: A medium-sized provincial organization
Affliation(s): Machinists, Fitters & Helpers Industrial Union #3, Marine Workers & Boilerworkers' Industrial Union #1, Shipwrights, Joiners & Caulkers' Industrial Union #9
Chief Officer(s):
George MacPherson, President
Quentin Del Vecchio, General Secretary
Membership: 1,100 + 3 locals;

Shoal Lake & District Chamber of Commerce
PO Box 176, Shoal Lake MB R0J 1Z0
Tel: 204-759-2215
pplace@mymts.net
www.facebook.com/105015103013460
Overview: A small local organization
Chief Officer(s):
Cory Luhowy, Manager
Tracey Myhill, President

Shock Trauma Air Rescue Society (STARS)
PO Box 570, 1441 Aviation Park NE, Calgary AB T2E 8M7
Tel: 403-295-1811; *Fax:* 403-275-4891
info@stars.ca
www.stars.ca
Overview: A small provincial organization founded in 1986
Mission: With a fleet of helicopters, STARS provides pre-hospital mobile emergency medical care through its focus on service, communications, education, training, research and consultation with the communities it serves. Its charitable registration # is: 118781103RR0001.
Chief Officer(s):
Brian Hesje, Chair
D. Gregory Powell, President & CEO
Finances: *Funding Sources:* donations
Publications:
- Horizons

Type: Newsletter; *Frequency:* 2 pa

Edmonton Base
Bldg. 16, 29 Airport Rd., Edmonton AB T5G 0W6
Tel: 780-447-5492; *Fax:* 780-447-5493
edmontonbase@stars.ca

Grande Prairie Base
10911 - 123 St., Grande Prairie AB T8V 7Z3
Tel: 780-830-7000; *Fax:* 780-830-7009
www.stars.ca
www.facebook.com/STARSairambulance
twitter.com/STARSambulance
www.youtube.com/starsairambulance
Chief Officer(s):
Greg Schmidt, GP Base Director, 780-830-7000, Fax: 780-830-7009
gschmidt@stars.ca

Lethbridge Office
#416, 10 St. North, Lethbridge AB T1H 2C7
Tel: 403-388-8214; *Fax:* 403-329-4101

Shoe Manufacturers' Association of Canada (SMAC) / Association des manufacturiers de chaussures du Canada
#203, 90, rue Morgan, Baie d'Urfe QC H9X 3A8
Tel: 514-457-3436; *Fax:* 514-457-8004
Overview: A medium-sized national organization founded in 1919
Mission: To represent & serve Canadian footwear manufacturers; To protect the Canadian domestic shoe industry
Chief Officer(s):
George P. Hanna, President
hanna@shoecanada.com
Membership: *Member Profile:* Footwear manufacturers throughout Canada
Activities: Monitoring developments in the Canadian footwear industry; Advocating on behalf of Canadian footwear manufacturers; Fostering a fair & competitive marketplace

Sholem Aleichem Community Inc. (SAC)
PO Box C105, 123 Doncaster St., Winnipeg MB R3N 2B2
Tel: 204-896-0456
sacommunity@gmail.com
www.sholemaleichemcommunity.ca
Overview: A small local organization
Mission: To preserve Jewish tradition & culture; To offer a secular humanistic approach to Jewish traditions & practices
Affliation(s): The Congress of Secular Jewish Organizations
Chief Officer(s):
Henry Shuster, Chair
Membership: *Fees:* $20 student; $30 individual; $50 family; *Member Profile:* Jewish people from Winnipeg, Manitoba; Individuals of non-Jewish backgrounds who wish to participate because of family connections, friendships, & personal interests
Activities: Fostering the application of humanistic values; Providing ethical training for children & educational programs for adults; Offering exposure to Jewish languages, arts, & culture; Organizing celebrations
Publications:
- Sholem Aleichem Community Newsletter

Type: Newsletter
Profile: Organization activities & forthcoming events

Shooting Federation of Canada (SFC) / Fédération de tir du Canada (FTC)
45 Shirley Blvd., Nepean ON K2K 2W6
Tel: 613-727-7483; *Fax:* 613-727-7487
info@sfc-ftc.ca
www.sfc-ftc.ca
Overview: A medium-sized national charitable organization founded in 1932
Mission: To represent firearms users in matters of legislation, shooting sports promotion, & program activities
Member of: International Shooting Sport Federation
Affliation(s): Canadian Shooting Sports Association
Chief Officer(s):
Asmir Arifovic, President
president@sfc-ftc.ca
Finances: *Funding Sources:* Sales; Donations; Government
Membership: 108 organizations; *Committees:* Coaching; National Officials Development; Commonwealth Games; Awards & Merits; High Performance
Activities: *Awareness Events:* National Smallbore Rifle Championships; National Trapshooting Championships; National Skeet Shooting Championships

Shooting Federation of Nova Scotia (SFNS)
PO Box 28023, Dartmouth NS B2W 6E2
e-mail: info@sfns.info
www.sfns.info
Overview: A small provincial organization founded in 1972
Member of: Sport Nova Scotia
Affliation(s): Shooting Federation of Canada
Chief Officer(s):
D. Beaulieu, Contact
Finances: *Annual Operating Budget:* Less than $50,000
12 volunteer(s)
Membership: 1600

Shorthorn Breeders of Manitoba Inc.
PO Box 54, Gladstone MB R0J 0T0
Tel: 204-870-0089
www.manitobashorthorns.com
www.facebook.com/296215440444692
Overview: A small provincial organization
Member of: Canadian Shorthorn Association
Chief Officer(s):
Monty Thomson, President
monty@hatfieldclydesdales.com
Susan Armbruster, Secretary, 204-859-2088

Shuswap Area Family Emergency Society (SAFE)
PO Box 1463, Salmon Arm BC V1E 4P6

Tel: 250-832-9616; Fax: 250-832-9516
safesociety@shaw.ca
www.safesociety.ca
Overview: A small local organization founded in 1979
Mission: To end violence against women & children in the Shuswap; To provide temporary accommodation; To offer support counselling for women & their children who are/have experienced violence
Member of: BC Council for Families
Finances: *Funding Sources:* Regional & provincial governments; Donations
Activities: Women's emergency shelter; Children Who Witness Abuse Program; Stopping the Violence Program; Youth sexual exploitation posters; Community based victim assistance; Police based victim assistance; *Awareness Events:* International Women's Day, March

Shuswap Association for Community Living (SACL)
4590 - 10 Ave. SW, Salmon Arm BC V1E 4M2
Tel: 250-832-3885; *Fax:* 250-832-1076
www.shuswap-a-c-l.com
Overview: A small local organization
Mission: To provide services, support and housing for people with intellectual disabilities and their families.
Chief Officer(s):
Joan Sturdy, Chair, 250-833-1397
joan_sturdy@telus.net
Jo-Anne Crawford, Executive Director, 250-832-1038
jcrawford@shuswap-a-c-l.com
Michele Weber, Program Director, 250-804-4211
mweber@shuswap-a-c-l.com
Finances: *Funding Sources:* donations; BC government; grants; fundraising events
Staff Member(s): 3
Activities: Vocational programs; leisure activities; housing assistance

Shuswap Columbia District Labour Council (SCDLC)
PO Box 1230, Revelstoke BC V0E 2S0
Tel: 250-832-8509; *Fax:* 250-832-8059
scdlabourcouncil@gmail.com
Overview: A small local organization overseen by British Columbia Federation of Labour
Mission: To advance the economic & social welfare of workers in British Columbia's Shuswap Columbia Regional District
Affliation(s): Canadian Labour Congress (CLC)
Chief Officer(s):
Michelle Cole, President
sahmof2iam@hotmail.com
Terry Coates, First Vice-President
Bill MacFarlane, Treasurer
bmacfarlane@hotmail.com
Membership: *Member Profile:* Unions in the Revelstoke & Salmon Arm area of British Columbia
Activities: Advocating for workers' rights in the Shuswap Columbia Regional District of British Columbia; Liaising with locally elected officials; Raising awareness of issues affecting workers, such as health & safety; Ensuring that provincial labour laws are enforced; Hosting a ceremony on the annual Day of Mourning to pay tribute to workers who were injured or killed on the job; Supporting local community organizations; Providing community information about employment;
Awards:
• William S. King Scholarship Trust (Scholarship)
Eligibility: A student entering post-secondary education to pursue a career working with people *Amount:* $500 *Contact:* SCDLC & Revelstoke NDP Club

Shuswap District Arts Council
PO Box 1181, Salmon Arm BC V1E 4P3
Tel: 250-832-6807; *Fax:* 250-832-6807
www.shuswapartscouncil.bc.ca
Overview: A small local organization founded in 1971
Member of: Assembly of BC Arts Councils; Thompson Okanagan Network of Arts Councils; BC Arts in Education Council; Canadian Conference of the Arts
Chief Officer(s):
Tracey Kutschker, Executive Director
Finances: *Annual Operating Budget:* $50,000-$100,000; *Funding Sources:* Provincial & local governments; donations; membership fees; fundraising
Staff Member(s): 1
Membership: 139; *Fees:* $15 Individual; $35 Arts groups; $50 Corporate; *Member Profile:* Amateur arts groups & individuals
Activities: Artwaves, summer school of the Arts; Community street banner project; Wow! Wednesdays on the Wharf, free summer concert series

Shuswap Lakes Tourism Association *See* Shuswap Tourism

Shuswap Naturalists
1740 - 16 St. NE, Salmon Arm BC V1E 3Z7
e-mail: info@shuswapnaturalists.org
www.shuswapnaturalists.org
Overview: A small local charitable organization founded in 1970
Mission: To promote the enjoyment of nature through environmental appreciation & conservation; to encourage wise use & conservation of natural resources & environmental protection.
Member of: Federation of BC Naturalists
Chief Officer(s):
Derek Beacham, President
Membership: *Fees:* $20 single; $30 family

Shuswap Rock Club
PO Box 235, Sorrento BC V0E 2W0
Tel: 250-955-6484
Overview: A small local organization
Member of: Lapidary, Rock & Mineral Society of British Columbia
Chief Officer(s):
Sylvia Repnow, Contact
shuswaprockclub@gmail.com
Activities: Rockhounding in thompson, Shuswap areas

Shuswap Tourism
PO Box 978, 781 Marine Park Dr. NE, Salmon Arm BC V1E 4P1
Tel: 250-833-5906
info@shuswaptourism.ca
www.shuswaptourism.ca
www.facebook.com/pages/Shuswap-Tourism/161797927239700
twitter.com/shuswaptourism
www.youtube.com/shuswaptourism
Previous Name: Shuswap Lakes Tourism Association
Overview: A small local organization founded in 1988
Mission: To promote the development of tourism by providing external & local marketing of the Shuswap Lakes Area
Member of: Thompson Okanagan Tourism Association
Finances: *Funding Sources:* Regional government
Membership: *Fees:* Free

Shwachman-Diamond Syndrome Canada
2152 Gatley Rd., Mississauga ON L5H 3L9
Toll-Free: 866-462-8907
info@shwachman.org
www.shwachman.org
Overview: A small national charitable organization
Mission: To raise funds to support research; to disseminate current medical information; to heighten awareness of SDS in the medical community to allow earlier diagnosis & treatment; to develop network of contacts & resources for people & families with SDS
Chief Officer(s):
Heather Norton, President
Finances: *Funding Sources:* Corporate & individual donations; Fund raising
Awards:
• PhD Fellowship (Scholarship)
Awarded annually

Sicamous & District Chamber of Commerce
PO Box 346, 314A Finlayson St., Sicamous BC V0E 2V0
Tel: 250-836-0002; *Fax:* 250-836-4368
sicamouschamber@cablelan.net
www.sicamouschamber.bc.ca
Overview: A small local organization
Finances: *Annual Operating Budget:* $50,000-$100,000; *Funding Sources:* Fundraising event; municipal fee for service
Staff Member(s): 2
Membership: 183 businesses; *Fees:* $125

Sickle Cell Association of Ontario (SCAO)
#202, 3199 Bathurst St., Toronto ON M6A 2B2
Tel: 416-789-2855; *Fax:* 416-789-1903
sicklecell@look.ca
www.sicklecellontario.ca
www.linkedin.com/company/2437730?trk=tyah
www.facebook.com/SickleCellCanada
twitter.com/SCA_O
Overview: A small provincial charitable organization founded in 1981
Mission: To serve the community as a recognized voluntary agency that endeavors to optimize the quality of life for individuals and families with sickle cell disease.
Chief Officer(s):
John Kirya, President
Finances: *Funding Sources:* Donations
Staff Member(s): 2
Membership: *Fees:* $15-35; *Committees:* Educational; Social Suport; Fundraising; Events; Public Policy
Activities: Public awareness; education, support groups; alternative methods of pain management; *Awareness Events:* World Sickle Cell Day, June; *Internships:* Yes; *Speaker Service:* Yes
Meetings/Conferences: • Sickle Cell Association of Ontario's 2015 Educational Conference, 2015, ON
Scope: Provincial

Sickle Cell Foundation of Alberta
PO Box 55041, Stn. New Knottwood, 1704 Millwoods Rd. SW, Edmonton AB T6K 3N0
Tel: 780-450-4943
scfoa@telus.ca
www.sicklecellfoundationofalberta.org
Overview: A small provincial organization
Mission: To promote awareness about sickle cell disorder in Alberta
Chief Officer(s):
Ekua Yorke, Founder & Coordinator

SIDA Moncton *See* AIDS Moncton

Sida Nouveau Brunswick *See* AIDS New Brunswick

Sidaction Mauricie
515, rue Ste-Cécile, Trois-Rivières QC G9A 1K9
Tél: 819-374-5740
information@sidactionmauricie.ca
www.sidactionmauricie.ca
Aperçu: *Dimension:* petite; *Envergure:* locale; Organisme sans but lucratif; fondée en 1990 surveillé par Canadian AIDS Society
Mission: Offrir des programmes d'éducation et de prévention au grand public et aux clientèles à risque, en collaboration avec les organismes gouvernementaux et communautaires qui oeuvrent aussi dans le domaine du Sida, et avec les personnes séropositives; l'organisme offre aussi un service de soutien aux personnes atteintes du VIH/Sida et à leurs proches
Membre de: Coalition des organismes communautaires québécois de lutte contre le Sida
Membre(s) du bureau directeur:
Hélène Neault, Adjointe à la coordination
Finances: *Budget de fonctionnement annuel:* Moins de $50,000
Membre: 1-99
Activités: *Stagiaires:* Oui; *Bibliothèque*

SIDALYS
3702, rue Ste-Famille, Montréal QC H2X 2L4
Tél: 514-842-4439; *Téléc:* 514-842-2284
sidasecours@hotmail.com
www.cocqsida.com
Nom précédent: Centre des services sida secours du Québec
Aperçu: *Dimension:* petite; *Envergure:* provinciale surveillé par Canadian AIDS Society
Membre de: Coalition des organismes communautaires québécois de lutte contre le sida (COCQ-SIDA)
Activités: Hébergement: Habitations Jean-Pierre Valiquette (appartements supervisés); Centre sida secours; Centre Amaryllis

Siding & Window Dealers Association of Canada (SAWDAC)
84 Adam St., Cambridge ON N3C 2K6
Tel: 519-651-2812; *Fax:* 519-658-4753
Toll-Free: 800-813-9616
info@sawdac.com
www.sawdac.com
Overview: A small national organization founded in 1988
Mission: To build consumer confidence in our association by delivering high standards of products, installations & business ethics

Sidney & North Saanich Board of Trade *See* Saanich Peninsula Chamber of Commerce

Sidney Lions Food Bank
PO Box 2281, Sydney BC V8L 3S8
Tel: 250-655-0679; *Fax:* 250-655-1130
fdbank@telus.net
www.sidneyfoodbank.com

Canadian Associations

Overview: A small local organization overseen by Food Banks British Columbia
Mission: To provide food & support to the needy
Member of: Food Banks British Columbia
Chief Officer(s):
Beverley Elder, Administrator
Finances: *Funding Sources:* Donations

Sierra Club of Canada (SCC) / Sierre club du Canada

#412, 1 Nicholas St., Ottawa ON K1N 7B7
Tel: 613-241-4611; *Fax:* 613-241-2292
Toll-Free: 888-810-4204
info@sierraclub.ca
www.sierraclub.ca
www.facebook.com/sierraclubcanada
twitter.com/SierraClubCan
www.youtube.com/sierraclubcanada
Overview: A medium-sized national charitable organization founded in 1992
Mission: To develop a diverse, well-trained grassroots network, working to protect the integrity of our global ecosystems; To focus on five overriding threats: loss of animal & plant species, deterioration of the planet's oceans & atmosphere, the ever-growing presence of toxic chemicals in all living things, destruction of our remaining wilderness, spiralling population growth & overconsumption
Member of: CANET; Green Budget Coalition; Canadian Renewable Energy Alliance
Affliation(s): Common Front on the World Trade Organization

Chief Officer(s):
John Bennett, Executive Director
Anowara Baqi, CFO
Tania Beriau, Development Director
Daniel Spence, Director, Communications
Finances: *Annual Operating Budget:* $500,000-$1.5 Million; *Funding Sources:* Foundations; Governments; Individual donors
Staff Member(s): 20
Membership: *Fees:* $50 regular; $25 student & senior/fixed income; $125 sustainer; $1,000 lifetime
Activities: Program Areas: Atmosphere & Energy; Health & Environment; Environmental Education; Protecting Biodiversity; Transition to a Sustainable Economy; *Internships:* Yes; *Rents Mailing List:* Yes
Publications:
• The RIO Report [a publication of the Sierra Club of Canada]
Type: Annual Report; *Frequency:* Annually
• SCAN - Sierra Club of Canada Activist News
Type: Newsletter

Atlantic Chapter
#533, 1657 Barrington St., Halifax NS B3J 2A1
Tel: 902-444-3113
atlanticcanadachapter@sierraclub.ca
atlantic.sierraclub.ca
www.facebook.com/sierraatlanticcanada
twitter.com/SierraClubACC
www.youtube.com/sierraclubcanada
Chief Officer(s):
Gretchen Fitzgerald, Director, 902-444-3113
gretchenf@sierraclub.ca

British Columbia Chapter
#302, 733 Johnson St., Victoria BC V8W 3C7
Tel: 250-386-5255; *Fax:* 250-386-4453
info@sierraclub.bc.ca
www.sierraclub.bc.ca
www.facebook.com/SierraClubBC
twitter.com/Sierra_BC
www.youtube.com/user/SierraClubofBC
Mission: To explore, enjoy & protect the country's forests, waters, wildlife & wilderness
Member of: Wild Salmon Coalition
Chief Officer(s):
George Heyman, Executive Director
george@sierraclub.bc.ca

Ontario Chapter
Evergreen Brickworks, #402, 550 Bayview Ave., Toronto ON M4W 3X8
Tel: 647-346-8744
ontariochapter@sierraclub.on.ca
ontario.sierraclub.ca
Affliation(s): Sierra Club - USA
Chief Officer(s):
Dan McDermott, Director

Prairie Chapter
10008 - 82nd Ave., 2nd Fl., Edmonton AB T6E 1Z3
Tel: 780-439-1160; *Fax:* 780-485-9640
prairiechapter@sierraclub.ca
p.sierraclub.ca
www.facebook.com/groups/117941398216232
twitter.com/SCPrairie
www.youtube.com/user/sierraprairie?feature=mhum
Mission: Program areas: energy; health communities; protecting biodiversity; training & support
Chief Officer(s):
Eriel Deranger, Chapter Director

Québec Chapter
1222, rue MacKay, Montréal QC H3G 2H4
Tél: 514-651-5847
quebec@sierraclub.ca
quebec.sierraclub.ca
Chief Officer(s):
Claude Martel, Directeur
claudem@sierraclub.ca

Sierra Club of Eastern Canada *See* Sierra Club of Canada

Sierra Legal Defence Fund *See* Ecojustice Canada Society

Sierra Youth Coalition (SYC) / Coalition Jeunesse Sierra

#406, 1 Nicholas St., Ottawa ON K1N 7B7
Tel: 613-241-1615; *Fax:* 613-241-2292
Toll-Free: 888-790-7393
info@syc-cjs.org
www.syc-cjs.org
www.facebook.com/sierrayouthcoalition
www.twitter.com/sierrayouth
Overview: A medium-sized local organization overseen by Sierra Club of Canada
Mission: To empower young people to become active community leaders who contribute to making Canada a more sustainable society
Chief Officer(s):
Gabriela Rappell, Acting National Director
director@syc-cjs.org
Finances: *Funding Sources:* Donations; Membership dues
Membership: 80 colleges & universities; 50 high schools; *Fees:* $12; *Member Profile:* Sierra Club of Canada members 25 or under & students of any age

Sierre club du Canada *See* Sierra Club of Canada

SIGMA Canadian Menopause Society

#205, 1089 West Broadway, Vancouver BC V6H 1E5
Tel: 604-736-7267; *Fax:* 604-736-7268
sigmamenopause@gmail.com
www.sigmamenopause.com
www.linkedin.com/pub/sigma-canadian-menopause-society/65/857/5a6
www.facebook.com/sigmacanadianmenopausesociety
twitter.com/sigmamenopause
www.youtube.com/user/SIGMACMS
Overview: A medium-sized national organization founded in 2008
Mission: To act as a group of family physicians, specialists & healthcare professionals interested in menopausal & postmenopausal health; to provide educational initiatives & information services to women going through menopause, in order to advance women's health.
Chief Officer(s):
Elaine Jolly, OC, MD, FRCSC, President
Christine Derzko, MD, FRCS(C), Vice-President
Marla Shapiro, MDCM, CCFP. MHS, Secretary
Michael Fortier, Treasurer
Chui Kin Yuen, MD, FRCS(C), FA, Executive Director
Membership: *Fees:* $105; *Member Profile:* Physicians, specialists & healthcare professionals

Sign Association of Canada (SAC) / Association canadienne de l'enseigne (ACE)

#301, 216 Chrislea Rd., Woodbridge ON L4L 8S5
Tel: 905-856-0000; *Fax:* 905-856-0064
Toll-Free: 877-470-9787
info@sac-ace.ca
www.sac-ace.ca
Overview: A small national organization founded in 1954
Mission: To represent & support association members
Member of: International Sign Association (ISA)
Chief Officer(s):
Bob Bronk, Executive Director, 416-628-6609
bronk@sac-ace.ca
Perry Brooks, President
perry@sac-ace.ca
Membership: *Fees:* Schedule available, based upon number of employees or annual gross sales to the sign industry in Canada; *Member Profile:* Sign manufacturing, installation, & maintenance companies; Sign industry suppliers & distributors & trade show exhibitors
Activities: Engaging in advocacy activities; Liaising with governments; Providing referrals to members; Offering educational seminars & training
Publications:
• Sign Association of Canada Membership Directory
Type: Directory

Atlantic Provinces Chapter
c/o Mattatall Signs, 80 Ilsley Ave., Dartmouth NS B3B 1L3
Tel: 902-468-8222; *Fax:* 902-468-2451
Chief Officer(s):
Justin Boudreau, Chapter President
jboudreau@mattatall.com

British Columbia Chapter
c/o Colortec, 4175 McConnell Dr., Burnaby BC V5A 3J7
Tel: 604-420-1718; *Fax:* 604-420-2591
Chief Officer(s):
Carlene Schoock, Chapter President
carlene@colortec.ca

Ontario Chapter
c/o ND Graphics, #1, 55 Interchange Way, Concord ON L4K 5W3
Tel: 416-663-6416; *Fax:* 416-663-5629
www.signsontario.com
Chief Officer(s):
Fred Elkins, Chapter President
fred@sac-ace.ca

Québec Chapter
#313, 315, Place d'Youville, Montréal QC H2Y 0A4
Tél: 514-876-4176
aqie.ca
www.facebook.com/aqiequebec
www.youtube.com/channel/UCkbJ1tuPGgwNJMI3sBGac3g/
Chief Officer(s):
Denis Barbeau, Président, 450-691-4907
Mélanie Arsenault, Directrice administrative

Saskatchewan Chapter
c/o Wolfecroft Signs, 806A - 43 St. East, Saskatoon SK S7K 3V1
Tel: 306-244-7739; *Fax:* 306-244-7759
www.sasksignassoc.ca
Chief Officer(s):
Sheldon Rioux, Chapter President
sheldon@sac-ace.ca

Sign Language Interpreters of the National Capital (SLINC)

c/o The Canadian Hearing Society, #600, 2197 Riverside Dr., Ottawa ON K1H 7X3
e-mail: info@slinc.ca
www.slinc.ca
Overview: A small local organization overseen by Association of Visual Language Interpreters of Canada
Mission: To promote & advance the interpreting profession in the National Capital Region of Canada
Member of: Association of Visual Language Interpreters of Canada (AVLIC)
Chief Officer(s):
Roxanne Whiting, President
president@slinc.ca

Signal Hill

PO Box 848, Stn. A, #112, 32868 Ventura Ave., Abbotsford BC V2T 7A2
Toll-Free: 877-774-4625
info@thesignalhill.com
www.thesignalhill.com
www.facebook.com/thesignalhill
twitter.com/TheSignalHill
www.youtube.com/thesignalhill
Overview: A small provincial charitable organization
Mission: To offer education about life issues, women's health, & human rights; To promote the value of human life
Chief Officer(s):
Neil Harker, Chair
James Borkowski, Executive Director
Monique van Berkel, Manager, Operations
Bev Sweeny, Bookkeeper
Finances: *Funding Sources:* Donations

Activities: Offering support to women & families with issues such as unplanned pregnancy, abortion, suicide, & euthanasia; Providing outreach resources
Awards:
• Cecelia Moore Award (Award)

The Sikh Foundation
#4900, 40 King St. West, Toronto ON M5H 4A2
Tel: 416-777-6697; *Fax:* 416-484-9656
Overview: A small national organization
Mission: Distributes literature regarding the Sikh religion to anyone who is interested.
Staff Member(s): 16

Sik-ooh-kotoki Friendship Society
1709 - 2nd Ave. South, Lethbridge AB T1J 0E8
Tel: 403-328-2414; *Fax:* 403-327-0087
sikooh@telusplanet.net
anfca.com/friendship-centres/lethbridge
Also Known As: Lethbridge Friendship Centre
Overview: A small local organization founded in 1969 overseen by Alberta Native Friendship Centres Association
Mission: To improve the quality of life for Aboriginal peoples in an urban environment by supporting self-determined activities which encourage equal access to, & participation in Canadian society & which respect & strengthen the increasing emphasis on Aboriginal cultural distinctiveness
Member of: Alberta Native Friendship Centres Association
Chief Officer(s):
Lynda First Rider, Executive Director
lydiafirstrider@yahoo.ca
Finances: *Funding Sources:* Federal & provincial government; Membership dues
Membership: 100-499

Silent Children's Mission
40 King Georges Rd., Toronto ON M8X 1L3
Tel: 905-428-6137; *Fax:* 416-231-6205
silentchildrenca@yahoo.com
Overview: A small international charitable organization
Mission: To serve impoverished children both internationally & in Canada
Affliation(s): Archdiocese of Toronto; Canadian Food for Children
Chief Officer(s):
Andrew Simone, Founder
Joan Simone, Founder
Francisca Burg-Feret, Contact

Silent Voice Canada Inc.
#300, 50 St. Clair Ave. East, Toronto ON M4T 1M9
Tel: 416-463-1104; *Fax:* 416-778-1876; *TTY:* 416-463-3928
silent.voice@silentvoice.ca
www.silentvoice.ca
Overview: A small national charitable organization founded in 1975
Mission: To serve deaf children, deaf youth & adults & their families in the GTA; to improve communication & relationships between the deaf & hearing in families & in our community; to provide services in a sign language environment
Member of: Catholic Charities of the Archdiocese of Toronto
Chief Officer(s):
Kelly MacKenzie, Executive Director
k.mackenzie@silentvoice.ca
Les Young, Chair
Finances: *Annual Operating Budget:* $500,000-$1.5 Million; *Funding Sources:* Catholic charities; City of Toronto
Staff Member(s): 9
Activities: *Awareness Events:* Deaf Awareness Day, June; *Library* by appointment

Silver Star Soaring Association
2331 Mount Tuam Cres., RR#2, Sorrento BC V0E 2W2
Tel: 250-675-2204
www.silverstarsoaring.org
Overview: A small local organization founded in 1999
Mission: To promote gliding in central Okanagan
Member of: Soaring Association of Canada
Chief Officer(s):
Bernie Boehnke, President

Silver Trail Chamber of Commerce
PO Box 268, Mayo YT Y0B 1M0
Tel: 867-332-1770
Overview: A small local charitable organization founded in 1977
Chief Officer(s):
Nancy Hager, President
Finances: *Annual Operating Budget:* Less than $50,000; *Funding Sources:* Government; local businesses
10 volunteer(s)
Membership: 20; *Fees:* $40; *Member Profile:* Local businesses
Activities: Promotion of businesses in the region

Simcoe & District Chamber of Commerce
Chamber Plaza, 95 Queensway West, Simcoe ON N3Y 2M8
Tel: 519-426-5867; *Fax:* 519-428-7718
www.simcoechamber.on.ca
www.linkedin.com/pub/simcoe-and-district-chamber-of-commerce/3a/3b0/78
twitter.com/SimcoeChamber
Overview: A small local organization founded in 1888
Chief Officer(s):
Dave Chuchill, President
Yvonne Di Pietro, General Manager
Membership: 350

Simcoe & District Real Estate Board
191 Queensway West, Simcoe ON N3Y 2M8
Tel: 519-426-4454; *Fax:* 519-426-9330
realsim@kwic.com
www.norfolk-mls.ca
www.facebook.com/sdreb
Overview: A small local organization overseen by Ontario Real Estate Association
Member of: Canadian Real Estate Association
Chief Officer(s):
Amie Ferris, President
president@norfolk-mls.ca
Membership: 140

Simcoe County Children's Aid Society
#7, 60 Bell Farm Rd., Barrie ON L4M 5G6
Tel: 705-726-6587; *Fax:* 705-726-9788
Toll-Free: 800-461-4236
www.simcoecas.com
Overview: A small local organization founded in 1894
Mission: To protect children and youth from maltreatment; promote the well-being of children and youth; strengthen families; and provide quality alternative care when necessary
Member of: Ontario Association of Children's Aid Societies
Chief Officer(s):
Susan Carmichael, Executive Director
Finances: *Annual Operating Budget:* Greater than $5 Million; *Funding Sources:* Provincial government; donations
Staff Member(s): 160; 140 volunteer(s)

Simcoe County Historical Association (SCHA)
PO Box 144, Barrie ON L4M 4S9
www.simcoecountyhistory.ca
Previous Name: Simcoe County Pioneer & Historical Society
Overview: A small local organization founded in 1891
Mission: To preserve the past in the present for the future
Member of: Ontario Historical Society
Chief Officer(s):
Mark Fisher, President
mwfisher2@hotmail.com
Gord Harris, Treasurer
gordon.harris67@gmail.com
Membership: *Fees:* $12 individual; $15 couple/family; *Member Profile:* Anyone interested in local history
Activities: Public meetings (8/yr); annual meeting; plaque unveilings

Simcoe County Jewish Association (SCJA) *See* Am Shalom

Simcoe County Law Association (SCLA)
Court House, 114 Worsley St., Barrie ON L4M 1M1
Tel: 705-739-6569; *Fax:* 705-728-8136
simlawlib@bellnet.ca
www.scla.ca
Also Known As: County of Simcoe Law Association
Overview: A small local organization founded in 1890
Chief Officer(s):
Ted Chadderton, President
Membership: 350; *Member Profile:* Lawyers in Simcoe County
Activities: *Library:* Simcoe County Law Library

Simcoe County Literacy Network *See* Simcoe/Muskoka Literacy Network

Simcoe County Parents of Multiples
Barrie ON
Tel: 705-733-3022
Other Communication: bulletwin@hotmail.com
simcoe@multiplebirthscanada.org
www.multiplebirthscanada.org/~barrie/web/index.html
Previous Name: Barrie Parents of Twins and More
Overview: A small local organization overseen by Multiple Births Canada
Mission: Offers support to parents of multiples (and parents-to-be).
Chief Officer(s):
Christina Chase-Nugent, Chair
Membership: *Fees:* $40

Simcoe County Pioneer & Historical Society *See* Simcoe County Historical Association

Simcoe Women's Wellness Centre Corporation
#232, 80 Bradford St., Barrie ON L4N 6S7
Tel: 705-721-5875; *Fax:* 705-721-5729
swwc@csolve.net
www.angelfire.com/vt2/womenshelter
Overview: A small local charitable organization founded in 1989
Mission: To promote a natural self-help approach to women's physical & emotional well-being; to provide resources including books, workshops & presentations about women's health concerns; to provide a well connected referral service on a local, provincial & national scale
Activities: Workshops; seminars on women issues; *Library* Open to public

Simcoe/Muskoka Literacy Network (SMLN)
#15, 575 West St. South, Orillia ON L3V 7N6
Tel: 705-326-7227; *Fax:* 705-326-7447
Toll-Free: 888-518-4788
simcoe.muskoka@literacynetwork.ca
literacynetwork.ca
Previous Name: Simcoe County Literacy Network
Overview: A small local charitable organization founded in 1994
Mission: To provide high-quality, basic skills training
Member of: Ontario Literacy Coalition; Community Literacy of Ontario; Movement for Canadian Literacy
Affliation(s): Laubach Literacy Ontario
Chief Officer(s):
Stephanie Hobbs, Executive Director
sahobbs@literacynetwork.ca
Staff Member(s): 2
Membership: *Member Profile:* Literacy & essential skills training provider within Simcoe County & Muskoka Region
Activities: Literacy services planning; communications; outreach & public education; information & referral service; clear language consultations; *Library*

Similkameen Chamber of Commerce
PO Box 490, Keremeos BC V0X 1N0
Tel: 250-499-5225
Overview: A small local organization
Finances: *Funding Sources:* Membership dues
Membership: 8

Similkameen Okanagan Organic Producers Association (SOOPA)
PO Box 577, Keremeos BC V0X 1N0
Tel: 250-499-5381; *Fax:* 250-499-5381
soopa@nethop.net
www.soopa.ca
Overview: A small local organization founded in 1985
Mission: To set & maintain high standards of organic food production; to encourage growers to develop their horticultural skills; to educate consumers & encourage other farmers to begin to use sustainable farming methods
Affliation(s): Certified Organic Associations of BC
Chief Officer(s):
Julie Hinton, Administrator
Guy Villecourt, President
Finances: *Annual Operating Budget:* Less than $50,000
Staff Member(s): 1; 15 volunteer(s)
Membership: 41 certified + 5 transitional + 7 associate; *Fees:* $200 certified & transitional depending on size of farm; $50 associate

Simmental Association of British Columbia
c/o Jan Wisse, 49420 Yale Rd., Chilliwack BC V2P 6H4
Tel: 604-794-3684
ww.simmental.com/bc.htm
Previous Name: British Columbia Simmental Association
Overview: A small provincial organization
Mission: To promote the breeding of Simmental cattle in BC.
Member of: Canadian Simmental Association
Chief Officer(s):

Jan Wisse, Secretary
Lorne Webster, President, 604-823-6797

The Simon Foundation for Continence Canada *See* The Canadian Continence Foundation

Simon Fraser Public Interest Research Group (SFPIRG)

#TC326, Simon Fraser University, Burnaby BC V5A 1S6
Tel: 778-782-4360
Other Communication: Board e-mail: board@sfpirg.ca
sfpirg@sfu.ca
www.sfpirg.ca
www.facebook.com/sfpirg
twitter.com/sfpirg
Also Known As: SFPIRG
Overview: A large local organization founded in 1981
Mission: To operate as a student funded & directed centre dedicated to environmental & social change
Affliation(s): Simon Fraser University
Chief Officer(s):
Kalamity Hildebrandt, Coordinator, Research
arx@sfpirg.ca
Shahaa Kakar, Coordinator, Media & Outreach
outreach@sfpirg.ca
Craig Pavelich, Coordinator, Administrative & Resource
admin@sfpirg.ca
Finances: *Annual Operating Budget:* $100,000-$250,000; *Funding Sources:* Student fees
Staff Member(s): 3
Membership: 30,000; *Fees:* Per semester: $3 full-time student; $1.50 part-time student; *Member Profile:* Students of Simon Fraser University, who support the centre through a small fee included in their tuition (students are free to opt out of this fee if they choose); *Committees:* Ancient Forests; Human Resources; Finance; Anti-Oppression; Grants
Activities: Forming Action Groups; research funding & grants; Action Research Exchange (ARX) program; *Internships:* Yes; *Library:* Social Justice Lending Library; Open to public
Awards:
• Usamah Ansari Creative Justice Award (Award)
Amount: $500
• Conferences & Workshops Fund (Grant)
Amount: $100
• Grants for Social & Environmental Work (Grant)
Amount: Up to $500 (small); $500-$1,000 (large)

Simon Fraser Society for Community Living (SFS)

204 Blue Mountain St., Coquitlam BC V3K 4H1
Tel: 604-525-9494; *Fax:* 604-525-3013
info@sfscl.org
www.sfscl.org
Also Known As: Simon Fraser Society
Previous Name: Simon Fraser Society for Mentally Handicapped People
Overview: A large local charitable organization founded in 1954
Mission: To provide choices & opportunities for children who require extra support, adults with intellectual abilities & their families
Member of: British Columbia Association for Community Living
Chief Officer(s):
Christine Scott, Executive Director
cscott@sfscl.org
Finances: *Annual Operating Budget:* Greater than $5 Million; *Funding Sources:* Donations; membership fees
Staff Member(s): 150; 60 volunteer(s)
Membership: 405 individual; *Fees:* $5 self advocate; $15 individual; $20 family; $25 organization/corporation; *Member Profile:* Open except for employees of society; can include individuals & corporations
Activities: Community fund-raisers; services for children/youth, families & adults; individual, family & community support; *Awareness Events:* Community Living Month, Oct.; *Internships:* Yes; *Speaker Service:* Yes; *Library* Open to public
Publications:
• Simon Says.. [a publication of the Simon Fraser Society for Community Living]
Type: Newsletter

Simon Fraser Society for Mentally Handicapped People *See* Simon Fraser Society for Community Living

Simon Fraser University Faculty Association (SFUFA) / Association des professeurs de l'Université Simon Fraser

Simon Fraser University, 8888 University Dr., Burnaby BC V5A 1S6
Tel: 778-782-4676
sfufaea@sfu.ca
www.sfufa.ca
Overview: A small local organization founded in 1965
Member of: Canadian Association of University Teachers; Confederation of Faculty Association of British Columbia
Chief Officer(s):
Glenn Chapman, President, 778-782-3814
glennc@sfu.ca
Brian Green, Officer, Membership Services
brian_green@sfu.ca
Melanie Lam, Office Manager
Membership: 500-999

Single Parent Association of Newfoundland (SPAN)

PO Box 21421, 472 Logy Bay Rd., St. John's NL A1A 5G6
Tel: 709-738-3401; *Fax:* 709-738-3406
span@spanl.ca
www.envision.ca/members/templates/template6.asp?ID=2468
Overview: A medium-sized provincial charitable organization founded in 1987
Mission: To provide information & referral services to single parents; To offer support & assistance in crisis situations
Chief Officer(s):
Yvette Walton, Executive Director
ywalton@spanl.ca
Elaine Balsom, Administrative Assistant
ebalsom@spanl.ca
Finances: *Funding Sources:* Government grants; Public donations
Staff Member(s): 9
Activities: Distributing clothing & food through an outlet; Organizing the Prom Dream Project for single parent families as well as the general public; Offering the Single Parent Employment Support Program; Providing peer support; Operating the Back to School Project to help school-age children of lower income, single parent families; Partnering with businesses & organizations to supply food & gifts at Christmastime; Offering parent effectiveness training; Publishing a cookbook of healthy, low-cost recipes; *Speaker Service:* Yes

Single Parents Association of Montréal *See* Single Persons Association of Montréal

Single Persons Association of Montréal / L'Association des Personnes Seules de Montréal (APS)

PO Box 3114, Stn. Lapierre, LaSalle QC H8N 3H2
Tel: 514-366-8600
spasource@bell.net
home.total.net/~spa
Also Known As: SPA Montréal
Previous Name: Single Parents Association of Montréal
Overview: A small local charitable organization founded in 1989
Mission: To support singles & single parents through a wide variety of social, sports & children's activities
Membership: 300; *Fees:* 30$; *Member Profile:* Single people 25 & older

Sioux Lookout & Hudson Association for Community Living *See* Community Living Sioux Lookout

Sioux Lookout Chamber of Commerce

PO Box 577, 11 First Ave. South, Sioux Lookout ON P8T 1A8
Tel: 807-737-1937; *Fax:* 807-737-1778
chamber@siouxlookout.com
www.siouxlookout.com
Overview: A small local organization founded in 1919
Mission: To promote Sioux Lookout area business
Member of: Northwestern Ontario Associated Chambers of Commerce
Chief Officer(s):
Matt Cairns, President
Staff Member(s): 1
Membership: 140

Sistering - A Woman's Place

962 Bloor St. West, Toronto ON M6H 1L6
Tel: 416-926-9762; *Fax:* 416-926-1932
info@sistering.org
www.sistering.org
Overview: A small local organization founded in 1981
Mission: Sistering is a women's organization that offers practical & emotional support through programs which enable them to take greater control over their lives. Guided by the principles of Anti-Racism/Anti-Oppression, Sistering works to change social conditions which endanger women's welfare
Chief Officer(s):
Sheryl Lindsay, Executive Director, 416-926-9762 Ext. 226
Finances: *Funding Sources:* Donations
Staff Member(s): 34
Activities: Drop-in centre & outreach program for homeless women; Services in English, Spanish & Mandarin

Sisters Adorers of the Precious Blood / Soeurs Adoratrices du Précieux Sang

301 Ramsay Rd., London ON N6G 1N7
Tel: 519-473-2499; *Fax:* 519-473-6590
www.pbsisters.on.ca
Overview: A small local charitable organization founded in 1861
Chief Officer(s):
Eileen Mary Walsh, General Superior

Sisters of Charity of Halifax (SC)

215 Seton Rd., Halifax NS B3M 0C9
Tel: 902-406-8077; *Fax:* 902-457-3506
communications@schalifax.ca
www.schalifax.ca
Overview: A small local organization founded in 1849
Mission: To develop a sensitivity to the oppressed through presence, prayer & ministry to others
Chief Officer(s):
Carrie Flemming, Advancement Associate
advancement@schalifax.ca
Ruth Jeppesen, Director, Communications
Membership: 400

Sisters of Saint Joseph of Pembroke (CSJ)

1127 Pembroke St. West, Pembroke ON K8A 5R3
Tel: 613-732-3694; *Fax:* 613-732-3319
infoPembroke@csjcanada.org
www.csjcanada.org
Overview: A small local organization founded in 1921
Mission: The Sisters of St. Joseph of Pembroke are a group of fifty Roman Catholic women religious based in eastern Ontario
Staff Member(s): 30; 5 volunteer(s)
Membership: 1-99

Sisters of Saint Joseph of Peterborough (CSJ)

PO Box 566, Stn. Mount St. Joseph, 1555 Monaghan Rd., Peterborough ON K9J 6Z6
Tel: 705-745-1307; *Fax:* 705-745-9219
contact@csjpeterborough.com
www.csjpeterborough.com
Overview: A small local charitable organization founded in 1890
Mission: To respond to the poor & most needy, particularly where the need is not already met
Chief Officer(s):
Helen Russell, Vocation Director
Membership: 80

Sisters of Saint Joseph of Sault Ste Marie

2025 Main St. West, North Bay ON P1B 2X6
Tel: 705-474-3800; *Fax:* 705-495-3028
stephanie.romiti@gmail.com
www.csjssm.ca
Overview: A small local organization
Mission: Lives & works that all people may be united with God & with one another
Chief Officer(s):
Shirley Anderson, General Superior
sanderson@csjssm.ca

Sisters of Saint Mary of Namur *Voir* Soeurs de Sainte-Marie de Namur

Sisters of the Child Jesus (SEJ) / Soeurs de l'Enfant-Jésus

318 Laval St., Coquitlam BC V3K 4W4
Tel: 604-939-7545; *Fax:* 604-939-7549
gpainchaud@shaw.ca
members.shaw.ca/gmlamy
Also Known As: Sisters of Instruction of the Child Jesus
Overview: A small local charitable organization founded in 1667
Mission: To be a presence of love to the Father & to others for the definite purpose of awakening & deepening the faith; to enable people to grow in the uniqueness of their person as created by God & to liberate themselves from all that prevents their being truly human; to bring hope & direction to contemporaries; to be at the service of the least favoured, the marginalized & those who have no voice in society
Chief Officer(s):
Gilberte Painchaud, Provincial Superior

Sisters of the Sacred Heart / Suore del Sacro Cuore di Ragusa
1 Edward St., Welland ON L3C 5H2
Tel: 905-732-4542
ssc@cogeco.net
www.sacredheartsisters.ca
Overview: A small local charitable organization founded in 1889
Mission: To live an apostolic life in the church & society through the works of beneficence among the poor & needy; To instruct & educate youth; To collaborate in parish pastoral work, especially through the teaching of catechism
Membership: 500-999
Activities: Day care, schools, orphanages & retirement homes for the elderly; Parish work; Home visits; Missions; Nursing

Sivananda Ashram Yoga Camp
673 - 8 Ave., Val Morin QC J0T 2R0
Tel: 819-322-3226
Toll-Free: 800-263-9642
hq@sivananda.org
www.sivananda.org
www.facebook.com/SivanandaYogaCamp
twitter.com/sivanandacamp
Previous Name: Yoga Vedanta Centre
Overview: A small international charitable organization founded in 1963
Mission: To practice classical Indian yoga.
Member of: International Sivananda Yoga Vedanta Centres
Finances: *Funding Sources:* Private donations
Activities: Daily classes; teachers' training course; Thai yoga massage certification course

Centre Sivananda de Yoga Vedanta de Montréal
5178, boul St-Laurent, Montréal QC H2T 1R8
Tél: 514-279-3545
montreal@sivananda.org
www.sivananda.org/montreal

Sivananda Yoga Vedanta Centre
77 Harbord St., Toronto ON M5S 1G4
Tel: 416-966-9642
toronto@sivananda.org
www.sivananda.org/toronto
www.facebook.com/sivanandatoronto
twitter.com/sivanandatoront

69'ers Club of Coombs *See* Parksville & District Rock & Gem Club

Sjögren's Syndrome Association *See* Association du Syndrome de Sjogren, Inc

Skate Canada / Patinage Canada
865 Shefford Rd., Ottawa ON K1J 1H9
Tel: 613-747-1007; *Fax:* 613-748-5718
Toll-Free: 888-747-2372
Other Communication: Membership e-mail: memberservices@skatecanada.ca
skatecanada@skatecanada.ca
www.skatecanada.ca
www.facebook.com/skatecanada
twitter.com/SkateCanada
www.youtube.com/channel/UCsc7hNfnY3b65mZqXkVKNZw
Also Known As: Canadian Figure Skating Association
Overview: A large national licensing charitable organization founded in 1914
Mission: To enable all Canadians to participate in skating throughout their lifetime for fun, fitness, & achievement
Member of: International Skating Union
Chief Officer(s):
Leanna Caron, President
Dan Thompson, Chief Executive Officer
Norm Proft, Director, Member Services
Barb MacDonald, Director, Corporate Communications
Michael Slipchuk, Director, High Performance
Finances: *Funding Sources:* User fees; Television events; Marketing; Membership fees
Staff Member(s): 50
Membership: *Fees:* $32 associate; $100 coaching; *Committees:* CEO Operational Review; Governance; External Relations; Membership Policy; Finance & Risk Management; Athlete Fund & Alumni; Officials Development; Coaching Development; Sections Coordinating; Hall of Fame & Heritage; High Performance Development; Officials Assignment & Promotion; Skating Programs Development; Strategic Planning Steering
Activities: *Speaker Service:* Yes

Alberta/NWT/Nunavut Section
11759 Groat Rd., Edmonton AB T5M 3K6
Tel: 780-415-0465; *Fax:* 780-427-1734
Toll-Free: 866-294-0663
info@skateabnwtnun.ca
www.skateabnwtnun.com
www.facebook.com/skateabnwtnun
twitter.com/SkateAB_NWT_NUN
Chief Officer(s):
Jessica Crighton, Coordinator, Communications & Events
jessica@skateabnwtnun.ca

British Columbia/Yukon Section
#2, 6501 Sprott St., Burnaby BC V5B 3B8
Fax: 604-205-6962
Toll-Free: 888-752-8322
www.skatinginbc.com
www.facebook.com/172540199441743
twitter.com/SkateBCYT
Chief Officer(s):
Ted Barton, Executive Director
ted.b@attglobal.net

Central Ontario Section
111 Snidercroft Rd., #A, Concord ON L4K 2J8
Tel: 905-760-9100; *Fax:* 905-760-9104
Toll-Free: 877-267-0081
www.skatecanada-centralontario.com
Chief Officer(s):
Gary B. Oswald, Executive Director
gary@skatecanada-centralontario.com

Eastern Ontario Section
PO Box 2209, 276 King St. West, Prescott ON K0E 1T0
Tel: 613-925-1441; *Fax:* 613-925-1314
administrator@skate-eos.on.ca
www.skate-eos.on.ca
www.facebook.com/114053658638501
Mission: EO administrates figure skating clubs in Ontario, southeast of a line from Severn Bridge to Point Alexander on the Ottawa River, following the Ontario border along the Ottawa River to the St. Lawrence River and Lake Ontario, to the eastern boundary of Ajax and north to Atherly and Severn Bridge. The section's clubs (90+) offer a variety of programs to their members (over 10,000): Learn to Skate & Recreational programs - CanSkate, CanPowerSkate; Figure Skating - STARSkate, CompetitiveSkate, Skating Development, CollegiateSkate; Adult Skating - AdultSkate; Synchronized Skating: Festival SynchroSkate. The clubs showcase their skaters with Carnivals, Ice Shows, and Exhibitions which are normally held at the end of the skating season. The section hosts competitions, offers seminars, clinics and camps for the skaters as well as training for coaches, judges & officials.
Chief Officer(s):
Barbara Hough, Office Administrator

Fédération de patinage artistique du Québec
4545, av Pierre-De-Doubertin, Montréal QC H1V 0B2
Tel: 514-252-3073; *Fax:* 514-252-3170
patinage@patinage.qc.ca
www.patinage.qc.ca
www.facebook.com/patinageqc
Chief Officer(s):
Any-Claude Dion, Directrice générale
acdion@patinage.qc.ca

Manitoba Section
145 Pacific Ave., Winnipeg MB R3B 2Z6
Tel: 204-925-5707; *Fax:* 204-925-5924
skate.admin@sportmanitoba.ca
www.mbskates.ca
Chief Officer(s):
Shauna Marling, Executive Director
skate.exec@sportmanitoba.ca

New Brunswick Section
#4, 299 Champlain St., Dieppe NB E1A 1P2
Tel: 506-855-1751; *Fax:* 506-855-1723
www.skatenb.org
Chief Officer(s):
Lise Auffrey-Arsenault, Executive Director
executivedirector@skatenb.org

Newfoundland/Labrador Section
1296A Kenmount Rd., Paradise NL A1L 1N3
Tel: 709-576-0509; *Fax:* 709-576-0549
skating@sportnl.ca
www.skating.nf.ca
twitter.com/SkateCanada_NL
Chief Officer(s):
Lori Brett, Executive Director

Northern Ontario Section
PO Box 130, #3, 6 Main St., Callander ON P0H 1H0
Tel: 705-752-4803; *Fax:* 705-752-5977
office@scno.net
www.scno.net
www.facebook.com/SkateCanadaNO
twitter.com/SkateCanadaNO
Chief Officer(s):
Traci Fong, Chair
chair@scno.net

Nova Scotia Section
5516 Spring Garden Rd., 4th Fl., Halifax NS B3J 3G6
Tel: 902-425-5450; *Fax:* 902-425-5606
skatecanadans@sportnovascotia.ca
www.skatecanada.ns.ca
Chief Officer(s):
Jill Knowles, Executive Director

Prince Edward Island Section
40 Enman Cres., Charlottetown PE C1E 1E6
Tel: 902-368-4985; *Fax:* 902-368-4548
skatecanadapei.ca
Chief Officer(s):
Mike Connolly, Executive Director
mconnolly@sportpei.pe.ca

Saskatchewan Section
2205 Victoria Ave., Regina SK S4P 0S4
Tel: 306-780-9245
sk.skate@sasktel.net
www.skatecanadasaskatchewan.com
Chief Officer(s):
Danielle Shaw, Executive Director

Western Ontario Section
237 Consortium Ct., London ON N6E 2S8
Tel: 519-686-0431; *Fax:* 519-686-0593
memberservice@skating-wos.on.ca
www.skating-wos.on.ca
www.facebook.com/pages/Skate-Canada-Western-Ontario/160795530609301
Chief Officer(s):
Steve Scherrer, Chair
scherrer@rogers.com

Skate Ontario
ON
www.skateontario.org
www.facebook.com/SkateOntario
twitter.com/SkateOntario
Also Known As: Ontario Figure Skating Association
Overview: A small provincial organization founded in 1982
Mission: To enable every citizen of the province to participate in skating through out his/her lifetime for fun &/or achievement
Chief Officer(s):
Tracey McCague-McElrea, Executive Director
tracey@skateontario.org
Wendy St. Denis, President
wendy.stdenis@skateontario.org
Membership: 75,000; *Member Profile:* Competitive & recreational skaters as well as coaches & officials; *Committees:* Events; Programs; Technical

Skeena Valley Naturalists
1677 Lupine St., Terrace BC V8G 0G1
Tel: 250-798-2535
weena@telus.net
Overview: A small local organization
Chief Officer(s):
Judy Chrysler, Director
Membership: 10; *Fees:* $15
Activities: Birdwatching; *Awareness Events:* Christmas Bird Count

Skeptics Canada *See* Association for Science & Reason

Ski de fond Canada *See* Cross Country Canada

Ski de fond Nouveau-Brunswick *See* Cross Country New Brunswick

Ski de fond Québec
4545, av Pierre-de Coubertin, Montréal QC H1V 0B2
Tel: 450-745-1888
info@skidefondquebec.ca
www.skidefondquebec.ca
Overview: A small provincial organization overseen by Cross Country Canada
Member of: Cross Country Canada

Ski Hawks Ottawa
c/o Bruce Meredith, 522 Hillcrest Ave., Ottawa ON K2A 2M9
Tel: 613-725-2472
www.cads-ncd.ca/skihawks/Skihawks_home.html
Overview: A small local charitable organization founded in 1978
Mission: To promote skiing to the visually impaired community
Member of: Canadian Association of Disabled Skiing - National Capital Division (CADS-NCD)
Chief Officer(s):
Bruce Meredith, Treasurer
brucemeredith@rogers.com
Carolyn Mitrow, President, 613-222-7718
cmitrow@gmail.com
Membership: *Member Profile:* Visually impaired skiers & snowboarders, aged 8 to 88, in all ability levels

Ski Jumping Canada (SJC) / Canada Saut à Ski
#418, 305 - 4625 Varsity Dr. NW, Calgary AB T3A 0Z9
e-mail: skijumpingcanada@shaw.ca
www.skijumpingcanada.com
www.facebook.com/SkiJumpingCanada
twitter.com/SkiJumpCanada
www.youtube.com/user/sskijump00
Overview: A small national organization
Mission: To be the national governing body for the sport of ski jumping in Canada.
Chief Officer(s):
Brent Morrice, Chair
Curtis Lyon, Director, High Performance

Ski nautique et planche Canada *See* Water Ski & Wakeboard Canada

Ski Québec alpin (SQA)
4545, av Pierre-de Coubertin, Montréal QC H1V 3R2
Tél: 514-252-3089; *Téléc:* 514-252-5282
www.skiquebec.qc.ca
www.facebook.com/skiqcalpin
twitter.com/SkiQuebecAlpin
www.youtube.com/channel/UCVQGzGbkN8J3tuPQD5WXIOw
Également appelé: Cross Country Québec
Aperçu: *Dimension:* moyenne; *Envergure:* provinciale; fondée en 1967
Mission: D'organiser et de gérer le ski alpin et concours
Membre de: Cross Country Canada
Membre(s) du bureau directeur:
Daniel Paul Lavallée, Directeur général, 514-252-3089 Ext. 3564
daniel@skiquebec.qc.ca
Éric Préfontaine, Directeur athlétique, 514-252-3089 Ext. 3621
eprefontaine@skiquebec.qc.ca
Sylvie Grenier, Responsable, Services comptables, 514-252-3089 Ext. 3565
comptabilité@skiquebec.qc.ca
Anthony Lamour, Responsable, Communications et du service aux partenaires, 514-252-3090
alamour@skiquebec.qc.ca
Membre(s) du personnel: 7
Membre: *Comités:* Haute Performance; Officiels

Skills Canada *See* Skills/Compétences Canada

Skills Canada / Compétences Canada
#201, 294 Albert St., Ottawa ON K1P 6E6
Tel: 343-883-7545; *Fax:* 613-691-1404
Toll-Free: 877-754-5226
skillscompetencescanada.com
www.facebook.com/skillscanada
twitter.com/Skills_Canada
www.youtube.com/user/SkillsCanadaOfficial
Overview: A medium-sized national organization
Mission: Actively promotes careers in skilled trades and technologies to Canadian youth.
Member of: World Skills International
Chief Officer(s):
Shaun Thorson, Chief Executive Officer
shaunt@skillscanada.com
Finances: *Funding Sources:* Public & private sponsorship
Staff Member(s): 14

Skills for Change (SfC)
791 St. Clair Ave. West, Toronto ON M6C 1B7
Tel: 416-658-3101
www.skillsforchange.org
www.linkedin.com/company/skills-for-change
www.facebook.com/SkillsforChange
twitter.com/skillsforchange
www.youtube.com/user/skillsforchange
Overview: A small local charitable organization founded in 1983
Mission: To provide services & training to immigrants & refugees to enter the Canadian workplace; to provide information & assistance to internationally-qualified professionals to enable them to find employment in their area of specialization
Member of: ONESTEP; Canadian Centre for Philanthropy; Ontario Council of Agencies Serving Immigrants; Advocates for Community Based Training & Education for Women
Affliation(s): Access to Professions & Trades; Women in Information Technology
Chief Officer(s):
Peter Perdue, Chair
Cheryl May, Executive Director
Finances: *Annual Operating Budget:* $3 Million-$5 Million; *Funding Sources:* United Way Toronto; Federal, provincial & municipal governments
Staff Member(s): 45; 60 volunteer(s)
Membership: 60; *Fees:* $10 individual; $20 groups/organizations; $250 corporate; *Committees:* Finance; Human Resources; Real Estate/Planning; Risk Management; Fundraising; Governance; Marketing/Communications; Strategic Planning
Activities: *Awareness Events:* diversity@work, Nov.; Pioneers for Change, June; *Library:* Employment Resource Centre; Open to public
Awards:
• New Pioneers Awards (Award)

Skills Unlimited (SKILLS)
201 Scott St., Winnipeg MB R3L 0L4
Tel: 204-474-2443
Overview: A small local charitable organization founded in 1962
Mission: To train & assist in finding employment for persons living with vocational disabilities
Affiliation(s): Winnipeg Chamber of Commerce
Chief Officer(s):
Ron Fortier, Contact
Activities: Centre of Learning providing quality vocational rehabilitation services; Skills Manufacturing, a private non-profit manufacturing facility employing handicapped people

Skills/Compétences Canada
#201, 294 Albert St., Ottawa ON K1P 6E6
Tel: 343-883-7545; *Fax:* 613-691-1404
Toll-Free: 877-754-5226
www.skillscanada.com
www.facebook.com/pages/Skills-Canada-Competences-Canada/11736117829828
twitter.com/Skills_Canada
www.youtube.com/user/SkillsCanadaOfficial
Previous Name: Skills Canada
Overview: A medium-sized national organization founded in 1989
Mission: To create dynamic synergies between industry, government, youth, educators & labour; to raise awareness of the value of a technical or skilled trade career; to champion & stimulate the development of technological & employability skills in Canadian youth to strengthen our competitive edge in the global marketplace
Chief Officer(s):
John Oates, President
Shaun Thorson, Chief Executive Officer
shaunt@skillscanada.com
Jennifer Cavanagh, Director, Communications
jenniferc@skillscanada.com
Staff Member(s): 14
Membership: 13 provincial/territorial organizations
Activities: *Awareness Events:* Canadian Skills Competition, May; World Skills Competition International, Aug.
Awards:
• Canadian Skills Competition (Award)
Awarded annually; is an olympic-style skills competition in over 40 skilled trades, technology & leadership contests, representing 6 industry sectors, designed to test skills required in technology & trade occupations; allows students access to newest technologies & communicate with industry experts who serve as mentors*Eligibility:* Students compete at the local, regional & provincial levels to win the right to represent their province at the national level *Amount:* Gold, silver & bronze medals

Alberta
#700, 10242 - 105 St., Edmonton AB T5J 3L5
Tel: 780-809-0746; *Fax:* 780-429-0009
www.skillsalberta.com
www.facebook.com/pages/Skills-Canada-Alberta/100249541386
twitter.com/skillsalberta
www.youtube.com/user/skillsalberta
Chief Officer(s):
Chris Browton, Executive Director
chrisb@skillscanada.com

British Columbia
3777 Kingsway, Vancouver BC V5H 3Z7
Tel: 604-432-4229; *Fax:* 604-433-1241
bc@skillscanada.com
www.skillscanada.bc.ca
www.facebook.com/pages/Skills-Canada-BC/28602593007
twitter.com/skillsbc
www.youtube.com/user/SkillsCanadaBC
Chief Officer(s):
Amber Papou, Executive Director

Manitoba
#31, 1313 Border St., Winnipeg MB R3H 0X4
Tel: 204-927-0250; *Fax:* 204-927-0258
www.skillsmanitoba.ca
www.facebook.com/skillscanadamanitoba
www.youtube.com/user/SkillsManitoba
Chief Officer(s):
Maria Pacella, Executive Director
mariapa@skillscanada.com

New Brunswick
#426, 527 Beaverbrook Ct., Fredericton NB E3B 1X6
Tel: 506-457-2762; *Fax:* 506-453-5317
newbrunswick@skillscanada.com
www.skillscanada.nb.ca
www.facebook.com/232663270114132
twitter.com/SkillsCanadaNB
Chief Officer(s):
Luc Morin, Executive Director

Newfoundland & Labrador
Town Square, 75 Barbour Dr., 2nd Fl., Mount Pearl NL A1N 2X3
Tel: 709-739-4172; *Fax:* 709-739-4198
newfoundland@skillscanada.com
www.skillscanada-nfld.com
www.facebook.com/skillscanadanewfoundlandandlabrador
twitter.com/Skills_NL
www.youtube.com/SkillsCanadaNL
Chief Officer(s):
Carole Ann Ryan, Executive Director

Northwest Territories
PO Box 1403, 5013 - 44th St., Yellowknife NT X1A 2P1
Tel: 867-873-8743
skillsnt@skillscanada.com
skillscanadanwt.org
www.facebook.com/pages/Skills-Canada-NWT/281827822861
twitter.com/skillsnt
www.youtube.com/user/skillsnt
Chief Officer(s):
Jan Fullerton, Executive Director

Nova Scotia
#7B, 800A Windmill Rd., Dartmouth NS B3B 1L1
Tel: 902-491-4640; *Fax:* 902-428-0112
info@skillsns.ca
skillsns.ca
www.facebook.com/SkillsNS
twitter.com/Skills_NS
www.youtube.com/channel/UCGwYvar8WCxD2neFGty8lSw
Chief Officer(s):
Robin Lorway, Acting Executive Director
robinlorway@skillsns.ca

Nunavut
PO Box 176, Iqaluit NU X0A 0H0
Tel: 867-979-7258; *Fax:* 867-979-2954
www.skillsnunavut.ca
www.facebook.com/pages/Skills-Canada-Nunavut/204380761652
twitter.com/skillsnunavut
Chief Officer(s):
Amanda Kilabuk, Executive Director
NUexecdir@skillscanada.com

Ontario
#11, 100 Campbell Ave., Kitchener ON N2H 4X8
Tel: 519-749-9899; *Fax:* 519-749-6322
Toll-Free: 888-228-5446
www.skillsontario.com
www.facebook.com/pages/Skills-Canada-Ontario/153697034656518

twitter.com/skillsontario
www.youtube.com/user/SkillsOntario
Chief Officer(s):
Gail Smyth, Executive Director
gsmyth@skillsontario.com

Prince Edward Island
140 Weymouth St., Charlottetown PE C1A 4Z1
Tel: 902-566-9352; *Fax:* 902-566-9505
www.skillscanada.pe.ca
Chief Officer(s):
Tawna MacLeod, Executive Director
tmacleod@hollandcollege.com

Québec Office of Compétences Québec
#30, 190, rue Dorchester, Québec QC G1K 9M6
Tel: 418-646-3534; *Fax:* 418-643-6336
info@competencesquebec.com
www.competencesquebec.com
www.facebook.com/people/Competences-Quebec/1185526209

Saskatchewan
2911D Cleveland Ave., Saskatoon SK S7K 8A9
Tel: 306-373-6035; *Fax:* 306-373-6036
www.skillscanadasask.com
Chief Officer(s):
Al Gabert, Executive Director
alg@skillscanada.com

Yukon
108 Lambert St., Whitehorse YT Y1A 1Z2
Tel: 867-668-2736; *Fax:* 867-668-2704
skillscanada@northwestel.net
www.skillsyukon.com
www.facebook.com/pages/Skills-Canada-Yukon/502471166484972
twitter.com/SkillsCanadaYT
Chief Officer(s):
Megan Freese, Executive Director
meganf@skillscanada.com

Skookum Jim Friendship Centre
3159 - 3rd Ave., Whitehorse YT Y1A 1G1
Tel: 867-633-7680; *Fax:* 867-668-4460
sjfcfriends@northwestel.net
www.skookumjim.com
www.facebook.com/pages/Skookum-Jim-Friendship-Centre/225218697517943
vimeo.com/user5226474
Overview: A small local organization founded in 1962 overseen by National Association of Friendship Centres
Mission: Committed to a vision of bettering the spiritual, emotional, mental & physical well being of First Nations peoples, fostering the way of Friendship & understanding between people
Chief Officer(s):
Marney Paradis, Executive Director, 867-633-7683
sjfcexecutive@northwestel.net
Staff Member(s): 17
Activities: Diversion Program; Prenatal Nutrition Outreach Program; Recreation Program; Traditional Training Program; Urban Multipurpose Aboriginal Youth Centre;

Sky Works Charitable Foundation
#240, 401 Richmond St. West, Toronto ON M5V 3A8
Tel: 416-536-6581; *Fax:* 416-536-7728
info@skyworksfoundation.org
www.skyworksfoundation.org
www.linkedin.com/company/1174113?trk=tyah
www.facebook.com/pages/skyworks-charitable-foundation
twitter.com/skyworksorg
Overview: A small national charitable organization founded in 1983
Mission: To operate as a non-profit educational documentary production organization; To produce documentary films that deal with contemporary social issues & are designed to encourage audiences to see the value of their own experiences & to take action on their own behalf
Chief Officer(s):
Laura Sky, Executive Director
Finances: *Annual Operating Budget:* $250,000-$500,000
Staff Member(s): 3; 15 volunteer(s)
Activities: Producing documentaries to raise questions, stimulate discussion & encourage audience particpation in social & community process; *Speaker Service:* Yes; *Library:* Film Library

Slave Lake & District Chamber of Commerce
PO Box 190, Slave Lake AB T0G 2A0
Tel: 780-849-3222; *Fax:* 780-849-6894
sldcc@telus.net
www.slavelake.ca
Overview: A small local organization
Mission: To serve & promote area businesses while promoting the positive attributes that will attract both business & families to our unique, energetic community
Member of: Alberta Chamber of Commerce
Chief Officer(s):
Laurie Renauer, Executive Director
Finances: *Funding Sources:* Municipal grant; membership fees; projects
Staff Member(s): 1; 15 volunteer(s)
Membership: 130+; *Fees:* $84-$446.25

Slave Lake Native Friendship Centre
416 - 6 Ave., Slave Lake AB T0G 2A2
Tel: 780-849-3039; *Fax:* 780-849-2402
slnfc2@gmail.com
anfca.com/friendship-centres/slave-lake
Overview: A small local organization founded in 1972 overseen by Alberta Native Friendship Centres Association
Mission: To be a leader in the community by implementing new programs/services that will serve the needs of the Aboriginal people in order to improve their self-reliance & well being
Member of: Alberta Native Friendship Centres Association
Chief Officer(s):
L. Cook, Executive Director

Sledge Hockey of Canada (SHOC)
c/o Hockey Canada, #N204, 801 King Edward Ave., Ottawa ON K1N 6N5
Tel: 613-562-5677; *Fax:* 613-562-5676
www.hockeycanada.ca
www.facebook.com/HCSledge
twitter.com/HC_Sledge
www.youtube.com/hcsledge
Overview: A small national organization
Mission: To promote & govern the sport of sledge hockey in Canada

Sleeping Children Around the World (SCAW)
28 Pinehurst Cres., Toronto ON M9A 3A5
Tel: 416-231-1841; *Fax:* 416-231-0120
Toll-Free: 866-321-1841
www.scaw.org
Overview: A small local charitable organization founded in 1970
Mission: To raise funds to provide bedkits for needy children in underdeveloped & developing countries (each bedkit consists of items such as a groundsheet, mattress, sheets, pyjamas, blanket or mosquito netting, sweater or other clothing, personal care items); 100% volunteer, both at its Canadian base & overseas
Chief Officer(s):
Linda Webb, Executive Director

Slocan District Chamber of Commerce (SDCC)
PO Box 448, New Denver BC V0G 1S0
e-mail: chamber@slocanlake.com
slocanlakechamber.com
www.linkedin.com/groups?home=&gid=4726589
Overview: A small local organization founded in 1911
Mission: To represent & advocate on behalf of its members
Chief Officer(s):
Amanda Murphy, Manager
Nikita Boroumand, President
Staff Member(s): 1
Membership: 147; *Fees:* $35 individual/non-profit; $60 business

Slo-Pitch Ontario Association (SPO)
#7, 8 Hiscott St., St. Catharines ON L2R 1C6
Tel: 905-646-7773; *Fax:* 905-646-8431
spoa@slopitch.org
www.slopitch.org
www.facebook.com/172816356093689
twitter.com/slopitchontario
www.youtube.com/user/slopitchontario
Overview: A medium-sized provincial organization founded in 1982 overseen by Softball Ontario
Mission: To institute & regulate slo-pitch softball in Ontario
Member of: Canadian Amateur Softball Association; Softball Ontario
Chief Officer(s):
Tom Buchan, CEO
tbuchan@slopitch.org
Ron Hawthorne, President, 613-831-8393
rhawthorne@slopitch.info
Finances: *Funding Sources:* Sponsors; Partners; Government grants; Team fees
Membership: *Fees:* Schedule available; *Member Profile:* Slo-pitch teams & leagues in Ontario

Slow Food Canada
Toll-Free: 866-266-6661
theresa@slowfoodvancouver.com
www.slowfood.ca
www.facebook.com/slowfoodcanada
twitter.com/SlowFoodCanada
Overview: A small national organization founded in 1989
Mission: To protect pleasures of the table from the homogenization of modern fast food & life
Member of: Slow Food International
Chief Officer(s):
Valerie Lugonja, Secretary
valerie@acanadianfoodie.com
Membership: 18 convivia; 600+ members; *Fees:* $40-$310
Activities: Convivia in Alberta, British Columbia, Ontario, Québec, Nova Scotia & Yukon

Small Business Association (SBA)
Ottawa ON
Tel: 613-627-4318
info@sba-canada.ca
sba-canada.ca
www.linkedin.com/groups?gid=3694685
www.facebook.com/SBA.Canada
twitter.com/sbacanada
Previous Name: Home Business Association of the National Capital Region
Overview: A small local organization founded in 1996
Mission: To facilitate networking & reduce isolation; to facilitate self-education, business development, growth, & sustainability; to become a public voice for self-employed entrepreneurs in the area
Finances: *Annual Operating Budget:* Less than $50,000; *Funding Sources:* Membership fees; donations; sponsorship
Staff Member(s): 6; 22 volunteer(s)
Membership: 200+; *Fees:* $100 individual; *Member Profile:* Self-employed & working from home or small office; *Committees:* Information Technology; Communications; Newsletter; Trade Show; Seminar; Public Relations; Membership
Activities: Seminars; trade shows; newsletters; networking breakfasts; mentoring program; *Speaker Service:* Yes

Small Business Centre (SBC)
316 Rectory St., 3rd Fl., London ON N5W 3V9
Tel: 519-659-2882; *Fax:* 519-659-7050
info@sbcentre.ca
www.sbcentre.ca
twitter.com/sbclondon
www.youtube.com/user/SBCLondon
Overview: A small local organization founded in 1986
Mission: To actively contribute to the econonomic development of London by supporting local entrepreneurs & small businesses
Chief Officer(s):
Steve Pellarin, Executive Director
spellarin@sbcentre.ca
Finances: *Funding Sources:* Municipal, provincial & federal governments
Activities: Seminars; workshops; Summer Company program; SEED program; Ontario Works program; Self Employment Benefit program; online resources; *Library:* Resource Centre

Small Explorers & Producers Association of Canada *See* Explorers & Producers Association of Canada

Small Investor Protection Association (SIPA)
PO Box 24008, Stratford PE C1B 2V5
Tel: 416-614-9128
sipa.toronto@sipa.ca
www.sipa.ca
Overview: A small national organization founded in 1999
Mission: To advocate on behalf of small investors in Canada
Chief Officer(s):
Stan I. Buell, President
Finances: *Funding Sources:* Membership fees; private donations
Membership: 600+
Activities: Reports & submissions to government & regulators; *Library:* SIPA Library; Open to public
Publications:
- SIPA [Small Investor Protection Association] Sentinel
Type: Newsletter; *Frequency:* bi-m.

Small Water Users Association of BC
4167 Highway 3A, Nelson BC V1L 6N1
Tel: 250-825-4308
smallwaterusers@shaw.ca
www.smallwaterusers.com
Overview: A medium-sized provincial organization founded in 2003
Mission: The Small Water Users Association of BC is a new non-profit society dedicated to serving the interests of small water systems (1 to 300 connections) throughout British Columbia.
Chief Officer(s):
Denny Ross-Smith, Executive Director
Membership: 258; *Fees:* $35 basic fee (+$1 per connection); $90 affiliate

Smart Commute
c/o Metrolinx, #600, 20 Bay St., Toronto ON M5J 2W3
Tel: 416-874-5900; *Fax:* 416-869-1794
info@smartcommute.ca
www.smartcommute.ca
www.linkedin.com/groups?home=&gid=2677721&trk=anet_ug_hm
www.facebook.com/pages/Smart-Commute/323016568512
twitter.com/SmartCommute
www.youtube.com/user/smartcommuteGTAH
Overview: A small local organization
Mission: To reduce the stress on our lives, roads & environment; to reduce traffic congestion & to take action on climate change through transportation efficiency
Chief Officer(s):
Aubrey Iwaniw, Acting Manager
Aubrey.Iwaniw@metrolinx.com
Finances: *Annual Operating Budget:* $500,000-$1.5 Million; *Funding Sources:* Transport Canada; Greater Toronto Area Municipalities
Membership: 100-499
Activities: *Awareness Events:* Bike to Work Day, May

Smart Serve Ontario
#105, 5405 Eglinton Ave. West, Toronto ON M9C 5K6
Tel: 416-695-8737; *Fax:* 416-695-0684
Toll-Free: 877-620-6082
info@smartserve.ca
www.smartserve.ca
Overview: A medium-sized provincial organization
Mission: To develop & deliver responsible server training to all individuals who serve alcohol beverages or work where alcohol beverages are served in the province of Ontario
Finances: *Funding Sources:* Government grants
Activities: Officially delivers the Responsible Beverage Service Training Progra for the Ontario hospitality industry

Smith-Ennismore Historical Society
PO Box 41, Bridgenorth ON K0L 1H0
Tel: 705-292-9430
sehs@sehs.on.ca
www.sehs.on.ca
Previous Name: Smith-Ennismore Township Historical Society
Overview: A small local charitable organization founded in 1983
Mission: To collect, preserve & exhibit material for the study of history & genealogy, especially the history & families of Smith-Ennismore-Lakefield; to locate & preserve historical sites in the area; to provide access to all available information to all ages; to assist families in research of their land & roots; to assist school students in research; to provide bus trips to historical sites & attractions in Central Ontario; to be involved & voice concern on environmental issues
Member of: Ontario Historical Society
Membership: *Fees:* $30 couple; $20 single
Activities: Monthly meetings; Jan. install new executive; *Library:* Smith-Ennismore Heritage Resource Centre
Awards:
• Community Citizen (Award)

Smith-Ennismore Township Historical Society *See* Smith-Ennismore Historical Society

Smithers Community Services Association (SCSA)
PO Box 3759, 3815-B Railway Ave., Smithers BC V0J 2N0
Tel: 250-847-9515
Toll-Free: 888-355-6222
general@scsa.ca
www.scsa.ca
www.facebook.com/298672643483861
Overview: A small local charitable organization founded in 1973
Mission: To provide services that enhance the quality of life; To promote equal opportunity for all people within the community
Member of: British Columbia Association for Community Living; BC Non-Profit Housing Association; BC Council for Families
Chief Officer(s):
Corol Johnson, Chair
Cathryn Olmstead, Executive Director
colmstead@scsa.ca
Finances: *Annual Operating Budget:* $1.5 Million-$3 Million
Staff Member(s): 40; 100 volunteer(s)
Membership: 50; *Fees:* $2 annual; $20 lifetime

Smithers District Chamber of Commerce
PO Box 2379, Smithers BC V0J 2N0
Tel: 250-847-5072; *Fax:* 250-847-3337
Toll-Free: 800-542-6673
info@smitherschamber.com
www.smitherschamber.com
Overview: A small local organization founded in 1923
Mission: To be the voice of business, promoting pride & growth in our community
Member of: BC Chamber of Commerce; Canadian Chamber of Commerce
Affliation(s): Northern BC Tourism Association
Chief Officer(s):
George Whitehead, President
Finances: *Annual Operating Budget:* $100,000-$250,000; *Funding Sources:* Membership fees; Fee for services; Tourism BC; HRDC
Staff Member(s): 2; 14 volunteer(s)
Membership: 9 individual + 196 corporate; *Fees:* Based on number of employees; *Committees:* Business Development; Finance; Operations; Member Services
Activities: *Library*

Smiths Falls & District Chamber of Commerce
Town Hall, 77 Beckwith St. North, Smiths Falls ON K7A 2B8
Tel: 613-283-1334; *Fax:* 613-283-4764
Toll-Free: 800-257-1334
sfchamber@smithfalls.ca
www.smithsfallschamber.ca
Overview: A small local organization
Chief Officer(s):
Victoria Ash, Manager
Ashley Lennox, Office Co-ordinator
Staff Member(s): 2; 16 volunteer(s)
Membership: 185

Smiths Falls & District Historical Society
11 Old Sly's Rd., Smiths Falls ON K7A 4T6
Tel: 613-283-6311
sfdhistoricalsociety@gmail.com
www.facebook.com/SmithsFallsDistrictHistoricalSociety
Overview: A small local organization founded in 1971
Member of: Ontario Historical Society
Finances: *Funding Sources:* Membership dues

Smoking & Health Action Foundation
#221, 720 Spadina Ave., Toronto ON M5S 2T9
Tel: 416-928-2900; *Fax:* 416-928-1860
toronto@nsra-adnf.ca
www.nsra-adnf.ca
twitter.com/nsra_adnf
Overview: A small local organization founded in 1974
Mission: To conduct public policy research & education designed to reduce tobacco-related disease & death
Chief Officer(s):
Lorraine Fry, Executive Director
Finances: *Funding Sources:* Federal government
Staff Member(s): 10; 50 volunteer(s)

Smoky Applied Research & Demonstration Association (SARDA)
PO Box 90, 701 Main St., Falher AB T0H 1M0
Tel: 780-837-2900; *Fax:* 780-837-8223
sarda@serbernet.com
www.areca.ab.ca/sardahome.html
twitter.com/SARDA6
Overview: A small local organization overseen by Agricultural Research & Extension Council of Alberta
Mission: To conduct agricultural research
Member of: Agricultural Research & Extension Council of Alberta
Chief Officer(s):
J.P. Pettyjohn, Manager
Shelleen Gerbig, Agrologist, AESA Program
shelleesarda@serbernet.com
Kabal Gill, Coordinator, Research Extension
gillsarda@serbernet.com
Membership: *Fees:* $50 individual; $100 corporate
Publications:
• Back Forty [a publication of the Smoky Applied Research & Demonstration Association]
Type: Newsletter

Smoky Lake & District Chamber of Commerce
PO Box 654, Smoky Lake AB T0A 3C0
Tel: 780-656-4347
smokylakechamber@mcsnet.ca
Overview: A small local organization
Chief Officer(s):
Wayne Taylor, President
Membership: *Member Profile:* Small businesses
Activities: *Speaker Service:* Yes

Smoky River Regional Chamber of Commerce
PO Box 814, 11 Centre Ave. SW, Falher AB T0H 1M0
Tel: 780-837-2188
office@smokyriverchamber.ca
www.smokyriverchamber.ca
Overview: A small local organization
Affliation(s): Alberta Chamber of Commerce; Canadian Chamber of Commerce
Membership: 71

Snow Crab Fishermans Inc.
c/o Carter Hutt, RR#2, Alberton PE C0B 1B0
Tel: 902-853-3332
Overview: A small provincial organization
Chief Officer(s):
Carter Hutt, President

Snowboard Association of Manitoba
4180 Henderson Hwy., East St Paul MB R2E 1B4
Overview: A small provincial organization overseen by Canadian Snowboard Federation
Mission: To be the provincial governing body of competitive snowboarding in Manitoba.
Member of: Canadian Snowboard Federation
Chief Officer(s):
Glenn Luff, Contact
gkluff@mymts.net

Snowboard Nova Scotia
#311, 5516 Spring Garden Rd., Halifax NS B3J 1G6
Tel: 902-425-5450; *Fax:* 902-425-5606
www.snowboardnovascotia.ca
www.facebook.com/SnowboardNovaScotia
Previous Name: Nova Scotia Snowboard Association
Overview: A small provincial organization overseen by Canadian Snowboard Federation
Mission: To be the provincial governing body of competitive snowboarding in Nova Scotia.
Member of: Canadian Snowboard Federation; Sport Nova Scotia
Chief Officer(s):
Karen Chassé, President
benmarc@ns.sympatico.ca
Kristin d'Eon, Technical Director
kdeon@accesswave.ca
Andrew Hayes, Administrative Coordinator
ahayes@sportnovascotia.ca

Snowboard Yukon
4061 - 4th Ave., Whitehorse YT Y1A 1H1
Tel: 867-332-2400
info@snowboardyukon.com
www.snowboardyukon.com
Overview: A medium-sized provincial organization overseen by Canadian Snowboard Federation
Mission: To organize & sanction events, train athletes & coaches, form & administer teams for out of territory competitions, & represent Yukon riders in the Canadian Snowboard Federation.
Member of: Canadian Snowboard Federation
Chief Officer(s):
Mary Binstead, Head Coach
mary@snowboardyukon.com

Snowmobilers Association of Nova Scotia (SANS)
5516 Spring Garden Rd., 4th Fl., Halifax NS B3J 3G6
Tel: 902-425-5450; *Fax:* 902-425-5606
www.snowmobilersns.com
Overview: A small provincial organization founded in 1976

Mission: To provide leadership & support to member snowmobile clubs so that they may enjoy quality recreational snowmobiling opportunities on a province-wide network of safe & well-developed snowmobile trails
Chief Officer(s):
Stan Slack, President
president@snowmobilersns.com
Membership: 21 member clubs; *Member Profile:* Snowmobile clubs

Snowmobilers of Manitoba Inc.

2121 Henderson Hwy., Winnipeg MB R2G 1P8
Tel: 204-940-7533; *Fax:* 204-940-7531
info@snoman.mb.ca
www.snoman.mb.ca
Also Known As: Snoman
Overview: A small provincial organization founded in 1975
Mission: To provide strong leadership & support to member clubs; to develop & maintain safe & environmentally responsible snowmobile trails; to further the enjoyment of organized snowmobiling throughout Manitoba
Affliation(s): Canadian Council of Snowmobile Organizations
Chief Officer(s):
Alan Butler, President
Ken Lucko, Executive Director
kenlucko@snoman.mb.ca
Finances: *Annual Operating Budget:* $500,000-$1.5 Million
Staff Member(s): 2; 2500 volunteer(s)
Membership: 2,500; *Fees:* $450
Meetings/Conferences: • Snowmobilers of Manitoba Inc. 2015 5th Annual Snoman Congress, 2015
Scope: Provincial

Soaring Association of Canada (SAC) / Association canadienne de vol à voile (ACVV)

c/o COPA National Office, 71 Bank St., 7th Fl., Ottawa ON K1P 5N2
Tel: 613-236-4901; *Fax:* 613-236-8646
sac@sac.ca
www.sac.ca
Overview: A medium-sized national organization founded in 1945
Mission: To promote, enhance & protect the sport of soaring in Canada; To provide information & services to the soaring community: licensing, medical requirements for glider pilots, aircraft certification, technical issues, courses & training, insurance plan, & services to clubs
Affliation(s): Aero Club of Canada; International Gliding Commission of the Fédération Aéronautique Internationale
Chief Officer(s):
Sylvain Bourque, President
bourques@videotron.ca
John Mulder, Vice-President & Secretary
johnmulder@shaw.ca
Finances: *Funding Sources:* Membership fees; Sales; Donations
40 volunteer(s)
Membership: 1,500 club affiliates; *Fees:* $60-$120; *Committees:* Air Cadets; Airspace; Archives/Historian; Contest Letters; FAI Awards; FAI Records; Fit Training & Safety; Free Flight; Insurance; Medical; Technical; Trophy Claims; World Contest; Flight Records
Activities: *Library* by appointment
Awards:
• Air Cadet Flying Scholarship (Scholarship)
• Corley Scholarship (Scholarship)
Publications:
• Free Flight
Type: Journal; *Frequency:* Quarterly; *Editor:* Tony Burton; *Price:* $30 Canada; $35 USA & overseas
Profile: The journal of the Soaring Association of Canada is indexed from 1968 to the present

Soaring Eagle Friendship Centre

PO Box 396, #2, 8 Gagnier St., Hay River NT X0E 1G1
Tel: 867-874-6581; *Fax:* 867-874-3362
www.facebook.com/SoaringEagleFriendshipCentre
Overview: A small local organization
Chief Officer(s):
Sharon Pekok, Executive Director

Soccer New Brunswick

#2, 125 Russ Howard Dr., Moncton NB E1C 0L7
Tel: 506-382-7529; *Fax:* 506-382-5621
admin@soccernb.org
www.soccernb.org
www.facebook.com/SoccerNb
twitter.com/SoccerNB
Also Known As: Soccer NB
Overview: A medium-sized provincial organization founded in 1965 overseen by Canadian Soccer Association
Mission: To foster & promote the development & growth of the sport of soccer in New Brunswick & to assure equitable accessibility through quality programs
Member of: Canadian Soccer Association
Chief Officer(s):
Marc Leger, Executive Director
exec@soccernb.org
Finances: *Annual Operating Budget:* $500,000-$1.5 Million; *Funding Sources:* Government; membership
Staff Member(s): 2; 9 volunteer(s)
Membership: 16,500

Soccer Nova Scotia (SNS)

210 Thomas Raddall Dr., Halifax NS B3S 1K3
Tel: 902-445-0265; *Fax:* 902-445-0258
admin@soccerns.ns.ca
www.soccerns.ns.ca
www.facebook.com/pages/Soccer-Nova-Scotia/290512917639108
twitter.com/SoccerNS
www.youtube.com/user/SoccerNovaScotia
Overview: A medium-sized provincial organization founded in 1913 overseen by Canadian Soccer Association
Mission: To promote the sport of soccer in Nova Scotia; To provide information & resources to aid player training, coaching education, & referee programs
Member of: Canadian Soccer Association
Chief Officer(s):
George Athanasiou, Chief Executive Officer
ceo@soccerns.ns.ca
Carman King, Officer, Referee Development
ref.services@soccerns.ns.ca
Membership: 27,000+ players; 2,500+ coaches; 700+ referees

Social Development Council Ajax-Pickering; Ajax/Pickering Social Development Council *See* Community Development Council Durham

Social Ecology Research Group *Voir* Groupe de recherche en écologie sociale

Social Investment Organization *See* Responsible Investment Association

Social Justice Committee / Comité pour la justice sociale

1857, rue de Maisonneuve ouest, Montréal QC H3H 1J9
Tel: 514-933-6797; *Fax:* 514-933-9517
info@sjc-cjs.org
www.s-j-c.net
Overview: A small local charitable organization founded in 1975
Mission: To work in solidarity with people in a number of southern countries & with Canadian & international organizations in the search for a more just & sustainable socio-economic system; To raise awareness of Canadians about the root causes of poverty & injustice in the world & how they are connected to us; To suggest ways by which we can work in cooperation with southern popular organizations
Chief Officer(s):
Ernie Schibli, Co-Founder & President
Derek MacCuish, Executive Director & Editor, Upstream Journal
Philippe Tousignant, Coordinator, Education Program
Doug Miller, Secretary
Dalila Benchaouche, Treasurer
Finances: *Annual Operating Budget:* $50,000-$100,000; *Funding Sources:* Canadian Development Agency; Members; General public
30 volunteer(s)
Membership: 100-499; *Member Profile:* Individuals who support the work of the Social Justice Committee financially or in other ways & who share a common concern to work for social change, particularly in the areas of human rights in Central America & socio-economic rights; Subscribers to the newsletter; Volunteers; *Committees:* Human Rights & Development; Debt & Environment; Resource Centre; Upstream Journal; Urgent Action Centre
Activities: *Speaker Service:* Yes; *Rents Mailing List:* Yes; *Library* Open to public

Social Planning & Research Council of BC (SPARC BC)

4445 Norfolk St., Burnaby BC V5G 0A7
Tel: 604-718-7733; *Fax:* 604-736-8697
Toll-Free: 888-718-7794
info@sparc.bc.ca
www.sparc.bc.ca
Overview: A medium-sized provincial charitable organization founded in 1966
Mission: To promote the social, economic & environmental well-being of citizens & communities; to advocate the principles of social justice, equality & the dignity & worth of all people in our multicultural society; to conduct research & planning for public information, education & citizen participation in developing social policies & programs
Member of: Canadian Council on Social Development
Affliation(s): Community Social Planning Network; BC Community Accessibility Network
Chief Officer(s):
Lorraine Copas, Executive Director
lcopas@sparc.bc.ca
Irene Willsie, President
Finances: *Funding Sources:* United Way; various project grants; membership fees; donations
Membership: *Fees:* $25 individual; $60 organization
Activities: Projects & programs: Parking permits for people with disabilities & advocacy on accessibility issues; education & social services; health; community economic development; income security/labour market policies; social planning/citizen participation; Social Development Research Program; Community Development Institute; *Speaker Service:* Yes; *Library* by appointment

Social Planning & Research Council of Hamilton

#103, 162 King William St., Hamilton ON L8R 3N9
Tel: 905-522-1148; *Fax:* 905-522-9124
sprc@sprc.hamilton.on.ca
www.sprc.hamilton.on.ca
www.facebook.com/sprchamilton
twitter.com/sprchamont
Overview: A small local organization founded in 1961
Mission: To improve the quality of life for all citizens of Hamilton-Wentworth
Chief Officer(s):
Don Jaffray, Executive Director
Purdeep Sangha, President
Finances: *Funding Sources:* United Way; municipal government
Staff Member(s): 17
Membership: *Fees:* $100 corporate; $50 non-profit; $25 individual; $10 students/unemployed

Social Planning Council for the North Okanagan (SPCNO)

c/o Community Futures North Okanagan, 3105 - 33rd St., Vernon BC V1T 9P7
Tel: 250-540-8572
info@socialplanning.ca
www.socialplanning.ca
Previous Name: North Okanagan Social Planning Council
Overview: A small local charitable organization founded in 1969
Mission: To facilitate & coordinate community planning & development by encouraging communication & cooperation amongst social, educational & health services in the North Okanagan
Chief Officer(s):
Annette Sharkey, Executive Director
Finances: *Funding Sources:* Provincial & municipal governments
Membership: *Member Profile:* Non-profit agencies, supportive individuals
Activities: Maintains a central information bureau & referral service; community services directory; volunteer bureau; community development; research; cancer prevention programs; *Library*

Social Planning Council of Cambridge & North Dumfries

#14, 55 Dickson St., Cambridge ON N1R 7A5
Tel: 519-623-1713; *Fax:* 519-267-4016
admin@spccnd.org
www.spccnd.org
www.facebook.com/220130431457527
twitter.com/SPCCND
Overview: A small local charitable organization founded in 1989
Mission: To actively participate in building & strengthening our community through research, analysis, facilitation & education
Chief Officer(s):
Linda Terry, Executive Director

Finances: *Funding Sources:* United Way; Ontario Trillium Foundation; City of Cambridge
Staff Member(s): 5
Activities: Community research & planning; Community development; Trend analyses; Policy analyses; Public education; Facilitation; *Library* by appointment

Social Planning Council of Kitchener-Waterloo

#300, 151 Frederick St., Kitchener ON N2H 2M2
Tel: 519-579-1096; *Fax:* 519-578-9185
Toll-Free: 877-579-3859
info@waterlooregion.org
www.waterlooregion.org
www.facebook.com/socialplanningcouncil
twitter.com/spcofkw
Overview: A small local charitable organization founded in 1966
Mission: To link services & people for the well-being of the community; to gather & manage comprehensive data on community needs & human services in Waterloo Region; to prepare & distribute information in meaningful & accessible ways to community citizens; to collaborate with others in developing a community which offers a desirable quality of life for all its citizens
Affiliation(s): Social Planning Network of Ontario; AIRS; Ontario Healthy Communities Coalition; InformCanada; InformOntario; Imagine Canada; Ontario Nonprofit Network
Chief Officer(s):
Trudy Beaulne, Executive Director
spckw@waterlooregion.org
Malcolm Waisman, Treasurer
Fahima Anwar, President
Finances: *Annual Operating Budget:* $250,000-$500,000; *Funding Sources:* Municipal Government; Regional Government; United Way; Publications; Fee for service
Staff Member(s): 7
Membership: 63 organizations; *Fees:* Schedule available; *Member Profile:* Community members & non-profit organziations; *Committees:* Board Development; Fundraising
Activities: Research & data management; Community information; Community building; *Library* Open to public
Awards:
- Sponsor Youth Leadership Award (Award)
- Sponsor Neighbourhood Community Spirit Award (Award)

Social Planning Council of Ottawa-Carleton (SPCO) / Conseil de planification sociale d'Ottawa-Carleton

790 Bronson Ave., Ottawa ON K1S 4G4
Tel: 613-236-9300; *Fax:* 613-236-7060
office@spcottawa.on.ca
www.spcottawa.on.ca
Previous Name: Ottawa Council of Social Agencies
Overview: A small local charitable organization founded in 1928
Mission: To provide the residents of Ottawa-Carleton with the means to exercise informed leadership on issues affecting their social & economic well-being
Member of: United Way of Ottawa-Carleton
Affiliation(s): District Health Council; Ontario Social Development Council
Chief Officer(s):
Diane Urquhart, Executive Director
dianneu@spcottawa.on.ca
Finances: *Funding Sources:* United Way; Municipal & provincial government; Various charitable organizations; User fees & contracts
Staff Member(s): 7; 91 volunteer(s)
Membership: *Fees:* $25 individual; $30 non-profit organization; $65 for profit organization; $200 10 year individual; $500 individual lifetime
Activities: *Library* Open to public

Social Planning Council of Sudbury Region (SPC) / Conseil de planification sociale Region de Sudbury

30 Ste. Anne Rd., Sudbury ON P3C 5E1
Tel: 705-675-3894
info@spcsudbury.ca
www.spcsudbury.ca
www.linkedin.com/company/1704612
www.facebook.com/SPC.Sudbury
twitter.com/SPCSudburyED
www.youtube.com/user/foodshed2011
Overview: A small local organization founded in 1991
Mission: To engage the diverse groups of the Sudbury community in a non-biased & interactive planning process aimed at improving the quality of life in the community
Member of: Social Planning Network of Ontario; Ontario Social Development Council; Canadian Council on Social Development
Chief Officer(s):
Annette Reszczynski, Interim Executive Director
Finances: *Funding Sources:* Municipal & provincial governments; Donations; Foundations
Staff Member(s): 7
Activities: Annual Options & Opportunities Employment Fair

Social Planning Council of Winnipeg

#300, 207 Donald St., Winnipeg MB R3C 1M5
Tel: 204-943-2561; *Fax:* 204-942-3221
info@spcw.mb.ca
www.spcw.mb.ca
ca.linkedin.com/company/social-planning-council-of-winnipeg
twitter.com/spcw1919
Overview: A small local organization
Mission: To identify & define social planning issues, needs & resources in the community; to develop & promote policy & program options to policy-makers; to support community groups & the voluntary human service sector; to raise community awareness of social issues & human service needs, social policy options & service delivery alternatives; to serve as a link between the three levels of government & community neighbourhoods
Chief Officer(s):
Dennis Lewycky, Executive Director
dlewycky@spcw.mb.ca
Membership: *Fees:* $20 individual, $50 organization, $100 sustaining

Social Planning Toronto (SPT)

#1001, 2 Carlton St., Toronto ON M5B 1J3
Tel: 416-351-0095; *Fax:* 416-351-0107
info@socialplanningtoronto.org
www.socialplanningtoronto.org
www.linkedin.com/company/social-planning-toronto
www.facebook.com/pages/Social-Planning-Toronto/139141580135
twitter.com/planningtoronto
plus.google.com/112933900589591472077
Overview: A small local organization
Mission: To promote community-based, social policy, planning & civic participation at both the local & city-wide levels through analysis & action-oriented research on social issues.
Chief Officer(s):
John Campey, Executive Director
jcampey@socialplanningtoronto.org
Maria Serrano, Director, Operations
mserrano@socialplanningtoronto.org
Finances: *Funding Sources:* City of Toronto; United Way; Ontario Trillium Foundation
Staff Member(s): 12
Membership: *Fees:* $5 students/seniors/unwaged; $25 individual; fee for organizations dependant on operating budget
Activities: Adversity Game; consulting services; custom research; fundraising resources; *Library* Open to public

Etobicoke Office
Applewood, The Shaver Homestead, #205, 450 The West Mall, Toronto ON M9C 1E9
Tel: 416-231-5499; *Fax:* 416-231-4608
Chief Officer(s):
Richard DeGaetano, Community Planner
rdegaetano@socialplanningtoronto.org

York/West Toronto Office
1652 Keele St., Toronto ON M6M 3W3
Tel: 416-652-9772; *Fax:* 416-652-7128
Chief Officer(s):
Yasmin Khan, Community Planner
kyasmin@socialplanningtoronto.org

Socialist Party of Canada (SPC) / Parti Socialiste du Canada

PO Box 4280, Victoria BC V8X 3X8
e-mail: spc@iname.com
www.worldsocialism.org/canada/
Overview: A small national organization founded in 1905
Mission: To promote the establishment of socialism - a system of society based upon the common ownership & democratic control of the means & instruments for producing & distributing wealth by & in the interest of society as a whole
Affiliation(s): World Socialist Movement
Chief Officer(s):
John Ayers, Contact
jpayers@sympatico.ca
Finances: *Annual Operating Budget:* Less than $50,000; *Funding Sources:* Membership fees; donations
3 volunteer(s)
Membership: 20; *Fees:* $25; *Member Profile:* Agreement with Object & Declaration of Principles; *Committees:* General Administrative Committee
Activities: *Speaker Service:* Yes; *Library* by appointment

Società Unita

1775 Islington Ave., Toronto ON M9P 3N2
Tel: 416-243-7319; *Fax:* 416-243-7319
info@teopoli.com
teopoli.com
twitter.com/teopoli
www.flickr.com/photos/60905934@N05
Also Known As: The United Society (The Mission)
Overview: A small local charitable organization founded in 1972
Mission: To promote peace, love, & unity, according to the Gospel & the teaching of the Roman Catholic Church
Affiliation(s): Archdiocese of Toronto
Chief Officer(s):
Joe Colalillo, Director
Finances: *Funding Sources:* Donations
Membership: *Member Profile:* Individuals, over the age of eighteen, who wish to follow the principles of peace, love, & unity, acccording to the Gospel & the teaching of the Roman Catholic Church
Activities: Encouraging religious & social activities for spiritual & moral growth; Providing assistance to the needy; Offering faith instruction, prayer groups, spiritual retreats, & spiritual pilgrimages; Operating the Teopoli Summer Experience for children at Teopoli, located in Muskoka; Providing a daily Catholic braodcast on Radio Teopoli, with programming such as Jesus the Listener, & The Good Samaritan;

Société Alzheimer Canada *See* Alzheimer Society Canada

Société Alzheimer d'Ottawa et Renfrew County *See* Alzheimer Society of Ottawa & Renfrew County

Société alzheimer du nouveau brunswick *See* Alzheimer Society of New Brunswick

Société Alzheimer Ontario *See* Alzheimer Society Ontario

Société Alzheimer Society Sudbury-Manitoulin (SASSM)

960B Notre Dame Ave., Sudbury ON P3A 2T4
Tel: 705-560-0603; *Fax:* 705-560-6938
Toll-Free: 800-407-6369
info@alzheimersudbury.ca
www.alzheimersudbury.ca
www.facebook.com/group.php?gid=448683941821858
Overview: A small local organization founded in 1985
Member of: Alzheimer Canada
Affiliation(s): Alzheimer Society of Ontario
Chief Officer(s):
Lorraine LeBlanc, Executive Director, 705-524-2024 Ext. 233, Fax: 705-560-6938
lleblanc@alzheimersudbury.ca
Lana Hodgins, Bookkeeper, 705-524-2024 Ext. 234, Fax: 705-560-6938
lhodgins@alzheimersudbury.ca
Anne Wurster, Coordinator, Office & Special Events
awurster@alzheimersudbury.ca
Finances: *Funding Sources:* Local Health Integration Network
Staff Member(s): 23; 85 volunteer(s)
Membership: 90; *Fees:* $10 students & seniors; $20 regular memberships; $50 patrons
Activities: *Awareness Events:* Awareness Dinner, January; *Speaker Service:* Yes; *Library:* Société Alzheimer Society Sudbury-Manitoulin Library; Open to public

Société anthroposophique au Canada *See* Anthroposophical Society in Canada

Société asiatique des partenaires Canada *See* South Asia Partnership Canada

Société bibliographique du Canada *See* Bibliographical Society of Canada

Société biblique canadienne *See* Canadian Bible Society

Société Canada-Japon de Montréal / Canada-Japan Society of Montréal

7375, rue Sagard, Montréal QC H2E 2S8
Tél: 514-721-0052
www.mtlinfo.ca/canada-japon
Aperçu: *Dimension:* petite; *Envergure:* locale; Organisme sans but lucratif; fondée en 1960

Mission: Faciliter les échanges entre les Canadiens et les Japonais
Membre(s) du bureau directeur:
Alice Bolduc, Présidente
Membre: 157
Activités: Démonstrations et activités artistiques; conférenciers; excursions; rencontres sociales

La Société canadienne d'Addison ***See*** The Canadian Addison Society

La société canadienne d'aérophilatélie ***See*** Canadian Aerophilatelic Society

Société canadienne d'agroéconomie ***See*** Canadian Agricultural Economics Society

Société canadienne d'allergie et d'immunologie clinique ***See*** Canadian Society of Allergy & Clinical Immunology

Société canadienne d'Anthropologie ***See*** Canadian Anthropology Society

Société canadienne d'apprentissage psychomoteur et de psychologie du sport ***See*** Canadian Society for Psychomotor Learning & Sport Psychology

Société canadienne d'association ***See*** Canadian Society of Association Executives

Société canadienne d'astronomie ***See*** Canadian Astronomical Society

Société canadienne d'Athérosclérose, de Thrombose et de Biologie Vasculaire ***See*** Canadian Society of Atherosclerosis, Thrombosis & Vascular Biology

Société canadienne d'autisme ***See*** Autism Society Canada

La Société canadienne d'éducation comparée et internationale ***See*** The Comparative & International Education Society of Canada

Société canadienne d'éducation par l'art ***See*** Canadian Society for Education through Art

Société canadienne d'endocrinologie et métabolisme ***See*** Canadian Society of Endocrinology & Metabolism

Société canadienne d'enregistrement des animaux ***See*** Canadian Livestock Records Corporation

Société canadienne d'épidémiologie et de biostatistique ***See*** Canadian Society for Epidemiology & Biostatistics

Société canadienne d'esthétique ***See*** Canadian Society for Aesthetics

Société canadienne d'étude du dix-huitième siècle ***See*** Canadian Society for Eighteenth-Century Studies

Société canadienne d'études ethniques ***See*** Canadian Ethnic Studies Association

Société canadienne d'évaluation ***See*** Canadian Evaluation Society

Société canadienne d'hématologie ***See*** Canadian Hematology Society

Société canadienne d'histoire de l'Église ***See*** Canadian Society of Church History

Société canadienne d'histoire de l'église catholique - Section anglaise ***See*** Canadian Catholic Historical Association - English Section

Société canadienne d'histoire de l'Église Catholique - Section française (SCHEC) / Canadian Catholic Historical Association - French Section

SCHEC, Université du Québec à Trois-Rivières, 3351, boul des Forges, Trois-Rivières QC G9A 5H7
Tél: 819-376-5011; *Téléc:* 819-376-5179
schec.cieq.ca
Aperçu: *Dimension:* moyenne; *Envergure:* nationale; fondée en 1933
Mission: Grouper les personnes intéressées à l'histoire de l'Église catholique au Canada; stimuler l'intérêt pour cette histoire dans le grand public; tenir des congrès annuels dans diverses régions du Canada afin de susciter un dialogue entre chercheurs participants et de promouvoir les travaux d'histoire régionale
Membre(s) du bureau directeur:
Lucia Ferretti, Président
Finances: *Budget de fonctionnement annuel:* Moins de $50,000
4 bénévole(s)
Membre: 150 individu; 100 institutionnel; *Montant de la cotisation:* 20$ étudiants; 40$ individu; 50$ institutionnel; *Critères d'admissibilite:* La Société compte des membres dans toutes les parties du Canada de même qu'en Europe et aux États-Unis; les membres peuvent être des individus, ou des institutions publiques ou privées, tels des dépôts d'archives, bibliothèques, diocèses, communautés religieuses
Meetings/Conferences: • Le congrès annuel, sept

Société canadienne d'histoire de la médecine ***See*** Canadian Society for the History of Medicine

Société Canadienne d'Histoire et Philosophie des Sciences ***See*** Canadian Society for the History & Philosophy of Science

Société canadienne d'histoire orale ***See*** Canadian Oral History Association

Société canadienne d'indexation ***See*** Indexing Society of Canada

Société canadienne d'ingénierie des services de santé ***See*** Canadian Healthcare Engineering Society

Société canadienne d'oncologie chirurgicale ***See*** Canadian Society for Surgical Oncology

Société canadienne d'onomastique ***See*** Canadian Society for the Study of Names

Société canadienne d'opthalmologie ***See*** Canadian Ophthalmological Society

Société canadienne d'otolaryngologie et de chirurgie cervico-faciale ***See*** Canadian Society of Otolaryngology - Head & Neck Surgery

Société canadienne de bioéthique ***See*** Canadian Bioethics Society

Société canadienne de cardiologie ***See*** Canadian Cardiovascular Society

Société canadienne de chimie ***See*** Canadian Society for Chemistry

Société canadienne de chirurgie plastique esthétique ***See*** Canadian Society for Aesthetic (Cosmetic) Plastic Surgery

Société canadienne de chirurgie vasculaire ***See*** Canadian Society for Vascular Surgery

Société canadienne de cytologie ***See*** Canadian Society of Cytology

Société canadienne de fertilité et d'andrologie ***See*** Canadian Fertility & Andrology Society

Société canadienne de génie agroalimentaire et de bioingénierie ***See*** Canadian Society for Bioengineering

Société canadienne de génie biomédical inc. ***See*** Canadian Medical & Biological Engineering Society

Société canadienne de génie chimique ***See*** Canadian Society for Chemical Engineering

Société canadienne de génie civil ***See*** Canadian Society for Civil Engineering

Société canadienne de génie mécanique ***See*** Canadian Society for Mechanical Engineering

Société canadienne de gériatrie ***See*** Canadian Geriatrics Society

Société canadienne de gestion de la nutrition ***See*** Canadian Society of Nutrition Management

Société canadienne de gestion en ingénierie ***See*** Canadian Society for Engineering Management

Société Canadienne de greffe de cellules souches hematopoietiques ***See*** Canadian Blood & Marrow Transplant Group

Société canadienne de l'asthme ***See*** Asthma Society of Canada

Société canadienne de l'énergie du sol ***See*** Earth Energy Society of Canada

La société canadienne de l'espace ***See*** Canadian Space Society

Société canadienne de l'hémochromatose ***See*** Canadian Hemochromatosis Society

Société canadienne de l'hémophilie ***See*** Canadian Hemophilia Society

Société canadienne de l'ouïe ***See*** Canadian Hearing Society

Société canadienne de la pivoine ***See*** Canadian Peony Society

Société canadienne de la santé et de la sécurité, inc. ***See*** Canadian Society of Safety Engineering, Inc.

Société canadienne de la santé internationale ***See*** Canadian Society for International Health

Société canadienne de la science du sol ***See*** Canadian Society of Soil Science

Société canadienne de la sclérose en plaques ***See*** Multiple Sclerosis Society of Canada

Société canadienne de la sclérose en plaques (Division du Québec) (SCSP) / Multiple Sclerosis Society of Canada (Québec Division)

Tour Est, #1010, 550, rue Sherbrooke ouest, Montréal QC H3A 1B9
Tél: 514-849-7591; *Téléc:* 514-849-8914
Ligne sans frais: 800-268-7582
info.qc@mssociety.ca
www.mssociety.ca/qc
Également appelé: SP - Québec
Aperçu: *Dimension:* moyenne; *Envergure:* provinciale; Organisme sans but lucratif; fondée en 1948
Mission: Soutenir la recherche sur la SP; offrir des services aux personnes atteintes de la maladie et à leurs familles; sensibiliser le public à la sclérose en plaques et maintenir les relations avec les gouvernements.
Membre de: Multiple Sclerosis Society of Canada
Affliation(s): Fédération internationale de la sclérose en plaques
Membre(s) du bureau directeur:
Louis Adam, Executive Director
Finances: *Budget de fonctionnement annuel:* $3 Million-$5 Million
Membre(s) du personnel: 30; 1000 bénévole(s)
Membre: 7 300; *Montant de la cotisation:* Gratuit pour personnes ayant la SP; 10$ par année pour les autres; *Critères d'admissibilite:* Personnes atteintes de SP et autres
Activités: 26 sections locales; *Evénements de sensibilisation:* Mois de la sensibilisation de la SP, mai; Marche de l'eSPoir; *Stagiaires:* Oui; *Service de conférenciers:* Oui; *Bibliothèque:* Centre de documentation; rendez-vous

La Société canadienne de la SLA ***See*** ALS Society of Canada

Société canadienne de la sûreté industrielle ***See*** Canadian Society for Industrial Security Inc.

Société canadienne de mathématiques appliquées et industrielles ***See*** Canadian Applied & Industrial Mathematics Society

Société canadienne de médecine interne ***See*** Canadian Society of Internal Medicine

Société canadienne de médecine transfusionnelle ***See*** Canadian Society for Transfusion Medicine

Société canadienne de météorologie et d'océanographie ***See*** Canadian Meteorological & Oceanographic Society

Société canadienne de néphrologie ***See*** Canadian Society of Nephrology

Société canadienne de neurologie ***See*** Canadian Neurological Society

Société canadienne de neurophysiologistes cliniques ***See*** Canadian Society of Clinical Neurophysiologists

Société canadienne de nutrition ***See*** Canadian Nutrition Society

Société canadienne de pédiatrie ***See*** Canadian Paediatric Society

Société canadienne de peintres en aquarelle ***See*** Canadian Society of Painters in Water Colour

Société Canadienne de Perfusion Clinique ***See*** Canadian Society of Clinical Perfusion

Société Canadienne de Philosophie de l'Education *See* Canadian Philosophy of Education Society

Société canadienne de physiologie *See* Canadian Physiological Society

Société canadienne de physiologie de l'exercice *See* Canadian Society for Exercise Physiology

Société canadienne de physiologie végétale *See* Canadian Society of Plant Physiologists

Société Canadienne de Phytopathologie *See* Canadian Phytopathological Society

Société canadienne de psychanalyse *See* Canadian Psychoanalytic Society

Société canadienne de psychologie *See* Canadian Psychological Association

Société canadienne de recherche opérationelle *See* Canadian Operational Research Society

Société canadienne de recherche sur le glaucome *See* Glaucoma Research Society of Canada

Société canadienne de recherches cliniques *See* Canadian Society for Clinical Investigation

Société canadienne de rhumatologie *See* Canadian Rheumatology Association

Société canadienne de schizophrénie *See* Schizophrenia Society of Canada

Société canadienne de science animale *See* Canadian Society of Animal Science

Société canadienne de science de laboratoire médical *See* Canadian Society for Medical Laboratory Science

Société canadienne de science horticole *See* Canadian Society for Horticultural Science

Société canadienne de soins intensifs *See* Canadian Critical Care Society

Société canadienne de technologie chimique *See* Canadian Society for Chemical Technology

Société canadienne de télédétection *See* Canadian Remote Sensing Society

Société canadienne de thoracologie *See* Canadian Thoracic Society

Société canadienne de transplantation *See* Canadian Society of Transplantation

Société canadienne de zoologie *See* Canadian Society of Zoologists

Société canadienne des anesthésiologistes *See* Canadian Anesthesiologists' Society

Société canadienne des auteurs, compositeurs et éditeurs de musique *See* Society of Composers, Authors & Music Publishers of Canada

La société canadienne des auteurs, illustrateurs et artistes pour enfants *See* Canadian Society of Children's Authors, Illustrators & Performers

Société canadienne des biologistes de l'environnement *See* Canadian Society of Environmental Biologists

Société canadienne des biomatériaux *See* Canadian Biomaterials Society

Société canadienne des bovins Dexter *See* Canadian Dexter Cattle Association

Société Canadienne des Bovins Red Poll *See* Canadian Red Poll Cattle Association

Société Canadienne des bovins Welsh Black *See* Canadian Welsh Black Cattle Society

Société canadienne des chirurgiens plasticiens *See* Canadian Society of Plastic Surgeons

Société canadienne des clinico-chimistes *See* Canadian Society of Clinical Chemists

Société canadienne des courtiers en douane *See* Canadian Society of Customs Brokers

Société Canadienne des Directeurs d'Association *See* Canadian Society of Association Executives

La Société canadienne des directeurs de club *See* Canadian Society of Club Managers

Société canadienne des éleveurs de bovins Highland *See* Canadian Highland Cattle Society

La Société canadienne des éléveurs de chèvres *See* Canadian Goat Society

La société canadienne des éleveurs de moutons *See* Canadian Sheep Breeders' Association

Société canadienne des études bibliques *See* Canadian Society of Biblical Studies

Société canadienne des études classiques *See* Classical Association of Canada

Société Canadienne des études juives *See* Canadian Society for Jewish Studies

La Société canadienne des études mésopotamiennes *See* The Canadian Society for Mesopotamian Studies

Société canadienne des infirmières et infirmiers en opthalmologie *See* Canadian Society of Ophthalmic Registered Nurses

Société canadienne des médecins de soins palliatifs *See* Canadian Society of Palliative Care Physicians

Société canadienne des médecins gestionnaires *See* Canadian Society of Physician Executives

Société canadienne des microbiologistes *See* Canadian Society of Microbiologists

Société canadienne des pharmaciens d'hôpitaux *See* Canadian Society of Hospital Pharmacists

La Société canadienne des relations publiques *See* Canadian Public Relations Society Inc.

Société Canadienne des Sciences du Cerveau, du Comportement et de la Cognition *See* Canadian Society for Brain, Behaviour & Cognitive Science

Société canadienne des sciences pharmaceutiques *See* Canadian Society for Pharmaceutical Sciences

Société canadienne des technologistes en orthopedie *See* Canadian Society of Orthopaedic Technologists

Société canadienne des technologues en cardiologie inc. *See* Canadian Society of Cardiology Technologists Inc.

Societe canadienne des therapeutes de la main *See* Canadian Society of Hand Therapists

La Société canadienne des thérapeutes respiratoires *See* Canadian Society of Respiratory Therapists

Société canadienne du cancer *See* Canadian Cancer Society

Société canadienne du cheval Thoroughbred *See* Canadian Thoroughbred Horse Society

Société canadienne du sang *See* Canadian Blood Services

Société canadienne du sida *See* Canadian AIDS Society

Société Canadienne du Sommeil *See* Canadian Sleep Society

Société canadienne du syndrome d'Angelman *See* Canadian Angelman Syndrome Society

Société canadienne du syndrome de Down *See* Canadian Down Syndrome Society

Société canadienne Galloway *See* Canadian Galloway Association

Société Canadienne pour Biosciences Moléculaires *See* Canadian Society for Molecular Biosciences

Société canadienne pour l'étude de l'éducation *See* Canadian Society for the Study of Education

La Société canadienne pour l'étude de l'enseignement supérieur *See* Canadian Society for the Study of Higher Education

Société canadienne pour l'étude de l'éthique appliquée *See* Canadian Society for the Study of Practical Ethics

Société canadienne pour l'Étude de l'Homme Vieillissant *See* Canadian Society for the Study of the Aging Male

Société canadienne pour l'étude de la religion *See* Canadian Society for the Study of Religion

Société canadienne pour la conservation de la nature *See* The Nature Conservancy of Canada

Société canadienne pour la distribution de la Bible *See* The Bible League of Canada

La société canadienne pour la protection la nature en israël *See* Canadian Society for the Protection of Nature in Israel

Société canadienne pour la recherche nautique *See* Canadian Nautical Research Society

Société Canadienne pour le Droit de Mourir *See* The Right to Die Society of Canada

Société canadienne pour le traitement de la douleur *See* Canadian Pain Society

Société canadienne pour les études italiennes *See* Canadian Society for Italian Studies

Société canadienne pour les traditions musicales *See* Canadian Society for Traditional Music

Société canadienne-française de radiologie (SCFR)

CP 216, Succursdale Desjardins, Montréal QC H5B 1G8
Tél: 514-350-5148; *Téléc:* 514-350-5147
courrier@scfr.qc.ca
www.arq.qc.ca
Aperçu: *Dimension:* petite; *Envergure:* provinciale; Organisme sans but lucratif; fondée en 1928
Membre de: Fédération des médecins spécialistes du Québec
Membre(s) du bureau directeur:
Bruno Morin, Président
Vahid Khairi, Secrétaire général
Finances: *Budget de fonctionnement annuel:* Moins de $50,000
Membre(s) du personnel: 1; 13 bénévole(s)
Membre: 550; *Montant de la cotisation:* 150$; *Critères d'admissibilite:* Tous les radiologistes du Québec
Activités: Développement professionnel continu des radiologues du Québec; *Stagiaires:* Oui; *Service de conférenciers:* Oui
Prix, Bouses:
• Prix Albert-Jutras
Amount: 1000$
• Prix Bernadette-Nogrady
• Prix d'Innovation et d'excellence Dr Jean-A.-Vézina
Amount: 5000$
• Prix Personnalité SCFR
Amount: 1000$

Société catholique de la Bible (SOCABI) / Catholic Bible Society

2000, rue Sherbrooke Ouest, Montréal QC H3H 1G4
Tél: 514-925-4300
www.interbible.org/socabi/index.html
Aperçu: *Dimension:* moyenne; *Envergure:* nationale; Organisme sans but lucratif; fondée en 1940
Mission: Rendre la bible accessible au plus grand nombre de personnes possible, en facilitant la lecture et la compréhension
Membre de: Association canadienne des périodiques catholiques
Affliation(s): World Catholic Federation for the Biblical Apostolate
Membre(s) du bureau directeur:
Dumais Marcel, Président
Finances: *Budget de fonctionnement annuel:* $100,000-$250,000
Membre(s) du personnel: 6; 3 bénévole(s)
Membre: 130; *Montant de la cotisation:* 45$ tous les trois ans; *Critères d'admissibilite:* Implication dans le pastorale biblique; *Comités:* Administration; Financement
Activités: Service de librairie; conférences sur cassettes; cours par correspondance; cours d'initiation et formation; voyage en Israël; retraites; publication d'articles; *Bibliothèque* Bibliothèque publique rendez-vous
Publications:
• Parabole
Type: Revue; *Frequency:* Bimensuel; *Editor:* Yves Guillemette, ptre
Profile: Revue bilique en ligne

Société chorale de Saint-Lambert *See* St. Lambert Choral Society

Société chorale de Saint-Lambert / St. Lambert Choral Society
CP 36546, Saint-Lambert QC J4P 2S8
Tél: 450-878-0200
info.choeur.scsl@gmail.com
www.chorale-stlambert.qc.ca
www.facebook.com/239010928525
Aperçu: *Dimension:* petite; *Envergure:* locale; fondée en 1919
Mission: De promouvoir et de recueillir une appréciation pour la musique chorale
Membre(s) du bureau directeur:
David Christiani, Directeur Artistique

Société collective de retransmission du Canada *See* Canadian Retransmission Collective

Société culturelle de la Baie des Chaleurs (SCBC)
CP 707, 45A, av. du Village, Campbellton NB E3N 1N5
Tél: 506-753-6494; *Téléc:* 506-753-7498
scbc@nb.aibn.com
www.scbc-campbellton.ca
www.facebook.com/scbc.campbellton
Aperçu: *Dimension:* petite; *Envergure:* locale; Organisme sans but lucratif; fondée en 1967
Mission: Faire rayonner la culture francophone et acadienne au Restigouche
Membre de: Conseil provincial des sociétés culturelles
Membre(s) du bureau directeur:
Conrad Bourque, Responsable de la programmation
Veronique Savoie-Levesque, Présidente
Finances: *Fonds:* Patrimoine canadien
Membre(s) du personnel: 1; 20 bénévole(s)
Membre: *Montant de la cotisation:* 10$ (carte de membre)
Activités: Spectacles et ateliers culturels

Société culturelle régionale Les Chutes (SCRLC)
215, rue Guimont, Grand Falls NB E3Y 1C7
Tél: 506-473-4329; *Téléc:* 506-473-9786
culturel@nb.aibn.com
www.societeculturelleregionaleleschutes.ca
Aperçu: *Dimension:* petite; *Envergure:* locale; Organisme sans but lucratif; fondée en 1986
Mission: Établir un réseau de communication et d'échange d'information dans le domaine culturel afin de promouvoir l'entente, la solidarité et le partage entre les communautés de la région des Chutes; favoriser le développement et l'épanouissement des artistes et artisans acadiens et francophones de la région des Chutes en mettant à leur disposition des informations sur les mécanismes de promotion et de diffusion de leur art; aider la personne dans sa démarche de perfectionnement culturel; appuyer et promouvoir les projets culturels, artistiques et artisanaux, et participer; maintenir des liens et favoriser des échanges avec d'autres organismes culturels de la province
Membre de: Conseil provincial des sociétés culturelles
Membre(s) du bureau directeur:
Nicole Levesque, Présidente
Nelly Kako, Agente de développement
Finances: *Budget de fonctionnement annuel:* Moins de $50,000; *Fonds:* Patrimoine canadien - Secrétariat à la Culture et au Sport
Membre(s) du personnel: 1; 15 bénévole(s)
Membre: 250; *Montant de la cotisation:* 6$ individu; 12$ famille
Activités: Foire du Cadeau; spectacles; cours; galerie d'art; *Evénements de sensibilisation:* Développement culturel

Société culturelle Sud-Acadie (SCSA)
CP 9056, Shédiac NB E4R 8W5
Tél: 506-860-0413
info@sudacadie.ca
www.sudacadie.ca
Aperçu: *Dimension:* petite; *Envergure:* locale; Organisme sans but lucratif; fondée en 1979
Mission: Promouvoir l'expression culturelle des acadiens et acadiennes de la région; planifier et réaliser des activités culturelles sur le territoire
Membre de: Conseil Provincial des sociétés culturelles
Membre(s) du bureau directeur:
Nathalie LeBlanc, Présidente
lanleb@rogers.com
Finances: *Budget de fonctionnement annuel:* $50,000-$100,000
15 bénévole(s)
Membre: 1-99
Activités: Organisation et support aux activités culturelles

Société d'adoption enfants du monde inc. *See* Children of the World Adoption Society Inc.

Société d'agriculture de Chicoutimi *Voir* Expo agricole de Chicoutimi

La Société d'aide à l'enfance des districts de Sudbury et de Manitoulin *See* Children's Aid Society of the Districts of Sudbury & Manitoulin

La Société d'aide à l'enfance Nipissing & Parry Sound *See* Children's Aid Society of the District of Nipissing & Parry Sound

Société d'animation du Jardin et de l'Institut botanique *Voir* Les Amis du Jardin botanique de Montréal

Société d'archéologie et de numismatique de Montréal / The Antiquarian & Numismatic Society of Montréal (ANSM)
280, rue Notre Dame Est, Montréal QC H2Y 1C5
Tél: 514-861-3708; *Téléc:* 514-861-8317
info@chateauramezay.qc.ca
www.chateauramezay.qc.ca
www.facebook.com/Chateau.Ramezay
twitter.com/chateauramezay
Également appelé: Musée du Château Ramezay
Aperçu: *Dimension:* petite; *Envergure:* locale; Organisme sans but lucratif; fondée en 1862
Mission: Conserver, mettre en valeur, et rendre accessible une collection axée principalement sur l'histoire de Montréal et du Québec et de mettre en oeuvre des activités et d'accueillir des manifestations liées de près à la vie culturelle de Montréal; préserver à des fins muséologiques et de conserver un édifice classé monument historique
Membre de: Association des musées canadiens; société des musées québécois
Membre(s) du bureau directeur:
André Delisle, Directeur général, Château Ramezay
Finances: *Fonds:* Ministère de la Culture et des Communications; Conseil des arts de Montréal; Ville de Montréal
Membre: *Critères d'admissibilite:* Majorité de retraités
Activités: Expositions; concerts; programmes éducatifs; activités familiales; *Stagiaires:* Oui; *Bibliothèque:* Recherches de niveau supérieur; rendez-vous
Prix, Bouses:
• Prix Mérite National (Prix)
• Prix Orange (Prix)
• Prix Coup d'État (Prix)
• Prix Ulysse (Prix)

Société d'Eczéma du Canada *See* Eczema Society of Canada

Société d'entomologie du Québec (SEQ)
Insectarium de Montréal, 4581, rue Sherbrooke est, Montréal QC H1X 2B2
registraire@seq.qc.ca
www.seq.qc.ca
www.facebook.com/groups/123516607707461
Aperçu: *Dimension:* petite; *Envergure:* provinciale; Organisme sans but lucratif; fondée en 1873
Mission: Promouvoir et soutenir l'intérêt et le développement de l'entomologie en matière de recherche, d'éducation et de conservation
Affliation(s): Société d'entomologie du Canada
Membre(s) du bureau directeur:
Jade Savage, Président
presidence@seq.qc.ca
Finances: *Budget de fonctionnement annuel:* Moins de $50,000
15 bénévole(s)
Membre: 230; *Montant de la cotisation:* 40$; *Critères d'admissibilite:* Entomologiste

Société d'études socialistes *See* Society for Socialist Studies

Société d'histoire d'Amos
222, 1er av est, Amos QC J9T 1H3
Tél: 819-732-6070; *Téléc:* 819-732-3242
societe.histoire@cableamos.com
www.societehistoireamos.com
Aperçu: *Dimension:* petite; *Envergure:* locale; fondée en 1952
Mission: Étudier et faire connaître l'histoire des familles, paroisses, institutions et industries de la MRC d'Abitibi; rechercher, conserver et rendre accessibles les documents qui témoignent de cette histoire
Membre de: Conseil de la culture d'Abitibi-Témiscamingue; Fédération des sociétés d'histoire du Québec
Membre(s) du bureau directeur:
Carmen Rousseau, Présidente
Finances: *Budget de fonctionnement annuel:* Moins de $50,000
2 bénévole(s)
Membre: 102; *Montant de la cotisation:* $15 individuel; $20 famille, organisme, entreprise
Activités: Expositions de photos; ateliers; conférences; circuit d'interprétation historique

Société d'histoire d'Asbestos
347, boul St-Luc, Asbestos QC J1T 2W4
Tel: 819-879-2198
sochisasbestos@gmail.com
histoireasbestos.wix.com
Overview: A small local organization founded in 1995

Société d'histoire Danville-Shipton
CP 518, Danville QC J0A 1A0
Tél: 819-839-2094
Aperçu: *Dimension:* petite; *Envergure:* locale; fondée en 1994
Mission: Colliger des documents, publications et photographies reliés à l'histoire de la région de Danville-Shipton; créer des archives
Membre(s) du bureau directeur:
J. Gilles Geoffroy, Président

Société d'histoire de Beloeil - Mont-Saint-Hilaire (SHBMSH)
CP 85010, Mont-Saint-Hilaire QC J3H 5W1
Tél: 450-446-5826
info@shbmsh.org
www.shbmsh.org
www.facebook.com/161940913845022
Aperçu: *Dimension:* petite; *Envergure:* locale; Organisme sans but lucratif; fondée en 1971
Mission: Promouvoir les recherches sur l'histoire de Beloeil, Mont-Saint-Hilaire et de la région avoisinante dans le but d'instruire la population et diffuser le résultat de ses recherches
Affliation(s): Fédération des sociétés d'histoire du Québec
Membre(s) du bureau directeur:
Alain Côté, Président
Membre: 249; *Montant de la cotisation:* 10$ conjoint; 20$ étudiant; 40$ général; 60$ corporatif; *Critères d'admissibilite:* Personnes intéressées à l'histoire
Activités: Conférences; présence dans le centre commercial local; *Service de conférenciers:* Oui; *Bibliothèque* Bibliothèque publique

Société d'histoire de Coaticook
34, rue Main Est, Coaticook QC J1A 1N2
Tel: 819-849-1023
info@societehistoirecoaticook.ca
www.societehistoirecoaticook.ca
Overview: A small local organization founded in 1995
Mission: Effectuer du collectage d'archives et de la recherche historique sur différents thèmes; faire de la conservation et de la restauration de documents historiques; établir un centre de documentation pluridisciplinaire et un fond d'archives et le rendre accessible à la population pour faciliter la recherche personnelle et collective; diffuser les recherches faites pour la société d'histoire
Activities: Recherches; conférences; déjeuners; expositions

Société d'histoire de Compton *See* Compton Historical Society

Société d'histoire de Georgeville *See* Georgeville Historical Society

Société d'histoire de Greenfrield Park
129, rue Greenfield, Greenfield Park QC J4V 2J6
Tél: 450-671-5141
Aperçu: *Dimension:* petite; *Envergure:* locale
Mission: De promouvoir l'histoire de Greenfield Park

Société d'histoire de l'Outaouais inc. (SHO)
CP 1007, Succ. B, 855, boul de la Gappe, Gatineau QC J8X 3X5
Tél: 613-562-5825; *Téléc:* 613-562-5198
Aperçu: *Dimension:* petite; *Envergure:* locale; fondée en 1968
Mission: Promotion de l'histoire et du patrimoine régional
Membre de: Fédération des sociétés d'histoire du Québec
Membre(s) du bureau directeur:
Michel Prévost, President
prevost@uottawa.ca
Finances: *Budget de fonctionnement annuel:* Moins de $50,000
10 bénévole(s)
Membre: 150; *Montant de la cotisation:* 20$
Activités: Visites commentées de divers secteurs historiques; remise de prix annuels du patrimoine; conférences

Société d'histoire de la Côte-des-Neiges (SHCDN)
Centre communautaire de loisir de la Côte-des-Neiges, 5347, ch de la Côte-des-Neiges, Montréal QC H3T 1Y4
Tél: 514-342-6754
Aperçu: *Dimension:* petite; *Envergure:* locale; fondée en 1982
Mission: Promotion de l'histoire et du patrimoine
Membre de: Fédération des sociétés d'histoire du Québec
Activités: Visites; expositions; publications; documentation

Société d'histoire de la Haute Gaspésie
675, boul Ste-Anne ouest, Sainte-Anne-des-Monts QC G4V 1T9
Tél: 418-763-7871
genealogie@globetrotter.net
Aperçu: *Dimension:* petite; *Envergure:* locale; Organisme sans but lucratif; fondée en 1970
Mission: Mettre en valeur tout ce qui a trait à l'histoire, la généalogie, l'archéologie et au patrimoine local et régional dans Haute-Gaspésie
Membre de: Fédération québécoise des sociétés de généalogie; Fédération des sociétés d'histoire du Québec
Membre(s) du bureau directeur:
Ghislain Lebeau, Contact
Activités: Imprimerie; reliure; musée; généalogie; *Bibliothèque:* Bibliothèque SHAM; Bibliothèque publique

Société d'histoire de la Haute-Yamaska (SHHY)
135, rue Principale, Granby QC J2G 2V1
Tél: 450-372-4500
info@shhy.info
www.shhy.info
Nom précédent: Société historique de Shefford
Aperçu: *Dimension:* petite; *Envergure:* locale; Organisme sans but lucratif; fondée en 1967
Mission: Promotion de l'histoire régionale et nationale; protection du patrimoine; conservation des archives régionales; service de généalogie
Membre de: Association des archivistes de Québec; Regroupement des services d'archives agrées; Réseau des archives du Québec
Membre(s) du bureau directeur:
René Beaudin, Président
Finances: *Budget de fonctionnement annuel:* $100,000-$250,000
Membre(s) du personnel: 2; 3 bénévole(s)
Membre: 100-499; *Montant de la cotisation:* 20$
Activités: *Bibliothèque:* Archives

Société d'histoire de la MRC de l'Assomption (SHRMCLASS)
CP 3147, 270, boul l'Ange-Gardien, L'Assomption QC J5W 4M9
Tél: 450-589-0233; *Téléc:* 450-589-2910
shmrclca@gmail.com
www.histoirequebec.qc.ca/membre_details.asp?idM=250
Aperçu: *Dimension:* petite; *Envergure:* locale; fondée en 1986
Mission: Sensibiliser la population à l'histoire; regrouper des personnes intéressées à l'histoire, à la généalogie et au patrimoine; inventorier, colliger et conserver tous les ouvrages, les documents, les objets, les souvenirs, etc. pouvant servir à l'histoire de la région et les rendre accessibles; favoriser l'étude, la recherche et la publication sur l'histoire.
Membre de: Fédération des sociétés d'histoire du Québec; Fédération québécoise des sociétés de généalogie
Membre(s) du bureau directeur:
Yolanda Gingras, Secrétaire
Natalie Myall, Vice-présidente
Yollande Masse, Trésorière
Josée Dufour, Secrétaire
Finances: *Budget de fonctionnement annuel:* Moins de $50,000
Membre: 160; *Montant de la cotisation:* 30$; 15$ 2e personne
Activités: Conférences mensuelles; expositions; *Bibliothèque:* Centre de documentation

Société d'histoire de La Prairie-de-la-Magdeleine (SHLM)
249, rue Sainte-Marie, La Prairie QC J5R 1G1
Tél: 450-659-1393
info@shlm.info
www.shlm.info
Aperçu: *Dimension:* petite; *Envergure:* locale; Organisme sans but lucratif; fondée en 1972
Mission: A comme objectif principal la préservation, la mise en valeur et la diffusion du patrimoine local et régional
Membre de: Association des archivistes du Québec
Affliation(s): Fédération des sociétés d'histoire du Québec; Réseau des Archives du Québec; Conseil culturel Montérégien
Membre(s) du bureau directeur:
Johanne Doyle, Coordonnatrice
Membre(s) du personnel: 1
Membre: *Montant de la cotisation:* 30$ individuel; 50$ familial; *Critères d'admissibilite:* Intérêt pour l'histoire et la généalogie
Activités: Conférences; expositions; généalogie; visites guidées; archéologie; mise en marché d'un logiciel d'archives: ARCHI-LOG; *Service de conférenciers:* Oui; *Bibliothèque:* Archives; Bibliothèque publique

Société d'histoire de la Rivière du Nord inc.
Maison de la culture Claude-Henri-Grignon, #206, 101, place du Curé-Labelle, Saint-Jérôme QC J7Z 1X6
Tél: 450-436-1511; *Téléc:* 450-436-1211
courriel@shrn.org
www.shrn.org
Aperçu: *Dimension:* petite; *Envergure:* locale; Organisme sans but lucratif; fondée en 1980
Mission: Mettre en valeur le patrimoine de la MRC Rivière-du-Nord
Membre de: Fédération des sociétés d'histoires du Québec
Membre(s) du bureau directeur:
Suzanne Marcotte, Présidente
Finances: *Budget de fonctionnement annuel:* Moins de $50,000
20 bénévole(s)
Membre: 35; *Montant de la cotisation:* 15$ individuel; 30$ bibliothèques/institutions; 100$ membre à vie
Activités: *Bibliothèque* rendez-vous

Société d'histoire de la Rivière Saint-Jean incorporée
715, rue Priestman, Fredericton NB E3B 5W7
www.franco-fredericton.com/shrsj/index.htm
Aperçu: *Dimension:* petite; *Envergure:* locale; fondée en 1981
Mission: Regrouper les personnes qui s'intéressent à l'histoire, en particulier à l'histoire acadienne le long de la rivière Saint-Jean; découvrir, collectionner et publier tout ce qui peut contribuer à mieux faire connaître et à valoriser cette histoire
Membre(s) du bureau directeur:
Bernard-Marie Thériault, Président
teriobm@gmail.com
Membre: *Montant de la cotisation:* 15$ individuel; 35$ collectif/bienfaiteur; 150$ vie
Activités: Rencontres; recherches; conférences publiques; consultations en histoire et en généalogie

La Société d'histoire de la Rivière-du-Nord
#206, 101, place du Curé-Labelle, Saint-Jérâme QC J7S 1X6
Tel: 450-436-1512
courriel@shrn.org
www.shrn.org
Overview: A small local organization
Mission: Soir une référence et un interlocuteur incontournable en matière d'histoire, ayant pignon sur rue dans un bâtiment patrimonial chaleureux, animé par une équipe conviviale de bénévoles, de permanents et de multiples partenaires.

Société d'histoire de la Seigneurie de Chambly (SHSC)
CP 142, 2445, av Bourgogne, Chambly QC J3L 4B1
Tél: 450-658-2666
shsc@societehistoirechambly.org
www.societehistoirechambly.org
Aperçu: *Dimension:* petite; *Envergure:* locale; Organisme sans but lucratif; fondée en 1979
Mission: Réunir des personnes intéressées par l'histoire de la seigneurie et la généalogie; faire des recherches pour mieux connaître cette histoire afin de diffuser soit par des conférences, la publication de cahiers et du bulletin Le Voltigeur
Affliation(s): Fédération des sociétés d'histoire du Québec; Société d'histoire de la Vallée du Richelieu
Membre(s) du bureau directeur:
Paul-Henri Hudon, Président
Finances: *Budget de fonctionnement annuel:* Moins de $50,000; *Fonds:* Ministère de la Culture et des Communications, députée de Chambly
Membre(s) du personnel: 1; 20 bénévole(s)
Membre: 205; *Montant de la cotisation:* 6$ étudiants; 25$ aînés; 30$ adultes; 40$ couples aînés; 45$ couples; 100$ entreprises; *Comités:* Écriture; Recherche sur l'histoire de Chambly
Activités: Conférences; réunion de généalogie publication d'un cahier annuellement; prêt de livres, magasin d'archives; *Bibliothèque* rendez-vous
Prix, Bouses:
• Concours d'histoire de la fondation Percy-W.-Foy (Prix)
Décernés pour des travaux de recherche en histoire locale

Société d'histoire de la Seigneurie de Monnoir (SHSM)
1800, rue du Pont, Marieville QC J3M 1J8
Tél: 450-460-6767
www.societehistoireseigneuriemonnoir.com
Aperçu: *Dimension:* petite; *Envergure:* locale; fondée en 1982
Membre: *Montant de la cotisation:* 5$ étudiant; 20$ adulte; 30$ couple

Société d'histoire de Lachine
Maison du Brasseur, 2901, boul Saint-Joseph, Lachine QC H8S 4B7
Tél: 514-634-9508
shl@genealogie.org
www.genealogie.org/club/shl
Aperçu: *Dimension:* petite; *Envergure:* locale; Organisme sans but lucratif; fondée en 1993
Mission: Faire connaître le riche patrimoine de la ville de Lachine; répondre à des demandes d'information concernant l'histoire locale, le patrimoine et la généalogie; maintenir d'étroites liaisons avec le Musée de la ville de Lachine; collaborer avec d'autres organismes culturels
Membre de: Fédération des sociétés d'histoire du Québec
Membre(s) du bureau directeur:
André Robichaud, Responsable
Activités: Conférences mensuelles; promenades historiques; expositions

Société d'histoire de Longueuil (SHL)
255, rue Saint-Charles est, Longueuil QC J4H 1B3
Tél: 450-674-0349
shl@societedhistoirelongueuil.qc.ca
www.societedhistoirelongueuil.qc.ca
www.youtube.com/user/societehistoirelong
Aperçu: *Dimension:* petite; *Envergure:* locale; Organisme sans but lucratif; fondée en 1971
Mission: Inventaire de tous les sujets à caractère historique (généalogique, archéologique, folklorique) se rapportant au territoire qui faisait partie de la baronnie de Longueuil; constitution d'archives, écrites, sonores, photographiques; protection du patrimoine bâti;l'association fête son 35e anniversaire le 24 nov. 2006
Membre(s) du bureau directeur:
Bruno Racine, Président
Activités: Conférences, expositions, visites et marches guidées; publications de plusieurs volumes sur l'histoire de Longueuil; publication de 33 cahiers d'histoire totalisant plus de 1 000 pages inédites; *Bibliothèque:* Maison André-Lamarre; rendez-vous

Société d'histoire de Louiseville inc.
#24, 121, rang de la Petite-Rivière, Louiseville QC J5V 2H3
Tél: 819-228-9656; *Téléc:* 819-228-0627
histoirelouiseville@hotmail.com
Nom précédent: Société d'histoire et de généalogie de Louiseville inc
Aperçu: *Dimension:* petite; *Envergure:* locale; fondée en 1981
Membre de: Fédération des sociétés d'histoire du Québec
Membre(s) du bureau directeur:
Mathieu Deschênes, Président
Membre: *Critères d'admissibilite:* Amateur et chercheur en histoire
Activités: Histoire régionale et généalogie; *Bibliothèque* Bibliothèque publique

Société d'histoire de Magog (SHM) / Magog Historical Society
95, rue Merry Nord, #002&024, Magog QC J1X 2E7
Tél: 819-868-6779; *Téléc:* 819-868-4016
info@histoiremagog.com
www.histoiremagog.com
www.facebook.com/SocieteDhistoireDeMagog
Également appelé: Histoire Magog
Aperçu: *Dimension:* petite; *Envergure:* locale; fondée en 1988
Mission: La mission se définit par la volonté de cueillir, traiter et diffuser l'informatique sur l'ensemble des documents et des objects de valeur historique et patrimoniale relatifs à la vie de nos populations. S'accomplit par la cueillette, traitement et diffusion de fonds d'archives et de collections diverses; par la mise en oeuvre de moyens visant la défense et la promotion du patrimoine régional; par la production de documentation et d'instruments de recherche; par la réalisation d'activités de promotion de notre culture historique; par un service offert à tous ceux et celles que l'histoire et la recherche intéressent
Membre de: Fédération des sociétés d'histoire du Québec; Conseil de la Culture de l'Estrie; Réseau des archives du

Québec; Conseil Canadien des Archives; Table des Archives de l'Estrie
Membre(s) du bureau directeur:
Paul-René Gilbert, Présidente
Pierre Rastoul, Coordonnateur
Membre(s) du personnel: 1; 20 bénévole(s)
Membre: 100; *Montant de la cotisation:* 20$ individuel; 25$ familial; 10$ étudiant; 100$ à vie; 100$ corporatif; *Comités:* Financement; Recrutement; Informatique; Activités; Gestion des archives et affaires légales; Rédaction et relations avec les médias
Activités: Expositions; ventes photographiques; panneaux d'interprétation; publication d'articles, chroniques historiques, brochures, outils promotionnels; *Evénements de sensibilisation:* Journées Nationales de la Culture

Société d'histoire de Missisquoi ***See*** Missisquoi Historical Society

Société d'histoire de Montarville (SHM)
1585, rue Montarville, Saint-Bruno-de-Montarville QC J3V 3T8
Tél: 450-653-3194
info@shmontarville.org
shmontarville.org
Aperçu: *Dimension:* petite; *Envergure:* locale; fondée en 1981
Mission: De préserver et de recherches sur l'histoire de Montarville
Membre(s) du bureau directeur:
Bernard Guilbert, Président, Conseil d'administration
Membre: *Montant de la cotisation:* 20$ individuelle; 30$ famille
Activités: Exposition photo; assemblée générale annuelle; *Evénements de sensibilisation:* Exposition annuelle sur le 24 juin

Société d'histoire de Rouyn-Noranda
CP 681, Rouyn-Noranda QC J9X 5C6
Tél: 819-762-2059
shrn08@hotmail.com
Aperçu: *Dimension:* petite; *Envergure:* locale; fondée en 1951

Société d'histoire de Sainte-Foy
CP 8586, Sainte-Foy QC G1V 4N5
Tél: 418-641-6301; *Téléc:* 418-641-6553
Aperçu: *Dimension:* petite; *Envergure:* locale; Organisme sans but lucratif; fondée en 1977
Mission: Faire connaître toutes les dimensions de l'histoire de l'ancienne ville de Sainte-Foy; sauvegarder les plus beaux éléments de son patrimoine
Membre de: Fédération des sociétés d'histoire du Québec
Membre(s) du bureau directeur:
Jean-Yves Landry, Contact
Finances: *Budget de fonctionnement annuel:* Moins de $50,000
10 bénévole(s)
Membre: 70; *Montant de la cotisation:* 20$; *Critères d'admissibilite:* Intérêt pour l'histoire locale; *Comités:* Archives; Archéologie; Conférences
Activités: Conférences mensuelles; recherches; *Service de conférenciers:* Oui; *Bibliothèque:* Centre d'Archives; rendez-vous

Société d'histoire de Saint-Hubert
CP 24, Saint-Hubert QC J3Y 4T1
Tél: 450-676-5385
Aperçu: *Dimension:* petite; *Envergure:* locale; fondée en 1984

Société d'histoire de Saint-Tite
410, rue du Couvent, Saint-Tite QC G0X 3H0
Tél: 418-365-7273
Aperçu: *Dimension:* petite; *Envergure:* locale
Membre(s) du bureau directeur:
Gilles Barbeau, Président

Société d'histoire de Sherbrooke (SHS) / Historical Society of Sherbrooke
275, rue Dufferin, Sherbrooke QC J1H 4M5
Tél: 819-821-5406; *Téléc:* 819-821-5417
info@histoiresherbrooke.com
www.histoiresherbrooke.com/en
Aperçu: *Dimension:* petite; *Envergure:* locale; Organisme sans but lucratif; fondée en 1927
Mission: Gérer un service d'archives privées et un centre d'interprétation; recueillir et conserver les collections d'archives, de les compléter et de les rendre accessibles aux chercheurs; initier et encourager la recherche en histoire régionale; interpréter et diffuser les résultats; favoriser les échanges avec d'autres institutions
Membre(s) du bureau directeur:
Josée Delage, Directrice
Hélène Liard, Archiviste
Finances: *Budget de fonctionnement annuel:* $250,000-$500,000; *Fonds:* Ville de Sherbrooke; gouvernement fédéral et québecois
Membre(s) du personnel: 4; 15 bénévole(s)
Membre: 350; *Montant de la cotisation:* 30$
Activités: Expositions; visites scolaires; publications; circuits à pied et en autobus; archives; *Bibliothèque:* Société d'histoire de Sherbrooke; Bibliothèque publique

Société d'histoire de Sillery (SHS)
CP 47051, Succ. Sheppard, Québec QC G1S 4X1
Tél: 418-641-6664
shs@videotron.ca
www.histoiresillery.org
www.facebook.com/pages/Société-dhistoire-de-Sillery/501293813255528
Aperçu: *Dimension:* petite; *Envergure:* locale; Organisme sans but lucratif; fondée en 1985
Mission: Interesser ses membres et le public de la région à l'histoire de Sillery et à l'histoire régionale
Membre de: Fédération des sociétés d'histoire du Québec; Quebec Anglophone heritage Network (QAHN); Table de concertation des Sociétés d"histoire de la Ville de Québec
Membre(s) du bureau directeur:
Louis Vallée, Président, 418-264-9068
jlvallee@cec.montmagny.qc.ca
Finances: *Budget de fonctionnement annuel:* Moins de $50,000
Membre(s) du personnel: 2; 22 bénévole(s)
Membre: 185; *Montant de la cotisation:* 25$ (résident de la Ville de Québec); 35$ (non résident), 10$ (étudiant); *Comités:* Publication de La Charcotte (2 fois par année); Protection du patrimoine; Recherche et bibliothèque; Activités spéciales
Activités: Conférences; excursions; expositions; soupers-conférence; *Stagiaires:* Oui; *Service de conférenciers:* Oui

La Société d'histoire de Toronto (LSHT)
CP 93, 552, rue Church, Toronto ON M4Y 2E3
Tél: 416-924-7631
info@sht.ca
www.sht.ca
www.flickr.com/photos/societedhistoire
Aperçu: *Dimension:* petite; *Envergure:* locale; Organisme sans but lucratif; fondée en 1984
Mission: Étudier et faire connaître l'histoire de l'Ontario et des franco-ontariens particulièrement celle de la région de Toronto; intéresser les chercheurs et le grand public à l'histoire régionale; encourager la recherche par la publication de travaux pertinents; veiller à la conservation de toutes les catégories de documents historiques écrits et non écrits
Membre de: Ontario Historical Society; Regroupement des Organismes du Patrimoine Franco-Ontarien
Affliation(s): The Toronto Historical Board
Membre(s) du bureau directeur:
Rolande Smith, Présidente
Finances: *Budget de fonctionnement annuel:* Moins de $50,000
25 bénévole(s)
Membre: 100; *Montant de la cotisation:* 25$
Activités: Conférences; visites guidés; publications; recherche; réunions mensuelles 3e mercredi du mois; *Stagiaires:* Oui; *Service de conférenciers:* Oui
Prix, Bouses:
• Prix Jean-Baptiste Rousseaux (Prix)

Société d'histoire de Val-d'Or ***Voir*** Société d'histoire et de généalogie de Val-d'Or

Société d'histoire de Warwick
154B, rue St-Louis, Warwick QC J0A 1M0
Tél: 819-358-6261
histoire@cablovision.com
fr-fr.facebook.com/SocieteHistoireWarwick
Aperçu: *Dimension:* petite; *Envergure:* locale; Organisme sans but lucratif; fondée en 1973
Mission: Protéger les biens à caractères historiques de notre municipalité, les conserver et sensibiliser la population à la richesse du patrimoine
Membre de: Fédération des Sociétés d'Histoire du Québec
Membre(s) du bureau directeur:
André Moreau, Président
Finances: *Budget de fonctionnement annuel:* Moins de $50,000
10 bénévole(s)
Membre: 147; *Montant de la cotisation:* 10$

Société d'histoire de Weedon
209, rue des Érables, Weedon QC J0B 3J0
Tél: 819-877-2917
admin@histoiredeweedon.info
histoiredeweedon.info
Aperçu: *Dimension:* petite; *Envergure:* locale; Organisme sans but lucratif; fondée en 1981
Mission: Retrouver l'histoire la plus complète de notre village; créer une banque d'information
Membre de: La Fédération des sociétés d' histoire du Québec
Membre(s) du bureau directeur:
Yves St-Pierre, Secrétaire
Lucie Vachon, Présidente
Membre: *Critères d'admissibilite:* Bénévole; intéressé à faire de la recherche en histoire
Activités: Expositions de photos anciennes agrandies; remise annuelle de certificats à des familles centenaires; en 2006, activités spéciales à l'occasion du 25e anniversaire de la société

Société d'histoire des Iles-Percées (SHIP)
CP 234, Boucherville QC J4B 5J6
Tél: 450-449-0790
pages.videotron.com/ship/
Aperçu: *Dimension:* petite; *Envergure:* locale; fondée en 1972
Membre(s) du bureau directeur:
Suzanne G. Carignan, Présidente, 450-449-0790
sgcarignan@yahoo.ca
10 bénévole(s)

Société d'histoire des Mille-Iles ***Voir*** Société d'histoire et de généalogie des Mille-Iles

Société d'histoire des Six Cantons
1093-c, rue St-André, Acton Vale QC J0H 1A0
Tél: 450-546-2093
Aperçu: *Dimension:* petite; *Envergure:* locale; fondée en 1977
Mission: Regrouper les amateurs d'histoire régionale; étudier et diffuser les connaissances
Membre de: Fédération des sociétés d'histoire du Québec
Membre(s) du bureau directeur:
Marie-Paule La Brèque, Présidente
Finances: *Budget de fonctionnement annuel:* Moins de $50,000
3 bénévole(s)
Membre: 60; *Montant de la cotisation:* 15$ individuel; 20$ familial; *Comités:* Toponomy; Genealogy
Activités: Expositions d'anciennes photographies, de vieux documents et d'artefacts; journée portes ouvertes dans les Archives; soirée d'identification d'objets patrimoniaux; *Bibliothèque* rendez-vous

Société d'histoire du Bas-Saint-Laurent (SHBSL)
c/o Université du Québec à Rimouski, 300, Allée des Ursulines, Rimouski QC G5L 3A1
Tél: 418-723-1986
lestuaire@uqar.ca
lestuaire.uqar.qc.ca
Aperçu: *Dimension:* petite; *Envergure:* locale; Organisme sans but lucratif; fondée en 1971
Mission: Promouvoir l'histoire régionale de l'est du Québec
Membre(s) du bureau directeur:
Jean-Rene Thuot, Directeur
Finances: *Budget de fonctionnement annuel:* Moins de $50,000
Membre: 1-99
Publications:
• L'Estuaire [a publication of the Société d'histoire du Bas-Saint-Laurent]
Type: Review *ISSN:* 1484-6969

Société d'histoire du Haut-Richelieu (SHHR)
CP 212, 203, rue Jacques-Cartier nord, Saint-Jean-sur-Richelieu QC J3B 6Z4
Tél: 450-358-5220
shhr@qc.aira.com
www.genealogie.org/club/shhr
Aperçu: *Dimension:* petite; *Envergure:* locale; Organisme sans but lucratif; fondée en 1979
Mission: Diffusion, conservation, protection de l'histoire et du patrimoine; gestion de la bibliothèque de généalogie et du centre d'archives privées
Affiliation(s): Fédération québécoise des sociétés de généalogie
Membre(s) du bureau directeur:
Nicole Poulin, Présidente
Finances: *Budget de fonctionnement annuel:* Moins de $50,000
Membre(s) du personnel: 2; 6 bénévole(s)
Membre: 200; *Montant de la cotisation:* 25$; *Critères d'admissibilite:* Historien-généalogiste
Activités: Publications de livres historiques; conférences; *Bibliothèque:* Bibliothèque privée; Bibliothèque publique

Société d'histoire du Lac-St-Jean/Maison des Bâtisseurs (SHL)

1671, Av du Pont Nord, Alma QC G8B 5G2
Tél: 418-668-2606; *Téléc:* 418-668-5851
Ligne sans frais: 866-668-2606
info@shlsj.org
www.shlsj.org
www.facebook.com/OdysseeDesBatisseurs
Aperçu: *Dimension:* petite; *Envergure:* locale; Organisme sans but lucratif; fondée en 1942
Mission: Acquérir, conserver, traiter et rendre accessible au public divers documents historiques et objets témoins de cette histoire, sur le territoire; diffuser et sensibiliser à la conservation et la mise en valeur par des publications de toutes natures et par la présentation d'expositions et d'interprétations à caractère historique, accessibles à l'ensemble de la population locale, régionale et touristique et ayant une qualité didactique et esthétique; éduquer par l'histoire et susciter l'intérêt pour la recherche, par la tenue d'activités pédagogiques et d'ateliers divers, et par le service de généalogie; protéger et aider à la conservation du patrimoine bâti par le SARP; favoriser le développement de services complémentaires qui augmentent l'autofinancement tout en respectant les orientations de la mission; provoquer et soutenir les initiatives de milieu en matière de sauvegarde, de restauration et de mise en valeur du patrimoine et de la culture régionale
Membre de: Fédération des sociétés d'historie du Québec; Société des musées québécois
Affliation(s): Société Musée Québec
Membre(s) du bureau directeur:
Alexandre Garon, Directeur général
Finances: *Budget de fonctionnement annuel:* $500,000-$1.5 Million; *Fonds:* Municipalité d'Alma
Membre(s) du personnel: 1; 10 bénévole(s)
Membre: 550; *Montant de la cotisation:* 25$ individuel; 15$ ainé; 15$ étudiant; 120$ collaborateur; 50$ associé; 600$ à vie; 40$ famille; *Comités:* Acquisitions; Finance; Généalogie; Projet
Activités: Musée; programme pédagogique; service d'archives; service d'aide à la rénovation patrimoniale; *Bibliothèque:* Bibliothèque du Service d'Archives; Bibliothèque publique

Société d'histoire du Témiscamingue

CP 1022, 8, rue Saint-Gabriel nord, Ville-Marie QC J0Z 3W0
Tél: 819-629-3533; *Téléc:* 819-629-2200
sht@cablevision.qc.ca
www.maisondufreremoffet.com
Aperçu: *Dimension:* petite; *Envergure:* locale; fondée en 1949
Membre(s) du bureau directeur:
Cécile Herbet
Finances: *Budget de fonctionnement annuel:* Moins de $50,000
Membre(s) du personnel: 1; 9 bénévole(s)
Membre: 180; *Montant de la cotisation:* 10$
Activités: *Listes de destinataires:* Oui

Société d'histoire et d'archéologie du Témiscouata

81, rue Caldwell, Cabano QC G0L 1E0
Tél: 418-854-2375; *Téléc:* 418-854-0416
Ligne sans frais: 866-242-2437
www.fortingall.ca/shatfr.php?id=109
Nom précédent: Société historique de Cabano, Inc.
Aperçu: *Dimension:* petite; *Envergure:* locale; fondée en 1967
Mission: Recherche et diffusion de l'histoire régionale; animation et gestion du site historique Fort Ingall
Membre de: La Société des musées québécois; Fédération des sociétés d'histoire du Québec
Membre(s) du bureau directeur:
Martin Simard, Président
Finances: *Budget de fonctionnement annuel:* $100,000-$250,000
7 bénévole(s)
Membre: 64; *Montant de la cotisation:* 10$

Société d'histoire et de généalogie de l'Ile Jésus (SHGIJ)

4300, boul Samson, Laval QC H7W 2G9
Tél: 450-681-9096; *Téléc:* 450-686-8270
info@shgij.org
www.shgij.org
Aperçu: *Dimension:* petite; *Envergure:* locale; Organisme sans but lucratif; fondée en 1963
Mission: Veiller à la préservation et à la diffusion du patrimoine lavallois, retracer et faire connaître notre histoire et stimuler le dynamisme des citoyens envers la généalogie
Membre de: Fédération des sociétés d'histoire du Québec; Réseau des Archives du Québec; Fédération des sociétés de généalogie du Québec
Membre(s) du bureau directeur:
Dominique Bodeven, Directrice générale
Membre(s) du personnel: 3
Membre: *Montant de la cotisation:* 10$ étudiant; 30$ particulier; 40$ famille; 60$ corporatif; 400$ membre à vie
Activités: Conférences et ateliers de généalogie; *Bibliothèque:* Centre de documentation;

Société d'histoire et de généalogie de la Matapédia

24, promenade de l'Hôtel-de-Ville, Amqui QC G5J 3E1
Tél: 418-629-4242
shgmma@cgocable.ca
www.genealogie.org/club/shgm
Aperçu: *Dimension:* petite; *Envergure:* locale; Organisme sans but lucratif; fondée en 1989 surveillé par Fédération québécoise des sociétés de généalogie
Mission: Favoriser la recherche et la connaissance de l'histoire de notre région; se familiariser avec la généalogie; fournir les outils pour retracer nos ancêtres
Membre(s) du bureau directeur:
René Pelletier, Président
Membre: 148; *Montant de la cotisation:* 30$ individuel; 40$ couple; 400$ membre à vie
Activités: *Service de conférenciers:* Oui

Société d'histoire et de généalogie de Louiseville inc *Voir* Société d'histoire de Louiseville inc.

Société d'histoire et de généalogie de Matane (SHGM) / Matane Historical & Genealogical Society

382, rue du Rempart, Matane QC G4W 2T7
Tél: 418-562-9766; *Téléc:* 418-562-9766
shgm@genealogie.org
www.shgmatane.org
fr-fr.facebook.com/shg.matane
Aperçu: *Dimension:* petite; *Envergure:* locale; Organisme sans but lucratif; fondée en 1950
Mission: Contribuer à la sauvegarde et à la mise en valeur du patrimoine régional sous tous ses aspects
Membre(s) du bureau directeur:
Louis Audet, Président
Finances: *Budget de fonctionnement annuel:* Moins de $50,000
20 bénévole(s)
Membre: 400; *Montant de la cotisation:* 25$ membre régulier; 35$ membre conjoint; 50$ membre corporations; 300$ membre à vie
Activités: *Bibliothèque* Bibliothèque publique

Société d'histoire et de généalogie de Rivière-du-Loup (SHGRDL)

67, rue du Rocher, Rivière-du-Loup QC G5R 1J8
Tél: 418-867-6604
info@shgrdl.org
www.shgrdl.org
Aperçu: *Dimension:* petite; *Envergure:* locale; Organisme sans but lucratif; fondée en 1987
Mission: Organiser, promouvoir et patronner des activités et manifestations historiques, généalogiques et culturelles; organiser et tenir des conférences, réunions, assemblées et expositions pour la promotion et la vulgarisation de l'histoire et de la généalogie; recueillir et classer vieux documents, contrats, photos, cartes postales, cartes mortuaires ou autres
Membre de: Fédération des sociétés d'histoire du Québec; Fédération des sociétés de généalogie du Québec
Membre(s) du bureau directeur:
Gilles Dubé, Président
gildub2@videotron.ca
Membre: *Montant de la cotisation:* 15$ membre associé; 30$ membre régulier; 50$ association; 525$ membre à vie
Activités: Soirée-conférence; déjeuner-conférence; publication de volumes historiques

Société d'histoire et de généalogie de Saint-Casimir

CP 127, 510, boul de la Montagne, Saint-Casimir QC G0A 3L0
shgsc@hotmail.com
www.genealogie.org/club/shgsc
Aperçu: *Dimension:* petite; *Envergure:* locale; Organisme sans but lucratif; fondée en 1996
Mission: Groupe les personnes intéressées à l'histoire et à la généalogie; publier, diffuser ou susciter la publication de tout article relatif à l'histoire familiale, municipale, régionale et à la généalogie
Membre de: Fédération québécoise des sociétés de généalogie
Membre(s) du bureau directeur:
Léo-Denis Carpentier, Président
Finances: *Budget de fonctionnement annuel:* Moins de $50,000
Membre: 143; *Montant de la cotisation:* 10$ membre associé; 15$ membre principal; 250$ membre à vie
Activités: *Bibliothèque:* Bibliothèque Jean-Charles-Magnan

Société d'histoire et de généalogie de Salaberry (SHGS)

80, rue St-Thomas, Salaberry-de-Valleyfield QC J6T 4J1
Tél: 450-371-0632
shgs2011@hotmail.fr
www.shgs.suroit.com
www.facebook.com/311946960934
Aperçu: *Dimension:* petite; *Envergure:* locale; Organisme sans but lucratif; fondée en 1991
Mission: Réunir les personnes intéressées par l'histoire, la généalogie et le patrimoine; renseigner la population sur ces sujets; faire fonctionner et animer un centre de documentation; faciliter la recherche et publier les résultats des recherches effectuées
Membre de: Fédération des sociétés d'histoire du Québec; Fédération des sociétés de généalogie du Québec
Membre(s) du bureau directeur:
Marie Royal, Présidente
marie.royal@sympatico.ca
Activités: Visites; atelier de généalogie; cours d'initiation à la généalogie; paléographie; conférences; *Bibliothèque:* Bibliothèque Armand-Frappier; Bibliothèque publique

Société d'histoire et de généalogie de Shawinigan-sud (SHGSS)

CP 1431, Shawinigan QC G9P 4R2
Tél: 819-537-5390
info@histoireshawinigan.com
www.histoireshawinigan.com
Aperçu: *Dimension:* petite; *Envergure:* locale; Organisme sans but lucratif; fondée en 1987
Mission: Regrouper les personnes intéressées à l'histoire et au patrimoine naturel de Shawinigan-Sud, ainsi qu'à la généalogie des familles et/ou individus qui composent sa population; rechercher, acquérir, conserver ou connaître tous les documents, objects, biens ou immeubles rattachés à l'histoire locale et à la généalogie des personnes; diffuser les connaissances historiques et généalogiques; promouvoir les recherches sur l'histoire de Shawinigan-Sud et l'origine de ses familles
Affliation(s): Fédération des sociétés d'histoire du Québec; Fédération québécoise des sociétés de généalogie
Membre(s) du bureau directeur:
Monique Duvot, Présidente
Activités: Salle de recherches historiques et généalogiques; rencontres culturelle; conférence; déjeuner-causerie; souper-reconnaissance excursion à caractère historique; ateliers de généalogie; *Bibliothèque*

Société d'histoire et de généalogie de Val-d'Or (SHGVD)

600, 7e Rue, Val-d'Or QC J9P 3P3
Tél: 819-874-7469; *Téléc:* 819-825-3062
shvd@ville.valdor.qc.ca
www.telebecinternet.com/histoirevd
Nom précédent: Société d'histoire de Val-d'Or
Aperçu: *Dimension:* petite; *Envergure:* locale; Organisme sans but lucratif; fondée en 1976
Mission: Recueillir, conserver et diffuser la documentation concernant l'histoire de Val-d'Or et de l'Abitibi
Membre de: Fédération des sociétés d'histoire du Québec; Commission de développement culturel de Val-d'Or; Conseil de la Culture de l'Abitibi-Témiscamingue
Membre(s) du bureau directeur:
Louiselle Alain, Présidente
Finances: *Budget de fonctionnement annuel:* $50,000-$100,000
Membre(s) du personnel: 2; 8 bénévole(s)
Membre: 90; *Montant de la cotisation:* 15$ invividuel; 20$ famille; 50$ corporatif
Activités: Histoire et généalogie; publication de livres historiques; *Stagiaires:* Oui; *Service de conférenciers:* Oui; *Bibliothèque*

Société d'histoire et de généalogie de Verdun

Centre culturel de Verdun, Salle Canadiana, 5955, av Bannantyne, Verdun QC H4H 1H6
Tél: 514-765-7174
shgv1@hotmail.com
www.ville.verdun.qc.ca/shgv/
Aperçu: *Dimension:* petite; *Envergure:* locale; fondée en 1995
Mission: Diffuser et mettre en valeur le patrimoine naturel et culturel de la ville de Verdun
Membre(s) du bureau directeur:

Denis Harton, Président
20 bénévole(s)
Membre: 100-499

Société d'histoire et de généalogie des Mille-Iles
Musée Joseph-Filion, 6, rue Blainville est, Sainte-Thérèse QC J7E 1L6
Tél: 450-434-9090
info@shgmi.ca
www.shgmi.ca
Également appelé: Musée régional Joseph-Filion
Nom précédent: Société d'histoire des Mille-Iles
Aperçu: *Dimension:* petite; *Envergure:* locale; Organisme sans but lucratif; fondée en 1939
Mission: Mise en valeur du patrimoine photographique écrit et bâti
Membre de: Fédération des sociétés d'histoire du Québec
Affiliation(s): Société des musées québécois
Membre(s) du bureau directeur:
J.G. Gilles Charron, Président
gramar@videotron.ca
Activités: Opération du Musée régional Joseph-Filion; *Service de conférenciers:* Oui; *Bibliothèque* rendez-vous

Société d'histoire et de généalogie des Pays-d'en-Haut, inc.
#27, 33, rue de l'Église, St-Sauveur-des-Monts QC J0R 1R0
Tél: 450-227-2669
shgph12@gmail.com
www.shgph.org
Aperçu: *Dimension:* petite; *Envergure:* locale
Membre(s) du bureau directeur:
Pierre Gravel, Président
Membre: 597

Société d'histoire et de généalogie des Quatre Lieux
1291, rang Double, Rougemont QC J0L 1M0
Tél: 450-469-2409
shgql@videotron.ca
www.quatrelieux.qc.ca
Aperçu: *Dimension:* petite; *Envergure:* locale; Organisme sans but lucratif; fondée en 1980
Mission: Valoriser l'importance de l'histoire, du patrimoine et de la généalogie auprès de la population. Acquérir, recevoir et conserver toute documentation sous divers formats, concernant l'histoire et le patrimoine des quatre municipalités et la généalogie de nos familles
Affliation(s): Fédération des Sociétés d'histoire du Québec
Membre(s) du bureau directeur:
Gilles Bachand, Président
gbachand@videotron.ca
Lucette Lévesque, Secrétaire-trésorière
lucettelevesque@sympatico.ca
Membre: 203; *Montant de la cotisation:* 30$ régulier; 10$ associé
Activités: Assemblées mensuelles; *Service de conférenciers:* Oui; *Bibliothèque*

Société d'histoire et de généalogie Maria-Chapdelaine
1024, rue des Copains, Dolbeau-Mistassini QC G8L 3N5
Tél: 418-276-4989; *Téléc:* 418-276-8156
mariachapdelaine@histoireetgenealogie.com
www.histoireetgenealogie.com
www.facebook.com/213010725404771
Aperçu: *Dimension:* petite; *Envergure:* locale; Organisme sans but lucratif; fondée en 1988
Mission: Recueillir et conserver tous les types de documents ayant une valeur historique et concernant les municipalités de la MRC Maria-Champdelaine
Membre(s) du bureau directeur:
Steeve Cantin, Directeur général
scantin@histoireetgenealogie.com
Jean-Marc Mailloux, Président
maillouxjmarc@videotron.ca
Membre(s) du personnel: 2
Membre: *Montant de la cotisation:* 20$ individu; 30$ supporteur; 50$ corporatif; 500$ vie
Activités: Centre d'archive; bibliothèque d'histoire et de généalogie; gestion documentaire; Numérisation professionnelle de documents; gestion archivistique; ateliers de généalogie; recherche historique et généalogique sur Internet; entreposage de documents; *Bibliothèque* Bibliothèque publique

Société d'histoire et de musée de Lennoxville-Ascot *Voir*
Lennoxville-Ascot Historical & Museum Society

Société d'histoire et généalogie du granit (SHGG)
CP 166, 252, rue Principale, St-Sébastien QC G0Y 1M0
Tél: 418-483-5473; *Téléc:* 819-652-2584
Autres numéros: Autre téléphone: 819-652-2285
shgssf@msn.com
www.shggranit.org
Aperçu: *Dimension:* petite; *Envergure:* locale; fondée en 2000
Mission: Recherches et documentation de l'histoire de la région. installés la région St-Sébastian
Membre de: Fédération histoire Québec; Fédération généalogie Québec
Membre(s) du bureau directeur:
Gilles Blouin, Président
gblouin@tellambton.net
Finances: *Budget de fonctionnement annuel:* Moins de $50,000; *Fonds:* Publication de volumes et cotisations des membres
Membre: 85; *Montant de la cotisation:* 15$ pour 1 an
Activités: Promotion de la conservation du patrimoine; Promotion de la conservation du patrimoine; Publication de BMS locales.; *Service de conférenciers:* Oui; *Bibliothèque:* Centre Paul VI

Société d'histoire naturelle de la vallée du St-Laurent *See*
St. Lawrence Valley Natural History Society

Société d'histoire régionale de Chibougamau (SHRC)
646, 3e Rue, Chibougamau QC G8P 1P1
Tél: 418-748-3124; *Téléc:* 418-748-3324
info@shrcnq.com
www.shrcnq.com
www.facebook.com/720678961296885
Aperçu: *Dimension:* petite; *Envergure:* locale
Membre(s) du bureau directeur:
Pierre Pelletier, Président
Membre(s) du personnel: 3
Membre: 51; *Montant de la cotisation:* 20$ individu/organisme à but non lucratif; 30$ entreprise privée

Société d'histoire régionale de Lévis
R-1, 9 Mgr-Gosselin, Lévis QC G6V 6J7
Tél: 418-837-2050; *Téléc:* 418-837-2050
histoirelevis@shrl.qc.ca
www.shrl.qc.ca
www.facebook.com/SHRL76
Aperçu: *Dimension:* petite; *Envergure:* locale; Organisme sans but lucratif; fondée en 1976
Mission: Grouper toutes les personnes intéressées à l'histoire régionale de Lévis et désireuses de participer à des rencontres, des études, des recherches et autres activités en vue de mieux connaître et faire connaître l'histoire de la région de Lévis, autrefois connue et désignée comme étant "la Seigneurie de Lauzon"
Membre de: Fédération des sociétés d'histoire du Québec
Membre(s) du bureau directeur:
Vincent Couture, Président
Gilbert Samson, Directeur général
Finances: *Budget de fonctionnement annuel:* Moins de $50,000; *Fonds:* Municipal
Membre(s) du personnel: 3; 10 bénévole(s)
Membre: 200+; *Montant de la cotisation:* 25$; *Critères d'admissibilite:* Interessé à la petite histoire régionale; *Comités:* Bulletin; Informatique; Conférence
Activités: Quatre conférences durant l'année; *Bibliothèque* rendez-vous

Société d'histoire régionale Deux-Montagnes (SHRDM)
CP 91, Succ. Bureau chef, Saint-Eustache QC J7R 4K5
info@shrdm.org
www.shrdm.org
www.facebook.com/shrdm2013
twitter.com/shrdm2013
Aperçu: *Dimension:* petite; *Envergure:* locale; Organisme sans but lucratif; fondée en 1961
Mission: Couvre la région de l'ancien comté de Deux-Montagnes, soit l'actuel territoire de la MRC de Deux-Montagnes et la MRC de Mirabel. Elle travaille activement à la diffusion de l'histoire de la région, à la sauvegarde et à la mise en valeur de son patrimoine bâti
Membre de: La Fédération des sociétés d'histoire du Québec; Conseil de la culture des Laurentides
Membre(s) du bureau directeur:
Vicki Onufriu, Présidente
Eric Poisson, Vice-pésident et trésorier
Membre: *Montant de la cotisation:* 15$ individu; 25$ couple; 50$ corporatif

Activités: Conférences; publication de dépliants; panneau d'interprétation historique; expositions; brunch du patrimoine; rallye
Prix, Bouses:
- Prix Claire-Yale (Prix)
- Mérite scolaire (Prix)

Société d'histoire St-Stanislas inc.
1480, rue Principale, Saint-Stanislas-de-Champlain QC G0X 3E0
Tél: 418-328-3255
www.saint-stanislas.ca/fr/societe-d-histoire_53.html
Aperçu: *Dimension:* petite; *Envergure:* locale; Organisme sans but lucratif; fondée en 1976
Mission: Recherche et diffusion de notre histoire et mise en valeur de notre patrimoine local
Membre de: Appartenance-Mauricie
Membre(s) du bureau directeur:
Ghislaine Brouillette, Présidente
Finances: *Fonds:* Conseil municipal de St-Stanislas; Caisse populaire de Moraine
Membre: *Critères d'admissibilite:* Personnes intéressées à l'histoire locale
Activités: Rencontres; brunch-récital annuel; expositions-photos; lancements de livres; compilations statistiques locales; aide aux généalogistes de partout; circuit patrimonial; *Bibliothèque:* Bibliothèque de la société d'histoire; Bibliothèque publique rendez-vous

Société d'horticulture de Saint-Lambert
600, av Oak, Saint-Lambert QC J4P 1T3
Tel: 450-671-4535
slhorticulturalsociety@yahoo.com
slhorticulturalsociety.org
Overview: A small local organization founded in 1894
Mission: Promouvoir l'étude et l'engagement dans des pratiques horticoles
Chief Officer(s):
Kevin Cuffling, Président, Conseil d'administration
Membership: *Fees:* 15$ individu; 25$ famille

Société d'horticulture et d'écologie de Boucherville (SOCHEB)
CP 302, Boucherville QC J4B 5J6
Tél: 450-641-8362; *Téléc:* 450-641-3013
socheb_boucherville@yahoo.ca
socheb.fsheq.org
Aperçu: *Dimension:* petite; *Envergure:* locale; fondée en 1996
Mission: Encourager des pratiques horticoles et aider à protéger l'environnement
Membre(s) du bureau directeur:
Olga Bosak, Présidente, Conseil d'administration
Membre: *Montant de la cotisation:* 30$ individuelle; 50$ famille

Société d'Horticulture et d'Écologie de Brossard (SHEB)
CP 50549, Succ. Carrefour Pelletier, Brossard QC J4X 2V7
sheb.brossard@gmail.com
www.shbrossard.org
www.facebook.com/SHBrossard
Aperçu: *Dimension:* petite; *Envergure:* locale; fondée en 1981
Mission: D'offrir des conseils éducatifs sur le jardinage
Membre(s) du bureau directeur:
Diane Doutre, Présidente, Conseil d'administration
Membre: *Montant de la cotisation:* 25$ personne ou couple

Société d'Horticulture et d'Écologie de Longueuil (SHELI)
205, ch. Chambly, Longueuil QC J4H 3L3
Tél: 450-646-2621
sheli_longueuil@yahoo.fr
sheli.ca
Aperçu: *Dimension:* petite; *Envergure:* locale; fondée en 1981
Mission: De promouvoir l'activité horticole et de préserver l'environnement
Membre(s) du bureau directeur:
Jean-René Gauthier, Président, Conseil d'administration
Membre: *Montant de la cotisation:* 20$
Activités: Conférences mensuellement; *Bibliothèque* rendez-vous

Société d'Horticulture et d'Écologie de Prévost (SHEP)
CP 611, Prévost QC J0R 1T0
Tél: 450-224-9252
shep.qc.com
Aperçu: *Dimension:* petite; *Envergure:* locale

Affliation(s): Fédération des Sociétés d'horticulture et d'écologie du Québec
Membre(s) du bureau directeur:
Florence Frigon, Présidente
Activités: Conférences; voyages horticoles; ateliers

Société d'investissement jeunesse (SIJ)
#720, 615, boul René Lévesque Ouest, Montréal QC H3B 1P5
Tél: 514-879-0558; *Téléc:* 514-879-0444
info-generales@sij.qc.ca
www.sij.qc.ca
Aperçu: *Dimension:* petite; *Envergure:* provinciale; Organisme sans but lucratif; fondée en 2001
Mission: La S.I.J. garantit des prêts aux entrepreneurs agés de 18 à 35 ans, qui désirent se lancer en affaires
Membre(s) du bureau directeur:
Hélène Desmarais, Présidente

La société de biophysique du Canada *See* Biophysical Society of Canada

Société de communication Atikamekw-Montagnais (SOCAM)
#600, 50, boul Chef Maurice-Bastien, 4e étage, Wendake QC G0A 4V0
Tél: 418-843-3873; *Téléc:* 418-845-4198
Ligne sans frais: 800-663-2611
socam@socam.net
www.socam.net
www.facebook.com/socam.net
Aperçu: *Dimension:* petite; *Envergure:* locale; fondée en 1983
Mission: Diffuser de l'information radiophonique en langue autochtone sur 14 communautés atikamekw, montagnaises et innu
Membre(s) du bureau directeur:
Bernard Hervieux, Directeur général
bhervieux@socam.net
Membre(s) du personnel: 13
Membre: 14 radios communautaires

Société de conservation de la Baie de l'Isle-Verte
CP 151, 371, rte 132 Est, L'Isle-Verte QC G0L 1K0
Tél: 418-898-2757
Aperçu: *Dimension:* petite; *Envergure:* locale; Organisme sans but lucratif; fondée en 1984
Mission: Mise en valeur de la réserve national de faune, patrimoine culturel, historique et naturel de l'Isle-Vertex; gestion de trois centres d'interprétation
Finances: *Fonds:* Gouvernement fédéral
Activités: Interprétation du marais salé, de la sauvagine et du baguage de la sauvagine; sentiers de randonnées pédestres

Société de Conservation du Patrimoine de Saint-François-de-la-Rivière-du-Sud inc.
534, ch Saint-François ouest, St-François-de-la-Rivière-du-Sud QC G0R 3A0
Tél: 418-259-7228; *Téléc:* 418-259-2056
patrimoine.st-franc@oricom.ca
www.patrimoinesaintfrancois.org
Aperçu: *Dimension:* petite; *Envergure:* locale; fondée en 1979
Mission: Prendre toute initiative, engager toute action propre à conserver les écrits, les imprimés, les objets, les organismes, les structures héritées du passé lointain ou récent
Membre(s) du bureau directeur:
Jacques Boulet, Président, 418-259-7805
apiboulet@videotron.ca
Membre: *Critères d'admissibilite:* Personnes intéressées à la conservation du patrimoine
Activités: Recherches historiques; publication de brochures, dépliants, guides

Société de coopération pour le développement international (SOCODEVI)
#160, 850, av Ernest-Gagnon, Québec QC G1S 4S2
Tél: 418-683-7225; *Téléc:* 418-683-5229
info@socodevi.org
www.socodevi.org
www.facebook.com/socodevi
twitter.com/socodevi
Aperçu: *Dimension:* moyenne; *Envergure:* internationale; Organisme sans but lucratif; fondée en 1985
Mission: Avec l'engagement de ses institutions membres, et par la mise en valeur de la formule coopérative ou d'autres formes associatives; contribue au développement durable des pays où elle intervient en ayant pour objectif que les populations se prennent en charge
Membre(s) du bureau directeur:
Réjean Lantagne, Directeur général
r.lantagne@socodevi.org
Finances: *Budget de fonctionnement annuel:* Plus de $5 Million
Membre(s) du personnel: 200
Membre: 20 entreprises coopératives et mutualistes; *Critères d'admissibilite:* Coopératives et mutuelles
Activités: *Bibliothèque*

Société de criminologie du Québec (SCQ)
#201, 2000, boul Saint-Joseph est, Montréal QC H2H 1E4
Tél: 514-529-4391; *Téléc:* 514-529-6936
crimino@societecrimino.qc.ca
www.societecrimino.qc.ca
www.facebook.com/SocieteCrimino
twitter.com/societecrimino
Aperçu: *Dimension:* moyenne; *Envergure:* provinciale; fondée en 1960
Mission: Mission: de contribuer à l'évolution du système de justice pénale, de favoriser les échanges & les débats entre tous les intéressés à l'avancement de la justice pénale, & de favoriser & encourager la recherche
Affliation(s): Canadian Criminal Justice Association
Membre(s) du bureau directeur:
Caroline Savard, Directrice générale
caroline.savard@societecrimino.qc.ca
Finances: *Budget de fonctionnement annuel:* $50,000-$100,000
Membre: 425; *Montant de la cotisation:* 50$ pour 1 an; 90$ pour 2 ans; *Critères d'admissibilite:* Toute personne concernée par l'administration de la justice pénale
Activités: *Bibliothèque* Bibliothèque publique

Société de développement des entreprises culturelles (SODEC)
#800, 215, rue Saint-Jacques, Montréal QC H2Y 1M6
Tél: 514-841-2200; *Téléc:* 514-841-8606
Ligne sans frais: 800-363-0401
info@sodec.gouv.qc.ca
www.sodec.gouv.qc.ca
www.facebook.com/SODEC.gouv.qc.ca
twitter.com/la_SODEC
Aperçu: *Dimension:* grande; *Envergure:* provinciale; fondée en 1995
Mission: La SODEC est une société du gouvernement du Québec qui relève du ministre de la Culture, des Communications et de la Condition féminine. Elle soutient la production et la diffusion de la culture québécoise dans le champ des industries culturelles.
Affliation(s): Ministère de la culture et des communications
Membre(s) du bureau directeur:
Jean Pronovost, Président du conseil
François Macerola, Président et chef de la direction
Finances: *Budget de fonctionnement annuel:* Plus de $5 Million
Membre(s) du personnel: 102
Activités: Gestion des programmes de soutien aux entreprises culturelle et cinéma
Publications:
- Info + SODEC [a publication of the Société de développement des entreprises culturelles]
Type: Newsletter
- VigiSODEC [a publication of the Société de développement des entreprises culturelles]
Type: Newsletter

Société de développement des périodiques culturels québécois (SODEP)
#716, 460, rue Ste-Catherine ouest, Montréal QC H3B 1A7
Tél: 514-397-8669; *Téléc:* 514-397-6887
info@sodep.qc.ca
www.sodep.qc.ca
www.facebook.com/sodep.qc.ca?ref=ts
twitter.com/cultureenrevues
Également appelé: Périodiques culturels québécois
Nom précédent: Association des Éditeurs de périodiques culturels québécois
Aperçu: *Dimension:* moyenne; *Envergure:* provinciale; fondée en 1978
Mission: Travailler à l'essor et au rayonnement des revues culturelles; établir et entretenir des liens avec le milieu de l'enseignement, les bibliothèques, les médias et les maisons de distribution; représenter et promouvoir les intérêts professionnels, éthiques et économiques des éditeurs; favoriser les échanges internationaux
Membre(s) du bureau directeur:
Éric Perron, Président
Isabelle Lelarge, Vice-président
Francine Bergeron, Directrice générale
Josiane Ouellet, Secrétaire-trésorier
Membre: 44; *Montant de la cotisation:* 250$; *Critères d'admissibilite:* Revues culturelles
Activités: *Listes de destinataires:* Oui

Société de développement économique du Saint-Laurent (SODES) / St. Lawrence Economic Development Council
271, rue de l'Estuaire, Québec QC G1K 8S8
Tél: 418-648-4572; *Téléc:* 418-648-4627
sodes@st-laurent.org
www.st-laurent.org
Aperçu: *Dimension:* petite; *Envergure:* locale; Organisme sans but lucratif; fondée en 1985
Mission: Promouvoir le St-Laurent comme axe de développement; protéger les intérêts de la communauté maritime du St-Laurent et la représenter auprès des gouvernements; rassembler la communauté maritime du St-Laurent et mettre à sa disposition un forum d'échange et de concertation
Membre(s) du bureau directeur:
Nicole Trépanier, Président
nicole.trepanier@st-laurent.org
Mélissa Laliberté, Directrice
melissa.laliberte@st-laurent.org
Laurie Grenier, Chargée, Communications
laurie.grenier@st-laurent.org
Pierrette Roy, Adjointe comptable
pierrette.roy@st-laurent.org
Finances: *Budget de fonctionnement annuel:* $100,000-$250,000
Membre(s) du personnel: 4
Membre: 80; *Montant de la cotisation:* Barème; *Comités:* Développement; Environnement; Réglementation; Tourisme; Assurances; Fiscalité municipale
Activités: Journée Maritime Québécoise; Prix du Saint-Laurent; *Stagiaires:* Oui; *Service de conférenciers:* Oui

Société de généalogie de Drummondville
555, rue des Écoles, Drummondville QC J2B 1J6
Tél: 819-474-2318
info@histoiredrummond.com
www.histoiredrummond.com
www.facebook.com/societehistoiredrummond
Également appelé: Société d'histoire de Drummondville
Aperçu: *Dimension:* petite; *Envergure:* locale; fondée en 1957
Mission: Réunir les amateurs de l'histoire régionale et encourager la recherche historique; promouvoir la conservation des monuments et sites historiques; organiser des conférences et expositions à portée historique; promouvoir la diffusion de l'histoire par des publications; organiser une bibliothèque de documents historiques
Membre de: Fédération des sociétés d'historie du Québec; Chambre de Commerce du Comté de Drummond
Membre(s) du bureau directeur:
Hélène Vallières, Directrice
Membre(s) du personnel: 2
Membre: 113; *Montant de la cotisation:* 12$ étudiant; 25$ individu; 35$ résident hors MRC; 100$ corporatif/vie
Activités: Conférences; expositions; services d'accueil et d'orientation de chercheurs; *Stagiaires:* Oui; *Service de conférenciers:* Oui; *Bibliothèque:* Archives

Société de généalogie de l'Outaouais
855, boul de la Gappe, Gatineau QC J8T 8H9
Tél: 819-243-0888; *Téléc:* 819-568-5933
sgo@genealogieoutaouais.com
www.genealogieoutaouais.com
Aperçu: *Dimension:* moyenne; *Envergure:* locale; fondée en 1978
Mission: Promouvoir la généalogie; donner des cours d'initiation à la recherche généalogique et en paléographie; collaborer avec le centre régional des archives nationales du Québec à Hull pour maintenir une bibliothèque spécialisée en généalogie et en histoire de la région
Affliation(s): Fédération québécoise des sociétés de généalogie
Membre(s) du bureau directeur:
Suzanne Bigras, Présidente
suzanne_bigras@hotmail.com
Membre: *Montant de la cotisation:* 35$ individu; 50$ couple; *Comités:* Reconnaissances
Activités: Ateliers et rencontres; *Evénements de sensibilisation:* Semaine nationale de la généalogie, novembre; *Service de conférenciers:* Oui; *Bibliothèque* Bibliothèque publique

Société de généalogie de la Beauce
#403, 250, 18e rue ouest, Saint-Georges QC G5Y 4S9

Tél: 418-228-3509
sgbce@globetrotter.net
genealogie.beauce.voila.net
Aperçu: *Dimension:* petite; *Envergure:* locale; Organisme sans but lucratif; fondée en 1996
Mission: Aider les membres dans leurs recherches généalogiques
Membre de: Fédération québécoise des sociétés de généalogie; Société de généalogie de Québec
Membre(s) du bureau directeur:
Jean Nicol Dubé, Président
Finances: *Budget de fonctionnement annuel:* Moins de $50,000
Membre(s) du personnel: 3; 8 bénévole(s)
Membre: 40; *Montant de la cotisation:* 20 $
Activités: Rencontre aux 2 semaines pour aider les membres en recherche; *Bibliothèque* Bibliothèque publique

Société de généalogie de la Jemmerais (SGLJ)
CP 82, Sainte-Julie QC J3E 1X5
Tél: 450-922-4466
sglj@genealogie.org
www.genealogie.org/club/sglj
Nom précédent: Club de généalogie de Sainte-Julie
Aperçu: *Dimension:* petite; *Envergure:* locale; Organisme sans but lucratif; fondée en 1994
Mission: Regrouper les personnes intéressées à la généalogie; faire connaître la généalogie et les activités connexes comme l'histoire, la paléographie, la démographie, la sociologie, l'héraldique; faire naître et soutenir l'intérêt de la population de la région pour la généalogie
Membre(s) du bureau directeur:
Anita de Chantal, Présidente
Membre: *Montant de la cotisation:* 20$ membre principal; 10$ membre associé
Activités: Visite organisées; conférences; ateliers; réunions mensuelles; cours d'initiation a la généalogie

Société de généalogie de la Mauricie et des Bois-Francs
#208, 1800, rue St-Paul, Trois-Rivières QC G9A 1J7
Tél: 819-376-2691
sgmbf@cgocable.ca
www.genealogie.org/club/sgmbf/sgmbf.htm
Aperçu: *Dimension:* petite; *Envergure:* locale; fondée en 1979
Membre de: Fédération québécoise des sociétés de généalogie
Membre(s) du bureau directeur:
Normand Houde, Président
Finances: *Budget de fonctionnement annuel:* Moins de $50,000
Membre: 425; *Montant de la cotisation:* 30$
Activités: *Bibliothèque* rendez-vous

Société de généalogie de Lanaudière
CP 221, Joliette QC J6E 3Z6
Tél: 450-756-1818
sgl@lanaudiere.net
www.sgl.lanaudiere.net
Aperçu: *Dimension:* petite; *Envergure:* locale; fondée en 1980
Mission: Regrouper en association les personnes intéressées à la généalogie et à la promotion de cet héritage
Membre de: la Fédération des sociétés d'histoire du Québec, la Fédération québécoise des sociétés de généalogie
Membre(s) du bureau directeur:
Jacques Gauthier, Président
Membre: *Montant de la cotisation:* 20$ étudiant; 40$ individuel; 75$ corporatif; 600$ membre à vie; *Comités:* Bibliothèque; Activités mensuelles; Finances; Registraire; Publications; Informatique; Sites Web

Société de généalogie de Longueuil
CP 21027, Succ. Jacques-Cartier, Longueuil QC J4J 5J4
Tél: 450-670-1869; *Téléc:* 450-670-1427
www.slongueuil.org
Aperçu: *Dimension:* petite; *Envergure:* locale; fondée en 1990
Mission: Regrouper les personnes intéressées à la recherche généalogique, à l'histoire des familles et à la petite histoire du Québec.
Membre de: Fédération québécoise des sociétés de généalogie
Membre(s) du bureau directeur:
Léandre Vachon, Président
Membre: *Montant de la cotisation:* 35$
Activités: Recherches généalogiques; cours; conférences; ateliers

Société de généalogie de Québec (SGQ)
CP 9066, Succ. Sainte-Foy, #3112, 1055, av du Séminaire, Québec QC G1V 4A8
Tél: 418-651-9127; *Téléc:* 418-651-2643
sgq@uniserve.com
www.sgq.qc.ca
Aperçu: *Dimension:* moyenne; *Envergure:* provinciale; Organisme sans but lucratif; fondée en 1961
Mission: Regrouper les personnes intéressées à promouvoir les recherches sur les histoires de familles des ancêtres et à répandre les connaissances généalogiques; favoriser la conservation des documents relatifs à la généalogie; être un lieu de conservation du patrimoine familial
Membre de: Fédération des sociétés de généalogie du Québec; Canadian Federation of Genealogical & Family Histories Societies Inc.
Membre(s) du bureau directeur:
André G. Bélanger, Président
Finances: *Budget de fonctionnement annuel:* $50,000-$100,000
50 bénévole(s)
Membre: 1 500; *Montant de la cotisation:* 20$ membre associé; 40$ membre principal; *Comités:* Bibliothèque; L'Ancêtre; Publications; Recherche généalogique; Généatique
Activités: Recherche en généalogie; formation; entraide; conférences; *Service de conférenciers:* Oui; *Bibliothèque:* Roland J. Auger Bibliothèque; rendez-vous

Société de généalogie de Saint-Eustache
Société de Généalogie de Saint-Eustache, 12, Chemin de la Grande-Côte, Saint-Eustache QC J7P 1A2
Tél: 450-974-5164
sgse@sgse.org
www.sgse.org
Aperçu: *Dimension:* petite; *Envergure:* locale; Organisme sans but lucratif; fondée en 1997
Mission: Faire connaître la généalogie à l'ensemble du territoire; regrouper toutes les personnes désireuses de partager leurs connaissances généalogiques et leur histoire de famille; publier des livres, revues, plaquettes historiques sur les familles de la région ou tout autre sujet d'intérêt pour les membres
Membre(s) du bureau directeur:
Claudette Giraldeau, Présidente
Membre: *Montant de la cotisation:* 25$ individuel; 30$ famille/couple
Activités: Centre de recherches; rencontres culturelles; cours d'initiation à la généalogie
Prix, Bouses:
- Prix Jacques-Labrie (Prix)

Pour travaux généalogiques

Société de généalogie des Cantons de l'Est (SGCE)
275, rue Dufferin, Sherbrooke QC J1H 4M5
Tél: 819-821-5414
sgce@libertel.org
www.sgce.qc.ca
Aperçu: *Dimension:* moyenne; *Envergure:* locale; Organisme sans but lucratif; fondée en 1968
Membre de: Fédération québécoise des sociétés de généalogie
Membre(s) du bureau directeur:
Réjean Roy, Présidente
Finances: *Budget de fonctionnement annuel:* Moins de $50,000
Membre(s) du personnel: 1; 28 bénévole(s)
Membre: 400; *Montant de la cotisation:* 20$ membre associé et étudiant; 30$ membre hors Québec; 40$ membre principal; 600$ membre à vie
Activités: Recherches; publication de répertoires généalogiques; *Service de conférenciers:* Oui; *Bibliothèque* Bibliothèque publique
Prix, Bouses:
- Prix Raymond Lambert (Prix)

Société de généalogie des Laurentides (SGL)
Bibliothèque C-E Garneau, 500, boul. des Laurentides, Saint-Jérôme QC J7Z 4M2
Tél: 450-553-1182
info@sglaurentides.org
www.genealogie.org/club/sglaurentides/
Aperçu: *Dimension:* petite; *Envergure:* locale; Organisme sans but lucratif; fondée en 1984
Membre(s) du bureau directeur:
Guy Constantineau, Présidente
7 bénévole(s)
Membre: 100; *Montant de la cotisation:* 35$ individuel; 55$ couple
Activités: Centre de recherches; cours d'initiation à la généalogie; conférences; visites historiques; banque de données; *Service de conférenciers:* Oui

Société de généalogie du Saguenay, inc. (SGS)
899 A, ch Sydenham, Chicoutimi QC G7H 2H4
Tél: 418-693-8266; *Téléc:* 418-698-1156
sgssaguenay@videotron.ca
sgsaguenay.ca/wp
Aperçu: *Dimension:* petite; *Envergure:* locale; Organisme sans but lucratif; fondée en 1979
Mission: Regrouper des personnes qui s'intéressent à la généalogie et à l'histoire de leur famille et favoriser des échanges entre elles; vulgariser les connaissances généalogiques et historiques par l'édition, les conférences, les cours, la recherche et la confection de documents; supporter les chercheurs locaux et régionaux en généalogie
Membre de: La Fédération québécoise des sociétés de généalogie
Membre(s) du bureau directeur:
Paul-Henri Croft, Président
croftph@videotron.ca
Finances: *Budget de fonctionnement annuel:* Moins de $50,000
Membre(s) du personnel: 1; 15 bénévole(s)
Membre: 250; *Montant de la cotisation:* 15$ étudiant; 35$ individu; 50$ couple; 400$ membre à vie; *Critères d'admissibilite:* Retraité et autres; *Comités:* Journal; Surveillance; Publicité; Informatique de la bibliothèque
Activités: Cours de généalogie; cours sur les logiciels de généalogie; *Evénements de sensibilisation:* Portes Ouvertes; *Bibliothèque:* Centre de Documentation

Société de généalogie et d'archives de Rimouski (SGAR)
#L-120, 110, rue de l'Évêché est, Rimouski QC G5L 1X9
Tél: 418-724-3242; *Téléc:* 418-724-3242
sghr@globetrotter.net
www.sgar.org
Nom précédent: Société généalogique de l'est du Québec
Aperçu: *Dimension:* moyenne; *Envergure:* locale; Organisme sans but lucratif; fondée en 1979
Mission: Organiser, promouvoir et patronner des activités et manifestations généalogiques, historiques et culturelles; inventorier, protéger et étudier le patrimoine; organiser et tenir des conférences, réunions, assemblées et expositions pour la promotion et la vulgarisation de la généalogie
Membre de: Fédération québécoise des sociétés de généalogie
Affliation(s): Centre de généalogie francophone d'Amérique (CGFA)
Membre(s) du bureau directeur:
Laurent Bérubé, Président
cethe@globetrotter.net
Pierre Rioux, Vice-président
pierre_rioux@uqar.qc.ca
Claude C. Fortin, Trésorier
clsy@cgocable.ca
Finances: *Budget de fonctionnement annuel:* Moins de $50,000
50 bénévole(s)
Membre: 22 sociétés; 30 membres à vie; 495 individu; 45 échanges divers; *Montant de la cotisation:* 20$ étudiant; 30$ individuel; 55$ couple; 600$ membre à vie
Activités: Atelier de généalogie, cours de généalogie; navigation sur internet; *Service de conférenciers:* Oui; *Bibliothèque:* Centre de recherche en généalogie; Bibliothèque publique

Société de généalogie et d'histoire de la région de Thetford-Mines
671, boul Frontenac ouest, Thetford Mines QC G6G 1N1
Tél: 418-338-8591
sghrtm@cegepth.qc.ca
www.genealogie.org/club/sghrtm
www.facebook.com/genealogiethetford?ref=ts&fref=ts
Aperçu: *Dimension:* petite; *Envergure:* locale; Organisme sans but lucratif
Mission: Favoriser l'entraide des membres, la recherche sur la généalogie et l'histoire des ancêtres et des familles; permettre la diffusion des connaissances généalogiques par la publication de répertoires généalogiques
Membre(s) du bureau directeur:
Pascal Binet, Président
Membre: *Montant de la cotisation:* 25$ individuel; *Critères d'admissibilite:* Personnes intéressées à la généalogie et à l'histoire; *Comités:* Revue; Informatique; Publicité; Recherche
Activités: Rencontres; études; recherches; publication d'articles, brochures, répertoires; banques de données; conférences; visites guidées

Société de généalogie Gaspésie-Les Iles
CP 6217, 80, boul de Gaspé, Gaspé QC G4X 2R7

Tél: 418-368-6438; *Téléc:* 418-368-1535
genealogie.gaspe@gmail.com
www.genealogie.org/club/sggi
Aperçu: *Dimension:* petite; *Envergure:* locale; Organisme sans but lucratif; fondée en 1990
Mission: Regrouper les personnes désireuses de partager des connaissances; publier des recherches en généalogie; organiser des sessions d'études et de formation en généalogie
Membre de: Fédération des Sociétés Généalogiques du Québec
Membre(s) du bureau directeur:
Serge Ouellet, Président
ouellet.serge@cgocable.ca
Finances: *Budget de fonctionnement annuel:* Moins de $50,000
Membre: 80; *Montant de la cotisation:* 20$

Société de généalogie Saint-Hubert
3500, rue Grand Boulevard, Longueuil (Saint-Hubert) QC J4T 0A1
Tél: 450-445-0080
www.sgsh.org
Aperçu: *Dimension:* petite; *Envergure:* locale; Organisme sans but lucratif; fondée en 1989
Mission: Mieux connaître et faire connaître la généalogie; faire découvrir les outils de recherche généalogique; favoriser la publication des recherches généalogiques
Membre de: Fédération québécoise des sociétés de généalogie
Membre(s) du bureau directeur:
Pierre Decelles, Président
Finances: *Budget de fonctionnement annuel:* Moins de $50,000
Membre: *Montant de la cotisation:* 25$ membre; 15$ conjoint
Activités: *Bibliothèque*

Société de l'aide à l'enfance d'Algoma *See* Children's Aid Society of Algoma

La Société de l'aide à l'enfance d'Ottawa *See* Children's Aid Society of Ottawa

Société de l'arthrite *See* Arthritis Society

Société de l'histoire des familles du Québec *See* Québec Family History Society

Société de l'information funéraire d'Ottawa *See* Funeral Information Society of Ottawa

Société de la médecine rurale du Canada *See* Society of Rural Physicians of Canada

Société de la SLA du Québec *Voir* ALS Society of Québec

Société de la thérapie respiratoire de l'Ontario *See* Respiratory Therapy Society of Ontario

Société de leucémie et lymphome du Canada *See* The Leukemia & Lymphoma Society of Canada

Société de Microscopie du Canada *See* Microscopical Society of Canada

Société de mise en marché des métiers d'art inc. *Voir* Conseil des métiers d'art du Québec (ind.)

Société de musique des universités canadiennes *See* Canadian University Music Society

Société de pharmacologie du Canada *See* Canadian Society of Pharmacology & Therapeutics

Société de philosophie du Québec (SPQ)
CP 217, Succ. B, Montréal QC H3B 3J7
Tél: 514-987-3000; *Téléc:* 514-987-6721
spq@uqam.ca
spq.uqam.ca
Aperçu: *Dimension:* petite; *Envergure:* provinciale; fondée en 1974
Membre de: La FISP; l'ASPLF
Membre(s) du bureau directeur:
Jean Leroux, Président
Finances: *Budget de fonctionnement annuel:* Moins de $50,000
15 bénévole(s)
Membre: 100-499; *Montant de la cotisation:* 30-195

Société de protection des animaux du Grand Moncton *See* Greater Moncton Society for the Prevention of Cruelty to Animals

Société de protection des forêts contre les insectes et maladies (SOPFIM)
1780, rue Semple, Québec QC G1N 4B8
Tél: 418-681-3381; *Téléc:* 418-681-0994
Ligne sans frais: 877-224-3381
www.sopfim.qc.ca
Aperçu: *Dimension:* petite; *Envergure:* provinciale; fondée en 1990
Mission: Protéger efficacement les forêts contre les insectes et les maladies, dans le respect de l'environnement, pour l'ensemble des utilisateurs et au bénéfice de toute la collectivité québécoise
Membre(s) du bureau directeur:
Jean-Yves Arsenault, Directeur général
j.arsenault@sopfim.qc.ca
Membre(s) du personnel: 12
Prix, Bouses:
• Bourse Wladimir-A.-Smirnoff (Bourse d études)
Octroyée à deux étudiants poursuivant leurs études universitaires dans le domaine de la lutte biologique contre les insectes ravageurs forestiers *Amount:* Deux bourses de 5 000$

Société de protection des infirmières et infirmiers du Canada *See* Canadian Nurses Protective Society

Société de protection des plantes du Québec / Québec Society for the Protection of Plants
QC
info@sppq.qc.ca
www.sppq.qc.ca
Aperçu: *Dimension:* petite; *Envergure:* provinciale; fondée en 1908
Mission: Vouée à la protection des plantes; regroupe des chercheurs universitaires et gouvernementaux, des agronomes, des biologistes, des ingénieurs forestiers, des technologistes, des étudiants, ainsi que toute personne intéressée à la protection des plantes.
Membre(s) du bureau directeur:
Sylvie Rioux, Présidente
sylvie.rioux@cerom.qc.ca
Vicky Toussaint, Secrétaire
vicky.toussaint@agr.gc.ca
Pierre-Antoine Thériault, Trésorier
tresorier@sppq.qc.ca
Membre: *Comités:* Promotion et recrutement; Bourses étudiantes; Futurs congrès; Nomenclature française des maladies des plantes du Canada; Phytoprotection; Fondation SPPQ; Congrès annuel; Les Échos phytosanitaires
Prix, Bouses:
• Bourse annuelle (Bourse d études)
Pour encourager les étudiantes et les étudiants à poursuivre des études graduées dans le domaine de la protection des végétaux *Amount:* 1 000$
• Prix W.E. Sackston (Prix)
Pour la meilleure communication étudiante présentée lors de son congrès annuel

Société de recherche sur le cancer *See* Cancer Research Society

Société de sauvetage *See* Lifesaving Society

Société de schizophrénie de l'Ontario *See* Schizophrenia Society of Ontario

Société de Schizophrénie de la Montérégie (SSM)
2510, rue Sainte-Hélène, Longueuil QC J4K 3V2
Tél: 450-677-4347; *Téléc:* 450-748-0503
www.schizophrenie-monteregie.com
Aperçu: *Dimension:* petite; *Envergure:* locale
Mission: Aider toute personne atteintes de schizophrénie et leurs familles d'améliorer leur qualité de vie et de sensibiliser aux problèmes de schizophrénie provoque
Membre(s) du bureau directeur:
Lucie Couillard, Présidente, Conseil d'administration
Activités: *Evénements de sensibilisation:* Cyclothon Écile-Nelligan (août)

Société de Théorie et de Culture existentialises et phénoménologique *See* Society for Existential & Phenomenological Theory & Culture

Société de toxicologie du Canada *See* Society of Toxicology of Canada

Société dentaire du Nouveau-Brunswick *See* New Brunswick Dental Society

Société des Acadiens et Acadiennes du Nouveau-Brunswick (SANB)
#204, 702, rue Principale, Petit-Rocher NB E8J 1V1
Tél: 506-783-4205; *Téléc:* 506-783-0629
Ligne sans frais: 888-722-2343
sanb@nb.aibn.com
www.saanb.org
www.facebook.com/sanb.ca
twitter.com/SANB2012
Aperçu: *Dimension:* moyenne; *Envergure:* provinciale; Organisme sans but lucratif; fondée en 1973 surveillé par Fédération des communautés francophones et acadienne du Canada
Mission: La Société vise à unir tous les Acadiens et Acadiennes du Nouveau-Brunswick et les sensibiliser aux problèmes sociaux, économiques, culturels et politiques qu'ils doivent affronter; s'occuper de tout sujet ayant trait à la protection et à la promotion des droits et à l'avancement des intérêts des Acadiens et Acadiennes du Nouveau-Brunswick; entretenir des liens aussi étroits que possible avec les groupements analogues des autres provinces canadiennes et de l'étranger.
Affliation(s): Société Nationale de l'Acadie
Membre(s) du bureau directeur:
Jeanne d'Arc Gaudet, Présidente
jeanne.darc.gaudet@UMoncton.ca
Bruno Godin, Directeur général
Finances: *Budget de fonctionnement annuel:* $500,000-$1.5 Million
Membre(s) du personnel: 8
Membre: 20 000+
Activités: *Stagiaires:* Oui; *Bibliothèque:* Centre de documentations

Région Acadie-Beauséjour
415 Notre Dame St., Dieppe NB E1A 2A8
Tél: 506-383-4427

Région Alnwick - Miramichi
300, ch Beaverbrook, Miramichi NB E1V 1A1
Tél: 506-622-6569; *Téléc:* 506-627-4592

Région du Nord/Nord-Est
#204, 702, rue Principale, Petit-Rocher NB E8J 1V7
Tél: 506-783-0620; *Téléc:* 506-783-0629
Ligne sans frais: 888-722-2343

Région du Sud-Ouest
info@franco-fredericton.com
www.franco-fredericton.com

Société des archives historiques de la région de l'Amiante (SAHRA)
671, boul Frontenac ouest, Thetford Mines QC G6G 1N1
Tél: 418-338-8591; *Téléc:* 418-338-3498
archives@cegepth.qc.ca
www.sahra.qc.ca
Aperçu: *Dimension:* petite; *Envergure:* locale; fondée en 1985
Mission: Recueillir, classer, conserver et rendre accessible au public les archives régionales
Membre(s) du bureau directeur:
Stéphane Hamann, Directeur-archiviste
Finances: *Budget de fonctionnement annuel:* $50,000-$100,000
Membre(s) du personnel: 2; 2 bénévole(s)

Société des artistes canadiens *See* Society of Canadian Artists

Société des attractions touristiques du Québec (SATQ)
4545, av Pierre-de Coubertin, Montréal QC H1V 0B2
Tél: 514-252-3037; *Téléc:* 514-254-1617
Ligne sans frais: 800-361-7688
info@satqfeq.com
www.attractionsevenements.com
www.facebook.com/satq.feq
twitter.com/SATQFEQ
Aperçu: *Dimension:* petite; *Envergure:* provinciale; Organisme sans but lucratif; fondée en 1991
Membre(s) du bureau directeur:
Pierre-Paul Leduc, Directeur général, 514-252-3037 Ext. 3475
pierre-paul.leduc@satqfeq.com
Camille Trudel, Président
camille.trudel@sympatico.ca
Membre(s) du personnel: 33
Activités: Promotion; formation; information; représentation; *Stagiaires:* Oui; *Listes de destinataires:* Oui

Société des Auteurs de Radio, Télévision et Cinéma (SARTEC) / Society of Writers in Radio, Television & Cinema
1229, rue Panet, Montréal QC H2L 2Y6
Tél: 514-526-9196; *Téléc:* 514-526-4124
information@sartec.qc.ca

www.sartec.qc.ca
twitter.com/SARTEC_auteur
vimeo.com/user8816585
Nom précédent: Société des auteurs, recherchistes, documentalistes et compositeurs
Aperçu: *Dimension:* moyenne; *Envergure:* nationale; fondée en 1949
Mission: Regroupe les auteurs de langue française oeuvrant au Canada dans les domaines de la radio, de la télévision, du cinéma ou de l'audiovisuel; a pour objet l'étude, la défense et le développement des intérêts économiques, sociaux et moraux de ses membres
Affiliation(s): International Affiliation of Writers Guilds (IAWG)
Membre(s) du bureau directeur:
Yves Légaré, Directeur général
ylegare@sartec.qc.ca
Sylvie Lussier, Présidente
Finances: *Budget de fonctionnement annuel:* $500,000-$1.5 Million
Membre(s) du personnel: 9
Membre: 1,300; *Montant de la cotisation:* 35$ stagiaire; 50$ associé; 85$ actif

Société des auteurs, recherchistes, documentalistes et compositeurs ***Voir*** Société des Auteurs de Radio, Télévision et Cinéma

Société des canadiennes dans la science et la technologie ***See*** Society for Canadian Women in Science & Technology

Société des chefs, cuisiniers et pâtissiers du Québec (SCCPQ)

CP 47536, Succ. Plateau Mont-Royal, Montréal QC H2H 2S8
Tél: 514-528-1083; *Téléc:* 514-528-1037
bureau-national@sccpq.ca
www.sccpq.ca
www.facebook.com/sccpq
twitter.com/SCCPQ
www.youtube.com/user/sccpq
Également appelé: Société des chefs du Québec
Aperçu: *Dimension:* moyenne; *Envergure:* provinciale; Organisme sans but lucratif; fondée en 1953
Mission: Mise en valeur et émulation de la profession; reconnaissance professionnelle au niveau national
Membre(s) du bureau directeur:
René Derrien, Président national
rene.derrien@hotmail.com
Patrick Gérôme, Secrétaire
patrick.gerome@baluchon.com
Finances: *Fonds:* Cotisations
Membre(s) du personnel: 1; 23 bénévole(s)
Membre: 800; *Montant de la cotisation:* 125$
Activités: Gala annuel, golf, salon, compétitions et concours

Société des chirurgiens cardiaques ***See*** Canadian Society of Cardiac Surgeons

Société des ciné amateurs canadiens ***See*** Society of Canadian Cine Amateurs

Société des collectionneurs d'estampes de Montréal (SCEM) / Montréal Print Collectors' Society (MPCS)

CP 324, Succ. NDG, Montréal QC H4A 3P6
www.mpcsscem.com
Aperçu: *Dimension:* petite; *Envergure:* locale; fondée en 1986
Mission: Regroupe des collectionneurs, des artistes et des marchands d'estampes anciennes et modernes
Membre: *Montant de la cotisation:* Individuel/le 60$, Couple 90$, Étudiant/e 30$
Activités: Huit conférences mensuelles; visites guidées aux musées; démonstrations de techniques;

La Société des comptables professionnels du Canada ***See*** The Society of Professional Accountants of Canada

Société des denturologistes du Nouveau-Brunswick ***See*** New Brunswick Denturists Society

Société des designers d'intérieurs du Québec ***Voir*** Association professionnelle des designers d'intérieur du Québec

Société des designers graphiques du Canada ***See*** Society of Graphic Designers of Canada

Société des designers graphiques du Québec (SDGQ)

#106, 7255 rue Alexandra, Montréal QC H2R 2Y9
Tél: 514-842-3960; *Téléc:* 514-842-4886
Ligne sans frais: 888-842-3960
infodesign@sdgq.ca
www.sdgq.ca
www.linkedin.com/groups?gid=1927274
www.facebook.com/sdgq.ca
twitter.com/SDGQ
Aperçu: *Dimension:* petite; *Envergure:* provinciale; Organisme sans but lucratif; fondée en 1972
Membre(s) du bureau directeur:
Philippe Lamarre, Président
Membre: *Critères d'admissibilité:* Professionnels en design graphique

Société des droits d'auteur du Front des artistes canadiens inc ***See*** Canadian Artists Representation Copyright Collective Inc.

Société des Écoles d'éducation internationale ***Voir*** Société des écoles du monde du BI du Québec et de la francophonie

Société des écoles du monde du BI du Québec et de la francophonie (SEBIQ)

2000, rue Lasalle, Longueuil QC J4K 3J4
Tél: 450-679-6618; *Téléc:* 450-679-9682
sec@sebiq.ca
www.sebiq.ca
Nom précédent: Société des Écoles d'éducation internationale
Aperçu: *Dimension:* petite; *Envergure:* provinciale; Organisme sans but lucratif; fondée en 1988
Mission: Favoriser la mise en commun des ressources et assurer la cohésion et l'uniformité de ses exigences dans plus de 125 établissements primaires, secondaires et collégiaux d'éducation internationale au Québec
Affiliation(s): Organisation du Baccalauréat International
Membre(s) du bureau directeur:
Louis Bouchard, Président, 450-679-9682
louisbouchard@sebiq.ca
Pierre Duclos, Directeur général, 450-679-6618
Finances: *Budget de fonctionnement annuel:* $500,000-$1.5 Million
Membre(s) du personnel: 7
Membre: 214; *Montant de la cotisation:* Barème; *Critères d'admissibilite:* Établissement scolaire primaire, secondaire, ou collégial; *Comités:* Varient selon les années
Activités: Perfectionnement du personnel des écoles; harmonisation de programmes internationaux au contexte québécois; rédaction de nouveaux programmes et de guides pédagogiques; délivrance d'un diplôme particulier

Société des écrivains canadiens ***Voir*** Écrivains Francophones d'Amérique

Société des éleveurs de bovins canadiens ***See*** Canadian Cattle Breeders' Association

Société des Éleveurs de Chevaux Canadiens ***See*** Canadian Horse Breeders' Association

Société des établissements de plein air du Québec (SEPAQ)

Place de la Cité, Tour Cominar, #1300, 2640 boul Laurier, Québec QC G1V 5C2
Tél: 418-686-4875; *Téléc:* 418-643-8177
Ligne sans frais: 800-665-6527
inforeservation@sepaq.com
www.sepaq.com
twitter.com/reseausepaq
www.youtube.com/user/ReseauSepaq
Nom précédent: Société des parcs de sciences naturelles du Québec
Aperçu: *Dimension:* petite; *Envergure:* provinciale
Mission: D'administrer et de développer des territoires naturels et des équipements touristiques qui lui sont confiés en vertu de sa loi constitutive; d'assurer l'accessibilité, la mise en valeur et la protection de ces équipements publics pour le bénéfice de sa clientèle, des régions du Québec et des générations futures
Membre(s) du bureau directeur:
Raymond Desjardins, Président-directeur général

Société des gynécologues oncologues du Canada ***See*** Society of Gynecologic Oncologists of Canada

Société des ingénieurs professionnels et associés ***See*** Society of Professional Engineers & Associates

Société des Jeux de l'Acadie Inc. (SJA)

#210, 702, rue Principale, Petit-Rocher NB E8J 1V1
Tél: 506-783-4207; *Téléc:* 506-783-4209
sja1@nbnet.nb.ca
www.jeuxdelacadie.org
www.facebook.com/societedesjeuxdelacadie
twitter.com/acajoux
www.youtube.com/user/AcajouxJeuxdelAcadie
Aperçu: *Dimension:* petite; *Envergure:* locale; Organisme sans but lucratif; fondée en 1981
Mission: Voir au maintien et au développement du Mouvement des Jeux de l'Acadie dans ses régions constituantes par l'entremise de rencontres sportives grâce à des ressources humaines, financières et des infrastructures adéquates
Membre de: Fondation des Jeux de l'Acadie inc.; Conseil économique du N.-B.; Sports N.-B.
Membre(s) du bureau directeur:
Mélanie McGrath, Présidente
Mylène Ouellet-LeBlanc, Directrice générale
sjadg@nb.aibn.com
Finances: *Budget de fonctionnement annuel:* $250,000-$500,000
Membre(s) du personnel: 4; 3500 bénévole(s)
Membre: 8; *Montant de la cotisation:* 30$; *Comités:* Développement sportif; Développement régional; Financement et Marketing
Activités: Programme Académie jeunesse; relations publiques, représentations et communications

Société des musées québécois (SMQ)

CP 8888, Succ. Centre-Ville, Montréal QC H3C 3P8
Tél: 514-987-3264; *Téléc:* 514-987-3379
info@smq.qc.ca
www.musees.qc.ca
www.facebook.com/museesadecouvrir
twitter.com/museesdecouvrir
Nom précédent: Association des musées de la province de Québec (1973)
Aperçu: *Dimension:* moyenne; *Envergure:* provinciale; fondée en 1958
Mission: Au service du développement de la muséologie au Québec
Membre de: AMC; ICOM
Membre(s) du bureau directeur:
Michel Perron, Directeur général
perron.michel@smq.qc.ca
Finances: *Budget de fonctionnement annuel:* $500,000-$1.5 Million; *Fonds:* Ministère de la Culture et des Communications du Québec; Tourisme Québec; Patrimoine canadien
Membre(s) du personnel: 11
Membre: 300 insitutionnel + 600 individu; *Montant de la cotisation:* barème 70$-$1500; *Comités:* Prix; Congrès; Comités AD HOC
Activités: Événements; congrès; formation et développement professionnel; informatisation des collections; *Stagiaires:* Oui
Publications:
• Musées à découvrir
Price: $20
Profile: Décrit 300 musées, lieux d'interprétation et centres d'exposition du Québec

Société des obstétriciens et gynécologues du Canada ***See*** Society of Obstetricians & Gynaecologists of Canada

Société des orchidophiles de Montréal

CP 57, Succ. NDG, Montréal QC H4A 3P4
info@orchidophilesmontreal.ca
orchidophilesmontreal.ca
www.facebook.com/136506563085346
Aperçu: *Dimension:* petite; *Envergure:* locale; fondée en 2011
Mission: Pour préserver les espèces d'orchidées menacées
Membre(s) du bureau directeur:
André Poliquin, Président
Membre: *Montant de la cotisation:* $35 individuel; $45 par couple
Activités: *Bibliothèque*

Société des Orchidophiles de Windsor ***See*** Windsor Orchid Society

Société des ornithologistes du Canada ***See*** Society of Canadian Ornithologists

Société des parcs de sciences naturelles du Québec ***Voir*** Société des établissements de plein air du Québec

Société des professeurs d'histoire du Québec inc. (SPHQ)

#202, 1319, ch de Chambly, Longueuil QC J4J 3X1
Tél: 514-242-1645
sphq.recitus.qc.ca
Aperçu: *Dimension:* moyenne; *Envergure:* provinciale; fondée en 1962

Mission: De promouvoir l'enseignement et la didactique de l'histoire au Québec; diffusion de moyens didactiques par revue et congrès; réseaux d'échanges de matériel
Affiliation(s): Conseil pédagogique interdisciplinaire du Québec
Membre(s) du bureau directeur:
Raymond Bédard, Président
raymondbedard@hotmail.com
Membre: *Montant de la cotisation:* 35$ étudiant(e)/retraité(e); 65$ enseignant(e); 75$ organisme/institution; *Critères d'admissibilite:* Regroupe des individus de l'ordre primaire, secondaire, collégial et universitaire ainsi que des organismes préoccupés par l'enseignement de l'histoire

Société des salles historiques *See* Historic Theatres' Trust

Société des sculpteurs de glace *See* Canadian Ice Carvers' Society

Société des sculpteurs du Canada *See* Sculptors Society of Canada

Société des techniciens et des technologues agréés du génie du Nouveau-Brunswick *See* New Brunswick Society of Certified Engineering Technicians & Technologists

Société des technologues en nutrition (STN)
CP 68568, Succ. Seugneuriale, 3333, rue du Carrefour, Québec QC G1C 0G7
Tél: 418-990-0309
info@stnq.ca
www.stnq.ca
ca.linkedin.com/groups/Société-technologues-nutrition-STN-4543978
Nom précédent: Association des techniciens et techniciennes en diététique du Québec
Aperçu: *Dimension:* moyenne; *Envergure:* provinciale; Organisme de réglementation; fondée en 1975
Mission: Signer des contrats collectifs de travail; surveiller la mise en application des conditions de travail des membres; promouvoir la défense et les intérêts économiques et professionnels des membres
Affiliation(s): Centrale des professionnelles et professionels de la santé (CPS)
Membre(s) du bureau directeur:
Sylvie Gignac, Présidente
Membre: *Montant de la cotisation:* 55$ étudiant; 110$ régulier; *Critères d'admissibilite:* Signature d'une carte d'adhésion; paiement d'une première cotisation syndicale de 2$

Société des traversiers du Québec (STQ)
Bureau de la traverse, 10, rue des Traversiers, Québec QC G1K 8L8
Tél: 418-643-8420; *Téléc:* 418-643-5178
Ligne sans frais: 877-787-7483
stq-quebec@traversiers.gouv.qc.ca
www.traversiers.gouv.qc.ca
Aperçu: *Dimension:* petite; *Envergure:* provinciale; fondée en 1971
Mission: Contribuer à la mobilité des personnes et des marchandises en assurant des services de transport maritime de qualité, sécuritaires et fiables, favorisant ainsi l'essor social, économique et touristique du Québec
Membre(s) du bureau directeur:
Jocelyn Fortier, Présidente/directrice générale
Finances: *Budget de fonctionnement annuel:* Plus de $5 Million
Membre: 100-499;

Traverse Isle aux Grues-Montmagny
125, chemin du Quai, L'Isle-aux-Grues QC G0R 1P0
Tél: 418-248-2379; *Téléc:* 418-248-9268

Traverse Isle-aux-Coudres-St-Joseph-de-la-Rive
1, ch de la Traverse, Isle-aux-Coudres QC G0A 3J0
Tél: 418-438-2743; *Téléc:* 418-438-2144
stq-iac@traversiers.gouv.qc.ca
Membre(s) du bureau directeur:
Christyan Dufour, Directeur

Traverse Matane-Baie-Comeau-Godbout
1410, rue Matane-sur-Mer, Matane QC G4W 3P5
Tél: 418-560-8616; *Téléc:* 418-560-8044
stq-matane@traversiers.gouv.qc.ca
Membre(s) du bureau directeur:
Greta Bédard, Directrice

Traverse Québec-Lévis
10, rue des Traversiers, Québec QC G1K 8L8
Tél: 418-643-8420; *Téléc:* 418-643-5178
stq-quebec@traversiers.gouv.qc.ca
Membre(s) du bureau directeur:
M. Jean Cantin, Directeur

Traverse Sorel-St-Ignace-de-Loyola
9, rue Élizabeth, Sorel-Tracy QC J3P 4G1
Tél: 450-742-3313; *Téléc:* 450-742-4307
stq-sorel@traversiers.gouv.qc.ca
Membre(s) du bureau directeur:
François Harvey, Directeur

Traverse Tadoussac-Baie-Ste-Catherine
98, rue du Bateau-Passeur, Tadoussac QC G0T 2A0
Tél: 418-235-4395; *Téléc:* 418-235-4357
stq-tadoussac@traversiers.gouv.qc.ca
Membre(s) du bureau directeur:
Carole Campeau, Directrice

La Société du Barreau du Manitoba *See* Law Society of Manitoba

Société du cancer du sein du Canada *See* Breast Cancer Society of Canada

Société du droit de reproduction des auteurs, compositeurs et éditeurs au Canada (SODRAC 2003) inc. (SODRAC) / Society for Reproduction Rights of Authors, Composers & Publishers Canada
1010, Tower B, 1470 Peel, Montréal QC H3A 1T1
Tél: 514-845-3268; *Téléc:* 514-845-3401
Ligne sans frais: 888-876-3722
sodrac@sodrac.ca
www.sodrac.ca
Aperçu: *Dimension:* moyenne; *Envergure:* internationale; Organisme sans but lucratif; Organisme de réglementation; fondée en 1985
Mission: Émettre au nom de ses membres des autorisations (licences); percevoir les sommes qui leur sont dues à la suite de la reproduction de leurs oeuvres; s'occuper de l'intérêt général de ses membres, notamment par une fonction conseil et des représentations au plan politique quand il s'agit par exemple de la révision de la loi sur le droit d'auteur
Affiliation(s): Bureau international des sociétés gérant les droits d'enregistrement et de reproduction mécanique; Confédération internationale des sociétés d'auteurs et compositeurs
Membre(s) du bureau directeur:
Alain Lauzon, Directeur général
Finances: *Budget de fonctionnement annuel:* $1.5 Million-$3 Million
Membre(s) du personnel: 40
Membre: 4 200; *Critères d'admissibilite:* Auteurs, compositeurs, et éditeurs canadiens; ayant aussi des droits étrangers (France, Italie, Espagne, Brésil, Autriche, etc.); les membres canadiens de la SODRAC sont représentés partout à l'étranger via des ententes de représentation conclues avec ses sociétés soeurs
Activités: *Service de conférenciers:* Oui

Société du Musée historique du Comté de Compton *See* Compton County Historical Museum Society

Société du patrimoine de Boucherville
566, boul. Marie-Victorin, Boucherville QC J4B 1X1
Tél: 450-449-0384; *Téléc:* 450-655-6577
secretaire@patrimoineboucherville.com
patrimoineboucherville.com
Aperçu: *Dimension:* petite; *Envergure:* locale; fondée en 1983
Mission: De promouvoir l'histoire et le patrimoine de Boucherville
Membre(s) du bureau directeur:
Madeleine Parenteau, Présidente, Conseil d'administration
Membre: *Montant de la cotisation:* 10$ individu; 25$ organisme à but non lucratif; 100$ société commerciale
Activités: *Evénements de sensibilisation:* Concert annuel (avril)

Société du syndrome de Turner *See* Turner's Syndrome Society

Société du timbre de Pâques de l'Ontario *See* The Easter Seal Society (Ontario)

Société éducative de visites et d'échanges au Canada *See* Society for Educational Visits & Exchanges in Canada

Société franco-manitobaine (SFM)
#106, 147, boul. Provencher, Saint-boniface MB R2H 0G2
Tél: 204-233-4915; *Téléc:* 204-977-8551
Ligne sans frais: 800-665-4443
sfm@sfm-mb.ca
www.sfm-mb.ca
Aperçu: *Dimension:* moyenne; *Envergure:* provinciale; Organisme sans but lucratif; fondée en 1968 surveillé par Fédération des communautés francophones et acadienne du Canada
Mission: Veiller à l'épanouissement de cette communauté
Membre(s) du bureau directeur:
Daniel Boucher, Président/Directeur général
Membre: 35 organismes probinciaux; *Critères d'admissibilite:* Age de 16 ans ou plus, comprenant le français et désirant vivre en français au Manitoba
Activités: *Service de conférenciers:* Oui

Société franco-ontarienne d'histoire et de généalogie *Voir* Réseau du patrimoine franco-ontarien

Société francophone de Victoria (SFV)
#200, 535 Yates St., Victoria BC V8W 2Z6
Tél: 250-388-7350; *Téléc:* 250-388-6280
Ligne sans frais: 888-388-7350
benevolat@francocentre.com
www.francocentre.com
www.facebook.com/francophonie.Victoria
Aperçu: *Dimension:* petite; *Envergure:* locale; Organisme sans but lucratif; fondée en 1941
Mission: Promouvoir, défendre et représenter les intérêts de la communauté francophone à Victoria et dans ses banlieues
Membre de: Fédération des francophones de la Colombie-Britannique
Membre(s) du bureau directeur:
Christian Francey, Directeur général
cfrancey@francocentre.com
Marylène Saumier Demers, Coordonnatrice culturel
marylenesd@francocentre.com
Randy Delisle, Responsable du secteur à l'emploi
rdelisle@francocentre.com
Valérie Dionne, Conseillère à l'emploi
vdionne@francocentre.com
Membre: 100-499; *Critères d'admissibilite:* Francophone ou francophile
Activités: *Evénements de sensibilisation:* Les beaux jeudis; Festival de la Francophonie de Victoria

Société généalogique canadienne-française (SGCF)
3440, rue Davidson, Montréal QC H1W 2Z5
Tél: 514-527-1010; *Téléc:* 514-527-0265
info@sgcf.com
www.sgcf.com
Aperçu: *Dimension:* moyenne; *Envergure:* internationale; Organisme sans but lucratif; fondée en 1943
Mission: Regrouper toutes les personnes désireuses de partager des connaissances généalogiques et leur histoire de famille par les conférences et la publication de travaux de recherche
Membre de: Fédération québécoise des sociétés de généalogie
Membre(s) du bureau directeur:
Gisèle Monarque, Présidente
gmonar@videotron.ca
Finances: *Budget de fonctionnement annuel:* $100,000-$250,000
Membre(s) du personnel: 1; 65 bénévole(s)
Membre: 3 700; *Montant de la cotisation:* 45$
Activités: *Evénements de sensibilisation:* Journées de la culture, oct.; *Service de conférenciers:* Oui; *Bibliothèque:* Maison de la Généalogie
Prix, Bouses:
• Prix Archange-Godbout (Prix)
Décerné à un chercheur pour l'ensemble de son oeuvre *Amount:* 1000$
• Prix Percy-W.-Foy (Prix)
Encourage et récompense le travail accompli par les généalogistes. Trois catégories: meilleur article publié dans la revue Mémoires; meilleur outil de recherche offert en don à la Société; meilleur ouvrage de recherche offert en don à la Société *Amount:* 500$

Société généalogique de Châteauguay
25, boul Maple, Châteauguay QC J6J 3P7
Tél: 450-698-3082
Aperçu: *Dimension:* petite; *Envergure:* locale; fondée en 1998
Mission: Favoriser la recherche généalogique et l'entraide entre ses membres ainsi que la diffusion de l'histoire de la vie des ancêtres ou de leurs familles
Membre(s) du bureau directeur:
Rémon Lecavalier, Président

Société généalogique de l'est du Québec *Voir* Société de généalogie et d'archives de Rimouski

Société Généalogique du Nouveau-Brunswick Inc. *See* New Brunswick Genealogical Society Inc.

La Société géographique royale du Canada *See* The Royal Canadian Geographical Society

Société histoire de Mouillepied

Bibliothèque de Saint-Lambert, 490, rue Mercille, 2e étage, Saint-Lambert QC J4P 2L5
Tél: 450-466-3910
Aperçu: *Dimension:* petite; *Envergure:* locale
Mission: De préserver et de découvrir l'histoire de St-Lambert

Société historique acadienne de la Baie Sainte-Marie

Université Sainte-Anne, 1695 route 1, Pointe-De-L'Église NS B0W 1M0
Tél: 902-769-2114
Aperçu: *Dimension:* petite; *Envergure:* locale; Organisme sans but lucratif; fondée en 1972
Mission: Promouvoir les études et recherches sur l'histoire acadienne dans notre milieu; il s'agit des sites historiques, d'anciens établissements, de cimetières, d'églises, et d'écoles
Affliation(s): Société acadienne de Clare
Membre(s) du bureau directeur:
Marc Lavoie, Président
Finances: *Budget de fonctionnement annuel:* Moins de $50,000
Membre: 100; *Montant de la cotisation:* 7$ individu; 10$ couple; 2$ étudiant

Société historique Alphonse-Desjardins (SHAD)

6, rue du Mont-Marie, Lévis QC G6V 1V9
Tél: 418-835-2090; *Téléc:* 418-835-9173
Ligne sans frais: 866-835-8444
shad@desjardins.com
www.desjardins.com/maisonalphonsedesjardins
www.facebook.com/MaisonAlphonseDesjardins
Également appelé: Maison Alphonse-Desjardins
Aperçu: *Dimension:* petite; *Envergure:* provinciale; Organisme sans but lucratif; fondée en 1979
Mission: Sauvegarder et mettre en valeur l'histoire et le patrimoine du Mouvement Desjardins et de son fondateur au bénéfice des générations actuelles et futures
Membre(s) du bureau directeur:
Marie Boissonneault, Directrice
maire.boissonneault@desjardins.com
Finances: *Budget de fonctionnement annuel:* $500,000-$1.5 Million; *Fonds:* Fédération des caisses Desjardins
Membre(s) du personnel: 14
Membre: 1-99
Activités: Visites guidées - gratuites et à l'année; publication de plusieurs volumes sur Alphonse Desjardins et l'histoire du Mouvement Desjardins; *Service de conférenciers:* Oui

Société historique Cavelier-de-LaSalle / Cavelier de Lasalle Historical Society

13A, rue Strathyre, LaSalle QC H8R 3P5
Tél: 514-364-9955; *Téléc:* 514-364-9955
www.csmb.qc.ca/shcavelier
Aperçu: *Dimension:* petite; *Envergure:* locale; fondée en 1965
Mission: Diffusion de l'histoire locale, de la généalogie; organisation de conférences; défense du patrimoine
Affliation(s): Fédération des sociétés d'histoire
Membre(s) du bureau directeur:
Cécile Duhamel, Président
Membre: *Montant de la cotisation:* 15$ individuel; 20$ familial; 5$ étudiant; 50$ corporatif; 150$ à bie; *Critères d'admissibilite:* Citoyen de la région de Montréal
Activités: Conférences, voyage ou excursion ou visite patrimoniale; *Bibliothèque:* Centre d'information; rendez-vous

Société historique d'Ottawa *See* Historical Society of Ottawa

Société historique de Bellechasse

8, av Commerciale, Saint-Charles-de-Bellechasse QC G0R 2T0
Tél: 418-887-3761
shb@shbellechasse.com
www.shbellechasse.com
Aperçu: *Dimension:* petite; *Envergure:* locale; Organisme sans but lucratif; fondée en 1985
Mission: Mettre en valleur l'histoire et le patrimoine de Bellechasse
Membre de: Fédération des sociétés d'histoire du Québec
Membre(s) du bureau directeur:
Jean-Pierre Lamonte, Président
Membre: 425+; *Montant de la cotisation:* 25$; 30$ familial; 45$ corporatif
Activités: Cours d'initiation en généalogie; *Service de conférenciers:* Oui; *Bibliothèque:* Bibliothèque généalogique BGI; rendez-vous

Société historique de Cabano, Inc. *Voir* Société d'histoire et d'archéologie du Témiscouata

Société historique de Charlesbourg

Maison Éphraïm-Bédard, 7655, ch Samuel, Charlesbourg QC G1H 7H4
Tél: 418-624-7745; *Téléc:* 418-624-7230
SHDC@live.ca
www.societe-historique-charlesbourg.org
Aperçu: *Dimension:* petite; *Envergure:* locale; Organisme sans but lucratif; fondée en 1983
Mission: Faire connaître l'histoire de Charlesbourg, mettre en valeur le patrimoin bâti et humain de Charlesbourg; offrir des services d'aide en généalogie et en informations cadastrales de Charlesbourg
Membre de: Fédération des sociétés d'histoire du Québec
Membre(s) du bureau directeur:
Jean Breton, Président
Finances: *Budget de fonctionnement annuel:* Moins de $50,000; *Fonds:* Statuaire de l'arrondissement Charlesbourg de la ville de Québec
9 bénévole(s)
Membre: 135; *Montant de la cotisation:* 20$; *Critères d'admissibilite:* Résidents adultes de Charlesbourg
Activités: Conférences mensuelles de septembre à avril; expositions; bulletins; *Stagiaires:* Oui; *Bibliothèque*

Société historique de Dorval / Dorval Historical Society

1335, ch du Bord-du-Lac, Dorval QC H9S 2E5
Tél: 514-633-4000
societehistoriquededorval.org
Aperçu: *Dimension:* petite; *Envergure:* locale; Organisme sans but lucratif; fondée en 1984
Mission: D'étudier et de préserver l'histoire de Dorval
Affliation(s): Fédération des sociétés d'histoire du Québec
Membre(s) du bureau directeur:
Michel Hébert, Président
Membre: *Montant de la cotisation:* 10$ résidents et non-résidents; *Critères d'admissibilite:* Surtout résidents de Dorval; retraités; intéressés à l'histoire locale
Activités: Expositions; kiosques; réunions mensuelles; conférences; visites patrimoniales

Société historique de Gloucester *See* Gloucester Historical Society

Société historique de Joliette-De Lanaudière

CP 354, 585, rue Archambault, Joliette QC J6E 2W7
Tél: 450-867-3183
shjlanaudiere@videotron.ca
societedhistoire.connexion-lanaudiere.ca
Aperçu: *Dimension:* petite; *Envergure:* locale; Organisme sans but lucratif; fondée en 1929
Mission: Faire des recherches historiques; rassembler et conserver des documents pour l'histoire spécifique de la ville de Joliette et de la région De Lanaudière; prot,ger le patrimoine par diverses interventions auprès des responsables des villes
Membre(s) du bureau directeur:
Claire L. Saint-Aubin, Présidente
Claude Amyot, Trésorier
Finances: *Budget de fonctionnement annuel:* Moins de $50,000
Membre: 52; *Montant de la cotisation:* 20$ individuel
Activités: Recherches; conférences; expositions; *Service de conférenciers:* Oui

Société historique de Kamouraska *Voir* Société historique de la Côte-du-Sud

La Société historique de l'Ontario *See* Ontario Historical Society

Société historique de la Côte-du-Sud

100, 4e av Painchaud, La Pocatière QC G0R 1Z0
Tél: 418-856-2104; *Téléc:* 418-856-2104
archsud@bellnet.ca
www.shcds.org
Nom précédent: Société historique de Kamouraska
Aperçu: *Dimension:* petite; *Envergure:* locale; fondée en 1948
Mission: Colliger et conserver tous les ouvrages, documents, objets, souvenirs, etc. pouvant servir à l'histoire de la région; regrouper les amateurs d'histoire régionale, afin de favoriser l'étude, la recherche et la publication; étudier, faire connaître et aimer notre histoire régionale; tirer de l'histoire régionale des leçons de fierté, d'attachement aux traditions et de vrai patriotisme qu'elle comporte
Membre de: Fédération des sociétés d'histoire du Québec
Membre(s) du bureau directeur:
Gaétan Godbout, Président
Finances: *Budget de fonctionnement annuel:* Moins de $50,000
9 bénévole(s)
Membre: 200; *Montant de la cotisation:* 10$ étudiant; 15$ régulier; 25$ institutionnel; 500$ et plus à vie; *Critères d'admissibilite:* 150
Activités: Journée d'histoire; *Événements de sensibilisation:* Journée d'histoire, sept.; *Bibliothèque:* Centre de documentation; Bibliothèque publique

Société historique de la Côte-Nord (SHCN)

2, place La Salle, Baie-Comeau QC G4Z 1K3
Tél: 418-296-8228
shcn@globetrotter.net
www.shcote-nord.org
www.facebook.com/215657145115493
Aperçu: *Dimension:* petite; *Envergure:* locale; Organisme sans but lucratif; fondée en 1947
Mission: Est un organisme de conservation, de préservation et de diffusion du patrimoine nord-côtier; met à la disposition des chercheurs ses fonds, ses collections et publications
Affliation(s): Groupe de préservation des vestiges subaquatiques de Manicouagan; Centre d'interprétation Le Bord du Cap de Natashquan
Membre(s) du bureau directeur:
Catherine Pellerin, Directrice-archiviste
catherine.pellerin@shcote-nord.org
Marc Champagne, Président
marcus_spartacus@hotmail.com
Finances: *Fonds:* Privé; Public
Membre(s) du personnel: 2
Membre: *Montant de la cotisation:* 30$
Activités: Généalogie; Archives; Exposition estivale; *Stagiaires:* Oui; *Service de conférenciers:* Oui; *Bibliothèque:* Bibliothèque Historique

Société historique de la région de Mont-Laurier (SHRML)

CP 153, 385, rue du Pont, Mont-Laurier QC J9L 3G9
Tél: 819-623-1900; *Téléc:* 819-623-7079
shghl@hotmail.ca
www.genealogie.org/club/shrml/
www.facebook.com/societedhistoire.deshauteslaurentides
Aperçu: *Dimension:* petite; *Envergure:* locale; Organisme sans but lucratif; fondée en 1975
Mission: Regrouper toutes les personnes qui s'intéressent à l'histoire, à la généalogie et au patrimoine de la région des Hautes-Laurentides
Membre de: Fédération des sociétés d'histoire du Québec; Réseau des archives du Québec
Membre(s) du bureau directeur:
Suzanne Guénette, Responsable administrative
Membre(s) du personnel: 2
Membre: *Montant de la cotisation:* 30$ individu; 50$ couple; *Critères d'admissibilite:* Individus avec interêt pour l'histoire et la généalogie
Activités: Circuits historiques guidés; publication de livres; recherches; expositions; *Bibliothèque* Bibliothèque publique
Prix, Bouses:
• Prix Méritas (Prix)
Implication exceptionnelle dans le monde de l'histoire
• Prix Alfred-Gamelin (Prix)
Sauvegarde du patrimoine bâti

Société historique de la Vallée de la Châteauguay

c/o Connie McClintock Wilson, 1588 1st Concession, Hinchinbrooke QC J0S 1A0
www.rootsweb.com/~qcchatea/shvc.htm
Aperçu: *Dimension:* petite; *Envergure:* locale; fondée en 1963
Mission: Soutenir la recherche et promouvoir le rayonnement et la conservation de l'histoire du sud-ouest du Québec
Membre(s) du bureau directeur:
Connie McClintock Wilson
12 bénévole(s)
Membre: 200; *Montant de la cotisation:* 10$; *Critères d'admissibilite:* Tous ceux qui s'intéressent à l'histoire de la Vallée

Société historique de la Vallée de la Gatineau *Voir* Gatineau Valley Historical Society

La Société historique de Nouvelle-Beauce (SHNB)

640, Notre-Dame sud, Sainte-Marie QC G6E 2W4
Tél: 418-387-7221; *Téléc:* 418-387-5454
museedelaviation@globetrotter.net
Aperçu: *Dimension:* petite; *Envergure:* locale; Organisme sans but lucratif; fondée en 1982

Mission: Promouvoir l'histoire des pionniers canadiens de langue française s'étant illustrés dans l'aviation civile au Québec. Maison Dupuis héberge le premier musée francophone de l'aviation civile en Amérique du Nord
Membre de: Conseil de la culture Chaudière Appalaches; Association touristique régionale de Chaudière Appalaches; Centre local de développement de la Nouvelle-Beauce
Finances: *Budget de fonctionnement annuel:* Moins de $50,000
10 bénévole(s)
Membre: 40; *Montant de la cotisation:* 10$; *Critères d'admissibilité:* Personnes intéressées à encourager la SHNB
Activités: *Bibliothèque*

Canadian Associations

Société historique de Pubnico-Ouest

CP 92, 898 Hwy. 335, West Pubnico NS B0W 3S0
Tél: 902-762-3380; *Téléc:* 902-762-0726
musee.acadien@ns.sympatico.ca
www.museeacadien.ca
www.facebook.com/101935276541461
Aperçu: *Dimension:* petite; *Envergure:* locale; Organisme sans but lucratif; fondée en 1973
Mission: L'étude de l'histoire du peuple acadien, en particulier celle de Pubnico-Ouest et du comté Yarmouth; le maintien du musée et du centre de recherche; le maintien et la présentation des artifacts et des archives qui s'y retrouvent
Membre de: Federation of Nova Scotian Heritage
Affliation(s): Community museums Nova Scotia
Finances: *Budget de fonctionnement annuel:* $50,000-$100,000
Membre(s) du personnel: 4; 50 bénévole(s)
Membre: 125; *Montant de la cotisation:* 10$
Activités: Gère musée et archives; conférences; réunions; visites guidées; soirée acadienne; expositions arts et métiers; *Bibliothèque:* Centre de recherche des archives "Père Clarence d'Entremont"

La Société historique de Québec

#158, 6, rue de la Vieille-Université, Québec QC G1R 5X8
Tél: 418-694-1020
shq1@bellnet.ca
www.societehistoriquedequebec.qc.ca
www.facebook.com/157594394301478
Aperçu: *Dimension:* moyenne; *Envergure:* provinciale; Organisme sans but lucratif; fondée en 1937
Mission: Étudier et diffuser l'histoire de la ville de Québec et de sa région; relever et mettre en valeur le patrimoine de la même région
Membre(s) du bureau directeur:
Jean Dorval, Président
Jean-François Caron, Trésorier
Doris Drolet, Secrétaire
Finances: *Fonds:* Ville de Québec
Membre: *Montant de la cotisation:* Barème; *Critères d'admissibilité:* Professionnels; étudiants; curieux; personnes ayant un intérêt pour l'histoire et le patrimoine
Activités: Publie plusieurs "Cahiers d'Histoire", calendriers, textes de conférences et cartes imprimées; *Bibliothèque* Bibliothèque publique

Société historique de Rivière-des-Prairies

9140, boul Perras, Montréal QC H1E 7E4
info@societe-historique-rdp.org
www.societe-historique-rdp.org
Aperçu: *Dimension:* petite; *Envergure:* locale; Organisme sans but lucratif; fondée en 1993
Mission: Promouvoir l'histoire locale
Membre de: Fédération des sociétés d'histoire du Québec
Membre(s) du bureau directeur:
Louise Bernard, Présidente
Membre: *Montant de la cotisation:* 10$ individu; 15$ famille; *Critères d'admissibilite:* Intéressés à l'histoire et au patrimoine

Société historique de Saint-Boniface (SHSB)

340, boul. Provencher, Saint-Boniface MB R2H 0G7
Tél: 204-233-4888; *Téléc:* 204-231-2562
shsb@shsb.mb.ca
www.shsb.mb.ca
www.facebook.com/234786813250213
Également appelé: Centre du patrimoine
Aperçu: *Dimension:* petite; *Envergure:* provinciale; Organisme sans but lucratif; fondée en 1902
Mission: Conserver et promouvoir le patrimoine, fruit de la présence des francophones dans l'Ouest canadien et en particulier au Manitoba
Membre(s) du bureau directeur:
Gilles Lesage, Directeur général
glesage@shsb.mb.ca
Michel Lagacé, Président
Membre(s) du personnel: 6
Activités: Service d'archives; gestion de lieux historiques; *Bibliothèque:* Centre de documentation; Bibliothèque publique

Société historique de Saint-Henri

521, Place Saint-Henri, 3 étage, Montréal QC H4C 2S1
Tél: 514-933-1318
shsth@cam.org
saint-henri.com
Aperçu: *Dimension:* petite; *Envergure:* locale; fondée en 1977
Membre: *Montant de la cotisation:* 10$ individuel; 15$ familial; 150$ à vie

Société historique de Saint-Romuald (SHSR)

2321, chemin du Fleuve, Saint-Romuald QC G6W 1X9
Tél: 418-834-3662
info@shstromuald.org
www.shstromuald.org
Aperçu: *Dimension:* petite; *Envergure:* locale; fondée en 1992
Mission: Protéger et mettre en valeur l'histoire et le patrimoine de St-Romuald
Membre de: Fédération des sociétés d'histoire du Québec
Membre(s) du bureau directeur:
Michel L'Hebreux, Président
Finances: *Budget de fonctionnement annuel:* Moins de $50,000
Membre(s) du personnel: 3; 9 bénévole(s)
Membre: 170; *Montant de la cotisation:* 10$; *Comités:* Diffusion; Toponymie
Activités: Conférences, expositions, publications; *Service de conférenciers:* Oui

Société historique de Shefford *Voir* Société d'histoire de la Haute-Yamaska

Société historique des Noirs de l'Ontario *See* Ontario Black History Society

Société historique du Canada *See* Canadian Historical Association

La Société historique du Cap-Rouge (SHCR)

4473, rue Saint-Félix, Québec QC G1Y 3A6
Tél: 418-641-6380; *Téléc:* 418-650-7505
info@shcr.qc.ca
www.shcr.qc.ca
Aperçu: *Dimension:* petite; *Envergure:* locale; Organisme sans but lucratif; fondée en 1974
Mission: Sensibiliser la population aux valeurs du patrimoine; faire connaître notre histoire et nos richesses patrimoniales
Affliation(s): Fédération des société d'histoire du Québec
Membre(s) du bureau directeur:
Emmanuel Rioux, Président
Louise Mainguy, Vice-Présidente
Louise Cloutier, Secrétaire
Yvon Lirette, Trésorier
Membre: *Montant de la cotisation:* 15$ régulier; 20$ couple; 5$ étudiant; 50$ collectif; 20$ couple; 150$ à vie; *Comités:* Le Saint-Brieuc; Envois postaux et archives administratives; Archives iconographiques; Prix Joseph-Bell-Forsyth; Activités; Centenaire du Tracel; Table de concertation de la ville; Vérification
Activités: Conférences; excursions; page jointe; *Stagiaires:* Oui; *Service de conférenciers:* Oui; *Bibliothèque* Bibliothèque publique rendez-vous

La Société historique du Comté de Brome *See* Brome County Historical Society

Société historique du comté de Richmond *See* Richmond County Historical Society

Société historique du Marigot inc *Voir* Société historique et culturelle du Marigot inc.

Société historique du Saguenay (SHS)

930, rue Jacques-Cartier est, Chicoutimi QC G7H 7K9
Tél: 418-549-2805; *Téléc:* 418-698-3758
shs@shistoriquesaguenay.com
www.shistoriquesaguenay.com
Aperçu: *Dimension:* moyenne; *Envergure:* locale; Organisme sans but lucratif; fondée en 1934
Mission: Colliger et conserver tout ce qui peut servir à la recherche sur un ou plusieurs aspects de la région du Saguenay-Lac-St-Jean; faire connaître et apprécier l'histoire régionale; assumer un leadership dans la conservation et la mise en valeur du patrimoine de la région
Membre de: Fédération des sociétés d'histoire du Québec
Membre(s) du bureau directeur:
Jean-Charles Dubé, Président
Finances: *Budget de fonctionnement annuel:* $50,000-$100,000
Membre(s) du personnel: 1; 7 bénévole(s)
Membre: 800; *Montant de la cotisation:* 30$ individuel; 40$ institution
Activités: Recherches (grille tarifaire); publications; reproductions; photocopies; conférences; veillées de Saguenayensia; *Événements de sensibilisation:* Semaine de la fierté régionale; Fête du Saguenay-Lac-Saint-Jean; *Service de conférenciers:* Oui; *Bibliothèque* Bibliothèque publique

Société historique et culturelle du Marigot inc.

440, ch de Chambly, Longueuil QC J4H 3L7
Tél: 450-677-4573; *Téléc:* 450-677-6231
shm@marigot.ca
marigot.ca
twitter.com/LeMarigot
Nom précédent: Société historique du Marigot inc
Aperçu: *Dimension:* petite; *Envergure:* locale; Organisme sans but lucratif; fondée en 1978
Mission: Promouvoir la protection du patrimoine
Membre de: Fédération des sociétés d'histoire du Québec
Membre(s) du bureau directeur:
Michel Pratt, Président
Finances: *Budget de fonctionnement annuel:* $50,000-$100,000; *Fonds:* Emploi-Québec; gouvernement fédéral et provincial
Membre(s) du personnel: 6; 8 bénévole(s)
Membre: 190; *Montant de la cotisation:* 20$ individus; 30$ familles; *Critères d'admissibilité:* Adulte
Activités: Conférences; visites guidées; café communautaire internet; *Service de conférenciers:* Oui; *Bibliothèque* rendez-vous

Société historique et généalogique de Trois-Pistoles, inc. (SHGTP)

Salle Philippe-Renouf, Centre culturel de Trois-Pistoles, CP 1586, 145-A, rue de l'Aréna, Trois-Pistoles QC G0L 4K0
Tél: 418-851-2105
info@shgtp.org
shgtp.org
Aperçu: *Dimension:* petite; *Envergure:* locale; Organisme sans but lucratif; fondée en 1977
Mission: Colliger et conserver tout document pertinent à notre histoire locale et/ou régionale; promouvoir la généologie locale et/ou régionale et celle des descendants des basques ayant immigré au Québec et en Acadie; maintenir et garder à jour une bibliothèque permettant la recherche généalogique et historique
Membre(s) du bureau directeur:
Robert Létourneau, Président
Finances: *Budget de fonctionnement annuel:* Moins de $50,000
Membre(s) du personnel: 1; 10 bénévole(s)
Membre: 210; *Montant de la cotisation:* 20$ régulier; 10$ étudiant
Activités: *Service de conférenciers:* Oui

Société historique Machault

134, boul Inter-Provincial, Pointe-à-la-Croix QC G0C 1L0
Tél: 418-788-5590
fr-ca.facebook.com/GouMic
Aperçu: *Dimension:* petite; *Envergure:* locale; Organisme sans but lucratif; fondée en 1983
Mission: Collectionner et conserver tous les ouvrages, objets, souvenirs pouvant servir à faire connaître le patrimoine de la Baie-des-Chaleurs; administrer et exploiter un centre d'interprétation historique
Membre de: Fédération des Sociétés d'histoire du Québec
Activités: Centre d'interpretation Maison Young - 1830; *Bibliothèque:* Centre d'information; rendez-vous

Société historique Pierre-de-Saurel inc. (SHPS)

6A, rue Saint-Pierre, Sorel-Tracy QC J3P 3S2
Tél: 450-780-5739; *Téléc:* 450-780-5743
histoire.archives@shps.qc.ca
www.shps.qc.ca
Aperçu: *Dimension:* petite; *Envergure:* locale; Organisme sans but lucratif; fondée en 1970
Mission: Grouper en association les personnes intéressées à la recherche historique; encourager la recherche historique; intéresser le public à l'histoire locale et régionale; favoriser la conservation de document, d'objets, de lieux et d'édifices historiques; publier des études et des document d'ordre historique
Membre(s) du bureau directeur:
Luc Poirier, Président
Olivier Bolduc, 450-780-5739 Ext. 3021
olivier.bolduc@shps.qc.ca

Finances: *Budget de fonctionnement annuel:* $100,000-$250,000; *Fonds:* ANQ; Ville de Sorel-Tracy; RAQ
Membre: 100-499; *Montant de la cotisation:* 25$
Activités: Conférences; expositions; *Stagiaires:* Oui; *Bibliothèque*

Société Huntington du Canada *See* Huntington Society of Canada

Société Huntington du Québec (SHQ) / Huntington Society of Québec (HSQ)

2300, boul René-Lévesque Ouest, Montréal QC H3H 2R5
Tél: 514-282-4272; *Téléc:* 514-937-0082
Ligne sans frais: 877-220-0226
shq@huntingtonqc.org
huntingtonqc.org
Aperçu: *Dimension:* petite; *Envergure:* provinciale; Organisme sans but lucratif; Organisme de réglementation; fondée en 1986 surveillé par Huntington Society Of Canada
Mission: Pour aider les personnes atteintes de la maladie de Huntington à faire face
Membre de: Huntington Society of Canada
Membre(s) du bureau directeur:
Francine Lacroix, Directrice générale
Membre(s) du personnel: 4
Activités: *Bibliothèque* Bibliothèque publique rendez-vous

Société internationale d'histoire de la médecine *See* International Society for the History of Medicine - Canadian Section

Société internationale de communication non-orale *See* International Society for Augmentative & Alternative Communication

Société internationale de droit du travail et de la sécurité sociale *See* International Society for Labour & Social Security Law - Canadian Chapter

Société internationale de recherches en chirologie inc. *See* International Society for Research in Palmistry Inc.

Société internationale des entreprises ÉCONOMUSÉ *Voir* Société internationale du réseau ÉCONOMUSÉE et Société ÉCONOMUSÉE du Québec

Société internationale du réseau ÉCONOMUSÉE et Société ÉCONOMUSÉE du Québec (SIRE) / International Economuseum Network Society

Maison Louis-S.-Saint-Laurent, 203, Grande-Allée est, Québec QC G1R 2H8
Tél: 418-694-4466; *Téléc:* 418-694-4410
info@economusees.com
www.economusees.com
www.facebook.com/SREQC
www.youtube.com/watch?v=jQJc3pT_qMg
Nom précédent: Société internationale des entreprises ÉCONOMUSÉ
Aperçu: *Dimension:* petite; *Envergure:* nationale; Organisme sans but lucratif; fondée en 1992
Mission: Conserver, développer et mettre en valeur les métiers et savoir-faire traditionnels selon le concept de l'économuséologie, en favorisant l'implantation d'entreprises ÉCONOMUSÉE à travers le pays, et ce, afin d'offrir au public un produit touristique et culturel de qualité
Membre(s) du bureau directeur:
Cyril Simard, Président directeur général
Finances: *Budget de fonctionnement annuel:* $500,000-$1.5 Million
Membre(s) du personnel: 6
Membre: 44; *Critères d'admissibilité:* Artisans

Bureau de l'Atlantique
#204, 25 Wentworth St., Dartmouth NS B2Y 2S7
Tél: 902-446-3409
Membre(s) du bureau directeur:
Tom Young, Regional Director

Société John Howard du Canada *See* The John Howard Society of Canada

La Société la Croix-Rouge canadienne *See* Canadian Red Cross

Société littéraire et historique de Québec *See* Literary & Historical Society of Québec

Société Logique

3210, rue Rachel est, Montréal QC H1W 1A4
Tél: 514-522-8284; *Téléc:* 514-522-2659
info@societelogique.org
www.societelogique.org
Aperçu: *Dimension:* petite; *Envergure:* provinciale; Organisme sans but lucratif; fondée en 1981
Mission: Promouvoir et intervenir dans le développement et la création d'environnements universellement accessibles
Affiliation(s): Confédération des organismes de personnes handicapées du Québec
Membre(s) du bureau directeur:
Jacques Dubois, Président
Finances: *Budget de fonctionnement annuel:* $250,000-$500,000; *Fonds:* Gouvernement provincial
Membre(s) du personnel: 10
Membre: 32
Activités: Consultation en aménagement et la promotion du concept d'accessibilité; recherche; formation; gestion immobilière; *Service de conférenciers:* Oui

Société Louis-Napoléon Dugal *Voir* Société Louis-Napoléon Dugal/Société Grande-Rivière

Société Louis-Napoléon Dugal/Société Grande-Rivière (SLND)

NB
Tél: 506-397-0930
sanbmc@nb.aibn.com
Nom précédent: Société Louis-Napoléon Dugal
Aperçu: *Dimension:* petite; *Envergure:* locale
Mission: Organisme qui prône un développement communautaire actif et positif. La Société Louis-Napoléon Dugal poursuit deux grands objectifs: Favoriser la vie en français au Madawaska & favoriser l'émancipation et l'épanouissement des francophones d'ici
Membre de: Société de l'Acadie du Nouveau-Brunswick (SANB)
Membre(s) du bureau directeur:
Maxime Caron, Coordonnatrice
Membre: 1,000-4,999

Société Makivik *See* Makivik Corporation

La societe Manitobaine de la SLA *See* ALS Society of Manitoba

Société mathématique du Canada *See* Canadian Mathematical Society

La Société Medicale Canadienne sur l'Addiction *See* Canadian Society of Addiction Medicine

Société médicale du Nouveau-Brunswick *See* New Brunswick Medical Society

La Société Mensa Canada *See* Mensa Canada Society

Société mondiale pour la protection des animaux *See* World Society for the Protection of Animals

Société Napoléonienne Internationale *See* International Napoleonic Society

Société nationale de bienfaisance en publicité *See* National Advertising Benevolent Society

Société nationale de l'Acadie (SNA)

307, rue Amirault Dieppe, Dieppe NB E1A 1G1
Tél: 506-853-0404; *Téléc:* 506-853-0400
www.snacadie.org
Aperçu: *Dimension:* moyenne; *Envergure:* nationale; Organisme sans but lucratif; fondée en 1881
Mission: Mène différentes activités sur les scènes interprovinciales et internationales afin de promouvoir et de défendre les droits et intérêts du peuple acadien
Membre(s) du bureau directeur:
Martin Arseneau, Directeur, Comunications
Membre: 8 réguliers, 4 affiliés; *Critères d'admissibilite:* Associations; *Comités:* Stratégie promotion d'artistes acadiens sur la scène internationale; Congrès Mondial Acadien; Commission Odyssée Acadienne
Prix, Bouses:
- Prix Littéraire France Acadie (Prix)
- Médaille Léger-Comeau (Prix)

Société nucléaire canadienne *See* Canadian Nuclear Society

Société numismatique d'Ottawa *See* Ottawa Numismatic Society

La Société Numismatique de Québec

CP 56036, Québec QC G1P 4P7
info@snquebec.ca
www.snquebec.ca
Aperçu: *Dimension:* petite; *Envergure:* provinciale; fondée en 1960
Mission: Regroupe des personnes d'origines variées et de situations diverses qui ont en commun leur intérêt pour la numismatique
Membre(s) du bureau directeur:
Pierre Minguy
Membre: *Montant de la cotisation:* $32 régulier; $15 internet; $45 Etats-Unis; $64 International
Activités: Bulletin; Réunions mensuelles; Exposition annuelle; Encan; *Bibliothèque*

La société numismatique de Vancouver *See* Vancouver Numismatic Society

Société Nunavummi Disabilities Makinnasuaqtiit *See* Nunavummi Disabilities Makinnasuaqtiit Society

Société ontarienne de gestion des déchets *See* Ontario Waste Management Association

Société ontarienne des arbitres et des régisseurs *See* Society of Ontario Adjudicators & Regulators

La société ontarienne des professionelles et professionnels de la nutrition en santé publique *See* Ontario Society of Nutrition Professionals in Public Health

La Société Opimian *See* Opimian Society

Société Parkinson - Region Maritime *See* Parkinson Society Maritime Region

Société Parkinson Canada *See* Parkinson Society Canada

Société Parkinson de l'est de l'Ontario *See* Parkinson Society of Eastern Ontario

Société Parkinson du Québec / Parkinson Society Québec

#1470, 550 rue Sherbrooke ouest, Montréal QC H3A 1B9
Tél: 514-861-4422; *Téléc:* 514-861-4510
Ligne sans frais: 800-720-1307
infos@parkinsonquebec.ca
www.parkinsonquebec.ca
Aperçu: *Dimension:* moyenne; *Envergure:* provinciale surveillé par Parkinson Society Canada
Membre(s) du bureau directeur:
Nicole Charpentier, Directrice générale
ncharpentier@parkinsonquebec.ca

Société Philatelique de Québec (SPQ)

CP 70076, Succ. Québec Centre, Québec QC G2J 0A1
societe.philatelique.quebec@s-p-q.org
www.s-p-q.org
Aperçu: *Dimension:* petite; *Envergure:* provinciale; fondée en 1929
Membre(s) du bureau directeur:
André Lafond, Président
Membre: 150
Activités: *Service de conférenciers:* Oui

Société planétaire pour l'assainissement de l'énergie *See* Planetary Association for Clean Energy, Inc.

Société pour enfants doués et surdoués (Ontario) *See* Association for Bright Children (Ontario)

Société pour l'étude de l'architecture au Canada *See* Society for the Study of Architecture in Canada

Société pour l'Étude de l'Égypte Ancienne *See* Society for the Study of Egyptian Antiquities

Société pour la nature et les parcs du Canada *See* Canadian Parks & Wilderness Society

Société pour la nature et les parcs du Canada, Section Québec *Voir* Canadian Parks & Wilderness Society

Société pour la promotion de l'enseignement de l'anglais, langue seconde, au Québec *See* Society for the Promotion of the Teaching of English as a Second Language in Quebec

Société pour les enfants handicapés du Québec (SEHQ) / Quebec Society for Disabled Children

2300, boul René-Lévesque ouest, Montréal QC H3H 2R5
Tél: 514-937-6171; *Téléc:* 514-937-0082
Ligne sans frais: 877-937-6171
sehq@enfantshandicapes.com

www.enfantshandicapes.com
www.facebook.com/enfantshandicapes
twitter.com/SEHQ
Aperçu: *Dimension:* moyenne; *Envergure:* provinciale; Organisme sans but lucratif; fondée en 1930 surveillé par Easter Seals Canada
Mission: Voué au bien-être des enfants handicapés et de leur famille; grâce aux contributions publiques qui lui sont versées et aux efforts conjugués de bénévoles et des permanents, la société offre des services directs et professionnels qui favorisent le développement personnel des enfants et leur intégration dans la communauté.
Membre(s) du bureau directeur:
Ronald Davidson, Directeur général, 877-937-6171 Ext. 210
rdavidson@enfantshandicapes.com
Carolle Desjardins, Directrice, Financement, 877-937-6171 Ext. 232
cdesjardins@enfantshandicapes.com
Nicole Amzallag, Séjours de groupes et classes nature, 877-937-6171 Ext. 212
namzallag@enfantshandicapes.com
Finances: *Budget de fonctionnement annuel:* $1.5 Million-$3 Million
Membre(s) du personnel: 65; 200 bénévole(s)
Membre: 1-99; *Montant de la cotisation:* Barème
Activités: *Evénements de sensibilisation:* Cabaret sur le Mont Royal, sept.; Classique Louis Coutu, sept.; Zone de Chute, sept.

Camp Papillon
210, av Papillon, Saint-Alphonse-Rodriguez QC J0K 2W0
Tel: 450-883-5642; *Fax:* 450-883-5642
Toll-Free: 877-937-6172
Membre(s) du bureau directeur:
Sylvianne Renaud, Directeur
srenaud@enfantshandicapes.com

La Société pour les troubles de l'humeur du Canada *See* Mood Disorders Society of Canada

Société Pro Musica Inc. / Pro Musica Society Inc.
#201, 3505, rue Ste-Famille, Montréal QC H2X 2L3
Tél: 514-845-0532; *Téléc:* 514-845-1500
Ligne sans frais: 877-445-0532
concerts@promusica.qc.ca
www.promusica.qc.ca
www.facebook.com/societepromusica
twitter.com/promusicamtl
Également appelé: La Société Pro Musica
Aperçu: *Dimension:* petite; *Envergure:* nationale; Organisme sans but lucratif; fondée en 1948
Mission: Promouvoir et présenter à Montréal la plus belle musique de chambre par les meilleurs interprètes d'ici et d'ailleurs; dans la série TOPAZE, promouvoir et offrir aux jeunes familles de meilleures conditions pour assister aux concerts avec un atelier d'animation musicale pour les enfants
Membre(s) du bureau directeur:
Louise-Andrée Baril, Directrice artistique
Monique Dubé, Directrice générale
Finances: *Fonds:* Conseil des arts et lettres du Québec; Conseil des arts de Montréal
Membre(s) du personnel: 2
Membre: *Critères d'admissibilité:* Adultes et étudiants agées de 15 à 85 ans

Société professionnelle des auteurs et des compositeurs du Québec (SPACQ)
#115, 4030, rue St-Ambroise, Montréal QC H4C 2C7
Tél: 514-845-3739; *Téléc:* 514-845-1903
Ligne sans frais: 866-445-3739
info@spacq.qc.ca
www.spacq.qc.ca
Aperçu: *Dimension:* petite; *Envergure:* nationale; Organisme sans but lucratif; fondée en 1981
Mission: Défendre les droits et les intérêts moraux, professionnels et économiques des auteurs et des compositeurs, ainsi que les droits qui se rapportent aux oeuvres, auprès des autorités gouvernementales.
Membre de: Confédération internationale des sociétés d'auteurs et compositeurs (CISAC)
Membre(s) du bureau directeur:
Pierre-Daniel Rheault, Directeur général
Sébastien Charest, Responsable, Formation permanente
scharest@spacq.qc.ca
Finances: *Budget de fonctionnement annuel:* $250,000-$500,000
Membre(s) du personnel: 5
Membre: 750; *Montant de la cotisation:* 75$; *Critères d'admissibilite:* Etre membre de la Société canadienne des auteurs, compositeurs et éditeurs de musique et/ou de la Société du droit de reproduction des auteurs, compositeurs et éditeurs du Canada
Activités: Ateliers de composition; *Stagiaires:* Oui; *Service de conférenciers:* Oui

La Société protectrice des animaux d'Ottawa *See* Ottawa Humane Society

Société protectrice des animaux du Nouveau-Brunswick *See* New Brunswick Society for the Prevention of Cruelty to Animals

Société Provancher d'histoire naturelle du Canada (SPHNC) / Provancher Society of Natural History of Canada
1400 rue de l'Aéroport, Québec QC G2G 1G6
Tél: 418-554-8636; *Téléc:* 418-831-8744
societe.provancher@gmail.com
www.provancher.qc.ca
www.facebook.com/groups/158959760781189
Aperçu: *Dimension:* petite; *Envergure:* provinciale; Organisme sans but lucratif; fondée en 1919
Mission: Société visant la protection de milieux naturels et l'éducation en sciences naturelles
Membre de: Reseau de milieux naturels protégés du Québec; Nature Québec; Institut Québécois de la Biodiversité
Membre(s) du bureau directeur:
Gilles Gaboury, Président
Eric-Yves Harvey, 1er Vice-Président
Louise Fortin, 2me Vice-Président
Michel Lepage, Secrétaire
André St-Hilaire, Trésorier
Elisabeth Bossert, Administratrice
Finances: *Budget de fonctionnement annuel:* $100,000-$250,000; *Fonds:* Cotisations des membres; dons; location de chalets
Membre(s) du personnel: 3; 25 bénévole(s)
Membre: 50 institutionnel; 1,500 individu; 30 associé; *Montant de la cotisation:* 70$ corporatif; 35$ famille; 30$ individu; *Critères d'admissibilite:* Amant de la nature, scientifiques
Activités: Visites guidées; inventaires fauniques; conférences sur la nature; location de chalets (Ile aux Basques); *Evénements de sensibilisation:* Marais Léon-Provancher, oct.

Société psoriasis du Canada *See* Psoriasis Society of Canada

Société québécoise d'espéranto (SQE) / Québec Esperanto Society (QES)
6358A, rue de Bordeaux, Montréal QC H2G 2R8
www.esperanto.qc.ca
Également appelé: Esperanto-Societo Kebekia
Aperçu: *Dimension:* petite; *Envergure:* provinciale; Organisme sans but lucratif; fondée en 1983 surveillé par Esperanto Association of Canada
Mission: Faire connaître et aider à l'apprentissage de l'espéranto; organiser des rencontres et favoriser l'utilisation de la langue; présenter les avantages de la langue et le mouvement mondial
Affiliation(s): Universala Esperanto-Asocio
Membre(s) du bureau directeur:
Normand Fleury, Président
Sylvano Auclair, Secrétaire-trésorier
silvano@esperanto.qc.ca
Membre: *Montant de la cotisation:* 25$
Activités: *Service de conférenciers:* Oui; *Bibliothèque* Bibliothèque publique rendez-vous

Société québécoise d'ethnologie (SQE)
Succ. #242, 310, boul Langelier, Québec QC G1K 5N3
Tél: 418-524-9090
info@sqe.qc.ca
www.sqe.qc.ca
Aperçu: *Dimension:* petite; *Envergure:* provinciale; Organisme sans but lucratif; fondée en 1975
Mission: Regroupe des personnes, professionnelles ou non de l'ethnologie, et des organismes intéressés à l'ethnologie et à la mise en valeur des patrimoines matériels et immatériels à des fins culturelles, sociales et scientifiques
Membre de: Fédération des sociétés d'histoire du Québec; Centre de valorisation du patrimoine vivant
Finances: *Budget de fonctionnement annuel:* Moins de $50,000
Membre: 1-99; *Montant de la cotisation:* 25$ individu; 15$ étudiant; 60$ institution; *Critères d'admissibilite:* Ethnologues; historiens
Prix, Bouses:
• Le prix Simone-Voyer (Prix)

Société Québécoise de droit international (SQDI)
Université du Québec à Montréal, CP 8888, Succ. Centre-Ville, Montréal QC H2L 4Y2
Tél: 514-987-3000; *Téléc:* 514-987-0115
info@sqdi.org
www.sqdi.org
www.linkedin.com/groups?gid=4184707
www.facebook.com/SocieteQuebecoisedeDroitInternational
twitter.com/SQDI_RQDI
Aperçu: *Dimension:* moyenne; *Envergure:* provinciale; fondée en 1982
Mission: De rassembler les gens qui sont intéressés à en apprendre sur le droit international et à en discuter, ainsi que de promouvoir le droit international au Québec
Membre(s) du bureau directeur:
Olivier Delas, Président, Conseil d'administration
Membre: Réguliers: 98; Étudiants: 301; Institutionels: 9
Activités: Conférences
Publications:
• Revue québécoise de droit international
Type: Revue; *Frequency:* Semestrielle
Profile: Articles présentera des études, des commentaires et des critiques de livres sur le droit international

Société québécoise de gériatrie (SQG)
a/s Mme Carole Labrie, 375, rue Argyll, Sherbrooke QC J1J 3H5
Tél: 819-346-9196; *Téléc:* 819-829-7145
clabrie.csss-iugs@ssss.gouv.qc.ca
www.sqgeriatrie.org
Aperçu: *Dimension:* petite; *Envergure:* provinciale; Organisme sans but lucratif; fondée en 1985
Membre(s) du bureau directeur:
Tamas Fülöp, Président
Finances: *Budget de fonctionnement annuel:* Moins de $50,000
Membre: 250; *Montant de la cotisation:* 50$; *Critères d'admissibilite:* Médecins et résidents
Activités: Congrès annuel

Société québécoise de l'autisme *Voir* Fédération québécoise de l'autisme et des autres troubles envahissants du développement

Société québécoise de la rédaction professionnelle (SQRP)
CP 18012, Succ. Ste-Rose, Laval QC H7L 6B2
Tél: 514-990-0430
info@sqrp.org
www.sqrp.org
www.linkedin.com/groups/SQRP-Société-québécoise-rédaction-professionne
www.facebook.com/172644542768672
Aperçu: *Dimension:* petite; *Envergure:* provinciale
Mission: Régrouper rédacteurs et rédactrices; établir des critères et évaluer la qualité de la rédaction des textes soumis; tenir un registre des membres; promouvoir la qualité de la rédaction et défendre les intérêts de la profession
Affliation(s): INTECOM
Membre(s) du bureau directeur:
Marie-Noël Pichelin, Présidente
Gilles Trudeau, Trésorier
Charles Allain, Secrétaire
Membre: *Montant de la cotisation:* Barème; *Critères d'admissibilite:* Examen d'agrément
Activités: *Service de conférenciers:* Oui

Société québécoise de la schizophrénie (SQS)
7401, rue Hochelaga, Montréal QC H1N 3M5
Tél: 514-251-4125; *Téléc:* 514-251-6347
Ligne sans frais: 866-888-2323
info@schizophrenie.qc.ca
www.schizophrenie.qc.ca
www.facebook.com/group.php?gid=116186171776523
twitter.com/SQSchizophrenie
Nom précédent: Association québécoise de la schizophrénie
Aperçu: *Dimension:* petite; *Envergure:* provinciale; Organisme sans but lucratif; fondée en 1988
Mission: Organisme communautaire dont les services et activités ont pour but d'apporter un soutien essentiel aux familles dont un être cher est atteint de schizophrénie; information, écoute, orientation et accompagnement font entre autres partie de notre mission
Membre de: Société canadienne de schizophrénie; Fédération des familles et amis de la personne atteinte de maladie mentale;

Association canadienne pour la santé mentale; Association québécoise pour la réadaptation psychosociale
Membre(s) du bureau directeur:
Francine Dubé, Directrice générale
fdube@schizophrenie.qc.ca
Finances: *Budget de fonctionnement annuel:* $100,000-$250,000
Membre(s) du personnel: 7
Membre: 500-999; *Critères d'admissibilité:* Famille et amis des personnes souffrant de schizophrénie
Activités: Conférences mensuelles de sept à juin

Société québécoise de lipidologie, de nutrition et de métabolisme *See* Québec Society of Lipidology, Nutrition & Metabolism Inc.

Société Québécoise de Psilogie inc (SQP)

375, boul Henri Bourassa ouest, Montréal QC H3L 1P2
Tél: 514-337-8292
Aperçu: *Dimension:* petite; *Envergure:* internationale; Organisme sans but lucratif; fondée en 1986
Mission: Études, échanges, rencontres traitant de psilogie pour favoriser la recherche, l'expérimentation, la publication; susciter la coopération entre les disciplines scientifiques; recueillir et gérer les fonds pour la poursuite des activités
Membre(s) du bureau directeur:
Philippe Mabilleau, Président et Porte-Parole
Finances: *Budget de fonctionnement annuel:* Moins de $50,000
Membre(s) du personnel: 10; 10 bénévole(s)
Membre: 3 institutionnel; 50 individu; 20 associé; *Montant de la cotisation:* 20$; *Critères d'admissibilité:* Chercheur sur base scientifique
Activités: *Bibliothèque* rendez-vous

Société québécoise de psychologie du travail (SQPTO)

533, rue de l'Atlantique, Mont-Saint-Hilaire QC J3H 0E8
Tél: 514-842-8178; *Téléc:* 514-842-8178
Ligne sans frais: 888-842-8178
permanence@sqpto.ca
www.sqpto.ca
www.facebook.com/sqpto
twitter.com/SQPTO
Également appelé: Société québécoise de psychologie du travail et des organisations
Aperçu: *Dimension:* petite; *Envergure:* provinciale; fondée en 1994
Membre(s) du personnel: 1; 3 bénévole(s)
Membre: 300; *Montant de la cotisation:* 125$, 40$ étudiants
Activités: Conférences, colloques, activite@s de formation;

Société québécoise de récupération et de recyclage

#200, 420, boul Charest est, Québec QC G1K 8M4
Tél: 418-643-0394; *Téléc:* 418-643-6507
Ligne sans frais: 800-807-0678
info@recyc-quebec.gouv.qc.ca
www.recyc-quebec.gouv.qc.ca
Également appelé: RECYC-QUÉBEC
Aperçu: *Dimension:* moyenne; *Envergure:* provinciale; Organisme sans but lucratif; fondée en 1990
Mission: Promouvoir, développer et de favoriser la réduction, le réemploi, la récupération et le recyclage des contenants, d'emballages, de matières ou de produits ainsi que leur valorisation dans une perspective de conservation des ressources
Membre(s) du bureau directeur:
Ginette Bureau, Président-directeur général
Johanne Riverin, Vice-présidente, Communications, sensibilisation et éducation
Finances: *Budget de fonctionnement annuel:* Plus de $5 Million
Activités: Coordination des activités de mise en valeur; gestion intégrée des pneux hors d'usage; gestion de la consigne sur les contenants à remplissage unique de bière ou de boissons gazeuses; développement des marchés et technologies dans le domaine de la mise en valeur des matières résiduelles; R&D; information, sensibilisation et éducation; promotion des produits québécois à contenu recyclé; publication de répertoires, guides, études et fiches; campagne sur la récupération des contenants à remplissage unique consignés; *Evénements de sensibilisation:* Semaine québécoise de réduction des déchets; *Stagiaires:* Oui

Bureau à Montréal
141, av du Président-Kennedy, 8e étage, Montréal QC H2X 1Y4
Tél: 514-352-5002; *Téléc:* 514-873-6542
Ligne sans frais: 800-807-0678

Société québécoise de science politique (SQSP)

a/s du Département de science politique, Université du Québec, CP 8888, Succ. Centre-Ville, Montréal QC H3C 3P8
Tél: 514-987-3000; *Téléc:* 514-987-0218
sqsp@er.uqam.ca
www.sqsp.uqam.ca
Aperçu: *Dimension:* petite; *Envergure:* provinciale
Mission: Favoriser l'avancement de la recherche et de l'enseignement en science politique; soutenir la diffusion des connaissances sur les phénomènes politiques
Membre de: Social Science Federation of Canada
Membre(s) du bureau directeur:
Daniel Salée, Président
Membre: *Montant de la cotisation:* 50$ étudiante; 60$ étudiante conjointe; 140$ régulière; 170$ régulière conjointe; *Critères d'admissibilité:* Professeurs et chercheurs en science politique
Activités: Congrès; colloques; conférences

Société québécoise de spéléologie (SQS)

4545, av Pierre-de Coubertin, Montréal QC H1V 0B2
Tél: 514-252-3006; *Téléc:* 514-252-3201
Ligne sans frais: 800-338-6636
info-sqs@speleo.qc.ca
www.speleo.qc.ca
www.facebook.com/101303566664
www.youtube.com/SPELEOSQS
Aperçu: *Dimension:* moyenne; *Envergure:* provinciale; Organisme sans but lucratif; fondée en 1970
Mission: De favoriser le développement de la spéléologie ainsi que la préservation du milieu cavernicole et de son environnement.
Membre de: Conseil québécois du Loisir; Regroupement Loisir Québec; Corporation de développement économique de l'Est; Science pour tous
Membre(s) du bureau directeur:
François Gélinas, Directeur général
fgelinas@speleo.qc.ca
Activités: *Stagiaires:* Oui; *Bibliothèque:* Centre de documentation

Société québécoise des auteurs dramatiques (SoQAD)

187, rue Sainte-Catherine, 3e étage, Montréal QC H2X 1K8
Tél: 514-596-3705; *Téléc:* 514-596-2953
soqad@aqad.qc.ca
www.aqad.qc.ca/indexsoqad.asp
Aperçu: *Dimension:* petite; *Envergure:* nationale; fondée en 1994
Mission: Défendre les intérêts matériels et moraux de ses mandants (auteurs lui ayant confié un mandat de gestion)
Affiliation(s): Association québécoise des auteurs dramatiques
Membre(s) du bureau directeur:
Marie-Louise Nadeau, Responsable du développement de la

Société québécoise des hostas et des hémérocalles (SQHH)

4101 est, rue Sherbrooke, Montréal QC H1X 2B2
Tél: 514-868-3078
info@millettephotomedia.com
sites.google.com/site/hostaquebec
Aperçu: *Dimension:* petite; *Envergure:* provinciale
Membre(s) du bureau directeur:
Réjean Millette, Président
Membre: *Montant de la cotisation:* 39$ individu 43$ famille

Société québécoise des psychothérapeutes professionnels (SQPP)

CP 68, Succ. Ahuntsic, Montréal QC H3L 3N5
Tél: 514-990-3403
info@sqpp.org
www.sqpp.org
Aperçu: *Dimension:* petite; *Envergure:* provinciale; fondée en 1991
Mission: Un regroupement multidisciplinaire de psychothérapeutes qui sont des professionnels de la psychothérapie régis par un code de déontologie; possèdent une formation académique universitaire ou son équivalent et une solide formation à la psychothérapie; ont accompli une démarche psychothérapeutique approfondie
Membre(s) du bureau directeur:
Andrée Thauvette-Poupart, Présidente
Finances: *Budget de fonctionnement annuel:* Moins de $50,000
8 bénévole(s)
Membre: 100-499
Activités: santé mentale

Société québécoise du dahlia

11, rue Bellerose, Dollard-des-Ormeaux, QC QC H9G 2A7
Tél: 450-747-6521
dahlia@videotron.qc.ca
www.sqdahlia.qc.ca
Aperçu: *Dimension:* petite; *Envergure:* locale; Organisme sans but lucratif; fondée en 1992
Mission: Regrouper les amateurs de dahlias et encourager la culture de cette plante; favoriser les échanges d'informations et de spécimens entre les membres
Affliation(s): American Dahlia Society; Fédération des Sociétés d'horticulture et d'Écologie du Québec; Société Canadienne du Glaïeul
Membre(s) du bureau directeur:
François Lefebvre, Président
flefebvre@videotron.qc.ca
Finances: *Budget de fonctionnement annuel:* Moins de $50,000
Membre(s) du personnel: 9
Membre: 100-499; *Montant de la cotisation:* 20$; *Critères d'admissibilité:* Amateurs de dahlias et de beaux jardins
Activités: Expositions; conférences; salons annuels; *Service de conférenciers:* Oui

Société québécoise pour l'étude de la religion

Université de Montréal, #490, 3333, Chemin Queen Mary, Montréal QC H3V 1A2
Tél: 514-343-6568; *Téléc:* 514-343-5738
Aperçu: *Dimension:* petite; *Envergure:* provinciale; fondée en 1989
Mission: Promouvoir la recherche, l'enseignement et la diffusion des connaissances dans les disciplines ayant pour objet l'étude de la religion
Membre(s) du bureau directeur:
Patrice Brodeur, Président
Membre: *Montant de la cotisation:* 50$ régulier; 25$ étudiant

Société québécoise pour la défense des animaux (SQDA) / Québec Society for the Defense of Animals (QSDA)

#102, 847, rue Cherrier, Montréal QC H2L 1H6
Tél: 514-524-1970
info@sqda.org
www.sqda.org
Aperçu: *Dimension:* moyenne; *Envergure:* provinciale; Organisme sans but lucratif; fondée en 1976 surveillé par Canadian Federation of Humane Societies
Mission: Faire connaître et respecter le monde animal par tous les moyens possibles; obtenir une législation modifiée pour la protection de toute espèce; Combattre la destruction de notre faune; exposer l'aberration de l'élevage intensif; Contrôler l'expérimentation animale
Affliation(s): The World Society for the Protection of Animals - England; The Royal Society for the Prevention of Cruelty to Animals - England; The Canadian Federation of Humane Societies; Société nationale pour la défense des animaux - France
Membre(s) du bureau directeur:
Ghislain A. Arsenault, Président
Membre: 500; *Montant de la cotisation:* 20$/an; 250$ bienfaiteur
Activités: *Evénements de sensibilisation:* Campagne annuelle de déménagement

Société royale d'astronomie du Canada *See* Royal Astronomical Society of Canada

La Société royale de philatélie du Canada *See* The Royal Philatelic Society of Canada

La Société royale du Canada *See* The Royal Society of Canada

La Société royale du Commonwealth du Canada *See* The Royal Commonwealth Society of Canada

Société royale héraldique du Canada *See* Royal Heraldry Society of Canada

Société Saint-Jean-Baptiste de Montréal (SSJBM)

82, rue Sherbrooke ouest, Montréal QC H2X 1X3
Tél: 514-843-8851; *Téléc:* 514-844-6369
www.ssjb.com
www.facebook.com/groups/84605646085
twitter.com/ssjbm
Aperçu: *Dimension:* moyenne; *Envergure:* provinciale; fondée en 1834
Mission: Une société nationale qui participe de façon non partisane à l'évolution politique, sociale, économique et culturelle du Québec par ses actions, ses études, ses interventions et ses

campagnes d'opinion
Membre de: Mouvement national des Québécoises et Québécois
Membre(s) du bureau directeur:
Mario Beaulieu, Président général
Membre(s) du personnel: 14
Membre: 15 000; *Montant de la cotisation:* 10 $; *Comités:* Comité de la fête nationale de la Saint-Jean
Activités: La Fondation Ludger-Duvernay; La Fondation Prêt d'Honneur; Fondation Langelier; Service d'Entraide
Prix, Bouses:
• Prix Séraphin-Marion (Prix)
Créé en 1984; décerné à une personnalité qui défend les droits de la francophonie hors-Québec
• Prix André-Guérin (Prix)
Créé en 1990; décerné à une personnalité canadienne-française qui s'illustre dans le domaine du cinéma et vidéo
• Prix Léon-Lortie (Prix)
Established 1987; awarded for achievement in the area of pure & applied sciences
• Prix Chomedey-de-Maisonneuve (Prix)
Créé en 1983; décerné à une personnalité dont les réalisations contribuent au rayonnement de Montréal
• Prix Maurice-Richard (Prix)
Established 1979; $1,500 & a medal awarded annually to a French Canadian in recognition of outstanding achievement in sports & athletics in serving the higher interests of the French Canadian people
• Prix Calixa-Lavallée (Prix)
Established 1959; $1,500 & a medal awarded annually to a French Canadian in recognition of outstanding achievement in music in serving the higher interests of the French Canadian people
• Prix Victor-Morin (Prix)
Créé en 1962; décerné à une personnalité canadienne-française qui s'illustre dans le domaine des arts de la scène
• Prix Esdras-Minville (Prix)
Créé en 1978; décerné à une personnalité canadienne-française qui s'illustre dans le domaine des sciences humaines
• Prix Bene Merenti De Patria (Prix)
Créée en 1923, cette médaille souligne les mérites d'un compatriote ayant rendu des services exceptionnels à la patrie. La maquette est l'oeuvre d'un artiste qui a préparé les chars allégoriques de nos grands défilés pendant de nombreuses années *Amount:* Médaille d'argent
• Prix Patriote de l'année (Prix)
Décerné à une personnalité qui s'est distinguée dans la défense des intérêts du Québec et de la démocratie des peuples, en mémoire des Patriotes des années 1830; créé en 1975
• Prix Ludger-Duvernay (Prix)
Le prix a été crée en 1944 afin de signaler les mérites d'un compatriote dont la compétence et le rayonnement dans le domaine intellectuel et littéraire servent les intérêts supérieurs de la nation québécoise; le prix est de 3 000 $, accompagne une médaille, et est attribué à tous les trois ans
• Prix Louis Philippe-Hébert (Prix)
Créé en 1971; décerné à une personnalité canadienne-française qui s'illustre dans le domaine des arts plastiques
• Prix Olivar-Asselin (Prix)
Established 1955; $1,500 & a medal awarded annually to a French Canadian in recognition of outstanding achievement in journalism in serving the higher interests of the French Canadian people

Société Saint-Jean-Baptiste du Centre du Québec

449, rue Notre-Dame, Drummondville QC J2B 2K9
Tél: 819-478-2519; *Téléc:* 819-472-7460
Ligne sans frais: 800-943-2519
info@ssjbcq.qc.ca
www.ssjbcq.qc.ca
Aperçu: *Dimension:* moyenne; *Envergure:* locale; Organisme sans but lucratif; fondée en 1944
Mission: Promouvoir le développement et l'unité du peuple québécois dans tous les aspects de la vie en société et dans ses intérêts les plus dignes en favorisant: son émancipation dans le domaine économique; son épanouissement dans le domaine culturel; sa réalisation dans le domaine politique; sa solidarité dans le domaine social; et, son perfectionnement dans le domaine spirituel
Affliation(s): Mouvement national des québécois et québécoises
Membre(s) du bureau directeur:
Yvon Camirand, Président
Finances: *Budget de fonctionnement annuel:* $500,000-$1.5 Million
Membre(s) du personnel: 6; 200 bénévole(s)
Membre: 33 000; *Montant de la cotisation:* 5$ individu
Activités: *Evénements de sensibilisation:* Francofête, mars; Concours J'affiche en français, mars
Prix, Bouses:
• Prix Lionel-Groulx (Prix)
Promotion de l'histoire ou du patrimoine québécois
• Prix Raymond-Beaudet (Prix)
Le dévouement et le nationalisme
• Prix Monseigneur-Parenteau (Prix)
Engagement communautaire et socioculturel

La Société Saint-Pierre

CP 430, 15584 Cabot Trail Highway, Cheticamp NS B0E 1H0
Tél: 902-224-2642; *Téléc:* 902-224-1579
lestroispignons@ns.sympatico.ca
www.lestroispignons.com
Également appelé: Les Trois Pignons
Aperçu: *Dimension:* petite; *Envergure:* locale; Organisme sans but lucratif; fondée en 1947
Mission: Vise à la conservation de notre héritage et à la promotion de l'aspect intellectuel, culturel, social et économique des Acadiens du Cap-Breton
Membre(s) du bureau directeur:
Lisette Aucoin-Bourgeois, Directrice générale
lisettebourgeois@ns.sympatico.ca
Finances: *Budget de fonctionnement annuel:* $100,000-$250,000
Membre(s) du personnel: 3; 100 bénévole(s)
Membre: 215; *Montant de la cotisation:* 10$ individuel; 15 famille; *Critères d'admissibilite:* Acadien/francophone
Activités: *Bibliothèque:* Centre de généalogie

Société Saint-Thomas-d'Aquin (SSTA)

5, av Maris Stella, Summerside PE C1N 6M9
Tél: 902-436-4881; *Téléc:* 902-436-6936
administration@ssta.org
www.ssta.org
www.facebook.com/SaintThomasdAquin
twitter.com/commSSTA
Aperçu: *Dimension:* petite; *Envergure:* provinciale; Organisme sans but lucratif; fondée en 1919
Mission: Travailler pour que tout Acadien, Acadienne ou francophone puissent vivre et s'épanouir (individuellement et collectivement) en français à l'Île-du-Prince-Édouard; regrouper les Acadiens, Acadiennes et francophones de l'Ile-du-Prince-Édouard au sein d'une même association; représenter ses membres auprès du gouvernement municipal, provincial et national; revendiquer leurs droits; établir et administrer un fonds devant servir d'aide financière aux étudiant(e)s acadiens, acadiennes et francophones de l'Ile-du-Prince-Édouard dans tous les secteurs; développer des relations amicales entre les Acadiens, Acadiennes et francophones de l'Ile-du-Prince-Édouard et les autres francophones du Canada et des pays étrangers
Affliation(s): SNA-Société Nationale de l'Acadie; FCFA-Fédération des communautés francophones et acadienne du Canada
Membre(s) du bureau directeur:
Jeannita Bernard, Directrice Générale par intérim
dg@ssta.org
Crystal Barriault, Contact
reception@ssta.org
Finances: *Budget de fonctionnement annuel:* $100,000-$250,000; *Fonds:* Gouvernement fédéral
Membre(s) du personnel: 6; 50 bénévole(s)
Membre: 17 institutionnel; 2,000 individu; *Montant de la cotisation:* $25 institutionnel; 30$ couple; $20 étudiant; $20 individu
Activités: La SSTA gère le programme de bourses de la Fondation acadienne d'aide aux étudiants et étudiantes

Comité du Carrefour Isle-Saint-Jean
5, promenade Acadienne, Charlottetown PE C1C 1M2
Tél: 902-368-1895; *Téléc:* 902-566-5989
accueil@carrefourisj.org
www.carrefourisj.org
Membre(s) du bureau directeur:
Émile Gallant, Président

Comité régional la Belle-Alliance ltée
5, av Maris Stella, Summerside PE C1N 6M9
Tél: 902-888-1681; *Téléc:* 902-888-1686
www.belle-alliance.ca
Membre(s) du bureau directeur:
Terry Couture, Président
tjcouture@edu.pe.ca

Comité régional Rév. S-E-Perrey
119, ch DeBlois, rte 157, Tignish PE C0B 2B0
Tél: 902-882-0475; *Téléc:* 902-882-0482
seperrey@seperrey.org
Membre(s) du bureau directeur:
Yvonne Deagle, Présidente
ydeagle@pei.sympatico.org

Conseil Acadien de Rustico
Centre acadien Grand Rustico, Rustico PE
Tél: 902-963-3252; *Téléc:* 902-963-3442
www.conseilacadien.com
Membre(s) du bureau directeur:
Michelle Pineau, Co-Présidente
michelle.pineau@conseilacadienrustico.org
Andy Gallant, Co-Président
andy.gallant@conseilacadienrustico.org

Conseil scolaire-communautaire Évangéline
CP 124, 1596, rte 124 Abram-Village, Wellington PE C0B 2E0
Tél: 902-854-2166; *Téléc:* 902-854-2981
csce@teleco.org
www.cscevangeline.ca
Membre(s) du bureau directeur:
Caroline Arsenault, Présidente

Le comité acadien et francophone de l'Est
CP 858, 95, rte 310, RR#4, Fortune PE C0A 2B0
Tél: 902-687-7179; *Téléc:* 902-687-7176
cafe@ssta.org
www.cafesouris.com
Membre(s) du bureau directeur:
Tina White, Présidente
tmwhite.edu.pe.ca

Société Santé en français (SSF)

#201, 291, rue Dalhousie, Ottawa ON K1N 7E5
Tél: 613-244-1889; *Téléc:* 613-244-0283
info@santefrancais.ca
www.santefrancais.ca
Aperçu: *Dimension:* moyenne; *Envergure:* nationale; fondée en 2002 surveillé par Fédération des communautés francophones et acadienne du Canada
Mission: Pour améliorer l'accès et la qualité des services de soins de santé en français au Canada
Affliation(s): Réseau de santé en français de Terre-Neuve-et-Labrador; Réseau Santé en français I.-P.-É; Réseau Santé - Nouvelle-Écosse; Réseau-action Communautaire; Réseau-action Formation et recherche; Réseau-action Organisation des services; Société Santé et Mieux-être en français du Nouveau-Brunswick; Réseau francophone de santé du Nord de l'Ontario; Réseau santé en français du Moyen-Nord de l'Ontario; Réseau franco-santé du Sud de l'Ontario; Réseau des services de santé en français de l'Est de l'Ontario; Conseil communauté en santé du Manitoba; Réseau Santé en français de la Saskatchewan
Membre(s) du bureau directeur:
Michel Tremblay, Directeur général, 613-244-1889 Ext. 232
m.tremblay@santefrancais.ca
Aurel Schofield, Président
Membre: 17 associations; *Critères d'admissibilite:* Les associations dont le but est d'améliorer les services de soins de santé en français, qui sont situés dans les provinces où la majorité ne parle pas français comme première langue

Société Santé et Mieux-être en français du Nouveau-Brunswick (SSMEFFNB)

CP 1764, Moncton NB E1C 9X6
Tél: 506-389-3351; *Téléc:* 506-389-3366
ssmefnb@nb.aibn.com
www.ssmefnb.ca
www.facebook.com/SSMEFNB
twitter.com/SSMEFNB
Aperçu: *Dimension:* petite; *Envergure:* provinciale surveillé par Société santé en français
Membre(s) du bureau directeur:
Gilles Vienneau, Directeur général

Société statistique du Canada *See* Statistical Society of Canada

Société St-Jean-Baptiste Richelieu-Yamaska (SSBRY)

151, rue Robert, Saint-Hyacinthe QC J2S 4L7
Tél: 450-773-8535; *Téléc:* 450-773-8262
Ligne sans frais: 888-773-8535
ssjb@maskatel.net
www.ssjbry.org
www.facebook.com/ssjbry

Aperçu: *Dimension:* moyenne; *Envergure:* locale; fondée en 1946
Mission: Coordination de la fête nationale du Québec
Affliation(s): Mouvement national des Québécois

Société St-Léonard du Canada *See* St. Leonard's Society of Canada

Société théologique canadienne *See* Canadian Theological Society

Société touristique des Autochtones du Québec (STAQ) / Québec Aboriginal Tourism Corporation
#220, 50, boul Maurice-Bastien, Wendake QC G0A 4V0
Tel: 418-843-5030
Toll-Free: 877-698-7827
info@tourismeautochtone.com
www.tourismeautochtone.com
www.facebook.com/TourismeAutochtoneQuebec
twitter.com/AutochtoneQC
www.youtube.com/user/TourismeAutochtone
Previous Name: Société touristique Innu
Overview: A small provincial organization
Mission: Créer, au moyen du tourisme, des activités propices au développement social et économique des communautés autochtones
Chief Officer(s):
Dave Laveau, Directeur général
dlaveau@tourismeautochtone.com
Staff Member(s): 6
Membership: *Fees:* Barème; *Member Profile:* Intervenants en tourisme des nations amérindiennes et inuites
Activities: Formation des ressources humaines en tourisme; banque d'informations; bulletins trimestriels; promotion et représentation du tourisme autochtone; commercialisation des produits

Société touristique Innu *See* Société touristique des Autochtones du Québec

Société zoologique de Montréal *See* Zoological Society of Montréal

Les Sociétés Canadiennes de Technologies Médicales *See* Canada's Medical Technology Companies

Society for Canadian Women in Science & Technology (SCWIST) / Société des canadiennes dans la science et la technologie
#311, 525 Seymour St., Vancouver BC V6B 3H7
Tel: 604-893-8657
esourcecentre@scwist.ca
www.scwist.ca
www.linkedin.com/groups?gid=1915550
www.facebook.com/167831516563792
twitter.com/SCWIST
Overview: A small national charitable organization founded in 1981
Mission: To promote equal opportunities for women in scientific, technical & engineering careers; to educate public about careers in science & technology particularly to improve social attitudes on the stereotyping of careers in science; to assist educators by providing current information on careers & career training in sciences & scientific policies
Chief Officer(s):
Rosine Hage-Moussa, President
Staff Member(s): 1
Membership: *Fees:* $100 sustaining; $60 professional; $20 student/retired/unemployed; *Member Profile:* Interest in promoting women in science & technology; *Committees:* Communications; Events; Fundraising; Grants; IWIS; ms infinity; Volunteer
Activities: 5-6 regular program meetings of various topics; collection of gender free science & mathematics examples of questions; Ms. Infinity & Hands On Math & Sciences held in May in community colleges & high schools throughout province; *Speaker Service:* Yes; *Library:* Resource Centre;

Society for Disability Arts & Culture *See* KickStart Disability Arts & Culture

Society for Educational Visits & Exchanges in Canada (SEVEC) / Société éducative de visites et d'échanges au Canada
#201, 1150 Morrison Dr., Ottawa ON K2H 8S9
Tel: 613-727-3832; *Fax:* 613-727-3831
Toll-Free: 800-387-3832
info@sevec.ca
www.sevec.ca
www.facebook.com/SEVECanada
twitter.com/sevec
www.youtube.com/user/SEVECanada
Previous Name: Bilingual Exchange Secretariat & Visites interprovinciales
Overview: A large national charitable organization founded in 1936
Mission: To create, facilitate & promote enriching educational opportunities within Canada for the development of mutual respect & understanding through programs of exploration in language & culture
Member of: Canadian Education Association
Chief Officer(s):
Mary Reeves, Chair
Françoise Gagnon, Executive Director
fgagnon@sevec.ca
Heather Daly, Director, Finance & Administration
hdaly@sevec.ca
Finances: *Annual Operating Budget:* Greater than $5 Million; *Funding Sources:* Canadian Heritage (Exchanges Canada); membership dues; individual corporate donations; cost recovery
Staff Member(s): 10; 50 volunteer(s)
Membership: 500; *Fees:* $50
Activities: *Speaker Service:* Yes
Awards:
• SEVEC Award of Merit (Award)

Society for Existential & Phenomenological Theory & Culture (EPTC) / Société de Théorie et de Culture existentialises et phénoménologique (TCEP)
www.eptc-tcep.net
Previous Name: Sartre Society of Canada
Overview: A small national organization founded in 1987
Affiliation(s): Humanities & Social Sciences Federation of Canada
Chief Officer(s):
Matthew King, President
mail.matthew.king@gmail.com
John Duncan, Treasurer
Activities: Invites papers & panel proposals in which any aspects of existential or phenomenological theory or culture are discussed; for example, papers or panels proposals dealing with theoretical or cultural issues in relation to contributions made by authors such as Kierkegaard, Nietzsche, Husserl, Heidegger, Levinas, Malraux, Sartre, Camus, Merleau-Ponty, or Beauvoir, & their critics
Meetings/Conferences: • Society for Existential & Phenomenological Theory & Culture 2015 Conference, June, 2015, Ottawa, ON

Society for International Ministries (SIM Canada)
10 Huntingdale Blvd., Toronto ON M1W 2S5
Tel: 416-497-2424; *Fax:* 416-497-2444
Toll-Free: 800-294-6918
info@sim.ca
www.sim.ca
www.facebook.com/SIMCANADA1
twitter.com/SIMCANADA1
www.youtube.com/simcanadavideo
Overview: A small international organization founded in 1893
Mission: To evangelize the unreached & minister to human need
Chief Officer(s):
Gregg Bryce, Executive Director
Finances: *Annual Operating Budget:* $3 Million-$5 Million
Staff Member(s): 30
Membership: 300
Activities: *Speaker Service:* Yes

Society for Manitobans with Disabilities Inc. (SMD)
825 Sherbrook St., Winnipeg MB R3A 1M5
Tel: 204-975-3010; *Fax:* 204-975-3073
Toll-Free: 866-282-8041; *TTY:* 204-784-3012
info@smd.mb.ca
smd.mb.ca
Overview: A large provincial charitable organization founded in 1946 overseen by Easter Seals Canada
Mission: To promote the full participation & equality of people with disabilities: To provide a full range of rehabilitation services; To facilitate the development of a receptive & supportive environment
Affiliation(s): Autism Society Manitoba
Chief Officer(s):
David L. Steen, Executive Director/President/CEO
Finances: *Annual Operating Budget:* Greater than $5 Million; *Funding Sources:* Provincial government; United Way; The March of Dimes; Easter Seals; fees
Activities: Providing a variety of services to children & adults with disabilities; *Speaker Service:* Yes; *Library:* Stephen Sparling Library; Open to public

Central Regional Office
#100, 30 Stephen St., Morden MB R6M 2G5
Tel: 204-822-7412; *Fax:* 204-822-7413
Toll-Free: 800-269-5451; *TTY:* 204-822-7412
smd.mb.ca

Eastman Regional Office
#5, 227 Main St., Steinbach MB R5G 1Y7
Tel: 204-326-5336; *Fax:* 204-326-9762
Toll-Free: 800-497-8196; *TTY:* 204-346-3998
smd.mb.ca

Interlake Regional Office
382 Main St., Selkirk MB R1A 1T8
Tel: 204-785-9338; *Fax:* 204-785-9340
Toll-Free: 888-831-4213; *TTY:* 204-482-5638
smd.mb.ca

Northern Regional Office
#303, 83 Churchill Dr., Thompson MB R8N 0L6
Tel: 204-778-4277; *Fax:* 204-778-4461
Toll-Free: 888-367-0268; *TTY:* 204-778-4277
smd.mb.ca

Parkland Regional Office
#411, 27 - 2 Ave. SW, Dauphin MB R7N 3E5
Tel: 204-622-2293; *Fax:* 204-622-2260
Toll-Free: 800-844-2307; *TTY:* 204-622-2293
smd.mb.ca

SMD Self-Help Clearinghouse
825 Sherbrook St., Winnipeg MB R3A 1M5
Tel: 204-975-3010; *Fax:* 204-975-3073
Toll-Free: 866-282-8041; *TTY:* 204-975-3012
smd.mb.ca
Mission: To foster collaboration & advocacy to assist self-help organizations

Westman Regional Office
#140, 340 - 9th St., Brandon MB R7A 6C2
Tel: 204-726-6157; *Fax:* 204-726-6499
Toll-Free: 800-813-3325; *TTY:* 204-726-6157
smd.mb.ca

Wheelchair Services
1111 Winnipeg Ave., Winnipeg MB R3E 0S2
Tel: 204-975-3250; *Fax:* 204-975-3240
Toll-Free: 800-836-5551; *TTY:* 204-975-3240
smd.mb.ca

Society for Mesopotamian Studies *See* The Canadian Society for Mesopotamian Studies

Society for Muscular Dystrophy Information International (SMDI)
PO Box 7490, Bridgewater NS B4V 2X6
Tel: 902-685-3961; *Fax:* 902-685-3962
smdi@auracom.com
www.nsnet.org/smdi
Overview: A medium-sized international charitable organization founded in 1983
Mission: To facilitate international contact by producing website, & publications (newsletters, books) & by the sharing of neuromuscular & disability information between those concerned with muscular dystrophy &/or allied disorders
Finances: *Funding Sources:* Donations; Membership dues
Membership: *Fees:* $25 individuals; $35 organizations

Society for Organic Urban Land Care (SOUL)
PO Box 281, 2530 Alberni Hwy., Coombs BC V0R 1M0
Tel: 250-386-7685
info@organiclandcare.org
www.organiclandcare.org
www.facebook.com/SOUL.Organic.Land.Care
Overview: A small national organization
Mission: SOUL was formed in response to the growing need for ecologically responsible land care practices. Our mission is to promote and support organic practices in our communities through education, certification and standardization.
Chief Officer(s):
Michael Cowan, President
Membership: 100; *Fees:* $30 public/professional; $250 supporting

Society for Personal Growth
Edmonton AB

Tel: 780-468-9435
prh@prh-canada.org
prh-canada.com
Overview: A small local charitable organization founded in 1984
Mission: To provide effective tools to foster personal growth & the emergence of the inner self; to help couples improve communication & build harmony & unity together; to facilitate the growth of parents & enable them to understand their children so they can live & grow harmoniously; to improve the quality of life in groups & in the workplace; to provide a place to achieve these objectives
Finances: *Funding Sources:* Regional government; Client fees
Activities: Personality & Human Relations (PRH) workshops; Couples & parenting workshops

Society for Quality Education (SQE)

57 Twyford Rd., Toronto ON M9A 1W5
Tel: 416-231-7247; *Fax:* 416-237-0108
Toll-Free: 888-856-5535
info@societyforqualityeducation.org
www.societyforqualityeducation.org
www.facebook.com/SQEducation
twitter.com/SQESocQualEd
Previous Name: Organization for Quality Education
Overview: A small local charitable organization
Mission: To advance public & private education in Canada by disseminating authoritative information on educational governance & methodology.
Chief Officer(s):
Doretta Wilson, Executive Director
Malkin Dare, President, 519-884-3166
Finances: *Funding Sources:* Foundations
Staff Member(s): 1
Activities: DVD on charter schools; Demonstration Remedial Reading Project; Comparison of Provincial Science Curricula; *Speaker Service:* Yes

Society for Reproduction Rights of Authors, Composers & Publishers Canada ***Voir*** Société du droit de reproduction des auteurs, compositeurs et éditeurs au Canada (SODRAC 2003) inc.

The Society for Safe & Caring Schools & Communities

11010 - 142 St., Edmonton AB T5N 2R1
Tel: 780-822-1500
office@sacsc.ca
safeandcaring.wordpress.com
www.facebook.com/safeandcaring
twitter.com/safeandcaring
www.youtube.com/safecaring
Overview: A small provincial organization
Mission: To encourage school practices that model & reinforce socially responsible & respectful behaviours, so that learning & teaching can take place in a safe & caring environment
Chief Officer(s):
Bev Esslinger, President
Marni Pearce, Executive Director
mpearce@sacsc.ca
Staff Member(s): 8
Membership: *Fees:* Free

Society for Socialist Studies (SSS) / Société d'études socialistes (SÉS)

c/o Kanchan Sarker, Sociology, Univ. of BC, Okanagan Campus, 3333 University Way, Kelowna BC V1V 1V7
Tel: 250-807-8707; *Fax:* 250-807-8001
admin@socialiststudies.ca
socialiststudies.ca
www.facebook.com/SocietyForSocialistStudies
Overview: A small national charitable organization founded in 1967
Mission: The Society creates, fosters, & publishes, academic & scholarly research & analysis in Canada, with emphasis on socialist, feminist, anti-racist, & ecological points of view.
Member of: Humanities & Social Science Federation of Canada
Chief Officer(s):
Kanchan Sarker, President
kanchan.sarker@ubc.ca
Murray Cooke, Vice-President
mcooke@yorku.ca
Matthew Brett, Secretary & Moderator, E-mail List
David Huxtable, Treasurer
huxtable@uvic.ca
Finances: *Funding Sources:* Membership fees
Membership: 350; *Fees:* $60 regular; $30 student/low incomed; $100 Canadian institution; US$100 foreign institutions; *Member Profile:* Membership includesany person underwriting the Society's purpose.; *Committees:* Canadian Federation of Humanities and Social Sciences Congress Programme Committee; Journal Editorial Committee
Activities: Organizes conferences, seminars, & workshops; publishes educational material; advances public education
Publications:
• Socialist Studies: Journal of the Society for Socialist Studies
Type: Journal; *Editor:* Sandra Rollings-Magnusson

Society for Technology & Rehabilitation ***See*** Ability Society of Alberta

Society for the Preservation & Encouragement of Barber Shop Quartet Singing in America Inc. ***See*** The Harmony Foundation

Society for the Preservation & Encouragement of Barber Shop Quartet Singing in America Inc. ***See*** The Harmony Foundation

Society for the Preservation of Old Mills - Canadian Chapter (SPOOM)

PO Box 352, 93 Woolwich St., Breslau ON N0B 1M0
Tel: 519-633-5577
spoomer@sympatico.ca
www.hips.com/spoomcanada
Overview: A small national organization founded in 1999
Mission: To promote interest in old mills, their history, function & preservation
Affliation(s): Society for the Preservation of Old Mills USA
Chief Officer(s):
Maryanne Szuck, Treasurer
Finances: *Annual Operating Budget:* Less than $50,000
Staff Member(s): 6
Membership: 100; *Fees:* $20; *Member Profile:* Anyone interested in old mills

Society for the Promotion of the Teaching of English as a Second Language in Quebec (SPEAQ) / Société pour la promotion de l'enseignement de l'anglais, langue seconde, au Québec

#2, 6818, Rue Saint-Denis, Montréal QC H2S 2S2
Tel: 514-271-3700; *Fax:* 514-271-4587
speaq@speaq.qc.ca
www.speaq.qc.ca
Overview: A medium-sized provincial charitable organization founded in 1976
Mission: To bring together persons engaged or interested in the teaching of English as a second language in Quebec; To promote & develop the professional & economic interests of its members; To create a favourable climate for the development of teaching English as a second language in Quebec//Promouvoir l'enseignement de l'anglais, langue seconde au Québec
Member of: Conseil pédagogique interdisciplinaire du Québec
Affliation(s): Teachers of English to Speakers of Other Languages, Inc; Canadian Association of Second Language Teachers; Society for Educational Visits & Exchanges in Canada
Chief Officer(s):
Micheline Schinck, President
Monique Mainella, Vice President
Finances: *Annual Operating Budget:* $100,000-$250,000; *Funding Sources:* Patrimoine Canada
Staff Member(s): 1; 7 volunteer(s)
Membership: 800; *Fees:* $10-$20; *Member Profile:* Individuals interested in the teaching of English as a second language
Activities: Annual Convention; *Awareness Events:* Intensig/Sugar Shack Smash; RASCALS Colloquium; SPEAQ Campus
Awards:
• Prix de la SPEAQ (Award)
• Prix du mérite en enseignement (Award)
• Prix du conseil d'administration (Award)

The Society for the Propagation of the Faith (SPF)

2219 Kennedy Rd., Toronto ON M1T 3G5
Tel: 416-699-7077; *Fax:* 416-699-9019
Toll-Free: 800-897-8865
missions@missionsocieties.ca
www.missionsocieties.ca
Overview: A small national charitable organization founded in 1889
Mission: To educate local clergy & religious men & women in developing countries
Chief Officer(s):
Alex Osei, C.S.Sp., National Director
Finances: *Annual Operating Budget:* $500,000-$1.5 Million; *Funding Sources:* Donations
Staff Member(s): 8
Activities: Funds the training of local clergy & religious missions; *Speaker Service:* Yes

Society for the Retired & Semi-Retired ***See*** Seniors Association of Greater Edmonton

Society for the Study of Architecture in Canada (SSAC) / Société pour l'étude de l'architecture au Canada (SEAC)

PO Box 2302, Stn. D, Ottawa ON K1P 5W5
e-mail: ssac.seac@gmail.com
canada-architecture.org
www.flickr.com/photos/ssac_photos
Overview: A small national organization founded in 1974
Mission: To promote the study of Canadian architecture including an examination of both historical & cultural issues relating to buildings, districts, cities & the cultural landscapes; to encourage the collection & preservation of Canada's architectural records; to encourage preservation of the built environment
Affliation(s): Society of Architectural Historians
Chief Officer(s):
Peter Coffman, President
Finances: *Annual Operating Budget:* $50,000-$100,000; *Funding Sources:* Membership dues; SSHRC
Membership: *Fees:* $35 student; $40 low income; $65 individual; $90 corporate; *Member Profile:* Individuals, organizations, institutions & corporations which have a particular interest in the study of architecture in Canada
Awards:
• Martin Eli Weil Award (Award)
Student essay competition on role of the built environment

Society for the Study of Egyptian Antiquities (SSEA) / Société pour l'Étude de l'Égypte Ancienne

PO Box 19004, Stn. Walmer, 360A Bloor St. West, Toronto ON M5S 3C9
Tel: 647-520-4339
info@thessea.org
www.thessea.org
www.facebook.com/SocietyfortheStudyofEgyptianAntiquities
Overview: A medium-sized international charitable organization founded in 1969
Mission: To stimulate interest in Egyptology; To assist with research & training in the field; To sponsor & promote archaeological expeditions to Egypt
Member of: Canadian Association of Learned Journals
Affliation(s): Canadian Institute in Egypt; Canadian Mediterranean Institute
Chief Officer(s):
Lyn Green, National President
Finances: *Funding Sources:* Membership fees; Donations; SSHRC Aid to Research & Transfer Journals
Membership: *Fees:* $30 student; $45 associate; $60 full; $80 library/institution; *Member Profile:* Individuals; Students; Institutions; *Committees:* Hospitality; Fieldwork & Research; Fundraising; Publications; Scholars' Colloquium; Symposium; Bylaws & Policy; Finance
Activities: Annual symposium; Main lecture series (4); Mini-lecture series; *Library*

Calgary Chapter
3008 Utah Dr. NW, Calgary AB T2N 4A1
Tel: 403-282-2153
info@calgaryssea.ca
calgaryssea.wordpress.com
Chief Officer(s):
Julius Szekrenyes, Chapter President

Chapitre de Montréal
CP 49022, Succ. Versailles, Montréal QC H1N 3T6
Tél: 514-353-4674; *Téléc:* 514-353-4674
info@sseamtl.org
www.sseamtl.org
Chief Officer(s):
Brigitte Ouellet, President

Vancouver Chapter
e-mail: vancouver@thessea.org
sseavancouver.wordpress.com
www.facebook.com/sseavancouver
twitter.com/VancouverSSEA
www.youtube.com/user/sseavancouver
Chief Officer(s):
Thomas H. Grenier, Chapter President

Society for the Treatment of Autism *See* Autism Treatment Services of Canada

Society of Canadian Artists (SCA) / Société des artistes canadiens (SAC)
Toronto ON
e-mail: info@societyofcanadianartists.com
www.societyofcanadianartists.com
Overview: A small national organization founded in 1957
Mission: To promote recognition of its member-artists through exhibitions, seminars, workshops, travelling shows
Chief Officer(s):
Josy Britton, President
josybritton@gmail.com
Peter Gough, Vice-President
petergough.art@bellaliant.net
Finances: *Annual Operating Budget:* Less than $50,000; *Funding Sources:* Membership dues
10 volunteer(s)
Membership: 311; *Fees:* $95 Elected members, $45 Associates; *Member Profile:* Professional visual artists & associate members; *Committees:* Membership; Exhibitions; Publicity; Website
Activities: An annual juried members' show; annual juried open show

Society of Canadian Cine Amateurs (SCCA) / Société des ciné amateurs canadiens
3 Wardrope Ave. South, Stoney Creek ON L8G 1R9
Tel: 905-662-4406
sccaonline.ca
Overview: A small national organization founded in 1968
Mission: To promote the arts & sciences of amateur film & video production; to foster & stimulate interest in amateur films & videos in Canada
Chief Officer(s):
Fred Briggs, President
pres@sccaonline.ca
Finances: *Annual Operating Budget:* Less than $50,000; *Funding Sources:* Membership fees; entry fees; donations
15 volunteer(s)
Membership: 130 + 12 clubs; *Fees:* $30; *Committees:* Executive; Honours; Nominations
Activities: *Speaker Service:* Yes

Society of Canadian Office Automation Professionals *See* Society of Collaborative Opportunities & Advancement of Professionals

Society of Canadian Ornithologists (SCO) / Société des ornithologistes du Canada (SOC)
a/s Thérèse Beaudet, SCO Membership Secretary, 1281, ch des Lièges, St-Jean de l'Ile d'Orléans QC G0A 3W0
e-mail: beaudet.lamothe@sympatico.ca
www.sco-soc.ca
Overview: A medium-sized national charitable organization founded in 1983
Mission: To support research to understand & conserve Canadian birds; To represent Canadian ornithologists
Chief Officer(s):
Erica Nol, President
enol@trentu.ca
Joe Nocera, Vice-President
joe.nocera@ontario.ca
Thérèse Beaudet, Membership Secretary
beaudet.lamothe@sympatico.ca
Pierre Lamothe, Treasurer
beaudet.lamothe@sympatico.ca
Finances: *Funding Sources:* Membership fees; Donations
Membership: 357; *Fees:* $10 students; $25 regular members; $35 international members; $50 sustaining members; $500 life members; *Member Profile:* Amateur & professional ornithologists
Activities: Connecting with other professional ornithological societies; Disseminating information about the birds of Canada; Offering grants to study birds
Awards:
• Jamie Smith Memorial Award (Award)
• Taverner Awards (Award)
• James L. Baillie Student Research Award (Award)
• Fred Cooke Student Research Award (Award)
• Doris Huestis Speirs Award (Award)
Meetings/Conferences: • Society of Canadian Ornithologists / Société des ornithologistes du Canada 2015 33rd Annual Meeting, 2015, Wolfville, NS
Scope: National
Publications:
• Avian Conservation & Ecology
Type: Journal
Profile: Published by the Society of Canadian Ornithologists / Société des ornithologistes du Canada & Bird Studies Canada
• Biology & Conservation of Forest Birds
Editor: A.W, Diamond; D.N. Nettleship
Profile: A series of manuscripts from a Society of Canadian Ornithologists / Société des ornithologistes du Canada meeting
• Picoides: Bulletin of the Society of Canadian Ornithologists / Bulletin de la Société des Ornithologistes du Canada
Type: Newsletter; *Editor:* Rob Warnock
Profile: President, committee, & meeting reports, announcements, award news, research articles,essays, book reviews, bird surveys, & conservation information

Society of Christian Schools in British Columbia (SCSBC)
Fosmark Centre, Trinity Western University, 7600 Glover Rd., Langley BC V2Y 1Y1
Tel: 604-888-6366; *Fax:* 604-888-2791
Other Communication: scsbc@twu.ca (Library & membership information)
contact@scsbc.ca
www.scsbc.ca
Previous Name: Southwest British Columbia League of Christian Schools
Overview: A small provincial organization founded in 1976
Mission: To serve Christian schools in British Columbia; To seek support in the provision of Christian education; To develop policies & curriculum outlines & units
Affliation(s): Christian Schools International (CSI); Christian Schools Canada (CSC); Christian Teachers Association of British Columbia; Christian Principals Association of British Columbia
Chief Officer(s):
Henry Contant, Executive Director, 604-888-6366 Ext. 104
leadership@scsbc.ca
Joanne Den Boer, Director of Learning, Preschool to Grade 5, 604-888-6366 Ext. 106
joanne@scsbc.ca
Bill de Jager, Director of Learning, Grades 6 - 13, 604-888-6366 Ext. 103
bill@scsbc.ca
Karen Bush, Coordinator, Communications & Publications, 604-888-6366 Ext. 101
karen@scsbc.ca
Membership: 1-99; *Member Profile:* Christian school campuses & societies in British Columbia
Activities: Monitoring government policies & regulations regarding Christian schoools, & advising schools about government relations; Promoting Christian education throughout British Columbia; Offering workshops; Publishing resource handbooks; Assisting new Christian schools & expanding schools; Supporting digital learning; *Library:* Society of Christian Schools in British Columbia Resource Library
Meetings/Conferences: • Society of Christian Schools in British Columbia 2015 Business & Development Conference, March, 2015, Cedar Springs Conference Center, Sumas, WA
Scope: Provincial
Publications:
• eBulletin
Type: Newsletter
Profile: Information, such as Ministry of Education updates, society policies, & forthcoming workshops & courses, sent regularly to member school board members, principals, curriculum coordinators, & preschooldirectors
• Educating for Life Today & Tomorrow: Resource Manual for High School Guidance
Type: Manual
• Educating toward Wisdom
Type: Booklet
Profile: A resource for curriculum leaders & administrators in Christian schools
• Educating with Heart & Mind: Principles for Curriculum in Christian Schools
Type: Booklet
Profile: A collection of biblical perspective statements
• For the Love of Your Child
Type: Booklet; *Number of Pages:* 20
Profile: Christian education information
• Good Teaching Comes from the Inside
Type: Booklet
Profile: Information for school leaders & teachers
• International Education Program: Student Coordinator Handbook
Type: Handbook
Profile: Information for schools initiating or restructuring an international student program
• La Joie de la langue française
Type: Booklet
Profile: A resource for both elementary & secondary French teachers
• Learning Together in the Middle
Type: Booklet
Profile: Renewing middle level education in Christian schools
• The Link
Type: Newsletter; *Frequency:* Quarterly
Profile: Information for Christian school, staff, & committee members, including new resources & school news & events
• Living, Loving, & Learning: A Kindergarten Handbook
Type: Handbook
Profile: A resource for kindergarten teachers in Christian schools
• Responding to a School Emergency
Type: Booklet
Profile: School emergency preparedness
• SCSBC Administrative Handbook
Type: Handbook
Profile: General guidelines to shape school policy & practice
• SCSBC Internal Control Checklist
Type: Booklet
Profile: Internal controls which may be suitable for SCSBC schools & other independent schools
• The SCSBC Language Arts Handbook
Type: Handbook
Profile: Fundamental principles for language arts education
• The SCSBC Visual Arts Activity Handbook
Type: Booklet
Profile: Direction for visual arts programs in Christian schools
• Serving All Children Well
Type: Booklet
Profile: Information for Christian educators

Society of Collaborative Opportunities & Advancement of Professionals (SCOAP)
c/o CATA Alliance, #416, 207 Bank St., Ottawa ON K2P 2N2
Tel: 613-236-6550; *Fax:* 613-236-8189
info@cata.ca
www.cata.ca/scoap
Previous Name: Society of Canadian Office Automation Professionals
Overview: A medium-sized national charitable organization founded in 1981
Mission: To explore the management, the use, & the impact of information in the knowledge-based society
Member of: Ottawa Centre for Research & Innovation (OCRI)
Chief Officer(s):
Kevin d'Entremont, Chair
Finances: *Annual Operating Budget:* Less than $50,000
Membership: 5,000; *Fees:* $95 individual; *Member Profile:* IT/IM professionals
Activities: Offering seminars; *Internships:* Yes; *Speaker Service:* Yes
Awards:
• SCOAP Awards of Excellence (Award)

Society of Composers, Authors & Music Publishers of Canada (SOCAN) / Société canadienne des auteurs, compositeurs et éditeurs de musique
41 Valleybrook Dr., Toronto ON M3B 2S6
Tel: 416-445-8700; *Fax:* 416-445-7108
Toll-Free: 800-557-6226
socan@socan.ca
www.socan.ca
www.facebook.com/SOCANmusic
twitter.com/SOCANmusic
www.youtube.com/SOCANmusic
Merged from: Performing Rights Organization of Canada Ltd. (PROCAN); Composers, Authors & Publishers Association
Overview: A large national licensing organization founded in 1990
Mission: SOCAN is the Canadian copyright collective that administers the performing rights of members & of affiliated international organizations by licensing the use of music in Canada
Chief Officer(s):
Stan Meissner, President
Eric Baptiste, CEO
David Wood, CFO
Randy Wark, CAO & Vice-President, Human Resources
Jennifer Brown, Vice-President, Licensing
France Lafleur, Vice-President, Membership

Janice Scott, Vice-President, Information Technology
Gilles M. Daigle, General Counsel, Legal Services
Finances: *Annual Operating Budget:* Greater than $5 Million; *Funding Sources:* Music performance licence fees
Staff Member(s): 200
Membership: 75,000; *Fees:* $50 one-time fee for publishers only; *Member Profile:* Music composer, author &/or publisher
Awards:
• Gordon F. Henderson/SOCAN Copyright Competition (Award)
Presented annually to a law student or articling lawyer for an essay on the subject of copyright & music*Deadline:* April *Amount:* $2,000
• SOCAN Awards (Award)
Established 1990 for the purpose of recognizing SOCAN creators & their contribution to Canadian music; presented at the annual Awards Dinner; only SOCAN member writers, composers & music publishers are eligible
• SOCAN Awards for Young Composers (Award)
Total of $17,500 awarded to encourage & recognize the creative talents of upcoming Canadian composers; The Sir Ernest MacMillan Awards for compositions for no fewer than 13 performers; The Serge Garant Awards for compositions for a minimum of three performers; The Pierre Mercure Awards for solo or duet compositions; The Hugh Le Caine Awards for compositions realized on tape with electronic means; The Godfrey Ridout Awards for choral compositions of any variety

Atlantic Division
Queen Square, #802, 45 Alderney Dr., Dartmouth NS B2Y 2N6
Tel: 902-464-7000; *Fax:* 902-464-9696
Toll-Free: 800-707-6226
Chief Officer(s):
Tim Hardy, Executive, Member & Industry Relations

Québec Division
#500, 600, boul de Maisonneuve Ouest, Montréal QC H3A 3J2
Tél: 514-844-8377; *Téléc:* 514-849-8446
Ligne sans frais: 800-797-6226
Chief Officer(s):
Geneviève Côté, Chief Québec Affairs Officer

West Coast Division
#504, 1166 Alberni St., Vancouver BC V6E 3Z3
Tel: 604-669-5569; *Fax:* 604-688-1142
Toll-Free: 800-937-6226

Society of Deaf & Hard of Hearing Nova Scotians (SDHHNS)

#117, 1657 Barrington St., Halifax NS B3J 2A1
Tel: 902-422-7130; *Fax:* 902-492-3864
Toll-Free: 800-516-5551; *TTY:* 902-422-7190
sdhhns@ns.sympatico.ca
www.sdhhns.org
Overview: A small local organization founded in 1980
Mission: To provide services that meet the needs of Deaf, hard of hearing and late deafened people with dignity, integrity and respect.
Chief Officer(s):
Frank O'Sullivan, Executive Director
fosullivan@ns.sympatico.ca
Rosalind Wright, Regional Manager, Cape Breton-Sydney Office
rwright@ns.aliantzinc.ca
Staff Member(s): 12
Membership: 58,000; *Fees:* $10 individual; $15 couple/family; $50 organization/business; $100 life; $150 life family; *Member Profile:* Deaf & hard of hearing people in Nova Scotia

The Society of Energy Professionals

2239 Yonge St., Toronto ON M4S 2B5
Tel: 416-979-2709; *Fax:* 416-979-5794
Toll-Free: 866-288-1788
society@thesociety.ca
www.thesociety.ca
Overview: A medium-sized provincial organization founded in 1948
Mission: To represent employees of Ontario's electricity industry; To ensure the best working conditions for members
Member of: Canadian Council of Professionals; Professional Employees' Network
Affliation(s): International Federation of Professional & Technical Engineers; Canadian Labour Congress / Congrès du travail du Canada; American Federation of Labour / Congress of Industrial Organizations, (AFL/CIO); UNI Global Union
Chief Officer(s):
Scott Travers, President, 416-979-2709 Ext. 5002
traverss@thesociety.ca
Michelle Johnston, Executive Vice-President, Policy, 416-979-2709 Ext. 5001
johnstonm@thesociety.ca
Dennis Minello, Executive Vice-President, Member Services, 416-979-2709 Ext. 3027
minellod@thesociety.ca
Rob Stanley, Executive Vice-President, Finance, 416-979-2709 Ext. 3019
stanleyr@thesociety.ca
Finances: *Funding Sources:* Membership dues
Membership: *Member Profile:* Professional members of the elctricity industry in Ontario, such as scientists, engineers, financial specialists, & supervisors

Society of Engineering Technicians & Technologists of Saskatchewan (SETTS) *See* Saskatchewan Applied Science Technologists & Technicians

Society of Engineering Technologists of BC *See* Applied Science Technologists & Technicians of British Columbia

Society of Graphic Designers of Canada (GDC) / Société des designers graphiques du Canada

Arts Court, 2 Daly Ave., Ottawa ON K1N 6E2
Tel: 613-567-5400; *Fax:* 613-564-4428
Toll-Free: 877-496-4453
info@gdc.net
www.gdc.net
www.linkedin.com/groups?home=&gid=124328
www.facebook.com/GDCNational
twitter.com/gdcntl
Overview: A large national charitable organization
Mission: To maintain a defined, recognized & competent body of graphic designers; To promote high standards of graphic design for benefit of Canadian industry, commerce, public service & education
Affliation(s): International Council of Graphic Design Associations
Chief Officer(s):
Roderick CJ Roodenburg, President
president@gdc.net
Melanie MacDonald, Administrative Director
Finances: *Annual Operating Budget:* Less than $50,000; *Funding Sources:* Membership dues; corporate
Staff Member(s): 1
Membership: 1,000; *Fees:* Schedule available; *Committees:* Icograde; Accreditation; Website; Ethics; Discipline; Constitutional; Sustainability; Sponsorship; Membership; Communications; Education & Scholarships
Activities: Student scholarships; *Rents Mailing List:* Yes
Awards:
• Veer Scholarship (Scholarship)
• Adobe Scholarship (Scholarship)
• Applied Arts Magazine Scholarship (Scholarship)
• Ray Hrynkow Scholarship (Scholarship)
• Canada Type Scholarship (Scholarship)
Publications:
• GDC Journal
Type: Journal; *Editor:* Matt Warburton

Alberta North Chapter
e-mail: president.abnorth@gdc.net
www.gdc.net/chapters/alberta_north.htm
www.facebook.com/groups/gdcabnorth
twitter.com/GDCABnorth
Chief Officer(s):
Ana Herrera, President

Alberta South Chapter
e-mail: president.absouth@gdc.net
www.gdc.net/chapters/alberta_south.htm
Chief Officer(s):
Naoko Masuda, President
president.absouth@gdc.net

Arctic Chapter
e-mail: president.arctic@gdc.net
www.gdc.net/chapters/arctic.htm
Chief Officer(s):
Jennifer Luckay, President

Atlantic Chapter
e-mail: president.atlantic@gdc.net
www.gdc.net/chapters/atlantic.htm
www.linkedin.com/groups/GDC-Atlantic-3062983/about
www.facebook.com/pages/GDCAtlantic/116595611710911
twitter.com/GDCAtlantic
Chief Officer(s):
Larry Burke, President
president.atlantic@gdc.net

British Columbia Mainland Chapter
e-mail: president.vibc@gdc.net
www.gdc.net/chapters/bc_mainland.htm
www.facebook.com/GDCBC
twitter.com/gdcbc
Chief Officer(s):
Andy Maier, President
president.bc@gdc.net

Manitoba Chapter
e-mail: president.mb@gdc.net
www.gdc.net/chapters/manitoba.php
Chief Officer(s):
Oliver Oike, President
president.mb@gdc.net

Saskatchewan North Chapter
e-mail: president.skn@gdc.net
www.gdc.net/chapters/saskatchewan_north.htm
Chief Officer(s):
Dave Nagy, President

Saskatchewan South Chapter
e-mail: president.sks@gdc.net
www.gdc.net/chapters/saskatchewan_south.htm
Chief Officer(s):
Rhea Leibel, President

Vancouver Island Chapter
e-mail: president.vibc@gdc.net
www.gdc.net/chapters/bc_vancouver_island.htm
Chief Officer(s):
Aaron Heppell, President

Society of Gynecologic Oncologists of Canada (GOC) / Société des gynécologues oncologues du Canada

780 Echo Dr., Ottawa ON K1S 5R7
Tel: 613-730-4192; *Fax:* 613-730-4314
Toll-Free: 800-561-2416
www.g-o-c.org
Overview: A small national organization founded in 1980
Mission: To improve the care of women with gynecologic cancer; to raise standards of practice in gynecologic oncology & to encourage ongoing research
Chief Officer(s):
Dianne Miller, President
Walter Gotlieb, Sec.-Treas.
Finances: *Annual Operating Budget:* $100,000-$250,000; *Funding Sources:* Membership fees; donations
Staff Member(s): 1
Membership: 170; *Fees:* $50 or $200, depending on membership category; *Member Profile:* Gyn-oncologists, medical, radiation oncologists, pathologists, nurse specialists, residents in fellowship training program, residents in ob-gyn programs; *Committees:* Practice Guidelines; Programme; Membership; Education; Government Relations
Activities: GOC Professional Continuing Development Meeting; GOC AGM; *Awareness Events:* Run for Her Life, June
Meetings/Conferences: • Society of Gynecologic Oncologists of Canada 36th Annual General Meeting, June, 2015, Québec City, QC
Scope: National
• Society of Gynecologic Oncologists of Canada 14th Annual Continuing Professional Development Meeting, May, 2015, Toronto, ON
Scope: National

Society of Incentive & Travel Executives of Canada

6519B Mississauga Rd., Mississauga ON L5N 1A6
Tel: 905-812-7483; *Fax:* 905-567-7191
office@sitecanada.org
www.sitecanada.org
Also Known As: SITE Canada
Overview: A small national organization
Mission: Worldwide organization of business professionals dedicated to the recognition & development of motivational & performance improvement strategies of which travel is a key component; it recognizes global cultural differences & practices in developing these strategies & serves as a prime networking & educational opportunity for its members
Chief Officer(s):
Leslie Wright, Secretariat
Pam Graham, President
pgraham@congresscan.com
Finances: *Funding Sources:* Membership fees; registration fees; advertising; sponsorship
Staff Member(s): 2; 20 volunteer(s)

Membership: 135; *Fees:* US$450; *Member Profile:* Involvement in the incentive travel industry; *Committees:* Meetings; Membership; Newsletter; Seminars; Social
Activities: *Rents Mailing List:* Yes
Awards:
• Crystal Awards (Award)
Annual competition recognizing outstanding incentive travel programs worldwide
• Lifetime Achievement Award (Award)
Voted as appropriate by the Board of Directors in acknoledgment of exceptional service to the industry
• Member of the Year (Award)
Annual award that recognizes one site member for outstanding contributions in a given year
• Certified Incentive Travel Executive (Award)
Certification that recognizes professionals who have demonsrated their extensive knowledge of the industry & achieved its highest standard of excellence

Society of Internet Professionals (SIP)
#305, 120 Carlton St., Toronto ON M5A 4K2
Tel: 416-891-4937
info@sipgroup.org
www.sipgroup.org
www.linkedin.com/groups/Society-Internet-Professionals-SIP-1509387
twitter.com/sipgroup
Overview: A small local organization founded in 1997
Mission: To represent the interests of internet professionals
Chief Officer(s):
Max Haroon, President
Membership: *Fees:* $100 individual; *Member Profile:* Accredited internet professionals
Activities: Online university; Accredited Internet Professional (AIP) Accreditation & Certification Program; symposiums; workshops; trade shows; *Internships:* Yes; *Speaker Service:* Yes; *Library:* Internet Resource Centre

Society of Kabalarians of Canada
1160 West 10th Ave., Vancouver BC V6H 1J1
Tel: 604-263-9551; *Fax:* 604-263-5514
Toll-Free: 866-489-1188
info1@kabalarians.com
www.kabalarians.com
Also Known As: Kabalarian Philosophy
Overview: A small international organization founded in 1963
Mission: To promote Kabalarian philosophy, which teaches a constructive way of life through the understanding of the Mathematical Principle, encouraging people to live a more progressive, constructive life.
Chief Officer(s):
Lorenda Bardell, President
Finances: *Funding Sources:* Donations; courses
Staff Member(s): 6
Activities: Public presentations, seminars, workshops; classes of study; *Speaker Service:* Yes; *Library:* Resource Centre; Open to public by appointment

Calgary
2618 Richmond Rd. SW, Calgary AB T3E 4M4
Tel: 403-246-0926
calgarycentre@kabalarians.com
www.kabalarians.com/calgary
Chief Officer(s):
Garett Willington, Representative
ronaye.willington@modelland.com

Edmonton
7764 - 83 Ave., Edmonton AB T6C 1A4
Tel: 780-466-7369
www.kabalarians.com/edmonton
Chief Officer(s):
Floyd Farrell, Representative

Society of Local Government Managers of Alberta
PO Box 308, 4629 - 54 Ave., Bruderheim AB T0B 0S0
Tel: 780-796-3836; *Fax:* 780-796-2081
www.clgm.net
Overview: A medium-sized provincial organization
Mission: To govern & promote the profession of municipal government managers
Chief Officer(s):
Linda M. Davies, Executive Director/Registrar
linda.davies@shaw.ca
Membership: *Committees:* Communications; Discipline; Practice Review; Professional Development; Registration; Planning Committee for the Municipal Administration Leadership Workshop

Society of Management Accountants of Alberta *See* CMA Canada - Alberta

Society of Management Accountants of British Columbia *See* CMA Canada - British Columbia

Society of Management Accountants of Nova Scotia *See* Certified Management Accountants of Nova Scotia

The Society of Management Accountants of Ontario *See* CMA Canada - Ontario

The Society of Notaries Public of British Columbia
PO Box 44, #1220, 625 Howe St., Vancouver BC V6C 2T6
Tel: 604-681-4516; *Fax:* 604-681-7258
Toll-Free: 800-663-0343
www.notaries.bc.ca
Overview: A medium-sized provincial organization founded in 1926
Mission: To ensure that its members provide high quality services to their clients
Chief Officer(s):
G.W. Wayne Braid, Chief Executive Officer/Secretary, 604-681-4516, Fax: 604-681-7258
Akash Sablok, President
Staff Member(s): 9

Society of Obstetricians & Gynaecologists of Canada (SOGC) / Société des obstétriciens et gynécologues du Canada
780 Echo Dr., Ottawa ON K1S 5R7
Tel: 613-730-4192; *Fax:* 613-730-4314
Toll-Free: 800-561-2416
helpdesk@sogc.com
www.sogc.org
Overview: A medium-sized national organization founded in 1944
Mission: To promote excellence in the practice of obstetrics & gynaecology; To produce national clinical guidelines for medical education on women's health issues; To promote optimal, comprehensive women's health care
Chief Officer(s):
Ward Murdock, President
Jennifer Blake, Chief Executive Officer
Membership: 3,000+; *Fees:* Schedule available; *Member Profile:* Gynaecologists; Obstetricians; Family physicians; Nurses; Nurse practitioners; Midwives; Allied health professionals; Students, enrolled in an undergraduate training program in a Canadian medical school, a family medical residency program, or a postgraduate training program in obstetrics & gynaecology; *Committees:* SOGC has over 50 committees, such as Aboriginal Health Initiatives; Canadian Paediatric & Adolescent Gynaecology & Obstetricians; Clinical Practice - Obstetrics; Clinical Practice - Gynaecology; Diagnostic Imaging; Ethics; Genetics; Infectious Disease; Reproductive Endocrinology Infertility; Maternal Fetal Medicine; RM Advisory; ALARM Committee; Junior Member; Maternal Fetal Medicine; Public Affairs Urogynaecology; Western Regional
Activities: Collaborating with other national & international organizations to improve health care; Providing continued professional development for physicians & health care providers, such as e-learning modules; Offering public education; Encouraging research; Engaging in advocacy activities; Presenting grants, awards. & fellowships;
Publications:
• Health News
Type: Newsletter
Profile: SOGC media reports & health news
• Healthy Beginnings
Profile: A guide to pregnancy & childbirth
• Journal of Obstetrics & Gynaecology Canada (JOGC)
Type: Journal; *Frequency:* Monthly; *Price:* Free with membership in the Society ofObstetricians & Gynaecologists of Canada
Profile: A peer-reviewed journal of obstetrics, gynaecology, & women's health, featuring original research articles,case reports, & reviews
• Sex Sense
Profile: A guide to contraception
• SOGC News
Type: Newsletter; *Frequency:* 10 pa
Profile: Society work & events, plus information about recent legislation & developments in women's health care
• What You Should Know About The Society of Obstetricians & Gynaecologists of Canada

Society of Ontario Adjudicators & Regulators (SOAR) / Société ontarienne des arbitres et des régisseurs
PO Box 22031, Stn. The Colonnade, Toronto ON M5S 1R0
Tel: 416-623-7454; *Fax:* 416-623-7437
information@soar.on.ca
soar.on.ca
www.linkedin.com/company/5355886
twitter.com/SOAR_News
Overview: A small provincial organization founded in 1993
Mission: To improve the administrative justice system
Affiliation(s): Canadian Council of Administrative Tribunals
Chief Officer(s):
Emanuela Heyninck, President
Daphne Simon, Executive Director
Membership: *Fees:* Free; *Member Profile:* Chairs, members & executive staff of administrative justice system agencies; *Committees:* Education; Advocacy & Innovation
Activities: Training; Conferences; Development of manuals; Model policies & guidelines

Society of Ontario Nut Growers (SONG)
RR#3, Niagara-on-the-Lake ON L0S 1J0
Tel: 905-935-9773; *Fax:* 905-935-6887
nuttrees@grimonut.com
www.songonline.ca
Overview: A medium-sized provincial organization founded in 1972
Mission: To promote the interests of nut growers; to encourage scientific research in the breeding & culture of nut-bearing plants suited to Ontario conditions; to disseminate information on propagation techniques & cultural practices
Member of: Northern Nut Growers Association
Affiliation(s): Eastern Chapter Society of Ontario Nut Growers
Chief Officer(s):
Ernie Grimo, Treasurer
Finances: *Annual Operating Budget:* Less than $50,000; *Funding Sources:* Membership fees; annual auction
5 volunteer(s)
Membership: 430 individual + 20 organizations; *Fees:* $12/yr; $30 - 3/yrs.; *Member Profile:* Growers & hobbyists
Activities: Meetings; technical presentations; nut tree auction; research

The Society of Professional Accountants of Canada (SPAC) / La Société des comptables professionnels du Canada
#1007, 250 Consumers Rd., Toronto ON M2J 4V6
Tel: 416-350-8145; *Fax:* 416-350-8146
Toll-Free: 877-515-4447
registrar@professionalaccountant.org
www.professionalaccountant.org
Overview: A medium-sized national organization founded in 1978
Mission: To provide ongoing education & to set qualifying standards, to ensure the professional competence of its members in the practice of accountancy
Chief Officer(s):
William O. Nichols, President
president@professionalaccountant.org
Finances: *Annual Operating Budget:* $50,000-$100,000
Membership: 300; *Fees:* $250; *Member Profile:* Individuals who have successfully completed mandatory accreditation examinations, adhered to the code of ethics, & provided evidence of at least three years of practical experience in accountancy
Activities: Professional development; employment referral service

Society of Professional Engineers & Associates (SPEA) / Société des ingénieurs professionnels et associés
#2, 2275 Speakman Dr., Mississauga ON L5K 1B1
Tel: 905-823-3606; *Fax:* 905-823-9602
www.spea.ca
Overview: A medium-sized national organization founded in 1974
Mission: To represent scientists, engineers, technologists, & tradespeople who work for Atomic Energy of Canada Limited (AECL) in Mississauga, Ontario & abroad
Chief Officer(s):
Michael Ivanco, President
Brian Girard, Chair, Membership
Vincent Tume, Secretary
Val Aleyaseen, Treasurer

Membership: 850; *Member Profile:* Scientists, engineers, technologists, & tradespeople who work for Atomic Energy of Canada Limited (AECL) in Mississauga, Ontario & abroad

Society of Public Insurance Administrators of Ontario (SPIAO)

c/o The Municipality Of Clarington, 40 Temperance St., Bowmanville ON L1C 3A6
e-mail: info@spiao.ca
www.spiao.ca
Overview: A small provincial organization founded in 1976
Mission: To exchange knowledge & pursue matters dealing with risk & insurance management; to promote cooperation among all local government bodies which have interests in the field of risk & insurance management; to encourage development of educational training programs; to collect & disperse information
Chief Officer(s):
Brian McEnhill, President
Nancy Taylor, Treasurer
Finances: *Annual Operating Budget:* Less than $50,000
6 volunteer(s)
Membership: 70 individuals; *Fees:* $100; *Member Profile:* Must work for any of three levels of government, board of education, library board, public utility, conservation authority or public housing authority
Activities: 2 one-day & 1 two-day workshops per year

Society of Rural Physicians of Canada (SRPC) / Société de la médecine rurale du Canada

PO Box 893, 269 Main St., Shawville QC J0X 2Y0
Fax: 819-647-2485
Toll-Free: 877-276-1949
info@srpc.ca
www.srpc.ca
Overview: A small national organization founded in 1993
Mission: To provide equitable medical care for rural communities; to provide sustainable working conditions for rural physicians
Affiliation(s): Canadian Medical Association; World Organization of Rural Doctors
Chief Officer(s):
John Soles, President
Lee Teperman, Administrative Officer
Finances: *Funding Sources:* Membership fees
Staff Member(s): 4
Membership: 3,000+; *Fees:* $390 individual; $100 associate; $50 retired; $20 resident; free - student; *Member Profile:* Rural M.D., medical student/resident; *Committees:* Emergency; Anesthesia; Nominations & Awards; Education; Specialist; Maternity Care; Rural Critical Care; International; Research; First Year in Practice
Activities: *Speaker Service:* Yes; *Library* by appointment
Meetings/Conferences: • Rural & Remote 2015, April, 2015, Fairmont Queen Elizabeth, Montreal, QC
Scope: International
Description: Includes the 23rd Annual Rural and Remote Medicine Course and the Second World Summit on Rural Generalist Medicine

Society of Saint Vincent de Paul *Voir* Conseil national Société de Saint-Vincent de Paul

The Society of St. Peter the Apostle (SPA)

2219 Kennedy Rd., Toronto ON M1T 3G5
Tel: 416-699-7077; *Fax:* 416-699-9019
Toll-Free: 800-897-8865
missions@missionsocieties.ca
www.missionsocieties.ca
Overview: A small national charitable organization founded in 1889
Mission: To educate local clergy & religious men & women in developing countries
Chief Officer(s):
Alex Osei, C.S.Sp., National Director
Finances: *Annual Operating Budget:* $500,000-$1.5 Million; *Funding Sources:* Donations
Staff Member(s): 8
Activities: Funds the training of local clergy & religious missions; *Speaker Service:* Yes

Society of St. Vincent de Paul - Toronto Central Council

240 Church St., Toronto ON M5B 1Z2
Tel: 416-365-5577; *Fax:* 416-364-2055
Other Communication: Camp e-mail: campinfo@ssvptoronto.ca
info@svdptoronto.org
www.svdptoronto.org
Overview: A small local charitable organization founded in 1850
Mission: To live the Gospel message by assisting the poor with love, respect, justice, & joy; To administer special works, including women's shelters, recovery homes, homes for the developmentally handicapped & mentally ill, & a camp for girls
Affliation(s): Archdiocese of Toronto
Chief Officer(s):
Bob Ossowski, President
Louise Coutu, Executive Director
Finances: *Funding Sources:* Donations
Membership: *Member Profile:* Individuals who are non-judgmental, compassionate, & giving, who wish to act on their faith by assisting those in need in this lay Catholic organization; Applicants must successfully complete the screening process, which includes a police check, references, & an interview; *Committees:* Advocacy; Addiction Recovery; Camp; Community Living; Election; Executive; Finance; Governance; Health & Safety; Prison Apostolate & Court Services; Resource; Shelter; Spirituality; Stores; Strategic Planning; Twinning
Activities: Delivering Christ's love, material assistance, respect, compassion, & hope to those in need; Offering home visitations; Operating the Marygrove Camp for girls; Providing housing & support to women in crisis; Supporting men & women recovering from addiction; Providing residential care for the developmentally handicapped; Offering low cost clothing; Supporting persons awaiting trial or in prison; Conducting members' conference meetings once or twice a month to grow in faith & to consult regarding ways to assist the needy
Publications:
• Volunteer Opportunities Handbook
Type: Handbook
Profile: Description, with contact information, of volunteer opportunities in special works

Society of the Plastics Industry of Canada *See* Canadian Plastics Industry Association

Society of Toxicology of Canada (STC) / Société de toxicologie du Canada

PO Box 55094, Montréal QC H3G 2W5
e-mail: stcsecretariat@mcgill.ca
www.stcweb.ca
Overview: A medium-sized national organization founded in 1964
Mission: To promote acquisition, facilitate dissemination & encourage utilization of knowledge in the science of toxicology
Affiliation(s): Canadian Federation of Biological Societies; International Union of Toxicology
Chief Officer(s):
Louise Winn, President
winnl@queensu.ca
Veronica Atehortua, Information Executive Secretary
Finances: *Funding Sources:* Membership fees
Membership: *Fees:* $100 regular; $30 retired/post-doctoral fellow/graduate student; *Member Profile:* Ordinary - qualified individual who has continuing professional interest in field of toxicology; associate - individual who has not satisfied requirement for ordinary membership; student - graduate student enrolled in postgraduate degree program with major emphasis on toxicology; *Committees:* Awards; Editorial/Newsletter; Education; Finance; Membership; Nominating; Science Policy; Scientific Program; Symposium; Web Site
Meetings/Conferences: • The Society of Toxicology of Canada Annual Symposium 2015, 2015
Scope: National

Society of Translators & Interpreters of British Columbia (STIBC)

PO Box 33, #511, 850 West Hastings St., Vancouver BC V6C 1E1
Tel: 604-684-2940; *Fax:* 604-684-2947
www.stibc.org
Overview: A medium-sized provincial licensing organization founded in 1981 overseen by Canadian Translators, Terminologists & Interpreters Council
Mission: To promote the interests of translators & interpreters in BC; to serve the public by applying a Code of Ethics members must comply with; by setting & maintaining high professional standards through education & certification
Chief Officer(s):
Golnaz Aliyarzadeh, President
Finances: *Annual Operating Budget:* $100,000-$250,000; *Funding Sources:* Membership dues
Staff Member(s): 2
Membership: 490; *Member Profile:* Persons with minimum 1 year experience as a translator or interpretor, and who have written & passed the Language Proficiency exam, the Admissions exam, & the Ethics exam

Society of Trust & Estate Practitioners (STEP)

#700, 1 Richmond St. West, Toronto ON M5H 3W4
Tel: 416-491-4949; *Fax:* 416-491-9499
Toll-Free: 877-991-4949
stepcanada@step.ca
www.step.ca
Overview: A medium-sized national licensing organization
Mission: To promote trust & estate work as a profession
Chief Officer(s):
Ian Worland, Chair, 604-631-1220, Fax: 604-683-6953
iworland@legacylawyers.ca
Membership: 18,500+ in 80 jurisdictions worldwide; *Member Profile:* Individuals working in the field of trusts & estates; *Committees:* Audit; Awards; Education; Governance; Member Services; National Conference; Nominations & Human Resources; Step Inside; Student Liaison; Trust & Estate Technical
Activities: Diploma covering major areas of estate planning (TEP designation)
Publications:
• STEP [Society of Trust & Estate Practitioners] Journal
Type: Journal
• STEP [Society of Trust & Estate Practitioners] Inside
Type: Newsletter
• STEP [Society of Trust & Estate Practitioners] Insider
Type: eNewsletter
• STEP [Society of Trust & Estate Practitioners] Directory & Yearbook
Type: Directory
• STEP [Society of Trust & Estate Practitioners] Marketing Brochures
Type: Brochures
Profile: Brochures include: Why Make a Trust? Why Make a Will? Why Make a Lasting Power of Attorney?
• Trust Quarterly Review
Type: Journal

Society of Urologic Surgeons of Ontario (SUSO)

#510, 3030 Lawrence Ave. East, Toronto ON M1P 2T7
Tel: 416-438-9948; *Fax:* 416-438-9590
executive@suso.ca
www.suso.ca
Overview: A small provincial organization
Mission: Dedicated to ensuring patient access to urological care with a commitment to excellence, education, research & sharing of information
Chief Officer(s):
Allan Toguri, Executive Director
Finances: *Funding Sources:* Sponsorships; Membership dues
Membership: *Fees:* $50 resident; $100 corresponding; $200 full; *Member Profile:* Doctors in a residency program in urology; Doctors registered with the Royal College of Physicians & Surgeons of Canada or the American Board of Urology

Society of Writers in Radio, Television & Cinema *Voir* Société des Auteurs de Radio, Télévision et Cinéma

Society Promoting Environmental Conservation (SPEC)

2060 Pine St., Vancouver BC V6J 4P8
Tel: 604-736-7732; *Fax:* 604-736-7115
admin@spec.bc.ca
www.spec.bc.ca
www.facebook.com/137945192900176
www.youtube.com/user/SPECbc
Overview: A medium-sized provincial charitable organization founded in 1969
Mission: To address environmental issues in British Columbia, with a focus on urban communities in the Lower Mainland & the Georgia Basin; To encourage policies that lead to urban sustainability
Chief Officer(s):
Rob Baxter, President
Oliver Lane, Coordinator
Finances: *Funding Sources:* Donations
Activities: Advocating for food safety & security; Providing public education programs; Reducing the use of hazardous pesticides
Meetings/Conferences: • Society Promoting Environmental Conservation Annual General Meeting 2015, 2015
Scope: Provincial

Publications:
• SPECTRUM [a publication of the Society Promoting Environmental Conservation]
Type: Newsletter
Profile: Society Promoting Environmental Conservation activities, news releases, upcoming events, & articles

Soeurs Adoratrices du Précieux Sang ***See*** Sisters Adorers of the Precious Blood

Soeurs Auxiliatrices
1637, rue St-Christophe, Montréal QC H2L 3W7
Tél: 514-522-4452; *Téléc:* 514-524-1448
auxiqc@point-net.com
Aperçu: *Dimension:* petite; *Envergure:* provinciale; fondée en 1856
Membre(s) du bureau directeur:
Maria-Paule Lebél
Suzanne Loiselle
Andrée Brosseau

Soeurs de l'Enfant-Jésus ***See*** Sisters of the Child Jesus

Les Soeurs de Sainte-Anne
1950, rue Provost, Lachine QC H8S 1P7
Tél: 514-637-3783; *Téléc:* 514-637-5400
accueil@ssacong.org
www.ssacong.org
Aperçu: *Dimension:* petite; *Envergure:* internationale; Organisme sans but lucratif; fondée en 1850
Mission: Impliquée dans l'éducation, les soins de santé, l'animation pastorale et sociale en divers milieux
Membre(s) du bureau directeur:
Marie Ellen King, Supérieure générale
Madeleine Lanoue, Secrétaire générale
Finances: *Budget de fonctionnement annuel:* $100,000-$250,000

Soeurs de Sainte-Marie de Namur / Sisters of Saint Mary of Namur
68, av Fairmont, Ottawa QC K1Y 1X5
Tél: 613-725-1510
sr.suzanneb@ssmn.ca
www.ssmn.ca
Aperçu: *Dimension:* petite; *Envergure:* internationale; Organisme sans but lucratif; fondée en 1819
Membre(s) du bureau directeur:
Réjeanne Roussel, Secrétaire-trésorière
Françoise Sabourin, Supérieure provinciale
Suzanne Martineau, Secrétaire-trésorière, 613-725-3427
ssmnproc@sympatico.ca
Finances: *Budget de fonctionnement annuel:* $250,000-$500,000
Membre: 1-99;

Soeurs de Saint-Joseph de Saint-Vallier (SSJ)
860, av Louis-Fréchette, Québec QC G1S 3N3
Tél: 418-683-9653; *Téléc:* 418-681-8781
ssjvallier1903@videotron.ca
www.saint-joseph-fed.org
Aperçu: *Dimension:* petite; *Envergure:* locale; fondée en 1683
Membre(s) du bureau directeur:
Berthe Fortin, Supérieure générale, 418-681-2989
Membre: 165

Soeurs missionnaires Notre-Dame des Anges / Missionary Sisters of Our Lady of the Angels
323, rue Queen, Sherbrooke QC J1M 1K8
Tél: 819-569-9248; *Téléc:* 819-569-9180
mindalen@videotron.ca
www.misnda.org
Aperçu: *Dimension:* petite; *Envergure:* internationale; Organisme sans but lucratif; fondée en 1922
Mission: The congregation is exclusively at the service of the missionary Church. Its specific mission is the formation of religious sisters, catechists and committed lay people. In addition, they respond to the needs of the local churches by working in the medical, social and educational fields when it is possible
Membre(s) du bureau directeur:
Fernande Leblanc, Contact
Membre: 142

Softball Manitoba
#321, 145 Pacific Ave., Winnipeg MB R3B 2Z6
Tel: 204-925-5673; *Fax:* 204-925-5703
softball@softball.mb.ca
www.softball.mb.ca
Also Known As: Softball Manitoba
Overview: A small provincial organization founded in 1965 overseen by Canadian Amateur Softball Association
Mission: To promote & develop softball at all levels by providing leadership, programs & services
Member of: Canadian Amateur Softball Association
Chief Officer(s):
Bill Finch, President
Membership: 15,000+ players & coaches; *Committees:* Finance; Facilities; Development; Umpire Development; Competition

Softball NB Inc. (SNB) / Softball Nouveau-Brunswick Inc.
4242 Water St., Miramichi NB E1N 4L2
Tel: 506-773-5343; *Fax:* 506-773-5630
Other Communication: Summer, Phone: 506-773-3507
www.softballnb.ca
www.facebook.com/210596526327
Also Known As: Softball New Brunswick
Overview: A medium-sized provincial organization founded in 1925 overseen by Canadian Amateur Softball Association
Mission: To foster, develop, promote & regulate the playing of amateur softball in New Brunswick
Member of: Canadian Amateur Softball Association
Chief Officer(s):
Bev Adams, President
adams@nb.sympatico.ca
Gail Gallant, Secretary-Treasurer
gail.gallant@rogers.com
Peter McLean, Executive & Technical Director
pmclean@nbnet.nb.ca
Finances: *Annual Operating Budget:* $50,000-$100,000
Staff Member(s): 1; 17 volunteer(s)
Membership: 350 teams; 225 officials; *Fees:* $75 per team
Activities: *Awareness Events:* Hall of Fame, 1st Sat. in June
Awards:
• Annual Recognition Awards (Award)

Softball Newfoundland & Labrador
PO Box 21165, #115, 183 Kenmount Rd., St. John's NL A1A 5B2
Tel: 709-576-7231; *Fax:* 709-576-7081
softball@sportnl.ca
www.softballnl.ca
Overview: A small provincial organization overseen by Canadian Amateur Softball Association
Member of: Canadian Amateur Softball Association
Chief Officer(s):
Ross Crocker, President

Softball Nouveau-Brunswick Inc. ***See*** Softball NB Inc.

Softball Nova Scotia
5516 Spring Garden Rd., 4th Fl., Halifax NS B3J 1G6
Tel: 902-425-5454; *Fax:* 902-425-5606
softballns@sportnovascotia.ca
www.softballns.ca
Overview: A small provincial organization overseen by Canadian Amateur Softball Association
Mission: To oversee the sport of softball in Nova Scotia.
Member of: Canadian Amateur Softball Association
Chief Officer(s):
Dave Houghton, President & CEO

Softball Ontario
3 Concorde Gate, Toronto ON M3C 3N7
Tel: 416-426-7150; *Fax:* 416-426-7368
info@softballontario.ca
www.softballontario.ca
www.facebook.com/SoftballOntario
twitter.com/SoftballOntario
Overview: A medium-sized provincial organization founded in 1971 overseen by Canadian Amateur Softball Association
Mission: To promote & develop the sport of softball for its athletes, officials & volunteers by providing programs & services at all levels of competitions
Member of: Canadian Amateur Softball Association
Affliation(s): Provincial Women's Softball Association (PWSA); Ontario Amateur Softball Association (OASA); Ontario Rural Softball Association (ORSA); Slo-Pitch Ontario Association (SPOA)
Chief Officer(s):
Wendy Cathcart, Executive Director
wcathcart@softballontario.ca
Staff Member(s): 5
Membership: 5 associations; *Committees:* Finance; Coaching; Participation; Scorekeeping; Fast Pitch & Slo-Pitch Umpire

Softball PEI (SPEI)
PO Box 1044, Charlottetown PE C1A 7M4
Tel: 902-569-4747; *Fax:* 902-569-3366
Toll-Free: 800-661-0797
softballpei.com
www.facebook.com/SoftballPEI33
twitter.com/SoftballPEI
Overview: A small provincial organization overseen by Canadian Amateur Softball Association
Mission: To promote & develop the sport of softball for all participating athletes in Prince Edward Island.
Member of: Canadian Amateur Softball Association
Chief Officer(s):
Alan Petrie, President, 902-393-0274
albob@pei.sympatico.ca
Activities: Umpire Program; Coaching & Athlete Development Program; Scorekeeping Program; Participation Program; Communication/Promotion; Resources;

Softball Québec
4545, av Pierre-de Coubertin, Montréal QC H1V 3R2
Tél: 514-252-3061; *Téléc:* 514-252-3134
softballqc@gmail.com
www.softballquebec.com
www.facebook.com/softballquebec
twitter.com/SoftballQuebec
Aperçu: *Dimension:* moyenne; *Envergure:* provinciale; Organisme sans but lucratif; fondée en 1970 surveillé par Canadian Amateur Softball Association
Mission: Promouvoir la pratique du softball sur le territoire du Québec; offrir aux athlètes, aux entraîneurs, aux officiels et aux administrateurs québécois un support technique et des services de qualité
Membre de: Canadian Amateur Softball Association
Membre(s) du bureau directeur:
Chantal Gagnon, Directrice générale
cgagnon@loisirquebec.qc.ca
Michel Nero, Président
mikeump@hotmail.com
Membre(s) du personnel: 5
Membre: 30,000
Activités: Programmes de formation pour officiels et entraîneurs; ligues; compétitions; *Stagiaires:* Oui

Softball Saskatchewan
2205 Victoria Ave., Regina SK S4P 0S4
Tel: 306-780-9235; *Fax:* 306-780-9483
info@softball.sk.ca
www.softball.sk.ca
Overview: A small provincial organization overseen by Canadian Amateur Softball Association
Mission: To make softball the number one choice for participation by athletes, coaches, parents and umpires.
Member of: Canadian Amateur Softball Association
Chief Officer(s):
Guy Jacobson, Executive Director
guy@softball.sk.ca

Softball Yukon
c/o Executive Director, 28 Evergreen Cres., Whitehorse YT Y1A 4X1
Tel: 867-667-4487
www.softballyukon.com
Overview: A small provincial organization overseen by Canadian Amateur Softball Association
Member of: Canadian Amateur Softball Association
Chief Officer(s):
George Arcand, Executive Director
garcand@northwestel.net

Software Human Resource Council (Canada) Inc. ***See*** Information & Communications Technology Council of Canada

SOHO Business Group (SOHO)
#1, 1680 Lloyd Ave., North Vancouver BC V7P 2N6
Toll-Free: 800-290-7646
questions@soho.ca
www.soho.ca
www.facebook.com/SOHObusinessgroup?ref=ts
twitter.com/sohomarketing
Overview: A medium-sized national organization founded in 1996
Mission: To provide a positive experience to small & medium sized businesses by developing special benefits, programs, &

events that focus on the growth & success of Canadian business & entrepreneurship
Chief Officer(s):
Moe Somani, Founder & Chief Executive Officer
Finances: *Funding Sources:* Membership fees
10 volunteer(s)
Membership: 5,000+; *Fees:* Schedule available; *Member Profile:* Small or home-based businesses with fewer than 25 employees
Activities: Offering seminars & networking events; *Speaker Service:* Yes

Soil Conservation Council of Canada (SCCC)
PO Box 998, Indian Head SK S0G 2K0
Tel: 306-972-7293; *Fax:* 306-695-3442
info@soilcc.ca
www.soilcc.ca
Overview: A medium-sized national charitable organization founded in 1987
Mission: To act as the voice of soil conservation in Canada
Chief Officer(s):
Glen Shaw, Executive Director, 306-972-7293
info@soilcc.ca
Don McCabe, President
Finances: *Funding Sources:* Corporations; Government
Membership: *Fees:* $35 individuals
Activities: Raising awareness about the causes of soil degradation; Presenting conservation issues to the government, private industry, producers, & the public; Delivering agriculture & environment programs for producers; Facilitating information exchange among researchers, government representatives, industry, & farmers; Partnering with similar organizations; *Awareness Events:* National Soil Conservation Week, April
Meetings/Conferences: • Conservation Agriculture 2015 7th World Congress (hosted by Soil Conservation Council of Canada with Conservation Agriculture Systems Alliance), 2015
Scope: International
Description: A gathering of world academic, industry, & producer leaders in conservation agriculture
Contact Information: Soil Conservation Council of Canada, Executive Director: Glen Shaw, E-mail: info@soilcc.ca
Publications:
• The Protector [a publication of the Soil Conservation Council of Canada]
Type: Newsletter
Profile: Up-to-date information about the Council's activities

Les soins de santé Sainte-Elizabeth *See* Saint Elizabeth Health Care

Soins et éducation à la petite enfance Nouveau-Brunswick *See* Early Childhood Care & Education New Brunswick

Sojourn House
101 Ontario St., Toronto ON M5A 2V2
Tel: 416-864-9136
info@sojournhouse.org
www.sojournhouse.org
www.facebook.com/pages/Sojourn-House-Canada/406404746088143
twitter.com/SojournHouse
Overview: A small local charitable organization
Mission: To offer safe & supportive emergency shelter, in Toronto, Ontario, for refugees from around the world; To assist refugees in building secure & productive lives in Canada
Chief Officer(s):
Gloria Nafziger, President
Finances: *Funding Sources:* Donations; City of Toronto; Government of Canada
Membership: *Fees:* $10 individual; $25 non profit organization; $50 for profit organization
Activities: Providing supportive counselling; Helping refugees in the re-settlement process; Liaising with government & non-governmental agencies; Assisting persons in identifying & accessing educational & employment opportunities; Connecting persons to ethno-cultural communities; Offering cultural orientation to Toronto & Canada
Publications:
• Sojourn House Newsletter
Type: Newsletter

Solbrekken Evangelistic Association of Canada
PO Box 44220, Stn. Garside, Edmonton AB T5V 1N6
Tel: 780-460-8444
mswm@shaw.ca
www.mswm.org
Also Known As: Max Solbrekken World Mission
Overview: A small national charitable organization founded in 1961
Mission: To promote the gospel
Affliation(s): Europa for Kristus, Oslo, Norway
Chief Officer(s):
Max Solbrekken, President
Donna Solbrekken, Secretary
Staff Member(s): 4; 6 volunteer(s)

Solo Swims of Ontario Inc. (SSO)
c/o Greg Taylor, 32 Coxwell Cres., Brantford ON N3P 1Z1
www.soloswims.com
Overview: A small provincial organization founded in 1975
Mission: To promote safety in marathon swimming in Ontario
Chief Officer(s):
Greg Taylor, President
gwc.taylor@sympatico.ca
Finances: *Funding Sources:* Provincial government
Membership: *Committees:* Advisory

Somali Immigrant Women's Association (SIWA)
1735 Kipling Ave, West, Toronto ON M9R 2V8
Tel: 416-741-7492
www.siwa.on.ca
Overview: A medium-sized provincial organization founded in 1997
Mission: To enhance the lives of Somali Canadians & immigrants in Ontario by motivating its members to actively participate in social service programs & by preserving their culture
Finances: *Funding Sources:* Federal, provincial & metro governments; foundations; donations
Activities: Immigration counselling & advocacy; translation services; orientation & workshops; ESL classes with daycare; support groups; job training; housing, welfare & legal services referrals

Somenos Marsh Wildlife Society
PO Box 711, Duncan BC V9L 3Y1
Tel: 250-746-7032
info@somenosmarsh.com
www.somenosmarsh.com
Overview: A small local organization
Mission: To preserve wetland habitat in Somenos Basin; to build wildlife viewing facilities
Member of: Cowichan Watershed Council; BC Environmental Network; Canadian Nature Federation
Chief Officer(s):
Paul Fletcher, President
Staff Member(s): 1; 30 volunteer(s)
Membership: 200; *Fees:* $20-$35

Somerset & District Chamber of Commerce
PO Box 64, Somerset MB R0G 2L0
Tel: 204-744-2011; *Fax:* 204-744-2170
somcdc@mts.net
Overview: A small local organization
Affliation(s): Manitoba Chamber of Commerce
Chief Officer(s):
Gilbert Mabon, President
Finances: *Funding Sources:* Membership dues
Membership: *Fees:* $20 individual; $50 business

Songwriters Association of Canada (SAC) / Association des auteurs-compositeurs canadiens
41 Valleybrook Dr., Toronto ON M3B 2S6
Tel: 416-961-1588; *Fax:* 416-961-2040
Toll-Free: 866-456-7664
sac@songwriters.ca
www.songwriters.ca
www.facebook.com/itallstartswithasong
twitter.com/songwritersofCa
www.youtube.com/songwriterscanada
Overview: A medium-sized national charitable organization founded in 1983
Mission: To protect & develop the creative & business environments for songwriters in Canada & around the world
Chief Officer(s):
Isabel Crack, Managing Director
isabel@songwriters.ca
Eddie Schwartz, President
Finances: *Funding Sources:* Canadian government; Heritage Canada; SOCAN
Staff Member(s): 5
Membership: 1,500; *Fees:* $60 regular; $30 students; $130 associate; *Member Profile:* Songwriters; composers; lyricists
Activities: Canadian song depository; song assessment service; songwriting workshops; songwriter showcases; songwriting competitions; Bluebird North Oct./Nov.; Date with a Tape; Song Stage; Songposium, Jan./Feb.; *Internships:* Yes; *Speaker Service:* Yes

Sonography Canada / Échographie Canada
PO Box 119, Kemptville ON K0G 1J0
Fax: 613-258-0899
Toll-Free: 877-488-0788
Other Communication: memberinfo@sonographycanada.ca
info@sonographycanada.ca
www.sonographycanada.ca
Merged from: Cnd. Assoc. of Registered Diagnostic Ultrasound Professionals & Cnd. Society of Diagnostic Medical
Overview: A small national organization founded in 2014
Mission: The national voice for diagnostic medical sonographers in Canada
Chief Officer(s):
Tom Hayward, Business Manager
THayward@sonographycanada.ca
Membership: 1-99; *Fees:* $70; *Committees:* National Education Advisory Committee; CJMS Editorial Board; Awards Committee; Examinations Committee
Meetings/Conferences: • Sonography Canada 2015 National Conference & Annual General Meeting, May, 2015, Delta Beauéjour, Moncton, NB
Scope: National
• Sonography Canada 2016 National Conference & Annual General Meeting, 2016
Scope: National
Publications:
• Canadian Journal of Medical Sonography
Type: Jounral; *Frequency:* Quarterly
Profile: CJMS is a combination of clinical and scientific content and is distributed to all members of Sonograhy Canada.

Sons of Scotland Benevolent Association
#801, 505 Consummers Rd., Toronto ON M2J 4V8
Tel: 416-482-1250; *Fax:* 416-482-9576
Toll-Free: 800-387-3382
info@sonsofscotland.com
www.sonsofscotland.com
Overview: A small local organization founded in 1876
Mission: Undertake & support activities which promote the elements of Scottish culture in Canada; honour the history & heritage of Scots in Canada; support & raise funds for charitable organizations; provide fraternal & insurance benefits for members
Chief Officer(s):
Robert Stewart, Executive Director
Finances: *Annual Operating Budget:* $500,000-$1.5 Million
Staff Member(s): 5
Membership: 4,490; *Fees:* $60

Sooke Food Bank Society
Sooke Community Hall, 2037 Eustace Rd., Sooke BC V0S 1N0
Tel: 250-642-7666
Overview: A small local organization

Sooke Harbour Chamber of Commerce
PO Box 18, #301, 2015 Shields Rd., Sooke BC V9Z 0E4
Tel: 250-642-6112
info@sookeharbourchamber.com
www.sookeharbourchamber.com
Overview: A small local organization founded in 1948
Member of: BC Chamber of Commerce
Chief Officer(s):
Scott Gertsma, President
Finances: *Annual Operating Budget:* Less than $50,000; *Funding Sources:* Membership dues
Membership: 205; *Fees:* $80-$180 business; $40 non-profit; $60 individual

Sooke Philharmonic Society
PO Box 767, Sooke BC V9Z 1H7
Tel: 250-419-3569
info@sookephil.ca
www.sookephil.ca
www.facebook.com/sookephil
twitter.com/sookephil
Overview: A small local organization overseen by Orchestras Canada
Mission: To promote & enhance the appreciation of music; to support & nurture musical talent in the community
Chief Officer(s):

Bob Whittlet, President

Soroptimist Foundation of Canada
c/o Treasurer, 2455 Cunningham Blvd., Peterborough ON K9H 0B2
www.soroptimistfoundation.ca
Overview: A small national charitable organization founded in 1963
Mission: To provide bursaries, scholarships & fellowships to Canadian students & Canadian schools, colleges & universities for the advancement of education & in particular to further the appreciation of social needs, & the study of community, national & international problems
Affliation(s): Soroptimist International of the Americas
Chief Officer(s):
Elizabeth Jane (BJ) Gallagher, Chair
chair@soroptimistfoundation.ca
Sheryl Hopkins, Treasurer
treasurer@soroptimistfoundation.ca
Lori Roblesky, Secretary
secretary@soroptimistfoundation.ca
Finances: *Annual Operating Budget:* $50,000-$100,000; *Funding Sources:* Donations; membership fees
5 volunteer(s)
Membership: 46 clubs; *Fees:* Schedule available
Activities: Soroptomist Grants for Females (only in Canada);
Awards:
• Grants for Women (Grant)
Amount: Four grants of $7,500 each
• Club Grants (Grant)
Amount: Seven grants of $1,000 each

SOS Children's Villages Canada / SOS Villages d'Enfants Canada
#240, 44 By Ward Market Square, Ottawa ON K1N 7A2
Tel: 613-232-3309
Toll-Free: 800-767-5111
info@soschildrensvillages.ca
www.soschildrensvillages.ca
www.facebook.com/105288666168351
www.youtube.com/user/soscanada1
Also Known As: SOS - Canada
Previous Name: Friends of SOS Children's Villages, Canada Inc.
Overview: A small international charitable organization founded in 1969
Mission: To assist SOS-Children's Villages in Canada & abroad through financial & operating support; to care for orphaned, abandoned & other children in need of long-term placement; to create opportunities for children to become happy, stable, responsible members of society
Member of: Canadian Child Welfare League
Affliation(s): SOS-Kinderdorf International
Chief Officer(s):
Boyd McBride, President & CEO
Finances: *Funding Sources:* Direct mail; special events
Staff Member(s): 10
Activities: *Internships:* Yes; *Speaker Service:* Yes

SOS Villages d'Enfants Canada *See* SOS Children's Villages Canada

SOSA Gliding Club
PO Box 81, 1144 Cooper Rd., Rockton ON L0R 1X0
Tel: 519-740-9328
sosa@sosaglidingclub.com
www.sosaglidingclub.com
www.linkedin.com/groups?viewMembers=&gid=3132977&sik=1276482950598
www.facebook.com/groups/2228522913
twitter.com/sosaglidingclub
Overview: A small local organization
Member of: Soaring Association of Canada
Chief Officer(s):
Herrie ten Cate, President
Herrie@SOSAGlidingClub.com

Sou'wester Coin Club
c/o Douglas B. Shand, PO Box 78, Shag Harbour, Shelburne County NS B0W 3B0
e-mail: info@souwestercoinclub.com
www.souwestercoinclub.com
Overview: A small local organization founded in 1992
Member of: Royal Canadian Numismatic Association
Chief Officer(s):
Douglas B. Shand, Contact

Soundstreams Canada
#200, 57 Spadina Ave., Toronto ON M5V 2J2
Tel: 416-504-1282; *Fax:* 416-504-1285
info@soundstreams.ca
www.soundstreams.ca
www.facebook.com/soundstreams
twitter.com/soundstreams
www.youtube.com/soundstreams
Overview: A small national charitable organization founded in 1981
Mission: To foster & promote the development of 20th century music & music by Canadian composers, through the sponsorship of concerts, musical theatre works for young audiences, festivals & special events, recording projects, the commissioning of new works by Canadian composers & touring of Canadian artists
Member of: Opera Canada; Orchestras Canada; Choirs Ontario
Chief Officer(s):
Chris Lorway, Executive Director
Staff Member(s): 7
Membership: *Committees:* Advisory; Encore Executive

Sources Foundation
882 Maple St., White Rock BC V4B 4M2
Tel: 604-531-6226; *Fax:* 604-531-2316
info@sourcesbc.ca
www.sourcesbc.ca
www.linkedin.com/company/sources
www.facebook.com/SourcesCommunityResourceCentres
twitter.com/sourcesbc
www.youtube.com/user/SourcesCommunity
Also Known As: Sources White Rock/South Surrey Food Bank
Previous Name: Peace Arch Community Services
Overview: A small local organization founded in 1978 overseen by Food Banks British Columbia
Mission: To raise funds for Sources BC, a comprehensive community service organization operating a food bank, programs for seniors, counselling services for youth & families, employment consultation
Member of: Food Banks British Columbia; British Columbians for Mentally Handicapped People
Chief Officer(s):
Harry White, President
David Young, Executive Director
dyoung@sourcesbc.ca
Activities: Training & workshops; counselling; food distribution

Souris & Glenwood Chamber of Commerce
PO Box 939, Souris MB R0K 2C0
e-mail: sourischamber@gmail.com
www.facebook.com/SourisGlenwoodChamber
Overview: A small local organization
Affliation(s): Manitoba Chamber of Commerce
Chief Officer(s):
Sande Denbow, President
Membership: 68
Activities: An interest in the well-being of Souris & area economically, educationally & recreationally; *Library* Open to public

Sous-Traitance Industrielle Québec (STIQ)
#900, 1080, côte du Beaver Hall, Montréal QC H2Z 1S8
Tél: 514-875-8789
Ligne sans frais: 888-875-8789
info@stiq.com
www.stiq.com
Aperçu: *Dimension:* moyenne; *Envergure:* provinciale; fondée en 1987
Membre(s) du bureau directeur:
Normand Voyer, Vice-président executive
nvoyer@stiq.com
Membre: 700; *Critères d'admissibilite:* Aéronautique; énergie; ressources; transport

South Asia Partnership Canada (SAP) / Société asiatique des partenaires Canada
#1210, One Nicholas St., Ottawa ON K1N 7B7
Tel: 613-241-1333; *Fax:* 613-244-3410
rharmston@sapcanada.org
www.sapcanada.org
Overview: A medium-sized international organization founded in 1981
Mission: To build a strong base of support for development in South Asia & encourage policies & programs that will benefit disadvantaged people there; to facilitate the sharing of ideas, experience & resources among organizations & the Canadian public on South Asian development; to mobilize Canadian support for & participation in the development programs of SAP International member organizations & their partners; to manage development programs
Member of: Canadian Council for International Cooperation; South Asia Partnership International
Chief Officer(s):
Richard Harmston, Executive Director
rharmston@sapcanada.org
Cliff Dick, President
Finances: *Annual Operating Budget:* $3 Million-$5 Million; *Funding Sources:* CIDA; membership dues; subscriptions; fees for services
Staff Member(s): 8
Membership: 22 institutional; *Fees:* $500; *Member Profile:* Agencies providing non-sectarian, financial support; interest in new approaches to development & established record of international development work
Activities: Forums; communication; network; policy advocacy; support human development in South Asia; *Internships:* Yes; *Speaker Service:* Yes; *Library:* Resource Centre

South Asian Centre of Windsor
#208, 225 Wyandotte St. West, Windsor ON N9A 5X1
Tel: 519-252-7447
info@southasiancentre.ca
www.southasiancentre.ca
Overview: A small local organization founded in 1986 overseen by Ontario Council of Agencies Serving Immigrants
Chief Officer(s):
Sushil Jain, President
sacw1968@gmail.com
Finances: *Funding Sources:* Private; federal & provincial government

South Asian Family Support Services *See* Settlement Assistance & Family Support Services

South Asian Women's Centre (SAWC)
8163 Main St., Vancouver BC V5X 3L2
Tel: 604-325-6637; *Fax:* 604-322-6675
sawc@asia.com
www.sawc.8m.com
Overview: A medium-sized local organization
Mission: The South Asian Women's Centre is a space for South Asian women to work actively for social change. The centre strongly believes that women can change their own lives and the lives of others in our communities, in our society, and even globally. The centre supports the development of non-oppressive attitudes and behaviours by critiquing and combating sexism, racism, homophobia, caste/classism, ageism and ableism.

South Cariboo Chamber of Commerce
PO Box 2312, #2, 385 Birch Ave., 100 Mile House BC V0K 2E0
Tel: 250-395-6124
www.southcariboochamber.org
Overview: A small local organization founded in 1978
Mission: To provide a united voice for business, committed to the enhancement of economic prosperity of the South Cariboo communities
Member of: BC Chamber of Commerce
Affliation(s): Canadian Chamber of Commerce
Chief Officer(s):
Tom Bachynski, President
tbachynski@centralgm.com
Finances: *Annual Operating Budget:* Less than $50,000; *Funding Sources:* Membership dues
Staff Member(s): 1; 2 volunteer(s)
Membership: 130; *Fees:* $117.50 based on 1-2 employees; *Member Profile:* Business owner, individual with interest in business
Activities: *Awareness Events:* Chamber of Commerce Week, Feb.; Small Business Week, Oct.; *Library:* Business Information Centre; Open to public by appointment

South Central Committee on Family Violence, Inc. (SCCFV)
PO Box 389, Winkler MB R6W 4A6
Tel: 204-325-9957; *Fax:* 204-325-5889; *Crisis Hot-Line:* 877-977-0007
sccfv@genesis-house.ca
genesishouseshelter.ca
Also Known As: Genesis House
Overview: A small local charitable organization founded in 1983
Mission: To provide a confidential service which includes a shelter for abused women & their children, supportive residential & non-residential programs & prevention through public

education to empower women & their children to make informed choices
Member of: Manitoba Association of Women's Shelters Inc.
Finances: *Funding Sources:* Provincial & federal governments; United Way; donations
Activities: Advocacy; Elder Abuse; Crisis & Long-Term Counselling; Follow-Up Service; Child Counselling; Support Groups; 2nd-Stage Housing; Referrals; Resource Centre; Speakers; Training; 24-hour Toll-Free Crisis Line; 24-hour Shelter for Abused Women & Their Children; *Library* by appointment

South Coast District Labour Council
PO Box 127, Marystown NL A0E 2M0
Tel: 709-279-3274; *Fax:* 709-279-4351
Overview: A small local organization
Member of: Newfoundland & Labrador Federation of Labour
Chief Officer(s):
Julie Mitchell, President
juliemitchell279@hotmail.com

South Cowichan Chamber of Commerce (SCCC)
#368, 2720 Mill Bay Rd., Mill Bay BC V0R 2P1
Tel: 250-743-3566; *Fax:* 250-743-5332
southcowichanchamber@shaw.ca
www.southcowichanchamber.org
Overview: A small local organization founded in 1982
Mission: To promote & improve trade & commerce & the economic, civic & social welfare of the district
Member of: BC Chamber Executives; BC Chamber of Commerce
Chief Officer(s):
Shauna Benson, Executive Director
Mike Hanson, President
bcporthose@gmail.com
Finances: *Annual Operating Budget:* Less than $50,000; *Funding Sources:* Membership dues; map advertising sales; showcase booths; auction
30 volunteer(s)
Membership: 130; *Fees:* $180-$775; *Committees:* Administration; Fundraising; Business Promotion; Local Issues; Tourism; Membership Services
Activities: Seasonal Info Centre; annual business showcase; Membership Directory; map; auction; group insurance; monthly meetings

South Delta Food Bank
5545 Ladner Trunk Rd., Delta BC V4K 1X1
Tel: 604-946-1967; *Fax:* 604-946-4944
info@ladnerlife.com
Overview: A small local organization overseen by Food Banks British Columbia
Member of: Food Banks British Columbia
Chief Officer(s):
Joe Van Essen, Contact

South Dundas Chamber of Commerce
PO Box 288, 91 Main St., Morrisburg ON K0C 1X0
Tel: 613-543-3982; *Fax:* 613-543-2971
managersdchamber@gmail.com
www.southdundaschamber.ca
Previous Name: Morrisburg & District Chamber of Commerce
Overview: A small local organization
Chief Officer(s):
Carl McIntyre, President
Staff Member(s): 1
Membership: 61; *Fees:* $60-$270

South East Asian Services Centre *See* Support Enhance Access Service Centre

South Eastern Alberta Archaeological Society *See* Archaeological Society of Alberta

South Essex Community Centre (SECC)
215 Talbot St. East, Leamington ON N8H 3X5
Tel: 519-326-8629; *Fax:* 519-326-1529
info@secc.on.ca
www.secc.on.ca
www.facebook.com/138831152979483
Overview: A medium-sized local organization founded in 1973
Mission: To preserve & improve the quality of life in the communities of South Essex by providing social planning &/or direct services to all individuals
Chief Officer(s):
Colleen Pearse, Chair
Finances: *Funding Sources:* Federal, provincial & municipal governments; United Way; fundraising; donations; membership dues
Membership: *Fees:* $10; *Member Profile:* Resident of South Essex 18 yrs of age & over
Activities: *Speaker Service:* Yes; *Rents Mailing List:* Yes; *Library:* Resource Centre; Open to public

South Etobicoke Community Legal Services (SECLS)
#210, 5353 Dundas St. West, Toronto ON M9B 6H8
Tel: 416-252-7218; *Fax:* 416-252-1474
secls@southetobicokelegal.ca
www.southetobicokelegal.ca
Overview: A small local charitable organization founded in 1982
Mission: To protect & promote the legal welfare of community members by offering services, unique to the community, through a network of volunteers & staff members, where language, financial hardship or disability will not act as barriers
Member of: Association of Community Legal Clinics of Ontario
Affliation(s): Toronto Refugees Affairs Council; Federation of Metro Tenants Ontario Council of Agencies Serving Immigrants
Staff Member(s): 5
Activities: *Speaker Service:* Yes

South Fraser Child Development Centre; Lower Fraser Valley Cerebral Palsy Association *See* Centre for Child Development

South Grenville Chamber of Commerce
950 Edward St. North, Prescott ON K0E 1T0
Tel: 613-213-1043
southgrenvillechamber@gmail.com
www.southgrenvillechamber.ca
Previous Name: Prescott Board of Trade; Prescott Chamber of Commerce; Prescott and District Chamber of Commerce
Overview: A small local organization founded in 1893
Member of: Canadian Chamber of Commerce; Ontario Chamber of Commerce
Chief Officer(s):
Dan Roddick, President
Jerone Taylor, President-Elect
Membership: 150; *Fees:* $65 1-5 employees; $90 6-15 employees; $135 16-30 employees; $165 31-50 employees; $215 51+ employees

South Huron Chamber of Commerce
PO Box 550, 414 Main St. South, Exeter ON N0M 1S6
Tel: 226-423-3028; *Fax:* 519-235-3141
www.shcc.on.ca
Overview: A small local organization
Chief Officer(s):
Steve Boles, Interim President & Treasurer

The South Journalists Club *See* Human Rights & Race Relations Centre

South Lake Community Futures Development Corporation
183 The Queensway South, Keswick ON L4P 2A3
Tel: 905-476-1244; *Fax:* 905-476-9978
Toll-Free: 866-606-1244
www.southlakecfdc.org
www.facebook.com/158511384227435
twitter.com/SouthLakeCFDC
Previous Name: Georgina Association for Business
Overview: A small local organization founded in 2004
Mission: A not-for-profit community based organization providing a variety of small business and community economic development services within the towns of East Gwillimbury, Georgina as well as Brock Township.
Member of: Ontario Association of Community Futures Development Corporation
Chief Officer(s):
Paul Nicholls, Chair
Peter Budero, General Manager
Staff Member(s): 3; 12 volunteer(s)

South Lake Simcoe Naturalists
PO Box 1044, Sutton West ON L0E 1R0
Tel: 416-722-8021
Overview: A small local organization founded in 1980
Mission: Conservation, education & recreation organization concerned with the study & experience of nature & the relationships between it & humans
Member of: Federation of Ontario Naturalists
Chief Officer(s):
Paul Harpley, President
Finances: *Annual Operating Budget:* Less than $50,000; *Funding Sources:* Federal & provincial governments; private
Membership: 100-499
Activities: Wildlife research; breeding bird census; South Lake Simcoe Wildlife Research Station (seasonal); lectures; outings; land use planning; *Internships:* Yes; *Speaker Service:* Yes

South Norwich Historical Society
PO Box 162, Otterville ON N0J 1R0
Tel: 519-879-6804
www.historicotterville.ca/info.shtml
Also Known As: Historic Otterville
Overview: A small local charitable organization founded in 1975
Mission: To encourage the discovery, collection & preservation of local history & buildings; to maintain a museum
Member of: Ontario Historical Society; Tourism Oxford
Chief Officer(s):
Gail Lewis, Contact
glewis@execulink.com
Finances: *Funding Sources:* Grants; fundraising
Activities: Operates an 1845 grist mill & 1881 Grand Trunk Railway Station; Motorcoach Tours of Otterville; *Awareness Events:* Welcome Back to Otterville, Nov.; Car Show, June; Country Fair, Sept.

South Okanagan Boundary Labour Council (SOBLC)
697 Martin St., Penticton BC V2A 5L5
Tel: 778-476-5771; *Fax:* 250-492-5540
soblc@shaw.ca
www.facebook.com/group.php?gid=42420073326
Overview: A small local organization
Mission: To act as the voice of union affiliates in the Penticton area of British Columbia; To advance the economic & social welfare of workers
Affliation(s): Canadian Labour Congress (CLC)
Chief Officer(s):
Brent Voss, President
soblc@shaw.ca
Renee van Uden, First Vice-President
redeye39@hotmail.com
Terry Green, Treasurer
terlingreen@shaw.ca
Colleen Wiens, Treasurer
Membership: 2,000; *Member Profile:* Members of unions from the South Okanagan region of British Columbia
Activities: Arranging events for International Workers' Day (May Day); Participating in the annual Day of Mourning for workers injured or killed on the job; Liaising with local council

South Okanagan Chamber Of Commerce
6431 Station St., Oliver BC V0H 1T0
Tel: 250-498-6321; *Fax:* 250-498-3156
www.sochamber.ca
www.facebook.com/182627531775650
twitter.com/southokchamber
www.youtube.com/user/SouthOKChamber
Previous Name: Oliver & District Chamber of Commerce
Overview: A small local organization founded in 1947
Mission: The Oliver Community Chamber of Commerce is the doorway to Wine Capital tourism information, as well as the place for local businesses to find chamber information.
Member of: Thompson Okanagan Tourism Association; BC Chamber of Commerce; Canadian Chamber of Commerce
Finances: *Annual Operating Budget:* $100,000-$250,000
Staff Member(s): 2; 8 volunteer(s)
Membership: 180; *Fees:* Schedule available
Activities: Festival of the Grape; Festival of the Tomato; *Library* Open to public

South Okanagan Immigrant & Community Services (SOICS)
508 Main St., Penticton BC V2A 5C7
Tel: 250-492-6299; *Fax:* 250-490-4684
admin@soics.ca
www.soics.ca
www.facebook.com/262859047105075
Previous Name: Penticton & District Multicultural Society
Overview: A small local organization founded in 1976
Mission: To build a community based upon mutual respect & full participation of people of all backgrounds through education, client advocacy & community programs
Member of: Affiliation of Multicultural Societies & Service Agencies of BC
Finances: *Annual Operating Budget:* $250,000-$500,000; *Funding Sources:* Grants; fundraising; donations; projects
Membership: 1-99

Activities: English as a Second Language; settlement & employment services; Settlement Worker in Schools (SWIS); learning centre

South Okanagan Real Estate Board (SOREB)
365 Van Horne St., Penticton BC V2A 8S4
Tel: 250-492-0626; *Fax:* 250-493-0832
www.soreb.org
www.facebook.com/151180668308444
twitter.com/soreb1
Overview: A small local organization founded in 1979 overseen by British Columbia Real Estate Association
Mission: To pursue excellence & professionalism in real estate, through quality education & high ethical standards; To protect the interest of the membership & the public
Member of: The Canadian Real Estate Association
Finances: *Funding Sources:* Membership fees
Membership: 300 realtors
Activities: *Library*

South Okanagan Similkameen Brain Injury Society (SOSBIS)
#2, 996 Main St., Penticton BC V2A 5E4
Tel: 250-490-0613; *Fax:* 250-490-3912
info@sosbis.com
www.sosbis.com
www.facebook.com/SOSBIS
Overview: A small local charitable organization
Mission: To assist survivors of acquired brain injuries & their families in acheiving independence & quality of life; To prevent brain injuries
Chief Officer(s):
Lisette Shewfelt, Executive Director
Finances: *Funding Sources:* United Way; Interior Health; Government of British Columbia; Donations
Staff Member(s): 10
Membership: *Member Profile:* Anyone living with the effects of acquired brain injury/stroke; anyone interested in supporting the purposes of the organization
Publications:
• Brain Waves
Type: Newsletter; *Frequency:* Quarterly
Profile: Organization news; upcoming events; stories; strategies to cope with acquired brain injury

South Okanagan Women in Need Society (SOWINS)
#303, 246 Martin St., Penticton BC V2A 5K3
Tel: 250-493-4366
Toll-Free: 800-814-2033
info@sowins.com
www.sowins.com
Overview: A small local charitable organization founded in 1981
Mission: To provide a secure haven, support & advocacy for women (& their children) who experience abuse; to work towards the prevention of violence/abuse in the South Okanagan area; to operate a Transition House which honours women & respects their experiences; to offer a supportive environment for women to explore their personal choices; to provide individual & community education & pre-employment services for eligibile abused women.
Affiliation(s): BC/Yukon Society of Transition Houses; Imagine Canada
Chief Officer(s):
Debbie Scarborough, Executive Director
Finances: *Funding Sources:* Provincial government; fundraising
Staff Member(s): 30; 100 volunteer(s)
Membership: *Fees:* $10 individual
Activities: Transition House; counselling for women in abusive relationships; children's group; Wings, secondhand store; *Speaker Service:* Yes

South Pacific Peoples Foundation *See* Pacific Peoples Partnership

South Peace AIDS Council of Grande Prairie; Society of the South Peace AIDS Council *See* HIV North Society

South Peace Community Arts Council
PO Box 2314, Dawson Creek BC V1G 4H4
Tel: 250-782-1164; *Fax:* 250-782-8801
dcagchin@pris.ca
www.southpeacearts.ca
www.facebook.com/pages/South-Peace-Community-Arts-Council/138320271866
Overview: A small local organization founded in 1969
Mission: To foster an interest and pride in the cultural heritage of the community by supporting and developing ongoing programs.
Member of: Assembly of BC Arts Councils
Chief Officer(s):
Melissa Holoboff, President
dcagchin@pris.ca

South Peace Community Resources Society (SPCRS)
PO Box 713, 10110 - 13th St., Dawson Creek BC V1G 4H7
Tel: 250-782-9174; *Fax:* 250-782-4167
Toll-Free: 866-712-9174
reception@spcrs.ca
www.spcrs.ca
www.facebook.com/spcrs.dawsoncreek
Overview: A small local charitable organization founded in 1974
Mission: To meet the social, educational & personal needs of the community by providing services that develop skills for living; To provide community & residential services; to meet the needs of children, youth & families, women who have experienced violence, victims of crime, adults with mental handicaps, children with special needs, couples & individuals experiencing trauma or difficulties in their life
Member of: British Columbia Association for Community Living; Federation of Child & Family Services; BC/Yukon Society of Transition Houses; BC Association for Specialized Victims Assistance Programs & Counselling
Chief Officer(s):
Jane Harper, Executive Director, 250-780-9174 Ext. 223, Fax: 250-782-4167
jharper@spcrs.ca
Finances: *Annual Operating Budget:* $3 Million-$5 Million
Staff Member(s): 80; 9 volunteer(s)
Membership: 50; *Fees:* $5; *Member Profile:* Victims of scrims; victims of family violence; special needs children; adults with disabilities & their families
Activities: Family Day; National Child Day; Little Black Dress Affair fundraiser; Youth Day; Community Living Month; White Ribbon Campaign; *Awareness Events:* December 6 Memorial; Take Back the Night; Community Living Week; International Women's Day; Family Week; *Internships:* Yes; *Speaker Service:* Yes; *Library:* Professional Resources Child Development; Open to public by appointment

South Peel Naturalists' Club (SPNC)
PO Box 69629, 109 Thomas St., Oakville ON L6J 7R4
Tel: 905-279-8807
mail@spnc.ca
www.spnc.ca
Overview: A small local organization founded in 1952
Member of: Federation of Ontario Naturalists
Affliation(s): Canadian Nature Federation
Chief Officer(s):
Don Morrison, President
Finances: *Annual Operating Budget:* Less than $50,000; *Funding Sources:* Membership fees; Donations
35 volunteer(s)
Membership: 200+; *Fees:* $25 individual; $30 family; $15 student; $20 senior family; $15 senior individual

South Queens Chamber of Commerce
Tel: 902-350-1826
secretary@southqueenschamber.com
www.southqueenschamber.com
www.facebook.com/191426127877
Overview: A small local organization
Chief Officer(s):
Barry Tomalin, President
Kevin Page, Treasurer
Monica Howard, Secretary

South Saskatchewan Community Foundation Inc.
3934 Gordon Rd., Regina SK S4S 6Y3
Tel: 306-751-4756; *Fax:* 306-751-4768
sscf@sasktel.net
www.sscf.ca
Previous Name: Regina Community Foundation
Overview: A small local charitable organization founded in 1969
Mission: Supports communities by managing & investing permanent endowment funds & donations & distributing the fund proceeds to charitable non-profit organizations
Member of: Community Foundations of Canada
Chief Officer(s):
Cindy Chamberlin, Manager, Donor Services & Administration
Finances: *Annual Operating Budget:* $50,000-$100,000
Staff Member(s): 2
Membership: 1-99

South Saskatchewan Youth Orchestra (SSYO)
PO Box 868, Lumsden SK S0G 3C0
Tel: 306-761-2576
www.ssyo.ca
twitter.com/SSYO4all
Overview: A small local organization founded in 1977 overseen by Orchestras Canada
Mission: To provide orchestral training to young musicians in Southern Saskatchewan
Member of: Saskatchewan Orchestral Association
Affliation(s): Regina Symphony Orchestra
Chief Officer(s):
Alan Denike, Music Director
Finances: *Funding Sources:* Membership fees; government grants; corporate donations; private donations
Membership: *Fees:* $50; $550 orchestra training; *Member Profile:* Serious musical students, most study privately, average age 15
Activities: 4-5 concerts a year; outreach programs; *Library:* Music Library;

South Shore Chamber of Commerce
PO Box 127, Crapaud PE C0A 1J0
Tel: 902-658-2738
Overview: A small local organization
Mission: To promote business in our community by sponsoring the Ice Fishing Derby, Walleye Classic, Canada Day Parade, Winter Fun Fest & Soap Box Derby
Member of: Saskatchewan Chamber of Commerce
Chief Officer(s):
Marion Miller, President
Finances: *Annual Operating Budget:* $50,000-$100,000
25 volunteer(s)
Membership: 82; *Fees:* $25

South Shore Genealogical Society
PO Box 901, 68 Bluenose Dr., Lunenburg NS B0J 2C0
Tel: 902-634-4794
Toll-Free: 866-579-4909
ssgsoc@hotmail.com
www.ssgs.ca
Overview: A small local organization founded in 1979
Mission: Dedicated to developing and providing genealogical information on the South Shore area (Lunenburg and Queens counties) of Nova Scotia.
Member of: Canadian Council of N.S. Archives
Chief Officer(s):
Paula Masson, Secretary
masson51@eastlink.ca
Finances: *Annual Operating Budget:* Less than $50,000; *Funding Sources:* Membership fees; Grants for summer student
25 volunteer(s)
Membership: 350; *Fees:* $15
Activities: *Library* Open to public

South Shore Genealogical Society
PO Box 901, 68 Bluenose Dr., Lunenburg NS B0J 2C0
Tel: 902-634-9610
Toll-Free: 866-579-4909
www.ssgs.ca
Overview: A small local organization founded in 1979
Mission: To preserve & research genealogical information regarding the South Shore
Chief Officer(s):
Stephen Ernst, President
stephen_a_ernst@hotmail.com
Membership: *Fees:* $20 single; $30 family

South Shore Reading Council (SSRC)
#4, 279 Hubert St., Greenfield Park QC J4V 1R9
Tel: 450-671-4375
info@ssrc.ca
ssrc.ca
Overview: A small local organization
Mission: To encourage English literacy among youth and adults, as well as to raise awareness about the levels of illiteracy rates to the public
Activities: Tutoring for adults; Lessons for children

South Shore Tourism Association *See* Destination Southwest Nova Association

South Shuswap Chamber of Commerce
PO Box 7, Blind Bay BC V0E 2W0
Tel: 250-675-3515; *Fax:* 250-675-3516
sorrentochamber@telus.net
www.southshuswapchamberofcommerce.org

www.facebook.com/224164024262712
twitter.com/SSCOC
Overview: A small local organization founded in 1985
Member of: Canadian Chamber of Commerce; British Columbia Chamber of Commerce
Chief Officer(s):
Judy Smith, President, 250-675-4801
jude@RDSweb.net
Nancy Kyle, Manager, 250-675-3515
Finances: *Annual Operating Budget:* Less than $50,000; *Funding Sources:* Membership fees; fundraising; grant
15 volunteer(s)
Membership: 100+; *Fees:* $95
Activities: *Library* Open to public

South Simcoe Community Information Centre
Town Square, PO Box 932, 39 Victoria St. East, Alliston ON L9R 1W1
Tel: 705-435-4900; *Fax:* 705-435-1106
contact@contactsouthsimcoe.ca
www.contactsouthsimcoe.ca
Overview: A small local organization founded in 1979 overseen by InformOntario
Mission: To work to create a community that is informed of available resources through the provision of information & referral, access to information technologies & partnership with others
Chief Officer(s):
Liz Beattie, Co-Executive Director
Sandra Mawby, Co-Executive Director
Finances: *Annual Operating Budget:* $100,000-$250,000
Staff Member(s): 12; 35 volunteer(s)

South Stormont Chamber of Commerce
PO Box 489, Ingleside ON K0C 1M0
Tel: 613-537-8344; *Fax:* 613-537-9439
info@sscc.on.ca
www.sscc.on.ca
Overview: A small local organization
Chief Officer(s):
Donna Primeau, President
Membership: *Fees:* $35-$280

South Surrey & White Rock Chamber of Commerce
#100, 15261 Russell Ave., White Rock BC V4B 2P7
Tel: 604-536-6844; *Fax:* 604-536-4994
admin@sswrchamber.ca
www.sswrchamberofcommerce.ca
www.facebook.com/293324054033157?sk=wall
twitter.com/SswrChamber
sswrchamber.tumblr.com
Overview: A small local organization founded in 1937
Mission: To promote business & economic growth on the peninsula
Member of: Canadian Chamber of Commerce
Affliation(s): BC Tourism
Chief Officer(s):
Cliff Annable, Executive Director, 604-536-6844 Ext. 6
cliff@sswrchamber.ca
Finances: *Annual Operating Budget:* $50,000-$100,000; *Funding Sources:* Provincial & local government; membership fees
Staff Member(s): 2; 20 volunteer(s)
Membership: 700
Activities: *Library:* Business Library; Open to public

South Wellington Coin Society (SWCS)
ON
www.w3design.com/swcs
Previous Name: Guelph Coin Club
Overview: A small local organization founded in 1997
Mission: To trade information on coins, medals, & tokens of interest to collectors; To increase awareness of Canadian history through numismatics
Affliation(s): Ontario Numismatic Association; Canadian Numismatic Association; London Numismatic Society
Membership: *Fees:* $10
Activities: Providing education through monthly meetings
Publications:
• SWCS Newsletter
Type: Newsletter
Profile: Club news & upcoming events

South West Community Care Access Centre
356 Oxford St. West, London ON N6H 1T3
Tel: 519-641-5519; *Fax:* 519-472-4045
Toll-Free: 800-811-5147; *TTY:* 519-473-9626
info-london@sw.ccac-ont.ca
www.ccac-ont.ca
Also Known As: South West CCAC
Overview: A small local charitable organization founded in 1970 overseen by InformOntario
Mission: Online directory of community & social services & resources for citizens of London & area
Affliation(s): London Health Sciences Centre; Middlesex-London Health Unit; St. Joseph's Health Care (London)
Chief Officer(s):
Lisa Misurak, Manager
Activities: Publications & printed resources; information technology; database of community services; community development, consultation & education

South Western Alberta Teachers' Convention Association (SWATCA)
c/o Roxane Holmes, 1215 - 19 Ave., Coaldale AB T1M 1A4
Tel: 403-308-8761
www.swatca.ca
twitter.com/swatca
Overview: A small provincial organization
Chief Officer(s):
Kim Yearous, President
Membership: *Committees:* Conference; Displays; Evaluation; Social; Website; Recruitment
Meetings/Conferences: • South Western Alberta Teachers' Convention Association 116th Annual Convention, February, 2015, University of Lethbridge, Lethbridge, AB
Scope: Provincial
Description: Theme: "Learning With E's"

Southam Foundation *See* Alva Foundation

Southeast Asia-Canada Business Council
5294 Imperial St., Burnaby BC V5J 1E4
Tel: 604-439-0779; *Fax:* 604-439-0284
info@aseancanada.com
www.aseancanada.com
Also Known As: Association of Southeast Asian Nations-Canada Business Council
Previous Name: ASEAN-Canada Business Council
Overview: A medium-sized international organization founded in 1987
Mission: To assist Canadian companies, especially small & medium sized enterprises (SMEs), to enter or expand their presence in the ASEAN market
Staff Member(s): 3
Membership: 50; *Fees:* $750

Southeast Environmental Association (SEA)
41 Woods Islands Hill, Montague PE C0A 1R0
Tel: 902-838-3351; *Fax:* 902-838-0610
seapei.org
Overview: A medium-sized provincial organization founded in 1992
Mission: To protect, maintain, and enhance the ecology of south eastern Prince Edward Island for the environmental, social, and economic well being of area residents.
Chief Officer(s):
Jackie Bourgeois, Executive Director
Lawrence Millar, Chair

Southeast Georgian Bay Chamber of Commerce
PO Box 70, 99 Lone Pine Rd., Port Severn ON L0K 1S0
Tel: 705-756-4863; *Fax:* 705-756-4863
info@segbay.ca
www.segbay.ca
www.facebook.com/SEGBAY
Previous Name: Honey Harbour/Port Severn District Chamber of Commerce
Overview: A small local organization
Chief Officer(s):
Marianne Braid, Manager
Membership: *Fees:* $69

South-East Grey Support Services (SEGSS)
PO Box 12, 24 Toronto St., Flesherton ON N0C 1E0
Tel: 519-924-3339; *Fax:* 519-924-3575
segss@bmts.com
www.southeastgreysupportservices.com
www.facebook.com/329076267124425
Overview: A small local organization founded in 1961
Mission: Provides and advocates for a full range of community-based services for individuals with intellectual disabilities including accommodation, employment, day program, planning and family supports.
Member of: Community Living Ontario
Chief Officer(s):
Maurice Voisin, Executive Director
Finances: *Funding Sources:* MCSS
Staff Member(s): 70
Publications:
• Grey Bruce Facilitation Network Newsletter [a publication of South-East Grey Support Services]
Type: Newsletter

Southern African Jewish Association of Canada (SAJAC)
PO Box 87510, 300 John St., Thornhill ON L3T 7R3
Tel: 416-499-2895
www.primequadrant.com/Sajac
Also Known As: SAJAC Seniors
Overview: A small international organization founded in 1979
Mission: A networking organization of Jewish ex-South Africans (including Zimbabwe) helping in the fields of job search, accommodation, seniors, & general information as needed by new immigrants
Chief Officer(s):
Thea Abramson, Chair
theabramson@yahoo.com
Colin Baskind, President, 416-733-8610
Membership: 100-499; *Member Profile:* Jewish people from Southern Africa now living in Toronto
Activities: Social activities for all Jewish ex-South Africans

Southern Alberta Brain Injury Society (SABIS)
#137, 2723 - 37th Ave. NE, Calgary AB T1Y 5R8
Tel: 403-521-5212; *Fax:* 403-283-5867
Toll-Free: 866-527-2247
sabis@sabis.ab.ca
www.sabis.ab.ca
www.twitter.com/SABISCalgary/
Overview: A small local charitable organization founded in 1985
Mission: To support adults with acquired brain injury, & their families, in southern Alberta; To provide lifelong services for adults with acquired brain injury; To assist persons with acquired brain injury to live as independently as possible in the community they choose
Chief Officer(s):
Joe Schreiber, Program Director
joe@sabis.ab.ca
Natasha Bodei, Director, Finance & Operations
natasha@sabis.ab.ca
Finances: *Funding Sources:* Donations; Fundraising
Membership: *Fees:* $10 individuals; $15 families; $20 professionals & non-profit agencies; $100 corporate members
Activities: Advocating, on behalf of persons affected by brain injury, for open & inclusive communities for all persons; Promoting optimal services for persons affected by brain injury; Developing personalized systems of support during recovery; Providing emotional support to persons with brain injury & their family members; Organizing peer support groups; Raising awareness of acquired brain injury & its causes & effects; Encouraging the further development of services & programs to support individuals affected by brain injury; *Awareness Events:* Brain Injury Awareness Month, June; *Library:* Southern Alberta Brain Injury Society Library
Publications:
• Southern Alberta Brain Injury Society Newsletter
Type: Newsletter; *Frequency:* Quarterly; *Price:* Free with membership in the Southern Alberta Brain Injury Society
• Southern Alberta Brain Injury Society Annual Report
Type: Yearbook; *Frequency:* Annually; *Price:* Free with membership in the Southern Alberta Brain Injury Society

Southern Alberta Brain Injury Society (SABIS)
#102, 2116 - 27th Ave. NE, Calgary AB T2E 7A6
Tel: 403-521-5212; *Fax:* 403-283-5867
sabis@sabis.ab.ca
www.sabis.ab.ca
www.facebook.com/226816920793215
twitter.com/SABISCalgary
Overview: A medium-sized local charitable organization founded in 1985
Mission: To promote lifelong support for persons with acquired brain injury, their families & support networks; community awareness of brain injury & optimal service delivery
Finances: *Funding Sources:* Membership dues; Fundraising; Donations

Membership: *Member Profile:* Survivors & families of brain injury; individual adults, families, professionals, non-profit agencies, corporations
Activities: No fees for services: counselling, referral, support groups, recreation & leisure activities, education & prevention of brain inury; *Awareness Events:* Astrid's Walk 'n' Roll, June; *Speaker Service:* Yes; *Library:* Multimedia Resource Centre

Southern Alberta Community Living Association (SACLA)
401 - 21A St. North, Lethbridge AB T1H 6L6
Tel: 403-329-1525; *Fax:* 403-329-1435
admin@sacla.ca
www.sacla.ca
Overview: A small local organization
Mission: To provide innovative supports to people with developmental disabilities & their families
Member of: Alberta Association of Rehab Centres
Chief Officer(s):
Sue Manery, Executive Director
sue.manery@sacla.ca
Finances: *Annual Operating Budget:* Greater than $5 Million

Southern Alberta Curling Association (SACA)
#720, 3 St. NW, Calgary AB T2N 1N9
Tel: 403-246-9300; *Fax:* 403-246-9349
curling@saca.ca
www.saca.ca
Overview: A small local organization overseen by Canadian Curling Association
Mission: To encourage active participation for residents of all ages in our communities by helping member curling clubs offer a wide variety of programs. To assist in providing opportunities to participate in curling.
Chief Officer(s):
Brent Syme, General Manager
brent@saca.ca
Stasia Perkins, Director, Clubs & Competitions
stasia@saca.ca

Southern Alberta Health Libraries Association (SAHLA)
c/o Lorraine Toews, Health Sciences Library, University of Calgary, 3330 University Dr. NW, Calgary AB T2N 4N1
e-mail: sahla.members@gmail.com
www.chla-absc.ca/sahla
Overview: A small local organization overseen by Canadian Health Libraries Association
Mission: To promote good health information service in southern Alberta; To encourage cooperation & communication among members; To promote educational development
Chief Officer(s):
Kathryn Ranjit, President
kathryn.ranjit@ucalgary.ca
Carrie Sherlock, Secretary
carrie.sherlock@topalbertadoctors.org
Michelle Lemieux, Treasurer
mrlemieu@ucalgary.ca
Membership: *Fees:* $15

Southern Alberta Post Polio Support Society (SAPPSS)
7 - 11 St. NE, Calgary AB T2E 4Z2
Tel: 403-265-5041; *Fax:* 403-265-0162
Toll-Free: 866-265-5049
sappss@shaw.ca
www.polioalberta.ca/sappss
Overview: A small local organization founded in 1988
Mission: To bring awareness about Post Polio Syndrome to the Southern Alberta community; to provide support for polio survivors

Southern Alberta Soaring Association
Warner AB
Tel: 403-527-9419
Overview: A small local organization
Mission: To promote gliding in southern Alberta
Chief Officer(s):
Ken Latam, Contact
latamken@yahoo.com
Membership: 21;

Southern First Nations Secretariat (SFNC)
22361 Austin Line, Bothwell ON N0P 1C0
Tel: 519-692-5868; *Fax:* 519-692-5976
Toll-Free: 800-668-2609
reception@sfns.on.ca
www.sfns.on.ca
Previous Name: London District Chief's Council
Overview: A small local organization
Mission: To provide a broad range of advisory & information services, technical & administrative support, & coordination of regional initiatives for Aboriginal peoples in southwestern Ontario
Affliation(s): Caldwell First Nation; Delaware First Nation; Munsee-Delaware First Nation; Oneida Nation; Kettle & Stoney Point First Nation; Aamjiwinaang First Nation; Chippewa of the Thames First Nation
Chief Officer(s):
Shirley Miller, Program Coordinator
Mike George, Executive Director
Staff Member(s): 27
Activities: Post-secondary counselling; technical services; financial & administrative services

Southern Georgian Bay Association of Realtors
243 Ste. Marie St., Collingwood ON L9Y 3K6
Tel: 705-445-7295; *Fax:* 705-445-7253
info@sgbrealtors.com
www.sgbrealtors.com
Overview: A small local organization overseen by Ontario Real Estate Association
Mission: To promote & support their members, as well as to provide them with knowledge to help them in the industry
Member of: The Ontario Real Estate Association; The Canadian Real Estate Association
Chief Officer(s):
Sandy Raymer, Executive Officer
Wayne Cornfield, President
Staff Member(s): 5
Membership: 500; *Member Profile:* Licensed realtors working in Midland, Penetanguishene, Elmvale, Port McNicoll, Victoria Harbour, Coldwater, Port Severn, Honey Harbour and Tiny, Tay, Springwater, Oro-Medonte, Severn, Georgian Bay Townships, Wasaga Beach, Collingwood, Clearview Township, The Blue Mountains, Meaford & Grey Highlands

Southern Georgian Bay Association of REALTORS©
243 Ste. Marie St., Collingwood ON L9Y 2K6
Tel: 705-445-7295; *Fax:* 705-445-7253
info@sgbREALTORS.com
www.sgbrealtors.com
Merged from: Georgian Triangle Real Estate Board & Southern Georgian Bay Real Estate Association
Overview: A small local organization overseen by Ontario Real Estate Association
Mission: To embrace new technologies, advancing quality education and high ethical standards in support of their membership while delivering MLS and real estate services consistant with the chaning regulations and market dynamics of our profession.
Member of: The Canadian Real Estate Association
Chief Officer(s):
Sandy Raymer, Executive Officer
Staff Member(s): 5
Membership: 500

Southern Georgian Bay Chamber of Commerce / Chambre de Commerce de la Baie Georgienne Sud
208 King St., Midland ON L4R 3L9
Tel: 705-526-7884
info@sgbchamber.ca
southerngeorgianbay.on.ca
www.linkedin.com/pub/sgb-chamber-of-commerce/17/620/b95
www.facebook.com/132190703477140
twitter.com/sgbchamber
Merged from: Penetanguishene-Tiny Chamber of Commerce; Midland Chamber of Commerce
Overview: A small local organization founded in 2003
Mission: To promote & to improve the commercial, professional, industrial, agricultural, economic, civic & social well-being of the district which includes the towns of Midland, Penetanguishene, & townships of Tiny & Tay.
Chief Officer(s):
Denise Hayes, General Manager
dhayes@sgbchamber.ca
Finances: *Funding Sources:* Membership dues; Fundraising
Staff Member(s): 3
Membership: 483; *Fees:* Schedule available; *Committees:* Membership
Activities: Tourism; Business Membership; Communication; *Rents Mailing List:* Yes

Penetanguishene Tourist Information Centre
(May-Oct.) Town Dock, 1 Main St., Penetanguishene ON L9M 1T1
Tel: 705-549-2232; *Fax:* 705-549-3743
ticinfo@penetanguishene.ca
www.penetanguishene.ca/en/discover/tourist-information-centre.asp
Chief Officer(s):
Courtney Parker, Coordinator, Tourism & Events
cparker@penetanguishene.ca

Southern Interior Construction Association (SICA)
#104, 151 Commercial Dr., Kelowna BC V1X 7W2
Tel: 250-491-7330; *Fax:* 250-491-3929
www.sica.bc.ca
www.linkedin.com/company/southern-interior-construction-association
www.facebook.com/SICABC
twitter.com/sicabc
www.youtube.com/user/SICA1969
Overview: A small local organization founded in 1969 overseen by Canadian Construction Association
Mission: To offer members' plans & specifications for viewing; to promote standard tendering practices
Member of: British Columbia Construction Association
Chief Officer(s):
William E. Everitt, Chief Operating Officer
Finances: *Funding Sources:* Membership dues
Staff Member(s): 12
Membership: 547; *Fees:* Schedule available

Southern Interior Local Government Association (SILGA)
c/o Alison Slater, 1996 Sheffield Way, Kamloops BC V2E 2M2
Tel: 250-374-3678; *Fax:* 250-374-3678
www.silga.ca
Previous Name: Okanagan Mainline Municipal Association; Okanagan Valley Municipal Association; Okanagan Valley Mayors & Reeves Association
Overview: A small local organization
Mission: To represent the municipalities & regional districts of the Okanagan Mainline area
Chief Officer(s):
Harry Kroeker, President
Marg Spina, First Vice-President
Tim Pennell, Second Vice-President
Alison Slater, Executive Director
alislater@shaw.ca
Membership: 36 municipalities; *Member Profile:* Elected officials from cities, towns, villages, districts, & regional districts in south central British Columbia
Activities: Working on water treatment standards issues; Organizing workshops for members; Liaising with the provincial & federal governments
Meetings/Conferences: • Southern Interior Local Government Association 2015 Annual General Meeting & Convention, April, 2015, Coast Hotel & Convention Centre, Kamloops, BC
Scope: Local

Southern Kings & Queens Chamber of Commerce *See* Eastern Prince Edward Island Chamber of Commerce

Southern Kings & Queens Food Bank Inc.
PO Box 1137, Montague PE C0A 1R0
Tel: 902-838-4234
Overview: A small local organization founded in 1988
Mission: To collect food & distribute to clients in need
Chief Officer(s):
Lawrence Power, Manager
Finances: *Funding Sources:* Fundraising; donations
6 volunteer(s)
Membership: 7; *Fees:* $1

Southern Kings Arts Council (SKAC)
PO Box 212, Montague PE C0A 1R0
Tel: 902-583-2888
southernkingsartscouncil.blogspot.ca
www.facebook.com/people/Southern-Kings-Arts-Council/100002014478545
Overview: A small local organization founded in 1980
Mission: To encourage & promote arts activities in the community.
Chief Officer(s):
Tom Rath, Contact, 902-962-3426
Finances: *Annual Operating Budget:* Less than $50,000
20 volunteer(s)

Membership: 25; *Fees:* $5 individual; $8 family; *Member Profile:* Any person interested in the arts who lives in the area

Southern Ontario Newsmedia Guild (SONG)
1253 Queen St. East, Toronto ON M4L 1C2
Tel: 416-461-2461; *Fax:* 416-461-5058
Toll-Free: 800-463-5797
info@song.on.ca
www.song.on.ca
Previous Name: Southern Ontario Newspaper Guild
Overview: A small local organization
Member of: Communications, Energy & Paperworkers Union of Canada
Chief Officer(s):
Paul Morse, President
paul@song.on.ca

Southern Ontario Newspaper Guild *See* Southern Ontario Newsmedia Guild

Southern Ontario Orchid Society
PO Box 88, Zephyr ON L0E 1T0
Tel: 905-640-5643; *Fax:* 905-640-0696
info@soos.ca
www.soos.ca
www.facebook.com/pages/Southern-Ontario-Orchid-Society/304367208791
Overview: A small local organization
Chief Officer(s):
Laura Leibgott, President
president@soos.ca
Membership: *Fees:* $25

Southern Ontario Seismic Network (SOSN)
c/o University of Western Ontario, London ON N6A 5B7
Tel: 519-661-3605; *Fax:* 519-661-3198
www.gp.uwo.ca
Overview: A small provincial organization
Mission: To obtain information on the seismicity and seismic hazards of a region of southern Ontario in which a number of nuclear power facilities are located.
Member of: POLARIS Network; Canadian National Seismograph Network
Chief Officer(s):
R.F. Mereu, Administrator
rmereu@uwo.ca

Southern Ontario Thunderbird Club
296 Village Green Ave., London ON N6J 3Z6
Tel: 519-471-8657
sotbirdclub.org
Overview: A small local organization founded in 1979
Mission: To preserve & enjoy Ford Thunderbird
Chief Officer(s):
Bob Ranick, Contact
Finances: *Annual Operating Budget:* Less than $50,000; *Funding Sources:* Membership fees
Membership: 180; *Fees:* $35

Southwest British Columbia League of Christian Schools *See* Society of Christian Schools in British Columbia

Southwestern Nova Scotia Fish Packers Association *See* Nova Scotia Fish Packers Association

Southwestern Ontario Adult Literacy Network See Literacy Link South Central

Southwestern Ontario Archivists' Association *See* Archives Association of Ontario

Southwestern Ontario Beekeepers' Association
c/o Mike Dodok, 108 London Dr., Chatham ON N7L 5J1
Tel: 519-351-8338
Overview: A small local organization
Mission: To help beekeepers in southwestern Ontario achieve excellence
Member of: Ontario Beekeepers' Association
Chief Officer(s):
Mike Dodok, President
dodoks@yahoo.ca
Membership: *Member Profile:* Beekeepers in southwestern Ontario
Activities: Offering workshops in beekeeping to educate members; Organizing meetings with guest speakers to inform members
Publications:
• Southwestern Ontario Beekeepers' Association Newsletter
Type: Newsletter
Profile: Association information, such as upcoming meetings

Southwestern Ontario Gliding Association (SOGA)
#6981, 7179 - 3 Line, Arthur ON N0G 1A0
soga.ca
Previous Name: K-W Hang Gliding Club; Hang-On-Tario
Overview: A medium-sized provincial organization founded in 1979
Mission: To organize hang gliding space & time for its members
Chief Officer(s):
John Pop, Contact
jpop@golden.net
Membership: *Fees:* $25 associate; $250 full/tow

Southwestern Ontario Health Library Information Network (SOHLIN)
c/o Medical Library, Windsor Regional Hospital, 1030 Ouellette Ave., Windsor ON N9A 1E1
www.chla-absc.ca/sohlin
Previous Name: Windsor Area Health Libraries Association; Windsor Hospitals Library Group
Overview: A small local organization founded in 1971 overseen by Canadian Health Libraries Association
Mission: To build communication lines among members; to provide opportunities for continued education & professional development
Member of: Canadian health Libraries Association
Chief Officer(s):
Jill McTavish, President
Jill.McTavish@lhsc.on.ca
Membership: *Fees:* $30 student; $40 first time; $50 regular

Sovereign Military Hospitaller Order of St-John of Jerusalem of Rhodes & of Malta - Canadian Association / Ordre souverain militaire hospitalier de St-Jean de Jérusalem, de Rhodes et de Malte - Association canadienne
#302, 1247 Kilborn Pl., Ottawa ON K1H 6K9
Tel: 613-731-8897; *Fax:* 613-731-1312
smomca@bellnet.ca
www.orderofmaltacanada.org
Previous Name: Association of Canadian Knights of the Sovereign Military Order of Malta
Overview: A medium-sized national charitable organization founded in 1953
Mission: To act as a Roman Catholic religious, chivalric & charitable organization; To provide assistance for: Good Shepherd Refuge, St. Francis, Second Mile Club, Providence Centre in Toronto, Czech Republic, Safe Motherhood Project, Nigeria, & ambulance brigades, Montréal, Cap-de-la-Madeleine, Ste. Anne de Beaupré
Affliation(s): Sovereign Military Order of Malta
Chief Officer(s):
Albert André Morin, President
Finances: *Annual Operating Budget:* $100,000-$250,000; *Funding Sources:* Donations
Staff Member(s): 1; 259 volunteer(s)
Membership: Over 12,500
Publications:
• Epistula
Type: Newsletter

Soyfoods Canada *See* Canadian Soybean Council

SPANCAN
#100, 596 Kingston Rd. West, Ajax ON L1T 3A2
Tel: 905-428-0700; *Fax:* 905-428-0690
spancan@idirect.ca
www.spancan.com
Overview: A small national organization founded in 1999
Affliation(s): Independent Lumber Dealers Cooperative
Chief Officer(s):
Mike Daniels, General Manager
mike2@idirect.ca
Staff Member(s): 4
Membership: 4; *Member Profile:* Home improvement retailers; wholesale distributor

Sparwood & District Chamber of Commerce
PO Box 1448, Aspen Dr., Sparwood BC V0B 2G0
Tel: 250-425-2423; *Fax:* 250-425-7130
Toll-Free: 877-485-8185
administrator@sparwoodchamber.bc.ca
www.sparwoodchamber.bc.ca
www.facebook.com/SparwoodChamber
Overview: A small local organization founded in 1983
Mission: To sustain existing business, enhance business opportunities & improve the economic, social, ecological & cultural well-being of the community
Member of: Canadian Chamber of Commerce; BC Chamber of Commerce
Chief Officer(s):
Muriel Stickney, President
Alayna Casselman, Administrator
Finances: *Annual Operating Budget:* $100,000-$250,000; *Funding Sources:* Membership dues; municipal & provincial governments
Staff Member(s): 5; 1 volunteer(s)
Membership: 112; *Fees:* $58.85 individual; sliding scale for businesses; *Member Profile:* Interest in community, business & or commerce; *Committees:* Community Events; Finance; Membership; Special Projects; Community Economic Development
Activities: Business information & visitor information centre; *Awareness Events:* Coal Miner Days; *Library:* Business Information Centre; Open to public by appointment

SPCA de l'ouest du Québec *See* SPCA of Western Québec

SPCA of Western Québec / SPCA de l'ouest du Québec
659, Auguste-Mondoux, Gatineau QC J9J 3K2
Tel: 819-770-7722; *Fax:* 819-770-7444
ahspca@storm.ca
www.aylmer-hull-spca.qc.ca
Also Known As: Society for the Prevention of Cruelty to Animals of Western Québec (Aylmer, Hull)
Overview: A small local charitable organization founded in 1977
Mission: A not-for-profit organization that cares for lost, abandoned and unwanted animals in the Outaouais; a "no-kill" animal shelter
Member of: Canadian Federation of Humane Societies
Chief Officer(s):
Alain Riel, Président
Finances: *Annual Operating Budget:* $100,000-$250,000; *Funding Sources:* Donations
Staff Member(s): 5; 25 volunteer(s)
Membership: 60; *Fees:* 25 $
Activities: Provides care & adoption program for lost & abandoned dogs, cats & rabbits in the Outaouais; partners with Petsmart (Merivale Rd., Ottawa) for adoptions

SPEC Association for Children & Families
c/o Community Culture Center, #101, 327 - 3rd St. West, Brooks AB T1R 0E7
Tel: 403-362-5056; *Fax:* 403-362-5090
home@spec.ab.ca
www.spec.ab.ca
Also Known As: SPEC: Support, Prevent, Educate, Counsel
Overview: A small local organization founded in 1978
Mission: To assist children & families in the Brooks area of Alberta to be healthy, nurtured, & safe; To encourage growth & education, from newborns to adults
Chief Officer(s):
Maureen Andruschak, Associate Executive Director, 403-362-5056 Ext. 247
maureen.andruschak@spec.ab.ca
Debbie Piper, Executive Director, 403-362-5056 Ext. 226
debbie.piper@spec.ab.ca
Finances: *Funding Sources:* Donations
Activities: Offering preventive services to children & families; Providing counselling & supportive services; Disseminating information, through the LINKS Community Information Centre; Coordinating programs, such as the Boys & Girls Club of Brooks & District, Parent LINK Centre, & Connections & Family Support Services

Special Education Association of British Columbia (SEA)
c/o British Columbia Teachers' Federation, #100, 550 West 6th Ave., Vancouver BC V5Z 4P2
www.seaofbc.ca
Overview: A small provincial organization overseen by British Columbia Teachers' Federation
Mission: To support teachers in providing quality education for students with special learning needs in British Columbia
Chief Officer(s):
BJ Foulds, President
bjfoulds@telus.net
Pearl Wong, Treasurer
pearlw@uniserve.com
Stephanie Koropatnick, Secretary
koropeople@shaw.ca

Karen Bell, Contact, Sponsorships
karbell@shaw.ca
Denise Chow, Contact, Membership & Chapters
denisechow@gmail.com
Alison Ogden, Contact, Publications
alisonogden@hotmail
Membership: *Fees:* $15 students & retired persons; $30 British Columbia Teachers' Federation members; $50.92 non-BCTF members; *Member Profile:* Teachers interested in supporting students with special needs
Activities: Offering professional development opportunities
Meetings/Conferences: • Special Education Association of British Columbia 2015 40th Annual Crosscurrents Conference, March, 2015, Sheraton Vancouver Airport Hotel, Richmond, BC
Scope: Provincial
Description: Sessions for regular & special education teachers, as well as administrators, teacher assistants, & parents
Contact Information: Conference Chair: Stephanie Koropatnick, E-mail: seaconferencechair@gmail.com
Publications:
• Crosscurrents
Type: Magazine; *Editor:* Alison Ogden
Profile: Original practical & theoretical articles about special education, plus reviews of publications, research, & methodologies

Special Interest Group on Computer Human Interaction (VanCHI)

PO Box 93672, Stn. Nelson Park, Vancouver BC V6E 4L7
Tel: 604-876-8985
chi-VanCHI@acm.org
www.sigchi.org
Overview: A small national organization overseen by Association for Computing Machinery
Mission: To provide a forum for discussion of all aspects of human-computer interaction; To advance education in human-computer interaction
Chief Officer(s):
Gerrit van der Veer, President
sigchi-president@acm.org
James Willock, Contact, Vancouver
Membership: *Member Profile:* Professionals, academics, & students who are interested in human-technology & human-computer interaction
Meetings/Conferences: • Computer Human Interaction 2015 Conference on Human Factors in Computing Systems, April, 2015, Seoul
Scope: International
Attendance: 2,500+
• Computer Human Interaction 2016 Conference on Human Factors in Computing Systems, 2016, San José, CA
Scope: International
Attendance: 2,500+
• Computer Human Interaction 2017 Conference on Human Factors in Computing Systems, 2017
Scope: International
Publications:
• Association for Computing Machinery Transactions on Computer-Human Interaction
Type: Journal; *Editor:* Shumin Zhai
• Interactions
Type: Magazine; *Editor:* Richard Anderson & Jon Kolko
• SIGCHI Bulletin
Type: Newsletter; *Editor:* Mark Apperley

Special Needs Planning Group

70 Ivy Cres., Stouffville ON L4A 5A9
Tel: 905-640-8285
www.specialneedsplanning.ca
Overview: A small local charitable organization founded in 1997
Mission: The "Special Needs" Planning Group is an organization that is made up entirely of parents of people with disabilities. They use a team approach to planning using Planners, Lawyers and Accountants, all of whom are specialists in planning for people with disabilities.
Chief Officer(s):
Graeme S. Treeby, Contact
graemetreeby@sympatico.ca

Special Olympics Alberta (SOA)

Percy Page Centre, 11759 Groat Rd., Edmonton AB T5M 3K6
Tel: 780-415-0719; *Fax:* 780-415-1306
Toll-Free: 800-444-2883
info@specialolympics.ab.ca
www.specialolympics.ab.ca
www.facebook.com/specialoalberta
twitter.com/SpecialOAlberta
Previous Name: Alberta Special Olympics Inc.
Overview: A medium-sized provincial charitable organization founded in 1980 overseen by Special Olympics Canada
Mission: To enrich the lives of Albertans with an intellectual disability, through sport
Chief Officer(s):
John Byrne, President & CEO
jbyrne@specialolympics.ab.ca
Finances: *Annual Operating Budget:* $500,000-$1.5 Million; *Funding Sources:* Donations; grants; fundraising events; sponsorship
Staff Member(s): 12; 1500 volunteer(s)
Membership: 3,000 athletes; 32 affiliates throughout Alberta; *Member Profile:* Athletes with intellectual disabilities; *Committees:* Strategic Development; Volunteer Management; New Community Development; New Sport Programs; Sport Development; Provincial Games; Team AB
Activities: 15 official sports including swimming, track & field, bowling (5 & 10 pin), floor hockey, powerlifting, soccer, softball, rhythmic gymnastics, speed skating, figure skating, alpine skiing, cross-country skiing & snowshoeing; also offers training in other sports including curling, basketball, equestrian, synchronized swimming, golf & pee wee programs (for those under 10); *Awareness Events:* Law Enforcement Torch Run; Sports Celebrities Festival; *Speaker Service:* Yes
Awards:
• Coach of the Year (Award)
• Administrator of the Year (Award)
• 5, 10, 15, 20 Year Service Award (Award)

Special Olympics BC (SOBC)

#210, 3701 East Hastings St., Burnaby BC V5C 2H6
Tel: 604-737-3078; *Fax:* 604-737-3080
Toll-Free: 888-854-2276
info@specialolympics.bc.ca
www.specialolympics.bc.ca
www.facebook.com/specialolympicsbc
twitter.com/sobcsociety
Previous Name: British Columbia Special Olympics
Overview: A medium-sized provincial charitable organization founded in 1980 overseen by Special Olympics Canada
Mission: The Association provides individuals with intellectual disability the opportunity to enhance their lives & celebrate personal achievement through positive sport experiences.
Member of: Special Olympics Canada
Affliation(s): Special Olympics International
Chief Officer(s):
Dan Howe, President & CEO, 604-737-3079
dhowe@specialolympics.bc.ca
Finances: *Funding Sources:* Donations; fundraising events; sponsors
Staff Member(s): 17; 3300 volunteer(s)
Membership: 4,300
Activities: Operates in 54 communities in British Columbia; *Speaker Service:* Yes
Awards:
• Athletic Achievement Award (Award)
• Spirit of Sport Award (Award)
• Howard Carter Award (Award)
• Grassroots Coach Award (Award)
• President's Award (Award)

Victoria
PO Box 31121, Stn. University Heights, Victoria BC V8N 6J3
Tel: 250-213-5467
www.victoriaspecialolympics.com
Chief Officer(s):
Kim Perkins, Coordinator, Public Relations
kim@kimperkins.ca
Kristina D'Sa, Secretary
specialo.kristinadsa@gmail.com

Special Olympics Canada (SOC) / Olympiques spéciaux Canada

#600, 21 St. Clair Ave. East, Toronto ON M4T 1L9
Tel: 416-927-9050; *Fax:* 416-927-8475
Toll-Free: 888-888-0608
www.specialolympics.ca
www.facebook.com/SpecialOCanada
twitter.com/SpecialOCanada
www.youtube.com/specialocanada
Previous Name: Canadian Special Olympics Inc.
Overview: A large national organization founded in 1969
Mission: To provide sport training & competition for people with a mental disability, at local, regional, provincial, national & international levels, year round
Affliation(s): Special Olympics International; The Order of United Commercial Travelers of America; The Sandbox Project
Chief Officer(s):
Dan Golberg, Chair
Sharon Bollenbach, Chief Executive Officer
Sarah Eyton, Vice President, Business Development & Marketing
Finances: *Funding Sources:* Foundations; Corporate sponsors; Individual donations
1630 volunteer(s)
Membership: 34,000 athletes; *Member Profile:* Mentally disabled Canadians
Activities: Offering national & international games; Providing coaching development

Special Olympics Manitoba (SOM)

#304, 145 Pacific Ave., Winnipeg MB R3B 2Z6
Tel: 204-925-5628; *Fax:* 204-925-5635
Toll-Free: 888-333-9179
som@specialolympics.mb.ca
www.specialolympics.mb.ca
www.facebook.com/117937068263657
twitter.com/SpecOManitoba
Previous Name: Manitoba Special Olympics
Overview: A small provincial charitable organization founded in 1980 overseen by Special Olympics Canada
Mission: To enrich the lives of Manitobans with an intellectual disability, through active participation in sport
Member of: Special Olympics Inc.
Chief Officer(s):
Simon Mundey, President & CEO
Finances: *Funding Sources:* Sport Manitoba; Various events
Staff Member(s): 13
Membership: *Fees:* $25 athlete; *Committees:* Human Resources; Marketing & Communications; Sport Program; Fundraising & Development
Activities: *Speaker Service:* Yes
Awards:
• Hall of Fame (Award)
• Sponsor of the Year (Award)
• Team of the Year (Award)
• Male Athlete of the Year (Award)
• Female Athlete of the Year (Award)
• Male Coach of the Year (Award)
• Female Coach of the Year (Award)
• Builder of the Year (Award)

Special Olympics New Brunswick

#103, 411 St. Mary's St., Fredericton NB E3B 8H4
Tel: 506-455-0404; *Fax:* 506-455-0410
infosonb@specialolympics.ca
www.specialolympicsnb.ca
www.facebook.com/specialolympicsnb
twitter.com/SpecialONB
Previous Name: New Brunswick Special Olympics
Overview: A small provincial charitable organization founded in 1979 overseen by Special Olympics Canada
Mission: To offer athletic programs to people with intellectual disabilites in New Brunswick
Chief Officer(s):
Josh Astle, Executive Director
jastle@specialolympicsnb.ca
Staff Member(s): 3
Membership: *Member Profile:* Athletes between 2 & 88 with an intellectual disabilities

Special Olympics Newfoundland & Labrador

#16B, 50 Pippy Pl., St. John's NL A1B 4H7
Tel: 709-738-1923; *Fax:* 709-738-0119
Toll-Free: 877-738-1913
sonl@sonl.ca
www.sonl.ca
Previous Name: Newfoundland-Labrador Special Olympics
Overview: A small provincial charitable organization founded in 1986 overseen by Special Olympics Canada
Mission: To provide sport, fitness & recreation programs for individuals with a mental handicap
Chief Officer(s):
Kevin Dunphy, Chair
Trish Williams, Executive Director
trishw@sonl.ca
Finances: *Annual Operating Budget:* $100,000-$250,000
Staff Member(s): 2; 250 volunteer(s)
Activities: *Awareness Events:* Provincial Winter & Summer Games

Special Olympics Northwest Territories (SONWT)
PO Box 1691, Yellowknife NT X1A 2N1
Tel: 867-446-2873
www.sonwt.ca
Previous Name: Northwest Territories Special Olympics
Overview: A small provincial organization founded in 1989 overseen by Special Olympics Canada
Mission: Special Olympics N.W.T. is the territorial sport governing body responsible for the delivery of sport for people with intellectual disabilities in the Northwest Territories.
Member of: Sport North; Special Olympics Canada
Chief Officer(s):
Lynn Elkin, Executive Director
lynn@sonwt.ca
Finances: *Funding Sources:* Law Enforcement Torch Run, public donations, grants, corporate sponsors and special fundraising events.

Special Olympics Nova Scotia (SONS)
#201, 5516 Spring Garden Rd., Halifax NS B3J 1G6
Tel: 902-429-2266; *Fax:* 902-425-5606
Toll-Free: 866-299-2019
www.sons.ca
www.facebook.com/SpecialONS
twitter.com/SpecialONS
Previous Name: Nova Scotia Special Olympics
Overview: A small provincial charitable organization founded in 1978 overseen by Special Olympics Canada
Mission: Special Olympics is a non-profit organization dedicated to providing year-round sports training and athletic competition in a variety of Olympic-type sports for children and adults with an intellectual disability.
Chief Officer(s):
Mike Greek, President/CEO
greekmr@sportnovascotia.ca
Staff Member(s): 4
Membership: 1700 athletes

Special Olympics Ontario (SOO)
#200, 65 Overlea Blvd., Toronto ON M4H 1P1
Tel: 416-447-8326; *Fax:* 416-447-6336
Toll-Free: 888-333-5515
www.specialolympicsontario.com
www.facebook.com/specialolympicsontario
www.youtube.com/specialolympicson
Previous Name: Ontario Special Olympics
Overview: A medium-sized provincial charitable organization founded in 1979 overseen by Special Olympics Canada
Mission: To provide sports training & competition for people with an intellectual disability through community-based programs
Chief Officer(s):
Glenn MacDonell, President & Chief Executive Officer
glennm@specialolympicsontario.com
Linda Ashe, Vice-President
lindaa@specialolympicsontario.com
Lynn Miller, Manager, Marketing Services
lynnm@specialolympicsontario.com
James Noronha, Manager, Program Services
jamesn@specialolympicsontario.com
Finances: *Annual Operating Budget:* Greater than $5 Million; *Funding Sources:* Private; corporate; service clubs; provincial government
Staff Member(s): 35; 9000 volunteer(s)
Membership: 19,000 athletes
Activities: Offers programs in the following sports: Alpine Skiing & Cross-Country Skiing; Snowshoeing; Speed Skating; Figure Skating; 5 & 10 Pin Bowling; Floor Hockey; Soccer; Swimming; Athletics; Basketball; Curling; Rhythmic Gymnastics; Powerlifting; Softball; Bocce; Golf; *Internships:* Yes; *Speaker Service:* Yes

Special Olympics Prince Edward Island (SOPEI)
PO Box 822, #240, 40 Enman Cres., Charlottetown PE C1A 7L9
Tel: 902-368-8919; *Fax:* 902-892-4553
Toll-Free: 800-287-1196
sopei@sopei.com
www.sopei.com
Previous Name: PEI Special Olympics
Overview: A small provincial charitable organization founded in 1987 overseen by Special Olympics Canada
Mission: To provide sport, recreation & fitness for the mentally disabled in PEI; to provide competitive opportunities for its members
Chief Officer(s):
Valerie Downe, Executive Director
vdowne@sopei.com
Finances: *Annual Operating Budget:* $100,000-$250,000
Staff Member(s): 2; 75 volunteer(s)
Membership: 235; *Member Profile:* Athletes with a mental disability; *Committees:* Program; Board of Directors

Special Olympics Saskatchewan
353 Broad St., Regina SK S4R 1X2
Tel: 306-780-9247; *Fax:* 306-780-9441
Toll-Free: 888-307-6226
sos@specialolympics.sk.ca
www.specialolympics.sk.ca
www.facebook.com/SOSaskatchewan
twitter.com/SpecialOSask
www.youtube.com/user/SpecialOSk
Previous Name: Saskatchewan Special Olympics Society
Overview: A small provincial organization overseen by Special Olympics Canada
Chief Officer(s):
Roger Dumont, Chief Executive Officer, 306-780-9277
rdumont@specialolympics.sk.ca

Special Olympics Yukon (SOY) / Les Jeux Olympiques Spéciaux du Yukon
#102, 221 Hanson St., Whitehorse YT Y1A 1H1
Tel: 867-668-6511; *Fax:* 867-667-4237
info@specialolympicsyukon.ca
www.specialolympicsyukon.ca
www.facebook.com/pages/Special-Olympics-Yukon/1914532843 18177
twitter.com/SpecialOYukon
Previous Name: Yukon Special Olympics
Overview: A medium-sized provincial charitable organization founded in 1981 overseen by Special Olympics Canada
Mission: To provide a full continuum of sport apportunities for Yukoners with a mental disability
Affliation(s): Special Olympics International
Chief Officer(s):
Serge Michaud, Executive Director
smichaud@specialolympicsyukon.ca
Thomas Gibbs, President
Staff Member(s): 3; 65 volunteer(s)
Membership: 100+; *Fees:* Schedule available; *Member Profile:* Individuals with a mental disability
Activities: *Awareness Events:* Sports Celebrities Dinner Auction; Golf Gala; Law Enforcement Torch Run
Awards:
- Most Improved Athlete of the Year (Award)
- Volunteer of the Year (Award)
- Sportsman of the Year (Award)

Specification Writers Association of Canada *See* Construction Specifications Canada

Spectacle aérienne d'Abbotsford *See* Abbotsford International Air Show Society

Spectra Community Support Services
#402, 7700 Hurontario St., Brampton ON L6Y 4M3
Tel: 905-459-8439; *Fax:* 905-459-3955; *Crisis Hot-Line:* 905-459-7777
info@spectrasupport.org
www.spectrasupport.org
www.linkedin.com/company/spectra-community-support-services
www.facebook.com/SpectraSupport
twitter.com/spectrasupport
Previous Name: Telecare Distress Centre Brampton
Overview: A small local charitable organization founded in 1973 overseen by Distress Centres Ontario
Mission: To provide a 24-hour-a-day telephone ministry to people in need; To aim to be a listening ministry, not a problem-solving, advice-giving institution
Affliation(s): Telecare Teleministries of Canada Inc.; Life Line International
Finances: *Funding Sources:* Region of Peel; United Way of Peel Region; Trillium Foundation; Central West LHIN
Activities: Distress line; TeleCheck seniors program; Multilingual lines; Peel Postpartum Family Support; Reassurance program; *Speaker Service:* Yes

Spectroscopy Society of Canada *See* Canadian Society for Analytical Sciences & Spectroscopy

Spectrum Society for Community Living
3231 Kingsway, Vancouver BC V5R 5K3
Tel: 604-323-1433; *Fax:* 604-321-4144
info@spectrumsociety.org
www.spectrumsociety.org
www.facebook.com/SpectrumSociety
twitter.com/SSCLSpectrum
Overview: A medium-sized local organization founded in 1987
Mission: To provide services to people with disabilities that will allow them to function more productively & independently in the community
Affliation(s): British Columbia Association for Community Living
Chief Officer(s):
Ernest Baatz, Co-Director
Susan Stanfield, Co-Director
Aaron Johannes, Co-Director
Finances: *Funding Sources:* Federal & provincial government; Fundraising
Staff Member(s): 37
Activities: *Library* by appointment

Speech & Hearing Association of Nova Scotia
PO Box 775, Stn. Halifax Central CRO, Halifax NS B3J 2V2
Tel: 902-423-9331
www.shans.ca
www.facebook.com/158487970888535
Overview: A medium-sized provincial charitable organization
Mission: To allow audiology & speech language pathology professionals to pursue professional development in order to benefit the public
Affliation(s): Canadian Association of Speech-Language Pathologists & Audiologists (CASLPA)
Chief Officer(s):
Cynthia Howroyd, President
president@shans.ca
Finances: *Funding Sources:* Membership dues

The Speech & Stuttering Institute
#2, 150 Duncan Mill Rd., Toronto ON M3B 3M4
Tel: 416-491-7771; *Fax:* 416-491-7215
info@speechandstuttering.com
www.speechandstuttering.com
Previous Name: Speech Foundation of Ontario
Overview: A medium-sized provincial charitable organization founded in 1977
Mission: To provide treatment of & foster the development of innovative speech/language therapy programs; to support education & research in communication disorders
Chief Officer(s):
Paul L'Heureux, Chair
Margit Pukonen, Program Director
Finances: *Annual Operating Budget:* $500,000-$1.5 Million; *Funding Sources:* Ministry of Health
Staff Member(s): 11; 4 volunteer(s)
Membership: 1-99; *Fees:* Schedule available; *Committees:* Development & Fundraising; Government Relations; London Centre; Public Relations; Toronto Children's Centre; Membership; Nominations; Professional Advisory Council; Stuttering Centre
Activities: Speech therapy groups; language therapy groups; consultation services; *Awareness Events:* Speech & Hearing Month, May; *Internships:* Yes; *Speaker Service:* Yes

Speech Foundation of Ontario *See* The Speech & Stuttering Institute

Speech Language Hearing Association of Alberta *See* Alberta College of Speech-Language Pathologists & Audiologists

Speech-Language & Audiology Canada (SAC) / Orthophonie et Audiologie Canada (OAC)
#1000, 1 Nicholas St., Ottawa ON K1N 7B7
Tel: 613-567-9968; *Fax:* 613-567-2859
Toll-Free: 800-259-8519
info@sac-oac.ca
www.sac-oac.ca
www.linkedin.com/groups/SAC-Members-4226965/about
www.facebook.com/sac.oac
www.twitter.com/sac_oac
www.youtube.com/channel/UCmg6LP26_eRR72hBEFfnRug
Previous Name: Canadian Association of Speech-Language Pathologists & Audiologists
Overview: A medium-sized national charitable organization founded in 1964
Mission: To support & represent the professional needs & development of speech-language pathologists & audiologists; to champion the needs of people with communication disorders
Affliation(s): International Association of Logopedics & Phoniatrics; International Society of Audiology; International Communication Project
Chief Officer(s):

Judy Meintzer, President, 613-567-9968 Ext. 262, Fax: 613-567-2859
pres@sac-oac.ca
Roula Baali, Treasurer
Joanne Charlebois, Chief Executive Officer, 613-567-9968 Ext. 262, Fax: 613-567-2859
joanne@sac-oac.ca
Jessica Bedford, Director, Communications and Marketing, 800-259-8519 Ext. 241
jessica@sac-oac.ca
Finances: *Annual Operating Budget:* $1.5 Million-$3 Million; *Funding Sources:* Membership fees
Staff Member(s): 14
Membership: 6,000+; *Member Profile:* Masters degree in S-LP or AUD; *Committees:* Awards and Recognition Committee; Audiology Clinical Certification Examination Committee; Speech-Language Pathology Clinical Certification Examination Committee; Clinical Research Grants Committee; Ethics Committee; Executive Committee; Expert Committee for Supportive Personnel Issues; Governance/Nominations Committee; Scholarship Committee; Standards Advisory Committee
Activities: *Awareness Events:* Speech and Hearing Month, May; *Speaker Service:* Yes
Awards:
• Isabel Richard Student Paper Award (Award)
Presented annually to two students, one in speech-language pathology & one in audiology, for outstanding research conducted in the course of their graduate program
• Student Excellence Awards (Award)
Presented to one outstanding student from each graduate program in speech-language pathology & audiology in Canada
• Promotions Awards (Award)
Presented to members or non-members who have contributed to the public awareness & understanding of human communication disorders in Canada
• National Certification Exam Award (Award)
• Eve Kassirer Award for Outstanding Professional Achievement (Award)
Presented to a member for his or her outstanding professional achievement in the areas of education, clinical services or administration at the national or international level
• Lifetime Achievement Award (Award)
Presented to an individual who is neither a speech-language pathologist nor an audiologist who has made significant contributions to the fields of speech-language pathology & audiology
• Mentorship Award (Award)
• Editor's Award (Award)
• Consumer Advocacy Award (Award)
• Award of Excellence for Interprofessional Collaboration (Award)
Meetings/Conferences: • Canadian Association of Speech-Language Pathologists & Audiologists 2015 Annual General Meeting, 2015
Scope: National
Publications:
• Canadian Association of Speech-Language Pathologists & Audiologists Communiqué
Type: Newsletter; *Frequency:* Quarterly; *Editor:* Krystle van Hoof *ISSN:* 0842-1196
• The Canadian Journal of Speech-Language Pathology & Audiology (CJSLPA)
Type: Journal; *Frequency:* Quarterly; *Accepts Advertising; ISSN:* 1913-200X
• CASLPA [Canadian Association of Speech-Language Pathologists & Audiologists] Membership Directory
Type: Directory

Speed Skate New Brunswick

NB
e-mail: speedskatenb@gmail.com
ssnb.homestead.com
Previous Name: New Brunswick Speed Skating Association
Overview: A small provincial organization overseen by Speed Skating Canada
Mission: The association provides members with access to coaching & chances to compete. It serves as a hub for information on the sport & for members to network.
Member of: Speed Skating Canada
Chief Officer(s):
Ray Harris, Chair
Peter Steele, Provincial Coach & Technical Director
psteele@nb.sympatico.ca

Speed Skate Nova Scotia

NS
www.speedskatens.ca
Previous Name: Nova Scotia Speed Skating Association
Overview: A small provincial organization overseen by Speed Skating Canada
Member of: Speed Skating Canada
Chief Officer(s):
Troy Myers, President, 902-527-6776
troymyers7@gmail.com

Speed Skate PEI

PO Box 383, Charlottetown PE C1A 7K7
Tel: 902-628-6606
info@speedskatepei.ca
www.speedskatepei.com
Previous Name: Prince Edward Island Speed Skating Association
Overview: A small provincial organization overseen by Speed Skating Canada
Mission: Supporting the sport of speedskating in PEI.
Member of: Speed Skating Canada
Chief Officer(s):
Rob Binns, President
rob@speedskatepei.ca
Alban Moran, Secretary
secretary@speedskatepei.ca

Speed Skating Canada (SSC) / Patinage de vitesse Canada

#402, 2781 Lancaster Rd., Ottawa ON K1B 1A7
Tel: 613-260-3669; *Fax:* 613-260-3660
ssc@speedskating.ca
www.speedskating.ca
Overview: A medium-sized national organization founded in 1887
Mission: To develop & promote long & short track speed skating in Canada; To prepare athletes, coaches, officials, & volunteers to make contributions to speed skating & to Canada's image abroad through development & international programs
Affliation(s): International Skating Union
Chief Officer(s):
John-Paul Cody-Cox, Chief Executive Officer
jpcodycox@speedskating.ca
Mark Mathies, Executive Director, Sport
mmathies@speedskating.ca
Patricia Brennan, Director, Finance & Administration
pbrennan@speedskating.ca
Douglas Duncan, Director, Leadership Eduation
dduncan@speedskating.ca
Phil Legault, Director, Communications
plegault@speedskating.ca
Finances: *Funding Sources:* Government; Sport Canada; Canadian Olympic Association; Sponsorships; Membership
50 volunteer(s)
Membership: 10,000; *Member Profile:* Participants in competitive or recreational speed skating; *Committees:* High Performance - Short Track & Long Track; Competitions Development; Club & Membership Development; Coaching Development; Officials Development
Activities: *Internships:* Yes; *Speaker Service:* Yes
Meetings/Conferences: • Speed Skating Canada 2015 Annual General Meeting, June, 2015, Winnipeg, MB
Scope: National
Description: A gathering of the organization's Board of Directors, branches, & committees
Publications:
• ING on the Edge Newsletter
Type: Newsletter

Spina Bifida & Hydrocephalus Association of British Columbia (SBHABC)

c/o BC Children's Hospital, 4480 Oak St., Vancouver BC V6H 3V4
Tel: 604-878-7000; *Fax:* 604-677-6608
sbhabc@shaw.ca
www.sbhabc.org
Previous Name: Lower Mainland Spina Bifida Association
Overview: A medium-sized provincial licensing charitable organization founded in 1977
Mission: To improve the quality of life of all individuals with spina bifada &/or hydrocephalus & their families, through awareness, education & research
Chief Officer(s):
Colleen Talbot, President
Pauline Dooley, Office Manager
Finances: *Annual Operating Budget:* $50,000-$100,000
Staff Member(s): 5
Membership: 250; *Fees:* $10; *Member Profile:* Adults, caregivers or families with a child with Spina Bifida &/or Hydrocephalus
Activities: *Awareness Events:* Spina Bifida Month, June
Meetings/Conferences: • Spina Bifida & Hydrocephalus Association of British Columbia 2015 Conference, 2015, BC
Scope: Provincial
Contact Information: sbhabc@shaw.ca

Spina Bifida & Hydrocephalus Association of Canada (SBHAC) / Association de spina-bifida et d'hydrocéphalie du Canada

#428, 167 Lombard Ave., Winnipeg MB R3B 0V3
Tel: 204-925-3650; *Fax:* 204-925-3654
Toll-Free: 800-565-9488
info@sbhac.ca
www.sbhac.ca
Overview: A medium-sized national charitable organization founded in 1981
Mission: To improve the quality of life of all individuals with spina bifida &/or hydrocephalus & their families through awareness, education, advocacy & research; to reduce the incidence of neural tube defects
Affliation(s): International Federation for Hydrocephalus & Spina Bifida
Chief Officer(s):
Colleen Talbot, President
Finances: *Annual Operating Budget:* $250,000-$500,000; *Funding Sources:* Donations; Special Events
Staff Member(s): 2; 20 volunteer(s)
Membership: 11 provincial member associations; *Fees:* $20 individual; or membership in provincial association; *Committees:* Adult/Advocacy; Fund Development; Bursary; Education; Public Awareness; Research; Policy & Governance; Volunteer Support
Activities: *Awareness Events:* Spina Bifida & Hydrocephalus Awareness Month, June; Hope Classic 2008, August; *Library:* SBHAC Library; Open to public by appointment
Awards:
• Two $1,000 bursaries per year (Scholarship)
• Research Grants (Grant)

Spina Bifida & Hydrocephalus Association of New Brunswick

1325 Mountain Rd., Moncton NB E1C 2T9
Tel: 506-857-9947
spinabifidanb@hotmail.com
Overview: A small provincial organization overseen by Spina Bifida & Hydrocephalus Association of Canada
Mission: To improve the quality of life of those persons who have spina bifida &/or hydrocephalus; to gather information on spina bifida & hydrocephalus & to disseminate it to all interested persons & organizations; to encourage research into the causes & to advance more effective treatment & care

Spina Bifida & Hydrocephalus Association of Northern Alberta (SBHANA)

PO Box 35025, 10818 Jasper Ave., Edmonton AB T5J 0B7
Tel: 780-451-6921; *Fax:* 888-881-7172
info@sbhana.org
www.sbhana.org
www.facebook.com/194855220556177
twitter.com/SBHANA1
Previous Name: Spina Bifida Association of Northern Alberta
Overview: A small provincial charitable organization founded in 1981
Mission: To enhance the lives of individuals & families affected with spina bifida &/or hydrocephalus through public awareness, education & research
Member of: Spina Bifida & Hydrocephalus Association of Canada; Alberta Disablility Forum; Albera Committee for Citizens with Disabilities
Chief Officer(s):
Cindy Smith, President
Darlene Cathcart, Program Manager
Finances: *Annual Operating Budget:* $100,000-$250,000
Staff Member(s): 2; 30 volunteer(s)
Membership: 250; *Fees:* $10; *Member Profile:* Parents/grandparents of children with spina bifida &/or hydrocephalus & adults affected with spina bifida &/or hydrocephalus; professionals; *Committees:* Social; Public Awareness; Fundraising; Newsletter; Education
Activities: Christmas party; June BBQ; parent support group; summer camp; *Awareness Events:* Spina Bifida and

Hydrocephalus Month, June; *Speaker Service:* Yes; *Library:* Resource Centre; by appointment
Awards:
• 2 Scholarships (Scholarship)
Scholarship for secondary students; schloarship for graduate research in related areas for University of Alberta students
Amount: $1,000

Spina Bifida & Hydrocephalus Association of Nova Scotia (SBHANS)
PO Box 341, Coldbrook NS B4R 1B6
Tel: 902-679-1124
Toll-Free: 800-304-0450
info@sbhans.ca
www.sbhans.ca
Overview: A small provincial charitable organization founded in 1984 overseen by Spina Bifida & Hydrocephalus Association of Canada
Mission: To eliminate spina bifida & hydrocephalus in newborns by promoting preventative measures; to help individuals with spina bifida &/or hydrocephalus to reach their full potential by promoting independence & improved quality of life
Membership: *Fees:* $10 individual/family
Activities: Newsletter, library service, workshops/conferences, resource kits; Slowpitch fundraising tournament; *Library*
Awards:
• Special Needs Fund (Grant)
Designed to alleviate some of the financial strain placed on parents of children with spina bifida & persons with spina bifida, when funds are not available from other sources*Eligibility:* Parents of children or persons with spina bifida &/or hydrocephlus; must be a member of Spina Bifida & Hydrocephalus Associaton of Nova Scotia or register at time of application
• Education Awards (Award)
To encourage & support students with spina bifida &/or hydrocephalus; to develop independence & responsibility for their future education; to assist students in pursuing higher education at university or other post secondary studies*Eligibility:* Canadian citizens who are residents of Nova Scotia who have spina bifida or hydrocephalus*Deadline:* April *Amount:* $500
Contact: Chairperson, Education Award Committee
• Bike/Vehicle Fund (Grant)
• Recreation Fund (Grant)

Cape Breton Chapter
20 Deanna Dr., Glace Bay NS B1A 6Y1
Tel: 902-849-4401
Chief Officer(s):
Blanche Murrant, President

Spina Bifida & Hydrocephalus Association of Ontario (SB&H)
PO Box 103, #1006, 555 Richmond St. West, Toronto ON M5V 3B1
Tel: 416-214-1056; *Fax:* 416-214-1446
Toll-Free: 800-387-1575
provincial@sbhao.on.ca
www.sbhao.on.ca
www.facebook.com/SpinaBifidaHydrocephalusOntario
twitter.com/SBH_Ontario
Overview: A medium-sized provincial charitable organization founded in 1973
Mission: To build awareness & drive education, research, support, care & advocacy to help find a cure while always continuing to improve the quality of life of all individuals with spina bifida &/or hydrocephalus
Affliation(s): Spina Bifida & Hydrocephalus Association of Canada
Chief Officer(s):
Joan Booth, Executive Director
jbooth@sbhao.on.ca
Finances: *Annual Operating Budget:* $250,000-$500,000
Staff Member(s): 7; 1003 volunteer(s)
Membership: *Fees:* $20 individual; $30 family/professional/associate; $30 corporate; *Committees:* Education; Fundraising; Finance & Audit
Activities: Toll-free telephone line to access support & information; support programs; scholarships programs; research programs; information materials; "Kids on the Block" Awareness Program; Folic Acid Awareness Program; educational workshops & conferences; advocacy; public awareness programs; *Awareness Events:* Spina Bifida & Hydrocephalus Month, June; *Speaker Service:* Yes; *Library:* Resource Lending Library; Open to public
Awards:
• Dr. E. Bruce Hendrick Scholarship Program (Scholarship)
• Luciana Spring Mascarin Bursary (Scholarship)

Spina Bifida & Hydrocephalus Association of Prince Edward Island
PO Box 3332, Charlottetown PE C0A 1R0
Tel: 902-628-8875
Overview: A small provincial charitable organization overseen by Spina Bifida & Hydrocephalus Association of Canada
Chief Officer(s):
Lurlean Palmer, Contact
lurleanpalmer@eastlink.ca

Spina Bifida & Hydrocephalus Association of South Saskatchewan
PO Box 37115, Stn. Landmark, Regina SK S4S 7K3
Tel: 306-586-2222
regina@sbhac.ca
Overview: A small provincial organization
Mission: To improve the quality of life for those afflicted with spina bifida &/or hydrocephalus
Member of: Spina Bifida & Hydrocephalus Association of Canada
Finances: *Funding Sources:* Fundraising; donations
Activities: *Library:* Family Resource Centre

North Chapter
351 Kenderdine Rd., Saskatoon SK S7N 3S9
Tel: 306-249-1362
lscherr2@sasktel.net
www.sbhasn.ca/Spina_Bifida.htm
Chief Officer(s):
Laura Scherr, President
lscherr2@shaw.ca

South Chapter
Saskatoon SK S4S 5L9
Tel: 306-586-2222
Mission: To improve the quality of life of all individuals with spina bifida and/or hydrocephalus and their families through awareness, education, advocacy and research, and to reduce the incidence of neural tube defects

Spina Bifida & Hydrocephalus Association of Southern Alberta (SBHASA)
PO Box 6837, Stn. D, Calgary AB T2P 2E9
www.sbhasa.ca
Previous Name: Spina Bifida Association of Southern Alberta
Overview: A small provincial charitable organization founded in 1981 overseen by Spina Bifida & Hydrocephalus Association of Canada
Mission: To raise awareness about spina bifida & hydrocephalus & to provide help to people & families who suffer from these conditions
Chief Officer(s):
Minh Ho, President
minh.ho@plainsmidstream.com
Membership: *Fees:* $10

Spina Bifida Association of Manitoba (SBAM)
#647, 167 Lombard Ave., Winnipeg MB R3B 0V3
Tel: 204-925-3653; *Fax:* 204-925-3654
manitoba.sbhac.ca
Overview: A small provincial charitable organization founded in 1965 overseen by Spina Bifida & Hydrocephalus Association of Canada
Mission: To provide resources & support to people & families suffering from spina bifida & hydrocephalus

Spina Bifida Association of Northern Alberta *See* Spina Bifida & Hydrocephalus Association of Northern Alberta

Spina Bifida Association of Southern Alberta *See* Spina Bifida & Hydrocephalus Association of Southern Alberta

Spinal Cord Injury Alberta
#305, 11010 - 101 St., Edmonton AB T5H 4B9
Tel: 780-424-6312; *Fax:* 780-424-6313
Toll-Free: 888-654-5444
edmonton@sci-ab.ca
www.sci-ab.ca
www.facebook.com/SpinalCordInjuryAlberta?ref=hl
twitter.com/scialberta
www.youtube.com/cpaalberta
Previous Name: Canadian Paraplegic Association (Alberta)
Overview: A medium-sized provincial organization overseen by Spinal Cord Injury Canada
Chief Officer(s):
Teren Clarke, Executive Director
Activities: Rehabilitation support & service coordination; Aboriginal Services, Information Service; Peer Program; Community Development
Publications:
• Spinal Columns
Type: Magazine; *Frequency:* Quarterly; *Accepts Advertising*; *Price:* $20
Profile: Articles on issues such as advocacy, transportation, employment, & relationships
• Wheel-e
Type: Newsletter; *Frequency:* Monthly
Profile: Association events & announcements

Calgary
5211 - 4th St. NE, Calgary AB T2K 6J5
Tel: 403-228-3001; *Fax:* 403-229-4271
calgary@sci-ab.ca

Fort McMurray
Gregoire Park Centre, 194 Grenfell Cres., Fort McMurray AB T9H 2M6
Tel: 780-743-0307; *Fax:* 403-743-4563
fortmcmurray@sci-ab.ca

Grande Prairie
10 Knowledge Way, Grande Prairie AB T8W 2V9
Tel: 780-532-3305; *Fax:* 780-539-3567
grandeprairie@sci-ab.ca

Lethbridge
#360, 515 - 7th St. South, Lethbridge AB T1J 2G8
Tel: 403-327-7577; *Fax:* 403-320-0269
lethbridge@sci-ab.ca

Lloydminster
PO Box 1691, Lloydminster AB S9V 1K6
Tel: 780-875-1046
lloydminster@sci-ab.ca

Medicine Hat
#26, 419 - 3rd St. SE, Medicine Hat AB T1A 0G9
Tel: 403-504-4001; *Fax:* 403-504-5172
medicinehat@sci-ab.ca

Red Deer
#103, 4719 - 48th Ave., Red Deer AB T4N 3T1
Tel: 403-341-5060; *Fax:* 403-343-1630
reddeer@sci-ab.ca

St. Paul
PO Box 653, St. Paul AB T0A 3A0
Tel: 780-645-5116; *Fax:* 780-645-5141
stpaul@sci-ab.ca

Spinal Cord Injury British Columbia (BCPA)
780 SW Marine Dr., Vancouver BC V6P 5Y7
Tel: 604-324-3611; *Fax:* 614-326-1229
Toll-Free: 877-324-3611
info@bcpara.org
sci-bc.ca
www.facebook.com/SpinalCordInjuryBC
twitter.com/sci_bc
www.youtube.com/user/BCParaplegic;
www.flickr.com/photos/80024115@N03
Previous Name: British Columbia Paraplegic Association; Canadian Paraplegic Association
Overview: A medium-sized provincial organization founded in 1957 overseen by Spinal Cord Injury Canada
Member of: BC SCI Community Services Network
Chief Officer(s):
Edward Milligan, Chair
Chris McBride, Executive Director
cmcbride@bcpara.org
Marion Patsis, Manager, Finance
mpatsis@bcpara.org
Finances: *Funding Sources:* Donations; Rick Hansen Man in Motion Foundation; BC Neurotrauma Initiative; Fundraising
Activities: Providing rehabilitation services; Engaging in advocacy activities; Administering the Youth: Bridges to the Future program; Presenting information & educational opportunities; Offering employment services; Arranging peer support; Providing grants to people with spinal cord injuries & other physical disabilities & to researchers who focus on community based rehabilitation & quality of life enhancement
Publications:
• Comming into Focus: People Living with Spinal Cord Injury in BC
Type: Report
• Paragraphic
Type: Magazine; *Frequency:* Quarterly; *Accepts Advertising*; *Price:* Free for BCPA supporting members & community partners

Profile: BCPA programs, research information, personal profiles, & updates from the GF Strong Rehabilitation Centre

Cranbrook
#102, 1617 Baker St., Cranbrook BC V1C 1B4
Tel: 250-417-0416; *Fax:* 250-417-0348
Toll-Free: 877-410-0416
Chief Officer(s):
Bill Roberts, Rehabilitation Consultant
wroberts@bcpara.org

Prince George
777 Kinsmen Pl., Prince George BC V2M 6Y7
Tel: 250-563-6942; *Fax:* 250-563-6992
info@sci-bc.ca
Chief Officer(s):
Patrick Harris, Supervisor, Regional Rehabilitation
pharris@bcpara.org
Joe Basnett, Rehabilitation Consultant
jbasnett@bcpara.org
Brandy McKay, Associate, Peer Program
bmckay@bcpara.org

Spinal Cord Injury Canada / Lésions Médullaires Canada

Varette Bldg., #512, 130 Albert St., Ottawa ON K1P 5G4
Tel: 613-723-1913; *Fax:* 613-723-1060
info@sciontario.org
www.sciontario.org
www.facebook.com/223239864405595
Also Known As: SCI Canada
Previous Name: Canadian Paraplegic Association
Overview: A medium-sized national charitable organization founded in 1945
Mission: To assist persons with spinal cord injuries & other physical disabilitieto to cope with the changes caused by their injury, to become independent & self-reliant, & to lead productive lives. The Canadian Paraplegic Association officially changed its name to Spinal Cord Injury Canada in 2012. Member associations are in the process of also changing their names & are aiming to share the Spinal Cord Injury title in 2013.
Chief Officer(s):
Eddie Joyce, President
Myrtle Jenkins-Smith, Vice-President/Secretary
Ron Swan, Treasurer
Finances: *Funding Sources:* Donations; Human Resources & Social Development Canada, Office of Disability Issues; Canadian International Development Agency; Corporate Partners
Activities: Offering the Self Advocacy Training Program; Counselling; Providing the National Peer Support Program; Participating in international development activities; Providing information about research, health, & assistive equipment; Fundraising
Publications:
• Canadian Paraplegic Association Annual Report
Type: Yearbook; *Frequency:* Annually
• The Complete Incomplete Resource
Price: $6
Profile: Resource dedicated to incomplete SCI
• Fire Safety for People with Disabilities
Price: $22
Profile: Fire safety training kit for people with disabilities & seniors
• Life After Spinal Cord Injury
Price: $30 non-members; $15 members
Profile: Information resource for persons with SCI & their family members
• Life Interrupted
Type: Manual
Profile: Practical information for youth, between the ages of 12 & 21, with SCI
• Opening Doors to Rehabilitation
Type: Manual
Profile: Information for professional counsellors who work with clients with mobility impairments
• Total Access
Type: Magazine; *Frequency:* Semiannually; *Price:* $19.99 Canada; $25 International
Profile: Information for people with spinal cord injury & other physical disabilities
• Workforce Participation Survey of Canadians with Spinal Cord Injuries
Type: Report

Spinal Cord Injury Newfoundland & Labrador (SCI NL)

PO Box 21284, #101, 396 Elizabeth Ave., St. John's NL A1A 5G6
Tel: 709-753-5901; *Fax:* 709-753-4224
Toll-Free: 877-783-5901
info@sci-nl.ca
sci-nl.ca
www.facebook.com/186403331430655
twitter.com/SCI_NL
Previous Name: Canadian Paraplegic Association - Newfoundland & Labrador
Overview: A medium-sized provincial organization overseen by Spinal Cord Injury Canada
Chief Officer(s):
Michael Burry, Executive Director
mburry@canparaplegic.org

Bay Roberts
PMC Professional Bldg., PO Box 1309, 25 Bareneed Rd., Bay Roberts NL A0A 1G0
Fax: 709-786-1441
Toll-Free: 877-634-0928

Corner Brook
PO Box 764, 1 Lester Ave., Corner Brook NL A2H 6G7
Fax: 709-634-7395
Toll-Free: 877-634-0928

Gander
Fraser Mall, 207 Airport Blvd., Gander NL A1V 1L7
Tel: 709-256-7077; *Fax:* 709-256-7047

Grand Falls - Windsor
#500, 4A Bayley St., Grand Falls-Windsor NL A2A 2T5
Fax: 709-489-8460
Toll-Free: 888-489-8410

Happy Valley - Labrador Office
PO Box 848, Stn. B, 21 Hamilton River Rd., Happy Valley NL A0P 1E0
Fax: 709-896-3716
Toll-Free: 877-596-3010

Marystown
PO Box 1296, #245, 247 Villa Marie Dr., Marystown NL A0E 2M0
Tel: 709-279-2790; *Fax:* 709-279-0919
Toll-Free: 877-792-2790

Spinal Cord Injury Ontario

520 Sutherland Dr., Toronto ON M4G 3V9
Tel: 416-422-5644; *Fax:* 416-422-5943
Toll-Free: 877-422-1112
info@sciontario.org
www.sciontario.org
www.facebook.com/sciontario.org
twitter.com/SCI_Ontario
Also Known As: SCI Ontario
Previous Name: Canadian Paraplegic Association Ontario
Overview: A medium-sized provincial organization founded in 1979 overseen by Spinal Cord Injury Canada
Mission: To act as the voice of persons with spinal cord injury in Ontario
Chief Officer(s):
Michael Gottlieb, Chair
Bill Adair, Executive Director
Membership: *Fees:* $10 individuals; $25 families
Activities: Delivers non-medical services to people with disabilities; Helping people integrate into the community; Increasing employment opportunities; Providing information services
Publications:
• Outspoken!
Type: Magazine; *Frequency:* Quarterly; *Price:* Free with membership
Profile: CPA Ontario services & activities

Barrie Office
#111, 80 Bradford St., Barrie ON L4N 6S7
Tel: 705-726-4546; *Fax:* 705-726-5054
Toll-Free: 800-870-5670
Chief Officer(s):
Heather Hollingshead, Coordinator

Hamilton Office
North Regional Rehabilitation Centre, #Bb1-3, 300 Wellington St., Hamilton ON L8N 3Z5
Tel: 905-383-0216; *Fax:* 905-383-5021
Toll-Free: 877-262-3366

Kingston Office
772 Blackburn Mews, Kingston ON K7P 2N7
Tel: 613-547-1391; *Fax:* 613-547-1393
Toll-Free: 866-220-7539

London Office
#3, 1111 Elias St., London ON N5W 5L1
Tel: 519-433-2331; *Fax:* 519-433-3987
Toll-Free: 866-433-9888

Mississauga/Halton; Peel/Dufferin Office
#175, 2 County Court Blvd., Brampton ON L6W 3W8
Tel: 905-459-6965
Toll-Free: 866-287-1689

Muskoka Office
PO Box 327, Kearney ON P0A 1M0
Tel: 705-636-5827; *Fax:* 705-636-7223

Ottawa Office
#104, 720 Belfast Rd., Ottawa ON K1G 0Z5
Tel: 613-723-1033; *Fax:* 613-723-1060
Toll-Free: 888-723-1033
• Spinal Columns: Ottawa Region Newsletter
Type: Newsletter; *Accepts Advertising*
Profile: Resources, upcoming events, & volunteer opportunities

Peterborough Office
PO Box 131, Warsaw ON K0L 3A0
Tel: 705-652-7496
Toll-Free: 888-643-2507

Sault St. Marie Office
260 Elizabeth St., Sault Ste Marie ON P6A 6J3
Tel: 705-759-0333; *Fax:* 705-759-0335
Toll-Free: 866-531-1513
Chief Officer(s):
Diane Morrell, Contact

Thunder Bay Office
1201 Jasper Dr., #B, Thunder Bay ON P7B 6R2
Tel: 807-344-3743; *Fax:* 807-344-9490
Toll-Free: 866-344-4159

Toronto - West Office
#306, 1120 Finch Ave., Toronto ON M3J 3H7
Tel: 416-241-1433; *Fax:* 416-241-2466
Toll-Free: 866-318-9990

Waterloo-Wellington Office
#1, 1382 Weber St. East, Kitchener ON N2A 1C4
Tel: 519-893-1267; *Fax:* 519-893-2585
Toll-Free: 888-893-1267

Windsor Office
c/o Western Campus, Windsor Regional Hospital, 1453 Prince Rd., Windsor ON N9C 3Z4
Tel: 519-253-7272; *Fax:* 519-253-7279
Toll-Free: 877-253-7279

Spirit of Sport Foundation *See* True Sport Foundation

Spiritans, the Congregation of the Holy Ghost

Laval House, 121 Victoria Park Ave., Toronto ON M4E 3S2
Tel: 416-691-9319; *Fax:* 416-691-8760
communications@spiritans.com
www.spiritans.com
www.youtube.com/profile?user=SpiritansTransCanada
Overview: A medium-sized national organization
Mission: Roman Catholic religious congregation specializing in education & mission
Chief Officer(s):
Paul McAuley, Contact
Membership: 3,000+

Spiritual Science Fellowship/International Institute of Integral Human Sciences (SSF-IIIHS)

PO Box 1387, Stn. H, 1974, rue de Maisonneuve ouest, Montréal QC H3G 2N3
Tel: 514-937-8359; *Fax:* 514-937-5380
info@iiihs.org
www.iiihs.org
www.facebook.com/SSF.IIIHS
twitter.com/SSF_IIIHS
Overview: A small local charitable organization
Mission: To provide spiritual services, educational programs, & pastoral ministrations for persons, regardless of religious background, who desire to understand experiences of psyche & spirit, & to dedicate themselves to personal spiritual growth & psychic development, in an atmosphere of informed free-thought & enquiry
Chief Officer(s):
Marilyn Z. Rossner
25 volunteer(s)
Membership: 10,000; *Fees:* $15; gifts
Activities: *Internships:* Yes; *Speaker Service:* Yes

Spiritwood Chamber of Commerce

PO Box 267, Spiritwood SK S0J 2M0
Tel: 306-883-2161
Overview: A small local organization
Chief Officer(s):
B. Fee, President
Yvette McGown, Secretary

Sport Alliance Ontario

3 Concorde Gate, Toronto ON M3C 3N7
Tel: 416-426-7000; *Fax:* 416-426-7381
www.sportalliance.com
www.facebook.com/115392235237272
twitter.com/talksportON
Previous Name: Ontario Sports & Recreation Centre Inc.
Overview: A large provincial organization
Mission: To provide facilities, services & business expertise to enable provincial sport, recreation & fitness organizations to serve the people of Ontario
Chief Officer(s):
Blair McIntosh, CEO, 416-426-7289
bmcintosh@sportallianceontario.com
Finances: *Annual Operating Budget:* Greater than $5 Million; *Funding Sources:* Provincial government & sport & recreation associations
Staff Member(s): 45
Activities: National Coaching Certificate Program; Female Athletics Motivation for Excellence Program; Fitness Ontario Leadership Program; Safety Recreation Resources Centre; Sport Injury, Prevention & Care Program; Skills programs for management volunteers; *Awareness Events:* 7th Annual KidSport Charity Golf Classic, August; *Internships:* Yes; *Library:* Sports & Recreation Resource Centre; Open to public
Awards:
• The Male Athlete Of The Year Award (Award)
• The Female Athlete Of The Year Award (Award)
• The Male Athlete With A Disability Of The Year Award (Award)
• The Female Athlete With A Disability Of The Year Award (Award)
• The Team Of The Year Award (Award)
• The Male Coach Of The Year Award (Award)
• The Female Coach Of The Year Award (Award)
• The Corporate Citation (Award)
• The Syl Apps Volunteer Achievement Award (Award)
• The Rolf Lund Jule Nisse Award (Award)
• The Sport Builder Award (Award)

Sport BC

#230, 3820 Cessna Dr., Richmond BC V7B 0A2
Tel: 604-333-3400; *Fax:* 604-333-3401
info@sportbc.com
sportbc.com
www.facebook.com/SportBC
twitter.com/SportBC
Overview: A medium-sized provincial organization founded in 1966
Mission: To provide leadership, direction, & support to member organizations in their delivery of sport opportunities to all British Columbians
Member of: Sport West
Chief Officer(s):
Pete Quevillon, Director, KidSport BC
Rob Newman, President & CEO
rob.newman@sportbc.com
Finances: *Annual Operating Budget:* $1.5 Million-$3 Million; *Funding Sources:* Provincial Funding; Membership Fees; Corporate Support, Event & Fundraising; Fee for Services; All Sport Insurance; SBC Insurance Operations
Staff Member(s): 7
Membership: 80 Associations; *Fees:* Schedule available; *Member Profile:* Non-profit society sport organization with province-wide representation; *Committees:* Finance & Audit
Activities: Participation & Excellence; KidSport Fund; Leadership; Sport Promotion; Advocacy; Organizations Development; *Internships:* Yes; *Speaker Service:* Yes
Awards:
• Community Sport Hero Awards (Award)
• President's Awards (Award)
• Athlete of the Year Awards (Award)

Sport Dispute Resolution Centre of Canada (SDRCC)

#950, 1080 Beaver Hall Hill, Montréal QC H2Z 1S8
Tel: 514-866-1245; *Fax:* 514-866-1246
Toll-Free: 866-733-7767
www.crdsc-sdrcc.ca
www.linkedin.com/company/sport-dispute-resolution-centre-of-canada
www.facebook.com/pages/SDRCC-CRDSC/424545007600467
Also Known As: ADRsportRED
Overview: A small national organization founded in 2004
Mission: To provide to the sport community a national alternative dispute resolution service for sport disputes
Chief Officer(s):
Allan J. Sattin, Chair
Marie-Claude Asselin, Executive Director
mcasselin@crdsc-sdrcc.ca

Sport for Disabled - Ontario; Paralympics Ontario *See* ParaSport Ontario

Sport interuniversitaire canadien *See* Canadian Interuniversity Sport

Sport Jeunesse / KidSport Québec

CP 1000, Succ. M, 4545, av Pierre-de Coubertin, Montréal QC H1V 3R2
Tél: 514-252-3114; *Téléc:* 514-254-9621
iducharme@sportsquebec.com
www.jeuxduquebec.com/Mes_premiers_Jeux-fr-13.php
Également appelé: Mes Premiers Jeux
Aperçu: *Dimension:* petite; *Envergure:* provinciale surveillé par KidSport Canada
Membre de: KidSport Canada; Sports Québec

Sport Manitoba

Sport for Life Centre, 145 Pacific Ave., Winnipeg MB R3B 2Z6
Tel: 204-925-5600; *Fax:* 204-925-5916
info@sportmanitoba.ca
www.sportmanitoba.ca
www.facebook.com/sportmb
twitter.com/SportManitoba
www.youtube.com/user/sportmanitoba
Previous Name: Manitoba Sports Federation Inc.
Overview: A large provincial organization founded in 1996
Mission: To create the best sport community in Canada through provision of resources to recognized sport organizations, enabling them to encourage participation in sport at all levels of skill & ability & to develop athletes of national & international calibre
Chief Officer(s):
Jeff Palamar, Chair
Jeff Hnatiuk, President & CEO
jeff.hnatiuk@sportmanitoba.ca
Tara Skibo, Communications/Public Relations Officer
tara.skibo@sportmanitoba.ca
Finances: *Funding Sources:* Provincial government
Staff Member(s): 45
Activities: Operating & overseeing the Sport for Life Centre; Coaching Manitoba; Sport Medicine Centre; Manitoba Sports Hall of Fame; KidSport Manitoba; Power Smart Manitoba Games; & Team Manitoba; *Awareness Events:* Polar Bear Dare; *Speaker Service:* Yes; *Library* by appointment
Awards:
• Athlete Assistance (Grant)
• Coaching Manitoba Bursary (Scholarship)
• Manitoba Foundation for Sports Scholarships (Scholarship)
• Princess Royal Pan Am Scholarship (Scholarship)
Publications:
• Sport for Life [a publication of Sport Manitoba]
Type: Newsletter

Sport Medicine & Science Council of Manitoba Inc.

145 Pacific Ave., Winnipeg MB R3B 2Z6
Tel: 204-925-5750; *Fax:* 204-925-5624
sport.med@sportmanitoba.ca
sportmed.mb.ca
twitter.com/smsc_mb
Overview: A small provincial organization
Mission: To meet the needs of Manitoba's sport, recreation and fitness communities through an organized cooperative forum of medical, paramedical and sport science provider groups
Chief Officer(s):
Russ Horbal, Presidnet
Activities: *Library:* Sport Medicine & Science Council of Manitoba Resource Library; Open to public

Sport Medicine Council of Alberta (SMCA)

Percy Page Centre, 11759 Groat Rd., Main Fl., Edmonton AB T5M 3K6
Tel: 780-415-0812; *Fax:* 780-422-3093
www.sportmedab.ca
twitter.com/SportMedAB
Overview: A medium-sized provincial licensing organization founded in 1983
Mission: To develop, promote & coordinate programs & services optimizing safe & healthful participation in sport & leisure activities for all Albertans
Member of: Sport Medicine
Chief Officer(s):
Steve Johnson, President
Barb Adamson, Executive Director
badamson@sportmedab.ca
Membership: *Fees:* $50 subscriber; $265 corporate; *Member Profile:* Athletic therapists & teachers; sport physiotherapists; sport medicine physicians; sport scientists (including exercise physiologists, sport nutrition specialists, sport psychologists); teams; clubs
Activities: Athletic first aid courses; taping & strapping; sport nutrition courses; medical supply sales; kit rentals; speakers bureau; resource library; *Internships:* Yes; *Speaker Service:* Yes

Sport Medicine Council of British Columbia *See* SportMedBC

Sport New Brunswick / Sport Nouveau-Brunswick

#13, 900 Hanwell Rd., Fredericton NB E3B 6A2
Tel: 506-451-1320; *Fax:* 506-451-1325
director@sportnb.com
www.sportnb.com
twitter.com/SportNB
Also Known As: Sport NB
Overview: A medium-sized provincial charitable organization founded in 1968
Mission: To promote the development of amateur sport in New Brunswick through services, programs, advocacy
Member of: Canadian Council of Provincial Territorial Sport Federations
Chief Officer(s):
Darcy McKillop, CEO
director@sportnb.com
Finances: *Annual Operating Budget:* $250,000-$500,000; *Funding Sources:* Provincial government; membership fees; corporate sponsorship
Staff Member(s): 3
Membership: 68 organizations with 120,000 participants; *Fees:* $114-$342
Activities: *Awareness Events:* McInnes Cooper Dragon Boat Festival; *Internships:* Yes; *Speaker Service:* Yes; *Library* by appointment

Sport Newfoundland & Labrador

PO Box 8700, 1296A Kenmount Rd., St. John's NL A1B 4J6
Tel: 709-576-4932; *Fax:* 709-576-7493
sportnl@sportnl.ca
www.sportnl.ca
www.facebook.com/sportnl
twitter.com/sportnl
Also Known As: Sport NL
Previous Name: Newfoundland & Labrador Amateur Sports Federation
Overview: A medium-sized provincial organization founded in 1972
Mission: To promote & advance amateur sport throughout Newfoundland & Labrador; to represent collective interests & goals of members; to provide various programs & services; to liaise & lobby with government, communities, media & other representative organizations; to provide direction & leadership on issues which affect members
Chief Officer(s):
Troy Croft, Executive Director
troy@sportnl.ca
Staff Member(s): 4
Membership: 45 provincial sport organizations; 70,000 individual

Sport North Federation

Don Cooper Building, PO Box 11089, 4908 - 49 St., Yellowknife NT X1A 3X7
Tel: 867-669-8326; *Fax:* 867-669-8327
Toll-Free: 800-661-0797
www.sportnorth.com
www.facebook.com/pages/Sport-North/279234862113396
twitter.com/SportNorth
www.youtube.com/user/SportNorthFederation
Previous Name: Northwest Territories Sport Federation
Overview: A small provincial organization founded in 1976 overseen by Athletics Canada
Mission: To represent NWT sports organizations
Member of: Athletics Canada

Chief Officer(s):
Maureen Miller, President
mmiller@sportnorth.com
Doug Rentmeister, Executive Director
drent@sportnorth.com
Staff Member(s): 10

Sport Nouveau-Brunswick *See* Sport New Brunswick

Sport Nova Scotia (SNS)
5516 Spring Garden Rd., 4th Fl., Halifax NS B3J 1G6
Tel: 902-425-5450; *Fax:* 902-425-5606
sportns@sportnovascotia.ca
www.sportnovascotia.ca
Overview: A medium-sized provincial organization founded in 1974
Mission: To promote the development of amateur sport in Nova Scotia through services, programs, advocacy & technical consultation
Chief Officer(s):
Jamie Ferguson, CEO
jferguson@sportnovascotia.ca
Finances: *Annual Operating Budget:* $1.5 Million-$3 Million; *Funding Sources:* Membership; sponsors; government
Staff Member(s): 17; 15 volunteer(s)
Membership: 86 groups + 150,000 individuals; *Fees:* $25-300

Sport Parachute Association of Saskatchewan
SK
Other Communication: Board of Directors, E-mail: bod@skydive.sk.ca
www.skydive.sk.ca
Overview: A small provincial organization overseen by Canadian Sport Parachuting Association
Member of: Canadian Sport Parachuting Association
Chief Officer(s):
Craig Skihar, President
stimpysplace@gmail.com
Jayson Pister, Vice-President
jay.pister@gmail.com

Sport PEI Inc.
PO Box 302, 40 Enman Cres., Charlottetown PE C1E 1E6
Tel: 902-368-4110; *Fax:* 902-368-4548
Toll-Free: 800-247-6712
Other Communication: Toll-Free Fax: 1-800-235-5687
sports@sportpei.pe.ca
www.sportpei.pe.ca
www.facebook.com/176050449103403
twitter.com/sportpei
Overview: A small provincial organization founded in 1973
Mission: To assist in the development & promotion of amateur sport in the province of Prince Edward Island; To offer services & programs to meet the needs of the membership
Chief Officer(s):
Ron Waite, President
Gemma Koughan, Executive Director
gkoughan@sportpei.pe.ca
Finances: *Annual Operating Budget:* $100,000-$250,000; *Funding Sources:* Government; private sector sponsorships
Staff Member(s): 13; 15 volunteer(s)
Membership: 6 corporate + 39 active + 17 affiliate + 11 honorary; *Fees:* Schedule available; *Member Profile:* Provincial sport organizations; *Committees:* Finance; Administration; Fundraising; Marketing; Sport Development
Activities: Provides advice to member associations; acts in consultative capacity with member associations; offers & administers fundraising opportunities for amateur sport in PEI; the ADL/Sport PEI Sport Achievement Program to honour achievement in sport in the province; ADL/Sport PEI Volunteer Recognition Program; Sport Leadership Program; Sport Scholarship Program; Kidsport; *Internships:* Yes; *Library* Open to public
Awards:
- Top Junior & Senior Male & Female Athletes of the Year (Award)
- Team, Coach, Administrator & Official of the Year (Award)
- Six scholarships to student athletes (Scholarship) *Amount:* $500 each
- All Around Intercollegiate Male & Female Masters (Award)

Sport Physiotherapy Canada (SPC)
#320, 4246 Albert St., Regina SK S4S 3R9
Tel: 613-748-5794
info@sportphysio.ca
www.sportphysio.ca
Previous Name: Sport Physiotherapy Division of the Canadian Physiotherapy Association
Overview: A small national organization founded in 1972
Mission: To promote professional development of members; To ensure high-quality health care for Canada's athletes
Member of: Canadian Physiotherapy Association; Sport Medicine Council of Canada
Chief Officer(s):
Suzanne Gorman, Chief Executive Officer
Membership: 1,200; *Member Profile:* Members can be physiotherapists, students, graduate / practising physiotherapists, or SPD-certified sport physiotherapists

Sport Physiotherapy Division of the Canadian Physiotherapy Association *See* Sport Physiotherapy Canada

Sport Scolaire Canada *See* School Sport Canada

Sport Yukon
4061 - 4 Ave., Whitehorse YT Y1A 1H1
Tel: 867-668-4236; *Fax:* 867-667-4237
news@sportyukon.com
www.sportyukon.com
www.facebook.com/237900786299653
twitter.com/sportyukon
Overview: A small provincial organization
Mission: To promote the development of amateur sport in the Yukon through services, programs, advocacy
Chief Officer(s):
Tracey Bilsky, Executive Director
tbilsky@sportyukon.com
Staff Member(s): 2
Membership: 68 clubs; *Fees:* $210

SportMedBC
#2350, 3713 Kensington Ave., Burnaby BC B5B 0A7
Tel: 604-294-3050; *Fax:* 604-294-3020
Toll-Free: 888-755-3375
info@sportmedbc.com
www.sportmedbc.com
www.facebook.com/sportmedbc
twitter.com/SportMedBC
www.youtube.com/user/SportMedBC
Previous Name: Sport Medicine Council of British Columbia
Overview: A small provincial organization founded in 1982
Chief Officer(s):
Alison Cristall, Executive Director, 604-294-3050 Ext. 102
alisonc@sportmedbc.com
Finances: *Annual Operating Budget:* $100,000-$250,000; *Funding Sources:* Service fees; grants
Staff Member(s): 6
Membership: 275; *Fees:* $30 individual
Activities: Injury Prevention; Athlete Development; Drug-free Sport

Sports à roulettes du Canada *See* Roller Sports Canada

Sports Car Club of British Columbia (SCCBC)
PO Box 3432, 33191 - 1 Ave., Mission BC V2V 4J5
Tel: 778-999-7769
marketing@sccbc.net
www.sccbc.net
www.facebook.com/147929071991449
twitter.com/SCC_BC
www.youtube.com/user/BSpecRacing
Overview: A small provincial charitable organization founded in 1951
Mission: To organize safe road race competition; to promote safe road conduct & to foster sportsmanship
Chief Officer(s):
Steve Hocaluk, President
president@sccbc.net
Finances: *Funding Sources:* Race entries; sponsors; membership dues
Membership: 300; *Fees:* $60 annually + $25 family members; $25 associate; *Committees:* Track Operations; Race Drivers; Executives

Sports Laval
#221, 3235, St-Martin Est, Laval QC H7E 5G8
Tél: 450-664-1917; *Téléc:* 450-664-7832
info@sportslaval.qc.ca
laval.rseq.ca
Également appelé: RSEQ Laval
Merged from: Association régionale du sport étudiant de Laval; La Commission Sports Laval
Aperçu: *Dimension:* petite; *Envergure:* locale; fondée en 2003
Mission: Mettre en ouvre des actions permettant aux différents sports de prendre place dans les communautés urbaines et scolaires lavalloises
Membre de: Réseau du sport étudiant du Québec
Affliation(s): Réseau du sport étudiant du Québec
Membre(s) du bureau directeur:
Martin Savoie, Directeur général
martin@sportslaval.qc.ca

Sports Medicine Council of Nova Scotia (SMCNS)
50 West Porters Lake Rd., Porters Lake NS B3E 1K2
Fax: 902-435-4491
Overview: A small provincial organization founded in 1989
Mission: To provide sport medicine services & education to the athletes & active Canadians of Nova Scotia; to maintain a registry of sport medicine providers, services & equipment in the province of Nova Scotia
Affiliation(s): Sport Medicine & Science Council of Canada
Finances: *Annual Operating Budget:* Less than $50,000; *Funding Sources:* Provincial government
2 volunteer(s)
Membership: 70 individual

Sports universitaires de l'Ontario *See* Ontario University Athletics

Sports-Québec
4545, av Pierre-de Coubertin, Montréal QC H1V 3R2
Tél: 514-252-3114; *Téléc:* 514-254-9621
sports@sportsquebec.com
www.sportsquebec.com
www.facebook.com/sportsquebec
twitter.com/sportsquebec
Aperçu: *Dimension:* moyenne; *Envergure:* provinciale; Organisme sans but lucratif; fondée en 1988
Mission: Assurer la synergie de ses membres et de ses partenaires du système sportif québécois et du système sportif canadien pour favoriser le développement et l'épanouissement de l'athlète et la promotion de la pratique sportive
Membre de: Canadian Council of Provincial & Territorial Sport Federation
Membre(s) du bureau directeur:
Alain Deschamps, Directeur général, 514-252-3114 Ext. 3621
adeschamps@sportsquebec.com
Isabelle Ducharme, Directrice, Programmes, 514-252-3114 Ext. 3624
iducharme@sportsquebec.com
Michelle Gendron, Coordonnatrice, Communications stratégiques, 514-252-3114 Ext. 3622
mgendron@sportsquebec.com
Membre: 900,000 personnes; *Critères d'admissibilite:* Ordinaires; Régionaux; Affinitaires
Activités: *Stagiaires:* Oui; *Bibliothèque:* Centre de documentation;

Springboard Dance
205 - 8th Ave. SE, 2nd Fl., Calgary AB T2G 0K9
Tel: 403-265-3230
springboardperformance.com
www.facebook.com/springboardYYC
twitter.com/springboardyyc
Overview: A small local charitable organization founded in 1988
Mission: To produce, create & perform intellectually & sensually stimulating modern dance
Affiliation(s): Alberta Dance Alliance; Canadian Dance Federation; Dance Current
Chief Officer(s):
Nicole Mion, Artistic Director & Curator
nicole@springboardperformance.com
Kari McQueen, Artistic Coordinator
kari@springboardperformance.com
Travis Wall, President
Finances: *Funding Sources:* Government
Staff Member(s): 9
Activities: *Internships:* Yes

Springdale & Area Chamber of Commerce
PO Box 37, 393 Little Bay Rd., Springdale NL A0J 1T0
Tel: 709-673-3837
www.townofspringdale.ca
Overview: A small local organization
Chief Officer(s):
Cyril Pelley, President
Glenn Seabright, Secretary
seabright.reception@nf.aibn.com

Springhill & Area Chamber of Commerce
PO Box 1030, Springhill NS B0M 1X0
Tel: 902-597-8462; *Fax:* 902-597-3839
audrey@surrette.com
www.springhillareachamber.com
Overview: A small local organization
Member of: Atlantic Provinces Chamber of Commerce
Chief Officer(s):
Frank Likely, President
fdlikely@yahoo.ca
Marcie Meekins, Secretary
amcprojects@eastlink.ca
Membership: 37; *Fees:* $20 individual; $50 corporate

Springtide Resources
#220, 215 Spadina Ave., Toronto ON M5T 2C7
Tel: 416-968-3422; *Fax:* 416-968-2026
info@womanabuseprevention.com
www.springtideresources.org
www.facebook.com/springtide.resources
twitter.com/Springtide_VAW
Previous Name: Education Wife Assault
Overview: A small local charitable organization founded in 1978
Mission: To increase public awareness of the many aspects of violence against women & its effect on children; to change the social conditions that subject women to abuse by providing training & resources proactively.
Member of: Volunteer Centre of Toronto; Association of Fundraising Professionals; Council of Agencies Serving South Asians.
Affliation(s): The National Action Committee on the Status of Women; Ontario Association of Interval & Transition Houses; Woman Abuse Council of Toronto
Chief Officer(s):
Marsha Sfeir, Executive Director
Finances: *Funding Sources:* Individual donors; foundations; churches; various levels of government.
Staff Member(s): 8
Membership: *Fees:* $25
Activities: Offering educational & training expertise; workshops & training programs; publications available in wide variety of languages; *Internships:* Yes; *Speaker Service:* Yes; *Library* Open to public by appointment

Springwater Chamber of Commerce
2231 Nursery Rd., Minesing ON L0L 1Y2
Tel: 705-797-7500
info@springwaterchamber.ca
www.springwaterchamber.ca
www.facebook.com/SpringwaterChamber
Overview: A small local organization
Member of: Canadian Chamber of Commerce; Ontario Chamber of Commerce
Chief Officer(s):
Mike Guilbault, President, 705-322-2223
mike@mgphotography.com
Membership: 109; *Fees:* $75

SPRINT Senior Care
140 Merton St., 2nd Fl., Toronto ON M4S 1A1
Tel: 416-481-0669; *Fax:* 416-481-9829
info@sprintseniorcare.org
sprintseniorcare.org
www.linkedin.com/company/sprint-senior-peoples-resources-in-north-toro
www.facebook.com/SPRINT.Senior.Care
twitter.com/SPRINT_Sr_Care
www.youtube.com/user/sprintseniorcare
Overview: A small local charitable organization
Mission: To offer community support services to seniors & their families in North Toronto
Chief Officer(s):
Stacy Landau, Executive Director
Publications:
• SPRINT News
Type: Newsletter; *Frequency:* Monthly

Spruce City Wildlife Association (SCWA)
1384 River Rd., Prince George BC V2L 5S8
Tel: 250-563-5437; *Fax:* 250-563-5438
info@scwa.bc.ca
www.scwa.bc.ca
Overview: A medium-sized local organization founded in 1970
Mission: To perform environmental acts that improve the BC wilderness
Member of: BC Wildlife Federation
Chief Officer(s):
Jim Glaicar, President
Membership: *Fees:* $50 individual; $60 family; $125 corporate; $40 student/senior

Spruce Grove & District Chamber of Commerce
PO Box 4210, 99 Campsite Rd., Spruce Grove AB T7X 3B4
Tel: 780-962-2561; *Fax:* 780-962-4417
www.sprucegrovechamber.com
Overview: A small local charitable organization founded in 1963
Mission: To develop a positive environment for successful business to profit; to foster confidence, progress & success through the synergy of professionalism, cooperation, respect, astute vision & leadership
Member of: Alberta Chamber of Commerce; Canadian Chamber of Commerce
Chief Officer(s):
Michelle Thiebaud, President
Robin Grayston, 1st Vice-President
Finances: *Annual Operating Budget:* $100,000-$250,000
Staff Member(s): 2
Membership: 450; *Fees:* $100-$325
Activities: *Internships:* Yes; *Speaker Service:* Yes; *Rents Mailing List:* Yes

Squamish & District Labour Committee (SDLC)
PO Box 424, Squamish BC V8B 0A4
Tel: 604-815-5133; *Fax:* 604-815-0811
sdlc2001@hotmail.com
Overview: A small local organization overseen by British Columbia Federation of Labour
Mission: To support workers' rights, strong social programs, & a sustainable environment in the Squamish & District region of British Columbia
Affliation(s): Canadian Labour Congress (CLC)
Chief Officer(s):
Lyle Fenton, President
Activities: Engaging in municipal political action; Liaising with local mayors & council members; Providing labour news for the Squamish area; Organizing a Day of Mourning ceremony to honour workers injured or killed on the job

Squamish & Howe Sound Chamber of Commerce; Chamber of Commerce Serving Squamish, Britannia Beach & Furry Creek *See* Squamish Chamber of Commerce

Squamish Chamber of Commerce
Squamish Adventure Centre, #102, 38551 Loggers Lane, Squamish BC V8B 0H2
Tel: 604-815-4994; *Fax:* 604-815-4998
Toll-Free: 866-333-2010
info@squamishchamber.com
www.squamishchamber.com
www.facebook.com/SquamishChamberofCommerce
twitter.com/SquamishChamber
www.youtube.com/spiritofsquamish
Previous Name: Squamish & Howe Sound Chamber of Commerce; Chamber of Commerce Serving Squamish, Britannia Beach & Furry Creek
Overview: A small local charitable organization founded in 1934
Mission: To enhance the quality of life in the community by actively supporting business, economic growth & diversification
Member of: Canadian Chamber of Commerce; BC Chamber of Commerce
Chief Officer(s):
Chris Pettingill, President
Finances: *Annual Operating Budget:* $250,000-$500,000; *Funding Sources:* Membership dues; fundraising; contracts
Staff Member(s): 3; 13 volunteer(s)
Membership: 400; *Fees:* $94.50-$380.10; *Committees:* Trade Fair; Tourism
Activities: Operates Visitors Info Centre; *Library:* Reference Library; Open to public

Squamish Food Bank
PO Box 207, 37978-3rd Ave, Garibaldi Highlands BC V0N 1T0
Tel: 604-848-4316
www.corridorconnector.org/region/group/squamish-food-bank
Overview: A small local organization overseen by Food Banks British Columbia
Mission: To provide food to community members experiencing hardship
Member of: Food Banks British Columbia
Chief Officer(s):
Susan Newman, President, 604-848-4316
Elca Tschol, Contact

Square & Round Dance Federation of Nova Scotia
c/o Ralph MacDonald, PO Box 16, Goshen NS B0H 1M0
Tel: 902-783-2731
www.chebucto.ns.ca
Overview: A small provincial organization founded in 1983 overseen by Canadian Square & Round Dance Society
Mission: To provide liaison between clubs & the provincial government; to suggest guidelines & provide an organizational framework for operating & coordinating activities of member clubs; to encourage cooperation in advertising, promoting & operating Square & Round Dance classes throughout the province of Nova Scotia; to support & supplement the work of the Association of Nova Scotia Square & Round Dance Teachers
Affiliation(s): Dance Nova Scotia
Chief Officer(s):
Paul Langille, Co-President
prlangille@eastlink.ca
Cathy Langille, Co-President
Membership: 30 member clubs; *Fees:* Schedule available; *Member Profile:* Couples interested in square & round dancing

Squash Alberta
3415 - 3rd Ave. NW, Calgary AB T2N 0M4
Tel: 403-270-7344; *Fax:* 403-270-8445
Toll-Free: 877-646-6566
www.squashalberta.com
Previous Name: Alberta Squash Racquets Association
Overview: A medium-sized provincial charitable organization founded in 1967 overseen by Squash Canada
Mission: To promote & facilitate the development of the sport of squash in Alberta
Member of: Squash Canada
Chief Officer(s):
Bob Grose, President
ambushbob@shaw.ca
Lynn Nixon, Executive Director
lynn@squashalberta.com
Finances: *Annual Operating Budget:* $100,000-$250,000; *Funding Sources:* Membership dues; programs; government grants
Staff Member(s): 2; 100 volunteer(s)
Membership: 1,600; *Fees:* $50 adult; $45 junior; $115 family

Squash British Columbia
4867 Ontario St., Vancouver BC V5V 3H4
Tel: 604-737-3084; *Fax:* 604-736-3527
info@squashbc.com
www.squashbc.com
www.facebook.com/squashbc
twitter.com/squashbc
Overview: A medium-sized provincial organization overseen by Squash Canada
Mission: To promote the growth of squash by providing orderly development opportunities for athletes, & encouraging participation through a variety of programs & activities organized by Squash BC & its partners
Member of: Sport BC; Squash Canada
Chief Officer(s):
Jonathan Money, President
Jordan Abney, Executive Director
jordan@squashbc.com
Membership: *Fees:* $45.92 individual; $22.40 student; $16.80 junior
Activities: *Library*

Squash Canada
#401, 2197 Riverside Dr., Ottawa ON K1H 7X3
Tel: 613-731-7385; *Fax:* 613-731-6291
info@squash.ca
www.squash.ca
www.facebook.com/squashcanada
twitter.com/squashcanada
www.youtube.com/user/Squashcanada2011
Previous Name: Canadian Squash Racquets Association
Overview: A large national charitable organization founded in 1913
Mission: To develop athletes, coaches & officials in the sport of squash; to set standards for squash in Canada; to promote growth & development in the sport across the country
Member of: World Squash Federation
Chief Officer(s):
Lolly Gillen, President
Danny Da Costa, Executive Director, 613-731-7385 Ext. 2301
ddacosta@squash.ca

Jamie Hickox, Director, Performance
performance@squash.ca
Whitney Fuller, Coordinator, Sport Development & Events, 613-731-7385 Ext. 2302
development@squash.ca
Finances: *Funding Sources:* Government; Donations; Sponsorship
Membership: *Member Profile:* Provincial/territorial clubs & members; *Committees:* High Performance; Squash Canada Officiating; Governance Review; Finance & Audit; Junior Development; Doubles; Masters; Patrons Fund; Community Endowment Fund; Nominations; Competitions; Coaching; Canada Games; Doubles Competition; Doubles Officiating
Publications:
• Canadian Squash News [a publication of Squash Canada]
Type: Newsletter

Squash Manitoba
145 Pacific Ave., Winnipeg MB R3B 2Z6
Tel: 204-925-5661; *Fax:* 204-925-5792
squash@sportmanitoba.ca
www.squashmb.org
Overview: A medium-sized provincial organization overseen by Squash Canada
Mission: To promote the game of squash in Manitoba, establish and enforce rules and programs for all levels of play.
Member of: Squash Canada
Affliation(s): Brandon squash & athletic centre; Dauphin Squash Club; University of Winnipeg; Winnipeg Squash Racquet Club; Winnipeg Winter Club
Chief Officer(s):
Lynn Colliou, Executive Director
Membership: *Fees:* $20

Squash Newfoundland & Labrador Inc.
PO Box 21254, St. John's NL A1A 5B2
e-mail: hongngee@gmail.com
www.hongngee.com/squashnl
Also Known As: Squash NL
Overview: A small provincial organization overseen by Squash Canada
Mission: To coordinate & promote the sport of squash in Newfoundland & Labrador.
Member of: Squash Canada
Chief Officer(s):
John Nichols, President

Squash Nova Scotia
PO Box 3010, Stn. Park Lane Centre, #401, 5516 Spring Garden Rd., Halifax NS B3J 3G6
Tel: 902-425-5450; *Fax:* 902-425-5606
www.squashns.ca
Overview: A medium-sized provincial organization overseen by Squash Canada
Mission: Fosters & promotes a squash community for players of all abilities from across the province to improve the profile of the sport & its enjoyment by its members.
Member of: Squash Canada
Chief Officer(s):
Alfred Seaman, President
Finances: *Annual Operating Budget:* Less than $50,000
Membership: 100-499; *Fees:* $15 student; $20 adult

Squash Ontario
3 Concorde Gate, Toronto ON M3C 3N7
Tel: 416-426-7201; *Fax:* 416-426-7393
info@squashontario.com
www.squashontario.com
www.facebook.com/SquashOntario
twitter.com/SquashOntario
www.youtube.com/squashontario
Overview: A medium-sized provincial organization founded in 1976
Mission: To act as the governing body for the sport of squash in Ontario; To develop & promote the sport of squash across Ontario; To provide an environment in which the sport of squash can thrive; To meet the needs of present & potential players
Chief Officer(s):
Mark Sachvie, President
msachvie@whiteoaksresort.com
Sherry Funston, Executive Director, 416-426-7202
sfunston@squashontario.com
Geoffrey Johnson, Program Coordinator, 416-426-7203
gjohnson@squashontario.com
Laura Mauer, Administrative Coordinator, 416-426-7201
lmauer@squashontario.com
Membership: *Committees:* Junior Advisory; High Performance; Masters'
Activities: Developing squash players, from beginners to elite athletes, as well as teams, coaches, & officials; Establishing & maintaining technical standards
Awards:
• Coaching Achievement Award (Award)
To recognize outstanding coaches in Ontario
• Special Achievement Award (Award)
To recognize a volunteer, player, coach, or official who has worked on behalf of the game of squash
• Corporate Special Achievement Award (Award)
To recognize outstanding contributions of corporations to the game of squash in Ontario
Publications:
• Policies & Procedures Manual
Type: Manual

Squash PEI
20 Massey Dr., Charlottetown PE C1E 1R6
Tel: 902-393-8663
squashpei.org
Overview: A small provincial organization overseen by Squash Canada
Mission: To promote squash in PEI; to provide competitive opportunities for members
Member of: Squash Canada; Sport PEI Inc.
Chief Officer(s):
Emily Brown, President
erc.brown@gmail.com
Kady Brown, Secretary
Ken Sampson, Treasurer
kensampson0@gmail.com

Squash Québec
4545, av Pierre-de Coubertin, Montréal QC H1V 0B2
Tél: 514-252-3062
info@sports-4murs.qc.ca
www.squash.qc.ca
Aperçu: *Dimension:* petite; *Envergure:* provinciale surveillé par Squash Canada
Mission: Promouvoir le développement du Squash au Québec en offrant différentes opportunités aux adeptes, tout en encourageant la participation sportive à travers un ensemble de services et de programmes
Membre de: Squash Canada
Membre(s) du bureau directeur:
Barry Faguy, Président
bfaguy@videotron.ca
Finances: *Budget de fonctionnement annuel:* $50,000-$100,000
Membre(s) du personnel: 2; 20 bénévole(s)
Membre: 5,000-14,999; *Montant de la cotisation:* 15$
Activités: *Stagiaires:* Oui

Squash Yukon
squashyukon.yk.ca
Overview: A small provincial organization overseen by Squash Canada
Member of: Squash Canada

Standardbred Breeders of Ontario Association (SBOA)
PO Box 371, Rockwood ON N0B 2K0
Tel: 519-856-4431
www.standardbredbreeders.com
Previous Name: Ontario Standardbred Improvement Association
Overview: A small provincial organization
Mission: To advocate on behalf of breeders; to establish races; to educate breeders
Chief Officer(s):
Walter Perkinson, President
Aimee Adams, Secretary-Treasurer & Administrator
aimee@sboa.info
Membership: *Fees:* $22.60
Activities: Annual banquet; holds races; regular column in Canadian Sportsman; New Owners Mentoring Program
Awards:
• Breeders Awards

Standardbred Canada (SC)
2150 Meadowvale Blvd., Mississauga ON L5N 6R6
Tel: 905-858-3060; *Fax:* 905-858-3111
www.standardbredcanada.ca
www.facebook.com/standardbred.canada
twitter.com/TrotInsider
www.youtube.com/user/jporchak
Merged from: The Canadian Trotting Association; The Canadian Standardbred Horse Society
Overview: A medium-sized national organization founded in 1909
Mission: To encourage & develop the breeding of Standardbred Horses
Chief Officer(s):
John Gallinger, President & CEO
jgallinger@standardbredcanada.ca
Val Boom, Manager, Member Services, Identification & Field Services
vboom@standardbredcanada.ca
Finances: *Annual Operating Budget:* $3 Million-$5 Million; *Funding Sources:* Membership & registration fees; horse sales
Staff Member(s): 45
Membership: 13,135; *Fees:* $55
Activities: *Rents Mailing List:* Yes; *Library:* Standardbred Canada Library; Open to public

Standing Conference of Organizations Concerned for Refugees *See* Canadian Council for Refugees

Stanley Park Ecology Society (SPES)
PO Box 5167, Vancouver BC V6B 4B2
Tel: 604-257-6908; *Fax:* 604-257-8378
info@stanleyparkecology.ca
www.stanleyparkecology.ca
www.facebook.com/StanleyPkEcoSoc
twitter.com/#!/StanleyPkEcoSoc
Overview: A small local organization founded in 1988
Mission: To encourage stewardship of our natural world through environmental education & action & by fostering awareness of the fragile balance that exists between urban populations & nature
Chief Officer(s):
Patricia Thomson, Executive Director, 604-718-6523
exec@stanleyparkecology.ca
Membership: *Fees:* $20 individual; $15 senior/junior/volunteer; $40 family

Stanstead Historical Society (SHS) / Musée Colby-Curtis
535 Dufferin Rd., Stanstead QC J0B 3E0
Tel: 819-876-7322; *Fax:* 819-876-7936
Other Communication: archives@colbycurtis.ca
info@colbycurtis.ca
www.colbycurtis.ca
Also Known As: The Colby-Curtis Museum/Carrollcroft
Overview: A small local charitable organization founded in 1929
Mission: To collect, preserve & pass on a knowledge & appreciation of all the people who have ever called the Border Region home
Member of: Canadian Museums Association; Société des musées quebecois
Affliation(s): Fédération des sociétés d'histoire du Québec
Chief Officer(s):
Sophie Cormier, Museum Director
Finances: *Annual Operating Budget:* $250,000-$500,000
Staff Member(s): 9; 25 volunteer(s)
Membership: 417; *Fees:* $15 individual; $20 family; $300 life; *Member Profile:* Seniors, local people & Americans
Activities: Victorian Tea Room & Garden; Boutique; *Internships:* Yes; *Speaker Service:* Yes; *Library:* Stanstead Historical Society Library; by appointment

Starlight Children's Foundation Canada
#809, 200 Consumers Rd., Toronto ON M2J 4R4
Tel: 416-642-5675; *Fax:* 416-642-5667
Toll-Free: 800-880-1004
info@starlightcanada.org
www.starlightcanada.org
www.linkedin.com/groups?gid=1414967
www.facebook.com/starlightcanada
twitter.com/StarlightCanada
www.youtube.com/CanadaStarlight
Overview: A medium-sized national charitable organization
Mission: To brighten the lives of seriously ill children & their families by providing both in-hospital & out-patient programs to enhance their ability to cope with the stress of illness
Chief Officer(s):
Brian J.H. Bringolf, Executive Director
brian@starlightcanada.ca

British Columbia Chapter
OddFellows' Hall, 1443 West 8th Ave., Vancouver BC V6H 1C9

Tel: 604-742-0272; *Fax:* 604-742-0274
heather@starlightcanada.org
Chief Officer(s):
Heather Burnett, Regional Coordinator
Calgary Chapter
8 Mount Norquay Gate SE, Calgary AB T2Z 2L3
Tel: 403-457-0344; *Fax:* 403-457-0384
laura.stow@starlightcanada.org
Chief Officer(s):
Laura Stow, Regional Coordinator
Montréal Chapter
105, 1375, rte Transcanadienne, Dorval QC H9P 2W8
Tel: 514-288-9474; *Fax:* 514-287-0635
Toll-Free: 888-782-7947
isabelle@starlightcanada.ca
Chief Officer(s):
Brian J.H. Bringolf, Executive Director
brian@starlightcanada.org
Ottawa Chapter
#204, 211 Bronson Ave., Ottawa ON K1R 6H5
Tel: 613-792-1268; *Fax:* 613-792-4220
chris@starlightcanada.org
Chief Officer(s):
Chris Baylis, Regional Coordinator

Start Right Coalition for Financial Literacy
PO Box 384, Pembroke ON K8A 6X6
Tel: 613-638-4313
Overview: A small local organization founded in 1998
Mission: To improve the financial literacy skills of youth ages 15 to 24
Chief Officer(s):
Michael Gulliver, Contact
Activities: Seminars to youth; website resources; newsletter; *Speaker Service:* Yes

Start2Finish
1295 North Service Rd., Burlington ON L7R 4M2
Tel: 905-319-1885; *Fax:* 905-319-3413
Toll-Free: 888-320-8844
info@start2finishonline.org
start2finishonline.org
www.facebook.com/pages/Start2Finish/235805049777065
twitter.com/EmpowrKids4Life
www.youtube.com/user/START2FINISHonline
Previous Name: Kidsfest
Overview: A small local organization founded in 2000
Mission: To provide the most vulnerable school children in grades 1 to 6 in Canada with school supplies, hygiene items & gift certificates for school clothing & shoes
Chief Officer(s):
Tracey Brophy, Chair
Brian Warren, CEO & Founder
Staff Member(s): 6
Activities: KidsFest Festival to raise money for our activities; annual dinner & auction; Spring Break - Reading Week; *Internships:* Yes; *Speaker Service:* Yes

Startup Canada
Ottawa ON
Tel: 613-316-6203
Other Communication: Alt. URL: startupblueprints.ca; Media E-mail: press@startupcan.ca
hello@startupcan.ca
www.startupcan.ca
www.linkedin.com/groups/Startup-Canada-Campaign-3895252
twitter.com/Startup_Canada
youtube.com/user/StartupCanada;
flickr.com/photos/62463248@N06
Overview: A large national organization founded in 2012
Mission: To be a national, grassroots, non-profit organization dedicated to strengthening & enhancing Canada's entrepreneurial culture.
Chief Officer(s):
Adam Chowaniec, Founding Chair
Victoria Lennox, Co-Founder & CEO
Cyprian Szalankiewicz, Co-Founder & Vice-President, Multimedia & Technology
250 volunteer(s)
Membership: 55,000 entrepreneurs + 400 partner organizations
Activities: Resources for Canadian entrepreneurs, including the Startup Connect network (www.startupconnect.ca)

Station Arts Centre Cooperative
PO Box 1078, Rosthern SK S0K 3R0
Tel: 306-232-5332; *Fax:* 306-232-5406
info@stationarts.com
www.stationarts.com
www.facebook.com/StationArts
Overview: A small local charitable organization founded in 1990
Mission: To promote the arts through education
Member of: Organization of Saskatchewan Arts Councils; Saskatchewan Arts Alliance; Saskatchewan Craft Council; Sask Culture; SK History & Folklore Society; Sask Tourism
Finances: *Annual Operating Budget:* $100,000-$250,000; *Funding Sources:* Federal & provincial grants; donations; rental; fundraising; tea room
Staff Member(s): 1; 50 volunteer(s)
Membership: 150; *Fees:* $15; *Committees:* Education; Fundraising; Maintenance; Performing; Tea Room; Theatre; Visual
Activities: Summer theatre; Christmas dinner concerts; winter concert series; spring concerts; juried art exhibits; tea room

Stationery & Office Equipment Guild of Canada Inc.; Stationers' Guild of Canada Inc. *See* Canadian Office Products Association

Statistical Society of Canada (SSC) / Société statistique du Canada
#209, 1725 St. Laurent Blvd., Ottawa ON K1G 3V4
Tel: 613-733-2662; *Fax:* 613-733-1386
Other Communication: admin@ssc.ca
info@ssc.ca
www.ssc.ca
Overview: A medium-sized national organization founded in 1977
Mission: To promote the development & use of statistics & probability; To ensure that decisions that affect society are based upon valid & appropriate statistics & interpretation; To encourage high standards for statistical education & practice
Chief Officer(s):
John Brewster, President
president@ssc.ca
John J. Koval, Treasurer
treasurer@ssc.ca
Julie Trépanier, Executive Secretary
secretary@ssc.ca
Membership: 900+; *Fees:* $15 students; $35 retired persons, spouses of regular members; $12510 regular membership; *Member Profile:* Canadian statisticians; *Committees:* Bilingualism; Election; Executive; Finance; Program; Publications; Accreditation; Accreditation Appeal; Awards; Award for Case Studies and Data Analysis; The Canadian Journal of Statistics Award; CRM-SSC Prize; Pierre Robillard Award; SSC Award for Impact of Applied & Collaborative Work; Student Presentation Award; Membership; Women in Statistics; Public Relations; Research; Statistical Education; AusCan Scholar; The Canadian Journal of Statistics Transition; Assessment of Meeting Arrangements; New Investigators; NSERC Liaison; Student Travel Awards
Activities: Increasing public awareness of the value of statistical thinking; Facilitating the exchange of ideas within the Canadian statistics community;
Awards:
• CRM-SSC Prize (Award)
• Founder Recognition Award (Award)
• Honorary Members Award (Award)
• SSC Service Award (Award)
• SSC Gold Medalists Award (Award)
• Pierre-Robillard Award (Award)
• The Canadian Journal of Statistics Award (Award)
Meetings/Conferences: • Statistical Society of Canada / Société statistique du Canada 2015 Annual Meeting, June, 2015, Dalhousie University, Halifax, NS
Scope: National
• Joint Statistical Meetings 2015, August, 2015, Seattle, WA
Scope: International
Description: Held jointly with the Statistical Society of Canada, American Statistical Association, the International Biometric Society (ENAR & WNAR), the International Chinese Statistical Association, the Institute of Mathematical Statistics, & the International Indian Statistical Association
• Joint Statistical Meetings 2016, July, 2016, Chicago, IL
Scope: International
Description: Held jointly with the Statistical Society of Canada, American Statistical Association, the International Biometric Society (ENAR & WNAR), the International Chinese Statistical Association, the Institute of Mathematical Statistics, & the International Indian Statistical Association
• Joint Statistical Meetings 2017, July, 2017, Baltimore, MD
Scope: International
Description: Held jointly with the Statistical Society of Canada, American Statistical Association, the International Biometric Society (ENAR & WNAR), the International Chinese Statistical Association, the Institute of Mathematical Statistics, & the International Indian Statistical Association
• Statistical Society of Canada / Société statistique du Canada 2014 Annual Meeting, 2016
Scope: National
• Joint Statistical Meetings 2018, 2018
Scope: International
Description: Held jointly with the Statistical Society of Canada, American Statistical Association, the International Biometric Society (ENAR & WNAR), the International Chinese Statistical Association, the Institute of Mathematical Statistics, & the International Indian Statistical Association
Publications:
• The Canadian Journal of Statistics / La revue canadienne de statistique
Type: Journal; *Frequency:* Quarterly; *Editor:* George P.H. Styan & Paul Gustafson; *Price:* $260
Profile: Research articles of interest to the statistical community
• SSC Handbook / Manuel de la SSC
Type: Handbook; *Number of Pages:* 98; *Editor:* Paul Cabilio
• SSC Liaison
Type: Newsletter; *Frequency:* Quarterly; *Accepts Advertising*; *Editor:* Larry K. Weldon
Profile: Society reports, announcements, conferences, & employment opportunities
• Statistical Society of Canada Membership Directory
Type: Directory
• Statistics Surveys
Editor: Richard Lockhart

Status of Women Council of the Northwest Territories (SWC)
Northwest Tower, PO Box 1320, 4th Fl., Yellowknife NT X1A 2L9
Tel: 867-920-6177; *Fax:* 867-873-0285
Toll-Free: 888-234-4485
council@statusofwomen.nt.ca
www.statusofwomen.nt.ca
www.facebook.com/113623588652526
twitter.com/StatusofWomenNT
Overview: A medium-sized provincial organization founded in 1990
Mission: To work towards equality for all NWT women, through public education & awareness, research, advocacy, community development, interagency cooperation, advice to government, & identification & development of opportunities for women
Member of: Status of Women Canada
Chief Officer(s):
Lorraine Phaneuf, Executive Director
lorraine@statusofwomen.nt.ca
Finances: *Annual Operating Budget:* $250,000-$500,000
Staff Member(s): 4
Membership: *Member Profile:* Represents all women through regional board members
Activities: *Awareness Events:* International Women's Day; March 8; Take Back the Night, Sept. 21; Family Violence Awareness Week, Oct.; *Library* Open to public
Awards:
• Wise Woman Award (Award)

St-Boniface chamber of Commerce *Voir* Chambre de commerce francophone de Saint-Boniface

Ste Rose & District Chamber of Commerce
PO Box 688, Ste Rose du Lac MB R0L 1S0
Tel: 204-447-2196; *Fax:* 204-447-2692
Overview: A small local organization founded in 1989
Mission: To represent & be the voice of our business community
Chief Officer(s):
Trevor Gates, President
Monica Lambourne, Contact
Finances: *Annual Operating Budget:* Less than $50,000; *Funding Sources:* Membership dues; fundraising
Staff Member(s): 1
Membership: 57; *Fees:* $80 company; $25 single; *Committees:* Main Street; Citizen on Patrol

Steel Structures Education Foundation
#200, 3760 14th Ave., Markham ON L3R 3T7

Tel: 905-944-1390; *Fax:* 905-946-8574
info@ssef-ffca.ca
www.ssef-ffca.ca
Overview: A small national organization founded in 1985
Mission: To further the application & use of steel in structures, through education; to produce educational videos on steel construction, in English & French
Affiliation(s): Canadian Institute of Steel Construction; Canadian Steel Construction Council
Chief Officer(s):
David MacKinnon, Executive Director
Staff Member(s): 6
Membership: 22 institutional;

Steelworkers Organization of Active Retirees (SOAR)

234 Eglinton Ave. East, 8th Fl., Toronto ON M4P 1K7
Tel: 416-487-1571; *Fax:* 416-482-5548
Toll-Free: 877-669-8792
info@usw.ca
www.usw.ca
Overview: A medium-sized national organization founded in 1985
Mission: To deal with the social, economic, educational, legislative & political developments & concerns of its members & spouses; to fight for the preservation of Social Security, Medicare, better health care protection, as well as for federal laws to better serve the elderly
Affiliation(s): United Steelworkers of America
Chief Officer(s):
Ken Neumann, National Director for Canada
Membership: 17,000

Steinbach Arts Council (SAC)

PO Box 3639, 304 - 2nd Ave., Steinbach MB R0A 2A0
Tel: 204-346-1077; *Fax:* 204-346-9777
www.steinbachartscouncil.ca
Overview: A small local organization founded in 1979
Mission: To enhance our quality of life through the arts
Member of: Manitoba Association of Community Arts Councils Inc.
Chief Officer(s):
Cindi Rempel-Patrick, Executive Director
director@steinbachartscouncil.ca
Finances: *Annual Operating Budget:* $100,000-$250,000
Staff Member(s): 4; 150 volunteer(s)
Membership: 300; *Fees:* $10 individual; $25 family; $30 affiliates; $100 corporate; *Member Profile:* Performing & visual artists & students; general public
Activities: Performing & visual arts in 60 programs as well as concert series; art & performing art programs

Steinbach Chamber of Commerce

#D4, 225 Reimer Ave., Steinbach MB R5G 2J1
Tel: 204-326-9566; *Fax:* 204-346-6600
www.steinbachchamberofcommerce.com
Overview: A small local organization founded in 1954
Member of: Manitoba Chamber of Commerce
Chief Officer(s):
Sjoerd Huese, President
Linda Peters, Executive Director
Finances: *Annual Operating Budget:* Less than $50,000
Staff Member(s): 1
Membership: 313; *Fees:* $110-$600

Stem Cell Network (SCN) / Réseau de cellules souches

#CCW-6189, 501 Smyth Rd., Ottawa ON K1H 8L6
Tel: 613-739-6675
info@stemcellnetwork.ca
www.stemcellnetwork.ca
www.facebook.com/CanadianStemCellNetwork
twitter.com/StemCellNetwork
vimeo.com/stemcellnetwork
Overview: A medium-sized national organization founded in 2001
Mission: To investigate the immense therapeutic potential of stem cells for the treatment of diseases currently incurable by conventional approaches
Member of: Networks of Centres of Excellence
Chief Officer(s):
Philip Welford, Executive Director
Lisa Willemse, Director of Communications
Staff Member(s): 8
Membership: *Committees:* Research Management

Step-By-Step Child Development Society

PO Box 47601, #1, 1020 Austin Ave., Coquitlam BC V3K 3P1
Tel: 604-931-1977
www.step-by-step.ca
Overview: A small local charitable organization founded in 1979
Mission: To provide preschool education to children requiring extra supports; to operate an equipment loans cupboard for children requiring specialized equipment; to provide physiotherapy & occupational therapy services to children; to provide outreach support services to neighbourhood child care centres; to promote inclusion of children needing extra supports
Member of: British Columbia Association Child Development & Rehabilitation
Chief Officer(s):
Carol Lloyd, Administrative Director
carol.lloyd@step-by-step.ca
Finances: *Funding Sources:* User fees
Membership: *Member Profile:* Parents; early childhood professionals
Activities: Public education; early intervention; *Library:* Step-by-Step Community Resource Room; Open to public

Stephan G. Stephansson Icelandic Society

PO Box 837, Markerville AB T0M 1M0
Tel: 403-728-3006; *Fax:* 403-728-3225
Toll-Free: 877-728-3007
admin@historicmarkerville.com
www.historicmarkerville.com
Also Known As: Historic Markerville Creamery
Overview: A small local charitable organization founded in 1974
Mission: To preserve & interpret history; to promote culture & community fellowship
Member of: Alberta Museums Association
Affiliation(s): Canadian Museums Association; Icelandic National League
Chief Officer(s):
Donna Nelson, President, 403-728-3438
Finances: *Annual Operating Budget:* $100,000-$250,000; *Funding Sources:* Fundraising; bingos; casino; donations
Staff Member(s): 1; 60 volunteer(s)
Membership: 150; *Fees:* $10 individual; $20 family; *Committees:* Finance/Budget Process; Policy; Personnel; Fundraising; Icelandic National League; Membership; Icelandic Picnic/Fjallkona; Gift Shop; Coffee Shop; Newsletter; Sponsorship; Volunteer Appreciation; Cheer; Truck; Insurance; Special Request; Museums Alberta; Promotion; Volunteer Management
Activities: Owns & operates the historic Markerville Creamery & Fensala Hall; auction; Icelandic picnic; Cream Day; Pioneer Days; Volunteer Breakfast; Christmas in Markerville; *Awareness Events:* Cream Day, Aug. 12

Stephen Leacock Associates

PO Box 854, Orillia ON L3V 6K8
Tel: 705-835-3218; *Fax:* 705-835-5171
www.leacock.ca
www.facebook.com/148060321915484
twitter.com/leacockmedal
Overview: A small national organization founded in 1946
Mission: To honour & promote Stephen Leacock & his body of writing
Chief Officer(s):
Michael Hill, President
mghill@rogers.com
Membership: *Fees:* $25 single; $35 family; *Committees:* Awards; Awards Dinner; Archives; Membership; Newspacket/Order of Mariposa; Planning; Publicity; Website & Social Media
Awards:
• The Order of Mariposa (Award)
Awarded occasionally to someone who has contributed significantly to humour in Canada, in other than the written word
• Stephen Leacock Memorial Medal (Award)
Established 1946 to encourage the writing & publishing of humorous works in Canada; given annually for the best Canadian book of humour published in the preceding year
Amount: Winner receives the medal & a cash award of $10,000 donated by TD Canada Trust

Stephenville Chamber of Commerce *See* Bay St. George Chamber of Commerce

Stettler & District Chamber of Commerce *See* Stettler Regional Board of Trade & Community Development

Stettler Regional Board of Trade & Community Development

6606 - 50th Ave., Stettler AB T0C 2L2
Tel: 403-742-3181; *Fax:* 403-742-3123
Toll-Free: 877-742-9499
info@stettlerboardoftrade.com
www.stettlerboardoftrade.com
www.facebook.com/StettlerRegionalBoardofTrade
Previous Name: Stettler & District Chamber of Commerce
Overview: A small local charitable organization founded in 1905
Mission: To work together to improve & promote trade, commerce & tourism & the economic, civil & social welfare of the district
Member of: Alberta Chambers of Commerce
Chief Officer(s):
Darrin Bosomworth, President, 403-742-1111
Aubrey Brown, Executive Director, 403-742-3181
executivedirector@stettlerboardoftrade.com
Finances: *Annual Operating Budget:* $50,000-$100,000
Staff Member(s): 3; 20 volunteer(s)
Membership: 148; *Fees:* $69.55-$144.45; *Committees:* Trade Show; Annual Awards Banquet; Energy Trade Show; Communications
Activities: AGM; Awards Banquet; Trade Show; Christmas Cash Cards Promotion; Santa Days; Tourist Information Centre

Stewart Historical Society

PO Box 402, 703 Brightwell St., Stewart BC V0T 1W0
Tel: 250-636-2568
stewartbcmuseum@gmail.com
Also Known As: Stewart Museum Infocenter
Overview: A small local charitable organization founded in 1976
Member of: North By NorthWest Tourism Association
Membership: *Fees:* $15 family; $10 adult; $7 student; $100 lifetime

Stewart-Hyder International Chamber of Commerce

PO Box 306, Stewart BC V0T 1W0
Tel: 250-636-9224; *Fax:* 250-636-2199
Overview: A small local organization founded in 1984
Member of: BC Chamber of Commerce; Northern BC Tourism Association; Better Business Bureau of Mainland BC; Yellowhead Highway Association; Ketchikan Visitors Bureaux
Finances: *Annual Operating Budget:* Less than $50,000; *Funding Sources:* Membership dues; municipal government
Membership: 50; *Fees:* $25 individual; $35-100 business
Activities: *Speaker Service:* Yes

Stonewall & District Chamber of Commerce

PO Box 762, Stonewall MB R0C 2Z0
Tel: 204-467-8377
info@stonewallchamber.com
www.stonewallchamber.com
Overview: A small local organization
Chief Officer(s):
Deborah Jensen, President
djensen@mts.net
Ryan Smith, CGA, Treasurer
rsmith.eprstonewall@shaw.ca
Finances: *Annual Operating Budget:* Less than $50,000
5 volunteer(s)
Membership: 60; *Fees:* $100; *Committees:* Education; Retail; Marketing

Stoney Creek Chamber of Commerce

21 Mountain Ave. South, Stoney Creek ON L8G 2V5
Tel: 905-664-4000; *Fax:* 905-664-7228
admin@chamberstoneycreek.com
www.chamberstoneycreek.com
www.linkedin.com/company/2485648?trk=tyah
www.facebook.com/chamberstoneycreek
twitter.com/CCStoneyCreek
www.youtube.com/ChamberStoneyCreek
Also Known As: Chambera Stoney Creek
Overview: A small local licensing organization founded in 1949
Mission: To grow business together
Member of: Canadian Chamber of Commerce; Ontario Chamber of Commerce
Chief Officer(s):
David Cage, Executive Director
Finances: *Annual Operating Budget:* $50,000-$100,000; *Funding Sources:* Membership dues
Staff Member(s): 1; 20 volunteer(s)
Membership: 400; *Fees:* $125-$300; *Member Profile:* Businesses in the area; *Committees:* Government; Communications; Special Events; Guest Speakers
Activities: *Awareness Events:* Citizen of the Year, May

Stoney Creek Historical Society (SCHS)
PO Box 66637, Stoney Creek ON L8G 5E6
e-mail: archives@stoneycreekhistorical
www.stoneycreekhistorical.ca
Overview: A small local charitable organization founded in 1908
Chief Officer(s):
Greg Armstrong, President
president@stoneycreekhistorical.ca
Membership: *Fees:* $10 individual; $18 family; $25 business
Activities: Battle of Stoney Creek re-enactment; monthly meetings Sept.-June with guest speakers; field trips to historical points of interest; *Library:* Stoney Creek Historical Society Library; by appointment

Stony Plain & District Chamber of Commerce
4815 - 44 Ave., Stony Plain AB T7Z 1V5
Tel: 780-963-4545; *Fax:* 780-963-4542
info@stonyplainchamber.com
www.stonyplainchamber.ca
Overview: A small local organization
Mission: To be a proactive leader & advocate for the promotion of business & community
Member of: Alberta Chamber of Commerce
Chief Officer(s):
John Gilchrist, President
president@stonyplainchamber.ca
Doug Lovsin, 1st Vice President
Tyler Randolph, 2nd Vice President
2ndvice@stonyplainchamber.ca
Finances: *Annual Operating Budget:* $100,000-$250,000; *Funding Sources:* Membership dues; fundraising
Staff Member(s): 2; 20 volunteer(s)
Membership: 480+; *Fees:* $90-$240
Activities: Trade show; phone directory; garage sales; mixers

Stormont, Dundas & Glengarry Historical Society
PO Box 773, Cornwall ON K6H 5T5
Tel: 613-936-0842; *Fax:* 613-936-0798
Overview: A small local charitable organization founded in 1920
Mission: To operate the local archives in the Cornwall Public Library & the United Counties Museum in the Wood House; to research, preserve, promote & inform the public about the history & archaeology of the counties of Stormont, Dundas & Glengarry for present & future generations
Affliation(s): Ontario Historical Society
Chief Officer(s):
Ian Bowering, Curator, The United Counties Museum
Finances: *Annual Operating Budget:* $100,000-$250,000; *Funding Sources:* Government & private
Staff Member(s): 2; 26 volunteer(s)
Membership: 150; *Fees:* $20
Activities: *Library:* Local History Room in the Cornwall Public Library; Open to public by appointment

Stormont, Dundas & Glengarry Law Association
29 Second St. West, Cornwall ON K6H 1G3
Tel: 613-932-5411; *Fax:* 613-932-0474
Toll-Free: 866-830-9118
sdglaw@on.aibn.com
Overview: A small local organization founded in 1988
Member of: Law Society of Upper Canada
Chief Officer(s):
Carolyn Goddard, Librarian
Staff Member(s): 1
Membership: 1-99
Activities: *Library:* Courthouse Library

Storytellers of Canada / Conteurs du Canada
#201, 192 Spadina Ave., Toronto ON M5T 2C2
e-mail: admin@storytellers-conteurs.ca
www.storytellers-conteurs.ca
www.facebook.com/210378645661591
twitter.com/storycanada
Overview: A small national organization
Mission: To promote storytelling across Canada; To support storytellers' work; To ensure the development of the art of storytelling
Chief Officer(s):
Ruth Stewart-Verger, Co-President
president@sc-cc.com
Donna Stewart, Co-President
president@sc-cc.com
Anne Kaarid, Administrator, 519-372-0623
admin@sc-cc.com
Marva Blackmore, Secretary
secretary@sc-cc.com
Alan Auyeung, Treasurer
treasurer@sc-cc.com
Membership: *Fees:* $45 individuals & organizations; *Member Profile:* Individuals & organizations across Canada who maintain & practice the oral tradition of storytelling
Activities: Advocating for storytellers; Facilitating communication among storytellers; Partnering with international storytelling organizations; Offering professional development opportunities; *Speaker Service:* Yes
Meetings/Conferences: • Storytellers of Canada 2015 Conference, July, 2015, Levis, QC
Scope: National
Contact Information: conference@storytellers-conteurs.ca
Publications:
• Notice Board
Type: Newsletter; *Frequency:* Monthly; *Editor:* Heather Whaley; *Price:* Free with membership in Storytellers of Canada
Profile: Events, products, & opportunities of interest to storytellers
• Le Raconteur
Type: Newsletter; *Frequency:* 3 pa; *Editor:* Kathy Bennett; *Price:* Free with membership in Storytellers of Canada
Profile: News & information distributed to all members of Storytellers of Canada
• Storytellers of Canada - Conteurs du Canada Membership Directory
Type: Directory

The Storytellers School of Toronto *See* Storytelling Toronto

Storytelling Toronto
#173, 601 Christie St., Toronto ON M6G 4C7
Tel: 416-656-2445; *Fax:* 416-656-8510
admin@storytellingtoronto.org
www.storytellingtoronto.org
Previous Name: The Storytellers School of Toronto
Overview: A small local organization
Mission: To support creative work in the art of storytelling
Chief Officer(s):
Paul Robert, President
Gail Nyoka, Office Manager
Activities: Offers courses; promotes & subsidizes the work of storytellers in education; produces the Toronto Festival of Storytelling; *Awareness Events:* Legless Stocking; Toronto Storytelling Festival
Awards:
• The Alice Kane Award (Award)
Eligibility: Supporters of Storytelling Toronto & members of Storytellers of Canada-Conteurs du Canada *Amount:* $1,000
• The Anne Smythe Travel Grant (Grant)
Eligibility: Supporters of Storytelling Toronto & members of Storytellers of Canada-Conteurs du Canada *Amount:* $500
Publications:
• Pippin [a publication of Storytelling Toronto]
Type: Newsletter; *Frequency:* Quarterly; *Editor:* Deborah Dunleavy

Strait Area Chamber of Commerce
#205, 609 Church St., Port Hawkesbury NS B9A 2X4
Tel: 902-625-1588; *Fax:* 902-625-5985
www.straitchamber.ca
Previous Name: Port Hawkesbury Chamber of Commerce
Overview: A small local organization founded in 1965
Member of: Nova Scotia Chamber of Commerce
Affliation(s): Atlantic Provinces Chamber of Commerce
Chief Officer(s):
Shannon MacDougall, Executive Director
Parker Stone, President
Finances: *Funding Sources:* Membership revenue; fundraising
Staff Member(s): 1; 19 volunteer(s)
Membership: 130+;

Straits-St. Barbe Chamber of Commerce
PO Box 119, Flowers Cove NL A0K 2N0
Tel: 709-456-2592
Overview: A small local organization

Strategic Leadership Forum (SLF)
165 Thamesview Cres., St. Mary's ON N4X 1E1
Tel: 416-628-8262
membership@slftoronto.com
strategicleadershipforum.camp9.org
www.linkedin.com/company/strategic-leadership-forum
www.facebook.com/SLFToronto
twitter.com/#%21/Letstalkstrat
Previous Name: The Planning Forum
Overview: A medium-sized national organization founded in 1950
Mission: To provide our community of members with an independent & intellectually challenging forum that delivers practical insights & interactions on strategic management & leadership
Chief Officer(s):
Augustin Manchon, President
Finances: *Annual Operating Budget:* $100,000-$250,000; *Funding Sources:* Membership fees; program fees; sponsorship revenue
Staff Member(s): 1; 24 volunteer(s)
Membership: 500; *Fees:* $295 executive; $175 academic; $1,180 corporate; *Member Profile:* Managers, directors, vice-presidents
Activities: Meetings: breakfast, luncheon, half-day, full-day & evening

Stratford & District Chamber of Commerce
55 Lorne Ave. East, Stratford ON N5A 6S4
Tel: 519-273-5250; *Fax:* 519-273-2229
info@stratfordchamber.com
www.stratfordchamber.com
www.facebook.com/100003043038197
twitter.com/stratfordchambr
Overview: A medium-sized local organization founded in 1860
Mission: To maintain & improve trade & commerce, conservation & good management of community resources; to promote the economic, commercial, industrial, tourist & convention, civic, agricultural & environmental welfare of the City of Stratford & the surrounding district
Member of: Ontario Chamber of Commerce; Canadian Chamber of Commerce
Affliation(s): Chamber of Commerce Executives of Canada
Chief Officer(s):
Garry Lobsinger, General Manager, 519-273-5252, Fax: 519-273-2229
manager@stratforddistrictchamber.com
Finances: *Funding Sources:* Membership dues & fundraising
Staff Member(s): 2; 16 volunteer(s)
Membership: 312; *Fees:* Schedule available; *Committees:* Membership Services; Legislative Action; Trade Show; Business Awards; Programs
Activities: Business lobby at all levels of government; seminars; information; publications

Stratford & District Labour Council
PO Box 661, 182 King St., Stratford ON N5A 6V6
Tel: 519-273-0300; *Fax:* 519-273-1051
stdflcnew@sympatico.ca
www.facebook.com/stratfordlabourcouncil
Overview: A small local organization founded in 1963 overseen by Ontario Fedearation of Labour
Member of: Ontario Federation of Labour
Chief Officer(s):
Dave Japper, President

Stratford Area Association for Community Living *See* Community Living Stratford & Area

Stratford Coin Club
PO Box 221, Gads Hill ON N0K 1J0
Tel: 519-271-3352
bcoins@rogers.com
Overview: A small local organization founded in 1960
Member of: Ontario Numismatic Association
Chief Officer(s):
Larry Walker, Executive, 519-271-3352
Finances: *Annual Operating Budget:* Less than $50,000; *Funding Sources:* Membership dues; coin show
Membership: 100

Stratford Musicians' Association, Local 418 of the American Federation of Musicians
PO Box 742, St. Mary's ON N4X 1B4
Tel: 519-301-2592
info@stratfordmusicians.org
www.stratfordmusicians.org
Overview: A small local organization founded in 1920
Mission: To unite the professional musicians in the jurisdiction who are eligible for membership; to provide services to members; to secure improved wages, hours, working conditions & other economic advantages; to establish terms & conditions for equitable & fair dealing among members
Affiliation(s): American Federation of Musicians of the United States & Canada
Chief Officer(s):

Grant Heywood, President
Stephanie Martin, Acting Secretary/Treasurer
Finances: *Annual Operating Budget:* Less than $50,000; *Funding Sources:* Membership & work dues
Staff Member(s): 2
Membership: 160; *Fees:* $108 regular; *Member Profile:* Instrumentalists & vocalists
Activities: *Speaker Service:* Yes; *Library* by appointment

Stratford Tourism Alliance (STA)
47 Downie St., Stratford ON N5A 1W7
Tel: 519-271-5140; *Fax:* 519-273-1818
Toll-Free: 800-561-7926
info@visitstratford.ca
www.welcometostratford.com
Previous Name: Tourism Stratford; Stratford & Area Visitors & Convention Bureau
Overview: A medium-sized local organization founded in 2007
Mission: A marketing organization promoting Stratford as a destination for leisure travelers & others; provides services to members, assistance, information & guidance to visitors, convention planners, & media contacts about the advantages of Stratford & surrounding area as a destination
Affliation(s): National Tour Association; Ontario Motor Coach Association
Chief Officer(s):
Eugene Zakreski, Executive Director
ezakreski@visitstratford.ca
Christina Phillips, Coordinator, On-line & Membership Programme
cphillips@visitstratford.ca
Cathy Rehberg, Coordinator, Marketing
crehberg@visitstratford.ca
Finances: *Annual Operating Budget:* $250,000-$500,000; *Funding Sources:* Municipal taxation; membership dues
Staff Member(s): 2; 20 volunteer(s)
Membership: 1,000-4,999
Activities: *Awareness Events:* Stratford Festival of Canada

Strathcona Archaeological Society *See* Archaeological Society of Alberta

Strathcona Christian Academy Society
1011 Clover Bar Rd., Sherwood Park AB T8A 4V7
Tel: 780-467-4752
karen.beaudet@spac.ca
www.scasociety.ca
Overview: A small local organization founded in 1980
Mission: To challenge students, through Christ-centred education, to know Jesus Christ as Savior & Lord in order to pursue a life of godly character, personal & academic excellence & service to others
Member of: Elk Island Public Schools
Chief Officer(s):
Jim Huth, Chair
Finances: *Annual Operating Budget:* $3 Million-$5 Million; *Funding Sources:* Regional Government
Staff Member(s): 47; 120 volunteer(s)

Strathcona Coin Discovery Group
c/o Ron Darbyshire, 4907 - 114 St., Edmonton AB T6H 3L5
Tel: 780-436-4335
coinguy@telus.net
Overview: A small local organization
Chief Officer(s):
Ron Darbyshire, Director

Strathcona Food Bank
255 Kaska Rd., Sherwood Park AB T8A 4E8
Tel: 780-449-6413
Overview: A small local charitable organization founded in 1983
Mission: To provide food and services to the needy in Strathcona.
69 volunteer(s)
Membership: 60

Strathcona Park Lodge & Outdoor Education Centre
PO Box 2160, Campbell River BC V9W 5C5
Tel: 250-286-3122; *Fax:* 250-286-6010
info@strathcona.bc.ca
www.strathcona.bc.ca
www.facebook.com/StrathconaParkLodge
twitter.com/strathconapark
www.youtube.com/user/strathconaparklodge
Also Known As: Canadian Outdoor Leadership Training Centre Ltd.
Overview: A medium-sized local organization founded in 1959
Mission: To teach the wonder, spirit & worth of people & the natural world through outdoor pursuits
Member of: Outdoor Recreation Council of British Columbia
Affliation(s): Sea Kayak Guides Alliance of BC; Tourism Association of Vancouver Island
Chief Officer(s):
Jamie Boulding, Executive Director
Christine Clarke, Executive Director
Finances: *Funding Sources:* Private
Activities: Kayaking; canoeing; sailing; ropes courses; rock climbing; mountaineering; hiking; backpacking; orienteering; wilderness ethics; survival; environmental education; *Library* Open to public

Strathmore & District Chamber of Commerce
510 Hwy. 1, Bay A1, Strathmore AB T1P 1K2
Tel: 403-901-3175; *Fax:* 403-901-1785
contactus@strathmoredistrictchamber.com
strathmoredistrictchamber.com
www.facebook.com/StrathmoreDistrictChamber
Overview: A small local organization founded in 1992
Mission: To advocate on behalf of its members
Chief Officer(s):
Joyce Bazant, Acting President
Membership: 87; *Fees:* Schedule available based on number of employees; *Member Profile:* Local businesses

Strathroy & District Chamber of Commerce
137 Frank St., Strathroy ON N7G 2R8
Tel: 519-245-7620; *Fax:* 519-245-9422
info@sdcc.on.ca
www.sdcc.on.ca
www.facebook.com/353157141060
Overview: A small local organization founded in 1940
Member of: Canadian Chamber of Commerce; Ontario Chamber of Commerce
Chief Officer(s):
Shannon Churchill, General Manager
Membership: 250; *Fees:* $210 1-4 employees/non-profit; $265 5-8 employees; $320 9-15 employees; $320+ 16+ employees

Street Haven at the Crossroads
87 Pembroke St., Toronto ON M5A 2N9
Tel: 416-967-6060; *Fax:* 416-924-6900
info@streethaven.com
www.streethaven.com
www.facebook.com/streethaven
twitter.com/StreetHaven
Overview: A small local charitable organization founded in 1965
Mission: To innovate and establish an integrated continuum of services which will improve the quality of life of women in need and bring creative solutions to their problems.
Chief Officer(s):
Joan Lauri, President

Street Kids International (SKI)
1210-20 Toronto St, Toronto ON M5C 2B8
Tel: 416-504-8994; *Fax:* 416-504-8977
Toll-Free: 800-387-5326
info@streetkids.org
www.streetkids.org
twitter.com/streetkidsintl
Overview: A small international charitable organization
Mission: To help children without homes around the world achieve dignity & self-reliance, health & security
Chief Officer(s):
Bindu Dhaliwal, Chair
Finances: *Annual Operating Budget:* $500,000-$1.5 Million
Staff Member(s): 6
Activities: *Internships:* Yes; *Library:* Resource Centre; by appointment

Streetsville Historical Society (SHS)
PO Box 7357, Mississauga ON L5M 3G3
Tel: 905-814-5958; *Fax:* 413-513-6789
Overview: A small local charitable organization founded in 1970
Mission: To collect, preserve, & promote interest in the history of Streetsville, one of the principal pioneer villages which form the nucleus of Mississauga
Member of: Ontario Historical Society
Affliation(s): Ontario Historical Society; City of Mississauga, Recreation & Parks Department
Chief Officer(s):
Malcolm Byard, President
mbyard@sympatico.ca
Bernice Cunningham, Vice President
bernice.two@hotmail.com
Finances: *Annual Operating Budget:* Less than $50,000; *Funding Sources:* Membership fees; Sale of publications; Provincial grant
9 volunteer(s)
Membership: 117; *Fees:* $10 single, $15 family or institution
Activities: Organizing displays at community fairs, such as Heritage Day; Hosting meetings throughout the year; *Speaker Service:* Yes; *Library:* SHS Archives; by appointment
Publications:
• SHS Bulletin
Type: Newsletter; *Frequency:* 4 times a year; *Editor:* Anne Byard

STRIDE
#26, 55 Ontario St. South, Milton ON L9T 2M3
Tel: 905-693-4252; *Fax:* 905-875-9262
stride@stride.on.ca
www.stride.on.ca
Also Known As: Supported Training & Rehabilitation in Diverse Environments
Overview: A small local organization
Chief Officer(s):
Anita Lloyd, Executive Director, 905-693-4252 Ext. 224
alloyd@stride.on.ca

Stroke Recovery Association of BC (SRABC)
#301, 1212 West Broadway, Vancouver BC V6H 3V1
Tel: 604-688-3603; *Fax:* 604-688-3660
Toll-Free: 888-313-3377
execdir@strokerecoverybc.ca
www.strokerecoverybc.ca
www.facebook.com/StrokeRecoveryBC
twitter.com/StrokeRecovBC
www.youtube.com/user/office814
Overview: A small provincial charitable organization founded in 1979
Mission: To encourage stroke survivors & their families as they adjust themselves to changes in their lives; to foster understanding of strokes within the community; to provide, through local Stroke Recovery branches throughout BC, a resource for stroke survivors living in the community
Chief Officer(s):
Casey Crawford, President
Membership: 1,000 individual; *Member Profile:* Stroke survivors, cargivers & volunteers
Activities: Support 40 community-based stroke recovery programs throughout BC; provides 2 camps for stroke survivors & family members; provides information; *Speaker Service:* Yes
Awards:
• Phyllis Delaney Life After Stroke Awards (Award)

Stroke Recovery Association of Manitoba Inc.
247 Provencher Blvd., #B, Winnipeg MB R2H 0G6
Tel: 204-942-2880; *Fax:* 204-944-1982
info@strokerecovery.ca
www.strokerecovery.ca
Overview: A small provincial organization overseen by Stroke Recovery Network
Mission: To help improve the lives of stroke victims and their families
Chief Officer(s):
April Takacs, President
Russ Down, Administrator
Staff Member(s): 2
Membership: *Committees:* Policy/Planning; Personnel; Finance; Fund-Raising; Public Relations & Special Events; Membership

Stroll of Poets Society
c/o Writers Guild of Alberta, 11759 Groat Rd., Edmonton AB T5M 3K6
Tel: 780-422-8174
www.strollofpoets.com
Overview: A small local organization founded in 1991
Mission: To address the need to promote poetry as an art form
Chief Officer(s):
Naomi Mcllwraith, Acting President
Membership: *Fees:* $20
Activities: Stroll Anthology; e-poem; festivals; series of public recitations of poetry

Strome & District Historical Society (SAM)
PO Box 151, Strome AB T0B 4H0
Tel: 780-376-3688
Also Known As: Strome Museum; Sodbusters Archives Museum
Overview: A small local charitable organization founded in 1987
Mission: To preserve the history of Western Canada, Village of Strome & area

Member of: Alberta Museum Association
Affliation(s): Alberta Historical Resource Foundation; Central Rural East Alberta Museums
Chief Officer(s):
Joan Brockhoff, Contact, 780-376-3546
Finances: *Annual Operating Budget:* Less than $50,000; *Funding Sources:* Donations; grants
50 volunteer(s)
Membership: 50; *Fees:* $5

Structural Pest Management Association of Alberta *See* Pest Management Association of Alberta

Structural Pest Management Association of British Columbia (SPMABC)
c/o Integrated Pest Supplies, #108, 360 Edworthy Way, New Westminster BC V3L 5T8
Tel: 604-520-9900; *Fax:* 604-522-5557
Toll-Free: 800-465-5511
info@spmabc.com
www.spmabc.com
Overview: A small provincial organization
Member of: Canadian Pest Management Association
Chief Officer(s):
Brett Johnston, President
Membership: 54; *Fees:* $295-$420

Structural Pest Management Association of Ontario (SPMAO)
#300, 1370 Don Mills Rd., Toronto ON M3B 3N7
Fax: 866-957-7378
Toll-Free: 800-461-6722
spmao@pestworld.org
www.spmao.ca
Previous Name: Ontario Pest Control Association
Overview: A small provincial organization founded in 1950
Mission: To help their members obtain professional licenses & remain up to date on industry policies & practices
Member of: Canadian Pest Management Association; National Pest Management Association (U.S.); Urban Pest Management Council of Canada
Chief Officer(s):
Greg Mulroney, Executive Coordinator
info@spmao.ca
Membership: 197; *Fees:* $425 active; $275 allied; $215 associate
Activities: Monthly meetings; annual conference; satellite meetings; *Library*

Student Christian Movement of Canada (SCM) / Mouvement d'étudiant(e)s chrétien(ne)s
#200, 310 Dupont Street, Toronto ON M5R 1V9
Tel: 416-463-7622
info@scmcanada.org
scmcanada.org
www.facebook.com/scmcanada
twitter.com/scmcanada
Overview: A medium-sized national charitable organization founded in 1921
Mission: National, ecumenical student organization; to encourage members in theological/social reflection & in actions for social change. Offices in Toronto & Winnipeg
Member of: World Student Christian Federation
Chief Officer(s):
Rick Garland, General Secretary
Finances: *Annual Operating Budget:* $50,000-$100,000
Staff Member(s): 2
Membership: 500; *Member Profile:* Groups at Canadian universities

Central Region
c/o Ecumenical Chaplain, 1125 Colonel By Dr., Ottawa ON K1S 5B6
Tel: 613-520-4449
carleton@scmcanada.org
www.scmcanada.org/carleton
Chief Officer(s):
Tom Sherwood, Chaplain

Eastern Region
Memorial University Of Newfoundland, #4010, University Centre, St. Johns NL A1C 5S7
Tel: 709-737-4376
mun@scmcanada.org
www.scmcanada.org/mun
Chief Officer(s):
Donna Lawrence, Chaplain

Western Region
PO Box 3015, Victoria BC V8W 3P2
Tel: 250-721-8338
victoria@scmcanada.org
www.scmcanada.org/victoria
Chief Officer(s):
Henri Lock, Chaplain

Student Legal Services of Edmonton
11011-88 Ave. NW, Edmonton AB T6G 0Z3
Tel: 780-492-2226; *Fax:* 780-492-7574
info@slsedmonton.com
www.slsedmonton.com
Overview: A small local charitable organization founded in 1971
Mission: As agents in Criminal & Civil Court, to provide free legal information & assistance to people who do not qualify for legal aid & are not able to afford a lawyer; legal research & education in issues of general community interest & concern; background work & suggestions for legal reform
Chief Officer(s):
Michael Whiting, Executive Coordinator
Finances: *Annual Operating Budget:* $250,000-$500,000
Staff Member(s): 2; 250 volunteer(s)
Membership: 287 student; 10 individual;

Student Life Education Company
255-55 St. Clair Ave West, Toronto ON M4V 2Y7
Tel: 416-243-1338; *Fax:* 416-967-6320
Toll-Free: 866-213-0311
info@studentlifeeducation.com
www.studentlifeeducation.com
Overview: A small local organization
Mission: To promote healthy decisions on the use or non-use of alcohol & other health issues
Chief Officer(s):
Michael Westcott, Chair

Sturgeon Falls Literacy Alliance *See* Literacy Alliance of West Nipissing

Subuddhi Deri Dasi *See* International Society for Krishna Consciousness (Toronto Branch)

Sudbury & District Association for Community Living *See* The City of Greater Sudbury Developmental Services

Sudbury & District Beekeepers' Association (SDBA)
Sudbury ON
Tel: 705-682-5925
www.sudburybeekeepers.com
www.facebook.com/1394362140801932
Overview: A small local organization founded in 1977
Mission: To serve beekeepers in the Sudbury area by helping them to develop their beekeeping skills
Member of: Ontario Beekeepers' Association
Chief Officer(s):
Wayne Leblanc, President
wleblanc@personainternet.com
Membership: *Fees:* $15 senior; $20 adult; $25 family; *Member Profile:* Apiarists in the Sudbury district, from beginners to commercial operators
Activities: Educating the public about apiaries & apiculture through displays at places such as the local farmers' market; Providing workshops & presentations to assist beekeepers; Creating opportunities for beekeepers to network; Organizing meetings at the Lo-Ellen Park Secondary School in Sudbury; *Library:* Sudbury & District Beekeepers' Association Library

Sudbury & District Labour Council
#209, 109 Elm St., Sudbury ON P3C 1T4
Tel: 705-674-1223
sdlc@persona.ca
sudburylabour.ca
Overview: A small local organization founded in 1957 overseen by Ontario Federation of Labour
Member of: Ontario Federation of Labour
Chief Officer(s):
John Closs, President

Sudbury Arts Council (SAC) / Conseil des arts de Sudbury
c/o AOE, 168 Elgin St., Sudbury ON P3E 3N5
Tel: 705-626-2787
sac.communicate@gmail.com
www.sudburyartscouncil.org
www.facebook.com/GuelphArtsCouncil
twitter.com/guelpharts
Overview: A small local charitable organization founded in 1974
Mission: To foster an environment that supports the arts at all levels; to enhance the quality of life adding to the vitality of the community by promoting an awareness & appreciation of the arts in all forms & to encourage the active pursuit of artistic excellence
Member of: Community Arts Ontario
Chief Officer(s):
Vicki Gilhula, President
vgilhula@gmail.com
Paddy O'Sullivan, Vice-President
Finances: *Funding Sources:* Government; fundraising
Staff Member(s): 1
Membership: 180; *Fees:* $20 regular/patron; $35 group; $50 business; *Member Profile:* Declared arts/culture interest
Activities: Promote arts & articulate relevance

Sudbury Community Service Centre Inc. / Centre de services communautaires de Sudbury
1166 Roy Ave., Sudbury ON P3A 3M6
Tel: 705-560-0430; *Fax:* 705-560-0440
Toll-Free: 800-685-1521
scsc@vianet.ca
www.sudburycommunityservicecentre.ca
www.youtube.com/channel/UCfXnydiEvAc1pf8QzXFbc1A
Overview: A small local charitable organization founded in 1972 overseen by Ontario Association of Credit Counselling Service
Mission: To provide support services to individuals with developmental disabilities & their families; To assist persons who are experiencing financial difficulties in the Greater Sudbury Area, as well as the Espanola & Parry Sound areas, through Credit Counselling Sudbury
Member of: Ontario Association of Credit Counselling Services
Finances: *Funding Sources:* Donations
Activities: Providing professional counselling services; Offering crisis management services for persons adapting to unexpected change; Providing case management services to help persons with developmental disabilities meet identified needs; Engaging in advocacy activities; Helping people resolve their debt & money management problems, through credit counselling, a Debt Management Program & negotiations with creditors; Teaching money management & budget planning skills

Sudbury Construction Association (SCA)
257 Beatty St., Sudbury ON P3C 4G1
Tel: 705-673-5619; *Fax:* 705-673-7910
sca@sudburyca.com
www.sudburyca.com
Overview: A small local organization founded in 1948 overseen by Canadian Construction Association
Mission: To provide labour relations for contractors & others in the construction industry.
Chief Officer(s):
Denis Shank, Executive Director
dshank@sudburyca.com
Staff Member(s): 3
Membership: 270; *Fees:* $625; *Member Profile:* Contractors; Manufacturers & Suppliers; Service Providers; Consulting Firms; Training & Personnel Providers

Sudbury Family Service *Voir* Service familial de Sudbury

Sudbury Manitoulin Children's Foundation
PO Box 1264, Stn. B, 84 Elgin St., Sudbury ON P3E 4S7
Tel: 705-673-2227; *Fax:* 705-673-8798
info@smcf.com
www.smcf.com
Overview: A small local charitable organization
Mission: Sponsors, promotes, devises, establishes, assists, develops & participates in measures & programs that will benefit children & families from the Sudbury-Manitoulin area
Chief Officer(s):
Anne Salter Dorland, Executive Director
Activities: Bursary Program; Send-a-Kid-to-Camp program

Sudbury Real Estate Board
190 Elm St., Sudbury ON P3C 1V3
Tel: 705-673-3388; *Fax:* 705-673-3197
sreb@vianet.on.ca
www.sudburyrealestateboard.on.ca
Overview: A small local organization overseen by Ontario Real Estate Association
Mission: To keep its members informed in order to better serve their customers
Member of: The Canadian Real Estate Association; Ontario Real Estate Association
Chief Officer(s):
Myra Lahti, Executive Officer, 705-673-3388

Membership: 300

Sudbury Rock & Lapidary Society (SRLS)
c/o 3171 Romeo St., Val Caron ON P3N 1G5
e-mail: mineral@isys.ca
www.ccfms.ca/Clubs/Sudbury
Overview: A small local organization founded in 1984
Mission: To promote rock, mineral, gem, & fossil collecting, & lapidary for both recreation & education
Member of: Central Canadian Federation of Mineralogical Societies
Chief Officer(s):
Roger Poulin, President, 705-897-6216
Ruth Debicki, Vice-President; Librarian
Ed Debicki, Secretary, 705-522-5140
ed.debicki@sympatico.ca
Gil Benoit, Treasurer
Membership: 85; *Fees:* $10 individual or family; *Member Profile:* Amateurs; Hobbyists; Professionals
Activities: Hosting monthly meetings from September to June; Offering courses in lapidary arts & silver smithing; Organizing field trips; *Awareness Events:* Annual Gem & Mineral Show, July; *Library:* Sudbury Rock & Lapidary Society Library
Publications:
• Nickel Basin Rockhound
Type: Newsletter; *Frequency:* 10 pa; *Number of Pages:* 10; *Editor:* Erv Mantler; *Price:* Free with Sudbury Rock & Lapidary Society membership
Profile: Information for Sudbury Rock & Lapidary Society members, published from Septemer to June

Sudbury Stamp Club
1779 Graywood Dr, Sudbury ON P3A 5S5
e-mail: biffandbetty@sympatico.ca
Also Known As: Sudbury Philatelic Society
Overview: A small local organization founded in 1946
Mission: To educate ourselves about philatelic matters & provide a forum for exchange & purchase of stamps & stamp supplies
Chief Officer(s):
Biff Pilon, Contact
Membership: 20; *Fees:* $10

Sudbury Symphony Orchestra Association Inc. (SSO) / Orchestre symphonique de Sudbury inc
303 York St., Sudbury ON P3E 2A5
Tel: 705-673-1280; *Fax:* 705-673-1434
info@sudburysymphony.com
www.sudburysymphony.com
ca.linkedin.com/company/sudbury-symphony-orchestra
www.facebook.com/SudburySymphony
twitter.com/SudburySymphony
www.youtube.com/sudburysymphony
Overview: A small local charitable organization founded in 1953 overseen by Orchestras Canada
Mission: To provide the opportunity for a broad spectrum of the public in the Sudbury Region & surrounding area to attend a stimulating program of concerts; to maintain an environment & organization which encourages artistic responsibility & commitment; to attract & maintain private & public funding in order to achieve accessibility & continuity through financial stability; to increase the awareness & appreciation of music in the community; to provide a vehicle for the participation in & ongoing development of the performance of orchestral music; to increase the awareness, appreciation & performance of Canadian music in the community
Member of: SOCAN
Chief Officer(s):
Victor Sawa, Artistic Director
Dawn Cattapan, Executive Director
Finances: *Funding Sources:* Ontario Arts Council; City of Greater Sudbury
Staff Member(s): 4
Awards:
• The Sudbury Symphony Littlehales Scholarship (Scholarship)
Awarded annually to the top student in the Junior Strings Class
• The Sudbury Symphony Emil First Memorial Scholarship (Scholarship)
Awarded annually to the top student in the Senior Strings Concerto Class

Sudbury Tourism
PO Box 5000, Stn. A, 200 Brady St., Sudbury ON P3A 5P3
Tel: 705-674-4455; *Fax:* 705-671-6767
Toll-Free: 877-304-8222
www.sudburytourism.ca
www.facebook.com/sudburytourism
twitter.com/sudburytourism
Overview: A small local organization
Member of: Tourism Industry Association of Canada
Chief Officer(s):
Bruno Fabris, Contact

Sudbury Youth Orchestra Inc.
PO Box 2241, Stn. A, Sudbury ON P3A 4S1
Tel: 705-566-8101
sudburyyouthorch@gmail.com
www.sudburyyouthorchestra.ca
Previous Name: Cambrian Youth Orchestra
Overview: A small local charitable organization founded in 1972 overseen by Orchestras Canada
Mission: To foster an appreciation of orchestral music; to create opportunities for orchestral performance; to provide access to education & training in an orchestral setting for the youth of Sudbury & area
Chief Officer(s):
Jamie Arrowsmith, Music Director
Membership: *Fees:* $90

Suicide Action Montréal (SAM)
2345, rue Bélanger, Montréal QC H2G 1C9
Tel: 514-723-3594
Toll-Free: 866-277-3553; *Crisis Hot-Line:* 514-723-4000
www.suicideactionmontreal.org
Overview: A small local charitable organization founded in 1984
Affliation(s): Canadian Association for Suicide Prevention
Chief Officer(s):
Simon Pierre Brodeur, Chair
Finances: *Annual Operating Budget:* $500,000-$1.5 Million
Staff Member(s): 24; 250 volunteer(s)
Membership: 260; *Fees:* $10; free for volunteers; *Member Profile:* Volunteers
Activities: Suicide prevention; bereaved; support group

Suicide Information & Education Centre *See* Centre for Suicide Prevention

Summer Street
72 Park St., New Glasgow NS B2H 5B8
Tel: 902-755-1745; *Fax:* 902-755-1956
www.summerstreet.ca
www.facebook.com/summerstr
twitter.com/SummStreet
Overview: A small local organization
Mission: To provide opportunities to people who have intellectual disabilities
Member of: DIRECTIONS Council for Vocational Services Society
Chief Officer(s):
Paula Irving, President
Bob Bennett, Executive Director
bob@summerstreet.ca
Finances: *Funding Sources:* Donations
Activities: Vocational activities & services include: catering, conference rooms, trophies & awards, & mailing & packaging

Summerhill Impact
30 Commercial Rd., Toronto ON M4G 1Z4
Tel: 416-922-2448; *Fax:* 416-922-1028
www.summerhillimpact.ca
www.linkedin.com/company/summerhill-group
www.facebook.com/SummerhillGroup
twitter.com/SummerhillTeam
www.youtube.com/summerhillgroup
Previous Name: Clean Air Foundation
Overview: A small national organization
Mission: To develop, implement, & manage public engagement programs & other strategic approaches that lead to measurable emission reductions, to improve air quality & protect the climate
Chief Officer(s):
Corey Diamond, Managing Director
Activities: Offering Car Heaven, Mow Down Pollution, Keep Cool, Switch Out, Energy Smarts, & Cool Shops

Summerland Chamber of Economic Development & Tourism (SCEDT)
PO Box 130, 15600 Hwy. 97, Summerland BC V0H 1Z0
Tel: 250-494-2686; *Fax:* 250-494-4039
info@summerlandchamber.com
www.summerlandchamber.com
www.facebook.com/161939953823991
twitter.com/SummerlandChmbr
www.youtube.com/user/scedt
Overview: A small local organization founded in 2000
Mission: To act as a voice for business interests; To represent & promote Summerland & area businesses to governments, community interest groups, businesses, other chambers, & business groups in the Okanagan Valley & British Columbia; To provide a forum for business interaction & membership services to the business community
Member of: BC Chamber of Commerce
Affliation(s): Economic Development Association of BC; Thompson/Okanagan Tourism Association
Chief Officer(s):
Arlene Fenrich, President
Finances: *Annual Operating Budget:* $100,000-$250,000; *Funding Sources:* Municipal business license fees; Tourism BC Grant
Staff Member(s): 4; 3 volunteer(s)
Membership: 800+; *Fees:* $50-225 based on type of business; $100 associate; *Member Profile:* Everyone with a business license in Summerland; *Committees:* Cultural Development; Economic Development; Festivals; Operations; Tourism; Communities in Bloom
Activities: Market Summerland; Sponsoring the visitor information centre; *Library:* Visitor Info Centre
Awards:
• Employee of the Year (Award)
• Arts Council Award (Award)
• Cultural Development Award (Award)
• Residential Light Up (Award)
• Best Old English Theme Display (Award)
• Best of Previous Light Up Winners (Award)
• Citizen of the Year (Award)
• Man of the Year (Award)
• Woman of the Year (Award)
• Community Service Award (Award)
• Sports (Award)
• Youth Award (Award)
• Business Excellence (Award)
• New Business of the Year (Award)
• Business Beautification (Award)

Summerland Community Arts Council (SCAC)
PO Box 1217, Summerland BC V0H 1Z0
Tel: 250-494-4494; *Fax:* 250-494-0055
admin@summerlandarts.com
summerlandarts.com
Overview: A small local charitable organization founded in 1981
Mission: To promote & facilitate the awareness & appreciation of the arts in Summerland
Member of: Assembly of BC Arts Councils; Okanagan Mainline Regional Arts Councils
Affliation(s): Corporation of Summerland
Chief Officer(s):
David Finnis, President
Sharry Schneider, Vice-President
Finances: *Annual Operating Budget:* $50,000-$100,000; *Funding Sources:* Province of BC; Corporation of District of Summerland; activiies
Staff Member(s): 1; 90 volunteer(s)
Membership: 100-499; *Fees:* Schedule available; *Member Profile:* Artists or friends of artists; *Committees:* Advocacy; Financial; Personnel; Art Centre; Arts Appreciation Award; Banner; Craft Sale; Entertainment; Finance; Gallery; Mainly Art Sale; Membership; Opportunities; Permanent Collection; Publicity; Art Reserve Fund; Summer Arts
Activities: Banner Program; entertainment series; art gallery; Mainly Arts Sale; summer arts program; bursaries; craft fair
Awards:
• Arts Appreciation Award (Award)
• Member Group Grants (Grant)
• Special Group Grants (Grant)

Summerland Community Food Bank
12583 Taylor Place, Summerland BC V0H 1Z0
Tel: 250-488-2099
donlev@shaw.ca
Overview: A small local organization
Chief Officer(s):
Leventine Adams, Contact, 250-488-2099

Summerland Museum & Heritage Society
PO Box 1491, 9521 Wharton St., Summerland BC V0H 1Z0
Tel: 250-494-9395; *Fax:* 250-494-9326
info@summerlandmuseum.org
www.summerlandmuseum.org
www.facebook.com/summerlandmuseum
Overview: A small local charitable organization founded in 1964

Mission: To collect, preserve & promote Summerland's valuable heritage
Member of: B.C. Museums Association; Archives Association of B.C.
Finances: *Funding Sources:* Municipal & provincial government; fundraising; Heritage Canada
Staff Member(s): 2
Activities: *Library:* Archives; Open to public

Summerside & Area Minor Hockey Association (SAMHA)
PO Box 1454, Summerside PE C1N 4K4
e-mail: info@summersideminorhockey.com
summersideminorhockey.com
Overview: A medium-sized local organization
Chief Officer(s):
Ewen Lamont, Registrar
registrar@summersideminorhockey.com
Gordie Montgomery, Technical Director
technical@summersideminorhockey.com

Sun Ergos, A Company of Theatre & Dance
130 Sunset Way, Priddis AB T0L 1W0
Tel: 403-931-1527; *Fax:* 403-931-1534
Toll-Free: 800-743-3351
waltermoke@sunergos.com
www.sunergos.com
www.facebook.com/SunErgosTheatreDance
twitter.com/sunergostheatre
www.youtube.com/user/sunergostheatre;
www.flickr.com/photos/sunergos
Also Known As: Sun.Ergos
Overview: A small local charitable organization founded in 1977
Mission: To witness, maintain & develop the ethnocultural roots of theatre & dance, without prejudice of race, creed, sex, or cultural background, to celebrate the differences & recognize the similarities among all peoples; to provide the best possible theatre & dance within the urban & rural communities, nationally & internationally
Member of: Canadian Actors' Equity Association; Alliance of Canadian Cinema, Television & Radio Artists (ACTRA)
Affliation(s): Western Arts Alliance; Arts Northwest; Montana Performing Arts Consortium; Arts MidWest; Arts Touring Alliance of Alberta; BC Touring; Wyoming Arts Alliance
Chief Officer(s):
Robert Greenwood, Artistic & Managing Director
Dana Luebke, Artistic & Production Director
dana.luebke@sunergos.com
Finances: *Annual Operating Budget:* $250,000-$500,000; *Funding Sources:* Performance fees; box office; grants
Staff Member(s): 2; 150 volunteer(s)
Membership: 150; *Fees:* $15-$35
Activities: 200-300 performances per year; residencies; workshops; master classes; *Speaker Service:* Yes

Sunbeam Sportscar Owners Club of Canada (SSOCC)
PO Box 15459, Vancouver BC V6B 5B2
e-mail: sunbeamcanada@hotmail.com
sunbeamcanada.org
Overview: A small national organization founded in 1978
Chief Officer(s):
Ohan Hovig Gurlekian, Contact
Finances: *Annual Operating Budget:* Less than $50,000; *Funding Sources:* Membership fees; advertising; regalia sales
Membership: 130; *Fees:* $30; *Member Profile:* Owner or enthusiast of British "Rootes Group" production automobile of any year
Activities: *Library* by appointment

Sunbury West Historical Society
110 Currie Lane, Fredericton Junction NB E5L 1X7
Tel: 506-368-2818
Also Known As: The Currie House Museum
Overview: A small local organization founded in 1986
Affliation(s): Association of Museums of New Brunswick
Activities: Operates The Currie House, built in 1900; Meetings: Third Thursday of every month except Jul., Aug., Dec at 7:30 pm at Currie House; *Library* by appointment

Sundre Chamber of Commerce
PO Box 1085, Sundre AB T0M 1X0
Tel: 403-638-3245
info@sundrechamber.com
www.sundrechamber.com
www.facebook.com/Sundre.Chamber.of.Commerce
twitter.com/SundreChamber#
Overview: A small local organization
Mission: To promote & enrich trade & commerce & stimulate the economic, civil & social welfare of the district
Member of: Alberta Chamber of Commerce
Membership: 120; *Fees:* Schedule available

Sunny South District Soccer Association
RR#8, Site 34, Comp 0, Lethbridge AB T1J 4P4
Tel: 403-894-2277
www.sunnysouthsoccer.com
Overview: A small local organization overseen by Alberta Soccer Association
Member of: Alberta Soccer Association
Chief Officer(s):
Paul Anwender, Executive Director
executivedirector@sunnysouthsoccer.com
Staff Member(s): 2

Sunrise Equestrian & Recreation Centre for the Disabled
See Sunrise Therapeutic Riding & Learning Centre

Sunrise Therapeutic Riding & Learning Centre
6920 Concession 1, RR#2, Puslinch ON N0B 2J0
Tel: 519-837-0558; *Fax:* 519-837-1233
Other Communication: Barn office phone: 519-827-0558, ext. 30
info@sunrise-therapeutic.ca
www.sunrise-therapeutic.ca
Also Known As: Sunrise
Previous Name: Sunrise Equestrian & Recreation Centre for the Disabled
Overview: A small local charitable organization founded in 1982
Mission: To develop the full potential of children & adults with disabilites & lead them closer to independence through therapy, recreation, horse riding, life skills & farm related activity programme
Member of: Canadian Therapeutic Riding Association; Ontario Therapeutic Riding Association
Affliation(s): Ontario's Promise
Chief Officer(s):
Ann Caine, Executive Director
ann@sunrise-therapeutic.ca
Lynne O'Brien, Manager, Operations & Volunteer
lynne@sunrise-therapeutic.ca
Finances: *Annual Operating Budget:* $250,000-$500,000; *Funding Sources:* Service clubs; foundations; industry; corporate; private; golf tournament; ride-a-thon
Staff Member(s): 7; 175 volunteer(s)
Membership: 250; *Fees:* $30; *Committees:* Finance; Fundraising; Public Relations/Marketing; Medical Advisory; Farm Management
Activities: Therapeutic riding; life skills program; Employment preparation courses for young adults with special needs; Therapeutic Riding Instructor Training School; integrated day camps; equestrian clinics; schooling shows; "Little Breeches" Club (4-7 years); education program for school groups (JK-3); monthly board & instructor meetings; Fall Open House; demonstrations at Royal Winter Fair; invitational horse shows; *Internships:* Yes; *Library:* Resource Centre for Instructor School; by appointment
Awards:
- Volunteer of the Year (Award)
- Sunrise Ambassador (Award)
- Outstanding Service Award (Award)

Sunshine Coast Arts Council (SCAC)
PO Box 1565, Sechelt BC V0N 3A0
Tel: 604-885-5412; *Fax:* 604-885-6192
sc_artscouncil@dccnet.com
www.suncoastarts.com/profiles/scartscouncil
www.facebook.com/sunshinecoastARTScouncil
Also Known As: Sunshine Coast Arts Centre
Overview: A small local charitable organization founded in 1966
Mission: To promote the arts on the Sunshine Coast; to increase & broaden the opportunities for public enjoyment of & participation in cultural activities
Member of: Assembly of Arts BC
Membership: *Fees:* $30 individual; $25 students/seniors; $35 family; $50 business/group; $100 corporate
Activities: 10-14 curated art exhibitions yearly; visual arts; performing arts; literary events; public garden; *Library* Open to public
Awards:
- Anne & Philip Klein Visual Arts Award (Award)
Eligibility: Applicants must be active in the visual arts field, age 65 or older & a resident of Sunshine Coast. Artists whose began pursuing their field later in life are preferred. *Amount:* $300
- Louise Baril Memorial Music Award (Award)
Eligibility: Advanced music students *Amount:* $300
- Gillian Lowndes Award (Award)
Eligibility: Applicants must show growth, innovation & sustained achievement in their field of art; they must be currently pursuing the arts & a resident of Sunshine Coast

Sunshine Coast Community Services Society (SCCSS)
PO Box 1069, 5638 Inlet Ave., Sechelt BC V0N 3A0
Tel: 604-885-5881; *Fax:* 604-885-9493
vickidobbyn@dccnet.com
www.sccss.ca
Overview: A small local organization founded in 1974
Mission: To build strength in individuals, family & community by planning & providing a range of social services
Chief Officer(s):
Vicki Dobbyn, Executive Director, 604-885-5881 Ext. 224
Finances: *Annual Operating Budget:* $1.5 Million-$3 Million; *Funding Sources:* Provincial government; federal government; provincial & federal housing grants; donations; fundraising
Staff Member(s): 79; 60 volunteer(s)
Membership: 56; *Fees:* $2 seniors; $8 family; $5 single
Activities: Services for children with special needs: paediatric occupational & physical therapy, infant development program, special services to children, supported child care, Variety Club Sunshine Coach, Kids in Motion Fund; Stopping the Violence: Yew Transition House, Thyme Second Stage program, Children who Witness Abuse, women's counselling service, women's support groups, Children's Sexual Abuse Treatment program; family & youth services: Project Parent, Nobody's Perfect, Parent-Tot Drop-In, & Parent support circles;

Sunshine Coast Labour Council
PO Box 1391, Gibsons BC V0N 1V0
Tel: 604-886-2733; *Fax:* 604-886-7650
info@sclc.ca
www.sclc.ca
www.facebook.com/group.php?gid=280412037266
Overview: A small local organization founded in 1986 overseen by Briitsh Columbia Federation of Labour
Mission: To defend the rights of workers on British Columbia's Sunshine Coast
Affliation(s): Canadian Labour Congress (CLC)
Chief Officer(s):
Stevo Knauff, President
stevoknauff@hotmail.com
Robert Hood, Vice-President
roberthood@dccnet.com
Glen Skidmore, Secretary
glens@dccnet.com
Marilyn Green, Treasurer
mgreen@dccnet.com
Membership: *Member Profile:* Unions in British Columbia communities, such as Howe Sound, Jervis Inlet, Port Mellon, & Earls Cove
Activities: Supporting member unions on strike; Participating in rallies & protests; Raising awareness of workers' issues, such as women's equality, workplace safety, & harassment; Providing educational opportunities for members; Organizing an annual memorial service to recognize the Day of Mourning for workers injured or killed at work; Providing local labour news

Sunshine Coast Natural History Society (SCNHS)
PO Box 543, Sechelt BC V0N 3A0
sunshinecoastnature.blogspot.ca
Previous Name: Sechelt Marsh Protective Society
Overview: A small local organization founded in 1978
Member of: Federation of BC Naturalists
Chief Officer(s):
Tony Greenfield, President
tony@whiskeyjacknaturetours.com
Finances: *Funding Sources:* Membership fees; municipal grant
Membership: 100; *Fees:* $30 single; $35 family
Activities: Monthly meetings; field trips; *Awareness Events:* Christmas Bird Count

Sunshine Dreams for Kids / Rayons de Soleil pour enfants
#100, 300 Wellingston St., London ON N6B 2L5
Tel: 519-642-0990; *Fax:* 519-642-1201
Toll-Free: 800-461-7935
info@sunshine.ca
www.sunshine.ca
www.facebook.com/SunshineFound
twitter.com/SunshineFound
www.youtube.com/user/SunshineFound

Also Known As: The Sunshine Foundation of Canada
Overview: A medium-sized national charitable organization founded in 1987
Mission: To fulfill the dreams of children between the ages of three & nineteen who are challenged by a severe physical disability or life-threatening illness
Chief Officer(s):
Adam Jean, President
Activities: *Awareness Events:* Annual Walk for Children's Dreams, June

Suore del Sacro Cuore di Ragusa *See* Sisters of the Sacred Heart

Superannuated Teachers of Ontario *See* The Retired Teachers of Ontario

Superior Greenstone Association for Community Living (SGACL)

PO Box 970, 206 Hogarth Ave., Geraldton ON P0T 1M0
Tel: 807-854-0775; *Fax:* 807-854-1047
Toll-Free: 888-434-4409
superior.greenstone.acl@bellnet.ca
www.sgacl.ca
Previous Name: Nipigon, Red Rock & District Association for Community Living
Overview: A small local charitable organization founded in 1968
Mission: That all persons live in a state of dignity, share in all elements of living in the community & have the opportunity to participate effectively
Member of: Community Living Ontario
Finances: *Annual Operating Budget:* $1.5 Million-$3 Million; *Funding Sources:* Ontario Ministry of Community & Social Services
Staff Member(s): 80; 15 volunteer(s)
Membership: 1-99; *Fees:* $2
Activities: *Awareness Events:* Flowers of Hope, March; Torch Run, Aug.

Superior International Junior Hockey League (SIJHL)

529 Dublin Ave., Thunder Bay ON P7B 5A1
Tel: 807-626-2316
sijhlmedia@gmail.com
www.sijhlhockey.com
www.facebook.com/SIJHL
twitter.com/SIJHL
Overview: A small local organization
Member of: Canadian Junior Hockey League
Chief Officer(s):
Ron Whitehead, President/Commissioner
Membership: 6 teams

Supply Chain Management Association (SCMA) / Association de la gestion de la chaîne d'approvisionnement (AGCA)

PO Box 112, #2701, 777 Bay St., Toronto ON M5G 2C8
Tel: 416-977-7111; *Fax:* 416-977-8886
Toll-Free: 888-799-0877
info@scmanational.ca
www.scmanational.ca
www.linkedin.com/groups/Supply-Chain-Management-Association-SCMA-28889
www.facebook.com/scmanational
twitter.com/scmanational
Merged from: Purchasing Management Association of Canada; Supply Chain & Logistics Association of Canada
Overview: A medium-sized national licensing organization founded in 2010
Mission: To advance strategic supply chain management by providing training, education, & professional development for supply chain management professionals in Canada
Affliation(s): Canadian Aborginal & Minority Supplier Council; Canadian Chamber of Commerce; Canadian Public Procurement Council; Canadian Supply Chain Sector Council; International Federation of Purchasing & Supply Management; Network for Business Sustainability
Chief Officer(s):
Cheryl Paradowski, President & CEO, 416-977-7111 Ext. 3125
cparadowski@pmac.ca
Cori Ferguson, Director, Public Affairs & Communications, 416-977-7111 Ext. 3129
cferguson@pmac.ca
Mike Whelan, Chair
Finances: *Funding Sources:* Membership dues
Staff Member(s): 14
Membership: 40,000+; *Fees:* Schedule available according to Institute &/or local District; *Member Profile:* Supply chain management professionals & enterprises in sectors including retail, manufacturing, transportation, distribution, government, natural resources, & service
Activities: Promoting standards of practice; Advocating for the profession; Developing partnerships; Providing networking opportunities;

Supply Chain Management Association - Alberta (SCMAAB)

Sterling Business Centre, #115, 17420 Stony Plain Rd., Edmonton AB T5S 1K6
Tel: 780-944-0355; *Fax:* 780-944-0356
Toll-Free: 866-610-4089
info@scmaab.ca
www.scmaab.ca
www.linkedin.com/groups?gid=4259963&trk=hb_side_g
www.facebook.com/332429763455410
twitter.com/SCMA_alberta
Previous Name: Alberta Institute Purchasing Management Association of Canada
Overview: A medium-sized provincial licensing organization founded in 1989 overseen by Supply Chain Management Association
Mission: To develop the profession by ensuring that professional status is accessible to all purchasing practitioners in the province; high standards of eligibility & professional conduct will be developed, maintained & enforced to enhance the profession & protect public interest in the province of Alberta
Chief Officer(s):
Allan To, President
ato@scmaab.ca
Finances: *Funding Sources:* Membership dues
Staff Member(s): 7
Membership: 1,650; *Fees:* $400; *Committees:* Registration; Practice Review; Discipline
Activities: *Speaker Service:* Yes
Awards:
- Fellowship Award (Award)
- Corporate Partner Award (Award)

Supply Chain Management Association - British Columbia (SCMABC)

#300, 435 Columbia St., New Westminster BC V3L 5N8
Tel: 604-540-4494; *Fax:* 604-540-4023
Toll-Free: 800-411-7622
info@scmabc.ca
www.scmabc.ca
www.linkedin.com/groups/Supply-Chain-Management-Association-SCMA-28889
www.facebook.com/scmanational
twitter.com/scmabc
Previous Name: British Columbia Institute of the Purchasing Management Association of Canada
Overview: A small provincial licensing organization founded in 1920 overseen by Supply Chain Management Association
Mission: BC Institute PMAC is an incorporated, not-for-profit association that maintains a code of ethics for the profession to regulate quality & integrity.
Chief Officer(s):
Barrie Lynch, Executive Director, 604-540-4494 Ext. 104
exec@scmabc.ca
Ron Wiebe, President
Membership: 750; *Fees:* $370 regular; $75 student
Meetings/Conferences: • 23rd Supply Chain Management Association - British Columbia Education Conference, September, 2015, Tigh-Na-Mara, Parksville, BC
Scope: Provincial

Supply Chain Management Association - Manitoba (SCMAMB)

#200, 5 Donald St., Winnipeg MB R3L 2T4
Tel: 204-231-0965; *Fax:* 204-233-1250
Toll-Free: 877-231-0965
info@scmamb.ca
www.scmamb.ca
www.linkedin.com/groups/SCMA-Manitoba-4546716
www.facebook.com/140785209269900
twitter.com/scmanational
Previous Name: Manitoba Institute of the Purhcasing Management Association of Canada; NPurchasing Management Association of Canada - Manitoba Institute
Overview: A small provincial licensing organization overseen by Supply Chain Management Association
Mission: SCMAMB is committed to offering a professional development program coupled with networking opportunities to advance supply chain management.
Chief Officer(s):
Jay Anderson, President
Rick Reid, Executive Director
Staff Member(s): 1
Membership: *Fees:* $410 regular; $45 student; $80 retired

Supply Chain Management Association - New Brunswick (SCMANB)

#402, 527 Dundonald St., Fredericton NB E3B 1X5
Tel: 506-458-9414
info@scmanb.ca
www.scmanb.ca
www.linkedin.com/groups?about=&gid=2888933
www.facebook.com/NBPMI
twitter.com/scmanational
Previous Name: New Brunswick Purchasing Management Institute
Overview: A small provincial licensing organization overseen by Supply Chain Management Association
Mission: NBPMI is dedicated to being the leading source of education, training, & development in the field of purchasing & supply chain management. It provides members with networking opportunities & offers them training for a Supply Chain Management Professional (SCMP) designation.
Chief Officer(s):
Ryan McPherson, President, 506-654-3280
president@scmanb.ca
Wendy Piercy, Administrator
Membership: 150; *Fees:* $365 regular; $0 student; *Member Profile:* Purchasing & supply management practioners, other business professionals, & students considering a career in the profession.
Activities: Training modules & interactive workshops

Supply Chain Management Association - Newfoundland & Labrador (SCMANL)

PO Box 29011, Stn. Torbay Road, St. John's NL A1A 5B5
Tel: 709-778-4033; *Fax:* 709-724-5625
info@scmanl.ca
www.scmanl.ca
www.linkedin.com/groups?about=&gid=2888933
www.facebook.com/scmanational
twitter.com/scmanational
Previous Name: Newfoundland & Labradour Institute of the Purchasing Management Association of Canada
Overview: A small provincial licensing organization overseen by Supply Chain Management Association
Mission: To deliver education, training, & professional development programs in the province, so members may earn a Supply Chain Management Professional (SCMP) designation
Chief Officer(s):
Shauna Clark, President
shaunak@nl.rogers.com
Membership: *Fees:* $295 regular; $147.50 regular discounted; $65 retired; $40 student; *Member Profile:* From all sectors of the economy, including retail, manufacturing, transportation, distribution, government, natural resources & service

Supply Chain Management Association - Northwest Territories (SCMANWT)

PO Box 2736, Yellowknife NT X1A 2R1
Tel: 867-873-9324
info@scmanwt.ca
www.scmanwt.ca
Previous Name: Northwest Territories Institute of the Purchasing Management Association of Canada
Overview: A small provincial licensing organization overseen by Supply Chain Management Association
Mission: A non profit organization registered with the Societies Act in the Northwest Territories. We provide information and Education leading to a professional designation as a C.P.P. (Certified Professional Purchaser) the only accredited and legally recognized designation in the fields of Purchasing and Supply Management in Canada.
Chief Officer(s):
John Vandenberg, President
Membership: *Fees:* $350 regular; $175 regular discounted; $32 student; $52.50 retired

Supply Chain Management Association - Nova Scotia (SCMANS)

PO Box 21, Stn. CRO, Halifax NS B3J 2L4
Tel: 902-425-4029; *Fax:* 902-431-7220
info@scmans.ca

www.scmans.ca
www.linkedin.com/groups?about=&gid=2888933
www.facebook.com/140785209269900
twitter.com/scmanational
Previous Name: Nova Scotia Institute of the Purchasing Management Association of Canada
Overview: A small provincial licensing organization overseen by Supply Chain Management Association
Mission: NSIPMAC delivers education, training & professional development programs in the province, so members may earn a Supply Chain Management Professional (SCMP) designation.
Chief Officer(s):
Joe McKenna, President
Membership: *Fees:* $370 regular; *Member Profile:* From all sectors of the economy, including retail, manufacturing, transportation, distribution, government, natural resources & service.

Supply Chain Management Association - Ontario (SCMAO)

PO Box 64, #2704, 1 Dundas St. West, Toronto ON M5G 1Z3
Tel: 416-977-7566; *Fax:* 416-977-4135
Toll-Free: 877-726-6968
info@scmao.ca
www.scmao.ca
www.linkedin.com/groups?gid=5139410&trk=my_groups-b-grp-v
twitter.com/SCMAOnt
www.youtube.com/user/OIPMAC
Previous Name: Ontario Institute of the Purchasing Management Association of Canada
Overview: A small provincial licensing organization overseen by Supply Chain Management Association
Mission: The preeminent supply chain managemen organisation in Ontario, supporting a growing global SCM community of over 20,00 active members and program participants in meeting their professional and lifelong learning goals. Their programs taught by leading North American academics and professional trainers, are designed to build/enhance the professional competence and strategic perspective of practitioners at all levels of career progression, from entry-, to mid-, to senior/executive levels of functional responsibility.
Chief Officer(s):
Kelly Duffin, Executive Director Ext. 2136
kduffin@scmao.ca
Meetings/Conferences: • The 18th Annual Supply Chain Management Association of Ontario Conference, 2015, ON
Scope: Provincial
Attendance: 400+

Supply Chain Management Association - Saskatchewan (SCMASK)

#221A, 3521 - 8th St. East, Saskatoon SK S7H 0W5
Tel: 306-653-8899; *Fax:* 306-653-8870
Toll-Free: 866-665-6167
info@scmask.ca
www.scmask.ca
www.linkedin.com/company/3549789?trk=tyah&trkInfo=tas%3As upply%20chain
www.facebook.com/SCMASK
twitter.com/SCMASK
Previous Name: Saskatchewan Institute of the Purchasing Management Association of Canada
Overview: A small provincial licensing organization overseen by Supply Chain Management Association
Mission: To promote & improve supply management practices in the profession through education & raising the awareness of the supply management profession within Saskatchewan
Chief Officer(s):
Nicole Burgess, Executive Director
nburgess@scmask.ca
Membership: 260; *Fees:* $450 regular; $225 regular discounted, student & retired; *Member Profile:* Supply chain management professionals
Activities: *Speaker Service:* Yes

Support aux Parents Uniques *See* Support to Single Parents Inc.

Support Enhance Access Service Centre (SEAS)

603 Whiteside Pl., Toronto ON M5A 1Y7
Tel: 416-362-1375; *Fax:* 416-362-4881
www.seascentre.org
www.youtube.com/user/SEASCentre
Previous Name: South East Asian Services Centre
Overview: A small local charitable organization founded in 1986
Mission: To promote individual well being, enhance family harmony and encourage community involvement in all walks of life through diverse programs, volunteer opportunities and community activities.
Member of: United Way
Chief Officer(s):
Rebecca Lee, Executive Director
Activities: Community support service; family service; senior service; volunteer service; youth service

The Support Network

#400, 10025 - 106 Street, Edmonton AB T5J 1G4
Tel: 780-482-0198; *Fax:* 780-488-1495; *Crisis Hot-Line:* 780-482-4357
admin@thesupportnetwork.com
www.thesupportnetwork.com
www.facebook.com/thesupportnetwork
twitter.com/EdmSupportNet
www.youtube.com/user/EdmontonCrisisCentre
Overview: A medium-sized local charitable organization founded in 1960
Mission: The Support Network strengthens individuals, families & the community, especially those who are experiencing crisis or distress, through support, information & education
Chief Officer(s):
Nancy McCalder, Executive Director
Finances: *Annual Operating Budget:* $500,000-$1.5 Million; *Funding Sources:* Government; United Way; donations; foundations
Staff Member(s): 49; 100 volunteer(s)
Membership: *Committees:* Board; Capital Campaign; Spirit Lifter Breakfast; Theresa Comrie Luncheon
Activities: 24-hour distress line; suicide prevention program; suicide bereavement services; 211 community service referral line; publications program; walk-in couselling; Youth One (youthone.com); volunteer program

Support Organization for Trisomy 18, 13 & Related Disorders

Toronto ON
Tel: 416-422-1393
www.trisomy.org
www.facebook.com/Trisomy.SOFT
Also Known As: SOFT Canada
Overview: A small national licensing charitable organization founded in 1989
Mission: To offer support to families whose children are born with any of the following disorders: Trisomy, Partial Trisomy, Mosaic (not every cell), deletion of all or part of a chromosome, single gene disorders, any other disorder which produces serious, multiple birth defects
Affliation(s): Easter Seals
Chief Officer(s):
Satinder Sahota, Local Contact
Finances: *Annual Operating Budget:* Less than $50,000
Membership: 7,200 families; *Fees:* $35; *Member Profile:* Families, friends or professionals associated with child with one of these disorders; child may be alive or deceased; *Committees:* Newsletter; Fundraising; Public Awareness; Professional Advisory; Information Services; Finance
Activities: Information about specific disorders; newsletters from Canada & the USA; access to an international database of children with rare disorders; *Speaker Service:* Yes

Support to Single Parents Inc. / Support aux Parents Uniques

178 rue Albert St, Moncton NB E1C 1B2
Tel: 506-858-1303; *Fax:* 506-855-4116
admin@supporttosingleparents.ca
www.supporttosingleparents.ca
www.facebook.com/Supporttosingleparents
Overview: A small local charitable organization founded in 1982
Mission: Provides leadership & sponsorship in developing programs & services to meet the needs of single parents, primarily women, teen mothers, expectant mothers, separated, widowed or divorced persons; designs & implements a broad range of adult workshops, educational & training programs; provides resource & referral services, public awareness, alliances & advocacy, & related physical & emotional support services; subsidized housing for single parents only
Affliation(s): Family Service Canada
Chief Officer(s):
Nancy Hartling, Executive Director Ext. 106
Brenda McMullen Brown, CEO
Finances: *Annual Operating Budget:* $100,000-$250,000; *Funding Sources:* Provincial government; United Way; donations & fundraising
Staff Member(s): 5; 35 volunteer(s)
Activities: *Speaker Service:* Yes; *Library* Open to public
Awards:
• The Family Award (Award)
• The Spiritus Award (Award)
• Certificate of Merit (Award)

Supporting Choices of People Edson (SCOPE)

4926 - 17 Ave., Edson AB T7E 1G4
Tel: 780-723-6100; *Fax:* 780-723-6100
scopel@telusplanet.net
Previous Name: Edson Association for the Developmentally Handicapped
Overview: A small local organization founded in 1974
Mission: To encourage the highest level of development of the individual; To promote normal opportunities for living in & integration within the community
Member of: Alberta Association for Community Living; Alberta Association of Rehabilitation Centres
Finances: *Annual Operating Budget:* $250,000-$500,000; *Funding Sources:* Government; fundraising
Staff Member(s): 21
Membership: 6; *Fees:* $5
Activities: *Awareness Events:* SCOPE Annual Telethon, Jan.

Surety Association of Canada (SAC) / Association canadienne de caution

#709, 6299 Airport Rd., Mississauga ON L4V 1N3
Tel: 905-677-1353; *Fax:* 905-677-3345
surety@surety-canada.com
www.surety-canada.com
www.twitter.com/suretyincanada
www.youtube.com/suretyincanada
Overview: A small national organization founded in 1992
Mission: The Surety Association of Canada is committed to the continued development and use of surety products throughout all jurisdictions of Canada
Chief Officer(s):
Steven D. Ness, President
sness@suretycanada.com
Staff Member(s): 2
Membership: *Member Profile:* Major bonding companies, members from the insurance brokerage community, legal fraternity and other industry related entities.

Surrey Association for Community Living (SACL)

17687 - 56A Ave., Surrey BC V3S 1G4
Tel: 604-574-7481; *Fax:* 604-574-4731
admin@commliv.com
www.commliv.com
www.facebook.com/212139572147037
Previous Name: The Surrey Association for the Mentally Handicapped
Overview: A small local charitable organization founded in 1958
Mission: To provide services & support for individuals with special needs & their families & advocate on their behalf; to create an inclusive, safe & caring community that values dignity & choices through committed leadership & guidance
Member of: British Columbia Association for Community Living
Chief Officer(s):
Louise Tait, Chair
Coreen Windbiel, Executive Director
Finances: *Annual Operating Budget:* $3 Million-$5 Million
Staff Member(s): 125; 50 volunteer(s)
Membership: 28; *Committees:* Audit & Policy Review; Governance; Monitoring
Activities: *Library* Open to public

The Surrey Association for the Mentally Handicapped *See* Surrey Association for Community Living

Surrey Board of Trade (SBOT)

#101, 14439 - 104 Ave., Surrey BC V3R 1M1
Tel: 604-581-7130; *Fax:* 604-588-7549
Toll-Free: 866-848-7130
info@businessinsurrey.com
www.businessinsurrey.com
www.facebook.com/pages/Surrey-Board-of-Trade/14153105258 1905
twitter.com/SBofT
Previous Name: Surrey Chamber of Commerce
Overview: A small local organization founded in 1918
Mission: To provide advocacy, resources, experience & networking to members & fosters best business practices to ensure growth & prosperity of members
Member of: BC Chamber of Commerce; Canadian Chamber of Commerce
Chief Officer(s):

Anita Huberman, Chief Executive Officer
anita@businessinsurrey.com
Bijoy Samuel, President
Gerard Breamault, Vice-President
Finances: *Funding Sources:* Membership fees; events; sponsorship
Staff Member(s): 8
Membership: 1,900; *Fees:* Schedule available; *Committees:* Crime & Justice; Environment & Natural Resources; Finance & Taxation; Internationl Affaris; Social Policy; Transport & Infrastructure; Finance; Governance; Ambassador; Education; Networking Golf; Police Officer of the Year Awards; Surrey Business Excellence Awards; Innovation
Activities: Monthly lunches & breakfasts; trade functions; forums; open houses/trade shows; awards; advocacy; networking; events; workshops; *Library:* Business Resource Centre; Open to public

Surrey Chamber of Commerce *See* Surrey Board of Trade

Surrey Food Bank
10732 City Pkwy., Surrey BC V3T 4C7
Tel: 604-581-5443; *Fax:* 604-588-8697
info@surreyfoodbank.org
www.surreyfoodbank.org
www.facebook.com/SurreyFoodBank
twitter.com/SurreyFoodBank
www.youtube.com/user/SurreyFoodBank
Overview: A small local charitable organization founded in 1983 overseen by Food Banks British Columbia
Mission: To help people help themselves by providing food hampers & alternatives to food lines such as community kitchens & food buying clubs
Member of: Food Banks British Columbia; Food Banks Canada; Surrey Chamber of Commerce
Affliation(s): Better Business Bureau
Chief Officer(s):
Glen Slobodian, President
Finances: *Annual Operating Budget:* $250,000-$500,000; *Funding Sources:* Public donations; foundation donations
Staff Member(s): 8; 75 volunteer(s)
Membership: 60; *Fees:* $5

Surrey Symphony Society (SSS)
#181, 6832 King George Blvd., Surrey BC V3W 4Z9
www.surreysymphony.com
www.facebook.com/surreysymphonysociety
Also Known As: Surrey Youth Orchestra
Overview: A small local organization founded in 1976 overseen by Orchestras Canada
Mission: To expand an appreciation of orchestral music among young musicians & to share this with the community through public performance
Chief Officer(s):
Catherine Francis, President
Heather Christiansen, General Manager
gm.surreysymphony@gmail.com
John Van Deursen, Youth Orchestra Conductor
Carla Birston, Intermediate Strings Conductor
Rick Dorfer, Junior Strings Conductor
Finances: *Annual Operating Budget:* Less than $50,000
Staff Member(s): 5; 8 volunteer(s)
Membership: 130 students; *Fees:* Schedule available
Activities: Weekly rehearsals; weekend workshop, Nov.; 1-day workshop, April; 2-3 public concerts; festival participation; *Library:* Resource Centre

Surrey-Delta Immigrant Services Society (SDISS)
#1107, 7330-137th St., Surrey BC V3W 1A3
Tel: 604-597-0205; *Fax:* 604-597-4299
www.dcrs.ca
Overview: A small local organization founded in 1978
Mission: To promote the independence of immigrants & to build strong culturally diverse communities
Member of: Affiliation of Multicultural Societies & Service Agencies of BC
Chief Officer(s):
Joseph Brown, President
Linda Howard, President
Finances: *Annual Operating Budget:* $3 Million-$5 Million; *Funding Sources:* Federal, provincial & service fees; United Way
Staff Member(s): 85; 150 volunteer(s)
Membership: 200; *Member Profile:* Any resident who supports the mission
Activities: Settlement services; community development; language training; interpretation & translation; job search services; *Internships:* Yes; *Speaker Service:* Yes

Awards:
• Cultural Diversity Awards for Business (Award)

Survivors of Abuse Recovering (SOAR)
PO Box 105, Kentville NS B4N 3V9
Tel: 902-679-7337
Toll-Free: 877-679-7627
info@survivorsofabuserecovering.ca
www.survivorsofabuserecovering.ca
Overview: A small local organization
Mission: To provide counselling service for survivors of childhood sexual abuse in Hants, Kings & Annapolis counties

SUS Foundation of Canada
620 Spadina Ave., Toronto ON M5S 2H4
www.susfoundation.ca
Also Known As: Cyc Foundation
Overview: A small national charitable organization founded in 1965
Mission: To fund educational & cultural projects
Member of: Ukrainian Self Reliance League of Canada
Affliation(s): Ukrainian Self Reliance Associations
Chief Officer(s):
William J. Strus, President
Finances: *Funding Sources:* Fundraising
Activities: *Library:* St. Vladimir Institute Library;

Sussex & District Chamber of Commerce
PO Box 4963, #2, 66 Broad St., Sussex NB E4E 5L2
Tel: 506-433-1845; *Fax:* 506-433-1886
sdcc@nb.aibn.com
sdccinc.org
Overview: A small local organization
Mission: To be a leading voice of business dedicated to enhancing opportunities for growth & development for our members & the community
Member of: Canadian Chamber of Commerce
Affliation(s): Atlantic Provinces Chambers of Commerce
Chief Officer(s):
Greg Zed, President
Pam Kaye, Administrator
Finances: *Annual Operating Budget:* Less than $50,000; *Funding Sources:* Membership fees
Staff Member(s): 1
Membership: 100

Sussex Sharing Club
PO Box 4196, 26 Eveleigh St., Sussex NB E4E 2N8
Tel: 506-433-6047
sussexsharingclub@nb.aibn.com
Overview: A small local charitable organization founded in 1986
Mission: To provide for those in need
Member of: Canadian Association of Food Banks; New Brunswick Association of Food Banks
Chief Officer(s):
Lois King, Administrator

Sustainability Project
2799 McDonald's Corners Rd., RR#3, Lanark ON K0G 1K0
Tel: 613-259-5022
sustain5@web.ca
www.sustainwellbeing.net
Also Known As: Guideposts for a Sustainable Future; Inviting Debate; 7th Generation Initiative
Overview: A small local organization founded in 1985
Mission: To collect, study, develop & teach ideas, information, technologies & customs that will help in the evolution of a sustainable society
Affliation(s): Ontario Environment Network; Canadian Environmental Network; Sierra Club of Canada
Chief Officer(s):
Mike Nickerson, Executive Director
Staff Member(s): 2
Activities: Life, Money & Illusion workshops

Sustainable Buildings Canada (SBC) / Bâtiments Durables Canada
#1801, 18 Eastern Ave., lower level, Toronto ON M5A 1H5
Tel: 416-364-0050; *Fax:* 416-364-0606
sbc@sbcanada.org
www.sbcanada.org
www.facebook.com/group.php?gid=118790911470730
twitter.com/SustBldgCan
Overview: A small national organization
Mission: To showcase to the world the Canadian cooperation that exists between the private sector & government, working together to implement innovative solutions to mitigate climate change, while serving the buildings industry
Chief Officer(s):
Lenard Hart, Chair
Michael Singleton, Executive Director

Sustainable Development Technology Canada (SDTC) / Technologies du développement durable Canada
#1850, 45 O'Connor St., Ottawa ON K1P 1A4
Tel: 613-234-6313; *Fax:* 613-234-0303
info@sdtc.ca
www.sdtc.ca
twitter.com/SDTC_TDDC
Overview: A medium-sized national organization founded in 2001
Mission: To create a healthy environment & a high quality of life for Canadians; To identify & fund technologies with strong competitive & environmental potential
Chief Officer(s):
Juergen Puetter, Chair
Vicky J. Sharpe, President & Chief Executive Officer
vj.sharpe@sdtc.ca
Rick Whittaker, Chief Technology Officer & Vice-President, Investments
Sailesh Thaker, Vice-President, Industry & Stakeholder Relations
Barry Wilson, Vice-President, Finance & Administration
David Minicola, Manager, Applications, 613-234-6313 Ext. 310
d.minicola@sdtc.ca
Patrice Breton, Director, Communications
p.breton@sdtc.ca
Finances: *Funding Sources:* Government of Canada
Membership: *Committees:* Corporate Governance; Human Resources; Project Review; Audit & Grant Investment
Publications:
• Sustainable Development Technology Canada Annual Report
Type: Yearbook; *Frequency:* Annually
• Sustainable Development Technology Canada Corporate Plan

Sustainable Kingston
184 Sydenham St., Kingston ON K7K 3M2
Tel: 613-544-2075
info@sustainablekingston.ca
sustainablekingston.ca
www.facebook.com/sustainablekingston
twitter.com/SustainableKtwn
www.pinterest.com/sustainablektwn/
Overview: A medium-sized local organization
Mission: Sustainable Kingston is a community-driven; non-profit organization that facilitates, connects and educates in order to drive initiatives as described in our city's Integrated Community Sustainability Plan (ICSP).
Chief Officer(s):
John Johnson, Executive Director
john@sustainablekingston.ca
Meetings/Conferences: • Green Building Symposium - Kingston, 2015, Kingston, ON
Scope: Local

Sustainable Urban Development Association (SUDA)
2637 Council Ring Rd., Mississauga ON L5L 1S6
Tel: 416-400-0553
mail@suda.ca
www.suda.ca
Overview: A medium-sized national organization
Mission: To foster a healthy natural environment by providing information about ways in which cities can become more efficient in the land, material, water and energy resources, and highly supportive of sustainable transportation.
Chief Officer(s):
John Banka, President

Svoboda Dance Festival Association
PO Box 664, North Battleford SK S9A 2Y9
Tel: 306-445-3732
Previous Name: Battlefords Dance Festival Association
Overview: A small local organization
Mission: To offer Ukranian dance instruction for all ages & skill levels
Chief Officer(s):
Marusia Kobrynsky, Co-President

Swampy Cree Tribal Council
PO Box 150, Hwy. 10 North, The Pas MB R9A 1K4

Tel: 204-623-3423; *Fax:* 204-623-2882
Toll-Free: 800-442-0459
www.swampycree.com
Overview: A small local organization founded in 1976
Mission: To vigorously pursue the object of fostering the social, economic and political well-being and development of member First Nation by formulating policy, administering programs and delivering services at a pace compatible with the level of development and aspirations of each First Nation.
Chief Officer(s):
Don Lathlin, Executive Director
dlathlin@swampycree.com
Staff Member(s): 40
Membership: *Member Profile:* Coalition of 8 tribal groups

Swan Hills Chamber of Commerce
PO Box 540, Swan Hills AB T0G 2C0
Tel: 780-333-4684
town@townofswanhills.com
www.townofswanhills.com
Overview: A small local organization
Member of: Alberta Chamber of Commerce
Chief Officer(s):
Rita Krawiec, Contact
Finances: *Annual Operating Budget:* Less than $50,000
Staff Member(s): 1; 10 volunteer(s)
Membership: 44; *Fees:* $15 homebase scale rate; *Committees:* Keyano Days; Tourist/Artists
Activities: *Awareness Events:* Keyano Days, last weekend in June; *Internships:* Yes; *Library* Open to public

Swan River Friendship Centre
PO Box 1448, 1413 Main St. East, Swan River MB R0L 1Z0
Tel: 204-734-9301; *Fax:* 204-734-3090
www.mac.mb.ca/swanriver/
Overview: A small local organization
Mission: To promote continuous public relations aimed at creating and developing mutual understanding and to improve relations between people of Indian descent and others
Chief Officer(s):
Elbert Chartrand, Executive Director

Swan Valley Chamber of Commerce
PO Box 1540, Swan River MB R0L 1Z0
Tel: 204-734-3102; *Fax:* 204-734-4342
chamberofcommerce@chamber8.ca
www.facebook.com/SwanValleyChamberOfCommerce
Overview: A small local organization
Mission: To promote local businesses & help them grow

The Swedish-Canadian Chamber of Commerce (SCCC)
#2109, 2 Bloor St. West, Toronto ON M4W 3E2
Tel: 416-925-8661
info@sccc.ca
www.sccc.ca
www.linkedin.com/groups?gid=3401296
www.facebook.com/SwedishCanadianChamber
twitter.com/SwedishCanadian
Overview: A small international organization founded in 1965
Mission: To promote trade, commercial, cultural & social contacts between Sweden & Canada
Member of: European Union Chambers of Commerce in Toronto (Eurocit)
Chief Officer(s):
Marie Larsson, Contact
Finances: *Funding Sources:* Membership dues; events; sponsorship; advertising

Sweet Adelines International - Westcoast Harmony Chapter
9574-160th St., Surrey BC V4N 2R6
Tel: 604-513-5991
info@westcoastsings.com
www.westcoastsings.com
www.facebook.com/WestcoastHarmonyChorus
twitter.com/WestcoastSings
Overview: A small local charitable organization founded in 1965
Mission: To promote a capella, close harmony style singing for women, with high performance & competitive standards
Chief Officer(s):
Anne Martenuik, Master Director
8 volunteer(s)
Activities: *Internships:* Yes

Swift Current Agricultural & Exhibition Association
PO Box 146, 1700 - 17th Ave. SE, Swift Current SK S9H 3V5
Tel: 306-773-2944; *Fax:* 306-773-7015
swiftcurrentex@sasktel.net
www.swiftcurrentex.com
Overview: A small provincial charitable organization founded in 1938
Mission: To facilitate education, entertainment, exhibitions & agricultural programs for the cultural & economic benefits of the community
Member of: Saskatchewan Association of Agricultural Societies & Exhibitions
Chief Officer(s):
Donna Sagin, General Manager
Stuart Smith, President
Finances: *Annual Operating Budget:* $500,000-$1.5 Million
Staff Member(s): 4; 500 volunteer(s)
Membership: 78; *Fees:* $5
Activities: Agricultural Fairs, Exhibitions, Livestock shows & sales, Trade shows

Swift Current Chamber of Commerce
145 - 1st Ave. NE, Swift Current SK S9H 2B1
Tel: 306-773-7268; *Fax:* 306-773-5686
info@swiftcurrentchamber.ca
www.swiftcurrentchamber.ca
www.linkedin.com/company/swift-current-&-district-chamber-of-commerce
Overview: A small local organization founded in 1908
Affliation(s): Saskatchewan Chamber of Commerce; Canadian Chamber of Commerce
Chief Officer(s):
Trevor Koot, Chair, 306-774-4113
tkoot@306invest.com
Finances: *Annual Operating Budget:* $100,000-$250,000; *Funding Sources:* Membership fees
Staff Member(s): 2; 20 volunteer(s)
Membership: 330; *Fees:* $205-$770 + GST
Activities: *Library*

Swift Current Creek Watershed Stewards (SCCWS)
PO Box 1088, Swift Current SK S9H 3X3
Tel: 306-778-5007; *Fax:* 306-778-5020
stewards@sccws.com
www.sccws.com
www.facebook.com/SwiftCurrentCreekWatershedStewards
Overview: A small local organization
Mission: To enhance water quality and stream health of the Swift Current Creek Watershed by promoting awareness and understanding among water users.
Chief Officer(s):
Arlene Unvoas, Executive Director

Swift Current United Way
PO Box 485, #203, 12 Cheadle St. West, Swift Current SK S9H 3W3
Tel: 306-773-4828; *Fax:* 306-773-4870
unitedway@sasktel.net
swiftcurrentunitedway.ca
www.facebook.com/swiftunitedway
www.twitter.com/swiftunitedway
www.youtube.com/user/SwiftUnitedWay
Overview: A small local organization overseen by United Way of Canada - Centraide Canada
Chief Officer(s):
Darla Lindbjerg, Executive Director

Swim Alberta
Percy Page Centre, 11759 Groat Rd., Edmonton AB T5M 3K6
Tel: 780-415-1780; *Fax:* 780-415-1788
office@swimalberta.ca
www.swimalberta.ca
Overview: A medium-sized provincial organization founded in 1963 overseen by Swimming Canada
Mission: To maintain a progressive athletic / club development program & a high performance program
Member of: Swimming Natation Canada
Chief Officer(s):
Doug Bird, President
dougbird@shaw.ca
Cheryl Humphrey, Executive Director
chumphrey@swimalberta.ca
Finances: *Funding Sources:* Membership fees; Sponsorships; Lottery
Staff Member(s): 4
Activities: *Speaker Service:* Yes; *Library* Open to public

Swim BC
PO Box 1749, Garibaldi Highlands BC V0N 1T0
Tel: 604-898-9100; *Fax:* 604-898-9200
www.swim.bc.ca
facebook.com/SwimBC
www.twitter.com/swimbcstaff
Overview: A small provincial organization founded in 1974 overseen by Swimming Canada
Mission: To provide the opportunity, leadership & means for members to achieve excellence in all areas of the sport of swimming
Member of: Swimming Canada
Chief Officer(s):
Mark Hahto, Executive Director
markschuett@swimbc.ca
Finances: *Annual Operating Budget:* $500,000-$1.5 Million; *Funding Sources:* Self-generated; provincial government
Staff Member(s): 4; 16 volunteer(s)
Membership: 8,000
Activities: *Library*

Swim Manitoba *See* Swim-Natation Manitoba

Swim Nova Scotia (SNS)
5516 Spring Garden Rd., Halifax NS B3J 1G6
Tel: 902-425-5450; *Fax:* 902-425-5606
www.swimnovascotia.com
Overview: A small provincial charitable organization overseen by Swimming Canada
Member of: Swimming Canada
Affliation(s): AthletesCAN
Chief Officer(s):
Sue Jackson, President
suejack01@yahoo.com
Bette El-Hawary, Executive Director
Finances: *Annual Operating Budget:* $50,000-$100,000
Staff Member(s): 1; 20 volunteer(s)
Membership: 2,800
Activities: Swim competitions & fundraising events

Swim Ontario
#206, 3 Concorde Gate, Toronto ON M3C 3N7
Tel: 416-426-7220; *Fax:* 416-426-7356
info@swimontario.com
www.swimontario.com
www.facebook.com/117335688316744
twitter.com/SwimOntario
Overview: A medium-sized provincial organization founded in 1922 overseen by Swimming Canada
Member of: Swimming Canada
Chief Officer(s):
Rick Hannah, President
rickhannah@aol.com
John Vadeika, Executive Director
john@swimontario.com
Staff Member(s): 5; 17 volunteer(s)
Membership: 10,000+ in 140+ clubs; *Committees:* Strategic Planning; Administration; Finance; Risk Management; Programme Policy
Activities: Learn-to-Swim; training for competitions & fitness;

Swim Saskatchewan
2205 Victoria Ave., Regina SK S4P 0S4
Tel: 306-780-9291; *Fax:* 306-525-4009
office@swimsask.ca
www.swimsask.ca
www.facebook.com/325400947571418
Overview: A medium-sized provincial organization overseen by Swimming Canada
Mission: To promote excellence through sport development, competition, education, training and strong member organizations.
Member of: Swimming Canada
Chief Officer(s):
Marj Walton, Executive Director, 306-780-9238
marjwalton@swimsask.ca
Staff Member(s): 3

Swim Yukon
4061 - 4th Ave., Whitehorse YT Y1A 1H1
sportyukon.com/member/swim-yukon
Overview: A medium-sized provincial organization
Mission: Swim Yukon is the Sport Governing Body for competitive swimming in the Yukon.
Member of: Sport Yukon
Affliation(s): Swimming Canada
Chief Officer(s):
Michael McArthur, President
mcarthurme@gmail.com

Activities: Swim meets

Swimming Canada / Natation Canada
#B140, 2445 St. Laurent Blvd., Ottawa ON K1G 6C3
Tel: 613-260-1348; *Fax:* 613-260-0804
natloffice@swimming.ca
www.swimming.ca
www.facebook.com/56320144853
twitter.com/SwimmingCanada
www.youtube.com/swimmingcanada
Overview: A large national organization founded in 1909
Mission: To direct & develop competitive swimming in Canada; To represent Canada in international organizations & events
Affliation(s): Aquatic Federation of Canada
Chief Officer(s):
Ahmed El-Awadi, CEO, 613-260-1348 Ext. 2007
Larry Clough, Director, Finance, 613-260-1348 Ext. 2008
Ken Radford, Director, Swimming Operations, 250-220-2537
Iain McDonald, Senior Manager, High Performance, 613-260-1348 Ext. 2010
Nathan White, Manager, Communications, 613-260-1348 Ext. 2002
Craig McCord, National Para-swimming Coach, 778-837-7328
Ken McKinnon, National Junior Coach, 613-260-1348 Ext. 2801
Finances: *Funding Sources:* Membership fees; Corporate sponsorships; Sport Canada; Canadian Olympic Association
21 volunteer(s)
Membership: Over 50,000
Activities: *Rents Mailing List:* Yes
Awards:
• Victor Davis Memorial Award (Award)
Annual awards from the Victor Davis Memorial Fund assist young Canadian swimmers to continue their training, education & pursuit of excellence at the international level of competition; recipients are determined by the Victor Davis Memorial Fund Awards Committee
• Administrator of the Year Award (Award)
Annual award presented to a volunteer, who has demonstrated outstanding commitment to the organization
• Official of the Year Award (Award)
Annual award recognizes outstanding service to Canadian swimming
• Club of the Year Award (Award)
Awards presented annually to three clubs
• Female/Male Swimmer of the Year (Award)
Annual awards recognize best international swimmers in the following categories: 1) able-bodied athletes, 2) athletes with a disability, & 3) long distance competitors; each winner receives a plaque & gift
• Coach of the Year (Award)
Annual awards recognize coaches of swimmers in the following categories: 1) able-bodied athletes; 2) athletes with a disability, & 3) long distance competitors; each winner receives a plaque & gift

Swimming New Brunswick / Natation Nouveau-Brunswick
#13, 900 Hanwell Rd., Fredericton NB E3B 6A3
Tel: 506-451-1323; *Fax:* 506-451-1325
www.swimnb.ca
Overview: A medium-sized provincial organization overseen by Swimming Canada
Member of: Swimming Canada
Chief Officer(s):
David Frise, President
dfrise@gmail.com
Pat Ketterling, Executive Director
300 volunteer(s)
Membership: 668; *Fees:* $12-70

Swimming Newfoundland & Labrador
1296A Kenmount Rd., Paradise NL A1L 1N3
Tel: 709-576-7946; *Fax:* 709-576-7493
swimnl@sportnl.ca
www.swimnl.nfld.net
www.facebook.com/swimmingNL
twitter.com/SwimmingNL
www.youtube.com/user/SwimmingNL
Overview: A medium-sized provincial organization founded in 1974 overseen by Swimming Canada
Member of: Swimming Canada
Chief Officer(s):
Eugene Murphy, Vice-President
Staff Member(s): 10

Swimming PEI *See* Swimming Prince Edward Island

Swimming Prince Edward Island
PO Box 302, Charlottetown PE C1A 7K7
Tel: 902-368-4548; *Fax:* 902-368-4548
Toll-Free: 800-247-6712
swimpei@sportpei.pe.ca
www.swimpei.com
Also Known As: Swim PEI
Previous Name: Swimming PEI
Overview: A small provincial charitable organization overseen by Swimming Canada
Member of: Swimming Canada
Finances: *Annual Operating Budget:* Less than $50,000
Staff Member(s): 1; 30 volunteer(s)
Membership: 200; *Fees:* $40; *Member Profile:* Ages 6-70; *Committees:* Finance; Coaching; Officials; Awards
Activities: Competitive swimming; swimming development; *Speaker Service:* Yes

Swim-Natation Manitoba
#209, 145 Pacific Ave., Winnipeg MB R3B 2Z6
Tel: 204-925-5778; *Fax:* 204-925-5624
swim@sportmanitoba.ca
www.swimmanitoba.mb.ca
twitter.com/Swim_Manitoba
Previous Name: Swim Manitoba
Overview: A medium-sized provincial organization founded in 1913 overseen by Swimming Canada
Mission: To produce fast swimmers & to make the experience a healthy, fun, exiting & rewarding adventure
Member of: Swimming Canada; Sport Manitoba
Chief Officer(s):
Darin Muma, Executive Director
swim.ed@sportmanitoba.ca
Nicole Parent, Program Coordinator
swim@sportmanitoba.ca
Finances: *Annual Operating Budget:* $250,000-$500,000
Staff Member(s): 3; 1500 volunteer(s)
Membership: 18 clubs + 1500 swimmers + 300 coaches + 1300 officials & volunteers; *Committees:* Advancement; Competition Hosting; Executive; Finance & Operations; Governance; Sport

Swiss Canadian Chamber of Commerce (Montréal) Inc. / Chambre de commerce Canado-Suisse (Montréal) Inc.
1572 Dr. Penfield Ave., Montréal QC H3G 1C4
Tel: 514-937-5822; *Fax:* 514-693-1032
info@cccsmtl.com
www.cccsmtl.com
Overview: A medium-sized international organization founded in 1969
Mission: D'assumer un rôle de premier plan dans la promotion des relations commerciales, industrielles et financières entre la Suisse et le Canada, tout en se concentrant sur l'est du Canada
Chief Officer(s):
Jean Serge Grisé, President
Staff Member(s): 1
Membership: 250

Swiss Canadian Chamber of Commerce (Ontario) Inc. (SCCC)
756 Royal York Rd., Toronto ON M8Y 2T6
Tel: 416-236-0039; *Fax:* 416-551-1011
sccc@swissbiz.ca
www.swissbiz.ca
www.linkedin.com/company/2231465
www.facebook.com/swiss.chamber
Overview: A medium-sized provincial organization founded in 1966
Mission: To assume a prominent role in promoting commercial, industrial & financial relations between Switzerland & Canada, with primary focus on membership in Ontario
Member of: Union of Swiss Chambers Abroad
Chief Officer(s):
Ernst Notz, President
Finances: *Funding Sources:* Annual dues; advertising in Info/Suisse
Membership: 88; *Fees:* Schedule available
Activities: Luncheons; networking evening; golf tournament; annual black tie dinner dance; annual spousal dinner cruise; *Speaker Service:* Yes

Swiss Club Saskatoon
349 Carlton Dr., Saskatoon SK S7H 3P2
Tel: 306-665-6039
swissclubsaskatoon@hotmail.com
Overview: A small provincial organization founded in 1979
Mission: To provide opportunities for Canadians of Swiss background to speak Swiss languages & dialects
Chief Officer(s):
Elisabeth Eilinger, Contact

Sydenham Field Naturalists (SFN)
PO Box 22008, Wallaceburg ON N8A 5G4
www.sydenhamfieldnaturalists.ca
Overview: A small local charitable organization founded in 1985
Mission: To preserve wildlife, promote public interest, cooperate with others with similar interests, consider matters of environmental concern
Member of: Federation of Ontario Naturalists; Canadian Nature Federation; Carolinian Canada
Chief Officer(s):
Denise Shephard, President
Finances: *Funding Sources:* Bingo profits; private donations; grants
Membership: 35-40; *Fees:* $10 student; $15 single; $25 family
Activities: Field trips; planting of native shrubs/wildflowers; indoor meetings; wood lot acquisition

Sydney & Area Chamber of Commerce (SACC)
275 Charlotte Street, Sydney NS B1P 1C6
Tel: 902-564-6453; *Fax:* 902-539-7487
www.sydneyareachamber.ca
www.facebook.com/sydneychamber
twitter.com/SydneyChamber
Overview: A small local organization
Chief Officer(s):
Adrian White, Executive Director
adrian@sydneyareachamber.ca
Finances: *Funding Sources:* Membership fees
Staff Member(s): 2
Membership: 500; *Fees:* $199 bronze; $299 silver; $699 gold; $1499 platinum
Activities: *Internships:* Yes; *Speaker Service:* Yes

Sydney & Louisburg Railway Historical Society / Le Musée de chemin de fer de Sydney à Louisburg
PO Box 225, Louisbourg NS B0A 1M0
Tel: 902-733-2720
Also Known As: S&L Museum
Overview: A small local organization founded in 1973
Mission: To commemorate the history of the S&L Railway by preserving & displaying the artifacts & documents which survive; to commemorate the people who worked for the S&L Railway; to explain the local & commercial history of the area which relates to the S&L Railway; to explain & commemorate the general themes of railway & transportation history & technology
Member of: Federation of the Nova Scotian Heritage; Heritage Canada
Activities: Annual reunion, Sept.; *Library:* Resource Centre; Open to public by appointment

Sylvan Lake Chamber of Commerce
PO Box 9119, Sylvan Lake AB T4S 1S6
Tel: 403-887-3048
info@sylvanlakechamber.com
www.sylvanlakechamber.com
www.facebook.com/172470262772131
Overview: A small local organization
Mission: To promote & contribute to the commercial, industrial, agricultural & civic progress of the Town of Sylvan Lake & district through the strength & participation of its members
Member of: Alberta Chamber of Commerce
Chief Officer(s):
Dwayne Stoesz, President
Finances: *Funding Sources:* Town grants; fundraising
Membership: *Fees:* Schedule available based on number of employees

Syme-Woolner Neighbourhood & Family Centre (SWNFC)
#3, 2468 Eglinton Ave. West, Toronto ON M6M 5E2
Tel: 416-766-4634; *Fax:* 416-766-8162
swoolner@symewoolner.org
www.symewoolner.org
Overview: A medium-sized local charitable organization founded in 1996
Mission: To create in the community a sense of belonging, to enable individuals, families and groups to support each other and build a better future.
Chief Officer(s):
Mark Neysmith, Executive Director
Finances: *Funding Sources:* City of Toronto, United Way
Staff Member(s): 42

Symphonie Nouveau-Brunswick *See* Symphony New Brunswick

Symphony New Brunswick / Symphonie Nouveau-Brunswick
Brunswick Square, 39 King St., Level III, Saint John NB E2L 4W3
Tel: 506-634-8379; *Fax:* 506-634-0843
symphony@nbnet.nb.ca
www.symphonynb.com
Previous Name: Saint John Symphony
Overview: A medium-sized provincial charitable organization founded in 1984 overseen by Orchestras Canada
Mission: To present high-quality, live orchestral & chamber music from all periods & to promote the appreciation of music through educational activities in New Brunswick
Affliation(s): American Federation of Musicians
Chief Officer(s):
Thomas J. Condon, President
Finances: *Annual Operating Budget:* $250,000-$500,000; *Funding Sources:* Canada Council; Province of NB
Staff Member(s): 3; 300 volunteer(s)
Membership: 500-999
Activities: Bravo & Virtuoso Series Concerts; Concerts for Kids; *Library*

Symphony Nova Scotia (SNS)
Park Lane Mall, PO Box 218, #301, 5657 Spring Garden Rd., Halifax NS B3J 3R4
Tel: 902-421-1300; *Fax:* 902-422-1209
info@symphonyns.ca
www.symphonynovascotia.ca
www.facebook.com/SymphonyNovaScotia
twitter.com/SymphonyNS
www.youtube.com/user/SymphonyNovaScotia
Overview: A small provincial charitable organization founded in 1983 overseen by Orchestras Canada
Mission: To enhance the quality of life of the citizens of Nova Scotia through high quality, professionally performed orchestral music
Chief Officer(s):
Christopher Wilkinson, Chief Executive Officer
ceo@symphonyns.ca
Finances: *Funding Sources:* Government; corporate & individual
Staff Member(s): 12
Membership: 27
Activities: Classical, baroque & pops concerts; Beer & Beethoven;

Symphony on the Bay
#300, 1100 Burloak, Burlington ON L7L 6B2
Tel: 905-526-6690
info@symphonyonthebay.ca
symphonyonthebay.com
www.facebook.com/119532624785141
twitter.com/SymphonyOnBay
www.youtube.com/channel/UC3N-Vqf9Yy304F5Q-mZ9leQ
Previous Name: McMaster Symphony Orchestra; Greater Hamilton Symphony Association
Overview: A small local charitable organization founded in 1973 overseen by Orchestras Canada
Mission: To enrich the cultural life of the Hamilton & surrounding area by maintaining a full-size community symphony orchestra; to perform a wide repertoire of symphonic music, including works by Canadian composers; to make great symphonic music accessible to a larger public by offering attractive concert programs at affordable prices
Member of: Hamilton Volunteer Centre
Affliation(s): Hamilton & Region Arts Council
Chief Officer(s):
James R. McKay, Music Director & Conductor
Karen Page, Manager, Orchestra Operations
Fonda Loft, President
Finances: *Funding Sources:* Government; foundations; corporate; private; fundraising
Staff Member(s): 5
Membership: 67; *Member Profile:* Audition for orchestra members
Activities: *Library* by appointment

Synchro Alberta
The Percy Page Centre, 11759 Groat Rd., Edmonton AB T5M 3K6
Tel: 780-415-1789; *Fax:* 780-415-0056
syncro@synchroalberta.com
www.synchroalberta.com
www.facebook.com/SynchroAlberta
Overview: A medium-sized provincial organization overseen by Synchro Canada
Member of: Synchro Canada
Chief Officer(s):
Jennifer Luzia, Executive Director
jluzia@synchroalberta.com
Staff Member(s): 2
Membership: 1200
Activities: Competitive & recreational meets

Synchro BC
c/o Fortius Athlete Development Centre, 3713 Kensington Ave., Burnaby BC V5B 0A7
www.synchro.bc.ca
Overview: A medium-sized provincial licensing organization overseen by Synchro Canada
Mission: To foster & promote a fully integrated Synchronized Swimming Sport System throughout BC, which will offer opportunities for excellence at all levels of participation from Recreational to International
Member of: Synchro Canada
Chief Officer(s):
Janice Birch, President
president@synchro.bc.ca
Finances: *Funding Sources:* Government; donations
Membership: 1,200; *Fees:* Schedule available
Activities: *Speaker Service:* Yes; *Rents Mailing List:* Yes

Synchro Canada
#401, 700 Industrial Ave., Ottawa ON K1G 0Y9
Tel: 613-748-5674; *Fax:* 613-748-5724
www.synchro.ca
www.facebook.com/synchrocanada
twitter.com/synchrocanada
www.youtube.com/synchrocanada
Previous Name: Canadian Amateur Synchronized Swimming Association
Overview: A medium-sized national charitable organization founded in 1968
Mission: To develop & operate the sport of synchronized swimming in Canada, through a variety of programs designed to develop athletes, coaches & officials
Chief Officer(s):
Catherine Gosselin-Després, CEO
catherine@synchro.ca
Isabelle Lecompte, Manager, High Performance
isabelle@synchro.ca
Staff Member(s): 7; 70 volunteer(s)
Membership: 5,000-14,999

Synchro Manitoba
145 Pacific Ave., Winnipeg MB R3B 2Z6
Tel: 204-925-5693; *Fax:* 204-925-5703
execdirector@synchromb.ca
www.synchromb.ca
Previous Name: Canadian Amateur Synchronized Swimming Association (Manitoba Section)
Overview: A small provincial organization founded in 1958 overseen by Synchro Canada
Mission: To promote, teach, foster, encourage, & improve, synchronized swimming in Manitoba; to regulate synchro swim in Manitoba in accordance with the constitution by-laws & rules
Member of: Synchro Canada
Affliation(s): Manitoba Sports Federation
Chief Officer(s):
Allison Gervais, Executive Director
execdirector@synchromb.ca
Staff Member(s): 2
Activities: *Library:* Resource Centre

Synchro New Brunswick
436 Young St., Saint John NB E2M 2V2
Tel: 506-672-2399; *Fax:* 506-672-6020
www.synchronb.ca
Overview: A medium-sized provincial organization overseen by Synchro Canada
Member of: Synchro Canada

Synchro Newfoundland & Labrador
c/o Sport Newfoundland & Labrador, 1296-A Kenmount Rd., Paradise NL A1L 1N3
Tel: 709-576-3397; *Fax:* 709-576-7493
admin@synchronl.com
www.synchronl.com
www.facebook.com/synchronl
twitter.com/synchronl
Overview: A small provincial organization overseen by Synchro Canada
Member of: Synchro Canada
Chief Officer(s):
Jennifer Folkes, President
synchronl@hotmail.ca
Natelle Tulk, Executive Director

Synchro Nova Scotia
5516 Spring Garden Rd., 4th Fl., Halifax NS B3J 1G6
Tel: 902-426-5454; *Fax:* 902-425-5606
synchro@sportnovascotia.ca
www.sportnovascotia.ca
www.facebook.com/pages/Synchro-Nova-Scotia/177261688979414
Overview: A medium-sized provincial organization overseen by Synchro Canada
Mission: To promote synchronized swimming throughout the province
Member of: Synchro Canada
Chief Officer(s):
Pam Kidney, Executive Director

Synchro PEI
c/o Sport PEI, PO Box 302, Charlottetown PE C1A 7K7
synchropei.goalline.ca
www.facebook.com/167646783276104
Also Known As: PEI Synchronized Swimming Association
Overview: A small provincial organization overseen by Synchro Canada
Member of: Synchro Canada
Chief Officer(s):
Desiree Oomen, Secretary
dmoomen@gmail.com

Synchro Saskatchewan
#209, 1860 Lorne St., Regina SK S4P 2L7
Tel: 306-780-9227; *Fax:* 306-780-9445
synchro.sk@sasktel.net
www.synchrosask.com
Overview: A small provincial organization overseen by Synchro Canada
Mission: To promote & develop synchronized swimming in Saskatchewan
Member of: Synchro Canada; SaskSport
Chief Officer(s):
Brenda Lyons, President
president@synchrosask.com
Kathleen Reynolds, Executive Director
Finances: *Annual Operating Budget:* $100,000-$250,000; *Funding Sources:* Saskatchewan Lottery Trust Fund
Staff Member(s): 3; 30 volunteer(s)
Membership: 1,200; *Fees:* $17; *Committees:* Finance; Marketing; Technical; Competitions; Officials; Marketing; Grassroot Programming

Synchro Swim Ontario
128 Galaxy Blvd., Toronto ON M9W 4Y6
Tel: 416-679-9522; *Fax:* 416-679-9535
synchroontario.com
www.facebook.com/SynchroSwimOntario
twitter.com/SynchroONTARIO
Overview: A medium-sized provincial licensing organization overseen by Synchro Canada
Mission: To oversee synchronized swimming in Ontario, including varsity competiton, competitive clubes & community recreation programs; to develop, promote, support & regulate synchronized swimming through the immplementation of an integrated sports system that is accessible to all Ontarians by providing opportunites for enjoyment & the pursuit of individual goals
Member of: Synchro Canada
Chief Officer(s):
Mary Dwyer, Executive Director, 416-679-9522 Ext. 222
mdwyer@synchroontario.com
Staff Member(s): 4
Membership: *Member Profile:* Athlete development at recreational through to elite levels; officials development; coach development; competition structures; *Committees:* Executive; Finance; High Performance; High Performance Hiring & Selection; Novice; Ontario Officials Management Team; Provincial Jury of Appeal; Technical Training & Development; Volunteer Management

Synchro Yukon Association
4061 - 4th Ave., Whitehorse YT Y1A 1H1
Tel: 867-668-7441
smduncan@northwestel.net
sportyukon.com/member/synchro-yukon-association
Overview: A medium-sized provincial organization overseen by Synchro Canada
Mission: To promote the sport of Synchronized Swimming in the Yukon.
Member of: Synchro Canada; Sport Yukon
Chief Officer(s):
Deborah Seal, President
debseal@hotmail.com

Synchro-Québec
4545, av Pierre-de Coubertin, Montréal QC H1V 0B2
Tél: 514-252-3087
Ligne sans frais: 866-537-3164
fnsq@synchroquebec.qc.ca
www.synchroquebec.com
www.facebook.com/synchro.quebec
twitter.com/synchroquebec
Nom précédent: Fédération de nage synchronisée
Aperçu: *Dimension:* moyenne; *Envergure:* provinciale; Organisme sans but lucratif surveillé par Synchro Canada
Mission: Planifier et supporter le développement de la nage synchronisée au Québec; administrer l'ensemble des compétitions qui se déroule au Québec; veiller au perfectionnement de ses entraîneurs, officiels et bénévoles
Membre de: Synchro Canada
Membre(s) du bureau directeur:
Diane Lachapelle, Directrice générale
dlachapelle@synchroquebec.qc.ca
Membre(s) du personnel: 4
Activités: *Stagiaires:* Oui

Syndicat canadien de la fonction publique ***See*** Canadian Union of Public Employees

Le Syndicat canadien des employées et employés professionnels et de bureau ***See*** Canadian Office & Professional Employees Union

Syndicat canadien des officiers de la marine marchande (FAT-COI/CTC) ***See*** Canadian Marine Officers' Union (AFL-CIO/CLC)

Syndicat catholique des ouvriers du textile de Magog ***Voir*** Syndicat des ouvriers du textile de Magog

Syndicat construction Côte-Nord (ind.) ***Voir*** Syndicat québécois de la construction

Syndicat de l'emploi et de l'immigration du Canada ***See*** Canada Employment & Immigration Union

Syndicat de la fonction publique de l'Alberta ***See*** Alberta Union of Provincial Employees

Syndicat de la fonction publique de l'Ile-du-Prince-Édouard ***See*** Prince Edward Island Union of Public Sector Employees

Syndicat de la fonction publique de la Nouvelle-Écosse ***See*** Nova Scotia Government & General Employees Union

Syndicat de la fonction publique de la Saskatchewan ***See*** Saskatchewan Government & General Employees' Union

Syndicat de la fonction publique du Québec inc. (ind.) (SFPQ) / Québec Government Employees' Union (Ind.)
5100, boul des Gradins, Québec QC G2J 1N4
Tél: 418-623-2424; *Téléc:* 418-623-6109
communication@sfpq.qc.ca
www.sfpq.qc.ca
Aperçu: *Dimension:* grande; *Envergure:* provinciale; fondée en 1962
Mission: Assurer la défense des intérêts économiques, politiques et sociaux des membres et le développement de leurs conditions de vie; faire la promotion des services publics comme moyen démocratique de répondre aux besoins de la population
Membre(s) du bureau directeur:
Lucie Martineau, Présidente général
Finances: *Budget de fonctionnement annuel:* $3 Million-$5 Million
Membre(s) du personnel: 105
Membre: 43 000 + 120 sections locales; *Comités:* Comité national des femmes; Comité national des jeunes
Activités: Recours; santé et sécurité au travail; assurances collectives; formation; publications de brochures, dépliants; *Bibliothèque:* Centre de documentation
Publications:
• Bulletin SFPQ Express
Type: Bulletin
• Journal SFPQ
Type: Journal

Abitibi - Témiscamingue - Nord du Québec
42, 7e rue, Rouyn-Noranda QC J9X 1Z7
Tél: 819-797-4254; *Téléc:* 819-797-4395
Ligne sans frais: 888-797-2844
alain.pomerleau@sfpq.qc.ca
www.sfpq.qc.ca/regions/abitibi-temiscamingue-nord-du-quebec
Membre(s) du bureau directeur:
Gabriel Bédard, Président régional, 819-797-4254
gabriel.bedard@sfpq.qc.ca

Bas Saint-Laurent - Côte Nord - Gaspésie et les Iles
159, rue St-Pierre, Matane QC G4W 2B8
Tél: 418-566-6591; *Téléc:* 418-566-8930
Ligne sans frais: 888-566-6591
nelson.carrier@sfpq.qc.ca
www.sfpq.qc.ca/regions/bas-laurent-gaspesie-cote-nord-les-iles
Membre(s) du bureau directeur:
Hélène Chouinard, Présidente régionale, 418-566-6591 Ext. 2002
helene.chouinard@sfpq.qc.ca

Centre du Québec-Estrie-Mauricie
2940, boul Lemire, Drummondville QC J2B 7J6
Tél: 819-475-0072; *Téléc:* 819-475-1188
Ligne sans frais: 800-561-5572
martine.charette@sfpq.qc.ca
www.monsyndicat.net
Membre(s) du bureau directeur:
Luc Légaré, Président régional, 819-475-0195
luc.legare@sfpq.qc.ca

Laurentides - Lanaudière - Outaouais
#204, 294, rue Labelle, 2e étage, Saint-Jérôme QC J7Z 5L1
Tél: 450-432-8800; *Téléc:* 450-432-0097
Ligne sans frais: 800-265-5693
rr5@sfpq.qc.ca
www.sfpq.qc.ca/regions/laurentides-lanaudiere-outaouais
Membre(s) du bureau directeur:
Sylvain Gendron, Président régional, 450-432-0011
sylvain.gendron@sfpq.qc.ca

Montérégie
#302, 3234 boulevard Taschereau, Greenfield Park QC J4V 2H3
Tél: 450-676-0357; *Téléc:* 450-676-0209
Ligne sans frais: 800-265-7445
normand.moreau@sfpq.qc.ca
www.sfpq.qc.ca/regions/monteregie
Membre(s) du bureau directeur:
Daniel Landry, Président régional
daniel.landry@sfpq.qc.ca

Montréal - Laval
#1005, 425, boul de Maisonneuve ouest, Montréal QC H3A 3G5
Tél: 514-844-4487; *Téléc:* 514-844-4619
sylvestre.jean-francois@sfpq.qc.ca
Membre(s) du bureau directeur:
Jean-François Sylvestre, Président régional

Québec - Chaudière-Appalaches
5100, boul des Gradins, Québec QC G2J 1N4
Tél: 418-623-9919; *Téléc:* 418-623-2286
Ligne sans frais: 800-382-6919
annie.dallaire@sfpq.qc.ca
www.sfpq.qc.ca/regions/quebec-chaudiere-appalaches
Membre(s) du bureau directeur:
Steve Dorval, Président régional, 418-623-9919 Ext. 101
steve.dorval@sfpq.qc.ca

Saguenay - Lac-St-Jean - Chibougamau - Charlevoix - Houte-Côte-Nord
2447, rue Saint-Dominique, Jonquière QC G7X 6K9
Tél: 418-548-5852; *Téléc:* 418-548-6777
Ligne sans frais: 800-561-5032
martine.duchesne@sfpq.qc.ca
Membre(s) du bureau directeur:
Brigitte Claveau, Présidente régionale, 418-548-5852
brigitte.claveau@sfpq.qc.ca

Syndicat de professionnelles et professionnels du gouvernement du Québec (SPGQ) / Union of Professional Employees of the Québec Government
7, rue Vallière, Québec QC G1K 6S9
Tél: 418-692-0022; *Téléc:* 418-692-1338
Ligne sans frais: 800-463-5079
courrier@spgq.qc.ca
www.spgq.qc.ca
www.facebook.com/lespgq
twitter.com/spgq
www.youtube.com/spgqinformation
Aperçu: *Dimension:* grande; *Envergure:* provinciale; fondée en 1966
Membre(s) du bureau directeur:
Richard Perron, Président
Jean Nadeau, Secrétaire
Finances: *Budget de fonctionnement annuel:* Plus de $5 Million
Membre(s) du personnel: 17
Membre: 20 000 + 35 sections locales; *Critères d'admissibilite:* professionnel; *Comités:* Électoral; surveillance; statuts et règlements; des femmes; griefs; classification, d'équité et de relativités salariales; avantages sociaux et de la retraite; santé et de sécurité du travail; d'information; d'action et de mobilisation; formation syndicale; personnes occasionnelles; sur la conciliation travail-famille; jeunes; régions
Activités: *Listes de destinataires:* Oui

Syndicat des Agents Correctionnels du Canada (CSN) (SACC-CSN) / Union of Canadian Correctional Officers (UCCO-CSN)
1601, av De Lorimier, Montréal QC H2K 4M5
Tel: 514-598-2263; *Fax:* 514-598-2943
Toll-Free: 866-229-5566
ucco-sacc@csn.qc.ca
www.ucco-sacc.csn.qc.ca
www.facebook.com/216852691687729
Overview: A medium-sized provincial organization founded in 1999
Chief Officer(s):
Kevin Grabosky, Président

Syndicat des agents de la paix en services correctionnels du Québec (ind.) (SAPSCQ) / Union of Prison Guards of Québec (Ind.)
4906, boul Gouin est, Montréal QC H1G 1A4
Tél: 514-328-7774; *Téléc:* 514-328-0889
Ligne sans frais: 800-361-3559
www.sapscq.com
Aperçu: *Dimension:* moyenne; *Envergure:* provinciale; Organisme sans but lucratif; fondée en 1982
Mission: Service syndical pour les agents de la paix en services correctionnels du Québec
Membre(s) du bureau directeur:
Stéphane Lemaire, Président national
s.lemaire@sapscq.com
Tony Vallières, Vice-président
t.vallieres@sapscq.com
Sylvain Maltais, Secrétaire général
s.maltais@sapscq.com
Membre(s) du personnel: 4
Membre: 2 085 particuliers; *Montant de la cotisation:* Barème; *Critères d'admissibilite:* Etre agent de la paix en services correctionnels du Québec

Syndicat des agents de maîtrise de Québectel (ind.) ***Voir*** Syndicat des agents de maîtrise de TELUS (ind.)

Syndicat des agents de maîtrise de TELUS (ind.) (SAMT) / TELUS Professional Employees Union (Ind.) (TPEU)
#605, 2, St-Germain est, Rimouski QC G5L 8T7
Tél: 418-722-6144; *Téléc:* 418-724-0765
info@samt.qc.ca
www.samt.qc.ca/apropos.php
Également appelé: SAMT - Section Locale 5144 du SCFP
Nom précédent: Syndicat des agents de maîtrise de Québectel (ind.)
Aperçu: *Dimension:* petite; *Envergure:* provinciale; fondée en 1980
Mission: La sauvegarde et la promotion des intérêts professionnels, scientifiques, économiques, sociaux, culturels et politiques de ses membres; faire bénéficier les membres et les travailleurs en général des avantages de l'entraide et des négociations collectives; obtenir pour ses membres un meilleur niveau de vie et de meilleures conditions de travail; représenter les membres auprès de l'employeur
Membre(s) du bureau directeur:

Harold Morrissey, Président
Lynda Fortin, Secrétaire
Finances: *Budget de fonctionnement annuel:* $100,000-$250,000
12 bénévole(s)
Membre: 580; *Montant de la cotisation:* 1.5% du salaire brut; *Critères d'admissibilite:* Etre salarié, avoir rempli et signé une fiche d'adhésion, avoir été accepté par le comité exécutif; *Comités:* Conseil syndical; Comités: Exécutif; Relations de travail; Retraite; Sécurité; Évaluation des Emplois; Équité en Matière d'Emploi; Négotiations

Syndicat des agricultrices d'Abitibi-Témiscamingue (SAAT)

970, av Larivière, Rouyn-Noranda QC J9X 4K5
Tél: 819-762-0833; *Téléc:* 819-762-0575
abitibi-temiscamingue@upa.qc.ca
Aperçu: *Dimension:* petite; *Envergure:* locale; fondée en 1987
Mission: L'étude, la défense et le développement des intérêts économiques, sociaux et moraux de ses membres
Membre de: Fédération de l'UPA d'Abitibi-Témiscamingue
Affiliation(s): Fédération des agricultrices du Québec
Membre(s) du bureau directeur:
Estelle Dorion, Présidente
Martine Delage, Secrétaire
Finances: *Budget de fonctionnement annuel:* Moins de $50,000; *Fonds:* Gouvernement provincial
Membre(s) du personnel: 1; 10 bénévole(s)
Membre: 25; *Montant de la cotisation:* 25$; *Critères d'admissibilite:* Agricultrices
Prix, Bouses:
• Hommage à l'agricultrice de l'année (Prix)

Syndicat des agricultrices de la Beauce

225, rang St Charles, Notre-Dame-Des-Pins QC G0M 1K0
Tél: 418-774-2330; *Téléc:* 418-774-2330
Aperçu: *Dimension:* petite; *Envergure:* locale; fondée en 1986
Affiliation(s): Fédération des agricultrices du Québec
Membre(s) du bureau directeur:
Manon Poulin, Secrétaire
15 bénévole(s)
Membre: 1-99

Syndicat des agricultrices de la Côte-du-Sud

#100, 1120, 6e av, La Pocatière QC G0R 1Z0
Tél: 418-856-3044; *Téléc:* 418-856-5199
Ligne sans frais: 800-463-8001
edube@upa.qc.ca
www.agricultrices.com
Nom précédent: Syndicat des agricultrices de la région de la Côte-du-Sud
Aperçu: *Dimension:* petite; *Envergure:* locale; Organisme sans but lucratif; fondée en 1987
Mission: En relation avec la planification stratégique de la Fédération des agricultrices du Québec soit: représenter toutes les agricultrices; susciter des échanges entre agricultrices; développer une prise de conscience individuelle et collective en agriculture, de l'agricultrice; participer aux orientations de l'agricultrice de la province
Affiliation(s): Fédération des Agricultrices du Québec
Membre(s) du bureau directeur:
Claire Lajoie, Présidente
Finances: *Budget de fonctionnement annuel:* Moins de $50,000
Membre: 60; *Montant de la cotisation:* 34 $

Syndicat des agricultrices de la région de la Côte-du-Sud ***Voir*** Syndicat des agricultrices de la Côte-du-Sud

Syndicat des agricultrices de la région de Nicolet ***Voir*** Syndicat des agricultrices du Centre du Québec

Syndicat des agricultrices du Centre du Québec (SACQ)

179, rang 10, Durham-Sud QC J0H 2C0
Tél: 819-858-2091; *Téléc:* 819-858-2091
sacqcentreduquebec@hotmail.com
Nom précédent: Syndicat des agricultrices de la région de Nicolet
Aperçu: *Dimension:* petite; *Envergure:* locale; Organisme sans but lucratif; fondée en 1987
Mission: Regrouper toutes les agricultrices reconnues ou non; les représenter, les informer, les conscientiser à leur place dans l'agriculture
Affiliation(s): Fédération des agricultrices du Québec
Membre(s) du bureau directeur:
Lucie Talbot, Présidente
Finances: *Budget de fonctionnement annuel:* Moins de $50,000; *Fonds:* Gouvernement provincial, fédéral
Membre(s) du personnel: 1; 50 bénévole(s)
Membre: 20 institutionnel; 200 individu; *Montant de la cotisation:* 30$; *Critères d'admissibilite:* Agricultrice impliquée sur la ferme; *Comités:* Agri-Elle
Activités: Quatre colloques annuels; Vidéo La Passion en 8 temps; *Evénements de sensibilisation:* Activité de formation; Forum, mars; Fête du 15e, avril

Syndicat des conseillères et conseillers de la CSQ (SCC-CSQ)

#100, 320, rue Saint-Joseph est, Québec QC G1K 9E7
Tél: 418-649-8888; *Téléc:* 418-649-8800
Ligne sans frais: 877-850-0897
www.lacsq.org/la-csq
Aperçu: *Dimension:* petite; *Envergure:* provinciale; Organisme de réglementation; fondée en 1970
Mission: Défense des membres
Membre(s) du bureau directeur:
Réjean Parent, Président
Finances: *Budget de fonctionnement annuel:* $50,000-$100,000
Membre: 80; *Montant de la cotisation:* 1% du salaire; *Critères d'admissibilite:* Avocats, pédagogues, conseillers en relations de travail
Activités: Santé; sécurité; solidarité; sélection; relations du travail; perfectionnements

Syndicat des douanes et de l'immigration ***See*** Customs & Immigration Union

Syndicat des employé(e)s de l'impôt ***See*** Union of Taxation Employees

Syndicat des employé(e)s de magasins et de bureau de la Société des alcools du Québec (ind.) (SEMB SAQ) / Québec Liquor Board Store & Office Employees Union (Ind.)

1065, rue St-Denis, Montréal QC H2X 3J3
Tél: 514-849-7754; *Téléc:* 514-849-7914
Ligne sans frais: 800-361-8427
info@semb-saq.com
www.semb-saq.com
www.facebook.com/semb.saq
Aperçu: *Dimension:* moyenne; *Envergure:* provinciale; fondée en 1964
Membre(s) du bureau directeur:
Katia Lelièvre, Présidente

Syndicat des employé(e)s des affaires des anciens combattants ***See*** Union of Veterans' Affairs Employees

Syndicat des employé(e)s de l'Université Laurentienne ***See*** Laurentian University Staff Union

Syndicat des employées de soutien de l'Université de Sherbrooke (SEESUS) / University of Sherbrooke Support Staff Union

Pavillon J.-S. Bourque, Université de Sherbrooke, #230, 2500, boul Université, Sherbrooke QC J1K 2R1
Tél: 819-821-7646; *Téléc:* 819-821-7627
seesus@usherbrooke.ca
www.seesus.ca
Aperçu: *Dimension:* moyenne; *Envergure:* locale; Organisme sans but lucratif; fondée en 1974
Affiliation(s): Syndicat canadien de la fonction publique
Membre(s) du bureau directeur:
Stéphane Caron, Président
Finances: *Budget de fonctionnement annuel:* $250,000-$500,000
Membre(s) du personnel: 3
Membre: 1 100; *Montant de la cotisation:* 1.68% du salaire brut; *Critères d'admissibilite:* Etre salarié de l'Université de Sherbrooke

Syndicat des employées et employés de la fonction publique de l'Ontario ***See*** Ontario Public Service Employees Union

Syndicat des employées et employés nationaux ***See*** Union of National Employees

Syndicat des employés d'hôpitaux ***See*** Hospital Employees' Union

Syndicat des employés d'indemnisation (ind.) ***See*** Compensation Employees' Union (Ind.)

Syndicat des employés des postes et des communications ***See*** Union of Postal Communications Employees

Syndicat des employés du secteur public de la Nouvelle-Écosse (CCU) ***See*** Nova Scotia Union of Public & Private Employees (CCU)

Syndicat des employés du Solliciteur général ***See*** Union of Solicitor General Employees

Syndicat des employés du Yukon ***See*** Yukon Employees Union

Syndicat des employés en radio-télédiffusion de Télé-Québec (CSQ) / Télé-Québec Television Broadcast Employees' Union

c/o Télé-Québec, 1000, rue Fullum, Montréal QC H2K 3L7
Tél: 514-529-2805
sert@colba.net
Aperçu: *Dimension:* petite; *Envergure:* provinciale
Membre(s) du bureau directeur:
Sylvain Leboeuf, Président
sleboeuf@telequebec.tv
Finances: *Budget de fonctionnement annuel:* $100,000-$250,000
Membre: 120 + 1 section locale; *Critères d'admissibilite:* Techniciens

Syndicat des employés énergie électrique Québec, inc. (SEEEQ)

1640, rue Hamilton, Alma QC G8B 4Z1
Tél: 418-668-2560; *Téléc:* 418-668-7969
www.seeeq.qc.ca
Aperçu: *Dimension:* petite; *Envergure:* locale; fondée en 1937
Membre(s) du bureau directeur:
Pierre Simard, Président
president@seeeq.qc.ca

Syndicat des employés et employées des syndicats et des organismes collectifs du Québec (SEESOCQ)

2600, rue de la Jachère, Québec QC G1C 5J9
information@seesocq.org
www.seesocq.org
Aperçu: *Dimension:* petite; *Envergure:* provinciale
Membre(s) du bureau directeur:
Richard Vennes, Président
presidence@seesocq.org
Ginette Boudreau, Trésorerie
tresorerie@seesocq.org
Myriam Lévesque, Secrétaire
secretaire@seesocq.org

Syndicat des enseignantes et enseignants Laurier ***See*** Laurier Teachers Union

Syndicat des enseignants de la Nouvelle-Écosse ***See*** Nova Scotia Teachers Union

Syndicat des fonctionnaires provinciaux et de service de la Colombie-Britannique ***See*** British Columbia Government & Service Employees' Union

Syndicat des infirmières de l'Ile-du-Prince-Édouard ***See*** Prince Edward Island Nurses' Union

Syndicat des infirmières de la Colombie-Britannique ***See*** British Columbia Nurses' Union

Syndicat des infirmières de la Saskatchewan ***See*** Saskatchewan Union of Nurses

Syndicat des infirmières de Terre-Neuve et du Labrador ***See*** Newfoundland & Labrador Nurses' Union

Syndicat des infirmières du Manitoba ***See*** Manitoba Nurses' Union

Syndicat des infirmières et infirmiers du Nouveau-Brunswick ***See*** New Brunswick Nurses Union

Syndicat des infirmières psychiatriques ***See*** Union of Psychiatric Nurses

Syndicat des ouvriers du textile de Magog

15, rue David, Magog QC J1X 2Z2
Tél: 819-843-4420; *Téléc:* 819-843-3320
synditexmagog@qc.aira.com
Nom précédent: Syndicat catholique des ouvriers du textile de Magog
Aperçu: *Dimension:* petite; *Envergure:* locale
Publications:
• STEP Equipment Directory
Type: Directory
Profile: Available in Spanish & Russian

• STEP Newsletter
Type: Newsletter; *Frequency:* Quarterly

Syndicat des pompiers et pompières du Québec (CTC) (SPQ) / Québec Union of Firefighters (CLC)
#3900, 565, boul Crémazie Est, Montréal QC H2M 2V6
Tél: 514-383-4698; *Téléc:* 514-383-6782
Ligne sans frais: 800-461-4698
www.spq-ftq.com
Nom précédent: Québec Federation of Professional Firefighters
Aperçu: *Dimension:* moyenne; *Envergure:* provinciale; fondée en 1945
Affiliation(s): FTQ
Membre(s) du bureau directeur:
Daniel Pépin, Président
dpepin@spq-ftq.com

Syndicat des producteurs de bois du Saguenay-Lac-Saint-Jean
3635, rue Panet, Jonquière QC G7X 8T7
Tél: 418-542-5666; *Téléc:* 418-542-4046
Ligne sans frais: 800-463-9176
info@spbsaglac.qc.ca
www.spbsaglac.qc.ca
Aperçu: *Dimension:* petite; *Envergure:* locale; Organisme sans but lucratif; fondée en 1955
Mission: La mise en marché; l'organisation du transport; l'aménagement; et la mise en application de programmes
Affiliation(s): Fédération des producteurs de bois du Québec
Membre(s) du bureau directeur:
Daniel Fillion, Directeur général
Finances: *Budget de fonctionnement annuel:* Plus de $5 Million*Fonds:* Gouvernement provincial
Membre(s) du personnel: 9; 65 bénévole(s)
Membre: 5 500; *Montant de la cotisation:* 25$

Syndicat des producteurs de chèvres du Québec (SPCQ)
555, boul Roland-Therrien, 4e étage, Longueuil QC J4H 4E7
Tél: 450-679-0540; *Téléc:* 450-463-5293
info@chevreduquebec.com
www.chevreduquebec.com
www.facebook.com/chevresduquebec.spcq
twitter.com/ChevreQC
Aperçu: *Dimension:* petite; *Envergure:* provinciale; fondée en 1982
Mission: Favoriser l'amélioration des revenus des producteurs caprins par le regroupement, la représentation et la défense des intérêts de l'ensemble des producteurs caprins du Québec; valoriser la profession des producteurs de chèvres; développer la production, la commercialisation et les marchés
Affiliation(s): Union des producteurs agricole
Membre(s) du bureau directeur:
Robert Camden, Président
Anass Soussi, Directeur général
Finances: *Fonds:* Ministère de l'Agriculture, Pêcheries et Alimentation
Membre(s) du personnel: 3
Membre: *Critères d'admissibilite:* Producteurs de chèvres; *Comités:* Lait; Boucherie; Mohair
Activités: Représentation des producteurs de chèvres du Québec; *Service de conférenciers:* Oui; *Listes de destinataires:* Oui

Syndicat des producteurs en serre du Québec (SPSQ)
Maison de l'UPA, #100, 555, boul Roland-Therrien, Longueuil QC J4H 3Y9
Tél: 450-679-0540; *Téléc:* 450-463-5296
spsq@upa.qc.ca
www.spsq.info
www.facebook.com/SyndicatDesProducteursEnSerre
twitter.com/SPSQ1
Aperçu: *Dimension:* petite; *Envergure:* locale; Organisme sans but lucratif; fondée en 1974
Mission: Défendre les intérêts des producteurs en serre du Québec
Membre(s) du bureau directeur:
Louis Dionne, Directeur géneral
ldionne@upa.gc.ca
Finances: *Budget de fonctionnement annuel:* $100,000-$250,000
Membre(s) du personnel: 4
Membre: 110; *Montant de la cotisation:* 170$ + superficie (m2) x 0,16$; *Critères d'admissibilite:* Producteur en serre
Activités: Semaine horticole (annuel); activités diverses;

Syndicat des professeures et professeurs de l'Université de Sherbrooke (SPPUS)
2500, boul Université, Sherbrooke QC J1K 2R1
Tél: 819-821-7656; *Téléc:* 819-821-7995
sppus@usherbrooke.ca
www.usherbrooke.ca/sppus
Aperçu: *Dimension:* petite; *Envergure:* locale; fondée en 1973
Mission: Voir à l'application de la convention collective; défendre les intérêts des membres
Affiliation(s): Fédération québécoise des professeures et professeurs d'universités
Membre(s) du bureau directeur:
Robert Tétrault, Secrétaire général
robert.tetrault@usherbrooke.ca
Finances: *Budget de fonctionnement annuel:* $250,000-$500,000
Membre(s) du personnel: 2
Membre: 450; *Critères d'admissibilite:* Professeur régulier; *Comités:* Comité de négociation; Conseil syndical

Syndicat des professeures et professeurs de l'Université du Québec à Chicoutimi (SPPUQAC)
#P2-1000, 555, boul de l'Université, Chicoutimi QC G7H 2B1
Tél: 418-545-5378; *Téléc:* 418-545-6659
sppuqac@uqac.ca
www.uqac.ca/sppuqac
Aperçu: *Dimension:* petite; *Envergure:* provinciale; fondée en 1969
Membre de: Fédération québécoise des professeures et professeurs d'université
Membre(s) du bureau directeur:
Lison Bergeron, Secrétaire
Finances: *Budget de fonctionnement annuel:* $100,000-$250,000
Membre(s) du personnel: 1; 5 bénévole(s)
Membre: 280; *Critères d'admissibilite:* Professeur(e)s

Syndicat des professeures et professeurs de l'Université du Québec à Hull *Voir* Syndicat des professeures et professeurs de l'Université du Québec en Outaouais

Syndicat des professeures et professeurs de l'Université du Québec à Rimouski (SPPUQAR)
#E230, 300, allée des Ursulines, Rimouski QC G5L 3A1
Tél: 418-724-1467; *Téléc:* 418-724-1559
sppuqar@uqar.ca
sppuqar.uqar.ca
Aperçu: *Dimension:* petite; *Envergure:* provinciale
Affiliation(s): Fédération québécoise des professeurs et professeurs d'université; Comité de liaison intersyndical de l'Université du Québec; Cartel intersyndical des régimes de retraite et d'assurances collectives
Membre(s) du bureau directeur:
Anne Giguère, Agente d'Administration
Mélanie Gagnon, Présidente
Membre: *Comités:* Exécutif; Griefs; Paritaire de développement et d'assistance pédagogiques; D'accès des femmes à la carrière professorale; Réseau sur les assurances collectives; Retraite; Institutionnel de suivi de la politique environnementale; Relations professionnelles; Affaires universitaires; Travail sur la modification des questionnaires d'évaluation de l'enseignement

Syndicat des professeures et professeurs de l'Université du Québec en Outaouais (SPUQO) / University of Québec in Hull Faculty Union
Pavillon Lucien Brault, CP 1250, Succ. Hull, 101, rue Saint-Jean-Bosco, Hull QC J8X 3X7
Tél: 819-595-3900; *Téléc:* 819-773-1877
spuqo@uqo.ca
twitter.com/SPUQO
Nom précédent: Syndicat des professeures et professeurs de l'Université du Québec à Hull
Aperçu: *Dimension:* petite; *Envergure:* locale; fondée en 1980 surveillé par Fédération québécoise des professeures et professeurs d'université
Mission: Protection des membres
Membre(s) du bureau directeur:
Elmustapha Najem, Présidente
Finances: *Budget de fonctionnement annuel:* $50,000-$100,000
Membre(s) du personnel: 1
Membre: 181; *Montant de la cotisation:* 1% du salaire; *Critères d'admissibilite:* Professeur, chercheur; *Comités:* Conseil exécutif; relations de travail

Syndicat des professeurs de l'État du Québec (ind.) (SPEQ) / Union of Professors for the Government of Québec (Ind.)
#1003, 2120, rue Sherbrooke Est, Montréal QC H2K 1C3
Tél: 514-525-7979; *Téléc:* 514-525-4655
Ligne sans frais: 877-525-7979
info@speq.org
www.speq.org
Aperçu: *Dimension:* moyenne; *Envergure:* provinciale; fondée en 1965
Mission: Pour représenter les fonctionnaires enseignants salariés.
Membre(s) du bureau directeur:
Claude Tanguay, Président
Membre: 900 + 21 sections locales

Syndicat des professeurs de l'Université Laval / Laval University Faculty Union
Pavillon Louis-Jacques Casault, Université Laval, CP 2208, #3339, 2325, rue de l'Université, Québec QC G1K 7P4
Tél: 418-656-2955; *Téléc:* 418-656-5377
spul@spul.ulaval.ca
www.spul.ulaval.ca
Aperçu: *Dimension:* petite; *Envergure:* locale
Membre(s) du bureau directeur:
Yves Lacouture, Président
Membre: 1 320

Syndicat des professeurs de l'Université Saint Mary *See* Saint Mary's University Faculty Union

Syndicat des professeurs et des professeures de l'Université du Québec à Trois-Rivières
Pavillon Ringuet, CP 500, #1115, 3351, boul des Forges, Trois-Rivières QC G9A 5H7
Tél: 819-376-5011; *Téléc:* 819-376-5209
syndicat_professeurs@uqtr.ca
www.sppuqtr.ca
Aperçu: *Dimension:* petite; *Envergure:* locale; Organisme sans but lucratif; fondée en 1970
Membre de: Fédération québécoise des professeures et professeurs d'université
Membre(s) du bureau directeur:
Pierre Baillargeon, Président
Denise Asselin, Secrétaire
Finances: *Budget de fonctionnement annuel:* $100,000-$250,000
Membre(s) du personnel: 3
Membre: 346; *Critères d'admissibilite:* Ötre professeur régulier de l'UQTR; *Comités:* services à la collectivité; affaires universitaires; préparation à la retraite relations de travail

Syndicat des professeurs et professeures de l'Université du Québec à Montréal (SPUQ)
Pavillon Hubert-Aquin, CP 8888, Succ. Centre-Ville, Montréal QC H3C 3P8
Tél: 514-987-6198; *Téléc:* 514-987-3014
spuq@uqam.ca
www.spuq.uqam.ca
Aperçu: *Dimension:* moyenne; *Envergure:* provinciale; fondée en 1971
Affiliation(s): Confédération des syndicats nationaux
Membre(s) du bureau directeur:
Michèle Nevert, Présidente
nevert.michele@uqam.ca
Pierre Lebuis, Secrétaire
lebuis.pierre@uqam.ca
Mario Houde, Trésorier
houde.mario@uqam.ca
Membre: 1 000

Syndicat des professionnelles et professionnels municipaux de Montréal (SPPMM)
#100, 281, rue Saint-Paul est, Montréal QC H2Y 1H1
Tél: 514-845-9646; *Téléc:* 514-844-3585
sppmm@sppmm.org
www.sppmm.org
Aperçu: *Dimension:* petite; *Envergure:* locale; fondée en 1965
Membre(s) du bureau directeur:
Gisèle Jolin, Présidente
Membre: 1 300; *Comités:* Assurances et les avantages sociaux; Communications; Caisse de retraite; Environnement et de la sécurité; Développement professionnel et productivité

Syndicat des professionnels et des techniciens de la santé du Québec (SPTSQ) / Québec Union of Health Professionals & Technicians

#850, 1001, rue Sherbrooke est, Montréal QC H2L 1L3
Tél: 514-521-4469; *Téléc:* 514-521-0086
Aperçu: *Dimension:* moyenne; *Envergure:* provinciale; Organisme sans but lucratif; fondée en 1973
Mission: Défense des intérêts socio-économiques de ses membres
Affiliation(s): Centrale des professionnelles et professionnels de la santé
Membre(s) du bureau directeur:
Carolle Dubé, Présidente
Finances: *Budget de fonctionnement annuel:* $250,000-$500,000
Membre: 750 + 145 unités; *Critères d'admissibilite:* Techniciens de la santé

Syndicat des salariés du contreplaqué de Sainte-Thérèse

CP 90, 15, boul Labelle, Sainte-Thérèse QC J7E 4H9
Tél: 450-435-6541; *Téléc:* 450-435-3814
info@commonwealthplywood.com
www.commonwealthplywood.com/fr/index.shtml
Aperçu: *Dimension:* petite; *Envergure:* locale
Membre de: Association canadienne du contreplaqué et du placage de bois dur

Syndicat des services du grain (CTC) *See* Grain Services Union (CLC)

Syndicat des services gouvernementaux *See* Government Services Union

Syndicat des technicien(ne)s et artisan(e)s du réseau français de Radio-Canada (ind.) (STARF) / CBC French Network Technicians' Union (Ind.)

1250, rue de la Visitation, Montréal QC H2L 3B4
Tél: 514-524-1100; *Téléc:* 514-524-6023
Ligne sans frais: 888-838-1100
secretariat@starf.qc.ca
www.starf.qc.ca
Aperçu: *Dimension:* moyenne; *Envergure:* nationale
Membre(s) du bureau directeur:
Benoît Celestino, Président
bcelestino@starf.qc.ca
Marie-Lou Faille, Secrétaire-trésorier
mlfaille@starf.qc.ca
Membre: *Comités:* Griefs nationaux; Supérieur inter-unités et comité mixte lettre d'entente 16; Formation; Conciliation travail; Harmonisation RC/PROFAC/STARF; Lettre d'entente 3; Équité en matière d'emplois

Syndicat des technologues en radiologie du Québec (ind.) (STRQ) / Union of Radiology Technicians of Québec

#850, 1001, rue Sherbrooke est, Montréal QC H2L 1L3
Tél: 514-521-4469; *Téléc:* 514-521-0086
Aperçu: *Dimension:* moyenne; *Envergure:* provinciale; fondée en 1965
Mission: Étude, développement et la défense des intérêts professionnels, économiques, sociaux et éducatifs de ses membres et particulièrement la négociation et l'application de conventions collectives.
Membre de: Centrale des Professionnelles et Professionnels de la Santé
Finances: *Budget de fonctionnement annuel:* $500,000-$1.5 Million
Membre(s) du personnel: 3
Membre: 3 050 + 142 units; *Montant de la cotisation:* 1.4% du salaire; *Critères d'admissibilite:* 85% femmes

Syndicat des travailleurs de l'environnement *See* Union of Environment Workers

Syndicat des travailleurs de la construction du Québec (CSD)

#300, 801, 4e rue, Québec QC G1J 2T7
Tél: 418-522-3918; *Téléc:* 418-529-6323
info@csdconstruction.qc.ca
www.csdconstruction.qc.ca
www.facebook.com/csdconstruction
twitter.com/csdconstruction
www.youtube.com/user/LaCSDConstruction
Également appelé: CSD - Construction
Aperçu: *Dimension:* moyenne; *Envergure:* provinciale; fondée en 1972
Mission: Défendre et promouvoir les intérêts sociaux et économiques de ses membres
Affiliation(s): Centrale des syndicats démocratiques
Membre(s) du bureau directeur:
Daniel Laterreur, Président
Guy Terrault, Vice-président
Gilles C. Coulombe, Secrétaire
Membre: *Critères d'admissibilite:* Travailleur en construction

Syndicat des travailleurs du Nord *See* Union of Northern Workers

Syndicat des travailleurs en télécommunications (CTC) *See* Telecommunications Workers' Union (CLC)

Syndicat des travailleurs et travailleuses des postes *See* Canadian Union of Postal Workers

Syndicat des travailleurs marins et de bacs de la Colombie-Britannique (CTC) *See* British Columbia Ferry & Marine Workers' Union (CLC)

Syndicat du Nouveau-Brunswick *See* New Brunswick Union

Syndicat du personnel technique et professionnel de la Société des alcools du Québec (ind.) (SPTP-SAQ) / Québec Liquor Board's Union of Technical & Professional Employees (Ind.)

905, rue de Lorimier, Montréal QC H2K 3V9
Tél: 514-873-5878; *Téléc:* 514-873-5896
intra.sptp-saq.ca
Aperçu: *Dimension:* petite; *Envergure:* provinciale; fondée en 1974
Membre(s) du bureau directeur:
Steve d'Agostino, Président
Patrick Bray, Vice-Président
Hélène Daneault, Directrice
Johanne Morrisseau, Directrice
Lisanne Racine, Directrice
Finances: *Budget de fonctionnement annuel:* $100,000-$250,000
Membre: 691 + 1 section locale; *Comités:* Assurances, communication, conciliation famille-travail, développement durable, dotation, entraide, finances, horaire, mobilisation, partenariat, santé sécurité au travail

Syndicat indépendant des briqueteurs et des maçons du Canada (CTC) *See* Bricklayers, Masons Independent Union of Canada (CLC)

Syndicat international des marins canadiens (FAT-COI/CTC) *See* Seafarers' International Union of Canada (AFL-CIO/CLC)

Syndicat interprovincial des ferblantiers et couvreurs, la section locale 2016 à la FTQ-Construction

#200, 8300, boul Métropolitain Est, Anjou QC H1K 1A2
Tél: 514-374-1515; *Téléc:* 514-448-2265
Ligne sans frais: 866-374-1515
info@ftq2016.org
www.ftq2016.org
Nom précédent: Association nationale des ferblantiers et couvreurs, section locale 2020 (CTC)
Aperçu: *Dimension:* moyenne; *Envergure:* provinciale; fondée en 1982
Mission: Voir à la promotion et à la défense des intérêts économiques et sociaux des membres; assurer l'intégrité du métier de ferblantier et couvreur en défendant sa jurisdiction professionnelle et en assurant sa sécurité d'emploi; représenter les travailleurs, que leur travail soit effectué à l'intérieur du chantier de construction ou non; cultiver des sentiments de solidarité parmis les travailleurs; obtenir des améliorations dans les conditions de travail de ses membres
Membre de: Canadian Labour Congress
Affiliation(s): Fédération des travailleurs et travailleuses du Québec - Construction
Membre(s) du bureau directeur:
Dorima Aubut, Directeur provincial
Membre(s) du personnel: 9
Membre: *Critères d'admissibilite:* Détenir carte de compétence requise

Montréal
#203, 3730, boul. Crémazie Est, Montréal QC H2A 1B4
Tél: 514-374-1515

Québec
#150, 5000, boul. des Gradins, Québec QC G2J 1N3
Tél: 418-624-2122; *Téléc:* 418-948-0798
Ligne sans frais: 866-624-2122
f.bouchard@ftq2016.org
Membre(s) du bureau directeur:
Gilles Caron, Président

Syndicat national de la santé *See* National Health Union

Syndicat national des cultivateurs *See* National Farmers Union

Syndicat national des employés de l'aluminium d'Alma inc.

Métallos local 9490, 830 rue des Pins ouest, Alma QC G8B 7R3
Tél: 418-662-7055; *Téléc:* 418-662-7354
www.staalma.org
Aperçu: *Dimension:* petite; *Envergure:* locale; fondée en 1943
Mission: Défense des membres
Membre de: Métallos local 9490
Membre(s) du bureau directeur:
Patrice Harvey, Président
Membre(s) du personnel: 9
Membre: 871; *Montant de la cotisation:* 1.40%

Syndicat national des employés de l'aluminium d'Arvida, inc.

1932, boul Mellon, Jonquière QC G7S 3H3
Tél: 418-548-4667; *Téléc:* 418-548-7942
www.sneaa.qc.ca
Aperçu: *Dimension:* petite; *Envergure:* locale; fondée en 1937
Membre(s) du bureau directeur:
Alain Gagnon, Président

Syndicat professionnel de la police municipale de Québec *Voir* Fraternité des Policiers et Policières de la Ville de Québec

Syndicat professionnel des diététistes *Voir* Syndicat professionnel des diététistes et nutritionnistes du Québec

Syndicat professionnel des diététistes et nutritionnistes du Québec (SPDNQ) / Québec Professional Union of Dieticians (Ind.)

2665, rue Beaubien est, Montréal QC H1Y 1G8
Tél: 514-725-5535; *Téléc:* 514-725-4433
Nom précédent: Syndicat professionnel des diététistes
Aperçu: *Dimension:* moyenne; *Envergure:* provinciale; fondée en 1970
Membre(s) du bureau directeur:
Claudette Péloquin-Antoun, Présidente
Membre: 1000; *Montant de la cotisation:* 1.5% du salaire; *Critères d'admissibilite:* Diététistes et nutritionnistes

Syndicat professionnel des homéopathes du Québec (SPHQ)

#106, 1600, av de Lorimier, Montréal QC H2K 3W5
Tél: 514-525-2037
Ligne sans frais: 800-465-5788
accueil@sphq.org
www.sphq.org
Aperçu: *Dimension:* petite; *Envergure:* provinciale; Organisme sans but lucratif; fondée en 1989
Membre(s) du bureau directeur:
Martine Jourde, Présidente
Membre(s) du personnel: 1; 7 bénévole(s)
Membre: 300+; *Montant de la cotisation:* 350$; 60$ étudiants; *Critères d'admissibilite:* Professionnels de la santé autonomes pratiquant l'homéopathie
Activités: Semaine de l'homéopathie; conférences; programmes de formation

Syndicat professionnel des ingénieurs d'Hydro-Québec (ind.) (SPIHQ) / Hydro-Québec Professional Engineers Union (Ind.)

#1400, 1255 rue University, Montréal QC H3B 3X1
Tél: 514-845-4239; *Téléc:* 514-845-0082
Ligne sans frais: 800-567-1260
spihq@spihq.qc.ca
www.spihq.qc.ca
Aperçu: *Dimension:* moyenne; *Envergure:* provinciale; fondée en 1964
Mission: Le Syndicat travaille pour la défense & le développement des intérêts économiques, sociaux, & professionnels des membres
Membre(s) du bureau directeur:
Jacqueline Pilote, Chef administration, 514-845-4239 Ext. 112
chefadmin@spihq.qc.ca
Carole Leroux, Présidente, 514-845-4239 Ext. 103
president@spihq.qc.ca

Finances: *Budget de fonctionnement annuel:* $500,000-$1.5 Million
Membre(s) du personnel: 3
Membre: 1 700

Syndicat professionnel des ingénieurs de la Ville de Montréal et de la CUM *Voir* Syndicat professionnel des scientifiques à pratique exclusive de Montréal

Syndicat professionnel des médecins du gouvernement du Québec (ind.) (SPMGQ) / Professional Union of Government of Québec Physicians (Ind.)

1390, rue du Père-Jamet, Sainte-Foy QC G1W 3G5
Tél: 418-266-4670
Aperçu: *Dimension:* petite; *Envergure:* provinciale; Organisme sans but lucratif; Organisme de réglementation; fondée en 1966
Mission: Représenter les médecins à l'emploi du gouvernement du Québec
Membre(s) du bureau directeur:
Christine Gagné, Présidente
Activités: Relations de travail, bien-être des membres;

Syndicat professionnel des scientifiques à pratique exclusive de Montréal (SPSPEM)

CP 96506, Succ. Montréal Gare Centrale, 895 De la Gauchetière ouest, Montréal QC H3B 5J8
secretaire@spspem.org
www.spspem.org
Nom précédent: Syndicat professionnel des ingénieurs de la Ville de Montréal et de la CUM
Aperçu: *Dimension:* petite; *Envergure:* locale
Mission: Établir des relations de travail ordonnées entre l'employeur et les salariés, et entre les membres eux-mêmes; défendre et développer les intérêts économiques, sociaux, moraux et professionnels de ses membres
Membre(s) du bureau directeur:
André Émond, Président
president@spspem.org
Membre: 200; *Critères d'admissibilite:* Ingénieur; arpenteur-géomètre; chimiste et médecin-vétérinaire à l'emploi de la ville de Montréal; société, organisme ou corporation accrédités

Syndicat professionnel des scientifiques de l'IREQ (SPSI)

#2008, 210, boul Montarville, Boucherville QC J4B 6T3
Tél: 450-449-9630; *Téléc:* 450-449-9631
spsi@spsi.qc.ca
www.spsi.qc.ca
Aperçu: *Dimension:* petite; *Envergure:* locale
Membre(s) du bureau directeur:
Michel Trudeau, Président
Membre: *Critères d'admissibilite:* Chercheurs et ingénieurs de l'Institut de recherche d'Hydro-Québec

Syndicat québécois de la construction (SQC) / North Shore Construction Inc. (Ind.)

2121, av Sainte-Anne, Saint-Hyacinthe QC J2S 5H5
Tél: 450-773-8833; *Téléc:* 450-773-2232
Ligne sans frais: 888-773-8834
info@sqc.ca
www.sqc.ca
www.facebook.com/SyndicatQuebecoisConstruction
Nom précédent: Syndicat construction Côte-Nord (ind.)
Aperçu: *Dimension:* moyenne; *Envergure:* provinciale; fondée en 1975
Membre(s) du bureau directeur:
Sylvain Gendron, Président

Syndicates of Co-Ownership Association of Québec *Voir* Association des syndicats de copropriété du Québec

Syrian Canadian Council (SCC)

#100, 5000 W, Jean-Talon St., Montréal QC H4P 1W9
Tel: 514-207-5315
Other Communication: montreal@syriancanadiancouncil.ca
contact@syriancanadiancouncil.ca
syriancanadiancouncil.ca
www.facebook.com/Syrian.Canadian.Council
twitter.com/sccfreedom
Overview: A medium-sized national organization founded in 2011
Mission: SCC is a non-profit organization dedicated to empowering the Syrian Canadian community through active defense of human rights and civil liberty for all Syrians and Canadians
Membership: *Fees:* $40

London Office
#130, 1326 Huron St., London ON N5V 2E2
Tel: 519-852-6353
london@syriancanadiancouncil.ca
Toronto Office
#278, 2325 Hurontario St., Toronto ON L5A 4K4
e-mail: gta@syriancanadiancouncil.ca
Vancouver Office
9040 No. 2 Rd., Richmond BC V7E 2C7
Tel: 778-987-0248
vancouver@syriancanadiancouncil.ca

Système informatisé sur les stagiaires post-MD en formation clinique *See* Canadian Post-MD Education Registry

The T. R. Meighen Foundation

#200, 12 Birch Ave., Toronto ON M4V 1C8
Tel: 416-413-1999; *Fax:* 416-413-0015
www.meighen.ca
Overview: A small provincial charitable organization founded in 1969
Mission: To encourage programs & initiatives that benefit at risk youth & families
Chief Officer(s):
Kate Pilgrim, Administrator
kpilgrim@meighen.ca
Finances: *Funding Sources:* Private donations

Taber & District Chamber of Commerce

4702 - 50 St., Taber AB T1G 2B6
Tel: 403-223-2265; *Fax:* 403-223-2291
tdcofc@telusplanet.net
www.taberchamber.com
Overview: A small local organization
Mission: To promote our businesses & community
Member of: Canadian Chamber of Commerce; Alberta Chamber of Commerce; Chinook Country Tourist Association
Chief Officer(s):
Bruce Warkentin, President
taberchamber.president@telus.net
Finances: *Annual Operating Budget:* $100,000-$250,000; *Funding Sources:* Membership dues; fundraising; events
Staff Member(s): 1; 16 volunteer(s)
Membership: 200; *Fees:* $75+GST
Activities: Trade Show; Rodeo Daze; Cornfest; Midnight Madness; Employment Program; Auction Sale; Small Business Owner of the Year; Outstanding Citizen Award; Shop Local Christmas Jackpot

Table d'Inter-Action du Quartier Peter-McGill

#215-216, 1857 De Maisonneuve Boulevard West, Montréal QC H3H 1J9
Tél: 514-934-2280; *Téléc:* 514-934-1002
interaction_petermcgill@bellnet.ca
petermcgill.org
www.facebook.com/interactionduquartierpetermcgill
Nom précédent: Table du Quartier Peter-McGill
Aperçu: *Dimension:* petite; *Envergure:* locale; fondée en 2003
Mission: Promouvoir un sens d'appartenance au quartier et une participation active à la vie communautaire; créer un lieu de parole pour améliorer la qualité de vie dans le quartier
Membre(s) du bureau directeur:
Stéphane Febbrari, Coordinator

Table de concertation du faubourg Saint-Laurent

250, rue Ontario Est, MontréAl QC H2X 1H4
Tél: 514-288-0404; *Téléc:* 514-288-7643
info@faubourgstlaurent.ca
www.faubourgstlaurent.ca
Aperçu: *Dimension:* petite; *Envergure:* locale; fondée en 1995
Mission: D'informer les citoyens de St Laurent des changements dans la région, ainsi que de veiller à ce que les préoccupations des citoyens soient entendues par les parties concernées
Membre(s) du bureau directeur:
Christine Caron, Coordonnatrice, 514-288-0404, Fax: 514-288-7643
direction@faubourgstlaurent.ca
Membre: 25; *Critères d'admissibilite:* Toute gens qui vie sue faubourg Saint-Laurent; Tout gens qui traille sue faubourg Saint-Laurent; tout groupe qui est impliqué dans des activités à caractère social, économique, éducatif ou culturel

Table des responsables de l'éducation des adultes et de la formation professionnelle des commissions scolaires du Québec (TRÉAQFP)

#210, 125, rue des Commissaires ouest, Québec QC G1K 1M7
Téléc: 418-781-0405
www.treaqfp.qc.ca
Aperçu: *Dimension:* moyenne; *Envergure:* provinciale; fondée en 1975
Membre(s) du bureau directeur:
Louise Dionne, Secrétaire générale, 418-686-4040 Ext. 5351
dionne.louise@treaqfp.qc.ca
Renée Blais, Agente, Développement en formation professionnelle, 418-755-1703
blais.renee@treaqfp.qc.ca
Diane Pouliot, Agente, Développement et de communication, 450-616-0565
pouliot.diane@treaqfp.qc.ca
Johanne Villeneuve, Agente, Bureau, 450-686-4040 Ext. 5350
villeneuve.johanne@treaqfp.qc.ca
Membre: 800

Table du Quartier Peter-McGill *Voir* Table d'Inter-Action du Quartier Peter-McGill

Table Tennis Canada / Tennis de Table Canada

18 Louisa St., Ottawa ON K1R 6Y6
Tel: 613-733-6272; *Fax:* 613-733-7279
ttcan@ttcan.ca
ttcan.ca
Previous Name: Canadian Table Tennis Association
Overview: A medium-sized national organization founded in 1937
Mission: To increase the popularity of the sport of table tennis through programs & activities; to increase participation in table tennis at all levels
Member of: International Table Tennis Federation
Affliation(s): Sports Council of Canada; International Table Tennis Federation
Chief Officer(s):
Tony Kiesenhofer, CEO
tonyk@ttcan.ca
Brian Ash, Director, Marketing
brian@ttcan.ca
Finances: *Annual Operating Budget:* $500,000-$1.5 Million; *Funding Sources:* Sponsorship; membership; government
Staff Member(s): 6
Membership: 20,000; *Committees:* Technical; Administrative
Activities: STIGA Canada Cup; Canadian Championships; Canadian Junior Championships; *Rents Mailing List:* Yes

Table Tennis Yukon

4061 - 4th Ave., Whitehorse YT Y1A 1H1
Tel: 867-668-3358
sportyukon.com/member/table-tennis-yukon
Overview: A small provincial organization overseen by Table Tennis Canada
Mission: To promote the sport of Table Tennis in the Yukon.
Member of: Table Tennis Canada; Sport Yukon
Affliation(s): International Table Tennis Federation
Chief Officer(s):
David Stockdale, President
stockdale@yknet.ca

Taekwondo Canada

#310, 1376 Bank St., Ottawa ON K1H 7Y3
Tel: 613-523-4134; *Fax:* 613-523-6651
info@wtfcanada.com
www.wtfcanada.com
www.facebook.com/Taekwondo.Canada
twitter.com/TKD_Canada
Overview: A medium-sized national organization
Mission: To develop, promote & govern the sport of Taekwondo in Canada.
Chief Officer(s):
Su Hwan Chung, President & Chair
president.wtfcanada@gmail.com
Eva Havaris, Chief Executive Officer
ehavaris@wtfcanada.com
Membership: *Committees:* Para Taekwondo; Audit; Finance; Sanction & Awards; Taekwondo Development; Nominating; Governance; High Performance; Strategic Planning
Activities: National Championships

Taekwondo Manitoba

#121, 1364 McPhillips St., Winnipeg MB R2X 2M4
Tel: 204-925-5682; *Fax:* 204-925-5703
www.taekwondomanitoba.ca
Previous Name: Manitoba Tae Kwon-Do Association
Overview: A small provincial organization
Mission: To promote & govern the sport of Taekwondo in Manitoba.

Chief Officer(s):
Jae Park, President
president@taekwondomanitoba.ca
Membership: *Committees:* Awards & Recognition; Finance; Membership; NCCP; Policy; Strategic Planning; Competition; Nominations; Referee

Tafelmusik Baroque Orchestra & Chamber Choir
PO Box 14, 427 Bloor St. West, Toronto ON M5S 1X7
Tel: 416-964-9562; *Fax:* 416-964-2782
info@tafelmusik.org
www.tafelmusik.org
www.facebook.com/tafelmusik.org?ref=ts
twitter.com/tafelmusik
www.youtube.com/user/tafelmusik1979
Also Known As: Tafelmusik
Overview: A medium-sized local organization founded in 1978 overseen by Orchestras Canada
Mission: Bringing baroque music to Toronto & the world, through concerts, recordings, & a music education programme
Chief Officer(s):
Andy Kenins, Chair
Finances: *Annual Operating Budget:* $1.5 Million-$3 Million
Staff Member(s): 17; 100 volunteer(s)
Membership: 800; *Fees:* Schedule available
Activities: *Internships:* Yes

Tahsis Chamber of Commerce
PO Box 278, 36 Rugged Mountain Rd., Tahsis BC V0P 1X0
Tel: 204-934-6425
info@tahsischamber.com
www.tahsischamber.com
Overview: A small local organization founded in 1938
Member of: BC Chamber of Commerce; Tourism Association of Vancouver Island
Chief Officer(s):
Tony Ellis, President
Silvie Keene, Secretary/Treasurer
Finances: *Annual Operating Budget:* Less than $50,000; *Funding Sources:* Membership dues; sales; municipality
Staff Member(s): 3
Membership: 34; *Fees:* $25 individual; $50 business
Activities: Tahsis Days; Great Walk

Taiwan Entrepreneurs Society Taipei/Toronto
#213, 885 Progress Ave., Toronto ON M1H 3G3
Tel: 416-439-9778; *Fax:* 416-439-9515
service@testt.com
www.testt.com
Overview: A small local organization

Taiwan Trade Center, Vancouver
Park Place, #120, 666 Burrard St., Vancouver BC V6C 2X8
Tel: 604-681-2787; *Fax:* 604-681-9886
vancouver@taitra.org.tw
vancouver.taiwantrade.com.tw
Overview: A medium-sized international organization
Mission: To help Taiwanese businesses & manufacturers grow in the international market
Affliation(s): Taiwan External Trade Development Council
Chief Officer(s):
Scott Yang, Director

Taiwanese Canadian Cultural Society (TCCS)
8853 Selkirk St., Vancouver BC V6P 4J6
Tel: 604-267-0901; *Fax:* 604-267-0903
van-office@tccs.ca
www.tccs.ca
Overview: A small local charitable organization founded in 1991
Mission: To educate & assist new immigrants; to contribute to multiculturalism; to introduce Taiwanese culture to Canadians
Member of: Taiwanese Canadian Cultural Society Collegiate Association
Affliation(s): Multicultural Societies & Service Agencies of BC
Chief Officer(s):
Peter Huang, Office Manager
peter.huang@tccs.ca
Staff Member(s): 4; 100 volunteer(s)
Membership: 3,400 families; *Fees:* $60 family; $48 single; $36 senior/student; *Member Profile:* Taiwanese Canadian immigrants
Activities: Taiwanese Cultural Festival; Lunar New Year in Taiwan Celebration; *Library:* TCCS Library

Tamil Catholic Community of Toronto (TCCT)
10 Parfield Dr., North York ON M1V 1H5
Tel: 416-499-0554
Overview: A small local charitable organization founded in 1987
Mission: To promote the Christian faith while preserving culture & heritage for future generations
Affliation(s): Archdiocese of Toronto
Finances: *Annual Operating Budget:* Less than $50,000
Activities: Pilgrimages; Christian holiday celebrations; seminars;

Tamil Eelam Society of Canada (TEOSC)
#1A, 1160 Birchmount Rd., Toronto ON M1P 2B8
Tel: 416-757-6043; *Fax:* 416-757-6851
ed@tesoc.org
www.tesoc.org
Also Known As: TESOC Multicultural Settlement Services
Overview: A medium-sized national organization founded in 1978
Mission: TESOC is dedicated to providing opportunities and services to newcomers and immigrants from the Tamil community and other ethno cultures. We are also committed to promote smooth integration into Canadian mainstream, by enhancing the lives of newcomers through programs designed for settlement, employment and personal growth.
Finances: *Funding Sources:* Citizenship and Immigration Canada

Tansi Friendship Centre Society
PO Box 418, Chetwynd BC V0C 1J0
Tel: 250-788-2996; *Fax:* 250-788-2353
reception@tansifcs.com
Overview: A small local organization overseen by Food Banks British Columbia
Member of: Food Banks British Columbia

Tanzer 22 Class Association
PO Box 11122, Stn. H, Nepean ON K2H 7T9
e-mail: president@tanzer22.com
www.tanzer22.com
Overview: A small national organization founded in 1971
Mission: To control quality & modifications in manufacture of Tanzer 22 yacht; To conduct social activities, including regional & local (fleet) meetings during winter, regattas & cruises during the summer; To provide technical help to all owners of Tanzer sail boats
Affliation(s): Canadian Yachting Association; United States Sailing Association
Finances: *Annual Operating Budget:* Less than $50,000
Staff Member(s): 1; 5 volunteer(s)
Membership: 400; *Fees:* $25; *Member Profile:* Owners of Tanzer 22 yachts + any other Tanzer sailboat owners

Tara Canada
PO Box 15270, Vancouver BC V6B 5B1
Tel: 604-298-4322
Toll-Free: 888-278-8272
information@taracanada.org
www.taracanada.org
Overview: A small national charitable organization
Mission: To provide information on the emergence of Maitreya, the World Teacher, & on transmission meditation, a specialized form of group meditation
Activities: *Speaker Service:* Yes

Taras H. Shevchenko Museum & Memorial Park Foundation
1614 Bloor St. West, Toronto ON M6P 1A7
Tel: 416-534-8662; *Fax:* 416-535-1063
shevchenkomuseum@bellnet.ca
www.infoukes.com/shevchenkomuseum
Also Known As: Shevchenko Museum
Overview: A small local organization founded in 1952
Mission: To perpetuate the memory & humanist philosophy of Taras Hryhorovich Shevchenko, (1814-1861), foremost poet, artist & revolutionary democrat of Urkaine, & to relate the conditions & contributions of the original Ukrainian immigration to Canada which began in 1891
Member of: Association of United Ukrainian Canadians
Affliation(s): Ontario Museum Association; Ontario Historical Society; Heritage Toronto
Chief Officer(s):
William Harasym, President, 416-762-9129
Finances: *Annual Operating Budget:* Less than $50,000
Staff Member(s): 1; 30 volunteer(s)
Membership: 1-99; *Committees:* Executive
Activities: AGM & monthly meetings; hosting visitors; special exhibitions; raising funds; Shevchenko's Birth, Museum Anniversary, March 9 & Sept. 8; *Speaker Service:* Yes; *Library:* Shevchenko Library; Open to public

Tarragon Theatre
30 Bridgman Ave, Toronto ON M5R 1X3
Tel: 416-531-1827
info@tarragontheatre.com
www.tarragontheatre.com
www.facebook.com/tarragontheatre
twitter.com/tarragontheatre
Overview: A small local charitable organization founded in 1971
Mission: To develop & produce new Canadian plays
Affliation(s): Professional Association of Canadian Theatres
Chief Officer(s):
Richard Rose, Artistic Director
Laura Dinner, President
Giles Meikle, Treasurer
Staff Member(s): 22

Taste of Nova Scotia
#240, 33 Ochterloney St., Dartmouth NS B2Y 4P5
Tel: 902-492-9291; *Fax:* 902-492-9286
Toll-Free: 800-281-5507
taste@tasteofnovascotia.com
www.tasteofnovascotia.com
www.facebook.com/TasteofNS
twitter.com/TasteofNS
www.youtube.com/user/TasteofNS
Overview: A small provincial organization
Mission: To promote its members & Nova Scotia as a leader in high quality culinary experiences.
Chief Officer(s):
Janice Ruddock, Executive Director
janice@tasteofnovascotia.com
Staff Member(s): 6
Membership: 140; *Member Profile:* Agricultural businesses; wineries; breweries; chocolate makers; meat & fish processors; jam & maple syrup producers & baked goods

Tavistock Chamber of Commerce
PO Box 670, Tavistock ON N0B 2R0
Tel: 519-655-2700
www.tavistock.on.ca/chamber.html
Overview: A small local organization
Chief Officer(s):
Andrew Raymer, President
araymer@dundeewealth.com
Membership: 25

TB Vets
1410 Kootenay St., Vancouver BC V5K 4R1
Tel: 604-874-5626
Toll-Free: 888-874-5626; *TTY:* 604-294-5610
info@tbvets.org
www.tbvets.org
twitter.com/tbvets
Overview: A medium-sized provincial charitable organization founded in 1946
Mission: Operates a key return service, with proceeds & donations going to respiratory disease research, treatments & education; annually sends out over 350,000 keytags to BC residents
Chief Officer(s):
Kandys Merola, Chair
Neil Mackie, General Manager
Finances: *Annual Operating Budget:* $1.5 Million-$3 Million; *Funding Sources:* Donations; Sponsorships
Publications:
• TB Vets e-newsletter
Type: Newsletter; *Frequency:* Quarterly

TD Friends of the Environment Foundation / Fondation des amis de l'environnement TD
TD Tower, 66 Wellington St., 17th Fl., Ottawa ON M5K 1A2
Toll-Free: 800-361-5333
tdfef@td.com
www.fef.td.com
Previous Name: Friends of the Environment Foundation
Overview: A medium-sized national charitable organization founded in 1990
Mission: To protect & preserve the Canadian environment
Chief Officer(s):
Natasha Alleyne-Martin, Manager, National Programs, 416-308-5047
natasha.martin@td.com
Ellen Dungen, Regional Manager, Saskatchewan & Manitoba
ellen.dungen@td.com
Cathy Jowsey, Regional Manager, Northern & Eastern Ontario
cathy.jowsey@td.com

Mandip Kharod, Regional Manager, British Columbia, Alberta, Yukon, & Northwest Territories
mandip.kharod@td.com
Amelie Picher, Regional Manager, Québec
amelie.picher@td.com
Yvetter Scrivener, Regional Manager, Central & Southwestern Ontario
yvette.scrivener@td.com
Farzana Syed, Regional Manager, Greater Toronto Area, Surrounding Region, & Atlantic Provinces
farzana.syed@td.com
Finances: *Funding Sources:* Donations
Membership: 1,000+
Activities: *Speaker Service:* Yes

Tea Association of Canada (TAC) / Association du thé du Canada

#602, 133 Richmond St. West, Toronto ON M5H 2L3
Tel: 416-510-8647
info@tea.ca
www.tea.ca
www.facebook.com/teaassociationofcanada
twitter.com/Canadatea
Overview: A medium-sized national organization founded in 1991
Mission: To represent & advance the interests of Canada's tea industry to all levels of government in an effort to improve the conditions under which the industry operates & to promote better business relations between the industry's players
Chief Officer(s):
Louise Roberge, President
Finances: *Funding Sources:* Membership fees; events
Membership: 1-99; *Fees:* Schedule available; *Member Profile:* Tea producing countries; tea packers; importers; retailers; businesses involved with tea trade; people who have completed the tea sommelier program; students enrolled in the tea sommelier program; people who are considering going into the tea business
Activities: *Internships:* Yes

Teachers of Home Economics Specialist Association

c/o G.W. Graham Middle-Secondary School, 45955 Thomas Rd., Chilliwack BC V2R 0B5
Tel: 604-847-0772; *Fax:* 604-824-0711
thesa.membership@gmail.com
www.bctf.ca/thesa
Overview: A small provincial organization
Member of: BC Teachers' Federation
Chief Officer(s):
Paula Aquino, President
Membership: *Fees:* Schedule available

Teaching Support Staff Union (TSSU)

Academic Quadrangle, Simon Fraser University, #5129/5130, 8888 University Dr., Burnaby BC V5A 1S6
Tel: 778-782-4735
tssu@tssu.ca
www.tssu.ca
www.facebook.com/TSSU.ca
twitter.com/TSSU
Overview: A medium-sized local organization founded in 1978
Mission: To represent teaching support staff during collective bargaining agreements & in employee-employer conflicts.
Affliation(s): Vancouver & District Labour Council
Chief Officer(s):
Melissa Roth, Organizer
Finances: *Funding Sources:* Membership dues
Membership: *Member Profile:* Tutor markers; sessional instructors; language instructors & teaching assistants; *Committees:* Finanace; Internal Relations; Social Justice; Grievance; Membership Mobilization; Executive; Steward's; Contract; General Membership

TEAL Manitoba

c/o Manitoba Teachers' Society, 191 Harcourt St., Winnipeg MB R3J 3H2
e-mail: dianaturner@shaw.ca
www.tealmanitoba.ca
Also Known As: Teachers of English as a Second Language in Manitoba
Previous Name: TESL Manitoba
Overview: A medium-sized provincial organization overseen by TESL Canada Federation
Chief Officer(s):
Kim Hewlett, President

Membership: *Fees:* $35-$45; $25 para-professional/assistant/volunteer; $20 student

Team Handball Ontario (THO)

Toronto ON
e-mail: info@handballontario.com
www.handballontario.com
www.facebook.com/TeamHandballOntario
Overview: A medium-sized provincial organization
Mission: To represent team handball in Ontario
Chief Officer(s):
Nick Cuddemi, President
Membership: *Fees:* $200 full4 $125 half season; $10 per drop in session; $25 social

TEAM of Canada Inc. (TEAM)

#372 - 16 Midlake Blvd. SE, Calgary AB T2X 2X7
Tel: 403-248-2344; *Fax:* 403-207-6025
Toll-Free: 800-295-4160
info@team.org
www.teamcanada.org
www.facebook.com/125163240888381
twitter.com/team
instagram.com/teammissions
Also Known As: The Evangelical Alliance Mission of Canada Inc.
Overview: A medium-sized international charitable organization founded in 1969
Mission: To help churches send missionaries to establish reproducing churches among the nations, to the Glory of God
Member of: Canadian Council of Christian Charities
Chief Officer(s):
Robert Hodge, Chairman
Scott Henson, Interim CEO
Finances: *Annual Operating Budget:* $1.5 Million-$3 Million
Staff Member(s): 6
Membership: 1-99
Activities: *Internships:* Yes; *Speaker Service:* Yes; *Library:* Resource Centre

Teamsters Canada (CLC) (TC)

#804, 2540, boul Daniel Johnson, Laval QC H7T 2S3
Tél: 450-682-5521; *Téléc:* 450-681-2244
Ligne sans frais: 866-888-6466
lantonin@teamsters.ca
www.teamsters-canada.org
www.facebook.com/TeamstersCanada
twitter.com/TeamstersCanada
twitter.com/TCYC1
Aperçu: *Dimension:* grande; *Envergure:* nationale; Organisme sans but lucratif; fondée en 1976
Affliation(s): International Brotherhood of Teamsters
Membre(s) du bureau directeur:
Robert Bouvier, Président
Don McGill, Vice-président, International
Tom Fraser, Vice-président, International
Finances: *Budget de fonctionnement annuel:* Plus de $5 Million
Membre(s) du personnel: 24
Membre: 125 000; 32 sections locales; *Montant de la cotisation:* barème; *Comités:* Youth
Prix, Bouses:
• The James R. Hoffa Memorial Scholarship Fund (Bourse d études)
Deadline: March 31 *Amount:* $1,000-$10,000

Central Region
Airway Centre, Phase 1, #252, 5945 Airport Rd., 2nd Fl., Mississauga ON L4V 1R9
Tel: 905-678-6652; *Fax:* 905-678-6178
www.teamsters.ca
Membre(s) du bureau directeur:
Ken Dean, Representative

Western Region
#204, 1867 West Broadway, Vancouver BC V6J 4W1
Tel: 604-736-3517; *Fax:* 604-736-3518
Membre(s) du bureau directeur:
Grant Coleman, Organizer

Teamsters Canada Rail Conference (TCRC) / Conference ferroviaire de Teamsters Canada (CFTC)

#1710, 130 Albert St., Ottawa ON K1P 5G4
Tel: 613-235-1828; *Fax:* 613-235-1069
info@teamstersrail.ca
www.teamstersrail.ca
Previous Name: Brotherhood of Locomotive Engineers
Overview: A medium-sized national organization
Chief Officer(s):
Rex Beatty, President
Staff Member(s): 1
Membership: 16,000 in 21 divisions; *Fees:* $15
Activities: *Library*

Teamwork Children's Services International

5983 Ladyburn Cres., Mississauga ON L5M 4V9
Tel: 905-542-1047
jchacha@teamworkchildrenservices.com
www.teamworkchildrenservices.com
Overview: A small international charitable organization
Mission: To provide orphaned & disadvantaged children in rural areas of Africa a safe & secure faith-based home environment; To provide the children with good health, education, & vocational training, enabling them to become self-supporting & productive citizens
Chief Officer(s):
Joel Chacha, Program Director
Finances: *Funding Sources:* Donations

The technical society of the Canadian Nuclear Association (CNA) *See* Canadian Nuclear Society

Technion Canada

#206, 970 Lawrence Ave. West, Toronto ON M6A 3B6
Tel: 416-789-4545; *Fax:* 416-789-0255
Toll-Free: 800-935-8864
info@technioncanada.org
www.technioncanada.org
www.linkedin.com/groups/Canadian-Technion-Society-4351525/about?trk=an
www.facebook.com/pages/Canadian-Technion-Society/120072721377514
Previous Name: Canadian Technion Society
Overview: A medium-sized national organization founded in 1943
Mission: To support Technion Israel Institute of Technology; to promote exchange of scientific information between Israel & Canada, scholarships, research, etc.
Chief Officer(s):
Marvin Ostin, National President
Cheryl Koperwas, National Executive Director
Edward Nagel, National Vice-President
Staff Member(s): 7
Membership: 5,000; *Fees:* $100
Activities: *Speaker Service:* Yes

Calgary Office
Tel: 403-238-5509
kaplanr@shaw.ca
www.technioncanada.org
Mission: To promote Canadian development and use of Technion educational facilities. The association supports those educators and scientists from Canada participating in Technion operations, as well as their Technion counter-parts involved in the exchange of scientific information and products of technical research and development.
Chief Officer(s):
Sandy Hurwitz, Director

Montréal Office
#3435, 6900 boul. Décarie, Montréal QC H3X 2T8
Tel: 514-735-5541; *Fax:* 514-737-9222
montreal@technioncanada.org
www.technioncanada.org
Mission: To promote Canadian development and use of Technion educational facilities. The group supports those educators and scientists from Canada participating in Technion operations, as well as their Technion counter-parts involved in the exchange of scientific information and products of technical research and development.
Chief Officer(s):
Anne Kalles, Director

TechnoCentre éolien / Wind Energy TechnoCentre

70, rue Bolduc, Gaspé QC G4X 1G2
Tél: 418-368-6162; *Téléc:* 418-368-4315
info@eolien.qc.ca
www.eolien.qc.ca
twitter.com/TCEolien
Aperçu: *Dimension:* petite; *Envergure:* provinciale; fondée en 2000
Mission: Le TechnoCentre éolien a pour mission de contribuer au développement d'une filière industrielle éolienne québécoise, compétitive à l'échelle nord-américaine et internationale, tout en mettant en valeur la Gaspésie-Iles-de-la-Madeleine au cour de ce créneau émergeant de l'économie du Québec.
Membre(s) du bureau directeur:

Frédéric Côté, directeur général
fcote@eolien.qc.ca
Meetings/Conferences: • 9e Colloque de l'industrie éolienne québécoise / Québec's 9th Wind Energy Conference, juin, 2015, Carleton-sur-Mer, QC
Scope: Provincial
Attendance: 200
Description: Les enjeux de la filière éolienne et l'innovation sous toutes ses formes sont au cour même de l'événement.
Contact Information: Twitter: twitter.com/TCEolien

TECHNOCompétences
#350, 550, rue Sherbrooke ouest, Montréal QC H3A 1B9
Tél: 514-840-1237
www.technocompetences.qc.ca
Aperçu: *Dimension:* moyenne; *Envergure:* provinciale; Organisme sans but lucratif
Mission: Favoriser le développement de la main-d'oeuvre et de l'emploi dans le secteur des technologies de l'information et des communications
Membre(s) du bureau directeur:
Sylvie Gagnon, Directrice générale

Technologies du développement durable Canada *See* Sustainable Development Technology Canada

TechNova
#308, 202 Brownlow Ave., Dartmouth NS B3B 1T5
Tel: 902-463-3236; *Fax:* 902-465-7567
Toll-Free: 866-723-8867
info@technova.ca
www.technova.ca
twitter.com/NSTechNova
Also Known As: Society of Certified Engineering Technicians & Technologists of Nova Scotia
Overview: A medium-sized provincial licensing organization founded in 1967 overseen by Canadian Council of Technicians & Technologists
Mission: To certify engineering & applied science technicians & technologists for the betterment of the public & the welfare of the environment
Chief Officer(s):
Eric Jury, President
Joe Simms, Executive Officer
Finances: *Funding Sources:* Memberships
Staff Member(s): 2
Membership: 1,357; *Fees:* $165 active; $110 associate; $75 non-active/retired; *Member Profile:* Technicians & technologists; *Committees:* Awards; Bylaw Enforcement

Tecumseh Community Development Corporation
311 Jubilee Rd., RR#1, Muncey ON N0L 1Y0
Tel: 519-289-2122; *Fax:* 519-289-5550
Toll-Free: 888-433-1533
info@tcdc.on.ca
www.tcdc.on.ca
Overview: A small local organization
Mission: To make available financial & management services to aboriginal entrepreneurs
Affliation(s): London District Chiefs Council
Chief Officer(s):
Caroline Ortiz, President
Finances: *Annual Operating Budget:* $250,000-$500,000
Staff Member(s): 5
Activities: *Library:* Seven Bands Community Futures Library; Open to public

Tecumseh Historical Society *See* Naval Museum of Alberta Society

Tecumseth & West Gwillimbury Historical Society
PO Box 171, Bond Head ON L0G 1B0
e-mail: pblackstock@sympatico.ca
stellent.ntpl.ca/historicalsociety/index.htm
Overview: A small local organization
Chief Officer(s):
P Blackstock, Contact

Tekeyan Armenian Cultural Association
825, rue Manoogian, Saint-Laurent QC H4N 1Z5
Tel: 514-747-6680; *Fax:* 514-747-6162
centretekeyan@bellnet.ca
Overview: A small local organization
Chief Officer(s):
Berge Manookian, Président

Tel-Aide Outaouais (TAO)
CP 7218, Succ. Vanier, Ottawa ON K1L 8E3
Tél: 819-776-2649; *Téléc:* 888-765-7040
info@tel-aide-outaouais.org
www.tel-aide-outaouais.org
Aperçu: *Dimension:* petite; *Envergure:* locale; Organisme sans but lucratif; fondée en 1974
Mission: Offrir un service d'écoute téléphonique en français pour toute personne ayant besoin d'aide, de soutien et de référence; développer et offrir des services d'écoute en français pour la population de l'Outaouais et de l'Ontario; favoriser l'implication sociale de la communauté par le biais du bénévolat; sensibiliser et éduquer le public à la nécessité d'être à l'écoute des gens vivant dans la détresse; susciter et entretenir des partenariats avec des organismes du milieu de la santé et des services sociaux; promouvoir les services de Tel-Aide Outaouais auprès de la population
Membre de: Ontario Association of Distress Centres; Association québécois de suicidologie
Affliation(s): Regroupement des organismes communautaires en santé mentale de l'Outaouais
Finances: *Budget de fonctionnement annuel:* $100,000-$250,000
Membre(s) du personnel: 4; 70 bénévole(s)
Membre: 10 doyen/membre à vie + 7 particuliers +; *Montant de la cotisation:* 20$
Activités: *Stagiaires:* Oui; *Service de conférenciers:* Oui

Telecare Distress Centre Brampton *See* Spectra Community Support Services

Telecommunications Employees Association of Manitoba (TEAM)
#200, 1 Wesley Ave., Winnipeg MB R3C 4C6
Tel: 204-984-9470; *Fax:* 204-231-2809
Toll-Free: 877-984-9470
team@teamunion.mb.ca
www.teamunion.mb.ca
www.facebook.com/teamunion161
twitter.com/teamunion161
Overview: A medium-sized provincial organization founded in 1972
Mission: To promote the interests of members; To advance the economic & social welfare of members
Chief Officer(s):
Misty Hughes-Newman, President
m.hughes-newman@teamunion.mb.ca
Bob Linsdell, Executive Director, 204-984-9471
bob.linsdell@teamunion.mb.ca
Wesley Emerson, Officer, Labour Relations, 204-984-9473
wesley.emerson@teamunion.mb.ca
Darlene Buan, Secretary
d.buan@teamunion.mb.ca
Membership: *Committees:* Communications; Finance; Governance; Pay & Benefits; Grievance
Activities: Presenting TEAM scholarships

Telecommunications Workers' Union (CLC) (TWU) / Syndicat des travailleurs en télécommunications (CTC) (STT)
Head Office, 5261 Lane St., Burnaby BC V5H 4A6
Tel: 604-437-8601; *Fax:* 604-435-7760
twu@twu-stt.ca
www.twu-stt.ca
Overview: A medium-sized national organization founded in 1980
Mission: To represent communications workers & workers in related fields
Affliation(s): Canadian Labour Congress; National Alliance of Communications Workers
Chief Officer(s):
Lee Riggs, President
Lee.Riggs@twu-stt.ca
Betty Carrasco, Vice-President
Betty.Carrasco@twu-stt.ca
Colin Brehaut, Secretary-Treasurer
colin.brehaut@twu-stt.ca
Membership: *Committees:* Constitution; Education; Finance; Convention; Pension; Clerical Job Classifications / Evaluations; Employment Equity; Health & Benefit Plan Trustees; Human Rights; Clerical Steering; Plant Steering; Technology; Contracting Out, Monitoring, & Action; Gay, Lesbian, Bisexual, Transgendered; National Health & Safety; Language & Cultural; Operator Services Steering; Political Action; Youth; Alberta (AFL); Ontario (OFL); British Columbia (BC FED); Quebec (FTQ); Canadian Labour Congress (CLC)
Activities: Negotiating collective agreements; Promoting fair wages; Protecting & improving benefits & working conditions

Telecommunities Canada Inc.
c/o President, #318, 210-1600 Kenaston Blvd., Winnipeg MB R3P 0Y4
www.tc.ca
Overview: A small national organization
Mission: To ensure that all Canadians are able to participate in community-based communications & electronic information services by promoting and supporting local community network initiatives; to represent & promote Canadian community networking movement at the national & international level
Chief Officer(s):
Clarice Leader, President
cleader@mb.e-association.ca

TelecomPioneers of Alberta
18 Primrose Place North, Lethbridge AB T1H 4K1
Tel: 403-329-3462
Also Known As: Chapter 46
Overview: A small provincial organization overseen by TelecomPioneers of Canada
Chief Officer(s):
Stan Mills, Manager
stananddee@shaw.ca

TelecomPioneers of Canada
PO Box 880, Halifax NS B3J 2W3
Fax: 902-484-5189
Toll-Free: 888-994-3232
www.telecompioneers.ca
Overview: A medium-sized national organization overseen by TelecomPioneers
Mission: The TelecomPioneers of Canada is a network of current and former telecom industry employees, their partners and their families and are commited to improving the quality of life in Canada's communities.
Chief Officer(s):
J. Michael Sears, President
Michael.sears@canadianpioneers.ca
Membership: *Fees:* $22

Telemiracle/Kinsmen Foundation Inc.
2217C Hanselman Ct., Saskatoon SK S7L 6A8
Tel: 306-244-6400; *Fax:* 306-653-5730
www.telemiracle.com
www.facebook.com/pages/Telemiracle/187556325811
twitter.com/Telemiracle
Overview: A small local charitable organization
Mission: To provide special needs equipment & medical assistance to people in Saskatchewan
Chief Officer(s):
Lori Klassen, Administrative Clerk

Telephone Aid Line Kingston (TALK)
PO Box 1325, Kingston ON K7L 5C6
Tel: 613-531-8529; *Fax:* 613-531-3312; *Crisis Hot-Line:* 613-544-1771
talk@kingston.net
www.telephoneaidlinekingston.com
www.facebook.com/228954140557393
Overview: A small local organization founded in 1973 overseen by Distress Centres Ontario
Mission: To aim to meet the needs of a diverse population by providing an empowering, empathetic, & safe environment through a phone service, community outreach, & education
Chief Officer(s):
Samuel DeKoven, Executive Director
Finances: *Funding Sources:* Grants; Donations
Activities: *Speaker Service:* Yes

Telephone Historical Centre (THC)
Prince of Wales Armouries Heritage Centre, PO Box 188, Stn. Main, #10440, 108 Ave., Edmonton AB T5J 2J1
Tel: 780-433-1010; *Fax:* 780-426-1876
thc3@telus.net
www.telephonehistoricalcentre.com
www.facebook.com/149652501779810
Previous Name: Edmonton Telephone Historical Information Centre Foundation
Overview: A small local charitable organization founded in 1987
Mission: To achieve the acquistion, researching, organization, documentation, display & storage of historical materials relating to the telephone in Edmonton & development of telephone technology in general; to preserve artifact/archival materials for historic documentation of local technological change in the telephone industry; to serve as a research resource for scholars & students, & as educational tool for the public, employees in the telecommunications industry & school children

Member of: Alberta Museums Association; Canadian Museums Association; International Association of Transport & Communications Museums
Affiliation(s): Canadian Association of Science Centres; AMA; CMA; IATM
Finances: *Annual Operating Budget:* $50,000-$100,000; *Funding Sources:* Corporations; membership dues; fundraising; grants
Staff Member(s): 3; 25 volunteer(s)
Membership: 130; *Fees:* By donation; *Member Profile:* Retired industry professionals; *Committees:* Fundraising; Programs; Volunteer Coordination
Activities: Collects & exhibits telephone artifacts; school programs; antique telephone show; *Awareness Events:* Science & Technology Week; *Library* Open to public by appointment

Télé-Québec Television Broadcast Employees' Union ***Voir*** Syndicat des employés en radio-télédiffusion de Télé-Québec (CSQ)

Television Bureau of Canada, Inc. (TVB) / Bureau de la télévision du Canada
#1005, 160 Bloor St. East, Toronto ON M4W 1B9
Tel: 416-923-8813; *Fax:* 416-413-3879
Toll-Free: 800-231-0051
tvb@tvb.ca
www.tvb.ca
twitter.com/TVB_CA
Also Known As: TVB of Canada Inc.
Overview: A medium-sized national organization founded in 1962
Mission: To promote sales, marketing & research of commercial television industry in Canada
Member of: Broadcast Executive Society; Broadcast Research Council
Affiliation(s): Television Bureau of Advertising - New York, USA
Chief Officer(s):
Rita Fabian, Chair
Theresa Treutler, President & CEO
Rhonda-Lynn Bagnall, Director, Telecaster Services
Duncan Robertson, Director, Media Insights & Research
Finances: *Funding Sources:* Membership, research & event fees
Staff Member(s): 18
Membership: 150+; *Fees:* Based on advertising revenues; *Member Profile:* Television networks, stations & representative organizations; *Committees:* Sales; Research; Digital
Activities: *Library* by appointment

Montréal Branch Office
7301, rue Beaubien Est, Montréal QC H1M 3X3
Tel: 514-284-0425
tvb@bellnet.ca
www.tvb.ca
Chief Officer(s):
Lyse Groleau, Senior Coordinator
lgroleau@tvb.ca

TELUS Professional Employees Union (Ind.) ***Voir*** Syndicat des agents de maîtrise de TELUS (ind.)

The Tema Conter Memorial Trust
PO Box 265, King City ON L7B 1A0
Fax: 905-893-1574
Toll-Free: 888-288-8036
info@tema.ca
www.tema.ca
www.linkedin.com/groups/Heroes-Are-Human-Tema-Conter-1569977
www.facebook.com/HeroesAreHuman
twitter.com/TEMATrust
www.youtube.com/tematrust
Overview: A small local organization
Mission: To educate emergency care workers about critical incident stress & post-traumatic stress disorder
Chief Officer(s):
Vince Savoia, Executive Director
Staff Member(s): 10
Awards:
• The Tema Conter Memorial Award (Scholarship)
To honor the memory of Tema Conter who was brutally raped & murdered in her Toronto apartment

Temagami & District Chamber of Commerce
PO Box 57, Stn. T, 7 Lakeshore Dr., Temagami ON P0H 2H0
Tel: 705-569-3344; *Fax:* 705-569-3344
Toll-Free: 800-661-7609
info@temagamiinformation.com
temagamiinformation.com
www.facebook.com/pages/Temagami-Chamber-of-Commerce/220034348098435
Overview: A small local organization founded in 1947
Member of: Ontario Chamber of Commerce; Almaguin Nipissing Travel Association
Chief Officer(s):
Ann Richmond, Office Manager
Hendrika Krygsman, President
Staff Member(s): 1
Membership: 1-99
Activities: Information centre; events; promotion of business & tourism; *Library:* Temagami Public Library

Temiskaming Cattlemen's Association (TCA)
RR#1, Belle Vallee ON P0J 1A0
Tel: 705-647-6860
bradie@parolink.net
www.cattle.guelph.on.ca/local/Temiskaming.asp
Overview: A small local organization
Mission: To provide dialogue between members & provincial agencies; to relay & discuss information on production, marketing & management; to direct & support promotion activities & policies
Member of: Ontario Cattlemen's Association
Chief Officer(s):
Brad Noyes, President, 705-647-6860
bradie@parolink.net
Mark Robilliard, Director
Staff Member(s): 1; 10 volunteer(s)
Membership: 150 individual

Temiskaming Environmental Action Committee (TEAC)
PO Box 541, New Liskeard ON P0J 1P0
Tel: 705-678-2404; *Fax:* 705-647-7511
Overview: A small local organization
Mission: To raise public awareness of environmental issues
Affiliation(s): Northwatch; Public Concern Temiskaming; Ontario Environmental Network
Chief Officer(s):
Terry Graves, Contact
Activities: *Speaker Service:* Yes

Temiskaming Law Association
PO Box 3020, 393 Main St., Haileybury ON P0J 1K0
Tel: 705-672-5655; *Fax:* 705-672-5070
Toll-Free: 877-672-5655
temk-law@ntl.sympatico.ca
Overview: A small local organization
Chief Officer(s):
Jackie Lefebvre, Library Assistant

Temiskaming Multiple Births / Naissances multiples Temiskaming
PO Box 2331, New Liskeard ON P0J 1P0
Toll-Free: 866-228-8824
temiskaming@multiplebirthscanada.org
www.temiskamingmultiplebirths.com
Overview: A small local organization founded in 1985 overseen by Multiple Births Canada

TemiskamingShores & Area Chamber of Commerce (TSACC)
PO Box 811, 883356 Hwy. 65 East, New Liskeard ON P0J 1P0
Tel: 705-647-5771; *Fax:* 705-647-8633
Toll-Free: 866-947-5753
info@tsacc.ca
www.tsacc.ca
www.facebook.com/Temiskaming.Shores.Area.Chamber
Previous Name: Tri-Town & District Chamber of Commerce
Overview: A small local organization
Member of: Ontario Chamber of Commerce
Chief Officer(s):
Lois Weston-Bernstein, Executive Director
manager@tsacc.ca
Staff Member(s): 2; 12 volunteer(s)
Membership: 235; *Fees:* $85-$345

Temple de la renommée des sports d'Ottawa ***See*** Ottawa Sports Hall of Fame Inc.

Temple de la renommée des sports du Canada ***See*** Canada's Sports Hall of Fame

Temple de la renommée olympique du Canada ***See*** Canadian Olympic Hall of Fame

Temple de la renommée sportive du N.-B. ***See*** New Brunswick Sports Hall of Fame

Tempus International ***See*** The Mighty Pen

Tennessee Walking Horse Association of Western Canada (TWHAWC)
c/o Ethel Mankow, Site 427, Box 1, Comp 4, RR#1, Drayton Valley AB T7A 2A1
www.twhawc.com
Overview: A small local organization founded in 1998
Mission: To promote the Tennessee Walking Horse breed in western Canada
Affiliation(s): Alberta Equestrian Federation; Tennessee Walking Horse Breeders' & Exhibitors' Association
Chief Officer(s):
Brent Bachman, President
bachman1@telusplanet.net
Lisa Adams, Vice-President
Koren LeVoir, Secretary
klmedia@shaw.ca
Ethel Mankow, Treasurer
mankow@live.com
Membership: *Fees:* $10 youth members; $25 single members; $40 family membership; *Member Profile:* Tennessee Walking Horse enthusiasts in western Canada
Activities: Sponsoring gaited clinics & shows; Organizing group trail rides; Arranging displays for local trade & equine fairs; Posting show results; Hosting regular membership meetings; Providing networking opportunities with other Walking Horse owners
Publications:
• Tennessee Walking Horse Association of Western Canada
Type: Newsletter
Profile: Issued every 2 months, featurring association activities & announcements

Tennis BC (TBC)
#204, 210 West Broadway, Vancouver BC V5Y 3W2
Tel: 604-737-3086; *Fax:* 604-737-3124
tbc@tennisbc.org
www.tennisbc.org
www.facebook.com/189016975927
twitter.com/TennisBC
www.youtube.com/user/TennisBC1
Previous Name: British Columbia Tennis Association
Overview: A medium-sized provincial organization founded in 1978 overseen by Tennis Canada
Member of: Tennis Performance Association (TPA); Tennis Canada
Chief Officer(s):
Sarah Dunbar, President
Sue Griffin, Executive Director
sue@tennisbc.org
Finances: *Funding Sources:* Government Sponsors; Tennis Canada; Sports Grants; Events; Member Clubs
Staff Member(s): 12
Membership: *Fees:* $45 adult; $26.50 junior; $102 family
Activities: *Library* Open to public

Tennis Canada
Rexall Centre, #100, 1 Shoreham Dr., Toronto ON M3N 3A6
Tel: 416-665-9777; *Fax:* 416-665-9017
Toll-Free: 877-283-6647
info@tenniscanada.com
www.tenniscanada.com
www.facebook.com/TennisCanada
twitter.com/Tennis_Canada
www.youtube.com/user/TCtenniscanada
Previous Name: Canadian Tennis Association
Overview: A large national organization founded in 1890
Mission: To stimulate participation & excellence in the sport at the local, provincial, national, & international levels; To provide encouragement, support, & leadership to organizations & individuals who seek to enhance the enjoyment, quality & image of Canadian tennis
Member of: International Tennis Federation; Canadian Olympic Association; Canadian Paralympic Committee; International Wheelchair Tennis Association
Chief Officer(s):
John LeBoutillier, Chair
Kelly D. Murumets, President & CEO
Eugène Lapierre, Senior Vice-President, Québec Professional Tennis
Hatem McDadi, Vice-President, Tennis Development
Finances: *Funding Sources:* Government
Membership: *Member Profile:* Provincial tennis association

Activities: Holding a number of championships; programs for all ages & abilities; *Awareness Events:* Rogers Cup tournament; Davis Cup; Fed Cup; *Internships:* Yes
Awards:
• Tennis Canada Excellence Awards (Award)
• Distinguished Service Awards (Award)
Publications:
• Tennis Canada Annual Report
Type: Yearbook; *Frequency:* Annually
• Topspin
Type: Newsletter; *Frequency:* Biweekly
Profile: Updated information to promote tennis in Canada
Montréal
Uniprix Stadium, 285 Faillon West, Montréal QC H2R 2W1
Tél: 514-273-1515; *Téléc:* 514-276-0070
Ligne sans frais: 866-338-2685

Tennis de Table Canada ***See*** Table Tennis Canada

Tennis Manitoba
#419, 145 Pacific Ave., Winnipeg MB R3B 2Z6
Tel: 204-925-5660; *Fax:* 204-925-5703
info@tennismanitoba.com
www.tennismanitoba.com
www.facebook.com/pages/Tennis-Manitoba/123417151011791
twitter.com/tennismanitoba
Also Known As: Manitoba Tennis Association
Overview: A medium-sized provincial organization founded in 1880 overseen by Tennis Canada
Mission: To stimulate participation & advancement in tennis by all Manitobans
Member of: Sport Manitoba; Tennis Canada
Chief Officer(s):
Mark Arndt, Executive Director
mark@tennismanitoba.com
Finances: *Funding Sources:* Provincial government; Manitoba Lotteries; Private sponsors
Membership: *Fees:* $20 adult; $10 junior

Tennis New Brunswick
PO Box 604, Fredericton NB E3B 5A6
Tel: 506-444-0885
tnb@tennisnb.net
www.tennisnb.net
www.facebook.com/TennisNewBrunswick
Overview: A medium-sized provincial organization overseen by Tennis Canada
Mission: To be the body governing the sport of tennis in the province
Member of: Sport NB; Tennis Canada
Chief Officer(s):
Dana Brown, President
Mark Thibault, Executive Director
Membership: *Fees:* $15-$40

Tennis Newfoundland & Labrador
PO Box 728, Stn. C, St. John's NL A1C 5L4
Tel: 709-722-3840
tennis@sportnl.ca
www.courtsidecanada.ca/communities/newfoundland_labrador
Previous Name: Newfoundland & Labrador Tennis Association
Overview: A medium-sized provincial organization overseen by Tennis Canada
Mission: To grow & promote the sport of tennis throughout Newfoundland & Labrador; To increase participation at levels consistent with the personal goals & aspirations of competitors in all age groups
Member of: Tennis Canada
Chief Officer(s):
Nancy Taylor, President
Bruce Crichton, Executive Director
Staff Member(s): 2

Tennis Northwest Territories ***See*** Northwest Territories Tennis Association

Tennis Québec (TQ)
285, rue Faillon ouest, Montréal QC H2R 2W1
Tél: 514-270-6060; *Téléc:* 514-270-2700
courrier@tennis.qc.ca
www.tennis.qc.ca
Nom précédent: Fédération québécoise de tennis
Aperçu: *Dimension:* moyenne; *Envergure:* provinciale; Organisme sans but lucratif; fondée en 1899 surveillé par Tennis Canada
Mission: Promotion et développement du tennis au Québec auprès de toutes les catégories d'âge et de tous les calibres
Membre de: Tennis Canada
Membre(s) du bureau directeur:
Réjean Genois, Président
Jean François Manibal, Directeur général
dg1@tennis.qc.ca
Finances: *Budget de fonctionnement annuel:* $500,000-$1.5 Million
Membre(s) du personnel: 8; 30 bénévole(s)
Membre: 35 000; *Montant de la cotisation:* 25$ pour une licence; *Comités:* Comité des entraîneurs; Commission des officiels; Commission d'enseignement
Activités: Remise des prix d'excellence; "Vive le Tennis"; Tournée sports experts; *Stagiaires:* Oui; *Service de conférenciers:* Oui; *Bibliothèque:* Centre d'information; Bibliothèque publique rendez-vous

Tennis Saskatchewan
2205 Victoria Ave., Regina SK S4P 0S4
Tel: 306-780-9410; *Fax:* 306-525-4009
tennissask@sasktel.net
www.tennissask.com
Previous Name: Saskatchewan Tennis Association
Overview: A medium-sized provincial organization founded in 1976 overseen by Tennis Canada
Mission: To advance tennis throughout Saskatchewan by stimulating participation & excellence in the sport; To provide players throughout Saskatchewan with systematic opportunities to participate in tennis & to achieve a level of competence consistent with their abilities & aspirations, with particular emphasis on youth; To stage tennis events; To produce teams & athletes capable of winning national championships
Member of: Tennis Canada
Affliation(s): Sask Sport Incorporated
Chief Officer(s):
Rory Park, Executive Director
Finances: *Funding Sources:* Saskatchewan Lotteries; Tennis Canada

Tennis Yukon Association
Whitehorse YT
Tel: 867-393-2621
tennisyukon@gmail.com
www.courtsidecanada.ca/communities/Yukon
Overview: A small provincial organization
Mission: To promote the sport of Tennis in the Yukon.
Chief Officer(s):
Stacy Lewis, President, 867-393-2621

The Teresa Group
#104, 124 Merton St., Toronto ON M4S 2Z2
Tel: 416-596-7703; *Fax:* 416-596-7910
info@teresagroup.ca
www.teresagroup.ca
www.facebook.com/120076698045376
twitter.com/TheTeresaGroup
Overview: A small local charitable organization founded in 1990 overseen by Canadian AIDS Society
Mission: Serves the needs of children & their families living with or affected by HIV/AIDS
Member of: Ontario AIDS Network; Canadian AIDS Society
Chief Officer(s):
Simone Shindler, Program Director
Finances: *Annual Operating Budget:* $250,000-$500,000; *Funding Sources:* Government & the private sector; fundraising
Staff Member(s): 10; 132 volunteer(s)
Membership: 100-499
Activities: *Awareness Events:* Scotiabank Charity Challenge, Oct.; *Speaker Service:* Yes; *Library* by appointment
Publications:
• Bye-Bye Secrets: A Book About Children Living With HIV or AIDS in their Family
Type: Book; *Number of Pages:* 36; *Price:* $14.95
Profile: The experiences of five girls, aged 8-12 years, who live with HIV/AIDS in their families.
• Early Intervention Programs for Children & Women Living with HIV & AIDS Leaflet
Type: Leaflet
Profile: Descriptions of the following: Pre-Natal, New Moms, Mom & Tots Groups, & The Formula Program
• Hopes, Wishes & Dreams: A Book of Art & Writing by Children Living with HIV/AIDS in their Family
Type: Book; *Number of Pages:* 40; *Price:* $14.95
Profile: Art, poetry & writings by children affected by HIV/AIDS
• How Do I Tell My Kids? A Disclosure Booklet About HIV/AIDS in the Family
Type: Booklet; *Number of Pages:* 48; *Price:* $5.00
Profile: A booklet for adults, designed to help with the process of telling their children that a family member has HIV.
• In Touch [a publication of The Teresa Group]
Type: Newsletter
• Programs & Services Booklet
Type: Brochure
Profile: This brochure outlines what The Teresa Group does.

Terrace & District Chamber of Commerce
4511 Keith Ave., Terrace BC V8G 1K1
Tel: 250-635-2063; *Fax:* 250-635-2573
terracechamber@telus.net
www.terracechamber.com
Overview: A small local organization founded in 1927
Mission: To be the recognized voice of business committed to the enhancement & development of the economic well-being of the Terrace area
Member of: BC Chamber of Commerce; Canadian Chamber of Commerce; Terrace Tourism Society
Chief Officer(s):
Janice Shaben, President
Carol Fielding, Executive Director
Finances: *Annual Operating Budget:* $100,000-$250,000; *Funding Sources:* Membership dues; special projects
Staff Member(s): 2; 15 volunteer(s)
Membership: 373; *Fees:* $120-$880 (depending on number of employees)
Activities: *Library:* Resource Centre; Open to public

Terrace & District Community Services Society
#200, 3219 Eby St., Terrace BC V8G 4R3
Tel: 250-635-3178; *Fax:* 250-635-6319
info@tdcss.ca
www.tdcss.ca
www.facebook.com/TDCSS
twitter.com/TDCSS_
Overview: A small local organization
Member of: British Columbia Association for Community Living
Chief Officer(s):
Marilyn Lissimore, Executive Director

Terrazzo Tile & Marble Association of Canada (TTMAC) / Association canadienne de terrazzo, tuile et marbre
#8, 163 Buttermill Ave., Concord ON L4K 3X8
Tel: 905-660-9640; *Fax:* 905-660-0513
Toll-Free: 800-201-8599
association@ttmac.com
www.ttmac.com
Overview: A small national organization founded in 1944
Mission: To standardize terrazzo, tile, marble, & stone installation techniques, so that the industry will grow & proper; To support the hardsurface industry & its members
Chief Officer(s):
Elaine Cook, Eastern Editor, The Analyst
elaine@ttmac.com
Finances: *Funding Sources:* Membership fees; Sponsorships
Membership: *Fees:* $145 - $405 professionals; $165 supplier & contractor branch offices; $3,000 affiliates; Schedule, based on volume, for contractors & suppliers; *Member Profile:* Professionals, such as architects, consultants, specifiers, designers, & engineers; Firms engaged in contracting to install terrazzo, tile, & stone products; Suppliers who sell or manufacture products, equipment, or services; Industry associations that want to be affiliated with Terrazzo Tile & Marble Association of Canada
Activities: Establishing guidelines; Promoting hardsurface products; Providing technical information to architects, specifiers, designers, & engineers; Testing; Conducting field inspections; Offering training opportunities; Providing networking occasions; *Library:* Terrazzo Tile & Marble Association of Canada Library
Meetings/Conferences:
• Terrazzo Tile & Marble Association of Canada 2015 Annual Convention, June, 2015, Chateaux Frontenac, Québec City, QC
Scope: National
Contact Information: E-mail: association@ttmac.com
Publications:
• The Analyst
Type: Newsletter; *Frequency:* Bimonthly; *Accepts Advertising;* *Editor:* Len Tompkins
Profile: Terrazzo Tile & Marble Association of Canada

developments, membership information, technical updates, business topics, training opportunities, & upcoming events
• Dimensional Stone Guide, Volume II
Type: Manual; *Price:* $150 members; $225 non-members
• Hard Surface Maintenance Guide
Type: Manual; *Price:* $10 members; $25 non-members
• Hardsurface
Type: Magazine; *Accepts Advertising*; *Editor:* Jeanne Fronda; *Price:* Free for TTMAC members & architectural & design firms across Canada
Profile: Feature articles written by experts in the field, award information, & forthcoming events
• Terrazzo Installation Manual
Type: Manual; *Price:* $25 members; $45 non-members
• Tile Installation Manual
Type: Manual; *Price:* $25 members; $45 non-members
• TTMAC E-news
Type: Newsletter
Profile: Happenings in the industry & the Terrazzo Tile & Marble Association of Canada, distributed free to all members

Burnaby (Western Branch)
#108, 3650 Bonneville Pl., Burnaby BC V3N 4T7
Tel: 604-294-6885; *Fax:* 604-294-2406
association@ttmac.com
www.ttmac.com
www.linkedin.com/company/terrazzo-tile-&-marble-association-of-canada
www.facebook.com/444656588885871
twitter.com/TTMACCanada
www.youtube.com/user/TTMACCanada
Chief Officer(s):
Ashley Petelycky, Office Manager
ashley@ttmac.com

Terre sans frontières (TSF) / World Without Borders

#23, 399, rue des Conseillers, La Prairie QC J5R 4H6
Tél: 450-659-7717; *Téléc:* 450-659-2276
Ligne sans frais: 877-873-2433
tsf@terresansfrontieres.ca
www.terresansfrontieres.ca
www.facebook.com/pageterresansfrontieres
www.youtube.com/user/TerreSansFrontieres
Merged from: Avions sans frontières; Prodeva
Aperçu: *Dimension:* petite; *Envergure:* internationale; Organisme sans but lucratif; fondée en 1981
Mission: Organisme de coopération internationale qui travaille dans la perspective de développement durable
Membre de: Canadian Council for International Cooperation
Affiliation(s): Association québécoise des organismes de coopération internationale (AQOCI)
Membre(s) du bureau directeur:
Joseph Bourgeois, Président
Robert Gonneville, Directeur général
Finances: *Budget de fonctionnement annuel:* Plus de $5 Million
Membre(s) du personnel: 15; 250 bénévole(s)
Membre: 121; *Montant de la cotisation:* 25$; *Comités:* Direction; Sélection de projets; Finances
Activités: Adduction d'eau et assainissement; éducation; transport aérien humanitaire; appui institutionnel; santé; agriculture; *Evénements de sensibilisation:* Journées Québécoises de la Solidarité Internationale; *Service de conférenciers:* Oui

Les Terre-Neuviens français *Voir* La Fédération des francophones de Terre-Neuve et du Labrador

The Terry Fox Foundation / La Fondation Terry Fox

#303, 46165 Yale Rd., Chilliwack BC V2P 2P2
Tel: 604-701-0246; *Fax:* 604-701-0247
national@terryfoxrun.org
www.terryfoxrun.org
www.facebook.com/TheTerryFoxFoundation
twitter.com/TerryFoxCanada
www.youtube.com/terryfoxcanada
Also Known As: Terry Fox Run
Overview: A large national charitable organization founded in 1980
Mission: To maintain the vision & principles of Terry Fox while raising money for cancer research through the annual Terry Fox Run, memoriam donations & planned gifts. All money raised by the Foundation is distributed through the National Cancer Institute of Canada
Chief Officer(s):
Bill Pristanski, Chair
Judith Fox-Alder, International Director
international@terryfoxrun.org
Finances: *Annual Operating Budget:* Greater than $5 Million
Activities: *Awareness Events:* Terry Fox Run, 2nd Sunday following Labour Day, Sept.; *Speaker Service:* Yes

Alberta/NWT/Nunavut Office
#D10, 6115 - 3rd St. SE, Calgary AB T2H 2L2
Tel: 403-212-1336; *Fax:* 403-212-1343
Toll-Free: 888-836-9786
abntnu@terryfoxrun.org
Chief Officer(s):
Rhonda Risebrough, Provincial Director

British Columbia/Yukon Office
2669 Shaughnessy St., Port Coquitlam BC V3C 3G7
Tel: 604-464-2666; *Fax:* 604-464-2664
Toll-Free: 888-836-9786
bcyukon@terryfoxrun.org
Chief Officer(s):
Donna White, Provincial Director

International Office
#303, 46167 Yale Rd., Chilliwack BC V2P 2P2
Tel: 604-701-0246; *Fax:* 604-701-0247
international@terryfoxrun.org
Chief Officer(s):
Judith Fox-Alder, International Director

Manitoba Office
1214 Chevrier Blvd., #A, Winnipeg MB R3T 1Y3
Tel: 204-231-5282; *Fax:* 204-321-5365
Toll-Free: 888-836-9786
mb@terryfoxrun.org
Chief Officer(s):
Tammy Ferrante, Provincial Director

New Brunswick/PEI Office
#493, 605 Prospect St., Fredericton NB E3B 6B8
Tel: 506-458-2618; *Fax:* 506-459-4572
Toll-Free: 888-836-9786
nbpei@terryfoxrun.org
Chief Officer(s):
Gwen Smith-Walsh, Provincial Director

Newfoundland & Labrador
#202, 835 Topsail Rd., Mount Pearl NL A1N 3J6
Tel: 709-576-8428; *Fax:* 709-747-7277
Toll-Free: 888-836-9786
nl@terryfoxrun.org
Chief Officer(s):
Heather Strong, Provincial Director

Nova Scotia Office
#203, 3600 Kempt Rd., Halifax NS B3K 4X8
Tel: 902-423-8131; *Fax:* 902-492-3639
Toll-Free: 888-836-9786
ns@terryfoxrun.org
Chief Officer(s):
Barbara Fickes, Provincial Director

Ontario Office
#900, 1200 Eglinton Ave. Wast, Toronto ON M3C 1H9
Tel: 416-924-8252; *Fax:* 416-924-6597
Toll-Free: 888-836-9786
ontario@terryfoxrun.org
Chief Officer(s):
Martha McClew, Provincial Director

Québec Office
#207, 10 Churchill Blvd., Greenfield Park QC J4V 2L7
Tel: 450-923-9747; *Fax:* 450-923-8468
Toll-Free: 888-836-9786
qc@terryfoxrun.org
Chief Officer(s):
Peter Sheremeta, Provincial Director

Saskatchewan Office
1812 - 9th Ave. North, Regina SK S4R 7T4
Tel: 306-757-1662; *Fax:* 306-757-7422
Toll-Free: 888-836-9786
sk@terryfoxrun.org
Chief Officer(s):
Robert Barr, Provincial Director

TESL Canada Federation (TESL Canada)

3751 - 21 St. NE, Calgary AB T2E 6T5
Tel: 403-538-7300; *Fax:* 403-538-7392
Toll-Free: 800-393-9199
info@tesl.ca
www.tesl.ca
Also Known As: Teaching English as a Second Language Canada Federation
Overview: A medium-sized national organization founded in 1978
Mission: To support the sharing of knowledge & experiences across Canada; To represents diverse interests in TESL nationally & internationally
Affliation(s): Teachers of English to Speakers of Other Languages (TESOL); Société pour la promotion de l'enseignement de l'anglais (langue seconde) au Québec
Chief Officer(s):
Sumana Barua, Executive Director
Ron Thomson, President
Membership: *Fees:* Schedule available; *Committees:* Executive; Standards Advisory; Journal Advisory; Governance & Policy; Finance; Testing; Professional Development; Research & Dissemination; Settlement Language National Network
Activities: *Internships:* Yes

TESL Manitoba *See* TEAL Manitoba

TESL New Brunswick

c/o English Language Programme, University of New Brunswick, PO Box 4400, Fredericton NB E3B 5A3
Toll-Free: 800-269-6719
Overview: A small provincial organization overseen by TESL Canada Federation
Chief Officer(s):
Alice Foley-Keats, President

TESL Newfoundland & Labrador (TESL NL)

c/o ESL Program, Memorial University of Newfoundland, St. John's NL A1B 3X9
Tel: 709-737-8054; *Fax:* 709-737-8282
arts-srv.arts.mun.ca/tesl
Overview: A small provincial organization overseen by TESL Canada Federation
Member of: TESL Canada Federation
Affliation(s): TESL Canada
Chief Officer(s):
Sonja Knutson, President
sknutson@mun.ca
Membership: *Fees:* $30; *Member Profile:* Teachers of English as a Second Language in Newfoundland & Labrador
Activities: Engaging in advocacy activities for ESL learners & issues; Offering professional development opportunities; Providing networking occasions; Sharing knowledge throughout the province; Hosting monthly meetings;

TESL Nova Scotia (TESLNS)

PO Box 36068, Halifax NS B3J 3S9
e-mail: teslnovascotia@gmail.com
tesl-nova-scotia.wikispaces.com
Also Known As: Teachers of English as a Second Language of Nova Scotia
Overview: A small provincial charitable organization founded in 1982 overseen by TESL Canada Federation
Mission: To advance communication & coordinating issues related to teaching English as a Second Language; To unify teachers & learners; To promote advocacy for ESL learners; To provide a forum for discussion & networking capabilities; To share knowledge in Nova Scotia
Member of: TESL Canada Federation
Chief Officer(s):
Andy de Champlain, President
Finances: *Annual Operating Budget:* Less than $50,000
100 volunteer(s)
Membership: 100; *Fees:* $45; *Member Profile:* Teachers of adults, elementary & secondary learners
Activities: Annual conference; monthly board meetings; professional development meetings; newsletter

TESL Ontario

#405, 27 Carlton St., Toronto ON M5B 1L2
Tel: 416-593-4243; *Fax:* 416-593-0164
Toll-Free: 800-327-4827
administration@teslontario.org
www.teslontario.org
www.linkedin.com/groups/TESL-Ontario-1813872
www.facebook.com/101601733235647
twitter.com/TESLOntario
Also Known As: Teachers of English as a Second Language Association of Ontario
Overview: A medium-sized provincial organization founded in 1972
Member of: TESL Canada Federation; TESOL International - Teachers of English to Speakers of Other Languages
Chief Officer(s):
Sheila Nicholas, Chair
Marilyn Johnston, Vice-Chair
Finances: *Annual Operating Budget:* $100,000-$250,000

Canadian Associations

Staff Member(s): 5; 50 volunteer(s)
Membership: 4,500; *Fees:* Schedule available; *Member Profile:* ESL professionals

TESL Prince Edward Island (TESL PEI)
c/o Webster Centre for Teaching & Learning, U of PEI, 550 University Ave., Charlottetown PE C1A 4P3
Tel: 902-566-6003
teslpei.ning.com
Overview: A small provincial organization overseen by TESL Canada Federation
Mission: To encourage & support the promotion of policies & programmes related to second language learning & teaching on Prince Edward Island
Member of: TESL Canada Federation
Chief Officer(s):
Christina Perry, President
cperry@upei.ca
Finances: *Funding Sources:* TESL Canada; membership fees
Membership: 1-99; *Fees:* $32; *Member Profile:* Individuals & groups actively involved or interested in the teaching of English as a Second Lanaguage

TESL Yukon
c/o E. Hurlburt, PO Box 5403, Haines Junction YT Y0B 1L0
dl1.yukoncollege.yk.ca/tesl
Overview: A small provincial organization founded in 1998 overseen by TESL Canada Federation
Membership: 16; *Member Profile:* Adults interested in English as a second language

Teslin Regional Chamber of Commerce
PO Box 181, Teslin YT Y0A 1B0
Tel: 867-390-2521; *Fax:* 867-390-2687
Overview: A small local organization
Chief Officer(s):
Wes Wirth, President

Tetra Society of North America
#318, 425 Carrall St., Vancouver BC V6B 6E3
Tel: 604-688-6464; *Fax:* 604-688-6463
Toll-Free: 877-688-8762
info@tetrasociety.org
www.tetrasociety.org
www.facebook.com/group.php?gid=63077456382
Overview: A small national charitable organization founded in 1992
Mission: To link volunteer engineers & technicians with persons with disabilities to create custom assistive devices to help them achieve greater independence
Member of: Sam Sullivan Disability Foundation, Volunteer Vancouver
Chief Officer(s):
Pat Tweedie, Provincial Coordinator
ptweedie@tetrasociety.org
Duane Geddes, Executive Director
Matthew Wild, National Coordinator
Finances: *Annual Operating Budget:* $100,000-$250,000
Staff Member(s): 2; 400 volunteer(s)
Membership: 1,000-4,999; *Member Profile:* Adults & children with disabilities
Activities: Monthly volunteer meetings; *Speaker Service:* Yes
Awards:
• Gizmo Awards (Award)

Teulon Chamber of Commerce
PO Box 235, Teulon MB R0C 3B0
Tel: 204-294-6171; *Fax:* 204-886-3232
Overview: A small local organization
Chief Officer(s):
Jan Lambourne, Chair
Linda Lamoureux, Secretary

Texada Island Chamber of Commerce
PO Box 249, Vananda BC V0N 3K0
Tel: 604-486-7597
Overview: A small local organization
Affliation(s): British Columbia Chamber of Commerce; Canadian Chamber of Commerce
Chief Officer(s):
Mave Leclair, President

Textile Federation of Canada *See* Canadian Textile Association

Textiles Human Resources Council (THRC)
#500, 222 Somerset St., Ottawa ON K2P 2G3
Tel: 613-230-7217; *Fax:* 613-230-1270
info@thrc-crhit.org
www.thrc-crhit.org
Overview: A small local organization founded in 1994
Mission: To develop innovative training & education solutions to respond to established & emerging human resources needs
Chief Officer(s):
John Saliba, Executive Director

Thalassemia Foundation of Canada
338 Falstaff Ave., Toronto ON M6L 3E7
Tel: 416-242-8425; *Fax:* 416-242-8425
info@thalassemia.ca
www.thalassemia.ca
Overview: A small national charitable organization founded in 1982
Mission: To raise public awareness of Thalassemia; To raise money for Thalassemia research & treatment; To support families of children with Thalassemia
Chief Officer(s):
Helen Ziavras, President

Thalidomide Victims Association of Canada (TVAC) / Association canadienne des victimes de la thalidomide (ACVT)
Centre commercial Joseph Renaud, #211, 6830, boul Joseph Renaud, Montréal QC H1K 3V4
Tel: 514-355-0811; *Fax:* 514-355-0860
Toll-Free: 877-355-0811
tvac.acvt@sympatico.ca
www.thalidomide.ca
Overview: A medium-sized national charitable organization founded in 1988
Mission: To monitor the drug thalidomide & to meet the needs of thalidomide survivors; to empower & enhance the quality of life of Canadian thalidomidors
Affliation(s): Council of Canadians with Disabilities; Canadian Centre for Philanthropy
Chief Officer(s):
Mercedes Benegbi, Executive Director
Membership: *Member Profile:* Persons born disabled as a consequence of the drug thalidomide
Activities: *Speaker Service:* Yes; *Library:* TVAC Resource Library; by appointment

Thames Region Ecological Association (TREA)
1017 Western Rd., London ON N6G 1G5
Tel: 519-672-5991; *Fax:* 519-645-0981
info@trea.ca
www.trea.ca
www.facebook.com/pages/TREA/165674636807720
twitter.com/TREAontario
www.youtube.com/user/londonbicyclefestiva
Overview: A small local charitable organization founded in 1986
Mission: Committed to educating ourselves & the community towards development of an ecologically responsible & sustainable future through awareness, reflection, caring & action
Member of: Grosvenor Lodge Resource Centre for Heritage & Environment
Affliation(s): Urban League of London; London Composts
Chief Officer(s):
Anne Arnott, President
Finances: *Annual Operating Budget:* Less than $50,000; *Funding Sources:* Government; membership fees; Compost Day
Staff Member(s): 1; 40 volunteer(s)
Membership: 60 individual; *Fees:* $20 individual
Activities: TREATop; waste group; home cocmposting program; TREATalk, tree planting; pesticide group; London Bicycle Festival; *Speaker Service:* Yes

Thames Valley Trail Association Inc. (TVTA)
c/o Grosvenor Lodge, 1017 Western Rd., London ON N6G 1G5
Tel: 519-645-2845; *Fax:* 519-645-0981
tvta.ca
www.facebook.com/theTVTA
twitter.com/TVTA_London_Ont
Overview: A small local charitable organization founded in 1969
Mission: To promote hiking; to develop & maintain the Thames Valley Trail; to cooperate with other environmental groups
Member of: Hike Ontario
Chief Officer(s):
Ruth Hoch, Co-Chair
Murray Hamilton, Co-Chair
Dave Potten, Co-Chair
Finances: *Funding Sources:* Membership dues
Membership: *Fees:* $25 individual; $35 family; $20 senior; *Member Profile:* All ages with an interest in hiking & recreational walking
Activities: Trail follows north branch of Thames River from Kilworth, the parks of London through neat farmlands & stands of hardwood to historic St. Marys (100 km); *Awareness Events:* Hike Ontario Day; *Speaker Service:* Yes; *Library:* Grosvenor Lodge Library; Open to public

Théâtre Action (TA)
203, 255, ch Montréal, Ottawa ON K1L 6C4
Tél: 613-745-2322; *Téléc:* 613-745-1733
theatreaction@franco.ca
www.theatreaction.ca/fr
www.facebook.com/TheatreActionON
twitter.com/TheatreActionON
Aperçu: *Dimension:* petite; *Envergure:* locale; fondée en 1972
Mission: Oeuvrer au développement du théâtre en Ontario
Membre de: Réseau Ontario; Alliance culturelle de l'Ontario; Theatre Canada
Affliation(s): Conseil des arts de l'Ontario, Ministère du patrimoine canadien, Ministère de l'Éducation de l'Ontario
Membre(s) du bureau directeur:
Pierre Simpson, Président
Finances: *Fonds:* Gouvernement de l'Ontario
Membre(s) du personnel: 5; 150 bénévole(s)
Activités: Prix et bourses; programmes de formation; *Evénements de sensibilisation:* Festival Franco-ontarien de théâtre
Prix, Bouses:
• Prix d'excellence artistique de Théâtre Action (Bourse d études)
Amount: 1 000$
• Bourse d'études Théâtre Action
Amount: 1 000$

Theatre Alberta Society
11759 Groat Rd., 3rd Fl., Edmonton AB T5M 3K6
Tel: 780-422-8162; *Fax:* 780-422-2663
Toll-Free: 888-422-8160
theatreab@theatrealberta.com
www.theatrealberta.com
www.facebook.com/TheatreAlberta
twitter.com/TheatreAlberta
Overview: A medium-sized provincial organization founded in 1985
Mission: To encourage the growth of theatre in Alberta through high quality support & training opportunities to theatre professionals, educators & community theatre practitioners
Chief Officer(s):
Keri Mitchell, Executive Director
keri@theatrealberta.com
Finances: *Funding Sources:* Alberta Foundation for the Arts
Staff Member(s): 7
Activities: *Library:* Theatre Alberta Library;

Theatre Calgary
220 - 9 Ave. SE, Calgary AB T2G 5C4
Tel: 403-294-7440; *Fax:* 403-294-7493
info@theatrecalgary.com
www.theatrecalgary.com
www.facebook.com/theatrecalgary
twitter.com/theatrecalgary
www.youtube.com/user/TheatreCalgary
Overview: A small local organization
Mission: To produce classical and modern theatre.
Chief Officer(s):
Mark Thompson, Chair
Dennis Garnhum, Artistic Director
Staff Member(s): 41

Théâtre de la Vieille 17
204, av King Edward, Ottawa ON K1N 7L7
Tél: 613-241-8562; *Téléc:* 613-241-9507
info@vieille17.ca
www.vieille17.ca
www.facebook.com/LaVieille17
twitter.com/theatrev17
vimeo.com/user8318968
Aperçu: *Dimension:* petite; *Envergure:* locale; fondée en 1979
Mission: Créer et diffuser des spectacles pour la jeunesse et pour les adultes à l'échelle régionale, nationale et internationale
Membre(s) du bureau directeur:
Esther Beauchemin, Directrice artistique et générale
eb@vieille17.ca
Membre(s) du personnel: 5

Théâtre des épinettes
55, rue Laframboise, Chibougamau QC G8P 2S5
Tél: 418-748-4682
Aperçu: *Dimension:* petite; *Envergure:* locale
Membre(s) du bureau directeur:
Guy Lalancette, Responsable
glalancette@tlb.sympatico.ca

Théâtre du Nouvel-Ontario (TNO)
21, boul Lasalle, Sudbury ON P3A 6B1
Tél: 705-525-5606
tno@letno.ca
www.letno.ca
www.facebook.com/pages/Theatre-du-Nouvel-Ontario/139137429438733
twitter.com/le_TNO
www.youtube.com/user/TheatreNouvelOntario
Aperçu: *Dimension:* petite; *Envergure:* locale; fondée en 1971
Mission: Dédié à la création, à la dramaturgie franco-ontarienne et à l'accueil d'oeuvres principalement canadiennes
Membre(s) du bureau directeur:
Geneviève Pineault, Directrice artistique
artistique@letno.ca
Membre(s) du personnel: 9
Activités: *Stagiaires:* Oui

Théâtre du Trillium
#5, 109, rue Murray, Ottawa ON K1N 5M5
Tél: 613-789-7643; *Téléc:* 613-789-7641
comm@theatre-trillium.com
www.theatre-trillium.com
www.facebook.com/theatredutrillium
twitter.com/theatretrillium
www.youtube.com/theatredutrillium
Aperçu: *Dimension:* petite; *Envergure:* locale
Mission: Pour effectuer des productions théâtrales contemporaines
Membre(s) du bureau directeur:
Anne-Marie White, Directrice artistique et générale
white@theatre-trillium.com
Membre(s) du personnel: 4
Activités: Trois productions grand public; laboratoire de mise en scène; spectacle pour adolescents

Théâtre français de Toronto
#610, 21, rue College, Toronto ON M5G 2B3
Tél: 416-534-7303
www.theatrefrancais.com
www.facebook.com/Theatrefrancais
twitter.com/theatrefrancais
www.youtube.com/LeTheatreFrancaisTfT
Également appelé: TFT
Aperçu: *Dimension:* petite; *Envergure:* provinciale; Organisme sans but lucratif
Mission: Le Théâtre français de Toronto est un théâtre professionnel de langue française, de répertoire et de création. Il s'adresse à tous les amateurs de théâtre en français, tant les francophones que les francophiles : ce faisant, il contribue au développement culturel et pédagogique de la communauté de Toronto. Théâtre français de Toronto is a professional French-language theatre presenting repertoire as well as new work. While appealing to all lovers of French-language theatre, it contributes to the cultural and educational development of Toronto's francophone community.
Membre(s) du bureau directeur:
Guy Mignault, Directeur artistique
gmignault@theatrefrancais.com
Ghislain Caron, Directeur administratif
gcaron@theatrefrancais.com
Finances: *Budget de fonctionnement annuel:* $500,000-$1.5 Million
Membre(s) du personnel: 11

Théâtre l'Escaouette
170, rue Botsford, Moncton NB E1C 4X6
Tél: 506-855-0001; *Téléc:* 506-855-0010
escaouette@nb.aibn.com
www.escaouette.com
www.facebook.com/escaouette
twitter.com/escaouette
www.youtube.com/user/escaouette
Aperçu: *Dimension:* petite; *Envergure:* locale; fondée en 1978
Mission: Pour effectuer productions acadiennes theatricial originaux
Membre(s) du bureau directeur:
Marcia Babineau, Direction artistique & codirection générale
marciababineau@nb.aibn.com
Finances: *Fonds:* Imperial Tobacco Canada
Membre(s) du personnel: 6

Théâtre la Catapulte
#4, 124, av King-Edward, Ottawa ON K1N 7L1
Tél: 613-562-0851; *Téléc:* 613-562-0631
communications@catapulte.ca
catapulte.ca
www.facebook.com/pages/Ottawa-ON/Theatre-la-Catapulte/221011962255
twitter.com/LaCatapulte
Aperçu: *Dimension:* petite; *Envergure:* locale; fondée en 1992
Mission: Le Théâtre la Catapulte est une compagnie professionnelle de création, de production et de diffusion enracinée en Ontario français, proposant aux adolescents et au grand public des expériences théâtrales audacieuses et éclectiques nourries par la fougue de la relève et par des artistes établis. Il assure à ses productions une diffusion importante dans la région d'Ottawa-Gatineau et dans l'ensemble du Canada tout en cultivant sa relation avec ses publics.
Membre de: ATFC, Théâtre Action, ACT
Membre(s) du bureau directeur:
Jean Stéphane Roy, Directeur artistique
jsroy@catapulte.ca
Maurice Demers, Président
Membre(s) du personnel: 5
Activités: *Stagiaires:* Oui

Théâtre la Seizième
#266, 1555, 7e av Ouest, Vancouver BC V6J 1S1
Tel: 604-736-2616; *Fax:* 604-736-9151
info@seizieme.ca
www.seizieme.ca
www.facebook.com/seizieme
twitter.com/seizieme
vimeo.com/seizieme
Overview: A small local organization founded in 1974
Mission: Promouvoir le théâtre professionnel francophone en Colombie-Britannique
Chief Officer(s):
Craig Holzschuh, Directeur général et artistique
Staff Member(s): 4
Activities: Ateliers d' art dramatique

Theatre Network (1975) Society
10708 - 124 St., Edmonton AB T5M 0H1
Tel: 780-453-2440; *Fax:* 780-453-2596
info@theatrenetwork.ca
theatrenetwork.ca
www.facebook.com/TheatreNetwork1975
twitter.com/Theatre_Network
www.youtube.com/user/TheatreNetworkEdm
Overview: A small local charitable organization founded in 1975
Mission: To promote original regional drama
Member of: Professional Association of Canadian Theatres (PACT)
Affliation(s): Edmonton Arts Council
Chief Officer(s):
Bradley Moss, Artistic Director
Staff Member(s): 16
Membership: *Committees:* Business Development & Outreach; Fundraising; Special Events/Projects; Building/Facility

Theatre New Brunswick (TNB)
55 Whitting Rd., Fredericton NB E3B 5Y5
Tel: 506-460-1381; *Fax:* 506-453-9315
general@tnb.nb.ca
www.tnb.nb.ca
www.facebook.com/pages/Theatre-New-Brunswick/37564223392
twitter.com/TheatreNB
www.youtube.com/user/theatreNB
Overview: A medium-sized provincial charitable organization founded in 1969
Mission: To provide live professional theatre to the people of New Brunswick by touring & performing in nine centres throughout the province; to entertain by providing quality theatre & acting as a theatrical resource for playwrights, actors & young people interested in the field
Chief Officer(s):
Susan Ready, General Manager
productionmanager@tnb.nb.ca
Activities: Mainstage Shows; Young Company; Workshops; Theatre School

Theatre Newfoundland Labrador
PO Box 655, Corner Brook NL A2H 6G1
Tel: 709-639-7238; *Fax:* 709-639-1006
www.theatrenewfoundland.com
www.facebook.com/pages/Theatre-Newfoundland-Labrador-TNL/71673366177
twitter.com/TheatreNL
Overview: A small provincial organization
Mission: To create & produce professional theatre which reflects the lives and dirversity of the audiences on the province's west coast, extending to labrador and across the island of Newfoundland.
Chief Officer(s):
Jeff Pitcher, Artistic Director
Staff Member(s): 6

Theatre Nova Scotia (TNS)
1113 Marginal Rd., Halifax NS B3H 4P7
Tel: 902-425-3876; *Fax:* 902-422-0881
theatrens@theatrens.ca
www.theatrens.ca
www.facebook.com/84236453845
twitter.com/TheatreNS
Previous Name: Nova Scotia Drama League
Overview: A medium-sized provincial charitable organization founded in 1949
Mission: To provide services, training & resources to professional & amateur theatre community throughout Nova Scotia
Member of: International Amateur Theatre Association
Affliation(s): Cultural Federation of NS; Professional Association of Canadian Theatres
Chief Officer(s):
Alexis Milligan, Chair
Nancy Morgan, Executive Director
Finances: *Funding Sources:* Government; Membership fees; fundraising
Staff Member(s): 6
Membership: *Fees:* $75 community/professional theatre/affiliate; $25 individual
Activities: Annual Robert Merritt Awards; Summer Theatre School Brochure; *Library*

Theatre Ontario
#350,401 Richmond St. West, Toronto ON M5V 3A8
Tel: 416-408-4556; *Fax:* 416-408-3402
info@theatreontario.org
www.theatreontario.org
Overview: A medium-sized provincial charitable organization founded in 1971
Mission: To promote the continued development of theatre arts & artists in Ontario; to support the continued development of vital & broadly accessible theatre training of the highest quality to all sectors of Ontario's theatre community; to encourage the continued development of high quality theatre & drama programs within the educational system of Ontario; to ensure that Ontario's community theatres & educators obtain access to the resources of professional theatre; to facilitate interaction & communication between community, educational & professional theatre
Member of: Association of Summer Theatres 'Round Ontario; Tourism Federation of Ontario; Toronto Association of Acting Studios; Acting & Modelling Information Service
Chief Officer(s):
Carol Beauchamp, Executive Director
carol@theatreontario.org
Finances: *Annual Operating Budget:* $250,000-$500,000; *Funding Sources:* Ontario Arts Council; Toronto Arts Council; Ontario Trillium Foundation
Staff Member(s): 7; 5 volunteer(s)
Membership: 1,000+; *Fees:* $65 - $195; *Member Profile:* People involved in the theatre community
Activities: Workshops; summer courses; showcase; publications; Theatre Ontario Festival, May; *Internships:* Yes; *Speaker Service:* Yes; *Library:* Resource Centre; Open to public
Awards:
- Sandra Tulloch Award (Award)
- Theatre Ontario Festival Awards (Award)
- Maggie Bassett Award (Award)

Théâtre populaire d'Acadie (TPA)
#302, 220, boul. St-Pierre Ouest, Caraquet NB E1W 1A5
Tél: 506-727-0920; *Téléc:* 506-727-0923
Ligne sans frais: 800-872-0920
tpa@tpacadie.ca
www.tpacadie.ca
www.facebook.com/tpacadie
www.youtube.com/tpacadie1

Aperçu: *Dimension:* petite; *Envergure:* provinciale; Organisme sans but lucratif; fondée en 1974
Mission: Créer, produire, diffuser et faire rayonner le théâtre d'ici et d'ailleurs
Membre de: Association des théâtres francophones du Canada; Conseil économique du Nouveau-Brunswick
Membre(s) du bureau directeur:
Maurice Arsenault, Directeur artistique et général
maurice@tpacadie.ca
Membre(s) du personnel: 6

Theatre Saskatchewan
402 Broad St., Regina SK S4R 1X3
Tel: 306-352-0797; *Fax:* 306-569-7888
www.theatresaskatchewan.com
Previous Name: Saskatchewan Community Theatre Inc.
Overview: A medium-sized provincial organization founded in 1933
Mission: To strive to build a strong foundation for theatre which allows all people in Saskatchewan accessibility to live drama
Chief Officer(s):
Melissa Brio, Executive Director
melissa@theatresaskatchewan.com
Membership: 53; *Fees:* $135 voting; $100 non-voting; $25+ associate; $10 subscription

Theatre Terrific Society
#430, 111 West Hastings St., Vancouver BC V6B 1H4
Tel: 604-222-4020; *Fax:* 604-669-2662
info@theatreterrific.ca
www.theatreterrific.ca
twitter.com/TheatreTerrific
www.youtube.com/user/theatreterrific
Overview: A small local charitable organization founded in 1985
Mission: To provide theatrical opportunities to people with disabilities
Member of: Alliance for Arts & Culture
Affliation(s): Volunteer Vancouver; Greater Vancouver Professional Theatre Association
Chief Officer(s):
Susanna Uchatius, Artistic Director
Finances: *Funding Sources:* Class fees; Corporate sponsors; Foundations; Government; Individuals
Staff Member(s): 1
Membership: *Fees:* $10
Activities: Courses in acting for people with mental & physical disabilities; professional theatre productions featuring artists with physical & mental disabilities; Annual free day of acting classes; *Speaker Service:* Yes; *Library* by appointment

Théâtres associés inc. (TAI)
#405, 1908, rue Panet, Montréal QC H2L 3A2
Tél: 514-842-6361; *Téléc:* 514-842-9730
info@theatresassocies.ca
www.theatresassocies.ca
Aperçu: *Dimension:* petite; *Envergure:* provinciale; Organisme sans but lucratif; fondée en 1985
Mission: Se faire la voix d'institutions théâtrales francophones québécoises
Membre(s) du bureau directeur:
Pierre Rousseau, Président
Suzanne Thomas, Secrétaire-Trésorière
Membre: 9; *Critères d'admissibilite:* Compagnie théatrale

Théâtres unis enfance jeunesse (TUEJ)
#217, 911, rue Jean-Talon Est, Montréal QC H2R 1V5
Tél: 514-380-2337
info@tuej.org
tuej.org
Aperçu: *Dimension:* petite; *Envergure:* provinciale; fondée en 1986
Mission: Défendre les intérêts des producteurs dans le domaine du théâtre pour la jeunesse
Membre de: Association québécoise des marionnettistes; Conseil Québécois du théâtre; Conseil québécois des Ressources humaines en Culture; RAPThéâtre
Affliation(s): Conseil québécois du Théâtre; Academie québécoise du Théâtre; Les Arts et la Ville; Conseil Québécois des ressources humaines en culture; RAPThéâtre
Membre(s) du bureau directeur:
Marie-Eve Huot, Présidente
Danielle Bergevin, Directrice générale
Membre: 30 actifs et 8 autres; *Montant de la cotisation:* 300$; *Critères d'admissibilite:* Théâtre professionnel; *Comités:* Action politique; Succession; Petite jauge; Conseil québécois du théâtre (CQT) auxquels TUEJ participe

Theatres' Trust *See* Historic Theatres' Trust

Thebacha Road Society Inc.
PO Box 147, Fort Smith NT X0E 0P0
Tel: 867-872-8400; *Fax:* 867-872-8401
townoffortsmith@northwestel.net
Overview: A small local organization
Chief Officer(s):
Peter Martselos, President
Richard Power, Economic Facilitator

Them Days Inc.
PO Box 939, Stn. B, 3 Courte Manche, Happy Valley-Goose Bay NL A0P 1E0
Tel: 709-896-8531; *Fax:* 709-896-4970
administrator@themdays.com
www.themdays.com
www.facebook.com/themdaysinc
twitter.com/themdays
Overview: A small local charitable organization founded in 1975
Mission: To keep the history of Labrador alive by documenting & preserving the "old ways & early days" of Labrador
Member of: Association of Newfoundland & Labrador Archivists; Newfoundland & Labrador Genealogical Society
Chief Officer(s):
Daphne Fudge, Administrator
Staff Member(s): 2
Activities: Records, documents, researches & publishes the oral, visual & written history of Labrador; conducts special projects of research, translation, consultation, maintenance of an archival collection & producation of publications on matters relating to Labrador history & culture; *Library* Open to public by appointment

Therapeutic Ride Algoma
2627 Second Line West, Sault Ste Marie ON P6A 6K4
Tel: 705-759-9282
therapeuticridealgoma@hotmail.ca
www.ridealgoma.com
Overview: A small local organization
Member of: Canadian Therapeutic Riding Association
Chief Officer(s):
Bob Trainor, President

The Therapeutic Touch Network (Ontario) *See* The Therapeutic Touch Network of Ontario

The Therapeutic Touch Network of Ontario (TTNO)
#4, 290 The West Mall, 4th Fl., Etobicoke ON M9C 1C6
Tel: 416-231-6824
ttno.membership@sympatico.ca
www.therapeutictouchontario.org
www.facebook.com/groups/ttnosm
twitter.com/TTNOntario
Previous Name: The Therapeutic Touch Network (Ontario)
Overview: A small provincial licensing organization founded in 1994
Mission: To promote the practice & acceptance of Therapeutic Touch as developed by Dolores Krieger & Dora Kunz
Chief Officer(s):
Doreen Sullivan, Contact
Alison Cooke, Contact
Shirley Allsworth, Contact
Finances: *Annual Operating Budget:* $100,000-$250,000; *Funding Sources:* Members' fees; fundraising; donations
Staff Member(s): 1
Membership: 1,009; *Fees:* $62 general; $79 recognized practitioner; $107 recognized teacher; *Member Profile:* Health professionals, therapists, counsellors, clergy, educators, veterinarians & Lay People; *Committees:* Practitioners; Teachers; Newsletter; Conference
Activities: TTNO Sponsored Practice Day, held throughout the year; Teacher Collective Days, held regionally; *Speaker Service:* Yes
Awards:
• The Therapeutic Touch Network of Ontario Scholarship Fund (Scholarship)
Publications:
• In Touch
Type: Newsletter

Theresians International - Canada
c/o Blessed Trinity Church, 3220 Bayview Ave., Toronto ON M2M 3R7
Tel: 905-763-7670
www.theresians.org
www.facebook.com/171787696166059
Also Known As: Theresians of Canada
Overview: A medium-sized international organization
Mission: To provide a nurturing, supportive, & spiritual environment for women
Affliation(s): Archdiocese of Toronto
Chief Officer(s):
Camila C.D. Nowakowski, Contact
cnowakowski@rogers.com
Finances: *Annual Operating Budget:* Less than $50,000

Thermal Environmental Comfort Association (TECA)
PO Box 73105, Stn. Evergreen RO, Surrey BC V3R 0J2
Tel: 604-594-5956; *Fax:* 604-594-5091
Toll-Free: 888-577-3818
training@teca.ca
www.teca.ca
Overview: A large provincial organization
Mission: To offer the residential heating, cooling and ventilation industry up-to-date training courses and a collective voice in local and provincial issues.
Chief Officer(s):
Kim Savage, Executive Director, 604-596-0595
Gary Fabbro, President, 604-299-1353
Kathryn Kubossek, Administrator
Membership: 298; *Fees:* $185-$350; $100 associate

Thermal Insulation Association of Alberta
#400, 1040 - 7 Ave. SW, Calgary AB T2P 3G9
Tel: 403-244-4487; *Fax:* 403-244-2340
info@tiaa.cc
www.tiaa.cc
Overview: A small provincial organization
Mission: To improve & elevate the technical & general knowledge of the mechanical insulation industry in Alberta, promoting excellence in manufacture, application, & installation of all insulation products & materials
Member of: Thermal Insulation Association of Canada
Chief Officer(s):
Mark Travors, Provincial President
Meetings/Conferences: • Thermal Insulation Association of Alberta Annual General Meeting & Banquet 2015, May, 2015, Red Deer, AB
Scope: Provincial

Thistletown Coin & Stamp Club *See* Mississauga-Etobicoke Coin Stamp & Collectibles Club

Thompson Chamber of Commerce
PO Box 363, 79 Selkirk Ave., Thompson MB R8N 1N2
Tel: 204-677-4155
Toll-Free: 888-307-0103
commerce@mts.net
www.thompsonchamber.ca
Overview: A small local organization founded in 1960
Mission: To promote the commercial, industrial & civic progress of the community
Member of: Manitoba Chamber of Commerce
Chief Officer(s):
Linda Markus, President
Finances: *Annual Operating Budget:* Less than $50,000; *Funding Sources:* Membership dues; fundraising
Staff Member(s): 1; 50 volunteer(s)
Membership: 230; *Fees:* Schedule available
Activities: *Rents Mailing List:* Yes

Thompson Crisis Centre
PO Box 1226, Thompson MB R8N 1P1
Tel: 204-677-9668; *Fax:* 204-677-9042; *Crisis Hot-Line:* 800-442-0613
www.thompsoncrisiscentre.org
Overview: A medium-sized local organization founded in 1977
Mission: To provide immediate assistance through a walk-in facility & a 24-hour emergency telephone service; to provide a safe place for the women & their children who are victims of physical/emotional abuse; to provide services to women & their children needing longer term support
Chief Officer(s):
Sue O'Brien, Chair
Activities: Emergency Program; Transition Program; 24-hour Crisis Line; Children's Program; Follow-up Program

Thompson Okanagan Tourism Association (TOTA)
2280-D Leckie Rd., Kelowna BC V1X 6G6
Tel: 250-860-5999; *Fax:* 250-860-9993
Toll-Free: 800-567-2275
info@totabc.com
www.totabc.org/corporatesite

www.facebook.com/totabc
twitter.com/totamedia
www.youtube.com/user/thompsonokanagan
Previous Name: Okanagan Similkameen Tourism Association
Overview: A medium-sized local organization founded in 1963 overseen by Council of Tourism Associations of British Columbia
Mission: To increase members' revenue & sustainability through cooperative marketing, ongoing education & government liaison
Member of: National Tour Association; American Bus Association
Chief Officer(s):
Glenn Mandziuk, CEO
ceo@totabc.com
Finances: *Annual Operating Budget:* $500,000-$1.5 Million; *Funding Sources:* Private; provincial & federal government
Staff Member(s): 10; 2 volunteer(s)
Membership: 400; *Fees:* $100+; *Committees:* Marketing; Personnel; Member Relations; Environment & Government Relations; Transportation; Community; Audit; Golf Marketing

Thompson Rivers University Faculty Association (TRUFA)

900 McGill Rd., Kamloops BC V2C 0C8
Tel: 250-374-3040; *Fax:* 250-374-6434
trufa@shawcable.com
trufa.tru.ca
Overview: A small local organization founded in 1974
Mission: To promote the professional standards set for its members at the university
Member of: Federation of Post-Secondary Educators of BC; Kamloops & District Labour Council
Affliation(s): Canadian Association of University Teachers; British Columbia Federation of Labour; Canadian Labour Congress
Chief Officer(s):
Jason Brown, President
trufa-pres@shawcable.com
Finances: *Funding Sources:* Membership dues
Membership: 650 faculty members; *Fees:* 1.5% of salary; *Committees:* Shop Stewards; Salary & Working Conditions; Human Rights; Status of Women; Equivalent Workload; Status of Non-Regular Faculty; Disability Management; Executive; Leave; Safety & Health; Education Policy; Pension Advocacy; Equity; Professional Development; Wellness; Consultative

Williams Lake
#1015, 1250 Western Ave., Williams Lake BC V2G 1H7
Tel: 250-392-8043
Chief Officer(s):
Barbara Bearman, Williams Lake Representative
bbearman@tru.ca

Thompson Rivers University Open Learning Faculty Association (TRUFOLA)

www.truolfa.ca
Previous Name: Faculty Association of the Open Learning Agency
Overview: A small local organization
Chief Officer(s):
John O'Brien, President, 250-852-6962
jobrien@tru.ca

Thompson Valley Rock Club

270 McGill Rd., Kamloops BC V2C 1M1
e-mail: tvrckamloops@gmail.com
www.tvrc.ca
Overview: A small local organization
Affliation(s): British Columbia Lapidary Society; Gem & Mineral Federation of Canada
Chief Officer(s):
Helen Lowndes, Club Contact, 250-314-1944
helow@telus.net
Membership: *Member Profile:* Rock hounding enthusiasts from Kamloops & the surrounding region
Activities: Hosting monthly meetings, except July & August; Providing workshops on topics such as cutting & polishing, wire wrapping, & faceting; Arranging field trips; *Speaker Service:* Yes
Publications:
• Chips & Chatter [a publication of the Thompson Valley Rock Club
Type: Newsletter; *Price:* Free with membership in the Thompson Valley Rock Club

Thompson, Nicola, Cariboo United Way

177 Victoria St., Kamloops BC V2C 1Z4
Tel: 250-372-9933; *Fax:* 250-372-5926
Toll-Free: 855-372-9933
office@unitedwaytnc.ca
www.unitedwaytnc.ca
www.facebook.com/unitedwaytnc
twitter.com/unitedwaytnc
www.youtube.com/unitedwaytnc
Previous Name: United Way of Kamloops & Region
Overview: A small local organization founded in 1959 overseen by United Way of Canada - Centraide Canada
Mission: To enable all citizens to join in a community wide effort to fund & provide in consort with others, effective delivery of health & social services & programs in response to the needs of the community
Chief Officer(s):
Brenda Aynsley, Executive Director
brenda@unitedwaytnc.ca
Finances: *Annual Operating Budget:* $500,000-$1.5 Million
Staff Member(s): 3; 800 volunteer(s)
Membership: 27 local service providers; *Fees:* $1 annually; *Committees:* Cabinet; Nominating; Advisory; Executive; Finance; Membership; Community Development
Activities: *Awareness Events:* Annual Golf Tournament, Aug.; Annual Kick Off Breakfast, Sept.

Thorhild Chamber of Commerce

PO Box 384, 638 - 6th Ave., Thorhild AB T0A 3J0
Tel: 780-398-2575; *Fax:* 780-398-2010
thorhildchamber@telus.net
Overview: A small local organization
Chief Officer(s):
John Dickey, President
Ed Cowley, Secretary
Membership: 29

Thornbury & District Chamber of Commerce *See* Blue Mountains Chamber of Commerce

Thorncliffe Neighbourhood Office

18 Thorncliffe Park Dr., Toronto ON M4H 1N7
Tel: 416-421-3054; *Fax:* 416-421-4269
info@thorncliffe.org
www.thorncliffe.org
Overview: A small local charitable organization overseen by Ontario Council of Agencies Serving Immigrants
Member of: Family Resource Association
Chief Officer(s):
Jehad Aliweiwi, Executive Director
jaliweiwi@thorncliffe.org
Staff Member(s): 14
Membership: *Committees:* Finance; Human Resource; Board Recruitment

Thorsby & District Chamber of Commerce

Thorsby AB
Overview: A small local organization
Chief Officer(s):
Mitch William, President
Activities: Trade fair; customer appreciation night; charity golf tournament;

Thousand Islands Watershed Land Trust (TIWLT)

19 Reynolds Rd., Landsdowne ON K0E 1L0
Tel: 613-659-4824
info@tiwlt.ca
tiwlt.weebly.com
Overview: A small local organization founded in 2007
Mission: To permanently protect land in the Thousand Islands watershed region through acquisition or conservation agreements, and to achieve good land management through stewardship agreements and education.
Chief Officer(s):
Dann Michols, President
Membership: *Fees:* $40-$100

Three Hills & District Chamber of Commerce

PO Box 277, Three Hills AB T0M 2A0
Tel: 403-443-5570
3hillschamber@gmail.com
threehillschamber.ca
Overview: A small local organization
Mission: To promote & improve commerce in the Three Hills District
Chief Officer(s):
Ross Gaehring, Acting President
ross.gaehring@kneehillhousing.com
Membership: 92

Three Sisters Scottish Festival Society

PO Box 8102, Canmore AB T1W 2T8
Tel: 403-678-9454; *Fax:* 403-678-3385
canmorehighlandgames@telus.net
www.canmorehighlandgames.ca
www.linkedin.com/company/seekers-media
www.facebook.com/festivalseekers
twitter.com/Canmorehighland
www.youtube.com/festivalseekers
Overview: A small local organization founded in 1991
Mission: Registered non-profit society with a mandate to promote and encourage Celtic culture in all its' forms; dance, music and sports, and to establish the Canmore Highland Games as an entertainment/cultural destination event.
Chief Officer(s):
Sandra McLeod, President
Ron Lewis, Vice-President
Doug Fraser, Secretary-Treasurer
Activities: *Awareness Events:* Canmore Highland Games, September; Tartan Day, April 6

The 3C Foundation of Canada / Fondation Canadienne des 3c

#200, 1 Hines Rd., Kanata ON K2K 3C7
Tel: 613-237-6690
info@3cfoundation.org
www.3cfoundation.org
Overview: A medium-sized national charitable organization
Chief Officer(s):
Michele Hepburn, President
michele@3cfoundation.org
Jessica Diener, Coordinator, Youth Programs
Finances: *Funding Sources:* Donations; fundraising
Membership: *Member Profile:* People living with Crohn's disease, colitis & colon cancer
Activities: The "IBDealing With It" program; Toilet Paper Flowers Campaign; *Awareness Events:* Gut Together, Oct.; Youth Gut Together; World IBD Day, May
Awards:
• The Abbott IBD Scholarship Program (Scholarship)

Thunder Bay & District Labour Council

#1, 929 Fort William Rd., Thunder Bay ON P7B 3A6
Tel: 807-345-2621; *Fax:* 807-345-1071
tbdlc@tbaytel.net
Previous Name: Fort William Trades & Labour Council
Overview: A medium-sized local organization overseen by Ontario Federation of Labour
Member of: Ontario Federation of Labour
Finances: *Funding Sources:* Membership fees
Activities: *Awareness Events:* Day of Mourning, April

Thunder Bay Adventure Trails

PO Box 29190, Thunder Bay ON P7B 6P9
Toll-Free: 800-526-7522
tbat_den@hotmail.com
Overview: A medium-sized local organization founded in 1990
Mission: To groom & maintain 700 kilometres of snowmobile trails, from Thunder Bay to Shabaqua
Member of: North Superior Snowmobile Association (NOSSA)
Chief Officer(s):
Marcel Gauthier, Club Executive
Lloyd Chaykowski, Club Executive
Harold Harkonen, Club Executive
Bradley Pollock, Club Executive
Membership: *Fees:* $200-before Dec.1; $250-after Dec.1; $100-3-day permit; $140-7-day permit; $125-classic permit

Thunder Bay Amateur Hockey Association *See* Hockey Northwestern Ontario

Thunder Bay Beekeepers' Association

#228, 1100 Memorial Ave., Thunder Bay ON P7B 4A3
Tel: 807-476-0927
www.thunderbaybeekeepersassociation.ca
www.facebook.com/128459093838912
Overview: A small local organization
Mission: To share information about beekeeping in the Thunder Bay area
Member of: Ontario Beekeepers' Association
Chief Officer(s):
Chris Carolan, President
chris.carolan@me.com
Membership: *Fees:* $25; *Member Profile:* Persons interested in apiculture in the Thunder Bay area
Activities: Promoting the beekeeping industry & educating the public in the Thunder Bay area by donating a bee journal to the

Canadian Associations

Thunder Bay Public Library; Creating educational displays, such as the association's demo hive, at places such as the local country market, in order to show the public the basics of beekeeping & how the public can sustain the population; Presenting workshops to share beekeeping skills & Knowledge; *Speaker Service:* Yes

Thunder Bay Chamber of Commerce (TBCC)

#102, 200 Syndicate Ave. South, Thunder Bay ON P7E 1C9
Tel: 807-624-2626; *Fax:* 807-622-7752
chamber@tbchamber.ca
www.tbchamber.ca
Overview: A medium-sized local organization founded in 1885
Mission: To serve the membership by providing leadership & influencing effective change for a healthy business environment
Affliation(s): Northwestern Ontario Associated Chambers of Commerce; Ontario Chamber of Commerce; Canadian Chamber of Commerce
Chief Officer(s):
Charla Robinson, President
charla@tbchamber.ca
Josh Tinkler-Josephi, Coordinator, Policy & Communications
josh@tbchamber.ca
Finances: *Annual Operating Budget:* $500,000-$1.5 Million; *Funding Sources:* Membership fees & special events
Staff Member(s): 8; 250 volunteer(s)
Membership: 1,000+; *Fees:* $205-$2705 based on number of employees; *Committees:* Board of Directors; Education, Training & Development; Environment; Chamber Executive; Finance; International Business; Nominating; Past Presidents; Quality Management; Shows (Home, Trade, Wedding Wishes); Small Business Development; Special Events; Transportation Week Luncheon & Activities
Activities: *Internships:* Yes; *Speaker Service:* Yes; *Library:* Office Library; Open to public
Awards:
• Secondary School Scholarships (Scholarship)
Amount: $1,000 & $500 respectively
• Business Excellence Awards (Award)
Categories: Employer of the Year; Employee of the Year; Best Service Industry; Best Retail Establishment; Best Hospitality Establishment; Ambassador's Award; Green Award; Looking Good Award

Thunder Bay Community Foundation

Ruttan Block, #17D, 4 Court St. South, Thunder Bay ON P7B 2W4
Tel: 807-475-7279; *Fax:* 807-684-0793
tbcf@tbaytel.net
www.tbcf.org
www.facebook.com/thunderbay.communityfoundation
twitter.com/@TBayCF
Previous Name: Thunder Bay Foundation
Overview: A small local charitable organization founded in 1971
Mission: To receive, maintain, manage, control & use donations for charitable purposes in the district of Thunder Bay to the benefit of children & youth services, alleviation of human suffering, & advancement of social work, education & cultural purposes
Member of: Community Foundations of Canada
Chief Officer(s):
Art Warwick, President
Rosy Brizi, Vice-President
Robert Mozzon, Secretary-Treasurer
Finances: *Funding Sources:* Donations
Membership: 1-99; *Committees:* Executive; Finance; Grants; Scholarships; Public Relations

Thunder Bay Counselling Centre

544 Winnipeg Ave., Thunder Bay ON P7B 3S7
Tel: 807-684-1880
community@tbaycounselling.com
www.tbaycounselling.com
www.facebook.com/134082413330347
Previous Name: Family Services Thunder Bay
Overview: A medium-sized local charitable organization founded in 1967
Mission: To provide community based support services to individuals, couples, & families in the Thunder Bay area; To offer confidential counselling
Member of: Ontario Association of Credit Couselling Services
Chief Officer(s):
Nancy Chamberlain, Executive Director
Finances: *Funding Sources:* Donations
Activities: Presenting courses on topics such as anger management, self-esteem, & stress reduction; Offering programs, such as Budgeting & Debt Management (e-mail: creditcounsellor@tbaycounselling.com), & Employee Assistance Programs (e-mail: corporate@tbaycounselling.com), featuring custom designed counselling solutions for businesses & employees; Disseminating promotional materials
Publications:
• The Solution Source
Type: Newsletter *ISSN:* 1481-2568
Profile: Issue topics include benefits of counselling, living with uncertainty, compassion fatigue, single parent families, & understanding teens & substance abuse

Thunder Bay District Municipal League (TBDML)

c/o Beth Stewart, 343 Parker Rd., Gillies Township, RR#1, Kakabeka Falls ON P0T 1W0
Tel: 807-476-0927; *Fax:* 807-622-8246
Overview: A small local organization founded in 1917
Mission: To improve services for its residents
Member of: Northwestern Ontario Municipal Association
Chief Officer(s):
Larry Hebert, President
Beth Stewart, Secretary-Treasurer
bstewart@tbaytel.net
Finances: *Funding Sources:* Municipal contributions
Membership: 19; *Fees:* Per capita; *Member Profile:* Municipalities dedicated to good local government

Thunder Bay Field Naturalists (TBFN)

PO Box 10037, Thunder Bay ON P7B 6T6
Tel: 807-474-6007
www.tbfn.net
Overview: A small local charitable organization founded in 1933
Mission: To promote the enjoyment of nature through environmental appreciation & conservation; to encourage wise use & conservation of natural resources; to promote environmental protection
Member of: Federation of Ontario Naturalists
Affliation(s): Thunder Cape Bird Observatory
Chief Officer(s):
Brian McLaren, President
bmclaren@lakeheadu.ca
Rob Foster, Vice-President
rfoster@tbaytel.net
Finances: *Annual Operating Budget:* $50,000-$100,000; *Funding Sources:* Membership fees; donations; grants
11 volunteer(s)
Membership: 200; *Fees:* $30 family; $25 single; $20 students/seniors; $350 life; *Member Profile:* Those interested in the study of nature & the environment; *Committees:* Nature Reserves; Bird Records; Peregrine Falcon Recovery; Bluebird Recovery
Activities: Adult & Junior Nature; oriented field trips; indoor lectures; *Speaker Service:* Yes

Thunder Bay Foundation *See* Thunder Bay Community Foundation

Thunder Bay Historical Museum Society (TBHMS)

425 Donald St. East, Thunder Bay ON P7E 5V1
Tel: 807-623-0801; *Fax:* 807-622-6880
info@thunderbaymuseum.com
www.thunderbaymuseum.com
Also Known As: Thunder Bay Museum
Overview: A small local charitable organization founded in 1908
Mission: To preserve, collect & interpret the heritage of Northwestern Ontario
Member of: Ontario Historical Society; Ontario Museum Association; Minnesota Historical Society; Canadian Museums Association
Chief Officer(s):
Tory Tronrud, Director
Finances: *Annual Operating Budget:* $250,000-$500,000
Staff Member(s): 6; 50 volunteer(s)
Membership: 1,000; *Fees:* $30 individual; $45 family; $100 business; $1,000 corporate; *Committees:* Publication; Programs & Plaques; Membership; Museum Development
Activities: Publications; lectures; craft classes; education; rotating exhibits; research services; outreach & extension; *Library* Open to public by appointment

Thunder Bay Indian Friendship Centre (TBIFC)

401 North Cumberland St., Thunder Bay ON P7A 4P7
Tel: 807-345-5840; *Fax:* 807-344-8945
www.tbifc.ca
Overview: A small local organization founded in 1964
Mission: To serve as a meeting place for the Native community in Thunder Bay, Ontario; To address issues that affect the lives of Native people
Member of: Ontario Federation of Indian Friendship Centres
Chief Officer(s):
Mark Hardy, President
Charlene Baglien, Secretary
Bonnie Wilson, Treasurer
Finances: *Funding Sources:* Donations
Membership: *Fees:* $1; *Member Profile:* Members of Aboriginal ancestry who live in Thunder Bay, Ontario; Corporations, partnerships, & other legal entities
Activities: Hosting seasonal feasts with the assistance of community elders; Providing programs & services such as the Children's Wellness Program, Anishnawbe Skills Development Program, Apatisiwin Employment Program, Aboriginal Healing & Wellness, the Urban Aboriginal Healthy Living Program, & the Life Long Care Program

Thunder Bay Law Association

277 Camelot St., Thunder Bay ON P7A 4B3
Tel: 807-344-3481; *Fax:* 807-345-9091
Toll-Free: 866-684-1186
tbla@tbaytel.net
www.tbla.on.ca
Overview: A small local organization
Chief Officer(s):
Catherine Walsh, Library Manager
Roy Karistedt, President
Finances: *Annual Operating Budget:* $100,000-$250,000; *Funding Sources:* Membership fees; Law Society of Upper Canada
Staff Member(s): 2
Membership: 200; *Committees:* Archives; Civil Liaison; Courthouse; Continuing Legal Education; Criminal Liaison; Family Liaison; Law DAy; Library; Personnel; Public Relations; REal Estate; Retention & Recruitment; Social; Website & Computers; Ad Hoc; Nominating; Public Service Awards
Activities: *Library:* District Courthouse Library; by appointment

Thunder Bay Minor Football Association (TBMFA)

535 Chapples Dr., Thunder Bay ON P7C 2V7
Tel: 807-251-5052
www.tbmfa.com
www.facebook.com/tbmfa.knights
twitter.com/TBMFAKNIGHTS
Overview: A small local organization founded in 2013
Mission: To run a football program for boys & girls ages 7-13 in Thunder Bay
Chief Officer(s):
Rob Thompson, President
Sarah Kuzik, Secretary
spkuzik@shaw.ca

Thunder Bay Minor Hockey Association (TBMHA)

#101, 212 East Miles St., Thunder Bay ON
Tel: 807-346-4510; *Fax:* 807-346-4511
www.tbmha.com
Overview: A small local organization
Chief Officer(s):
Larry Busniuk, President
Membership: *Committees:* Finance; Playing & Ice; Rules & Input; Grievance; Awards & Public Relations; Draft Committee; Harrassment & Abuse; Risk Management

Thunder Bay Multicultural Association (TBMA)

17 North Court St., Thunder Bay ON P7A 4T4
Tel: 807-345-0551; *Fax:* 807-345-0173
Toll-Free: 866-831-1144
www.tbma.ca
Overview: A small local organization founded in 1972 overseen by Ontario Council of Agencies Serving Immigrants
Mission: To promote the concept of multiculturalism; to encourage cultural awareness, appreciation, & cooperation; to preserve cultural freedom, heritage, & cultural identity
Finances: *Funding Sources:* Federal government; provincial government; fundraising
Membership: *Member Profile:* Ethnocultural groups of region
Activities: Interpretation/translation; settlement services; community programs; newcomer services; educational materials; website; *Library* Open to public

Thunder Bay Musicians' Association

1111 East Victoria Ave., Thunder Bay ON P7C 1B7
Tel: 807-622-1062; *Fax:* 807-622-3961
local591@tbaytel.net
www.afm.org/locals/info/number/591
Overview: A small local organization founded in 1970
Mission: To promote live music

Chief Officer(s):
Garry Agostino, President
Finances: *Annual Operating Budget:* Less than $50,000
Staff Member(s): 1
Membership: 286; *Fees:* $112

Thunder Bay Physical & Sexual Assault Crisis Centre *See* Thunder Bay Sexual Assault / Sexual Abuse Counselling & Crisis Centre

Thunder Bay Police Association (TBPA) / Association de la police de Thunder Bay
McIntyre Centre, PO Box 29035, Thunder Bay ON P7B 6P9
Tel: 807-344-8336; *Fax:* 807-344-8337
Overview: A small local organization
Member of: Police Association of Ontario
Chief Officer(s):
Greg Stephenson, Contact
Activities: Raising funds for service-oriented organizations in Thunder Bay, Ontario;

Thunder Bay Public Affairs - Visitors & Convention Department *See* Tourism Thunder Bay

Thunder Bay Real Estate Board
1141 Barton St., Thunder Bay ON P7B 5N3
Tel: 807-623-5011; *Fax:* 807-623-3056
info@thunderbay-MLS.on.ca
www.thunderbay-mls.on.ca
Overview: A small local organization founded in 1971 overseen by Ontario Real Estate Association
Chief Officer(s):
Diane Erickson, President, 807-473-7443
Mark Boudreau, Director, Education & Membership Committees, 807-223-6215

Thunder Bay Regional Arts Council (TBRAC)
#100, 105 South May St., Thunder Bay ON P7E 1B1
Tel: 807-623-6544; *Fax:* 807-623-2821
www.thunderbayculture.com
Overview: A small local charitable organization founded in 1982
Mission: To enrich the quality of life by promoting & encouraging the development of arts & cultural activities
Member of: Volunteer Thunder Bay; Community Arts Ontario
Chief Officer(s):
Janis Swanson, Office Administrator
Finances: *Annual Operating Budget:* Less than $50,000
Staff Member(s): 1; 30 volunteer(s)
Membership: 150; *Fees:* $25-75; *Member Profile:* Artists; cultural organizations; arts supporters; *Committees:* Arts Alive; Mayor's Arts Luncheon; Website; Newsletter
Activities: Arts awareness; arts promotion; *Library:* Artist Resource Centre; Open to public

Thunder Bay Sexual Assault / Sexual Abuse Counselling & Crisis Centre
385 Mooney St., Thunder Bay ON P7B 5L5
Tel: 807-345-0894; *Fax:* 807-344-1981; *Crisis Hot-Line:* 807-344-4502
tbcounselling@tbsasa.org
www.tbsasa.org
Previous Name: Thunder Bay Physical & Sexual Assault Crisis Centre
Overview: A small local organization overseen by Canadian Association of Sexual Assault Centres
Mission: To provide help & support to victims of sexual assault & their family that allows them to overcome their trauma
Member of: Ontario Federation of Mental Health & Addiction Program; Thunder Bay Chamber of Commerce
Finances: *Funding Sources:* Ontario Ministry of Health & Long-Term Care; Ontario Ministry of the Attorney General
Staff Member(s): 10

Thunder Bay Symphony Orchestra Association (TBSO)
PO Box 29192, Thunder Bay ON P7B 6P9
Tel: 807-474-2284; *Fax:* 807-622-1927
info@tbso.ca
www.tbso.ca
www.facebook.com/ThunderBaySymphonyOrchestra
www.youtube.com/user/ThunderBaySymphony
Overview: A small local charitable organization founded in 1960 overseen by Orchestras Canada
Mission: To maintain & nurture a professional, regional orchestra of artistic integrity & excellence; to offer a variety of programs to enrich & encourage the widest possible audience; to support the development of local young musicians
Member of: Orchestras Ontario
Chief Officer(s):
Paul Inksetter, President
Shannon Whidden, General Manager
gm@tbso.ca
Arthur Post, Music Director
Finances: *Funding Sources:* Canada Council; City of Thunder Bay; ticket sales; Ontario Arts Council
Staff Member(s): 11
Activities: *Library:* Music Library

Thunderbird Friendship Centre
PO Box 430, 301 Beamish Ave. West, Geraldton ON P0T 1M0
Tel: 807-854-1060; *Fax:* 807-854-0861
Toll-Free: 888-854-1060
www.tbfc.ca
Overview: A small local organization founded in 1971
Mission: To provide a meeting place for the Aboriginal & non-Aboriginal people of the Geraldton, Ontario area
Member of: Ontario Federation of Indian Friendship Centres
Membership: *Fees:* $1
Activities: Offering cultural, educational, recreational, & social programs; Providing services in the areas of prenatal nutrition, healthy living, & career development

Thyroid Foundation of Canada / La Fondation canadienne de la Thyroïde
c/o National Treasurer, PO Box 9, Manotick ON K4M 1A2
Fax: 514-630-9815
Toll-Free: 800-267-8822
www.thyroid.ca
Overview: A medium-sized national charitable organization founded in 1980
Mission: To provide leadership to the fight against thyroid disease
Chief Officer(s):
Mabel Miller, President
Donna Miniely, Treasurer
Finances: *Annual Operating Budget:* $50,000-$100,000; *Funding Sources:* Health Canada; donations; membership fees
Staff Member(s): 2; 1000 volunteer(s)
Membership: 4,000 individual; *Fees:* Schedule available
Activities: *Awareness Events:* Thyroid Month, June
Awards:
• Diana Meltzer Abramsky Research Fellowship (Scholarship)
• Summer Student Scholarship (Scholarship)

Tides Canada Foundation
#400, 163 Hastings St. West, Vancouver BC V6B 1H5
Tel: 604-647-6611
Toll-Free: 866-780-6611
info@tidescanada.org
www.tidescanada.org
facebook.com/tidescanada
twitter.com/tidescanada
Overview: A small national charitable organization founded in 2000
Mission: To create partnerships with donors & charitable organizations to grow resources for social change & environmental stability
Member of: Canadian Environmental Grantmakers Network; Canadian Centre for Philanthropy
Chief Officer(s):
Ross McMillan, President & CEO
Finances: *Annual Operating Budget:* $500,000-$1.5 Million
Staff Member(s): 10
Awards:
• Tides Canada Grant (Grant)
To charities that are addressing issues like climate change, wilderness protection, marine conservation, aboriginal issues, poverty, and international development

Toronto Office
#360, 215 Spadina Ave., Toronto ON M5T 2C7
Tel: 416-481-8652
Toll-Free: 866-780-6611

Tiger Hills Arts Association Inc. (THAA)
McFeetors Centre, 103 Broadway St., Holland MB R0G 0X0
Tel: 204-526-2063; *Fax:* 204-526-2105
thaa@mymts.net
www.tigerhillsarts.com
www.facebook.com/tigerhillsarts
Overview: A small local charitable organization
Mission: To promote lifetime involvement in the visual, performing & literary arts through the development of a varied program of cultural activities in the Tiger Hills area
Member of: Manitoba Association of Community Arts Councils Inc.
Chief Officer(s):
Catheryn Pedersen, Executive Director
Finances: *Annual Operating Budget:* $100,000-$250,000
Staff Member(s): 2; 200 volunteer(s)
Membership: 95; *Fees:* $15 individual; $30 family
Activities: Arts & cultural programs; *Library*
Awards:
• Arts Career Scholarship (Scholarship)
Amount: $1,000
• Talent Search Scholarship (Scholarship)
Amount: $1,000

Tikinagan Child & Family Services
PO Box 627, 63 King St., Sioux Lookout ON P8T 1B1
Tel: 807-737-3466; *Fax:* 807-737-3543
Toll-Free: 800-465-3624
www.tikinagan.org
Previous Name: Tikinagan North Child & Family Services
Overview: A small local organization founded in 1984
Member of: Association of Native Child & Family Services Agencies of Ontario
Chief Officer(s):
Michael Hardy, Executive Director
Finances: *Annual Operating Budget:* Greater than $5 Million; *Funding Sources:* Ministry of Community & Social Services
Staff Member(s): 100
Membership: 10

Tikinagan North Child & Family Services *See* Tikinagan Child & Family Services

Tilbury & District Chamber of Commerce
PO Box 1299, 17 Superior St., Tilbury ON N0P 2L0
Tel: 519-682-3040
tbia.dcc@pppoe.ca
www.tilburyontario.com/Chamber
www.facebook.com/217527424926762
twitter.com/TilburyOntario
Overview: A small local organization
Mission: To promote commercial business in our local community; to improve commerce & industry in local community
Member of: Ontario Chamber of Commerce
Chief Officer(s):
Kathy Cottingham, Chair
kcottingham@mnsi.net
Natalie Whittal, Executive Director & Coordinator, Events
Finances: *Annual Operating Budget:* Less than $50,000; *Funding Sources:* Membership fees; donations
9 volunteer(s)
Membership: 120; *Fees:* $35-$210
Activities: *Awareness Events:* Tilbury Family Fest, June; *Library:* Tilbury Odette Memorial Library; Open to public

Tillicum Centre - Hope Association for Community Living
1166 - 7 Ave., Hope BC V0X 1L4
Tel: 604-869-2565; *Fax:* 604-869-2565
tillicum@telus.net
Previous Name: Hope Association for Community Living
Overview: A small local organization founded in 1964
Mission: To provide service to mentally & physically challenged adults in the community of Hope
Member of: British Columbia Association for Community Living
Finances: *Annual Operating Budget:* Less than $50,000
Activities: Life skills; recreation; academic activities

Tillicum Haus Native Friendship Centre
927 Haliburton St., Nanaimo BC V9R 6N4
Tel: 250-753-4417; *Fax:* 250-753-8122
admin@tillicumhaus.ca
www.tillicumhaus.ca
Overview: A small local organization
Chief Officer(s):
Grace Elliott-Nielsen, Executive Director

Tillsonburg & District Association for Community Living
96 Tillson Ave., Tillsonburg ON N4G 3A1
Tel: 519-842-9000; *Fax:* 519-842-7628
info@communitylivingtillsonburg.ca
www.communitylivingtillsonburg.ca
Overview: A small local organization
Member of: Community Living Ontario
Chief Officer(s):
Virginia Armstrong, President

Tillsonburg & District Multi-Service Centre (TDMSC)

Livingston Centre, 96 Tillson Ave., Tillsonburg ON N4G 3A1
Tel: 519-842-9008; *Fax:* 519-842-4727
info@multiservicecentre.com
www.multiservicecentre.com
www.facebook.com/109475662455610
twitter.com/multisercen
Previous Name: Information Tillsonburg
Overview: A small local charitable organization founded in 1977
Mission: To provide human support resources
Chief Officer(s):
Bill Hett, Executive Director & CEO
Maureen Vandenberghe, Coordinator, Communications & Development
Staff Member(s): 7
Activities: Volunteer Recognition, May; Employee Recognition, summer/fall; Donor Recognition, Nov.; *Speaker Service:* Yes

Tillsonburg Coin Club

c/o Ralph Harrison, 36 Hamps Cres., Tillsonburg ON N4G 4Z3
Tel: 519-842-8790
Overview: A small local organization
Chief Officer(s):
Ralph Harrison, Treasurer
rchar@sympatico.ca

Tillsonburg District Chamber of Commerce

Tillsonburg ON
www.tillsonburgchamber.ca
Overview: A small local organization founded in 1976
Mission: To promote our community & to be a source of information
Chief Officer(s):
Sheryl Williams, President, 519-688-1072
Suzanne Renken, General Manager, 519-688-3737
suzanne@tillsonburgchamber.ca
Finances: *Annual Operating Budget:* Less than $50,000
Membership: 115; *Fees:* $120-350

Tillsonburg District Real Estate Board

#202, 1 Library Lane, Tillsonburg ON N4G 4W3
Tel: 519-842-9361; *Fax:* 519-688-6850
tburgreb@bellnet.ca
www.tburgreb.ca
Overview: A small local organization founded in 1968 overseen by Ontario Real Estate Association
Mission: To provide its members with the tools they need to best serve the public
Member of: The Canadian Real Estate Association; The Ontario Real Estate Association
Chief Officer(s):
Lindsay Morgan, President
lindsay@morganrealty.ca
Membership: 99

Tim Horton Children's Foundation

RR#2, 264 Glen Morris Rd. East, St George ON N0E 1N0
Tel: 519-448-1248; *Fax:* 519-448-1415
thcf_info@timhortons.com
www.timhortonchildrensfoundation.com
www.facebook.com/timhortonchildrensfoundation
Overview: A medium-sized national organization founded in 1975
Mission: Dedicated to fostering within our children the quest for a brighter future
Chief Officer(s):
Victoria Caves, Youth Leadership Program Registrar
caves_victoria@timhortons.com
Activities: Operates 6 camps

Timberline Trail & Nature Club

701 - 105th Ave., Dawson Creek BC V1G 2K5
Tel: 250-782-7680
www.timberlinetrailandnature.com
www.facebook.com#timberlinetrailandnature
Overview: A small local organization founded in 1973
Mission: To promote the enjoyment of nature through environmental appreciation & conservation; To encourage wise use & conservation of natural resources & environmental protection
Member of: Federation of BC Naturalists
Chief Officer(s):
Meredith Thornton, Contact
mthorntnpris.ca
Membership: 15; *Fees:* $25
Meetings/Conferences: • Timberline Trail & Nature Member Meeting, Third Wednesday of every month, South Peace Secondary School Library, Dawson Creek, BC

Timbres de Pâques Canada *See* Easter Seals Canada

Les Timbres de Pâques N.-B. *See* Easter Seals New Brunswick

Times Change Women's Employment Service

#1704, 365 Bloor St. East, Toronto ON M4W 3L4
Tel: 416-927-1900; *Fax:* 416-927-1900
women@timeschange.org
www.timeschange.org
www.facebook.com/timeschangeWES?v=wall
Overview: A small local charitable organization founded in 1974
Member of: Ontario Council of Agencies Serving Immigrants
Finances: *Funding Sources:* Employment Ontario; Ontario Women's Directorate; United Way Toronto; Private donations
Staff Member(s): 10; 20 volunteer(s)
Membership: 150; *Fees:* $5 unemployed; $10 employed; *Member Profile:* Clients; Supporters
Activities: Providing group workshops in career planning & job search techniques; Offering individual educational counselling; Providing computers, by appointment, for practice or preparing cover letters & resumes; Arranging job matching & placement; *Library:* Times Change Women's Employment Service Resource Centre; Open to public by appointment

Timmins & Area Women in Crisis Support & Information Centre on Violence Against Women (TAWC)

355 Wilson Ave., Timmins ON P4N 2T7
Tel: 705-268-8380; *Fax:* 705-268-3332
info@tawc.ca
www.tawc.ca
www.facebook.com/TAWCTimmins
Previous Name: Rape Crisis Centre Timmins
Overview: A small local charitable organization founded in 1992
Mission: To assist survivors of sexual violence & to promote the establishment of social & political structures free of sexual violence & exploitation
Member of: Ontario Coalition of Rape Crisis Centres
Chief Officer(s):
Becky Mason, Contact, 705-268-8381
becky@tawc.ca
Finances: *Annual Operating Budget:* $100,000-$250,000; *Funding Sources:* Ministry of the Attorney General; Ministry of Community & Social Services
Staff Member(s): 20; 12 volunteer(s)
Membership: *Member Profile:* Women 16 & over
Activities: Advocacy; counselling; crisis line; referrals; workshops; speakers; family court support; transitional housing support; women's shelter; *Awareness Events:* Take Back the Night March, Sept.; Sexual Assault Awareness Month, May; International Women's Day, March 8; *Internships:* Yes; *Library:* Timmins & Area Women in Crisis Library; Open to public

Timmins Chamber of Commerce / Chambre de commerce de Timmins

PO Box 985, 76 McIntyre Rd., Timmins ON P4N 7H6
Tel: 705-360-1900; *Fax:* 705-360-1193
admin@timminschamber.on.ca
www.timminschamber.on.ca
www.facebook.com/TimminsChamber
twitter.com/TimminsChamber
Overview: A small local organization founded in 1949
Mission: To encourage growth in our community by promoting business opportunities
Member of: Ontario Chamber of Commerce; Canadian Chamber of Commerce
Chief Officer(s):
Rob Galloway, President
Keitha Robson, Manager
Finances: *Annual Operating Budget:* $250,000-$500,000; *Funding Sources:* Membership dues; licence bureau; fundraising
Staff Member(s): 8; 1 volunteer(s)
Membership: 830; *Fees:* Schedule available; *Committees:* Transportation; Business Development; Economic Development; Marketing; Tourism; Sustainable Energy & Environment
Activities: Tourist Information Centre; Licensing Bureau (drivers & vehicles); Annual Dinner, fall; *Internships:* Yes

Timmins Coin Club

c/o Randy Maass, PO Box 466, Timmons ON P4N 7E3
Overview: A small local organization
Chief Officer(s):
Randy Maass, President
nifinder@hotmail.com

Timmins Family Counselling Centre, Inc. / Centre de Counselling Familial de Timmins inc.

#310, 60 Wilson Ave., Timmins ON P4N 2S7
Tel: 705-267-7333; *Fax:* 705-268-6850
www.timminsfamilycounselling.com
Overview: A small local charitable organization founded in 1979
Mission: To provide high quality therapeutic services in regards to maintaining & improving the functioning of families, couples & the individual; aims to promote education & development in the community & intercedes for the client's rights with a goal of impro0ing the quality of life in Timmins & its surrounding areas
Chief Officer(s):
Nathalie Parnell, Executive Director
Staff Member(s): 10
Activities: Presentation to EAP clients; presentations in the community of Timmins & surrounding areas; *Internships:* Yes; *Speaker Service:* Yes; *Library* by appointment

Timmins Native Friendship Centre

316 Spruce St. South, Timmins ON P4N 2M9
Tel: 705-268-6262; *Fax:* 705-268-6266
reception@tnfc.ca
www.tnfc.ca
www.facebook.com/TimminsNativeFriendshipCentre?ref=tn_tnmn
Overview: A small local organization
Mission: To provide a culturally sensitive, helpful environment for Aboriginal & non-Aboriginal people in Timmins, Ontario; To improve the quality of life for Aboriginal & non-Aboriginal people in the Timmins community
Member of: Ontario Federation of Indian Friendship Centres
Chief Officer(s):
Veronica Nicholson, Executive Director
vnicholson@tnfc.ca
Roseanne Ross, Director, Finance
rross@tnfc.ca
Rena Buhler, Worker, Urban Aboriginal Healthy Lifestyles Program
rbuhler@tnfc.ca
Micheline Hunter, Worker, Aboriginal Healthy Babies, Healthy Children
mhunter@tnfc.ca
Karen Innes, Worker, Aboriginal Prenatal Nutrition
kinnes@tnfc.ca
Debbie Lovelace, Worker, Aboriginal Family Support
dlovelace@tnfc.ca
Crystal Moore, Worker, Life Long Care
cmoore@tnfc.ca
Lisa Wesley, Worker, Indigenous Children's Wellness
lwesley@tnfc.ca
Sinclair Williams, Worker, Aboriginal Alcohol & Drugs
siwilliams@tnfc.ca
Activities: Offering programs in areas such as nutrition, literacy & basic skills, academic upgrading, & career development

Timmins Real Estate Board

225 Algonquin Blvd. East, Timmins ON P4N 1B4
Tel: 705-268-5451; *Fax:* 705-264-6420
boards.mls.ca/timmins/
Overview: A small local organization overseen by Ontario Real Estate Association
Finances: *Annual Operating Budget:* $100,000-$250,000; *Funding Sources:* Membership dues
Staff Member(s): 2
Membership: 80

Timmins Symphony Orchestra

PO Box 1365, Timmins ON P4N 7N2
Tel: 705-267-1006; *Fax:* 705-267-1006
info@timminssymphony.com
www.timminssymphony.com
www.facebook.com/TimminsSymphonyOrchestra
twitter.com/timminssymphony
Overview: A small local organization founded in 1979 overseen by Orchestras Canada
Chief Officer(s):
Suzanne Robichaud, Manager, Operations

Tir-à-l'arc Moncton Archers Inc.

Moncton NB
Tel: 506-382-3522
Previous Name: Moncton Archers & Bowhunters Association
Overview: A small local organization founded in 1968

Mission: To enjoy the sport of archery & bowhunting; To promote saftey in each sport
Affliation(s): New Brunswick Archery Association; Canadian Archery Association
Chief Officer(s):
John Langelaan, Director
johnlangelaan@hotmail.com

Tire and Rubber Association of Canada (TRAC) / L'Association canadienne du pneu et du caoutchouc

Plaza 4, #100, 2000 Argentia Rd., Mississauga ON L5N 1W1
Tel: 905-814-1714; *Fax:* 905-814-1085
info@rubberassociation.ca
www.tracanada.ca
www.linkedin.com/company/the-rubber-association-of-canada
twitter.com/GTRadials
Previous Name: The Rubber Association of Canada
Overview: A large national organization founded in 1920
Mission: To upgrade & maintain good industry/government working relations; to explore ways of improving industry competitiveness & efficiency; To promote safety in members' products, in their use & in the workplace; To promote expansion & profitability of Canadian rubber manufacturing units; To enhance standing of Canadian rubber industry worldwide; To provide members with industry marketing statistics
Chief Officer(s):
Glenn Maidment, President
glenn@rubberassociation.ca
Ralph Warner, Director, Operations
ralph@rubberassociation.ca
Antonia Issa, Communications Manager
Finances: *Annual Operating Budget:* $250,000-$500,000; *Funding Sources:* Membership dues
Staff Member(s): 4
Membership: 24 corporate; *Fees:* Based on volume of product; *Member Profile:* Manufacturers of products made from rubber; suppliers; importers; *Committees:* Customs & Tariffs; General Rubber Products; Human Resources; Occupational Health & Safety; Workers' Compensation; Environment; Tire Statistical; Tire Technical; Scrap Tire
Activities: *Speaker Service:* Yes
Meetings/Conferences: • Tire and Rubber Association 2015 Tire & Rubber Summit, 2015
Scope: National
• Tire and Rubber Association 2016 Symposium, 2016
Scope: National

Tire Stewardship BC Association (TSBC)

PO Box 5366, 1627 Fort St., 4th Fl., Victoria BC V8R 6S4
Tel: 250-598-9112; *Fax:* 250-598-9119
Toll-Free: 866-759-0488
www.tirestewardshipbc.ca
Overview: A small provincial organization founded in 2006
Mission: The Tire Stewardship BC Association was founded by the Rubber Association of Canada, The Retail Council of Canada and the Western Canada Tire Dealers. In 2007 the New Car Dealers Association joined the Association. TSBC is governed by a Board that is made up of representatives from these four organizations
Chief Officer(s):
Don Blythe, Chair
Glenn Maidment, Secretary

Tisdale & District Chamber of Commerce

PO Box 219, Tisdale SK S0E 1T0
Tel: 306-873-4257; *Fax:* 306-873-4241
Overview: A small local organization
Staff Member(s): 1; 12 volunteer(s)
Membership: 100; *Fees:* Schedule available; *Member Profile:* Local businesses
Activities: Community events; Customer Service Training; Community Promotion

Title Insurance Industry Association of Canada (TIIAC) / Association canadienne des compagnies d'assurance titres (ACCAT)

PO Box 866, 31 Adelaide St. East, Toronto ON M5C 2K1
e-mail: info@tiiac-accat.com
www.tiiac-accat.com
Overview: A small national organization
Mission: To represent the interests of the title insurance industry in Canada
Chief Officer(s):
Paul Zappala, President
Membership: 4 companies; *Member Profile:* Federally regulated title insurers

Activities: Education for members; advocation

Tiverton Board of Trade

PO Box 629, 3083 Hwy. 217, Tiverton NS B0V 1G0
Tel: 902-839-2853
tivertonboardoftrade@hotmail.com
Overview: A small local organization

Tobermory & District Chamber of Commerce

PO Box 250, Tobermory ON N0H 2R0
Tel: 519-596-2452; *Fax:* 519-596-2452
Other Communication: Visitor Information e-mail: info@tobermory.com
chamber@tobermory.org
www.tobermory.org
Overview: A small local organization founded in 1977
Mission: To promote the trade & commerce of the business community; to encourage the economic, civic & social welfare of the district
Member of: Bruce County Tourism Association; Bruce Peninsula Tourist Association
Affliation(s): Central Bruce Peninsula Chamber of Commerce; South Bruce Peninsula Chamber of Commerce; Manitoulin Chamber of Commerce; Manitoulin Tourism Association; Sauble Beach Chamber of Commerce
Finances: *Annual Operating Budget:* Less than $50,000; *Funding Sources:* Membership dues; municipal government; fundraising
Staff Member(s): 1; 45 volunteer(s)
Membership: 100; *Fees:* $100-300

Tofield & District Chamber of Commerce

PO Box 967, Tofield AB T0B 4J0
www.tofieldalberta.ca/business/chamber-of-commerce
Overview: A small local organization
Mission: To advocate for businesses in the town of Tofield, Alberta & the surrounding area
Affliation(s): Alberta Chambers of Commerce
Chief Officer(s):
David Williamson, President
Davidw@sdi-team.ca
Greg Litwin, Vice-President
Calvin Andringa, Secretary
Janet Trotno, Treasurer
Membership: *Fees:* $60
Activities: Participating in & sponsoring local events, such as the Sherwood Park Trade Show & the Small Business Week celebration
Publications:
• Tofield & Area Business & Services Directory
Type: Directory
Profile: Detailed listings of local businesses

Tofield Historical Society

PO Box 1082, Tofield AB T0B 4J0
Tel: 780-662-3269
www.tofieldalberta.ca/recreation/attractions/museum
Also Known As: Tofield Museum
Overview: A small local organization founded in 1961
Member of: Museums Alberta
Finances: *Funding Sources:* Donations; grants; fundraising
Activities: Canada Day Open House; Strawberry Social, Aug.

Tofino-Long Beach Chamber of Commerce

PO Box 249, 1426 Pacific Rim Hwy., Tofino BC V0R 2Z0
Tel: 250-725-3414; *Fax:* 250-725-3296
info@tofinochamber.org
www.tofinochamber.org
twitter.com/tofinochamber
Overview: A small local charitable organization
Mission: To promote a healthy & responsible environment for businesses operating in or relocating to the Tofino Long Beach & Clayoquot Sound Region
Chief Officer(s):
Don Travers, President
tofino@remotepassages.com
Gord Johns, Executive Director
Finances: *Annual Operating Budget:* $50,000-$100,000
Staff Member(s): 1; 10 volunteer(s)
Membership: 225; *Fees:* $130
Activities: Pacific Rim Whale Festival; Clayoquot Shorebird Festival; Edge to Edge Marathon; Clayoquot Oyster Festival

Top of Lake Superior Chamber of Commerce

PO Box 402, Nipigon ON P0T 2P0
e-mail: chamber@topoflakesuperior.com
www.topoflakesuperior.com

Overview: A small local organization founded in 1988
Member of: Canadian Chamber of Commerce; Ontario Chamber of Commerce
Chief Officer(s):
Brigitte Tremblay, Coordinator, 807-887-4147
bdtremblay@shaw.ca
Staff Member(s): 2
Membership: 96

Toronto *See* Juvenile Diabetes Research Foundation

Toronto & District Square & Round Dance Association

c/o Bob & Betty Beck, 62 Tupper Dr., Thorold ON L2V 4C8
Tel: 905-227-7264
www.td-dance.ca
Overview: A small local organization founded in 1951
Mission: To promote, encourage & foster wider knowledge of square & round dancing; to provide for mutual exchange of philosophy & material pertaining to square & round dancing between callers, teachers, & leaders; to improve quality of square & round dancing; to encourage use of standards of uniformity relating to square & round dancing
Member of: Ontario Square & Round Dance Federation
Affliation(s): Canadian Square & Round Dance Society
Chief Officer(s):
Sharron Hall, Co-President
president@td-dance.ca
Wayne Hall, Co-President
president@td-dance.ca
Finances: *Funding Sources:* Membership fees; dances; convention
Activities: *Internships:* Yes; *Speaker Service:* Yes; *Library:* Resource Centre; by appointment

Toronto & York Region Labour Council

#407, 15 Gervais Dr., Toronto ON M3C 1Y8
Tel: 416-441-3663; *Fax:* 416-445-8405
council@labourcouncil.ca
www.labourcouncil.ca
Previous Name: Labour Council of Metropolitan Toronto & York Region
Overview: A medium-sized local organization overseen by Ontario Feeration of Labour
Member of: Ontario Federation of Labour
Chief Officer(s):
John Cartwright, President
jcartwright@labourcouncil.ca

Toronto Academy of Dentistry

#207, 970 Lawrence Ave. West, Toronto ON M6A 3B6
Tel: 416-967-5649; *Fax:* 416-967-5081
admin@tordent.com
www.tordent.com
Overview: A small provincial organization founded in 1890
Mission: To provide leadership & service to both the profession & the community; to advance the art & science of dentistry; to promote the highest ideals of dental practice; to cultivate harmony & good fellowship among its fellows & among the members of the dental profession
Chief Officer(s):
Mara Busca-Bedford, Executive Director
Staff Member(s): 3
Membership: 1,800; *Member Profile:* Dentists

Toronto Action for Social Change

PO Box 73620, 509 St. Clair Ave. West, Toronto ON M6C 1C0
Tel: 416-651-5800
tasc@web.ca
www.homesnotbombs.ca/tasc.htm
Also Known As: Homes Not Bombs
Overview: A small local organization
Mission: Building community through non-violent action

Toronto Alliance for the Performing Arts (TAPA)

#350, 401 Richmond St. West, Toronto ON M5V 3A8
Tel: 416-536-6468; *Fax:* 416-536-3463
Toll-Free: 800-541-0499
www.tapa.ca
Previous Name: Toronto Theatre Alliance
Overview: A medium-sized local organization founded in 1980
Mission: To foster greater respect & support for the arts by advocating on behalf of Canadian theatre & dance, representing all cultural backgrounds, to government, supporters, & the general public; to provide services which enhance the artistic, technical, & administrative development of members

Affiliation(s): Professional Association of Canadian Theatres (PACT), Theatre Ontario
Chief Officer(s):
Jacoba Knaapen, Executive Director
jacobak@tapa.ca
Alexis Da Silva-Powell, Manager, Corporate Partnerships & Membership
alexisdsp@tapa.ca
Sandra Lefrançois, Manager, Dora
sandral@tapa.ca
Kevin John Macdonald, Manager, Operations
kevinm@tapa.ca
Bill Van Heerden, Manager, Sales
billvh@tapa.ca
Finances: *Funding Sources:* Grants from Toronto Arts Council & Ontario Arts Council
Staff Member(s): 6; 80 volunteer(s)
Membership: 187 professional theatre, dance & opera companies; *Fees:* Sliding scale; *Committees:* Government; corporate & private sector sponsorship; self-generated revenue
Activities: Runs ticket outlet in the downtown Toronto theatre district (TO Tix); provides professional development workshops/seminars Sept.-June (through the TAPA trade series).; *Internships:* Yes; *Rents Mailing List:* Yes
Awards:
• Dora Mavor Moore Awards (Award)
Established 1979; celebrating excellence in Toronto theatre, 35 awards in large, medium & small theatre divisions, Theatre for Young Audiences & New Choreography
• Silver Ticket Award (Award)

Toronto Animated Image Society (TAIS)
#102, 60 Atlantic Ave., Studio 9, Toronto ON M6K 1X9
Tel: 416-533-7889
tais.animation@gmail.com
www.tais.ca
www.facebook.com/group.php?gid=2396817462
twitter.com/TAIS_Animation
Overview: A small local organization founded in 1984
Mission: To facilitate the growth of animation artists, craftsmen, & others interested in the art of animation through the sharing of ideas & information on animation; to be a support group for the individual as part of a pool of talent from which to draw
Chief Officer(s):
Madi Piller, President
Membership: *Fees:* $40 individual; $150 studio

Toronto Area Gays & Lesbians Phoneline & Crisis Counselling (TAGL)
PO Box 632, Stn. F, Toronto ON M4Y 2N6
Tel: 416-964-6600
Toll-Free: 877-964-6677
Overview: A small local charitable organization founded in 1975
Mission: To operate a telephone information & peer counselling line for gays & lesbians
Affiliation(s): Gay Lesbian & Bisexual Access Coalition
Finances: *Annual Operating Budget:* Less than $50,000
30 volunteer(s)
Membership: 1-99

Toronto Art Therapy Institute (TATI)
#103, 66 Portland St., Toronto ON M5V 2M6
Tel: 416-924-6221; *Fax:* 416-924-0156
www.tati.on.ca
Overview: A small local charitable organization founded in 1968
Mission: To train individuals who want to become art therapists; to develop a preventative program for children & adolescents at risk & to offer art therapy
Affiliation(s): Lesley College, Cambridge, MA
Chief Officer(s):
Peter J. Carrington, President
Helene Burt, Executive Director
Staff Member(s): 25
Membership: *Committees:* Academic; Admission
Activities: Training program; workshops & information meetings; *Library*
Awards:
• Martin Fischer Memorial Thesis Prize (Award)

Toronto Arts Council (TAC)
Toronto ON
e-mail: mail@torontoartscouncil.org
www.torontoartscouncil.org
Overview: A medium-sized local charitable organization founded in 1974
Mission: To support the development, accessibility & excellence of the arts in Toronto; on behalf of the city, offers grants programs to the city's arts organizations & professional artists
Chief Officer(s):
Claire Hopkinson, Executive Director
claire@torontoartscouncil.org
Finances: *Annual Operating Budget:* Greater than $5 Million
Staff Member(s): 12; 29 volunteer(s)
Membership: 130; *Member Profile:* Artists; city councillors; arts supporters; *Committees:* Literary; Dance; Visual Arts/Media Arts; Music; Community Arts; Theatre
Activities: *Library* by appointment

Toronto Arts Council Foundation (TACF)
141 Bathurst St., Toronto ON M5V 2R2
Tel: 416-392-6800; *Fax:* 416-392-6920
mail@torontoartscouncil.org
www.torontoartscouncil.org
www.facebook.com/TorontoArts
twitter.com/TorontoArts
Overview: A medium-sized local charitable organization founded in 1995
Mission: To create a Toronto-based repository for legacies & other gifts from individuals, families, corporations or trusts that wish to support the arts in Toronto
Chief Officer(s):
John McKellar, Chair
Lydia Perovic, Executive Assistant
Claire Hopkinson, Executive Director
Finances: *Annual Operating Budget:* $250,000-$500,000
400 volunteer(s)
Membership: 5,300; *Member Profile:* Arts supporters in Toronto
Activities: Mayor's Arts Awards Lunch, Oct.
Awards:
• William Kilbourn Award (Award)
Awarded every second year to an individual performer, teacher, administrator, or creator in any arts discipline, including architecture & design, whose work is a celebration of life through the arts in Toronto *Amount:* $5,000
• Muriel Sherrin Award (Award)
$10,000 cash prize presented to an artist or creator who has made a contribution to the cultural life ot Toronto through outstanding achievement in music. The recipient will also have participated in international initiatives, including touring, study abroad & artist exchanges. Awarded every second year
• Rita Davies Award (Award)
$5,000 cash prize presented to a Toronto artist, volunteer or administrator who has demonstrated creative leadership in the development of arts & culture in Toronto. Awarded every second year
• Margo Bindhardt Award (Award)
$10,000 cash prize presented every second year to Toronto artist or administrator whose leadership & vision, whether through their creative work or cultural activism, have had a significant impact on the arts in Toronto & for whom the cash prize will make a difference

Toronto Artscape Inc.
#224, 174 East Liberty St., Toronto ON M6K 3P6
Tel: 416-392-1038; *Fax:* 416-535-6260
info@torontoartscape.on.ca
www.torontoartscape.org
www.facebook.com/TorontoArtscape
twitter.com/Artscape
www.youtube.com/torontoartscape;
www.flickr.com/photos/artscape
Also Known As: Artscape Non-Profit Homes Inc.
Overview: A medium-sized local organization founded in 1986
Mission: To provide affordable living &/or working space for artists for the relief of poverty & the advancement of education, culture, art & other purposes beneficial to the community
Member of: Parkdale/Liberty Economic Development Corp.; Liberty Village Business Improvement Area; Queen West Gallery District; Ontario Non-Profit Housing Association
Chief Officer(s):
Robert J. Foster, Chair
Tim Jones, President & CEO
tim@torontoartscape.on.ca
Leslie Najgebauer, Director, Administration
leslie@torontoartscape.on.ca
Finances: *Annual Operating Budget:* $500,000-$1.5 Million; *Funding Sources:* City of Toronto; Ministry of Municipal Affairs & Housing; Laidlaw Foundation; Toronto Arts Council
Staff Member(s): 8; 12 volunteer(s)
Activities: Acquisition, funding, development & management of property; liaison, information & outreach services; consulting services; provision of programs & services for artists & the non-profit, charitable, education & government sectors; *Awareness Events:* Inside Artscape; Art for Art's Sake Fundraising Event

Gibraltar Point Centre for Artscape
443 Lakeshore Ave., Toronto Island ON
Tel: 416-392-1030
www.torontoartscape.org/artscape-gibraltar-point
Chief Officer(s):
Susan Serran, Director, Arts Programs & Services

Toronto Association for Business Economics Inc. (TABE)
PO Box 955, 31 Adelaide St. East, Toronto ON M5C 2K3
Tel: 647-693-7418; *Fax:* 416-352-5627
tabe@cabe.ca
www.cabe.ca/chapters/TABE
twitter.com/TABE_Economics
Overview: A small local organization founded in 1965 overseen by Canadian Association for Business Economics
Mission: To promote a better understanding of economic issues; to contribute to the professional development of members; to encourage the availability of economic information & to broaden awareness of business economics; to recognize achievement of business economists
Member of: Canadian Association for Business Economics
Chief Officer(s):
Ingrid Porter, Executive Director
Jane Voll, President
jvoll@bankofcanada.ca
Finances: *Funding Sources:* Membership fees
Membership: *Fees:* $80 full; $160 national CABE members; $30 student
Activities: Luncheons, workshops & quarterly study sessions; *Speaker Service:* Yes

Toronto Association for Community Living *See* Community Living Toronto

Toronto Association for Democracy in China (TADC)
#407, 253 College St., Toronto ON M5T 1R5
Tel: 416-592-5406
www.tadc.ca
Overview: A small international organization founded in 1989
Chief Officer(s):
Cheuk Kwan, Chair
Finances: *Funding Sources:* Donations
Membership: 100-499; *Committees:* Lobbying; Education; Publicity
Activities: *Speaker Service:* Yes

Toronto Association for Learning & Preserving the History of WWII in Asia
#305, 85 Scarsdale Rd., Toronto ON M3B 2R2
Tel: 416-299-0111; *Fax:* 866-248-5290
www.torontoalpha.org
www.linkedin.com/company/1563278
www.facebook.com/torontoalpha
www.youtube.com/ALPHAtoronto
Overview: A small local organization
Mission: To achieve peace & reconciliation with the understanding of the history of World War II in Asia
Chief Officer(s):
Flora Chong, Executive Director
Staff Member(s): 6

Toronto Association of Acting Studios (TAAS)
c/o Theatre Ontario, #210, 215 Spadina Ave., Toronto ON M5T 2C7
Tel: 416-408-4556; *Fax:* 416-408-3402
info@theatreontario.org
www.torontoactingstudios.com
Overview: A small local organization founded in 1984
Mission: To offer a wide variety of high-quality approaches to the craft of acting & related theatrical skills
Chief Officer(s):
Vrenia Ivonoffski, Chair
Membership: 31; *Fees:* $125

Toronto Association of Law Libraries (TALL)
PO Box 1042, Stn. TDC, 77 King St. West, Toronto ON M5K 1P2
www.talltoronto.ca
www.facebook.com/TorontoAssociationOfLawLibraries
Overview: A small local organization founded in 1979
Mission: To represent & support members of the legal community in Toronto & the surrounding region

Chief Officer(s):
Pamela Bakker, President
John Bolan, Vice-President
Leanne Notenboom, Secretary
Eve Leung, Treasurer
Laura Knapp, Coordinator, Administration
talladmin@gmail.com
Membership: *Fees:* $34.65 students; $52.50 general & associate members; *Member Profile:* Members of the Toronto & surrounding area legal community, representing corporate law libraries, law firms, law societies, court houses, academia, government, & legal publishers; *Committees:* Education; Information Technology; Publisher Liaison; Salary Survey; Newsletter Editorial Board; Union List; Audit; Election; Photographers Group
Activities: Informing members of new information sources & emerging technologies; Facilitating the exchange of ideas & information among Toronto area law libraries through the TALL Listserv; Developing continuing educational programs; Advocating for members; Conducting surveys of salaries & benefits in the Toronto region legal community; Providing an interlibrary loan list for members; Offering networking opportunities
Publications:
• TALL Directory of Law Libraries
Type: Directory; *Frequency:* Annually; *Price:* Subscription based upon the size of an organization
Profile: Law library & personnel contact information, plus special subject collections & services provided to external users
• TALL Newsletter
Frequency: Quarterly; *Price:* Free with Toronto Association of Law Libraries membership
Profile: Communications for members of the Toronto Association of Law Libraries
• Toronto Association of Law Libraries Union List of Periodicals
Frequency: Biennially; *Price:* Free with Toronto Association of Law Libraries membership

Toronto Association of Synagogue & Temple Administrators

c/o Beth Tikvah Synagogue, 3080 Bayview Ave., Toronto ON M5N 5L3
Tel: 416-221-3433
Overview: A small local organization
Chief Officer(s):
Doris Alter, President
doris@bethtikvahtoronto.org
Finances: *Annual Operating Budget:* Less than $50,000
Membership: 12; *Fees:* $50; *Member Profile:* Executive directors of synagogues & temples

Toronto Association of Systems & Software Quality (TASSQ)

1489 Agnew Rd., Mississauga ON L5J 3G8
Tel: 905-822-6645
admin@toronto-assq.com
www.tassq.org
www.linkedin.com/groups/Toronto-Association-Systems-Software-Quality-9
www.facebook.com/TASSQorg
twitter.com/TASSQ_Online
Overview: A small local organization founded in 1993
Mission: To promote quality assurance in the information technology industry
Chief Officer(s):
Joe Larizza, President
Membership: *Fees:* $100 individual; $500 corporate; $1200 media sponsorship; $2500 platinum media sponsorship

Toronto Autosport Club (TAC)

49 Monkswood Cres., Newmarket ON L3Y 2J9
e-mail: registrar@torontoautosportclub.ca
www.torontoautosportclub.ca
Overview: A small local organization founded in 1956
Member of: Canadian Association of Rally Sport; Canadian Association Sport Clubs - Ontario Region; Rally Sport Ontario
Chief Officer(s):
Rob McAuley, President
rob@rmcauley.ca
Finances: *Annual Operating Budget:* Less than $50,000; *Funding Sources:* Membership fees; contract sports events
80 volunteer(s)
Membership: 80; *Fees:* $50; *Member Profile:* People who compete in car racing & rallying
Activities: Autosports; rallying-auto; racing-ice & autoslalom; *Speaker Service:* Yes

Toronto Baptist Ministries

1585 Yonge St., Toronto ON M4T 1Z9
Tel: 416-425-9472; *Fax:* 416-922-1807
office@torontobaptistministries.org
www.torontobaptistministries.org
Overview: A small local organization overseen by Canadian Baptists of Ontario and Quebec
Mission: To support their member churches
Member of: Canadian Baptists of Ontario & Quebec
Chief Officer(s):
Jim Parker, Moderator
bethanychurch@sympatico.ca
Staff Member(s): 2
Membership: 85 churches; *Member Profile:* Baptist churches in the Greater Toronto Area

Toronto Bicycling Network

PO Box 279, #200, 131 Bloor St. West, Toronto ON M5S 1R8
Tel: 416-760-4191
info@tbn.ca
www.tbn.ca
Overview: A small local organization founded in 1983
Chief Officer(s):
Brian Mclean, President
Membership: 850
Activities: Leisure Wheeler Rides; Easy Roller Rides; Tourist & Short Tourist Rides; Sportif Rides; Country Cruise Rides; Snails & Spice Ride; cross-country skiing; in-line skating; ice skating & hiking;

Toronto Biotechnology Initiative (TBI) / L'Initiative torontoise de biotechnologie

#109, 1 Concorde Gate, Toronto ON M3C 3N5
Tel: 416-426-7293; *Fax:* 416-426-7280
admin@ontbio.org
Overview: A small local organization founded in 1989
Mission: To further biotechnology in the Greater Toronto Area; to further TBI as a leading Canadian biotechnology organization; to further the Greater Toronto Area as a major international centre for biotechnology
Affiliation(s): Biotechnology Industry Organization; Council of Biotechnology Centres; BIOTECanada
Chief Officer(s):
Ali Ibrahimi, Manager, Communications & Membership
Finances: *Annual Operating Budget:* $50,000-$100,000; *Funding Sources:* Membership fees
Membership: 400; *Fees:* $200 regular; $100 student; *Committees:* Biofinance; Breakfast Meetings; Education; Membership; Public Interest Forum; Regulatory; Technology Transfer
Activities: Biofinance (events, awards dinner); Bioscan newsletter; community service award; education; entrepreneurship program; international program; monthly meetings; public interest forum; regulatory affairs

Toronto Blues Society (TBS)

#B04, 910 Queen St. West, Toronto ON M6J 1G6
Tel: 416-538-3885; *Fax:* 416-538-6559
Toll-Free: 866-871-9457
Other Communication: www.myspace.com/torontobluessociety
info@torontobluessociety.com
www.torontobluessociety.com
www.facebook.com/groups/8407237433
twitter.com/TOBluesSociety
www.youtube.com/user/TorontoBluesSociety
Overview: A small local organization founded in 1985
Mission: To foster an appreciation & awareness of the blues as a musical form, thereby giving blues music a higher profile within the music industry & the larger community; to educate, inform & represent the interest of its members
Member of: Folk Alliance North America; Ontario Council of Folk Festivals; The Blues Foundation
Chief Officer(s):
Jordan Safer, Office Manager & Coordinator, Events
Finances: *Annual Operating Budget:* $50,000-$100,000; *Funding Sources:* Toronto Arts Council; SOCAN Foundation; Ontario Arts Council
Staff Member(s): 1; 100 volunteer(s)
Membership: 600; *Fees:* $30 general; $45 charter; $65 family; $125 institutional; *Committees:* Executive; Internet; Programming; Newsletter; Volunteer
Activities: Maple Blues Awards; Women's Blues Revue; New Talent Search

The Toronto Board of Trade

PO Box 60, 1 First Canadian Place, Toronto ON M5X 1C1
Tel: 416-366-6811; *Fax:* 416-366-2444
www.bot.com
www.linkedin.com/groups?gid=35950
www.facebook.com/TorontoBoardOfTrade
twitter.com/torontobot
www.youtube.com/user/TorontoBoardofTrade
Also Known As: World Trade Centre - Toronto
Overview: A large local organization founded in 1845
Mission: To build a better community through business leadership by providing business services, advocating public policy positions, participating in community partnerships & facilitating economic & business development
Chief Officer(s):
Bill MacKinnon, Chair
Carol Wilding, President & CEO, 416-862-4536
ceo@bot.com
Jacqueline Baptist, Vice-President, Marketing & Communications, 416-862-4525
jbaptist@bot.com
Paul Gallucci, Vice-President, Sales & Member Services, 416-862-4561
pgallucci@bot.com
Richard Joy, Vice-President, Policy & Government Relations, 416-862-4519
rjoy@bot.com
Finances: *Annual Operating Budget:* Greater than $5 Million; *Funding Sources:* Membership fees
Staff Member(s): 305
Membership: 10,500; *Fees:* Schedule available: 7 different membership classes; *Committees:* Policy & Advocacy; Economic Development; Infrastructure; Municipal Performance; Liveability
Activities: *Speaker Service:* Yes; *Rents Mailing List:* Yes; *Library:* Worksite;

West End Office
JPR Suite, Skyway Business Park, 170 Attwell Dr., 3rd Fl., Toronto ON M9W 5Z5
Tel: 416-798-6811; *Fax:* 416-798-2499

Toronto Cat Rescue

PO Box 41175, Stn. Rockwood, Mississauga ON L4W 5C9
Tel: 416-538-8592
info@torontocatrescue.ca
www.torontocatrescue.ca
www.facebook.com/TorontoCatRescue
twitter.com/TorontoCatRescu
Overview: A small local charitable organization founded in 1994
Mission: To help cats escape situations of abuse or neglect, or euthanasia at a pound
Chief Officer(s):
Heather Brown, Contact
Finances: *Annual Operating Budget:* $500,000-$1.5 Million
500+ volunteer(s)

Toronto Centre for Community Learning & Development (CCL&D)

269 Gerrard St. East, 2nd Fl., Toronto ON M5A 2G3
Tel: 416-968-6989; *Fax:* 416-968-0597
info@tccld.org
www.tccld.org
www.facebook.com/torontoccld
twitter.com/TorontoCCLD
Previous Name: East End Literacy
Overview: A small local organization founded in 1979
Mission: To encourage literacy skills, employability skills, independent living skills, & community capacity building
Chief Officer(s):
Alfred Jean-Baptiste, Executive Director
Staff Member(s): 11
Membership: *Committees:* Communications
Activities: Creating community engagement through innovative training; Offering programs, such as academic upgrading & the immigrant women integration program; Collaborating with other organizations to develop individual skills & community

Toronto CFA Society; Toronto Society of Financial Analysts
See CFA Society Toronto

Toronto Chapter of the International Association of Printing House Craftsmen

#806, 170 - 6A The Donway West, Toronto ON M3C 2E8
Tel: 905-895-4141
www.iaphc.ca
Also Known As: Toronto IAPHC
Overview: A small local organization founded in 1921

Mission: To group people within the printing industry together, & to promote the industry
Member of: International Association of Printing House Craftsmen
Chief Officer(s):
Bill Kidd, President
b.kidd@rogers.com
Membership: *Member Profile:* Graphic arts
Activities: Monthly education meetings; golf tournament; dinner & dance

Toronto Child Psychoanalytic Program *See* Canadian Institute for Child & Adolescent Psychoanalytic Psychotherapy

Toronto Coin Club (TCC)
c/o 128 Silverstone Dr., Toronto ON M6V 3G7
e-mail: info@torontocoinclub.ca
www.torontocoinclub.ca
Overview: A small local organization founded in 1936
Mission: To promote coin collecting & provide a discussion forum for its members
Member of: Royal Canadian Numismatic Association; Ontario Numismatic Association

Toronto Community Care Access Centre
#305, 250 Dundas St. West, Toronto ON M5T 2Z5
Tel: 416-506-9888; *Fax:* 416-506-0374
Toll-Free: 866-243-0061; *TTY:* 416-506-1512
toronto_ccac@toronto.ccac-ont.ca
www.torontoccac.com
Previous Name: Home Care Program for Metropolitan Toronto
Overview: A medium-sized local organization founded in 1964
Mission: To coordinate & deliver health & social care to all people in Metro Toronto who are sick or disabled; to enhance the quality of their lives & enable them to remain at home; to provide & coordinate an appropriate range of services to meet the diverse needs (health & social) of individuals & families
Member of: Canadian Home Care Association; Ontario Home Care Programs Association
Chief Officer(s):
Stacey Daub, CEO
Nancy Dudgeon, Chair
Finances: *Annual Operating Budget:* $3 Million-$5 Million
Membership: *Committees:* Executive; Planning; Nominating; Patient Care; Community Relations; Finance & Audit; Human Relations
Activities: Nursing; physiotherapy; occupational therapy; speech pathology; social work services; homemaking; medical equipment; laboratory work; drugs; oxygen; transporation

Toronto Community Employment Services
#201, 2221 Yonge St., Toronto ON M4S 2B4
Tel: 416-488-0084; *Fax:* 416-488-3743
service@tces.on.ca
www.toronto-jobs.org
www.linkedin.com/company/toronto-community-employment-services
Previous Name: Immigrant Women's Job Placement Centre
Overview: A small local organization founded in 1978 overseen by Ontario Council of Agencies Serving Immigrants
Mission: To provide placement & employment services
Chief Officer(s):
Andrea de Shield, Chair

Toronto Community Foundation (TCF)
#1603, 33 Bloor St. East, Toronto ON M4W 3H1
Tel: 416-921-2035; *Fax:* 416-921-1026
info@tcf.ca
www.tcf.ca
Also Known As: TCF
Previous Name: Community Foundation for Greater Toronto
Overview: A medium-sized local charitable organization founded in 1983
Mission: To connect philanthropic individuals and families to charitable organizations in Toronto. TCF invests charitable gifts from donors into income-earning endowment funds, and makes grants from the earnings to support a range of charities
Chief Officer(s):
John B. MacIntyre, Chair
Rosalyn Morrison, VP, Community Initiatives
Carol Turner, VP, Finance
Finances: *Annual Operating Budget:* Greater than $5 Million
Staff Member(s): 9

The Toronto Consort
427 Bloor St. West, Toronto ON M5S 1X7
Tel: 416-966-1045; *Fax:* 416-966-1759
info@torontoconsort.org
www.torontoconsort.org
www.facebook.com/155552007809
www.youtube.com/thetorontoconsort
Overview: A small international charitable organization founded in 1972
Mission: To perform & promote music of the Middle Ages & the Renaissance
Finances: *Annual Operating Budget:* $250,000-$500,000
Staff Member(s): 5; 35 volunteer(s)
Membership: 300; *Fees:* $50-$1,000+
Activities: Concerts; Educational events; Recordings; Broadcasts

Toronto Construction Association
70 Leek Cres., Richmond Hill ON L4B 1H1
Tel: 416-499-4000; *Fax:* 416-499-8752
www.tcaconnect.com
Overview: A small local organization founded in 1867 overseen by Canadian Construction Association
Mission: To develop & promote excellence within the construction industry of the Greater Toronto Area
Affliation(s): International Council for Building Research Studies & Documentation
Chief Officer(s):
Chris Fillingham, Chair
cfillingham@stantec.com
John G. Mollenhauer, President & CEO
jmollenhauer@tcaconnect.com
Kim F. McKinney, Executive Vice-President
kmckinney@tcaconnect.com
Staff Member(s): 35
Membership: 2,200 member companies; *Member Profile:* Companies involved in the construction industry; *Committees:* Allied Professions Division; Building a Better Business; Construct Canada Trade Show; Construction Careers Development & Marketing; Entertainment; Environmental; General Contractors Division; Government Relations; Industry Practices; Manufacturer, Supply & Service Division; Membership Retention & Development; Plans Room & EPR Users; The Construction Institute of Canada Accreditation; The Construction Institute of Canada Professional Development; Trade Contractors Division; Young Construction Executives' Club

Mississauga
#122, 1900 Minnesota Ct., Mississauga ON L5N 3C9
Tel: 905-567-1077; *Fax:* 905-567-4114
Chief Officer(s):
Kristina Kouznetsova, Office Administrator
kkouznetsova@tcaconnect.com

Toronto Council Fire Native Cultural Centre
439 Dundas St. East, Toronto ON M5A 2B1
Tel: 416-360-4350
cdo@councilfire.ca
www.councilfire.ca
Previous Name: Council Fire Native Cultural Centre
Overview: A small local organization founded in 1978
Mission: To provide cultural & social services to Aboriginal people
Chief Officer(s):
Andrea Chrisjohn, Board Designate
andrea@cfis.ca
Membership: *Member Profile:* To provide counselling, material assistance & other direct services to First Nations people & to encourage & enhance spiritual & personal growth

Toronto Council of Hazzanim (Cantors)
3080 Bayview Ave., Toronto ON M2N 6E1
Tel: 647-201-3956
info@torontohazzanim.com
www.torontohazzanim.com
www.facebook.com/hazzanim
Also Known As: Cantorial Clergymen of Ontario
Overview: A small local organization
Mission: To represent cantors from all denominations of Judaism; to provide funds for cantorial scholarships, Jewish music, etc.
Chief Officer(s):
Tibor Kovari, President

Toronto Cricket Umpires' & Scorers' Association (TCU&SA)
Toronto ON
www.tcuandsa.org
Overview: A small local organization
Mission: To train Canadian cricket umpires & scorers.
Chief Officer(s):
Arnold Madeela, President
arnold.maddela@gmail.com
Ashcook Brijcoomar, Vice-President, 905-850-3016
abrijcoomar@hotmail.com
Muhammad Haroon, Secretary, 647-284-4857
mharoon2376@gmail.com
Mike Henry, Treasurer, 416-209-9812
mikenhenry@rogers.com

Toronto Crime Stoppers
40 College St., Toronto ON M5G 2P6
Tel: 416-222-8477
Toll-Free: 800-222-8477
www.222tips.com
www.facebook.com/1800222TIPS
twitter.com/1800222TIPS
www.youtube.com/user/1800222TIPS
Overview: A small local organization
Mission: Partnership of the public, police & media that provides the community with a proactive program for people to assist the police anonymously to solve crimes & thereby, to contribute to an improved quality of life
Chief Officer(s):
Lorne Simon, Chair
Activities: *Awareness Events:* Crime Stoppers Month, Jan.

Toronto Cultural Youth Orchestra *See* Canadian Sinfonietta Youth Orchestra

Toronto Curling Association (TCA)
#6A-1409, 170 The Donway West, Toronto ON M3C 2E8
Tel: 416-657-2425
general@torontocurling.com
www.torontocurling.com
www.facebook.com/torontocurling
twitter.com/torontocurling
Overview: A small local organization founded in 1964
Mission: To promote curling in the Greater Toronto Area
Chief Officer(s):
Hugh Murphy, President
president@torontocurling.com
Membership: 24 clubs

Toronto Dance Theatre (TDT)
80 Winchester St., Toronto ON M4X 1B2
Tel: 416-967-1365; *Fax:* 416-963-4379
info@tdt.org
www.tdt.org
www.facebook.com/torontodancetheatre
twitter.com/TDTWinch
www.youtube.com/TorontoDanceTheatre
Overview: A small international charitable organization founded in 1968
Mission: To develop Canadian dance works of art; to perform nationally & internationally; to explore new ideas in choreographic expression while embracing the fresh & vital aspects of inherited traditions
Member of: Canadian Conference of the Arts; Canadian Dance Assembly; Toronto Theatre Alliance; PACT
Chief Officer(s):
Andrea Vagianos, Managing Director
andrea@tdt.org
Christopher House, Artistic Director
Finances: *Funding Sources:* Municipal, federal & provincial governments; corporate; individuals; foundations
Staff Member(s): 23
Activities: Creation & performance of original Canadian choreography; *Internships:* Yes

Toronto District Beekeepers' Association (TDBA)
#005, 10350 Yonge St., Richmond Hill ON L4C 3K9
e-mail: info@torontobeekeepers.org
www.torontobeekeepers.org
Overview: A small local organization founded in 1911
Mission: To assist beekeepers in the Toronto area; To improve the beekeeping industry
Member of: Ontario Beekeepers' Association
Chief Officer(s):
André Flys, Contact
andreflys@sympatico.ca
Membership: *Member Profile:* Professional & hobby apiarists in the Toronto area
Activities: Promoting the honey bee industry; Providing education about the industry; Liaising with the Ministry of Agriculture to share information; Organizing meetings with guest

speakers, including research professors & manufacturers & suppliers of beekeeping equipment; Offering networking opportunities for beekeepers
Publications:
• Toronto District Beekeepers' Association Newsletter
Type: Newsletter; *Frequency:* Monthly
Profile: Association updates & meeting announcements

Toronto Downtown Jazz Society
82 Bleecker St., Toronto ON M4X 1L8
Tel: 416-928-2033; *Fax:* 416-928-0533
tdjs@tojazz.com
www.torontojazz.com
www.facebook.com/torontojazzfest
twitter.com/torontojazzfest
Overview: A small local charitable organization founded in 1987
Mission: To produce the Toronto Downtown Jazz Festival, as well as many other events & programs to further develop jazz talent & audience appreciation; To operate as a registered charity (No. 12969 0269 RR0001); To promote community involvement, artistic excellence, & outstanding production standards
Chief Officer(s):
Patrick Taylor, CEO/Executive Producer
Josh Grossman, Artistic Director
Finances: *Funding Sources:* Donations

Toronto Endometriosis Network *See* The Endometriosis Network

Toronto Entertainment District Residental Association (TEDRA)
Toronto ON
e-mail: info@torontoedra.ca
www.torontoedra.ca
www.facebook.com/TorontoEDRA
Overview: A small local organization founded in 2012
Mission: Engages local residents & businesses regarding concerns of area development, traffic congestion, government services, and circumstances that affect property values & quality of life.
Chief Officer(s):
Mike Yen, Executive Director
mike@TorontoEDRA.ca
Membership: *Member Profile:* Residents who inhabit Toronto's Entertainment District.

Toronto Entomologists Association (TEA)
c/o Chris Rickard, Treasurer, 16 Mount View Ct., Collingwood ON L9Y 5A9
e-mail: info@ontarioinsects.org
www.ontarioinsects.org
Overview: A small local charitable organization founded in 1969
Mission: To maintain an interest in the insects, particularly the butterflies & moths of Ontario; To record life histories, changes in distribution, unusual records, etc., of Ontario butterflies & moths
Member of: Federation of Ontario Naturalists
Chief Officer(s):
Glenn Richardson, President
glennr@personainternet.com
Finances: *Annual Operating Budget:* Less than $50,000; *Funding Sources:* Membership fees; donations
Membership: 170; *Fees:* $15 student; $25 individual; $30 family; *Member Profile:* Amateur insect enthusiasts; professionals
Activities: Butterfly counts

Toronto Environmental Alliance (TEA)
#201, 30 Duncan St., Toronto ON M5V 2C3
Tel: 416-596-0660; *Fax:* 416-596-0345
tea@torontoenvironment.org
www.torontoenvironment.org
www.facebook.com/TOenviro
Overview: A small local organization founded in 1988
Mission: To bring together groups & individuals who share the common goal of making the communities of Greater Toronto area operate in an ecologically sustainable manner
Member of: Ontario Environmental Network
Chief Officer(s):
Franz Hartmann, Executive Director
franz@torontoenvironment.org
Finances: *Annual Operating Budget:* $250,000-$500,000
Staff Member(s): 7; 200 volunteer(s)
Membership: 8,000; *Fees:* Free; *Committees:* Water; Climate Change; Waste; Smog; Transit
Activities: *Library* by appointment

Toronto Esperanto Circle *See* Esperanto-Rondo de Toronto

Toronto Esperanto-Klubo *See* Esperanto-Rondo de Toronto

Toronto Fashion Incubator (TFI)
Exhibition Place, 285 Manitoba Dr., Toronto ON M6K 3C3
Tel: 416-971-7117; *Fax:* 416-971-6717
tfi@fashionincubator.com
www.fashionincubator.com
Overview: A medium-sized local organization founded in 1987
Mission: To provide business solutions to new & established members of the fashion industry in Toronto
Chief Officer(s):
Ben Barry, Chair
Susan Langdon, Executive Director
Finances: *Funding Sources:* Sponsors
Activities: *Library:* TFI Resource Centre
Awards:
• The Suzanne Rogers Award for Best New Label (Award)
Amount: $25,000

Toronto Field Naturalists (TFN)
#1519, 2 Carlton St., Toronto ON M5B 1J3
Tel: 416-593-2656
office@torontofieldnaturalists.org
www.torontofieldnaturalists.org
www.facebook.com/TorontoFieldNaturalists
Overview: A medium-sized local charitable organization founded in 1923
Mission: To promote the enjoyment & preservation of nature; To raise public interest in natural history
Chief Officer(s):
Bob Kortright, President
Walter Weary, Secretary-Treasurer
Finances: *Funding Sources:* Membership fees; Donations
Membership: *Fees:* $20 youth; $30 single seniors; $40 adults & senior families; $50 families
Activities: Partnering with organizations such as Ontario Nature, Toronto Green Community, Toronto Parks & Recreation, & the Toronto & Region Conservation Authority; Engaging in advocacy activities; Organizing monthly talks by experts on natural history topics
Meetings/Conferences: • Toronto Field Naturalists 2015 Monthly Talks: Mosses, Mooses and Mycorrhizas, February, 2015, University of Toronto, Northrop Frye Building, Toronto, ON
Scope: Local
Description: This lecture discusses the connections between mosses, mooses, fungi & forest ecosystems
Contact Information: E-mail: office@torontofieldnaturalists.org
• Toronto Field Naturalists 2015 Monthly Talk: What the *#&! Is a Bioblitz?, March, 2015, University of Toronto, Northrop Frye Building, Toronto, ON
Scope: Local
Description: This lecture focuses on bioblitzes & the information they provide about our natural surroundings.
Contact Information: E-mail: office@torontofieldnaturalists.org
• Toronto Field Naturalists 2015 Monthly Talk: Climate Change Effects on Pollinators, April, 2015, University of Toronto, Northrop Frye Building, Toronto, ON
Scope: Local
Description: This lecture examines the results that climate change has on bees, wildflowers blooming times & plant-pollinator interactions
Contact Information: E-mail: office@torontofieldnaturalists.org
• Toronto Field Naturalists 2015 Monthly Talk: Toronto's Urban Forests, May, 2015, University of Toronto, Northrop Frye Building, Toronto, ON
Scope: Local
Description: This lecture explains the state of the forests in Toronto
Contact Information: E-mail: office@torontofieldnaturalists.org
Publications:
• Toronto Field Naturalist
Type: Newsletter; *Frequency:* 8 pa
Profile: Information about nature in Toronto, environmental issues, & the organization's upcoming activities

Toronto Film Society (TFS)
173B Front St. East, Toronto ON M5A 3Z4
Tel: 416-785-0335
info@torontofilmsociety.com
torontofilmsociety.org
www.facebook.com/pages/Toronto-Film-Society/138608787942
twitter.com/TorFilmSociety
www.youtube.com/channel/UCIeKdJTKBEXiw97oC10mxjw
Overview: A small local charitable organization founded in 1948
Mission: To encourage & promote the study, appreciation & use of motion & sound pictures & television as educational & cultural factors in the city of Toronto, its vicinity & elsewhere; to encourage & promote motion & sound pictures through private showings of selected films of an artistic or experimental nature
Affliation(s): British Film Institute; American Film Institute
Chief Officer(s):
Barry Chapman, President
Finances: *Funding Sources:* Membership fees
Membership: *Fees:* Schedule available; *Member Profile:* 18 years of age minimum
Activities: Screening of vintage sound & silent films; two weekend seminars; *Speaker Service:* Yes; *Library:* TFS Archives; by appointment

Toronto Financial Services Alliance (TFSA)
#1800, 55 University Ave., Toronto ON M5J 2H7
Tel: 416-933-6780; *Fax:* 416-933-6799
info@tfsa.ca
www.tfsa.ca
www.linkedin.com/company/toronto-financial-services-alliance
twitter.com/TFSAweb
Overview: A small local organization founded in 2001
Mission: To build Toronto's financial cluster into a "top ten" global financial services centre; to foster collaboration between the three levels of government, the financial services industry & academia.
Chief Officer(s):
Janet L. Ecker, President & CEO
Catherine Chandler-Crichlow, Executive Director, Centre of Excellence in Financial Services Education
Matt Hobbs, Vice-President, Sector Growth & Business Development
Karen Tam, Vice-President, Finance & Operations
Membership: 61; *Member Profile:* Government bodies, financial services companies & academic institutions
Activities: Operating the Centre of Excellence in Financial Services Education

Toronto Finnish-Canadian Seniors Centre
795 Eglinton Ave. East, Toronto ON M4G 4E4
Tel: 416-425-4134; *Fax:* 416-425-6319
reception@suomikoti.ca
www.suomikoti.ca
Also Known As: Suomi-Koti, Toronto
Overview: A small local organization founded in 1982
Mission: To provide multi-lingual care & services, housing & activities for the Finnish community
Chief Officer(s):
Juha Mynttinen, Administrator, 416-425-4134 Ext. 243
Finances: *Funding Sources:* Government; private
Membership: *Member Profile:* Individuals of Finnish descent
Activities: Exercise; pool; sauna; seniors' programs; outings

Toronto Free-Net (TFN)
#406, 600 Bay St., Toronto ON M5G 1M6
Tel: 416-204-9257; *Fax:* 416-273-2677
office@torfree.net
www.torfree.net
Also Known As: torfree.net
Overview: A small local organization founded in 1994
Chief Officer(s):
Iain Calder, President & Manager
Finances: *Funding Sources:* Donations; service subscriptions
Staff Member(s): 12; 35 volunteer(s)
Membership: 50,000 registered
Activities: Community Network supplying ISP services on by-donation basis, tiered access plans including DSL high speed, IP, remote LAN administration, & cystom programming services; *Library*

Toronto French Book Fair *Voir* Salon du livre de Toronto et Festival des écrivains

Toronto Gaelic Learners Association
43 Norbrook Cres., Toronto ON M9V 4P7
Other Communication: Registration e-mail: register@torontogaelic.ca
fios@torontogaelic.ca
www.torontogaelic.ca
Also Known As: CLUINN
Overview: A small provincial organization founded in 1995
Mission: To encourage education in the Scottish Gaelic language
Chief Officer(s):
Janice Chan, Contact

Membership: *Member Profile:* Teachers & organizers of Scottish Gaelic language classes
Activities: Offering non-credit Scottish Gaelic language classes at St. Michael's College, University of Toronto; Presenting scholarships to students

Toronto General & Western Hospital Foundation
R. Fraser Elliot Bldg., #5S-801, 190 Elizabeth St., Toronto ON M5G 2C4
Tel: 416-340-3935; *Fax:* 416-340-4864
Toll-Free: 877-846-4483
foundation@uhn.ca
www.tgwhf-uhn.ca
Previous Name: Toronto Hospital Foundation
Overview: A small local charitable organization
Chief Officer(s):
Tennys J.M. Hanson, President & CEO

Toronto Health Libraries Association (THLA)
c/o Melissa Paladines (Treasurer), Credit Valley Hospital, 2200 Eglinton Ave. West, Toronto ON L5M 2N1
www.thla.ca
Overview: A small local organization founded in 1965 overseen by Canadian Health Libraries Association
Mission: To promote the provision of quality library service to the health community; to encourage communication & cooperation among members & to foster their professional development; to consult & collaborate with other professional, technical & scientific organizations in matters of mutual interest
Affiliation(s): Ontario Hospital Libraries Association
Chief Officer(s):
Sheila Lecroix, President, 416-535-8501 Ext. 6982
president@thla.ca
Finances: *Annual Operating Budget:* Less than $50,000; *Funding Sources:* Membership dues
Membership: 150; *Fees:* $25 individual; $15 student/retired/unemployed; *Member Profile:* Professional association for health librarians
Meetings/Conferences: • Toronto Health Libraries Association 2015 Annual General Meeting, 2015, Toronto, ON
Scope: Local

Toronto Historical Board *See* Heritage Toronto

Toronto Hospital Foundation *See* Toronto General & Western Hospital Foundation

Toronto Humane Society (THS)
11 River St., Toronto ON M5A 4C2
Tel: 416-392-2273; *Fax:* 416-392-9978
communications@torontohumanesociety.com
torontohumanesociety.com
www.facebook.com/8666187799
twitter.com/THS_tweet
Overview: A large local organization founded in 1887 overseen by Canadian Federation of Humane Societies
Mission: To promote the humane care & protection of all animals & to prevent cruelty & suffering
Affiliation(s): OSPCA
Chief Officer(s):
David Bronskill, BA, MA, LL.B, Chair
Marcie Laking, President
Jennifer Downe, Vice-President
Lisa Gibbens, BA, MISt, Secretary
Finances: *Funding Sources:* Donations
500 volunteer(s)
Membership: 3,000; *Fees:* $30; *Committees:* Adoption; Audit & Finance; Canine Animal Welfare; Feline Animal Welfare; Fundraising; Membership; Nominating & Governance; Spay/Neuter; Spay/Neuter Clinic; Special Species Animal Welfare; Volunteer
Activities: Providing shelter for animals; Conducting investigations; Offering education; Arranging adoptions; Providing emergency rescues; Rehabilitating wildlife; Offering lost & found & foster care services; Microchipping; Providing a spaying & neutering service; *Awareness Events:* Be Kind to Animals Week

Toronto Institute of Medical Technology *See* The Michener Institute for Applied Health Sciences

Toronto Insurance Women's Association (TIWA)
PO Box 861, 31 Adelaide St. East, Toronto ON M5C 2K1
Tel: 416-359-8739
www.tiwa.org
Overview: A small local organization founded in 1960
Mission: To educate and assist its members in reaching their potential both professionally and personally, promote the spirit of friendship and service in the industry, and encourage and foster high ethical standards in business and social relations
Member of: Canadian Association of Insurance Women
Chief Officer(s):
Betty Hornick, President, 416-288-5889, Fax: 416-288-9295
betty_hornick@avivacanada.com
10 volunteer(s)
Membership: 150; *Fees:* $65; *Committees:* Bulletin; Meeting Co-ordinator; Golf Tournament; Membership; Education; Program; Insurance Fundamentals; Publicity; Awards; Wine & Cheese
Activities: Monthly dinner meetings; *Awareness Events:* Annual Wine & Cheese; Annual Golf Tournament

Toronto International Film Festival Inc. (TIFF)
TIFF Bell Lightbox, 250 King St. West, Toronto ON M5V 3K5
Tel: 416-599-8433
Toll-Free: 888-599-8433
customerrelations@tiff.net
www.tiff.net
www.facebook.com/TIFF
twitter.com/search/%23TIFF
www.youtube.com/user/tiff
Overview: A medium-sized international charitable organization founded in 1976
Mission: To lead in creative & cultural discovery through the moving image
Chief Officer(s):
Paul Atkinson, Chair
Finances: *Annual Operating Budget:* Greater than $5 Million; *Funding Sources:* Donations; Sponsorships
Staff Member(s): 600; 2000 volunteer(s)
Membership: *Fees:* $99 individual; $150 family/dual; $400 contributor; $600 principal; *Committees:* Sprockets Educational Advisory
Activities: Offering Cinematheque Ontario, a screening program of the classics of world cinema; Organizing Film Circuit, which provides films to formerly under-serviced areas; Coordinating Reel Talk, which offers preview screenings of films, followed by informal discussions; Providing specialized industry programming & project development; *Awareness Events:* Toronto International Film Festival, September; Sprockets Toronto International Film Festival for Children, April; Canada's Top Ten (a selection of the best Canadian films of the year); *Library:* Film Reference Library

Toronto Japanese Association of Commerce & Industry
PO Box 104, #122, 20 York Mills Rd., Toronto ON M2P 2C2
Tel: 416-360-0235; *Fax:* 416-360-0236
office@torontoshokokai.org
www.torontoshokokai.org
Overview: A medium-sized local organization
Mission: To promote business relations between Canada & Japan through the activities of the members of the Japanese School of Toronto Shokokai Inc. (commonly known as the Hoshuko).
Chief Officer(s):
Tetsuo Komuro, President
Yukio Arita, Executive Director & Secretary
Membership: *Fees:* $700 + $170 per member regular; $350 + $85 per member associate; $200 individual
Activities: Business luncheons & information sessions; newsletter; New Year's reception; *Awareness Events:* Charity Golf Tournament, May

Toronto Jewish Film Society (TJFS)
c/o Miles Nadal Jewish Community Centre, 750 Spadina Ave., Toronto ON M5S 2J2
Tel: 416-924-6211; *Fax:* 416-924-0442
www.milesnadaljcc.ca
Overview: A small local charitable organization founded in 1978
Mission: Celebration of Jewish film; exposure of film artists; forum for promotion of Jewish film & relevant issues
Affliation(s): Miles Nadal Jewish Community Centre
Chief Officer(s):
Mark Clamen, Co-Chair
Shirley Kumove, Co-Chair
Esther Arbeid, Contact
esthera@mnjcc.org
Membership: *Fees:* $100; $60 young adult
Activities: 8 Yearly screenings sold as a subscription series, includes speakers & Q&A session

Toronto Jewish Free Loan Cassa *See* Jewish Free Loan Toronto

Toronto Latvian Concert Association (TLK)
Tel: 416-512-7348
music.lv@sympatico.ca
www.torontolatvianconcerts.com
Overview: A small local charitable organization founded in 1959
Mission: To promote 4 concert season with Latvian performers & to provide an opportunity to hear music by composers of Latvian origin
Chief Officer(s):
Arvids Purvs, President
Finances: *Annual Operating Budget:* Less than $50,000; *Funding Sources:* Subscription fees; ticket sale; donations
10 volunteer(s)
Membership: 300; *Fees:* $100 subscription to 4 concerts; $90 seniors; $45 students

Toronto Law Office Management Association (TLOMA)
43 Daniel Ct., Markham ON L3P 4B8
Tel: 416-410-0979; *Fax:* 905-427-5115
www.tloma.com
Overview: A small local organization founded in 1968
Mission: To offer forum for legal administrators to learn about their industry
Chief Officer(s):
Janice Rooney, President
janice.rooney@fmc-law.com
Membership: 420 individuals from over 225 law firms; *Fees:* $275; *Member Profile:* Law firm administrators
Activities: Education & professional development;

Toronto Lawyers Association (TLA)
Court House Library, 361 University Ave., Toronto ON M5G 1T3
Tel: 416-327-5700; *Fax:* 416-947-9148
info@tlaonline.ca
www.tlaonline.ca
www.linkedin.com/groups/Toronto-Lawyers-Association-440200 2
www.facebook.com/pages/Toronto-Lawyers-Association/124864 490954414
twitter.com/tlavoice
Previous Name: Metropolitan Toronto Lawyers Association; County of York Law Association
Overview: A small local organization founded in 1885
Mission: Provides lawyers with key services; timely & relevant information; education about issues & opportunities affecting members; advocacy on behalf of the profession
Chief Officer(s):
Chris Matthews, President
Christopher Wayland, Secretary
Joseph Neuberger, Treasurer
Miriam Young, Vice-President
Joan Rataic-Lang, Executive Director, 416-927-6012
jrataiclang@tlaonline.ca
Cybil Stephens, Membership Services Coordinator, 416-327-5702
cstephens@tlaonline.ca
Finances: *Annual Operating Budget:* $500,000-$1.5 Million; *Funding Sources:* Membership dues; library services
Staff Member(s): 2; 24 volunteer(s)
Membership: 1,000-4,999; *Fees:* $99.44; *Member Profile:* Lawyers; judges
Activities: *Library:* County Court House Library; Open to public

The Toronto Mendelssohn Choir
#404, 720 Bathurst St., Toronto ON M5S 2R4
Tel: 416-598-0422
admin@tmchoir.org
www.tmchoir.org
www.facebook.com/TMChoir
twitter.com/TMChoir
www.youtube.com/user/TOMendelssohnChoir
Overview: A small local charitable organization founded in 1894
Chief Officer(s):
Cynthia Hawkins, Executive Director
manager@tmchoir.org
Finances: *Funding Sources:* Box office; donations; government; sponsorship
Staff Member(s): 7
Activities: *Library* by appointment

Toronto Montessori Institute (TMI)
8569 Bayview Ave., Richmond Hill ON L4B 3M7
Tel: 905-889-6882; *Fax:* 905-886-6516
tmi@tmsschool.ca
www.tmi.edu
Previous Name: Toronto Montessori Teacher Training Institute

Overview: A small local charitable organization founded in 1971
Mission: Engages in training Montessori teachers; competent in the curriculum, committed to working in a spirit of mutual respect, towards the fulfillment of each child's potential
Member of: Montessori Accreditation Council for Teacher Education
Affliation(s): Canadian Council of Montessori Administrators
Chief Officer(s):
Nancy Coyle, Director
ncoyle@torontomontessori.ca
Finances: *Annual Operating Budget:* $500,000-$1.5 Million; *Funding Sources:* Student fees
Staff Member(s): 5

Toronto Montessori Teacher Training Institute *See* Toronto Montessori Institute

Toronto Musicians' Association (TMA)
#500, 15 Gervais Dr., Toronto ON M3C 1Y8
Tel: 416-421-1020; *Fax:* 416-421-7011
Toll-Free: 800-762-3444
info@tma149.ca
www.torontomusicians.org
www.facebook.com/146633580744
twitter.com/TMA149
Overview: A medium-sized local organization founded in 1887
Mission: To represent professional musicians in all facets of music in the greater Toronto area; To offer legal protection, assistance, & advice; To help musicians have a successful professional career
Member of: American Federation of Musicians
Chief Officer(s):
Jim Biros, Executive Director, 416-421-1020 Ext. 235
jbiros@tma149.ca
Finances: *Funding Sources:* Membership dues
Staff Member(s): 12
Membership: 3,500

Toronto Ornithological Club (TOC)
Toronto ON
e-mail: info@torontobirding.ca
www.torontobirding.ca
Overview: A small local charitable organization founded in 1934
Mission: To afford opportunities for the meeting together of ornithologists at regular intervals for discussion; to facilitate cooperation in ornithological studies; to review & report on ornithological topics; to establish a liaison between members & visiting naturalists
Member of: Federation of Ontario Naturalists
Chief Officer(s):
Jeremy Hatt, Councillor, Membership
membership@torontobirding.ca
Finances: *Annual Operating Budget:* Less than $50,000
Membership: 150+; *Fees:* $25; *Committees:* Outings; Records; Editorial; Archives; Conservation
Activities: Bird outings; High Park hawk watch; fall field day

Toronto Paramedic Association
c/o Toronto Emergency Medical Services, 4330 Dufferin St., Toronto ON M3H 5R9
Tel: 416-410-9453; *Fax:* 416-410-9453
Toll-Free: 866-708-3888
torontoparamedic.com
Overview: A small local organization founded in 1992
Mission: To support the paramedic community and focus on paramedic advancements in patient care.
Member of: Ontario Paramedic Association
Chief Officer(s):
Geoff MacBride, President
president@torontoparamedic.com
Activities: *Awareness Events:* EMS Week, May

Toronto Parents of Multiple Births Association (TPOMBA)
#356, 1920 Ellesmere Rd., Toronto ON M1H 3G1
Tel: 416-760-3944
info@tpomba.org
www.tpomba.org
www.facebook.com/TorontoParentsOfMultipleBirthsAssociation
twitter.com/TPOMBA
plus.google.com/u/0/b/116137137302949869664
Previous Name: Toronto Parents of Twins Club
Overview: A small local organization founded in 1976
Mission: To provide guidance & help to adjust to multiple birth situations through educational meetings, support groups, social events for families & adults, & member services; to enable families to cope with their unique situation & therefore lead a full life
Chief Officer(s):
Camille Kloppenburg, President
Membership: 500+; *Fees:* $42; *Member Profile:* Parents of twins, triplets, quads, quints & more
Activities: *Awareness Events:* New & Expectant Parents Nights; Toddler Nights; *Library* by appointment

Toronto Parents of Twins Club *See* Toronto Parents of Multiple Births Association

Toronto Philharmonia
PO Box 705, Stn. U, Toronto ON M8Z 5P9
Tel: 647-348-5828
office@torontophilharmonia.com
torontophilharmonia.com
Previous Name: North York Symphony Association
Overview: A small local charitable organization founded in 1971 overseen by Orchestras Canada
Mission: To provide quality, affordable classical music to City of Toronto & to Ontario communities on tour
Affliation(s): Ontario Federation of Symphony Orchestras
Chief Officer(s):
Uri Mayer, Artistic Director
Finances: *Funding Sources:* Ticket sales; government grants; sponsorships; donations
Membership: *Member Profile:* Professional musicians
Activities: Adopt-a-School Program; Partners in Music Program; Annual Viennese Ball, April/May; *Library:* Music Library

Toronto Police Accountability Coalition (TPAC)
#206, 401 Richmond St. West, Toronto ON M5V 3A8
Tel: 416-977-5097
info@tpac.ca
www.tpac.ca
Overview: A small local organization
Mission: To encourage debate about police issues & to make the police accountable to the public.

Toronto Police Association (TPA) / Association de la police de Toronto
180 Yorkland Blvd., Toronto ON M2J 1R5
Tel: 416-491-4301; *Fax:* 416-494-4948
information@tpa.ca
www.tpa.ca
Previous Name: Metropolitan Toronto Police Association
Overview: A medium-sized local organization
Chief Officer(s):
Mike McCormack, President
Douglas Corrigan, Vice-President
Membership: 7,450 uniform & civilian members

Toronto Press & Media Club
#101, 1755 Rathburn Rd. East, Mississauga ON L4W 2M8
e-mail: info@torontopressclub.net
www.torontopressclub.net
www.facebook.com/TorontoPressAndMediaClub
Overview: A medium-sized provincial organization founded in 1882
Chief Officer(s):
Ed Patrick, President
Finances: *Funding Sources:* Membership dues; sponsorships; donations
Membership: *Member Profile:* Journalism; public relations; communications
Awards:
• National Newspaper Awards (Award)
Established 1949; awarded annually to print men & women employed regularly on the staffs of Canadian daily newspapers
• Canadian News Hall of Fame (Award)
Toronto Press Club is custodian of the Hall of Fame dedicated to those people who have contributed regularly to journalism as staffers
• Norman DePoe Memorial Scholastic Fund (Scholarship)
A bursary awards program to students in the media

Toronto Professional Fire Fighters Association
39 Commissioners St., Toronto ON M5A 1A6
Tel: 416-466-1167; *Fax:* 416-466-6632
mail@torontofirefighters.org
www.torontofirefighters.org
twitter.com/tpffa
Overview: A small local organization
Chief Officer(s):
Ed Kennedy, President

Toronto Public Library Foundation
789 Yonge St., Toronto ON M4W 2G8
Tel: 416-393-7123; *Fax:* 416-397-5999
foundation@torontopubliclibrary.ca
tplfoundation.ca
www.facebook.com/tplfoundation
twitter.com/TPL_Foundation
www.youtube.com/tplfoundation
Overview: A medium-sized local charitable organization founded in 1997
Mission: Provides essential resources for the enhancement of Toronto Public Library and allocates funds to priority needs not supported by municipal funding.
Chief Officer(s):
Rumball Heather, President
hrumball@torontopubliclibrary.ca

Toronto Public Spaces Initiative (TPSI)
Toronto ON
e-mail: info@publicspaces.ca
publicspaces.ca
www.facebook.com/254649407883843
twitter.com/TOpublicspace
Overview: A small local organization founded in 2001
Mission: Dedicated to enhancing public space through research, policy analysis, and service provision.
Chief Officer(s):
Jayme Turney, CEO

Toronto PWA Foundation (TPWAF)
200 Gerrard St East, 2nd Fl, Toronto ON M5A 2E6
Tel: 416-506-1400; *Fax:* 416-506-1404
info@pwatoronto.org
www.pwatoronto.org
Also Known As: Toronto People With AIDS Foundation
Previous Name: People with AIDS Foundation
Overview: A small local charitable organization founded in 1987 overseen by Canadian AIDS Society
Mission: To promote the health & well-being of all people living with HIV/AIDS by providing accessible, direct & practical services
Member of: Ontario AIDS Network
Chief Officer(s):
Murray Jose, Executive Director
mjose@pwatoronto.org
Finances: *Annual Operating Budget:* $500,000-$1.5 Million; *Funding Sources:* All levels of government; fundraising; private donations; honorarium
Staff Member(s): 15; 150 volunteer(s)
Membership: 1,000-4,999
Activities: *Awareness Events:* AIDS Awareness Week; *Speaker Service:* Yes; *Library:* Treatment Resource Centre; Open to public

Toronto Real Estate Board (TREB)
1400 Don Mills Rd., Toronto ON M3B 3N1
Tel: 416-443-8100
www.torontorealestateboard.com
www.facebook.com/TorontoRealEstateBoard
twitter.com/TREBhome
www.youtube.com/TREBChannel
Overview: A large local organization founded in 1920 overseen by Ontario Real Estate Association
Member of: The Canadian Real Estate Association
Chief Officer(s):
Dianne Usher, President
Membership: 35,000; *Fees:* Schedule available; *Member Profile:* Registration under the Real Estate & Business Brokers Act; course of education determined from time to time by directors; Members are specialists in industrial & commercial real estate, appraisals & property management
Activities: *Speaker Service:* Yes; *Library:* Resource Centre; Open to public by appointment

Toronto Renaissance & Reformation Colloquium (TRRC)
c/o Germaine Warkentin, Victoria College, University of Toronto, #205, 73 Queen's Park Cres., Toronto ON M5S 1K7
www.crrs.ca
Overview: A small local organization founded in 1965
Affliation(s): International Federation of Societies & Institutes for the Study of the Renaissance
Chief Officer(s):
Germaine Warkentin, Director
g.warkentin@utoronto.ca
Finances: *Annual Operating Budget:* Less than $50,000; *Funding Sources:* Membership fees

Staff Member(s): 2
Membership: 1-99; *Fees:* $12
Activities: Presents a lecture series; *Speaker Service:* Yes; *Library:* Centre for Renaissance & Reformation Studies

Toronto Renewable Energy Co-operative (TREC)
#405, 401 Richmond St. W., Toronto ON M5V 3A8
Tel: 416-977-5093; *Fax:* 416-306-6476
Toll-Free: 866-560-9463
info@trec.on.ca
www.trec.on.ca
www.facebook.com/TRECCoop
twitter.com/TRECcoop
Overview: A small local organization founded in 1998
Mission: A non-profit organization of citizens dedicated to renewable energy & energy conservation
Member of: Canadian Renewable Energy Alliance
Affliation(s): Toronto District School Board; Ontario Trillium Foundation; Ontario Power Authority Conservation Fund; Toronto Atmospheric Fund; Community Power Fund; Ontario Sustainable Energy Ass'n
Chief Officer(s):
Judy Lipp, Executive Director
jlipp@trec.on.ca
Finances: *Funding Sources:* Donations
Activities: Community energy projects; interactive, hands-on education; Green City Bike Tours; Green Collar Career program; Our Power solar initiative; solar home tours; round table discussions; Bruce County wind energy co-operative project

Toronto Sheet Metal & Air Handling Group; Environmental Sheet Metal Association Toronto *See* Toronto Sheet Metal Contractors Association

Toronto Sheet Metal Contractors Association (TSMCA)
#26, 30 Wertheim Ct., Richmond Hill ON L4B 1B9
Tel: 905-886-9627; *Fax:* 905-886-9959
shtmetal@bellnet.ca
www.tsmca.org
Previous Name: Toronto Sheet Metal & Air Handling Group; Environmental Sheet Metal Association Toronto
Overview: A medium-sized local organization
Member of: Ontario Sheet Metal & Air Handling Group
Chief Officer(s):
Jim Warner, President, 416-749-6031, Fax: 416-749-4673
jwarner@modernniagara.com
Finances: *Annual Operating Budget:* $250,000-$500,000; *Funding Sources:* Collective Agreement Assessment
Staff Member(s): 5
Membership: 102 individual

Toronto Sinfonietta
400 St. Clair Ave. East, Toronto ON M4T 1P5
Tel: 416-488-8057
info@torontosinfonietta.com
www.torontosinfonietta.com
Also Known As: Polish Canadian Society of Music
Overview: A small local organization overseen by Orchestras Canada
Chief Officer(s):
Matthew Jaskiewicz, Music Director
jaskiewicz@sympatico.ca

Toronto Soaring Club
c/o President, 58 River Ridge Rd., Barrie ON L4N 7E8
Tel: 705-735-4422
www.toronto-soaring.ca
Overview: A small local organization
Member of: Soaring Association of Canada
Chief Officer(s):
Dave Ellis, President
dellis82@rogers.com

Toronto Society of Model Engineers (TSME)
Toronto ON
e-mail: tsmeexec@gmail.com
sites.google.com/site/tsmeweb
Overview: A small local organization founded in 1933
Mission: To encourage the art & craft of model building in such areas as live steam locomotives, stationary engines, gas engines, ships, aircraft, clocks & models of all kinds
Membership: *Fees:* $35; *Member Profile:* Open to modellers, craftsmen & those with an interest in creating working models
Activities: Monthly meetings & special functions; participates in "Hobby Show" at International Centre in Nov.; *Library:* TSME Library

Awards:
• Herb Jordan Award (Award)

Toronto Symphony Orchestra (TSO)
212 King St. West, 6th Fl., Toronto ON M5H 1K5
Tel: 416-593-7769; *Fax:* 416-977-2912
www.tso.ca
www.facebook.com/group.php?gid=52219459772
twitter.com/TorontoSymphony
www.youtube.com/TorontoSymphony
Overview: A large local organization founded in 1922 overseen by Orchestras Canada
Mission: To present concerts of both established & new music at the highest artistic standard possible, while recognizing audiences' needs; to play a role in the development of future musicians & audiences
Chief Officer(s):
George Lewis, Chair
Andrew R. Shaw, President/CEO
ashaw@tso.ca
Finances: *Annual Operating Budget:* Greater than $5 Million; *Funding Sources:* Box Office; individual & corporate donations; Canada Council; Ontario Arts Council; City of Toronto
Staff Member(s): 38; 450 volunteer(s)
Membership: *Committees:* Volunteer Committee
Activities: *Awareness Events:* Mozart Festival; New Creations Festival; *Internships:* Yes; *Library:* TSO Library; by appointment
Awards:
• TSYO Awards (Award)

Toronto Symphony Youth Orchestra (TSYO)
212 King St. West, 6th Fl., Toronto ON M5H 1K5
Tel: 416-593-7769; *Fax:* 416-977-2912
www.tso.ca
Overview: A small local organization founded in 1974 overseen by Orchestras Canada
Affliation(s): Toronto Symphony Orchestra
Chief Officer(s):
Rachel Robbins, Manager
rrobbins@tso.ca
Membership: *Member Profile:* Orchestral musicians 22 & under
Activities: Perform minimum three full orchestra concerts per season; *Library:* TSYO Library

Toronto Theatre Alliance *See* Toronto Alliance for the Performing Arts

Toronto Training Board *See* Toronto Workforce Innovation Group

Toronto Transportation Society (TTS)
PO Box 5187, Stn. A, Toronto ON M5W 1N5
www.torontotransportationsociety.org
Overview: A small local organization founded in 1973
Chief Officer(s):
Kevin Nichol, President
Richard Hooles, Vice-President
Robert Giles, Secretary
Robert Lubinski, Treasurer
Finances: *Funding Sources:* Membership fees
Membership: *Fees:* $25 CDN Canadians; $30 USD USA residents; $45 CDN international; *Member Profile:* Transportation enthusiasts with an interest in buses, streetcars, railways, & subways
Activities: Hosting monthly meetings; Organizing a Memorabilia Night, featuring an auction of transit collections; Arranging charters using unique transit vehicles
Publications:
• Transfer Points
Type: Newsletter; *Frequency:* 10 pa; *Editor:* Adam Zhelka; *Price:* Free with membership in the Toronto Transportation Society
Profile: Transportation related news, historic articles, photographs, & happenings in the Greater Toronto Area

Toronto Ukraina Sports Association
#75, 6 Point Rd., Toronto ON M8Z 2X3
Tel: 416-535-0681
postmaster@ukrainasports.com
www.ukrainasports.com
Overview: A small local organization founded in 1948
Mission: To promote an interest in sports among its members
Chief Officer(s):
Constantino Czoli, Contact
choli66@hotmail.com

Toronto Users Group for Power Systems
#850, 36 Toronto St., Toronto ON M5C 2C5
Tel: 905-607-2546
admin@tug.ca
www.tug.on.ca
www.facebook.com/groups/13354906396
Overview: A small local organization founded in 1985
Mission: To promote knowledge of IBM Power Systems
Chief Officer(s):
Léo Lefebvre, President
leo@tug.ca
Glenn Gundermann, Vice-President
ggundermann@tug.ca
Bob Lesiw, Vice-President
blesiw@gesco.ca
Jay Burford, Secretary
jburford@rogers.com
Kumar Rajendra, Treasurer
rajendra.kumar@aonbenfield.com
Finances: *Funding Sources:* Sponsorships
Membership: 350+ corporations
Activities: Hosting regular meetings for members
Publications:
• TUG [Toronto Users Group] Buzz
Type: Newsletter; *Price:* Free
Profile: Updates from the Toronto Users Group plus forthcoming events

Toronto Vegetarian Association (TVA)
17 Baldwin St., 2nd Fl., Toronto ON M5T 1L1
Tel: 416-544-9800; *Fax:* 416-544-9094
tva@veg.ca
www.veg.ca
www.facebook.com/group.php?gid=2249192685
twitter.com/torontoveg
Overview: A small local charitable organization founded in 1945
Mission: To help Torontonians adopt & maintain a healthy, ethical & ecological vegetarian lifestyle
Member of: Vegetarian Union of North America; International Vegetarian Union
Chief Officer(s):
Fraser Gibson, President
Finances: *Annual Operating Budget:* $100,000-$250,000; *Funding Sources:* Donations, advertising, exhibitor fees
Staff Member(s): 2; 300 volunteer(s)
Membership: 1,200; *Fees:* Donation min. $20
Activities: *Awareness Events:* Annual Vegetarian Food Festival, early Sept.; *Speaker Service:* Yes; *Library:* Resource Centre; Open to public

Toronto Women in Film & Television *See* Women in Film & Television - Toronto

Toronto Workforce Innovation Group (TWIG)
#350, 215 Spadina Ave., Toronto ON M5T 2C7
Tel: 416-934-1653; *Fax:* 416-934-1654
info@workforceinnovation.ca
www.workforceinnovation.ca
www.linkedin.com/groups?mostPopular=&gid=3160513
www.facebook.com/TOworkforce
twitter.com/TOworkforce
www.youtube.com/user/tworkforceinnovation
Previous Name: Toronto Training Board
Overview: A small local organization
Mission: To ensure that there are available workers for Toronto industries
Member of: Workforce Planning Ontario
Chief Officer(s):
Karen Lior, Executive Director
karen@workforceinnovation.ca
Staff Member(s): 3

Toronto Zoo
361A Old Finch Ave., Toronto ON M1B 5K7
Tel: 416-392-5929
www.torontozoo.com
www.facebook.com/TheTorontoZoo
Previous Name: Zoological Society of Metropolitan Toronto
Overview: A small local organization founded in 1969
Mission: To support the Toronto Zoo in its efforts to conserve species diversity through conservation, education, & research
Affliation(s): Canadian Association of Zoos, Parks & Aquariums; American Association of Zoos, Parks & Aquariums; Canadian Centre for Philanthropy
Chief Officer(s):
Raymond Cho, Chair
John Tracogna, Chief Executive Officer

Finances: *Annual Operating Budget:* $500,000-$1.5 Million; *Funding Sources:* Grants; Events; Corporate; Memberships; Bequests
Staff Member(s): 5; 45 volunteer(s)
Membership: 20,000; *Fees:* Schedule available; *Committees:* Executive; Finance; Sponsorship
Activities: *Rents Mailing List:* Yes

The Toronto-Calcutta Foundation
2 Leland Ave., Toronto ON M8Z 2X5
www.toronto-calcutta.org
www.facebook.com/pages/Toronto-Calcutta-Foundation/191539797524369
www.twitter.com/torontocalc
www.youtube.com/user/TorCalFoundation#p/u
Overview: A small international charitable organization founded in 1988
Mission: To establish medical clinics for the improverished citizens of Calcutta, & of other cities of India; to establish schools for impoverished children in Calcutta, & in other cities of India; to protect animals & to provide for their welfare in Calcutta, & in other cities of India; to provide & to supervise developmental aid to alleviate the poverty of inhabitants of the provincial states in India, & of other countries of the Indian sub-continent
Chief Officer(s):
Arun Palit, President
Tapan Mazumder, Secretary
Membership: *Fees:* $25 regular; $100 five-year; $500 benefactor

Touch Football Ontario (TFO)
21 Bird Cres., Ajax ON L1S 5G3
Tel: 416-399-8792
Other Communication: touchfootballontario.wordpress.com
info@tfont.com
www.tfont.com
Overview: A medium-sized provincial organization
Mission: To organize touch football games among amateur teams in Ontario; to represent the sport within the province
Chief Officer(s):
Russ Henderson, President
president@tfont.com
Staff Member(s): 5
Membership: *Member Profile:* Touch football teams

Tourette Syndrome Foundation of Canada (TSFC) / La Fondation canadienne du syndrome de Tourette
#175, 5945 Airport Rd., Mississauga ON L4V 1R9
Tel: 905-673-2255; *Fax:* 905-673-2638
Toll-Free: 800-341-3120
tsfc@tourette.ca
www.tourette.ca
www.facebook.com/TSFCanada
twitter.com/TSFCanada
www.youtube.com/TSFCanada
Overview: A medium-sized national charitable organization founded in 1976
Mission: Through education, advocacy, self-help, & the promotion of research, the TSFC assists individuals affected by Tourette Syndrome & its associated disorders.
Member of: Canadian Brain Tissue Bank; Canadian Centre for Philanthropy; Volunteers Canada
Affliation(s): Health Charities Council of Canada
Chief Officer(s):
Lynn McLarnon, Executive Director
lynn@tourette.ca
Finances: *Funding Sources:* Membership dues; Fundraising programs & activities; Donations; Project funding
Membership: *Fees:* $45 individual; $65 family
Activities: *Speaker Service:* Yes; *Library:* Resource Centre; by appointment
Awards:
• National Volunteer Awards (Award)
Publications:
• The Green Leaflet [a publication of the Tourette Syndrome Foundation of Canada]
Type: Newsletter; *Frequency:* 3 pa
• NewsFlash [a publication of the Tourette Syndrome Foundation of Canada]
Type: Newsletter
• Twitch Times [a publication of the Tourette Syndrome Foundation of Canada]
Type: Newsletter; *Frequency:* Monthly

Tourette Syndrome Foundation of Canada (TSFC)
#175, 5945 Airport Rd., Mississauga ON L4V 1R9
Tel: 905-673-2255; *Fax:* 905-673-2638
Toll-Free: 800-361-3120
tsfc@tourette.ca
www.tourette.ca
www.facebook.com/TSFCanada
twitter.com/TSFCanada
www.youtube.com/TSFCanada
Overview: A large national charitable organization
Mission: To educate & increase public awareness about Tourette Syndrome
Activities: *Awareness Events:* Trek for Tourette, March
Publications:
• It's Your Move!
Type: Course
Profile: Personal development program aimed at helping youth with Tourette deal with their challenges
• Understanding Tourette Syndrome
Type: Handbook
Profile: Comprehensive information regarding Tourette Syndrome

Tourism Brantford
Brantford Visitor & Tourism Centre, 399 Wayne Gretzky Pkwy., Brantford ON N3R 8B4
Tel: 519-751-9900; *Fax:* 519-751-2617
Toll-Free: 800-265-6299
tourism@brantford.ca
www.discoverbrantford.com
Previous Name: Brantford Tourism & Convention Services
Overview: A small local organization founded in 1990
Mission: To ensure quality visitor services through awareness, education, marketing & communications; to enhance the development of the tourism industry as an economic generator & to enhance the quality of life in our community
Member of: Southern Ontario Travel Organization; Ontario Motor Coach Association
Chief Officer(s):
John Frabotta, Director, Economic Development & Tourism Services
Donna Clements, Acting Manager, Tourism & Marketing
dclements@brantford.ca
Finances: *Annual Operating Budget:* $250,000-$500,000; *Funding Sources:* Municipal government; grants; partnerships
Staff Member(s): 7; 15 volunteer(s)
Membership: *Committees:* Tourism Advisory; Tournament Capital of Ontario; Brantford Cultural Network
Activities: Step-on-Guide Service; *Awareness Events:* Discover Brant - Tourism Awareness Week; Doors Open Brant

Tourism Burlington
414 Locust St., Burlington ON L7S 1T7
Tel: 905-634-5594; *Fax:* 905-634-7220
Toll-Free: 877-499-9989
info@tourismburlington.com
www.tourismburlington.com
www.linkedin.com/groups?gid=4070362
www.facebook.com/TourismBurlington
twitter.com/burlingtontour
www.youtube.com/user/TourismBurlington
Also Known As: Burlington Visitor & Convention Bureau
Overview: A small local organization founded in 1988
Mission: To increase tourism, resulting in economic benefits through utilization of recreational, cultural, commercial & personal resources
Member of: Meeting Planners International; Tourism Industry Association of Canada
Chief Officer(s):
Pam Belgrade, Executive Director
Victor Szeverenyi, Chair
Finances: *Annual Operating Budget:* $250,000-$500,000; *Funding Sources:* Grants; co-op marketing; souvenir sales
Membership: *Committees:* Marketing
Activities: Tourism Awareness & Media Reception; Tourism Open House, June; *Library*
Awards:
• Tourism Ambassador Award (Award)

Tourism Calgary
#200, 238 - 11 Ave. SE, Calgary AB T2G 0X8
Tel: 403-263-8510; *Fax:* 403-262-3809
Toll-Free: 800-661-1678
www.visitcalgary.com
www.facebook.com/visitcalgary
twitter.com/calgary
Also Known As: Calgary Convention & Visitors Bureau
Previous Name: Calgary Tourist & Convention Bureau
Overview: A medium-sized local organization founded in 1957
Mission: A non-profit destination marketing organization, providing services to members to promote Calgary as a destination for travel industry professionals, as well as leisure & business travelers
Member of: Tourism Industry Association of Canada; Canadian Association of Convention & Visitor Bureaux; International Association of Convention & Visitors Bureaus; Western Association of Convention & Visitors Bureaus
Chief Officer(s):
Randy Williams, President & CEO
Finances: *Annual Operating Budget:* $3 Million-$5 Million; *Funding Sources:* 46% public + 54% private
Staff Member(s): 32; 200 volunteer(s)
Membership: 600 institutional; 350 individual
Activities: White Hat Awards; Stampede Breakfast; Golf Tournament; *Library* by appointment

Tourism Canmore Kananaskis
PO Box 8608, 907 - 7th Ave., Canmore AB T1W 2V3
Tel: 403-678-1295; *Fax:* 403-678-1296
tourismcanmore.com
www.facebook.com/TourismCanmore
twitter.com/TourismCanmore
Overview: A small local organization
Mission: To promote tourism in the Town of Canmore
Membership: *Fees:* Schedule available
Activities: *Awareness Events:* Canmore Nordic Festival, Nov.-Dec.

Tourism Cape Breton
PO Box 1448, Sydney NS B1P 6R7
Tel: 902-563-4636
Toll-Free: 888-562-9848
dcb@dcba.ca
www.cbisland.com
www.facebook.com/TourismCB
twitter.com/TourismCB
www.youtube.com/user/CBTourism
Previous Name: Cape Breton Tourist Association
Overview: A small local organization founded in 1996
Member of: Tourism Industry Association of Canada: Tourism Industry Association of Nova Scotia
Activities: Festivals & Events Line 1-888-562-9848 (May-Oct.)

Tourism Goderich
57 West St., Goderich ON N7A 2K5
Tel: 519-524-6600; *Fax:* 519-524-1466
Toll-Free: 800-280-7637
www.goderich.ca
Overview: A small local organization

Tourism Hamilton
28 James St. North, Hamilton ON L8R 2K1
Tel: 905-546-2666; *Fax:* 905-546-2667
Toll-Free: 800-263-8590
tourism@hamilton.ca
www.tourismhamilton.com
www.facebook.com/TourismHamilton
twitter.com/tourismhamilton
www.youtube.com/user/HamiltonTourism
Previous Name: Greater Hamilton Tourism & Convention Services
Overview: A small local organization
Mission: To promote & increase the tourism & convention industries in Greater Hamilton
Member of: Tourism Industry Association of Canada; Canadian Society of Association Executives; Canadian Association of Visitor & Convention Bureaus; International Association of Visitor & Convention Bureaus
Chief Officer(s):
Susan Monarch, Manager
susan.monarch@hamilton.ca
Staff Member(s): 12

Tourism Industry Association of BC *See* Council of Tourism Associations of British Columbia

Tourism Industry Association of Canada (TIAC) / Association de l'industrie touristique du Canada (AITC)
#600, 116 Lisgar St., Ottawa ON K2P 0C2
Tel: 613-238-3883; *Fax:* 613-238-3878
info@tiac.travel
www.tiac-aitc.ca
twitter.com/tiac_aitc
Overview: A large national organization founded in 1931

Mission: To enhance Canada's tourism industry by removing regulatory & legislative barriers to growth
Chief Officer(s):
David F. Goldstein, President/CEO
dgoldstein@tiac.travel
David Lauer, Manager, Communications, 613-238-9400
dlauer@tiac.travel
Finances: *Annual Operating Budget:* $1.5 Million-$3 Million; *Funding Sources:* Membership dues
Staff Member(s): 12
Membership: 300 primary members; *Committees:* Policy; Conference; PTTIA; Rendez-Vous Canada
Activities: Talking with TIAC Forums; Issue Forum; Talking Tourism Symposium
Awards:
• InterContinental Hotels Group Employee of the Year Award (Award)
• Via Rail Canada Community Service Award (Award)
Given to an individual who as a volunteer has demonstrated an outstanding effort in serving tourism locally, provincially or nationally
• Delta Hotels and Resorts Traveller Experience Award (Award)
Recognizes the outstanding front-line employee who has shown exemplary dedication within their organization
• National Cultural Tourism Award (Award)
• Parks Canada Sustainable Tourism Award (Award)
• CTHRC Award for Excellence in Human Resources Development (Award)
Recognizes individuals that have demonstrated a commitment to professionalism in the Canadian tourism workforce
• WestJet Social Media Initiative of the Year Award (Award)
• Metro Toronto Convention Centre Event of the Year Award (Award)
• Deloitte Innovator of the Year Award (Award)
• Air Canada Business of the Year Award (Award)
• Hilton Worldwide Small or Medium-sized Business of the Year Award (Award)

Tourism Industry Association of New Brunswick Inc. (TIANB) / Association de l'industrie touristique du Nouveau-Brunswick inc. (AITNB)

#440, 500 Beaverbrook Ct., Fredericton NB E3B 5X4
Tel: 506-458-5646; *Fax:* 506-459-3634
Toll-Free: 800-668-5313
info@tianb.com
www.tianb.com
www.facebook.com/pages/TIANB-AITNB/127475440600650?sk=wall&filter=12
twitter.com/tianb_aitnb
Previous Name: Hospitality New Brunswick
Overview: A medium-sized provincial organization founded in 1978
Mission: To act as the provincial tourism & hospitality organization of New Brunswick, existing to fulfill the needs of its membership, in cooperation with both private & public sector partners; committed to be a representative, industry driven organization which provides leadership & direction, making tourism & hospitality the leading & most viably sustainable industry in New Brunswick
Member of: Tourism Industry Association of Canada; Hotel Association of Canada; Canadian Tourism Human Resource Council; Provincial Territorial Tourism Industry Association
Chief Officer(s):
Ron Drisdelle, Executive Director, 506-458-5646
Ron@tianb.com
Kathy Weir, President, 506-882-2349
Finances: *Annual Operating Budget:* $500,000-$1.5 Million
Staff Member(s): 10; 22 volunteer(s)
Membership: 600; *Fees:* Schedule available; *Member Profile:* Businesses having anything to do with the tourism industry in New Brunswick; *Committees:* Tourism strategy; National HR product quality; Emerit certification
Activities: Annual golf tournament, Sept.; *Awareness Events:* Annual meeting & conference, May; Provincial Tourism Awareness Week, June; *Library* Open to public
Awards:
• TIANB Scholarship Program (Scholarship)
• Business Recognition (Award)
• Pioneer Award (Award)

Tourism Industry Association of Nova Scotia (TIANS)

2089 Maitland St., Halifax NS B3K 2Z8
Tel: 902-423-4480; *Fax:* 902-422-0184
Toll-Free: 800-948-4267
information_central@tians.org
www.tians.org
www.facebook.com/tians.nsthrc
Overview: A medium-sized provincial organization founded in 1977
Mission: To lead, support, represent & enhance the Nova Scotia tourism industry
Member of: Tourism Industry Association of Canada; Canadian Tourism Human Resource Council
Affiliation(s): Innkeepers Guild of Nova Scotia; Adventure Tourism Association of Nova Scotia; Campground Owners Association of Nova Scotia; Metropolitan Area Tourism Association; Nova Scotia Bed & Breakfast Association
Chief Officer(s):
Darlene Grant Fiander, President
darlene@tourism.ca
Glenn Squires, Chair
James Miller, Secretary/Treasurer
Finances: *Funding Sources:* Membership; projects
Staff Member(s): 11
Membership: *Fees:* Schedule available based on sales per year; *Member Profile:* Tourism industry services providers
Activities: Advocacy; Trend Applications; Long-term planning; seminars; Sustainable Tourism Project; NS Ecotourism Development Foundation; Standards & Certification; Tourism Careers for Youth; SuperHost Atlantic; It's Good Business; Accessible Service Nova Scotia; Discover Tourism Month; Career Awareness/Expos; Tourism/Hospitality Business Employment Inventory; festivals & events; *Internships:* Yes; *Speaker Service:* Yes; *Rents Mailing List:* Yes; *Library:* Business/Career Centre; Open to public
Awards:
• Scholarship (Scholarship)
Renewable for 2nd $1,000 based on performance awarded to Nova Scotia student choosing post-secondary tourism education *Amount:* $1,000
• Scholarship (Scholarship)
Amount: $750

Tourism Industry Association of PEI (TIAPEI)

PO Box 2050, 25 Queen St., 3rd Fl., Charlottetown PE C1A 7N7
Tel: 902-566-5008; *Fax:* 902-368-3605
Toll-Free: 866-566-5008
tiapei@tiapei.pe.ca
www.tiapei.pe.ca
www.facebook.com/tiapei
twitter.com/tiapei
Overview: A small provincial organization
Mission: To represent tourism related businesses, associations, institutions, & individuals; to encourage tourism to & within PEI
Member of: Tourism Industry Association of Canada
Chief Officer(s):
Donald Cudmore, Executive Director
dcudmore@tiapei.pe.ca
Finances: *Annual Operating Budget:* $1.5 Million-$3 Million
Staff Member(s): 10
Activities: *Awareness Events:* Awards Gala & Tourism Conference (March); *Library* Open to public
Meetings/Conferences: • Tourism Industry Association of PEI 2015 Annual General Meeting, 2015

Tourism Industry Association of the NWT *See* Northwest Territories Tourism

Tourism Industry Association of the Yukon

#3, 1109 - 1st Ave., Whitehorse YT Y1A 5G4
Tel: 867-668-3331; *Fax:* 867-667-7379
info@tiayukon.com
www.tiayukon.com
www.facebook.com/232432356772503
Also Known As: TIA Yukon
Previous Name: Yukon Visitor's Association
Overview: A medium-sized provincial organization founded in 1972
Mission: To represent all sectors & businesses of the tourism industry; to foster & promote travel in Yukon; to encourage increase & improvement of visitor facilities, services & attractions; to enhance & stimulate business climate in industry; to enhance awareness of importance of tourism; to design & deliver marketing programs
Member of: Tourism Industry Association of Canada
Chief Officer(s):
Krista Prochazka, Executive Director
krista.prochazka@tiayukon.com
Staff Member(s): 4
Membership: 270 corporate

Tourism Kelowna

#214, 1626 Richter St., Kelowna BC V1Y 2M3
Tel: 250-861-1515
Toll-Free: 800-663-4345
info@tourismkelowna.com
www.tourismkelowna.com
www.facebook.com/TourismKelowna
twitter.com/Tourism_Kelowna
www.youtube.com/user/TourismKelowna
Previous Name: Kelowna Visitor & Convention Bureau
Overview: A small local organization founded in 1990
Mission: To attract visitors by positioning Kelowna as a unique & diverse year-round destination for the benefit of our community
Chief Officer(s):
Nancy Cameron, CEO
nancy@tourismkelowna.com
Staff Member(s): 13
Membership: *Member Profile:* Tourism businesses
Activities: Marketing & sales

Tourism London

696 Wellington Rd. South, London ON N6C 4R2
Toll-Free: 800-265-2602
www.londontourism.ca
www.facebook.com/tourismlondon
twitter.com/tourism_london
www.youtube.com/tourismlondonontario
Overview: A small local organization founded in 1997
Mission: To promote London through co-operative partnerships as the tourism, sports tourism & meeting destination of choice resulting in positive economic impact on the city of London
Chief Officer(s):
Deb Harvey, President
dharvey@grandtheatre.com
Finances: *Funding Sources:* City of London; membership fees; co-op promotions; sponsorship
Activities: *Speaker Service:* Yes
Awards:
• Hotel & Food Services Scholarship (Scholarship)
Location: Fanshawe College
• Tourism London Award (Award)
• Hospitality Scholarship (Scholarship)
Location: Fanshawe College

Tourism Moncton / Tourisme Moncton

City Hall, City of Moncton, 655 Main St., Moncton NB E1C 1E8
Toll-Free: 800-363-4558
tourism@moncton.ca
tourism.moncton.ca
www.facebook.com/139158706094720
twitter.com/TourismMoncton
www.youtube.com/user/TourismMoncton;
flickr.com/photos/tourismmoncton
Overview: A small local organization
Mission: To position Moncton as the preferred visitor, convention & meeting destination in Atlantic Canada
Chief Officer(s):
Louise D'Amours, Manager, Destination Sales, 506-389-5913, Fax: 506-859-2629
louise.d'amours@moncton.ca

Tourism Nanaimo

104 Front St., Nanaimo BC V9R 5H7
Tel: 250-591-1551
Toll-Free: 800-663-7337
info@tourismnanaimo.com
tourismnanaimo.com
www.facebook.com/TourismNanaimo
twitter.com/TourismNanaimo
www.youtube.com/channel/UCNSBLKQoxvnLDliuzZ7T3Aw
Overview: A small local organization
Mission: To promote & enhance Nanaimo as a regional supply, service & accommodation base for the business & recreational traveller
Member of: Team Canada; American Bus Association; National Tour Association
Affliation(s): Tourism Association of Vancouver Island; Tourism BC
Chief Officer(s):
Sasha Angus, CEO
sasha.angus@investnanaimo.com
Finances: *Funding Sources:* City of Nanaimo; provincial government; membership fees
Staff Member(s): 7

Activities: Destination marketing; operates city infocentre, convention sales; *Speaker Service:* Yes

Tourism Prince Albert
3700 - 2 Ave. West, Prince Albert SK S6W 1A2
Tel: 306-953-4385; *Fax:* 306-922-8687
Toll-Free: 877-868-7470
visitorpatourism@sasktel.net
www.princealberttourism.com
www.facebook.com/PrinceAlbertTourism
twitter.com/PAtourism
Previous Name: Prince Albert Tourism & Convention Bureau Inc.
Overview: A small local organization
Finances: *Annual Operating Budget:* $50,000-$100,000
Staff Member(s): 2
Membership: 1-99
Activities: *Library* Open to public

Tourism Prince George
#101, 1300 - 1st Ave., Prince George BC V2L 2Y3
Tel: 250-562-3700; *Fax:* 250-564-9807
Toll-Free: 800-668-7646
tourismpg.com
www.facebook.com/tourismpg
twitter.com/TourismPG
www.youtube.com/user/TourismPrinceGeorge
Overview: A small provincial organization
Mission: To promote Prince George as a prime northern tourist destination; to help citizens & visitors in Prince George plan their vacations
Member of: Initiatives Prince George; Canadian Society of Association Executives; Canadian Sport Tourism Association
Affiliation(s): Northern BC Tourism Association; Yellowhead Highway Association
Chief Officer(s):
Erica Hummel, Chief Executive Officer, 250-649-3218
hummel@tourismpg.com
Finances: *Funding Sources:* Municipal government
Staff Member(s): 5

Tourism Red Deer (TRD)
#101, 4200 Hwy. 2, Red Deer AB T4N 1E3
Tel: 403-346-0180; *Fax:* 403-346-5081
info@tourismreddeer.net
www.tourismreddeer.net
www.facebook.com/tourismreddeer
twitter.com/VisitRedDeer
www.youtube.com/user/TourismRedDeer
Also Known As: Visit Red Deer
Overview: A small local organization founded in 1987
Mission: To develop & promote tourism in Red Deer in cooperation with industry partners
Member of: Tourism Industry Association of Canada; Canadian Association of Visitor & Convention Bureau
Chief Officer(s):
Liz Taylor, Executive Director
liz@tourismreddeer.com
RJ Steenstra, Chair
Finances: *Funding Sources:* City of Red Deer; membership dues; revenue from services & activities
Staff Member(s): 6
Membership: *Fees:* Schedule available; *Member Profile:* Interest in tourism industry in Red Deer
Awards:
• Red Hat Awards (Award)

Tourism Rockies *See* Kootenay Rockies Tourism

Tourism Saint John / Bureau de tourisme et de congrés de Saint John
PO Box 1971, Saint John NB E2L 4L1
Tel: 506-658-2990; *Fax:* 506-632-6118
Toll-Free: 866-463-8639
visitsj@saintjohn.ca
www.tourismsaintjohn.com
www.facebook.com/DiscoverSaintJohn
twitter.com/visitsaintjohn
www.youtube.com/user/discoversaintjohn
Previous Name: Saint John Visitor & Convention Bureau
Overview: A medium-sized local organization overseen by Tourism Industry Association of New Brunswick Inc.
Mission: To position Saint John as the premier all-season, visitor, meeting & event destination on New Brunswick's Bay of Fundy; to generate revenues & publicity for the city of Saint John & its tourism operators & businesses through increased visitation, service excellence & the provision of advice & partnering opportunities
Member of: Tourism Industry Association of Canada
Chief Officer(s):
Ross Jefferson, Executive Director
Staff Member(s): 6
Membership: *Fees:* $75
Activities: Destination marketing & promotion

Tourism Sarnia Lambton (TSL)
556 Christina St. North, Sarnia ON N7T 5W6
Tel: 519-336-3232; *Fax:* 519-336-3278
Toll-Free: 800-265-0316
info@tourismsarnialambton.com
www.tourismsarnialambton.com
www.facebook.com/tourismsarnialambton
www.youtube.com/user/VisitSarniaLambton?feature=watch
Previous Name: Convention & Visitors Bureau of Sarnia/Lambton
Overview: A small local organization founded in 2000
Mission: To promote tourism to Lambton County, creating economic value for the entire community
Member of: National Tour Association; American Bus Association; Ontario Motor Coach Association; Canadian Society of Association Executives
Chief Officer(s):
Leona Allen, Office Administrator
Marlene Wood, General Manager
mwood@tourismsarnialambton.com
Finances: *Annual Operating Budget:* $500,000-$1.5 Million; *Funding Sources:* Municipal government; Chamber of Commerce; fundraising
Staff Member(s): 7; 100 volunteer(s)

Tourism Saskatoon
#101, 202 Fourth Ave. North, Saskatoon SK S7K 0K1
Tel: 306-242-1206; *Fax:* 306-242-1955
Toll-Free: 800-567-2444
info@tourismsaskatoon.com
www.tourismsaskatoon.com
www.facebook.com/tourismsaskatoon
twitter.com/visitsaskatoon
www.youtube.com/tourismsaskatoon
Also Known As: Saskatoon Visitor & Convention Bureau
Overview: A small local organization
Mission: To operate as Saskatoon's destination management organization, maximizing the economic benefit for Saskatoon through tourism
Member of: Tourism Industry Association of Canada
Affiliation(s): Tourism Saskatchewan
Chief Officer(s):
Todd Brandt, CEO
tbrandt@tourismsaskatoon.com
Finances: *Annual Operating Budget:* $500,000-$1.5 Million
Staff Member(s): 9; 20 volunteer(s)
Membership: 430; *Fees:* $150-$1,400; *Member Profile:* All sectors in tourism industry

Tourism Simcoe County
Simcoe County Museum, 1151 Hwy. 26 West, Minesing ON L0L 1Y2
Toll-Free: 800-487-6642
tourism@simcoe.ca
discover.simcoe.ca
www.facebook.com/TourismSimcoeCounty
twitter.com/simcoecountytsc
Previous Name: Huronia Tourism Association
Overview: A small local organization founded in 1969
Mission: The association promotes & develops the tourism industry of Simcoe County & area.
Member of: Tourism Industry Association of Canada
Chief Officer(s):
Kathryn Stephenson, Manager, Tourism
kathryn.stephenson@simcoe.ca
Diana Coulson, Coordinator, Marketing & Communications
gayle.mckay@simcoe.ca
Finances: *Funding Sources:* Membership dues; grants
Staff Member(s): 3
Membership: *Member Profile:* Tourism-based businesses
Activities: Brochure distribution program; border run program

Tourism Stratford; Stratford & Area Visitors & Convention Bureau *See* Stratford Tourism Alliance

Tourism Thunder Bay
PO Box 800, 53 Water St. South, Thunder Bay ON P7C 5K4
Tel: 807-625-2564; *Fax:* 807-625-3789
Toll-Free: 800-667-8386; *TTY:* 807-622-2225
rtarnowski@thunderbay.ca
www.visitthunderbay.com
www.Facebook.com/visitthunderbay
twitter.com/visitthunderbay
Also Known As: City of Thunder Bay - Tourism Division
Previous Name: Thunder Bay Public Affairs - Visitors & Convention Department
Overview: A medium-sized local organization founded in 1970
Mission: To market Thunder Bay as a destination for individuals & groups
Member of: American Bus Association; National Tour Association
Chief Officer(s):
Paul Pepe, Tourism Manager, 807-625-3880
ppepe@thunderbay.ca
Rose Marie Tarnowski, Convention & Visitor Services Coordinator
rtarnowski@thunderbay.ca
Finances: *Annual Operating Budget:* $500,000-$1.5 Million; *Funding Sources:* Municipality; Ontario Tourism
Staff Member(s): 5
Activities: Product development & training; visitor services; Marketing; Convention Services; *Awareness Events:* Doors Open Thunder Bay; Thunder Bay Children's Festival; Thunder Bay Blues Festival; *Internships:* Yes; *Speaker Service:* Yes

Tourism Toronto (TCVA)
Toronto Convention & Visitors Association, PO Box 126, 207 Queen's Quay West, Toronto ON M5J 1A7
Tel: 416-203-2600; *Fax:* 416-203-6753
Toll-Free: 800-499-2514
Other Communication: hr@torcvb.com
toronto@torcvb.com
www.torontotourism.com
www.facebook.com/visittoronto
www.twitter.com/seetorontonow
www.youtube.com/seetorontonow
Also Known As: Toronto Convention & Visitors Association
Previous Name: Metropolitan Toronto Convention & Visitors Association
Overview: A large local organization founded in 1926
Mission: To promote Toronto as a convention & visitor destination; To position Toronto as one of the world's great cities & a year-round destination for leisure & business
Member of: Tourism Industry Association of Canada
Affiliation(s): International Association of Convention & Visitor Bureaux; Toronto Board of Trade; American Society of Association Executives
Chief Officer(s):
David Whitaker, President/CEO
Andrew Weir, Vice-President, Communications
aweir@torcvb.com
Finances: *Annual Operating Budget:* Greater than $5 Million
Staff Member(s): 65
Membership: 1,000; *Member Profile:* Located in or near Toronto; interested in accessing convention & visitor markets; *Committees:* Finance; Convention Services Council; Attractions Council; Public Relations; Marketing
Activities: *Internships:* Yes; *Speaker Service:* Yes; *Rents Mailing List:* Yes; *Library:* Information Centre; Open to public by appointment

Tourism Vancouver/Greater Vancouver Convention & Visitors Bureau
The Greater Vancouver Convention & Visitors Bureau, #210, 200 Burrard St., Vancouver BC V6C 3L6
Tel: 604-682-2222; *Fax:* 604-682-1717
www.tourismvancouver.com
www.facebook.com/insidevancouver
www.twitter.com/myvancouver
Overview: A large local organization founded in 1902
Mission: To lead the cooperative effort of positioning Greater Vancouver as a preferred travel destination in all targeted markets worldwide, thereby creating opportunities for member & community sharing of the resulting economic, environmental, social & cultural benefits
Member of: Tourism Industry Association of Canada; Council of Tourism Association of BC
Affiliation(s): Canadian Association of Convention & Visitors Bureaus
Chief Officer(s):
Rick Antonson, President/CEO, 604-631-2888
Paul Vallee, Exec. Vice-President, 604-631-1815
Ted Lee, CFO, 604-631-2807
Finances: *Annual Operating Budget:* Greater than $5 Million
Staff Member(s): 80; 200 volunteer(s)

Membership: 1,000; *Fees:* $400+

Tourism Victoria/Greater Victoria Visitors & Convention Bureau

Administration Office, #200, 737 Yates St., Victoria BC V8W 1L6
Tel: 250-953-2033; *Fax:* 250-382-6539
Toll-Free: 800-663-3883
info@tourismvictoria.com
www.tourismvictoria.com
www.facebook.com/tourismvictoriafan
twitter.com/victoriavisitor
www.youtube.com/user/TourismVictoriaBC
Overview: A medium-sized local organization founded in 1974 overseen by Council of Tourism Associations of British Columbia
Mission: To oversee the development & promotion of the tourism industry in Greater Victoria
Member of: International Association of Convention & Visitors Bureaus
Chief Officer(s):
Paul Nursey, President & CEO
Alan Paige, Vice-President, Strategy Management & CFO
Finances: *Annual Operating Budget:* $3 Million-$5 Million; *Funding Sources:* Membership dues; government grants; fundraising; 2% hotel tax for external marketing
Membership: 750+; *Member Profile:* Must conform to municipal bylaws, applicable provincial & federal legislation; *Committees:* Sales & Marketing; Finance & Membership; Transportation
Activities: Marketing; convention sales & services; tour & travel; visitor services; tourism advocacy; *Speaker Service:* Yes
Awards:
• Tourism Victoria Bursary (Scholarship)

Tourism Windsor Essex Pelee Island

City Centre, #103, 333 Riverside Dr. West, Windsor ON N9A 5K4
Tel: 519-253-3616; *Fax:* 519-255-6192
Toll-Free: 800-265-3633
info@tourismwindsoressex.com
www.visitwindsoressex.com
www.facebook.com/visitwindsoressex
twitter.com/TWEPI
www.youtube.com/user/visitwindsoressex
Previous Name: Convention & Visitors Bureau of Windsor, Essex County & Pelee Island
Overview: A medium-sized local organization founded in 1980
Mission: Helps make the most of your visit to Windsor, Essex County & Pelee Island.
Member of: Tourism Industry Association of Canada; National Tour Association; American Bus Association
Chief Officer(s):
Gordon Orr, Chief Executive Officer, 800-265-3633 Ext. 4334
gorr@tourismwindsoressex.com
Staff Member(s): 14

Tourism Yorkton

PO Box 460, Yorkton SK S3N 2W4
Tel: 306-783-8707
tourismyorkton@sasktel.net
www.tourismyorkton.com
Overview: A small local organization founded in 1984
Mission: To promote, advance & encourage tourism, conventions, visitor & special events industry
Affliation(s): Saskatchewan Tourism Authority
Activities: *Speaker Service:* Yes

Tourisme Abitibi-Témiscamingue

#100, 155, av Dallaire, Rouyn-Noranda QC J9X 4T3
Tél: 819-762-8181; *Téléc:* 819-762-5212
Ligne sans frais: 800-808-0706
info@tourisme-abitibi-temiscamingue.org
www.abitibi-temiscamingue-tourism.org
www.facebook.com/TourismeAbitibiTemiscamingue
twitter.com/tourismeAT
www.vimeo.com/atrat
Également appelé: Association touristique de l'Abitibi-Témiscamingue
Aperçu: *Dimension:* petite; *Envergure:* locale; Organisme sans but lucratif surveillé par Associations touristiques régionales associées du Québec
Mission: Promotion du tourisme en Abitibi-Témiscamingue
Membre de: ATR associées du Québec

Tourisme Baie-James (TBJ) / James Bay Tourism

CP 134, 1252, rte 167 sud, Chibougamau QC G8P 2K6
Tél: 418-748-8140; *Téléc:* 418-748-8150
Ligne sans frais: 888-748-8140
info@tourismebaiejames.com
www.tourismebaiejames.com
Aperçu: *Dimension:* petite; *Envergure:* locale; Organisme sans but lucratif surveillé par Associations touristiques régionales associées du Québec
Mission: Assure dans le cadre de ses responsabilités corporatives, des mandats en matière de concertation régionale, d'accueil, d'information, de signalisation, de promotion et de développement touristique
Membre(s) du bureau directeur:
Luc Letendre, Président
Finances: *Budget de fonctionnement annuel:* $250,000-$500,000
Membre(s) du personnel: 5; 11 bénévole(s)
Membre: 133; *Montant de la cotisation:* Barème

Tourisme Bas-Saint-Laurent

148, rue Fraser, 2e étage, Rivière-du-Loup QC G5R 1C8
Tél: 418-867-1272; *Téléc:* 418-867-3245
Ligne sans frais: 800-563-5268
info@bassaintlaurent.ca
bassaintlaurent.ca
www.facebook.com/tourismebassaintlaurent
Également appelé: Association touristique régionale du Bas-Saint-Laurent
Aperçu: *Dimension:* moyenne; *Envergure:* locale; Organisme sans but lucratif; fondée en 1978 surveillé par Associations touristiques régionales associées du Québec
Mission: Accueil, développement et promotion touristique
Membre(s) du bureau directeur:
Pierre Laplante, Directeur général
pierrelaplante@bassaintlaurent.ca
Finances: *Budget de fonctionnement annuel:* $500,000-$1.5 Million
Membre(s) du personnel: 8
Membre: 450; *Critères d'admissibilite:* Industrie touristique
Activités: *Stagiaires:* Oui

Tourisme Cantons-de-l'Est

20, rue Don-Bosco sud, Sherbrooke QC J1L 1W4
Tél: 819-820-2020; *Téléc:* 819-566-4445
Ligne sans frais: 800-355-5755
info@atrce.com
www.cantonsdelest.com
www.facebook.com/cantonsdelest
twitter.com/cantonsdelest
Également appelé: Association touristique des Cantons-de-l'Est
Aperçu: *Dimension:* moyenne; *Envergure:* locale; fondée en 1978 surveillé par Associations touristiques régionales associées du Québec
Mission: A pour mission de faire de la région des Cantons-de-l'Est une des meilleures destinations touristique du Québec en toutes saisons
Affliation(s): Tourisme Québec
Membre(s) du bureau directeur:
Alain Larouche, Directeur général
Francine Patenaude, Directrice, Marketing & développement
Finances: *Budget de fonctionnement annuel:* $3 Million-$5 Million; *Fonds:* Promotion coopérative
Membre(s) du personnel: 15
Membre: 525; *Montant de la cotisation:* 340$; *Comités:* Marketing; Club exportateur

Tourisme Centre-du-Québec

20, boul Carignan Ouest, Princeville QC G6L 4M4
Tél: 819-364-7177; *Téléc:* 819-364-2120
Ligne sans frais: 888-816-4007
info@tourismecentreduquebec.com
www.tourismecentreduquebec.com
www.linkedin.com/company/tourisme-centre-du-qu-bec
www.facebook.com/Tourismecentreduquebec
twitter.com/CentreduQuebec
www.youtube.com/TourismCentreduQc
Aperçu: *Dimension:* petite; *Envergure:* locale surveillé par Associations touristiques régionales associées du Québec
Membre(s) du bureau directeur:
Yves Zahra, Directeur général
Membre(s) du personnel: 8

Tourisme Chaudière-Appalaches (ATCA)

800, autoroute Jean-Lesage, Saint-Nicolas QC G7A 1E3
Tél: 418-831-4411; *Téléc:* 418-831-8442
Ligne sans frais: 888-831-4411
info@chaudiereappalaches.com
www.chaudiereappalaches.com
www.facebook.com/ChaudiereAppalaches
twitter.com/ChaudApp
Nom précédent: Association touristique Chaudière-Appalaches
Aperçu: *Dimension:* moyenne; *Envergure:* locale; Organisme sans but lucratif; fondée en 1976 surveillé par Associations touristiques régionales associées du Québec
Mission: Favoriser le développement et la promotion de l'industrie touristique de son territoire tout en contribuant à la réussite des entreprises qui en sont membres
Membre(s) du bureau directeur:
Richard Moreau, Director général
rmoreau@chaudiereappalaches.com
Finances: *Budget de fonctionnement annuel:* $500,000-$1.5 Million
Membre(s) du personnel: 10
Membre: 500; *Montant de la cotisation:* Barème
Activités: Promotion touristique;

Tourisme Gaspésie

1020, boul Jacques-Cartier, Québec QC G5H 0B1
Tél: 418-775-2223; *Téléc:* 418-775-2234
Ligne sans frais: 800-463-0323
info@tourisme-gaspesie.com
www.tourisme-gaspesie.com
ca.linkedin.com/company/tourisme-gasp-sie
www.facebook.com/gaspesiejetaime
twitter.com/gaspesiejetaime
www.youtube.com/Gaspesiejetaime
Également appelé: Association touristique régionale de la Gaspésie
Aperçu: *Dimension:* moyenne; *Envergure:* locale; fondée en 1978 surveillé par Associations touristiques régionales associées du Québec
Mission: Orienter et favoriser la promotion, le développement et l'activité touristique dans le meilleur intérêt de la Gaspésie; promouvoir, organiser et coordonner divers programmes de promotion et de développement touristique ayant comme conséquence d'accroître la clientèle touristique et prolongation des séjours dans la Gaspésie
Membre de: Tourisme Québec
Membre(s) du bureau directeur:
Joëlle Ross, Directrice générale
joeller@tourisme-gaspesie.com
Christine St-Pierre, Responsable des communications
christine@tourisme-gaspesie.com
Finances: *Budget de fonctionnement annuel:* $500,000-$1.5 Million
Membre(s) du personnel: 7
Membre: 529; *Comités:* Salons promotionnels; motoneige; guide touristique

Tourisme Harricana *Voir* Maison du Tourisme

Tourisme Iles de la Madeleine

128, ch Principal, Cap-aux-Meules QC G4T 1C5
Tél: 418-986-2245; *Téléc:* 418-986-2327
Ligne sans frais: 877-624-4437
info@tourismeilesdelamadeleine.com
www.tourismeilesdelamadeleine.com
www.facebook.com/tourismeilesdelamadeleine
twitter.com/ATRIM
www.youtube.com/TourismeIDM
Nom précédent: Association touristique des Iles-de-la-Madeleine
Aperçu: *Dimension:* moyenne; *Envergure:* locale surveillé par Associations touristiques régionales associées du Québec
Mission: Regrouper les entreprises de l'industrie touristique de l'archipel afin d'accroître les efforts de développement et de promotion
Membre(s) du bureau directeur:
Michel Bonato, Directrice générale, 418-986-2245 Ext. 225
direction@tourismeilesdelamadeleine.com
Finances: *Fonds:* Tourisme Québec
Activités: Salons consommateurs; bourses et foires professionnelles; tournées de presse; voyage de familiarisation; publicité; publication du guide touristique officiel et des brochures promotionnelles

Tourisme Lanaudière

3568, rue Church, Rawdon QC J0K 1S0
Tél: 450-834-2535; *Téléc:* 450-834-8100
Ligne sans frais: 800-363-2788
info@lanaudiere.ca
www.lanaudiere.ca/fr/
www.facebook.com/tourismelanaudiere
twitter.com/tourlanaud
Également appelé: Association touristique de Lanaudière

Aperçu: *Dimension:* moyenne; *Envergure:* locale; Organisme sans but lucratif; fondée en 1978 surveillé par Associations touristiques régionales associées du Québec
Mission: Faire la promotion, développement, commercialisation de l'offre touristiques de la région auprès des clienteles des différents marchés; améliorer l'accueil & l'information touristique
Membre(s) du bureau directeur:
Évangéline Richard, Présidente
Finances: *Budget de fonctionnement annuel:* $500,000-$1.5 Million
Membre(s) du personnel: 8
Membre: 360; *Montant de la cotisation:* Barème; *Critères d'admissibilite:* Organismes touristiques & municipalités
Activités: Développement et promotion touristique;

Tourisme Laval

480, Promenade du Centropolis, Laval QC H7T 3C2
Tél: 450-682-5522; *Téléc:* 450-682-7304
info@tourismelaval.com
www.tourismelaval.com
www.facebook.com/tourismelaval
twitter.com/TourismeLaval
www.youtube.com/user/tourismelaval
Aperçu: *Dimension:* petite; *Envergure:* locale surveillé par Associations touristiques régionales associées du Québec
Mission: De promouvoir Laval comme destination touristique
Membre(s) du bureau directeur:
Geneviève Roy, Directrice générale
groy@tourismelaval.com
Yves Legault, Président
yves.legault@collegeletendre.qc.ca
Membre(s) du personnel: 11

Tourisme Mauricie

CP 100, Shawinigan QC G9N 8S1
Tél: 819-536-3334; *Téléc:* 819-536-3373
Ligne sans frais: 800-567-7603
info@tourismemauricie.com
www.tourismemauricie.com
www.facebook.com/tourismemauricie
twitter.com/mauricie
www.youtube.com/tourismemauricie
Également appelé: Association touristique régionale de la Mauricie
Aperçu: *Dimension:* moyenne; *Envergure:* locale; Organisme sans but lucratif; fondée en 1977 surveillé par Associations touristiques régionales associées du Québec
Mission: De promouvoir la ville de Maurice comme une destination touristique
Membre(s) du bureau directeur:
André Nollet, Directeur général
direction@tourismemauricie.com
Membre(s) du personnel: 11

Tourisme Moncton *See* Tourism Moncton

Tourisme Montérégie

#10, 8940, boul Leduc, Brossard QC J4Y 0G4
Tél: 450-466-4666; *Téléc:* 450-466-7999
Ligne sans frais: 866-469-0069
info@tourisme-monteregie.qc.ca
www.tourisme-monteregie.qc.ca
www.facebook.com/pages/Tourisme-Monteregie/283759343997
twitter.com/tourmonteregie
Également appelé: Association touristique régionale de la Montérégie
Aperçu: *Dimension:* moyenne; *Envergure:* locale; fondée en 1978 surveillé par Associations touristiques régionales associées du Québec
Membre(s) du bureau directeur:
Josée Juliener, Directrice générale
jjulien@tourisme-monteregie.qc.ca
François Trépanier, Directeur, Communications
ftrepanier@tourisme-monteregie.qc.ca
Finances: *Budget de fonctionnement annuel:* $1.5 Million-$3 Million
Membre(s) du personnel: 13
Membre: 378; *Comités:* Stratégique d'orientation marketing; Route des cidres; Route des vins; Cyclotourisme
Activités: *Stagiaires:* Oui; *Service de conférenciers:* Oui; *Listes de destinataires:* Oui

Tourisme Montréal/Office des congrès et du tourisme du Grand Montréal / Greater Montréal Convention & Tourism Bureau

CP 979, Montréal QC H3C 2W3
Tél: 514-873-2015; *Téléc:* 514-864-3838
Ligne sans frais: 877-266-5687
info@tourisme-montreal.org
www.tourism-montreal.org
www.facebook.com/Montreal
twitter.com/montreal
www.youtube.com/user/TourismeMontreal
Également appelé: Tourisme Montréal
Aperçu: *Dimension:* moyenne; *Envergure:* locale; Organisme sans but lucratif; fondée en 1919 surveillé par Associations touristiques régionales associées du Québec
Mission: De promouvoir Montréal comme une destination touristique populaire
Membre de: Tourism Industry Association of Canada
Affliation(s): Canadian Society of Association Executives
Membre(s) du bureau directeur:
Yves Lalumière, Président et directeur général
Membre: 750
Activités: *Stagiaires:* Oui; *Service de conférenciers:* Oui; *Bibliothèque*

Tourisme Ottawa *See* Ottawa Tourism

Tourisme Outaouais

103, rue Laurier, Gatineau QC J8X 3V8
Tél: 819-778-2222; *Téléc:* 819-778-7758
Ligne sans frais: 800-265-7822
info@tourisme-outaouais.ca
www.tourismeoutaouais.ca
www.facebook.com/tourismeoutaouais
twitter.com/TourOutaouais
www.youtube.com/tourismeoutaouais
Également appelé: Association touristique de l'Outaouais
Aperçu: *Dimension:* petite; *Envergure:* locale; Organisme sans but lucratif; fondée en 1981 surveillé par Associations touristiques régionales associées du Québec
Mission: Prospérité économique de la région par le développement et la promotion du produit touristique; structurer, organiser, orchestrer tout projet susceptible de générer des activités touristiques à retombées économiques importantes; assumer un accueil de qualité et une diffusion de l'information
Membre(s) du bureau directeur:
Louise Boudrias, Présidente, 819-775-9070
lboudrias@videotron.ca
Gilles Picard, Directeur général
gpicard@tourisme-outaouais.ca
Finances: *Budget de fonctionnement annuel:* $1.5 Million-$3 Million
Membre(s) du personnel: 22
Membre: 465; *Montant de la cotisation:* 150-1500; *Critères d'admissibilite:* Hébergement, plein air, restaurants, services professionnels, festivals, attractions touristiques
Activités: Gala des Grands Prix du Tourisme; *Evénements de sensibilisation:* Semaine Nationale du Tourisme

Tourisme Sherbrooke; Société de développement économique de la région sherbrookoise - Tourisme *Voir* Destination Sherbrooke

Tournoi de Soccer de Victoriaville

CP 393, Victoriaville QC G6P 6T2
Tél: 819-752-2878
admin@soccervicto.com
www.soccervicto.com
Aperçu: *Dimension:* petite; *Envergure:* locale

Town of York Historical Society (TYHS)

260 Adelaide St. East, Toronto ON M5A 1N1
Tel: 416-865-1833; *Fax:* 416-865-9414
tfpo@total.net
www.townofyork.com
www.facebook.com/TOs1stPO
twitter.com/TOs1stPO
Also Known As: Toronto's First Post Office (TFPO)
Overview: A small local charitable organization founded in 1983
Mission: To research, interpret & promote the history of the Town of York & early Toronto, with emphasis on the role of postal service in communications of Upper Canada, & the surviving built environment
Member of: Ontario Museum Association; Canadian Museum Associations; Ontario Historical Society; Green Tourism Association; Attractions Ontario; Toronto Historical Association; Heritage Canada Foundation
Affliation(s): La Société d'histoire de Toronto; Toronto Region, Architectural Conservancy; Cabbagetown Preservation Association
Chief Officer(s):
Janet Walters, Director/Curator, Toronto's First Post Office
Finances: *Funding Sources:* Municipal & provincial government; postal retail outlet; donations; membership fees
Staff Member(s): 2
Membership: *Fees:* $25 single; $40 family; $250 life
Activities: Operates Toronto's First Post Office; exhibits; school tours; *Library:* Town of York Historical Association Library; by appointment

Township of Clarence Minor Hockey Association (TCMHA)

PO Box 212, Clarence Creek AB K0A 1N0
clarencehockey.ca
Overview: A small local organization
Mission: To govern & promote minor hockey in Clarence
Chief Officer(s):
Linda Thompson, President
castorpresident@gmail.com

Township of Oro-Medonte History Committee

Oro-Medonte Township Office, PO Box 100, Oro Station ON L0L 2X0
Tel: 705-487-2171
kirkland@csolve.net
www.oro-medonte.ca
Overview: A small local organization founded in 1955
Mission: To research & promote local history
Chief Officer(s):
Allan Howard, Chair
jallenhoward@xplornet.ca
Activities: Organizing exhibitions of historical artifacts & photographs
Publications:
• Bayview Memorial Park
Type: Book; *Price:* $1.50
• The Hills of Oro & Other Landmarks
Type: Book; *Price:* $3.00
• Kith 'n Kin
Type: Book; *Price:* $37.00
• Knox Presbyterian Church
Type: Book; *Price:* $3.15
• Medonte: A Township Remembered
Type: Book; *Price:* $37.00
• Monty Leigh Remembers
Type: Book; *Price:* $8.35
• Oro African Church
Type: Book; *Price:* $15.00
• Story of Oro
Type: Book; *Price:* $13.65
• Visible Past
Type: Book; *Price:* $17.85

Townshippers' Association (TA) / Association des Townshippers

#100, 257, rue Queen, Sherbrooke QC J1M 1K7
Tel: 819-566-5717; *Fax:* 819-566-0271
Toll-Free: 866-566-5717
ta@townshippers.qc.ca
www.townshippers.qc.ca
twitter.com/townshippersTA
Overview: A medium-sized local organization founded in 1979
Mission: To promote the interests of the English-speaking community in the historical Eastern Townships; to strengthen the cultural identity of this community; to encourage the full participation of the English-speaking population in the community at large
Member of: Québec Community Groups Network; Québec Anglophone Heritage Network; Community Health & Social Services Network
Chief Officer(s):
Ingrid Marini, Executive Director
Gerald Cutting, President
Finances: *Annual Operating Budget:* $250,000-$500,000; *Funding Sources:* Canadian Heritage; membership fees; donations; diverse grants
Staff Member(s): 9; 100 volunteer(s)
Membership: 4,000; *Fees:* $15 individual; $25 family; $100 lifetime; *Member Profile:* English speakers in the historical Eastern Townships; *Committees:* Communications; Health & Social Services; Community & Culture; Membership; Townshippers of Tomorrow; Knowledge Base
Activities: *Awareness Events:* Townshippers' Day, Sept.; Outstanding Townshippers Banquet & AGM, June; *Library:* Resource Centre; Open to public
Awards:
• Outstanding Townshippers Awards (Award)

• Townships Leaders of Tomorrow Awards (Award)

Lac-Brome Office
#3, 584 Knowlton Rd., Lac-Brome QC J0E 1V0
Tel: 450-242-4421; *Fax:* 450-242-5870
Toll-Free: 877-242-4421
kw@townshippers.qc.ca

Toxics Watch Society of Alberta (TWS)
1-6328A - 104 St. NW, Edmonton AB T6H 2K9
Tel: 780-439-1912
www.toxwatch.ca
Overview: A small provincial organization founded in 1986
Mission: To promote reduction in the common use of toxic substances & zero discharge of toxic wastes; to ensure clean air & water & safe food for Albertans; to facilitate sustainable communities & environmental citizenship
Member of: Alberta Environmental Network; Canadian Environmental Network
Affliation(s): Environmental Resource Centre; Tomorrow Foundation for a Sustainable Future
Activities: Public Information Service; *Library:* Resource Library; Open to public

T.P.U.G.
258 Lake Promenade, Toronto ON M8W 1B3
e-mail: info@tpug.ca
www.tpug.ca
Also Known As: Toronto PET Users Group Inc.
Overview: A small local organization founded in 1978
Mission: To promote the effective use of Commodore computers
Chief Officer(s):
Ian McIntosh, Secretary
Ernie Chorny, President
Finances: *Annual Operating Budget:* Less than $50,000
Membership: *Fees:* $10; *Member Profile:* Users of Commodore machines & operating systems

Trade Facilitation Office Canada / Bureau de promotion du commerce Canada
#300, 56 Sparks St., Ottawa ON K1P 5A9
Tel: 613-233-3925; *Fax:* 613-233-7860
Toll-Free: 800-267-9674
info@tfocanada.ca
www.tfocanada.ca
www.linkedin.com/company/tfo-canada
twitter.com/TFOcan
Also Known As: TFO Canada
Overview: A small international organization founded in 1980
Mission: To help improve the economic well-being of developing countries through increased integration into the global economy
Chief Officer(s):
Brian Mitchell, Executive Director, 613-233-3925 Ext. 31
Finances: *Funding Sources:* Government; international development agencies; private
Staff Member(s): 10; 2 volunteer(s)
Membership: 1-99
Activities: Provides free assistance to exporters from developing countries to find markets in Canada & to importers who wish to locate new sources of products from over 120 countries; provides training & related assistance in export marketing, trade policy & investment prospecting to developing & transition countries on a fee-for-service basis; *Internships:* Yes; *Speaker Service:* Yes

Traffic Injury Research Foundation (TIRF) / Fondation de recherches sur les blessures de la route
#200, 171 Nepean St., Ottawa ON K2P 0B4
Tel: 613-238-5235; *Fax:* 613-238-5292
Toll-Free: 877-238-5235
tirf@tirf.ca
www.tirf.ca
Overview: A medium-sized national charitable organization founded in 1964
Mission: To reduce traffic related deaths & injuries, through the design, promotion, & implementation of prevention programs & policies based on sound research
Chief Officer(s):
Robyn D. Robertson, President & CEO
Sara Oglestone, Manager, Marketing & Communications
Finances: *Annual Operating Budget:* $500,000-$1,5 Million; *Funding Sources:* Memberships; donations
Staff Member(s): 11
Membership: 100 corporate + 125 individual
Activities: Projects include: Distracted Driving; Drinking & Driving; Trends & Statistics; Trucks; Young & Novice Drivers; *Speaker Service:* Yes; *Library:* Resource Centre; Open to public

Trager Canada
PO Box 2903, Richmond Hill ON L4E 1A8
Toll-Free: 888-724-3788
admin@trager.ca
www.trager.ca
Previous Name: Trager Practitioners of S. Central Ontario
Overview: A small national licensing organization founded in 1981
Mission: To support & encourage the expanding practice of the Trager Approach & Mentastics movement re-education in Canada
Member of: Trager International
Chief Officer(s):
Sandra Yanover, Chair
Chris Bruels, Administrator
Finances: *Annual Operating Budget:* Less than $50,000
Staff Member(s): 1; 15 volunteer(s)
Membership: 75; *Fees:* $225; *Member Profile:* Certified practitioners of Trager Psychophysical Integration & students; *Committees:* Ethics; Newsletter; Website Development
Activities: Provides information about Trager bodywork/movement education; referrals; *Speaker Service:* Yes

Trager Practitioners of S. Central Ontario *See* Trager Canada

Trail & District Chamber of Commerce
#200, 1199 Bay Ave., Trail BC V1R 4A4
Tel: 250-368-3144; *Fax:* 250-368-6427
Other Communication: Member Services e-mail: tcoc2@netidea.com
tcocm@netidea.com
www.trailchamber.bc.ca
Overview: A small local organization
Mission: To provide leadership in the growth of a progressive & financially strong community, by assisting members in improving their competitiveness
Member of: British Columbia Chamber of Commerce; British Columbia Rockies Tourist Association; Better Business Bureau
Chief Officer(s):
Lisa Gregorini, President
Norm Casler, Executive Director
Finances: *Annual Operating Budget:* $100,000-$250,000; *Funding Sources:* Fee for service
Staff Member(s): 2
Membership: 210; *Fees:* Schedule available; *Member Profile:* Local businesses in Trail, British Columbia & the surrounding area; *Committees:* Membership; Greater Trail Community Events & Promotions; Special Events
Activities: Organizing business events & a trade show; *Library* Open to public

Trail & Ultra Running Association Of The Yukon (TURAY)
4061 - 4th Ave., Whitehorse YT Y1A 1H1
Tel: 867-333-0983; *Fax:* 867-667-4237
sportyukon.com
Overview: A small provincial organization
Chief Officer(s):
Nancy Thomson, President
nancy.thomson@cbc.ca

Trail Association for Community Living
PO Box 131, 1565B Bay Ave., Trail BC V1R 4L3
Tel: 250-368-3503; *Fax:* 250-368-5559
tacl@telus.net
www.taclkootenays.com
Overview: A small local organization
Mission: To help & support people with developmental disabilities, providing them with a higher quality of life
Member of: Kootenay Society for Community Living
Chief Officer(s):
Nancy Gurr, Executive Director
Staff Member(s): 5
Membership: *Fees:* $5 individual; $10 organization; $100 lifetime

Trail Riders of the Canadian Rockies
PO Box 6742, Stn. D, Calgary AB T2P 2E6
Tel: 403-874-4408
admin@trail-rides.ca
trailridevacations.com
www.facebook.com/189174017824540
Overview: A small local organization founded in 1923
Mission: To encourage travel on horseback through the Canadian Rockies; to foster the maintenance & improvement of old trails & the building of new trails; to promote good fellowship among those who visit & live in the Canadian Rockies; to encourage the appreciation of outdoor life & the study & conservation of mountain ecology; to assist in every way possible to ensure the preservation of the National Parks of Canada for the use & enjoyment of the public; to cooperate with other organizations with similar aims
Chief Officer(s):
Robert Vanderzweerde, Secretary-Treasurer
Finances: *Funding Sources:* Ride sales; membership fees
Membership: *Fees:* $35

Trail Riding Alberta Conference (TRAC)
PO Box 44, RR#4, Site 5, Lacombe AB T4L 2N4
Tel: 403-782-7363
office@trailriding.ca
www.trailriding.ca
Overview: A small provincial organization
Mission: To promote long-distance horse riding
Affliation(s): Canadian Long Distance Riding Association
Chief Officer(s):
Ken Vanderwekken, President
Finances: *Funding Sources:* Fundraising; membership fees; ride fees
Membership: 166; *Fees:* $25
Activities: Three divisions: novice, intermediate & open; three categories within each: junior, lightweight & heavyweight.; *Speaker Service:* Yes; *Library:* Long Distance Info; Open to public

La Trame
CP 845, Succ. Desjardins, Montréal QC H5B 1B9
Tél: 514-374-0227
la.trame@hotmail.com
la-trame.ca
Aperçu: *Dimension:* petite; *Envergure:* locale
Mission: Regroupement pour lesbiennes dans le domaine des arts, de la culture et du loisir
Membre(s) du bureau directeur:
Mireille Robillard, Contact
Membre: *Montant de la cotisation:* 20$
Activités: Rencontres, expositions, sorties

Trans Canada Trail Foundation (TCTF) / Fondation du sentier transcanadien
#300, 321 de la Commune West, Montréal QC H2Y 2E1
Tel: 514-485-3959; *Fax:* 514-485-4541
Toll-Free: 800-465-3636
info@tctrail.ca
www.tctrail.ca
www.linkedin.com/company/trans-canada-trail
www.facebook.com/transcanadatrail
twitter.com/#!/TCTrail
www.youtube.com/user/TheTransCanadaTrail
Overview: A medium-sized national charitable organization founded in 1992
Mission: To promote & coordinate the planning, designing & building of a continuous, shared-use recreation trail that winds its way through every Province & Territory
Chief Officer(s):
Jane Murphy, National Director of Trail, 800-465-3636 Ext. 4355
jmurphy@tctrail.ca
Gay Decker, Director of Communications, 800-465-3636 Ext. 4350
gdecker@tctrail.ca
Amparo Jardine, Director of Development, 800-465-3636 Ext. 4349
AJardine@tctrail.ca
Finances: *Annual Operating Budget:* $250,000-$500,000; *Funding Sources:* Public donations
Staff Member(s): 11; 1 volunteer(s)
Membership: 2,500; *Fees:* $75-150
Activities: Trail-building; trail locators & signage; guidebooks & maps

Trans Canada Yellowhead Highway Association (TCYHA)
77 Airport Rd., Edmonton AB T5G 0W6
Tel: 780-761-3800
members@yellowheadit.com
www.transcanadayellowhead.com
Previous Name: Yellowhead Highway Association
Overview: A small local organization founded in 1947
Mission: To improve highway infrastructure & promote tourism along the TransCanada/Yellowhead highway corridor

Chief Officer(s):
Loranne Martin, President
Finances: *Annual Operating Budget:* $100,000-$250,000
Staff Member(s): 3; 1 volunteer(s)
Membership: 390; *Member Profile:* Municipal, commercial, & corporate organizations & individuals; *Committees:* Marketing; Resources

Trans-Canada Advertising Agency Network (T-CAAN)

#504, 4001 Bayview Ave., Toronto ON M2M 3Z7
Tel: 416-221-6984; *Fax:* 416-221-8260
wwsr@rogers.com
www.tcaan.ca
Also Known As: T-CAAN
Overview: A medium-sized national organization founded in 1963
Mission: To serve & support its members in every type of marketing & communications endeavour; Focuses on advertising, communications, & marketing
Affliation(s): Intermarket Agency Network (IAN)
Chief Officer(s):
Bill Whitehead, Managing Director
Finances: *Annual Operating Budget:* Less than $50,000; *Funding Sources:* Membership fees
Membership: 28 corporate; *Fees:* $2000; *Member Profile:* Advertising agencies
Publications:
• E-Tattler
Frequency: bi-monthly; *Editor:* Phil Chant
Profile: For members only

Trans-Himalayan Aid Society (TRAS)

#720, 999 West Broadway, Vancouver BC V5Z 1K5
Tel: 604-224-5133; *Fax:* 604-738-4080
tras@portal.ca
www.tras.ca
Overview: A small international organization founded in 1962
Mission: To help the people of the Himalayas to help themselves; to aid in poverty alleviation by giving basic health care, education for employment, skills, tools & basic inputs for agricultural development; to promote environmentally sound development by fostering understanding for conservation & ecologically sustainable development; to foster & strengthen the links between Canadians & the people of the Himalayas through non-government agencies
Chief Officer(s):
Armila C. Shakya, Office Manager
Staff Member(s): 1; 300 volunteer(s)
Membership: 375; *Fees:* $20

Transition House Association of Nova Scotia (THANS)

#215, 2099 Gottingen St., Halifax NS B3K 3B2
Tel: 902-429-7287; *Fax:* 902-429-0561
coordinator@thans.ca
www.thans.ca
Overview: A medium-sized provincial organization
Mission: The Transition House Association of Nova Scotia (THANS) member organizations provide transitional services to women (and their children) who are experiencing violence and abuse, including culturally relevant services to Mi'kmaw people. THANS eleven member organizations work with women and their children in thirteen locations across Nova Scotia.
Chief Officer(s):
Pamela Harrison, Provincial Coordinator

Transitions

#100, Carleton Dr., St Albert AB T8N 7L1
Tel: 780-458-7371; *Fax:* 780-460-7078
info@transitions-ab.org
www.transitions-ab.org
www.facebook.com/transitions.stalbert
twitter.com/Transitions_ab
Previous Name: Transitions Rehabilitation Association of St. Albert & District; St. Albert Association for People with Disabilities
Overview: A small local organization
Mission: To offer support services to individuals with developmental delays & disabilities of all ages & their families in St. Albert, Sturgeon County & Northwest Edmonton
Chief Officer(s):
Bev Janzen, President
Paul Fujishige, Executive Director
Activities: *Awareness Events:* Jump Start, Jan.; Roy Financial Mayor's Walk for Charity

Transitions Rehabilitation Association of St. Albert & District; St. Albert Association for People with Disabilities

See Transitions

The Transplantation Society (TTS)

International Headquarters, #605, 1255, rue University, Montréal QC H3B 3V9
Tel: 514-874-1717; *Fax:* 514-874-1716
info@tts.org
www.tts.org
Overview: A medium-sized international organization
Mission: To provide global leadership in transplantation; To develop the science & clinical practice
Chief Officer(s):
Gerhard Opelz, President
Ron Shapiro, Vice-President
Hans Sollinger, Senior Treasurer
Filomena Picciano, Director, Professional Services
Jean-Pierre Mongeau, Director, Headquarter Services
Membership: *Committees:* Global Data Dictionary; Women in Transplantation; Global Alliance for Transplantation; Section Presidents Liaison; Basic Science; Medawar Prize; Congress Organizing; Membership; Ethics; Education; Communications; Executive
Activities: Providing continuing education; Offering guidance on the ethical practice
Meetings/Conferences: • The Transplantation Society 2015 Transplant Science Symposium, November, 2015, Mantra Lorne, Lorne
Scope: International
Contact Information: URL: www.tss2015.org
Publications:
• Transplantation: The Official Journal of The Transplantation Society
Type: Journal; *Frequency:* Semimonthly
Profile: Advances in transplantation, in areas such as cell therapy & islet transplantation, clinical transplantation, experimental transplantation,immunobiology & genomics, & xenotransplantation
• Tribune
Type: Newsletter; *Frequency:* 3 pa; *Editor:* Henrik ekberg
Profile: Society news, meeting reviews, & feature articles

Transport 2000 Canada

See Transport Action Canada

Transport Action Canada

Bronson Centre, PO Box 858, Stn. B, #303, 211 Bronson Ave., Ottawa ON K1P 5P9
Tel: 613-594-3290; *Fax:* 613-594-3271
info@transport-action.ca
www.transport-action.ca
Previous Name: Transport 2000 Canada
Overview: A medium-sized national charitable organization founded in 1976
Mission: National federation of environmental & consumer groups concerned about the importance of transportation on our environment & quality of life; to inform Canadians of the need for a coherent national transport policy which recognizes that conservation of resources must be a priority & that access to good public transportation is a right of all Canadians; to work for the improvement & greater use of bus & rail transportation in the interests of public safety, social equity & the protection of the environment; to press for the coordination of all transport services for the benefit of users; to demand more attention to the needs of pedestrians, cyclists & public transport users; to maximize the use of the energy-efficient rail & marine modes for the shipment of freight.
PUBLICATIONS: National Transport Newsletter.
Affiliation(s): Transport 2000 International
Chief Officer(s):
David Jeanes, President
Justin Bur, VP East
Peter Lacey, VP West
Tony Turritin, Secretary
Klaus Beltzner, Treasurer
Bert Titcomb, Manager
Finances: *Annual Operating Budget:* $50,000-$100,000; *Funding Sources:* Donations
15 volunteer(s)
Membership: 1,500; *Fees:* $35 regular; $30 senior; $50 family; $75 affiliate non-profit; $170corporate
Activities: Research, public education & advocacy, representation of the consumer interests before federal, provincial, municipal public hearings & regulatory bodies, direction of consumer complaints to public carriers; *Speaker Service:* Yes; *Library* Open to public

Transportation Association of Canada (TAC) / Association des transports du Canada (ATC)

2323 St. Laurent Blvd., Ottawa ON K1G 4J8
Tel: 613-736-1350; *Fax:* 613-736-1395
secretariat@tac-atc.ca
www.tac-atc.ca
Previous Name: Canadian Good Roads Association; Roads & Transportation Association of Canada
Overview: A large national organization founded in 1914
Mission: To promote the provision of safe, efficient, effective & environmentally sustainable transportation services in support of Canada's social & economic goals; To act as a neutral forum for the discussion of transportation issues & matters; to act as a technical focus in the highway transportation area
Chief Officer(s):
Sarah Wells, Executive Director, 613-736-1350 Ext. 226
Meena Peruvemba, Director, Finance & Administration
mperuvemba@tac-atc.ca
Sarah Wells, Director, Technical Programs
swells@tac-atc.ca
Erica Andersen, Director, Communications & Member Services
eandersen@tac-atc.ca
John Law, President
Joseph K. Lam, Vice-President
Alex Turnbull, Treasurer
Finances: *Annual Operating Budget:* Greater than $5 Million
Staff Member(s): 20; 500 volunteer(s)
Membership: 550 corporate; *Fees:* Schedule available; *Committees:* Technical & Research; Editing & Publications; Rules of the Road; Project; Technical Steering; Asphalts Advisory; Operations; Pavements; Structures; Aviation; Conference Technical Program; Geometric Design; Goods Movement; Soils & Materials; Traffic; Transit Planning; Technology
Activities: *Library:* Transportation Information Service; by appointment
Meetings/Conferences: • Transportation Association of Canada 2015 Conference & Exhibition, September, 2015, PEI Convention Centre, Charlottetown, PE
Scope: National

Trauma Association of Canada (TAC) / Association canadienne de traumatologie

c/o Trauma Services, Foothills Medical Centre, 1403 - 29 St. NW, Calgary AB T2N 2T9
Tel: 403-944-2888; *Fax:* 403-944-8799
info@traumacanada.org
www.traumacanada.org
twitter.com/TraumaCanada
Overview: A small national organization founded in 1984
Mission: To promote the highest standards of care for the injured patient; To encourage research & education related to trauma
Member of: Royal College of Physicians & Surgeons of Canada
Chief Officer(s):
Sandro Rizoli, President
sandro.rizoli@sw.ca
Natalie Yanchar, Secretary
natalie.yanchar@iwk.nshealth.ca
Morad Hameed, Treasurer
morad.hameed@vch.ca
Membership: *Member Profile:* Physicians; Surgeons; Allied health care professionals; Canadian community; *Committees:* Canadian Forces Medical Liaison; Education; Guidelines; Injury Prevention / Surveillance; International Issues / Disasters; Nomination; Paediatrics; Publication; Research; Scientific Programme
Activities: Engaging in advocacy activities; Facilitating professional & community education in the field of injury prevention; Participating in community disaster response planning; Developing & maintaining a National Trauma Registry; Establishing guidelines for Trauma Centres
Meetings/Conferences: • Trauma 2015: Trauma Association of Canada Annual Scientific Meeting & Conference, April, 2015, Westin Calgary, Calgary, AB
Scope: National
Publications:
• Trauma Association of Canada Newsletter
Type: Newsletter; *Frequency:* Semiannually

Travel Health Insurance Association of Canada (THIA)

#300, 191 John St., Toronto ON M5T 1X3
e-mail: info@thiaonline.com
www.thiaonline.com
twitter.com/thiaonline

Overview: A medium-sized national organization founded in 1998
Mission: To be the leading voice for travel insurance in Canada
Chief Officer(s):
Alex Bittner, President
Membership: 381 individuals; *Fees:* $125 individual; $525 corporate; *Member Profile:* Travel insurers, brokers, underwriters, re-insurers, emergency assistance companies, air ambulance companies & allied services in the travel insurance field
Activities: Seminars; annual conferences; continuing education sessions

Travel Industry Council of Ontario (TICO)
West Tower, #402, 2700 Matheson Blvd., Mississauga ON L4W 4V9
Tel: 905-624-6241; *Fax:* 905-624-8631
Toll-Free: 888-451-8426
tico@tico.ca
www.tico.ca
www.facebook.com/ticontario
www.youtube.com/user/ticoinfo
Overview: A medium-sized provincial organization
Mission: To promote a fair & informed marketplace where consumers can be confident in their travel purchases; To promote fair & ethical competition in the industry, support a Code of Ethics; To maintain & enforce programs that provide for consumer compensation in specific circumstances; To promote an expected level of education as a criterion for registration & encourage legislative & regulatory amendments aimed at industry professionalism & consumer confidence
Chief Officer(s):
Michael Pepper, President & CEO
Finances: *Funding Sources:* Registration fees
Staff Member(s): 25
Membership: 2,500 travel retailers & wholesalers; *Committees:* Audit; Executive; Business Strategy; Governance; Legislative & Regulatory Review; Complaints; Education Standards; Expanded Converage; Compensation Fund; Consumer Advisory
Publications:
• TICO [Travel Industry Council of Ontario] Talk
Type: Newsletter; *Frequency:* Quarterly
Profile: Information distributed to all Ontario registered travel retailers & travel wholesalers
• TICO [Travel Industry Council of Ontario] Education Standards Study Manual
Type: Manual
Profile: Every person in Ontario who works for a retail travel agency & sells travel services or provides travel advice to the public must meet TICO'seducation standards
• TICO [Travel Industry Council of Ontario] Annual Report
Type: Manual
Profile: An outline of activities, the performance of the council, & a financial report for each fiscal year

Travel Manitoba
Dept. SA6, 155 Carlton St., 7th Fl., Winnipeg MB R3C 3H8
Tel: 204-927-7838
Toll-Free: 800-665-0040
www.travelmanitoba.com
www.facebook.com/TravelManitoba
twitter.com/travelmanitoba
www.youtube.com/TravelManitoba
Overview: A medium-sized provincial organization
Mission: To contribute to Manitoba's economic well-being by facilitating & supporting the growth & development of tourism in harmony with the environment & in partnership with all stakeholders
Chief Officer(s):
Colin Ferguson, President & CEO
coferguson@travelmanitoba.com
Finances: *Annual Operating Budget:* Greater than $5 Million
Staff Member(s): 32
Activities: *Library:* Industry, Trade & Tourism Business Library

Travel Media Association of Canada (TMAC)
c/o TO Corporate Services, #255, 55 St. Clair Ave. West, Toronto ON M4V 2Y7
Tel: 416-934-0599; *Fax:* 416-967-6320
info@travelmedia.ca
www.travelmedia.ca
www.facebook.com/306419759424463
twitter.com/TravelMediaCA
Overview: A small national organization founded in 1994
Mission: Brings together travel media & tourism industry members to foster excellence, uphold ethical standards, & promote professional development
Chief Officer(s):
Michelle Sponagle, President, 519-442-6605
m.sponagle@sympatico.ca
Finances: *Annual Operating Budget:* $50,000-$100,000
Staff Member(s): 1
Membership: 460; *Fees:* $175 industry; $125 media; *Member Profile:* Journalists & industry dealing with travel; *Committees:* Awards; chapter liaison; communications; conference; finance; governance; handbook; industry membership; listserv; media membership; membership benefits; national newsletter; profesional development; revenue generation; volunteer
Awards:
• Travel Media Association of Canada Awards (Award)
Honours members with the best travel writing and photography.
Amount: $1000 each
Meetings/Conferences: • Travel Media Association of Canada 2015 Conference & AGM, June, 2015, Holiday Inn Peterborough Waterfront, Peterborough, ON
Scope: National
• Travel Media Association of Canada 2016 Conference & AGM, 2016
Scope: National

Travellers' Aid Society of Toronto (TAS)
Union Station, PO Box 102, 65 Front St. West, Toronto ON M5J 1E6
Tel: 416-366-7788; *Fax:* 416-366-0829
TAID668@gmail.com
www.travellersaid.ca
Also Known As: Travellers'Aid
Overview: A small local charitable organization founded in 1903
Mission: To provide a base of needed information for travellers as well as shelter & other help in crisis situations
Member of: Tourism Toronto; Volunteer Centre of Toronto/Etobicoke; Green Tourism; Travellers Assistance Services of Toronto
Affliation(s): Travellers Aid International
Finances: *Annual Operating Budget:* $50,000-$100,000; *Funding Sources:* Donations; government; corporations & individuals
Staff Member(s): 8; 185 volunteer(s)
Activities: Finds accommodation for travellers; works with social agencies in assisting immigrants & refugees; acts as a link between stranded travellers & social service agencies; operates information booths at all terminals at the Lester B. Pearson Airport, Toronto Coach Terminal & Union Railway Station; *Speaker Service:* Yes

La Traversée - Centre d'aide et de lutte contre les agressions à caractère sexuel de la Rive-Sud
CP 36569, Saint-Lambert QC J4P 3S8
Tél: 450-465-5263; *Téléc:* 450-465-1990
info@latraversee.qc.ca
www.latraversee.qc.ca
Aperçu: *Dimension:* petite; *Envergure:* locale; Organisme sans but lucratif; fondée en 1984
Membre(s) du bureau directeur:
Catherine Audrain, Directrice générale
Membre(s) du personnel: 13; 20 bénévole(s)

Treasury Management Association of Canada - British Columbia *See* Association for Financial Professionals - Vancouver

Treasury Management Association of Canada - Toronto
1698 Flamborough Circle, Mississauga ON L5M 3M7
Tel: 416-629-2871; *Fax:* 416-981-3282
admin@tmac-toronto.ca
tmac-toronto.ca
Also Known As: TMAC - Toronto
Overview: A small local organization overseen by Association for Financial Professionals
Mission: To act as a resource & advocate for Canadian corporate treasurers
Member of: Association for Financial Professionals
Chief Officer(s):
Linda Hartley, President
linda.hartley@scotiabank.com
David Balmer, Vice-President/Treasurer
davidb@calyxinc.com
Vivien Hall-Cho, Administrator
Laurie Jackson, Contact, Membership
ljackson@edc.ca
Membership: 200; *Fees:* $446.35; *Member Profile:* Treasury professionals from mid-market corporations, crown corporations, banks, investment dealers, finance & trust companies, software vendors, management consultants & government organizations
Activities: Events; job postings

Treaty & Aboriginal Land Stewards Association of Alberta (TALSAA)
c/o Piikani Nation, PO Box 70, Brocket AB T0K 0H0
Tel: 403-965-3807; *Fax:* 403-965-2214
Overview: A small provincial organization founded in 2000 overseen by National Aboriginal Lands Managers Association
Chief Officer(s):
Lance Yellow Face, Contact
Staff Member(s): 1

Treaty & Aboriginal Rights Research Centre of Manitoba Inc.
#300, 153 Lombard Ave., Winnipeg MB R3B 0T4
Tel: 204-943-6456; *Fax:* 204-942-3202
Also Known As: TARR Centre of Manitoba
Overview: A small local organization
Chief Officer(s):
Ralph Abramson, Contact

Tree Canada Foundation / Arbres Canada
#1, 470 Somerset St. West, Ottawa ON K1R 5J8
Tel: 613-567-5545; *Fax:* 613-567-5270
info@treecanada.ca
www.treecanada.ca
www.facebook.com/pages/Tree-Canada/172923782752077
twitter.com/TreeCanada
www.youtube.com/user/treecanada1
Overview: A small national organization founded in 1992
Mission: To provide education, technical support, resources & financial support through working partnerships to encourage Canadians to plant & care for trees in our urban & rural environment in an effort to help reduce the harmful effects of carbon dioxide emissions
Chief Officer(s):
Michael Rosen, President
mrosen@treecanada.ca
Staff Member(s): 11
Activities: *Speaker Service:* Yes
Awards:
• Awards (Grant)
National tree-planting & tree-care program designed to offset the problem of global warming; provides technical advice & financial assistance to qualifying partners for certain planting costs & for buying trees; partners are expected to contribute cash &/or in-kind services *Eligibility:* Groups interested in tree-planting programs

T.R.E.E. Foundation for Youth Development / Fondation pour le développement de la jeunesse T.R.E.E.
#520, 5250, rue Ferrier, Montréal QC H4P 1L4
Tel: 514-731-3419; *Fax:* 514-731-4999
Also Known As: TREE
Overview: A small national charitable organization
Mission: To receive & maintain general & special funds & apply from time to time all or part thereof &/or the income from these funds, by making gifts, grants, contributions & donations, for charitable, educational or research purposes with relation to youth in general
Chief Officer(s):
Peter L. Clement, Executive Director
Terence J. McQuillan, Chair, Board of Directors
Membership: 1-99

Trees Winnipeg
1539 Waverley St., Winnipeg MB R3T 4V7
Tel: 204-832-7188; *Fax:* 204-986-4050
office@treeswinnipeg.org
www.savetheelms.mb.ca
Previous Name: Coalition to Save the Elms
Overview: A medium-sized local charitable organization founded in 1992
Mission: To protect, preserve, & promote the urban forest & environment
Chief Officer(s):
Gerry Engel, President
Kerienne La France, Executive Director
Richard Westwood, Secretary-Treasurer
Finances: *Funding Sources:* Donations
Membership: 10,000; *Fees:* $25 preferred; $15 regular/renewal

Activities: Providing public workshops; Organizing a treebanding program; *Awareness Events:* Arbor Day, June; Adopt-a-Tree Program; *Speaker Service:* Yes
Publications:
• Manitoba Elm Survival Guide
Type: Guide
• Tree Owner's Manual
Type: Manual
• The Urban Forester
Type: Newsletter; *Frequency:* Quarterly
Profile: Information for Tree Winnipeg supporters & interested parties

Treherne Chamber of Commerce
c/o Town of Treherne / RM of South Norfolk, PO Box 30, 215 Broadway St., Treherne MB R0G 2V0
Tel: 204-723-2044; *Fax:* 204-723-2719
www.treherne.ca
www.facebook.com/112659625415420
Overview: A small local organization
Chief Officer(s):
Keith Sparling, President, 204-723-2565

Trent Hills & District Chamber of Commerce
PO Box 376, 51 Grand Rd., Campbellford ON K0L 1L0
Tel: 705-653-1551; *Fax:* 705-653-1629
Toll-Free: 888-653-1556
info@trenthillschamber.ca
www.trenthillschamber.ca
www.twitter.com/THchamber
Previous Name: Campbellford-Seymour Chamber of Commerce
Overview: A small local organization founded in 1921
Mission: To promote the commercial, industrial, agricultural, social, civic & tourism interests of the community
Chief Officer(s):
Nancy Allanson, Executive Director
Finances: *Annual Operating Budget:* $50,000-$100,000; *Funding Sources:* Regional Government
Staff Member(s): 3; 12 volunteer(s)
Membership: 190 individual; *Fees:* $85-$175 business

Trent Port Historical Society
55 King St., Trenton ON K8V 3V9
Tel: 613-394-1333
Overview: A small local charitable organization founded in 1980
Mission: To encourage research into area history; to promote public interest in history; to preserve artifacts, buildings & lands of historical significance to the area
Member of: Ontario Historical Society
Chief Officer(s):
Shawn Ellis, President
trentonshawn@hotmail.com
Finances: *Funding Sources:* Donations; fundraising
Activities: Restoration of Trenton Town Hall - 1861 & Trent Port Museum

Trent University Faculty Association (TUFA) / Association des professeurs de l'Université Trent
Champlain College, c/o TUFA Office, Peterborough ON K9J 7B8
Tel: 705-748-1011; *Fax:* 705-748-1651
tufa@trentu.ca
www.trentfaculty.ca
Overview: A small local organization founded in 1980
Mission: To protect & enhance the professional interests of the university faculty & librarians, especially ensuring that the collective agreement is properly administered; to ensure that members develop & practise their expertise & are rewarded suitably both in monetary & nonmonetary aspects
Affliation(s): Canadian Association of University Teachers; Ontario Confederation of University Faculty Associations
Chief Officer(s):
Marcus Harvey, Executive Director
Finances: *Annual Operating Budget:* $100,000-$250,000; *Funding Sources:* Membership dues
Staff Member(s): 1
Membership: 312; *Member Profile:* Fulltime, tenured, librairians & sessionals

Trent Valley Association of Baptist Churches
ON
e-mail: trentvalleybaptists@gmail.com
Overview: A small local organization overseen by Canadian Baptists of Ontario and Quebec
Member of: Canadian Baptists of Ontario & Quebec
Chief Officer(s):
Chris Taylor, Moderator
edmisonbaptist@gmail.com
Membership: *Member Profile:* Baptist churches in the Trent Valley Area

Trenton & District Association for Community Living *See* Community Living Quinte West

Trenton & District Chamber of Commerce *See* Quinte West Chamber of Commerce

Trenton Art Club
c/o Dufferin Centre, 344 Dufferin Ave., Trenton ON K8V 5N1
Tel: 613-392-7743
Overview: A small local organization
Chief Officer(s):
Amy Worrick, Treasurer
Finances: *Funding Sources:* Fundraising

Trenton Care & Share Food Bank
38 Guelph St., Trenton ON K8V 4G4
Tel: 613-394-5551; *Fax:* 613-394-0508
caresharefoodbank@bellnet.ca
www.trentonfoodbank.ca
www.facebook.com/129719410433462?fref=ts
twitter.com/TrentonFoodBank
Also Known As: Trenton Foodbank
Overview: A small local organization founded in 1985
Member of: Ontario Association of Food Banks; Canadian Association of Food Banks
Chief Officer(s):
Al Teal, Manager
Staff Member(s): 1; 27 volunteer(s)

Trial Lawyers Association of British Columbia (TLABC)
#1111, 1100 Melville St., Vancouver BC V6E 4A6
Tel: 604-682-5343; *Fax:* 604-682-0373
Toll-Free: 888-558-5222
tla-info@tlabc.org
www.tlabc.org
Overview: A medium-sized provincial organization founded in 1980
Chief Officer(s):
Carla Terzariol, Executive Director & CEO
Staff Member(s): 6
Membership: 910; *Member Profile:* Trial lawyers
Activities: *Speaker Service:* Yes

Triathlon British Columbia
PO Box 34098, Stn. D, Vancouver BC V6J 4M1
Tel: 604-736-3176; *Fax:* 604-736-3180
info@tribc.org
www.tribc.org
www.facebook.com/TriathlonBC
Also Known As: Triathlon BC
Overview: A small provincial organization overseen by Triathlon Canada
Mission: To be the provincial governing body of triathlon, duathlon, aquathon & winter triathlon in British Columbia.
Member of: Triathlon Canada
Chief Officer(s):
Les Pereira, President
Allan Prazsky, Executive Director

Triathlon Canada
#106, 3 Concorde Gate, Toronto ON M3C 3N7
Tel: 416-426-7180; *Fax:* 416-426-7294
info@triathloncanada.com
www.triathloncanada.com
www.facebook.com/148631098541373
twitter.com/TriathlonCanada
Previous Name: National Federation for the Sports of Triathlon, Duathlon & Aquathlon in Canada
Overview: A small national organization
Mission: To function as the National Federation for triathlon & duathlon in Canada, & to represent Canada internationally; to promote the triathlon & duathlon, both competitive & non-competitive in Canada; to encourage support of Triathlon Canada programmes by the public generally; to provide guidance, information & assistance to the provincial triathlon associations, zones & clubs in respect to these objects & in the development of programmes for competitive & non-competitive triathletes & duathletes; to affiliate all provincial associations to Triathlon Canada who are the Provincial Sports Governing Bodies, or who are in the process of becoming the Provincial Sports Governing Bodies in their province; to organize training courses for triathletes, duathletes, coaches & administrators to national & international standards; to promote other multi-disciplined endurance events & excluding the traditional decathlon, pentathlon, heptathlon, modern pentathlon & biathlon, which are part of existing National Federations
Chief Officer(s):
Alan Trivett, CEO & Secretary General
alan.trivett@triathloncanada.com

Triathlon Manitoba
c/o Sport for Life Centre, 145 Pacific Ave., Winnipeg MB R3B 2Z6
Tel: 204-925-5636; *Fax:* 204-925-5703
www.triathlon.mb.ca
www.facebook.com/TriathlonManitoba
www.twitter.com/MBTri
Overview: A small provincial organization overseen by Triathlon Canada
Mission: To be the provincial governing body of triathlon in Manitoba.
Member of: Triathlon Canada; Sport Manitoba
Chief Officer(s):
Kevin Freedman, Executive Director
kevin.freedman@triathlon.mb.ca

Triathlon New Brunswick
PO Box 22053, Stn. Landsdowne, Saint John NB E2K 4T7
Tel: 506-848-1144
www.trinb.ca
www.facebook.com/175501629145477
twitter.com/TriathlonNB
Also Known As: Triathlon NB
Overview: A small provincial organization overseen by Triathlon Canada
Mission: To be the provincial governing body of triathlon in New Brunswick.
Member of: Triathlon Canada
Chief Officer(s):
Paul Lavoie, President
lavoiep19@gmail.com
Jim Johnson, Executive Director
jimejohnson@gmail.com

Triathlon Newfoundland & Labrador
PO Box 872, Stn. C, St. John's NL A1C 5L7
e-mail: admin@trinl.com
www.trinl.com
www.facebook.com/triathlon.nl
twitter.com/trinl
Also Known As: TriNL
Overview: A small provincial organization overseen by Triathlon Canada
Mission: To be the governing body for the sport of triathalon in Newfoundland & Labrador
Member of: Triathlon Canada
Affliation(s): International Triathlon Union
Chief Officer(s):
Rob Coleman, President
president@trinl.com
Membership: *Fees:* $10 youth/one event; $20 adult

Triathlon Nova Scotia
c/o Sport Nova Scotia, 5516 Spring Garden Rd., 4th Fl., Halifax NB B3J 1G6
Tel: 902-425-5450; *Fax:* 902-425-5606
triathlon@sportnovascotia.ca
www.trins.ca
www.facebook.com/175501629145477
twitter.com/TriathlonNB
Overview: A small provincial organization overseen by Triathlon Canada
Mission: To be the provincial governing body of triathlon in Nova Scotia.
Member of: Triathlon Canada; Sport Nova Scotia

Triathlon PEI
40 Enman Cres., Charlottetown PE C1A 7K7
e-mail: triathlonpei@gmail.com
www.tripei.com
www.facebook.com/groups/217742304907740
twitter.com/triathlonpei
Overview: A small provincial organization founded in 2012 overseen by Triathlon Canada
Mission: To be the provincial governing body of triathlon in Prince Edward Island.
Member of: Triathlon Canada
Chief Officer(s):
Jamie Nickerson, President

Triathlon Québec
CP 1000, Succ. M, 4545, av Pierre-de Coubertin, Montréal QC H1V 3R2
Tél: 514-252-3121
info@triathlonquebec.org
www.triathlonquebec.org
www.facebook.com/132997480092478
twitter.com/triathlonquebec
Aperçu: *Dimension:* petite; *Envergure:* provinciale; fondée en 1985 surveillé par Triathlon Canada
Membre de: Triathlon Canada
Affliation(s): Triathlon Canada
Membre(s) du bureau directeur:
Sébastien Gilbert-Corlay, Directeur des opérations
sgilbert-corlay@triathlonquebec.org
Finances: *Budget de fonctionnement annuel:* $250,000-$500,000
Membre(s) du personnel: 3; 20 bénévole(s)
Membre: 1 100
Activités: *Stagiaires:* Oui

Tribuna Noastra *Voir* Fondation roumaine de Montréal

Tri-Cities Chamber of Commerce Serving Coquitlam, Port Coquitlam & Port Moody
1209 Pinetree Way, Coquitlam BC V3B 7Y3
Tel: 604-464-2716
info@tricitieschamber.com
www.tricitieschamber.com
Previous Name: Chamber of Commerce Serving Coquitlam, Port Coquitlam, Port Moody
Overview: A small local organization
Mission: To support, educate, & promote business interests in our community
Member of: Canadian Chamber of Commerce; BC Chamber of Commerce
Chief Officer(s):
Michael Hind, Executive Director
michaelh@tricitieschamber.com
Finances: *Annual Operating Budget:* $100,000-$250,000
Staff Member(s): 3; 14 volunteer(s)
Membership: 700; *Fees:* $257.25-$1,580.25; *Committees:* Economic Affairs; Membership; Transportation; Information Technology; Events; Welcome Committee; Speakers; Ambassador
Activities: Golf; auction; ball; business expo; luncheons; Business AM; Business After Hours;

Tri-County Soccer Association
c/o Fran Glenn, #41, 10 Woodcrest Ln., Fort Saskatchewan AB T8L 0C7
e-mail: tricounty.district@yahoo.ca
www.tricountysoccer.net
Overview: A small local organization overseen by Alberta Soccer Association
Member of: Alberta Soccer Association
Chief Officer(s):
Fran Glenn, President
tricouny.president@yahoo.ca

Tri-County Women's Centre
12 Cumberland St., Yarmouth NS B5A 3K3
Tel: 902-742-0085; *Fax:* 902-742-6068
Toll-Free: 877-742-0085
tcwc@tricountywomenscentre.org
www.tricountywomenscentre.org
Overview: A small local organization founded in 2002
Mission: To support, enrich & empower the lives of women in Nova Scotia

The Trident Mediation Counselling & Support Foundation
PO Box 8148, Canmore AB T1W 2T9
Tel: 403-678-2918; *Fax:* 732-601-2918
info@tridentfoundation.net
www.tridentfoundation.net
Also Known As: TRIDENT
Overview: A small local charitable organization founded in 1999
Mission: Covers the disciplines of social work, law, conflict management & education; focuses on policy & practice in social development, conflict management & training services
Chief Officer(s):
Jennifer Geary, Contact
Finances: *Annual Operating Budget:* Less than $50,000
Staff Member(s): 2; 1 volunteer(s)
Membership: 11; *Fees:* Fee for service
Activities: Conflict management; mediation; on-line dispute resolution; public speaking; counselling; marriage & family therapy; consultancy; research & policy development; distance education; *Speaker Service:* Yes

Trillium Automobile Dealers' Association (TADA)
85 Renfrew Dr., Markham ON L3R 0N9
Tel: 905-940-6232; *Fax:* 905-940-6235
Toll-Free: 800-668-6510
info@tada.ca
www.tada.ca
www.facebook.com/group.php?gid=149581915142339
twitter.com/tada_gr
Merged from: Toronto Automobile Dealers' Association; Ontario Automobile Dealers' Association
Overview: A medium-sized provincial organization
Member of: Canadian Automobile Dealers Association
Chief Officer(s):
Brenda Sachdev, Contact, 905-940-8421
brendas@tada.ca
Membership: 340 Dealers; *Member Profile:* New franchise automobile dealers

Trillium Gift of Life Network
#900, 522 University Ave., Toronto ON M5G 1W7
Tel: 416-363-4001; *Fax:* 416-363-4002
Toll-Free: 800-263-2833
www.giftoflife.on.ca
www.linkedin.com/company/1426658
www.facebook.com/TrilliumGiftofLife
twitter.com/TrilliumGift
Previous Name: Multiple Organ Retrieval & Exchange Program of Ontario
Overview: A medium-sized provincial organization founded in 1988
Mission: To enable every Ontario resident to make an informed decision to donate organs & tissue; to support healthcare professionals in implementing their wishes; maximize organ & tissue donation in Ontario in a respectful & equitable manner through education, research, services & support
Chief Officer(s):
Ronnie Gavsie, President & CEO
Activities: Administers computer system that lists transplant patients & matches donated organs; promotes public awareness; *Awareness Events:* Organ Donor Awareness Week; *Speaker Service:* Yes

Trillium Health Partners Foundation
2200 Eglinton Ave. West, Mississauga ON L5M 2N1
Tel: 905-813-4123; *Fax:* 905-813-4334
foundation@trilliumhealthpartners.ca
www.trilliumgiving.ca
www.facebook.com/TrilliumHealthPartnersFoundation
twitter.com/trilliumhealth
www.youtube.com/user/TrilliumHeroes
Merged from: Trillium Health Centre Foundation; Credit Valley Hospital Foundation
Overview: A small local charitable organization founded in 2013
Mission: To help raise funds for the Credit Valley Hospital, the Mississauga Hospital & the Queensway Health Centre in order to provide patients with improved health care services & to fund research
Chief Officer(s):
Steve Hoscheit, President & CEO
Steve.Hoscheit@trilliumhealthpartners.ca
Staff Member(s): 30
Activities: Fundraising

Trinity Historical Society Inc.
PO Box 8, Trinity NL A0C 2S0
Tel: 709-464-3599; *Fax:* 709-464-3599
info@trinityhistoricalsociety.com
www.trinityhistoricalsociety.com
www.facebook.com/thsoc
Overview: A small local organization founded in 1964
Mission: To operate the Trinity Museum, Green Family Forge, Lester-Garland House, the Cooperage & the Court House, Gaol & General Building

Tri-Town & District Chamber of Commerce *See* TemiskamingShores & Area Chamber of Commerce

Trochu Chamber of Commerce
PO Box 771, Trochu AB T0M 2C0
Overview: A small local organization
Chief Officer(s):
Wanda Jones, Vice-President
Membership: *Fees:* $50

Trois-Rivières Real Estate Board *Voir* Chambre immobilière de la Mauricie Inc.

Tropicana Community Services Organization
1385 Huntingwood Dr., Toronto ON M1S 3J1
Tel: 416-439-9009
www.tropicanacommunity.org
Overview: A small local organization founded in 1969 overseen by Ontario Council of Agencies Serving Immigrants
Mission: To work for the creation of a harmonious, multicultural society; to develop youth participation & leadership; to recruit & develop volunteers; to advocate & provide access to counselling for youth
Chief Officer(s):
Sharon Shelton, Executive Director

Trotskyist League of Canada / Ligue trotskyste du Canada
PO Box 7198, Stn. A, Toronto ON M5W 1X8
Tel: 416-593-4138
spartcan@on.aibn.com
www.icl-fi.org
Overview: A small national organization
Member of: International Communist League
Chief Officer(s):
John Masters, President

Troubles d'apprentissage - Association de l'Alberta *See* Learning Disabilities Association of Alberta

Troubles d'apprentissage - Association de l'Ontario *See* Learning Disabilities Association of Ontario

Troubles d'apprentissage - Association de la Colombie-Britannique *See* Learning Disabilities Association of British Columbia

Troubles d'apprentissage - Association de la Saskatchewan *See* Learning Disabilities Association of Saskatchewan

Troubles d'apprentissage - Association de Manitoba *See* Learning Disabilities Association of Manitoba

Troubles d'apprentissage - Association du Nouveau-Brunswick *See* Learning Disabilities Association of New Brunswick

La Troupe du Jour (LTDJ)
914, 20e rue Ouest, Saskatoon SK S7M 0Y4
Tél: 306-244-1040
communication@latroupedujour.ca
www.latroupedujour.ca
Aperçu: *Dimension:* petite; *Envergure:* locale; fondée en 1985
Mission: La Troupe du Jour Inc. develops professional and community French-language theatre through the creation of new works, training, performance, and outreach. La Troupe du Jour is dedicated to the development of French-language theatre in Saskatchewan.
Membre(s) du bureau directeur:
Denis Rouleau, Directeur artistique et général
artistique@latroupedujour.ca
Membre(s) du personnel: 5

Trout Unlimited Canada (TUC)
#160, 6712 Fisher St. SE, Calgary AB T2H 2A7
Tel: 403-221-8360; *Fax:* 403-221-8368
Toll-Free: 800-909-6040
tuc@tucanada.org
www.tucanada.org
www.facebook.com/pages/Trout-Unlimited-Canada/170262052986490
twitter.com/TUCanada1
www.youtube.com/user/TroutUnlimitedCanada
Overview: A small national charitable organization founded in 1972
Mission: To promote the conservation & wise use of trout & other coldwater fisheries & their watersheds, through the undertaking of habitat restoration & enhancement, research, management, & public education
Chief Officer(s):
Jeff Surtees, CEO, 403-221-8363
jsurtees@tucanada.org
Dean Orlando, CFO, 403-221-8373
DOrlando@tucanada.org
Finances: *Annual Operating Budget:* $500,000-$1.5 Million
Staff Member(s): 10; 1000 volunteer(s)
Membership: 4,000; *Fees:* $30

Activities: Yellow Fish Road Program; Adopt a Trout; Aquatic Renwal Program; educational programs; *Library* by appointment

Trowel Trades Canadian Association, Local 100 (CLC) *Voir* Association canadienne des métiers de la truelle, section locale 100 (CTC)

Truck Loggers Association (TLA)
#725, 815 Hastings St. West, Vancouver BC V6C 1B4
Tel: 604-684-4291; *Fax:* 604-684-7134
contact@tla.ca
www.tla.ca
www.linkedin.com/company/the-truck-loggers-association
www.facebook.com/TruckLoggersAssociation
www.twitter.com/truckloggerBC
Overview: A medium-sized provincial organization founded in 1942
Affliation(s): Pacific Logging Congress
Chief Officer(s):
Dwight Yochim, Executive Director, 604-684-4291 Ext. 1
dwight@tla.ca
Finances: *Annual Operating Budget:* $500,000-$1.5 Million
Staff Member(s): 5; 17 volunteer(s)
Membership: 600 institutional; *Member Profile:* TO give the independent loggers a collective voice in the changes taking place in society and the forest industry; To share information about newly developing logging machines, methods, and technology.
Meetings/Conferences: • 72nd Truck Loggers Association Convention & Trade Show, 2015
Scope: National

Truck Training Schools Association of Ontario Inc. (TTSAO)
Fax: 519-858-0920
Toll-Free: 866-475-9436
training@ttsao.com
www.ttsao.com
Overview: A small provincial licensing organization founded in 1992
Mission: To provide the trucking industry with the highest quality driver training programs for entry level individuals that earn & maintain public confidence, adhering to sound & ethical business practices
Affliation(s): Ontario Trucking Association; Ministry of Education, Ministry of Transportation
Chief Officer(s):
Yvette Lagrois, President
Finances: *Annual Operating Budget:* $100,000-$250,000
Staff Member(s): 7
Membership: 75; *Fees:* Schedule available
Activities: *Internships:* Yes

Truckers Association of Nova Scotia (TANS)
#3, 779 Prince St., Truro NS B2N 1G7
Tel: 902-895-7447; *Fax:* 902-897-0487
Toll-Free: 800-232-6631
contact@tans.ca
www.tans.ca
Overview: A medium-sized provincial organization founded in 1968
Mission: Promotes all matters aiding the development and improvement of the trucking industry and the allied trades in Nova Scotia, including social, recreational, benevolent, educational and charitable activities. In addition, the Truckers Association of Nova Scotia makes presentations to government and other regulatory bodies in relation to the economic welfare of the trucking industry and is the main proponent in gaining access to the provincial haul rates and beneficial changes to the contract specifications used by the contractors
Member of: The Transportation Sector of Voluntary Planning
Affliation(s): Atlantic Provinces Trucking Association of Nova Scotia
Chief Officer(s):
Taunia MacAdam, Executive Director

True Sport Foundation / Fondation sport pur
#350, 955 Green Valley Cres., Ottawa ON K2C 3V4
Tel: 613-526-6043; *Fax:* 613-521-3134
info@truesport.ca
www.truesportfoundation.ca
Previous Name: Spirit of Sport Foundation
Overview: A small national charitable organization founded in 1993
Mission: To ensure that sport makes a positive contribution to Canadian society, to our athletes & to the physical & moral development of Canada's youth; to bring together leading organizations to promote, celebrate & recognize sporting excellence
Member of: Canadian Centre for Ethics in Sport; Athletics Canada
Chief Officer(s):
Peter Leyser, Executive Director
pleyser@truesport.ca
Finances: *Annual Operating Budget:* $250,000-$500,000
Staff Member(s): 3; 14 volunteer(s)
Membership: 1-99
Awards:
• Canadian Sport Awards (Award)

Truro & Area Outreach Project; Pictou County AIDS Coalition *See* The Northern AIDS Connection Society

Truro & District Chamber of Commerce (TDCOC)
PO Box 54, 605 Prince St., Truro NS B2N 1G2
Tel: 902-895-6328; *Fax:* 902-897-6641
www.truroChamber.com
www.facebook.com/tdcoc
twitter.com/TruroCoC
Overview: A medium-sized local charitable organization founded in 1890
Mission: To be the principal advocate for business in Truro & the Colchester Region in matters of economic, social & political importance
Member of: Nova Scotia Chamber; Atlantic Provinces Chamber; Canadian Chamber
Chief Officer(s):
Tim Tucker, Executive Director, 902-895-6328, Fax: 902-897-6641
Ted Jordan, President
Finances: *Annual Operating Budget:* $50,000-$100,000; *Funding Sources:* Membership dues
Staff Member(s): 2; 25 volunteer(s)
Membership: 300 corporate + 6 institutional + 4 senior/lifetime + 21 individual; *Fees:* Schedule available; *Member Profile:* Must do business in the community
Activities: Advocacy; networking; educational events; community events; Chamber Group Insurance Plan; Chamber Credit Card Discount Program; member-to-member discounts; *Awareness Events:* Home & Country Living Show; Chamber Golf Tournament; Annual General Banquet; *Library* by appointment
Awards:
• Chamber Business Person of the Year Award (Award)

Truro Art Society
36 Arthur St., Truro NS B2N 4X9
truroartsociety.ca
Overview: A small local organization founded in 1969
Mission: To promote the arts in Truro & vicinity
Chief Officer(s):
Janice Stewart, President
Membership: *Fees:* $25 adult; $35 family; $10 student

Tuberous Sclerosis Canada Sclérose Tubéreuse (TSCST)
#125, 92 Calpan Ave., Barrie ON L9N 0Z7
Toll-Free: 800-347-0252
TSCanadaST@gmail.com
www.tscanada.ca
www.twitter.com/TSCANADA1
Overview: A small national charitable organization founded in 1990
Mission: To provide information & support to tuberous sclerosis victims & their families; to promote & improve professional & public awareness, education & research regarding this disease
Affliation(s): Tuberous Sclerosis Alliance (USA); Tuberous Sclerosis Association (GB); Tuberous Sclerosis International (The Netherlands)
Chief Officer(s):
Andrew Duffy, Chair
Finances: *Annual Operating Budget:* Less than $50,000; *Funding Sources:* Fundraising; donations
15 volunteer(s)
Membership: 150; *Fees:* $25
Activities: *Awareness Events:* Tuberous Sclerosis Awareness Month, May

Tunisian Canadian Chamber of Commerce *Voir* Chambre de commerce Canado-Tunisienne

Tunnelling Association of Canada (TAC) / Association canadienne des tunnels
8828 Pigott Rd., Richmond ON V7A 2C4
Tel: 604-241-1297; *Fax:* 604-241-1399
admin@tunnelcanada.ca
www.tunnelcanada.ca
Overview: A medium-sized national organization
Mission: To promote Canadian tunnelling & underground excavation technologies, & safe design, construction & maintenance; to facilitate information exchange; to represent the tunnelling community in matters of public & technical concern; to publish a Canadian registry of tunnels, underground excavations & similar works
Member of: Canadian Geotechnical Society
Chief Officer(s):
Derek Zoldy, Secretary-Treasurer
secretary@tunnelcanada.ca
Rick Staples, President
president@tunnelcanada.ca
12 volunteer(s)
Membership: 350 individual, student & corporate members; *Fees:* $50 individual; $15 student; $250 corporate
Meetings/Conferences: • Tunnelling Association of Canada 2015 Conference, 2015
Scope: National
Contact Information: Wayne Gibson, Conference Manager

Turkey Farmers of Canada (TFC) / Les éleveurs de dindon du Canada (ÉDC)
Bldg. One, #202, 7145 West Credit Ave., Mississauga ON L5N 6J7
Tel: 905-812-3140; *Fax:* 905-812-9326
www.turkeyfarmersofcanada.ca
www.facebook.com/TastyTurkey
twitter.com/tastyturkey
Previous Name: Canadian Turkey Marketing Agency
Overview: A medium-sized national organization founded in 1974
Mission: To develop & strengthen the Canadian Turkey market through an effective supply management systems that stimulates growth & profitability for stakeholders
Member of: Canadian Federation of Agriculture
Affliation(s): Further Poultry Processors Association of Canada; Canadian Poultry & Egg Processors Council
Chief Officer(s):
Mark Davies, Chair
Finances: *Funding Sources:* Turkey producer levies
Publications:
• CTMA Annual Report
Type: Yearbook; *Frequency:* Annually
Profile: Produced for the Federal Minister of Agriculture & Agri-Food, National Farm Products Council, & CTMA members
• Eye on the Industry
Frequency: Biweekly
Profile: Currents happenings & news related to the Canadian turkey industry
• Plume
Frequency: 4-6 pa
Profile: Current events, & industry issues, for all Canadian turkey producers, government, regulatory associations, & industry affiliates

Turkey Farmers of New Brunswick / Les Éleveurs de dindons du Nouveau-Brunswick
#103, 277 Main St., Fredericton NB E3A 1B1
Tel: 506-452-8103; *Fax:* 506-451-2121
nbturkey@nb.aibn.com
Previous Name: New Brunswick Turkey Marketing Board
Overview: A small provincial organization
Chief Officer(s):
Larry Slipp, Chair
Louis Martin, Secretary-Manager

Turks & Caicos Development Organization of Canada
3501, 50 Aurora Crt., Toronto ON M1W 2M6
Tel: 416-760-0908; *Fax:* 416-760-0908
www.turksandcaicoscanada.ca
Overview: A small international organization founded in 1987
Mission: To promote closer ties between Canada & the Turks & Caicos Islands & to assist Canadians interested in vacationing, investing, retiring, or starting a business in the Turks & Caicos Islands
Chief Officer(s):
Ian A. Stuart, Vice-President & General Manager
ianstuart@turksandcaicoscanada.ca
Staff Member(s): 3
Membership: 735 individual

Turner's Syndrome Society (TSS) / Société du syndrome de Turner
#9, 30 Clearly Ave., Ottawa ON K2A 4A1
Tel: 613-321-2267; *Fax:* 613-321-2268
Toll-Free: 800-465-6744
info@turnersyndrome.ca
www.turnersyndrome.ca
www.facebook.com/TurnerSyndromeSocietyOfCanada
Overview: A small national charitable organization founded in 1981
Mission: To improve the quality of life for individuals & families affected by Turner's Syndrome; to strive to accomplish this through providing public & professional awareness about the needs & concerns of individuals with Turner's Syndrome & their families through the development of communication networks to provide mutual support
Chief Officer(s):
Krista Kamstra-Cooper, President
Finances: *Funding Sources:* Government; direct mail; donations; fundraising
Membership: *Fees:* $15 student; $30 individual; $40 family; $50 health professional/institution
Activities: *Library* by appointment

Tweed & Area Historical Society
PO Box 665, 40 Victoria St. North, Tweed ON K0K 3J0
Tel: 613-478-3989; *Fax:* 613-478-6457
tweedheritageinfo@on.aibn.com
Also Known As: Tweed Heritage Centre
Overview: A small local charitable organization founded in 1988
Mission: To research, document, preserve & promote the heritage (past, present, natural built) of the Tweed area.
Member of: Ontario Historical Society; Ontario Genealogical Society
Chief Officer(s):
Evan Morton, Curator
Finances: *Annual Operating Budget:* $50,000-$100,000; *Funding Sources:* Donations; Grants; Fees
Staff Member(s): 1; 10 volunteer(s)
Membership: 37; *Fees:* $40 families; $25 individuals
Activities: Tours; research; local arts & crafts; Art Gallery; Museum; Archives, Genealogy; *Speaker Service:* Yes; *Library:* Tweed Heritage Centre; Open to public

Tweed Chamber of Commerce
PO Box 988, Tweed ON K0K 3J0
Tel: 613-813-2784
tweedcoc@yahoo.ca
www.tweed-chamber.ca
Overview: A small local organization
Chief Officer(s):
Richard Rashotte, President
Membership: 52; *Fees:* $80

Twins Plus Association of Brampton
218 Ecclestone Dr., Brampton ON L6X 3P9
Tel: 905-799-4658
brampton@multiplebirthscanada.org
www.twinsplus.ca
www.facebook.com/MultipleBirthsBrampton
twitter.com/BramptonTwins
Overview: A small local organization overseen by Multiple Births Canada
Mission: A not-for-profit support and social group for expectant parents, parents and families of twins, triplets, or multiples living in Brampton, Caledon, Georgetown, Acton, Milton, Bolton, Orangeville and surrounding areas.
Membership: *Fees:* $30
Activities: *Library*

Twins, Triplets & More Association of Calgary (TTMAC)
Bay #16, 1215 Lake Sylvan Dr. SE, Calgary AB T2J 3Z5
Tel: 403-274-8703
info@ttmac.org
www.ttmac.org
www.facebook.com/groups/88356987184
Previous Name: Calgary Parents of Multiple Births Association
Overview: A small local organization founded in 1970
Mission: To improve & promote the health & well-being of expectant multiple birth families & families with multiple births
Finances: *Annual Operating Budget:* Less than $50,000
60 volunteer(s)
Membership: 500 families; *Fees:* $35 family; *Committees:* Breastfeeding Support; Health Support; Membership Services; Social, Resources & Zone Support
Activities: Prenatal classes; new parents info sessions; women's retreats; children's Halloween & Christmas parties; BBQs; two playgroups; bi-annual sale; coffee parties; *Library* by appointment

Two Planks & a Passion Theatre Association (TP&aP)
PO Box 190, 555 Ross Creek Rd., Canning NS B0P 1H0
Tel: 902-582-3842; *Fax:* 902-582-7943
mail@twoplanks.ca
www.twoplanks.ca
www.facebook.com/104539126303588
twitter.com/rosscreek
www.youtube.com/user/rosscreektv
Overview: A small provincial organization founded in 1992
Mission: To develop & present high quality, professional theatre both regionally & nationally which reflects Canadian life, with strong roles for women; to develop & build an artistic centre in Canning, NS, accessible to both the local community & to artists of all disciplines & residencies
Member of: Professional Association of Canadian Theatres; Nova Scotia Professional Theatre Alliance
Affliation(s): Playwrights Union of Canada
Chief Officer(s):
Ken Schwartz, Artistic Director
artisticdirectors@twoplanks.ca
Finances: *Funding Sources:* Canada Council; NS Dept. of Education & Culture; NS Arts Council; Canadian Heritage; foundations
Membership: *Fees:* $15 individual; $25 family
Activities: Theatre productions & tours; theatre workshops; fundraising & community events

Two/Ten Charity Trust of Canada Inc. / Deux/Dix
PO Box 306, Stn. Westmount, Montréal QC H3Z 2T5
Tel: 450-671-3604; *Fax:* 450-671-0166
dclandry@videotron.ca
www.twotencanada.ca
Also Known As: Two/Ten Foundation of Canada
Overview: A small national charitable organization founded in 1989
Mission: To promote services to members of the Canadian footwear & allied industries
Member of: Two/Ten International Footwear Foundation
Chief Officer(s):
Laurie Weston, President
Diane Cappella, Sec.-Treas.
Robert Yama, Chairman
Finances: *Annual Operating Budget:* Less than $50,000; *Funding Sources:* Fundraising; corporate donations
Membership: 400; *Fees:* $390; *Member Profile:* Shoe industry related; *Committees:* Bursary Program; Social Service Programs

211 Southwest Ontario
#410, 400 City Hall Sq., Windsor ON N9A 7K6
Tel: 519-258-0247; *Fax:* 519-256-3311
Toll-Free: 866-686-0045; *TTY:* 866-488-9311
info@211southwestontario.ca
Previous Name: Information Windsor
Overview: A small local charitable organization founded in 1966
Mission: To provide leadership in the collection, management & dissemination of community service information for all consumers within the Greater Windsor region
Chief Officer(s):
Jennifer Tanner, Project Manager
Finances: *Funding Sources:* United Way/Centraide Windsor-Essex County; sale of publications, labels, lists, data sets
Activities: Help desk services; community online database; publications; list & label production; broadcast announcement service; data leasing; professional management services; educational programs for human service workers & call centres; Golf Drop Raffle Event, Aug.; *Speaker Service:* Yes; *Rents Mailing List:* Yes; *Library* Open to public

2-Spirited People of the First Nations (TPFN)
#202, 593 Yonge St., Toronto ON M4Y 1Z4
Tel: 416-944-9300; *Fax:* 416-944-8381
info@2spirits.com
www.2spirits.com
Previous Name: Gays & Lesbians of the First Nations
Overview: A medium-sized national organization founded in 1989
Mission: To create a place where Aboriginal 2-Spirited people can grow & learn together as a community, fostering a positive, self-sufficient image, honouring our past & building a future; to work together toward bridging the gap between the 2-Spirited, Lesbian, Gay, Bisexual & Transgendered community & our Aboriginal identity
Member of: Ontario AIDS Network; Toronto Aboriginal Social Services Association; Canadian Aboriginal AIDS Network
Chief Officer(s):
Art Zoccole, Executive Director Ext. 222
art@2spirits.com
Finances: *Annual Operating Budget:* $250,000-$500,000; *Funding Sources:* Ontario Ministry of Health; Health Canada; Aboriginal Healing & Wellness Strategy
Staff Member(s): 3; 30 volunteer(s)
Membership: 189; *Fees:* Schedule available; *Member Profile:* Full (Aboriginal, Homosexual); Associate (non-Aboriginal); *Committees:* Lesbian & Gay Pride Day
Activities: 2-Spirits HIV/AIDS education & prevention program; counselling; client support programs

Tyndale St-Georges Community Centre / Centre Communautaire Tyndale St-Georges
870 Richmond Sq., Montréal QC H3J 1V7
Tel: 514-931-6265; *Fax:* 514-931-1343
info@tyndalestgeorges.com
www.tyndalestgeorges.ca
Overview: A medium-sized local organization founded in 1927
Mission: Tyndale St-Georges Community Centre is a not-for-profit charitable organization, providing services to more than 2,000 members of the Little Burgundy community through programs extending from pre-school to adult development without regard to race or religious affiliation.
Chief Officer(s):
Jen de Combe, Executive Director
jendecombe@tyndalestgeorges.com

U'mista Cultural Society
PO Box 253, Alert Bay BC V0N 1A0
Tel: 250-974-5403; *Fax:* 250-974-5499
Toll-Free: 800-690-8222
info@umista.ca
www.umista.org
www.facebook.com/pages/Umista-Cultural-Society/125883764163342
Overview: A medium-sized local charitable organization founded in 1974
Mission: To collect, preserve & exhibit native artifacts of cultural, artistic & historic value to the Kwakwaka'wakw; to promote & foster carving, dancing, ceremonial & other cultural/artistic activities engaged in by the Kwakwaka'wakw; to collect, record & make available information & records relating to the language & history of the Kwakwaka'wakw; to promote, build & maintain facilities for carrying out the above aims; to recover from other institutions & individuals artifacts & records of cultural, artistic & historic value to the Kwakwaka'wakw
Member of: Canadian Museums Association; British Columbia Museums Association; First Nations Confederacy of Cultural Education Centres
Finances: *Funding Sources:* Federal & provincial government; private; sales
Membership: *Fees:* $20 Canadian individual; $35 Canadian family; $35 international individual; $70 international family; *Member Profile:* Ordinary membership open to any person who can trace ancestry to a member of any tribe of the Kwakwaka'wakw; persons eligible to become ordinary members become honourary members at age 65; persons not eligible to become ordinary members may become individual or family members upon payment of a small annual fee
Activities: The U'mista Cultural Centre disseminates cultural, historic & artistic information about the Kwakwaka'wakw by means of travelling exhibits, cooperation with researchers, distribution of films, participation in conferences & the distribution of newsletters, etc.; Language Retention Programs (including Kwak'wala language books & tapes, & an Oral History Project); Big House rebuilding; Potlatch Collection; *Speaker Service:* Yes; *Library* Open to public

UBC Alumni Association
6251 Cecil Green Park Rd., Vancouver BC V6T 1Z1
Tel: 604-822-3313; *Fax:* 604-822-8928
Toll-Free: 800-883-3088
alumni.association@ubc.ca
www.alumni.ubc.ca
www.linkedin.com/groups?home=&gid=59693
www.facebook.com/ubcalumni?ref=ts
www.twitter.com/ubcalumni
www.youtube.com/ubcalumni
Overview: A large provincial organization founded in 1946

Mission: To use our unique position to serve our alumni, the university & its students by fostering communications, life-long relationships, networking & access to resources that enrich the lives of alumni, the students & advance the reputation of the university
Member of: Canadian Council for the Advancement of Education (CCAE); Council for Advancement & Support of Education (CASE)
Chief Officer(s):
Jeff Todd, Executive Director
jeff.todd@ubc.ca
Finances: *Annual Operating Budget:* $500,000-$1.5 Million; *Funding Sources:* Marketing of alumni services & programs; travel programs; university grant
Staff Member(s): 13; 250 volunteer(s)
Membership: 225,000; *Member Profile:* Graduate of UBC; *Committees:* Board; Governance; Advocacy; Regional Networks; Marketing & Communications; Awards; Dinner; Young Alumni
Activities: Communications; Reunions; Recognition; University Liaison; Alumni Reunion Weekend; Member Services
Awards:
- Blythe Eagles Volunteer Leadership Award (Award)
- Outstanding Student Award (Award)
- Alumni Award for Research (Award)
- Faculty Citation Community Service Award (Award)
- Lifetime Achievement Award (Award)
- Regional Network Volunteer Service Award (Award)
- Alumni Award of Distinction (Award)
- Outstanding Young Alumnus Award (Award)
- Honorary Alumnus Award (Award)

Publications:
- Trek

Type: Magazine

Ucluelet Chamber of Commerce (UCOC)
PO Box 428, 200 Main St., Ucluelet BC V0R 3A0
Tel: 250-726-4641; *Fax:* 250-726-4611
info@uclueletinfo.com
www.uclueletinfo.com
Overview: A small local organization founded in 1947
Member of: Tourism BC; BC Chamber of Commerce
Chief Officer(s):
Marny Saunders, General Manager
Finances: *Annual Operating Budget:* $50,000-$100,000
Staff Member(s): 3
Membership: 110; *Fees:* $131.25-$210
Activities: Edge to Edge Marathon; Winter Festival; Pacific Rim Whale Festival; *Library:* Business Library; Open to public

UJA Federation of Greater Toronto
4600 Bathurst St., Toronto ON M2R 3V2
Tel: 416-635-2883; *Fax:* 416-635-9565
Toll-Free: 888-635-2424
info@ujafed.org
www.jewishtoronto.net
www.facebook.com/UJAFederationToronto?sk=app_184498014941265
twitter.com/ujafederation
Also Known As: United Jewish Appeal
Previous Name: The Jewish Federation of Greater Toronto
Overview: A large local organization founded in 1994
Mission: To preserve & strengthen Jewish life in Toronto, Canada & Israel, through philanthropic, volunteer & professional leadership. The UJA is committed to social justice on behalf of the Jewish poor & vulnerable locally & internationally, to strengthening ties with Israel & its people, to supporting Israel's struggle to meet its social welfare needs, to combatting antisemitism in all its forms around the world, to nurturing shared values with Canadians of all faiths, to promoting Jewish education, to building a vibrant Jewish communal life. The following Pillars identify main areas of focus for UJA: Jewish Education & Identity; Strategic Planning & Community Engagement; Integrated Development; Operations & Corporate Relations; Business & Finance
Affliation(s): Toronto Jewish Library; Board of Jewish Education; Committee for Yiddish; Holocaust Centre of Greater Toronto; Jewish Information Service of Greater Toronto; Ontario Jewish Archives; Bathurst JCC & Miles Nadal JCC; Jewish Family & Child Service; Hillel of Greater Toronto; Bernard Betel Centre for Creative Living; Jewish Immigrant Aid Services Toronto; Jewish Vocational Services Toronto, Jewish Russian Community Centre
Chief Officer(s):
Ted Sokolsky, President & CEO
Richard Venn, Chair
Finances: *Funding Sources:* Corporate partners, private donations
Activities: *Awareness Events:* Campaign for Our Jewish Future; Tomorrow Campaign

Ukrainian Canadian Civil Liberties Association (UCCLA)
PO Box 275, 3044 Bloor St. West, Toronto ON M8X 2Y8
e-mail: pr@uccla.ca
www.uccla.ca
www.facebook.com/group.php?gid=160615690635396
twitter.com/UCCLA
Overview: A small national organization founded in 1984
Mission: To promote the interests of the Ukrainian Canadian community & educate the general public about the Ukrainian experience in Canada & about contemporary Ukrainian issues; to articulate & defend the civil liberties & human rights of Canadians of Ukrainian heritage & to provide objective information on Ukraine & Ukrainians to the media, government & general public
Chief Officer(s):
John B. Gregorovich, Chair
Finances: *Annual Operating Budget:* Less than $50,000
25 volunteer(s)
Membership: 1,000-4,999; *Member Profile:* Canadian Ukrainians
Activities: Publish occasional booklets for eductional purposes in English with Ukrainian & French abstracts; prepare & install historical markers relevant to Ukrainian history; *Speaker Service:* Yes

Ukrainian Canadian Committee *See* Ukrainian Canadian Congress

Ukrainian Canadian Congress (UCC) / Congrès des ukrainiens canadiens
#203, 952 Main St., Winnipeg MB R2W 3P4
Tel: 204-942-4627; *Fax:* 204-947-3882
Toll-Free: 866-942-4627
ucc@ucc.ca
www.ucc.ca
www.facebook.com/pages/Ukrainian-Canadian-Congress/195065046451
twitter.com/ukrcancongress
www.youtube.com/user/UkrainianCanCongress
Previous Name: Ukrainian Canadian Committee
Overview: A large national charitable organization founded in 1940
Mission: To protect, promote & enhance cultural identity of Ukrainians throughout Canada & beyond; to maintain, develop & enhance Ukrainian culture & language as integral elements of Canada's multicultural mosaic; to encourage participation of Ukrainian Canadians in cultural, social, economic, & political life in Canada; to actively advance better communication, understanding & mutual respect between Ukrainian Canadians & other ethnocultural communities; to foster sense of unity, cohesiveness & cooperation among member organizations
Member of: Canadian Ethnocultural Council; Ukrainian World Congress
Affliation(s): Ukrainian Catholic Brotherhood; Ukrainian Self-Reliance Association (Orthodox); Ukrainian National Federation; League of Ukrainian Canadians; Ukrainian Canadian Professional & Business Federation
Chief Officer(s):
Paul Grod, President
Membership: 29 organizations; *Fees:* Schedule available; *Member Profile:* Member organizations; *Committees:* 125th Anniversary; Awards & Recognition; Canada & Ukraine; Community Development; Communications; Finance; Governance; Immigration & Resettlement; Internment; Multiculturalism; National Sports; Fundraising; National Arts Council; National Holodomor Awareness; National Holodomor Education; National School Council; National Youth Advisory Council; 200th Anniversary of Shevchenko's Birthday
Activities: *Awareness Events:* Holodomor Awareness Week, November; *Internships:* Yes; *Library* Open to public
Awards:
- Shevchenko Medal Award (Award)

Recognizes individuals of Ukrainian and non-Ukrainian descent, as well as institutions and organizations, for their outstanding national contribution towards the development of the Ukrainian Canadian community.
- Youth Leadership Award of Excellence (Award)

Alberta Provincial Council
#8, 8103 - 127 Ave., Edmonton AB T5C 1R9
Tel: 780-414-1624; *Fax:* 780-414-1626
uccab@shaw.ca
www.uccab.ca
www.facebook.com/UCCAPC
Chief Officer(s):
Barbara Hlus, President
British Columbia Provincial Council
Vancouver BC
www.infoukes.com/uccbc/
Mission: To protect & develop the Ukranian culture in BC
Montréal Branch
6175 - 10 Ave., Montréal QC H1Y 2H5
Tel: 514-593-1000
www.uccmontreal.org
Chief Officer(s):
Zorianna Hrycenko-Luhova, President
Saskatchewan Provincial Council
4 - 2345 Ave. C North, Saskatoon SK S7L 5Z5
Tel: 306-652-5850; *Fax:* 306-665-2127
Toll-Free: 888-652-5850
uccspc@ucc.sk.ca
www.ucc.sk.ca
Chief Officer(s):
Slawko Kindrachuk, President
s.kindrachuk@ucc.sk.ca
Danylo Puderak, Executive Director
danylo.puderak@ucc.sk.ca
Toronto Branch
#208, 145 Evans Ave., Toronto ON M8Z 5X8
Tel: 416-323-4772
ucctoronto@bellnet.ca
www.ucctoronto.ca
Chief Officer(s):
Oksana Rewa, President
Nadia Sydorenko, Office Administrator

Ukrainian Canadian Foundation of Taras Shevchenko
#202, 952 Main St., Winnipeg MB R2W 3P4
Tel: 204-944-9128; *Fax:* 204-944-9135
Toll-Free: 866-524-5314
lesia@shevchenkofoundation.ca
www.shevchenkofoundation.ca
Also Known As: Shevchenko Foundation
Overview: A medium-sized national charitable organization founded in 1963
Mission: To promote & advance Ukrainian culture in Canada
Member of: Ukrainian Canadian Congress
Chief Officer(s):
Lesia Szwaluk, Executive Director
Finances: *Annual Operating Budget:* $250,000-$500,000; *Funding Sources:* Donations & bequests
Staff Member(s): 1
Membership: 1,000-4,999
Awards:
- Kobzar Literary Award (Award)

Ukrainian Canadian Research & Documentation Centre (UCRDC) / Centre canadien-ukrainien de recherches et de documentation
620 Spadina Ave., Toronto ON M5S 2H4
Tel: 416-966-1819; *Fax:* 416-966-1820
info@ucrdc.org
www.ucrdc.org
Overview: A small national charitable organization founded in 1986
Mission: To collect, store & promote information pertaining to Ukrainian historical events & Ukrainian Canadian experiences
Member of: Ukrainian Canadian Congress
Affliation(s): St. Vladimir Institute
Chief Officer(s):
Jurij Darewych, Chair & President
Finances: *Funding Sources:* Private donations; sale of films & publications; sponsorship
Activities: Oral history; travelling exhibition; produce film about Ukraine during WWII; *Internships:* Yes; *Library:* Research & Documentation Centre; by appointment

Ukrainian Canadian Social Services (Toronto) Inc
2445 Bloor St. West, Toronto ON M6S 1P7
Tel: 416-763-4982; *Fax:* 416-763-3997
toradmin@ucss.info
tor.ucss.info
Overview: A small local charitable organization founded in 1960
Mission: To provide social services to individuals & families of Ukrainian background who experience language & cultural

barriers
Affliation(s): Ukrainian Canadian Social Services Inc. of Canada
Chief Officer(s):
Tatiana Wanio, President
Lydia Cymbaluk, Executive Director
Finances: *Funding Sources:* All levels of government; Donations; Fund raising
Staff Member(s): 4
Membership: 246 individual; 9 organizational; *Fees:* $25 individual; $50 organization; *Committees:* Audit; Nominating
Activities: Social & cultural services for seniors; friendly visiting; income tax clinic

Ukrainian Fraternal Society of Canada (UFSC)
235 McGregor St., Winnipeg MB R2W 4W5
Tel: 204-568-4482; *Fax:* 204-589-6411
Toll-Free: 800-988-8372
info@ufsc.ca
www.ufsc.ca
Overview: A small national licensing organization founded in 1921
Member of: Canadian Fraternal Association
Chief Officer(s):
Boris Salamon, President
Donna Smigelsky, Manager
Finances: *Annual Operating Budget:* $250,000-$500,000
Staff Member(s): 1
Membership: 995; *Member Profile:* Ukrainian Canadians only; *Committees:* Donations; Scholarship
Activities: *Library* by appointment
Awards:
• Provincial Scholarships (Award)
5 Annual provincial scholarships of $500
Meetings/Conferences: • 22nd Convention of the Ukrainian Fraternal Society of Canada, 2015
Scope: National

Ukrainian Genealogical & Historical Society of Canada (UGHSC)
PO Box 56, Blaine Lake SK S0J 0J0
Tel: 306-497-2770; *Fax:* 306-497-2770
ukrainiangenealogist@sasktel.net
ukrainiangenealogist.tripod.com
Also Known As: UGHS of Canada
Overview: A small national charitable organization founded in 1979
Mission: To encourage individuals & families to record their family tree; to research & collect family histories, genealogies & data pertinent to Ukraine's diasporas
Member of: Federation of Eastern European Family History Societies
Chief Officer(s):
Walter Rusel, President
Finances: *Annual Operating Budget:* Less than $50,000
42 volunteer(s)
Membership: 100-499
Activities: Library is mobile & visiting local events throughout North America; society is involved in "village identifying" 880 microfilms from Lviv, Ukraine; *Library:* Prosvita; Open to public by appointment

Ukrainian Orthodox Church of Canada
Ecumenical Patriarchate, 9 St. John's Ave., Winnipeg MB R2W 1G8
Tel: 204-586-3093; *Fax:* 204-582-5241
Toll-Free: 877-586-3093
consistory@uocc.ca
www.uocc.ca
Overview: A large national organization founded in 1918
Chief Officer(s):
Metropolitan Yurij, Primate
metropolitan@uocc.ca
Victor Lakusta, Chancellor & Chair, Presidium
chancellor@uocc.ca
Membership: 120,000
Activities: *Speaker Service:* Yes; *Library* Open to public by appointment
Publications:
• Visnyk/Herald [a publication of Ukrainian Orthodox Church of Canada]
Type: Newspaper; *Editor:* Marusia Kaweski

Eastern Eparchy
3281 Cindy Cres., Mississauga ON L4Y 3S7
Tel: 905-206-9372; *Fax:* 905-206-9373
uocceast@rogers.com
www.uocc.ca/en-ca/contact

Western Eparchy
11404 - 112 Ave., Edmonton MB T5G 0H6
Tel: 780-455-1938; *Fax:* 780-454-5287
admin@uocc-we.ca
www.uocc-we.ca
Chief Officer(s):
Ilarion, Bishop, Edmonton & the Western Eparchy
rudnyk1@telus.net

Ukrainian World Congress / Congrès mondial des ukrainiens
#207, 145 Evans Ave., Toronto ON M8Z 5X8
Tel: 416-323-3020; *Fax:* 416-323-3250
congress@look.ca
www.ukrainianworldcongress.org
www.facebook.com\130772870318563
Overview: A medium-sized international organization
Mission: To be an umbrella organization for Ukrainian associations outside Ukraine
Chief Officer(s):
Eugene Czolij, President

Ultimate Canada
4382 Shelbourne St., Vancouver BC V8N 3G3
Toll-Free: 888-691-1080
info@canadianultimate.com
www.canadianultimate.com
www.facebook.com/UltimateCanada
twitter.com/Ultimate_Canada
Previous Name: Canadian Ultimate Players Association
Overview: A medium-sized national charitable organization founded in 1993
Mission: To be the governing body for the sport of ultimate in Canada.
Chief Officer(s):
Danny Saunders, Executive Director
ed@canadianultimate.com
Finances: *Annual Operating Budget:* $50,000-$100,000; *Funding Sources:* Membership dues
Staff Member(s): 4; 50 volunteer(s)
Membership: 800; *Fees:* $30 junior; $55 regular
Activities: *Awareness Events:* Canadian National Championships; Canadian National University Championships
Publications:
• CUPA Connection
Type: Newsletter

Ultralight Pilots Association of Canada (UPAC) / Association canadienne des pilotes d'avions ultra-légers
907289 Township Rd. 12, RR#4, Bright ON N0J 1B0
Tel: 519-684-7628
info@upac.ca
www.upac.ca
Overview: A small national organization
Mission: To promote ultralight aviation in Canada
Chief Officer(s):
K. Lubitz, President
Finances: *Annual Operating Budget:* Less than $50,000; *Funding Sources:* Membership fees
10 volunteer(s)
Membership: 500+; *Fees:* $40 individual; $60 family; *Member Profile:* Interest in ultralight aviaton
Activities: Video library for members; *Library:* Video Library

Uncles & Aunts at Large
11031 - 124 St. NW, Edmonton AB T5M 0J5
Tel: 780-452-5791; *Fax:* 780-453-6914
info@unclesatlarge.ab.ca
www.unclesatlarge.ab.ca
Overview: A small local organization founded in 1967
Mission: To provide mentoring services to children of single parent homes

Underwater Archaeological Society of British Columbia (UASBC)
c/o Vancouver Maritime Museum, 1905 Ogden Ave., Vancouver BC V6J 1A3
www.uasbc.com
vimeo.com/uasbc
Overview: A small provincial charitable organization founded in 1975
Mission: To promote the science of underwater archaeology; to conserve, preserve & protect the maritime heritage lying beneath our coastal & inland waters
Member of: Outdoor Recreation Council of British Columbia
Finances: *Funding Sources:* Membership dues; government; corporate
Activities: Archaeological site surveys, heritage awareness promotion; operates 4 chapters in Vancouver, Victoria, Kootenay & Okanagan; *Speaker Service:* Yes; *Library:* Archives; by appointment

Underwater Council of British Columbia (UCBC)
BC
e-mail: underwatercouncil.bc@gmail.com
www.underwatercouncilbc.org
www.youtube.com/user/TheUCBC
Overview: A small provincial organization
Mission: To represent recreational divers in British Columbia.
Chief Officer(s):
Paul Sim, President

Underwriters' Laboratories of Canada (ULC) / Laboratoires des assureurs du Canada
7 Underwriters Rd., Toronto ON M1R 3A9
Tel: 416-757-3611; *Fax:* 416-757-8727
Toll-Free: 866-937-3852
customerservice@ulc.ca
www.ul.com
Overview: A medium-sized national organization founded in 1920
Mission: To support domestic governmental product safety regulations, & works with international safety systems to help further trade with adherence to local safety requirements.
Affliation(s): Underwriters Laboratories Inc., Northbrook IL
Chief Officer(s):
Keith E. Williams, President & CEO
Finances: *Funding Sources:* Fee for service
Activities: *Library*

Montréal Site
#330, 6505, rte Transcanada, Saint-Laurent QC H4T 1S3
Tél: 514-363-5941; *Téléc:* 514-363-7014
customerservice@ulc.ca

Ottawa Site
#200, 440 Laurier Ave. West, Ottawa ON K1R 7X6
Tél: 613-755-2729; *Téléc:* 613-231-5977
customerservice@ulc.ca
Chief Officer(s):
Annette Wetmore, CCA Liaison

Vancouver Site
#130, 13775 Commerce Pkwy., Richmond BC V6V 2V4
Tel: 604-214-9555; *Fax:* 604-214-9550
customerservice@ulc.ca

Unemployed Help Centre (UHC)
6955 Cantelon Dr., Windsor ON N8T 3J9
Tel: 519-944-4900; *Fax:* 519-944-9184
uhc@uhc.ca
www.uhc.ca
www.facebook.com/UHC.Windsor
twitter.com/@uhc_
Overview: A small local charitable organization founded in 1977
Mission: To assist, inform & advise on problems related to being unemployed; to assist the unemployed in dealing with Canada Employment & Immigration, E.I.; Social Services & other appropriate community service agencies; to provide a phone-in service for the unemployed; to promote community projects that assist disadvantaged people; to offer relief to the poor; to solicit funds by way of donations, grants, bequests, lotteries & other similar methods
Member of: Ontario Association of Food Banks; Ontario Association of Help Centres
Chief Officer(s):
Pamela Pons, Contact
Finances: *Annual Operating Budget:* $1.5 Million-$3 Million; *Funding Sources:* Government grants; United Way; fundraising
Staff Member(s): 26; 25 volunteer(s)
Activities: Vocational Counselling; Literacy/Numeracy; Closure & Downsizing; On-the-job Training; Human Resources; Job Line; Food Bank; Income Tax; Pre-employment Preparation Services; Resource Centre; *Library:* Information Resource Centre; Open to public
Awards:
• Minister's Award of Excellence (Award)

UNICEF Canada / Comité UNICEF Canada
Canada Sq., #1100, 2200 Yonge St., Toronto ON M4S 2C6
Tel: 416-482-4444; *Fax:* 416-482-8035
Toll-Free: 800-567-4483

Other Communication: communityevents@unicef.ca
secretary@unicef.ca
www.unicef.ca
www.linkedin.com/company/unicef-canada
www.facebook.com/UNICEF-Canada
twitter.com/UNICEFLive
www.youtube.com/user/unicefcanada
Also Known As: Canadian UNICEF Committee
Overview: A large national charitable organization founded in 1955
Mission: To raise funds to help ensure the survival, growth & long term development of the world's children
Member of: UNICEF International
Chief Officer(s):
David Morley, President & CEO
Noella Milne, Chair
Christopher Simard, Secretary
Finances: *Annual Operating Budget:* Greater than $5 Million; *Funding Sources:* General public; government grants
Staff Member(s): 62; 3276 volunteer(s)
Membership: 1,200; *Committees:* Communication; Education for Development; Direct Mail; Finance & Administration; International Program; Marketing; Youth
Activities: *Awareness Events:* UNICEF Fund Drive - Halloween, Oct. 31; National UNICEF Day, October 31; *Speaker Service:* Yes; *Library* by appointment

UNICEF Alberta
#140, 301 - 14th St. NW, Calgary AB T2N 2A1
Tel: 403-270-2857; *Fax:* 403-283-0115
Toll-Free: 800-819-0889
Chief Officer(s):
Holly Davidson, Regional Davidson

UNICEF Atlantic
#103, 11 Thornhill Dr., Dartmouth NS B3B 1R9
Tel: 902-422-6000; *Fax:* 902-425-3002
Toll-Free: 877-786-4233
Chief Officer(s):
John Humble, Regional Director

UNICEF British Columbia
#201, 3077 Granville St., Vancouver BC V6H 3J9
Tel: 604-874-3666; *Fax:* 604-874-5411
Toll-Free: 800-381-4343
Chief Officer(s):
Shirley Kepper, Regional Director, British Columbia

UNICEF Ontario - Toronto
#1100, 2200 Yonge St., Toronto ON M4S 2C6
Tel: 416-482-4444; *Fax:* 416-482-8035
Toll-Free: 800-567-4483
Chief Officer(s):
Jacqueline Jones, Regional Director

UNICEF Ottawa-Carleton
#1206, 1 Nicholas St., Ottawa ON K1N 7B7
Tel: 613-233-1561; *Fax:* 613-235-3522

UNICEF Prairies
#323, 112 Market Ave., Winnipeg MB R3B 0P4
Tel: 204-477-4600; *Fax:* 204-477-4040
Toll-Free: 866-888-6088
Chief Officer(s):
Tricia Schers, Regional Director

UNICEF Québec - Montréal
#21C, 1100, rue de la Gauchetière ouest, Montréal QC H3B 2S2
Tel: 514-288-5134; *Fax:* 514-288-7243
qc.secretaire@unicef.ca

UNICEF Québec Metropolitain
160, rue Saint-Joseph est, Québec QC G1K 3A7
Tel: 418-683-3017; *Fax:* 418-683-2590

Unifarm *See* Wild Rose Agricultural Producers

UNIFOR
205 Placer Ct., Toronto ON M2H 3H9
Tel: 416-497-4110
Toll-Free: 800-268-5763
communications@unifor.org
www.unifor.org
www.facebook.com/UniforCanada
twitter.com/UniforTheUnion
www.youtube.com/user/UniforCanada
Previous Name: National Automobile, Aerospace, Transportation & General Workers Union of Canada, Canadian Auto Workers, Communications, Energy & Paperworkers
Overview: A large national organization founded in 2013
Mission: To improve the working conditions & general economic & social conditions of Canadian workers in the industries of: aerospace, mining, fishing, auto & specialty vehicle assembly, auto parts, hotels, airlines, rail, education, hospitality, retail, road transportation, health care, manufacturing, shipbuilding, & others
Affliation(s): TCA-Quebec
Chief Officer(s):
Jerry Dias, National President
president@unifor.org
Peter Kennedy, National Secretary-Treasurer
treasurer@unifor.org
Michel Ouimet, Québec Director
michel.ouimet@unifor.org
Finances: *Funding Sources:* Membership dues
Staff Member(s): 200
Membership: 300,000 +
Activities: *Library*
Meetings/Conferences: • 2015 Unifor National Retail and Wholesale Workers Conference, March, 2015, Unifor Family Education Centre, Port Elgin, ON
Scope: National
• 2015 Unifor Pride Conference, April, 2015, Unifor Family Education Centre, Port Elgin, ON
Scope: National
Publications:
• Contact
Type: Newsletter; *Frequency:* Weekly
Profile: News about the union, mailed to local union leaders & the media
• Eduaction
Type: Newsletter
Profile: Information about Port Elgin courses

Chatham Office
200 Riverview Dr., Chatham ON N7M 5Z8
Tel: 519-354-5800; *Fax:* 519-354-8290
Toll-Free: 800-204-3121
chatham@unifor.org

Dartmouth
#101, 238 Brownlow Ave., Dartmouth NS B3B 2B4
Tel: 902-468-5687
unifor@unifor.org

Drummondville
Place Royale, #120, 1125, boul St-Joseph, Drummondville QC J2C 2C8
Tel: 819-478-0111; *Fax:* 819-478-7772
Toll-Free: 877-478-0111
drummondville@unifor.org

Edmonton
#60, 9703 - 41 Ave., Edmonton AB T6E 6M9
Tel: 780-448-5865; *Fax:* 780-486-0671
Toll-Free: 800-890-9608
alberta@unifor.org

Halifax Office
63 Otter Lake Crt., 2nd Fl., Halifax NS B3S 1M1
Tel: 902-455-9327; *Fax:* 902-454-9473
Toll-Free: 800-565-1272
halifax@unifor.org

Jonquiere
#120, 2679 boul. Du Royaume, Jonquiere QC G7S 5T1
Tel: 418-548-7075
Toll-Free: 800-268-4808
uniforquebec@unifor.org

Kitchener
5 Executive Pl., Kitchener ON N2P 2N4
Tel: 519-893-4873
Toll-Free: 800-265-2884
kitchener@unifor.org

Kitchener Office
5 Executive Pl., Kitchener ON N2P 2N4
Tel: 519-893-4873; *Fax:* 519-893-9908
Toll-Free: 800-265-2884
kitchener@unifor.org

London Office
140 Pine Valley Blvd., London ON N6K 3X3
Tel: 519-649-2552; *Fax:* 519-649-7355
Toll-Free: 800-265-1891
london@unifor.org

Mississauga
#510, 5915 Airport Rd., Mississauga ON L4V 1T1
Tel: 905-678-0800
Toll-Free: 800-268-9040
unifor@unifor.org

Moncton
55 Highfield St., Moncton NB E1C 5N2
Tel: 506-857-8647
unifor@unifor.org

Montréal
#1101, 545 boul. Cremazie est, Montréal QC H2M 2V1
Tel: 514-384-9000
uniforquebec@unifor.org

Montréal Office
#10100, 565, boul Crémazie est, Montréal QC H2M 2W1
Tel: 514-389-9223; *Fax:* 514-389-4450
Toll-Free: 800-361-0483
uniforquebec@unifor.org

New Westminster
326 - 12th St., 2nd Fl., New Westminster BC V3M 4H6
Tel: 604-522-7911; *Fax:* 604-522-8975
Toll-Free: 800-665-3553
newwestminster@unifor.org

Ottawa
5 Gurdwara Dr., Ottawa ON K2E 7X6
Tel: 613-523-0434; *Fax:* 613-523-2375
Toll-Free: 800-982-2601
ottawa@unifor.org

Ottawa
301 Laurier Ave. West, Ottawa ON K1P 6M6
Tel: 613-230-5200
Toll-Free: 877-230-5201
unifor@unifor.org

Port Elgin Office (Family Education Centre)
c/o Family Education Centre, RR#1, Bruce County Rd. 25, 115 Shipley Ave., Port Elgin ON N0H 2C5
Tel: 519-389-3200; *Fax:* 519-389-3222
Toll-Free: 800-265-3735
confcentre@unifor.org

Québec
#275, 5000 boul. Des Gradins, Québec QC G2J 1N3
Tel: 418-624-5320
uniforquebec@unifor.org

Québec Office
#110, 5000, boul des Gradins, Québec QC G2J 1N3
Tel: 418-622-5261; *Fax:* 418-621-1183
Toll-Free: 800-561-5261
uniforquebec@unifor.org

Regina
2365 - 13th Ave., Regina SK S4P 0V8
Tel: 306-777-0000
regina@unifor.org

St Catharines
#7B, 318 Ontario St., St Catharines ON L2R 5L8
Tel: 905-687-1841; *Fax:* 905-684-3741
Toll-Free: 800-663-9983
stcatherines@unifor.org

St. John's
#302, 55 Bond St., St. John's NL A1C 1S9
Tel: 709-753-7191; *Fax:* 709-753-7197
sydney@unifor.org

St. John's
NAPE Building, 330A Portugal Cove Pl., St. John's NL A1A 4Y5
Tel: 709-726-5667
unifor@unifor.org

Sarnia
900 Devine St., Sarnia ON N7T 1X5
Tel: 519-332-4102
unifor@unifor.org

Sydney
4 Hugh St., Sydney NS B1P 1V7
Tel: 902-562-3857; *Fax:* 902-539-0519
Toll-Free: 800-591-7523
sydney@unifor.org

Thunder Bay
#100, 979 Alloy Dr., Thunder Bay ON P7B 5Z8
Tel: 807-344-1122; *Fax:* 807-344-1133
Toll-Free: 866-832-1122
thunderbay@unifor.org

Thunder Bay
516 South High St., Thunder Bay ON P7B 3M3
Tel: 807-346-1742
unifor@unifor.org

Trois Rivières
7080 rue Marion, Trois-Rivières QC G9A 6G4
Tel: 819-378-4696
unifor@unifor.org

Vancouver
#540, 1199 West Pender St., Vancouver BC V6E 2R1
Tel: 604-682-6501
unifor@unifor.org

Windsor
2345 Central Ave., 2nd Fl., Windsor ON N8W 4J1
Tel: 519-944-5866
Toll-Free: 800-465-0974
windsor@unifor.org

Windsor Office
2345 Central Ave., 2nd Fl., Windsor ON N8W 4J1
Tel: 519-944-5866; *Fax:* 519-944-6431
Toll-Free: 800-465-0974
windsor@unifor.org

Winnipeg
1376 Grant Ave., 2nd Fl., Winnipeg MB R3M 3Y4
Tel: 204-489-0355; *Fax:* 204-487-2201
Toll-Free: 800-665-7492
winnipeg@unifor.org

Winnipeg
#203, 275 Broadway Ave., Winnipeg MB R3C 4M6
Tel: 204-988-1400
unifor@unifor.org

UniforACL
c/o Unifor Local 2289, #100, 6300 Lady Hammond Rd., Halifax NS B3K 2R6
Tel: 902-425-2440; *Fax:* 902-422-4647
Toll-Free: 800-565-2289
unifor-acl.ca
Merged from: Telephone Employee's Union
Overview: A medium-sized provincial organization
Chief Officer(s):
Penny Fawcett, Chair
penny.fawcett@cep2289.ca
Membership: 4 locals

Uniform Law Conference of Canada (ULCC) / Conference pour l'harmonisation des lois au Canada (CHLC)
c/o 622 Hochelaga St., Ottawa ON K1K 2E9
Tel: 613-747-1695; *Fax:* 613-941-9310
conference@ulcc.ca
www.ulcc.ca
Overview: A small national organization founded in 1935
Mission: To facilitate & promote the harmonization & improvements to laws throughtout Canada by developing, at the request of the constituent jurisdictions, Uniform Acts, Model Acts, Statements of Legal Principles, Proposals to Change Laws & other documents deemed appropriate to meet the demands that are presented to it by the constituent jurisdictions from time to time
Chief Officer(s):
C. Lynn Romeo, President
lynn.romeo@gov.mb.ca
Marie Bordeleau, Executive Director
Finances: *Annual Operating Budget:* $50,000-$100,000
Staff Member(s): 1
Membership: 14; *Member Profile:* Canada, the Provinces & Territories are constituent jurisdictions of the Conference; *Committees:* Criminal Section; Civil Section
Activities: Annual Conference, research
Meetings/Conferences: • Uniform Law Conference of Canada 2015 Conference, August, 2015, Explorer Hotel, Yellowknife, NT
Scope: National
Contact Information: Executive Director, Marie Bordeleau, marie.bordeleau@ulcc-chlc.ca

Union canadienne des employés des transports *See* Union of Canadian Transportation Employees

Union canadienne des travailleurs en communication (ind.) / Canadian Union of Communication Workers (Ind.)
502, 90e av, LaSalle QC H8R 2Z7
Tél: 514-595-9095; *Téléc:* 514-595-8911
Aperçu: *Dimension:* moyenne; *Envergure:* locale
Membre: 1 700 + 3 sections locales

L'Union culturelle des Franco-Ontariennes (UCFO)
#302, 450, rue Rideau, Ottawa ON K1N 5Z4
Tél: 613-741-1334; *Téléc:* 613-741-8577
Ligne sans frais: 877-520-8226
ucfo@on.aibn.com
www.unionculturelle.ca
Aperçu: *Dimension:* moyenne; *Envergure:* provinciale; Organisme sans but lucratif; fondée en 1936
Mission: Améliorer les conditions et les réalités sociales des femmes francophones de l'Ontario; faciliter l'épanouissement de la femme tout en favorisant son autonomie
Membre de: Réseau canadien de développement économique communautaire; Table féministe francophone de concertation provinciale de l'Ontario; Assemblée de la francophonie de l'Ontario
Membre(s) du bureau directeur:
Madeleine Chabot, Présidente provinciale
Membre: *Critères d'admissibilité:* 14 ans et plus; femme; francophone

Union des artistes (UDA) / Artists' Union
#400, 1441, boul. René-Lévesque ouest, Montréal QC H3G 1T7
Tél: 514-288-6682; *Téléc:* 514-285-6789
info@uda.ca
www.uda.ca
www.facebook.com/75AnsDeLUnionDesArtistes?notif_t=page_new_likes
twitter.com/udaquebec
Aperçu: *Dimension:* grande; *Envergure:* provinciale; fondée en 1937
Mission: Identification, étude, défense et développement des intérêts économiques, sociaux et moraux de ses membres
Membre de: Fédération internationale des acteurs
Membre(s) du bureau directeur:
Sophie Prègent, Président
Sylvie Brousseau, Directrice générale
Finances: *Budget de fonctionnement annuel:* $3 Million-$5 Million
Membre(s) du personnel: 70
Membre: +12 000 membres actifs et stagiaires; *Montant de la cotisation:* 125$ + 2,5%; *Comités:* Comité permanent des femmes artistes interprètes; Comité permanent d'éthique; Comité permanent du secrétariat général; Comité du doublage; Comité sur les relations agents - artistes; Comité sur le cinéma autogéré (artisanal); Comité sur l'accessibilité au travail; Comité minorités ethniques; Comité du congrès; Comité du 75e anniversaire; Comité Variétés scène / Comité Variétés phonogramme; Comité consultatif sur la formation continue

Union des associations des professeurs des universités de l'Ontario *See* Ontario Confederation of University Faculty Associations

Union des cultivateurs franco-ontariens (UCFO)
2474 rue Champlain, Clarence Creek ON K0A 1N0
Tél: 613-488-2929; *Téléc:* 613-488-2541
Ligne sans frais: 877-425-8366
info@ucfo.ca
www.ucfo.ca
www.facebook.com/UCFO.ca
Aperçu: *Dimension:* petite; *Envergure:* provinciale; Organisme sans but lucratif; fondée en 1929
Mission: Regrouper les franco-ontariens et les franco-ontariennes qui oeuvrent dans le secteur agricole; concerter pour la protection de nos droits; promouvoir nos intérêts; informer notre communauté; appuyer les institutions et groupements qui favorisent notre développement; développer notre sentiment et fierté; stimuler le développement social et économique des régions agricoles et rurales
Membre(s) du bureau directeur:
Marc Laflèche, Président
Simon Durand, Directeur exécutif
sdurand@ucfo.ca
Marc-André Tessier, Agent, Communication et développement du leadership
communication@ucfo.ca
Finances: *Budget de fonctionnement annuel:* $100,000-$250,000
Membre(s) du personnel: 5; 10 bénévole(s)
Membre: 500; *Montant de la cotisation:* 15$ membre régulier; 35$ membre auxiliaire; *Critères d'admissibilité:* Agriculteurs, agricultrices de l'Ontario
Activités: Formation agricole

Union des écrivaines et écrivains québécois (UNEQ)
3492, av Laval, Montréal QC H2X 3C8
Tél: 514-849-8540; *Téléc:* 514-849-6239
Ligne sans frais: 888-849-8540
ecrivez@uneq.qc.ca
www.uneq.qc.ca
www.facebook.com/152536222994
twitter.com/Ecrivains_QC
Aperçu: *Dimension:* moyenne; *Envergure:* provinciale; fondée en 1977
Mission: Élaborer des politiques et administrer des programmes en vue de favoriser le développement de la littérature québécoise et sa diffusion au Québec comme à l'étranger, en vue également de faire reconnaître la profession d'écrivain de telle sorte que les intérêts moraux, sociaux et économiques des auteurs soient respectés
Membre(s) du bureau directeur:
Danièle Simpson, Présidente
Francis Farley-Chevrier, Directeur général
ffc@uneq.qc.ca
Membre(s) du personnel: 8
Membre: 1,500 écrivains; *Montant de la cotisation:* 140$ titulaire; 115$ associé/adhérent; 100$ doyen titulaire/adhérent/associé; 50$ débutant; *Critères d'admissibilité:* Les membres doivent avoir publié au moins deux livres (d'au moins 48 pages, publiés par une maison d'édition reconnue et qu'ils appartiennent à l'un ou l'autre des genres suivants: le roman, le récit, la nouvelle; la poésie; le théâtre; l'essai), dont l'un doit être pendant les dix années précédentes; membres adhérents doivent avoir publié une oeuvre; *Comités:* Trans-Québec; Sur le numérique; Membres associés
Activités: Tournées-rencontres; tournées dans les écoles; parrainage; festival de la littérature; animation à la maison des écrivains; centre de documentation virtuel: www.litterature.org; *Bibliothèque:* Bibliothèque L'Ile; Bibliothèque publique

Union des employés de la Défense nationale *See* Union of National Defence Employees

Union des municipalités du Nouveau-Brunswick *See* Union of Municipalities of New Brunswick

Union des municipalités du Québec (UMQ)
#680, 680, rue Sherbrooke ouest, Montréal QC H3A 2M7
Tél: 514-282-7700; *Téléc:* 514-282-8893
info@umq.qc.ca
www.umq.qc.ca
twitter.com/UMQuebec
Aperçu: *Dimension:* grande; *Envergure:* provinciale; Organisme sans but lucratif; fondée en 1919
Mission: Au bénéfice des citoyens, représenter les municipalités auprès du gouvernement et contribuer à l'efficience de gestion des municipalités.
Membre de: Fédération canadienne des municipalités
Affliation(s): Conseil du patronat du Québec; Fédération canadienne des municipalités
Membre(s) du bureau directeur:
Pierre Prévost, Directeur général par intérim
Robert Coulombe, Président
r.coulombe@ville.maniwaki.qc.ca
Finances: *Budget de fonctionnement annuel:* $3 Million-$5 Million
Membre(s) du personnel: 35
Membre: 300; *Montant de la cotisation:* 0,46$ per capita; *Critères d'admissibilité:* Toutes les municipalités du Québec
Activités: Formation des élus et des gestionnaires municipaux; *Stagiaires:* Oui; *Service de conférenciers:* Oui; *Listes de destinataires:* Oui; *Bibliothèque*

Union des municipalités régionales de comté et des municipalités locales du Québec *Voir* Fédération Québécoise des Municipalités

Union des pêcheurs des Maritimes (CTC) *See* Maritime Fishermen's Union (CLC)

Union des producteurs agricoles (UPA)
#100, 555, boul. Roland-Therrien, Longueuil QC J4H 3Y9
Tél: 450-679-0530
upa@upa.qc.ca
www.upa.qc.ca
www.facebook.com/pageUPA
twitter.com/upaqc
www.youtube.com/user/upa1972
Aperçu: *Dimension:* grande; *Envergure:* provinciale; fondée en 1924 surveillé par Canadian Federation of Agriculture
Mission: Promouvoir, défendre et développer les intérêts professionnels, économiques, sociaux et moraux des producteurs agricoles et forestiers, sans distinction de race, de nationalité, de sexe, de langue et de croyance
Membre de: Fédération canadienne des producteurs de lait
Membre(s) du bureau directeur:
Marcel Groleau, Président
Finances: *Budget de fonctionnement annuel:* $3 Million-$5 Million
Membre: 43 000;

Union des tenanciers de bars du Québec (UTBQ)
3800, rue Notre-Dame Ouest, Montréal QC H4C 1P9
Tél: 514-937-0531
info@utbq.ca
utbq.ca

Aperçu: *Dimension:* petite; *Envergure:* provinciale; fondée en 2006
Mission: Représenter de façon active et responsable ses membres afin de défendre leurs droits en tant que tenanciers de bars
Membre: 683; *Critères d'admissibilite:* Les propriétaires de bars

Union géophysique canadienne *See* Canadian Geophysical Union

Union internationale pour les livres de jeunesse *See* International Board on Books for Young People - Canadian Section

Union mondiale des aveugles *See* World Blind Union

Union of British Columbia Indian Chiefs
#500, 342 Water St., Vancouver BC V6B 1B6
Tel: 604-684-0231; *Fax:* 604-684-5726
ubcic@ubcic.bc.ca
www.ubcic.bc.ca
www.facebook.com/UBCIC
twitter.com/UBCIC
www.youtube.com/UBCIC
Overview: A medium-sized provincial charitable organization founded in 1969
Mission: To settle land claims & aboriginal rights in BC; to improve the social, economic, health, education of Aboriginal people in BC; to provide a political voice for Aboriginal people in BC
Member of: Assembly of First Nations; World Council of Indigenous Peoples
Chief Officer(s):
Stewart Phillip, President
Activities: *Library* Open to public by appointment

Union of British Columbia Municipalities (UBCM)
#60, 10551 Shellbridge Way, Richmond BC V6X 2W9
Tel: 604-270-8226; *Fax:* 604-270-9116
www.ubcm.ca
twitter.com/UBCM
Overview: A medium-sized provincial organization founded in 1905
Mission: To provide a common voice for local government
Member of: Federation of Canadian Municipalities
Chief Officer(s):
Mary Sjostrom, President
Gary MacIsaac, Executive Director
gmacisaac@ubcm.ca
Marie Crawford, Associate Executive Director
mcrawford@ubcm.ca
Anna-Maria Wijesinghe, Manager, Member & Association Services
amwijesinghe@ubcm.ca
Finances: *Annual Operating Budget:* $500,000-$1.5 Million
Staff Member(s): 20
Membership: 161 municipalities + 29 regional districts; *Committees:* Community Economic Development; Community Safety; Convention; Environment; First Nations; Healthy Communities; Presidents; Resolutions
Activities: *Awareness Events:* Local Government Awareness Week, May; *Speaker Service:* Yes; *Library* Open to public
Awards:
• Community Excellence Awards (Award)
• Long Service Awards (Award)
Meetings/Conferences: • Union of British Columbia Municipalities 2015 Annual Convention, September, 2015, Vancouver Convention & Exhibition Centre, Vancouver, BC
Scope: Provincial
• Union of British Columbia Municipalities 2016 Annual Convention, September, 2016, Penticton Trade & Convention Centre, BC
Scope: Provincial
• Union of British Columbia Municipalities 2017 Annual Convention, September, 2017, Vancouver Convention & Exhibition Centre, Vancouver, BC
Scope: Provincial
• Union of British Columbia Municipalities 2018 Annual Convention, 2018, BC
Scope: Provincial
• Union of British Columbia Municipalities 2019 Annual Convention, September, 2019, Vancouver Convention & Exhibition Centre, Vancouver, BC
Scope: Provincial

Union of Calgary Cooperative Employees (UCCE)
#123, 2723 - 37 Ave. NE, Calgary AB T1Y 5R8
Tel: 403-299-6700; *Fax:* 403-299-6710
reception@ucce.info
www.ucce.info
Also Known As: Calco Club
Overview: A small local organization
Mission: To represent members employed in occupations ranging from trades, janitorial, clerical, and technical in the field of retail grocery
Chief Officer(s):
Shelly Winters, President

Union of Canadian Correctional Officers *See* Syndicat des Agents Correctionnels du Canada (CSN)

Union of Canadian Transportation Employees (UCTE) / Union canadienne des employés des transports (UCET)
#702, 233 Gilmour St., Ottawa ON K2P 0P2
Tel: 613-238-4003; *Fax:* 613-236-0379
www.ucte.com
Overview: A medium-sized national organization overseen by Public Service Alliance of Canada (CLC)
Mission: The Union represents members working in the public & private sectors of the Canadian transportation industry (ports, airports, NAV Canada, pilotage authorities, transportation companies, canals, the Dept. of Transport, lighthouses, ships and Canadian Coast Guard bases)
Chief Officer(s):
Gardenia Li, Finance & Administration Officer
Membership: 7,500 + 90 locals

Union of Energy, Mines & Resources Employees *See* Natural Resources Union

Union of Environment Workers (UEW) / Syndicat des travailleurs de l'environnement (STE)
2181 Thurston Dr., Ottawa ON K1G 6C9
Tel: 613-736-5533; *Fax:* 613-736-5537
www.uew-ste.ca
www.facebook.com/pages/Union-of-Environment-Workers/111345079011371
twitter.com/UEWCanada
Overview: A medium-sized national organization founded in 1972 overseen by Public Service Alliance of Canada (CLC)
Mission: To protect their members by ensuring safe working conditions & fair wage rights & benefits
Chief Officer(s):
Luc Paquette, Service Officer
Luc.paquette@uew-ste.ca
Staff Member(s): 4
Membership: 5,700 + 40 Locals; *Member Profile:* Employees in the departments of Environment, Fisheries and Oceans & the Canadian Forest Service; *Committees:* Staff Relations; By-Laws & Policies; Strategies & Planning; Honours and Awards; Environment; Finance & Planning; Collective Bargaining; Convention; Our Fish

Union of Injured Workers of Ontario, Inc.
2888 Dufferin St., Toronto ON M6B 3S6
Tel: 416-785-8787; *Fax:* 416-785-6390
Overview: A medium-sized provincial organization founded in 1974
Mission: Serving injured workers & their families; advocacy, counselling, information & referral
Affliation(s): Ontario Network of Injured Workers Groups
Chief Officer(s):
Philip Biggin, Executive Director
pbiggin@hotmail.com
Finances: *Annual Operating Budget:* $100,000-$250,000; *Funding Sources:* Unions; government
Staff Member(s): 3; 25 volunteer(s)
Membership: 2,500; *Fees:* $30 optional

Union of Municipalities of New Brunswick (UMNB) / Union des municipalités du Nouveau-Brunswick
#4, 79 Main St., Rexton NB E4W 1Z9
Tel: 506-523-7991; *Fax:* 506-523-7992
umnb@nb.aibn.com
www.umnb.ca
Merged from: Association of the Villages of New Brunswick; Towns of New Brunswick Association
Overview: A medium-sized provincial organization founded in 1995
Mission: To unite the municipalities of New Brunswick through their respective councils into a body whose common efforts shall be devoted solely to the achievement of that which is the common good of all
Member of: Federation of Canadian Municipalities
Chief Officer(s):
Tom Gillett, Director, 506-339-6128
Finances: *Annual Operating Budget:* $50,000-$100,000; *Funding Sources:* Membership dues
Staff Member(s): 1; 40 volunteer(s)
Membership: 56

Union of National Defence Employees (UNDE) / Union des employés de la Défense nationale (UEDN)
#700, 116 Albert St., Ottawa ON K1P 5G3
Tel: 613-594-4505; *Fax:* 613-594-8233
Toll-Free: 866-594-4505
www.unde-uedn.com
twitter.com/UNDEUEDN
www.youtube.com/channel/UCHq7kXfLm2OP2EpPj4L58DA
Overview: A medium-sized national organization overseen by Public Service Alliance of Canada (CLC)
Mission: To represent the interests of their members & ensure safe working conditions for them
Chief Officer(s):
John MacLennan, National President
Membership: 18,000 + 80 locals

Union of National Employees (UNE) / Syndicat des employées et employés nationaux (SEN)
#900, 150 Isabella St., Ottawa ON K1S 1V7
Tel: 613-560-4364; *Fax:* 613-560-4208
Toll-Free: 800-663-6685
une-sen.org
www.facebook.com/Union.NE.Syndicat.EN
twitter.com/my_UNE
www.youtube.com/user/UnionNESyndicatEN
Overview: A medium-sized national organization overseen by Public Service Alliance of Canada (CLC)
Mission: To protect their members by ensuring safe working conditions & fair wage rights & benefits
Chief Officer(s):
Georges St-Jean, Acting Coordinator & Finance Officer
georges.stjean@une-sen.org
Staff Member(s): 24
Membership: 26,000; *Committees:* By-laws and Policies; Collective Bargaining; Communications, Education, Honours & Awards; Finance & Human Resources; Francophone; Locals & Membership; National Executive Disciplinary

Union of Northern Workers / Syndicat des travailleurs du Nord
#200, 5112 - 52 St., Yellowknife NT X1A 3Z5
Tel: 867-873-5668; *Fax:* 867-920-4448
Toll-Free: 877-906-4447
hq@unw.ca
www.unw.ca
twitter.com/UNW_NWT
Previous Name: Northwest Territories Public Service Association
Overview: A medium-sized national organization overseen by Public Service Alliance of Canada (CLC)
Mission: To represent the interests of its members in contract negotiatons & grievances
Chief Officer(s):
Todd Parsons, President
Staff Member(s): 13
Membership: 4,000 + 18 locals

Union of Nova Scotia Indians (UNSI)
47 Maillard St., Membertou NS B1S 2P5
Tel: 902-539-4107; *Fax:* 902-564-2137
rec@unsi.ns.ca
www.unsi.ns.ca
Overview: A medium-sized provincial organization founded in 1969
Mission: To promote welfare & progress of Native people in Nova Scotia; to liaise with all Native people on relevant issues; to defend & advise on Native rights; to cooperate with Native & non-Native agencies & organizations to the benefit of Nova Scotia Native people
Chief Officer(s):
Joe B. Marshall, Executive Director
Finances: *Annual Operating Budget:* $1.5 Million-$3 Million
Staff Member(s): 21
Membership: *Member Profile:* Individual who is registered as an Indian pursuant to the Indian Act

Union of Nova Scotia Municipalities (UNSM)
#1106, 1809 Barrington St., Halifax NS B3J 3K8

Tel: 902-423-8331; *Fax:* 902-425-5592
info@unsm.ca
www.unsm.ca
Overview: A medium-sized provincial organization founded in 1905
Mission: To research, promote & represent provincial interests of local government
Member of: Federation of Canadian Municipalities
Chief Officer(s):
Betty MacDonald, Executive Director
bmacdonald@unsm.ca
Judy Webber, Event Planner/Financal Officer
jwebber@unsm.ca
Finances: *Annual Operating Budget:* $250,000-$500,000; *Funding Sources:* Membership dues
Staff Member(s): 3; 20 volunteer(s)
Membership: 455 individual; *Member Profile:* Elected to municipal office
Activities: *Library* by appointment

Union of Ontario Indians (UOI)

Nipissing First Nation, 1 Miigizi Mikan, North Bay ON P1B 8J8
Tel: 705-497-9127; *Fax:* 705-497-9135
Toll-Free: 877-702-5200
info@anishinabek.ca
www.anishinabek.ca
www.facebook.com/AnishinabekNation
twitter.com/anishnation
www.youtube.com/user/AnishinabekNation
Also Known As: Anishinabek Nation
Overview: A large provincial organization founded in 1949
Mission: The UOI represents 42 First Nations throughout the province of Ontario from Golden Lake in the east, Sarnia in the south, Thunder Bay and Lake Nipigon in the north. The 42 First Nations have an approximate combined population of 42,000 citizens, one third of the province of Ontario's aboriginal population.
Chief Officer(s):
Patrick Madahbee, Grand Council Chief
Finances: *Annual Operating Budget:* $3 Million-$5 Million
Staff Member(s): 24
Membership: 42 First Nations
Activities: *Speaker Service:* Yes; *Library* Open to public
Publications:
• Anishinabek News
Type: Newspaper

Union of Postal Communications Employees (UPCE) / Syndicat des employés des postes et des communications (SEPC)

#701, 233 Gilmour St., Ottawa ON K2P 0P2
Tel: 613-560-4342; *Fax:* 613-594-3849
sepc-upce@psac.com
www.upce.ca
Overview: A medium-sized national licensing organization overseen by Public Service Alliance of Canada (CLC)
Mission: Represents Canada Post members employed in administrative, clerical, technical & professional capacities
Chief Officer(s):
Patty Ducharme, National Executive Vice President, 613-560-4310, Fax: 613-567-0385
ducharp@psac.com
Finances: *Annual Operating Budget:* $1.5 Million-$3 Million
Staff Member(s): 4
Membership: 2,900 + 24 locals

Union of Prison Guards of Québec (Ind.) *Voir* Syndicat des agents de la paix en services correctionnels du Québec (ind.)

Union of Professional Employees of the Québec Government *Voir* Syndicat de professionnels et professionnelles du gouvernement du Québec

Union of Professors for the Government of Québec (Ind.) *Voir* Syndicat des professeurs de l'État du Québec (ind.)

Union of Psychiatric Nurses / Syndicat des infirmières psychiatriques

#211, 20644 Eastleigh Cres., Langley BC V3A 4C4
Tel: 604-530-9253; *Fax:* 604-530-9653
Toll-Free: 877-931-2471
www.upnbc.org
Previous Name: Union of Registered Psychiatric Nurses of British Columbia
Overview: A medium-sized provincial organization founded in 1966
Mission: To represent its members' interests & promote the Psychiatric Nursing profession
Affliation(s): BC Government Employees Union; BC Federation of Labour; BC Nurses Union
Chief Officer(s):
Dan Murphy, President
Garnet Zimmerman, Executive Director
gzimmerman@upnbc.org
Finances: *Funding Sources:* Membership dues
Staff Member(s): 7
Membership: 1000 + 5 locals;

Union of Radiology Technicians of Québec *Voir* Syndicat des technologues en radiologie du Québec (ind.)

Union of Registered Psychiatric Nurses of British Columbia *See* Union of Psychiatric Nurses

Union of Solicitor General Employees (USGE) / Syndicat des employés du Solliciteur général (SESG)

#603, 233 Gilmour St., Ottawa ON K2P 0P2
Tel: 613-232-4821; *Fax:* 613-232-3311
www.usge-sesg.com
Overview: A medium-sized national organization overseen by Public Service Alliance of Canada (CLC)
Chief Officer(s):
Stan Stapleton, National President
Membership: 15,000 + 140 locals; *Committees:* National Health & Safety Advisory

Union of Spiritual Communities of Christ

1876 Brilliant Rd., Castlegar BC V1N 4K2
Tel: 250-365-3613; *Fax:* 250-365-5477
info@iskra.ca
iskra.ca
Overview: A small national organization
Mission: The Union of Spiritual Communities of Christ (USCC) is a registered Canadian charitable society dedicated to the sustainability and enrichment of the Doukhobor Life-Concept based on the Law of God and the Teachings of Jesus Christ
Chief Officer(s):
Stephanie Swetlishoff, Editor
Barry Verigin, Editor

Union of Taxation Employees (UTE) / Syndicat des employé(e)s de l'impôt (SEI)

#800, 233 Gilmour St., Ottawa ON K2P 0P2
Tel: 613-235-6704; *Fax:* 613-234-7290
www.ute-sei.org
www.facebook.com/pages/Union-of-Taxation-Employees/125402707475856
Overview: A medium-sized national organization founded in 1967 overseen by Public Service Alliance of Canada (CLC)
Chief Officer(s):
Robert Campbell, National President
Staff Member(s): 15
Membership: 27,000 + 51 locals; *Committees:* Bargaining; By-Laws; Call Centre; Communications; Employee Assistance Program; Equal Opportunities; Executive; Finance; Harassment; Health & Safety; Honours & Awards; National Union-Management; Political Action; Staffing; Technological Change; Workforce Adjustment

Union of Veterans' Affairs Employees (UVAE) / Syndicat des employé(e)s des affaires des anciens combattants (SEAC)

#703, 233 Gilmour St., Ottawa ON K2P 0P2
Tel: 613-560-5460; *Fax:* 613-237-8282
uvae-seac.ca
Overview: A small national organization overseen by Public Service Alliance of Canada (CLC)
Mission: To represent the interests of employees of Veterans' Affairs Canada
Chief Officer(s):
Carl Gannon, National President
gannonc@psac.com
Membership: 2,600;

Union Paysanne

CP 515, Succ. Bureau Chef, Saint-Hyacinthe QC J2S 7B8
Tél: 450-774-7692; *Téléc:* 450-774-9404
paysanne@unionpaysanne.com
www.unionpaysanne.com
www.facebook.com/443010025581
twitter.com/UnionPaysanne
Aperçu: *Dimension:* moyenne; *Envergure:* provinciale
Mission: A pour but de regrouper en une force collective organisée et représentative tous ceux qui sont en faveur d'une agriculture et d'une alimentation paysannes pour faire contrepoids au monopole de représentation syndicale et au puisant lobby de l'industrie agro-alimentaire et des promoteurs du libre échange en faveur d'un modèle industriel d'agriculture
Membre(s) du bureau directeur:
Maxime Laplante, Président
Membre: *Montant de la cotisation:* 60$

Union philatélique de Montréal

7110, av 8e, Montréal QC H2A 3C4
Tél: 514-274-0480
ncaron@philatelie-upm.com
www.philatelie-upm.com
Aperçu: *Dimension:* petite; *Envergure:* locale
Membre de: Royal Philatelic Society of Canada
Membre(s) du bureau directeur:
Normand Caron

Union québécoise de réhabilitation des oiseaux de proie (UQROP) / Québec Raptor Rehabilitation Network

CP 246, Saint-Hyacinthe QC J2S 7B6
Tél: 450-773-8521; *Téléc:* 450-778-8125
info@uqrop.qc.ca
www.uqrop.qc.ca
www.facebook.com/166157060085717
Aperçu: *Dimension:* petite; *Envergure:* provinciale; fondée en 1987
Mission: Conservation des oiseaux de proie & de leurs habitats naturels par la réhabilitation d'oiseaux blessés & l'éducation du public
Membre(s) du bureau directeur:
Guy Fitzgerald, Président et directeur
Membre(s) du personnel: 4
Membre: *Critères d'admissibilité:* Ornithologues
Activités: *Stagiaires:* Oui; *Service de conférenciers:* Oui

Union québécoise des infirmières et infirmiers (UQII) / Québec Union of Nurses

9405, rue Sherbrooke est, Montréal QC H1L 6P3
Tél: 514-356-8888; *Téléc:* 514-356-9999
uqii@csq.qc.net
Aperçu: *Dimension:* moyenne; *Envergure:* provinciale; Organisme sans but lucratif; fondée en 1988
Mission: L'UQII assure la représentation de ses membres, donne aux syndicats une structure politique et fournit, en collaboration avec la CSQ, des services aux membres en matière de relations de travail, de professionnel, de négociation et de formation
Affliation(s): Centrale des syndicats du Québec (CSQ)
Membre(s) du bureau directeur:
Monique Bélanger, Présidente
Finances: *Budget de fonctionnement annuel:* $100,000-$250,000
Membre(s) du personnel: 1
Membre: 7 000 infirmières; *Critères d'admissibilite:* Infirmières; infirmières auxiliaire; inhalothérapeutes
Activités: *Service de conférenciers:* Oui

Union québécoise du bison

#100, 555, boul Roland-Therrien, Longueuil QC J4H 3Y9
Tel: 450-679-0530; *Fax:* 450-670-4867
www.bisonquebec.com
Overview: A small provincial organization
Member of: Canadian Bison Association
Chief Officer(s):
Jean-Luc Chouinard, President
jl_chouinard@videotron.ca

Union québécoise pour la conservation de la nature *Voir* Nature Québec

Union Saint Laurent Grands Lacs *See* Great Lakes United

Unison Health & Community Services

1651 Keele St., Toronto ON M6M 3W2
Tel: 416-653-5400; *Fax:* 416-653-1696
unisonhcs.org
www.facebook.com/UnisonHCS
twitter.com/unisonhcs
www.youtube.com/user/UnisonHCS
Overview: A small local organization founded in 1973 overseen by Ontario Council of Agencies Serving Immigrants
Mission: To provide services to the public to help improve their lives
Chief Officer(s):

Janak Jass, Chair
Finances: *Annual Operating Budget:* Greater than $5 Million
Staff Member(s): 226; 150 volunteer(s)
Membership: *Fees:* $1

Unisphere (Cross-Cultural) Learner Centre ***See*** Unisphere Global Resource Centre

Unisphere Global Resource Centre
101 - 6 St. SE, Medicine Hat AB T1A 1G7
Tel: 403-529-2656
unispheregrc@gmail.com
nonprofit.memlane.com/unisphere
Previous Name: Unisphere (Cross-Cultural) Learner Centre
Overview: A small local charitable organization
Mission: To create a climate in which the sharing of cultures can be experienced & where vital global issues are discussed with openness; to provide a place for all peoples to develop as informed world citizens through sharing of ideas, experiences, & friendship; to identify & develop sensitive awareness to the values of all cultures through dialogue, with a view to cross-cultural enrichment; to work towards a better understanding of the essential inter-relatedness, culturally & economically, of all nations; to "think globally"
Member of: LEARN; MH Volunteerism in Action; Southeastern Alberta Racial & Community Harmony Society
Membership: *Fees:* $6 student/senior; $15 individual; $25 family; $40 organization
Activities: World Food Day; Spring Fundraiser; *Speaker Service:* Yes; *Library* Open to public

UNITE HERE Canada
OFL Bldg., 15 Gervais Dr., 3rd Fl., Toronto ON M3C 1Y8
Tel: 416-384-0983; *Fax:* 416-384-0991
info@uniteherecanada.org
www.uniteherecanada.org
Merged from: UNITE; HERE
Overview: A large national organization
Chief Officer(s):
Nick Worhaug, Canadian Director
Paul Clifford, Executive/International Vice-President
Karen Grella, International Vice-President
Amarjeet Kaur Chhabra, Media Contact, 416-856-9587
achhabra@unitehereloca175.org
Membership: 50,000 in Canada; 250,000 total across the USA & Canada; *Member Profile:* Represents workers in: hotels, casinos, apparel & textile manufacturing, apparel distribution centers, apparel retail, industrial laundries, foodservice, airport concessions, & restaurants

Edmonton-Calgary Chapter
Local 47, 10643 - 105 St., Edmonton AB T5H 2X1
Tel: 780-426-7890; *Fax:* 780-426-5098
Toll-Free: 888-801-4373
info@local47.net
www.local47.net
Chief Officer(s):
Ian Robb, President/Administrator

Ottawa Chapter
Local 261, #2, 200 Cooper St., Ottawa ON K2P 0G1
Tel: 613-238-8136; *Fax:* 613-238-5499
local261@aol.com
Chief Officer(s):
Karen Grella, Secretary-Treasurer

Ottawa Chapter
Local 272, c/o Frank Ryan Senior Elementary School, #222, 128 Chesterton Dr., Nepean ON K2E 5T8
Tel: 613-228-9991; *Fax:* 613-228-9909

Regina Chapter
Local 41, 1317 - 9th Ave. North, Regina SK S4R 0E6
Tel: 306-781-8157; *Fax:* 306-543-3856

St. John's Chapter
c/o National Headquarters, OFL Bldg., 15 Gervais Dr., 3rd Fl., Toronto ON M3C 1Y8
Tel: 416-384-0983; *Fax:* 416-384-0991
info@uniteherecanada.org
Mission: Contact UNITE HERE Canada's National Headquarters for information on Local 779 St. John's

Toronto Chapter
Local 75, OFL Bldg., 15 Gervais Dr., 3rd Fl., Toronto ON M3C 1Y8
Tel: 416-384-0983; *Fax:* 416-384-0991
info@unitehereloca175.org
www.unitehereloca175.org
www.facebook.com/UniteHereLocal75
twitter.com/UniteHere75
Chief Officer(s):
Lis Pimentel, President
lpimentel@unitehereloca175.org

Vancouver & Vicinity Chapter
Local 40, #100, 4853 East Hastings St., Burnaby BC V5C 2L1
Tel: 604-291-8211; *Fax:* 604-291-2676
www.unitehereloca140.org
www.facebook.com/129648666837
twitter.com/UniteHere40
www.youtube.com/user/UniteHereL40
Chief Officer(s):
Jim Pearson, President
Shelly Ervin, Secretary-Treasurer
Mike Casey, Supervisor

United Appeal of Ottawa-Carleton ***See*** United Way/Centraide Ottawa

United Baptist Convention of the Maritime Provinces ***See*** Convention of Atlantic Baptist Churches

The United Brethren Church in Canada
501 Whitelaw Rd., Guelph ON N1K 1E7
Tel: 519-836-0180; *Fax:* 519-821-8385
www.ubcanada.org
Previous Name: Ontario Conference, Church of the United Brethren in Christ
Overview: A small national charitable organization founded in 1856
Mission: To organize groups of people into congregations to worship God; to make effective application of principles of righteousness in the Society
Member of: Church of the United Brethren in Christ, International
Affliation(s): Evangelical Fellowship of Canada
Chief Officer(s):
Brian K. Magnus, Bishop
Finances: *Annual Operating Budget:* $50,000-$100,000; *Funding Sources:* Donations
Staff Member(s): 1
Membership: 12 churches; *Fees:* Schedule available; *Member Profile:* Personal knowledge of God through faith in Christ; desire to live a life conforming to biblical principles
Activities: *Library:* At Emmanuel Bible College Library

United Church of Canada (UCC) / L'Église Unie du Canada
#300, 3250 Bloor St. West, Toronto ON M8X 2Y4
Tel: 416-231-5931; *Fax:* 416-231-3103
Toll-Free: 800-268-3781
Other Communication: Voice Mail 416-231-7680
info@united-church.ca
www.united-church.ca
www.facebook.com/UnitedChurchCda
twitter.com/UnitedChurchCda
www.youtube.com/unitedchurchofcanada
Overview: A large national charitable organization founded in 1925
Mission: To foster the spirit of unity in the hope that this sentiment of unity may in due time, so far as Canada is concerned, take shape in a Church which may fittingly be described as national
Member of: Canadian Council of Churches; World Council of Churches; Canadian Council for International Cooperation; World Methodist Council
Affliation(s): United Church of Canada Foundation
Chief Officer(s):
Gary Paterson, Moderator
moderator@united-church.ca
Nora Sanders, General Secretary
nsanders@united-church.ca
Finances: *Annual Operating Budget:* Greater than $5 Million; *Funding Sources:* Voluntary givings; sales; bequests; investment income; foundation
Staff Member(s): 5000
Membership: 650,000; *Member Profile:* Baptism & profession of faith in Jesus Christ as Saviour & Lord
Activities: *Speaker Service:* Yes
Publications:
• The United Church Observer
Type: Magazine; *Frequency:* Monthly; *Accepts Advertising*; *Editor:* David Wilson; *Price:* $25/year within Canada; $35/year outside of Canada

Alberta & Northwest Conference
9911 - 48th Ave., Edmonton AB T6E 5V6
Tel: 780-435-3995; *Fax:* 780-438-3317
coffice@anwconf.com
www.anwconf.com
Chief Officer(s):
Lynn Maki, Executive Secretary, 780-435-3995 Ext. 224

All Native Circle Conference
367 Selkirk Ave., Winnipeg MB R2W 2M3
Tel: 204-582-5518; *Fax:* 204-582-6649
allnative@ancconline.ca

Bay of Quinte Conference
PO Box 700, 67 Mill St., Frankford ON K0K 2C0
Tel: 613-398-1051; *Fax:* 613-398-8894
Toll-Free: 888-759-2444
officeadmin@bayofquinteconference.ca
www.bayofquinteconference.ca
Chief Officer(s):
Bill Smith, Executive Secretary
execsec@bayofquinteconference.ca

British Columbia Conference
4383 Rumble St., Burnaby BC V5J 2A2
Tel: 604-431-0434; *Fax:* 604-431-0439
Toll-Free: 800-934-0434
reception@bc.united-church.ca
bc.united-church.ca
Chief Officer(s):
Doug Goodwin, Executive Secretary
dgoodwin@bc.united-church.ca

Hamilton Conference
PO Box 100, Carlisle ON L0R 1H0
Tel: 905-659-3343; *Fax:* 905-659-7766
office@hamconf.org
www.hamconf.org
www.facebook.com/HamiltonConference
twitter.com/HamiltonConfere
Chief Officer(s):
Fred Monteith, Executive Secretary
fmonteith@hamconf.org

London Conference
#111, 747 Hyde Park Rd., London ON N6H 3S3
Tel: 519-672-1930; *Fax:* 519-439-2800
office@londonconference.ca
www.londonconference.ca
www.youtube.com/channel/UCwXE33RTsKxV-isk-Ffr_CA
Chief Officer(s):
Cheryl-Ann Stadelbauer-Sampa, Executive Secretary
c-a@londonconference.ca

Manitoba & Northwestern Ontario Conference
#1622-B, St. Mary's Rd., Winnipeg MB R2M 3W7
Tel: 204-233-8911; *Fax:* 204-233-3289
Toll-Free: 866-860-9662
office@confmnwo.mb.ca
www.mnwo.united-church.ca
www.facebook.com/confmnwo
twitter.com/MNWOConference
www.youtube.com/user/UCCMNWOCONFERENCE/videos
Chief Officer(s):
Bill Gillis, Acting Executive Secretary
bgillis@confmnwo.mb.ca

Manitou Conference
319 McKenzie Ave., North Bay ON P1B 7E3
Tel: 705-474-3350; *Fax:* 705-497-3597
office@manitouconference.ca
manitouconference.ca
www.facebook.com/manitouconference
Chief Officer(s):
Will Kunder, Executive Secretary
wkunder@manitouconference.ca

Maritime Conference
21 Wright St., Sackville NB E4L 4P8
Tel: 506-536-1334; *Fax:* 506-536-2900
info@marconf.ca
www.marconf.ca
www.facebook.com/329299033776135
twitter.com/maritimeconf
www.youtube.com/user/maritimeconference
Chief Officer(s):
Catherine H. Gaw, Executive Secretary
cgaw@marconf.ca

Newfoundland & Labrador Conference
320 Elizabeth Ave., St. John's NL A1B 1T9
Tel: 709-754-0386; *Fax:* 709-754-8336
unitedchurch@nfld.net
www.newlabconf.com
Chief Officer(s):

Faith March-McCuish, Executive Secretary
executivesecretary@nfld.net
Saskatchewan Conference
418A McDonald St., Regina SK S4N 6E1
Tel: 306-721-3311; *Fax:* 306-721-3171
ucskco@sasktel.net
www.sk.united-church.ca
Chief Officer(s):
Bill Doyle, Executive Secretary
Synode Montréal & Ottawa Conference
225-50e ave., Lachine QC H8T 2T7
Tel: 514-634-7015; *Fax:* 514-634-2489
www.synodemontrealettawa.ca
Chief Officer(s):
Rosemary Lambie, Executive Secretary
Toronto Conference
65 Mayall Ave., Toronto ON M3L 1E7
Tel: 416-241-2677; *Fax:* 416-241-2689
Toll-Free: 800-446-4729
www.torontoconference.ca
www.facebook.com/196221203732363
twitter.com/TorontoConferen
Chief Officer(s):
David Allen, Executive Secretary
dallen@united-church.ca

United Church of Canada Foundation / Église Unie du Canada

#300, 3250 Bloor St. West, Toronto ON M8X 2Y4
Tel: 416-231-5931; *Fax:* 416-231-3103
Toll-Free: 866-340-8223
fdn@united-church.ca
www.unitedchurchfoundation.ca
Overview: A large national charitable organization founded in 2002
Mission: To help sustain the United Church of Canada
Affliation(s): United Church of Canada
Chief Officer(s):
Peter Harder, Chair
David Armour, President
Finances: *Annual Operating Budget:* $3 Million-$5 Million
Membership: *Committees:* Audit; Governance; Joint Grants; Investment
Activities: Managing 40 endowments; grants & scholarships
Awards:
• W. Norman McLeod Scholarship (Scholarship)
To promote, advance & encourage theological education *Amount:* $500-$1,500
• McGeachy Senior Scholarship (Scholarship)
To develop leaders for the United Church of Canada
• Davidson Trust Award (Award)
To acknowledge excellence of scholarship & theological teaching *Amount:* $5,000
• Clifford Elliott Rural Ministry Award (Award)
To enable study at the Saskatoon Theological Union's Institute for Rural Ministry *Amount:* $5,000
• Alfred J. Mitchell Trust (Grant), Lectureships & Research or Educational Bursaries
• James Robertson Memorial Trust (Grant), Lectureships & Research or Educational Bursaries
• Rowntree Scholarship (Scholarship), Lectureships & Research or Educational Bursaries
• Victor Blatherwick Memorial Bursary (Grant), Lectureships & Research or Educational Bursaries
• Bill & Anna Jentzsch Endowment Bursary (Grant), Lectureships & Research or Educational Bursaries
• Watkins Fund for Innovative Ministries with Senior Adults (Grant), Innovative Programs for Seniors
• Ann Baker Estate Trust (Grant), Innovative Programs for Seniors
• Watkins Fund (Grant), Programs for Children/Anti-Poverty
• Wesley C. Smith Fund for Innovative Programs & Projects in Addressing Poverty & Children at Risk (Grant), Programs for Children/Anti-Poverty
• Living Spirit Fund/Davey Family Fund (Grant), General
• Peace & Justice Fund/Brian & Belva Piercy Fund (Grant), General
• Faith & Mission Fund (Grant), General
• Leadership Fund (Grant), General

United County Beekeepers

QC
Tel: 514-630-6336
ucba@hotmail.ca
www.ucbabee.com
Overview: A small local organization
Mission: To assist beekeepers in the United County of Ontario by providing education & information
Member of: Ontario Beekeepers' Association
Chief Officer(s):
John McCraig, Contact
Membership: *Member Profile:* Apiarists in Ontario's United County

United Empire Loyalists' Association of Canada (UELAC)

Dominion Office, The George Brown House, #202, 50 Baldwin St., Toronto ON M5T 1L4
Tel: 416-591-1783
uelac@uelac.org
www.uelac.org
www.facebook.com/UELAC
twitter.com/uelac
Also Known As: UEL Association
Overview: A medium-sized national charitable organization founded in 1914
Mission: To unite together descendants of those families who, as a result of the American revolutionary war, sacrificed their homes in retaining their loyalty to the British Crown; to keep alive the knowledge of the early contributions of hundreds of thousands of Loyalists of many cultures, creeds & colours
Chief Officer(s):
Bonnie Schepers, President
Barbara J. Andrew, Sr. Vice-President
Membership: 664; *Member Profile:* Descent from or interest in United Empire Loyalists
Activities: Educational Program; Loyalist Burial Sites; True Millennium Projects; Poetry-Essay Collections; *Library:* Reference Library

Abegweit Branch
288 Maple Ave., Summerside PE C1N 2H3
Tel: 902-436-3355
www.islandregister.com/uel.html
Chief Officer(s):
Mary Bradshaw, Branch Genealogist
Bay of Quinte Branch
PO Box 112 RR#1, 54 Park Rd., Bath ON K0H 1G0
Tel: 613-373-2632
1784@uel.ca
www.uelmain.aboutyourcommunications.com
Bicentennial Branch
41 Erie St., Kingsville ON N9Y 1N1
Tel: 519-733-6686
info@uelbicentennial.org
www.uelbicentennial.org
Chief Officer(s):
Pat Haynes, Branch President
info@uelbicentennial.org
Calgary Branch
Calgary AB
e-mail: davidhongisto@shaw.ca
Chief Officer(s):
David Hongisto, President
Chilliwack Branch
46486 Uplands Dr., Chilliwack BC V2R 4M5
e-mail: ksdargatz@shaw.ca
www.uelac.org/Chilliwack
Chief Officer(s):
Shirley Dargatz, President
Col. Edward Jessup Branch
RR#4, North Augusta ON K0G 1R0
Tel: 613-924-2928
myrtlejohnston@hotmail.com
Chief Officer(s):
Myrtle Johnston, President
Col. John Butler Branch
ON
Tel: 905-892-3420
rcraig@beacon.org
www.coljohnbutleruel.com
Chief Officer(s):
Rodney Craig, Genealogist
Edmonton Branch
c/o 9304 Ottewell Rd., Edmonton AB T6B 2C9
e-mail: robertrogers@shaw.ca
members.shaw.ca/edmonton_uela/
Chief Officer(s):
Robert Rogers, President
Governor Simcoe Branch
315 Carlton St., Toronto ON M5A 2L6
Tel: 416-921-7756
doug.grant@insurance-canada.ca
www.uelgovsimcoe.org
Chief Officer(s):
Doug Grant, Genealogist
Grand River Branch
#12, 590 Millbank Dr., London ON N6E 2H2
Tel: 519-893-5631
paul_gray@rogers.com
www.grandriveruel.ca
twitter.com/GrandRiverUELAC
Chief Officer(s):
Paul Gray, President, 519-893-5631
paul_gray@rogers.com
Halifax-Dartmouth Branch
Dartmouth NS
e-mail: lewis001@ns.sympatico.ca
Chief Officer(s):
Lewis Perry, President
Hamilton Branch
#62-175 Fiddler's Green Rd, Ancaster ON L9G 4X7
Tel: 905-648-6519
g.oakes@sympatico.ca
www.uel-hamilton.com
Chief Officer(s):
Lloyd Oakes, President
Heritage Branch
383, av Clarke, Montréal QC H3Z 2E7
Tel: 514-937-3274; *Fax:* 514-398-4659
RWilkins@blg.com
Chief Officer(s):
Robert C. Wilkins, President
Kawartha Branch
1482 Monahan Rd, Peterborough ON K9J 5N2
e-mail: dthompson@nexicom.net
www.uelac.org/Kawartha/index.php
Chief Officer(s):
Doreen Thompson, President
Kingston Branch
PO Box 635, Kingston ON K7L 4X7
Tel: 613-546-2256
pgdreal@kos.net
www.uelac.org/Kingston
Chief Officer(s):
Dean Taylor, President
Little Forks Branch
PO Box 67, 5955 Route Gilbert Hyatt, Lennoxville QC J1M 1Z3
Tel: 819-346-6746
Chief Officer(s):
Beverly Loomis, President
London & South-Western District Branch
983 Dalhousie Dr., London ON N6K 1M8
www.uelac.org/londonuel
Chief Officer(s):
June Klassen, President
Manitoba Branch
120 Eugenie St., Winnipeg MB R2H 0X7
Tel: 204-489-7180
uelmanitoba@gmail.com
www.uelmanitoba.ca
Chief Officer(s):
Peter Rogers, President
New Brunswick Branch
PO Box 484, Saint John NB E2L 3Z8
e-mail: membership@uelac-nb.ca
www.uelac-nb.ca
Chief Officer(s):
Dave Laskey, President
Regina Branch
SK
Tel: 306-646-4952
gerry.pat@sasktel.net
www.uelac.org/Saskatchewan
Chief Officer(s):
Pat Adair, President
St. Lawrence Branch
PO Box 607, 3 Augusta St., Morrisburg ON K0C 1X0
e-mail: Lynnecook@personainternet.com
Chief Officer(s):
Carol Goddard, President

Sir Guy Carleton Branch
PO Box 5104, 1547 Merivale Rd., Nepean ON K2C 3H4
Tel: 613-225-6377
carletonuel@hotmail.com
www.uelac.org/Carletonuel

Sir John Johnson Centennial Branch
QC
Tel: 450-293-6342
jmccaw@citenet.net
www.uelac.org/sirjohnjohnson
Chief Officer(s):
Rod Riordon, President
Rod@Riordon.ca

Thompson/Okanagan Branch
PO Box 1441, Vernon BC V1T 6N7
Tel: 250-549-3646
sally_harrison@telus.net
www.members.shaw.ca/thompsonokanagan/index.htm
Chief Officer(s):
Sally Harrison, President
sally_harrison@telus.net

Toronto Branch
#300, 40 Scollard St., Toronto ON M5R 3S1
Tel: 416-489-1783; *Fax:* 416-489-3664
torontouel@bellnet.ca
www.ueltoronto.ca
Chief Officer(s):
Karen Windover, President

Vancouver Branch
#616-9210 Salish Court, Burnaby BC V3J 7C4
e-mail: vancouver@uelac.org
www.uelac.org/Vancouver
Chief Officer(s):
Carl Stymiest, President

Victoria Branch
BC
e-mail: haroldmorgan@shaw.ca
www.uelac.org/uelvictoria
Chief Officer(s):
Harold Morgan, Privacy Offier, 250-248-2066

United Food & Commercial Workers Canada (UFCW CANADA)

#300, 61 International Blvd., Toronto ON M9W 6K4
Tel: 416-675-1104; *Fax:* 416-675-6919
ufcw@ufcw.ca
www.ufcw.ca
www.facebook.com/ufcwcanada
twitter.com/ufcwcanada
www.youtube.com/user/UFCWCanada
Overview: A large national organization
Mission: One of Canada's largest private sector unions
Chief Officer(s):
Paul Meinema, National President
pmeinema@ufcw.ca
Membership: 197,000 + 143 locals
Awards:
- Beggs-Dowling-Mathieu Scholarships Program (Scholarship)
- Migrant Workers Scholarships Program (Scholarship)

Atlantic Canada
220, 1550 Bedford Hwy., Bedford NS B4A 1E6
Tel: 902-832-1935; *Fax:* 902-832-0186
ufcw@eastlink.ca
Chief Officer(s):
Mark Dobson, Regional Director, Eastern Provinces

Quebec Council
#720, 1100, boul Crémazie Est, Montréal QC H2P 2X2
Tel: 514-326-8822; *Fax:* 514-326-1226
Chief Officer(s):
Anouk Collet, Regional Director, Québec
anouk.collet@tuac.ca

Western Canada
PO Box 21056, Stn. Westwood Plateau, Coquitlam BC V3E 3P9
Tel: 604-269-3511; *Fax:* 604-909-1701
Chief Officer(s):
Nancy Quiring, Regional Director, Western Provinces
nancy.quiring@ufcw.ca

United Generations Ontario (UGO) / Générations Unies Ontario

#604B, 1185 Eglinton Ave. East, Toronto ON M3C 3C6
Tel: 416-426-7115; *Fax:* 416-426-7388
info@intergenugo.org
Overview: A small provincial charitable organization founded in 1993
Mission: To promote programs that bring young & old together in a spirit of cooperation, mutual support, shared affection & regard; to empower people to take a constructive part in the life of their own communities & to create a vital volunteer exchange in caring & sharing
Member of: Ontario Community Support Association; Canadian Centre for Philanthropy; Vanier Institute of the Family
Affliation(s): Ontario Gerontological Association; Older Adults Association of Ontario; BC Council for Families; Canadian Health Network
Finances: *Funding Sources:* Membership dues; Canadian Living Foundation; Trillium; corporate sponsors
Membership: *Member Profile:* Interest &/or active in intergenerational activities
Activities: *Speaker Service:* Yes

United Independent Contractors' Group of Ontario *See* Merit OpenShop Contractors Association of Ontario

United Jewish Peoples' Order (UJPO)

The Winchevsky Centre, 585 Cranbrooke Ave., Toronto ON M6A 2X9
Tel: 416-789-5502; *Fax:* 416-789-5981
Other Communication: www.winchevskycentre.org
info@winchevskycentre.org
www.ujpo.org
www.facebook.com/WinchevskyCtr
Overview: A small local organization founded in 1926
Mission: To develop a secular approach to social & cultural matters, the Jewish heritage, & the Yiddish language; To promote peace & social justice in Canada & the world; To support universal human rights & gender & ethnic equality
Affliation(s): Canadian Peace Alliance; Congress of Secular Jewish Organizations; North American Federation of Secular Humanistic Jews; International Institute of Secular Humanistic Jews
Chief Officer(s):
Maxine Hermolin, Executive Director
mhermolin@winchevskycentre.org
Activities: Sponsoring secular Jewish education & cultural groups
Publications:
- UJPO [United Jewish People's Order] News

Type: Newsletter; *Editor:* UJPO National Board of Directors
Profile: Regional reports, articles, & upcoming events

United Macedonians Organization of Canada (UMOC)

PO Box 66517, 686 McCowan Rd., Toronto ON M1J 3N8
Tel: 416-490-0181; *Fax:* 416-490-0398
info@unitedmacedonians.org
www.unitedmacedonians.org
Overview: A medium-sized national organization founded in 1959
Mission: Uniting Canadians of Macedonian origin with the purpose of maintaining the Macedonian heritage & preserving it by passing it to the next generation
Member of: Canadian Ethnocultural Council; Canadian Cultural Council
Chief Officer(s):
Dragi Stojkovski, President
Borche Kulevski, Secretary
Finances: *Annual Operating Budget:* Less than $50,000
Membership: 5,000; *Fees:* $20
Activities: Delchef Night, Feb.; *Awareness Events:* Ilinden Picnic (National Day), Aug.; *Library:* Canadian Macedonian Historical Society Library
Awards:
- Student Scholarship (Award)

United Mennonite Educational Institute (UMEI)

614 Mersea Rd. 6, Leamington ON N8H 3V8
Tel: 519-326-7448; *Fax:* 519-326-0278
umei@mnsi.net
www.umei.on.ca
Overview: A medium-sized national organization founded in 1945
Mission: To provide a strong academic education in a Christian environment
Member of: Canadian Association of Mennonite Schools (CAMS)
Affliation(s): Mennonite Secondary Education Council
Chief Officer(s):
Sonya Bedal, Principal
Finances: *Annual Operating Budget:* $500,000-$1.5 Million
Staff Member(s): 10

United Nations Association in Canada (UNAC) / Association canadienne pour les Nations Unies (ACNU)

#300, 309 Cooper St., Ottawa ON K2P 0G5
Tel: 613-232-5751; *Fax:* 613-563-2455
info@unac.org
www.unac.org
www.linkedin.com/company/1177974?trk=prof-exp-company-name
twitter.com/UNACanada
Flickr: www.flickr.com/photos/106512533@N07
Also Known As: UNA - Canada
Overview: A medium-sized international charitable organization founded in 1946
Mission: To study international problems & Canada's relationship to them as a member of the UN & its related agencies; To foster mutual understanding, goodwill & cooperation between the people of Canada & those of other countries, with the object of promoting peace & justice; To study possible courses of action in the field of international affairs; To work for support by the government & the people of Canada for desirable policies; To provide information on & stimulate public interest in the UN & its various agencies which have been established for direct or indirect promotion of international order, justice & security; To foster national commitment to principles of multilateralism & international cooperation
Affliation(s): World Federation of United Nations Associations
Chief Officer(s):
Kathryn White, Executive Director
Finances: *Annual Operating Budget:* $500,000-$1.5 Million; *Funding Sources:* Individual donations; corporate support; government grants
Staff Member(s): 12; 200 volunteer(s)
Membership: 100 corporate + 12,000 individual; *Fees:* Suggested minimum of $25
Activities: Projects include: Healthy Children, Healthy Communities; Model United Nations; United Nations Professional Placement Programme; *Awareness Events:* UN Day, Oct. 24; Canadian International Model United Nations Conference; *Library:* Resource Centre; Open to public
Awards:
- Pearson Peace Medal (Award)

Awarded to a Canadian who has contributed significantly to humanitarian causes

Calgary
PO Box 6593, Stn. D, Calgary AB T2Z 2M3
e-mail: unac.calgary@gmail.com
calgary.unac.org
www.facebook.com/group.php?gid=7390276814&ref=ts
Chief Officer(s):
Michael Gretton, President

Edmonton
c/o C. Mensah, Grant MacEwan College, 10700 - 104 Ave., Edmonton AB T5J 4S2
Tel: 780-432-6531; *Fax:* 780-497-5308
edmonton@unac.org
www.edmonton.unac.org
www.facebook.com/unacedmonton
twitter.com/unacanadayeg

Greater Montréal Office
a/s #J-4350, Université du Québec à Montréal, CP 8888, Succ. Centre-Ville, Montréal QC H3C 3P8
Tél: 514-987-8743; *Téléc:* 514-987-0249
acnu@uqam.ca
Chief Officer(s):
Michèle Bertrand, Présidente

Hamilton
173 Dundurn St. South, Hamilton ON L8P 4K5
Tel: 905-527-0470
info@hamilton.unac.org
hamilton.unac.org
Chief Officer(s):
Brian Reid, President

Kootenay Region
PO Box 760, Grand Forks BC V0H 1H0
Tel: 250-442-8252; *Fax:* 250-442-3433

National Capital Region
#300, 309 Cooper St., Ottawa ON K2P 0G5
Tel: 613-232-5751; *Fax:* 613-563-2455
info@ncrb.unac.org
ncrb.unac.org

Québec Office
c/o Institut Québécois des Hautes Études Internationales (IQHEI), #5458, Pavillon Charles-de-Koninck, Université Laval, Québec QC G1K 7P4
infos@acnu-quebec.org
Chief Officer(s):
Daniel Atangana, Président

Quinte & District
221 Charles St., Belleville ON K8N 3M3
Tel: 613-966-3928; *Fax:* 613-966-3928
globalperspectives@cogeco.ca
Chief Officer(s):
Aruna Alexander, President

Saguenay/Lac-St-Jean
a/s UQAC, Département des sciences humaines, 555, boul de l'Université, Chicoutimi QC G7H 2B1
Tél: 418-545-5011; *Téléc:* 418-545-5012
jules_dufour@uqac.uquebec.ca
Chief Officer(s):
Jules Dufour, Président

St. John's
c/o Ian McMaster, 3 Ross Rd., Paradise NL A1A 1M2
e-mail: unacnl@yahoo.ca
Chief Officer(s):
Lesley Herridge, Contact

Saskatoon
c/o John Parry, President, Saskatoon SK
Tel: 306-664-3698
johnparry@shaw.ca

Toronto Office
PO Box 26008, 2345 Yonge St., Toronto ON M4P 3E0
Tel: 416-467-4672
info@to.unac.org
to.unac.org
Chief Officer(s):
Ali Khachan, President, 416-467-4672

Vancouver Office
2305-867 Hamilton St., Vancouver BC V6B 6B7
Tel: 604-732-0448; *Fax:* 604-736-8963
unacvancouver@gmail.com
edmonton.unac.org
Chief Officer(s):
Chrystal Coleman, President
cc@chrystalcoleman.com

Victoria Office
c/o France Gilbert, #200, 535 Yates St., Victoria BC V8W 2Z6
Tel: 250-388-7350
unac.victoria@gmail.com
Chief Officer(s):
Nora Curry, Contact

Winnipeg Office
c/o Univ. of Winnipeg Library, 515 Portage Ave., Winnipeg MB R3B 2E9
Tel: 204-586-0173; *Fax:* 204-783-8910
unacwinnipeg@gmail.com
www.unacwinnipeg.ca

United Nations Educational, Scientific & Cultural Organization: Canadian Commission for UNESCO
PO Box 1047, 150 Elgin St., Ottawa ON K1P 5V8
Tel: 613-566-4414; *Fax:* 613-566-4405
Toll-Free: 800-263-5588
www.unesco.ca
Overview: A medium-sized international organization
Mission: To act as a forum for governments & civil society, & to mobilize the participation of Canadian organizations & committed individuals in UNESCO's mandated areas: education, natural & social sciences, culture & communication & information
Chief Officer(s):
Louise Filiatrault, Secretary General
Staff Member(s): 13
Membership: 330; *Member Profile:* Government department, institutions & individuals; *Committees:* Membership

United Nations Entity for Gender Equality & the Empowerment of Women - National Committee Canada
#502, 331 Cooper St., Ottawa ON K2P 0G5
Tel: 613-234-8252
info@unwomencanada.org
www.unwomencanada.org
www.facebook.com/unwomencanada
twitter.com/unwomencanada
Overview: A medium-sized international organization
Mission: To advance the status of women worldwide by working to make sure women have more rights, reducing AIDS & HIV transmission, ending violence against women& improving gender equality
Chief Officer(s):
Almas Jiwani, President
Membership: *Fees:* $25 student; $50 individual; $1000 corporate; *Committees:* Pubic Relations; Social Media; Fundraising & Outreach; Newsletter; Communications; Executive Advisory

United Nations Environment Programme - Multilateral Fund for the Implementation of the Montréal Protocol
#4100, 1000, de la Gauchetière ouest, Montréal QC H3B 4W5
Tel: 514-282-1122; *Fax:* 514-282-0068
secretariat@unmfs.org
www.multilateralfund.org
Overview: A medium-sized international organization
Mission: To assist developing countries party to the Montréal Protocol whose annual per capita consumption & production of Ozone Depleting Substances (ODS) is less than 0.3 Kg to comply with the control measures of the Protocol
Chief Officer(s):
Eduardo Ganem, Chief Officer

United Nations Environment Programme - Secretariat of the Convention on Biological Diversity
#800, 413, rue St-Jacques, Montréal QC H2Y 1N9
Tel: 514-288-2220; *Fax:* 514-288-6588
secretariat@biodiv.org
www.cbd.int
www.facebook.com/UNBiodiversity
twitter.com/cbdnews
www.youtube.com/user/chmcbd
Overview: A medium-sized international organization
Mission: The Convention on Biological Diversity was inspired by the world community's growing commitment to sustainable development. It represents a dramatic step forward in the conservation of biological diversity, the sustainable use of its components, and the fair and equitable sharing of benefits arising from the use of genetic resources.
Chief Officer(s):
Braulio Ferreira de Souza Dias, Executive Secretary, 514-287-7002
Braulio.Dias@cbd.int

United Nations High Commissioner for Refugees
#401, 280 Albert St., Ottawa ON K1P 5G8
Fax: 613-230-1855
Toll-Free: 877-232-0909
withyou@unhcr.ch
www.unhcr.ca
www.facebook.com/UNHCRCanada
twitter.com/UNHCRCanada
www.youtube.com/user/storytellingunhcr
Also Known As: UNHCR Canada
Overview: A medium-sized international organization
Mission: To monitor Canada's intake & treatment refugees; to create awareness about the status of refugees worldwide

United Native Friendship Centre (UNFC)
PO Box 752, Fort Frances ON P9A 3N1
Tel: 807-274-8542; *Fax:* 807-274-4110
Toll-Free: 877-496-9034
inquiry@unfc.org
www.unfc.org
Overview: A small local charitable organization founded in 1973
Mission: To enhance the lives of Native & non-Native peoples; to serve aboriginal people with special services in the fields of social, educational, & cultural development while at the same time building a bridge of understanding between Native & non-Native people
Member of: Ontario Federation of Indian Friendship Centres
Chief Officer(s):
Sheila McMahon, Executive Director
sheilamcmahon@vianet.ca
Staff Member(s): 24
Membership: *Fees:* $5 individual; $10 family
Activities: Operates Family Resource Centre/Youth Centre: 807/274-0561; *Library*
Awards:
• Claude Bruyere Memorial Bursary (Award)
For local Aboriginal high school student

Circle of Life Centre
616 Mowat Ave., Fort Frances ON P9A 3N1
Tel: 807-274-3762; *Fax:* 807-274-4067

United Native Nations Society
#6, 534 Cedar St., Campbell River BC V9W 2V6
Tel: 250-287-9249
administration@unitednativenation510.com
www.unitednativenation510.com
Overview: A small local organization overseen by Congress of Aboriginal Peoples
Chief Officer(s):
Bill Williams, Contact

United Nurses of Alberta (UNA) / Infirmières unies de l'Alberta
700-11150 Jasper Ave., Edmonton AB T5K 0L1
Tel: 780-425-1025; *Fax:* 780-426-2093
Toll-Free: 800-252-9394
nurses@una.ab.ca
www.una.ab.ca
www.facebook.com/UnitedNurses
twitter.com/unitednurses
www.youtube.com/user/UnitedNursesAlberta
Previous Name: Provincial Staff Nurses Committee
Overview: A large provincial organization founded in 1977
Mission: To advance the social, economic & general welfare of nurses & other allied personnel
Member of: Canadian Labour Congress; Alberta Federation of Labour; Canadian Federation of Nurses Unions; Alberta District Labour Councils
Chief Officer(s):
Heather Smith, President
Finances: *Annual Operating Budget:* Greater than $5 Million; *Funding Sources:* Membership dues
Staff Member(s): 35
Membership: 24,000 + 170 locals; *Fees:* 1.3% of gross salary; *Committees:* Communications; Education; Finance; Legislative; Occupational Health & Safety; Pensions; Political Action; Steering
Activities: *Library*
Awards:
• UNA Nursing Education Scholarship (Scholarship)
Eligibility: Applicants must be related to a UNA member in good standing, complete an application form and write a short essay responding to the question "Over the past 35 years, how has the United Nurses of Alberta made a difference in the work lives of Alberta Nurses?"*Deadline:* October 15 *Amount:* $750 (11); $1,000 (1)

Southern Alberta Regional Office
#300, 1422 Kensington Rd. NW, Calgary AB T2N 3P9
Tel: 403-237-2377; *Fax:* 403-263-2908
Toll-Free: 800-661-1802
calgaryoffice@una.ab.ca
www.una.ab.ca

United Ostomy Association of Canada *See* Ostomy Canada Society

United Party of Canada
119 Oakcrest Dr., Keswick ON L4P 3J2
Tel: 905-476-0000
www.unitedpartyofcanada.com
Overview: A small national organization
Chief Officer(s):
Robert (Bob) Kesic, Leader

United Senior Citizens of Ontario Inc. (USCO)
3033 Lakeshore Blvd. West, Toronto ON M8V 1K5
Tel: 416-252-2021; *Fax:* 416-252-5770
Toll-Free: 888-320-2222
office@uscont.ca
www.uscont.ca
Overview: A large provincial organization founded in 1961
Mission: To further the interests & promote the welfare of the senior population in Ontario; To provide for an exchange of ideas for member groups; To assist in the formation of senior citizens clubs
Chief Officer(s):
Bernard Jordan, President
Finances: *Annual Operating Budget:* $50,000-$100,000; *Funding Sources:* Membership fees
Staff Member(s): 3; 20 volunteer(s)
Membership: 300,000 individual + 1,000 clubs; *Fees:* $20 individual; $25 couple; $2 per club member
Publications:
• The Voice
Type: Newsletter

United Services Institute of New Brunswick *See* Royal United Services Institute of New Brunswick

United Steelworkers Local 1-424
#100, 1777 - 3rd Ave., Prince George BC V2L 3G7
Tel: 250-563-7771; *Fax:* 250-563-0274
Toll-Free: 800-565-3641
usw1-424@telus.net
www.steelworkers1-424.ca
Also Known As: United Steelworkers Local 1-424
Previous Name: Northern Interior Wood Workers Association
Merged from: International Woodworkers of America (Canada); United Steelworkers of America
Overview: A small local organization founded in 1937
Chief Officer(s):
Frank Everitt, President
frank@usw1-424.ca
Brian O'Rourke, Financial Secretary
brian@usw1-424.ca

United Synagogue of Conservative Judaism, Canadian Region (USCJ)
#508, 1000 Finch Ave. West, Toronto ON M3J 2V5
Tel: 416-667-1717; *Fax:* 416-667-1881
Toll-Free: 800-417-1332
canadian@uscj.org
Overview: A medium-sized provincial organization
Chief Officer(s):
Irit Printz, Youth Director, 647-931-4833
printz@uscj.org
David Schild, Office Manager
canadian@uscj.org

United Synagogue Youth (USY)
1700 Bathurst St., Toronto ON M5P 3K3
Tel: 416-667-1717; *Fax:* 416-667-1881
ecrusy@uscj.org
www.ecrusy.org
Also Known As: ECRUSY
Overview: A medium-sized international organization
Mission: To offer opportunities to Jewish Youth to continue to strengthen their identification with Judaism and with the synagogue; To develop a programme based on personality development, needs, and interests of the Jewish teenager.
Chief Officer(s):
Max Marmer, Director, Youth Activities
marmer@uscj.org
Staff Member(s): 1

United Transportation Union (AFL-CIO/CLC) - Canada
71 Bank St., 7th Fl., Ottawa ON K1P 5N2
Tel: 613-747-7979; *Fax:* 613-747-2815
Overview: A medium-sized national organization
Member of: United Transportation Union (AFL-CIO/CLC), Cleveland USA

United Ukrainian Charitable Trust
2445 Bloor St. West, Toronto ON M6S 1P7
Tel: 416-763-4982; *Fax:* 416-763-3997
toradmin@ucss.info
Overview: A small local charitable organization
Mission: To provide financial assistance to Ukrainian institutions involved in charitable work & in cultural & educational programming in the Toronto area
Chief Officer(s):
Maria Tarnavskyj, President, Ukrainian Canadian Social Services (Toronto)

United Utility Workers' Association (UUWA)
1207 - 20 Ave. NW, Calgary AB T2M 1G2
Tel: 403-284-4521; *Fax:* 403-282-1598
info@uuwac.org
www.uuwac.org
Previous Name: Calgary Power Employees Association; TransAlta Employees' Association
Overview: A medium-sized national organization founded in 1943
Mission: To represent employees in the energy secotr
Chief Officer(s):
Chuck Pozzo, Chief Executive Officer
Grace Thostenson, Manager, Business
Membership: 1,400; *Member Profile:* Employees in the energy sector, such as meter readers, power line technicians, designers, & administrators
Activities: Offering training courses

United Way Central & Northern Vancouver Island
3156 Barons Rd., Nanaimo BC V9T 4B5
Tel: 250-729-7400; *Fax:* 250-729-8084
info@uwcnvi.ca
www.uwcnvi.ca
www.facebook.com/UWCNVI
www.twitter.com/UWCNVI
www.youtube.com/user/UnitedWayCNVI
Previous Name: United Way of Nanaimo & District
Overview: A small local charitable organization founded in 1958 overseen by United Way of Canada - Centraide Canada
Mission: To improve lives by engaging individuals & mobilizing collective action
Member of: Nanaimo & Ladysmith Chambers of Commerce
Chief Officer(s):
Signy Madden, Executive Director
signy@uwcnvi.ca
Finances: *Annual Operating Budget:* $250,000-$500,000; *Funding Sources:* Annual fundraising campaign
Staff Member(s): 3; 100 volunteer(s)
Membership: 1,000 voting members + 28 agencies
Activities: *Internships:* Yes

United Way Elgin-St. Thomas
300 South Edgeware Rd., St Thomas ON N5P 4L1
Tel: 519-631-3171; *Fax:* 519-631-9253
office@stthomasunitedway.ca
www.stthomasunitedway.ca
www.facebook.com/UnitedWayElginStThomas
Previous Name: Elgin-St.Thomas United Way Services
Overview: A small local charitable organization founded in 1957 overseen by United Way of Canada - Centraide Canada
Mission: To be a leader in improving the quality of life for all people in Elgin County.
Member of: St. Thomas & District Chamber of Commerce; Canadian Association of Gift Planners
Chief Officer(s):
George Dryburgh, President
Paul Shaffer, Executive Director
Finances: *Annual Operating Budget:* $500,000-$1.5 Million; *Funding Sources:* Annual campaign; fundraising
Staff Member(s): 3; 200 volunteer(s)
Activities: Fundraising on behalf of 23 member agencies; *Awareness Events:* Aylmer StairClimb, Nov.; Timken StairClimb for United Way, Nov.; *Speaker Service:* Yes

United Way for the City of Kawartha Lakes (UWVC)
50 Mary St. West, Lindsay ON K9V 2N6
Tel: 705-878-5081; *Fax:* 705-878-0475
office@ckl.unitedway.ca
www.ckl.unitedway.ca
www.facebook.com/UWCKL
twitter.com/unitedwayckl
Previous Name: United Way of Victoria County (UWVC)
Overview: A medium-sized local charitable organization founded in 1983 overseen by United Way of Canada - Centraide Canada
Mission: To promote the organized capacity of people & groups in Victoria County to care for each other
Chief Officer(s):
Penny Barton Dyke, Executive Director
pbartondyke@ckl.unitedway.ca
Finances: *Annual Operating Budget:* $250,000-$500,000; *Funding Sources:* Private & corporate donations; fundraising; special events
Staff Member(s): 2
Membership: 1-99
Activities: *Speaker Service:* Yes

United Way of Amherst *See* United Way of Cumberland County

United Way of Barrie/South Simcoe *See* United Way of Greater Simcoe County

United Way of Belleville & District *See* United Way of Quinte

United Way of Brandon & District Inc.
Scotia Towers, 201-1011 Rosser Ave., Brandon MB R7A 0L5
Tel: 204-571-8929; *Fax:* 204-727-8939
office@brandonuw.ca
www.brandonuw.ca
www.facebook.com/UnitedWayBrandon
Also Known As: Brandon & District United Way
Overview: A small local organization founded in 1966 overseen by United Way of Canada - Centraide Canada
Chief Officer(s):
Cynamon Mychasiw, Interim CEO
Staff Member(s): 3; 785 volunteer(s)
Activities: *Library*

United Way of Burlington & Greater Hamilton
177 Rebecca St., Hamilton ON L8R 1B9
Tel: 905-527-4543; *Fax:* 905-527-5152
uway@uwaybh.ca
www.uwaybh.ca
www.facebook.com/unitedwaybh
twitter.com/UnitedWayBH
Previous Name: United Way of Burlington, Hamilton-Wentworth
Overview: A small local charitable organization overseen by United Way of Canada - Centraide Canada
Mission: To empower a diverse community to achieve positive social development
Chief Officer(s):
Len Lifchus, CEO
llifchus@uwaybh.ca

Burlington Office
#107, 3425 Harvester Rd., Burlington ON L7N 3N1
Tel: 905-635-3138; *Fax:* 905-632-1918
uway@uwaybh.ca

United Way of Burlington, Hamilton-Wentworth *See* United Way of Burlington & Greater Hamilton

United Way of Calgary & Area
#600, 105 - 12 Ave SE, Calgary AB T2G 1A1
Tel: 403-231-6265; *Fax:* 403-355-3135
uway@calgaryunitedway.org
www.calgaryunitedway.org
www.linkedin.com/companies/united-way-of-calgary-and-area
www.facebook.com/calgaryunitedway
twitter.com/UnitedWayCgy
www.youtube.com/calgaryunitedway
Overview: A small local organization overseen by United Way of Canada - Centraide Canada
Mission: To invest in 250 programs offered by 130 agencies in Calgary, Airdrie, Cochrane, High River, Okotoks & Strathmore
Chief Officer(s):
Lucy Miller, President
Finances: *Annual Operating Budget:* Greater than $5 Million
Staff Member(s): 63; 1000 volunteer(s)
Membership: Over 50,000

United Way of Cambridge & North Dumfries
150 Main St., 2nd Fl., Cambridge ON N1R 6P9
Tel: 519-621-1030; *Fax:* 519-621-6220
www.uwcambridge.on.ca
www.facebook.com/142106829162378?ref=sgm
twitter.com/uwcambridge
Overview: A small local charitable organization founded in 1940 overseen by United Way of Canada - Centraide Canada
Mission: To enhance the quality of life in Cambridge & North Dumfries by caring for & contributing to community needs
Chief Officer(s):
Ron Dowhaniuk, Executive Director
ron@uwcambridge.on.ca
Finances: *Annual Operating Budget:* $1.5 Million-$3 Million; *Funding Sources:* Workplace campaign; corporate; individual
Staff Member(s): 10; 1200 volunteer(s)
Membership: 5,000-14,999; *Fees:* Donations
Activities: *Speaker Service:* Yes

United Way of Canada - Centraide Canada
#404, 56 Sparks St., Ottawa ON K1P 5A9
Tel: 613-236-7041; *Fax:* 613-236-3087
Toll-Free: 800-267-8221
info@unitedway.ca
www.centraide.ca
ca.linkedin.com/company/united-way-centraide-canada
www.facebook.com/UnitedWayCentraide
twitter.com/UnitedWayCanada
www.youtube.com/UnitedWayofCanada
Also Known As: Centraide Canada - United Way of Canada
Overview: A large national charitable organization
Mission: To increase the organized capacity of people to care for one another
Affliation(s): United Way International
Chief Officer(s):
Peter Doig, Chair
Al Hatton, President/CEO
Finances: *Annual Operating Budget:* $3 Million-$5 Million; *Funding Sources:* Conducts no campaign for funds; supported by fees paid by members
Staff Member(s): 22; 24 volunteer(s)

Membership: 100-499
Activities: *Library*

United Way of Cape Breton
245 Charlotte St., Sydney NS B1P 6W4
Tel: 902-562-5226; *Fax:* 902-562-5721
unitedway@ns.aliantzinc.ca
www.sydney.unitedway.ca
www.facebook.com/UnitedWayOfCapeBreton
Overview: A small local organization overseen by United Way of Canada - Centraide Canada
Chief Officer(s):
Brenda Durrah, Executive Director

United Way of Central Alberta
4811 - 48th St., Red Deer AB T4N 1S6
Tel: 403-343-3900; *Fax:* 403-309-3820
info@caunitedway.ca
www.caunitedway.ca
Overview: A small local charitable organization founded in 1965 overseen by United Way of Canada - Centraide Canada
Mission: To improve lives & build community by engaging individuals & mobilizing collective action
Chief Officer(s):
Robert J. Mitchell, Chief Executive Officer
Finances: *Annual Operating Budget:* $500,000-$1.5 Million; *Funding Sources:* Corporate & individual donations
Staff Member(s): 4; 700 volunteer(s)
Membership: 1,500; *Committees:* Campaign; Citizen Review; Marketing; Planned Giving; Board of Directors
Activities: *Speaker Service:* Yes

United Way of Chatham-Kent County
PO Box 606, 425 McNaughton Ave. West, Chatham ON N7M 5K8
Tel: 519-354-0430; *Fax:* 519-354-9511
info@uwock.ca
uwock.ca
www.facebook.com/UnitedWayofChathamKent
twitter.com/UnitedWayCK
www.youtube.com/user/UnitedWayChathamKent
Previous Name: United Way of Kent County
Overview: A small local charitable organization founded in 1948 overseen by United Way of Canada - Centraide Canada
Mission: To build the organized capacity of people to care for one another
Chief Officer(s):
William Steep, President
Karen Kirkwood-Whyte, CEO
karen@uwock.ca
Finances: *Annual Operating Budget:* $1.5 Million-$3 Million; *Funding Sources:* Corporate donations; employee payroll deductions; individual gifts; special events
Staff Member(s): 13; 200 volunteer(s)
Membership: 5,000-14,999
Activities: AGM; kick-off event; fundraising; *Speaker Service:* Yes

United Way of Cornwall & District *See* United Way of Stormont, Dundas & Glengarry

United Way of Cranbrook & Kimberley
PO Box 657, 930 Baker St., Cranbrook BC V1C 4J2
Tel: 250-426-8833; *Fax:* 250-426-5455
office@cranbrook.unitedway.ca
www.cranbrook.unitedway.ca
Overview: A small local charitable organization founded in 1969 overseen by United Way of Canada - Centraide Canada
Mission: To ensure the effective raising & allocation of charitable funds for community based social services that are in the best interest of the community
Chief Officer(s):
Donna Brady Fields, Executive Director
Finances: *Annual Operating Budget:* Less than $50,000
Staff Member(s): 1; 30 volunteer(s)
Membership: *Fees:* Donation
Activities: Hole-in-One Extravaganza; *Awareness Events:* Day of Caring

United Way of Cumberland County
PO Box 535, 43 Prince Arthur St., Lower Level, Amherst NS B4H 4A1
Tel: 902-667-2203; *Fax:* 902-667-3819
unitedway.cumberland@ns.aliantzinc.ca
amherst.unitedway.ca
Previous Name: United Way of Amherst
Overview: A small local organization overseen by United Way of Canada - Centraide Canada
Chief Officer(s):
Judi Giroux, Chair

United Way of Durham Region
345 Simcoe St. South, Oshawa ON L1H 4J2
Tel: 905-436-7377; *Fax:* 905-436-6414
mail@unitedwaydr.com
www.unitedwaydr.com
www.facebook.com/profile.php?id=100001589175198
Overview: A small local organization founded in 1940 overseen by United Way of Canada - Centraide Canada
Chief Officer(s):
Cindy Murray, Executive Director
Robert Howard, Campaign Director
Staff Member(s): 6
Activities: *Speaker Service:* Yes

Ajax Office
144 Old Kingston Rd., Ajax ON L1S 2Z9
Tel: 905-686-0606
Chief Officer(s):
Edna Klazek, Executive Director

United Way of Elrose & District Corp.
PO Box 443, Elrose SK S0L 0Z0
Tel: 306-378-2921
delhart@hotmail.com
Previous Name: Elrose & District United Appeal
Overview: A small local organization overseen by United Way of Canada - Centraide Canada
Chief Officer(s):
Jack Elliott, Chair

United Way of Estevan
PO Box 611, Estevan SK S4A 2A5
Tel: 306-634-7375
www.unitedwayofestevan.com
Overview: A small local organization founded in 1967 overseen by United Way of Canada - Centraide Canada
Chief Officer(s):
Lori Buchanan, Executive Director
executivedirector@unitedwayofestevan.com
Membership: *Committees:* Banking; Community Building; Entertainment; Facilities; Finance & Allocations; Food Services; Fundraising; History; Phones & Cameras; Public Relations; Production; Raffle; Security

United Way of Fort McMurray
The Redpoll Centre, #200, 10010 Franklin Ave., Fort McMurray AB T9H 2K6
Tel: 780-791-0077; *Fax:* 780-791-0088
redpollcentre@fmunitedway.com
fmunitedway.com
www.facebook.com/142299649181047
twitter.com/FMUnitedWay
Overview: A small local charitable organization founded in 1979 overseen by United Way of Canada - Centraide Canada
Mission: To provide effective support for social health & welfare services in the community of Fort McMurray
Chief Officer(s):
Barb Jewers, President
Trevor Sheppard, Director, Communications
communications@fmunitedway.com
Finances: *Annual Operating Budget:* $500,000-$1.5 Million; *Funding Sources:* Corporate & employee donations
Staff Member(s): 3; 850 volunteer(s)
Membership: 20 funded agencies; *Member Profile:* Registered charity; volunteer component; *Committees:* Allocations; Campaign

United Way of Greater Moncton & Southeastern New Brunswick (UWGMSENB) / Centraide de la région du Grand Moncton et du Sud-Est du NB Inc. (CGMSENB)
#T210, 22 Church St., Moncton NB E1C 0P7
Tel: 506-858-8600; *Fax:* 506-858-0584
office@moncton.unitedway.ca
www.gmsenbunitedway.ca
www.facebook.com/UnitedWayGMSENBCentraideGMSENB
twitter.com/unitedwaygmsenb
www.flickr.com/photos/unitedwaygmsenb
Previous Name: United Way/Centraide of the Moncton Region
Overview: A small local charitable organization founded in 1953 overseen by United Way of Canada - Centraide Canada
Mission: To raise funds to increase the organized capacity of people to care for one another
Chief Officer(s):
Debbie McInnis, Executive Director
dmcinnis@moncton.unitedway.ca
Finances: *Annual Operating Budget:* $100,000-$250,000
Staff Member(s): 9; 2000 volunteer(s)
Membership: 1-99

United Way of Greater Saint John Inc.
61 Union St., 2nd Fl., Saint John NB E2L 1A2
Tel: 506-658-1212; *Fax:* 506-633-7724
www.unitedwaysaintjohn.com
www.facebook.com/21724743048
www.twitter.com/SJUnitedWay
www.youtube.com/UnitedWaySJ
Overview: A small local charitable organization founded in 1958 overseen by United Way of Canada - Centraide Canada
Chief Officer(s):
Wendy MacDermott, Executive Director
wendy.unitedway@nb.aibn.com
Finances: *Annual Operating Budget:* $100,000-$250,000; *Funding Sources:* Corporate; individual donations
Staff Member(s): 4; 2000 volunteer(s)
Membership: 400 corporate + 25 institutional + 30,000 individual; *Fees:* Schedule available; *Committees:* Agency Relations Allocations; Public Relations/Marketing; Strategic Planning; Labour
Activities: *Speaker Service:* Yes

United Way of Greater Simcoe County
1110 Hwy. 26, Midhurst ON L0L 1X0
Tel: 705-726-2301; *Fax:* 705-726-4897
info@UnitedWayGSC.ca
www.unitedwaygsc.ca
www.linkedin.com/pub/united-way-of-greater-simcoe-county/20/44/6a3
www.facebook.com/UnitedWayofGreaterSimcoeCounty?ref=ts&sk=wall
twitter.com/greatersimcoeco
www.youtube.com/user/UnitedWaySimcoeCty
Previous Name: United Way of Barrie/South Simcoe
Overview: A small local charitable organization founded in 1960 overseen by United Way of Canada - Centraide Canada
Mission: United Way of Greater Simcoe County has been making a difference in our community for over 47 years by assessing local needs and distributing resources to help those most in need.
Member of: Barrie Chamber of Commerce
Chief Officer(s):
Alison Pickard, CEO, 705-726-2301 Ext. 2026
apickard@unitedwaygsc.ca
Finances: *Annual Operating Budget:* $500,000-$1.5 Million; *Funding Sources:* Community
Staff Member(s): 5; 400 volunteer(s)
Membership: 21 agencies; *Committees:* Allocations; Communications; Executive; Campaign Cabinet
Activities: Food for Thought; Simcoe County Alliance to End Homelessness; Partners for Success by Six; 211 Information; Training & Consulting Services; *Internships:* Yes; *Speaker Service:* Yes; *Library* by appointment

United Way of Guelph, Wellington & Dufferin
85 Westmount Rd., Guelph ON N1H 5J2
Tel: 519-821-0571; *Fax:* 519-821-7847
info@unitedwayguelph.com
www.unitedwayguelph.com
www.facebook.com/unitedwayguelph
twitter.com/uwguelph
Previous Name: Guelph & Wellington United Way Social Planning Council
Overview: A small local charitable organization founded in 1945 overseen by United Way of Canada - Centraide Canada
Chief Officer(s):
Ken Dardano, Executive Director
ken@unitedwayguelph.com
Staff Member(s): 9; 750 volunteer(s)
Activities: *Library* Open to public

United Way of Haldimand-Norfolk
45 Kent St. North, Simcoe ON N3Y 3L5
Tel: 519-426-5660; *Fax:* 519-426-0017
Toll-Free: 866-792-7394
uw@unitedwayhn.on.ca
www.unitedwayhn.on.ca
www.facebook.com/UnitedWayOfHaldimandAndNorfolk?ref=ts&fref=ts
twitter.com/UWayHaldimand
Previous Name: Norfolk Community Chest

Overview: A small local charitable organization founded in 1946 overseen by United Way of Canada - Centraide Canada
Mission: To improve people's lives & to strengthen the community
Chief Officer(s):
Evelyn Nobbs, Executive Director
Finances: *Annual Operating Budget:* $100,000-$250,000
Staff Member(s): 2; 500 volunteer(s)
Membership: 1,000-4,999; *Committees:* Campaign Planning; Administration; Allocations
Activities: Amazing Race, Aug.; Mini Putt Marathon, Sept.; *Speaker Service:* Yes

United Way of Halifax Region
Royal Bank Bldg., 46 Portland St., 7th Fl.., Dartmouth NS B2Y 1H4
Tel: 902-422-1501; *Fax:* 902-423-6837
info@unitedwayhalifax.ca
www.unitedwayhalifax.ca
www.facebook.com/UnitedWayHalifaxRegion
twitter.com/UWHalifax
Previous Name: Metro United Way (Halifax-Dartmouth)
Overview: A medium-sized local charitable organization founded in 1924 overseen by United Way of Canada - Centraide Canada
Mission: To strengthen neighbourhoods & communities by providing programs & services that link people & resources, encourage participation & increase giving
Chief Officer(s):
Catherine J. Woodman, President/CEO
cjwoodman@unitedwayhalifax.ca

United Way of Halton Hills
PO Box 286, Georgetown ON L7G 4Y5
Tel: 905-877-3066; *Fax:* 905-877-3067
office@unitedwayofhaltonhills.ca
www.unitedwayofhaltonhills.ca
Overview: A small local charitable organization founded in 1986 overseen by United Way of Canada - Centraide Canada
Mission: To provide leadership in the raising & responsible allocation of funds to meet human needs & to improve social conditions in a caring community
Chief Officer(s):
Janet Foster, Executive Director
Finances: *Annual Operating Budget:* Less than $50,000
Staff Member(s): 1; 300 volunteer(s)
Membership: 1-99
Activities: 18 member agencies

United Way of Kamloops & Region *See* Thompson, Nicola, Cariboo United Way

United Way of Kent County *See* United Way of Chatham-Kent County

United Way of Kingston, Frontenac, Lennox & Addington
417 Bagot St., Kingston ON K7K 3C1
Tel: 613-542-2674; *Fax:* 613-542-1379
uway@unitedwaykfla.ca
www.unitedwaykfla.ca
www.facebook.com/unitedwaykfla
twitter.com/unitedwaykfla
www.youtube.com/unitedwaykfla
Overview: A small local charitable organization overseen by United Way of Canada - Centraide Canada
Mission: To strengthen & support the organized capacity of our diverse community to care for one another
Chief Officer(s):
Bhavana Varma, President & CEO
bvarma@unitedwaykfla.ca
Finances: *Annual Operating Budget:* $100,000-$250,000; *Funding Sources:* Annual campaign; endowment fund interest
Staff Member(s): 6; 1000 volunteer(s)
Membership: 1-99; *Fees:* Donation
Activities: Campaign kick-off; Fare for Friends; Country 96, 36-hour Radiothon; *Speaker Service:* Yes

United Way of Kitchener-Waterloo & Area
Marsland Centre, #801, 20 Erb St. West, Waterloo ON N2L 1T2
Tel: 519-888-6100; *Fax:* 519-888-7737
info@uwaykw.org
www.uwaykw.org
www.facebook.com/uwaykw
twitter.com/UnitedWayKW
www.youtube.com/user/UwayKW
Overview: A small local charitable organization founded in 1941 overseen by United Way of Canada - Centraide Canada
Mission: Through collaboration, build on our community's resources & strengthen our capacity to improve the quality of life for all
Member of: Kitchener-Waterloo Chamber of Commerce
Chief Officer(s):
Daniela Seskar-Hencic, Board Chair
Jan Varner, CEO
jvarner@uwaykw.org
Finances: *Annual Operating Budget:* $3 Million-$5 Million; *Funding Sources:* Donations
Staff Member(s): 12; 3000 volunteer(s)
Membership: 25,000+; *Fees:* $10 donation; *Member Profile:* An individual who makes a financial donation of $10 or more; *Committees:* Campaign; Allocations; Admissions; Planned Giving; Finance/Human Resources; Nominating; Policy Development & Governance
Activities: *Internships:* Yes; *Speaker Service:* Yes

United Way of Lanark County
15 Bates Dr., Carleton Place ON K7C 4J8
Tel: 613-253-9074; *Fax:* 888-249-9075
www.lanarkunitedway.com
www.linkedin.com/company/united-way-of-lanark-county
www.facebook.com/pages/United-Way-Lanark-County/124650764256245
twitter.com/UWLanarkCounty
www.youtube.com/UnitedWayofCanada
Overview: A small local organization overseen by United Way of Canada - Centraide Canada
Chief Officer(s):
Fraser Scantlebury, Executive Director
fscantlebury@lanarkunitedway.com
Staff Member(s): 3

United Way of Leeds & Grenville
PO Box 576, 42 George St., Brockville ON K6V 5V7
Tel: 613-342-8889; *Fax:* 613-342-8850
www.uwlg.org
www.facebook.com/pages/United-Way-Leeds-Grenville/132810080337
www.youtube.com/user/UnitedWayLeedsGrenv
Overview: A small local licensing charitable organization founded in 1957 overseen by United Way of Canada - Centraide Canada
Chief Officer(s):
Judi Baril, Executive Director
judi.baril@uwlg.org
Finances: *Annual Operating Budget:* $500,000-$1.5 Million
Staff Member(s): 2
Membership: 27; *Committees:* Allocations; Administrative; Long Range Planning; Policy & Procedures; Sub Allocation; Marketing & Publicity
Activities: *Speaker Service:* Yes; *Library* Open to public

United Way of Lethbridge & South Western Alberta
1277 - 3 Ave. South, Lethbridge AB T1J 0K3
Tel: 403-327-1700; *Fax:* 403-317-7940
uwaysw@telusplanet.net
www.lethbridgeunitedway.ca
Overview: A small local charitable organization overseen by United Way of Canada - Centraide Canada
Mission: To build a better community by organizing the capacity of people to care for one another
Chief Officer(s):
Jeff McLarty, Executive Director
jmclarty@lethbridgeunitedway.ca
Finances: *Annual Operating Budget:* $100,000-$250,000; *Funding Sources:* Campaigns & special events
Staff Member(s): 2; 140 volunteer(s)
Membership: 3,000; *Fees:* $1; *Committees:* Budget Allocation; Nominating; Special Events; Community Development; Campaign

United Way of London & Middlesex
409 King St., London ON N6B 1S5
Tel: 519-438-1721; *Fax:* 519-438-9938
uwl@uwlondon.on.ca
www.uwlondon.on.ca
www.facebook.com/unitedwaylm
twitter.com/unitedwaylm
Overview: A small local charitable organization founded in 1965 overseen by United Way of Canada - Centraide Canada
Mission: To exercise leadership in coordinating people & organizations to assist those in need in our community
Chief Officer(s):
Andrew Lockie, CEO
alockie@uwlondon.on.ca
Finances: *Annual Operating Budget:* $3 Million-$5 Million
Staff Member(s): 15; 3000 volunteer(s)
Membership: 985 corporate + 43,966 individual; *Fees:* $10 minimum donation; *Committees:* Community Services; Finance; Resource Development; Nominations; External Review; Executive
Activities: Annual fundraising campaign; *Speaker Service:* Yes

United Way of Medicine Hat, Redcliff & District *See* United Way of South Eastern Alberta

United Way of Milton
PO Box 212, 1 Chris Hadfield Way, Milton ON L9T 4N9
Tel: 905-875-2550; *Fax:* 905-875-2402
office@miltonunitedway.ca
www.miltonunitedway.ca
www.linkedin.com/groups?gid=2558626
www.facebook.com/pages/United-Way-of-Milton/147869698556418
twitter.com/unitedwaymilton
www.youtube.com/unitedwaymilton
Overview: A small local charitable organization founded in 1982 overseen by United Way of Canada - Centraide Canada
Mission: To act as a voluntary fundraising organization to serve the people of the Milton area, reaching out for & with the recognized charitable agencies to ensure human services that enhance the quality of life in our community
Chief Officer(s):
Kate Williamson, CEO
kwilliamson@miltonunitedway.ca
Staff Member(s): 2; 150 volunteer(s)

United Way of Morden & District Inc.
114 Nelson St., Morden MB R6M 1S2
Tel: 204-822-6992
mordendistrictuw@gmail.com
Overview: A small local organization overseen by United Way of Canada - Centraide Canada
Mission: To serve as an umbrella group representing 17 charitable agencies in Morden & perform only one community-wide canvassing campaign on their behalf
Chief Officer(s):
Cindy Kolwalski, Chair
Finances: *Annual Operating Budget:* Less than $50,000; *Funding Sources:* Manitoba lotteries

United Way of Nanaimo & District *See* United Way Central & Northern Vancouver Island

United Way of Niagara Falls & Greater Fort Erie
MacBain Community Ctr., 7150 Montrose Rd., Niagara Falls ON L2H 3N3
Tel: 905-354-9342; *Fax:* 905-354-2717
unitedw@vaxxine.com
www.unitedwayniagara.org
www.facebook.com/UnitedWayNFGFE
Overview: A small local organization founded in 1942 overseen by United Way of Canada - Centraide Canada
Chief Officer(s):
Carol Stewart-Kirkby, Executive Director
carolsk@vaxxine.com
Staff Member(s): 3; 250 volunteer(s)

United Way of North Okanagan Columbia Shuswap
3304 - 30th Ave., Vernon BC V1T 2C8
Tel: 250-549-1346; *Fax:* 250-549-1357
Toll-Free: 866-448-3489
unitedwaynocs@shaw.ca
www.unitedwaynocs.com
www.facebook.com/226411234037024
twitter.com/unitedwaynocs
Previous Name: North Okanagan United Way
Overview: A small local charitable organization founded in 1961 overseen by United Way of Canada - Centraide Canada
Mission: To promote a healthy, caring inclusive community; To strenghten our community's capacity to address social issues
Member of: Vernon Chamber of Commerce
Chief Officer(s):
Linda Yule, Executive Director
Finances: *Funding Sources:* Donations; fundraising; payroll deductions; special events

United Way of Oakville (UWO)
#200, 466 Speers Rd., Oakville ON L6K 3W9
Tel: 905-845-5571; *Fax:* 905-845-0166
info@uwoakville.org

www.uwoakville.org
www.linkedin.com/company/united-way-oakville
www.facebook.com/UnitedWayOakville
twitter.com/uwoakville
www.youtube.com/user/UnitedWayofOakville
Overview: A medium-sized local charitable organization founded in 1955 overseen by United Way of Canada - Centraide Canada
Mission: To bring people & resources together to strengthen the Oakville community
Chief Officer(s):
Brad Park, CEO
brad@uwoakville.org
John Armstrong, Chair
Finances: *Annual Operating Budget:* $3 Million-$5 Million; *Funding Sources:* Fundraising Campaign; leadership giving; sponsorship
Staff Member(s): 16; 200 volunteer(s)
Membership: *Committees:* Finance & Audit; Human Resources; Governance; Campaign Cabinet
Activities: Campaign Kick-Off; Annual Bathtub Race; Golf Tournament; Day of Caring; *Internships:* Yes; *Speaker Service:* Yes

United Way of Oxford
#5, 65 Springbank Ave. North, Woodstock ON N4S 8V8
Tel: 519-539-3851; *Fax:* 519-539-3209
Toll-Free: 877-280-1391
info@unitedwayoxford.ca
www.unitedwayoxford.ca
www.facebook.com/pages/United-Way-of-Oxford/36680758990
twitter.com/UnitedWayOxford
www.youtube.com/watch?v=txDpzdNm0Jk
Overview: A small local organization overseen by United Way of Canada - Centraide Canada
Mission: To build the organized capacity of the community to care for one another
Member of: United Way of Ontario
Chief Officer(s):
Kelly Gilson, Executive Director
kelly@unitedwayoxford.ca
Finances: *Annual Operating Budget:* $500,000-$1.5 Million
Staff Member(s): 4; 200 volunteer(s)
Membership: *Fees:* Donation
Activities: Fundraising; fund distribution

United Way of Peel Region
PO Box 58, #408, 90 Burnhamthorpe Rd. West, Mississauga ON L5B 3C3
Tel: 905-602-3650; *Fax:* 905-602-3651; *TTY:* 905-602-3653
www.unitedwaypeel.org
www.linkedin.com/company/657177
www.facebook.com/unitedwaypeel
twitter.com/Unitedwaypeel
www.youtube.com/user/unitedwaypeel
Overview: A large local charitable organization founded in 1967 overseen by United Way of Canada - Centraide Canada
Mission: United Way of Peel Region was established in 1967 and serves the communities of Mississauga, Brampton and Caledon, improving social conditions so that everyone can thrive. United Way provides a strong voice for social change that strengthens communities and improves lives.
Chief Officer(s):
Shelley White, President/ CEO
swhite@unitedwaypeel.org
Shirley Crocker, Vice President, Finance & Administration
scrocker@unitedwaypeel.org
Doris Mohrhardt, Vice President, Communications & Marketing
dmohrhardt@unitedwaypeel.org
Anita Stellinga, Vice President, Community Investment
astellinga@unitedwaypeel.org
Finances: *Annual Operating Budget:* $3 Million-$5 Million; *Funding Sources:* Campaign pledges; donations; gifts in kind
Staff Member(s): 29
Membership: 36,000; *Fees:* $10; *Committees:* Agency & Community Services; Campaign Cabinet
Activities: Fair Share for Peel Task Force; *Awareness Events:* Campaign Kickoff; Lexus Golf Tournament; Roll Around Square One
Awards:
- Welcome to United Way Award (Award)
- Employee Campaign Chair (ECC) of the Year (Award)
- Outstanding Agency Campaign Award (Award)
- Outstanding Corporate Campaign Award (Award)
- Outstanding Employee Campaign Award (Award)
- Leading the Way Campaign Award (Award)
- Best National Employee Campaign Award (Award)
- Labour Award of Distinction (Award)

United Way of Perth-Huron
32 Erie St., Stratford ON N5A 2M4
Tel: 519-271-7730; *Fax:* 519-273-9350
Toll-Free: 877-818-8867
perthhuron@unitedway.ca
www.perthhuron.unitedway.ca
www.linkedin.com/groups?gid=3966504&trk=group-name
www.facebook.com/UWPH1
www.twitter.com/UnitedWayPH
www.youtube.com/user/UnitedWPH?feature=watch
Previous Name: United Way of Stratford-Perth
Overview: A small local charitable organization founded in 1967 overseen by United Way of Canada - Centraide Canada
Mission: To strengthen & support the ability of the people of our community to care for one another
Affliation(s): Perth County Community Development Council; Local Voices
Chief Officer(s):
Ryan Erb, Executive Director
rerb@perthhuron.unitedway.ca
Ron Cameron, President
Finances: *Annual Operating Budget:* $250,000-$500,000; *Funding Sources:* Workplace campaigns; special events; individual donations
Staff Member(s): 3; 50 volunteer(s)
Membership: 17 organizations; *Member Profile:* Funded, not for profit agencies; *Committees:* Board of Directors; Campaign Cabinet; Program Review & Allocations
Activities: Fundraising & allocation to agencies, building awareness of emerging community needs; *Awareness Events:* Kick-Off Luncheon; *Speaker Service:* Yes

United Way of Peterborough & District
277 Stewart St., Peterborough ON K9J 3M8
Tel: 705-742-8839; *Fax:* 705-742-9186
office@uwpeterborough.ca
www.uwpeterborough.ca
www.facebook.com/15103169591
twitter.com/UnitedWayPtbo
Overview: A medium-sized local charitable organization founded in 1941 overseen by United Way of Canada - Centraide Canada
Mission: To improve lives & build community by engaging individuals & mobilizing collective action; to provide resources, services & programs for community leadership
Chief Officer(s):
Jim Russell, CEO
jrussell@uwpeterborough.ca
Finances: *Annual Operating Budget:* $250,000-$500,000; *Funding Sources:* Community fundraising
Staff Member(s): 9; 2400 volunteer(s)
Membership: 34 agencies; *Fees:* Donation; *Committees:* Allocations; Campaign; Finance
Activities: Campaign kick-off, Sept.; fundraising; *Speaker Service:* Yes

United Way of Pictou County
Victoria Plaza, PO Box 75, #1, 342 Stewart St., New Glasgow NS B2H 5E1
Tel: 902-755-1754; *Fax:* 902-755-0853
info@pictoucountyunitedway.ca
www.pictoucountyunitedway.ca
www.facebook.com/UWPictouCounty
twitter.com/UWPictouCo
Overview: A small local charitable organization founded in 1960 overseen by United Way of Canada - Centraide Canada
Mission: To strengthen communities by facilitating programs & services that link people & resources; encourage participation; increase giving
Chief Officer(s):
Jessica Smith, Executive Director
jessica@pictoucountyunitedway.ca
Finances: *Annual Operating Budget:* $100,000-$250,000
Staff Member(s): 2
Membership: 1-99

United Way of Prince Edward Island / Centraide PEI
180 Kent St., Charlottetown PE C1A 7K4
Tel: 902-894-8202; *Fax:* 902-894-9643
Toll-Free: 877-902-4438
inquiries@peiunitedway.com
www.peiunitedway.com
www.facebook.com/pages/United-Way-of-PEI/398947502165?ref=nf
www.twitter.com/uwpei
Overview: A small provincial charitable organization founded in 1962 overseen by United Way of Canada - Centraide Canada
Mission: To provide funds needed to meet community needs & build stronger communities
Chief Officer(s):
David Hennessey, Executive Director
dhennessey@peiunitedway.com
Kris O'Brien, President
Finances: *Annual Operating Budget:* $500,000-$1.5 Million; *Funding Sources:* Corporate, individual donations
Staff Member(s): 3; 2300 volunteer(s)
Membership: 20,000; *Member Profile:* All donors; *Committees:* Board of Directors; Executive; Campaign Cabinet
Activities: *Speaker Service:* Yes

United Way of Quinte
PO Box 815, #2, 48 Dundas St. West, Belleville ON K8P 1A3
Tel: 613-962-9531; *Fax:* 613-962-4165
www.unitedwayofquinte.ca
www.facebook.com/UnitedWayofQuinte
twitter.com/unitedwayquinte
Previous Name: United Way of Belleville & District
Overview: A small local charitable organization founded in 1959 overseen by United Way of Canada - Centraide Canada
Mission: To provide leadership in a collaborative endeavor with our member agencies & others to increase the capacity of our community to respond to human service needs
Member of: United Way Ontario
Chief Officer(s):
Rosemary Judd-Archer, Chair
Judi Gilbert, Executive Director
jgilbert@unitedwayofquinte.ca
Tambra Patrick-MacDonald, Director, Finance & Administration
tmacdonald@unitedwayofquinte.ca
Finances: *Annual Operating Budget:* $500,000-$1.5 Million; *Funding Sources:* Donations
Staff Member(s): 3; 850 volunteer(s)
Membership: 43 agencies
Activities: Fundraising; information & referral; monthly community forum;

United Way of Regina
1440 Scarth St., Regina SK S4R 2E9
Tel: 306-757-5671; *Fax:* 306-522-7199
office@unitedwayregina.ca
www.unitedwayregina.ca
www.facebook.com/UnitedWayRegina?ref=stream
twitter.com/unitedwayregina
Overview: A small local charitable organization founded in 1935 overseen by United Way of Canada - Centraide Canada
Mission: To improve lives & to build the community by engaging individuals & mobilizing collective action
Chief Officer(s):
Joanne Grant, CEO
jgrant@unitedwayregina.ca
Finances: *Annual Operating Budget:* $1.5 Million-$3 Million; *Funding Sources:* Fundraising
Staff Member(s): 11; 3500 volunteer(s)
Membership: 37 funded agencies + 100 registered agencies; *Committees:* Allocations/Admissions; Campaign; Audit; Nominations; Resource Devlopment
Activities: AGM; Tribute Luncheon; *Awareness Events:* Day of Caring; Vital Link Dinner; *Speaker Service:* Yes; *Library:* Volunteer Regina Resource Centre; Open to public

United Way of St Catharines & District
#3, 80 King St., Ground Fl., St Catharines ON L2R 7G1
Tel: 905-688-5050; *Fax:* 905-688-2997
office@stcatharines.unitedway.ca
www.unitedwaysc.ca
www.facebook.com/148938585140989
twitter.com/UWStCathDis
Overview: A small local charitable organization founded in 1953 overseen by United Way of Canada - Centraide Canada
Mission: To increase the organized capacity of people to care for one another
Chief Officer(s):
Frances Hallworth, Executive Director
fhallworth@stcatharines.unitedway.ca
Finances: *Annual Operating Budget:* $500,000-$1.5 Million; *Funding Sources:* Fundraising
Staff Member(s): 10
Membership: 20,000; *Fees:* $10 donation or more
Activities: *Internships:* Yes; *Speaker Service:* Yes

United Way of Sarnia-Lambton
PO Box 548, 420 East St. North, Sarnia ON N7T 6Y5
Tel: 519-336-5452; *Fax:* 519-383-6032
info@theunitedway.on.ca
www.theunitedway.on.ca
Overview: A small local charitable organization founded in 1959 overseen by United Way of Canada - Centraide Canada
Mission: To generate resources enabling the community to respond to human care priorities in Sarnia-Lambton
Chief Officer(s):
Dave Brown, Executive Director
dave@theunitedway.on.ca
Finances: *Annual Operating Budget:* $250,000-$500,000; *Funding Sources:* Annual fall fundraising campaign
Staff Member(s): 5; 2000 volunteer(s)
Membership: 28 local agencies; *Committees:* Campaign Cabinet; Community Investment
Activities: *Speaker Service:* Yes

United Way of Saskatoon & Area
#100, 506 - 25 St. East, Saskatoon SK S7K 4A7
Tel: 306-975-7700; *Fax:* 306-244-0583
office@unitedwaysaskatoon.ca
www.unitedwaysaskatoon.ca
Overview: A small local organization overseen by United Way of Canada - Centraide Canada
Chief Officer(s):
Sheri Benson, Executive Director
sbenson@unitedwaysaskatoon.ca

United Way of Sault Ste Marie & District
7A Oxford St., Sault Ste Marie ON P6B 1R7
Tel: 705-256-7476; *Fax:* 705-759-5899
uwssm@ssmunitedway.ca
www.ssmunitedway.ca
www.facebook.com/pages/United-Way-of-Sault-Ste-Marie/172581389458207
Overview: A small local organization founded in 1957 overseen by United Way of Canada - Centraide Canada
Mission: To improve lives & build community by engaging individuals & mobilizing collective action
Member of: Chamber of Commerce of Sault Ste Marie
Affliation(s): United Way of Ontario; Regional Professional Advisory Council
Chief Officer(s):
Gary Vipond, CEO
Finances: *Annual Operating Budget:* $500,000-$1.5 Million; *Funding Sources:* 99% donations + 1% government
Staff Member(s): 5; 450 volunteer(s)
Membership: 23; *Fees:* Donation; *Committees:* Community Services; Volunteer Centre; Labour
Activities: Public assistance coordination; Charity Golf Scramble; Starlight Filmfest; Old Tyme Fair & Picnic, June; Annual Fall Campaign, Sept.-Nov.; *Speaker Service:* Yes; *Library:* Campaign & Volunteer Centre; by appointment

United Way of Slave Lake Society
PO Box 1985, Slave Lake AB T0G 2A0
Tel: 780-849-7290
gdungsym@telus.net
Overview: A small local organization overseen by United Way of Canada - Centraide Canada

United Way of South Eastern Alberta
PO Box 783, Stn. M, #101, 928 Allowance Ave., Medicine Hat AB T1A 7G7
Tel: 403-526-5544; *Fax:* 403-526-5244
utdway@telus.net
www.utdway.ca
www.facebook.com/163245983449
twitter.com/UnitedWaySEAB
Previous Name: United Way of Medicine Hat, Redcliff & District
Overview: A small local organization overseen by United Way of Canada - Centraide Canada

United Way of South Georgian Bay
PO Box 284, #9, 275 First St., Collingwood ON L9Y 3Z5
Tel: 705-444-1141; *Fax:* 705-444-0981
admin@unitedwaysgb.ca
Previous Name: Collingwood & District United Way
Overview: A small local charitable organization founded in 1969 overseen by United Way of Canada - Centraide Canada
Mission: To serve the south Georgian Bay area by promoting, supporting & facilitating the organized capacity of people to help one another
Chief Officer(s):
Debbie Kesheshian, Executive Director
Finances: *Annual Operating Budget:* Less than $50,000; *Funding Sources:* Donations
16 volunteer(s)
Membership: 500-999

United Way of Stormont, Dundas & Glengarry / Centraide de Stormont, Dundas & Glengarry
PO Box 441, Stn. Case Postale, Cornwall ON K6H 5T2
Tel: 613-932-2051; *Fax:* 613-932-7534
info@unitedwaysdg.com
www.unitedwaysdg.com
www.facebook.com/209841445745076
twitter.com/unitedwaysdg
Previous Name: United Way of Cornwall & District
Overview: A small local charitable organization founded in 1944 overseen by United Way of Canada - Centraide Canada
Mission: To improve lives & build our community by working together
Chief Officer(s):
Kimberley Lauzon-Desjardin, Program Development Director
Heather Paquette, President
Karen Turchetto, Executive Director
Finances: *Annual Operating Budget:* $50,000-$100,000; *Funding Sources:* Fundraising
Staff Member(s): 3; 500 volunteer(s)
Membership: 500-999
Activities: Variety of fundraisers to raise money to fund 18 agencies; *Speaker Service:* Yes

United Way of Stratford-Perth *See* United Way of Perth-Huron

United Way of the Alberta Capital Region
15132 Stony Plain Rd., Edmonton AB T5P 3Y3
Tel: 780-990-1000; *Fax:* 780-990-0203
united@myunitedway.ca
myunitedway.ca
www.facebook.com/myUnitedWay
www.twitter.com/myunitedway
www.youtube.com/uwacr
Overview: A large local charitable organization founded in 1941 overseen by United Way of Canada - Centraide Canada
Mission: To bring people & resources together to build caring, vibrant communities
Chief Officer(s):
Lynne Duncan, Chair
Anne Smith, Secretary/Treasurer
Finances: *Annual Operating Budget:* Greater than $5 Million; *Funding Sources:* Donations
Staff Member(s): 53; 5000 volunteer(s)
Membership: 1,000-4,999; *Fees:* Donation; *Committees:* Nominating; Appeal; Compensation; Officers; Audit
Activities: *Awareness Events:* United Way Campaign Kick Off, Sept. 22
Publications:
• WE Magazine
Type: Magazine

United Way of the Central Okanagan & South Okanagan/Similkameen
#202, 1456 St. Paul St., Kelowna BC V1Y 2E6
Tel: 250-860-2356; *Fax:* 250-868-3206
info@unitedwaycso.com
unitedwaycso.com
www.facebook.com/unitedwaycso
twitter.com/UnitedWayCSO
www.youtube.com/user/UnitedWayCSO
Overview: A medium-sized local charitable organization founded in 1950 overseen by United Way of Canada - Centraide Canada
Mission: To increase the organized capacity of people in our community to care for one another
Chief Officer(s):
Marla O'Brien, Executive Director
marla@unitedwaycso.com
Angela Pomeroy, Development Associate
angela@unitedwaycso.com
Finances: *Annual Operating Budget:* $500,000-$1.5 Million; *Funding Sources:* Donations
Staff Member(s): 5; 100 volunteer(s)
Membership: 5,000-14,999
Activities: September Kick-Off Breakfast; Golf Tournament; Drive-Thru Breakfast; Fundraising Campaign; Leadership Development Program; Volunteer Leadership Development Program; *Speaker Service:* Yes

United Way of the Fraser Valley (UWFV)
Sweeney Neighbourhood Centre, #208, 33355 Bevan Ave., Abbotsford BC V2S 0E7
Tel: 604-852-1234; *Fax:* 604-852-2316
Toll-Free: 888-251-7777
info@uwfv.bc.ca
www.uwfv.bc.ca
www.facebook.com/unitedwayfraservalley
www.twitter.com/unitedwayfv
Overview: A small local charitable organization founded in 1985 overseen by United Way of Canada - Centraide Canada
Mission: To promote the organized capacity of people to care for one another
Chief Officer(s):
Wayne Green, Executive Director
wayne@uwfv.bc.ca
Finances: *Annual Operating Budget:* $500,000-$1.5 Million; *Funding Sources:* Donations
Staff Member(s): 4; 400 volunteer(s)
Membership: 25; *Member Profile:* Charitable health & social service agencies; *Committees:* Agency Relations & Allocations; Community Development; Campaign
Activities: Volunteer training; fundraising; community development; *Speaker Service:* Yes

United Way of the Lower Mainland
4543 Canada Way, Burnaby BC V5G 4T4
Tel: 604-294-8929
info@uwlm.ca
www.uwlm.ca
www.linkedin.com/groups?about=&gid=4196396
www.facebook.com/UnitedWayoftheLowerMainland
www.twitter.com/uwlm
www.youtube.com/user/UnitedWayVancouver
Overview: A small local organization overseen by United Way of Canada - Centraide Canada
Chief Officer(s):
Michael McKnight, President & CEO
michaelm@uwlm.ca

United Way of Trail & District
803B Victoria St., Trail BC V1R 3T3
Tel: 250-364-0999; *Fax:* 250-364-1564
www.traildistrictunitedway.com
Overview: A small local charitable organization founded in 1928 overseen by United Way of Canada - Centraide Canada
Mission: To raise funds which are allocated to 26 affiliated non-profit organizations
Chief Officer(s):
Jodi LeSergent, President
Finances: *Annual Operating Budget:* $100,000-$250,000; *Funding Sources:* Donations; fundraising
Staff Member(s): 1; 200 volunteer(s)
Membership: 3,000; *Fees:* $25; *Committees:* Budget; Publicity; Campaign; Nominating; Fundraising; Special Events
Activities: *Awareness Events:* Campaign Kickoff Event; *Library* Open to public

United Way of Victoria County (UWVC) *See* United Way for the City of Kawartha Lakes

United Way of Windsor-Essex County
#A1, 300 Giles Blvd. East, Windsor ON N9A 4C4
Tel: 519-258-0000; *Fax:* 519-258-2346
united@weareunited.com
www.weareunited.com
www.facebook.com/unitedway.windsoressex
twitter.com/UnitedWayWE
Overview: A small local charitable organization overseen by United Way of Canada - Centraide Canada
Mission: To promote & strengthen the organized capacity of people to care for one another
Chief Officer(s):
Sheila Wisdom, Executive Director
Staff Member(s): 25; 25 volunteer(s)
Membership: 15,000-49,999
Activities: *Speaker Service:* Yes

United Way of Winnipeg / Winnipeg Centraide
580 Main St., Winnipeg MB R3B 1C7
Tel: 204-477-5360; *Fax:* 204-453-6198
info@unitedwaywinnipeg.mb.ca
www.unitedwaywinnipeg.mb.ca
www.facebook.com/unitedwaywinnipeg
twitter.com/unitedwaywpg
www.youtube.com/user/uwaywinnipeg

Overview: A small local organization founded in 1965 overseen by United Way of Canada - Centraide Canada
Mission: To support & strengthen the organized capacity of people to care for one another
Chief Officer(s):
Susan Lewis, President & CEO
Staff Member(s): 30; 8000 volunteer(s)
Membership: 75,000; *Fees:* Donation
Activities: *Speaker Service:* Yes

United Way of York Region (UWYR)
#200, 80F Centurian Dr., Markham ON L3R 8C1
Tel: 905-474-9974; *Fax:* 905-474-0051
Toll-Free: 877-241-4516
info@uwyr.on.ca
www.uwyr.on.ca
www.facebook.com/unitedwayyork?sk=wall
twitter.com/unitedwayyork
www.youtube.com/user/UnitedWayYorkRegion
Overview: A medium-sized local charitable organization founded in 1974 overseen by United Way of Canada - Centraide Canada
Mission: To improve the quality of life in the communities of York Region; to ascertain & address critical human needs by fostering innovative, responsible & inclusive partnerships of financial & other resources
Chief Officer(s):
Daniele Zanotti, CEO
dzanotti@uwyr.on.ca
Finances: *Annual Operating Budget:* $500,000-$1.5 Million; *Funding Sources:* Corporate, employee, & individual donations
Staff Member(s): 16; 1600 volunteer(s)
Membership: 605; *Fees:* $10; *Member Profile:* Subscribing, Honorary, Patron or organizational members who donate to the United Way or pay membership dues; *Committees:* Board of Directors; Fund Distribution; Campaign Cabinet; Chinese Community Council; Marketing; Finance; Citizen Review Panels; Community Leadership Resources Advisory; Human Resources
Activities: *Library:* Sam Bowman Resource Library; by appointment
Awards:
• Douglas E. Lear Memorial Award for Volunteer of the Year (Award)

United Way South Niagara (UWSN) / Centraide de Niagara Sud
Seaway Mall, 800 Niagara St., Welland ON L3C 5Z4
Tel: 905-735-0490; *Fax:* 905-735-5432
office@southniagara.unitedway.ca
www.unitedwaysouthniagara.ca
www.facebook.com/pages/United-Way-of-South-Niagara/227801910292
twitter.com/UnitedWaySN
www.youtube.com/UWSouthNiagara
Overview: A medium-sized local charitable organization founded in 1964 overseen by United Way of Canada - Centraide Canada
Finances: *Funding Sources:* Donations; Fundraising
Staff Member(s): 4; 500 volunteer(s)
Membership: *Committees:* Allocations; Campaign; Communications & Marketing; Executive; Planning
Activities: Distributing funds for programs & services; Contributing to community development

United Way Toronto
26 Wellington St. East, 2nd Fl., Toronto ON M5E 1W9
Tel: 416-777-2001; *Fax:* 416-777-0962; *TTY:* 416-359-2083
www.unitedwaytoronto.com
www.facebook.com/group.php?gid=108587420188
twitter.com/unitedwayto
www.youtube.com/user/uwtoronto
Previous Name: Red Feather United Appeal; United Way of Greater Toronto
Overview: A medium-sized local organization founded in 1956 overseen by United Way of Canada - Centraide Canada
Mission: To meet urgent human needs & improve social conditions by mobilizing the community's volunteer & financial resources in a common cause of caring
Chief Officer(s):
Susan McIsaac, President & CEO
Yezdi Pavri, Chair
Finances: *Annual Operating Budget:* Greater than $5 Million; *Funding Sources:* Corporate & individual donations
Staff Member(s): 148; 2000 volunteer(s)
Membership: 126
Activities: Annual fundraising compaign on behalf of 200 agencies; Leaps & Bounds Walkathon, Sept. 11.; CN Tower Climb, Oct.; Bay Street Rat Race, June; *Internships:* Yes; *Speaker Service:* Yes; *Library* by appointment
Awards:
• Spirit Awards (Award)
Given each year in the following categories: Canvasser of the Year; Employee Campaign Coordinators of the Year; Leadership Giving Campaign Award; Corporate Support Awards; First-Time Corporate & Employee Giving Award; Employee Campaign Awards; Labour Participation Award; Agency Employee Campaign Award; Public Service Employee Campaign Award; Student Campaign Awards; Public Awareness Award
• Get in the Way Awards (Award)

United Way/Centraide (Central NB) Inc.
#400, 1133 Regent St., Fredericton NB E3B 3Z2
Tel: 506-459-7773; *Fax:* 506-451-1104
office@unitedwaycentral.com
www.unitedwaycentral.com
www.facebook.com/148382218531358
twitter.com/JessieUnitedWay
www.youtube.com/UnitedWayCentralNB
Previous Name: United Way/Centraide Fredericton Inc.
Overview: A small local charitable organization founded in 1960 overseen by United Way of Canada - Centraide Canada
Mission: To be a leader in helping to create & sustain a caring & healthy community
Chief Officer(s):
Steven Fletcher, President
Brian Duplessis, Executive Director
bduplessis@nb.aibn.com
Finances: *Annual Operating Budget:* $500,000-$1.5 Million; *Funding Sources:* Corporate; general public
Staff Member(s): 4
Membership: 33
Activities: Fundraising; Community Need Survey; Allocation of Funds

United Way/Centraide Fredericton Inc. *See* United Way/Centraide (Central NB) Inc.

United Way/Centraide of the Moncton Region *See* United Way of Greater Moncton & Southeastern New Brunswick

United Way/Centraide Ottawa (UW/CO)
363 Coventry Rd., Ottawa ON K1K 2C5
Tel: 613-228-6700; *Fax:* 613-228-6730
info@unitedwayottawa.ca
www.unitedwayottawa.ca
www.linkedin.com/company/united-way-centraide-ottawa
www.facebook.com/unitedwayottawa
twitter.com/UnitedWayOttawa
www.youtube.com/user/unitedwayottawa
Previous Name: United Appeal of Ottawa-Carleton
Overview: A small local charitable organization founded in 1933 overseen by United Way of Canada - Centraide Canada
Mission: To bring people & resources together to build a strong, healthy, safe community for all; to build & support a network of high priority, results-oriented community services; to offer leadership in bringing the community together; to excel in fundraising; to invest resources & charitable funds in partnership with the community; to inform & engage community stakeholders
Chief Officer(s):
Michael Allen, President/CEO
Finances: *Funding Sources:* Donations
Activities: *Speaker Service:* Yes

United Way/Centraide Sudbury & District
#E6, 105 Elm St., Sudbury ON P3C 1T3
Tel: 705-560-3330
www.unitedwaysudbury.com
www.facebook.com/UWSudNip
twitter.com/UWSudNip
Overview: A small local charitable organization founded in 1982 overseen by United Way of Canada - Centraide Canada
Mission: To increase the organized capacity of people to care for one another through effective fundraising & allocation of these funds
Chief Officer(s):
Michael Cullen, Executive Director
edirector@unitedwaysudbury.com
Finances: *Funding Sources:* Donations
Staff Member(s): 15
Activities: *Speaker Service:* Yes

United World Colleges
Lester B. Pearson College of the Pacific, 650 Pearson College Dr., Victoria BC V9C 4H7
Tel: 250-391-2411
alumni@pearsoncollege.ca
www.pearsoncollege.ca
www.linkedin.com/groups?gid=49277&home=
www.facebook.com/PearsonUWC
twitter.com/PCUWC
www.youtube.com/user/PearsonUWC
Also Known As: Pearson College
Overview: A medium-sized international charitable organization founded in 1974
Mission: To encourage young people to become responsible citizens, politically & environmentally aware, committed to the ideals of peace, justice, understanding & cooperation, & to the implementation of these ideals through action & personal example
Member of: United World Colleges International
Chief Officer(s):
David B. Hawley, Director
Finances: *Funding Sources:* Governments; corporations; foundations; individuals
Staff Member(s): 72
Membership: 200; *Fees:* All students attend on full scholarship; *Member Profile:* Students from over 100 countries are brought together after being competitively selected by committees in their own countries; they generally have completed the equivalent of 11 years of North American schooling & are between the ages of 16 & 18; *Committees:* Student selection committees are established in each province/territory & in 136 countries
Activities: *Internships:* Yes; *Speaker Service:* Yes; *Library* by appointment

United Wushu Association of Ontario *See* WushuOntario

Unity & District Chamber of Commerce
PO Box 834, Unity SK S0K 4L0
Tel: 306-228-2688; *Fax:* 306-228-2185
www.townofunity.com
Overview: A small local organization
Chief Officer(s):
Helena Long, President
Kristine Moon, Treasurer

Universal Negro Improvement Association of Montreal (UNIA)
2741 rue Notre-Dame, Montréal QC H3J 1N9
Tel: 514-846-0049
Overview: A small local organization

Universal Youth Foundation
#301, 2800 Hwy. 7, Concord ON L4K 1W8
Tel: 905-326-9732; *Fax:* 905-695-0801
info@universalyouthfoundation.org
www.universalyouthfoundation.org
Overview: A small international organization founded in 2005
Mission: To provide educational assistance to children & youth in need throughout the world by funding schools & teachers, with the goal of creating & inspiring a new generation of leaders
Chief Officer(s):
Mario Cortellucci, Founder & Chairman

Universities Art Association of Canada (UAAC) / Association d'art des universités du Canada (AAUC)
189 Mill Ridge Rd., Arnprior ON K7S 3G8
Tel: 613-622-5570; *Fax:* 613-622-0671
uaac@gozoom.ca
www.uaac-aauc.com
www.facebook.com/UAACAAUC
Overview: A small national organization founded in 1974
Mission: To provide a national voice for its membership
Member of: Humanities & Social Sciences Federation of Canada
Affiliation(s): Comité International d'histoire de l'art
Chief Officer(s):
Anne Whitelaw, President
anne.whitelaw@concordia.ca
Finances: *Annual Operating Budget:* Less than $50,000; *Funding Sources:* National government
Staff Member(s): 1
Membership: 50 institutional + 400 individual; *Fees:* $225 institutional; $55 student; $115 full; $80 unaffiliate; *Member Profile:* Art historians & artists who teach in Canadian universities & colleges, independent scholars & other art professionals

Meetings/Conferences: • Universities Art Association of Canada Conference 2015, 2015
Scope: National

University College of Cape Breton Faculty Association of University Teachers *See* Cape Breton University Faculty Association

University College of the Fraser Valley Faculty & Staff Association (UFV FSA)
33844 King Rd., Abbotsford BC V2S 7M8
Tel: 604-854-4530; *Fax:* 604-853-9540
FSA.Info@ufv.ca
www.ufv-fsa.ca
Overview: A small local organization
Chief Officer(s):
Virginia Cook, President, 604-854-4516
virginia.cooke@ufv.ca
Jonathan Hughes, Faculty Vice-President, 604-504-7441 Ext. 4687
jonathan.hughes@ufv.ca
Martin Kelly, Staff Vice-President, 604-504-7441 Ext. 4781
martin.kelly@ufv.ca
Sean Parkinson, Secretary-Treasurer, 604-504-7441 Ext. 4301
sean.parkinson@ufv.ca
Membership: 500-999;

University Counselling & Placement Association *See* Canadian University & College Counselling Association

University of Alberta Library & Information Studies Alumni Association (LISAA)
c/o School of Library and Information Studies, #3, 20 Rutherford South, Edmonton AB T6G 2J4
Tel: 780-492-4578; *Fax:* 780-492-2430
www.slis.ualberta.ca/peoplegroups/alumni.aspx
Overview: A small provincial organization
Chief Officer(s):
Hanne Pearce, President
president@lisaa.ca

University of Alberta Non-Academic Staff Association *See* Non-Academic Staff Association for the University of Alberta

University of Alberta South East Asian Students' Association (SEASA)
#SUB 040T, Basement, University of Alberta, Edmonton AB T6G 2R3
e-mail: seasa@ualberta.ca
www.ualberta.ca/~seasa
Previous Name: Federation of Asian Students (FAS)
Overview: A small local organization founded in 1996
Mission: To unite & support southeast Asian students who attend the University of Alberta; To assist members to adapt in a Canadian environment
Finances: *Funding Sources:* Fundraising; Sponsorships
Membership: *Member Profile:* Full-time, part-time, & alumni Southeast Asian students of the University of Alberta; Individuals interested in the services of the association
Activities: Offering cultural, educational, recreational, & social activities; Promoting cultural awareness amongst students & the Edmonton community; Providing study buddies
Publications:
• South East Asian Students' Association Newsletter
Type: Newsletter; *Frequency:* Monthly
Profile: Association information for members each month from September to April

University of Alberta Students' Union
Students' Union Building, University of Alberta, #2-900, 8900 - 114 St. NW, Edmonton AB T6G 2J7
Tel: 780-492-4241; *Fax:* 780-492-4643
su@su.ualberta.ca
www.su.ualberta.ca
www.facebook.com/UAlbertaSU;
www.facebook.com/uasuevents
twitter.com/ualbertaSU
www.youtube.com/ualbertaSU
Overview: A medium-sized local organization
Chief Officer(s):
Rory Tighe, President
Andy Cheema, Vice-President, Operations & Finance
Emerson Csorba, Vice-President, Academic
Farid Iskandar, Vice-President, External
Colten Yamagishi, Vice-President, Student Life

University of British Columbia Faculty Association (UBCFA) / Association des professeurs de l'Université de la Colombie-Britannique
University of British Columbia, #112, 1924 West Mall, Vancouver BC V6T 1Z2
Tel: 604-822-3883; *Fax:* 604-222-0174
faculty.association@ubc.ca
www.facultyassoc.ubc.ca
Overview: A medium-sized local organization founded in 1920
Mission: To provide information and support in workplace issues; To advocate on behalf of it members on a wide variety of issues; To provide workshops and seminars.
Chief Officer(s):
Deena Rubuliak, Executive Director, 604-822-3301
deena.rubuliak@ubc.ca
Staff Member(s): 7
Membership: 3,200; *Member Profile:* Faculty members; *Committees:* Bargaining Prepation; Librarians & Archivists; Member Services & Grievance; Okanagan Faculty; Sessional Faculty; Status of Women

University of British Columbia Symphony Orchestra
c/o School of Music, University of British Columbia, 6361 Memorial Rd., Vancouver BC V6T 1Z2
Tel: 604-822-3113; *Fax:* 604-822-4884
www.music.ubc.ca/student-ensembles/symphony-orchestra.html
Also Known As: UBC Symphony Orchestra
Overview: A small local organization overseen by Orchestras Canada
Mission: The 90-member orchestra performs symphonic works from the 18th, 19th and 20th centuries.
Chief Officer(s):
Jesse Read, Director

University of Calgary Faculty Association / Association des professeurs de l'Université de Calgary
Math Sciences, University of Calgary, #220, 2500 University Dr. NW, Calgary AB T2N 1N4
Tel: 403-220-5722; *Fax:* 403-284-1976
faculty.association@tucfa.com
www.tucfa.com
Overview: A medium-sized local organization
Mission: To promote and protect Faculty Interests; To represent the Faculty in the councils of the University; To provide information to members and to negotiate the Collective Agreement with the Board of Governors.
Member of: Canadian Association of University Teachers (CAUT); Confederation of Alberta Faculty Associations (CAFA)
Chief Officer(s):
Sheila Miller, Executive Director
sheila.miller@tucfa.com
Staff Member(s): 7
Membership: *Member Profile:* CAUT is a defender of academic freedom and works actively in the public interest to improve the quality and accessibility of post-secondary education in Canada; CAFA promotes the quality of education in the province and the well-being of Alberta universities and their academic staff.; *Committees:* Election; Executive; Personnel; Joint Liaison

University of Guelph Food Service Employees Association (UGFSEA)
Drew Hall, University of Guelph, Guelph ON N1G 2W1
Tel: 519-824-4120; *Fax:* 519-837-9302
Previous Name: Hospitality Food Service Employees Association
Overview: A small local organization

University of Guelph Professional Staff Association / Association du personnel professionelle de l'Université de Guelph
University Centre, University of Guelph, #158, 50 Stone Rd. East, Guelph ON N1G 2W1
Tel: 519-824-4120
psa@uoguelph.ca
psa.uoguelph.ca
Previous Name: University of Guelphy Staff Association
Overview: A medium-sized local organization
Mission: To promote the interests of its members
Chief Officer(s):
Kent Percival, Chair, 519-824-4120 Ext. 56397
percival@uoguelph.ca
Membership: *Fees:* $10.00/month; *Member Profile:* To promote career enhancement and development programs to members; To partecipate in the review and negotiation of salary and benefit improvements

University of Guelphy Staff Association *See* University of Guelph Professional Staff Association

University of Lethbridge Faculty Association (ULFA) / Association des professeurs de l'Université de Lethbridge
#D620, 4401 University Dr., Lethbridge AB T1K 3M4
Tel: 403-329-2578; *Fax:* 403-329-2113
www.ulfa.ca
Overview: A small local organization founded in 1967
Mission: To ensure academic freedom of membership; To bargain collectively on behalf of membership
Member of: Canadian Association of University Teachers; Confederation of Alberta Faculty Associations
Chief Officer(s):
Brenda Rennie, Executive Director, 403-329-2328, Fax: 403-329-2113
rennie@uleth.ca
John Usher, President, 403-329-2759, Fax: 403-329-2038
john.usher@uleth.ca
Trevor Harrison, Vice-President, 403-329-2552, Fax: 403-329-2085
trevor.harrison@uleth.ca
Jon Doan, Secretary-Treasurer, 403-332-5208, Fax: 403-380-1839
jon.doan@uleth.ca
Finances: *Funding Sources:* Membership dues
Membership: 100-499; *Fees:* Mill rate multiplied by actual salary; *Committees:* Economic Benefits; Academic Welfare; Executive; Grievance
Awards:
• ULFA Academic Scholarship (Award)

University of Manitoba Faculty Association (UMFA) / Association des professeurs de l'Université du Manitoba
#100, 29 Dysart Rd., Winnipeg MB R3T 2M7
Tel: 204-474-8272; *Fax:* 204-474-7548
faum@umfa.ca
www.umfa.ca
Overview: A medium-sized local organization founded in 1965
Mission: To promote the well-being of the university community; to defend academic freedom; To promote the collective & individual interests of members
Member of: National Union of CAUT (NUCAUT), Manitoba Labour Federation (MFL)
Affliation(s): Canadian Association of University Teachers (CAUT), Manitoba Organization of Faculty Associations (MOFA), National Union of CAUT (NUCAUT); Manitoba Labour Federation (MFL); Winnipeg Labour Council (WLC)
Chief Officer(s):
Linda Guse, Executive Director
lguse@umfa.ca
Finances: *Funding Sources:* Membership fees
Staff Member(s): 5
Membership: *Member Profile:* CLC advocates for human and civil rights, academic freedom and freedom of speech.The MFL is an important ally in lobbying the provincial government and in advocating for legislative amendments.; *Committees:* Collective Agreement; Status of Women; Board of Representatives; Reserve Fund; UMFA Staff Benefits; Workplace Health & Safety
Activities: Collective bargaining, Employee-employer relations, Higher Education Issues

University of New Brunswick Employees Association (UNBEA)
PO Box 4400, Fredericton NB E3B 5A3
Tel: 506-453-4504; *Fax:* 506-453-4954
unbea@unb.ca
www.unbea.ca
Overview: A small local organization founded in 1992
Mission: To act as the bargaining unit for two groups of employees at the University of New Brunswick
Chief Officer(s):
Marc Prosser, President
Membership: 320; *Member Profile:* General labour, trades, allied services, audio-visual & security (GLTA); secretaries, accountants, library assistants & clerks (SALAC)

University of Prince Edward Island Faculty Association (UPEIFA) / Association des professeurs de l'Université de l'Ile-du-Prince-Edouard
University of Prince Edward Island, Main Bldg., #315, 550 University Ave., Charlottetown PE C1A 4P3
Tel: 902-566-0438; *Fax:* 902-566-6043
upeifa@upeifa.org
www.upeifa.org

Overview: A small local organization founded in 1969
Mission: To encourage academic discussion among members; to provide full support for all activities; to maintain & improve quality & stature of members; to provide for student-faculty discussion on matters of mutual concern
Member of: Canadian Association of University Teachers
Chief Officer(s):
Betty Jeffery, President
Finances: *Annual Operating Budget:* Less than $50,000
Membership: 230 individual; *Fees:* Schedule available; *Member Profile:* Full-time faculty of University of Prince Edward Island; part-time teaching faculty; *Committees:* Executive; Awards & Scholarships; Hessian Merit Award; Merit Award; Communications; Equity; Social; Research & Advocacy; Nominating; Health & Safety Steering; University Joint Benefits Advisory; Joint Benefits Management; UPEI Questions

University of Québec in Hull Faculty Union *Voir* Syndicat des professeures et professeurs de l'Université du Québec en Outaouais

University of Regina Faculty Association (URFA) / Association des professeurs de l'Université de Regina

University of Regina, #122, Campion College, Regina SK S4S 0A2
Tel: 306-585-4378; *Fax:* 306-585-5208
urfa@uregina.ca
www.urfa.uregina.ca
Overview: A small local organization founded in 1977
Affiliation(s): Canadian Association of University Teachers (CAUT)
Chief Officer(s):
Gary Tompkins, Chair
Chair.URFA@uregina.ca
Richard Buettner, Chair, Grievance
Grievance.URFA@uregina.ca
Mairin Barnabé, Officer, Member Services
Mairin.Barnabe@uregina.ca
Debbie Sagel, Professional Officer
Debbie.Sagel@uregina.ca
Finances: *Funding Sources:* Union dues
Membership: 500-999
Activities: *Library*

University of Saskatchewan Arts Council (USAC)

#488, Williams Bldg., Centre for Continuing & Distance Education, University of Saskatchewan, Saskatoon SK S7N 5C8
Tel: 306-966-5530
community.arts@usask.ca
ccde.usask.ca/uscad/usac
www.facebook.com/CCDEUniversityofSaskatchewan
Also Known As: U of S Arts Council
Overview: A small local charitable organization founded in 1993
Mission: To promote lifelong learning in the arts & culture
Member of: Organization of Saskatchewan Arts Councils
Chief Officer(s):
Val Miles, Program Manager
Finances: *Annual Operating Budget:* Less than $50,000; *Funding Sources:* Membership fees; special events; programs; grants
Staff Member(s): 2; 20 volunteer(s)
Membership: 250; *Fees:* $25 individual; $30 family; $15 student; *Member Profile:* Art students

University of Saskatchewan Faculty Association (USFA) / Association des professeurs de l'Université de la Saskatchewan

Education Bldg., University of Saskatchewan, #20, 28 Campus Dr., Saskatoon SK S7N 0X1
Tel: 306-966-5609; *Fax:* 306-966-8807
usfa@usaskfaculty.ca
www.usaskfaculty.ca
Overview: A medium-sized provincial organization founded in 1952
Mission: To attain highest standards of excellence through teaching, scholarship, & research; To encourage climate of freedom, responsibility & mutual respect
Affiliation(s): Saskatchewan Association of University Teachers; Saskatchewan Federation of Labour
Chief Officer(s):
Tammy Stieb, Administrative Secretary
Tammy.Stieb@usask.ca
Doug Chivers, Chair
Finances: *Funding Sources:* Membership dues
Staff Member(s): 4
Membership: 1,100; *Fees:* Mil rate of 8.5%; *Member Profile:* Full time faculty members; *Committees:* Negotiating; Executive; Committee on Committees; Trustees of the Contingency Trust Fund; Trustees of the VGLI Trust Fund; Communications; Constitutuin; External Relations; Financial Appeal; Grievance; Member Development; Planning & Assessment; University Administrative Practice; Status of Visible Minorities; Women's Issues; Charitable Donations; Collective Negotiating; Joint Benefits; Management of the Agreemen; Joint Grievance; Pension; Occupational Health
Publications:
• University of Saskatchewan Faculty Association Faculty Guide
Type: Guide
Profile: A guide to help answer questions of USFA members
• USFA [University of Saskatchewan Faculty Association] E-Letter
Type: Newsletter
Profile: Association news & issues

University of Sherbrooke Support Staff Union *Voir* Syndicat des employées de soutien de l'Université de Sherbrooke

University of the Philippines Alumni Association of Toronto (UPAA Toronto)

c/o Paulina Corpuz, 30 Minerva Ave., Toronto ON M1M 0C3
Tel: 647-477-8722
www.upaatoronto.org
Previous Name: U.P. Alumni Association in Metro Toronto
Overview: A small local organization founded in 1977
Mission: To facilitate communication among University of the Philippines alumni members in the Greater Toronto Area; To promote the interests of members; To offer programs that promote the personal & professional growth of members
Chief Officer(s):
Rose Tijam, President
Marlene Mogado, Vice-President
Rheea Liboro, Secretary
Alice Herrera, Treasurer
Marie Garingalao, Officer, Public Affairs & Communications
Finances: *Funding Sources:* Membership fees; Charitable donations; Fundraising
Membership: *Fees:* $25 2 years; $50 5 years; *Member Profile:* Canadian residents who have earned at least 30 units of graduate education from the University of the Philippines; Residents of Canada who have earned a minimum of 60 units of post secondary education from the University of the Philippines; Canadian residents who are graduates of the University of the Philippines secondary school; Persons who are former faculty members or administrative staff of the University of the Philippines; Parents & spouses of regular members; Individuals who are members of other University of the Philippines alumni associations outside Ontario
Activities: Presenting educational activities; Hosting social & cultural events, such as reunions; Facilitating professional & business networking opportunities; Involving members in University of the Philippines activities; Posting jobs; Organizing discussion-forums on issues of interest to the Filipino & Canadian communities; Establishing a mentoring program for new immigrant alumni; Participating in social issues, such as protests against racism; Assisting disaster victims in the Philippines; Partnering with other organizations
Awards:
• Most Outstanding UPAA Member Award (Award)
To honour exceptional alumni for remarkable achievements
• Most Outstanding UP Graduate Award (Award)
• University of the Philippines Alumni Association of Toronto Scholarship (Award)
Publications:
• University of the Philippines Alumni Association of Toronto Members' Diretory
Type: Directory; *Price:* Free with membership in University of the Philippines Alumni Association of Toronto

University of Toronto Faculty Association (UTFA) / Association des professeurs de l'Université de Toronto

#419, 720 Spadina Ave., Toronto ON M5S 2T9
Tel: 416-978-3351; *Fax:* 416-978-7061
www.utfa.org
Overview: A medium-sized local organization founded in 1971
Mission: To promote the welfare of the current & retired faculty members & librarians of the University of Toronto, the University of St. Michael's College, the University of Trinity College, & Victoria University; To advance the interests of teachers, researchers & librarians in Canadian universities
Member of: Canadian Association of University Teachers
Affiliation(s): Ontario Confederation of University Faculty Associations
Chief Officer(s):
Scott Prudham, President, 416-978-4613
prudham@utfa.org
Cynthia Messenger, Vice-President, Grievances, 416-978-4640
cynthia.messenger@utoronto.ca
Staff Member(s): 7
Membership: 1,000-4,999; *Fees:* 0.75% of salary; $50/year retired members; *Member Profile:* University of Toronto academics & retired members; *Committees:* Salary, Benefit & Pensions; Grievance; Status of Women; Appointments; University & External Affairs; Teaching Stream; Librarians; Equity; Membership; Financial Advisory; Office Staff Relations; Nominating; Constitutional Review; Apportionment
Activities: *Library*

University of Toronto Institute for Aerospace Studies

Faculty of Applied Science & Engineering, 4925 Dufferin St., Toronto ON M3H 5T6
Tel: 416-667-7700; *Fax:* 416-667-7799
www.utias.utoronto.ca
Overview: A medium-sized national organization founded in 1949
Mission: UTIAS is a graduate studies and research institute, forming part of the faculty of Applied Science and Engineering at the University of Toronto.
Affiliation(s): Canadian Aeronautics & Space Institute; Institute for Space & Terrestrial Science; Canadian Space Agency; Intelligent Sensing for Innovative Structures Canada
Chief Officer(s):
D.W. Zingg, Director
dwz@oddjob.utias.utoronto.ca
H.T. Liu, Associate Director
liu@utias.utoronto.ca
O.L. Gülder, Associate Director
ogulder@utias.utoronto.ca
Staff Member(s): 55
Membership: 68
Activities: *Library*

University of Toronto Menorah Society *See* Hillel of Greater Toronto

University of Toronto Native Students Association (NSA)

First Nations House, Borden Building North, 563 Spadina Ave., 3rd Fl., Toronto ON M5S 2J7
Tel: 416-978-1042; *Fax:* 416-978-1893
nsa.exec@utoronto.ca
www.fnh.utoronto.ca
Overview: A small local organization
Mission: To create social & cultural networks of students through feasts, social gatherings, conferences and cultural events; to support events run through other students' organizations both in the university & in broader Canadian communities; to advocate on behalf of Indigenous issues in Canada.
Chief Officer(s):
Sarah Nanibush, Crane Clan Leader

University of Toronto Symphony Orchestra

Faculty of Music, University of Toronto, 80 Queen's Park Cres., Toronto ON M5S 2C5
Tel: 416-978-3733; *Fax:* 416-946-3353
performance.music@utoronto.ca
www.music.utoronto.ca
Overview: A small local organization overseen by Orchestras Canada
Chief Officer(s):
David Briskin, Conductor
Finances: *Annual Operating Budget:* Less than $50,000
Membership: 1-99
Activities: *Library*

University of Toronto, Faculty of Information Alumni Association (FISAA)

140 St. George St., Toronto ON M5S 3G6
Tel: 416-978-3234; *Fax:* 416-978-5762
alumni@ischool.utoronto.ca
www.ischool.utoronto.ca
www.linkedin.com/groups/Faculty-Information-Alumni-Association-Univers
www.facebook.com/iSchoolAlumniTO
twitter.com/iSchoolAlumniTO
Overview: A small local organization founded in 1929

Mission: The Association represents all the graduates of the Faculty of Information, University of Toronto.
Affliation(s): University of Toronto Alumni Association
Chief Officer(s):
Kate MacDonald, President
fiaapresident@gmail.com
Membership: 6,700; *Member Profile:* All are graduates of the Faculty of Information Sciences; *Committees:* Social Events; Social Media & Website; Job Shadowing; Ask-an-Alum Mentoring; Grants & Awards; Bertha Bassam Lecture Event Planning
Activities: *Internships:* Yes

University of Victoria Faculty Association / Association des professeurs de l'Université de Victoria

#102 University House 2, University of Victoria, PO Box 3060, Stn. CSC, Victoria BC V8W 3R4
Tel: 250-721-7939; *Fax:* 250-721-8873
uvicfa@uvic.ca
dev.uvicfa.ca/index.html
Also Known As: UVIC Faculty Association
Overview: A medium-sized local organization founded in 1979
Mission: To maintain & promote the professional & material status of members; To promote the welfare of the University of Victoria; To further the cause of higher education
Affliation(s): Confederation of University Faculty Associations of BC; Canadian Association of University Teachers
Chief Officer(s):
Doug Baer, President
baer@uvic.ca
Jeff McKeil, Executive Director
Staff Member(s): 2
Membership: *Fees:* Schedule available; *Member Profile:* UVIC Faculty - full-time; librarians; *Committees:* Nominations & Elections; Equity; Constitution & Bylaws; Executive; Disability; Librarians; Senior Instructors; Advising & Dispute Resolution; Compensation & Benefits

University of Waterloo Staff Association (UWSA)

#3603, Davis Centre, 200 University Ave. West, Waterloo ON N2L 3G1
Tel: 519-888-4567
staffasc@uwaterloo.ca
www.adm.uwaterloo.ca/infostaf/index.html
www.linkedin.com/groups?gid=3741942
twitter.com/UWStaffAssoc
Overview: A small local organization
Chief Officer(s):
Carlos Mendes, President
Gail Spencer, Executive Manager
gspencer@uwaterloo.ca

University of Western Ontario Staff Association (UWOSA)

#255, University Community Centre, London ON N6A 3K7
Tel: 519-661-2111
mhay2@uwo.ca
www.uwosa.ca
Overview: A small local organization founded in 1967
Chief Officer(s):
John Critchley, President
jcritchley@uwosa.ca
Karen Foullong, Vice-President
karen@uwosa.ca
Staff Member(s): 1; 40 volunteer(s)
Membership: 1,200; *Fees:* 1.25% gross earnings; *Member Profile:* Unionized administrative & technical staff

University of Western Ontario Symphony Orchestra (UWOSO)

Faculty of Music, University of Western Ontario, 1151 Richmond St. North, London ON N6A 3K7
Tel: 519-661-2043; *Fax:* 519-661-3531
music@uwo.ca
www.music.uwo.ca
Overview: A small local organization founded in 1968 overseen by Orchestras Canada
Finances: *Annual Operating Budget:* Less than $50,000
Staff Member(s): 2
Membership: 93
Activities: *Library:* UWO Music Library

University of Winnipeg Faculty Association (UWFA) / Association des professeurs de l'Université de Winnipeg

Sparling Hall, University of Winnipeg, #4M56, 515 Portage Ave., 3rd Fl., Winnipeg MB R3B 2E9
Tel: 204-786-9430; *Fax:* 204-774-3068
uwfa@uwinnipeg.ca
www.uwfa.ca
Overview: A small local organization founded in 1981
Member of: Canadian Association of University Teachers
Chief Officer(s):
Lisa McGifford, B.A., LLB, Executive Director
l.mcgifford@uwinnipeg.ca
Marissa Dudych, B.A., Administrative Assistant
ma.dudych@uwinnipeg.ca
Membership: 100-499; *Fees:* Mill rate; *Member Profile:* Continuing, tenured & probationary academic staff, librarians & academic staff on contract

University Settlement Recreation Centre (USRC)

23 Grange Rd., Toronto ON M5T 1C3
Tel: 416-598-3444
universitysettlement.ca
Overview: A small local organization founded in 1910 overseen by Ontario Council of Agencies Serving Immigrants
Affliation(s): Toronto Association of Neighbourhood Services
Chief Officer(s):
David Prendergast, Executive Director
david.prendergast@universitysettlement.ca
Ena Mulic, Administrative Assistant
ena.mulic@universitysettlement.ca
Finances: *Annual Operating Budget:* $3 Million-$5 Million; *Funding Sources:* Government; United Way; Foundations
Staff Member(s): 270; 300 volunteer(s)
Activities: Other locations: Employment & Training Dept.; ESL & Language Dept.; Toronto Chinatown Safety Centre

University Singers *See* Richard Eaton Singers

Unparty: The Consensus-Building Party

#418, 8120 Colonial Dr., Richmond BC V7C 4V2
Tel: 778-896-3571; *Fax:* 604-637-2189
unparty.ca
Also Known As: Unparty
Previous Name: People's Senate Party
Overview: A small provincial organization founded in 2011
Mission: To promote consensus government over adversarial party politics.
Chief Officer(s):
Mike Donovan, Party Leader
mikedonovan2011@gmail.com

U.P. Alumni Association in Metro Toronto *See* University of the Philippines Alumni Association of Toronto

Upper Ottawa Valley Beekeepers' Association

c/o Murray Borer, RR#2, Renfrew ON K7H 2Z5
Tel: 613-432-3432
Overview: A small local organization
Mission: To serve members by disseminating information about beekeeping practices in the Upper Ottawa Valley; To promote the beekeeping industry locally
Chief Officer(s):
Murray Borer, President, 613-432-3432
Membership: *Member Profile:* Apiarists in the Upper Ottawa Valley
Activities: Creating opportunities for member beekeepers to network;

Upper Ottawa Valley Chamber of Commerce

PO Box 1010, 611 TV Tower Rd., Pembroke ON K8A 6Y6
Tel: 613-732-1492; *Fax:* 613-732-5793
manager@uovchamber.com
www.upperottawavalleychamber.com
www.facebook.com/UOVCC
twitter.com/UOVCC
www.youtube.com/user/UOVCC
Previous Name: Pembroke & Area Chamber of Commerce
Overview: A small local organization founded in 1955
Mission: To promote commerce, the cooperation of tourist organizations, business & industry, consumers, government, agriculture & service groups; to give informed, responsible leadership in tourism, publicity, planning, education, civic action, beautification, special events & free enterprise
Member of: Canadian Chamber of Commerce; Ontario Chamber of Commerce; Ottawa Valley Tourist Association
Finances: *Annual Operating Budget:* $50,000-$100,000; *Funding Sources:* Membership dues; non-dues revenue
Staff Member(s): 1; 16 volunteer(s)
Membership: 260; *Fees:* $105-$515 based on number of employees; *Committees:* Education; Communications/PR; Membership; Social Events; Awards Gala; Voice of Business; Policy & Procedures; Zoomer Entrepreneur Peer Group
Activities: Business improvement seminars; Business After Hours; annual golf tournament
Awards:
• Upper Ottawa Valley Chamber of Commerce Achievement Awards (Award)

Upper Thames River Conservation Authority

1424 Clarke Rd., London ON N5V 5B9
Tel: 519-451-2800; *Fax:* 519-451-1188
infoline@thamesriver.on.ca
www.thamesriver.on.ca
www.facebook.com/UpperThamesRiverConservationAuthority
twitter.com/UTRCAMarketing
www.youtube.com/user/UTRCA
Previous Name: Upper Thames River Conservation Foundation
Overview: A small local organization founded in 1947
Mission: To establish and undertake, in the area in which it has jurisdiction, a program designed to further the conservation, restoration, development and management of natural resources other than gas, oil, coal and minerals
Chief Officer(s):
Jane Boyce, Chair
Ian Wilcox, General Manager/Sec.-Treas.
wilcoxi@thamesriver.on.ca
Staff Member(s): 60; 6 volunteer(s)

Upper Thames River Conservation Foundation *See* Upper Thames River Conservation Authority

Urban Alliance on Race Relations (UARR)

#507, 302 Spadina Ave., Toronto ON M5T 2E7
Tel: 416-703-6607; *Fax:* 416-703-4415
info@urbanalliance.ca
www.urbanalliance.ca
Overview: A medium-sized local charitable organization founded in 1975
Mission: To promote a stable & healthy multiracial environment in the community, by creating awareness of current issues, assisting institutions to develop solid policies & practices, & promoting full participation by the community to dismantle barriers to equal opportunity
Chief Officer(s):
Sharon Simpson, President
sharon.uarr@gmail.com
Yumei Lin, Administrative Assistant
Finances: *Annual Operating Budget:* Less than $50,000; *Funding Sources:* Donations; Municipal government; Foundations
Staff Member(s): 2; 50 volunteer(s)
Membership: 300; *Fees:* $25 general; $50 sustaining; $100 benefactor; $1,000 life; $10 senior/student; *Committees:* Volunteer
Activities: Annual Employment Equity Forum & Career Fair; Anti-Racism Response Network; seminars, workshops & conferences; research studies; *Awareness Events:* Annual Golf Day; *Internships:* Yes; *Speaker Service:* Yes; *Library* Open to public
Awards:
• Urban Alliance on Race Relations (Award)
Presented biennially, next presentation 2006
• President's Award (Award)
Presented biennially, next presentation 2006

Urban Development Institute - Calgary

#360, 999 - 8th St. SW, Calgary AB T2R 1J5
Tel: 403-531-6250; *Fax:* 403-531-6252
www.udicalgary.com
www.facebook.com/pages/UDI-Calgary/548065425208738
twitter.com/udicalgary
Overview: A small local organization
Chief Officer(s):
Michael Flynn, Executive Director

Urban Development Institute Greater Edmonton Chapter

Birks Bldg., #324, 10113 - 104 St., Edmonton AB T5J 1A1
Tel: 780-428-6146; *Fax:* 780-425-9548
info@udiedmonton.com
www.udiedmonton.com
Overview: A small local organization founded in 1958

Chief Officer(s):
Rick Preston, Executive Director

Urban Development Institute of Canada (UDI) / Institut de développement urbain du Canada
200-602 West Hastings St., Vancouver BC V6B 1P2
Tel: 604-669-9585; *Fax:* 604-689-8691
info@udi.org
www.udi.bc.ca
www.facebook.com/UDIBC
twitter.com/udibc
www.youtube.com/UDIPacific
Overview: A large national organization
Mission: To promote wise, efficient & productive urban growth; To be an effective voice of the land development & property management industry at all levels of government; To serve as a forum for the exchange of knowledge, experience & research on land use planning & development
Chief Officer(s):
Anne McMullin, President & CEO
Jeff Fisher, Vice President
jfisher@udi.org
Finances: *Annual Operating Budget:* $500,000-$1.5 Million; *Funding Sources:* Membership dues
Staff Member(s): 10
Membership: 1,500 corporations; *Fees:* Schedule available; *Committees:* Tax & Legal; Planning; Housing Affordability; Environmental; Transportation & Infrastructure; News & Events
Activities: *Speaker Service:* Yes; *Library* by appointment

Urban Development Institute of Nova Scotia
#150, 1083 Queen St., Halifax NS B3H 1M2
Tel: 902-442-5017; *Fax:* 902-431-7220
udi@udins.ca
www.udins.ca
Also Known As: UDI of Nova Scotia
Overview: A medium-sized provincial organization
Mission: To represent the interests of the development industry & related professions
Chief Officer(s):
Ben Young, President
Membership: 50; *Fees:* $595 supplier & government; $895 associate; $1,195 builder; $1,495 developers; *Committees:* Technical; Membership; Finance; Public Relations/Communications

Urban Municipal Administrators' Association of Saskatchewan (UMAAS)
PO Box 730, Hudson Bay SK S0E 0Y0
Tel: 306-865-2261; *Fax:* 306-865-2800
umaas@sasktel.net
www.umaas.ca
Overview: A medium-sized provincial organization founded in 1974
Chief Officer(s):
Richard Dolezsar, Executive Director
rdolezsar@sasktel.net
Finances: *Annual Operating Budget:* Less than $50,000; *Funding Sources:* Membership; convention; donations
Membership: 350+; *Fees:* Schedule available; *Member Profile:* Local government administration certificate; employment in urban municipal government in Saskatchewan; *Committees:* Education; Discipline; Advisory; Administration; Convention

Urban Music Association of Canada (UMAC)
#210, 675 King St. West, Toronto ON M5V 1M9
Tel: 416-916-2874; *Fax:* 416-504-7343
umacgoturb@gmail.com
Overview: A small national organization founded in 1996
Mission: The Urban Music Association of Canada (UMAC) is the voice of Canada's urban entertainment scene. It is a member-driven, non-profit organization dedicated to building the domestic and international profile of Canadian urban music
Chief Officer(s):
Will Strickland, President
Activities: Workshops, artist showcases, networking events

Urban Native Indian Education Society *See* NEC Native Education College Society

Urban Pest Management Council of Canada / Conseil canadien de la lutte antiparasitaire en milieu urbain
#627, 21 Four Seasons Pl., Toronto ON M9B 6J8
Tel: 416-622-9771; *Fax:* 416-622-6764
www.urbanpestmanagement.ca
Overview: A medium-sized national organization
Mission: The Urban Pest Management Council of Canada represents the manufacturers, formulators, distributors and allied associations of specialty pest management products, for the consumer or professional markets used in turf, ornamental, pest management, forestry, aquatic, vegetation management and other non-food/fibre applications
Chief Officer(s):
Pierre Petelle, Contact, 613-230-9811 Ext. 3222

Urology Nurses of Canada
c/o 62 Barrie St., Kingston ON K7L 3J7
e-mail: membership@unc.org
www.unc.org
Overview: A small national organization
Mission: To promote the specialty of urologic nursing in Canada by promoting education, research & clinical practice.
Affliation(s): Canadian Urological Association; Canadian Nurses' Association
Chief Officer(s):
Gina Porter, President
president@unc.org
LuAnn Pickard, Secretary
secretary@unc.org
Nancy Carson, Treasurer
treasurer@unc.org
Membership: *Fees:* $50 regular; $25 students; *Member Profile:* Nurses & other allied health care professionals; Corporations, foundations, & associations
Activities: Maintaining & promoting standards of care; Raising the profile of urologic nursing; Promoting communication among members
Awards:
• Editorial Award (Award)
$1,000 for written or co-editor of paper, article or editorial concerning urological nursing practice, education or research in one of the sub specialities of urodynamic, biofeedback, endourology, sexual health uro-oncology or incontinence *Amount:* $1000
• Research Award (Award)
$1,000 towards research related to urological nursing practice or subspecialities of urodynamic, biofeedback, endourology, sexual health uro-oncology or incontinence *Amount:* $1000
• Scholarship Award (Award)
$1,000 towards student enrolled in full or part time study related to the practice of nursing *Amount:* $1000
Publications:
• Pipeline
Type: Newsletter; *Frequency:* Semiannually; *Editor:* Brenda Bonde

Calgary
Calgary AB

Edmonton
Chief Officer(s):
Elizabeth Smits, Contact
lizsmits@shaw.ca

Halifax
Halifax NS
Chief Officer(s):
Liette Connor, Contact
liette.connor@cdha.nshealth.ca

Kingston
Chief Officer(s):
Sylvia Robb, Contact
sylviamrobb@gmail.com

Montréal
Montréal QC
Chief Officer(s):
Raquel DeLeon, Contact
raquel.deleon@muhc.mcgill.ca

New Brunswick
Chief Officer(s):
Gina Porter, Contact
gina.porter@rogers.com

Newfoundland & Labrador
Chief Officer(s):
Sue Hammond, Contact
hammond_so@yahoo.ca

Ottawa
Chief Officer(s):
Susan Freed, Contact
freeds@teksavvy.com
Nancy Bauer, Secretary
Judy St. Germain, Treasurer

Toronto
Chief Officer(s):
Frances Stewart, Contact
bladderqueen@hotmail.com

Victoria
Chief Officer(s):
Jill Jeffery, Contact
jpjeffery@shaw.ca

USC Canada
#705, 56 Sparks St., Ottawa ON K1P 5B1
Tel: 613-234-6827; *Fax:* 613-234-6842
Toll-Free: 800-565-6872
info@usc-canada.org
www.usc-canada.org
www.facebook.com/78368904729
twitter.com/usccanada
www.youtube.com/user/USCCanada
Also Known As: Unitarian Service Committee of Canada
Overview: A medium-sized international charitable organization founded in 1945
Mission: Committed to enhancing human development through an international partnership of people linked in the challenge to reduce poverty
Member of: Canadian Council for International Cooperation
Chief Officer(s):
Lauren Viot, Director, International Programs
Sheila Petzold, Director, Communications
Martin Settle, Director, Finance & Human Resources
Susan Walsh, Executive Director
Finances: *Annual Operating Budget:* Greater than $5 Million; *Funding Sources:* Support from the general public; bequests; foundations & corporations; investment income; government
Staff Member(s): 22
Membership: 1,000; *Member Profile:* Membership is offered to individuals supporting USC through volunteer or financial means; *Committees:* Finance; Executive; Programs
Activities: Communications/Media Program; Development Education Program to raise awareness about development issues & their impact on our lives in Canada; Fundraising & Volunteer Program; Overseas Program to work in partnership with people in the developing world to build self-reliant communities; *Speaker Service:* Yes; *Rents Mailing List:* Yes; *Library* by appointment

USC Canada
#705, 56 Sparks St., Ottawa ON K1P 5B1
Tel: 613-234-6827; *Fax:* 613-234-6842
Toll-Free: 800-565-6872
Other Communication: fundraising@usc-canada.org
info@usc-canada.org
usc-canada.org
www.facebook.com/pages/USC-Canada-Seeds-of-Survival/78368904729
twitter.com/usccanada
www.flickr.com/photos/usc-canada
Overview: A large national charitable organization
Mission: USC Canada promotes vibrant family farms, strong rural communities, and healthy ecosystems around the world. With engaged Canadians and partners in Africa, Asia, and Latin America, they support programs, training, and policies that strengthen biodiversity, food sovereignty, and the rights of those at the heart of resilient food systems - women, indigenous peoples, and small-scale farmers.
Chief Officer(s):
Susan Walsh, Executive Director

Used Car Dealers Association of Manitoba / Association des marchands de voitures d'occasion du Manitoba
PO Box 53023, RPO South St. Vital, Winnipeg MB R2N 3X2
Tel: 204-254-1891
Toll-Free: 877-386-8232
info@mucda.mb.ca
www.mucda.mb.ca
Overview: A small provincial organization founded in 1991
Mission: To enhance & improve the automobile industry in Manitoba for the benefit of the Province's consumers through identifying public agenda issues affecting the industry and contributing to the decision-making process.
Membership: *Member Profile:* Independent used car dealers
Activities: Scholarship Program

Used Car Dealers Association of Ontario (UCDA)
230 Norseman St., Toronto ON M8X 6A2

Tel: 416-231-2600; *Fax:* 416-232-0775
Toll-Free: 800-268-2598
web@ucda.org
www.ucda.org
Overview: A medium-sized provincial organization founded in 1984
Mission: To enhance the image of the industry through member education, consumer awareness of the benefits members provide, & mediation of consumer/dealer disputes
Affliation(s): International Auto Theft Investigators; National Independent Automobile Dealers Association
Chief Officer(s):
Robert G. Beattie, Executive Director
Steve Peck, President
Finances: *Annual Operating Budget:* $1.5 Million-$3 Million; *Funding Sources:* Membership dues; services
Staff Member(s): 19
Membership: 4,359; *Fees:* $200; *Member Profile:* Registered motor vehicle dealers engaging in used vehicle sales in Ontario
Activities: *Speaker Service:* Yes

Utility Contractors Association of Ontario, Inc. (UCA)

PO Box 762, Oakville ON L6K 0A9
Tel: 905-847-7305; *Fax:* 905-412-0339
www.uca.on.ca
Overview: A medium-sized provincial organization founded in 1968
Mission: To negotiate & administer collective agreements with operating engineers & labourers in Ontario's utility sector
Chief Officer(s):
Rene Beaudry, President
Barry Brown, Executive Director
bbrown@uca.on.ca
Glen Hansen, Treasurer
Membership: 10 contractor members + 34 associate (supplier) members
Activities: Organizing networking events; Recognizing exellence in safety through the presentation of awards
Meetings/Conferences: • Utility Contractors Association of Ontario 2015 Annual Convention, 2015, ON
Scope: Provincial
Description: An event with guest speakers & networking activities for association members & their guests
Publications:
• The Conduit [a publication of the Utility Contractors Association of Ontario]
Type: Newsletter; *Frequency:* Semiannually
Profile: Association news, action dates, & industry information

Uxbridge & District Chamber of Commerce ***See*** **Uxbridge Chamber of Commerce**

Uxbridge Chamber of Commerce

PO Box 810, 2 Campbell Dr., Uxbridge ON L9P 0A3
Tel: 905-852-7683; *Fax:* 905-852-2632
info@uxcc.ca
www.uxcc.ca
Previous Name: Uxbridge & District Chamber of Commerce
Overview: A small local organization
Mission: Association exists to represent all businesses in Uxbridge Township
Chief Officer(s):
Angela Horne, President
Finances: *Annual Operating Budget:* Less than $50,000
Staff Member(s): 1; 6 volunteer(s)
Membership: 80; *Fees:* $150

Uxbridge Conservation Association (UCA)

RR#3, Kirkfield ON K0M 2B0
Tel: 905-852-3044
Overview: A small local organization founded in 1987
Affliation(s): Ontario Environment Network; Durham Environment Network
Chief Officer(s):
Dave Martin, Contact
Finances: *Annual Operating Budget:* Less than $50,000
6 volunteer(s)
Membership: *Fees:* $10 student; $15 individual

Uxbridge Historical Centre

PO Box 1301, 7239 Conc. 6, Uxbridge ON L9P 1N5
Tel: 905-852-5854
museum@town.uxbridge.on.ca
www.uxbridgehistoricalcentre.com
www.facebook.com/uxbridgehistoricalcentre
twitter.com/UxbridgeMuseum
Previous Name: Uxbridge-Scott Museum & Archives
Overview: A small local organization founded in 1972
Mission: To collect, preserve & display artifacts, photographs, documents & buildings which record & illustrate the community & daily life of early & successive generations of residents of the Uxbridge-Scott area; to maintain, display & interpret this collection in a museum comprised of local historic buildings or replicas; to promote understanding of the local heritage & encourage research of local history & families, through educational programs, research, outreach & special events
Affliation(s): Ontario Museum Association
Finances: *Annual Operating Budget:* $50,000-$100,000
Staff Member(s): 2; 20 volunteer(s)
Membership: *Fees:* $10 student; $15 single; $25 family; $125 patron; $250 sponsor; $500 partner
Activities: Steam Threshing & Heritage Days; *Library:* Archives; Open to public

Uxbridge-Scott Museum & Archives ***See*** **Uxbridge Historical Centre**

Vaad Harabonim (Orthodox Rabbinical Council)

3600 Bathurst St., Toronto ON M6A 2C9
Tel: 416-787-1631; *Fax:* 416-785-5378
Also Known As: Rabbinical Council of Ontario
Overview: A small provincial organization founded in 1982
Mission: To serve & guide the Jewish community
Finances: *Annual Operating Budget:* Less than $50,000
Membership: 40

Vaccination Risk Awareness Network Inc. (VRAN)

PO Box 169, Winlaw BC V0G 2J0
e-mail: info@vaccinechoicecanada.com
www.vran.org
www.facebook.com/330700720307290
twitter.com/vran_canada
Overview: A small national organization
Mission: To provide information about the potential risks & side-effects of vaccines; To foster a multi-disciplinary approach to child & family health; To uphold the right of persons to exercise informed consent
Finances: *Funding Sources:* Donations
Membership: *Fees:* Donation
Publications:
• Vaccination Risk Awareness Network Newsletter
Type: Newsletter; *Frequency:* 3 pa; *Price:* Free with membership in the Vaccination Risk Awareness Network
Profile: Information about the educational & outreach work of the organization

Vaccine & Infectious Disease Organization (VIDO)

University of Saskatchewan, 120 Veterinary Rd., Saskatoon SK S7N 5E3
Tel: 306-966-7465; *Fax:* 306-966-7478
info@vido.org
www.vido.org
Previous Name: Veterinary Infectious Disease Organization
Overview: A medium-sized international organization founded in 1975
Mission: To serve the livestock & poultry industry by conducting animal health related research; communicating livestock management techniques & information; facilitating the transfer of technology for international commercial development; to be recognized as an international biotechnology leader in the development of innovative vaccines & vaccine delivery systems, & to be a preferred partner in the development & commercialization of products for use by the food animal industry; to retain leaders in product discovery & strive for excellence in establishing partnerships at all levels of industry (producers, governments, universities, bio- pharmaceutical companies & other research institutions in the biopharmaceutical industry)
Chief Officer(s):
Andrew Potter, Director & CEO
Finances: *Funding Sources:* Livestock & poultry industries; charitable foundations; federal & provincial granting donations
Activities: 50,000 square foot research facility; a 160 acre research farm; specific pathogen-free isolation facilities, & state of the art virology, bacteriology, biochemistry & immunology laboratories

Val-d'Or Native Friendship Centre ***Voir*** **Centre d'amitié autochtone de Val-d'Or**

Valemount & Area Chamber of Commerce (VACC)

PO Box 690, Valemount BC V0E 2Z0
Tel: 250-566-0061; *Fax:* 250-566-0061
info@valemountchamber.com
www.valemountchamber.com
www.facebook.com/152151818151811
Overview: A small local organization
Mission: To promote local businesses through educational activities
Member of: BC Chamber of Commerce
Chief Officer(s):
Christine Latimer, Chair
Finances: *Funding Sources:* Donations; membership dues
Membership: *Fees:* $75 business; $40 associate

Valhalla Wilderness Society (VWS)

PO Box 329, New Denver BC V0G 1S0
Tel: 250-358-2333; *Fax:* 250-358-2748
info@vws.org
www.vws.org
Overview: A small local charitable organization founded in 1975
Mission: To raise awareness of environmental issues such as wildlife conservation & the protection of forests
Finances: *Funding Sources:* Donations
Membership: *Fees:* $10
Activities: Participating in advocacy activities; Working with scientists & researchers, such as forest ecologists, wildlife biologists, botanists, & hydrologists; Providing information about environmental issues; Working with Aboriginal people on issues of environmental & social justice
Publications:
• Valhalla Wilderness Society Year-End Newsletter
Type: Newsletter; *Frequency:* Annually; *Price:* Free with membership in the Valhalla Wilderness Society
Profile: A report to members about the society's campaigns & activities

Valley Chamber of Commerce

#200, 131 Pleasant St., Grand Falls NB E3Y 1G6
Tel: 506-473-1905; *Fax:* 506-475-7779
gfcocgs@nbnet.nb.ca
www.grandfalls.com
Previous Name: Grand Falls, Saint-André & Drummond Chamber of Commerce; Grand Falls & Region Chamber of Commerce
Overview: A small local organization
Chief Officer(s):
Melanie Ouellette-Toner, Directrice générale
Mimi Rioux, Secrétaire
Finances: *Annual Operating Budget:* Less than $50,000
Staff Member(s): 1; 16 volunteer(s)
Membership: 113

Valley Family Resource Centre Inc.

#1, 110 Richmond St., Woodstock NB E7M 2N9
Tel: 506-325-2299; *Fax:* 506-328-8896
woodstock@frc-crf.com
frc-crf.com/woodstock
Previous Name: Atlantic Alliance of Family Resource Centres
Overview: A small local organization
Chief Officer(s):
Anne-Marie Hayes, Director

Valley Native Friendship Centre Society ***See*** **Hiiye'yu Lelum Society House of Friendship**

Valleyview Chamber of Commerce

PO Box 1020, Valleyview AB T0H 3N0
Tel: 780-524-4535
info@valleyviewchamber.ca
www.valleyviewchamber.ca
Overview: A small local organization
Mission: To focus on meeting the needs & expectations of retail & service businesses, industries, local consumers, & travellers in Valleyview, Alberta
Chief Officer(s):
Evan Heynemans, President
Membership: 39; *Fees:* $99 not-for-profit; $125 for profit; *Member Profile:* Local businesses

Valoris for Children & Adults of Prescott-Russell / Valoris pour enfants et adultes de Prescott-Russell

PO Box 248, 173, Old Hwy 17, Plantagenet ON K0B 1L0
Tel: 613-673-5148; *Fax:* 613-673-4800
Toll-Free: 800-675-6168
www.seapr.ca
Previous Name: Prescott & Russell Association for Community Living
Overview: A small local organization

Member of: Community Living Ontario
Chief Officer(s):
Gabrielle Cadieux, President

Valoris pour enfants et adultes de Prescott-Russell *See* Valoris for Children & Adults of Prescott-Russell

The Van Horne Institute for International Transportation & Regulatory Affairs

2500 University Dr. NW, Calgary AB T2N 1N4
Tel: 403-220-8455; *Fax:* 403-282-4663
vanhorne@ucalgary.ca
www.vanhorne.info
Overview: A small international organization founded in 1991
Mission: To contribute to public policy development & education in the areas of transportation & regulated industries.
PUBLICATIONS: On-Trac.
Affliation(s): University of Calgary; University of Alberta; Southern Alberta Institute of Technology
Chief Officer(s):
Peter C. Wallis, President & CEO, 403-220-3967
pcwallis@ucalgary.ca
Bryndis Whitson, Manager, Strategic Development & Member Relations, 403-220-2114
bwhitson@ucalgary.ca
Gerald Maier, Chairman
Finances: *Annual Operating Budget:* Less than $50,000; *Funding Sources:* Private sector
Staff Member(s): 4
Membership: 60; *Member Profile:* Government; industry; education; *Committees:* Centre for Transportation; Centre for Regulatory Affairs; Centre for Innovation & Communication
Activities: Transporation research & education; programs to assist in improving the efficiency & equity of transportation & regulated industries; *Speaker Service:* Yes; *Rents Mailing List:* Yes; *Library* Open to public

Vancouver & District Labour Council (VDLC)

Maritime Labour Centre, #20, 1880 Triumph St., Vancouver BC V5L 1K3
Tel: 604-254-0703; *Fax:* 604-254-0701
office@vdlc.ca
www.vdlc.ca
www.facebook.com/vancouver.labourcouncil
Overview: A large local organization founded in 1889 overseen by British Columbia Federation of Labour
Mission: To act as the voice of the labour movement in Vancouver & the surrounding district
Affliation(s): Canadian Labour Congress (CLC)
Chief Officer(s):
Joey Hartman, President
president@vdlc.ca
Terry Engler, First Vice-President
ken1004@telus.net
Stephen Von Sychowski, Second Vice-President
Paul Sihota, Treasurer
Membership: 65,000 workers; *Member Profile:* 118 affiliated local unions in the Greater Vancouver area
Activities: Promoting the interests of local affiliates; Assisting unions on strike; Organizing political action; Working for social justice

Vancouver Aboriginal Friendship Centre Society (VAFCS)

1607 East Hastings St., Vancouver BC V5L 1S7
Tel: 604-251-4844; *Fax:* 604-251-1986
info@vafcs.org
www.vafcs.org
Overview: A small local charitable organization founded in 1963
Mission: To meet the needs of aboriginal people making a transition to the urban community by providing social, cultural & recreational programs
Chief Officer(s):
John Webster, President
Tami Omeasoo, Vice-President/Treasurer
Staff Member(s): 25; 6 volunteer(s)
Membership: 100-499; *Fees:* $1
Activities: *Internships:* Yes

Vancouver Art Gallery Association (VAG)

750 Hornby St., Vancouver BC V6Z 2H7
Tel: 604-662-4700; *Fax:* 604-682-1086
customerservice@vanartgallery.bc.ca
www.vanartgallery.bc.ca
www.facebook.com/VancouverArtGallery
twitter.com/VanArtGallery
Overview: A small local organization founded in 1931
Mission: A place for people to meet to experience inspiration, meaning & pleasure through visual art
Affliation(s): Canadian Museum Association; British Columbia Museums Association; American Federation of Arts
Chief Officer(s):
Bruce Wright, Chair, Board of Trustees
Kathleen Bartels, Director
Finances: *Annual Operating Budget:* Greater than $5 Million; *Funding Sources:* Private; corporate; grants; foundations; government
Staff Member(s): 100; 300 volunteer(s)
Membership: 10,000; *Fees:* $35 student; $60 individual; $90 household; $40 senior; $60 senior couple
Activities: Exhibitions, children's programs, school tours & workshops; *Library* Open to public

The Vancouver Art Therapy Institute

1575 Johnston St., Vancouver BC V6H 3R9
Tel: 604-681-8284; *Fax:* 604-331-8262
vatimail@telus.net
www.vati.bc.ca
Overview: A small local charitable organization founded in 1982
Mission: To train art therapists at the graduate level; to provide art therapy as a service; to educate the public about the efficiency of art therapy
Member of: Canadian Art Therapy Association; BC Art Therapy Association
Chief Officer(s):
Sarah Van Norman, Director
Finances: *Annual Operating Budget:* $100,000-$250,000
Staff Member(s): 10
Membership: 1-99
Activities: Master of Counselling with Art Therapy Program; Advanced Diploma Program; *Internships:* Yes

Vancouver Association for the Survivors of Torture (VAST)

2618 East Hastings St., Vancouver BC V5K 1Z6
Tel: 604-299-3539; *Fax:* 604-299-3523
Toll-Free: 866-393-3133
office@vast-vancouver.ca
www.vast-vancouver.ca
Overview: A small local charitable organization founded in 1986
Mission: To encourage & to promote the well-being of people who have survived torture &/or political violence
Member of: Affiliation of Multicultural Societies & Service Agencies of BC; Canadian Council for Refugees; Vancouver Refugee Council; BC Human Rights Coalition; International Rehabilitation Council for Torture Victims
Affliation(s): Vancouver Multicultural Society
Chief Officer(s):
Christine Thomas, Executive Director
Finances: *Annual Operating Budget:* $100,000-$250,000; *Funding Sources:* Membership fees; provincial & municipal government; United Nations; private donations
Staff Member(s): 7; 20 volunteer(s)
Membership: 1-99
Activities: *Awareness Events:* International Day in Support of Victims of Torture, June 26; *Internships:* Yes; *Speaker Service:* Yes; *Library* by appointment

Vancouver Association of Chinese Canadians (VACC)

2639 Kingsford Ave., Burnaby BC V5B 4L7
Tel: 604-421-2983
www.freewebs.com/vacc/
Overview: A small local organization founded in 1992
Mission: To advocate for the rights of all Canadians, particularly Chinese Canadians and encourage their full and equal participation in Canadian society
Member of: Chinese Canadian National Council
Chief Officer(s):
Sid Tan, President
sidtan@vcn.bc.ca
Finances: *Annual Operating Budget:* Less than $50,000
Staff Member(s): 2
Membership: 1-99; *Fees:* $50 corporate; $30 non-profit; $10 adult; $5 students & seniors
Activities: *Speaker Service:* Yes

Vancouver Association of Law Libraries (VALL)

c/o Rebecca Slave, Courthouse Libraries BC, 800 Smithe St., Vancouver BC V6Z 2E1
Tel: 604-660-2841
www.vall.vancouver.bc.ca
twitter.com/VALLBC
Overview: A small provincial organization founded in 1988
Mission: To be a forum for information exchange & continuing education
Chief Officer(s):
Sarah Sutherland, President
ssutherland@canlii.org
Larisa Titova, Vice-President, 604-631-4210
larisa.titova@blakes.com
Membership: *Fees:* $35 regular; free for students; *Member Profile:* Individuals working in or associated with law libraries; *Committees:* Program

Vancouver Ballet Society

Scotiabank Dance Theatre, 677 Davie St., Level 6, Vancouver BC V6B 2G6
Tel: 604-681-1525; *Fax:* 604-681-7732
vbs@telus.net
vancouverballetsociety.ca
www.facebook.com/VancouverBalletSocietyvbs
Overview: A medium-sized local charitable organization founded in 1946
Mission: To promote further interest in the art of classical ballet & contemporary dance through education, encouragement & assistance
Member of: Canadian Magazine Publishers Association; Volunteer Vancouver; BC Association of Magazine Publishers
Chief Officer(s):
Maureen Allen, President
Finances: *Funding Sources:* BC Arts Council; Vancouver Foundation; Canada Council; individuals
Staff Member(s): 4
Membership: *Fees:* $20 dance student; $40 individual; $50-$99 contributing; $100-$249 sustaining; *Member Profile:* Dance enthusiasts
Activities: Master Dance Classes; Spring Dance Seminar; *Library*

The Vancouver Board of Trade

World Trade Centre, #400, 999 Canada Place, Vancouver BC V6C 3E1
Tel: 604-681-2111; *Fax:* 604-681-0437
contactus@boardoftrade.com
www.boardoftrade.com
www.facebook.com/VancouverBoardofTrade
twitter.com/BoardofTrade
Previous Name: World Trade Centre Vancouver
Overview: A small local organization
Mission: To promote, enhance & facilitate the development of the region as a Pacific centre for trade, commerce & travel
Member of: Canadian Chamber of Commerce; World Trade Centres Association
Chief Officer(s):
Iain Black, President & CEO
ceo@boardoftrade.com
Staff Member(s): 35
Membership: 5,800; *Committees:* Advanced Technology; Business & Arts; Communications; Community Affairs; Contract Club; Economic Development & Environment; Government Budget & Finance; Membership & Marketing; Leaders of Tomorrow; Urban Transportation
Activities: Speakers Programs; Business After Business; networking roundtables, seminars & workshops; *Speaker Service:* Yes

Vancouver Botanical Gardens Association *See* VanDusen Botanical Garden Association

Vancouver Central Council *See* Conseil national Société de Saint-Vincent de Paul

Vancouver Chinatown Merchants Association

508 Taylor St., Vancouver BC V6B 2T2
Tel: 604-682-8998; *Fax:* 604-682-8939
vcma@vancouver-chinatown.com
Overview: A small provincial organization founded in 1981
Mission: To acquire best benefits for the Chinese merchants & the whole community
Member of: Vancouver Chinatown BIA Society
Affliation(s): Tourism Vancouver
Finances: *Annual Operating Budget:* $250,000-$500,000; *Funding Sources:* Membership fees; fundraising
Staff Member(s): 3; 50 volunteer(s)
Membership: 230; *Fees:* $100
Activities: Vancouver Chinatown Night Market; Chinese New Year Parade

Vancouver Club of Printing House Craftsmen (VCPHC)
c/o Dennis Kratoska, G.A. Roedde Ltd., #3, 12840 Bathgate Way, Richmond BC V6V 1Z4
Tel: 604-270-3302; *Fax:* 604-270-4347
www.vcphc.org
Overview: A small local organization founded in 1929
Member of: International Association of Printing House Craftsmen
Chief Officer(s):
Michael Smith, President
sales@minuteman-vancouver.com
Dennis Kratoska, Treasurer
dennis@garoedde.com
Membership: 120; *Fees:* $180 + $30 initiation fee; *Committees:* Advisory; Gallery; Bulletin; Education; Entertainment; Membership; Programs

Vancouver Community College Faculty Association (VCCFA) / Association des professeurs de Collège Communautaire de Vancouver
#401, 402 Pender St. West, Vancouver BC V6B 1T6
Tel: 604-688-6210; *Fax:* 604-688-6219
info@vccfa.ca
www.vccfa.ca
Overview: A small local organization
Chief Officer(s):
Frank Cosco, President, 604-838-9428
Membership: 500-999

Vancouver Community Network (VCN)
Help Desk, #705, 333 Terminal Ave., Vancouver BC V6A 4C1
Tel: 778-724-0826; *Fax:* 855-299-0647
Other Communication: Complaints e-mail: abuse@vcn.bc.ca
help@vcn.bc.ca
www.vcn.bc.ca
www.facebook.com/vancouvercommunitynetwork
twitter.com/VCN_Community
Overview: A small local organization founded in 1993
Mission: The Vancouver Community Network owns, operates & promotes a free, publicly accessible, non-commercial, community computer utility in the Lower Mainland of BC which provides a public space on the Internet
Member of: BC Community Network Association
Finances: *Funding Sources:* Membership fees; project funding
Staff Member(s): 2; 50 volunteer(s)
Membership: 9,750 registered users; 2,700 members
Activities: Web community index; modem lines; public access terminals; training; *Internships:* Yes
Publications:
• The VCN [Vancouver Community Network] User News
Type: Newsletter
Main Office & Webteam
#280, 111 West Hastings St., Vancouver BC V6B 1H4

Vancouver Consultants
PO Box 48232, Stn. Bentall Centre, Vancouver BC V7X 1A1
Tel: 604-562-1746; *Fax:* 604-583-7132
mailbox@vancouverconsultants.com
www.vancouverconsultants.com
Overview: A small local organization founded in 2000
Mission: To provide a virtual directory of consultants in Vancouver; to facilitate & enhance opportunities for independent consultants & the market
Chief Officer(s):
Ian Marshall, Partner/Associate, 604-512-1265
ian@vancouverconsultants.com
Dave Schulte, Partner
Membership: *Fees:* Free basic; $9.95-$299.95 basic plus-platinum

Vancouver Cultural Alliance *See* Alliance for Arts & Culture

Vancouver East Cultural Centre *See* The Cultch

Vancouver Electric Vehicle Association (VEVA)
PO Box 3456, 349 West Georgia St., Vancouver BC V6B 3Y4
e-mail: info@veva.bc.ca
www.veva.bc.ca
www.linkedin.com/groups?home=&gid=4741516
www.facebook.com/vancouverelectricvehicleassociation
twitter.com/vevabc
www.youtube.com/user/VEVAEVTV/
Overview: A small local organization founded in 1987
Mission: To promote the development of clean alternative transportation with a focus on electric vehicles
Chief Officer(s):
Bruce Stout, President
pres@veva.dhs.org
Robert Shaw, Treasurer
treasurer@veva.dhs.org
Membership: *Fees:* $25; $10 students

Vancouver Elementary School Teachers' Association (VESTA)
2915 Commercial Dr., Vancouver BC V5N 4C8
Tel: 604-873-8378; *Fax:* 604-873-2652
www.bctf.ca/vesta
Overview: A small local organization
Chief Officer(s):
Glen Hansman, President
gerry@vesta.ca

Vancouver Executives Association
#400, 601 West Broadway, Vancouver BC V5Z 4C2
Tel: 604-684-0660; *Fax:* 604-205-5490
exec@vanex.com
www.vanex.com
Also Known As: VANEX
Overview: A small local organization founded in 1920
Mission: To promote business & share ideas with trusted business leaders in a non-competive environment
Member of: International Executives Association
Chief Officer(s):
Linda Enns, Executive Director
Staff Member(s): 1
Membership: 92

Vancouver Folk Song Society (VFSS)
e-mail: vanfolksong@gmail.com
www.folksongsociety.org
Overview: A small local organization founded in 1959
Mission: To encourage the study & enjoyment of all aspects of the folk music of Canada & other countries; to promote the publication & performance of folk music
Chief Officer(s):
Pat Howard, President
banjomamapat@gmail.com
Finances: *Annual Operating Budget:* Less than $50,000; *Funding Sources:* Membership fees
Membership: 150 individual; *Fees:* $15 individual; $20 families
Activities: *Library* by appointment

Vancouver Foundation
PO Box 12132, #1200, 555 West Hastings St., Vancouver BC V6B 4N6
Tel: 604-688-2204; *Fax:* 604-688-4170
info@vancouverfoundation.bc.ca
www.vancouverfoundation.bc.ca
www.facebook.com/pages/Vancouver-Foundation/78713406917
twitter.com/vancouverfdn
Overview: A small national charitable organization founded in 1943
Mission: To fund special programs or capital projects of non-profit organizations in British Columbia; concerned with the mental, physical, moral, educational, & cultural well-being of residents of British Columbia
Chief Officer(s):
Faye Wightman, President & CEO

Vancouver Francophone Cultural Centre *Voir* Le Centre culturel francophone de Vancouver

Vancouver Grain Exchange
#100, 1111 Hastings St. West, Vancouver BC V6E 2J3
Tel: 604-685-0141; *Fax:* 604-681-4364
vge@bcmarine.org
Overview: A small local organization
Chief Officer(s):
Andrew Knapman, Contact

Vancouver Guild of Puppetry
Overview: A small local organization
Member of: Alliance for Arts & Culture
Chief Officer(s):
Miryana Heath, President
miryana@shaw.ca

Vancouver Holocaust Centre Society - A Museum for Education & Remembrance (VHEC)
#50, 950 West 41st Ave., Vancouver BC V5Z 2N7
Tel: 604-264-0499; *Fax:* 604-264-0497
info@vhec.org
www.vhec.org
www.facebook.com/140874547755
twitter.com/VHolocaustCntr
Also Known As: Vancouver Holocaust Education Centre
Overview: A small provincial charitable organization founded in 1983
Mission: To provide educational programs, commemorative services, lecture series, exhibits, archives (documents & artifacts), oral history program; to maintain an education centre containing an archives & teaching museum
Member of: Canadian Museum Association; Association of Holocaust Organizations
Chief Officer(s):
Ed Lewin, President
Nina Krieger, Executive Director
Finances: *Annual Operating Budget:* $250,000-$500,000; *Funding Sources:* Membership fees, donations, grants
Staff Member(s): 10
Activities: *Library* Open to public

Vancouver Humane Society (VHS)
#303, 8623 Granville St., Vancouver BC V6P 5A2
Tel: 604-266-9744; *Fax:* 604-266-1311
info@vancouverhumanesociety.bc.ca
www.vancouverhumanesociety.bc.ca/home.html
www.facebook.com/VancouverHumaneSociety
twitter.com/vanhumane
Overview: A small local organization founded in 1987
Mission: To promote public awareness of animal welfare problems; to ensure & promote the fair & proper treatment of animals; to accept & solicit funds for education about animal welfare; to disburse funds for care & veterinary treatment of animals in need
Chief Officer(s):
Liberty Mulkani, President
Debra Probert, Executive Director
debra@vancouverhumanesociety.bc.ca
Finances: *Annual Operating Budget:* $100,000-$250,000
Staff Member(s): 3; 27 volunteer(s)
Membership: 23 individual;

Vancouver International Children's Festival
402 - 873 Beatty St., Vancouver BC V6B 2M6
Tel: 604-708-5655; *Fax:* 604-708-5661
Other Communication: www.flickr.com/photos/vankidsfest
info@childrensfestival.ca
www.childrensfestival.ca
www.facebook.com/KidsFest
twitter.com/VICF
www.youtube.com/user/VanKidsFest
Previous Name: Canadian Institute of the Arts for Young Audiences
Overview: A small national charitable organization founded in 1975
Mission: To provide performing arts programs to young people in a festival environment; To encourage critical thinking & a lifelong interest in learning, the arts & cultural development
Member of: Vancouver Cultural Alliance; Canadian Children's Festival Association
Chief Officer(s):
Tom Stulberg, Chair
Katharine Carol, Artistic & Executive Director
Finances: *Annual Operating Budget:* $500,000-$1.5 Million; *Funding Sources:* Corporate; government; private sector; earned revenue; consulting
Staff Member(s): 7; 1400 volunteer(s)
Membership: 84; *Fees:* $5

Vancouver Island Advanced Technology Centre (VIATeC)
#2659 Douglas St., 2nd Fl., Victoria BC V8T 5M2
Tel: 250-483-3214
www.viatec.ca
www.facebook.com/VIATeC
twitter.com/VIATeC
www.flickr.com/photos/viatec
Overview: A small local organization founded in 1989
Mission: To promote & enhance the development of the advanced technology industry on Vancouver Island; to be the first place contacted by people who require information or assistance related to the development or application of advanced technology; to act as liaison with industry, government & educational organizations to ensure that Vancouver Island's potential for growth in the advanced technology industry is fully realized
Affliation(s): Canadian Advanced Technology Association
Chief Officer(s):

Art Aylesworth, Executive Chair
Dan Gunn, Executive Director
dgunn@viatec.ca
Georgia Cowell, Manager, Member Relations
gcowell@viatec.ca
Staff Member(s): 5
Membership: 400; *Fees:* $20 student; $100 individual; $370 + $5 per employee organization; $2,625 sustaining; *Member Profile:* Persons, companies, organizations & agencies within Vancouver Island's advanced technology community
Activities: Information or assistance related to the development or application of advanced technology

Vancouver Island Construction Association
1075 Alston St., Victoria BC V9A 3S6
Tel: 250-388-6471; *Fax:* 250-388-5183
Toll-Free: 877-847-6471
www.vicabc.ca
twitter.com/VICA_BC
www.youtube.com/user/VICA1075
Overview: A small local organization founded in 1912 overseen by Canadian Construction Association
Mission: To support & provide educational opportunities for its memebers
Member of: British Columbia Construction Association
Chief Officer(s):
Greg Baynton, Chief Executive Officer
gregbaynton@vicabc.ca
Angus Macpherson, Chair
Staff Member(s): 9
Membership: 500+; *Fees:* Schedule available; *Committees:* General Contractor; Trade Contractor; Social & Networking; Construction Careers; Standards & Practices; VICA U40

Vancouver Island Construction Association (VICA)
1075 Alston St., Victoria BC V9A 3S6
Tel: 250-388-6471; *Fax:* 250-388-5183
Toll-Free: 877-847-6471
www.vicabc.ca
twitter.com/VICA_BC
Overview: A small local organization founded in 1912
Mission: To serve & promote the business life of members & the construction industry; To be the recognized voice & authority of Victoria's construction industry
Affiliation(s): British Columbia Construction Association; Canadian Construction Association
Chief Officer(s):
Greg Baynton, President
gregbaynton@vicabc.ca
Finances: *Annual Operating Budget:* $250,000-$500,000
Staff Member(s): 3
Membership: 275; *Fees:* $1195-$1,675 per company based on volume of business; *Member Profile:* ICI sectors; *Committees:* General Contractor; Trade Contractor; Social and Networking; Construction Careers; Standards and Practices; Young Construction Leaders
Activities: AGM; Christmas Lunch; golf tournament; educational seminars

Nanaimo Office
#5, 1850 Northfield Rd., Nanaimo BC V9S 3B3
Tel: 250-758-1841; *Fax:* 250-758-1286

Vancouver Island Crisis Society
PO Box 1118, Nanaimo BC V9R 6E7
Tel: 250-753-2495; *Fax:* 250-753-2475; *Crisis Hot-Line:* 888-494-3888
info@vicrisis.ca
www.vicrisis.ca
www.facebook.com/pages/Vancouver-Island-Crisis-Society/178964375571662
Overview: A small local charitable organization founded in 1970
Member of: British Columbia Crisis Line Association
Affliation(s): Canadian Association of Suicide Prevention; American Association of Suicidology
Finances: *Funding Sources:* Municipal government; Provincial government; Private donations
Staff Member(s): 20; 40 volunteer(s)
Membership: 55; *Fees:* $20 individuals; *Member Profile:* Board members; Community members; Volunteers; *Committees:* Training Development
Activities: *Awareness Events:* Crisis Line Awareness Week, last week of arch

Vancouver Island Danish-Canadian Club
e-mail: vidanclub@shaw.ca
Overview: A small local organization founded in 1989
Mission: A club for Danes to meet other Danes
Member of: Federation of Danish Associations in Canada
Finances: *Annual Operating Budget:* Less than $50,000; *Funding Sources:* Membership fees; party tickets
10 volunteer(s)
Membership: 180; *Fees:* $15; *Member Profile:* Danish by birth, descent or marriage
Activities: 3 annual parties; cultural meetings

Vancouver Island Miniature Horse Club (VIMHC)
c/o Catherine Royle, 2918 Glen Eagles Rd., Shawnigan Lake BC V0R 2W1
Tel: 250-743-2755; *Fax:* 250-743-2785
kinsol@shaw.ca
www.bcminiaturehorseclubs.com/viclubinfo.htm
Overview: A small local organization
Chief Officer(s):
Gerry Breckon, President, 250-743-1183
lombardfarm@shaw.ca
Lesley Roy, Vice-President, 250-749-4767
les_roy@telus.net
Dawn Nedzelsk, Secretary, 250-544-6114
dawn.nedzelski@viha.ca
Finances: *Funding Sources:* Sponsorships; Membership fees
Membership: *Fees:* $5 youth members under age 18; $25 adult members; $30 families; *Member Profile:* Miniature horse owners & breeders on Vancouver Island
Activities: Organizing meetings & educational activities for members; Hosting & participating in shows for miniature horses; Presenting awards
Publications:
• Vancouver Island Miniature Horse Club Newsletter
Type: Newsletter; *Editor:* David Hollebone
Profile: Club activities, announcements, & upcoming events for members

Vancouver Island Prostate Cancer Research Foundation
#107, 1027 Pandora Ave., Victoria BC V8V 3P6
Tel: 250-920-0772
vip@viprostate.org
Overview: A small local charitable organization
Mission: To support prostate cancer patients, by finding better methods of treatment & increasing the quality of life for prostate cancer sufferers
Affiliation(s): Canadian Prostate Cancer Network
Membership: *Member Profile:* Prostate cancer patients, survivors, spouses & others

Vancouver Island Public Interest Research Group (VIPIRG)
University of Victoria, SUB Room B122, PO Box 3035, Stn. CSC, Victoria BC V8W 3P3
Tel: 250-472-4386
info@vipirg.ca
www.vipirg.ca
www.facebook.com/VIPIRG
twitter.com/VIPIRG
Overview: A medium-sized local organization
Mission: Combines original research on emerging social & environmental issues with education, advocacy & action for positive change; research is directly relevant to community; projects developed in partnership & consultations with other groups; research internship program, training workshops, resource library & other programming
Member of: BC Environmental Network; Canadian Centre for Policy Alternatives
Chief Officer(s):
Meghan Jezewski, Internal Coordinator
Staff Member(s): 3
Membership: *Fees:* $3 full-time students; $1.50 part-time students; $2 graduate students; $10 community member; *Member Profile:* All University of Victoria students are automatically members & community members
Activities: Research projects leading to lobbying, education, activism & advocacy on emerging social justice & environmental issues; research internship program; *Internships:* Yes; *Speaker Service:* Yes; *Library:* VIPIRG Alternative Resource Library; Open to public

Vancouver Island Real Estate Board (VIREB)
6374 Metral Dr., Nanaimo BC V9T 2L8
Tel: 250-390-4212; *Fax:* 250-390-5014
info@vireb.com
www.vireb.com
www.linkedin.com/pub/vancouver-island-real-estate-board/4a/926/332
www.facebook.com/117416804932
twitter.com/vireb
Overview: A small local organization founded in 1966 overseen by British Columbia Real Estate Association
Mission: To provide cost-effective tools, services & information necessary to foster professionalism & maintain the realtor's position as the primary focus in the real estate industry
Member of: The Canadian Real Estate Association
Chief Officer(s):
Guy Bezeau, President
Bill Benoit, CAE, Executive Officer
bbenoit@vireb.com
Darrell Paysen, Manager, Member Services
dpaysen@vireb.com
Finances: *Annual Operating Budget:* $1.5 Million-$3 Million; *Funding Sources:* Members monthly assessment
Staff Member(s): 13; 50 volunteer(s)
Membership: 1,000+; *Member Profile:* Licensed as realtor
Activities: *Speaker Service:* Yes
Awards:
• REALTORS Care Awards (Award)

Vancouver Island Rock & Alpine Garden Society (VIRAGS)
PO Box 33012, #3, 310 Goldstream Ave., Victoria BC V9B 6K3
Tel: 250-389-1397
ua024@victoria.tc.ca
www.virags.ca
Overview: A small local organization
Mission: VIRAGS is a club of plant lovers living near Victoria, British Columbia, who visit, study, photograph, draw & grow alpine plants, bog dwellers & woodlanders, whether native or exotic
Chief Officer(s):
Yvonne Rorison, Contact, 250-519-0269
Membership: *Fees:* $20
Activities: Field trips; garden shows

Vancouver Island Society for Disabled Artists
#304, 1550 Church Ave., Victoria BC V8P 2H1
Tel: 250-472-2917
Overview: A small local organization founded in 1995
Mission: To support artists with disabilities by creating an art gallery in Victoria British Columbia so artists can showcase their art work
Chief Officer(s):
Garry Curry
Alistair Green, 250-721-1516
Membership: *Fees:* $20
Activities: Project for the 2010 Winter Olympics, Whistler BC

Vancouver Island Symphony
PO Box 661, Nanaimo BC V9R 5L9
Tel: 250-754-0177; *Fax:* 250-754-0165
admin@vancouverislandsymphony.com
www.vancouverislandsymphony.com
www.facebook.com/vanislesymphony
Overview: A small local charitable organization founded in 1995 overseen by Orchestras Canada
Mission: To promote & present orchestra music in the Central Vancouver Island Region
Chief Officer(s):
Margot Holmes, Executive Director
Jae Valentine, Administrator
admin@vancouverislandsymphony.com
Activities: *Speaker Service:* Yes

Vancouver Island University Faculty Association (VIUFA)
Building 360, #108, 900 Fifth St., Nanaimo BC V9R 5S5
Tel: 250-740-6339; *Fax:* 250-753-9713
www.viufa.ca
Overview: A small local organization
Member of: Federation of Post-Secondary Educators of British Columbia (FPSE)
Chief Officer(s):
Marni Stanley
Manjeet Uppal, Vice-President
Johnny Blakeborough, Secretary-Treasurer
Judy Benner, Office Manager
Membership: *Committees:* Contract Negotiating; Personnel Stewards; Professional & Scholarly Development; Status of Women; Status of Non-Regular Faculty; Human Rights & International Solidarity

Vancouver Island Vegetarian Association (VIVA)
c/o Morgan Andrews, 2523 Wark St., Victoria BC V8T 4G7

www.islandveg.com
www.facebook.com/islandveg
Overview: A small local organization founded in 1980
Mission: To promote awareness of vegetarianism on Vancouver Island
Chief Officer(s):
Trevor Murdock, Chair
Sandra Carlson, Secretary
Morgan Andrews, Treasurer
Finances: *Funding Sources:* Donations
Activities: Providing education about vegetarianism; Offering a library of cookbooks at the Overleaf Cafe - Bookshop in Victoria, British Columbia; *Awareness Events:* Victoria Vegan Festival; *Library:* Vancouver Island Vegetarian Association Library; Open to public
Publications:
• Vancouver Island Vegetarian Association Newsletter
Type: Newsletter; *Editor:* Sarat Collings
Profile: Information about association activities, events, book reviews, & recipes

Vancouver Jewish Film Festival Society (JFAS)
6184 Ash St., Vancouver BC V5Z 3G9
Tel: 604-266-0245; *Fax:* 604-266-0244
film@vjff.org
www.vjff.org
Overview: A small local charitable organization founded in 1986
Mission: To provide Jewish cultural & heritage programs, exhibits & performances for the Jewish community & general public; to provide information on artists & performing groups; to maintain records on locally owned Judaica
Chief Officer(s):
Bridget Sacks, President & Chair
Robert Albanese, Executive Director
Finances: *Funding Sources:* Donations; programs; fundraising; government grants
Activities: Annual Vancouver Jewish Film Festival, May; cultural programs; *Speaker Service:* Yes; *Rents Mailing List:* Yes

Vancouver Maritime Museum
1905 Ogden Ave., Vancouver BC V6J 1A3
Tel: 604-257-8300; *Fax:* 604-737-2621
info@vancouvermaritimemuseum.com
www.vancouvermaritimemuseum.com
www.facebook.com/vanmaritime
twitter.com/vanmaritime
www.youtube.com/channel/UChBhyY0K-sOpAr32kQz306w
Overview: A small local organization founded in 1959
Mission: Canada's principal maritime museum on the Pacific, located in the heart of Canada's greatest part, Vancouver, at the gateway to the Pacific
Member of: Council of American Maritime Museums; International Congress of Maritime Museums; Canadian Museums Association; British Columbia Museums Association; Historic Naval Ships Association
Chief Officer(s):
Ken Burton, Executive Director
director@vancouvermaritimemuseum.com
Finances: *Funding Sources:* Municipal & provincial governments; private
Staff Member(s): 32; 62 volunteer(s)
Membership: *Fees:* $60 family; $40 individual; $35 senior
Activities: Educational Programs; Conferences; Exhibits; *Internships:* Yes; *Speaker Service:* Yes; *Rents Mailing List:* Yes

Vancouver Moving Theatre (VMT)
PO Box 88270, Stn. Chinatown, Vancouver BC V6A 4A4
Tel: 604-628-5672
vancouvermovingtheatre@shaw.ca
www.vancouvermovingtheatre.com
www.facebook.com/pages/Vancouver-Moving-Theatre/1899867 27692739
twitter.com/VanMovTheatre
Overview: A small local charitable organization founded in 1983
Mission: To develop a new form of interdisciplinary art influenced by the Pacific Rim culture of Vancouver; to present services & products to affirm the importance of art in questions of healing, humanity & the soul
Member of: Vancouver Professional Theatre Alliance; Vancouver Dance Centre; Vancouver Cultural Alliance
Chief Officer(s):
Savannah Walling, Artistic Director
Terry Hunter, Executive Director
Finances: *Funding Sources:* City of Vancouver; provincial government; foundations

Activities: Performances; workshops; demonstrations; lectures; articles; performing & miscellaneous cultural services; *Speaker Service:* Yes; *Library* by appointment

Vancouver Multicultural Society (VMS)
1254 - West 7th Ave., Vancouver BC V6H 1B6
Tel: 604-731-4648
vmsbc@telus.net
www.vmsbc.com
Previous Name: Vancouver Multicultural Society of British Columbia
Overview: A small local charitable organization founded in 1974
Mission: To raise awareness of & conduct public education in cross-cultural relations & multiculturalism with the object of preserving & fostering cultural heritages; To advocate on issues related to multiculturalism, human rights, race relations, & cross-cultural understanding
Chief Officer(s):
John Halani, President, 604-687-6631
jhalani@telus.net
Membership: *Fees:* $25 Youth/Senior; $30 Individual; $75 Non-profit Organization; $100 Corporate; *Member Profile:* Applications must be reviewed by Membership Committee Chairperson & accepted/not accepted at regular Board of Directors meetings

Vancouver Multicultural Society of British Columbia *See* Vancouver Multicultural Society

Vancouver Museum Commission *See* Vancouver Museum Society

Vancouver Museum Society
1100 Chestnut St., Vancouver BC V6J 3J9
Tel: 604-736-4431; *Fax:* 604-736-5417
guestservices@museumofvancouver.ca
www.museumofvancouver.ca
www.facebook.com/MuseumofVancouver
twitter.com/Museumofvan
www.youtube.com/user/MuseumofVancouver
Previous Name: Vancouver Museum Commission
Overview: A small local charitable organization founded in 1894
Mission: To interpret the natural & cultural history of Vancouver including all its cultural constituents
Chief Officer(s):
Hugh Bulmer, Chair
Nancy Noble, CEO
Finances: *Annual Operating Budget:* $1.5 Million-$3 Million; *Funding Sources:* Federal; provincial; municipal; fundraising
Staff Member(s): 30; 200 volunteer(s)
Membership: 500; *Fees:* Schedule available
Activities: Bus tours; school programs; adult programs; *Speaker Service:* Yes; *Library* by appointment

Vancouver Musicians' Association (VMA)
#100, 925 West 8th Ave., Vancouver BC V5Z 1E4
Tel: 604-737-1110; *Fax:* 604-734-3299
Toll-Free: 800-644-2899
wmorris@afm.org
www.vma145.ca
Overview: A medium-sized local organization founded in 1901
Member of: American Federation of Musicians of the United States & Canada
Affiliation(s): Vancouver Trades & Labour Council
Chief Officer(s):
David G. Brown, President
dbrown@vma145.ca
Staff Member(s): 5
Membership: 1,900+; *Fees:* $136.50; *Member Profile:* Professional musicians

Vancouver Natural History Society *See* Nature Vancouver

Vancouver New Music (VNM)
837 Davie St., Vancouver BC V6Z 1B7
Tel: 604-633-0861; *Fax:* 604-633-0871
info@newmusic.org
www.newmusic.org
www.facebook.com/group.php?gid=145832458818903
twitter.com/vannewmusic
Also Known As: Vancouver New Music Society
Overview: A medium-sized local charitable organization founded in 1973
Mission: Regarded as Western Canada's major producer of contemporary music & sonic art, dedicated to the outstanding performance of the music of our time; fostering connections within the community to bring new music to a wider audience; commissions & premieres new works by Canadian composers; produces music-theatre, leading electroacoustic music, international composers & performers; produces an annual Vancouver New Music Festival; explores the interaction of contemporary music with other disciplines
Member of: Opera America; Opera.ca; Alliance for Arts & Culture; Vancouver Music Alliance; Canadian New Music Network; Independent Media Arts Alliance
Affliation(s): Canadian Music Centre
Chief Officer(s):
Giorgio Magnanensi, Artistic Director
David Murphy, President
Heather McDermid, Manager, Marketing & Communications
heather@newmusic.org
Jim Smith, Managing Producer
jim@newmusic.org
Jason Dubois, Production Manager
jason@newmusic.org
Finances: *Annual Operating Budget:* $250,000-$500,000; *Funding Sources:* Government grants; charitable gaming; corporate sponsorships; foundation grants; donations
Staff Member(s): 10; 31 volunteer(s)
Membership: 183; *Committees:* Education, Advocacy, Personel, Artistic Advisory, Marketing, Fundraising, Volunteer, Nominating
Activities: Annual concert series; musical festival (third week of Oct.); biennial music theatre production; lectures & workshops with visiting artists; *Library:* Musical Score Archive; by appointment

Vancouver Numismatic Society (VNS) / La société numismatique de Vancouver
c/o Brian Grant Duff, 434 Richards St., Vancouver BC V6B 2Z3
Tel: 604-684-4613; *Fax:* 604-684-4618
collect@direct.ca
Overview: A small local organization founded in 1955
Mission: To promote the collection & study of coins, tokens, medals & paper money
Member of: Canadian Numismatic Association
Affliation(s): British Columbia Numismatic Association; Pacific Northwest Numismatic Association
Chief Officer(s):
Brian Grant Duff, Contact
Peter Moogk, Contact, 604-228-9445
Finances: *Annual Operating Budget:* Less than $50,000; *Funding Sources:* Membership fees & revenue from annual collectors' fair
Membership: 1-99; *Member Profile:* Currency collectors
Activities: Monthly meetings for currency collectors; annual show to display & sell old & modern examples of currency; *Library* Open to public by appointment

Vancouver Opera (VOA) / Association de l'opéra de vancouver
1945 McLean Dr., Vancouver BC V5N 3J7
Tel: 604-682-2871; *Fax:* 604-682-3981
tickets@vancouveropera.ca
www.vancouveropera.ca
www.facebook.com/vancouveropera
twitter.com/VancouverOpera
www.youtube.com/user/vancouveropera
Previous Name: Vancouver Opera Association
Overview: A large local charitable organization founded in 1958
Mission: To share the power of opera with all who are open to receiving it, through superior performances & meaningful education programs for all ages
Member of: Opera America; Opera.ca
Affliation(s): Canadian Actors' Equity Association; IATSE; AFM
Chief Officer(s):
James W. Wright, General Director
jwright@vancouveropera.ca
Finances: *Annual Operating Budget:* Greater than $5 Million; *Funding Sources:* Earned revenue; fundraising; government grants
Staff Member(s): 27; 117 volunteer(s)
Membership: 6,500; *Fees:* Subscription; donation; *Member Profile:* Subscribers & donors; *Committees:* Individual Giving; Corporate Advisors; Planned Giving; Finance; Executive; Special Events
Activities: 4 fully staged opera productions at the Queen Elizabeth Theatre (20+ performances + 1 or 2 concerts per year); VO Ensemble performances in schools & the community; *Internships:* Yes; *Library:* Music Library

Vancouver Opera Association *See* Vancouver Opera

Vancouver Orchid Society
PO Box 42025, Stn. Marpole, Vancouver BC V6B 6S6

e-mail: info@vancouverorchidsociety.ca
www.vancouverorchidsociety.ca
Overview: A small local organization founded in 1946
Mission: To promote & widen knowledege of orchids
Chief Officer(s):
Margaret Prat, President
Membership: *Fees:* $20 students; $30 regular

Vancouver Paleontological Society (VanPS)
#12 8171 Steveson Hwy., Richmond BC V7A 1M4
www.vcn.bc.ca/vanps
Overview: A small local organization
Mission: To promote public awareness of our fossil heritage; to promote safe & responsible fossil collecting; to provide educational information about ancient life through field trips, presentations & displays; to bring together amateurs & professionals who share a common interest in fossils
Member of: BC Paleontological Alliance
Chief Officer(s):
Jim Haggart, Chair
Jim.Haggart@NRCan-RNCan.gc.ca
Finances: *Annual Operating Budget:* Less than $50,000
Membership: 62; *Fees:* $35; *Member Profile:* Amateur & professional paleontologists
Activities: Monthly lectures; field trips

Vancouver Peretz Institute; Vancouver Peretz Shule ***See*** Peretz Centre for Secular Jewish Culture

Vancouver Philharmonic Orchestra (VPO)
PO Box 27503, Stn. Oakridge, Vancouver BC V5Z 4M4
Tel: 604-878-9989
vpo@vcn.bc.ca
www.vanphil.ca
www.facebook.com/83282488987
Overview: A small local charitable organization founded in 1964 overseen by Orchestras Canada
Chief Officer(s):
Chris Buchner, President
Joan Carne, Treasurer
Jin Zhang, Music Director
Anne Worthington, Contact, Memberships
Finances: *Annual Operating Budget:* Less than $50,000;
Funding Sources: Ticket sales; grants; donations; fundraising
Staff Member(s): 2; 20 volunteer(s)
Membership: 1-99
Activities: Offers five concerts a year; provides an opportunity for serious amateur musicians to study & perform; *Internships:* Yes

Vancouver Pro Musica
PO Box 78077, Stn. Grandview, Vancouver BC V5N 5W1
Tel: 604-688-6407
info@vancouverpromusica.ca
www.vancouverpromusica.ca
www.facebook.com/vancouver.promusica
twitter.com/vanpromusica
Overview: A small local charitable organization founded in 1984
Mission: To promote musical life in British Columbia by holding concerts
Chief Officer(s):
Craig Day, President
Martin Ritter, Vice-President
John L. Baker, Treasurer
Finances: *Annual Operating Budget:* Less than $50,000;
Funding Sources: Donations
10 volunteer(s)
Membership: 40; *Member Profile:* Vancouver-based composers active in various aspects of new music
Activities: Sonic Boom Concert Series (spring); Further East/Further West Concert Series (fall);

Vancouver Professional Theatre Alliance ***See*** Greater Vancouver Professional Theatre Alliance

Vancouver Rape Relief & Women's Shelter
PO Box 21562, 1424 Commercial Dr., Vancouver BC V5L 5G2
Tel: 604-872-8212; *TTY:* 604-877-0958; *Crisis Hot-Line:* 604-877-8212
info@rapereliefshelter.bc.ca
www.rapereliefshelter.bc.ca
Overview: A small local charitable organization founded in 1973
Mission: To stop violence against woman; to give women survivors emotional support after a sexual assault; to house battered women & their children
Member of: Canadian Association of Sexual Assault Centres; BC/Yukon Transition House Society
Finances: *Annual Operating Budget:* $250,000-$500,000;
Funding Sources: Provincial government; fundraising
Activities: 24 hour rape crisis centre; shelter for battered women; peer counselling; advocacy & accompaniment; support group; *Awareness Events:* Take Back the Night, Dec. 6 Memorial; *Speaker Service:* Yes; *Library* by appointment

Vancouver Recital Society (VRS)
#304, 873 Beatty St., Vancouver BC V6B 2M6
Tel: 604-602-0363; *Fax:* 604-602-0364
vrs@vanrecital.com
vanrecital.com
www.facebook.com/vancouverrecitalsociety
twitter.com/vanrecital
www.youtube.com/user/vanrecital
Overview: A small local organization founded in 1980
Chief Officer(s):
Jean Hodgins, President
Niamh Small, Director, Communications & Marketing
niamhsmall@vanrecital.com
Staff Member(s): 5

Vancouver Regional Construction Association (VRCA)
3636 - 4th Ave. East, Vancouver BC V5M 1M3
Tel: 604-294-3766; *Fax:* 604-298-9472
www.vrca.bc.ca
Previous Name: Amalgamated Construction Association of British Columbia
Overview: A medium-sized provincial organization founded in 1965
Mission: To promote construction investment & efficiency in the BC construction industry; to represent all sectors of the industry to government & the public
Member of: British Columbia Construction Association
Affiliation(s): Canadian Construction Association
Chief Officer(s):
Keith Sashaw, President
Finances: *Annual Operating Budget:* $500,000-$1.5 Million;
Funding Sources: Membership dues; sale of documents
Staff Member(s): 9; 50 volunteer(s)
Membership: 650 organizations; *Fees:* Schedule available; *Committees:* Membership; Arbitration; Education; Special Events; Awards; Life Member; Standard Practices
Activities: *Library*
Awards:
- Safety Awards (Award)
- General Contractor Award (Award)
- Trade Contractor Award (Award)
- Mechanical Contractor Award (Award)
- Electrical Contractor Award (Award)
- Outstanding Woman in Construction Award (Award)

Vancouver Soaring Association
PO Box 3251, Vancouver BC V6B 3X9
Tel: 604-869-7211
www.vsa.ca
twitter.com/vancouversoaring
Overview: A small local organization
Member of: Soaring Association of Canada

Vancouver Society of Financial Analysts ***See*** CFA Society Vancouver

Vancouver Society of Immigrant & Visible Minority Women (VSIVMW)
#204, 2524 Cypress St., Vancouver BC V6J 3N2
Tel: 604-731-9108; *Fax:* 604-731-9117
vsivmw@amssa.org
Overview: A small local organization
Mission: To assist immigrant & visible minority women; to advocate & facilitate their empowerment; to create an awareness of their rights & to help them access equal opportunities in Canadian society; a voice for the concerns & issues facing immigrant & visible minority women, at grassroots & professional levels; provides education, services, referrals, research, & advocacy; promotes multiculturalism & harmony for all cultures
Finances: *Annual Operating Budget:* $50,000-$100,000
Membership: 1-99
Activities: Referral services; workshops & seminars; sponsors research projects in area of needs of immigrant women; *Library* Open to public

Vancouver Status of Women (VSW)
2652 East Hastings St., Vancouver BC V5K 1Z6
Tel: 604-255-6554; *Fax:* 604-255-7508
womencentre@vsw.ca
www.vsw.ca
Overview: A small local organization founded in 1971
Mission: To ensure that women participate fully in the social, political & economic life of our communities; to work for women's full equality in these areas by addressing barriers of patriarchy, racism, poverty, male violence against women, heterosexism, ablism, classism, imperialism & anti-Jewish oppression; all of which profoundly impact the lives of women
Affliation(s): National Action Committee on the Status of Women
Chief Officer(s):
Patricia E. Aguilar-Zeleny, Coordinator
Finances: *Annual Operating Budget:* $100,000-$250,000;
Funding Sources: Regional government
Staff Member(s): 7; 50 volunteer(s)
Membership: 50 institutional + 30 student + 300 individual; *Fees:* $1-$50 based on sliding scale

The Vancouver Summer Festival Society
#402, 873 Beatty St., Vancouver BC V6B 2M6
www.musicfestvancouver.ca
www.facebook.com/mfestvan
twitter.com/mfestvan
www.youtube.com/mfestvan
Also Known As: MusicFest Vancouver
Overview: A small local charitable organization founded in 1997
Mission: To present a summer music celebration that explores the connections between cultures, centuries & people; internationally acclaimed artists from around the globe join forces with some of Canada's best performers in over 40 concerts featuring classical music, world music & jazz
Member of: Tourism Vancouver
Chief Officer(s):
Morris Biddle, President
Finances: *Annual Operating Budget:* $1.5 Million-$3 Million;
Funding Sources: Public & private donations; Earned revenue
Activities: Presents a 2 week summer music festival of classical music, world & jazz, plus a year-round concert series across BC

Vancouver Symphony Society (VSO)
#500, 833 Seymour St., Vancouver BC V6B 0G4
Tel: 604-684-9100; *Fax:* 604-684-9264
customerservice@vancouversymphony.ca
www.vancouversymphony.ca
Overview: A small local charitable organization founded in 1919 overseen by Orchestras Canada
Mission: Provides stewardship for the Vancouver Symphony Orchestra to achieve recognition as one of Canada's highest quality symphony orchestras; to perform at all times with artistic distinction & thereby enrich BC's quality of life; to expand the enjoyment & appreciation of the finest orchestral music of the past & present
Member of: Alliance for Arts & Culture
Chief Officer(s):
Jeff Alexander, President & CEO
Mary-Ann Moir, Vice-President, Finance & Administration
Finances: *Annual Operating Budget:* Greater than $5 Million
Staff Member(s): 28; 70 volunteer(s)
Membership: 1,000-4,999
Activities: *Library:* VSO Library

Vancouver TheatreSports League (VTSL)
1502 Duranleau St., Vancouver BC V6H 3S4
Tel: 604-738-7013; *Fax:* 604-738-8013
info@vtsl.com
www.vtsl.com
www.facebook.com/VanTheatreSport
twitter.com/VanTheatreSport
Overview: A small local organization founded in 1980
Mission: To challenge & inspire the community by growing & exploring exceptional improv-based work
Chief Officer(s):
Jay Ono, Executive Director
Staff Member(s): 14

Vancouver Women's Health Collective
29 West Hastings St., Vancouver BC V6B 1G4
Tel: 604-736-5262
vwhc.centre@gmail.com
www.womenshealthcollective.ca
Overview: A small local charitable organization founded in 1972
Mission: Raises awareness for women's health issues; provides information on women's health
Chief Officer(s):
Caryn Duncan, Executive Director

Finances: *Funding Sources:* Donations; Membership Fees; Grants; Fundraising; Gaming revenue
Staff Member(s): 2
Membership: *Fees:* $10-25 individual; $50 organization

Vancouver Youth Symphony Orchestra Society (VYSO)

3214 - 10 Ave. West, Vancouver BC V6K 2L2
Tel: 604-737-0714; *Fax:* 604-737-0739
vyso@telus.net
www.vyso.com
www.facebook.com/113486838664675
Previous Name: Junior Symphony Society
Overview: A small local charitable organization founded in 1930 overseen by Orchestras Canada
Mission: To provide orchestral training & experience to music students in Greater Vancouver & the Lower Mainland from beginner to advanced level career student
Member of: Alliance for Arts & Culture
Chief Officer(s):
Roger Cole, Artistic Director
Holly Littleford, Orchestra Manager
vyso@telus.net
Finances: *Annual Operating Budget:* $100,000-$250,000; *Funding Sources:* G
overnment; corporate & private donations; tuition fee; concert revenue; fundraising
Staff Member(s): 2; 200 volunteer(s)
Membership: 240; *Fees:* $20; *Member Profile:* Audition for membership & placement
Activities: Orchestral training; public concerts; *Library*

Vancouver, Coast & Mountains Tourism Region

#270, 1651 Commercial Dr., Vancouver BC V5l 3Y3
Tel: 604-739-9011; *Fax:* 604-739-0153
Toll-Free: 800-667-3306
info@vcmbc.com
www.604pulse.com
www.facebook.com/vcmbc
twitter.com/vcmbc
Overview: A small local organization founded in 1972 overseen by Council of Tourism Associations of British Columbia
Mission: To create tourist experinces for travellers
Chief Officer(s):
Kevan Ridgway, President & CEO, 604-638-6930, Fax: 604-739-0153
kevan@vcmbc.com
Doleen Dean, Visitor Services
doleen@vcmbc.com
Finances: *Annual Operating Budget:* $1.5 Million-$3 Million
Staff Member(s): 10; 25 volunteer(s)
Membership: 3500
Activities: *Internships:* Yes; *Speaker Service:* Yes

Vanderhoof & District Chamber of Commerce *See* Vanderhoof Chamber of Commerce

Vanderhoof Chamber of Commerce

PO Box 126, 2353 Burrard Ave., Vanderhoof BC V0J 3A0
Tel: 250-567-2124; *Fax:* 250-567-3316
Toll-Free: 800-752-4094
info@vanderhoofchamber.com
www.vanderhoofchamber.com
www.facebook.com/119783441393384
twitter.com/VisitVanderhoof
Previous Name: Vanderhoof & District Chamber of Commerce
Overview: A small local organization
Mission: To provide a strong voice for the future of business, industry & the professional community
Member of: Canadian Chamber of Commerce
Affliation(s): BC Chamber of Commerce
Chief Officer(s):
Jessi Wilson, President
Nicole Armstrong, Executive Director
manager@vanderhoofchamber.com
Staff Member(s): 4; 12 volunteer(s)
Membership: 240 individual; *Fees:* $84-$470.40; *Committees:* Agriculture; Beautification; Bylaws & Policy; Education; Finance; Forestry; Future Planning; Health; Membership; Mining; Nechako Watershed Council; Nominating; Retail; Special Events; Tourism; Trade Show
Activities: *Awareness Events:* Pumpkin Walk, Oct.; Parade of Lights, Dec.; *Rents Mailing List:* Yes; *Library* Open to public

VanDusen Botanical Garden Association (VBGA)

5251 Oak St., Vancouver BC V6M 4H1
Tel: 604-257-8666
volunteer@vandusen.org
www.vandusengarden.org
www.facebook.com/210746535227
Previous Name: Vancouver Botanical Gardens Association
Overview: A small local charitable organization founded in 1965
Mission: To support & promote VanDusen Gardens as an outstanding botanical garden; to act as a source & focus of excellence in botanical/horticultural plant conservation & education; to enhance & perpetuate the Garden as a place of beauty, pleasure & inspiration for all
Affliation(s): American Association of Botanical Gardens & Arboretums
Chief Officer(s):
Harry Jongerden, Garden Director
harry.jongerden@vancouver.ca
Judy Aird, Volunteer Director
volunteer@vandusen.org
Nancy Wong, Director, Public Relations
media@vandusen.org
Finances: *Annual Operating Budget:* $500,000-$1.5 Million; *Funding Sources:* Membership fees; private donations; special events
Staff Member(s): 18; 1200 volunteer(s)
Membership: 9,000; *Fees:* Schedule available
Activities: *Library:* VanDusen Library
Publications:
• The Bulletin [a publication of the VanDusen Botanical Garden Association]
Type: Newsletter; *Frequency:* Quarterly

Vanier Institute of The Family (VIF) / Institut Vanier de la famille

94 Centrepointe Dr., Ottawa ON K2G 6B1
Tel: 613-228-8500; *Fax:* 613-228-8007
info@vanierinstitute.ca
www.vanierinstitute.ca
www.facebook.com/vanierinstitute
twitter.com/vanierinstitute
Overview: A medium-sized national charitable organization founded in 1965
Mission: To create awareness of, & to provide leadership on the importance & strengths of families in Canada, & the challenges families face in all their diverse structures; information from the institute's research, consultation & policy development is conveyed through advocacy, education & communications vehicles to elected officials, policymakers, educators, the media, the public & Canadian families themselves
Chief Officer(s):
Nora Spinks, Chief Executive Officer
CEO@vanierinstitute.ca
David Northcott, Chair
Finances: *Annual Operating Budget:* $500,000-$1.5 Million; *Funding Sources:* Foundation; project funding
Staff Member(s): 8
Membership: *Committees:* Finance & Investment; Nominations; Special Events; Human Resources
Activities: *Speaker Service:* Yes

Vanscoy & District Agricultural Society

PO Box 35, Vanscoy SK S0L 3J0
Tel: 306-493-2388; *Fax:* 306-956-3136
vanscoyag@gmail.com
www.vanscoyanddistrictagsociety.ca
Overview: A small local organization founded in 1983
Mission: To improve agriculture & the quality of life in the community by educating members & the community; To provide a community forum for discussion of agricultural issues; to encourage the conservation of natural resources
Member of: Saskatchewan Association of Agricultural Societies & Exhibitions
Chief Officer(s):
Shelley Sowter, Administrator
Quinten Odnokon, President
Finances: *Funding Sources:* Saskatchewan lotteries; fundraising
100 volunteer(s)
Membership: 200; *Fees:* $1
Activities: Rodeo; Taste of RM; Perennial Exchange; fair;

Variety - The Children's Charity (Ontario)

3701 Danforth Ave., Toronto ON M1N 2G2
Tel: 416-699-7167; *Fax:* 416-367-0028
info@varietyontario.ca
www.varietyontario.ca
Previous Name: Variety Club of Ontario, Tent 28
Overview: A medium-sized provincial organization founded in 1945
Mission: To improve the quality of life for children with disabilities & their integration into society
Member of: Variety Clubs International
Affliation(s): Variety Village; Variety Ability Systems Inc.
Chief Officer(s):
John Wilson, CEO
jwillson@varietyontario.ca
Finances: *Annual Operating Budget:* Greater than $5 Million; *Funding Sources:* Events; private & corporate donations
Staff Member(s): 120
Membership: 5,644
Activities: Gold Heart Day Campaign; Blue Jay Kids Day; Sunshine Games; Sports Festival; Blue Jays Luncheon; Lieutenant Governor's Games

Variety - The Children's Charity of BC

4300 Still Creek Dr., Burnaby BC V5C 6C6
Tel: 604-320-0505
Toll-Free: 800-310-5437
info@variety.bc.ca
www.variety.bc.ca
www.facebook.com/variety.bc.ca
twitter.com/VarietyBC
www.youtube.com/user/VarietyBC
Also Known As: Variety Club
Overview: A medium-sized provincial charitable organization founded in 1965
Mission: To raise funds throughout the province of B.C. for the benefit of B.C.'s children with special needs; to provide funds for capital costs; to create new centres or improve existing facilities & purchase specialized equipment
Member of: Variety Clubs International
Chief Officer(s):
Bernice Scholten, Executive Director
Finances: *Funding Sources:* Special events & annual telethon
Membership: *Fees:* $75
Activities: Sunshine Coaches; Electro Limb Program; Talking Computers Program; Child Development Centres; Variety's Parks for Special Children; Outings for Variety's Kids; Variety B.C. Lifeline; grants to other organizations dedicated to helping children with special needs; *Awareness Events:* Annual "Show of Hearts" Telethon; Market & Auction; Boat for Hope; *Speaker Service:* Yes

Variety - The Children's Charity of Manitoba, Tent 58 Inc.

#2 - 1313 Border St., Winnipeg MB R3H 0X4
Tel: 204-982-1050; *Fax:* 204-475-3198
admin@varietymanitoba.com
www.varietymanitoba.com
Overview: A medium-sized provincial charitable organization founded in 1979
Member of: Variety International - The Children's Charity
Finances: *Funding Sources:* Corporate support; Special events; Individual donations
Staff Member(s): 5; 300 volunteer(s)
Membership: 150; *Committees:* Celebrity Dinner; Gold Heart; Golf; Scholarship; Special Needs
Activities: *Awareness Events:* Gold Heart Day, February
Awards:
• Gold Heart Humanitarian of the Year Award (Award)

Variety Club of Northern Alberta, Tent 63

#1205 Energy Square, 10109 - 106th St., Edmonton AB T5J 3L7
Tel: 780-448-9544; *Fax:* 780-448-9289
Overview: A small local organization
Mission: Raises funds for the children of Northern Alberta who have disabilities or are disadvantaged
Chief Officer(s):
Sue McEachern, Executive Director

Variety Club of Ontario, Tent 28 *See* Variety - The Children's Charity (Ontario)

Variety Club of Southern Alberta

Calgary AB
Tel: 403-228-6168
info@varietyalberta.ca
www.varietyalberta.ca
www.facebook.com/VarietyAlberta
Overview: A small local charitable organization founded in 1982
Mission: To provide disabled & disadvantaged children with the means to enjoy quality life experiences; to support research for below the knee amputee children; to provide assistance &

bursaries to children in special situations
Affliation(s): Variety Children's Lifeline
Finances: *Funding Sources:* Membership dues; fundraising
Activities: Variety at Work; Special Celebrity Dinner & Dance; Calgary Stampeder Football Game; Variety Children's Holiday Toylift; Variety Children's Park

Vasculitis Foundation Canada (WGSG)

#446, 425 Hespeler Rd., Cambridge ON N1R 8J6
Toll-Free: 877-572-9474
contact@vasculitis.ca
www.vasculitis.ca
Also Known As: Wegener's Granulomatosis Support Group of Canada
Overview: A small national charitable organization founded in 1998
Mission: To provide emotional & informational support to patients with WG; to assist them & their families in understanding the disease & recovery process, to educate the public about WG, & to support research into the cause, control & cure of WG
Affliation(s): Canadian Order of Rare Disorders (CORD); Wegeners Granulomatosis Association International
Chief Officer(s):
Ann Turuta, Interim President
ann_turuta@hotmail.com
Finances: *Annual Operating Budget:* Less than $50,000; *Funding Sources:* Membership fees; Donations; Bequests
6 volunteer(s)
Membership: *Fees:* $25 CDN membership; $70 dual Mmbership; *Member Profile:* To encourage and support research efforts for the cause and cure for all forms of Vasculitis; To establish rapport with all known Vasculitis patients and try to alleviate the isolation of having an uncommon, life-threatening disease; To assist Vasculitis patients and their families with clinical information and coping strategies, to help them develop a strong and positive outlook.
Activities: *Awareness Events:* Annual Picnic

Vatnabyggd Icelandic Club of Saskatchewan Inc.

www.inlofna.org/Elfros/Vatnabyggd.html
Overview: A small provincial organization founded in 1981
Mission: To foster & promote good citizenship among people of Icelandic origin; to foster & promote knowledge of the Icelandic language, literature & other Icelandic cultural heritage
Member of: Icelandic National League of North America
Affliation(s): Multicultural Council of Saskatchewan
Chief Officer(s):
Christie Dalman, President, 306-554-2267
dalman@sasktel.net
Stella Stephanson, Secretary, 306-328-2077
Finances: *Funding Sources:* Membership fees; raffles; events; Multicultural Council of Saskatchewan
Membership: 210; *Fees:* $5 individual; $10 family

Vaughan Chamber of Commerce (VCC)

#2, 25 Edilcan Dr., Vaughan ON L4K 3S4
Tel: 905-761-1366; *Fax:* 905-761-1918
info@vaughanchamber.ca
www.vaughanchamber.ca
Overview: A medium-sized local organization founded in 1977
Mission: To be the voice of business working together to promote & improve business in the City of Vaughan
Member of: Ontario Chamber of Commerce; Canadian Chamber of Commerce
Chief Officer(s):
Paula Curtis, President & CEO
paula@vaughanchamber.ca
Joanne Taibi, Accounting
joanne@vaughanchamber.ca
Finances: *Annual Operating Budget:* $100,000-$250,000; *Funding Sources:* Membership fees; fundraising
Staff Member(s): 5; 60 volunteer(s)
Membership: 900; *Fees:* Schedule available; *Committees:* Government Liaison; Program Services; Social; Training & Education
Activities: Networking; education & training
Awards:
- Business Achievement Awards (Award)

Vecova Centre for Disability Services & Research

3304 - 33 St. NW, Calgary AB T2L 2A6
Tel: 403-284-1121; *Fax:* 403-284-1146
info@vecova.ca
www.vecova.ca
www.linkedin.com/company/vecova
www.facebook.com/Vecova
twitter.com/Vecova
www.youtube.com/user/Vecovadisability
Previous Name: Vocational & Rehabilitation Research Institute
Overview: A large national charitable organization founded in 1966
Mission: To be leaders in innovative services & research that support persons with disabilities to live as contributing & valued members of the community
Member of: Alberta Association of Rehabilitation Centres
Affliation(s): University of Calgary
Chief Officer(s):
John Lee, CEO
Neil MacKenzie, Chair
Finances: *Annual Operating Budget:* Greater than $5 Million; *Funding Sources:* Alberta Community Development; City of Calgary; donations; fundraising; Canada Mortgage & Housing
Staff Member(s): 370; 100 volunteer(s)
Membership: 50; *Fees:* $15 individual; $20 family; $10 associate
Activities: *Speaker Service:* Yes; *Library:* Dr. Randy Tighe Resource Centre; Open to public

Vegetable & Potato Producers' Association of Nova Scotia *See* Horticulture Nova Scotia

Vegetable Growers' Association of Manitoba (VGAM)

PO Box 894, Portage la Prairie MB R1N 3C4
Tel: 204-857-4581; *Fax:* 204-239-0260
vgamveggies@hotmail.com
www.vgam.ca
Overview: A small provincial organization founded in 1953
Mission: To support Manitoba's vegetable growers
Member of: Canadian Horticultural Council
Chief Officer(s):
Todd Giffin, President
Finances: *Funding Sources:* Membership fees
Activities: Providing information to assist members

Vegetarians of Alberta Association (VOA)

9605 - 82 Ave., Edmonton AB T6C 0Z9
Tel: 780-439-8725
info@vofa.ca
www.vofa.ca
Overview: A small provincial organization founded in 1989
Mission: To promote & advance a vegetarian diet in North America based on the proven health, environmental, animal welfare & spiritual benefits
Member of: Alberta Environment Network Society
Affliation(s): North American Vegetarian Society
Chief Officer(s):
Dayna McIntyre, President
Laura-Lynn Johnston, Vice-President
Finances: *Annual Operating Budget:* Less than $50,000
25 volunteer(s)
Membership: 300 individual; *Fees:* $15 student & senior; $25 individual; $30 family; $150 life single; $175 life family; *Member Profile:* Open to anyone sympathetic to our goals
Activities: November cook-off competition; Edmonton Earth Day; speakers; *Internships:* Yes; *Speaker Service:* Yes; *Library:* VOA Resource Library; Open to public

Vegreville & District Chamber of Commerce

PO Box 877, 5009 - 50 Ave., Vegreville AB T9C 1R9
Tel: 780-632-2771; *Fax:* 780-632-6958
vegchamb@telusplanet.net
www.vegrevillechamber.com
Overview: A small local organization founded in 1906
Mission: To build & perpetuate confidence in business enterprise to a level where, willingly & enthusiastically they risk resources to achieve economic success
Member of: Alberta Chambers of Commerce
Chief Officer(s):
Rhonda Tkachuk, President
Elaine Kucher, General Manager
Finances: *Annual Operating Budget:* $50,000-$100,000; *Funding Sources:* Membership fees; fundraising events
Staff Member(s): 1; 13 volunteer(s)
Membership: 149; *Fees:* Based on number of employees; *Member Profile:* Retail; automotive; industry; professionals; *Committees:* Economic Development; Finance/Personnel; Publicity/Promotions/Tourism; Agriculture; Social/Entertainment/Attendance
Activities: Fundraisers; Awards Night; Christmas Events
Awards:
- Citizen of the Year (Award)
- Junior Citizen of the Year (Award)
- Senior Citizen of the Year (Award)
- Small Business Owner of the Year (Award)
- Farm Family of the Year (Award)

Vegreville Association for Living in Dignity (VALID)

4843 - 49th St., Vegreville AB T9C 1K7
Tel: 780-632-2418; *Fax:* 780-632-3882
www.valid-assoc.org
Previous Name: Vegreville Association for the Handicapped
Overview: A small local charitable organization
Mission: To provide excellence in programs founded upon individual strengths & needs; to be a person-centered organization that believes in every individual's ability to succeed
Member of: Alberta Council of Disability Services
Chief Officer(s):
Jody Nicholson, Executive Director
jody@valid-assoc.org
Finances: *Funding Sources:* Fundraising
Staff Member(s): 2
Membership: *Member Profile:* 18 years of age & older
Activities: Residential services; community support; community access program; employment preparation & placement; recycling program; second chance store; family intervention services; *Library*
Awards:
- Helping Hands Award (Award)
- Staff Recognition of Excellence Award (Award)
- Marg Imesch Memorial Award of Excellence (Award)

Vegreville Association for the Handicapped *See* Vegreville Association for Living in Dignity

Vehicle Information Centre of Canada *See* Insurance Bureau of Canada

Vela Microboard Association of British Columbia

#100, 17564 - 56A Ave., Surrey BC V3S 1G3
Tel: 604-575-2588; *Fax:* 604-575-2589
info@microboard.org
www.microboard.org
www.facebook.com/VelaCanada
Overview: A small local organization
Mission: Helps offer people with developmental challenges subsidized housing in the Greater Vancouver area.
Chief Officer(s):
Linda Perry, Executive Director
Evan Thomas, President

Velo Halifax Bicycle Club

PO Box 125, Dartmouth NS B2Y 3Y2
e-mail: cycling@chebucto.ns.ca
www.velohalifax.com
Overview: A medium-sized local organization founded in 1974
Chief Officer(s):
Terry Walker, President, 902-835-8045
teddymw@hotmail.com
Membership: *Fees:* $30

Vélo New Brunswick

536 McAllister Rd., Riverview NB E1B 4G1
www.velo.nb.ca
www.facebook.com/VeloNB
Overview: A small provincial organization founded in 1993 overseen by Cycling Canada Cyclisme
Mission: To promote all aspects of the activity of bicycling, competitive & recreational, both on & off the road
Member of: Cycling Canada Cyclisme
Affliation(s): Sport New Brunswick
Chief Officer(s):
Kelly Murray, President
Kelly.Murray@velo.nb.ca
Michelle Chase, Vice-President
Michelle.Chase@velo.nb.ca
Sheila Colbourne, Executive Director
Sheila.Colbourne@velo.nb.ca

Vélo Québec

Maison des cyclistes, 1251, rue Rachel Est, Montréal QC H2J 2J9
Tél: 514-521-8356; *Téléc:* 514-521-5711
Ligne sans frais: 800-567-8356
www.velo.qc.ca
www.facebook.com/VeloQuebec
twitter.com/VeloQuebec
instagram.com/veloquebec
Aperçu: *Dimension:* moyenne; *Envergure:* provinciale; fondée en 1967
Mission: µ promouvoir l'utilisation du vélo à travers le Québec

Membre(s) du bureau directeur:
Suzanne Lareau, Directrice générale
Membre: *Montant de la cotisation:* 41$
Activités: *Stagiaires:* Oui; *Service de conférenciers:* Oui

VeloNorth Cycling Club
4061 - 4th Ave., Whitehorse YT Y1A 1H1
Tel: 867-633-2279
www.velonorth.ca
Overview: A small provincial organization
Mission: To encourage safe bicyle riding for sport, recreation & fitness.
Affliation(s): Contagious Mountain Bike Club
Chief Officer(s):
Elijah Buffalo, President
Bill Curtis, Treasurer
wcurtis@northwestel.net

Venezuelan Association for Canadian Studies / Asociación Venezolana de Estudios Canadienses
Apartado 3-F, Piso 3, Final Calle Chama, Mérida, Estado Mérida Venezuela
Overview: A small international organization founded in 1991
Mission: To foster an awareness of Canada; to promote the study of Canada & to contribute to the body of research in Canadian Studies
Chief Officer(s):
Diego R. Zamvrano-Nieto, President
dzambran@cantv.net
Activities: Nine Canadian Studies centres distributed in the different regions of Venezuela

Vera Perlin Society
PO Box 7114, 6 Logy Bay Rd., St. John's NL A1A 1J3
Tel: 709-739-6017; *Fax:* 709-739-5532
veraperlinsociety@nfld.net
www.veraperlinsociety.ca
Overview: A small local organization founded in 1954
Mission: To secure & provide quality services & support for all developmentally handicapped citizens & their families in the St. John's & surrounding area, enabling them to participate in all areas of community living
Affliation(s): Newfoundland Association for Community Living
Chief Officer(s):
Marilyn Wall, Employment Manager
Finances: *Funding Sources:* Regional government
Membership: 250 individual; *Fees:* $2 individual

Vermilion & District Chamber of Commerce
4606 - 52 St., Vermilion AB T9X 0A1
Tel: 780-853-6593; *Fax:* 780-853-1740
www.vermilionchamber.ca
Overview: A small local charitable organization founded in 1906
Member of: Alberta Chamber of Commerce; Canadian Chamber of Commerce
Chief Officer(s):
Marlene Beattie, 1st Vice-President
Finances: *Annual Operating Budget:* $100,000-$250,000; *Funding Sources:* Membership dues; fundraising
Staff Member(s): 2; 13 volunteer(s)
Membership: 110; *Fees:* Schedule available; *Member Profile:* Business people & others interested; *Committees:* Finance/Administration; Retail Promotions; Membership/Speakers; Economic Development; Hire-a-Student
Awards:
- Vermilion Chamber of Commerce Award (Award)

Vermilion Association for Persons with Disabilities
4921 - 51 Ave., Vermilion AB T9X 1S8
Tel: 780-853-4121; *Fax:* 780-853-2840
focus@telusplanet.net
Also Known As: FOCUS
Overview: A small local charitable organization founded in 1959
Mission: To branch out in response to community needs; To empower people to meet their needs
Member of: Alberta Association for Community Living; Alberta Association of Rehabilitation Centers; Alberta Association for Services to Children & Families
Chief Officer(s):
Marlene Beattie, Chair
Finances: *Annual Operating Budget:* $1.5 Million-$3 Million; *Funding Sources:* PDD Board; productive enterprise; donations; Children's Authority; HRDC
Staff Member(s): 58
Membership: 8; *Fees:* $10; *Committees:* Finance; Advocacy; Resource; Program; Fundraising

Awards:
- Individual Award (Award)
- Andre Turgeon Award (Award)
- Community Partner Award (Award)
- Extra Mile Award (Award)
- Professional Award (Award)
- Friends of Focus Award (Award)
- Staff Excellence Award (Award)

Vermilion Forks Field Naturalists
e-mail: princetonartscouncilbc@gmail.com
www.princetonarts.ca/Vermilion_Forks_Field_Naturalists.html
Overview: A small local organization
Chief Officer(s):
Cathie Yingling, President, 250-295-4802
cathieyingling@gmail.com
Ken Heuser, Vice-President, 250-295-7647
Joan Kelly, Secretary, 250-295-7743
Linda Neumann, Treasurer, 250-295-7013
Membership: 84; *Fees:* $25

Vernon & Enderby Food Bank
3303 - 32 Ave., Vernon BC V1T 2M7
Tel: 250-549-1314; *Fax:* 250-549-7344
Overview: A small local organization overseen by Food Banks British Columbia
Member of: Food Banks British Columbia
Chief Officer(s):
David MacBain, Contact
david.macbain@shawcable.com

Vernon Community Arts Council (VCAC)
2704A Hwy. 6, Vernon BC V1T 5G5
www.vernonartscouncil.ca
Also Known As: Vernon Arts Centre
Overview: A small local organization founded in 1970
Mission: To foster, encourage & support fine arts activites in the Vernon area, & in particular in School District No. 22 (Vernon); to stimulate & encourage the development of fine arts projects & activitites; to act as a clearing house on such projects & activities; to help & coordinate the work & programs of cultural groups in the district; to bring to the attention of civic & provincial authorities the cultural needs of the community; to increase & broaden the opportunities for Vernon & district citizens to enjoy & participate in cultural activities; to render services to all participating groups; to interpret the work of such groups to the community, enlist pubic understanding & to foster interest & pride in the cultural heritage of the district
Member of: Assembly of BC Arts Councils
Chief Officer(s):
David Foster, President
fostersfollies@shaw.ca
Michael Wardlow, Treas.
mwardlow@shaw.ca
Finances: *Annual Operating Budget:* $100,000-$250,000
Staff Member(s): 4; 20 volunteer(s)
Membership: 250; *Fees:* $20 individual; $30 business/family; $50 group
Activities: Art workshops for all ages; cultural special events; *Library* Open to public by appointment

Vernon Japanese Cultural Society (VJCS)
4895 BellaVista Rd., Vernon BC
Tel: 250-545-4162
vjcsannouncement@gmail.com
www3.telus.net/aubcom/VJCS.HTM
Overview: A small local organization founded in 1940
Member of: National Association of Japanese Canadians
Membership: 150-200; *Fees:* $10 individual; $20 family

Vernon Jubilee Hospital Foundation
2101 - 32nd St., Vernon BC V1T 5L2
Tel: 250-558-1362; *Fax:* 250-558-4133
www.vjhfoundation.org
www.facebook.com/home.php#%21/group.php?gid=4036069459
0
Overview: A small local charitable organization founded in 1981
Mission: To raise capital funds for Vernon Jubilee Hospital
Chief Officer(s):
Sue Beaudry, Director, Development
sue.beaudry@interiorhealth.ca
Staff Member(s): 3

Vernon Lapidary & Mineral Club
c/o Vernon Community Arts Centre, 2704A Hwy. #6, Vernon BC V1T 5G5
www.vernonlapidary.org
Overview: A small local organization founded in 1959
Chief Officer(s):
Dan Gillies, President, 250-542-4234
Joy Gillies, Secretary
Phylicia O'Brien, Treasurer; Contact, Membership
Membership: *Fees:* $20 individuals; $30 families
Activities: Hosting nonthly meetings, except July & August; Offering lapidary workshops to members; *Awareness Events:* Vernon Lapidary Show & Sale

Vernon Tourism
701 Hwy. 97 South, Vernon BC V1B 3W4
Tel: 250-542-1415
Toll-Free: 800-665-0795
info@vernontourism.com
www.vernontourism.com
www.youtube.com/tourismvernon
www.facebook.com/Tourism.Vernon
twitter.com/tourismvernon
Also Known As: Greater Vernon Visitors & Convention Bureau
Overview: A small local organization founded in 1991
Mission: To promote Vernon & the North Okanagan to the vacationing public
Affliation(s): Greater Vernon Tourism Association
Chief Officer(s):
Michelle Jefferson, Manager, Tourism Services, 250-550-3649
Finances: *Annual Operating Budget:* $100,000-$250,000
Staff Member(s): 2

Vernon Women's Transition House Society
PO Box 625, Vernon BC V1T 6M6
Fax: 250-549-3347; *Crisis Hot-Line:* 250-542-1122
transition@telus.net
Overview: A small local organization founded in 1977
Mission: To provide temporary accommodation in a safe, supportive environment, to women & their children who have experienced abusive relationships; to provide information & referrals to appropriate counselling agencies & to provide a program for young unwed mothers, including support groups
Member of: British Columbia Federation of Child & Family Services
Finances: *Funding Sources:* Provincial government
Staff Member(s): 6; 6 volunteer(s)
Membership: 40 individual + 25 associate

Vert l'Aventure Plein Air
#204, 321, rue Père Marquette, Québec QC G1S 1Y9
Tél: 418-687-2396
vertlaventure@videotron.ca
vertlaventurepleinair.com
Aperçu: *Dimension:* petite; *Envergure:* locale
Mission: De réunir des gens qui aiment les activités de plein air et à organiser des randonnées
Activités: Randonnées; Voyages

Vertes boisées du fjord
#304, 129, rue Jacques Cartier Est, Chicoutimi QC G7H 1Y4
Tél: 418-973-4261; *Téléc:* 418-543-7270
vertsboises@lvbf.org
www.lvbf.org
twitter.com/LVBFjord
Aperçu: *Dimension:* petite; *Envergure:* locale
Mission: De protéger et de préserver les forêts urbain dans la région du Saguenay
Membre(s) du bureau directeur:
Julien Petitclerc, Président, Conseil d'administration
Membre: *Montant de la cotisation:* 10$

Vêtement Québec *See* Apparel Quebec

Veterinary Infectious Disease Organization *See* Vaccine & Infectious Disease Organization

Vetta Chamber Music Society
PO Box 19148, Stn. 4th Ave., Vancouver BC V6K 4R8
Tel: 604-430-9527
Toll-Free: 866-863-6250
info@vettachambermusic.com
vettachambermusic.com
www.facebook.com/VettaChamber
twitter.com/VettaChamber
Overview: A small local organization
Member of: Vancouver Cultural Alliance
Chief Officer(s):
Les Tullock, President
Joan Blackman, Artistic Director

VHA Home HealthCare

#500, 30 Soudan Ave., Toronto ON M4S 1V6
Tel: 416-489-2500; *Fax:* 416-482-8775
Toll-Free: 888-314-6622
www.vha.ca
Also Known As: Visiting Homemakers Association
Overview: A large local charitable organization founded in 1925
Mission: To be a leading not-for-profit provider of community-based, client-centred health & support services in the Greater Toronto Area
Member of: United Way
Chief Officer(s):
John Macfarlane, Chair
Carol Annett, President/CEO
Finances: *Annual Operating Budget:* Greater than $5 Million
Staff Member(s): 1500
Membership: 1-99

Via Prévention

#301, 6455, boul Jean-Talon Est, Montréal QC H1S 3E8
Tél: 514-955-0454; *Téléc:* 514-955-0449
Ligne sans frais: 800-361-8906
info@viaprevention.com
www.viaprevention.com
Aperçu: *Dimension:* moyenne; *Envergure:* provinciale; fondée en 1982
Mission: Pour protéger les personnes qui travaillent dans les transports, de l'Entreposage et de l'environnement en leur donnant une formation en santé et sécurité routière
Membre(s) du bureau directeur:
Alain Lajoie, Directeur général
Membre(s) du personnel: 10

ViaSport

#1000, 510 Burrard St., Vancouver BC V6C 3A8
Tel: 778-331-8642; *Fax:* 778-327-5199
Toll-Free: 866-427-2010
Other Communication: Media, E-mail: media@viasport.ca
info@viasport.ca
www.viasport.ca
twitter.com/ViaSport_
Overview: A medium-sized provincial organization
Mission: To provide the opportunity for participation in sports for all British Columbians, at every age & level of skill.
Chief Officer(s):
Cathy Priestner Allinger, CEO
cathyp@viasport.ca
Activities: Funding & grants
Awards:
- Aboriginal Youth Sport Legacy Fund (Grant)
- BC Ferries Sport Experience Program (Grant)
- Funding for Girls & Women in Sport (Grant)
- Local Sport Program Development Fund (Grant)
- Hosting BC Grant Program (Grant)
- BC Sport Participation Program (Grant)
- Sport on the Move (Grant)
- Northern BC Sport Equipment Grant (Grant)

Coaches ViaSport
#1000, 510 Burrard St., Vancouver BC V6C 3A8
Tel: 778-331-8642; *Fax:* 778-327-5199
Toll-Free: 800-335-3120
Coaches@ViaSport.ca
www.viasport.ca/coaches
Mission: To act as the provincial representative for coaches in British Columbia
Affliation(s): Coaching Association of Canada
Chief Officer(s):
Eric Sinker, Manager, Coaching & Leadership Development
eric@viasport.ca

Victims of Violence Canadian Centre for Missing Children (VOV)

#340, 117 Centrepointe Dr., Ottawa ON K2G 5X3
Tel: 613-233-0052; *Fax:* 613-233-2712
Toll-Free: 888-606-0000
vofv@victimsofviolence.on.ca
www.victimsofviolence.on.ca
www.facebook.com/205047429517768
Overview: A small provincial charitable organization founded in 1984
Mission: To help crime victims regain control of their lives by reducing fear & trauma; to prevent future victimization through crime prevention information; to strengthen local efforts to assist crime victims & witnesses
Affliation(s): National Organization for Victim Assistance - Washington DC; RCMP Missing Children's Registry
Chief Officer(s):
Gary Rosenfeldt, Executive Director
Finances: *Annual Operating Budget:* Less than $50,000; *Funding Sources:* Fundraising; donations; memoriam donations
Staff Member(s): 5; 6 volunteer(s)
Membership: 1,000+; *Member Profile:* Concerned citizens; primary or secondary victim of violent crime including attempted homicide & homicide-survivors
Activities: Courtroom Support; information re: criminal justice system for victims; information booklets; *Speaker Service:* Yes; *Rents Mailing List:* Yes; *Library:* Research Library; Open to public by appointment

Victoria Association for Community Living ***See*** Community Living Victoria

Victoria Cool Aid Society

#102, 749 Pandora Ave., Victoria BC V8W 1N9
Tel: 250-383-1977
society@coolaid.org
www.coolaid.org
www.facebook.com/VicCoolAid
twitter.com/VicCoolAid
www.youtube.com/VicCoolAid
Overview: A medium-sized local charitable organization founded in 1958
Mission: To provide shelter, housing & community health services to the most disadvantages in the community
Chief Officer(s):
Alan Rycroft, Contact, 250-414-4781, Fax: 250-383-1639
Finances: *Annual Operating Budget:* Greater than $5 Million
Staff Member(s): 145; 40 volunteer(s)
Membership: 1-99

Victoria County Association for Community Living ***See*** Community Living Kawartha Lakes

Victoria County Historical Society

Old Gaol Museum, PO Box 187, 50 Victoria Ave. North, Lindsay ON K9V 4S1
Tel: 705-324-3404; *Fax:* 705-454-3043
Toll-Free: 866-747-2010
info@victoriacountyhistoricalsociety.ca
www.victoriacountyhistoricalsociety.ca
Overview: A small local charitable organization founded in 1957
Mission: To collect, preserve, exhibit, & publish information about the history of Ontario's County of Victoria
Chief Officer(s):
John Macklem, President
Bill Bateman, Vice-President
Charles Cooper, Secretary
Howard Jackmam, Treasurer
Katherine Mathias, Publicist
Finances: *Funding Sources:* Admission fees; Fundraising
Membership: *Fees:* $20 individual; $30 family; $100 corporate or patron
Activities: Operating the Olde Gaol Museum; Maintaining a gallery of historical portraits; Promoting study of the history of the County of Victoria; Hosting a speaker series
Publications:
- VCHS [Victoria County Historical Society] Newsletter
Type: Newsletter
Profile: Information about the speakers series, meetings, membership, & exhibits

Victoria County Humane Society ***See*** Ontario Society for the Prevention of Cruelty to Animals

Victoria County Society for the Prevention of Cruelty to Animals

2238 Rte. 109, Arthurette NB E7H 4C2
Tel: 506-356-1117
www.facebook.com/VictoriaCountySpca
Also Known As: Victoria County SPCA
Overview: A small local charitable organization
Member of: Canadian Federation of Humane Societies

Victoria Epilepsy & Parkinson's Centre Society

#202, 1640 Oak Bay Ave., Victoria BC V8R 1B2
Tel: 250-475-6677; *Fax:* 250-475-6619
help@vepc.bc.ca
www.headwayvictoria.com
www.facebook.com/vepc.victoria
twitter.com/VEPC
Overview: A small local charitable organization founded in 1983
Mission: To provide education & support services to those affected by epilepsy or Parkinson's Disease, individuals & family members; to promote excellence in care through collaboration with the health care community, to increase public understanding of these conditions & expand awareness & support of the services provided
Affliation(s): Canadian Epilepsy Alliance
Chief Officer(s):
Barbara Gilmore, Executive Director
bgilmore@vepc.bc.ca
Finances: *Annual Operating Budget:* $250,000-$500,000; *Funding Sources:* United Way of Greater Victoria, Vndekerkhove Family Foundation, grants
Staff Member(s): 6; 200 volunteer(s)
Membership: 200 institutional + 800 individual; *Fees:* by donation; *Committees:* Parkinson's Advisory; Epilepsy Advisory
Activities: Support, knowledge, advocacy, public awareness; *Awareness Events:* Purple Day for Epilepsy, March 26; Parkinson's Month, April; *Speaker Service:* Yes; *Library:* Vandekerkhove Library; Open to public

Victoria Hospitals Foundation (VHF)

1952 Bay St., Victoria BC V8R 1JB
Tel: 250-519-1750; *Fax:* 250-519-1751
vhf@viha.ca
www.victoriahf.ca
www.facebook.com/VictoriaHF?ref=ts
Previous Name: Greater Victoria Hospitals Foundation
Overview: A small local charitable organization founded in 1989
Mission: Raises funds for Victoria's major hospitals: Victoria General & Royal Jubilee which also serve the entire Vancouver Island
Affliation(s): Vancouver Island Health Authority
Chief Officer(s):
Melanie McKenzie, Executive Director
Finances: *Funding Sources:* Donations; Foundations; Corporations; Fundraising
Staff Member(s): 15
Activities: Visions - annual fundraising event
Publications:
- InTouch
Type: Newsletter; *Frequency:* Quarterly
Profile: Relays news about funding activities & priorities at the hospitals

Victoria International Development Education Association (VIDEA)

1200 Deeks Pl., Victoria BC V8P 5S7
e-mail: info@videa.ca
www.videa.ca
www.linkedin.com/company/videa-victoria-international-development-educ
twitter.com/VIDEAvictoria
www.youtube.com/user/Videavids1
Overview: A small international charitable organization founded in 1977
Mission: To increase awareness of international development issues, particularly those affecting Third World countries
Member of: Canadian Council for International Cooperation
Affliation(s): BC Council for International Cooperation
Chief Officer(s):
Elvira Perrella, Chair
Lynn Thornton, Executive Director
Finances: *Annual Operating Budget:* $100,000-$250,000
Staff Member(s): 3
Membership: 490 senior/lifetime; *Fees:* $15 students, low income, elderly; $25 individual; $50 organizational; *Committees:* Schools; Resource Centre; Public Programs; Personnel
Activities: *Internships:* Yes; *Speaker Service:* Yes; *Library:* Resource Centre; Open to public

Victoria Jazz Society

PO Box 39083, RPO James Bay, Victoria BC V8V 4X8
Tel: 250-388-4423; *Fax:* 250-388-4407
info@jazzvictoria.ca
jazzvictoria.ca
www.facebook.com/VicJazzSociety
twitter.com/VicJazzSociety
Overview: A small local organization founded in 1981
Mission: The Victoria Jazz Society is a professional arts organization committed to presenting the highest quality of jazz possible to our community, by presenting music in performance, with acclaimed musicians. The Victoria Jazz Society's primary activity is to produce two major multi-day music festivals in the summer, TD Victoria International JazzFest and the Vancouver Island Blues Bash, as well as a series of concerts from September to May, all featuring international, national and regional jazz artists.
Chief Officer(s):

Darryl Mar, Artistic/Executive Director
Membership: *Fees:* $10 student; $15 senior; $25 individual; $40 couple/family

Victoria Labour Council (VLC)

#219, 2750 Quadra St., Victoria BC V8T 4E8
Tel: 250-384-8331; *Fax:* 250-384-8381
vlcbc@telus.net
www.victorialabour.ca
www.facebook.com/group.php?gid=7809013259
Overview: A small local organization overseen by British Columbia Federation of Labour
Mission: To advance the economic & social welfare of workers in Victoria, British Columbia
Affliation(s): Canadian Labour Congress (CLC)
Chief Officer(s):
Mike Eso, President
mike.eso@bcgeu.ca
Stan Dzbik, Secretary-Treasurer
stan.dzibik@telus.net
Kim Manton, Secretary
kimmanton@shaw.ca
Membership: *Member Profile:* Locals of national unions affiliated to the Canadian Labour Congress
Activities: Supporting local community organizations, such as the United Way; Providing local labour news; Engaging in municipal political action; Advocating for workers' issues, such as wages & safe working conditions; Organizing rallies for issues such as public services; Marking International Woman's Day; Participating in campaigns, such as Women's Economic Equality Campaign

Victoria Lapidary & Mineral Society (VLMS)

PO Box 5114, Stn. B, Victoria BC V8R 6N3
e-mail: vlms@vlms.ca
www.islandnet.com/~vlms
Overview: A small local organization
Affliation(s): British Columbia Lapidary Society; Gem & Mineral Federation of Canada
Chief Officer(s):
Gilles Lebrun, Contact, Field Trips, 250-382-6119
Finances: *Funding Sources:* Annual auction of used equipment & lapidary material
Membership: 100; *Fees:* $25 individuals; $35 couples; $40 families; *Member Profile:* Individuals with an interest in rocks, crystals, minerals, lapidary arts, or earth sciences in Victoria, British Columbia
Activities: Providing lapidary & silversmithing courses; Hosting monthly meetings with guest speakers; Planning field trips; *Awareness Events:* Rock & Gem Show; *Library:* Victoria Lapidary & Mineral Society Library
Publications:
• Victoria Lapidary & Mineral Society Newsletter
Type: Newsletter; *Price:* Free, if e-mailed; $15 for mailing
Profile: Information for VLMS members

Victoria Medical Society (VMS)

Eric Martin Pavillion, #190, 2334 Trent St., Victoria BC V8R 4Z3
Tel: 250-598-6021; *Fax:* 250-370-8274
administrator@victoriamedicalsociety.org
www.victoriamedicalsociety.org
Overview: A small local organization founded in 1895
Mission: To promote good health & act as an advocate on health issues; to promote good & appropriate medical practice in accord with the Code of Ethics; to promote the good name of medicine; to promote medical education; to promote fellowship & good relations within the profession & with the public; to help, as much as possible, any member in distress from any cause; to advocate for any doctor or group of doctors subjected to injustice; to mediate, when requested, in disputes & differences between local medical groups or individuals (mediation & advocacy does not apply to cases under the jurisdiction of the College of Physicians & Surgeons of BC); to cooperate with the BCMA, CMA & College of Physicians & Surgeons of BC
Affliation(s): BC College of Physicians & Surgeons; BC Medical Association
Chief Officer(s):
C. Peter Innes, President
vicmedso@telus.net
Membership: 100-499; *Fees:* $135 ordinary; $25 associate (retired); *Member Profile:* Practicing & retired physicians
Activities: Education & social; annual dinner; Listerian Oration

Victoria Musicians' Association *See* Musicians' Association of Victoria & the Islands, Local 247, AFM

Victoria Native Friendship Centre (VNFC)

231 Regina Ave., Victoria BC V8Z 1J6
Tel: 250-384-3211; *Fax:* 250-384-1586
online@vnfc.ca
www.vnfc.ca
Overview: A small local organization founded in 1969
Mission: To meet the needs of Native people in the greater Victoria area by providing them with services & information designed to enhance their traditional values
Member of: United Way; Association of Aboriginal Post-Secondary Institutions
Chief Officer(s):
Bruce Parisian, Executive Director
brucep@vnfc.ca
Finances: *Funding Sources:* Federal, provincial & Aboriginal organizations; charitable foundations; corporations; local business
Staff Member(s): 40; 150 volunteer(s)
Membership: 80; *Fees:* $1
Activities: Wellness Clinic; Health services; family services; intervention programs;

Victoria Natural History Society

PO Box 5220, Stn. B, Victoria BC V8R 6N4
www.vicnhs.bc.ca
Overview: A small local organization founded in 1944
Mission: To stimulate active interest in natural history; to study & protect flora & fauna & their habitats
Member of: Federation of BC Naturalists
Affliation(s): Canadian Nature Federation
Chief Officer(s):
Darren Copley, President, 250-479-6622
dccopley@telus.net
Finances: *Funding Sources:* Membership fees
Membership: 750; *Fees:* $30 Regular; $35 Family; $25 senior; $20 student
Activities: Christmas Bird Count; *Speaker Service:* Yes; *Library* Open to public

Victoria Numismatic Society

PO Box 39028, Stn. James Bay Postal Outlet, Victoria BC V8V 4X8
e-mail: victoriacoinclub@yahoo.ca
victoriacoinclub.webs.com
Overview: A small local organization founded in 1955
Mission: To promote coin & money collecting
Membership: *Fees:* $20; $15 junior

Victoria Orchid Society

1199 Tattersall Dr., Victoria BC V8P 1Y8
www.victoriaorchidsociety.ca
www.facebook.com/groups/103631859679933/members/
Overview: A small local organization
Chief Officer(s):
Ingrid Ostrander, President
ifl@telus.net
Membership: 153; *Fees:* $15 single; $20 family

Victoria Particular Council *See* Conseil national Société de Saint-Vincent de Paul

Victoria Peace Centre *See* Victoria Peace Coalition

Victoria Peace Coalition (VPC)

victoriapeacecoalition.org
www.facebook.com/128112807259174
twitter.com/peace_victoria
Previous Name: Victoria Peace Centre
Overview: A small provincial organization founded in 2001
Mission: To raise awareness on a wide range of issues, such as Palestine, Iraq, & Missile Defence; to promote education through research & the publishing of brochures
Finances: *Annual Operating Budget:* Less than $50,000
20 volunteer(s)
Membership: 100-499
Activities: *Awareness Events:* Earth Walk, April; *Speaker Service:* Yes

Victoria READ Society

#201 & 202, 990 Hillside Ave., Victoria BC V8T 2A1
Tel: 250-388-7225; *Fax:* 250-386-8330
info@readsociety.bc.ca
www.readsociety.bc.ca
www.linkedin.com/company/703924
www.facebook.com/209661882291
twitter.com/READSociety
Also Known As: READ Learning Centre
Previous Name: Victoria Reading Evaluation & Development Society
Overview: A small local charitable organization founded in 1976
Mission: To help children & adults improve & upgrade their basic reading, writing & math skills in a supportive small class; also literacy, English as a Second Language
Member of: ASPECT; ELSA-Net; International Reading Association; Literacy BC; Volunteer Victoria
Chief Officer(s):
Carol J. Carman, Chair
Claire Rettie, Executive Director
crettie@readsociety.bc.ca
Finances: *Annual Operating Budget:* $500,000-$1.5 Million; *Funding Sources:* Federal government; provincial government; corporate sponsorship; fees for service; foundations
Staff Member(s): 23; 130 volunteer(s)
Membership: 30 individual; *Fees:* $10 individual; *Committees:* READ Festival; Bursary; Finance; Personnel; Fundraising
Activities: READ Festival - an annual "Poetry Bash" to benefit children's literacy programs; Bursary Fund program to subsidize tuition for children's programming; Scrabble Scramble for Literacy; Random Acts of Poetry

Victoria Reading Evaluation & Development Society *See* Victoria READ Society

Victoria Real Estate Board (VREB)

3035 Nanaimo St., Victoria BC V8T 4W2
Tel: 250-385-7766; *Fax:* 250-385-8773
info@vreb.org
www.vreb.org
Overview: A small local organization founded in 1921 overseen by British Columbia Real Estate Association
Mission: To promote & enhance the use of the real estate services that its members provide to the public
Member of: The Canadian Real Estate Association
Chief Officer(s):
David Corey, Executive Officer, 250-920-4658
Carol Crabb, President, 250-477-7291
Finances: *Annual Operating Budget:* $1.5 Million-$3 Million
Staff Member(s): 15
Membership: 1,153; *Member Profile:* Realtors
Activities: Continuing education; leadership; *Library:* Resource Centre

Victoria Riding for Disabled Association *See* Victoria Therapeutic Riding Association

Victoria Society for Humanistic Judaism (VSHJ)

3636 Shelbourne St., Victoria BC V8P 4H2
Tel: 250-658-5836
info@vshj.ca
vshj.ca
Overview: A small local organization
Mission: To preserve Jewish heritage, culture, & customs within a non-theistic environment
Affliation(s): Congress of Secular Jewish Organizations; Leadership Conference of Secular & Humanistic Jews; Canadian Jewish Congress
Chief Officer(s):
Larry Gontovnick, President
Membership: *Fees:* $100 single; $150 family; *Member Profile:* Persons of Jewish descent; Persons who wish to identify with the history, culture, & ethical values of Jewish people
Activities: Hosting meetings twice a month at the Jewish Community Centre in Victoria; Discussing topics relevant to Humanism; Providing educational programs for children; Offering life cycle events to members; Celebrating major Jewish holidays with secularly meaningful programs

Victoria Symphony Society

#610, 620 View St., Victoria BC V8W 1J6
Tel: 250-385-6515; *Fax:* 250-385-7767
boxoffice@victoriasymphony.ca
www.victoriasymphony.ca
www.facebook.com/victoriasymphony
twitter.com/VicSymphony
Overview: A small local charitable organization founded in 1941 overseen by Orchestras Canada
Mission: To advance musical culture; to advance musical education among younger members of community; to encourage, foster, & promote performance of Canadian & other contemporary musicians
Chief Officer(s):
Marsha Hanen, President
Mitchell Krieger, Executive Director

Tania Miller, Music Director
Finances: *Annual Operating Budget:* $3 Million-$5 Million; *Funding Sources:* Government; corporate; individual
Staff Member(s): 13; 150 volunteer(s)
Membership: 5,000 individual; *Fees:* Schedule available; *Member Profile:* Donation of $25 or more; subscription to any series
Activities: *Library:* Music Library

Victoria Therapeutic Riding Association (VTRA)
PO Box 412, Brentwood Bay BC V8M 1R3
Tel: 778-426-0506
vtra.ca
www.facebook.com/VictoriaTherapeuticRidingAssociation
Previous Name: Victoria Riding for Disabled Association
Overview: A small local charitable organization founded in 1982
Mission: To provide a therapeutic riding program for children & adults with disabilities to promote their physical, psychological, & social well-being
Member of: Canadian Therapeutic Riding Association
Affliation(s): B.C. Therapeutic Riding Association; Horse Council of British Columbia; Volunteer Victoria; Canadian Therapeutic Riding Association's; Association of Fundraising Professionals
Chief Officer(s):
Carol Hubberstey, President
Sue Colgate, Executive Director
Finances: *Funding Sources:* Service club; fund-raising events; foundations
Staff Member(s): 4; 100 volunteer(s)
Membership: *Fees:* $20 individual; $200 life; $10 riders
Publications:
• The Stable Voice [a publication of Victoria Therapeutic Riding Association]
Type: Newsletter; *Frequency:* q.

Victoria Youth Empowerment Society
533 Yates St., Victoria BC V8W 1K7
Tel: 250-383-3514; *Fax:* 250-383-3812
office_manager@vyes.ca
www.vyes.ca
Merged from: Alliance Club; Association for Street Kids
Overview: A small local charitable organization founded in 1992
Mission: To assist youth to remove themselves from the high risk environment of the street & make the transition to healthier & more constructive life situations; To help youth make positive choices which will prevent involvement in at risk behaviour or connection with the street scene
Member of: Federation of Child & Family Services of BC; United Way
Chief Officer(s):
Pat Griffin, Executive Director
Finances: *Annual Operating Budget:* $1.5 Million-$3 Million; *Funding Sources:* Ministry of Social Services; Ministry of Health; United Way; churches; fun-raising; individual contributions
Staff Member(s): 60
Membership: *Fees:* $10
Activities: Souper Bowls; Mayor's Golf Classic Tournament; daytime/evening drop-in centre; information; referrals; advocacy; counselling; housing; outreach; workshops; employment;

Victorian Order of Nurses for Canada (VON Canada) / Infirmières de l'Ordre de Victoria du Canada
110 Argyle Ave., Ottawa ON K2P 1B4
Tel: 613-233-5694; *Fax:* 613-230-4376
Toll-Free: 888-866-2273
national@von.ca
www.von.ca
www.linkedin.com/company/von-canada
twitter.com/VON_Canada
www.youtube.com/VONCanadaFD
Overview: A medium-sized national charitable organization founded in 1897
Mission: To be a leader in the delivery of innovative comprehensive health & social services & to influencing the development of health & social policy in Canada; to meet rapidly changing social & external challenges
Chief Officer(s):
Judith Shamian, President & CEO
John Gallinger, Chief Operationg Officer
Finances: *Annual Operating Budget:* $1.5 Million-$3 Million
Staff Member(s): 5000; 9000 volunteer(s)
Activities: Offers a wide range of community health care solutions

Victorian Studies Association of Western Canada
LLPA Department, Douglas College, University of Victoria, #2635, 700 Royal Ave., New Westminster BC V3M 5Z5
web.uvic.ca/vsawc
twitter.com/vsawc
Overview: A medium-sized local organization founded in 1972
Mission: To promote the interest & activity of scholars in the study of Victorian Britain & the British Empire & to promote a sense of a community among scholars in Western Canada, where distance often makes informal & frequent meetings with colleagues & access to major libraries difficult
Chief Officer(s):
Ryan Stephenson, Contact
stephensonr@douglascollege.ca
Membership: *Fees:* $50 faculty; $30 students
Activities: Annual fall conference, Sept./Oct.
Meetings/Conferences: • Victorian Studies Association of Western Canada 2015 Conference, April, 2015, Manteo Lakeside Resort, Kelowna, BC
Scope: National

VideoFACT, A Foundation to Assist Canadian Talent *See* MuchFACT

Vidéographe
4550, rue Garnier, Montréal QC H2J 3S7
Tél: 514-521-2116; *Téléc:* 514-521-1676
info@videographe.qc.ca
www.videographe.qc.ca
www.facebook.com/124501969721
twitter.com/Videographe
Aperçu: *Dimension:* petite; *Envergure:* provinciale; fondée en 1971
Mission: Favoriser le développement de la pratique de la vidéo en soutenant autant les jeunes auteurs dans le cadre de la réalisation de leurs premières oeuvres, que les vidéastes professionnels dans la pratique et la reconnaissance de leur art; cette mission s'articule autour d'un triple mandat: faciliter l'accès à la production, à la création et à la recherche en arts médiatiques; soutenir la pratique professionnelle, notamment en assurant la distribution des oeuvres vidéographiques et une juste rétribution des droits aux artistes; permettre l'ouverture de marchés par le biais d'activités multiples en diffusion et de rencontres interactives
Membre de: Alliance de la vidéo et du cinéma indépendant; Conseil québécois des arts médiatiques; Culture Montréal
Membre(s) du bureau directeur:
Etienne Desrosiers, Président
Fortner Anderson, Directeur général
fanderson@videographe.qc.ca
Finances: *Budget de fonctionnement annuel:* $500,000-$1.5 Million
Membre(s) du personnel: 8; 15 bénévole(s)
Membre: 263; *Montant de la cotisation:* 112,88$ individu; 225,75$ institution; *Comités:* Programmation; Co-Production
Activités: *Stagiaires:* Oui

Vides Canada
178 Steeles Ave. East, Markham ON L3T 1A5
Tel: 416-803-3558
videscanada.ca
www.facebook.com/videscanada
www.flickr.com/photos/57388169@N05
Overview: A small international charitable organization founded in 1987
Mission: To improve the lives of underpriviledged children; to train volunteers & send them to developing countries in order to help the children who live there
Chief Officer(s):
Jeannine Landra, Director
jeanninefma@videscanada.ca

Vie autonome Canada *See* Independent Living Canada

VieCanada *See* LifeCanada

Vietnamese Association, Toronto (VAT)
1364 Dundas St. West, Toronto ON M6J 1Y2
Tel: 416-536-3611; *Fax:* 416-536-8364
info@vatoronto.ca
www.vatoronto.ca
Overview: A small local charitable organization founded in 1972 overseen by Vietnamese Canadian Federation
Mission: To promote unity, fraternity, & mutual assistance among members of the community through social, educational, & cultural activites
Chief Officer(s):
Manh Nguyen, Executive Director
manh@vatoronto.ca
Maxwell Vo Ngoc Thach, President
Finances: *Annual Operating Budget:* $250,000-$500,000; *Funding Sources:* Federal, provincial & municipal government
Staff Member(s): 16; 30 volunteer(s)
Membership: *Fees:* $10
Activities: Settlement and adaptation programs; employment counselling; computer tutorials; tai chi; health and community workshops; *Awareness Events:* TET, Lunar New Year Festival

Vietnamese Canadian Federation (VCF) / Fédération vietnamienne du Canada
2476 Regatta Ave., Ottawa ON K2J 5V6
Tel: 780-708-0876; *Fax:* 780-425-0799
lhnvc1980vcf@gmail.com
www.vietfederation.ca
www.facebook.com/vietnamesecanadian.centre
twitter.com/VietCdnCentre
www.flickr.com/photos/vietnamesecanadianfederationcentre
Previous Name: Canadian Federation of Vietnamese Associations of Canada
Overview: A medium-sized national licensing charitable organization founded in 1980
Mission: To provide focal point for activities of the Vietnamese community in the National Capital Region & across Canada; to serve as resource centre on Vietnamese culture & issues related to resettlement & integration of Vietnamese refugees & immigrants in Canada; to maintain solidarity among the Vietnamese associations across Canada; to harmonize their activities for a better achievement of their common objectives; to work for the preservation & development of Vietnamese culture & for the enrichment of Canadian culture; to foster the spirit of mutual help & community responsibility
Member of: World Federation of Vietnamese Associations Overseas
Affliation(s): Canadian Ethnocultural Council
Finances: *Funding Sources:* Canadian Heritage; membership fees; Vietnamese community
Membership: *Member Profile:* Vietnamese community organizations
Activities: *Internships:* Yes; *Speaker Service:* Yes; *Library:* Vietnamese Canadian Centre; Open to public

Les Vieux Brachés de Longueuil
Centre Communcauture Le Traint d'Union, 3100, rue Mosseau, Longueuil QC J4L 4P2
Tél: 450-647-1107
vieuxbranches@hotmail.com
cctu.ca
Aperçu: *Dimension:* petite; *Envergure:* locale; fondée en 1996
Mission: Pour faire discouveries, répondre aux questions et résoudre les problèmes concernant les ordinateurs
Membre(s) du bureau directeur:
Robert Bujold, Président, Consil d'administration
Membre: 200; *Montant de la cotisation:* 25$; *Critères d'admissibilite:* Les adultes qui ont 50 ou plus anées qui sont intéressés à en apprendre sur les ordinateurs
Activités: *Evénements de sensibilisation:* Dîner de Noël

Viking Economic Development Committee (VEDC)
PO Box 369, Viking AB T0B 4N0
Tel: 780-336-3466
info@viking.ca
www.townofviking.ca
Overview: A small local organization
Mission: To promote the community of Viking
Chief Officer(s):
Jackie Fenton, Chief Administrative Officer
Finances: *Funding Sources:* Town of Viking; fundraising
12 volunteer(s)
Membership: 12

Villa Charities Inc. (Toronto District)
901 Lawrence Ave. West, Toronto ON M6A 1C3
Tel: 416-789-7011; *Fax:* 416-789-3951
www.villacharities.com
Previous Name: Italian Canadian Benevolent Corporation (Toronto District)
Overview: A medium-sized provincial charitable organization founded in 1971
Mission: To develop social programs that enhance the lives of their senior members & promote Italian heritage
Affliation(s): Villa Colombo Services for Seniors; Columbus Centre; VITA Community Living Services; Caboto Terrace; Casa DelZotto; Casa Abruzzo; Villa Colombo Vaughan Di Poce Centre
Chief Officer(s):

Nina Perfetto, Chair
Pal Di Iulio, Chief Executive Officer
paldi@villacharities.com
Stefanie Polsinelli, Media Contact
spolsinelli@villacharities.com
Membership: 8 organizations
Activities: *Library:* Alberto DiGiovanni Library

Columbus Centre
901 Lawrence Ave. West, Toronto ON M6A 1C3
Tel: 416-789-7011; *Fax:* 416-789-3951
Chief Officer(s):
Nick Sgro, Chair
Pal Di Iulio, Executive Director
Ugo Di Federico, Administrator

Villa Colombo Services for Seniors
40 Playfair Ave., Toronto ON M6B 2P9
Tel: 416-789-2113; *Fax:* 416-789-5435
Chief Officer(s):
Nick Manocchio, President & Chair
Fernando Scopa, CEO & Exec. Dir.

Villa Colombo Vaughan - Di Poce Centre
10443 Hwy. 27, Vaughan ON L0J 1C0
Tel: 289-202-2222; *Fax:* 289-202-2000
Chief Officer(s):
Sam Ciccolini, Chair
Valeria De Simone, Acting Administrator

VITA Community Living Services
4301 Weston Rd., Toronto ON M9L 2Y3
Tel: 416-749-6234; *Fax:* 416-749-1456
www.vitacls.org/vita/index.asp
Chief Officer(s):
Paul Mior, President
Manuela Dalla-Nora, Executive Director
mdallanora@vitacls.org

Village International Sudbury (VIS)
900 Lasalle Blvd., Sudbury ON P3A 5W8
Tel: 705-524-2999
villageinternationalsudbury@hotmail.com
www.northernontario.org/vi/
Overview: A small local organization founded in 1989
Mission: Imports products from 25 different countries
Member of: Global Education Centres of Ontario
Finances: *Annual Operating Budget:* $100,000-$250,000; *Funding Sources:* Crafts sale
Staff Member(s): 2; 25 volunteer(s)
Membership: 175; *Fees:* $10-20
Activities: *Library*

Villages internationaux d'enfants *See* Children's International Summer Villages (Canada) Inc.

Vilna & District Chamber of Commerce
PO Box 542, Vilna AB T0A 3L0
Tel: 780-636-3615
Overview: A small local organization
Affiliation(s): Alberta Chamber of Commerce; Canadian Chamber of Commerce

Vinok Worldance
PO Box 4867, Edmonton AB T6E 5G7
Tel: 780-454-3739; *Fax:* 780-454-3436
vinok@vinok.ca
www.vinok.ca
www.facebook.com/vinok.worldance
twitter.com/VinokWorldance
Overview: A small local organization founded in 1988
Mission: To present music & dances of the world to audiences all across Canada; to reflect world dance as a way of celebrating life, involving dance, music, song, improvisation & the expression of a people
Finances: *Funding Sources:* The Canada Council; The Alberta Foundation for the Arts; City of Edmonton; Edmonton Arts Council
Activities: Theatre productions; educational programs; workshops; special event performances

Vintage Locomotive Society Inc.
PO Box 33021, RPO Polo Park, Winnipeg MB R3G 3N4
Tel: 204-832-5259; *Fax:* 866-751-2348
info@pdcrailway.com
www.pdcrailway.com
Also Known As: Prairie Dog Central Steam Train
Overview: A small local charitable organization founded in 1968
Mission: To collect, restore for operation & maintain steam locomotives & rolling stock of early part of twentieth-century; to provide source of historical information relating to origin & past operation of acquired equipment & buildings
Chief Officer(s):
Paul Newsome, General Manager
Finances: *Annual Operating Budget:* $250,000-$500,000
170 volunteer(s)
Membership: 170 individuals; *Fees:* $25 full; $15 junior; $40 family; *Committees:* Restoration-Locomotive; Restoration-Coaches; Painting; Sign Work; Public Relations; Advertising; Photography; Operations & Maintenance
Activities: *Speaker Service:* Yes

Vintage Road Racing Association (VRRA)
c/o Karen Duncan, Membership Secretary, 499 Fiddick Rd., Brighton ON K0K 1H0
Tel: 613-475-9052
vrramembership@gmail.com
www.vrra.ca
www.facebook.com/vrra.ca
twitter.com/VRRACANADA
Overview: A medium-sized national organization founded in 1980
Mission: To promote & maintain the sport & traditions of racing classic & vintage machines
Chief Officer(s):
Mike Vinten, President
m.vinten@sympatico.ca
Karen Duncan, Membership Secretary
Membership: *Fees:* $75 racing member; $30 non-racing member; *Member Profile:* Amateur & ex-professional racers; mechanics; bike builders; bike owners; racing fans
Activities: Races; newsletter
Awards:
• Rookie of the Year (Award)
• Most Improved Rider (Award)
• President's Award (Award)
• Most Meritorious Award (Award)
• Roger Beaumont Award (Award)
• Dorman Diesel Award (Award)
• Mary McCaw Award (Award)
• Sportsman of the Year Award (Award)
• Winner of the #1 Plate (Award)
• The Peter Sheppard Women's Trophy (Award)
• The John McCaw Memorial Sportsman Award (Award)
Publications:
• The Baffled Muffler [a publication of the Vintage Road Racing Association]
Type: Newsletter; *Editor:* Malcolm & Janice Lake

Vintners Quality Alliance
#1601, 1 Yonge St., Toronto ON M5E 1E5
Tel: 416-367-2002; *Fax:* 416-367-4044
info@vqaontario.ca
www.vqaontario.com
Overview: A medium-sized national organization founded in 1989
Mission: To establish standards of quality & designations for wines produced in Ontario
Chief Officer(s):
Laurie Macdonald, Executive Director
laurie.macdonald@vqaontario.ca
Ken Douglas, President & Chair
Finances: *Annual Operating Budget:* $250,000-$500,000
Staff Member(s): 6
Membership: 44 institutional

Viol-secours inc.
3293 - 1e av, Québec QC G1L 3R2
Tél: 418-522-2120; *Téléc:* 418-522-2130
www.violsecours.qc.ca
Aperçu: *Dimension:* petite; *Envergure:* locale; Organisme sans but lucratif; fondée en 1976
Mission: Venir en aide à toute femme, adolescente ou enfant ayant subi une situation d'agression à caractère sexuel en offrant divers services: intervention téléphonique, accompagnement médico-légal et juridique, suivi individuel et de groupe
Affiliation(s): Regroupement québécois des CALACS

Virden & District Chamber of Commerce *See* Virden Community Chamber of Commerce

Virden Community Arts Council
425 - 6th Ave. South, Virden MB R0M 2C0
Tel: 204-748-3014; *Fax:* 204-748-6985
vcaccp@mts.net
www.virdencommunityarts.ca
Overview: A small local charitable organization founded in 1981
Mission: To encourage the development of an interest in & appreciation for the visual, literary, performing & functional arts by providing appropriate programming & facilities within the Fort la Bosse School Division
Member of: Manitoba Arts Network; Dance Manitoba
Chief Officer(s):
Tina Williams, President
Finances: *Annual Operating Budget:* $100,000-$250,000; *Funding Sources:* Manitoba Culture, Heritage & Tourism; Enbridge Pipelines; municipal; private donations
65 volunteer(s)
Membership: 130; *Fees:* $5 individual; $10 organizations/commercial enterprises; *Member Profile:* Keen interest in the arts with some desire to actively participate; *Committees:* Costume Closet; Exhibitions; Fundraising/Membership; Publicity; Scholarship; Performing Arts
Activities: Performances; travelling exhibitions; workshops & classes; films; *Library:* Costume Closet; by appointment
Awards:
• High School Scholarship, General Scholarship, Peace Garden Scholarship (Scholarship)
• High School Scholarship, General Scholarship, Peace Garden Scholarship (Scholarship)

Virden Community Chamber of Commerce
PO Box 899, 425 - 6th Ave. South, Virden MB R0M 2C0
Tel: 204-851-1551; *Fax:* 604-608-9110
info@virdenchamber.ca
www.virdenchamber.ca
Previous Name: Virden & District Chamber of Commerce
Overview: A small local organization
Member of: Manitoba Chamber of Commerce
Affiliation(s): Virden Wallace Community Development Corp.; Virden Employment Skills Centre Inc., Virden Agricultural Society; Virden Indoor Rodeo
Chief Officer(s):
Dave Wowk, President
Finances: *Annual Operating Budget:* Less than $50,000; *Funding Sources:* Membership dues; grants
16 volunteer(s)
Membership: 100; *Fees:* Based on number of employees; *Committees:* Budget; Constitution & Incorporation; Membership; Promotion; Sign; Special Events; Western Rodeo
Activities: Tourist Booth; Youth Job Centre; Rainbow Promo; Rodeo Promo; Xmas Promo

Viscount Cultural Council Inc. (VCC)
PO Box 186, Neepawa MB R0J 1H0
Tel: 204-476-3232
Other Communication: VCCBoard1@gmail.com
viscount@mts.net
www.neepawavcc.ca
www.facebook.com/profile.php?id=100001507473370
Also Known As: Manawaka Gallery
Overview: A small local charitable organization founded in 1976
Mission: To enrich the leisure time of the citizens of Neepawa & the surrounding area by offering instruction in visual & performing arts & crafts by operating an art gallery & by bringing performing artists to the community
Member of: Manitoba Arts Network
Chief Officer(s):
Brenda Kryschuk, Administrator
Finances: *Annual Operating Budget:* $50,000-$100,000
Staff Member(s): 1; 12 volunteer(s)
Membership: 150-200; *Fees:* $10 student; $12 adult; $20 family; *Committees:* Exhibition; Performance; Craft Sale; Personnel; Program
Activities: Craft sale, Nov.; music lessons; dance lessons; workshops on quilting; drawing
Awards:
• VCC Art Award (Award)

Vision Institute of Canada (VIC)
York Mills Centre, #110, 16 York Mills Rd., Toronto ON M2P 2E5
Tel: 416-224-2273; *Fax:* 416-224-9234
visioninstitute.optometry.net
Previous Name: Optometric Institute of Toronto
Overview: A medium-sized national charitable organization founded in 1981
Mission: To improve the quality of vision care in the community; to provide eye & vision care to persons with special needs
Chief Officer(s):
Paul Chris, Executive Director
Catherine Chiarelli, Chief of Clinical Services

Finances: *Funding Sources:* Fundraising; corporate; OHIP billings
Activities: *Internships:* Yes; *Speaker Service:* Yes; *Library:* Bobier-Fisher-Lyle Vision Science Library; by appointment

Vision Mondiale *See* World Vision Canada

Vision of Love Ministry - Canada
51 Harland Cres., Ajax ON L1S 1K1
Tel: 416-546-4669; *Fax:* 206-888-3164
info@visionoflove.ca
www.visionoflove.ca
Also Known As: Vision 2000
Overview: A small provincial organization founded in 1996
Mission: To manifest God's love & enrich the local Catholic faith; To share time & musical & artistic talent at churches & Christian gatherings, especially within the Catholic Charismatic Renewal & lay organizations
Affliation(s): Archdiocese of Toronto; Renewal Ministries CCRER/CCRSO; Radio Maria; Mission SOS - Toronto; Living Waters and Fr. Trevor Nathasingh - Trinidad; Multi-Cultural Christian Communities
Chief Officer(s):
Tony Gosgnach, Contact
tonygmusician@visionoflove.ca
Danny Nelson, Contact
danny@visionoflove.ca
Finances: *Funding Sources:* Sponsorships
Membership: 30+; *Member Profile:* Members are part of a Christian community of artists, who desire to live the contemplative Christian faith & serve with love, through music & the arts; Participants must acknowledge "Jesus Christ is Lord"
Activities: Providing music & worship with the arts for Catholic liturgies, renewal programs, pastoral groups, parishes, churches, & youth; Offering praise & worship music in a range of styles, such as rock, blues, jazz, folk, Gospel, Latin, & reggae; Producing CDs & DVDs; Tutoring; Providing Christian artwork

VISION TV
64 Jefferson Ave., Toronto ON M6K 1Y4
Tel: 416-368-3194; *Fax:* 416-368-9774; *TTY:* 416-216-6311
www.visiontv.ca
www.facebook.com/visiontelevision
twitter.com/visiontv
Overview: A medium-sized national charitable organization founded in 1988
Mission: To reflect & illuminate the full spectrum of faith & religious beliefs which make up Canada's diverse society; To build bridges of knowledge & understanding between faiths & cultures; To provide paid access to all eligible religious & faith communities & broadcast ministries; To broadcast non-sectarian programs based on values, ethics, & spirituality concerning a wide variety of issues & themes
Member of: Canadian Association of Broadcasters; North American Interfaith Network
Affliation(s): North American Broadcasters Association
Chief Officer(s):
Znaimer Moses, Executive Producer
Finances: *Funding Sources:* Sale of airtime; Advertising; Cable fees
3 volunteer(s)

Visual Arts Newfoundland & Labrador (VANL-CARFAC)
Devon House, 59 Duckworth St., St. John's NL A1C 1E6
Fax: 709-738-7304
Toll-Free: 877-738-7303
vanl-carfac@nf.aibn.com
vanl-carfac.com
twitter.com/VisualArtistsNL
Overview: A small provincial organization overseen by Canadian Artists' Representation
Mission: To raise the socio-economic status of artists
Chief Officer(s):
Gerri Lynn Mackey, Chair
Dave Andrews, Executive Director
Awards:
• The Long Haul Award (Award)
Amount: $1,000 + lifetime membership
• The Large Year Award (Award)
Amount: $1,000
• The Emerging Visual Artist Award (Award)
Amount: $1,000
• The Kippy Goins Award (Award)
Amount: Original artwork by Michael Pittman
• The Critical Eye Award (Award)
Amount: $1,000

Visual Arts Nova Scotia (VANS)
1113 Marginal Rd., Halifax NS B3H 4P7
Tel: 902-423-4694; *Fax:* 902-422-0881
Toll-Free: 866-225-8267
vans@visualarts.ns.ca
www.visualarts.ns.ca
www.facebook.com/VisualArtsNovaScotia
twitter.com/visualartsns
Overview: A medium-sized provincial charitable organization founded in 1976
Mission: To promote a better understanding of arts & artists in Nova Scotia; to provide practical assistance to artists; to act in an advisory capacity to public & private interests
Member of: Canadian Conference of the Arts; Cultural Federations of Nova Scotia; Nova Scotia Cultural Network; Art Gallery of NS
Affliation(s): Nova Scotia College of Art & Design; Visual Arts of Ontario; Canadian Conference of the Arts
Chief Officer(s):
Briony Carros, Executive Director
director@visualarts.ns.ca
Finances: *Funding Sources:* Fundraising; Membership; Programs; Grants
Staff Member(s): 3
Membership: *Fees:* $40 individual; $60 group; $75 corporate; $35 senior; $30 student; $55 family; $45 international; *Member Profile:* Working artists; art students; educators; critics; curators; galleries & corporate patrons
Activities: Exhibitions; Information; Slide Registry; Equipment Rentals; Workshops; *Library:* Video & Slide Library, Resource Centre; Open to public by appointment

Vitesse
#210, 359 Terry Fox Dr., Ottawa ON K2K 2E7
Tel: 613-254-9880; *Fax:* 613-254-9881
info@vitesse.ca
www.vitesse.ca
Also Known As: Re-Skilling Canada/Réorientation professionnelle Canada
Overview: A small provincial organization
Mission: Retrains & re-skills science & engineering graduates to take advantage of current & emerging opportunities in software engineering, photonics, bioinformatics, microelectronics, wireless communications, & related fields
Chief Officer(s):
Hamid Rahbar, President & CEO
hamid.rahbar@vitesse.ca

Vocational & Rehabilitation Research Institute *See* Vecova Centre for Disability Services & Research

Vocational Rehabilitation Association of Canada (VRA Canada)
#310, 4 Cataraqui St., Kingston ON K7K 1Z7
Tel: 613-507-5530; *Fax:* 888-441-8002
Toll-Free: 888-876-9992
info@vracanada.com
www.vracanada.com
www.linkedin.com/groups?home=&gid=374132
www.facebook.com/VRACanada
twitter.com/VRACanada
Previous Name: Canadian Association of Rehabilitation Professionals Inc.
Overview: A small national organization founded in 1970
Mission: To support members in promoting & providing the professional delivery of rehabilitation services
Member of: Commission on Rehabilitation Counselor Certification
Affliation(s): Canadian Association for Vocational Evaluation & Work Adjustment
Chief Officer(s):
Lesley McIntyre, President
lesley@ircrehab.com
Finances: *Funding Sources:* Membership fees
Membership: *Fees:* $275 associate; $325 professional; $200 new graduate; $137.50 student; *Member Profile:* Vocational rehabilitation professionals
Activities: *Rents Mailing List:* Yes
Meetings/Conferences: • Vocational Rehabilitation Association of Canada 2015 National Conference, June, 2015, Delta Hotel Ottawa, Ottawa, ON
Scope: National

Alberta Society
Calgary AB
e-mail: vrac.ab@gmail.com
Chief Officer(s):
Shelley Langstaff, President

Atlantic Society
PO Box 757, 14 Weymouth Street, Charlottetown PE C1A 7L7
Tel: 902-569-7730; *Fax:* 902-368-6359
amaxwell@wcb.pe.ca
www.vraatlantic.com
Chief Officer(s):
Ann Maxwell, BBA, RRP, President

British Columbia Society
#102, 211 Columbia St., Vancouver BC V6A 2R5
Tel: 604-681-0296; *Fax:* 604-681-4545
office@vracanadabc.ca
www.vracanadabc.ca
Chief Officer(s):
Audrey Robertson, President

Manitoba Society
VRAC Manitoba, c/o 299 Truro Street, Winnipeg MB R3J 2A2
Tel: 204-799-8842
kerrihiebert@mts.net
vracanada.com/manitoba.php
Chief Officer(s):
Kerri Hiebert, Contact

Ontario Society
#310, 4 Cataraqui St., Kingston ON K7K 1Z7
Tel: 613-507-5530; *Fax:* 888-441-8002
Toll-Free: 888-876-9992
info@vracanadaon.com
www.vracanadaon.com
Chief Officer(s):
Addie Greco-Sanchez, President

Saskatchewan Society
1440 Broadway Ave., Regina SK S4P 1E2
Tel: 306-522-8571
Chief Officer(s):
Rhonda Teichreb, Contact

Voice for Animals Humane Society
PO Box 68119, 162 Bonnie Doon Mall, Edmonton AB T6C 4N6
Tel: 780-490-0905; *Fax:* 780-922-5287
info@v4a.org
www.v4a.org
Also Known As: V4A
Previous Name: Voice for Animals Society
Overview: A small provincial organization founded in 1997
Mission: To raise awareness of animal cruelty issues through education, lobbying, speakers & peaceful protests
Member of: Zoocheck Canada
Affliation(s): World Society for the Protection of Animals; Canadian Coalition for Farm Animals
Chief Officer(s):
Tove Reece, Contact
treece@v4a.org
Finances: *Annual Operating Budget:* Less than $50,000
30 volunteer(s)
Membership: 500; *Fees:* $20
Activities: Animal protection & advocacy

Voice for Animals Society *See* Voice for Animals Humane Society

VOICE for Hearing Impaired Children
#704, 161 Eglinton Ave. East, Toronto ON M4P 1J5
Tel: 416-487-7719; *Fax:* 416-487-7423
Toll-Free: 866-779-5144
info@voicefordeafkids.com
www.voicefordeafkids.com
www.facebook.com/VOICEforHearingImpairedChildren
twitter.com/VOICE4DEAFKIDS
Overview: A small provincial charitable organization founded in 1972
Mission: To ensure that all hearing impaired children have the right to develop their ability to listen & speak & have access to services which will enable them to listen & speak
Member of: Canadian Society of Association Executives
Affliation(s): Alexander Graham Bell Association
Chief Officer(s):
Lori Nikkel, Executive Director
lori@voicefordeafkids.com
Finances: *Annual Operating Budget:* $250,000-$500,000; *Funding Sources:* Private - foundations, corporations, individuals, special events; Golf Tournament & Theatre Night
Staff Member(s): 4; 200 volunteer(s)
Membership: 1,000 individual; *Fees:* $65; *Member Profile:* Parents & professionals in support of deaf & hard of hearing children; *Committees:* Education; Health

Activities: Service provider for Ontario Infant Hearing Program; *Speaker Service:* Yes; *Library* by appointment

Voice of English-speaking Québec (VEQ) / La Voix des anglophones de Québec
Pavillion Jeffery Hale, #2141, 1270, ch Sainte-Foy, Québec QC G1S 2M4
Tel: 418-683-2366; *Fax:* 418-688-3273
info@veq.qc.ca
www.veq.qc.ca
www.facebook.com/114198115271356
Overview: A small provincial organization founded in 1981
Mission: Dedicated to the preservation of a dynamic, English-speaking community in the Québec City & Chaudière-Appalaches regions, & to the promotion of that community's interests
Chief Officer(s):
Helen Walling, President
Jean-Sébastien J. Gignac, Executive Director
Finances: *Funding Sources:* Canadian Heritage's Official Languages Programme
Staff Member(s): 2; 50 volunteer(s)
Membership: 1,300+
Activities: Demographic research;

Voices for Children
#207, 12 Birch Ave., Toronto ON M4V 1C8
Tel: 416-489-5485; *Fax:* 416-489-5204
Toll-Free: 877-489-5485
info@voicesforchildren.ca
www.offordcentre.com/VoicesWebsite/index.htm
Overview: A small provincial charitable organization
Mission: To speak up for children & youth in Ontario
Chief Officer(s):
Cathy Vine, Executive Director
cathy@voicesforchildren.ca
Finances: *Funding Sources:* Child Development Institute; Margaret & Wallace McCain Family Foundation; Scotia Capital; Donations
Staff Member(s): 6

Voile Canada *See* Sail Canada

Voitures anciennes du Québec inc. (VAQ)
#200, 270, boul Sir-Wilfred-Laurier, Beloeil QC J3G 447
Tél: 514-990-9111; *Téléc:* 450-464-5368
voituresanciennes@bellnet.ca
www.vaq.qc.ca
Aperçu: *Dimension:* moyenne; *Envergure:* provinciale; fondée en 1974
Mission: Préservation de la voiture ancienne au Québec.
Membre(s) du bureau directeur:
Léo Gravelle, Président
Marie-Pier Charest, Coordonnatrice
Finances: *Budget de fonctionnement annuel:* $50,000-$100,000
Membre(s) du personnel: 1; 15 bénévole(s)
Membre: 2 000+; *Montant de la cotisation:* 59.95$
Activités: Expositions de voitures de collection durant la période estivales et publication d'un magazine mensuel de 56 pages en couleurs

La Voix des anglophones de Québec *See* Voice of English-speaking Québec

Volkssport Association of Alberta (VAA)
PO Box 131, #3, 11 Bellerose Dr., St Albert AB T8N 5C9
Tel: 780-998-1033
walksalot2@shaw.ca
walkalberta.ca
Overview: A small provincial charitable organization founded in 1987
Mission: To promote fun, fitness, & friendship through physical activity, specifically walking
Chief Officer(s):
Kathleen Parr, President
Finances: *Annual Operating Budget:* Less than $50,000
Membership: 100-499; *Committees:* Advertising & Publicity; Alberta Materials; Alberta Sanction; Booklet; Event Calendar; Event; Fundraising; Merchandise Sales; Newcomer Program; Newsletter; Public Relations & Communications; Refreshment/Social
Activities: Group walks; swimming, cycling, & skiing events

Volkssport Association of British Columbia (VABC)
1231 Hewlett Pl., Victoria BC V8S 4P6
Tel: 250-598-4316
vabc@volkssportingbc.ca
www.volkssportingbc.ca
Overview: A small provincial organization
Mission: To promote health, fitness, & friendship through stress-free exercise
Member of: Canadian Volkssport Federation
Affliation(s): Victoria International Walking Festival Society
Chief Officer(s):
Beverley Cattrall, President
beverley.cattrall@telus.net
Brenda Dudfield, Vice-President, 604-584-1900
dudfield@shaw.ca
Membership: *Committees:* Sanction; Webpage; Materials; Publicity & Marketing
Activities: Group walks
Publications:
• Volkssporting BC [a publication of the Volksport Association of British Columbia]
Type: Newsletter; *Editor:* Janet Lewis

Volleyball Alberta
Percy Page Centre, 11759 Groat Rd., Edmonton AB T5M 3K6
Tel: 780-415-1703; *Fax:* 780-415-1700
info@albertavolleyball.com
www.albertavolleyball.com
www.facebook.com/VolleyballAlberta
Overview: A medium-sized provincial charitable organization founded in 1974 overseen by Volleyball Canada
Mission: To promote volleyball in Alberta; To provide competitive opportunities for members
Affliation(s): Federation of Outdoor Volleyball Associations
Chief Officer(s):
Terry Gagnon, Executive Director, 587-273-1513, Fax: 587-273-1514
tgagnon@volleyballalberta.ca
Jim Plakas, Director, Technical
jplakas@volleyballalberta.ca
Staff Member(s): 8
Membership: *Member Profile:* Active in volleyball; *Committees:* Athlete Development; Business Development; High Performance; Leadership; Nominations/Awards
Activities: *Internships:* Yes; *Rents Mailing List:* Yes

Volleyball BC
Harry Jerome Sports Centre, 7564 Barnet Hwy., Burnaby BC V5A 1E7
Tel: 604-291-2007; *Fax:* 604-291-2602
contact@volleyballbc.ca
www.volleyballbc.ca
www.facebook.com/pages/Volleyball-BC/236547563024786
twitter.com/VolleyballBC
instagram.com/volleyballbc
Also Known As: British Columbia Volleyball Association
Overview: A medium-sized provincial organization founded in 1965 overseen by Volleyball Canada
Mission: To promote volleyball in British Columbia; To provide competitive opportunities for members
Chief Officer(s):
Chris Densmore, Executive Director, 604-291-2007 Ext. 223
execdirector@volleyballbc.ca
Chris Berglund, Director, Technical & High Performance, 604-291-2007 Ext. 222
cberglund@volleyballbc.ca
Jenny Graham, Manager, Programs, 604-291-2007 Ext. 225
jgraham@volleyballbc.ca
Dave Brewin, Manager, Marketing & Communications, 604-291-2007 Ext. 226
communications@volleyballbc.ca
Staff Member(s): 12
Membership: *Committees:* Beach Players; Finance & Audit; Governance; High Performance; Nominations; Regional Development

Volleyball Canada (VC)
National Office, #1A, 1084 Kenaston St., Ottawa ON K1B 3P5
Tel: 613-748-5681; *Fax:* 613-748-5727
info@volleyball.ca
www.volleyball.ca
www.facebook.com/VolleyballCanada
twitter.com/VBallCanada
Also Known As: Canadian Volleyball Association
Overview: A large national charitable organization founded in 1953
Mission: To lead the growth of & excellence in the sport of volleyball for all Canadians
Affliation(s): International Volleyball Federation; Canadian Olympic Association; Coaching Association of Canada
Chief Officer(s):
Debra Armstrong, President
Mark Eckert, Executive Director
meckert@volleyball.ca
James Sneddon, Director, Domestic Development
jsneddon@volleyball.ca
Linden Leung, Director, Finance & Operations
linden@volleyball.ca
Finances: *Funding Sources:* Membership dues; Fundraising; Merchandise & publications sale; Government; Sponsorships
Staff Member(s): 31
Membership: *Member Profile:* Athletes, officials; *Committees:* Domestic Development; National Championships; Sitting Volleyball; High Performance Management; National Referee; Alumni & Awards; National Registration Systems Project Management; National Registration System Operation Group; Nominations & Elections; Finance & Audit; Legal; Ethics; External Relations
Activities: Offering National Championships for Indoor & Beach Volleyball & National Team Challenge Cup (for Provincial Teams); Providing coaching certification & education programs; Producing publications & videos; Coordinating international & national officials programs; Hosting international events; Marketing & promoting volleyball to the corporate community & the media; *Internships:* Yes; *Rents Mailing List:* Yes
Awards:
• Hall of Fame: Athlete, Builder, Coach, Referee, Team (Award)
• Annual Awards: Special Recognition, Referee of the Year, Coach of the Year, Contributor of the Year (Award)

Volleyball New Brunswick
#13, 900 Hanwell Rd., Fredericton NB E3B 6A3
Tel: 506-451-1346; *Fax:* 506-451-1325
vnb@nb.aibn.com
www.vnb.nb.ca
www.facebook.com/volleyballnb
twitter.com/volleyballnb
instagram.com/volleyballnb
Also Known As: VNB
Overview: A medium-sized provincial organization overseen by Volleyball Canada
Mission: To promote volleyball in New Brunswick; To provide competitive opportunities for members
Chief Officer(s):
James Cress, President
Ryley Boldon, Executive Director
Monica Jones, Coordinator, Program
vnbcoordinator@nb.aibn.com
Staff Member(s): 2
Membership: *Fees:* Schedule available; *Committees:* Executive; Officials; Beach; Senior; Age Class; Female High Performance; Male High Performance; Coaching

Volleyball Nova Scotia
5516 Spring Garden Rd., 4th Fl., Halifax NS B3J 1G6
Tel: 902-425-5450
vns@sportnovascotia.ca
www.volleyballnovascotia.ca
www.facebook.com/Volleyballnovascotia
twitter.com/volleyballNS
Overview: A medium-sized provincial organization founded in 1965 overseen by Volleyball Canada
Mission: To promote volleyball in Nova Scotia; To provide competitive opportunities for members
Chief Officer(s):
Dave Swetnam, President, 902-817-7262
dswetnam@eastlink.ca
Michelle Aucoin, Executive Director, 902-476-4668
vns@sportnovascotia.ca
Shane St-Louis, Director, Technical, 902-225-9926
volleyballtd@sportnovascotia.ca
Staff Member(s): 3

Volleyball Nunavut
NCC Building, PO Box 440, Baker Lake NU X0C 0A0
Tel: 867-793-3301; *Fax:* 867-793-3321
volleyballnunavut.ca
Overview: A medium-sized provincial organization founded in 1999 overseen by Volleyball Canada
Mission: To promote volleyball in Nunavut & provide programs throughout the territory
Member of: Sport & Recreation Nunavut
Chief Officer(s):
Scott Schutz, Executive Director
scott@volleyballnunavut.ca
Finances: *Funding Sources:* Sport & Recreation Nunavut

Volleyball Prince Edward Island
PO Box 302, Charlottetown PE C1A 7K7
Tel: 902-569-0583; *Fax:* 902-368-4548
Toll-Free: 800-247-6712
www.volleyballpei.com
Overview: A small provincial organization overseen by Volleyball Canada
Mission: To promote volleyball in PEI; to provide competitive opportunities for members
Affliation(s): Sport PEI
Chief Officer(s):
Cheryl Crozier, Executive Director, 902-569-0583
cgcrozier@sportpei.pe.ca
Krista Walsh, President
Harvey Mazerolle, Vice-President
Finances: *Funding Sources:* Government grants; membership fees; fund-raising
Membership: *Member Profile:* Coaches & players
Activities: *Rents Mailing List:* Yes

Volleyball Yukon
4061 - 4th Ave., Whitehorse YT Y1A 1H1
Tel: 867-334-4592; *Fax:* 867-667-4237
volleyballyukon@gmail.com
www.volleyballyukon.com
www.facebook.com/pages/Volleyball-Yukon/283652915006482
Overview: A small provincial organization overseen by Volleyball Canada
Mission: To promote volleyball in the Yukon; to provide competitive opportunities for its members
Chief Officer(s):
Peter Grundmanis, President

Vols d'espoir *See* Hope Air

Voluntas Dei Institute *Voir* Institut Voluntas Dei

Volunteer Alberta
Birks Bldg., #217, 10113 - 104 St., Edmonton AB T5J 1A1
Tel: 780-482-3300; *Fax:* 780-482-3310
Toll-Free: 877-915-6336
volab@volunteeralberta.ab.ca
www.volunteeralberta.ab.ca
Overview: A medium-sized provincial organization
Mission: Building the capacity of the voluntary sector by strategically connecting leaders, organizations, & networks to ensure Albertans are engaged in creating vibrant & progressive communities
Chief Officer(s):
Kim McClymont, President
Angela Keibel, Vice-President
Membership: *Fees:* $50 affiliate; $80 associate; $125 volunteer centre

Volunteer BC
c/o Volunteer Richmond Information Services, #190, 7000 Minoru Blvd., Vancouver BC V6Y 3Z5
Tel: 604-873-5877
volunteerbc@gmail.com
www.volunteerbc.bc.ca
twitter.com/volunteerbc
Overview: A medium-sized provincial organization
Mission: To strengthen the growth & development of voluntary action in British Columbia
Chief Officer(s):
Lawrie Portigal, President
Stacy Ashton, Vice-President
Membership: *Fees:* $25 individual; $35 volunteer centres/voluntary organizations; *Member Profile:* Volunteer centres; provincial voluntary organizations; individuals

Volunteer Bureau of Montreal *Voir* Centre d'action bénévole de Montréal

Volunteer Canada / Bénévoles Canada
353 Dalhousie St. 3rd floor, Ottawa ON K1N 7G1
Tel: 613-231-4371; *Fax:* 613-231-6725
Toll-Free: 800-670-0401
info@volunteer.ca
www.volunteer.ca
www.facebook.com/VolunteerCanada
twitter.com/VolunteerCanada
www.youtube.com/VolunteerCanada
Previous Name: Canadian Association of Volunteer Bureaux Centres
Overview: A medium-sized national organization
Mission: To support volunteerism & civic participation through special projects & programs
Staff Member(s): 20
Membership: 86+ volunteer centres
Activities: Canada Volunteerism Initiative; *Awareness Events:* National Volunteer Week, April

Volunteer Centre of Charlotte County Inc.
PO Box 271, 199 Union St., St Stephen NB E3L 2X2
Tel: 506-466-4995; *Fax:* 506-465-0988
Overview: A small local organization
Member of: Canadian Association of Food Banks; Canadian Association of Volunteer Centres
Finances: *Funding Sources:* Donations
Staff Member(s): 2
Activities: Services for under-employed families

Volunteer Centre of Guelph/Wellington
#1, 46 Cork St. East, Guelph ON N1H 2W8
Tel: 519-822-0912; *Fax:* 519-822-1389
Toll-Free: 866-693-3318
info@volunteerguelphwellington.on.ca
www.volunteerguelphwellington.on.ca
www.linkedin.com/company/volunteer-centre-of-guelph-wellington
www.facebook.com/VolunteerGW
twitter.com/volunteergw
Previous Name: Guelph Information
Overview: A small local charitable organization founded in 2001 overseen by InformOntario
Mission: The Centre strives to build a vibrant, volunteer-based community. It offers programs to assist non-profit organizations find & maintain a force of capable volunteer workers.
Chief Officer(s):
Christine Oldfield, Interim Executive Director, 519-822-0912 Ext. 222
coldfield@volunteerguelphwellington.on.ca
Finances: *Funding Sources:* Federal, provinicial, municipal governments; foundations & corporations; public donations
Staff Member(s): 7
Membership: 107; *Fees:* $175
Activities: Leadership program for non-profit management; Community Information Guelph, a community news database to connect programs & volunteers; Snow Angels, to help senior/disabled people with snow removal; *Awareness Events:* National Volunteer Week; *Rents Mailing List:* Yes; *Library:* Volunteer Centre Resource Library; Open to public

Volunteer Circle of the National Gallery of Canada / Cercle des bénévoles du Musée des beaux-arts du Canada
c/o National Gallery of Canada, PO Box 427, Stn. A, 380 Sussex Dr., Ottawa ON K1N 9N4
Tel: 613-990-0130
info@gallery.ca
www.gallery.ca/en/about/volunteers.php
Overview: A small national charitable organization founded in 1958
Mission: To raise funds for the National Gallery; to provide activities for members & to provide ancillary volunteer assistance to the Gallery
Member of: Canadian Museum Association
Finances: *Annual Operating Budget:* $50,000-$100,000
Staff Member(s): 1; 300 volunteer(s)
Membership: 100-499
Awards:
• Volunteer Awards (Award)
Given annually for 100 hrs., 500 hrs, 1,000 hrs, 2,000 hrs cumulative volunteer service

Volunteer Grandparents (VIP)
#203, 2101 Holdom Ave., Burnaby BC V5B 0A4
Tel: 604-736-8271; *Fax:* 604-294-6814
info@volunteergrandparents.ca
www.volunteergrandparents.ca
Also Known As: Volunteers for Intergenerational Programs Society
Previous Name: Volunteer Grandparents Society of Canada
Overview: A small local charitable organization founded in 1973
Mission: To support & encourage multigenerational relationships & the concept of extended family by matching screened volunteers (50+) with families with children between the age of 3-14
Member of: Volunteer Vancouver; BC Council of Families; Go Volunteer.ca
Affliation(s): Volunteer Burnaby
Chief Officer(s):
Stephen Sjoberg, President
Finances: *Annual Operating Budget:* Less than $50,000; *Funding Sources:* Provincial Gaming
Staff Member(s): 1; 100 volunteer(s)
Membership: 1-99; *Fees:* $5; *Committees:* Executive
Activities: Family Match Program; school grandparent program; ambassador program;

Volunteer Grandparents Society of Canada *See* Volunteer Grandparents

Volunteer Management Professionals of Canada (VMPC)
#9, 380 Champlain St., Dieppe NB E1A 1P3
e-mail: info@vmpc.ca
www.vmpc.ca
Overview: A small national licensing organization founded in 1980
Chief Officer(s):
Charles Allain, President
President@vmpc.ca
Membership: *Committees:* Advocacy and Professional Standards; Certification; Communications; Information Technology; Membership; Professional Development
Meetings/Conferences: • 2015 Volunteer Management Professionals of Canada National Conference, June, 2015, Edmonton, AB
Scope: National

Volunteer Red Deer
Community Village, 4728 Ross St., Red Deer AB T4N 1X2
Tel: 403-346-4636; *Fax:* 403-340-8193
info@volunteerreddeer.ca
volunteerreddeer.ca
Previous Name: Red Deer Landlord & Tenant Services
Overview: A small local organization
Mission: To meet the needs of the citizens of Red Deer & Central Alberta through strengthening the non-profit sector
Chief Officer(s):
Bill Farr, Chair
Finances: *Funding Sources:* Provincial government; municipal government

Vonda Chamber of Commerce
c/o Vonda Hometown Insurance Brokers, PO Box 285, Vonda SK S0K 4N0
Tel: 306-258-2134; *Fax:* 306-258-2244
Overview: A small local organization
Chief Officer(s):
A. Bussiere, President
Robert Lalonde, Secretary
rlalonde@sasktel.net

Voyageur Trail Association (VTA)
PO Box 20040, 150 Churchill Blvd., Sault Ste Marie ON P6A 6W3
Toll-Free: 877-393-4003
info@voyageurtrail.ca
www.voyageurtrail.ca
www.facebook.com/voyageurtrailassociation
Overview: A small local charitable organization founded in 1973
Mission: The Voyageur Trail Association remains today as a trail building and maintenance organization to a trail building-and-hiking organization with several public outings held throughout the year in various clubs
Member of: Hike Ontario
Affliation(s): Great Lakes Forestry Research; Pukaskwa National Park; Lake Superior Provincial Park; Rainbow Falls Provincial Park; Nipigon River Recreational Trail; Charity Village
Chief Officer(s):
Gail Andrew, Treasurer
Susan Graham, President
Finances: *Funding Sources:* Membership fees & donations
Membership: *Fees:* $30 family; $25 adult; $10 student
Activities: Trail follows the clear waters of North Channel to the cold granite coast of Lake Superior (640 km completed; 470+ km planned)

Vraies femmes du Canada *See* REAL Women of Canada

Vrais Copains *See* Best Buddies Canada

Vues d'Afrique (Les Journées africaines et créoles). *Voir* Vues d'Afriques - Les Journées du cinéma africain et créole

Vues d'Afriques - Les Journées du cinéma africain et créole (VA)
#3100, 100, rue Sherbrooke est, Montréal QC H2X 1C3

Tél: 514-284-3322; *Téléc:* 514-845-0631
www.vuesdafrique.org
www.facebook.com/vuesdafrique
Nom précédent: Vues d'Afrique (Les Journées africaines et créoles).
Aperçu: *Dimension:* petite; *Envergure:* internationale; Organisme sans but lucratif; fondée en 1984
Mission: Est une force dans l'action nationale et internationale pour le soutien des cultures comme outil de développement harmonieux des sociétés du Nord et du Sud; organiser des activités grand public qui contribuent à faire connaître les cultures africaines et créoles, et développer des partenariats entre le Canada et les pays du Sud dans le domaine des industries culturelles
Membre de: Conseil des festivals jumelés
Finances: *Budget de fonctionnement annuel:* $500,000-$1.5 Million
Membre(s) du personnel: 15; 150 bénévole(s)
Membre: 1-99
Activités: Festival de films, avril; *Stagiaires:* Oui; *Bibliothèque:* IMPAC; rendez-vous
Prix, Bouses:
- Prix de la communication interculturelle documentaire (Prix)
- Prix Vues d'Afrique (Prix)
- Prix ONF (Prix)
- Bourse pour la meilleure production indépendante (Brouse)
- Prix de la communication interculturelle long métrage (Prix)
- Prix de la communication interculturelle court métrage (Prix)
- Prix Images de Femmes (Prix)

Vulcan & District Chamber of Commerce
Vulcan AB
e-mail: info@vulcantourism.com
www.vulcanchamber.com
Also Known As: Vulcan Business Development & Tourism
Overview: A small local organization
Mission: To promote, educate & develop Vulcan & district businesses & their community
Member of: Alberta Chamber of Commerce
Chief Officer(s):
Dwayne Hill, President
Karen Currie, Vice-President
Finances: *Annual Operating Budget:* Less than $50,000; *Funding Sources:* Membership fees; fund-raising
30 volunteer(s)
Membership: 40; *Fees:* $40; *Member Profile:* Small business owner; *Committees:* Tourism; Economic Development
Activities: Spock Days; Moonlight Madness; Fly in Breakfast; *Speaker Service:* Yes; *Rents Mailing List:* Yes; *Library:* Economic Development Centre

Vulcan & District Fish & Game Club
PO Box 301, Vulcan AB T0L 2B0
Tel: 403-485-6744
Overview: A small local organization
Member of: Alberta Fish & Game Association
Chief Officer(s):
Doug McIntyre, Treasurer

Vulcan Business Development Society (VBDS)
PO Box 1205, 110 - 1st Ave. South, Vulcan AB T0L 2B0
Tel: 403-485-4100; *Fax:* 403-485-3143
www.vulcanbusiness.ca
Overview: A small local organization
Mission: To assist the existing businesses in their development and to encourage new businesses.
Chief Officer(s):
Gordon Nelson, President
Paul Taylor, Vice-President
Finances: *Funding Sources:* Membership fees; fund-raising

The W. Garfield Weston Foundation
c/o George Weston Ltd., #2001, 22 St. Clair Ave. East, Toronto ON M4T 2S3
Tel: 416-922-2500; *Fax:* 416-967-7949
info@westonfoundation.org
www.westonfoundation.org
Overview: A medium-sized national organization
Mission: Focuses on education (through a scholarship & bursary program), conservation (via habitat conservation projects through national organizations only), & trustee-initiated grants (for which applications are not accepted)
Chief Officer(s):
Susan Cohen, Executive Director

W. Maurice Young Centre for Applied Ethics (CAE)
University of British Columbia, #227, 6356 Agricultural Rd., Vancouver BC V6T 1Z1
Tel: 604-822-8625; *Fax:* 604-822-8627
www.ethics.ubc.ca
Previous Name: Centre for Applied Ethics
Overview: A small local organization founded in 1993
Mission: An interdisciplinary research centre focused on health care practices, new technologies & business & professional procedures
Chief Officer(s):
David Silver, Acting Director
david.silver@ubc.ca
Finances: *Annual Operating Budget:* $50,000-$100,000
Membership: 1-99
Activities: Research projects;

Wabamun District Chamber of Commerce Society
PO Box 29, Wabamun AB T0E 2K0
Tel: 780-892-4665
wabamun.chamber@xplornet.com
www.wabamunchamber.org
www.facebook.com/249125105187278?ref=hl
Overview: A small local organization
Chief Officer(s):
Vicki Specht, President

Wainwright & District Chamber of Commerce
PO Box 2997, #203, 1006 - 4th Ave., Wainwright AB T9W 1S9
Tel: 780-842-4910; *Fax:* 780-842-6061
exec@wdchamber.com
www.wdchamber.com
Overview: A small local organization founded in 1959
Member of: Alberta Chambers of Commerce
Chief Officer(s):
Sheri Ducolon, President
Shawna Batten, Executive Director
Staff Member(s): 1
Membership: 200+

Wakaw & District Board of Trade
PO Box 188, Wakaw SK S0K 4P0
www.townofwakaw.com/boardoftrade.html
Overview: A small local organization
Mission: Group of local Business Owners who work together with various clubs and organizations to promote the Town of Wakaw and its business community
Chief Officer(s):
Laurianne Osmak, President & Secretary, 306-233-5330
Sandi Draude, Vice-President

Waldorf School Association of Kelowna
PO Box 29093, Stn. Okanagan Mission, 429 Collett Rd., Kelowna BC V1W 4A7
Tel: 250-764-4130; *Fax:* 250-764-4139
info@kelownawaldorfschool.com
www.kelownawaldorfschool.com
Overview: A small local organization founded in 1981
Chief Officer(s):
Dana Bodnar, Administrator
Staff Member(s): 16; 20 volunteer(s)
Membership: 35 individual;

Walker Lynch Foundation
72 Railside Rd., Toronto ON M3A 1A3
Tel: 416-449-5464; *Fax:* 416-449-9165
Overview: A small national charitable organization
Chief Officer(s):
Walker Lynch, Contact

Walker Mineralogical Club (WMC)
c/o Department of Natural History, Royal Ontario Museum, 100 Queens Park, Toronto ON M5S 2C6
e-mail: info@walkermineralogicalclub.com
www.walkermineralogicalclub.com
Overview: A small local organization founded in 1937
Member of: Central Canadian Federation of Mineralogical Societies
Chief Officer(s):
Don Caldwell, Treasurer
Bill Lechner, Contact, Membership Services
Finances: *Funding Sources:* Fundraising
Membership: *Fees:* $15 juniors (ages 14-18); $25 singles; $35 families; *Committees:* Auction; Banquet; Field Trip
Activities: Hosting monthly meetings featuring guest speakers with expertise in mineralogy or geology; Organizing field trips; Arranging an annual mineral specimen auction
Publications:
- Walker Club SourceBook [a publication of the Walker Mineralogical Club]
Type: Handbook
Profile: Information about club activities for new members of the Walker Mineralogical Club
- The Walker Mineralogical Club Newsletter
Type: Newsletter; *Frequency:* Monthly; *Editor:* Heidi Tomes
Profile: Articles about mineralogy

Walkerton & District Chamber of Commerce
PO Box 1344, 101 Durham St., Walkerton ON N0G 2V0
Tel: 519-881-3413; *Fax:* 519-881-4009
Toll-Free: 888-820-9291
chamberinfo@wightman.ca
www.brockton.ca/chamber.php?area=cm&pc=CH00
Overview: A small local organization founded in 1956
Mission: To foster & develop trade & commerce, & the further improvement of the economic, civic & social welfare of our district
Member of: Ontario Chamber of Commerce; Ontario Business Improvement Association
Affliation(s): Ontario Chamber of Commerce
Chief Officer(s):
Tracey Cassidy, Chamber Manager
Dennis Moran, President, 519-881-0835
Neil Kirstine, Vice-President, 519-881-2551
Finances: *Annual Operating Budget:* $100,000-$250,000; *Funding Sources:* Membership fees
Staff Member(s): 2; 11 volunteer(s)
Membership: 220; *Fees:* $150; *Committees:* Image; Promotions
Activities: Business improvement; town beautification; tourist guide; Santa Parade; *Library:* Walkerton Tourist Information Centre;

Walkerton & District Community Support Services ***See*** Community Living Walkerton & District

Walkley Centre / Association des familles unies de la rue Walkley
6650 ch de la Côte-St.-Luc, Montréal QC H4V 1G8
Tel: 514-872-1391
walkley.center@gmail.com
www.facebook.com/pages/Walkley-Center-Centre-Walkley/206990426007754
Overview: A small local organization
Mission: Community Centre serving families in the Notre-Dame-de-Grâce borough of Montréal

Wallaceburg & District Chamber of Commerce
152 Duncan St., Wallaceburg ON N8A 4E2
Tel: 519-627-1443; *Fax:* 519-627-1485
Toll-Free: 888-545-0558
info@wallaceburgchamber.com
www.wallaceburgchamber.com
www.facebook.com/WallaceburgDistrictChamber
twitter.com/Wburgchamber
Overview: A small local organization
Chief Officer(s):
Carmen McGregor, President
Tina Fraleigh, Office Administrator
Membership: *Fees:* Schedule available
Publications:
- Wallaceburg & District Chamber of Commerce Newsletter
Type: Newsletter

Wallaceburg & District Council for the Arts ***See*** Wallaceburg Arts Council

Wallaceburg & District Historical Society, Inc.
505 King St., Wallaceburg ON N8A 1J1
Tel: 519-627-8962; *Fax:* 519-627-9859
wallaceburg.museum@kent.net
www.kent.net/wallaceburg-museum
Overview: A small local charitable organization founded in 1973
Mission: To collect, preserve, research, exhibit, & intrepret a collection of historical artifacts
Member of: Ontario Museums Association; Ontario Historical Society; Architectural Conservancy of Ontario; Wallaceburg Chamber of Commerce; Heritage Sarnia-Lambton
Finances: *Annual Operating Budget:* $100,000-$250,000
Staff Member(s): 3; 122 volunteer(s)
Membership: 221; *Fees:* $15 single; $20 family
Activities: Operates the Wallaceburg & District Museum; *Library* Open to public

Wallaceburg & Sydenham District Association for Community Living ***See*** Community Living Wallaceburg

Wallaceburg Arts Council
PO Box 20077, Stn. James St., Wallaceburg ON N8A 5G1
Tel: 519-627-1607
Previous Name: Wallaceburg & District Council for the Arts
Overview: A small local charitable organization founded in 1980
Mission: To stimulate awareness & appreciation for the arts in Wallaceburg & district by organizing, promoting, & operating shows for local artists, sponsoring appearance of provincial on-tour performers, coordinating planned cultural events, raising funds for operation of the Council &/or events it will support or create, supporting local art & artists, sponsoring, organizing or promoting clinics & workshops for benefit of local artists
Affiliation(s): Ontario Arts Council
Chief Officer(s):
Dave Babbitt, Contact, 519-627-9803
Finances: *Annual Operating Budget:* Less than $50,000
Membership: 50; *Member Profile:* Divided into 4 classes: artists (amateur or professional) - produce any work of art or craft; patrons - appreciate artistic endeavours produced by others; junior patrons - 16 years of age or under & appreciate artistic endeavours; sponsors - interests similar to the Council

Walpole Island Heritage Centre
RR#3, Wallaceburg ON N8A 4K9
Tel: 519-627-1475; *Fax:* 519-627-1530
heritage@web.net
Also Known As: Nin-Da-Waab-Jig
Overview: A small local organization
Affiliation(s): Centre for Indigenous Environmental Resources
Chief Officer(s):
Joyce Johnson, Director
joyce.johnson@wifn.org

The War Amputations of Canada / Les Amputés de guerre du Canada
2827 Riverside Dr., Ottawa ON K1V 0C4
Tel: 613-731-3821; *Fax:* 613-731-3234
Toll-Free: 800-465-2677
customerservice@waramps.ca
www.waramps.ca
www.facebook.com/TheWarAmps
twitter.com/thewaramps
www.youtube.com/warampsofcanada
Also Known As: The War Amps
Overview: A medium-sized national charitable organization founded in 1919
Mission: To provide a wide range of assistance to all Canadian war amputees & child amputees; promotes the advancement of prosthetics & prosthetic research through grants to facilities undertaking research in field of prosthetics
Member of: National Council of Veteran Associations
Chief Officer(s):
David Saunders, Chief Operating Officer
Danita Chisholm, Executive Director, Communications
Activities: Child Amputee Program (CHAMP) financially assists child amputees & their families & provides counselling & pays travel & accommodation expenses to prosthetic centres; Key Tag Service provides employment & fund-raising capabilities to war amputees; Play Safe Program promotes child safety; Matching Mothers Program matches families whose children have similar amputations for purposes of counselling & information; Provides public awareness films about amputee sports & child safety, & Canada's military history; *Speaker Service:* Yes

Warden Woods Community Centre
74 Firvalley Ct., Toronto ON M1L 1N9
Tel: 416-694-1138; *Fax:* 416-694-1161
www.wardenwoods.com
www.facebook.com/pages/Warden-Woods-Community-Centre/12257770090
twitter.com/WardenWoodsCC
www.flickr.com/photos/80046247@N07
Overview: A medium-sized local charitable organization founded in 1970
Mission: Warden Woods is a charitable community centre in Scarborough offering programmes to families, seniors, youth.
Chief Officer(s):
Ginelle Skerritt, Executive Director
Finances: *Funding Sources:* United Way; Provincial & municipal government
300 volunteer(s)
Membership: *Fees:* $5

Wasaga Beach Chamber of Commerce
PO Box 394, 550 River Rd. West, Wasaga Beach ON L9Z 1A4
Tel: 705-429-2247; *Fax:* 705-429-1407
Toll-Free: 866-292-7242
info@wasagainfo.com
www.wasagainfo.com
Overview: A small local organization founded in 1938
Mission: To promote & improve trade & commerce, as well as the economic, civic & social welfare of the district
Affiliation(s): Canadian Chamber of Commerce; Ontario Chamber of Commerce
Chief Officer(s):
Trudie McCrea, Office Manager
Staff Member(s): 3
Membership: *Fees:* Schedule available
Activities: Annual business awards, April;

Wasagaming Arts Council *See* Wasagaming Community Arts Inc.

Wasagaming Chamber of Commerce
PO Box 621, Onanole MB R0J 1N0
e-mail: info@discoverclearlake.com
www.discoverclearlake.com
Overview: A small local organization
Mission: To help promote local businesses & their growth
Chief Officer(s):
Scott Gowler, President
Bob Bickerton, Treasurer
Membership: 67

Wasagaming Community Arts Inc.
PO Box 98, 110 Wasagaming Dr., Wasagaming MB R0J 2H0
Tel: 204-848-2993; *Fax:* 204-848-2993
Previous Name: Wasagaming Arts Council
Overview: A small local charitable organization founded in 1979
Mission: To provide a creative learning experience for children & adults; to develop in individuals an appreciation of nature & positive attitude toward the environment; to create meaningful work experience for students & volunteers; to interpret the work of cultural groups & to enlist public interest & understanding
Member of: Manitoba Association of Community Arts Councils Inc.
Affiliation(s): Wasagaming Chamber of Commerce
Finances: *Annual Operating Budget:* Less than $50,000
Staff Member(s): 4; 15 volunteer(s)
Membership: 1-99; *Committees:* Membership; Exhibitions; Gallery Shop; Building
Activities: Exhibitions; adult & youth workshops in the visual arts & crafts; children's arts/craft classes; community arts resource; *Internships:* Yes

Washademoak Region Chamber of Commerce
Cambridge-Narrows NB
Tel: 506-488-8091
www.w-rcc.ca
www.facebook.com/WashademoakRegionChamberOfCommerce
Overview: A small local organization
Mission: To provide a forum that enables businesses to meet, exchange ideas, identify issues, & formulate plans of action to increase awareness & commerce for businesses within the region
Chief Officer(s):
David Craw, President, 506-488-8091
djcraw@xplornet.ca
Vince Lalond, Vice-President
slivers@xplornet.ca
Membership: 30; *Fees:* $30

Waskesiu Chamber of Commerce
PO Box 216, Waskesiu Lake SK S0J 2Y0
Tel: 306-663-5140; *Fax:* 306-663-5448
wakesiuchamber@sasktel.net
www.waskesiulake.ca
Overview: A small local organization
Chief Officer(s):
G.A. Wilson, Manager
G.J.P. Bueckert, President

Waswanipi Cree Model Forest
3 Rte 113, Waswanipi QC J0Y 3C0
Tel: 819-753-2900; *Fax:* 819-753-2904
Overview: A small local organization
Member of: Canadian Model Forest Network
Chief Officer(s):
Rhonda Oblin, General Manager

Watch Tower Bible & Tract Society of Canada
PO Box 4100, Georgetown ON L7G 4Y4
Tel: 905-873-4100; *Fax:* 905-873-4554
www.watchtower.org
Also Known As: Jehovah's Witnesses
Overview: A medium-sized national organization
Mission: To serve Jehovah's Witnesses in Canada
Chief Officer(s):
Kenneth Little, President

Water Environment Association of Ontario (WEAO)
PO Box 176, Milton ON L9T 4N9
Tel: 416-410-6933; *Fax:* 416-410-1626
julie.vincent@weao.org
www.weao.org
Previous Name: Pollution Control Association of Ontario
Overview: A medium-sized provincial organization founded in 1971
Mission: To advance the water environment industry; To promote sound public policy
Member of: Water Environment Federation (WEF)
Affiliation(s): Canadian Water & Wastewater Association
Chief Officer(s):
Catherine Jefferson, Executive Director, 416-410-6933 Ext. 2, Fax: 416-657-7006
catherine.jefferson@weao.org
Julie A. Vincent, Executive Administrator, 416-410-6933 Ext. 1, Fax: 416-410-1626
julie.vincent@weao.org
Anne Baliva, Admin. Assistant, 416-410-6933 Ext. 1, Fax: 416-410-1626
anne.baliva@weao.org.com
John Presta, Treasurer
john.presta@region.durham.on.ca
Finances: *Funding Sources:* Membership fees; Sponsorships
Staff Member(s): 3; 150 volunteer(s)
Membership: 1,400; *Member Profile:* Technical & professional individuals committed to the preservation & enhancement of Ontario's water environment, such as scientists, operators, engineers, & students; Employees of consulting firms, industries, equipment manufacturers, municipalities, colleges & universities, & provincial & federal government agencies; *Committees:* Asset Management; Communications; Conference; Environmental, Health, Safety & Security; Government Affairs; New Professionals; Operations Challenge; Promotions & Events Planning; Public Education; Residuals & Biosolids; Water for People - Canada; Wastewater Collection Systems; Wastewater Treatment & Technology
Activities: Delivering services to members; Providing a forum for members to interact for educational & professional advancement; Increasing public understanding; Promoting careers in the water environment industry; *Library*
Awards:
• Exemplary Biosolids Management Award (Award)
To recognize biosolides practitioners who go beyond the normal requirements in the practice of managing biosolids *Contact:* Water Environment Association of Ontario, PO Box 176, Milton, ON, L9T 4N9
• Geoffrey T. G. Scott Memorial Award (Award)
To honour outstanding leadership & inspiration in the water environment industry
• Golden Manhole Award (Award), WEAO Golden Manhole Society Selection Committee
• Water Environment Association of Ontario Scholarship (Scholarship)
To recognize outstanding students in the water quality field in Ontario*Deadline:* October
Meetings/Conferences: • Water Environment Association of Ontario 2015 44th Annual Technical Symposium & Exhibition, April, 2015, Toronto Congress Centre, Toronto, ON
Scope: Provincial
Description: A conference featuring technical sessions, a keynote speaker, a student program, an awards presentation, & networking opportunities
Contact Information: Chair, Conference Committee: Frank Farkas, E-mail: farkas.f@spdsales.com
• Water Environment Association of Ontario 2016 45th Annual Technical Symposium & Exhibition, April, 2016, Scotiabank Convention Centre, Niagara Falls, ON
Scope: Provincial
Description: A conference featuring technical sessions, a keynote speaker, a student program, an awards presentation, & networking opportunities
Contact Information: Chair, Conference Committee: Frank Farkas, E-mail: farkas.f@spdsales.com
• Water Environment Association of Ontario 2017 46th Annual Technical Symposium & Exhibition, April, 2017, Ottawa

Convention Centre, Ottawa, ON
Scope: Provincial
Description: A conference featuring technical sessions, a keynote speaker, a student program, an awards presentation, & networking opportunities
Contact Information: Chair, Conference Committee: Frank Farkas, E-mail: farkas.f@spdsales.com
Publications:
• INFLUENTS [a publication of the Water Environment Association of Ontario]
Type: Magazine; *Frequency:* Quarterly; *Accepts Advertising;* *Editor:* Cole Kelman
Profile: Features on current issues, educational articles, project profiles, people in the news, committee reports, events, & marketplacedevelopments

Water Polo Canada (WPC)
1084 Kenaston St., #1A, Ottawa ON K1B 3P5
Tel: 613-748-5682; *Fax:* 613-748-5777
office@waterpolo.ca
www.waterpolo.ca
www.facebook.com/193992167322377
twitter.com/waterpolocanada
www.youtube.com/waterpolocanada
Also Known As: Canadian Water Polo Association
Overview: A medium-sized national organization founded in 1976
Mission: To promote growth in sport of water polo in Canada; to administer Canada's high performance programs (Olympics, Pan Am Games, etc.) in water polo
Affliation(s): Aquatic Federation of Canada
Chief Officer(s):
Martin Goulet, Executive Director, 613-748-5682 Ext. 322
mgoulet@waterpolo.ca
Finances: *Funding Sources:* Government; sponsors; members
Staff Member(s): 15
Membership: *Member Profile:* Water polo participant or team
Activities: *Internships:* Yes

Water Polo New Brunswick (WPNB)
NB
waterpolonb.ca
Overview: A medium-sized provincial organization overseen by Water Polo Canada
Member of: Water Polo Canada
Chief Officer(s):
JC Besner, President
president@waterpolonb.ca

Water Polo Newfoundland (WPNL)
NL
waterpolonl.ca
Overview: A medium-sized provincial organization overseen by Water Polo Canada
Member of: Water Polo Canada

Water Polo Nova Scotia
c/o Sport Nova Scotia, #311, 5516 Spring Garden Rd., Halifax NS B3J 1G6
Tel: 902-425-5450; *Fax:* 902-425-5606
info@waterpolonovascotia.ca
pwpa.ca
www.facebook.com/332153633464854
Previous Name: Provincial Water Polo Association
Overview: A small provincial organization founded in 2006 overseen by Water Polo Canada
Mission: To promote the sport of water polo in Nova Scotia
Member of: Water Polo Canada
Chief Officer(s):
Chris Nichols, Chair
chris@waterpolonovascotia.ca
Andrew Hayes, PSO Administration Coordinator

Water Polo Québec ***Voir*** **Fédération de Water-Polo du Québec**

Water Polo Saskatchewan Inc. (WPS)
1860 Lorne St., Regina SK S4P 2L7
Tel: 306-780-9260; *Fax:* 306-780-9467
admin@wpsask.ca
www.wpsask.ca
www.facebook.com/waterpolosask
Previous Name: Saskatchewan Water Polo Association
Overview: A small provincial organization overseen by Water Polo Canada
Member of: Water Polo Canada

Finances: *Funding Sources:* Saskatchewan Lotteries; self-help projects

Water Ski - Wakeboard Manitoba (WSWM)
#415, 145 Pacific Ave., Winnipeg MB R3B 2Z6
Tel: 204-925-5700; *Fax:* 204-925-5792
info@wswm.ca
www.wswm.ca
www.flickr.com/photos/wswm/sets/
Overview: A small provincial organization founded in 1956 overseen by Sport Manitoba
Mission: To meet the needs of all those interested in the sport of water skiing by providing the resources necessary to help them achieve their goals & to encourage fun, friendship, fitness & fair play for skiers at all ability levels
Member of: Water Ski & Wakeboard Canada
Chief Officer(s):
Alanna Boudreau, Executive Director
Mark Mueller, President
Finances: *Funding Sources:* Provincial grants
Membership: *Fees:* $35 regular; $75 family; $5 associate
Activities: Slalom, tricks and jump water skiing; barefoot water skiing; wakeboarding; adaptive skiing;

Water Ski & Wakeboard Alberta (WSWA)
Percy Page Centre, 11759 Groat Rd., Edmonton AB T5M 3K6
Tel: 780-415-0088; *Fax:* 780-422-2663
Toll-Free: 866-258-2754
info@wswa.ca
www.wswa.ca
www.facebook.com/WaterSkiWakeboardAlberta
twitter.com/WaterskiWakeAB
Previous Name: Water Ski Alberta
Overview: A small provincial organization founded in 1967
Mission: To promote participation & excellence in the sport of water skiing & wakeboarding in Alberta
Member of: Alberta Sport Council; Water Ski & Wakeboard Canada
Affliation(s): International Water Ski Federation
Chief Officer(s):
Peter Peebles, President
peterpeebles@gmail.com
Melanie Oliver, Executive Director
melanie@wswa.ca
Finances: *Funding Sources:* Alberta government; fundraising (casinos) membership fees; program fees
Membership: 1,000; *Fees:* $40

Water Ski & Wakeboard British Columbia (WSWBC)
PO Box 56011, 1511 Admiral's Rd., Victoria BC V9A 2P8
Toll-Free: 888-696-6677
info@wswbc.org
www.wswbc.org
twitter.com/WSWBC
Previous Name: BC Water Ski Association
Overview: A medium-sized provincial charitable organization founded in 1969
Mission: To promote organized towed water sports in British Columbia
Member of: Water Ski & Wakeboard Canada
Chief Officer(s):
Kim McKnight, Executive Director
Shawn Shorsky, President, 250-479-7828
Finances: *Funding Sources:* Government; advertising sales; fundraisings
Membership: 1,250; *Fees:* $40 active single; $80 family
Activities: Provincial championships; Protour; *Internships:* Yes
Awards:
• Kim de Macedo Skier Achievement Award (Award)
• Coach of the Year (Award)
• Official of the Year (Award)
• Curtis McDonell Memorial Trophy (Award)

Water Ski & Wakeboard Canada (WSWC) / Ski nautique et planche Canada
#210, 223 Colonnade Rd. South, Ottawa ON K2E 7K3
Tel: 613-526-0685; *Fax:* 613-526-4380
info@waterski-wakeboard.ca
www.waterski-wakeboard.ca
www.facebook.com/164160506956549
twitter.com/wswc_canada
www.youtube.com/user/TheWSWCanada
Previous Name: Canadian Water Ski Association
Overview: A medium-sized national charitable organization
Mission: To promote & organize competitive Canadian towed water sports
Chief Officer(s):
Paul Melnuk, Chair
David Patterson, Chief Executive Officer
david@waterski-wakeboard.ca
Finances: *Annual Operating Budget:* $500,000-$1.5 Million
Staff Member(s): 4
Membership: 4,500; *Committees:* Water Ski; Wakeboard; Barefoot; Adaptive Towed Water Sports; Athlete Development; Coaching; Safety; Waterways; Hall of Fame

Water Ski & Wakeboard Saskatchewan (WSWS)
SK
Tel: 306-931-2901
info@wswsask.com
wswsask.com
www.facebook.com/wswsask
twitter.com/wswsask
Previous Name: Saskatchewan Water Ski Association
Overview: A small provincial organization
Mission: To promote & develop towed water spoorts in Saskatchewan
Member of: Water Ski & Wakeboard Canada; Sask Sport Inc.
Membership: *Fees:* $25 recreational; $30 competitive; $45 recreational family; $50 competitive family
Activities: All activity & advocacy related to towed water sports; tournaments
Awards:
• Male Athlete of the Year (Award)
• Female Athlete of the Year (Award)
• Rookie of the Year (Award)
• Wakeboarder of the Year (Award)
• Most Improved Skier of the Year (Award)
• Most Improved Wakeboarder (Award)

Water Ski Alberta ***See*** Water Ski & Wakeboard Alberta

WaterCan / Eau Vive
321 Chapel St., Ottawa ON K1N 7Z2
Tel: 613-230-5182; *Fax:* 613-230-0712
Toll-Free: 800-370-5658
info@watercan.com
www.watercan.com
www.facebook.com/watercan
twitter.com/WaterCanCharity
www.youtube.com/Watercancontest
Overview: A small international charitable organization founded in 1987
Mission: To support integrated water supply, sanitation, & hygiene promotion projects that assist rural communities & the urban poor in Africa
Member of: Canadian Water Resources Association; Canadian Water & Wastewater Association
Chief Officer(s):
George Yap, Executive Director
Bonnie Kirkwood, Administrative Assistant
Erinn Steringa, Coordinator, Communications & Development
George Yap, Program Director
Amyn Hyder Ali, Financial Officer
Finances: *Annual Operating Budget:* $500,000-$1.5 Million; *Funding Sources:* Direct mail; special events; corporate donations; private donations; government grants; foundations
Staff Member(s): 7; 200 volunteer(s)
Membership: 1-99
Activities: Partnerships with local/indigenous organizations; technical training; knowledge networks in the international water & sanitation sector; education activities to raise awareness on the health & development benefits of clean water in the developing world; *Awareness Events:* World Water Day, March 22; *Library* Open to public by appointment

Waterford & Townsend Historical Society
c/o Spruce Row Museum, PO Box 504, 159 Nichol St., Waterford ON N0E 1Y0
Tel: 519-443-5659
Overview: A small local organization
Chief Officer(s):
Alison Bell, President
Membership: *Fees:* $10

Waterfront Regeneration Trust
#227, 4195 Dundas St. West, Toronto ON M8X 1Y4
Tel: 416-943-8080; *Fax:* 416-943-8068
info@wrtrust.com
www.waterfronttrail.org
Overview: A medium-sized local organization founded in 1988
Mission: To expand, promote and enhance the Waterfront Trail and Greenway of Lake Ontario and the St. Lawrence River.
Chief Officer(s):

Marlaine Koehler, Executive Director
mk@wrtrust.com
David Crombie, Founding Chair
Staff Member(s): 4

Waterloo Coin Society (WCS)
PO Box 40044, Stn. Waterloo Square, 75 King St. South, Waterloo ON N2J 4V1
Tel: 519-745-3104
pbecker1964-wcspresident@yahoo.ca
www.waterloocoinsociety.com
www.facebook.com/groups/6373988231
Overview: A small local organization founded in 1959
Mission: To offer our members a monthly educational meeting in addition to the opportunity to buy, sell & evaluate their numismatic items
Member of: Ontario Numismatic Association; Royal Canadian Numismatic Association
Chief Officer(s):
Robb McPherson, President
president@waterloocoinsociety.com
Brent Mackie, Vice-President
vicepresident@waterloocoinsociety.com
Finances: *Annual Operating Budget:* Less than $50,000; *Funding Sources:* Membership dues; auction fees; show
Membership: 150; *Fees:* $10 Individual; $5 Junior; $15 Family
Activities: Monthly educational meeting; 40 lot numismatic auction; youth program; *Library:* WCS Library; by appointment

Waterloo Historical Society (WHS)
c/o Kitchener Public Library, 85 Queen St. North, Kitchener ON N2H 2H1
e-mail: whs@whs.ca
www.whs.ca
www.facebook.com/waterloohs
Overview: A medium-sized local charitable organization founded in 1912
Mission: To foster the recognition of our region's unique heritage & to diligently encourage its preservation
Affliation(s): Ontario Historical Society; Waterloo Regional Heritage Foundation
Chief Officer(s):
Marion Roes, President
Finances: *Annual Operating Budget:* Less than $50,000; *Funding Sources:* Membership; provincial government; Waterloo Regional Heritage Foundation
15 volunteer(s)
Membership: 300; *Fees:* $25
Activities: At least four public meetings per year; *Speaker Service:* Yes; *Library* Open to public

Waterloo Regional Arts Council Inc. (WRAC)
PO Box 1122, Stn. C, 141 Whitney Pl., Kitchener ON N2G 4G1
Tel: 519-744-4552; *Fax:* 519-744-9342
www.artsportalwr.ca
Overview: A small local licensing charitable organization founded in 1980
Mission: To promote & support the arts in order to enrich & enliven all the communities of the Waterloo Region; To serve artists & organizations of all discipines & traditions
Member of: Chamber of Commerce; Community Arts Onatio; CARFAC
Chief Officer(s):
Martin de Groot, Executive Director
Finances: *Annual Operating Budget:* $50,000-$100,000
Staff Member(s): 3; 50 volunteer(s)
Membership: 50 group + 100 individual; *Fees:* $10 affiliate; $15 student & senior; $20 individual; $35 joint; $40 organization; *Member Profile:* Artists in all disciplines (professional); *Committees:* Communication; Programming; Municipal Liaison; Personnel; Facilities; Membership; Nomination
Activities: Workshops, Artvote; studio tour; Poetry on the Way; cultural directory; *Speaker Service:* Yes

Waterloo Regional Heritage Foundation (WRHF)
Regional Admin. Building, PO Box 9051, Stn. C, 150 Frederick St., 2nd Fl., Kitchener ON N2J 4J3
Tel: 519-575-4493; *Fax:* 519-575-4481
wrhf@regionofwaterloo.ca
www.wrhf.org
Overview: A small local organization founded in 1973
Mission: To act as funding & support umbrella for organizations throughout the Region of Waterloo to preserve its heritage
Member of: Heritage Canada
Chief Officer(s):
Sandy Rung, Chair
Mike Grivicic, Administrative Contact
gmike@region.waterloo.on.ca
Finances: *Annual Operating Budget:* $100,000-$250,000; *Funding Sources:* Regional Municipality of Waterloo
Staff Member(s): 2
Membership: 18; *Committees:* Allocations & Finance; Awards; Communications
Activities: *Awareness Events:* Heritage Day
Awards:
• Regional Award for Heritage Research (Scholarship)
For M.A. or Ph.D. student, resident of, or registered at a university in, the Waterloo region

Waterloo Regional Labour Council (WRLC)
#203, 120 Ottawa St., Kitchener ON N2H 3K5
Tel: 519-743-8301; *Fax:* 519-743-9460
www.wrlc.ca
Overview: A small local organization founded in 1941 overseen by Ontario Federation of Labour
Member of: Ontario Federation of Labour
Chief Officer(s):
Len Carter, President
Staff Member(s): 1; 20 volunteer(s)
Membership: 15,000-49,999
Activities: *Speaker Service:* Yes

Waterloo Regional Police Association / Association de la police de Waterloo
1128 Rife Rd., Cambridge ON N1R 5S3
Tel: 519-622-0771; *Fax:* 519-622-5194
info@wrpa.org
www.wrpa.org
Overview: A small local organization
Mission: To promote the interests of members & maintain interest in active membership
Chief Officer(s):
Bruce Tucker, President

Waterloo, Wellington, Dufferin & Grey Building & Construction Trades Council (WWDGBCTC)
#172, 55 Northfield Dr. East, Waterloo ON N2K 3T6
Tel: 519-503-2347; *Fax:* 519-579-4076
www.yourlocaltrades.ca
Previous Name: Kitchener-Waterloo Building & Construction Trades Council
Overview: A small local organization
Mission: To work together with local union contractors to build & work on construction projects
Member of: AFL-CIO
Affliation(s): Provincial Building & Construction Trades Council of Ontario
Membership: 5,000+

Waterski & Wakeboard New Brunswick (NBWSWBA)
NB
Tel: 506-832-0307
info@nbwswba.com
www.nbwswba.com
Also Known As: NB Waterski
Overview: A small provincial organization
Mission: To promote organized pulled watersports in the province of New Brunswick.
Member of: Water Ski & Wakeboard Canada
Chief Officer(s):
Anthony Hourihan, President
Kyla Jonah-Hourihan, Vice-President
Kevin Hourihan, Treasurer
Harry Booth, Director, Membership & Tournament
Membership: *Fees:* $20 individual; $40 family

Waterton Natural History Association (WNHA)
PO Box 145, Waterton Park AB T0K 2M0
Tel: 403-859-2624; *Fax:* 403-859-2624
www.wnha.ca
Overview: A small local charitable organization founded in 1983
Mission: To further the understanding & appropriate use of Waterton Lakes National Park; to provide & publish materials relevant to Waterton/Glacier International Peace Park
Member of: Canadian Parks Partnership; Alberta Museums Association; Alberta Historical Society; Canadian Booksellers Association
Chief Officer(s):
Gina Sydenham, Chair
Finances: *Annual Operating Budget:* $50,000-$100,000; *Funding Sources:* Fund-raising
Staff Member(s): 10; 20 volunteer(s)
Membership: 395; *Fees:* $20 individual lifetime; $25 family lifetime
Activities: Museum upgrade

Waterton Park Chamber of Commerce & Visitors Association
PO Box 55, Waterton Lakes National Park AB T0K 2M0
Tel: 403-859-2224; *Fax:* 403-859-2650
waterton.info@pc.gc.ca
www.mywaterton.ca/community-chamber.cfm
Overview: A small local organization
Chief Officer(s):
Rod Kretz, President

Watrous & District Chamber of Commerce
PO Box 906, Watrous SK S0K 4T0
Tel: 306-946-3353; *Fax:* 306-946-3966
townofwatrous.com/chamber
Overview: A small local organization
Chief Officer(s):
Brenda Reichert, Secretary

Watrous Area Arts Council
102 - 3rd Ave. East, Watrous SK S0K 4T0
Tel: 306-946-1333
www.townofwatrous.com/artscouncil.htm
www.facebook.com/247519998694936
Overview: A small local charitable organization founded in 1979
Mission: To present performing & visual arts to the community of Watrous & surrounding areas
Member of: Organization of Saskatchewan Arts Councils
Finances: *Annual Operating Budget:* Less than $50,000
10 volunteer(s)
Membership: 1-99

Watson & District Chamber of Commerce
PO Box 686, Watson SK S0K 4V0
Tel: 306-287-3636; *Fax:* 306-287-3601
Overview: A small local organization
Chief Officer(s):
Michael Becker, President
Debbie A Schwartz, Treasurer

Watson Lake Chamber of Commerce
c/o Town Office, PO Box 590, 710 Adela Trail, Watson Lake YT Y0A 1C0
Tel: 867-536-8000; *Fax:* 867-536-7522
twl@northwestel.net
www.watsonlake.ca/business-services/chamber-of-commerce
Overview: A small local organization
3 volunteer(s)
Membership: 37; *Fees:* $120 full; *Member Profile:* Business community

Wawatay Native Communications Society
PO Box 1180, 16 - 5th Ave., Sioux Lookout ON P8T 1B7
Tel: 807-737-2951; *Fax:* 807-737-3224
Toll-Free: 800-243-9059
reception@wawatay.on.ca
www.wawataynews.ca
ca.linkedin.com/company/wawatay-native-communications-society
www.facebook.com/wawataynews
Also Known As: Wawatay News Online
Overview: A medium-sized national organization founded in 1974
Mission: To preserve & promote aboriginal languages & cultures with the use of modern technology in radio, television & newspaper
Member of: Nishnawbe-Aki Nation
Affliation(s): Grand Council Treaty #3; Robinson-Superior Treaty Area
Chief Officer(s):
Lenny Carpenter, Publisher/Editor
Membership: 49 first nations communities; *Member Profile:* 48 First Nations Communities of Nishnawbe-Aski Nation
Activities: *Internships:* Yes; *Speaker Service:* Yes; *Library* Open to public

Waypoint centre de soins de santé mentale *See* Waypoint Centre for Mental Health Care

Waypoint Centre for Mental Health Care / Waypoint centre de soins de santé mentale
500 Church St., Penetanguishene ON L9M 1G3
Tel: 705-549-3181
info@waypointcentre.ca
www.waypointcentre.ca

Overview: A small local organization founded in 2008
Mission: To provide acute & longer-term psychiatric inpatient & outpatient services to Simcoe County, Dufferin County & Muskoka/Parry Sound
Chief Officer(s):
John McCullough, Chair
Carol Lambie, President & CEO
Finances: *Funding Sources:* Catholic Health Corporation of Ontario
Staff Member(s): 10

Webgrrls Canada

c/o Webgrrls International, #314, 119 West 72nd St., New York NY 10023 USA
Fax: 866-935-1188
Toll-Free: 888-932-4775
www.webgrrls.com
Overview: A medium-sized international organization
Mission: To serve as a learning & networking resource for women in & interested in new media & the internet

Calgary
www.webgrrls.com

Nova Scotia
NS
www.webgrrls.com/novascotia.ca/

Vancouver
e-mail: vancouver-canada@webgrrls.com
www.webgrrls.com/vancouver.ca

Welcome Hall Mission *See* Mission Bon Accueil

Welfare Committee for the Assyrian Community in Canada

#102, 964 Albion Rd., Toronto ON M9V 1A7
Tel: 416-741-8836; *Fax:* 416-741-8836
assyrianwelfare@aol.com
Previous Name: Assyrian Association
Overview: A small national charitable organization founded in 1989
Mission: To sponsor Assyrian refugees for admission into Canada; To provide support for the settlement of Assyrian refugees; To offer referrals & general information
Member of: Canadian Council for Refugees
Chief Officer(s):
Mizra Shmoli, Chair & Executive Director
Finances: *Annual Operating Budget:* $50,000-$100,000
Staff Member(s): 1; 5 volunteer(s)
Membership: 80

Welland & District Labour Council

c/o Bob McCallion, 16 Steel St., Welland ON L3B 3L9
Tel: 905-732-3103
Overview: A small local organization overseen by Ontario Feeration of Labour
Member of: Ontario Federation of Labour
Chief Officer(s):
Bob McCallion, Chair

Welland County Law Association

102 East Main St., Welland ON L3B 3W6
Tel: 905-734-3174; *Fax:* 905-734-1883
wcla@execulink.com
www.execulink.com/~wellaw
Overview: A small local organization
Staff Member(s): 1; 12 volunteer(s)
Membership: 150
Activities: *Library:* R. Boak Burns Law Library

Welland District Association for Community Living *See* Community Living Welland Pelham

The Welland/Pelham Chamber of Commerce / La Chambre de commerce de Welland/Pelham

32 East Main St., Welland ON L3B 3W3
Tel: 905-732-7515; *Fax:* 905-732-7175
www.wellandpelhamchamber.com
twitter.com/doloresfabiano
Overview: A small local organization founded in 1889
Chief Officer(s):
Verne Milot, President
Dolores Fabiano, Executive Director
dolores@iaw.on.ca
Finances: *Annual Operating Budget:* $100,000-$250,000
Membership: 350; *Fees:* $178.82-$2,258.90

Wellesley & District Board of Trade

c/o Wendy Sauder, Wellesley Service Centre, 1220 Queens Bush Rd., Wellesley ON N0B 2T0
Tel: 519-656-3494
wellesleyboardoftrade@gmail.com
wellesleyboardoftrade.com
Overview: A small local organization
Member of: Canadian Chamber of Commerce; Ontario Chamber of Commerce
Chief Officer(s):
Chris Franklin, President
Membership: 21; *Fees:* $175 non-business; $250 business

Wellington County Beekeepers' Association

Guelph ON
Tel: 519-824-4012
Overview: A small local organization
Mission: To promote apiculture education
Chief Officer(s):
Bill Higgins, Contact
whiggins@sympatico.ca
Membership: *Member Profile:* Commercial & hobbyist beekeepers in Wellington County
Activities: Organizing regular meetings; Providing networking opportunities for local beekeepers; Teaching the proper care & maintenance of hives & correct harvesting techniques; Arranging delivery of beekeeping supplies for the group, such as polypropylene

Wellington County Historical Society (WCHS)

PO Box 5, Fergus ON N1M 2W7
guelpharts.ca/wellingtoncountyhistsoc
Overview: A small local charitable organization founded in 1928
Mission: To preserve, promote & publicize the history of Wellington County; to assist with the Wellington County Museum & Archives
Affliation(s): Ontario Historical Society
Chief Officer(s):
Ron Hattle, President, 519-546-3450
Jude Dowling, Director, Membership, 519-787-0408
Finances: *Annual Operating Budget:* Less than $50,000; *Funding Sources:* Membership fees; donations; local & provincial grants
Membership: 250; *Fees:* $20 Canada; $25 USA; *Committees:* Program & Publicity; Publications; Membership; Constitution; Historical Research & Records
Publications:
• Wellington County History [a publication of the Wellington County Historical Society]
Type: Journal; *Frequency:* Annual

Wellington Law Association

Court House, 74 Woolwich St., Guelph ON N1H 3T9
Tel: 519-763-6365; *Fax:* 519-763-6847
Toll-Free: 866-893-5220
wellington@on.aibn.com
www.wellingtonlaw.org
Overview: A small local organization
Member of: County & District Law Presidents Association
Chief Officer(s):
John Kerr, Librarian
lawlibwell@gmail.com
Finances: *Annual Operating Budget:* $50,000-$100,000; *Funding Sources:* Provincial government; membership fees
Staff Member(s): 1
Membership: 151 individual
Activities: *Library:* Wellington Law Library; by appointment

Wells & District Chamber of Commerce

PO Box 123, Wells BC V0K 2R0
Tel: 250-994-3223; *Fax:* 250-994-3223
Toll-Free: 877-451-9355
president@wellschamber.ca
www.wellsbc.com
www.facebook.com/groups/185864013016
twitter.com/mt_trails
Overview: A small local organization founded in 1936
Mission: To promote Wells, Barkerville & Bowron Lake business community
Member of: BC Chamber of Commerce
Chief Officer(s):
Norma Collins, President
Finances: *Annual Operating Budget:* Less than $50,000
Staff Member(s): 1; 20 volunteer(s)
Membership: 40
Activities: *Awareness Events:* Fred Wells Days

Wellspring Cancer Support Foundation / Fondation Wellspring pour les personnes atteintes de cancer

#300, 2 Adelaide St West, Toronto ON M5H 1L6
Tel: 416-961-1928; *Fax:* 416-323-6330
feedback@wellspring.ca
www.wellspring.ca
Overview: A medium-sized provincial charitable organization
Chief Officer(s):
Nancy Wilson, Chair
Activities: Five centres that provide emotional & psychological support, free of charge, to individuals & families living with cancer

Welsh Pony & Cob Association of Ontario (WPCAO)

c/o Paula Dalgarno, 125 Hazelwood Dr., Whitby ON L1N 3L7
Tel: 905-728-4802
WPCAO2014@gmail.com
wpcao.com
www.facebook.com/112049522224451
Overview: A small provincial organization overseen by Welsh Pony & Cob Society of Canada
Mission: To promote Welsh Ponies & Cobs in Ontario
Chief Officer(s):
Rose Reid, President, 905-260-2848
Alice McKeen, Vice-President, 905-786-1059
Jessica Figas, Secretary, 905-431-5620
Paula Dalgarno, Treasurer
Membership: *Fees:* $20 junior; $35 regular; $60 family; *Member Profile:* Welsh Ponies & Cob enthusiasts in Ontario
Activities: Offering networking opportunities; Supporting clinics; Operating the annual Canadian All Welsh Show; Holding the annual Champion of Champions competition; Providing an annual High Point Awards program; Offering information about the breed
Publications:
• Welsh Pony & Cob Association of Ontario Newsletter
Type: Newsletter; *Frequency:* Quarterly; *Editor:* Bev Fantauzzi
Profile: Information about Ontario events

Welsh Pony & Cob Society of Canada (WPCSC)

PO Box 119, Alliston ON L94 1T9
Tel: 705-435-3210; *Fax:* 705-435-5936
welshponyandcobsociety@bellnet.ca
www.welshponyandcob.org
Overview: A small international organization founded in 1979
Mission: To oversee the registration of Welsh ponies
Affliation(s): Canadian Livestock Records Corporation
Chief Officer(s):
Mary Cork, President
Duane Stewart, Vice-President
Jennifer Parsons, Secretary
Ray Dabrowski, Treasurer, 416-431-7624, Fax: 416-431-9844
raydabrowski@rogers.com
Membership: 400; *Fees:* $20 junior members, 18 years & under; $40 individuals, over age 18, as well as corporate members; $350 life members, over age 50; $500 life members; *Member Profile:* Individuals, companies, partnerships, associations, & syndicates interested in the Welsh pony breed in Canada, the United States, & Great Britain
Activities: Maintaining registration certificates & other official records of the society; Participating in shows
Publications:
• Canadian Stud Book
Type: Book; *Frequency:* Annually
Profile: Details of every Welsh pony registered in Canada
• Welsh in Canada
Type: Magazine; *Frequency:* Quarterly; *Accepts Advertising*
Profile: Society meeting highlights, financial statements, transfer lists, awards, ratings, Welsh pony stories, farm & breeder profiles, & forthcoming events

Welsh Pony & Cob Society of Saskatchewan

c/o Alana Longman, PO Box 36, Harris SK S0L 1K0
Tel: 306-656-2051
Overview: A small provincial organization overseen by Welsh Pony & Cob Society of Canada
Mission: To promote the Welsh pony breed in Saskatchewam
Chief Officer(s):
Alana Longman, Contact
alana@ch-equestrian.com
Membership: *Member Profile:* Welsh pony breeders & other interested persons in Saskatchewan

The West Bend Community Association (TWBCA)

c/o Secretary, 33 Kenneth Ave., Toronto ON M6P 1J1
www.thewestbend.ca
Previous Name: Dundas West Residents Association
Overview: A small local organization
Mission: To help promote & improve the community of West Bend in Toronto

Membership: *Fees:* $10

West Central Alberta Real Estate Board
162 Athabasca Ave., Hinton AB T7V 2A5
Tel: 780-865-7511; *Fax:* 780-865-7517
wcareb@shaw.ca
boards.mls.ca/wcab
Previous Name: Hinton-Edson & District Real Estate Board
Overview: A small local organization founded in 1978 overseen by Alberta Real Estate Association
Member of: Alberta Real Estate Association; The Canadian Real Estate Association
Staff Member(s): 1
Membership: 110

West Central Forage Association (WCFA)
PO Box 360, #1, 5013 - 50 Ave., Evansburg AB T0E 0T0
Tel: 780-727-4447; *Fax:* 780-727-4424
Toll-Free: 866-725-4447
www.areca.ab.ca/wcfahome.html
www.facebook.com/103583293026991
Overview: A small local organization founded in 1978 overseen by Agricultural Research & Extension Council of Alberta
Mission: To share knowledge, conduct applied research & extension activities, & demonstrate new agricultural technology & production practices
Member of: Agricultural Research & Extension Council of Alberta
Chief Officer(s):
Bob Kidd, President
Carla Amonson, Manager
manager@westcentralforage.com
Membership: *Fees:* $20
Publications:
• Forage Views [a publication of the West Central Forage Association]
Type: Newsletter; *Frequency:* Monthly

West Coast Amateur Musicians' Society (WCAMS)
5468 Walter Place, Burnaby BC V5G 4K3
Tel: 604-586-9486
info@wcams.com
www.wcams.com
Overview: A small local charitable organization founded in 1981
Mission: To operate a summer music camp for adult amateur musicians & their families; to provide skills development (sight reading) session for chorus & orchestra; to provide workshops for singers & instrumentalists of all ages & all levels of ability
Chief Officer(s):
Sara Brusse, President
Elena Miller, Vice-President
Finances: *Annual Operating Budget:* $50,000-$100,000
30 volunteer(s)
Membership: 250; *Fees:* $45 institutional; $15 student/senior; $30 individual; $50 family; *Member Profile:* Amateur instrumentalists & singers; *Committees:* Fundraising; Publicity; Festival Operations; Workshops
Activities: West Coast Summer Music Festival, workshops; *Library:* Music Library;

West Coast Book Prize Society
#901, 207 West Hastings St., Vancouver BC V6B 1H7
Tel: 604-687-2405; *Fax:* 604-687-2435
info@bcbookprizes.ca
www.bcbookprizes.ca
www.facebook.com/pages/The-BC-Book-Prizes/109460751791
twitter.com/bcbookprizes
pinterest.com/bcbookprizes
Overview: A small provincial organization founded in 1985
Mission: To celebrate writers from British Columbia through the BC Book Prizes; to bridge the gap between writing & publishing
Chief Officer(s):
Bryan Pike, Executive Director
bryan@rebuscreative.com
Staff Member(s): 4
Membership: *Fees:* $20
Awards:
• The Christie Harris Illustrated Children's Literature Prize (Award), BC Book Prizes
• Dorothy Livesay Poetry Prize (Award), BC Book Prizes
Awarded to the author of the best work of poetry; the writer must have lived in BC for three of the preceding five years
• The Sheila A. Egoff Children's Prize (Award), BC Book Prizes
Awarded to the author of the best book for young people aged 16 & under; the author or illustrator must have lived in BC for three of the preceding five years
• The Bill Duthie Booksellers' Choice Prize (Award), BC Book Prizes
Awarded for the best book in terms of public appeal, initiative, design, production & content; the book must have been published in BC
• The Roderick Haig-Brown Regional Prize (Award), BC Book Prizes
Awarded to the author of the book that contributes most to the enjoyment & understanding of BC; the book may deal with any aspect of the province & should epitomize the BC experience
• The Ethel Wilson Fiction Prize (Award), BC Book Prizes
Awarded to the author of the best work of fiction; the writer must have lived in BC for three of the preceding five years
• The Hubert Evans Non-Fiction Prize (Award), BC Book Prizes
Awarded to the author of the best original non-fiction literary work (philosophy, belles lettres, biography, history, etc.); the writer must have lived in BC for three of the preceding five years
• Lieutenant Governor's Award of Literary Excellence (Award), BC Book Prizes

West Coast Domestic Workers' Association (WCDWA)
#302, 119 West Pender St., Vancouver BC V6B 1S5
Tel: 604-669-4482; *Fax:* 604-669-4482
Toll-Free: 888-669-4482
info@wcdwa.ca
www.wcdwa.ca
Overview: A medium-sized local organization founded in 1987
Mission: West Coast Domestic Workers' Association is a non-profit association that provides free legal assistance in the form of advocacy, support and counselling to live-in caregivers based in British Columbia.
Chief Officer(s):
virginie Francoeur, Lawyer and Executive Director
Staff Member(s): 5
Membership: 525; *Fees:* $25-$30

West Coast Environmental Law (WCEL)
#200, 2006 West 10th Ave., Vancouver BC V6J 2B3
Tel: 604-684-7378; *Fax:* 604-684-1312
Toll-Free: 800-330-9235
admin@wcel.org
www.wcel.org
www.facebook.com/WCELaw
twitter.com/WCELaw
Overview: A medium-sized local charitable organization founded in 1974
Mission: To safeguard the environment through law; To help British Columbians access legal assistance to protect the environment
Chief Officer(s):
Jessica Clogg, Executive Director & Senior Counsel, 604-601-2501
jessica_clogg@wcel.org
Lucy Hough, Director, Development, 604-601-2509
lucy_hough@wcel.org
Todd Monge, Manager, Environmental Dispute Resolution Fund & Communications, 604-601-2503
todd_monge@wcel.org
Finances: *Funding Sources:* Law Foundation of British Columbia & other foundations; Independent donations
Staff Member(s): 8
Activities: Publishing policy papers; Offering legal advice; *Library:* West Coast Environmental Law; Open to public
Awards:
• Dr. Andrew Thompson Award (Award)
Meetings/Conferences: • West Coast Environmental Law 2015 Annual General Meeting, 2015
Scope: Provincial
Description: The appointment of board members takes place each year
Publications:
• Legal e-Brief
Type: Newsletter; *Frequency:* Monthly
Profile: Information about topical environmental law issues, plus explanations of new & existing laws & policies
• West Coast Environmental Law Annual Report
Type: Yearbook; *Frequency:* Annually

West Coast Railway Association (WCRA)
PO Box 2790, Stn. Term., Vancouver BC V6B 3X2
Tel: 604-681-4403; *Fax:* 604-876-4104
Toll-Free: 800-722-1233
info@wcra.org
www.wcra.org
Overview: A small local charitable organization founded in 1961
Mission: Collects, preserves, restores, operates & exhibits artifacts relating to the history of railways, especially those of BC; the West Coast Railway Heritage Park in Squamish BC develops educational exhibits on railway heritage for all age groups; the tour program encourages the public to travel today's railways to see Canada
Member of: Association of Rail Museums; Tourist Railroad Association
Chief Officer(s):
Gerry Burgess, Executive Director
board@wcra.org
Finances: *Annual Operating Budget:* $500,000-$1.5 Million; *Funding Sources:* Tours; government grants; donations; fundraising; foundation
Staff Member(s): 12; 150 volunteer(s)
Membership: 1500; *Fees:* Schedule available; *Member Profile:* Interest in railways past & present; *Committees:* Museum; Tours; Collections; Motive Power; Children; Education
Activities: Develops & operates West Coast Railway Heritage Park in Squamish B.C. - collection of over 60 locomotives, freight & passenger cars; operates tour progr
m; other community event; Day out with Thoma, June; *Speaker Service:* Yes; *Library:* Archives; Open to public by appointment

West Elgin Chamber of Commerce
PO Box 276, Rodney ON N0L 2C0
e-mail: secretary@westelginchamber.ca
www.westelginchamber.ca
Overview: A small local organization overseen by Ontario Chamber of Commerce
Mission: To promote & improve trade & commerce, the economic, civil & social welfare of the district
Chief Officer(s):
Bill Denning, President
Finances: *Funding Sources:* Membership fees
Membership: *Committees:* Membership; Downtown Improvement; Business & Education; Welcome; Tourism & Special Events; New Business Development
Activities: *Speaker Service:* Yes

West Elgin Historical & Genealogical Society
c/o Dutton-Dunwich Public Library, 236 Shackleton St., Dutton ON N0L 1J0
Tel: 519-785-0177
westelgin.g.h.s@altavista.net
Overview: A small local organization
Chief Officer(s):
Norma Schnekenburger, Contact
normaatng@golden.net

West Elgin Nature Club
PO Box 7, West Lorne ON N0L 2P0
Tel: 519-768-2691
www.naturallyelgin.org
Overview: A small local organization
Member of: Federation of Ontario Naturalists
Chief Officer(s):
Joan Neil, Contact
Membership: *Fees:* $8 individual; $10 family

West Grey Chamber of Commerce
PO Box 800, 144 Garafraxa St. South, Durham ON N0G 1R0
Tel: 519-369-5750
westgreychamber@gmail.com
westgreychamber.ca
Previous Name: Durham & District Chamber of Commerce
Overview: A small local organization founded in 1978
Mission: To promote the town of Durham with our tourist information centre; to work with Business Improvement Association to promote town events & promotions; to provide members with an opportunity to obtain insurance through the Ontario Chamber of Commerce.
Member of: Ontario Chamber of Commerce
Affliation(s): Durham Business Improvement Association
Chief Officer(s):
Maggie Harrison, President
Finances: *Annual Operating Budget:* Less than $50,000; *Funding Sources:* Membership dues
Staff Member(s): 1; 8 volunteer(s)
Membership: 56; *Fees:* $100; *Committees:* Finance; Membership; Newsletter

West Hants Chamber of Commerce; Windsor Board of Trade *See* Avon River Chamber of Commerce

West Hants Historical Society (WHHS)
PO Box 2335, 281 King St., Windsor NS B0N 2T0

Tel: 902-798-4706
whhs@ns.aliantzinc.ca
westhantshistoricalsociety.ca
www.facebook.com/141349919273121
Also Known As: West Hants Museum
Overview: A small local charitable organization founded in 1973
Mission: To collect, record, & preserve the history of West Hants; To initiate & promote programs to further historic interest in West Hants; To compile & publish local historical data from material collected; To collect, frame, catalogue & display photos of local historical interest; To develop display areas on specific subjects; To compile graveyard inscriptions
Member of: Federation of the Nova Scotian Heritage
Affiliation(s): Heritage Trust of Nova Scotia
Chief Officer(s):
Jeff Barrett, President
Garnet Clark, Vice-President
Isabel Palmeter, Secretary
Membership: *Fees:* $10 individual; $15 couple; $100 corporate
Activities: Operates Genealogy Centre; Heritage Banquet; Museum Day; *Library* Open to public

West Island Black Community Association (WIBCA)
48C - 4th Ave. South, Roxboro QC H8Y 2M2
Tel: 514-683-3925; *Fax:* 514-683-7649
admin@wibca.org
www.wibca.org
www.facebook.com/wibca.montreal
twitter.com/WIBCAMontreal
Overview: A small local organization founded in 1982
Mission: To respond to the needs of the community; to help our young people achieve their highest potential
Membership: *Committees:* Cultural & Social; Education; Finance; Membership; Seniors'; Youth, Sports & Recreation

West Island Chamber of Commerce *Voir* Chambre de commerce de l'Ouest-de-l'Ile de Montréal

West Island Chamber of Commerce
#602, 1000 St. Jean Blvd., Pointe-Claire QC H9R 5P1
Tel: 514-697-4228; *Fax:* 514-697-2562
info@wimcc.ca
ccoim.ca
www.facebook.com/CCOIM.WIMCC
Overview: A small local organization founded in 1978
Member of: Canadian Chamber of Commerce
Chief Officer(s):
Éric Léouzon, President
Joseph Huza, Executive Director
jhuza@wimcc.ca
Membership: 481; *Fees:* $224.20 1-10 employees; $316.18 11-24 employees; $431.16 25-49 employees; $603.62 50+ employees; *Committees:* Acolades Gala; Discover the Stars

West Island Youth Symphony Orchestra *Voir* Orchestre symphonique des jeunes du West Island

West Kootenay District Labour Council
101 Baker St., Nelson BC V1L 4H1
Tel: 250-352-9223; *Fax:* 250-352-9223
Overview: A small local organization overseen by British Columbia Federation of Labour
Mission: To promote the interests of affiliates in the West Kootenay region of Biritish Columbia; To advance the economic & social welfare of workers
Chief Officer(s):
Patsy Harmston, President
patsyharmston@shaw.ca
Bruce Northcott, First Vice-President
Andy Chernoff, Secretary
Jean Poole, Treasurer
Activities: Organizing a Day of Mourning ceremony, to pay tribute to workers injured or killed on the job; Participating in rallies; Supporting community organizations

West Kootenay Naturalists Association
c/o Esther Brown, 415 Olivia Cres., Trail BC V1R 1A6
Tel: 250-368-3663
www.kootenaynaturalists.org
Overview: A small local organization founded in 1973
Mission: To promote the enjoyment of nature through environmental appreciation & conservation; to encourage wise use & conservation of natural resources & environmental protection.
Member of: Federation of BC Naturalists
Affiliation(s): Creston Valley Wildlife Management Area
Chief Officer(s):
Peter Wood, President, 250-359-7107
Finances: *Funding Sources:* Donations; membership fees
Membership: *Fees:* $30 single; $46 family
Activities: Botany & ornithology hikes; scenic hikes, skiing/snow shoeing; trail maintenance; bird counts; Violin Lake Conservation Project; educational presentations; Waldie Island Heron Project
Awards:
• Selkirk College Foundation Bursary (Scholarship)

West Kootenay Regional Arts Council (WKRAC)
PO Box 103, #2, 619B Front St., Nelson BC V1L 5P7
Tel: 250-352-2421; *Fax:* 250-352-2420
Toll-Free: 800-850-2787
wkrac@telus.net
www.wkartscouncil.com
Overview: A small local charitable organization founded in 1980
Member of: Assembly of BC Arts Councils; BC Touring Council; Canadian Conference of the Arts; Columbia Kootenay Cultural Alliance
Chief Officer(s):
Krista Patterson, Executive Director
Finances: *Annual Operating Budget:* Less than $50,000; *Funding Sources:* Grant; BC Arts Council; Columbia Basin Trust
Staff Member(s): 1; 10 volunteer(s)
Membership: 12 community arts councils; *Fees:* $45; *Member Profile:* Arts councils & regional cultural organizations; *Committees:* Regional Events Producers
Activities: Workshops; advocacy; delivery agent for Columbia Basin Trust arts, culture & heritage funding sector; *Library:* Lending Library; by appointment

West Kootenay Women's Association
420 Mill St., Nelson BC V1L 4R9
Tel: 250-352-9916
info@nelsonwomenscentre.com
www.nelsonwomenscentre.com
Also Known As: Nelson & District Women's Centre
Overview: A small local organization founded in 1974
Mission: To provide & promote educational & cultural activities to promote the status of women
Member of: West Kootenay Women's Council; VAWIR; Women's Health Council
Affiliation(s): National Action Committee on the Status of Women
Chief Officer(s):
Maibrit Sorensen, Chair
Tasha Bassingthwaighte, Executive Director
Finances: *Annual Operating Budget:* $50,000-$100,000; *Funding Sources:* National & provincial government; private donations
Staff Member(s): 3; 25 volunteer(s)
Membership: 200 individual; *Fees:* $15-30 sliding scale
Activities: *Awareness Events:* Dec. 6 Memorial; Anti-Violence Prevention Week; Take Bak the Nigth; *Library:* Women's Centre Library; Open to public

West Lincoln Chamber of Commerce
PO Box 555, 270 Station St., Smithville ON L0R 2A0
Tel: 905-957-1606; *Fax:* 905-957-4628
www.westlincolnchamber.com
Overview: A small local charitable organization founded in 1950
Mission: To strengthen the municipality industrially, commercially & economically
Member of: Canadian Chamber of Commerce
Chief Officer(s):
David Hominuk, President
Lynn Thomas, Executive Director
Finances: *Annual Operating Budget:* Less than $50,000; *Funding Sources:* Membership; events
Staff Member(s): 1; 6 volunteer(s)
Membership: 206; *Fees:* $209.05; *Member Profile:* Businesses
Activities: *Library* Open to public
Publications:
• West Lincoln Chamber of Commerce Newsletter
Type: Newsletter

West Lincoln Historical Society & Archives (WLHS)
Restored Smithville Train Station, PO Box 797, 288 Station St., Smithville ON L0R 2A0
Tel: 905-957-0138
archives@wlhs.info
www.wlhs.info
Overview: A small local organization
Mission: Dedicated to the preservation & restoration of the Smithville train station
Chief Officer(s):
Edna Phillips, President
Eileen Moore, Vice-President
Everett Lampman, Chairperson of Membership
Membership: *Fees:* $10 individual; $15 family; *Committees:* Membership; Program

West Muskoka Chamber of Commerce *See* Muskoka Lakes Chamber of Commerce

West Neighbourhood House
588 Queen St. West, 2nd Fl., Toronto ON M6J 1E3
Tel: 416-532-7586; *Fax:* 416-504-3047
info@westnh.org
www.westnh.org
www.facebook.com/StChristopherHouse
twitter.com/WestNHouse
Previous Name: St. Christopher House Adult Literacy Program
Overview: A small local organization founded in 1977
Mission: To provide various social leaning programs to children & adults
Affliation(s): Metro Toronto Movement for Literacy; Ontario Literacy Coalition
Chief Officer(s):
Maureen Fair, Executive Director
Finances: *Funding Sources:* Municipal, provincial & federal government; Local businesses; Clubs; Foundations; Individual donors
Staff Member(s): 235; 1400 volunteer(s)

West Niagara Second Stage Housing & Counselling
PO Box 1115, Beamsville ON L0R 1B0
Tel: 905-309-1477; *Fax:* 905-309-1877
debbie@wnss.org
www.wnss.org
Overview: A small local charitable organization founded in 1998
Mission: To provide safe, low cost housing to women & children & provide them with the tools to progress to independent living
Activities: Provides interim housing & counselling to women & their children leaving situations of family violence

West Nipissing Association for Community Living *See* Community Living West Nipissing

West Nipissing Chamber of Commerce / Chambre de commerce de Nipissing Ouest
200 Main St., #B, Sturgeon Falls ON P2B 1P2
Tel: 705-753-5672; *Fax:* 705-580-5672
wnchamber@gmail.com
www.westnipissingchamber.ca
Overview: A small local organization founded in 1951
Mission: To promote businesses in West Nipissing & strengthen commerce
Chief Officer(s):
Greg Demers, President
Mike Bozzer, Project Manager
chamberpm@gmail.com
Staff Member(s): 2; 9 volunteer(s)

West Prince Chamber of Commerce
PO Box 220, 455 Main St., Alberton PE C0B 1B0
Tel: 902-853-4555
chamber@resourceswest.pe.ca
Overview: A small local organization
Chief Officer(s):
John Lane, President
Elmer Arsenault, Vice-President

West Region Tribal Council Cultural Education Centre
21 - 4th Ave. NW, Dauphin MB R7N 1H9
Tel: 204-638-8225; *Fax:* 204-638-8062
Overview: A small provincial organization

West Scarborough Neighbourhood Community Centre
313 Pharmacy Ave., Toronto ON M1L 3E7
Tel: 416-755-9215
www.wsncc.org
Overview: A small local organization
Mission: To provide neighbourhood programs & services designed to enhance the well-being of people in the context of their community, culture & environment
Member of: Boys & Girls Clubs of Ontario
Finances: *Annual Operating Budget:* $250,000-$500,000; *Funding Sources:* Government; United Way; donations
Staff Member(s): 32; 400 volunteer(s)
Membership: 5,000+;

West Shore Arts Council (WSAC)
PO Box 28090, RPO Can West, Victoria BC V9B 6R8
Tel: 250-478-2286; *Fax:* 250-478-5591
info@westshorearts.org
www.westshorearts.org
Previous Name: Western Communities Arts Council
Overview: A small local organization founded in 1988
Mission: To encourage creative participation & excellence in visual & performing arts; to provide information & promote public interest; to bring the artistic needs of the community to the attention of governing authorities; to advocate arts education
Member of: Assembly of BC Arts Councils
Chief Officer(s):
Gail Nash, President
Finances: *Annual Operating Budget:* Less than $50,000; *Funding Sources:* Membership; Donations; Government Grants
Staff Member(s): 1; 20 volunteer(s)
Membership: 125; *Fees:* $10 individual; $15 family, $20 groups; *Member Profile:* Individual, group/organizations involved in the Arts; *Committees:* Scholarship; Events; Funding
Activities: Monthly meetings, annual visual art show; periodic literary & music evenings events; trade shows; *Library* by appointment

West Shore Chamber of Commerce
2830 Aldwynd Rd., Victoria BC V9B 3S7
Tel: 250-478-1130; *Fax:* 250-478-1584
chamber@westshore.bc.ca
www.westshore.bc.ca
Overview: A small local organization founded in 1955
Mission: To promote a strong economic & social environment for Victoria's West Shore
Member of: BC Chamber of Commerce; Canadian Chamber of Commerce
Chief Officer(s):
Dan Spinner, CEO
dspinner@westshore.bc.ca
Lindsay Vogan, Manager, Operations
lwilson@westshore.bc.ca
Finances: *Annual Operating Budget:* $100,000-$250,000; *Funding Sources:* Membership dues; municipalities; auction; golf tournament
Staff Member(s): 2; 12 volunteer(s)
Membership: 400; *Fees:* Schedule available; *Committees:* Economic Development; Education; Media; Professional Development; Tourism; Events; WestShore Healthy Communities Initiative Climate Action WestShore
Activities: *Awareness Events:* Fire Truck Parade, December; *Internships:* Yes; *Speaker Service:* Yes

West Toronto Junction Historical Society (WTJHS)
c/o Annette Street Public Library, 145 Annette St. Lower Level, Toronto ON M6P 1P3
Tel: 416-763-3161
junctionhistorical@gmail.com
wtjhs.ca
twitter.com/WTJHS
Overview: A small local charitable organization founded in 1980
Mission: The West Toronto Junction Historical Society is a non-profit, charitable, volunteer organization. Incorporated in 1981 as an affiliate of the Ontario Historical Society
Member of: Ontario Historical Society; Heritage Canada; Architectural Conservancy of Ontario (Toronto Region); Archives Association of Ontario; Toronto Historical Association
Chief Officer(s):
Neil Ross, President
Finances: *Annual Operating Budget:* Less than $50,000; *Funding Sources:* Donations; grants; house tour; book sales
Staff Member(s): 1; 20 volunteer(s)
Membership: 477; *Fees:* $20 single; $30 family; *Member Profile:* Interest in local history
Activities: Walking tours; speakers & slideshows at meetings, research projects; exhibits; *Library* Open to public
Publications:
• The Leader & Recorder [a publication of the West Toronto Junction Historical Society]
Type: Newsletter; *Frequency:* Quarterly

West Toronto Stamp Club
Fairfield Seniors' Centre, 80 Lothian Ave., Etobicoke ON
Tel: 416-231-2248
gaerfieldportch@westtorontostampclub.org
Overview: A small local organization
Mission: To promote the hobby to collectors of all ages; to gain knowledge and experience in the various fields of the Hobby; to acquire new and dispose of postal material; to foster friendship among collectors
Chief Officer(s):
Garfield Portch, Contact
Staff Member(s): 5
Membership: 1,000-4,999
Activities: Study Group Session; Regular Meetings and Auctions; Discussion Group Sessions; Exhibitions; Award winning; Stamp Dealers; Social Events.

West Vancouver Chamber of Commerce
#401, 100 Park Royal, West Vancouver BC V7T 1A2
Tel: 604-926-6614; *Fax:* 604-925-7220
info@westvanchamber.com
www.westvanchamber.com
www.linkedin.com/company/west-vancouver-chamber-of-commerce
www.facebook.com/WestVanChamber
twitter.com/westvanchamber
Overview: A medium-sized local organization
Mission: To promote, enhance, & facilitate business in our community
Chief Officer(s):
Leagh Gabriel, Executive Director, 604-926-6614
leagh@westvanchamber.com
Membership: 100-499

West Vancouver Community Arts Council
1570 Argyle Ave., West Vancouver BC V7V 1A4
Tel: 604-925-7292; *Fax:* 604-922-8924
westvanartscouncil@shaw.ca
www.silkpurse.ca
Overview: A small local charitable organization founded in 1968
Mission: To champion the arts as fundamental to a vital community by encouraging an environment in which all the arts can be created, shared, & celebrated
Member of: Assembly of BC Arts Councils
Affliation(s): West Vancouver Chamber of Commerce; Alliance of the Arts
Chief Officer(s):
Sara Baker, Executive Director
Finances: *Annual Operating Budget:* Less than $50,000
Staff Member(s): 1; 55 volunteer(s)
Membership: 250; *Fees:* $35 family; $30 individual; $20 senior; $50 group
Activities: Music & Muffins-monthly concerts; Spoken Word award readings from the Canada Council-monthly; Cercle Francophone French readings; evening classical music concerts; *Internships:* Yes; *Speaker Service:* Yes

West Vancouver Community Foundation
775 - 15th St., West Vancouver BC V7T 2S9
Tel: 604-925-8153; *Fax:* 604-925-8154
westvanfoundation@telus.net
www.westvanfoundation.com
Overview: A small local charitable organization founded in 1979
Mission: To improve the quality of life in West Vancouver; to assist organizations & people through grants & awards, with special emphasis on health, education, the arts, social services & West Vancouver's physical environment
Member of: Community Foundations of Canada
Chief Officer(s):
Gerry Humphries, Chair
Delaina Bell, Executive Director
Finances: *Annual Operating Budget:* $50,000-$100,000; *Funding Sources:* Donations
Staff Member(s): 1; 40 volunteer(s)
Membership: 17; *Committees:* Finance & Audit; Grants; Investment; Marketing & Communications; Nominations; Fund Development; Community Leadership
Activities: Fundraising event
Awards:
• Gertrude Lawson Scholarship in Education (Scholarship)
Awarded annually to a Grade 12 graduating student, orginarily a resident of West Vancouver, who is continuing wth studies in the field of Education at a post-secondary institution in BC*Eligibility:* Evidence of high academic standing & community service *Amount:* $1,200
• Faris Family Scholarship (Scholarship)
Awarded annually to a Grade 12 graduating student, ordinarily a resident of West Vancouver, who is planning to attend university in BC*Eligibility:* Must provide evidence of high academic standing & community service *Amount:* $6,000 ($1,500/yr for 4 years)
• James A. Inkster Leadership Award (Award)
Presented annually to a West Vancouver Grade 12 graduating student who has shown leadership & enthusiasm for extra-curricular activities as well as a vigorous school spirit, academic performance is not a factor *Amount:* $500
• Christina Lawson Scholarship in Music/Drama (Scholarship)
Awarded annually to a Grade 12 graduating student, ordinarily a resident of West Vancouver, who will be involved in music/drama pursuits at a post-secondary institution in Canada or the United States; perference given to students in a Canadian institution*Eligibility:* Evidence of high academic standing & community service *Amount:* $1,200
• Bradley T. Bowles Scholarship (Scholarship)
Awarded annually to a West Vancouver Secondary Grade 12 graduating student continuing with post-secondary study*Eligibility:* Applicant must present evidence of superior athletic performance, high academic standing, leadership & school spirit as well as community service *Amount:* $1,000
• West Vancouver Community Foundation Grant (Grant)
Awarded annually*Eligibility:* To local non-profit projects or community programs with an emphasis on health, education, the arts, social services and the improvement of West Vancouver's physical environment.*Deadline:* Feb. 15, 2013

West Vancouver Municipal Employees' Association (WVMEA) / Association des employés municipaux de Vancouver-Ouest
#118, 2419 Bellevue Ave., West Vancouver BC V7V 4T4
Tel: 604-925-7447; *Fax:* 604-926-7059
info@wvmea.com
www.wvmea.com
Overview: A small local organization
Chief Officer(s):
Judy Shaughnessy, President
Staff Member(s): 3
Membership: 650+

West World Holiday Exchange; WorldHomes Holiday Exchange *See* HomeLink International Home Exchange

The Wesleyan Church of Canada - Atlantic District
1830 Mountain Rd., Moncton NB E1G 1A9
Tel: 506-383-8326; *Fax:* 506-383-8333
office@atlanticdistrict.com
www.atlanticdistrict.com
Overview: A medium-sized local organization
Chief Officer(s):
David W. LeRoy, District Superintendent

The Wesleyan Church of Canada - Central Canada District
3545 Centennial Road, Lyn ON K0E 1M0
Tel: 613-877-2087
Central.Canada.District.Office@gmail.com
www.ccdwesleyan.ca
Also Known As: The Wesleyan Methodist Church of Canada
Overview: A medium-sized national charitable organization founded in 1897
Mission: To create a context that produces healthy churches
Affliation(s): Tyndale Seminary; World Hope International; World Relief Canada; Bethany Bible College; Outreach Canada; Evangelical Fellowship of Canada
Chief Officer(s):
Peter Rigby, District Superintendent
Finances: *Annual Operating Budget:* $500,000-$1.5 Million; *Funding Sources:* District churches
Staff Member(s): 3
Membership: 1,736; *Member Profile:* Covenant members & community members
Activities: *Internships:* Yes

Westbank & District Chamber of Commerce
2372 Dobbin Rd., Westbank BC V4T 2H9
Tel: 250-768-3378; *Fax:* 250-768-3465
Toll-Free: 866-768-3378
admin@westbankchamber.com
www.westbankchamber.com
www.facebook.com/westbank.chamber
twitter.com/WestbankDCC
Also Known As: Westbank Info Centre
Overview: A small local organization founded in 1947
Mission: To pursue activities that enhance the social & economic prosperity of our community
Member of: BC Chamber of Commerce
Chief Officer(s):
Craig Brown, President
Karen Beaubier, Chamber Liaison Officer
Staff Member(s): 1

Membership: 465; *Fees:* Schedule available; *Committees:* Membership; Events; Advocacy; Finance
Activities: *Rents Mailing List:* Yes
Awards:
• Key Business Awards (Award)

Westcoast Association of Visual Language Interpreters (WAVLI)

PO Box 41542, 923 - 12th St., New Westminster BC V3M 6L1
www.wavli.com
www.facebook.com/wavli.britishcolumbia
twitter.com/WAVLI
Overview: A small local organization founded in 1987 overseen by Association of Visual Language Interpreters of Canada
Mission: Committed to advancing the profession of sign language interpretation & to ensuring that our members provide British Columbians with exceptional standards of practice
Member of: Association of Visual Language Interpreters of Canada (AVLIC)
Chief Officer(s):
Caroline Tetreault, President
Brenda Carmichael, Vice-President
Finances: *Funding Sources:* Membership fees; Fundraising
Membership: *Member Profile:* Sign language interpreters & those supporting goals of the association; *Committees:* Fundraising; Membership; Newsletter; Professional Development; Professional Standards; Public Relations; Technology

Western Arctic Liberal Association

PO Box 965, Yellowknife NT XIA 2N7
Tel: 867-445-2377; *Fax:* 867-766-4915
Overview: A medium-sized provincial organization

Western Association of Broadcast Engineers (WABE)

#300, 8120 Beddington Blvd. NW, Calgary AB T3K 2A8
Tel: 403-630-4907; *Fax:* 403-295-3135
info@wabe.ca
www.wabe.ca
www.linkedin.com/company/western-association-of-broadcast-engineers
Overview: A medium-sized local organization
Chief Officer(s):
Brian Mayer, President
brian.mayer@shawmedia.ca

Western Association of Broadcasters (WAB)

#507, 918 - 16th Ave. NW, Calgary AB T2M 0K3
Toll-Free: 877-814-2719
Other Communication: Toll-Free Fax: 1-877-814-2749
info@wab.ca
www.wab.ca
Overview: A medium-sized provincial organization
Mission: To represent private television & radio stations in Alberta, Saskatchewan & Manitoba.
Chief Officer(s):
Tom Newton, President
Meetings/Conferences: • Western Association of Broadcasters Conference 2015, June, 2015, Fairmont Banff Springs Hotel, Banff, AB
Scope: Provincial

Western Ayrshire Club

Cobble Hill BC
Tel: 250-743-6192; *Fax:* 250-743-6190
Overview: A medium-sized provincial organization founded in 1928
Mission: To promote the breeding of Ayrshire cattle in British Columbia; to promote the dairy farming industry & the Ayrshire dairy cow as the most economical, productive, profitable & efficient dairy cow to the farmer
Member of: Ayrshire Canada
Chief Officer(s):
Olivier Balme, Director

Western Barley Growers Association (WBGA)

Agriculture Centre, 97 East Lake Ramp NE, Airdrie AB T4A 0C3
Tel: 403-912-3998; *Fax:* 403-948-2069
wbga@wbga.org
www.wbga.org
Overview: A medium-sized local organization founded in 1973
Mission: To provide farmers with an informed & effective voice in the agriculture industry of Western Canada
Chief Officer(s):
Doug Robertson, President
dougarob@gmail.com
Douglas McBain, Treasurer
dkmcbain@lincsat.com
Tom Hewson, Saskatchewan Vice-President
hewws@sasktel.net
Membership: *Fees:* $200; *Member Profile:* Farmers; industry-related to agriculture; end users
Activities: *Rents Mailing List:* Yes
Meetings/Conferences: • Western Barley Growers Association 38th Annual Convention, February, 2015, Deerfoot Inn, Calgary, AB
Scope: Provincial

Western Block Party

PO Box 24052, 4420 West Saanich Rd., Victoria BC V8Z 7E7
Tel: 250-479-6270; *Fax:* 250-479-3294
www.westernblockparty.com
www.facebook.com/group.php?gid=37548613733#
Overview: A small national organization
Chief Officer(s):
Paul St. Laurent, Leader

Western Board of Music *See* Conservatory Canada

Western Boreal Growth & Yield Association

c/o Renewable Resources, #861, GSB, University of Alberta, Edmonton AB T6G 2H1
Tel: 780-492-1879; *Fax:* 780-492-4323
phil.comeau@ualberta.ca
www.rr.ualberta.ca
Also Known As: WESBOGY Association
Overview: A small local organization
Mission: To conduct research projects that contribute to the development & dissemination of growth & yield modeling technology for both natural & regenerated stands growing in the boreal mixedwood region, primarily aspen & spruce
Chief Officer(s):
Phil Comeau, Chair

Western Canada B&B Innkeepers Association *See* British Columbia Bed & Breakfast Innkeepers Guild

Western Canada Children's Wear Markets (WCCWM)

#245, 1868 Glen Dr., Vancouver BC V6A 4K4
Tel: 604-634-0909; *Fax:* 888-595-9360
www.wccwm.com
Overview: A small local organization founded in 1967 overseen by Canadian Association of Wholesale Sales Representatives
Mission: To provide showcases for children's & maternity goods
Member of: CAWS
Affliation(s): WCCM
Chief Officer(s):
Doug Fulton, President
doug@fultonsales.com
Finances: *Funding Sources:* Advertising; Markets
Membership: 18;

Western Canada Concept Party of BC

PO Box 101, 255 Menzies St., Victoria BC V8V 2G6
Tel: 250-727-3438; *Fax:* 250-479-3294
dougchristie@shaw.ca
www.westcan.org
www.facebook.com/group.php?gid=37548613733#
www.youtube.com/DHChristie
Also Known As: Western Canada Concept
Overview: A small local organization
Chief Officer(s):
Doug Christie, Founder and Leader

Western Canada Family Child Care Association of British Columbia (WCFCCA) *See* British Columbia Family Child Care Association

The Western Canada Group of Chartered Engineers (WCGCE)

www.wcgce.org
Overview: A medium-sized local organization founded in 1987
Mission: To provide a series of technical meetings & visits programs; to act as a liaison between local engineers & British engineering institutes
Affliation(s): Institutions of Civil, Mechanical, Structural, Electrical & Chemical Engineers, London UK
Chief Officer(s):
Andrzej Nawrocki, Chair
David Harvey, Vice-Chair
Membership: 1,000 individual

Western Canada Irish Dancing Teachers Association (WCIDTA)

c/o Deirdre Penk-O'Donnell, Penk O'Donnell School of Irish Dance, Vancouver BC
Tel: 604-921-0700
www.wcidta.ca
Overview: A small provincial organization founded in 1964
Mission: To administer & regulate Irish dancing in British Columbia, Alberta, Saskatchewan, & Manitoba; To ensure the quality of competitive Irish dancing standards in the western Canadian region
Member of: An Coimisiun le Rinci Gaelacha (the governing body of Irish dancing); Irish Dancing Teachers Association of North America
Chief Officer(s):
Deirdre Penk-O'Donnell, Regional Director
Membership: *Member Profile:* Registered teachers (TCRG) & adjudicators (ADCRG) in British Columbia, Alberta, Saskatchewan, & Manitoba who are also members of the An Coimisiun le Rinci Gaelacha & the Irish Dancing Teachers Association of North America
Activities: Promoting Irish dancing throughout western Canada

Western Canada Roadbuilders Association

c/o Manitoba Heavy Construction Association, #3, 1680 Ellice Ave., Winnipeg MB R3H 0Z2
Tel: 204-947-1379; *Fax:* 204-943-2279
www.wcrhca.org
Overview: A medium-sized local organization founded in 1975 overseen by Canadian Construction Association
Mission: To represent four western provincial roadbuilders & heavy construction associations at the provincial & federal level
Affliation(s): Roads & Transportation Association of Canada
Chief Officer(s):
Chris Lorenc, President
clorenc@mhca.mb.ca
Membership: 4 member associations; *Member Profile:* British Columbia Roadbuilders & Heavy Construction Association, Alberta Roadbuilders & Heavy Construction Association, Saskatchewan Heavy Construction Association, Manitoba Heavy Construction Association
Meetings/Conferences: • Western Canada Roadbuilders and Heavy Construction Association's 2015 Annual Convention, February, 2015, Hapuna Beach Prince Hotel, Island of Hawaii, HI
Scope: Provincial
Contact Information: Chris Lorenc, SHCA President; Phone: 204-947-1379; clorenc@mhca.mb.ca

Western Canada Theatre Company Society (WCT)

PO Box 329, 1025 Lorne St., Kamloops BC V2C 5K9
Tel: 250-372-3216; *Fax:* 250-374-7099
www.wctlive.ca
www.facebook.com/pages/Western-Canada-Theatre/227054654008534
twitter.com/wctlive
www.youtube.com/user/wctkamloops
Also Known As: Western Canada Theatre
Overview: A small provincial charitable organization founded in 1975
Mission: To provide the regional community with challenging professional theatre; to entertain, educate, enrich & interact with the cultural mosaic of its community; to promote & assist the performing arts through the provision of educational, theatrical & artistic opportunities & services & through the management & operation of facilities
Affliation(s): Professional Association of Candian Theatres
Chief Officer(s):
Lori Marchand, General Manager
lori@wctlive.ca
Finances: *Funding Sources:* Regional government; federal government; City of Kamloops; private donations; box office sales
Staff Member(s): 30
Activities: 5 mainstage productions; 2-4 second stage productions; *Internships:* Yes

Western Canada Tire Dealers Association (WCTD)

PO Box 58047, Stn. Chaparral, Calgary AB T2X 3V2
Tel: 403-264-3179; *Fax:* 403-264-3176
www.wctd.ca
twitter.com/WestCanTire
Overview: A medium-sized local organization founded in 1962
Mission: To establish standards of excellence for members; To promote a professional image in the industry; To act as a unified voice in dealings with government agencies & equipment

distributors; To inform members of advancements in products & services
Chief Officer(s):
Andy Nagy, Contact
andy@wctda.ca
Membership: 900+; *Fees:* $100; *Member Profile:* Independent tire dealers & retreaders from the Yukon, Northwest Territories, British Columbia, Alberta, Saskatchewan, Manitoba, & western Ontario; Manufacturers; Distributors; Exporters; Dealer support services
Activities: Maintaining standards of excellence for tire dealers; Providing a forum for members to discuss issues within the industry; Assisting members to develop beneficial business plans; Representing members on scrap tire boards across western Canada; Offering the Tire Certification Training Program to train employees, plus seminars on various subjects
Awards:
• Western Canada Tire Dealers Academic Scholarship (Scholarship)
Amount: 5 scholarships of $2,000 each *Contact:* Dan Harper, Chair, WCTD Scholarship Committee, Address: 948 Jim Common Dr. North, Sherwood Park, AB, T8H 1Y3
• WCTD Hall of Fame (Award)
To recognize individuals who have made outstanding contributions for the betterment of the industry
Publications:
• Tracker
Type: Newsletter; *Frequency:* 5 pa; *Accepts Advertising*
Profile: Informative stories, guest editorials from industry leaders, & special reports on issues, for small to medium-sized enterprises throughout western Canada

Western Canada Water (WCW)

PO Box 1708, 240 River Ave., Cochrane AB T4C 1B6
Tel: 403-709-0064; *Fax:* 403-709-0068
Toll-Free: 877-283-2003
member@wcwwa.ca
www.wcwwa.ca
Overview: A medium-sized local organization founded in 1948
Mission: To advance support for water professionals throughout western Canada
Affiliation(s): Alberta Water & Wastewater Operator Association (AWWOA); Manitoba Water & Wastewater Association (MWWA); Municipal Service & Suppliers Association (MSSA); Northern Territories Water & Waste Association (NTWWA); Saskatchewan Water & Wastewater Association (SWWA); Western Canada Water Environment Association (WCWEA)
Chief Officer(s):
Audrey Arisman, Executive Director, 403-709-0064, Fax: 403-709-0068
aarisman@wcwwa.ca
Membership: 4,000; *Committees:* Alberta Provincial Council; Saskatchewan Provincial Council; Manitoba Provincial Council; Joint Operators; Conference Planning; Editorial
Activities: Offering education & training
Meetings/Conferences: • Western Canada Water 2015 67th Annual Conference & Exhibition, September, 2015, Winnipeg, MB
Scope: Provincial
Attendance: 500+
Description: Information & a showcase of products & services for delegates from the Western Canada Water marketplace, such as utility managers & operators, municipal & provincial government representatives, & consulting engineers
Contact Information: Western Canada Water, Toll-Free Phone: 1-877-283-2003, Toll-Free Fax: 1-877-283-2007, E-mail: member@wcwwa.ca
• Western Canada Water 2016 68th Annual Conference & Exhibition, October, 2016, Telus Convention Centre, Calgary, AB
Scope: Provincial
Attendance: 500+
Description: Informative sessions, an exhibition, & networking opportunities for utility managers & operators, consulting engineers, & municipal & provincial government representatives
Contact Information: Western Canada Water, Toll-Free Phone: 1-877-283-2003, Toll-Free Fax: 1-877-283-2007, E-mail: member@wcwwa.ca
• Western Canada Water 2017 69th Annual Conference & Exhibition, September, 2017, TCU Place, Saskatoon, SK
Scope: Provincial
Attendance: 500+
Description: A technical program, a keynote speaker, & a trade show for delegates from Western Canada Water
Contact Information: Western Canada Water, Toll-Free Phone: 1-877-283-2003, Toll-Free Fax: 1-877-283-2007, E-mail: member@wcwwa.ca
• Western Canada Water 2018 70th Annual Conference & Exhibition, September, 2018, Winnipeg Convention Centre, Winnipeg, MB
Scope: Provincial
Attendance: 500+
Description: A technical program, a keynote speaker, & a trade show for delegates from Western Canada Water
Contact Information: Western Canada Water, Toll-Free Phone: 1-877-283-2003, Toll-Free Fax: 1-877-283-2007, E-mail: member@wcwwa.ca
• Western Canada Water 2019 71st Annual Conference & Exhibition, September, 2019, Shaw Conference Center, Edmonton, AB
Scope: Provincial
Attendance: 500+
Description: A technical program, a keynote speaker, & a trade show for delegates from Western Canada Water
Contact Information: Western Canada Water, Toll-Free Phone: 1-877-283-2003, Toll-Free Fax: 1-877-283-2007, E-mail: member@wcwwa.ca
• Western Canada Water 2020 72nd Annual Conference & Exhibition, 2020
Scope: Provincial
Attendance: 500+
Description: A technical program, a keynote speaker, & a trade show for delegates from Western Canada Water
Contact Information: Western Canada Water, Toll-Free Phone: 1-877-283-2003, Toll-Free Fax: 1-877-283-2007, E-mail: member@wcwwa.ca
• Western Canada Water 2021 73rd Annual Conference & Exhibition, 2021
Scope: Provincial
Attendance: 500+
Description: A technical program, a keynote speaker, & a trade show for delegates from Western Canada Water
Contact Information: Western Canada Water, Toll-Free Phone: 1-877-283-2003, Toll-Free Fax: 1-877-283-2007, E-mail: member@wcwwa.ca
• Western Canada Water 2022 74th Annual Conference & Exhibition, September, 2022, Calgary, AB
Scope: Provincial
Attendance: 500+
Description: A technical program, a keynote speaker, & a trade show for delegates from Western Canada Water
Contact Information: Western Canada Water, Toll-Free Phone: 1-877-283-2003, Toll-Free Fax: 1-877-283-2007, E-mail: member@wcwwa.ca
Publications:
• Western Canada Water
Type: Magazine; *Frequency:* Quarterly; *Accepts Advertising*; *Editor:* Terry Ross (terry@kelman.ca) *ISSN:* 1483-7730; *Price:* Free with Western Canada Water membership
Profile: Theme issues, plus regular departments such as the president's message, the calendar of events, going green, news from the field, the minister's forum, & a newproduct showcase
• Western Canada Water Member Newsletter
Type: Newsletter
Profile: Membership information & news about forthcoming events

Western Canada Wilderness Committee (WCWC)

PO Box 2205, Station Terminal, Vancouver BC V6B 3W2
Tel: 604-683-8220; *Fax:* 604-683-8229
Toll-Free: 800-661-9453
info@wildernesscommittee.org
www.wildernesscommittee.org
www.facebook.com/wildernesscommittee
twitter.com/wildernews
Also Known As: Wilderness Committee
Overview: A large international charitable organization founded in 1980
Mission: To work for the protection of Canadian & the Earth's wilderness through research & education; to promote the principles which achieve ecologically sustainable communities
Chief Officer(s):
Beth Clarke, Director, Development & Program
Gwen Barlee, Director, Policy
Joe Foy, Director, National Campaign
Finances: *Annual Operating Budget:* $1.5 Million-$3 Million; *Funding Sources:* Donations; membership dues; merchandise sales; grants
Staff Member(s): 25; 300 volunteer(s)
Membership: 26,000; *Fees:* $35 individual (Canada); $50 international/family
Activities: Research; education; slide shows; events; trailbuilding; speaking tours; conferences; media relations; *Speaker Service:* Yes; *Library* by appointment

Manitoba Field Office
#3, 303 Portage Ave., Winnipeg MB R3B 2B4
Tel: 204-942-9292; *Fax:* 204-949-1527
contactmb@wildernesscommittee.org
wildernesscommittee.org/manitoba
www.facebook.com/WildernessCommitteeManitoba
twitter.com/WilderNewsMB
Chief Officer(s):
Eric Reder, Campaign Director

Toronto Office
#209, 425 Queen St. West, Toronto ON M5V 2A5
Tel: 416-849-6520

Vancouver Island - Mid-Island Office
PO Box 442, Qualicum Beach BC V3W 2B5
Tel: 250-752-6585
www.cathedragrovecanyon.com
Chief Officer(s):
Annette Tanner, Contact

Victoria Office & Outreach Centre
#202, 3 Fan Tan Alley, Victoria BC V8W 3G9
Tel: 250-388-9292; *Fax:* 250-388-9223
vi_info@wildernesscommittee.org
wildernesscommittee.org/victoria
www.facebook.com/groups/vi.wildernesscommittee

Western Canadian Association of Bovine Practitioners (WCABP)

226E Wheeler St., 2nd Fl., Saskatoon SK S7P 0A9
Fax: 306-956-0607
Toll-Free: 866-269-8387
info@wcabp.com
www.wcabp.com
Overview: A medium-sized national organization
Chief Officer(s):
Kerri-Rae Millar, President, 204-822-4333
kes113@mail.usask.ca
Membership: 250+; *Fees:* $200 active; $16 student
Meetings/Conferences: • 2015 Western Canadian Association of Bovine Practitioners Conference, January, 2015, Sheraton CAvalier Hotel, Saskatoon, SK
Scope: National

Western Canadian Miniature Horse Club (WCMHC)

c/o Charlene Bier, PO Box 1475, Vulcan AB T0L 2B0
www.wcmhc.ca
Overview: A small local organization founded in 1985
Mission: To encourage the breeding & exhibition of Canadian stock, as defined by the American Miniature Horse Association Standard of Perfection & the American Miniature Horse Registry Standard of Perfection; To develop & promote the miniature horse breed
Affiliation(s): American Miniature Horse Association (AMHA); American Miniature Horse Registry (AMHR)
Chief Officer(s):
Bill Clark, President
wcmhclub@gmail.com
Scott Rempel, Vice-President
rempel44@telus.net
Sonja Marinoske, Secretary
minirose@telusplanet.net
Charlene Bier, Treasurer
charlene@doubletreefarms.ca
Membership: *Fees:* $10 associate & youth members; $35 single memberships; $40 family memberships; *Member Profile:* Any person with an interest in the miniature horse breed; Members do not need to own a horse & do not need to live in western Canada
Activities: Presenting show results; Cooperating with other horse associations; Arranging exhibits about miniature horses; Providing showing & judges' clinics
Publications:
• WCMHC Newsletter
Type: Newsletter; *Editor:* Cindy Hunter; *Price:* Free with Western Canadian Miniature Horse Club membership

Western Canadian Music Alliance (WCMA)

#340, 955 Portage Ave., Winnipeg MB R3G OP9
Tel: 204-943-8485; *Fax:* 204-453-1594
breakoutwest.ca
www.facebook.com/groups/60923781123
twitter.com/breakoutwest

Previous Name: Prairie Music Alliance
Overview: A large local organization founded in 1999
Mission: The music industry associations of Manitoba, Alberta, and Saskatchewan work in tandem towards the shared vision of developing the infrastructure of the independent music industry in Western Canada.
Affliation(s): Alberta Recording Industry Association; Saskatchewan Recording Industry Association; Manitoba Audio Recording Industry Association
Chief Officer(s):
Rick Fenton, Executive Director
rick@breakoutwest.ca
Activities: Prairie Music Week; Music Awards; *Awareness Events:* BreakOut West
Awards:
• Prairie Music Awards (Award)
Annual Awards in the following categories: Recording Engineer of the Year, Record Producer of the Year, Recording Studio of the Year, Record Company of the Year, Publishing Company of the Year, Best Compilation Album of the Year, Best Album Design of the Year, Best Music Score of the Year, Best Music Video, Best Booking Agent, Manager of the Year, & Musician of the Year; also Annual Awards for Prairie artists in the following categories: People's Choice Award, Female/Male Recording Artist of the Year, Group Recording of the Year, Most Promising Artist, Best Pop/Light Rock, Best Rock/Heavy Metal, Best Alternative, Best Country, Best Blues/R&B/Soul, Best Roots/Traditional/Ethnic, Best Rap/Dance/Rhythm, Best Jazz, Best Classical Performance

Western Canadian Opera Society
PO Box 5105, Vancouver BC V6B 4A9
Tel: 604-942-6646
info@operaclub.net
www.operaclub.net
Also Known As: The Opera Club
Overview: A small local charitable organization founded in 1974
Mission: To educate the public about opera through a series of illustrated lectures; one special annual lecture by a nationally known expert in Opera (Western Canadian Opera Lecture)
Membership: *Fees:* $45 individual; $85 double; *Member Profile:* Opera-goers & enthusiasts living in the Greater Vancouver, BC area
Activities: Eight monthly lectures; bus trips to operas outside Vancouver lower mainland; annual special lecture presented by expert in opera

Western Canadian Shippers' Coalition (WCSC)
31 Centennial Pkwy., Delta BC V4L 2C3
Tel: 604-943-8984; *Fax:* 604-943-8936
contact@westshippers.com
www.westshippers.com
twitter.com/Westshippers
www.youtube.com/user/Rhobot?feature=mhee
Overview: A medium-sized provincial organization
Member of: a
Chief Officer(s):
Ian May, Chair
Membership: 21; *Member Profile:* Companies & associations involved in the transportation industry in western Canada

Western Canadian Wheat Growers
3602 Taylor St. East, Bay 6A, Saskatoon SK S7H 5H9
Tel: 306-586-5866; *Fax:* 306-244-4497
Other Communication: Alt. Phone: 306-955-0356
info@wheatgrowers.ca
www.wheatgrowers.ca
Previous Name: Palliser Wheat Growers Association
Overview: A medium-sized national organization founded in 1970
Mission: To promote changes that improve the wheat industry for its members
Chief Officer(s):
Blair Rutter, Executive Director, 204-256-2353, Fax: 204-256-2357
brutter@wheatgrowers.ca
Membership: *Fees:* $25 students; $238.10 farmers; $500 agribusiness; *Member Profile:* Wheat farmers in Western Canada

Western Communities Arts Council *See* West Shore Arts Council

Western Convenience Store Association (WCSA)
AB
Tel: 778-987-4440
Toll-Free: 800-734-2487
andrew@conveniencestores.ca
www.thewcsa.com
www.linkedin.com/groups/Western-Convenience-Stores-Association-4191541
Overview: A medium-sized provincial organization overseen by Canadian Convenience Store Association
Mission: To represent convenience store retailers in Manitoba, Saskatchewan, Alberta, British Columbia, Yukon, Northwest Territories & Nunavut
Affliation(s): Canadian Convenience Stores Association; Ontario Convenience Stores Association; Association Québécoise des dépanneurs en alimentation; Atlantic Convenience Stores Association
Chief Officer(s):
Andrew Klukas, President
andrew@conveniencestores.ca
Finances: *Funding Sources:* Membership fees
Membership: *Member Profile:* Major convenience store companies; independent owners; food retailers; suppliers & wholesalers; gasoline & automotive product vendors

Western Employers Labour Relations Association
#203, 27126 Fraser Hwy., Langley BC V4W 3P6
Tel: 604-857-5540; *Fax:* 604-857-5547
Previous Name: Metal Industries Association
Overview: A medium-sized local organization founded in 1967
Mission: To provide employee relations services for both union & non-union employers

Western Fair Association (WFA)
PO Box 7550, 316 Rectory St., London ON N5Y 5P8
Tel: 519-438-7203
Toll-Free: 800-619-4629
contact@westernfairdistrict.com
www.westernfairdistrict.com
www.facebook.com/westernfairdistrict
twitter.com/WesternFair
Overview: A small local charitable organization founded in 1867
Mission: To create unique experiences that build positive memories
Member of: International Association of Fairs & Expositions; Canadian Association of Fairs & Exibitions
Affliation(s): Ontario Horse Racing Industry
Chief Officer(s):
Hugh Mitchell, Chief Executive Officer
Finances: *Annual Operating Budget:* Greater than $5 Million
Staff Member(s): 80; 175 volunteer(s)
Membership: 243; *Member Profile:* Agriculture, civic, city representatives & individuals
Activities: Presenting horse racing, IMAX-theatre, an annual fair, banquets, a 4 pad ice arena, & trade, consumer, & agricultural related shows;

Western Fertilizer & Chemical Dealers Association *See* Canadian Association of Agri-Retailers

Western Front Society
303 East 8th Ave., Vancouver BC V5T 1S1
Tel: 604-876-9343; *Fax:* 604-876-4099
admin@front.bc.ca
www.front.bc.ca
www.facebook.com/pages/Western-Front/164127636934501
twitter.com/western_front
Overview: A small local charitable organization founded in 1974
Mission: Artist-run centre that focuses on the production & presentation of new art
Member of: Pacific Association of Artist Run Centres; Museums Associations Canada; Alliance for Arts & Culture
Chief Officer(s):
Kate Armstrong, President
Caitlin Jones, Executive Director
caitlinjones@front.bc.ca
Finances: *Annual Operating Budget:* $250,000-$500,000; *Funding Sources:* National, provincial & municipal government; private
Staff Member(s): 11; 60 volunteer(s)
Membership: 250 individual; *Fees:* $40 individual; $100 sustaining; *Member Profile:* Artists; patrons; litterati; *Committees:* Personnel; Budget, Access & Outreach; Building; Communications; Fund-raising
Activities: Offers programs of exhibition, performance art, video production, computer graphics, telecommunications, poetry, dance & music; through a residency program, local, national & international artists are invited to create new works in this interdisciplinary environment; *Internships:* Yes; *Library* by appointment

Western Grain Elevator Association
#2240, 360 Main St., Winnipeg MB R3C 3Z3
Tel: 204-942-6835; *Fax:* 204-943-4328
wgea@mts.net
Overview: A small local organization
Chief Officer(s):
Wade Sobkowich, Executive Director
Staff Member(s): 3
Membership: 10 institutional; *Member Profile:* Major grain handling & sales companies

Western Hockey League (WHL)
Father David Bauer Arena, 2424 University Dr. NW, Calgary AB T2N 3Y9
Tel: 403-693-3030; *Fax:* 403-693-3031
info@whl.ca
www.whl.ca
www.facebook.com/WHLHockey
twitter.com/theWHL
Overview: A medium-sized local organization founded in 1966
Mission: To remain the world's premiere major junior hockey league by continuing to provide the best player development & educational opportunities while enhancing the entertainment value of the game for our fan base
Member of: Canadian Hockey League
Chief Officer(s):
Ron Robison, Commissioner
Staff Member(s): 12
Membership: Comprised of 22 hockey teams in Western Canada & the northwest United States

Western Independence Party of Sakatchewan (WIP)
PO Box 1797, Melville SK S0A 2P0
e-mail: wipsk@gmail.com
www.wipsk.com
Overview: A small provincial organization founded in 2003
Chief Officer(s):
Dana Armason, Party Leader
Frank Serfas, President

Western Independent Adjusters' Association
c/o Russell Fitzgerald, Kernaghan Adjusters Limited, #203, 4246 97 St. NW, Edmonton AB T6E 5Z9
www.ciaa-adjusters.ca
Overview: A small provincial organization overseen by Canadian Independent Adjusters' Association
Chief Officer(s):
Russell Fitzgerald, President, 780-488-2371, Fax: 780-488-0243
rfitzgerald@kernaghan.com

Western Institute for the Deaf & Hard of Hearing (WIDHH)
2125 West 7th Ave., Vancouver BC V6K 1X9
Tel: 604-736-7391; *Fax:* 604-736-4381; *TTY:* 604-736-2527
info@widhh.com
www.widhh.com
www.facebook.com/92914429597
twitter.com/widhh
Also Known As: Western Institute
Overview: A small provincial charitable organization founded in 1956
Mission: To address the needs of the deaf, deafened & hard of hearing individuals by providing products, services & programs that work towards ensuring accessibility to their environment which is equal to that of the hearing public
Member of: United Way; Better Business Bureau
Chief Officer(s):
Ruth Warick, President
Susan Masters, Executive Director
masters@widhh.com
Staff Member(s): 39
Membership: *Fees:* $15; $100 life; *Member Profile:* Deaf & hard of hearing
Activities: Public displays; *Library*

Western Inter-College Conference (WICC) *See* Alberta Colleges Athletic Conference

Western Magazine Awards Foundation (WMAF)
#102, 211 Columbia St., Vancouver BC V6A 2R5
Tel: 604-945-3711
info@westernmagazineawards.ca
www.westernmagazineawards.ca
www.facebook.com/WesternMagazineAwards
twitter.com/WesternMagAward
Also Known As: The Westerns
Overview: A small local organization

Mission: To recognize exceptional work in the Western Canadian magazine industry.
Chief Officer(s):
Jane Zatylny, President
Kate Cockerill, Executive Director
Staff Member(s): 1
Awards:
• The Western Magazine Awards (Award)
Editorial excellence in western Canadian magazine writing, photography, illustration & art direction

Western Newfoundland Model Forest *See* Model Forest of Newfoundland & Labrador

Western Québec Literacy Council (WQLC) / Conseil d'alphabétisation de l'ouest du Québec
PO Box 266, 381, route 148, Shawville QC J0X 2Y0
Tel: 819-647-3112; *Fax:* 819-647-3188
Toll-Free: 888-647-3112
info@wq-literacy.org
www.wq-literacy.org
www.facebook.com/199249413439491
Overview: A small local charitable organization founded in 1984
Mission: To give free lessons in reading, writing & mathematics, in English, to adults in the Western Québec region; to train volunteer tutors; to sensitize the public about the problem of illiteracy & to offer support to tutors & students
Affiliation(s): Literacy Volunteers of Québec; Laubach Literacy of Canada
Chief Officer(s):
Marilee DeLombard, Executive Director
Norma J. DesRosiers, President
Finances: *Annual Operating Budget:* $50,000-$100,000; *Funding Sources:* Provincial & federal government; private funding
Staff Member(s): 3; 100 volunteer(s)
Membership: 75 individual; *Fees:* $5 institutional; $5 individual; $5 associate

Western Red Cedar Lumber Association (WRCLA)
Pender Place 1, #1501, 700 West Pender St., Vancouver BC V6C 1G8
Tel: 604-684-0266; *Fax:* 604-687-4930
Toll-Free: 866-778-9096
wrcla@wrcla.org
www.wrcla.org
www.facebook.com/RealCedar
twitter.com/RealCedar
www.youtube.com/user/WRCLA
Overview: A small local organization founded in 1954
Mission: Trade association representing quality producers of Western Red Cedar lumber products in BC & the Pacific Northwest states; members are dedicated to producing quality siding, decking, paneling, outdoor & other specialty cedar products
Chief Officer(s):
Peter Lang, General Manager
Staff Member(s): 5
Membership: 22; *Fees:* Based on shipments; *Member Profile:* Producers of Western Red cedar

Western Refederation Party of BC; Western Independence Party of BC *See* British Columbia Refederation Party

Western Retail Lumber Association (WRLA)
Western Retail Lumber Association Inc., #1004, 213 Notre Dame Ave., Winnipeg MB R3B 1N3
Tel: 204-957-1077; *Fax:* 204-947-5195
Toll-Free: 800-661-0253
wrla@wrla.org
www.wrla.org
Overview: A medium-sized local organization founded in 1890
Mission: To serve & promote needs & common interests of lumber, building materials & hard goods industry on the Prairies
Chief Officer(s):
Gary Hamilton, Executive Director
Dwight Dixon, President
Membership: *Fees:* Schedule available
Meetings/Conferences: • Western Retail Lumber Association 2015 Prairie Showcase Buying Show & Convention, January, 2015, Calgary, AB
Scope: Provincial
Contact Information: Caren Kelly, Marketing Manager, E-mail: Ckelly@wrla.org
• Western Retail Lumber Association 2016 Prairie Showcase Buying Show & Convention, January, 2016, Calgary, AB
Scope: Provincial
Contact Information: Caren Kelly, Marketing Manager, E-mail: Ckelly@wrla.org
• Western Retail Lumber Association 2017 Prairie Showcase Buying Show & Convention, January, 2017, Calgary, AB
Scope: Provincial
Contact Information: Caren Kelly, Marketing Manager, E-mail: Ckelly@wrla.org
• Western Retail Lumber Association 2018 Prairie Showcase Buying Show & Convention, 2018
Scope: Provincial
Publications:
• The YardStick [a publication of the Western Retail Lumber Association]
Type: Magazine; *Frequency:* 6 pa

Western Silvicultural Contractors' Association (WSCA)
#720, 999 West Broadway, Vancouver BC V5Z 1K5
Tel: 604-736-8660; *Fax:* 604-738-4080
info@wsca.ca
www.wsca.ca
Overview: A medium-sized local organization founded in 1980
Mission: Dedicated to improving working conditions, quality of life and safety for all silviculture workers.
Chief Officer(s):
John Betts, Executive Director
Finances: *Annual Operating Budget:* $50,000-$100,000
Staff Member(s): 2; 15 volunteer(s)
Membership: 75; *Fees:* Schedule available; *Member Profile:* Silvicultural contractors

The Western Stock Growers' Association (WSGA)
PO Box 179, 900 Village Lane, Okotoks AB T1S 1Z6
Tel: 403-250-9121
office@wsga.ca
www.wsga.ca
Overview: A medium-sized local organization founded in 1896
Mission: To support & protect livestock growers by lobbying the government on legislation & proposed new legislation; to promote environmentally sound range management practices
Chief Officer(s):
Phil Rowland, President
Staff Member(s): 1
Membership: 1,200; *Fees:* $150-$500; *Member Profile:* Stockmen
Meetings/Conferences: • Western Stock Growers' Association Annual General Meeting 2015, 2015
Scope: Provincial

Western Transportation Advisory Council (WESTAC)
#401, 899 Pender St. West, Vancouver BC V6C 3B2
Tel: 604-687-8691; *Fax:* 604-687-8751
infoservices@westac.com
www.westac.com
www.linkedin.com/company/2275285?trk=tyah
www.facebook.com/181099878620851
twitter.com/WESTAC
Overview: A small local organization founded in 1973
Mission: To advance Western Canadian economy through the improvement of the region's transportation system.
Chief Officer(s):
Lisa Baratta, Director, Strategy
Ruth Sol, President
Marcella Szel, Chairman (Executive Committee)
Lois Jackson, Chairman of the Board
Finances: *Annual Operating Budget:* $500,000-$1.5 Million; *Funding Sources:* Membership fees; project fees; professional services fees
Staff Member(s): 4
Membership: 52 corporate; *Fees:* Revenue-related scale; *Member Profile:* Carriers; shippers; ports & terminals; labour unions; government
Activities: *Library* by appointment

Westerner Park
4847A - 19th St., Red Deer AB T4R 2N7
Tel: 403-343-7800; *Fax:* 403-341-4767
askus@westerner.ab.ca
www.westernerpark.ca
www.facebook.com/westernerpark
twitter.com/westernerpark
www.youtube.com/westernerpark
Also Known As: The Westerner Exposition Association
Overview: A small local charitable organization founded in 1891
Mission: To take a leadership role in providing superior services, programs, & events benefiting Central Alberta
Member of: Canadian Association of Fairs & Exhibitions; International Association of Fairs & Exhibitions
Chief Officer(s):
John Harms, Chief Executive Officer & General Manager, 403-309-0200
jharms@westerner.ab.ca
Staff Member(s): 22
Activities: Westerner Days Fair & Exposition; Agritrade Farm Expo

Westgen
PO Box 40, 6681 Glover Rd., Milner BC V0X 1T0
Tel: 604-530-1141; *Fax:* 604-534-3036
Toll-Free: 800-563-5603
www.westgen.com
Previous Name: BC Artificial Insemination Centre
Overview: A small provincial charitable organization founded in 1943
Mission: To provide Semex Alliance Genetics & other value-added products & services which enhance herd improvement to livestock producers in western Canada
Member of: Semex Alliance
Chief Officer(s):
Brent Belluk, General Manager
gm@westgen.com
Darcie Kaye, Marketing Manager
dkaye@westgen.com
Finances: *Annual Operating Budget:* Greater than $5 Million
Staff Member(s): 46
Membership: 1,400; *Fees:* $5; *Member Profile:* Dairy & beef producers in Western Canada

Westhaven-Elmhurst Community Association
7405 Harley Ave., Montréal QC H4B 1Y2
Tel: 514-872-6134
westhavencenter@hotmail.com
www.westhavenndg.com
www.facebook.com/WesthavenNDG
Overview: A small local organization founded in 1972
Mission: To offer recreational & social programs & activities to the community on a year-round basis

Westlock & District Chamber of Commerce
PO Box 5917, Westlock AB T7P 2P7
Tel: 780-307-3251
www.facebook.com/282139025132580
Overview: A small local organization
Member of: Alberta Chamber of Commerce
Chief Officer(s):
Ben Kellert, President
John Bosman, Vice-President
jbosman@newcap.ca
Finances: *Annual Operating Budget:* Less than $50,000; *Funding Sources:* Membership dues; fundraising
75 volunteer(s)
Membership: 78; *Fees:* $75 individual; $125 business; $15 senior/student; *Committees:* Agriculture; Economic Development; Fund-raising; Membership
Activities: Christmas Liteup; Best Bloomin' Town in the West program; *Awareness Events:* Small Business Week; Seniors Week

Westmorland Historical Society (WHS)
4974 Main St., Dorchester NB E4K 2Z1
Tel: 506-379-6633
www.keillorhousemuseum.com
Overview: A small local organization founded in 1961
Mission: To preserve the past for the future

Westmount Historical Association (WHA) / Association historique de Westmount
Westmount Public Library, 4574, rue Sherbrooke ouest, Montréal QC H3Z 1G1
Tel: 514-989-5510
info@westmounthistorical.org
www.westmounthistorical.org
Overview: A small local charitable organization founded in 1944
Mission: To collect, preserve, & interpret the history of Westmount, Québec; To promote awareness of local history; To encourage research about local cultural & social development
Finances: *Funding Sources:* Donations; Membership fees
Membership: *Fees:* $20 individuals; $30 families; $100 patrons; $250 corporate
Activities: Presenting lectures on topics related to heritage; Offering walking tours of Westmount; *Library:* Westmount Historical Association Archives; Open to public by appointment

Publications:
• The Westmount Historian
Type: Newsletter; *Frequency:* Semiannually
Profile: Articles about the history of Westmount, Québec & association events

Weston Historical Society
1901 Weston Rd., Toronto ON M9N 3P5
Tel: 416-249-6663
westonhistoricalsociety@rogers.com
www.welcometoweston.ca/whs
Overview: A small local organization
Chief Officer(s):
Eva Ferguson, Contact, 416-235-0845, *Fax:* 416-487-7126
Mary Lou Ashbourne, Contact, 416-247-4354, *Fax:* 416-247-3519
mashbour@idirect.com

Westport & Rideau Lakes Chamber of Commerce
PO Box 157, #2, 36 Main St., Westport ON K0G 1X0
Tel: 613-273-2929; *Fax:* 613-273-2929
wrlcc@rideau.net
www.westportrideaulakes.on.ca
www.facebook.com/#!/WestportRideauLakesChamberOfCommerce
twitter.com/WRLCC
Overview: A small local charitable organization founded in 1960
Chief Officer(s):
Colin Horsfall, President
Finances: *Annual Operating Budget:* Less than $50,000; *Funding Sources:* Membership fees; donations
12 volunteer(s)
Membership: 130; *Fees:* $125-$175; *Member Profile:* Local businesses & services

Westward Goals Support Services Inc.
4611 - 48th St., Rocky Mountain House AB T4B 1B7
Tel: 403-845-2922; *Fax:* 403-845-2277
wwgoals@telusplanet.net
www.westwardgoals.ca
Overview: A small local organization founded in 1991
Mission: To assist mentally handicapped/brain injured persons in maximizing independence through supported programs; to offer residential support, community networking & outreach support for adults; to provide children with outreach & family support, including in-home support, rehabilitation aides & host family services
Chief Officer(s):
Heather Pengelly, Executive Director
Finances: *Annual Operating Budget:* $500,000-$1.5 Million; *Funding Sources:* Provincial government
Staff Member(s): 47

Wetaskiwin & District Association for Community Service (WDACS)
5211 - 54 St., Wetaskiwin AB T9A 1T2
Tel: 780-352-2241; *Fax:* 780-352-8558
info@wdacs.ca
Overview: A small local organization founded in 1964
Mission: To provide services to persons with disabilities thereby promoting quality of life, individual choices, respect, personal growth & development
Affliation(s): Alberta Association of Rehabilitation Centres
Chief Officer(s):
Marilyn Conner, Executive Director
m.conner@wdacs.ca
Lavern Buchert, President
Finances: *Annual Operating Budget:* $1.5 Million-$3 Million; *Funding Sources:* Regional government
Staff Member(s): 65; 30 volunteer(s)
Membership: 1-99
Activities: Annual Pumpkin Ball

Wetaskiwin Chamber of Commerce (WCC)
4910 - 55A St., Wetaskiwin AB T9A 2R7
Tel: 780-352-8003; *Fax:* 780-352-6226
www.wetaskiwinchamber.ca
Overview: A small local organization founded in 1929
Mission: To foster sustainable business development & growth in the Wetaskiwin area
Member of: Alberta Chamber of Commerce; Canadian Chamber of Commerce; Economic Developers Association of Alberta
Chief Officer(s):
Randy Plant, President
Alan Greene, Executive Director
Allan Halter, Secretary
Petra Erhardt, Treasurer
Finances: *Annual Operating Budget:* $100,000-$250,000; *Funding Sources:* Business license revenue
Staff Member(s): 3
Membership: 688; *Fees:* $20; *Committees:* Ambassadorship; Marketing; Policy; Strategic Planning; Technology; Tourism
Activities: *Speaker Service:* Yes

Weyburn & District Labour Council
PO Box 1204, Weuburn SK S4H 2L5
Tel: 306-842-7938
Overview: A small local organization overseen by Saskatchewan Federation of Labour
Mission: To promote the interests of affiliates in Weyburn, Saskatchewan, & the surrounding area; To advance the economic & social welfare of workers
Affliation(s): Canadian Labour Congress (CLC)
Chief Officer(s):
Wanda Bartlett, President
wbartlett@sasktel.net
Activities: Presenting educational opportunities; Coordinating local campaigns & events, such as a ceremony on the annual Day of Mourning, for workers who have suffered workplace injury, illness, or death; Promoting occupational health & safety; Supporting community organizations, such as the Envision Counselling & Support Centre

Weyburn & District United Way
PO Box 608, Weyburn SK S4H 2K7
Tel: 306-842-7880
weyburn.unitedway@accesscomm.ca
www.weyburnunitedway.com
www.facebook.com/197260380295115
Overview: A small local charitable organization overseen by United Way of Canada - Centraide Canada
Chief Officer(s):
Gary Erickson, President
Finances: *Annual Operating Budget:* Less than $50,000; *Funding Sources:* Donations
Membership: 1-99

Weyburn Agricultural Society
PO Box 699, Weyburn SK S4H 2K8
Tel: 306-842-4052; *Fax:* 306-842-1469
agsociety@accesscomm.ca
www.weyburnagsociety.com
Overview: A small local charitable organization founded in 1908
Mission: To promote agriculture; to act as a liaison between the rural & urban population; To promote education on agriculture-related subjects
Member of: Saskatchewan Association of Agricultural Societies & Exhibitions
Affliation(s): Western Canada Fairs; Canadian Association of Exhibitions
Chief Officer(s):
Treva Tollefson, President
Finances: *Annual Operating Budget:* $50,000-$100,000
Staff Member(s): 1; 250 volunteer(s)
Membership: 36 senior/lifetime; 120 individual; *Fees:* Schedule available; *Member Profile:* Interest in agriculture; *Committees:* Attractions; Commercial; Hospitality; Gates; Horse; Cattle; 4H Youth; 4H Calf; Publicity
Activities: *Awareness Events:* Weyburn Agricultural Society Fair, July; Weyburn Rodeo, Aug.

Weyburn Chamber of Commerce
#11, 3rd St. NE, Weyburn SK S4H OW5
Tel: 306-842-4738; *Fax:* 306-842-0520
info@weyburnchamber.com
www.weyburnchamber.com
twitter.com/WeyburnChamber
Overview: A small local organization
Mission: To assume a leadership role in business & community growth by promoting programs designed to strengthen & expand the potential of business within the trading area; To enhance the general welfare & prosperity of the Weyburn area
Affliation(s): Saskatchewan Chamber of Commerce
Chief Officer(s):
Jeff Chessal, President
Finances: *Annual Operating Budget:* Less than $50,000; *Funding Sources:* Membership fees; special projects
Staff Member(s): 1
Membership: 146; *Fees:* $107.25 base rate + $8 for every full-time employee; *Member Profile:* Local business & industry; *Committees:* Economic Development; Government Issues & Education; Public Relations; Membership
Activities: Business Cleanup Competition; local promotions; parades; *Speaker Service:* Yes; *Rents Mailing List:* Yes
Awards:
• Golden Spike Award (Award)
Presented yearly to a member of the community who has contributed to growth & improvement by participating on volunteer committees
• Two scholarships a year (Scholarship)
• Golden Sheaf Award (Award)
To recognize excellence in farming achievement & to help foster rural-urban understanding & consideration
• Golden Service Award (Award)

Weyburn Group Homes Society Inc
209 Lorraine St., Weyburn SK S4H 1R9
Tel: 306-842-6686; *Fax:* 306-842-1586
Overview: A small local organization founded in 1975
Chief Officer(s):
Bernice Erickson, Executive Director
Finances: *Annual Operating Budget:* $250,000-$500,000
Staff Member(s): 15; 11 volunteer(s)

Weymouth Historical Society
c/o Maurine Mullen, RR#3, Weymouth NS B0W 3T0
Tel: 902-837-5185
Overview: A small local organization
Chief Officer(s):
Leota Lewis, President, 902-837-5185
Maurine Mullen, Secretary, 902-837-5593
Membership: 30 individual; *Fees:* $5 individual
Activities: Thursday teas held July-Sept.

Wheelchair Sports Alberta
11759 Groat Rd., Edmonton AB T5M 3K6
Tel: 780-427-8699
Toll-Free: 888-453-6770
wsa1@telus.net
www.abwheelchairsport.ca
Overview: A small provincial organization
Mission: To develop wheelchair sports throughout Alberta
Member of: Canadian Wheelchair Sports Association
Chief Officer(s):
Mike Sandomirsky, Executive Director
Membership: *Fees:* $10 board/coach/official; $25 athlete; $30 family; *Member Profile:* Any athlete, club, official, coach or board member

Wheelchair Sports Association of Newfoundland & Labrador (WSANL)
40 Imogene Cres., Paradise NL A1L 1E8
Tel: 709-782-0487
Overview: A small provincial organization
Member of: Canadian Wheelchair Sports Association
Chief Officer(s):
Gary Power, President
gpower@cwsa.ca

Where the Rivers Meet *See* Sagitawa Friendship Centre

Whistler Chamber of Commerce
#201, 4230 Gateway Dr., Whistler BC V0N 1B4
Tel: 604-932-5922; *Fax:* 604-932-3755
chamber@whistlerchamber.com
www.whistlerchamber.com
www.facebook.com/whistlerchamber
twitter.com/whistlerchamber
Overview: A small local organization founded in 1966
Mission: To serve its members & promote the businesses of Whistler; To provide leadership in monitoring & directing the local economy; To lobby on behalf of business in Whistler; To provide Whistler businesses with networking opportunities; to provide training opportunities & recognition programs for employer/employees to ensure service excellence throughout the Resort
Member of: BC Chamber of Commerce
Chief Officer(s):
Mechthild Facundo, Manager
Fiona Famulak, President, 604-932-5922 Ext. 22
Finances: *Annual Operating Budget:* $500,000-$1.5 Million; *Funding Sources:* Membership dues; municipal; sponsorships
Staff Member(s): 5
Membership: 800; *Fees:* $240; *Committees:* Finance; Membership Development; Service; Events; Landlord/Tenant Task Force; Strategic Planning; Employee Housing; Governance & Nominating; Business Readiness
Activities: American Express Employee Recognition Program; Whistler Spirit Program; Canada Day; monthly luncheons;

Business 2 Business; Women of Whistler; Whistler Card; *Library* Open to public

Whistler Food Bank
PO Box 900, 6195 Lorimer Rd., Whistler BC V0N 1B0
Tel: 604-935-7717; *Fax:* 604-932-0599
foodbank@mywcss.org
Overview: A small local organization overseen by Food Banks British Columbia
Member of: Food Banks British Columbia
Chief Officer(s):
Sara Jennings, Contact

Whistler Resort Association (WRA)
4010 Whistler Way, Whistler BC V0N 1B4
Tel: 604-932-3928; *Fax:* 604-932-7231
Toll-Free: 888-869-2777
www.whistler.com
www.facebook.com/gowhistler
twitter.com/gowhistler
www.youtube.com/gowhistler
Also Known As: Tourism Whistler
Overview: A small local organization founded in 1979
Mission: To develop strategic partnerships, positioning Whistler as a preferred resort destination in all target markets; To successfully grow the business; To improve the value provided to stakeholders; To create a climate for growth & development of staff within the organization
Chief Officer(s):
Suzanne Denbak, President
Finances: *Annual Operating Budget:* Greater than $5 Million
Staff Member(s): 88
Membership: 6,000; *Fees:* Schedule available; *Member Profile:* Having a business in Whistler/owners of resort land

Whitby Chamber of Commerce (WCC)
128 Brock St. South, Whitby ON L1N 4J8
Tel: 905-668-4506; *Fax:* 905-668-1894
info@whitbychamber.org
www.whitbychamber.org
www.linkedin.com/company/whitby-chamber-of-commerce
www.facebook.com/93725729133
twitter.com/whitbychamber
Overview: A medium-sized local organization founded in 1928
Mission: To act as the recognized voice of business for Whitby; To provide leadership & innovation of services & programs in support of members & the community, through advocacy, networking, education, communication, government liaison, value-added programs, & leadership opportunities
Member of: Canadian Chamber of Commerce; Ontario Chamber of Commerce
Chief Officer(s):
Tracy Hanson, Chief Executive Officer
tracy@whitbychamber.org
Finances: *Annual Operating Budget:* $250,000-$500,000; *Funding Sources:* Membership fees; Events
Staff Member(s): 2; 80 volunteer(s)
Membership: 800; *Fees:* $200 average; *Committees:* Government Relations; Business Development; Programs & Events; Community Development; Marketing & Communications
Activities: Hosting an annual general meeting, monthly networking breakfasts, evening meetings, an annual golf tournament, the Monday Night Golf League, the Peter Perry Business Achievement Awards Gala, a President's Ball, & the Annual Mayor's Luncheon; Organizing training & mentoring programs
Awards:
- Peter Perry Citizen of the Year (Award)
- Scholarships (Scholarship)

Two scholarships presented to children of Chamber members or children of employees of Chamber members in full time post secondary education program *Amount:* $1,000
- Business Person Achievement Award (Award)
- Young Entrepreneur Achievement Awaard (Award)
- Business Achievement Award (Award)

Whitchurch-Stouffville Chamber of Commerce
PO Box 1500, 6176 Main St., Stouffville ON L4A 8A4
Tel: 905-642-4227; *Fax:* 905-642-8966
chamber@whitchurchstouffville.ca
www.whitchurchstouffville.ca
www.facebook.com/100780059972589
Overview: A small local organization founded in 1977
Mission: To promote & improve trade & commerce & the economic, civic & social welfare of the district
Member of: Ontario Chamber of Commerce; Canadian Chamber of Commerce
Chief Officer(s):
Penny Reid, Chair, 905-640-3131
Edward Nelles, Executive Director
Finances: *Annual Operating Budget:* $50,000-$100,000; *Funding Sources:* Membership dues; social events; golf tournament; trade show; event sponsorship
Staff Member(s): 3; 1 volunteer(s)
Membership: 205; *Fees:* $182-$494.95; *Member Profile:* Small & medium sized businesses; *Committees:* Tourist; Networking
Activities: Golf tournament; networking breakfasts; *Library:* Tourist Information Centre
Awards:
- Heritage Award (Award)
- Business of the Year (Award)
- Business Entrepreneur of the Year (Award)
- Corporate Citizen of the Year (Award)
- Young Entrepreneur (Award)

The White Ribbon Campaign
#203, 365 Bloor St. East, Toronto ON M4W 3L4
Tel: 416-920-6684; *Fax:* 416-920-1678
Toll-Free: 800-328-2228
info@whiteribbon.ca
www.whiteribbon.ca
www.facebook.com/whiteribboncampaign
twitter.com/whiteribbon
Overview: A medium-sized national charitable organization founded in 1991
Mission: Men working to end men's violence against women; to bring about positive behaviour & attitude shifts that will contribute to ending violence against women through public education, advocacy activities & encourage the efforts of men to gather men around the issue
Chief Officer(s):
Raymond Ludwin, Chair
Finances: *Annual Operating Budget:* $250,000-$500,000
Staff Member(s): 4
Membership: 1,000-4,999; *Fees:* $10
Activities: Education & Action Kit; workbook, lesson plans for educators; *Awareness Events:* White Ribbon Campaign, Nov. 25 - Dec. 6

White River District Historical Society
PO Box 583, 200 Elgin St., White River ON P0M 3G0
Tel: 807-822-2657; *Fax:* 807-822-1920
museum@nwconx.net
www.nwconx.net/~museum
Overview: A small local organization
Member of: Ontario Museum Association
Finances: *Annual Operating Budget:* Less than $50,000
3 volunteer(s)
Membership: 40; *Fees:* $10 single; $20 family
Activities: Winnie's Hometown Festival; Perfect Pie Contest; Museum & Gift Shop

White Rock & Surrey Naturalists
Surrey BC
Overview: A small local charitable organization
Mission: To promote the enjoyment of nature through environmental appreciation & conservation; to encourage wise use & conservation of natural resources & environmental protection
Member of: Federation of BC Naturalists
Chief Officer(s):
Viveka Ohman, Contact, Christmas Bird Count
ohmanv@inspection.gc.ca
Lynn Pollard, Contact, Youth Program, 604-531-6307
jacquielynn@telus.net
Liz Walker, Contact
swalker3@shaw.ca
Finances: *Annual Operating Budget:* Less than $50,000
42 volunteer(s)
Membership: 120; *Fees:* $27 single; $37 family; *Committees:* Conservation; Education
Activities: Natural history walks & hikes; conservation & education activities;

Whitecourt & District Chamber of Commerce
Synergy Business Centre, PO Box 1011, 4907 - 52 Ave., Whitecourt AB T7S 1N9
Tel: 780-778-5363; *Fax:* 780-778-2351
manager@whitecourtchamber.com
www.whitecourtchamber.com
www.facebook.com/whitecourtchamber
Overview: A medium-sized local organization founded in 1980
Mission: To promote trade & commerce & the economic, civic & social welfare of the district
Member of: Canadian Chamber of Commerce
Affliation(s): Alberta Chamber of Commerce
Chief Officer(s):
Pat VanderBurg, General Manager
Neil Shewchuk, President
Finances: *Funding Sources:* Membership fees; projects & promotions
Staff Member(s): 1
Membership: 240; *Fees:* Schedule available; *Member Profile:* Associations; corporations; societies; partnerships or estates
Activities: Business Information Library; *Speaker Service:* Yes; *Library:* Chamber Resource Library; Open to public

Whitecourt Fish & Game Association
PO Box 3, Whitecourt AB T7S 1N3
www.wfga.ca
Overview: A small local licensing charitable organization
Member of: Alberta Fish & Game Association
Affliation(s): Alberta Bow Hunting Association
Chief Officer(s):
Rick Fetch, President
president@wfga.ca
Ron Brown, Vice-President
vicepresident@wfga.ca
Finances: *Annual Operating Budget:* Less than $50,000
Membership: 100; *Fees:* $25 regular; $15 associate; $35 family; $25 range passes
Activities: Archery & gun ranges; hunter education; 3D archery shoots; birdhouse building

Whitehorse Chamber of Commerce (WCC)
#101, 302 Steele St., Whitehorse YT Y1A 2C5
Tel: 867-667-7545; *Fax:* 867-667-4507
business@whitehorsechamber.ca
www.whitehorsechamber.ca
Overview: A medium-sized local organization founded in 1948
Mission: To promote & improve trade & commerce; to contribute to the economic, civic & social well-being of Whitehorse
Member of: Canadian Chamber of Commerce
Affliation(s): Yukon Chamber of Commerce; Tourism Industry Association of Yukon
Chief Officer(s):
Rick Karp, President
president@whitehorsechamber.ca
Finances: *Annual Operating Budget:* $100,000-$250,000; *Funding Sources:* Membership fees; fund-raising
Staff Member(s): 2
Membership: 400; *Fees:* $185.38 Individual; *Committees:* Membership; Government Relations; Fundraising; WCB issues
Activities: Chamber luncheons; Business After Hours; Fair Exchange; Planter Box Program; lobbying on behalf of business community; *Rents Mailing List:* Yes

Whitehorse Cross Country Ski Club
#200, 1 Sumanik Dr., Whitehorse YT Y1A 6J6
Tel: 867-668-4477
info@xcskiwhitehorse.ca
www.xcskiwhitehorse.ca
Overview: A small provincial organization
Mission: To maintain high-quality ski trails & facilities, maintain a safe environment, ensure the long-term viability of the club & secure land tenure for the Yukon's trail system.
Chief Officer(s):
Claude Chabot, Executive Director
ed@xcskiwhitehorse.ca
Mike Gladish, Operations Manager
manager@xcskiwhitehorse.ca
Membership: *Fees:* $195-$215

Whitehorse Glacier Bears Swim Club
4061 - 4th Ave., Whitehorse YT Y1A 1H1
Tel: 867-667-6220
whseglacierbears@yahoo.ca
www.whitehorseglacierbears.ca
Overview: A small local organization
Mission: To promote competitive swimming.
Chief Officer(s):
Shelby Workman, President
workman@northwestel.net

Whitehorse Minor Hockey Association (WMHA)
4061 - 4th Ave., Whitehorse YT Y1A 1H1
Tel: 867-393-4698; *Fax:* 867-667-4237
whseminorhockey@gmail.com
www.whitehorseminorhockey.ca
Overview: A medium-sized provincial organization

Mission: Promotes and coordinates minor hockey leagues in Whitehorse.
Member of: Sport Yukon
Affliation(s): Yukon Amateur Hockey Association
Chief Officer(s):
Carl Burgess, President
carl.whitehorse@gmail.com
Kim King, Manager
Membership: *Committees:* Policy & Discipline; Sponsorship/Grants; House League; Mustangs; Online Communications; Fundraising/Bingo/Cantina

Whitehorse Minor Soccer Association (WMS)
4061 - 4th Ave., Whitehorse YT Y1A 1H1
Tel: 867-667-2445
wms@sportyukon.com
www.yukonsoccer.yk.ca/minor
Overview: A medium-sized provincial organization founded in 1977
Mission: Provides low-cost, easily accessible indoor & outdoor soccer opportunities to the youth of Whitehorse.
Member of: Sport Yukon
Chief Officer(s):
Gerald Haase, President
Hanne Hoefs, Administrator

Whitehorse Women's Hockey Association (WWHA)
4061 - 4th Ave., Whitehorse YT Y1A 1H1
e-mail: wwhayukon@gmail.com
whitehorsewomenshockey.com
www.facebook.com/whitehorsewomenshockeyassn
Overview: A small local organization founded in 1993
Mission: To administer women's hockey in Whitehorse.
Chief Officer(s):
Hodgins Joelle, President

Whitewater Historical Society
2022 Foresters Falls Rd., Foresters Falls ON K0J 1V0
Tel: 613-646-2622
info@rossmuseum.ca
www.rossmuseum.ca
Previous Name: Ross Township Historical Society of Whitewater Region; Ross Township Historical Society
Overview: A small local organization founded in 1985
Mission: To promote & preserve local history & collections of the Township of Whitewater Region
Finances: *Funding Sources:* Ontario Trillium Foundation; Ministry of Culture of Ontario; Donations
Membership: *Fees:* $10 individuals; $15 families
Activities: Operating the Ross Museum in Foresters Falls, which consists of the Ross House, the former Ross Township Fire Hall, a drive shed, & St. Aidan's Church; Organizing & maintaining the records of the Whitewater region for researchers; *Library:* Ross Museum Resource Centre; Open to public

Whitewater Ontario
411 Carnegie Beach Rd., Port Perry ON L9L 1B6
Tel: 905-985-4585; *Fax:* 905-985-5256
Toll-Free: 888-322-2849
info@whitewaterontario.ca
www.whitewaterontario.ca
www.facebook.com/whitewaterontario
Overview: A small provincial organization overseen by CanoeKayak Canada
Mission: Whitewater Ontario is the sport governing body in the province, & represents provincial interests within the national body CanoeKayak Canada.
Member of: CanoeKayak Canada
Chief Officer(s):
Steve Pomeroy, President
spomeroy@rogers.com
Membership: *Fees:* $30 adult; $15 junior; $30 family; $1,000 life

Whole Village
20725 Shaws Creek Rd., Caledon ON L7K 1L7
Tel: 519-941-1099
info@wholevillage.org
www.wholevillage.org
www.facebook.com/group.php?gid=6413163738
twitter.com/WholeVillageEco
www.youtube.com/watch?v=SUzdnR6dqwM&feature=plcp
Overview: A small local organization founded in 1996
Mission: To create an example of sustainable living
Member of: Ecovillage Network of Canada; Canadian Cohousing Network; Canadian Organic Growers
Affliation(s): National Farmers Union; Ecological Farm Association of Ontario
Finances: *Annual Operating Budget:* $100,000-$250,000; *Funding Sources:* Membership fees; member loans; grants
55 volunteer(s)
Membership: 25; *Fees:* $10/month or $120/year; *Committees:* Legal/Financial; Communications; Education; Farm; Community Dynamics
Activities: Sustainable agriculture; green construction; community development; *Internships:* Yes; *Speaker Service:* Yes

Wiarton South Bruce Peninsula Chamber of Commerce
PO Box 68, Wiarton ON N0H 2T0
Tel: 519-534-4009
info@wiartonchamber.ca
www.wiartonchamber.ca
Also Known As: Wiarton & District Chamber of Commerce
Overview: A small local organization founded in 1991
Mission: To act as the collective voice of area businesses; To promote growth & prosperity of members in the community
Member of: Bruce Peninsula Tourism
Affliation(s): Wiarton BIA
Chief Officer(s):
Mel Rinehart, President
10 volunteer(s)
Membership: 120; *Fees:* $130-$310, based on number of employees; *Committees:* Membership

Wiccan Church of Canada
The Occult Shop, 1373 Bathurst St., Toronto ON M5R 3J1
e-mail: info@wcc.on.ca
www.wcc.on.ca
Overview: A small national organization founded in 1979
Mission: To assist practicing Wiccans in achieving a spiritual balance that brings them into true harmony with the Gods.
Chief Officer(s):
Richard James, Priest
richard@wcc.on.ca

Wikwemikong Anishinabe Association for Community Living
11 Fox Lake Rd., Wikwemikong ON P0P 2J0
Tel: 705-859-2147; *Fax:* 705-859-2147
coliving@amtelecom.net
Overview: A small local organization
Member of: Community Living Ontario

WIL Employment Connections
141 Dundas St., 4th Fl., London ON N6A 1G3
Tel: 519-663-0774; *Fax:* 519-663-5377
careerinformation@wil.ca
www.wil.ca
www.linkedin.com/company/676963
www.facebook.com/wilemploymentconnections
twitter.com/wilemployment
Previous Name: Women Immigrants of London
Overview: A small local organization founded in 1984
Mission: To offer employment help for new immigrants, the unemployed & employers
Member of: Ontario Network of Employment Skills Training Projects
Chief Officer(s):
Anne Langille, Executive Director
Finances: *Funding Sources:* Federal; provincial; private sector
Staff Member(s): 51
Membership: *Committees:* Steering

Wilberforce Project
PO Box 11479, Edmonton AB T5J 3K5
Tel: 780-421-7747; *Fax:* 888-492-9375
Toll-Free: 877-880-5433
office@wilberforceproject.ca
thewilberforceproject.ca
Previous Name: Alberta Pro Life Alliance Association
Overview: A small provincial organization founded in 1986
Mission: To educate Albertans on pro-life & pro-family issues; to mobilize citizens to effect changes in government policy relating to sanctity of life issues
Chief Officer(s):
Dale Bullock, President
Rosey Rosenke, Executive Director
Staff Member(s): 2
Membership: *Fees:* $25
Activities: *Library* Open to public

Publications:
• The Rose
Type: Newsletter; *Frequency:* Quarterly

Wild Bird Care Centre (WBCC)
PO Box 11159, Nepean ON K2H 7T9
Tel: 613-828-2849; *Fax:* 613-828-2194
mojo@wildbirdcarecentre.org
www.wildbirdcarecentre.org
Overview: A medium-sized national organization founded in 1981
Mission: To assess, treat, and rehabilitate sick, orphaned, or injured wild birds before releasing them back to the wild.
Chief Officer(s):
Kathy Nihei, Founder
Membership: *Fees:* $25 single; $40 family; $15 student/senior; $50 school; $100 business; $1000+ corporate/patron

Wild Blueberry Association of North America (WBANA) / Association des bleuets sauvages de l'Amérique du Nord (ABSAN)
81 Woodmere Dr., Upper Kinsclear NB E3E 1T8
Tel: 506-363-3606
wildblueberries@gwi.net
www.wildblueberries.com
www.facebook.com/wildblueberries
twitter.com/WildBBerries4U
www.youtube.com/user/WildBlueberries4u
Overview: A medium-sized international organization founded in 1981
Mission: To extend awareness & promote use of wild blueberries on domestic & overseas markets
Finances: *Funding Sources:* Dues; government co-op programs
Activities: *Speaker Service:* Yes

Wild Blueberry Producers Association of Nova Scotia (WBPANS)
PO Box 119, 168 Dakota Rd., Debert NS B0M 1G0
Tel: 902-662-3306; *Fax:* 902-662-3284
wbpans@ns.aliantzinc.ca
www.nswildblueberries.com
Overview: A medium-sized provincial organization founded in 1970
Mission: To encourage the production & consumption of wild blueberries; to provide a viable & sustainable industry for Nova Scotia blueberry producers
Affliation(s): Wild Blueberry Association of North America
Finances: *Funding Sources:* Membership dues; interest income
Membership: *Member Profile:* Must be a producer of wild blueberries
Awards:
• Scholarship (Scholarship)
Amount: $750

Wild Rose Agricultural Producers
5033 - 52 St., Lacombe AB T4L 2A6
Tel: 403-789-9151; *Fax:* 780-789-9152
Toll-Free: 855-789-9151
info@wrap.ab.ca
www.wrap.ab.ca
www.facebook.com/122046961202493
twitter.com/WildRoseGFO
Previous Name: Unifarm
Overview: A medium-sized provincial organization founded in 1996
Mission: To represent its members at the regional, provincial & national level for the benefit of agriculture; to create an atmosphere of cooperation & communication to ensure that areas of common concern among all producers are dealt with to the benefit of agriculture as a whole
Chief Officer(s):
Sheryl Rae, Executive Director
Membership: 1,000-4,999; *Fees:* $140 producer; $65 associate

Wild Rose Ball Hockey Association
Edmonton AB
e-mail: wrbha@telus.net
www.wrballhockey.com
Overview: A small provincial organization
Member of: Canadian Ball Hockey Association
Chief Officer(s):
Connie Liosis, Executive Director

Wild Rose Draft Horse Association (WRDHA)
c/o Barb Stephenson, PO Box 96, Turner Valley AB T0L 2A0
Tel: 403-933-5765
www.wrdha.com

Overview: A small provincial organization founded in 1994
Mission: To act as a unified voice for the draft horse industry in Alberta
Chief Officer(s):
Barb Stephenson, Secretary
dbsteph@telusplanet.net
Membership: *Fees:* $20 single members; $25 family members; *Member Profile:* Draft horse enthusiasts in Alberta
Activities: Hosting events, such as 4-H Draft Horse Events, the Annual Wild Rose Draft Horse Sale, & the Alberta Draft Horse Improvement; Sponsoring other events, such as the Calgary Stampede; Offering a Wild Rose Draft Horse Futurity to showcase pedigreed Clydesdale, Percheron, Belgian, Suffolk, & Shire breeding stock; Posting show results; Providing educational programs
Awards:
• Wild Rose Draft Horse Association Youth Scholarship (Scholarship)
Eligibility: Members of the Wild Rose Draft Horse Association between the ages of 15 & 21

Wild Rose Economic Development Corporation *See* Community Futures Wild Rose

Wilderness Canoe Association (WCA)
PO Box 91068, 2901 Bayview Ave., Toronto ON M2K 2Y6
Tel: 416-223-4646
info@wildernesscanoe.ca
www.wildernesscanoe.ca
Overview: A small local organization founded in 1973
Mission: Organization of individuals interested in wilderness travel, mainly by canoe, kayak, and backpacking and, in winter, by skis and snowshoes
Member of: Federation of Ontario Naturalists
Chief Officer(s):
David Young, Chair
chair@wildernesscanoe.ca
Finances: *Annual Operating Budget:* Less than $50,000
Membership: 750; *Fees:* $35 single; $45 family
Activities: Winter pool training sessions; Paddle the Don River; year-round outings; *Awareness Events:* Wine & Cheese, Nov.; Paddlers' Club Night, Feb.
Publications:
• Nastawgan Journal [a publication of the Wilderness Canoe Association]
Type: Journal; *Frequency:* Quarterly; *Editor:* Aleks Gusev

Wilderness Tourism Association (WTA)
PO Box 423, Cumberland BC V0R 1S0
Tel: 250-336-2862; *Fax:* 250-336-2861
admin@wilderness-tourism.bc.ca
www.wilderness-tourism.bc.ca
Overview: A small local organization founded in 1999
Mission: To protect a land base for the wilderness tourism industry
Chief Officer(s):
Brian Gunn, President
Evan Loveless, Executive Director
Sam Purin, Director, Membership & Development
Jim DeHart, Secretary
Gilles Valade, Treasurer
Finances: *Funding Sources:* Membership fees; Donations
Membership: 100-499; *Fees:* Schedule available; *Member Profile:* Wilderness tourism operators in British Columbia, such as businesses & community DMOs; Educational institutions; Industry suppliers
Activities: Engaging in advocacy activities; Providing education
Meetings/Conferences: • Wilderness Tourism Association 2015 Summit & Annual General Meeting, 2015
Scope: Provincial
Description: Informative sessions & workshops about nature based tourism

Wilderness Tourism Association of the Yukon (WTAY)
#4, 1114 - 1st Ave., Whitehorse YT Y1A 1A3
Tel: 867-668-3369; *Fax:* 867-668-3370
info@wtay.com
wtay.com
Overview: A small provincial organization
Mission: To represent the wilderness & adventure tourism industry in the Yukon Territory, Canada; to provide marketing, advocacy, research, consultation, referral & education resources.
Affliation(s): Yukon Wild
Chief Officer(s):
Felix Geithner, President
Membership: 68; *Fees:* $125; *Committees:* Environment; Legislation; Marketing; Research; Education

Wildlife Foundation of Manitoba; Fort Whyte Centre for Environmental Education *See* FortWhyte Alive

Wildlife Habitat Canada (WHC) / Habitat faunique Canada (HFC)
#207, 120 Iber Rd., Ottawa ON K2S 1E9
Tel: 613-722-2090; *Fax:* 613-722-3318
Toll-Free: 800-669-7919
www.whc.org
www.facebook.com/124492716000
twitter.com/WildlifeHCanada
Overview: A medium-sized national organization founded in 1984
Mission: To promote the conservation, restoration & enhancement of wildlife habitat to retain diversity, distribution & abundance of wildlife; To provide a funding mechanism for the conservation, restoration & enhancement of wildlife habitat in Canada; To foster coordination & leadership in the conservation, restoration & enhancement of wildlife habitat in Canada
Chief Officer(s):
Pierre Vary, Director, Finance & Administration, 613-722-2090 Ext. 201
pvary@whc.org
Finances: *Funding Sources:* Donations
Activities: *Rents Mailing List:* Yes

Wildlife Haven Rehabilitation Centre
PO Box 49, Glenlea MB R0G 0S0
Tel: 204-883-2122; *Fax:* 204-883-2582
www.mwro.mb.ca
Previous Name: Manitoba Wildlife Rehabilitation Organization
Overview: A small provincial charitable organization founded in 1984
Mission: To maintain & preserve the province's wildlife; to receive & professionally handle injured & orphaned native wildlife; to promote public education in wildlife conservation & appreciation; to establish & maintain a Wildlife Rehabilitation Centre; to stimulate & conduct applied noninvasive research; to record data & preserve materials pertaining to rehabilitation & captive breeding of endangered species
Member of: International Wildlife Rehabilitation Council
Finances: *Annual Operating Budget:* $50,000-$100,000
Staff Member(s): 3; 40 volunteer(s)
Membership: 550; *Fees:* $50 family; $30 individual; *Member Profile:* Individuals with an appreciation for wildlife & nature; all ages; *Committees:* Education; Fundraising; Relocation
Activities: Education; rehabilitation; *Internships:* Yes; *Speaker Service:* Yes

Wildlife Preservation Canada (WPC) / Conservation de la faune au Canada
RR#5, 5420 Hwy. 6 North, Guelph ON N1H 6J2
Tel: 519-836-9314
Toll-Free: 800-956-6608
admin@wildlifepreservation.ca
www.wildlifepreservation.ca
www.facebook.com/WildlifePreservationCanada
twitter.com/WPCWild911
Previous Name: Wildlife Preservation Trust Canada
Overview: A medium-sized national charitable organization founded in 1985
Mission: To save endangered animal species from extinction in Canada & internationally
Chief Officer(s):
Elaine Williams, Executive Director
elaine@wildlifepreservation.ca
Ian Glen, President
Jessica Steiner, Recovery Biologist
Finances: *Annual Operating Budget:* $500,000-$1.5 Million
Membership: *Committees:* Conservation; Communications; Strategic Funding; Nominations
Activities: Providing training & outreach programs; Administering conservation grants
Publications:
• Home on the Range [a publication of Wildlife Preservation Canada]
Type: Newsletter
Profile: Updates on the Eastern Loggerhead Shrike recovery program
• On the Edge [a publication of Wildlife Preservation Canada]
Type: Newsletter; *Frequency:* 3 pa
Profile: Information about recovery & conservation efforts of Wildlife Preservation Canada
• Wildlife Preservation Canada Annual Report
Type: Yearbook; *Frequency:* Annually
Profile: Financial highlights & donation information

Wildlife Preservation Trust Canada *See* Wildlife Preservation Canada

Wildlife Rescue Association of British Columbia (WRA)
5216 Glencarin Dr., Burnaby BC V5B 3C1
Tel: 604-526-2747; *Fax:* 604-524-2890; *Crisis Hot-Line:* 604-526-7275
info@wildliferescue.ca
www.wildliferescue.ca
www.facebook.com/group.php?gid=335147280556
twitter.com/WRAofBC
Previous Name: Lower Mainland Wildlife Rescue Association
Overview: A medium-sized provincial charitable organization founded in 1979
Mission: To rehabilitate wildlife; To promote the welfare of wild animals in the urban environment
Chief Officer(s):
Rose Hamilton, Senior Executive Consultant
Heather Gill, Administrator
Stefanie Broad, Coordinator, Volunteers
Johanna Thompson, Officer, Education
Yolanda Brooks, Manager, Communications
yolanda@wildliferescue.ca
Linda Bakker, Team Leader, Wildlife Rehabilitation
Janelle Stephenson, Coordinator, Care Centre
Membership: *Fees:* $15 students & seniors; $25 individuals; $35 families; $250 businesses & life memberships
Activities: Providing education & outreach services
Publications:
• To the Rescue [a publication of the Wildlife Rescue Association of British Columbia]
Type: Newsletter; *Frequency:* 3 pa; *Accepts Advertising*; *Editor:* Yolanda Brooks
Profile: Educational information, success stories, care centre news, forthcoming events, donation information, campaigns, & avolunteer update from the association

Wildrose Alliance Party
#408, 919 Centre St. NW, Calgary AB T2E 2P6
Tel: 403-769-0999; *Fax:* 866-620-4791
Toll-Free: 888-262-1888
www.wildrose.ca
www.facebook.com/teamwildrose
twitter.com/TeamWildrose
www.youtube.com/WildroseTV
Also Known As: Wildrose
Overview: A large provincial organization
Chief Officer(s):
Heather Forsyth, Interim Party Leader
David Yager, President
Finances: *Funding Sources:* Membership purchases; Donations
Membership: *Fees:* $10 per year

Wildrose Polio Support Society
132 Warwick Rd. NW, Edmonton AB T5X 4P8
Tel: 780-428-8842; *Fax:* 780-475-7968
wpss@polioalberta.ca
www.polioalberta.ca/wildrose
Overview: A small local organization founded in 1999
Mission: To bring awareness about Post Polio Syndrome to the Southern Alberta community; to provide support for polio survivors
Chief Officer(s):
Marleen Henley, President
Membership: *Fees:* $15 individual; $25 couple; *Member Profile:* Polio survivors from Edmonton & northern Alberta; *Committees:* Events; Casino; Telephone; Outreach; Fundraising; Nominations; Newsletter; Membership; Web; Birthdays

Wilfrid Laurier University Faculty Association (WLUFA) / Association des professeurs de l'Université Wilfrid-Laurier
Wilfrid Laurier University, #114, 202 Regina St. North, Waterloo ON N2L 3C5
Tel: 519-884-1970; *Fax:* 519-888-9721
wlufa@wlu.ca
www.wlufa.ca
Overview: A small local organization founded in 1988
Member of: Ontario Confederation of University Faculty Associations; Canadian Association of University Teachers
Chief Officer(s):

Sheila McKee-Protopapas, Executive Director, 519-884-1970 Ext. 2367
smckeeprotopapas@wlu.ca
Linda Watson, Senior Administrative Assistant, 519-884-1970 Ext. 2603
lwatson@wlu.ca
Membership: 100-499

Wilfrid Laurier University Symphony Orchestra

Faculty of Music, 75 University Ave. West, Waterloo ON N2L 3C5
Tel: 519-884-0710; *Fax:* 519-884-5285
Overview: A small local organization overseen by Orchestras Canada
Mission: To train music students to be musicians who have solid knowledge of music theory & history, & are competent performers
Member of: Canadian University Music Society; Association of Canadian Choral Conductors; Choirs Ontario
Chief Officer(s):
Paul Pulford, Conductor
Membership: *Member Profile:* Faculty of music students

William Morris Society of Canada (WMSC)

87 Government Rd., Toronto ON M8X 1W4
Tel: 416-233-7686
info@wmsc.ca
www.wmsc.ca
Overview: A small national charitable organization founded in 1981
Mission: To foster knowledge about the life & work of William Morris (1834-1896), the nineteenth-century English artist, writer, & craftsman
Affiliation(s): William Morris Society - Great Britain & US
Finances: *Annual Operating Budget:* Less than $50,000
15 volunteer(s)
Membership: 200; *Fees:* $45 - $55
Activities: Lectures; tours; trips; symposia
Publications:
• The Canadian Society Newsletter [a publication of the William Morris Society of Canada]
Type: Newsletter; *Frequency:* s-a.
• The Journal [a publication of the William Morris Society of Canada]
Frequency: s-a.

William W. Creighton Youth Services

PO Box 10632, 1014 Oliver Rd., Thunder Bay ON P7B 6V1
Tel: 807-345-4456; *Fax:* 807-345-1635
www.creightonyouth.com
Overview: A small local organization
Mission: To provide youth justice services under the Child & Family Services Act & the Youth Criminal Justice Act
Chief Officer(s):
Keith Zehr, Executive Director
Staff Member(s): 23

Williams Lake & District Association for the Mentally Handicapped *See* Williams Lake Association for Community Living

Williams Lake & District Chamber of Commerce

1660 Broadway South, Williams Lake BC V2G 2W4
Tel: 250-392-5025; *Fax:* 250-392-4214
Toll-Free: 877-967-5253
info@williamslakechamber.com
www.williamslakechamber.com
www.facebook.com/williams.centre
Overview: A small local organization founded in 1949
Mission: To represent the business community by providing services, benefits, & leadership for positive growth
Affliation(s): BC Chamber of Commerce; Canadian Chamber of Commerce; Cariboo Chilcotin Coast Tourism Association
Chief Officer(s):
Jason Ryll, President
Claudia Blair, Executive Director
Finances: *Annual Operating Budget:* $100,000-$250,000; *Funding Sources:* Municipal, provincial & federal government; private
Staff Member(s): 2
Membership: 300; *Fees:* Schedule available; *Committees:* Business Excellence Awards
Activities: *Library:* Business Info Centre; Open to public
Awards:
• Business Excellence Awards (Award)

Williams Lake Association for Community Living (WLACL)

51 South 4th Ave., Williams Lake BC V2G 1H2
Tel: 250-395-4489; *Fax:* 250-398-7623
www.wlacl.org
Previous Name: Williams Lake & District Association for the Mentally Handicapped
Overview: A small local charitable organization founded in 1961
Mission: To provide services to adults with mental handicaps to integrate them into the community & further their independence
Member of: British Columbia Association for Community Living
Chief Officer(s):
Ian McLaughlin, Executive Director
ian.mclaughlin@shaw.ca
Finances: *Funding Sources:* Ministry of Children & Family Services; sales
Activities: Recreational; Educational; Supported Living; Community Employment; Community Housing

Williams Lake Field Naturalists

1305A Borland Rd., Williams Lake BC V2G 5K5
Tel: 250-392-7680
muskratexpress@midbc.com
www.williamslakefieldnaturalists.ca
Overview: A small local charitable organization
Mission: To promote the enjoyment of nature through environmental appreciation, education & conservation; To encourage wise use & conservation of natural resources & environmental protection; To administer the Scout Island Nature Centre in Williams Lake
Member of: Federation of BC Naturalists
Chief Officer(s):
Fred McMechan, President
Membership: *Fees:* $22 individual; $27 family
Activities: *Library* Open to public

Williams Lake Stampede Association

PO Box 4076, Williams Lake BC V2G 2V2
Tel: 250-398-8388; *Fax:* 250-398-7701
Toll-Free: 800-717-6336
info@williamslakestampede.com
www.williamslakestampede.com
www.facebook.com/WilliamsLakeStampede
www.youtube.com/WilliamsLakeStampede
Overview: A small local organization
Chief Officer(s):
Fred Thomas, President

Willow Beach Field Naturalists (WBFN)

PO Box 421, Port Hope ON L1A 3W4
willowbeachfieldnaturalists.org
Overview: A small local charitable organization founded in 1953
Mission: To protect & enhance the natural heritage of Northumberland County & surrounding areas; to develop knowledge of our natural heritage; to record & share this knowledge; to encourage the preservation, renewal & enhancement of our natural heritage
Member of: Ontario Nature
Finances: *Annual Operating Budget:* Less than $50,000; *Funding Sources:* Membership fees; donations
Membership: 200; *Fees:* $25 individual; $35 family; *Member Profile:* Interest in all aspects of nature & conservation
Activities: Monthly meetings; outings; bird counts; breeding bird atlas
Publications:
• The Curlew [a publication of the Willow Beach Field Naturalists]
Type: Newsletter

Willowdale Community Legal Services

106, 245 Fairview Mall Dr., Toronto ON M2J 4T1
Tel: 416-492-2437
willowdalelegal.com
Overview: A small local organization overseen by Ontario Council of Agencies Serving Immigrants
Mission: To provide free legal advice, assistance and representation to low-income residents living in a specified area
Finances: *Funding Sources:* Legal Aid Ontario

Wilno Heritage Society

c/o Beverly A. Glofcheskie, PO Box 232, 6 Biernacki Mountain Rd., Barry's Bay ON K0J 1B0
e-mail: heritage@wilno.org
www.wilno.org
Overview: A small local organization founded in 1998
Mission: To commemorate the past, recognize contributions by our ancestors; to support & augment existing Polish language studies for our students; to preserve the Kaszubian customs & traditions
Chief Officer(s):
Peter Glofcheskie, President
peter.glofcheskie@gmail.com
Mike Coulas, Vice-President
Teenie Mask, Secretary
christinemask@hotmail.com
Ursula Jeffrey, Treasurer
ujeffrey@rogers.com
10 volunteer(s)
Membership: *Fees:* $10 single; $15 family; $25 sponsor
Activities: Compiling genealogy of Polish Kashub Canadians; promoting Kashub language & culture; *Awareness Events:* Canadian Polish Kashub Festival, 1st Sat. in May

Wind Athletes Canada

PO Box 29047, Stn. Portsmouth, Kingston ON K7M 8W6
www.windathletes.ca
www.facebook.com/windathletes
twitter.com/windathletes
www.youtube.com/user/windathletescanada
Overview: A medium-sized national organization
Mission: To promote the sport of sailing in Canada; to provide funding to the Canadian Sailing Team
Finances: *Funding Sources:* Fundraising
Activities: Training programs

Wind Energy TechnoCentre *Voir* TechnoCentre éolien

Windermere District Historical Society

PO Box 2315, Invermere BC V0A 1K0
Tel: 250-342-9769
wvmuseum@cyberlink.bc.ca
www.windermerevalleymuseum.ca
Also Known As: Windermere Valley Museum & Archives
Overview: A small local charitable organization founded in 1965
Mission: To preserve & display pioneer artifacts & record local history
Member of: BC Museums Association; BC Heritage; BC Archives Association
Chief Officer(s):
Margaret Christensen, President
Joan George, Secretary
Finances: *Annual Operating Budget:* Less than $50,000; *Funding Sources:* Admissions; membership dues; municipal grant
Staff Member(s): 2; 20 volunteer(s)
Membership: 120; *Fees:* $20 friends of the museum; *Committees:* Displays; Acquisitions; Building
Activities: Historical displays; Heritage Day luncheons; historical talks, slides & videos; school programs & field trips; *Library:* Archives; Open to public

Windfall Ecology Centre

93A Industrial Pkwy. South, Aurora ON L4G 3V5
Tel: 905-727-0491; *Fax:* 905-727-0491
Toll-Free: 866-280-4431
Other Communication: Alt. phone: 416-465-6333
info@windfallcentre.ca
www.windfallcentre.ca
www.facebook.com/windfallcentre
twitter.com/windfallcentre
www.youtube.com/user/WindfallCentre
Overview: A medium-sized provincial organization founded in 1998
Mission: To educate & advocate in the areas of energy conservation, renewable energy production, water protection and leadership development.
Affliation(s): Green Communities Canada; Ontario Trillium Foundation; Ontario Sustainable Energy Association; Ashoka; TD Friends of the Environment
Chief Officer(s):
Brent Kopperson, Executive Director
Staff Member(s): 7
Activities: Programs for youth; First Nations joint projects; Well Aware and other water protection programs; Safe Routes to School, and ecoDriver; projects in wind energy, solar energy, and geothermal energy; Windfall Home Energy Assessment program; *Awareness Events:* Windfall Ecology Festival, June; *Internships:* Yes
Meetings/Conferences: • 14th Annual Windfall Ecology Festival, 2015
Description: Electric vehicles, infrastructure development and practical information on how to incorporate electric mobility into your organization and strategy planning.

Contact Information: Fraser Damoff, Program Coordinator; fdamoff@windfallcentre.ca; Phone: 905-727-0491 ex.123.

Windigo First Nations' Council
PO Box 299, 160 Alcona Dr., Sioux Lookout ON P8T 1A3
Tel: 807-737-1585; *Fax:* 807-737-3133
Toll-Free: 800-465-3621
info@windigo.on.ca
www.windigo.on.ca
Overview: A small local organization
Mission: To develop programs & services that respond to the needs of the Band members within the six communities of the Windigo area; to negotiate with other levels of government on various aspects of First Nations' jurisdiction & control
Chief Officer(s):
Frank McKay, CEO & Council Chair
Staff Member(s): 28

Windsor & District Baseball Umpires Association (WDBUA)
Windsor ON
www.windsorumpires.ca
twitter.com/WDBUA
Also Known As: Windsor Umpires
Overview: A small local organization
Mission: To train, instruct & evaluate members.
Affliation(s): Baseball Ontario; Baseball Canada; Sun Parlour Baseball Association
Chief Officer(s):
Matthew Tyler, President
president@windsorumpires.ca
Scott Scantlebury, Secretary
secretary@windsorumpires.ca

Windsor & District Black Coalition of Canada
PO Box 1381, Stn. A, Windsor ON N9A 4J4
Tel: 519-252-2561
contact@blackcoalition.com
www.blackcoalition.com
Overview: A small local organization founded in 1980
Mission: To see that the Black people of Windsor achieve full social, cultural, political & economic participation in the shaping of a humane society, & they benefit fully from this society; to eradicate all forms of racism & discrimination in Windsor & area
Member of: Federation of Race Relations Organizations
Chief Officer(s):
Marc Taylor, President
10 volunteer(s)
Membership: 350; *Fees:* $20 individual, $35 family; *Committees:* Fundraising; Program; Public Relations; Social Action
Activities: *Awareness Events:* Black History Month, Feb.; International Day for Elimination of Racial Discrimination, March 21

Windsor & District Labour Council
#200, 3450 Ypres Ave., Windsor ON N8W 5K9
Tel: 519-252-8281; *Fax:* 519-252-2906
wdlc_office@bellnet.ca
www.wdlc.ca
Also Known As: CAW Local 44
Overview: A small local organization founded in 1986 overseen by Ontario Federation of Labour
Member of: Ontario Federation of Labour
Chief Officer(s):
Dino Chiodo, President
Tullio DiPonti, Financial Secretary

Windsor Area Health Libraries Association; Windsor Hospitals Library Group *See* Southwestern Ontario Health Library Information Network

Windsor Association for the Deaf (WAD)
c/o Shoppers Drug Mart, PO Box 28036, 500 Tecumseh Rd. East, Windsor ON N8X 2S2
Other Communication: Fan Page: www.facebook.com/deafwad
deafwad@gmail.com
sites.google.com/site/deafwad
www.facebook.com/wad.deaf
Overview: A small local organization
Mission: Social & recreational activities for persons deafened or hard of hearing; provides social gatherings; offers special events & traveling sports tournaments; promotes the welfare of deaf members, preserves Deaf Culture & ASL, offers social interaction between cultures, encourage the promotion of Deaf Awareness; offer workshops for deaf, hearing, & parents of deaf children & deaf parents of hearing children
Chief Officer(s):
Ken Borckway, President
wadpresident1@gmail.com
Gary Vassallo, Vice-President
wasvicepresident2@gmail.com
Judy Kraemer, Treasurer
wadtreasurer3@gmail.com
Membership: *Fees:* $20 single; $10 student

Windsor Association of Moldmakers *See* Canadian Association of Moldmakers

Windsor Catholic Family Service Bureau *See* Family Services Windsor-Essex Counselling & Advocacy Centre

Windsor Coin Club
#505, 5060 Tecumseh Rd. East, Windsor ON N8T 1C1
Tel: 519-735-0727
info@windsorcoinclub.com
www.windsorcoinclub.com
Overview: A small local organization founded in 1951
Chief Officer(s):
Brett Irick, President
Membership: *Fees:* $15 regular; $12 seniors; free for children 16 & under

Windsor Community Living Support Services *See* Community Living Windsor

Windsor Construction Association
2880 Temple Dr., Windsor ON N8W 5J5
Tel: 519-974-9680; *Fax:* 519-974-3854
construction@wca.on.ca
www.wca.on.ca
Overview: A medium-sized local organization founded in 1918
Mission: To unite, inform & strengthen those in the construction industry
Member of: Council of Ontario Construction Associations; Windsor Chamber of Commerce
Affliation(s): Heavy Construction Association of Windsor
Chief Officer(s):
Charlie Hotham, President, 519-945-0001
chotham@hothambuildingmaterials.com
Davide Petretta, Vice President, 519-727-1292
info@petcon.net
Finances: *Funding Sources:* Membership dues
Membership: 400 corporate; *Fees:* Schedule available; *Member Profile:* Construction related company; professional services
Activities: *Library*

Windsor Electrical Contractors Association
#202, 2880 Temple Dr., Windsor ON N8W 5J5
Tel: 519-974-3411; *Fax:* 519-974-9923
weca@meshgroup.ca
www.weca.ca
Overview: A small local organization
Mission: To foster and advance the interests of those who are engaged in any branch of the Electrical Construction Industry; to represent the members of the Association in any matters pertaining to the Electrical Construction Industry, and to enter into such agreements as may appear to be in the best interests of the Electrical Construction Industry
Chief Officer(s):
Jim Kennedy, Executive Director

Windsor Federation of Musicians
#307, 52 Chatham St., Windsor ON N9A 5M6
Tel: 519-258-2288; *Fax:* 519-258-9041
winfdmus@mnsi.net
www.afm.org/locals/info/number/566
Also Known As: Local 566 AFM
Overview: A small local organization founded in 1911
Member of: Federation of Musicians of the United States & Canada
Chief Officer(s):
Chris Borshuk, President
Staff Member(s): 2
Membership: 300

Windsor Islamic Association (WIA)
c/o Windsor Mosque, 1320 Northwood Dr., Windsor ON N9E 1A4
Tel: 519-966-2355
wia@windsormosque.com
www.wiao.org
www.facebook.com/windsormosque
Overview: A small local organization founded in 1964
Mission: Serves a population of over 25,000 Muslims in the Windsor locality
Affliation(s): World Muslim League
Chief Officer(s):
Muhammad Khalid Raana, President
president@windsormosque.ca
Abdallah Shamisa, Vice-President
Majed Mahmoud, Secretary
Activities: Prayer services; funeral services; marriages; Qura'an memorization; Arabic language lessons; teachings about Islam; live broadcast

Windsor Orchid Society / Société des Orchidophiles de Windsor
c/o Betty Levar, 1822 Chilver Rd., Windsor ON N8W 2T8
www.windsororchidsociety.ca
Overview: A small local organization
Chief Officer(s):
Deb Boersma, President
Membership: *Fees:* $20 single; $25 family; *Committees:* Archives; Budget; Conservation; Fundraising; Hospitality; Library; Membership; Newsletter; Photographer; Program; Raffles & Prizes; Special Orders & Supplies; Website; Welcoming; Winter Social

Windsor Police Association (WPA) / Association de la police de Windsor
548 Windsor Ave., Windsor ON N9A 1J5
Tel: 519-969-0510; *Fax:* 519-969-6064
windsorpa@on.aibn.com
www.windsorpa.ca
Overview: A small local organization founded in 1967
Mission: To represent member's interests in regards to all aspects of their collective agreements with the Windsor Police Service Board and issues in general with policing in the community
Member of: Police Association of Ontario; Canadian Police Association
Chief Officer(s):
Ed Parent, President
eparent@on.aibn.com

Windsor Public Library Adult Literacy Program
850 Ouellette Ave., Windsor ON N9A 4M9
Tel: 519-255-6770; *Fax:* 519-255-7207; *TTY:* 519-252-4775
www.windsorpubliclibrary.com
Previous Name: Windsor Volunteers for Literacy
Overview: A small local organization founded in 1980
Affliation(s): Laubach Literacy of Canada
Chief Officer(s):
Christine Dean, Co-ordinator
adultlit@windsorpubliclibrary.com
Finances: *Funding Sources:* Municipal government; Ministry of Training, Colleges & Universities
Activities: Tutors & learners meet on a one-on-one basis in the literacy & basic skills levels one & two

Windsor Sexual Assault Crisis Centre *See* Sexual Assault Crisis Centre of Essex County Inc.

Windsor Symphony Orchestra (WSO)
487 Ouellette Ave., Windsor ON N9A 4J2
Tel: 519-973-1238
Toll-Free: 888-327-8327
www.windsorsymphony.com
Overview: A medium-sized local charitable organization founded in 1947 overseen by Orchestras Canada
Mission: To enrich community life & serve as an educational resource through high quality live performance of orchestral music
Member of: Ontario Federation of Symphony Orchestras
Affliation(s): American Symphony Orchestra League
Chief Officer(s):
Barb Kuker, President
Stephen Savage, First Vice President
Sandra Aversa, Second Vice President
Finances: *Annual Operating Budget:* $500,000-$1.5 Million; *Funding Sources:* Ticket sales; government grants; community support; special events; volunteer association
Staff Member(s): 12; 150 volunteer(s)
Membership: 500; *Fees:* $65; *Committees:* Artistic Planning; Development; Education & Youth; Executive; Finance; Marketing; Outreach; Strategic Planning; Youth Chorus
Activities: *Awareness Events:* Great-West Life Community Concert; Gift of Music Concerts; *Internships:* Yes; *Library* by appointment

Windsor University Faculty Association (WUFA) / Association des professeurs de l'Université Windsor
Kerr House, 366 Sunset Ave., Windsor ON N9B 3P4
Tel: 519-253-3000; *Fax:* 519-977-6154
wufa@uwindsor.ca
www.wufa.ca
www.facebook.com/215414038490229
twitter.com/_WUFA
Overview: A small local organization founded in 1963
Mission: To act as the exclusive bargaining agent for all academic staff & librarians at the University of Windsor at any stages of their career whether it be employed on a permanent or limited term contract, full-time or sessional appointment, tenure-track or tenured, arriving or departing.
Affliation(s): Canadian Association of University Teachers; Ontario Confederation of University Faculty Associations; National Union of the Canadian Association of University Teachers; Canadian Labour Congress
Chief Officer(s):
Brian E. Brown, President
brown2v@uwindsor.ca
Membership: *Member Profile:* Professors; sessional instructors; librarians; *Committees:* Grievance; Health & Safety; Negotiating; Retirement & Benefits; Sessional; Status of Women, Diversity & Equity Action

Windsor Volunteers for Literacy *See* Windsor Public Library Adult Literacy Program

Windsor Women Working with Immigrant Women (WWWWIW)
500 Ouelette Ave., 3rd Floor, Windsor ON N9A 1B3
Tel: 519-973-5588; *Fax:* 519-973-1534
info@wwwwiw.org
www.wwwwiw.org
Overview: A small local charitable organization founded in 1981 overseen by Ontario Council of Agencies Serving Immigrants
Mission: To assist first generation Canadians to be full & productive members of society
Affliation(s): Teachers of English as a Second Language; National Action Committee on the Status of Women
Chief Officer(s):
Padmini Raju, Executive Director, 519-973-5588 Ext. 11
padmini@wwwwiw.org
Sandra McLean, EAS Coordinator, 519-973-5588 Ext. 17
sandra@wwwwiw.org
Philippine Ishak, Coordinator, 519-973-5588 Ext. 21
philippine@wwwwiw.org
Scholastica Lyanga, Project Manager, 519-973-5588 Ext. 19
scholastica@wwwwiw.org
Finances: *Annual Operating Budget:* $50,000-$100,000
Staff Member(s): 10; 20 volunteer(s)
Membership: 1-99
Activities: LINC classes; Women's Circle; In-Depth, support & group counselling; citizenship class; support services; introduction to self-employment; child care

Windsor/Essex County Parents of Multiple Births Association
7515 Forest Glade Dr., Windsor ON N8T 3P5
Tel: 519-948-5545
Other Communication: suppor@PombaWindsor.com
windsor.essex@multiplebirthscanada.org
www.pombawindsor.com
Overview: A small local organization overseen by Multiple Births Canada
Mission: To improve and promote the health and well-being of multiple birth families before, during and after pregnancy.
Chief Officer(s):
Christine Prieur, Co-President
Valerie Hodgins, Co-President
Membership: *Fees:* $40; *Member Profile:* Parents of twins, triplets and higher order multiples
Activities: *Library*

Windsor-Essex *Voir* Réseau du patrimoine franco-ontarien

Windsor-Essex Children's Aid Society (WECAS)
1671 Riverside Dr. East, Windsor ON N8Y 5B5
Tel: 519-256-1171; *Fax:* 519-256-2739
Toll-Free: 800-265-4844
foundation@wecas.on.ca
www.wecaf.on.ca
Overview: A small local organization founded in 1899
Mission: Dedicated to the well being & safety of every child by advocating for & partnering with our children, families & communities
Member of: Ontario Association of Children's Aid Societies
Chief Officer(s):
William Bevan, Executive Director
Staff Member(s): 400; 250 volunteer(s)
Activities: Summer camps; holiday assistance programs; independent living program; public education

Windsor-Essex County Real Estate Board
3020 Deziel Dr., Windsor ON N8W 5H8
Tel: 519-966-6432; *Fax:* 519-966-4469
info@windsorrealestate.com
www.windsorrealestate.com
www.facebook.com/wecrealtors
twitter.com/wecrealtors
www.youtube.com/wecrealtors
Previous Name: Border Cities Real Estate Board
Merged from: **Windsor Real Estate Board; South Essex Real Estate Board**
Overview: A small local organization founded in 1918 overseen by Ontario Real Estate Association
Member of: Canadian Real Estate Association
Chief Officer(s):
Krista Del Gatto, Executive Officer
Activities: *Library*

Windsor-Essex Down Syndrome Parent Association
#206, 5060 Tecumseh Rd. East, Windsor ON N8T 1C1
Tel: 519-973-6486
info@upaboutdown.org
www.upaboutdown.org
Also Known As: Up About Down
Overview: A small local charitable organization founded in 1990
Mission: To enhance the lives of individuals with Down syndrome & their families; To provide positive & accurate information through advocacy & education thereby raising awareness throughout the community
Membership: *Member Profile:* Parents of children with Down syndrome

Windsor-Essex Regional Chamber of Commerce
2575 Ouellette Place, Windsor ON N8X 1L9
Tel: 519-966-3696
info@windsorchamber.org
www.windsorchamber.org
www.linkedin.com/groups?home=&gid=2762020
www.facebook.com/125412597496221
twitter.com/WERCofC
Overview: A medium-sized local organization founded in 1876
Mission: To serve the business community of Windsor & district by providing networking opportunities, & by communicating positions & opinions on government policy & other issues on behalf of its membership.
Member of: Ontario Chamber of Commerce; Canadian Chamber of Commerce; Better Business Bureau
Chief Officer(s):
Carolyn Brown, Chair
Matt Marchand, President & CEO
mmarchand@windsorchamber.org
Finances: *Funding Sources:* Membership fees
Staff Member(s): 10
Membership: 1,200; *Committees:* After Business; BEA; Transportation; Environment & Energy; Membership
Activities: *Library* Open to public

Windsor-Essex Therapeutic Riding Association (WETRA) / Association d'équitation thérapeutique Windsor-Essex
3323 North Maklen Rd., RR#2, Essex ON N8M 2X6
Tel: 519-726-7682; *Fax:* 519-726-4403
wetra@on.aibn.com
www.wetra.ca
Overview: A small local charitable organization founded in 1969
Mission: To improve the quality of life of physically, emotionally, mentally challenged persons through equine related therapy
Member of: Canadian Therapeutic Riding Association
Affliation(s): Ontario Therapeutic Riding Association
Chief Officer(s):
Sue Klotzer, Program Director
sueklotzer@wetra.ca
Finances: *Annual Operating Budget:* $100,000-$250,000; *Funding Sources:* United Way; Donations; Bingo
Staff Member(s): 7; 80 volunteer(s)
Membership: 200 riders
Activities: Offering therapeutic riding & horse shows; Hosting an open house, benefit horse show, & golf tournament; *Awareness Events:* Ride-a-Thon, March

Wine Council of Ontario
PO Box 4000, 4890 Victoria Ave. North, Vineland ON L0R 2E0
Tel: 905-684-8070; *Fax:* 905-562-1993
info@winesofontario.org
winecountryontario.ca
www.facebook.com/WineCountryOntario
twitter.com/winecountryont
Overview: A medium-sized provincial organization founded in 1974
Mission: A non-profit trade association which plays a leadership role in the marketing, promotion, and future directions of the Ontario wine industry
Chief Officer(s):
Magdalena Kaiser-Smit, Director, Public Relations, Marketing & Tourism
magdalena@winesofontario.org
Finances: *Annual Operating Budget:* $500,000-$1.5 Million; *Funding Sources:* Membership dues
Staff Member(s): 9
Membership: Represents 81 winery properties; *Fees:* $1,000 + marketing fee

Wine Writers' Circle of Canada
PO Box 545, Stn. Etobicoke B, Toronto ON M9W 5L4
Tel: 416-410-0086
www.winewriterscircle.ca
Overview: A small local organization founded in 1985
Mission: To provide a forum for information sharing, education & maintenance of professional standards in the wine writer & educator professions
Chief Officer(s):
Sadie Darby, Administrator
Staff Member(s): 2; 4 volunteer(s)
Membership: 35 individual; *Fees:* $150
Activities: *Rents Mailing List:* Yes

Wings & Heros
10 Pridham Cres., Angus ON L0M 1B2
Tel: 705-424-4213; *Fax:* 705-424-3907
admin@wingsandheros.com
www.wingsandheros.com
www.facebook.com/205054412999
Also Known As: Mentors In Motion
Overview: A small national organization
Mission: To promote the concept of NetWeaving for business women; to help business women connect with people they can trust
Membership: *Fees:* $50

Winkler & District Chamber of Commerce
185 Main St., Winkler MB R6W 1B4
Tel: 204-325-9758; *Fax:* 204-325-8290
chamber@winkleronline.com
www.winklerchamber.com
Overview: A small local organization founded in 1922
Mission: To represent the business community by providing & coordinating activities that support a vibrant business environment
Member of: Manitoba & Canadian Chamber of Commerce
Chief Officer(s):
Kenton Doerksen, President
kdoerksen@gtp.mb.ca
Myrna Hildebrand, Vice-President
mhildebrand@hcu.mb.ca
Brenda Storey, Executive Director, 204-325-9758 Ext. 102
brenda@winkleronline.com
Dianne Frieson, Manager, 204-325-9758 Ext. 100
chamber@winkleronline.com
Finances: *Annual Operating Budget:* $100,000-$250,000; *Funding Sources:* City of Winkler
Staff Member(s): 1; 18 volunteer(s)
Membership: 240; *Fees:* $50-$300
Awards:
• P.W. Enns Business Achievement Awards (Award)

Winkler & District United Way
PO Box 1528, Winkler MB R6W 4B4
Tel: 204-829-3843
unitedway.wix.com/winkleranddistrict
www.facebook.com/152819198203?ref=nf
Overview: A small local organization overseen by United Way of Canada - Centraide Canada

Winnipeg Association of Non-Teaching Employees (WANTE) / Association des employés non enseignants de Winnipeg
#111, 1555 St. James St., Winnipeg MB R3H 1B5

Tel: 204-953-0250; *Fax:* 204-953-0259
wante@wante.org
www.wante.org
Overview: A small local organization
Chief Officer(s):
Gale Hladik, President
Membership: *Fees:* $5 one time fee

Winnipeg Association of Public Service Officers (WAPSO) / Association des agents de services au public de Winnipeg
#2705, 83 Garry St., Winnipeg MB R3C 4J9
Tel: 204-925-4120; *Fax:* 204-925-4128
wapsoadmin@mts.net
www.wapso.ca
Overview: A medium-sized local organization founded in 1969
Chief Officer(s):
Robert Young, Executive Director
Andrew Weremy, President
Alex Regiec, 1st Vice-President
Michael Robinson, 2nd Vice-President
Finances: *Annual Operating Budget:* $250,000-$500,000; *Funding Sources:* Membership dues
Staff Member(s): 4; 15 volunteer(s)
Membership: 625; *Member Profile:* Supervisory, professionals & administrative

Winnipeg Board of Trade *See* Winnipeg Chamber of Commerce

Winnipeg Branch *See* Manitoba Genealogical Society Inc.

Winnipeg Building & Construction Trades Council *See* Manitoba Building & Construction Trades Council

Winnipeg Centraide *See* United Way of Winnipeg

Winnipeg Chamber of Commerce (WCC) / Chambre de commerce de Winnipeg
#100, 259 Portage Ave., Winnipeg MB R3B 2A9
Tel: 204-944-8484; *Fax:* 204-944-8492
info@winnipeg-chamber.com
www.winnipeg-chamber.com
www.linkedin.com/company/the-winnipeg-chamber-of-commerce?trk=fc_badge
www.facebook.com/WpgChamber
twitter.com/wpgchamber
www.youtube.com/wpgchamber
Previous Name: Winnipeg Board of Trade
Overview: A medium-sized local organization founded in 1873
Mission: To act as the voice of business in Winnipeg; To foster an environment in which Winnipeg businesses can proper
Chief Officer(s):
David Angus, President & Chief Executive Officer, 204-944-3301
dangus@winnipeg-chamber.com
Chuck Davidson, Vice-President, Policy, 204-944-3316
cdavidson@winnipeg-chamber.com
Karen Weiss, Vice-President, Finance & Operations, 204-944-3305
kweiss@winnipeg-chamber.com
Christine Ens, Director, Membership & Marketing, 204-944-3313
cens@winnipeg-chamber.com
Wendy Stephenson, Director, Strategic Initiatives, 204-944-3317
wstephenson@winnipeg-chamber.com
Stacia Franz, Coordinator, Communications, 204-944-3306
sfranz@winnipeg-chamber.com
Marion Wong, Coordinator, Information, 204-944-8484
info@winnipeg-chamber.com
Finances: *Funding Sources:* Membership dues; Sponsorships
Membership: 2,060+ companies, representing close to 90,000 employees; *Fees:* Schedule available, based upon number of full-time Winnipeg employees
Activities: Promoting Winnipeg businesses; Engaging in lobbying & advocacy activities
Awards:
• The Winnipeg Chamber of Commerce Spirit of Winnipeg Awards (Award)
The following categories will be recognized for innovation: small businesses, with revenues less than $10 million; medium businesses, with revenues of $10-$75 million; large businesses, with revenues over $75 million; start-up businesses, that have been operating for under three years; not-for-profit organizations; & charities*Location:* Winnipeg, Manitoba*Deadline:* December
Meetings/Conferences: • Winnipeg Chamber of Commerce 2015 6th Annual Spirit of Winnipeg Awards, March, 2015, Winnipeg, MB
Scope: Provincial
Description: A presentation of awards to honour innvoation in Winnipeg
Contact Information: Events Coordinator: Yanik Ottenbreit, Phone: 204-944-3306, E-mail: yottenbreit@winnipeg-chamber.com
• Winnipeg 2015 State of the City Address, 2015, Winnipeg, MB
Scope: Provincial
Attendance: 1,100
Description: A presentation by Mayor Brian Bowman
Contact Information: Events Coordinator: Yanik Ottenbreit, Phone: 204-944-3306, E-mail: yottenbreit@winnipeg-chamber.com
• Winnipeg Chamber of Commerce 2015 25th Annual Golf Clssic, June, 2015, Winnipeg, MB
Scope: Provincial
Description: An annual golf tournament since 1990.
Contact Information: Events Coordinator: Yanik Ottenbreit, Phone: 204-944-3306, E-mail: yottenbreit@winnipeg-chamber.com
• Winnipeg Chamber of Commerce 2015 Annual General Meeting, October, 2015, Winnipeg, MB
Scope: Provincial
Description: An examination of the organization's goals & objectives & finances
Contact Information: Events Coordinator: Yanik Ottenbreit, Phone: 204-944-3306, E-mail: yottenbreit@winnipeg-chamber.com
Publications:
• The Chamber Connected [a publication of the Winnipeg Chamber of Commerce]
Type: Newsletter; *Frequency:* 3 pa; *Accepts Advertising*
Profile: Chamber happenings, policies, events, & new members
• The Chamber E-Wire: The E-Newsletter of the Winnipeg Chamber of Commerce
Type: Newsletter; *Frequency:* Weekly; *Accepts Advertising*
Profile: Chamber issues, actions, & events
• Marketplace: Innovation, Strategy, & Leadership [a publication of the Winnipeg Chamber of Commerce]
Type: Magazine; *Frequency:* Bimonthly; *Accepts Advertising*; *Editor:* Jon Waldman
Profile: Chamber news, profiles, columns, & feature articles
• Winnipeg Chamber Member Directory
Type: Directory; *Accepts Advertising*
Profile: A directory to connect users with trusted member companies of the Winnipeg Chamber of Commerce
• Winnipeg Chamber of Commerce Annual Report
Type: Yearbook; *Frequency:* Annually
Profile: A year-in-review summary in conjunction with the annual general meeting

Winnipeg Clinic Employees Association (WCEA)
c/o Winnipeg Clinic, 425 St. Mary Ave., Winnipeg MB R3C 0N2
Tel: 204-782-6861; *Fax:* 204-957-1860
Overview: A small local licensing organization founded in 1981
Chief Officer(s):
Sherryl Dillabough, President
sherryld@gosympatico.ca
Finances: *Annual Operating Budget:* Less than $50,000
Membership: 150; *Fees:* $5 biweekly; *Member Profile:* Medical support staff

Winnipeg Construction Association
1447 Waverly St., Winnipeg MB R3T 0P7
Tel: 204-775-8664; *Fax:* 204-783-6446
wca@winnipegconstruction.ca
www.winnipegconstruction.ca
Also Known As: Manitoba Construction Association
Overview: A medium-sized local organization overseen by Canadian Construction Association
Mission: To encourage a high level of standards among the construction industry in Manitoba & to promote the industry as a whole
Member of: Canadian Construction Association
Chief Officer(s):
Ryan Einarson, President
Ronald Hambley, Executive Vice-President
Membership: 700+; *Fees:* $2400 regular; $875 professional/associate; *Member Profile:* Commercial contractors & suppliers in Manitoba

Winnipeg Executives Association (WEA)
#503, 386 Broadway Ave., Winnipeg MB R3C 3R6
Tel: 204-947-9766
weaadmin@wpgexecs.ca
www.wpgexecs.ca
Overview: A small international organization founded in 1923
Mission: To enhance, develop & promote business opportunities available to our members through networking & direct contacts with Winnipeg's business leaders in a spirit of fellowship & friendship
Chief Officer(s):
Geoff Powell, Executive Director
gap@strauss.ca
Finances: *Annual Operating Budget:* $100,000-$250,000; *Funding Sources:* Membership dues
Staff Member(s): 1
Membership: 125; *Fees:* $1134; *Member Profile:* Owners, presidents; *Committees:* Membership; Programme; Attendance; Leads
Activities: Golf Days; Presidents Ball; Holiday Party; Associates Day; Spouse/Guest Day; Inspirational Day

Winnipeg Film Group (WFG)
#304, 100 Arthur St., Winnipeg MB R3B 1H3
Tel: 204-925-3456; *Fax:* 204-942-6799
info@winnipegfilmgroup.com
www.winnipegfilmgroup.com
Overview: A small local charitable organization founded in 1974
Mission: To enhance the art of film by providing equal opportunities to make, view & discuss film within a greater artistic & social community
Member of: Independent Film & Video Alliance; Artspace
Chief Officer(s):
Cecilia Araneda, Executive Director
cecilia@winnipegfilmgroup.com
Staff Member(s): 14
Membership: *Fees:* Schedule available; *Member Profile:* Independent filmmakers; *Committees:* Community Engagement; Finance; Board Development
Activities: Workshops; screenings; film production assistance; grants to filmmakers; distribution; promotion; *Library*

Winnipeg Foundation
#1350, One Lombard Pl., Winnipeg MB R3B 0X3
Tel: 204-944-9474; *Fax:* 204-942-2987
Toll-Free: 877-974-3631
info@wpgfdn.org
www.wpgfdn.org
www.facebook.com/wpgfdn
www.twitter.com/winnipegfdn
www.youtube.com/user/winnipegfoundation
Overview: A small local charitable organization founded in 1921
Mission: Community trust for charitable, educational & cultural purposes in Greater Winnipeg
Chief Officer(s):
Richard L. Frost, CEO
Staff Member(s): 11

Winnipeg Gliding Club (WGC)
PO Box 1255, Winnipeg MB R3C 2Y4
Tel: 204-735-2868
info@wgc.mb.ca
www.wgc.mb.ca
Overview: A small local organization
Mission: The Winnipeg Gliding Club is a non-profit organization dedicated to the promotion of gliding and soaring
Member of: Soaring Association of Canada
Membership: 70; *Fees:* $25-$450
Awards:
• The Cracked Head Award (Award)
Eligibility: Tow pilots

Winnipeg Harvest Inc.
1085 Winnipeg Ave., Winnipeg MB R3E 0S2
Tel: 204-982-3663; *Fax:* 204-775-4180
info@winnipegharvest.org
www.winnipegharvest.org
www.facebook.com/profile.php?id=529150187#!/wpgharvest
twitter.com/WinnipegHarvest
www.youtube.com/results?search_query=winnipeg+harvest&aq=f
Overview: A small local charitable organization founded in 1984
Mission: To collect & distribute food to feed those in our community who struggle to feed themselves & their families & to maximize public awareness of hunger while working towards long term solutions to hunger & poverty
Affliation(s): Canadian Association of Food Banks
Chief Officer(s):
Jody Hecht, President
Finances: *Annual Operating Budget:* $500,000-$1.5 Million
Staff Member(s): 12; 200 volunteer(s)

Activities: Food Bank; Share Your Thanks, Oct.; Hunger Count, fall; *Speaker Service:* Yes; *Library* Open to public

Winnipeg Humane Society (WHS)
45 Hurst Way, Winnipeg MB R3T 0R3
Tel: 204-982-2021; *Fax:* 204-663-9401
reception@humanesociety.mb.ca
www.winnipeghumanesociety.ca
www.facebook.com/WinnipegHumaneSociety
twitter.com/thewhs
Overview: A small provincial charitable organization
Mission: To protect animals from suffering & promoting their welfare & dignity
Member of: Canadian Federation of Humane Societies
Chief Officer(s):
Bill McDonald, Executive Director
Nancy McQuade, President
Patricia Nesbitt, Vice-President
Staff Member(s): 50; 250 volunteer(s)

Winnipeg Labour Council
#504, 275 Broadway Ave., Winnipeg MB R3C 4M6
Tel: 204-942-0522; *Fax:* 204-942-7396
info@winnipeglabour.ca
www.winnipeglabour.ca
www.facebook.com/pages/Winnipeg-Labour-Council/291591290865352
twitter.com/DaveSour
Overview: A small local organization
Chief Officer(s):
Dave Sauer, President
sauer@winnipeglabour.ca

Winnipeg Musicians' Association
#201, 180 Market Ave. East, Winnipeg MB R3B 0P7
Tel: 204-943-4803; *Fax:* 204-943-5029
wma190@mts.net
winnipegmusicians.ca
Also Known As: AFM Local 190
Overview: A small local organization founded in 1902
Member of: American Federation of Musicians of the United States & Canada
Chief Officer(s):
Cornelius Godri, President
James Jay Harrison, Vice-President
Tony Cyre, Secretary-Treasurer
Staff Member(s): 2
Membership: 600; *Fees:* $170 yearly dues; $136 initiation fee; *Member Profile:* Professional musicians of Manitoba

Winnipeg Ostomy Association (WOA)
#204, 825 Sherbrook St., Winnipeg MB R3A 1M5
Tel: 204-234-2022
woainfo@mts.net
www.ostomy-winnipeg.ca
Overview: A small local charitable organization founded in 1972 overseen by Canadian Ostomy Society
Mission: To assist people with ostomy & related surgeries in Winnipeg and the surrounding area
Chief Officer(s):
Lorrie Pismenny, President
Finances: *Funding Sources:* Membership dues; donations
Membership: 280; *Fees:* $40
Publications:
• Inside Out
Type: Newsletter; *Frequency:* 6 pa

Winnipeg Philatelic Society (WPS)
PO Box 1425, Winnipeg MB R3C 2Z1
Tel: 204-896-3800
rpenko@shaw.ca
www.wps.mb.ca
Also Known As: Winnipeg Stamp Club
Overview: A small local organization founded in 1900
Chief Officer(s):
R. Stanley, President
R. Thompson, Vice-President
J. Lipsey, Secretary
Finances: *Funding Sources:* Membership dues
5 volunteer(s)
Membership: 160; *Fees:* $35; $25 senior/spouse; $15 junior; $350 life
Activities: *Library*

Winnipeg Police Association (WPA) / Association de la police de Winnipeg
#70, 81 Garry St., Winnipeg MB R3C 4J9
Tel: 204-957-1579; *Fax:* 204-949-1674
info@wpa.mb.ca
www.winnipegpoliceassociation.ca
www.facebook.com/169240943135061
twitter.com/wpgwpa
pinterest.com/winnipegpolicea
Overview: A medium-sized local organization founded in 1972
Mission: To support its members & act as the bargaining agent in all contractual matters
Member of: Canadian Police Association
Affliation(s): Manitoba Police Association; Alberta Federation of Police Associations; Calgary Police Association; Edmonton Police Association; British Columbia Federation of Police Officers; Vancouver Police Union; Winnipeg Police Credit Union; Winnipeg Police Service; New Brunswick Police Association; Police Association of Nova Scotia; Royal Newfoundland Constabulary Association; Durham Regional Police Association; Ontario Provincial Police Association; Ottawa Police Association; Peel Regional Police Association; Police Association of Ontario; Toronto Police Association; Montreal Police Brotherhood
Chief Officer(s):
Mike Sutherland, President
Membership: 1,400+ individual; *Member Profile:* Police officers & support staff
Activities: *Speaker Service:* Yes

Winnipeg Real Estate Board (WREB)
1240 Portage Ave., Winnipeg MB R3G 0T6
Tel: 204-786-8854; *Fax:* 204-784-2343
websupport@winnipegrealtors.ca
www.winnipegrealtors.ca
www.youtube.com/user/winnipegrealtors
Overview: A medium-sized local organization founded in 1903 overseen by Manitoba Real Estate Association
Mission: To serve members & to promote the benefits of organized real estate
Member of: The Canadian Real Estate Association
Affliation(s): Winnipeg Chamber of Commerce
Finances: *Funding Sources:* Membership dues
Membership: *Member Profile:* Real estate salespeople & brokers
Activities: Citizens Hall of Fame; Housing Opportunity Partnership; *Library*
Awards:
• Citizens Hall of Fame (Award)
• Board Builders Awards (Award)
• Medallion Awards (Award)
• Rookie of the Year (Award)
• Community Services & Commercial Awards (Award)
• Member Recognition (25 year & 35 year) (Award)

Winnipeg Society of Financial Analysts *See* CFA Society Winnipeg

Winnipeg Symphony Orchestra Inc. (WSO)
#101, 555 Main St., Winnipeg MB R3B 1C3
Tel: 204-949-3999; *Fax:* 204-956-4271
lmarks@wso.mb.ca
www.wso.mb.ca
www.facebook.com/WinnipegSymphony
twitter.com/WpgSymphony
www.youtube.com/WinnipegSymphony
Overview: A large local charitable organization founded in 1948 overseen by Orchestras Canada
Mission: To perform a wide variety of orchestral music including classical, contemporary, pop & children's music in Manitoba & Northwestern Ontario
Chief Officer(s):
Timothy E. Burt, Chair & President
Alexander Mickelthwate, Music Director
lmarks@wso.mb.ca
Trudy Schroeder, Executive Director
tschroeder@wso.mb.ca
Finances: *Annual Operating Budget:* Greater than $5 Million; *Funding Sources:* Federal, provincial & municipal governments; corporate & individual donors
Staff Member(s): 100; 100 volunteer(s)
Membership: 5,000-14,999; *Committees:* Women's
Activities: Annual new music festival; *Library:* Music Library;

Winnipeg Tribal Council *See* Keewatin Tribal Council

Winnipeg Vegetarian Association (WVA)
PO Box 2721, Stn. Main, Winnipeg MB R3C 4B3
Tel: 204-889-5789
wva@ivu.org
www.ivu.org/wva/
Overview: A small local organization founded in 1993
Mission: To foster & encourage vegetarianism through social & educational events
Member of: Vegetarian Union of North America
Affliation(s): North America Vegetarian Society; American Vegan Society
Chief Officer(s):
Dennis Bayomi, Founder/Coordinator
Finances: *Annual Operating Budget:* Less than $50,000; *Funding Sources:* Membership fees
11 volunteer(s)
Membership: 150+; *Fees:* $10-100 individual; $15-150 family; $5-50 senior/student; *Member Profile:* Vegetarian or interest in becoming vegetarian; *Committees:* Health Professionals; Restaurants
Activities: *Awareness Events:* World Vegetarian Day, Oct. 1; World Vegetarian Month, Oct.; National Nutrition Month, March; *Speaker Service:* Yes

Winnipeg Youth Orchestras
Winnipeg MB
Tel: 204-284-0074
administrator@winnipegyouthorchestras.ca
www.winnipegyouthorchestras.ca
www.facebook.com/winnipegyouthorchestras
Also Known As: Junior Strings; Youth Concert Orchestra; Youth Symphony Orchestra
Previous Name: Manitoba Schools' Orchestra
Overview: A large local organization founded in 1923 overseen by Orchestras Canada
Chief Officer(s):
Nancy Read, Contact
nancy15@mymts.net

Winnipeg's Contemporary Dancers
#204, 211 Bannatyne Ave., Winnipeg MB R3B 3P2
Tel: 204-452-0229
wcd@mts.net
www.winnipegscontemporarydancers.ca
www.facebook.com/WpgContemps
twitter.com/WpgContemps
plus.google.com/107457430919121766901
Previous Name: Contemporary Dancers Canada
Overview: A small local charitable organization founded in 1964
Mission: To create a place on the local, national and international arts landscape that enables vital intersections, linkages and exchange among dance creators, dance interpreters, spectators and communities
Chief Officer(s):
Kathy Fenton, General Manager

WinSport Canada
88 Canada Olympic Rd. SW, Calgary AB T3B 5R5
Tel: 403-247-5452; *Fax:* 403-286-7213
info@coda.ca
www.winsportcanada.ca
www.facebook.com/CanadaOlympicPark
twitter.com/winsportcanada
Previous Name: Calgary Olympic Development Association
Overview: A small local organization founded in 1956
Mission: WinSport Canada is a not-for-profit association that develops & sustains the sporting facilities of Canada Olympic Park. It supports national sports organizations & subsidizes unique facilities used by top athletes & the public.
Member of: Calgary Society of Associations Executives
Affliation(s): Canadian Olympic Committee; Canadian Paralympic Committee
Chief Officer(s):
Trevor Nakka, Chair
Staff Member(s): 260; 200 volunteer(s)
Activities: Fundraising for Canada Wins, a winter sports institute;

Wired Woman Society
#395, 280 Nelson St., Vancouver BC V6B 2E2
Tel: 604-605-8825; *Fax:* 604-648-9521
vancouver@wiredwoman.com
www.wiredwoman.com
Overview: A small local organization
Mission: To create an open environment that encourages women to explore opportunities in information technology & to build successful careers that will allow them to play a positive role in the growth & development of the information age
Chief Officer(s):
Marnie Larson, President
Staff Member(s): 4

Activities: Networking opportunities; career resources; community & academic presentations; role-modeling & mentoring for members

Wolfville Historical Society
259 Main St., Wolfville NS B4P 1C6
Tel: 902-542-9775
randallhouse@live.ca
www.wolfvillehs.ednet.ns.ca
Overview: A small local charitable organization founded in 1941
Mission: To operate the Randall House Museum
Chief Officer(s):
John Vaillancourt, President
Heather Watts, Archivist, 902-542-0307
Membership: *Fees:* $20 individual; $30 family
Activities: *Library:* Wolfville Historical Society Photograph Archive; Open to public
Publications:
• Wolfville Historical Society Newsletter
Type: Newsletter
Profile: News & events of the society

Wolseley & District Chamber of Commerce
PO Box 519, Wolseley SK S0G 5H0
Tel: 306-698-2252; *Fax:* 306-698-2750
www.wolseleychamber.net
Overview: A small local organization
Chief Officer(s):
S. Harris, Secretary
gsharris@sasktel.net
W. Stewart Scott, Chair

Wolverines Wheelchair Sports Association
10 Knowledge Way, Grande Prairie AB T8W 2V9
Tel: 780-402-3331; *Fax:* 780-402-3318
info@gpwolverines.com
www.gpwolverines.com
Overview: A small local organization founded in 1990
Mission: To provide people with disabilities the opportunity to engage in physcial & recreational activities.
Membership: *Fees:* Schedule available

The Women & Environments Education & Development Foundation ***See*** Women's Healthy Environments Network

Women Business Owners of Manitoba (WBOM)
PO Box 2748, Winnipeg MB R3C 4B3
Tel: 204-775-7981; *Fax:* 204-897-8094
info@wbom.ca
www.wbom.ca
www.linkedin.com/groups?mostPopular=&gid=2573420
www.facebook.com/WomenBusinessOwnersOfManitoba
Overview: A small provincial organization
Mission: Supports & inspires excellence, learning & growth in business
Chief Officer(s):
Lucy Camara, President
lcamara@olatechcorp.com
Tracy Ducharme, Vice-President
tracy@veritus.ca
Membership: 165; *Fees:* $399 regular; $1,575 corporate; $399 friend
Activities: *Awareness Events:* Annual Golf Tournament
Awards:
• Manitoba Woman Entrepreneur of the Year Award (Award)

Women Educating in Self-Defense Training (WEST)
Tel: 604-876-6390
wenlido.west@gmail.com
wenlido-west.webs.com
Also Known As: Wenlido WEST
Overview: A small provincial organization founded in 1976
Affliation(s): Women in Self-Defense Education
Finances: *Annual Operating Budget:* Less than $50,000
3 volunteer(s)
Membership: 20; *Fees:* $15
Activities: Teaching self-defense to women & their children; *Speaker Service:* Yes

Women Entrepreneurs of Saskatchewan Inc. (WE)
#108, 502 Cope Way, Saskatoon SK S7T 0G3
Tel: 306-477-7173; *Fax:* 306-477-7175
Toll-Free: 800-879-6331
info@womenentrepreneurs.sk.ca
www.womenentrepreneurs.sk.ca
www.linkedin.com/company/1277529
www.facebook.com/womenentrepreneurssk
Overview: A medium-sized provincial organization founded in 1995
Mission: To provide programs & service to women who are considering a business, starting a business, or operating an existing business
Member of: Women's Enterprise Initiative
Affliation(s): Western Economic Diversification Canada
Chief Officer(s):
Irene Boychuk, Chair
8 volunteer(s)
Membership: 800; *Fees:* $75 full; $25 associate
Activities: Offering training & seminars & financing; *Library:* Resource Centre for Members; Open to public
Awards:
• Member of the Year (Award)
Publications:
• The Bulletin [a publication of the Women Entrepreneurs of Saskatchewan Inc.]
Type: Newsletter; *Frequency:* Monthly
Profile: Information about the association plus training events & conferences across Saskatchewan
• Women Entrepreneurs of Saskatchewan Inc.'s Annual Report
Type: Yearbook; *Frequency:* Annually
Profile: Contents include financial statements & the auditor's report

Regina Office
100 - 1925 Rose St., Regina SK S4P 3P1
Tel: 306-359-9732; *Fax:* 306-359-9739
Toll-Free: 800-879-6331

Women Expanding Business Network of Lanark County
Tel: 613-253-1802
lanarkcountyweb@rogers.com
www.facebook.com/lanarkweb
Overview: A small local organization founded in 1998
Mission: To connect & educate business women in Lanark County
Activities: Meetings; showcases; groups; keynote speakers

Women for Recreation, Information & Business (WRIB)
PO Box 1155, Stn. F, 50 Charles St. East, Toronto ON M4Y 2T8
Tel: 416-925-9872
social@wrib.ca
www.wrib.ca
Overview: A small local organization founded in 1991
Mission: To provide social, business & informational networking environment for lesbians, bisexual, transsexual & transgendered women with common goals & interests
Chief Officer(s):
Dee Paul, Chair
chair@wrib.ca
Membership: *Fees:* $36 single membership

Women Immigrants of London ***See*** WIL Employment Connections

Women in a Home Office
PO Box 369, #440, 10816 Macleod Trail South, Calgary AB T2J 5N8
Tel: 403-726-0785
Toll-Free: 800-615-7685
info@womeninahomeoffice.com
www.womeninahomeoffice.com
Overview: A small local organization founded in 2000
Mission: To support women working in a home based business &/or from a home office through network events, workshops, etc. on & off-line
Membership: *Fees:* $99; *Member Profile:* Chapters in Alberta, Manitoba & Ontario

Women in Capital Markets (WCM) / Les femmes sur les marchés financiers
#202, 720 Spadina Ave., Toronto ON M5S 2T9
Tel: 416-502-3614; *Fax:* 416-929-5256
admin@wcm.ca
www.wcm.ca
Overview: A small national organization founded in 1995
Mission: To enable capital markets professionals to reach their greatest potential for success; to advance woment within Canadian financial services
Chief Officer(s):
Kathryn Smith, Chair
Jennifer Reynolds, President
Finances: *Annual Operating Budget:* $100,000-$250,000; *Funding Sources:* Founding firms; sponsors; membership dues
Staff Member(s): 2; 100 volunteer(s)
Membership: 1200+; *Fees:* $197.75 full; $141.25 associate; $96.05 out of town member; $28.25 student; *Member Profile:* Professionals working in Capital Markets; Students; *Committees:* Awards; Benchmarking; Executive Coaching; External & Joint Events; Golf; High School Liaison; Marketing & Communications; Membership; Mentorship Program; Senior Women's Network; Sponsorship; University Connections; Vinifera; Website
Activities: Education & outreach; mentorship program;

Women In Crisis (Algoma) Inc. (WIC)
23 Oakland Ave., Sault Ste Marie ON P6A 2T2
Tel: 705-759-1230; *Fax:* 705-759-3239
Toll-Free: 877-759-1230
adminassist@wicalgoma.com
Also Known As: Oakland Place
Overview: A small local organization founded in 1979
Mission: To work towards the elimination of violence against women & their children; to provide a range of direct & indirect services for women who have or currently are experiencing abuse in their lives; to work within a feminist perspective to provide programs which facilitate the claiming of power by women
Affliation(s): Ontario Association of Interval & Transition Houses
Chief Officer(s):
E. Dale Kenney, Director, Community Relations & Finance
Norma Elliott, Director, Programs & Staff
Finances: *Annual Operating Budget:* $500,000-$1.5 Million; *Funding Sources:* Provincial government; United Way; Ministry of Health
Staff Member(s): 38
Membership: *Committees:* MCSS; MDF Housing; United Way; Bequests/Donation

Women in Film & Television - Toronto
#601, 110 Eglinton Ave. East, Toronto ON M4P 2Y1
Tel: 416-322-3430; *Fax:* 416-322-3703
wift@wift.com
www.wift.com
www.linkedin.com/groups/Women-in-Film-Television-Toronto-2908431
www.facebook.com/WIFT.Toronto
twitter.com/WIFT
vimeo.com/wift
Also Known As: WIFT-T
Previous Name: Toronto Women in Film & Television
Overview: A medium-sized provincial charitable organization founded in 1984
Mission: To provide year-round training programs, industry events, & professional awards for women & men in Canadian screen based media
Affliation(s): Women in Film Chapters (worldwide)
Chief Officer(s):
Prentiss Fraser, Chair
Heather Webb, Executive Director
Finances: *Annual Operating Budget:* $250,000-$500,000; *Funding Sources:* Membership fees; government; corporate; donations
Staff Member(s): 5; 50 volunteer(s)
Membership: 850; *Fees:* $148.75 full; $106.25 associate; $144.50 friend; $42.50 Senior/student; *Member Profile:* Open to all women working in any facet of the film & television industry residing in Ontario; Friend category for both women & men who don't qualify for other membership categories but wish to take part in WIFT-T's programs; *Committees:* Professional Development, Member Services, Special Events, Fundraising, Profile & Policy
Activities: Professional development workshops; monthy networking breakfasts; advanced training courses; annual awards gala; booths at industry events; *Library:* Resource Centre; by appointment
Awards:
• The Crystal Awards - Annual Outstanding Achievement Awards (Award)

Women in Film & Television Alberta (WIFT-A)
c/o Luanne Morrow, Borden Ladner Gervais, #1000 Canterra Tower, 400 3rd Ave. SW, Calgary AB T2P 4H2
e-mail: admin@wifta.ca
www.wifta.ca
www.linkedin.com/groups/WIFTA-Women-in-Film-Television-4165901
www.facebook.com/groups/51921469116/
twitter.com/WIFTAlberta

Also Known As: WIFT Alberta
Overview: A medium-sized provincial organization
Mission: WIFT-A is a non-profit organization that promotes and assists the professional development, equitable treatment, recognition of achievements and the creation of new opportunities for professionals, especially women in the film, video, multimedia and television industries
Chief Officer(s):
Kathy Fedori, President
Coralie Braum, Vice-President
Astrid Kuhn, Treasurer
Membership: *Fees:* $32.50 voting members; $37.50 non-voting members; $17.50 student

Women in Film & Television Vancouver (WIFTV)
Dominion Building, #306, 207 West Hastings St., Vancouver BC V6B 1H7
Tel: 604-685-1152; *Fax:* 604-685-1124
info@womeninfilm.ca
www.womeninfilm.ca
www.facebook.com/Womeninfilm
twitter.com/WIFTV
www.youtube.com/user/wiftv
Overview: A medium-sized provincial organization founded in 1989
Mission: To support, advance, promote & celebrate the professional development & achievements of women working in British Columbia's film, television, video & multimedia industries
Member of: Women in Film & Television International; Alliance for Arts & Culture
Chief Officer(s):
Rachelle Chartrand, President
Michelle Billy Povill, Vice-President
Christine Larsen, Secretary
Finances: *Annual Operating Budget:* $100,000-$250,000
Staff Member(s): 2; 200 volunteer(s)
Membership: 750; *Fees:* $78.75-$157.50; *Member Profile:* Directors; writers; producers; actors; crew; *Committees:* Advocacy; Fundraising
Activities: Mentorship Program; Walking Talking Heads seminar; Career Cafe Seminars; Producers, Actors, Writers & Directors Workshops; Flash Forward; Film Festival for International Women's Day; Spotlight Gala; networking breakfasts; *Internships:* Yes; *Speaker Service:* Yes
Awards:
- Spotlights Awards Gala (Award)
- Artistic Merit Award (Award)
- WIFVV Scholarships (Award)

Women in Food Industry Management (WFIM)
c/o ADM Milling Company, 7585 Danbro Cres., Mississauga ON L5N 6P9
Fax: 905-883-9840
admin@wfim.ca
www.wfim.ca
Overview: A small national organization founded in 1984
Mission: To build a network of contacts among women at the management level in the food industry, for the exchange of ideas & information of importance to the industry & the members; tTo promote& encourage personal growth of members
Chief Officer(s):
Barbara Onyskow, Chair
Membership: *Fees:* $100

Women of the Word - Toronto (WOW)
536 Cunningham Dr., Maple ON L6A 2H2
Tel: 905-832-3275
blessingsmagazine@hotmail.ca
www.blessingsmagazine.ca
Overview: A medium-sized international organization
Mission: To inspire, teach, & help women grow in the Catholic community
Affliation(s): Archdiocese of Toronto
Chief Officer(s):
Mary Filangi, Publisher
mary.filangi@sympatico.ca
Finances: *Annual Operating Budget:* Less than $50,000
Activities: Publishing the "Blessings" magazine
Publications:
- Blessings [a publication of Women of the Word - Toronto]
Type: Magazine; *Editor:* Daniela Di Panfilo

Women on the Rise Telling her Story (WORTH)
5775 rue Saint-Jacques, Montréal QC H4A 2E8
Tel: 514-485-7418; *Fax:* 514-485-7418
womenontherise@bellnet.ca
Overview: A medium-sized local organization
Mission: To promote the well-being of women and their children, especially in the Black anglophone community, by offering them self-help activities and encouraging them to develop their potential.
Chief Officer(s):
Grace Campbell, Director

Women Who Excel Inc. (WWE)
9 Woodbridge Rd., Hamilton ON L8K 3C6
Tel: 905-547-7135; *Fax:* 905-547-7135
Toll-Free: 800-363-0268
info@womenwhoexcel.com
www.womenwhoexcel.com
Overview: A small local organization founded in 1989
Mission: To promote women in business & to get more business
Member of: Oakville Chamber of Commerce; Burlington Chamber of Commerce; Hamilton Chamber of Commerce
Chief Officer(s):
Christine Whitlock, President/Publisher
Finances: *Funding Sources:* User fees; memberships; advertising
Membership: 52; *Fees:* $60; *Member Profile:* Women in home-based or small retail businesses; organizations; media; politics
Activities: Networking dinners, breakfasts, & bingos to find & make contacts with other women in the Hamilton-Wentworth & Halton Regions; mini trade shows; seasonal fashion shows; *Internships:* Yes; *Speaker Service:* Yes; *Rents Mailing List:* Yes; *Library* Open to public by appointment

Women's & Gender Studies et Recherches Féministes (WGSRF)
c/o Rachel Bergen, Dept. of Women's Studies, University of Victoria, PO Box 3045, Stn. CSC, Victoria BC V8W 3P4
Other Communication: membership@cwsaacef.com
generalinfo@cwsaacef.com
www.wgsrf.com
Previous Name: Canadian Women's Studies Association / L'association canadienne des études sur les femmes (CWSA / ACÉF)
Overview: A small national organization founded in 1982
Mission: To foster & promote women's & gender studies as an academic field
Member of: Canadian Federation for the Humanities & Social Sciences
Chief Officer(s):
Annalee Lepp, President
Katie Aubrecht, Secretary
Rhiannon Bury, Treasurer
Finances: *Funding Sources:* Membership fees; Donations
Membership: *Fees:* $15 students & unwaged persons; $26 individuals (retired or low income); $70 individuals (waged 100,000); $100 individuals (waged $100,000); *Member Profile:* Women's & gender studies practitioners in Canada; Undergraduate & graduate students; Community activists; Policy researchers; *Committees:* Conference Program; Conference Local Organizing; Outstanding Scholarship Prize; Undergraduate Essay Prize; Graduate Essay Prize; Communications

Women's Art Association of Canada (WAAC)
23 Prince Arthur Ave., Toronto ON M5R 1B2
Tel: 416-922-2060
administration@womensartofcanada.ca
www.womensartofcanada.ca
Overview: A small national charitable organization founded in 1887
Mission: To provide scholarships for the arts through the following schools & colleges: The Royal Conservatory of Music of Toronto; The Ontario College of Art; The Faculty of Music, University of Toronto; The National Ballet School; Sheridan College
Membership: 7; *Fees:* $225 regular; $75 out of town/student
Activities: Fundraising events; art shows; recitals; *Library* by appointment

Women's Art Resource Centre (WARC)
#122, 401 Richmond St. West, Toronto ON M5V 3A8
Tel: 416-977-0097
warc@warc.net
www.warc.net
Also Known As: WARC Gallery
Overview: A small national organization founded in 1984
Staff Member(s): 3; 5 volunteer(s)
Activities: *Library*

Women's Association of the Mining Industry of Canada
c/o Vi Andersen, President, 140 Shanty Bay Rd., Barrie ON L4M 1E3
e-mail: scholarships@cogeco.ca
www.pdac.ca/wamic
Overview: A small national organization founded in 1921
Mission: To promote friendship among women whose interests are connected with the mining industry; to render service where possible to the mining industry or those connected therewith; & to participate in work which relates to the well-being of Canadian residents
Chief Officer(s):
Vi Andersen, President
Membership: 270 individual; *Fees:* $17 individual
Awards:
- National Geophysics Scholarship
Eligibility: Awarded annually to an undergraduate student who has attained the highest academic average on completion of third year in an accredited geophysics program at a qualified Canadian university*Deadline:* June 4 *Amount:* $1,000
- National Scholarship
Eligibility: Awarded annually to an undergraduate student enrolled in any of the above accredited programs at a qualified Canadian university who has attained the highest academic average on completion of third year*Deadline:* June 4 *Amount:* $1,000
- The Wood Bursary
Eligibility: Awarded annually to third and fourth year undergraduate students who can demonstrate financial need and who are enrolled in an accredited mining related program in a Canadian university. This bursary can be continued through re-application providing the scholar maintains good academic standing and the need prevails*Deadline:* June 4 *Amount:* $6,000

Women's Business Network of Ottawa (WBN)
#200, 435 St. Laurent Blvd., Ottawa ON K1K 2Z8
Tel: 613-749-5975; *Fax:* 613-745-8753
info@womensbusinessnetwork.ca
www.womensbusinessnetwork.ca
www.linkedin.com/groups?gid=2967196
www.facebook.com/WBNOttawa
twitter.com/WBN_Ottawa
Overview: A small local organization founded in 1981
Mission: To be the leading vehicle for business women to build business relationships; achieve success; celebrate their accomplishments & have fun doing it
Chief Officer(s):
Lynda Carter, President
lycarter@deloitte.ca
Finances: *Annual Operating Budget:* Less than $50,000
Staff Member(s): 1
Membership: 150; *Fees:* $220; *Member Profile:* Women business owners in commission sales or senior managers; *Committees:* Golf; Membership; Marketing & Communications; Events & Programming; Sponsorship
Activities: Monthly meetings; *Speaker Service:* Yes
Awards:
- Business Woman of the Year (Award)
- Businesswoman's achievement award (Award)

Women's Canadian Historical Society of Ottawa *See* Historical Society of Ottawa

The Women's Centre
#229, 1515 Rebecca St., Oakville ON L6G 5G8
Tel: 905-847-5520; *Fax:* 905-847-7413
www.haltonwomenscentre.org
www.facebook.com/pages/The-Halton-Womens-Centre/191885775004
twitter.com/HalWomensCentre
www.flickr.com/photos/haltonwomenscentre
Also Known As: Halton Women's Centre
Overview: A small local organization founded in 1991
Mission: To make a positive difference in the lives of women in transition, crisis or distress
Membership: *Fees:* $15

Women's Centre of Montréal / Centre des femes de Montréal
3585, rue St Urbain, Montréal QC H2X 2N6
Tél: 514-842-1066; *Téléc:* 514-842-1067
Autres numéros: emploi@centredesfemmesdemtl.org
cfmwcm@centredesfemmesdemtl.org
www.centredesfemmesdemtl.org
Aperçu: *Dimension:* petite; *Envergure:* locale; Organisme sans but lucratif; fondée en 1973

Mission: To provide front line services to women to promote their personal, social, psychological, & economic autonomy; To facilitate the integration of women into the labour market
Membre(s) du bureau directeur:
Johanne Bélisle, Executive Director
Finances: *Fonds:* Donations
Membre: *Montant de la cotisation:* $5
Activités: Offering services in English, French, Arabic, Spanish, & Creole; Providing workshops & presentations by employers; Offering a Community Internet Access Centre; Providing a professional clothing kiosk
Publications:
• Women's Centre of Montréal Annual Report
Type: Yearbook; *Frequency:* Annually

Women's Centre of Montreal / Centre des femmes de Montréal
3585, rue Saint-Urbain, Montréal QC H2X 2N6
Tél: 514-842-1066; *Téléc:* 514-842-1067
cfmwcm@centredesfemmes.com
www.centredesfemmesdemtl.org
Aperçu: *Dimension:* moyenne; *Envergure:* locale; fondée en 1973
Mission: The mission of the Women's Centre of Montréal is to provide services to help women help themselves. To accomplish its mission, the Centre offers educational and vocational training, information, counselling and referral services. The Centre communicates women's concerns to the public and acts as a catalyst for change regarding women's issues.
Membre(s) du bureau directeur:
Johanne Bélisle, Directrice générale
300 bénévole(s)
Membre: *Montant de la cotisation:* 5 $

Women's Counselling & Referral & Education Centre (WCREC)
#303B, 489 College St., Toronto ON M6G 1A5
Tel: 416-534-8458; *Fax:* 416-534-1704
generalmail@wcrec.org
www.plasmalife.com/WCRECsite/index.html
Overview: A medium-sized local charitable organization founded in 1976
Mission: To promote the mental & emotional well-being of women; To provide free community-based, alternative, non-medical mental health services in Toronto & in other areas through contact by phone & e-mail
Chief Officer(s):
Barbara Heron, President
Finances: *Funding Sources:* Ministry of Health & Long-Tem Care; City of Toronto
Staff Member(s): 19
Membership: *Fees:* $0 - $25; *Member Profile:* Women interested in feminist, anti-racist, & anti-oppression politics & activism
Activities: Offering referrals to counsellors, therapists, support groups, & other community organizations; Providing information & educational services to empower women

Women's Enterprise Centre of Manitoba / Centre d'entreprise des femmes du Manitoba
#100, 207 Donald St., Winnipeg MB R3C 1M5
Tel: 204-988-1860; *Fax:* 204-988-1871
Toll-Free: 800-203-2343
wecinfo@wecm.ca
www.wecm.ca
Previous Name: Manitoba Women's Enterprise Centre
Overview: A small provincial organization founded in 1994
Mission: To assist Manitoba women to start or expand businesses; to raise awareness of entrepreneurship & self-employment as a career option for girls & women
Member of: Women Business Owner of Manitoba; Winnipeg Chamber of Commerce; Manitoba Chamber of Commerce
Chief Officer(s):
Sandra Altner, CEO
Staff Member(s): 12
Activities: Business seminars; business advice; loan program; *Speaker Service:* Yes

Women's Executive Network (WXN) / Réseau des femmes exécutives (RFE)
#502, 180 Bloor St. West, Toronto ON M5S 2V6
Tel: 416-361-1475; *Fax:* 416-361-1652
Toll-Free: 866-465-3996
sbartley@wxnetwork.com
www.wxnetwork.com
Overview: A medium-sized national organization founded in 1997
Mission: Dedicated to the advancement & recognition of executive-minded women in the workplace
Chief Officer(s):
Pamela Jeffery, Founder, 416-361-1475 Ext. 224
pjeffery@wxnetwork.com
Melanie Walker, Vice President, Strategy and Program Development, International
mwalker@wxnetwork.com
Membership: *Fees:* $50

Women's Healthy Environments Network (WHEN)
#400, 215 Spadina Ave., Toronto ON M5T 2C7
Tel: 416-928-0880; *Fax:* 416-644-0116
office@womenshealthyenvironments.ca
www.womenshealthyenvironments.ca
www.facebook.com/WHENonlinex
twitter.com/WHENonline
www.youtube.com/user/WHENwomen
Previous Name: The Women & Environments Education & Development Foundation
Overview: A medium-sized national charitable organization founded in 1987
Mission: To provide a forum for communication; to conduct research on issues relating to women in their environments of planning, health, ecology, workplace design, community development & urban & rural sociology & economy
Affliation(s): National Action Committee on the Status of Women
Chief Officer(s):
Enida Kule, Chair
Finances: *Funding Sources:* Government; corporate; private foundations
Staff Member(s): 1
Activities: *Speaker Service:* Yes; *Library:* WEED Resource Centre;

Women's Institutes of Nova Scotia (WINS)
90 Research Dr., Bible Hill NS B6L 2R2
Tel: 902-843-9467; *Fax:* 902-896-7276
novascotiawi@eastlink.ca
www.gov.ns.ca/agri/wins
Overview: A medium-sized provincial organization founded in 1913 overseen by Federated Women's Institutes of Canada
Mission: To provide women with opportunities to enhance their lives through community service & involvement, education & leadership development
Member of: Federated Women's Institutes of Canada
Affliation(s): Associated Country Women of the World
Chief Officer(s):
Linda Munro, President
Finances: *Funding Sources:* Membership fees; grants; project funding

Women's Inter-Church Council of Canada (WICC) / Conseil oecuménique des chrétiennes du Canada
47 Queen's Park Cres. East, Toronto ON M5S 2C3
Tel: 416-929-5184; *Fax:* 416-929-4064
wicc@wicc.org
www.wicc.org
www.facebook.com/WICCanada
Overview: A medium-sized national organization founded in 1918
Mission: To focus on national & international issues affecting women, growth in ecumenism, action for social justice, & the sharing of spirituality & prayer
Chief Officer(s):
Patricia Burton-Williams, Executive Director
burton-williams@wicc.org
Finances: *Funding Sources:* World Day of Prayer offerings
Membership: *Member Profile:* Representatives from the Anglican Church of Canada, the Canadian Baptist Ministries, the Christian Church (Disciples of Christ), the Evangelical Lutheran Church in Canada, the Mennonite Central Committee, the Presbyterian Church in Canada, the Religious Society of Friends, the Roman Catholic Church, the Salvation Army, & the United Church of Canada; Membership is by appointment & election; *Committees:* Program; Communications; Membership & Nominating; Finance
Activities: Establishing the Ecumenical Network for Women's Justice; Preparing policy statements on issues such as racial justice & health care; Granting funds for a variety of projects that benefit women & children in Canada & around the world; Coordinating the Fellowship of the Least Coin program in Canada; Providing education, such as theology workshops
Awards:
• World Day of Prayer Grant (Grant)
Eligibility: Canadian ecumenical organizations; local women's groups in Canada; national & international organizations supporting local initiatives with & on behalf of women; denominational groups that have ecumenical outreach serving women within the wider community*Deadline:* March 1 *Amount:* $500-$5000
Meetings/Conferences: • Women's Inter-Church Council of Canada 2015 Annual General Meeting, 2015
Scope: National
Publications:
• Riding the Waves
Type: Newsmagazine; *Frequency:* 3x/yr.
Profile: Updates on the work of the Women's Inter-Church Council of Canada, including results of project grants & forthcoming events; Bible study; Book review; Youth page; Issues important to women of faith

Women's International League for Peace & Freedom (WILPF)
c/o Bruna Nota, #901, 70 Mill St., Toronto ON M5A 4R1
Tel: 416-203-1402
www.wilpfinternational.org/canada
Overview: A small international organization founded in 1915
Mission: To unite women throughout the world into a force working to put an end to war; to work for social, economic & political equality for all people in all nations.
Chief Officer(s):
Marlene LeGates, President
mlegates33@gmail.com
Membership: *Fees:* $35
Activities: *Internships:* Yes

Women's Legal Education & Action Fund (LEAF) / Fonds d'action et d'éducation juridiques pour les femmes (FAEJ)
#401, 260 Spadina Ave., Toronto ON M5T 2E4
Tel: 416-595-7170; *Fax:* 416-595-7191
Toll-Free: 888-824-5323
info@leaf.ca
www.leaf.ca
www.facebook.com/23825817618
twitter.com/LEAFNational
Overview: A medium-sized national charitable organization founded in 1985
Mission: The Fund promotes equality for women, primarily by using the gender equality provisions of the Canadian Charter of Rights & Freedoms. It sponsors test cases before the Canadian courts, human rights commissions & government agencies on behalf of women, & provides public education on the issue of gender equality.
Chief Officer(s):
Michelle Bullas, Chair
Diane O'Reggio, Executive Director, 416-595-7170 Ext. 225
d.oreggio@leaf.ca
Kim Stanton, Legal Director, 416-595-7170 Ext. 223
k.stanton@leaf.ca
Staff Member(s): 16
Membership: 2,500
Activities: *Library*

LEAF Halifax
Halifax NS
e-mail: halifax@leaf.ca

LEAF Sudbury
Sudbury ON
e-mail: sudbury@leaf.ca
Chief Officer(s):
Carol Stos, Contact

West Coast LEAF
#555, 409 Granville St., Vancouver BC V6C 1T2
Tel: 604-684-8772
Toll-Free: 866-737-7716
info@westcoastleaf.org
www.westcoastleaf.org
www.facebook.com/WestCoastLEAF
twitter.com/WestCoast_LEAF
Chief Officer(s):
Kasari Govender, Executive Director

Women's Missionary Society (WMS)
Tel: 416-441-1111
Toll-Free: 800-619-7301
www.wmspcc.ca
Overview: A medium-sized national organization overseen by Presbyterian Church in Canada

Mission: To encourage people of the Presbyterian Church in Canada to be involved in local & world mission
Member of: Presbyterian Church in Canada
Chief Officer(s):
Sarah Kim, Executive Director
skim@presbyterian.ca
Membership: *Member Profile:* Women who belong to the Presbyterian Church in Canada
Publications:
• Glad Tidings [a publication of the Women's Missionary Society]
Type: Magazine; *Editor:* Colleen Wood

Women's Musical Club of Toronto (WMCT)
#203A, 56 The Esplanade, Toronto ON M5E 1A7
Tel: 416-923-7052
wmct@wmct.on.ca
www.wmct.on.ca
Overview: A small local charitable organization founded in 1899
Mission: To provide fine chamber music; to give a series of afternoon concerts of international standard; To award a number of scholarships & a triennial national career development award for young Canadian musicians
Chief Officer(s):
Julia Smith, President
Finances: *Annual Operating Budget:* $50,000-$100,000
90 volunteer(s)
Membership: 420 individual; *Fees:* $165; *Member Profile:* By subscription for concert series; *Committees:* Concert; Membership; Finance; Career Development Award; Honourary Board Members
Activities: Annual "Music in the Afternoon" concert series; *Library:* Archives: housed at Toronto Reference Library, Special Collection; Open to public
Awards:
• WMCT Career Development "Artist of the Year" Award (Award)
• WMCT Centennial Foundation Graduate Fellowship, Faculty of Music, University of Toronto (Award)
• Entrance Scholarship - Faculty of Music, University of Toronto (Scholarship)
• WMCT Centennial Scholarship - Faculty of Music, University of Toronto (Scholarship)
• Ottilie M. Gunning Memorial Scholarship - The Royal Conservatory (Scholarship)

Women's Network PEI
PO Box 233, 40 Enman Cres., Charlottetown PE C1A 7K4
Tel: 902-368-5040; *Fax:* 902-368-5039
Toll-Free: 888-362-7373
www.wnpei.org
www.facebook.com/wnpei
Overview: A medium-sized provincial organization founded in 1984
Mission: To strengthen & support the efforts of PEI women to improve their status in society
Member of: National Action Committee on the Status of Women (NAC); Prince Edward Island Literacy Alliance Inc.
Chief Officer(s):
Michelle MacCallum, Executive Director
michelle@wnpei.org
Finances: *Annual Operating Budget:* $100,000-$250,000; *Funding Sources:* Advertising; sales; subscriptions; fees; government; private donations
Staff Member(s): 4; 50 volunteer(s)
Membership: 270; *Fees:* $15
Activities: Referral service; project related work; *Internships:* Yes

Women's Sexual Assault Helpline & Outreach Services *See* Women's Support Network of York Region

Women's Soccer Association of Lethbridge (WSAL)
4401 University Dr., Lethbridge AB T1K 3M4
Tel: 403-329-2232
www.losa.ca
twitter.com/wsal_soccer
Overview: A small local organization founded in 2001
Chief Officer(s):
Ilsa Wong, President

Women's Support Network of York Region (WSAH)
#109, 1110 Stellar Dr., Newmarket ON L3Y 7B7
Tel: 905-895-3646; *Fax:* 905-895-6542
Toll-Free: 800-263-6734
generalinfo@womenssupportnetwork.ca
www.womenssupportnetwork.ca
Also Known As: Women's Helpline
Previous Name: Women's Sexual Assault Helpline & Outreach Services
Overview: A small local charitable organization founded in 1992
Mission: Dedicated to eliminating sexual violence
Affliation(s): Ontario Coalition of Rape Crisis Centres
Finances: *Annual Operating Budget:* $250,000-$500,000; *Funding Sources:* Provincial government; United Way; Fund raising; Ontario Trillium Foundation
Staff Member(s): 7; 40 volunteer(s)
Membership: 1-99; *Committees:* Violence Against Women Coordinating Committee
Activities: Crisis hotline; *Awareness Events:* International Women's Day; Take Back the Night, Dec. 6; Sexual Assault Awareness & Prevention Month, May; *Speaker Service:* Yes; *Library* Open to public

Wood Buffalo Environmental Association (WBEA)
#100, 330 Thickwood Blvd., Fort McMurray AB T9K 1Y1
Tel: 780-799-4420
info@wbea.org
www.wbea.org
www.facebook.com/321509804531241
twitter.com/WBEA1
www.youtube.com/user/WoodBuffaloEnvAssoc?feature=watch
Overview: A small local organization
Mission: To provide state of the art air monitoring system that meets the needs of residents and stakeholders in the Wood Buffalo Region.
Chief Officer(s):
Kevin Percy, Executive Director
Diane Phillips, President
Membership: 28 corporate

Wood Buffalo Food Bank *See* Fort McMurray Food Bank

Wood Energy Technology Transfer Inc. (WETT)
#1, 189 Queen St. East, Toronto ON M5A 1S2
Tel: 416-968-7718; *Fax:* 416-968-6818
Toll-Free: 888-358-9388
WETT@funnel.ca
www.wettinc.ca
Overview: A medium-sized national organization founded in 1993
Mission: To promote the safe & effective use of wood burning systems, WETT maintains a training program designed to confirm & recognize the knowledge & skills of practising wood energy professionals; to provide training to new people entering the industry; to provide training to non-industry professionals such as inspectors; to provide training to specialty audiences such as volunteer firefighters & carpenters in remote communities
Chief Officer(s):
Anthony Laycock, Executive Director
Finances: *Annual Operating Budget:* $100,000-$250,000; *Funding Sources:* Membership dues; member services
Staff Member(s): 2
Membership: 1,400; *Fees:* $40-$75
Activities: Administers Wood Energy Technical Training Program for providers, installers, inspectors & cleaners of wood heat services

Wood Manufacturing Council (WMC) / Conseil des fabricants de bois (CFB)
#302, 1390 Prince of Wales Dr., Ottawa ON K2C 3N6
Tel: 613-567-5511; *Fax:* 613-567-5411
wmc@wmc-cfb.ca
www.wmc-cfb.ca
www.facebook.com/pages/Wood-Manufacturing-Council/119407547397
twitter.com/#!/careersinwood
Overview: A medium-sized national organization
Mission: To plan, develop & implement human resources strategies that support the long-term growth & competitiveness of Canada's advanced wood products manufacturing industry & meet the developmental needs of its workforce
Chief Officer(s):
Mike McClements, Chairman
Finances: *Funding Sources:* Federal government

Wood Pellet Association of Canada (WPAC)
PO Box 2989, 1877 Upper McKinnon Rd., Revelstoke BC V0E 2S0
www.pellet.org
Overview: A medium-sized national organization
Mission: The Wood Pellet Association of Canada is a member-driven organization advancing the interests of Canadian wood pellet producers.
Chief Officer(s):
Gordon Murray, Executive Director, 250-837-8821
gord@pellet.org
Meetings/Conferences: • Wood Pellet Association of Canada 2015 Conference & AGM, 2015
Scope: National

Wood Preservation Canada (WPC) / Préservation du bois Canada
#202, 2141 Thurston Dr., Ottawa ON K1G 6C9
Tel: 613-737-4337; *Fax:* 613-247-0540
www.woodpreservation.ca
Previous Name: Canadian Institute of Treated Wood
Overview: A medium-sized national organization founded in 1955
Mission: To represent, support & promote the treated wood industry in Canada

Wood Product Group
700 McLeod Ave., Fredericton NB E3B 1V5
Overview: A medium-sized local organization
Mission: To represent, promote & advance the interests of specialty & value-added wood product companies in Atlantic Canada
Chief Officer(s):
Fred Nott, President & CEO

Woodgreen Community Centre
#100, 815 Danforth Ave., Toronto ON M4J 1L2
Tel: 416-645-6000
info@woodgreen.org
www.woodgreen.org
Overview: A small local organization founded in 1937 overseen by Ontario Council of Agencies Serving Immigrants
Mission: To promote self-sufficiency & reduce poverty
Chief Officer(s):
Brian Smith, President & CEO
Finances: *Annual Operating Budget:* Greater than $5 Million; *Funding Sources:* United Way; government
Staff Member(s): 650; 1000 volunteer(s)
Membership: *Fees:* $20 or more donation

Woodland Cultural Centre (WCC)
PO Box 1506, 184 Mohawk St., Brantford ON N3T 5V6
Tel: 519-759-2650; *Fax:* 519-759-2445
Toll-Free: 866-412-2202
museum@woodland-centre.on.ca
www.woodland-centre.on.ca
www.facebook.com/WoodlandCulturalCentre
twitter.com/woodlandcc
www.youtube.com/user/woodlandcc1972
Overview: A small local charitable organization founded in 1972
Mission: To preserve the values & practices of First Nation cultures through the storage & exhibits of First Nation National Treasures; to bring about acceptable positive change in our communities & in the interaction with western Euro-society; to provide a place where people can receive teachings & guidance from our First Nation existence; to instill pride in self, children & our existence as Nations in the world community
Member of: Mohawks of the Bay of Quinte; Mohawks of Wahta; Six Nations of the Grand River
Chief Officer(s):
Janis Monture, Executive Director
jamonture@woodland-centre.on.ca
Paula Whitlow, Museum Director
pwhitlow@woodland-centre.on.ca
Virve Wiland, Library Technician
librarywoodland@yahoo.com
Finances: *Annual Operating Budget:* $500,000-$1.5 Million
Staff Member(s): 20; 30 volunteer(s)
Membership: 25,000; *Member Profile:* First Nations Peoples; *Committees:* Education; Marketing
Activities: Museum; art gallery; library; First Nations languages; *Awareness Events:* Snowsnake Tournament, Jan/Feb.; Ancestors in the Archives, Feb & Sept.; Christmas Craft Fair, 1st Sat in Nov.; *Internships:* Yes; *Speaker Service:* Yes; *Library:* Woodland Culture Centre Library; Open to public

Woodstock & District Chamber of Commerce *See* Woodstock District Chamber of Commerce

Woodstock & District Developmental Services (WDDS)
212 Bysham Park Dr., Woodstock ON N4T 1R2

Tel: 519-539-7447; *Fax:* 519-539-7332
info@wdds.ca
www.wdds.ca
www.facebook.com/363364180390260
www.youtube.com/user/WDDS212BYSHAM
Overview: A small local charitable organization founded in 1959
Mission: Committed to supporting lifelong opportunities for individuals & their families; To strive for independent living in the community through services, partnership & advocacy
Affiliation(s): Ontario Agencies Supporting Individuals with Special Needs
Chief Officer(s):
Nancy Springstead, President
John F. Bedell, CEO
jbedell@wdds.ca
Kathy Straus, Director, Operations
kstraus@wdds.ca
Finances: *Annual Operating Budget:* Greater than $5 Million
Staff Member(s): 170; 120 volunteer(s)
Membership: 74; *Fees:* $10 member; $1,000 life; *Member Profile:* Volunteers; parents; consumers; general public
Activities: Sport Celebrity Dinner; *Awareness Events:* Flower of Hope Campaign, May; Christmas Tea, Dec.

Woodstock Coin Club

PO Box 20128, Woodstock ON N4S 8X8
Tel: 519-537-5914
Overview: A small local organization
Member of: Royal Canadian Numismatic Association
Chief Officer(s):
John Tuffnail, President

Woodstock District Chamber of Commerce

476 Peel St., 3rd Fl., Woodstock ON N4S 1K1
Tel: 519-539-9411; *Fax:* 519-456-1611
info@woodstockchamber.on.ca
www.woodstockchamber.on.ca
Previous Name: Woodstock & District Chamber of Commerce
Overview: A small local organization
Mission: To support businesses in their efforts to be successful & grow
Chief Officer(s):
Ted Beynen, President
Martha Dennis, General Manager
Membership: 271; *Fees:* Schedule available; *Committees:* Executive; Finance; Business & Industry; Programs & Events; Communications & Public Relations; Energy Conservation & Innovation

Woodstock Field Naturalists

PO Box 20037, Stn. Woodstock Centre, Woodstock ON N4S 8X8
e-mail: woodstockfnc@gmail.com
www.execulink.com/~wfnc
Overview: A small local organization founded in 1934
Mission: To promote the enjoyment of nature; to learn about natural history; To promote preservation of the environment through active participation in conservation projects
Member of: Federation of Ontario Naturalists
Chief Officer(s):
Roger Boyd, President
rogeboyd@oxford.net
Membership: *Fees:* $20 individual; $25 family

Woodstock-Ingersoll & District Real Estate Board

#6, 65 Springbank Ave. North, Woodstock ON N4S 8V8
Tel: 519-539-3616; *Fax:* 519-539-1975
admin@widreb.ca
woodstockingersolldistrictrealestateboard.com
Overview: A small local organization founded in 1956 overseen by Ontario Real Estate Association
Member of: The Canadian Real Estate Association
Chief Officer(s):
Nicole Bowman, Executive Officer
nicole@widreb.ca
Finances: *Funding Sources:* Membership dues
Membership: 200

Woodview Mental Health & Autism Services

69 Flatt Rd., Burlingotn ON L7R 3X5
Tel: 905-689-4727; *Fax:* 905-689-2474
wcc@woodview.ca
woodview.ca
www.facebook.com/woodviewmha
twitter.com/WoodviewWLC
www.youtube.com/user/WoodviewMHA
Overview: A small local organization
Mission: To provide services & support to youth & adults with Autism Spectrum Disorder, in order to help them live more independently
Chief Officer(s):
Cindy I'Anson, Executive Director
cianson@woodview.ca
Finances: *Annual Operating Budget:* Greater than $5 Million; *Funding Sources:* Provincial government; donations

Woolwich Community Services (WCS)

73 Arthur St. South, Elmira ON N3B 2M8
Tel: 519-669-5139; *Fax:* 519-669-4210
Toll-Free: 800-661-7918
wcs@execulink.com
www.woolwichcommunityservices.com
Overview: A small local organization founded in 1974 overseen by InformOntario
Mission: To help people find solutions to social, legal, health, government & environmental problems; To define unmet needs in the community & communicate with appropriate agencies or organizations about such needs; To initiate action toward solutions when appropriate agencies do not exist in the community, including direct assistance, organizing & coordinating
Chief Officer(s):
Don Harloff, Executive Director
Finances: *Annual Operating Budget:* $250,000-$500,000
Staff Member(s): 9; 100 volunteer(s)
Activities: Thrift Store; Parent & Child Resource Centre; Growing Together; Family Violence Prevention; Care-Ring; Christmas Goodwill; Food Bank; support to Low German speaking Mennonites; Youth Centre; *Speaker Service:* Yes; *Library:* Kids & I Resource Centre; Open to public

The Workers' Educational Association of Canada

#205, 157 Carlton St., Toronto ON M5A 2K2
Tel: 416-923-7872; *Fax:* 416-923-7896
info@weacanada.ca
www.weacanada.ca
Also Known As: WEA Canada
Overview: A small national charitable organization founded in 1917
Member of: International Federation of Worker Education Associations
Chief Officer(s):
Wendy Terry, Administrator & Manager
Finances: *Annual Operating Budget:* $100,000-$250,000
Staff Member(s): 3; 25 volunteer(s)
Membership: 1-99; *Fees:* $15
Activities: *Library:* Resource Centre; by appointment
Publications:
• Learning Curves
Type: Newspaper; *Frequency:* 8 times a year; *Editor:* Anne McDonagh

Working Women Community Centre (WWCC)

533A Gladstone Ave., Toronto ON M6H 3J1
Tel: 416-532-2824; *Fax:* 416-532-1065
admin@workingwomencc.org
www.workingwomencc.org
www.linkedin.com/company/1357713
www.facebook.com/WorkingWomenCommunityCentre
twitter.com/workingwomencc
www.youtube.com/channel/UCnArFwwXd3I1sJJAuBAQwvQ
Overview: A small local charitable organization founded in 1975 overseen by Ontario Council of Agencies Serving Immigrants
Mission: To increase the self-sufficiency of Portuguese, Spanish-speaking & African women of Metro Toronto through the provision of settlement adaptation, education, language & citizenship acquisition, & general support; to break down employment barriers by meeting educational training needs of immigrant women; to act as a resource to the immigrant community & community at large in Metro Toronto
Affliation(s): Portuguese Interagency Network; Hispanic Council; Advocates for Community-Based Training & Education
Chief Officer(s):
Marcie Ponte, Executive Director
marcie@workingwomencc.org
Lorraine Boucher, President
Membership: *Member Profile:* Immigrant women from communities served
Activities: Counselling; peer support groups; employment; seniors program; LINC-ESL; Computer classes; Ontario Works Placement; *Library* Open to public

Workplace Safety & Prevention Services (WSPS)

Centre for Health & Safety Innovation, 5110 Creekbank Rd., Mississauga ON L4W 0A1
Tel: 905-614-1400; *Fax:* 905-614-1414
Toll-Free: 877-494-9777
customercare@wsps.ca
www.wsps.ca
Previous Name: Safe Workplace Promotion Services Ontario
Merged from: Industrial Accident Prevention Association; Ontario Service Safety Alliance; Farm Safety Association
Overview: A large provincial organization founded in 2010
Mission: WSPS is a not-for-profit organization with a mandate to meet the health & safety needs of businesses in the agricultural, manufacturing & service industries. It provides programs, products & services for the prevention of injury & illness.
Affliation(s): Amalgamated Industry Groups - Ceramics & Stone Accident Prevention Association; Chemical Industries Accident Prevention Association; Food Products Accident Prevention Association; Grain, Feed & Fertilizer Accident Prevention Association; Leather, Rubber & Tanners Accident Prevention Association; Metal Trades Accident Prevention Association; Printing Trades Accident Prevention Association; Textile & Allied Industries Accident Prevention Association; Woodworkers' Accident Prevention Association; High Tech; Offices & Related Services
Chief Officer(s):
Elizabeth Mills, CEO
Finances: *Funding Sources:* Ministry of Labour, WSIB employer premiums
Membership: 154,000 employers
Activities: *Library:* Information Centre; Open to public by appointment
Meetings/Conferences: • Partners in Prevention 2015 National Conference: Health & Safety Conference & Trade Show, April, 2015, The International Centre, Mississauga, ON
Scope: National
Publications:
• HSO Network Magazine
Type: Magazine; *Frequency:* q.; *Price:* Free to members
Profile: Updates on health & safety resources, special events & product promotions
• Network News
Type: Newsletter; *Frequency:* monthly; *Price:* Free to members
Profile: Occupational health & safety news; notices & alerts on products, services & events

Workshop Council of Nova Scotia *See* DIRECTIONS Council for Vocational Services Society

World Accord

#1C, 185 Frobisher Dr., Waterloo ON N2V 2E6
Tel: 519-747-2215; *Fax:* 519-747-2644
Toll-Free: 800-525-3545
dbarth@worldaccord.org
www.worldaccord.org
www.facebook.com/pages/World-Accord/11974905918
Overview: A small international organization founded in 1980
Mission: To bring people together; to partnership with God, the environment & people around the world; to respond to needs & opportunities that recognize the worth & dignity of all.
Chief Officer(s):
David Barth, Executive Director
dbarth@worldaccord.org
Finances: *Annual Operating Budget:* $500,000-$1.5 Million
Staff Member(s): 4
Activities: Fastathon; *Internships:* Yes; *Speaker Service:* Yes

World Amateur Muay Thai Association of Canada (WAMTAC)

164 Macatee Pl., Cambridge ON N1R 6Z8
Tel: 519-584-5426
info@wamtac.org
www.wamtac.org
Overview: A medium-sized national organization
Mission: To govern amateur muay thai in Canada
Affliation(s): World Muay Thai Council; Olympic Committee of Asia; General Association of International Sports Federations
Chief Officer(s):
Khan Phady, President
Membership: *Fees:* $500 club; $50 coach/athlete/official

World Anti-Doping Agency

Stock Exchange Tower, PO Box 120, #1700, 800, Place Victoria, Montréal QC H4Z 1B7
Tel: 514-904-9232; *Fax:* 514-904-8650
media@wada-ama.org

www.wada-ama.org
www.facebook.com/wada.ama
twitter.com/wada_ama
www.youtube.com/wadamovies
Overview: A medium-sized international organization founded in 1999
Mission: To promote & coordinate at international level the fight against doping in sport in all forms
Chief Officer(s):
Craig Reedie, President
Membership: *Committees:* Executive; Athlete; Education; Finance & Administration; Health, Medical & Research

World Arm Wrestling Federation (WAF)

c/o Lise Blanchard, 1216 Campeau Cres., Rockland ON K4K 1B4
Other Communication: Sponsorship, E-mail: sponsorship@worldarmwrestlingfederation.com
waf@worldarmwrestlingfederation.com
www.worldarmwrestlingfederation.com
Overview: A medium-sized international organization

World Association for Christian Communication (WACC) / Association mondiale pour la communication

308 Main St., Toronto ON M4C 4X7
Tel: 416-691-1999; *Fax:* 416-691-1997
info@waccglobal.org
www.waccglobal.org
www.linkedin.com/company/world-association-for-christian-communication
www.facebook.com/WACCglobal?ref=ts
twitter.com/waccglobal
vimeo.com/waccglobal
Overview: A small international charitable organization founded in 1975
Mission: Communication for social change is promoted by WACC through advocacy, education, training, & the creation & sharing of knowledge. Areas of chief concern include media diversity, equal & affordable access to communication & knowledge, media & gender justice, & the relationship between communication & power.
Member of: UNESCO; ACT Alliance
Chief Officer(s):
Karin Achtelstetter, General Secretary
ka@waccglobal.org
Dennis Smith, President
David M. Wanless, Treasurer
Staff Member(s): 12
Membership: 1,000-4,999; *Fees:* US$120 corporate; US$40 personal; US$10 student; *Member Profile:* Individuals, churches, church-related agencies, media producers, educational institutions, secular communication organizations, & persons who share WACC's mission
Activities: *Speaker Service:* Yes; *Library* by appointment
Publications:
• Media Development
Type: Journal; *Frequency:* Quarterly; *Price:* US$40 individual; US$50-US$75 libraries & institutions
Profile: Theory & practice of communication worldwide
• No-Nonsense Guides
Number of Pages: 6
Profile: Different aspects of communication for practitioners & activists

World at Work

PO Box 4520, Stn. A, Toronto ON M5W 4M4
Tel: 480-951-9191; *Fax:* 480-483-8352
Toll-Free: 877-951-9191
customerrelations@worldatwork.com
www.worldatwork.org
www.linkedin.com/groups?about=&gid=84761
www.facebook.com/WorldatWorkAssociation
twitter.com/worldatwork
www.youtube.com/worldatworktv
Previous Name: Canadian Compensation Association
Overview: A medium-sized national organization founded in 1985
Mission: To promote the education of compensation & benefits professionals
Member of: Canadian Council of Human Resource Associations
Chief Officer(s):
Anne Ruddy, President
Marcia Rhodes, Contact, Media Relations
marcia.rhodes@worldatwork.org
Finances: *Annual Operating Budget:* $500,000-$1.5 Million
Membership: 1,625 individual; *Fees:* Schedule available; *Member Profile:* Must be in the human resources profession; *Committees:* Conference; Education; Communications
Activities: *Rents Mailing List:* Yes

World Blind Union / Union mondiale des aveugles

1929 Bayview Ave., Toronto ON M4G 3E8
Tel: 416-486-9698; *Fax:* 416-486-8107
info@wbuoffice.org
www.worldblindunion.org
twitter.com/BlindUnion
Overview: A medium-sized international organization founded in 1984
Mission: To speak on behalf of blind and partially sighted persons of the world, representing 285 million blind and visually impaired persons from 190 countries
Member of: Vision Alliance
Chief Officer(s):
Rina Prasarani, Secretary General
rinalamsyah@gmail.com
Arnt Holte, President
arnt.holte@blindeforbundet.no
Penny Hartin, Chief Executive Officer
penny.hartin@wbuoffice.org
Membership: 500+ organizations; *Committees:* Right to Read; Mobility & Transport; Technology; Human Rights & Advocacy; Employment; Development; Diversity; Languages Strategy; Finance; Policy Review; Constitution; Membership Fee; Resource Generation; Nominations; World Braille Council

World Conference on Religion & Peace (Canada) (WCRP)

#490-1, 333 Queen Mary Rd., Montréal QC H3Z 1A2
Tel: 450-478-3904
www.religionsforpeace.org
Also Known As: Religions for Peace (Canada)
Overview: A medium-sized national organization founded in 1975
Mission: To establish peace & justice at the local, national & international levels; to encourage members to work together with like-minded organizations on issues of social & economic justice, human rights, ecological harmony, arms limitation & nuclear disarmament; to aim for world peace through interfaith dialogue & applied ethics
Affliation(s): World Conference on Religion & Peace (International)
Chief Officer(s):
Pascale Frémond, President
pascale.fremond@videotron.ca
20 volunteer(s)
Membership: 100-499; *Fees:* $100 institutional; $10 student; $25 individual; $15 senior
Activities: Meetings; occasional conferences; newsletter;

World Energy Council - Canadian Member Committee *See* Energy Council of Canada

World Federalist Movement - Canada (WFMC)

#207, 145 Spruce St., Ottawa ON K1R 6P1
Tel: 613-232-0647; *Fax:* 613-563-0017
wfcnat@web.ca
www.worldfederalistscanada.org
www.facebook.com/pages/World-Federalist-Movement-Canada/14694450199518
twitter.com/WFMCanada
Overview: A small national organization founded in 1948
Mission: Education, research, political support for strengthening the United Nations & rule of law in world affairs
Member of: Canadian Council for International Cooperation; Coalition for the International Criminal Court; International Civil Society Forum for Democracy; Canadian Peacebuilding Coordinating Committee; Canadian Network to Abolish Nuclear Weapons; Climate Action Network
Affliation(s): World Federalist Movement
Chief Officer(s):
Warren Allmand, President
allmandw@gmail.com
Fergus Watt, Executive Director
ferguswatt@worldfederalistscanada.org
Simon Rosenblum, Chair
Finances: *Annual Operating Budget:* $100,000-$250,000
Staff Member(s): 2
Membership: 2,200; *Fees:* $150 contributor; $60 household; $40 individual; $15 limited income; *Committees:* Policy; Finance; Environment
Activities: *Speaker Service:* Yes; *Rents Mailing List:* Yes

World Federation of Chiropractic (WFC) / La Fédération mondiale de chiropratique

#203, 1246 Yonge St., Toronto ON M4N 1W5
Tel: 416-484-9978; *Fax:* 416-484-9665
info@wfc.org
www.wfc.org
www.facebook.com/391186181003637
Overview: A medium-sized international organization founded in 1988
Member of: Council of International Organizations of Medical Sciences (CIOMS)
Affliation(s): World Health Organization (WHO)
Chief Officer(s):
David Chapman-Smith, Secretary-General

World Federation of Hemophilia (WFH) / Fédération mondiale de l'hémophilie (FMH)

#1010, 1425, boul René-Lévesque Ouest, Montréal QC H3G 1T7
Tel: 514-875-7944; *Fax:* 514-875-8916
wfh@wfh.org
www.wfh.org
www.facebook.com/wfhemophilia
twitter.com/wfhemophilia
www.youtube.com/user/WFHcommunications
Overview: A medium-sized international licensing organization founded in 1963
Mission: To introduce, improve & maintain care for people with hemophilia & related blood disorders around the world
Affliation(s): World Health Organization; International Society of Blood Transfusion; International Committee on Thrombosis & Haemostasis; International Society of Haematology; Société internationale de chirurgie orthopédique (SICOT)
Chief Officer(s):
Elizabeth Myles, Chief Operating Officer
Finances: *Annual Operating Budget:* Greater than $5 Million
Staff Member(s): 38
Membership: 127 countries; *Committees:* Dental; International External Quality Assessment Scheme; Laboratory Sciences; Musculoskeletal; Nurses; Psychosocial; Treatment Product Safety, Supply & Access; International Hemophilia Training Centre; von Willebrand Disease and Rare Bleeding Disorders; Data & Demographics; Research
Activities: Health care development programs; humanitarian aid; data collection; public affairs; publications;

World Federation of Ukrainian Engineering Societies (WFUES)

27 Newell Ct., Toronto ON M9A 4T9
Tel: 416-235-2610; *Fax:* 416-240-9095
jgk@the-wire.com
Overview: A medium-sized international organization founded in 1973
Mission: To maintain Ukrainian engineering tradition & culture; To publish Ukrainian engineering news; To organize conferences & seminars on technical subjects; To exchange information on technology & facilitate technology transfer
Chief Officer(s):
J.G. Kurys, President
Finances: *Annual Operating Budget:* Less than $50,000; *Funding Sources:* Membership fees
Staff Member(s): 4; 6 volunteer(s)
Membership: 5,000 individuals; *Fees:* Schedule available; *Member Profile:* Licensed professional engineer in respective country; *Committees:* Environmental; Educational; Social Events
Activities: *Speaker Service:* Yes

World Federation of Ukrainian Women's Organizations (WFUWO)

#206, 2118A Bloor St. West, Toronto ON M6S 1M8
Tel: 416-762-2066; *Fax:* 416-762-2077
www.wfuwo.org
Overview: A medium-sized national charitable organization founded in 1948
Mission: A charitable association that works for the betterment of Ukrainian women
Member of: ECOSOC, UNICEF, NGO
Affliation(s): Ukrainian World Congress; General Federation of Women's Clubs; World Movement of Mothers; International Council of Women; International Alliance of Women
Chief Officer(s):
Marika Szkambara, President
Finances: *Annual Operating Budget:* Less than $50,000
Staff Member(s): 1; 10 volunteer(s)
Membership: 15,000-49,999; *Fees:* $150 institutional; $10 individual; *Committees:* The Arts; Cultural Affairs; Education;

Canadian Associations

International Relations; Social Welfare; Organization; Press & Publication; Programming; Women's Studies

World Home Bible League *See* The Bible League of Canada

World Hypertension League (WHL)

Faculty of Health Sciences, Blusson Hall, Simon Fraser University, #11016, 8888 University Dr., Burnaby BC V5A 1S6
Tel: 778-782-6952; *Fax:* 778-782-5927
www.worldhypertensionleague.org
Overview: A large international organization founded in 1984
Mission: To promote the detection, control & prevention of arterial hypertension in populations; To assist national bodies by providing internationally applicable programs
Member of: International Society of Hypertension
Affliation(s): Canadian Coalition for High Blood Pressure Prevention & Control; WHO
Chief Officer(s):
Liu Lisheng, M.D., President
chlhypt@163bj.com
Arun Chockalingam, Secretary General
whlsec@sfu.ca
Finances: *Annual Operating Budget:* $100,000-$250,000; *Funding Sources:* Membership dues; grants
10 volunteer(s)
Membership: 74 regular + 18 associate + 3 supporting; *Fees:* US$375; *Member Profile:* Must be a league, society or national body
Activities: Hypertension Management Audit Project; hypertension control in developing countries; international workshop on patient education; cooperative patient education project; conference every two years; *Awareness Events:* World Kidney Day, March; World Hypertension Day, May; *Speaker Service:* Yes; *Rents Mailing List:* Yes; *Library* Open to public
Publications:
• WHL [World Hypertension League] Newsletter
Type: Newsletter; *Frequency:* q.; *Editor:* Dr. Daniel T. Lackland

World Inter-Action Mondiale; Ottawa-Hull Learner Centre *See* One World Arts

The World Job & Food Bank Inc. (WJFB)

#104, 820 - 10th St., Calgary AB T2P 2X1
Tel: 403-457-0416; *Fax:* 403-457-0493
info@wjfb.org
www.wjfb.org
Previous Name: Global Food Bank Association Inc.
Overview: A medium-sized international charitable organization founded in 1985
Mission: To alleviate poverty, chronic unemployment, disease, hunger, homelessness & the causes of same, in Canada & less developed countries
Member of: Council of Alberta NGOs
Chief Officer(s):
Joseph Edison, CEO
jedison@wjfb.org
Linda Zhou, Director, International Programs
Finances: *Funding Sources:* Corporations; foundations & clubs; churches; general public
Activities: Jobs for the unemployed; hope for children; health care for families; food for the hungry; surplus food & goods for the poor; "Brown Bagging for Calgary Street Kids" program; has over 60 development projects in 15 developing countries; *Speaker Service:* Yes

World Literacy of Canada (WLC) / Alphabétisation mondiale Canada

#281, 401 Richmond St. West, Toronto ON M5V 3A8
Tel: 416-977-0008; *Fax:* 416-977-1112
info@worldlit.ca
www.worldlit.ca
www.facebook.com/worldlit
twitter.com/WorldLit
www.youtube.com/user/worldliteracycanada
Overview: A medium-sized international charitable organization founded in 1955
Mission: To promote international development & social justice through support of community-based programs that emphasize adult literacy & non-formal education
Chief Officer(s):
Ken Setterington, President
Jasmine Gill, Vice-President
Virginia Bosomworth, Secretary
Mamta Mishra, Executive Director
mamta@worldlit.ca
Finances: *Funding Sources:* CIDA; private sector; donors
Staff Member(s): 4

Activities: KAMA Poetry Reading Series; *Awareness Events:* International Women's Day, March; The World on the Street, Sept.; *Internships:* Yes; *Speaker Service:* Yes

World Masters Judo Association

16 Frankfort Grove, Jacksons Point ON L0E 1L0
Tel: 416-580-1885; *Fax:* 905-722-5330
www.masterathlete.com
Also Known As: International Masters Judo
Overview: A medium-sized international charitable organization
Activities: Organizing the World Masters Judo Championship; *Awareness Events:* World Masters Judo Championship

A World of Dreams Foundation Canada / La Fondation canadienne un monde de rêves

#3575, 6900, boul déCarie, Montréal QC H3A 3L4
Tel: 514-985-3003; *Fax:* 514-985-9280
Toll-Free: 800-567-7254
info@awdreams.com
www.awdreams.com
Overview: A small national charitable organization founded in 1987
Mission: To fulfill dreams for chronically, critically & terminally ill children
Chief Officer(s):
Lora Cianci, Director
Finances: *Annual Operating Budget:* $250,000-$500,000; *Funding Sources:* Fundraising; corporate & private donations
Staff Member(s): 1; 20 volunteer(s)
Membership: 11; *Member Profile:* Business; entrepreneurs; lawyers; medical doctors
Activities: Fundraising events: wine & cheese party, golf tournaments, Bowl-a-Thons, comedy nights, BBQ party, softball tournaments

World Organization of Building Officials (WOBO)

155 Bearspaw Meadows, Calgary AB T3L 2M3
Tel: 403-239-2889; *Fax:* 403-547-4546
channan@telus.net
www.wobo-un.org/home.html
Overview: A medium-sized international organization founded in 1984
Mission: To improve the quality of life & resource optimization internationally, through the development, exchange & application of knowledge & experience, affecting the health, safety, welfare & usefulness of the built environment; To promote safeguards from potential hazards & to recommend solutions for preventing fire risks in existing buildings or buildings under construction; To promote the concept of standardizing construction training, materials, equipment & appliances; To promote the unification of legislation pertaining to the administration & enforcement of codes & standards; To update the development of technology
Member of: Habitat International Coalition
Affliation(s): Special conservative status with the Economic & Social Council of the United Nations, the United Nations Industrial Development Organization, the United Nations Habitat Human Settlements Program, & the Department of Information of the United Nations
Chief Officer(s):
Omkar Nath Channan, Founding President & Governor
Finances: *Annual Operating Budget:* $50,000-$100,000; *Funding Sources:* Membership fees
Membership: 22 country members; 600 individual members; *Fees:* US$30 individuals; US$175 group; *Member Profile:* Individual members consist of individuals interested in codes related to construction, fire safety, property maintenance, development, land use, enforcement, administration, inspection, investigations, testing, designs, surveys, appraisals, education & other such disciplines connected therewith directly or indirectly; Group members consist of government units, agencies, departments, corporations, bureaus, professional institutes, associations & organizations, which administer, formulate, or enforce laws, codes or standards relating to construction, fire safety, property maintenance, development, land use, research, inspections, testing, designs, standards, investigations, surveys, manufacture or education.
Activities: *Internships:* Yes; *Speaker Service:* Yes

World Organization Ovulation Method Billings Inc.

1506 Dansey Ave., Coquitlam BC V3K 3J1
Tel: 604-936-4472; *Fax:* 604-936-5690
www.woomb.ca
Also Known As: WOOMB Canada Inc.
Overview: A small international organization founded in 1982
Mission: To teach fertility awareness & natural family planning
Affliation(s): WOOMB International - Australia
Finances: *Funding Sources:* Donations

Membership: *Member Profile:* Trained teachers of OM Billings; natural family plannings; supportive individuals/groups
Activities: *Speaker Service:* Yes

World Potato Congress

Farm Centre, #101, 420 University Ave., Charlottetown PE C1A 7Z5
Tel: 902-368-8885; *Fax:* 902-628-2225
info@potatocongress.org
www.potatocongress.org
Also Known As: WPC Inc.
Overview: A small international organization founded in 1991
Mission: Dedicated to supporting the global growth and development of the potato
Chief Officer(s):
Allan Parker, President & CEO
kartsar@me.com
David Thompson, Vice-President
dathompson@pei.sympatico.ca
Staff Member(s): 1
Membership: *Member Profile:* Group of volunteer directors representing potato jurisdictions around the world; *Committees:* Intl. Advisory; Awards

World Renew (CRWRC)

PO Box 5070, Stn. LCD 1, 3475 Mainway, Burlington ON L7R 3Y8
Tel: 905-336-2920
Toll-Free: 800-730-3490
info@worldrenew.net
www.worldrenew.net
www.facebook.com/worldrenew
twitter.com/worldrenew_net
www.youtube.com/user/CRWRCComm
Previous Name: Christian Reformed World Relief Committee
Overview: A large international charitable organization founded in 1962
Mission: To engage God's people in redeeming resources & developing gifts in collaborative activities of love, mercy, justice, & compassion
Member of: Canadian Foodgrains Bank; Canadian Council of Christian Charities; Canadian Council for International Cooperation.
Affliation(s): Christian Reformed Church in North America
Chief Officer(s):
James Joossee, President
Ida Mutoigo, Director, 905-336-2920 Ext. 4303
imutoigo@worldrenew.net
Iona Buisman, Contact, Missionary Partnerships & Volunteer Opportunities, 905-336-2920 Ext. 321
ibuisman@crwrc.org
Judy Eising, Contact, Donations & Planned Giving, 905-336-2920 Ext. 297
jeising@crwrc.org
Renee Scobel, Contact, Church Relations, 905-336-2920 Ext. 237
rscobel@crwrc.org
Kristen VanderBerg, Contact, Communications, 905-336-2920 Ext. 305
kvanderberg@crwrc.org
Finances: *Funding Sources:* Christian Reformed Churches; CIDA; Other denominations
Membership: 15,000-49,999
Activities: *Awareness Events:* World Hunger Week, November; *Internships:* Yes; *Speaker Service:* Yes; *Library:* CRWRC Development Education Library; Open to public

World Sikh Organization of Canada (WSO)

1183 Cecil Ave., Ottawa ON K1H 7Z6
www.worldsikh.org
www.facebook.com/WSOCanada
twitter.com/WorldSikhOrg
Overview: A medium-sized international organization founded in 1984
Mission: To foster understanding & goodwill amongst all nations, creeds & races; To promote & protect the rights of humanity as articulated in UN declarations & covenants
Affliation(s): World Sikh Organization (International)
Chief Officer(s):
Amritpal Singh Shergill, President
Kulmit Singh Sangha, Senior Vice-President
Rupinder Kaur Dhaliwal, Director, Administration
Jagdeep Singh Mann, Director, Finance
100 volunteer(s)
Membership: 15,000-49,999; *Fees:* $1,000 institutional; $10 student/associate; $100 individual

Activities: *Library* Open to public by appointment

World Society for the Protection of Animals (WSPA) / Société mondiale pour la protection des animaux
#960, 90 Eglinton Ave. East, Toronto ON M4P 2Y3
Tel: 416-369-0044; *Fax:* 416-369-0147
Toll-Free: 800-363-9772
wspa@wspa.ca
www.wspa.ca
www.facebook.com/group.php?gid=143249880633
www.twitter.com/wspacanada
www.youtube.com/wspacanada
Overview: A large international charitable organization founded in 1953
Mission: To promote effective means for the prevention of cruelty to, & relief of suffering of animals in any part of the world; 15 offices worldwide
Chief Officer(s):
Peter Davies, Director General
Finances: *Annual Operating Budget:* $1.5 Million-$3 Million; *Funding Sources:* General public
Staff Member(s): 9; 20 volunteer(s)
Membership: 900 member organizations in 150 countries; *Fees:* $25
Publications:
• WSPA News
Type: Newsletter; *Frequency:* Biannually

World Trade Centre Atlantic Canada (WTCAC)
PO Box 955, Halifax NS B3J 2V9
Tel: 902-424-5054
info@tclns.com
wtcac.tradecentrelimited.com
Overview: A small international organization
Mission: To provide Atlantic Canadian companies with export trade training & assistance & give them access to the World Trade Centers Association network. It is operated by Trade Centre Ltd.
Member of: World Trade Centers Association
Affliation(s): 300 World Trade Centres in 85 countries
Chief Officer(s):
Scott Ferguson, President & CEO, Trade Centre Ltd.
Membership: 189

World Trade Centre Montréal (WTCM)
#6000, 380, rue St-Antoine Ouest, Montréal QC H2Y 3X7
Tél: 514-871-4002; *Téléc:* 514-849-3813
Ligne sans frais: 877-590-4040
wtcmontreal@ccmm.qc.ca
www.btmm.qc.ca/en/international
Également appelé: WTC Montréal
Aperçu: *Dimension:* moyenne; *Envergure:* nationale; Organisme sans but lucratif; fondée en 1984
Mission: Appuyer, former et conseiller les entreprises, associations, institutions et organismes de développement économiques dans leurs démarches sur les marchés internationaux
Membre de: World Trade Centre Association
Affiliation(s): Chambre de commerce du Montréal Metropolitain
Membre(s) du bureau directeur:
Michel Leblanc, Président et chef de la direction
Lise Aubin, Vice-présidente, Exploitation & Administration
Finances: *Fonds:* Développement économique Canada
Membre: 7,000
Activités: Missions commerciales; services de préparation à l'exportation; ateliers de formation en commerce international; *Listes de destinataires:* Oui

World Trade Centre Vancouver *See* The Vancouver Board of Trade

World University Service of Canada (WUSC) / Entraide universitaire mondiale du Canada (EUMC)
1404 Scott St., Ottawa ON K1Y 2N2
Tel: 613-798-7477; *Fax:* 613-798-0990
Toll-Free: 800-267-8699
wusc@wusc.ca
www.wusc.ca
www.linkedin.com/groups/WUSC-EUMC-Alumni-2441658
www.facebook.com/wusc.ca
twitter.com/worlduniservice
www.youtube.com/wusceumc
Overview: A large international charitable organization founded in 1939
Mission: We believe that all peoples are entitled to the knowledge & skills necessary to contribute to a more equitable world; to foster human development & global understanding through education & training
Affliation(s): Canadian Council for International Cooperation
Chief Officer(s):
Chris Eaton, Executive Director
ceaton@wusc.ca
Ravi Gupta, Associate Executive Director
ravi@wusc.ca
Finances: *Annual Operating Budget:* Greater than $5 Million; *Funding Sources:* Canadian International Development Agency; overseas governments; international agencies
Staff Member(s): 60; 400 volunteer(s)
Membership: 4,000+; *Member Profile:* Universities & colleges; students; alumni; development workers
Activities: International seminars to give Canadian students personal exposure to issues & problems of development; through Local Committees, WUSC has sponsored more than 800 student refugees from Africa, Central America, Asia & the Middle East since 1978; administers a variety of scholarship programs on behalf of the Government of Canada & a number of developing countries which bring pre-selected students from Latin America, Africa, the Carribean & Asia for study or technical skills upgrading at universities & colleges in Canada; *Internships:* Yes
Awards:
• Annual WUSC Alumni Award (Award)
To recognize the outstanding contribution of an individual who has demonstrated dedication and long-time commitment to the organization.

World Vision Canada (WVC) / Vision Mondiale
1 World Dr., Mississauga ON L5T 2Y4
Tel: 905-565-6100; *Fax:* 866-219-8620
Toll-Free: 866-595-5550
info@worldvision.ca
www.worldvision.ca
www.facebook.com/WorldVisionCan
twitter.com/worldvisioncan
www.youtube.com/WorldVisionCanada
Overview: A large international charitable organization founded in 1950
Mission: An international partnership of Christians committed to the poor; a Christian relief organization dedicated to children, families and communities, with a mission to overcome poverty and injustice, and serve all people regardless of religion, race, ethnicity or gender; active in 90+ countries around the world.
Member of: Canadian Council for International Cooperation; Ontario Council for International Cooperation
Affliation(s): Evangelical Fellowship of Canada
Chief Officer(s):
Dave Toycen, President & CEO
Finances: *Annual Operating Budget:* Greater than $5 Million; *Funding Sources:* 89% private + 11% government
Staff Member(s): 500; 660 volunteer(s)
Membership: 100-499
Activities: Child sponsorship; development projects (reforestation, income generation, etc.); emergency relief & rehabilitation; the 30-Hour Famine (annual fundraising event); Neighbourlink builds networks, mobilizes volunteers & connects people in need with local resources; Chinese ministries (to raise awareness among the ethnic Chinese community in Canada about needs); *Awareness Events:* National 30-Hour Famine, April; *Internships:* Yes; *Speaker Service:* Yes; *Library:* Resource Centre; by appointment
Publications:
• ChildView
Type: Magazine

Alberta Office
PO Box 76067, #240, 70 Shawville Blvd. SE, Calgary AB T2Y 2Z9
Tel: 403-254-6460
Toll-Free: 877-254-6460
Chief Officer(s):
John Goulding, Area Manager
john_goulding@worldvision.ca

British Columbia Office
20586 - 87A Ave., Langley BC V1M 3X2
Tel: 604-882-9757
Toll-Free: 877-626-7423
Chief Officer(s):
Kevin Garratt, Area Manager
kevin_garratt@worldvision.ca

Central Ontario Office
91 Brunswick Ave., Markham ON L6C 2E6
Tel: 905-887-6093; *Fax:* 905-887-6094
maria_drossos@worldvision.ca
Chief Officer(s):
Maria Drossos, Area Manager

Corporate & Foundations Office
1 World Dr., Mississauga ON L5T 2Y4
Tel: 905-565-6100; *Fax:* 866-219-8620
Toll-Free: 866-595-5550
info@worldvision.ca
Chief Officer(s):
Jenny Jarvis, Area Manager
jenny_jarvis@worldvision.ca

World Wildlife Fund - Canada (WWF-Canada) / Fonds mondial pour la nature
#410, 245 Eglinton Ave. East, Toronto ON M4P 3J1
Tel: 416-489-8800; *Fax:* 416-489-3611
Toll-Free: 800-267-2632
ca-panda@wwfcanada.org
www.wwf.ca
www.facebook.com/WWFCanada
twitter.com/wwfcanada
www.youtube.com/wwfcanada
Overview: A large international charitable organization founded in 1967
Mission: To conserve wild animals, plants & habitats for their own sake & the long-term benefit of people; to protect the diversity of life on earth; to stop, & eventually reverse, the accelerating degradation of our planet's natural environment, & to help build a future in which humans live in harmony with nature
Affliation(s): World Wide Fund for Nature (International)
Chief Officer(s):
Roger Dickhout, Chair
Monte Hummel, President Emeritus
Darcy Dobell, Vice-President, Pacific Conservation
Arlin Hackman, Chief Conservation Officer & Vice-President, Conservation
Sara Oates, CFO & Vice-President, Finance & Administration
Robert Rangeley, Vice-President, Atlantic Region
Christina Topp, Vice-President, Marketing & Communications
Finances: *Annual Operating Budget:* Greater than $5 Million; *Funding Sources:* Individuals; corporate donations; government; foundations
Staff Member(s): 80
Membership: 64,000; *Fees:* Donation of $26 or more; *Committees:* Management
Activities: Endangered Species Recovery Fund; Marine, Forests & Trade Biodiversity; Arctic; *Awareness Events:* National Sweater Day, Feb.; Earth Hour, March; CN Tower Climb, April; *Rents Mailing List:* Yes
Awards:
• Endangered Species Recovery Fund (Grant)
Sponsors high-priority conservation projects to assist the recovery of endangered wildlife & their natural habitats. This program is under review*Eligibility:* Must be affiliated with a non-governmental organization or non-profit body with a mandate for conservation*Deadline:* January
• Endangered Spaces Campaign Local Action Fund (Grant)
Sponsors site-specific, public awareness activities to advance protection of terrestrial & marine areas across Canada*Eligibility:* Must be affiliated with a non-governmental organization or non-profit body with a mandate for conservation*Deadline:* November *Contact:* Project Manager, Jarmila Becka Lee
Publications:
• World Wildlife Fund - Canada E-Newsletter
Type: Newsletter

Halifax
Duke Tower, #1202, 5251 Duke St., Halifax NS B3J 1P3
Tel: 902-482-1105; *Fax:* 902-487-1107

Inuvik
PO Box 1019, 191 Mackenzie Rd., 2nd Fl., Inuvik NT X0E 0T0
Tel: 867-777-5343

Iqaluit
Bldg. 959A, PO Box 1750, Iqaluit NU X0A 0H0
Tel: 867-979-7298; *Fax:* 867-979-7109

Montréal
#340, 50, rue Ste-Catherine ouest, Montréal QC H2X 3V4
Tél: 514-394-1106

Ottawa
#400, 30 Metcalfe St., Ottawa ON K1P 5L4
Tel: 613-232-8706; *Fax:* 613-232-4181

Prince Rupert
PO Box 362, #3, 437 - 3rd Ave. West, Prince Rupert PE V8J 3P9

Tel: 250-624-3705; *Fax:* 250-624-3725
pacificmarine@wwfcanada.org
St. John's
TD Place, #305, 140 Water St., St. John's NL A1C 6H6
Tel: 709-722-9453; *Fax:* 709-726-0931
Vancouver
#1588, 409 Granville St., Vancouver BC V6T 1T2
Tel: 604-678-5152; *Fax:* 604-678-5155

World Without Borders *Voir* Terre sans frontières

World's Poultry Science Association - Canadian Branch
Agricultural Bldg., Dept. of Animal & Poultry Science, Univ. of SK, #6D34, 51 Campus Dr., Saskatoon SK S7N 5A8
Tel: 306-966-2492; *Fax:* 306-966-4155
karen.schwean@usask.ca
Overview: A small national organization
Chief Officer(s):
K.V. Schwean-Lardner, Contact

Worldwide Association of Business Coaches (WABC)
c/o WABC Coaches Inc., PO Box 215, Saanichton BC V8M 2C3
www.wabccoaches.com
www.linkedin.com/groups?about=&gid=3262807
twitter.com/wabccoaches
Overview: A small international organization
Mission: To develop, advance & promote the emerging profession of business coaching, worldwide
Chief Officer(s):
Wendy Johnson, President/CEO
Membership: *Fees:* US$195 individual affiliate; US$395 individual regular; *Committees:* Ethics & Integrity

World-Wide Bible Study Association
PO Box 98590, 873 Jane St., Toronto ON M6N 4C0
e-mail: richard.kruse@sympatico.ca
www.ibcschool.ca
Also Known As: International Bible Correspondence School
Overview: A small local organization founded in 1968
Chief Officer(s):
Richard Kruse, Director
Staff Member(s): 1; 25 volunteer(s)

Worldwide Church of God Canada *See* Grace Communion International Canada

Worldwide Marriage Encounter
72 Amelia St., Toronto ON M4X 1E1
Toll-Free: 800-795-5683
Overview: A small local organization founded in 1971
Mission: To renew the sacraments of Matrimony & Holy Orders
Affliation(s): Archdiocese of Toronto
Chief Officer(s):
Mike & Cora Bryce, Contact, 905-896-2958
cora-mikebryce@sympatico.ca
Finances: *Funding Sources:* Donations
Membership: *Member Profile:* Persons who are validly married, & who have attended a Worldwide Marriage Encounter weekend experience in one of the seven secretariats (Africa, Asia, Europe, Latin America, Pacific, Canada, USA); Members become part of a pro-marriage movement in the Catholic Church
Activities: Programming for married couples, including enrichments, peer support, community activities, & social events

Worsley Chamber of Commerce
PO Box 181, Worsley AB T0H 3W0
Tel: 780-685-3943; *Fax:* 780-685-2115
Overview: A small local organization

Wrestling Nova Scotia
NS
www.wrestlingnovascotia.ca
Overview: A small provincial organization overseen by Canadian Amateur Wrestling Association
Chief Officer(s):
Joe Beckerman, Chair
joe@slots-online.ca
Josh Albright, President, 902-446-9093
joshuraw@hotmail.com
Mike Hielman, Vice-President, 888-431-3059
dylan59@ns.sympatico.ca

Wrestling PEI
c/o Sport PEI, PO Box 302, 40 Enman Crescent, Charlottetown PE C1A 7K7
Tel: 902-368-4262; *Fax:* 902-368-4548
sports@sportpei.pe.ca
www.wrestlingpei.ca
Overview: A small provincial organization overseen by Canadian Amateur Wrestling Association
Mission: To promote wrestling in PEI; to provide competitive opportunities for members
Member of: Wrestling Canada
Chief Officer(s):
Glen Flood, Executive Director
gflood@sportpei.pe.ca
Staff Member(s): 1
Activities: Canada Games; Provincials; Atlantics; Nationals

Writers Guild of Canada (WGC)
#401, 366 Adelaide St. West, Toronto ON M5V 1R9
Tel: 416-979-7907; *Fax:* 416-979-9273
Toll-Free: 800-567-9974
info@wgc.ca
www.wgc.ca
twitter.com/WGCtweet
Overview: A small national organization founded in 1991
Mission: Voice of professional Canadian screenwriters; to lobby on their behalf; to protect their interests; to raise the profile of screenwriters & screenwriting
Member of: International Affiliation of Writers Guilds
Affliation(s): Coalition of Canadian Audio-Visual Unions
Chief Officer(s):
Jill Golick, President
j.golick@wgc.ca
Maureen Parker, Executive Director
m.parker@wgc.ca
Finances: *Funding Sources:* Union member supported
Staff Member(s): 18
Membership: 1,900; *Fees:* $350 initiation; $150 annual; *Member Profile:* Screenwriters with at least one writing credit in the WGC's jurisdiction
Activities: Script Registration Service; contract negotiation, administration & enforcement, policy & lobbying on behalf of screenwriters
Awards:
• Canadian Screenwriting Awards (Award)
Publications:
• Canadian Screenwriter [a publication of the Writers Guild of Canada]
Type: Magazine; *Frequency:* 3 pa

Writers' Alliance of Newfoundland & Labrador (WANL)
Haymarket Square, #208, 223 Duckworth St., St. John's NL A1C 6N1
Tel: 709-739-5215
Toll-Free: 866-739-5215
wanl@nf.aibn.com
wanl.ca
www.facebook.com/writersalliance
twitter.com/WANL
Overview: A small provincial organization founded in 1987
Mission: To enhance the quality of writing in Newfoundland & Labrador through such programmes as workshops, meetings, readings; to encourage & develop public awareness & appreciation for the work of writers in Newfoundland & Labrador
Member of: Access Copyright; Canadian Writers' Summit
Chief Officer(s):
Alison Dyer, Executive Director
Finances: *Funding Sources:* Federal, provincial & municipal government grants
Staff Member(s): 2
Membership: 400+; *Fees:* Free youth; $25 students/unemployed/retired; $55 adult; *Member Profile:* Writers & anyone interested in the writing/publishing industry
Activities: *Speaker Service:* Yes
Awards:
• Provincial Book Awards (Award)
Poetry & Non-Fiction categories *Amount:* $1,250 in each category

The Writers' Development Trust *See* The Writers' Trust of Canada

Writers' Federation of New Brunswick (WFNB)
#151, 527 Dundonald St., Fredericton NB E3B 1X5
Tel: 506-260-3564
info@wfnb.ca
www.wfnb.ca
www.facebook.com/writersfederation
twitter.com/WritersNB
Overview: A small provincial organization founded in 1983
Mission: To promote New Brunswick writing; to assist writers of New Brunswick at all stages of their development by providing services; to uphold the right to free artistic expression; to provide additional educational services to schools & libraries; to contribute to the enhancement of literary arts
Member of: CANCOPY
Finances: *Funding Sources:* Provincial government; sponsors; membership fees; Canada Council
Membership: 235 individual; *Member Profile:* Published amateur
Activities: Annual Literary Competition; manuscript reading service; Writers-in-Schools program; Literary Festival; *Library* by appointment
Awards:
• The Sheree Fitch Prize (Award)
Open to youth, 14-18 years of age; entries will alternate between fiction & poetry *Amount:* 1st - $150; 2nd - $100; 3rd - $50
• The Richards Prize (Award)
For a collection of short stories, a short novel, or a substantial portion of a longer novel *Amount:* $400
• The Alfred G. Bailey Prize (Award)
For poetry manuscript not previously published *Amount:* $400

Writers' Federation of Nova Scotia (WFNS)
1113 Marginal Rd., Halifax NS B3H 4P7
Tel: 902-423-8116; *Fax:* 902-422-0881
talk@writers.ns.ca
www.writers.ns.ca
www.facebook.com/groups/7093286492
twitter.com/WFNS
Overview: A medium-sized provincial charitable organization founded in 1975
Mission: To foster creative & professional writing; to provide advice & assistance to writers; to encourage greater public recognition of Nova Scotia writers
Affliation(s): Cultural Federation of Nova Scotia; Writers' Trust; Access Copyright; Canadian Children's Book Centre; International Board on Books for Youth
Finances: *Annual Operating Budget:* $250,000-$500,000; *Funding Sources:* Federal & provincial government support; fundraising; earned income
Staff Member(s): 2; 100 volunteer(s)
Membership: 30 student + 20 senior/lifetime + 800 individual; *Fees:* $20-$40
Activities: Atlantic Writing Awards; readings; workshops; mentorships; *Internships:* Yes; *Speaker Service:* Yes; *Library* Open to public
Awards:
• Thomas H. Raddall Atlantic Fiction Prize (Award)
Honours the best fiction writing by an Atlantic Canadian writer *Amount:* $10,000
• Evelyn Richardson Memorial Literary Trust Award (Award)
Award was established in 1978 to recognize outstanding work in non-fiction by a Nova Scotian writer (native or resident) *Amount:* $2,000
• Atlantic Poetry Prize (Award)
Amount: $2,000

The Writers' Guild of Alberta (WGA)
Percy Page Centre, 11759 Groat Rd., Edmonton AB T5M 3K6
Tel: 780-422-8174; *Fax:* 780-422-2663
Toll-Free: 800-665-5354
mail@writersguild.ab.ca
www.writersguild.ab.ca
www.facebook.com/139496766118754
twitter.com/WritersGuildAB
Overview: A medium-sized provincial charitable organization founded in 1980
Mission: To provide a meeting ground & collective voice for the writers of Alberta; to promote excellence in writing in Alberta
Affliation(s): Manitoba Writers' Guild; Federation of BC Writers; Saskatchewan Writers' Guild; Writers' Union of Canada; Newfoundland & Labrador Guilds; Periodical Writers' Association of Canada; League of Canadian Poets
Chief Officer(s):
Carol Holmes, Executive Director
cholmes@writersguild.ab.ca
Patricia MacQuarrie, President
Julie Sedivy, Vice-President
Finances: *Annual Operating Budget:* $250,000-$500,000
Staff Member(s): 16
Membership: 5 associate + 450 individual + 350 student + 20 senior/lifetime; *Fees:* $70 annually; $40 seniors/students; *Committees:* Awards; Annual General Meeting; Newsletter;

Promote Alberta Writing; Professional Standards; Retreats; Workshop
Activities: *Awareness Events:* Alberta Book Awards Gala; *Library* Open to public
Awards:
• Annual Awards Program (Award)
Established 1982 to recognize excellence in writing by Alberta authors; published books may be entered in any of the following categories: Children's Literature (any genre), Drama, Novel, Non-Fiction, Poetry, Short Fiction, Best First Book; winners receive $1000 cash award

Calgary Office
Lord Denning House, #509, 20th Ave. SW, Calgary AB T2S 0E7
Tel: 403-265-2226; *Fax:* 403-234-9532
mail@writersguild.ab.ca

The Writers' Trust of Canada

#200, 90 Richmond St. East, Toronto ON M5C 1P1
Tel: 416-504-8222; *Fax:* 416-504-9090
info@writerstrust.com
www.writerstrust.com
www.facebook.com/writerstrust
twitter.com/writerstrust
Previous Name: The Writers' Development Trust
Overview: A small national organization founded in 1976
Mission: Is a national charitable organization providing support to writers through various programs & awards; celebrates the talents & achievements of our country's writers; is committed to exploring & introducing to future generations the traditions that will enrich our common literary heritage & strengthen Canada's cultural foundations
Chief Officer(s):
Peter Kahnert, Chair
Don Oravec, Executive Director
doravec@writerstrust.com
Amanda Hopkins, Program Coordinator
ahopkins@writerstrust.com
Finances: *Funding Sources:* Business sponsors; individuals; government
Staff Member(s): 5
Membership: 1-99
Activities: Canada Book Day; Great Literary Dinner Party; Great Literary Awards; Politics & the Pen; Small Literary Dinner Parties; *Awareness Events:* Canada Book Week, April
Awards:
• The Thomas Raddall Atlantic Fiction Award (Award)
Presented in conjunction with the Writers' Federation of Nova Scotia to an Atlantic writer for a work of fiction published in the previous year *Amount:* $5,000
• The W.O. Mitchell Literary Prize (Award)
Presented annually to a writer who has produced an outstanding body of work, has acted during his/her career as a "caring mentor" for writers*Eligibility:* Has published a work of fiction or had a new stage play produced during the three-year period specified for each competition; every third year the prize will be awarded to a writer who works in French*Location:* $15,000
• Vicky Metcalf Prize for Children's Literature (Award)
Awarded annually to an author of children's literature, either fiction, non-fiction, picture books or poetry, not for a single book, but for a body of work, unless, in the opinion of the jury, there is no author worthy of the award that year *Amount:* $15,000
• Rogers Writers' Trust Fiction Prize (Award)
Annually to the author of the work of fiction published in the previous year that in the opinion of the judges, shows the best literary merit *Amount:* $15,000
• McClelland & Stewart Journey Prize (Award)
Awarded annually to a new & developing writer *Amount:* $10,000
• Matt Cohen Award (Award)
For a lifetime of distinguished work by a Canadian writer, working in either poetry or prose, writing in either French or English who has dedicated their life to writing as a primary pursuit *Amount:* $20,000
• The Matt Cohen Award (Award)
Amount: $20,000
• The Writers' Trust of Canada/McClelland & Stewart Journey Prize (Award)
Amount: $10,000
• The Bronwen Wallace Memorial Award (Award)
Awarded annually to a Canadian writer under the age of 35 who is not yet published in book form; award alternates each year between poetry & short fiction *Amount:* $1,000
• The Writers Trust of Canada's Shaughnessy Cohen Award for Political Writing (Award)
Sponsored by CTV awarded to a non-fiction book of outstanding literary merit that enlarges our understanding of contemporary Canadian political & social issues *Amount:* $10,000
• The Drainie-Taylor Biography Prize (Award)
Awarded annually for the best work of biography, autobiography or personal memoir *Amount:* $10,000
• The Timothy Findley Award (Award)
Awarded annually to a male Canadian writer for a body of work & in hope of future contributions *Amount:* $15,000
• Pearson Writers' Trust Non-Fiction Prize (Award)
Awarded annually to the author of the work of non-fiction published in the previous year that, in the opinion of the judges, shows the best literary merit *Amount:* $15,000
• The Marian Engel Award (Award)
Established 1986; awarded annually to a female Canadian writer, for a body of work & in hope of future contributions *Amount:* $15,000
• The Vicky Metcalf Award for Children's Literature (Award)
Amount: $15,000

The Writers' Union of Canada (TWUC)

#600, 460 Richmond St. West, Toronto ON M5V 1Y1
Tel: 416-703-8982; *Fax:* 416-504-9090
info@writersunion.ca
www.writersunion.ca
www.facebook.com/thewritersunionofcanada
twitter.com/twuc
Overview: A medium-sized national organization founded in 1973
Mission: To unite writers for the advancement of their common interests; to foster writing in Canada; to maintain relations with publishers; to exchange information among members; to safeguard the freedom to write & to publish; to advance good relations with other writers & their organizations in Canada & all parts of the world
Member of: Book & Periodical Council
Affliation(s): Canadian Copyright Licensing Agency; Canadian Conference of the Arts; Cultural Human Resources Council
Chief Officer(s):
Harry Tnurston, Chair
John Degen, Executive Director
jdegen@writersunion.ca
Finances: *Funding Sources:* Member dues; Canada Council; Ontario Arts Council; Ontario Ministry of Tourism, Culture & Recreation
Staff Member(s): 7
Membership: 2,000; *Fees:* $205; *Member Profile:* Canadian citizen or landed immigrant who has had a trade book published by a commercial or university press
Activities: Writers in the Schools Program; National Public Readings Program; Manuscript Evaluation Service; Contract Evaluation Service; Contract Negotiation Service; *Speaker Service:* Yes
Awards:
• Postcard Story Competition (Award)
Amount: $500
• Writing for Children Competition (Award)
Amount: $1,500
• Short Prose Competition for Developing Writers (Award)
Amount: $2,500
• Postcard Story Competition (Award)
• Danuta Gleed Literary Award (Award)
Awarded to a Canadian writer for the best first collection of published short stories in the English language *Amount:* $10,000

Pacific Regional Office
PO Box 45052, Stn. Ocean Park, Surrey BC V4A 9L1
Tel: 604-535-8288; *Fax:* 604-535-8288
twucpacific@shaw.ca
Chief Officer(s):
Judy Villeneuve, Co-ordinator

WTF Taekwondo Federation of British Columbia

c/o Grand Master Dae Lim, #3, 511 Cottonwood Ave., Coquitlam BC V3J 2R4
Tel: 604-939-8232
wtfbccanada@gmail.com
taekwondobc.com
Also Known As: BC Taekwondo Federation
Overview: A small provincial organization
Mission: To be the governing body of taekwondo in British Columbia; sanctioned to send athletes to the Olympic Games, World Taekwondo Championships, World Junior Taekwondo Championships, World Cup Taekwondo Games, Pan-American Games, Canadian National Championships & Canadian Junior National Championships.
Member of: WTF Taekwondo Canada; Sport BC
Affliation(s): International Olympic Committee
Chief Officer(s):
Dae Lim, President
Tony Kook, Secretary General, 604-986-5558
northshoretkd@shaw.ca

WushuCanada

2370 Midland Ave., #B25, Toronto ON M1S 5C6
Tel: 416-321-5913
info@wushucanada.com
wushucanada.com
www.facebook.com/pages/WushuCanada/211084358925927
twitter.com/WushuCanada
Previous Name: Confederation of Canadian Wushu Organizations
Overview: A small national organization
Mission: To promote & develop the Olympic sport of Wushu in Canada

WushuOntario

2370 Midland Ave., #B25-22, Toronto ON M1S 5C6
Tel: 416-321-5913
www.wushuontario.ca
Previous Name: United Wushu Association of Ontario
Overview: A small provincial organization founded in 1997
Mission: To govern & promote Wushu in Ontario

WWOOF Canada (WWOOF Canada)

4429 Carlson Rd., Nelson BC V1L 6X3
Tel: 250-354-4417
wwoofcan@shaw.ca
www.wwoof.ca
Also Known As: Willing Workers on Organic Farms, World Wide Opportunities on Organic Farms
Overview: A small national organization founded in 1985
Mission: WWOOF Aims to get firsthand experience of organic farming & gardening and to lend a helping hand wherever needed
Member of: WWOOF International Federation
Finances: *Annual Operating Budget:* Less than $50,000
Staff Member(s): 1; 2000 volunteer(s)
Membership: 20,000; *Fees:* $45
Activities: WWOOFing is a cultural exchange & a helping exchange; *Internships:* Yes

Wycliffe Bible Translators of Canada, Inc. (WBTC)

4316 - 10th St. NE, Calgary AB T2E 6K3
Tel: 403-250-5411; *Fax:* 403-250-2623
Toll-Free: 800-463-1143
info@wycliffe.ca
www.wycliffe.ca
www.linkedin.com/WycliffeBibleTranslatorsCanada
www.facebook.com/WycliffeCanada
twitter.com/wycliffe_canada
www.youtube.com/wycliffecanada;
www.godtube.com/wycliffecanada
Also Known As: Wycliffe Canada
Overview: A large national charitable organization founded in 1968
Mission: To serve minority language groups worldwide by fostering an understanding of God's Word through Bible translation, while encouraging literacy, education & stronger communities
Member of: Wycliffe Global Alliance
Affliation(s): Wycliffe Bible Translators International; Summer Institute of Linguistics; Canada Institute of Linguistics; Wycliffe Associates Canada
Chief Officer(s):
Jannice Moore, Chair
Roy Eyre, President
roy.eyre@wycliffe.ca
Finances: *Annual Operating Budget:* Greater than $5 Million; *Funding Sources:* Charitable donations; CIDA funding for literacy projects
Staff Member(s): 400; 75 volunteer(s)
Membership: 400 individual
Activities: Overseas Bible translation & literacy programs; *Internships:* Yes; *Speaker Service:* Yes; *Library:* Resource Centre; Open to public
Meetings/Conferences: • Wycliffe Bible Translators of Canada Inc. 2015 Annual General Meeting, 2015
Scope: National
Publications:
• Prayer Alive [a publication of Wycliffe Bible Translators of Canada Inc.]
Type: Newsletter; *Frequency:* Quarterly
• Word Alive [a publication of Wycliffe Bible Translators of Canada Inc.]

Type: Magazine; *Frequency:* Quarterly; *Editor:* Dwayne Janke; *Price:* Donation of $16 annually
Profile: Feature stories about the Bible translation movement
Eastern Region Office
#4, 14 Steinway Blvd., Etobicoke ON M9W 6M6
Tel: 416-675-6473; *Fax:* 416-675-7504
Toll-Free: 866-702-5273
toronto_office_canada@wycliffe.ca
Chief Officer(s):
Paul Hooper, Office Manager
paul_hooper@wycliffe.ca
Western Canada Office
7600 Glover Rd., Langley BC V2Y 1Y1
Tel: 604-881-1011; *Fax:* 604-513-2128
info@wycliffe.ca

Wynyard & District Chamber of Commerce
PO Box 508, Wynyard SK S0A 4T0
Tel: 306-554-2551; *Fax:* 306-554-3851
Overview: A small local organization
Chief Officer(s):
E.A. Zahayko, President
D. Johannesson, Secretary
Finances: *Annual Operating Budget:* Less than $50,000; *Funding Sources:* Membership dues
40 volunteer(s)
Membership: 87; *Fees:* $85; *Committees:* Social; Agriculture; Economic Development
Activities: *Speaker Service:* Yes

X Changes Artists' Gallery & Studios Society
#6E, 2333 Government Street, Victoria BC V8T 4P4
Tel: 250-382-0442
www.xchangesgallery.org
Overview: A small local organization founded in 1981
Chief Officer(s):
Richard Motchman, President
Staff Member(s): 7; 20 volunteer(s)
Membership: 20 individual; *Fees:* $30 - annual

Xplor Canada Association
#100, 445 Apple Creek Blvd., Markham ON L3R 9X7
Tel: 416-204-0011; *Fax:* 888-256-8868
Toll-Free: 888-258-0335
info@xplorcanada.org
www.xplorcanada.org
www.linkedin.com/groups?gid=1851072
www.facebook.com/groups/7356267451
twitter.com/Xplorcanada
Also Known As: Xplor
Overview: A small national organization founded in 1985
Mission: To provide an international forum to educate organizations & enable professionals to build & share knowledge concerning solutions, tools & processes for communicating customized information
Affliation(s): Xplor International
Chief Officer(s):
Dennis Quon, President
quond@gilmore.ca
Sandi Gilbert, Vice-President
sandi.gilbert@ccistrategic.com
Paul Abdool, Treasurer
pabdool@ikon.com
Franklin Friedmann, President, Eastern Chapter
franklin@ca.ibm.com
Sandi Gilbert, President, Western Chapter
sandi.gilbert@ccistrategic.com
Larry Henry, Acting President, Central Chapter
larry.henry@canadapost.postescanada.ca
Finances: *Funding Sources:* Membership dues; conference fees
Staff Member(s): 2; 35 volunteer(s)
Membership: 500; *Fees:* $50 student; $199 associate; $290 individual; $1,100 corporate; $5,600 corporate plus; *Member Profile:* Organizations that develop & use the technology of the document systems industry
Activities: Electronic Document Professional certification (EDP); *Speaker Service:* Yes
Awards:
• Xplorer of the Year (Award)
• Innovator of the Year (Award)

Yamaska Literacy Council (YLC) / Conseil d'alphabétisation de Yamaska
#203, 505 South St., Cowansville QC J2K 2X9
Tél: 450-263-7503; *Téléc:* 450-263-7209
Ligne sans frais: 866-337-7503
yamaskalit@endirect.qc.ca
www.yamaskaliteracy.ca
Aperçu: *Dimension:* petite; *Envergure:* locale; Organisme sans but lucratif
Mission: The Yamaska Literacy Council trains volunteers to help adults improve their literacy skills
Affliation(s): Laubach Literacy of Canada-Québec; Literacy Volunteers of Québec; Québec English Literacy Alliance; The Literacy Foundation
Membre(s) du bureau directeur:
Martha Shufelt, President
Wendy Seys, Coordinator
Finances: *Budget de fonctionnement annuel:* $50,000-$100,000; *Fonds:* Regional government
Membre(s) du personnel: 2; 40 bénévole(s)
Membre: 1-99

Yarmouth & Area Chamber of Commerce (YCC)
PO Box 532, #1, 342 Main St., Yarmouth NS B5A 4B4
Tel: 902-742-3074; *Fax:* 902-749-1383
info@yarmouthchamberofcommerce.com
www.yarmouthchamberofcommerce.com
www.linkedin.com/groups?about=&gid=2910385
www.facebook.com/YarmouthNSChamber
Overview: A medium-sized local organization founded in 1892
Mission: To promote a positive economic & business climate in Yarmouth county
Member of: Canadian Chamber of Commerce; Atlantic Provinces Chamber of Commerce
Chief Officer(s):
Dave Hall, President
Karen Churchill, 1st Vice-President
Mike Mercier, 2nd Vice-President
Finances: *Annual Operating Budget:* Less than $50,000; *Funding Sources:* Membership dues; fee for service; magazine publications
Membership: 200; *Fees:* $20-$310; *Committees:* Transportation; Membership; Economic Development
Awards:
• The Royal Bank Partners in Education Award (Award)

Yarmouth County Historical Society
22 Collins St., Yarmouth NS B5A 3C8
Tel: 902-742-5539; *Fax:* 902-749-1120
ycmuseum@eastlink.ca
yarmouthcountymuseum.ednet.ns.ca
www.facebook.com/92402018979
Also Known As: Yarmouth County Museum & Archives
Overview: A small local charitable organization founded in 1935
Mission: To collect and preserve historical data, records and objects of interest, to erect historical markers, and generally to promote interest in Yarmouth County history.
Member of: Federation of the Nova Scotian Heritage; Canadian Museums Association; Council of Nova Scotia Archives
Chief Officer(s):
Nadine Gates, Director/Curator
Finances: *Annual Operating Budget:* $100,000-$250,000; *Funding Sources:* Membership dues; provincial government; gift shop
Staff Member(s): 2; 100 volunteer(s)
Membership: 385; *Fees:* $20 individual; $40 family
Activities: Historical programs; genealogy; *Speaker Service:* Yes; *Library:* Yarmouth County Museum Archives; Open to public

Yarmouth County Tourist Association
PO Box 477, Yarmouth NS B5A 4B4
Tel: 902-742-5355; *Fax:* 902-742-1967
www.aboutyarmouth.com
Overview: A small local organization founded in 1979
Chief Officer(s):
Wendy Muise, Executive Director
Finances: *Funding Sources:* Municipal government
Staff Member(s): 1
Membership: 125

Yarmouth Food Bank Society
390 Main St., Yarmouth NS B5A 2A3
Tel: 902-742-0918
Overview: A small local charitable organization founded in 1987
Member of: Nova Scotia Food Bank Association; Atlantic Alliance of Food Banks & C.V.A.'s
Chief Officer(s):
Bill Carter, Contact
Finances: *Annual Operating Budget:* Less than $50,000; *Funding Sources:* Fundraising
Staff Member(s): 14; 14 volunteer(s)
Membership: 1-99; *Fees:* $100
Activities: Food drives; *Speaker Service:* Yes

Yasodhara Ashram Society
PO Box 9, Kootenay Bay BC V0B 1X0
Tel: 250-227-9224; *Fax:* 250-227-9494
Toll-Free: 800-661-8711
info@yasodhara.org
www.yasodhara.org
Overview: A small international charitable organization founded in 1963
Mission: To maintain a centre for adults engaged in a life of spiritual intent; to provide instruction in & opportunities for religious & spiritual practice
Finances: *Annual Operating Budget:* $500,000-$1.5 Million
15 volunteer(s)
Membership: 125; *Fees:* $25
Activities: *Internships:* Yes; *Speaker Service:* Yes; *Library* by appointment

The Yellow Dog Project
#5 4646 Riverside Dr., Red Deer AB T4N 6Y5
Tel: 403-342-0187
info@theyellowdogproject.com
www.theyellowdogproject.com
www.facebook.com/TheYellowDogProject
twitter.com/YellowDogProj
pinterest.com/yellowdogproj/
Overview: A small international organization
Mission: To educate the public and dog owners to identify dogs needing space, promote appropriate contact of dogs and assist dog parents to identify their dog as needing space.

Yellowhead East Business Development Corporation (YEBDC)
PO Box 249, 5028 - 50 Ave., Sangudo AB T0E 2A0
Tel: 780-785-2900; *Fax:* 780-785-3337
Toll-Free: 800-556-0328
Overview: A small local organization
Mission: To provide a single window of opportunity through which businesses & other entities can access information, resources, financial assistance & training in order to foster economic development, resulting in job creation
Chief Officer(s):
Roxanne Harper, Manager
rharper@yebdc.ab.ca
Finances: *Funding Sources:* National government
Staff Member(s): 40; 14 volunteer(s)

Yellowhead Emergency Shelter for Women Society
PO Box 6401, Hinton AB T7V 1X7
Tel: 780-865-4359; *Fax:* 780-865-7151
Toll-Free: 800-661-0937; *Crisis Hot-Line:* 780-865-5133
yeswomen@shaw.ca
Overview: A small local organization
Mission: To offer temporary safe accommodation for abused women & their children & 24-hour telephone & walk-in counselling; To offer outreach & public education
Finances: *Funding Sources:* Provincial government

Yellowhead Highway Association *See* Trans Canada Yellowhead Highway Association

Yellowknife Association for Community Living (YKACL)
PO Box 981, 4912 - 53 St., Yellowknife NT X1A 2N7
Tel: 867-920-2644; *Fax:* 867-920-2348
info@ykacl.ca
www.ykacl.ca
www.facebook.com/124566867584059
Overview: A small provincial charitable organization overseen by Canadian Association for Community Living
Mission: To promote the welfare of people with handicaps & their families; to lobby on behalf of people with developmental disabilities in the Northwest Territories; to ensure that every person in Northwest Territories has access to supports to live with dignity & to participate in the community of his/her choice
Member of: Canadian Association for Community Living
Chief Officer(s):
Lynn Elkin, Executive Director, 867-920-2644, Fax: 768-920-2348
ed@ykacl.ca
Pamela Weeks-Beaton, President
president@ykacl.ca
Claudia Parker, Vice-President
Finances: *Funding Sources:* Canadian & GNWT governments
Staff Member(s): 23

Activities: *Library* Open to public

Yellowknife Chamber of Commerce
#21, 4910 - 50th Ave., 3rd Fl., Yellowknife NT X1A 1C4
Tel: 867-920-4944; *Fax:* 867-920-4640
generalmanager@ykchamber.com
www.ykchamber.com
www.facebook.com/pages/Yellowknife-Chamber-of-Commerce/194561107260153
twitter.com/intent/user?screen_name=YKChamber
Overview: A medium-sized local organization founded in 1947
Member of: Canadian Chamber of Commerce; NWT Chamber of Commerce
Chief Officer(s):
Tim Doyle, Executive Director
Finances: *Annual Operating Budget:* $250,000-$500,000; *Funding Sources:* Membership & service fees
Staff Member(s): 3; 18 volunteer(s)
Membership: 400; *Fees:* Schedule available; *Committees:* Education; Environment; Municipal Affairs; Government Affairs; Business Development; Member Services
Activities: Public awareness; business advocacy; Spring Trade Show; Small Business Week; *Speaker Service:* Yes; *Library* by appointment

Yellowknife Real Estate Board
#201, 5204 - 50 Ave., Yellowknife NT X1A 1E2
Tel: 867-920-4624; *Fax:* 867-873-6387
boards.mls.ca/yellowknife
Overview: A small local organization
Member of: The Canadian Real Estate Association

Yellowknife Shooting Club (YKSC)
PO Box 2931, Yellowknife NT X1A 2R2
yellowknifeshootingclub.ca
Overview: A small local organization founded in 1961
Mission: Safe shooting of all types for firearms for sport & recreational purposes
Affliation(s): NWT Federation of Shooting Sports; Shooting Federation of Canada; NRA
Chief Officer(s):
Scott Cairns, President, 867-669-9220
Bud Rhyndress, Vice-President, 867-873-6209
Membership: *Fees:* $170 individual; $280 family; $10 youth; *Member Profile:* Firearms owners & users
Activities: Caribou Carnival; Wolverine Days; fun shoot; media shoot; turkey shoot; Sight-In Days

YMCA ASK! & YMCA ASCC *See* ASK! Community Information Centre (LAMP)

YMCA Canada
#601, 1867 Younge St., Toronto ON M4S 1Y5
Tel: 416-967-9622; *Fax:* 416-967-9618
www.ymca.ca
www.facebook.com/YMCACanada
twitter.com/YMCA_Canada
Also Known As: The National Council of Young Men's Christian Associations of Canada
Overview: A large national charitable organization founded in 1851
Mission: Dedicated to the growth of all persons in spirit, mind & body, & in a sense of responsibility to each other & the global community; fosters & stimulates the development of strong member associations & advocates on their behalf regionally, nationally & internationally
Affliation(s): Canadian Centre for Philanthropy; Canadian Child Care Federation; Canadian Coalition for the Rights of Children; Canadian Council for International Cooperation; Canadian Council on Children & Youth; Canadian Recreational Canoeing Association; Coalition on National Voluntary Organizations; Conference Board of Canada; Huronia Tourism Association; National Fitness Leadership Advisory Committee; National Life Guard Service; National Voluntary Health Agencies; National Youth Serving Agencies; Partnership Africa Canada; Resorts Ontario; Royal Life Saving Society; Voluntary Sector Round Table
Chief Officer(s):
Scott Haldane, President/CEO
Marilyn Kapitany, Chair
Finances: *Annual Operating Budget:* Greater than $5 Million
Staff Member(s): 17; 3000 volunteer(s)
Membership: 1.8 million participants annually; *Member Profile:* 45 YMCAs + 8 YMCA/YWCAs
Activities: Camps; leadership development; child care; health & fitness programs; *Awareness Events:* YMCA Healthy Kids Day, May-June
Awards:
- Fellowship of Honour (Award)
- YMCA Hall of Fame (Award)
- YMCA Canada Educational Awards (Award)

Brockville & Area YMCA-YWCA
345 Park St., Brockville ON K6V 5Y7
Tel: 613-342-7961; *Fax:* 613-342-8223
ymca@brockvilley.com
www.brockvilley.com
www.facebook.com/163865009971
twitter.com/YMCABrockville
Chief Officer(s):
Kim Charteris, Interim CEO
kcharteris@brockvilley.com

Family YMCA of Windsor - Essex County
500 Victoria Ave., Windsor ON N9A 4M8
Tel: 519-258-9622; *Fax:* 519-258-9629
windsor@ymca.ca
ymcawo.ca/windsor-essex-contact
www.facebook.com/12860181433
Chief Officer(s):
Giles Denis, Contact, 519-258-9622 Ext. 225
dgiles@ymcawo.ca

National Capital Region YMCA - YWCA de la région de la capitale nationale
180 Argyle Ave., Ottawa ON K2P 1B7
Tel: 613-237-1320; *Fax:* 613-788-5052
www.ymcaywca.ca
www.facebook.com/ymcaywca
twitter.com/YMCAYWCA_Ottawa
www.youtube.com/user/ymcaywcaottawa
Chief Officer(s):
Deirdre Speers, President & CEO

Northern Alberta YMCA
#300, 10030 - 102A Ave., Edmonton AB T5J 0G5
Tel: 780-425-9622; *Fax:* 780-428-9469
edmonton.ymca.ca
www.facebook.com/82802289395
Chief Officer(s):
Nick Parkinson, President & CEO
nparkinson@edmonton.ymca.ca

Owen Sound Family YMCA
700 10th Street East, Owen Sound ON N4K 0C6
Tel: 519-376-0484; *Fax:* 519-376-0487
Toll-Free: 800-265-3711
membership@ymcaowensound.on.ca
www.ymcaowensound.on.ca
Chief Officer(s):
Gayle Graham, CEO, 519-376-0484 Ext. 204
ggraham@ymcaowensound.on.ca

Timmins Family YMCA
376 Poplar Ave., Timmins ON P4N 4S4
Tel: 705-360-4381; *Fax:* 705-360-4382
info@timminsymca.org
www.timminsymca.org
Chief Officer(s):
Wayne Bozzer, Executive Director
wbozzer@timminsymca.org

YMCA - YWCA of Brantford
143 Wellington St., Brantford ON N3S 3Y8
Tel: 519-752-6568; *Fax:* 519-759-8431
brantford_membership@ymca.ca
www.ymcahbb.ca
Chief Officer(s):
Lisa Roddie, General Manager
lisa_roddie@ymca.ca

YMCA - YWCA of Moose Jaw
220 Fairford St. East, Moose Jaw SK S6H 6H2
Tel: 306-692-0688; *Fax:* 306-694-5034
www.moosejawymca.ca
www.facebook.com/mjymca
Chief Officer(s):
Jana Bollinger, President

YMCA - YWCA of Saint John
130 Broadview Ave., Saint John NB E2L 5C5
Tel: 506-634-4860; *Fax:* 506-634-0783
admin@saintjohny.com
www.saintjohny.com
www.facebook.com/SaintJohnY
twitter.com/Y_SaintJohn
Chief Officer(s):
Jill Keliher, Director

YMCA - YWCA of the Central Okanagan
375 Hartman Rd., Kelowna BC V1X 2M9
Tel: 250-491-9622; *Fax:* 250-765-7962
info@ymca-ywca.com
www.ymcaokanagan.ca
Chief Officer(s):
Sharon Peterson, CEO
speterson@ymca-ywca.com

YMCA - YWCA of Winnipeg
3550 Portage Ave., Winnipeg MB R3K 0Z8
Tel: 204-832-7002; *Fax:* 204-889-9002
info@ymcaywca.mb.ca
www.ywinnipeg.ca
www.facebook.com/ywinnipeg
twitter.com/YWinnipeg
www.youtube.com/user/YWinnipeg
Chief Officer(s):
Kent Paterson, President & CEO

YMCA of Barrie
22 Grove St. West, Barrie ON L4N 1M7
Tel: 705-726-6421; *Fax:* 705-726-0508
barrie@ymcaofsimcoemuskoka.ca

YMCA of Belleville & Quinte
433 Victoria Ave., Belleville ON K8N 2G1
Tel: 613-966-9622; *Fax:* 613-962-9247
info@bellevilleymca.ca
www.bellevilleymca.ca
Chief Officer(s):
Robert J. Gallagher, CEO

YMCA of Brandon
231 - 8th St., Brandon MB R7A 3X2
Tel: 204-727-5456; *Fax:* 204-726-0995
info@ymcabrandon.com
www.ymcabrandon.com
Chief Officer(s):
Lon Culling, CEO

YMCA of Calgary
101 - 3 St. SW, 2nd Fl., Calgary AB T2P 4G6
Tel: 403-237-9622; *Fax:* 403-269-4661
nkaminer@calgary.ymca.ca
www.ymcacalgary.org
www.facebook.com/146637995640
Chief Officer(s):
Helene Weir, President & CEO, 403-781-1670
hweir@calgary.ymca.ca

YMCA of Cape Breton
399 Charlotte St., Sydney NS B1P 1E3
Tel: 902-562-9622; *Fax:* 902-564-2063
info@cbymca.com
www.cbymca.com
www.facebook.com/YMCAcapebreton
Chief Officer(s):
Andre Gallant, CEO

YMCA of Chatham-Kent
101 Courthouse Lane, Chatham ON N7L 0B5
Tel: 519-360-9622; *Fax:* 519-360-9629
www.ymcaswo.ca/membership_branches-ymca_of_chathamkent.php
Chief Officer(s):
Amy Wadsworth, General Manager, 519-360-9622 Ext. 103

YMCA of Chilliwack
45844 Hocking Ave., Chilliwack BC V2P 1B4
Tel: 604-792-3371; *Fax:* 604-792-7298
chilliwack@gv.ymca.cag
www.vanymca.org/centres/chilliwack
twitter.com/ChilliwackYMCA
Chief Officer(s):
Yvonne Comfort, General Manager

YMCA of Collingwood & District
PO Box 592, 200 Hume St., Collingwood ON L9Y 4E8
Tel: 705-445-5705; *Fax:* 705-445-7732
ymcaofsimcoemuskoka.ca/health_fitness_recreation/collingwood.html
Chief Officer(s):
Rob Armstrong, CEO, 705-726-9622 Ext. 437

YMCA of Cumberland
PO Box 552, 92 Church St., Amherst NS B4H 4A1
Tel: 902-667-9112; *Fax:* 902-661-4692
info@cumberland.ymca.ca
www.ymcaofcumberland.com
www.facebook.com/29565029610
Chief Officer(s):
Trina Clarke, CEO
tclarke@ymcaofcumberland.com

YMCA of Exploits Valley
13 Prices Ave., Grand Falls-Windsor NL A2B 1C9

Tel: 709-489-9622; *Fax:* 709-489-8404
shaunette_skinner@exploitsvalley.ymca.ca
www.exploitsvalleyymca.ca
www.facebook.com/2263448125
Chief Officer(s):
Shaunette Skinner, Contact

YMCA of Fort Erie
1555 Garrison Rd., Fort Erie ON L2A 1P8
Tel: 905-871-9622; *Fax:* 905-871-9228
www.ymcaofniagara.org/membership_branches-fort_erie.php

YMCA of Fredericton
570 York St., Fredericton NB E3B 3R2
Tel: 506-462-3000; *Fax:* 506-462-3007
www.ymcafredericton.nb.ca
www.facebook.com/260446094448
twitter.com/FrederictonYMCA
Mission: To encourage the health of individuals & communities; To serve people of all ages, backgrounds & abilities through all stages of life
Member of: Fredericton Chamber of Commerce
Chief Officer(s):
Barb Ramsay, CEO
barb.ramsay@ymcafredericton.org
Ruth Claybourn, Manager, Family Services
Ruth.Claybourn@ymcafredericton.org
Lisa Hanson-Ouellette, Manager, Member Services
Lisa.Hanson-Ouellette@ymcafredericton.org

YMCA of Greater Halifax/Dartmouth
#306, 5670 Spring Garden Road, Halifax NS B3J 1H6
Tel: 902-423-4261
www.ymcahrm.ns.ca
Chief Officer(s):
Bette Watson-Borg, CEO
bette_watson-borg@ymca.ca

YMCA of Greater Moncton
30 War Veterans Ave., Moncton NB E1C 0B3
Tel: 506-857-0606; *Fax:* 506-859-8198
info@ymcamoncton.com
www.ymcamoncton.ca
www.facebook.com/107599097472
Chief Officer(s):
Zane Korytko, CEO
zane.korytko@ymcamoncton.com

YMCA of Greater Montréal
1435, rue Drummond, 4e étage, Montréal QC H3G 1W3
Tel: 514-849-5331; *Fax:* 514-849-5863
ymcamontreal.qc.ca/centres_en.htm
Chief Officer(s):
Stéphanie Vaillancourt, CEO

YMCA of Greater Toronto
#300, 2200 Yonge St., Toronto ON M4S 2C6
Tel: 416-928-9622; *Fax:* 416-928-2030
memberservices@ymcagta.org
www.ymcagta.org
www.facebook.com/YMCAGTA
twitter.com/ymcagta
www.youtube.com/user/ymcagta
Chief Officer(s):
Medhat Mahdy, President & CEO

YMCA of Greater Vancouver
100 - 5055 Joyce Street, Vancouver BC V5R 6B2
Tel: 604-681-9622; *Fax:* 604-688-0220
info@gv.ymca.cag
www.vanymca.org
Chief Officer(s):
Stephen Butz, President & CEO

YMCA of Greater Victoria
851 Broughton St., Victoria BC V8W 1E5
Tel: 250-386-7511; *Fax:* 250-380-1933
memberservices@victoriay.com
www.victoriay.com
www.facebook.com/13153669353503
Chief Officer(s):
Jennie Edgecombe, CEO
jedgecombe@victoriay.com

YMCA of Hamilton/Burlington/Brantford
79 James St. South, Hamilton ON L8P 2Z1
Tel: 905-529-7102; *Fax:* 905-529-6682
hamilton_downtown@ymca.ca
www.ymcahbb.ca
Chief Officer(s):
Jim Commerford, CEO, 905-317-4919
jim_commerford@ymca.ca

YMCA of Humber Community
PO Box 836, 2 Herald Ave., Corner Brook NL A2H 6H6
Tel: 709-639-9676; *Fax:* 709-634-9622
www.humbercommunityymca.ca
Chief Officer(s):
Christine Young, CEO

YMCA of Kingston
100 Wright Cres., Kingston ON K7L 4T9
Tel: 613-546-2647; *Fax:* 613-549-0654
contact@kingston.ymca.ca
www.kingston.ymca.ca
Chief Officer(s):
Mary Kloosterman, CEO
mary_kloosterman@kingston.ymca.ca

YMCA of Lethbridge
515 Stafford Dr. South, Lethbridge AB T1J 2L3
Tel: 403-327-9622; *Fax:* 403-320-6475
ymca@lethbridgeymca.org
www.lethbridgeymca.org
Chief Officer(s):
Jennifer Petracek-Kolb, CEO
jennifer@lethbridgeymca.org

YMCA of London
382 Waterloo St., London ON N6B 2N8
Tel: 519-667-3300; *Fax:* 519-433-8527
www.ymcawo.ca
Chief Officer(s):
Shaun Elliott, CEO
selliott@ymcawo.ca

YMCA of Lunenburg County
75 High St., Bridgewater NS B4V 1V8
Tel: 902-543-9622; *Fax:* 902-543-6545
jill_sutherland@ymca.ca
www.ymcalunenburgcounty.org
Chief Officer(s):
Yvonne Smith, CEO
yvonne_smith@ymca.ca

YMCA of Medicine Hat
770 1st St. SE, Medicine Hat AB T1A 0B4
Tel: 403-529-4733; *Fax:* 403-529-4734
www.ymca-medicinehat.org
www.facebook.com/122710295708
Chief Officer(s):
Scott Richter, CEO
scott@medicinehatymca.ca

YMCA of Midland
Little Lake Park, PO Box 488, 560 Little Lake Park Rd., Midland ON L4R 4L3
Tel: 705-526-7828; *Fax:* 705-526-8735
www.ymcaofsimcoemuskoka.ca/health_fitness_recreation/midland.html

YMCA of Niagara
43 Church Street, St. Catharines ON L2R 7E1
Tel: 905-646-9622; *Fax:* 905-646-4213
www.ymcaofniagara.org
Chief Officer(s):
Stephen Butz, CEO

YMCA of North Bay
186 Chippewa St. West, North Bay ON P1B 6G2
Tel: 705-497-9622; *Fax:* 705-474-5116
www.ymcanorthbay.com
www.facebook.com/ymcanorthbay
Chief Officer(s):
Kim Kanmacher, CEO

YMCA of Northumberland
339 Elgin St. West, Cobourg ON K9A 4X5
Tel: 905-372-0161; *Fax:* 905-377-8940
www.ymcanorthumberland.com
www.facebook.com/93308676120
Chief Officer(s):
Eunice Kirkpatrick, CEO, 905-372-4318 Ext. 310
ekirkpatrick@ymcanorthumberland.com

YMCA of Oakville
410 Rebecca St., Oakville ON L6K 1K7
Tel: 905-845-3417; *Fax:* 905-842-6792
customerservice@oakville.ymca.ca
www.ymcaofoakville.com
www.linkedin.com/company/ymca-of-oakville
www.facebook.com/YMCAOakville
twitter.com/YMCAOakville
Chief Officer(s):
Kyle Barber, President & CEO

YMCA of Orillia
300 Peter St. North, Orillia ON L3V 5A2
Tel: 705-325-6168; *Fax:* 705-325-0243
orillia@ymcaofsimcoemuskoka.ca
www.ymcaofsimcoemuskoka.ca
Chief Officer(s):
Gilda Evely, General Manager
gilda_evely@ymca.ca

YMCA of Peterborough
123 Aylmer St. South, Peterborough ON K9J 3H8
Tel: 705-748-9622; *Fax:* 705-741-3719
kelly_wilson@ymca.ca
www.peterboroughymca.org
twitter.com/YMCA_of_Ptbo
Chief Officer(s):
Robert Gallagher, CEO
bob_gallagher@ymca.ca

YMCA of Pictou County
RR #3, 2756 Westville Rd., New Glasgow NS B2H 5C6
Tel: 902-752-0202; *Fax:* 902-755-3446
frontdesk@pcymca.ca
www.pcymca.ca
www.facebook.com/YMCAPictouCounty
Chief Officer(s):
Dave MacIntyre, General Manager

YMCA of Prince George
PO Box 1808, 2020 Massey Dr., Prince George BC V2L 4V7
Tel: 250-562-9341; *Fax:* 250-564-2474
info@pgymca.bc.ca
www.pgymca.bc.ca
www.facebook.com/NBCYMCA
twitter.com/NBCY
www.youtube.com/user/PGYMCA
Chief Officer(s):
Amanda Alexander, CEO, 250-562-9341 Ext. 116

YMCA of Regina
2400 - 13th Ave., Regina SK S4P 0V9
Tel: 306-757-9622; *Fax:* 306-525-5508
ymcaregina.squarespace.com
www.facebook.com/YMCARegina
Chief Officer(s):
Randy Klassen, CEO
rklassen@regina.ymca.ca

YMCA of St. John's
PO Box 21291, 84 Elizabeth Ave., St. John's NL A1A 5G6
Tel: 709-726-9622; *Fax:* 709-576-0410
www.ynortheastavalon.com
www.linkedin.com/groups/YMCA-Northeast-Avalon-1903327
www.facebook.com/348363604436
twitter.com/@YMCAofNEA
Chief Officer(s):
Jason Brown, President & CEO
jbrown@ynortheastavalon.com

YMCA of St Thomas - Elgin
20 High St., St Thomas ON N5R 5V2
Tel: 519-631-2418; *Fax:* 519-631-4131
www.ymcawo.ca
Chief Officer(s):
Katie Payler, General Manager, 519-631-2418 Ext. 226
kpayler@ymcawo.ca

YMCA of Sarnia - Lambton
1015 Finch Dr., Sarnia ON N7S 8G5
Tel: 519-336-9622; *Fax:* 519-336-7818
Chief Officer(s):
Ian Foss, General Manager

YMCA of Saskatoon
25 - 22nd St. East, Saskatoon SK S7K 0C7
Tel: 306-652-7515; *Fax:* 306-652-2828
ymca@ymcasaskatoon.org
www.ymcasaskatoon.org
Chief Officer(s):
Dean Dodge, CEO

YMCA of Sault Ste Marie
235 McNabb St., Sault Ste Marie ON P6B 1Y3
Tel: 705-949-3133; *Fax:* 705-949-3344
info@ssmymca.ca
www.sault.ymca.ca
Chief Officer(s):
Kim Caruso, CEO
kim.caruso@ssmymca.ca

YMCA of Stratford - Perth
204 Downie St. South, Stratford ON N5A 1X4
Tel: 519-271-0480; *Fax:* 519-271-0489
cathy_clay@ymca.ca
www.stratfordperthymca.com
Chief Officer(s):

Mimi Price, CEO
mimi_price@ymca.ca

YMCA of Sudbury
140 Durham St., Sudbury ON P3E 3M7
Tel: 705-673-9136; *Fax:* 705-675-8777
memberservices@sudbury.ymca.ca
www.sudbury.ymca.ca
www.facebook.com/YMCASudbury
Chief Officer(s):
Kim Kanmacher, CEO

YMCA of Summerside
212 Green St., Summerside PE C1N 1Y4
Tel: 902-436-3446; *Fax:* 902-436-4935
mail@ymcapei.ca
www.ymcapei.ca
Chief Officer(s):
Ron Perry, President

YMCA of ville de Québec/Québec City
650, Wilfrid-Laurier, Québec QC G1R 2L4
Tel: 418-522-0800
ymca02@globetrotter.net
Chief Officer(s):
Claude Gagné, CEO

YMCA of Wood Buffalo
Westwood Centre, 221 Tundra Dr., Fort McMurray AB T9H 4Z7
Tel: 780-790-9622; *Fax:* 780-743-4045
nahanni_alma@ymca.ca
www.ymca.woodbuffalo.org
www.facebook.com/FortMcMurrayYmcaWoodbuffalo
twitter.com/YMCAWoodBuffalo
instagram.com/ymcawoodbuffalo
Chief Officer(s):
Nahanni Alma, Senior Director, Membership Sales & Service, 780-790-9622 Ext. 226

YMCA of Yarmouth
PO Box 86, 275 Main St., Yarmouth NS B5A 4B1
Tel: 902-742-7181; *Fax:* 902-742-7676
denise_reid@ymca.ca
www.ymcayarmouth.net
www.facebook.com/YmcaYarmouth
Chief Officer(s):
Yvonne Smith, CEO
Yvonne_Smith@ymca.ca

YMCAs of Cambridge & Kitchener-Waterloo
#203, 460 Frederick Street, Kitchener ON N2H 2P5
Tel: 519-584-7479
ymcacambridge@ymca.ca
www.ymcacambridgekw.ca
Chief Officer(s):
John Haddock, CEO, 519-584-7479 Ext. 200

YMCA-YWCA of Guelph
130 Woodland Glen Dr., Guelph ON N1G 4M3
Tel: 519-824-5150; *Fax:* 519-824-4729
contact@guelphy.org
www.guelphy.org
Chief Officer(s):
Bonk Jim, CEO

YMCA-YWCA of Kamloops
400 Battle St., Kamloops BC V2C 2L7
Tel: 250-372-7725; *Fax:* 250-372-3023
dharris@kamloopsy.org
www.kamloopsy.org
Chief Officer(s):
Colin Reid, CEO, 250-372-7725 Ext. 202
creid@kamloopsy.org

YMCA Immigrant & Community Services
256 Hespeler Rd., Cambridge ON N1R 3H3
Tel: 519-621-1621
newcomers@ckwymca.ca
www.ymcaimmigrantservices.ca
www.facebook.com/YMCAImmigrant
Previous Name: Cambridge Multicultural Centre
Overview: A small local organization founded in 1985 overseen by Ontario Council of Agencies Serving Immigrants
Mission: To promote integration of newcomers & first Canadians
Activities: Settlement; *Speaker Service:* Yes

YMCA of Cambridge *See* YMCA Canada

YMCA of Edmonton *See* YMCA Canada

YMCA of Montréal *See* YMCA Canada

Yoga Association of Alberta (YAA)
Percy Page Centre, 11759 Groat Rd., Edmonton AB T5M 3K6
Tel: 780-427-8776; *Fax:* 780-427-0524
yaa@yoga.ca
www.yoga.ca
www.facebook.com/yogaalberta
Overview: A small provincial charitable organization founded in 1976
Mission: To offer yoga activities to the public; to provide coordination & support to yoga enthusiasts
Chief Officer(s):
Debbie Spence, Executive Director
Finances: *Annual Operating Budget:* $250,000-$500,000; *Funding Sources:* Government grant
Staff Member(s): 7; 100 volunteer(s)
Membership: 1,200; *Fees:* $10 associate; $25 individual; $300 life; *Committees:* Teacher Training Program; Outreach
Activities: *Internships:* Yes

Yoga Vedanta Centre *See* Sivananda Ashram Yoga Camp

Yonge Street Mission (YSM)
306 Gerrard St. East, Toronto ON M5A 2G7
Tel: 416-929-9614; *Fax:* 416-929-7204
Toll-Free: 800-416-5111
info@ysm.ca
www.ysm.ca
www.facebook.com/YongeStreetMission
twitter.com/YSM_TO
Overview: A medium-sized local charitable organization founded in 1896
Mission: To bring God's peace, love, & justice to people living with economic, social, & spiritual poverty in Toronto
Chief Officer(s):
Angela Draskovic, President & CEO
Shirlene Courtis, Chief Development Officer
Rick Tobias, Mission Community Advocate
Brent Mitchell, Mission Program Officer
Paul Davidson, Mission Administrative Officer
Finances: *Annual Operating Budget:* Greater than $5 Million; *Funding Sources:* Donations; churches; individuals; businesses; foundations; grants
Staff Member(s): 120; 4000 volunteer(s)
Activities: Recreation; education; social & family events; relief; housing; *Internships:* Yes; *Speaker Service:* Yes

York and Metro Toronto Region *See* Junior Achievement of Canada

York Pioneer & Historical Society
PO Box 45026, 2482 Yonge St., Toronto ON M4P 3E3
Tel: 416-961-4420
www.yorkpioneers.org
Overview: A small provincial charitable organization founded in 1869
Mission: To unite descendants of those who immigrated to original county of York & others interested in preserving & perpetuating such historical recollections, incidents, documents & pictorial illustrations relating to early settlement of this district of Ontario
Member of: Ontario Historical Society
Chief Officer(s):
John Marshall, President
Finances: *Annual Operating Budget:* Less than $50,000
Staff Member(s): 1; 40 volunteer(s)
Membership: 7 corporate + 94 lifetime + 160 individual; *Fees:* Schedule available; *Committees:* Editorial; Eversley Church; Scadding Cabin; Program; Publicity
Activities: Operates Scadding Cabin Museum; *Library*

York Region Athletic Association (YRAA)
#1038, 44 Main St. South, Unionville ON L3R 2E4
Tel: 905-470-1551; *Fax:* 905-470-9092
www.yraa.com
twitter.com/yraa_news
Overview: A small local organization
Mission: To offer athletics in York Region high schools
Chief Officer(s):
Scot Angus, President
scot.angus@yrdsb.edu.on.ca

York Region Children's Aid Society
Kennedy Place, 16915 Leslie St., Newmarket ON L3Y 9A1
Tel: 905-895-2318; *Fax:* 905-895-2113
Toll-Free: 800-718-3850
inquiries@YorkCAS.org
www.yorkcas.on.ca
Also Known As: York Region CAS
Previous Name: Children & Family Services for York Region
Overview: A small local charitable organization
Mission: To protect children & promote a safe, healthy & caring environment for them in partnership with our diverse community
Member of: Ontario Association of Children's Aid Societies
Chief Officer(s):
Tammy Ward, President
Bruce Herridge, Vice-President
Patrick Lake, Executive Director
Finances: *Annual Operating Budget:* Greater than $5 Million; *Funding Sources:* Provincial government
Staff Member(s): 270; 200 volunteer(s)
Membership: 1-99; *Fees:* $10 individual; $25 family; *Member Profile:* Must have an interest in the welfare of children; work &/or live in York Region; 18 years or over; *Committees:* Finance; Planning; Governance; Policy; Quality Assurance
Activities: *Awareness Events:* Purple Ribbon Campaign for Child Abuse Prevention; *Speaker Service:* Yes

York Region Law Association
50 Eagle St. West, Newmarket ON L3Y 6B1
Tel: 905-895-2018; *Fax:* 905-853-7678
Toll-Free: 800-221-8864
bdykstra@yorklaw.ca
www.yorklaw.ca
Overview: A small local organization
Chief Officer(s):
Norman Panzica, President
npanzica@rogers.com
William Doodnauth, Treasurer
wdoodnauth@monteithbaker.com
Staff Member(s): 5

York Regional Police Association (YRPA) / Association régionale de la police de York
600 Stonehaven Ave., Newmarket ON L3X 2M4
Tel: 905-830-4947; *Fax:* 905-898-7282
yrpa@rogers.com
www.yrpa.on.ca
Overview: A small local organization founded in 1971
Member of: Police Association of Ontario; Canadian Police Association
Chief Officer(s):
John Miskiw, President
Staff Member(s): 8
Membership: 2,200

York Rose & Garden Society *See* Greater Toronto Rose & Garden Horticultural Society

York Soaring Association
Airfield, 7296, 5th Line, RR#1, Bellwood ON NOB 1J0
Tel: 519-848-3621
www.yorksoaring.com
www.facebook.com/yorksa
Overview: A small local organization founded in 1961
Member of: Soaring Association of Canada
Chief Officer(s):
Stan Martin, President
Walter Chemla, Founder
Finances: *Annual Operating Budget:* $250,000-$500,000
10 volunteer(s)
Membership: 100-499
Activities: Soaring & gliding facilities; advanced training of glider pilots

York Symphony Orchestra Inc.
PO Box 355, Richmond Hill ON L4C 4Y6
Tel: 416-410-0860
yorksymphonyorchestra@hotmail.com
www.yorksymphony.ca
www.facebook.com/pages/York-Symphony-Orchestra/292050064166541
twitter.com/yorksymphony
Previous Name: Richmond Hill Symphony
Overview: A small local charitable organization founded in 1961 overseen by Orchestras Canada
Mission: To provide musical enjoyment for audiences & musicians, with the goal of being recognized & supported throughout the region
Affliation(s): York Symphony Youth Orchestra
Chief Officer(s):
Gregory Burton, Music Director
Finances: *Annual Operating Budget:* $50,000-$100,000
Activities: *Speaker Service:* Yes

York Technology Alliance (YTA)
7271 Warden Ave., Markham ON L3R 5X5
e-mail: info@yorktech.ca
www.yorktech.ca
Overview: A small local organization founded in 1982
Mission: To provide a community for technology companies to connect & grow
Chief Officer(s):
Dan Duffy, Chair
Patrick Shaw, Executive Director, 905-415-4558 Ext. 3104
patshaw@yorktech.ca
Ryan Ellis, Manager, Membership, 905-415-4558 Ext. 3102
ryanellis@yorktech.ca
Pamela Montgomery, Coordinator, Events, 905-415-4558 Ext. 3106
pamela.m@yorktech.ca
Finances: *Funding Sources:* Sponsorships
Activities: Offering learning & networking opportunities

York University Faculty Association (YUFA) / Association des professeurs de l'Université York
240 York Lanes, 4700 Keele St., Toronto ON M3J 1P3
Tel: 416-736-5236; *Fax:* 416-736-5850
yufa@yorku.ca
www.yufa.ca
Overview: A medium-sized local organization founded in 1962
Mission: To promote the welfare of the university as an institution of higher learning & the welfare of academic staff including the regulation of employment relations between the University & its academic staff
Affliation(s): Ontario Council of Faculty Associations; Canadian Association of University Teachers
Chief Officer(s):
Arthur Hilliker, President
Mary Kandiuk, Vice President Internal
Craig Heron, Vice President External
Staff Member(s): 4
Membership: 1,400; *Member Profile:* Appointed to full-time teaching or librarian; *Committees:* Compensatrion; Pension; Equity; Grievance; Community Projects

York University Staff Association / Association du personnel de l'Université York
East Office Bldg., 190 Albany Rd., 2nd Fl., Toronto ON M3J 1P3
Tel: 416-736-5109; *Fax:* 416-736-5519
yusapuy@yorku.ca
www.yusapuy.org
www.facebook.com/YorkUniversityStaffAssociation
www.youtube.com/user/CCUchannel
Also Known As: YusApuY
Overview: A medium-sized local organization founded in 1975
Member of: Equal Pay Coalition; York Community Coalition
Affliation(s): Confederation of Canadian Unions
Chief Officer(s):
Giulio Malfatti, President
Finances: *Funding Sources:* Membership dues
Staff Member(s): 2
Membership: 2,500+; *Member Profile:* Clerical, technical, computer & laboratory staff; *Committees:* Bargaining; Communications; Constitution & Policy; Grievance; Grievance; Job Evaluation; Nominations; Health & Safety
Activities: *Speaker Service:* Yes; *Library* Open to public

York-Grand River Historical Society
c/o Mary V. Nelles, #4, 1 Peebes St., Caledonia ON N3W 1J6
Previous Name: Seneca Centennial Committee
Overview: A small local organization founded in 1974
Mission: To support, encourage & facilitate the conservation, protection & promotion of the heritage of the community
Member of: Ontario Historical Society
Affliation(s): Golden Horseshoe Antique Society
Chief Officer(s):
Mary V. Nelles, Contact
Finances: *Annual Operating Budget:* Less than $50,000; *Funding Sources:* Membership fees; Heritage Organization Development Grant
10 volunteer(s)
Membership: 30; *Fees:* $5; *Member Profile:* Interest in local history
Activities: Interested in putting up signs to mark former local sites

Yorkton & District Labour Council (YDLC)
180A Broadway St. West, Yorkton SK S3N 0M6
Tel: 603-621-8948
Overview: A small local organization overseen by Saskatchewan Federation of Labour
Mission: To promote the interests of affiliates in Yorkton, Saskatchewan & the surrounding region; To advance the economic & social welfare of workers
Affliation(s): Canadian Labour Congress (CLC)
Chief Officer(s):
Mary Ann Fererko, President, 306-783-2234
mfederko@sasktel.net
Activities: Presenting educational opportunities; Hosting a ceremony on the annual Day of Mourning for workers killed & injured on the job; Raising awareness of occupational health & safety; Supporting community organizations

Yorkton & District United Way Inc.
180 Broadway St. West, #A, Yorkton SK S3N 0M6
Tel: 306-621-8948
bpohorelic@sasktel.net
Overview: A small local charitable organization founded in 1982 overseen by United Way of Canada - Centraide Canada
Mission: To unite & facilitate community fundraising on behalf of our membership of local, charitable organizations
Chief Officer(s):
Brian Pohorelic, Chair
Lisa Washington, Secretary
Finances: *Annual Operating Budget:* Less than $50,000
Activities: Community donations; *Awareness Events:* Helping Hand Campaign

Yorkton Chamber of Commerce
PO Box 1051, Hwy. 9 South, Yorkton SK S3N 2X3
Tel: 306-783-4368; *Fax:* 306-786-6978
yorktonchamber@sasktel.net
www.chamber.yorkton.sk.ca
Overview: A small local organization founded in 1898
Mission: To represent the interests of business & encourage economic development
Member of: Canadian Chamber; City Economic Development Commission; Saskatchewan Chamber of Commerce
Affliation(s): Saskatchewan Economic Developers Association
Chief Officer(s):
Rob Irvine, President
ron.irvine@accesscomm.ca
Guy Gendreau, Exec. Vice-President
ycp@sasktel.net
Finances: *Annual Operating Budget:* Less than $50,000; *Funding Sources:* Membership fees; sponsored Spring Trade show
Staff Member(s): 1; 16 volunteer(s)
Membership: 275; *Fees:* $25-240; *Committees:* Finance; Education; Membership; Public Relations; Environmental Scanning; Economic Development
Activities: Business Awards Program; Dine-a-night
Awards:
• Celebrate Success Awards (Award)

Yorkton Friendship Centre
139 Dominion Ave., Yorkton SK S3N 1S3
Tel: 306-782-2822; *Fax:* 306-782-6662
Overview: A small local organization
Chief Officer(s):
Darlene Langan, Executive Director

Yorkton Real Estate Association Inc. (YREA)
#040, 41 Broadway West, Yorkton SK S3N 0L6
Tel: 306-783-3067; *Fax:* 306-782-3231
yrea@sasktel.net
Overview: A small local organization founded in 1969 overseen by Saskatchewan Real Estate Association
Mission: To promote a high level of professionalism among members by providing leadership in the real estate industry & in the community
Member of: The Canadian Real Estate Association
Chief Officer(s):
Judy Pfeifer, Executive Officer
Ron Skinner, President
ronskinner@royallepage.ca
Finances: *Annual Operating Budget:* Less than $50,000; *Funding Sources:* Membership fees
Staff Member(s): 1
Membership: 30; *Fees:* Annual/quarterly/monthly; *Member Profile:* Brokers; salespeople; affiliate members; *Committees:* Education; Professional Standards; PAC; Public Relations; Nominating; Financial
Activities: Fundraising for Kidney Foundation, Yorkton Big Brothers & Big Sisters

Yorkton Short Film & Video Festival (YSFVF)
49 Smith St. East, Yorkton SK S3N 0H4
Tel: 306-782-7077; *Fax:* 306-782-1550
info@goldensheafawards.com
www.yorktonshortfilm.org
Also Known As: Golden Sheaf Awards
Overview: A small local charitable organization founded in 1947
Member of: Saskatchewan Motion Picture Association
Chief Officer(s):
Randy Goulden, Executive Director
Staff Member(s): 2; 55 volunteer(s)
Membership: 189; *Fees:* $5
Activities: Canada's Golden Sheaf Awards Competition

Yorkton Society for the Prevention of Cruelty to Animals Inc.
79 - 7th Ave. South, Yorkton SK S3N 3V1
Tel: 306-783-4080; *Fax:* 306-783-4080
Other Communication: After hours: 306-786-1799
www.facebook.com/241196172557900
Also Known As: Yorkton SPCA
Overview: A small local organization founded in 1977
Mission: To help find homes for animals in the shelter & to educate people so that they may become better pet owners
Member of: Canadian Federation of Humane Societies

Young Alberta Book Festival Society *See* Young Alberta Book Society

Young Alberta Book Society (YABS)
Percy Page Ctr., 2nd Fl., 11759 Groat Rd., Edmonton AB T5M 3K6
Tel: 780-422-8232; *Fax:* 780-422-8239
info@yabs.ab.ca
www.yabs.ab.ca
www.facebook.com/youngalbertabooksociety
twitter.com/YABStweet
Previous Name: Young Alberta Book Festival Society
Overview: A small provincial charitable organization founded in 1985
Mission: To foster literacy & a love of reading among young people in Alberta by providing access to Albertan literary artists and their work.
Member of: Edmonton Arts Council; Professional Arts Coalition of Edmonton
Affliation(s): Canadian Children's Book Centre
Chief Officer(s):
Stephanie Gregorwich, Executive Director, 780-422-8232
Finances: *Annual Operating Budget:* $250,000-$500,000; *Funding Sources:* Provincial Government; Municipal Government; Sponsorship; Donations
Staff Member(s): 2; 70 volunteer(s)
Membership: 250; *Fees:* $50
Activities: Taleblazers Festival, annual month-long tour of literary artists; Story Avenue, two day writing workshop for grades 5-7; WordPower, week-long series writing workshops in rural communities; *Library:* Canadian Children's Book Centre Collection; by appointment
Awards:
• Charles Allard Award (Award)
Teachers & librarians must explain the struggles they face when encouraging their students to read, & how a presentation from an author of their choice would benefit their students. The society selects 10 winners, who will receive a visit from that author. Eligibility: Teachers & librarians
• Martyn Godfrey Young Writers Award (Award)
Students must submit a 500 - 1500 word humour story or graphic novel. One winner in grade 4-6 and one winner in grade 7-9 is chosen to receive a visit from an anuthor, a selection of book & an e-reader*Eligibility:* Alberta students in grades 4 to 9*Deadline:* January 6

Young Bar Association of Montréal *Voir* Association du jeune barreau de Montréal

Young Guard *See* Hashomer Hatzair

Young People's Theatre (YPT)
165 Front St. East, Toronto ON M5A 3Z4
Tel: 416-862-2222
online@youngpeoplestheatre.ca
www.youngpeoplestheatre.ca
www.facebook.com/LKTYPYoungPeoplesTheatre
twitter.com/YPTToronto
www.youtube.com/user/YoungPeoplesTheatre
Previous Name: Lorraine Kimsa Theatre for Young People
Overview: A medium-sized local charitable organization founded in 1966

Mission: To make a positive impact on the intellectual, social, & emotional development of young people; To produce plays for young audiences; To operate a year-round drama school for youth
Chief Officer(s):
Nancy J. Webster, Executive Director
Alexis Buset, Technical Director
Allen MacInnis, Artistic Director
Rick Banville, Director, Production
Jill Ward, Manager, Education & Participation
Marilyn Hamilton, Director, Marketing
Finances: *Funding Sources:* Ticket sales; Donations; Corporate sponsorships
Staff Member(s): 43

Your Political Party of BC (YPP)
194 Turtlehead Rd., Belcarra BC V3H 4P1
Tel: 604-805-3547; *Fax:* 604-939-5564
ypp@yppofbc.com
www.yppofbc.com
Also Known As: Your Party
Overview: A small provincial organization
Mission: The party advocates more transparency and accountability in government.
Chief Officer(s):
James Filippelli, Party founder & Leader

Youth Assisting Youth (YAY)
#401, 5734 Yonge St., Toronto ON M2M 4E7
Tel: 416-932-1919; *Fax:* 416-932-1924
Toll-Free: 877-932-1919
mail@yay.org
www.yay.org
Overview: A medium-sized local charitable organization founded in 1976
Mission: To implement Special Friend/Mentor program; matching mature, responsible youth (ages 16-29) with children (ages 6-15) experiencing social, emotional &/or cultural adjustment problems; To prevent delinquency by providing positive role models & friendship; to promote healthy growth & development of young people, strengthening families & responding to & supporting changing community needs
Finances: *Annual Operating Budget:* $500,000-$1.5 Million; *Funding Sources:* Government; United Way; corporations; foundations; service clubs; events; individuals; gaming
Staff Member(s): 18; 450 volunteer(s)
Membership: 70 corporate + 25 institutional + 450 volunteers; *Fees:* $25; *Committees:* Executive; Finance; Youth Leadership; Policy & Procedure; Fundraising; Information & Technology
Activities: *Internships:* Yes; *Speaker Service:* Yes

York Region
#401, 5743 Yonge St., Toronto ON M2M 4E7
Tel: 416-932-1919; *Fax:* 416-932-1924
Toll-Free: 877-932-1919
www.yay.org
Chief Officer(s):
Sally Spencer, Chief Executive Officer
sspencer@yay.org

Youth Ballet & Contemporary Dance of Saskatchewan Inc. (YBCS) / Les ballets de la jeunesse Saskatchewan
1106 McNiven Ave., Regina SK S4S 3X3
Tel: 306-352-9908; *Fax:* 306-585-2565
ybcs@sasktel.net
www.youthballet.com
www.linkedin.com/company/youth-ballet-and-contemporary-dance-of-saskat
www.facebook.com/368852441211
twitter.com/youthballet
Overview: A small provincial charitable organization founded in 1983
Mission: To enable the youth of Saskatchewan to develop to their highest potential in classical ballet & contemporary dance, by providing superior training & support; to enhance public appreciation of dance
Member of: Dance Saskatchewan; Dance & the Child International; Sask Culture; Sask Arts Alliance
Chief Officer(s):
Michelle McMillan, Artistic Director
Brenda Bancescu, Executive Director
Finances: *Funding Sources:* Grants; fundraising; school fees
Staff Member(s): 4

Youth Bowling Canada (YBC)
c/o Bowl Canada, #10A, 250 Shields Ct., Markham ON L3R 9W7
Tel: 905-479-1560; *Fax:* 905-479-8613
Toll-Free: 888-269-5922
info@bowlcanada.ca
www.youthbowling.ca
www.facebook.com/youthbowlingcanada
twitter.com/ybcbowling
Previous Name: National Youth Bowling Council
Overview: A small national organization founded in 1963 overseen by Bowling Proprietors' Association Of Canada
Mission: YBC is a program operating under the auspices of the Bowling Proprietors' Association of Canada (Bowl Canada), a not-for-profit organization comprised of 500 member centres across the country. The YBC league is divided in 5-pin & 10-pin, & further broken down in 3 age groups: bantam, junior & senior.
Chief Officer(s):
Paul Oliveira, Executive Director, Bowl Canada
paul@bowlcanada.ca
Membership: *Fees:* $15 registration; $5-10/week

Youth Challenge International (YCI)
PO Box 1205, #313, 555 Richmond St. West, Toronto ON M5V 3B1
Tel: 416-504-3370; *Fax:* 416-504-3376
Toll-Free: 877-504-3370
generalinfo@yci.net
www.yci.org
www.facebook.com/yci.org
twitter.com/youthchallenge
www.youtube.com/profile?user=YCICanada
Overview: A small international charitable organization founded in 1989
Mission: To promote young people's active, responsible & continuing participation in the issues of local & global development; to promote & support the establishment of a YCI global network, with partners in developed & developing regions of the world; to foster increased international cooperation between individuals, communities, service organizations, governments & agencies by focusing expertise & materials upon locally indentified problems in developing regions
Chief Officer(s):
Stephen Brown, Chair & President
Bryan Cox, Executive Director
Finances: *Annual Operating Budget:* $500,000-$1.5 Million; *Funding Sources:* Private sources; foundations; government
Staff Member(s): 13; 200 volunteer(s)
Membership: 100-499; *Committees:* Social Justice; Global Development Education
Activities: Challenger Programme offers youth an opportunity for personal development through four challenges - selection, preparation, field project & returning home; a 10-week field programme followed by the transformation of skills into civic action in their home communities

Youth Emergency Shelter Society of Edmonton *See* Youth Empowerment & Support Services

Youth Empowerment & Support Services (YESS)
9310 - 82 Ave., Edmonton AB T6C 0Z6
Tel: 780-468-7070; *Fax:* 780-466-1374
yess@yess.org
www.yess.org
www.facebook.com/YESSorg
twitter.com/YESSorg
www.youtube.com/user/YESSorg
Previous Name: Youth Emergency Shelter Society of Edmonton
Overview: A small local charitable organization founded in 1981
Mission: To provide food, shelter, clothing & support to youth at risk 15-19 who have no other viable living alternatives or who is in immediate risk or jeopardy; to provide multiple services for troubled families & homeless youth, including mediation, counselling, advocacy & shelter; to operate START House, a longer term facility for young people requiring support to become independent; also one of four joint partners involved in the Inner City Youth Housing Project; Outreach is provided through the Armoury Youth Centre which also runs programms during the day.
Member of: Alberta Association of Services for Children & Families; Association of Fundraising Professionals
Chief Officer(s):
René Cloutier, President
Deb Cautley, Executive Director
deb.cautley@yess.org
Finances: *Annual Operating Budget:* $3 Million-$5 Million; *Funding Sources:* Provincial government; United Way; private donations;sponsorship
Staff Member(s): 85; 350 volunteer(s)
Membership: 200; *Fees:* $20
Activities: Growing Dreams; Homeless for a Night; Great Expectations, Annual Golf Tournment; *Awareness Events:* Cornflake Breakfast & Annual Campaign, Dec-Jan; Annual General Meeting, June; Homeless for a Night, June; *Internships:* Yes; *Speaker Service:* Yes

Youth Flight Canada (YFC)
10 Courtwood Pl., Toronto ON M2K 1Z9
Tel: 416-223-6487
www.youthflight.ca
Also Known As: Youth Flight Canada Education Fund
Previous Name: YouthFlightCanada
Overview: A small national charitable organization founded in 1995
Mission: To inspire, to motivate, to educate, to foster self-esteem within challenged & disadvantaged youth
Member of: Freedom's Wings Canada
Affliation(s): Canadian Paraplegic Association, Ontario; K-W Access Ability
Chief Officer(s):
Charles Petersen, Chairman
Walter Chmela, Treasurer
Peter Foster, Executive Director
pede.foster@rogers.com
Finances: *Annual Operating Budget:* Less than $50,000; *Funding Sources:* Public & corporate donations; Ontario Trillium Foundation
40 volunteer(s)
Membership: 1-99
Activities: Flight programs for challenged & disadvantaged youth & adults; "Inspiration Flights" & pilot training for persons with disabilities: www.freedomswings.ca; flying scholarships for youth; *Internships:* Yes; *Speaker Service:* Yes
Awards:
• YFC Soaring Bursary (Scholarship)

Youth for Christ - Canada
PO Box 93008, #135, 19705 Fraser Highway, Langley BC V3A 8H2
Tel: 604-595-2498; *Fax:* 604-595-2473
Toll-Free: 800-899-9322
info@yfccanada.com
www.yfccanada.com
Overview: A medium-sized national organization
Mission: To impact every young person in Canada with the person, work & teachings of Jesus Christ & discipling them into the Church
Chief Officer(s):
Dave Brereton, National Director
Shirley Loewen, Office Manager
Activities: Responsible, effective & culturally sensitive evangelism of youth, communicating & caring in ways that are relevant to this generation

Youth in Care Canada
#332, 207 Bank St., Ottawa ON K2P 2N2
Tel: 613-230-8945; *Fax:* 613-230-8945
Toll-Free: 800-790-7074
info@youthincare.ca
www.youthincare.ca
Previous Name: National Youth in Care Network
Overview: A medium-sized national charitable organization founded in 1986
Mission: To increase the awareness of the needs of youth in & from government care by researching the issues & presenting the results to youth, professionals & the general public through publications & speaking engagements; To provide emotional support to youth in or from government care & to guide the development of youth in care groups
Chief Officer(s):
Adam Diamond, President
adam@youthincare.ca
Sheila Nyamaizi, Administrative Coordinator
sheila@youthincare.ca
Finances: *Funding Sources:* Government; corporate; foundation; membership fees
Staff Member(s): 2
Membership: *Fees:* $60 individual; $300 organization; $20 alumni; *Member Profile:* Youth in & from care; adults; organizations

Activities: Ken Dryden Scholarship; research & advocacy; leadership & training; *Internships:* Yes; *Speaker Service:* Yes; *Rents Mailing List:* Yes; *Library* Open to public

Youth Media Alliance (AMJ) / Alliance Médias Jeunesse (AET)

#107, 1400, boul René-Lévesque est, Montréal QC H2L 2M2
Tel: 514-597-5417; *Fax:* 514-597-5205
alliance@ymamj.org
www.ymamj.org
www.facebook.com/150380741707933
twitter.com/YMAMJ
www.youtube.com/alliancemediasjeunes
Previous Name: The Children's Broadcast Institute
Overview: A medium-sized national charitable organization founded in 1974
Mission: To promote the production & carriage of quality Canadian television programming for children; to ensure the development of critical viewing skills so that families are able to use media more effectively in the home; to promote awareness of the need to help young people make the most of their experience of television & other screen-based media
Chief Officer(s):
Chantal Brown, Executive Director
cbowen@ymamj.org
Finances: *Annual Operating Budget:* $250,000-$500,000; *Funding Sources:* Membership dues; Endowment Fund; project grants
Staff Member(s): 2
Membership: 100-499; *Fees:* $100 individual; $600-$3,000 organization; *Member Profile:* Among its members are parents, producers, educators, broadcasters, researchers, advertisers, writers & performers; *Committees:* Executive; Awards; Communications; Strategic Planning
Activities: Media Literacy Workshop Kit; professional development seminars; annual awards of excellence; research; publications; submissions & presentations; *Awareness Events:* Children's Television Festival (and Media); Prime Time Parent Workshop Kit; *Speaker Service:* Yes; *Library* Open to public by appointment
Awards:
• Awards of Excellence (Award)
For children's TV programs produced in Canada

Youth Now on Track Program (YNOT)

2300 Sheppard Ave. West, #LL17, Toronto ON M9M 3A2
Tel: 647-427-4989; *Fax:* 647-430-5814
info@ynotservices.org
www.ynotservices.org
Overview: A small local organization
Mission: To help youth who have had trouble with the law in the forms of prevention and intervention, in order to help these youth avoid such problems in the future
Membership: *Member Profile:* People ages 12 - 24 who have existing problems with the law
Activities: *Awareness Events:* Award & Fundraising Dinner (October); Family Day (December)

Youth Science Canada (YSC) / Sciences jeunesse Canada (SJC)

#213, 1550 Kingston Rd., Pickering ON L1V 1C3
Tel: 416-341-0040; *Fax:* 866-613-2542
Toll-Free: 866-341-0040
info@youthscience.ca
youthscience.ca
www.facebook.com/ysc.sjc
twitter.com/YouthScienceCan
www.youtube.com/user/YOUTHSCIENCECANADA
Previous Name: Youth Science Foundation Canada
Overview: A small national charitable organization founded in 1966
Mission: YSF assists Canadian youth to develop skills & knowledge for excellence in science & technology.
Chief Officer(s):
Reni Barlow, Executive Director
reni.barlow@youthscience.ca
Malcolm Butler, Chair
Mayur Gahdia, Treasurer
Jennifer Gerritsen, Secretary
Finances: *Funding Sources:* Corporate; government agencies
Staff Member(s): 2
Membership: 100-499; *Fees:* $50 adult; $25 full-time post-secondary students; *Member Profile:* Members are those who support the development of youth science, technology, & innovation.
Activities: Provides programs to increase awareness & involvement of youth in science and technology; sets standards for scientific experimentation by young people; promotes the creation & support of science fairs; engages scientists, educators, parents, & leading public & private sector organizations in the development of a national science & technology network of Canadian youth; *Awareness Events:* Youth Science Month, March; Invent the Future, October; Canada-Wide Science Fair, May; *Library:* Resource Centre

Youth Science Foundation Canada *See* Youth Science Canada

Youth Singers of Calgary (YSC)

1371 Hastings Cres. SE, Calgary AB T2G 4C8
Tel: 403-234-9549; *Fax:* 403-234-9590
yscadmin@youthsingers.org
www.youthsingers.org
www.facebook.com/pages/Youth-Singers-of-Calgary/25384252673
twitter.com/YouthSingers
www.youtube.com/user/YouthSingersCalgary
Overview: A small local charitable organization founded in 1985
Mission: To develop & deliver a comprehensive choral program for young performers; to train them in the performance of classical music, jazz, folk & contemporary music, musical theatre & dance
Member of: Alberta Choral Federation; Arts Touring Alliance; Canadian Choral Conductors Association
Affliation(s): Calgary Chamber of Commerce
Chief Officer(s):
Keith Heilman, Financial Administrator/Office Mgr.
keith@youthsingers.org
Shirley Penner, CEO & Artistic Director
srpenner@shaw.ca
Finances: *Funding Sources:* Alberta Foundation for the Arts; Calgary Region Arts Foundation; corporate sponsors; individual dono
Staff Member(s): 9
Activities: *Internships:* Yes; *Library:* Music Library

Youth Without Shelter (YWS)

6 Warrendale Ct., toronto ON M9V 1P9
Tel: 416-748-0110; *Fax:* 416-748-2169
communications@yws.on.ca
www.yws.on.ca/about-us/a-safe-haven
www.linkedin.com/company/2345421?trk=tyah
www.facebook.com/pages/Youth-Without-Shelter-YWS/111734105730?sk=wall
twitter.com/YWSToronto
www.youtube.com/user/YouthWithoutShelter
Overview: A small local charitable organization founded in 1986
Mission: Help youth aged 16 to 24 develop to their fullest potential by providing shelter and counselling.
Affliation(s): Youth Empowerment & Support Services, Edmonton
Chief Officer(s):
Wendy Horton, Executive Director
12 volunteer(s)

YouthFlightCanada *See* Youth Flight Canada

YOUTHLINK

747 Warden Ave., Toronto ON M1L 4A8
Tel: 416-967-1773; *Fax:* 416-967-7515
info@youthlink.ca
www.youthlink.ca
www.facebook.com/142606382418105
twitter.com/youthlinkto
Overview: A small local charitable organization founded in 1914
Mission: To support vulnerable youth in making positive life choices
Member of: Ontario Association of Children's Mental Health Centres
Chief Officer(s):
Janice Hayes, Executive Director
Sandy Mundy, President
Finances: *Annual Operating Budget:* $1.5 Million-$3 Million; *Funding Sources:* Ministry of Community & Social Services; City of Toronto; Ontario Ministry of Health; United Way; Big Sister Thrift Shop; individuals; corporations
Staff Member(s): 60; 100 volunteer(s)
Membership: 250; *Fees:* $30 general; $10 youth; $100 friend; $250 patron; *Member Profile:* Volunteers come from a variety of backgrounds & disciplines including graduate students; former clients & community volunteers; *Committees:* Agency Operations; Social Advocacy; Client Services & Human Resources; Board
Activities: Individual, family & group counselling; school-based prevention programs & community education; case management & coordination of support services to young people with developmental disabilities & their families; residential & co-op programs; *Library*
Awards:
• Big Sisters Legacy Fund Bursary (Grant)
• Karen Positano Bursary (Grant)

North West Scarborough Youth Centre
#410, 3850 Finch Ave. East, Toronto ON M1T 3T6
Tel: 416-502-9293; *Fax:* 416-502-0047

Pathways to Education - Scarborough Village
#1, 3471 Kingston Rd., 2nd Fl., Toronto ON M1M 1R4
Tel: 647-351-0091; *Fax:* 647-351-0092

Yukon Aboriginal Sport Circle (YASC)

2166 - 2nd Ave., Whitehorse YT Y1A 4P1
Tel: 867-668-2840; *Fax:* 867-668-6577
aboriginalsport@yasc.ca
www.yasc.ca
www.facebook.com/343599029002109
twitter.com/yukonasc
Merged from: **Yukon Aboriginal Sport Development Office Interim Steering Committee & YIGSC**
Overview: A medium-sized provincial organization founded in 1990
Mission: The Yukon Aboriginal Sport Circle is a non-profit society dedicated to the advancement of Aboriginal recreation and sport in the Yukon through a variety of programs to increase participation and skill levels and to increase awareness.
Member of: Sport Yukon
Chief Officer(s):
Gael Marchand, Executive Director
ed@yasc.ca
Justin Ferbey, President
Membership: *Member Profile:* The Yukon Aboriginal Sport Circle is a non-profit society dedicated to the advancement of Aboriginal recreation and sport in the Yukon.

Yukon Aboriginal Women's Council

#202, 307 Jarvis St., Whitehorse YT Y1A 2H3
Tel: 867-667-6162; *Fax:* 867-668-7539
admin@yawc.ca
yawc.ca
Overview: A small provincial organization founded in 1983 overseen by Native Women's Association of Canada
Mission: To create equal opportunities for Aboriginal women by implementing programs aimed to improving their quality of life
Chief Officer(s):
Marian Horne, President
Staff Member(s): 2

Yukon Agricultural Association

#203, 302 Steele St., Whitehorse YT Y1A 2E5
Tel: 867-668-6864; *Fax:* 867-393-3566
admin@yukonag.ca
www.yukonag.ca
Overview: A small provincial organization founded in 1974
Mission: To provide resources and opportunities to agricultural producers in the Yukon.
Chief Officer(s):
Mike Blumenschein, President
Bev Buckway, Executive Director
Staff Member(s): 2
Membership: *Fees:* $10; *Member Profile:* Agricultural producers in the Yukon

Yukon Amateur Boxing Association

1201A Grove St., Whitehorse YT Y1A 4E1
Tel: 867-335-3831
www.facebook.com/100624973327745
Overview: A small provincial organization overseen by Canadian Amateur Boxing Association
Mission: To govern the sport of boxing in the Yukon Territory.
Member of: Canadian Amateur Boxing Association
Chief Officer(s):
Jess Staffen, Head Coach
jess_staffen@yahoo.com

Yukon Amateur Hockey Association (YAHA)

4061 - 4th Ave., Whitehorse YT Y1A 1H1
Tel: 867-393-4501
yaha@sportyukon.com
www.yukonhockey.ca
Overview: A small provincial organization

Mission: The Yukon Amateur Hockey Association is the sports governing body for amateur hockey in the Yukon.
Member of: British Columbia Amateur Hockey Association; Sport Yukon
Chief Officer(s):
Kim King, Manager

Yukon Amateur Radio Association (YARA)
49 Liard Rd, Whitehorse YT Y1A 3L3
Tel: 867-667-2570
swilliamson@northwestel.net
yara.ca
Overview: A small provincial organization founded in 1976
Mission: To represent all amateur radio operators in Yukon; to promote the exciting hobby of amateur radio; to be of service to the public in case of emergency
Member of: Radio Amateurs of Canada
Chief Officer(s):
Scott Williamson, President (VY1SW)
Finances: *Annual Operating Budget:* Less than $50,000; *Funding Sources:* Yukon Government Emergency Measures; Yukon Lotteries
20 volunteer(s)
Membership: 20; *Fees:* $50; *Member Profile:* Amateur radio certificate
Activities: Sport Yukon Klondike International Road Relay; Chilkat Bicycle Relay
Awards:
• Amateur of the Year (Award)

Yukon Amateur Speed Skating Association
4061 - 4th Ave., Whitehorse YT Y1A 1H1
Tel: 867-660-5347
www.shorttrack06.com
Also Known As: Whitehorse Rapids Speed Skating Club
Overview: A small provincial organization
Chief Officer(s):
Malcolm Taggart, President
mtaggart@northwestel.net
Phil Hoffman, Secretary & Head Coach, 867-633-5984
philh@northwestel.net

Yukon Art Society (YAS)
#15, 305 Main St., Whitehorse YT Y1A 2B4
Tel: 867-667-4080; *Fax:* 867-667-4099
reception@artsunderground.ca
www.artsunderground.ca
www.facebook.com/ArtsUnderground
Also Known As: Arts Underground
Overview: A small local organization founded in 1970
Mission: To promote Yukon artists through shows & workshops
Chief Officer(s):
Cass Collins, Contact, Exhibitions & Programs
programs@artsunderground.ca
Leslie Leong, Contact, Administration
admin@artsunderground.ca
Finances: *Annual Operating Budget:* $50,000-$100,000; *Funding Sources:* Provincial government
Staff Member(s): 2; 25 volunteer(s)
Membership: 140 individual; *Fees:* $45 institutional; $15 student; $25 individual; $35 family; *Member Profile:* All walks of life from ages 12-87; *Committees:* Road Show; Auction
Activities: Arts in the Park Events; Rendezvous Show; Points of View Show; Artist of the Month Shows; workshops; *Internships:* Yes; *Rents Mailing List:* Yes; *Library:* Yukon Art Society Library; Open to public

Yukon Arts Centre (YAC)
PO Box 16, Whitehorse YT Y1A 5X9
Tel: 867-667-8575; *Fax:* 867-393-6300
www.yukonartscentre.com
www.facebook.com/YukonArtsCentre
twitter.com/YukonArtsCentre
Overview: A medium-sized provincial organization
Mission: To promote, stimulate & nurture the Arts throughout the Yukon; to create educational & developmental programmes, to maintain & manage the Yukon Arts Centre to the benefit of Yukon artists & audiences
Chief Officer(s):
Patrick Michael, Chair
Deborah Bartlette, Vice-Chair
Finances: *Funding Sources:* Provincial government

Yukon Association for Children & Adults with Learning Disabilities *See* Learning Disabilities Association of Yukon Territory

Yukon Association for Community Living (YACL)
PO Box 31478, Whitehorse YT Y1A 6K8
Tel: 867-667-4606; *Fax:* 867-668-8169
yaclwhse@northwestel.net
Overview: A medium-sized provincial organization founded in 1964 overseen by Canadian Association for Community Living
Mission: To promote the welfare of people with intellectual disabilities & their families; To ensure that every person in the Yukon has access to supports necessary to live with dignity & to participate fully in the community of his/her choice
Member of: Canadian Association for Community Living
Chief Officer(s):
Chris Hale, President
Vicki Wilson, Coordinator
Finances: *Funding Sources:* Federal, territorial & municipal government; Fundraising; National CACL; Yukon lotteries; United Way
50 volunteer(s)
Membership: 50; *Fees:* $1; *Committees:* Public Awareness; Fundraising; Policy; Personnel; Finance
Activities: *Library:* YACL Resource Library
Awards:
• Nicki Henry Award (Award)

Yukon Badminton Association
4061 - 4th Ave., Whitehorse YT Y1A 1H1
Tel: 867-393-4343
Overview: A small provincial organization overseen by Badminton Canada
Chief Officer(s):
Michael Muller, President
muller@northwestel.net
Yesh Sharma, Youth Coordinator, 867-456-4120

Yukon Broomball Association (YBA)
4061 - 4th Ave., Whitehorse YT Y1A 1H1
Tel: 867-668-3589
biz@yukonbroomball.com
www.yukonbroomball.com
Previous Name: Yukon Broomball League
Overview: A medium-sized provincial organization overseen by Ballon sur glace Broomball Canada
Mission: To promote & facilitate Broomball in the Yukon Territory.
Member of: Ballon sur glace Broomball Canada; Sport Yukon
Chief Officer(s):
Milford Allain, President
Membership: 6 teams

Yukon Broomball League *See* Yukon Broomball Association

Yukon Canoe & Kayak Club
c/o Sport Yukon, 4061 - 4 Ave., Whitehorse YT Y1A 1H1
e-mail: current@yckc.ca
www.yckc.ca
Overview: A small provincial organization founded in 1961
Membership: *Fees:* $20 adult; $10 child; $40 family
Activities: White water rafting; kayak polo;

Yukon Chamber of Commerce (YCC)
#101, 307 Jarvis St., Whitehorse YT Y1A 2H3
Tel: 867-667-2000; *Fax:* 867-667-2001
Toll-Free: 800-661-0543
ycc@yukonchamber.com
www.yukonchamber.com
Overview: A medium-sized provincial charitable organization founded in 1985
Mission: To create a climate conducive to a strong private sector economy by providing leadership & representation
Member of: Canadian Chamber of Commerce
Chief Officer(s):
Sandy Babcock, President & CEO
Finances: *Annual Operating Budget:* $250,000-$500,000; *Funding Sources:* Territorial government; self-generated
Staff Member(s): 5
Membership: 150+; *Fees:* Varies with size of business & affiliations with other chambers; *Member Profile:* Business sector & associations
Activities: *Library:* Canada Yukon Business Service Centre; Open to public

Yukon Chamber of Mines (YCM)
3151B - 3rd Ave., Whitehorse YT Y1A 1G1
Tel: 867-667-2090; *Fax:* 867-668-7127
info@yukonminers.ca
www.yukonminers.ca
Overview: A medium-sized provincial organization founded in 1959
Mission: To provides services to members, with a focus on the mining industry; To promote responsible exploration & sustainable mining practices
Affliation(s): Mining Association of Canada
Chief Officer(s):
Mark Ayranto, President
Hugh Kitchen, Vice President
Finances: *Funding Sources:* Membership fees; Government funding
Membership: 350; *Fees:* $50 individual; $120-$6000 other
Activities: *Library* Open to public
Meetings/Conferences: • Yukon Chamber of Mines 2015 43rd Annual Yukon Geoscience Forum & Trade Show, 2015
Scope: Provincial
Description: A conference for the mining & exploration industry, featuring technical events, short courses, & exhibits
Contact Information: E-mail: admin@yukonminers.ca

Yukon Child Care Association (YCCA)
PO Box 31103, Whitehorse YT Y1A 5P7
Tel: 867-668-5130
ycca1974@gmail.com
www.yukonchildcareassociation.org
www.facebook.com/YukonCCA
twitter.com/YukonChildCare
Overview: A medium-sized provincial organization founded in 1974
Mission: To develop a high quality, universally accessible, & affordable child care system in the Yukon; To represent caregivers & families
Affliation(s): Canadian Child Care Federation
Chief Officer(s):
Cyndi Desharnais, President
Activities: Arranging inspections & enforcing regulations; Advocating on behalf of child care providers in the Yukon; Liaising with the territorial government; Encouraging parental involvement; Hosting child care conferences; Educating the public about child care

Yukon Church Heritage Society (YCHS)
PO Box 31461, Whitehorse YT Y1A 6K8
Tel: 867-668-2555; *Fax:* 867-667-6258
logchurch@klondiker.com
yukonmuseums.ca/museum/oldlog/oldlog.html
Also Known As: Old Log Church Museum
Overview: A small provincial charitable organization founded in 1982
Mission: To promote & preserve church history in the Yukon
Member of: Yukon Historical & Museums Association
Affliation(s): Canadian Museums Association
Chief Officer(s):
Taryn Parker, Director/Curator
Linda Thistle, President
Finances: *Annual Operating Budget:* $50,000-$100,000
Staff Member(s): 1; 8 volunteer(s)
Membership: 25; *Fees:* $15 student/senior; $20 adult; $30 family
Activities: Operates Old Log Church Museum; *Library* Open to public by appointment

Yukon Conservation Society (YCS)
302 Hawkins St., Whitehorse YT Y1A 1X6
Tel: 867-668-5678; *Fax:* 867-668-6637
ycs@ycs.yk.ca
www.yukonconservation.org
Overview: A small provincial charitable organization founded in 1968
Mission: To pursue ecosystem well-being throughout the Yukon & beyond
Chief Officer(s):
Karen Baltgailis, Executive Director
Georgia Greetham, Coordinator, Office
Sue Kemmett, Coordinator, Forestry
Anne Middler, Coordinator, Energy
Lewis Rifkind, Coordinator, Mining
Finances: *Funding Sources:* Membership fees; Donations
Membership: 400; *Fees:* $10 students; $25 individuals & corporate or business memberships; $40 families; *Committees:* Personnel Standing Committee; Executive Standing Committee; Finance Standing Committee; Membership / Fundraising Standing Committee; Energy & Climate Change Working Group; Forestry Working Group; Habitat & Wildlife Working Group; Mining Working Group; Whitehorse Area Issues Working Group

Activities: Influencing environmental policy in the North; Providing environmental educational programs; Raising environmental awareness & the realization that human well-being is dependent upon fully functioning healthy ecosystems; *Library:* Yukon Conservation Society Library; Open to public by appointment
Meetings/Conferences: • Yukon Conservation Society 2015 Annual General Meeting, 2015, YT
Scope: Provincial
Contact Information: Phone: 867-668-5678
Publications:
• Walk Softly
Type: Newsletter; *Frequency:* Quarterly; *Editor:* Georgia Greetham; *Price:* Free with Yukon Conservation Society membership; $25 non-members
Profile: Information about current & upcoming issues & events

Yukon Contractors Association (YCA)
103A-103 Platinum Rd., Whitehorse YT Y1A 5M3
Tel: 867-335-0374; *Fax:* 867-668-3985
Overview: A medium-sized provincial organization

Yukon Council of Archives (YCA)
PO Box 31089, Whitehorse YT Y1A 5P7
Fax: 867-393-6253
yukoncnclarch@gmail.com
www.yukoncouncilofarchives.ca
Overview: A small provincial organization founded in 1986 overseen by Canadian Council of Archives
Mission: To facilitate the development of the archival system in the Yukon; To make recommendations about the system's operation & financing; To develop & facilitate implementation & management of programs to assist the archival community; To communicate archival needs & concerns to decision-makers, researchers & the general public
Membership: *Fees:* $25 institution; $20 general; $10 individual; *Member Profile:* Engaged or interested in archival practice; *Committees:* Education; Grants; Membership; Archives Week; Yukon Archival Advisory Program

Yukon Council of the Canadian Physiotherapy Association
www.yukonphysiotherapy.org
Overview: A medium-sized provincial organization overseen by Canadian Physiotherapy Association
Mission: To unite members of the profession
Member of: Canadian Physiotherapy Association
Chief Officer(s):
Susan Rubinoff, President
susan.rubinoff@northwestel.net
Finances: *Funding Sources:* Membership dues; educational activities
Membership: 30+; *Fees:* $60 Territorial fee
Activities: *Awareness Events:* National Physiotherapy Month, April 20 - May 20
Publications:
• Yukon Council of Canadian Physiotherapy Association Newsletter
Type: Newsletter; *Frequency:* a.

Yukon Council on Aging (YCOA)
4061B - 4th Ave., Whitehorse YT Y1A 1H1
Tel: 867-668-3383; *Fax:* 867-668-6745
Toll-Free: 866-582-9707
ycoa@yknet.yk.ca
www.yukon-seniors-and-elders.org/yukoncouncil
Also Known As: Seniors Information Centre
Overview: A small provincial organization founded in 1977
Mission: The YCOA is a volunteer organization of Yukon seniors administered by a Board of Directors elected from its membership
Chief Officer(s):
Connie Dublenko, President
Finances: *Annual Operating Budget:* $50,000-$100,000
Staff Member(s): 2; 20 volunteer(s)
Membership: 250; *Fees:* $10; *Member Profile:* 55 years of age & older; *Committees:* Advocacy; Health; Housing: Research
Activities: Information workshops; home & yard maintenance program; rural yukon pension workshops; *Library* Open to public

Yukon Curling Association (YCA)
4061 - 4th Ave., Whitehorse YT Y1A 1H1
Tel: 867-668-7121; *Fax:* 867-667-4237
www.yukoncurling.ca
Overview: A small provincial organization founded in 1974 overseen by Canadian Curling Association
Affliation(s): Watson Lake Curling Club; Mayo Curling Club
Chief Officer(s):
Linden Mattie, Executive Director
executivedirector@yukoncurling.ca
10 volunteer(s)
Membership: 1,000; *Member Profile:* Seniors; masters; adults; juniors; youth; little rockers

Yukon Denturist Association
#1, 106 Main St., Whitehorse YT Y1A 2A7
Tel: 867-668-6818; *Fax:* 867-668-6811
Overview: A small provincial organization overseen by Denturist Association of Canada

Yukon Employees Union (YEU) / Syndicat des employés du Yukon
#201, 2285 - 2nd Ave., Whitehorse YT Y1A 1C9
Tel: 867-667-2331; *Fax:* 867-667-6521
Toll-Free: 888-938-2331
contact@yeu.ca
www.yeu.ca
www.facebook.com/YukonEmployeesUnion
twitter.com/YEUPSAC
www.youtube.com/user/YukonEmployeesUnion
Overview: A medium-sized provincial organization founded in 1965 overseen by Public Service Alliance of Canada (CLC)
Mission: To unite all members of the Alliance over which this Union has jurisdiction into a single union capable of acting on their behalf; to obtain through democratic means for all members the best possible standards of wages, salaries & other conditions of employment, & to protect the interests, rights & privileges of all such employees
Chief Officer(s):
Steve Geick, President
Laura Hureau, Executive Director
Staff Member(s): 7
Membership: 4,000 + 19 locals; *Committees:* Women's; Health & Safety; Visible Minority; Aboriginal Peoples; Pride; Access
Activities: *Library*

Yukon Family Services Association *See* Many Rivers Counselling & Support Services

Yukon Federation of Labour (YFL) / Fédération du travail du Yukon
#102, 106 Strickland St., Whitehorse YT Y1A 2J5
Tel: 867-456-8250; *Fax:* 867-668-3426
yfl@yukonfed.com
www.yukonfed.com
www.facebook.com/pages/Yukon-Federation-of-Labour/137821525367
twitter.com/yukonworkers
Overview: A medium-sized provincial organization founded in 1980 overseen by Canadian Labour Congress
Mission: To advocate on behalf of its memebers
Chief Officer(s):
Vikki Quocksister, President

Yukon Film Society (YFS)
212 Lambert St., Whitehorse YT Y1A 1Z4
Tel: 867-393-3456; *Fax:* 867-393-3456
yfs@yukonfilmsociety.com
www.yukonfilmsociety.com
Overview: A small provincial organization founded in 1984
Mission: To present independent and alternative media art works to Yukon audiences and to support the production and distribution of works by Yukon media artists.
Chief Officer(s):
Noel Sinclair, President
Zoë Toupin, General Manager
Finances: *Funding Sources:* membership fees; rental fees; screenings
Staff Member(s): 2; 9 volunteer(s)
Membership: *Fees:* $30 production; $5 exhibition
Activities: Available Light Film Festival; Film screenings;

Yukon First Nations Party
PO Box 6, Burwash YT Y0B 1V0
Tel: 867-841-4180
Overview: A small provincial organization founded in 2011
Mission: The party believes in sustaining the traditional laws of respect, honour, love, compassion, and harmony.
Finances: *Funding Sources:* Donations

Yukon First Nations Tourism Association (YFNTA)
#1, 1109 - 1st Ave., Whitehorse YT Y1A 5G4
Tel: 867-667-7698; *Fax:* 867-667-7527
admin@yfnta.org
www.yfnta.org
Overview: A small provincial organization

Yukon Fish & Game Association (YFGA)
509 Strickland St., Whitehorse YT Y1A 2K5
Tel: 867-667-4263; *Fax:* 867-667-4237
www.yukonfga.ca
Overview: A medium-sized provincial organization founded in 1945 overseen by Canadian Wildlife Federation
Mission: To ensure the long-term management of fish, wildlife, & outdoor recreational resources in the Yukon; To improve wildlife habitat
Chief Officer(s):
Paul Jacobs, President
Gord Zealand, Executive Director
yfgaexdir@klondiker.com
Jillian Mclellan, Office Administrator
yfga@klondiker.com
Finances: *Funding Sources:* Membership fees; Donations; Sponsorships
Membership: *Fees:* $30 singles; $35 families; $500 corporate & lifetime membership
Activities: Providing hunter education & ethics development; Promoting proper catch & release; Meeting with government regarding fish & wildlife issues; Promoting sportsmanship; Managing the Whitehorse Rapids fish ladder & tourist facility; Overseeing the operation of a salmon hatchery
Meetings/Conferences: • Yukon Fish & Game Association 2015 Annual Banquet, Awards & Dance, January, 2015, High Country Inn Convention Center, Whitehorse, YT
Contact Information: Yukon Fish & Game Association Office, Phone: 867-667-4263, E-mail: yfga@klondiker.com
Publications:
• Outdoor Edge [a publication of the Yukon Fish & Game Association]
Type: Newsletter; *Frequency:* Bimonthly; *Accepts Advertising*; *Price:* Free with Yukon Fish & Game Association membership
Profile: A publication sent to more than 450 households in the Yukon & throughout Canada

Yukon Foundation
PO Box 31622, Whitehorse YT Y1A 6L2
Tel: 867-393-2454
yukonfoundation@klondiker.com
www.yukonfoundation.com
Overview: A small provincial organization founded in 1980
Mission: To promote educational advancement and scientific or medical research for the enhancement of human knowledge; provide support intended to contribute to the mental, cultural and physical well-being of residents of Yukon; and promote the cultural heritage of Yukon.
Chief Officer(s):
Sophie Partridge, Executive Director

Yukon Freestyle Ski Association
4061 - 4th Ave., Whitehorse YT Y1A 1H1
Tel: 867-393-3369
yukonfreeski@gmail.com
www.yfsa.ca
www.facebook.com/239011292821887
Overview: A small provincial organization overseen by Canadian Freestyle Ski Association
Mission: To promote & facilitate freestyle skiing in the Yukon Territory.
Member of: Canadian Freestyle Ski Association; Sport Yukon
Chief Officer(s):
Lynda Harlow, President
lynda.harlow@yec.yk.ca

Yukon Golf Association
4061 - 4th Ave., Whitehorse YT Y1A 1H1
Tel: 867-633-3364; *Fax:* 867-393-3051
sportyukon.com/member/yukon-golf-association
Overview: A small provincial organization
Mission: The Yukon Golf Association is an organization that enhances opportunities for all Yukonners in their pursuit of excellence & in their enjoyment of participation.
Chief Officer(s):
Gordon Zealand, President
zealandg@northwestel.net

Yukon Green Party
PO Box 31603, Whitehorse YT Y1A 6L2
Tel: 867-633-6334; *Fax:* 867-633-3392
yukongreenparty@gmail.com
www.yukongreenparty.ca
Overview: A small provincial organization overseen by Green Party of Canada

Membership: *Fees:* $5

Yukon Gymnastics Association
4061 - 4th Ave., Whitehorse YT Y1A 1H1
Tel: 867-456-7896; *Fax:* 867-668-6922
yukongymnastic.com
Overview: A small provincial organization
Member of: Canadian Gymnastics Federation
Chief Officer(s):
Shannon Albisser, President
shannonalbisser@yahoo.ca

Yukon Historical & Museums Association (YHMA)
3126 - 3 Ave., Whitehorse YT Y1A 1E7
Tel: 867-667-4704; *Fax:* 867-667-4506
info@heritageyukon.ca
heritageyukon.ca
twitter.com/Yukonheritage
Overview: A medium-sized provincial charitable organization founded in 1977
Mission: To preserve & foster an appreciation of the Yukon's history & culture; to act as forum for other museum & heritage organizations in the region
Member of: Canadian Museums Association
Affliation(s): Heritage Canada; BC Heritage Trust
Chief Officer(s):
Nancy Oakley, Executive Director
Finances: *Funding Sources:* Membership fees; territorial & municipal governments
Membership: 44 individual + 28 institutional + 15 commercial; *Fees:* Schedule available; *Member Profile:* Interest in preserving & promoting heritage; *Committees:* Heritage Training Fund; Joint Marketing; Awards; Advocacy; Membership; Newsletter; Conference
Activities: Yukon Lifestyles program which involves oral history, photography & building documentation as ways of preserving & recording Yukon buildings; Historical Maps series; Heritage Lecture series; Heritage awards which honour contributions to the preservation of the Yukon heritage by individuals, organizations & businesses; *Library:* YHMA Reference Centre; by appointment
Awards:
• YHMA Heritage Award (Award)

Yukon Horse & Rider Association (YHRA)
PO Box 31482, Whitehorse YT Y1A 6K8
e-mail: yukonhorseandriderassociation@gmail.com
www.yhra.ca
www.facebook.com/186825158005753
Overview: A medium-sized provincial organization
Mission: The YHRA is dedicated to the sport of horseback riding in the Yukon Territory, Canada. The Association aims to encourage good horsemanship & help promote interest in the light horse industry.
Chief Officer(s):
Jody Mackenzie-Grieve, President
Membership: 100+; *Fees:* $35 senior; $25 junior; $60 family; *Committees:* Events; Development

Yukon Indian Hockey Association (YIHA)
PO Box 31769, Whitehorse YT Y1A 6L3
Tel: 867-456-7294; *Fax:* 867-456-7290
yihahockey@gmail.com
www.yiha.ca
www.facebook.com/169614299786
Overview: A medium-sized provincial organization founded in 1984
Mission: To establish a hockey league in the Yukon to enable Native athletes to compete with other Canadian Provinces & Territories in the sport.
Chief Officer(s):
Jeanie Dendys, President

Yukon Kennel Club
Whitehorse YT
Tel: 867-668-6960
YukonKennelClub@gmail.com
www.yukonkennelclub.com
www.facebook.com/YukonKennelClub
Overview: A small provincial organization
Member of: Canadian Kennel Club
Membership: *Fees:* $25

Yukon Law Foundation
PO Box 31789, Whitehorse YT Y1A 6L3
Tel: 867-667-7500; *Fax:* 867-393-3904
info@yukonlawfoundation.com
www.yukonlawfoundation.com
Overview: A small local organization founded in 1985
Mission: The objects of the Foundation are to maintain & manage a fund accumulated primarily from the interest on lawyers' trust accounts
Member of: Association of Canadian Law Foundation
Chief Officer(s):
Mike Reynolds, Chair
Deana Lemke, Executive Director
execdir@yukonlawfoundation.com
Finances: *Annual Operating Budget:* $100,000-$250,000
Staff Member(s): 1; 6 volunteer(s)
Activities: *Library:* Law Library; Open to public

Yukon Learn Society (YLS)
107 Main St., Whitehorse YT Y1A 2A7
Tel: 867-668-6280; *Fax:* 867-633-4576
Toll-Free: 888-668-6280
learn@yukonlearn.com
www.yukonlearn.com
www.facebook.com/155488232762
Overview: A small provincial charitable organization founded in 1983
Mission: To provide adult literacy services; promote literacy awareness; to be the voice representing & uniting literacy in the Yukon
Member of: Movement for Canadian Literacy
Chief Officer(s):
Peter Morawsky, President
Amar Dhillon, Vice-President
Debbie Parent, Executive Director, 867-668-6280 Ext. 222
Finances: *Annual Operating Budget:* $100,000-$250,000
Staff Member(s): 4; 80 volunteer(s)
Membership: 128
Activities: *Awareness Events:* PGI Golf Tournament, June; International Literacy Day, Sept.; Yukon Literacy Week, Oct.; Family Literacy Day, Jan.; *Library:* Yukon Learn Library; Open to public
Awards:
• Tutor of the Year (Award)
• Learner of the Year (Award)
• Volunteer of the Year (Award)

Yukon Liberal Party
PO Box 183, #108 Elliot St., Whitehorse YT Y1A 2C6
Tel: 867-667-4748; *Fax:* 867-667-4720
Other Communication: secretary@ylp.ca
info@ylp.ca
www.ylp.ca
www.facebook.com/pages/Yukon-Liberal-Party/220062241344288
Overview: A small provincial organization overseen by The Liberal Party of Canada
Chief Officer(s):
Sandy Silver, Leader
Devin Bailey, President
President@ylp.ca

Yukon Medical Association
5 Hospital Rd., Whitehorse YT Y1A 3H7
Tel: 867-393-8749
yma@yukondoctors.ca
www.yukondoctors.ca
Overview: A medium-sized provincial organization overseen by Canadian Medical Association
Mission: A voluntary association of Yukon doctors; advocates on behalf of members; promotes professionalism in medical practice & accessibility to quality health care for Yukoners
Affiliation(s): British Columbia Medical Association
Chief Officer(s):
Rao Tadepalli, President
Finances: *Annual Operating Budget:* $50,000-$100,000
Membership: 60; *Fees:* $900

Yukon Mine Training Association (YMTA)
2099 - 2nd Ave., Whitehorse YT Y1A 1B5
Tel: 867-633-6463
Toll-Free: 877-986-4637
info@ymta.org
ymta.org
Overview: A medium-sized provincial organization
Mission: To maximize employment opportunities emerging from the growth of the mining and related resource sectors in the North for First Nations and other Yukoners.
Chief Officer(s):
P. Jerry Asp, Chair
Sascha Weber, Executive Director

Yukon Order of Pioneers (YOOP)
PO Box 31693, Whitehorse YT Y1A 6L3
Tel: 867-993-6441
yukon-seniors-and-elders.org/yukonorder/yukonorder.home.htm
Overview: A small provincial organization
Mission: To protect its members, & to unite those members in the strong tie of Brotherhood & to preserve the names of all Yukon Pioneers on its rolls & to collect & preserve the literature & incidents of the Order's history
Chief Officer(s):
Mark Castellarin, President
Membership: *Member Profile:* Men over 20 years old in the Yukon Territory

Yukon Orienteering Association (YOA)
4061 - 4th Ave., Whitehorse YT Y1A 1H1
Tel: 867-335-2287
info@yukonorienteering.ca
www.yukonorienteering.ca
Overview: A small provincial organization
Mission: To provide both friendly & quality competitive orienteering opportunities in Yukon, & encourage the development & growth of the sport of orienteering where possible
Member of: Canadian Orienteering Federation
Chief Officer(s):
Afan Jones, President
Bob Sagar, Vice-President
Membership: *Fees:* $5; *Member Profile:* Male & female, 0-70 yrs old, enjoys outdoors
Activities: Kids Running Wild; Yukon Orienteering Team; Yukon Championships; clinics;
Publications:
• Legends [a publication of the Yukon Orienteering Association]
Type: Newsletter

Yukon Outdoors Club (YOC)
4061 - 4th Ave., Whitehorse YT Y1A 1H1
e-mail: yukonoutdoorsclub@gmail.com
www.yukonoutdoorsclub.ca
Overview: A small provincial organization founded in 1980
Mission: To co-ordinate trips that promote the enjoyment of the outdoors.
Membership: *Fees:* $10 single; $15 family

Yukon Outfitters' Association (YOA)
#4B, 302 Steele St., Whitehorse YT Y1A 2C5
Tel: 867-668-4118; *Fax:* 867-668-4120
info@yukonoutfitters.net
www.yukonoutfitters.net
Overview: A small provincial organization
Mission: To conserve, maintain & enhance the Yukon wildlife & their habitat on a sustained basis for the benefit & pleasure of all Yukoners including hunters
Affliation(s): Safari Club International; Foundation for North American Wild Sheep
Finances: *Annual Operating Budget:* $50,000-$100,000
Staff Member(s): 1; 18 volunteer(s)
Membership: 18; *Member Profile:* Yukon outfitters & associates
Activities: *Speaker Service:* Yes

Yukon Party
PO Box 31113, Whitehorse YT Y1A 5P7
Tel: 867-668-6505
info@yukonparty.ca
yukonparty.ca
Overview: A small provincial organization founded in 2011
Chief Officer(s):
Darrell Pasloski, Party Leader
Finances: *Funding Sources:* Donations

Yukon Prospectors' Association (YPA)
3151B - 3rd Ave., Whitehorse YT Y1A 1G1
www.yukonprospectors.ca
Overview: A small provincial organization
Mission: To promote and advocate for the mining industry and miners of the Yukon Territory
Chief Officer(s):
Mike Power, President

Yukon Public Legal Education Association (YPLEA)
PO Box 2799, Yukon College, Whitehorse YT Y1A 5K4
Tel: 867-668-5297
Toll-Free: 866-667-4305
www.yplea.com

Overview: A medium-sized provincial organization founded in 1984
Mission: To provide free legal information to Yukoners & promote greater accessibility to the legal system
Finances: *Annual Operating Budget:* $50,000-$100,000
Staff Member(s): 2; 7 volunteer(s)
Membership: *Fees:* $10
Activities: *Speaker Service:* Yes

Yukon RCMP Veteran's Association
PO Box 314 63, Whitehorse YT Y1A 6K8
www.yukonrcmpvets.ca
Overview: A medium-sized provincial organization
Mission: To represent members' interests on pension and benefits issues, and provide a formal communications link to the RCMP
Chief Officer(s):
Helmer Hermanson, President

Yukon Real Estate Association
3 Bonanza Pl., Whitehorse YT Y1A 5M4
Tel: 867-633-5565; *Fax:* 867-667-7005
admin@yrea.ca
www.yrea.ca
Overview: A small provincial organization founded in 1977
Mission: To promote interest in marketing of real estate in all its aspects & to advance & improve relations of members of society with public
Member of: The Canadian Real Estate Association
Membership: 5 corporate

Yukon Registered Nurses Association (YRNA)
#204, 4133 - 4th Ave., Whitehorse YT Y1A 1H8
Tel: 867-667-4062; *Fax:* 867-668-5123
admin@yrna.ca
www.yrna.ca
www.facebook.com/190306321094679
twitter.com/YrnaExec
Overview: A medium-sized provincial licensing organization founded in 1993 overseen by Canadian Nurses Association
Mission: To establish & promote standards of practice for registered nurses; to regulate nursing practice & to advance professional excellence; to speak out on health care issues; to advocate for the development of healthy public policy in the interest of the public.
Chief Officer(s):
Joy Peacock, Executive Director
exec.director@yrna.ca
Sean Secord, President
Finances: *Funding Sources:* Membership fees
Staff Member(s): 2
Membership: *Fees:* $717 practising; $105 non-practising; $189 associate plus; $238 special practice; $52.50 student; *Committees:* Registration; Complaints; Discipline; Nursing Practice; Education Approval; Nominations; Education Fund Management; Nurse Practitioner Advisory
Activities: *Library* Open to public
Publications:
• Nurses' Notes
Type: Newsletter; *Frequency:* Quarterly

Yukon River Marathon Paddlers Association
4061 - 4th Ave., Whitehorse YT Y1A 1H1
Tel: 867-333-5628; *Fax:* 888-959-3846
info@yukonriverquest.com
www.yukonriverquest.com
www.facebook.com/186123281403836
Also Known As: Yukon River Quest
Overview: A small provincial organization
Mission: To govern the Yukon River Quest canoe & kayak race.
Chief Officer(s):
Carl Rumscheidt, President
Membership: *Fees:* $10 regular; $50 lifetime
Activities: *Awareness Events:* Yukon River Quest, June

Yukon Schools' Athletic Association (YSAA)
YT
www.yesnet.yk.ca/ysaa/index.html
Overview: A medium-sized provincial organization founded in 1996 overseen by School Sport Canada
Mission: To encourage participation of students in inter school athletics, emphasize interschool athletics as an integral part of the total educational process & plan, promote, supervise & administer a program of inter-school athletics in all approved competitions.
Member of: School Sport Canada
Chief Officer(s):
Marc Senécal, President
marc.senecal@yesnet.yk.ca
James Shaw, Vice-President
james.shaw@yesnet.k.ca
Ron Billingsley, Secretary/Treasurer
ron.billingsley@yesnet.yk.ca
Awards:
• Ben Sheardown Award for Coaching Excellence (Award)

Yukon Schutzhund Association
Whitehorse YT
e-mail: yukon.schutzhund@gmail.com
www.facebook.com/yukonysa
Overview: A small provincial organization founded in 2002
Mission: To promote dog training for the sport of Schutzhund in the Yukon Territory.
Member of: German Shepherd Schutzhund Club of Canada

Yukon Shooting Federation
4061 - 4th Ave., Whitehorse YT Y1A 1H1
Tel: 867-633-6202
sportyukon.com/member/yukon-shooting-federation
Overview: A small provincial organization
Mission: To promote & facilitate air rifle & air pistol shooting in the Yukon Territory.
Member of: Sport Yukon
Chief Officer(s):
David Wipp, President
Nora Trombley, Treasurer
trombley@northwestel.net
Activities: Junior Shooters Program

Yukon Ski Division *See* Cross Country Yukon

Yukon Soccer Association
4061 - 4th Ave., Whitehorse YT Y1A 1H1
Tel: 867-633-4625; *Fax:* 867-667-4237
yukonsoccer@sportyukon.com
www.yukonsoccer.yk.ca
Overview: A small provincial organization overseen by Canadian Soccer Association
Mission: The Yukon Soccer Association is the sport governing body for the sport of soccer in the Yukon Territory. It is a volunteer based organization that coordinates & administers various programs devoted to the promotion & development of soccer.
Member of: Canadian Soccer Association
Chief Officer(s):
Kim King, Sport Administrator
Tony Gaw, Technical Director
chile07@northwestel.net

Yukon Sourdough Rendezvous Society
PO Box 31721, Whitehorse YT Y1A 6L3
Tel: 867-667-2148; *Fax:* 867-668-6755
www.yukonrendezvous.com
www.facebook.com/yukonrendezvous
twitter.com/YukonRendezvous
Overview: A small local organization
Mission: Society that organizes the Yukon Sourdough Rendezvous festival
Chief Officer(s):
Marj Eschak, President
Doris Wurfbaum, Vice-President, Public Relations
Jon Solberg, Executive Director

Yukon Special Olympics *See* Special Olympics Yukon

Yukon Speech-Language Pathology & Audiology Association (YSLPAA)
c/o 80 Falcon Dr., Whitehorse YT Y1A 6C7
e-mail: yslpaa@gmail.com
Overview: A small provincial organization
Mission: Supports and represents the professional needs of speech-language pathologists, audiologists and supportive personnel in the Yukon.
Chief Officer(s):
Karen Rach, President

Yukon Teachers' Association (YTA) / Association des enseignantes et des enseignants du Yukon
2064 - 2 Ave., Whitehorse YT Y1A 1A9
Tel: 867-668-6777; *Fax:* 867-667-4324
Toll-Free: 866-668-2097
admin@yta.yk.ca
www.yta.yk.ca
Overview: A medium-sized provincial organization founded in 1955 overseen by Canadian Teachers' Federation
Mission: To promote & support public education; To represent the professional & economic needs of Yukon educators
Chief Officer(s):
Katherine Mackwood, President
pres@yta.yk.ca
Douglas Rody, General Secretary
gensec@yta.yk.ca
Finances: *Funding Sources:* Fees & funding from employers
Staff Member(s): 6
Membership: *Member Profile:* Teachers; Assistants; Tutors; Native language instructors; *Committees:* Ethics
Awards:
• Mary Gartside Scholarship (Scholarship)
• Elijah Smith Scholarship (Scholarship)
• Doris Stanbraten Scholarship (Scholarship)
• YTA 50th Anniversary Bursary (Scholarship)
• Yukon Retired Teachers Alumni Scholarship (Scholarship)
• The Alice Elston Award (Award)
Eligibility: Any person whose contributions the association or education warrants special recognition*Deadline:* February
Publications:
• YTA [Yukon Teachers' Association] Benefit Guide
Type: Guide
• YTA [Yukon Teachers' Association] Handbook
Type: Handbook
• YTA [Yukon Teachers' Association] Notes
Type: Newsletter; *Frequency:* Monthly

Yukon Territory Environmental Network
302 Hawkins St., Whitehorse YT Y1A 1X6
Tel: 867-668-5678; *Fax:* 867-668-6637
yukonenvironet@gmail.com
Previous Name: Nornet-Yukon
Overview: A small provincial organization overseen by Canadian Environmental Network
Chief Officer(s):
Susan Davis, Coordinator

Yukon Tourism Education Council (YTEC)
#C, 202 Strickland St., Whitehorse YT Y1A 2J8
Tel: 867-667-4733; *Fax:* 867-667-2688
yukontec@internorth.com
www.yukontec.com
Overview: A small provincial organization
Mission: To foster industry led development of a professional tourism workforce
Chief Officer(s):
Darlene Doerksen, Chief Executive Officer
Staff Member(s): 3
Activities: Providing education & training
Publications:
• Yukon Tourism Education Council Newsletter
Type: Newsletter; *Frequency:* Monthly

Yukon Trappers Association
4194A - 4th Ave., Whitehorse YT Y1A 1JB
Tel: 867-667-7091; *Fax:* 867-667-7330
yukonfur@yknet.ca
Overview: A small provincial charitable organization founded in 1972
Mission: To assist trappers in all aspects of the trapping & marketing of their furs
Chief Officer(s):
Wendy Fournier, President
Finances: *Annual Operating Budget:* $100,000-$250,000; *Funding Sources:* Government contracts
Staff Member(s): 2; 6 volunteer(s)
Membership: 175; *Fees:* $30; $200 corporate
Activities: Retail store specializing in locally handcrafted products, as well as tanned fur; *Library:* Yukon Trappers Library; Open to public

Yukon Underwater Diving Association (YUDA)
YT
www.yukonweb.com/community/yuda
Overview: A small provincial organization
Mission: The Yukon Underwater Diving Association (YUDA) is a non-profit organization created by sport divers to promote the sport of underwater diving in the Yukon, Northern British Columbia & South East Alaska.
Chief Officer(s):
Allyn Lyon, President
alyon@yukon.net
Doug Davidge, Contact
ddavidge@yknet.yk.ca

Yukon Visitor's Association *See* Tourism Industry Association of the Yukon

Yukon Weightlifting Association
4061 - 4th Ave., Whitehorse YT Y1A 1H1
Tel: 867-334-7007
sportyukon.com/member/yukon-weightlifting-association
www.facebook.com/YukonWeightlifting
Overview: A small provincial organization
Mission: To promote & facilitate competitive weightlifting in the Yukon Territory.
Member of: Sport Yukon
Chief Officer(s):
Kim Haehnel, President
frozenveggies@hotmail.com
Jeane Lassen, Development Coordinator
jeanelassen@gmail.com

YWCA Canada / Association des jeunes femmes chrétiennes du Canada
104 Edward St., 1st Fl., Toronto ON M5G 0A7
Tel: 416-962-8881; *Fax:* 416-962-8084
national@ywcacanada.ca
www.ywcacanada.ca
www.facebook.com/ywcacanada
twitter.com/YWCA_Canada
Also Known As: Young Women's Christian Association of Canada
Overview: A large national charitable organization founded in 1893
Mission: A charitable, voluntary organization which coordinates the YWCA movement in Canada, and has a mission to advocate for the equity and equality rights and needs of women. The YWCA works actively to raise awareness on the prevention of violence against women, and the need for universal, accessible and quality child care.
Affliation(s): Selective: Canadian Policy Research Network; National Council of Women; National Youth Serving Organizations; Women's Future Fund; Canadian Centre for Philanthropy; National Action Committee on the Status of Women
Chief Officer(s):
Elizabeth Bourns, President
Paulette Senior, CEO
psenior@ywcacanada.ca
Lynne Kent, President
Keitha McClocklin, Vice President
Colette Prévost, Vice President
Finances: *Annual Operating Budget:* $500,000-$1.5 Million; *Funding Sources:* Affiliation fees; donations; grants; sponsorships
Staff Member(s): 11; 50 volunteer(s)
Membership: 34 associations; *Fees:* Schedule available; *Committees:* Executive; Finance; International Cooperation; Nominating; Youth Engagement
Activities: Largest provider of shelter & non-profit housing; second largest provider of childcare; adult education; long-term supportive housing, residences; programs to end violence against women; job & life-skills training; leadership development; wellness programs; youth services; fitness activities; international development education; *Awareness Events:* YWCA Week Without Violence, Oct.; Rose Button Campaign, Dec.; Women of Distinction Awards; *Internships:* Yes; *Speaker Service:* Yes; *Library* by appointment

Community YWCA of Muskoka
440 Ecclestone Dr., Bracebridge ON P1L 1Z6
Tel: 705-645-9827; *Fax:* 705-645-4804
www.ywcamuskoka.com
www.facebook.com/muskoka.yw
twitter.com/YWCAMuskoka
Chief Officer(s):
Hannah Lin, Executive Director

YWCA Niagara Region
183 King St., St Catharines ON L2R 3J5
Tel: 905-988-3528; *Fax:* 905-988-3739
info@ywcaniagararegion.ca
www.ywcaniagararegion.ca
www.facebook.com/YWCANiagaraRegion
twitter.com/YWCA_Niagara
Chief Officer(s):
Elisabeth Zimmermann, Executive Director
ezimmermann@ywcaniagararegion.ca

YWCA Northeast Avalon
PO Box 21291, St. John's NL A1A 5G6
Tel: 709-726-9622; *Fax:* 709-576-0410
www.ynortheastavalon.com
www.linkedin.com/groups?about=&gid=1903327
www.facebook.com/pages/YWCA-of-Northeast-Avalon/348363604436
twitter.com/YMCAofNEA
Chief Officer(s):
Jason Brown, CEO/President
jbrown@ynortheastavalon.com

YWCA of Banff
PO Box 520, 102 Spray Ave., Banff AB T1L 1A6
Tel: 403-762-3560; *Fax:* 403-762-3202
crc@ywcabanff.ab.ca
www.ywcabanff.ab.ca
Mission: To empower women and their communities through leadership, advocacy, and provision of meaningful services
Chief Officer(s):
Kerry-Lee Schulteis, Executive Director

YWCA of Brandon
148 - 11th St., Brandon MB R7A 4J4
Tel: 204-571-3680; *Fax:* 204-571-3687
ywca2@wcgwave.ca
www.ywcabrandon.com
www.facebook.com/YWCABrandon
twitter.com/YWCABrandon
Chief Officer(s):
Karen Peto, Executive Director
kpeto@wcgwave.ca

YWCA of Calgary
320 - 5th Ave. SE, Calgary AB T2G 0E5
Tel: 403-263-1550; *Fax:* 403-263-4681; *Crisis Hot-Line:* 403-266-0707
communications@ywcaofcalgary.com
www.ywcaofcalgary.com
www.facebook.com/pages/YWCA-of-Calgary/10150115104400262
twitter.com/ywcaofcalgary
www.youtube.com/ywcaofcalgary
Chief Officer(s):
Sue Tomney, Chief Executive Officer

YWCA of Durham
33 McGrigor St., Oshawa ON L1H 1X8
Tel: 905-576-6356; *Fax:* 905-576-0816
www.ywcadurham.org
Chief Officer(s):
Kim Beatty, President

YWCA of Edmonton
Empire Building, #400, 10080 Jasper Ave., Edmonton AB T5J 1V9
Tel: 780-423-9922; *Fax:* 780-488-6077
information@ywcaofedmonton.org
www.ywcaofedmonton.org
www.facebook.com/pages/YWCA-Edmonton/109755395744949
twitter.com/ywcaedmonton
www.flickr.com/photos/ywcaedmonton
Chief Officer(s):
Hilary Anaka, President

YWCA of Guelph
130 Woodland Glen Dr., Guelph ON N1G 4M3
Tel: 519-824-5150; *Fax:* 519-824-4729
contact@guelphy.org
www.guelphy.org
www.facebook.com/pages/YMCA-YWCA-of-Guelph/306629139364333
twitter.com/YGuelph
Chief Officer(s):
Jim Bonk, CEO
jim_bonk@ymca.ca

YWCA of Halifax
1239 Barrington St., Halifax NS B3J 1Y2
Tel: 902-423-6162; *Fax:* 902-444-3568
www.ywcahalifax.com
www.facebook.com/ywcahalifax
twitter.com/YWCAHalifax
www.youtube.com/user/YWCAHalifax
Chief Officer(s):
Miia Suokonautio, Executive Director
m.suokonautio@ywcahalifax.com

YWCA of Hamilton
75 MacNab St. South, Hamilton ON L8P 3C1
Tel: 905-522-9922
www.ywcahamilton.org
www.facebook.com/pages/YWCA-Hamilton/130462810309052
Chief Officer(s):
Denise Doyle, Chief Executive Officer
ddoyle@ywcahamilton.org

YWCA of Kitchener-Waterloo
153 Frederick St., Kitchener ON N2H 2M2
Tel: 519-576-8856; *Fax:* 519-576-0129
general@ywcakw.on.ca
www.ywcakw.on.ca
www.facebook.com/ywcakw
twitter.com/YWCA_KW
Chief Officer(s):
Tracy Van Kalsbeek, President

YWCA of Lethbridge & District
604 - 8th St. South, Lethbridge AB T1J 2K1
Tel: 403-329-0088; *Fax:* 403-327-9112; *Crisis Hot-Line:* 403-320-1881
inquiries@ywcalethbridge.org
www.ywcalethbridge.org
www.facebook.com/pages/YWCA-of-Lethbridge-and-District/21516367559
Chief Officer(s):
Kristine Cassie, CEO

YWCA of Moncton
#T310, 22 Church St., Moncton NB E1C 0P7
Tel: 506-855-4349; *Fax:* 506-855-3320
info@ywcamoncton.com
www.ywcamoncton.com
www.facebook.com/ywcamoncton
twitter.com/ywcamoncton
www.ywcamoncton.tumblr.com
Chief Officer(s):
Jewell Mitchell, Executive Director
jmitchell@ywcamoncton.com

YWCA of Montréal
1355, boul René-Lévesque Ouest, Montréal QC H3G 1T3
Tel: 514-866-9941; *Fax:* 514-866-4866
info@ydesfemmesmtl.org
www.ydesfemmesmtl.org
www.linkedin.com/company/fondation-y-des-femmes-de-montr-al
www.facebook.com/pages/Le-Y-des-femmes-de-Montreal/122110488922
twitter.com/YWCA_mtl
www.youtube.com/user/YWCAMTL
Chief Officer(s):
Hélène Lépine, Présidente-directrice générale

YWCA of Peterborough, Victoria & Haliburton
216 Simcoe St., Peterborough ON K9H 2H7
Tel: 705-743-3526; *Fax:* 705-745-4654; *TTY:* 705-743-4015; *Crisis Hot-Line:* 800-461-7656
info@ywcapeterborough.org
www.ywcapeterborough.org
www.facebook.com/ywcapeterborough
twitter.com/YWCAPtbo
Chief Officer(s):
Lynn Zimmer, Executive Director
lzimmer@ywcapeterborough.org

YWCA of Pictou County
2756 Westville Rd., RR#3, New Glasgow NS B2H 5C6
Tel: 902-752-0202; *Fax:* 902-755-3446
frontdesk@pcymca.ca
www.pcymca.ca
www.facebook.com/YMCAPictouCounty
Chief Officer(s):
Dave MacIntyre, Chief Executive Officer

YWCA of Prince Albert
1895 Central Ave., Prince Albert SK S6V 4W8
Tel: 306-763-8571; *Fax:* 306-763-8165
ywcaprincealbert.ca
Chief Officer(s):
Donna Brooks, Chief Executive Officer
donnabrooks.ywca@sasktel.net

YWCA of Regina
1940 McIntyre St., Regina SK S4P 2R3
Tel: 306-525-2141; *Fax:* 306-525-2171
ywcaregina@ywcaregina.com
www.ywcaregina.com
Chief Officer(s):
Deanna Elias-Henry, Executive Director
deanna@ywcaregina.com

YWCA of Saint John
130 Broadview Ave., Saint John NB E2L 5C5

Tel: 506-693-9622; *Fax:* 506-634-4180
www.saintjohny.com
www.facebook.com/SaintJohnY
twitter.com/Y_SaintJohn
Chief Officer(s):
Shilo Boucher, CEO/President

YWCA of St. Thomas Elgin
16 Mary St. West, St Thomas ON N5P 2S3
Tel: 519-631-9800; *Fax:* 519-631-6411
Toll-Free: 800-461-0954
ywcastthomaselgin@bellnet.ca
www.ywcastthomaselgin.org
www.facebook.com/pages/YWCA-St-Thomas-Elgin/17454590 2575534
twitter.com/YWCAStThomas
Chief Officer(s):
Marla Champion, Executive Director

YWCA of Saskatoon
510 - 25th St. East, Saskatoon SK S7K 4A7
Tel: 306-244-0944; *Fax:* 306-653-2468
info@ywcasaskatoon.com
www.ywcasaskatoon.com
www.facebook.com/ywcasaskatoon
twitter.com/YWCASaskatoon
Chief Officer(s):
Deb Parker-Loewen, President

YWCA of Sudbury
370 St. Raphael St., Sudbury ON P3B 4K7
Tel: 705-673-4754; *Fax:* 705-688-1727
ywcasudbury.ca
Chief Officer(s):
Marlene Gorman, Executive Director
m.gorman@ywcasudbury.ca

YWCA of Thompson
39 Nickel Rd., Thompson MB R8N 0Y5
Tel: 204-778-6341; *Fax:* 204-778-5308
www.ywcathompson.ca
www.facebook.com/pages/YWCA-Thompson/282578048442 942
Chief Officer(s):
Elaine McGregor, Executive Director
ywcaexdir@mymts.net

YWCA of Vancouver
535 Hornby St., Vancouver BC V6C 2E8
Tel: 250-895-5800
enquire@ywcavan.org
www.ywcavan.org
www.linkedin.com/company/ywca-metro-vancouver
www.facebook.com/pages/YWCA-Vancouver/268163004562
twitter.com/YWCAVAN
www.youtube.com/user/YWCAVancouver
Chief Officer(s):
Janet Austin, CEO

YWCA of Western Ontario
382 Waterloo St., London ON N6B 2N8
Tel: 519-667-3306; *Fax:* 519-433-8527
www.ymcawo.ca
www.facebook.com/CentreBranchYMCALondon
twitter.com/yourYMCAWO
www.youtube.com/mylondony
Chief Officer(s):
Shaun Elliott, CEO

YWCA of Winnipeg
3550 Portage Ave., Winnipeg MB R3K 0Z8
Tel: 204-947-3044
www.ywinnipeg.ca
www.facebook.com/ywinnipeg
twitter.com/YWinnipeg
www.youtube.com/user/YWinnipeg
Chief Officer(s):
Kent Paterson, President & CEO

YWCA of Yellowknife
PO Box 1679, Yellowknife NT X1A 2P3
Tel: 867-920-2777; *Fax:* 867-873-9406
info@ywcanwt.ca
www.ywcanwt.ca
www.facebook.com/122130201165447
twitter.com/YWCAYK
Chief Officer(s):
Lyda Fuller, Executive Director

YWCA Québec
855, av Holland, Québec QC G1S 3S5
Tél: 418-683-2155; *Téléc:* 418-683-5526
info@ywcaquebec.qc.ca
www.ywcaquebec.qc.ca
www.facebook.com/ywcaquebec
twitter.com/ywcaqc
www.facebook.com/ywcaquebec
Chief Officer(s):
Katia de Pokomandy-Morin, Directrice générale
directiongenerale@ywcaquebec.qc.ca

YWCA Toronto
87 Elm St., Toronto ON M5G 0A8
Tel: 416-961-8100; *Fax:* 416-961-7739
Toll-Free: 888-843-9922
info@ywcatoronto.org
www.ywcatoronto.org
www.facebook.com/pages/YWCA-Toronto/29472659546
twitter.com/YWCAToronto
Chief Officer(s):
Heather McGregor, CEO

YWCAs of Cambridge & Kitchener-Waterloo
#203, 460 Frederick St., Kitchener ON N2H 2P5
Tel: 519-584-7479; *Fax:* 519-576-6223
info@ckwymca.ca
www.ymcacambridgekw.ca
www.linkedin.com/company/ymcas-of-cambridge-&-kitchener-waterloo
www.facebook.com/YMCAsofCandKW
twitter.com/ymcasofcandkw
www.youtube.com/YMCAsofCandKW
Chief Officer(s):
John Haddock, Chief Executive Officer

YWCA December 6 Fund of Toronto
87 Elm St., Toronto ON M5G 0A8
Tel: 416-961-8101; *Fax:* 416-961-7739
Toll-Free: 888-843-9922
dec6@ywcatoronto.org
www.dec6fund.ca
Overview: A small local organization founded in 1994
Mission: To raise money to help women build lives free of violence
Chief Officer(s):
Yvonne Avila, Registrar
Finances: *Funding Sources:* United Way; Canadian Women's Foundation; donations
Activities: Provide interest free loans to women fleeing abuse

YWCA of Banff Programs & Services
PO Box 520, 102 Spray Ave., Banff AB T1L 1A6
Tel: 403-760-3200; *Fax:* 403-760-3234
yps@ywcabanff.ab.ca
ywcabanff.ab.ca
www.facebook.com/YWCABanff
twitter.com/YWCABanff
Previous Name: Planned Parenthood Banff; Banff YWCA Community Resource Centre
Overview: A small local charitable organization founded in 1987
Mission: The Centre's primary focus is on safe, affordable housing and family violence prevention through education, programming, events, resource management and crisis intervention. It can arrange emergency access to shelter and provide referrals to community services.
Affliation(s): Society Against Family Violence
Chief Officer(s):
Susan Kennard, President
Connie MacDonald, Chief Executive Director
Staff Member(s): 5
Membership: 100-499; *Fees:* $25/yr.; $50/3 yrs.
Activities: *Awareness Events:* Week Without Violence; International Women's Day; Walk a Mile in Her Shoes; *Library:* YWCA of Banff Programs & Serives

YWCA Westman Women's Shelter
148 - 11 St., Brandon MB R7A 4J4
Tel: 204-727-3644; *Fax:* 204-726-1793; *Crisis Hot-Line:* 877-977-0007
ywca2@wcgwave.ca
Overview: A small local charitable organization founded in 1978
Mission: To provide women with safe shelter, supportive counselling, advocacy, education & awareness of alternatives to violence
Finances: *Funding Sources:* Provincial government; United Way; grants; donations
Activities: *Speaker Service:* Yes

Zane Cohen Centre for Digestive Diseases Familial Gastrointestinal Cancer Registry (FGICR)
Mount Sinai Hospital, Zane Cohen Centre, PO Box 24, 60 Murray St., Toronto ON M5T 3L9
Tel: 416-586-4800; *Fax:* 416-586-5924
Toll-Free: 877-586-5112
zcc@mtsinai.on.ca
www.zanecohencentre.ca
Previous Name: Familial GI Cancer Registry
Overview: A small local organization founded in 1980
Mission: The Registry is an interdisciplinary program dedicated to the specialty care of families affected with rare forms of inherited colorectal cancer.
Publications:
• Network [a publication of the Familial Gastrointestinal Cancer Registry]
Type: Newsletter; *Editor:* Terri Berk

Zeballos Board of Trade
c/o Village of Zeballos, PO Box 127, Zeballos BC V0P 2A0
Tel: 250-761-4229; *Fax:* 250-761-4331
adminzeb@recn.ca
www.zeballos.com
Overview: A small local organization founded in 1938
Member of: BC Chamber of Commerce
Finances: *Annual Operating Budget:* Less than $50,000; *Funding Sources:* Membership dues
4 volunteer(s)
Membership: 1-99

Zenon Park Board of Trade
c/o Zenon Park Credit Union, PO Box 250, 735 Main St., Zenon Park SK S0E 1W0
Tel: 306-767-2434; *Fax:* 306-767-2224
Overview: A small local organization
Chief Officer(s):
Seline Favreau, Secretary
Allen Georget, President

Zhahti Koe Friendship Centre
PO Box 209, Fort Providence NT X0E 0L0
Tel: 867-699-3801; *Fax:* 867-699-4355
zhahti@ssimicro.com
Overview: A small local organization

La Zone Boxe 49
95, rue Merrill, Chibougamau QC G8P 1C3
Tél: 418-770-6315
boxe49@hotmail.ca
Nom précédent: Club de boxe Chibougamau
Aperçu: *Dimension:* petite; *Envergure:* locale
Membre(s) du bureau directeur:
David Pelletier, Président

ZOOCHECK Canada Inc.
788 1/2 O'Connor Dr., Toronto ON M4B 2S6
Tel: 416-285-1744
zoocheck@zoocheck.com
www.zoocheck.com
www.facebook.com/pages/Zoocheck/118864269587
Overview: A small national charitable organization founded in 1984
Mission: Zoocheck works to improve wildlife protection in Canada and to end the abuse, neglect and exploitation of individual wild animals through: investigation & research; public education & awareness campaigns; capacity building initiatives; legal programs; legislative actions.
Finances: *Funding Sources:* Donations
Activities: *Speaker Service:* Yes; *Rents Mailing List:* Yes

Zoological Society of Manitoba *See* Assiniboine Park Conservancy

Zoological Society of Metropolitan Toronto *See* Toronto Zoo

Zoological Society of Montréal / Société zoologique de Montréal
#525, 117, rue Ste-Catherine ouest, Montréal QC H3B 1H9
Tel: 514-845-8317
contact@zoologicalsocietymtl.org
www.zoologicalsocietymtl.org
Overview: A small local organization founded in 1964
Mission: To promote & develop interest in & knowledge of wildlife; To encourage the study of biology & nature sciences; To encourage the protection of wildlife
Finances: *Funding Sources:* Fundrasing, donations, member dues
Membership: 500; *Fees:* $35 individual; $55 family

Activities: Field trips; monthly meetings; *Speaker Service:* Yes

Zoroastrian Associaton of Québec *See* Association Zoroastrianne de Québec

Zoroastrian Society of Ontario (ZSO)

3590 Bayview Ave., Toronto ON M2M 3S6
Tel: 416-225-7771
secretary@zso.org
www.zso.org
Overview: A small provincial charitable organization founded in 1971
Mission: Meeting the religious & cultural needs of the Zoroastrian community of Ontario
Affliation(s): Federation of North American Zoroastrian Associations
Chief Officer(s):
Sam M. Vesuna, President
Kevin Mancherjee, Exec. Vice-President
Fram Sethna, Treasurer
Mehroo Chothia, Secretary
Finances: *Annual Operating Budget:* $100,000-$250,000; *Funding Sources:* Membership fees; donations; investment income
Staff Member(s): 1; 200 volunteer(s)
Membership: 1,000; *Fees:* $70 family; $40 individual; $20 seniors & students; *Member Profile:* Zoroastrians living in Ontario; *Committees:* 15 sub-committees reporting to elected executive committee of 9
Activities: Religious, cultural, youth, religious classes, seniors activities; sponsors 100th Scout Group; *Library:* ZSO Library; by appointment
Awards:
• Volunteer of the Year (Award)
4 volunteer awards given per year

Zurich & Association District Chamber of Commerce

PO Box 189, Zurich ON N0M 2T0
Tel: 519-236-4717
www.zurich-ontario-canada.com
Overview: A small local organization
Mission: The mission of the Zurich and District Chamber of Commerce is to serve as the Voice of Business, to promote and enhance economic prosperity and quality of life in Zurich and District
Chief Officer(s):
Phillip Knight, President
Joyce McBeath, Secretary
Finances: *Annual Operating Budget:* Less than $50,000
Membership: 25; *Fees:* $25

Zwiazek Nauczycielstwa Polskiego w Kanadzie *See* Polish Teachers Association in Canada

Foreign Associations

Academic Pediatric Association (APA)
6728 Old McLean Village Dr., McLean VA 22101 USA
Tel: 703-556-9222; *Fax:* 703-556-8729
info@academicpeds.org
www.ambpeds.org
www.facebook.com/AcademicPeds
twitter.com/academicpeds
Overview: A large international organization
Mission: To improve the health of children & adolescents; To provide leadership in education of child health professionals; To engage in research & disseminate knowledge
Chief Officer(s):
Marge Degnon, Executive Director
marge@academicpeds.org
Connie Mackay, Associate Director
connie@academicpeds.org
Nui Dhepyasuwan, Research Associate
nui@academicpeds.org
Membership: *Fees:* In-Training, $50; Non-Physician, $125; Physician, $250
Awards:
• Child Advocacy Award (Award)
• APA Public Policy & Advocacy Award (Award)
• Global Health Research Award (Award)
• Health Care Delivery Award (Award)
• Michael Shannon Award (Award)
• Teaching Program Award (Award)
• Research Award (Award)
Meetings/Conferences:
• Pediatric Academic Societies' 2015 Annual Meeting, April, 2015, San Diego, CA
Scope: International
Description: An international meeting focussing on research in child health
Contact Information: Address: #7B, 3400 Research Forest Dr., The Woodlands, TX, 77381, USA; Phone: 281-419-0052; Fax: 281-419-0082
• Pediatric Academic Societies' 2016 Annual Meeting, April, 2016, Baltimore, MD
Scope: International
Description: An international meeting focussing on research in child health
Contact Information: Address: #7B, 3400 Research Forest Dr., The Woodlands, TX, 77381, USA; Phone: 281-419-0052; Fax: 281-419-0082
• Pediatric Academic Societies' 2017 Annual Meeting, May, 2017, San Francisco, CA
Scope: International
Description: An international meeting focussing on research in child health
Contact Information: Address: #7B, 3400 Research Forest Dr., The Woodlands, TX, 77381, USA; Phone: 281-419-0052; Fax: 281-419-0082
• Pediatric Academic Societies' 2018 Annual Meeting, May, 2018, Toronto, ON
Scope: International
Description: An international meeting focussing on research in child health
Contact Information: Address: #7B, 3400 Research Forest Dr., The Woodlands, TX, 77381, USA; Phone: 281-419-0052; Fax: 281-419-0082
• Pediatric Academic Societies' 2019 Annual Meeting, April, 2019, Baltimore, MD
Scope: International
Description: An international meeting focussing on research in child health
Contact Information: Address: #7B, 3400 Research Forest Dr., The Woodlands, TX, 77381, USA; Phone: 281-419-0052; Fax: 281-419-0082
• Pediatric Academic Societies' 2020 Annual Meeting, May, 2020, Philadelphia, PA
Scope: International
Description: An international meeting focussing on research in child health
Contact Information: Address: #7B, 3400 Research Forest Dr., The Woodlands, TX, 77381, USA; Phone: 281-419-0052; Fax: 281-419-0082
• Pediatric Academic Societies' 2021 Annual Meeting, 2021
Scope: International
Description: An international meeting focussing on research in child health
Contact Information: Address: #7B, 3400 Research Forest Dr., The Woodlands, TX, 77381, USA; Phone: 281-419-0052; Fax: 281-419-0082
Publications:
• APA Focus
Type: Newsletter; *Frequency:* Bimonthly; *Price:* Free with Academic Pediatric Association membership
• APA Journal: Academic Pediatrics
Type: Journal; *Frequency:* Bimonthly; *Editor:* Peter Szilagyi, MD, MPH; *Price:* Free with Academic Pediatric Association membership
Profile: The peer-reviewed publication is the official journal of the Academic Pediatric Association, featuring research & educational information for health professionalswho care for children

Académie européenne des sciences, des arts et des lettres (AESAL) / European Academy of Sciences, Arts & Humanities
60, rue Monsieur le Prince, Paris 75006 France
Téléc: 33-4-93-34-05-06
www.europeanacademysciencesartsandletters.com
Aperçu: *Dimension:* moyenne; *Envergure:* internationale; Organisme sans but lucratif; fondée en 1980
Mission: De coopérer bénévolements avec L'UNESCO dans ses domaines de compétence
Affliation(s): Relation formelle avec l'UNESCO
Membre(s) du bureau directeur:
Nicole D'Agaggio Lemaire, Secrétaire Perpétuelle
nilemaire@wanadoo.fr
Membre: *Critères d'admissibilite:* Personnalités choisies pour leur polyvalence, principalement au sein des Académies Nationales, et parmi les Lauréats des Grands Prix Internationaux, comme le Prix Nobel, le Prix Erasme

Academy of Management (AOM)
PO Box 3020, Briarcliff Manor NY 10510-8020 USA
Tel: 914-923-2607; *Fax:* 914-923-2615
www.aomonline.org
www.linkedin.com/groups?gid=102523
facebook.com/AOMConnect
twitter.com/AOMConnect
Overview: A large international organization founded in 1936
Mission: To create & disseminate knowledge about management & organizations
Chief Officer(s):
Anne S. Tsui, President, 480-965-3999
R. Duane Ireland, Vice President & Program Chair, Management, 979-862-3963
Membership: 17,707; *Member Profile:* Scholars from 106 nations
Meetings/Conferences:
• Academy of Management 2015 Annual Meeting, August, 2015, Vancouver Convention Centre, Vancouver, BC
Scope: International
Attendance: 10,000+
Description: Sharing of research and expertise in all management disciplines through distinguished speakers, competitive paper sessions, symposia, panels, workshops, & special programs for doctoral students
Contact Information: Assistant Director of Meetings: Taryn Fiore, E-mail: tfiore@pace.edu
• Academy of Management 2016 Annual Meeting, August, 2016, Anaheim, CA
Scope: International
Attendance: 10,000+
Description: Sharing of research and expertise in all management disciplines through distinguished speakers, competitive paper sessions, symposia, panels, workshops, & special programs for doctoral students
Contact Information: Assistant Director of Meetings: Taryn Fiore, E-mail: tfiore@pace.edu
• Academy of Management 2017 Annual Meeting, August, 2017, Atlanta, GA
Scope: International
Attendance: 10,000+
Description: Sharing of research and expertise in all management disciplines through distinguished speakers, competitive paper sessions, symposia, panels, workshops, & special programs for doctoral students
Contact Information: Assistant Director of Meetings: Taryn Fiore, E-mail: tfiore@pace.edu
Publications:
• Academy of Management Annals
Type: Book; *Frequency:* Annually
Profile: Advances in various management fields, with critical research reviews, for academic scholars in management & professionals in allied fields
• Academy of Management Annual Meeting Proceedings
Type: Yearbook; *Frequency:* Annually
• Academy of Management Journal (AMJ)
Type: Journal; *Frequency:* 6 pa; *Accepts Advertising*; *Editor:* Michael Malgrande
Profile: Research for management scholars
• Academy of Management Learning & Education (AMLE)
Type: Journal; *Frequency:* Quarterly; *Accepts Advertising*; *Editor:* Michael Malgrande
Profile: Issues in the fields of management learning & education for scholars, educators, program directors, deans at academic institutions, & practitioners intraining & corporate education
• Academy of Management Member Directory
Type: Directory
• Academy of Management News
Type: Newsletter; *Frequency:* Quarterly
Profile: Association announcements, news, professional opportunities, & meetings
• Academy of Management Perspectives (AMP)
Type: Journal; *Frequency:* Quarterly; *Accepts Advertising*; *Editor:* Susan Zaid
Profile: Formerly the Academy of Management Executive, the journal features advances in management theory & research & articles about the process of managing an organization
• Academy of Management Review (AMR)
Type: Journal; *Frequency:* Quarterly; *Accepts Advertising*; *Editor:* Susan Zaid
Profile: Theory development, conceptual work, articles about organizations & their role in society, & reviews of literature

Action Mondiale des Parlementaires ***See*** Parliamentarians for Global Action

AdvaMed
#800, 701 Pennsylvania Ave. NW, Washington DC 20004-2654 USA
Tel: 202-783-8700; *Fax:* 202-783-8750
info@advamed.org
www.advamed.org
www.linkedin.com/company/79166
www.facebook.com/AdvaMed
twitter.com/advamedupdate
www.youtube.com/advamedupdate
Also Known As: Advanced Medical Technology Association
Overview: A small international organization
Mission: To promote procedures that encourage ethical practices & easier access to technology in the medical industry.
Chief Officer(s):
José E. Almedia, President/CEO
Staff Member(s): 75
Membership: 300 companies; *Member Profile:* Medical technology firms; professional service firms that support and directly benefit the medical industry; emerging growth companies

Aerospace & Electronic Systems Society (AESS)
445 Hoes Lane, Piscataway NJ 08854-1331 USA
Tel: 732-981-0060; *Fax:* 732-981-1721
customer-service@ieee.org
www.ieee-aess.org
Overview: A medium-sized international organization founded in 1965 overseen by Institute of Electrical & Electronics Engineers Inc.
Mission: To advance the art of the design, integration, test & analysis of large, complex systems consisting of major subsystems
Chief Officer(s):
Hugh Griffiths, President
h.griffiths@ieee.org
Finances: *Annual Operating Budget:* $500,000-$1.5 Million; *Funding Sources:* Membership dues; conferences
100 volunteer(s)
Membership: 8,500; *Fees:* $25; *Member Profile:* IEEE members; *Committees:* Formal Methods in System Design; Gyro & Accelerometer; Integrated Avionics; Radar; Satellite Navigation; Space Systems; System Engineering; Target Tracking & Sensor Fusion

AFCOM
742 East Chapman Ave., Orange CA 92866 USA
Tel: 714-997-7966; *Fax:* 714-997-9743
afcom@afcom.com
www.afcom.com
Previous Name: Association for Computer Operations Management
Overview: A medium-sized local organization founded in 1980

Mission: To enable data center professionals to share industry best practices by providing a forum for dissemination of criticial information; to provide education on key data center management issues; to provide the industry's most comprehensive insight & analysis in key areas affecting all data-intensive organizations & to be the most comprehensive & effective resource available to the overall data community
Chief Officer(s):
Jill Yaoz, President
jyaoz@afcom.com
Finances: *Annual Operating Budget:* $500,000-$1.5 Million; *Funding Sources:* Membership dues; conference dues; trade show sales
Staff Member(s): 17
Membership: 2,500; *Fees:* USD $255 Individual; USD $585 site; USD $866 Corporate; *Committees:* Membership advisory

African Literature Association (ALA) / Association Africane de Literature

c/o Hobart & William Smith Colleges, 300 Pulteney St., Geneva NY 14456 USA
Tel: 315-781-3491; *Fax:* 315-781-3822
headquarters@africanlit.org
www.africanlit.org
Overview: A medium-sized international organization founded in 1975
Mission: To promote the study & teaching of African literatures in their broad social, historical, & political dimensions. Aims for a constructive interaction between scholars & artists, the worldwide understanding & appreciation of African literatures, & the continual refinement of the tools & methods of African literary study
Member of: African Studies Association
Chief Officer(s):
James McCorkle, Director, 315-781-3491, Fax: 315-781-3822
mccorkie@africanlit.org
Soraya Mekerta, President, 404-270-5531
president@africanlit.org
Tejumola Olaniyan, Vice-President
vice-president@africanlit.org
Finances: *Annual Operating Budget:* Less than $50,000; *Funding Sources:* Membership dues; subscriptions
Membership: 600; *Fees:* US$20-$100; $5 African Student; $120 Sponsor; $1500 Life; *Member Profile:* Scholars; teachers; writers; *Committees:* Awards; Constitution & Policy; Finance; Issues; Media Relations; Publications; Teaching & Research; Travel Grants
Activities: *Rents Mailing List:* Yes

African Wildlife Foundation (AWF)

#120, 1400 Sixteenth St. NW, Washington DC 20036 USA
Tel: 202-939-3333; *Fax:* 202-939-3332
Toll-Free: 888-494-5354
africanwildlife@awf.org
www.awf.org
www.facebook.com/AfricanWildlifeFoundation
twitter.com/AWF_Official?ref=nf
www.youtube.com/AfricanWildlife
Overview: A large international organization
Mission: To promote conservation of Africa's wildlife & natural resources; to promote belief that the survival of African wildlife lies in a working knowledge of the relationship between man, his economics & his environment; to promote, establish & support grassroots & institutional programs in conservation education, wildlife management & training, & management of threatened conservation areas; to manage projects aimed at saving endangered species (eg. the African Elephant, Mountain Gorilla, Rhinoceros)
Chief Officer(s):
Patrick J. Bergin, CEO
Helen W. Gichohi, President
Jeff Chrisfield, CFO
Staff Member(s): 120
Publications:
• African Heartland News
Type: Newsletter; *Frequency:* Quarterly
Profile: For AWF's technical partners
• African Wildlife News
Type: Newsletter; *Frequency:* Quarterly
Profile: For AWF members

Agence internationale de l'énergie atomique *See* International Atomic Energy Agency

Agence spatiale européenne *See* European Space Agency

AIM Global (AIM)

One Landmark North, #203, 20399 Rte. 19, Cranberry Township PA 16066 USA
Tel: 724-742-4470; *Fax:* 724-742-4476
info@aimglobal.org
www.aimglobal.org
Previous Name: Automatic Identification Manufacturers
Overview: A small international charitable organization founded in 1972
Mission: To stimulate the understanding, adoption & use of AIM technology by providing timely, unbiased & commercial-free news & information
Chief Officer(s):
Mary Lou Bosco, Chief Operating Officer
marylou@aimglobal.org
Staff Member(s): 2
Membership: 95; *Member Profile:* Providers & users of technologies, systems, & services that capture, manage & integrate accurate data into larger information management systems; *Committees:* Internet of Things; RFID Experts Group; Technical Symbologies; Unique Device Identification Initiative-AIM North America; UID Suppliers Alliance AIM North America
Activities: Sponsor of frontline solution shows; standards developer in Bar code & RFID; liaison member ISO SC31; *Speaker Service:* Yes
Awards:
• Don Percival Award (Award)
• Richard R. Dilling Award (Award)

Air & Waste Management Association (A&WMA) / Association pour la prévention de la contamination de l'air et du sol

One Gateway Center, 420 Fort Duquesne Blvd., 3rd Fl., Pittsburgh PA 15222-1435 USA
Tel: 412-232-3444; *Fax:* 412-232-3450
Toll-Free: 800-270-3444
info@awma.org
www.awma.org
www.linkedin.com/company/445959
www.facebook.com/groups/33499462923
twitter.com/AirandWaste
Previous Name: Air Pollution Control Association
Overview: A large international organization founded in 1907
Mission: To improve environmental knowledge & decisions; To assist members in critical environmental decision making & professional development; To provide a neutral forum for exchanging information & developing networking opportunities; To increase public education & outreach
Member of: International Union of Air Pollution Prevention & Environmental Protection Associations
Affliation(s): Canadian Prairie & Northern Section (www.cpans.org); Ontario Section (www.awma.on.ca); Québec Section (www.apcas.qc.ca); Ottawa Valley Chapter (www.awma-ovc.ca); Pacific Northwest International Section (www.pnwis.org)
Chief Officer(s):
Merlyn L. Hough, President
Jim Powell, Executive Director/Secretary, 412-904-6007
jpowell@awma.org
Amy Gilligan, Treasurer
Membership: 5,000+ in 65 countries; *Fees:* $40 students; $75 emeritus members; $105 young professional members; $200 individuals; $480 primary organizational members; *Member Profile:* Environmental professionals; *Committees:* Councils: Education; Sections & Chapters; Technical; Young Professionals
Awards:
• S. Smith Griswold Outstanding Air Pollution Control Official Award (Award)
• Frank A. Chambers Excellence in Air Pollution Control Award (Award)
Awarded to individuals who make an exceptional contribution to any technical aspect of air pollution control
• Richard Beatty Mellon Environmental Stewarship Award (Award)
Presented to a person who has made a civic contribution to a field related to the mission & objectives of the association
• Charles W. Gruber Association Leadership Award (Award)
• Lyman A. Ripperton Environmental Educator Award (Award)
Presented to teachers who inspire students to achieve excellence in professional & social endeavours; recipients are educators from some field related to the mission & objectives of the association
• J. Deane Sensenbaugh Environmental Technology Award (Award)
Presented every year to a firm, company, or corporation that has made outstanding achievements in air pollution control or waste management; the recipient's contribution to the state of the art must be one that has been recognized & accepted in the field
• Richard I. Stessel Waste Management Award (Award)
• Honorary A&WMA Membership (Award)
• Fellow A&WMA Membership (Award)
• Outstanding Young Professional Award (Award)
Meetings/Conferences:
• Air & Waste Management Association 2015 Annual Conference & Exhibition, June, 2015, Raleigh Convention Center, Raleigh, NC
Scope: International
Contact Information: URL: ace2015.awma.org
Publications:
• Air & Waste Management Association Membership Directory
Type: Directory
Profile: Contact information for members
• EM, The Magazine for Environmental Managers
Type: Magazine; *Frequency:* Monthly; *Accepts Advertising*; *Price:* $180 individuals; $265 nonprofit organization & government agencies; $405 all others
Profile: Management, policy, & regulatory perspective
• Journal of the Air & Waste Management Association
Type: Journal; *Frequency:* Monthly; *Editor:* Tim Keener
Profile: Peer reviewed, technical environmental journal

Air Pollution Control Association *See* Air & Waste Management Association

Airports Council International - Pacific Region

Unit 5, 2/4, Airport World Trade Centre, 1 Sky Plaza Road, Hong Kong Intl. Airport, Hong Kong Hong-Kong
Tel: 852-2180-9449; *Fax:* 852-2180-9462
info@aci-asiapac.aero
www.aci-asiapac.aero
Also Known As: ACI-Pacific
Overview: A medium-sized international organization founded in 1992
Mission: To foster cooperation among member airports & with other partners in world aviation, including governmental, airlines & aircraft manufacturing organizations; to provide the travelling public with an air transport system that is safe, secure, efficient & environmentally compatible
Member of: Airports Council International
Chief Officer(s):
Tan Sri Bashir Ahmad Abdul Majid, President
Staff Member(s): 3
Membership: 50 regional; 550 worldwide; *Fees:* Airports, dependent upon size; US$1,500 associates

Alcoholic Beverage Medical Research Foundation (ABMRF)

#310, 1200-C Agora Dr., Bel Air MD 21014 USA
Toll-Free: 800-688-7152
info@abmrf.org
www.abmrf.org
www.linkedin.com/company/1137768
www.facebook.com/AlcoholResearch?ref=ts
twitter.com/AlcoholResearch
Also Known As: The Foundation for Alcohol Research
Overview: A small international organization founded in 1982
Chief Officer(s):
Mack C. Mitchell, President
Lisa Hoffberger, Director, Development & Communications
Erin Teigen, Director, Research & Grants Programs
Activities: International conferences

Alliance for Sustainability

Hillel Centre, 1521 University Ave. SE, Minneapolis MN 55414 USA
Tel: 612-331-1099; *Fax:* 612-379-9004
iasa@mtn.org
www.afors.org
Also Known As: International Alliance for Sustainable Agriculture
Overview: A medium-sized international charitable organization founded in 1983
Mission: Supporting ecologically sound, economically viable, socially just & humane projects on a personal, organizational & planetary level
Chief Officer(s):
Sean Gosiewski, Program Director
sean@allianceforsustainabilty.com
Finances: *Annual Operating Budget:* Less than $50,000; *Funding Sources:* Membership; foundations; donors;

corporations; religious groups; fundraising; revenue from public speaking, sale of publications, shirts, & buttons
Staff Member(s): 1; 5 volunteer(s)
Membership: 800; *Fees:* $25; *Member Profile:* Farmers; consumers; business & government leaders; environmentalists; educators & scientists
Activities: Natural Step Network meetings; introductory presentations; slide shows; seminars; support projects overseas; *Internships:* Yes; *Speaker Service:* Yes *Library:* Sustainability Resource Center; Open to public

Alliance for the Wild Rockies (AWR)
PO Box 505, Helena MT 59624 USA
Tel: 406-459-5936
awr@wildrockiesalliance.org
www.wildrockiesalliance.org
www.facebook.com/148406678172
twitter.com/awr_nrepa
www.myspace.com/awrnrepa
Overview: A medium-sized international organization founded in 1988
Mission: To protect wildlands & wildlife habitat in the Wild Rockies Bioregion, containing parts of Alberta, British Columbia, Montana, Idaho, Wyoming, Oregon, Washington; to protect threatened, endangered & sensitive species; to promote sound ecosystem protection & sustainable economic development; to promote ecosystem-based land management based on scientific principles
Chief Officer(s):
Gary Macfarlane, President
Finances: *Annual Operating Budget:* $250,000-$500,000; *Funding Sources:* Membership dues; fundraising; donations; foundations
Staff Member(s): 2; 10 volunteer(s)
Membership: 3,500 individual + 1,000 organizational; *Fees:* (USD) Habitat Sponsor: $25; Watershed Sponsor: $50; Ecosystem Sponsor: $100; Bioregion Sponsor: $1000
Activities: *Internships:* Yes *Library:* Ecosystem Defense; Open to public

Alliance internationale de tourisme / International Touring Alliance
2 ch de Blandonnet, Geneva 1215 Switzerland
Tel: 41-22-544-4500; *Fax:* 41-22-544-4550
ait-admin@fia.com
www.ait-touringalliance.com
Overview: A small international organization founded in 1898
Mission: Represents motoring organizations & touring clubs around the world
Affiliation(s): Canadian Automobile Association
Chief Officer(s):
Werner Kraus, President
Membership: 117 member associations in 96 countries

Alliance of Foam Packaging Recyclers *See* EPS Industry Alliance

The Aluminum Association
#600, 1525 Wilson Blvd., Arlington VA 22209 USA
Tel: 703-358-2960; *Fax:* 703-358-2961
www.aluminum.org
www.facebook.com/AluminumAssociation?v=wall
www.twitter.com/AluminumNews
Previous Name: Aluminum Recycling Association
Overview: A small national organization
Mission: To enhance aluminum's position in a world of proliferating materials, increase its use as the "material of choice" remove impediments to its fullest use & assist in achieving the industry's environmental, societal, & economic objectives
Chief Officer(s):
Heidi Biggs Brock, President
hbrock@aluminum.org
Membership: *Member Profile:* Producers of primary aluminum, recyclers & semi-fabricated aluminum products, as well as suppliers to the industry

Aluminum Recycling Association *See* The Aluminum Association

Amalgamated Transit Union (AFL-CIO/CLC) / Syndicat uni du transport (FAT-COI/CTC)
5025 Wisconsin Ave. NW, Washington DC 20016 USA
Tel: 202-537-1645; *Fax:* 202-244-7824
Toll-Free: 888-240-1196
www.atu.org
www.facebook.com/ATUInternational
twitter.com/ATUComm
www.youtube.com/user/stpatuorg
Overview: A medium-sized international organization
Mission: The Amalgamated Transit Union fights for the interests of its members and promotes mass transit.
Chief Officer(s):
Lawrence J Hanley, President
Oscar Owens, Sec.-Treas.
Membership: *Member Profile:* Transit workers

Canadian Council
#210, 61 International Blvd., Toronto ON M9W 6K4
Tel: 416-679-8846; *Fax:* 416-679-9195
director@atucanada.ca
www.atucanada.ca
www.facebook.com/199638993399029
twitter.com/atu_cc
www.youtube.com/user/atucanadiancouncil/videos
Chief Officer(s):
Stan Dera, Canadian Director

Amateur Athletic Union (AAU)
PO Box 22049, Lake Buena Vista FL 32830 USA
Tel: 407-934-7200; *Fax:* 407-934-7242
Toll-Free: 800-228-4872
www.aausports.org
www.facebook.com/realaau
twitter.com/therealaau
www.youtube.com/therealaauvideo
Overview: A large national organization founded in 1888
Mission: To offer a lifelong progression of amateur sports programs for persons of all ages, races & creeds, thereby enhancing the physical, mental & moral development of amateur athletes; to promote good sportsmanship, good citizenship & safety
Chief Officer(s):
Henry Forrest, President
Finances: *Funding Sources:* Membership dues
1000 volunteer(s)
Membership: 650,000; *Fees:* Schedule available
Activities: Conducts programs & works with other sports organizations to benefit amateur athletes; conducts recognition programs for outstanding amateur athletes; publishes an extensive line of handbooks & brochures on individual sports; *Internships:* Yes; *Rents Mailing List:* Yes *Library*
Awards:
- AAU James E. Sullivan Memorial Award (Award)
Honors an outstanding amateur athlete in the United States. *Contact:* Pam Kirby Marshall, sullivan@aausports.org

American Academy for Cerebral Palsy & Developmental Medicine (AACPDM)
#1100, 555 East Wells St., Milwaukee WI 53202 USA
Tel: 414-918-3014; *Fax:* 414-276-2146
info@aacpdm.org
www.aacpdm.org
www.facebook.com/aacpdm
twitter.com/aacpdm
Overview: A medium-sized international organization founded in 1947
Mission: The multidisciplinary scientific society fosters & stimulates education & research in cerebral palsy & developmental medicine for the welfare of patients & their families.
Affiliation(s): Canadian Cerebral Palsy Association
Chief Officer(s):
Darcy Fehlings, President
Tracy Burr, Executive Director
Staff Member(s): 4
Membership: *Fees:* US$285 fellow; US$45 international corresponding; US$35 resident, trainee or student; *Committees:* Awards; Publications; Communications; Complex Care; Education; Lifespan Care; Adapted Sports & Recreation; Advocacy; International Affairs; Research; Memebership
Activities: *Library*
Awards:
- Clinical Research Planning Grant (Grant)
- Academy IAC Scholarship (Scholarship)
- Student Travel Scholarship (Scholarship)
- AACPDM Mentorship Award (Award)

Meetings/Conferences:
- American Academy for Cerebral Palsy & Developmental Medicine 71st Annual Meeting, September, 2017, Palais des congrès de Montréal, Montreal, QC
Scope: International

Publications:
- AACPDM [American Academy for Cerebral Palsy & Developmental Medicine] Newsletter
Type: Newsletter; *Frequency:* Quarterly
- Developmental Medicine & Child Neurology
Type: Journal
Profile: Peer reviewed journal

American Academy of Arts & Sciences
Norton's Woods, 136 Irving St., Cambridge MA 02138 USA
Tel: 617-576-5000; *Fax:* 617-576-5050
www.amacad.org
www.facebook.com/americanacad
twitter.com/americanacad
www.youtube.com/americanacad
Overview: A small international organization founded in 1780
Mission: To conduct a series of multidisciplinary studies & projects
Member of: American Council of Learned Societies
Affiliation(s): International Institute of Applied Systems Analysis
Chief Officer(s):
Jonathan F. Fanton, President
Don M. Randel, Chair
Membership: 4,600 USA + 600 foreign honorary; *Fees:* Schedule available; *Member Profile:* Membership based on distinction in a given field or profession
Activities: The Committee on International Security Studies; Science & Global Security; Social Policy & American Institutions; Humanities & Culture; Education
Awards:
- Scholar-Patriot Award (Award)
- Francis Amory Prize (Award)
- Talcott Parsons Prize (Award)
- George & May Sarton Fellowship (Award)
- The Emerson-Thoreau Prize in Literature (Award)
- Humanistic Studies Award (Award)
- Rumford Prize (Award)

American Academy of Neurology (AAN)
201 Chicago Ave., Minneapolis MN 55415 USA
Tel: 612-928-6000; *Fax:* 612-454-2746
Toll-Free: 800-879-1960
memberservices@aan.com
www.aan.com
www.linkedin.com/groups?gid=2386034
www.facebook.com/AmericanAcademyofNeurology
twitter.com/AANMember
www.youtube.com/AANChannel
Overview: A large international organization
Mission: To advance the art & science of neurology; To promote the best possible care for patients with neurological disorders
Chief Officer(s):
Catherine M. Rydell, Executive Director & CEO
crydell@aan.com
Christine E. Phelps, Deputy Executive Director
cphelps@aan.com
Timothy Engel, Chief Financial Officer
tengel@aan.com
Christopher M. Keran, Chief Membership & Strategy Officer
ckeran@aan.com
Jason Kopinski, Chief Officer, Marketing & Technology
jkopinski@aan.com
Rod Larson, Chief Health Policy Officer
rlarson@aan.com
Membership: 20,000+; *Member Profile:* Medical specialists dedicated to improving the care of patients with neurological diseases; *Committees:* Disclosures; Archives; AAN Audit; AEI Audit; Board Planning; Bylaws; Committee on Sections; Editors-in-Chief; Education; Ethics, Law, & Humanities; Executive; Finance; Government Relations; Grievance; Investment; Journal Arbitration; Medical Economics & Management; Meeting Management; Membership; Nominations; Practice; Science
Activities: Advocating for ethical, high-quality neurological care; Providing professional education programs to physicians & allied health professionals; Supporting clinical & basic research in the neurosciences & related fields; Offering information to patients
Meetings/Conferences:
- American Academy of Neurology 2015 67th Annual Meeting, April, 2015, Walter E. Washington Convention Center, Washington, DC
Scope: International
Attendance: 12,000+
Description: Education, science, & practice programs & exhibits
Contact Information: Member Services, E-mail: memberservices@aan.com

Foreign Associations

Publications:
• AANnews [a publication of the American Academy of Neurology]
Type: Newsletter; *Frequency:* Monthly; *Price:* Free with American Academy of Neurology membership
Profile: American Academy of Neurology & practice information
• American Academy of Neurology Patient Education Series
Type: Books
Profile: Information & treatment options for patients & caregivers
• Continuum: Lifelong Learning in Neurology
Frequency: Bimonthly; *Editor:* Aaron E. Miller, MD
Profile: A self-study continuing medical education publication
• Neurology
Type: Journal; *Editor:* Robert A. Gross, MD, PhD, FAAN
Profile: The official scientific journal of the American Academy of Neurology, directed to physicians concerned with diseases & conditions of the nervous system
• Neurology Now
Type: Magazine; *Frequency:* Bimonthly
Profile: Updated & important information for neurology patients, families, & caregivers
• Neurology Today
Type: Newspaper; *Frequency:* Biweekly
Profile: Clinical, policy, research, & practice news, for neurologists

American Academy of Religion (AAR)

#300, 825 Houston Mill Rd., Atlanta GA 30329-4205 USA
Tel: 404-727-3049; *Fax:* 404-727-7959
info@aarweb.org
www.aarweb.org
www.facebook.com/256288333448
twitter.com/AARWeb
Overview: A medium-sized national charitable organization founded in 1909
Mission: To promote research, teaching & scholarship in the field of religion; to be dedicated to furthering knowledge of religion & religious institutions in all their forms & manifestations
Member of: American Council of Learned Societies
Chief Officer(s):
John R. Fitzmier, Executive Director & Treasurer
jfitzmier@aarweb.org
Otto A. Maduro, President
Warren G. Frisina, Secretary
Staff Member(s): 16
Membership: 10,000+; *Fees:* Schedule available; *Member Profile:* Teachers; Research scholars; *Committees:* Academic Relations; Executive; Finance; Graduate Student; International Connections; Nominations; Program; Publications; Public Understanding of Religion; Regions; Status of Racial & Ethnic Minorities in the Profession; Status of Women in the Profession; Teaching & Learning; Theological Education Steering Committee
Activities: Sustainability Task Force; Status of Lesbian, Gay, Bisexual, & Transgendered Persons in the Profession; Awards for Excellence in the Study of Religion Book Award Juries; History of Religions Jury; Research Grants Jury; *Speaker Service:* Yes
Awards:
• Book Awards (Award)
For scholarly publications that contribute to the study of religion
• Journalism Awards (Award)
For best in-depth reporting on topics related to religion
• Ray L. Hart Service Award (Award)
• Martin E. Marty Public Understanding of Religion Award (Award)
• AAR Award for Excellence in Teaching (Award)
• Religion and the Arts Award (Award)
• Annual Meeting Travel Grants (Grant)
• Wabash Center For Teaching & Learning In Theology & Religion (Grant)
• Regional Development Grants (Award)
Meetings/Conferences:
• Annual Meeting
Description: Meeting bringing together thousands of professors & students, authors & publishers, religious leaders & interested laypersons for academic sessions, meetings & workshops in the fields of religious studies & theology
Publications:
• In the Field
Type: Newsletter
Profile: Calls for papers, grant news, conference announcements, & other opportunities for scholars of religion
• Journal of the American Academy of Religion
Type: Journal; *Frequency:* Quarterly
Profile: Scholarly articles of world religious traditions & methodologies
• Openings: Employment Opportunities for Scholars of Religion
Accepts Advertising

American Anthropological Association (AAA)

Stn. 600, 2300 Clarendon Blvd., Arlington VA 22201 USA
Tel: 703-528-1902; *Fax:* 703-528-3546
www.aaanet.org
Group-AmericanAnthropologicalAssociation
www.facebook.com/AmericanAnthropologicalAssociation
twitter.com/AmericanAnthro
blog.aaanet.org
Overview: A medium-sized international organization founded in 1902
Member of: American Council of Learned Societies; International Union of Anthropological & Ethnological Sciences
Affliation(s): World Council of Anthropological Associations
Chief Officer(s):
Ed Liebow, Executive Director
eliebow@aaanet.org
Elaine Lynch, Deputy Executive Director/CFO
elynch@aaanet.org
Finances: *Annual Operating Budget:* $3 Million-$5 Million
Staff Member(s): 21
Membership: 11,000; *Fees:* Schedule available; *Member Profile:* Persons with a professional or scholarly interest; *Committees:* Nominations; Finance; Annual Meeting Program; Awards; Association Operations; Scientific Communications; Public Policy; Ethics; Human Rights; Minority Issues in Anthropology; Status of Women in Anthropology
Activities: Publisher of American Anthropologist and Anthropology News, of 20+ Specialized Journals; host of Anthrosource, Digital Archive of the Discipline; organizer; *Internships:* Yes *Library* Open to public by appointment
Awards:
• Franz Boas Award (Award)
• AIME Award (Award)
• McGraw Hill Award (Award)
• Textor Award (Award)
Meetings/Conferences:
• American Anthropological Association 2015 Annual Meeting, November, 2015, Colorado Convention Center, Denver, CO
Scope: International
Contact Information: Director, American Anthropological Association & Section Meetings: Jason G. Watkins, E-mail: jwatkins@aaanet.org; Meeting Planner: Carla Fernandez, E-mail: cfernandez@aaanet.org
• American Anthropological Association 2016 Annual Meeting, November, 2016, Minneapolis Convention Center, Minneapolis, MN
Scope: International
Contact Information: Director, American Anthropological Association & Section Meetings: Jason G. Watkins, E-mail: jwatkins@aaanet.org; Meeting Planner: Carla Fernandez, E-mail: cfernandez@aaanet.org
• American Anthropological Association 2017 Annual Meeting, November, 2017, Marriott Wardman Park Hotel & Omni Shoreham Hotel, Washington, DC
Scope: International
Contact Information: Director, American Anthropological Association & Section Meetings: Jason G. Watkins, E-mail: jwatkins@aaanet.org; Meeting Planner: Carla Fernandez, E-mail: cfernandez@aaanet.org

American Antiquarian Society (AAS)

185 Salisbury St., Worcester MA 01609-1634 USA
Tel: 508-755-5221; *Fax:* 508-753-3311
library@mwa.org
www.americanantiquarian.org
Overview: A small national organization founded in 1812
Mission: To maintain a research library of American history & culture in order to collect, preserve & make available for study the printed record of the United States; specializes in the American period to 1877
Member of: American Council of Learned Societies
Chief Officer(s):
Sidney Lapidus, Chair
Ellen S. Dunlap, President
Finances: *Annual Operating Budget:* Greater than $5 Million
Staff Member(s): 60; 5 volunteer(s)
Membership: 1,021; *Member Profile:* Contributions to advancement of historical scholarship in America
Activities: Public lectures & seminars on the history of the book & the copies related to the collections; grants & fellowships; research; public programs; *Library*

American Association for Justice (AAJ)

#200, 777 - 6th St., NW, Washington DC 20001 USA
Tel: 202-965-3500
Toll-Free: 800-424-2725
Other Communication: media.replies@justice.org
membership@justice.org
www.justice.org
Previous Name: Association of Trial Lawyers of America (ATLA); National Association of Claimants' Compensation Attorneys (NACCA)
Overview: A large international organization
Mission: To promote a fair & effective justice system; To support the work of attorneys
Chief Officer(s):
Gary M. Paul, President
Lipsen Linda, Chief Executive Officer, 202-965-3500 Ext. 8305
linda.lipsen@justice.org
Membership: *Fees:* From $15 to $525, see website
Awards:
• AAJ Paralegal of the Year Award (Award)
• Steven J. Sharp Public Service Award (Award)
• Community Champion Award (Award)
• Soaring Eagles Award (Award)
• Marie Lambert Award (Award)
• F. Scott Baldwin Award (Award)
• Joe Tonahill Award (Award)
• Wiedemann & Wysocki Award (Award)
• Alia Herrera Memorial Scholarship (Scholarship)
• The Richard D. Hailey Law Student Scholarship (Scholarship)
• Trial Advocacy Scholarship (Scholarship)
• Leesfield Scholarship (Scholarship)
• Mike Eidson Scholarship (Scholarship)
Meetings/Conferences:
• American Association for Justice 2015 Annual Convention, July, 2015, Montréal Convention Center, Montréal, QC
Scope: International
• American Association for Justice 2016 Winter Convention, February, 2016, Boca Raton Beach Club, Boca Raton, FL
Scope: International
Publications:
• American Association for Justice Member Directory
Type: Directory
Profile: Directory listings of AAJ membership for public & AAJ members
• Law Reporters
Accepts Advertising; *Editor:* Christine Mollenauer
Profile: Products Liability Law Reporter; Professional Negligence Law Reporter; Class Action Law Reporter; Motor Vehicle Law Reporter
• Trial
Type: Magazine; *Frequency:* Monthly; *Accepts Advertising*; *Editor:* Julie Gannon Shoop; *Price:* Free with AAJ membership
Profile: Trial focuses on a specific theme each month, such as employment law, products liability, & medical negligence

American Association for the Advancement of Science (AAAS)

1200 New York Ave. NW, Washington DC 20005 USA
Tel: 202-326-6440
Other Communication: media@aaas.org;
development@aaas.org
membership@aaas.org
www.aaas.org
Overview: A large national organization founded in 1848
Mission: To advance science, engineering, & innovation around the world to benefit all people; To provide a voice for science on societal issues
Affliation(s): 262 affiliated societies & academies of science
Chief Officer(s):
Nina V. Fedoroff, Chair
Phillip A. Sharp, President
Alan I. Leshner, Chief Executive Officer
David E. Shaw, Treasurer
Staff Member(s): 300
Membership: *Member Profile:* Open to all
Activities: Offering international programs; Providing science education; Publishing books & reports; Promoting the integrity of science & its responsible use in public policy; Facilitating communication among scientists, engineers, & the public; Raising public engagement with science & technology
Awards:
• AAAS Philip Hauge Abelson Prize
• AAAS Award for International Scientific Cooperation
• AAAS Award for Public Understanding of Science and Technology

- AAAS Mentor Award
- AAAS Scientific Freedom and Responsibility Award
- AAAS Science Journalism Award

Meetings/Conferences:
• American Association for the Advancement of Science 2015 Annual Meeting, February, 2015, San Jose, CA
Scope: International
Description: Information for scientists, engineers, educators, & policy-makers
Contact Information: Phone: 202-326-6450; Fax: 202-289-4021; E-mail: meetings@aaas.org; Director, Meetings & Public Engagement: Tiffany Lohwater, E-mail: tlohwate@aaas.org
• American Association for the Advancement of Science 2016 Annual Meeting, February, 2016, Washington, DC
Scope: International
Description: Information for scientists, engineers, educators, & policy-makers
Contact Information: Phone: 202-326-6450; Fax: 202-289-4021; E-mail: meetings@aaas.org; Director, Meetings & Public Engagement: Tiffany Lohwater, E-mail: tlohwate@aaas.org
• American Association for the Advancement of Science 2017 Annual Meeting, February, 2017, Boston, MA
Scope: International
Description: Information for scientists, engineers, educators, & policy-makers
Contact Information: Phone: 202-326-6450; Fax: 202-289-4021; E-mail: meetings@aaas.org; Director, Meetings & Public Engagement: Tiffany Lohwater, E-mail: tlohwate@aaas.org
• American Association for the Advancement of Science 2018 Annual Meeting, February, 2018, Austin, TX
Scope: International
Description: Information for scientists, engineers, educators, & policy-makers
Contact Information: Phone: 202-326-6450; Fax: 202-289-4021; E-mail: meetings@aaas.org; Director, Meetings & Public Engagement: Tiffany Lohwater, E-mail: tlohwate@aaas.org

Publications:
• AAAS [American Association for the Advancement of Science] Annual Report
Type: Yearbook; *Frequency:* Annually
• AAAS [American Association for the Advancement of Science] Advances
Type: Newsletter
Profile: A members only newsletter with updates on American Association for the Advancement of Science research
• AAAS [American Association for the Advancement of Science] Policy Alert
Type: Newsletter; *Frequency:* Weekly
Profile: News about science policy
• Science [a publication of the American Association for the Advancement of Science]
Type: Journal; *Frequency:* Weekly; *Editor:* Bruce Alberts
Profile: Original scientific research & global news
• Science Books & Films [a publication of the American Association for the Advancement of Science]
Type: Journal
Profile: A critical review journal of educational materials for science teachers
• Science Roundup [a publication of the American Association for the Advancement of Science]
Type: Newsletter
Profile: A members only newsletter with updates on American Association for the Advancement of Science research & programs
• Science Signaling [a publication of the American Association for the Advancement of Science]
Type: Journal; *Frequency:* Weekly; *Editor:* Michael B. Yaffe, M.D., Ph.D *ISSN:* 1937-9145
Profile: Information for experts & novices in cell signaling
• Science Translational Medicine [a publication of the American Association for the Advancement of Science]
Type: Journal; *Editor:* Katrina L. Kelner, Ph.D.
Profile: Information for basic translational, & clinical research practitioners & trainees

American Association for the Advancement of Slavic Studies (ASEEES)

University of Pittsburgh, #203C Bellefield Hall, Pittsburgh PA 15260-6424 USA
Tel: 412-648-9911; *Fax:* 412-648-9815
aseees@pitt.edu
aseees.org
Previous Name: American Association for the Advancement of Slavic Studies (AAASS)
Overview: A medium-sized national organization founded in 1948 overseen by American Council of Learned Societies
Mission: To advance knowledge about Russia, Central Eurasia & Eastern/Central Europe
Affliation(s): Central Slavic Conference; Mid-Atlantic Conference; Midwest Slavic Conference; New England Slavic Association; Rocky Mountain Western Slavic Studies Association; Southern Conference on Slavic Studies; Southwest Slavic Association; Western Slavic Association
Chief Officer(s):
Lynda Park, Executive Director
lypark@pitt.edu
Judith Deutsch Kornblatt, President
jkornbla@wisc.edu
Membership: 3,500 individual & 40 institutions; *Fees:* Schedule available
Awards:
• AAASS Distinguished Contributions Award (Award)

American Association for the Advancement of Slavic Studies (AAASS) *See* American Association for the Advancement of Slavic Studies

American Association for Thoracic Surgery (AATS)

#221U, 900 Cummings Center, Beverly MA USA
Tel: 978-927-8330; *Fax:* 978-524-8890
www.aats.org
Overview: A medium-sized international organization founded in 1917
Mission: To promote scholarship & scientific research in thoracic & cardiovascular surgery
Chief Officer(s):
Alec Patterson, President
Membership: 1,200+; *Member Profile:* Cardiothoracic surgeons from 37 countries
Activities: Offering continuing medical education
Meetings/Conferences:
• American Association for Thoracic Surgery 95th Annual Meeting, April, 2015, Washington State Convention & Trade Ctr., Seattle, WA
Scope: International
Attendance: 4,000
Description: Education in the field of thoracic & cardiovascular surgery, for cardiothoracic surgeons, physicians in related specialties, allied health professionals, fellows & residents in cardiothoracic & general surgical training programs, as well as medical students with an interest in cardiothoracic surgery
• American Association for Thoracic Surgery 96th Annual Meeting, May, 2016, Baltimore Convention Center, Baltimore, MD
Scope: International
Attendance: 4,000
Description: Education in the field of thoracic & cardiovascular surgery, for cardiothoracic surgeons, physicians in related specialties, allied health professionals, fellows & residents in cardiothoracic & general surgical training programs, as well as medical students with an interest in cardiothoracic surgery
• American Association for Thoracic Surgery 97th Annual Meeting, April, 2017, Boston Hynes Convention Centere, Boston, MA
Scope: International
Description: Education in the field of thoracic & cardiovascular surgery, for cardiothoracic surgeons, physicians in related specialties, allied health professionals, fellows & residents in cardiothoracic & general surgical training programs, as well as medical students with an interest in cardiothoracic surgery
Publications:
• Journal of Thoracic & Cardiovascular Surgery
Type: Journal; *Editor:* Lawrence H. Cohn, MD
Profile: Original articles about the chest, heart, lungs, & great vessels where surgical intervention is indicated
• Operative Techniques in Thoracic & Cardiovascular Surgery: A Comparative Atlas
Editor: Fred A. Crawford, MD
Profile: Technique-based articles in cardiovascular & thoracic surgery by renowned surgeons in the field
• Pediatric Cardiac Surgery Annual
Type: Journal; *Frequency:* Annually; *Editor:* Thomas L. Spray, MD
Profile: Developments in pediatric cardiac surgery
• Seminars in Thoracic & Cardiovascular Surgery
Type: Journal; *Editor:* David H. Adams; Michael A. Maddaus
Profile: Topics & issues faced by practising surgeons in clinical practice
• Thoracic Surgery News
Type: Newspaper; *Frequency:* 10 pa; *Editor:* Yolonda L. Colson, MD
Profile: News of general thoracic surgery, adult cardiac surgery, transplantation, & congenital heart disease

American Association of Bovine Practitioners (AABP)

PO Box 3610, #802, 3320 Skyway Dr., Auburn AL 36831-3610 USA
Tel: 334-821-0442; *Fax:* 334-821-9532
aabphq@aabp.org
www.aabp.org
Overview: A medium-sized international organization
Mission: To enhance the professional lives of international veterinarians; To improve the well-being of cattle; To help the economic success of cattle owners
Chief Officer(s):
Roger Saltman, President
M. Gatz Riddell, Executive Vice-President
mgriddell@aabp.org
Membership: *Member Profile:* International veterinarians engaged in the general field of bovine medicine or those who are interested in bovine medicine; Honorary members are persons who have made outstanding contributions to bovine practice; Veterinary students; *Committees:* Amstutz Scholarship; Animal Welfare; Beef Production Management; Biological Risk Management & Preparedness; Bovine Respiratory Disease; Food Quality, Safety, & Security; Distance Education; Information Management; Lameness; Milk Quality & Udder Health; Membership; Nutrition; Pharmaceutical & Biological Issues; Reproduction
Activities: Offering continuing education programs; Providing networking opportunities with fellow veterinarians; Improving career opportunities in bovine medicine; Increasing awareness of issues in the cattle industry; Promoting leadership on critical issues in the cattle business
Meetings/Conferences:
• The American Association of Bovine Practitioners 2015 Annual Conference, September, 2015, New Orleans, LA
Scope: International
• The American Association of Bovine Practitioners 2016 Annual Conference, September, 2016, Charlotte, NC
Scope: International
• The American Association of Bovine Practitioners 2017 Annual Conference, September, 2017, Omaha, NE
Scope: International
• The American Association of Bovine Practitioners 2018 Annual Conference, September, 2018, Phoenix, AZ
Scope: International
Publications:
• American Association of Bovine Practitioners Newsletter
Type: Newsletter; *Frequency:* Monthly; *Price:* Free with American Association of Bovine Practitioners membership
Profile: Updates from the association
• American Association of Bovine Practitioners Annual Membership Directory
Type: Directory; *Frequency:* Annually; *Price:* Free with American Association of Bovine Practitioners membership
• The Bovine Practitioner
Type: Journal; *Frequency:* Semiannually; *Accepts Advertising*; *Price:* Free with American Association of Bovine Practitioners membership
• Proceedings of the American Association of Bovine Practitioners Annual Conference
Type: Yearbook; *Frequency:* Annually; *Price:* Free with American Association of Bovine Practitioners membership

American Association of Naturopathic Physicians (AANP)

#250, 818 - 18th St., NW, Washington DC 20006 USA
Tel: 202-237-8150; *Fax:* 202-237-8152
Toll-Free: 866-538-2267
member.services@naturopathic.org
www.naturopathic.org
www.facebook.com/theAANP
twitter.com/AANP
Overview: A small international organization
Mission: Represents licensed or licensable naturopathic physicians who are graduates of four-year, residential graduates programs
Affliation(s): Canadian Association of Naturopathic Doctors; College of Naturopathic Doctors of Alberta; British Columbia Naturopathic Association; Manitoba Naturopathic Association; New Brunswick Association of Naturopathic Doctors; Newfoundland and Labrador Association of Naturopathic Doctors; Nova Scotia Association of Naturopathic Doctors; Ontario Association of Naturopathic Doctors; Prince Edward

Foreign Associations

Island Association of Naturopathic Doctors; Quebec Association of Naturopathic Medicine; Saskatchewan Association of Naturopathic Practitioners; Yukon Naturopathic Association
Chief Officer(s):
Kasra Pournadeali, President
Membership: 2000 (students & physicians)
Awards:
• Physician of the Year
• Corporation of the Year
• President's Award
• Vis Award
Meetings/Conferences:
• American Association of Naturopathic Physicians 2015 Annual Conference, August, 2015, Oakland Marriott, Oakland, CA
Scope: International

American Association of Neuromuscular & Electrodiagnostic Medicine (AANEM)

2621 Superior Dr. NW, Rochester MN 55901 USA
Tel: 507-288-0100; *Fax:* 507-288-1225
aanem@aanem.org
www.aanem.org
Overview: A medium-sized international organization founded in 1953
Mission: To advance neuromuscular, musculoskeletal, & electrodiagnostic medicine; To increase members' knowledge of neurophysiology, pathophysiology, instrumentation, & electrodiagnostic medicine; To improve the quality of patient care
Chief Officer(s):
Shirlyn A. Adkins, Executive Director
sadkins@aanem.org
Megan Fogelson, Director, Health Policy & Advocacy
mfogelson@aanem.org
Brenda L. Riggott, Director, Marketing & Communications
briggott@aanem.org
Darren Burchill, Manager, Professional Standards & Membership
dburchill@aanem.org
Membership: 5,187; *Member Profile:* Physicians who diagnose & treat patients with disorders of the muscless & nerves
Activities: Liaising with other organizations; Providing educational programs; Encouraging research
Meetings/Conferences:
• American Association of Neuromuscular & Electrodiagnostic Medicine 2015 62nd Annual Meeting, October, 2015, Hawaii Convention Center & Hilton Hawaiian Village, Honolulu, HI
Scope: International
Contact Information: Director, Meetings: Denae Brennan, E-mail: dbrennan@aanem.org
• American Association of Neuromuscular & Electrodiagnostic Medicine 2016 63rd Annual Meeting, September, 2016, Hilton New Orleans, New Orleans, LA
Scope: International
Contact Information: Director, Meetings: Denae Brennan, E-mail: dbrennan@aanem.org
• American Association of Neuromuscular & Electrodiagnostic Medicine 2017 64th Annual Meeting, September, 2017, JW Marriott Desert Ridge, Phoenix, AZ
Scope: International
Contact Information: Director, Meetings: Denae Brennan, E-mail: dbrennan@aanem.org
Publications:
• AANEM [American Association of Neuromuscular & Electrodiagnostic Medicine] News
Type: Newsletter; *Frequency:* Quarterly
Profile: Association activities, science in brief, legislative issues, & information about coding
• Muscle & Nerve
Type: Journal; *Accepts Advertising ISSN:* 0148-639X
Profile: Readership includes neurologists, physiatrists, & physical & rehabilitative medical specialists

American Association of Opticians *See* American Optometric Association

The American Association of Petroleum Geologists (AAPG)

PO Box 979, 1444 South Boulder, Tulsa OK 74101-0979 USA
Tel: 918-584-2555; *Fax:* 918-560-2665
Toll-Free: 800-364-2274
postmaster@aapg.org
www.aapg.org
linkd.in/AAPG_Group
www.facebook.com/AAPGeologists
twitter.com/AAPG
www.youtube.com/AAPGweb
Overview: A small national organization
Affliation(s): Canadian Society of Petroleum Geologists
Chief Officer(s):
Richard (Rick) D. Fritz, Executive Director
Scott W. Tinker, President
Activities: *Library:* AAPG Library; Open to public
Awards:
• Grants-in-Aid (Scholarship)
Postgraduate research projects leading to the M.S. degree in geology, geophysics, engineering, environmental studies, earth sciences, chemistry, mineralogy or science for Canadian, landed immigrant or visa students *Amount:* $2,000 maximum

American Association on Intellectual & Developmental Disabilities (AAIDD)

#200, 501 - 3rd St. NW, Washington DC 20001 USA
Tel: 202-387-1968; *Fax:* 202-387-2193
aaidd.org
www.linkedin.com/groups/American-Association-on-Intellectual-Developme
www.facebook.com/350322627779
twitter.com/_aaidd
www.youtube.com/user/aaiddvideos
Previous Name: American Association on Mental Retardation
Overview: A large international organization founded in 1876
Mission: To provide leadership in the field of intellectual & developmental disabilities throughout the world.
Chief Officer(s):
James R. Thompson, PhD, President
Margaret A. Nygren, EdD, Executive Director & CEO
mnygren@aaidd.org
Paul D. Aitken, CPA, Director
pdaitken@aaidd.org
Finances: *Funding Sources:* Membership fees; donations
Membership: 5,000 in the USA; present in 55 countries worldwide; *Fees:* $50 international electronic; $75 basic; $125 classic
Activities: Publications; annual conference; webinars; e-learning & continuing professional education; Supports Intensity Scale
Meetings/Conferences:
• 139th American Association on Intellectual & Developmental Disabilities Annual Meeting, June, 2015, Galt House of Louisville, Louisville, KY
Scope: International
Publications:
• American Journal on Intellectual & Developmental Disabilities
Type: Journal; *Frequency:* Bimonthly *ISSN:* 1944-7558
Profile: Scientific, scholarly & archival journal for original contributions of knowledge of intellectual disability, including its causes, treatment &prevention.
• Inclusion
Type: Journal; *Frequency:* Bimonthly *ISSN:* 2326-6988
Profile: Peer-reviewed journal that discusses strategies that promote the inclusion of people with intellectual & developmental disabilities in society.
• Intellectual & Developmental Disabilities
Type: Journal; *Frequency:* Bimonthly *ISSN:* 1934-9556
Profile: Peer-reviewed journal of policy, practices & perspectives.

American Association on Mental Retardation *See* American Association on Intellectual & Developmental Disabilities

The American Astronautical Society (AAS)

#102, 6352 Rolling Mill Pl., Springfield VA 22152-2370 USA
Tel: 703-865-0020; *Fax:* 703-866-3526
aas@astronautical.org
www.astronautical.org
www.facebook.com/AmericanAstronauticalSociety
twitter.com/astrosociety
www.youtube.com/user/astrosociety
Overview: A medium-sized international organization founded in 1954
Mission: To promote professional support & interaction in astronautical sciences (rocketry, spaceflight, space medicine, international cooperation)
Member of: International Astronautical Federation; American Association for the Advancement of Science
Chief Officer(s):
James Kirkpatrick, Executive Director, 703-866-0020
jkirkpatrick@astronautical.org
Lyn D. Wigbels, President
Finances: *Annual Operating Budget:* $500,000-$1.5 Million
Staff Member(s): 2; 40 volunteer(s)
Membership: 1,500; *Fees:* $100 USD individual, affiliate; $50 USD retired, teacher, student;S$115 USD senior member; schedule corporate; *Member Profile:* Space professionals & enthusiasts; *Committees:* Space Flight Mechanics; Guidance & Control; International Program; History
Activities: National Conference; Goddard Symposium; Van Braun Symposium; technical meetings; ISS Conference
Awards:
• Industrial Leadership Award (Award)
• Space Flight Award (Award)
• Flight Achievement Award (Award)
• Carl Sagan Memorial Award (Award)
• Victor A. Prather Award (Award)
• Lloyd V. Berkner Award (Award)
• Randolph Lovelace II Award (Award)
• Melbourne W. Boynton Award (Award)
• Dirk Brouwer Award (Award)
• John F. Kennedy Astronautics Award (Award)
• Eugene M. Emme Astronautical Literature Award (Award)
• Military Astronautics Award (Award)

American Bankers Association (ABA)

1120 Connecticut Ave. NW, Washington DC 20036 USA
Toll-Free: 800-226-5377
custserv@aba.com
www.aba.com
www.linkedin.com/company/american-bankers-association
www.facebook.com/AmericanBankersAssociation
twitter.com/ABABankingNews
www.youtube.com/user/AmericanBankersAssn
Overview: A medium-sized national organization
Mission: To represent banks of all sizes on issues of national importance for financial institutions & their customers
Chief Officer(s):
Jeff L. Plagge, Chair
Frank Keating, President & CEO

American Birding Association, Inc. (ABA)

1618 West Colorado Ave., Colorado Springs CO 80904 USA
Tel: 719-578-9703; *Fax:* 719-578-1480
Toll-Free: 800-850-2473
member@aba.org
www.americanbirding.org
www.facebook.com/birders
twitter.com/aba
www.youtube.com/user/AmericanBirding
Overview: A large national organization founded in 1969
Mission: To provide leadership to field birders by increasing their knowledge, skills & enjoyment of birding & by contributing to bird conservation
Member of: Partners in Flight; American Bird Conservancy; Bird Conservation Alliance
Chief Officer(s):
Louis M. Morrell, Chair
Jeffrey A. Gordon, President
jgordon@aba.org
Finances: *Annual Operating Budget:* $500,000-$1.5 Million
Staff Member(s): 18
Membership: 22,000; *Fees:* US$55 individual; US$63 family
Activities: Youth Education; Conservation Programs; *Rents Mailing List:* Yes *Library* Open to public
Awards:
• ABA Roger Tory Peterson Award Promoting the Cause of Birding (Award)
• ABA Chandler Robbins Award Education/Conservation (Award)
• ABA Claudia Wilds Award Distinguished Service (Award)
• ABA Robert Ridgway Award Publications in Field Ornithology (Award)
• ABA Ludlow Griscom Award Outstanding Contributions in Regional Ornithology (Award)
Publications:
• Big Day Report & List Report [a publication of American Birding Association, Inc.]
Frequency: Annual
Profile: Formerly in print, now the Report is online
• Birding [a publication of American Birding Association, Inc.]
Type: Magazine; *Frequency:* s-m.; *Editor:* Ted Floyd
• Gear Guide [a publication of American Birding Association, Inc.]
Frequency: Annual
• North American Birds [a publication of American Birding Association, Inc.]
Type: Journal; *Frequency:* q.; *Editor:* Ned Brinkley
• Winging It [a publication of American Birding Association, Inc.]
Type: Newsletter; *Editor:* Michael Retter

American Cave Conservation Association (ACCA)

PO Box 409, 119 East Main St., Horse Cave KY 42749 USA
Tel: 270-786-1466; *Fax:* 270-786-1467
acca@cavern.org
caveconservation.com
Also Known As: American Cave & Karst Center
Overview: A small international organization founded in 1977
Mission: To protect & preserve caves, karstlands & groundwater; to bring together information about cave & karst resources from across the nation & make it available to those who are working to protect these resources
Chief Officer(s):
David G. Foster, Executive Director
acca@cavern.org
Staff Member(s): 4
Membership: *Fees:* Regular: $25; Internation: $30; Student: $15; Family: $35, Supporter: $50; Sustainer: $100; Guarantor: $200; Benefactor: $500; Patron: $1000
Activities: Operates National Cave Management Training program & The American Cave Museum; provides outreach educational programs; constructs cave gates; *Library* by appointment
Publications:
• American Caves

American Chemistry Council (ACC)

700 Second St. NE, Washington DC 20002 USA
Tel: 202-249-7000; *Fax:* 202-249-6100
www.americanchemistry.com
Overview: A medium-sized national organization
Chief Officer(s):
Calvin M. Dooley, President & Chief Executive Officer
Raymond J. O'Bryan, Chief Financial Officer & CAO
Dell Perelman, Chief of Staff & General Counsel
Roger D. Bernstein, Vice-President, State Affairs & Grassroots
Walter Moore, Vice-President, Federal Affairs
Steve Russell, Vice-President, Plastics
Robert J. Simon, Vice-President, Chemical Products & Technology & Chlorine Chemistry
Michael P. Walls, Vice-President, Regulatory & Technical Affairs
Anne Womack Kolton, Vice-President, Communications
Activities: Conducting research & development activities

American College of Chest Physicians (ACCP)

3300 Dundee Rd., Northbrook IL 60062-2348 USA
Tel: 847-498-1400; *Fax:* 847-498-5460
Toll-Free: 800-343-2227
www.chestnet.org
Overview: A medium-sized international organization founded in 1935
Mission: To improve cardiopulmonary health & critical care worldwide; To promote the prevention & treatment of diseases of the chest
Chief Officer(s):
Paul A. Markowski, CEO & Executive Vice-President
P. Stratton Davies, Chief Financial Officer & Sr. Vice-President, Finance
Darlene Buczak, Senior Vice-President, Organizational Affairs
Ed Dellert, Senior Vice-President, Clinical Education, Informatics, & Research
David H. Eubanks, Senior Vice-President, Business & Development
Stephen Welch, Senior Vice-President, Communications
Membership: *Member Profile:* USA & Canadian physicians, who are board-certified specialists in chest medicine, surgery, or critical care medicine, & who devote a major portion of their practice to diseases of the chest; International physicians, recognized in their community in disciplines related to chest medicine, surgery, or critical care medicine; Physicians who are interested in cardiopulmonary medicine or surgery, critical care, or related disciplines; Physicians-in-Training; Allied health members, such as nonphysician health professionals or administrators; *Committees:* International Education; Council of Committees; Bylaws; CHEST Scientific Program; Education; Ethics; Finance; Government Relations; Health and Science Policy; International Nominations; Marketing; Membership; Nominating; Practice Management; Scientific Presentations & Awards; Quality Improvement
Activities: Providing educational opportunities; Encouraging research; Liaising with government agencies
Meetings/Conferences:
• American College of Chest Physicians Conference: CHEST 2015, October, 2015, Palais des congrès (Convention Centre), Montréal, QC
Scope: International
Description: A chest medicine conference for health professionals such as cardiologists, critical care physicinas, general medicine physicians, ICU medical directors, pulmonologists, pediatric pulmonologists, sleep medicine physicians, anesthesiologists, practice administrators, respiratory therapists, advanced practice nurses, & registered nurses
• American College of Chest Physicians Conference: CHEST 2016, 2016
Scope: International
Description: Educational sessions, CME credits, clinical instruction, & networking opportunities for health professionals
Publications:
• ACCP [American College of Chest Physicians] Critical Care Medicine Board Review
ISBN: 978-0-916609-76-4
Profile: Review chapters developed to complement the American College of Chest Physicians Critical Care Medicine Board Review course,directed toward an audience of physicians in critical care & pulmonary medicine, emergency departments, anesthesiology, & surgery, as well as nurses & respiratory therapists
• ACCP [American College of Chest Physicians] Pulmonary Medicine Board Review
ISBN: 978-0-916609-77-1
Profile: A text covering current pulmonary literature & management strategies for critically ill patients, written for physicians & fellows incritical care pulmonary medicine, as well as advanced critical care nurse practitioners & respiratory therapy practitioners
• ACCP [American College of Chest Physicians] Sleep Medicine Board Review
ISBN: 978-0-916609-75-7
Profile: Review chapters of major topics from the American College of Chest Physicians Sleep Medicine Board Review course, intended for physiciansin sleep medicine, physicians in pulmonary medicine, neurologists, respiratory therapists, & nurses
• ACCP [American College of Chest Physicians] / AAP Pediatric Pulmonary Board Review
ISBN: 978-0-916609-85-6
Profile: Review chapters of major topics from the American College of Chest Physicians / American Academy of Pediatrics PediatricPulmonary Medicine Board Review course, of interest to pediatric pulmonologists, family physicians, pediatric intensivists, allergists, & general pediatricians
• CHEST [a publication of the American College of Chest Physicians]
Type: Journal; *Frequency:* Monthly; *Accepts Advertising*; *Editor:* Richard S. Irwin, MD, FCCP *ISSN:* 0012-3692
Profile: Original research in the multidisciplinary specialties of chest medicine, of interest to specialists in pulmonology,critical care medicine, sleep medicine, thoracic surgery, cardiorespiratory interactions, & related specialists
• Chest Physician
Type: Newspaper; *Frequency:* Monthly; *Accepts Advertising*; *Editor:* Paul A. Selecky, MD, FCCP
Profile: News from chest medicine specialties, clinical information, American College of Chest Physicians activities, & updoming events

American Concrete Institute (ACI)

PO Box 9094, 38800 Country Club Dr., Farmington MI 48333-9094 USA
Tel: 248-848-3700; *Fax:* 248-848-3701
www.concrete.org
www.facebook.com/AmericanConcreteInstitute
twitter.com/concreteaci
Overview: A large international licensing organization founded in 1905
Mission: To gather & disseminate technical information relating to the design & construction of concrete & its properties
Chief Officer(s):
James K. Wight, President
Ronald G. Burg, Executive Vice-President
ron.burg@concrete.org
Finances: *Annual Operating Budget:* Greater than $5 Million
Staff Member(s): 96
Membership: 20,000 individuals in 120 countries; *Committees:* Many committees grouped into the following categories: Board; Certification; Convention; Education; International; & Technical
Activities: Offering 18 certification programs; many publications relating to the concrete industry
Awards:
• ACI Foundation Awards (Award)
• Paper Awards (Award)
• Personal Awards (Award)
• Chapter Activities Award (Award), Other Awards
• Delmar L. Bloem Distinguished Service Award (Award), Other Awards
• ACI Commemorative Lecture Series (Award), Other Awards
• Young Professional Essay Contest (Award), Other Awards
• Scholarships & Fellowships (Scholarship)
Meetings/Conferences:
• American Concrete Institute Spring 2015 Convention: Concrete Endures, April, 2015, Marriott & Kansas City Convention Center, Kansas City, MO
Scope: International
• American Concrete Institute Fall 2015 Conference: Spanning the Globe, November, 2015, Sheraton, Denver, CO
Scope: International
• American Concrete Institute Spring 2016 Convention: Concrete Endures, April, 2016, Hyatt & Frontier Airlines Center, Milwaukee, WI
Scope: International
• American Concrete Institute Fall 2016 Conference: Spanning the Globe, October, 2016, Marriott Philadelphia, Philadelphia, PA
Scope: International
• American Concrete Institute Spring 2017 Convention, March, 2017, Renaissance Center, Detroit, MI
Scope: International
• American Concrete Institute Fall 2017 Conference, October, 2017, Disneyland Hotel, Anaheim, CA
Scope: International
Publications:
• ACI [American Concrete Institute] Materials Journal
Type: Journal
• ACI [American Concrete Institute] Structural Journal
Type: Journal
• Concrete International [a publication of the American Concrete Institute]
Type: Magazine; *Frequency:* Monthly
• Manual of Concrete Practice [a publication of the American Concrete Institute]
Type: Journal; *Price:* $681.50 non-members; $409 ACI Members
• The Sustainable Concrete Guide - Applications [a publication of the American Concrete Institute]
Type: Guide
• The Sustainable Concrete Guide - Strategies & Examples [a publication of the American Concrete Institute]
Type: Guide

Alberta Chapter
c/o Alison Dowling, Graham Group Ltd, 8404 McIntyre Rd., Edmonton AB T6E 6V3
www.aci-alberta.org
Mission: To gather & disseminate technical information relating to the design & construction of concrete & its properties
Chief Officer(s):
Alison Dowling, President, 780-577-7032, Fax: 780-485-3888
alisond@graham.ca
John McClafferty, Vice-President, 780-917-7241, Fax: 780-917-7086
John.McClafferty@stantec.com
Shaun Radomski, Secretary-Treasurer, 403-387-1744, Fax: 403-569-0737
shaun.radomski@amec.com

Atlantic Chapter
PO Box 20110, RPO King's Pl., Fredericton NB E3B 6Y8
Tel: 709-722-7023; *Fax:* 709-722-7353
michael.lio@lafarge-na.com
www.concrete.org
Chief Officer(s):
Corey Boland, President, 506-458-1444 Ext. 659, Fax: 506-462-7646
Robert Simpson, Secretary, 506-444-5106, Fax: 506-457-6714
Robert.Simpson@gnb.ca
R. Harry Olive, Treasurer, 506-452-7000, Fax: 506-452-0112
harry.olive@stantec.com

British Columbia Chapter
c/o Darlene C. Lane, 6547 Inverness St., Vancouver BC V5X 4G1
Tel: 604-734-0184
Chief Officer(s):
Kyle Gilmour, President, 604-261-2226, Fax: 604-648-9728
kgilmour@lehighcement.com
Emlyn Alexandra L., Vice-President, 604-324-8280, Fax: 604-324-8899
a.emlyn@kryton.com

Darlene C. Lane, Secretary-Treasurer
darclane@telus.net
Eastern Ontario & Quebec Chapter
c/o Pierre-Louis Maillard, #304, 334, rue Notre Dame est, Laval QC H2Y 1C7
Tel: 514-678-8247
aciquebec@hotmail.com
www.aciquebec.com
Chief Officer(s):
Luc Desmeules, President, 418-667-2060 Ext. 140, Fax: 418-667-2068
ldesmeules@cqi.ca
Martin Lemieux, Vice-President, 450-674-4901, Fax: 450-674-3370
lemieux.martin@qualitas.qc.ca
Pierre-Louis Maillard, Executive Manager, 514-678-8247
p.lmaillard@videotron.ca
Manitoba Chapter
c/o Lafarge Canada Inc., 185 Dawson Rd., Winnipeg MB R2J 0S6
Tel: 204-943-7501; *Fax:* 204-943-7507
www.concrete.org/CHAPTERS/chap.asp?cid=c087
Chief Officer(s):
Derek Mizak, President
derek.m@ckpeng.com
Rick Pelletier, Vice-President, 204-233-7135
Ontario
110 Belfield Rd., Toronto ON M9W 1G1
Tel: 416-245-4720; *Fax:* 416-242-2727
www.aciontario.com
Chief Officer(s):
Alain Belanger, Secretary-Treasurer
abelanger@nca.ca

American Council for an Energy-Efficient Economy (ACEEE)

#600, 529 14th St. NW, Washington DC 20045-1000 USA
Tel: 202-507-4000; *Fax:* 202-429-2248
www.aceee.org
www.facebook.com/67449893973
twitter.com/ACEEEdc
Overview: A medium-sized national organization founded in 1980
Mission: To advance energy-conserving technology & policies; to assist utilities & regulators to implement cost-effective conservation programs; to support the adoption of comprehensive new policies for increasing energy efficiency; to show how energy efficiency improvements can protect the environment; to analyse & promote technologies & policies for increasing vehicle fuel efficiency & reducing vehicle use; to help developing & Eastern European countries undertake energy efficiency programs
Chief Officer(s):
Steven Nadel, Executive Director, 202-507-4011
snadel@aceee.org
Activities: *Library*

American Council for Québec Studies (ACQS)

c/o University of Maine, 213 Little Hall, Orono ME 04469 USA
acqs2@maine.edu
www.southalabama.edu/acqs
Previous Name: Northeast Council for Québec Studies
Overview: A small international organization founded in 1981
Mission: The ACQS promotes the study of Québec in the United States through the publication of its Québec Studies journal and the sponsorship of the biennial conference.
Chief Officer(s):
Leslie Choquette, President
lchoquet@assumption.edu
Membership: *Fees:* US$100; *Member Profile:* American scholars & others with teaching, research, &/or business interests in Québec & French Canada, or with an active interest in Québec's history, literature, politics, language and culture.
Activities: biennial conference
Meetings/Conferences:
• American Council for Québec Studies Biennial Conference, November, 2016, Westin Portland Harborview, Portland, ME
Publications:
• Québec Studies
Type: academic journal

American Council of Learned Societies

633 Third Ave., 8th Fl, New York NY 10017-6795 USA
Tel: 212-697-1505; *Fax:* 212-949-8058
www.acls.org
www.facebook.com/acls1919
www.twitter.com/acls1919
www.pinterest.com/acls1919
Overview: A large international organization founded in 1919
Mission: The advancement of humanistic studies in all fields of learning in the humanities & the social sciences & the maintenance & strengthening of relations among the national societies devoted to such studies
Chief Officer(s):
Pauline Yu, President
paulineyu@acls.org
Finances: *Funding Sources:* Private grants, endowment income, annual subscriptions from university and college Associates,government contracts, individual gifts
Membership: *Member Profile:* Restricted to organizations

American Dialect Society (ADS)

Duke University Press, PO Box 90660, Durham NC 27708-0660 USA
Tel: 919-688-5134
Toll-Free: 888-651-0122
administrator@americandialect.org
www.americandialect.org
www.linkedin.com/groups?about=&gid=103237
www.facebook.com/americandialect
twitter.com/americandialect
Overview: A medium-sized national organization founded in 1889
Mission: To study the English language in North America
Member of: American Council of Learned Societies
Chief Officer(s):
Jesse Sheidlower, President
Allan A. Metcalf, Executive Secretary
aallan@aol.com
Finances: *Funding Sources:* Membership dues
Membership: *Fees:* $60 regular; $25 student; *Member Profile:* Interest in the English language in North America & other languages as they interact with it
Activities: Publishes the journal American Speech; Sponsors sessions at the national conventions of the Dictionary Society of North America; Holds an annual meeting at the annual meeting of the Linguistic Society of America; *Rents Mailing List:* Yes
Awards:
• Presidential Honorary Memberships for Outstanding Students (Award)

American Economic Association (AEA)

#305, 2014 Broadway, Nashville TN 37203 USA
Tel: 615-322-2595; *Fax:* 615-343-7590
aeainfo@vanderbilt.edu
www.aeaweb.org
twitter.com/AEAJournals
Overview: A medium-sized national organization founded in 1888
Mission: The encouragement of economic research, especially the historical & statistical study of the actual conditions of industrial life; the issue of publications on economic subjects; the encouragement of perfect freedom of economic discussion
Member of: American Council of Learned Societies
Affiliation(s): International Economic Association
Chief Officer(s):
William D. Nordhaus, President
Peter L. Rousseau, Secretary-Treasurer
Regina H. Montgomery, Administrative Director
Finances: *Annual Operating Budget:* $1.5 Million-$3 Million
Membership: 18,000 individual; *Fees:* Schedule available; *Committees:* Editorial Appointments; Audit; Budget & Finance; Oversight of Operations & Publishing; Economic Education; Economic Statistics; Government Relations; Honors & Awards; Status of Minority Groups in the Economics Profession; Status of Women in the Economics Profession; Nominating; Registry of Random Controlled Trial
Activities: *Rents Mailing List:* Yes
Awards:
• Distinguished Fellows (Award)
• John Bates Clark Medal (Award)
• Francis A. Walker Medal (Award)
Publications:
• AEJ: Applied Economics
Type: Journal
• AEJ: Economic Policy
Type: Journal
• AEJ: Macroeconomics
Type: Journal
• AEJ: Microeconomics
Type: Journal
• The American Economic Review
Type: Journal
• The Journal of Economic Literature
Type: Journal
• The Journal of Economic Perspectives
Type: Journal

American Electroplaters & Surface Finishers Society (AESF) / Association des galvanoplastes d'Amérique

#500, 1155 - 15th St. NW, Washington DC 20005 USA
Tel: 202-457-8404; *Fax:* 202-530-0659
passante@nasf.org
www.nasf.org/
Overview: A medium-sized international organization founded in 1909
Mission: To advance the science of electroplating & surface finishing
Chief Officer(s):
Phil Assante, Member Relations, 703-887-7235
Finances: *Annual Operating Budget:* $500,000-$1.5 Million; *Funding Sources:* Membership dues; publications; education events
Staff Member(s): 6
Membership: 3,500 individual; *Fees:* Individual: $100-125; Student: $62.50; Institutional: $375; Corporate: $375-10,100 (dependent upon business size); *Member Profile:* Technical; professional; doctorate; managers; owners; job shop personnel; *Committees:* Over 25 technical/membership/social
Activities: *Library* Open to public
Publications:
• Plating & Surface Finishing
Type: Magazine; *Frequency:* Monthly; *Editor:* Dr. James Lindsay

American Farmland Trust (AFT)

#800, 1200 - 18th St. NW, Washington DC 20036 USA
Tel: 202-331-7300; *Fax:* 202-659-8339
info@farmland.org
www.farmland.org
www.facebook.com/AmericanFarmland
www.twitter.com/farmland
Overview: A large national charitable organization founded in 1980
Mission: To stop the loss of productive farmland & to promote farming practices that lead to a healthy environment
Chief Officer(s):
Miranda M. Kaiser, Chair
Membership: 20,000; *Fees:* $25
Activities: Public education; technical assistance in policy development; direct farmland protection projects; sustainable agriculture projects
Publications:
• American Farmland
Type: Magazine; *Frequency:* Biannually

American Federation of Labor & Congress of Industrial Organizations (AFL-CIO) (AFL-CIO) / Fédération Américaine du travail et congrès des organisations industrielles (FAT-COI) (FAT-COI)

815 - 16th St. NW, Washington DC 20006 USA
Tel: 202-637-5000; *Fax:* 202-637-5058
www.aflcio.org
www.facebook.com/aflcio
twitter.com/AFLCIO
www.youtube.com/user/AFLCIONow
Overview: A large international organization
Chief Officer(s):
Richard Trumka, President
Elizabeth Shuler, Sec.-Tres.
Arlene Holt Baker, Executive Vice-President
Membership: 13,700,000 + 90 affiliated unions
Activities: Operating as one of the largest labour bodies in the United States;

American Federation of Musicians of the United States & Canada (AFL-CIO/CLC) (AFM) / Fédération des musiciens des États-Unis et du Canada (FAT-COI/CTC)

#600, 1501 Broadway, New York NY 10036 United States
Tel: 212-869-1330; *Fax:* 212-764-6134
www.afm.org
www.facebook.com/afm.org
twitter.com/MusiciansUnion
Overview: A medium-sized international organization founded in 1896

Mission: The largest organization in the world which represens of professional musicians in both Canada and the US. Helps in negotiating fair agreements, protectingownership of recorded music, securing benefits such as health care and pension or lobbying our legislators. AFM is committed to raising industry standards and placing the professional musician in the foreground of the cultural landscape.
Chief Officer(s):
Ray Hair, President
Staff Member(s): 9
Membership: 15,000; *Member Profile:* Professional musicians

Canadian Office
#202, 150 Ferrand Dr., Toronto ON M3C 3E5
Tel: 416-391-5161; *Fax:* 416-391-5165
afmcan@afm.org
www.afm.org
www.facebook.com/afm.org
twitter.com/MusiciansUnion
www.myspace.com/afmorg;
www.youtube.com/user/MusiciansUnion
Chief Officer(s):
Bill Skolnik, Canadian Vice-President
bskolnik@afm.org

American Fisheries Society (AFS)
5410 Grosvenor Lane, Bethesda MD 20814-2199 USA
Tel: 301-897-8616; *Fax:* 301-897-8096
www.fisheries.org
www.facebook.com/group.php?gid=39804224812
twitter.com/AmFisheriesSoc
www.flickr.com/photos/americanfisheriessociety
Overview: A large international organization founded in 1870
Mission: To advance fisheries science & the conservation of renewable aquatic resources; To promote & evaluate the educational, scientific, & technological development & advancement of all branches of fisheries science & practice, including aquatic biology, engineering, economics, fish culture, limnology, oceanography, & technology; To gather & disseminate technical & other information on fish, fishing, fisheries, & all phases of fisheries science & practice; To encourage the teaching of all phases of fisheries science
Chief Officer(s):
Bill Franzin, President
Gus Rassam, Executive Director
Finances: *Annual Operating Budget:* $1.5 Million-$3 Million; *Funding Sources:* Donations; Grants; Membership fees; Publication sales
Staff Member(s): 24
Membership: 8,500+ fisheries & aquatic science professionals & students; *Fees:* $80 North America; $95 outside North America; *Member Profile:* Open to anyone interested in the progress of fisheries science & education & the conservation & management of fisheries resources; *Committees:* Arrangements; Award of Excellence; Board of Appeals; Board of Professional Certification; Budget & Finance; Continuing Education; Mail Ballot Tally; Membership; Membership Concerns; Names of Fishes; Names of Aquatic Invertebrates; Nominating; Program; Publications Overview; Resolutions; Resource Policy; Time & Place
Activities: *Rents Mailing List:* Yes
Awards:
• The Meritorious Service Award (Award)
Given to an individual for loyalty, dedication & meritorious service to the society over a long period of time, & for exceptional commitment to the society's programs, ideals, objectives, & long-term goals
• The Distinguished Service Award (Award)
Given in recognition of outstanding service to the society
• The AFS Award of Excellence (Award)
Given to recognize outstanding scientists in the fields of fisheries & aquatic biology
• The Carl R. Sullivan Fisheries Conservation Award (Award)
Given annually to an individual or organization, professional or non-professional, for outstanding contributions to the conservation of fishery resources
• Award for Excellence in Fisheries Education (Award)
Presented annually to an individual to recognize excellence in organized teaching & advising in a field of fisheries
• J. Frances Allen Scholarship (Scholarship)
Awarded annually to a female Ph.D. student whose research emphasis is in an area of fisheries science*Eligibility:* Must be an AFS member
• Honourary Membership (Award)
Awarded to individuals who have achieved outstanding professional or other attainments or have given outstanding service to the Society
• Presidents' Fishery Conservation Award (Award)
Presented annually, one or more awards if warranted, in one of two categories: (1) an AFS individual or unit or (2) a non-AFS individual or entity, for a singular accomplishment or activity that advances aquatic resource conservation at the regional or Society level
• William E. Ricker Resource Conservation Award (Award)
Given to any entity for a singular accomplishment or activity in resource conservation that is significant at the U.S., continental, or international level
• Excellence in Public Outreach (Award)
Awarded annually to an AFS member who goes "the extra mile" in sharing the value of fisheries science/research with the general public through the popular media & other communication channels
• Fish Culture Hall of Fame (Award)
Inductees will have made significant contributions to the advancement of fish culture in the United States
Meetings/Conferences:
• American Fisheries Society Annual Meeting, August, 2015, Portland, OR
Scope: International
Contact Information: URL: 2015.fisheries.org
• American Fisheries Society Annual Meeting, August, 2016, Kansas City, MO
Scope: International
Publications:
• Fisheries
Editor: Sarah Gilbert Fox
Profile: Monthly Magazine

American Forest & Paper Association (AF&PA)
#800, 1111 - 19th St. NW, Washington DC 20036 USA
Tel: 202-463-2700
Toll-Free: 800-878-8878
Other Communication: membership@afandpa.org
info@afandpa.org
www.afandpa.org
Previous Name: American Paper Institute
Overview: A large international organization founded in 1993
Mission: To act as a leading voice for the forest products industry
Chief Officer(s):
Alexander Toeldte, Chair
Donna A. Harman, President & Chief Executive Officer
Jan Poling, Vice-President, General Counsel & Secretary
Membership: 157; *Member Profile:* Companies & associations that produce forest, paper, & wood products; *Committees:* North American Forest Carbon Standards; Environment Resource; Energy Resource; Air Quality; Printing-Writing; Timber Purchasers
Activities: Providing advice & counsel about the forest products industry; Operating a statistics program in the paper & packaging industry;

American Foundry Society (AFS)
1695 North Penny Lane, Schaumburg IL 60173 USA
Tel: 847-824-0181; *Fax:* 847-824-2174
Toll-Free: 800-537-4237
www.afsinc.org
www.linkedin.com/groups?gid=1796048
www.facebook.com/americanfoundrysociety
twitter.com/AmerFoundrySoc
Previous Name: American Foundrymen's Society
Overview: A medium-sized international organization founded in 1896
Mission: To promote the interests of the metalcasting industry before the legislative & executive branches of the federal government.
Member of: International Committee of Foundry Technical Association (CIATF)
Chief Officer(s):
Jerry Call, Executive Vice-President, 847-825-0181 Ext. 255
jcall@afsinc.org
Membership: 7,700; *Fees:* Schedule available; *Member Profile:* Metalcasting facilities, diecasters & industry suppliers
Activities: *Speaker Service:* Yes; *Rents Mailing List:* Yes
Library Open to public

British Columbia Chapter
#15, 18503 - 97 Ave., Surrey BC V4N 3N9
Tel: 604-888-0181
www.afsbc.ca
www.linkedin.com/groups?homeNewMember=&gid=2259332
www.facebook.com/280931248600222
twitter.com/AFSBC
Chief Officer(s):
David Lalonde, Chair
dlalonde@almacg.ca

Manitoba Chapter
MB

Ontario Chapter
555 Bay St. North, Hamilton ON L8L 1H1
afsontario@bell.net
afsontario.ca
Chief Officer(s):
John Papaionnou, Chair
Crystal Burkholder, Secretary-Treasurer

American Foundrymen's Society *See* American Foundry Society

American Galvanizers Association (AGA)
#108, 6881 South Holly Circle, Centennial CO 80112 USA
Tel: 720-554-0900; *Fax:* 720-554-0909
Toll-Free: 800-468-7732
aga@galvanizeit.org
www.galvanizeit.org
Overview: A medium-sized national organization founded in 1935
Chief Officer(s):
Philip G. Rahrig, Executive Director
Finances: *Annual Operating Budget:* $500,000-$1.5 Million
Staff Member(s): 9; 30 volunteer(s)
Membership: 125 corporate; *Fees:* Professional: $65; Associate: $1575; Sustaining: $4200-13,125; *Member Profile:* Galvanizers & industry suppliers
Activities: Technical meeting every Sept./Oct.
Awards:
• Excellence in Hot-Dip Galvanizing Annual Award (Award)

American Guild of Variety Artists (AFL-CIO) (AGVA) / Guilde américaine des artistes de variétés (FAT-COI)
363 - 7 Ave., 17th Fl., New York NY 10001-3904 USA
Tel: 212-675-1003; *Fax:* 212-633-0097
Other Communication: Alternate e-mail: agvany@aol.com
agva@agvausa.com
www.agvausa.com
www.facebook.com/171985806179829
Overview: A large national organization founded in 1939
Mission: To represent performing artists & stage managers for live performances in the variety field
Member of: Associated Actors & Artistes of America
Affliation(s): AFL-CIO
Chief Officer(s):
Rod McKuen, President & CEO
Susanne K. Doris, Sec.-Treas.
sdoris@agvausa.com
Finances: *Funding Sources:* Membership dues
Staff Member(s): 20
Membership: 5,000+; *Fees:* US$72-US$795 based on earnings; *Committees:* AGVA Sick & Relief Fund; Membership

American Hiking Society (AHS)
1422 Fenwick Lane, Silver Spring MD 20910 USA
Tel: 301-565-6704; *Fax:* 301-565-6714
Toll-Free: 800-972-8608
info@americanhiking.org
www.americanhiking.org
www.facebook.com/AmericanHiking
twitter.com/AmericanHiking
Overview: A medium-sized international organization founded in 1977
Mission: To promote & protect foot trails & the hiking experience
Chief Officer(s):
Gregory A. Miller, President
gmiller@americanhiking.org
Lynn Scarlett, Chair
Finances: *Annual Operating Budget:* $500,000-$1.5 Million
Staff Member(s): 8
Membership: 5,000; *Fees:* $30
Activities: Maintains a public information service to provide hikers & other trail users with facts regarding facilities, organizations, & how to make best use of trails while protecting the environment; work trips; Trails for All Americans project; National Trails Day; Winter Trails; Advocacy Week; *Awareness Events:* National Trails Day, June; *Rents Mailing List:* Yes

American Historical Association (AHA)
400 A St. SE, Washington DC 20003-3889 USA

Tel: 202-544-2422; *Fax:* 202-544-8307
info@historians.org
www.historians.org
www.linkedin.com/groups?about=&gid=3810333
www.facebook.com/AHAhistorians
twitter.com/ahahistorians
Overview: A medium-sized international organization founded in 1884
Mission: To promote historical studies, the collection & preservation of historical documents & artifacts, & the dissemination of historical research
Member of: American Council of Learned Societies
Affliation(s): Comité international des sciences historiques
Chief Officer(s):
Anthony Grafton, President
Jim Grossman, Executive Director
Finances: *Annual Operating Budget:* $3 Million-$5 Million
Staff Member(s): 22
Membership: 13,420 individual + 4,100 institutional; *Fees:* Schedule available; *Member Profile:* Interest in history; *Committees:* Women Historians; Minority Historians; Graduate Education; Graduate Students; Part-time & Adjunct Employment; Public History; Task Force on Graduate Education; Intellectual Property Rights; Nominating; Affiliated Societies; Prizes & Awards; Professional Division; Teaching Division
Activities: *Rents Mailing List:* Yes
Awards:
• Book Awards & Prizes (Award)
See www.theaha.org/prizes

American Hotel & Lodging Association (AHLA)
#600, 1201 New York Ave. NW, Washington DC 20005-3931 USA
Tel: 202-289-3100; *Fax:* 202-289-3199
Toll-Free: 888-743-2515
informationcenter@ahla.com
www.ahla.com
www.linkedin.com/pub/american-hotel-lodging-association/6/870/a22
www.facebook.com/hotelassociation
twitter.com/ahla
Previous Name: American Hotel & Motel Association
Overview: A small international organization
Mission: To provide national representation for the lodging industry with services including public relations, image management, education & training, research & information.
Affliation(s): Ontario Hotel & Motel Association
Chief Officer(s):
John Fitzpatrick, Chair
Katherine Lugar, President & CEO
klugar@ahla.com
Finances: *Funding Sources:* Membership dues; sponsorship
Staff Member(s): 26
Membership: 12,000+; *Fees:* Schedule available; *Member Profile:* Stakeholders in the lodging industry, including individual hotel property members, hotel companies, student and faculty members, and industry suppliers; *Committees:* Audit, Certification & Credentials; Communications; Sustainability; Executive; Financial Management; Food & Beverage; Governmental Affairs; Human Resrouces; Labor Relations; Lodging Industry Rating Advisory; Resort; Risk Management

American Hotel & Motel Association *See* American Hotel & Lodging Association

American Humane Association (AHA)
#360, 1400 - 16th St. NW, Washington DC 20036 USA
Toll-Free: 800-227-4645
info@americanhumane.org
www.americanhumane.org
www.facebook.com/americanhumane
twitter.com/americanhumane
www.youtube.com/americanhumane
Overview: A large international organization founded in 1877
Mission: To prevent cruelty, abuse, neglect & exploitation of children & animals & to assure that their interests & well-being are fully, effectively & humanely guaranteed by an aware & caring society
Chief Officer(s):
Robin R. Ganzert, President & CEO
Finances: *Annual Operating Budget:* $3 Million-$5 Million; *Funding Sources:* Individual contributions; foundation grants; state & federal contracts
Staff Member(s): 23
Membership: 2,000; *Fees:* $59 individual; $119 organization
Activities: Management workshops; fundraising; public relations; education/outreach; animal care facilities; cruelty investigation; *Awareness Events:* Be Kind to Animals Week
Library by appointment
Awards:
• Meacham Foundation Memorial Grant (Grant)
• Second Chancer Fund (Grant)
• Red Star Emergency Grant (Grant)
Publications:
• Protecting Animals
Type: Journal; *Frequency:* Quarterly
• Protecting Children
Type: Journal; *Frequency:* Quarterly

American Industrial Hygiene Association (AIHA)
#777, 3141 Fariview Park Dr., Falls Church VA 22042 USA
Tel: 703-849-8888; *Fax:* 703-207-3561
infonet@aiha.org
www.aiha.org
www.linkedin.com/groups?gid=101603
www.facebook.com/aihaglobal
twitter.com/AIHA
www.youtube.com/user/IHValue
Overview: A medium-sized international organization founded in 1939
Mission: To serve the needs of occupational & environmental health professionals; To achieve high professional standards; To promote certification of industrial hygienists
Chief Officer(s):
Peter J. O'Neil, Executive Director, 703-846-0760
poneil@aiha.org
Staff Member(s): 61
Membership: 10,000; *Fees:* Schedule available; *Member Profile:* International occupational & environmental health & safety professionals, who practise industrial hygiene in industry, academic institutions, government, & independent organizations
Activities: Administering education programs; Operating laboratory accreditation programs based on high international standards; Providing networking opportunities; Engaging in advocacy activities
Meetings/Conferences:
• American Industrial Hygiene Conference & Exposition 2015, May, 2015, Salt Lake City, UT
Scope: International
Contact Information: Assistant Manager, Meetings: Lindsay Padilla, Phone: 703-846-0754, lpadilla@aiha.org
Publications:
• American Industrial Hygiene Association Member Directory
Type: Directory
• Journal of Occupational & Environmental Hygiene
Type: Journal; *Accepts Advertising*; *Editor:* Sheila Brown
Profile: A peer-reviewed publication to enhance the knowledge & practice of occupational & environmental hygiene & safety
• The Synergist
Type: Magazine; *Frequency:* Monthly; *Accepts Advertising*; *Editor:* Ed Rutkowski
Profile: Information about the occupational & environmental health & safety fields & the industrial hygiene profession, including industry trends, government activities, technical information, &association news

American Institute of Plant Engineers *See* Association for Facilities Engineering

American Iron & Steel Institute (AISI)
#800, 25 Massachusetts Ave. NW, Washington DC 20001 USA
Tel: 202-452-7100; *Fax:* 202-463-6573
webmaster@steel.org
www.steel.org
www.facebook.com/pages/American-Iron-and-Steel-Institute/86935184929
twitter.com/aisisteel
www.youtube.com/user/AISIsteel
Overview: A small international organization
Mission: To advance steel as the material of choice and to enhance the competitiveness of member companies and the North American steel industry.
Chief Officer(s):
Thomas J. Gibson, President & CEO
Membership: *Member Profile:* Producer companies - including integrated, electric furnace & reconstituted mills; associate companies - suppliers to or customers of the industry; affiliate organizations - downstream steel producers of products such as cold rolled strip, pipe & tube, coated sheet

American Library Association (ALA)
50 East Huron St., Chicago IL 60611 USA
Fax: 312-440-9374
Toll-Free: 800-545-2433
Other Communication: membership@ala.org
ala@ala.org
www.ala.org
www.facebook.com/group.php?gid=107691181566
Overview: A large international organization founded in 1876
Mission: To develop & improve library & information services & the profession of librarianship; To enhance learning; To ensure access to information for all
Chief Officer(s):
Keith Michael Fiels, Executive Director
kfiels@ala.org
Cathleen J. Bourdon, Associate Executive Director
cbourdon@ala.org
Donald E. Chatham, Associate Executive Director
dchatham@ala.org
John F. Chrastka, Director, Membership Development
jchrastka@ala.org
Alex Companio, Director, Operations & Support
acompanio@ala.org
Denise Davis, Director, Office of Research & Statistics
dmdavis@ala.org
Mark R. Gould, Director, Public Information Office
mgould@ala.org
Alan Inouye, Director, Office for Information Technology Policy
ainouye@alawash.org
Sandra C. Lee, Director, Planning & Budgeting
slee@ala.org
Membership: *Member Profile:* Individuals & organizations interested in libary & information science & library service; *Committees:* Accreditation; Advisory; Appointments; Awards; Chapter Relations; Conference; Constitution & Bylaws; Elections; Human Resource Development & Recruitment Advisory; Information Technology Policy Advisory; Literacy; Literacy & Outreach Services Advisory; Membership; Nominating; Public & Cultural Programs Advisory; Research & Statistics; Rural, Native & Tribal Libraries; Scholarships & Study Grants; Training, Orientation & Leadership Development; Website Advisory
Activities: Promoting libraries & information services; Providing professional development opportunities; awards, bursaries and scholarships
Meetings/Conferences:
• American Library Association 2015 Midwinter Meeting & Exhibits, January, 2015, Chicago, IL
Scope: International
Description: A meeting for librarians, support staff, trustees, & retirees, offering discussion groups, committee meetings, speakers, & exhibits
Contact Information: Registration Customer Service, Phone: 1-800-974-3084, E-mail: ala@experient-inc.com
• American Library Association 2015 Annual Conference, June, 2015, San Francisco, CA
Scope: International
Description: A program for people in the library & information services field, offering speakers, educational programs, committee meetings, & exhibits
Contact Information: Registration Customer Service, Phone: 1-800-974-3084, E-mail: ala@experient-inc.com
• American Library Association 2016 Midwinter Meeting & Exhibits, January, 2016, Boston, MA
Scope: International
Description: An annual gathering of those in the library & information services community, highlighting committee meetings, discussion groups, speakers, & exhibits
Contact Information: Registration Customer Service, Phone: 1-800-974-3084, E-mail: ala@experient-inc.com
• American Library Association 2016 Annual Conference, June, 2016, Orlando, FL
Scope: International
Description: A conference providing speakers, educational programs, committee meetings, & exhibits related to library & information services
Contact Information: Registration Customer Service, Phone: 1-800-974-3084, E-mail: ala@experient-inc.com
• Public Library Association (a division of the American Library Association) 2016 Biennial Conference, April, 2016, Denver, CO
Scope: International
Description: The multi-day event offers nearly 200 education programs, social events that include author luncheons and networking receptions, and an exhibits hall featuring the latest in products and services.

Contact Information: Registration Customer Service, Phone: 1-800-974-3084, E-mail: ala@experient-inc.com
• American Library Association 2017 Annual Conference, June, 2017, Chicago, IL
Scope: International
Description: Highlights include a variety of speakers, educational programs, committee meetings, & exhibits
Contact Information: Registration Customer Service, Phone: 1-800-974-3084, E-mail: ala@experient-inc.com
• American Library Association 2017 Midwinter Meeting & Exhibits, January, 2017, Atlanta, GA
Scope: International
Description: A library & information service meeting presenting speakers, discussion groups, exhibits, & committee meetings
Contact Information: Registration Customer Service, Phone: 1-800-974-3084, E-mail: ala@experient-inc.com
• Public Library Association (a division of the American Library Association) 2018 Biennial Conference, March, 2018, Philadelphia, PA
Scope: International
Description: The multi-day event offers nearly 200 education programs, social events that include author luncheons and networking receptions, and an exhibits hall featuring the latest in products and services.
Contact Information: Registration Customer Service, Phone: 1-800-974-3084, E-mail: ala@experient-inc.com
• American Library Association 2018 Annual Conference, June, 2018, New Orleans, LA
Scope: International
Description: A conference providing speakers, educational programs, committee meetings, & exhibits related to library & information services
• American Library Association 2018 Midwinter Meeting & Exhibits, February, 2018, Denver, CO
Scope: International
Description: A library & information service meeting presenting speakers, discussion groups, exhibits, & committee meetings
Contact Information: Registration Customer Service, Phone: 1-800-974-3084, E-mail: ala@experient-inc.com
• American Library Association 2019 Midwinter Meeting & Exhibits, January, 2019, Seattle, WA
Scope: International
Description: A library & information service meeting presenting speakers, discussion groups, exhibits, & committee meetings
Contact Information: Registration Customer Service, Phone: 1-800-974-3084, E-mail: ala@experient-inc.com
• American Library Association 2019 Annual Conference, June, 2019, Washington, DC
Scope: International
Description: A conference providing speakers, educational programs, committee meetings, & exhibits related to library & information services
• American Library Association 2020 Annual Conference, June, 2020, Chicago, IL
Scope: International
Description: A conference providing speakers, educational programs, committee meetings, & exhibits related to library & information services
• American Library Association 2020 Midwinter Meeting & Exhibits, January, 2020, Philadelphia, PA
Scope: International
Description: A library & information service meeting presenting speakers, discussion groups, exhibits, & committee meetings
Contact Information: Registration Customer Service, Phone: 1-800-974-3084, E-mail: ala@experient-inc.com
• American Library Association 2021 Midwinter Meeting & Exhibits, January, 2021, Indianapolis, IN
Scope: International
Description: A library & information service meeting presenting speakers, discussion groups, exhibits, & committee meetings
Contact Information: Registration Customer Service, Phone: 1-800-974-3084, E-mail: ala@experient-inc.com
• American Library Association 2021 Annual Conference, June, 2021, San Francisco, CA
Scope: International
Description: A conference providing speakers, educational programs, committee meetings, & exhibits related to library & information services
Publications:
• American Libaries
Type: Magazine; *Frequency:* 10 pa *ISSN:* 0002-9769; *Price:* Free with payment ofAmerican Library Association dues
Profile: Topics include association & international news, conference highlights, professional development opportunities, advocacy, intellectual freedom, legislation, & technology
• Book Links
Type: Magazine; *Frequency:* Quarterly; *Editor:* Laura Tillotson
Profile: A quarterly supplement to Booklist, with articles & thematic bibliographies of interest to youth librarians, school library media specialists, teachers, reading specialists, & curriculumcoordinators
• Booklist
Type: Magazine; *Frequency:* 22 pa; *Accepts Advertising*; *Price:* $109.95 / year; $126.95 Canada & international
Profile: Reviews of books, media, & reference sources for collection development
• Guide to Reference
Profile: An annotated guide to reference sources, organized by academic discipline
• Library Technology Reports
Type: Newsletter; *Accepts Advertising*
Profile: The most recent information about library technology
• Smart Libraries (formerly Library Systems Newsletter)
Type: Newsletter; *Frequency:* Monthly; *Accepts Advertising*; *Editor:* Dan Freeman
Profile: Articles related to library technology

American Lung Association (ALA)
Washington Office, #800, 1301 Pennsylvania Ave. NW, Washington DC 20004 USA
Tel: 202-785-3355; *Fax:* 202-452-1805
Toll-Free: 800-732-9339
info@lungusa.org
www.lungusa.org
www.facebook.com/lungusa
twitter.com/lungassociation
www.youtube.com/user/americanlung
Overview: A large international charitable organization founded in 1904
Mission: To prevent lung disease & promote lung health
Affliation(s): American Thoracic Society
Chief Officer(s):
Kathryn A. Forbes, Chair
Finances: *Annual Operating Budget:* Greater than $5 Million; *Funding Sources:* Donations; Grants
Staff Member(s): 105
Membership: 130,000 volunteers

American Management Association (AMA)
1601 Broadway, New York NY 10019 USA
Tel: 212-586-8100; *Fax:* 212-903-8168
Toll-Free: 800-262-9699
customerservice@amanet.org
www.amanet.org
www.linkedin.com/company/12230
www.facebook.com/176633092380292
twitter.com/amanet
Overview: A large international organization founded in 1923
Mission: American Management Association is a world leader in professional development, advancing the skills of individuals to drive business success
Chief Officer(s):
Edward T. Reilly, President & CEO
Vivianna Guzman, CFO & Treasurer
John Wright, President/ Managing Director, Canada
Staff Member(s): 750
Membership: 70,000

American Marketing Association (AMA)
#5800, 311 Wacker Dr. South, Chicago IL 60606 USA
Tel: 312-542-9000; *Fax:* 312-542-9001
info@ama.org
www.ama.org
twitter.com/marketing_power
Overview: A medium-sized international organization founded in 1937
Mission: To urge & assist the personal & professional development of members; to advance the science & ethical practice of the marketing discipline
Finances: *Annual Operating Budget:* $3 Million-$5 Million; *Funding Sources:* Membership fees; publications; conferences
Staff Member(s): 60
Membership: 38,000; *Fees:* $205 first year + $175 renewal
Activities: *Library* Open to public

Montréal Chapter
#925, 2015, rue Peel, Montréal QC H3A 1T8
Tél: 514-842-5681; *Téléc:* 514-842-8836
info@apcm.biz
www.communicationmarketing.org
www.linkedin.com/groups?gid=100675
www.facebook.com/apcm.biz
Chief Officer(s):
Nathalie Dupont, Présidente

Toronto Chapter
c/o Managing Matters, #202, 720 Spadina Ave., Toronto ON M5S 2T9
Tel: 416-944-9529
contact@ama-toronto.com
www.ama-toronto.com
www.linkedin.com/groups?gid=72166
www.facebook.com/AMAToronto
twitter.com/amatoronto
Mission: To increase the impact and value of marketing to its members and helps connect its members to Toronto marketing and business professionals and the world's largest marketing community, the American Marketing Association.
Chief Officer(s):
Craig Lund, President

American Medical Association
515 North State St., Chicago IL 60610 USA
Tel: 312-464-5000; *Fax:* 312-464-5543
Toll-Free: 800-621-8335
www.ama-assn.org
www.linkedin.com/groups?mostPopular=&gid=76194&trk=myg_ugrp_ovr
www.facebook.com/AmericanMedicalAssociation
twitter.com/AmerMedicalAssn
plus.google.com/107410187242660838577
Overview: A large international organization founded in 1847
Chief Officer(s):
Michael D. Maves, Exec. Vice President & CEO
Membership: *Fees:* Physician: $84-420; Intern/Resident/Fellow: $45-160; Student: $20-68
Activities: Council on Scientific Affairs - major contributions in the area of environmental health; Dept. of Environmental, Public & Occupational Health (these responsibilities are now with the Dept. of Risk Assessment in the Division of Biomedical Science)
Awards:
• Nathan Davis Awards for Outstanding Government Service (Award)
Spotlights legislators, public health officials, researchers and state and local executives who put health care at the forefront of their civic efforts.
• Jordan Fieldman, MD, Award (Award)
• Joan F. Giambalvo Memorial Scholarship (Scholarship)
To advance the progress of women in the medical profession and strengthening the ability of the AMA to identify and address the needs of women physicians and medical students.
• Healthy Living Grants (Grant)
Supports grassroots health education programs to develop school and community-based solutions to behavioral health challenges.
• Healthy Communities/Healthy America Fund (Grant)
Supports to physician-led free clinics across the country.
Amount: $10,000-$25,000
Publications:
• JAMA [The Journal of the American Medical Association]
Type: Journal

American Musicological Society (AMS)
6010 College Station, Brunswick ME 04011-8451 USA
Tel: 207-798-4243; *Fax:* 207-798-4254
Toll-Free: 877-679-7648
ams@ams-net.org
www.ams-net.org
Overview: A large international organization founded in 1934
Mission: To advance research in the various fields of music as a branch of learning & scholarship
Member of: American Council of Learned Societies
Affliation(s): International Musicological Society
Chief Officer(s):
Robert Judd, Executive Director
Anne Walters Robertson, President
Al Hipkins, Office Manager
Finances: *Funding Sources:* Membership dues; Endowments; Gifts
Staff Member(s): 3
Membership: 3,600 individual + 1,200 institutional; *Fees:* Schedule available; *Member Profile:* Persons with an interest in the advancement of research in various fields of music; *Committees:* Annual Meeting; Committees; Communications; Development; Membership & Professional Development; Awards; Nominating; Publications; AMS-MLA Joint RISM; Chapter Activities; Career-Related Issues; Cultural Diversity; Graduate Education Steering; History of the Society; Obituaries;

Moderated Electronic Discussion List; Status of Women; Finance
Awards:
• The Alfred Einstein Award (Award)
Musical article of exceptional merit by a scholar in the early stages of his/her career
• The Noah Greenburg Award (Award)
For outstanding performance projects
• The Otto Kinkeldey Award (Award)
For outstanding work of musicological scholarship (senior scholar)
• Lewis Lockwood Award (Award)
For outstanding work of musicological scholarship (early stages)
• Claude V. Palisca Award (Award)
For outstanding edition or translation
• Alvin H. Johnson AMS 50 Dissertation-year Fellowships (Award)
• Howard Mayer Brown Fellowships (Award)
For minority graduate study in musicology
• Paul Pisk Award (Award)
For outstanding paper at annual meeting by graduate student
• H. Colin Slim Award (Award)
For outstanding article in musicology (senior scholar)
• Ruth A. Solie Award (Award)
For outstanding collection of essays
• Robert M. Stevenson Award (Award)
For outstanding scholarship in Iberian music
• Philip Brett Award (Award)
For oustanding work in gay, lesbian, bisexual, and transgender/transsexual studies
• M. Elizabeth C. Bartlet Fund for Research in France (Grant)
• Committee on Cultural Diversity Travel Fund (Grant)
• Janet Levy Fund for Independent Scholars (Grant)
• Harold S. Powers World Travel Fund (Grant)
• Eugene K. Wolf Travel Fund for European Research (Award)
Publications:
• AMS Directory
Type: Directory; *Frequency:* Annually
• AMS Newsletter
Type: Newsletter; *Frequency:* Semiannually
• AMS Studies in Music
Editor: Mary Hunter
• Journal of the American Musicological Society
Type: Journal; *Frequency:* 3 pa; *Accepts Advertising*; *Author:* Bruce Alan Brown; *Editor:* Annegret Fauser *ISSN:* 0003-0139; *Price:* $47 per issue
Profile: One of the premier journals in the field of publishing scholarship from all fields of musical inquiry from historical musicology,critical theory, music analysis, iconography & organology, to performance practice, aesthetics & hermeneutics, ethnomusicology, gender & sexuality, & popular music

New York - St. Lawrence Chapter
691 Carlaw Ave, Toronto ON M4K 3K8
Tel: 416-462-9715
kschult5@uwo.ca
Chief Officer(s):
Jim Davis, Chair
Kirsten M. Schultz, Sec.-Treas.

American Newspaper Guild *See* The Newspaper Guild (AFL-CIO/CLC)

American Numismatic Society (ANS)

75 Varick St., 11th Fl., New York NY 10013 USA
Tel: 212-571-4470; *Fax:* 212-571-4479
info@numismatics.org
www.numismatics.org
www.facebook.com/AmericanNumismaticSociety
twitter.com/ANSCoins/
Overview: A large national organization founded in 1858
Member of: American Council of Learned Societies
Affliation(s): Commission internationale de numismatique; Fédération internationale de la médaille
Chief Officer(s):
Ute Wartenberg Kagan, Executive Director
Jeffrey Benjamin, Treasurer
Finances: *Annual Operating Budget:* $500,000-$1.5 Million
Staff Member(s): 15; 7 volunteer(s)
Membership: 1,875 individual + 112 institutional; *Fees:* $35 student; $55-$100 associate; $110 fellow; $150-$500 institution; *Member Profile:* Serious interest in numismatics
Activities: *Internships:* Yes *Library:* The Francis D. Campbell Library
Awards:
• Huntington Medal Award (Award)
• Saltus Medal Award (Award)
Publications:
• American Journal of Numismatics
Type: Journal; *Editor:* Oliver Hoover
• ANS Magazine
Type: Magazine; *Editor:* Peter van Alfen
• Colonial Newsletter
Type: Newsletter; *Editor:* Oliver Hoover

American Optometric Association (AOA)

243 North Lindbergh Blvd., 1st Fl., St. Louis MO 63141-7881 USA
Tel: 314-991-4100; *Fax:* 314-991-4101
Toll-Free: 800-365-2219
www.aoa.org
Previous Name: American Association of Opticians
Overview: A large national organization founded in 1898
Mission: To advance the quality, availability & accessibility of eye, vision & related health care; To represent the profession of optometry; To enhance & promote the independent & ethical decision making of its members; To assist doctors of optometry in practicing successfully in accordance with the highest standards of patient care
Member of: World Council of Optometry
Affliation(s): Canadian Association of Optometrists
Chief Officer(s):
Ronald L. Hopping, President
RLHopping@aoa.org
Finances: *Annual Operating Budget:* Greater than $5 Million; *Funding Sources:* Membership dues
Staff Member(s): 90; 360 volunteer(s)
Membership: 34,500; *Fees:* $628; *Member Profile:* Active members generally are doctors of optometry; they become members of AOA only through membership in an affiliated (state) optometric association
Activities: *Awareness Events:* Save Your Vision Month, March; Diabetes Awareness Month, Nov.; *Internships:* Yes; *Rents Mailing List:* Yes *Library* Open to public
Awards:
• Young Optometrist of the Year (Award)
Recognizes those individuals (who have been active prctice less than 10 years) who show leadership skills when serving their profession, patients & community
• Apollo Award (Award)
Recognizes individuals, organizations or institutions who have performed a signigicant public service for the visual welfare of others
• Distinguished Service (Award)
Recognizes an individual doctor of optometry who has distinguished him/herself within the profession for unusually significant contributions & outstanding achievements contributing to the advancement for the profession of optometry
• Optometrist of the Year (Award)
Recognizes the deserving individual doctor of optometry for performance of outstanding services on behalf of the profession & to the visual welfare of the public
Publications:
• Optometry
Type: Journal; *Frequency:* Monthly

American Ornithologists' Union (AOU)

5405 Villa View Dr., Farmington NM 87402 USA
Tel: 505-326-1579
aou@aou.org
www.aou.org
Overview: A medium-sized national organization founded in 1883
Mission: To be devoted to the scientific study of birds in North America
Chief Officer(s):
Scott Gillihan, Executive Director
John R. Faaborg, President
president@aou.org
Sara R. Morris, Secretary
secretary@aou.org
Membership: 4,500; *Fees:* Regular: $85; Student: $27; Lifetime: $2550
Activities: Supporting individual research projects; Providing funds for graduate students to attend annual meetings; Presenting several annual awards for excellence in research; *Rents Mailing List:* Yes
Awards:
• William Brewster Memorial Award
• Elliott Coues Award
• Ned K. Johnson Young Investigator Award
• Ralph W. Schreiber Conservation Award
• Marion Jenkinson AOU Service Award
Publications:
• The Auk [a publication of the American Ornithologists' Union]
Type: Journal; *Frequency:* Quarterly
Profile: A journal of ornithology

American Paper Institute *See* American Forest & Paper Association

American Philological Association (APA)

University of Pennsylvania, #201E, 220 South 40th St., Philadelphia PA 19104-3512 USA
Tel: 215-898-4975; *Fax:* 215-573-7874
apaclassics@sas.upenn.edu
apaclassics.org
www.facebook.com/APAClassics
twitter.com/apaclassics
Overview: A large international organization founded in 1869
Mission: To ensure an adequate number of well-trained, inspirational Classics teachers at all levels, kindergarten through graduate school; To give Classics scholars & teachers the tools they need to preserve & extend our knowledge of classical civilization & to communicate that knowledge as widely as possible; To develop the necessary infrastructure to achieve these goals & to make the APA a model for other societies confronting similar challenges
Member of: American Council of Learned Societies; International Federation of Classical Studies
Affliation(s): International Federation of Classical Studies
Chief Officer(s):
Adam D. Blistein, Executive Director, 215-898-4975
blistein@sas.upenn.edu
Denis Feeney, President
Kathryn J. Gutzwiller, President-Elect
Finances: *Annual Operating Budget:* $500,000-$1.5 Million
Staff Member(s): 3; 300 volunteer(s)
Membership: 3,000; *Fees:* Schedule available; *Member Profile:* Open; *Committees:* Committee on Classical Tradition & Reception; Ancient & Modern Performance
Activities: *Speaker Service:* Yes
Awards:
• The President's Award of the APA (Award)
• The Charles J. Goodwin Award of Merit (Award)
• Distinguished Service Awards (Award)
• Awards for Excellence in the Teaching of Classics at the College Level (Award)
• Awards for Excellence in Teaching at the Precollegiate Level (Award)
• APA Outreach Prize (Award)
Meetings/Conferences:
• American Philological Association 146th Annual Meeting, January, 2015, New Orleans, LA
Scope: International
• American Philological Association 147th Annual Meeting, January, 2016, San Francisco, CA
Scope: International
• American Philological Association 148th Annual Meeting, January, 2017, Toronto, ON
Scope: International
• American Philological Association 149th Annual Meeting, January, 2018, Boston, MA
Scope: International
• American Philological Association 150th Annual Meeting, January, 2019, San Diego, CA
Scope: International
Publications:
• Transactions of the American Philological Association (TAPA)
Profile: The official research publication of the APA, reflects the wide range and high quality of research currently undertaken by classicists.

American Planning Association (APA)

#750 West, 1030 15th St. NW, Washington DC 20005-1503 USA
Tel: 202-872-0611; *Fax:* 202-872-0643
customerservice@planning.org
www.planning.org
www.linkedin.com/groups?gid=116818
www.facebook.com/AmericanPlanningAssociation
twitter.com/APA_Planning
www.youtube.com/user/AmericanPlanningAssn
Overview: A large national organization founded in 1909
Mission: To provide members with systematic ways to work on problems in common & to affect national planning policies
Chief Officer(s):
Mitch Silver, President
Paul Farmer, Executive Director

Finances: *Annual Operating Budget:* $3 Million-$5 Million
Staff Member(s): 66
Membership: 29,000
Activities: Environment, Natural Resources & Energy Division - to bring sound planning principles to the protection, management or conservation of environmental, natural & energy resources, as well as national forests & public lands; Small town & Rural Planning Division - oriented toward improving the quality & extent of planning in small communities & rural areas with a focus on protection of natural resources; *Rents Mailing List:* Yes *Library:* APA Library; by appointment
Awards:
• Judith McManus Price Scholarship (Scholarship)
Eligibility: Undergraduate or graduate planning students; Women and minority (African American, Hispanic American, or Native American) students enrolled in an approved Planning Accreditation Board (PAB) planning program who are citizens of the United States, intend to pursue careers as practicing planners in the public sector, and are able to demonstrate a genuine financial need*Deadline:* April 30*Amount:* $2,000 - $4,000 *Contact:* Kriss Blank, kblank@planning.org
• Charles Abrams Scholarship (Scholarship)
Eligibility: A student who is enrolled in a graduate planning program leading to a master's degree in one of the five schools at which Charles Abrams taught and who has been nominated by the program's department chair.*Deadline:* April 30 *Contact:* Kriss Blank, kblank@planning.org
Publications:
• JAPA [The Journal of the American Planning Association]
Type: Journal
• Planning
Type: Magazine

American Political Science Association (APSA)
1527 New Hampshire Ave. NW, Washington DC 20036-1206 USA
Tel: 202-483-2512; *Fax:* 202-483-2657
apsa@apsanet.org
www.apsanet.org
www.linkedin.com/groups?gid=154534&trk=hb_side_g
www.facebook.com/likeAPSA
twitter.com/apsatweets
Overview: A large national organization founded in 1903
Mission: To provide members with services to facilitate research, teaching, & professional development
Member of: American Council of Learned Societies; Consortium of Social Science Associations; National Humanities Alliance
Affliation(s): International Political Science Association
Chief Officer(s):
Michael Brintrall, Executive Director
brintnall@apsanet.org
Finances: *Funding Sources:* Membership dues; fees; sales; endowments; grants
Staff Member(s): 24
Membership: 13,000 individual + 3,000 institutional; *Fees:* $40 - $316; *Member Profile:* Interest in political science
Activities: Programs: International Exchange, Congressional Fellowship, Graduate Minority Fellowship; Projects: Task Forces, Minority Identification; The Ralph Bunche Summer Institute for Black Undergraduates
Awards:
• Dissertation Awards (Award)
• Paper & Article Awards (Award)
• Book Awards (Award)
• Career Awards (Award)
• Goodnow Awards (Award)
• Teaching Award & Campus Teaching Award (Award)
• Organized Section Awards (Award)
Publications:
• American Political Science Review
Profile: Quarterly Journal
• Perspectives on Politics
Profile: Quarterly Journal
• PS: Political Science & Politics
Profile: Quarterly peer-reviewed journal focusing on contemporary politics

American Psychological Association (APA)
750 First St. NE, Washington DC 20002-4242 USA
Tel: 202-336-5500; *Fax:* 202-335-5997
Toll-Free: 800-374-2721
executiveoffice@apa.org
www.apa.org
www.linkedin.com/groups?gid=58284
www.facebook.com/AmericanPsychologicalAssociation
www.twitter.com/apa
plus.google.com/109392714004041510585
Overview: A large international organization founded in 1892
Mission: To advance psychology as a science, profession & as a means of promoting human welfare
Member of: American Council of Learned Societies
Chief Officer(s):
Suzanne Bennett Johnson, President
Norman Anderson, CEO
Finances: *Annual Operating Budget:* $3 Million-$5 Million; *Funding Sources:* Membership dues; publications
Staff Member(s): 560
Membership: 156,000 members & affiliates; *Fees:* Schedule available; *Member Profile:* Must have doctoral degree based in part upon a psychological dissertation or based on other evidence of proficiency in psychological scholarship; *Committees:* Election; Ethics; Finance; APA Fellows; Advancement of Professional Practice; American Psychological Association of Graduate Students; Psychology Teachers at Community Colleges; Aging; Animal Research and Ethics; Children, Youth and Families; Disability Issues in Psychology; Division/APA Relations; Early Career Psychologists; International Relations in Psychology; Human Resources; Rural Health; Women in Psychology; Continuing Education
Activities: An extensive range of publications; *Rents Mailing List:* Yes *Library* by appointment
Meetings/Conferences:
• American Psychological Association 2015 Convention, August, 2015, Toronto, ON
Scope: International

American Public Gardens Association (APGA)
351 Longwood Rd., Kennet Square PA 19348 USA
Tel: 610-708-3010; *Fax:* 610-444-3594
www.publicgardens.org
Overview: A medium-sized international organization founded in 1940
Mission: To support North American botanical gardens & arboreta, public horticultural organizations, their staff & trustees by: promoting the value of botanical gardens, arboreta & public horticultural organizations involved in the display, study & conservation of plants for public benefit; setting, promoting & recognizing professional standards; facilitating the exchange of information; advocating the collective interests of the association's members; promoting membership services
Chief Officer(s):
Casey Sclar, Interim Executive Director, 610-708-3016
csclar@publicgardens.org
Finances: *Annual Operating Budget:* $250,000-$500,000; *Funding Sources:* Membership dues; meetings; publication sales
Staff Member(s): 8
Membership: 2,400; *Fees:* $65-80 regular; $35 student; $50 library subscription; institutional dues based on operating budget; *Member Profile:* Anyone who works or volunteers for public gardens, zoos, horticultural societies, arboreta or historic house gardens
Activities: *Internships:* Yes; *Rents Mailing List:* Yes *Library* by appointment
Publications:
• The Public Garden
Profile: Quarterly Magazine

American Public Works Association (APWA)
#700, 2345 Grand Blvd., Kansas City MO 64108-2625 USA
Tel: 816-472-6100; *Fax:* 816-472-1610
Toll-Free: 800-848-2792
apwa@apwa.net
www.apwa.net
www.facebook.com/AmericanPublicWorksAssociation
twitter.com/apwatweets
www.youtube.com/apwatv
Overview: A medium-sized international organization founded in 1938
Mission: To provide high quality public works goods & services
Chief Officer(s):
Peter King, Executive Director
pking@apwa.net
Julie Burrell, Director, Human Resources / Office Services, 816-595-5280
jburrell@apwa.net
Finances: *Annual Operating Budget:* Greater than $5 Million; *Funding Sources:* Membership dues; Federal grants; Products
Staff Member(s): 50; 250 volunteer(s)
Membership: 26,000; *Fees:* Schedule available; *Member Profile:* Public agencies, private sector companies, & individuals engaged in public works services; *Committees:* Transportation; Solid Waste; Water Resources; Engineering & Technology; Management & Leadership; Emergency Management; Fleet Services; Facilities & Grounds; Utility & Public Right of Way

American Rhododendron Society (ARS)
PO Box 525, Niagara Falls NY 14304 USA
Tel: 416-424-1942; *Fax:* 905-262-1999
www.rhododendron.org
Overview: A small international charitable organization
Mission: To encourage interest in and to disseminate information about the genus Rhododendron.
Chief Officer(s):
Laura Grant, Executive Director
lauragrant@arsoffice.org
Finances: *Annual Operating Budget:* Less than $50,000; *Funding Sources:* Membership dues; plant sales
50 volunteer(s)
Membership: 400; *Fees:* $35; *Member Profile:* Growers of rhododendrons
Activities: Bulletins; flower shows; plant sales;

American Rivers
#1400, 1101 - 14th St. NW, Washington DC 20005 USA
Tel: 202-347-7550; *Fax:* 202-347-9240
outreach@americanrivers.org
www.americanrivers.org
www.facebook.com/AmericanRivers
twitter.com/AmericanRivers
www.youtube.com/AmericanRivers
Previous Name: American Rivers Conservation Council
Overview: A medium-sized national organization founded in 1973
Mission: To preserve & restore America's river systems; to foster a river stewardship ethic
Chief Officer(s):
William Robert (Bob) Irvin, President
Swep Davis, Chair
Finances: *Annual Operating Budget:* $1.5 Million-$3 Million
Staff Member(s): 25; 7 volunteer(s)
Membership: *Fees:* $20
Activities: Policy manuals; *Internships:* Yes; *Speaker Service:* Yes

American Rivers Conservation Council *See* American Rivers

American Society for Aesthetic Plastic Surgery (ASAPS)
c/o Renato Saltz, M.D., FACS, 5445 South Highland Dr., Salt Lake City UT 84117 USA
Tel: 801-274-9500; *Fax:* 801-274-9515
Toll-Free: 888-272-7711
Other Communication: media@surgery.org
findasurgeon@surgery.org
www.surgery.org
Overview: A medium-sized international organization founded in 1967
Mission: To advance the science, art, & safe practice of aesthetic plastic surgery among qualified plastic surgeons
Chief Officer(s):
Renato Saltz, President
rsaltz@saltzplasticsurgery.com
Jeffrey M. Kenkel, Vice-Presidnet
James A. Matas, Treasurer
Leo R. McCafferty, Secretary
Adeena Babbitt, Manager, Media Relations, 212-921-0500, Fax: 212-921-0011
media@surgery.org
Membership: 2,400; *Member Profile:* Plastic surgeons from the United States, certified by the American Board of Plastic Surgery; Plastic surgeons from Canada certified in plastic surgery by the Royal College of Physicians & Surgeons of Canada; Plastic surgeons from several other countries, who specialize in cosmetic plastic surgery
Activities: Providing both medical & public education; Advocating for patients; Publishing annual statistics; *Speaker Service:* Yes
Meetings/Conferences:
• American Society for Aesthetic Plastic Surgery 2015 Annual Meeting, May, 2015, Palais des congrès (Convention Centre), Montréal, QC
Scope: International
Publications:
• Aesthetic Surgery Journal
Type: Journal; *Accepts Advertising*; *Editor:* Foad Nahai, MD
ISSN: 1090-820X

Profile: A peer-reviewed international journal which focuses on scientific developments & clinical techniques in aesthetic surgery
• Beautiful Choice Newsletter
Type: Newsletter

American Society for Bone & Mineral Research (ASBMR)

#800, 2025 M St. NW, Washington DC 20036-3309 USA
Tel: 202-367-1161; *Fax:* 202-367-2161
Other Communication: publications@asbmr.org
asbmr@asbmr.org
www.asbmr.org
www.facebook.com/ASBMR
twitter.com/ASBMR
Overview: A medium-sized international organization
Mission: To promote study in the field of bone & mineral metabolism
Chief Officer(s):
Sundeep Khosia, President
Ann L. Elderkin, Executive Director
Douglas Fesler, Associate Executive Director
Matt Croll, Senior Director, Finance
Robert Fulcher, Director, Publications
Amy Goetz, Director, Marketing & Communications
Deborah Kroll, Director, Development
Gretchen Bretsch, Manager, Projects
Membership: 4,000; *Member Profile:* Clinical & experimental scientists involved in the study of bone & mineral metabolism; Physicians; Other healthcare practitioners; *Committees:* Advocacy; Ancillary Program; Annual Meeting Program; Education; Ethics Advisory; Executive; Finance; Membership Development; Nominating; Professional Practice; Publications; Representatives to Other Groups; Science Policy; Women in Bone & Mineral Research; ASBMR Task Force on Atypical Femoral Fractures
Activities: Engaging in advocacy activities; Interacting with government agencies & related societies
Meetings/Conferences:
• American Society for Bone & Mineral Research 2018 Annual Meeting, September, 2018, Palais des congrès de Montréal, Montréal, QC
Scope: International
Description: Plenary & poster sessions, panel discussions, & networking events
Contact Information: E-mail: asbmr@asbmr.org
Publications:
• ASBMR [American Society for Bone & Mineral Research] e-news
Type: Newsletter; *Frequency:* Monthly
Profile: Information from the American Society for Bone & Mineral Research, including upcoming events, grant announcements, membership benefits, committee & task forcehighlights, & program updates
• Journal of Bone & Mineral Research
Type: Journal; *Accepts Advertising*; *Editor:* Thomas L. Clemens, Ph.D.
Profile: Up-to-date basic & clinical research in the pathophysiology & treatment of bone & mineral disorders
• Primer on the Metabolic Bone Diseases & Disorders of Mineral Metabolism
Type: Primer; *Editor:* Clifford Rosen, M.D.; *Price:* A free copy & on-line access for American Society for Bone & Mineral Research members
Profile: A resource for scientists & students seeking an overview of the bone & mineral field, as well as for clinicians who care forpatients with disorders of bone & mineral metabolism

American Society for Environmental History (ASEH)

Interdisciplinary Arts & Sciences Program, University of Washington, PO Box 358436, 1900 Commerce St., Tacoma WA 98402-3100 USA
Tel: 206-465-0630
director@aseh.net
www.aseh.net
www.facebook.com/78043136293
www.youtube.com/watch?v=ewX25rVu0EY
Overview: A small international charitable organization founded in 1977
Mission: To promote interdisciplinary study of past environmental change; to promote the study of environmental history in all disciplines
Member of: American Council of Learned Societies
Affliation(s): International Consortium of Environmental History Organizations
Chief Officer(s):
Gregg Mitman, President
Membership: *Committees:* Executive; Nominating; Diversity; Outreach; Conference Site Selection; Publications; Education; Conference Program; Conference Local Arrangements; George Perkins Marsh Prize; Alice Hamilton Prize; Rachel Carson Prize; Leopold-Hidy Prize; H-Evironment
Awards:
• Leopold-Hidy Prize for Best Article in Environmental History (Award)
• Alice Hamilton Prize for Best Article, Outside the journal, Environmental History (Award)
• Rachel Carson Prize for Best Dissertation in Environmental History (Award)
• George Perkins March Prize for Best Book in Environmental History (Award)
Publications:
• ASEH [American Society for Environmental History] News
Type: Newsletter; *Frequency:* Quarterly
• Environmental History
Type: Journal
Profile: Published jointly with the Forest History Society

American Society for Information Science & Technology (ASIS&T)

#850, 8555 - 16th St., Silver Spring MD 20910 USA
Tel: 301-495-0900; *Fax:* 301-495-0810
Other Communication: membership@asis.org
asis@asis.org
www.asis.org
www.facebook.com/pages/ASIST/209226365809427
twitter.com/asist_org
Overview: A small international organization founded in 1937
Mission: To advance the information sciences & related applications of information technology by providing focus, opportunity, & support to information professionals & organizations
Member of: American Library Association
Chief Officer(s):
Harry W. Bruce, President
harryb@uw.edu
Richard B. Hill, Executive Director
rhill@asis.org
Janice Hatzakos, Director, Finance & Administration
jan@asis.org
Staff Member(s): 8
Membership: 4,000; *Fees:* US$140 regular; US$40 student; US$70 retired; US$800 corporate; US$650 institutional; US$65 Entry/Transitional Professionals; *Member Profile:* Information professionals; *Committees:* Executive; Budget & Finance; Awards & Honors; Constitution & Bylaws; Information Science Education; International Relations; Leadership; Membership; Nominations; Communications & Publications; Standards

American Society for Legal History (ASLH)

c/o Western Michigan University, 4301 Friedmann Hall, Kalamazoo MI 49008-5334 USA
Fax: 269-387-4651
www.aslh.net
Overview: A small international organization founded in 1956
Mission: To promote study, research & publication in the worldwide history of law & legal institutions
Member of: American Council of Learned Societies
Affliation(s): American History Association
Chief Officer(s):
Rebecca J. Scott, President-Elect
Michael Grossberg, President
grossber@indiana.edu
Sally Hadden, Secretary
sally.hadden@wmich.edu
Finances: *Funding Sources:* Membership dues; donations; advertisements; mailing lists
Membership: *Fees:* Schedule available; *Committees:* Conferences & the Annual Meeting; Cromwell Prizes; Documentary Preservation; Finance; Graduate Student Outreach; Honours; Willard Hurst Memorial Fund; Local Arrangements; Membership; Paul L. Murphy Award; Nominating; Kathryn T. Preyer Memorial; Annual Meeting Program; Projects & Proposals; Publications; John Phillip Reid Book Award; Research Fellowships & Awards; Surrency Prize; Sutherland Prize
Activities: Publishes, in conjunction with UNC press, monograph series "Studies in Legal History"; *Rents Mailing List:* Yes
Publications:
• Law and History Review
Editor: David S. Tanenhaus *ISSN:* 0738-2480
Profile: Journal, issued three times per year

American Society for Parenteral & Enteral Nutrition (ASPEN)

#412, 8630 Fenton St., Silver Spring MD 20910 USA
Tel: 301-587-6315; *Fax:* 301-587-2365
Toll-Free: 800-727-4567
aspen@nutr.org
www.nutritioncare.org
www.facebook.com/nutritioncare.org
twitter.com/aspenweb
Overview: A medium-sized international organization founded in 1976
Mission: To advance the science & practice of nutrition support therapy; To improve patient care
Chief Officer(s):
Debra Ben Avram, Chief Executive Officer
debrab@nutritioncare.org
Patrick McGary, Chief Operating Officer
patrickm@nutritioncare.org
Staff Member(s): 17
Membership: 5,500+; *Fees:* Schedule available; *Member Profile:* Individuals from around the world who are involved in the provision of clinical nutrition therapies, such as dietitians, physicians, nurses, pharmacists, & other health professionals
Publications:
• Journal of Parenteral & Enteral Nutrition
Type: Journal; *Frequency:* Bimonthly; *Accepts Advertising*; *Price:* Free with membership in the American Society for Parenteral & EnteralNutrition
Profile: Original peer-reviewed studies about basic & clinical research in the field of nutrition & metabolic support
• Nutrition in Clinical Practice
Type: Journal; *Frequency:* Bimonthly; *Accepts Advertising*; *Price:* Free with membership in the American Society for Parenteral & Enteral Nutrition
Profile: Multidisciplinary peer-reviewed articles for the clinical practice professional

American Society for Quality (ASQ)

PO Box 3005, 600 Plankinton Ave. North, Milwaukee WI 53203 USA
Tel: 414-272-8575; *Fax:* 414-272-1734
Toll-Free: 800-248-1946
help@asq.org
www.asq.org
www.linkedin.com/groups?gid=3633
www.facebook.com/ASQ
twitter.com/ASQ
www.youtube.com/user/ASQhq
Overview: A large international organization founded in 1946
Mission: The American Society for Quality (ASQ) advances learning, quality improvement, & knowledge exchange to improve business results, & to create better workplaces & communities worldwide
Chief Officer(s):
James J. Rooney, Chair
jrooney@absconsulting.com
Paul Borwaski, CEO
pborawski@asq.org
Finances: *Annual Operating Budget:* Greater than $5 Million
Staff Member(s): 225; 600 volunteer(s)
Membership: 150,000 individual & corporate; *Fees:* $27 student; $81 associate; $139 full; *Committees:* Technical Forums/Divisions: Quality Management; Aviation, Space & Defense; Automotive; Chemical & Process Industries; Electronics & Communications; Textile & Needle Trades; Food, Drug, & Cosmetics; Inspection; Biomedical; Energy & Environmental; Statistics; Human Development & Leadership; Software; Customer-Supplier; Service Industries; Quality Audit; Health Care; Measurement Quality; Design & Construction; Education; Advanced Manufacturing; Community Quality Councils; Government; Product Safety & Liability Prevention; Reliability; Six Sigma; Teamwork & Participation
Activities: Instruction, home study classes, courses taught by highly qualified instructors from business, industry, & academia; *Speaker Service:* Yes *Library:* Quality Information Center; Open to public

Edmonton Section
PO Box 2426, 10035 - 105 St., Edmonton AB T5J 2V6
info@asqedmonton.org
www.asqedmonton.org/
Chief Officer(s):
Viswanathan Ganapahy, Chair
chair@asqedmonton.org

Kitchener Section
Kitchener ON

www.asqkitchener.org
Mission: To create awareness of the need for quality, to promote research & development of standards, and to provide educational opportunities to ensure product and service excellence.
Chief Officer(s):
Jane Martin, Chair
chair@asqkitchener.org

London Section
PO Box 40034, Stn. Argyle, 1905 Dundas St. East, London ON N5W 5Z5
Tel: 519-951-5234
www.asqlondon.on.ca
Chief Officer(s):
Keith Harasyn, Chair
kharasyn@invacare.com

Nova Scotia Section
#100, 424 Sunnyside Place, 1600 Bedford Hwy., Halifax NS B4A 1E8
Tel: 902-445-5905; *Fax:* 902-445-5730
info@asq411.org
www.asq411.org/index.html
Chief Officer(s):
Vishal Bhardwaj, Chair
vb_109@yahoo.com

Saskatchewan Section
Saskatoon SK
info@asqsask.org
www.facebook.com/pages/ASQ-Saskatchewan/105726962829232

Toronto Section
#307, 2275 Lakeshore Blvd. West, Toronto ON M8V 3Y3
Tel: 416-352-6047
information@asqtoronto.org
www.asqtoronto.org/
Mission: To function as a volunteer resource for learning, networking and fellowship for members, organizations and the community interested in and with a passion for Quality.
Chief Officer(s):
Tonis Kilp, Chair
chair@asqtoronto.org

Vancouver Section
Vancouver BC
www.asq.bc.ca
www.linkedin.com/groups?gid=3789010
www.facebook.com/pages/ASQ-Vancouver-section-408/148764348511754
twitter.com/ASQVancouver
vimeo.com/asqvancouver
Chief Officer(s):
David Muncaster, Chair
chair@asq.bc.ca

Windsor Section
3478 Wells St., Windsor ON N9C 1T5
Tel: 519-254-5587; *Fax:* 519-967-0748
www.asqwindsor.org/
Chief Officer(s):
Graham Young, Chair
graham.young@pernod-ricard-canada.com

American Society for Theatre Research (ASTR)
PO Box 1798, Boulder CO 80306-1798 USA
Tel: 303-530-1838; *Fax:* 303-530-1839
Toll-Free: 888-530-1838
www.astr.org
Overview: A medium-sized international organization founded in 1956
Mission: To promote the cause of theatre as a field for serious scholarly study & research
Member of: American Council of Learned Societies
Affliation(s): International Federation for Theatre Research
Chief Officer(s):
Rhonda Blair, President
Finances: *Annual Operating Budget:* $50,000-$100,000
Staff Member(s): 1
Membership: 750 individual; *Fees:* Individual: $115; Retired: $40; Student: $35; Institution: $225; *Member Profile:* Students; professors; independent scholars of theatre
Activities: *Rents Mailing List:* Yes
Awards:
• Errol Hill Award (Award)
Awarded for the most outstanding work on African-American theatre
• Barnard Hewitt Award (Award)
Given in conjuction with the University of Illinois for the best book in theatre history to be published by a North American or on a North American topic
• Gerald Kahan Scholars Prize (Award)
Given for the best article by an emerging scholar
• Biennial Sally Banes Publication Prize
• Selma Jeanne Cohen Conference Presentation Award
• Distinguished Scholar Award
Publications:
• Theatre Survey
Editor: Martin Puchner
Profile: Theatre history journal

American Society of Association Executives (ASAE)
1575 I St. NW, Washington DC 20005 USA
Tel: 202-371-0940; *Fax:* 202-371-8315
Toll-Free: 888-950-2723
pr@asaecenter.org
www.asaecenter.org
Overview: A large national organization founded in 1920
Mission: To advance the value of voluntary associations to society & to support the professionalism of the individuals who lead them
Chief Officer(s):
Joseph M. McGuire, Chair
jmcguire@aham.org
Finances: *Annual Operating Budget:* Greater than $5 Million
Staff Member(s): 140; 37 volunteer(s)
Membership: 21,000 executives + 10,000 organizations
Activities: *Internships:* Yes; *Rents Mailing List:* Yes *Library*
Awards:
• The Key Award (Award)
Honours a CEO who has demonstrated exceptional leadership skills*Deadline:* April 1
• The Professional Performance Award (Award)
Honours top-level executives for their contributions*Deadline:* April 1
• The Academy of Leaders Award (Award)
Awarded to industry partners & consultants who have supported the association community in an outstanding way*Deadline:* April 1
Publications:
• AMC Connection [a publication of American Society of Association Executives]
Type: Newsletter; *Frequency:* q.
• Association Law & Policy [a publication of American Society of Association Executives]
Type: Newsletter; *Frequency:* Monthly
• Associations Now [a publication of American Society of Association Executives]
Type: Magazine; *Frequency:* Monthly
• Communication News [a publication of American Society of Association Executives]
Type: Newsletter; *Frequency:* s-m.
• Component Relations [a publication of American Society of Association Executives]
Type: Newsletter; *Frequency:* s-m.
• Consultants Connection [a publication of American Society of Association Executives]
Type: Newsletter; *Frequency:* q.
• Dollars & Cents [a publication of American Society of Association Executives]
Type: Newsletter; *Frequency:* s-m.
• Executive IdeaLink [a publication of American Society of Association Executives]
Type: Newsletter; *Frequency:* s-m.
• Global Link [a publication of American Society of Association Executives]
Type: Newsletter; *Frequency:* s-m.
• Government Relations [a publication of American Society of Association Executives]
Type: Newsletter; *Frequency:* s-m.
• Marketing Insights [a publication of American Society of Association Executives]
Type: Newsletter; *Frequency:* s-m.
• Meetings & Expositions [a publication of American Society of Association Executives]
Type: Newsletter; *Frequency:* s-m.
• Membership Developments [a publication of American Society of Association Executives]
Type: Newsletter; *Frequency:* q.
• Professional Development Forum Online [a publication of American Society of Association Executives]
Type: Newsletter; *Frequency:* q.
• TechnoScope [a publication of American Society of Association Executives]
Type: Newsletter; *Frequency:* s-m.

American Society of Colon & Rectal Surgeons
#550, 85 West Algonquin Rd., Arlington Heights IL 60005 USA
Tel: 847-290-9184; *Fax:* 847-290-9203
ascrs@fascrs.org
www.fascrs.org
Overview: A medium-sized international organization
Mission: To advance the science & practice of the treatment of patients with diseases & disorders that affect the colon, rectum, & anus
Chief Officer(s):
James Fleshman, President
John Pemberton, Vice-President
Steven Wexner, Secretary
Alan G. Thorson, Treasurer
Membership: 2,600+; *Member Profile:* Colon & rectal surgeons & other professionals; *Committees:* Awards; Bylaws; Continuing Education; Credentials; CREST; Finance & Management; Fundraising Steering; History of ASCRS; Hospitality; Local Arrangements; Maintenance of Certification; Membership; Planned Giving; Professional Outreach; Program; Public Relations; Quality Assessment & Safety; Regional Society; Residents; Self Assessment; Socioeconomic; Standards; Website; Young Surgeons
Activities: Assuring high quality research; Promoting education for the prevention & management of disorders of the colon, rectum, & anus
Meetings/Conferences:
• American Society of Colon & Rectal Surgeons 2015 Annual Meeting, May, 2015, Hynes Convention Center & Sheraton Boston Hotel, Boston, MA
Scope: International
Attendance: 1,500+
Description: Courses, workshops, symposia, lectures, & scientific sessions for surgeons
Contact Information: Director, Exhibits: Jean Foellmer, jeanfoellmer@fascrs.org
Publications:
• ASCRS [American Society of Colon & Rectal Surgeons] News
Type: Newsletter; *Frequency:* Semiannually
Profile: Information from the society of interest to its members

American Society of Echocardiography (ASE)
#310, 2100 Gateway Centre Blvd., Morrisville NC 27560 USA
Tel: 919-861-5574; *Fax:* 919-882-9900
ase@asecho.org
www.asecho.org
www.linkedin.com/groups/American-Society-Echocardiography-55219
www.facebook.com/asecho
twitter.com/ase360
www.youtube.com/user/AmericanSocietyofEch
Overview: A medium-sized international organization founded in 1975
Mission: To promote excellence in cardiovascular ultrasound & its application to patient care
Chief Officer(s):
Benjamin Byrd, President
president@asecho.org
Robin L. Wiegerink, Chief Executive Officer
rwiegerink@asecho.org
Membership: 16,000+; *Fees:* Schedule available; *Member Profile:* Heart & circulation ultrasound specialists, such as physicians, scientists, lab managers, sonographers & retirees who live in the United States, Canada, & Mexico; International specialists; Medical & sonogrpahy students; *Committees:* Advocacy; Awards; CME; Bylaws & Ethics; Education; FASE; Finance, Strategy & Development; Guidelines and Standards; Industry Relations; Information Technology; Management/Executive; Membership Steering; Nominating; Research; Research Awards; Scientific Sessions Program
Activities: Providing education; Engaging in advocacy activities; Encouraging research

American Society of Heating, Refrigerating & Air Conditioning Engineers (ASHRAE)
1791 Tullie Circle NE, Atlanta GA 30329 USA
Tel: 404-636-8400; *Fax:* 404-321-5478
Toll-Free: 800-527-4723
ashrae@ashrae.org
www.ashrae.org
www.facebook.com/106136469528

twitter.com/ashraenews
www.youtube.com/user/ASHRAEvideo
Overview: A medium-sized international organization founded in 1894
Mission: To advance heating, ventilation, air conditioning & refrigeration; To promote a sustainable environment through research, standards writing, publishing & continuing education.
Chief Officer(s):
William Bahnfleth, President
Jeff H. Littleton, Executive Vice President
Staff Member(s): 32
Membership: 54,000; *Fees:* $196 Regular/Student/Associate; $52 Affiliate; *Committees:* Advocacy; Finance; Nominating; Planning; Society Rules; Membership Promotion; Research Promotion; Chapter Technology Transfer; Student Activities; Conferences & Expositions; Young Engineers in ASHRAE; Honors & Awards; Publishing & Education; Historical; Certification; Electronic Communications; Professional Development; Handbook; Publications; Research Administration; Environmental Health; Standards; Refrigeration; Technical Activities
Awards:
• ASHRAE Engineers Grant-in-Aid (Scholarship)
Graduate level studies in the areas of heating, cooling, refrigeration, air conditioning, energy conservation, air quality*Deadline:* February *Amount:* $6,000 US; 12 awards available *Contact:* Manager of Research, ASHRAE
Meetings/Conferences:
• 15th Annual International Conference for Enhanced Building Operations (ICEBO), 2015
Scope: International
Description: A global forum providing technology transfer, best practices, education and excellent networking opportunities for those who insist upon using the latest innovative solutions to enhance operations and maximize the efficiency and productivity of their buildings.
Contact Information: Alissa Simpson, Conference Manager; alissasimpson@tees.tamus.edu; Website: icebo.tamu.edu
Publications:
• ASHRAE [American Society of Heating, Refrigerating & Air Conditioning Engineers] Journal
Type: Journal; *Frequency:* Monthly

British Columbia Chapter
#111, 3790 Canada Way, Burnaby BC V5C 4S2
ashrae.bc.ca/bc
Chief Officer(s):
Kim Rosval, President
krosval@modern-systems.com

Chapitre de Québec Chapter
CP 8652, Succ. Ste-Foy, Québec QC G1V 4N6
info@ashraequebec.org
www.ashraequebec.org
Chief Officer(s):
Alexis T. Gagnon, Président
atg@evap-techmtc.com

Chapitre Montréal Chapter
CP 81, Boucherville QC J4B 5E6
Tél: 450-449-3667
info@ashrae-mtl.org
www.ashraemontreal.org
Chief Officer(s):
Anthony Jonkov, Président, 514-783-9865 Ext. 2232, Fax: 514-783-9614
president@ashrae-mtl.org

Halifax Chapter
Halifax NS
ASHRAE.Halifax@gmail.com
sites.google.com/site/ashraehalifax/
Chief Officer(s):
Darrell Amirault, President

Hamilton Chapter
Hamilton ON
www.vaxxine.com/ashrae
Chief Officer(s):
Reaz Usmanali, President
reaz.usmanali@jci.com

London Chapter
London ON
londoncanada.ashraechapters.org
Chief Officer(s):
Jamie Kruspel, President, 519-200-2197
jamie.kruspel@td.com

Manitoba Chapter
MB
ashrae.mb@gmail.com
www.ashraemanitoba.ca
Chief Officer(s):
Stephen Norsworthy, President, 204-786-8080
stephen.norsworthy@snclavalin.com

New Brunswick/PEI Chapter
PO Box 1629, Moncton NB E1C 9X4
www.ashraenbpei.com
twitter.com/AshraeNBPEI
Chief Officer(s):
Camille Chevarie, President, 506-857-8708

Northern Alberta Chapter
PO Box 42066, Stn. Milbourne, Edmonton AB T6K 4C4
ashraenac.org
Chief Officer(s):
Tom Jacknisky, President, 780-452-1800
president@ashraenac.org

Ottawa Valley Chapter
PO Box 21088, 1166 Bank St., Ottawa ON K1S 5N1
contact@ashrae.ottawa.on.ca
www.ashrae.ottawa.on.ca
Chief Officer(s):
Roderic Potter, President
rod@rodders.com

Regina Chapter
PO Box 3958, 2200 Saskatchewan Dr., Regina SK S4P 0B5
regina.ashraechapters.org
Chief Officer(s):
Alana Yip, President
alana.yip@sasktel.net

Saskatoon Chapter
Saskatoon SK
Tel: 306-477-0678
reply@ashraesaskatoon.ca
www.ashraesaskatoon.ca
www.facebook.com/ashraesaskatoon
Chief Officer(s):
Blake Erb, President, 306-242-3663

Southern Alberta Chapter
PO Box 76006, Calgary AB T2Y 2Z9
chapter.administrator@sac-ashrae.com
www.sac-ashrae.com
Chief Officer(s):
Brad Bond, President
president@sac-ashrae.com

Toronto Chapter
#201, 2800 Skymark Ave., Mississauga ON L4W 5A6
Tel: 905-602-4714
www.torontoashrae.com
www.linkedin.com/groups/ASHRAE-Toronto-Chapter-2792724
www.facebook.com/pages/Toronto_ASHRAE/284670984877500
twitter.com/torontoashrae
Chief Officer(s):
David Benedetti, President
dbenedetti@deltacontrols.com
Sabrina Tai, Contact
stai@hrai.ca

Vancouver Island Chapter
BC
Tel: 250-478-8885; *Fax:* 250-478-8827
www.ashrae.bc.ca/vi
Chief Officer(s):
Mark Stitt, President

Windsor Chapter
Windsor ON
windsor.ashraechapters.org
Chief Officer(s):
Mason Hoppe, President, 519-966-1550
Dan Castellan, Contact, 519-253-3000 Ext. 2164, Fax: 519-561-1404
danc@uwindsor.ca

American Society of International Law (ASIL)
2223 Massachussetts Ave. NW, Washington DC 20008 USA
Tel: 202-939-6000; *Fax:* 202-797-7133
services@asil.org
www.asil.org
www.facebook.com/AmericanSocietyofInternationalLaw
twitter.com/asilorg
www.youtube.com/asil1906
Overview: A medium-sized international organization founded in 1906 overseen by American Council of Learned Societies
Affiliation(s): International Law Students' Association (same address)
Chief Officer(s):
Elizabeth Andersen, Exec. Vice-President & Exec. Dir.
eandersen@asil.org
Finances: *Annual Operating Budget:* $1.5 Million-$3 Million; *Funding Sources:* Membership dues; publications; grants
Staff Member(s): 18
Membership: 4,000 individual; *Fees:* Schedule available; *Member Profile:* Scholars; practitioners; government officials; international civil servants; students; *Committees:* Interest Groups: Africa; Antartic Law; Dispute Resolution; Human Rights; Intellectual Property Law; International Criminal Law; International Economic Law; International Environmental Law; International Health Law; International Law in Domestic Courts; International Legal Theory; International Organizations; International Security; International Space Law; International Tax Law; Law in the Pacific Rim Region; Lieber Society on the Law of Armed Conflict; New Professionals; Private International Law; Rights of Indigenous People; Status of Minorities & Other Communities; Teaching International La
Activities: *Rents Mailing List:* Yes *Library*

American Society of Lubrication Engineers *See* Society of Tribologists & Lubrication Engineers

American Society of Mechanical Engineers (ASME)
3 Park Ave., New York NY 10016-5990 USA
Tel: 800-843-2763*Tel:* 973-882-1170
customercare@asme.org
www.asme.org
www.facebook.com/ASME.org
twitter.com/ASMEmembership
Overview: A large international organization founded in 1880
Mission: To promote the art, science, & practice of multidisciplinary engineering; To focus on the technical, educational, & research issues of the engineering & technology community; To help the engineering community develop solutions to improve the quality of life
Chief Officer(s):
Thomas G. Loughlin, Executive Director
execdirector@asme.org
Marc Goldsmith, President
marc@mgallc.net
Warren DeVries, Secretary-Treasurer
wdevries@umbc.edu
David Soukup, Managing Director, Governance, 212-591-7397
soukupd@asme.org
Finances: *Funding Sources:* Publications; Meetings; Standards accreditation
Membership: 120,000+ in 150+ countries; *Fees:* Schedule available; *Member Profile:* Students; Engineers; Technical professionals; Researchers; Project managers; Academic leaders; Corporate executives; *Committees:* Finance & Investment; Honors; Organization & Rules; Past Presidents; Governance & Strategy; Executive Director Evaluation & Staff Compensation
Activities: Promoting multidisciplinary engineering & allied science throughout the world; Engaging in research; Liaising with government; Enabling knowledge sharing; Offering continuing education & professional development in mechanical engineering; Maintaining codes & standards; Promoting the technical competency of members; Offering a mentoring program; *Library:* American Society of Mechanical Engineers e-Library
Awards:
• Service Awards (Award)
• Achievement Awards (Award)
• Literature Awards (Award)
• Unit Awards (Award)
• ASME Fellow (Award)
• ASME Scholarships (Scholarship)
Meetings/Conferences:
• American Society of Mechanical Engineers 2015 International Mechanical Engineering Congress & Exposition, November, 2015, Hilton of the Americas and George R. Brown Convention Center, Houston, TX
Scope: International
Contact Information: Jimmy Le, Phone: 212-591-7116; Fax: 212-591-7856; LeJ2@asme.org
• American Society of Mechanical Engineers 2016 International Mechanical Engineering Congress & Exposition, November, 2016, Phoenix Convention Center, Phoenix, AZ
Scope: International
Contact Information: Jimmy Le, Phone: 212-591-7116; Fax: 212-591-7856; LeJ2@asme.org

• American Society of Mechanical Engineers 2017 International Mechanical Engineering Congress & Exposition, November, 2017
Scope: International
Publications:
• Applied Mechanics Reviews
Type: Journal; *Frequency:* Bimonthly; *Editor:* Harry Dankowicz
ISSN: 0003-6900
Profile: An international review journal featuring topics such as heat transfer, vibration, & dynamics
• ASME [American Society of Mechanical Engineers] Capitol Update
Type: Newsletter; *Frequency:* Weekly
Profile: Legislative & regulatory news of interest to the engineering community
• History & Heritage Newsletter [a publication of the American Society of Mechanical Engineers]
Type: Newsletter; *Frequency:* Semiannually
Profile: Notable accomplishments in mechanical engineering history
• Journal of Applied Mechanics
Type: Journal; *Frequency:* Bimonthly; *Editor:* Yonggang Huang
ISSN: 0021-8936
Profile: Peer-reviewed research papers covering subjects such as wave propagation, turbulence, stress analysis, structures, hydraulics, & flow & fracture
• Journal of Biomechanical Engineering
Type: Journal; *Frequency:* Monthly; *Editor:* Beth Winkelstein
ISSN: 0148-0731
Profile: Research papers on topics such as cellular mechanics, the design & control of biological systems, bioheat transfer, biomaterials, & biomechanics
• Journal of Computational & Nonlinear Dynamics
Type: Journal; *Frequency:* Quarterly; *Editor:* Ahmed A. Shabana, Ph.D. *ISSN:* 1555-1415
Profile: Technical briefs & research papers cover bio-mechanical dynamics, design & design optimization dynamical analysis & method, vehicular dynamics,stability, & aerospace applications
• Journal of Computing & Information Science in Engineering
Type: Journal; *Frequency:* Quarterly; *Editor:* Bahram Ravani
ISSN: 1530-9827
Profile: Research papers & technical briefs about virtual environments & haptics, tolerance mondeling & computational metrology, reverse engineering,& internet-aided design, manufacturing, & commerce
• Journal of Dynamic Systems, Measurement, & Control
Type: Journal; *Frequency:* Bimonthly; *Editor:* Karl Hedrick *ISSN:* 0022-0434
Profile: Articles on design innovation, research papers, & technical briefs address aerospace systems, energy systems & control, manufacturing technology,power systems, production systems, signal processing, & transportation
• Journal of Electronic Packaging
Type: Journal; *Frequency:* Quarterly; *Editor:* Bahgat Sammakia
ISSN: 1043-7398
Profile: Papers to address mechanical, materials, & reliability problems encountered in the design, manufacturing, & operation of electronic, optoelectronic, & photonicsystems
• Journal of Energy Resources Technology
Type: Journal; *Frequency:* Quarterly; *Editor:* Hameed Metghalchi
ISSN: 0195-0738
Profile: Research on topics such as extraction of energy from natural resources, enerty resource recovery from biomass & solid wastes, technology for energygenerations, offshore & deepwater mechanics, petroleum engineering, natural gas technology, & rock & material mechanics for energy resources
• Journal of Engineering for Gas Turbines & Power
Type: Journal; *Frequency:* Monthly; *Editor:* Dilip R. Ballal *ISSN:* 0742-4795
Profile: Technical briefs & research examine nuclear engineering, coal, biomass & alternative fuels, energy production & conversion, & oil & gasapplications
• Journal of Engineering Materials & Technology
Type: Journal; *Frequency:* Quarterly; *Editor:* Hussein M. Zbib
ISSN: 0094-4289
Profile: Topics include environmental effects, fatigue, fracture, high temperature creep, & phase transformations in materials
• Journal of Fluids Engineering
Type: Journal; *Frequency:* Monthly; *Editor:* Malcolm J. Andrews
ISSN: 0098-2202
Profile: Contents include cavitation erosion, flow in biolgical systems, fluid transients & wave motion, naval hydrodynamics, pumps, pipelines, turbines, propulsion systems,& water hammers
• Journal of Fuel Cell Science & Technology
Type: Journal; *Frequency:* Bimonthly; *Editor:* Nigel M. Sammes
ISSN: 1550-624X
Profile: Subjects include durability & damage tolerance, aging, system design & manufacturing, & fuel cell applications
• Journal of Heat Transfer
Type: Journal; *Frequency:* Monthly; *Editor:* Terrence W. Simon
ISSN: 0022-1481
Profile: Featuring research on environmental issues, low temperature & the Arctic, aircraft, & energy technology & systems
• Journal of Manufacturing Science & Engineering
Type: Journal; *Frequency:* Bimonthly; *Editor:* Y. Lawrence Yao
ISSN: 1087-1357
Profile: Subjects include rail transportation, inspection & quality control, material removal by machining, production systems optimization, textileproduction, & sensors
• Journal of Mechanical Design
Type: Journal; *Frequency:* Monthly; *Editor:* Panos Y. Papalambros *ISSN:* 1050-0472
Profile: Technical briefs & research papers address design theory & methodology, design automation, & design of direct contact systems
• Journal of Mechanisms & Robotics
Type: Journal; *Frequency:* Quarterly; *Editor:* J. Michael McCarthys *ISSN:* 1942-4302
Profile: Research covers the theory, algorithms, & applications for robotic & machine systems
• Journal of Medical Devices
Type: Journal; *Frequency:* Quarterly; *Editor:* Arthur G. Erdman; Gerald E. Miller *ISSN:* 1932-6181
Profile: Design innovation articles & research papers focus upon new medical devices or instrumentation that improve diagnostic interventional & therapeutictreatments
• Journal of Micro & Nano Manufacturing
Type: Journal
• Journal of Microelectromechanical Systems (MEMS)
Type: Journal; *Frequency:* 6 pa.; *Editor:* William Trimmer
• Journal of Nanotechnology in Engineering & Medicine
Type: Journal; *Frequency:* Quarterly; *Editor:* Vijay K. Varadan
ISSN: 1949-2944
Profile: The impact of nanotechnology upon medicine & the direction of research & development
• Journal of Offshore Mechanics & Arctic Engineering
Type: Journal; *Frequency:* Quarterly; *Editor:* Solomon C. Yim
ISSN: 0892-7219
Profile: Articles highlight Arctic exploration & drilling, permafrost engineering & Arctic thermal design, offshore structures, ice structure interaction, &marine geotechnique
• Journal of Pressure Vessel Technology
Type: Journal; *Frequency:* Bimonthly; *Editor:* G. E. Otto Widera
ISSN: 0094-9930
Profile: Technology reviews & research papers cover codes & standards, pressure vessel & piping, fatigue & fracture prediction, elevated temperature analysis &design, lifeline earthquake engineering, & safety & reliability
• Journal of Solar Energy Engineering
Type: Journal; *Frequency:* Quarterly; *Editor:* Gilles Flamant
ISSN: 0199-6231
Profile: Research papers & technical information about solar collectors, solar optics, solar chemistry & bioconversion, solar thermal power, energy storage, conservation,solar buildings, solar space applications, wind energy, emerging technologies, & energy policy
• Journal of Thermal Science & Engineering Applications
Type: Journal; *Frequency:* Quarterly; *Editor:* Michael Jensen
ISSN: 1948-5085
Profile: Subjects addressed include applications in areas such as defense systems, aerospace systems, energy systems, refrigeration & air conditioning,petrochemical processing, combustion systems, & medical systems
• Journal of Tribology
Type: Journal; *Frequency:* Quarterly; *Editor:* Michael Khonsari
ISSN: 0742-4787
Profile: Technical information & research cover tribological systems, bearing design & technology, gears, seals, & friction & wear
• Journal of Turbomachinery
Type: Journal; *Frequency:* Quarterly; *Editor:* David C. Wisler
ISSN: 0889-504X
Profile: Research papers examine fluid dynamics & heat transfer phenomena in compressor & turbine components
• Journal of Vibration & Acoustics
Type: Journal; *Frequency:* Bimonthly; *Editor:* Noel C. Perkins
ISSN: 1048-9002
Profile: Subjects include areas such as machinery dynamics & noise, structural acoustics, acoustic emission, noise control, & vibration suppression
• ME Today [a publication of the American Society of Mechanical Engineers]
Type: Newsletter; *Frequency:* Quarterly
Profile: Information of interest to early career engineers
• Mechanical Engineering [a publication of the American Society Of Mechanical Engineers]
Type: Magazine; *Frequency:* Monthly; *Editor:* John G. Falconi
Profile: Engineering trends & breakthroughs
• Member Savvy [a publication of the American Society of Mechanical Engineers]
Type: Newsletter; *Frequency:* Monthly
Profile: The benefits of membership in the American Society of Mechanical Engineer
• Standards & Certification Update [a publication of the American Society of Mechanical Engineers]
Type: Newsletter; *Frequency:* Quarterly
Profile: Information about American Society of Mechanical Engineers standards & certification activities, including newpublications, professional development, & conformity assessment

American Society of Mining & Reclamation (ASMR)

3134 Montavesta Rd., Lexington KY 40502-3548 USA
Tel: 859-351-9032; *Fax:* 859-335-6529
ces.ca.uky.edu/asmr
Overview: A medium-sized international charitable organization founded in 1983
Mission: To encourage any agency, institution, organization, or individual in their efforts to protect, re-establish or enhance the surface resources of land disturbances associated with mineral extraction; to promote, support & assist in research & studies; to encourage communication between the research scientist, regulatory agencies, organizations & others who seek assistance; to promote & support related educational programs
Affliation(s): International Affiliation of Land Reclamationists
Chief Officer(s):
Bruce Buchanan, President
Finances: *Annual Operating Budget:* $50,000-$100,000;
Funding Sources: Membership dues
Staff Member(s): 1; 1 volunteer(s)
Membership: 400; *Fees:* $100 sustaining; $50 regular; $10-25 student; *Member Profile:* Sustaining - agency, department, organization, corporation, or individual representation; regular - individual representation; student - full-time students at accredited colleges; *Committees:* Publication Policy & Review Board; Awards; National Meeting; Membership; Memorial Scholarship Fund; National Register of Research & Demonstration
Activities: Small independent professional groups affiliated with the Society have been organized to concentrate on a particular aspect of surface mining or reclamation: International Tailings Reclamation, Landscape Architecture, Soil & Overburden, Ecology, Geotechnical Engineering, Meter Management, Forestry & Wildlife
Awards:
• Reclamation Researcher of the Year (Award)
Awarded to research scientists who have made substantive contributions to the advancement of reclamation science &/or technology, or contributed meaningful information relating to the economic, social, environmental or ecological effects of surface mining
• William T. Plass Award (Award)
Awarded irregularly; recognizes outstanding contributions in the areas of mining, teaching, research, &/or regulating authority as they relate to land reclamation. Those nominated should be recognized nationally & internationally for their contibutions covering a significant portion of their career
• Reclamationist of the Year (Award)
Awarded to individuals demonstrating outstanding accomplishments in the practical application or evaluation of reclamation technology

American Society of Neuroradiology (ASNR)

#207, 2210 Midwest Rd., Oak Brook IL 60523 USA
Tel: 630-574-0220; *Fax:* 630-574-0661
jgantenberg@asnr.org
www.asnr.org
Overview: A medium-sized international organization
Mission: To develop standards for the training & practice of neuroradiologists; To promote understanding of neuroradiology among patients & other professionals & public agencies
Chief Officer(s):
James B. Gantenberg, Executive Director & CEO

Angelo Artemakis, Director, Communications & Media Management
aartemakis@asnr.org
Ken Cammarata, Director, Specialty Societies & Member Services
kcammarata@asnr.org
Margaret Klys, Director, Clinical Practice Services
mklys@asnr.org
Membership: *Member Profile:* Radiologists certified by the Royal College of Physicians & Surgeons of Canada, the American Board of Radiology, the American Osteopathic College of Radiology, or other boards or tribunals; Neuroradiologists, radiologists, or physicians with an interest in neuroradiology; Physicists (PhD) or neuroscientists (MS, PhD) with an interest in or position relevant to neuroradiology or radiology; Member in training
Activities: Fostering research in neuroradiology; Promoting an exchange of ideas among neuroradiologists; Disseminating knowledge; Cooperating with other branches of medicine & allied sciences
Meetings/Conferences:
• American Society of Neuroradiology 2015 53rd Annual Meeting, April, 2015, Sheraton Chicago Hotel & Towers, Chicago, IL
Scope: International
Contact Information: Director, Scientific Meetings: Lora Tannehill, E-mail: ltannehill@asnr.org; Manager, Scientific Meetings: Valerie Geisendorfer, E-mail: vgeisendorfer@asnr.org
• American Society of Neuroradiology 2016 54th Annual Meeting, May, 2016, Washington Marriott Wardman Park, Washington, DC
Scope: International
Contact Information: Director, Scientific Meetings: Lora Tannehill, E-mail: ltannehill@asnr.org; Manager, Scientific Meetings: Valerie Geisendorfer, E-mail: vgeisendorfer@asnr.org
• American Society of Neuroradiology 2017 55th Annual Meeting, April, 2017, Long Beach Convention & Entertainment Center, Long Beach, CA
Scope: International
Contact Information: Director, Scientific Meetings: Lora Tannehill, E-mail: ltannehill@asnr.org; Manager, Scientific Meetings: Valerie Geisendorfer, E-mail: vgeisendorfer@asnr.org
• American Society of Neuroradiology 2018 56th Annual Meeting, May, 2018, Vancouver Convention Centre, Vancouver, BC
Scope: International
Contact Information: Director, Scientific Meetings: Lora Tannehill, E-mail: ltannehill@asnr.org; Manager, Scientific Meetings: Valerie Geisendorfer, E-mail: vgeisendorfer@asnr.org
• American Society of Neuroradiology 2019 57th Annual Meeting, May, 2019, Hynes Convention Center, Boston, MA
Scope: International
Contact Information: Director, Scientific Meetings: Lora Tannehill, E-mail: ltannehill@asnr.org; Manager, Scientific Meetings: Valerie Geisendorfer, E-mail: vgeisendorfer@asnr.org
• American Society of Neuroradiology 2020 58th Annual Meeting, 2020
Scope: International
Contact Information: Director, Scientific Meetings: Lora Tannehill, E-mail: ltannehill@asnr.org; Manager, Scientific Meetings: Valerie Geisendorfer, E-mail: vgeisendorfer@asnr.org
Publications:
• American Journal of Neuroradiology
Type: Journal; *Frequency:* 10 pa; *Number of Pages:* 200
Profile: Peer-reviewed original research papers, review articles, & technical notes

American Society of Pediatric Hematology / Oncology (ASPHO)
#300, 8735 West Higgins Rd., Chicago IL 60631 USA
Tel: 847-375-4716; *Fax:* 847-375-6483
info@aspho.org
www.aspho.org
Overview: A medium-sized international organization founded in 1974
Mission: To promote optimal care of children & adolescents with blood disorders & cancer; To advance research, education, treatment, & professional practice
Chief Officer(s):
A. Kim Ritchey, President
Cynthia Porter, Executive Director
cporter@aspho.org
Staff Member(s): 14
Membership: 1,800; *Fees:* Schedule available; *Committees:* Advocacy; Certification & Continuing Education; Clinical Practice Guidelines; Communications; Finance; Joint ASPHO-SIOP Journal; Membership; Nominating; Practice; Professional Development; Program; Review Course; Training Directors Steering
Activities: Providing a forum for the exchange of ideas; Offering professional development opportunities
Publications:
• Pediatric Blood & Cancer
Type: Journal; *Frequency:* Monthly; *Editor:* Robert J. Arceci, MD PhD
Profile: Official journal of the American Society of Pediatric Hematology / Oncology & the International Society of Pediatric Oncology

American Society of Piano Technicians *See* Piano Technicians Guild Inc.

American Society of Plant Biologists (ASPB)
15501 Monona Dr., Rockville MD 20855-2768 USA
Tel: 301-251-0560; *Fax:* 301-279-2996
info@aspb.org
www.aspb.org
Overview: A medium-sized international organization founded in 1924
Mission: To advance the plant sciences; To promote the development & outreach of plant biology as a pure & applied science
Chief Officer(s):
Crispin Taylor, Executive Director
ctaylor@aspb.org
Staff Member(s): 24
Membership: 5,000; *Fees:* $140 regular; $70 postdoctoral; $45 graduate student; $35 undergraduate member; *Member Profile:* Plant biology researchers, educators, & students from any nation; Any person concerned with the physiology, molecular biology, environmental biology, cell biology, & biophysics of plants; *Committees:* Awards; Constitution & Bylaws; Education; Executive; International; Membership; Minority Affairs; Nominating; Operations Subcommittee; Program; Publications; Women in Plant Biology
Publications:
• ASPB [American Society of Plant Biologists] News
Type: Newsletter; *Frequency:* Bimonthly; *Price:* Free for American Society Of Plant Biologists members; $30 non-members
• The Plant Cell
Type: Journal; *Frequency:* Monthly; *Accepts Advertising*; *Editor:* John Long *ISSN:* 1040-4651
Profile: Primary research in the plant sciences
• Plant Physiology
Type: Journal; *Frequency:* Monthly; *Accepts Advertising*; *Editor:* John Long *ISSN:* 0032-0889
Profile: Physiology, biochemistry, cellular & molecular biology, genetics, biophysics, & environmental biology of plants

American Society of Plastic Surgeons (ASPS)
444 East Algonquin Rd., Arlington Heights IL 60005 USA
Tel: 847-228-9900
media@plasticsurgery.org
www.plasticsurgery.org
www.facebook.com/PlasticSurgeryASPS
twitter.com/ASPS_News
Overview: A medium-sized international organization founded in 1931
Mission: To advance quality care to plastic surgery patients; To promote high standards of training, professionalism, ethics, physician practice, & research
Affliation(s): Plastic Surgery Educational Foundation (PSEF)
Chief Officer(s):
Robert X. Murphy, President
Michael D. Costelloe, Executive Vice-President
Karen Craven, Vice-President, Communications & External Affairs
Finances: *Annual Operating Budget:* Less than $50,000
Membership: 7,000+; *Fees:* Schedule available; *Member Profile:* Plastic surgeons, certified by the Royal College of Physicians & Surgeons of Canada or the American Board of Plastic Surgery, who perform cosmetic & reconstructive surgery
Activities: Advocating for patient safety; Providing public education about plastic surgery; Publishing informational brochures
Publications:
• Plastic & Reconstructive Surgery: Journal of the American Society of Plastic Surgeons
Type: Journal; *Frequency:* Monthly; *Editor:* Rod J. Rohrich, M.D. *ISSN:* 0032-1052

American Society of Plumbing Engineers (ASPE)
2980 River Rd. South, Des Plaines IL 60018 USA
Tel: 847-296-0002; *Fax:* 847-296-2963
info@aspe.org
www.aspe.org
Overview: A medium-sized international organization founded in 1964
Chief Officer(s):
Jim Kendzel, Executive Director Ext. 222
jkendzel@aspe.org
Membership: 6,500

British Columbia Chapter
PO Box 2201, Vancouver BC V6B 3W2
sites.google.com/site/aspebcchapter
Chief Officer(s):
Happy Wong, President
hwong@fwdeng.ca

Chapitre de Montréal
CP 20024, 8610, Boul St-Laurent, MontréAl QC H2P 3A4
Tél: 514-237-6559; *Téléc:* 514-383-8760
montreal.aspe.org
Chief Officer(s):
Patrick Lavoie, Président, 514-735-5651
patricklavoie@snclavallin.com

Québec
PO Box 56071, Stn. Père-LelièVre, Québec QC G1P 4P7
www.aspequebec.com
Chief Officer(s):
Dave Morin, Président, 418-654-9600
dave.morin@roche.ca

American Society of Regional Anesthesia & Pain Medicine (ASRA)
#1714, 239 - 4 Ave., Pittsburgh PA 15222 USA
Tel: 412-471-2718
Toll-Free: 855-795-2772
asraassistant@kenes.com
www.asra.com
www.linkedin.com/groups?gid=4797719
www.facebook.com/228281927234196
twitter.com/asra_society
Overview: A medium-sized international organization founded in 1923
Mission: To assure excellence in patient care utilizing regional anesthesia & pain medicine; To investigate the scientific basis of the specialty
Chief Officer(s):
Joseph M. Neal, President
Angie Stengel, Executive Secretary
astengel@kenes.com
Membership: 4,000; *Fees:* Schedule available; *Member Profile:* Physicians; Scientists; *Committees:* Audit; Finance; Communications; Continuing Medical Education; Membership; Newsletter; Research; Scientific Educational Planning; Resident Section
Activities: Providing professional development activities
Publications:
• ASRA [American Society of Regional Anesthesia & Pain Medicine] News
Type: Newsletter; *Frequency:* Quarterly; *Editor:* Colin McCartney, M.B., F.R.C.A.
Profile: Society news, articles, & meeting reviews
• ASRA [American Society of Regional Anesthesia & Pain Medicine] E-News
Type: Newsletter
Profile: Society announcements, including information about meetings, workshops, awards
• Regional Anesthesia & Pain Medicine
Type: Journal; *Frequency:* Bimonthly; *Editor:* Joseph M. Neal, M.D.
Profile: Peer-reviewed scientific & clinical studies

American Society of Safety Engineers (ASSE)
1800 East Oakton St., Des Plaines IL 60018-2187 USA
Tel: 847-699-2929; *Fax:* 847-768-3434
customerservice@asse.org
www.asse.org
www.facebook.com/ASSESafety
www.twitter.com/asse_safety
Overview: A large international organization founded in 1911
Mission: To promote the advancement of the safety profession & to foster the technical, scientific, managerial & ethical knowledge, skills & competency of safety professionals
Affliation(s): Canadian Society of Safety Engineering, Inc.
Chief Officer(s):

Fred J. Fortman, Executive Director
Staff Member(s): 60
Membership: 30,000; *Fees:* Regular: $160; Student: $135
Activities: Providing a Professional Development Conference & Exposition; Offering continuing education & training seminars; Presenting technical publications & audio-visual training courses; *Awareness Events:* National Safety Week, June; *Rents Mailing List:* Yes
Awards:
• Fellow Honor (Award)
• Edgar Monsanto Queeny Safety Professional of the Year (Award)
• The ASSE Dr. William E. Tarrants Outstanding Safety Educator Award (Award)
• Charles v. Culbertson Outstanding Volunteer Service Award (Award)
• American Society of Safety Engineers President's Award (Award)
• Outstanding Student Section Award (Award)
• ASSE Chapter of the Year (Award)
• Practice Specialty Recognition Award (Award)
• Best Technical Publication Award (Award)
• Thomas F. Bresnahan Standards Medal (Award)
Publications:
• Profofessional Safety
Profile: Monthly journal

American Society of Travel Agents
#200, 1101 King St., Alexandria VA 22314 USA
Tel: 703-739-2782
askasta@asta.org
www.asta.org
Overview: A medium-sized national organization
Chief Officer(s):
Nina Meyer, Chair & President
nrmmeyer@gmail.com
Tony Gonchar, Chief Executive Officer
tgonchar@asta.org
John I. Lovell, Vice-President & Secretary
jlovell@bretontravel.com
Scott Pinheiro, Treasurer
scott@santacruztravel.com

American Sociological Association (ASA)
#600, 1430 K St., Washington DC 20005 USA
Tel: 202-383-9005; *Fax:* 202-638-0882; *TTY:* 202-638-0981
executive.office@asanet.org
www.asanet.org
www.facebook.com/AmericanSociologicalAssociation
twitter.com/ASANews
Overview: A medium-sized national organization founded in 1905
Mission: The non-profit association strives to advance sociology as a scientific discipline & profession serving the public good.
Member of: American Council of Learned Societies; Consortium of Social Science Associations
Affliation(s): International Sociological Association
Chief Officer(s):
Sally T. Hillsman, Executive Officer
Frank Olin Wright, President
Membership: 14,000; **Fees:** Schedule available; *Member Profile:* College & university faculty; researchers; students; practitioners; *Committees:* Awards; Committees; Executive Office & Budget; Nominations; Professional Ethics; Publications; Sections; Program; Status of Persons with Disabilities in Sociology; Status of Gay, Lesbian, Bisexual & Transgendered Persons in Sociology; Status of Racial & Ethnic Minorities in Sociology; Status of Women in Sociology; Book Award Selection; W.E.B. Bois Career of Distinguished Scholarship Award Selection; Dissertation Award Selection; Excellence in Reporting of Social Issues Selection; Cox-Johnson-Frazier Award; Practice of Sociology Award; Public Understanding of Sociology Award; Teaching Award
Activities: *Rents Mailing List:* Yes *Library* by appointment
Awards:
• Jessie Bernard Award (Award)
• Cox-Johnson-Frazier Award (Award)
• Excellence in the Reporting of Social Issues Award (Award)
• Distinguished Career Award for the Practice of Sociology (Award)
• Distinguished Contributions to Teaching Award (Award)
• Distinguished Book Award (Award)
• Dissertation Award (Award)
• Award for the Public Understanding of Sociology (Award)
• W.E.B. DuBois Career of Distinguished Scholarship Award (Award)
Meetings/Conferences:
• 2017 American Sociological Association Annual Meeting, August, 2017, Palais des congrès de Montréal, Montréal, QC
Scope: International
Publications:
• American Sociological Review
Type: Journal; *Frequency:* Bimonthly; *Accepts Advertising*; *Editor:* Randy Hodson; Vincent Roscigno *ISSN:* 0003-1224; *Price:* $40member; $25 student member; $220 institution
Profile: Original works of interest to the sociology discipline in general, new theoretical developments, results of research, & methodological innovations
• ASA Rose Series in Sociology
Profile: Specific substantive areas in sociology
• City & Community
Type: Journal; *Frequency:* Quarterly; *Accepts Advertising*; *Editor:* Anthony M. Orum *ISSN:* 1535-6841; *Price:* $41 member; $21 student member; $76 non-member; $301 institution
Profile: Journal of the ASA Section on Community & Urban Sociology with research & theory on topics such as community studies, immigration, rural communities, social networks, socialsupport, suburbia, spatial studies, studies that connect specific places to general forces, urban movements, & urban history
• Contemporary Sociology
Type: Journal; *Frequency:* Bimonthly; *Accepts Advertising*; *Editor:* Valerie Jenness; J. Stepan-Norris *ISSN:* 0094-3061; *Price:* $40 member; $25 student member;$220 institution
Profile: A journal of reviews & critical discussions of recent works in sociology& related disciplines of interest to sociologists
• Contexts
Type: Magazine; *Frequency:* Quarterly; *Accepts Advertising*; *Editor:* Jeff Goodwin; James M. Jasper *ISSN:* 1536-5042; *Price:* $40 member; $25 student member; $50 non-member; $176 non-member institution
Profile: Original essays
• Footnotes
Type: Newsletter; *Frequency:* 9 pa; *Accepts Advertising*; *Editor:* Sally T. Hillsman *ISSN:* 0749-6931; *Price:* Free with membership; $40 non-member
Profile: Feature stories, calls for papers, meeting calendar, funding opportunities, obituaries, & the ASA Official Reports and Proceedings
• Journal of Health & Social Behavior
Type: Journal; *Frequency:* Quarterly; *Accepts Advertising*; *Editor:* Peggy A. Thoits *ISSN:* 0022-1465; *Price:* $40 member; $25 student member; $185 institution
Profile: A medical sociology journal with empirical & theoretical articles that apply sociological concepts & methods to the understanding of health and illness & theorganization of medicine & health care
• Social Psychology Quarterly: The Journal of Microsociologies
Type: Journal; *Frequency:* Quarterly; *Accepts Advertising*; *Editor:* Gary Alan Fine *ISSN:* 0190-2725; *Price:* $40 member; $25 student member; $185 institution
Profile: Theoretical & empirical papers on the link between the individual & society
• Sociological Methodology
Frequency: Annually; *Accepts Advertising*; *Editor:* Yu Xie *ISSN:* 0081-1750; *Price:* $50 member; $40 student member; $256 institution
Profile: Methodological papers of interest to the field of sociology
• Sociological Theory
Type: Journal; *Frequency:* Quarterly; *Accepts Advertising*; *Editor:* J. Adam; J.C. Alexander, P. Gorski *ISSN:* 0735-2751; *Price:* $40 member; $25 student member; $262 institution
Profile: Articles about social thought, including new theories, history of theory, metatheory, formal theory construction, & syntheses of existing bodies of theory
• Sociology of Education
Type: Journal; *Frequency:* Quarterly; *Accepts Advertising*; *Editor:* Barbara Schneider *ISSN:* 0038-0407; *Price:* $40 member; $25 student member; $185 institution
Profile: Studies in the sociology of education & human social development
• Teaching Sociology
Type: Journal; *Frequency:* Quarterly; *Accepts Advertising*; *Editor:* Elizabeth Grauerholz *ISSN:* 0092-055X; *Price:* $40 member; $25 student member; $185 institution
Profile: Articles, notes, & reviews to assist sociology teachers

American Studies Association (ASA)
#301, 1120 - 19th St. NW, Washington DC 20036 USA
Tel: 202-467-4783; *Fax:* 202-467-4786
Toll-Free: 800-548-1748
asastaff@theasa.net
www.theasa.net
Overview: A large international charitable organization founded in 1951
Mission: To enable people of diverse interests to exchange ideas about American life; members approach American culture from many directions but have in common the desire to view America as a whole rather than from the perspective of a single discipline
Member of: American Council of Learned Societies
Affliation(s): Canadian Association for American Studies
Chief Officer(s):
John F. Stephens, Executive Director
Finances: *Annual Operating Budget:* $500,000-$1.5 Million
Staff Member(s): 2
Membership: 5,000 individual; *Fees:* $20-99, dependent upon income; *Member Profile:* Persons with an interdisciplinary interest in American culture; institutions sympathetic to the aims of the association; *Committees:* American Studies Programs; Electronic Projects; Publications; Secondary Education; International; Minority Scholars; Regional Chapters; Students; Women's; Prize; Annual Meeting; Local Arrangements
Activities: American Studies Curriculum Resources (ASCR) makes available course outlines & bibliographies ranging from introductory American Studies courses to graduate seminars on special topics; supports & assists programs for teaching American Studies abroad, encourages the exchange of teachers & students, & maintains informal relations with American Studies associations in 50 countries; *Rents Mailing List:* Yes
Awards:
• Mary C. Turpie Prize (Award), Annual Awards Program
For outstanding contribution to teaching, advising & program development
• John Hope Franklin Publication Prize (Award), Annual Awards Program
For the best published book in American Studies
• Ralph Henry Gabriel Dissertation Prize (Award), Annual Awards Program
For the best completed dissertation in American Studies
• Carl Bode-Norman Holmes Pearson Prize (Award), Annual Awards Program
For outstanding contribution to American Studies
• Wise-Susman Prize (Award), Annual Awards Program
For the best student paper presented at the annual meeting
• Lora Romero First Book Publication Prize (Award), Annual Awards Program
Publications:
• American Quarterly
Profile: Academic Journal

American Thyroid Association
#550, 6066 Leesburg Pike, Falls Church VA 22041 USA
thyroid@thyroid.org
www.thyroid.org
Overview: A medium-sized international organization founded in 1923
Mission: To promote health & understanding of thyroid biology; To encourage innovation in research on physiology, diseases, & thyroid molecular & cell biology; To guide public policies on the causes, diagnosis, & management of thyroid diseases & related disorders
Chief Officer(s):
Gregory A. Brent, President
Richard T. Kloos, Chief Operating Officer & Secretary
Barbara (Bobbi) R. Smith, Executive Director
bsmith@thyroid.org
Adonia C. Coates, Director, Meetings & Program Services
acoates@thyroid.org
Charles Emerson, Editor, Thyroid
thyroideditor@umassmed.edu
Ernest Mazzaferri, Editor, Clinical Thyroidology
editorclinthy@thyroid.org
Membership: 900; *Member Profile:* Internatioanal scientists & physicians who are engaged in researching & treating thyroid diseases; *Committees:* Awards; Patient Education & Advocacy; Bylaws; Clinical Affairs; Program; Ethics; Publications; Finance & Audit; History & Archives; Public Health; International Thyroid Congress (ITC) Coordinating Committee; Program Organizing; Public Relations; Internet Communications; Research; Lab Services; Surgical Affairs; Membership; Nominating; Trainees & Career Advancement
Activities: Promoting the prevention of thyroid disorders; Engaging in advocacy activities for thyroid specialists; Supporting education of scientists, physicians, & other health care professionals; Collaborating with other thyroid societies

Meetings/Conferences:
• American Thyroid Association 2015 85th Annual Meeting, October, 2015, Walt Disney Swan & Dolphin Resort, Orlando, FL
Scope: International
Attendance: 1,000+
Description: Held each autumn, the meeting includes platform presentations, lectures, symposia, discussion groups, posters, exhibits, & opportunities for networking
Publications:
• Clinical Thyroidology
Type: Journal; *Frequency:* 3 pa; *Editor:* Ernest Mazzaferri; *Price:* Free
Profile: A summary of & expert commentary on recently published clinical & preclinical thyroid literature from around the world
• Signal
Type: Newsletter; *Frequency:* 3 pa; *Editor:* Peter Kopp, M.D.
Profile: American Thyroid Association happenings, such as policies, leaders, & meetings, as well as thyroid-related issues
• Thyroid
Type: Journal; *Frequency:* Monthly; *Editor:* Charles Emerson; *Price:* Free with membership in the American thyroid association
Profile: A peer-reviewed journal, covering subjects such as the molecular biology of the thyroid gland & the clinical management of thyroid disorders

American Vegan Society (AVS)

PO Box 369, 56 Dinshah Lane, Malaga NJ 08328-0908 USA
Tel: 856-694-2887; *Fax:* 856-694-2288
www.americanvegan.org
Overview: A small international charitable organization founded in 1960
Mission: To advocate a diet without any animal products (no meat, fish, fowl, no animal broths, fat, or gelatin; no eggs, milk, cheese; no honey) on ethical & healthful grounds, & a lifestyle excluding use of animals products such as fur, leather, wool, or silk
Affliation(s): North American Vegetarian Society; Vegetarian Union of North America; International Vegetarian Union; The Vegan Society (England)
Membership: *Fees:* USD$20; USD$10 low income/student
Publications:
• American Vegan
Profile: Quarterly magazine

American Vintners Association *See* WineAmerica

American Water Resources Association (AWRA)

PO Box 1626, 4 Federal St. West, Middleburg VA 20118-1626 USA
Tel: 540-687-8390; *Fax:* 540-687-8395
info@awra.org
www.awra.org
www.linkedin.com/groups?gid=769747&trk=myg_ugrp_ovr
www.facebook.com/pages/American-Water-Resources-Association/1114740355
twitter.com/AWRAHQ
Overview: A large national organization founded in 1964
Mission: To advance research, planning, management, development & education in water resources; provides a focal point for the collection, organization & dissemination of ideas & information in the physical, biological, economic, social, political, legal & engineering aspects of water-related problems; to provide a forum for communication among disciplines with a common interest in water supply, quality, use, development & conservation
Chief Officer(s):
Kenneth D. Reid, Executive Vice President
ken@awra.org
Michael J. Kowalski, Director, Operations
mike@awra.org
Finances: *Annual Operating Budget:* $500,000-$1.5 Million
Staff Member(s): 8
Membership: 3,000 worldwide; *Fees:* Schedule available; *Member Profile:* Regular - persons interested in any aspect of water resources; student - full-time student engaged in study of any aspect of water resources at a college or university; institutional - universities, governmental agencies & institutions; corporate - consulting firms & business concerns
Activities: Technical Committees provide a focus for special interests; *Rents Mailing List:* Yes
Awards:
• Fellow Member Award (Award)
• Honorary Member Award (Award)
• Icko Iben Award (Award)
• Henry P. Caulfield, Jr., Medal (Award)
• Mary H. Marsh Medal (Award)
• Sandor C. Csallany Award (Award)
• William C. Ackermann Medal (Award)
• A. Ivan Johnson Award (Award)
• IWRM Award (Award)
• Outstanding State Section Award (Award)
• Outstanding Student Chapter Award (Award)
• Richard A. Herbert Memorial Scholarship (Scholarship)
Eligibility: AWRA member; full-time undergraduate student*Deadline:* April *Amount:* $2,000
Publications:
• JAWRA [Journal of the American Water Resources Association]
Type: Journal

American Water Works Association (AWWA)

6666 West Quincy Ave., Denver CO 80235 USA
Tel: 303-794-7711; *Fax:* 303-347-0804
Toll-Free: 800-926-7337
custsvc@awwa.org
www.awwa.org
www.linkedin.com/groups?gid=733277&trk=hb_side_g
www.facebook.com/AmericanWaterWorksAssociation
twitter.com/AWWAACE
www.youtube.com/user/AmericanWaterWorks
Overview: A large international organization founded in 1881
Mission: To advance public health & safety through the improvement of water quality & supply throughout North America & beyond; To provide standards for the design, manufacturing, installation, & performance of water industry products; To advance & protect the interests of the water industry
Chief Officer(s):
Charles F. Anderson, President
Dave E. Rager, Treasurer
David B. LaFrance, Executive Director
Susan Franceschi, Chief Membership Officer
Robert Huff, Chief Information Officer
Kevin Mann, Chief Financial Officer
April DeBaker, Director, Conferences & Events
adebaker@awwa.org
Liz Haigh, Director, Publishing
Jane Johnson, Director, Sales & Research
jjohnson@awwa.org
Cynthia Lane, Director, Engineering & Technical Services
rmartinez@awwa.org
Membership: 60,000+; *Fees:* Schedule available; *Member Profile:* Treatment plant operators & managers; Scientists; Environmentalists; Manufacturers; Academics; Regulators; Others interested in water supply & public health; *Committees:* 250 committees
Activities: Providing information about the water industry; *Library:* American Water Works Association Water Library
Meetings/Conferences:
• American Water Works Association 2015 134th Annual Conference & Exposition, June, 2015, Anaheim, CA
Scope: International
Description: An annual meeting providing technical sessions, an exhibit hall, & networking opportunities for water professionals
Contact Information: American Water Works Association, Phone: 800-926-7337, Fax: 303-347-0804, E-mail: awwamktg@awwa.org
• American Water Works Association 2016 135th Annual Conference & Exposition, June, 2016, Chicago, IL
Scope: International
Description: Offering a technical program, professional development activities, & exhibitors for the worldwide water community
Contact Information: American Water Works Association, Phone: 800-926-7337, Fax: 303-347-0804, E-mail: awwamktg@awwa.org
• American Water Works Association 2017 136th Annual Conference & Exposition, June, 2017, Philadelphia, PA
Scope: International
Description: A technical program & exhibits for association members & associated professionals
Contact Information: American Water Works Association, Phone: 800-926-7337, Fax: 303-347-0804, E-mail: awwamktg@awwa.org
• American Water Works Association 2018 137th Annual Conference & Exposition, June, 2018, Las Vegas, NV
Scope: International
Description: Technical programs, workshops, poster sessions, seminars, continuing education units, & exhibits for the international water community
Contact Information: American Water Works Association, Phone: 800-926-7337, Fax: 303-347-0804, E-mail: awwamktg@awwa.org
• American Water Works Association 2019 138th Annual Conference & Exposition, June, 2019, Denver, CO
Scope: International
Description: Presenting water research & best practices of interest to international water professionals
Contact Information: American Water Works Association, Phone: 800-926-7337, Fax: 303-347-0804, E-mail: awwamktg@awwa.org
• American Water Works Association 2020 139th Annual Conference & Exposition, June, 2020, Orlando, FL
Scope: International
Description: An annual meeting of water professionals, featuring technical programs & exhibits to foster sustainability
Contact Information: American Water Works Association, Phone: 800-926-7337, Fax: 303-347-0804, E-mail: awwamktg@awwa.org
• American Water Works Association 2021 140th Annual Conference & Exposition, 2021
Scope: International
Description: An international gathering of thousands of water professionals, featuring a technical program, workshops, seminars, & exhibits
Contact Information: American Water Works Association, Phone: 800-926-7337, Fax: 303-347-0804, E-mail: awwamktg@awwa.org
Publications:
• American Water Works Association Officers & Committee Directory
Type: Directory
Profile: Director, trustee, officer, & staff management information, plus the AWWA strategic plan & statements of policy
• AWWA [American Water Works Association] Standards
Profile: A print set of the current standards of the American Water Works Association
• Journal AWWA [American Water Works Association]
Type: Journal; *Frequency:* Monthly; *Editor:* Marcia Lacey *ISSN:* 1551-8833; *Price:* Free with individual, utility, & service provider membership in AWWA
Profile: Peer-reviewed information about water quality, resources, & supply, in addition to professional & scholarly articles about themanagement & operation of water utilities
• Opflow [a publication of the American Water Works Association]
Type: Magazine; *Frequency:* Monthly; *Accepts Advertising*; *Editor:* John Hughes *ISSN:* 1551-8701; *Price:* Free with individual, utility, & service provider membership in AWWA
Profile: Practical publication for water supply operators
• The Water Dictionary: A Comprehensive Reference of Water Terminology
Type: Book; *Number of Pages:* 716; *Editor:* Nancy McTigue; *ISBN:* 978-1-58321-741-2
Profile: Definitions for 15,000 water-related words, acronyms, & formulas

American Wilderness Alliance *See* American Wildlands

American Wildlands (AWL)

PO Box 6669, #418, 321 East Main St., Bozeman MT 59771 USA
Tel: 406-586-8175
www.facebook.com/pages/American-Wildlands/188400107836676
Previous Name: American Wilderness Alliance
Overview: A medium-sized international organization founded in 1977
Mission: To insure the responsible management & protection of forests, wildlife, wilderness, wetlands, watersheds, rivers & fisheries
Finances: *Annual Operating Budget:* $250,000-$500,000
Staff Member(s): 6; 6 volunteer(s)
Membership: 2,500; *Fees:* $40
Activities: *Internships:* Yes; *Speaker Service:* Yes; *Rents Mailing List:* Yes

American Wire Producers Association (AWPA)

#211, 801 North Fairfax St., Alexandria VA 22314-1757 USA
Tel: 703-299-4434; *Fax:* 703-299-9233
info@awpa.org
www.awpa.org
www.facebook.com/332838850061
Overview: A small international organization founded in 1981
Mission: Leading voice of the ferrous wire & wire products industry in North America

Staff Member(s): 5
Membership: 91; *Member Profile:* Wire producers in the United States, Canada & Mexico; *Committees:* PC Strand; Nail; Stainless; Membership

American Zoo & Aquarium Association (AZA)

#710, 8403 Colesville Rd., Silver Spring MD 20910-3314 USA
Tel: 301-562-0777; *Fax:* 301-562-0888
Other Communication: wildexplorer.org
www.aza.org
www.facebook.com/AssociationOfZoosAndAquariums
twitter.com/zoos_aquariums
Overview: A medium-sized national organization founded in 1924
Mission: To help preserve the world's rare & endangered species; to advance zoological parks & aquariums through conservation, education, scientific studies & recreation; to cooperate with government agencies & international conservation groups in matters dealing with the health & welfare of wildlife in captivity
Affliation(s): World Wildlife Fund - USA; Species Survival Commission of IUCN - World Conservation Union; Captive Breeding Specialist Group; International Species Information System; Wildlife Conservation International; American Committee for International Conservation; Centre for Marine Conservation; International Union of Directors of Zoological Gardens; International Association of Zoo Educators
Chief Officer(s):
Jim Maddy, President & CEO
Finances: *Annual Operating Budget:* $500,000-$1.5 Million
Staff Member(s): 20
Membership: 5,500; *Fees:* Associate: $70; Affiliate: $95; Fellow: $195; *Member Profile:* Comprises zoological institutions, related organizations, societies, zoological staff employees, commercial concerns that provide products & services to zoological facilities & other interested individuals; open to anyone interested in animal welfare, protection of wildlife & the development of better zoos & aquariums for the good of animals & people; *Committees:* Accreditation; Animal Data Information Systems; Animal Health; Animal Welfare; Aquatic Advisory; Board of Regents; Charter & Bylaws; Conference; Conservation Education; Diversity; Ethics; Field Conservation; Finance & Investments; Government Affairs; Honors & Awards; Information Trends; Marketing; Membership; National Awareness Campaign; Nominating; Operations; Public Relations; Wildlife Conservation & Management
Activities: Species Survival Plan - a strategy for the long-term survival of certain endangered species; International Species System (ISIS) - to promote healthy gene pools; computerized inventory of over 60,000 living animals in order to enable zoos to locate the best individuals for their breeding programs; *Rents Mailing List:* Yes

Amnesty International

International Secretariat, 1 Easton St., London WC1X 0DW United Kingdom
Tel: 44-20-7413-5500; *Fax:* 44-20-7956-1157
www.amnesty.org
www.facebook.com/amnestyglobal
twitter.com/AmnestyOnline
www.youtube.com/amnestyinternational
Overview: A large international organization
Mission: A worldwide movement which is independent of any government, political grouping, ideology, economic interest or religious creed; it plays a specific role within the overall spectrum of human rights work; the activities of the organization focus on the promotion of the Universal Declaration of Human Rights; it seeks the release of men & women detained anywhere for their beliefs, colour, sex, ethnic origin, language or religion, provided they have not used or advocated violence - these are termed prisoners of conscience; it advocates fair & early trials for all political prisoners & works on behalf of such persons detained without charge or without trial; it opposes the death penalty & torture or other cruel, inhuman or degrading treatment or punishment of all prisoners without reservation
Affliation(s): Amnesty International, Canadian Section (English Speaking); Amnistie internationale, Section canadienne (Francophone)
Chief Officer(s):
Salil Shetty, Secretary General
Membership: *Committees:* International Executive
Activities: *Library:* Virutal Library; Open to public

Antarctic & Southern Ocean Coalition (ASOC)

1630 Connecticut Ave., 3rd Fl., Washington DC 20009 USA
Tel: 202-234-2480; *Fax:* 202-387-4823
antarctica@igc.org
www.asoc.org
www.facebook.com/38924681853
twitter.com/ASOC1
Also Known As: Secretariat, The Antarctica Project
Overview: A medium-sized international organization founded in 1977
Mission: To protect the biological diversity & pristine wilderness of Antarctica, including its oceans & marine life; to work for the passage of strong measures which protect the marine ecosystem from the harmful effects of overfishing; to ensure that the integrity of the southern ocean whale sanctuary is maintained & internationally respected
Affliation(s): World Wildlife Fund Canada; World Society for the Protection of Animals; Friends of the Earth; Greenpeace; Sierra Club
Chief Officer(s):
Jim Barnes, Executive Director
Finances: *Annual Operating Budget:* $250,000-$500,000; *Funding Sources:* Foundation grants; membership dues
Staff Member(s): 9; 2 volunteer(s)
Membership: 235
Activities: Conducts legal & policy research & analysis; testifies at Congressional hearings; produces educational materials; works with the key users of Antarctica, including scientists, tourists, & governments, to ensure that activities have a minimal environmental impact; attends all Antarctic Treaty Consultative Meetings & all CCAMLR meetings; *Library* by appointment

The Antiochan Orthodox Christian Archdiocese of North America

Antiochan Orthodox Christian Archdiocese, PO Box 5238, Englewood NJ 07631-5238 USA
Tel: 201-871-1355; *Fax:* 201-871-7954
archdiocese@antiochian.org
www.antiochian.org
Overview: A small national organization founded in 1875
Mission: The Antiochan Orthodox Community in Canada is under the jurisdiction of the Patriarch of Antioch & all the East, with headquarters in Damascus, Syria. There are five churches in Canada & eight missions. The headquarters for all churches in North America is the Antiochan Orthodox Christian archdiocese, in Englewood, New Jersey, under Archbishop Philip Salica
Affliation(s): Canadian (Can-Am) Region
Chief Officer(s):
Philip Saliba, Archpriest
Staff Member(s): 4; 6 volunteer(s)
Membership: 275 parishes, 19 in Canada

Antique Automobile Club of America (AACA)

501 West Governor Rd., Hershey PA 17033 USA
Tel: 717-534-1910; *Fax:* 717-534-9101
general@aaca.org
www.aaca.org
Overview: A medium-sized international organization founded in 1935
Chief Officer(s):
Steven L. Moskowitz, Executive Director
Jack Armstrong, Secretary-Treasurer
Membership: 62,000; *Fees:* $35
Activities: *Library*
Publications:
• Antique Automobile
Type: Magazine; *Frequency:* Bimonthly; *Accepts Advertising*; *Editor:* West Peterson
Profile: Information for members of hte Antique Automobile Club of America

Lord Selkirk Region
305 Carpathia Rd., Winnipeg MB R3N 1T2
Mission: To futher the interest in and preserving of antique automobiles, and the promotion of sportsmanship and of good fellowship amoung all AACA members.
Chief Officer(s):
James Drummond, President

Ontario Region
116 Longwter Chase, Unionville ON L3R 6C4
www.aacaontario.ca
Mission: To further the interest in and preserving of antique automobiles and the promotion of sportsmanship and good fellowship among all AACA members.
Member of: Antique Automobile Club of America
Chief Officer(s):
Andrew Sommers, President
andrewsommers@sympatico.ca

Archaeological Institute of America (AIA) / Institut Archéologique d'Amérique

Boston University, 656 Beacon St., 6th Fl, Boston MA 02215-2006 USA
Tel: 617-353-9361; *Fax:* 617-353-6550
aia@aia.bu.edu
www.archaeological.org
www.facebook.com/Archaeological.Institute
twitter.com/archaeology_aia
youtube.com/archaeologytv
Overview: A large international charitable organization founded in 1879
Mission: To encourage & support archaeological research & publication; To encourage protection of world's cultural heritage
Member of: American Council of Learned Societies
Affliation(s): Fédération internationale des associations d'études classiques
Chief Officer(s):
Peter Herdrich, CEO
pherdrich@aia.bu.edu
Elizabeth Bartman, President
Finances: *Annual Operating Budget:* Greater than $5 Million; *Funding Sources:* Membership dues; donations; subscription income
Staff Member(s): 25
Membership: 9,000; *Fees:* Schedule available; *Committees:* AIA Tours; American Committee on the Corpus Vasorum Antiquorum; Archaeology in Higher Education; Archives; Audit; Conservation & Site Preservation; Corresponding Members; Development; Digital Technology; Education; Executive; Fellowship; Gold Medal; Governance; Lecture Program; Museums and Exhibitions; Nominating; Personnel; Professional Responsibilities; Publication Subvention; Societies
Activities: Provides over 250 lectures within the US each year; *Speaker Service:* Yes; *Rents Mailing List:* Yes
Awards:
• The Harriet Pomerance Fellowship (Scholarship)
Given to a resident of the US or Canada for travel to the Mediterranean area to pursue a scholarly project in Aegean Bronze Age archaeology
• The Olivia James Traveling Fellowship (Scholarship)
Provides funds to citizens or permanent residents of the US for travel & study in Greece, the Aegean Islands, Sicily, Southern Italy, Turkey, or Iraq
• Colburn Fellowship (Scholarship)
• S. Woodruff Fellowship (Scholarship)
• Undergraduate Teaching Award (Award)
• Society Outreach Grant (Grant)
• Pomerance Science Medal (Award)
• Joukowsky Distinguished Service Award (Award)
• Jane C. Waldbaum Field School Scholarship (Scholarship)
• James R. Wiseman Book Award (Award)
• Holton Book Award (Award)
• Graduate Student Paper Award (Award)
Publications:
• American Journal of Archaeology
Editor: Naomi Norman
Profile: Quarterly academic journal
• Archaeology
Editor: Peter A. Young
Profile: Bi-monthly magazine

ARMA International

#450, 11880 College Blvd., Overland Park KS 66215 USA
Tel: 913-341-3808; *Fax:* 913-341-3742
Toll-Free: 800-422-2762
hq@armaintl.org
www.arma.org
www.linkedin.com/company/arma-international
twitter.com/ARMA-INT
Overview: A large international organization
Chief Officer(s):
Marilyn Bier, Chief Executive Officer
Komal Gulich, President
Staff Member(s): 30
Membership: 5,000-14,999
Awards:
• Distinguished Service Award (Award)
• Chapter of the Year Award (Award)
• Chapter Member of the Year Award (Award)
• Chapter Newsletter of the Year Award (Award)
• Chapter Website of the Year Award (Award)
• Special Project Award (Award)
• Christine Zanotti Award for Excellence in Non-Serial Publications (Award)

- Chapter Innovation Award (Award)
- Chapter Leader of the Year (Award)
- Chapter Merit Award (Award)
- Chapter Participation Award (Award)
- Membership Recruitment Award (Award)

Meetings/Conferences:
- ARMA Annual Conference & Expo 2016, June, 2016, Halifax Annual Conference, Halifax, NS

Attendance: 600
Publications:
- Information Management

Type: Magazine

Art Libraries Society of North America (ARLIS/NA)

Technical Enterprises, Inc., 7044 - 13th St. South, Oak Creek WI 53154 USA
Tel: 414-908-4954; *Fax:* 414-768-8001
Toll-Free: 800-817-0621
info@arlisna.org
www.arlisna.org
www.linkedin.com/groups/ARLIS-NA-2590950
www.facebook.com/ARLISNA
twitter.com/ARLIS_NA
Overview: A medium-sized international organization founded in 1972
Mission: To promote & support art librarianship & image management.
Affiliation(s): American Library Association; Arbeitsgemeinschaft der Kunst und Museumsbibliotheken; ARLIS/Australia & New Zealand; ARLIS/Netherlands; ARLIS/Norden; ARLIS/United Kingdom & Ireland; Association of Architecture School Librarians; College Art Association; International Federation of Library Associations and Institutions; Japan Art Documentation Society, Tokyo; Museum Computer Network; Society of American Archivists; Society of Architectural Historians; Sous-section des Bibliothèques d'art, Association des bibliothécaires français; Visual Resources Association
Chief Officer(s):
Gregory P.J. Most, President
g-most@nga.gov
Carole Ann Fabian, Vice-President/President-Elect
caf2140@columbia.edu
Eric Wolf, Secretary
ewolf@menil.org
Deborah Barlow Smedstad, Treasurer
dbarlowsmedstad@mfa.org
Daniel Payne, Canadian Member-at-Large
dpayne@ocadu.ca
Staff Member(s): 1; 100 volunteer(s)
Membership: 1100; *Fees:* $30 USD students; $60 USD retired & unemployed; $90 USD introductorroy; $120 USD individuals; *Member Profile:* Art information professionals; *Committees:* Awards; Cataloging Advisory; Communications & Publications; Development; Diversity; Finance; International Relations; Membership; Nominating; Professional Development; Public Policy; Strategic Planning; Virtual Conference Advisory Group
Activities: Networking; Publishing; Communicating; Presenting scholarships & awards
Meetings/Conferences:
- 43rd Annual Conference of the Art Libraries Society, March, 2015, Fort Worth, TX

Description: The conference provides the opportunity for professionals involved in art librarianship to meet, learn and share their knowledge of the field. It also allows them to explore exhibitions & interact with vendors involved with art libraries.
Contact Information: Program Co-Chair: Catherine Essinger; cwessinger@uh.edu; Program Co-Chair: Lynn Wexler; lwexler@mfah.org
- 44th Annual Conference of the Art Libraries Society, 2016

Description: The conference provides the opportunity for professionals involved in art librarianship to meet, learn and share their knowledge of the field. It also allows them to explore exhibitions & interact with vendors involved with art libraries.
Publications:
-
- Art Documentation

Type: Journal; *Frequency:* Twice yearly; *Editor:* Judy Dyki; *Price:* Included with membership
Profile: The official journal of the Art Libraries Society of North America. It features articles that pertain to art librarianship & visual resources curatorship.
- Handbook & List of Members

Type: Yearbook; *Frequency:* Annually

Montreal Chapter
c/o Patrick Black, UQAM. Local A-2113, PO Box 8889, Stn. Centre-Ville, Montréal QC H3C 3P3
Tel: 514-987-3000
arlismoq@yahoo.com
www.arlismoq.ca
Chief Officer(s):
Paul Handa, Chairman

Northwest Chapter
c/o Marilyn Nasserden, university of Calgary, 2500 University Dr. NW, Calgary AB T2N 1N4
nw.arlisna.org
www.facebook.com/pages/ARLIS-NA-Northwest-Chapter/175582815809442
Chief Officer(s):
Clément Déziel, Président

Ontario Chapter
c/o Melissa Bruno, Faculty of Information, University of Toronto, #211, 140 St. George St., Toronto ON M5S 3G6
arlison.org
www.linkedin.com/groups/ARLIS-NA-Ontario-Chapter-4846604/about
www.facebook.com/ARLISNA.Ontario
twitter.com/ARLIS_ON

Asia-Pacific Centre for Environmental Law (APCEL)

Faculty of Law, Ntl. University of Singapore, Eu Tong Sen Bldg., 469G Bukit Timah Rd., Singapore 259776 Singapore
Tel: 65-6516-6246; *Fax:* 65-6872-1937
lawapcel@nus.edu.sg
law.nus.edu.sg/apcel/
Overview: A small international organization founded in 1996
Chief Officer(s):
Lye Lin Heng, Director
lawlyelh@nus.edu.sg
Shirley Mak, Secretary
lawmaksy@nus.edu.sg

ASM International

9639 Kinsman Rd., Materials Park OH 44073-0002 USA
Tel: 440-338-5151; *Fax:* 440-338-4634
Toll-Free: 800-336-5152
memberservicecenter@asminternational.org
www.asminternational.org
Also Known As: American Society for Metals
Overview: A medium-sized international organization founded in 1913
Mission: To gather, process & disseminate technical information; to foster understanding & application of engineered materials; to provide career support & education for business & information systems professionals
Chief Officer(s):
Mark F. Smith, President
Finances: *Annual Operating Budget:* $500,000-$1.5 Million
Staff Member(s): 100
Membership: 36,000 worldwide; *Fees:* US$113; US$15 Student; *Member Profile:* Business or systems professional
Activities: *Rents Mailing List:* Yes

Asociacion Nacional de Directores y Ejecutivos de Organismos Empresariales y Profesionales

Colonia Cuauhtemoc, Manuel Maria Contreras 133, 2o piso, Mexico 6500 Mexico
Overview: A medium-sized national organization
Chief Officer(s):
Miguel Angel García Paredes, Director General

Asociación mexicana de estudios sobre Canadá (AMEC) / Mexican Association of Canadian Studies (MACS)

Av. Tepeyac 4800, col. Prados Tepeyac, Zapopan JA 4800 Mexico
Tel: 52 (33) 3134-0800
www.amec.com.mx
www.facebook.com/CANADA.AMEC?sk=wall
twitter.com/amec_canada
Overview: A small international organization founded in 1992
Mission: To foster the study & interest on Canada in Mexico through the promotion of several academic, cultural & scientific activities to increase the knowledge & awareness of that country
Member of: International Council for Canadian Studies
Chief Officer(s):
Ricardo Cortez Amezcua, Presidente
ricardo.cortez@amec.com.mx
Jorge Antonio Hernández Velázquez, Secretario
jhernandez@amec.com.mx
Membership: 233

Asociación Nacional de la Industria Química, A.C *See* National Association of the Chemistry Industry

Assemblée mondiale de la jeunesse *See* World Assembly of Youth

Associação Brasileira de Estudos Canadense (ABECAN) / Brazilian Association for Canadian Studies

Centro Universitário la Salle, 2288 Victor Barreto Ave., Canoas RS 92010-000 Brazil
Tel: 55-51-3476-8411
abecan@abecan.org.br
www.abecan.org.br
www.facebook.com/abecan
Overview: A small international charitable organization founded in 1991
Mission: To promote the gathering of researchers interested in culture, science and technology in Canada, and their relation to those of Brazil; to contribute to the excellence and disclosure of Canadian Studies; to serve as a source of intelligence among Brazilian communities interested in studying Canadian topics
Member of: International Council for Canadian Studies
Chief Officer(s):
Monique Vandressen, President
Membership: 198; *Fees:* $40 students; $75 professors, researchers & institutions
Activities: Organizing conferences, seminars, meetings, conferences, studies and research; promote publications; establish agreements and trade cooperation in the fields of competence; support activities related to the Brazilian stock market analysis while studying in Canada; *Internships:* Yes; *Speaker Service:* Yes

Associated Country Women of the World

Mary Sumner House, 24 Tufton St., London SW1P 3RB United Kingdom
Tel: 44-20-7799-3875; *Fax:* 44-20-7340-9950
Other Communication: Blog: acwwnews.blogspot.co.uk
info@acww.org.uk
www.acww.org.uk
www.facebook.com/133340763410423
twitter.com/acww_news
www.youtube.com/user/ACWWnews
Overview: A large international organization
Mission: To raise the standards of living & education of women & their families all over the world through community development projects & training; To promote international goodwill, friendship & understanding between women everywhere; To work for equal opportunites for women by the elimination of discrimination because of gender, race, nationality, religion or marital status; To act as a forum on international affairs for rural women, speaking for them with an informed voice in the Councils of the world
Chief Officer(s):
May Kidd, World President
Membership: *Fees:* £20 annual; £50 three-year; *Committees:* Promotion & Publications; United Nations; Projects
Activities: Funding more than 900 projects around the world, including the Water for All Fund, the Women Feed the World Fund, & the Projects Fund
Publications:
- ACWW [Associated Country Women of the World] Annual Report

Type: Yearbook; *Frequency:* Annually
- All About ACWW [Associated Country Women of the World]

Type: Brochure
- The Country Woman [a publication of the Associated Country Women of the World]

Type: Magazine; *Frequency:* q.
Profile: Up-to-date association news & stories

Association Africaine de Literature *See* African Literature Association

Association britanniques d'études canadiennes *See* British Association for Canadian Studies

Association Canado-Américaine (ACA)

55 South Commercial St., Manchester NH 03101 USA
Tél: 603-624-1351; *Téléc:* 603-625-1214
Ligne sans frais: 855-712-7482
info@aca-assurance.org
www.aca-assurance.com
Également appelé: ACA Assurance
Aperçu: *Dimension:* moyenne; *Envergure:* internationale; Organisme sans but lucratif; fondée en 1896

Mission: Union des personnes d'ascendance ou d'affinité française et catholique en Amérique, leur avancement spirituel, civique, culturel, social et économique et la préservation de la langue et la culture française
Membre de: National Fraternal Congress of America
Membre: *Critères d'admissibilite:* Franco américain et canadien
Activités: Fraternelles: voyages; sorties; cabane à sucre; *Service de conférenciers:* Oui *Bibliothèque:* ACA Assurance

Association d'études canadiennes dans les pays de langue allemande *See* Association for Canadian Studies in German-Speaking Countries

Association d'Études Canadiennes en Europe Centrale *See* Central European Association for Canadian Studies

Association d'études canadiennes en Israel *See* Israel Association for Canadian Studies

Association de l'endometriose inc. *See* Endometriosis Association, Inc.

Association des études canadiennes aux Pays-Bas *See* Association for Canadian Studies in the Netherlands

Association des galvanoplastes d'Amérique *See* American Electroplaters & Surface Finishers Society

Association des joueurs de la Ligue majeure de baseball (ind.) *See* Major League Baseball Players' Association (Ind.)

Association for Asian Studies - USA (AAS)

#310, 825 Victors Way, Ann Arbor MI 48108 USA
Tel: 734-665-2490; *Fax:* 734-665-3801
mpaschal@asian-studies.org
www.asian-studies.org
www.facebook.com/104663456241055
Previous Name: Far Eastern Association Inc.
Overview: A small international organization founded in 1941
Member of: American Council of Learned Societies
Chief Officer(s):
Thongchai Winichakul, President
twinicha@wisc.edu
Mrinalini Sinha, Vice-President
sinha@umich.edu
Finances: *Annual Operating Budget:* $500,000-$1.5 Million; *Funding Sources:* Membership fees; endowment
Staff Member(s): 10
Membership: 8,500; *Fees:* Schedule available; *Member Profile:* Interest in Asian studies
Publications:
• Journal of Asian Studies
Author: Jeffrey Wasserstrom
Profile: Quarterly academic journal

Association for Canadian Studies in Argentina

Universidad Nacional del Comahue, PO Box 8300, Avenida Argentina 1400, Neuquen, Provincia del Neuquen 4.924175 Argentina
Tel: 0299-4490-305
info@asaec.com
Also Known As: Asociación Argentina de Estudios Canadienses
Overview: A small international organization founded in 1997
Chief Officer(s):
Alicia Garro, Secretariat
asaec@fibertel.com.ar

Association for Canadian Studies in Australia & New Zealand (ACSANZ)

University of Wollongong, PO Box U163, Wollongong, New South Wales 2500 Australia
info@acsanz.org.au
www.acsanz.org.au
www.facebook.com/189197111101161
Overview: A small international organization founded in 1982
Mission: To encourage Canadian studies within Australia & New Zealand
Member of: International Council for Canadian Studies
Chief Officer(s):
Robyn Morris, President
robynm@uow.edu.au
Debra Dudek, Acting Treasurer
debrad@uow.edu.au
Membership: 200+; *Fees:* AUD$85 individual; AUD$50 student

Association for Canadian Studies in China (ACSC)

c/o School of History & Culture, Shandong University, 27 Shanda Rd. South, Jinan, Shandong Province 250100 China
Tel: 86-531-8836-4661; *Fax:* 86-531-8836-51697
Overview: A small international charitable organization founded in 1984
Mission: To promote a better understanding of Canada; to offer recommendations on Canadian affairs & policies to the Chinese government; to foster improved business relations between Canada & China.
Finances: *Funding Sources:* Business donations; government
Activities: *Speaker Service:* Yes *Library:* Canadian Studies Library; Open to public

Association for Canadian Studies in German-Speaking Countries (GKS) / Association d'études canadiennes dans les pays de langue allemande

c/o Universität Trier, Fachbereich III - Geschichte, Trier 54286 Germany
Tel: 49-0-651-201-2178
gks@kanada-studien.de
www.kanada-studien.org
Overview: A small international organization founded in 1980
Mission: To promote scholarship in Canadian studies to strengthen the cultural relations & understanding between Canada & German-speaking countries.
Member of: International Council for Canadian Studies
Chief Officer(s):
Ursula Lehmkuhl, President
lehmkuhl@uni-trier.de
Caroline Rosenthal, Vice-President
caroline.rosenthal@uni-jena.de
Bernhard Metz, Treasurer
bernhard.metz@t-online.de
Finances: *Funding Sources:* Membership fees; donations; grants
Membership: 538; *Fees:* 25 Euros student/unemployed; 70 Euros regular
Activities: *Speaker Service:* Yes
Awards:
• GKS Awards (3) (Award)

Association for Canadian Studies in Ireland (ACSI) / Association irlandaise d'étude canadiennes

c/o School of Languages and Literatures, University College Dublin, Belfield, Dublin 4 Ireland
www.canadianstudiesireland.com
Also Known As: An Cumann Le Léann Ceanadach in Éirinn
Overview: A small international organization founded in 1982
Mission: To promote the knowledge of Canada in Ireland & encourage the creation of new universities & the pursuit of research
Member of: International Council for Canadian Studies
Chief Officer(s):
Michael Brophy, President
michael.brophy@ucd.ie
Membership: *Member Profile:* Academics with an interest in Canada
Activities: *Speaker Service:* Yes

Association for Canadian Studies in the Netherlands (ACSN) / Association des études canadiennes aux Pays-Bas

Bosweg 12, Nijmegen 6523 NM Netherlands
Tel: 31-243234525
acsn@upcmail.nl
www.acsn.nl
Overview: A small international charitable organization founded in 1985
Mission: The promotion of teaching & research about Canada in the humanities & social sciences at post-secondary level
Member of: International Council for Canadian Studies; European Network for Canadian Studies
Chief Officer(s):
Conny J. Steenman-Marcusse, President
Amanda Helderman, Secretary
acsn@amandahelderman.com
Finances: *Annual Operating Budget:* Less than $50,000
5 volunteer(s)
Membership: 140; *Fees:* 27 Euro; 13.50 Euro students; 100 Euro companies/associations; *Member Profile:* Academic
Activities: Conferences, seminars, lecture tours, publicizing; *Speaker Service:* Yes *Library*

Association for Canadian Studies in the United States (ACSUS)

#350, 2030 - M St. NW, Washington DC 20036 USA
Tel: 202-223-9007; *Fax:* 202-775-0061
info@acsus.org
www.acsus.org
www.facebook.com/group.php?v=wall&gid=47952082556
Overview: A medium-sized international charitable organization founded in 1971
Mission: To raise awareness & understanding of Canada
Chief Officer(s):
David Archibald, Executive Director
Doug Nord, President
Michael Broadway, Vice-President
Nadine Fabbi, Secretary-Treasurer
Membership: *Fees:* Schedule available based on income; *Member Profile:* Scholars, professionals, & institutions dedicated to improving understanding of Canada in the United States; *Committees:* Membership; Development; Rufus Z. Smith Prize; Nominations & Elections; Graduate Student; Distinguished Dissertation Award; Jeanne Kissner Award; Affiliates; Status of Women & Diversity; Outreach
Activities: Supporting the teaching of Canadian studies; Promoting research; Engaging in advocacy activities;
Awards:
• ACSUS Distinguished Dissertation Award (Award)
Awarded biennially to honour outstanding doctoral research on Canada at United States institutions
• Jeanne Kissner Undergraduate Essay Award (Award)
• The Thomas O. Enders Endowment (Grant)
To encourage advanced scholarship on Canada & Canadian - United States relations on divese bilateral issues
• The Rufus Z. Smith Prize (Award)
Awarded for the best article in The American Review of Canadian Studies during the two years prior to the biennial conference at which it is awarded
• The Donner Medal in Canadian Studies (Award)
Awarded biennially for distinguished achievement, scholarship, & program innovation in the area of Canadian studies in the United States
Meetings/Conferences:
• Association for Canadian Studies in the United States (ACSUS) 2016 Biennial Colloquium, 2016
Scope: International
Description: An examination of an interdisciplinary topic during a meeting held at a Canadian location
Contact Information: Executive Director: David Archibald, E-mail: info@acsus.org
• Association for Canadian Studies in the United States (ACSUS) 23rd Biennial Conference, 2015
Scope: International
Description: Speakers & panels presenting research & information about Canada across all disciplines
Contact Information: Executive Director: David Archibald, E-mail: info@acsus.org
Publications:
• American Review of Canadian Studies
Type: Journal; *Frequency:* Quarterly; *Editor:* Dr. John L. Purdy & Kathy Reigstad *ISSN:* 0272-2011
Profile: A refereed, multidisciplinary journal, featuring Canada's art, culture, history, economics & politics from an American perspective
• Think Canada!
Type: Newsletter; *Frequency:* Semiannually
Profile: Covering developments in Canada - United States academic relations, as well as the associated institutions & personalities

Association for Childhood Education International (ACEI)

#300, 1101 - 16 St. NW, Washington D.C. 20036 USA
Tel: 202-372-9986; *Fax:* 202-372-9989
Toll-Free: 800-423-3563
headquarters@acei.org
www.acei.org
www.facebook.com/ACEIpage
twitter.com/ACEI_info
Previous Name: International Kindergarten Union
Overview: A medium-sized international organization founded in 1892
Mission: To promote & support the optimal education & development of children, from infancy through middle childhood, in the global community; to influence the professional growth of educators, & the efforts of others who are committed to the needs of children in a changing society
Member of: Alliance for Curriculum Reform; National Council for Accreditation of Teacher Education (NCATE); United Nations; National Committee on the Rights of the Child

Chief Officer(s):
Diane Whitehead, Executive Director
Carrie Whaley, President
cwhaley@uu.edu
Finances: *Funding Sources:* Membership dues; sales of publications; conferences
Membership: *Fees:* Schedule available; *Member Profile:* Educators & persons interested in children's education, rights & well-being; *Committees:* Nominations; Finance; Awards; Program; Special Advisory
Activities: *Speaker Service:* Yes
Awards:
• Outstanding Member Service Award (Award)
• Elizabeth Breathwaite Mini-Grants (Grant)
Implementation of outstanding educational experiences for children
• Elizabeth Breathwaite Student Leadership Award (Award)
Available to college students who are ACEI members
• ACEI Friends of Children Award (Award)
• Nancy Bartlett Hitch Student Scholarship Award (Scholarship)
• Patty Smith Hill Award (Award)
• Roll of Honor (Award)
• Best Professional Development Workshop / Conference Award (Award)
• Best Use of ACEI Materials Award (Award)
• Branch Excellence Award (Award)
• Best Publicity Award (Award)
• Best Communications Award (Award)
• Best Global Focus Award (Award)
• Best Mentor Program (Award)
• Best Fundraiser Award (Award)
• Best New Branch Award (Award)
• Best Children's Event / Community Service (Award)
• Outstanding Branch Member Service Award (Award)
• Branch Development Grant (Grant)
• Local Conference Grant (Grant)
• International Development Fund Grant (Grant)
• Presidents' Council Awards / Grants (Award)
Publications:
• ACEI Exchange
Type: Newsletter; *Frequency:* 5 pa
• Childhood Education
Type: Journal; *Frequency:* Bimonthly
• Focus on Elementary
Frequency: Quarterly; *Price:* US$15 members
Profile: Ages 7 to 10
• Focus on Inclusive Education
Frequency: Quarterly; *Price:* US$15 members
Profile: For teachers of children with special needs
• Focus on Infants & Toddlers
Frequency: Quarterly; *Price:* US$15 members
Profile: Ages birth to 3
• Focus on Middle School
Frequency: Quarterly; *Price:* US$15 members
Profile: Ages 11 to 13
• Focus on Pre-K & K
Frequency: Quarterly; *Price:* US$15 members
Profile: Ages 4 to 6
• Focus on Teacher Education
Frequency: Quarterly; *Price:* US$15 members
Profile: For teacher educators
• Journal of Research in Childhood Education
Type: Journal; *Frequency:* Quarterly; *Price:* US$79 members
• Retirees' Review
• Student Connection

Association for Computer Operations Management *See* AFCOM

Association for Computing Machinery (ACM)
PO Box 30777, Stn. General Post Office, #701, 2 Penn Plaza, New York NY 10121-0701 USA
Tel: 212-626-0500; *Fax:* 212-944-1318
Toll-Free: 800-342-6626
acmhelp@acm.org
www.acm.org
Overview: A medium-sized international organization
Mission: To advance computing as a science & profession
Membership: *Member Profile:* Professionals; Libraries; Institutions; Students
Activities: Providing career resources, including access to online books; Publishing over 40 publications; Presenting over 100 special interest group conferences
Publications:
• Communications of the ACM
Type: Magazine; *Frequency:* Monthly

Association for Facilities Engineering (AFE)
#500, 12801 Worldgate Dr., Herndon VA 20170 USA
Tel: 571-203-7171; *Fax:* 571-766-2142
info@afe.org
www.afe.org
www.linkedin.com/groups?home=&gid=1770033
twitter.com/FacilitiesEng
Previous Name: American Institute of Plant Engineers
Overview: A large international organization founded in 1954
Mission: To further professional interests of plant engineers; to aid in the development of this branch of engineering in the West; to cooperate with like-minded organizations around the world
Chief Officer(s):
Larry Ross, CPE, President & Chair
Larry.Ross@erickson.com
Kate Kerrigan, CPMM, Chair, AFE Foundation
Wayne P. Saya, Sr., CPE, Executive Director
waynesaya@afe.org
Finances: *Annual Operating Budget:* $1.5 Million-$3 Million
Staff Member(s): 8; 300 volunteer(s)
Membership: 5,000; *Fees:* Schedule available; *Member Profile:* People employed in plant or facility engineering, managing, operation, education with engineering OREQ degree & 4 years supervisory experience; *Committees:* Membership; Finance; Professional Development
Activities: *Rents Mailing List:* Yes
Publications:
• Facilities Engineering Journal [a publication of Association for Facilities Engineering]
Type: Journal
• Weekly Headlines [a publication of Association for Facilities Engineering]
Type: Journal; *Frequency:* Weekly

Association for Financial Professionals (AFP)
#750, 4520 East West Hwy., Bethesda MD 20814
Tel: 301-907-2862; *Fax:* 301-907-2864
afp@afponline.org
www.afponline.org
www.linkedin.com/groups/Association-Financial-Professionals-AFP-81522
twitter.com/afponline
www.youtube.com/afponline
Overview: A large international licensing organization
Mission: To operate as a global resource & advocate for financial professionals; To raise the stature & visibility of members, by offering them products & services
Chief Officer(s):
Anthony Scaglione, Chair
Membership: *Fees:* $495; *Member Profile:* Executives in the financial services industry
Activities: Providing professional development activities & networking opportunities; annual conference; newsletters; research & economic data; administering the Certified Treasury Professional & Certified Corporate FP&A Professional credentials
Meetings/Conferences:
• Association for Financial Professionals 2015 Annual Conference, October, 2015, Denver, CO
Scope: National
Publications:
• AFP [Association for Financial Professionals] Payments
Type: Newsletter; *Frequency:* Monthly
• AFP [Association for Financial Professionals] EconWatch
Type: Newsletter; *Frequency:* Weekly
• AFP [Association for Financial Professionals] Exchange
Type: Magazine
• FP&A Newsletter [a publication of the Association for Financial Professionals]
Type: Newsletter; *Frequency:* Monthly
• Futures in Finance [a publication of the Association for Financial Professionals]
Type: Newsletter; *Frequency:* Monthly
• Risk! [a publication of the Association for Financial Professionals]
Type: Newsletter; *Frequency:* Monthly

Association for Jewish Studies - USA (AJS)
15 West 16th St., New York NY 10011-6301 USA
Tel: 917-606-8249; *Fax:* 917-606-8222
ajs@ajs.cjh.org
www.ajsnet.org
www.facebook.com/119828850063
twitter.com/jewish_studies
Overview: A medium-sized national organization founded in 1969
Mission: Promote, maintain, & improve teaching, research, & related endeavors in Jewish Studies in colleges, universities & other institutions of higher learning
Member of: American Council of Learned Societies
Chief Officer(s):
Rona Sheramy, Executive Director
Staff Member(s): 3
Membership: 1,800; *Fees:* Schedule available; *Member Profile:* Individuals whose full-time vocation is devoted to either teaching or research in academic Jewish studies or related endeavors in academic Jewish studies

Association for Preservation Technology International (APT)
#200, 3085 Stevenson Dr., Springfield IL USA
Tel: 217-529-9039; *Fax:* 888-723-4242
Other Communication: admin@apti.org
info@apti.org
www.apti.org
Overview: A medium-sized international organization founded in 1968
Mission: To promote technology to conserve & maintain historic structures & their sites for future appreciation & use
Chief Officer(s):
Anne T. Sullivan, President
Kyle Normandin, Secretary-Treasurer
Nathela Chatara, Administrative Director
Membership: *Member Profile:* Conservators; Preservationists; Curators; Historians; Architects; Architects; Engineers; Technicians; *Committees:* Executive; Chapters; Conference; Finance; Membership; Nominating; Outreach; Partnerships; Publications; Student Scholarships; Training & Education; Codes for Historic Resources; Modern Heritage; Preservation Engineering; Sustainable Preservation
Activities: Facilitating the exchange of ideas; Providing training for members
Meetings/Conferences:
• Association for Preservation Technology International 2015 Annual Conference, November, 2015, The Clubhouse on Baltimore, Kansas, MO
Scope: International
Attendance: 1,000
Description: Training & networking opportunities plus exhibits of interest to an international audience of persons involved in the application of methods & materials to conserve historic structures
• Association for Preservation Technology International 2016 Annual Conference, October, 2016, Hilton Palacio del Rio, San Antonio, TX
Scope: International
Attendance: 1,000
Description: Training & networking opportunities plus exhibits of interest to an international audience of persons involved in the application of methods & materials to conserve historic structures
Publications:
• APT Bulletin: The Journal of Preservation Technology
Type: Journal; *Frequency:* 3 pa; *Editor:* Diana S. Waite
Profile: Peer-reviewed articles about preservation techniques, including case studies, international debates, & reviews of preservation-related books
• Communiqué [a publication of the Association for Preservation Technology International]
Type: Newsletter; *Frequency:* Quarterly; *Accepts Advertising*; *Editor:* Erin Brasell; *Price:* Free with membership in the Association for Preservation Technology International
Profile: Member news, including preservation experience, resources, chapter information, grants, awards, conference reviews, &forthcoming events
• Preservation Technology Primer
Type: Guide; *Price:* $45 members; $50 non-members
Profile: Articles about preservation practice that have been published in the APT Bulletin

Association française d'études canadiennes (AFEC) / French Association for Canadian Studies (FACS)
Institut des Amérique, 175, rue du Chevaleret, Paris 75013 France
afec@msha.fr
www.afec33.asso.fr
Aperçu: *Dimension:* petite; *Envergure:* internationale; Organisme sans but lucratif; fondée en 1976
Mission: Promotion des études canadiennes en France: en toutes disciplines; Recherches avec rédaction des thèses par les chercheurs/étudiants
Membre de: International Council for Canadian Studies

Membre(s) du bureau directeur:
Jean-Michel Lacroix, Président
Annick Monnerie, Secrétariat, Attachée culturelle
Membre(s) du personnel: 1
Membre: 400; *Montant de la cotisation:* 45 euros; 50 euros à l'étranger; *Critères d'admissibilite:* Professeur d'universités, chercheurs, étudiants-chercheurs
Activités: *Service de conférenciers:* Oui *Bibliothèque*

Association France-Québec

94, rue de Courcelles, Paris 75008 France
Tél: 01-45-54-35-37
accueil@francequebec.fr
francequebec.fr
www.facebook.com/AssociationFranceQuebec
twitter.com/AssoFrQc
Aperçu: *Dimension:* petite; *Envergure:* internationale; Organisme sans but lucratif; fondée en 1968
Mission: De regrouper des associations régionales; De coordonner non seulement l'ensemble des actions et des activités qui intéressent les adhérents et les Régionales, mais elle assure également la liaison avec tous les partenaires de la coopération franco-québécoise
Affiliation(s): Association Québec-France
Membre(s) du bureau directeur:
Marc Martin, Président
president@francequebec.fr
Membre(s) du personnel: 5
Membre: 3500
Activités: Programmes d'échanges intermunicipaux; stages professionnels; pommes; tabac; tournée culturelle; prix littéraire; *Stagiaires:* Oui

Association francophone internationale des directeurs d'établissements scolaires (AFIDES)

c/o Anne Macherel Rey, Lycee Jean-Piaget, Ecole Supérieure de commerce, Rue des Beaux-Arts 30, Neuchâtel 2000 Switzerland
Tél: 514-383-7335
www.afides.ch
Aperçu: *Dimension:* moyenne; *Envergure:* internationale; fondée en 1983
Mission: PromouVoir les échanges entre les responsables francophones d'établissements scolaires pour répondre à des besoins de perfectionnement international par la coopération et les échanges
Membre de: UNESCO - Comité de liaison des ONG avec l'Agence de la Francophonie
Membre(s) du bureau directeur:
Anne Macherel Rey, Présidente
Anne.MacherelRey@rpn.ch
Membre: 1,000-4,999; *Critères d'admissibilite:* Toute personne qui exerce un rôle de direction dans un ou plusieurs établissements scolaires, sous le titre de directeur, directeur adjoint, principal adjoint, proviseur, censeur ou sous toute autre appellation pour les responsabilités identiques

Association internationale d'histoire économique *See* International Economic History Association

Association internationale de droit pénal (AIDP) / International Association of Penal Law

12, rue Charles Fourier, Paris 75013 France
Tél: 33(0)1.79.25.45.76; *Téléc:* 33(0)1.55.04.92.89
ridp-irpl@penal.org
www.penal.org
Aperçu: *Dimension:* petite; *Envergure:* internationale; fondée en 1924
Mission: L'A.I.D.P. s'est toujours souciée des problèmes de droit pénal international et de la responsabilité des auteurs de crimes internationaux
Membre(s) du bureau directeur:
José Luis de la Cuesta, Président
Finances: *Budget de fonctionnement annuel:* $50,000-$100,000
Membre(s) du personnel: 1
Membre: 3 000 dans 97 pays; *Montant de la cotisation:* Barème

Association internationale de la critique littéraire (AICL)

Paris France
www.aicl-fr.com
Aperçu: *Dimension:* petite; *Envergure:* internationale; Organisme sans but lucratif; fondée en 1970
Mission: Favoriser le rapprochement entre les cultures; favoriser par des rencontres internationales, les échanges culturels, les traductions, en particulier des littératures en langues de petite diffusion
Affliation(s): UNESCO
Membre(s) du bureau directeur:
Daniel Leuwers, Président
Finances: *Fonds:* Cotisations
Membre: 84; *Critères d'admissibilite:* Écrivains et critiques
Activités: Colloques; congrès; *Stagiaires:* Oui; *Listes de destinataires:* Oui

Association internationale de pédiatrie *See* International Pediatric Association

Association internationale de relations professionnelles *See* International Labour & Employment Relations Association

Association internationale de signalisation maritime *See* International Association of Marine Aids to Navigation & Lighthouse Authorities

Association Internationale de Théâtre Amateur *See* International Amateur Theatre Association

Association internationale des bibliothèques, archives et de documentation musicaux *See* International Association of Music Libraries, Archives & Documentation Centres

Association internationale des débardeurs (FAT-COI/CTC) *See* International Longshoremen's Association (AFL-CIO/CLC)

Association internationale des éducateurs pour la paix du monde *See* International Association of Educators for World Peace - USA

Association internationale des études arméniennes *See* International Association for Armenian Studies

Association internationale des études patristiques (AIEP) / International Association for Patristic Studies (IAPS)

60 Mississippi River Blvd. South, Saint Paul MN 55105 USA
secaiep@duq.edu
www.aiep-iaps.org
Aperçu: *Dimension:* moyenne; *Envergure:* internationale; fondée en 1965
Mission: Chercheurs et professeurs qui s'intéressent à l'antiquité chrétienne au général
Membre(s) du bureau directeur:
Michael Slusser, Secrétaire général
slusser@duq.edu
Carol Harrison, Présidente
carol.harrison@durham.ac.uk
Finances: *Budget de fonctionnement annuel:* Moins de $50,000
Membre: 740; *Montant de la cotisation:* US$17; *Critères d'admissibilite:* Interessé aux pères de l'Eglise; *Comités:* Executive
Activités: *Listes de destinataires:* Oui

Association internationale des machinistes et des travailleurs de l'aérospatiale *See* International Association of Machinists & Aerospace Workers

Association internationale des métiers alliés de l'imprimerie *See* International Allied Printing Trades Association

Association internationale des pompiers (FAT-COI/CTC) *See* International Association of Fire Fighters (AFL-CIO/CLC)

Association internationale des sociologues de langue française (AISLF)

AISLF - Université de Toulouse-Le Mirail, 5, allée Antonio Machado, Toulouse F-31058 France CEDEX 9
Tél: 33-561-50-43-74; *Téléc:* 33-561-50-43-74
aislf@univ-tlse2.fr
w3.aislf.univ-tlse2.fr/spip/index.php
Aperçu: *Dimension:* moyenne; *Envergure:* internationale; Organisme sans but lucratif; fondée en 1958
Mission: Regroupe des sociologues et d'autres spécialistes en sciences sociales donnant une orientation sociologique à leurs travaux, quelle que soit leur nationalité, à condition qu'ils utilisent le français pour une part notable dans leur activité scientifique
Affiliation(s): UNESCO - Agence de la Francophonie
Membre(s) du bureau directeur:
Marc-Henry Soulet, Secrétaire général de l'AISLF
marc-henry.soulet@unifr.ch
Odile Saint-Raymond, Secrétaire générale adjointe
odile.saint-raymond@univ-tlse2.fr
André Petitat, Présidente de l'AISLF
andre.petitat@unil.ch
Finances: *Fonds:* Cotisations et subventions
Membre: 1 500 membres en 60 pays; *Critères d'admissibilite:* Sociologues travaillant majoritairement en français
Activités: Colloques; tables rondes; congrès; publications; comités de recherche et groupes de travail internationaux
Prix, Bouses: • Prix du Jeune sociologue (Prix)
Attribué lors de chaque congrès à un premier ouvrage; montant 1000 EURO
Publications:
• SociologieS: Revue de l'Association internationale des sociologues de langue française
Type: Journal; *Editor:* Marc-Henry Soulet *ISSN:* 1992-2655

Association internationale des travailleurs de ponts, de fer structural et ornemental (FAT-COI) *See* International Association of Bridge, Structural, Ornamental & Reinforcing Iron Workers (AFL-CIO)

Association internationale des travailleurs du métal en feuilles (FAT-COI/FCT) *See* Sheet Metal Workers' International Association (AFL-CIO/CFL)

Association internationale du droit nucléaire *See* International Nuclear Law Association

Association internationale permanente des congrès de navigation (AIPCN) / Permanent International Association of Navigation Congresses (PIANC)

Bâtiment Graaf de Ferraris, 11ième étage, boul du Roi Albert II, 20 - Boîte 3, Bruxelles B-1000 Belgique
Tél: 32-2-553-7161; *Téléc:* 32-2-553-7155
info@pianc-aipcn.org
www.pianc-aipcn.org
be.linkedin.com/pub/pianc-international/61/386/2a
www.facebook.com/175978305876451
twitter.com/PIANC1
Également appelé: The World Association for Waterborne Transport Infrastructure
Aperçu: *Dimension:* petite; *Envergure:* internationale; fondée en 1885
Mission: Pour fournir des informations à ses membres, de fournir un réseau de personnes impliquées dans le transport international par voie d'eau
Membre de: Union des Associations Internationales; Union des Associations Techniques Internationales; Comité Scientifique pour les Recherches Hydrologiques
Membre(s) du bureau directeur:
Geoffrey Caude, Président
president@painc.org
Louis Van Schel, Secrétaire général
secretary.general@pianc.org
André Châteauvert, Représentant canadien
chateauverta@dfo-mpo.gc.ca
Membre(s) du personnel: 4
Membre: 2,000 individuels; 450 corporations; *Montant de la cotisation:* 95 E individu; 35 E étudiant; 475-950 E corporatif

Association irlandaise d'étude canadiennes *See* Association for Canadian Studies in Ireland

Association nordique d'études canadiennes *See* Nordic Association for Canadian Studies

Association of American Geographers (AAG)

1710 - 16 St. NW, Washington DC 20009-3198 USA
Tel: 202-234-1450; *Fax:* 202-234-2744
gaia@aag.org
www.aag.org
Overview: A medium-sized national organization founded in 1904
Mission: To advance professional studies in geography & to encourage the application of geographic research in education, government & business; to promote discussion among its members & with scholars in related fields; to support the publication of scholarly studies
Member of: American Council of Learned Societies
Chief Officer(s):
Douglas Richardson, Executive Director
drichardson@aag.org
Finances: *Annual Operating Budget:* $1.5 Million-$3 Million
Staff Member(s): 10
Membership: 7,100 individual + 800 institutional; *Fees:* Schedule available; *Member Profile:* Members include students & professionals with backgrounds in a wide variety of geographic subfields such as urban geography, geographic information systems, cartography, remote sensing, historical geography, geomorphology, political geography, planning, environmental studies, & area studies
Activities: Specialty groups (comprised of geographers who share a professional interest in a systematic or topical specialty or in a major region of the world) sponsor sessions at the annual

Foreign Associations

meetings, publish newsletters or other communications, & develop workshops & other projects to advance their professional interests; AAG manages several funded projects; AAG supports special symposia; *Internships:* Yes; *Rents Mailing List:* Yes
Publications:
• The Professional Geographer
Editor: Sharmistha Bagchi-Sen
Profile: Annual journal

Association of American Publishers
71 - 5th Ave., 2nd Fl., New York NY 10003-3004 USA
Tel: 212-255-0200; *Fax:* 212-255-7007
www.publishers.org
twitter.com/AmericanPublish
Overview: A large national organization
Mission: To expand the market for American books & other published works in all media; to promote the status of publishing in the United States & throughout the world; To nutre creativity by protecting & strengthening intellectual property rights, especially copyright; To promote intellectual freedom & to oppose all forms of censorship, at home & abroad
Chief Officer(s):
Ronald G. Gunn, Chair
Tom Allen, President & CEO
tallen@publishers.org
Membership: 300 companies; *Fees:* Schedule available; *Committees:* Core Committees: Compensation Survey Steering; Publishing Latino Voices for America Task Force; Smaller & Independent Publishers; Paper Issues Working Group; Get Caught Reading Marketing Task Force; Freedom to Read; Educational Programs; Diversity/Recruit & Retain; Statistics; Tax; Trade Publishers Executive; Trade Libraries Joint Committee with ALA/ALCTS; AAP Core Copyright Committees; AAP Core International Committees; AAP Digital Issues Committees; AAP Higher Education Committees; AAP Professional/Scholarly Publishing Division Committees; AAP School Division Committees
Activities: Operates Bookjobs.com; Book Donation Initiative program

Association of Americans & Canadians in Israel (AACI)
Glassman Family Center, PO Box 53349, 37 Pierre Koenig, Jerusalem 91533 Israel
Tel: 972-2-566-1181; *Fax:* 972-2-566-1186
info@aaci.org.il
www.aaci.org.il
www.facebook.com/aacipage
Overview: A small international charitable organization founded in 1951
Mission: To provide a range of services to its members, whether new immigrants or long-time, English-speaking residents of Israel
Member of: Council of Immigrant Associations in Israel; Volunteer Sector Directorate
Chief Officer(s):
Helen Har-Tal, Contact
Finances: *Annual Operating Budget:* $500,000-$1.5 Million; *Funding Sources:* Jewish Agency for Israel; membership fees; grants; fundraising
Staff Member(s): 18; 1000 volunteer(s)
Membership: 20,000; *Member Profile:* North Americans of all ages, all religious streams, with no political affiliations; *Committees:* Absorption; Development; Finance; Membership; Legal; Loans & Mortgages
Activities: Employment Resource Center; loans; advice on legal, tax, banking, translation matters; senior outreach; library for visually impaired
Awards:
• Knesset Prize for Improving Quality of Life in Israel (Award)

Association of Children's Prosthetic-Orthotic Clinics (ACPOC)
#727, 6300, North River Rd., Rosemont IL 60018-4226 USA
Tel: 847-698-1637; *Fax:* 847-823-0536
acpoc@aaos.org
www.acpoc.org
Overview: A small international organization founded in 1978
Mission: To provide prosthetic-orthotic care for children with limb loss or orthopaedic disabilities.
Chief Officer(s):
David B. Rotter, President
Membership: *Fees:* US$90 corresponsing; US$125 non-physician; US$200 physician; *Member Profile:* Orthopaedic Surgeons; PTs; DO; Prosthetists; Orthotists; OTs; Nurses

Association of Christian Schools International (ACSI)
PO Box 65130, 731 Chapel Hills Dr., Colorado Springs CO 80962-5130 USA
Tel: 719-528-6906; *Fax:* 719-531-0631
info@acsi.org
www.acsi.org
www.facebook.com/ACSIUSA
twitter.com/ACSIUS
Overview: A medium-sized international organization founded in 1978
Mission: ACSI is an association of Protestant schools. It strives for school improvement, professional development & a provision of resources to enable Christian educators & schools worldwide to effectively prepare students for life.
Chief Officer(s):
Brian S. Simmons, President
Finances: *Funding Sources:* Membership fees
Membership: 5300 schools/colleges in 100 countries; *Fees:* Schedule available; *Member Profile:* Christian school; affirmation of ACSI statement of faith
Activities: Teacher conferences; student leadership conferences; board/administrator conferences; district principals meetings; music events; professional development days; *Speaker Service:* Yes

Eastern Canada Office
1 Wenden Ct., RR#2, Minesing ON L0L 1Y2
Tel: 705-728-7344; *Fax:* 705-728-4401
acsiec@sympatico.ca
www.acsiec.org
www.facebook.com/ACSIEC
Chief Officer(s):
Mark Kennedy, Regional Director

Western Canada Office
PO Box 3460, 44 Willow Brook Dr. NW, Airdrie AB T4B 2J5
Tel: 403-948-2332; *Fax:* 403-948-2395
www.acsiwc.org
www.facebook.com/ACSIWC
twitter.com/HillsPhilip
Chief Officer(s):
Philip Hills, Regional Director
phills@acsiwc.org

Association of Construction Inspectors (ACI)
PO Box 879, Palm Springs CA 92263 USA
Tel: 760-327-5284; *Fax:* 760-327-5631
Toll-Free: 877-815-4174
support@assoc-hdqts.org
www.aci-assoc.org
www.linkedin.com/groups/Association-Construction-Inspectors-4463001
Overview: A medium-sized international organization
Mission: To provide professional designation to construction inspectors; education & marketing information to members
Member of: International Association Managers
Membership: *Fees:* Schedule available; *Member Profile:* Construction inspectors
Activities: *Internships:* Yes; *Speaker Service:* Yes; *Rents Mailing List:* Yes

Association of Environmental Engineering & Science Professors (AEESP)
#600, 1211 Connecticut Ave. NW, Washington D.C. IL 20036 USA
Tel: 202-640-6591; *Fax:* 202-223-5537
www.aeesp.org
Overview: A medium-sized international organization founded in 1963
Mission: To assist members in the development & dissemination of knowledge in environmental engineering & science; to strengthen & advance the environmental field through cooperation amongst academic & other communities
Chief Officer(s):
Jennifer G. Becker, President
jgbecker@mtu.edu
Brian Schorr, Manager, Business Office
bschorr@aeesp.org
Membership: 700; *Fees:* $15 student; $60 affiliate; $50 assistant professor; $75 associate professor; $100 full professor; *Committees:* Administrative Handbook; Arrangements; Audit; Awards; Conference Selection; Education; Government Affairs; Internet Resources; Lecturers; Liaison; Membership & Demographics; Nominating; Publications; Strategic Planning; Student Services; Sustaining Member Stewardship
Activities: *Rents Mailing List:* Yes

Association of Fish & Wildlife Agencies
#725, 444 North Capitol St. NW, Washington DC 20001 USA
Tel: 202-624-7890; *Fax:* 202-624-7891
info@fishwildlife.org
www.fishwildlife.org
www.facebook.com/FishWildlifeAgencies
twitter.com/fishwildlife
Previous Name: International Association of Fish & Wildlife Agencies
Overview: A small international organization founded in 1902
Mission: To guide its members toward long term conservation of renewable natural resources by employing conservation science & research.
Chief Officer(s):
Ron Regan, Executive Director
rregan@fishwildlife.org
Dan Forster, President
Staff Member(s): 26
Membership: 142; *Member Profile:* Conservationists; Governments & government agencies; Regional associations; Organizations with similar objectives or supportive of the Association; Sportsmen; Individuals with varied backgrounds; *Committees:* Agricultural Conservation; Amphibian & Reptile; Annual Meeting/Awards/Nominating; Audit; Bird Conservation; Budget Conservation; Climate Change; Drug Approval Working Group; Education/Outreach/Diversity; Energy and Wildlife Policy; Executive; Federal and Tribal Relations; Fish & Wildlife Health; Fish and Wildlife Trust Funds; Fisheries/Water Resources Policy; Hunting/Shooting Sports Participation; International Relations; Invasive Species; Joint Federal/State Joint Policy Task Force on Federal Assistance Policy; Wildlife Resource Policy; Teaming with wildlife; Sustainable Wildlife Use
Activities: All bird conservation; Agency information database; Automated wildlife data systems; Conservation education; Conservation Leadership Institute; Farm Bill program; Furbearer management; International relations; Legislation; National Fish Habitat Action Plan; Science & Research; Teaming with wildlife; Wildlife conflict

Association of Fundraising Professionals (AFP)
#300, 4300 Wilson Blvd., Arlington VA 22203
Tel: 703-684-0410; *Fax:* 703-684-0540
Toll-Free: 800-666-3863
Other Communication: Canadian Membership: cdnmembership@afpnet.org
afp@afpnet.org
www.afpnet.org
www.linkedin.com/company/878282
www.facebook.com/AFPFan
twitter.com/afpihq
Previous Name: National Society of Fund Raising Executives
Overview: A large international organization founded in 1960
Mission: To promote stewardship, donor trust & effective & ethical fundraising
Chief Officer(s):
Bob Carter, Chair
Derek Fraser, Chair, AFP Canadian Council
Andrew Watt, President & CEO
awatt@afpnet.org
Membership: 30,000 in 233 chapters worldwide; *Fees:* $250 professional & associate; $75 young professional; $75 retired; $35 collegiate; $50 global e-membership; $150-$5,000 corporate; all + dues; *Member Profile:* Fundraising professionals, including development directors, fundraising consultants, grant writers, volunteer fundraisers, foundation executives& others
Activities: Conferences; publications; online resource centre; seminars & networking events; professional development opportunities; *Awareness Events:* National Philanthropy Day, November 15
Awards:
• Changing our World/Simms Awards for Outstanding Youth in Philanthropy (Award)
Ages 5-17 & Ages 18-23
• Community Counselling Service (CCS) Award for Outstanding Fundraising Professional (Award)
• Freeman Philanthropic Services Award for Outstanding Corporation (Award)
• Award for Outstanding Philanthropist (Award)
• Award for Outstanding Foundation (Award)
• Award for Outstanding Volunteer Fundraiser (Award)
• Barbara Marion Award for Outstanding Service to AFP (Award)
• Awards for Excellence in Fundraising (Award)
• Skystone Ryan Prize for Research on Fundraising & Philanthropy (Award)
• Charles R. Stephens Excellence in Diversity Award (Award)

Publications:
• Advancing Philanthropy [a publication of the Association of Fundraising Professionals]
Type: Magazine; *Frequency:* Quarterly
• AFP [Association of Fundraising Professionals] eWire
Type: eNewsletter; *Frequency:* Weekly
• AFP [Association of Fundraising Professionals] Fund Development Series
Type: Books
Profile: Career resource publications
• AFP [Association of Fundraising Professionals] Ready reference Series
Type: Booklets
Profile: Information on topics relevant to the industry
• Kaleidoscope [a publication of the Association of Fundraising Professionals]
Type: Newsletter; *Frequency:* Quarterly
• Te Informa [a publication of the Association of Fundraising Professionals]
Type: eNewsletter; *Frequency:* Quarterly
Profile: Spanish-language covering issues relevant to Mexico/Latin American countries

Calgary & Area Chapter
#300, 5 Richard Way SW, Calgary AB T3E 7M8
Tel: 403-297-1033; *Fax:* 403-724-0091
afp@telus.net
afpcalgary.afpnet.org
Chief Officer(s):
Lorie Abernethy, President
Stephanie McWilliam, Contact

Canada South Chapter
c/o AFP Greater Toronto Chapter, #412, 250 King St. East, Toronto ON M5A 4L5
info@afpcanadasouth.com
www.afpcanadasouth.com
ca.linkedin.com/pub/afp-canada-south-chapter/25/4b7/527
www.facebook.com/AFPCanadaSouth
twitter.com/AFPCanadaSouth
www.youtube.com/user/afpcanadasouth
Chief Officer(s):
Fedela Falkner, President
ffalkner@uwindsor.ca
Amanda Gellman, Contact, Government Relations, 519-253-3000 Ext. 4141
Pat Valleau, Contact, Membership & Mentoring, 519-973-4411 Ext. 33966
pat.valleau@wrh.on.ca

Cape Breton Chapter
Cape Breton NS

Central Alberta Chapter
AB

Edmonton & Area Chapter
PO Box 4355, Spruce Grove AB T7X 3B5
info@afpedmonton.ca
www.afpedmonton.ca
www.linkedin.com/groups/AFP-Edmonton-Area-Chapter-3796360
www.facebook.com/AFPEdmonton
twitter.com/AFPEdmonton
Chief Officer(s):
Adam Zawadiuk, President
adamz@nait.ca
Neil Luipasco, Director, Membership
nluipasco@citadeltheatre.com
Heather Manning, Administrator

Golden Horseshoe Chapter
ON
afpgoldenhorseshoe.org
www.linkedin.com/groups/AFP-Golden-Horseshoe-Chapter-2781017
www.facebook.com/344066545713
twitter.com/AFPGolden
Chief Officer(s):
Clark Trevor, President
trevor.clark@alzda.ca
Lorie Colledge, Vice-President, Membership
lcolledge@shrinenet.org

Greater Toronto Chapter
#412, 260 King St. East, Toronto ON M5A 4L5
Tel: 416-941-9212; *Fax:* 416-941-9013
Toll-Free: 800-796-7373
info@afptoronto.org
www.afptoronto.org
www.youtube.com/AFPToronto

Affliation(s): International Society of Fund Raising Executives
Chief Officer(s):
Susan A. Storey, President
sstorey@kciphilanthropy.com
Cynthia Quigley, Administrator
cquigley@afptoronto.org

Manitoba Chapter
PO Box 644, 395 Kensington St., Winnipeg MB R3C 2K3
Tel: 204-832-1512; *Fax:* 204-897-8094
www.afpmanitoba.ca
www.facebook.com/AFPManitoba
twitter.com/afpmanitoba
Chief Officer(s):
Tania Douglas, President
tdouglas3@hsc.mb.ca
Lise Carbonneau, Administrator
whirlwind@shaw.ca

Newfoundland & Labrador Chapter
NL
afp.nlchapter@gmail.com
www.facebook.com/146912222014068
Chief Officer(s):
Nancy Hollett, Contact, 709-753-0423
nhollett@nl.rogers.com

Nova Scotia Chapter
PO Box 33009, Halifax NS B3L 4T6
afpnovascotia@gmail.com
www.afpns.afpnet.org
Chief Officer(s):
Carol Murray-Rodriguez, President, 902-420-9124

Okanagan Chapter
#554, 101 - 1865 Dilworth Dr., Kelowna BC V1Y 9T1
Tel: 250-979-6652
afpokanagan@gmail.com
afpokanagan.afpnet.org
Chief Officer(s):
Chantelle Funk, President
chantelle.funk@bccancer.bc.ca
Shannon Jolly, Contact, Membership
sjolley@bc.cancer.ca

Ottawa Chapter
c/o Sarah Zgraggen, The Willow Group, 1485 Laperriere Ave., Ottawa ON K1Z 7S8
Tel: 613-590-1412
secretariat@afpottawa.ca
afpottawa.afpnet.org
www.facebook.com/AFPOttawa
twitter.com/AFPOttawa
Chief Officer(s):
Daniel Brunette, President
dbrunette@cfo-fcoa.ca
Sarah Zgraggen, Administrator

Québec Chapter
QC
Tél: 514-918-6572
afpquebec@gmail.com
afpquebec.afpnet.org
Chief Officer(s):
Denis Lalonde, Président
dlalonde@quebec.cancer.ca
Julie-Anne Houdayer, Gestionnaire

Regina Chapter
PO Box 613, Regina SK S4P 3A3
afpregina@gmail.com
afpsaskatoon.afpnet.org
www.facebook.com/afpregina
twitter.com/AFPRegina
Chief Officer(s):
Cindy Kobayashi, President
ckobayashi@habitatregina.ca
Ticia Starkes-Heward, Director, Membership
ticia.starkes-heward@sasktel.net

Saskatoon Chapter
Saskatoon SK
afpsaskatoon.afpnet.org
Chief Officer(s):
Jen Pederson, President
jenniferapederson@gmail.com
Kathleen Crowther, Chair, Membership
Kathleen.crowther@usask.ca

South Eastern Ontario Chapter
PO Box 1695, Kingston ON K7L 5J6
afpseo@gmail.com
afpseo.afpnet.org
www.facebook.com/afpseo.afpnet.org
twitter.com/AFP_SEO
Chief Officer(s):
Lisa Riley, Contact & Board Member, 613-533-6000 Ext. 7895
lisa.riley@queensu.ca

Southern Chapter
AB
afp.southernalberta@gmail.com
www.facebook.com/AFPSouthernAlbertaChapter
Chief Officer(s):
Lori Gusdorf, AFP Staff Liaison
LGusdorf@afpnet.org

Vancouver Chapter
#720, 999 West Broadway, Vancouver BC V5Z 1K5
Tel: 604-736-1010; *Fax:* 604-738-4080
info@afpvancouver.org
www.afpvancouver.org
www.facebook.com/afpvancouver
twitter.com/AFPVancouver
Chief Officer(s):
Shantal Cashman, President
Karline Mark-Eng, Contact

Vancouver Island Chapter
1075 Portage Rd., Victoria BC V8Z 1L1
Tel: 250-217-0772
afp.vancouverisland@gmail.com
afpvancouverisland.afpnet.org
www.linkedin.com/groups?home=&gid=7452371
www.facebook.com/afp.vi
twitter.com/AFP_VI
Chief Officer(s):
Carly Milloy, President
carlymilloy@shaw.ca
Monica Powell, Administrator
monicapowell@shaw.ca

Association of Great Lakes Outdoor Writers (AGLOW)

PO Box 35, Benld IL 62009 USA
Toll-Free: 877-472-4569
aglowinfo.org
www.facebook.com/145249282212242
Overview: A small local organization founded in 1954
Mission: Dedicated to communicating the outdoor experience in word & image
Chief Officer(s):
Josh Lantz, Executive Director
josh@sandcreek-media.com
P.J. Perea, President
pperea@nwtf.net
Finances: *Annual Operating Budget:* Less than $50,000; *Funding Sources:* Membership dues; fundraising
Staff Member(s): 2
Membership: 330; *Fees:* $45-135
Meetings/Conferences:
• Association of Great Lakes Outdoors Writers Fall Conference 2015, September, 2015, Minneapolis, MN
Scope: Local

Association of Holocaust Organizations (AHO)

PO Box 230317, Hollis NY 11423 USA
Tel: 516-582-4571
ahoinfo@att.net
www.ahoinfo.org
Overview: A medium-sized international organization founded in 1985
Mission: To serve as a network of organizations & individuals for the advancement of Holocaust programs, education, awareness & research
Chief Officer(s):
William L. Shulman, President
Susan Myers, Vice-President
Finances: *Annual Operating Budget:* Less than $50,000; *Funding Sources:* Membership dues
Membership: 209 organizations

Association of Personal Computer Users Groups (APCUG)

PO Box 671294, Dallas TX 75367-1294 USA
Toll-Free: 800-558-6867
apcug2.org
Overview: A medium-sized national organization founded in 1990

Mission: To help user groups offer better services to their members
Chief Officer(s):
Marie Vesta, President
Membership: 400+ groups; 300,000 individuals; *Fees:* US$50

Association of Postconsumer Plastic Recyclers (APR)

#500 West, 1001 - G St. NW, Washington DC 20001 USA
Tel: 202-316-3046
info@plasticsrecycling.org
www.plasticsrecycling.org
www.linkedin.com/groups?home=&gid=3176812&trk=anet_ug_hm
www.facebook.com/694931163886120
Overview: A small national organization founded in 1992
Mission: The Association represents companies who acquire, reprocess & sell post-consumer plastic. It strives to enhance the plastics recycling industry by promoting cooperative testing for the development of new packaging, improving the quality of plastics, encouraging better recycling guidelines, & presenting awards for advancements in the industry.
Chief Officer(s):
Steve Alexander, Executive Director
salexander@cmrgroup4.com
Finances: *Annual Operating Budget:* $100,000-$250,000; *Funding Sources:* Related associations; membership dues
Staff Member(s): 1
Membership: 103; *Fees:* $800-3,500; *Member Profile:* PCR reclaimers; *Committees:* Market Development; Technical; Executive
Activities: Design for Recyclability Programs; Champions for Change

Association of Research Libraries (ARL)

#800, 21 Dupont Circle NW, Washington DC 20036 USA
Tel: 202-296-2296; *Fax:* 202-872-0884
webmgr@arl.org
www.arl.org
www.linkedin.com/company/association-of-research-libraries
www.facebook.com/association.of.research.libraries
twitter.com/ARLnews
www.youtube.com/ARLvideo
Overview: A medium-sized international organization founded in 1932
Mission: To identify & influence forces affecting the future of research libraries in the process of scholarly communication
Member of: American Library Association
Affliation(s): Coalition for Networked Information; Office of Management Services; Scholarly Publishing & Academic Resources Coalition
Chief Officer(s):
Carol Pitts Diedrichs, President
Elliott Shore, Executive Director
elliott@arl.org
Finances: *Funding Sources:* Membership dues
Staff Member(s): 23
Membership: 125 research libraries; *Committees:* Executive; Coalition for Networked Information; Diversity & Leadership; Membership; Nominating; Statistics & Assessment; Influencing Public Policies; Advancing Scholarly Communication; Transforming Research Libraries; AAUP/ARL Working Group on University Press/Research Library Collaboration; Research Library Leadership Fellows (RLLF) Program Sponsors Advisor; Coalition for Networked Information; LibQUAL; Scholarly Publishing & Academic Resources Coalition
Activities: Promotes equitable access to & effective use of recorded knowledge in support of teaching, research, scholarship & community service

Association of Retail Travel Agents (ARTA)

4320 North Miller Rd., Scottsdale AZ 85251-3606 USA
Fax: 866-743-2087
Toll-Free: 866-369-8969
www.arta.travel
Overview: A medium-sized international organization founded in 1963
Mission: To represent travel agents in North America
Chief Officer(s):
Nancy Linares, Chair
Membership: *Fees:* $99 individual; $250 agency; $1000 lifetime; *Member Profile:* Travel agents in the USA & Canada

Association of Telehealth Service Providers (ATSP)

#400, 4702 SW Scholls Ferry Rd., Portland OR 97225-2008 USA
Tel: 503-922-0988; *Fax:* 315-222-2402
www.atsp.org
Overview: A small international organization founded in 1996
Mission: To improve health care through growth of the telehealth industry
Chief Officer(s):
William Engle, Executive Director

Association of Trial Lawyers of America (ATLA); National Association of Claimants' Compensation Attorneys (NACCA) *See* American Association for Justice

Association pour l'amélioration des cultures biologiques (international) *See* Organic Crop Improvement Association (International)

Association pour la prévention de la contamination de l'air et du sol *See* Air & Waste Management Association

Associazione Italiana di Studi Canadesi *See* Italian Association for Canadian Studies

Australian Association for Environmental Education (AAEE)

PO Box 996, Cotton Tree 4558 Australia
Tel: 61 7 5479 1424
admin@aaee.org.au
www.aaee.org.au
Overview: A small national organization founded in 1980
Mission: To promote environmental education
Chief Officer(s):
Phil Smith, President
rephilled@hotmail.com
Finances: *Annual Operating Budget:* $50,000-$100,000; *Funding Sources:* Fees; grants; sponsorship; subsidies
Staff Member(s): 1; 30 volunteer(s)
Membership: 500; *Fees:* $90-$99 individual; $120 family; $240 corporate; $140 school/NGO; $896-$985 lifetime; *Member Profile:* Professionals; *Committees:* Special interest groups

Australian Bankers' Association Inc.

56 Pitt St., Level 3, Sydney NSW 2000 Australia
Tel: 61-2-8298-0417; *Fax:* 61-2-8298-0402
www.bankers.asn.au
twitter.com/austbankers
www.youtube.com/user/AustralianBankers
Overview: A medium-sized national organization
Mission: To improve the economic well-being of Australians by fostering a banking system recognized as one of the safest, dynamic & most efficient in the world
Chief Officer(s):
Michael Smith, Chair

Australian Society of Association Executives Ltd. (AuSAE)

PO Box 752, Stones Corner, QLD 4120 Australia
Tel: 61 1 300 5764 6576; *Fax:* 61 7 3319 6056
info@ausae.org.au
www.ausae.org.au
twitter.com/AuSAENews
Overview: A small national organization founded in 1954
Mission: To provide support, networking services, & industry information to association managers in the business, professional, technical, trade, sporting, welfare, religious, educational & finance sectors.
Chief Officer(s):
Tony Steven, President
belinda@ausae.org.au
Belinda Moore, Chief Executive Officer
Finances: *Funding Sources:* Membership fees
Staff Member(s): 6
Membership: *Fees:* Schedule available
Activities: Networking functions; seminars; trade fairs

Austrian-Canadian Society

c/o Wolf Theiss, Schubertring 6, Vienna 1010 Austria
info@austria-canada.com
www.austria-canada.com
Overview: A small international organization founded in 2003
Mission: To improve the relationships between Austria & Canada in a sustainable manner; to forge contacts in the fields of traditional diplomacy, business, science, & culture.
Chief Officer(s):
Heinz Seitinger, President
president@austria-canada.com
Membership: *Fees:* 15 euros student; 50 euros regular; 75 euros family/couple

Automatic Identification Manufacturers *See* AIM Global

Badminton World Federation (BWF)

Amoda Bldg., #17.05, 22 Jalan Imbi, L. 17, Kuala Lumpur 55100 Malaysia
Tel: 603-2141 7155; *Fax:* 603-2143 7155
bwf@bwfbadminton.org
www.bwfbadminton.org
www.facebook.com/bwfbadminton
twitter.com/bwfmedia
Previous Name: International Badminton Federation (IBF)
Overview: A medium-sized international organization founded in 1934
Mission: To control the game of badminton, from an international aspect, in all countries; to uphold the Laws of Badminton as at present adopted
Chief Officer(s):
Poul-Erik Høyer, President
pe.hoyer@bwfbadminton.org
Finances: *Funding Sources:* Subscriptions & sponsorships
Membership: 180 nationally organized bodies; *Committees:* Continental Confederations; IOC & International Relations; Administration; Events; Development & Sport for All; Marketing; Finance; Para-Badminton
Awards:
• Hall of Fame (Award)
Periodic for exceptional achievements by players/administration
• Herbert Scheele Trophy (Award)
Awarded periodically for outstandingly eceptional achievements
• Eddy Choong Player of the Year Award (Award)
Annual award for achieving outstanding results
• Certificate of Commendation (Award)
Awarded semi-annually for commercial & external organisations who contribute to badminton
• Distinguished Associates Award (Award)
Annual awared for major support in the development of badminton
• Distinguished Service Award (Award)
Semi-annual award for long or distinguished services to badminton
• Meritorious Sevice Award (Award)
Awarded semi-annually for long & meritorious services to badminton

Barbershop Harmony Society

110 - 7th Ave. North, Nashville TN 37203-3704 USA
Tel: 615-823-9339; *Fax:* 615-313-7620
Toll-Free: 800-876-7464
info@barbershop.org
www.barbershop.org
www.facebook.com/barbershopharmonysociety
twitter.com/barbershopnews
www.youtube.com/user/BarbershopHarmony
Previous Name: Society for the Preservation & Encouragement of Barber Shop Quartet Singing in America Inc.
Overview: A medium-sized international charitable organization founded in 1938
Mission: To perpetuate the old American institution, the barbershop quartet; to promote & encourage vocal harmony & good fellowship among its members by the formation of local chapters & districts; to encourage & promote the education of its members & the public in music appreciation
Affliation(s): British Association of Barbershop Singers; Barbershop Harmony Australia; Barbershop in Germany; Dutch Association of Barbershop Singers; Finnish Association of Barbershop Singers; Irish Association of Barbershop Singers; New Zealand Association of Barbershop Singers; Spanish Association of Barbershop Singers; Society of Nordic Barbershop Singers; Southern Part of Africa Tonsorial Singers
Chief Officer(s):
Marty Monson, CEO & Executive Director
mmonson@barbershop.org
Staff Member(s): 36
Membership: 25,000 in the United States & Canada; *Fees:* $115
Activities: Annual, local, district, state, national & international contests in quartet & chorus singing; *Library:* Old Songs Library

Bear Biology Association *See* International Association for Bear Research & Management

Bibliographical Society of America (BSA)

PO Box 1537, Stn. Lennox Hill, New York NY 10021 USA
Tel: 212-452-2710; *Fax:* 212-452-2710
bsa@bibsocamer.org
www.bibsocamer.org
Overview: A small international organization founded in 1904

Mission: To study books & manuscripts as physical objects; to promote bibliographical research through meetings, lectures, fellowship programs & the publishing of books & journals
Member of: American Council of Learned Societies
Chief Officer(s):
Martin Antonetti, President
Michèle E. Randall, Executive Director
Membership: *Fees:* $20 student; $65 individual; $100 institution/contributing; $250 sustaining; $1250 lifetime; *Member Profile:* Interest in bibliographical projects & problems; *Committees:* Audit; Fellowship; Finance; Program; Publications
Activities: *Rents Mailing List:* Yes
Awards:
• Mitchell Prize (Award)
For bibliography or documentary work on early British periodicals or newspapers *Amount:* $1000 + 1 year's membership
• Schiller Prize (Award)
Bibliographical work on pre-20th-Century children's books *Amount:* $2000 + 1 year's membership
• St. Louis Mercantile Library Prize (Award)
Bibliographical work on American history and literature; awarded every 3 yrs. *Amount:* $2000 + 1 year's membership
Publications:
• The Papers of the Bibliographical Society of America
Type: journal

Bonn Agreement (BONN)
Victoria House, 37-63 Southampton Row, London WC1B 4DA United Kingdom
Tel: 44-20-7430-5200; *Fax:* 44-20-7430-5225
secretariat@bonnagreement.org
www.bonnagreement.org
Overview: A small international organization founded in 1969
Mission: To provide a cooperation forum for dealing with accidental marine pollution of the North Sea & marine pollution aerial surveillance
Chief Officer(s):
M. Michel Aymeric, Chair
Staff Member(s): 3
Membership: 9 European & EU countries; *Fees:* Annual contribution

Brazilian Association for Canadian Studies *See* Associação Brasileira de Estudos Canadense

British Association for Canadian Studies (BACS) / Association britanniques d'études canadiennes
#212, South Block, Senate House, University of London, Malet St., London WC1E 7HU United Kingdom
Tel: 020 7862 8687; *Fax:* 020 7117 1875
canstuds@gmail.com
www.canadian-studies.net
twitter.com/Canada_BACS
Overview: A small international charitable organization founded in 1975
Mission: To act as a forum for Canadian studies in the United Kingdom
Member of: International Council for Canadian Studies
Chief Officer(s):
Jodie Robson, Administrator
Membership: *Fees:* $30 students & unwaged persons; $60 regular members; *Member Profile:* Persons with an interest in the study of Canada
Awards:
• British Association for Canadian Studies Travel Awards (Award)
To enable qualified British scholars make academic visits to Canada
Meetings/Conferences:
• British Association for Canadian Studies (BACS) 2015 40th Annual Conference, April, 2015, British Library Conference Centre, London
Scope: International
Description: Distinguished speakers on a great range of topics
Contact Information: Conference Manager: Luke Flanagan, E-mail: lukeflanagan@btinternet.com
Publications:
• British Association for Canadian Studies Newsletter
Type: Newsletter
Profile: Upcoming events & information from the association
• British Journal of Canadian Studies
Type: Journal; *Frequency:* Semiannually; *Editor:* Dr. Heather Norris Nicholson
Profile: Articles & book reviews

The Brontë Society
Brontë Parsonage Museum, Haworth, Keighley, West Yorkshire BD22 8DR United Kingdom
Tel: 44-1535-642-323; *Fax:* 44-1535-647-131
bronte@bronte.org.uk
www.bronte.info
Overview: A medium-sized international charitable organization founded in 1893
Mission: To bring closer together all who honour the Brontë sisters; to act as the guardian of such letters, writings & personal belongings as could be acquired for the Museum; to foster interest in the Brontës' writing & lives through education programs, publications & exhibitions
Affiliation(s): Alliance of Literary Societies
Chief Officer(s):
Andrew McCarthy, Director
Bonnie Greer, President
Finances: *Annual Operating Budget:* $500,000-$1.5 Million; *Funding Sources:* Museum admissions; society subscriptions
Staff Member(s): 35; 10 volunteer(s)
Membership: 2,500; *Fees:* 18.50 Pounds UK & Europe; rest of the world 27.50 Pounds; 10.50 Pounds students; 5 Pounds Angrians; *Committees:* Finance; Membership; Museum Education
Activities: *Library:* Brontë Parsonage Library; by appointment
Awards:
• Heritage Education Trust - The Sandford Award (Award)

Brotherhood of Maintenance of Way Employees (AFL-CIO/CLC) / Fraternité des préposés à l'entretien des voies (FAT-COI/CTC)
41475 Gardenbrook Rd., Novi MI 48375-1328 USA
Tel: 248-662-2660; *Fax:* 248-662-2659
www.bmwe.org
Overview: A medium-sized international organization
Chief Officer(s):
Fred N. Simpson, President
fns@bmwe.org
Membership: 12,110 + 133 locals

Building Materials Reuse Association (BMRA)
PO Box 47776, Chicago IL 60647 USA
Tel: 773-340-2672
contact@bmra.org
www.bmra.org
Previous Name: Used Building Materials Association
Overview: A medium-sized national organization
Mission: To represent companies & organizations in the United States & Canada involved in the acquisition &/or redistribution of used building materials
Chief Officer(s):
Brad Guy, President
Membership: *Fees:* $95; *Member Profile:* Companies & organizations involved in the acquisition &/or redistribution of used building materials

Building Owners & Managers Association International (BOMA)
#800, 1101 - 15th St. NW, Washington DC 20005 USA
Tel: 202-408-2662; *Fax:* 202-326-6377
info@boma.org
www.boma.org
Overview: A medium-sized international organization founded in 1907
Chief Officer(s):
Henry Chamberlain, APR, FASAE, CAE, President & COO
Finances: *Annual Operating Budget:* Greater than $5 Million
Staff Member(s): 29
Membership: 16,500 individuals & companies

Bureau international de la paix *See* International Peace Bureau

Bureau international des poids et mesures (BIPM)
Pavillon de Breteuil, Sévres F-92312 France
Tél: 33-1-45-07-70-00
webmaster@bipm.org
www.bipm.fr
Aperçu: *Dimension:* petite; *Envergure:* internationale; fondée en 1875
Mission: Établir les étalons fondamentaux et les échelles des principales grandeurs physiques et conserver les prototypes internationaux; effectuer la comparaison des étalons nationaux et internationaux; assurer la coordination des techniques de mesure correspondantes; to ensure world-wide uniformity of measurements & their traceability to the International System of Units (SI)
Membre(s) du bureau directeur:
Martin Milton, Directeur
Membre: *Comités:* International des Poids et Mesure; Consultatif de l'acoustique, des ultrasons et des vibrations; Consultatif d'électricité et magnétisme; Consultatif des longueurs; Consultatif pour la masse et les grandeurs apparentées; Consultatif pour la quantité de matière - métrologie en chimie; Consultatif des rayonnements ionisants; Consultatif de thermométrie; Consultatif du temps et des fréquences; Consultatif des unités; Commun pour les guides en métrologie; Mixte des organisations régionales de métrologie et du BIPM; Commun pour la traçabilité en médecine de laboratoire
Activités: *Bibliothèque*

Bureau of International Recycling (BIR)
24, av Franklin Roosevelt, Brussels 1050 Belgium
Tel: 32-2-627-5770; *Fax:* 32-2-627-5773
bir@bir.org
www.bir.org
Overview: A medium-sized international organization founded in 1948
Mission: To promote recycling & a recyclability, thereby conserving natural resources, protecting the environment, & facilitating free trade of recyclables in an environmentally sound manner
Chief Officer(s):
Björn Grufman, President
Membership: 890+; *Fees:* 2,000€ regular; 2,400€ gold; 1,000€ subsidiaries

Business & Institutional Furniture Manufacturer's Association (BIFMA)
#150. 678 Front Ave. NW, Grand Rapids MI 49504-5368 USA
Tel: 616-285-3963; *Fax:* 616-285-3765
email@bifma.org
www.bifma.org
www.linkedin.com/company/BIFMA
twitter.com/BIFMA
Overview: A medium-sized international organization founded in 1973
Chief Officer(s):
Roxanne DeBoer, Contact
Staff Member(s): 6
Membership: 245 companies

Campaign Against Arms Trade (CAAT)
#4, 5-7 Weeks Terrace, London N4 3JU UK
Tel: 44-20728-10297
enquiries@caat.org.uk
www.caat.org.uk
www.facebook.com/campaignagainstarmstrade
twitter.com/wwwcaatorguk
www.youtube.com/wwwcaatorguk
Overview: A small international organization founded in 1974
Mission: To end the international arms trade; to pursue security by promoting the idea that funds should be funnelled, not into military interests, but into such causes of insecurity as social inequality & climate change.
Chief Officer(s):
Andrew Smith, Media Coordinator
media@caat.org.uk
Activities: *Speaker Service:* Yes *Library* by appointment

Canada - United States Trade Center (CUSTAC)
Dept. of Geography, Univ. of Buffalo, 105 Wilkeson Quadrangle, Buffalo NY 14261-0055 USA
Tel: 716-645-2722; *Fax:* 716-645-2329
geog@buffalo.edu
www.custac.buffalo.edu
Previous Name: International Center for Canadian-American Trade
Overview: A small international organization
Mission: CUSTAC conducts applied & policy-oriented research on the nature of Canada-US commercial relations with respect to trade, capital investment, border management, & regulatory conditions. Specifically, one of its main functions is to assist in the development of the trade corridor between Western New York & Southern Ontario. It also lobbies governments for equitable environments, suitable for stable, economic transactions between the 2 countries.
Chief Officer(s):
McConnell James, Associate Director
geojem@acsu.buffalo.edu
Activities: Conducting seminars & workshops; developing university courses; *Library:* Information Library;

Foreign Associations

Canadian Bull Riders Association *See* Professional Bull Riders Inc

Canadian Cultural Centre *Voir* Centre culturel canadien

Canadian Decorating Products Association *See* Paint & Decorating Retailers Association Canada

Canadian Norwegian Business Association (CNBA)

PO Box 449, Sandvika N-1302 Norway
Tel: 47-928-68-757
post@cnba.no
www.cnba.no
Overview: A small international organization
Mission: To strengthen the business & cultural ties between Canada & Norway
Chief Officer(s):
Kristian Kristiansen, Administrator
Membership: *Fees:* $200 student; $500 individual; $2,500 corporate

The Canadian Philatelic Society of Great Britain

12 Milchester House, Staveley Rd., Meads Eastbourne BN20 7JX United Kingdom
Tel: 01323-438-964
cpsofgb@hotmail.com
www.canadianpsgb.org.uk
Overview: A small national organization founded in 1946
Mission: The study of the philately of Canada, including provinces which were separate colonies prior to Confederation
Chief Officer(s):
Derrick Scoot, President
J.M. Wright, Secretary
Finances: *Annual Operating Budget:* Less than $50,000; *Funding Sources:* Membership fees
Membership: 420; *Fees:* £16 or $39 CAN or US$39; *Member Profile:* Members mostly in UK, Canada & USA
Activities: Two auctions, March & at Sept. convention; *Library* by appointment

Can-Am Border Trade Alliance

PO Box 929, Lewiston NY 14092 USA
Tel: 716-754-8824; *Fax:* 716-754-8824
canambta@aol.com
canambta.org
Overview: A medium-sized international organization
Mission: To maximize global commercial activity and ensure continued growth of two-way cross border trade along the entire common U.S./Canadian border and assure efficient, productive border crossing capabilities; and also to provide unified leadership for border concern, operations and needs and to act as an effective, proactive and focused border issues resource.
Chief Officer(s):
James D. Phillips, President & CEO
Membership: *Fees:* Schedule available

Carrying Capacity Network (CCN)

PO Box 457, San Francisco CA 94104-0457 USA
Tel: 202-296-4548; *Fax:* 202-296-4609
Toll-Free: 800-466-4866
info@carryingcapacity.org
www.carryingcapacity.org
Overview: A large international organization founded in 1989
Mission: "Carrying Capacity" refers to the number of individuals who can be supported without degrading the physical, ecological, cultural & social environment (ie without reducing the ability of the environment to sustain the desired quality of life over the long term); CCN functions as a clearinghouse of information for participants, a forum for discussion of controversial issues & as a catalyst for cooperation among diverse groups involved in carrying capacity issues; CCN's objective is to facilitate the understanding of the crucial linkages between population & the environment by exchanging information, disseminating news & encouraging cooperation among environmental, resource conservation, growth control & population stabilization organizations & activists
Finances: *Annual Operating Budget:* $500,000-$1.5 Million
Staff Member(s): 8
Membership: *Fees:* $20 senior/student; $25 adult; $40 sustaining; $100 major; $250 sponsor; $500 benefactor; $1,000 patron
Activities: Resource Bank (a catalogue of resources to aid participants in their search for information); Speakers/Writers Bureau (a database of individuals & organizations that would speak or write on the wide range of carrying capacity issues); *Speaker Service:* Yes

Cátedra de Estudios sobre Canadá / Chair of Canadian Studies

Universidad de la Habana, Edificio Varona (altos), Flasco Cuba, Havana 10400 Cuba
Overview: A small international organization founded in 1994
Mission: The Chair promotes in Cuba knowledge of the history & current socio-economic reality of Canada, as well as facilitating knowledge in Canada of Cuba. It coordinates & promotes scientific/technical & cultural exchange & the development of joint activities between the University of Havana & Canadian institutions.
Member of: International Council for Canadian Studies (ICCS)
Chief Officer(s):
Beatriz Diaz, President
beatriz@flacso.uh.cu

Catholic Biblical Federation (CBF) / Fédération biblique catholique (FBC)

St. Ottilien 86941 Germany
Tel: 49-8193-716900; *Fax:* 49-8193-716999
gensec@c-b-f.org
www.c-b-f.org
Overview: A small international charitable organization founded in 1969
Affliation(s): Catholic Biblical Association of Canada
Chief Officer(s):
Alexander Schweitzer, General Secretary
Staff Member(s): 6
Membership: 300+ in 130 countries
Activities: Workshops; Plenary Assembly

Cell Stress Society International (CSSI)

91 North Eagleville Rd., Storrs CT 06269-3125 USA
Tel: 860-486-5709; *Fax:* 860-486-5709
cellstress.uconn.edu
Overview: A medium-sized international organization
Mission: To promote stress response research & the dissemination of information; To encourage clinical & industrial applications of research
Member of: Society of the International Union of Biological Sciences
Chief Officer(s):
Graham Pockley, President
Helen Neumann, General Secretary
Membership: 230; *Fees:* US$55 student/member from developing countries; US$240 regular membership; US$1,000 lifetime membership
Activities: Supporting young scientists in the field of stress response; Cooperating with related organizations; Increasing public awarness of advances in stress response research
Publications:
• Cell Stress & Chaperones: An Integrative Journal of Stress Biology & Medicine
Type: Journal; *Editor:* Lawrence E. Hightower *ISSN:* 1355-8145; *Price:* Free with membership in Cell Stress Society International

Center for Health, Environment & Justice (CHEJ)

PO Box 6806, Falls Church VA 22040-6806 USA
Tel: 703-237-2249; *Fax:* 703-237-8389
chej@chej.org
www.chej.org
www.facebook.com/CHEJfans
twitter.com/CHEJ
www.youtube.com/CHEJtv
Previous Name: Citizens Clearinghouse for Hazardous Wastes
Overview: A medium-sized national charitable organization founded in 1981
Mission: To help communities win environmental justice
Chief Officer(s):
Lois Marie Gibbs, Executive Director/Founder
Sharon Franklin, Finance/Administrative Director
Finances: *Annual Operating Budget:* $500,000-$1.5 Million; *Funding Sources:* Membership dues; donations
Staff Member(s): 14
Membership: 25,000 individual + 7,500 groups; *Fees:* $30 individual; $100 group
Activities: Provides science, organizing & technical assistance to citizens concerned with dioxin, toxic waste, chemical poisons, etc. in their communities; site visits by staff; 130+ self-help guides & fact packs; campaigns: Stop Dioxin Exposure; childproofing communities; BESAFE; *Awareness Events:* March into Spring, March; *Internships:* Yes; *Speaker Service:* Yes *Library* Open to public

Center for Holocaust & Genocide Studies (CHGS)

Social Sciences Bldg., Univ. of Minnesota, #214, 267 - 19th Ave. South, Minneapolis MN 55455 USA
Tel: 612-624-9007
chgs@umn.edu
www.chgs.umn.edu
www.facebook.com/chgsumn
twitter.com/chgsumn
www.youtube.com/CHGSumn
Overview: A small local organization founded in 1997
Mission: To serve as an independent, academic, resource institution for information & teaching about the Holocaust & contemporary aspects of genocide; to act as consultants to universities, news media, & civic organizations; to support secondary-school classroom educators through workshops & curriculum materials.
Member of: Association of Holocaust Organizations
Affiliation(s): Genocide Watch; Acgis Trust
Chief Officer(s):
Alejandro Baer, Director
abaer@umn.edu
Finances: *Funding Sources:* Donations
Staff Member(s): 3
Activities: Virtual exhibitions; memorials, testaments; reading & discussion groups; *Internships:* Yes; *Speaker Service:* Yes *Library* Open to public

Center for Marine Conservation; Center for Environmental Education *See* The Ocean Conservancy

Center for Plant Conservation

PO Box 299, St. Louis MO 63166-0299 USA
Tel: 314-577-9450; *Fax:* 314-577-9465
cpc@mobot.org
www.centerforplantconservation.org
Overview: A medium-sized international organization founded in 1984
Mission: To create a systematic, comprehensive national program of plant conservation, research & education within existing institutions, as a complement to the preservation of genetic diversity through habitat protection; to strengthen its collaborative ties with countries contiguous to the US & its territories - Canada, Mexico & nations of the Greater Antilles; to develop & maintain comprehensive & broadly accessible information systems, national networks & databases concerning the biology, horticulture & conservation status of all nationally endangered native plants of the US
Chief Officer(s):
Kathryn Kennedy, President & Executive Director
Staff Member(s): 3
Membership: *Fees:* Schedule available
Activities: The National Collection of Endangered Species consists of living plant materials collected from the wild, representing to the greatest extent possible the genetic diversity found in natural populations; Participating Institutions - affiliated botanical gardens & arboreta around the US; Priority Regions - areas facing a major plant extinction crisis; Integrated Conservation; Conservation Research; Information & Data Systems; Economic Plant Research; International Conservation

Center for Psychology & Social Change; Center for Psychological Studies in the Nuclear Age *See* John E. Mack Institute

Central European Association for Canadian Studies (CEACS) / Association d'Études Canadiennes en Europe Centrale

Institut de Langues et Littératures Romanes, Université Masaryk, A. Nováka 1, Brno 60200 Czech Republic
Tel: 420-542-128-309; *Fax:* 420-542-128-238
www.cecanstud.cz
www.facebook.com/groups/330011670458880/
Overview: A small international organization founded in 2003
Mission: The CEACS brings together university teachers, researchers and students from the Central European region who are doing work related to Canada
Chief Officer(s):
Diana Yankova, President
yankova@nlcv.net
Rodica Albu, Secretary
rr_albu@yahoo.co.uk
Membership: 165; *Member Profile:* Members from Bulgaria, Croatia, the Czech Republic, Hungary, Romania, Serbia & Montenegro, Slovakia & Slovenia

Centre culturel canadien / Canadian Cultural Centre

5, rue de Constantine, Paris 75007 France

Tél: 33-144-432-190; *Téléc:* 33-144-432-199
info@canada-culture.org
www.canadainternational.gc.ca
www.facebook.com/198305393540697
twitter.com/cc_canadien
www.youtube.com/user/CCCanadienParis
Aperçu: *Dimension:* petite; *Envergure:* internationale; fondée en 1970
Mission: Les services culturels de l'Ambassade du Canada appuient et présentent plusieurs aspects de l'activité culturelle canadienne en France; de nombreuses manifestations culturelles sont organisées par les services des arts de la scène, des industries culturelles et des arts visuels conjointement avec des organismes français à Paris et en province, à l'occasion de festivals, de spectacles, de sorties de films, de livres ou de disques
Affiliation(s): Canadian Conference of the Arts
Finances: *Budget de fonctionnement annuel:* $100,000-$250,000
Membre(s) du personnel: 16
Activités: *Service de conférenciers:* Oui *Bibliothèque* Bibliothèque publique

Centre d'Études Canadiennes de l'Université Libre de Bruxelles ***See*** Centre d'Études Nord-Américaines de l'Université Libre de Bruxelles

Centre d'Études Nord-Américaines de l'Université Libre de Bruxelles

Faculté de Philosophie et Lettres, Univ. Libre de Bruxelles, Stn. 175/01, 50, av F.D. Roosevelt, Brussels 1050 Belgium
Tel: 32-2-650-3807; *Fax:* 32-2-650-3919
mlebrun@admin.ulb.ac.be
www.ulb.ac.be//cena
Previous Name: Centre d'Études Canadiennes de l'Université Libre de Bruxelles
Overview: A small international organization founded in 1982
Chief Officer(s):
Serge Jaumain, Director
sjaumain@ulb.ac.be
Membership: *Member Profile:* Professors, primarily in the humanities, & experts in fields as varied as literature, sociology, law, history, media & computer science
Activities: Research topics: the coexistence of linguistic communities & its impact on history, politics, sociology & culture; the secularization of society (in particular Québec society); relations between Belgium & Canada since the late nineteenth century; Belgian immigration to Canada; gender studies; anglophone & francophone literatures; the economic & institutional evolution of the two states; comparative analysis of museums; & the status of artists

Centre du Commerce International ***See*** International Trade Centre

Centre for Environmental Law & Development ***See*** Foundation for International Environmental Law & Development

Centre international d'informations de sécurité et de santé au travail ***See*** International Occupational Safety & Health Information Centre

La Chaine bleue mondiale ***See*** World Blue Chain for the Protection of Animals & Nature

Chair of Canadian Studies ***See*** Cátedra de Estudios sobre Canadá

Chambre de Commerce Internationale ***See*** International Chamber of Commerce

Chartered Accountants Institute of Bermuda (ICAB)

Sofia House, 48 Church St., 1st Fl., Hamilton HM 12 Bermuda
Tel: 441-292-7479; *Fax:* 441-295-3121
info@icab.bm
www.icab.bm
Overview: A small international organization founded in 1973 overseen by Chartered Professional Accountants Canada
Mission: To build a reputation of reliability on behalf of members among the public
Chief Officer(s):
Annarita G. Marion, JP, CA, President & CEO
agwmarion@icab.bm
Finances: *Funding Sources:* Membership dues
Staff Member(s): 4
Membership: *Fees:* Schedule available; *Committees:* Applications Review; Nominating; Professional Development; Student Affairs; Professional Practice; Public Awareness
Activities: *Internships:* Yes

Chartered Institute of Logistics & Transport (CILT)

Earlstrees Court, Earlstrees Rd., Corbyn NN17 4AX UK
Tel: 44-0-1536-740-100; *Fax:* 44-0-1536-740-101
www.ciltinternational.org
www.linkedin.com/groups?about=&gid=780717
Previous Name: Chartered Institute of Transport
Overview: A medium-sized international charitable organization founded in 1919
Mission: To promote, encourage & coordinate the study & advancement of the science & art of transportation in all its branches
Affliation(s): Integrated in UK with Institute of Logistics UK section now titled Institute of Logistics & Transport
Chief Officer(s):
Dorothy Chan, President
Finances: *Annual Operating Budget:* Greater than $5 Million; *Funding Sources:* Membership dues
Staff Member(s): 21
Membership: 33,000 worldwide; *Fees:* Schedule available; *Member Profile:* Professionals in transport & logistics; *Committees:* Membership; Education
Activities: Providing education programs, lecture meetings, & training; Presenting transport reports; *Speaker Service:* Yes *Library:* Chartered Institute of Logistics & Transport Library; Open to public

Chartered Institute of Public Finance & Accountancy (CIPFA)

3 Robert St., London WC2N 6RL United Kingdom
Tel: 020 7543 5600; *Fax:* 020 7543 5700
customerliaison@cipfa.org
www.cipfa.org.uk
www.linkedin.com/company/cipfa
www.facebook.com/CIPFA.org
twitter.com/cipfa
Overview: A medium-sized international organization
Mission: To promote high performance in public financial services; To advance public finance; To support improved public financial services
Chief Officer(s):
Jaki Salisbury, President
Rob Whiteman, Chief Executive
Adrian Pulham, Director, Education & Membership
Membership: 14,000; *Member Profile:* Persons in public finance
Activities: Providing information & guidance; Offering professional, financial, & management development programs; Providing consultancy services; Collaborating other accountancy bodies, the public sector, & donors;
Publications:
• Chartered Institute of Public Finance & Accountancy Annual Report & Accounts
Type: Yearbook; *Frequency:* Annually
• Public Finance Magazine
Type: Magazine; *Frequency:* Weekly

Chartered Institute of Transport ***See*** Chartered Institute of Logistics & Transport

Chevaliers de Colomb ***See*** Knights of Columbus

Children's Tumor Foundation (CTF)

95 Pine St., 16th Fl., New York NY 10005 USA
Tel: 212-344-6633; *Fax:* 212-747-0004
Toll-Free: 800-323-7938
info@ctf.org
www.ctf.org
www.facebook.com/childrenstmrfdn
twitter.com/childrenstumor
Previous Name: National NF Foundation
Overview: A medium-sized national charitable organization founded in 1978
Mission: To sponsor research to find the cause of & cure for both types of NF - NF1 & NF2; to promote clinical activities which assure individuals with NF ready access to the highest calibre of medical care; to develop programs to increase public awareness of NF; to provide support services for patients & families, with referrals to qualified healthcare professionals
Member of: International NF Association
Affliation(s): NF Associations worldwide
Chief Officer(s):
John W. Risner, President
Finances: *Annual Operating Budget:* $3 Million-$5 Million
Staff Member(s): 2; 1000 volunteer(s)
Membership: 50,000+; *Fees:* $40
Activities: *Awareness Events:* NF Awareness Month, May; *Speaker Service:* Yes

Christian Peace Conference (CPC)

PO Box 136, Prokopova 4, Praha 3, Praha 13011 Czech Republic
Tel: 420-2-2278-1800; *Fax:* 420-2-2278-1801
christianpeace@volny.cz
www.volny.cz/christianpeace/cpc
Overview: A small international organization founded in 1958
Finances: *Funding Sources:* Fundraising; donations; membership fees
Membership: *Member Profile:* Churches; groups; individuals
Publications:
• CPC [Christian Peace Conference] Information
Type: Magazine; *Frequency:* Bimonthly

Christian Science / La Première Église du Christ, Scientiste

The First Church of Christ, Scientist, 210 Massachusetts Ave., Boston MA 02115 USA
Tel: 617-450-2000
Toll-Free: 800-775-2775
Other Communication: www.marybakereddylibrary.org
info@churchofchristscientist.org
christianscience.com
twitter.com/cschurches
plus.google.com/104001952392468849471
Also Known As: The Mother Church
Overview: A large international organization founded in 1879
Mission: Christian Scientists believe in one God, the Bible & in Christ Jesus as the Messiah. They believe that the application of the laws of God are practical & provable, hence scientific.
Chief Officer(s):
Channing Walker, President
Russ Gerber, Manager, Committee on Publication
Finances: *Annual Operating Budget:* Greater than $5 Million; *Funding Sources:* Donations
Staff Member(s): 850
Membership: 2,200 churches in over 70 countries; *Fees:* Per capita tax of not less than 1$; *Member Profile:* The Church is open to those who are "believer(s) [of] the doctrines of [the] Christian Science textbook: Science & Health with Key to the Scriptures, by Rev. Mary Baker Eddy."
Activities: Sunday worship services, Wednesday testimonial meetings; Sunday School for children; worldwide speakers bureau; retail book stores; Christian Science Reading Rooms; Christian Science programs & Weekly Bible Lessons are broadcast on public media; *Internships:* Yes; *Speaker Service:* Yes *Library:* Mary Baker Eddy Library for the Betterment of Humanity; Open to public by appointment
Publications:
• The Christian Science Journal
Type: Magazine; *Frequency:* Monthly
Profile: www.spirituality.com/journal
• The Christian Science Monitor
Type: Newspaper; *Frequency:* Weekly; *Editor:* Marshall Ingwerson; *Price:* Print & digital: $5.99/mth. Digital: $4.99/mth.
Profile: Weekly review of global news & ideas

Citizens Clearinghouse for Hazardous Wastes ***See*** Center for Health, Environment & Justice

CIVICUS: World Alliance for Citizen Participation

PO Box 933, 24 Gwigwi Mrwebi St., Johannesburg 2135 South Africa
Tel: +27 11 833 5959; *Fax:* +27 11 833 7997
Other Communication: membership@civicus.org
info@civicus.org
www.civicus.org
Overview: A small international organization
Mission: To strengthen citizen action & civil society around the globe towards a more just & equitable world; To promote the rights of citizens to organize & act collectively; To foster interaction between civil society & other institutions
Chief Officer(s):
Ingrid Srinath, Secretary General
Katsuji Imata, Deputy Secretary General, Programs
Sebastian Njagi Runguma, Manager, Planning & Learning
Sandra Pires, Manager, Membership
Devendra Tak, Manager, Communications & Media
Membership: 450+; *Member Profile:* Citizens from 110 countries, including individuals, youth, business associates, citizen organizations, & nongovernmental grantmaking organizations
Activities: Advocating for citizen participation; Amplifying the opinions of ordinary people; Increasing the effectiveness of civil society organizations

Meetings/Conferences:
• CIVICUS: World Alliance for Citizen Participation 2015 World Assembly, 2015
Scope: International
Publications:
• Affinity Group of National Associations (AGNA) Newsletter
Type: Newsletter
• Civil Society Index (CSI) Newsletter
Type: Newsletter; *Frequency:* Quarterly
Profile: Project updates
• Civil Society Watch (CSW) Monthly Bulletin
Type: Newsletter; *Frequency:* Monthly
• e-CIVICUS [a publication of CIVICUS: World Alliance for Citizen Participation]
Type: Newsletter; *Frequency:* Weekly
Profile: Developments in civil society organizations around the world

Clean Water Action
#400, 1010 Vermont Ave. NW, Washington DC 20005-4918 USA
Tel: 202-895-0420; *Fax:* 202-895-0438
Other Communication: blog.cleanwateraction.org
cwa@cleanwater.org
www.cleanwateraction.org
www.facebook.com/pages/Clean-Water-Action/22907478728?ref=nf
twitter.com/cleanh2oaction
www.youtube.com/cleanwateraction
Overview: A large international organization founded in 1971
Mission: A national organization of diverse people and groups working together for clean water, protection of health, creation of jobs and making democracy work for environmental causes.
Chief Officer(s):
Robert Wendelgass, President & CEO
bwendelgass@cleanwater.org
Membership: 1,200,000

Climate Institute
900 - 17 St. NW, Washington D.C. 20006 USA
Tel: 202-552-4723; *Fax:* 202-737-6410
info@climate.org
www.climate.org
Overview: A medium-sized international charitable organization founded in 1986
Mission: To help maintain the balance between climate & life on earth; To strive to be a source of objective, reliable information & a trustworthy facilitator of dialogue among scientists, policy makers, business executives, & citizens
Chief Officer(s):
John Topping, President
jtopping@climate.org
Crispin Tickell, Chair
Finances: *Funding Sources:* Foundation; US government; Corporations
Staff Member(s): 12
Membership: *Member Profile:* Scientists & environmentalists of many nationalities
Activities: *Internships:* Yes; *Speaker Service:* Yes *Library* by appointment
Publications:
• Climate Alert
Editor: Corrine Kisner
Profile: Quarterly Newsletter
• Sudden & Disruptive Climate Change: Exploring the Real Risks & How We Can Avoid Them
Type: Book; *Editor:* Michael C. MacKracken et al.
Profile: An outline of the risks of & solutions to climate change

Club de Madrid / Club of Madrid
Palacio del Marqués de Cañete, Calle Mayor, 69, Planta 1, Madrid 28013 Spain
Tel: 34-911-548-230; *Fax:* 34-911-548-240
clubmadrid@clubmadrid.org
www.clubmadrid.org
www.facebook.com/pages/Club-de-Madrid/134400549949023
twitter.com/CLUBdeMADRID
www.youtube.com/clubmadrid
Overview: A small international organization founded in 2001
Mission: To contribute to strengthening democracy in the world
Chief Officer(s):
Carlos Westendrop, Secretary General
Vike-Freiberga Vaira, President
Membership: *Member Profile:* Former heads of state & government; representatives of constituent foundations

Club of Madrid *See* Club de Madrid

Coalition for Education in the Outdoors
c/o State University of New York College at Cortland, PO Box 2000, Cortland NY 13045-0900 USA
Tel: 607-753-4968; *Fax:* 607-753-5982
outdoored@outdooredcoalition.org
www.outdooredcoalition.org
Overview: A medium-sized international organization founded in 1987
Mission: To assist in identifying the networking needs of its affiliates & to seek ways to meet those needs
Chief Officer(s):
Charles H. Yaple, Executive Director
Membership: *Fees:* Schedule available; *Member Profile:* A network of agencies, institutions, associations, centres, businesses & organizations linked & communicating in support of the broad purposes of education in, for, & about the outdoors
Activities: *Speaker Service:* Yes
Publications:
• Taproot
Profile: Quarterly Journal

Coalition for International Criminal Court (CICC)
c/o WFM, 708 - 3rd Ave., 24th Fl., New York NY 10017 USA
Tel: 212-687-2863; *Fax:* 212-599-1332
cicc@coalitionfortheicc.org
www.iccnow.org
www.facebook.com/CoalitionfortheInternationalCriminalCourt
twitter.com/_CICC
www.flickr.com/photos/coalitionforicc
Overview: A large international organization
Mission: To advocate for a fair, effective,& independent international criminal court
Chief Officer(s):
William R. Pace, Covernor
Jelena Pia-Comella, Program Director
Membership: 2,500+ NGOs in 150 countries
Publications:
• Africa Update
Type: Newsletter; *Frequency:* Biannually
Profile: ICC developments in relation to Africa
• Asia Update
Type: Newsletter; *Frequency:* Biannually
Profile: ICC developments in relation to Asia
• The Bulletin
Frequency: Biannually
Profile: Featuring timely updates about the work of the ICC and the CICC
• The Monitor
Frequency: Biannually
Profile: Available in English, French and Spanish

CODA International Training (CIT)
ADKC Centre, Whitstable House, Silchester Rd., London W10 6SB UK
Tel: 44-208-960-8888
www.coda-international.org.uk
Previous Name: Tecnica England
Overview: A small international charitable organization founded in 1986
Mission: To work in partnership with civil society organisations from Latin America, Southern Africa & the Middle East, enabling skill transfer through volunteers who provide training & consultancy in developing countries, with the aim of promoting economic & social equality, & sustainable change without dependency. It is a registered charity in the U.K.
Affiliation(s): tecNICA Canada; Women and Law in Southern Africa (WLSA); KwaZulu Natal; Guatemala Community Movement (GCM); East Jerusalem YMCA; Confederation of Salvadorean Workers; Nicaraguan Association for Community Integration
Chief Officer(s):
Kevin Caulfield, Chair
Samira Yussuf, Executive Director
Finances: *Funding Sources:* Comic Relief; DFID; MRDF; Big Lottery Fund; Hilden Foundation; UNISON/UIDF; Individual donors
Staff Member(s): 2
Activities: Capacity building; health clinics; literacy projects; women's groups; electronics; traffic engineering; preventive health database development; economic issues; English as a Foreign Language;

Coffin-Lowry Syndrome Foundation (CLSF)
675 Kalima Pl. NW, Issaquah WA 98027 USA
Tel: 425-427-0939
coffinlowry@gmail.com
clsf.info
Overview: A small international organization founded in 1991
Mission: To serve as a clearinghouse of information on the syndrome, a support group for parents with CLS children & a general forum for exchanging experiences, advice & information with other CLS families; to seek to become a visible group in the medical, scientific, educational & professional communities in order to facilitate referrals of newly diagnosed individuals, & to encourage medical & behavioural research in order to improve methods of social integration of CLS individuals
Chief Officer(s):
Mary C. Hoffman, Chairperson
Finances: *Annual Operating Budget:* Less than $50,000; *Funding Sources:* Donations
Membership: 100-499

Colonial Waterbird Society *See* The Waterbird Society

Comité international des Sports des Sourds *See* International Committee of Sports for the Deaf

Comité international pour la documentation du Conseil international des musées *See* International Committee for Documentation of the International Council of Museums

Comité maritime international (CMI) / International Maritime Committee
Ernest Van Dijckkaai 8, Antwerpen B-2000 Belgium
Tel: 32-3-231-1331; *Fax:* 32-3-231-1333
info@comitemaritime.org
www.comitemaritime.org
Overview: A medium-sized international organization founded in 1897
Mission: To contribute by all appropriate means & activities to the unification of maritime law
Affliation(s): Canadian Maritime Law Association
Chief Officer(s):
Stuart Hetherington, President
swh@cbp.com.au
John Hare, Secretary General
john.hare@uct.ac.za
Membership: 53 associations; *Committees:* Audit; CMI Charitable Trust; CMI Archives; CMI Young Memvers; Collection of Outstanding Contributions; Conferrences/Seminars; Constitution; Genera; Average Interest Rates; Interpretation of International Organizations; Jurisprudence Database; National Associations; Nominating; Planning; Promotion of Maritime Conventions; PUblications & Website
Activities: *Library:* CMI-Secretariat; Open to public by appointment

Commission des Grands Lacs *See* Great Lakes Commission

Commission internationale de diplomatique
a/s École nationale des Chartes, 19, rue de la Sorbonne, Paris F-75005 France
Tél: 00-33-1-5542-7500; *Téléc:* 00-33-1-5542-7509
cidipl.org
Également appelé: Internal Commission of the Comité international des sciences historiques
Aperçu: *Dimension:* petite; *Envergure:* internationale; Organisme sans but lucratif; fondée en 1971
Mission: Organiser des réunions de spécialistes dans les sciences auxiliaires de l'histoire, notamment l'analyse de l'authenticité des chartes de l'ancien régime (diplomatique).
Membre(s) du bureau directeur:
Olivier Guyotjeannin, Président
ogj@wanadoo.fr
Thérèse de Hemptinne, Secrétaire générale
Therese.deHemptinne@Gent.be
Membre: 77; *Critères d'admissibilite:* Historien, spécialisé en diplomatique

Commission internationale de l'éclairage *See* International Commission on Illumination

Commission internationale de la santé au travail *See* International Commission on Occupational Health

Commission internationale des irrigations & du drainage *See* International Commission on Irrigation & Drainage

Commission Internationale du Genie Rural *See* International Commission of Agricultural & Biosystems Engineering

Commission on Sustainable Development (CSD)
Dept. of Economic & Social Affairs, UN Secretariat Bldg., #405, 42nd East St., New York NY 10017 USA

Tel: 212-963-8102; *Fax:* 212-963-4260
dsd@un.org
sustainabledevelopment.un.org
Mission: To operate as a functional commission of the UN Economic & Social Council, composed of members elected for terms of office for three years; To meet annually; To be guided by a multi-year (2004-2017) program of work which outlines seven two-year cycles, with each two-year cyle focused on themes; To review progress at the international, regional & national levels in the implementation of recommendations & commitments contained in Agenda 21 & the Rio Declaration on Environment & Development
Chief Officer(s):
Nikhil Seth, Director
Membership: *Member Profile:* Members of the intergovernmental body are elected by the Economic & Social Council from memberstates of the United Nations & its specialized agencies
Activities: Promoting dialogue & building partnerships for sustainable development with governments, the international community & the major groups who have a role to play in the transition toward sustainable development, including women, youth, indigenous peoples, non-governmental organizations, local authorities, workers & trade unions, business & industry, the scientific community & farmers

Committee for the National Institutes for the Environment ***See*** National Council for Science & the Environment

Committee on Nutrition in the Commonwealth ***See*** Commonwealth Human Ecology Council

Commonwealth Association of Surveying & Land Economy (CASLE)

c/o Faculty of Environment & Technology, Univ. of West England, Coldharbour Lane, Bristol BS16 1QY United Kingdom
Tel: 44-117-328-3036
www.casle.org
Overview: A medium-sized international organization founded in 1969
Mission: To maintain & strengthen professional links between Commonwealth countries, with the aim of assisting each country to achieve the scale, quality & integrity of surveying services that it requires; to foster the establishment of professional societies in countries where none exists & to promote their usefulness for the public advantage
Chief Officer(s):
Chitra Weddikkara, President
chitra.weddikkara@gmail.com
Susan M. Spedding, Secretary General
susan.spedding@uwe.ac.uk
Finances: *Annual Operating Budget:* $50,000-$100,000
Membership: 40 societies; *Member Profile:* Open to leading society in each surveying discipline in each Commonwealth country; *Committees:* Management Board
Activities: Conferences/seminars; research into sustainable development

Commonwealth Geographical Bureau (CGB)

c/o Dept. of Geography, Universitt of Otago, PO Box 56, Dunedin New Zealand
www.commonwealthgeography.org
Overview: A small international organization founded in 1968
Mission: To promote the study & practice of geography at all levels within the Commonwealth, especially in developing countries
Affiliation(s): International Geographical Union
Chief Officer(s):
Tony Binns, President
j.a.binns@geography.otago.ac.nz
Nigel Walford, Treasurer
nwalford@kingston.ac.uk
Finances: *Funding Sources:* Commonwealth Foundation; Trusts
Membership: *Member Profile:* Commonwealth geographers
Activities: Organizing workshops

Commonwealth Human Ecology Council (CHEC)

Church House, 4 Hurlingham Studios, Ranelagh Gardens, London SW6 3PA United Kingdom
Tel: 44-20-3689-0979
contact@checinternational.org
www.checinternational.org
www.facebook.com/247748745381618
twitter.com/CwHumanEcology
Previous Name: Committee on Nutrition in the Commonwealth
Overview: A medium-sized international charitable organization founded in 1969
Mission: To challenge governments to create policies in support of ecological & sustainable communities
Affliation(s): In consultative status with UN ECOSOC (Economic & Social Council)
Finances: *Funding Sources:* Commonwealth Foundation; UK Government; UK Lottery; Comic Relief
Membership: *Member Profile:* Government; non-government; professionals; cross section of communities & civil society

Commonwealth Parliamentary Association (CPA)

Secretariat, Westminster House, #700, 7 Millbank, London SW1P 3JA United Kingdom
Tel: 44-20-7799-1460; *Fax:* 44-20-7222-6073
hq.sec@cpahq.org
www.cpahq.org
en-gb.facebook.com/CPAHQ
twitter.com/cpa_secretariat
www.flickr.com/photos/cpa_hq
Previous Name: Empire Parliamentary Association
Overview: A medium-sized international charitable organization founded in 1911
Mission: To promote knowledge & understanding of the constitutional, legislative, economic, social & cultural systems within a parliamentary democratic framework
Chief Officer(s):
William F. Shija, Secretary General
Membership: 17,000; *Member Profile:* British Commonwealth members of parliament & legislature; *Committees:* Executive
Activities: *Internships:* Yes *Library:* Parliamentary Information & Reference Centre; by appointment
Publications:
• The Parliamentarian
Editor: Andrew Imlach; *Price:* £34 annual subscription; £11 per issue
Profile: Quarterly journal

Canadian Branch
House of Commons, PO Box 743, Ottawa ON K1A 0A6
Tel: 613-992-2093; *Fax:* 613-995-0212
cpa@parl.gc.ca
www.parl.gc.ca
Chief Officer(s):
Elizabeth Kingston, Association Secretary

Commonwealth Pharmaceutical Association ***See*** Commonwealth Pharmacists Association

Commonwealth Pharmacists Association (CPA)

1 Lambeth High St., London SE1 7JN United Kingdom
Tel: 44-20-7572-2216; *Fax:* 44-20-7572-2504
admin@commonwealthpharmacy.org
www.commonwealthpharmacy.org
www.facebook.com/509918019095288
Previous Name: Commonwealth Pharmaceutical Association
Overview: A small international organization founded in 1969
Mission: To facilitate the dissemination of knowledge & information about the professional practice of pharmacy & the pharmaceutical sciences; to foster a high standard of control over the quality & distribution of drugs by professional means, & by encouraging the implementation of appropriate legislation
Affiliation(s): Canadian Pharmaceutical Association
Chief Officer(s):
Raymond Anderson, President
Membership: 34; *Fees:* £15; *Member Profile:* Pharmaceutical societies, associations & boards within the Commonwealth
Activities: Symposiums; *Library:* Information Centre;

Compressed Gas Association, Inc. (CGA)

#103, 14501 George Carter Way, Chantilly VA 20151 USA
Tel: 703-788-2700; *Fax:* 703-961-1831
Other Communication: customerservice@cganet.com
cga@cganet.com
www.cganet.com
Overview: A small international organization founded in 1913
Mission: To develop & promote safety standards for the industrial gas industry
Membership: *Member Profile:* Manufacturers, suppliers, distributors, & transporters of gases, cryogenic liquids, & related products in Canada & the United States; *Committees:* Canadian Cylinder Specification; Canadian Medical, Food, & Beverage Gases & Equipment; Canadian Pressure Vessels & Piping Sys.; Canadian Health, Safety, & Environment; Canadian Transportation; Acetylene; Atmospheric Gases & Equipment; Bulk Distribution Equipment & Standards; Carbon Dioxide; Compressed Gas Emergency Action Plan; Cylinder Specifications; Cylinder Valve; Distribution & Fleet Safety; Environmental; Food Gases; Hazard Comm.; Hazardous Materials Codes; Hydrogen Tech.; HYCO; Industrial Gases Apparatus; Liquefied Petroleum Gas; Medical Equipment; Medical Gases; Security; Safety/Health
Activities: Working with governmental agencies to produce standards & regulations; Promoting compliance with regulations in the workplace; Providing access to educational publications & videos; Offering networking opportunities
Awards:
• Compressed Gas Association Safety Awards
Meetings/Conferences:
• Compressed Gas Association Canada Annual Meeting 2015, April, 2015, Palm Beach Gardens, FL
Scope: National
Publications:
• Compressions [a publication of the Compressed Gas Association]
Type: Newsletter; *Frequency:* Quarterly; *Price:* Free with Compressed Gas Association membership
Profile: Association & industry news

Concerned Educators Allied for a Safe Environment (CEASE)

55 Frost St., Cambridge MA 2140 USA
Tel: 617-661-8347
info@peaceeducators.org
www.peaceeducators.org
www.facebook.com/peace.educators
Overview: A small national organization founded in 1979
Mission: To create safe world for children; to seek to end the violence in society & remove the root causes of violence by advocating for peace, justice & economic opportunity
Member of: Survival Education Fund
Affiliation(s): National Association for the Education of Young Children
Chief Officer(s):
Lucy Stroock
Susan Hopkins
Chris Lamm
Lucy Stroock, Sec.-Treas.
Finances: *Annual Operating Budget:* Less than $50,000; *Funding Sources:* Subscriptions; membership dues; donations
6 volunteer(s)
Membership: 1,000; *Fees:* $10; $5 student; *Member Profile:* Early childhood educators & trainers
Activities: Workshops; seminars

Confédération internationale de sages-femmes ***See*** International Confederation of Midwives

Conférence des Nations Unies sur le commerce et le développement ***See*** United Nations Conference on Trade & Development

Congrès mondiaux du pétrole ***See*** World Petroleum Congress

Conseil international d'études de l'Europe centrale et orientale (Canada) ***See*** International Council for Central & East European Studies (Canada)

Conseil international de la musique ***See*** International Music Council

Conseil International des Agences Bénévoles ***See*** International Council of Voluntary Agencies

Conseil international des Monuments et des Sites ***See*** International Council on Monuments & Sites

Conseil international des musées ***See*** International Council of Museums

Conseil international des sciences de l'animal de laboratoire ***See*** International Council for Laboratory Animal Science

Conseil international du droit de l'environnement ***See*** International Council of Environmental Law

Conseil Mondial de l'Energie ***See*** World Energy Council

Conservation International (CI)

#500, 2011 Crystal Dr., Arlington VA 22202 USA
Tel: 703-341-2400
Toll-Free: 800-429-5660
www.conservation.org
www.facebook.com/conservation.intl
twitter.com/ConservationOrg
Overview: A large international charitable organization founded in 1987

Mission: To conserve the Earth's living natural heritage, our global biodiversity, & to demonstrate that human societies are able to live harmoniously with nature
Chief Officer(s):
Peter Seligmann, Chairman/Chief Executive Officer
Russell A. Mittermeier, President
Barbara DiPietro, CFO
Finances: *Annual Operating Budget:* Greater than $5 Million; *Funding Sources:* Private; government; agencies; foundations
Staff Member(s): 1200
Membership: 5,000; *Fees:* $35; *Member Profile:* Scientists; economists; communicators; educators; conservation professionals
Activities: Center for Applied Biodiversity Science; Critical Ecosystem Partnership Fund; Global Conservation Fund; Center for Environmental Leadership in Business; Field Support; Resources & Communications; *Internships:* Yes *Library*

Consortium of Multiple Sclerosis Centers (CMSC)
359 Main St., #A, Hackensack NJ 07601 USA
Tel: 201-487-1050; *Fax:* 201-678-2290
info@mscare.org
www.mscare.org
twitter.com/mscare
Also Known As: Consortium of MS Centers
Overview: A medium-sized international organization founded in 1986
Mission: To maximize the ability of multiple sclerosis healthcare professionals to improve the quality of life for people affected by multiple sclerosis; To provide information about the most current research results, clinical trials, treatments, & patient education programs
Chief Officer(s):
Colleen Harris, President
June Halper, Executive Director
Rachelle Ramirez, Manager, Special Projects
Kelly Walters, Manager, Business
Tina Trott, Coordinator, Education
Membership: *Fees:* $600 full & associate members; $350 liaison; $150 individual physicians; $100 individual health professionals; $25 student health professionals; *Member Profile:* Multiple sclerosis healthcare providers & researchers from North America; *Committees:* Executive; Advocacy & Scholarship; By-Laws; Clinical Care; Finance; Education; Program; Research
Activities: Improving the quality of care for patients with multiple sclerosis through international, multidisciplinary communication; Offering networking opportunities; *Speaker Service:* Yes
Publications:
• Consortium of Multiple Sclerosis Centers Membership Directory
Type: Directory; *Price:* Free with Consortium of Multiple Sclerosis Centers membership
• International Journal of Multiple Sclerosis Care
Type: Journal; *Frequency:* Quarterly; *Accepts Advertising*; *Editor:* Lael A. Stone, MD
Profile: Peer-reviewed clinical & original research articles on topics of interest to multiple sclerosis healthcare providers

Consortium on Peace Research, Education & Development; Peace Studies Association *See* Peace & Justice Studies Association

Consultative Group on International Agricultural Research (CGIAR)
The World Bank, MSN P6-601, 1818 H Street NW, Washington DC 20433 USA
Tel: 202-473-8951; *Fax:* 202-473-8110
cgiar@worldbank.org
www.cgiar.org
www.facebook.com/CGIARConsortium
twitter.com/CGIAR
Overview: A medium-sized international organization founded in 1971
Mission: To achieve sustainable food security and reduce poverty in developing countries through scientific research and research-related activities in the fields of agriculture, forestry, fisheries, policy, and environment.
Chief Officer(s):
Frank Rijsberman, CEO
Staff Member(s): 1000
Activities: *Library:* Information Center; by appointment

Consumers International (CI)
24 Highbury Cres., London N5 1RX United Kingdom
Tel: 44-20-7226-6663; *Fax:* 44-20-7354-0607
consint@consint.org
www.consumersinternational.org
Overview: A medium-sized international organization founded in 1960
Mission: To protect consumer interests worldwide through institution building, education, research & lobbying of international decision making bodies
Chief Officer(s):
Helen McCallum, Contact
Finances: *Annual Operating Budget:* $1.5 Million-$3 Million; *Funding Sources:* Membership fees; Project funding
Staff Member(s): 80
Membership: links the activities of more than 220 consumer groups in 115 countries; *Fees:* Schedule available
Activities: Special services available only to IOCU members, volunteers, correspondents, networks & participants of like-minded organizations: Consumer Alert (a hazard notification issued by the Consumer Interpol; Consumer Interpol seeks to protect consumers from hazardous products, technologies & wastes); Consumer Interpol Memo (disseminates news on health & safety issues); Pesticide Monitor (disseminates information on the work of the Pesticide Action Network, a global network which aims to curb indiscriminate use; *Internships:* Yes; *Speaker Service:* Yes

Controlled Release Society (CRS)
3340 Pilot Knob Rd., St. Paul MN 55121 USA
Tel: 651-454-7250; *Fax:* 651-454-0766
crs@scisoc.org
www.controlledrelease.org
Overview: A medium-sized international organization
Mission: To advance the science & technology of controlled release throughout the world
Chief Officer(s):
Steven C. Nelson, Executive Vice-President
snelson@scisoc.org
Amy Hope, Vice-President, Operations
ahope@scisoc.org
Barbara Mock, Vice-President, Finance
bmock@scisoc.org
Membership: 3,000; *Member Profile:* Individuals from industry, academia, & government, from over 50 countries, who are involved in the field of controlled release; *Committees:* Awards Committees; Bioactive Materials Track Program; Board of Scientific Advisors; Books Advisory Board; Books Subcommittee; Chapter; China Initiative Subcommittee; Consumer & Diversified Products; CRS Foundation; CRS Journal Subcommittee; Marketing; Educational Workshop / Satellite Meeting Reviewe; Meetings; Membership & Development; Newsletter Subcommittee; Nominating; Planning & Finance; Regulatory Ad Hoc; Veterinary; Webcast; Young Scientist; Young Scientist Mentorship / Protege Subcommittee
Activities: Promoting & sponsoring educational opportunities; Advocating in regulatory affairs; Supporting 16 international chapters & 4 student chapters; Offering a peer to peer network; Informing members of breakthroughs in science & technology
Meetings/Conferences:
• Controlled Release Society 2015 42nd Annual Meeting & Exposition, July, 2015, Edinburgh International Conference Centre, Edinburgh
Scope: International
Contact Information: Meeting Manager: Tressa Patrias, tpatrias@scisoc.org
• Controlled Release Society 2016 43rd Annual Meeting & Exposition, July, 2016, Washington State Convention Center, Seattle, WA
Scope: International
Contact Information: Meeting Manager: Tressa Patrias, tpatrias@scisoc.org
Publications:
• Controlled Release Society Membership Directory
Type: Directory
• Controlled Release Society Newsletter
Type: Newsletter; *Accepts Advertising*; *Price:* Free with membership in theControlled Release Society
Profile: Featuring a patent watch on fields of controlled release, information on scientific publications, & techical information in the field of drug delivery
• Journal of Controlled Release
Type: Journal; *Editor:* K. Park
Profile: Original research about controlled release & the delivery of drugs & other biologically active agents

Canadian Local Chapter
Michael R. Doschak, President, University of Alberta, 2121 Dentistry/Pharmacy Centre, Edmonton AB T6G 2N8
Tel: 780-492-8758
cccrs.secretary@gmail.com
www.cc-crs.com
Mission: To promote education in the science & technology of controlled release
Michael R. Doschak, President

Cordage Institute (CI)
#1019, 994 Old Eagle School Rd., Wayne PA 19087 USA
Tel: 610-971-4854; *Fax:* 610-971-4859
info@cordageinstitute.com
www.ropecord.com
Overview: A small national organization founded in 1920
Mission: The Institue serves the operating, trade, government, liaison & technical needs of the cordage, rope, twine & netting industry.
Chief Officer(s):
Luis Padilla, President
Peter M. Lance, Executive Director
pete@mmco1.com
Finances: *Funding Sources:* Membership dues; sale of publications
Membership: 1-99; *Fees:* Schedule available; *Member Profile:* Members are manufacturers, producers, & resellers of cordage, rope, & twine. Categories of membership include regular, associate, affiliate, reseller, specialty supplier, technical, & academic.; *Committees:* Technical; Inter-Association Liaison
Publications:
• Ropecord News
Frequency: Quarterly; *Price:* US$45 North America; US$95 International
Profile: New products & applications; trade & legal issues; markets; technical information

Council of Biology Editors *See* Council of Science Editors

Council of Great Lakes Governors (CGLG)
#2700, 20 North Wacker Dr., Chicago IL 60606 USA
Tel: 312-407-0177; *Fax:* 312-407-0038
cglg@cglg.org
www.cglg.org
Overview: A small international organization founded in 1990
Mission: To facilitate economic growth in the Great Lakes region, including Ontario, Québec, & the Great Lakes states of Illinois, Indiana, Michigan, Minnesota, New York, Ohio, Pennsylvania, & Wisconsin
Chief Officer(s):
Mitchell E. Daniels, Co-Chair; Governor of Indiana
Pat Quinn, Co-Chair; Governor of Illinois
David Naftzger, Executive Director
dnaftzger@cglg.org
Toby McCarrick, Executive Director, Great Lakes USA
tmccarrick@cglg.org
Zoë Munro, Program Manager
zmunro@cglg.org
Michael Piskur, Program Manager
mpiskur@cglg.org
Finances: *Funding Sources:* Donations
Activities: Hosting webinars for Great Lakes companies; Leading multi-sector trade missions
Publications:
• The Compass [a publication of the Council of Great Lakes Governors]
Type: Newsletter; *Frequency:* Quarterly
Profile: Information about the ongoing work of the Council of Great Lakes Governors, such as trade missions & trade offices

Council of Science Editors
#304, 10200 W. 44th Ave., Wheat Ridge CO 80033 USA
Tel: 720-881-6046; *Fax:* 303-422-8894
cse@councilscienceeditors.org
www.councilscienceeditors.org
www.linkedin.com/groups?gid=3103324&trk=hb_side_g
www.facebook.com/CouncilofScienceEditors?ref=ts
twitter.com/CScienceEditors
Previous Name: Council of Biology Editors
Overview: A small international organization
Mission: To improve communications in the life sciences; to educate authors, editors & publishers; to promote effective communication practices in primary & secondary publishing in any form
Chief Officer(s):
David Stumph, Executive Director

Membership: 1,200; *Fees:* $164; $43 student; *Committees:* Awards and Honors; Editorial Policy; Education; Finance; Marketing; Membership; Nominating; Program; Publications; Research; Science Editor; Scientific Style and Format; Short Courses & Workshops; Social Media; Sponsorship; Web

Council on Hemispheric Affairs (COHA)

1250 Connecticut Ave. NW. #1C, Washington DC 20036 USA
Tel: 202-223-4975; *Fax:* 202-223-4979
coha@coha.org
www.coha.org
www.linkedin.com/in/councilonhemisphericaffairs
www.facebook.com/council.on.hemispheric.affairs
twitter.com/cohastaff
pinterest.com/cohadc
Overview: A medium-sized international organization founded in 1975
Mission: To monitor US-Canadian-Latin American relations in the areas of economics, politics, human rights, trade & diplomacy through public statements, critical analyses & media appearances
Chief Officer(s):
Larry Birns, Director
Finances: *Funding Sources:* Subscription revenue; private donations
Activities: Issue press releases, submit op-eds to national newspapers for publication; publish biweekly Washington Report on the Hemisphere; provide congressional testimony & media resource; representatives frequently appear on radio & tv programs to analyze news stories; *Internships:* Yes; *Speaker Service:* Yes *Library*

The Cousteau Society (TCS) / Société Cousteau

#707E, 732 Eden Way North, Chesapeake VA 23320 USA
Tel: 212-532-2588
communication@cousteau.org
www.cousteau.org
www.youtube.com/user/cousteauenglish
Overview: A large international charitable organization founded in 1973
Mission: Dedicated to the protection & wise management of natural resources & the improvement of life for present & future generations; to promote an increased awareness & knowledge of the beauty & fragility of the planet's resources
Chief Officer(s):
Francine Cousteau, President
Finances: *Annual Operating Budget:* Greater than $5 Million; *Funding Sources:* Membership fees; production contracts
Staff Member(s): 32; 5 volunteer(s)
Membership: 50,000 worldwide including sister organization Equipe Cousteau; *Fees:* $30 individual; $40 family
Activities: Produces television films, filmstrips & books on important environmental concerns for the general public

Croplife International

PO Box 35, 326 Louise Ave., Brussels 1050 Belgium
Tel: 32-2-542-0410; *Fax:* 32-2-542-0419
croplife@croplife.org
www.croplife.org
www.facebook.com/CropLifeIntl
twitter.com/croplifeintl
www.youtube.com/croplifeint
Previous Name: Global Crop Protection Federation; International Group of National Associations of Manufacturers of Agrochemical Products
Overview: A medium-sized international charitable organization
Mission: To act as an ambassador for the pan science industry, encouraging understanding & dialogue whilst promoting agricultural technology in the context of sustainable development
Chief Officer(s):
Howard Minigh, President & CEO
howard.minigh@croplife.org
Staff Member(s): 21
Membership: 23; *Member Profile:* Regional crop protection associations

Cruise Lines International Association, Inc. (CLIA)

#400, 910 SE 17th St., Fort Lauderdale FL 33316 USA
Tel: 754-224-2200; *Fax:* 754-224-2250
info@cruising.org
www.cruising.org
www.facebook.com/CLIAFan
twitter.com/CruiseFacts
Merged from: International Council of Cruise Lines (ICCL)
Overview: A large international organization founded in 1975
Mission: To promote & develop the cruise industry; To serve as a non-governmental consultative organization to the International Maritime Organization, an agency of the United Nations; To foster a safe, secure, & healthy cruise ship environment
Affliation(s): 16,000 travel agencies
Chief Officer(s):
Christine Duffy, CEO & President
Membership: 26 cruise lines; 14,000 travel agencies; 100 executive members; *Member Profile:* Major cruise lines that serve North America
Activities: Providing education & training to travel agent members
Meetings/Conferences:
• Cruise3sixty 2015, April, 2015, Broward County Convention Center, Fort Lauderdale, FL
Scope: International
Description: An annual cruise conference hosted by Cruise Lines International Association, Inc., including educational training & networking opportunities.
Contact Information: Registration Coordinator: Tim Chau, Phone: 949-457-1545 ext. 122, Fax: 949-457-1281, E-mail: tchau@mjpa.com; URL: www.cruise3sixty.com
Publications:
• Cruise Industry Source Book
Type: Guidebook
Profile: Profiles of CLIA's member cruise lines & general information about CLIA

Cyclic Vomiting Syndrome Association (CVSA)

#106, 10520 Blue Mound Rd. West, Milwaukee WI 53226 USA
Tel: 414-342-7880; *Fax:* 414-342-8980
cvsa@cvsaonline.org
www.cvsaonline.org
www.facebook.com/CyclicVomitingSyndromeAssociation
Overview: A medium-sized international charitable organization founded in 1993
Chief Officer(s):
Ruth Novak, Contact
cvsa@cvsaonline.org
Carol Warner, Canadian Contact
cdwarner2@gmail.com
Kathleen Adams, President
Finances: *Annual Operating Budget:* $50,000-$100,000; *Funding Sources:* Membership fees; grants; donations
Staff Member(s): 1; 100 volunteer(s)
Membership: 800; *Fees:* US$35-225; *Member Profile:* Families; professionals
Activities: Support; education; research; *Speaker Service:* Yes

Dangerous Goods Advisory Council

#740, 1100 H St. NW, Washington DC 20005 USA
Tel: 202-289-4550; *Fax:* 202-289-4074
info@dgac.org
www.hmac.org
www.linkedin.com/groups?gid=2474343&trk=hb_side_g
www.facebook.com/dangerousgoodsadvisorycouncil
twitter.com/dgac_hmac
Also Known As: Hazardous Materials Advisory Council
Overview: A medium-sized international organization founded in 1978
Mission: To promote improvement in the safe transportation of hazardous materials/dangerous goods globally by providing education, assistance & information to the private & public sectors, through our unique status with regulatory bodies, & the diversity & technical strengths of our membership
Affliation(s): Canadian Government
Chief Officer(s):
Vaughn Arthur, President
Gail Cooley, Office Manager
Membership: *Fees:* Schedule available; *Member Profile:* Shippers; carriers; container manufacturers & reconditioners; emergency response/waste clean-up companies; trade associations

DES Action USA

PO Box 7296, Jupiter FL 33468 USA
Toll-Free: 800-337-9288
info@desaction.org
www.desaction.org
www.facebook.com/pages/DES-Action-USA/148293015181338
Overview: A small national charitable organization founded in 1979
Mission: To provide public & physician education on special health needs of those exposed to the synthetic estrogen diethylstilbestrol (DES)
Chief Officer(s):
Fran Howell, Executive Director
Finances: *Annual Operating Budget:* $50,000-$100,000
Staff Member(s): 3
Membership: 1,000-4,999; *Fees:* $40

Development Innovations and Networks *Voir* Innovations et réseaux pour le développement

Dictionary Society of North America (DSNA)

Buffalo State College, Dept. of English, Ketchum Hall 326, 1300 Elmwood Ave., Buffalo NY 14222 USA
Tel: 716-878-4049; *Fax:* 716-878-5700
dsnaadmin@gmail.com
www.dictionarysociety.com
www.facebook.com/dsnaoffice
Overview: A small international charitable organization founded in 1975
Member of: American Council of Learned Societies; National Humanities Alliance
Chief Officer(s):
David Barnhart, President
Lisa Berglund, Executive Secretary
Finances: *Annual Operating Budget:* Less than $50,000
Staff Member(s): 1
Membership: 400; *Fees:* US$60 North America; US$70 elsewhere; *Member Profile:* Academics; professional lexicographers; bibliophiles
Activities: Biennial meeting
Awards:
• Laurence Urdang-DSNA Award (Award)

Direct Marketing Association (DMA)

1120 Avenue of the Americas, New York NY 10036-6700 USA
Tel: 212-768-7277; *Fax:* 212-302-6714
customerservice@the-dma.org
www.the-dma.org
www.linkedin.com/groups?gid=1620437
www.facebook.com/pages/Direct-Marketing-Association-DMA/60905377232?r
twitter.com/dma_usa
Overview: A large international organization
Chief Officer(s):
Linda A. Woolley, Acting President & CEO
Finances: *Funding Sources:* Membership dues
Staff Member(s): 120
Membership: 3,600
Activities: *Speaker Service:* Yes; *Rents Mailing List:* Yes *Library* by appointment

Ducks Unlimited Inc. (DU)

1 Waterfowl Way, Memphis TN 38120 USA
Tel: 901-758-3825
Toll-Free: 800-453-8257
www.ducks.org
www.facebook.com/DucksUnlimited
twitter.com/ducksunlimited
www.youtube.com/ducksunlimitedinc
Overview: A medium-sized international organization founded in 1937
Mission: To fulfill the annual life cycle needs of North American waterfowl by protecting, enhancing, restoring & managing important wetlands & associated uplands
Chief Officer(s):
Dale Hall, Chief Executive Officer
Membership: *Fees:* $35
Publications:
• Ducks Unlimited Magazine
Editor: Tom Fulgham
Profile: Bimonthly magazine

Earth Island Institute (EII)

#460, 2150 Allston Way, Berkeley CA 94704-1375 USA
Tel: 510-859-9100; *Fax:* 510-859-9091
Other Communication:
plus.google.com/104299409429481130063
www.earthisland.org
www.facebook.com/groups/26250703694
twitter.com/earthisland
Overview: A large international organization founded in 1982
Mission: To develop innovative projects for the conservation, preservation & restoration of the global environment
Chief Officer(s):
Martha Davis, President
John Knox, Executive Director, 510-859-9108
johnknox@earthisland.org
Finances: *Annual Operating Budget:* $3 Million-$5 Million; *Funding Sources:* Membership dues; grants; contributions

Staff Member(s): 65; 25 volunteer(s)
Membership: 15,000; *Fees:* US$25 regular; US$15 student/limited income
Activities: Operating more than 40 projects, including: Baikal Watch; Borneo Project; Campaign to Safeguard America's Waters; Centre for Safe Energy; Global Service Corps; International Marine Mammal Project; Women's Earth Alliance; *Library* by appointment
Awards:
• Brower Youth Awards (Award)
Amount: $3,000
Publications:
• Earth Island Journal
Type: Magazine; *Frequency:* q.
• IslandWire [a publication of Earth Island Institute]
Type: Newsletter
Profile: Campaign updates

Earthwatch Europe

256 Banbury Rd., Oxford OX2 7DE United Kingdom
Tel: 44-1865-318-838; *Fax:* 44-1865-311-383
info@earthwatch.org.uk
www.earthwatch.org/europe
Overview: A large international charitable organization
Mission: To engage people worldwide in scientific field research & education
Chief Officer(s):
Nigel Winser, Executive Director
Ed Wilson, President & CEO
Finances: *Annual Operating Budget:* Greater than $5 Million
Staff Member(s): 50; 5 volunteer(s)
Membership: 5,000-14,999
Activities: *Internships:* Yes; *Speaker Service:* Yes
Awards:
• Earthwatch Research Grants (Grant)
To engage people worldwide in scientific field research and education to promote the understanding and action necessary for a sustainable environment.

East African Wild Life Society (EAWLS)

PO Box 20110-00200, Nairobi 00200 Kenya
Tel: 254-20-387-4145; *Fax:* 254-20-387-0335
info@eawildlife.org
www.eawildlife.org
www.facebook.com/eawildlife
twitter.com/SwaraMag
Overview: A medium-sized international organization founded in 1956
Mission: To promote the conservation & wise use of wildlife & the environment in East Africa
Member of: World Conservation Union
Chief Officer(s):
Michael Gachanja, Executive Director
Finances: *Funding Sources:* Membership fees; shop fund; donations
Membership: *Fees:* Schedule available
Activities: Education & awareness; advocacy; monitoring of species; field projects; *Speaker Service:* Yes *Library* by appointment

Eastern Apicultural Society of North America, Inc. (EAS)

c/o Loretta Surprenant, PO Box 300, Essex NY 12936 USA
Tel: 518-963-7593; *Fax:* 518-963-7593
secretary@easternapiculture.org
www.easternapiculture.org
Overview: A medium-sized international organization founded in 1955
Mission: To educate the beekeeping community in eastern the eastern United States & Canada; To promote honey bee culture; To encourage excellent bee research
Chief Officer(s):
Jim Bobb, Chair
chairman@easternapiculture.org
Kim Flottum, President
president2009@easternapiculture.org
Loretta Surprenant, Secretary
secretary@easternapiculture.org
John Tulloch, Treasurer
treasurer@easternapiculture.org
Membership: *Fees:* $25 / year individuals & families; $50 / year provincial, state, county, & regional associations; $250 life membership; *Member Profile:* Beginning & advanced beekeepers from the eastern United States & Canada
Activities: Sponsoring awards for graduate students & bee researchers; Offering modest research grants
Meetings/Conferences:
• Eastern Apicultural Society of North America 2015 Annual Conference & Short Course, August, 2015, University of Guelph, Guelph, ON
Scope: International
Attendance: 500
Description: Annual business meeting, lectures, workshops, short courses, & vendor displays for beginning & advanced beekeepers
Publications:
• EAS Journal
Type: Journal; *Frequency:* Quarterly; *Accepts Advertising*;
Editor: Kathy Summers-Flottum
Profile: Society news, including executive reports, meetings, & honey shows

Ecological Society of America (ESA)

#700, 1990 M St. NW, Washington D.C. 20036 USA
Tel: 202-833-8773; *Fax:* 202-833-8775
esahq@esa.org
www.esa.org
www.linkedin.com/groups?home=&gid=1233137
www.facebook.com/esa.org
twitter.com/esa_org
www.youtube.com/user/ESAVideos
Overview: A medium-sized international organization founded in 1915
Mission: To stimulate & publish research on the interrelations of organisms & their environment; to facilitate an exchange of ideas among those interested in ecology; to instill ecological principles in the decision-making of society at large; provides Professional Certification which constitutes recognition by the Society that an applicant meets the minimum educational, experience & ethical standards adopted by ESA for professional ecologists
Affliation(s): American Association for the Advancement of Science; American Institute of Biological Sciences; National Resources Council; National Research Council; Council of Scientific Society Presidents; Renewable Natural Resources Foundation
Chief Officer(s):
Katherine S. McCarter, Executive Director
ksm@esa.org
Staff Member(s): 36
Membership: 10,000; *Fees:* Schedule available; *Member Profile:* Ecologists
Activities: Maintains sections for ecologists with special needs & interests: Paleoecology, Aquatic, Physiological, Statistical, Applied Ecology, Vegetation, Education, Long-Term Studies; Professional Certification (constitutes recognition by the Society that an applicant meets the minimum educational experience & ethical standards adopted by ESA for professional ecologists); *Internships:* Yes; *Rents Mailing List:* Yes
Awards:
• The Mercer Award (Award)
Given for outstanding paper published by a young ecologist
• The MacArthur Award (Award)
Given for outstanding research contributions by an established ecologist
• The Cooper Award (Award)
Given for the best paper in geobotany, physiographic ecology, etc.
• The Whittaker Travel Fellowship (Award)
Brings a leading foreign scientist to America
• The E. Lucy Braun Award (Award)
• The Murray F. Buell Award (Award)
Outstanding paper presented orally at the ESA Annual meeting by an undergraduate
• Eminent Ecologist Award (Award)
Given to senior ecologist for distinguished contributions
• Corporate Award (Award)
Given to a corporation, business, program or individual of a company for incorporating sound ecological concepts in operating procedures

Education International (EI) / Internationale de l'Education

5, boul du Roi Albert II, 8 étage, Brussels B1210 Belgium
Tel: 32-2-224-0611; *Fax:* 32-2-224-0606
headoffice@ei-ie.org
www.ei-ie.org
Also Known As: Internacional de la Educación
Previous Name: World Confederation of Organizations of the Teaching Profession
Overview: A large international organization founded in 1993
Mission: To further the cause of organizations of teachers & education employees; To promote status, interests & welfare of members & defend their trade union & professional rights; To promote peace, democracy, social justice, equality & the application of the Universal Declaration on Human Rights through the development of education & the collective strength of teachers & education employees; To seek & maintain recognition of the trade rights of workers in general & of teachers & education employees in particular
Member of: NGO in formal associate relations with UNESCO, ILO; contacts with UN, WHO, UNAIDS, OECD, TUAC-OECD, IMF, World Bank, CONGO; associated with ICFTU
Chief Officer(s):
Susan Hopgood, President
Fred van Leeuwen, General Secretary
David Edwards, Deputy General Secretary
Charlie Lennon, Deputy General Secretary
Finances: *Funding Sources:* Membership dues
Staff Member(s): 30
Membership: 30,000,000 in 400 national member organizations in 270 countries; *Member Profile:* Education personnel from all sectors of education, from pre-school to university; *Committees:* Experts on Membership; Advisory Bodies; Status of Women; Finance; Constitution & By-laws
Activities: *Awareness Events:* World Teachers' Day, Oct. 5
Library: Resource Centre; by appointment
Meetings/Conferences:
• Education International 7th World Congress, July, 2015, Ottawa Convention Centre, Ottawa, ON
Scope: International
Publications:
• Worlds of Education
Editor: Nancy Knickerbocker *ISSN:* 1998-3433
Profile: Bi-monthly magazine

Electrochemical Society (ECS)

Bldg. D, 65 South Main St., Pennington NJ 08534-2839 USA
Tel: 609-737-1902; *Fax:* 609-737-2743
ecs@electrochem.org
www.electrochem.org
www.linkedin.com/groups/ECS-74067
www.facebook.com/TheElectrochemicalSociety
twitter.com/ECSorg
Overview: A medium-sized international organization
Mission: To provide information about the latest scientific & technical advancements in the electrochemical field
Chief Officer(s):
Roque J. Calvo, Executive Director
roque.calvo@electrochem.org
Staff Member(s): 25
Membership: 8,000; *Fees:* $105 individual; $25 student; *Member Profile:* Individuals with a a bachelor's degree in natural science or engineering, or relevant work experience in electrochemistry or allied subjects; Students who are full-time undergraduate or graduates registered for a degree in natural science or engineering; Corporate members; *Committees:* Executive Committee of the Board of Directors; Education; Finance; Honors & Awards; Individual Membership; Nominating; Technical Affairs; Tellers of Election; Ways & Means; Audit; Education; Ethical Standards; Sponsorship
Activities: Offering networking opportunities among scientists & engineers
Publications:
• ECS Transactions
Type: Journal; *Editor:* John W. Weidner *ISSN:* 1938-5862
Profile: Proceedings from ECS meetings & ECS-sponsored meetings
• Electrochemical & Solid-State Letters
Type: Journal; *Frequency:* Monthly; *Editor:* Dennis W. Hess *ISSN:* 1099-0062
Profile: Research & development in the field of solid-state & electrochemical science & technology
• Interface
Type: Magazine; *Frequency:* Quarterly; *Accepts Advertising*; *Editor:* Mary Yess *ISSN:* 1064-8208; *Price:* Free with membership in The Electrochemical Society
Profile: For individuals in the field of solid-state & electrochemical science and technology
• Journal of The Electrochemical Society
Type: Journal; *Frequency:* Monthly; *Number of Pages:* 450; *Editor:* Daniel A. Scherson *ISSN:* 0013-4651
Profile: Peer-reviewed journal, with 70 articles each month
• Meeting Abstracts
Type: Journal *ISSN:* 1091-8213
Profile: Extended abstracts of the technical papers presented at the spring & fall meetings of ECS

Emeric & Ilana Csengeri Institute for Holocaust Studies *See* Rosenthal Institute for Holocaust Studies

Emotions Anonymous
PO Box 4245, St. Paul MN 55104-0245 USA
Tel: 651-647-9712; *Fax:* 651-647-1593
info2gh99jsd@emotionsanonymous.org
www.emotionsanonymous.org
Overview: A small local organization
Mission: To help people overcome emotional difficulties

Empire Parliamentary Association *See* Commonwealth Parliamentary Association

Endometriosis Association, Inc. (EA) / Association de l'endométriose inc.
International Headquarters, 8585 North 76th Pl., Milwaukee WI 53223 USA
Tel: 414-355-2200; *Fax:* 414-355-6065
endo@endometriosisassn.org
www.endometriosisassn.org
www.facebook.com/EndoAssn
Overview: A large international charitable organization founded in 1980
Mission: To establish network for women with endometriosis to share information & mutual support; to educate women, families, friends, & community about endometriosis & about living with this chronic disease; to promote & conduct research on endometriosis; to provide advocacy for women with endometriosis, when necessary, either on an individual or on a group level; to support groups & chapters in Canadian centers
Member of: Society of Obstetricians & Gynacologists of Canada; Canadian Fertility/Andrology Society
Chief Officer(s):
Mary Lou Ballweg, President/Executive Director
Finances: *Annual Operating Budget:* $500,000-$1.5 Million; *Funding Sources:* Membership dues; literature sales; donations; grants
Staff Member(s): 5; 1170 volunteer(s)
Membership: 5,000 worldwide; *Fees:* $35 member; $45 associate; *Member Profile:* Women & girls who have or had endometriosis; associate membership also available for physicians & families; *Committees:* Millennium Campaign for the Cure Coordinating Committee; Endowment Fund Steering Committee; Asians in North America Outreach Council; Nurses Council; Black Outreach Council; Hispanic Outreach Council; Lesbian Outreach Council; Teen Outreach Council
Activities: Sponsors educational events; provides one-on-one support & crisis call assistance; coordinates international network of women, physicians & self-help groups; awards research grants; publications & books; teen program; *Awareness Events:* Endometriosis Awareness Week, last full week in March; *Internships:* Yes *Library*
Publications:
• The Endometriosis Sourcebook
Type: Book; *Author:* Mary Lou Ballweg; *Price:* $12.95
• Endometriosis: The Complete Reference for Taking Charge of Your Health
Type: Book; *Author:* Mary Lou Ballweg; *Price:* $15,95
• Overcoming Endometriosis
Type: Book

Entertainment Merchants Association - International Head Office (EMA)
#400, 16530 Ventura Blvd., Encino CA 91436-4551 USA
Tel: 818-385-1500; *Fax:* 818-385-0567
emaoffice@entmerch.org
www.entmerch.org
www.linkedin.com/company/entertainment-merchants-associatio n
www.facebook.com/135312479836292
Previous Name: Video Software Dealers Association
Overview: A small international organization founded in 1981
Mission: To protect, promote & provide a forum for all those engaged in the rental & sale of packaged and digitally delivered home entertainment
Chief Officer(s):
Crossan (Bo) Andersen, President/CEO
Sean Bersell, Vice-President, Public Affairs
Carrie Dieterich, Vice-President, Marketing & Industry Relations
Mark Fisher, Executive Vice President
Finances: *Annual Operating Budget:* $3 Million-$5 Million
Staff Member(s): 10
Membership: 200 members representing 35,000 retail outlets in the U.S. and 45,000 around the world; *Member Profile:* DVD and online video and video game retailers, distributors & suppliers
Activities: *Awareness Events:* Game Supply for Interactive Entertainment; Digital Media Pipeline; GamePlan Summit

EnviroLink
PO Box 8102, Pittsburgh PA 15217 USA
websupport@envirolink.org
www.envirolink.org
Overview: A medium-sized international organization founded in 1991
Mission: To promote a sustainable society by connecting individuals and organizations through communication technologies.

Environmental Bankers Association (EBA)
#410, 510 King St., Alexandria VA 22314 USA
Tel: 703-549-0977; *Fax:* 703-548-5945
eba@envirobank.org
www.envirobank.org
Overview: A medium-sized international organization founded in 1994
Mission: To assist the financial services industry in developing environmental risk management policies & procedures
Chief Officer(s):
Rick Ferguson, President, Policy
richardr.ferguson@usbank.com
Sharon Valverde, Vice-President, Programs
sharon.s.valverde@chase.com
Tacy Telego, Co-Executive Director
Tacytelego@envirobank.org
D. Jeffrey Telego, Co-Executive Director
jefftelego@envirobank.org
Membership: *Fees:* Schedule available based upon asset size of financial institutions; *Member Profile:* Members of the financial services industry, such as bank & non-bank financial institutions, asset management firms, insurers, & those who provide services to them; Environmental consultants, appraisers, environmental attorneys, & environmental information management firms; *Committees:* Policy; Finance & Budget; Communications & Programs; Business Development & Membership; Legal & ASTM; Trust; Risk Management; Global Sustainability Issues; Technical
Activities: Facilitating networking opportunities

Environmental Defense
Membership & Public Information, #600, 1875 Connecticut Ave., NW, Washington DC 20009 USA
Tel: 212-505-2100; *Fax:* 212-505-2375
Toll-Free: 800-684-3322
www.edf.org
www.linkedin.com/company/environmental-defense
www.facebook.com/EnvDefenseFund
twitter.com/EnvDefenseFund
Previous Name: Environmental Defense Fund
Overview: A large international organization founded in 1967
Mission: To protect environmental rights for all people — clean air, clean water, healthy food, & flourishing ecosystems; To work to create practical solutions, guided by science, that win lasting political, economic & social support
Chief Officer(s):
Fred Krupp, President
Finances: *Annual Operating Budget:* Greater than $5 Million; *Funding Sources:* Donations; foundations
Staff Member(s): 340
Membership: 750,000+
Activities: Areas of focus include climate, oceans, ecosystems & health
Publications:
• Earth: The Sequel - The Race to Reinvent Energy and Stop Global Warming
Number of Pages: 256; *Author:* Fred Krupp, Miriam Horn; *Price:* $24.95

Environmental Defense Fund *See* Environmental Defense

Environmental Industry Associations *See* National Waste & Recycling Association

Environmental Information Association
#306, 6935 Wisconsin Ave., Chevy Chase MD 20815-6112 USA
Tel: 301-961-4999; *Fax:* 301-961-3094
Toll-Free: 888-343-4342
info@eia-usa.org
www.eia-usa.org
Previous Name: National Asbestos Council
Overview: A small international organization
Mission: To protect public health & safety; To provide information about environmental health hazards to occupants of buildings, industrial sites, & other facility operations
Chief Officer(s):
Michael W Schrum, President
mwschrum@terracon.com
Brent Kynoch, Managing Director
bkynoch@eia-usa.org
Joy Finch, Secretary
joy.finch@gvltec.edu
Kevin Cannan, Treasurer
ktc@aac-contracting.com
Kim Goodman, Manager, Membership & Marketing
kgoodman@kynoch.com
Kelly Ruttman, Manager, Development & Communications
krutt@kynoch.com
Membership: *Fees:* $1,000 executive; $500 organization; $125 individual; *Committees:* Conference; Membership / Marketing; Publications; Strategic Planning; Training; Asbestos; EMS / ESA; Indoor Air Quality; Lead Paint; Sampling & Analysis
Activities: Offering professional development opportunities; Providing networking events
Publications:
• Indoor Environment Connections
Type: Newsletter; *Price:* Free with Environmental Information Association membership
• Inside EIA [Environmental Information Association]
Type: Newsletter; *Accepts Advertising*; *Price:* Free with Environmental Information Association membership
• Net News [a publication of the Environmental Information Association]
Type: Newsletter; *Frequency:* Weekly; *Price:* Free with Environmental Information Association membership

Environmental Law Institute
#620, 2000 L St. NW, Washington DC 20036 USA
Tel: 202-939-3800; *Fax:* 202-939-3868
law@eli.org
www.eli.org
www.linkedin.com/company/environmental-law-institute
www.facebook.com/35601332048
twitter.com/ELIORG
Overview: A medium-sized international organization
Mission: To advance environmental protection by improving law, policy & management; to research pressing problems; to educate professionals & citizens about the nature of these issues; to convene all sectors in forging effective solutions; to achieve society's goals for improving the health of the biosphere & its inhabitants
Chief Officer(s):
John Cruden, President
cruden@eli.org
Finances: *Annual Operating Budget:* Greater than $5 Million; *Funding Sources:* Subscriptions; fees; grants
Staff Member(s): 56
Membership: 100-499; *Fees:* Schedule available
Activities: *Internships:* Yes; *Speaker Service:* Yes *Library*

Epilepsy Foundation of America (EFA)
8301 Professional Place, Landover MD 20785-7223 USA
Tel: 301-459-3700; *Fax:* 301-577-4941
Toll-Free: 800-332-1000
ContactUs@efa.org
www.epilepsyfoundation.org
www.facebook.com/EpilepsyFoundationofAmerica
twitter.com/epilepsyfdn
www.youtube.com/epilepsyfoundation
Overview: A small national charitable organization founded in 1967
Mission: To work for people affected by seizures through research, education, advocacy & service
Affliation(s): Epilepsy Canada
Chief Officer(s):
Eric R. Hargis, President & CEO
Finances: *Funding Sources:* Charitable contributions; donations
Staff Member(s): 61
Membership: *Fees:* $25
Activities: *Awareness Events:* Epilepsy Month, Nov.; *Speaker Service:* Yes *Library:* NEL National Epilepsy Library; by appointment

EPS Industry Alliance (EPS-IA)
#201, 1298 Cronson Blvd., Crofton MD 21114 USA
Tel: 410-451-8340; *Fax:* 410-451-8343
info@epsindustry.org
www.epspackaging.org

www.facebook.com/EPSRecycling
twitter.com/EPSRecycle
Previous Name: Alliance of Foam Packaging Recyclers
Overview: A small international organization founded in 2012
Mission: To provide leadership to the EPS foam packaging industry through activities that promote the development of recycling; To maintain a network for the collection, reprocessing, & reuse of foam packaging
Member of: Institute of Packaging Professionals
Finances: *Funding Sources:* Manufacturers of expanded polystyrene packaging
Membership: 45; *Fees:* $1,000-$36,000

Eurographics - European Association for Computer Graphics (EG)

Stn. 2926, Goslar 38629 Germany
Fax: 49-532-1676-2998
secretary@eg.org
www.eg.org
Also Known As: Eurographics
Overview: A small international organization founded in 1979
Mission: To serve the needs of professionals working in computer graphics & such related fields as scientific visualization, human-computer interfaces, windowing systems, computer-aided design & image analysis; to promote the exchange of information & skills on a global scale.
Affliation(s): Gesellschaft für Informatik; NGI; NORSIGD; ACM SIGGRAPH
Chief Officer(s):
Werner Purgathofer, Chair
wp@cg.tuwien.ac.at
Werner Hansmann, Treasurer
hansmann@informatik.uni-hamburg.de
David Duce, Secretary
daduce@brookes.ac.uk
Membership: *Fees:* 870 Euro organzations; *Member Profile:* Primarily Europeans, but membership is worldwide; researchers, developers, educators, & those who work in the computer graphics industry, both as users & providers of computer graphics hardware, software, & applications
Activities: Annual conference, workshops, tutorials; *Speaker Service:* Yes

Canada Branch
c/o Dept. of Computer Science, Univ. of Victoria, PO Box 3055, Stn. CSC, Victoria BC V8W 3P6
Tel: 250-472-5760; *Fax:* 250-472-5708
ca-chapter@eg.org
Chief Officer(s):
Brian Wyvill, Chair

European Academy of Sciences, Arts & Humanities *Voir* Académie européenne des sciences, des arts et des lettres

European Association of Geoscientists & Engineers (EAGE)

PO Box 59, Houten 3990 DB Netherlands
Tel: 31-88-995-5055; *Fax:* 31-30-634-3524
eage@eage.org
www.eage.org
Overview: A medium-sized international organization founded in 1951
Mission: To promote exploration geophysics; to foster fellowship & cooperation among those working, studying, or being otherwise interested in the field; comprised of EAEG Division (formerly European Association of Exploration Geophysicists) & EAPG Division (formerly European Association of Petroleum Geoscientists & Engineers)
Affliation(s): Society of Exploration Geophysicists
Chief Officer(s):
Gladys Gonzalez, President
board@eage.org
Membership: 17,000; *Fees:* €50 general; €25 student; *Committees:* Technical Program; Awards; Publications; Research; Membership & Co-operation; Education; Student Affairs; Improved Oil Recovery; ECMOR; PACE
Activities: *Speaker Service:* Yes *Library* by appointment

European Direct Marketing Association *See* Federation of European Direct & Interactive Marketing

European Geophysical Union *See* European Geosciences Union

European Geosciences Union (EGS)

Luisenstr. 37, Munich 80333 Germany
Tel: 49-89-2180-6549; *Fax:* 49-87-2180-17855
info@egu.eu
www.egu.eu
www.linkedin.com/company/european-geosciences-union
www.facebook.com/EuropeanGeosciencesUnion
twitter.com/EuroGeosciences
www.youtube.com/user/EuroGeosciencesUnion
Previous Name: European Geophysical Union
Overview: A medium-sized international organization founded in 2002
Mission: To promote geophysics including planetary & space sciences by assisting cooperation among scientists, laboratories, institutes & individual research workers
Affliation(s): Canadian Geophysical Union
Chief Officer(s):
Günter Blöschl, President
president@egu.eu
Philippe Courtial, Executive Secretary
executive-secretary@egu.eu
Membership: 12,500; *Fees:* 20€ regular; 10€ student/retired; 500€ life; *Member Profile:* Scientists; *Committees:* Awards; Education; Finance; Nominations; Outreach; Programme; Publications; Topical Events
Activities: Organization of conferences; meetings & workshops; publication of scientific journals & books

European Photochemistry Association

c/o A.N. Nesmeyanov Institute of Organoelement, Vavilova str. 28, Moscow 119991 Russia
Tel: 7-499-135-8098; *Fax:* 7-499-135-5085
www.photochemistry.eu
Overview: A medium-sized international organization founded in 1970
Mission: To promote & encourage the international development of photochemistry & related subjects with special reference to European & neighbouring countries
Chief Officer(s):
Werner Nau, Chair
w.nau@jacobs-university.de
Membership: 439; *Fees:* 30 euros regular; 15 euros student; *Member Profile:* Scientists
Publications:
• Photochemical & Photobiological Sciences
Type: Journal; *Frequency:* Monthly; *Editor:* Sarah Ruthven

European Society of Association Executives (ESAE)

63 D'auderghem Ave., Brussels 1040 Belgium
Tel: 32-2-280-4696; *Fax:* 32-2-282-9353
office@esae.org
esae.org
Overview: A medium-sized international organization
Membership: *Fees:* Schedule available

European Society of Gynaecological Oncology (ESGO)

c/o Kenes Intl., PO Box 1726, 1-3 rue Chantepoulet, Geneva CH-1211 Switzerland
Tel: 41-22-906-9150; *Fax:* 41-22-732-2850
info@esgo.org
www.esgo.org
Overview: A medium-sized international organization founded in 1983
Mission: To promote international & cultural communications between gynaecologists, pathologists, surgeons, oncologists, radiotherapists, & other specialists of disciplines related & pertaining to gynaecological oncology; to promote clinical & basic research investigations & spreading of knowledge in gynaecological oncology
Member of: European board & College Obstectrics & Gynecology
Affliation(s): Federation of European Cancer Societies
Chief Officer(s):
Nicoletta Colombo, President
nicoletta.colombo@ieo.it
Finances: *Annual Operating Budget:* Less than $50,000; *Funding Sources:* Membership fees
Staff Member(s): 7; 7 volunteer(s)
Membership: 600; *Fees:* US$50; *Member Profile:* Interest in the field of gynaecological oncology; *Committees:* By-Laws; Newsletter; Federal; Prognostic Factors; Breast Cancer; Screening; Education; Membership

European Solidarity Towards Equal Participation of People / Solidarité européenne pour une égale participation des peuples

115, rue Stévin, Brussels B-1000 Belgium
Tel: 32-2-231-1659; *Fax:* 32-2-230-3780
admin@eurostep.org
www.eurostep.org
www.facebook.com/Eurostep
Also Known As: EUROSTEP
Overview: A small international organization founded in 1990
Mission: To co-ordinate the policy work of its members at European level & to influence the policy & practice of the European Union; with a focus on the EU's cooperation with other countries, particularly in Africa, Asia, & Latin America, Eurostep uses its membership base in 15 European countries & the secretariat located in Brussels to present common policy approaches to the European Commission, European Parliament & Member States governments
Chief Officer(s):
Simon Stocker, Director
Finances: *Annual Operating Budget:* $250,000-$500,000
Activities: *Internships:* Yes

European Space Agency (ESA) / Agence spatiale européenne

8-10, rue Mario Nikis, Paris 75738 France
Tel: 33-1-5369-7654; *Fax:* 33-1-5369-7560
Other Communication:
www.flickr.com/photos/europeanspaceagency
contactesa@esa.int
www.esa.int
twitter.com/esa
www.youtube.com/esa
Merged from: European Space Research Organization (ESRO); European Organization for the Development & Constructio
Overview: A large international organization founded in 1975
Mission: To provide for & to promote, for exclusively peaceful purposes, cooperation among European States in space research & technology & their space applications, with a view to their being used for scientific purposes & for operational space applications systems
Affliation(s): Canadian Space Agency
Chief Officer(s):
Jean-Jacques Dordain, Director General
Finances: *Annual Operating Budget:* $1.5 Million-$3 Million
Staff Member(s): 2000
Membership: 18 member states
Publications:
• ESA [European Space Agency] Annual Report
Type: Yearbook
• ESA [European Space Agency] Bulletin
Type: Newsletter

The Facial Pain Association (TNA)

602, 408 W. University Ave., Gainesville FL 32601 USA
Tel: 352-384-3600; *Fax:* 352-384-3606
Toll-Free: 800-923-3608
tnanational@tna-support.org
www.tna-support.org
www.facebook.com/facialpainassociation
twitter.com/facialpainassoc
Previous Name: Trigeminal Neuralgia Association
Overview: A large international charitable organization founded in 1990
Mission: To bring people with trigeminal neuralgia & related facial pain conditions together to share their experience & reduce their isolation; to serve as resource/pooling centre for information on trigeminal neuralgia; to provide mutual aid, support & encouragement to those afflicted, their families & other caring individuals; to increase public/professional awareness, visibility & better understanding of the disorder
Member of: National Organization for Rare Disorders (NORD)
Affliation(s): Centre for Non-Profit Corporations
Chief Officer(s):
John Koff, Chief Executive Officer
jkoff@tna-support.org
Finances: *Annual Operating Budget:* $250,000-$500,000; *Funding Sources:* Individual; foundations
Staff Member(s): 5; 200 volunteer(s)
Membership: 30,000; *Member Profile:* Patients with Trigeminal Neuralgia or related facial pain problems; *Committees:* Education
Activities: Ontario-Thunder Bay Support Group: Pam Kubala, 807/767-0022, kubala@tbaytel.net; Support Group: Carol Horvat, 905/687-8562, chorvat1@cogeco.ca; Dana & Daniel Lavrence, 905/886-7563, lavrence@sprint.ca; Norman/Nora Kudrenecky, 519/743-4579, Lezlie Wilson, 705/649-0883; Toronto, Gary Bannister, 416/234-5488; Dana Laurence, 905/886-7563, laurence@sprint.ca; Montreal/SW Québec Support Group: Sy Moskowitz, 514/934-0909,

symoss@sympatico.ca; Lethbridge-Alberta Support Group: Marion Guzik, 403/327-7668, mguzik@telus.net

Far Eastern Association Inc. ***See*** Association for Asian Studies - USA

Fédération Américaine du travail et congrès des organisations industrielles (FAT-COI) ***See*** American Federation of Labor & Congress of Industrial Organizations (AFL-CIO)

Fédération biblique catholique ***See*** Catholic Biblical Federation

Fédération des musiciens des États-Unis et du Canada (FAT-COI/CTC) ***See*** American Federation of Musicians of the United States & Canada (AFL-CIO/CLC)

Fédération internationale de bobsleigh et de tobogganing (FIBT)

Maison du Sport, Avenue de Rhodanie 54, Lausanne 1007 Switzerland
Tél: 41-21-601-51-01; *Téléc:* 41-21-601-79-23
office@fibt.com
www.fibt.com
www.linkedin.com/groups/FIBT-Fédération-International-de-Bobsleigh-189
www.facebook.com/128374647314728
twitter.com/FIBT
www.youtube.com/user/bobskeletv
Aperçu: *Dimension:* petite; *Envergure:* internationale; fondée en 1923
Affiliation(s): Canadian Amateur Bobsleigh & Tobogganing Association
Membre(s) du bureau directeur:
Ivo Ferriani, Président
Ermanno Gardella, Secrétaire général

Fédération Internationale de Camping et de Caravanning (FICC) / International Federation of Camping & Caravanning (IFCC)

18-24, rue des Colonies, bte 9, Brussels B-1000 Belgium
Tél: 32-2-513-87-82; *Téléc:* 32-2-513-87-83
info@ficc.org
www.ficc.be
Aperçu: *Dimension:* grande; *Envergure:* internationale; fondée en 1933
Mission: To promote camping & caravanning worldwide
Membre(s) du bureau directeur:
Joao Alves Pereira, President
Membre(s) du personnel: 1
Membre: 1,800,000; *Montant de la cotisation:* 300 Euro; 600 Euro; 900 Euro; *Comités:* Youth; Asia Pacific; North America; Technical; Environmental

Fédération internationale de hockey (FIH) / International Hockey Federation

Rue du Valentin 61, Lausanne CH-1004 Switzerland
Tél: 41-21-641-0606; *Téléc:* 41-21-641-0607
info@fih.ch
www.fih.ch
www.facebook.com/fihockey
twitter.com/FIH_Hockey
www.youtube.com/user/fihockey
Aperçu: *Dimension:* moyenne; *Envergure:* internationale; fondée en 1924
Mission: The federation works in co-operation with both the national and continental organisations to ensure consistency and unity in hockey around the world. The FIH not only regulates the sport, but is also responsible for its development and promotion so as to guarantee a secure future for hockey
Affiliation(s): Field Hockey Canada
Membre(s) du bureau directeur:
Leandro Negre, President
Membre(s) du personnel: 26
Membre: 5 federations; *Comités:* Appointments; Athletes; Competitions; Risk & Compliance; Rules; Umpiring; Equipment Advisory Panel; High Performance & Coaching Advisory Panel; Judicial Commission; Medical Advisory Panel

Fédération Internationale de l'Art Photographique (FIAP)

37, rue Chanzy, Paris 75011 France
Tél: 331-43-723-724; *Téléc:* 331-43-723-728
fiap@fiap.net
www.fiap.net
www.facebook.com/315152355167952
Aperçu: *Dimension:* petite; *Envergure:* internationale; Organisme sans but lucratif; fondée en 1950
Mission: PromouVoir la photographie par une collaboration internationale dans tous les domaines photographiques afin de créer des liens d'amitié entre toutes les fédérations affiliées en contribuant ainsi à l'évolution d'un climat de confiance entre les peuples dans le but de consolider la paix dans le monde
Affiliation(s): Canadian Association for Photographic Art
Membre(s) du bureau directeur:
Riccardo Busi, Président
busi.fiap@gmail.com
Membre: 85; *Critères d'admissibilite:* Regroupe plus de 85 fédérations nationales dans les cinq continents et répresente les intérêts de plus d'un demi million de photographes individuels, amateurs pour la plupart; FIAP compte aussi des membres individuels dans ILFIAP (club local) et IRFIAP (association régionale)
Activités: Salons photographiques; *Bibliothèque* Bibliothèque publique

Fédération internationale de Laiterie ***See*** International Dairy Federation

Fédération Internationale de Luge de Course (FIL) / International Luge Federation

Rathausplatz 9, Berchtesgaden 83471 Germany
Tél: 49-86-526-6960; *Téléc:* 49-86-526-6969
office@fil-luge.org
www.fil-luge.org
Aperçu: *Dimension:* petite; *Envergure:* internationale; fondée en 1957
Mission: Promotion et participation aux compétitions de la luge dans le monde; organise des championnats du monde, des coupes du monde, des championnats régionaux; organise des cours et séminaires pour des arbitres et des entraîneurs
Affiliation(s): Canadian Luge Association
Membre(s) du bureau directeur:
Josef Fendt, Président
Svein Romstad, Secrétaire général
Finances: *Budget de fonctionnement annuel:* $250,000-$500,000
Membre(s) du personnel: 5
Membre: 49
Activités: *Bibliothèque*

Fédération internationale de natation amateur ***See*** International Amateur Swimming Federation

Fédération Internationale de Volleyball ***See*** International Volleyball Association

Fédération internationale des Amis de la Terre ***See*** Friends of the Earth International

Fédération internationale des architectes paysagistes ***See*** International Federation of Landscape Architects

Fédération internationale des associations de producteurs de films (FIAPF) / International Federation of Film Producers' Associations

9, rue de l'Échelle, Paris 75001 France
Tél: 33-1-44-77-97-50; *Téléc:* 33-1-44-77-97-55
info@fiapf.org
www.fiapf.org
Aperçu: *Dimension:* petite; *Envergure:* internationale; fondée en 1933
Mission: Pour défendre les droits de propriété des producteurs et d'influencer la mise en ouvre des lois de copyright afin d'éviter le piratage
Affiliation(s): Canadian Film & Television Association
Membre(s) du bureau directeur:
Luis Alberto Scalella, President
Membre: 32 organisations

Fédération Internationale des Associations de Professeurs de Sciences ***See*** International Council of Associations for Science Education

Fédération internationale des femmes de carrières libérales et commerciales ***See*** International Federation of Business & Professional Women

Fédération internationale des géomètres ***See*** International Federation of Surveyors

Fédération internationale des hôpitaux ***See*** International Hospital Federation

Fédération internationale des industries textiles ***See*** International Textile Manufacturers Federation

Fédération internationale des ingénieurs et techniciens (FAT-COI/CTC) ***See*** International Federation of Professional & Technical Engineers (AFL-CIO/CLC)

Fédération internationale des mouvements d'agriculture biologique ***See*** International Federation of Organic Agriculture Movements

Fédération Internationale des Producteurs Agricoles ***See*** International Federation of Agricultural Producers

Fédération internationale des professeurs de français (FIPF)

1, av Léon-Journault, Sèvres-Cedex F-92310 France
Tél: 33-1-46-26-53-16; *Téléc:* 33-1-46-26-81-69
secretariat@fipf.org
www.fipf.org
Aperçu: *Dimension:* moyenne; *Envergure:* internationale; Organisme sans but lucratif; fondée en 1969
Mission: Regrouper toutes les associations de professeurs de français et toutes les personnes chargées de l'enseignement du français dans le monde; favoriser la mise en commun de leurs expériences et de leurs recherches pédagogiques en vue de promouVoir l'enseignement du français et d'améliorer les conditions générales et particulières de cet enseignement; susciter et faciliter entre ses membres les échanges de toute nature
Membre de: UNESCO
Affiliation(s): Association des professeurs de français des universités et collèges du Canada; Alliance ontarienne des professeurs d'immersion; Association québécoise des professeurs de français; Association québécoise des enseignants de français langue seconde
Membre(s) du bureau directeur:
Martine Defontaine, Secrétaire générale
Dario Pagel, Président
Membre: 90 000
Publications:
• Dialogues et cultures
Type: Annuaire; *Frequency:* Annually
• Échanges
Type: Bulletin
• Le français dans le monde

Fédération internationale des professions immobilières (FIABCI) / International Real Estate Federation

17, rue Dumont d'Urville, Paris F-75116 France
Tel: 33-1-73-79-58-30; *Fax:* 33-1-73-79-58-33
info@fiabci.com
www.fiabci.org
Overview: A medium-sized international charitable organization founded in 1951
Mission: Pour aider les membres réparties leur réputation à l'échelle internationale
Chief Officer(s):
Patricia Delaney, Secrétaire général
delaney@fiabci.com
Membership: 100 associations; *Committees:* Africa Region; Americas Region; Asia-Pacific; Europe & Near East; Membership; Conference; Finance; Nominations; Young Members; International Organisations; Exchanges; Environment & Legislation; Education; Forums; Marketing & Networking
Activities: *Internships:* Yes

Fédération Internationale des Sociétés de la Croix-Rouge & du Croissant-Rouge ***See*** International Federation of Red Cross & Red Crescent Societies

Fédération Internationale des Traducteurs (FIT) / International Federation of Translators (IFT)

REGUS, 57 rue d'Amsterdam, Paris 75008 France
secretariat@fit-ift.org
www.fit-ift.org
Aperçu: *Dimension:* petite; *Envergure:* internationale; Organisme sans but lucratif; fondée en 1953
Mission: De rassembler les organisations de traducteurs existant dans les divers pays, de susciter et de favoriser la constitution de telles organisations dans les pays où il n'en existe pas encore; de fournir aux organisations membres les informations et les conseils susceptibles de leur être utiles; d'établir, entre toutes les organisations membres, la bonne entente favorable aux intérêts des traducteurs et de contribuer à aplanir les différences qui pourraient s'élever entre ces organisations; de défendre les droits moraux et matériels des traducteurs dans le monde
Membre de: UNESCO

Affliation(s): Canadian Translators, Terminologists & Interpreters Council
Membre(s) du bureau directeur:
Izabel Arocha, Secrétaire général
secgen@fit-ift.org
Finances: *Budget de fonctionnement annuel:* $50,000-$100,000
Membre(s) du personnel: 1; 50 bénévole(s)
Membre: 120; *Montant de la cotisation:* Barème; *Critères d'admissibilite:* Toute organisation professionnelle de traducteurs ayant un caractère représentatif peut demander son admission comme membre ordinaire; les groupements qui s'intéressent aux activités et à la promotion des objectifs de la FIT, mais ne répondent pas entièrement aux qualités requises pour être membre ou ne souhaitent pas le devenir, peuvent postuler en qualité de membres associés ou membres observateurs
Activités: *Service de conférenciers:* Oui

Fédération internationale du personnel des services publics *See* International Federation of Employees in Public Service

Fédération internationale pour l'habitation, l'urbanisme et l'aménagement des territoires *See* International Federation for Housing & Planning

Fédération internationale pour la recherche en histoire des femmes *See* International Federation for Research in Women's History

Fédération mondiale des concours internationaux de musique (FMCIM) / World Federation of International Music Competitions (WFIMC)

104, rue de Carouge, Geneva CH-1205 Switzerland
Tél: 41-22-321-3620; *Téléc:* 41-22-781-1418
fmcim@fmcim.org
www.fmcim.org
www.facebook.com/FMCIM.WFIMC
Aperçu: *Dimension:* petite; *Envergure:* internationale; fondée en 1957
Mission: Favoriser la coordination des activités des concours membres; aider les jeunes lauréats de concours membres à se faire connaître; maintenir un lien amical entre les membres de la Fédération
Membre de: Conseil international de la musique (UNESCO)
Affliation(s): Union Européenne des Concours de Musique pour la Jeunesse; Fédération Française des Festivals Internationaux de Musique; Jeunesses Musicales International; European Broadcasting Union; L'Association Internationale des Agents Artistiques; The International Society for the Performing Arts
Membre(s) du bureau directeur:
Glen Kwok, Président
Marianne Granvig, Secrétaire générale
Membre(s) du personnel: 2
Membre: 120 compétitions musicales internationales

Fédération mondiale des sourds *See* World Federation of the Deaf

Fédération mondiale pour la santé mentale *See* World Federation for Mental Health

Fédération mondiale pour les études sur le future *See* World Futures Studies Federation

Federation of European Direct & Interactive Marketing (FEDMA)

Av. Ariane 5, 4th Fl., Brussels 1200 Belgium
Tel: 32-2-779-4268; *Fax:* 32-2-778-9922
www.fedma.org
Previous Name: European Direct Marketing Association
Overview: A medium-sized international organization founded in 1997
Mission: To promote & defend the interests & to advance the image, status & prestige of direct marketing in Europe; to build the business of cross-border direct marketing by representation within the European Union institutions & through its vast network of contacts & businesses from within & outside Europe
Affliation(s): Canadian Direct Marketing Association; Canadian Advertising Foundation
Chief Officer(s):
Ivan Vandermeersch, Secretary General
ivan@fedma.org
Staff Member(s): 10
Membership: 350 in 36+ countries; *Fees:* 1.000 to 29.000 EUR; *Member Profile:* Users & suppliers of direct marketing services; *Committees:* Task Forces & Councils
Activities: Information on the European market, European legislation & legal issues, postal regulations, lists availability; providing networking & business links, organizing conferences & seminars; *Library*
Awards:
• Best of Europe DM Awards (Award)

Federation of Sewage Works Associations; Federation of Sewage & Industrial Wastes Associations; Water Pollution Control Federation *See* Water Environment Federation

Federation of Swiss Association Executives

Boul. de Pérolles 18 A, Fribourg 1700 Switzerland
Tel: 41-31-390-99-09; *Fax:* 41-31-390-99-03
info@verbandssekretaere.ch
www.verbandssekretaere.ch
Also Known As: Vereinigung Schweizischer Verbandssekretäre
Overview: A medium-sized national organization
Chief Officer(s):
Barbara Gutzwiller, Chair

Fellowship of Reconciliation (FOR)

PO Box 271, Nyack NY 10960 USA
Tel: 845-358-4601; *Fax:* 845-358-4924
for@forusa.org
forusa.org
www.facebook.com/FORUSA
twitter.com/FORpeace
www.youtube.com/FellowshipUSA
Overview: A medium-sized international organization founded in 1914
Mission: To replace violence, war, racism & economic injustice with nonviolence, peace & justice; committed to active nonviolence as a transforming way of life & as a means of radical change; to educate, train, rebuild coalitions & engage in nonviolent & compassionate actions locally, nationally & globally
Member of: International Fellowship of Reconciliation
Chief Officer(s):
Kristin Stoneking, Executive Director
kstoneking@forusa.org
Staff Member(s): 23
Membership: *Member Profile:* Clergy; teachers; students; peace activists
Activities: Peacemaker Training for young adults; non-violence training; peacebuilder delegations to Palestine/Israel; Campaign of Conscience for the Iraqi People; The Decade for a Culture of Peace & Nonviolence for the Children of the World; publications; sale of cards, calendars & gifts; *Internships:* Yes; *Speaker Service:* Yes *Library:* FOR Peace Library; Open to public by appointment
Awards:
• Martin Luther King, Jr. Award (Award)
• Pfeffer Peace Prize (Award)

Financial Planning Association (FPA)

#600, 7535 East Hampden Ave., Denver CO 80231 USA
Tel: 303-759-4900; *Fax:* 303-759-0749
Toll-Free: 800-322-4237
member.services@onefpa.org
www.plannersearch.org
www.facebook.com/FinancialPlanningAssociation
twitter.com/fpassociation
Overview: A medium-sized international organization founded in 1969
Mission: To provide leadership & advocacy for persons who need, support, & deliverprofessional financial planning services; To advance the financial planning profession
Chief Officer(s):
Lauren Schadle, Chief Executive Officer
Membership: 28,500+; *Member Profile:* Members of the financial planning community
Activities: Offering diverse educational opportunities; Liaising with legislative & regulatory bodies, financial services firms, & consumer interest organizations; *Awareness Events:* Financial Planning Week, October
Publications:
• FPA SmartBrief
Type: Newsletter; *Frequency:* Weekly; *Price:* Free for Financial Planning Association members
Profile: Government & industry updates for the financial planning community
• Journal of Financial Planning
Type: Journal; *Frequency:* Monthly; *Accepts Advertising; Editor:* Lance Ritchlin; *Price:* Free with membership in the Financial Planning Association; $119 U.S.non-members
Profile: Articles, interviews, & peer-reviewed technical contributions for financial planners & advisers

Fondation pour la conservation de l'environnement *See* Foundation for Environmental Conservation

Fonds mondial pour la nature *See* World Wildlife Fund - USA

Foodservice & Packaging Institute (FPI)

201 Park Washington Crt., Falls Church VA 22046 USA
Tel: 703-538-3550; *Fax:* 703-241-5603
fpi@fpi.org
www.fpi.org
www.linkedin.com/company/1680721?trk=tyah
www.facebook.com/pages/Foodservice-Packaging-Institute/133857106247
www.twitter.com/fpihq
Overview: A small national organization founded in 1933
Chief Officer(s):
Lynn Dyer, President
ldyer@fpi.org
Jennifer Goldman, Manager, Membership & Meetings, 703-538-3553
jgoldman@fpi.org
Lynn Rosseth, Director, Market Development & Programs
Finances: *Annual Operating Budget:* $500,000-$1.5 Million; *Funding Sources:* Membership fees
Staff Member(s): 3
Membership: 25; *Fees:* Varies by sales; *Member Profile:* Serves the single-use foodservice packaging industry; is the material-neutral trade association for manufacturers, suppliers & distributors of single-use foodservice packaging products; *Committees:* Market Development; Marketing & Communications; Public Affairs; Safety Management; Technical; Standards Council
Activities: Market development; marketing & communications; member services; public affairs & technical programs

Foundation for Environmental Conservation (FEC) / Fondation pour la conservation de l'environnement

1148 Moiry Switzerland
Fax: 41-21-8666-6616
envcons@ncl.ac.uk
www.ncl.ac.uk/icef
Overview: A small international organization founded in 1975
Mission: To undertake, in cooperation with appropriate individuals, organizations & other groups, all possible activities to further environmental conservation & global sustainability
Chief Officer(s):
Nicholas V.C. Polunin, Editor
Membership: *Committees:* Awards
Activities: International Conferences on Environmental Future (ICEFs); specialist workshops;

Foundation for International Environmental Law & Development (FIELD)

Cityside House, 40 Adler St, 3rd Fl., London E1 1EE United Kingdom
Tel: 44-20-7096 0277; *Fax:* 44-20-7388-2826
www.field.org.uk
www.facebook.com/474981202565918
twitter.com/FIELDLegal
Previous Name: Centre for Environmental Law & Development
Overview: A small international organization founded in 1989
Mission: To help vulnerable countries, communities, & campaigners negotiate for fairer international environmental laws
Chief Officer(s):
Joy Hyvarinen, Executive Director
Finances: *Annual Operating Budget:* $500,000-$1.5 Million; *Funding Sources:* Foundations; Consultancy work
Staff Member(s): 13; 8 volunteer(s)
Membership: *Member Profile:* Public international lawyers
Activities: *Internships:* Yes *Library*

Fraternité des préposés à l'entretien des voies (FAT-COI/CTC) *See* Brotherhood of Maintenance of Way Employees (AFL-CIO/CLC)

Fraternité internationale des chaudronniers, constructeurs de navires en fer, forgerons, forgeurs et aides (FAT-COI) *See* International Brotherhood of Boilermakers, Iron Ship Builders, Blacksmiths, Forgers & Helpers (AFL-CIO)

Fraternité internationale des ouvriers en électricité (FAT-COI/FCT) *See* International Brotherhood of Electrical Workers (AFL-CIO/CFL)

Fraternité internationale des teamsters (FAT-COI/CTC) *See* International Brotherhood of Teamsters (AFL-CIO/CLC)

Fraternité unie des charpentiers et menuisiers d'Amérique (FAT-COI/CTC) ***See*** United Brotherhood of Carpenters & Joiners of America (AFL-CIO/CLC)

French Association for Canadian Studies ***Voir*** Association française d'études canadiennes

Friends Historical Association (FHA)

Quaker Collection, Haverford College, 370 Lancaster Ave., Haverford PA 19041-1392 USA
Tel: 610-896-1161; *Fax:* 610-896-1102
fha@haverford.edu
www.haverford.edu/library/fha/
Overview: A medium-sized international charitable organization founded in 1873
Mission: To promote the study, preservation & publication of material relating to the history of the Religious Society of Friends
Affliation(s): Conference of Quaker Historians & Archivists
Chief Officer(s):
Kenneth Carroll, President
Joelle Bertolet, Office Manager
Finances: *Annual Operating Budget:* Less than $50,000; *Funding Sources:* Membership dues; subscriptions; donations
Staff Member(s): 1; 21 volunteer(s)
Membership: 800; *Fees:* $15; *Member Profile:* Friends & interested historians; *Committees:* Membership; Publication; Historical Research; Finance; Curatorial; Development
Activities: Pilgrimages to historic Friends Meetings; lectures; *Rents Mailing List:* Yes
Publications:
• Quaker History
Type: Journal; *Frequency:* Semiannually; *Editor:* Charles L. Cherry

Friends Historical Society - London (FHS)

c/o Friends House, 173 Euston Rd., London NW1 2BJ United Kingdom
Tel: 44 020 7663 1094; *Fax:* 44 020 7663 1001
Overview: A small international organization founded in 1903
Mission: To encourage the study of Quaker history
Member of: Association of Denominational Historical Societies & Cognate Libraries
Finances: *Funding Sources:* Membership fees
Membership: 400;

Friends of Animals (FoA)

#205, 777 Post Rd., Darien CT USA
Tel: 203-656-1522; *Fax:* 203-656-0267
Toll-Free: 800-321-7387
info@friendsofanimals.org
friendsofanimals.org
www.facebook.com/FriendsOfAnimalsOrg
twitter.com/pferal
www.youtube.com/user/FriendsofAnimals
Overview: A large national charitable organization founded in 1957
Mission: To free animals from cruelty & institutionalized exploitation around the world; works to cultivate a respectful view of nonhuman animals, free-living & domestic. Branch offices in New York & Victoria, BC.
Chief Officer(s):
Carol Fleischmann, Chair
Priscilla Feral, President
feral@friendsofanimals.org
Finances: *Annual Operating Budget:* $3 Million-$5 Million; *Funding Sources:* Membership dues; bequests; grants; donations
Staff Member(s): 23; 185 volunteer(s)
Membership: 200,000; *Fees:* US$25; $30 international
Activities: Low-cost spay/neuter program; anti-fur, anti-wolf & anti-ivory campaigns; opposes all hunting & & international animal trade; supports marine mammal protection; assists & supports programs in Africa for chimpanzees & other animals; anti-vivisection; advocates vegan, plant-based diets
Publications:
• ActùionLine [a publication of Friends of Animals]
Type: Magazine

Canadian Office
PO Box 50024, #15, 1594 Fairfield Rd., Victoria BC V8S 5L8
Tel: 250-588-0482
www.thevictoriavegan.com
twitter.com/FoA_Victoria
• The Victoria Vegan [a publication of Friends of Animals, Canadian Office]
Editor: Dave Shishkoff
Profile: Newsletter archived on website

Friends of the Earth International (FoEI) / Fédération internationale des Amis de la Terre

International Secretariat, PO Box 19199, Amsterdam 1000 GD Netherlands
Tel: 31-20-622-1369
foei@foei.org
www.foei.org
twitter.com/FoEint
www.youtube.com/user/FriendsoftheEarthInt
Also Known As: Amigos de la Tierra
Overview: A medium-sized international organization founded in 1971
Mission: To promote that environmental problems do not respect geographical & political boundaries; To cooperate with other organizations; To raise awareness that environmental, social, economic & political issues are interdependent; To encourage positive alternatives to policies & practices which cause ecological degradation
Member of: International Union for the Conservation of Nature
Affliation(s): International Rivers Network; Rainforest Action Network; Rainforest Information Centre; EcoPeace; Action for Solidarity, Equality Environment & Development Europe
Chief Officer(s):
Jagoda Munic, Chair
Dave Hirsch, International Coordinator
Pauline Vincenten, Office Coordinator
Finances: *Funding Sources:* Fees; Donations; Subsidies
Membership: 74 national groups, comprised of 5,000 local groups with over 2 million members; *Member Profile:* Envrionmental organizations
Activities: Workshops on specific campaigns; Political lobbying; Information distribution;

La Fundación Canadá ***See*** Spanish Association for Canadian Studies

The Galpin Society

37 Townsend Dr., St. Albans, Herts AL3 5RF UK
administrator@galpinsociety.org
www.galpinsociety.org
Overview: A medium-sized international charitable organization founded in 1946
Mission: To study the history & construction of musical instruments
Chief Officer(s):
Graham Wells, Chair
grahamwhwells@aol.com
Finances: *Funding Sources:* Membership dues
Membership: *Fees:* Schedule available
Activities: Symposia, AGM & meetings abroad

The Geneva Association

53 Route de Malagnou, Geneva CH-1208 Switzerland
Tel: 41-22-707-6600; *Fax:* 41-22-736-7536
secretariat@genevaassociation.org
www.genevaassociation.org
www.linkedin.com/groups?gid=3792189
twitter.com/TheGenevaAssoc
Also Known As: International Association for the Study of Insurance Economics
Overview: A small international organization founded in 1973
Mission: To research the growing economic importance of world-wide insurance activities in the major sectors of the economy
Chief Officer(s):
Anna Maria D'Hulster, Secretary General & Managing Direct
Membership: 90; *Member Profile:* CEOs of the most important insurance companies in Europe, North America, South America, Asia, Africa & Australia

Geochemical Society

c/o Earth & Planetary Sciences Department, Washington University, #CB 11691, Brookings Dr., St. Louis MO 63130-4899 USA
Tel: 314-935-4131; *Fax:* 314-935-4121
gsoffice@geochemsoc.org
www.geochemsoc.org
Overview: A medium-sized international organization
Mission: To encourage the application of chemistry to the solution of geological & cosmological problems
Affliation(s): American Association for the Advancement of Science; International Union of Geological Sciences; Council of Scientific Society Presidents; Geological Society of America
Chief Officer(s):
Martin Goldhaber, President
mgold@usgs.gov
Samuel Mukasa, Vice-President
mukasa@umich.edu
Neil Sturchio, Secretary
sturchio@uic.edu
Louise Criscenti, Treasurer
ljcrisc@sandia.gov
Seth Davis, Manager, Business
seth.davis@geochemsoc.org
Membership: *Member Profile:* An international membership with interests in fields such as high & low-temperature geochemistry, fluid-rock interaction, organic geochemistry, petrology, isotope geochemistry, & meteoritics; *Committees:* Joint Publications; Nominations; Program; V.M. Goldschmidt Award; F.W. Clarke Award; C.C. Patterson Award; Geochemical Fellows; OGD Executive; Alfred Treibs Award; OGD Best Paper Award; AAAS Liaison
Meetings/Conferences:
• Goldschmidt Conference 2015, August, 2015, Prague
Scope: International
Attendance: 3,000+
Description: An international conference on geochemistry
• Goldschmidt Conference 2016, June, 2016, Yokohama
Scope: International
Attendance: 3,000+
Description: An international conference on geochemistry
• Goldschmidt Conference 2017, 2017
Scope: International
Attendance: 3,000+
Description: An international conference on geochemistry
Publications:
• Elements Magazine [a publication of the Geochemical Society]
Type: Journal; *Frequency:* Bimonthly; *Price:* Free with membership in the Geochemical Society
Profile: Theme issues with peer-reviewed invited papers related to the mineral & geochemical sciences
• GCA: Geochimica et Cosmochimica Acta
Type: Journal; *Frequency:* Biweekly; *Editor:* Dr. Frank Podosek
Profile: Scientific contributions related to geochemistry & cosmochemistry
• G-Cubed (Geochemistry, Geophysics, Geosystems)
Type: Journal
Profile: Research papers on the chemistry, physics, & biology of earth & planetary processes
• Geochemical News
Type: Newsletter; *Frequency:* Quarterly; *Editor:* Stephen Komor
Profile: News of the Geochemical Society
• Geochemical Society Special Publication Series
Profile: Scientifically significant collections of related, original papers on topics such as magmatic processes, fluid-mineral interactions, stable isotope geochemistry, mineralspectroscopy, mantle petrology, & volcanic, geothermal, & ore-forming fluids

The G.K. Chesterton Institute for Faith & Culture

Seton Hall University, 400 South Orange Ave., South Orange NJ 07079-2687 USA
Tel: 973-275-2431; *Fax:* 973-275-2594
chestertoninstitute@shu.edu
www.shu.edu/catholic-mission/chesterton-index.cfm
www.facebook.com/121042177917463
Overview: A medium-sized international charitable organization founded in 1974
Mission: To promote a critical interest in all aspects of the life & work of G.K. Chesterton
Chief Officer(s):
Ian Boyd, President
boydjian@shu.edu
Finances: *Annual Operating Budget:* $50,000-$100,000
Staff Member(s): 4
Membership: 237 institutional; 1,800 individual; *Fees:* $38 individual
Publications:
• The Chesterton Review
Editor: Ian Boyd; *Price:* $38 subscription
Profile: Quarterly journal

Glass Packaging Institute (GPI)

#510, 700 North Fairfax St., Alexandria VA 22314 USA
Tel: 703-684-6359; *Fax:* 703-299-1543
info@gpi.org
www.gpi.org
www.facebook.com/chooseglass
www.twitter.com/chooseglass
Overview: A medium-sized national organization founded in 1919
Mission: The trade association representing the North American glass container industry.

Chief Officer(s):
Lynn M. Bragg, President
Awards:
• Clear Choice Awards, Glass Packaging Institute
Awards for consumer product goods manufacturers who expand the fronteirs of glass packaging design my using glass containers in innovatibe ways *Contact:* Kristen LeKander, kristen@lindberggrp.com; 703/778-7644

Glass, Molders, Pottery, Plastic & Allied Workers International Union (AFL-CIO/CLC) (GMP) / Union internationale des travailleurs du verre, mouleurs, poterie, plastique et autres (FAT-COI/CTC)

PO Box 607, 608 East Baltimore Pike, Media PA 19063-0607 USA
Tel: 610-565-5051; *Fax:* 610-565-0983
gmpiu@gmpiu.org
www.gmpiu.org
Also Known As: GMP International Union
Overview: A medium-sized international organization founded in 1842
Mission: To create relationships that create more resources for its members
Affliation(s): AFL-CIO; Canadia Labour Congress
Chief Officer(s):
Bruce R. Smith, President
David Doyle, Executive Director, Canada
Finances: *Funding Sources:* Membership dues
Membership: 250+ unions

Global Crop Protection Federation; International Group of National Associations of Manufacturers of Agrochemical Products *See* Croplife International

Government Finance Officers Association (GFOA)

#2700, 203 North LaSalle St., Chicago IL 60601-1210 USA
Tel: 312-977-9700; *Fax:* 312-977-4806
inquiry@gfoa.org
www.gfoa.org
Overview: A medium-sized international organization founded in 1906
Mission: To serve the public finance profession in the the United States & Canada
Chief Officer(s):
Jeffrey Esser, Executive Director & CEO
Kenneth L. Rust, President
John Jurkash, Chief Financial Officer, Financial Administration
Membership: 17,600+; *Fees:* Schedule available, based upon population of city or county; *Member Profile:* State, provincial, & local finance officers, in the United States & Canada, who are involved in the management of government financial resources; *Committees:* Governmental Budgeting & Fiscal Policy; Accounting, Auditing, & Financial Reporting; Canadian Issues; Economic Development & Capital Planning; Retirement & Benefits Administration; Governmental Debt Management; Treasury & Investment Management
Activities: Providing opportunities for continuing education; Conducting research; Providing recommended practices for the government finance profession; Publishing over 75 books about government finance, as well as specialty newsletters on the topics of accounting, auditing, and financial reporting, cash management, & pension & benefit issues; Offering technical inquiry services for members; *Library:* GFOA Reference Library
Awards:
• Certificate of Achievement for Excellence in Financial Reporting (CAFR) (Award)
Established in 1945, the certificate is designed to recognize & encourage excellence in financial reporting by state & local governments
• Popular Annual Financial Reporting Award (PAFR) (Award)
To encourage governments to produce reports that make financial data more accessible to those who need less detailed information than what is traditionally found in CAFRPs
• Awards for Excellence (Award)
Recognizes contributions to the practice of government finance that exemplify outstanding financial management; awarded in the following categories: accounting, auditing, & financial reporting, budgeting & financial planning, cash managment & investments, captial finance & debt administration, pensions & benefits, management & service delivery, enterprise financial systems & technology
• Canadian Award for Financial Reporting (CANFR) (Award)
• Distinguished Budget Awards (Award)
Meetings/Conferences:
• Government Finance Officers Association 2015 109th Annual Conference, May, 2015, Philadelphia, PA
Scope: International
Attendance: 4,100+
Contact Information: Manager, Communications: Natalie Laudadio, Phone: 312-977-9700, ext. 2298
• Government Finance Officers Association 2016 110th Annual Conference, May, 2016, Toronto, ON
Scope: International
Attendance: 4,100+
Contact Information: Manager, Communications: Natalie Laudadio, Phone: 312-977-9700, ext. 2298
• Government Finance Officers Association 2017 111th Annual Conference, May, 2017, Denver, CO
Scope: International
Attendance: 4,100+
Contact Information: Manager, Communications: Natalie Laudadio, Phone: 312-977-9700, ext. 2298
• Government Finance Officers Association 2018 112th Annual Conference, May, 2018, St. Louis, MO
Scope: International
Attendance: 4,100+
Contact Information: Manager, Communications: Natalie Laudadio, Phone: 312-977-9700, ext. 2298
• Government Finance Officers Association 2019 112th Annual Conference, 2019
Scope: International
Contact Information: Manager, Communications: Natalie Laudadio, Phone: 312-977-9700, ext. 2298
Publications:
• Government Finance Officers Association Membership Newsletter
Type: Newsletter; *Frequency:* Semimonthly; *Accepts Advertising*; *Editor:* Marcy Boggs
• Government Finance Officers Association Professional Magazine
Type: Magazine; *Frequency:* Bimonthly

Government Refuse Collection & Disposal Association *See* Solid Waste Association of North America

Grain Elevator & Processing Society (GEAPS)

4248 Park Glen Rd., Minneapolis MN 55416 USA
Tel: 952-928-4640; *Fax:* 952-929-1318
info@geaps.com
www.geaps.com
www.linkedin.com/groups/Grain-Elevator-Processing-Society-GEAPS-389535
www.facebook.com/GEAPS
twitter.com/GEAPSinfo
Overview: A medium-sized international organization founded in 1937
Mission: To provide a forum for the analysis & exchange of information affecting the industries; to advance educational & professional qualifications of the members; to represent the interests of the members in governmental activities; to foster good business ethics & social responsibility throughout the membership; to communicate with the trade media & general public concerning the issues of interest to the members & the industries; to provide technical information on grain handling & storage
Chief Officer(s):
David Krejci, Executive Vice-President
Finances: *Funding Sources:* Membership dues; publications
Staff Member(s): 11
Membership: *Fees:* US$185 regular; $0 student; *Member Profile:* Individuals across the grain operations industry worldwide
Activities: Publications; education & training; trade shows; conferences; *Speaker Service:* Yes; *Rents Mailing List:* Yes

Graphic Communications International Union *See* International Brotherhood of Teamsters

Great Lakes Commission / Commission des Grands Lacs

Eisenhower Corporate Park, #100, 2805 Industrial Way South, Ann Arbor MI 48104-6791 USA
Tel: 734-971-9135; *Fax:* 734-971-9150
www.glc.org
Mission: The Commission is a binational, public agency dedicated to the use, management & protection of water, land & other natural resources of the Great Lakes-St. Lawrence system. In partnership with 8 Great Lakes states & provinces of Ontario & Québec, the Commission applies sustainable development principles addressing issues of resource management, environmental protection, transportation & sustainable development. The Commission provides information on public policy issues; a forum for developing & coordinating public policy; & a unified, system-wide voice to advocate member interests.
Chief Officer(s):
Kenneth G. Johnson, Chair
Tim A. Eder, Executive Director
teder@glc.org

The Great Lakes Research Consortium (GLRC)

SUNY College of Environmental Science & Forestry, 253 Baker Labs, 1 Forestry Dr., Syracuse NY 13210 USA
Tel: 315-470-6720; *Fax:* 315-470-6970
glrc@esf.edu
www.esf.edu/glrc
Overview: A medium-sized international organization founded in 1986
Mission: To facilitate research & scholarship on Great Lakes problems; to provide opportunities for training & education of students; to disseminate important information & research findings
Chief Officer(s):
Greg Boyer, Executive Director
glboyer@esf.edu
Heather Carringon, Coordinator, Great Lakes Research Consortium
Finances: *Annual Operating Budget:* $100,000-$250,000
Staff Member(s): 2
Membership: 18 institutional; *Fees:* $500-1,000 per campus; *Member Profile:* New York State colleges & universities + 9 Ontario universities
Activities: Speakers exchange; task forces; small grants program; annual student/faculty conferences; *Speaker Service:* Yes

Greenpeace International

Ottho Heldringstraat 5, Amsterdam 1066 AZ Netherlands
Tel: 31-20-718-2000; *Fax:* 31-20-718-2002
Other Communication: pinterest.com/greenpeace
supporter.services.int@greenpeace.org
www.greenpeace.org
www.facebook.com/greenpeace.international
twitter.com/Greenpeace
www.youtube.com/greenpeacevideo
Also Known As: Stichting Greenpeace Council
Overview: A large international organization founded in 1971
Mission: To protect the environment from the threats of pollution, global warming, & the depletion of natural resources; To protect endangered species, such as whales, dolphins, & seals
Chief Officer(s):
Ana Toni, Chair
Kumi Naidoo, Executive Director
Finances: *Annual Operating Budget:* $1.5 Million-$3 Million
Staff Member(s): 175
Membership: 40 countries
Activities: Campaigning; non-violent direct action; publishing environmental reports
Publications:
• Greenpeace Annual Report
Type: Yearbook

Greenpeace USA

#300, 702 H St. NW, Washington DC 20001 USA
Tel: 202-462-1177; *Fax:* 202-462-4507
Toll-Free: 800-326-0959
info@wdc.greenpeace.org
www.greenpeaceusa.org
www.facebook.com/greenpeaceusa
twitter.com/greenpeaceusa
www.youtube.com/profile?user=greenpeaceusa
Overview: A large international charitable organization founded in 1971
Mission: To use non-violent confrontation to expose global environmental problems & to promote solutions essential to a green & peaceful future; to protect biodiversity in all its forms; to end the nuclear threat & promote global disarmament
Affliation(s): Greenpeace International
Chief Officer(s):
Kumi Naidoo, International Executive Director
Phil Radford, Executive Director
Finances: *Annual Operating Budget:* Greater than $5 Million
Membership: 4 million; *Fees:* $30
Activities: *Internships:* Yes; *Speaker Service:* Yes; *Rents Mailing List:* Yes

Awards:
• Diversity Scholarship (Scholarship)
Amount: $1,750 (2)

Guilde américaine des artistes de variétés (FAT-COI) *See* American Guild of Variety Artists (AFL-CIO)

La Guilde des journalistes (FAT-COI/CTC) *See* The Newspaper Guild (AFL-CIO/CLC)

Hawk Migration Association of North America (HMANA)

PO Box 721, Plymouth NH 03264 USA
info@hmana.org
www.hmana.org
www.facebook.com/278725758995
twitter.com/hmanahawkwatch
Overview: A medium-sized international organization founded in 1974
Mission: To conserve raptor populations through the scientific study, enjoyment & appreciation of hawk migration
Chief Officer(s):
Carolyn Hoffman, Chair
Staff Member(s): 2
Membership: 600+; *Fees:* US$25 student; US$35 individual; US$55 family; US$60 organization; US$100 benefactor; corporate US$300; US$700 life supporting; *Committees:* RPI; Development; Data; Conservation; Tour
Activities: *Speaker Service:* Yes

Healthcare Information & Management Systems Society (HIMSS)

#1700, 33 West Monrnoe St., Chicago IL 60603-5616 USA
Tel: 312-664-4467; *Fax:* 312-664-6143
Other Communication: membership@himss.org;
policy@himss.org
himss@himss.org
www.himss.org
www.linkedin.com/groups?about=&gid=93115
www.facebook.com/pages/HIMSS/142288373333
twitter.com/himss
www.youtube.com/himss
Overview: A large international organization
Mission: To provide worldwide leadership in the optimal use of healthcare information technology & management systems in order to improve healthcare
Chief Officer(s):
Willa Fields, Chair
H. Stephen Lieber, President & Chief Executive Officer
slieber@himss.org
R. Norris Orms, Exec. Vice-President, COO & Executive Dir., HIMSS Foundation
norms@himss.org
Carla Smith, Executive Vice-President
csmith@himss.org
Jeremy Bonfini, Executive Vice-President, Global Services
jbonfini@himss.org
Membership: 20,000+; *Fees:* Individual, $160; Chapter-Only, $30; Student, $30; *Committees:* Public Policy; Ambulatory IS; Annual Conference Education; Career Services; Distance Education; Interoperability; Innovation; Physician; Privacy & Security
Awards:
• HIMSS Nicholas E. Davies Award of Excellence (Award)
• Stage 7 Award (Award)
• Richard P. Covert, PhD, LFHIMSS Scholarship for Management Systems (Scholarship)
Meetings/Conferences:
• Healthcare Information & Management Systems Society 2015 Annual Conference, April, 2015, Chicago, IL
Scope: International
Attendance: 38,000+
Contact Information: URL: www.himssconference.org
Publications:
• The Digital Office
Type: Newsletter; *Frequency:* Monthly; *Price:* Free with HIMSS membership
Profile: Information about health information technology & electronic medical records
• Financial Edge
Type: Newsletter; *Frequency:* Monthly; *Price:* Free with HIMSS membership
Profile: HIMSS' financial systems e-newsletter, with current issues & trends related to financial systems & other technologies in healthcare
• Healthcare IT News
Type: Newspaper; *Frequency:* Monthly; *Price:* Free with HIMSS membership
Profile: Features the HIMSS Insider newsletter, plus information about advocacy, education, & HIMSS happenings
• HIMSS [Healthcare Information & Management Systems Society] Weekly Insider
Type: Newsletter; *Frequency:* Weekly; *Price:* Free with HIMSS membership
Profile: Current news from HIMSS, member profiles, & interviews
• HIMSS [Healthcare Information & Management Systems Society] Conference Proceedings
Frequency: Annually
Profile: Proceedings from the annual HIMSS conference & exhibition
• HIMSS [Healthcare Information & Management Systems Society] Clinical Informatics Insights
Type: Newsletter; *Frequency:* Monthly; *Price:* Free with HIMSS membership
Profile: Comprehensive articles about informatics across the continuum of care
• HIMSS [Healthcare Information & Management Systems Society] Pulse on Public Policy
Type: Newsletter; *Frequency:* Monthly; *Price:* Free with HIMSS membership
Profile: Information for HIMSS members, policymakers, regulators, & interested stakeholders
• HIMSS [Healthcare Information & Management Systems Society] HIELights
Type: Newsletter; *Frequency:* Monthly; *Price:* Free with HIMSS membership
Profile: Issues pertaining to health information exchange & regional health information organizations
• Journal of Healthcare Information Management
Type: Journal; *Frequency:* Quarterly; *Accepts Advertising*; *Editor:* M.A. Annecharico, Exec. Director; *Price:* Free with HIMSS membership
Profile: Peer-reviewed journal for healthcare information & management systems professionals

Hedge Fund Association Canada (HFA)

c/o HFA, #900, 2875 NE 191st St., Aventura FL 33180 USA
Tel: 305-935-7296; *Fax:* 305-405-8858
info@thehfa.org
www.thehfa.org
Overview: A small national organization founded in 1996
Member of: International Hedge Fund Association
Chief Officer(s):
Mitch Ackles, President, 646-657-9230
mitch@hedgefundpr.net
Lara Block, Executive Director & Secretary
Membership: *Fees:* $1000-$2000

Heiser Program for Research in Leprosy & Tuberculosis

c/o The New York Community Trust, 909 - 3rd Ave., New York NY 10022 USA
Tel: 212-686-0010; *Fax:* 212-532-8528
Overview: A small international charitable organization
Mission: To award grants to fund research into leoprosy, tuberculosis & their bacterial agents to find measures for prevention & cure.
Chief Officer(s):
Gilla Kaplan, Chair, Scientific Advisory Committee
Len McNally, Director
lm@nyct-cfi.org
Membership: *Committees:* Scientific Advisory
Awards:
• Postdoctoral Research Fellowships (Scholarship)
Eligibility: Applicants should have an M.D., Ph.D., or equivalent degree; Although there is no age limit, candidates should be at an early stage of postdoctoral research training*Deadline:* March 1 *Amount:* $80,000 over 2 years
• Research Grants (Grant)
Eligibility: Applications should come from laboratories that have experience in leprosy research & have demonstrable, ongoing interactions with corresponding laboratories in endemic regions.*Deadline:* prelim. report, Mar. 25 *Amount:* $50,000 renewable for 2nd year

HelpAge International (HAI)

PO Box 70156, London WC1A 9GB United Kingdom
Tel: 44-20-7278-7778; *Fax:* 44-207-148-7623
info@helpage.org
www.helpage.org
www.facebook.com/HelpAgeInternational
twitter.com/helpage
www.youtube.com/helpage
Overview: A medium-sized international charitable organization founded in 1983
Mission: To campaign on behalf of the world's older population & provide expertise & grants to older people's organisations in 70 developing countries-assisting them to help the most disadvantaged lead independent lives
Affliation(s): Help the Aged - Canada
Chief Officer(s):
Cynthia Cox Roman, Chair
Toby Porter, Chief Executive Officer
Membership: 100+; *Member Profile:* Non-profit organizations working with/for older people
Activities: Works via a network of development, research, community-based & social service organisations that share a common mission to improve the lives of disadvantaged older people; combines support for partners & members, direct programme implementation, research & advocacy; involved in the fomulation of national & international strategies on aging; *Library*
Awards:
• Leslie Kirkley Award (Award)
Given to support a particularly innovative programme or individual activity focusing either on direct service delivery, a policy/advocacy initiative, or work in particularly difficult circumstances

Holocaust Memorial Foundation of Illinois (HMFI)

9603 Woods Dr., Skokie IL 60077 USA
Tel: 847-967-4800
info@ilhmec.org
www.ilholocaustmuseum.org
www.facebook.com/IHMEC
twitter.com/ihmec
pinterest.com/ihmec
Also Known As: Illinois Holocaust Museum & Education Center
Overview: A medium-sized international organization founded in 1981
Mission: To ensure the continuance of an open & free society where human rights are respected & preserved
Member of: Association of Holocaust Organizations
Chief Officer(s):
Richard S. Hirschhaut, Executive Director, Illinois Holocaust Museum & Education Center
Fritzie Fritzshall, President
Membership: *Fees:* Schedule available
Activities: Provides teacher training courses for college credits; exhibits; tapes oral histories of survivors/liberators of the Holocaust; provides speakers & programming on an outreach basis to schools & the community; documentary film production; development of curriculum & educational resource material; *Internships:* Yes; *Speaker Service:* Yes *Library* Open to public

Housing Inspection Foundation (HIF)

PO Box 879, Palm Springs CA 92263 USA
Toll-Free: 877-743-6806
support@assoc-hdqts.org
www.hif-assoc.org
Overview: A medium-sized international organization
Member of: International Association Managers
Membership: *Fees:* Schedule available; *Member Profile:* Housing inspectors

Human Anatomy & Physiology Society (HAPS)

PO Box 2945, 251 S.L. White Blvd., LaGrange GA 30241-2945 USA
Tel: 800-448-4277; *Fax:* 706-883-8215
admin@hapsweb.org
www.hapsweb.org
Overview: A medium-sized international organization
Mission: To promote excellence in the teaching of human anatomy & physiology
Chief Officer(s):
Larry Spraggs, Executive Director
lspraggs@hapsweb.org
Shanan Molnar, Manager, Business
Robin Hurst, Coordinator, Membership, & Administrator, Website & ListServe
webmaster@hapsweb.org
Tom Lancraft, Editor, Website Content, 727-341-4797
webeditor@hapsweb.org
Membership: *Member Profile:* Any person in Canada, the United States, & the rest of the world, with an interest in anatomy & physiology education

Activities: Encouraging research; Providing position statements in areas such as animal & cadaver use; Facilitating communication among teachers of human anatomy & physiology; Providing professional development programs; Communicating with other educational & scientific organizations; Awarding grants & scholarships for anatomy & physiology students & instructors
Meetings/Conferences:
• Human Anatomy & Physiology Society 2015 29th Annual Conference, May, 2015, Hyatt Regency San Antonio Riverwalk, San Antonio, TX
Scope: International
Description: An international conference, featuring workshops & networking opportunities
Contact Information: Phone: 1-800-448-4277; info@hapsconnect.org
Publications:
• HAPS-EDucator
Frequency: Quarterly
Profile: Teaching tips for anatomy & physiology instructors

Human Life International (HLI) / Vie Humaine Internationale

4 Family Life Lane, Front Royal VA 22630 USA
Fax: 540-622-6247
Toll-Free: 800-549-5433
Other Communication: www.vidahumana.org
hli@hli.org
www.hli.org
www.facebook.com/HumanLifeInternational
twitter.com/HumanLifeIntnl
www.youtube.com/user/HLICommunications#p/u
Overview: A small international organization
Mission: To bring the pro-life & pro-family message to countries throughout the world
Chief Officer(s):
Shenan J. Boquet, President
Membership: 8,000

The Humane Society of the United States (HSUS)

2100 L St. NW, Washington DC 20037 USA
Tel: 202-452-1100
membership@humanesociety.org
www.humanesociety.org
www.facebook.com/humanesociety
twitter.com/HumaneSociety
Overview: A large national organization founded in 1954
Mission: To prevent the abuse of all animals; to promote the protection of endangered species
Affliation(s): Doris Day Animal League; Humane Society International; Humane Society Legislative Fund; Humane Society University; Humane Society Veterinary Medical Association; Humane Society Wildlife Land Trust; The Fund for Animals
Chief Officer(s):
Wayne Pacelle, President & CEO
Michael Markarian, Chief Program & Policy Officer
Andrew Rowan, CIO/CSO
Finances: *Annual Operating Budget:* $3 Million-$5 Million
Staff Member(s): 165
Membership: 1.6 million members & constituents; *Fees:* Donation
Activities: *Library* by appointment
Meetings/Conferences:
• Taking Action for Animals 2016, 2016
Scope: National
Description: An educational conference meant to inspire people to help animals. Topics covered include factory farming & animal fighting.
Contact Information: URL: takingactionforanimals.org
• Animal Care Expo 2015, March, 2015, New Orleans, LA
Scope: National
Description: An educational conference meant to inspire people to help animals. Topics covered include factory farming & animal fighting.
Contact Information: URL: www.animalsheltering.org/expo
Publications:
• All Animals [a publication of The Humane Society of the United States]
Type: Magazine; *Frequency:* s-m.
Profile: Stories about the HSUS & the humane movement
• Animal Sheltering [a publication of The Humane Society of the United States]
Type: Magazine; *Frequency:* s-m.
Profile: The magazine is intended for animal care workers
• Kind News [a publication of The Humane Society of the United States]
Type: Magazine; *Number of Pages:* 8
Profile: The magazine teaches kindness & respect for animals & their habitats, & is meant for children from kindergarten to grade six

Hydrographic Society *See* International Federation of Hydrographic Societies

IEEE Microwave Theory & Techniques Society (MTT-S)

5829 Bellanca Dr., Elkridge MD 21075 USA
Tel: 410-796-5866; *Fax:* 410-796-5829
www.mtt.org
www.linkedin.com/groups?home=&gid=51393
www.facebook.com/312882368791765?ref=hl
twitter.com/MTTSEnewsletter
Overview: A large international organization
Mission: To promote the advancement of microwave theory & its applications, by focussing on scientific, technical, & industrial activities; To enhance the quality of life for all people, through the development & application of microwave technology
Chief Officer(s):
Nicholas J. Kolias, President
Edward C. Niehenke, Ombudsman
e.niehenke@ieee.org
J. Michael Golio, Area Editor, Publications
m.golio@ieee.org
Membership: 11,000+; *Member Profile:* Persons who are members of the IEEE, a technical professional association; Individual members should have competence in the field of engineering, computer science, information technology, the physical sciences, biological & medical sciences, mathematics, technical communications, education, management, law, or policy; *Committees:* Computer-Aided Design; Microwave Acoustics; Microwave Photonics; Terahertz Technology & Applications; Microwave High-Power Techniques; Microwave & Millimeter-Wave Integrated Circuits; Microwave & Millimeter-Wave Solid State Devices; Filters & Passive Components; Digital Signal Processing; Biological Effects & Medical Applications; Microwave Measurements; Microwave & Millimeter-Wave Packaging and Manufacturing; Microwave Ferrites & Ferroelectrics; Microwave Low-Noise Techniques; Microwave Field Theory; Microwave Systems; HF-VHF-UHF Technology; Microwave Superconductivity; Tech. Business Issues
Activities: Distributing knowledge; Supporting professional development; *Speaker Service:* Yes
Meetings/Conferences:
• Microwave Theory & Techniques Society IEEE Wireless & Microwave Technology Conference (WAMICON), April, 2015, Hilton Cocoa Beach Oceanfront, Cocoa Beach, FL
Scope: International
• Microwave Theory & Techniques Society International Microwave Symposia 2015, May, 2015, Phoenix, AZ
Scope: International
Description: Technical papers; Workshops; Trade show
• Microwave Theory & Techniques Society International Microwave Symposia 2016, May, 2016, San Francisco, CA
Scope: International
Description: Technical papers; Workshops; Trade show
• Microwave Theory & Techniques Society International Microwave Symposia 2017, June, 2017, Honolulu, HI
Scope: International
Description: Technical papers; Workshops; Trade show
• Microwave Theory & Techniques Society International Microwave Symposia 2018, June, 2018, Philadelphia, PA
Scope: International
Description: Technical papers; Workshops; Trade show
• Microwave Theory & Techniques Society International Microwave Symposia 2019, June, 2019, Boston, MA
Scope: International
Description: Technical papers; Workshops; Trade show
• Microwave Theory & Techniques Society International Microwave Symposia 2020, June, 2020, Los Angeles, CA
Scope: International
Description: Technical papers; Workshops; Trade show
• Microwave Theory & Techniques Society International Microwave Symposia 2021, June, 2021, Atlanta, GA
Scope: International
Description: Technical papers; Workshops; Trade show
• Microwave Theory & Techniques Society International Microwave Symposia 2022, 2022
Scope: International
Description: Technical papers; Workshops; Trade show
Publications:
• IEEE Microwave & Wirelss Component Letters
Type: Journal; *Frequency:* Monthly; *Editor:* Dr. George E. Ponchak
Profile: Articles about microwave/millimeter-wave technology, with an emphasis on devices, components, circuits, guided wave structures, & systems & applicationscovering the frequency spectrum
• IEEE Microwave Magazine
Type: Magazine; *Accepts Advertising*; *Price:* Free with IEEE Microwave Theory and Techniques Society membership
Profile: Feature articles, application notes, news of the IEEE Microwave Theory & Techniques Society, a conference calendar, & reviews of interest to professionals in the field of microwave theory &techniques
• Transactions
Type: Journal; *Editor:* Amir Mortazawi; Dylan Williams
Profile: Articles about engineering & theory associated with microwave circuits & guided wave structures

Illuminating Engineering Society of North America (IESNA)

120 Wall St., 17th Fl., New York NY 10005-4001 USA
Tel: 212-248-5000; *Fax:* 212-248-5017
ies@ies.org
www.iesna.org
www.linkedin.com/groups?mostPopular=&gid=3790528
www.facebook.com/140309826005859
twitter.com/IllumEngSoc
Overview: A medium-sized international organization founded in 1906
Mission: To improve the lighted environment by bringing together those with lighting knowledge & by translating that knowledge into artforms that benefit the public
Chief Officer(s):
Paul Mercier, President
Finances: *Annual Operating Budget:* Greater than $5 Million
Staff Member(s): 19
Membership: 8,000; *Fees:* US$170 associate; US$550 individual subscribing member; US$75 associate EP; US$20 student; *Member Profile:* Designers; engineers; architects; utilities; *Committees:* Knowledge; Membership; Public Relations; Programs; Emerging Professionals; Students; IIDA
Activities: *Rents Mailing List:* Yes
Awards:
• International Illuminating Design Awards (Award)

Fiddlehead Section
c/o John Randall, 26 Robby St., Douglas NB E3G 8B4
Tel: 506-292-3821; *Fax:* 506-852-9118
Chief Officer(s):
John Randall, President
john.randall@focuselectrical.com

Montréal Section
CP 66012, Succ. Haut-Anjou, Anjou QC H1J 3B8
Tél: 514-277-1438; *Téléc:* 514-277-0494
ies-montreal@videotron.ca
montreal.iesna.net
Chief Officer(s):
Christiane de Cesare, Présidente, 514-825-7501

National Capital Section
c/o Gabriel Mackinnon, #1, 109 Murray St., Ottawa ON K1N 5M5
Tel: 613-241-1822
iesottawa.ca
Chief Officer(s):
Andrew MacKinnon, President
andrew@gabrielmackinnon.com

Northumberland Section
c/o R.E. LeBlanc Consultants, #425, 236 St. George St., Moncton NB E1C 1W1
Tel: 506-858-0950; *Fax:* 506-856-6304
info@viziwiz.com
northumberland.iesna.net
Chief Officer(s):
David Knickle, President
releblanc@releblanc.com

Toronto Section
c/o Cree Canada, #3, 6889 Rexwood Rd., Mississauga ON L4V 1R2
Fax: 800-890-7507
Toll-Free: 800-473-1234
ies@iestoronto.org
www.iestoronto.org
www.linkedin.com/groups?home=&gid=4948047
Chief Officer(s):

Brenda Quies, President
Winnipeg Section
PO Box 33081, Stn. Polo Park, Winnipeg MB R3G 0W4
Tel: 204-694-0000; *Fax:* 204-694-0433
winnipeg.iesna.net
Chief Officer(s):
Greg Macdonald, President
gmacdonald@hi-techsales.ca

IMCS Pax Romana

7 Impasse Reille, Paris 75014 France
Tél: 33-014-544-7075; *Téléc:* 33-014-284-0453
office@imcs-miec.org
www.imcs-miec.org
Également appelé: International Catholic Organization
Nom précédent: International Movement of Catholic Students; International Catholic Movement for Intellectual & Cultural Affairs
Aperçu: *Dimension:* grande; *Envergure:* internationale; fondée en 1921
Mission: Aims, through its various professional & intellectual commitments in society & the Church, to engage in pro-active dialogue between Christian faith & cultures in order to promote the evangelization of cultures & the inculturation of the Gospel for the realization of the Kingdom of God
Affiliation(s): Mouvement d'étudiants chrétiens du Québec; Association of Canadian Catholic Students
Membre(s) du bureau directeur:
Charles Ochero, International President
president@imcs-miec.org
Activités: Pax Romana has consultative status with the United Nations Economic & Social Council, UNESCO & the European Council, & has accredited representatives to those organisations in New York, Vienna, Paris, Geneve & Strasbourg
Publications:
• Forum
Type: Magazine

Indian Association for Canadian Studies (IACS)

101 Dwarkamai, 25/B Pratapgunj, Vadodara 390 002 India
www.iacs-ind.com
Overview: A small international organization founded in 1985
Mission: The Association promotes & encourages teaching, research & publications related to Canadian & Indo-Canadian Studies, especially with regard to interdisciplinary, multidiscipllinary & comparative approaches.
Affiliation(s): International Council for Canadian Studies
Chief Officer(s):
Jaydipsinh K. Dodia, President
Membership: 806

Industrial Fabrics Association International (IFAI)

1801 County Rd. BW, Roseville MN 55113-4061 USA
Tel: 651-222-2508; *Fax:* 651-631-9334
Toll-Free: 800-225-4324
Other Communication: membership@ifai.com
generalinfo@ifai.com
www.ifai.com
Overview: A medium-sized international organization founded in 1912
Mission: To represent the specialty fabrics & technical textiles industry; To contribute to the prosperity of the specialty fabrics industry
Chief Officer(s):
Stephen M. Warner, President & Chief Executive Officer, 800-486-3978
Mary J. Hennessy, Vice-President, Communications & Publishing, 800-319-3133
Kathy J. Mattson, Vice-President, Member Services, 800-272-1852
Steven C. Rider, Vice-President, Finance & Administration, 800-225-6915
Membership: 2,100; *Member Profile:* Companies involved in the specialty fabrics & technical textiles industry from 58 countries, including manufacturers of end products, equipment, & hardware, as well as suppliers of fibre & fabric
Activities: Promoting the specialty fabrics industry; Providing educational opportunities, such as hands-on training workshops; Disseminating research reports & other information to members; Creating networking opportunities
Publications:
• Fabric Architecture
Type: Magazine; *Frequency:* Bimonthly; *Editor:* Bruce N. Wright
Profile: Articles about designing with fabric, for architects, designers, specifiers, contractors, & developers
• Fabric Graphics
Type: Magazine; *Frequency:* Bimonthly; *Editor:* Chris P. Tschida
Profile: Information about the use of textiles as a printing medium, with applications for fabric & the technology
• Geosynthetics
Type: Magazine; *Frequency:* Bimonthly; *Editor:* Ron W. Bygness
Profile: Geosynthetic products, design, & applications
• InTents
Type: Magazine; *Frequency:* Bimonthly; *Editor:* Sigrid A. Tornquist
Profile: Information focussing on tents, fabric structures, & accessories tenters need
• Marine Fabricator
Type: Magazine; *Frequency:* Bimonthly; *Editor:* Kelly R. Frush; Chris P. Tschida
Profile: Techniques of marine craftsmanship & upholstery for marine shop professionals
• Review Buyer's Guide
Type: Yearbook; *Frequency:* Annually
• Specialty Fabrics Review
Type: Magazine; *Frequency:* Monthly; *Editor:* Galynn D. Nordstrom; Janet L. Preus; *Price:* Free with membership in Industrial Fabrics Association International
Profile: Information for specialty fabric professionals
• Upholstery Journal
Type: Journal; *Frequency:* Bimonthly; *Editor:* Kelly R. Frush; Chris P. Tschida
Profile: Educational information about the craft & business of upholstery, for persons involved in the after furniture, marine, automotive, & commercial upholstery markets

Industrial Truck Association (ITA)

#460, 1750 K St. NW, Washington DC 20006 USA
Tel: 202-296-9880; *Fax:* 202-296-9884
www.indtrk.org
Overview: A medium-sized international organization
Mission: Represents the manufacturers of lift trucks & their suppliers who do business in Canada, the United States or Mexico
Chief Officer(s):
William Montwieler, Executive Director
Finances: *Annual Operating Budget:* $1.5 Million-$3 Million
Staff Member(s): 5
Membership: 100; *Fees:* Varies; *Member Profile:* Manufacturers of forklifts & suppliers

Infectious Diseases Society of America (IDSA)

#300, 1300 Wilson Blvd., Arlington VA 22209 USA
Tel: 703-299-0200; *Fax:* 703-299-0204
membership@idsociety.org
www.idsociety.org
www.facebook.com/IDSociety
twitter.com/idsainfo
www.flickr.com/photos/idsociety
Overview: A large international organization
Mission: To improve the health of individuals, communities, & society; To promote excellence in education, research, public health, prevention, & patient care
Chief Officer(s):
Thomas G. Slama, President
Barbara Murray, Vice-President
Kathryn M. Edwards, Secretary
Cynthia L. Sears, Treasurer
Membership: *Member Profile:* Physicians; Scientists; Health care professionals who specialize in infectious diseases
Meetings/Conferences:
• IDWeek 2015, October, 2015, San Diego, CA
Scope: International
Contact Information: URL: www.idweek.org
• Infectious Diseases Society of America Annual Meeting 2015, 2015
Scope: International
Publications:
• Clinical Infectious Diseases
Type: Journal
Profile: State-of-the-art clinical articles, medical & legal issues, review articles, & studies in infectious disease research
• IDSA [Infectious Diseases Society of America] News
Type: Newsletter
Profile: Society activities, education, research, & prevention & treatment advances
• Journal of Infectious Diseases
Type: Journal
Profile: Original research about the pathogenesis, diagnosis, & treatment of infectious diseases

INFORM Inc.

5 Hanover Sq., 19th Fl., New York NY 10004 USA
Tel: 212-361-2400; *Fax:* 212-361-2412
ramsey@informinc.org
www.informinc.org
www.facebook.com/199694845376
twitter.com/informinc
Overview: A medium-sized international charitable organization founded in 1974
Mission: To examine the effects of business practices on the environment & human health
Member of: Earthshare
Chief Officer(s):
Virginia Ramsey, Executive Director
Finances: *Annual Operating Budget:* $1.5 Million-$3 Million; *Funding Sources:* Individual donors; Foundations; Government; Corporate contributions; Book sales
Staff Member(s): 25; 5 volunteer(s)
Membership: 1,000; *Fees:* $35
Activities: Researching strategies to prevent chemical hazards & to develop sustainable products & practices; *Internships:* Yes; *Speaker Service:* Yes

Information Systems Audit & Control Association *See* ISACA

Information Systems Security Association (ISSA)

#119-333, 9220 SW Barbur Blvd., Portland OR 97219 USA
Tel: 206-388-4584; *Fax:* 206-299-3366
Toll-Free: 866-349-5818
www.issa.org
Overview: A medium-sized international organization founded in 1984
Mission: To provide education forums, publications & peer interaction opportunities that enhance the knowledge, skill & professional growth of its members; to be a global voice of information security
Chief Officer(s):
Lyn Trainer, Managing Director
ltrainer@issa.org
Finances: *Annual Operating Budget:* $500,000-$1.5 Million
17 volunteer(s)
Membership: 11,000; *Fees:* $95
Activities: *Rents Mailing List:* Yes
Ottawa Chapter
PO Box 71002, 174 Bank St., Ottawa ON K2P 1W6
communications@issa-ottawa.ca
www.issa-ottawa.ca
www.linkedin.com/groups?home=&gid=873227
Chief Officer(s):
Doug Lawrence, ISSA Chapter President
Vancouver Chapter
Vancouver BC
info@vancouver-issa.org
www.vancouver-issa.org
Chief Officer(s):
Eva Kuiper, ISSA Chapter President

Innovations et réseaux pour le développement (IRED) / Development Innovations and Networks

CP 116, 3, rue Varembé, Genève 1211-20 Suisse
Tél: 41-22-734-17-16; *Téléc:* 41-22-740-00-11
info@ired.org
www.ired.org
Aperçu: *Dimension:* grande; *Envergure:* internationale; Organisme sans but lucratif; fondée en 1981
Membre(s) du bureau directeur:
Nkiko Nsengimana, Président
Finances: *Budget de fonctionnement annuel:* $250,000-$500,000
Membre: 250 individus; 1 000 associations partenaires
Activités: Facilite les échanges d'expériences Sud-Sud, Sud-Nord, Nord-Sud; aide à la création et au développement de réseaux locaux et nationaux, d'unions et de fédérations de groupements; organise, avec ses partenaires, des appuis techniques dans les domaines de la formation, de la gestion et de l'organisation, des technologies appropriées, des négociations, etc., de façon à renforcer les institutions promues à tous les niveaux; *Bibliothèque:* Centre de documentation; rendez-vous
Publications:
• IRED [Innovations et réseaux pour le développement] Newsletter en ligne
Type: Newsletter

Institut africain international *See* International African Institute

Institut Archéologique d'Amérique *See* Archaeological Institute of America

Institut de recherche des Nations Unies pour le développement social ***See*** United Nations Research Institute for Social Development

L'Institut des vérificateurs internes ***See*** The Institute of Internal Auditors

Institut international de l'ocean ***See*** International Ocean Institute

L'Institut International de Statistique ***See*** International Statistical Institute

Institut pour une synthése planétaire ***See*** Institute for Planetary Synthesis

Institute for Alternative Agriculture ***See*** Wallace Center, Winrock International

Institute for Folklore Studies in Britain & Canada (IFSBAC)

c/o National Centre for English Cultural Tradition, University of Sheffield, Sheffield S10 2TN UK
Tel: 44-114-222-2000
Overview: A small international organization founded in 1986
Mission: To promote the study of folklore in Britain & Canada through teaching, research, archive development & publication; to encourage & engage in research on all aspects of folklore & related disciplines. A cooperative endeavour between the University of Sheffield & Memorial University of Newfoundland
Chief Officer(s):
P.S. Smith, Co-Director, Memorial University of Newfoundland
J.C. Beal, Co-Director, University of Sheffield
Activities: Heritage interpretation; *Internships:* Yes *Library:* IFSBAC Library; by appointment

Institute for Local Self-Reliance (ILSR)

#570, 2001 S St. NW, Washington DC 20009 USA
Tel: 202-898-1610
info@ilsr.org
www.ilsr.org
Overview: A medium-sized international organization founded in 1974
Mission: To provide innovative strategies & models to support environmentally sound community development; To work with citizens & policymakers to meet local needs; To provide the tools to increase economic effectiveness, to reduce waste & decrease impacts on the environment, & provide for local ownership of infrastructure & resources
Affliation(s): Healthy Building Network; Black Environment Justice Network; GrassRoots Recycling Network
Chief Officer(s):
Neil Seldman, President
nseldman@ilsr.org
David Morris, Vice-President
dmorris@ilsr.org
Sarah Pickell, Director, Finance
dmorris@ilsr.org
Brenda Platt, Director, Waste to Wealth & Sustainable Plastics Program
Stacy Mitchell, Senior Researcher
smitchell@ilsr.org
Finances: *Funding Sources:* Foundations; Individuals; Speaking; Technical assistance
1 volunteer(s)
Activities: *Internships:* Yes; *Speaker Service:* Yes

Institute for Planetary Synthesis (IPS) / Institut pour une synthèse planétaire

PO Box 171, Chatelaine, Geneva CH-1211 Switzerland
Tel: 41-22-733-88-76; *Fax:* 41-22-733-88-76
ipsbox@ipsgeneva.com
www.ipsgeneva.com
Overview: A small international organization founded in 1981
Mission: To reawaken an awareness of spiritual values in daily life; to promote planetary awareness, leading to planetary citizenship; to analyze & solve world problems on a basis of spiritual values
Member of: Adult Learning Documentation & Information Network (UNESCO Institute for Education)
Affliation(s): Canadian Peace Research & Education Association; Center Light; Earth Day International; Earth Concert Project; Expanding Boundaries; International Peace Committee; Peal for Peace; Planetary Initiative; Responsibility International Canada
Chief Officer(s):
Alice Boainain-Schneider, IPS UN Representative
Activities: *Speaker Service:* Yes; *Rents Mailing List:* Yes *Library:* Ten Seed-Group Documentation Centre; by appointment

Institute of Electrical & Electronics Engineers Inc. (IEEE)

445 Hoes Lane, Piscataway NJ 8855 USA
Tel: 732-981-0060; *Fax:* 732-981-9667
customer-service@ieee.org
www.ieee.org
www.linkedin.com/groups?home=&gid=23804
www.facebook.com/IEEE.org
twitter.com/IEEEorg
Overview: A large international organization founded in 1884
Mission: The world's largest technical professional society; to advance theory & practice of electrical engineering, electronics, radio & allied branches of engineering & related arts & sciences; to publish documents in order to enhance the quality of life for all peoples through improved public awareness of the influences & applications of its technologies; to advance the standing of the engineering profession & its members; to provide leadership in areas ranging from aerospace, computers & communications to biomedical technology, electric power & consumer electronics
Chief Officer(s):
Gordon W. Day, President & CEO
Staff Member(s): 800; 30 volunteer(s)
Membership: 365,000 worldwide; 39 technical societies; 4 councils; *Fees:* Schedule available
Activities: Has published more than 130 transactions, magazines & journals; global network of over 90 branches worldwide, providing local focus for engineering, including events, lectures & company visits; *Internships:* Yes *Library*

Institute of Food Technologists (IFT)

#1000, 525 West Van Buren, Chicago IL 60607 USA
Tel: 312-782-8424; *Fax:* 312-782-8348
Toll-Free: 800-438-3663
info@ift.org
www.ift.org
www.linkedin.com/groups/Institute-Food-Technologists-IFT-36409
www.facebook.com/events/193978063950994
twitter.com/IFT
www.youtube.com/user/IFTlive
Overview: A large international organization founded in 1939
Mission: To advance food & health through science
Chief Officer(s):
John Ruff, President
Kelley Ahuja, CAO
kahuja@ift.org
Mark Barenie, CFO
mbarenie@ift.org
Jerry Bowman, Vice-President, Communications & Media Relations
jmbowman@ift.org
Will Fisher, Vice-President, Science & Policy Initiatives
wfisher@ift.org
Amanda Perl, Vice-President, Development
aperl@ift.org
Finances: *Funding Sources:* Membership fees; Sponsorships
Membership: *Member Profile:* Food science & technology professionals from over 90 countries
Activities: Engaging in advocacy activities; Fostering technology development & supporting innovation in food science; Facilitating the exchange of information & ideas among the food community; Offering professional development activities; Increasing the understanding & application of the science of food; Publishing science reports of interest to members, government officials, scientific constituencies, government officials, the media, & the public; Publishing books through IFT Press, a joint publishing venture with Wiley-Blackwell
Awards:
• IFT Achievement Awards (Award)
• Marcel Loncin Research Prize (Award)
• Feeding Tomorrow Scholarships (Scholarship)
• Congressional Support for Science Award (Award)
• IFT Fellows (Grant)
Meetings/Conferences:
• Institute of Food Technologists 2015 Annual Wellness Conference, 2015
Scope: International
Description: Informative presentations plus exhibits of interest to food industry professionals in product development, brand management, & marketing
• Institute of Food Technologists 2015 Annual Meeting & Food Expo, July, 2015, McCormick Place South, Chicago, IL
Scope: International
Attendance: 21,500+
Description: The largest annual food science forum & exposition, featuring presentation from experts of research institutions, government agencies, & companies, of interest to food scientists, suppliers, & marketers from around the globe
• Institute of Food Technologists 2016 Annual Meeting & Food Expo, July, 2016, McCormick Place South, Chicago, IL
Scope: International
Description: An annual gathering of thousands of food professionals from around the world to participate in scientific sessions, poster sessions, the IFT Food Expo, an awards celebration, & networking events
Publications:
• Comprehensive Reviews in Food Science & Food Safety
Type: Journal; *Frequency:* Bimonthly; *Editor:* Daryl B. Lund
Profile: A peer-reviewed journal, covering topics such as nutrition, physiology, microbiology, engineering, & regulations
• Eat Your Words
Type: Newsletter; *Frequency:* Monthly
Profile: Food science & technology stories for new professionals in the industry
• Express Connect
Type: Newsletter; *Frequency:* Monthly
Profile: Happenings at the Institute of Food Technologists, for members only
• Food Technology
Type: Magazine; *Frequency:* Monthly; *Accepts Advertising*; *Editor:* Bob Swientek (bswientek@ift.org)
Profile: Industry news, research developments, consumer product innovations, & professional opportunities
• Institute of Food Technologists Annual Meeting & Food Expo Preview
Type: Newsletter; *Frequency:* Annually
Profile: A preview of the annual educational event, which attracts food scientists, technologists, sellers, & buyers from around the globe
• Institute of Food Technologists Annual Meeting & Food Expo Wrap-up
Type: Newsletter; *Frequency:* Annually
Profile: A review of the annual event, which features over 21,500 attendees, as well as more than 900 exhibitors who present recent products & innovations inthe food industry
• Journal of Food Science
Type: Journal; *Frequency:* 9 pa; *Editor:* Daryl B. Lund (dlund@cals.wisc.edu)
Profile: A peer-reviewed journal, featuring original research, & reviews of all aspects of food science
• Journal of Food Science Education
Type: Journal; *Editor:* Daryl B. Lund (dlund@cals.wisc.edu)
Profile: Information of interest to persons in the field of food science education at all levels, including primary, secondary, undergraduate & graduate,continuing, & workplace education
• Nutraraceutical Newsletter
Type: Newsletter
Profile: News & current research from the nutraceutical & functional foods sector
• The Weekly Newsletter
Type: Newsletter; *Frequency:* Weekly
Profile: Industry news & highlights from the food science, technology, & regulatory sectors
• The World of Food Science
Type: Journal; *Editor:* Ken Buckle (k.buckle@unsw.edu.au)
Profile: A publication of current research on sensors & biosensors & its potential application in the food & technology industry, presented to readers by the Institute ofFood Technologists & the International Union of Food Science & Technology

Institute of Industrial Engineers (IIE)

#200, 3577 Parkway Lane, Norcross GA 30092 USA
Tel: 770-449-0461; *Fax:* 770-441-3295
cs@iienet.org
www.iienet2.org
www.linkedin.com/groups?mostPopular=&gid=75670
www.facebook.com/group.php?gid=26148220561
twitter.com/iienet
Overview: A large national licensing organization founded in 1948
Mission: To advance the technical & managerial excellence of industrial engineers, concerned with the design, installation & improvement of integrated systems of people, material, information, equipment & energy

Affliation(s): Organized into three societies: Society for Health Systems (SHS); Society for Engineering & Management Systems (SEMS); Aerospace & Defense Society (ADS)
Chief Officer(s):
Don Greene, Executive Director
Finances: *Annual Operating Budget:* $3 Million-$5 Million
Staff Member(s): 35
Membership: 24,000 internationally in 200 senior & 140 university chapters; *Fees:* $30-$139 USD; *Committees:* Divisions: Energy, Environment & Plant Engineering; Engineering Economy; Ergonomics; Facilities Planning & Design; Financial Services; Industrial & Labour Relations; Operations Research; Quality Control & Reliability; Utilities; Work Measurement & Methods Engineering; Interest Groups; Computer & Information Systems; Consultants; Electronics Industry; Engineering Design; Government; Maintenance; Process Industries; Production & Inventory Control; Retail; Transportation & Distribution
Activities: Provides continuing education opportunities through professional trade books, periodicals, journals, technical publications, conferences, seminars & workshops; Conferences: International Industrial Engineering, Industrial Engineering Research & International Maintenance; Material Handling Management Course; Management, Maintenance, Quality & Manufacturing Seminars; *Speaker Service:* Yes; *Rents Mailing List:* Yes *Library* by appointment
Awards:
• Albert G. Holzman Distinguished Educator Award (Award), Educator Awards
Outstanding educators who have contributed to industrial engineering.
• Innovations in Curriculum Award (Award), Educator Awards
Outstanding innovation in the design or presentation of an accredited IE, ISE, IEOR, or similar engineering curriculum
• Dr. Hamed K. Eldin Outstanding Early Career IE in Academia Award (Award), Educator Awards
Individuals in academia who have shown outstanding characteristics.
• Captains of Industry Award (Award), Leadership Awards
Business or government leaders who successfully used industrial engineering in the workplace.
• Fellow Award (Award), Leadership Awards
Leaders who have made significant, nationally recognized contributions to industrial engineering.
• Frank and Lillian Gilbreth Industrial Engineering Award (Award), Leadership Awards
Individuals who distinguished themselves through contributions to mankind.
• Outstanding Middle Career IE Leadership Award for Business/Industry (Award), Leadership Awards
Individuals working in industry who have excelled in their role as a practicing manager/leader within their organization.
• Outstanding Achievement in Management Award (Award), Leadership Awards
Executives contributing to the profession through innovative use of its methods.
• Outstanding Early Career IE in Business/Industry (Award), Leadership Awards
Honoring leadership, professionalism, and potential.
Meetings/Conferences:
• Institute of Industrial Engineers Annual IE Conference & Expo 2015, May, 2015, Renaissance Nashville Hotel, Nashville, TN
Scope: International

The Institute of Internal Auditors (IIA) / L'Institut des vérificateurs internes

247 Maitland Ave., Altamonte Springs FL 32701-4201 USA
Tel: 407-937-1111; *Fax:* 407-937-1101
customerrelations@theiia.org
www.theiia.org
www.linkedin.com/groups?home=&gid=107948
www.facebook.com/TheInstituteofInternalAuditors
twitter.com/theiia
Overview: A large national organization founded in 1941
Mission: To provide leadership for the global profession of internal auditing; To advocate for the profession's value
Chief Officer(s):
Richard F. Chambers, President & CEO
Finances: *Funding Sources:* Membership dues; Sale of products & services
Membership: 180,000+ in 160 chapters; *Fees:* Schedule available; *Member Profile:* Regular individual members; Educators; Students; Retired individuals; Government; Groups
Activities: Networking; Training; Professional guidance & certification; Audit Career Center; Compiling & disseminating information; *Awareness Events:* International Internal Audit Awareness Month, May; *Speaker Service:* Yes
Awards:
• North American Membership Award (Award)
Eligibility: Recognizes chapters that use innovative techniques to find and recruit members*Deadline:* August
Meetings/Conferences:
• 2015 Institute of Internal Auditors 2015 International Conference, July, 2015, Vancouver Convention Centre, Vancouver, BC
Scope: International
Publications:
• CAE Bulletin
Type: Newsletter; *Frequency:* s-m; *Price:* Free to Audit Executive Center members
Profile: News & guidance for chief audit executives.
• Certification Corner
Type: Newsletter; *Frequency:* Quarterly; *Price:* Free to public
Profile: Developments in The IIA's certificate programs.
• IIA [The Institute of Internal Auditors] SmartBrief
Type: Newsletter; *Price:* Free to public
Profile: Market news & issues
• IIA [The Institute of Internal Auditors] Connection
Type: eNewsletter; *Price:* Free to members
Profile: Internal audit news; guidance, research, training, services, events, & certification.
• Internal Auditor
Type: Magazine; *Frequency:* Bimonthly; *Accepts Advertising*; *Editor:* Anne Millage; *Price:* $75 U.S.A. & Canada; $99 outside North America
Profile: Information for professionals in internal auditing
• Tone at the Top
Type: Newsletter; *Frequency:* Quarterly; *Price:* Free to public
Profile: Information on risk, internal control, governance, ethics, & the changing role of internal auditing for executive management, boards of directors, & audit committees.
• Your Career Compass
Type: Guide; *Frequency:* Quarterly; *Number of Pages:* 52; *Price:* Free to members
Profile: Knowledge, tools, & resources for career growth. Replaced IIA Today & Your Training Compass Resource Guide.

Institute of Packaging Professionals (IoPP)

#123, 1833 Centre Point Circle, Naperville IL 60563 USA
Tel: 800-432-4085
info@iopp.org
www.iopp.org
www.linkedin.com/groups?gid=77086&mostPopular=
www.facebook.com/groups/253022814142
twitter.com/IoPP_Pros
www.youtube.com/user/iopppack1
Overview: A medium-sized national organization
Mission: To create networking & educational opportunities to help packaging professionals succeed
Chief Officer(s):
Barbara Dykes, Manager, Member Services, 630-544-5050 Ext. 114
bdykes@iopp.org
Finances: *Funding Sources:* Corporate sponsors
Membership: 5,000; *Fees:* $150; *Member Profile:* Packaging professionals
Publications:
• IoPP [Institute of Packaging Professionals] Update
Type: Newsletter; *Frequency:* Biweekly
Profile: Institute information, such as awards competitions, scholarships, publications surveys, & professional development activities

Institute of Scrap Recycling Industries, Inc. (ISRI)

#600, 1615 I St. NW, Washington DC 20036-5610 USA
Tel: 202-662-8500; *Fax:* 202-626-0900
www.isri.org
www.linkedin.com/company/563629
www.facebook.com/isri1987
twitter.com/ISRI
www.youtube.com/user/ISRI1987
Overview: A medium-sized national organization
Mission: To provide education, advocacy, compliance training; to promote public awareness of the value & importance of recycling to the produciton of the world's goods & services
Chief Officer(s):
Robin K. Wiener, President
robinwiener@isri.org
Staff Member(s): 34
Membership: 1,250; 21 chapters across the US; *Fees:* Schedule available; *Member Profile:* North American companies that process, broker & consume srap commodities; associate memberships available for international members outside Canada, Mexico & the US, as well as to equipment & service providers of the scrap recycling industry
Activities: *Internships:* Yes; *Speaker Service:* Yes

Institute of Transportation Engineers (ITE)

#600, 1627 Eye St. NW, Washington DC 20006 USA
Tel: 202-785-0060; *Fax:* 202-785-0609
ite_staff@ite.org
www.ite.org
www.linkedin.com/groups?gid=166463
www.facebook.com/74169838900
twitter.com/ITEHQ
plus.google.com/116119105398656508668
Overview: A large international organization founded in 1930
Mission: To facilitate the application of technology & scientific principles for modes of ground transportation
Chief Officer(s):
Rock E. Miller, International President
Membership: 10,750; *Member Profile:* Transportation professionals with the responsibilities for meeting mobility & safety needs, such as transportation educators, researchers, consultants, planners, & engineers
Activities: Promoting professional development; Supporting education; Encouraging research; Increasing public awareness; Exchanging professional information
Awards:
• Daniel B. Fambro Student Paper Award (Award)
• Student Chapter Award (Award)
• Burton W. Marsh Distinguished Service Award (Award)
• Theodore M. Matson Memorial Award (Award)
• Wilbur S. Smith Distinguished Transportation Educator Award (Award)
• Innovative Intermodal Solutions for Urban Transportation Paper Award in Memory of Daniel W. Hoyt (Award)
• Past Presidents' Award for Merit in Transportation (Award)
• District and Section Newsletter Award (Award)
• Section Activities Award (Award)
• Transportation Achievement Award (Award)
Meetings/Conferences:
• Institute of Transportation Engineers 2015 Technical Conference & Exhibit, March, 2015, Westin La Paloma, Tucson, AZ
Scope: International
Contact Information: Contact, Registration Information: Sallie C. Dollins, E-mail: sdollins@ite.org; Contact, Technical Program: Eunice Chege, E-mail: echege@ite.org; Contact, Exhibits: Christina Garneski, E-mail: cgarneski@ite.org; Contact, Paper Submittals: Eunice Chege, E-mail: echege@ite.org
• Institute of Transportation Engineers 2015 Annual Meeting & Exhibit, August, 2015, Westin Diplomat, Hollywood, FL
Scope: International
Contact Information: Contact, Registration Information: Sallie C. Dollins, E-mail: sdollins@ite.org; Contact, Technical Program: Eunice Chege, E-mail: echege@ite.org; Contact, Exhibits: Christina Garneski, E-mail: cgarneski@ite.org; Contact, Paper Submittals: Eunice Chege, E-mail: echege@ite.org
• Institute of Transportation Engineers 2016 Annual Meeting & Exhibit, August, 2016, Anaheim Convention Center, Anaheim, CA
Scope: International
Contact Information: Contact, Registration Information: Sallie C. Dollins, E-mail: sdollins@ite.org; Contact, Technical Program: Eunice Chege, E-mail: echege@ite.org; Contact, Exhibits: Christina Garneski, E-mail: cgarneski@ite.org; Contact, Paper Submittals: Eunice Chege, E-mail: echege@ite.org
• Institute of Transportation Engineers 2016 Technical Conference & Exhibit, 2016
Scope: International
• Institute of Transportation Engineers 2017 Annual Meeting & Exhibit, July, 2017, Sheraton Centre Toronto, Toronto, ON
Scope: International
Contact Information: Contact, Registration Information: Sallie C. Dollins, E-mail: sdollins@ite.org; Contact, Technical Program: Eunice Chege, E-mail: echege@ite.org; Contact, Exhibits: Christina Garneski, E-mail: cgarneski@ite.org; Contact, Paper Submittals: Eunice Chege, E-mail: echege@ite.org
• Institute of Transportation Engineers 2018 Annual Meeting & Exhibit, 2018
Scope: International
Publications:
• Context Sensitive Solutions in Designing Major Urban Thoroughfares for Walkable Communities
Profile: An ITE Proposed Recommended Practice

- Parking Generation: An ITE Informational Report
- Traffic Engineering Handbook
- Traffic Signal Timing Manual
- Transportation Impact Analyses for Site Development: An ITE Proposed Recommended Practice
- Transportation Planning Handbook
- Trip Generation: An ITE Informational Report
- Urban Street Geometric Design Handbook

Institution of Mechanical Engineers (IMechE)

1 Birdcage Walk, London SW1H 9JJ United Kingdom
Tel: 44-(0)20-7222-7899; *Fax:* 44-(0)20-7222-4557
enquiries@imeche.org
www.imeche.org
www.linkedin.com/e/vgh/2265081/
www.facebook.com/imeche
twitter.com/imeche
Overview: A medium-sized international organization founded in 1847
Mission: To educate, train & promote the professional development of engineers; to act as an international centre for technology transfer in mechanical engineering
Chief Officer(s):
Rod Smith, President
president@imeche.org
Finances: *Annual Operating Budget:* $3 Million-$5 Million; *Funding Sources:* Subscriptions & earnings
Staff Member(s): 180
Membership: 75,000+
Activities: *Speaker Service:* Yes *Library* by appointment

Instrument Society of America *See* The Instrumentation, Systems & Automation Society of America

The Instrumentation, Systems & Automation Society of America (ISA)

PO Box 12277, 67 T.W. Alexander Dr., Research Triangle Park NC 27709 USA
Tel: 919-549-8411; *Fax:* 919-549-8288
info@isa.org
www.isa.org
www.linkedin.com/groups?gid=137598
www.facebook.com/InternationalSocietyOfAutomation
twitter.com/ISA_Interchange
www.flickr.com/photos/isaautomation
Previous Name: Instrument Society of America
Overview: A large international charitable organization founded in 1945
Mission: To be the foremost worldwide society involved with the science & application of measurement & control technologies; To advance members' competence, professionalism & recognition
Affliation(s): American Association for the Advancement of Science; American Institute of Physics; International Measurement Confederation; National Institute for Certification in Engineering Technologies; National Inventors Hall of Fame; American National Standards Institute; American Society of Mechanical Engineers; Fluid Controls Institute; Institute of Electrical & Electronic Engineers
Chief Officer(s):
Patrick Gouhin, Executive Director
pgouhin@isa.org
Ken Hilgers, Director, Finance & Administration, Customer Service, & Facility Operations, 919-990-9435
khilgers@isa.org
Finances: *Funding Sources:* Membership dues; Sales of books; Magazine ads; Training courses; Exhibit space; Conference registration
5000 volunteer(s)
Membership: 40,000; *Fees:* $85
Activities: *Speaker Service:* Yes; *Rents Mailing List:* Yes *Library* by appointment
Awards:
- Educational Foundation Scholarship (Scholarship)
Eligibility: Full-time college or university students in either a graduate, undergraduate, or 2 yr. degree program with at least an overall GPA of 2.5 on a 4.0 scale. Students should be enrolled in a program in automation and control or a closely related field.
- ISA Executive Board Scholarship (Scholarship)
Eligibility: Past and present members of ISA's Executive Board. Preference is given to applicants with demonstrated leadership capabilities.
- ISA Technical Division Scholarships (Scholarship)
- J.R. (Bob) Connell Memorial Scholarship (Scholarship)
Eligibility: Students enrolled in Engineering Technology-related courses of study at the Northern Alberta Institute of Technology and the University of Alberta.
- Norman E. and Mary-Belle Huston Scholarship (Scholarship)
- Bob and Mary Ives Scholarship (Scholarship)
- Paros-Digiquartz Endowment (Scholarship)
Amount: $2,000
- Daris and Gerald Wilbanks Endowment (Scholarship)

Interamerican Association of Securities Commissions & Similar Agencies *See* International Organization of Securities Commissions

Inter-American Society for Chemotherapy (IASC)

Auguero 1248, Buenos Aires 1425 Argentina
Tel: 54-1-963-4040; *Fax:* 54-1-963-4141
hmoore@compudata.com.ar
Overview: A small international organization founded in 1985
Mission: To bring together scientists in North, Central & South America involved in various approaches to the control of infectious dieseases & cancer; recent emphaiss has been on biological response modifiers & on alternative medicine
Member of: International Society of Chemotherapy
Chief Officer(s):
F.G. Gercovich, Secretary
Michael Ussery, President
Finances: *Annual Operating Budget:* Less than $50,000
6 volunteer(s)
Membership: 208; *Fees:* $25; *Member Profile:* PhD, MD researchers in chemotherapy of infectious disease & cancer

Intermodal Association of North America (IANA)

#1100, 11785 Beltsville Dr., Calverton MD 20705 USA
Tel: 301-982-3400; *Fax:* 301-982-4815
info@intermodal.org
www.intermodal.org
Overview: A medium-sized international organization founded in 1991
Mission: To represent the combined interests of intermodal freight transportation companies & their suppliers
Chief Officer(s):
Joanne F. Casey, President/CEO
joni.casey@intermodal.org
Thomas J. Malloy, Vice-President, Policy & Communications
tom.malloy@intermodal.org
Constance M. Sheffield, Vice-President, Administration & Programs
connie.sheffield@intermodal.org
James R. Morrow, Assistant Vice-President, Member Services
james.morrow@intermodal.org
Debbie Sasko, Assistant Vice-President, Contract Administration Services
debbie.sasko@intermodal.org
Membership: 700; *Committees:* Conference Planning; Education & Training; Electronic Business Solutions; Maintenance & Repair, Operations & P.R.

International Academy of Cytology (IAC)

c/o Secretary General, PO Box 1347, Freiburg 79013 Germany
Tel: 49-761-292-3801; *Fax:* 49-761-292-3802
centraloffice@cytology-iac.org
www.cytology-iac.org
Overview: A medium-sized international organization founded in 1957
Mission: To further knowledge in the field of cytopathology
Affiliation(s): European Federation of Cytology Societies; African Society of Cytology - West African; African Society of Cytology - East African; Argentinian Society of Cytology; Australian Society of Cytology; Austrian Society for Applied Cytology; Belgian Society of Clinical Cytology; Bolivian Society of Cytology; Brazilian Society of Cytopathology; British Association für Cytopathology; Canadian Society of Cytology - Société Canadienne de Cytologie; Chilean Society of Cytology; Chinese Academy of Clinical Cytology; Chinese Society of Cytopathology; Colombian Association of Cytology
Chief Officer(s):
Philippe Vielh, President
Fernando Schmitt, Secretary/Treasurer
Finances: *Funding Sources:* Membership dues; international congress
Membership: 1,574; *Fees:* Schedule available; *Committees:* Executive; Membership; Nominating; International Board of Cytopathology; Continuing Education; International Cytotechnology Award; International Cytopathology Award; Budget & Finance; Constitutuin & Bylaws; Cytotechnology Registration & Renewal; Cytotechnology; Congress Organization; Future Congress Site Selection; Liaison
Activities: International Congresses every 3 years
Awards:
- The George L. Wied Life-Time Achievement in Cytologic Research Award (Award)
- The International Cytotechnology of the Year Award (Award)
- The James W. Reagan Lecture Award (Award)
- The Maurice Goldblatt Cytology Award (Award)
- The Kazumasa Masubuchi Life-Time Achievement in Clinical Cytology (Award)

International African Institute (IAI) / Institut africain international

School of Oriental & African Studies, Thornhaugh St., Russell Square, London WC1H 0XG United Kingdom
Tel: 44-020-7898-4420; *Fax:* 44-020-7898-4419
iai@soas.ac.uk
www.internationalafricaninstitute.org
Previous Name: International Institute of African Languages & Cultures
Overview: A small international charitable organization founded in 1926
Mission: To facilitate communication between scholars within the continent & Africans throughout the world on issues that are of direct relevance to the peoples of this region
Chief Officer(s):
Philip Burnham, Honorary Director
V.Y. Mudimbe, Chairman
Staff Member(s): 3
Membership: *Committees:* Council; Publications
Activities: Encourages the study of African society; bibliographies of Africa (evaluation of the degree to which the results of African research are included in bibliographies & databases); IAI seminars, held usually in Africa, bringing together small groups of African & non-African scholars to explore innovative themes

International Alliance of Dietary/Food Supplement Associations (IADSA)

50, rue de l'Association, Brussels B-1000 Belgium
Tel: 32-2-209-1155; *Fax:* 32-2-223-3064
secretariat@iadsa.be
www.iadsa.org
Overview: A medium-sized international organization founded in 1998
Mission: To represent the views of the industry in the shaping of global policies & regulations that affect dietary supplements; focus on regional & national regulatory programs, scientific research, & technical program for quality assurance in manufacturing of supplements.
Chief Officer(s):
Peter Zambetti, Chairman
Membership: 54 dietary supplement associations representing 20,000 companies worldwide

International Alliance of Theatrical Stage Employees, Moving Picture Technicians, Artists & Allied Crafts of the U.S., Its Territories & Canada (IATSE)

1430 Broadway, 20th Fl., New York NY 10018 USA
Tel: 212-730-1770; *Fax:* 212-921-7699
webmaster@iatse-intl.org
www.iatse-intl.org
www.facebook.com/iatse
www.twitter.com/iatse
www.flickr.com/groups/iatse
Overview: A large international organization founded in 1893
Mission: Union representing workers in the entertainment industry.
Chief Officer(s):
Matthew D. Loeb, International President
John M. Lewis, Director, Canadian Affairs
Membership: 113,000; *Member Profile:* Members in live theater, motion picture and television production, trade shows and exhibitions, television broadcasting, and concerts as well as the equipment and construction shops that support all these areas of the entertainment industry.
Awards:
- Richard F. Walsh/Alfred W. Di Tolla/ Harold P. Spivak Foundation Scholarship (Scholarship)
Eligibility: The son/daughter of a member of the IATSE; high school senior at the time of application; applying to accredited college/university
Publications:
- Official Bulletin
Type: Bulletin; *Frequency:* Quarterly

• The Organizer
Type: Newsletter

Canadian Office
511 Adelaide St. W., Toronto ON M5V 1T4
Tel: 416-364-5565; *Fax:* 416-364-5987
iatse58@iatse58.org
www.iatse58.org
Mission: Local 58
Chief Officer(s):
Jim Brett, President
president@iatse58.org

International Allied Printing Trades Association / Association internationale des métiers alliés de l'imprimerie

6210 No. Capitol St., NW, Washington DC 20011 USA
Tel: 202-882-3000
Overview: A small international organization founded in 1911
Mission: Member Unions: Graphic Communications International Union; Printing, Publishing & Media Workers Sector of Communications Workers of America
Chief Officer(s):
William J. Boarman, President
Robert Lacey, Sec.-Treas.
6 volunteer(s)
Membership: 32 local councils

International Amateur Swimming Federation (IASF) / Fédération internationale de natation amateur (FINA)

Av. de l'Avant-Poste 4, Lausanne 1005 Switzerland
Tel: 41-21-310-4710; *Fax:* 41-21-312-6610
www.fina.org
www.linkedin.com/company/952149
www.facebook.com/fina1908
twitter.com/fina1908
www.youtube.com/user/fina1908
Overview: A large international organization founded in 1908
Mission: To promote and encourage the development of swimming in all possible manifestations throughout the world
Chief Officer(s):
Paolo Barelli, Hon. Secretary
Julio C. Maglione, President
Cornel Marculescu, Executive Director
Membership: 171 national federations; *Committees:* Technical Swimming, Diving, Water Polo; Technical Synchronized Swimming; Technical Open Water Swimming; Medical; Masters; Doping Panel; Press Commission
Meetings/Conferences:
• 16th FINA World Championships 2015 - Kazan, Russia, July, 2015, Kazan
Scope: International
• 17th FINA World Championships 2017, July, 2017, Guadalajara
Scope: International
Publications:
• FINA [International Amateur Swimming Federation] Newsletter
Type: Newsletter

International Amateur Theatre Association (IATA) / Association Internationale de Théâtre Amateur (AITA)

c/o The Questors Theatre, 19, Dorset Ave., Southall, Middlesex, London UB2 4HF United Kingdom
Tel: 372-641-8405; *Fax:* 372-641-8406
secretariat@aitaiata.org
www.aitaiata.org
Overview: A small international organization founded in 1952
Mission: To propagate & protect dramatic art by all theatrical groups of the world devoted, without remuneration, to artistic & cultural aims; to promote those activities common to its members; to coordinate the action of its members in their purpose of enriching human experience & educating people through the medium of theatre; to facilitate international exchanges between all groups belonging to the amateur theatre
Affliation(s): Theatre Canada
Chief Officer(s):
Paddy O'Dwyer, President
odwyerpaddy@gmail.com
Finances: *Annual Operating Budget:* $50,000-$100,000
Staff Member(s): 1; 1 volunteer(s)
Membership: 100-499

International Archery Federation *See* World Archery Federation

International Arctic Science Committee (IASC)

Telegrafenberg A43, Postdam DE-14473 Germany
Tel: 49-331-288-2214; *Fax:* 49-331-288-2215
iasc@iasc.info
iasc.info
www.facebook.com/groups/343786799008379
Overview: A large international organization founded in 1990
Mission: To encourage & facilitate cooperation in all aspects of arctic research, in all countries engaged in arctic research & in all areas of the arctic region; to provide scientific advice on arctic issues including environmental & technological matters
Affliation(s): Canadian Polar Commission
Chief Officer(s):
David Hik, President
Jackie Grebmeier, Vice-President
Volker Rachold, Executive Secretary
Finances: *Annual Operating Budget:* $250,000-$500,000; *Funding Sources:* Government of Norway: the IASC Secretariat
Staff Member(s): 2; 150 volunteer(s)
Membership: 18 countries; *Fees:* $7,000-9,000; *Member Profile:* Significant arctic research for a period of at least 5 years
Activities: Circum-Arctic research planning; 12 project groups; Developing Arctic EIA Guidelines under the Arctic Environmental Protection Strategy & International Arctic Environmental Data Directory; *Awareness Events:* Arctic Science Summit Week; *Internships:* Yes

International Arthurian Society - North American Branch / Société internationale arthurienne

c/o French Dept. of Modern Languages, Literatures & Linguistics, University of Oklahoma, #202, 780 Van Vleet Oval, Norman OK 73019-0250 USA
Tel: 405-325-6181; *Fax:* 405-325-0103
lwhalen@ou.edu
Overview: A medium-sized international organization founded in 1948
Mission: To foster research in all areas of the Arthurian legend
Chief Officer(s):
Logan Whalen, Contact
Finances: *Annual Operating Budget:* Less than $50,000; *Funding Sources:* Membership dues
1 volunteer(s)
Membership: 350; *Fees:* $US50 regular; $US60 contributing; $US75 patron; $US30 student; $US40 emeritus; $US500 life
Activities: *Rents Mailing List:* Yes

International Association for Armenian Studies (IAAS) / Association internationale des études arméniennes (AIEA)

c/o Université de Genève, Centre de Recherches Arménologiques, 5 Candolle Rd., Geneva CH 1211 Switzerland
Tel: 41-22-379-7210; *Fax:* 41-21-802-5543
aiea.fltr.ucl.ac.be/AIEAfr/Accueil.html
Overview: A small international charitable organization founded in 1981
Mission: To promote Armenian studies
Affliation(s): International Union for Oriental & Asian Studies
Chief Officer(s):
Valentina Calzolari, President
valentina.calzolari@unige.ch
Membership: *Fees:* US$32 individual; US$20 associate; US$17 student; *Member Profile:* Armenologues
Activities: *Library:* AIEA Library

International Association for Bear Research & Management (IBA)

c/o Terry While, USGS-SAFL, University of Tennessee, 274 Ellington Hall, Knoxville TN 37996 USA
Fax: 865-974-3555
www.bearbiology.com
Also Known As: IUCN/SSC Bear Specialist Group
Previous Name: Bear Biology Association
Overview: A small international charitable organization founded in 1968
Mission: To support the scientific management of bears & their habitats, through research & distribution of information
Chief Officer(s):
Frank van Manen, President
vanmanen@utk.edu
Harry Reynolds, Vice-President, Americas
hreynolds@reynoldsalaska.com
Diana Doan-Crider, Secretary
d-crider@tamu.edu
Cecily Costello, Treasurer
ccostello@bresnan.net
Membership: 550+ from 50+ countries; *Member Profile:* Professional biologists with an interest in bears; Wildlife managers; Others dedicated to the conservation of all bear species; *Committees:* Conference; Publications; Membership; Website
Activities: Encouraging communication & collaboration across scientific disciplines; Increasing public awareness & understanding of bear ecology; Maintaining high standards of professional ethics; Building an endowment & a future funding base; Sponsoring workshops & conferences on bear ecology, management, & biology
Awards:
• Research & Conservation Grants (Grant)
• Experience & Exchange Grants (Grant)
Publications:
• International Bear News
Type: Newsletter; *Frequency:* Quarterly; *Editor:* Tanya Rosen
ISSN: 1064-1564; *Price:* Free for members of the International Association forBear Research & Management
Profile: Articles about biology, conservation, & management of the world's eight bear species, plus reviews of books on bears
• Ursus [a publication of the International Association for Bear Research & Management]
Type: Journal; *Frequency:* Semiannually; *Editor:* Richard B. Harris; *Price:* Free for members of theInternational Association for Bear Research & Management
Profile: A peer-reviewed journal with articles on all aspects of bear management & research worldwide

International Association for Cross-Cultural Psychology (IACCP)

School of Humanites & Social Science, University, Campus Ring 1, HJacobs, Bremen D-28759 Germany
Tel: 49-421-200-3401; *Fax:* 49-421-200-3303
k.boehnke@iu-bremen.de
www.iaccp.org
twitter.com/iaccp
Overview: A small international organization founded in 1972
Mission: To facilitate communication among persons interested in cross-cultural psychology issues
Affliation(s): International Union of Psychological Science
Chief Officer(s):
William Gabrenya, Secretary General
gabrenya@fit.edu
Yoshi Kashima, President
ykashima@unimelb.edu.au
Sharon Glazer, Treasurer
sharon.glazer@usa.net
Finances: *Funding Sources:* Membership fees; Journal revenues
Membership: 800+; *Fees:* US$20 -$85 based upon income; *Member Profile:* Academic psychologists & social scientists from over 65 countries
Awards:
• Harry & Pola Triandis Doctoral Thesis Award (Award)
• Witkin-Okonji Memorial Fund Award (Award)
Publications:
• Cross-Cultural Psychology Bulletin
Type: Journal; *Editor:* William K. Gabrenya Jr.; *Price:* Free to IACCP members
• Journal of Cross-Cultural Psychology
Type: Journal; *Frequency:* Bimonthly; *Editor:* David Matsumoto
ISSN: 0022-0221
Profile: Papers focussing on the interrelationships between culture & psychological processes

International Association for Earthquake Engineering (IAEE)

Central Office, Ken chiku-kaikan Bldg., 3rd Fl., Minatoku Shiba 5, Chome 26-20, Tokyo 108-0014 Japan
Fax: 81-3-3453-0428
secretary@iaee.or.jp
www.iaee.or.jp
Overview: A medium-sized international organization founded in 1963
Mission: To promote international cooperation among scientists, engineers & other professionals in the broad field of earthquake engineering through interchange of knowledge, ideas, results of research & practical experience
Chief Officer(s):
Manabu Yoshimura, Secretary General
Polat Gulkan, President
Staff Member(s): 2
Membership: 54 countries

International Association for Ecology (INTECOL)

Dean of Faculty of Pure Science, Dept. of Animal & Plant Sciences, Univ. of Sheffield, Sheffield S10 2TN United Kingdom

kimeuns@kookmin.ac.kr
www.intecol.net
Overview: A medium-sized international organization founded in 1967
Mission: To promote the development of the science of ecology & the application of ecological principles to global needs; to collect, evaluate & disseminate information about ecology; to promote international actions in ecological research
Member of: Union of Biological Societies
Chief Officer(s):
Alan P. Covich, President
Membership: 1,000; *Fees:* $25

International Association for Environmental Hydrology (IAEH)

2607 Hopeton Dr., San Antonio TX 78230 USA
Tel: 201-984-7583; *Fax:* 201-564-8581
hydroweb@gmail.com
www.hydroweb.com
Overview: A medium-sized international organization founded in 1991
Mission: To provide a place to share technical information & exchange ideas; To provide a source of inexpensive tools for the environmental hydrologist, especially hydrologists & water resource engineers in developing countries
Membership: 450; *Fees:* US$75
Publications:
• Journal of Environmental Hydrology
Type: Journal; *Frequency:* Monthly *ISSN:* 1058-3912
Profile: Covering the fields of hydrology, environmental hydrology, urban hydrology, groundwater, groundwater pollution, groundwater contamination, & groundwater remediation

International Association for Great Lakes Research (IAGLR)

4840 South State Rd., Ann Arbor MI 48108 USA
Tel: 734-665-5303; *Fax:* 734-741-2055
office@iaglr.org
www.iaglr.org
www.facebook.com/iaglr
twitter.com/iaglr
Overview: A small international organization
Mission: To promote all aspects of Great Lakes research & the dissemination of research information through publications & meetings
Chief Officer(s):
Wendy Foster, Business Manager
Jerome Marty, President
president@iaglr.org
Membership: *Fees:* Schedule available; *Committees:* Awards; Conference; Endowment; Membership; Nominations; Outreach; Publications; Website
Activities: Annual four-day Conference on Great Lakes Research to exchange information on all aspects of research applicable to the understanding of large lakes of the world & to the human societies surrounding them
Awards:
• IAGLR Scholarship (Scholarship)
To a M.Sc or PhD student whose proposed research topic is relevant to large lake research *Amount:* US$2,000
• Norman S. Baldwin Fishery Science Scholarship (Scholarship)
Amount: US$1,000
• Chandler-Misener Award (Award)
Presented annually to the author(s) of the paper in the current volume of the peer reviewed Journal of Great Lakes Research judged to be "most notable"
• Anderson-Everett Award (Award)
Recognizes important & continued contributions to the Association
• Editor's Award (Award)
Presented for outstanding support of the Journal's review process
• IAGLR-Hydrolab Student Paper & Poster Awards (Award)
Offered for the best oral & poster presentations given by students at the annual conference; co-sponsored by Hydrolab Inc. *Amount:* US$250 & one year membership in association
• Paul W. Rodgers Scholarship (Scholarship)
Awarded annually to senior undergraduate, masters or doctoral student who wishes to pursue a future in research, conservation, education, communication, management or other knowledge-based activity pertaining to the Great Lakes *Amount:* US$2,000

International Association for Human Resource Information Management (IHRIM)

PO Box 1086, Burlington MA 01803 USA
press@ihrim.org
www.ihrim.org
Overview: A medium-sized international charitable organization founded in 1985
Mission: To operate as a clearinghouse for the HRIM industry; To enable members to achieve strategic objectives through the integration of information technology & human resource management
Chief Officer(s):
Lynne Mealy, President & Chief Executive Officer
lmealy@ihrim.org
Jean Andrews, Manager, Membership Marketing & Vendor Relations, 800-804-3983 Ext. 3
jandrews@ihrim.org
Laurie Carantit, Manager, Marketing & Communications, 800-804-3983 Ext. 4
lcarantit@ihrim.org
Michelle Czosek, Manager, Education & Special Programs, 800-804-3983 Ext. 2
mczosek@ihrim.org
Karen Murray, Manager, Membership Programs, 800-804-3983 Ext. 1
kmurray@ihrim.org
Finances: *Funding Sources:* Membership fees
Membership: 5,000; *Fees:* US$295; schedule
Activities: *Speaker Service:* Yes

International Association for Human Resource Information Management (IHRIM)

PO Box 1086, Burlington MA 01803 USA
Toll-Free: 800-804-3983
moreinfo@ihrim.org
www.ihrim.org
www.linkedin.com/groups?gid=741637&trk=hb_side_g
www.facebook.com/45721367331
twitter.com/IHRIM
Overview: A large international organization founded in 1980
Mission: To be the leading global source of knowledge for the application of human resource information & technology to improve organizational effectiveness
Chief Officer(s):
Lynne Mealy, President & CEO
lmealy@ihrim.org
Nov Omana, Chair
nmomana@ihrim.org
Finances: *Funding Sources:* Membership dues; conferences; seminars
Staff Member(s): 12
Membership: 4,000; *Fees:* Schedule available
Activities: *Rents Mailing List:* Yes
Awards:
• IHRIM Chairman's Award (Award)
• IHRIM Ambassador Award (Award)
• IHRIM Summit Award (Award)
• IHRIM Partners Award (Award)

International Association for Hydrogen Energy (IAHE)

#303, 5794 40th St. SW, Miami FL 33155 USA
info@iahe.org
www.iahe.org
Overview: A medium-sized international organization
Mission: To provide information about the role of hydrogen energy
Chief Officer(s):
T. Nejat Veziroglu, President
veziroglu@iahe.org
David Sanborn Scott, Vice-President, North America
davidsanbornscott@scottpoint.ca
Ayfer Veziroglu, Comptroller
ayfer@iahe.org
Membership: *Member Profile:* Professional persons in fields related to hydrogen energy; Laypersons with an interest in hydrogen energy; IAHE Fellows; Emeritus members; Students
Meetings/Conferences:
• 6th World Hydrogen Technology Convention (WHTC 2015), 2015, Sydney
Scope: International
Attendance: 1,000+
Description: A conference of the International Association for Hydrogen Energy, for the hydrogen & fuel cell community, featuring an exhibition with hydrogen & fuel cell applications from research institutions & companies
• 21st World Hydrogen Energy Conference (WHEC 2016), 2016, Zaragoza
Scope: International
Description: A biennial conference of the International Association for Hydrogen Energy
• 7th World Hydrogen Technology Convention (WHTC 2017), 2017, Prague
Scope: International
Attendance: 1,000+
Description: A conference of the International Association for Hydrogen Energy, for the hydrogen & fuel cell community, featuring an exhibition with hydrogen & fuel cell applications from research institutions & companies
Publications:
• International Journal of Hydrogen Energy
Type: Journal; *Editor:* Emre A. Veziroglu; *ISBN:* 0360-3199
Profile: Ideas in the field of hydrogen energy for environmentalists, chemists, energy researchers, energy companies, & engineering students

International Association for Impact Assessment (IAIA)

1330 - 23rd St. South, #C, Fargo ND 58103-3705 USA
Tel: 701-297-7908; *Fax:* 701-297-7917
info@iaia.org
www.iaia.org
www.linkedin.com/company/international-association-for-impact-assessme
www.facebook.com/iaia.impact.assessment
www.youtube.com/iaiachannel
Overview: A small international organization founded in 1980
Mission: To be a forum for advancing innovation, development & communication of best practice in impact assessment; to promote the development of local & global capacity for the application of environmental assessment in which sound science & full public participation provide a foundation for equitable & sustainable development
Affliation(s): International Society of City & Regional Planners; Environment Institute of Australia & New Zealand; South Asian Regional Environment Assessment Association; Japan Society for Impact Assessment; Chinese Association of Environmental Protection Industry
Chief Officer(s):
Rita R. Hamm, Chief Executive Officer, 701-297-7912
rita@iaia.org
Greg Radford, President, 613-798-1300
gradford@essa.com
Finances: *Funding Sources:* Membership fees; meeting registration
Staff Member(s): 6
Membership: 1,600 in more than 120 countries; *Fees:* US$110 individual (base rate); US$55 student; US$1,000 standard corporate; US$5,000 stewardship corporate; *Member Profile:* Corporate planners & managers; public interest advocates; government planners & administrators; private consultants & policy analysts; college teachers; students
Activities: Presentation of papers, posters, plenary sessions, exhibits, technical tours, pre-meeting training courses
Awards:
• Corporate (Award)
• Best Poster (Award)
• Global Environment (Award)
• Regional (Award)
• Institutional (Award)
• Individual (Award)
• IAPA Best Paper (Award)
• Outstanding Service to IAIA (Award)
• Rose-Hulman Award (Award)

International Association for Neo-Latin Studies (IANLS)

c/o Raija Sarasti-Wilenius, Institutum classicum, PB 24, SF-00014 University of Helsinki, Finland
Tel: 358405457597
www.ianls.org
Overview: A small international organization
Mission: To study & promote Neo-Latin studies
Affliation(s): Fédération internationale des langues et littératures modernes
Chief Officer(s):
Craig Kallendorf, President
kalendrf@tamu.edu
Jan Papy, Treasurer
jan.papy@arts.kuleuven.be
Finances: *Funding Sources:* Membership dues
Membership: 100-499; *Fees:* 40 Euro; *Member Profile:* Interest in all branches of Neo-Latin studies

International Association for Patristic Studies *Voir* Association internationale des études patristiques

International Association for Public Participation (IAP2)
#124 PMB 54, 13762 Colorado Blvd., Thornton CO 80602 USA
Tel: +61 8 8120 0669; *Fax:* 1-303-255-2382
iap2hq@iap2.org
www.iap2.org
www.facebook.com/group.php?gid=11982150193
Previous Name: International Association of Public Participation Practitioners
Overview: A medium-sized international organization founded in 1990
Mission: To serve the learning needs of members through events, publications, & communication technology; To advocate for public participation throughout the world; to promote research; To provide technical assistance
Chief Officer(s):
Moira Deslandes, Executive Director
moira@iap2.org
Geoff Wilson, President
president@iap2.org
Antonietta Cacciani, Manager, Professional Development
antonietta@iap2.org
Membership: 1,100; *Fees:* $975 individual; *Member Profile:* Public participation designers & facilitators; Policymakers; Project managers; Representatives from government agencies; Members of advocacy groups & professional organizations; trainers; Mediators; Citizen activists

International Association for the Study of Pain (IASP)
IASP Secretariat, #501, 111 Queen Anne Ave. North, Seattle WA 98109-4955 USA
Tel: 206-283-0311; *Fax:* 206-283-9403
iaspdesk@iasp-pain.org
www.iasp-pain.org
www.facebook.com/IASP.pain
twitter.com/IASPPAIN
Overview: A medium-sized international charitable organization founded in 1973
Mission: To provide a professional forum for science, practice, & education in the field of pain
Member of: World Federation of Neurology; World Federation of Ageing
Affiliation(s): Canadian Pain Society; World Health Organization
Chief Officer(s):
Katherine Kreiter, Executive Director
kreiter@iasp-pain.org
Troels S. Jensen, President
Harald Breivik, Secretary
Fernando Cervero, Treasurer
Finances: *Funding Sources:* Membership dues; Meetings; Book sales; Journal royalties; Donations
Membership: 6,900+ in 108 countries; *Fees:* Schedule available; *Member Profile:* All professionals involved in pain research, diagnosis, or treatment, including scientists, clinicians, health care providers, & policy makers
Activities: Special interest groups include the following: Acute Pain; Pain & Pain Management in Non-Human Species; Pain in Childhood; Pain in Older Persons; Pain Related to Torture, Organized Violence, and War; Pain & the Sympathetic Nervous System; Systematic Reviews in Pain Relief; Clinical-Legal Issues; Systematic Reviews in Pain; Placebo; Sex Gender & Pain; Orofacial Pain; Neuropathic Pain; Urogenital Pain; & Pain & Movement; *Rents Mailing List:* Yes
Awards:
• Patrick D. Wall Young Investigator Award (Award)
• IASP Trainee Research Prize (Award)
• John J. Bonica Trainee Fellowship (Scholarship)
• IASP Research Symposium Grant (Grant)
• Collaborative Research Grants (Grant)
• John J. Bonica Distiguished Lecture (Award)
Publications:
• IASP Newsletter
Type: Newsletter; *Frequency:* Quarterly
Profile: Activities of IASP, its chapters, & special interest groups for members
• PAIN
Type: Journal; *Frequency:* 18 pa
Profile: Peer-reviewed, original research on the nature, mechanisms, & treatment of pain
• Pain: Clinical Updates
Type: Newsletter
Profile: Details about pain therapy for clinicians, patients & families

International Association of Administrative Professionals (IAAP)
PO Box 20404, 10502 NW Ambassador Dr., Kansas City MO 64195-0404 USA
Tel: 816-891-6600; *Fax:* 816-891-9118
service@iaap-hq.org
www.iaap-hq.org
www.linkedin.com/groups?about=&gid=97764&trk=anet_ug_grppro
www.facebook.com/iaaphq
twitter.com/iaap
Previous Name: Professional Secretaries International
Overview: A large international organization founded in 1981
Mission: To effect increased productivity, career development & quality of work life within office environments by providing opportunities for educational, personal & professional growth; To be the acknowledged, recognized leader of office professionals & to enhance their individual & collective value, image, competence & influence
Affliation(s): American Society for Training & Development
Chief Officer(s):
Judith Yannarelli, President
Jay Donohue, Executive Director
Finances: *Annual Operating Budget:* $1.5 Million-$3 Million
Staff Member(s): 20
Membership: 22,000 and over 500 chapters; *Fees:* $50 student; $83 professional; $180 associate; *Member Profile:* Professional - employed secretary or certified professional secretary recipient or employed teacher of business education; student - enrolled student of business education; associate - individual, firm or educational institution which sustains objectives; *Committees:* Bylaws & Standing Rules; Nominations; CPS Service; Education & Program; Student Advisory; Membership; Retirement Centre; Bulletin Award; Public Relations; Executive Advisory Board Ad Hoc Committee
Activities: *Internships:* Yes; *Speaker Service:* Yes; *Rents Mailing List:* Yes *Library*
Meetings/Conferences:
• International Association of Administrative Professionals 2015 International Education Forum & Annual Meeting, July, 2015, Kentucky International Convention Center, Louisville, KY
Scope: International
Attendance: 1,200+
Description: Education workshops
• International Association of Administrative Professionals 2016 International Education Forum & Annual Meeting, 2016
Scope: International
Description: Education workshops
Publications:
• OfficePro
Type: Magazine

International Association of Agricultural Economists (IAAE)
#1100, 555 East Wells St., Milwaukee WI 53202 USA
Tel: 414-918-3199; *Fax:* 414-276-3349
iaae@execinc.com
www.iaae-agecon.org
Overview: A medium-sized international organization founded in 1929
Mission: To foster the application of agricultural economics to improve rural economic & social conditions; to advance knowledge of agriculture's economic organization; to facilitate communication & information exchange among those concerned with rural welfare
Affliation(s): Canadian Council - International Association of Agricultural Economists
Chief Officer(s):
Johan Swinnen, President
jo.swinnen@econ.kuleuven.be
Walter J. Armbruster, Secretary-Treasurer, 630-271-1679, Fax: 630-908-3384
walt@farmfoundation.org
Finances: *Annual Operating Budget:* $50,000-$100,000
Membership: 1,700; *Fees:* US$60-US$175; *Member Profile:* A worldwide confederation of agricultural economists & others concerned with agricultural economic problems
Activities: *Rents Mailing List:* Yes

International Association of Assembly Managers, Inc. *See* International Association of Venue Managers, Inc.

International Association of Bridge, Structural, Ornamental & Reinforcing Iron Workers (AFL-CIO) / Association internationale des travailleurs de ponts, de fer structural et ornemental (FAT-COI)
#400, 1750 New York Ave. NW, Washington DC 20006 USA
Tel: 202-383-4800; *Fax:* 202-638-4856
iwmagazine@iwintl.org
www.ironworkers.org
www.facebook.com/unionironworkers
twitter.com/TheIronworkers
www.youtube.com/user/IronworkersIMPACT
Overview: A medium-sized international organization
Mission: This union represents ironworkers and works for employment oppourtunties, fair pay, health and welfare benefits, continuing education, and other workers' rights since 1896.
Chief Officer(s):
Walter Wise, General President
Membership: 15,300 + 23 locals

International Association of Business Communicators (IABC)
#1900, 601 Montgomery St., San Francisco CA 94111 USA
Tel: 415-544-4700; *Fax:* 415-544-4747
Toll-Free: 800-776-4222
member_relations@iabc.com
www.iabc.com
www.linkedin.com/company/26095
www.facebook.com/IABCWorld
twitter.com/iabc
www.youtube.com/iabclive
Overview: A large international organization founded in 1970
Mission: To lead in use of information technology; To unite a diverse global network; To provide lifelong learning & research; To share ethical & effective performance standards & global best practices
Chief Officer(s):
Russell L. Grossman, Chair
Carlos Fulcher, Executive Director
cfulcher@iabc.com
Finances: *Annual Operating Budget:* $3 Million-$5 Million
Staff Member(s): 22
Membership: 14,000; *Committees:* Executive; Accreditation
Activities: *Speaker Service:* Yes; *Rents Mailing List:* Yes *Library* by appointment
Awards:
• Gold Quill Awards (Award)
• Excellence in Communication Leadership (EXCEL) Award (Award)
Awarded to individuals who foster excellence in organizational communication*Deadline:* February 10
• Fellow Award (Award)
For outstanding leadership, professional accomplishment & service to IABC & the profession*Deadline:* January 27
• Chairman's Award (Award)
Awarded to one or more individuals who have worked behind the scenes to benefit both the IABC & the profession
Publications:
• Communication World (CW) [a publication of the International Association of Business Communicators]
Type: Magazine; *Price:* $150 non-member
• CW Bulletin [a publication of the International Association of Business Communicators]
Type: Newsletter; *Editor:* Natasha Nicholson

Calgary Chapter
#400, 1040 - 7 Ave. SW, Calgary AB T2P 2G9
Tel: 403-270-4222; *Fax:* 403-244-2340
calgary-info@iabc.com
calgary.iabc.com
www.linkedin.com/groups/IABC-Calgary-4958331
www.facebook.com/IABC.Calgary
twitter.com/IABCyyc
Chief Officer(s):
Jennifer de Vries, President
Calgary-executive@iabc.com

Toronto Chapter
#1, 189 Queen St. East, Toronto ON M5A 1S2
Tel: 416-968-0264; *Fax:* 416-968-6818
toronto-info@iabc.com
toronto.iabc.com
www.linkedin.com/groups?gid=1878089
www.facebook.com/IABCToronto
twitter.com/IABCtoronto
www.youtube.com/user/IABCToronto
Mission: To help members achieve their personal & career aspirations by providing quality programmes & services that

advance the standards & practices of communication, & that enable members to help their organizations realize their goals
Chief Officer(s):
Stephanie Engel, President
toronto-president@iabc.com

International Association of Chiefs of Police (IACP)
#200, 44 Canal Center Plaza, Alexandria VA 22314 United States
Tel: 703-836-6767; *Fax:* 703-836-4543
www.fncpa.ca
www.facebook.com/TheIACP
twitter.com/TheIACP
www.youtube.com/theiacp
Overview: A medium-sized international organization founded in 1893
Mission: To promote improved police services, & cooperation & exchange of information among police chiefs throughout the world
Chief Officer(s):
Michael Wagers, Contact, State & Provincial Police
wagers@theiacp.org
Membership: *Committees:* Membership Benefits; Conference; Foundation; Communications; Training; Management Assistance; State & Provincial Services

International Association of Educators for World Peace - USA (IAEWP) / Association internationale des éducateurs pour la paix du monde
Mastin Lake Station, PO Box 3282, Huntsville AB 35810 USA
Tel: 256-534-5501; *Fax:* 256-536-1018
iaewp.net
Overview: A medium-sized international organization founded in 1969
Mission: To promote international understanding & world peace through education; to protect the environment from man-made pollution; to safeguard human rights; to encourage disarmament & development
Member of: United Nations (ECOSOC); UNDPI; UNICEF; UNCED; UNESCO
Affiliation(s): International Association of Educators for World Peace - National Office
Chief Officer(s):
Charles Mercieca, President
Willard Von De Bogart, Intl. Liaison & Public Relations
Finances: *Annual Operating Budget:* Less than $50,000; *Funding Sources:* Donations
Staff Member(s): 30
Membership: 35,000 in 92 countries; *Fees:* $45
Activities: Conventions; peace education studies & programs; gives more than 20 awards; *Speaker Service:* Yes; *Rents Mailing List:* Yes *Library:* Research Centre; by appointment
Awards:
- Diploma of Leadership (Award)
- Diploma of Scholarship (Award)
- Mahatma Gandi Peace Prize (Award)
- World Peace Academy Diploma (Award)
- Albert Einstein Peace Award (Award)
- Albert Schweitzer Humanitarian Award (Award)
- Ambassador of Peace Award (Award)
- Fountain of Universal Peace Award (Award)
- Diploma of Honour (Award)

International Association of Environmental Analytical Chemistry (IAEAC)
c/o Dr. Montserrat Filella, Institut F.- A. Forel, Route de Suisse, Versoix 1290 Switzerland
Tel: 41 22 379 03 00; *Fax:* 41 22 379 03 29
iaeac@dplanet.ch
www.iaeac.com
Overview: A small international organization founded in 1977
Mission: To support regular exchange of experiences between experts in the field of analytical chemistry of pollutants & related areas; To orient its members about recent advances in the field; To address relevant problems of environmental analysis & on questions related to environmental protection & control
Chief Officer(s):
Montserrat Filella, Secretary
montserrat.filella@unige.ch
José A.C. Broekaert, President
jose.broekaert@chemie.uni-hamburg.de
Staff Member(s): 1
Membership: 110-130; *Fees:* SFR 110-300

International Association of Fire Fighters (AFL-CIO/CLC) (IAFF) / Association internationale des pompiers (FAT-COI/CTC)
#300, 1750 New York Ave. NW, Washington DC 20006-5395 USA
Tel: 202-737-8484; *Fax:* 202-737-8418
membership@iaff.org
www.iaff.org
www.facebook.com/IAFFonline
twitter.com/iaffnewsdesk
Overview: A large international organization founded in 1918
Mission: To establish professional standards for the North American fire service with active political & legislative programs, & with experts in the fields of occupational health & safety, fire-based emergency medical services & hazardous materials training; to provide a voice in the development & implementation of new training & equipment; to work to ensure the staffing of fire & EMS departments
Chief Officer(s):
Harold A. Schaitberger, General President
Thomas H. Miller, General Secretary-Treasurer
Tim Burns, Press Secretary, 202-824-1566
tburn@iaff.org
Membership: 300,000+ fire fighters & paramedics in the U.S. & Canada + 3,200 affiliates; *Member Profile:* full-time professional fire fighters & paramedics
Activities: *Library*
Awards:
- The International Association of Fire Fighters Media Awards Contest (Award)

Publications:
- International Fire Fighter [a publication of the International Association of Fire Fighters (AFL-CIO/CLC)]

Type: Magazine; *Frequency:* 5 pa

Canadian Office
#403, 350 Sparks St., Ottawa ON K1R 7S8
Tel: 613-567-8988; *Fax:* 613-567-8986
www.iaff.org/canada
Mission: To represent Canada's professional fire fighters and work towards better working conditions & wages; 4 district Vice Presidents respresent regions of Canada
Chief Officer(s):
Scott Marks, Asst. to President, Canadian Operations
smarks@iaff.org

International Association of Fish & Wildlife Agencies *See* Association of Fish & Wildlife Agencies

International Association of Hydrogeologists (IAH)
IAH Secretariat, PO Box 4130, Stn. Goring, Reading RG8 6BJKOA 1L0 UK
Tel: +44 870 762 4462; *Fax:* +44 870 762 8462
info@iah.org
www.iah.org
Overview: A medium-sized international organization founded in 1956
Mission: To advance the science of hydrogeology & exchange hydrogeologic information internationally
Affiliation(s): UNESCO; International Union of Geological Sciences
Chief Officer(s):
John Chilton, Executive Manager, IAH Secretariat
jchilton@iah.org
Membership: 4,000 in 135 countries; 300 in Canada
Meetings/Conferences:
- International Association of Hydrogeologists 2015 42nd Congress: Hydrogeology: Back to the Future, September, 2015, Rome

Scope: International
Description: Presented in partnership with the Ministry of Energy, Mines, Water & Environment & the International Institute for Water & Sanitation
Contact Information: organizing@iah2015.org; URL: www.iah2015.org

International Association of Judges (IAJ) / Union internationale des magistrats (UIM)
Palazzo di Giustizia, Piazza Cavour, Rome 00193 Italy
Tel: 39-066-883-2213; *Fax:* 39-066-871-1195
secretariat@iaj-uim.org
www.iaj-uim.org
Overview: A small international organization founded in 1953
Mission: To defend the independence of the judiciary; to promote the exchange of cultural relations between judges of different countries; the IAJ has full consultative status with the Council of Europe, the International Labour Office, & the UN Economic & Social Council
Affliation(s): Council of Europe; International Labour Office; UN Economic & Social Council
Chief Officer(s):
Giacomo Oberto, Secretary General
secretariat@iaj-uim.org
Gerhard Reissner, President
Cristina Crespo, First Vice-President
Finances: *Funding Sources:* Membership fees
Membership: 81 national associations of judges; *Member Profile:* National associations of judges which represent the judiciary of their country; *Committees:* Presidency Committee
Activities: Meetings & exchanges of information & experiences
Awards:
- Justice in the World Award (Award)

International Association of Machinists & Aerospace Workers (IAMAW) / Association internationale des machinistes et des travailleurs de l'aérospatiale
Machinists Bldg., 9000 Machinists Pl., Upper Marlboro MD 20772-2687 USA
Tel: 301-967-4500
www.iamaw.ca
www.facebook.com/machinistsunion
twitter.com/machinistsunion
Overview: A small international organization
Mission: To work as the negotiating body for its members
Chief Officer(s):
R. Thomas Buffenbarger, President
Membership: 720,000 across North America
Publications:
- IAM Journal for Fighting Machinists

Type: Journal
Profile: International Association of Machinists news & stories

Canadian Office
#707, 15 Gervais Dr., Toronto ON M3C 1Y8
Tel: 416-386-1789
Toll-Free: 877-426-1426
info@iamaw.ca
www.iamaw.ca
twitter.com/iamawcanada
www.youtube.com/user/IAMAWCanada
Chief Officer(s):
Dave Ritchie, General Vice-President, Canada

International Association of Marine Aids to Navigation & Lighthouse Authorities (IALA) / Association internationale de signalisation maritime (AISM)
10, rue des Gaudines, St-Germain-en-Laye 78100 France
Tel: 33-1-3451-7001; *Fax:* 33-1-3451-8205
contact@iala-aism.org
www.iala-aism.org
Overview: A small international organization founded in 1957
Mission: To ensure that the movements of vessels are safe, fast & economical by developing ways to improve navigation aides & maritime traffic
Finances: *Annual Operating Budget:* $3 Million-$5 Million; *Funding Sources:* Membership dues; Publications; Seminars & workshops; IALA Conferences; World Wide Academy
Staff Member(s): 12
Membership: 280; *Fees:* 14,000 Euros national; 5,700 Europs industrial; 2,730 Euros associate; *Member Profile:* Services de signalisation maritime; ports maritimes; fabricants d'équipement; consultants; *Committees:* Aids to Navigation Management; Engineering, Environmental and Preservation; e-Navigation; Vessel Traffic Service
Activities: Radionavigation commissions; Operating engineering services; various seminars - conferences; exhibitions every 4 years; *Library* by appointment

International Association of Museums of Arms & Military History *See* International Committee of Museums & Collections of Arms & Military History

International Association of Music Libraries, Archives & Documentation Centres (IAML) / Association internationale des bibliothèques, archives et de documentation musicaux
c/o Roger Flury, Music Room, National Library of New Zealand, PO Box 1467, Wellington 6001 New Zealand
Tel: +64 4 474 3039; *Fax:* +64 4 474 3035
www.iaml.info
Overview: A small international organization founded in 1951
Mission: To promote the activities of music libraries, archives, & documentation centres nationally & internationally; To encourage

international cooperation; To support projects in music bibliography, music documentation, & music library & information science
Member of: International Federation of Library Associations & Institutions (IFLA); International Council on Archives (ICA); European Bureau of Library, Information & Documentation Associations (EBLIDA); International Music Council (IMC)
Affiliation(s): International Association of Sound Archives (IASA); International Association of Music Information Centres (IAMIC)
Chief Officer(s):
Roger Flury, Secretary General
roger.flury@natlib.govt.nz
Kathryn Adamson, Treasurer
Membership: 2,000 individual & institutional members from 45 countries; *Member Profile:* Music & audio-visual librarians; Music archivists; Documentation specialists; Musicologists; Music publishers; Music dealers; Major music collections; *Committees:* Constitution; Copyright; Information Technology; Outreach; Programme; Publications
Activities: Supporting members' interests;
Meetings/Conferences:
• International Association of Music Libraries, Archives & Documentation Centres 2015 64th Annual Conference, June, 2015, New York City, NY
Scope: International
Description: Educational sessions, social & cultural programs, & exhibits of interest to international music librarians, archivists, & documentation specialists
• International Association of Music Libraries, Archives & Documentation Centres 2016 65th Annual Conference, July, 2016, Rome
Scope: International
Description: Presenting association committee & national branch meetings, guest speakers, & informative sessions related to music librarianship
Publications:
• Fontes artis musicae
Type: Journal; *Frequency:* Quarterly; *Editor:* Maureen Buja, PhD
Profile: Articles related to music librarianship, documentation, bibliography, & musicology, available only to association members
• IAML Newsletter
Type: Newsletter; *Accepts Advertising*; *Editor:* Brian McMillan
Profile: Association & country reports, plus articles

International Association of Penal Law ***Voir*** Association internationale de droit pénal

International Association of Physicians in Audiology

c/o Dept. of Audiology, H:S Bispebjerg Hospital, Copenhagen University Hospital, Copenhagen DK 2400 Denmark
secretary@iapa-online.org
www.iapa-online.org
Overview: A small international organization founded in 1980
Mission: To promote & improve clinical, ethical & scientific standards in the field of audiological medicine
Chief Officer(s):
Konrad S. Konradsson, Secretary
Linda M. Luxon, President
Finances: *Annual Operating Budget:* Less than $50,000
Membership: 200; *Fees:* Euro50; *Member Profile:* Medically qualified in audiology

International Association of Ports & Harbours (IAPH)

7F South Tower, New Pier Takeshiba, 1-16-1 Kaigan, Minato-Ku, Tokyo 105-0022 Japan
Tel: 81-3-5403-2770; *Fax:* 81-3-5403-7651
info@iaphworldports.org
www.iaphworldports.org
www.facebook.com/iaphworldports
Overview: A large international organization founded in 1955
Mission: To promote the development of the international port & maritime industry by fostering cooperation among members in order to build a more cohesive partnership among the world's ports & harbors, thereby promoting peace in the world & the welfare of mankind; to ensure that the industry's interests & views are represented before international organizations involved n the regulation of international trade & transportation & incorporated in the regulatory initiatives of these organizations; & to collect, analyse, exchange & distribute information on developing trends in international trade, transportation, ports & the regulations of these industries
Affiliation(s): International Maritime Organization; United Nations Conference on Trade & Development; United Nations Economic & Social Council; Permanent International Association of Navigation Congresses; International Cargo Handling Coordination Association; International Maritime Pilots Association; International Association of Independent Tanker Owners; Baltic & International Martime Council
Chief Officer(s):
Susumu Naruse, Secretary General
Geraldine Knatz, President
Finances: *Annual Operating Budget:* $1.5 Million-$3 Million; *Funding Sources:* Membership fees
Staff Member(s): 7
Membership: 360; *Fees:* Schedule available; *Member Profile:* 90 maritime countries are represented; *Committees:* Executive; Communication & Community Relations; Port Finance & Economics; Port Safety & Security; Port Environment; Legal; Port Planning & Development; Port Operations & Logistics; Trade Facilitation & Port Community System; Conference; Finance; Constitution & By-Laws; Membership; Long Range Planning/Review
Activities: *Library*
Awards:
• Essay Contest Award (Award)
• IAPH Information Technology Award (Award)
• IAPH Training Scholarship (Scholarship)

International Association of Professional Congress Organizers (IAPCO)

Brambles House, Colwell Rd., freshwater PO40 9SL UK
Tel: 44 1983 755546
info@iapco.org
www.iapco.org
twitter.com/IAPCO
Overview: A small international organization founded in 1968
Mission: To undertake & promote the study of theoretical & practical aspects of international congresses; To develop a programme of educational courses through its Institute for Congress Management Training; To undertake research work concerning all problems confronting professional organizers of international meetings, & to seek & promote relevant solutions; To further the recognition of the profession of congress organizer
Affiliation(s): IAPCO Training Academy
Chief Officer(s):
Sarah Storie-Pugh, Administrator
Staff Member(s): 1
Membership: 6 individual + 67 corporate (includes 5 corporate Canadian); *Fees:* 2,200 euro; *Member Profile:* Professional congress organizing companies; individuals employed by the congress dept. of associations & companies; freelance individuals engaged on a permanent basis in the organization of international meetings; must have been responsible for 10 international meetings attended by representatives of more than 3 different countries, of at least 4 days' duration, & at least 5 of which have been attended by at least 400 delegates
Activities: Responsible for the activities of the Institute for Congress Management Training (ICMT) which offers a comprehensive programme of training seminars

International Association of Public Participation Practitioners ***See*** International Association for Public Participation

International Association of Rebekah Assemblies

c/o The Sovereign Grand Lodge IOOF, 422 Trade St., Winston-Salem NC 27101 USA
Tel: 336-725-6037; *Fax:* 336-773-1066
Toll-Free: 800-766-1838
iarasec@aol.com
www.ioof.org/rebekahs.html
Overview: A medium-sized international organization founded in 1914
Mission: The Rebekah lodges are the female auxiliary of the Independent Order of Odd Fellows, but are open to both women and men.
Finances: *Annual Operating Budget:* $250,000-$500,000; *Funding Sources:* Donations
Staff Member(s): 2
Membership: 97,000
Activities: Arthritis Telethon

International Association of Sedimentologists (IAS)

c/o Universita' di Sassari, Via Piandanna 4, Sassari 07100 Italy
www.sedimentologists.org
Overview: A medium-sized international organization founded in 1952
Mission: To promote the study of sedimentology by publication, discussion & comparison of research results; to encourage the interchange of research, particularly where international cooperation is desirable; to promote integration with other disciplines. Canadian Correspondent: Dr. A. Guy Plint, Dept. of Earth Sciences, University of Western Ontario, London, ON N6A 5B7, email gplint@uwo.ca
Member of: International Union of Geological Sciences
Chief Officer(s):
Vincenzo Pascucci, General Secretary, Universita' di Sassari
pascucci@uniss.it
Poppe de Boer, President, Utrecht University
pdeboer@geo.uu.nl
Marc De Batist, Treasurer, Ghent University, Belgium
marc.debatist@ugent.be
Finances: *Annual Operating Budget:* $500,000-$1.5 Million; *Funding Sources:* Membership dues; sales of books
Staff Member(s): 1
Membership: 1,700; *Fees:* EUR 30 full member; EUR 15 student
Publications:
• Basin Research
Type: Journal
Profile: Published by Blackwell
• Journal of Petroleum Geology
Type: Journal
Profile: Published by Blackwell
• Sedimentology
Type: Journal
Profile: Published by Blackwell

International Association of Theoretical and Applied Limnology; Societas Internationalis Limnologiae, SIL ***See*** International Society of Limnology

International Association of University Professors of English (IAUPE)

Fribourg Switzerland
iaupe.secretarygeneral@gmail.com
www.iaupe.org
Overview: A small international organization founded in 1951
Mission: To promote the development of English studies at the university level on a worldwide basis
Affiliation(s): Fédération internationale des langues et littératures modernes
Chief Officer(s):
Thomas Austenfeld, Secretary General & Treasurer
Jane Roberts, President
Finances: *Funding Sources:* Membership dues
Membership: 500; *Member Profile:* University professors of English Language &/or Literature; other scholars of distinction in these & related fields; *Committees:* Executive; International
Publications:
• IAUPE Bulletin
Type: Newsletter; *Editor:* A. Breeze

International Association of Venue Managers, Inc. (IAVM)

#100, 635 Fritz Dr., Coppell TX 75019-4442 USA
Tel: 972-906-7441; *Fax:* 972-906-7418
membership@iavm.org
www.iavm.org
www.linkedin.com/IAVMgroup
www.facebook.com/IAVMWHQ
twitter.com/IAVMWHQ
Previous Name: International Association of Assembly Managers, Inc.
Overview: A medium-sized international organization founded in 1924
Mission: To provide leadership & to educate; to inform & to cultivate friendships among individuals involved in the management, operation & support of venues
Chief Officer(s):
Vicki Hawarden, CMP, President/CEO, 972-906-7441, Fax: 972-906-7418
vicki.hawarden@IAVM.org
Finances: *Annual Operating Budget:* $3 Million-$5 Million; *Funding Sources:* Membership dues; conferences; trade show; seminars; services; IAVM Foundation
Staff Member(s): 25
Membership: 3,900; *Fees:* $445; *Member Profile:* Managers of arenas & stadiums, performing arts venues, convention & conference centres, fairs, race tracks. Allied companies provide products & services used by venue managers.
Activities: *Awareness Events:* Venue Connect - Annual conference & trade show; *Internships:* Yes; *Rents Mailing List:* Yes

International Association on Water Quality; International Association on Water Pollution Research & Control *See* International Water Association

International Atomic Energy Agency (IAEA) / Agence internationale de l'énergie atomique

Vienna International Centre, PO Box 100, Wagramer Strasse 5, Vienna A-1400 Austria
Tel: 43-1 2600-0; *Fax:* 43-1 2600-7
official.mail@iaea.org
www.iaea.org
www.facebook.com/iaeaorg
twitter.com/iaeaorg
www.youtube.com/user/IAEAvideo
Overview: A large international organization founded in 1957
Mission: An independent intergovernmental organization within the UN system; to accelerate & enlarge the contribution of atomic energy to peace, health & prosperity throughout the world; to ensure that assistance provided is not used to further any military purpose
Affliation(s): United Nations
Chief Officer(s):
Yukiya Amano, Director General
Janice Dunn Lee, Deputy Director General, Management
Finances: *Annual Operating Budget:* Greater than $5 Million; *Funding Sources:* Member states contributions
Staff Member(s): 2300
Membership: 158 sovereign states; *Fees:* Percentage of share of regular budget is fixed by UN General Assembly; *Member Profile:* Intergovernmental organization; *Committees:* Board of Governors composed of 35 member states
Activities: Verification in framework of Nuclear Non-Proliferation Treaty (NPT) that over 1,000 nuclear facilities in over 60 non-nuclear weapon states are used for peaceful purposes only; *Library* by appointment
Publications:
• Animal Production & Health Newsletter [a publication of the International Atomic Energy Agency]
Type: Newsletter; *Editor:* Gerrit Johannes Viljoen *ISSN:* 1011-2529
• Education & Training in Radiation, Transport & Waste Safety Newsletter
Type: Newsletter; *Editor:* Andrea Luciani *ISSN:* 2304-5744
• Food & Environmental Protection Newsletter [a publication of the International Atomic Energy Agency]
Type: Newsletter; *Editor:* David Henry Byron *ISSN:* 1020-6671
• Fuel Cycle & Waste Newsletter [a publication of the International Atomic Energy Agency]
Type: Newsletter; *Editor:* Hiroko Ratcliffe *ISSN:* 1816-9287
• IAEA [International Atomic Energy Agency] Bulletin
Type: Magazine
• Insect Pest Control Newsletter [a publication of the International Atomic Energy Agency]
Type: Newsletter; *Editor:* Jorge Hendrichs *ISSN:* 1011-274X
• Nuclear Data Newsletter [a publication of the International Atomic Energy Agency]
Type: Newsletter; *Editor:* Janet Roberts *ISSN:* 0257-6376
• Nuclear Fusion [a publication of the International Atomic Energy Agency]
Type: Journal; *Editor:* Sophy Le Masurier
• Nuclear Information & Knowledge [a publication of the International Atomic Energy Agency]
Type: Newsletter; *Editor:* Bruna Lecossois *ISSN:* 1819-9186
• Nuclear Power Newsletter [a publication of the International Atomic Energy Agency]
Type: Newsletter; *Editor:* Elisabeth Dyck *ISSN:* 1816-9295
• Water & Environment News [a publication of the International Atomic Energy Agency]
Type: Newsletter; *Editor:* Luis Jesus Araguas Araguas *ISSN:* 1020-7120
• XRF Newsletter [a publication of the International Atomic Energy Agency]
Type: Newsletter *ISSN:* 1608-4632

International Badminton Federation (IBF) *See* Badminton World Federation

International Bar Association (IBA)

10 St. Bride St., 4th Fl., London EC4A 4AD United Kingdom
Tel: 44-20-7842-0090; *Fax:* 44-20-7842-0091
member@int-bar.org
www.ibanet.org
www.linkedin.com/company/international-bar-association
twitter.com/ibanews
Overview: A large international organization founded in 1947
Mission: The development of international law reform is influenced by the IBA. The organization also shapes the future of the legal profession throughout the world. It is divided into the Legal Practice Division & the Public & Professional Interest Division.
Affliation(s): Canadian Bar Association
Chief Officer(s):
Akira Kawamura, President
David W. Rivkin, Secretary-General
Almudena Arpón de Mendívil, Treasurer
Mark Ellis, Executive Director
Membership: 45,000 individual lawyers + 200 bar associations & law societies; *Fees:* Schedule available; *Member Profile:* International legal practitioners; Bar associations; Law societies; *Committees:* Academic & Professional Development; Anti-Corruption; Antitrust; Arbitration; Art, Cultural Institutions & Heritage Law; Aviation Law; Banking Law; Business Crime; Client Protection; Closely Held & Growing Business Enterprises; Communications Law; Construction Projects; Consumer Litigation; Corporate & M&A Law; Corporate Social Responsibility; Criminal Law; Discrimination Law; Employment & Industrial Relations Law; Environment, Health & Safety Law; Family Law; Healthcare & Life Sciences Law; Human Rights Law; Immigration & Nationality Law; Indigenous Peoples; Insurance; and others...
Activities: Providing members with access to timely information; Establishing & operating IBA institutions such as the Bar Issues Commission, the Human Rights Institute, the Southern Africa Litigation Centre, & the International Legal Assistance Consortium; Supporting the independence of the judiciary & human rights for lawyers
Meetings/Conferences:
• International Bar Association 2015 Annual Conference, October, 2015, Vienna
Scope: International
Description: An opportunity to network, generate new business & participate in professional development programs
Contact Information: Web Site: www.ibanet.org/Conferences/Vienna2015.aspx
Publications:
• Business Law International [a publication of the International Bar Association]
Type: Journal; *Frequency:* 3 pa; *Editor:* Wayne McArdle & Audley Sheppard *ISSN:* 1467 632X; *Price:* $385
Profile: Issues of interest to the international commercial, legal, & academiccommunity
• Competition Law International [a publication of the International Bar Association]
Type: Journal; *Frequency:* 3 pa; *Editor:* Dan Swanson *ISSN:* 1817-5708; *Price:* $215
Profile: Journal of the Antitrust & Trade Law Section of the IBA
• Construction Law International [a publication of the International Bar Association]
Type: Magazine; *Frequency:* Quarterly; *Editor:* Emily Silvester; *Price:* $196
Profile: Magazine of the IBA International Construction Projects Committee
• Convergence [a publication of the International Bar Association]
Type: Journal; *Frequency:* Semiannually; *Editor:* John J. Lynch *ISSN:* 1817-5694
Profile: Journal of the Intellectual Property, Communications & Technology Section of the International Bar Association
• Dispute Resolution International [a publication of the International Bar Association]
Type: Journal; *Frequency:* Semiannually; *Editor:* Lawrence S. Schaner *ISSN:* 2075-5333; *Price:* $238
Profile: Journal of the Dispute Resolution Section of the Legal Practice Division of the IBA
• IBA Global Insight [a publication of the International Bar Association]
Type: Magazine; *Frequency:* Bimonthly *ISSN:* 2221-5859; *Price:* $196
Profile: Articles about legal & business issues, IBA initiatives, & activities
• The In-House Perspective [a publication of the International Bar Association-
Type: Magazine; *Frequency:* Quarterly; *Editor:* Tom Bangay *ISSN:* 1814 0408; *Price:* $196
Profile: Magazine of the IBA Corporate Counsel Forum
• Insolvency & Restructuring International [a publication of the International Bar Association]
Type: Journal; *Editor:* Jennifer Stam; Karen O'Flynn; *Price:* $196
Profile: Issues of interest to the international legal business community
• Journal of Energy & Natural Resources Law [a publication of the International Bar Association]
Type: Journal; *Frequency:* Quarterly; *Editor:* Don C. Smith *ISSN:* 0264-6811; *Price:* $612

International Board on Books for Young People (IBBY) / Union internationale pour les livres de jeunesse

Nonnenweg 12, Postfach, Basel CH-4003 Switzerland
Tel: 41-61-272-29-17; *Fax:* 41-61-272-27-57
ibby@ibby.org
www.ibby.org
Overview: A small international organization founded in 1953
Mission: To promote international understanding through children's books; To strives to give children everywhere access to books with high literary & artistic standards
Member of: UNESCO; UNICEF; International Federation of Library Associations
Affliation(s): International Board on Books for Young People - Canadian National Section
Chief Officer(s):
Ahmad Redza Ahmad Khairuddin, President
aredza@gmail.com
Liz Page, Executive Director
liz.page@ibby.org
Forest Zhang, Deputy Director, Administration
forest.zhang@ibby.org
Finances: *Funding Sources:* Membership dues; Donations; Sponsorships; Fundraising
Membership: 70 national sections; *Fees:* Schedule available; *Member Profile:* Countries with developed book publishing & literacy programs; Countries with few professionals in children's book publishing; Members in national sections include authors, illustrators, publishers, editors, translators, journalists, critics, teachers, university professors, students, librarians, booksellers, social workers, & parents
Activities: Advocating for children's books; Encouraging the publication & distribution of quality children's books; Providing support & training for those involved with children & children's literature; Encouraging research in the field; Establishing the IBBY Documentation Centre of Books for Disabled Young People; *Awareness Events:* International Children's Book Day, April 2
Awards:
• IBBY Honour List Diplomas (Award)
A biennial selection of outstanding, recently published books, honouring writers, translators, & illustrators from IBBY member countries
• IBBY-Asahi Reading Promotion Award (Award)
Presented every two years to a group or institution which, by its outstanding activities, is judged to be making a lasting contribution to reading programs for children & young people
• Hans Christian Andersen Awards (Award)
Awards include the Hans Christian Andersen Author Award & the Hans Christian Andersen Illustrator Award
• Jella Lepman Medal (Award)
An award named after the founder of IBBY & presented to those who have made lastin gcontribution to children's literature
Meetings/Conferences:
• International Board on Books for Young People 2016 35th International Congress, August, 2016, Auckland
Scope: International
Description: A biennial congress, hosted by an IBBY national section, for IBBY members & people involved in children's books & reading development from around the world. This year's theme is "Literature in a Multi-linguistic Society."
• International Board on Books for Young People 2018 36th International Congress, 2018
Scope: International
Publications:
• Bookbird: A Journal of International Children's Literature
Type: Journal; *Frequency:* Quarterly; *Editor:* Sylvia Vardell; Catherine Kurkjian *ISSN:* 0006 7377
Profile: A refereed journal to communicate ideas to readers interested in international children's literature
• A Bridge of Children's Books
Profile: The autobiography of Jella Lepman, the founder of IBBY
• IBBY Honour List
Type: Catalogue; *Frequency:* Biennially; *Editor:* Liz Page; Forest Zhang
Profile: A presentation of outstanding, recently published books selected by national section in the categories of writing, translating, & illustrating
• IBBY Newsletter
Type: Newsletter

Profile: News from IBBY national sections, the IBBY executive committee, the IBBY World Congress, plus information about IBBY projects, workshops, & awards
• Outstanding Books for Young People with Disabilities
Type: Catalogue
Profile: An international selection of titles recommended by the IBBY Documentation Centre of Books for Disabled Young People

International Bottled Water Association (IBWA)
#650, 1700 Diagonal Rd., Alexandria VA 22314 USA
Tel: 703-683-5213; *Fax:* 703-683-4074
Toll-Free: 800-928-3711
info@bottledwater.org
www.bottledwater.org
www.facebook.com/bottledwatermatters
twitter.com/BottledWaterOrg
www.youtube.com/user/BottledWaterMatters
Overview: A large international organization founded in 1958
Mission: To assure that safe, clean, good-tasting bottled water is produced & marketed to consumers
Chief Officer(s):
Joseph K. Doss, President
jdoss@bottledwater.org
Membership: 1,200; *Fees:* Schedule available
Activities: IBWA works closely with its member companies & with government officials; takes active role at all levels of local, state & federal governments to assist in the development of regulations for bottled water
Awards:
• Environmental Sustainability Award (Award)
• Route Salesperson of the Year Award (Award)
• Plant Manager of the Year Award (Award)
• Kristin Safran Directors' Award (Award)
• Supplier of the Year Award (Award)

International Brotherhood of Boilermakers, Iron Ship Builders, Blacksmiths, Forgers & Helpers (AFL-CIO) (IBB) / Fraternité internationale des chaudronniers, constructeurs de navires en fer, forgerons, forgeurs et aides (FAT-COI)
753 State Ave., Kansas City KS 66101 USA
Tel: 913-371-2640; *Fax:* 913-281-8101
www.boilermakers.org
Also Known As: Boilermakers
Overview: A large international organization founded in 1880
Mission: To represent workers employed in shipbuilding, manufacturing, railroads, cement, mining & related industries
Chief Officer(s):
Newton B. Jones, International President
ipjones@boilermakers.org
Finances: *Funding Sources:* Membership dues; Investments
Staff Member(s): 85
Membership: *Committees:* Departments: Accounting, Audit, Communications, Education & Training, Government Affairs, Industrial Health & Safety, Industrial Sector Services, Information Technology, Membership, Organizing, Research & Collective Bargaining Services
Activities: *Library*

Burlington (Toronto Lodge 128)
1035 Sutton Dr., Burlington ON L7L 5Z8
Tel: 905-332-0128; *Fax:* 905-332-9057
info@ibblocal128.org
128.boilermaker.ca

Burnaby (Vancouver Lodge 359)
4514 Dawson St., Burnaby BC V5C 4C1
Tel: 604-291-7531; *Fax:* 604-291-9265
memberservices@boilermakers359.org
www.boilermakers359.org

Calgary (Lodge 146)
11055 - 48 St. SE, Calgary AB T2C 1G8
Tel: 403-253-6976; *Fax:* 403-252-4187
www.boilermakers.ca

Edmonton (Lodge 146)
15220 - 114 Ave., Edmonton AB T5M 2Z2
Tel: 780-451-5992; *Fax:* 780-451-3927
info@boilermakers.ca
www.boilermakers.ca
Chief Officer(s):
Joseph Maloney, International Vice-President, Western Canada

Holyrood (Lodge 203)
PO Box 250, Holyrood NL A0A 2R0
Tel: 709-229-7958; *Fax:* 709-229-7300
dryan@nf.aibn.com

Montréal (Lodge 271)
1205, boul St. Jean Baptiste, Montréal QC H1B 4A2
Tel: 514-327-6135; *Fax:* 514-327-7294
local271@videotron.ca

Regina (Lodge 555)
214 - 4th Ave. East, Regina SK S4N 4Z6
Tel: 306-949-4452; *Fax:* 306-543-9339
local555@sasktel.net
www.boilermakerslocal555.org

Saint John (Lodge 73)
345 King William Rd., Saint John NB E2M 7C9
Tel: 506-634-7386; *Fax:* 506-634-0411
bm73@nbnet.nb.ca
www.boilermaker73.ca
Chief Officer(s):
Edward Power, International Vice-President, Eastern Canada

Thunder Bay (Lodge 555)
878A Tungsten St., Thunder Bay ON P7B 6J3
Tel: 807-623-8186; *Fax:* 807-623-9294
bmtbay@tbaytel.net
www.boilermakerslocal555.org

Truro (Lodge 73)
124 Parkway Dr., Truro Heighs NS B6L 1N8
Tel: 902-897-7306; *Fax:* 902-897-7305
bm73@ns.aliantzinc.ca
www.boilermaker73.ca

Victoria (Lodge 191)
802 Esquimalt Rd., Victoria BC V9A 3M4
Tel: 250-383-4196; *Fax:* 250-386-4688
lodge191adm@shaw.ca

Winnipeg (Lodge 555)
110 Haarsma Rd., East St. Paul MB R2E 0M8
Tel: 204-987-9200; *Fax:* 204-987-9219
local555@escape.ca
www.boilermakerslocal555.org

International Brotherhood of Electrical Workers (AFL-CIO/CFL) (IBEW) / Fraternité internationale des ouvriers en électricité (FAT-COI/FCT)
900 Seventh St. NW, Washington DC 20001 USA
Tel: 202-833-7000; *Fax:* 202-728-7676
www.ibew.org
www.facebook.com/IBEWFB
twitter.com/IBEW_IP
www.flickr.com/photos/58797631@N07
Overview: A large international organization founded in 1891
Mission: To represent members from a wide variety of fields, including utilities, construction, telecommunications, broadcasting, manufacturing, railroads & government
Chief Officer(s):
Robert W. Pierson, Chair, 708-449-9000, Fax: 708-449-9001
Edwin d. Hill, International President
Salvatore J. Chilia, International Secretary-Treasurer
Finances: *Annual Operating Budget:* $3 Million-$5 Million; *Funding Sources:* Membership dues
Staff Member(s): 198
Membership: 675,000
Activities: *Library* by appointment

Canadian Office
#300, 1450 Meyerside Dr., Mississauga ON L5T 2N5
Tel: 905-564-5441; *Fax:* 905-564-8114
ivpd_01@ibew.org
www.ibew.org/1stDistrict
Mission: The IBEW was founded in 1891, our first local union organized in Canada was Local Union 93, Ottawa, in 1899. The IBEW represents 725,000 members throughout Canada, United States, Panama, and Puerto Rico. The International Head Office is located in Washington, D.C. which houses our Museum, Archives, and state of the art computer and research departments.

International Brotherhood of Painters & Allied Trades (AFL-CIO/CFL) *See* International Union of Painters & Allied Trades

International Brotherhood of Teamsters (AFL-CIO/CLC) / Fraternité internationale des teamsters (FAT-COI/CTC)
25 Louisiana Ave. NW, Washington DC 20001 USA
Tel: 202-624-6800
www.teamster.org
Overview: A large international organization founded in 1903
Mission: The Teamsters are known as the champion of freight drivers and warehouse workers, but have organized workers in virtually every occupation imaginable, both professional and non-professional, private sector and public sector
Chief Officer(s):
James P. Hoffa, General President
Ken Hall, General Sec.-Treas.
Membership: 1,400,000 + 568 locals
Publications:
• Teamster
Type: Magazine; *Frequency:* Quarterly

Graphic Communications Conference
25 Louisianna Ave. NW, Washington DC 20001 USA
Tel: 202-624-6800
teamster.org/divisions/graphic-communications
Mission: To represent the interests of those who print, produce & design numerous publications, including major newspapers, magazines, books, brochures & catalogues.
Chief Officer(s):
George Tedeschi, President

International Caterers Association (ICA)
3601 East Joppa Rd., Baltimore MD 21234 USA
Tel: 418-931-8100; *Fax:* 418-931-8111
www.internationalcaterers.org
www.facebook.com/internationalcaterers
twitter.com/icacater
instagram.com/icacater
Merged from: Canadian Association of Caterers; National Caterers Association
Overview: A small international organization founded in 1981
Mission: To support, promote & improve all aspects of the business through publications, education, & demonstrations
Chief Officer(s):
Jennifer Perna, President
Paula Kreuzburg, Executive Director
paulak@internationalcaterers.org
Staff Member(s): 3
Membership: *Fees:* US$290 caterer; US$350 vendor; *Member Profile:* Licensed, professional off-premise & on-premise caterers, with liability insurance & food premises regularly inspected by a regional health department
Activities: Seminars, workshops & demonstrations on catering sales & marketing, regional & state of the art cuisine, event management, & legal issues; *Speaker Service:* Yes

International Center for Canadian-American Trade *See* Canada - United States Trade Center

International Centre for Research in Agroforestry (ICRAF) *See* World Agroforestry Centre

International Chamber of Commerce (ICC) / Chambre de Commerce Internationale
38, cours Albert 1er, Paris 75008 France
Tel: 33-149-53-28-28; *Fax:* 33-149-53-28-59
icc@iccwbo.org
www.iccwbo.org
Overview: A medium-sized international organization founded in 1919
Mission: Serving as the voice of world business, the ICC champions the global economy as a force for economic growth, job creation, & prosperity.
Affliation(s): United Nations; World Trade Organization
Chief Officer(s):
Dawn Chardonnal, Communications Manager
Marcus Wallenberg, Chair
Finances: *Funding Sources:* Membership fees; services & publications income
Membership: 5,000-14,999; *Fees:* US$1,500 local chambers of commerce, local companies, professional individuals; US$3,000 national chambers of commerce, national trade associations; *Member Profile:* Corporations & companies in all sectors of every size in more than 130 countries; National professional & sectoral associations; Business & employers federations; Law firms & consultancies; Chambers of commerce; Individuals involved in international business; *Committees:* National Committees assist their membership in formulating positions on international issues of relevance to them & ensuring that these views are represented effectively through the ICC to governments & international organizations
Activities: Setting rules & standards; Promoting growth & prosperity; Advocating for international business; Providing practical services to business; Fighting commercial crime

International Climbing & Mountaineering Federation *See* Union internationale des associations d'alpinisme

International Coalition of Fisheries Associations (ICFA)

c/o National Fisheries Institute, #700, 7918 Jones Branch Dr., McLean VA 22102 USA
Tel: 703-752-8880; *Fax:* 703-752-7583
www.icfa.net
Overview: A small international organization founded in 1988
Mission: To provide a unified voice for the world's commercial fishing industries in international forums; to preserve & maintain the oceans as a major source of food for the people of the world
Affliation(s): Fisheries Council of Canada
Membership: 1,000

International Commission for the Conservation of Atlantic Tunas (ICCAT)

Calle Corazón de María, 8, 6th Fl., Madrid 28002 Spain
Tel: 34-914-165-600; *Fax:* 34-914-152-612
info@iccat.int
www.iccat.int
Overview: A medium-sized international organization
Chief Officer(s):
Driss Meski, Executive Secretary
driss.meski@iccat.int
Juan Antonio Moreno, Department Head, Administration & Finance
juan.antonio@iccat.int
Staff Member(s): 25

International Commission of Agricultural & Biosystems Engineering / Commission Internationale du Genie Rural (CIGR)

c/o Dr. Takaaki Maekawa, School of Life & Environmental Sciences, 1-1-1 Tennodai, University of Tsukuba, Tsukuba, Ibaraki Japan
Tel: +81-29-875-6380; *Fax:* +81-29-875-6381
biopro@sakura.cc.tsukuba.ac.jp
www.cigr.org
Overview: A medium-sized international organization
Mission: To ensure food security & the sustainable use of natural resources, through the application of principles of technology & engineering science
Chief Officer(s):
Soren Pedersen, President
Takaaki Maekawan, Secretary General
biopro@sakura.cc.tsukuba.ac.jp
Yutaka Kitamura, Secretary
kitamura@sakura.cc.tsukuba.ac.jp
Membership: *Member Profile:* National organizations, such as the Canadian Society for Bioengineering; Regional organizations; Individuals; Corporations
Activities: Providing networking opportunities for regional & national societies of agricultural engineering, as well as for private & public companies & individuals throughout the world
Meetings/Conferences:
• International Commission of Agricultural & Biosystems Engineering 2016 4th International Conference of Agricultural Engineering (CIGR-AgEng2016), June, 2016, Aarhus
Scope: International
• International Commission of Agricultural & Biosystems Engineering XIX 2018 World Congress, April, 2018, Antalya
Scope: International
Publications:
• Agricultural Engineering International: The CIGR Journal of Scientific Research & Development
Type: Journal; *Editor:* Fedro S. Zazueta Ranahan
• CIGR [Commission Internationale du Genie Rural] Newsletter / Bulletin de la CIGR
Type: Newsletter; *Frequency:* Quarterly
Profile: Available in English, French, Arabic, Chinese, Russian, & Spanish

International Commission on Illumination (ICI) / Commission internationale de l'éclairage (CIE)

Kegelgasse 27, Vienna A-1030 Austria
Tel: 43-1-714-31870; *Fax:* 43-1-714-318718
ciecb@ping.at
www.cie.co.at
Also Known As: Internationale Beleuchtungs Kommission
Overview: A medium-sized international organization founded in 1910
Mission: To promote international cooperation & exchange of information among member countries on all matters relating to the science & art of lighting; to develop basic standards & procedures of metrology in the fields of light & lighting
Chief Officer(s):
Martina Paul, General Secretary
Membership: 39 national committees + 4 individual; *Committees:* CIE's National Committees have the responsibility for decisions on all matters relating to the organization; the composition of the National Committees varies from country to country, but each is required to represent & have the cooperation of all organizations having an interest in light & lighting
Activities: Technical committees; Publication of technical reports & standards; organizaing symposia

International Commission on Irrigation & Drainage (ICID) / Commission internationale des irrigations & du drainage

48 Nyaya Marg, Chanakyapuri, New Delhi 110021 India
Tel: 91-11-26116837; *Fax:* 91-11-26115962
icid@icid.org
www.icid.org
Overview: A small international organization founded in 1950
Mission: To stimulate & promote development & application of arts, sciences & techniques of engineering, agriculture, economics, ecology & social science in managing water & land resources for irrigation, drainage, flood control & river training &/or for research in a more comprehensive manner adopting up-to-date techniques; to help produce more food from irrigated agriculture on a global basis to alleviate want & hunger without disturbing the environment adversely
Affliation(s): International Commission on Irrigation & Drainage - Canadian National Committee
Chief Officer(s):
Avinash C. Tyagi, Secretary General
tyagi@icid.org
S.A. Kulkarni, Executive Secretary
kulkarni@icid.org
Staff Member(s): 25
Membership: 107 countries
Activities: *Library*

International Commission on Occupational Health (ICOH) / Commission internationale de la santé au travail (CIST)

INAIL, Italian Workers' Compensation Authority, Occupational Medicine, Via Fontana Candida 1, Monteporzio Catone, Rome I-00040 Italy
Tel: 39-06-941-815-06; *Fax:* 39-06-941-815-56
icoh@inail.it
www.icohweb.org
Overview: A small international organization founded in 1906
Mission: To foster scientific progress, knowledge & development of occupational health & safety in all its aspects
Affliation(s): International Association of Agricultural Medicine & Rural Health; International Federation of Associations of Specialists in Occupational Safety & Industrial Hygiene; International Social Security Association; ISSA International Section on Prevention of Occupational Risks in the Iron & Metal Industry
Chief Officer(s):
Kazutaka Kogi, President
k.kogi@isl.or.jp
Sergio Iavicoli, Secretary General
S.Iavicoli@inail.it
Finances: *Annual Operating Budget:* $100,000-$250,000
Staff Member(s): 2
Membership: 1,900 individual + 19 sustaining + 31 affiliate (in 93 countries); *Member Profile:* Individual & collective members; sustaining - organization, society, industry, or enterprise; affiliate - professional organization or a scientific society; *Committees:* 36 scientific committees & working groups
Activities: International congresses; special meetings; collaboration with international & national bodies & societies having similar aims;

International Committee for Documentation of the International Council of Museums (ICOM-CIDOC) / Comité international pour la documentation du Conseil international des musées (CIDOC)

Maison de l'UNESCO, Stn. Cedex 15, 1 rue Miollis, Paris France
Tel: 33-01-47-34-0500; *Fax:* 33-01-43-06-7862
www.icom.museum
Overview: A medium-sized international organization founded in 1956
Mission: To provide better methods & standards for the recording of museum information
Member of: International Council of Museums
Chief Officer(s):
Hans-Martin Hinz, President
Finances: *Funding Sources:* Membership stipend from ICOM 8 volunteer(s)
Membership: 750; *Member Profile:* Professionals working in museums documentation & information; *Committees:* 11 Working Groups - Archaeological Sites; Conceptual Reference Model; Contemporary Art; Digital Preservation; Documentation Standards; Ethno; Iconography; Internet; Multimedia; Museum Information Centres; Services
Activities: *Speaker Service:* Yes *Library:* Centre de documentation; by appointment

International Committee of Museums & Collections of Arms & Military History (ICOMAM)

c/o Secretary Mathieu Willemsen, Conservateur Armes à feu1, Legermuseum, Korte Geer 1, Delft NL-2611 Netherlands
Tel: 31 (0) 15 21 52 622; *Fax:* 31 (0) 15 21 52 608
secretary@icomam.icom.museum
www.klm-mra.be/icomam
Previous Name: International Association of Museums of Arms & Military History
Overview: A small international organization founded in 1957
Mission: To establish & maintain contact between museums & similar institutions within the range of interest of historical weapons & militaria, & to foster the study of objects within those fields
Affliation(s): ICOM (International Council of Museums)
Chief Officer(s):
Mathieu Willemsen, Secretary
Piet De Gryse, President
Membership: 265; *Member Profile:* Senior managers of collections of arms & militaria open to the public

International Committee of Sports for the Deaf (ICSD) / Comité international des Sports des Sourds (CISS)

PO Box 3441, Frederick MD 21701-3441 USA
Fax: 499-255-0436
office@ciss.org
www.deaflympics.com
www.facebook.com/Deaflympics
twitter.com/deaflympics
Also Known As: International Deaflympics
Overview: A medium-sized international charitable organization founded in 1924
Member of: International Olympic Committee; General Assembly of International Sports Federations
Affliation(s): Canadian Deaf Sports Association
Chief Officer(s):
Rukhledev Valery, President
president@ciss.org
Membership: 109 countries; *Member Profile:* National Deaf Sports Federations
Activities: Deaflympics; Deaf World Championships; *Internships:* Yes

International Committee on Alcohol, Drugs & Traffic Safety (ICADTS)

2901 Baxter Rd., Ann Arbor MI 48109-2050 USA
Tel: +31 734-764-6504; *Fax:* +41 734-936-1081
www.icadts.org
Overview: A small international organization founded in 1963
Mission: To reduce traffic related deaths & injuries by designing, promoting & implementing effective programs & policies, based on sound research
Chief Officer(s):
Jean Thatcher Shope, ICADTS Secretary
jshope@umich.edu
Finances: *Funding Sources:* Charitable donations; Memberships; Project grants; Contracts

International Computer Games Association (ICGA)

c/o David N.L. Levy, 34 Courthope Rd., Hampstead, London NW3 2LD England
info@icga.org
ilk.uvt.nl/icga
Overview: A small international organization founded in 1977
Mission: To promote computer games; To share technical knowledge; To foster developments in the man-machine area
Chief Officer(s):
David N.L. Levy, President
davidlevylondon@yahoo.com
Yngvi Björnsson, Vice-President
yngvi@ru.is
Hiroyuki Iida, Secretary-Treasurer
iida@jaist.ac.jp
Finances: *Funding Sources:* Membership fees; Sponsorships

Membership: *Fees:* US$50
Activities: Encouraging cooperation between computer game researchers; Supporting computer games tournament organizers & computer games organizations; Holding the World Computer-Chess Championships & the Computer Olympiads
Publications:
• ICGA Journal
Type: Journal; *Frequency:* Quarterly; *Price:* Free with membership in the International Computer Games Association
Profile: Featuring reports of computer-computer & man-machine events

International Confederation for Plastic Reconstructive & Aesthetic Surgery (IPRAS)

Zita Congress SA, PO Box 155, 1st km Peanias Markopoulou Ave, Peania Attica 190 02 Greece
Tel: (30) 211 100 1770-1; *Fax:* (30) 210 664 2216
zita@iprasmanagement.com
www.ipras.org
www.facebook.com/349996668374109
Overview: A large international organization founded in 1955
Mission: To promote plastic surgery both scientifically & clinically; To further education
Chief Officer(s):
Zacharias Kaplanidis, Executive Director
zacharias.kaplanidis@iprasmanagement.com
Maria Petsa, Assistant Executive Director
maria.petsa@iprasmanagement.com
Membership: Over 50,000; *Member Profile:* Plastic & aesthetic surgeons; Residents in training; Hand surgeons; Micro surgeons; Burn specialists
Meetings/Conferences:
• 18th World Congress of the International Confederation for Plastic Reconstructive & Aesthetic Surgery 2015, July, 2015, Hofburg Palace, Vienna
Scope: International
Contact Information: URL: www.ipras2015.com
Publications:
• Glovalplast
Type: Newsletter; *Frequency:* Annually
• IPRAS Journal
Type: Journal

International Confederation for Thermal Analysis & Calorimetry (ICTAC)

SONY Inst. of Higher Education, Dept. of Informatics & Media Tech., Atsugi, Kanagawa 243-8501 Japan
Tel: 81-46-247-3131; *Fax:* 81-46-250-8936
www.ictac.org
Overview: A large international organization founded in 1965
Mission: To promote the use of thermal analysis in science & technology; to strengthen the collaboration between scientists & technicians from different parts of the world
Member of: International Union of Pure & Applied Chemistry
Chief Officer(s):
Andrzej Malecki, President
malecki@agh.edu.pl
Riko Ozao, Membership Secretary
ozao@ei.shohoku.ac.jp
Finances: *Annual Operating Budget:* Less than $50,000
6 volunteer(s)
Membership: 500 full + 5,000 affiliate; *Fees:* US$20 student; US$100 individual; US$200 corporate; US$320 affiliate with less than 100 members; US$480 affiliate with more than 100 members; *Member Profile:* Open to scientists & technicians who are involved in thermal analysis; *Committees:* ICTAC Advisory; ICTAC Scientific Awards; ICTAC Congress Organising; Education; Environmental Safety; Geosciences; Kinetics; Lifetime Prediction of Materials; Nomenclature; Pharmaceuticals; Polymers; Sample Controlled Thermal Analysis; Standardization; Temperature Modulated Calorimetry; Thermal Analysis Combined Approach to Food Work; Thermal Reactivity; Thermochemistry
Activities: Scientific congress every four years
Awards:
• TA Instruments-ICTAC Award (Award), ICTAC Scientific Awards
• SETARAM - ICTAC Award for Calorimetry (Award), ICTAC Scientific Awards
• ICTAC Young Scientist Award (Award), ICTAC Scientific Awards
• ICTAC Honorary Lifetime Membership (Award), ICTAC Service Awards
• Robert Mackenzie Memorial Lectureship (Award)
• ICTAC Travel Grants (Award)

International Confederation of Midwives (ICM) / Confédération internationale de sages-femmes

Laan van Meerdervoort 70, The Hague 2517 AN Netherlands
Tel: 31-70-3060-520; *Fax:* 31-70-3555-651
info@internationalmidwives.org
www.internationalmidwives.org
www.linkedin.com/company/international-confederation-of-midwives-icm-
www.facebook.com/InternationalConfederationofMidwives
twitter.com/world_midwives
Previous Name: International Union of Midwives
Overview: A medium-sized international charitable organization founded in 1919
Mission: To advance, worldwide, the aims & aspirations of midwives in the attainment of improved outcomes for women in their childbearing years, their newborn, & their families, wherever they reside
Affiliation(s): Association of Ontario Midwives; Alberta Association of Midwives; Midwives Association of British Columbia
Chief Officer(s):
Agneta S. Bridges, Secretary General
Finances: *Annual Operating Budget:* $250,000-$500,000;
Funding Sources: Capitation fees; fundraising
Staff Member(s): 6; 2 volunteer(s)
Membership: 90 member associations worldwide; *Fees:* Based on number of midwives in association; *Member Profile:* Independent associations of midwives, or midwives groups within other organizations, provided that the midwives group is autonomous & responsible for the affairs of midwifery; *Committees:* Council; Executive; Board of Management
Activities: Safe Motherhood workshops; triennial congresses; *Library* by appointment

International Confederation of Principals (ICP)

ICP Secretariat, 68 Martin St., Heidelberg, Victoria 3084 Australia
Tel: + 61 3 9326 8077; *Fax:* + 61 3 9326 8147
www.icponline.org
Overview: A medium-sized international organization
Mission: To support the professional development & work of school leaders from over forty countries; To act as the voice for school education
Chief Officer(s):
Andrew Blair, President
ablair@vassp.org.au
Ted Brierley, Executive Secretary
brierted@optusnet.com.au
Lisa Vincent, Regional Representative, Americas, 613-962-9295 Ext. 2119, Fax: 613-962-1047
lvincent@hpedsb.on.ca
Membership: 40+ school leadership associations; *Member Profile:* School leadership organizations from five continents, with constitutions in agreement with the ICP constitution
Activities: Enhancing the professionalism of school leaders; Providing professional learning for school leaders; Offering access to current educational research; Encouraging equal opportunities for young people; Developing curricula that promotes international understanding
Meetings/Conferences:
• International Confederation of Principals (ICP) 12th World Convention, August, 2015, Helsinki
Scope: International
Attendance: 2,000+
Description: A convention of interest to principals vice-principals, education leaders, academics, researchers, policy makers, & government representatives from around the world
Contact Information: Executive Secretary: Toni Lehtinen, E-mail: icp2015@surefire.fi; URL: www.confedent.fi/icp2015
Publications:
• International Confederation of Principals Newsletter
Type: Newsletter
Profile: Executive news & information from around the world

International Continence Society (ICS)

19 Portland Sq., Bristol BS2 8SJ United Kingdom
Tel: +44 117 9444881; *Fax:* +44 117 9444882
info@icsoffice.org
www.icsoffice.org
Overview: A medium-sized international organization
Mission: To further education, clinical practice, & scientific research; To remove the stigma of incontinence
Chief Officer(s):
Jacques Corcos, General Secretary
Ajay Singla, Treasurer
Avicia Burchill, Manager, Administration
Membership: *Member Profile:* Medical professionals; *Committees:* Children's; Continence Promotion; Education; Ethics; Executive; Fistula; Meetings; Neuro-urology Promotion; Nursing; Physiotherapy; Publications & Communications; Scientific; Standardization
Activities: Providing educational opportunities; *Speaker Service:* Yes
Meetings/Conferences:
• International Continence Society (ICS) 2015 45th Annual Scientific Meeting, October, 2015, Palais des congrès de Montréal, Montréal, QC
Scope: International
Description: Educational workshops & a scientific meeting for urological, gynaecological, physiotherapy, & nursing professionals. This year's meeting is held jointly with the International Urogynecological Association.
Publications:
• ICS [International Continence Society] Newsletter
Type: Newsletter; *Price:* Free with International Continence Society membership
• International Continence Society Membership Directory
Type: Directory
Profile: Continence professionals throughout the world
• Neurourology & Urodynamics
Type: Journal; *Frequency:* Bimonthly; *Price:* Free with International Continence Society membership

International Cooperative Alliance (ICA)

PO Box 2100, 150, Route de Ferney, Geneva 1211 Switzerland
Tel: 41-22-929-8838; *Fax:* 41-22-798-4122
ica@ica.coop
ica.coop
Overview: A medium-sized international organization founded in 1895
Mission: To unite, represent & serve cooperatives worldwide
Chief Officer(s):
Ivano Barberini, President
Membership: 233 national & international cooperative
Meetings/Conferences:
• 2016 International Summit of Cooperatives, 2016
Scope: International
Contact Information: info@intlsummit.coop

International Council for Applied Mineralogy (ICAM)

Federal Institute for Geosciences & Natural Resources, B4.15 Inorganic Geochemistry, Stilleweg 2, Hannover D-30655 Germany
Tel: 49-511-643-2565; *Fax:* 49-511-643-3685
icam2000@bgr.de
www.bgr.de/icam
Overview: A small international organization founded in 1981
Mission: To promote scientific & technical interests of applied mineralogy by providing an international forum for exchange of ideas
Affliation(s): National Mineralogical Association - USA, Australia, South Africa, Europe, Brazil, South America, Poland; International Mineralogical Association
Chief Officer(s):
Dieter Rammlmair, Secretary General
rammlmair@bgr.de
Finances: *Annual Operating Budget:* Less than $50,000;
Funding Sources: Meeting registrations; donations
Membership: 20; *Member Profile:* Professionals in the field

International Council for Archaeozoology (ICAZ)

c/o University Of Sheffield, Department of Archaeology, Northgate House, West St., Sheffield S1 4ET England
icaz@alexandriaarchive.org
www.alexandriaarchive.org/icaz/
Overview: A small international charitable organization founded in 1976
Mission: To develop & stimulate archaeozoological research; To strengthen cooperation among archaeozoologists; To foster cooperation with archaeologists & scientists working in related fields; To promote high ethical & scientific standards for archaeozoological work
Affliation(s): International Union of Prehistoric & Protohistoric Sciences
Chief Officer(s):
László Bartosiewicz, President
h10459bar@ella.hu
Umberto Albarella, Secretary
u.albarella@sheffield.ac.uk
Finances: *Annual Operating Budget:* Less than $50,000;
Funding Sources: Membership fees

Membership: 383; *Fees:* US$15; *Member Profile:* University staff; museums; freelance; *Committees:* Working Groups; Fish Remains; Bird Remains; Archaeozoology of Southwestern Asia & Adjacent Areas; Camelid; Animal Pathology; Worked Bone; North Atlantic Bioarchaeological Organization

International Council for Central & East European Studies (Canada) (ICCEES) / Conseil international d'études de l'Europe centrale et orientale (Canada)

c/o Dept. Government & International Relations, University of Sydney, Sydney NSW 2006 Australia
Tel: 61-2-9351 3090; *Fax:* 61-2-9351 3624
www.iccees.org
Overview: A small international organization founded in 1974
Mission: To foster study of East European affairs & to encourage dissemination of this knowledge among specialists; To create an international community of scholars.
Affliation(s): American Assoc. for the Advancement of Slavic Studies; Assoc. hellénique d'études Slaves; Associazione Italiana degli Slavisti; Australasian Assoc. for the Study of the Socialist Countries; Australia & New Zealand Slavists' Association; British Association for Soviet, Slavonic & East European Studies; Canadian Association of Slavists; Centre Belge D'Études Slaves; Deutsche Gesellschaft für Osteuropakunde; Dutch Slavists' Assoc.; Finnish Institute for Russian & East European Studies; Institut d'études slaves; Irish Slavists' Association; Israeli Association of Slavic & East European Studies
Chief Officer(s):
Graeme Gill, President
graeme.gill@sydney.edu.au
Andrii Krawchuk, Member, Canada
AKrawchuk@usudbury.ca
Finances: *Annual Operating Budget:* Less than $50,000
5 volunteer(s)
Membership: 8,000 in 18 national associations; *Fees:* US$1; *Member Profile:* Professor; researcher; *Committees:* Executive
Activities: *Speaker Service:* Yes

International Council for Laboratory Animal Science (ICLAS) / Conseil international des sciences de l'animal de laboratoire

40 Washington St., Brussels 1050 Belgium
info@iclas.org
www.iclas.org
Overview: A small international organization founded in 1956
Mission: To promote the humane use of animals in research through recognition of ethical principles & scientific responsibilities; to be an advocate for the advancement of laboratory animal science & biological research resources throughout the world; to promote international collaboration as a worldwide resource of knowledge in laboratory animal science; to promote the production & monitoring of high-quality laboratory animals by establishing standards & providing support resources
Affliation(s): Canadian Association for Laboratory Animal Science
Chief Officer(s):
Patri Vergara, President
Cynthia Pekow, Acting Secretary General
Membership: 30 national; 33 scientific; 5 union; 21 associate; 2 institutional; *Fees:* Schedule available; *Committees:* Communications; Education & Training; Finance; Europe Regional; Africa Regional; Americas Regional; Asia Regional; Australia & New Zealand Regional; Harmonization; Membership; Ethics & Animal Welfare
Activities: Scientific meetings; reference & monitoring centres; training courses; publications
Meetings/Conferences:
• XVI International Council for Laboratory Animal Science General Assembly & 54th Annual Symposium, May, 2015, Palais des congrès de Montréal, Montréal, QC
Scope: International

International Council for Local Environmental Initiatives (ICLEI)

World Secretariat, Kaiser-Friedrich-Str. 7, Bonn 53113 Germany
Tel: 49-228-97-62-99-00; *Fax:* 49-228-97-62-99-01
iclei@iclei.org
www.iclei.org
Overview: A small international organization founded in 1990
Mission: To build & serve a worldwide movement of local governments to achieve tangible improvements in global environmental & sustainable development conditions through cumulative local actions
Affliation(s): International Union of Local Authorities
Chief Officer(s):
Gino Van Begin, Secretary General
Monika Zimmermann, Deputy Secretary General
Finances: *Funding Sources:* Membership dues; project funding
Membership: *Fees:* Schedule available; *Committees:* Executive; Regional Executive; Management
Activities: *Library* by appointment

International Council for the Exploration of the Sea (ICES)

H.C. Andersens Blvd. 44-46, Copenhagen VDK-1553 Denmark
Tel: 45-3338-6700; *Fax:* 45-3393-4215
info@ices.dk
www.ices.dk
Overview: A medium-sized international organization
Mission: To coordinate research & monitor activities to understand the marine environment & resources & man's impact upon them, including the identification of priority marine contaminants, their distribution, transport & effects; to provide advice regarding marine resources & pollution to member governments & international regulatory commissions; to publish & disseminate the results of research
Chief Officer(s):
Gerd Hubold, General Secretary
David Gillis, ICES Delegate, Canada
dave.gillis@dfo-mpo.gc.ca
Ariane Plourde, ICES Delegate, Canada
ariane.plourde@dfo-mpo.gc.ca

International Council of Associations for Science Education (ICASE) / Fédération Internationale des Associations de Professeurs de Sciences (FIAPS)

info@icaseonline.net
www.icaseonline.net
Overview: A small international organization founded in 1973
Mission: To improve science education worldwide by assisting member organizations
Affliation(s): Canadian Association for Science Education
Chief Officer(s):
Beverley Cooper, Secretary
bcooper@waikato.ac.nz
Teresa J. Kennedy, President
tkennedy@uttyler.edu
Dennis Chisman, Treasurer
Finances: *Annual Operating Budget:* Less than $50,000; *Funding Sources:* Membership fees
Staff Member(s): 1; 14 volunteer(s)
Membership: 155 organizations; *Fees:* Schedule available; *Member Profile:* Organization involved in science education
Activities: Project 2000+, providing appropriate science & technology education for all; exchange of teaching resources; science education research & its application in teaching; exchanges of science teaching personnel

International Council of Ballroom Dancing *See* World Dance Council Ltd.

International Council of Environmental Law (ICEL) / Conseil international du droit de l'environnement (CIDE)

Godesberger Allee 108-112, Bonn D-53175 Germany
Tel: 49-228-2692-240; *Fax:* 49-228-2692-251
icel@intlawpol.org
www.i-c-e-l.org
Overview: A small international organization founded in 1969
Mission: Promoting the exchange of information on the legal, administrative and policy aspects of environmental conservation and sustainable development, to support new initiatives in this field, and to encourage advice and assistance through its network.
Member of: The World Conservation Union
Chief Officer(s):
Wolfgang E. Burhenne, Executive Governor
Finances: *Funding Sources:* Donations
Membership: 340
Activities: ICEL Reference to Environmental Policy & Law Literature; Bulletin online; *Library* by appointment

International Council of Museums (ICOM) / Conseil international des musées

Maison de l'UNESCO, 1, rue Miollis, Cedex 15, Paris 75732 France
Tel: 33-1-47-34-05-00; *Fax:* 33-1-43-06-78-62
secretariat@icom.museum
www.icom.museum
Overview: A medium-sized international organization founded in 1946
Mission: To communicate to society the conservation & continuation of the world's natural & cultural heritage, present & future, tangible & intangible
Affliation(s): International Association of Agricultural Museums; Association of Museums of the Indian Ocean; Commonwealth Association of Museums; International Association of Arms & Military History Museums; International Association of Transport & Communications Museums; International Confederation of Architectural Museums; International Congress of Maritime Museums; Museums Association of the Caribbean; International Movement for a New Museology; Association of European Open-Air Museums; Southern Africa Development Community Association of Museums & Monuments; International Society of Libraries & Museums
Chief Officer(s):
Julien Anfruns, Director General
Hans Martin Hinz, President
Dominique Ferriot, Treasurer
Membership: 24,000 in 150 countries; *Member Profile:* Museum professionals; museums; *Committees:* 117 national committees; 30 international committees
Activities: Reinforcing regional cooperative networks; Providing professional training & exchange; Promoting professional ethics; Fighting against illicit traffic of cultural property; Protecting world heritage; Increasing public awareness of museums; Training personnel; *Awareness Events:* International Museums Day, May 18 *Library* by appointment
Publications:
• ICOM News
Type: Newsletter; *Frequency:* Quarterly; *Editor:* Lysa Hochroth; *Price:* Free to ICOM members

International Council of Ophthalmology (ICO)

#10, 945 Green St., San Francisco CA 94133 USA
Fax: 415-409-8411
info@icoph.org
www.icoph.org
www.linkedin.com/company/713250
www.facebook.com/InternationalCouncilOphthalmology
twitter.com/intlcounciloph
Overview: A small international charitable organization founded in 1857
Mission: To advocate the prevention & treatment of preventable blindness in developing nations; to support the International Agency for the Prevention of Blindness & Vision 2020: Right to Sight with WHO; to support educational competency in ophthalmologic education worldwide; to evaluate & coordinate standardization in ophthalmology; to support ophthalmologic interchange through supranational organizations & international congresses
Member of: International Federation of Ophthalmological Societies
Affliation(s): Canadian Ophthalmological Society
Chief Officer(s):
Kathleen Miller, Executive Director
kmiller@icoph.org
Bruce E. Spivey, President
Finances: *Funding Sources:* Membership dues
Staff Member(s): 12
Membership: 120 national ophthalmological societies; *Fees:* Sliding scale based on national members; *Member Profile:* Recognized world ophthalmic leaders; *Committees:* Education; Advocacy; Accreditation & Certification; Continuing Professional Development; Curricula & Expectations for Training Programs; Teaching the Teachers; Technologies for Teaching & Learning; Training Teams to Meet Public Needs; Ethics; Eye Care Delivery; Examinations; Examinations Educational Advisors & Steering; Fellowship; G.O.H. Naumann Award; Guidelines; Society & Leadership Development; Strategic Planning
Activities: Oversight of educational, professional & scientific interchange worldwide in ophthalmology
Awards:
• Gonin Medal (Award)
• International Duke Elder Medal (Award)
• Jules Francois Golden Medal (Award)
• Ophthalmic Pathology Award (Award)

International Council of Prison Medical Services *See* World Health Organization Health in Prisons Programme

International Council of Voluntary Agencies (ICVA) / Conseil International des Agences Bénévoles

26-28, av Guiseppe Motta, Geneva CH-1202 Switzerland
Tel: 41-22-950-9600; *Fax:* 41-22-950-9609
secretariat@icva.ch
www.icva.ch

Overview: A large international organization founded in 1962
Mission: To promote & advocate for human rights & a humanitarian perspective in global debates & responses
Affliation(s): Standing invitee of UN's Inter-Agency Standing Committee (IASC)
Chief Officer(s):
Penny Lawrence, Chair
Ed Schenkenberg van Mierop, Executive Director
ed.schenkenberg@icva.ch
Finances: *Annual Operating Budget:* $250,000-$500,000; *Funding Sources:* Membership dues; governments; foundations
Staff Member(s): 3; 2 volunteer(s)
Membership: 75+ agencies; *Fees:* Schedule available; *Member Profile:* International & regional voluntary agencies, national umbrella groups, major national non-government organizations
Activities: Mobilizing of voluntary agencies on humanitarian assistance, human rights; facilitation of voluntary agency action on these concerns; representation of collective voluntary agency views on these matters

International Council on Jewish Social & Welfare Services

c/o AJJDC, 711 Third Ave., New York NY 10017-4014 USA
Tel: 212-687-6200; *Fax:* 212-370-5467
Also Known As: INTERCO
Overview: A medium-sized international organization

International Council on Monuments & Sites (ICOMOS) / Conseil international des Monuments et des Sites

#49, 51, rue de la Fédération, Paris 75015 France
Tel: 33-1-45-67-67-70; *Fax:* 33-1-45-66-06-22
secretariat@icomos.org
www.icomos.org
twitter.com/icomos
Overview: A medium-sized international organization founded in 1965
Mission: ICOMOS works for the conservation and protection of cultural heritage places, with a focus on the application of theory, methodology and scientific techniques for conservation.
Chief Officer(s):
Gustavo Araoz, President
Bernadette Bertel-Rault, Secretary General
Staff Member(s): 9; 2 volunteer(s)
Membership: 9,500 worldwide; *Member Profile:* Architects & specialists in the conservation & renovation of built heritage
Activities: *Library:* UNESCO-ICOMOS Documentation Centre; Open to public

International Curling Federation *See* World Curling Federation

International Dairy Federation (IDF) / Fédération internationale de Laiterie (FIL)

70B Auguste Reyers Blvd., Brussels 1030 Belgium
Tel: 32-2-325-6740; *Fax:* 32-2-325-6741
info@fil-idf.org
www.fil-idf.org
www.linkedin.com/company/2265490
twitter.com/FIL_IDF
Overview: A small international organization founded in 1903
Mission: To promote through international cooperation & consultation, the solution of scientific, technical & economic problems in the international dairy field
Member of: International Council of Scientific Unions
Chief Officer(s):
Nico van Belzen, Director General
nvanbelzen@fil-idf.org
Pierre Doyle, Executive Director, IDF Canada
pierre.doyle@agr.gc.ca
Staff Member(s): 11
Membership: 48 national committees; *Committees:* Science & Programming Coordination
Activities: Scientific & technical cooperation within dairy sector; *Library* by appointment

International Economic History Association / Association internationale d'histoire économique

c/o University of Tuebingen, Department of Economic History, Mohlstrasse 36, Tuebingen 72074 Germany
Tel: 49 7071 29 72985; *Fax:* 49 7071 29 5119
ieha@uni-tuebingen.de
www.uni-tuebingen.de/ieha/
Overview: A small international organization
Mission: To unite economic historians from countries in Africa, America, Asia, Europe and Oceania.
Affliation(s): Comité international des sciences historiques
Chief Officer(s):
Jan Luiten van Zanden, President
Membership: 45; *Member Profile:* Associations involved with economic history; *Committees:* Local Organizing; Executive

International Ergonomics Association

Department of Industrial Engineering, National Tsing Hua University, 101, Sec. 2 Guang Fu Rd., Hsinchu 30013 Taiwan
Tel: 886-3-574-2649; *Fax:* 886-3-572-6153
www.iea.cc
Overview: A small international organization
Mission: To elaborate & advance ergonomics science & practice & to improve the quality of life by expanding its scope of application & contribution to society
Chief Officer(s):
Eric Min-yang Wang, Secretary General
mywang@ie.nthu.edu.tw
Membership: *Committees:* Policy & Planning; Professional Standards & Education; Science, Technology & Practice; Communications & Public Relations; Industrially Developing Countries; Awards
Awards:
- K.U. Smith Student Paper Award (Award)
- IEA/Liberty Mutual Prize in Occupational Safety & Ergonomics (Award)
- IEA Fellow Award (Award)
- Distinguished Service Award (Award)
- Outstanding Educators Award (Award)
- Award for Promotion of Ergonomics in Industrially Developing Countries (Award)
- Ergonomics Development Award (Award)
- President's Award (Award)

International Erosion Control Association (IECA)

#3500, 3401 Quebec St., Denver CO 80207 USA
Tel: 1-303-640-7554; *Fax:* 866-308-3087
Toll-Free: 800-455-4322
ecinfo@ieca.org
www.ieca.org
www.facebook.com/erosioncontrol
Overview: A medium-sized international organization founded in 1972
Mission: Serves as a global resource for environmental education & exchange of information; represents, leads & unifies a diverse group of people worldwide who share a common responsibility for the causes, prevention & control of erosion
Chief Officer(s):
Philip Handley, President
Finances: *Annual Operating Budget:* $500,000-$1.5 Million; *Funding Sources:* Membership dues; conferences; courses; publications
Staff Member(s): 10
Membership: 3,500 members in 52 countries; *Fees:* Schedule available; *Member Profile:* 17 Professional Fields of Practice: Academic, Consultant, Contractor, Developer, Engineer, Government Agency, Landscape Architect, Library, Mining, Non-Profit, Publisher, Ski Industry, Supplier, Utility Company, & Other
Activities: Professional development courses; field trips & tours throughout the world; training bureau; scholarship program; research grant program & an erosion control material standards program; *Speaker Service:* Yes

International Facility Management Association (IFMA)

#900, 800 Gessner Rd., Houston TX 77024-4257 USA
Tel: 713-623-4362; *Fax:* 713-623-6124
ifma@ifma.org
www.ifma.org
www.linkedin.com/groups?gid=38141
www.facebook.com/InternationalFacilityManagementAssociation
twitter.com/IFMA
www.youtube.com/ifmaglobal
Overview: A small international charitable organization founded in 1980
Mission: To lead & sustain progress of the facility management profession
Affliation(s): Facility Management Nederland; Health Care Institute; Bulgarian Facility Management Association; British Institute of Facilities Management; Facilities Management Association of Australia; American Society for Healthcare Engineering; ASHRAE; Building & Construction Authority; European Facility Management Network; German Facility Management Association; Japan Facility Management Association; Society of American Military Engineers; South African Facilities Management Association; U.S. Environmental Protection Agency; U.S. Green Building Council
Chief Officer(s):
Tony Keane, President & CEO
tony.keane@ifma.org
Andrea E. Sanchez, Director, Communications
andrea.sanchez@ifma.org
Finances: *Funding Sources:* Dues; educational programs; publications
Staff Member(s): 11
Membership: 23,000+; *Fees:* US$179 professional; US$179 associate; US$10 student; US$100 retired; US$99 young professional; *Member Profile:* Facility management executives, consultants & suppliers; real estate executives; security experts; designers
Activities: Certification, education, research, trade shows, publications, lobbying; *Speaker Service:* Yes; *Rents Mailing List:* Yes

International Federation for Cell Biology (IFCB)

www.ifcbiol.org
Overview: A medium-sized international organization founded in 1972
Mission: To promote cooperation & to contribute to the advancement of cell biology in all its branches
Affliation(s): International Union of Biological Sciences; International Cell Research Organization
Chief Officer(s):
Denys Wheatley, President, United Kingdom
pat028@abdn.ac.uk
Hernandez F. Carvalho, Secretary General, Brazil
hern@unicamp.br
Membership: 15 member organizations representing 60 nations; *Fees:* US$200

International Federation for Home Economics (IFHE)

Kaiser - Friedrich - Strasse 13, Bonn D - 53113 Germany
Tel: 49-0-228-921-2590; *Fax:* 49-0-228-921-2591
office@ifhe.org
www.ifhe.org
Overview: A small international charitable organization founded in 1908
Mission: To provide an international forum for home economists; To develop & express the home economics concerns for individuals, families, & households at the United Nations & among other international non-governmental organizations, whose interests parallel those of home economics
Affliation(s): Canadian Home Economics Association
Chief Officer(s):
Carol Warren, Presidnet
Elisabeth Leicht-Eckardt, Treasurer General
Membership: *Fees:* €50 individual; €25 individuals in developing countries; €20 students; €250 organization; *Member Profile:* Individuals & students participating in practise, education or research of home economics or who are interested in these topics; Professional associations, universities, schools, & other organizations involved in home economics; Businesses & industries concerned with home economics; *Committees:* Executive; United Nations; Finance; Membership; IFHE Congress; Young Professionals Network; Publication & Communication; Think Tank; Research; Project Assessment; Senior Advisory; Accredition/Certification; Partnerships; Consumers & Sustainable Development; Family (and Gender); Food Security & Nutrition & Nutritional Health; Home Economics Policies in Education and Training; Household Technology & Sustainability; IFHE International Business Group; Institutional & Hospitality Management; Outreach to Central & East European Countries; Textiles & Design
Activities: Promoting continuing education; Providing opportunities for global networking; *Library:* National Archives; Open to public
Publications:
- Home Economics News

Type: Newsletter; *Frequency:* Quarterly

International Federation for Housing & Planning (IFHP) / Fédération internationale pour l'habitation, l'urbanisme et l'aménagement des territoires (FIHUAT)

Binckhorstlaan 36, M04-03, The Hague 2516 BE Netherlands
Tel: 31-70-324-4557; *Fax:* 31-70-328-2085
info@ifhp.org
www.ifhp.org
www.facebook.com/50479462167
twitter.com/ifhp
Previous Name: International Garden Cities & Town Planning Association

Overview: A medium-sized international organization founded in 1913
Mission: To plan & organize activities; To create opportunities for an exchange of professional knowledge & experience
Chief Officer(s):
Derek Martin, Secretary General
d.martin@ifhp.org
Membership: 500-999; *Member Profile:* Organizations or individuals who support the aims & objectives of IFHP, & who wish to participate in a worldwide network
Activities: Offering conferences, seminars, symposia, & study tours; Organizing student & film & video competitions
Publications:
• IFHP [International Federation for Housing & Planning] Membership List & Directory
Type: Directory; *Number of Pages:* 77; *Price:* Free for members only

International Federation for Medical & Biological Engineering (IFMBE)

office@ifmbe.org
www.ifmbe.org
Overview: A medium-sized international organization founded in 1959
Mission: To reflect the interests & initiatives of national affiliated organizations; to generate & disseminate information of interest to the medical & biological engineering community & international organizations; to provide an international forum for the exchange of ideas & concepts; to encourage & foster research & application of medical & biological engineering knowledge & techniques in support of life quality & cost-effective health care; to stimulate international cooperation & collaboration on medical & biological engineering matters; to encourage educational programs that develop scientific & technical expertise in medical & biological engineering. IFMBE Secretariat currently located in Stockholm, Sweden.
Affiliation(s): International Union of Physical & Engineering Sciences in Medicine; International Organization for Medical Physics
Chief Officer(s):
Herbert F. Voigt, President, Boston University, USA
hfv@bu.edu
Ratko Magjarevic, Vice President, University of Zagreb, Croatia
ratko.magjarevic@fer.hr
Staff Member(s): 2
Membership: 48 countries; *Fees:* Schedule available; *Committees:* Finance; Constitution & Bylaws; Secretaries; Working Groups: Asian Pacific Activities; Developing Countries; European Activities; Women in MBE; Regional Liaisons; International Liaisons; Nominating; Publication & Publicity; Federation Journal
Meetings/Conferences:
• World Congress on Medical Physics and Biomedical Engineering 2015, June, 2015, Toronto, ON
Scope: International
Description: The Congresses are scheduled on a three-year basis and aligned with Federation's General Assembly meeting at which elections are held.
• World Congress on Medical Physics and Biomedical Engineering 2018, 2018, Prague
Scope: International
Description: The Congresses are scheduled on a three-year basis and aligned with Federation's General Assembly meeting at which elections are held.

International Federation for Research in Women's History (IFRWH) / Fédération internationale pour la recherche en histoire des femmes (FIRHF)

Dept. of Philosophy & Social Sciences, St. Kliment Ohridski University of Sofia, 15 Tsar Osvoboditel Blvd., Sofia 1504 Bulgaria
krasi@sclg.uni-sofia.bg
www.ifrwh.com
Overview: A small international organization founded in 1990
Mission: To promote women's history around the world
Member of: International Committee for Historical Sciences
Chief Officer(s):
Clare Midgley, President
c.c.midgley@shu.ac.uk
Finances: *Annual Operating Budget:* Less than $50,000
Membership: 36; *Fees:* 20 pounds/$30; *Member Profile:* National committees on women's history
Activities: Conferences; publications

International Federation of Accountants (IFAC)

545 Fifth Ave., 14th Fl., New York NY 10017 USA
Tel: 212-286-9344; *Fax:* 212-286-9570
Communications@ifac.org
www.ifac.org
www.linkedin.com/company/ifac
www.facebook.com/InternationalFederationOfAccountants
twitter.com/IFAC_Update
www.youtube.com/user/IFACMultimedia
Overview: A medium-sized international organization founded in 1977
Mission: Worldwide development & enhancement of an accountancy profession with harmonized standards, able to provide services of consistently high quality in the public interest
Affiliation(s): Canadian Institute of Chartered Accountants; Certified General Accountants Association of Canada; Society of Management Accountants of Canada
Chief Officer(s):
Warren Allan, President
Olivia Kirtley, Deputy President
Fayezul Choudhury, Chief Executive Officer
Laura Wilker, Director, Communications
LauraWilker@ifac.org
Staff Member(s): 12
Membership: 179; *Member Profile:* National accountancy bodies; *Committees:* Compliance Advisory Panel; Developing Nations; Nominating; Professional Accountancy Organization Development; Professional Accountants in Business; Small & Medium Practices; Transnational Auditors

International Federation of Agricultural Producers (IFAP-FIPA) / Fédération Internationale des Producteurs Agricoles

60, rue Saint-Lazare, Paris F-75009 France
Tel: 33-1-45-26-05-53; *Fax:* 33-1-48-74-72-12
www.ifap.org
www.facebook.com/profile.php?id=1215442884
twitter.com/worldfarmers
Overview: A medium-sized international organization founded in 1946
Mission: To secure the fullest cooperation between organizations of agricultural primary producers in meeting the optimum nutritional & consumptive requirements of the peoples of the world & in improving the economic & social status of all who live by & on the land
Affiliation(s): Canadian Federation of Agriculture
Chief Officer(s):
David King, Secretary General
david.king@ifap.org
Ajay Vashee, President, (Zambia)
Finances: *Annual Operating Budget:* $500,000-$1.5 Million
Staff Member(s): 10
Membership: 120 farmers' organizations in 79 countries; *Member Profile:* Representative of farmers at the national level; *Committees:* African Regional; Asia Regional; Mediterranean Regional; Agricultural Cooperatives; Women in Agriculture; Development Cooperation; Latin America & the Caribbean

International Federation of Aircraft Technology & Engineering *See* International Federation of Airworthiness

International Federation of Airworthiness (IFA)

14 Railway Approach, East Grinstead, West Sussex RH19 1BP United Kingdom
Tel: 44-1342-301-788; *Fax:* 44-1342-317-808
www.ifairworthy.com
Previous Name: International Federation of Aircraft Technology & Engineering
Overview: A medium-sized international charitable organization founded in 1975
Mission: Dedicated to improving aviation safety by increasing international communications, awareness & cooperation on all aspects of airworthiness particularly continuing airworthiness
Member of: Flight Safety Foundation; Aeronautical Repair Station Association
Chief Officer(s):
John W. Saull, Executive Director
Maurice E. Hare, Deputy Executive Director/Treasurer
Finances: *Annual Operating Budget:* $50,000-$100,000; *Funding Sources:* Membership fees
10 volunteer(s)
Membership: 115 corporate; *Fees:* US$800; *Member Profile:* Corporate bodies; *Committees:* Technical; Executive Council; Scholarship
Activities: Organizes Annual Technical Conferences on Air Safety; updates IFA members on proposed changes to airworthiness requirements & procedures; provides a forum for discussion of airworthiness problems; establishes IFA opinion on outstanding airworthiness problems; IFA Newsextra (emailed) newsletter
Awards:
• IFA Whittle Safety Award (Award)

International Federation of Beekeepers' Associations

Corso Vittorio Emanuele 101, Rome I-00186 Italy
Tel: 39-06-685-2286; *Fax:* 39-06-685-2287
apimondia@mclink.it
www.apimondia.org
Also Known As: APIMONDIA
Overview: A medium-sized international organization founded in 1897
Mission: Working with beekeepers' associations, scientific bodies, & individuals involved in apiculture, APIMONDIA promotes apicultural development in all countries, scientifically, ecologically, socially & economically.
Affiliation(s): Canadian Honey Council
Chief Officer(s):
Gilles Ratia, President
gilles@apiservices.com

International Federation of Business & Professional Women (IFBPW) / Fédération internationale des femmes de carrières libérales et commerciales

PO Box 2042, Stn. Fitzroy, Victoria 3065 Australia
Other Communication: Membership e-mail: member.services@bpw-international.org
presidents.office@bpw-international.org
www.bpw-international.org
www.facebook.com/bpw.international
Also Known As: BPW International
Overview: A large international organization founded in 1930
Mission: To organize business & professional women in all parts of the world to use their combined abilities & strengths for the attainment of the following objectives: To work for equal opportunities & status for women in the economic, civil & political life of all countries & the removal of discrimination; To encourage women & girls to acquire eduction, occupational training & advanced education & use their occupational capacities & intelligence for the advantage of others as well as themselves; To improve the position of women in business, trade & the professions, & in the economic life of their countries; To stimulate & encourage in women a realization & acceptance of their responsibilities to the community - locally, nationally & internationally; To work for high standards of service in business & the professions; To promote worldwide friendship, cooperation & understanding between business & professional women
Affiliation(s): Canadian Federation of Business & Professional Women's Clubs
Chief Officer(s):
Freda Miriklis, President
Angela McLeod, Director, Public Relations & Communications
pr.manager@bpw-international.org
Finances: *Annual Operating Budget:* $250,000-$500,000; *Funding Sources:* Membership dues
Staff Member(s): 2
Membership: 95 countries; *Fees:* 5 Pound Sterling per member; *Member Profile:* Women employed in business, professions or entrepreneurial; *Committees:* Arts & Culture; Agriculture; Business, Trade & Technology; Development, Training & Employment; Environment & Sustainable Development; Finance; Health; Legislation; Membership; Projects; Public Relations; UN Status of Woman; Young BPW
Activities: Involved in the INSTRAW Women's Training Centre, UNIFEM, Project 5-O International, ILO Training Centre, Women's World Banking & over 50 other on-going projects around the world; *Speaker Service:* Yes *Library:* IFBPW Archive Centre; by appointment
Awards:
• Badge of Honour (Award)
• Gertrude Mongella Award (Award)
• Jennifer Cox Trophy (Award)
Publications:
• International Federation of Business & Professional Women E-News
Type: Newsletter
• International Federation of Business & Professional Women Annual Report
Type: Yearbook

International Federation of Camping & Caravanning *Voir* Fédération Internationale de Camping et de Caravanning

International Federation of Clinical Chemistry & Laboratory Medicine (IFCC)
Via Carlo Farini 81, Milan 20159 Italy
Tel: +39 0266809912; *Fax:* +39 0260781846
ifcc@ifcc.org
www.ifcc.org
Overview: A small international organization
Mission: To enhance the scientific level & the quality of diagnosis & therapy for patients throughout the world
Chief Officer(s):
Graham Beastall, President
gbeastall@googlemail.com
Howard Morris, Vice-President
Howard.Morris@unisa.edu.au
Sergio Bernardini, Secretary
bernardini@med.uniroma2.it

International Federation of Employees in Public Service (INFEDOP) / Fédération internationale du personnel des services publics
Blijde Inkomstlaan 1-5, Avenue de la Joyeuse Entrée 1-5, Brussels B-1040 Belgium
Tel: 32-2-2303-865; *Fax:* 32-2-2311-472
info@infedop-eurofedop.com
www.eurofedop.org
Overview: A medium-sized international licensing organization
Affliation(s): World Confederation of Labour
Chief Officer(s):
Bert Van Caelenberg, Secretary General
Finances: *Annual Operating Budget:* $250,000-$500,000
Staff Member(s): 6; 3 volunteer(s)
Membership: *Member Profile:* Trade Unions

International Federation of Film Producers' Associations
Voir Fédération internationale des associations de producteurs de films

International Federation of Hardware & Housewares Association (IHA)
c/o North American Retail Hardware Association, #300, 6325 Digital Way, Indianapolis IN 46278 USA
Tel: 317-275-9400; *Fax:* 317-375-9403
Toll-Free: 800-772-4424
iha@nrha.org
www.nrha.org
Overview: A small international organization founded in 1909
Mission: To inform, educate & influence
Chief Officer(s):
Bill Lee, Secretary General
blee@nrha.org
Finances: *Funding Sources:* Subscriptions
Staff Member(s): 2
Membership: 35; *Member Profile:* National hardware retail organizations
Activities: *Internships:* Yes; *Speaker Service:* Yes; *Rents Mailing List:* Yes

International Federation of Health Information Management Associations (IFHIMA)
College of Health & Human Services, Indiana University Northwest, 3400 Broadway St., Gary IN 46408 USA
www.ifhima.org
Previous Name: International Federation of Health Records Organizations
Overview: A medium-sized international organization
Mission: To improve health/medical record practices in member countries; to be a forum for the exchange of information relating to health records & information technology
Member of: World Health Organization
Affliation(s): Canadian Health Record Association
Chief Officer(s):
Margaret Skurka, President
mskurk@iun.edu
Membership: 1-99; *Fees:* Rate per capita

International Federation of Health Records Organizations
See International Federation of Health Information Management Associations

International Federation of Human Genetics Societies (IFHGS)
c/o Vienna Medical Academy, Alserstrasse 4, Vienna 1090 Austria
Tel: +43 1 405 13 83 22; *Fax:* +43 1 407 82 74
ifhgs@medacad.org
www.ifhgs.org
Overview: A small international organization founded in 1996
Mission: To facilitate communication throughout the international community of human geneticists
Chief Officer(s):
Stephen Lam, President
ts_lam@dh.gov.hk
Membership: 58 societies; *Member Profile:* International professional human genetics societies
Activities: Sharing information about research, education, & clinical services; Encouraging interaction between workers in genetics fields & in related scientific fields

International Federation of Hydrographic Societies
PO Box 103, Plymouth PL4 7YP United Kingdom
Tel: 44-175-222-3512; *Fax:* 44-175-222-3512
helen@hydrographicsociety.org
www.hydrographicsociety.org
Previous Name: Hydrographic Society
Overview: A small international charitable organization founded in 1972
Mission: To promote the science of surveying afloat & related sciences; to promote better education & training of persons engaged or intending to engage in the study of hydrography & related sciences; to accumulate, extend & disseminate information, knowledge & expertise
Finances: *Annual Operating Budget:* $100,000-$250,000
Staff Member(s): 1; 10 volunteer(s)
Membership: From over 70 countries; *Fees:* Available on application; *Member Profile:* Individuals & organizations with an interest in any aspect of surveying afloat; *Committees:* Educational Award Scheme
Activities: Publications, conferences, seminars, workshops

International Federation of Landscape Architects (IFLA) / Fédération internationale des architectes paysagistes
c/o Christine Bavassa, Tour Louise - Ave Louise 149/24, Brussels 1050 Belgium
Tel: 32-0-497-63-05-50
admin@iflaonline.org
www.iflaonline.org
Also Known As: IFLA
Overview: A small international charitable organization founded in 1948
Mission: To develop the profession of landscape architecture; To assist in identifying & preserving the intricate balance of ecological systems; To promote education & encourage scientific research in landscape architecture; To assist all levels of government in establishing & improving legislation connected with the profession of landscape architecture
Chief Officer(s):
Radmila Fingerova, Secretary-General
secgen@iflaonline.org
Desiree Martinez Uriarte, President
IFLA_president@iflaonline.org
John Easthope, Treasurer
john@jea.com.au
Membership: 1-99; *Member Profile:* National associations of professional landscape architects, individuals & corporations; *Committees:* Executive; Finance; Foundation
Activities: Offering world congresses, regional conferences, symposia & seminars; Organizing an international student design competition & educational programs
Publications:
• Guide to International Opportunities in Landscape Architecture, Education & Internships
Profile: Listing of international opportunities sorted by country
• IFLA Journal
Type: Journal; *Editor:* Thomas Jakob
Profile: Selected articles from landscape architecture magazines from around the world

International Federation of Library Associations & Institutions (IFLA)
PO Box 95312, The Hague 2509 CH Netherlands
Tel: 31-70-314-0884; *Fax:* 31-70-383-4827
ifla@ifla.org
www.ifla.org
www.linkedin.com/groups/IFLA-796937?gid=796937
www.facebook.com/pages/IFLA/115229368506017
twitter.com/IFLA
www.youtube.com/user/iflahq
Overview: A medium-sized international organization founded in 1927
Mission: To promote international cooperation, research, & development in all fields of library activity & information service
Affliation(s): Gold partners: Australian Science; Elsevier; Emerald; De Gruyter Saur; Intech; nbd/biblion; OCLC; Sage; SirsiDynix. Silver partners: BRILL; Cambridge U. Press; Gale Cengage Learning; Bronze partners: AXIELL Library Group; Annual Reviews; ebrary; Harrassowitz Booksellers & Subscription Agents; Ingressus; Innovative Interfaces Inc.; ProQuest; Schulz Bibliothekstechnik GmbH; Springer
Chief Officer(s):
Jennefer Nicholson, Secretary General
Sinikka Sipilä, President
sinikka.sipila@fla.fi
Donna Scheeder, President-Elect
dscheeder@crs.loc.gov
Frédéric Blin, Treasurer
frederic.blin@bnu.fr
Finances: *Funding Sources:* Membership fees; Sponsorship contributions; Revenues from sales of publications; Foundation grants
Membership: 1,500+; *Fees:* Schedule available; *Member Profile:* Members include library associations, libraries, information centres, library schools, school libraries, bibliographical & research institutes, students, & information professionals; *Committees:* Executive; Professional
Activities: Providing a forum for information specialists throughout the world to exchange ideas
Awards:
• IFLA / OCLC (Online Computer Library Center) Early Career Development Fellowship (Award)
• Margreet Wijnstroom Fund for Regional Library Development (Award)
Supports IFLA's regional offices, involves librarians from the developing world in the work of IFLA's professional groups, & supports projects in the developing world
• Dr. Shawky Salem Conference Grant (Grant)
Enables an expert in library science from an Arabic country to attend an IFLA conference
• Guust Van Wesemael Literacy Prize (Award)
Sponsors a public or school library in a developing country to purchase books for literacy promotion
• Harry Campbell Conference Attendance Grant (Grant)
• IFLA International Marketing Award (Award)
Publications:
• IFLA Directory
Type: Directory; *Frequency:* Biennially
Profile: Overview of IFLA's professional structure & activities, & a comprehensive list of names & contact details for all IFLA officers & members
• IFLA Journal
Type: Journal; *Frequency:* Quarterly; *Editor:* Stephen Parker
ISSN: 0340-0352
Profile: IFLA activities & articles
• IFLA's Annual Report
Type: Yearbook; *Frequency:* Annually
Profile: Resolutions, projects, meetings, summaries from the annual conference, finances, membership objectives, & reports on professional activities

International Federation of Medical Students' Associations (IFMSA)
c/o World Medical Association, B.P. 63 012 12 Ferney-Voltaire, Cedex France
gs@ifmsa.org
www.ifmsa.org
www.linkedin.com/in/ifmsa
www.facebook.com/ifmsa
twitter.com/@ifmsa
plus.google.com/ifmsa
Overview: A large international organization founded in 1951
Mission: To represent & serve medical students worldwide; To offer future physicians an understanding of current global health challenges
Chief Officer(s):
Josko Mise, President
president@ifmsa.org
Fredrik Johansson, Vice President, External Affairs
vpe@ifmsa.org
Dimitris Stathis, Vice President, Internal Affairs
vpi@ifmsa.org
Salma M. Hassan Abdalla, Secretary General
secgen@ifmsa.org
Membership: 97 national member organizations; *Member Profile:* Medical students' associations from around the world; *Committees:* Public Health; Professional Exchanges; Medical Education; Reproductive Health including AIDS; Research Exchange; Human Rights & Peace
Activities: Providing a forum for discussion for medical students

Publications:
• IFMSA Bulletin
IFMSA-Quebec
QC
Tel: 438-838-0594
www.ifmsa.qc.ca
www.facebook.com/ifmsaquebec
twitter.com/ifmsa_quebec
www.youtube.com/ifmsaquebec
Chief Officer(s):
Claudel P. Desrosiers, President
president@ifmsa.qc.ca

International Federation of Multiple Sclerosis Societies *See* Multiple Sclerosis International Federation

International Federation of Organic Agriculture Movements (IFOAM) / Fédération internationale des mouvements d'agriculture biologique

Charles-de-Gaulle-Str.5, Bonn 53113 Germany
Tel: 49-228-926-5010; *Fax:* 49-228-926-5099
headoffice@ifoam.org
www.ifoam.org
Overview: A small international charitable organization founded in 1972
Mission: To lead, assist, & unite the organic movement in its full diversity; To promote the worldwide adoption of ecologically, socially, & economically sound systems that are based on the principles of organic agriculture
Member of: Consumers Choice Council
Affliation(s): Association interprofessionnelle pour le développement agrobiologique; Canadian Organic Growers; International Development Research Center; Ecological Agriculture Projects; Université écologique internationale; Mouvement pour l'agriculture biologique au Québec
Finances: *Annual Operating Budget:* $500,000-$1.5 Million
Staff Member(s): 10
Membership: 750 member organizations & corporate associates in 105 countries; *Fees:* Schedule available; *Committees:* Standards; Third World; Accreditation; Criteria Revision
Activities: *Internships:* Yes; *Speaker Service:* Yes *Library* by appointment

International Federation of Physical Medicine & Rehabilitation *See* International Society of Physical & Rehabilitation Medicine

International Federation of Professional & Technical Engineers (AFL-CIO/CLC) (IFPTE) / Fédération internationale des ingénieurs et techniciens (FAT-COI/CTC)

#701, 501 3rd St. NW, Washington DC 20001 USA
Tel: 202-239-4880; *Fax:* 202-239-4881
Other Communication: research@ifpte.org
generalinfo@ifpte.org
www.ifpte.org
www.linkedin.com/groups?gid=70495
www.facebook.com/IFPTE
twitter.com/IFPTE
Overview: A large international organization founded in 1918
Mission: To represent employees in a wide variety of occupations in the technical, administrative & professional fields
Affliation(s): AFL-CIO; Canadian Labour Congress; IMF; UNI; PSI
Chief Officer(s):
Gregory J. Junemann, President
Finances: *Annual Operating Budget:* $3 Million-$5 Million; *Funding Sources:* Per capita tax from local unions
Staff Member(s): 15
Membership: 80,000; *Member Profile:* Professional, technical & administrative employees
Publications:
• Outlook
Type: Magazine
Canadian Office - Local 160
2239 Yonge St., Toronto ON M4S 2B5
Tel: 416-979-2709; *Fax:* 416-979-5794
Toll-Free: 866-288-1788
society@thesociety.ca
www.thesociety.ca
Member of: Canadian Council of Professionals; Professional Employees' Network
Chief Officer(s):
Misty Hughes-Newman, Canadian Area Vice President (MB)
m.hughes-newman@teamunion.mb.ca
Andrew Müller, Canadian Area Vice President (ON)

International Federation of Red Cross & Red Crescent Societies / Fédération Internationale des Sociétés de la Croix-Rouge & du Croissant-Rouge

Petit Saconnex, PO Box 372, 17, ch des Crêts, Geneva CH-1211 19 Switzerland
Tel: 41-22-730-42-22; *Fax:* 41-22-733-03-95
secretariat@ifrc.org
www.ifrc.org
www.facebook.com/RedCrossRedCrescent
twitter.com/Federation
www.youtube.com/user/ifrc
Overview: A small international organization founded in 1919
Mission: The International Federation of Red Cross and Red Crescent Societies is the world's largest humanitarian organization, providing assistance without discrimination as to nationality, race, religious beliefs, class or political opinions
Affliation(s): Canadian Red Cross Society
Chief Officer(s):
Bekele Geleta, Secretary General
Membership: 186 member Red Cross and Red Crescent societies

International Federation of Surveyors (IFS) / Fédération internationale des géomètres (FIG)

Kalvebod Brygge 31-33, Copenhagen 1780 Denmark
Tel: 45 3886 1081; *Fax:* 45 3886 0252
FIG@fig.net
www.fig.net
Overview: A medium-sized international organization founded in 1878
Mission: To ensure that the disciplines of surveying and all who practise them meet the needs of the markets and communities that they serve.
Affliation(s): Canadian Institute of Surveying and Mapping
Chief Officer(s):
CheeHai Teo, President
chteo.surveyor@gmail.com
Staff Member(s): 1; 7 volunteer(s)
Membership: 200,000;

International Federation of Translators *Voir* Fédération Internationale des Traducteurs

International Flying Farmers (IFF)

PO Box 309, Mansfield IL 61854 USA
Tel: 217-489-9300; *Fax:* 217-489-9280
iff1944@hotmail.com
www.internationalflyingfarmers.org
Overview: A medium-sized international organization founded in 1944
Mission: To provide a personalized, unique & economical opportunity to experience agriculture & aviation in a family environment in Canada & the United States
Chief Officer(s):
Marilyn Brohman, President
Staff Member(s): 1
Membership: 1,100; *Fees:* US$60 per family

International Foster Care Organisation (IFCO)

26 Red Lion Square, London WC1R 4AG UK
Tel: +44 (0)208 144 7571
ifco@ifco.info
www.ifco.info
www.facebook.com/IFCO.info
twitter.com/IFCOinfo
Overview: A medium-sized international charitable organization
Mission: To promote family-based solutions for out-of-home children; To support family foster care throughout the world; To provide advice to governmental & non-governmental organizations about the development & improvement of family-based substitute care
Member of: Eurochild; NGO Group for the United Nations Convention Rights of the Child
Chief Officer(s):
Volodymyr Kuzmynskyi, President
Jean Kennedy, Vice-President
Lacy Kendrick Burk, Secretary
Colin Chatten, Treasurer
Membership: *Fees:* Schedule available
Activities: Advising foster care associations; Sharing news & developments from around the globe; Training trainers in aspects of foster care; Establishing regional networks for the sharing of ideas
Meetings/Conferences:
• International Foster Care Organisation 2015 World Conference, November 2015, 2015, Star Events Centre, Sydney
Scope: International
Description: A biennial conference, featuring a youth program, workshops, & plenary sessions about quality care solutions for children & youth living in out-of-home care
Contact Information: Website: www.ifco2015.com
Publications:
• IFCO Magazine
Type: Magazine; *Frequency:* Quarterly
Profile: Foster care news from around the world, including projects, research, insights, & upcoming events
• Stakeholders in Foster Care
Type: Study; *Editor:* Shanti George & Nico van Oudenhoven
Profile: An examination of fost care, in the context of family, social networks, non-governmental organizations, & the state
• The Unfolding of The Wings of Foster Care
Type: Book
Profile: A collection of contributions from the 2003 International Foster Care Organisation conference

International Foundation of Employee Benefit Plans

PO Box 69, 18700 West Bluemound Rd., Brookfield WI 53045 USA
Tel: 262-786-6700; *Fax:* 262-786-8670
Toll-Free: 888-334-3327
pr@ifebp.org
www.ifebp.org
www.linkedin.com/groups?gid=1875051
www.facebook.com/IFEBP?ref=search
twitter.com/IFEBP
www.youtube.com/user/IFEBP
Overview: A large international organization founded in 1954
Mission: Dedicated exclusively to employee benefits & compensation education
Chief Officer(s):
Michael Wilson, CEO
mwilson@ifebp.org
Finances: *Annual Operating Budget:* Greater than $5 Million; *Funding Sources:* Membership dues; fees for services
Staff Member(s): 140
Membership: 34,000; *Fees:* US$625 corporate; US$295 individual; *Member Profile:* Trust fund representations & corporate benefits professionals
Activities: *Awareness Events:* National Employee Benefits Day, April 2; *Internships:* Yes *Library*
Publications:
• Benefits Magazine
Type: Magazine; *Frequency:* Monthly
Profile: Features articles by experienced benefits professionals on topics concerning multiemployer, public employer, single employer and corporate benefit plans.
• Benefits Quarterly
Type: Magazine; *Frequency:* Quarterly
Profile: Offers comprehensive benefits coverage from a corporate perspective.
• Plans & Trust
Type: Magazine; *Frequency:* Bimonthly
Profile: Provides an in-depth look at benefits issues, and reviews federal and provincial legal decisions and legislative developments.

International Game Developers Association (IGDA)

19 Mantua Rd., Mount Royal NJ 08061 USA
Tel: 856-423-2990; *Fax:* 856-423-3420
contact@igda.org
www.igda.org
www.linkedin.com/in/baldwinjames
www.facebook.com/IGDA.org
twitter.com/twistededge
Overview: A small international organization
Mission: To strengthen & bring together the international game development community while effecting change to benefit that community.
Affliation(s): Canadian Chapters: Calgary www.igda.org/calgary; Montréal www.igda.org/montreal; Ottawa www.igda.org/ottawa; Toronto www.igda.org/toronto, Jason MacIsaac, Contact; Vancouver www.igda.org/vancouver, James Everett, Contact
Chief Officer(s):
Dustin Clingman, Chair
James Baldwin, Operations Coordinator

International Garden Cities & Town Planning Association *See* International Federation for Housing & Planning

International Genetics Federation (IGF)
Dept. of Evolution & Ecology, University of California - Davis, 1 Shields Ave., Davis CA 95616-8554 USA
Tel: 530-752-4085; *Fax:* 530-752-1449
info@meiosis.org
www.meiosis.org
Overview: A small international organization founded in 1968
Mission: To promote the advancement of the science of genetics
Member of: International Union of Biological Sciences
Affliation(s): Genetics Society of Canada
Chief Officer(s):
Alfred Nordheim, President
alred.nordheim@uni-tuebingen.de
Charles H. Langley, Secretary-General
chlangley@ucdavis.edu
Membership: 63 national genetics societies

International Geographic Union (IGU) / Union géographique internationale
2246N Pollard St., Arlington VA 22207-3805 USA
Fax: 703-527-3227
www.igu-online.org
Overview: A small international organization founded in 1922
Mission: The IGU has the following objectives: to promote the study of geographical problems; to initiate & coordinate geographical research; to provide for the participation of geographers in the work of international organizations; to facilitate the collection & diffusion of geographical data & documentation; & to promote international standardization or compatibility of methods, nomenclature & symbols employed in geography.
Member of: International Social Science Council
Affliation(s): International Council of Science
Chief Officer(s):
Michael Meadows, Secretary-General
mmeadows@mweb.co.za
Adalberto Vallega, President
Membership: 1-99
Activities: *Library:* Archives, Royal Geographical Society in London
Awards:
• Planet & Humanity Medal (Award)
• Laureat d'Honneur of the IGU (Award)
Publications:
• IGU [International Geographic Union] Newsletter
Type: Newsletter; *Frequency:* Quarterly; *Editor:* Ronald F. Abler
Profile: Announcements, information, calls for participation in scientific events, programs, & projects

International Geosynthetics Society (IGS)
IGS Secretariat, #4, 1934 Commerce Lane, Jupiter FL 33458 USA
Tel: 561-768-9489; *Fax:* 561-828-7618
igssec@geosyntheticssociety.org
www.geosyntheticssociety.org
Overview: A medium-sized international organization founded in 1984
Mission: To be dedicated to the scientific & engineering development of geotextiles, geomembranes, related products & associated technologies
Chief Officer(s):
Diana Davis, Secretariat
igssec@geosyntheticssociety.org
Jorge G. Zornberg, President
zornberg@mail.utexas.edu
Russell Jones, Vice-President
Fumio Tatsuoka, Past President
Elizabeth Peggs, Secretary
Peter Legg, Treasurer
Finances: *Funding Sources:* Membership dues
Staff Member(s): 1; 10 volunteer(s)
Membership: 41 chapters; 3,000+ individuals; 161 corporate members; *Fees:* Schedule available; *Member Profile:* Geosynthetics professionals; *Committees:* Awards; Chapters; Corporate; Education; Technical
Activities: *Library*
Publications:
• IGS (International Geosynthetics Society) News
Type: Newsletter; *Editor:* Gerhard Bräu
Profile: General information for IGS members, news from IGS chapters, conference reports, & a calendar of events

International Heavy Haul Association (IHHA)
2808 Forest Hills Crt., Virginia Beach 23454-1236 USA
Tel: 757-496-8288; *Fax:* 757-496-2622
www.ihha.net
Overview: A large international organization
Mission: To pursue excellence in heavy haul railway operations, engineering, technology & maintenance
Chief Officer(s):
Michael Roney, Chair
W. Scott Lovelace, CEO
scottlovelace@verizon.net
Finances: *Funding Sources:* Membership fees; Sponsorships
Membership: *Member Profile:* Railway organizations; National & state organizations; Private railway systems; Advocates for the world's heavy haul rail operations; *Committees:* Finance; Strategic Planning
Activities: Organizing specialist seminars & specialist technical sessions; Offering networking opportunities
Awards:
• Heavy Haul of Fame Award (Award)
• Best Paper Award (Award)
Meetings/Conferences:
• International Heavy Haul Association 2015 Specialist Technical Session, 2015, Perth
Scope: International
Description: A conference offered every four years to examine heavy haul operation issues. This year's tentative theme is "Operational Excellence."
• International Heavy Haul Association 2017 International Conference, 2017
Scope: International
Description: An international conference, scheduled every four years, featuring meetings covering the complete spectrum of heavy haul subjects, as well as technical tours
Publications:
• Guidelines To Best Practices For Heavy Haul Railway Operations - Infrastructure Construction & Maintenance Issues
Price: $125
• Guidelines To Best Practices For Heavy Haul Railway Operations - Wheel & Rail Interface Issues
Price: $80
• International Heavy Haul Association Conference Proceedings

International Hockey Federation *Voir* Fédération internationale de hockey

International Hospital Federation (IHF) / Fédération internationale des hôpitaux
Immeuble JB SAY, 13, ch du Levant, Ferney-Voltaire F-01210 France
Tel: 33-450-426-000; *Fax:* 33-450-426-001
info@ihf-fih.org
www.ihf-fih.org
Overview: A medium-sized international charitable organization founded in 1947
Mission: To provide the opportunity for exchange of information, education, experience relevant to the provision of high-quality health services in member countries; to promote modern management techniques to improve efficiency; to participate in & encourage research & experimentation in hospital & health service planning & management; to collect & disseminate international health service data; to serve as advocate for hospital & related health service organizations in world health affairs
Affliation(s): World Health Organization
Chief Officer(s):
Eric de Roodenbeke, CEO
Staff Member(s): 7
Membership: 1,500; *Member Profile:* Hospital organizations; ministries of health; individuals in any health care profession; companies engaged in supplying goods & services to the health care industry
Activities: Publications, meetings; networking; *Rents Mailing List:* Yes

International Hotel & Restaurant Association (IH&RA)
42 Ave. General Guisan, Lausanne 1009 Switzerland
Tel: 41-21-711-4283; *Fax:* 41-21-711-4285
ihra@live.com
www.ih-ra.com
www.facebook.com/group.php?gid=260181355823
Overview: A large international charitable organization founded in 1946
Mission: To promote & defend the interests of the hotel & restaurant industry worldwide
Chief Officer(s):
Ghassan Aidi, President & CEO
ghassan.aidi@ih-ra.com
Finances: *Annual Operating Budget:* $500,000-$1.5 Million
Staff Member(s): 5; 50 volunteer(s)
Membership: Over 50,000; *Member Profile:* National hotel & restaurant associations; international & national hotel & restaurant chains
Activities: *Speaker Service:* Yes

International Humanist & Ethical Union (IHEU) / Union internationale humanite et laique
1 Gower St., London WC1E 6HD United Kingdom
Tel: 44-870-288-7631; *Fax:* 44-870-288-7631
office-iheu@iheu.org
www.iheu.org
Overview: A medium-sized international organization founded in 1952
Mission: To bring into active association groups & individuals throughout the world interested in promoting ethical & scientific humanism, understood as a dedication to responsibility for human life by maintenance, furtherance, & development of human values, cultivation of science, loyalty to democratic principles in all social relations, & practice of good faith, without reliance upon authority or dogma; to work with international agencies & outstanding personalities engaged in promoting human well-being, especially through education & cultural programs
Affliation(s): Humanist Association of Canada
Chief Officer(s):
Sonja Eggerickx, President, (Belgium)
Jack Jeffery, 1st Vice President, (United Kingdom)
Finances: *Annual Operating Budget:* $100,000-$250,000
Staff Member(s): 2; 15 volunteer(s)
Membership: 100 organizations; *Member Profile:* Rationalists; humanists; secularists; humanist organizations; *Committees:* Committee on Religious Abuse of Children; Committee on Declaration of Humanist Values
Activities: World Congress; *Internships:* Yes; *Speaker Service:* Yes

International Husserl & Phenomenological Research Society
1 Ivy Pointe Way, Hanover NH 3755 USA
Tel: 802-295-3487; *Fax:* 802-295-5963
Overview: A small international organization founded in 1968
Mission: To pursue interdisciplinary research along the lines of phenomenological philosophy; to unfold a philosophy/phenomenology of life answering the needs of our times
Member of: The World Institute for Advanced Phenomenological Research & Learning (USA)
Chief Officer(s):
Anna-Teresa Tymieniecka, President
Thomas Ryba, Vice-President
Finances: *Annual Operating Budget:* $50,000-$100,000; *Funding Sources:* Membership fees; publications
5 volunteer(s)
Membership: 700 in 25 countries; *Fees:* $65
Activities: *Library* by appointment

International Ice Hockey Federation (IIHF)
Brandschenkestrasse 50, Zurich CH-8027 Switzerland
Tel: 41-44-562-22-00; *Fax:* 41-44-562-22-29
office@iihf.com
www.iihf.com
www.facebook.com/294239820899
twitter.com/IIHFHockey
Overview: A large international organization founded in 1908
Mission: To govern, develop & promote ice & in-line hockey throughout the world; To develop & control international ice & in-line hockey; To promote friendly relations among the member national associations; To operate in an organized manner for the good order of the sport
Member of: Association of International Olympic Winter Sports Federations
Affliation(s): Hockey Canada
Chief Officer(s):
René Fasel, President
Horst Lichtner, General Secretary
Staff Member(s): 32
Membership: 73 national associations; *Member Profile:* National ice hockey associations & in-line hockey associations; *Committees:* Athletes; Competition &Inline; Co-ordination; Development & Coaching; Disciplinary; Event; Facilities; Historical; Legal; Medical; Officiating; Player Safety Consulting

Group; Social & Environment; Strategic Consulting Group; Women's; Asian Strategic Planning Group
Activities: *Internships:* Yes; *Speaker Service:* Yes *Library:* Hockey Hall of Fame, Toronto Canada; Open to public

International Industrial Relations Association *See* International Labour & Employment Relations Association

International Industry Working Group (IIWG)
International Air Transport Association, PO Box 416, Route de l'Aéroport 33 1215, 15 Airport, Geneva Switzerland
www.iata.org/whatwedo/workgroups/Pages/iiwg.aspx
Overview: A small international organization founded in 1970
Mission: To promote & develop an open exchange of information to minimize interface problems through well-informed design, development & operation of both aircraft & airports; to study jointly solutions to major problems which impede the development of the air transport system
Chief Officer(s):
Koos Noordeloos, Chair
Colin Spear, Secretariat
spearc@iata.org
Membership: 50; *Member Profile:* Aircraft & aeroengine manufacturers; airlines & airport authorities

International Institute for Applied Systems Analysis (IIASA)
Schlossplatz 1, Laxenburg A-2361 Austria
Tel: 43-2236-807-0; *Fax:* 43-2236-71-313
inf@iiasa.ac.at
www.iiasa.ac.at
www.facebook.com/IIASA
twitter.com/IIASAVienna
Overview: A medium-sized international organization founded in 1972
Mission: To initiate & support individual & collaborative research on problems associated with social, economic, technological & environmental change, & thereby assist scientific, industrial & policy communities throughout the world in tackling such problems; current principal focus: scientific study of sustainability & the human dimensions of global change; to bring together scientists from various countries & disciplines to conduct research in a setting that is non-political & scientifically rigorous; to provide policy-oriented research results that deal with issues transcending national boundaries; to coordinate research projects, working in collaboration with worldwide networks of researchers, policy makers & research organizations
Member of: International Council for Science; International Federation of Institutes for Advanced Study
Affliation(s): Canadian Committee for IIASA
Chief Officer(s):
Detlof von Winterfeldt, Director
detlof@iiasa.ac.at
Finances: *Annual Operating Budget:* Greater than $5 Million
Staff Member(s): 180
Membership: 16; *Member Profile:* International & national research & policy institutes, organizations, & universities; *Committees:* Executive; Finance; Program; Membership; Advisory; Science; Steering
Activities: Policy-relevant research carried out by international, interdisciplinary teams, based on the following related themes: 1. Energy & Technology, including studies of environmentally compatible energy strategies, economic transition & integration, decision analysis & support, dynamic systems, & risk, modeling & policy; 2. Natural Resources & the Environment, including modeling land-use & land-cover changes in Europe & Northern Asia, sustainable boreal forest resources, transboundary air pollution, & adaptive dynamics; *Library* by appointment
Awards:
• Young Scientists Summer Program (Award)
• Young Postdoctoral Fellows Program (Award)
• Peccei & Mikhalevich Scholarship (Award)
• Luis Donaldo Colosio Fellowship (Award)

International Institute for Audio-Visual Communication & Cultural Development *See* International Research Institute for Media, Communication & Cultural Development

International Institute for Conservation of Historic & Artistic Works (IIC)
#209, 3 Birdcage Walk, Westminster, london SW1H 9JJ UK
Tel: +44 (0)20 7799 5500; *Fax:* +44 (0)20 7799 5800
iic@iiconservation.org
www.iiconservation.org
Overview: A medium-sized international organization founded in 1950
Mission: To coordinate & improve the knowledge, methods, & working standards needed to protect, preserve & maintain the condition & integrity of historic & artistic works
Chief Officer(s):
Graham Voce, Executive Secretary
iic@iiconservation.org
Valerie Compton-Taylor, Membership Secretary
membership@iiconservation.org
Membership: *Fees:* £49 individual; £19 student; £70 fellow; £170 institution; *Member Profile:* Restorers; Conservators; Conservation scientists; Educators; Students; Architects; Collection managers; Curators; Art historians; Cultural heritage professionals

International Institute for Energy Conservation (IIEC)
#100, 10005 Leamoore Lane, Vienna VA 22181 USA
Tel: 703-281-7263; *Fax:* 703-938-5153
iiecdc@iiec.org
www.iiec.org
www.linkedin.com/company/international-institute-for-energy-conservati
Overview: A medium-sized international organization founded in 1984
Mission: To bring the power of sustainable energy solutions to developing countries & economies in transition
Chief Officer(s):
Robert L. Pratt, Chair
Felix Gooneratne, Chief Executive Officer

International Institute of African Languages & Cultures *See* International African Institute

International Institute of Fisheries Economics & Trade (IIFET)
Agricultural & Resource Economics, Oregon State University, 220 Ballard Hall, Corvallis OR 97331-3601 USA
Tel: 541-737-1416; *Fax:* 541-737-2563
iifet@oregonstate.edu
www.oregonstate.edu/Dept/IIFET/
Overview: A small international charitable organization founded in 1982
Mission: To promote discussion of factors which affect international trade in seafoods & fisheries policy questions
Chief Officer(s):
Dan Holland, President
dholland@gmri.org
Ann L. Shriver, Executive Director
ann.l.shriver@oregonstate.edu
Staff Member(s): 2
Membership: 100-499; *Fees:* $75 regular; $25 student; $500 corporate/institutional; *Member Profile:* International Fisheries Economists; *Committees:* Executive
Activities: *Rents Mailing List:* Yes

International ISBN Agency
c/o EDItEUR, 39-41 North Rd., London N7 9DP United Kingdom
Tel: +44(0)20 7503 6418
info@isbn-international.org
www.isbn-international.org
Overview: A medium-sized international organization founded in 1972
Mission: To promote, coordinate and supervise the worlwide use of the ISBN (International Standard Book Number) system; to act in an advisory role to group agencies
Affliation(s): Canadian ISBN Agency
Chief Officer(s):
Stella Griffiths, Executive Director
Finances: *Annual Operating Budget:* Less than $50,000
Staff Member(s): 3
Membership: 156 countries
Activities: *Library* Open to public

International Kindergarten Union *See* Association for Childhood Education International

International Labour & Employment Relations Association (ILERA) / Association internationale de relations professionnelles (AIRP)
c/o DIALOGUE, International Labour Office, 22, Geneva CH-1211 Switzerland
Tel: 41-22-799-73-71; *Fax:* 41-22-799-87-49
iira@ilo.org
www.ilo.org/public/english/iira
Previous Name: International Industrial Relations Association
Overview: A large international organization founded in 1966
Mission: To promote the study of industrial relations throughout the world by encouraging the establishment of national associations of IR (Industrial Relations) specialists; to faciliate the spread of information in the field of IR; to organize regional & worldwide congresses & to publish their proceedings; to promote international research by organizing study groups on IR topics
Affliation(s): Association canadienne de relations industrielles
Chief Officer(s):
Evance Kalula, President
evance.kalula@uct.ac.za
Moussa Oumarou, Secretary
oumarou@ilo.org
Finances: *Funding Sources:* Membership dues
Staff Member(s): 1
Membership: 39 full + 47 institutional + 1,000 individual; *Fees:* US$25 individual; US$60 institutional; US$40, US$65, US$100 full; *Member Profile:* Full members - national or regional (a group of countries in the same geographical area) industrial relations associations whose primary purpose is research in the industrial relations field, or committees where such associations do not exist; Institutional associate members - universities & colleges or departments thereof & other research institutes concerned with the study of industrial relations; Individual associate members - persons engaged in industrial relations research or teaching, as well as practitioners in the industrial relations field; *Committees:* Executive
Activities: World Congress convened every 3 years; IIRA members can take part in any of the following study groups - Industrial Relations as a field & industrial relations theory; Technological change & industrial relations; Equality in pay & employment; Worker's participation; Public policy & industrial relations; Urban labour markets in developing countries; The rights of employees & industrial justice; Pay systems; Flexible work patterns; Trade unions in the future; Theory & practice of negotiations; Human resource management
Awards:
• Luis Aparicio Prize (Award)
To recognize the contribution of emerging scholars in the fields of work, employment, labour & employment relations
Meetings/Conferences:
• 17th International Labour & Employment Relations Association World Congress, 2015, Cape Town
Scope: International
Publications:
• ILERA [International Labour & Employment Relations Association] Newsletter
Type: Newsletter

International Labour Organization (ILO)
4, route des Morillons, Geneva CH-1211 Switzerland
Tel: 41-22-799-6111; *Fax:* 41-22-798-8685
ilo@ilo.org
www.ilo.org
www.facebook.com/ILO.ORG
twitter.com/ilonews
www.youtube.com/ilotv
Overview: A large international organization founded in 1919
Mission: To bring governments, employers & trade unions together for united action in the cause of social justice & better living conditions everywhere; supports efforts by the international community & by individual nations to achieve full employment, raise living standards, share the fruits of progress fairly, protect the life & health of workers, & to promote cooperation between workers & employers in order to improve production & working conditions; the ILO employs a tripartite structure (dialogue among governments, workers' & employers' organizations) in order to interpret the aims & aspirations of each country, reflect its preoccupations & reach realistic decisions based on the social & economic situations of the countries concerned; the ILO cooperates with other organizations of the international community
Chief Officer(s):
Guy Ryder, Director General
Finances: *Annual Operating Budget:* Greater than $5 Million
Staff Member(s): 2700
Membership: 185 member states + worker & employer organizations; *Committees:* Freedom of Association; Application of Standards
Activities: Setting international labour standards; technical cooperation; publications & research; *Internships:* Yes; *Speaker Service:* Yes *Library* Open to public
Meetings/Conferences:
• XXI Congress on Safety & Health at Work - Global Forum for Prevention, September, 2017
Scope: International

Description: The World Congress is a forum for the exchange of knowledge, practices & experiences for anyone involved with or interested in health & safety in the workplace.
Publications:
• World of Work [a publication of the International Labour Organization]
Type: Magazine; *Frequency:* 3 pa. *ISSN:* 1020-0010

International Ladies' Garment Workers' Union (AFL-CIO/CLC); Union of Needletrades, Industrial & Textile Employees *See* UNITE HERE

International Law Association (ILA)
Charles Clore House, 17 Russell Sq., London WC1B 5JD United Kingdom
Tel: 44-20-7323-2978; *Fax:* 44-20-7323-3580
info@ila-hq.org
www.ila-hq.org
Overview: A medium-sized international organization founded in 1873
Mission: Dedicated to the study, elucidation & advancement of international law, public & private, the study of comparative law, the making of proposals for the solution of conflicts of law & for the unification of law, & the furthering of international understanding & goodwill
Chief Officer(s):
David J.C. Wyld, Secretary General
Finances: *Funding Sources:* Membership fees; grants; appeals
Staff Member(s): 1
Membership: 3,700; *Committees:* Space Law; International Monetary Law; International Human Rights Law & Practice; Water Resources Law; International Commercial Arbitration; Legal Aspects of Sustainable Development; Refugee Procedures; Legal Aspects of Inter-Country Adoption & Protection of the Family; Extraterritorial Jurisdiction; International Securities Regulation; Cultural Heritage Law; International Law in Municipal Courts; Regional Economic Development Law; Arms Control & Disarmament Law; Feminism & International Law; Extradition & Human Rights; International Civil & Commercial Litigation; International Trade Law

International League of Dermatological Societies (ILDS)
Wilan House, 4 Fitroy Sq., London W1T 5HQ United Kingdom
Tel: 44 20 7388 6515; *Fax:* 44 20 7388 3123
admin@ilds.org
web.ilds.org
Overview: A medium-sized international organization founded in 1888
Mission: To stimulate the cooperation of societies of dermatology and societies interested in all fields of cutaneous medicine and biology throughout the world; encourage the worldwide advancement of dermatological education, care, and sciences; promote personal and professional relations among the dermatologists of the world; represent dermatology in commisions and international health organizations; and organize a World Congress of Dermatology every five years and to sponsor additional international educational and scientific activities.
Membership: *Fees:* Schedule available; *Member Profile:* Members of national & international societies of dermatology; *Committees:* Executive; International Foundation for Dermatology; Finance; Membership & Communications; World Congress of Dermatology Programme; Awards; Commissions & International Health Organization
Activities: *Speaker Service:* Yes

International Leisure Information Network (LINK) *See* World Leisure & Recreation Association

International Lilac Society
c/o Karen McCauley, Treasurer, 325 West 82nd St., Chaska MN 55318
Tel: 952-443-3703
ILSExecVP@gmail.com
www.internationallilacsociety.org
Overview: A small international organization
Mission: To promote & stimulate interest in the genus Syringa
Chief Officer(s):
Nicole Jordan, President
njordan236@aol.com
Brad Bittorf, Executive Vice-President
ilsexecvp@gmail.com
Karen McCauley, Treasurer & Membership Secretary
mccauleytk@aol.com

International Liver Cancer Association (ILCA)
300, av de Tervueren, Brussels B-1150 Belgium
Tel: +32 (0)2 789 2345; *Fax:* +32 (0)2 743 1550
info@ilca-online.org
www.ilca-online.org
www.linkedin.com/groups/International-Liver-Cancer-Association-ILCA-46
www.facebook.com/InternationalLiverCancerAssociation
twitter.com/ILCAnews
Overview: A small international organization
Mission: To advance research in the pathogenesis, prevention, & treatment of liver cancer
Chief Officer(s):
Géraldine Damar, Executive Officer
Peter Galle, President
Staff Member(s): 7
Membership: *Fees:* Schedule available; *Member Profile:* International researchers, physicians, & allied professionals involved in liver cancer; *Committees:* Executive; Membership; Web Site; Counsensus Guidelines
Activities: Educating healthcare professionals & the general public; Increasing understanding of liver cancer

International Longshore & Warehouse Union (CLC) / Syndicat international des débardeurs et magasiniers (CTC)
1188 Franklin St., 4th Fl., San Francisco CA 94109 USA
Tel: 415-775-0533; *Fax:* 415-775-1302
www.ilwu.org
Overview: A small international charitable organization
Mission: To represent the rights of their members, who work in the warehouse industry
Chief Officer(s):
Robert McEllrath, President

Canadian Office
#180, 111 Victoria Ave., Vancouver BC V5L 4C4
Tel: 604-254-8141; *Fax:* 604-254-8183
www.ilwu.ca
www.youtube.com/TheILWUCanada
Affliation(s): Retail Wholesale Union of BC; Retail Wholesale Department Store Union of SK; Grain Services Union of SK
Chief Officer(s):
Mark Gordienko, President
president@ilwu.ca

International Longshoremen's Association (AFL-CIO/CLC) (ILA) / Association internationale des débardeurs (FAT-COI/CTC)
5000 West Side Ave., North Bergen NJ 07047 USA
Tel: 212-425-1200; *Fax:* 212-425-2928
ilaunion.org
Overview: A small international organization founded in 1892
Chief Officer(s):
Harold Daggett, President
hdaggett@ilaunion.org
Robert E. Gleason, Sec.-Treas.
Membership: 65,000+

Canadian Division
15070, rue Notre-Dame est, Montréal QC H1A 1W6
Tel: 514-644-0509
Chief Officer(s):
Raymond Desgagnes, Vice President
raymond_desgagnes@yahoo.ca

International Luge Federation *Voir* Fédération Internationale de Luge de Course

International Maritime Committee *See* Comité maritime international

International Maritime Organization (IMO) / Organisation maritime internationale
4 Albert Embankment, London SE1 7SR United Kingdom
Tel: 44-20-7735-7611; *Fax:* 44-20-7587-3210
Other Communication: www.flickr.com/photos/imo-un
info@imo.org
www.imo.org
www.facebook.com/IMOHQ
twitter.com/imohq
www.youtube.com/user/IMOHQ
Overview: A large international organization founded in 1948
Mission: To encourage the adoption of high standards in matters concerning maritime safety, security, efficiency of navigation & control of marine pollution from ships
Chief Officer(s):
Koji Sekimizu, Secretary General
Lee Adamson, Manager, Public Information
Finances: *Annual Operating Budget:* Greater than $5 Million; *Funding Sources:* Government
Staff Member(s): 300
Membership: 170 member states + 3 associate; *Fees:* Based on shipping fleet tonnage; *Committees:* Maritime Safety; Marine Environment Protection; Legal; Technical Cooperation; Facilitation
Activities: *Awareness Events:* Day of the Seafarer, June *Library* by appointment
Awards:
• International Maritime Prize (Award)
Amount: US$1,000 + travel expenses

International Masters Games Association (IMGA)
Maison du Sport International, Avenue de Rhodanie 54, Lausanne 1007 Switzerland
Tel: 41-216018171; *Fax:* 41-216018173
info@imga.ch
www.imga.ch
www.facebook.com/134323223278024
twitter.com/IMGALausanne
www.youtube.com/user/TheIMGA
Overview: A large international organization founded in 1995
Mission: To govern the World Masters Games
Chief Officer(s):
Kai Holm, President, Board of Governors
Jens V. Holm, CEO
Membership: *Member Profile:* International Sports Federations participating in the World Masters Games
Activities: World Masters Games; European Masters Games

International Medical Informatics Association (IMIA)
c/o Health On the Net, Chemin du Petit-Bel-Air 2, Chêne-Bourg, Geneva CH-1225 Switzerland
Tel: 41-22-3727249
imia@imia-services.org
www.imia-medinfo.org
www.facebook.com/pages/IMIA/191053744240749
twitter.com/IMIAtweets
Overview: A small international organization founded in 1989
Mission: To promote informatics in health care & biomedical research; To advance international cooperation; To stimulate research, development & education; To disseminate & exchange information
Chief Officer(s):
Antoine Geissbuhler, President
Elizabeth Borycki, Vice-President, IMIA North America
Peter J. Murray, CEO
Staff Member(s): 2

International Migration Service *See* International Social Service

International Movement of Catholic Students; International Catholic Movement for Intellectual & Cultural Affairs *Voir* IMCS Pax Romana

International Music Council (IMC) / Conseil international de la musique
1, rue Miollis, Paris 75732 CEDEX 15 France
Tel: 33-145-684-850; *Fax:* 33-145-684-866
www.imc-cim.org
Overview: A medium-sized international organization founded in 1949
Mission: To monitor the availability of access to music for all; To support endeavours which assure & secure this right; To inform widely about music & the right to it; To exercise advocacy when & where needed; To aim at contributing to the development & strengthening of friendly working relations between all the musical cultures of the world, on the basis of their absolute equality, mutual respect, & appreciation; To concern itself with musical creativity, education, performance, broadcasting & promotion, research & documentation, the status of musicians, & various other aspects of musical life
Chief Officer(s):
Paul Dujardin, President
Silja Fischer, Secretary General
Finances: *Funding Sources:* UNESCO; Membership fees; A number of governments & broadcasting organizations provide most of the funds required for the Rostra & recordings
Membership: 65 national music councils + 50 international & regional music organizations; *Fees:* Schedule available
Activities: Working on the effects of globlization upon music mainly through a new action & reflection program entitled "May Musics"; Promoting international & regional Rostra, which are designed to promote local cultures, bring recognition to living composers, promote the career of young performers, & offer

performance interchange opportunities for musicians & musics from all regions of the world; *Library* by appointment
Awards:
• IMC/UNESCO International Music Prize (Award)
Awarded by competition to eminent personalities in all fields of music & to important national or international institutions for their exceptional contribution to musical life

International Network for Environmental Management (INEM)
Osterstrasse 58, Hamburg 20259 Germany
Tel: 49-89-18935-200; *Fax:* 49-89-18935-199
www.inem.org
Overview: A small international organization founded in 1991
Mission: To be committed to the implementation of environmental management in businesses worldwide, including small- & medium-sized enterprises; To promote clean technologies
Chief Officer(s):
Ludwig Karg, Chair
L.Karg@INEM.org
Membership: *Member Profile:* Autonomous & non-profit business associations concerned with environmental management

International Network for Social Network Analysis (INSNA)
c/o JulNet Solutions, LLC, 3327B US Rte. 60 East, Huntington WV 25705 USA
Tel: 304-523-9700; *Fax:* 304-523-9701
www.insna.org
www.facebook.com/INSNA
twitter.com/SocNetAnalysts
Overview: A small international organization founded in 1978
Chief Officer(s):
John Skvoretz, President
Membership: *Member Profile:* Researchers interested in social network analysis

International Northwest Aviation Council (INAC)
PO Box 5178, Helena MT 59604 USA
Overview: A medium-sized international organization
Mission: To foster & promote the development of civil aviation in Canada & the United States; to encourage the development of airports, improve navigational aids & safety installations within the Provinces, States & Territories; to maintain a cooperative liaison with Federal, Provincial, State & Territorial governments in all matters affecting aviation in Canada & the United States; to promote the simplification of air regulation; to develop alliances among aviation organizations; to provide a voice for regional, local & small airports; to support aviation education through scholarships to deserving aviation students
Chief Officer(s):
Judy Gifford, Contact
judyg@spokaneairports.net

International Nuclear Law Association (INLA) / Association internationale du droit nucléaire
Square de Meeûs 29, Brussels B-1000 Belgium
Tel: 32-2-547-5841; *Fax:* 32-2-503-0440
info@aidn-inla.be
www.aidn-inla.be
Overview: A small international organization founded in 1970
Mission: To promote international studies of legal problems related to the peaceful use of nuclear energy
Chief Officer(s):
Rafael Manovil, President
Patrick Reyners, Secretary General
Staff Member(s): 2
Membership: 500; *Committees:* Safety and Regulation; Nuclear Liability and Inurance; International Nuclear Trade; Radiological Protection; Waste Management; Radioisotopes

International Occupational Safety & Health Information Centre / Centre international d'informations de sécurité et de santé au travail
International Labour Office/CIS, 4 route des Morillons, Geneva CH-1211 Switzerland
Tel: 41-22-799-61-11; *Fax:* 41-22-798-86-85
www.ilo.org/cis/
Also Known As: Centro Internacional de Informacion sobre Seguridad y Salud en el Trabajo
Overview: A small international organization founded in 1959
Mission: To collect & disseminate world information that can contribute to the prevention of occupational accidents & diseases
Affiliation(s): Canadian Centre for Occupational Health & Safety; Canada Safety Council; Institut de recherche en santé et en sécurité de travail - Québec
Membership: 104 national centres; 2 regional centres; 44 collaborating centres
Activities: CIS Information Service (personalized searches on any OSH topic); CIS factual microcomputer databases (covering important OSH topics); CIS Information Sheets (chemical, medical, technical, ergonomic); CIS microfiche service (reproduction of abstracted documents no longer obtainable from original sources); Directory of OSH Institutions (complete international OSH contact information); CIS Glossary of OSH Terms (OSH words & expressions: English, French, Spanish, German, Russian); CIS Bibliographies; *Library* Open to public

International Ocean Institute (IOI) / Institut international de l'ocean
PO Box 3, Gzira GZR 1000 Malta
Tel: 356-21-346-529; *Fax:* 356-21-346-502
ioihq@ioihq.org.mt
www.ioinst.org
Overview: A small international organization founded in 1972
Mission: To promote education, training & research to enhance the peaceful uses of ocean space & its resources, their management & regulation as well as the protection & conservation of the marine environment, guided by the principle of the common heritage of mankind
Chief Officer(s):
Awni Behnam, President
awni.behnam@ioihq.org.mt
Finances: *Annual Operating Budget:* $1.5 Million-$3 Million; *Funding Sources:* Donations; UN & government funding agencies; private foundations; endowment fund
Staff Member(s): 35; 200 volunteer(s)
Membership: 25 operational centres worldwide; *Committees:* Directors; Governing Board
Activities: Policy research; training; advisory services; *Speaker Service:* Yes *Library:* IOI, Malta HQ Library

International Ombudsman Institute
c/o Austrian Ombudsman Board, PO Box 20, Singerstrasse 17, Vienna A-1015 Austria
Tel: 43/1/512 93 88; *Fax:* 43/1/512 93 88-200
ioi@volksanw.gv.at
www.theioi.org
Overview: A small international organization
Mission: To make an objective investigation into complaints from the public about the administration of government
Chief Officer(s):
Beverley A. Wakem, DNZM, CBE, President
Peter Kostelka, Secretary General

International Order of the King's Daughters & Sons
PO Box 1017, Chautauqua NY 14722-1017 USA
Tel: 716-357-4951; *Fax:* 716-357-3762
iokds5@windstream.net
www.iokds.org
Overview: A large international organization founded in 1886
Mission: Interdenominational organization of Christians
Chief Officer(s):
Joyce S. Cote, President
orderpresident24@comcast.net
Membership: 5,000; *Fees:* $25 ages 17 & up; $2 under age 18; *Committees:* By-laws; Chautauqua Building; Editorial; Headquarters; Long Range Development & Planning; Membership Extension; New Horizons; Special Projects; Nominating
Activities: Scholarship program; support of mission work;
Awards:
• Around the World Scholarships (Scholarship)
• Chautauqua Scholarships (Scholarship)
• Health Careers Scholarships (Scholarship)
• New Horizons Scholarships (Scholarship)
• North American Indian Scholarships (Scholarship)
• Student Ministry Scholarships (Scholarship)
Publications:
• The Silver Cross [a publication of the International Order of the King's Daughters & Sons]
Editor: Vince Ciarlo

British Columbia Branch
938 Eloery St., Victoria BC V9A 4S1
Chief Officer(s):
Katherine Morettin, Treasurer

New Brunswick Branch
48 Fairview Dr., Fredericton NB E3C 1L1
Chief Officer(s):
Elizabeth Galey, Student Ministry Director

Ontario Branch
#330, 567 Cambridge St., Ottawa ON K1S 4J5
Tel: 613-235-1147
Chief Officer(s):
Dorothy Hobbs, President

International Organic Inspectors Association (IOIA)
PO Box 6, Broadus MT 59317 USA
Tel: 406-436-2031; *Fax:* 406-436-2031
ioia@ioia.net
www.ioia.net
www.facebook.com/margaret.scoles.3
Also Known As: Independent Organic Inspectors Association
Overview: A small international organization founded in 1991
Mission: To address issues & concerns relevant to organic inspectors, to provide quality inspector training & to promote integrity & consistency in the orgnic certification process
Chief Officer(s):
Margaret Scoles, Executive Director
Staff Member(s): 6
Membership: 250 from 41 countries; *Member Profile:* Organic farm, livestock & process inspectors dedicated to verification of organic production practices

International Organisation of La Francophonie *Voir* Organisation internationale de la Francophonie

International Organization for Standardization (ISO) / Organisation internationale de normalisation
PO Box 56, 1, ch. de la Voie-Creuse, Geneva 20 1211 Switzerland
Tel: 41-22-749-01-11; *Fax:* 41-22-733-34-30
central@iso.org
www.iso.org
www.linkedin.com/company/iso-international-organization-for-standardiz
www.facebook.com/isostandards
twitter.com/isostandards
plus.google.com/+iso#+iso/posts
Overview: A small international organization founded in 1947
Mission: To promote the development of standardization & related activities in the world with a view to facilitating the international exchange of goods & services; developing cooperation in the spheres of intellectual, scientific, technological & economic activity; the results of ISO's technical work are published as "International Standards"
Affliation(s): Standards Council of Canada
Chief Officer(s):
Terry Hill, President
Sadao Takeda, Vice-President, Policy
Finances: *Funding Sources:* 62% member bodies + 38% subscriptions + publications income + other services
Staff Member(s): 154
Membership: 162; *Member Profile:* National body, representative of standardization in its country; *Committees:* 192 technical committees which develop international standards in a wide range of technological areas; the secretariat for a number of committees is held by the ISO member body for Canada (Standards Council of Canada, Ottawa)
Activities: *Library:* Reference Library; Open to public

International Organization of Scenographers, Theatre Architects & Technicians
#A, 2nd Floor, No.7, Sec.2, Renai Rd., Taipei 10055 Taiwan
Tel: 886(0)2 77260088; *Fax:* 886(0)2 77260808
secretariat@oistat.org
www.oistat.nl
Overview: A medium-sized international organization
Mission: To bring together and represent those who work as Scenographers, Theatre Architects & Technicians.
Affliation(s): Canadian Institute for Theatre Technology
Chief Officer(s):
Louis Janssen, President
louis@theateradvies.nl
Chang Wei-Wen, Executive Director
executivedirector@oistat.org

International Organization of Securities Commissions (IOSCO) / Organisation internationale des commissions de valeurs (OICV)
C/ Oquendo 12, Madrid 28006 Spain
Tel: 34-91-417-55-49; *Fax:* 34-91-555-93-68
Other Communication: Press/Media Enquiries e-mail: press@iosco.org
mail@iosco.org
www.iosco.org
twitter.com/IOSCOPress

Previous Name: Interamerican Association of Securities Commissions & Similar Agencies
Overview: A large international organization founded in 1983
Mission: To cooperate together to ensure a better regulation of the markets, on both the domestic & international level, in order to maintain just & efficient securities markets; To exchange information in order to promote development of domestic markets; To unite efforts to establish standards & effective surveillance of international securities transactions; To provide mutual assistance to ensure the integrity of the markets by rigorous application of standards & by effective enforcement against offences
Chief Officer(s):
David Wright, Secretary General
Tajinder Singh, Deputy Secretary General
Finances: *Annual Operating Budget:* $500,000-$1.5 Million; *Funding Sources:* Membership dues
Staff Member(s): 8
Membership: 145; *Fees:* 10.100 Euros; *Member Profile:* Ordinary - securities commission or similar governmental agency, self-regulatory organization when there is no governmental regulatory agency; Associate - association that assembles the public regulatory bodies having jurisdiction in subdivisions of a country, when the national regulatory body is already a member or any other regulatory body, with exception of a self-regulatory body, recommended by the Executive Committee; Affiliate - international organization with universal or regional scope or organization recommended by the Executive Committee & recommended self-regulatory organizations; *Committees:* Executive; Technical Committee on International Transactions; Emerging Markets; Consultative (Self-Regulatory Organizations); Interamerican Regional; European Regional; Asia-Pacific Regional; Africa-Middle East Regional
Activities: On-the-job training program; IOSCO Educational Program; *Library* Open to public
Meetings/Conferences:
• International Organization of Securities Commissions / Organisation internationale des commissions de valeurs Annual Conference 2015, June, 2015, London
Scope: International

International Orienteering Federation (IOF)

Radiokatu 20, Slu FIN-00093 Finland
Tel: 358-9-3481-3112; *Fax:* 358-9-3481-3113
iof@orienteering.org
www.orienteering.org
www.facebook.com/IOFarena
Overview: A small international organization founded in 1961
Mission: To promote & develop the outdoor sport of orienteering
Affliation(s): Canadian Orienteering Federation
Chief Officer(s):
Barbro Rönnberg, Secretary General
barbro.ronnberg.iof@orienteering.org
Anna Jacobson, Assistant to the Secretary General
anna.jacobson(at) orienteering.org
Staff Member(s): 2
Membership: 70 member countries; *Committees:* Discipline: Foot Orienteering; Ski Orienteering; Mountain Bike Orienteering; Trail Orienteering; Specialist: Rules; Map; IT; Environment; Medical

International Orthoptic Association (IOA)

c/o Moorfields Eye Hospital, City Rd., London EC1V 2PD
United Kingdom
webmaster@internationalorthoptics.org
www.internationalorthoptics.org
linkedin.com/groups/International-Orthoptic-Association-IOA-4119567
Overview: A large international organization founded in 1967
Mission: To promote the science of orthoptics throughout the world; To maintain & improve standards of education, training, & orthoptic practice
Chief Officer(s):
Karen McMain, President
president@internationalorthoptics.org
Bronia Unwin, Secretary
secretary@internationalorthoptics.org
Jane Tapley, Treasurer
treasurer@internationalorthoptics.org
Membership: 15 full member countries + 5 associate member countries (20,000 orthoptists); *Member Profile:* National professional orthoptic associations; Individual orthoptists; Ophthalmologists; Affiliate members; *Committees:* Finance; International Relations; Membership; Public Relations; Scientific; Terminology; Website
Activities: Providing information to national orthoptic bodies & individual orthoptists; Engaging in advocacy activities regarding issues of importance to the orthoptic profession; Offering networking opportunities
Meetings/Conferences:
• XIIIth International Orthoptic Congress 2016, June, 2016, Westin Harbour Castle Hotel, Rotterdam
Scope: International
Description: Plenary sessions, exhibitions, & educational activities
Contact Information: Web Site: www.ioacongress2016.org; E-mail: IOA2016@congrex.com

International Pacific Halibut Commission (IPHC)

#300, 2320 West Commodore Way, Seattle WA 98199-1287 USA
Tel: 206-634-1838; *Fax:* 206-632-2983
www.iphc.int
www.facebook.com/InternationalPacificHalibutCommission
twitter.com/iphcinfo
www.youtube.com/user/IPHCStaff
Overview: A medium-sized international organization founded in 1923
Mission: Mandated to research and manage Pacific halibut stocks, within the Convention waters of the U.S. and Canada.
Chief Officer(s):
Bruce M. Leaman, Executive Director
Staff Member(s): 29

International Papillomavirus Society (IPVS)

#1714, 239 - 4 Ave., Pittsburgh PA 15222 USA
Tel: 412-471-1981; *Fax:* 412-471-7503
www.ipvsoc.org
Overview: A medium-sized international organization
Mission: To facilitate research on human & animal papillomaviruses & their associated diseases; To promote the translation of research into applications & policies
Chief Officer(s):
Joel Palefsky, President
jpalefsky@medicine.ucsf.edu
Tracey Escamilla, Account Manager
tescamilla@kenes.com
W. Martin Kast, Secretary-Treasurer, 323-442-3870, Fax: 323-442-7760
Martin.Kast@med.usc.edu
Membership: *Member Profile:* Biomedical scientists & physicians engaged in papillomavirus research
Activities: Providing professional communication; Offering public education; Presenting training opportunities
Publications:
• International Papillomavirus Society Membership Directory
Type: Directory

International Peace Bureau (IPB) / Bureau international de la paix

41 Zurich Rd., Geneva 1201 Switzerland
Tel: 41-22-731-64-29; *Fax:* 41-22-738-94-19
mailbox@ipb.org
www.ipb.org
www.facebook.com/ipb1910
twitter.com/IntlPeaceBureau
www.youtube.com/user/ipb1910
Overview: A small international organization founded in 1892
Mission: To serve the cause of peace by the promotion of international cooperation & the non-violent & peaceful solution of international conflicts
Affiliation(s): Voice of Women; Act for Disarmament Coalition
Chief Officer(s):
Colin Archer, Secretary General
Reiner Braun, Co-President
Ingeborg Breines, Co-President
Staff Member(s): 3
Membership: *Fees:* Schedule available; *Member Profile:* Full - non-aligned & independent peace organizations; associate (non-voting) - other organizations working for peace as one of their aims (ie. labour unions, churches, cultural organizations); individual - persons who support the work of the IPB; *Committees:* Steering
Activities: Peace education; nuclear weapons; landmines; arms trade; European security; conflicts/human rights; international law; environment; women; Geneva connections; *Library* Open to public

International Peat Society (IPS)

Kauppakatu 19 D 31, Jyväskylä FIN-40100 Finland
Tel: 358-40-418-4075; *Fax:* 358-14-3385-410
ips@peatsociety.org
www.peatsociety.org
Overview: A small international organization founded in 1968
Mission: IPS works toward the advancement & communication of scientific, technical, & social knowledge for the wise use of peatlands & peat.
Affliation(s): UNESCO
Chief Officer(s):
Jaakko Silpola, Secretary General
Markku Mäkelä, President
markku.makela@gsf.fi
Membership: 1,450 from 36 countries; *Fees:* Schedule available; *Member Profile:* Scientific, industrial, commercial, & other organizations; Individuals interested in the study, conservation, & utilization of peat & peatlands
Activities: Organizing congresses, symposia & workshops; Publishing scientific publications; *Library*
Awards:
• Wim Tonnis Peat Award (Award)
Meetings/Conferences:
• International Peat Society Annual Meetings and International Peat Technology Conference 2015, June, 2015, Tullamore Court Hotel, Tullamore
Scope: International
Contact Information: URL: www.peatsociety.org/tullamore2015
• 2015 IPS-ISHS Peat in Horticulture, September, 2015, Vienna
Scope: International
• 15th International Peat Congress: Peatland in Harmony - Agriculture, Industry, Nature, August, 2016, Kuching
Scope: International
Publications:
• Mires & Peat
Type: Journal; *Editor:* Dr. Olivia Bragg; Prof. Jack Rieley
Profile: A joint scientific journal of the International Peat Society & the International Mire Conservation Group, featuring peer-reviewed academic papers on research related tomires, peatlands, & peat throughout the world
• Peat News
Type: Newsletter; *Frequency:* Monthly; *Editor:* Susann Warnecke
• Peatlands International
Type: Magazine; *Frequency:* Semiannually; *Accepts Advertising*; *Number of Pages:* 60; *Price:* Free for members
Profile: Background reports on peat & peatlands, reviews of conferences & books, research findings, business reports, & internal information about the IPS
• Proceedings
Profile: Proceedings of IPS conferences, symposia, & workshops

International Pediatric Association (IPA) / Association internationale de pédiatrie

141 Northwest Point Blvd., Elk Grove Village IL 60007-1098 USA
www.ipa-world.org
www.facebook.com/InternationalPediatricAssociation
twitter.com/ipaworldorg
Overview: A large international organization founded in 1910
Mission: To promote the physical, mental, & social health of all children; To realize high standards of health for newborns, children, & adolescents in all countries of the world
Chief Officer(s):
Sergio Cabral, President
William J. Keenan, Executive Director
Membership: *Member Profile:* Regional pediatric societies; International pediatric specialty societies; National pediatric societies; *Committees:* Advocacy & Government Affairs; Archives & Alumni; Communication; Education; Ethics; Finance & Fundraising; Governance & Constitution; Membership; Newsletter
Meetings/Conferences:
• 28th International Pediatric Association Congress of Pediatrics 2016, August, 2016, Vancouver, BC
Scope: International
Publications:
• IPA Quarterly Newsletter
Type: Newsletter; *Frequency:* Quarterly; *Editor:* Dr. Swati Y. Bhave

International PEN / PEN International

Brownlow House, 50/51 High Holborn, London WC1V 6ER
United Kingdom
Tel: +44(0) 20 7405 0338; *Fax:* +44(0) 20 7405 0339
info@pen-international.org
www.pen-international.org

www.facebook.com/peninternational
twitter.com/pen_int
Overview: A medium-sized international charitable organization founded in 1921
Mission: To promote friendship & goodwill among writers everywhere, regardless of their political or other views; to fight for freedom of expression & to defend vigorously writers suffering from oppressive regimes whether of the extreme right or the extreme left
Affliation(s): Canadian PEN Centre; Centre québécois du PEN international
Chief Officer(s):
Laura McVeigh, Executive Director
Laura.McVeigh@pen-international.org
Finances: *Annual Operating Budget:* $100,000-$250,000; *Funding Sources:* Membership dues
Staff Member(s): 4
Membership: 14,000; 144 Centres in 102 countries worldwide; *Fees:* US$12; *Member Profile:* All qualified writers regardless of nationality, race, colour, or religion; each centre, being autonomous, sets its own membership qualifications; *Committees:* Writers in Prison Committee; Writers for Peace; Translation & Linguistic Rights; Women Writers' Committee
Activities: *Library:* PEN Global Library (at Slovak PEN); Open to public

International Permafrost Association (IPA)

c/o H. Lantuit, Alfred Wegener Institute for Polar & Marine Research, Telefrafenberg A43, Potsdam 14473 Germany
Tel: +49-331-288-2162; *Fax:* +49-331-288-2188
contact@ipa-permafrost.org
ipa.arcticportal.org
twitter.com/ipapermafrost
Overview: A medium-sized international organization founded in 1983
Mission: To disseminate knowledge concerning permafrost; To promote cooperation among persons & national or international organizations engaged in scientific investigation & enginering work on permafrost
Affliation(s): International Union of Geological Science
Chief Officer(s):
Hugues Lantuit, International Secretariat
Hugues.Lantuit@awi.de
Hans-W. Hubberten, President
hans-wolfgang.hubberten@awi.de
Hanne H. Christiansen, Vice-President
hanne.christiansen@unis.no
Antoni G. Lewkowicz, Vice-President
alewkowi@uottawa.ca
Membership: *Committees:* Standing Committee on Data, Information & Communications; International Advisory Committee for ICOP
Activities: Assembling the following working groups: Antarctic Permafrost & Periglacial Environments; Coastal & Offshore Permafrost Dynamics; Cryosol; Glaciers & Permafrost Hazards in High Mountain Slopes; Isotopes & Geochemistry of Permafrost; Periglacial Landforms, Processes & Climate; Permafrost & Climate; Planetary Permafrost & Astrobiology; Permafrost Engineering
Meetings/Conferences:
• International Permafrost Association 2016 11th International Conference on Permafrost, 2016, Potsdam
Scope: International
Description: The conference will be held in early summer
Contact Information: E-mail: contact@ipa-permafrost.org
Publications:
• Frozen Ground: The News Bulletin of the International Permafrost Association
Type: Yearbook; *Frequency:* Annually *ISSN:* 2076-7463
Profile: Member news, current events, working group & task force reports, calendar, & publications
• Permafrost & Periglacial Processes
Type: Journal; *Frequency:* Semiannually
Profile: Reports from the International Permafrost Association
• Proceedings of the International Conferences on Permafrost
Type: Yearbook; *Frequency:* Annually
Profile: Peer-reviewed conference proceedings

International Plant Nutrition Institute (IPNI)

#550, 3500 Parkway Lane, Norcross GA 30092 USA
Tel: 770-447-0335; *Fax:* 770-448-0439
info@ipni.net
www.ipni.net
Previous Name: Potash & Phosphate Institute/Potash & Phosphate Institute of Canada
Overview: A medium-sized international organization founded in 1935
Mission: To assist in the design & implementation of agronomic research; to obtain scientific facts & education programs to tell those facts about balanced fertilization, particularly in relation to agricultural production systems; to conduct & provide on-site support of field experiments worldwide
Chief Officer(s):
Terry L. Roberts, President
troberts@ipni.net
Tom Jensen, Northern Great Plains Director, (Saskatchewan)
tjensen@ipni.net
Tom Bruulsema, N. American-Northeastern Director, (Ontario)
tom.bruulsema@ipni.net
Finances: *Annual Operating Budget:* Greater than $5 Million; *Funding Sources:* North American potash & phosphate producers; Government of Saskatchewan
Staff Member(s): 6
Membership: 16 corporate; 6 affiliate companies; *Member Profile:* North American potash or phosphate producer
Activities: *Library* Open to public
Awards:
• Robert E. Wagner Award (Award)
• J. Fielding Reed PPI Fellowship (Scholarship)

Northern Great Plains Region - Saskatoon
#102-411 Downey Rd., Saskatoon SK S7N 4L8
Tel: 306-652-3467; *Fax:* 306-664-8941
Chief Officer(s):
Tom Jensen, Director

International Plant Propagators Society, Inc. (IPPS)

4 Hawthorn Court., Castle PA 17015-7930 USA
Tel: 717-243-7685; *Fax:* 717-243-7691
Secretary@ipps.org
www.ipps.org
Overview: A medium-sized international organization founded in 1951
Mission: To seek & share information about the art & science of plant propagation
Chief Officer(s):
David Cliffe, Chair
d.cliffe@bigpond.net.au
Finances: *Annual Operating Budget:* $100,000-$250,000; *Funding Sources:* Membership dues
Membership: 3,200 individual; *Fees:* Varies with region; *Member Profile:* Open to individuals for commercial purposes or to those involved in research, teaching or extension activities

International Primary Care Respiratory Group (IPCRG)

c/o Samantha Louw, PO Box 11961, Westhill AB32 9AE Scotland
Tel: 44-1224-743-753; *Fax:* 44-1224-743-753
BusinessManager@theipcrg.org
www.theipcrg.org
Overview: A medium-sized international organization
Mission: To represent international primary care perspectives in respiratory medicine; To raise standards of care worldwide
Chief Officer(s):
Siân Williams, Executive Officer
Activities: Engaging in collaborative research; Disseminating best practice information; Providing educational opportunities
Publications:
• Primary Care Respiratory Journal
Type: Journal
Profile: Original research papers, review, & discussion papers on respiratory conditions commonly found in primary & community settings in countries around the world

International Primate Protection League (IPPL)

PO Box 766, Summerville SC 29484 USA
Tel: 843-871-2280; *Fax:* 843-871-7988
info@ippl.org
www.ippl.org
Overview: A medium-sized international charitable organization founded in 1973
Mission: To encourage & contribute to a better understanding of matters relating to the conservation of non-human primates & their habitats; to promote relevant training & educational activities with reference to non-human primates; to promote & enhance the welfare of non-human primates; to support primate protection projects; to investigate smuggling of primates
Member of: Monitor Consortium; Summit for the Animals; International Union for Conservation of Nature; Civicus
Chief Officer(s):
Dianne Taylor-Snow, Chair
Shirley McGreal, Executive Director
Jean Martin, Secretary-Treasurer
Finances: *Annual Operating Budget:* $500,000-$1.5 Million; *Funding Sources:* Membership dues; foundation grants; bequests
Staff Member(s): 7; 4 volunteer(s)
Membership: 15,000 in over 60 countries; *Fees:* $20 regular; $10 student; $50 sustaining; $100 patron

International Reading Association (IRA)

PO Box 8139, 800 Barksdale Rd., Newark DE 19714-8139 USA
Tel: 302-731-1600; *Fax:* 302-731-1057
Toll-Free: 800-336-7323
customerservice@reading.org
www.reading.org
www.linkedin.com/company/59530
www.facebook.com/pages/International-Reading-Association/81491751082
twitter.com/Readingtoday
Overview: A large international organization founded in 1956
Mission: IRA promotes high levels of literacy for all. Work of the Association includes the following: improving the quality of reading instruction by studying the reading process & teaching techniques; disseminating reading research through conferences, journals & other publications; & encouraging a lifetime reading habit. The Association advocates for policy, curriculum & education reform that supports both teachers & learners. It also encourages collaboration among professionals internationally.
Chief Officer(s):
Jill Lewis-Spector, President
jlewisprof1@yahoo.com
Marcie Craig Post, Executive Director
exec@reading.org
Membership: 100,000; *Fees:* US$39 basic; $29 online; $24 student; schedule for developing economies; *Committees:* Bylaws & Resolutions; Citations & Awards; Council & Affiliate Services; Government Relations; Intellectual Freedom; International Development; Professional Standards & Ethics; Program; Publications; Studies & Research; Ad Hoc Committees; Commissions
Activities: *Awareness Events:* International Literacy Day - Sept. 8 *Library:* Ralph C. Staiger Library; by appointment
Publications:
• Journal of Adolescent & Adult Literacy
Type: Journal; *Frequency:* 8 pa; *Editor:* Tom Bean; Helen Harper
Profile: Literacy journal published exclusively for teachers of older learners
• Lectura y Vida
Type: Journal; *Frequency:* Quarterly
Profile: A Spanish journal
• Reading Online
Type: Electronic Journal *ISSN:* 1096-1232
Profile: Literacy practice & research in classrooms serving students aged 5 to 18
• Reading Research Quarterly
Type: Journal; *Editor:* David Bloome; Ian Wilkinson
Profile: Reports of important studies, multidisciplinary research, & various modes of investigation; diverse viewpoints on literacy practices, teaching, &learning
• The Reading Teacher
Type: Journal; *Frequency:* 8 pa; *Editor:* Robert B. Cooter; J. Helen Perkins
• Reading Today
Type: Newspaper; *Frequency:* Bimonthly

International Real Estate Federation *See* Fédération internationale des professions immobilières

International Real Estate Institute (IREI)

PO Box 879, 810 North Farrell Dr., Palm Springs CA 92263 USA
Tel: 760-327-5284; *Fax:* 760-327-5631
Toll-Free: 877-743-6799
support@assoc-hdqts.org
www.irei-assoc.org
Overview: A medium-sized international organization founded in 1967
Member of: International Association Managers
Chief Officer(s):
Snehal Jardosh, Member, Advisory Council
Bill Merrell, Member, Advisory Council
Staff Member(s): 14; 4 volunteer(s)
Membership: 2,800; *Fees:* US$195; *Member Profile:* International real estate professionals

International Reference Centre for Community Water Supply & Sanitation *See* IRC International Water & Sanitation Centre

International Research Group on Wood Protection (IRG)
PO Box 5609, Stn. Drottning Kristinas väg 67, Stockholm SE-114 86 Sweden
Tel: 46-8-101-453; *Fax:* 46-8-108-081
irg@sp.se
www.irg-wp.com
www.linkedin.com/groups/International-Research-Group-on-Wood-4161596
www.facebook.com/142224589156224
Overview: A small international organization founded in 1969
Mission: To promote research throughout the world on the subject of wood protection; to facilitate collaborative research projects; to promote the exchange of technical information on wood protection
Chief Officer(s):
Jöran Jermer, Secretariat
joran.jermer@sp.se
Finances: *Funding Sources:* Membership & conference fees; sponsorships
Membership: *Fees:* 900 SEK (Swedish Kroner) - regular; 450 SEK - student; *Member Profile:* Open to all persons with appropriate qualifications or research experience who are active or interested in wood protection research; *Committees:* Executive; Finance; Scientific Program; Ron Cockcroft Award; IRG Travel Awards; Communications
Activities: 4-day conference; workshops; plenary meetings; *Rents Mailing List:* Yes *Library* by appointment
Awards:
• IRG Travel Awards (Grant)
• Ron Cockcroft Award (Grant)
Travel grant for younger scientists, PhD students to attend annual meeting

International Research Institute for Media, Communication & Cultural Development
Marxergasse 48/8, Vienna A-1030 Austria
Tel: 431-236-29-23; *Fax:* 431-236-39-2399
office@mediacult.at
www.mediacult.at
Also Known As: Mediacult
Previous Name: International Institute for Audio-Visual Communication & Cultural Development
Overview: A small international licensing organization founded in 1969
Mission: To observe & to document the influence of new media technologies on cultural development; to produce research findings to serve as decision-making aids to cultural & media policy makers
Chief Officer(s):
Alfred Smudits, Honorary Secretary General
smudits@mediacult.at
Finances: *Annual Operating Budget:* $100,000-$250,000; *Funding Sources:* State subsidies
Staff Member(s): 3
Membership: 64
Activities: Research in music & new communication technologies in the arts; consultancy; *Library* by appointment

International Sanitary Supply Association, Inc. (ISSA)
7373 Lincoln Ave. North, Lincolnwood IL 60712-1799 USA
Tel: 847-982-0800; *Fax:* 847-982-1012
Toll-Free: 800-225-4772
info@issa.com
www.issa.com
www.linkedin.com/groups?gid=1799553
www.facebook.com/issaworldwide
twitter.com/issaworldwide
Previous Name: National Sanitary Supply Association
Overview: A large international organization founded in 1923
Mission: To link resources & expertise of everyone in the cleaning & maintenance products industry through an ongoing program of training & education, regional & national conferences, publications & the industry's largest annual trade show; to act as one voice before government agencies; to increase product quality, service & value to the customer; to promote the highest standards of public health & sanitation
Chief Officer(s):
John P. Garfinkel, Executive Director
Barbara Bornmann, Executive Assistant
barbara@issa.com
Finances: *Annual Operating Budget:* Greater than $5 Million; *Funding Sources:* Convention revenue; membership dues; educational materials
Staff Member(s): 24; 15 volunteer(s)
Membership: 5,700 companies in 83 countries; *Fees:* Schedule available; *Member Profile:* Firms which have been continuously engaged in the manufacture &/or distribution of cleaning & maintenance supplies & related products & services; classes of membership are distributor, wholesaler, manufacturer, associate, manufacturer representative, publisher; *Committees:* ISSA/INTERCLEAN; YES Coordinators
Activities: *Awareness Events:* Operation Clean Sweep *Library*

International Seed Federation (ISF)
ISF Secretariat, ch du Reposoir 7, 1260, Nyon Switzerland
Tel: +41 22 365 44 20; *Fax:* +41 22 365 44 21
isf@worldseed.org
www.worldseed.org
www.facebook.com/153497914694532?ref=ts&fref=ts
twitter.com/IntSeedFed
www.youtube.com/user/isfprochannel
Overview: A medium-sized international organization
Mission: To represent the interests of the international seed industry; To serve as an international forum for the world seed trade & plant breeders' community
Chief Officer(s):
Marcel Bruins, Secretary General
Radha Ranganathan, Director, Technical Affairs
Piero Sismondohan, Director, Seed Technology & Trade
Membership: *Member Profile:* National seed associations & seed companies from more than seventy developed & developing countries
Activities: Interacting with public & private institutions related to the international seed trade; Providing procedural rules for dispute settlement & trade rules; Publishing seed trade statistics
Publications:
• International Seed Federation Newsletter
Type: Newsletter; *Frequency:* Quarterly
• International Seed Federation World Seed Congress Report
Type: Report; *Frequency:* Annually

International Skating Union (ISU) / Union Internationale de Patinage
Chemin de Primerose 2, Lausanne 1007 Switzerland
Tel: 41-21-612-6666; *Fax:* 41-21-612-6677
info@isu.ch
www.isu.org
www.facebook.com/isuofficial
www.youtube.com/user/SkatingISU/featured
Overview: A small international organization founded in 1892
Mission: To regulate, control & promote the sports of figure & speed skating & their organized development on the basis of friendship & mutual understanding between sportsmen & women & to broaden interest in figure & speed skating sports by increasing their popularity, improving their quality & increasing the number of participants throughout the world
Chief Officer(s):
Fredi Schmid, Director General
Finances: *Annual Operating Budget:* Greater than $5 Million
Staff Member(s): 11; 60 volunteer(s)
Membership: 73; *Fees:* 300 Swiss francs; *Member Profile:* National skating associations
Activities: Administration of figure skating & speed skating sports throughout the world

International Snowmobile Manufacturers Association (ISMA)
#170, 1640 Haslett Rd., Haslett MI 48840 USA
Tel: 517-339-7788; *Fax:* 517-339-7798
ismasue@aol.com
www.snowmobile.org
Overview: A medium-sized international organization founded in 1995
Mission: To educate the public on safe snowmobiling benefits
Chief Officer(s):
Edward J. Klim, President
Finances: *Annual Operating Budget:* $250,000-$500,000
Staff Member(s): 2
Activities: *Library* Open to public

International Social Service (ISS) / Service social international
32 Quai du Seujet, Geneva 1201 Switzerland
Tel: 41-22-906-77-00; *Fax:* 41-22-906-77-01
info@iss-ssi.org
www.iss-ssi.org
Previous Name: International Migration Service
Overview: A small international organization founded in 1924
Mission: To assist individuals who, as a consequence of voluntary or forced migration or other social problems of an international character have to overcome personal or family difficulties, the solution of which requires coordinated action in several countries or in some cases only in the country of residence of the person concerned; to study from an international standpoint, the conditions & consequences of migration in relation to individual & family life, & as a result of these studies make appropriate recommendations
Member of: NGO Committee on UNICEF; ICSW
Affliation(s): International Social Service Canada
Chief Officer(s):
Jean Ayoub, Secretary General
Doug Lewis, President
Finances: *Funding Sources:* Membership fees; project grants
Membership: 4 associations/affiliated bureaus; 140 correspondants
Activities: *Library:* International Reference Centre for the Rights of Children Deprive; by appointment

International Society for Affective Disorders (ISAD)
c/o Caroline Holebrook, Institute of Psychiatry, King's College London, PO72 De Crespigny Park, Denmark Hill, London SE5 8AF UK
Tel: +44 (0) 20 7848 0295; *Fax:* +44 (0) 20 7848 0298
Other Communication: help@isad.org.uk
enquiry@isad.org.uk
www.isad.org.uk
twitter.com/ISADTweet
Overview: A large international charitable organization founded in 2001
Mission: To advance research into affective disorders through all relevant scientific disciplines
Chief Officer(s):
Sidney Kennedy, President
Allan Young, Treasurer
John Rush, Regional Representative, North America (Canada & the United States)
Caroline Holebrook, Administrator
caroline.holebrook@iop.kcl.ac.uk
Finances: *Funding Sources:* Sponsorships
Membership: *Member Profile:* Researchers; Clinicians; Members of recognized advocacy groups; *Committees:* Executive; Membership; Education; External Affairs; Programme
Activities: Engaging in advocacy activities; Promoting networking & the exchange of ideas
Meetings/Conferences:
• International Society for Affective Disorders 8th Biennial Conference 2016, 2016
Scope: International
Publications:
• Journal of Affective Disorders
Type: Journal; *Editor:* Cornelius Katona; Hagop Akiskal

International Society for Burn Injuries (ISBI)
c/o Administrator, 2172 Hwy. 181 South, Floresville TX 781114 USA
Fax: 830-216-4101
lizals@tgti.net
www.worldburn.org
Overview: A small international organization founded in 1965
Mission: To disseminate knowledge; to stimulate burn prevention
Chief Officer(s):
Elisabeth Greenfield McManus, Administrator, Fax: 830-947-3142
lizals@tgti.net
Richard L. Gamelli, President
rgamell@luc.edu
Nicole S. Gibran, Regional Representative, North America
burnadmn@u.washington.edu
Membership: *Member Profile:* Specialists in burn care; *Committees:* Executive; Burn Care; Research; Industry; Disaster Planning; Lab Services; Rehabilitation; Prevention; Nursing
Activities: Collaborating with WHO; Assisting the organization of educational courses
Publications:
• Burns
Type: Journal; *Price:* Free with ISBI membership

International Society for Business Education (ISBE) / Société internationale pour l'enseignement commercial (SIEC)
#100, 6302 Mineral Point Rd., Madison WI 53705 USA

Tel: 608-273-8467
secretary@siec-isbe.org
www.siec-isbe.org
Overview: A small international organization founded in 1901
Mission: To bridge the gap between business education & the world of business on an international scale
Chief Officer(s):
Judith Olson-Sutton, General Secretary
secretary@siec-isbe.org
Finances: *Annual Operating Budget:* Less than $50,000; *Funding Sources:* Membership dues
Staff Member(s): 1
Membership: 2,000; *Fees:* Schedule available; *Member Profile:* Business educators; individuals interested in business education; *Committees:* Network; Pedagogical
Awards:
• Annual Research Award (Award)

International Society for Ecological Economics (ISEE)

c/o Secretariat, PO Box 44194, West Allis WI 53214 USA
Tel: 1-414-453-0030; *Fax:* 1-973-273-2178
secretariat@isecoeco.org
www.isecoeco.org
www.facebook.com/iseeorg
twitter.com/ISEEORG
Overview: A medium-sized international organization founded in 1989
Mission: To extend & integrate the study & management of ecology & economics
Chief Officer(s):
Marina Fischer-Kowalski, President
Anne Carter Aitken, Treasurer/Secretariat
Finances: *Annual Operating Budget:* $100,000-$250,000; *Funding Sources:* Membership fees; grants
Membership: 2,008; *Fees:* $15-$130; *Committees:* Executive

International Society for Ecological Modelling (ISEM)

PMB 255, 550 M Ritchie Hwy., Severna Park MD 21146 USA
www.isemna.org
Overview: A small international organization founded in 1975
Mission: To promote the international exchange of ideas, scientific results, & general knowledge in the area of the application of systems analysis & simulation in ecology & natural resource management
Chief Officer(s):
Sven E. Jorgensen, President
msijapan@hotmail.com
Membership: *Fees:* $10 student; $20 individual; $100 institution

International Society for Environmental Epidemiology (ISEE)

c/o ISEE Secretariat, JSI Research & Training Institute, 44 Farnsworth St., Boston MA 2210 USA
Tel: 617-482-9485; *Fax:* 617-482-0617
www.iseepi.org
Overview: A small international organization founded in 1989
Mission: To provide a forum for the discussion of problems unique to the study of health & the environment, such as environmental exposures, health effects, methodology, environment-gene interactions, & ethics & law
Member of: International Society of Exposure Analysis
Chief Officer(s):
Verónica Vieira, Secretary-Treasurer
vvieira@uci.edu
Francine Laden, President
francine.laden@channing.harvard.edu
Francine Laden, Sec.-Treas.
francine.laden@channing.harvard.edu
Membership: 500-999; *Fees:* US$220 full member; US$145 basic; US$55 developing country & student; *Member Profile:* Members include epidemiologists, toxicologists, exposure analysts & others with an interest in environmental epidemiology, from academia, local, state & federal government, industry, & community organizations.; *Committees:* Nominations; Annual Conference; Awards; Membership; Communications; Ethics & Philosophy; Capacity Building in Developing Countries
Activities: *Rents Mailing List:* Yes
Awards:
• The ISEE Research Integrity Award (Award)
Recognizes those who have remained true to the core values of the profession by maintaining objectivity in protecting the public health interest above any other interest *Contact:* Daniel Wartenberg, Chair, Awards Committee, dew@eohsi.rutgers.edu
• Rebecca James Baker Memorial Prize (Award)
Eligibility: Graduate level students & new investigators who are within three years of completing their degree *Contact:* Irva Hertz-Picciotto, Co-Chair, ihp@ucdavis.edu
• John Goldsmith Award for Outstanding Conributions to Environmental Epidemiology (Award)
Recognizes environmental epidemiologist who seve as models of excellence in research, unwavering promotion of environmental health, & integrity*Deadline:* March *Contact:* Daniel Wartenberg, Chair, Awards Committee, dew@eohsi.rutgers.edu
Publications:
• Epidemiology
Type: Journal; *Frequency:* Bimonthly; *Editor:* Allen J. Wilcox
ISSN: 1044-3983
Profile: A peer-reviewed scientific journal featuring original research on the full spectrum of epidemiologic topics
• International Society for Environmental Epidemiology Directory of Members
Type: Directory
Profile: Includes all ISEE members

International Society for Environmental Ethics (ISEE)

c/o Allen Thompson, Dept. of Philosophy, Oregon State University, 102C Hovland Hall, Corvallis OR 97331-3902 USA
enviroethics@hotmail.com
enviroethics.org
www.facebook.com/EnvironmentalEthics
twitter.com/EnviroEthics
plus.google.com/u/0/105320470303657467396?prsrc=3
Overview: A small international organization founded in 1990
Chief Officer(s):
Phil Cafaro, President, 970-491-2061, Fax: 970-491-4900
philip.cafaro@colostate.edu
Ben Hale, Vice-President, 303-735-3624, Fax: 303-735-1576
bhale@colorado.edu
William Grove-Fanning, Secretary
Allen Thompson, Treasurer, 541-737-5654, Fax: 541-737-2571
allen.thompson@oregonstate.edu
Membership: *Fees:* $25 regular membership (US); $15 students (US); $25 regular international member
Activities: Providing information about environmental ethics; Maintaining a bibliography on environmental ethics; Offering educational events
Publications:
• Environmental Ethics Syllabus Project
Editor: Robert Hood *ISSN:* 1564-001
Profile: Information about courses in environmental philosophy & environmental ethics
• International Society for Environmental Ethics Newsletter
Frequency: 3 pa; *Editor:* Mark Woods; *Price:* Free with International Society for Environmental Ethics membership
Profile: Society activities & announcements, plus articles

International Society for Eye Research

PO Box 193940, San Francisco CA 94119 USA
Tel: 415-561-8569; *Fax:* 415-561-8531
mail@iser.org
www.iser.org
www.facebook.com/ISERPage
twitter.com/iserworld
Overview: A medium-sized international organization founded in 1968
Mission: To support & sustain excellent eye & vision research around the globe
Chief Officer(s):
Steven J. Fliesler, President
fliesler@buffalo.edu
Membership: 356; *Fees:* Schedule available; *Member Profile:* Vision research scientists from over 34 countries; *Committees:* Membership
Activities: Engaging in international collaboration; Offering networking opportunities
Publications:
• Experimental Eye Research
Type: Journal
Profile: Original research papers in the following sections: Aqueous Humor & Blood Flow; Cornea & Ocular Surface; Lens & Retina; & Choroid

International Society for Human & Animal Mycology (ISHAM)

Dept. of Haematology, Radboud University Nijmegen Medical Centre, Geert Grootplein Zuid 8, Nijmegen 6525 GA Netherlands
Tel: 31-24-361-9987; *Fax:* 31-24-354-2080
www.isham.org
Overview: A small international organization founded in 1960
Mission: To be devoted to all aspects of the field of medical mycology (fungal diseases of man & animals)
Chief Officer(s):
Peter Donnelly, General Secretary
Membership: 1000+

International Society for Human Rights (ISHR)

Borsigallee 9, Frankfurt am Main 60388 Germany
Tel: 49-(0)69-420 108-0; *Fax:* 49-(0)69-420 108-33
info@ishr.org
www.ishr.org
Overview: A medium-sized international organization founded in 1972
Mission: To assist isolated individuals or groups striving for human rights; to help divided families & those persecuted for religious beliefs
Member of: Liaison Committee of NGOs enjoying consultative status with eh Council of Europe
Affliation(s): United Nations, Dept. of Public Information; African Commission on Human Peoples' Rights
Chief Officer(s):
Marat Zakhidov, President
Finances: *Funding Sources:* Membership dues; donations; projects
Membership: 30,000 people in 38 countries
Activities: *Internships:* Yes

International Society for Magnetic Resonance in Medicine (ISMRM)

2030 Addison St., 7th Fl., Berkeley CA 94704 USA
Tel: 510-841-1899; *Fax:* 510-841-2340
info@ismrm.org
www.ismrm.org
Previous Name: Society of Magnetic Resonance
Merged from: Society of Magnetic Resonance in Medicine; Society of Magnetic Resonance Imaging
Overview: A medium-sized international organization founded in 1994
Mission: To further the development & application of magnetic resonance techniques in medicine & biology; To promote research, development, & applications in the field
Chief Officer(s):
Roberta A. Kravitz, Executive Director
roberta@ismrm.org
Jennifer Olson, Associate Executive Director
jennifer@ismrm.org
Robert Goldstein, Director, Education
bob@ismrm.org
Kristina King, Director, Membership & Study Groups
kristina@ismrm.org
Jerushaa Rich, Registrar
jerusha@ismrm.org
Membership: 6,000+; *Member Profile:* Clinicians; Physicists; Engineers; Biochemists; Technologists; *Committees:* Executive; Board of Trustees; Committee for Affiliated Sections - SMRT; Annual Meeting Program; Awards; Education; Finance; Governance; Historical Archives; Nominating; Publications; Safety; Workshop & Study Group Review; Ad Hoc Committee on Standards for Quantitative MR; Ad Hoc Committee on Sustainability; Ad Hoc Committee on Web-Based Services
Activities: Promoting communication; Developing continuing education
Meetings/Conferences:
• International Society for Magnetic Resonance in Medicine 2015 23rd Scientific Meeting & Exhibition, May, 2015, Toronto, ON
Scope: International
Description: Featuring the 24th Annual Meeting of the Section for Magnetic Resonance Technologists
Contact Information: Director, Meetings: Sandra Daudlin, E-mail: sandra@ismrm.org; Coordinator, Meetings: Melisa Martinez, E-mail: melisa@ismrm.org
• International Society for Magnetic Resonance in Medicine 2016 24th Scientific Meeting & Exhibition, May, 2016
Scope: International
Description: Featuring the 25th Annual Meeting of the Section for Magnetic Resonance Technologists
Contact Information: Director, Meetings: Sandra Daudlin, E-mail: sandra@ismrm.org; Coordinator, Meetings: Melisa Martinez, E-mail: melisa@ismrm.org
• International Society for Magnetic Resonance in Medicine 2017 25th Scientific Meeting & Exhibition, April, 2017, Honolulu, HI
Scope: International
Description: Featuring the 26th Annual Meeting of the Section for Magnetic Resonance Technologists
Contact Information: Director, Meetings: Sandra Daudlin, E-mail:

sandra@ismrm.org; Coordinator, Meetings: Melisa Martinez, E-mail: melisa@ismrm.org
• International Society for Magnetic Resonance in Medicine 2018 26th Scientific Meeting & Exhibition, April, 2018, Paris
Scope: International
Description: Featuring the 26th Annual Meeting of the Section for Magnetic Resonance Technologists
Contact Information: Director, Meetings: Sandra Daudlin, E-mail: sandra@ismrm.org; Coordinator, Meetings: Melisa Martinez, E-mail: melisa@ismrm.org
• International Society for Magnetic Resonance in Medicine 2019 27th Scientific Meeting & Exhibition, May, 2019, Montreal, QC
Scope: International
Description: Featuring the 26th Annual Meeting of the Section for Magnetic Resonance Technologists
Contact Information: Director, Meetings: Sandra Daudlin, E-mail: sandra@ismrm.org; Coordinator, Meetings: Melisa Martinez, E-mail: melisa@ismrm.org
• International Society for Magnetic Resonance in Medicine 2020 28th Scientific Meeting & Exhibition, 2020
Scope: International
Description: Featuring the 29th Annual Meeting of the Section for Magnetic Resonance Technologists
Publications:
• Journal of Magnetic Resonance Imaging
Type: Journal; *Editor:* C. Leon Partain, M.D., Ph.D.
Profile: Basic & clinical research, plus educational & review articles related to the diagnostic applications of magnetic resonance
• Magnetic Resonance in Medicine
Type: Journal; *Editor:* Michael B. Smith
Profile: Original investigations concerned with the development & use of nuclear magnetic resonance & electron paramagnetic resonance techniques for medical applications
• MR Pulse
Type: Newsletter
Profile: Society updates & announcements

International Society for Music Education (ISME)

#148, 45 Glenferrie Rd., Malvern VA 3144 Australia
Tel: 61-8-9386-2654; *Fax:* 61-8-9386-2658
isme@isme.org
www.isme.org
www.facebook.com/136976192999210
twitter.com/official_isme
www.youtube.com/user/isme1953
Overview: A medium-sized international charitable organization founded in 1953
Mission: To serve as a network for the music educators, music researchers & students, & music therapists of the world; to build & maintain a worldwide community of music educators characterized by mutual respect & support
Member of: International Music Council
Affliation(s): UNESCO
Chief Officer(s):
Margaret Barrett, President
Liane Hentschke, Chair of ISME 2014
Finances: *Annual Operating Budget:* $50,000-$100,000; *Funding Sources:* Membership dues; conference revenue; sponsorship
Staff Member(s): 1
Membership: 1,330; *Fees:* Based on the Human Development Index determined by the United Nations; *Member Profile:* Individuals, institutions, organizations; *Committees:* Research; Education of the Professional Musician; Music in Schools & Teacher Education; Music in Special Education, Music Therapy & Music Medicine; Community Music Activity; Music in Cultural, Educational & Mass Media Policies; Early Childhood Music Education; Instrumental/Studio Pedagogy
Meetings/Conferences:
• 32nd World Conference of the International Society for Music Education, 2016
Scope: International
Description: Listening to the Musical Diversity of the World

International Society for Neurochemistry (ISN)

c/o Kenes International, #1, 3, rue de Chantepoulet, Geneva 1211 Switzerland
Tel: 41-22-906-9151; *Fax:* 41-22-732-2607
www.neurochemistry.org
www.facebook.com/205062269527045
twitter.com/ISN_secretariat
Overview: A medium-sized international organization founded in 1965
Mission: To facilitate the worldwide advance of neurochemistry & related neuroscience disciplines; to foster the education & development of neurochemists, particularly of young & emerging investigators
Chief Officer(s):
Alois Saria, President
alois.saria@i-med.ac.at
Monica J. Carson, Secretary
Kazuhiro Ikenaka, Treasurer
ikenaka@nips.ac.jp
Membership: *Fees:* $60 full; $25 student; *Member Profile:* Ordinary - past & present record of neurochemical research; associate - interest in neurochemical aspects of subjects; junior - under the age of 30 with a less than four years' postdoctoral experience; *Committees:* Rules; Aid and Education in Neurochemistry; Travel Grant; Advanced School; Finance; Schools Initiative; Biennial Program; Conference; Publication; Advanced School
Activities: Biennial international meetings

International Society for Pediatric & Adolescent Diabetes (ISPAD)

c/o KIT, Kurfürstendamm 71, 10709, Berlin Germany
Tel: +49 30 24603210; *Fax:* +49 30 24603200
secretariat@ispad.org
www.ispad.org
Overview: A medium-sized international organization
Mission: To promote research, science, education, & advocacy in childhood & adolescent diabetes
Chief Officer(s):
Lynda K. Fisher, President
lfisher@chla.usc.edu
Ragnar Hanas, Secretary General
ragnar.hanas@vgregion.se
Kenneth J. Robertson, Treasurer
kjr@diabetes-scotland.org
Membership: *Fees:* $50 emeritus membership; $100 regular members; *Member Profile:* Persons with scientific & clinical expertise in childhood & adolescent diabetes
Meetings/Conferences:
• International Society for Pediatric & Adolescent Diabetes 2015 41st Annual Meeting, October, 2015, Brisbane
Scope: International
Description: A scientific meeting featuring paper, poster, & plenary sessions, workshops, & symposia
Contact Information: URL: www.ispad-apeg.com
Publications:
• International Society for Pediatric & Adolescent Diabetes Membership Directory
Type: Directory
Profile: A listing of society members with contact information
• ISPAD [International Society for Pediatric & Adolescent Diabetes] Newsletter
Type: Newsletter
Profile: Society activities, including meeting reviews, educational opportunities, forthcoming events
• Pediatric Diabetes
Type: Journal; *Price:* Free with International Society for Pediatric & Adolescent Diabetes memberships

International Society for Performance Improvement (ISPI)

PO Box 13035, Silver Spring MD 20910-2753 USA
Tel: 301-587-8570; *Fax:* 301-587-8573
info@ispi.org
www.ispi.org
www.linkedin.com/ISPIGlobal
www.facebook.com/ISPI1962
twitter.com/ISPI1962
www.youtube.com/user/ISPITube
Overview: A medium-sized international organization founded in 1962
Mission: To improve the performance of individuals & organizations through the application of human performance technology
Chief Officer(s):
April Davis, Executive Director
april@ispi.org
Finances: *Annual Operating Budget:* $500,000-$1.5 Million
Staff Member(s): 4
Membership: 50 institutional + 200 student + 6,000 individual; *Fees:* Schedule available; *Member Profile:* Performance technologists, training directors, human resources managers, instructional technologists, human factors practitioners, project managers, & organizational consultants
Activities: *Rents Mailing List:* Yes

International Society for Plant Pathology

c/o Secretary General, PO Box 412, Jamison ACT 2612 Australia
Tel: 61-2-62515658
www.isppweb.org
twitter.com/Food_Security
Overview: A small international charitable organization founded in 1968
Mission: To promote the worldwide development of plant pathology & the dissemination of knowledge about plant diseases & plant health management
Member of: International Union of Biological Sciences; International Union of Microbiological Sciences
Chief Officer(s):
M. Lodovica Gullino, President
issp.president@isppweb.org
Thomas Evans, Treasurer
ispp.treasurer@isppweb.org
Membership: *Member Profile:* Open to persons interested in or involved in plant pathology

International Society for Rock Mechanics (ISRM)

c/o Laboratório Nacional de Engenharia Civil, 101 Av. do Brasil, Lisbon 1700-066 Portugal
Tel: 351-21-844-3419; *Fax:* 351-21-844-3021
secretariat.isrm@lnec.pt
www.isrm.net
Overview: A medium-sized international organization founded in 1962
Mission: The non-profit scientific association encourages & coordinates international cooperation in the area of rock mechanics. It maintains liaison with other organizations dealing with fields of science related to rock mechanics, such as geology, geophysics, soil mechanics, mining engineering, petroleum engineering & civil engineering.
Member of: International Union of Geological Societies
Affliation(s): Canadian Rock Mechanics Association; Canadian Geotechnical Society
Chief Officer(s):
Luís Lamas, Secretary General
llamas@lnec.pt
John A. Hudson, President
john.a.hudson@gmail.com
Finances: *Funding Sources:* Membership fees; Grants that do not impair the Society's free action
Membership: 5,000 members + 46 national groups; *Member Profile:* Rock mechanics practitioners & corporations; *Committees:* Joint Technical Committee on Landslides & Engineered Slopes; Joint Technical Committee on Representation of Geo-engineering Data in Electronic Form; Joint Technical Committee on Education & Training; Joint Technical Committee on Professional Practice; Joint Technical Committee on Sustainable Use of Underground Space; Joint Technical Committee on Ancient Monuments & Historical Sites; Joint Technical Committee on Soft Rocks & Indurated Soils
Activities: Encouraging teaching, research, & advancement of knowledge in rock mechanics; Operating commissions for studying scientific & technical matters; Sponsoring international & regional symposia; *Library* by appointment
Awards:
• Rocha Medal (Award)
For an outstanding doctoral thesis
• Müller Award (Award)
For distinguished contributions to the profession of rock mechanics and rock engineering
Meetings/Conferences:
• International Society for Rock Mechanics 13th International Congress on Rock Mechanics, 2015, Montréal, QC
Scope: International
Publications:
• International Journal of Rock Mechanics & Mining Sciences
Type: Journal
• ISRM [International Society for Rock Mechanics] News Journal
Type: Journal
Profile: Information about technology related to rock mechanics & news on activities in the rock mechanics community
• ISRM [International Society for Rock Mechanics] Newsletter
Type: Newsletter
• Journal of Rock Mechanics & Rock Engineering
Type: Journal

International Society for Sexually Transmitted Diseases Research (ISSTDR)

c/o Basil Donovan, The Kirby Institute, University of New South Wales, Sidney Australia
www.isstdr.org

Overview: A medium-sized international organization founded in 1977
Mission: To promote research on sexually transmitted diseases
Chief Officer(s):
Michel Alary, Chair & President
michel.alary@uresp.ulaval.ca
Activities: Facilitating the timely exchange of information among researchers; Hosting a biennial, interdisciplinary scientific meeting to address the breadth of research on sexually transimitte diesease
Meetings/Conferences:
• International Society for Sexually Transmitted Diseases Research 21st Meeting, September, 2015, Brisbane Convention and Exhibition Centre, Brisbane
Scope: International
Attendance: 1,000
Description: To address the range of the biomedical, behavioral, & social sciences related to all sexually transmitted diseases, including HIV infection
• International Society for Sexually Transmitted Diseases Research World STI & HIV Congress 2017, 2017, Rio de Janeiro
Scope: International
Description: To address the range of the biomedical, behavioral, & social sciences related to all sexually transmitted diseases, including HIV infection

International Society for Soil Mechanics & Foundation Engineering *See* International Society for Soil Mechanics & Geotechnical Engineering

International Society for Soil Mechanics & Geotechnical Engineering (ISSMGE) / Société Internationale de Mécanique des Sols et de la Géotechnique (SIMSG)

City University, Northampton Square, London EC1V 0HB United Kingdom
Tel: 44-20-7040-8154; *Fax:* 44-20-7040-8832
secretariat@issmge.org
www.issmge.org
Previous Name: International Society for Soil Mechanics & Foundation Engineering
Overview: A medium-sized international organization
Affliation(s): International Society for Soil Mechanics & Geotechnical Engineering - Canadian Section; Canadian Geotechnical Society
Chief Officer(s):
R. N. (Neil) Taylor, Secretary General
Roger Frank, President
Finances: *Annual Operating Budget:* $250,000-$500,000
Membership: 15,000-49,999; *Committees:* 25 active international Technical Committees working in various specialist areas of geotechnics

International Society for Telemedicine & eHealth

c/o AMTS Luzern, Luzerner Kantonsspital, Luzern 16 CH - 6000 Switzerland
telemedicine@skynet.be
www.isft.net
Overview: A small international organization
Mission: To facilitate the international dissemination of knowledge & experience in telemedicine & e-health & to provide access to recognized experts in the field worldwide
Chief Officer(s):
Andy Fischer, President
president@isfteh.org
Membership: *Fees:* $100

International Society for the Sociology of Religion *Voir* Société internationale de sociologie des religions

International Society for the Study of Medieval Philosophy *Voir* Société internationale pour l'étude de la philosophie médiévale

International Society for the Study of the Lumbar Spine (ISSLS)

c/o Institute for Clinical Sciences, Sahlgrenska Academy, PO Box 426, #MG301, 2075 Bayview Ave., Gothenburg SE-405 30 Sweden
Tel: 46-31-786-44-36
www.issls.org
Overview: A small international organization founded in 1974
Chief Officer(s):
Kazuhisa Takahashi, President
Katarina Olinder Eriksson, Administrator
katarina.olinder@gu.se

Staff Member(s): 1
Membership: 230

International Society for Vascular Behavioural & Cognitive Disorders

c/o Newcastle University Campus for Ageing & Vitality, NIHR Biomedical Research Building, 1st Fl., Newcastle upon Tyne NE4 5PL United Kingdom
Tel: 44-191-248-1352; *Fax:* 44-191-248-1301
vascogsoc@gmail.com
www.vas-cog.org
Also Known As: The Vas-Cog Society
Overview: A medium-sized international organization founded in 2001
Mission: To study the vascular causes of various brain disorders, by bringing together diverse basic sciences & clinical research interests
Chief Officer(s):
Christopher Chen, Chair
Raj Kalaria, Secretariat
Finances: *Funding Sources:* Sponsorships
Membership: 193; *Fees:* £60 regular; £40 student; *Committees:* By-law; Program; Executive; Scientific; Nominating
Activities: Training researchers; Disseminating information; Raising awareness of various brain disorders & other behavioural disorders & their prevention & treatment; Advocating for patients
Meetings/Conferences:
• International Society for Vascular Behavioural & Cognitive Disorders 2015 VasCog Congress, September, 2015, Tokyo
Scope: International

International Society of Arboriculture

PO Box 3129, Champaign IL 61826-3129 USA
Tel: 217-355-9411; *Fax:* 217-355-9516
Toll-Free: 888-472-8733
isa@isa-arbor.com
www.isa-arbor.com
www.linkedin.com/groups?mostPopular=&gid=1953660
www.facebook.com/InternationalSocietyofArboriculture
twitter.com/ISArboriculture
www.youtube.com/user/ISAAdmin
Overview: A medium-sized international organization founded in 1924
Mission: To foster research & education that promotes the care & the benefits of trees
Chief Officer(s):
Terrence Flanagan, President
terry@teragan.com
Jim Skiera, Executive Director
jskiera@isa-arbor.com
Staff Member(s): 44
Membership: *Fees:* $0 student; $65 senior; $130 professional; $500 patron; *Committees:* Annual Conference Program; Awards; Best Management Practices; Development; Educational Goods & Services; Finance/Audit; Goverenance & Bylaws; Hispanic; International Safety; International Tree Climbing Championship; Membership; Nominating & Elections; Plant Appraisal & Valuation; Public Relations & Marketing; Science & Research

International Society of Biometeorology (ISB) / Société internationale de biométéorolgy

c/o Dept. of Geography, Univ. of Wisconsin-Milwaukee, PO Box 413, Milwaukee WI 53201-0413 USA
Tel: 414-229-6611; *Fax:* 414-229-3981
www.biometeorology.org
Overview: A small international organization founded in 1956
Mission: To promote international collaboration of physicists, biologists, meteorologists & other scientists & the development of the field of meteorology in relation to humans, animals & plants
Chief Officer(s):
Glenn McGregor, President
g.mcgregor@auckland.ac.nz
Jonathan M. Hanes, Secretary
jmhanes@uwm.edu
Finances: *Funding Sources:* Membership fees
Membership: *Fees:* US$85 regular; US$60 retired/student
Activities: *Library:* ISB Archive

International Society of Chemotherapy for Infection & Cancer (ISC)

c/o Dept. of Preclinical & Clinical Pharmacology, Viale Pieraccini 6, Florence 50139 Italy
Tel: 39-055-427-1265; *Fax:* 39-055-427-1265
www.ischemo.org
Overview: A medium-sized international organization founded in 1961
Mission: To advance the education & science of chemotherapy.
Chief Officer(s):
Teresita Mazzei, President
teresita.mazzei@unifi.it
Ian Gould, Secretary General
i.m.gould@abdn.ac.uk
Membership: 94 member societies worldwide; *Committees:* Hamao Umezawa Memorial Award; Tom Bergan Memorial Award; John David Williams Memorial Award; Masaaki Ohkoshi Award; Young Investigator Travel Awards; IASC Awards; Publication/Communication: IJAA; Publication/Communication: Website; Disease Management Series
Activities: Conferences; research & special projects

International Society of Citriculture (ISC)

Dept. of Botany & Plant Sciences, University of California, Riverside CA 92521-0124 USA
Tel: 951-827-4663; *Fax:* 951-827-4437
iscucr@ucr.edu
www.crec.ifas.ufl.edu/societies/ISC
Overview: A large international organization founded in 1976
Mission: To promote & encourage research, exchange of information & education, in all aspects of citrus production, harvesting, handling, & distribution of both fresh fruit & products
Affliation(s): International Society for Horticultural Science
Chief Officer(s):
Luis Navarro, President
lnavarro@ivia.es
Carol J. Lovatt, Sec.-Treas.
Finances: *Funding Sources:* Membership dues; Sales of congress proceedings
Membership: 1,000-4,999; *Fees:* US$30/4 years; *Member Profile:* Any individual, corporation, unincorporated association, or organization interested in an aspect of citrus culture, handling, marketing, processing, transportation, research, or education
Publications:
• ISC [International Society of Citriculture] Proceedings
Profile: Papers presented at previous meetings
• ISC [International Society of Citriculture] Newsletter
Type: Newsletter
Profile: Archived newsletters from 1995-2003

International Society of City & Regional Planners

PO Box 983, The Hague 2501 CZ Netherlands
Tel: 31-70-346-2654; *Fax:* 31-70-361-7909
isocarp@isocarp.org
www.isocarp.org
Also Known As: ISOCARP
Overview: A small international licensing organization founded in 1965
Mission: To improve cities & territories through planning practice, training, education, & research
Affliation(s): UNESCO; Council of Europe; UN/ECOSOC; UNCHS/Habitat
Chief Officer(s):
Milica Bajic Brkovic, President
Alex Macgregor, Secretary General
Manfred Schrenk, Treasurer
Finances: *Funding Sources:* Membership fees
Membership: 100-499; *Fees:* Schedule available; *Member Profile:* Professional planners; Stakeholders involved in the development & maintenance of the built environment
Activities: Promoting the planning profession; Facilitating exchange between planners from different countries; Providing information on major planning issues; Evaluating developments & trends in planning practice
Awards:
• Gerd Albert Award (Award)
• Routledge Prize (Award)
Poster congress prize
Meetings/Conferences:
• 50th ISOCARP Congress, 2015
Scope: International
Publications:
• International Manual of Planning Practice (IMPP)
Editor: Judith Ryser; Teresa Franchini
Profile: Reference guide to the key features of the spatial planning systems
• International Society of City & Regional Planners Annual Congress Report
Type: Yearbook; *Frequency:* Annually
Profile: Final report of each congress

• ISOCARP [International Society of City & Regional Planners] NET
Type: Newsletter; *Editor:* Judy van Hemert
• ISOCARP [International Society of City & Regional Planners] Review
Profile: Complement to the research efforts prepared for the annual ISOCARP Congresses

International Society of Friendship & Good Will (ISFGW) / Société internationale d'amitié et de bonne volonté

3119 Lassiter St., Durham NC 27707-3888 USA
www.friendshipandgoodwill.org
Overview: A small international organization founded in 1978
Mission: To encourage & foster advancement of international understanding, better human relations, friendship, goodwill & peace through world fellowship of men & women; to promote the teaching & learning of Esperanto & to collaborate with national & international Esperanto associations
Chief Officer(s):
D. Gary Grady, President
dgary@mindspring.com
Finances: *Annual Operating Budget:* Less than $50,000; *Funding Sources:* Membership dues; donations
Staff Member(s): 2
Membership: 46 Canadian; *Fees:* Members pay whatever they can afford
Activities: *Speaker Service:* Yes; *Rents Mailing List:* Yes

International Society of Hypertension (ISH)

ISH Secretariat, Hampton Medical Conferences Ltd., 113-119 High St., Hampton Hill, Middlesex TW12 1NJ United Kingdom
Tel: +44 (0) 20 8979 8300; *Fax:* +44 (0) 20 8979 6700
secretariat@ish-world.com
www.ish-world.com
Overview: A medium-sized international charitable organization
Mission: To advance scientific knowledge in all aspects of research; To promote application of research to the prevention & management of heart disease & stroke in hypertension and related cardiovascular diseases
Affliation(s): Canadian Hypertension Society; World Hypertension League; American Society of Hypertension; Council for High Blood Pressure Research of the AHA; Cuban National Committee for the Study of Hypertension; Hypertension societies throughout Africa, The Middle East, Asia, Australasia, Europe, & South America
Chief Officer(s):
Stephen Harrap, President
Ernesto Schiffrin, Vice-President
Rhian Touyz, Secretary
Louise Burrell, Treasurer
Membership: 800; *Member Profile:* Clinicians, academic scientists, & researchers in hypertension & cardiovascular disease from around the globe
Meetings/Conferences:
• International Society of Hypertension 26th Scientific Meeting, September, 2016, Seoul
Scope: International
Description: Scientific program & exhibition
• International Society of Hypertension 27th Scientific Meeting, 2018
Scope: International
Description: Scientific program & exhibition
Publications:
• Hypertension News
Type: Newsletter; *Frequency:* Quarterly; *Price:* Free with International Society of Hypertension membership
• Journal of Hypertension
Type: Journal; *Frequency:* Monthly; *Price:* Free with International Society of Hypertension membership
Profile: Primary papers from experts, authoritative reviews, recent developments, special reports, & time-sensitive information

International Society of Indoor Air Quality & Climate (ISIAQ)

c/o Gina Bendy, 2548 Empire Grade, Santa Cruz CA 95060 USA
Tel: 831-426-0148; *Fax:* 831-426-6522
info@isiaq.org
www.isiaq.org
Overview: A medium-sized international organization founded in 1992
Mission: To support the establishment of healthy, productivity-encouraging indoor environments
Chief Officer(s):
Richard Shaughnessy, President
rjstulsau@aol.com
Anne Hyvärinen, Secretary
anne.hyvarinen@thl.fi
Carl-Gustaf Bornehag, Treasurer
carl-gustaf.bornehag@kau.se
Finances: *Funding Sources:* Membership fees; Donations; Sponsorships
Membership: *Fees:* US $15 - $30 /year students; US $135 / year individuals; US $700 / year corporate members; *Member Profile:* Individuals, such as scientist involved in indoor air quality research, occupational health professionals, government & regulatory professionals, & architects; Corporations; Students; *Committees:* Task force on the control of moisture & mould problems in cold climate; Task force on the vocabulary of the indoor air sciences; Task force on the IAQ & climate in cultural & heritage collections; Task force on the criteria for cleaning of air handling systems; Task force on the performance of portable air cleaners; Task force on the education for healthier buildings; Task force on the effect of the indoor environment on productivity in offices; Task force on indoor air research & building practice
Activities: Facilitating international & interdisciplinary communication; Liaising with governments & other agencies with interests in indoor environment;
Meetings/Conferences:
• International Society for Environmental Epidemiology 27th Annual Conference, August, 2015, Sao Paolo
Scope: International
Contact Information: contact@isee2015.org; URL: www.isee2015.org
Publications:
• Indoor Air: The International Journal of Indoor Environment & Health
Type: Journal; *Frequency:* Bimonthly; *Accepts Advertising*; *Editor:* Jan Sundell; William Nazaroff; *Price:* Free with International Society of Indoor Air Quality & Climate membership
Profile: Original research about indoor environments
• International Society of Indoor Air Quality & Climate Conference Proceedings
Profile: Proceedings of Healthy Buildings & Indoor Air conferences
• International Society of Indoor Air Quality & Climate Task Force Reports
• International Society of Indoor Air Quality & Climate Newsletter
Type: Newsletter; *Accepts Advertising*; *Price:* Free with International Society of Indoor Air Quality & Climate membership
Profile: Society activities
• Vocabulary of the Indoor Air Sciences

International Society of Limnology (IATAL) / Societas Internationalis Limnologiae (SIL)

c/o Denise L. Johnson, 5020 Swepsonville-Saxapahaw Road, Graham NC 27253 USA
Tel: 336-376-9362; *Fax:* 336-376-8825
www.limnology.org
Previous Name: International Association of Theoretical and Applied Limnology; Societas Internationalis Limnologiae, SIL
Overview: A medium-sized international organization founded in 1922
Mission: To promote communication between limnologists of all countries & all disciplines to increase understanding of inland aquatic ecosystems & their management.
Affliation(s): Canadian Society of Limnology
Chief Officer(s):
Yves Prairie, President, (Canada)
prairie.yves@uqam.ca
Tamar Zohary, General Secretary-Treasurer, (Israel)
tamarz@ocean.org.il
Membership: *Fees:* Schedule available; *Member Profile:* Open to those with an interest in limnology, the study of inland water ecosystems (rivers, lakes, streams, reserVoir s, fish ponds, aquifers, & bogs); Members have varied interests which include physics of water movements, water chemistry, plankton & water plants, invertebrate ecology, fish & fisheries, watershed & reserVoir management, pollution of inland waters, & modelling of aquatic ecosystems; *Committees:* Baldi Memorial; International; Kilham Memorial; Naumann-Thienemann Medal; Nominating; Publication Advisory; Awards; Executive; Regions & Meetings Countries

International Society of Physical & Rehabilitation Medicine (ISPRM)

kloosterstraat 5, Assenede B-9960 Belgium
Tel: 32-9-344-3959; *Fax:* 32-9-344-4010
centraloffice@isprm.org
www.isprm.org
Previous Name: International Federation of Physical Medicine & Rehabilitation
Overview: A medium-sized international organization founded in 1999
Mission: To work with practitioners to improve the quality of life of people with impairments & disabilities
Member of: World Health Organization
Chief Officer(s):
Werner van Cleemputte, Executive Director
werner@medicongress.com
Gerold Stucki, President
gerold.stucki@paranet.ch
Jorge Lains, Secretary
jorgelains@sapo.pt
John Olver, Treasurer
john.olver@epworth.org.au
Membership: 1,000-4,999; *Fees:* Schedule available; *Member Profile:* Practitioners of physical & rehabilitation medicine; *Committees:* Audit & Finance; Awards; Bylaws; Congress; Education; International Education & Development Fund; Faculty Student Educational Exchange; Membership; News & Views; Nominating; Sponsorship
Activities: Improving the knowledge, skills, & attitudes of physicians in understanding impairments & disabilities; Facilitating rehabilitation medicine input to international health organizations; Influencing rehabilitation policies & activities; Facilitating research activities
Publications:
• International Society of Physical & Rehabilitation Medicine Congress Abstracts
• The Journal of Rehabilitation Medicine
Type: Journal; *Frequency:* 8 pa; *Editor:* Professor Gunnar Grimby
Profile: International peer-review scientific journal of original articles, reviews, case reports, brief communications, special reports, letters to the editor, &editorials
• News & Views [a publication of the International Society of Physical & Rehabilitation Medicine]
Type: Newsletter; *Frequency:* Monthly; *Editor:* Nicholas Christodoulou

International Society of Radiographers & Radiological Technologists (ISRRT)

143 Bryn Pinwydden, Pentwyn, Cardiff, Wales CF2 7DG United Kingdom
Tel: 44-2920-735-037; *Fax:* 44-2920-540-551
Other Communication: World Radiography Day URL: www.worldradiographyday.org
www.isrrt.org
Overview: A large international charitable organization founded in 1959
Mission: To advance radiation medicine technology through international communication & sponsorship of professional activities
Affliation(s): World Health Organization; United Nations
Chief Officer(s):
Michael D. Ward, Ph.D., RT(R), F, President, 314-362-9155, Fax: 314-362-9250
mward@bjc.org
A. Yule, OBE, JP, DSc, Secretary General
isrrt.yule@btopenworld.com
Terry Ell, MRT(NM), Ph.D., Council Member, Canada, 403-944-1161, Fax: 403-944-1161
terry.ell@albertahealthservices.ca
Finances: *Annual Operating Budget:* $100,000-$250,000; *Funding Sources:* Membership fees; donations; conferences
Staff Member(s): 5; 30 volunteer(s)
Membership: 75 countries; 350,000 radiographers; *Fees:* Schedule available; *Member Profile:* National radiation medicine technology societies; associate - individuals who support objectives
Activities: *Awareness Events:* World Radiography Day, Nov.
Meetings/Conferences:
• 19th ISRRT World Congress in Seoul, South Korea, October, 2016, Coex Center, Seoul
Scope: International
Description: Hosted by the South Korean Society of Radiographers.
Contact Information: isrrt.yule@btinternet.com, URL: isrrt2016.kr
• 20th ISRRT World Congress, 2018
Scope: International

Publications:
• News & Views from Around the World [a publication of the International Society of Radiographers & Radiological Technologists]
Type: Newsletter; *Frequency:* 2 pa.; *Editor:* Rahcel Bullard *ISSN:* 1027-0671

International Society of Soil Science *See* International Union of Soil Sciences

International Society of Surgery (ISS) / La Société internationale de Chirurgie (SIC)

c/o Allveco AG, PO Box 1527, Netzibodenstrasse 34, Pratteln CH-4133 Switzerland
Tel: 41-61-815-9666; *Fax:* 41-61-811-4775
surgery@iss-sic.ch
www.iss-sic.com
Overview: A medium-sized international organization founded in 1902
Mission: To contribute to the advancement of the science & art of surgery by researching & discussing surgical problems, through congresses, courses, & publications
Chief Officer(s):
Jean-Claude Givel, Secretary General
givel@cabchirvisc.ch
Victor Bertschi, Administrative Director
victor.bertschi@iss-sic.ch
Finances: *Funding Sources:* Membership dues; Congress
Membership: 1,000-4,999; *Member Profile:* Medical doctors who have received training in a field of surgery & are or have been engaged in a career involving a recognized field of surgery; Non-medical scientists involved in medical research related to surgery; *Committees:* Executive; Editorial; Program
Activities: *Awareness Events:* International Surgical Week, Sept.
Awards:
• ISS/SIC Prize (Award)
• Robert Danis Prize (Award)
• René Leriche Prize (Award)
• ISS/SIC Honorary Membership (Award)
Publications:
• International Society of Surgery Newsletter
Type: Newsletter; *Frequency:* Semiannually
• World Journal of Surgery: The Official Journal of the International Society of Surgery/Société Internationale de Chirurgie
Type: Journal; *Editor:* John G. Hunter, M.D. *ISSN:* 0364-2313
Profile: Authoritative scientific reports in the fields of clinical &experimental surgery, surgical education, & socioeconomic aspects of surgical care

International Sociological Association (ISA)

Faculty of Political Science & Sociology, University Complutense, Madrid 28223 Spain
Tel: 34-913-527-650; *Fax:* 34-913-524-945
isa@isa-sociology.org
www.isa-sociology.org
www.facebook.com/180226035354843
twitter.com/isa_sociology
www.youtube.com/user/isasociotube
Overview: A small international organization founded in 1949
Mission: To represent sociologists; to advance sociological knowledge
Member of: International Social Science Council
Chief Officer(s):
Michel Burawoy, President
Izabela Barlinska, Executive Secretary
Membership: 5,000; *Fees:* Schedule available; *Committees:* Executive; Research Coordinating; National Associations Liaison; Programme; Publications; Finance & Membership; Research

International Soil Reference & Information Centre (ISRIC)

PO Box 353, #101, Droevendaalsesteeg 3, Wageningen 6700 AJ Netherlands
Tel: 31-317-483-735
soil.isric@wur.nl
www.isric.org
Overview: A small international organization founded in 1966
Mission: To contribute to the challenge of providing sufficient food for the growing world populations while preserving the biophysical potential of natural resources & minimizing environmental degradation
Member of: World Data Centres of International Council of Sciences; World Data Centre for Soils
Affliation(s): Wageningen University & Research Centre
Chief Officer(s):
Ir P.S. Bindraban, Director
Prem.Bindraban@wur.nl
Finances: *Annual Operating Budget:* $500,000-$1.5 Million; *Funding Sources:* Dutch government, international/bilateral project donor organizations
Staff Member(s): 25
Membership: 1-99
Activities: *Library* Open to public by appointment

International Solar Energy Society (ISES)

International Headquarters, Villa Tannheim, Wiesentalstrasse 50, Freiburg 79115 Germany
Tel: 49-761-459-06-0; *Fax:* 49-761-459-06-99
hq@ises.org
www.ises.org
www.facebook.com/InternationalSolarEnergySociety
Overview: A medium-sized international charitable organization founded in 1954
Mission: A United Nations accredited NGO, with members in 50+ countries worldwide; goals include the promotion of renewable energy, with solar energy being a focus, sustainable development, and research
Member of: International Renewable Energy Alliance
Chief Officer(s):
Eduardo A. Rincón Mejia, Secretary, (Mexico)
rinconsolar@hotmail.com
Monica V. Oliphant, President, (Australia)
oliphant@adam.com.au
Staff Member(s): 8
Membership: 4,000; *Fees:* Schedule available; *Member Profile:* Persons engaged in the research development & utilisation of solar energy & persons who have an interest in advancing the purposes of the society
Activities: All aspects of solar energy, including characteristics, effects & methods of use; international congresses on solar energy
Awards:
• Achievement through Action Award (Award)
Monetary, biennial; awarded to an individual, a group, or corporate body that has made an important contribution to the harnessing of solar energy for practical use or is proposing a new concept, development or product for the same purpose
• Farrington Daniel Award (Award)
Recognition for outstanding intellectual leadership in the field of solar energy
Publications:
• Solar Energy
Type: Journal; *Frequency:* Monthly; *Editor:* Dr. D. Yogi Goswami

International Solid Waste Association (ISWA)

Auerspergstrasse 15, Top 41, Vienna 1080 Austria
Tel: +43 1 253 6001; *Fax:* +43 1 523 6001 99
iswa@iswa.dk
www.iswa.org
www.facebook.com/group.php?gid=123367611068687
Overview: A medium-sized international organization founded in 1931
Mission: To promote efficiency in environmental practice
Chief Officer(s):
Hermann Koller, Managing Director
hkoller@iswa.org
Greg Vogt, Managing Director
gvogt@iswa.dk
Gerfried Habenicht, Manager, Communications
Niels Jorn Hahn, President
njh@r98.dk
Alfred Holzschuster, Manager, Finance & Member Services
Morten Sandbakken, Treasurer
morten.sandbakken@fias.no
Rachael Williams, Technical Manager
Finances: *Funding Sources:* Sponsorships
Membership: *Member Profile:* Non-profit waste management associations representing the waste management industry in a particular country; Organizations or companies associated with or working in the field of waste management
Activities: Promoting professionalism; Supporting developing countries
Publications:
• Global News [a publication of the International Solid Waste Association]
Type: Newsletter
Profile: Contents include news from the association president, conference information, awards, news from around the world, & forthcoming events
• International Solid Waste Association Conference Proceedings
Type: Yearbook; *Frequency:* Annually
Profile: Information from the International Solid Waste Association Annual Congress, the Beacon Conference, & other conferences organized by the association
• International Solid Waste Association Annual Report
Type: Yearbook; *Frequency:* Annually
• Waste Management & Research
Type: Journal; *Frequency:* Monthly; *Editor:* Jens Aage Hansen
Profile: The theory & practice of waste management & research
• Waste Management World
Type: Magazine; *Frequency:* Bimonthly; *Accepts Advertising*; *Editor:* Tom Freyberg
Profile: Incorporates the International Directory of Solid Waste Management, with a listing of ISWA members & waste management companies

International Statistical Institute (ISI) / L'Institut International de Statistique

PO Box 24070, The Hague 2490 AB Netherlands
Tel: 31-70-337-5737; *Fax:* 31-70-3860025
isi-web.org
www.facebook.com/435104499838038
twitter.com/IntStat
Overview: A medium-sized international licensing charitable organization founded in 1885
Mission: Seeks to develop & improve statistical methods & their application through the promotion of international activity & co-operation
Affliation(s): International Association of Survey Statisticians; Bernoulli Society; International Association for Statistical Computing; International Association for Official Statistics; International Association for Statistical Education; International Society for Business & Industrial Statistics; The International Environmetrics Society
Chief Officer(s):
Vijayan N. Nair, President
Ada van Krimpen, Director
Finances: *Annual Operating Budget:* $500,000-$1.5 Million; *Funding Sources:* Membership fees
Staff Member(s): 9; 2 volunteer(s)
Membership: 2,000 ISI; 3,000 in specialised sections; *Fees:* Schedule available; *Member Profile:* Honorary - elected from the ranks of ordinary members in recognition of their contributions to statistics merit special honour; Elected - elected by virtue of their distinguished contributions to the development or application of statistical methods; ex officio - occupants of certain positions in official national statistical agencies & international organizations designated by the Council or are the representatives of organizations affiliated with the Institute; corporate - national & international statistical agencies to certain cultural, educational, & scientific institutions, & to commercial, industrial & business enterprises which share or support the aims of the Institute; *Committees:* Numerous
Activities: Project implementation; cooperation with the UN; technical advice & assistance; project funding; training; conferences; publications; *Rents Mailing List:* Yes *Library* by appointment

International Student Pugwash (SPUSA)

c/o Student Pugwash USA, #704, 1015 - 18th St. NW, Washington DC 20036 USA
Tel: 202-419-8900; *Fax:* 202-429-8905
Toll-Free: 800-969-2784
spusa@spusa.org
www.spusa.org
www.facebook.com/pages/Student-Pugwash-USA/14128095074
twitter.com/StudentPugwash
www.youtube.com/StudentPugwashUSA
Overview: A medium-sized international organization founded in 1979
Mission: To build a committment among young people to integrate social concerns into their academic, professional & personal lives; to educate young people on the relevance of science & technology to their own lives & its ability to shape the future of the global community
Affliation(s): Science for Peace International
Chief Officer(s):
Sharlissa Moore, President
smoore@spusa.org
Finances: *Annual Operating Budget:* $100,000-$250,000
Staff Member(s): 5; 3 volunteer(s)
Membership: 50 chapters in the US; 15 chapters abroad

Activities: International & National Conferences; Chapter Program (at over 120 colleges, universities & high schools); New Careers Program; PUGWASHinton Seminars; *Internships:* Yes; *Rents Mailing List:* Yes

International Tennis Federation (ITF)

Bank Lane, Roehampton, London SW15 5XZ United Kingdom
Tel: 44-20-8878-6464; *Fax:* 44-20-8392-4744
www.itftennis.com
www.facebook.com/InternationalTennisFederation
twitter.com/ITF_Tennis
www.youtube.com/OfficialITFTennis
Overview: A medium-sized international organization founded in 1913
Affliation(s): Tennis Canada
Chief Officer(s):
Francesco Ricci Bitti, President
Juan Margets, Executive Vice-President
Staff Member(s): 53
Membership: 205 nations; *Fees:* Schedule available
Activities: Grand Slam tennis events; Davis Cup; Grand Slam Cup

International Textile Manufacturers Federation (ITMF) / Fédération internationale des industries textiles

Wiedingstrasse 9, Zurich CH-8055 Switzerland
Tel: 41-44-283-6380; *Fax:* 41-44-283-6389
secretariat@itmf.org
www.itmf.org
Overview: A medium-sized international organization founded in 1904
Mission: To provide a neutral forum for the textile industries of the world; to act as clearinghouse of ideas, information & experience; to act as the spokesman for the industry in matters relating to raw materials (cotton & man-made fibres); to provide a safeguard for the interests of the textile industry in world affairs; to maintain official liaison status with various intergovernmental organizations; also enjoys consultative status with the Economic & Social Council of the United Nations; maintains permanent liaison with private national & international textile & fibre organizations
Affliation(s): Food & Agriculture Organization; WTO; International Cotton Advisory Committee; International Labour Organization; the Organization for Economic Cooperation & Development; United Nations Industrial Development Organization; the World Bank
Chief Officer(s):
Christian P. Schindler, Director General
Josué C. Gomes da Silva, President
Finances: *Funding Sources:* Membership fees
Staff Member(s): 1
Membership: 17 members; 14 associates; 35 corporate; *Member Profile:* Full - associations & other trade organizations of manufacturers of textiles; Associate - organizations allied to textile industry; the Federation's members are not the individual textile enterprises, but the trade associations in the countries concerned; corporate membership possible since 2000; *Committees:* Joint Cotton; Management; Spinners; Statistical; Home Textile Producers; Cotton Testing Methods; Man-Made Fibres

International Titanium Association (ITA)

#100, 11674 Huron St., Northglenn CO 80234 USA
Tel: 303-404-2221; *Fax:* 303-404-9111
ita@titanium.org
www.titanium.org
Overview: A large international organization founded in 1984
Mission: To connect the public with titanium specialists throughout the world, who can offer technical & sales assistance
Chief Officer(s):
Jennifer Simpson, Executive Director
jsimpson@titanium.org
Stacey Blicker, Contact, Member Services
sblicker@titanium.org
Membership: 195 companies; *Fees:* Schedule available based on previous year's shipments (producers), receipts (users & consumers); $500-$4,500 non-voting; *Committees:* Education; Safety; Conference Planning; Trade Show; Achievement Award; Grant; Applications
Activities: Offering titanium literature; Sponsoring educational workshops & seminars
Awards:
• Titanium Achievement Award (Award)
• Ti Applications Development Award (Award)
Meetings/Conferences:
• Titanium Europe 2015, May, 2015, Hilton Birmingham Metropole Hotel, Birmingham
Scope: International
Contact Information: Jennifer Cunningham, Planner; E-mail: jcunningham@titanium.org
• Titanium USA 2015, October, 2015, Rosen Shingle Creek Golf Resort, Orlando, FL
Scope: International
Publications:
• Titanium Update Newsletter
Type: Newsletter; *Price:* Free
Profile: Titanium news, awards, & membership information

International Touring Alliance *See* Alliance internationale de tourisme

International Trade Centre (ITC) / Centre du Commerce International (CCI)

Palais des Nations, 54-56 Rue de Montbrillant, Geneva CH-1211 Switzerland
Tel: 41-22-730-0111; *Fax:* 41-22-733-4439
itcreg@intracen.org
www.intracen.org
Overview: A small international organization founded in 1964
Mission: Trade promotion for developing countries
Affliation(s): Joint subsidiary organ of WTO & the United Nations
Chief Officer(s):
Patricia Francis, Executive Director
Finances: *Funding Sources:* United Nations organization
Staff Member(s): 30
Activities: Institutional infrastructure for trade promotion & export development; product & market research, development & promotion; import operations & techniques; human resource development for trade promotion

International Trade Union Confederation (ITUC)

5 Boul du Roi Albert II, Bte 1, Brussels B-1210 Belgium
Tel: 32 (0)2 224 0211; *Fax:* 32 (0)2 201 5815
info@ituc-csi.org
www.ituc-csi.org
www.facebook.com/pages/ITUC/20556338116
twitter.com/ituc
www.youtube.com/ituccsi
Previous Name: World Confederation of Labour
Overview: A large international organization founded in 1920
Mission: The ITUC's primary mission is the promotion and defence of workers' rights and interests, through international cooperation between trade unions, global campaigning and advocacy within the major global institutions
Member of: International Labour Organization
Chief Officer(s):
Sharan Burrow, General Secretary
Michel Sommer, President
Staff Member(s): 40
Membership: Affiliates in 155 countries & territories; *Fees:* Schedule available
Activities: Trade unions solidarity; social/human rights; consultative status to UN organization; *Speaker Service:* Yes *Library:* Documentation Service; by appointment

International Trademark Association (INTA)

655 Third Ave., 10th Fl., New York NY 10017-5617 USA
Tel: 212-642-1700; *Fax:* 212-768-7796
info@inta.org
www.inta.org
www.linkedin.com/groups?gid=69899
www.facebook.com/home.php?#!/GoINTA?ref=ts
twitter.com/_INTA
Previous Name: U.S. Trademark Association
Overview: A large international organization founded in 1878
Mission: Dedicated to the support & advancement of trademarks & related intellectual property concepts as essential elements of effective national & international commerce through advocacy, communication, education & service to members
Chief Officer(s):
Alan C. Drewsen, Executive Director
Toe Su Aung, President & Chair
Lucy Nichols, Treasurer
J. Scott Evans, Secretary
Finances: *Annual Operating Budget:* $3 Million-$5 Million; *Funding Sources:* Membership dues; publications; seminars, forums & other meetings
Staff Member(s): 28
Membership: 3,500; *Fees:* Schedule available; *Member Profile:* Trademark owner or supplier; *Committees:* Brief Amicus; Trademark Management; Education; Communications; Finance; Forums; International: Management; Membership; Nominating; Planning; Publications; US Legislation; Information Resources ADR; Industry Advisory Council; Public Relations
Activities: Trademark Hotline - free information service available to the press 212/768-9886 between 2:00 pm & 5:00 pm weekdays (excluding holidays); *Speaker Service:* Yes *Library* Open to public by appointment
Awards:
• President's Award (Award)
The President's Award recognizes individuals who over the course of their career have made outstanding contributions to INTA and to the trademark profession.
• Volunteer Service Awards (Award)
Advancement of Trademark Law; Advancement of Committee or Subcommittee Objectives; Advancement of the Association; Pro Bono Legal Services to an Individual; Pro Bono Legal Services to a Member Organization*Eligibility:* Subcommittee chairs, committee members and non-committee volunteers
Meetings/Conferences:
• The International Trademark Association's 137th Annual Meeting 2015, May, 2015, San Diego, CA
Scope: International
Contact Information: meetings@inta.org; URL: www.inta.org/2015AM

International Union Against Cancer (IUAC) / Union internationale contre le cancer (UICC)

62, rte de Frontenex, Geneva 1207 Switzerland
Tel: 41-22-809-1811; *Fax:* 41-22-809-1810
info@uicc.org
www.uicc.org
Overview: A small international organization founded in 1933
Mission: To advance scientific & medical knowledge in research, diagnosis, treatment & prevention of cancer & to promote all other aspects of the campaign against cancer throughout the world; emphasis on professional & public education
Affliation(s): Canadian Cancer Society
Chief Officer(s):
David Hill, President
Cary Adams, Executive Director
Finances: *Annual Operating Budget:* $3 Million-$5 Million; *Funding Sources:* Membership dues; national subscription; foundations; corporations; individuals
Staff Member(s): 20
Membership: 300+; *Fees:* Schedule available; *Member Profile:* Voluntary organizations; cancer leagues & societies, cancer research &/or treatment centres & institutes; cancer patient associations &, in some countries Ministries of Health
Activities: Extensive fellowships programme; international symposia; training courses; advisory visits; capacity building; tobacco control; prevention & early detection; knowledge transfer; *Awareness Events:* UICC International No Smoking Days; World Cancer Day (February 4th) *Library*
Awards:
• Reach To Recovery International Theresa Lasser Award (Award)
• Reach to Recovery International Medal (Award)

International Union for Conservation of Nature (IUCN)

28, rue Mauverney, Gland 1196 Switzerland
Tel: 41-22-999-0000; *Fax:* 41-22-999-0002
Other Communication: www.flickr.com/photos/iucnweb
mail@iucn.org
www.iucn.org
www.facebook.com/iucn.org
twitter.com/IUCN
www.youtube.com/user/IUCN
Previous Name: The World Conservation Union; International Union for Conservation of Nature & Natural Resources
Overview: A large international organization founded in 1948
Mission: To find solutions to environment & development challenges; To conserve the integrity & diversity of nature; To ensure the use of natural resources is equitable & ecologically sustainable
Chief Officer(s):
Zhang Xinsheng, President
president@iucn.org
Patrick de Henry, Treasurer
Finances: *Funding Sources:* Member organizations; Governments; Foundations; Bilateral & multilateral agencies; Corporations

Staff Member(s): 1000
Membership: 1,200+ government organizations & NGOs + 11,000 volunteer scientist from over 160 countries; *Member Profile:* Government organizations; NGOs; Volunteer scientists
Activities: Supporting scientific research; Managing field projects; Coordinatingpersons & organization to develop & implement policies, laws, & best practices; Publishing over 100 books, reports, documents, & guidelines each year
Awards:
• John C. Phillips Memorial Medal (Award)
To recognize outstanding service in international conservation
• Harold Jefferson Coolidge Memorial Medal (Award)
To recognize the outstanding conservation contributions of one conservation professional
• Honorary membership of IUCN (Award)
To recognize the outstanding contributions of two or three individuals to furthering the goals of the IUCN
Publications:
• Arborvitae [a publication of the International Union for Conservation of Nature]
Type: Newsletter; *Frequency:* 3 pa
Profile: Issues affecting how forest resources are used & governed
• Building Bridges [a publication of the International Union for Conservation of Nature]
Type: Newsletter; *Frequency:* Quarterly
Profile: Conservation & the private sector
• Conservation Made Clear [a publication of the International Union for Conservation of Nature]
Type: Newsletter; *Frequency:* Monthly
Profile: Information about environmental issues & sustainable solutions
• European Newsletter [a publication of the International Union for Conservation of Nature]
Type: Newsletter; *Frequency:* q.
Profile: Provides updates on IUCN's work in Europe
• Off the Shelf [a publication of the International Union for Conservation of Nature]
Type: Newsletter; *Frequency:* Monthly
Profile: International Union for Conservation of Nature's latest & most notable publications
• UNFCCC Newsletter
Type: Newsletter; *Frequency:* Semiannually
Profile: International Union for Conservation of Nature's contributions to the UN Framework Convention on Climate Change
• World Conservation [a publication of the International Union for Conservation of Nature]
Type: Magazine; *Frequency:* 2 - 3 pa
Profile: An examinations of conservation, development, economics, & society

International Union of Academies *Voir* Union académique internationale

International Union of Anthropological & Ethnological Sciences (IUAES) / Union internationale des sciences anthropologiques et ethnologiques
1-2 Yamadaoka, Suita, Osaka 565-0871 Japan
Tel: 81-06-6879-8085
iuaes@glocol.osaka-u.ac.jp
www.iuaes.org
Overview: A small international organization founded in 1948
Mission: To develop international scientific & professional cooperation in the fields of anthropology & ethnology; to foster the development of scientific & professional institutions internationally & regionally; to stimulate scientific & professional cooperation among institutions devoted to the relevant fields of knowledge; to develop appropriate roles for anthropology & ethnology in international inter-disciplinary scientific endeavours
Affliation(s): International Council for Philosophy & Humanistic Studies; International Social Science Council; International Council of Scientific Unions; International Council of Museums
Chief Officer(s):
Peter J.M. Nas, President
Junji Koizumi, Secretary General
Finances: *Funding Sources:* Membership fees; ISSC subvention
Membership: 200; *Fees:* US$50 institutes (first time); US$35 institutes (continuing)

International Union of Architects *Voir* Union internationale des architectes

International Union of Basic & Clinical Pharmacology (IUPHAR)
c/o Dr. S.J. Enna, University of Kansas Medical Center, PO Box 3051, Stn. MRRC Mail Stop, 3901 Rainbow Blvd., Kansas City KS 66160 USA
Tel: 913-588-7533; *Fax:* 913-588-7373
IUPHAR@kumc.edu
www.iuphar.org
Previous Name: International Union of Pharmacology
Overview: A large international organization founded in 1959
Mission: To foster international cooperation in pharmacology by promoting cooperation between societies representing pharmacology & related disciplines throughout the world; sponsoring international & regional congresses & meetings; encouraging international cooperation & free exchange of scientists & of ideas in research; acting as a body through which pharmacologists can participate with scientists from other disciplines; promoting programmes of public awareness on pharmacological issues
Chief Officer(s):
Patrick du Souich, President
S.J. Enna, Secretary-General
Finances: *Annual Operating Budget:* $100,000-$250,000; *Funding Sources:* National Pharmacological Societies; benefactors
Membership: 54 associations internationally; *Member Profile:* Academic & industrial pharmacologists; *Committees:* Executive; Nominating; Membership; Receptor Nomenclature and Drug Classification
Awards:
• Young Investigator Awards (Award)
Publications:
• Pharmacology International
Type: Newsletter; *Frequency:* Biannually

International Union of Biological Sciences (IUBS) / Union internationale des sciences biologiques
Secretariat, Bat 442 Université Paris-Sud 11, Orsay cedex, Paris 91405 France
Tel: 33-1-69-15-50-27; *Fax:* 33-1-69-15-79-47
secretariat@iubs.org
www.iubs.org
twitter.com/IUBS_bio
Overview: A medium-sized international charitable organization founded in 1919
Mission: To promote the study of biological sciences; to initiate, facilitate & coordinate research & other scientific activities that require international cooperation; to ensure the discussion & dissemination of the results of cooperative research; to promote the organization of international conferences & to assist in the publication of their reports
Chief Officer(s):
Nathalie Fomproix, Executive Director
Staff Member(s): 2
Membership: 31 ordinary + 96 scientific (associations, societies or commissions); *Fees:* Schedule available; *Member Profile:* National science academies; International scientific organizations
Activities: *Speaker Service:* Yes
Publications:
• Biology International
Type: Journal; *Frequency:* Quarterly

International Union of Bricklayers & Allied Craftworkers (AFL-CIO/CFL) (BAC) / Union internationale des briqueteurs et métiers connexes (FAT-COI/FCT)
620 F St. NW, Washington DC 20004 USA
Tel: 202-783-3788
Toll-Free: 888-880-8222
askbac@bacweb.org
www.bacweb.org
www.facebook.com/IUBAC
twitter.com/IUBAC
www.youtube.com/user/BACInternational
Overview: A small international organization founded in 1865
Mission: To improve the quality of life of their members
Chief Officer(s):
James Boland, President
Canadian Office
141 Laurier Ave. West, #A, Ottawa ON K1P 5J3
Tel: 613-233-7920
Toll-Free: 877-276-7771
www.bacweb.org/canada/index.php
Mission: To improve their members' quality of life- on and off the job- through access to fair wages, good benefits, safe working conditions, and solidarity among members.
Chief Officer(s):
Oliver Swan, Co-Chair, Canadian Congress
James Boland, Co-Chair, Canadian Congress

International Union of Crystallography (ICUr)
c/o Executive Secretariat, 2 Abbey Sq., Chester CH1 2HU United Kingdom
Tel: 44 1244 345431; *Fax:* 44 1244 344843
execsec@iucr.org
www.iucr.org
Overview: A small international organization founded in 1947
Mission: To promote international cooperation in crystallography; To contribute to all aspects of crystallography; To standardize methods, symbols, nomenclatures, & units
Membership: *Member Profile:* Adhering bodies, such as the Canadian National Committee for Crystallography; Regional associates, such as the American Crystallographic Association; Scientific associates such as the International Organization of Crystal Growth; Other bodies whose interests overlap with the aims & activities of the union, such as the International Council for Science; *Committees:* Aperiodic Crystals; Biological Macromolecules; Charge, Spin & Momentum Densities; Crystal Growth & Characterization of Materials; Crystallographic Computing; Crystallographic Nomenclature; Crystallographic Teaching; Crystallography in Art & Cultural Heritage; Electron Crystallography; High Pressure; Inorganic & Mineral Structures; International Tables; Journals; Mathematical & Theoretical Crystallography; Neutron Scattering; Powder Diffraction; Small-Angle Scattering; Structural Chemistry; Synchrotron Radiation; XAFS
Activities: Encouraging publication of crystallographic research throughout the world
Meetings/Conferences:
• International Union of Crystallography 24th Triennial Congress & General Assembly, August, 2017, Hyderabad International Convention Centre, Hyerabad
Scope: International
Publications:
• Biological Crystallography
Type: Journal
Profile: Research papers & short communications
• Crystal Structure Communications
Type: Journal
Profile: Organic, inorganic, & metal-organic compounds
• Foundations of Crystallography
Type: Journal
Profile: Research papers & book reviews
• Journal of Applied Crystallography
Type: Journal
Profile: Research papers, computer programs, laboratory notes, & meetings
• Journal of Synchrotron Radiation
Type: Journal
Profile: Facility information, research papers, short communications, current events & meetings
• Structural Biology & Crystallization Communications
Type: Journal
Profile: Structural communications
• Structural Science
Type: Journal
Profile: Research papers
• Structure Reports
Type: Journal
Profile: Organic, inorganic, & metal-organic compounds
• World Directory of Crystallographers
Type: Directory
Profile: Contact information & research interests

International Union of Elevator Constructors (IUEC) / Union internationale des constructeurs d'ascenseurs
7154 Columbia Gateway Dr., Columbia MD 21046 USA
Tel: 410-953-6150; *Fax:* 410-953-6169
iuechdq@aol.com
www.iuec.org
Overview: A medium-sized international organization founded in 1901
Chief Officer(s):
Frank J. Christensen, General President
Larry McGann, General Secretary-Treasurer
Finances: *Funding Sources:* Membership dues
Staff Member(s): 17
Membership: 25,000 members in the U.S. & Canada

Local 50 - Toronto
400 Westney Rd. South, Ajax ON L1S 6M6
Tel: 416-754-2424; *Fax:* 905-686-7355
www.iuec50.org
Chief Officer(s):
Terry Shannon, President

International Union of Forest Research Organizations (IUFRO) / Union internationale des instituts de recherches forestières

IUFRO Secretariat, Marxergasse 2, Vienna A-1140 Austria
Tel: 43-1-877-01-510; *Fax:* 43-1-877-01-5150
office@iufro.org
www.iufro.org
twitter.com/iufro
www.youtube.com/user/IUFRO
Overview: A medium-sized international organization founded in 1892
Mission: To promote international cooperation in scientific studies embracing the whole field of research related to forestry & forest products by facilitating exchanges of ideas, methods, data & results among researchers throughout the world
Chief Officer(s):
Alexander Buck, Executive Director
buck@iufro.org
Niels Elers Koch, President, (Denmark)
nek@life.ku.dk
Membership: 15,000 scientists in 700 member organizations in 110 countries worldwide; *Fees:* Schedule available; *Member Profile:* Open to organizations conducting research related to forestry, including government agencies, universities, private institutions, natural resource associations; associate - individuals
Activities: Environmental change; forests in sustainable mountain development; internet resources; sustainable forest management; management & conservation of forest gene resources; water & forests; on-line reference library; *Library* Open to public
Awards:
• Student Award for Excellence in Forest Service (Award)
• Distinguished Service Award (Award)
• Honorary Membership (Award)
• Scientific Achievement Award (Award)
• Outstanding Doctoral Research Award (Award)

International Union of Geodesy & Geophysics (IUGG) / Union géodésique et géophysique internationale

Helmholtz Centre Potsdam, GFZ German Research Centre for Geosciences, Telegrafenberg, A17, Potsdam 14473 Germany
Fax: 49-331-288-1759
secretariat@iugg.org
www.iugg.org
www.facebook.com/InternationalUnionGeodesyGeophysics
Overview: A medium-sized international organization founded in 1919
Mission: To promote & coordinate studies of the Earth & its environment in space
Chief Officer(s):
Franz G. Kuglitsch, Secretariat
secretariat@iugg.org
Membership: 70 member countries; *Member Profile:* 8 member associations: International Assn of Cryospheric Sciences; International Assn of Geodesy; International Assn of Geomagnetism & Aeronomy; International Assn of Hydrological Sciences; International Assn of Meteorology & Atmospheric Sciences; International Assn of the Physical Sciences of the Ocean; International Assn of Seismology & Physics of the Earth's Interior; and International Assn of Volcanology & Chemistry of the Earth's Interior; *Committees:* Capacity Building & Education; Membership Issues; Honours & Recognition; Visioning; Nominating; Site Evaluation; Statutes & ByLaws; Resolution

International Union of Microbiological Societies

Centralbureau voor Schimmelcultures, PO Box 85167, Utrecht 3508AD Netherlands
Tel: 31-30-21-22-600; *Fax:* 31-30-251-2097
www.iums.org
Overview: A small international organization
Affiliation(s): International Council of Scientific Unions
Chief Officer(s):
Robert A. Samson, Secretary General
r.samson@cbs.knaw.nl
Membership: *Member Profile:* National & international societies & other organizations having a common interest in microbiological sciences
Meetings/Conferences:
• International Union of Microbiological Societies 2015 XV Congress, 2015
Scope: International
Description: Meetings of the three divisions of the International Union of Microbiological Societies

International Union of Midwives *See* International Confederation of Midwives

International Union of Nutritional Sciences

c/o Institute of Nutritional Sciences, University of Vienna, Althanstrasse 14, Vienna A-1090 Vienna Austria
Tel: 43-1-4277-54901; *Fax:* 43-1-4277-9549
IUNS@kenes.com
www.iuns.org
Overview: A medium-sized international organization founded in 1948
Mission: To accomplish extensive international cooperation among scientists in nutrition-related research & education
Chief Officer(s):
Anna Lartey, President
aalartey@ug.edu.gh
Catherine Geissler, Secretary General
catherine.geissler@kcl.ac.uk
Finances: *Funding Sources:* International Council of Scientific Unions; UNESCO; membership
Membership: *Committees:* Nominating

International Union of Operating Engineers (AFL-CIO/CFL) / Union internationale des opérateurs de machines lourdes (FAT-COI/FCT)

1125 - 17 St. NW, Washington DC 20036 USA
Tel: 202-429-9100; *Fax:* 202-778-2613
www.iuoe.org
Overview: A small international organization
Chief Officer(s):
James T. Callahan, President
Membership: 400,000 + 138 locals

Local 772
Mount James Square, #401, 1030 Upper James St., Hamilton ON L9C 6X6
Tel: 905-527-5250; *Fax:* 905-527-6336
Toll-Free: 800-286-0422
iuoe772hamilton@shaw.ca
www.iuoe772.org
Mission: To serve members in Hamilton & Ottawa

International Union of Painters & Allied Trades (IUPAT) / Syndicat international des peintres et métiers connexes

7234 Parkway Dr., Hanover MD 21076 USA
Tel: 410-564-5900
mail@iupat.org
www.iupat.org
www.facebook.com/iupat?sk=friends#!/iupat?fref=ts
twitter.com/goiupat
www.youtube.com/GoIUPAT
Previous Name: International Brotherhood of Painters & Allied Trades (AFL-CIO/CFL)
Overview: A small international organization founded in 1887
Chief Officer(s):
Kenneth E. Rigmaiden, President
Robert Kucheran, Vice-President
Membership: 160,000; *Member Profile:* Active & retired members of the finishing trades industry

District Council 28 - British Columbia
7621 Kingsway, Burnaby BC V3N 3C7
Tel: 604-524-8334; *Fax:* 604-524-8011
Toll-Free: 800-866-1527
www.dc38.ca
www.facebook.com/IUPATdc38
twitter.com/DC38Trades
www.flickr.com/photos/dc38
Mission: District Council 38 includes the Painters' Union Local 138, the Glaziers' Union Local 1527, the Drywall Finishers' Union Local 2009, and the Lathers and Allied Trades Local 163. Offices in Burnaby, Victoria and Prince George
Chief Officer(s):
David Holmes, Business Manager & Secretary-Treasurer

International Union of Pharmacology *See* International Union of Basic & Clinical Pharmacology

International Union of Pure & Applied Chemistry (IUPAC)

IUPAC Secretariat, Bldg. 19, PO Box 13757, 104 T.W. Alexander Park, Research Triangle Park NC 27709-3757 USA
Fax: 919-485-8706
secretariat@iupac.org
www.iupac.org
Overview: A small international organization founded in 1919
Mission: To advance the worldwide aspects of the chemical sciences & to contribute to the application of chemistry in the service of mankind
Member of: International Council of Scientific Unions
Affliation(s): World Health Organization; UN Food & Agricultural Organization; United Nations Education, Scientific & Cultural Organization; International Organization for Standardization; Organization internationale de métrologie légale
Chief Officer(s):
Kazuyuki Tatsumi, President
John D. Petersen, Executive Director
jpetersen@iupac.org
Finances: *Annual Operating Budget:* $1.5 Million-$3 Million
Staff Member(s): 6; 1000 volunteer(s)
Membership: 49 National Adhering Organizations which represent the chemists of different member countries; *Fees:* Variable - min. US$1,400; *Member Profile:* Adhering organizations are the members of the Union & they may be a national chemical council, a national society representing chemistry, a national academy of science, or any institution or association of institutions representative of national chemical interests; *Committees:* Divisions: Physical & Biophysical, Inorganic, Organic & Biomolecular, Polymer, Analytical, Chemistry & the Environment, Chemistry & Human Health, Chemical Nomenclature & Structure Representation; Standing Committees: Chemical Research Applied to World Needs, Chemistry Education, Chemistry & Industry, Printed & Electronic Publications, Terminology Nomenclature & Symbols, Finance, Project, Evaluation
Awards:
• Financial Support for Symposia & Conferences in Scientifically Emerging Regions (Award)
• IUPAC Prize for Young Chemists (Award)

International Union of Societies for Biomaterials Science & Engineering (IUSBSE)

c/o Prof. Nicholas A. Peppas, The University of Texas at Austin, #C-0400, 1 University Station, Austin TX 78712-0231 USA
Tel: 512-471-6644; *Fax:* 512-471-8227
peppas@che.utexas.edu
www.worldbiomaterials.org
Overview: A medium-sized international organization
Mission: To advance biomaterials, surgical implants, prosthetics, artificial organs, tissue engineering, & regenerative medicine
Chief Officer(s):
Nicholas A. Peppas, President
Membership: *Member Profile:* National & multi-national groups from Canada, the United States, the European Union, China, Japan, Korea, India, & Australia
Meetings/Conferences:
• Biomaterials 2016 10th World Congress, May, 2016, Palais des congrès (Convention Centre), Montréal, QC
Scope: International

International Union of Soil Sciences (IUSS) / Union internationale de la science du sol

c/o University of Wisconsin, Department of Soil Science, 1525 Observatory Dr., Madison WI 53706-1299 USA
www.iuss.org
www.facebook.com/unionsoilsciences
Previous Name: International Society of Soil Science
Overview: A medium-sized international charitable organization founded in 1924
Mission: To promote soil science & give support to soil scientists
Member of: International Council of Scientific Unions
Affiliation(s): Canadian Society of Soil Science
Chief Officer(s):
Jae Yang, President, (Korea)
yangjay@kangwon.ac.kr
Aldred Hartemink, Secretary General
hartemink@wisc.edu
Finances: *Funding Sources:* Membership fees
Membership: *Member Profile:* National soil science societies; *Committees:* Awards & Prizes; Budget & Finances; Statutes & Bylaws
Activities: *Rents Mailing List:* Yes *Library*

International Union of Theoretical & Applied Mechanics (IUTAM)

Centre de Mathématiques et de Leurs Applications, Ecole Normale Supérieure de Cachan, Cachan 94235 France
Tel: 33-14-740-5900; *Fax:* 33-14-740-5901
iutam.org
Overview: A large international organization founded in 1947
Mission: To carry out & promote scientific work in mechanics & related sciences
Chief Officer(s):
Viggo Tvergaard, President
Frederic Dias, Secretary General
Finances: *Annual Operating Budget:* $100,000-$250,000; *Funding Sources:* Membership fees; grants
Membership: 45 nations; *Member Profile:* National Committees of Mechanics; *Committees:* Congress; 2 Symposia - Panels
Activities: *Internships:* Yes *Library* Open to public
Publications:
• International Union of Theoretical & Applied Mechanics Newsletter
Type: Newsletter
• International Union of Theoretical & Applied Mechanics Annual Report
Type: Yearbook
• IUTAMM [International Union of Theoretical & Applied Mechanics] - A Short History
Type: Book; *Editor:* S. Juhasz; *ISBN:* 3-540-50043-X
• Mechanics at the Turn of the Century [a publication of the International Union of Theoretical & Applied Mechanics]
Type: Report; *Editor:* W. Schiehlen & L. van Wijngaarden; *ISBN:* 3-8265-7714-0

International Union, United Automobile, Aerospace & Agricultural Implement Workers of America (UAW) / Syndicat international des travailleurs unis de l'automobile, de l'aérospatiale et de l'outillage agricole d'Amérique

8000 East Jefferson Ave., Detroit MI 48214 USA
Tel: 313-926-5000
Toll-Free: 800-243-8829
www.uaw.org
www.facebook.com/uaw.union
twitter.com/uaw
www.youtube.com/uaw
Overview: A small international organization founded in 1935
Mission: To act as the collective bargaining body for its members, negotiating for wages & benefits.
Chief Officer(s):
Dennis Williams, President
Gary Casteel, Sec.-Treas.
Membership: 390,000 active members; 600,000 retired members; 750 locals;

UAW Local 251 - Wallaceburg, ON
88 Elm Dr. South, Wallaceburg ON N8A 5E7
Tel: 519-627-1629; *Fax:* 519-627-2055
Toll-Free: 800-646-5437
local251@uaw.ca
www.canadianuaw.ca
Chief Officer(s):
Bill Pollock, President

International Vegetarian Union (IVU) / Union internationale végéterienne

Shropshire United Kingdom
manager@ivu.org
www.ivu.org
www.facebook.com/InternationalVegUnion
Overview: A small international organization founded in 1908
Mission: To further vegetarianism worldwide by promoting knowledge of vegetarianism as a means of advancing the spiritual, moral, mental, physical & economic well-being of mankind; to promote research into all aspects of vegetarianism; to encourage the formation of vegetarian organizations & cooperation amongst them
Affliation(s): Toronto Vegetarian Association
Chief Officer(s):
Dilip Barman, Regional Representative, North America
Membership: *Member Profile:* Vegetarian societies subscribing to the vegetarian ethic whose executive authority is vested exclusively in vegetarians; Associate - organization which is in sympathy with animal welfare, humanitarian, health or similar relevant objectives
Activities: *Speaker Service:* Yes

International Virtual Assistants Association

#400, 2360 Corporate Circle, Henderson NV 89074 USA
Toll-Free: 877-440-2750
www.ivaa.org
www.linkedin.com/groups?gid=695327&trk=myg_ugrp_ovr
www.facebook.com/IVAA.org
www.twitter.com/ivaa_org
www.youtube.com/user/IVAAVirtualAssistant
Overview: A small international organization
Mission: Dedicated to the professional education & development of members, & to educating the public on the role & function of the Virtual Assistant
Chief Officer(s):
Kathy Colaiacovo, President, 877-440-2750 Ext. 712
president@ivaa.org
Membership: *Member Profile:* Independent entrepreneur providing administrative, creative &/or technical services, utilizing advanced technological modes of communication & data delivery
Activities: Offers IVAA Certified Virtual Assistant (CVA) exam

International Volleyball Association / Fédération Internationale de Volleyball (FIVB)

Château Les Tourelles, Edouard-Sandoz 2-4, Lausanne 1006 Switzerland
Tel: 41-21-345-3535; *Fax:* 41-21-345-3545
info@fivb.org
www.fivb.ch
www.facebook.com/FIVB.InternationalVolleyballFederation
twitter.com/fivbvolleyball
www.youtube.com/videofivb
Overview: A small international organization founded in 1947
Affiliation(s): Canadian Volleyball Association
Chief Officer(s):
Ary S. Graça Filho, President
Carlos Luiz Martins, General Director
Staff Member(s): 20
Membership: 211;

International Warehouse Logistics Association (IWLA)

#260, 2800 South River Rd., Des Plaines IL 60018 USA
Tel: 847-813-4699; *Fax:* 847-813-0115
email@iwla.com
www.iwla.com
Overview: A medium-sized international organization founded in 1997
Mission: To encourage, promote, & further the use of public warehousing & distribution services among potential existing users; to establish & enforce adherence to appropriate industry operating standards; to provide forum for members to meet, study & discuss problems & opportunities of common interest; to encourage a spirit of cooperation in the implementation of solutions & the pursuit of those opportunities; to make representations to governments at all levels & their regulatory agencies for benefit of the industry, members & their clients; to provide vehicle for industry-related educational services. The Canadian Council represents the interests of Canadian member companies & provides a forum to share resources & information about the Canadian warehousing & 3PL industry.
Chief Officer(s):
Paul Verst, Chair
Steve DeHaan, President & CEO
sdehaan@IWLA.com
John Levi, Executive Director, Canadian Council
jlevi@primus.ca
Finances: *Funding Sources:* Membership dues; interest; programs
Staff Member(s): 9
Membership: *Committees:* Canadian Council; Education Advisory; Executive; Government Affairs; Insurance & Legal Affairs; IWLA Convention & Expo Planning; Nominating; Partner Member; Political Action; Warehouse Membership
Activities: *Speaker Service:* Yes

International Water Association (IWA)

Alliance House, 12 Caxton St., London SW1H 0QS United Kingdom
Tel: 44-20-7654-5500; *Fax:* 44-20-7654-5555
water@iwahq.org
www.iwahq.org
www.linkedin.com/company/international-water-association
twitter.com/IWAwaternews
Previous Name: International Association on Water Quality; International Association on Water Pollution Research & Control
Overview: A large international organization founded in 1999
Mission: To advance the science & practice of water management internationally
Chief Officer(s):
Glen Daigger, President & Chair
Ger Bergkamp, Interim Executive Director
ger.bergkamp@iwahq.org
Finances: *Annual Operating Budget:* $250,000-$500,000
Staff Member(s): 20
Membership: 9,000; *Committees:* Executive; Finance & Investment; Renumeration; Program; Publications; Young Professionals
Activities: Wastewater treatment processes; hazardous wastes & source control; impacts of pollutants on receiving waters; environmental restoration
Meetings/Conferences:
• 6th IWA-ASPIRE Conference & Exhibition 2015, September, 2015, Beijing
Scope: International
Contact Information: Congress Web Site: www.iwaaspire2015.org
• International Water Association World Water Congress & Exhibition 2016, September, 2016, Brisbane
Scope: International
Description: Provides international water experts the change to explore the science & practice of water management
• International Water Association World Water Congress & Exhibition 2018, 2018
Scope: International
Description: Provides international water experts the change to explore the science & practice of water management
Publications:
• Hydrology Research [a publication of the International Water Association]
Type: Journal; *Editor:* Ian Littlewood & Chong-Yu Xu *ISSN:* 0029-1277
Profile: Official journal of the Nordic Association for Hydrology, British Hydrological Society, German HydrologicalSociety, & Italian Hydrological Society
• Journal of Hydroinformatics [a publication of the International Water Association]
Type: Journal; *Editor:* Professor Dragan Savic *ISSN:* 1464-7141
Profile: Devoted to the application of information technology to problems of the aquatic environment
• Journal of Water & Health [a publication of the International Water Association]
Type: Journal; *Editor:* Morteza Abbaszadegan *ISSN:* 1477-8920
Profile: Promotes research into the challenges of harnessing water for health in developing & developed countries
• Journal of Water Reuse & Desalination [a publication of the International Water Association]
Type: Journal; *Frequency:* q.; *Editor:* Blanca Jiménez Cisneros *ISSN:* 2220-1319
• Journal of Water Supply: Research and Technology - Aqua [a publication of the International Water Association]
Type: Journal; *Editor:* Rolf Gimbel *ISSN:* 0003-7214
Profile: Research & development in water supply technology & management
• Journal of Water, Sanitation & Hygiene for Development [a publication of the International Water Association]
Type: Journal; *Editor:* Barbara Evans *ISSN:* 2043-9083
Profile: Science, policy & practice of drinking-water supply, sanitation & hygiene
• Water Asset Management International [a publication of the International Water Association]
Type: Newsletter; *Editor:* Dr. John Bridgeman *ISSN:* 1814-5434
Profile: Asset management in water & wastewater utilities
• Water Practice & Technology [a publication of the International Water Association]
Type: Journal; *Editor:* Dr.-Ing. Burkhard Teichgräber *ISSN:* 1751-231X
Profile: Online journal under the control of the Water Science & Technology Editorial Board
• Water21 [a publication of the International Water Association]
Type: Magazine; *Frequency:* 6 pa. *ISSN:* 1561-9508
Profile: Official magazine of the International Water Association

International Whaling Commission (IWC)

The Red House, 135 Station Rd., Impington, Cambridge CB24 9NP United Kingdom
Tel: 44-1223-233-971; *Fax:* 44-1223-232-876
secretariat@iwcoffice.org
iwc.int
Overview: A medium-sized international organization founded in 1946
Mission: To keep under review & revise as necessary those measures which provide for the complete protection of certain species of whales; to designate specified areas as whale sanctuaries; to set limits on the maximum numbers of whales

which may be taken in one season; to prescribe open & closed seasons & areas for whaling; to set limits on the size of whales that may be killed; to prohibit the capture of suckling calves & female whales accompanied by calves; to encourage, coordinate & fund whale research; to publish results of research & other scientific research; to promote studies into related matters. Canada is not currently a member.
Chief Officer(s):
Simon Brockington, Secretariat
secretariat@iwc.int
Membership: 89 whaling governments; *Member Profile:* Open to any country in the world that formally adheres to the 1946 Convention; *Committees:* Scientific; Finance & Administration; Conservation; Aboriginal Subsistence Whaling; Infractions; Working Group on Whale Killing Methods & Associated Welfare Issues
Activities: *Speaker Service:* Yes *Library* Open to public by appointment

International Wildlife Rehabilitation Council (IWRC)
PO Box 3197, Eugene OR 97403 USA
Tel: 866-871-1869
Toll-Free: 866-871-1869
info@iwrc-online.org
www.iwrc-online.org
www.linkedin.com/companies/the-international-wildlife-rehabilitation-c
www.facebook.com/theiwrc
twitter.com/theiwrc
Overview: A small international charitable organization founded in 1972
Mission: To further knowledge & experience in the field of wildlife rehabilitation, through education, networking, & professional standards of review; to preserve our wildlife & its habitat
Chief Officer(s):
Kai Williams, Executive Director
director@theiwrc.org
Finances: *Annual Operating Budget:* $250,000-$500,000; *Funding Sources:* Membership dues; course fees; private donations; sales of literature; annual conference
Staff Member(s): 3; 12 volunteer(s)
Membership: 1,850; *Fees:* $49 individual; $59 family; $75 organization; $32 library; *Member Profile:* Individual - persons actively working in the field of wildlife rehabilitation in administration, conservation, management, education, research, humane work, or veterinary or allied professional practice; Family - two or more active rehabilitators residing at the same address; Organizational/Institutional - non-profit corporations or public agencies affiliated with a branch of local, state, or federal government actively supporting or operating wildlife rehabilitation programs; Affiliate/Corporate - small & large businesses or foundations that are not actively involved in wildlife rehabilitation but wish to provide financial support for IWRC programs; Library/Agency: Accredited library or government, state, provincial agency
Activities: Nationwide certification program which includes a series of hands-on training seminars in state-of-the-art wildlife rehabilitation techniques, from beginner through advanced levels

International Wine & Food Society (IWFS)
The Naval & Military Club, 4 St James's Square, London SW1J 4JU United Kingdom
Tel: 44-20-7827-5732; *Fax:* 44-20-7827-5733
sec@iwfs.org
www.iwfs.org
Overview: A medium-sized international organization founded in 1933
Mission: To bring together & serve all who believe that a right understanding of good food & wine is an essential part of personal contentment & health, & that an intelligent approach to the pleasures & problems of the table offers far greater rewards than the mere satisfaction of appetite
Chief Officer(s):
Yvonne Wallis, Chair, Council of Management
David R. Felton, Chair, Americas
Membership: 6,000+ members in 130 branches; *Committees:* Wines; European & African; Asian Pacific Zone; Board of Governors of the Americas
Activities: *Library:* Guildhall Library; Open to public by appointment

Edmonton Branch
Edmonton AB
Chief Officer(s):
Bruce Ambrose, President

Kitchener-Waterloo
Waterloo ON
www.rjengineering.com/iwfs
Chief Officer(s):
Julien J. Hradecky, Contact
JJHrad@golden.net

Montréal Branch
Montréal QC
Chief Officer(s):
Louis Villeneuve, Contact
louis.villeneuve@iwfsmontreal.com

Niagara Branch
St Catharines ON

Toronto Branch
Toronto ON
Tel: 416-725-0425
info@iwfstoronto.org
www.iwfstoronto.org
Chief Officer(s):
Chris Tierney, Contact
ctiern@gmail.com

Vancouver Branch
#1201, 1169 Cordova St. West, Vancouver BC V6C 3T1
Tel: 604-620-9008
info@iwfsvancouver.com
www.iwfsvancouver.com
www.facebook.com/128978526019
Chief Officer(s):
James Robertson, President

Victoria Branch
Victoria BC

International Women's Forum (IWF)
#460, 2120 L St. NW, Washington DC 20037 USA
Tel: 202-387-1010; *Fax:* 202-387-1009
iwf@iwforum.org
www.iwforum.org
Overview: A small international organization founded in 1982
Mission: To advance women's leadership across careers, cultures & continents
Chief Officer(s):
Ludmila Shvetsova, President
Membership: 5,500; *Member Profile:* Female leaders

International WWOOF Association
PO Box 2675, Lewes BN7 1RB United Kingdom
www.wwoof.org
Also Known As: World-Wide Opportunities on Organic Farms
Overview: A small international organization
Mission: To help those who would like to volunteer on organic farms internationally
Chief Officer(s):
Amanda Pearson, Administrator
amanda@wwoof.net

Internationale de l'Education *See* Education International

Internationale des services publics *See* Public Services International

Inter-Parliamentary Union (IPU) / Union interparlementaire
PO Box 330, 5, ch du Pommier, Geneva CH-1218 Switzerland
Tel: 41-22-919-41-50; *Fax:* 41-22-919-41-60
postbox@mail.ipu.org
www.ipu.org
twitter.com/IPUparliament
Overview: A large international organization founded in 1889
Mission: To foster contacts, coordination & exchange of experience among parliaments & parliamentarians of all countries; To consider questions of international interest & concern; To contribute to the defence & promotion of human rights; To contribute to the better knowledge of the working of representative institutions & to the strengthening & development of their means of action
Affliation(s): Canadian Inter-Parliamentary Group
Chief Officer(s):
Abdelwahad Radi, President
Anders B. Johnsson, Secretary General
Finances: *Annual Operating Budget:* $3 Million-$5 Million; *Funding Sources:* Assessed contributions from National Groups
Staff Member(s): 33
Membership: 162 full + 10 associate; *Member Profile:* Parliaments of sovereign states (National Groups of parliamentarians); *Committees:* Peace & International Security; Democracy & Human Rights; Sustainable Development, Finance & Trade; Human Rights of Parliamentarians; Middle East Questions; Facilitators for Cyprus; Promote Respect for International Humanitarian Law; Advisory Group of the IPU Committee on United Nations Affairs; Advisory Group on HIV/AIDS & Maternal, Newborn & Child Health; Women Parliamentarians; Gender Partnership Group
Activities: *Library* Open to public

IRC International Water & Sanitation Centre
PO Box 82327, The Hague 2508 EH Netherlands
Tel: 31-70-304-4000; *Fax:* 31-70-304-4044
www.irc.nl
Previous Name: International Reference Centre for Community Water Supply & Sanitation
Overview: A small international organization founded in 1968
Mission: The IRC helps people in developing countries to get the best water & sanitation services they can afford
Chief Officer(s):
L. de Waal, Chairman, Supervisory Board
Michel van der Leest, Office Coordinator, Services Section
Finances: *Annual Operating Budget:* $1.5 Million-$3 Million
Staff Member(s): 38
Activities: *Internships:* Yes *Library* by appointment

ISACA
#1010, 3701 Algonquin Rd., Rolling Meadows IL 60008 USA
Tel: 847-253-1545; *Fax:* 847-253-1443
news@isaca.org
www.isaca.org
www.linkedin.com/groups/ISACA-Official-3839870?home=&gid=3839870&trk=a
www.facebook.com/ISACAHQ
twitter.com/ISACANews
Previous Name: Information Systems Audit & Control Association
Overview: A large international organization founded in 1967
Mission: To be the recognized global leader in IT governance, control, & assurance
Chief Officer(s):
Bevin Callan, Contact, Membership, 847-660-5600
Megan Mortiz, Contact, Chapter Relations, 847-660-5587
Deborah Vohasek, Contact, Media Relations, 847-660-5566
Linda Wogelius, Contact, Research, 847-660-5562
Finances: *Annual Operating Budget:* $50,000-$100,000; *Funding Sources:* Membership dues; Education; Certification exam
Membership: 86,000 worldwide in 175 chapters
Activities: *Speaker Service:* Yes; *Rents Mailing List:* Yes
Publications:
• ISACA Journal
Type: Journal; *Frequency:* Bimonthly

Israel Association for Canadian Studies (IACS) / Association d'études canadiennes en Israel
c/o Halbert Centre for Canadian Studies, Faculty of Social Sciences, Hebrew University of Jerusalem, Jerusalem 91905 Israel
Tel: 972-2-588-1344; *Fax:* 972-2-582-6267
mscanada@mscc.huji.ac.il
Overview: A small international organization founded in 1985
Mission: To promote, develop, & expand Canadian Studies in Israel; to encourage the teaching of courses with Canadian content & engage in research on Canada & Canadian issues within Israeli universities
Member of: International Council for Canadian Studies
Affliation(s): Association of Canadian Studies
Chief Officer(s):
Daniel Ben-Natan, President
Finances: *Annual Operating Budget:* $50,000-$100,000
Staff Member(s): 2
Membership: 370; *Member Profile:* University faculty; students; civil servants; journalists; general public; *Committees:* Executive
Activities: Biennial international conference, public lecture series, research grants, publications, library facilities, resource & information; *Speaker Service:* Yes *Library*

Italian Association for Canadian Studies / Associazione Italiana di Studi Canadesi
c/o Oriana Palusci, Vis Duomo, 219, Università di Napoli 'L'Orientale', Napoli 80138 Italy
Tel: 0039-816909840; *Fax:* 0039-81-204639
Also Known As: AISC
Overview: A small international organization founded in 1979
Mission: To promote Canadian Studies in Italy, encouraging collaboration & scholarly publishing, promoting & maintaining academic & cultural links with Canada & sponsoring

conferences, seminars & courses related to the study of Canada
Affliation(s): International Council for Canadian Studies
Chief Officer(s):
Oriana Palusci, President
opalusci@unior.it
Finances: *Annual Operating Budget:* $50,000-$100,000; *Funding Sources:* Canadian government; charities
Staff Member(s): 9; 2 volunteer(s)
Membership: 206; *Fees:* 22 euros
Activities: Organizes seminars, conferences & conventions; sponsors Canadianist cultural activities in Italy
Awards:
• Italian Association of Canadian Studies Award (Award)

The Jane Goodall Institute for Wildlife Research, Education & Conservation (JGI)
#550, 1595 Spring Hill Rd., Vienna VA 22182 USA
Tel: 703-682-9220; *Fax:* 703-682-9312
www.janegoodall.org
www.facebook.com/janegoodallinst
twitter.com/JaneGoodallInst
www.youtube.com/user/JaneGoodallInstitute
Overview: A small international organization founded in 1977
Mission: To increase primate habitat conservation; to increase awareness of, support for & training in issues related to our relationship with each other, the environment & other animals (leading to behaviour change); to expand non-invasive research program on chimpanzees & other primates; to promote activities that ensure the well-being of chimpanzees, other primates & animal welfare activities in general
Chief Officer(s):
Mary Humphrey, Chief Executive Officer
Chris Fanning, Vice President, Finance
Activities: Gombe Stream Research Centre; ChimpanZoo Project; reforestation projects; conservation centres; educational & communcation resources

Japanese Association for Canadian Studies
c/o Meiji University, 1-1 Kanda-Surugadia, Chiyoda, Tokyo 101-8301 Japan
Tel: 81-3-3219-5822; *Fax:* 81-3-3219-5822
jacsmeiji@jacs.jp
www.jacs.jp/English/index.html
Overview: A small international organization founded in 1979
Mission: To promote Canadian studies research, teaching & publishing in Japan
Member of: International Council for Canadian Studies
Chief Officer(s):
Naoharu Fujita, President
Membership: 265; *Fees:* 7,000 yen; *Member Profile:* University teachers, research fellows of institutes, graduate students, government officials, journalists & business people

John E. Mack Institute
PO Box 7046, Boulder CO 80306 USA
info@johnemackinstitute.org
www.johnemackinstitute.org
Previous Name: Center for Psychology & Social Change; Center for Psychological Studies in the Nuclear Age
Overview: A medium-sized international charitable organization founded in 1982
Mission: To explore the frontiers of human experience; to serve the transformation of individual consciousness; to further the evolution of the paradigms by which we understand human identity.
Affliation(s): Consultative status with the Economic & Social Council at the UN
Chief Officer(s):
Will Bueché, Contact, 303-875-5394
Finances: *Funding Sources:* Membership dues; donations; grants
Activities: Integrative Healing Research Program; Ecopsychology Institute; Marine Advocacy Program; United Nations Program; Balkans Trauma Project; Program for Extraordinary Experience Research; Psychospiritual Institute; *Speaker Service:* Yes; *Rents Mailing List:* Yes

Joubert Syndrome Foundation
#252, 414 Hungerford Dr., Rockville MB 20850 USA
Tel: 614-864-1362
joubertfoundation@joubertfoundation.com
www.joubertfoundation.com
www.facebook.com/groups/179994158677513/?bookmark_t=group
twitter.com/jsrdf
Overview: A small international charitable organization founded in 1992
Mission: To serve as an international network of parents who share knowledge, experience & emotional support; to educate physicians & their support teams; to increase awareness & understanding of Joubert Syndrome; to provide support to families who have loved ones diagnosed with Joubert Syndrome
Chief Officer(s):
Karen Tompkins, President
president@jsrdf.org
Finances: *Annual Operating Budget:* Less than $50,000
8 volunteer(s)
Membership: 350; *Fees:* US$35; $40 international; *Member Profile:* Interested professionals & affected persons & their families
Activities: Networking list of affected families; biennial conference; development & maintenance of database

Junior Chamber International (JCI)
15645 Olive Blvd., Chesterfield MO 63017 USA
Tel: 636-449-3100; *Fax:* 636-449-3107
Other Communication: www.flickr.com/groups/1513948@N23
www.jci.cc
www.facebook.com/pages/JCI/35159638460
twitter.com/jcinews
www.youtube.com/user/pzjci
Merged from: Lions Clubs International
Overview: A large international organization founded in 1944
Mission: To contribute to the advancement of the community through service & volunteer projects, encouraging the development of leadership skills among youth for the benefit of the community
Affliation(s): United Nations; UN Global Compact; International Chamber of Commerce-World Chambers Federation; UN Foundation; United Nations Educational, Scientific & Cultural Organization; Pan American Health Organization
Chief Officer(s):
Kentaro Hadara, President
Finances: *Annual Operating Budget:* $3 Million-$5 Million
Staff Member(s): 40
Membership: 100+ countries + 5,000 communities + 200,000 individuals; *Member Profile:* Young professionals & entrepreneurs between ages 18 & 40
Activities: *Speaker Service:* Yes
Publications:
• Be Better [a publication of Junior Chamber International]
Type: Newsletter
• JCI [Junior Chamber International] World Congress Report
Type: Report
• JCI [Junior Chamber International] Impact Update
Type: Newsletter

Kitchen Cabinet Manufacturers Association (KCMA)
1899 Preston White Dr., Reston VA 20191-5435 USA
Tel: 703-264-1690; *Fax:* 703-620-6530
www.kcma.org
twitter.com/KCMAorg
Overview: A small international organization founded in 1955
Mission: To serve & represent kitchen, bath & other residential cabinet manufacturers & suppliers in the US & Canada
Chief Officer(s):
C. Richard Titus, Executive Vice-President
dtitus@kcma.org
Membership: 360 in US & Canada; *Member Profile:* Manufacturers of kitchen cabinets, bath vanities; countertop fabricators; goods & services suppliers; *Committees:* Government & Regulatory Affairs; Standards; Environmental Stewardship Program; Marketing; Associates; Entrepreneurs Council

Knights of Columbus / Chevaliers de Colomb
1 Columbus Plaza, New Haven CT 06510 USA
Tel: 203-752-4000; *Fax:* 203-752-4118
info@kofc.org
www.kofc.org
www.facebook.com/pages/Knights-of-Columbus/75774105475
twitter.com/kofc
www.youtube.com/knightsofcolumbus
Also Known As: K of C
Overview: A large international charitable organization founded in 1882
Mission: To render pecuniary aid to members & their families; To render mutual aid & assistance to sick, disabled & needy members; To promote social & intellectual intercourse among members; To promote & conduct educational, charitable, religious, social welfare, war relief & welfare, & public relief work
Member of: Canadian Life & Health Insurance Association; Canadian Fraternal Association
Chief Officer(s):
Carl A. Anderson, Supreme Knight
Dennis Savoie, Deputy Supreme Knight
Charles E. Maurer, Supreme Secretary
Finances: *Annual Operating Budget:* Greater than $5 Million
Staff Member(s): 650
Membership: 228,812 individuals + 1,873 groups in Canada; 1,678,205 individuals + 12,522 groups worldwide; *Fees:* Varies by province & state; *Member Profile:* Male aged 18+ & practicing Catholics in Union with the Holy See
Activities: *Library:* Archives; by appointment
Awards:
• Percy J. Johnson Endowed Scholarships (Scholarship)
Eligibility: Young men who demonstrate financial need.
• Matthews and Swift Educational Trust Scholarships (Scholarship)
• Vocations Scholarships (Scholarship)
• Mexico, Philippines and Puerto Rico Scholarships (Scholarship)
• Anthony J. LaBella Endowed Scholarships (Scholarship)
• Frank L. Goularte Endowed Scholarships (Scholarship)

Laborers' International Union of North America (AFL-CIO/CLC) (LiUNA) / Union internationale des journaliers d'Amérique (FAT-COI/CTC)
905 - 16 St. NW, Washington DC 20006 USA
Tel: 202-737-8320; *Fax:* 202-737-2754
communications@liuna.org
www.liuna.org
www.facebook.com/LaborersInternationalUnionofNorthAmerica
twitter.com/LIUNA
www.youtube.com/user/liunavideo
Overview: A large international organization founded in 1903
Mission: Union fighting for better wages and benefits, safer jobsites, more successful employers, and a strong voice for the people.
Affliation(s): American Federation of Labour & Congress of Industrial Organizations; Canadian Labour Congress
Chief Officer(s):
Richard Metcalf, Director, Corporate Affairs, 202-942-2269
Richard Greer, Director, Strategic Communications
Membership: 500,000 + 629 locals

Canadian Office
44 Hughson St. South, Hamilton ON L8N 2A7
Tel: 905-522-7177; *Fax:* 905-522-9310
www.liuna.org
Mission: Members run the Laborers' Union through their day-to-day activism and election of officers. The Central & Eastern Canada Region office, located in Hamilton, includes locals in Ontario, Québec, New Brunswick, Nova Scotia, Prince Edward Island & Newfoundland & Labrador. The regional office also coordinates the trusteeship for Local 183, the largest construction local in North America.
Chief Officer(s):
Joseph S. Mancinelli, Vice President & Regional Manager, Central & Eastern Canada Region
joseph@liuna.ca
Leo D'Agostini, International Representative
leo@liuna.ca
Phil Hambrook, International Representative
Gerry Varricchio, Regional Organizing Coordinator
gerry@liuna.ca
Daniel P. Randazzo, Legal Counsel
randazzo@liuna.ca
Joe Missori, International Representative

Ladies' Golf Union (LGU)
The Scores, St. Andrews, Fife KY16 9AT United Kingdom
Tel: 44-13-34-475811; *Fax:* 44-13-34-472818
www.lgu.org
www.facebook.com/ladiesgolfunion
twitter.com/LadiesGolfUnion
Overview: A small international organization founded in 1893
Mission: To uphold the rules of golf; to advance & safeguard the interests of ladies' golf & to decide all doubtful & disputed points in connection therewith; to maintain LGU Scratch Score System; to employ the funds of the LGU in such a manner as shall be deemed best for the interests of ladies' golf, with power to borrow or raise money for the same purpose; to promote, maintain & regulate international events, championships & competitions held under the LGU regulations & to promote the interests of Great Britain & Ireland in ladies' international golf; to promulgate, maintain, enforce & publish such regulations as may

be considered necessary
Affliation(s): Canadian Ladies' Golf Association
Chief Officer(s):
Brigid McCaw, President
Shona Malcolm, CEO
Staff Member(s): 8
Membership: 2,750 clubs; *Committees:* Finance & General Purposes; International Selection; Rules & Regulations; Scratch Score; Training
Activities: *Library* by appointment

Land Trust Alliance (LTA)

#1100, 1660 L St. NW, Washington DC 20036 USA
Tel: 202-638-4725; *Fax:* 202-638-4730
info@lta.org
www.lta.org
www.facebook.com/landtrustalliance
twitter.com/ltalliance
Overview: A large international organization founded in 1982
Mission: To strengthen the land trust movement & ensure that land trusts have the information, skills & resources they use to save land
Chief Officer(s):
Rand Wentworth, President
rwentworth@lta.org
Mary Pope Hutson, Exec. Vice President
mpmhutson@lta.org
Marilyn Ayres, Chief Operating
mayres@lta.org
Finances: *Annual Operating Budget:* $3 Million-$5 Million
Staff Member(s): 32
Membership: 1,000
Activities: *Awareness Events:* National Land Trust Rally; *Internships:* Yes
Awards:
• Allen Morgan Award for Excellence in Membership Development (Award)
Publications:
• Saving Land
Type: Magazine; *Frequency:* Quarterly; *Number of Pages:* 40

Latin American Studies Association (LASA)

416 Bellefield Hall, University of Pittsburgh, Pittsburgh PA 15260 USA
Tel: 412-648-7929; *Fax:* 412-624-7145
lasa@pitt.edu
lasa.international.pitt.edu
Overview: A medium-sized international organization founded in 1966
Mission: To foster the concerns of all scholars interested in Latin American studies; to encourage more effective training, teaching & research in connection with such studies; to provide a forum for dealing with matters of common interest to scholars & individuals concerned with Latin American studies
Member of: American Council of Learned Societies; National Council of Area Studies Associations
Chief Officer(s):
Milagros Pereyra-Rojas, Executive Director
Finances: *Funding Sources:* Membership dues; congresses; donations from members
Staff Member(s): 6
Membership: 7,000+ worldwide; *Fees:* Schedule available; *Member Profile:* Interest in Latin American studies
Awards:
• Bryce Wood Book (Award)
• Diskin Award (Award)
• Kalman Silbert Memorial Award (Award)
• Media Award (Award)
• Premio Iberoamericano Book Award (Award)

Lawson Wilkins Pediatric Endocrine Society *See* Pediatric Endocrine Society

La Leche League International (LLLI)

957 North Plum Grove Rd., Schaumburg IL 60173 USA
Tel: 847-519-7730; *Fax:* 847-696-0460
Toll-Free: 800-525-3243
www.llli.org
Overview: A medium-sized international organization founded in 1956
Mission: To help mothers worldwide to breastfeed through mother-to-mother support, encouragement, information & education; to promote a better understanding of breastfeeding as an important element in the healthy development of the baby & mother.
Affliation(s): United Nations Children's Fund (UNICEF); World Health Organization (WHO); World Alliance for Breastfeeding Action (WABA)
Chief Officer(s):
Cynthia Garrison, Co-Chair
Lydia de Raad, Co-Chair
Membership: *Fees:* $25; *Member Profile:* Breastfeeding mothers or parents; *Committees:* Health Advisory; Legal Advisory; Management Advisory
Activities: Annual Seminar For Physicians; Workshops for Lactation Consultants; Biennial International Conference; Annual World Walk for Breastfeeding; *Library:* Center for Breastfeeding Information

Linguistic Society of America (LSA)

#211, 1325 - 18 St. NW, Washington DC 20036-6501 USA
Tel: 202-835-1714; *Fax:* 202-835-1717
lsa@lsadc.org
www.linguisticsociety.org
www.facebook.com/LingSocAm
twitter.com/LingSocAm
www.flickr.com/photos/lingsocam/
Overview: A large international organization founded in 1924
Mission: The Linguistic Society of America is the major professional society in the United States that is exclusively dedicated to the advancement of the scientific study of language
Member of: American Council of Learned Societies
Affliation(s): Permanent International Committee of Linguists
Chief Officer(s):
Ellen Kaisse, President
Alyson Reed, Executive Director
areed@lsadc.org
Finances: *Annual Operating Budget:* $500,000-$1.5 Million
Staff Member(s): 3
Membership: 4,593 individual + 2,060 institutional; *Fees:* Schedule available; *Member Profile:* Interest in the advancement of the scientific study of language
Activities: *Internships:* Yes

Lions Clubs International

300 - 22nd St. West, Oak Brook IL 60523-8842 USA
Tel: 630-571-5466
Other Communication: flickr.com/photos/lionsclubsorg
www.lionsclubs.org
www.linkedin.com/groupRegistration?gid=64494
www.facebook.com/lionsclubs
twitter.com/lionsclubsorg
www.youtube.com/user/lionsclubsorg
Overview: A large international organization
Mission: World's largest service club organization; 46,000 clubs in 193 countries including Canada
Chief Officer(s):
Wayne A. Madden, International President

Publications:
• Lion
Type: Magazine; *Frequency:* Quarterly
Profile: Published in 21 languages.

Major League Baseball Players' Association (Ind.) / Association des joueurs de la Ligue majeure de baseball (ind.)

12 East 49th St., 24th Fl., New York NY 10017 USA
Tel: 212-826-0808; *Fax:* 212-752-4378
feedback@mlbpa.org
www.mlb.com/pa
twitter.com/MLB_PLAYERS
Overview: A medium-sized international organization
Mission: To represent and protect the interests of professional baseball players in the United States.
Chief Officer(s):
Tony Clark, Executive Director
Martha Child, CAO
Marietta DiCamillo, Chief Financial Officer
Membership: 80 + 2 locals (in Canada)
Activities: Baseball Card Clubhouse; Baseball Tomorrow Fund; Rookie Career Development; *Awareness Events:* Players Choice Awards

Master Brewers Association of The Americas (MBAA)

3340 Pilot Knob Rd., St. Paul MN 55121-2097 USA
Tel: 651-454-7250; *Fax:* 651-454-0766
mbaa@mbaa.com
www.mbaa.com
www.facebook.com/MasterBrewers
twitter.com/masterbrewers
Overview: A large international organization founded in 1887
Mission: To advance brewing, fermentation, & allied industries
Chief Officer(s):
Horace B. Cunningham, President
hcunningham@coldspringbrewingco.com
Ruth Ellen Martin, Treasurer
ruth@sierranevada.com
Membership: 1,000-4,999; *Fees:* Schedule available; *Member Profile:* Professionals in the fermentation & brewing industry; *Committees:* ASBC/MBAA Steering; Beer Specialist Certification Program; Board of Governor Representatives; Bylaws; Committee Chairs; Communicator; Education; Executive; Finance; Heritage; International Brewers Symposium Planning; MBAA Global Emerging Issues; Membership; Nominating; Publications; Technical; Technical Quarterly Editorial Board; Website
Activities: Developing continuing education programs; Advocating knowledge exchange; Disseminating information; *Speaker Service:* Yes
Awards:
• Lifetime Membership (Award)
• Award of Honor (Award)
• Award of Merit (Award)
• Distinguished Life Award (Award)
• Service Award (Award)
• William A. Hipp Scholarship (Scholarship)
• Brewery Excellence Recognition Award (Award)
• Inge Russell Best Paper Award (Award)
Meetings/Conferences:
• Master Brewers Association Annual Conference 2015, October, 2015, Jacksonville, FL
Scope: International
Publications:
• Master Brewers Association of The Americas Technical Quarterly
Frequency: Quarterly; *Accepts Advertising*
Profile: Papers covering technical aspects of brewing ingredients, the brewing process, brewing by-products, brewery ecological matters, beer packaging, beer flavor, &physical stability
• The MBAA [Master Brewers Association of The Americas] Communicator
Type: Newsletter; *Frequency:* Quarterly; *Accepts Advertising*
• Your Master Brewers News
Type: Newsletter; *Frequency:* Monthly
Profile: Association activities, upcoming events; topics of interest to the brewing community

District Eastern Canada
c/o Labatt Breweries, 50 Labatt Street, La Salle QC H8R 3E7
Tel: 514-364-8048; *Fax:* 514-364-8113
www.mbaa.com/Districts/EasternCanada/default.htm
Chief Officer(s):
Peter G. Delamont, District President
Marc Poirier, District Secretary, 819-758-5229, Fax: 819-758-5220
marcp@selwarwick.com
Marie Lajeunesse, District Treasurer, 514-694-4700, Fax: 514-694-4119
marie.lajeunesse@casco.ca

District Western Canada
c/o Canadian Malting Barley Technical Centre, #1365, 303 Main St., Winnipeg MB R3C 3G7
Tel: 204-983-1981; *Fax:* 204-984-5843
www.mbaa.com/Districts/WesternCanada/default.htm
Chief Officer(s):
Robert McCaig, District President
rmccaig@cmbtc.com
Douglas R. Wilkie, District Secretary
doug.wilkie@malteurop.com

Ontario District
c/o Sleeman Breweries Ltd., 551 Clair Rd. West, Guelph ON N1L 1E9
Tel: 519-822-1834; *Fax:* 519-822-0430
www.mbaa.com/Districts/Ontario/default.htm
Chief Officer(s):
James A. McGregor, District President
james.mcgregor@molsoncoors.com
Cate L. McFalls, District Secretary
cmcfalls@sleeman.ca
James C. Rowe, District Treasurer
mbactreasurer@gmail.com

Medical Library Association (MLA)

#1900, 65 East Wacker Pl., Chicago IL 60601-7246 USA

Tel: 312-419-9094; *Fax:* 312-419-8950
info@mlahq.org
www.mlanet.org
www.linkedin.com/company/medical-library-association
www.facebook.com/MedicalLibraryAssn
twitter.com/MedLibAssn
www.youtube.com/user/MedLibrAssoc
Overview: A large national organization founded in 1898
Mission: The nonprofit, educational organization provides lifelong educational opportunities, supports a knowledgebase of health information research, & works with partners worldwide to promote the importance of quality information for improved health to the health care community & the public.
Chief Officer(s):
Jane Blumenthal, AHIP, President
janeblum@umich.edu
Carla J. Funk, Executive Director
funk@mlahq.org
Finances: *Annual Operating Budget:* $3 Million-$5 Million
Staff Member(s): 14; 4000 volunteer(s)
Membership: 4,000+; *Fees:* $185 regular; $120 introductory & international; $110 annual salary under $30,000, & affiliate; $45 student; *Member Profile:* Health sciences information professionals & institutions; *Committees:* Administrative & Board; Awards; Books Panel; Bylaws; Continuing Education; Credentialing; Executive; Governmental Relations; Grants & Scholarships; JMLA Editorial; Joseph Leiter NLM/MLA Lectureship; Librarians Without Borders Advisory; Membership; National Program; Nominating; Oral History; Professional Recruitment & Retention; Scholarly Communications; Technology Advisory
Activities: *Awareness Events:* National Medical Librarians Month, Oct.; Medical Information Week, Apr.
Awards:
• Virginia L. & William K. Beatty Volunteer Service Award (Award)
• Estelle Brodman Award for the Academic Medical Librarian of the Year (Award)
• Lois Ann Colaianni Award for Excellence & Achievement in Hospital Librarianship (Award)
• Louise Darling Medal for Distinguished Achievement in Collection Development in the Health Sciences (Award)
• Janet Doe Lectureship (Award)
• Ida & George Eliot Prize (Award)
• Fellows & Honorary Members (Award)
• Carla J. Funk Governmental Relations Award (Award)
• Murray Gottlieb Prize (Award)
• T. Mark Hodges International Service Award (Award)
• Joseph Leiter NLM/MLA Lectureship (Award)
• Majors/MLA Chapter Project of the Year (Award)
• Lucretia W. McClure Excellence in Education Award (Award)
• John P. McGovern Award Lectureship (Award)
• Marcia C. Noyes Award (Award)
• Michael E. DeBakey Library Services Outreach Award (Award)
• MLA Award for Distinguished Public Service (Award)
• President's Award (Award)
• Rittenhouse Award (Award)
• Section Project of the Year Award (Award)
• Thomson Reuters/Frank Bradway Rogers Information Advancement Award (Award)
Meetings/Conferences:
• Medical Library Association 2015 Annual Meeting & Exhibition, May, 2015, Austin, TX
Scope: International
• Medical Library Association 2016 Annual Meeting & Exhibition, May, 2016, Toronto, ON
Scope: International
• Medical Library Association 2017 Annual Meeting & Exhibition, May, 2017, Seattle, WA
Scope: International
• Medical Library Association 2018 Annual Meeting & Exhibition, May, 2018, Atlanta, GA
Scope: International
• Medical Library Association 2019 Annual Meeting & Exhibition, May, 2019, Chicago, IL
Scope: International
• Medical Library Association 2020 Annual Meeting & Exhibition, 2020
Scope: International
Publications:
• Journal of the Medical Library Association (JMLA)
Type: Journal; *Frequency:* Quarterly
• MLA [Medical Library Association] FOCUS
Type: Newsletter
• MLA [Medical Library Association] News
Type: Newsletter; *Frequency:* 10 pa
• MLA [Medical Library Association] Style Guide
Type: Manual

Medieval Academy of America

104 Mount Aubrun St., 5th Fl., Cambridge MA 02138 USA
Tel: 617-491-1622; *Fax:* 617-492-3303
info@medievalacademy.org
www.medievalacademy.org
Overview: A large international organization founded in 1925
Mission: The largest professional organization in the world devoted to medieval studies; promotes and supports research, publication, and teaching in all aspects of medieval studies: art, archaeology, history, law, literature, music, philosophy, religion, science, social and economic institutions.
Member of: American Council of Learned Societies
Affliation(s): Fédération internationale des instituts d'études médiévales
Chief Officer(s):
Alice-Mary Talbot, President
alicemarytalbot@gmail.com
Maryanne Kowaleski, First Vice President
kowaleski@fordham.edu
Membership: 5,000-14,999; *Fees:* $70 individual; $30 student; *Member Profile:* Individuals & institutions with interests in the Middle Ages; *Committees:* Centers & Regional Associations; Electronic Resources; AHA Program; Professional Development; Committees; Finance; Graduate Student; Kalamazoo Program; Mart Advisory Board; Nominating; Publications Advisory Board; Haskins Medal; John Nicholas Brown Prize; Van Courtlandt Elliott Prize
Activities: *Rents Mailing List:* Yes
Awards:
• Haskins Medal (Award)
For a distinguished book
• John Nicholas Brown Prize (Award)
For a distinguished first book or monograph *Amount:* $1,000
• Van Courtlandt Elliott Prize (Award)
For a distinguished first article *Amount:* $500
• Graduate Student Research Grants (Grant)
Amount: $2,000
• Cara Grants (Grant)
Amount: $1,000
• CARA Tuition Scholarships (Scholarship)
• Medieval Academy Dissertation Grants (Grant)
Publications:
• Medieval Academy News
Type: Newsletter; *Frequency:* 3 pa; *Editor:* Mary-Jo Arn
• Medieval Academy of America Member Directory
Type: Directory
• Speculum [a publication of the Medieval Academy of America]
Type: Journal; *Frequency:* Quarterly; *Accepts Advertising*; *Editor:* Paul E. Szarmach

Meeting Planners International ***See*** Meeting Professionals International

Meeting Professionals International (MPI)

#1700, 3030 Lyndon B. Johnson Freeway, Dallas TX 75234-2759 USA
Tel: 972-702-3000; *Fax:* 972-702-3070
feedback@mpiweb.org
www.mpiweb.org
www.linkedin.com/groups?gid=46450&trk=hb_side_g
www.facebook.com/MPIfans
twitter.com/mpi
youtube.com/mpihq
Previous Name: Meeting Planners International
Overview: A large international organization founded in 1972
Mission: To position meetings as a primary communications vehicle & a critical component of an organization's success; To lead the industry by serving the diverse needs of all people with a direct interest in the outcome of meetings; To educate & prepare members for their changing roles in the greater business world; To validate relevant knowledge & skills while simultaneously demonstrating a commitment to meeting excellence. Canadian office: 6519-B Mississauga Rd., Mississauga, ON L5N 1A6; phone: 905-286-4807, fax: 905-567-7191
Member of: American Society of Association Executives; Convention Liaison Council; Unity Team
Chief Officer(s):
Kevin Hinton, Chair
Finances: *Annual Operating Budget:* Greater than $5 Million
Staff Member(s): 66
Membership: 17,199 in 65 countries; *Fees:* $315; *Member Profile:* Planners, suppliers & students of the meetings industry; *Committees:* MPI Board of Directors; MPI Foundation Board of Trustees; Awards; Education; Government Affairs; Marketing; Nominating; Special Interest Group Council (Association Meeting Management; Corporate Meeting Planners; Management; Independent Meeting Planners; Sales & Marketing); Canadian Council; European Council; Intl. Chapter Leadership Council
Activities: *Speaker Service:* Yes *Library:* Resource Centre; Open to public
Publications:
• One+
Type: Magazine; *Frequency:* Monthly; *Editor:* Blair Potter

Canadian Office
6519B Mississauga Rd., Mississauga ON L5N 1A6
Tel: 905-286-4807; *Fax:* 905-567-7191
mpicanada@mpiweb.org
Chief Officer(s):
Leslie Wright, Director, Canadian Operations

Métallurgistes unis d'Amérique (FAT-COI/CTC) ***See*** United Steelworkers of America (AFL-CIO/CLC)

Mexican Association of Canadian Studies ***See*** Asociación mexicana de estudios sobre Canadá

Middle East Studies Association of North America (MESA)

University of Arizona, 1219 Santa Rita Ave. North, Tucson AZ 85721-0410 USA
Tel: 520-621-5850
sbs-mesa@email.arizona.edu
mesa.arizona.edu
Overview: A medium-sized international charitable organization founded in 1966
Mission: To promote high standards of scholarship & instruction; to facilitate communication among scholars through meetings & publications; to promote cooperation among persons & organizations concerned with the scholarly study of the Middle East
Member of: American Council of Learned Societies; National Humanities Alliance
Chief Officer(s):
Amy W. Newhall, Executive Director/Treasurer
newhall@u.arizona.edu
Fred M. Donner, President
sjoseph@ucdavis.edu
Finances: *Annual Operating Budget:* $250,000-$500,000; *Funding Sources:* Membership dues; contributions
Staff Member(s): 5
Membership: 3,000 individual + 70 institutional; *Fees:* US$45-$135 individual (based on income); $40 student; $500 institutional; *Member Profile:* Scholars & others interested in the study of the Middle East; *Committees:* Ethics; Academic Freedom; Finance; Book Award; Dissertation Awards; Publications; Electronic Communication
Activities: Academic conferences; publications; *Rents Mailing List:* Yes
Publications:
• International Journal of Middle East Studies
Editor: Judith Tucker; Sylvia Whitman
Profile: Quarterly academic journal

Mineurs unis d'Amérique (CTC) ***See*** United Mine Workers of America (CLC)

Modern Language Association of America (MLA)

26 Broadway, 3rd Fl., New York NY 10004-1789 USA
Tel: 646-576-5000; *Fax:* 646-458-0030
www.mla.org
Also Known As: Modern Language Association
Overview: A medium-sized international organization founded in 1883 overseen by American Council of Learned Societies
Mission: To share the results of scholarly activity & teaching experiences with colleagues; To discuss trends in the study & teaching of language & literature
Affliation(s): Fédération internationale des langues et littératures modernes
Chief Officer(s):
Marianne Hirsch, President
Rosemary G. Feal, Executive Director
rfeal@mla.org
Membership: 30,000 individual; *Fees:* Schedule available; *Member Profile:* Persons professionally interested in modern languages & literature
Activities: Publishing books & journals; *Rents Mailing List:* Yes

Meetings/Conferences:
• 130th Modern Language Association (MLA) Annual Convention, January, 2015, Vancouver Convention Centre, Vancouver, BC
Scope: Provincial
Publications:
• ADE Bulletin
Type: Journal
• ADFL Bulletin
Type: Journal
• MLA International Bibliography
Type: Bibliography
Profile: Print & online
• Profession
Type: Journal; *Frequency:* Annually

Monte Cassino Society

c/o White Horses, Meadway, East Looe, Cornwall PL13 1JT United Kingdom
www.montecassinosociety.org
Overview: A small international organization
Mission: To further an interest in the experiences of those who took part in the battles of Monte Cassino & in the Italian Campaign
Chief Officer(s):
Judith Coote, Contact, England
jude@whlooe.eclipse.co.uk
Membership: *Fees:* Free for veterans & spouses; £12 in the UK for children of veterans or others interested in the society

Mouvement féderalist mondial *See* World Federalist Movement

Multinational Association for Supportive Care in Cancer (MASCC)

Herredsvejen 2, Hiller³d DK-3400 Denmark
Tel: 45-4820-7022; *Fax:* 45-4821-7022
www.mascc.org
www.linkedin.com/groups/MASCC-ISOO-Supportive-Care-in-5128277
www.facebook.com/589292597781443
twitter.com/CancerCareMASCC
www.youtube.com/user/MASCCorg
Overview: A medium-sized international organization founded in 1990
Mission: To promote research & education in all aspects of supportive care for patients with cancer
Chief Officer(s):
Åge Schultz, Executive Director
aschultz@mascc.org
Membership: *Fees:* Schedule available; *Member Profile:* Physicians; Nurses; Dentists; Pharmacists; Psychologists; Social workers; Dieticians; Infectious disease specialists; Educators; Representatives from industry and non-profit sectors; *Committees:* Awards; Finance; Governance; Guidelines; Membership; Publications; Nominations; Communications
Activities: Providing recent scientific & social information on medical, surgical, nursing, & psycho-social supportive care for cancer patients in all stages of their disease; Organizing research & education through study groups; Encouraging networking among disciplines
Publications:
• MASCC E-News
Type: Newsletter; *Frequency:* Quarterly
Profile: Recent information about organizational changes, deadlines, surveys, & study groups for Multinational Association for Supportive Care in Cancer members
• MASCC Society News
Type: Newsletter; *Frequency:* Monthly; *Editor:* Lisa Schulmeister; Snezana Bosnjak
Profile: Published on the web & in the back of the SCC journal
• Supportive Care in Cancer: The Journal of MASCC
Type: Journal; *Frequency:* Monthly; *Editor:* Fred Ashbury; *Price:* Free with MASCC / ISOO membership
Profile: Original work, reviews, consensus papers, guidelines, & short communications

Multiple Sclerosis International Federation (MSIF)

Skyline House, 200 Union St., 3rd Fl., London SE1 0LX United Kingdom
Tel: 44-20-7620-1911; *Fax:* 44-20-7620-1922
info@msif.org
www.msif.org
www.facebook.com/110033075774139
twitter.com/MSIntFederation
Previous Name: International Federation of Multiple Sclerosis Societies
Overview: A medium-sized international charitable organization founded in 1967
Mission: To link the work of national MS societies worldwide; to eliminate MS & its devastating effects; to promote global research, exchange of information, advocacy & development of new & existing MS societies
Affliation(s): Multiple Sclerosis Society of Canada
Chief Officer(s):
Peer Baneke, CEO
Finances: *Annual Operating Budget:* $1.5 Million-$3 Million; *Funding Sources:* Member societies; subscriptions; corporate, foundation & individual donations
Staff Member(s): 6
Membership: 42; *Fees:* Variable; *Committees:* Board Membership; Finance & Audit; Fundraising; Council; Nominating; CEO Advisory Group; Int'l Medical & Scientific Board; Persons with MS Int'l Committee; Secretariat
Activities: MS Global Dinner Party

NACE International (NACE)

1440 South Creek Dr., Houston TX 77084-4906 USA
Tel: 281-228-6200; *Fax:* 281-228-6300
Toll-Free: 800-797-6223
firstservice@nace.org
www.nace.org
www.linkedin.com/groups?gid=868097&goback=%2Egna_868097
www.facebook.com/NACEinternational
twitter.com/NACEtweet
Previous Name: The National Association of Corrosion Engineers
Overview: A large international licensing charitable organization founded in 1943
Mission: To protect people, assets & the environment from the effects of corrosion. Northern Area sections include: Atlantic Canada, B.C., Calgary, Canadian National Capital Section, Edmonton, Montreal, Saskatchewan & Toronto
Chief Officer(s):
Bob Chalker, Executive Director
Jenny Been, Section Secretary/Treasurer, Northern Area
jenny.been@arc.ab.ca
Scott MacIntyre, Area Membership Chairman, Northern Area
scott.amc@ns.aliantzinc.ca
Finances: *Annual Operating Budget:* Greater than $5 Million; *Funding Sources:* Membership dues; registration fees; publication sales
Staff Member(s): 65
Membership: 19,000 members in 100 countries; *Fees:* $130; *Member Profile:* Engineers & others involved in corrosion prevention & control
Activities: Technical training & certification; technical conferences; standards, publications & software; *Speaker Service:* Yes; *Rents Mailing List:* Yes *Library* Open to public
Awards:
• R.A. Brannan Award (Award)
• A.B. Campbell Award (Award)
• CORROSION Best Paper Award (Award)
• T.J. Hull Award (Award)
• Frank Newman Speller Award (Award)
• H.H. Uhlig Award (Award)
• Willis Rodney Whitney Award (Award)
• Distinguished Organization Award (Award)
• Distinguished Service Award (Award)
• Technical Achievement Award (Award)
Publications:
• CorrDefense
Type: Magazine
• Corrosion Journal
Type: Journal; *Frequency:* Monthly
• InspectThis!
Type: Newsletter
• Materials Performance (MP)
Type: Journal; *Frequency:* Monthly
• NACE Corrosion Press
Type: Newsletter
• Stay Current
Type: Newsletter; *Frequency:* Monthly

Canadian Region - Atlantic Canada Section
c/o AMC Atlantic Met Consulting Ltd., #106, 11 Morris Dr., Dartmouth NS B3B 1M2
Tel: 902-405-3600
Chief Officer(s):
Glenn McRae, Section Trustee
gmcrae@mae.carleton.ca

Canadian Region - British Columbia Section
c/o Terasen Gas Inc., 3700 2nd Ave., Burnaby BC V5C 6S4
Chief Officer(s):
Scott Bowing, Section Chair
scott.bowing@terasengas.com

Canadian Region - Calgary Section
c/o Husky Energy, 707 8th Ave. SW, Calgary AB T2P 3G7
Tel: 403-840-1913
Chief Officer(s):
Thane Schaffer, Section Chair
chair@nacecalagry.com

Canadian Region - Edmonton Section
c/o CSI Coating Systems Inc., 556 Stewart Cres. SW, Edmonton AB T6X 0A8
Tel: 780-955-2856
Chief Officer(s):
Glenn MacIntosh, Section Chair

Canadian Region - Montréal Section
c/o CPI Corrosion Ltd., #300, 1200, boul St-Martin ouest, Laval QC H7S 2E4
Tél: 514-342-2828
Chief Officer(s):
Stephanie Dontigny, Section Chair

Canadian Region - National Capital Section
c/o CANMET Materials Technology Laboratory, 183 Longwood South, Hamilton ON L8P 0A5
Tel: 905-645-0688
Chief Officer(s):
Sankara Papavinasam, Section Chair
spapavin@nrcan.gc.ca

Canadian Region - Toronto Section
c/o Kinectrics Inc., #215, 800 Kipling Ave., Toronto ON M8Z 6C4
Tel: 416-207-6000
Chief Officer(s):
Joseph Beutler, Section Chair

NAFSA: Association of International Educators

1307 New York Ave. NW, 8th Fl., Washington DC 20005-4701 USA
Tél: 202-737-3699; *Fax:* 202-737-3657
Other Communication: publications@nafsa.org; govrel@nafsa.org
inbox@nafsa.org
www.nafsa.org
www.linkedin.com/groups?gid=71923
www.facebook.com/nafsa
twitter.com/nafsa
Overview: A large international organization founded in 1948
Mission: To promote international education; To offer professional development opportunities
Chief Officer(s):
Marlene Johnson, Executive Director & CEO
marlenej@nafsa.org
Membership: 5,000-14,999; *Fees:* Regular, $370; Associate, $123
Activities: Providing networking opportunities; Building government & public awareness of the role of international education
Meetings/Conferences:
• NAFSA's 2015 Annual Conference & International Education Expo, May, 2015, Boston, MA
Scope: International
Publications:
• International Educator Magazine
Type: Magazine; *Frequency:* Bimonthly; *Accepts Advertising*; *Editor:* Elaina Loveland
• Journal of Studies in International Education
Type: Journal; *Editor:* Hans de Wit; *Price:* $20/yr. members; $84/yr. non-members
Profile: Peer-reviewed historical, analytical, & experimental research in the field of international education
• NAFSA: Association of International Educators Membership Directory
Type: Directory
• NAFSA.news
Type: Newsletter; *Frequency:* Weekly
Profile: Developments in international education, resources, policy developments, & conferences for NAFSA members only
• Policy Brief
Frequency: Irregular
Profile: Policy news & analysis on international education issues

Foreign Associations

National Alopecia Areata Foundation (NAAF)
14 Mitchell Blvd., San Rafael CA 94903 USA
Tel: 415-472-3780; *Fax:* 415-472-5343
info@naaf.org
www.naaf.org
www.facebook.com/47066008907
twitter.com/NAAF_Org
www.youtube.com/user/naaforg?feature=watch
Overview: A medium-sized international charitable organization founded in 1981
Mission: To support research to find a cure or acceptable treatment for aropecia areata; to support those with the disease & educate the public about aropecia areata
Member of: National Health Council; National Organization of Rare Disorders; BBB Wise Giving Alliance Accredited Charities; Dermatology Nurses' Association; Coalition of Skin Diseases; Research America
Affiliation(s): Society for Investigative Dermatology; American Academy of Dermatology; National Institute for Arthritis & Musculoskeletal & Skin Diseases
Chief Officer(s):
Vicki Kalabokes, President/CEO
Finances: *Annual Operating Budget:* $500,000-$1.5 Million
Staff Member(s): 7; 180 volunteer(s)
Membership: 65,000 on database, not a membership organization
Activities: *Awareness Events:* Alopecia Areata Awareness Month, Sept.

National Asbestos Council *See* Environmental Information Association

National Association for Environmental Education (UK) (NAEE)
University of Wolverhampton, Walsall Campus, Gorway Rd., Walsall WS1 3BD United Kingdom
Tel: 44-922-631-200
info@naee.org.uk
www.naee.org.uk
www.facebook.com/NAEEUK
twitter.com/NAEE_UK
Overview: A medium-sized international charitable organization founded in 1965
Mission: To promote environmental education for sustainability in the formal education sector by teachers for teachers
Member of: Council for Environmental Education
Chief Officer(s):
William Scott, President
Finances: *Annual Operating Budget:* Less than $50,000; *Funding Sources:* Dept. of Environment grant; membership dues; publication sales
Staff Member(s): 2
Membership: 1,000; *Fees:* 50 Pounds overseas; 40 Pounds Europe; 30 Pounds UK; *Member Profile:* Educationalists
Activities: Conferences & courses which attempt to further environmental education in both its natural & human setting; seminars on current topics; publications; *Speaker Service:* Yes *Library*

National Association for Environmental Management (NAEM)
#1002, 1612 K St. NW, Washington DC 20006 USA
Tel: 202-986-6616; *Fax:* 202-530-4408
Toll-Free: 800-391-6236
programs@naem.org
www.naem.org
www.linkedin.com/groups?home=&gid=151419
www.facebook.com/NAEM.org
twitter.com/thegreentie
Overview: A large international organization founded in 1990
Mission: To promote global sustainability; To advance environmental stewardship; To establish safe & healthy workplaces
Chief Officer(s):
Carol Singer Neuvelt, Executive Director
csinger@naem.org
Virginia Hoekenga, Deputy Director
Virginia@naem.org
Mike Mahanna, Manager, Programs
mike@naem.org
Elizabeth Ryan, Manager, Interactive Media & Communications
elizabeth@naem.org
Membership: *Fees:* $1,500-$7,500; *Member Profile:* Corporate environmental, health & safety, & sustainability decision-makers
Activities: Conducting research; Creating a knowledge sharing network; Offering educational webinars
Meetings/Conferences:
• National Association for Environmental Management 2015 Conference: Metrics and Materiality for EHS and Sustainability Reporting, 2015
Scope: International
Description: An international gathering of environmental, health & safety, & sustainability practitioners, with opportunities for benchmarking, best-practice sharing, & networking
Contact Information: E-mail: programs@naem.org
• National Association for Environmental Management 2015 23rd Annual EHS Management Forum, 2015
Scope: International
Attendance: 500+
Description: Environmental, health & safety, & sustainability practitioners gain the opportunity to exchange ideas, participate in interactive sessions, & hear timely keynote presentations
Contact Information: E-mail: programs@naem.org
Publications:
• Affiliates Council Guide [a publication of the National Association for Environmental Management]
Type: Guide
Profile: A guide to finding a service provider or consultant
• Green TIPS Guide
Type: Guide
Profile: A resource to engage others about a company's sustainability goals
• NAEM [National Association for Environmental Management] Network E-News
Type: Newsletter; *Frequency:* Biweekly
Profile: Relevant news for environmental, health & safety, & sustainability professionals

National Association for Information Destruction (NAID)
#350, 1951 W Camelback Rd., Phoenix AZ 85015 USA
Tel: 602-788-6243; *Fax:* 602-788-4144
info@naidonline.org
www.naidonline.org
www.linkedin.com/groups?gid=3957595&trk=hb_side_g
www.facebook.com/NAIDHQ
twitter.com/NAIDinc
www.youtube.com/user/NAIDTV
Overview: A small international organization
Mission: NAID is the international, non-profit trade association of the information destruction industry. Its members are companies and individuals involved in providing information destruction services. NAID's mission is to educate business, industry and government of the importance of destroying discarded information and the value of contract destruction services
Chief Officer(s):
Robert Johnson, Executive Director
rjohnson@naidonline.org
Membership: *Fees:* Schedule available; *Member Profile:* Includes 50+ Canadian companies

National Association for PET Container Resources (NAPCOR)
PO Box 1327, Sonoma CA 95476 USA
Tel: 707-996-4207; *Fax:* 707-935-1998
Toll-Free: 800-762-7267
information@napcor.com
www.napcor.com
www.facebook.com/173626632687722?sk=wall
Overview: A small national organization founded in 1987
Mission: To promote the usage of PET packaging & to facilitate the collection of PET plastic containers
Chief Officer(s):
Rick Moore, Executive Director
rmoore@napcor.com
Finances: *Funding Sources:* Membership dues
Membership: 13; *Member Profile:* PET bottle manufacturers & suppliers to the PET industry

National Association of Addiction Treatment Providers
#129, 313 West Liberty St., Lancaster PA 17603-2748 USA
Tel: 717-392-8480; *Fax:* 717-392-8481
www.naatp.org
Overview: A small international organization founded in 1978
Mission: To promote, assist & enhance the delivery of ethical, effective, research-based treatment for alcoholism & other drug addictions; to provide its members & the public with accurate, responsible information & other resources related to the treatment of these diseases; to advocate for increased access to & availability of quality treatment for those who suffer from alcoholism & other drug addictions; to work in partnership with other organizations & individuals that share NAATP's mission & goals
Affiliation(s): Fifteen treatment centres in Canada
Chief Officer(s):
Michael E. Walsh, President/CEO
mwalsh@naatp.org
Membership: 250

National Association of College Auxiliary Services (NACAS)
PO Box 5546, 7 Boar's Head Lane, Charlottesville VA 22905-5546 USA
Tel: 434-245-8425; *Fax:* 434-245-8453
info@nacas.org
www.nacas.org
Overview: A medium-sized international organization founded in 1969
Mission: To provide information & opportunity for auxiliary service professionals
Chief Officer(s):
Bob Hassmiller, Chief Executive Officer, 434-245-8425 Ext. 222
bob@nacas.org
Jeff Perdue, Deputy Executive Director, 434-245-8425 Ext. 223
jeff@nacas.org
Abby Tammen, Associate Executive Director, 434-245-8425 Ext. 238
abby@nacas.org
Heather W. Brown, Director, Business Partner Services, 434-245-8425 Ext. 228
heather@nacas.org
Anne P. Munson, Director, Education & Membership Services, 434-245-8425 Ext. 235
anne@nacas.org
Membership: 835 USA institutions + 69 Canadian institutions + 5 overseas institutions; *Member Profile:* International college auxiliary service professionals; Non-academic campus support services such as bookstores, food services, housing, recreation services, & security
Activities: Offering professional development opportunities
Meetings/Conferences:
• National Association of College Auxiliary Services 2015 47th Annual Conference, November, 2015, San Antonio, TX
Scope: International
Publications:
• College Services
Type: Magazine; *Frequency:* Quarterly; *Accepts Advertising*
• NACAS Quarterly
Type: Newsletter; *Frequency:* Quarterly
Profile: Current events, member news, professional development activities, & brief articles of interest to college auxiliary services professionals

National Association of Collegiate Directors of Athletics (NACDA)
24651 Detroit Rd., Westlake OH 44145 USA
Tel: 440-892-4000; *Fax:* 440-892-4007
www.nacda.com
www.facebook.com/nacda
twitter.com/nacda
Overview: A small international organization founded in 1965
Mission: To serve as the professional association for those in the field of intercollegiate athletics administration; To serves as a vehicle for networking, the exchange of information, & advocacy on behalf of the profession
Chief Officer(s):
Bob Vecchione, Executive Director
bvecchione@nacda.com
Membership: 6,100 individuals; 1,600 institutions; *Fees:* Schedule available; *Member Profile:* Collegiate athletics administrators in the United States, Canada, & Mexico
Activities: Providing educational opportunities;

The National Association of Corrosion Engineers *See* NACE International

National Association of Environmental Professionals (NAEP)
PO Box 460, Collingswood NJ 08108 USA
Tel: 856-283-7816; *Fax:* 856-210-1619
naep@bowermanagementservices.com
www.naep.org
www.linkedin.com/groups/National-Association-Environmental-Professiona
www.facebook.com/267926723515

Overview: A medium-sized national organization founded in 1975
Mission: To promote a code of ethics & standard of practice among environmental professionals
Chief Officer(s):
Harold Draper, President
Ron Deverman, President
deverman415@comcast.net
Tim Bower, Managing Director, 856-283-7816
Finances: *Annual Operating Budget:* $100,000-$250,000
Staff Member(s): 2; 30 volunteer(s)
Membership: 2,000; *Fees:* US$150 general membership; *Committees:* Education; Membership; Awards; Conference; NAEP Operations; Chapters; Environmental Policy; Communications
Activities: *Rents Mailing List:* Yes
Awards:
• NAEP Presidential Award For Excellence (Award)

National Association of Railroad Passengers (NARP)
#300, 505 Capitol Court NE, Washington D.C. 20002-7706 USA
Tel: 202-408-8362; *Fax:* 202-408-8287
narp@narprail.org
www.narprail.org
www.facebook.com/narprail
twitter.com/narprail
plus.google.com/110252908993287069826
Overview: A medium-sized national charitable organization founded in 1967
Mission: To encourage & promote a more balanced US transporation system including promotion of federal & state policies beneficial to all forms of rail service, urban rail transit, rural public transporation & intermodal terminals
Affliation(s): Transport 2000 Ltd.
Chief Officer(s):
Ross Capon, President
Finances: *Funding Sources:* Membership dues
Staff Member(s): 6
Membership: *Fees:* Schedule available
Activities: *Rents Mailing List:* Yes *Library*
Awards:
• George Felton Golden Spike Award (Award)

National Association of Real Estate Appraisers (NAREA)
PO Box 879, Palm Springs CA 92263 USA
Fax: 760-327-5631
Toll-Free: 877-815-4172
support@assoc-hdqts.org
www.narea-assoc.org
Overview: A medium-sized international organization founded in 1966
Member of: International Association Managers
Membership: 10,000 (includes Canadian); *Fees:* US$155-295
Activities: *Library:* National Association of Real Estate Appraiser's Library
Publications:
• The Apprisal Times
Type: Newsletter; *Frequency:* q.

National Association of Review Appraisers & Mortgage Underwriters (NARAMU)
PO Box 879, 810 Farrell Dr. North, Palm Springs CA 92263 USA
Tel: 760-327-5284; *Fax:* 760-327-5631
Toll-Free: 877-743-6805
Other Communication: Alt. E-mail: support@assoc-hdqts.org
info@naramu.org
www.naramu.org
Overview: A medium-sized international organization founded in 1975
Member of: International Association Managers
Affliation(s): National Association of Real Estate Appraisers
Chief Officer(s):
Bill Merrell, Member, Advisory Council
Membership: 4,200; *Fees:* US$245; US$205 associate; *Member Profile:* Review Appraisers

National Association of Sanitarians *See* National Environmental Health Association

National Association of Secondary School Principals (NASSP)
1904 Association Dr., Reston VA 20191-1537 USA
Tel: 703-860-0200; *Fax:* 703-476-5432
Toll-Free: 800-253-7746
membership@nasps.org
www.nassp.org
www.facebook.com/principals
twitter.com/NASSP
edWeb.net
Overview: A medium-sized international organization founded in 1916
Mission: Leading Schools
Affliation(s): Canadian Association of Principals
Chief Officer(s):
David Vodila, President
Gerald N. Tirozzi, Executive Director
Membership: *Member Profile:* Middle level & high school principals; assistant principals; aspiring school leaders from across the United States & more than 45 countries around the world

National Association of Teachers of Singing (NATS)
#401, 9957 Moorings Dr., Jacksonville FL 32257 USA
Tel: 904-992-9101; *Fax:* 904-262-2587
info@nats.org
www.nats.org
www.linkedin.com/company/nat%27l-assoc.-of-teachers-of-singing-nats-
www.facebook.com/OfficialNATS
twitter.com/OfficialNATS
www.youtube.com/user/OfficialNATS
Overview: A small international organization founded in 1944
Mission: To encourage the highest standards of the vocal art & of ethical principles in the teaching of singing; to promote vocal education & research at all levels, both for the enrichment of the general public & for the professional advancement of the talented
Member of: National Music Council
Chief Officer(s):
Allen Henderson, Executive Director
allen@nats.org
Deborah L. Guess, Director of Operations
deborah@nats.org
Kathryn Protor Duax, President
president@nats.org
Norman Spivey, President Elect
presidentelect@nats.org
Carole Blankenship, Vice-President
vpnatsaa@nats.org
Finances: *Annual Operating Budget:* $500,000-$1.5 Million
Staff Member(s): 6; 22 volunteer(s)
Membership: 14 regions in United States & Canada; *Fees:* US$100-110; *Member Profile:* Teachers of singing
Activities: *Internships:* Yes; *Rents Mailing List:* Yes

National Association of Television Program Executives (NATPE)
5757 Wilshire Blvd., Penthouse 10, Los Angeles CA 90036-3681 USA
Tel: 310-453-4440; *Fax:* 310-453-5258
info@natpe.org
www.natpe.org
www.facebook.com/NATPE
twitter.com/NATPE
Overview: A medium-sized international organization
Mission: Dedicated to the creation, development & distribution of televised programming in all forms, across all platforms; develops & nurtures opportunities for buying, selling & sharing of content & ideas
Chief Officer(s):
Rick Feldman, President & CEO, 310-857-1621

National Association of the Chemistry Industry / Asociación Nacional de la Industria Química, A.C (ANIQ)
Angel Urraza No. 505, Col del Valle, Mexico 03100 DF Mexico
Tel: 52-55-5230-5100; *Fax:* 52-55-5230-5107
anavarrete@aniq.org.mx
www.aniq.org.mx
Overview: A medium-sized national organization
Mission: To promote the sustainable development of the chemical sector, in harmony with the environment that surrounds it, as well as to look for joint solutions to common problems by dialogue & agreement, under strict rules of ethics & supported by specialized services, consulting, information, negotiation & diffusion
Chief Officer(s):
Miguel Benedetto Alexanderson, President
Finances: *Annual Operating Budget:* $500,000-$1.5 Million; *Funding Sources:* Membership fees & services
Staff Member(s): 50
Membership: 223; *Member Profile:* Chemical producers & distributors; *Committees:* International Trade; Human Resources; Logistics & Transportation; Environment; Safety & Health; Communication & Information
Activities: National Forum of the Chemical Industry; *Internships:* Yes; *Speaker Service:* Yes; *Rents Mailing List:* Yes *Library:* ANIQ's Information Centre; Open to public

National Association of Towns & Townships (NATaT)
#300, 1130 Connecticut Ave., Washington DC 20036 USA
Tel: 202-454-3950; *Fax:* 202-331-1598
www.natat.org
www.facebook.com/168130923318590
Overview: A large national organization founded in 1976
Mission: To help improve the quality of life for suburban and non-metro communities.
Chief Officer(s):
Jennifer Jimo, Federal Director
jimo@tfgnet.com.
Finances: *Annual Operating Budget:* $500,000-$1.5 Million
Staff Member(s): 5
Membership: 13,000 towns; *Member Profile:* Small, generally rural, communities
Activities: Offers technical assistance, educational services & public policy support to local government officials from small communities across the USA; conducts research & develops public policy recommendations through National Center for Small Communities; *Awareness Events:* America's Town Meeting, 1st week Sept.
Publications:
• Washington Report
Type: Newsletter
Profile: A focus on legislative issues of importance to small governments.

National Association of Watch & Clock Collectors, Inc. (NAWCC)
514 Poplar St., Columbia PA 17512-2130 USA
Tel: 717-684-8261; *Fax:* 717-684-0878
research@nawcc.org
www.nawcc.org
Overview: A large international organization founded in 1943
Mission: To stimulate interest in timepieces; to collect & preserve horological materials & information; to work with others in exhibiting timepieces; to encourage timepiece collection; to disseminate information on timepieces; to facilitate timepiece markets.
Chief Officer(s):
J. Steven Humphrey, Executive Director
shumphrey@nawcc.org
Chuck Auman, Controller
cauman@nawcc.org
Finances: *Annual Operating Budget:* $1.5 Million-$3 Million
Staff Member(s): 37
Membership: 29,000; *Fees:* Schedule available
Activities: *Library:* NAWCC Library

British Columbia Chapter
Heritage Hall, 3102 Main St., Vancouver BC V5T 3G7
community.nawcc.org/chapter121/home
Chief Officer(s):
John Connolly, President
joco@dccnet.com
Dennis Radage, Secretary
clocks@telus.net

Calgary Chapter
609 Rideau Rd. SW, Calgary AB T2S 0S2
Tel: 403-238-2808
jim40@shaw.ca
www.cawcca.com
Chief Officer(s):
Bryn Quinlan, President
bryn@jvairanderson.com
Jim Johnson, Secretary
jim40@shaw.ca

Kingston - Quinte Timekeepers
49 Princess St., Kingston ON K7L 1A3
www.jolenet.com/QT/join.html
Chief Officer(s):
Jolene Tycholiz, Contact
jolene@jolenet.com

Montréal Association of Watch & Clock Collectors

1673, St-Jean-Baptiste, Nicolet QC J3T 1G8
community.nawcc.org/chapter187/home
Chief Officer(s):
Peter Kushnir, President
Ottawa Valley Chapter
The Ottawa Citizen, 1101 Baxter Rd., Ottawa ON K2C 3Z3
chapter111.gary@yahoo.ca
www.ottawaclocksandwatches.ca
Chief Officer(s):
Wally Clemens, President
• Bytown Times [a publication of the National Association of Watch & Clock Collectors, Ottawa Valley Chapter]
Type: Newsletter; *Frequency:* 5 pa
Southwestern Ontario
Royal Canadian Legion, Branch 501 Lambeth, 7097 Kilbourne Rd., London ON N6P 1K5
Tel: 519-652-3412
www.nawcc92.mysite.com
Chief Officer(s):
Janet Clarke, Executive Member, 705-645-9938
Toronto Chapter
Travelodge Airport Hotel, 925 Dixon Rd., Etobicoke ON M9W 1J8
Tel: 416-674-2222
info@torontochapter33.ca
www.torontochapter33.ca
Chief Officer(s):
Bob Pritzker, President
timeman@live.com
John Farnan, Secretary
john@cogeco.ca

National Association of Women in Construction (NAWIC)

327 South Adams St., Fort Worth TX 76104 USA
Tel: 817-877-5551; *Fax:* 817-877-0324
Toll-Free: 800-552-3506
nawic@nawic.org
www.nawic.org
www.facebook.com/nawicnational
Overview: A large international organization founded in 1955
Mission: To promote & support the advancement & employment of women in the construction industry
Chief Officer(s):
Dede Hughes, Executive Vice President
dedeh@nawic.org
Debra M. Gregoire, Vice-President
Finances: *Annual Operating Budget:* $500,000-$1.5 Million; *Funding Sources:* Membership dues; sponsorship
Staff Member(s): 9
Membership: 6,000; *Fees:* $36 student-at-large; $46 student chapter; $146 international; $211 active and member-at-large; $286 corporate; *Member Profile:* Women employed in construction & construction-related fields
Activities: *Speaker Service:* Yes *Library*
Awards:
• NAWIC Founders' Scholarship (Scholarship)
Amount: $1,000-$2,000
Publications:
• The NAWIC Image
Type: Magazine

National Audubon Society, Inc. (NAS)

225 Varick St., New York NY 10014 USA
Tel: 212-979-3000
Other Communication: Membership e-mail: audubon@emailcustomerservice.com
www.audubon.org
www.facebook.com/NationalAudubonSociety
twitter.com/AudubonSociety
www.youtube.com/user/NationalAudubon
Overview: A large national charitable organization founded in 1905
Mission: To conserve & restore natural ecosystems, focusing on birds, other wildlife & their habitats for the benefit of humanity & the earth's biological diversity
Chief Officer(s):
B. Holt Thrasher, Chair
David Yarnold, President & CEO
Susan Lunden, COO
Membership: 500,000; *Fees:* $20 USA; $45 Canada; $50 international
Activities: Seminars, educational events & workshops on various conservation topics
Publications:
• Audubon Magazine [a publication of the National Audubon Society, Inc.]
Type: Magazine; *Frequency:* s-m.
Profile: The magazine is a century old, & reaches 1.8 million readers
• Audubon Wingspan [a publication of the National Audubon Society, Inc.]
Type: Newsletter
Profile: Photographs, conservation news, & more
• National Audubon Society, Inc. Annual Report
Type: Yearbook; *Frequency:* Annual

National Bison Association (NBA)

#200, 8690 Wolff Ct., Westminster CO 80031 USA
Tel: 303-292-2833; *Fax:* 303-845-9081
info@bisoncentral.com
www.bisoncentral.com
www.facebook.com/125262637531750
Overview: A medium-sized international organization founded in 1975
Mission: To promote the production, marketing & preservation of bison
Affliation(s): Canadian Bison Association
Chief Officer(s):
Dave Carter, Executive Director
david@bisoncentral.com
Peter Cook, President
pcookbuffaloman@aol.com
Finances: *Funding Sources:* Membership dues; sales; donations
Staff Member(s): 4
Membership: 1,000+; *Fees:* Schedule available; *Member Profile:* Active - actively involved in production, management &/or marketing of bison; associate - non-owner of bison, interested in bison; *Committees:* Bison Registry; Commercial Marketers; Conservation; Finance; GTSS Consignors; Government Relations; Grass-Fed Bison; Heritage; Membership; Promotions; State & Regional; Winter Conference; Youth/Education
Activities: Gold Trophy Show & Sale; *Internships:* Yes
Publications:
• Bison World Magazine
Type: Journal; *Frequency:* Quarterly

National Coalition Against the Misuse of Pesticides (NCAMP)

#200, 701 East St. SE, Washington DC 20003 USA
Tel: 202-543-5450; *Fax:* 202-543-4791
info@beyondpesticides.org
www.beyondpesticides.org
www.facebook.com/beyondpesticides
twitter.com/bpncamp
www.youtube.com/bpncamp
Overview: A medium-sized national organization founded in 1981
Mission: To address the issue of hazards of pesticide use; to provide the public with clearinghouse of information on pesticides & pesticides issues; to promote alternative forms of pest management
Chief Officer(s):
Jay Feldman, Executive Director
jfeldman@beyondpesticides.org
Finances: *Annual Operating Budget:* $250,000-$500,000
Staff Member(s): 4; 1 volunteer(s)
Membership: 1,400
Activities: *Speaker Service:* Yes *Library*

National Conferences of Firemen & Oilers (SEIU)

1023 - 15th St. NW, 10th Fl., Washington DC 20005 USA
Tel: 202-962-0981; *Fax:* 202-872-1222
mail@ncfo.org
www.ncfo.org
Overview: A small international organization founded in 1898
Chief Officer(s):
John R. Thacker, President
Dean Devits, Secretary-Treasurer

National Council for Science & the Environment (NCSE)

#250, 1101 17th St. NW, Washington DC 20036 USA
Tel: 202-530-5810; *Fax:* 202-628-4311
info@ncseonline.org
www.ncseonline.org
www.linkedin.com/company/national-council-for-science-and-the-environm
www.facebook.com/167494469941852
twitter.com/NCSEonline
www.youtube.com/user/NCSEonline
Previous Name: Committee for the National Institutes for the Environment
Overview: A medium-sized national organization founded in 1990
Mission: Improving the scientific basis for environmental decision making
Affliation(s): Council of Environmental Deans & Directors; National Commission on Science for Sustainable Forestry
Chief Officer(s):
Peter D. Saundry, Executive Director
peter@ncseonline.org
Finances: *Annual Operating Budget:* $500,000-$1.5 Million
Staff Member(s): 12; 10 volunteer(s)
Membership: *Member Profile:* Open to any concerned individual or organization
Activities: National Conference on Science Policy & the Environment; education & outreach programs; *Library:* National Library for the Environment

National Council of Philippine American Canadian Accountants (NCPACA)

c/o Ed Ortiz, #2-N, 333 South Des Plaines St., Chicago IL 60661 USA
Tel: 312-876-1900; *Fax:* 312-876-1911
NCPACAWebmaster@ncpaca.org
www.ncpaca.org
Overview: A medium-sized international organization founded in 1984
Mission: To promote the continuing education of Filipino Canadian accountants; To promote high professional standards; To liaise with other international organizations
Affliation(s): Philippine Certified Public Accountants of Greater Chicago; Philippine American Society of CPAs; Filipino American Accountants of Texas; Association of Filipino American Accountants; Association of Filipino American Accountants; Philippine Institute of Certified Public Accountants, USA; Filipino American Association of CPAs; Filipino American Institute of Accountants; Association of Filipino Canadian Accountants; Association of Filipino Canadian Accountants
Chief Officer(s):
Chris Banagan, President
chris.banagan@verizon.net
Leonora Galleros, Executive VP & President-Elect
Marlo Mallari, Secretary
Lucy Macabenta, Treasurer
Imelda Bautista, Public Relations Officer
Membership: 10 organizations; *Member Profile:* Filipino professional accounting organizations
Activities: Annual convention; professional development;
Awards:
• NCPACA College Scholarship Grant (Scholarship)

National Court Reporters Association (NCRA)

8224 Old Courthouse Rd., Vienna VA 22182-3808 USA
Tel: 703-556-6272; *Fax:* 703-556-6291
Toll-Free: 800-272-6272; *TTY:* 703-556-6289
Other Communication: testing@ncrahq.org
msic@ncrahq.org
www.ncraonline.org
www.linkedin.com/groups/Court-Reporting-Captioning-Group-79508
www.facebook.com/NCRAfb
twitter.com/NCRA
www.youtube.com/user/NCRAonline
Overview: A large international organization founded in 1899
Mission: To promote excellence in the reporting & captioning professions; To support those who capture & convert the spoken word to text to achieve professional expertise
Chief Officer(s):
Tami Smith, RPR, CPE, President
Sarah Nageotte, RDR, CRR, CBC, Vice-President
Stephen A. Zinone, PRP, Secretary-Treasurer
James M. Cudahy, CAE, Executive Director & CEO
Finances: *Funding Sources:* Membership fees; NCRA store
Membership: *Member Profile:* Participating members, such as freelance, official, hearing, legislative, & caption reporters; Associate members, such as instructors, retired reporters, proofreaders, attorneys, & transcriptionists; Students, enrolled in a stenographic court reporting program or a scoping program; *Committees:* Captioning Community of Interest; Professional Ethics; Constitution & Bylaws; Contests; CAPR Item Writing; CAPR Realtime Certification; CAPR Test Advisory; CAPR Verification; Distinguished Service Award; Firm Owners

Community of Interest; Freelance Community of Interest; Membership Marketing; National Committee of State Associations; Nominating; Officials Community of Interest; Realtime Systems Administrator; Technology Evaluation; Trial Presentation Certificate
Activities: Offering educational opportunities
Awards:
• Fellows of the Academy of Professional Reporters (Award)
To honour extraordinary qualifications & experiences in shorthand reporting
• Distinguished Service Award (Award)
To recognize work by individual members for the benefit of the reporting profession
• Endorsers of the Year (Award)
To recognize the participating or registered member who endorses the most new members
• CASE Award of Excellence (Award)
To recognize dedication to students & extraordinary contributions to reporter education
Publications:
• Certification News [a publication of the National Court Reporters Association]
Type: Newsletter
• Court Reporter Sourcebook [a publication of the National Court Reporters Association]
Type: Yearbook; *Frequency:* Annually; *Accepts Advertising*
Profile: A listing of court reporters, with their credentials & specialties
• EventFlash [a publication of the National Court Reporters Association]
Type: Newsletter
• Journal of Court Reporting [a publication of the National Court Reporters Association]
Type: Journal; *Frequency:* Monthly; *Accepts Advertising*; *Price:* Free with membership in the National Court Reporters Association
Profile: Activities of the National Court Reporters Association & information related to court reporting & captioning sent to associationmembers & other reporting & captioning professionals
• NCRA [National Court Reporters Association] News
Type: Newsletter
Profile: Current events of the National Court Reporters Association
• NewsFlash [a publication of the National Court Reporters Association]
Type: Newsletter
• TechTracker [a publication of the National Court Reporters Association]
Type: Newsletter
Profile: Articles about the effects of technology on the reporting & captioning profession, as well as technology in the news

National Education Association

1201 - 16th St. NW, Washington DC 20036-3290 USA
Tel: 202-833-4000; *Fax:* 202-822-7974
Other Communication: www.flickr.com/photos/nea-hq
www.nea.org
www.facebook.com/NEA.ORG
twitter.com/neamedia
www.facebook.com/NEA.ORG
Overview: A large national organization founded in 1857
Mission: To promote the cause of quality public education & advance the profession of education; To expand the rights & further the interest of educational employees & advocate human, civil & economic rights for all
Chief Officer(s):
Dennis Van Roekel, President
John C. Stocks, Executive Director
Membership: 3.2 million; *Fees:* Schedule available; *Committees:* Executive
Awards:
• The Gloria Barron Prize for Young Heroes (Award)
Deadline: April 30
• CGPS State & Local Project Grants (Grant)
Deadline: January 8
• Ezra Jack Keats Minigrants (Award)
Deadline: March 15
• Minority Community Organizing & Partnerships Grants (Grant)
Deadline: February 1
• NEA Foundation Grants (Grant)
Deadline: February 1
• NEA Friend of Education Award (Award)
Deadline: April 1
• NEA HIN: Ryan White HIV Prevention Awards (Award)
Deadline: January
• NEA Human & Civil Rights Awards (Award)
Deadline: December 10
• NEA State Media Grants (Grant)
Deadline: Ongoing
• NEA Student Organizing & Assistance Resources (SOAR) Grants (Grant)
Deadline: November 30
Publications:
• Higher Education Advocate [a publication of the National Education Association]
Type: Newsletter; *Frequency:* 5 pa
Profile: Post-secondary education trends, legislation, resource material & news
• NEA [National Education Association] E-Newsletter
Type: Newsletter
• NEA [National Education Association] Today Magazine
Type: Magazine; *Editor:* Steven Grant
• The NEA [National Education Association] Almanac of Higher Education
Type: Directory; *Frequency:* Annual
Profile: Up-to-date information on the entire scope of American higher education
• This Active Life [National Education Association]
Type: Magazine
Profile: Intended for active retired educators
• Thought & Action [a publication of the National Education Association]
Type: Journal; *Frequency:* Annual
Profile: Theoretical & practical information on issues in higher education; readership of 150,000
• Tomorrow's Teachers [a publication of the National Education Association]
Type: Magazine
Profile: Intended for student members & those new to the teaching profession

National Environmental Health Association (NEHA)

#1000N, 720 South Colorado Blvd., Denver CO 80246 USA
Tel: 303-756-9090; *Fax:* 303-691-9490
Toll-Free: 866-956-2258
staff@neha.org
www.neha.org
www.facebook.com/NEHA.org
twitter.com/nehaorg
Previous Name: National Association of Sanitarians
Overview: A medium-sized national charitable organization founded in 1937
Mission: To advance the environmental health & protection professional, in order to improve the environment throughout the world & provide a more healthful quality of life for all
Chief Officer(s):
Nelson Fabian, Executive Director
nfabian@neha.org
Mel Knight, President
melknight@sbcglobal.net
Brian Collins, President Elect
brianc@plano.gov
Staff Member(s): 26
Membership: 4,500+; *Member Profile:* Environmental health practitioners in both the public & private sectors; Academia; Uniformed services, employed mainly by health departments
Activities: Providing national credential programs; Advocating for the profession; Offering networking opportunities; Working cooperatively with other national professional societies & government agencies
Meetings/Conferences:
• National Environmental Health Association 2015 79th Annual Conference & Exhibition, 2015
Scope: International
Contact Information: Toll-Free Phone: 866-956-2258; Fax: 303-691-9490; E-mail: staff@neha.org
Publications:
• Journal of Environmental Health
Type: Journal; *Frequency:* 10 pa; *Accepts Advertising*; *Editor:* Nelson Fabian
Profile: Current issues, peer-reviewed research, products, & services in the area or environmental health

National Ground Water Association (NGWA)

601 Dempsey Rd., Westerville OH 43081 USA
Tel: 614-898-7791; *Fax:* 614-898-7786
Toll-Free: 800-551-7379
ngwa@ngwa.org
www.ngwa.org
www.linkedin.com/groups?home=&gid=4204578
www.facebook.com/NGWAFB
twitter.com/ngwatweets
www.youtube.com/user/NGWATUBE
Overview: A medium-sized international organization founded in 1948
Mission: To advance the expertise of all ground water professionals & furthering ground water awareness & protection through education & outreach
Member of: Advisory Committee on Water Information; American National Standards Institute; Coalition for National Science Funding; Geological Society of America; Global Water Partnership; Groundwater Foundation; International Union of Geological Sciences; Source Water Collaborative; U.S. Water Alliance
Chief Officer(s):
Kevin McCray, Chief Executive Officer
kmmcray@ngwa.org
Finances: *Annual Operating Budget:* Greater than $5 Million
Membership: *Fees:* Schedule available; *Member Profile:* Ground water scientists & engineers; water well drillers; pump installers; suppliers & manufacturers; *Committees:* Geothermal Heat Pump Technical; Government Affairs; Membership Standing; Professional Development; Public Awareness; Publishing and Information Products; Standard Development Oversight; Water Systems Technical
Activities: *Speaker Service:* Yes *Library:* National Ground Water Information Centre
Awards:
• Outstanding Project in Ground Water Protection Award (Award)
• Outstanding Project in Ground Water Remediation Award (Award)
• Life Member Awards (Award)
• M. King Hubbert Award (Award)
• Oliver Award (Award)
• Outstanding Project in Ground Water Supply Award (Award)
• Robert Storm Interdivisional Cooperation Award (Award)

National Horse Protection Coalition *See* National Horse Protection League

National Horse Protection League

PO Box 318, Chappaqua NY 10514 USA
Tel: 202-293-0570
Previous Name: National Horse Protection Coalition
Overview: A medium-sized national organization
Finances: *Annual Operating Budget:* $250,000-$500,000

National Institute of Governmental Purchasing, Inc. (NIGP)

151 Spring St., Herndon VA 20170-5223 USA
Tel: 703-736-8900; *Fax:* 703-635-2326
Toll-Free: 800-367-6447
customercare@nigp.org
www.nigp.org
www.linkedin.com/groups?home=&gid=1800364
www.facebook.com/OfficialNIGP
twitter.com/OfficialNIGP
Overview: A medium-sized national organization founded in 1944
Mission: To develop, support & promote the public procurement profession through premier educational & research programs, professional support & advocacy initiatives
Member of: International Federation of Purchasing & Supply Management
Affliation(s): National Association of Purchasing Card Professionals; National Council for Public Procurement and Contracting; National Purchasing Institute
Chief Officer(s):
Rick Grimm, Chief Executive Officer
rgrimm@nigp.org
Finances: *Funding Sources:* Membership dues; services (education & technical/audit services)
Staff Member(s): 32
Membership: 2,600 member agencies, representing 16,000 individuals in the U.S., Canada & elsewhere; *Fees:* Schedule available; *Member Profile:* Organizational or Agency membership provides the operational & administrative framework for the Institute, but individual, affiliate & associate memberships are available
Activities: *Speaker Service:* Yes; *Rents Mailing List:* Yes *Library:* Procurement Information Exchanges;
Awards:
• Lewis E. Spangler Education & Professional Development Foundation (Scholarship)

Provides scholarships, grants & loans to students & the public purchasing professionals of the NIGP

National Marine Manufacturers Association (NMMA)
#2050, 231 South LaSalle St., Chicago IL 60604 USA
Tel: 312-946-6200
www.nmma.org
Overview: A medium-sized international organization
Mission: To create, promote & protect an environment where members can achieve financial success through excellence in manufacturing, in selling, and in servicing their customers.
Affliation(s): National Association of Boat Manufacturers; National Association of Marine Products & Services; Association of Marine Engine Manufacturers
Chief Officer(s):
Thomas Dammrich, President, 312-946-6220
tdammrich@nmma.org
Sara Anghel, Vice President, Government Relations and Public Affairs (Canada), 905-951-4048
sanghel@nmma.org
Finances: *Funding Sources:* Membership fees & shows
Membership: *Fees:* Schedule available; *Member Profile:* Canadian/American manufacturer, distributor, or retailer of boating-related products
Activities: *Internships:* Yes

National NF Foundation ***See*** Children's Tumor Foundation

National Oil Recyclers Association ***See*** NORA, An Association of Responsible Recyclers

National Organization for Rare Disorders, Inc. (NORD)
PO Box 1968, 55 Kenosia Ave., Danbury CT 06813-1968 USA
Tel: 203-744-0100; *Fax:* 203-798-2291
Toll-Free: 800-999-6673; *TTY:* 203-797-9590
orphan@rarediseases.org
www.rarediseases.org
twitter.com/rarediseases
www.youtube.com/raredisorders
Overview: A large international organization founded in 1983
Mission: To identify, treat & cure rare diseases through programs of education, services & research
Affliation(s): 127 national voluntary agencies for rare disorders
Chief Officer(s):
Michael D. Scott, Chair
Carolyn Asbury, Vice-Chair
Josephine Grima, Secretary
Finances: *Funding Sources:* Public donations; grants
Staff Member(s): 35; 10 volunteer(s)
Membership: *Fees:* $30; *Committees:* Medical Advisory
Activities: Education; patient advocacy and mentorship programs; *Library* Open to public

National Parks Conservation Association (NPCA)
#700, 777 6th St. NW, Washington DC 20001-3723 USA
Tel: 202-223-6722; *Fax:* 202-659-0650
Toll-Free: 800-628-7275
npca@npca.org
www.npca.org
www.facebook.com/NationalParks
twitter.com/npca
Overview: A large national organization founded in 1919
Mission: America's only private, non-profit advocacy organization dedicated to protecting, preserving & enhancing the National Park system; to protect & improve the quality of parks & to promote an understanding of, appreciation for, & sense of personal commitment to parklands
Chief Officer(s):
Thomas C. Kiernan, President
Theresa Pierno, Executive Vice-President
Finances: *Annual Operating Budget:* Greater than $5 Million
Membership: 460,000; *Fees:* $25; $18 students

National Psoriasis Foundation - USA
#300, 6600 SW 92nd Ave., Portland OR 97223-7195 USA
Tel: 503-244-7404; *Fax:* 503-245-0626
Toll-Free: 800-723-9166
getinfo@psoriasis.org
www.psoriasis.org
www.facebook.com/National.Psoriasis.Foundation
twitter.com/NPF
www.youtube.com/user/PsoriasisFoundation
Overview: A medium-sized international charitable organization founded in 1968
Mission: To improve the quality of life of people who have psoriasis & psoriatic arthritis; to promote, through education & advocacy, awareness & understanding, ensure access to treatment & support research that will lead to effective management & ultimately a cure
Member of: International Federation of Psoriasis Associations
Affliation(s): Canadian Psoriasis Foundation
Chief Officer(s):
Randy Beranek, President/CEO
Finances: *Annual Operating Budget:* Greater than $5 Million; *Funding Sources:* Donations
Activities: *Awareness Events:* Psoriasis Awareness Month, Aug.; *Internships:* Yes *Library*

National Recycling Coalition, Inc. (NRC)
1220 L St. NW, Washington DC 20005 USA
Tel: 202-618-2107
info@nrcrecycles.org
nrcrecycles.org
Overview: A small national organization founded in 1978
Mission: To advance & improve recycling, source reduction, composting & reuse by providing technical information, education, training, outreach & advocacy services to its members in order to conserve resources & benefit the environment
Affliation(s): California Resource Recovery Association; Northern California Recycling Association; Recycling Council of Alberta; Indiana Recycling Coalition; North Carolina Recycling Association; Oklahoma Recycling Association; Association of Oregon Recyclers; Pennsylvania Resources Council; Arizona Recycling Coalition; Arkansas Recycling Coalition; RECARIBE; Colorado Association for Recycling; Connecticut Recyclers Coalition; Recycle Florida Today; Illinois Recycling Association; Iowa Recycling Association; Kansas Recyclers Association; Louisiana Recycling Association
Chief Officer(s):
Mark Lichtenstein, Executive Director
MarkL@nrcrecycles.org
Margretta Morris, Vice-President/Treasurer
Meg@nrcrecycles.org
Staff Member(s): 7
Membership: 5,000+
Activities: *Internships:* Yes

National Sanitary Supply Association ***See*** International Sanitary Supply Association, Inc.

National Society of Fund Raising Executives ***See*** Association of Fundraising Professionals

National Solid Wastes Management Association (NSWMA)
#300, 4301 Connecticut Ave. NW, Washington DC 20008 USA
Tel: 202-244-4700; *Fax:* 202-966-4824
Toll-Free: 800-424-2869
www.nswma.org
www.facebook.com/group.php?gid=130041787022156
Overview: A medium-sized international organization founded in 1962
Mission: To promote the environmentally responsible, efficient, profitable, & ethical management of waste
Chief Officer(s):
Bruce J. Parker, President & Chief Executive Officer
bparker@nswma.org
David Biderman, General Counsel & Director, Safety
davidb@nswma.org
Christine Hutcherson, Director, Member Services
chutcherson@nswma.org
Alice Jacobsohn, Director, Education
alicej@nswma.org
Thom Metzger, Director, Communications & Public Affairs
tmetzger@nswma.org
Ed Repa, Director, Environmental Programs
erepa@nswma.org
Catherine Maimon, Manager, Meetings
cmaimon@nswma.org
Membership: *Member Profile:* For-profit companies in North America that provide solid, hazardous, & medical waste collection, recycling, & disposal services; Companies that provide professional & consulting services to the waste services industry
Activities: Offering educational & training opportunities; Engaging in research; Facilitating networking; *Library:* National Solid Wastes Management Association Library
Publications:
• NSWMA [National Solid Wastes Management Association] e-News
Type: Newsletter
Profile: Timely information to help businesses make decisions

National Space Society (NSS)
#500, 1155 15th St. NW, Washington DC 20005 USA
Tel: 202-429-1600; *Fax:* 202-530-0659
Other Communication: Membership e-mail: members@nss.org
nsshq@nss.org
www.nss.org
www.linkedin.com/groups?trk=anet_ug_hm&gid=164840&home
www.facebook.com/NSS
twitter.com/nss
www.youtube.com/user/NationalSpaceSociety
Overview: A large international organization
Mission: To promote social, economic, technological & political change, to advance the day when humans will live & work in space
Affliation(s): Calgary Space Frontier Society; Niagara Peninsula Space Frontier Society
Chief Officer(s):
Hugh Downs, Chair, Board of Governors
Mark Hopkins, Chair, Executive Committee
Kirby Ikin, Chair, Board of Directors
Ken Money, President
Membership: 22,000; *Fees:* Schedule available; *Committees:* Executive
Activities: *Speaker Service:* Yes; *Rents Mailing List:* Yes
Meetings/Conferences:
• The National Space Society's 34th Annual International Space Development Conference, May, 2015, Hyatt Regency, Toronto, ON
Scope: International
Description: Discussions of the future of space exploration
Publications:
• Ad Astra [a publication of the National Space Society]
Type: Magazine; *Frequency:* q.
Profile: News & photography related to space exploration
• To the Stars International Quarterly [a publication of the National Space Society]
Type: Magazine; *Frequency:* q.; *Price:* Free
Profile: Online magazine for space enthousiasts

National Waste & Recycling Association (NWRA)
#300, 4301 Connecticut Ave., Washington DC 20008 USA
Tel: 202-244-4700; *Fax:* 202-966-4818
Toll-Free: 800-424-2869
www.envasns.org
www.facebook.com/130041787022156?ref=ts
twitter.com/NSWMA
www.youtube.com/user/envasns
Previous Name: Environmental Industry Associations
Overview: A medium-sized national organization
Mission: The National Waste & Recycling Association is the trade association that represents the private sector solid waste and recycling industry. It was formerly known as the Environmental Industry Associations (EIA), National Solid Wastes Management Association (NSWMA) and the Waste Equipment Technology Association (WASTEC).
Chief Officer(s):
Bruce J. Parker, President & CEO
bparker@nswma.org

National Wildlife Federation (NWF)
PO Box 1583, Merrifield VA 22116-1583 USA
Tel: 703-438-6000; *Fax:* 703-438-6035
Toll-Free: 800-822-9919
www.nwf.org
www.facebook.com/NationalWildlife
twitter.com/nwf
www.youtube.com/user/NationalWildlife
Overview: A large national organization founded in 1936
Mission: NWF advances common-sense conservation policies through advocacy, education & litigation in concert with affiliate groups & other like-minded organizations across the country & around the world; efforts focus on the conservation of wildlife & wild places & the health of the environment upon which we all depend, with special emphasis on wetlands, water quality, endangered habitats, land stewardship & sustainable communities
Chief Officer(s):
Larry J. Schweiger, President & CEO
Finances: *Annual Operating Budget:* Greater than $5 Million; *Funding Sources:* Memberships; donations; bequests; magazine subscriptions; sales of nature education materials
Staff Member(s): 600
Membership: Over 4 million members & supporters + 46 affiliated organizations + 11 field office locations; *Fees:* $15+
Activities: *Awareness Events:* National Wildlife Week; *Internships:* Yes; *Rents Mailing List:* Yes *Library*

Awards:
• The National Conservation Achievement Awards (Award) Program that recognizes outstanding individual & group achievements in conservation
Meetings/Conferences:
• 2015 for National Wildlife Federation's 79th Annual Meeting, May, 2015, National Conservation Training Center, Shepherdstown, WV
Scope: International

New Music USA
#312, 90 John St., New York NY 10038 USA
Tel: 212-645-6949; *Fax:* 646-490-0098
info@newmusicusa.org
www.newmusicusa.org
www.facebook.com/NewMusicUSA
twitter.com/NewMusicUSA
Merged from: American Music Centre; Meet The Composer
Overview: A medium-sized national organization founded in 2011
Mission: To promote the creation, performance & appreciation of American contemporary music
Chief Officer(s):
Ed Harsh, President & CEO
eharsh@newmusicusa.org
Frederick Peters, Chair

Newsletter Publishers Association *See* Specialized Information Publishers Association

The Newspaper Guild (AFL-CIO/CLC) (TNG) / La Guilde des journalistes (FAT-COI/CTC)
501 Third St. NW, 6th Fl., Washington DC 20001-2797 USA
Tel: 202-434-7177; *Fax:* 202-434-1472
guild@cwa-union.org
www.newsguild.org
www.facebook.com/TheNewspaperGuildCWA
twitter.com/news_guild
www.flickr.com/photos/69542346@N05/
Previous Name: American Newspaper Guild
Overview: A large international organization founded in 1933
Mission: The Guild is primarily a media union whose members are diverse in their occupations, but who share the view that the best working conditions are achieved by people who have a say in their workplace
Affliation(s): International Federation of Journalists
Chief Officer(s):
Bernard J. Lunzer, President
blunzer@cwa-union.org
Carol D. Rothman, Sec.-Treas.
crothman@cwa-union.org
Finances: *Annual Operating Budget:* $3 Million-$5 Million; *Funding Sources:* Membership dues
Staff Member(s): 32
Membership: 34,000; *Member Profile:* Media employer
Activities: *Library* by appointment

The Ninety-Nines Inc./International Organization of Women Pilots
4300 Amelia Earhart Rd., #A, Oklahoma City OK 73159 USA
Tel: 405-685-7969*Tel:* 33-1-405-685-7969; *Fax:* 405-685-7985; *Fax:* 33-1-405-685-7985
Toll-Free: 800-994-1929
PR@ninety-nines.org
www.ninety-nines.org
www.facebook.com/100905045593
Also Known As: 99's
Overview: A small international charitable organization founded in 1929
Mission: To promote world fellowship through flight; to provide networking & scholarship opportunities for women & aviation education in the community; to preserve the unique history of women in aviation
Chief Officer(s):
Kathy Fox, Governor, East Canada Section
Angelee Skywork, Governor, West Canada Section
Martha Phillips, President
president@ninety-nines.org
Membership: *Fees:* US$65 for US; US$57 Canadian; US$44 other countries; US$35 US/Canadian associate; US$30 international associate; *Member Profile:* Women pilots
Activities: *Speaker Service:* Yes *Library:* 99s Museum of Women Pilots

NORA, An Association of Responsible Recyclers (NORA)
#201, 7250 Heritage Village Plaza, Gainesville VA 20155 USA
Tel: 703-753-4277; *Fax:* 703-733-2445
www.noranews.org
www.linkedin.com/groups?gid=1675687
Previous Name: National Oil Recyclers Association
Overview: A medium-sized national licensing organization founded in 1985
Member of: American Society of Association Executives
Chief Officer(s):
Scott D. Parker, Executive Director
sparker@noranews.org
Finances: *Annual Operating Budget:* $250,000-$500,000
Staff Member(s): 4
Membership: 200 companies; *Fees:* Based on company type; *Member Profile:* Liquid recyclers & vendors; *Committees:* Membership; Marketing; Conference; Governmental Affairs; Parts cleanin; Chemical Recycling; Used Oil Recycling; Ethics/Standards; Strategic Planning; Associate Advisory
Activities: *Rents Mailing List:* Yes

Nordic Association for Canadian Studies (NACS) / Association nordique d'études canadiennes
Department of English, Turku University, Turku 20014 Finland
Fax: 385-2-333-5630
www.hum.au.dk/nacs
Overview: A small international organization founded in 1984
Mission: To promote Canadian studies in the five Nordic countries: Denmark, Finland, Iceland, Norway & Sweden
Member of: International Council for Canadian Studies
Chief Officer(s):
Janne Korkka, Contact
jkorkka@utu.fi
Staff Member(s): 3; 2 volunteer(s)
Membership: 320; *Fees:* 17 euros
Activities: *Library:* Canadian Collection

North American Association for Environmental Education (NAAEE)
#540, 2000 P St. NW, Washington DC 20036 USA
Tel: 202-419-0412; *Fax:* 202-419-0415
bredy@naaee.org
www.naaee.org
www.facebook.com/126762430689361
twitter.com/NAAEEStaff
Overview: A medium-sized international organization founded in 1971
Mission: To promote education about environmental issues
Chief Officer(s):
Judy Braus, Executive Director, 202-419-0414
jbraus@naaee.org
Finances: *Funding Sources:* Donations
Membership: *Member Profile:* Practitioners in the fields of environmental education, outdoor education, & conservation education; Students in the field of environmental education
Activities: Providing professional development events; Offering networking opportunities
Publications:
• Conservation Education & Outreach Techniques
Number of Pages: 496; *Author:* S. Jacobson; M. McDuff; M.C. Monroe; *ISBN:* 0-19-856772-3
Profile: Case sudies & application exercises
• EE News [a publication of the North American Association for Environmental Education]
Type: Newsletter
• Elementary School Teachers' Beliefs About Teaching Environmental Education
Number of Pages: 48; *Author:* S. Middlestadt; R. Ledsky; *ISBN:* 1-884008-76-3
• Environmental Education at the Early Childhood Level
Number of Pages: 126; *Editor:* R. Wilson; *ISBN:* 1-884008-14-3
• Environmental Education in the Schools: Creating a Program That Works!
Number of Pages: 500; *Author:* J. Braus; D. Wood; *ISBN:* 1-884008-08-9
• Environmental Education Research, Special Issue on Significant Life Experiences
Number of Pages: 114; *Editor:* T. Tanner; *ISBN:* 1350-4622
• Environmental Education Undergraduate & Graduate Programs & Faculty in the United States
Author: Michaela Zint; Aimee Giles; *ISBN:* 1-884008-79-B
• Environmental Education: Academia's Response
Number of Pages: 96; *Author:* E. Kormondy; P.B. Corcoran; *ISBN:* 1-884008-51-8
• Environmental Literacy in the United States: What Should Be...What Is...Getting from Here to There
Number of Pages: 80; *Editor:* T. Volk; W. McBeth; *ISBN:* 1-884008-73-9
• Evaluating Your Environmental Education Programs: A Workbook for Practitioners
Author: J.A. Ernst; M.C. Monroe; B. Simmons
Profile: Case sudies & application exercises
• A Field Guide to Environmental Literacy: Making Strategic Investments in Environmental Education
Number of Pages: 110; *Author:* J.L. Elder; *ISBN:* 1-884008-87-9
• NAAEE [North American Association for Environmental Education] Communicator
Type: Newsletter
• North American Association for Environmental Education Conference Proceedings
• Preparing Effective Environmental Educators
Type: Monograph; *Number of Pages:* 89; *Editor:* Dr. Bora Simmons; *ISBN:* 1-884008-88-7
• Using a Logic Model to Review & Analyze an Environmental Education Program
Type: Monograph; *Number of Pages:* 72; *Editor:* Thomas C. Marcinkowski; *ISBN:* 1-884008-86-0
• What's Fair Got To Do With It: Diversity Cases from Environmental Educators
Number of Pages: 119; *Editor:* Tania J. Madfes; *ISBN:* 0-914409-20-4

North American Association of Central Cancer Registries, Inc. (NAACCR, Inc.)
2121 West White Oaks Dr., #B, Springfield IL 62704-7412 USA
Tel: 217-698-0800; *Fax:* 217-698-0188
info@naaccr.org
www.naaccr.org
Overview: A small international organization
Mission: To develop & promote data standards for cancer registration; To provide certification for population-based registries; To promote the use of cancer surveillance data & systems for cancer control
Chief Officer(s):
Maria J. Schymura, President
Betsy A. Kohler, Executive Director
Karen Knight, Treasurer
Membership: *Committees:* Bylaws; Nominating; Communications; Program; Data Evaluation & Certification; Registry Operations; Data Use & Research; Education; Uniform Data Standards; Information & Technology; GIS; Interoperability; Cancer Registration; Scientific Editorial Board; Institutional Review Board
Activities: Promoting epidemiologic research; Providing educational & training opportunities; Publishing data from central cancer registries; Promoting public health programs to reduce the burden of cancer
Meetings/Conferences:
• North American Association of Central Cancer Registries 2015 Annual Conference: First in Flight: Launching a New Era in Cancer Surveillance, June, 2015, Westin Charlotte, Charlotte, NC
Scope: International
Attendance: 450
• North American Association of Central Cancer Registries 2016 Annual Conference, June, 2016, St. Louis, MI
Scope: International
Attendance: 450
• North American Association of Central Cancer Registries 2017 Annual Conference, June, 2017, Albuquerque, NM
Scope: International
Attendance: 450
Publications:
• NAACCR Narrative
Type: Newsletter; *Frequency:* Quarterly
Profile: NAACCR updates, reports, & education & training calendar

North American Butterfly Association (NABA)
4 Delaware Rd., Morristown NJ 7960 USA
naba@naba.org
www.naba.org
www.facebook.com/153175048034815
Overview: A small international organization
Mission: To increase public enjoyment & conservation of butterflies; To work to save butterfly species throughout North America
Chief Officer(s):
Jeffrey Glassberg, President
Membership: *Fees:* $US30 regular; $US40 family; *Member Profile:* The largest group of people in North America (Canada, United States & Mexico) interested in butterflies

North American Conference on British Studies (NACBS)

c/o University of Colorado Denver, PO Box 173364, Stn. 182, Denver CO 80217 USA
Tel: 303-556-2896; *Fax:* 303-556-6037
www.nacbs.org
Overview: A medium-sized international organization founded in 1950
Mission: To pursue the study of British civilization
Affliation(s): American Historical Association
Chief Officer(s):
Marjorie Levine-Clark, Executive Secretary
marjorie.levine-clark@ucdenver.edu
Membership: *Fees:* Schedule available; *Member Profile:* Interest in British studies; *Committees:* Executive; Nominating
Awards:
• Huntington Library Fellowship (Scholarship)
Annual, for at least one month of study in the collections of the Huntington Library in San Marino, California *Amount:* $1,800
• John Ben Snow Foundation Book Prize (Award)
Annual, for the best book in any field of British Studies before 1800 *Amount:* $1,000
• British Council Book Prize (Award)
Annual, for the best book in any field of British Studies after 1800 *Amount:* $1,000
• Walter D. Love Article Prize (Award)
Annual, for the best article or article-length study in any field of British Studies *Amount:* $150
• Dissertation-Year Fellowship (Scholarship)
Annual, for study in British archives & collections *Amount:* $5,000
Publications:
• Journal of British Studies
Editor: Anna Clark
Profile: Quarterly academic journal

North American Die Casting Association (NADCA)

#101, 3250 Arlington Heights Rd., Arlingotn Heights IL 60004 USA
Tel: 847-279-0001; *Fax:* 847-279-0002
nadca@diecasting.org
www.diecasting.org
www.linkedin.com/company/north-american-die-casting-association
www.facebook.com/84385559055
www.youtube.com/user/NADCAvideos
Previous Name: Society of Die Casting Engineers
Overview: A small international organization founded in 1954
Mission: To promote the industry & its members
Chief Officer(s):
Daniel Twarog, President
twarog@diecasting.org
Membership: *Fees:* US$85 individual; $25 student; corporate fee by sales volume; *Member Profile:* Custom die casters; Captive die casters; Suppliers to the industry

Ontario Chapter
ON
Chief Officer(s):
Eric V. Klaassen, Chair
Boris Lukezic, Secretary
lukezic@yahoo.com

North American Insulation Manufacturers Association (NAIMA)

#310, 44 Canal Center Plaza, Alexandria VA 22314 USA
Tel: 703-684-0084; *Fax:* 703-684-0427
insulation@naima.org
www.naima.org
Overview: A medium-sized national organization founded in 1933
Affliation(s): NAIMA Canada
Chief Officer(s):
Ken Mentzer, President
Finances: *Annual Operating Budget:* $3 Million-$5 Million
Staff Member(s): 10
Membership: 16

North American Lincoln Red Association

c/o Sarah Pedelty, 9724 County Rd. 138 SE, Chatfield MN 55923 USA
Tel: 507-867-9041; *Fax:* 507-867-4852
www.lincolnred.org
Also Known As: Lincoln Red Association of North America
Overview: A small international organization founded in 2004
Mission: To develop & regulate the breeding of Lincoln Red cattle in Canada & the United States; To carry out a system of registration for Lincoln Red cattle
Affliation(s): Canadian Livestock Records Corporation
Chief Officer(s):
Scott McClinchey, President, 519-928-3106
hlm.dvm@sympatico.ca
Sarah Pedelty, Secretary, 507-867-9041
sarahpedelty@yahoo.com
Membership: 1-99; *Fees:* $80 / year; $15 junior membership (up to 18 years of age); $800 life membership; *Member Profile:* Breeders & ownders of Lincoln Red cattle in Canada & the United States; *Committees:* Executive; Pedigree; Breed Improvement; Special Committees:
Activities: Compiling statistics related to the Lincoln Red cattle industry; Publishing data related to Lincoln Red cattle; Assisting & supervising persons engaged in the breeding of Lincoln Red cattle; Inspecting herds or private breeding records of breeders
Publications:
• The Lincoln Letter
Type: Newsletter; *Frequency:* Y
Profile: Association announcements, president's report, & meeting information

North American Piedmontese Association (NAPA)

1740 Co. Rd 185, Ramah CO 80832 USA
Tel: 306-329-8600
NAPA@yourlink.ca
www.piedmontese.org
Overview: A small international organization founded in 2000
Mission: To offer registry services to Piedmontese breeders throughout Canada & the United States; to develop & improve the Piedmontese breed; to promote & preserve fullblood Piedmontese cattle
Affliation(s): Canadian Livestock Records Corporation
Chief Officer(s):
Vicki Johnson, NAPA Executive Director
Membership: *Fees:* $90; *Member Profile:* Canadian & American Piedmontese breeders

North American Riding for the Handicapped Association *See* Professional Association of Therapeutic Horsemanship International

North American Society for Oceanic History (NASOH)

Texas Christian University, Department Of History, PO Box 297260, Fort Worth TX 76129 USA
www.nasoh.org
Overview: A small international organization founded in 1974
Mission: To provide a forum for maritime history; To study & promote naval & maritime history; To promote exchange of information among its members & others interested in history of seas, lakes & inland waterways; To call attention to books, articles, other publications & documents pertinent to naval & maritime history; to work with local, regional, national & international organizations as well as appropriate government agencies towards goal of fostering a more general awareness & appreciation for North America's naval & maritime heritage
Chief Officer(s):
Warren Reiss, President
Finances: *Annual Operating Budget:* Less than $50,000
Membership: 220; *Fees:* $65 US individual/corporate; $18 US student
Awards:
• John Lyman Book Awards (Award)
• Jack Bauer Award (Award)

North American Society of Adlerian Psychology (NASAP)

614 Old West Chocolate Ave., Hershey PA 17033 USA
Tel: 717-579-8795; *Fax:* 717-533-8616
info@alfredadler.org
www.alfredadler.org
Overview: A medium-sized international organization
Mission: To promote the teaching, understanding, & application of the core concepts of Adlerian (Individual) Psychology; To maintain the principles of Adlerian Psychology; To foster research, knowledge, & training; To operate according to the Codes of Ethics of the American Psychological Association, the International Coach Federation, & the National Board of Certified Counselors
Affliation(s): Adler Graduate School of Minesota; Adler International Learning Inc.; Adler School of Professional Psychology; Aderian Psychology Association of British Columbia; Adlerian Society of Arizona; Adlerian Student Affiliate; Alfred Adler Institute of New York; ALFREDS - Adler Learning Federation for Research, Education & Delivery of Services; Central PA Society of Adlerian Psychology; Georgia Society of Adlerian Psychology; McAbee Adlerian Psychology Society (MAPS); Parent Encouragement Program (PEP); South Carolina Society of Adlerian Psychology; The Individual Psychology Society - Chicago (TIPS)
Chief Officer(s):
Becky LaFountain, Executive Director
Al Milliren, Chair, Education & Professional Development Committee
Joyce A. DeVoss, Treasurer
Membership: *Fees:* $25 students; $35 associates; $45 retired persons; $55 family members; $135 individuals & affiliate organizations; *Member Profile:* Psychologists; Psychiatrists; Cousellors; Educators; Community organizations; Parents
Activities: Encouraging scientific inquiry & the growth of Adlerian Psychology; Developing & supporting training centres & educational opportunities; Providing a home study course; Awarding the NASAP Certificate of Adlerian Studies; Expanding the availability of counselling & family enrichment programs, based on Adlerian Psychology; Networking with other organizations in the fields of psychology & education; *Speaker Service:* Yes
Meetings/Conferences:
• North American Society of Adlerian Psychology 2015 63rd Annual Conference, May, 2015, Philadelphia, PA
Scope: International
Description: Educational & networking opportunities for members of the North American Society of Adlerian Psychology
Contact Information: E-mail: info@alfredadler.org
Publications:
• Family!
Type: Newsletter; *Frequency:* Bimonthly; *Editor:* Bryna Gamson
Profile: A publication of the NASAP Family Education Section

• North American Society of Adlerian Psychology Newsletter
Type: Newsletter; *Editor:* Susan Belangee

North Atlantic Salmon Conservation Organization (NASCO)

11 Rutland Sq., Edinburgh EH1 2AS United Kingdom
Tel: 44-131-228-2551; *Fax:* 44-131-228-4384
hq@nasco.int
www.nasco.int
Overview: A medium-sized international organization
Mission: To promote the conservation, restoration, enhancement & rational management of salmon stocks in North Atlantic
Chief Officer(s):
Mary Collingan, President
Peter Hutchinson, Secretary
Staff Member(s): 3
Membership: 6; *Member Profile:* National & multi-national governments; *Committees:* Finance & Administration

Northeast Council for Québec Studies *See* American Council for Québec Studies

Northeast Modern Language Association (NeMLA)

c/o Dr. Elizabeth Abele, Dept. of English, Nassau Community College, One Education Dr., Garden City NY 11530-6793 USA
nemlasupport@gmail.com
www.nemla.org
Overview: A small international organization founded in 1967
Chief Officer(s):
Elizabeth Abele, Executive Director
northeast.mla@gmail.com
Simona Wright, President
simona@tcnj.edu
William Waddell, First Vice-President
bwaddell@sjfc.edu
Finances: *Funding Sources:* Membership fees
Membership: *Fees:* $167 full-time faculty, registration & membership; $106 independent scholars; *Member Profile:* Professionals in English, French, German, Italian, Spanish, & other modern languages, such as professors & students at colleges & universities in eastern Canada & the northeast United States
Activities: Supporting research in modern languages through fellowship programs
Meetings/Conferences:
• Northeast Modern Language Association 2014 45th Annual Convention, April, 2015, Harrisburg, PA
Scope: International
Contact Information: Executive Director: Elizabeth Abele, E-mail: northeast.mla@gmail.com

Publications:
• Modern Language Studies
Type: Newsletter; *Frequency:* Semiannually; *Editor:* Laurence Roth (roth@susqu.edu); *Price:* $15members; $20 individuals; $30 institutions
Profile: Articles, essays, & reviews, plus information from the Northeast Modern Language Association, including conference highlights & previews, awards, & board news
• NeMLA Italian Studies
Type: Journal; *Frequency:* Annually; *Editor:* Simona Wright; *Price:* $15
Profile: Critical studies on Italian language pedagogy, literature, linguistics, culture, & cinema

Northeast Organic Farming Association (NOFA)

Massachusetts Chapter, 411 Sheldon Rd., Barre MA 01005 USA
Tel: 978-355-2853; *Fax:* 978-355-4046
info@nofamass.org
www.nofamass.org
www.facebook.com/NOFAMass
twitter.com/nofamass
www.flickr.com/photos/46485133@N08
Overview: A small local charitable organization founded in 1982
Mission: To educate members & the general public about the benefits of local organic systems based on complete cycles, natural materials & minimal waste for the health of individual beings, communities & the living planet
Chief Officer(s):
Julie Rawson, Executive & Education Director
julie@nofamass.org
Finances: *Annual Operating Budget:* $500,000-$1.5 Million; *Funding Sources:* Private donations; membership dues; conference fees
Staff Member(s): 15
Membership: 1,200; *Fees:* US$40 individual; US$25 low income; US$50 family/institution/small farm; US$75 large farm/business; US$125 premier business; US$250 supporting
Activities: Educational conferences & workshops; videos on organic growing; information about apprenticeship programs matching farms seeking workers with people wanting to learn organic methods; Organic Food Guide map listing organic farmers in Massachusetts; bulk order of soil amendments; genetic engineering awareness; *Speaker Service:* Yes

Northwest Coalition for Alternatives to Pesticides (NCAP)

PO Box 1393, Eugene OR 97440-1393 USA
Tel: 541-344-5044; *Fax:* 541-344-6923
www.pesticide.org
www.facebook.com/pesticide.free
twitter.com/_ncap
www.youtube.com/user/NCAPVids
Overview: A medium-sized local charitable organization founded in 1977
Mission: Works to protect the health of people & the environment by advancing alternatives to pesticides
Chief Officer(s):
Kim Leval, Executive Director
kleval@pesticide.org
Betty McArdle, President
Finances: *Annual Operating Budget:* $250,000-$500,000; *Funding Sources:* Grants; donations
Staff Member(s): 9; 10 volunteer(s)
Membership: 2,300; *Fees:* $25; $15 limited income; $50 associate
Activities: Clean water for salmon; public education; sustainable agriculture; pesticide free parks; inert ingredient disclosure; *Internships:* Yes *Library* Open to public

Northwest Wall & Ceiling Bureau (NWCB)

1032A NE 65th St., Seattle WA 98115 USA
Tel: 206-524-4243; *Fax:* 206-524-4136
info@nwcb.org
www.nwcb.org
www.facebook.com/nwcb1
Overview: A medium-sized international organization founded in 1946
Mission: To serve professionals in the wall & ceiling industry from northwestern United States & western Canada
Chief Officer(s):
Jim Dunham, President
jim@vanderlipco.com
Robert Drury, Executive Director
bob@nwcb.org
Tiina Freeman, Director, Communications & Events
tiina@nwcb.org
Karen Morales, Manager, Office
karen@nwcb.org
Terry Kastner, Technical Consultant
terry@nwcb.org
Membership: *Member Profile:* Manufacturers; Suppliers & distributors; Subcontractors; Labour organizations
Activities: Providing information, such as technical information & advice, to help members operate their businesses effectively; Offering continuing education, through workshops & seminars; Facilitating networking opportunities, for the exchange of experiences & ideas; Providing promotion & marketing to help members market their products & services;
Meetings/Conferences:
• Northwest Wall & Ceiling Bureau 2015 Annual Convention & Trade Show, April, 2015, Rancho Mirage, CA
Scope: International
Description: Informative seminars & exhibits, plus networking opportunities, for persons in the northwestern wall & ceiling industry
Contact Information: Director, Communications & Events: Tiina Freeman, E-mail: tiina@nwcb.org; Exhibitor & Sponsorship Information, Phone: 206-524-4243
• Northwest Wall & Ceiling Bureau 2016 Annual Convention & Trade Show, April, 2016, San Diego, CA
Scope: International
Description: Informative seminars & exhibits, plus networking opportunities, for persons in the northwestern wall & ceiling industry
Contact Information: Director, Communications & Events: Tiina Freeman, E-mail: tiina@nwcb.org; Exhibitor & Sponsorship Information, Phone: 206-524-4243
Publications:
• Change Order
Type: Newsletter; *Frequency:* Quarterly; *Accepts Advertising*; *Editor:* Tiina Freeman (tiina@nwcb.org)
Profile: Organization activities, regional updates, convention & trade show highlights, technical information, new products, & awards
• Impacts to Labor Productivity in Steel Framing & the Installation & Finishing of Gypsum Wallboard
Price: $199 members; $299non-members
Profile: A study testing variables generated by industry experts against labour productivity in over 200 sample projects
• Northwest Wall & Ceiling Bureau Membership Directory
Type: Directory
• Stucco Resource Guide & CD-ROM
Type: Manual; *Price:* $65 members; $85 non-members
Profile: A comprehensive, updated manual for designing & building with stucco, produced with industry experts
• Walls & Ceilings
Type: Magazine

Nuclear Information & Resource Service (NIRS)

#340, 6930 Carroll Ave., Tacoma Park MD 20912 USA
Tel: 301-270-6477; *Fax:* 301-270-4291
nirsnet@nirs.org
www.nirs.org
www.facebook.com/26490791479
twitter.com/nirsnet
www.youtube.com/user/nirsnet
Overview: A small international organization founded in 1978
Mission: To raise awareness about the effects of nuclear power
Affliation(s): Nuclear Awareness Project
Chief Officer(s):
Tim Judson, Executive Director
Staff Member(s): 6
Activities: *Internships:* Yes; *Speaker Service:* Yes *Library* by appointment

The Ocean Conservancy

1300 19th St. NW, 8th Fl., Washington DC 20036 USA
Tel: 202-429-5609; *Fax:* 202-872-0619
Toll-Free: 800-519-1541
info@oceanconservancy.org
www.oceanconservancy.org
www.facebook.com/oceanconservancy
twitter.com/OurOcean
www.youtube.com/user/oceanconservancy
Previous Name: Center for Marine Conservation; Center for Environmental Education
Overview: A large international organization founded in 1972
Mission: To protect ocean ecosystems & conserve the global abundance & diversity of marine wildlife
Chief Officer(s):
Janis Searles Jones, President & CEO
jjones@oceanconservancy.org
Finances: *Annual Operating Budget:* $3 Million-$5 Million; *Funding Sources:* Bequests; contributions; grants
Staff Member(s): 40
Membership: 110,000; *Fees:* Schedule available
Activities: Policy oriented research; promotion of public awareness through education; *Internships:* Yes

The Oceanography Society

PO Box 1931, Rockville MD 20849-1931 USA
Tel: 301-251-7708; *Fax:* 301-251-7709
info@tos.org
www.tos.org
www.linkedin.com/company/the-oceanography-society?trk=hb_tab_compy_id_
www.facebook.com/274812976299?v=wall
twitter.com/TOSOceanography
Overview: A small international organization founded in 1988
Chief Officer(s):
Jennifer Ramarui, Executive Director
Publications:
• Oceanography
Editor: Dr. Ellen Kappel *ISSN:* 1042-8275
Profile: Monthly magazine; peer reviewed

Office & Professional Employees International Union (AFL-CIO/CLC) / Union internationale des employés professionnels et de bureau (FAT-COI/CTC)

80 - 8 Ave., 20th Fl., New York NY 10011 USA
Tel: 800-346-7348
www.opeiu.org
Overview: A small international organization
Chief Officer(s):
Michael Goodwin, President
Membership: 125,000

Opera America Inc.

330 Seventh Ave., 16th Fl., New York NY 10001 USA
Tel: 212-796-8620; *Fax:* 212-796-8631
info@operaamerica.org
www.operaamerica.org
www.facebook.com/operaamerica
twitter.com/operaamerica
Overview: A medium-sized international organization founded in 1970
Mission: To support professional opera companies in North America; to promote opera as an exciting & accessible art form to all segments of society; to develop a national climate conducive to increased public & private support
Affliation(s): Canadian Conference of the Arts
Chief Officer(s):
Marc A. Scorca, President & CEO
mscorca@operaamerica.org
Finances: *Annual Operating Budget:* $500,000-$1.5 Million
Staff Member(s): 18
Membership: 2,000 individual; 200 company; 300 affiliate & business; *Fees:* Schedule available; *Member Profile:* Professional opera companies; affiliate companies; individuals; the media & funding communities; government agencies, representing Australia, Asia, Europe & South America; *Committees:* Affirmative Action; Annual Conference; Development; Education; Executive; Fellowship; Information Service; Opera for a New America
Activities: *Speaker Service:* Yes; *Rents Mailing List:* Yes *Library*

Optimist International

4494 Lindell Blvd., St. Louis MO 63108 USA
Tel: 314-371-6000; *Fax:* 314-371-6006
Toll-Free: 800-500-8130
headquarters@optimist.org
www.optimist.org
www.facebook.com/optimist.international
www.youtube.com/user/OptimistIntl
Overview: A medium-sized international organization
Membership: 100,000+; *Fees:* US$25.80-$49.62, based on economic standing of home country

Organic Crop Improvement Association (International) (OCIA) / Association pour l'amélioration des cultures biologiques (international)

1340 North Cotner, Lincoln NE 68505 USA

Tel: 402-477-2323; *Fax:* 402-477-4325
info@ocia.org
www.ocia.org
Also Known As: OCIA International
Overview: A medium-sized international licensing organization founded in 1988
Mission: To support all farmers with the technical knowledge, skills & organizational aids they need to develop workable crop management systems capable of supplying the growing market demand for organic foods; to provide third party certification of organic foods
Member of: Organic Trade Association
Affliation(s): International Federation of Organic Agriculture Movements; Japan Agriculture Standards; US National Organic Program; Conseil des Appelations Agroalimentaires du Québec; Costa Rica Ministry of Agriculture & Livestock; ISO Guide 65
Chief Officer(s):
Peggy Linzmeier, President
Finances: *Annual Operating Budget:* $1.5 Million-$3 Million; *Funding Sources:* Member-owned & funded
Staff Member(s): 30
Membership: 3,000+; *Fees:* US$75 corporate & chapter level; individual chapter membership fees vary; *Member Profile:* Farmers, processors & merchants who are committed to seeking alternatives to conventional chemical & energy-intensive food system; *Committees:* By-Laws; Crop Improvement; Finance; Inspector Accreditation; Internal Review; Certification Analysis; International Certification; International Standards; Chapter Licensing; Promotions; AGMM; Canadian Organic Regulatory Committee; Research & Education
Activities: *Speaker Service:* Yes

Organic Food Production Association of North America *See* Organic Trade Association

Organic Trade Association (OTA)

#413, 28 Vernon St., Brattleboro VT 05301 USA
Tel: 802-275-3800; *Fax:* 802-275-3801
www.ota.com
Previous Name: Organic Food Production Association of North America
Overview: A medium-sized international organization founded in 1985
Mission: To encourage global sustainability through promoting & protecting the growth of diverse organic trade
Member of: International Federation of Organic Agriculture Movements
Chief Officer(s):
Christine Bushway, Executive Director
Finances: *Annual Operating Budget:* $500,000-$1.5 Million; *Funding Sources:* Membership fees; merchandise sales; fundraising
Staff Member(s): 22; 20 volunteer(s)
Membership: 1,500; *Fees:* Based on revenues; *Member Profile:* Organic food processors; certifiers; distributors; organic farm organizations; consultants; farmers; retail outlets; restaurants; *Committees:* Legislative; Quality Assurance; Marketing; International Relations; Organic Certifiers Council; Organic Fiber Council; Organic Suppliers Advisory Council; Canadian Council
Activities: Organic Harvest Month; *Awareness Events:* Organic Harvest Month, Sept.; *Speaker Service:* Yes

Organisation de coopération et de développement économique *See* Organization for Economic Co-operation & Development

Organisation internationale de la Francophonie (OIF) / International Organisation of La Francophonie (IOF)

19-21 avenue Bosquet, Paris 75007 France
Tél: (33) 1 44 37 33 00; *Téléc:* (33) 1 45 79 14 98
www.francophonie.org
twitter.com/OIFfrancophonie
Aperçu: *Dimension:* grande; *Envergure:* internationale; fondée en 1970
Mission: L'OIF a pour objectif de contribuer à améliorer le niveau de vie de ses populations en les aidant à devenir les acteurs de leur propre développement. Elle apporte à ses États membres un appui dans l'élaboration ou la consolidation de leurs politiques et mène des actions de politique internationale et de coopération multilatérale, conformément aux 4 grandes missions tracées par le Sommet de la Francophonie.
Membre(s) du bureau directeur:
Michaëlle Jean, Secrétaire générale
Finances: *Budget de fonctionnement annuel:* Plus de $5 Million
Membre: 77 États et gouvernements membres

Organisation internationale de normalisation *See* International Organization for Standardization

Organisation internationale des commissions de valeurs *See* International Organization of Securities Commissions

Organisation maritime internationale *See* International Maritime Organization

Organisation météorologique mondiale *See* World Meteorological Organization

Organisation mondiale de la santé *See* World Health Organization

Organisation mondiale du mouvement scout *See* World Organization of the Scout Movement

Organisation Mondiale pour la Systémique et la Cybernétique *Voir* World Organisation of Systems & Cybernetics

Organization for Economic Co-operation & Development (OECD) / Organisation de coopération et de développement économique (OCDE)

2, rue André-Pascal, Paris 75775 France
Tel: 33-1-45-24-82-00; *Fax:* 33-1-45-24-85-00
www.oecd.org
www.facebook.com/theOECD
twitter.com/oecd
www.youtube.com/oecd; www.flickr.com/photos/oecd
Overview: A large international organization founded in 1961
Mission: To achieve the highest sustainable economic growth & employment; To promote economic & social welfare throughout the OECD area by coordinating the policies of its member countries; To stimulate & harmonize its members' efforts in favour of developing countries
Member of: International Organization of Securities Commissions - Canada
Affliation(s): International Energy Agency (IEA); Nuclear Energy Agency
Chief Officer(s):
Angel Gurría, Secretary General
Finances: *Annual Operating Budget:* Greater than $5 Million
Staff Member(s): 2500
Membership: 34 member countries
Activities: Provides a forum for monitoring economic trends & coordinating economic policies among its member countries: the free-market democracies of North America, Western Europe & the Pacific; provides the largest source of comparative data on the industrial economies in the world; produces a wide range of publications, economic surveys, statistics, analyses & policy recommendations
Publications:
• OECD [Organization for Economic Co-operation & Development] Observer
Type: Magazine

Organization of American Historians (OAH)

Indiana University, 112 North Bryant Ave., Bloomington IN 47408-4141 USA
Tel: 812-855-7311; *Fax:* 812-855-0696
help@oah.org
www.oah.org
www.linkedin.com/company/444102
www.facebook.com/TheOAH
twitter.com/The_OAH
Overview: A medium-sized international charitable organization founded in 1907
Mission: To promote teaching & scholarship about the history of the United States, both before & after its formation as a nation-state
Member of: American Council of Learned Societies
Chief Officer(s):
Alice Kessler-Harris, President
Katherine Finley, Executive Director
kmfinley@oah.org
Finances: *Annual Operating Budget:* $1.5 Million-$3 Million
Staff Member(s): 27
Membership: 11,000; *Fees:* Schedule available; *Member Profile:* Interest in promotion of historical study & research in American history; *Committees:* Access to Documents & Open Information; Status of Minority Historians & Minority History; Public History; Teaching; Status of Women in the Historical Profession; Community Colleges; International; Membership; Nominating; National Park Service; Program
Activities: *Internships:* Yes; *Speaker Service:* Yes; *Rents Mailing List:* Yes
Awards:
• Japanese Fellowship (Grant)
Deadline: December
• Louis Pelzer Memorial Award (Award)
Best essay in American history by a graduate student*Deadline:* November *Amount:* $500
• Tachau Teacher of the Year Award (Award)
Deadline: December *Amount:* $1,000
• Frederick Jackson Turner Award (Award)
Deadline: October *Amount:* $1,000
• Willi Paul Adams Award (Award)
Best article (annual) and best book (biennial) on American history published in languages other than English*Deadline:* May 1 *Amount:* $1,000
• ABC-CLIO America: History And Life Award (biennial) (Award)
Deadline: December *Amount:* $750
• Binkley-Stephenson Award (Award)
For the best article in the JAH from the previous year *Amount:* $500
• Avery O. Craven Award (Award)
Most original book on the Civil War or Era of Reconstruction*Deadline:* October *Amount:* $500
• Merle Curti Award (Award)
Deadline: October *Amount:* $2,000
• Huggins-Quarles Awards (Award)
Deadline: December *Amount:* $1,000
• Ray Allen Billington Prize (biennial) (Award)
Best book on American frontier history*Deadline:* October *Amount:* $1,000
• Ellis W. Hawley Prize (Award)
Best book-length historical study of U.S. politics from the Civil War to the present *Deadline:* October *Amount:* $500
• Richard W. Leopold Prize (biennial) (Award)
Deadline: October *Amount:* $1,500
• Lerner-Scott Prize (Award)
Best doctoral dissertation in U.S. women's history*Deadline:* December *Amount:* $1,000
• James A. Rawley Prize (Award)
Best book dealing with the history of race relations in the U.S.*Deadline:* October *Amount:* $1,000
• Erik Barnouw Award (Award)
Deadline: December *Amount:* $1,000
• OAH/IEHS John Higham Travel Grants (Grant)
Amount: $500
• Liberty Legacy Fdn. Award (Award)
Amount: $2,000
• White House Historical Assn. Fellowships (Award)
Amount: $2,000/month
Publications:
• Journal of American History
Editor: Edward T. Linenthal
Profile: Quarterly scholarly journal

Oslo & Paris Commissions *See* OSPAR Commission

OSPAR Commission (OSPAR)

#37, 63 Southampton Row, London WC1B 4DA United Kingdom
Tel: 44-207-430-5200; *Fax:* 44-207-242-3737
secretariat@ospar.org
www.ospar.org
Previous Name: Oslo & Paris Commissions
Overview: A small international organization founded in 1998
Mission: To control pollution of marine environment of the Northeast Atlantic
Chief Officer(s):
Darius Campbell, Executive Secretary
darius.campbell@ospar.org
Finances: *Funding Sources:* Membership
Staff Member(s): 12
Membership: 15 European countries & EU
Activities: Protection of the marine environment NE Atlantic

Pacific NorthWest Economic Region (PNWER)

World Trade Center West, #460, 2200 Alaskan Way, Seattle WA 98121 USA
Tel: 206-443-7723; *Fax:* 206-443-7703
www.pnwer.org
www.facebook.com/147636495253612
twitter.com/PNWER
Previous Name: Pacific Northwest Legislative Leadership
Overview: A medium-sized local organization founded in 1989
Mission: To promote greater collaboration among the seven state & provincial members in order to enhance the economic competitiveness of the region in international & domestic markets

Chief Officer(s):
Matt Morrison, Chief Executive Officer
matt.morrison@pnwer.org
Staff Member(s): 8
Membership: *Member Profile:* Consists of the Pacific Northwestern states of Alaska, Idaho, Montana, Oregon & Washington & the provinces of Alberta, British Columbia & the Yukon Territory; includes Legislators, Governors/Premiers & private sector individuals
Activities: 9 Working Groups; *Internships:* Yes

Pacific Northwest Legislative Leadership *See* Pacific NorthWest Economic Region

Paint & Decorating Retailers Association Canada (PDRA)

1401 Triad Center Dr., St. Peters MO 63376 USA
Tel: 636-326-2636
info@pdra.org
www.pdra.org
www.facebook.com/PaintDecoratingRetailerMagazine
twitter.com/PaintDecoRetail
Previous Name: Canadian Decorating Products Association
Overview: A large national organization founded in 1949
Mission: To educate, promote & represent the interests of decorating products dealers in Canada
Affliation(s): National Decorating Products Association
Chief Officer(s):
Jeff Baggaley, President, 519-455-6400
colorcompany@rogers.com
Dan Simon, Executive Vice-President & Publisher
dan@pdra.org
Larry DeWitt, Senior Director, Art & Marketing
larry@pdra.org
Renée Nolte, Director, Finance & Human Resources
renee@pdra.org
Membership: 100 associate + 450 retail; *Fees:* Schedule available
Activities: Education for dealers; trade shows; *Library* Open to public
Meetings/Conferences:
• Paint & Decorating Retailers Association Canada Paint & Accessories Show at the National Hardware Show 2015, May, 2015
Scope: National
Publications:
• Paint & Decorating Retailer [a publication of Paint & Decorating Retailers Association Canada]
Type: Magazine; *Frequency:* Monthly; *Accepts Advertising*

Pan American Center for Sanitary Engineering & Environmental Sciences (CEPIS)

Urbanizacion Camacho, La Molina, PO Box 4337, Calle Los Pinos 259, Lima 12 Peru
Tel: 51-1-437-1077; *Fax:* 51-1-437-8289
Overview: A large international organization founded in 1968
Mission: To cooperate with the countries of the Americas to evaluate & manage environmental risk factors that, directly or indirectly, affect the health of the population
Finances: *Funding Sources:* PAHO; WHO; Peruvian government; other
Staff Member(s): 90
Membership: Governments of 48 countries & territories
Activities: Carries out programs aimed at strengthening national capacities for protecting environmental health & the management of risks derived from man-made contamination; *Library* Open to public

Paperboard Packaging Council

#1508, 1350 Main St., Springfield MA 01103-1670 USA
Tel: 413-686-9191; *Fax:* 413-747-7777
www.ppcnet.org
www.linkedin.com/groups?gid=1134757&mostPopular=&trk=tya
h
www.facebook.com/paperboard.packaging.3?ref=ts
twitter.com/ppcnet
Overview: A large national organization
Mission: To represent paperboard packaging converters & industry suppliers
Chief Officer(s):
Ben Markens, President, 413-686-9181
ben@ppcnet.org
Lou Kornet, Chief of Staff & Vice-President, 413-686-9180
lou@ppcnet.org
Kim Guarnaccia, Director, Marketing & Communications, 413-686-9183
kim@ppcnet.org
Jennie Markens, Director, Next Generation Leaders, 413-686-9191
jen@ppcnet.org
Emily Rae, Director, Member Services & Manager, Marketing Communications, 413-686-9185
emily@ppcnet.org
Susan Martins, Controller, 413-686-9192
susan@ppcnet.org
Finances: *Funding Sources:* Membership fees
Activities: *Speaker Service:* Yes
Awards:
• The Volunteer Leader Award (Award)
• The PPC Service Award (Award)
• The Safety Boxscore Award (Award)
• The National Paperboard Packaging Competition Awards (Award)

Parents Without Partners Inc. (PWP)

1100-H Brandywine Blvd., Zanesville OH 43701-7303 USA
Fax: 561-395-8557
Toll-Free: 800-637-7974
Intl.pres@parentswithoutpartners.org
www.parentswithoutpartners.org
Overview: A large international organization founded in 1957
Mission: To provide single parents & their children with an opportunity for enhancing personal growth, self-confidence & sensitivity towards others by offering an environment for support, friendship & the exchange of parenting techniques
Chief Officer(s):
Janet Gallinati, President
Intl.pres@parentswithoutpartners.org
Finances: *Annual Operating Budget:* $250,000-$500,000
Membership: 30,000 + 300 chapters in Canada & US; *Fees:* $20-$40 annually; *Member Profile:* A person must be the parent of one or more living sons or daughters, & be single by reason of death, divorce, separation or never married, or other reason which may be deemed acceptable by PWP
Activities: Various activities for parent & family at each chapter; Spring conference
Awards:
• Distinguished Service to Children Award (Award)
Awarded annually to a person or group that has made a great contribution to children's welfare
• Family Individual Talent Awards Program (Award)
Presented annually in all arts-related categories to member children & teens
• PWP Scholarships (Scholarship)
Cash awards presented to member teens to help with college expenses *Amount:* $750
• Single Parent of the Year Award (Award)
Awarded annually to an outstanding member parent
Meetings/Conferences:
• Parents Without Parents Convention 2015, July, 2015, Nashville, TN
Scope: National

Coquitlam Chapter
Surrey BC V3N 5B7
Tel: 604-616-6315
pwp722@gmail.com
www.pwpcanada.com

Mississauga Valley Chapter
PO Box 29623, RPO Central Parkway, Mississauga ON L5A 4H2
Tel: 905-278-0111; *Crisis Hot-Line:* 416-463-9355
pwpmississauga@yahoo.com
www.pwpcanada.com

New Dawn Chapter
PO Box 69011, RPO Rosedale, Hamilton ON L8K 5R4
Tel: 905-544-4444
general@pwphamilton.com
www.pwpcanada.com

Royal City Chapter
c/o Florence Boys, 73 Knightwood Blvd., Guelph ON N1E 3W5
Tel: 519-823-0227
guelphpwp@hotmail.com
www.pwpcanada.com

Stepping Stone (Winnipeg) Chapter
PO Box 1756, Winnipeg MB R3C 2Z9
Tel: 204-957-7172
pwp.winnipeg@gmail.com
www.pwpcanada.com

Toronto Chapter
Toronto ON
Tel: 416-489-2221; *Crisis Hot-Line:* 416-463-9355
info@pwptoronto.com
www.pwpcanada.com

Parents, Families & Friends of Lesbians & Gays (PFLAG)

#660, 1828 L St. NW, Washington DC 20036-5112 USA
Tel: 202-467-8180; *Fax:* 202-467-8194
info@pflag.org
www.pflag.org
Overview: A medium-sized national organization founded in 1981
Mission: To promote the health & well-being of gay, lesbian, bisexual & transgendered persons, their families & friends, through: support, to cope with an adverse society; education, to enlighten an ill-informed public; & advocacy, to end discrimination & to secure equal civil rights; provides opportunity for dialogue about sexual orientation & gender identity, & acts to create a society that is healthy & respectful of human diversity
Chief Officer(s):
David Horowitz, President
Jean Hodges, Vice-President
Finances: *Annual Operating Budget:* $1.5 Million-$3 Million
Staff Member(s): 17
Membership: 200,000; *Fees:* $50
Activities: *Internships:* Yes; *Speaker Service:* Yes

Parliamentarians for Global Action (PGA) / Action Mondiale des Parlementaires

#1604, 211 East 43 St., New York NY 10017 USA
Tel: 212-687-7755; *Fax:* 212-687-8409
info@pgaction.org
www.pgaction.org
Previous Name: Parliamentarians for World Order
Overview: A medium-sized international organization founded in 1979
Mission: To service parliamentarians, informing them on issues of global security, including but not confined to disarmament, peacekeeping, economic development & the environment, & assisting them in cooperative efforts to resolve such problems; to approach governments with suggested courses of action
Affliation(s): Parliamentarians for Global Action - Canadian Section
Chief Officer(s):
Shazia Z. Rafi, Secretary-General
sg@pgaction.org
Finances: *Annual Operating Budget:* $500,000-$1.5 Million; *Funding Sources:* Individual donors; foundations; institutes; governments
Staff Member(s): 14; 5 volunteer(s)
Membership: 1,400 individuals from 100 parliaments; *Fees:* US$50; *Committees:* Executive
Activities: Nuclear test ban & non-proliferation; United Nations peacekeeping & collective security; sustainable development (including environmental security & international economic reform); international law & global institutions (focussing on the creation of an International Criminal Court); a parliamentary initiative for democracy; special programme on Africa
Awards:
• Defender of Democracy Award
Presented to individuals who have made significant progress in strengthening democracy and democratic principles

Parliamentarians for World Order *See* Parliamentarians for Global Action

Peace & Justice Studies Association (PJSA)

Poulton Hall, Georgetown University, #130, 1421 - 37th St. NW, Washington DC 20057 USA
www.peacejusticestudies.org
Previous Name: Consortium on Peace Research, Education & Development; Peace Studies Association
Overview: A medium-sized national organization founded in 2001
Mission: To bring together researchers, educators & activists working for the peaceful resolution of conflict
Affliation(s): International Peace Research Association; Canadian Peace Research & Education Association; Center for UN Reform; Council on Peace Research in History; Consejo Latinoamericano de Investigadores para la Paz; National Peace Institute Foundation; National Conference on Peacemaking & Conflict Resolution; International Studies Association; American Association for the Advancement of Science; Pan-American Council on Peace Research

2 volunteer(s)
Membership: 650 individual + 150 institutional; *Fees:* Schedule available; *Member Profile:* Individual - includes students, K-12 educators, conflict resolution practitioners, peace activists, university professors, clergy; institutional - includes peace studies programs at colleges & universities, religious organizations, community centres, professional associations, institutes & foundations, activist organizations; *Committees:* Arts & Media; Conference; Conflict Resolution; Cross-Cultural; Feminisms & Gender Issues; Finance; LesBiGay Friends & Allies; Nonviolence; Peace Action; Peace Education; Peace & Justice Resource Centers; Peace Research; Religion & Ethics; Student Peace Network; University Peace Studies
Activities: *Internships:* Yes; *Speaker Service:* Yes; *Rents Mailing List:* Yes

Pediatric Endocrine Society (PES)
6728 Old McLean Village Dr., McLean VA 22101 USA
Tel: 703-556-9222; *Fax:* 703-556-8729
info@pedsendo.org
www.pedsendo.org
Previous Name: Lawson Wilkins Pediatric Endocrine Society
Overview: A medium-sized international organization
Mission: To promote the acquisition of knowledge about endocrine & metabolic disorders, from conception through adolescence
Chief Officer(s):
David B. Allen, President
George K. Degnon, Executive Director
Christy McGinty Levine, Association Manager
Peter Lee, Secretary
John Kirkland, Treasurer
Membership: 900+; *Member Profile:* Persons who represent the disciplines of pediatric endocrinology; *Committees:* Awards; Drug & Therapeutics; Membership; Program; Ethics; History; Organizational Liaison; Public Policy; Finance & Audit; Nominating; Development; History; Honors; International Scholars; Maintenance of Certification in Endocrinology; Study Network of Pediatric Endocrinology
Activities: Promoting research into endocrine disorders; Disseminating information about endocrine & metabolic disorders; Encouraging continuing education
Meetings/Conferences:
• Pediatric Endocrine Society 2015 Annual Meeting, April, 2015, San Diego, CA
Scope: International
Description: A conference for persons who represent the disciplines of pediatric endocrinology
Contact Information: E-mail: info@pedsendo.org
• Pediatric Endocrine Society 2016 Annual Meeting, April, 2016, Baltimore, MD
Scope: International
Description: Original science abstract sessions, poster sessions, plenary sessions, business meetings, topic symposia, workshops, & exhibits
Contact Information: E-mail: info@pedsendo.org
• Pediatric Endocrine Society 2017 Annual Meeting, May, 2017, San Francisco, CA
Scope: International
Description: A yearly spring conference, featuring lectures, topic symposia, business meetings, plenary sessions, exhibits, & opportunities for networking
Contact Information: E-mail: info@pedsendo.org
• Pediatric Endocrine Society 2018 Annual Meeting, May, 2018, Toronto, ON
Scope: International
Description: An annual gathering of persons from the disciplines of pediatric endocrinology, including business meetings, lectures, topic symposia, poster sessions, workshops, exhibits, & social activities
Contact Information: E-mail: info@pedsendo.org
• Pediatric Endocrine Society 2019 Annual Meeting, April, 2019, Baltimore, MD
Scope: International
Description: An annual opportunity for medical education for those engaged in the disciplines of pediatric endocrinology
Contact Information: E-mail: info@pedsendo.org
• Pediatric Endocrine Society 2020 Annual Meeting, May, 2020, Philadelphia, PA
Scope: International
Description: An annual continuing education event, featuring speaker presentations, a scientific program, poster sessions, exhibits, & networking occasions for persons who represent the field of pediatric endocrinology
Contact Information: E-mail: info@pedsendo.org
• Pediatric Endocrine Society 2021 Annual Meeting, 2021
Scope: International
Publications:
• Pediatric Endocrine Society Membership Directory
Type: Directory
• PES Newsletter
Type: Newsletter
Profile: Pediatric Endocrine Society news, including award winners, meeting reviews, forthcoming meetings, & workshops

PEN International ***See*** International PEN

People for the Ethical Treatment of Animals (PETA)
501 Front St., Norfolk VA 23510 USA
Tel: 757-622-7382; *Fax:* 757-628-0457
Other Communication: pinterest.com/officialpeta
www.peta.org
www.linkedin.com/in/ingridnewkirk
www.facebook.com/officialpeta
twitter.com/peta
www.youtube.com/profile?user=officialpeta
Overview: A large international charitable organization founded in 1980
Mission: To protect animals from exploitation & cruelty; To bring positive changes in the ways humans regard other species; to expose animal abuse so it will not be perpetuated; To promote a world in which animals are respected & people are aware of & concerned with how their daily decisions affect the lives of other sentient beings
Chief Officer(s):
Ingrid E. Newkirk, President
Lisa Lange, Senior Vice-President, Communications
Finances: *Annual Operating Budget:* Greater than $5 Million; *Funding Sources:* Contributions
Staff Member(s): 180; 40 volunteer(s)
Membership: 3,000,000+; *Fees:* US$16; $25 Cdn.
Activities: International campaigns on vegetarianism, against animal testing, against fur & dissection, against animal abuse in the entertainment industry; *Internships:* Yes; *Rents Mailing List:* Yes *Library:* PETA Library; Open to public

Permanent International Association of Navigation Congresses ***Voir*** Association internationale permanente des congrès de navigation

Pesticide Action Network North America (PANNA)
#1200, 1611 Telegraph Ave., Oakland CA 94612 USA
Tel: 510-788-9020; *Fax:* 415-981-1991
panna@panna.org
www.panna.org
www.facebook.com/pesticideactionnetwork
twitter.com/pesticideaction
www.youtube.com/user/pannavideo
Overview: A medium-sized international charitable organization founded in 1984
Mission: Works to replace pesticide use with ecologically sound & socially just alternatives; links local & international consumer, labor, health, environment & agriculture groups into an international citizens' action network; network challenges the global proliferation of pesticides, defends basic rights to health & environmental quality & works to insure the transition to a just & viable society
Chief Officer(s):
Jennifer Sokolove, President
Monica Moore, Founding Executive Director
Steve Scholl-Buckwald, CFO & Managing Director
Finances: *Annual Operating Budget:* $1.5 Million-$3 Million; *Funding Sources:* Grants & individual donors
Staff Member(s): 21; 5 volunteer(s)
Membership: 225 affiliate organizations; *Fees:* US$35 organizations with paid staff; US$20 all volunteer organizations
Activities: Campaign to stop pesticide drift; documenting pesticide body burden; holding corporations accountable for the use & promotion of pesticides & genetically engineered crops; campaign to transform agricultural development through the International Assessment of Agricultural Science & Technology for Development; California & Midwest pesticide use reduction; public education; farmworkers' rights campaign; promotion of alternatives to pesticides; *Internships:* Yes *Library* by appointment

Piano Technicians Guild Inc. (PTG)
4444 Forest Ave., Kansas City KS 66106 USA
Tel: 913-432-9975; *Fax:* 913-432-9986
ptg@ptg.org
www.ptg.org
www.facebook.com/pianotechniciansguild
twitter.com/pianotechguild
www.youtube.com/user/PTGHomeOffice
Previous Name: American Society of Piano Technicians
Merged from: National Association of Piano Tuners
Overview: A medium-sized international organization founded in 1957
Mission: To promote the highest possible standards of piano service by providing members with opportunities for professional development, by recognizing technical competence through examinations & by advancing the interests of its members
Member of: International Association of Piano Builders & Technicians (IAPBT)
Chief Officer(s):
Barbara Cassaday, Executive Director
barbara@ptg.org
Staff Member(s): 7
Membership: 4,000; *Member Profile:* Individuals with a professional or vocational interest in piano technology
Activities: *Library:* The Stephen S. Jellen Library; by appointment

Calgary Chapter
Calgary AB
Tel: 403-995-3284
www.calgaryptg.com
Chief Officer(s):
Colin Meckelburg, President
gcmeck@gmail.com

The Planetary Society (TPS)
85 South Grand, Pasadena CA 91105 USA
Tel: 626-793-5100; *Fax:* 626-793-5528
Other Communication: www.flickr.com/photos/77417785@N05
tps@planetary.org
www.planetary.org
www.facebook.com/planetarysociety
twitter.com/exploreplanets
www.youtube.com/planetarysociety
Overview: A large international organization founded in 1980
Mission: To educate & inform the general public about planetary exploration & the search for extraterrestrial life
Member of: Coalition for Space Exploration; Space Exploration Alliance; International Astronautical Federation; American Association for the Advancement of Science; International Year of Astronomy; United Nations
Chief Officer(s):
Daniel T. Geraci, Chair
Jim Bell, President
Bill Nye, CEO
Finances: *Annual Operating Budget:* $1.5 Million-$3 Million; *Funding Sources:* Dues; donations
Staff Member(s): 20
Membership: 100,000; *Fees:* $37 US; $40 Canada; $57 international
Activities: Multimedia resources; various space-related projects; contests; *Internships:* Yes; *Rents Mailing List:* Yes *Library:* Resource Library
Publications:
• E-News [a publication of The Planetary Society]
Type: Newsletter
• The Planetary Report [a publication of The Planetary Society]
Type: Magazine; *Frequency:* q.; *Editor:* Amir Alexander
Profile: Coverage of discoveries on Earth & other planets

Plastic Loose Fill Council (PLFC)
#201, 1298 Cronson Blvd., Crofton MD 21114 USA
Crisis Hot-Line: 800-828-2214
www.loosefillpackaging.com
Overview: A small national organization founded in 1991
Mission: Promoted the reuse of plastic packing peanuts through its national collection program the Peanut Hotline, with over 240 drop-off sites.
Chief Officer(s):
John D. Mellott
Membership: 4; *Member Profile:* Manufacturers of expanded polystyrene loose fill packaging
Activities: Operates the Peanut Hotline, the consumer reuse program in US for plastic packaging peanuts;

Polish Association for Canadian Studies (PACS)
c/o Dr. Marcin Gabrys, Institute of American Studies & Polish Diaspora, Jagiellonian University, Rynek Glówny 34, Cracow 31-010 Poland
Tel: 48 12 4325060
ptbk@uj.edu.pl
www.ptbk.org.pl
Overview: A small international organization founded in 1998

Mission: To promote activities in favour of the development of Canadian studies in all scholarly areas; to spread knowledge about Canada & to develop contacts with scholars & academics researching into Canadian studies & all people interested in any form of expanding knowledge about Canada
Chief Officer(s):
Marcin Gabrys, President
Tomasz Soroka, Secretary
Activities: Four Canadian Studies Centres in Poland

Polystyrene Packaging Council (PSPC)
1300 Wilson Blvd., 8th Fl., Arlington VA 22209 USA
Tel: 703-741-5649; *Fax:* 703-741-5651
pspc@plastics.org
www.polystyrene.org
Overview: A small international organization overseen by American Chemistry Council
Mission: To promote & defend the polystyrene industry by providing a forum for issues of importance to the polystyrene industry; keeping markets free by eliminating or amending anti-polystyrene legislation & regulation & avoiding future burdensome polystyrene legislation/regulation; & serving as the polystyrene industry communications voice to selected audiences & the general public
Chief Officer(s):
Michael H. Levy, Director
Finances: *Annual Operating Budget:* $500,000-$1.5 Million
Staff Member(s): 2
Membership: 9; *Fees:* Schedule available; *Member Profile:* Major suppliers & manufacturers of polystyrene products

Population Connection (PC)
#500, 2120 L St. NW, Washington DC 20037 USA
Tel: 202-332-2200; *Fax:* 202-332-2302
Toll-Free: 800-767-1956
info@populationconnection.org
www.populationconnection.org
www.facebook.com/PopulationConnection
twitter.com/popconnect
www.youtube.com/user/populationconnection
Previous Name: Zero Population Growth
Overview: A large international organization founded in 1968
Mission: To advocate progressive action to stabilize world population at a level that can be sustained by Earth's resources
Chief Officer(s):
Marianne Gabel, Chair
John Seager, President & CEO
john@popconnect.org
Finances: *Annual Operating Budget:* $3 Million-$5 Million; *Funding Sources:* Memberships; foundations; private donations
Staff Member(s): 40; 20 volunteer(s)
Membership: 30,000; *Fees:* $25
Activities: Encourages better media coverage of population issues; Teachers PETNet (Population Education Trainers Network); roving reporters; legislative alert; campus organizing; *Speaker Service:* Yes
Publications:
• Congressional Report Card [a publication of Population Connection]
Type: Report; *Frequency:* Annual
• The Reporter [a publication of Population Connection]
Type: Magazine; *Frequency:* 3 pa; *Editor:* Marian Starkey
Profile: Covers environmental, social & health-related topics

Potash & Phosphate Institute/Potash & Phosphate Institute of Canada *See* International Plant Nutrition Institute

POWERtalk International
PO Box 13260, Tauranga New Zealand
Tel: 64 7 579 9972; *Fax:* 64 7 579 9976
info@powertalkinternational.com
powertalkinternational.com
Also Known As: International Training in Communication
Overview: A medium-sized international organization founded in 1938
Mission: International Training in Communication & POWERtalk International developed from the International Toastmistress Clubs in the U.S. It's mission is to be a world leader in the promotion of opportunities for quality training in communication & leadership skills
Chief Officer(s):
Margaret Sutherland, International President
Mary Flentge, Secretary, (Netherlands)
Membership: Clubs in 15 countries
Activities: *Speaker Service:* Yes

Atlantic Canada
Fredericton NB
Tel: 506-453-8643
dennis.m@corknb.ca
itc-northeast.tripod.com/fredericton
Chief Officer(s):
Shelley Petley, Contact
shelley.petley@unb.ca
Québec/Ontario
North Bay ON
Tel: 705-474-8660
itc-northeast.tripod.com/northbay
Chief Officer(s):
Karen Sherry, President
Geraldine Lightfoot, Contact
gerryvl@thot.net
Western Canada
Winnipeg MB
sbgeorge@mts.net

La Première Église du Christ, Scientiste *See* Christian Science

Professional Association of Therapeutic Horsemanship International (PATH)
PO Box 33150, Denver CO 80233 USA
Tel: 303-452-1212; *Fax:* 303-252-4610
Toll-Free: 800-369-7433
www.pathintl.org
Previous Name: North American Riding for the Handicapped Association
Overview: A medium-sized international charitable organization founded in 1969
Mission: Promotes the benefit of the horse riding for individuals with physical, emotional & learning disabilities
Chief Officer(s):
Kay Green, CEO
kgreen@pathintl.org
Membership: 1,000-4,999; *Fees:* $355-$2000

Professional Bull Riders Inc
101 West Riverwalk, Pueblo CO 81003 USA
Tel: 719-242-2800; *Fax:* 719-242-2855
admin@pbrnow.com
pbrnow.com
www.facebook.com/PBR
twitter.com/PBR
www.youtube.com/user/PBRNow
Previous Name: Canadian Bull Riders Association
Overview: A small international organization founded in 1992
Chief Officer(s):
Randy Bernard, CEO
Ty Murray, President
Publications:
• Pro Bull Rider Magazine
Profile: Bi-monthly magazine

Professional Secretaries International *See* International Association of Administrative Professionals

Programme des nations unies pour l'environnement *See* United Nations Environment Programme

Project Management Institute (PMI)
14 Campus Blvd., Newtown Square PA 19073-3299 USA
Tel: 610-356-4600; *Fax:* 610-356-4647
Toll-Free: 855-746-4849
customercare@pmi.org
www.pmi.org
www.linkedin.com/groups?gid=2784738
www.facebook.com/PMInstitute
twitter.com/pminstitute
www.youtube.com/PMInstitute
Overview: A medium-sized international organization founded in 1969
Mission: To advance the state-of-the-art of the practice of managing projects & programs; To advocate acceptance of project management as a profession & discipline
Chief Officer(s):
Gregory Balestrero, President/CEO
Finances: *Annual Operating Budget:* Greater than $5 Million
Staff Member(s): 90
Membership: 265,000 worldwide; *Fees:* US$129 individual; US$60 retiree; US$40 student
Meetings/Conferences:
• Project Management Institute Global Congress 2015, May, 2015, London
Scope: International
Description: Professional development, information sharing, exhibit viewing, & neworking opportunities

Durham Highlands
info@pmi-dhc.ca
www.pmi-dhc.ca
www.linkedin.com/groups?gid=2228530
Chief Officer(s):
Susan Carroll-Clark, President
president@pmi-dhc.ca
Kitchener, Waterloo, Cambridge, Guelph & Areas
PO Box 24041, Stn. Highland West, Kitchener ON N2N 5P1
Tel: 519-489-2882
www.pmi-ctt.org
Chief Officer(s):
Marc Blanchette, President
Lakeshore
#361, 6-2400 Dundas Street West, Mississauga ON L5K 2R8
Toll-Free: 855-764-2193
info@pmi-lakeshore.org
www.pmi-lakeshore.org
www.linkedin.com/groups?gid=1299437
Chief Officer(s):
Rishi Kumar, Chair
Kelly Ann Pauly, President
Lévis-Québec
#375, 3175, ch des Quatre-Bourgeois, Québec QC G1W 2K7
Tel: 418-780-5383; *Fax:* 418-681-7408
secretariat@pmiquebec.qc.ca
www.pmiquebec.qc.ca
www.linkedin.com/groups?gid=1385577
www.facebook.com/pmiquebec
Chief Officer(s):
Eric Maquennehan, Président
Manitoba
PO Box 1857, Winnipeg MB R3C 3R1
Tel: 204-943-0717
communications@pmimanitoba.org
www.pmimanitoba.org
www.linkedin.com/groups?gid=2961710
twitter.com/pmiManitoba
Chief Officer(s):
Debbie Wilgosh, President
president@pmimanitoba.org
Montréal
#520, 630 Sherbrooke Ouest, Montréal QC H3A 1E4
Tel: 514-861-8788
www.pmimontreal.org
www.linkedin.com/in/pmimontreal
www.facebook.com/144996582182759
twitter.com/pmimontreal
Chief Officer(s):
Benoît Lalonde, Président
New Brunswick
#199, 126C Hampton Rd., Rothesay NB E2E 2N6
communications@pminb.ca
www.pminb.ca
www.linkedin.com/groups?home=&gid=148712
twitter.com/PMINB
Chief Officer(s):
Warren Long, President
president@pminb.ca
Newfoundland & Labrador
#358, 38 Pearson St., St. John's NL A1A 3R1
info@pminl.ca
www.pminl.ca
www.linkedin.com/groups?gid=3702248
Chief Officer(s):
Nicole Strong, President
North Saskatchewan
PO Box 278, #8B, 3110 - 8th St. East, Saskatoon SK S7H 0W2
Tel: 306-220-0330
info@pminorthsask.com
www.pminorthsask.com
Chief Officer(s):
Hemant Anand, President
president@pminorthsask.com
Northern Alberta
PO Box 11868, Stn. Main, Edmonton AB T5J 3K9
info@pminac.com
www.pminac.com
twitter.com/PMINAC2012
Chief Officer(s):

Harold Eggert, President
president@pmiinac.com
Nova Scotia
PO Box 34054, Halifax NS B3J 3J8
Tel: 902-423-1764; *Fax:* 902-484-6697
www.pmi.ns.ca
Chief Officer(s):
Paul Dean, President
Ottawa Valley
#256, 1568 Merivale Rd., Ottawa ON K2G 5Y7
Tel: 613-569-6236; *Fax:* 613-569-2854
www.pmiovoc.org
Chief Officer(s):
Derek Hughes, President
Regina/South Saskatchewan
PO Box 3181, Regina SK S4P 3G7
www.pmisouthsask.org
Chief Officer(s):
Dawn Kobayashi, President
South Western Ontario
PO Box 583, Stn. B, London ON N6A 4W3
Tel: 226-377-0012
president@pmiswoc.org
www.pmiswoc.org
www.linkedin.com/groups?home=&gid=2425554
www.facebook.com/pmiswoc
twitter.com/pmiswoc
Chief Officer(s):
Danelle Peddell, President, 519-636-3605
president@pmiswoc.org
Southern Alberta
#400, 1040 - 7th Ave. SW, Calgary AB T2P 3G9
Tel: 403-244-4487; *Fax:* 403-244-2340
news@pmisac.com
www.pmisac.com
www.linkedin.com/groups?gid=79052
www.facebook.com/PMISAC
twitter.com/pmi_sac
Chief Officer(s):
Laurel Sim, President
president@pmisac.com
Southern Ontario
#300, 1370 Don Mills Rd., Toronto ON M3B 3N7
Tel: 416-381-4058; *Fax:* 416-441-0591
info@soc.pmi.on.ca
www.soc.pmi.on.ca
www.linkedin.com/groups?gid=48405
www.facebook.com/pmi.soc
twitter.com/PMI_SOC
www.youtube.com/PMInstitute
Chief Officer(s):
Felix Moshkovich, President
Vancouver Island
#8208, 706 Yates St., Victoria BC V8W 3R8
Tel: 250-356-5390
membership@pmivi.org
www.pmivancouverisland.com
twitter.com/pmivi
Chief Officer(s):
Calin Somosan, President
president@pmivi.org
West Coast
membership@pmi.bc.ca
www.pmi.bc.ca
Chief Officer(s):
Richard Brodowski, President
president@pmi.bc.ca

Public Services International (PSI) / Internationale des services publics

Centre d'Aumard, 45, av Voltaire, BP 9, F-01211, Ferney-Voltaire Cedex France
Tel: 330-450-406-464; *Fax:* 330-450-407-320
Other Communication: www.flickr.com/photos/psi_isp_iska
psi@world-psi.org
www.world-psi.org
www.facebook.com/56171560717
twitter.com/PSIglobalunion
www.youtube.com/user/PSIglobalunion
Overview: A large international organization founded in 1907
Mission: The international trade union federation which represents public sector trade unions in countries around the world; has consultative status with ECOSOC & observer status with other UN bodies such as UNCTAD & UNESCO
Chief Officer(s):
Dave Prentis, President
Rosa Pavanelli, General Secretary
Finances: *Annual Operating Budget:* Greater than $5 Million
Staff Member(s): 74
Membership: Represents over 20 million workers from 587 unions in 146 countries worldwide; *Fees:* 0.89 CHF/member, countries with above average GDP/capita; 0.27 CHF others; *Committees:* 4 regions within each of which are Regional, Regional Conference, & Woman's committees
Activities: National reports; conferences
Publications:
• FOCUS on public services [a publication of Public Services International]
Type: Magazine; *Editor:* Teresa Marshall *ISSN:* 1023-3431
• Youth to Youth [a publication of Public Services International]
Type: Magazine
Profile: News bulletin for young members in the Asia Pacific region

The Publishers Association (PA)

29B Montague St., London WC1B 5BW United Kingdom
Tel: 44-20-7691-9191; *Fax:* 44-20-7691-9199
mail@publishers.org.uk
www.publishers.org.uk
Overview: A medium-sized national organization founded in 1896
Mission: To represent the British book publishing industry; to negotiate & liaise with the government of the UK, the Commission of the EEC & other bodies in the book trade in the UK & in other countries; to collect essential data about the British publishing industry & its markets
Member of: International Publishers Association; Federation of European Publishers; National Book Committee; British Copyright Council
Chief Officer(s):
Richard Mollet, Chief Executive
Finances: *Annual Operating Budget:* $500,000-$1.5 Million
Staff Member(s): 19
Membership: 200; *Fees:* Sliding scale; *Committees:* Operates through three divisions: Book Development Council International (responsible for developing Britain's overseas markets); Educational Publishers Council (school markets); Council of Academic & Professional Publishers (responsible for tertiary, business & professional areas of publishing)

Rainforest Action Network (RAN)

#300, 425 Bush St., San Francisco CA 94108 USA
Tel: 415-398-4404; *Fax:* 415-398-2732
answers@ran.org
www.ran.org
www.facebook.com/rainforestactionnetwork
twitter.com/ran
www.youtube.com/user/ranvideo
Overview: A medium-sized international organization founded in 1985
Mission: To protect the Earth's rainforests & support the rights of their inhabitants through campaigns that work to bring corporate & government policies into alignment with popular support for rainforest conservation
Member of: Friends of the Earth International
Affliation(s): 150 Rainforest Action Groups (RAGs) in the US & Europe; the RAGs are informally affiliated with RAN, receiving support materials, but no funding; RAGs organize local community actions
Chief Officer(s):
James D. Gollin, President
Lindsey Allen, Executive Director
Finances: *Funding Sources:* 45% membership; 55% grants & donations
Staff Member(s): 35
Activities: Oil Exploration Campaign; Old Growth Wood Consumption Campaign; Traditional Forest Peoples Campaign; Education Campaign; Grass Roots Team; Zero Emissions Campaign; Global Finance Campaign; *Awareness Events:* World Rainforest Week; *Internships:* Yes *Library*

Rainforest Alliance (RA)

233 Broadway, 28th Fl., New York NY 10279 USA
Tel: 212-677-1900; *Fax:* 212-677-2187
info@ra.org
www.rainforest-alliance.org
www.facebook.com/8895898655
twitter.com/RnfrstAlliance
www.youtube.com/user/rainforestalliance
Overview: A medium-sized international charitable organization founded in 1987
Mission: To protect ecosystems & the people & wildlife that depend on them by transforming land-use practices, business practices & consumer behavior
Chief Officer(s):
Tensie Whelan, President
Finances: *Annual Operating Budget:* Greater than $5 Million
Staff Member(s): 300
Membership: 35,000; *Fees:* $35+ donation
Activities: *Internships:* Yes; *Rents Mailing List:* Yes

Red Hat Society Inc.

431 South Acacia Ave., Fullerton CA 92831 USA
Tel: 714-738-0001
Toll-Free: 866-386-2850
info@redhatsociety.com
www.redhatsociety.com
www.linkedin.com/company/1175774
www.facebook.com/RedHatSocietyPage
twitter.com/redhatsociety
Overview: A medium-sized international organization
Mission: To offer women an opportunity to have fun with kindred spirits
Affliation(s): 32 chapters across Canada (www.redhatchapters.com)
Membership: *Fees:* US$39 Queen; $US20 regular; *Member Profile:* Pink Hatters (pink hats & lavender clothing) - women younger than 50; Red Hatters - women 50 & older

Renaissance Society of America (RSA)

Graduate School & University Center, City University of New York, #5400, 365 Fifth Ave., New York NY 10016-4309 USA
Tel: 212-817-2130; *Fax:* 212-817-1544
rsa@rsa.org
www.rsa.org
Overview: A medium-sized international organization founded in 1954
Member of: American Council of Learned Societies
Affliation(s): International Federation of Renaissance Societies & Institutes
Chief Officer(s):
John Monfasani, Executive Director
Finances: *Annual Operating Budget:* $50,000-$100,000
Staff Member(s): 4
Membership: 3,000 individual + 1,200 institutional; *Fees:* Schedule available; *Member Profile:* Interest in the Renaissance Period
Awards:
• William Nelson Prize (Award)
$600 for best manuscript submitted to Renaissance Quarterly
• Phyllis Goodhart Gordan Book Prize (Award)
Annual book prize of $1,000
• Paul Oskar Kristeller Lifetime Achievement Award (Award)
Honours a scholar for lifetime achievement
• RSA Research Grants (Award)
Amount: 10 grants of $2,000 each

Renewable Natural Resources Foundation (RNRF)

5430 Grosvenor Lane, Bethesda MD 20814-2142 USA
Tel: 301-493-9101; *Fax:* 301-493-6148
info@rnrf.org
www.rnrf.org
Overview: A small national charitable organization founded in 1972
Mission: To advance sciences & public education in renewable natural resources; to promote the application of sound, scientific practices in managing & conserving renewable natural resources; to foster coordination & cooperation among professional, scientific & educational organizations having leadership responsibilities for renewable natural resources; to develop a Renewable Natural Resources Center
Chief Officer(s):
Robert D. Day, Executive Director
Staff Member(s): 5
Membership: 12; *Member Profile:* Professional & scientific societies with interest in natural resources
Activities: Public policy roundtables, national congresses, annual awards, quarterly journal, internship program; *Internships:* Yes
Awards:
• Outstanding Achievement Award (Award)
• Excellence in Journalism Award (Award)

Resource Recycling Inc.

PO Box 42270, Portland OR 97242-0270 USA

Tel: 503-233-1305; *Fax:* 503-233-1356
info@resource-recycling.com
www.resource-recycling.com
www.facebook.com/ResourceRecycling
twitter.com/rrecycling
Overview: A medium-sized international organization founded in 1982
Chief Officer(s):
Cara Bergeson, Publisher & Conference Manager
cara@resource-recycling.com
Finances: *Annual Operating Budget:* $500,000-$1.5 Million
Staff Member(s): 8
Activities: *Rents Mailing List:* Yes
Publications:
• Resource Recycling
Editor: Jerry Powell; *Price:* $52 annual subscription
Profile: Monthly magazine

Retail, Wholesale & Department Store Union (AFL-CIO/CLC) (RWDSU) / Union des employés de gros, de détail et de magasins à rayons (FAT-COI/CTC)

30 East 29 St., New York NY 10016 USA
Tel: 212-684-5300; *Fax:* 212-779-2809
info@rwdsu.org
www.rwdsu.org
www.facebook.com/pages/Retail-Wholesale-and-Department-Store-Union-RWD
twitter.com/RWDSU
www.youtube.com/RetailUnion
Overview: A large international organization founded in 1937
Mission: The Retail, Wholesale and Department Store Union, UFCW, CLC, represents workers throughout much of the United States and Canada. RWDSU members work in a wide variety of occupations that range from food processing to retail to manufacturing to service and health care
Chief Officer(s):
Jack Wurm, Sec.-Treas.
Stuart Appelbaum, President
Membership: 7,000 individuals + 12 locals + 1 joint council in Canada
Activities: *Internships:* Yes
Awards:
• Alvin E. Heaps Memorial Scholarship (Scholarship)

Rocky Mountain Elk Foundation Canada

5705 Grant Creek, Missoula MT 59808 USA
Tel: 406-523-4500
Toll-Free: 800-225-5355
www.rmef.org
facebook.com/RMEF1
twitter.com/RMEF
youtube.com/elkfoundation
Overview: A small local organization founded in 1984
Mission: To ensure the future of elk, other wildlife & their habitat

The Rocky Mountain Institute (RMI)

2317 Snowmass Creek Rd., Snowmass CO 81654 USA
Tel: 970-927-3851; *Fax:* 970-927-3420
media@rmi.org
www.rmi.org
www.linkedin.com/company/rocky-mountain-institute
www.facebook.com/RockyMtnInst
twitter.com/RockyMtnInst
www.youtube.com/user/RockyMtnInstitute
Overview: A medium-sized national organization founded in 1982
Mission: To foster the efficient & sustainable use of resources as a path to global security; focuses on five program areas - energy, water, agriculture, economic renewal, security; stresses understanding the interconnections between resource issues, honoring people's integrity, seeking ideas that transcend ideology & harnessing the problem-solving power of free-market economics
Chief Officer(s):
Michael Potts, President & CEO
Marty Pickett, Executive Director & General Counsel
Finances: *Annual Operating Budget:* Greater than $5 Million; *Funding Sources:* Personal donations; grants
Staff Member(s): 45
Membership: 23,000; *Fees:* $10
Activities: *Internships:* Yes; *Speaker Service:* Yes *Library* by appointment

Rosenthal Institute for Holocaust Studies

c/o Graduate Center of the City Univ. of New York, #5301, 365 - 5th Ave., New York NY 10016 USA
Tel: 212-817-1949
web.gc.cuny.edu/dept/cjstu/pages/Holocaust.html
Previous Name: Emeric & Ilana Csengeri Institute for Holocaust Studies
Overview: A small international organization founded in 1979
Mission: To conduct research revolving Holocaust
Member of: Centre for Jewish Studies
Chief Officer(s):
Randolph L. Braham, Director
rbraham@gc.cuny.edu
Activities: *Library* by appointment

Rotary International

One Rotary Center, 1560 Sherman Ave., Evanston IL 60201 USA
Tel: 847-866-3000; *Fax:* 847-328-8554
Toll-Free: 866-976-8279
contact.center@rotary.org
www.rotary.org
www.linkedin.com/groups?gid=858557
www.facebook.com/pages/Rotary-International/7268844551
twitter.com/rotary
www.youtube.com/user/RotaryInternational
Overview: A large international organization
Mission: To support its member clubs in fulfilling the Object of Rotary by fostering unity among member clubs, strengthening & expanding rotary around the world, communicating worldwide the work of Rotary & providing a system of international administration
Chief Officer(s):
Sakuji Tanaka, President
Membership: 1.2 million belonging to 33,000 clubs in 200 countries
Awards:
• Rotary Youth Leadership Awards (RYLA) (Award)
Meetings/Conferences:
• 106th Rotary International Convention, June, 2015, SÆo Paulo
Scope: International

The Royal Commonwealth Society

7 Lion Yard, Tremadoc Road, London SW4 7NQ United Kingdom
Tel: 44-0-20-7766-9200
info@thercs.org
thercs.org
www.linkedin.com/company/royal-commonwealth-society
www.facebook.com/thercs
twitter.com/TheRCSLondon
www.youtube.com/user/TheRCSociety
Previous Name: Royal Empire Society
Overview: A small international organization founded in 1868
Mission: To promote an understanding of the nature & working of the Commonwealth & of the factors which shape the lives of its peoples & the policies of its governments
Chief Officer(s):
Michael Lake, Director
michael.lake@thercs.org
Staff Member(s): 8

Royal Empire Society *See* The Royal Commonwealth Society

The Royal Scottish Country Dance Society (RSCDS)

12 Coates Cres., Edinburgh EH3 7AF UK
Tel: 44-0131-225-3854; *Fax:* 44-0131-225-7783
info@rscds.org
www.rscds.org
www.facebook.com/RSCDS
twitter.com/rscdsdancescot
www.youtube.com/user/TheRSCDS
Overview: A medium-sized international charitable organization founded in 1923
Mission: To preserve & further the practice of traditional Scottish Country Dancing; to provide or assist in providing special education or instruction in the practice of Scottish Country Dances
Chief Officer(s):
Elizabeth Foster, Executive Officer/Secretary
elizabeth.foster@rscds.org
Staff Member(s): 6
Membership: *Committees:* Education & Training; Membership Services; Youth Services

Burlington Branch
#416, 2085 Amherst Heights Dr., Burlington ON L7P 5C2
Tel: 905-331-7846
Chief Officer(s):
Susan Dilworth, Secretary
sdilworth1@bell.net

Calgary Branch
PO Box 1471, Stn. M, Calgary AB T2P 2L6
secretary@rscdscalgary.org
www.rscdscalgary.org
Chief Officer(s):
Ann Vanderwal, Secretary
Debby Henderson, President
president@rscdscalgary.org

Hamilton Branch
57 Foxborough Dr., Ancaster ON L9G 4Y8
Tel: 905-304-5437
www.rscdshamilton.org
Chief Officer(s):
Lynn Taplay, Secretary
letaplay@sympatico.ca

Kingston Branch
40 Murray Pl., Kingston ON K7N 1P6
Tel: 613-384-2597
www.rscdskingston.org
Chief Officer(s):
Mary Clipperton, Secretary
maryclipperton@yahoo.ca

Kitchener-Waterloo Branch
PO Box 40029, Stn. Waterloo Town Square, Waterloo ON N2J 4V1
Tel: 519-894-6995
secretaryws@rscds.kitchener.on.ca
www.rscds.kitchener.on.ca
Chief Officer(s):
Lynn Dramnitzki, Secretary

London Branch
PO Box 33012, 900 Oxford St. East, London ON N5Y 5A1
Tel: 519-641-3929
www.rscdslondoncanada.org
Chief Officer(s):
Margaret Campbell, Secretary
mecampbell517@gmail.com

Medicine Hat Branch
PO Box 447, Stn. Main, Medicine Hat AB T1A 7G2
Tel: 403-526-4599
rscdsmh@gmail.com
nonprofit.memlane.com/scottish
Chief Officer(s):
Stewart Kennedy, President

Montréal Branch
4435 Coronation Ave., Montreal QC H4B 2C3
Tel: 514-288-0992
info@scdmontreal.org
www.scdmontreal.org
Chief Officer(s):
Holly Boyd, Secretary
secretary@scdmontreal.org

Ottawa Branch
4385 Rainforest Dr., Ottawa ON K1V 1L4
Tel: 613-822-2252
chair@rscdsottawa.ca
www.rscdsottawa.ca
www.facebook.com/109552889062566
Chief Officer(s):
Jo Anne Thorp, Secretary
secretary@rscdsottawa.ca

St. John's Branch
PO Box 23097, Stn. Churchill Square, St. John's NL A1B 4J9
Tel: 709-754-1703
www.rscdsstjohns.ca
Chief Officer(s):
Catherine Wright, Chair
catherinewright@hotmail.com

Saskatchewan Branch
312 Willow St., Saskatoon SK S7J 0C6
Tel: 306-244-8283
info@rscdssask.org
www.rscdssask.org
Chief Officer(s):
Bob McNaughton, Secretary

Toronto Branch
#113, 942 Yonge St., Toronto ON M4W 3S8
Tel: 416-923-4392
www.rscdstoronto.org
Chief Officer(s):

Nancy White, Secretary
nawhite15@gmail.com
Vancouver Branch
8886 Hudson St., Vancouver BC V6P 4N2
secretary@rscdsvancouver.org
www.rscdsvancouver.org
Chief Officer(s):
Vicki Downey, Secretary, 604-298-9695
Vancouver Island Branch
PO Box 30123, Stn. Reynolds, 3943C Quadra St., Victoria BC V8X 1J5
viscds@shaw.ca
viscds.ca
Chief Officer(s):
Janet Yonge, Secretary
jebazett@gmail.com
Dora Dempster, President, 250-598-0207
dorademspter@shaw.ca
Windsor Branch
8444 Jerome St., Windsor ON N8S 4S1
Tel: 519-944-6823
www.rscdswindsor.org
Chief Officer(s):
June Dey, Contact, 519-974-1363
jbdey@cogeco.ca
Winnipeg Branch
821 Parkhill St., Winnipeg MB R2Y 0V4
Tel: 204-488-7386; *Fax:* 204-837-7346
info@rscdswinnipeg.ca
www.rscdswinnipeg.ca
Chief Officer(s):
Agnes Brydon, Secretary

The Royal Society for the Encouragement of Arts, Manufactures & Commerce (RSA)

8 John Adam St., London WC2N 6EZ United Kingdom
Tel: 44-020-7930-5115; *Fax:* 44-020-7839-5805
general@rsa.org.uk
www.rsa.org.uk
www.facebook.com/theRSAorg
twitter.com/theRSAorg
Overview: A medium-sized international charitable organization founded in 1754
Mission: To encourage the development of a principled, prosperous society & the release of human potential
Chief Officer(s):
Matthew Taylor, Chief Executive
Philip Duke of Edinburgh, President
Finances: *Annual Operating Budget:* $3 Million-$5 Million; *Funding Sources:* Membership fees; sponsorship for projects; conference facilities
Staff Member(s): 50
Membership: 27,000 fellows worldwide; *Committees:* Audit, Risk & Governance; Environment; Arts Advisory Group; Marketing Panel; History, Records & Collections Panel; Finance & General Purpose
Activities: *Library* by appointment

Rubber Manufacturers Association (RMA)

#900, 1400 K St. NW, Washington DC 20005 USA
Tel: 202-682-4800
info@rma.org
www.rma.org
Previous Name: The Scrap Tire Management Council
Overview: A small national organization founded in 1990
Mission: To advocate on behalf of the rubber products industry
Chief Officer(s):
Charles A. Cannon, President/CEO
Membership: *Member Profile:* Tire group companies include tire manufacturers & retread & repair material suppliers; Elastomer Products Group companies include manufacturers of non-tire elastomer products & suppliers of raw materials & machinery
Activities: Producing publications on consumer tire information, the market, industry standards, government affairs, safety, scrap tire activities, & tire service professionals; *Awareness Events:* National Tire Safety Week, June
Publications:
• Rubber Manufacturers Association Member Directory
Type: Directory
Profile: RMA member company contact & product information

Russian Association of Canadian Studies

Russian Academy of Sciences, 2/3 Khlebny Pereulok, Moscow 121814 Russia
Tel: 7-095-202-3084; *Fax:* 7-095-202-3016
racs@yandex.ru
Overview: A small international organization
Mission: Promotes study, research, teaching & publication about Canada in all academic disciplines
Member of: International Council for Canadian Studies
Chief Officer(s):
Tatiana Shchukina, Executive Director
Sergei Rogov, President
Membership: 160

Salt Institute

Fairfax Plaza, #600, 700 North Fairfax St., Alexandria VA 22314-2040 USA
Tel: 703-549-4648; *Fax:* 703-548-2194
info@saltinstitute.org
www.saltinstitute.org
www.facebook.com/ALittleSalt
twitter.com/WithALittleSalt
www.youtube.com/user/SaltGuru
Overview: A medium-sized national organization founded in 1914
Mission: To advocate fpr responsible salt use, enabling improved quality of water, healthy nutrition, & safe roadways.
Affliation(s): Transportation Association of Canada
Chief Officer(s):
Lori Roman, President
lori@saltinstitute.org
Jorge Amselle, Director, Communications
Finances: *Funding Sources:* Membership dues
Staff Member(s): 4
Membership: 37; *Fees:* Based on salt sales by company; *Member Profile:* Manufacturers, producers & sellers of sodium chloride
Activities: *Speaker Service:* Yes *Library*
Awards:
• Excellence in Storage Award (Award)

SCOPE for People with Cerebral Palsy

6 Market Rd., London N7 9PW United Kingdom
Tel: 0-20-7619-7100
response@scope.org.uk
www.scope.org.uk
www.linkedin.com/companies/165883
www.facebook.com/scope
twitter.com/scope
www.youtube.com/user/scopestories
Previous Name: The Spastics Society
Overview: A small international organization founded in 1952
Mission: To enable men, women & children with cerebral palsy & associated disabilities to claim their rights, lead fulfilling & rewarding lives & play a full part in society; to provide activities & services which respond to individuals' needs, choices & rights
Affliation(s): Canadian Cerebral Palsy Association
Chief Officer(s):
Richard Hawkes, Chief Executive
Finances: *Funding Sources:* Individual; corporate; events
Membership: *Committees:* Resources; Development; Audit
Activities: Creates housing, education & employment opportunities; provides expert & loving care; supports families, carers & self-help groups; *Speaker Service:* Yes *Library* Open to public by appointment

The Scrap Tire Management Council *See* Rubber Manufacturers Association

Screen Actors Guild - American Federation of Television & Radio Artists (SAG-AFTRA)

5757 Wilshire Blvd., 7th Fl., Los Angeles CA 90036-3600 USA
Tel: 323-954-1600
Toll-Free: 855-724-2387
sagaftrainfo@sagaftra.org
www.sagaftra.org
www.facebook.com/SAGAFTRA
twitter.com/SAGAFTRA
www.youtube.com/user/SAGAFTRATV
Merged from: Screen Actors Guild; American Federation of Television & Radio Artists
Overview: A small international organization founded in 2012
Mission: To ensure that its members receive fair wages, health benefits & work in safe conditions; to work to protect their members from exploitation
Member of: AFL-CIO
Chief Officer(s):
David White, National Executive Director
Mathis Dunn, Associate National Executive Director
Membership: 165,000; *Fees:* $198 + 1.575% of earnings under SAG-AFTRA from $1 to $500,000; *Member Profile:* Actors; announcers; broadcast journalists; DJs; news writers; news editors; program hosts; puppeteers; recording artists; singers; stunt performers; voiceover artists
New York Office
1900 Broadway, 5th Fl., New York NY 10023 USA
Tel: 212-944-1030

Screenprinting & Graphic Imaging Association International *See* Specialty Graphic Imaging Association

Sea Shepherd Conservation Society - USA (SSCS)

PO Box 2616, Friday Harbor WA 98250 USA
Tel: 360-370-5650; *Fax:* 360-370-5651
info@seashepherd.org
www.seashepherd.org
www.linkedin.com/company/590176?trk=tyah
www.facebook.com/seashepherdconservationsociety
twitter.com/seashepherd
www.youtube.com/seashepherd
Overview: A large international charitable organization founded in 1977
Mission: A direct action organization to protect dolphins, whales, seals & other marine life
Chief Officer(s):
Paul Watson, Founder & President
Carla Robinson, Administrative Director
Farley Mowat, Honorary Chair
Finances: *Annual Operating Budget:* $500,000-$1.5 Million; *Funding Sources:* Grants, public contributions
Staff Member(s): 5; 40 volunteer(s)
Membership: 30,000 worldwide; *Fees:* $25
Activities: Research, documentation & enforcement of international marine conservation law; *Rents Mailing List:* Yes *Library:* Sea Shepherd Media Library
Publications:
• Sea Shepard Log
Type: Newsletter; *Frequency:* Annual
Profile: Contains educational information on marine issues, updates on current laws and legislation, and updates on Sea Shepherd programs and activities.

SEDS - USA

M.I.T., 77 Massachusetts Ave., Rm. W20-445, Cambridge MA 02139-4307 USA
Tel: 617-253-8897; *Fax:* 617-253-8897
chair@seds.org
www.seds.org
www.facebook.com/sedsusa
twitter.com/sedsusa
Also Known As: Students for the Exploration & Development of Space
Overview: A medium-sized international organization founded in 1980
Mission: To operate as an international student-run space interest group, with chapters in Canada, the United States, South America, Europe, & Asia; To educate students & the public about space & space-related issues
Chief Officer(s):
Daniel Pastuf, Chair
Finances: *Funding Sources:* Chapter dues; corporate donations
Membership: 40 chapters; *Fees:* $25 chapter
Activities: Hosts an international conference; offers a space information e-mail network (SEDSNEWS) & a communications e-mail link for members internationally (SEDSLINK);

Service Employees International Union (AFL-CIO/CLC) / Union internationale des employés des services (FAT-COI/CTC)

1800 Massachusetts Ave. NW, Washington DC 20036 USA
Tel: 202-730-7000; *Fax:* 202-898-3402
Toll-Free: 800-424-8592; *TTY:* 202-730-7481
Other Communication: www.flickr.com/photos/seiu
www.seiu.org
www.facebook.com/SEIU
twitter.com/SEIU
www.youtube.com/user/SEIU
Overview: A large international organization
Mission: SEIU is focused on uniting workers in 3 sectors: healthcare, property services, & public services. The union aims to improve the lives of its members, their families, & the services they provide.
Chief Officer(s):
Mary Kay Henry, President
Finances: *Annual Operating Budget:* Greater than $5 Million

Membership: 3 million
Activities: *Internships:* Yes; *Speaker Service:* Yes *Library* by appointment

SEIU Healthcare
125 Mural St., Richmond Hill ON L4B 1M4
Tel: 905-695-1767; *Fax:* 905-695-1768
Toll-Free: 800-267-7348
info@seiuhealthcare.ca
www.seiu.ca
www.facebook.com/SEIUHealthcareCanada
twitter.com/seiucanada
www.youtube.com/user/seiulocal1canada
Chief Officer(s):
Sharleen Stewart, President

Service social international *See* International Social Service

Seva Foundation
1786 - 5th St., Berkeley CA 94710 USA
Tel: 510-845-7382; *Fax:* 510-845-7410
Toll-Free: 877-764-7382
www.seva.org
www.facebook.com/seva.foundation
twitter.com/Seva_Foundation
Overview: A small international charitable organization founded in 1979
Mission: To prevent & relieve suffering; to generate hope through compassionate action
Chief Officer(s):
Jack Blanks, Executive Director
Staff Member(s): 30

Sheet Metal & Air Conditioning Contractors' National Association (SMACNA)
PO Box 221230, 4201 Lafayette Center Dr., Chantilly VA 20153-1230 USA
Tel: 703-803-2980; *Fax:* 703-803-3732
info@smacna.org
www.smacna.org
www.facebook.com/SMACNA
Overview: A large international organization founded in 1943
Finances: *Funding Sources:* Membership dues; Industry fund
Staff Member(s): 34
Membership: 1,800
Meetings/Conferences:
• Sheet Metal and Air Conditioning Contractors' National Association (SMACNA) 72nd Annual Convention, September, 2015, The Broadmoor Hotel, Colorado Springs, CO
Scope: National
Contact Information: SMACNAConvention@cmrus.com; Phone: 800-336-9704
• Sheet Metal and Air Conditioning Contractors' National Association (SMACNA) 73rd Annual Convention, October, 2016, JW Marriott Desert Ridge, Phoenix, AZ
Scope: National
Contact Information: SMACNAConvention@cmrus.com; Phone: 800-336-9704
• Sheet Metal and Air Conditioning Contractors' National Association (SMACNA) 74th Annual Convention, 2017
Scope: National
Contact Information: SMACNAConvention@cmrus.com; Phone: 800-336-9704

Sheet Metal Workers' International Association (AFL-CIO/CFL) (SMWIA) / Association internationale des travailleurs du métal en feuilles (FAT-COI/FCT)
1750 New York Ave. NW, 6th Fl., Washington DC 20006 USA
Toll-Free: 800-457-7694
www.smwia.org
www.facebook.com/smartunion
twitter.com/smwia
Overview: A small international organization
Mission: To establish & maintain desirable working conditions for its members, & is their collective bargaining agent.
Affiliation(s): American Federation of Labor & Congress of Industrial Organizations; Canadian Labour Congress
Chief Officer(s):
Joseph J. Nigro, General President
Membership: 150,000; *Member Profile:* Men & women employed in the United States, Canada & Puerto Rico, working in the construction, manufacturing, service, railroad & shipyard industries

Canadian Office
190 Thames Rd. East, Exeter ON N0M 1S3

Sierra Club
85 Second St., 2nd Fl., San Francisco CA 94105-3441 USA
Tel: 415-977-5500; *Fax:* 415-977-5797
information@sierraclub.org
www.sierraclub.org
www.facebook.com/SierraClub
twitter.com/sierra_club
Overview: A large international organization founded in 1892
Mission: To promote conservation of the natural environment by influencing public policy decisions - legislative, administrative, legal & electoral; to explore, enjoy & protect the wild places of the earth; to practise & promote the responsible use of the earth's ecosystems & resources; to educate & enlist humanity to protect & restore the quality of the natural & human environment; to use all lawful means to carry out these objectives at the federal, state & local levels
Chief Officer(s):
Michael Brune, Executive Director
Robin Mann, President
Finances: *Annual Operating Budget:* $3 Million-$5 Million
Membership: 1,300,000; *Fees:* $15-$100
Activities: Conservation Programs (lobbying, expert testimony, grassroots activism, public education on major conservation campaigns); Sierra Book Clubs (nearly 600 titles published - 100 Bush St., 13th Fl., San Francisco, CA 94104 415/291-1600); Outings; *Awareness Events:* John Muir Day, April 21 *Library*
Publications:
• Sierra
Type: Magazine

Sjogren's Syndrome Foundation Inc. (SSF)
#325, 6707 Democracy Blvd., Bethesda MD 20817 USA
Tel: 301-530-4420; *Fax:* 301-530-4415
Toll-Free: 800-475-6473
tms@sjogrens.org
www.sjogrens.org
www.facebook.com/SjogrensSyndromeFoundation
twitter.com/MoistureSeekers
Also Known As: The Moisture Seekers
Overview: A medium-sized international charitable organization founded in 1983
Mission: To educate patients & their families about Sjogren's syndrome; to increase public & professional awareness of Sjogren's syndrome; to encourage research into new treatments & a cure; provides patients practical information & coping strategies that minimize the effects of Sjogren's syndrome; Foundation is clearing house for medication information & is the recognized national advocate for Sjogren's syndrome
Chief Officer(s):
Steven Taylor, CEO
staylor@sjogrens.org
Desiree Roell, BC Support Group Leader, 250-838-9378
Betty Ponder, NB Contact, 506-450-9929
Ginette Texier, Montreal Support Group Leader, 514-934-3666
Lee Durdon, Ontario Support Group Leader, 888-558-0950
Joan Williams, Newfoundland Contact, 709-579-9272
Finances: *Annual Operating Budget:* $1.5 Million-$3 Million; *Funding Sources:* Membership dues; contributions
Staff Member(s): 9
Membership: 6,000 internationally; *Fees:* US$32 US; US$38 Canada; US$45 Overseas
Activities: *Library* by appointment

Slow Food
Piazza XX Settembre, 5, Bra 12042 Italy
Tel: 39-0172-419-611; *Fax:* 39-0172-421-293
international@slowfood.com
www.slowfood.com
www.facebook.com/slowfoodinternational
twitter.com/SlowFoodHQ
Overview: A medium-sized international organization founded in 1986
Mission: To protect the pleasures of the table from the homogenization of modern fast food & life; to promote gastronomic culture; to develop taste education; to conserve agricultural biodiversity & to protect traditional foods at risk of extinction
Chief Officer(s):
Carlo Petrini, Founder
Membership: 85,000; 800 convivia in 132 countries

Small Publishers Association of North America (SPAN)
PO Box 9725, Colorado Springs CO 80932-0725 USA
Tel: 719-924-5534; *Fax:* 719-213-2602
info@spannet.org
www.spannet.org
Overview: A medium-sized international organization founded in 1996
Mission: To advance the image & profits of independent publishers & authors, through education & marketing opportunities
Chief Officer(s):
Brian Jud, Executive Director
Membership: *Member Profile:* Independent publishers, self publishers, & authors in Canada & the USA

Snack Food Association
#650, 1600 Wilson Blvd., Arlington VA 22209 USA
Tel: 703-836-4500; *Fax:* 703-836-8262
Toll-Free: 800-628-1334
sfa@sfa.org
www.sfa.org
Overview: A medium-sized international organization founded in 1937
Mission: To provide value for members by offering services & relationship building that strengthen the performance of member companies & support industry growth
Chief Officer(s):
James A. McCarthy, President & CEO
jmccarthy@sfa.org
Membership: 800+ companies worldwide;

Societas Internationalis Limnologiae *See* International Society of Limnology

Société Cousteau *See* The Cousteau Society

Société des tribologistes et ingénieurs en lubrification *See* Society of Tribologists & Lubrication Engineers

Société internationale arthurienne *See* International Arthurian Society - North American Branch

Société internationale d'amitié et de bonne volonté *See* International Society of Friendship & Good Will

Société internationale de biométéorolgy *See* International Society of Biometeorology

La Société internationale de Chirurgie *See* International Society of Surgery

Société Internationale de Mécanique des Sols et de la Géotechnique *See* International Society for Soil Mechanics & Geotechnical Engineering

Société internationale de sociologie des religions (SISR) / International Society for the Sociology of Religion (ISSR)
c/o Giuseppe Giordan, General Secretary, Università di Padova, Dipartimento di Sociologia, Via cesarotti, 10, Padova 35123 Italy
Tél: +39.049.8274325; *Téléc:* +39.049.657508
www.sisr.org
Aperçu: *Dimension:* petite; *Envergure:* internationale; fondée en 1948
Membre(s) du bureau directeur:
Giuseppe Giordan, Secrétaire générale
generalsecretary.issr@unipd.it
Finances: *Budget de fonctionnement annuel:* Moins de $50,000; *Fonds:* Cotisations des membres
2 bénévole(s)
Membre: 300; *Montant de la cotisation:* 106 E; *Critères d'admissibilite:* En sciences sociales des religions

Société internationale pour l'enseignement commercial *See* International Society for Business Education

Société internationale pour l'étude de la philosophie médiévale (SIEPM) / International Society for the Study of Medieval Philosophy
Universitat Freiburg, Philosophisches Seminar, Werthmannplatz 3, Freiburg D-79085 Germany
Tél: 49-761-203-2439; *Téléc:* 49-761-203-9260
www.siepm.uni-freiburg.de
Aperçu: *Dimension:* moyenne; *Envergure:* internationale; fondée en 1958
Mission: A pour but la coordination des recherches scientifiques sur la pensée médiévale
Membre(s) du bureau directeur:
Maarten Hoenen, Secrétaire général
Josep Puig Montada, Chair
Membre: 660; *Montant de la cotisation:* 35 Euro
Activités: *Bibliothèque*

Society for Adolescent Health & Medicine (SAHM)
#100, 111 Deer Lake Rd., Deerfield IL 60015 USA
Tel: 847-753-5226; *Fax:* 847-480-9282
sahm@adolescenthealth.org
www.adolescenthealth.org
www.facebook.com/adolescenthealth.medicine
twitter.com/SAHMtweets
www.youtube.com/SAHMAdolescentHealth
Overview: A medium-sized international organization founded in 1968
Mission: To advance the physical & psychosocial health & well-being of adolescents & young adults; To improve the delivery of health services for adolescents; To promote the field of adolescent medicine & health
Chief Officer(s):
Susan Tibbitts, Executive Director
Ryan Norton, Director, Administration
Kasia Chalko, Manager, Marketing Communications
Staff Member(s): 9
Membership: *Fees:* Schedule available; *Member Profile:* Healthcare professionals, from a wide range of disciplines from thirty countries, who want to learn more about adolescent health; *Committees:* Awards; Clinical Services; Communications & Media Relations; FSAHM Review; Development; Diversity; Education; Multidisciplinary Membership; Research; Work Force
Activities: Engaging in advocacy activities; Promoting optimal health; Providing professional development activities; Researching
Publications:
• Journal of Adolescent Health
Type: Journal; *Frequency:* Monthly; *Editor:* Charles E. Irwin, Jr., M.D., FSAM; *Price:* Free with Society forAdolescent Medicine membership dues
Profile: Peer-reviewed articles on clinical medicine, public health policy, youth development, international health, & behavioral science
• SAM Newsletter
Type: Newsletter; *Frequency:* Quarterly
Profile: News from programs & members, presidential messages, announcements, committee reports, special interest group reports, professional development opportunities, & chapter activities

Society for Conservation Biology (SCB)
1017 O St. NW, Washington DC 20001-4229 USA
Tel: 202-234-4133; *Fax:* 703-995-4633
info@conbio.org
www.conbio.org
www.facebook.com//227557507333973
twitter.com/Society4ConBio
www.youtube.com/user/society4conbio
Overview: A medium-sized international organization founded in 1985
Mission: To advance the scientific study of the phenomena that affect the maintenance, loss, & restoration of biological diversity; To promote the practice of conserving biological diversity
Chief Officer(s):
Geri Unger, Executive Director, 202-234-4133 Ext. 102
gunger@conbio.org
Membership: 10,000+; *Member Profile:* Persons from around the world, who are interested in the study & conservation of biological diversity, such as conservation workers, educators, government workers, resource managers, & students
Activities: Providing recommendations about policies to advance the conservation of biological diversity; Developing educational programs; Providing mentorship opportunities in the field of conservation; Facilitating networking with the professional community
Publications:
• Conservation
Type: Magazine; *Frequency:* Quarterly; *Accepts Advertising*; *Editor:* Kathryn A. Kohm
Profile: Conservation articles for members of the Society for Conservation Biology
• Conservation Biology
Type: Journal; *Frequency:* Bimonthly; *Editor:* Erica Fleishman
ISSN: 0888-8892
Profile: Information about conservation science for members of the Society for Conservation Biology
• Conservation Letters, A Journal of the Society for Conservation Biology
Type: Journal; *Editor:* Corey Bradshaw
Profile: Empirical, theoretical, & interdisciplinary research about the conservation of biological diversity worldwide
• SCB [Society for Conservation Biology] Newsletter
Type: Newsletter; *Frequency:* Quarterly; *Editor:* Sharon Collinge; *Price:* Free with membership in the Society for Conservation Biology

Society for Ecological Restoration International (SER)
1017 O St. NW, Washington DC 20001 USA
Tel: 202-299-9518; *Fax:* 270-626-5485
info@ser.org
www.ser.org
www.linkedin.com/groups/Society-Ecological-Restoration-4076378
www.facebook.com/SocietyforEcologicalRestoration
twitter.com/SERestoration
Overview: A medium-sized international organization founded in 1988
Mission: To promote ecological restoration as a means of sustaining the diversity of life; To reestablish an ecologically healthy relationship between nature & culture
Chief Officer(s):
Steve Bosak, Executive Director
steve@ser.org
Levi Wickwire, Manager, Program
levi@ser.org
Leah Bregman, Manager, Membership & Communications
leah@ser.org
Staff Member(s): 5
Membership: *Fees:* Schedule available; *Member Profile:* Individuals & organizations involved in ecologically-sensitive repair & the management of ecosystems, such as scientists, ecological consultants, planners, engineers, teachers, growers, & natural areas managers; *Committees:* Executive; Assessment; Board Development; Finance; Science & Policy
Activities: Raising public awareness of restoration; Facilitating communication among restorationists; Encouraging research; Providing input to discussions of public policy
Awards:
• John Rieger Award (Award)
Awarded to those that have dedicated their time & skills to the advancement of ecological restoration &/or to the devleopment of the Society
• Model Project Award (Award)
Recognizes those restoration projects that have truly advanced with craft of ecosystem restoration & upon which future projects may well be modeled
• Full Circle Award (Award)
Awarded to those indigenous people whose projects have brought ecosystems full circle, returning them to their condition prior to the impacts caused by non-indigenous peoples
• Project Facilitation Award (Award)
Awarded in recognition of well-conceived & properly initiated ecosystem restoration projects that may require or significantly benefit from supplemental funding
• Theodore M. Sperry Award (Award)
Recognizes achievement in those elements & approaches that improve restoration programs
• Communication Award (Award)
Acknowledges the importance of all forms of communication that advance the goals of the Society
Publications:
• Ecological Restoration
Type: Journal; *Frequency:* Quarterly; *Price:* Included with Society for Ecological Restoration International membership
Profile: Philosophical essays & summaries of current projects & techniques
• Restoration Ecology
Type: Journal; *Frequency:* Quarterly
Profile: Peer-reviewed scientific & technical research articles on topics of restoration & ecological principles
• Restore [a publication of the Society for Ecological Restoration International]
Type: Newsletter; *Frequency:* Weekly
Profile: Annotated links to news stories from around the globe
• Society for Ecological Restoration International Newsletter
Type: Newsletter; *Frequency:* Quarterly
Profile: Up-to-date information for members about the Society & it chapters

British Columbia Branch
c/o Montane Environmental Services, #A, 258 Robertson St.,
Victoria BC V8S 3X5
m_giasson@shaw.ca
Chief Officer(s):
Moss Giasson, Contact

Ontario Branch
ON
info@serontario.org
www.serontario.org
Chief Officer(s):
Stephen Murphy, Chair
chair@serontario.org
Amanda Newell, Contact
communications@serontario.org

Society for Environmental Graphic Design (SEGD)
#400, 1000 Vermont Ave. NW, Washington DC 20005 USA
Tel: 202-638-5555; *Fax:* 202-478-2286
segd@segd.org
www.segd.org
www.linkedin.com/groups?gid=1806064
www.facebook.com/SEGDcommunity
twitter.com/segd
Overview: A medium-sized international organization
Mission: To promote graphic design & educate the public about the graphic design community
Chief Officer(s):
Clive Roux, Chief Executive Officer, 202-638-5555
clive@segd.org
Ann Makowski, Chief Operating Officer, 202-638-5555
ann@segd.org
Jill Ayers, President
Staff Member(s): 10
Membership: *Fees:* Schedule available; *Member Profile:* Individuals who work in the planning, design, fabrication, & implementation of communications in the built environment
Activities: Fostering research; Providing educational resources; Refining standards of practice; Collaborating across various design disciplines; Offering referrals to fabricators or designers; Providing networking opportunities
Publications:
• segdDESIGN: The International Journal of Environmental Graphic Design
Type: Journal; *Frequency:* Quarterly; *Accepts Advertising*; *Editor:* Pat Matson Knapp
Profile: Information about the people, research, technologies, materials, & resources that influence communications in the built environment
• Society for Environmental Graphic Design Membership Directory
Type: Directory

Society for Ethnomusicology (SEM)
Business Office, #005, Morrison Hall, Indiana University, 1165 East 3rd St., Bloomington IN 47405-3700 USA
Tel: 812-855-6672; *Fax:* 812-855-6673
sem@indiana.edu
webdb.iu.edu/sem/scripts/home.cfm
Overview: A medium-sized international organization founded in 1955
Member of: American Council of Learned Societies
Chief Officer(s):
Steve Stuempfle, Executive Director
semexec@indiana.edu
Membership: 1,108 individual + 929 institutional; *Fees:* $60-$105 individual; $40 student; *Member Profile:* Interest in the field of ethnomusicology

Society for Information Management (SIM)
#C, 15000 Commerce Parkway, Mount Laurel NJ 08054 USA
Tel: 856-380-6807
sim@simnet.org
www.simnet.org
www.linkedin.com/groups?gid=1812580
twitter.com/SIMInt
www.youtube.com/user/societyofIM
Overview: A medium-sized international organization founded in 1968
Mission: To support IT leaders by increasing the knowledge base of SIM members & associates; giving back to local communities; being the voice of the IT commhnity on critical issues; developing the next generation of effective IT leaders
Chief Officer(s):
Patricia A. Coffey, Chair
Amy Williams, Chief Staff Executive, 856-642-4417
Membership: 3,500; *Fees:* $190 individual; $95 non-profit/academic

Society for Research in Child Development (SRCD)
#401, 2950 South State St., Ann Arbor MI 48104 USA

Tel: 734-926-0600; *Fax:* 734-926-0601
info@srcd.org
www.srcd.org
www.linkedin.com/company/society-for-research-in-child-development
www.facebook.com/143127176115
twitter.com/SRCDtweets
Overview: A medium-sized international organization founded in 1933
Mission: To promote multidisciplinary research in the field of human development; To encourage applications of research findings
Chief Officer(s):
Lonnie Sherrod, Executive Director, 734-926-0611, Fax: 734-926-0601
sherrod@srcd.org
Susan Lennon, Deputy Executive Director, 734-926-0619, Fax: 734-926-0601
slennon@srcd.org
Staff Member(s): 17
Membership: 5,400+; *Fees:* Schedule available; *Member Profile:* Multidisciplinary professionals, such as practitioners, researchers, & human development professionals, from more than 50 countries; *Committees:* Ethic & Racial Issues; History; International Affairs; Policy & Communications; Programs; Publications; Audit; Awards; Equity & Justice; Finance; Interdisciplinary; Nominations; Student & Early Career Council; Teaching
Activities: Facilitating the exchange of information among scientists & other professionals
Meetings/Conferences:
• Society for Research in Child Development 2015 Biennial Meeting, March, 2015, Philadelphia, PA
Scope: International
Contact Information: Biennial Meeting Planner: Hailey Buck, Phone: 734-926-0613, Fax: 734-926-0601, E-mail: hkbuck@srcd.org, biennialmeeting@srcd.org
Publications:
• Child Development
Type: Journal; *Accepts Advertising*; *Editor:* Detra Davis
Profile: Topics in child development from the fetal period through adolescence
• Child Development Perspectives
Type: Journal; *Editor:* Detra Davis
Profile: Emerging trends or conclusions within domains of developmental research
• Developments
Type: Newsletter; *Frequency:* Quarterly; *Accepts Advertising*
• Monographs of Society for Research in Child Development
Frequency: 3-4 pa; *Editor:* Detra Davis
Profile: In-depth research studies in child development & related disciplines
• Social Policy Report
Editor: Amy D. Glaspie

Society for Research on Nicotine & Tobacco (SNRT)

2424 American Lane, Madison WI 53704 USA
Tel: 608-443-2462; *Fax:* 608-443-2474
info@srnt.org
www.srnt.org
Overview: A small international organization
Mission: To generate new knowledge about nicotine
Chief Officer(s):
Bruce Wheeler, Executive Director, 608-443-2462 Ext. 143
Dianne Benson, Financial Contact, 608-443-2462 Ext. 147
Membership: *Member Profile:* Full members possess training beyond the undergraduate level, plus at least one peer-reviewed publication on nicotine, tobacco-control, or a related topic; Affiliate members possess a documented interest in some aspect of research on nicotine or tobacco-control; Retired full members; Students; *Committees:* Awards; Development; Finance; Membership; Nominations; Program; Publications; Training; Website
Activities: Encouraging scientific research on on public health efforts for the prevention & treatment of cigarette & tobacco use; Sponsoring publications & scientific meetings on the effects of nicotine; Engaging in advocacy activities;
Meetings/Conferences:
• 2015 Society for Research on Nicotine and Tobacco 20th Annual Meeting, February, 2015, Philadelphia Marriott Hotel, Philadelphia, PA
Scope: International
Contact Information: Jane Shepard; meetings@srnt.org
Publications:
• Nicotine & Tobacco Research: The Journal of SRNT [Society for Research on Nicotine & Tobacco]
Type: Journal; *Frequency:* Monthly *ISSN:* 1462-2203
Profile: Peer reviewed articles about the study of nicotine & tobacco
• Society for Research on Nicotine & Tobacco Annual Meeting Abstracts
Type: Yearbook; *Frequency:* Annually
• SRNT [Society for Research on Nicotine & Tobacco] Newsletter
Type: Newsletter; *Editor:* Karen Cropsey
Profile: Current society information for members, featuring reviews, meetings, publications, position openings, & funding news
• SRNT [Society for Research on Nicotine & Tobacco] Membership Directory
Type: Directory

Society for Technical Communication (STC)

#300, 9401 Lee Hwy., Fairfax VA 22031 USA
Tel: 703-522-4114; *Fax:* 703-522-2075
www.stc.org
www.linkedin.com/groups?gid=2926
www.facebook.com/stc.org
twitter.com/stc_org
www.youtube.com/user/society4techcomm
Overview: A medium-sized international organization
Mission: To work together in a spirit of community to promote & develop professional technical communication
Chief Officer(s):
Chris Lyons, Executive Director, 571-366-1901
chris.lyons@stc.org
Membership: 16,000 worldwide; *Member Profile:* Technical writers; editors; graphic designers; multimedia artists; web & intranet page information designers; translators; others that make technical information understandable & available to those who need it

Alberta Chapter
#494, 3553 - 31 St. NW, Calgary AB T2L 2K7
secretary@stc-alberta.org
www.stc-alberta.org/wp
www.linkedin.com/groups/STC-Alberta-3904559?trk=myg_ugrp_ovr
twitter.com/#STCAlberta
Mission: Represents technical communicators within Alberta, Saskatchewan, and the Northwest Territories.
Chief Officer(s):
Jessie Channey, President
president@stc-alberta.org

Canada West Coast Chapter
#415, 2416 Main St., Vancouver BC V5T 3E2
secretary@stc-alberta.org
stcwestcoast.ca
www.linkedin.com/groups/STC-Canada-West-Coast-122291/about
www.facebook.com/stccwc
twitter.com/stccwc
Mission: To provide knowledge and to build connection between peers in order to strengthen the role of technical communication in industry.
Chief Officer(s):
Aaron Fultz, President, 604-347-6521
president@stcwestcoast.ca

Manitoba Chapter
MB
www.stcmanitoba.org
Chief Officer(s):
Andrew Quarry, President
andrewquarry@shaw.ca

Southwestern Ontario Chapter
ON
www.stc-soc.org
www.linkedin.com/company/southwestern-ontario-chapter-stc
www.facebook.com/279888462067083
twitter.com/STC_SOC
www.youtube.com/watch?v=ARkkVuxwz-c
Chief Officer(s):
Rob Cundari, President
rcundari@technicallywrite.ca

Society for the History of Technology (SHOT)

c/o Dept. of Science, Technology & Society, University of Virginia, PO Box 400744, Charlottesville VA 22904-4744 USA
Tel: 434-987-6230; *Fax:* 434-975-2190
shot@virginia.edu
www.historyoftechnology.org
www.facebook.com/historyoftechnology
Overview: A large national organization founded in 1958
Mission: To promote the historical study of technology & its relation to politics, economics, labor, business, the environment, public policy, science, & the arts
Member of: American Council of Learned Societies
Affliation(s): American Association for the Advancement of Science; American Historical Association
Chief Officer(s):
Ron Kline, President
rrk1@cornell.edu
Bruce Seely, Vice President
bseely@mtu.edu
Finances: *Annual Operating Budget:* Less than $50,000
Membership: 1,500 individual + 1,000 institutional; *Fees:* $60 individual; *Member Profile:* Persons with an interest in the development of technology & its relations with society & culture; *Committees:* Nominating; Editorial; Awards; Finance; Sites; Program; International Scholars
Activities: Special interest groups; Young Scholars Travel Support; Secondary Education Project
Awards:
• Leonardo da Vinci Medal (Award)
For outstanding contribution to the history of technology, through research, teaching, publications, and other activities
• Sidney Edelstein Prize (Award)
Recognizing outstanding scholarly work in the history of technology.
• Sally Hacker Prize (Award)
Established in 1999 to honor exceptional scholarship that reaches beyond the academy toward a broad audience.
• Abbot Payson Usher Prize (Award)
Awarded annually to honor the best scholarly work published under the auspices of SHOT.
• Joan Cahalin Robinson Prize (Award)
Awarded for the best-presented paper at the SHOT annual meeting by a scholar of any age presenting for the first time.
• Samuel Eleazar and Rose Tartakow Levinson Prize (Award)
For an original essay in the history of technology that examines technology within the framework of social or intellectual history.
• IEEE Life Members' Prize in Electrical History (Award)
For the best article in the history of electrotechnology-power, electronics, telecommunications, and computer science.
• Dibner Award for Excellence in Museum Exhibits (Award)
Recognizing museums and exhibits that interpret the history of technology, industry, and engineering to the general public.
• Eugene S. Ferguson Prize (Award)
For original reference works that support future scholarship in the history of technology.
Publications:
• Technology and Culture
Type: Journal

Society for the Preservation & Encouragement of Barber Shop Quartet Singing in America Inc. *See* Barbershop Harmony Society

Society for the Prevention of Cruelty to Animals International (SPCA)

PO Box 8682, New York NY 10001 USA
www.spcai.org
www.facebook.com/pages/SPCA-International/336727290576
twitter.com/SPCAINT
Also Known As: SPCA International
Overview: A large international charitable organization founded in 2006
Mission: To advocates for humane laws; To promote humane education & public awareness of the humane treatment of animals; To assist animals in areas of conflict and disaster
Finances: *Funding Sources:* Fundraising; Public donations

Society for the Study of Pathophysiology of Pregnancy

www.gestosis.ge
Also Known As: Organisation Gestosis
Overview: A medium-sized international organization founded in 1969
Mission: To spread knowledge about EPH-Gestosis, training, exchange of information amongst scientists; to standartize nomenclature, classification & definition of EPH - Gestosis
Affliation(s): International Federation of Social Workers; International Federation for Medical & Biological Engineering; Canadian Public Health Association; Society of Obstetricians & Gynaecologists of Canada
Chief Officer(s):

Sanjay Gupte, Secretary General
guptehospital@gmail.com
Finances: *Annual Operating Budget:* Less than $50,000
Membership: 4,500; *Fees:* US$50; *Member Profile:* MDs, RNs, midwives, social workers; *Committees:* O.G. Press; Consulting; Steering
Activities: Annual meetings; discussion groups; congresses; exchange of scientists; postgraduate training; *Internships:* Yes; *Speaker Service:* Yes *Library* by appointment

Society of Actuaries (SOA)
#600, 475 North Martingale Rd., Schaumburg IL 60173 USA
Tel: 847-706-3500; *Fax:* 847-706-3599
customerservice@soa.org
www.soa.org
twitter.com/soasupport
Overview: A medium-sized international organization
Mission: To advance actuarial knowledge & improve decision making to benefit society
Chief Officer(s):
Errol Cramer, President
Greg Heidrich, Executive Director
gheidrich@soa.org
Membership: 24,000 worldwide; *Member Profile:* Actuaries in the United States, Canada & worldwide; *Committees:* Admissions; Audit; Employers; Finance; International; Issues Advisory; Leadership Development; Leadership Team; Learning Strategy Task Force; Marketing Executive; Nominating; Policy; Research Executive; Risk
Activities: Professional development; education; research
Publications:
• The Actuary Magazine [a publication of the Society of Actuaries]
Type: Magazine; *Frequency:* bi-m.
• The Future Actuary [a publication of the Society of Actuaries]
Type: Newsletter; *Frequency:* q.
• In Touch: Your Canadian Connection [a publication of the Society of Actuaries]
Type: Newsletter; *Frequency:* q.
• The North American Actuarial Journal [a publication of the Society of Actuaries]
Type: Journal
• SOA [Society of Actuaries] Candidate Connect
Type: eNewsletter
• SOA [Society of Actuaries] News Weekly
Type: eNewsletter

Society of Architectural Historians (SAH)
1365 North Astor St., Chicago IL 60610-2144 USA
Tel: 312-573-1365; *Fax:* 312-573-1141
info@sah.org
www.sah.org
www.linkedin.com/company/1359199?trk=tyah
www.facebook.com/289376327346
twitter.com/sah1365
sahcommunities.groupsite.com/main/summary
Overview: A large international organization founded in 1940
Mission: To advance knowledge & understanding of the history of architecture, design, landscape & urbanism worldwide
Member of: American Council of Learned Societies
Chief Officer(s):
Abigail Van Slyck, President
Ken Breisch, 1st Vice-President
Ken Tadashi, 2nd Vice-President
Pauline Saliga, Executive Director
psaliga@sah.org
Staff Member(s): 5
Membership: 3,500; *Fees:* Schedule available; *Member Profile:* Interest in past, present & future architecture
Activities: *Internships:* Yes
Awards:
• Founder's Award (Award)
Awarded each year to a young scholar for the best article on the history of architecture published each year in the Society's Journal
• Spiro Kostof Book Award (Award)
Awarded each year for a work in any discipline that has made the greatest contribution to our understanding of the physical environment published in English worldwide during the previous two years
• Alice Davis Hitchcock Book Award (Award)
Awarded each year for the publication of the most distinguished work of scholarship in the history of architecture by a North American Scholar during the preceding two years
• Antoinette Forrester Downing Award (Award)
Awarded each year for excellence in architectural surveys published during the previous two years
• Architectural Exhibition Catalogue Award (Award)
Awarded each year in recognition of excellence in architectural exhibition catalogue publication during the previous two years
• SAH Membership Grant for Emerging Professionals (Grant)
Awarded each year in recognition of excellence in architectural exhibition catalogue publication during the previous two yearsEligibility: Entry-level college and university professors and other new professionals engaged in the study of the built environment.
Meetings/Conferences:
• 68th Society of Architectural Historians Annual Conference, April, 2015, Chicago, IL
Scope: International
• 69th Society of Architectural Historians Annual Conference, April, 2016, Pasadena, CA
Scope: International
• 70th Society of Architectural Historians Annual Conference, June, 2017, Glasgow
Scope: International
• 71st Society of Architectural Historians Annual Conference, 2018
Scope: International

Society of Association Executives of the Philippines
c/o Tourism Promotions Board, PO Box EA-459, 4/F, Legaspi Towers, 300 Roxas Blvd., Manila 1004 Philippines
Tel: 632-525-9318; *Fax:* 632-521-6165
pcvcnet@dotpcvc.gov.ph
www.dotpcvc.gov.ph
Overview: A medium-sized national organization

Society of Bead Researchers (SBR)
PO Box 13719, Portland OR 97213 USA
www.beadresearch.org
Overview: A small international organization founded in 1981
Mission: To foster serious research on beads of all materials & periods; to expedite dissemination of resultant knowledge
Chief Officer(s):
Bill Billeck, President
billeckb@si.edu
Alice Scherer, Secretary-Treasurer
alice@europa.com
Karlis Karklins, Editor, Journal
karlis4444@gmail.com
Finances: *Annual Operating Budget:* Less than $50,000; *Funding Sources:* Membership dues
9 volunteer(s)
Membership: 3 senior/lifetime + 275 individuals; *Fees:* US$20; US$30 overseas; *Member Profile:* Anyone conducting research on beads, or interested in subject
Activities: *Rents Mailing List:* Yes

Society of Cardiovascular Anesthesiologists (SCA)
2209 Dickens Rd., Richmond VA 23230-2005 USA
Tel: 804-282-0084; *Fax:* 804-282-0090
sca@societyhq.com
www.scahq.org
www.facebook.com/210665095719456
Overview: A large international organization
Mission: To promote excellence in clinical care & research in perioperative care for patients undergoing cardiothoracic & vascular procedures
Chief Officer(s):
Scott T. Reeves, President
reevess@musc.edu
Linda Shore-Lesserson, Secretary-Treasurer
lshore@montefiore.org
Membership: 6,000+; *Fees:* Fellow, $40; Resident, $40; Membership, $210; Active/Associate/Career Scientist, $175; *Member Profile:* International cardiac, thoracic, & vascular anesthesiologists; *Committees:* Bylaws & Procedures; Economics & Governmental Affairs; Educational Liaison; Electronic Communications; Ethics; Interdisciplinary Professional Practice; International; Membership; Newsletter; Nominating; Publications; Research
Activities: Providing continuing medical education for physicians, through accreditation from the Accreditation Council for Continuing Medical Education; Offering networking opportunities with the leading physicians & practitioners in the field of cardiovascular anesthesiology; Publishing monographs
Meetings/Conferences:
• SCA/STS Critical Care Symposium, April, 2015, Washington Marriott Marquis, Washington, DC
Scope: International
Description: Hosted jointly by the Society of Cardiovascular Anesthesiologists & the Society of Thoracic Surgeons.
• Society of Cardiovascular Anesthesiologists 4th Annual Thoracic Anesthesia Symposium 2015, April, 2015, Washington Marriott Marquis, Washington, DC
Scope: International
• Society of Cardiovascular Anesthesiologists 37th Annual Meeting 2015, April, 2015, Washington Marriott Marquis, Washington, DC
Scope: International
• Society of Cardiovascular Anesthesiologists Echo 18th Annual Comprehensive Review & Update of Perioperative Echo, March, 2015, Loews Atlanta Hotel, Atlanta, GA
Scope: International
• Society of Cardiovascular Anesthesiologists 19th Annual Comprehensive Review & Update of Perioperative Echo 2016, 2016
Scope: International
Publications:
• Annual Update of Cardiopulmonary Bypass
Type: Yearbook; *Frequency:* Annually
• SCA [Society of Cardiovascular Anesthesiologists] Bulletin
Type: Newsletter; *Frequency:* Bimonthly
• Society of Cardiovascular Anesthesiologists Annual Meeting Syllabi
Type: Yearbook; *Frequency:* Annually
• TEE Review Courses [a publication of the Society of Cardiovascular Anesthesiologists]

Society of Die Casting Engineers *See* North American Die Casting Association

Society of Environmental Toxicology & Chemistry (SETAC)
SETAC Asia / Pacific, SETAC Latin America, & SETAC North America, 1010 - 12th Ave. North, Pensacola FL 32501-3370 USA
Tel: 850-469-1500; *Fax:* 850-469-9778
setac@setac.org
www.setac.org
Overview: A small international organization founded in 1979
Mission: To develop principles & practices for the protection, enhancement, & management of sustainable environmental quality
Chief Officer(s):
Mike Mozur, Executive Director
mike.mozur@setac.org
Linda Fenner, Manager, Finance
linda.fenner@setac.org
Mimi Meredith, Manager, Publications
mimi.meredith@setac.org
Bruce Vigon, Manager, Scientific Affairs
bruce.vigon@setac.org
Membership: *Member Profile:* Individuals & institutions involved in environmental research, development, & education, as well as the management & regulation of natural resources; *Committees:* Awards & Fellowships; Development; Education; Endowment Fund; Finance; Long-range Planning; Meetings; Membership; Mentoring; Nominations; Regional Chapters; Short Courses; Student Activities; Student Council; Technical
Awards:
• SETAC/ABC Laboratories Environmental Education Award (Award)
Given to an individual, group, organization, or coporation for significant contributions to environmental education
• SETAC Government Service Award (Award)
Recognizes exemplary dedication & service by a scientist or scientific organization toward promoting the collective application of environmental toxicology & chemistry to risk assessment in a governent function
• Environmental Toxicology & Chemistry Best Student Paper Award (Award)
Recognizes the best paper published by a student in ET&C during the last year
• SETAC/Battelle Best Student Platform & Poster Presentation Awards (Award)
Given to the best student platform & poster presentations at the SETAC annual meetings*Eligibility:* Must be a member of SETAC
• Rachel Carson Award (Award)
Given to an individual who has substantially increased public awareness & understanding of an issue concerning contaminants in the environment *Eligibility:* Recipient's action must result in a redefintion of environmental policies & practices

• Herb Ward Exceptional Service Award (Award)
Given to SETAC members who have performed long-term, exceptionally high-quality service for SETAC
• SETAC Founders Awards (Award)
Given to a person with an outstanding career who has made clearly identifiable contributions in the environmental sciences that are consistent with the goals of SETAC
• SETAC Student Travel Awards Program (Award)
Provides travel support assistance for graduate students to attend the SETAC annual meeting
• SETAC Program for North American Minority Students & Mentors (Award)
Program introduces North American minority students &/or their faculty mentors to the Society & the professional opportunities offered in the fields of environmental toxicoloy, environmental chemistry & risk assessment *Amount:* Selected individuals receive 1 year membership to the Society & funds to support their travel
• SETAC/Taylor & Francis Advanced Training Fellowship (Grant)
To provide pre-doctoral or post-doctoral scholars the opportunity to expand their research skills & grantsmanship through specialized training not available at their institution
• SETAC/Roy F. Weston Environmental Chemistry Award (Award)
Given to a scientist under the age of 40 for contributions made to the field of environmental chemistry
• SETAC/EA Engineering Jeff Black Award (Award)
Eligibility: SETAC members & masters students who have been accepted to or are participating in an environmental science or engineering award *Amount:* US$2,000 & certificate
Meetings/Conferences:
• Society of Environmental Toxicology & Chemistry North America 2015 36th Annual Meeting, November, 2015, Salt Palace Convention Center, Salt Lake City, UT
Scope: International
Attendance: 2,300
• Society of Environmental Toxicology & Chemistry North America 2016 37th Annual Meeting, November, 2016, Minneapolis, MN
Scope: International
Attendance: 2,300
Publications:
• Environmental Toxicology & Chemistry
Type: Journal; *Editor:* C.H. Ward *ISSN:* 0730-7268
• Integrated Environmental Assessment & Management
Type: Journal; *Editor:* Richard J. Wenning *ISSN:* 1551-3777
• Society of Environmental Toxicology & Chemistry Annual Report
Type: Yearbook; *Frequency:* Annually

Society of Fire Protection Engineers (SFPE)

#620E, 7315 Wisconsin Ave., Bethesda MD 20814 USA
Tel: 301-718-2910; *Fax:* 301-718-2242
www.sfpe.org
www.facebook.com/careers.sfpe.org
twitter.com/SFPEAnnualMtg
Overview: A medium-sized international organization founded in 1950
Mission: To advance the practice & science of fire protection engineering & its allied fields; to maintain a high ethical standard among its members; to foster fire protection engineering education
Chief Officer(s):
Allan Freedman, Executive Director, 301-915-9723
Finances: *Annual Operating Budget:* $500,000-$1.5 Million
Staff Member(s): 6
Membership: 4,500; *Fees:* US$195
Activities: *Rents Mailing List:* Yes

British Columbia Chapter
BC
www.sfpe.bc.ca
Chief Officer(s):
John Ivison, President, 778-989-1909
executive@sfpe.bc.ca

Conseil St-Laurent
St-Laurent QC
www.sfpe-st-lawrence-quebec.com
Chief Officer(s):
Gilles Carrier, President
g.carrier@pgaexperts.com

National Capital Region
c/o Mark Ramlochan, #200, 440 Laurier Ave. West, Ottawa ON K1R 7X6
eng.sfpe.org/Chapters/CanadaNCR
www.linkedin.com/groups?home=&gid=4783650
Chief Officer(s):
Robert Salvador, President
robert.salvador@labour-travail.gc.ca

Southern Ontario Chapter
Toronto ON
info@sfpesoc.com
www.sfpesoc.com
Chief Officer(s):
Ed Koe, President
president@sfpesoc.com

Society of Magnetic Resonance *See* International Society for Magnetic Resonance in Medicine

Society of Motion Picture & Television Engineers (SMPTE)

3 Barker Ave, 5th Fl., White Plains NY 10601 USA
Tel: 914-761-1100; *Fax:* 914-761-3115
membership@smpte.org
www.smpte.org
www.linkedin.com/groups?mostPopular=&gid=71716
www.facebook.com/smpteconnect
twitter.com/smpteconnect
www.youtube.com/user/smpteconnect;
www.flickr.com/photos/smpte
Overview: A medium-sized international organization founded in 1916
Chief Officer(s):
Aylsworth Wendy, President
Robert P. Seidel, Executive Vice-President
Jean-Claude Krelic, Chair, Montréal/Québec Section
Paul Roeser, Chair, Toronto Section
Barbara Lange, Executive Director
Finances: *Annual Operating Budget:* $1.5 Million-$3 Million;
Funding Sources: Membership dues; educational programs
Staff Member(s): 20; 200 volunteer(s)
Membership: 10,000 worldwide (800 in Canada); *Fees:* $135

SMPTE Toronto
Toronto ON
Tel: 416-642-4304
www.smptetoronto.org
Chief Officer(s):
Paul Briscoe, Chair
Tony Meerakker, Secretary-Treasurer

Society of Petroleum Engineers (SPE)

PO Box 833836, 222 Palisades Creek Dr., Richardson TX 75083-3868 USA
Tel: 972-952-9393; *Fax:* 972-952-9435
Toll-Free: 800-456-6863
spedal@spe.org
www.spe.org
www.linkedin.com/groups?about=&gid=57660
www.facebook.com/spemembers
twitter.com/SPE_Events
www.youtube.com/user/2012SPE?feature=mhee
Overview: A large international organization founded in 1957
Mission: To collect, disseminate & exchange technical knowledge concerning the exploration, development & production of oil & gas resources & related technologies for the public benefit; provide opportunities for professionals to enhance their technical & professional competence
Chief Officer(s):
Mark A. Rubin, Executive Director
execdir@spe.org
Egbert Imomoh, President
president@spe.org
Finances: *Annual Operating Budget:* $3 Million-$5 Million
Staff Member(s): 87
Membership: 79,000+ (active operations in some 50 countries); *Fees:* $10-$90; *Member Profile:* Managers, engineers, operating personnel & scientists engaged in the exploration, drilling & production sectors of the global oil & gas industry; *Committees:* Student Development; Global Training; Distinguished Lecturer; Membership; Forum Series Coordinating; DAA For PE Faculty; Education & Accreditation; Oil & Gas Reserves; Editorial Review; Twenty Five Year Club; TIG Coordinating; Research & Development; Young Professional Coordinating; SPE Energy Information; Sustainability; Robert Earll McConnell; Online Communities Advisory; Awards
Activities: *Speaker Service:* Yes Library
Awards:
• Health Safety Social Resp. & Environ. Award (Award)
• ReserVoir Description & Dynamics Award (Award)
• Drilling Engineering Award (Award)
• Production & Operations Award (Award)
• Management & Information Award (Award)
• Carll, Lucas & Uren Award (Award)
• DeGolyer & Distinguished Service Award (Award)
• Completions Optimization & Technology Award (Award)
• Charles F. Rand Memorial Gold Medal (Award)
Publications:
• JPT [Journal of Petroleum Technology]
Type: Journal
• Oil Gas Facilities
Type: Magazine
• TWA [The Way Ahead]
Type: Magazine

Society of Plastics Engineers (SPE)

13 Church Hill Rd., Newtown CT 06470 USA
Tel: 203-775-0471; *Fax:* 203-775-8490
info@4spe.org
www.4spe.org
www.linkedin.com/groups?gid=857357
www.facebook.com/SocietyofPlasticsEngineers
twitter.com/SPEANTEC
Overview: A large international organization founded in 1942
Mission: To promote the scientific & engineering knowledge related to plastics
Chief Officer(s):
Russell C. Broome, President
rbroome@4spe.org
Membership: 20,000 in 70+ countries; *Fees:* US$31 student; US$144 individual; *Member Profile:* Engineers, scientists, & other plastics professionals, including technicians, salespeople, marketers, retailers, & representatives from tertiary industries
Activities: *Library:* Online Technical Library; by appointment
Awards:
• The SPE Foundation General Scholarships (Scholarship)
• The SPE Foundation Special Scholarships (Scholarship)
• The SPE Foundation General Grants (Grant)
• Thermoforming Equipment Grants (Grant)
• Blow Molding Equipment Grants (Grant)
• SPE Plastivan Grants (Grant)
Meetings/Conferences:
• Society of Plastics Engineers 2015 International Polyolefins Conference, February, 2015, Hilton Houston North Hotel, Houston, TX
Scope: International
Attendance: 600+
Description: This year's theme is "Four Decades of Advancing Polyolefin Technology"
Contact Information: Sponsorship contact: Brandon Cleary, E-mail: brandon@birchplastics.com; Publicity contact: David Hansen, E-mail: david.hansen47@yahoo.com
• Society of Plastics Engineers 2015 Thermoset Conference, February, 2015, Le Parker Méridien, Palm Springs, CA
Scope: International
Contact Information: RSVP contact: Shelane Nunnery, Phone: 630-247-6733, E-mail: shelane@gvineme.com; URL: www.spetopcon.com
• Society of Plastics Engineers 2015 GPEC Conference, February, 2015, Hyatt Regency, Dallas, TX
Scope: International
Contact Information: URL: www.plasticsrecycling.com
• Society of Plastics Engineers 2015 ANTEC Orlando Conference, March, 2015, Orange County Convention Center, Orlando, FL
Scope: International
• Society of Plastics Engineers 2015 ANTEC Brussels Conference, September, 2015, Brussels
Scope: International
• Society of Plastics Engineers 2015 24th Annual Thermoforming Conference, August, 2015, Renaissance Schaumburg Convention Center, Atlanta, GA
Scope: International
Contact Information: Conference Coordinator, Lesley Kyle, Phone: 914-671-9524, thermoformingdivision@gmail.com
• Society of Plastics Engineers 2015 RETEC Conference, October, 2015, Indianapolis Westin, Indianapolis, IN
Scope: International
Description: This year's theme is Show Your Colours
• Society of Plastics Engineers Annual Blow Molding Conference 2015, October, 2015, Sheraton Station Square, Pittsburgh, PA
Scope: International
Publications:
• Journal of Vinyl & Additive Technology [a publication of the Society of Plastics Engineers]
Type: Journal; *Frequency:* Quarterly *ISSN:* 1083-5601

• Plastics Engineering [a publication of the Society of Plastics Engineers]
Type: Magazine; *Frequency:* 10 pa; *Accepts Advertising*
Profile: Industry news & perspectives, developments in machinery, processing, & materials technology
• Polymer Composites [a publication of the Society of Plastics Engineers]
Type: Journal; *Frequency:* Bimonthly *ISSN:* 0272-8397
• Polymer Engineering & Science [a publication of the Society of Plastics Engineers]
Type: Journal; *Frequency:* Monthly *ISSN:* 0032-3888

Ontario Section
Tel: 416-740-5300; *Fax:* 416-740-2227
plem@pms-c.com
www.speontario.ca
Chief Officer(s):
Phil Lem, President, 905-271-8402

Québec Section
#146, 75, boul. de Mortagne, Boucherville QC J4B 6Y4
Tel: 450-641-5179; *Fax:* 450-641-5105
spequebec@polymtl.ca
www.polymtl.ca/spequebec
Chief Officer(s):
Caroline Vachon, President

Society of the Plastics Industry, Inc. (SPI)
#1000, 1667 K St. NW, Washington DC 20006 USA
Tel: 202-974-5200; *Fax:* 202-296-7005
www.plasticsindustry.org
www.facebook.com/pages/NPE/214402080959
twitter.com/SPI_4_Plastics
Overview: A large international organization founded in 1937
Mission: To be a world class trade association representing the entire plastics industry in a way that promotes the development of the plastics industry & enhances the public's understanding of its contributions while meeting the needs of society & providing value to its members
Chief Officer(s):
William R. Carteaux, President & CEO
Phyllis Hortie, Contact, Trade Shows & Conferences
Finances: *Annual Operating Budget:* Greater than $5 Million
Staff Member(s): 65
Membership: 1,100; *Member Profile:* Members represent the entire plastics supply chain; *Committees:* Finance, Administration & Membership; Communications & Marketing Advisory; Equipment Statistics; Nominating; NPE Executive; Special Committees
Activities: Operates 12 divisions: Epoxy Resin Systems Task Group, Film & Bag Federation, Food, Drug & Cosmetic Packaging Materials, Fluropolymers, Machinery, Molders, Moldmakers, Organic Peroxide Producers Safety, Sheet Producers, Structural Plastics, Thermoforming Institute, Vinyl Formulators; *Library:* Plastics Data Source
Meetings/Conferences:
• Society of the Plastics Industry, Inc. Spring 2015 National Board Conference, 2015
Scope: National

Society of Toxicology (SOT)
#300, 1821 Michael Faraday Dr., Reston VA 20190 USA
Tel: 703-438-3115; *Fax:* 703-438-3113
sothq@toxicology.org
www.toxicology.org
Overview: A large international organization
Mission: To advance the science of toxicology; To promote the acquisition & utilization of knowledge in toxicology; To protect public health
Chief Officer(s):
Jon C. Cook, President
Rosibel Alvarenga, Contact, Membership & Customer Service, 703-438-3115 Ext. 1432
rosibel@toxicology.org
Betty Eidemiller, Contact, Teacher & Student Inquiries, 703-438-3115 Ext. 1430
bettye@toxicology.org
Martha Lindauer, Contact, Press & Media Inquiries, 703-438-3115 Ext. 1640
martha@toxicology.org
Membership: *Member Profile:* Scientists from academic institutions, government, & industry who practice toxicology
Meetings/Conferences:
• Society of Toxicology 54th Annual Meeting & ToxExpo, March, 2015, San Diego Convention Center, San Diego, CA
Scope: International
Attendance: 6,500
Description: Toxicology meeting & exhibition
Contact Information: Phone: 703-438-3115; Fax: 703-438-3113; E-mail: sothq@toxicology.org
• Society of Toxicology 55th Annual Meeting & ToxExpo, March, 2016, Ernest N. Morial Convention Center, New Orleans, LA
Scope: International
Attendance: 6,500
Description: Toxicology meeting & exhibition
Contact Information: Phone: 703-438-3115; Fax: 703-438-3113; E-mail: sothq@toxicology.org
• Society of Toxicology 56th Annual Meeting & ToxExpo, March, 2017, Baltimore Convention Center, Baltimore, MD
Scope: International
Attendance: 6,500
Description: Toxicology meeting & exhibition
Contact Information: Phone: 703-438-3115; Fax: 703-438-3113; E-mail: sothq@toxicology.org
• Society of Toxicology 57th Annual Meeting & ToxExpo, 2018
Scope: International
Description: Toxicology meeting & exhibition
Contact Information: Phone: 703-438-3115; Fax: 703-438-3113; E-mail: sothq@toxicology.org
Publications:
• Communiqué [a publication of the Society of Toxicology]
Type: Newsletter; *Frequency:* Quarterly; *Accepts Advertising*
Profile: Society of Toxicology news; Member spotlight; Regional chapters, specialty sections, & special interest groups; Annual meeting; Science news
• Preliminary Program [a publication of the Society of Toxicology]
Accepts Advertising
Profile: Information about the annual meeting program, a registration form, & housing information
• Society of Toxicology Membership Directory
Accepts Advertising
Profile: Names, addresses, & e-mail addresses for more than 6,000 SOT members
• ToxExpo Directory
Accepts Advertising
• ToxSci Journal
Type: Journal

Society of Tribologists & Lubrication Engineers / Société des tribologistes et ingénieurs en lubrification
840 Busse Hwy., Park Ridge IL 60068-2302 USA
Tel: 847-825-5536; *Fax:* 847-825-1456
information@stle.org
www.stle.org
www.linkedin.com/groups?gid=1928646&trk=myg_ugrp_ovr
www.facebook.com/pages/STLE/35069018863
twitter.com/@stle_tribology
www.youtube.com/user/STLEMedia?feature=mhee
Previous Name: American Society of Lubrication Engineers
Overview: A large international organization founded in 1987
Mission: To promote study of tribology, friction, wear & lubrication; To function as resource for distribution of new information & techniques
Chief Officer(s):
Edward Salek, Executive Director
esalek@stle.org
Membership: *Member Profile:* Professionals; *Committees:* Nominations; Rules; Finance; Technical; Operations; Annual Meeting Program; Fellows; Young Tribologists; Wear Technical; Tribotesting Technical; Organization & Operations
Activities: *Speaker Service:* Yes; *Rents Mailing List:* Yes
Awards:
• STLE International Award (Award)
• Vic Joll Award (Award)
• Outstanding Section Awards (Award)
• The W.K. Stair Membership Award (Award)
Publications:
• Tribology & Lubrication Technology (TLT)
Type: Magazine
Profile: For members

Alberta Section
AB
Tel: 780-591-5339
Chief Officer(s):
Terrence Lee Veenstra, Chair
tveenstra@suncor.com

Hamilton Section
PO Box 47623, 1183 Bartin St. East, Hamilton ON L8H 7S7
Tel: 905-671-2355
Chief Officer(s):
Mike Deckert, Chair
mdeckert@flocomponents.com

Manitoba/North-West Ontario Section
MB

Toronto Section
c/o Lorne Brock, 421 Wallace St., Wallaceburg ON N8A 1L5
Tel: 705-321-1192; *Fax:* 519-628-5688
www.torontostle.com
Chief Officer(s):
Wayne Mackwood, Chair
wayne.mackwood@chemtura.com

Society of Women Engineers
#1675, 203 N La Salle St., Chicago IL 60601 USA
Tel: 312-596-5223
Toll-Free: 877-793-4636
hq@swe.org
societyofwomenengineers.swe.org
Overview: A medium-sized international organization founded in 1950
Chief Officer(s):
Betty A. Shanahan, Executive Director & CEO
Membership: *Fees:* $100

Soil & Water Conservation Society (SWCS)
945 SW Ankeny Rd., Ankeny IA 50023-9723 USA
Tel: 515-289-2331; *Fax:* 515-289-1227
swcs@swcs.org
www.swcs.org
Overview: A large international organization founded in 1945
Mission: To promote the conservation of soil, water, & related resources; To promote an ethic that recognizes the interdependence of people & the environment
Chief Officer(s):
Jim Gulliford, Executive Director, 515-289-2331 Ext. 113, Fax: 515-289-1227
jim.gulliford@swcs.org
Jim Bruce, Representative, Canadian Policy, 613-731-5929
jpbruce@sympatico.ca
Dewayne Johnson, Director, Professional Development, 515-289-2331 Ext. 114, Fax: 515-289-1227
dewayne.johnson@swcs.org
Cammie Callen, Specialist, Membership Services, 515-289-2331 Ext. 118, Fax: 515-289-1227
memberservices@swcs.org
Membership: 5,000-14,999; *Fees:* $220 Presidents Club; $145 leader; $90 conservationist; $30 student; *Member Profile:* Researchers; Administrators; Educators; Planners; Technicians; Legislators; Farmers & ranchers; Local conservation officials; Consultants; Students
Awards:
• Donald A. Williams Soil Conservation Scholarship (Scholarship)
Offered to members wanting to improve their professional competency*Deadline:* April 1 *Amount:* $1,500
• Kenneth E. Grant Research Scholarship (Scholarship)
For graduate level research*Deadline:* Spring
Meetings/Conferences:
• Soil & Water Conservation Society 69th Annual International Conference, July, 2015, Sheraton Four Seasons Hotel, Greensboro, NC
Scope: International
Publications:
• The Journal of Soil and Water Conservation (JSWC)
Type: Journal; *Frequency:* Bimonthly; *Editor:* Oksana Gieseman
ISSN: 0022-4561
Profile: A multidisciplinary journal of natural resource conservation research, practice, policy, and perspectives.

Solid Waste Association of North America (SWANA)
#700, 1100 Wayne Ave., Silver Spring MD 20910 USA
Fax: 301-589-7068
Toll-Free: 800-467-9262
info@swana.org
www.swana.org
www.linkedin.com/groups?home=&gid=45037
www.facebook.com/MySWANA
twitter.com/SWANA
Previous Name: Government Refuse Collection & Disposal Association
Overview: A medium-sized international organization founded in 1961
Mission: To serve individuals & communities responsible for the operation & management of solid waste management systems; To advance professional standards in the field through training programs, technical assistance, & education

Member of: International Solid Waste Association; Federation of Canadian Municipalities
Chief Officer(s):
John Skinner, Executive Director & CEO, 240-494-2254
Finances: *Annual Operating Budget:* $3 Million-$5 Million; *Funding Sources:* Membership dues; publications
Staff Member(s): 22
Membership: 8,000; *Fees:* US$62 student; US$72 retired; US$183 public sector; US$243 small business; US$343 private sector; *Committees:* Technical; Recycling & Special Waste Management; Communication, Education & Marketing; Collection & Transfer; Landfill; Landfill Gas; Planning & Management; Waste-to-Energy
Activities: Technical divisions: collection & transfer, waste-to-energy, landfill gas management, landfill management, planning & management, special waste management; waste reduction, recycling & composting, communication, education & marketing; publications; trade shows & conferences; *Internships:* Yes *Library* Open to public
Awards:
• Excellence Awards (Award)
SWANA's Excellence Awards Program recognizes outstanding solid waste programs and facilities that advance the practice of environmentally and economically sound solid waste management through their commitment to utilizing effective technologies and processes in system design and operations, advancing worker and community health and safety, and implementing successful public education and outreach programs.

Atlantic Canada Chapter
#100, 137 Chainlake Dr., Halifax NS B3S 1V3
Fax: 902-450-2008
info@atcanswana.org
www.atcanswana.org
Chief Officer(s):
Nicole Haverkort, President, 902-232-2563, Fax: 902-533-4909
nicole@erswm.ca
Gerry Isenor, Executive Director, 902-404-7723, Fax: 902-444-6348
gisenor@eastlink.ca
Christopher Shortall, Treasurer, 902-450-4000
cshortall@dillon.ca

Northern Lights Chapter
PO Box 3317, Sherwood Park AB T8H 2T2
Tel: 780-496-5614; *Fax:* 866-698-8203
info@swananorthernlights.org
www.swananorthernlights.org
Mission: To serve commmunities & individuals responsible for the operation of municipal solid waste management systems
Chief Officer(s):
Sheri Praski, Executive Director
sheri.praski@swananorthernlights.org
Dick Ellis, President
dick.ellis@swananorthernlights.org
Sheila Reithmayer, Administrator, 780-496-5614
sheila.reithmayer@swananorthernlights.org
Bud Latta, Treasurer
bud.latta@swananorthernlights.org

Ontario Chapter
PO Box 9, Hillsdale ON L0L 1V0
Tel: 705-835-3560; *Fax:* 705-835-6224
www.swanaon.org
Chief Officer(s):
John Lackie, Executive Director
j.lackie@sympatico.com

Pacific Chapter - BC & Yukon
PO Box 47007, #15, 555 West 12th Ave., Vancouver BC V5Z 3X0
Tel: 250-538-0110; *Fax:* 250-538-0120
Toll-Free: 800-648-2560
info@swanabc.org
www.swanabc.org
twitter.com/SWANAPacific
Chief Officer(s):
Ralph Bischoff, Executive Director

Solidarité européenne pour une égale participation des peuples *See* European Solidarity Towards Equal Participation of People

Soroptimist International of the Americas (SIA)
1709 Spruce St., Philadelphia PA 19103-6103 USA
Tel: 215-893-9000; *Fax:* 215-893-5200
siahq@soroptimist.org
www.soroptimist.org
www.facebook.com/69575569890
twitter.com/soroptimist
www.youtube.com/siahq
Overview: A large international charitable organization founded in 1921
Mission: To maintain high ethical standards in business & professional life; To strive for human rights for all people & in particular, to advance the status of women; To develop a spirit of friendship & unity among Soroptomists of all countries; To develop interest in community, national & international affairs; To contribute to international understanding & universal friendship
Member of: Soroptimist International
Chief Officer(s):
Nancy Montvydas, Senior Director, Development, 215-893-9000 Ext. 125
Nicole Simmons, Director, Membership, 215-893-9000 Ext. 139
Staff Member(s): 20
Membership: 38,000+; *Fees:* $48; *Member Profile:* Business & professional women
Activities: *Library:* Soroptimist Archives
Awards:
• Women's Opportunity Awards (Award)
Improve the lives of women by giving them the resources they needto improve their education, skills, & employment prospects
• Violet Richardson Award (Award)
Honor girls who donate their time & energy to causes that make the community & world a better place
• Soroptimist Club Grants for Women & Girls (Grant)
Intended to help clubs meet community need by improving their financial resources
Meetings/Conferences:
• Soroptimist 43rd Biennial Convention 2016, July, 2016, Walt Disney World Dolphin Hotel, Orlando, FL
Scope: International
Publications:
• Best for Women [a publication of Soroptimist International of the Americas]
Type: Magazine; *Frequency:* 3 pa; *Editor:* Jessica Puterbaugh

Southeast Asian Ministers of Education Organization (SEAMEO)
Mom Luang Pin Malakul Centenary Bldg., 920 Sukhumvit Rd., Bangkok 10110 Thailand
Tel: 66-2-391-0144; *Fax:* 66-2-381-2587
secretariat@seameo.org
www.seameo.org
Overview: A medium-sized international organization founded in 1965
Mission: To enhance a regional understanding, cooperation & unity of purpose among member countries & achieve a better quality of life through the establishment of networks & partnerships, the provision of an intellectual forum for policy makers & experts, & the development of regional centres of excellence for the promotion of sustainable human resource development
Affiliation(s): International Council for Open & Distance Education
Chief Officer(s):
Witaya Jeradechakul, Secretariat Director
Edilberto de Jesus, Director
Finances: *Annual Operating Budget:* $500,000-$1.5 Million
Staff Member(s): 32
Membership: 11 states + 8 associate member countries
Activities: *Internships:* Yes *Library* Open to public
Awards:
• Jasper Fellowship (Scholarship)

Spanish Association for Canadian Studies / La Fundación Canadá
Espronceda 40, Madrid 28003 Spain
Tel: 34-91-441-1895; *Fax:* 34-91-399-2378
secretaria@estudioscanadienses.org
www.estudioscanadienses.org
Overview: A small international organization founded in 1988
Mission: To promote interdisciplinary research in Canadian Studies; to encourage the exchange of knowledge between members; to establish international relations with other Canadian Studies associations; to develop linkages between Canadian & Spanish universities; to cultivate an interest in Canada among students of Spanish universities; & to promote Canadian activities in Spanish society

The Spastics Society *See* SCOPE for People with Cerebral Palsy

Special Libraries Association (SLA)
331 South Patrick St., Alexandria VA 22314-3501 USA
Tel: 703-647-4900; *Fax:* 703-647-4901
Other Communication: membership@sla.org
cschatz@sla.org
www.sla.org
www.linkedin.com/company/sla
www.facebook.com/slahq
twitter.com/slahq
Overview: A medium-sized international organization founded in 1909
Mission: To promote & strengthen information professionals from around the globe
Chief Officer(s):
Janice R. Lachance, Chief Executive Officer
janice@sla.org
Linda Broussard, Chief Community Officer, 703-647-4938
lbroussard@sla.org
Quan O. Logan, Chief Technology Officer, 703-647-4928
qlogan@sla.org
Doug Newcomb, Chief Policy Officer, 703-647-4923
dnewcomb@sla.org
Membership: *Member Profile:* Persons in the information profession from around the world; Library & information science students; *Committees:* Annual Conference Advisory Council; Awards & Honours; Bylaws; Association Governance; Cataloguing; Diversity Leadership Development Program; Emergency Preparedness & Recovery Advisory Council; Finance; First Five Years Advisory Council; Information Ethics Advisory Council; Information Outlook Advisory Council; Nominating; Professional Development Advisory Council; Public Policy Advisory Council; Research & Development; Scholarship; Student Group - SAAAC; Technical Standards; Virtual World Advisory Council
Activities: Providing professional development opportunities, including online education programs; Offering networking opportunities; Engaging in advocacy activities
Awards:
• Diversity Leadership Development Program Award (Scholarship)
• Special Libraries Association Student & Academic Affairs Advisory Council Merit Awards (Scholarship)
• Dow Jones Leadership Award (Award)
• Fellow of the Special Libraries Association (Award)
• John Cotton Dana Award (Award)
• Special Libraries Association Presidential Citations (Award)
• Professional Award (Award)
• Rose L. Vormelker Award (Award)
• Special Libraries Association Rising Star Award (Award)
• Special Libraries Association Hall of Fame (Award)
• J.J. Keller Innovations in Technology Award (Award)
• Dialog Member Achievement Award (Award)
Meetings/Conferences:
• Special Libraries Association 2015 Annual Conference & INFO-EXPO, June, 2015, Boston, MA
Scope: International
Description: A meeting featuring educational sessions, keynote speakers, & exhibitors of interest to information professionals from around the world
Contact Information: Director, Events: Caroline Hamilton, Phone: 703-647-4949, E-mail: chamilton@sla.org; Director, Marketing & Exhibits: Jeff Leach, Phone: 703-647-4922, E-mail: jleach@sla.org
• Special Libraries Association 2016 Annual Conference & INFO-EXPO, 2016, Philadelphia, PA
Scope: International
Description: A gathering of information professionals, providing informative educational sessions, keynote speakers, & exhibitors
Contact Information: Director, Events: Caroline Hamilton, Phone: 703-647-4949, E-mail: chamilton@sla.org; Director, Marketing & Exhibits: Jeff Leach, Phone: 703-647-4922, E-mail: jleach@sla.org
Publications:
• Information Outlook
Type: Magazine; *Frequency:* Monthly
Profile: News & information on trends & practices in the information profession
• SLA Connections
Type: Newsletter; *Frequency:* Weekly
Profile: News & information from the Special Libraries Association, including executive updates, learning center information, public policy issues, & conferences

• SLA Member Directory
Type: Directory
Profile: Organization of members by name, organization, city, country, & chapter

Eastern Canada
PO Box 549, Stn. B, 800 René-Lévesque Blvd. West, Montréal QC H3B 3K3
ecanada.sla.org
www.linkedin.com/groups/SLA-Section-de-lest-du-4587961/about
www.facebook.com/groups/11088485637/
twitter.com/SLAsec
Mission: To represent the interests of information professionals in Eastern Canada.

Toronto
c/o Claire Lysnes, PricewaterhouseCoopers, 145 King St. West, Toronto ON M5H 1V8
Tel: 416-941-8383
slatoronto@yahoo.ca
toronto.sla.org
www.linkedin.com/groups?home=&gid=1961919
www.facebook.com/slatoronto
www.twitter.com/slatoronto
www.youtube.com/user/SLAVideos
Mission: To represent the interests of information professionals from Toronto & the surrounding region
Chief Officer(s):
Claire Lysnes, President
clysnes@gmail.com
Heather Brunstad, Director, Programming
hbrunstad@hotmail.com
Gillian Horwood, Director, First 5 Years
gillian.horwood@utoronto.ca
Shelley McBride, Director, Membership
Shelley.McBride@canadabusiness.ca
Laura Warner, Director, Technology
Laura.Warner@dal.ca
Emmeline Hobbs, Secretary
hobbsey@gmail.com
Jan Dawson, Treasurer
jan_dawson@hotmail.com
• The Toronto Chapter SLA Courier
Type: Newsletter; *Frequency:* Quarterly; *Accepts Advertising*; *Editor:* Caroline Chung
Profile: Chapter reports plus information about continuing education & networking opportunities

Western Canada
Vancouver BC
vancouver@wcanada.sla.org
wcanada.sla.org
www.linkedin.com/groups?home=&gid=2200726
twitter.com/SLAWCC
www.flickr.com/groups/slawcc
Mission: To represent the interests of information professionals in Western Canada.
Chief Officer(s):
Warren Schmidt, President

Special Olympics International
1133 - 19th St. NW, Washington DC 20036-3604 USA
Tel: 202-628-3630; *Fax:* 202-824-0200
Toll-Free: 800-700-8585
info@specialolympics.org
www.specialolympics.org
www.facebook.com/SpecialOlympics
twitter.com/SpecialOlympics
www.youtube.com/SpecialOlympicsHQ
Overview: A large international organization
Mission: To offer year-round training & athletic competition for more than one million athletes in nearly 150 countries
Affliation(s): Canadian Special Olympics Inc.
Chief Officer(s):
J. Brady Lum, President & COO
Activities: *Awareness Events:* Eunice Kennedy Shriver Day

Specialized Information Publishers Association (SIPA)
#260, 8229 Boone Boulevard, Vienna VA 22182 USA
Tel: 703-992-9339; *Fax:* 703-992-7512
Toll-Free: 800-356-9302
www.sipaonline.com
Previous Name: Newsletter Publishers Association
Overview: A medium-sized international organization founded in 1977
Mission: To advance the interests of for-profit subscription newsletter publishers & specialized information services; to provide information & services that enhance the ability of members to build & manage profitable newsletter publishing ventures
Chief Officer(s):
Matt Salt, Executive Director
Finances: *Annual Operating Budget:* $500,000-$1.5 Million
Staff Member(s): 5
Membership: 600; *Fees:* $295-$14,995 based on company revenue
Activities: Label & Copyright; Penny-Wise Office Products; two annual conferences, Dec. & June; *Internships:* Yes; *Speaker Service:* Yes; *Rents Mailing List:* Yes *Library* by appointment

Specialty Graphic Imaging Association (SGIA)
10015 Main St., Fairfax VA 22031-3489 USA
Tel: 703-385-1335; *Fax:* 703-273-0456
Toll-Free: 888-385-3588
sgia@sgia.org
www.sgia.org
www.linkedin.com/groups?gid=101519
www.facebook.com/400183973373526
twitter.com/SGIA_community
Previous Name: Screenprinting & Graphic Imaging Association International
Overview: A large international organization founded in 1948
Mission: To to provide the tools & information needed so that imaging professionals can make the best possible business decisions
Affliation(s): Screen Printing Association of Korea; Screenprinting & Graphic Imaging Association of Japan; South Africa Screen Printing Association; China Screenprinting & Graphic Imaging Association; Screenprinting & Graphic Imaging Association of Australia; Screenprinting & Graphic Imaging Association of the Philippines
Chief Officer(s):
Lynn Krinsky, Chair
Michael Mockridge, Treasurer
Finances: *Funding Sources:* Membership fees; seminar, conferences & expositions
Membership: 1,000-4,999; *Fees:* $300+; *Member Profile:* Printers; Suppliers to screen printers
Activities: SGIA Information Network; *Speaker Service:* Yes *Library*
Awards:
• Dave Swormstedt Sr. Memorial Award (Award)
For the best published article or technical paper written for any aspect of the screen printing industry *Contact:* Marci Kinter, marcik@sgia.org
• Howard Parmele Award (Award)
Awarded to an individual with an ongoing commitment to improve the screen printing & graphic imaging industry's products, services & image
• Golden Image/André Schellenberg Awards (Award)
"Best in Show" & "Best in Creativity" awards given to participants in this competition of the best & most creative imaged products for all avenues of the specialty imaging marketplace
• SGIA Product of the Year (Award)
For the best equipment & supplies currently on the market
Publications:
• Buyer's Guide [a publication of the Specialty Graphic Imaging Association]
Profile: SGIA member suppliers who provide screen printers & graphic imagers
• SGIA [Specialty Graphic Imaging Association] News
Type: Newsletter; *Frequency:* Monthly
• SGIA [Specialty Graphic Imaging Association] Journal
Type: Journal; *Frequency:* Quarterly

Steel Can Recycling Institute *See* Steel Recycling Institute

Steel Recycling Institute (SRI)
680 Andersen Dr., Pittsburgh PA 15220 USA
Tel: 412-922-2772
www.recycle-steel.org
www.facebook.com/envirometal
twitter.com/envirometal
www.youtube.com/envirometal
Previous Name: Steel Can Recycling Institute
Overview: A medium-sized international organization founded in 1988
Mission: To promote the recycling of steel products
Chief Officer(s):
Gregory Crawford, Executive Director

Stockholm Environment Institute (SEI)
Kräftriket 2B, Stockholm SE-106 91 Sweden
Tel: 46-8-674-7070
info@sei-international.org
www.sei-international.org
Overview: A medium-sized international organization founded in 1988
Mission: International research institute focusing on local, regional & global environmental issues
Chief Officer(s):
Johan Kuylenstierna, Centre Director
johan.kuylenstiernaSE@sei-international.org
Finances: *Annual Operating Budget:* Greater than $5 Million; *Funding Sources:* Government; other sources in Sweden, UK, USA
Staff Member(s): 60; 2 volunteer(s)
Activities: *Internships:* Yes; *Speaker Service:* Yes *Library* by appointment

Sustainable Forestry Initiative Inc.
#700, 900 - 17th St. NW, Washington DC 20006 USA
Tel: 202-596-3450; *Fax:* 202-596-3451
info@sfiprogram.org
www.sfiprogram.org
twitter.com/sfiprogram
www.youtube.com/user/SFIProgram
Overview: A large international charitable organization founded in 1994
Mission: To promote sustainable forest management; To maintain & improve the sustainable forestry certification program
Chief Officer(s):
Robert A. (Bob) Luoto, Chair
Kathy Abusow, President & CEO, 613-722-8734
Kathy.abusow@sfiprogram.org
Rick Cantrell, Vice-President & COO, 864-653-7224
Rick.Cantrell@sfiprogram.org
Eli Weissman, Senior Director, Conservation Partnerships, 202-596-3452
Eli.Weissman@sfiprogram.org
Danny Karch, Director, Green Building, 450-242-1233
danny.karch@sfiprogram.org
Activities: Promoting research to improve forestry practices
Awards:
• SFI President's Award (Award)
• SFI Implementation Committee Achievement Award (Award)
• Leadership in Conservation Award (Award)
• Dr. Sharon Haines Memorial Award for Innovation & Leadership in Sustainability (Award)
Meetings/Conferences:
• Sustainable Forestry Initiative 2015 Annual Conference, October, 2015, Lake Tahoe, CA
Scope: International
Description: Educational sessions, business meetings, the presentation of annual SFI awards, & networking opportunities
Publications:
• Sustainable Forestry Initiative Newsletter
Type: Newsletter; *Frequency:* Bimonthly
Profile: Recent information about the SFI program, including conservation grants updates, new certifications, & program statistics

Syndicat international des débardeurs et magasiniers (CTC) *See* International Longshore & Warehouse Union (CLC)

Syndicat international des peintres et métiers connexes *See* International Union of Painters & Allied Trades

Syndicat international des travailleurs unis de l'automobile, de l'aérospatiale et de l'outillage agricole d'Amérique *See* International Union, United Automobile, Aerospace & Agricultural Implement Workers of America

Syndicat uni du transport (FAT-COI/CTC) *See* Amalgamated Transit Union (AFL-CIO/CLC)

Teachers of English to Speakers of Other Languages, Inc. (TESOL)
#500, 1925 Ballenger Ave., Alexandria VA 22314 USA
Tel: 703-836-0774; *Fax:* 703-836-7864
info@tesol.org
www.tesol.org
www.facebook.com/tesol.assn
Overview: A medium-sized national organization founded in 1966
Mission: To ensure excellence in English language teaching to speakers of other languages
Affliation(s): 42 organizations in the US; 51 outside the US

Chief Officer(s):
Rosa Aronson, Executive Director Ext. 505
raronson@tesol.org
Paul Gibbs, Director of Publishing
Finances: *Annual Operating Budget:* $3 Million-$5 Million
Staff Member(s): 23
Membership: 13,000 teachers, teachers-in-training, administrators, researchers, materials writers, curriculum developers; *Fees:* $75; *Committees:* Awards; Nominations; Professional Development; Publications; Rules & Resolutions; Sociopolitical Concerns; Serial Publications; Standards
Activities: Members choose a primary interest section: ESL in Adult, Bilingual, Elementary Education or Higher Education; ESL in Secondary Schools; Applied Linguistics; Computer-Assisted Language Learning; English as a Foreign Language; Intensive English Programs; Materials Writers; Program Administration; Refugee Concerns; Research; Teacher Education; Video; International Teaching Assistants

Teachers Without Borders
PO Box 25067, Seattle WA 98165 USA
Tel: 206-623-0394; *Fax:* 425-491-7070
info@twb.org
www.teacherswithoutborders.org
www.linkedin.com/groups?home=&gid=1713607
www.facebook.com/teacherswithoutborders
twitter.com/teachersnetwork
www.youtube.com/user/TeachersWB
Overview: A medium-sized international organization founded in 2000
Mission: To invite, gather, distill, synthesize, & disseminate the best collective wisdom from teacher leaders from every culture to make all teachers even more effective in contributing to the creation of a world that works for all
Chief Officer(s):
Fred Mednick, Founder
mednick@teacherswithoutborders.org
Staff Member(s): 7
Activities: Nine offices around the world

Technology Services Industry Association (TSIA)
#200, 17065 Camino San Bernardo, San Diego CA 92127 USA
Tel: 858-674-5491
info@tsia.com
www.tsia.com
Overview: A large international organization
Mission: To further the knowledge, understanding, & career development of executives, managers, & professionals from around the globe in the high-tech & other emerging services & support industries
Chief Officer(s):
J.B. Wood, President & CEO
Thomas Lah, Executive Director
Stephen Smith, CFO & Vice-President, Operations
Awards:
• Vision Awards (Award)
• Star Awards (Award)
• TechBEST Awards (Award)
• TechBEST Awards (Award)
Publications:
• Inside Technology Services [a publication of AFSM International]
Type: Journal; *Frequency:* q.
• TSIA [Technology Services Industry Association] News
Type: Newsletter; *Frequency:* Monthly

Tecnica England *See* CODA International Training

TelecomPioneers
1801 California St., 44th Fl., Denver CO 80202 USA
Tel: 303-571-1200; *Fax:* 303-572-0520
Toll-Free: 800-872-5995
info@pioneersvolunteer.org
www.telecompioneers.org
www.facebook.com/pages/Pioneers-Volunteer-Network/111882325524028
Also Known As: Pioneers
Previous Name: Telephone Pioneers of America
Overview: A large international organization founded in 1911
Mission: TelecomPioneers is the largest industry-related volunteer organizationin the world, comprising of over 600,000 current and retired telecommunications employees who have joined together to make their communities better places to live and work.
Chief Officer(s):
Charlene Hill, Executive Director
chill@pioneersvolunteer.org
Membership: 620,000
Publications:
• PioneersPress
Type: Newsletter

Telephone Pioneers of America *See* TelecomPioneers

Tellus Institute
11 Arlington St., Boston MA 02116-3411 USA
Tel: 617-266-5400; *Fax:* 617-266-8303
info@tellus.org
www.tellus.org
Overview: A medium-sized international charitable organization founded in 1976
Mission: To conduct a diverse program of research, consulting, & communications; To address policy & planning issues in such areas as energy, water, waste, & land use for a sustainable world for future generations
Member of: Stockholm Environment Institute
Chief Officer(s):
Paul Raskin, President
praskin@tellus.org
David McAnulty, Administrative Director
dmac@tellus.org
Finances: *Funding Sources:* Government agencies; Foundations; Non-governmental organizations
2 volunteer(s)
Activities: Conducting research; Analyzing problems & evaluating options for technological & institutional change;

TOPS Club, Inc.
PO Box 070360, 4575 South Fifth St., Milwaukee WI 53207-0360 United States
Tel: 414-482-4620
wondering@tops.org
www.tops.org
Also Known As: Take Off Pounds Sensibly
Overview: A small provincial organization
Mission: To help overweight persons attain & maintain their goal weight
Chief Officer(s):
Sandra Seidlitz, Area Coordinator, AB, BC, MB, NT, NU, ON, SK, YT
Debra-Ann MacLean, Area Coordinator, NB, NL, NS, PE, QC
Activities: Numerous chapters in Canada

Travailleurs unis des transports (FAT-CIO/CTC) *See* United Transportation Union (AFL-CIO/CLC)

Trigeminal Neuralgia Association *See* The Facial Pain Association

UFI - The Global Association of the Exhibition Industry (UFI)
17 rue Louise Michel, Levallois-Perret F-92300 France
Tél: 33-1-46-39-75-15; *Téléc:* 33-1-46-39-75-01
info@ufi.org
www.ufi.org
twitter.com/ufilive
Nom précédent: Union des foires internationales
Aperçu: *Dimension:* moyenne; *Envergure:* internationale; Organisme sans but lucratif; fondée en 1925
Membre(s) du bureau directeur:
Paul Woodward, Directeur général
pw@ufi.org
Finances: *Budget de fonctionnement annuel:* $500,000-$1.5 Million
Membre(s) du personnel: 10
Membre: 298 institutionnels; 395 associations; 18 partenaires; *Critères d'admissibilite:* Organisations et associations de foires/salons; gestionnaires de parcs; partenaires de l'Industrie des Foires/Salons
Activités: *Stagiaires:* Oui

UNEP - World Conservation Monitoring Centre (UNEP-WCMC)
219 Huntingdon Rd., Cambridge CB3 0DL United Kingdom
Tel: 44-1223-277-314; *Fax:* 44-1223-277-136
info@unep-wcmc.org
www.unep-wcmc.org
Previous Name: World Conservation Monitoring Centre
Overview: A small international charitable organization founded in 1988
Mission: To provide information services on conservation & sustainable use of the world's living resources; to help others to develop information system on their own
Affliation(s): United Nations Environment Programme
Chief Officer(s):
Jonathan Hutton, Director
Staff Member(s): 50; 10 volunteer(s)
Activities: *Library* by appointment

Union académique internationale (UAI) / International Union of Academies
Palais des Académies, 1, rue Ducale, Brussels B-1000 Belgium
Tél: 32-2-550-2200; *Téléc:* 32-2-550-2205
info@uai-iua.org
www.uai-iua.org
Aperçu: *Dimension:* grande; *Envergure:* internationale; Organisme sans but lucratif; fondée en 1919
Membre de: Conseil international de la philosophie et des sciences humaines; UNESCO
Affliation(s): Société Royale du Canada
Membre(s) du bureau directeur:
Janusz Koslowski, Président
janusz.kozlowski@uj.edu.pl
Hervé Hasquin, Secrétaire général
herve.hasquin@cfwb.be
Finances: *Budget de fonctionnement annuel:* $50,000-$100,000
Membre: 50 pays; *Montant de la cotisation:* US$250 - US$2,500; *Comités:* Comités des candidatures
Activités: 60 entreprises scientifiques internationales; *Bibliothèque*

Union des employés de gros, de détail et de magasins à rayons (FAT-COI/CTC) *See* Retail, Wholesale & Department Store Union (AFL-CIO/CLC)

Union des foires internationales *Voir* UFI - The Global Association of the Exhibition Industry

Union géodésique et géophysique internationale *See* International Union of Geodesy & Geophysics

Union géographique internationale *See* International Geographic Union

Union internationale contre le cancer *See* International Union Against Cancer

Union internationale de la presse francophone (UPF)
3, Cité Bergère, Paris 75009 France
Tél: 33-1-47-70-02-80; *Téléc:* 33-1-48-24-26-32
fr-fr.facebook.com/114481718630592
Nom précédent: Union internationale des journalistes et de la presse de langue française
Aperçu: *Dimension:* petite; *Envergure:* internationale; Organisme sans but lucratif; Organisme de réglementation; fondée en 1950
Mission: Défendre et rapprocher les journalistes, les éditeurs de la presse francophone; entreprendre toutes actions d'entraide et de solidarité
Membre de: Organisation internationale de la Francophonie; UNESCO; Parlement européen de Strasbourg
Membre(s) du bureau directeur:
Georges Gros, Secrétaire général
Finances: *Budget de fonctionnement annuel:* $500,000-$1.5 Million
Membre(s) du personnel: 7; 5 bénévole(s)
Membre: 3 000; *Montant de la cotisation:* 50$; *Critères d'admissibilite:* Journaliste
Activités: Expositions sur la Presse; *Stagiaires:* Oui; *Service de conférenciers:* Oui *Bibliothèque:* La Pressothèque; Bibliothèque publique
Prix, Bouses: • Prix de la Libre Expression (Prix)
Est décerné à un journaliste qui a "dans un environnement difficile, maintenu son indépendance malgré les atteintes à sa personne"

Union internationale de la science du sol *See* International Union of Soil Sciences

Union Internationale de Patinage *See* International Skating Union

Union internationale des architectes (UIA) / International Union of Architects (IUA)
33, av du Maine, Paris 75755 France
Tél: 33-1-45-24-36-88; *Téléc:* 33-1-45-24-02-78
uia@uia-architectes.org
www.uia-architectes.org/
www.facebook.com/161916773874971
Aperçu: *Dimension:* moyenne; *Envergure:* internationale; fondée en 1948

Mission: Unir les architectes de tous les pays du monde
Finances: *Budget de fonctionnement annuel:* $500,000-$1.5 Million
Membre(s) du personnel: 7
Membre: 124 pays; *Critères d'admissibilite:* Organisations nationales d'architectes
Activités: *Listes de destinataires:* Oui
Prix, Bouses: • UIA Gold Medal (Prix)
Awarded to a living architect in recognition of his/her life's work & contribution to mankind, to society & to the promotion of the art of architecture; awarded every three years
• Auguste Perret Prize (Prix)
Awarded every three years for technology applied to architecture
• Jean Tschumi Prize (Prix)
Awarded every three years for architectural criticism &/or education
• Sir Robert Matthew Prize (Prix)
Awarded every three years for improvement in the quality of human settlements
• Sir Patrick Abercrombie Prize (Prix)
Awarded every three years for town Planning & territorial development

Union internationale des associations d'alpinisme (UIAA) / International Climbing & Mountaineering Federation

PO Box 23, Monbijoustrasse 61, Bern CH-3000 Switzerland
Tel: 41-(0)31-370-18-28; *Fax:* 41-(0)31-370-18-38
office@uiaa.ch
www.theuiaa.org
www.facebook.com/theuiaa
twitter.com/UIAAmountains
www.youtube.com/uiaabern
Overview: A medium-sized international organization founded in 1932
Mission: To study & solve all problems in connection with mountaineering in general & particularly those of an international nature; To contribute to the development & promotion of mountaineering on an international level
Affliation(s): Alpine Club of Canada; Fédération québecoise de la montagne
Chief Officer(s):
Vrijlandt Frits, President
Membership: 80 institutional from 50 countries; *Member Profile:* National alpine associations from all over the world; *Committees:* Management; Mountaineering; Sports; Access; Anti-Doping; Ice Climbing; Medical; Mountain Protection; Safety; Youth

Union internationale des briqueteurs et métiers connexes (FAT-COI/FCT) *See* International Union of Bricklayers & Allied Craftworkers (AFL-CIO/CFL)

Union internationale des constructeurs d'ascenseurs *See* International Union of Elevator Constructors

Union internationale des employés des services (FAT-COI/CTC) *See* Service Employees International Union (AFL-CIO/CLC)

Union internationale des employés professionnels et de bureau (FAT-COI/CTC) *See* Office & Professional Employees International Union (AFL-CIO/CLC)

Union internationale des instituts de recherches forestières *See* International Union of Forest Research Organizations

Union internationale des journaliers d'Amérique (FAT-COI/CTC) *See* Laborers' International Union of North America (AFL-CIO/CLC)

Union internationale des journalistes et de la presse de langue française *Voir* Union internationale de la presse francophone

Union internationale des magistrats *See* International Association of Judges

Union internationale des opérateurs de machines lourdes (FAT-COI/FCT) *See* International Union of Operating Engineers (AFL-CIO/CFL)

Union internationale des sciences anthropologiques et ethnologiques *See* International Union of Anthropological & Ethnological Sciences

Union internationale des sciences biologiques *See* International Union of Biological Sciences

Union internationale des travailleurs du verre, mouleurs, poterie, plastique et autres (FAT-COI/CTC) *See* Glass, Molders, Pottery, Plastic & Allied Workers International Union (AFL-CIO/CLC)

Union internationale des travailleurs et travailleuses unis de l'alimentation et du commerce *See* United Food & Commercial Workers' International Union

Union internationale humanite et laique *See* International Humanist & Ethical Union

Union internationale pour les livres de jeunesse *See* International Board on Books for Young People

Union internationale végéterienne *See* International Vegetarian Union

Union interparlementaire *See* Inter-Parliamentary Union

Union mondiale des organisations féminines catholiques (UMOFC) / World Union of Catholic Women's Organizations (WUCWO)

76, rue de Saints-Pères, Paris F-75007 France
Tél: 33-1-45-44-27-65; *Téléc:* 33-1-42-84-04-80
wucwoparis@wanadoo.fr
www.wucwo.org
Aperçu: *Dimension:* grande; *Envergure:* internationale; fondée en 1910
Mission: PromouVoir l'apport des femmes catholiques à la communauté ecclésiale et humaine; étudier et encourager la participation des femmes dans la mission d'évangélisation de l'Église; promouVoir une action qui rend les femmes capables de mieux remplir leur rôle dans l'Église et dans la société
Membre de: Conférence des Organisations Internationales Catholiques (OIC)
Affiliation(s): Catholic Women's League of Canada; Ukrainian Catholic Women's League of Canada; Association féminine d'éducation d'action sociale; Mouvement des femmes chrétiennes - Inter-Montréal
Membre(s) du bureau directeur:
Maria Giovanna Ruggieri, Présidente générale
wucwopregen@gmail.com
Liliane Stevenson, Secrétaire générale
wucwosecgen@gmail.com
Membre(s) du personnel: 3
Membre: Over 50,000; *Critères d'admissibilite:* Organisation féminine catholique ayant 3 ans d'existance; *Comités:* Commissions Permanentes - Droits Humains; Développement et Coopération; Femmes et Église; Famille; Oecuménisme; Comités permanents - Finances; Statutes et Procédures; Communication, Information et Publications; International
Activités: Groupe de travail sur la violence contre les femmes, santé et prises de décisions; éducation; droits humains
Publications:
• Voix de Femmes [a publication of Union mondiale des organisations féminines catholiques]
Type: Newsletter

Union mondiale ORT *See* World ORT Union

Union of International Associations (UAI)

Rue Washington 40, Brussels B-1050 Belgium
Tel: 32-2-640-1808; *Fax:* 32-2-643-6199
uia@uia.be
www.uia.org
Overview: A large international organization founded in 1910
Mission: The Union of International Associations (UIA) - non-profit, apolitical, independent, and non-governmental - is a scientific research institute and documentation centre
Chief Officer(s):
Anne-Marie Boutin, President
Staff Member(s): 20
Publications:
• Yearbook of International Organizations

UNITE HERE

275 - 7th Ave., New York NY 10001-6708 USA
Tel: 212-265-7000; *Fax:* 212-265-3415
tsnyder@unitehere.org
www.uniteunion.org
www.facebook.com/UniteHere?v=wall
twitter.com/unitehere
Previous Name: International Ladies' Garment Workers' Union (AFL-CIO/CLC); Union of Needletrades, Industrial & Textile Employees
Overview: A large international organization founded in 1995
Mission: To represent workers in the following major sectors: apparel & textile manufacturing, apparel distribution centers, apparel retail, industrial laundries, hotels, casinos, foodservice, airport concessions, & restaurants
Chief Officer(s):
Tom Snyder, Communications
D. Taylor, President
Membership: 450,000 active members and more than 400,000 retirees throughout North America

United Association of Journeymen & Apprentices of the Plumbing & Pipe Fitting Industry of the United States & Canada (UA)

3 Park Place, Annapolis MD 21401 USA
Tel: 410-269-2000; *Fax:* 410-267-0262
ua.org
www.facebook.com/pages/United-Association/103644036958
twitter.com/UAPoliticalEd
www.youtube.com/uaweb901
Also Known As: United Association
Overview: A large international organization founded in 1889
Mission: The union for plumbers, fitters, welders & HVAC Service Techs
Chief Officer(s):
William P. Hite, General President
Patrick R. Perno, General Sec.-Treas.
Stephen F. Kelly, Assistant General President
Staff Member(s): 100
Membership: 300 unions with 340,000 members

Canadian Office
442 Gilmour St., Ottawa ON K2P 0R8
Tel: 613-565-1100; *Fax:* 613-562-1200
www.uacanada.ca
www.facebook.com/uacanadamembers
twitter.com/UACanada
www.youtube.com/user/theuacanada
Chief Officer(s):
John Telford, Canadian Affairs Director
john.telford@uacanada.ca

United Brotherhood of Carpenters & Joiners of America (AFL-CIO/CLC) / Fraternité unie des charpentiers et menuisiers d'Amérique (FAT-COI/CTC)

101 Constitution Ave. NW, Washington DC 20001 USA
Tel: 202-546-6206; *Fax:* 202-543-5724
webmaster@carpenters.org
www.carpenters.org
Overview: A large international organization
Chief Officer(s):
Douglas J. McCarron, General President
Membership: 56,000 + 121 locals

United Food & Commercial Workers' International Union (UFCW) / Union internationale des travailleurs et travailleuses unis de l'alimentation et du commerce

1775 K St. NW, Washington DC 20006 USA
Tel: 202-223-3111; *Fax:* 202-466-1562
ufcw@ufcw.ca
www.ufcw.org
www.facebook.com/ufcwinternational
twitter.com/UFCW
youtube.com/UFCWInternational;
flickr.com/photos/ufcwinternational
Overview: A large international organization founded in 1979
Mission: Empowering workers to unite & find their voice.
Chief Officer(s):
Joseph T. Hansen, International President
Anthony M. Perrone, International Secretary-Treasurer
Membership: 1,300,000; *Member Profile:* People working primarily in grocery & retail stores, & in the food processing & meat packing industries.

United Mine Workers of America (CLC) / Mineurs unis d'Amérique (CTC)

#200, 18354 Quantico Gateway Dr., Triangle VA 22172-1179 USA
Tel: 703-291-2400
www.umwa.org
Overview: A small international organization
Chief Officer(s):
Cecil Roberts, President

Canada
33 Gallant St., Glace Bay NS B1A 1T2
Tel: 902-849-8692
umwa@ns.sympatico.ca
www.umwa.org

Mission: The union represents U.S. & Canadian coal miners, clean coal technicians, health care workers, truck drivers, manufacturing workers & public employees
District 26
33 Gallant St., Glace Bay NS B1A 1T2
Tel: 902-849-8692
umwa@ns.sympatico.ca
www.umwa.org

United Mitochondrial Disease Foundation (UMDF)
#201, 8085 Saltsburg Rd., Pittsburgh PA 15239 USA
Tel: 412-793-8077; *Fax:* 412-793-6477
Toll-Free: 888-317-8633
info@umdf.org
www.umdf.org
Overview: A small international organization founded in 1995
Mission: To promote research & education for the diagnosis, treatment & cure of mitochondrial disorders & to provide support to affected individuals & families
Chief Officer(s):
Charles A. Mohan, CEO/Executive Director
chuckm@umdf.org
Charles A. Mohan, Jr., CEO
Staff Member(s): 10; 100 volunteer(s)
Membership: 1,045; *Fees:* US$50; *Member Profile:* Unification of the COX Foundation, PALS (People Affected by Leigh's Syndrome), & the National Leigh's Disease Foundation; *Committees:* Scientific Advisory; Executive; Governence; Symposium
Activities: Research grants; *Library* Open to public

United Nations Centre for Human Settlements (Habitat) *See* United Nations Human Settlements Programme (Habitat)

United Nations Conference on Trade & Development (UNCTAD) / Conférence des Nations Unies sur le commerce et le développement (CNUCED)
Palais des Nations, 8-14, av de la Paix, Geneva 10 1211 Switzerland
Tel: 41-22-917-1234; *Fax:* 41-22-917-0057
Other Communication: www.flickr.com/photos/53390373@N06
info@unctad.org
www.unctad.org
twitter.com/unctad
www.youtube.com/user/UNCTADOnline
Overview: A large international organization founded in 1964
Mission: Fostering sustainable growth & development in developing countries & countries in transition through analytical & operational activities in the areas of trade & related development issues, such as finance, technology, investment, enterprise development, & environment
Chief Officer(s):
Supachai Panitchpakdi, Secretary General
sgo@unctad.org
Finances: *Annual Operating Budget:* Greater than $5 Million
Staff Member(s): 394
Membership: 194 countries
Activities: Promotes & examines the participation of developing countries in international trade & investment; monitors the implementation of the UN Programme of Action for the Least Developed Countries (LDCs); analyzes trends in foreign direct investment & their impact on development; strengthens the service sector capacity in developing countries; promotes the integration of trade, environment & development; reduces commodity dependence through diversification & risk management; faciliates trade; *Internships:* Yes; *Speaker Service:* Yes *Library*

United Nations Development Programme (UNDP)
One United Nations Plaza, New York NY 10017 USA
Tel: 212-906-5000
Other Communication: publications.queries@undp.org
UNDP-newsroom@undp.org
www.undp.org
www.facebook.com/UNDP
twitter.com/undp
www.youtube.com/user/undp/featured
Overview: A medium-sized international organization
Mission: To help the United Nations become a powerful & cohesive force for sustainable human development; To focus its own resources on a series of objectives central to sustainable human development: democratic governance, poverty reduction, crisis prevention & recovery, energy & environment, information & communications technology & HIV/AIDS: To help developing countries attract & use aid effectively; To promote the protection of human rights & the empowerment of women
Chief Officer(s):
Helen Clark, Administrator
Rekha Thapa, Secretary
William Warner, Senior Editor, 212-906-5389
Soohyun Kim, Specialist, Reports & Policy, 212-906-5151

United Nations Environment Programme (UNEP) / Programme des nations unies pour l'environnement
Regional Office for North America (RONA), #506, 900 - 17th St. NW, Washington DC 20006 USA
Tel: 202-785-0465; *Fax:* 202-785-2096
www.rona.unep.org
www.facebook.com/unep.org
twitter.com/unep
www.youtube.com/unepandyou
Overview: A large international organization founded in 1972
Mission: To provide leadership & encourage partnership in caring for the environment by inspiring, informing & enabling nations & peoples to improve their quality of life without compromising that of future generations
Affiliation(s): Canadian Committee for UNEP
Chief Officer(s):
Amy Fraenkel, Regional Director
Elisabeth Guilbaud-Cox, Senior Programme Officer & Head, Communications
Finances: *Annual Operating Budget:* Greater than $5 Million; *Funding Sources:* UN member countries; private sector
Staff Member(s): 20
Activities: Development of environmental law; collection & dissemination of environmental data; assistance to developing countries; *Awareness Events:* World Environment Day, June 5; *Internships:* Yes; *Speaker Service:* Yes
Publications:
• Our Planet [a publication of the United Nations Environment Programme]
Type: Magazine
Profile: Topics regarding environmentally sustainable development
• Tunza [a publication of the United Nations Environment Programme]
Type: Magazine
Profile: Magazine aimed at youth
• The UNEP [United Nations Environment Program] Year Book
Type: Yearbook

United Nations Human Settlements Programme (Habitat)
PO Box 30030, Nairobi 00100 Kenya
Tel: 254-20-6623-120; *Fax:* 254-20-6234-77
infohabitat@unhabitat.org
www.unhabitat.org
www.facebook.com/pages/UN-HABITAT/127012777443
twitter.com/unhabitat
www.youtube.com/user/epitunhabitat
Also Known As: UN-HABITAT
Previous Name: United Nations Centre for Human Settlements (Habitat)
Overview: A large international organization
Mission: The United Nations Human Settlements Programme, UN-HABITAT, is the United Nations agency for human settlements. It is mandated by the UN General Assembly to promote socially and environmentally sustainable towns and cities with the goal of providing adequate shelter for all
Chief Officer(s):
Joan Clos, Executive Director
Aisa Kirabo Kacyira, Deputy Exec. Dir. & Ass't Sec.-Gen.
Publications:
• Publications Catalogue [a publication of the United Nations Human Settlements Programme (Habitat)]

United Nations Industrial Development Organization (UNIDO)
Vienna International Centre, PO Box 300, Wagramerstr. 5, Vienna A-1400 Austria
Tel: 43-1-26026-0; *Fax:* 43-1-269-2669
unido@unido.org
www.unido.org
www.facebook.com/UNIDO.HQ
twitter.com/UNIDO
www.youtube.com/user/UNIDObeta
Overview: A large international organization founded in 1966
Mission: To relieve poverty by fostering productivity growth; to help developing countries & countries in transition in their fight against marginalization in the globalized world; to mobilize knowledge, skills, information & technology to promote productive employment, a competitive economy & a sound environment
Chief Officer(s):
Kandeh K. Yumkella, Director General
Finances: *Annual Operating Budget:* Greater than $5 Million; *Funding Sources:* Regular & operational budgets; special contributions for technical cooperation activities
Staff Member(s): 700
Membership: 174 member states; *Fees:* Regular & operational budgets; Special contributions for technical cooperation activities; *Member Profile:* States ratifying the UNIDO Constitution; *Committees:* Governing Bodies: Director-General; Member States; General Conference; Industrial Development Board; Program & Budget Committee
Activities: Business Plan is to strengthen industrial capacities; cleaner & sustainable industrial development; focused on least developed countries, in particular Africa, on agro-based & industries & small & medium enterprises; *Awareness Events:* Africa Industrialization Day; *Internships:* Yes

United Nations Research Institute for Social Development (UNRISD) / Institut de recherche des Nations Unies pour le développement social
Palais des Nations, Geneva CH-1211 Switzerland
Tel: 41-22-917-3020; *Fax:* 41-22-917-0650
info@unrisd.org
www.unrisd.org
www.linkedin.com/company/unrisd
www.facebook.com/UNRISD
twitter.com/unrisd
www.youtube.com/unrisd
Overview: A small international organization founded in 1963
Mission: Engages in multi-disciplinary research on the social dimensions of contemporary problems affecting development; attempts to provide governments, development agencies, grassroots organizations & scholars with a better understanding of how development policies & processes of economic, social & environmental change affect different social groups; works in affiliation with a wide range of international, national & regional organizations
Chief Officer(s):
Sarah Cook, Director
Peter Utting, Deputy Director
Finances: *Annual Operating Budget:* $3 Million-$5 Million; *Funding Sources:* Voluntary grants from governments, & a variety of national & international grant-giving bodies
Staff Member(s): 20; 10 volunteer(s)
Membership: 1-99
Activities: Cross-country, multidisciplinary research on six themes: Civil Society & Social Movements; Identities, Conflict & Cohesion; Social Policy & Development; Gender & Development; Democracy, Governance & Well-Being; Markets, Business & Regulation; *Internships:* Yes

United Steelworkers of America (AFL-CIO/CLC) / Métallurgistes unis d'Amérique (FAT-COI/CTC)
5 Gateway Center, Pittsburgh PA 15222 USA
Tel: 412-562-2400
Other Communication:
www.flickr.com/photos/unitedsteelworkers
webmaster@uswa.org
www.usw.org
www.facebook.com/steelworkers
twitter.com/steelworkers
www.youtube.com/steelworkers
Also Known As: Steelworkers
Overview: A large international organization
Affiliation(s): AFL-CIO; Alliance for American Manufacturing; Blue Green Alliance; National College Players Association; Sierra Club; Steelworkers Organization of Active Retirees; Transortation Trades Department; Union Sportsmen Alliance; Union Veterans Council; United Students Againts Sewatshops; We Can Solve It
Chief Officer(s):
Leo W. Gerard, International President
Stan Johnson, International Secretary-Treasurer
Membership: 1.2 million active & retired; *Member Profile:* Members from the following industries: Metals; Manufacturing; Paper & Forestry Products; Chemical Industry; Pharmacies & Pharmaceuticals; Public Employee Council; Mining; Energy & Utilities
Publications:
• FrontLines [a publication of United Steelworkers of America (AFL-CIO/CLC)]
Type: Newsletter

• The Oilworker [a publication of United Steelworkers of America (AFL-CIO/CLC)]
Type: Newsletter
• Pulp Truth [a publication of United Steelworkers of America (AFL-CIO/CLC)]
Type: Newsletter
• SOAR in Action [a publication of United Steelworkers of America (AFL-CIO/CLC)]
Type: Newsletter
• USW@Work [a publication of United Steelworkers of America (AFL-CIO/CLC)]
Type: Magazine

USWA Canadian National Office
234 Eglinton Ave. East, 8th Fl., Toronto ON M4P 1K7
Tel: 416-487-1571; *Fax:* 416-482-5548
Toll-Free: 877-669-8792
info@usw.ca
www.usw.ca
Mission: To enhance members' economic security & human well-being by negotiating strong collective agreements by playing progressive role in Canada's social & political affairs
Affliation(s): IMF International Metalworkers' Federation; American Federation of Labour
Chief Officer(s):
Ken Neuman, Canadian National Director
kneuman@usw.ca

United Transportation Union (AFL-CIO/CLC) (UTU) / Travailleurs unis des transports (FAT-CIO/CTC)
#340, 24950 Country Club Blvd., North Olmsted OH 44070-5333 USA
Tel: 216-228-9400; *Fax:* 216-228-5755
www.utu.org
Overview: A medium-sized international organization founded in 1969
Chief Officer(s):
Malcolm B. Futhey Jr., International President
president@utu.org

United Way of America
701 North Fairfax St., Alexandria VA 22314-2045 USA
Tel: 703-836-7112; *Fax:* 703-683-7840
www.liveunited.org
www.facebook.com/UnitedWay
twitter.com/live_united
www.youtube.com/user/UnitedWayPSAs
Overview: A large international organization
Mission: United Way of America is the national organization dedicated to leading the United Way movement
Chief Officer(s):
Brian A. Gallagher, President & CEO
Awards:
• Student United Way Awards (Award)

Universal Esperanto Association ***See*** Universala Esperanto-Asocio

Universala Esperanto Asocio
Stn. BJ, Nieuwe Binnenweg 176, Rotterdam 3015 Netherlands
Tel: 31-10-436-1044; *Fax:* 31-10-436-1751
info@uea.org
www.uea.org
Previous Name: World Esperanto Association
Overview: A medium-sized international charitable organization founded in 1908 overseen by Esperanto Association of Canada
Mission: To promote the use of the international language Esperanto; to work toward the solution to the language problem within international relations; to help improve human relations by making every effort to diminish national, racial, religious, & political tensions; to promote solidarity among all Esperantists & respect for all people
Finances: *Funding Sources:* Membership fees; donations
Staff Member(s): 10; 3 volunteer(s)
Membership: More than 20,000 individual & associated in 117 countries; *Fees:* $13 in Canada; *Member Profile:* Working knowledge of the language Esperanto; *Committees:* The Honorable Patrons Committee; The UEA Committees A,B,C
Activities: Information services; the UEA-UN office (#1, 777 United Nations Plaza, New York NY 10017); The Centre for Terminology; The Centre for Research & Documentation of the World Language Problems; The World Pen Club; *Awareness Events:* Zamenhofa Tago, Dec. 15; International Friendship Week, last week of Feb.; *Speaker Service:* Yes *Library:* Bibliotego "Hodler"; by appointment

Universala Esperanto-Asocio (UEA) / Universal Esperanto Association
Nieuwe Binnenweg 176, Rotterdam 3015 BJ Netherlands
Tel: 31-10-436-1044; *Fax:* 31-10-436-1751
info@uea.org
www.uea.org
Overview: A medium-sized international organization founded in 1908
Mission: To promote the use of Esperanto as a solution of the language problem in international relations; to improve the spiritual & material relations between the peoples of the world
Affliation(s): Canadian Esperanto Association
Chief Officer(s):
Renato Corsetti, Chair
Osmo Buller, General Director
Finances: *Annual Operating Budget:* $250,000-$500,000;
Funding Sources: Membership fees
Staff Member(s): 9; 2 volunteer(s)
Membership: 6,050 individual + 12,200 in 65 national affiliates + 50 national youth organizations + 77 interest groups; *Fees:* 9 euros; *Member Profile:* People with a working knowledge of Esperanto
Activities: World Esperanto Congress; *Library:* Hector Hodler Library; Open to public

The Uranium Institute ***See*** World Nuclear Association

Urban & Regional Information Systems Association (URISA)
#680, 701 Lee St., Des Plaines IL 60016 USA
Tel: 847-824-6300; *Fax:* 847-824-6363
info@urisa.org
www.urisa.org
Overview: A small international organization founded in 1963
Mission: To support the effective application of information technology; to provide a means for the exchange of information among members & others; to develop members' skills & knowledge relating to information management technology & systems; provides ongoing educational programs about Geographic Information Systems (GIS) & automated information management within all levels of government & a wide cross-section of the private sector (GIS - computer based technology that captures, stores, analyzes & displays information about places on the earth's surface; more than 80 percent of all information used by local governments is geographically referenced; with GIS any location, any point on the map can become an index to cultural, economic, environmental, demographic & political information about that location)
Chief Officer(s):
Al Butler, President
Finances: *Annual Operating Budget:* $1.5 Million-$3 Million
Staff Member(s): 9
Membership: 3,500; *Fees:* US$132; *Member Profile:* IT professionals in all levels of government

British Columbia Chapter
PO Box 608, #101, 1001 West Broadway, Vancouver BC V6H 4E4
news@urisabc.org
www.urisabc.org
Mission: To promote the use of spatial information technologies
Chief Officer(s):
Dan Toncon, President, 604-436-6854
Dan.Tancon@metrovancouver.org
Drew Rifkin, Vice-President, 604-501-9985 Ext. 294
drew.rifkin@safe.com
Robert Schultz, Treasurer, 604-264-2238
treasurer@urisabc.org
• Urban & Regional Information Systems Association British Columbia Chapter Newsletter
Type: Newsletter; *Editor:* Jerry Maedel

URISA Alberta
PO Box 76137, 468 Southgate Shopping Centre NW, Edmonton AB T6H 4M6
Tel: 780-492-3318; *Fax:* 780-464-8116
www.urisab.org
Chief Officer(s):
Randy Williamson, President
president@urisab.org

URISA Ontario
15 Thornlea Rd., Thornhill ON L3T 1X2
Tel: 416-338-2219; *Fax:* 905-709-0764
newmember@urisaoc.ca
www.urisaoc.ca
Chief Officer(s):
Sandra Crutcher, Executive Director
execdirector@urisaoc.ca

URISA Québec
CP 32255, Succ. Waverly, Montréal QC H3L 3X1
Tél: 514-382-3873; *Téléc:* 514-382-9534
www.agmq.qc.ca
Chief Officer(s):
Marc Bélair, President
mbelair@gazmetro.com
Gilles Boislard, Direction générale
gilles.boislard@videotron.ca
Jasmine Ratté, Service aux membres
jasmine.ratte@agmq.qc.ca

U.S. Committee for Refugees & Immigrants (USCRI)
#350, 2231 Crystal Dr., Arlington VA 22202-3711 USA
Tel: 703-310-1130; *Fax:* 703-769-4241
uscri@uscridc.org
www.refugees.org
www.facebook.com/USCRI
twitter.com/USCRIDC
Overview: A large international organization founded in 1958
Mission: To defend the basic human rights of refugees, most fundamentally, the principle of nonrefoulement - no forced return of a person with a well-founded fear of persecution to his or her homeland; To defend the rights of asylum seekers to a fair & impartial determination of their status; To defend the right to decent & humane treatment for all internally displaced persons
Member of: Immigration & Refugee Services of America
Chief Officer(s):
Scott Wu, Chair
Lavinia Limón, President & CEO
Jeff Fahey, Global Ambassador
Finances: *Annual Operating Budget:* $500,000-$1.5 Million;
Funding Sources: Foundations; individuals & corporations
Staff Member(s): 12; 12 volunteer(s)
Activities: Work includes refugee resettlement, refugee rights, child migrants & human trafficking; *Internships:* Yes; *Speaker Service:* Yes; *Rents Mailing List:* Yes *Library*

U.S. Green Building Council
#500, 2101 L Street NW, Washington DC 20037 USA
Tel: 202-742-3792
Toll-Free: 800-795-1747
leedinfo@usgbc.org
www.usgbc.org
Overview: A medium-sized national organization
Mission: To promote buildings that are environmentally responsible, profitable & healthy places to live & work
Chief Officer(s):
S. Richard Fedrizzi, President & CEO
Scot Horst, Senior Vice-President LEED
Judith Webb, Senior Vice-President, Marketing & Communications
Staff Member(s): 5
Membership: 15,000+; *Fees:* Schedule available; *Committees:* Executive; Finance; Governance
Activities: Promotes LEED, Leadership in Energy & Environmental Design, green building rating system, a voluntary consensus-based national standard for developing high-performance, sustainable buildings

U.S. Trademark Association ***See*** International Trademark Association

Used Building Materials Association ***See*** Building Materials Reuse Association

Video Software Dealers Association ***See*** Entertainment Merchants Association - International Head Office

Vie Humaine Internationale ***See*** Human Life International

The Vinyl Institute (VI)
#390, 1737 King St., Alexandria VA 22314 USA
Tel: 571-970-3400; *Fax:* 571-970-3271
www.vinylinfo.org
twitter.com/VinylinDesign
www.youtube.com/user/vinylinstitute
Overview: A small local organization founded in 1982
Mission: Clearinghouse for information about vinyl's environmental performance
Chief Officer(s):
Richard M. Doyle, President, 571-970-3372
ddoyle@vinylinfo.org

Wallace Center, Winrock International
#500, 2121 Crystal Dr., Arlington VA 22202 USA
Tel: 703-302-6500; *Fax:* 703-302-6512
wallace@winrock.org
www.wallacecenter.org
Previous Name: Institute for Alternative Agriculture
Overview: A small national charitable organization founded in 1983
Mission: To serve as publisher of reliable scientific information on alternative agriculture; to sponsor research & education outreach programs; to be a voice for alternative agriculture; to act as a contact for farmers & others who seek information on diversified, sustainable farming systems; to encourage & facilitate the adoption of low-cost, resource-conserving & environmentally sound farming methods
Chief Officer(s):
Erin Caricofe, Program Assistant
John Fisk, Director
Finances: *Annual Operating Budget:* $500,000-$1.5 Million
Staff Member(s): 10
Membership: 995; *Fees:* US$16 individual; *Member Profile:* Farmers, researchers, Extension personnel, policy makers & consumers
Activities: Research; policy analysis & development; education & outreach; scientific & general audience publications; symposia

Warmer Bulletin - Residua Ltd.
Yellow Cottage, Draughton, Skipton, North Yorkshire BD23 6EA United Kingdom
Tel: 44-0-1756-711-363; *Fax:* 44-0-1756-711-360
info@resourcesnotwaste.org
www.resourcesnotwaste.org
Previous Name: Warmer Campaign (World Action for Recycling Materials & Energy from Rubbish)
Overview: A medium-sized international charitable organization founded in 1984
Mission: To collect & disseminate information on household waste, its minimization, reuse, recycling & energy from waste
Chief Officer(s):
Steve Read, Chair
Staff Member(s): 4
Membership: 2,000; *Fees:* Depends on location & status
Activities: *Library* Open to public by appointment

Warmer Campaign (World Action for Recycling Materials & Energy from Rubbish) ***See*** Warmer Bulletin - Residua Ltd.

Water Environment Federation (WEF)
601 Wythe St., Alexandria VA 22314-1994 USA
Tel: 703-684-2400; *Fax:* 703-684-2492
Toll-Free: 800-666-0206
comments@wef.org
www.wef.org
www.facebook.com/WaterEnvironmentFederation
twitter.com/WEForg
Previous Name: Federation of Sewage Works Associations; Federation of Sewage & Industrial Wastes Associations; Water Pollution Control Federation
Overview: A large international organization founded in 1928
Mission: To ensure clean water for the protection of public health; To advance the water profession
Chief Officer(s):
Cordell Samuels, President
Jeff Eger, Executive Director, 703-684-2430
jeger@wef.org
Linda Kelly, Director, Communications, 703-684-2448
lkelly@wef.org
Staff Member(s): 100
Membership: 36,000 individuals + 75 affiliated associations; *Member Profile:* Water quality professionals from around the globe; *Committees:* Air Quality & Odor Control; Audit; Automation & Info Tech; Awards & recognitions; Collection Systems; Constitution & Bylaws; Disinfection & Public Health; Government Affairs; Groundwater; Industrial Wastewater; International Coordination; Laboratory Practices; Literature Review; Manufacturers & Representatives; Membership; Municipal Wastewater Treatment Design; Nominating; Operations Challenge; Plant Operations & Maintenance; Professional Development; Program; Public Communication & Outreach; Research & Innovation; Residuals & Biosolids; and others...
Activities: Providing water quality information; offering networking opportunities; online Knowledge Center for members; *Library:* WEF Knowledge Center
Meetings/Conferences:
• 2015 Water & Wastewater Leadership Center, March, 2015, University of North Carolina at Chapel Hill, Chapel Hill, NC
Scope: International
• Collection Systems 2015: Collection Systems Taking Center Stage - Seize the Opportunity, April, 2015, Duke Energy Convention Center, Cincinnati, OH
Scope: International
• Water Environment Federation and American Water Works Association (AWWA) The Utility Management Conference 2015, February, 2015, Hyatt Regency Austin, Austin, TX
Scope: International
Description: Water and wastewater managers and utility professionals will gather to hear the latest in cutting edge approaches and practices, techniques and case studies in all aspects of utility management.
Contact Information: Phone: 703-684-2400 ext. 7010; confinfo@wef.org
• Water Environment Federation Residuals and Biosolids 2015: The Next Generation of Science, Technology & Management, June, 2015, Walter E. Washington Convention Center, Washington, DC
Scope: International
Description: A specialty conference on residuals and biosolids management.
• Water Environment Federation 2015 Design-Build for Water/Wastewater Conference, March, 2015, Henry B. Gonzalez Convention Center, San Antonio, TX
Scope: International
• Water Environment Federation WEFTEC 2015: 88th Annual Water Environment Federation Technical Exhibition & Conference, September, 2015, McCormick Place, Chicago, IL
Scope: International
Attendance: 18,000
Description: Educational & training opportunities, plus an exhibition by more than 750 companies
Contact Information: Membership Information, Toll-Free Phone: 1-800-666-0206, International Phone: +44 120-679-6351 or 571-830-1545
• Water Environment Federation WEFTEC 2016: 89th Annual Water Environment Federation Technical Exhibition & Conference, September, 2016, New Orleans Morial Convention Center, New Orleans, LA
Scope: International
Attendance: 18,000
Description: An annual educational & networking event drawing water quality experts from around the world
Contact Information: Membership Information, Toll-Free Phone: 1-800-666-0206, International Phone: +44 120-679-6351 or 571-830-1545
Publications:
• Water Environment & Technology [a publication of the Water Environment Federation]
Type: Magazine; *Accepts Advertising*; *Editor:* Melissa Jackson
Profile: Information for water professionals such as regulatory & legislative impacts, technologies, solutions, & professionaldevelopment activities
• Water Environment Laboratory Solutions [a publication of the Water Environment Federation]
Type: Newsletter; *Editor:* Steve Spicer (sspicer@wef.org)
Profile: Contents include equipment use, sample tracking, quality control, analytical methods, &certification
• Water Environment Regulation Watch [a publication of the Water Environment Federation]
Type: Newsletter; *Frequency:* Monthly
Profile: Reports of federal government actions related to water quality
• Water Environment Research [a publication of the Water Environment Federation]
Type: Journal; *Frequency:* Monthly; *Editor:* Anthony Krizel;
Price: $100 (print only) withWater Environment Federation membership
Profile: Peer-reviewed research papers related to pollution control, water quality, & management
• WEF [Water Environment Federation] Highlights
Type: Newsletter; *Editor:* Jennifer Fulcher (jfulcher&wef.org)
Profile: Water Environment Federation activities & information for members
• World Water [a publication of the Water Environment Federation]
Type: Magazine
Profile: An international magazine focussing on water issues, such as groundwater, wastewater, sludge, desalination, & treatment
• World Water: Water Reuse & Desalination [a publication of the Water Environment Federation]
Type: Magazinr; *Frequency:* Monthly
Profile: Technical, scientific, policy, public health & financial aspects to water reuse & desalination

The Waterbird Society
c/o ONSA, #680, 5400 Bosque Blvd., Waco TX 76710-4446 USA
www.waterbirds.org
Previous Name: Colonial Waterbird Society
Overview: A small international organization founded in 1976
Mission: To study & conserve all aquatic birds
Affliation(s): Ornithological Council; American Bird Conservancy
Chief Officer(s):
Katharine Parsons, President
kparsons@massaudubon.org
Susan Elbin, Vice-President & President-Elect
selbin@nycaudubon.org
Clay Green, Secretary
claygreen@txstate.edu
Christine Custer, Treasurer
christine_custer@usgs.gov
Finances: *Funding Sources:* Membership dues
Membership: *Fees:* $45 students; $55 regular members; $60 families; $1000 lifetimes members (Fees include copies of the paper journal); *Member Profile:* Persons interested in studying & monitoring aquatic birds; *Committees:* Archives; Membership; Nominations; Bylaws; Finance & Investment; Research Awards; Conservation; Publications; Future Meetings; Outreach & Communications; Recognition Awards; Research Awards; Students Activities
Activities: Facilitating communication among persons who study waterbirds
Publications:
• Waterbirds
Type: Journal; *Frequency:* 3 pa; *Editor:* Dr. Robert W. Elner
Profile: Papers about biology, conservation, & techniques for study of the world's waterbirds, such as wading birds, seabirds, waterfowl, & shorebirds

Weed Science Society of America (WSSA)
PO Box 7050, Lawrence KS 66044-8897 USA
Fax: 785-843-1274
Toll-Free: 800-627-0629
wssa@allenpress.com
www.wssa.net
www.linkedin.com/groups?gid=5020473&goback=.gmp_5020473
www.facebook.com/189815314505652
twitter.com/WorldOfWeeds
Overview: A small national organization
Mission: To protect the environment through the use of safe & efficient weed control practices; to facilitate the exchange of information about weeds & their control; to enhance professionalism among scientists in teaching, extension & research
Chief Officer(s):
Joyce Lancaster, Executive Secretary
jlancaster@allenpress.com

Western Finance Association (WFA)
c/o Professor Duane Seppi, Tepper School of Business, Carnegie Mellon University, Pittsburgh PA 15213 USA
Tel: 412-268-2298
wfa@andrew.cmu.edu
www.westernfinance.org
Overview: A medium-sized international organization
Mission: To improve teaching & scholarship; To enable communication among members
Chief Officer(s):
Francis Longstaff, President
Duane Seppi, Secretary-Treasurer
Membership: *Fees:* $150 lifetime membership; $50 three year membership; *Member Profile:* Academicians & practitioners with an interest in the development & application of research in finance
Activities: Disseminating information

WineAmerica
#500, 1015 - 18 St. NW, Washington DC 20036 USA
Tel: 202-783-2756
www.wineamerica.org
www.facebook.com/102925946431027
Also Known As: The National Association of American Wineries
Previous Name: American Vintners Association

Overview: A medium-sized international organization founded in 1978
Mission: To encourage the dynamic growth & development of American wineries & winegrowing through the advancement & advocacy of sound public policy
Chief Officer(s):
Edward O'Keefe, Chair
Mark Chandler, Executive Director
mchandler@wineamerica.org
Staff Member(s): 3
Membership: 600+; *Fees:* Schedule available

Women's Environment & Development Organization (WEDO)

355 Lexington Ave., 3rd Fl., New York NY 10017 USA
Tel: 212-973-0325; *Fax:* 212-973-0335
www.wedo.org
www.facebook.com/WEDOworldwide
twitter.com/wedo_worldwide
www.youtube.com/wedoworldwide;
www.flickr.com/photos/wedoworldwide
Overview: A medium-sized international organization founded in 1989
Mission: To empower women to be equal & active decision makers in environment & development matters
Chief Officer(s):
Monique Essed Fernandes, Chair
Activities: Monitor Implementation (focuses on specific recommendations for women); Outreach & Leadership (to help women become policy makers as well as policy monitors); Education & Communications; *Internships:* Yes

World Agroforestry Centre

PO Box 30677, United Nations Ave., Gigiri, Nairobi 00100 Kenya
Tel: 254 20 7224000; *Fax:* 254 20 7224001
Other Communication: www.flickr.com/photos/icraf
worldagroforestry@cgiar.org
www.worldagroforestry.org
www.facebook.com/worldagroforestry
twitter.com/ICRAF
www.youtube.com/user/WorldAgroforestry
Previous Name: International Centre for Research in Agroforestry (ICRAF)
Overview: A large international organization founded in 1977
Mission: To improve human welfare by alleviating poverty, increasing cash income, improving food & nutritional security, & enhancing environmental resilience in the tropics; To conduct strategic & applied research, in partnership with national agricultural systems, for more sustainable & productive land use. Programmes in Africa, India, Sri Lanka, Bangladesh, Indonesia, the Philippines, Viet Nam, Thailand, China, Brazil & Peru.
Member of: Consultative Group on International Agricultural Research
Chief Officer(s):
Eric Tollens, Chair
Tony Simons, Director General
Finances: *Annual Operating Budget:* Greater than $5 Million; *Funding Sources:* Donations; foundations
Staff Member(s): 402
Activities: *Awareness Events:* Field Days; *Rents Mailing List:* Yes *Library:* ICRAF Library; by appointment

World Aquaculture Society (WAS)

143 J.M. Parker Coliseum, LSU, Baton Rouge LA 70803-0001 USA
Tel: 225-578-3137; *Fax:* 225-578-3493
carolm@was.org
www.was.org
Previous Name: World Mariculture Society
Overview: A medium-sized international organization founded in 1970
Mission: To secure, evaluate, promote & distribute educational, scientific & technological advancement of aquaculture & mariculture throughout the world
Affliation(s): Aquaculture Association of Canada; European Acquaculture Association; Asian Fisheries Society; KOSFAS; Aquaculture Association of South Africa; Sociedad Brasileira de Acicultura; Indonesian Aquaculture Society; Society of Aquaculture Professionals (India); Malaysian Fisheries Society; Egyptian Aquaculture Society; Spanish Aquaculture Association; Aquaculture Without Frontiers; IAFI
Chief Officer(s):
Lorenzo Juarez, President
lorenzojuarez@yahoo.com
Staff Member(s): 2
Membership: 3,000+ direct & affiliated; *Fees:* $65 individual; $255 corporate; $45 student; sustaining $105

World Arabian Horse Organization (WAHO)

Newbarn Farmhouse, Forthampton, Gloucestershire GL19 4QD United Kingdom
Tel: 44-1684-274-455; *Fax:* 44-1684-274-422
waho@btconnect.com
www.waho.org
Overview: A medium-sized international charitable organization founded in 1972
Mission: To acquire, promote & facilitate the acquisition & dissemination of knowledge or information in all or any countries directly or indirectly concerning horses of the Arabian breed
Affliation(s): Canadian Arabian Horse Registry
Chief Officer(s):
Katrina Murray, Executive Secretary
Finances: *Annual Operating Budget:* $50,000-$100,000; *Funding Sources:* Membership fees; Donations
Staff Member(s): 1
Membership: 64 countries; *Fees:* $60 associate; $40 individual; $400 life; *Member Profile:* Big M - Registering Authorities; associate - affiliates; individual associate - individual supporters
Activities: Conference held every two years; *Library:* Arabian Horse Stud Books of the World; by appointment

World Archery Federation

Maison du Sport International, Avenue de Rhodanie 54, Lausanne 1007 Switzerland
Tel: 41-21-614-3050; *Fax:* 41-21-614-3055
info@archery.org
www.worldarchery.org
www.facebook.com/WorldArcheryPage
twitter.com/worldarchery
www.youtube.com/archerytv
Previous Name: International Archery Federation
Overview: A small international organization founded in 1931
Mission: To promote & encourage archery throughout the world in conformity with the Olympic principles; to frame & interpret FITA rules & regulations; to arrange for the organization of World Championships; to confirm & maintain world record scores & Olympic Games record scores; to maintain complete lists of scores from FITA Championships & Olympic Games
Member of: International Olympic Committee
Affliation(s): Federation of Canadian Archers Inc.
Chief Officer(s):
Ugur Erdener, President
uerdener@hacettepe.edu.tr
Tom Dielen, Secretary General
tdielen@archery.org
Finances: *Annual Operating Budget:* $500,000-$1.5 Million
Staff Member(s): 8; 70 volunteer(s)
Membership: 141 countries; *Member Profile:* National federations; *Committees:* Athletes; Elections Procedure; Coaches; Manuals; Information from Judges & Coaches; Constitution & Rules; Field Archery; Judges; Medical & Sport Sciences; Para-Archery; Target Archery; Technical

World Assembly of Youth (WAY) / Assemblée mondiale de la jeunesse

World Youth Complex, Jalan Lebuh Raya, Melaka 75450 Malaysia
Tel: 603-232-1871; *Fax:* 603-232-7271
office@way.org.my
www.way.org.my
www.facebook.com/pages/World-Assembly-of-Youth/106962109342582
Overview: A small international organization founded in 1950
Mission: An international coordinating body of national youth councils & organizations throughout the world; seeks to increase interracial respect & to foster international understanding & cooperation; to facilitate the collection of information about the needs & problems of youth; to disseminate information about the methods, techniques, activities of youth organizations; to support & encourage the national youth movement of self-governing countries in their struggle for attainment of self-government
Affliation(s): Canada World Youth
Chief Officer(s):
Datuk Ir. Idris Haron, President
Membership: 90 countries
Activities: *Rents Mailing List:* Yes

World Association for World Federation *See* World Federalist Movement

World Association of Industrial & Technological Research Organizations (WAITRO)

c/o SIRIM Berhad, PO Box 7035, 1 Persiaran Dato'Menteri, Section 2, Shah Alam 40700 Malaysia
Tel: 603-544-6635; *Fax:* 603-544-6735
info@waitro.sirim.my
www.waitro.org
Overview: A small international organization founded in 1970
Mission: To be the leading global network of research & technological organizations through collaboration & knowledge sharing for sustainable development; encourage & facilitate transfer of research results & technical know-how; promote exchange of experience in research & technology management; enhance capabilities in management of research & technological organizations; identify & promote fields of research suitable for international collaboration, new opportunities & markets; promote technological research & capability building in developing countries
Affliation(s): Research & Productivity Council; Centre de recherche industrielle du Québec; International Development Research Centre; Canadian International Development Agency; BC Research
Chief Officer(s):
R.K. Khandal, President
Charles Kwesiga, 1st Vice-President
Eckhart Bierdümpel, 2nd Vice-President
Membership: 157; *Member Profile:* Technical membership - laboratories & other organizations actively engaged in industrial & technological research & development; sustaining membership - bodies active in encouraging & promoting technological research & assisting the Association with financial support or by otherwise advancing its aims

World Association of Sleep Medicine (WASM)

#110, 3270 - 19 St. NW, Rochester MN 55901 USA
Tel: 507-316-0084; *Fax:* 877-659-0760
info@wasmonline.org
www.wasmonline.org
www.facebook.com/wasmf
Overview: A medium-sized international organization
Mission: To advance knowledge about sleep health throughout the world; To improve sleep health; To encourage prevention of sleep disorders; To act as bridge between different sleep societies & cultures; To encourage standards of practice for sleep medicine
Chief Officer(s):
Richard Allen, President
Membership: *Fees:* $55; *Member Profile:* Healthcare professionals, active in the field of sleep medicine, from around the world; *Committees:* Education; Bylaws; Membership; Scientific Affairs; Nominating; Awards Publication; Executive; World Sleep Day
Activities: Encouraging education & research in sleep medicine around the world; Facilitating the exchange of clinical information & scientific studies; Advancing knowledge of sleep & its disorders among the public
Publications:
• Sleep Medicine Worldwide: Sleep Health around the World
Type: Newsletter; *Editor:* Liborio Parrino; Robert Thomas

World Association of Veteran Athletes *See* World Masters Athletics

World Blue Chain for the Protection of Animals & Nature / La Chaine bleue mondiale

Avenue de Visé 39, Brussels B-1170 Belgium
Tel: 32-2-673-5230; *Fax:* 32-2-672-0947
contact@bwk-cbm.be
www.bwk-cbm.be
Also Known As: Blauwe Wereldketen
Overview: A medium-sized international organization founded in 1962
Mission: Protection of animals by inspections, propaganda & cultural education
Member of: World Society for Protection of Animals
Finances: *Annual Operating Budget:* $250,000-$500,000
Staff Member(s): 9; 250 volunteer(s)
Membership: 35,000 individual; *Fees:* 7.50, 12.50, 30.00 euros
Activities: *Library* Open to public by appointment

World Business Council for Sustainable Development (WBCSD)

4, ch de Conches, Geneva 1231 Switzerland
Tel: 41-22-839-3100; *Fax:* 41-22-839-3131
info@wbcsd.org

www.wbcsd.ch
twitter.com/wbcsd
Overview: A small international organization
Mission: To provide business leadership as a catalyst for change toward sustainable development; to promote the role of eco-efficiency, innovation & corporate social responsibility
Affiliation(s): The EXCEL Partnership (Canada)
Chief Officer(s):
Peter Bakker, President & CEO
Bakker@wbcsd.org
Peter White, COO
white@wbcsd.org
Membership: 170 companies in 35 countries

World Chambers Federation (WCF)

38 cours Albert 1er, Paris 75008 France
Tel: 33-149-532-944; *Fax:* 33-149-533-079
wcf@iccwbo.org
www.iccwbo.org/wcf
www.linkedin.com/company/international-chamber-of-commerce
www.facebook.com/pages/ICC-World-Chambers-Federation/267170160003753
twitter.com/WorldChambers
www.youtube.com/user/03WCF
Overview: A large international organization founded in 1951
Affiliation(s): Specialized div. of International Chamber of Commerce
Chief Officer(s):
Anthony Parkes, Director
Staff Member(s): 160
Membership: *Member Profile:* Chambers of commerce worldwide
Awards:
• World Business and Develoment Awards (Award)
• Business for Peace Awards (Award)
• Institute of World Business Law Prize (Award)
Meetings/Conferences:
• 10th International Chamber of Commerce International Mediation Competition, February, 2015, Paris
Scope: International

World Citizen Foundation (WCF)

#905, 211 East 43rd St., New York NY 10017 USA
www.worldcitizen.org
Previous Name: World Citizens Assembly
Overview: A large international organization founded in 1975
Mission: To raise awareness in the general public around the world to the need for world citizenship & the global rule of law as the foundation of a future World Democracy to legitimately enforce basic human rights & solve common global problems
Chief Officer(s):
Troy Davis, President
Finances: *Annual Operating Budget:* Less than $50,000; *Funding Sources:* Fundraising
Activities: School of Democracy Project

World Citizens Assembly ***See*** World Citizen Foundation

World Coal Institute (WCI)

Heddon House, 5th Fl., #149, 151 Regent St., London W1B 4JD United Kingdom
Tel: 44 (0) 20 7851 0052; *Fax:* 44 (0) 20 7851 0061
info@worldcoal.org
www.worldcoal.org
twitter.com/WorldCoal
www.youtube.com/worldcoal
Overview: A small international organization founded in 1985
Mission: To promote the use of coal as an economic & environmentally sound energy source; to provide a voice for coal in international debates on energy & the environment; to improve public awareness of the merits & importance of coal as the single largest source of fuel for the generation of electricity; to ensure that decision makers, & public opinion generally, are fully informed on the advances in modern clean coal technology; to widen understanding of the vital role that metallurgical coal fulfills in the worldwide production of steel; to support other sectors of the worldwide coal industry
Chief Officer(s):
Milton Catelin, Chief Executive
Christine Copley, Senior Manager
Zhang Xiwu, Chair
Finances: *Annual Operating Budget:* $500,000-$1.5 Million
Staff Member(s): 4
Membership: 20; *Committees:* Executive; Standing
Activities: *Library*

World Confederation for Physical Therapy (WCPT)

Victoria Charity Centre, 11 Belgrave. Rd., London SW1V 1RB United Kingdom
Tel: 44-20-7931-6465; *Fax:* 44-20-7931-6494
info@wcpt.org
www.wcpt.org
www.linkedin.com/company/world-confederation-for-physical-therapy-wcpt
www.facebook.com/116826698351147
twitter.com/WCPT1951
www.youtube.com/user/theWCPT
Overview: A small international charitable organization founded in 1951
Mission: To better global health by encouraging high standards of physical therapy research, education & practice, by supporting communication & by collaborating with national & international organisations.
Affiliation(s): Canadian Physiotherapy Association
Chief Officer(s):
Brenda J. Myers, Secretary General
Finances: *Funding Sources:* Membership fees
Membership: 107 Member Organisations
Activities: Establishing new standards & networks; Collecting data; Sharing expertise; Supporting investigation of workforce & migration issues; *Awareness Events:* International Physical Therapy Day, Sept.
Publications:
• WCPT News
Type: Newsletter; *Frequency:* Quarterly
Profile: News from member organizations, regions & subgroups, reports on WCPT initiatives, executive committee & general meeting decisions, & opinion articles on international issues relevant to the profession

World Confederation of Labour ***See*** International Trade Union Confederation

World Confederation of Organizations of the Teaching Profession ***See*** Education International

World Conservation Monitoring Centre ***See*** UNEP - World Conservation Monitoring Centre

The World Conservation Union; International Union for Conservation of Nature & Natural Resources ***See*** International Union for Conservation of Nature

World Council of Churches

PO Box 2100, 150, rte de Ferney, Geneva CH-1211 Switzerland
Tel: 41-22-791-6111; *Fax:* 41-22-791-0361
oikoumene.org
Overview: A medium-sized international organization
Affiliation(s): International Council of World Religions & Cultures
Chief Officer(s):
Olav Fykse Tveit, General Secretary

World Council of Credit Unions, Inc. (WOCCU)

PO Box 2982, 5710 Mineral Point Rd., Madison WI 53705-4493 USA
Tel: 608-395-2000; *Fax:* 608-395-2001
mail@woccu.org
www.woccu.org
www.linkedin.com/company/world-council-of-credit-unions
www.facebook.com/woccu
twitter.com/woccu
www.youtube.com/user/WOCCU/featured
Overview: A large international organization founded in 1971
Mission: To promote the sustainable growth & expansion of credit unions & financial cooperatives worldwide; to provide technical assistance & trade association services to members
Affiliation(s): Credit Union Central of Canada; International Cooperative Banking Assoc.; Assoc. of British Credit Unions Ltd.; Assoc. of Asian Confederation of Credit Unions; Caribbean Confederation of Credit Unions; Confederacion Latinoamericana de Cooperativas de Ahorro y Credito; Credit Union National Association; CUNA Caribbean Insurance Society Ltd; CUNA Mutual Group; Credit Union Services Corp. (Australia) Ltd.; ECCU Assurance Company Ltd.; Irish League of Credit Unions; International Raiffeisen Union; National Assoc. of Cooperative Savings & Credit Unions; National Credit Union Federation of Korea
Chief Officer(s):
Grzegorz Bierecki, Chair
Manfred Alfonso Dasenbrock, Secretary
Brian Branch, President & CEO
Finances: *Annual Operating Budget:* Greater than $5 Million; *Funding Sources:* Membership dues; grants
Staff Member(s): 59
Membership: Over 50,000; *Member Profile:* Represents the largest credit union cooperative network in the world: over 56,000 credit unions in more than 103 countries, with over 207 million members.
Activities: Information; education; advocacy; leadership & technical services; Global Credit Union Network, an international clearinghouse for credit unions, offers affiliated credit unions access to resources produced by other members, electronically links credit union movements & leaders together from across the globe; *Awareness Events:* International Credit Union Day, 3rd Thursday in Oct.; *Internships:* Yes *Library:* Information Resource Centre; Open to public
Awards:
• Distinguished Service Award (Award)
Meetings/Conferences:
• 2015 World Credit Union Conference, July, 2015, Denver, CO
Scope: International
Contact Information: URL: cuindenver2015.org
Publications:
• Credit Union World [a publication of the World Council of Credit Unions, Inc.]
Type: Magazine; *Frequency:* Annually
Profile: Highlights credit union developments, & provides information & WOCCU members, products & services

World Curling Federation (WCF)

74 Tay St., Perth PH2 8NP Scotland
Tel: 44-173-845-1630; *Fax:* 44-173-845-1641
info@worldcurling.org
www.worldcurling.org
www.linkedin.com/company/world-curling-federation
www.facebook.com/WorldCurlingFederation
twitter.com/worldcurling
www.youtube.com/user/WorldCurlingTV
Previous Name: International Curling Federation
Overview: A medium-sized international organization founded in 1966
Mission: To represent curling internationally & to facilitate the growth of the sport through a network of member nations
Member of: General Association of International Sports Federations (GAISF)
Chief Officer(s):
Kate Caithness, President
Bent Ånund Ramsfjell, Vice-President
Colin Grahamslaw, Secretary General
Staff Member(s): 11
Membership: 53 member associations; *Member Profile:* National associations
Activities: World & World Junior & World Senior Curling Championships, Men & Women; World Wheelchair Curling Championship, Mixed teams

World Dance Council Ltd. (WDC)

WDC Centre, 4 Dorset Gardens Mitcham, Surrey CR4 1LX England
Tel: 44-7590-061170
competitivedance@wdcdance.com
www.wdcdance.com
Previous Name: International Council of Ballroom Dancing
Overview: A small international organization founded in 1950
Affiliation(s): International Dance Organization
Chief Officer(s):
Hannes Emrich, Company & General Secretary
gensec@wdcdance.com
Staff Member(s): 3
Membership: 50; *Committees:* Dance Sport; Social Dance

World Darts Federation (WDF)

4 Byron Plavce, Croespenmaen, Crumlin, Newpoint NP11 3BP Wales
Tel: 44 1495 247732; *Fax:* 44-774-704-8025
www.dartswdf.com
www.facebook.com/159256067495664?sk=wall
twitter.com/wdfdarts
Overview: A small international organization founded in 1976
Mission: The WDF is a non-political, non-racial and non-profit making organization dedicated toward achieving and maintaining the highest possible standard of presentation and organization, around the world
Affiliation(s): National Darts Federation of Canada
Chief Officer(s):
Roy Price, President
president@dartswdf.com

Kelvin James, Vice-President
kelvindjames@optusnet.com.au
Dave Alderman, Secretary General
daveralderman@dartswdf.com
Membership: 250,000 players representing 60 nations;

World Energy Council (WEC) / Conseil Mondial de l'Energie (CME)

Regency House, 1-4 Warwick St., 5th Fl., London W1B 5LT
United Kingdom
Tel: 44-20-7734-5996; *Fax:* 44-20-7734-5926
info@worldenergy.org
www.worldenergy.org
www.linkedin.com/company/world-energy-council
twitter.com/WECouncil
Overview: A small international organization founded in 1923
Mission: To promote the sustainable supply & use of energy for the greatest benefit of all
Chief Officer(s):
Pierre Gadonneix, Chair
Finances: *Annual Operating Budget:* $3 Million-$5 Million
Staff Member(s): 14
Membership: 92 member countries; *Fees:* Variable; *Member Profile:* Commercial; government; non-government
Activities: Energy; energy conservation; *Library:* Information Services; by appointment

World Esperanto Association *See* Universala Esperanto Asocio

World Federalist Movement (WFM) / Mouvement féderalist mondial

708 - 3rd Ave., 24th Fl., New York NY 10017 USA
Tel: 212-599-1320; *Fax:* 212-599-1332
info@wfm-igp.org
www.wfm-igp.org
www.facebook.com/worldfederalist
twitter.com/worldfederalist
Previous Name: World Association for World Federation
Overview: A medium-sized international organization founded in 1947
Mission: To work for justice, peace & sustainable prosperity; to promote an end to the rule of force through a world governed by law, based on strengthened & democratized world institutions
Affliation(s): World Federalists of Canada
Chief Officer(s):
William Pace, Executive Director
Membership: 31 organizations
Activities: Conferences; seminars; policy research; publishing of papers & monographs; lobbying; *Library*

World Federation for Mental Health (WFMH) / Fédération mondiale pour la santé mentale

PO Box 807, Occoquan VA 22125 USA
Tel: 703-313-8680; *Fax:* 703-490-6926
info@wfmh.com
www.wfmh.org
www.facebook.com/WFMH1
twitter.com/WFMHDC
Overview: A large international charitable organization founded in 1948
Mission: To promote mental health through advocacy, transfer of knowledge & consultation; to prevent or reduce the incidence & disabling consequences of mental illness throughout the world
Affliation(s): World Health Organization
Chief Officer(s):
George Christodoulou, President
Ellen R. Mercer, Vice-President, Program Development
John Bowis, Vice-President, Government
Larry Cimino, Corporate Secretary
Finances: *Annual Operating Budget:* $250,000-$500,000; *Funding Sources:* Membership dues; grants
Staff Member(s): 5; 2 volunteer(s)
Membership: 3,107 individuals + 290 organizations; *Fees:* Schedule available; *Member Profile:* Psychiatrists; psychologists; mental health consultants; lay people
Activities: *Awareness Events:* World Mental Health Day, Oct. 10

World Federation of International Music Competitions *Voir* Fédération mondiale des concours internationaux de musique

World Federation of Occupational Therapists (WFOT)

PO Box 30, Forrestfield 6058 Australia
Fax: 61-8-9453-9746
admin@wfot.org.au
www.wfot.org.au
Overview: A small international organization founded in 1952
Mission: To promote occupational therapy & international cooperation; To maintain the ethics of the profession & to advance the practice & standards; To promote internationally recognized standards for the education of the profession; to facilitate international exchange & placement of therapists & students; To facilitate the exchange of information & publications; To promote research
Affliation(s): Council of Occupational Therapists of the European Community
Chief Officer(s):
E. Sharon Brintnell, President
Susan Baptiste, Vice-President
Samantha Shann, Vice-President, Finance
Marilyn Pattison, Executive Director
Finances: *Annual Operating Budget:* Less than $50,000; *Funding Sources:* Membership fees
Membership: 55 national associations; *Fees:* Schedule available; *Member Profile:* Occupational therapists; *Committees:* Education & Research; Promotion & Development; Executive Programes; International Cooperation; Standards & Quality
Activities: *Speaker Service:* Yes *Library*

World Federation of the Deaf (WFD) / Fédération mondiale des sourds

PO Box 65, Helsinki FIN-00401 Finland
Tel: 358-9-580-3573; *Fax:* 358-9-580-3572
info@wfdeaf.org
www.wfdeaf.org
www.facebook.com/Wfdeaf.org
Overview: A medium-sized international organization founded in 1951
Mission: To promote the unification of national associations, federations & other organizations of & for deaf people at both regional & international levels; to ensure that the government in each country observe all international declarations & recommendations on human rights & the rights of deaf persons & other persons with disabilities; to promote the creation & development of national organizations of deaf people & organizations providing services to deaf people where such organizations do not exist; to disseminate scientific & legal materials about deafness & the current needs of deaf people; to promote the coordination & conduct of research & studies in all fields of deafness, including other categories of hearing loss; to facilitate the efforts of deaf people to make contributions to cultural enrichment in every country
Affliation(s): Disabled Persons International; International Sign Language Association; International Federation of the Hard of Hearing; Rehabilitation International; International Committee of Sport for the Deaf; World Blind Union; Inclusion International; World Federation of Deaf Blind; United Nations; World Health Organization; International Labor Organization; UN Educational, Scientific & Cultural Organization (UNESCO); World Association of Sign Language Interpreters
Chief Officer(s):
Colin Allen, President
Wilma Newhoudt-Druchen, Vice-President
Torun Eklund, Development Officer
Finances: *Funding Sources:* Regular membership fees; contributions, donations & government or foundation grants
Staff Member(s): 5
Membership: 184 Ordinary - national associations of the deaf; *Member Profile:* Ordinary; associate; individual
Activities: *Awareness Events:* International Week of the Deaf, 4th week of Sept.; *Internships:* Yes; *Speaker Service:* Yes

World Fellowship of Orthodox Youth

Syndesmos General Secretariat, PO Box 66051, Holargos 15510 Greece
Tel: 30-210-656-0991; *Fax:* 30-210-656-0992
syndesmos@syndesmos.org
www.syndesmos.org
Also Known As: Syndesmos
Overview: A small international organization founded in 1953
Mission: To serve as a bond of unity among Orthodox youth movements, organisations & theological schools around the world, promoting a consciousness of the catholicity of the Orthodox faith; to foster relations, coordination & mutual aid among them; to promote among young people a full understanding of the Orthodox faith & the mission of the Church in the contemporary world & an active participation of youth in ecclesial life; to promote a way of life founded in eucharistic communion, in the Gospel & in patristic teaching, for witness & service to the world; to assist & promote Orthodox effocrts for visible Christian unity & for positive relations with people of other faiths; to encourage reflection & action on issues affecting the lives of Orthodox Christians & the local churches; to be an instrument for furthering cooperation & deeper communion between the Orthodox Church & the Oriental Orthodox Churches
Chief Officer(s):
Christopher D'Aloisio, President
christophedaloisio@hotmail.com
Tony El Soury, Vice-President
telsoury@Tidm.net.lb
Tsimouris Spyros, Secretary General
Finances: *Annual Operating Budget:* $50,000-$100,000; *Funding Sources:* Orthodox churches; Orthodox church organisations; council of Eurpoe; European Christina Diakonia age
Staff Member(s): 2; 4 volunteer(s)
Membership: 121 organizations in 42 countries; *Fees:* $500 affiliated; *Member Profile:* Christian Orthodox youth organizations & theological schools; *Committees:* Publications
Activities: Orthodox youth camps, festivals, encounters, seminars, consultations, conferences, training courses, workshops; *Internships:* Yes *Library*

World Future Society (WFS)

#450, 7910 Woodmont Ave., Bethesda MD 20814-3032 USA
Tel: 301-656-8274; *Fax:* 301-951-0394
Toll-Free: 800-989-8274
info@wfs.org
www.wfs.org
www.facebook.com/146987498680054
twitter.com/WorldFutureSoc
Overview: A medium-sized international organization founded in 1966
Mission: The nonpartisan scientific & educational association serves as a clearinghouse for ideas about the future, including forecasts, recommendations, & alternative scenarios.
Chief Officer(s):
Timothy C. Mack, President
Kenneth W. Harris, Secretary
Kenneth W. Hunter, Treasurer
Finances: *Funding Sources:* Membership fees
Membership: 25,000 in over 80 countries; *Fees:* $49; *Member Profile:* Persons who would like to know more about what the future will hold, including sociologists, scientists, corporate planners, educators, students, & retirees
Activities: *Speaker Service:* Yes
Publications:
• Future Survey
Frequency: Monthly; *Editor:* Michael Marien; *Price:* $109 individuals; $165 institutions
Profile: Abstract of books, articles, & reports about the future
• Future Times
• Futures Research Quarterly
Type: Journal; *Frequency:* Quarterly; *Editor:* Timothy Mack; *Price:* $85 individuals; $110 institutions
Profile: Refereed journal with articles, news items, reprints of classic papers, & reviews of selected new books or reports for those professionals involved with the theory, methodology,practice, & use of futures research
• Futurist Update
Type: Newsletter; *Frequency:* Monthly; *Editor:* Cindy Wagner
Profile: News & previews from the Society
• The Futurist
Type: Magazine; *Frequency:* Bimonthly; *Accepts Advertising*; *Editor:* Cindy Wagner; *Price:* $49
Profile: Feature articles, news briefs, & book reviews

World Futures Studies Federation (WFSF) / Fédération mondiale pour les études sur le future

c/o Evelyne Koenig, 35, bis rue du Château, Lauw 68290 France
secretariat@wfsf.org
www.wfsf.org
www.linkedin.com/company/1590066
www.facebook.com/109772375809270
Overview: A small international organization founded in 1973
Mission: To promote & encourage futures studies in different disciplines & areas; to provide a forum for generating ideas concerning the future; to stimulate awareness of the need for future studies in governments & international organizations, as well as other decision making & educational groups & institutions; to resolve problems at local, national & global levels; to assist with national & global futures research activities; to encourage the democratization of future-oriented thinking & acting

Chief Officer(s):
Jennifer Gidley, President
Annie Ferguson, Secretariat Director
Finances: *Funding Sources:* Membership fees; UNESCO
Membership: *Fees:* Schedule available; *Member Profile:* Members are institutes & individuals from more than 70 countries from all regions, sectors & ideological perspectives of the world; they come from many disciplines & include scholars, policy makers & other people seriously involved in futures studies; membership is open to students
Activities: Coordinates research in the following: education towards the future; cultural aspects of the futures of peace; futures of political institutions; futures of communication & information; changing structures of social support; futures of development; methods of social forecasting & design

World Health Organization (WHO) / Organisation mondiale de la santé (OMS)

20, av Appia, 27, Geneva CH-1211 Switzerland
Tel: 41-22-791-21-11; *Fax:* 41-22-791-31-11
info@who.int
www.who.int
www.linkedin.com/company/world-health-organization
www.facebook.com/WorldHealthOrganization
twitter.com/WHONEWS
Overview: A large international organization founded in 1948
Mission: To attain for all peoples the highest possible level of health
Chief Officer(s):
Joy St. John, Chairman, Executive Board
Margaret Chan, Director General
Membership: 194 member states
Activities: Global strategy to achieve optimal health for all peoples of the world is based on the primary health care approach, involving the following components: education concerning prevailing health problems, proper food supply & nutrition, safe water & sanitation, maternal & child health, immunization against major infectious diseases, prevention & control of local diseases, appropriate treatment of common diseases & injuries, provision of essential drugs; *Awareness Events:* World Health Day, April 7; World No-Tobacco Day, May 31; World AIDS Day, Dec. 1; World TB (Tuberculosis) Day, March
Awards:
• The Léon Bernard Foundation Prize (Award)
• Dr. A.T. Shousha Foundation Prize & Fellowship (Award)
• Jacques Parisot Foundation Fellowship (Award)
• Ihsan Dogramaci Family Health Foundation Prize (Award)
• The Sasakawa Health Prize (Award)
• Dr. Comlan A.A. Quenum Prize for Public Health (Award)
• Francesco Pocchiari Fellowship (Award)
• United Arab Emirates Health Foundation Prize (Award)
• Down Syndrome Research Prize in the Eastern Mediterranean Region (Award)
• The State of Kuwait Prize for Research in Health Promotion (Award)
• The Dr. LEE Jong-wook Memorial Prize for Public Health (Award)
Publications:
• International Classification of Diseases [a publication of the World Health Organization]
Profile: A diagnostic tool for epidemiology, health management & clinical purposes
• International Health Regulations [a publication of the World Health Organization]
Profile: Rules to enhance national, regional & global public health security
• The International Pharmacopoeia [a publication of the World Health Organization]
Profile: To harmonize global quality specifications for selected pharmaceutical products, excipients & dosage forms
• International Travel & Health [a publication of the World Health Organization]
Type: Report
Profile: Information on health risks for travellers
• The World Health Report [a publication of the World Health Organization]
Type: Report
Profile: An expert assessment of global health
• World Health Statistics [a publication of the World Health Organization]
Type: Report
Profile: Recent health statistics for member states

World Health Organization Health in Prisons Programme (HIPP)

c/o WHO Regional Office for Europe, Scherfigsvej 8, Copenhagen DK-2100 Denmark
Tel: 45-39-17-17-17; *Fax:* 45-39-17-18-18
postmaster@euro.who.int
www.euro.who.int
Previous Name: International Council of Prison Medical Services
Overview: A small international organization founded in 1995
Chief Officer(s):
Lars Moller, Programme Manager, Alcohol & Illicit Drugs
lmo@euro.who.int
Stefan Enggist, Technical Officer, Prisons & Health
stg@euro.who.int

World Leisure & Recreation Association (WLRA)

#203, Wellness / Recreation Centre, University of Northern Iowa, Cedar Falls IA 50614-0241 USA
Tel: 319-273-6279; *Fax:* 319-273-5958
secretariat@worldleisure.org
www.worldleisure.org
www.facebook.com/159197134114790
Previous Name: International Leisure Information Network (LINK)
Overview: A medium-sized international charitable organization founded in 1956
Mission: To discover & foster conditions best permitting leisure to serve as a force to optimize individual & collective well-being
Affliation(s): UNESCO & other UN agencies
Finances: *Annual Operating Budget:* $100,000-$250,000; *Funding Sources:* Donations; membership fees; projects; grants; subsidies
Membership: 1,000; *Fees:* Schedule available
Activities: Education; Management; Research; Tourism; Centre of Excellence; Professional Services; Women & Gender; Access & Inclusion; Voluntarism; Low; Older Persons; Children & Youth; World Congress; *Speaker Service:* Yes

World Lottery Association (WLA)

c/o Interkantonale Landeslotterie, Swisslos, Lange Gasse 20, PO Box CH-4002, Basel Switzerland
Tel: +41 61 284 1502; *Fax:* +41 61 284 1350
info@world-lotteries.org
www.world-lotteries.org
Overview: A medium-sized international organization founded in 1999
Mission: To control runaway gambling; To protect territorial integrity & promote the role of state-licensed lotteries as generators of funds for good causes
Chief Officer(s):
Jean-Luc Moner-Banet, President
moner-banet@loro.ch
Rebecca Paul Paul Hargrove, Senior Vice-President, 615-324-6501, Fax: 615-324-6537
rebecca.p.hargrove@tnlottery.com
Membership: 138 regular + 61 associate; *Fees:* US$5,000-10,000 based on sales level of the lottery; *Member Profile:* Restricted to state lotteries & suppliers of goods or services to lotteries; *Committees:* Strategic Development; Corporate Social Responsibility; Audit; Nominating; New Media/Cross-Border; Security & Risk Management; RFP Standardization; GRADE Sub-Committee; Training Program; Supplier Relations; WLA Conventions; Bylaws
Activities: *Library:* Centre de documentation de Loto-Québec; Open to public by appointment
Awards:
• The WLA Advertising Awards (Award)
• The Guy Simonis Lifetime Achievement Award (Award)

World Mariculture Society *See* World Aquaculture Society

World Masters Athletics

c/o Stan Perkins, 4 Lawnton St., Daisy Hill QLD 4127 Australia
Tel: 61 7 3209 1131; *Fax:* 61 7 3209 1131
info@world-masters-athletics.org
www.world-masters-athletics.org
twitter.com/wmaforlife
Previous Name: World Association of Veteran Athletes
Overview: A small international organization founded in 1977
Mission: To organize, regulate and administer athletics for masters (women and men of not less than thirty-five years of age); To sanction World Masters' Athletic Championships and other international masters athletic competitions; To ratify and register world masters five-year age-group records and maintain data on other outstanding athletic performances by masters; To foster international friendship, understanding and co-operation through masters athletics
Member of: International Association of Athletic Federations
Chief Officer(s):
Stan Perkins, President
stanperkins@me.com
Finances: *Annual Operating Budget:* $100,000-$250,000
Membership: 140; *Member Profile:* National Athletic Federations; *Committees:* Stadia; Non-Stadia; Medical & Anti-doping; Women's; Law & Legislation
Activities: Athletics/track & field for veterans & masters;

World Meteorological Organization (WMO) / Organisation météorologique mondiale (OMM)

Information & Public Affairs, PO Box 2300, 7 bis, av de la Paix, Geneva 2, Geneva CH-1211 Switzerland
Tel: 41-22-730-8111; *Fax:* 41-22-730-8181
cpa@wmo.int
www.wmo.int
www.facebook.com/pages/World-Meteorological-Organization/71741701887
twitter.com/WMOnews
www.youtube.com/wmovideomaster
Overview: A medium-sized international organization founded in 1950
Mission: Coordinates global scientific activity to allow prompt & accurate weather information & other services for public, private & commercial use; contributes to the safety of life & property, the socio-economic development of nations & the protection of the environment; disaster mitigation & reduction
Chief Officer(s):
David Grimes, President, (Canada)
Antonio Divino Moura, 1st Vice-President, (Brazil)
Mieczyslaw S. Ostojski, Ph.D., 2nd Vice-President, (Poland)
Abdalah Mokssit, 3rd Vice-President, (Morocco)
Finances: *Annual Operating Budget:* Greater than $5 Million; *Funding Sources:* Member governments
Staff Member(s): 246
Membership: 191 governments; *Fees:* Assessed contributions; *Committees:* WMO Congress; Executive Council; Regional Associations; Technical
Activities: World Weather Watch; World Climate; Atmospheric Research & Environment; Applications of Meteorology; Hydrology & Water Resources; Education & Training; Technical Cooperation; Regional; *Library:* WMO Technical Library; Open to public
Meetings/Conferences:
• Arctic Observing Summit 2015, April, 2015, Cape Town
Scope: International
Description: The Arctic Observing Summit (AOS) is a high-level, summit that aims to provide community-driven, science-based guidance for the design, implementation, coordination and sustained long-term (decades) operation of an international network of arctic observing systems.

World Nuclear Association (WNA)

Carlton House, 22A St. James's Sq., London SW1Y 4JH United Kingdom
Tel: 44-20-7451-1520; *Fax:* 44-20-7839-1501
wna@world-nuclear.org
www.world-nuclear.org
www.linkedin.com/company/world-nuclear-association
www.facebook.com/worldnuclearassociation
twitter.com/WorldNuclear
www.youtube.com/user/WorldNuclear
Previous Name: The Uranium Institute
Overview: A medium-sized international charitable organization founded in 2001
Mission: To promote the use of nuclear energy for peaceful purposes; to provide a forum for research & debate on economic & political issues affecting the nuclear industry; to play a central role in the collection, analysis & communication of information on all aspects of the industry & related subjects
Chief Officer(s):
John B. Ritch, Director General
Tim Gitzel, Chair
Jean-Jacques Gautrot, Vice-Chair
Finances: *Annual Operating Budget:* $1.5 Million-$3 Million
Staff Member(s): 17
Membership: 165; *Fees:* Schedule available; *Member Profile:* Uranium producers, electrical utilities, fuel processing, handling & trading companies, government organizations
Activities: *Library:* Information Library; Open to public

World Organisation of Systems & Cybernetics (WOSC) / Organisation Mondiale pour la Systémique et la Cybernétique (OMSC)

North Place, #3, 30 Nettleham Rd., Lincoln LN2 1RE United Kingdom
Tél: 44-1522-589-252
wosc.co
www.facebook.com/WOSC.org
twitter.com/WOSC_
Aperçu: *Dimension:* petite; *Envergure:* internationale; fondée en 1969
Membre(s) du bureau directeur:
Raul Espejo, Director General
r.espejo@syncho.org
Robert Vallée, President
r.vallee@afscet.asso.fr
Membre: 24 institutions; *Critères d'admissibilite:* Federation of national associations & institutions devoted to systems or cybernetics, with English, French & Russian as official languages
Activités: Operates Norbert Wiener Institute

World Organization of the Scout Movement (WOSM) / Organisation mondiale du mouvement scout

World Scout Bureau/Bureau Mondial du Scoutisme, PO Box 91, rue du Pré-Jérôme 5, Geneva 1211-4 Switzerland
Tel: 41-22-705-1010; *Fax:* 41-22-705-1020
worldbureau@scout.org
www.scout.org
www.facebook.com/WOSM.OMMS?v=wall
twitter.com/worldscouting
www.youtube.com/worldscouting
Overview: A large international organization
Mission: The Scout Movement is a voluntary non-political educational movement for young people open to all without distinction of gender, origin, race or creed
Affliation(s): Scouts Canada; Association des Scouts du Canada
Chief Officer(s):
Luc Panissod, Secretary General
Membership: 28 million; *Member Profile:* Young people & adults in 217 countries & territories
Awards:
• Scouts of the World Award (Award)
To encourage a stronger involvement of young people in the development of society by making them more aware of the present world issues.*Eligibility:* Ages 15 to 26 years

World ORT Union (ORT) / Union mondiale ORT

ORT House, 126 Albert St., London NW1 7NE United Kingdom
Tel: 44-20-7446-8500; *Fax:* 44-20-7446-8650
wo@ort.org
www.ort.org
Overview: A medium-sized international charitable organization founded in 1921
Mission: The education & training organization works for the advancement of Jewish people to cope with the complexities & uncertainties of their environment. Through state-of-the-art technology ORT fosters self-sufficiency, mobility, & a sense of identity.
Affliation(s): Canadian ORT Federation; Women's Canadian ORT
Chief Officer(s):
Robert Singer, Director General
Finances: *Funding Sources:* Donations
Activities: Providing vocational training & technical assistance; Supporting non-sectarian economic & social development in under-developed regions of the world
Publications:
• The 1880 Scoiety Newsletter
Type: Newsletter; *Editor:* Stefan Bialoguski
Profile: ORT news & projects of interest to major donors
• The Next Generation Newsletter
Type: Newsletter
Profile: News, events, & information for ORT's new lay-leadership
• The World ORT Report
Type: Yearbook; *Frequency:* Annually
Profile: ORT's activities around the world
• World ORT Times
Type: Newspaper; *Editor:* Stefan Bialoguski *ISSN:* 1681-648X
Profile: World ORT news, events, activities, updates, & celebrations

World Packaging Organization (WPO)

#123, 1833 Centre Point Circle, Naperville IL 60563 USA
Tel: 630-596-9007; *Fax:* 630-544-5055
info@worldpackaging.org
www.worldpackaging.org
www.linkedin.com/groups?gid=2602547
twitter.com/WorldPackOrg
www.flickr.com/photos/worldpackorg/
Overview: A medium-sized international organization founded in 1968
Chief Officer(s):
Carl Olsmats, General Secretary
carl.olsmats@stfi.se
Membership: 2,614

World Petroleum Congress (WPC) / Congrès mondiaux du pétrole

#1, 1 Duchess St., 4th Fl., London W1W 6AN United Kingdom
Tel: 44-20-7637-4958
info@world-petroleum.org
www.world-petroleum.org
Overview: A medium-sized international organization founded in 1933
Mission: To help the oil industry in the development of petroleum resources & the use of petroleum products for the benefit of mankind; to promote petroleum science & technology; to encourage the application of scientific advances & the transfer of technology
Affliation(s): IEA; OPEN; United Nations
Chief Officer(s):
Pierce Riemer, Director General
pierce@world-petroleum.org
Randy Gossen, President
Finances: *Funding Sources:* Membership dues; royalties; levy on registration
Staff Member(s): 4
Membership: 57 countries; *Fees:* Schedule available; *Member Profile:* Major oil producing & consuming nations of the world; each country has a National Committee made up of representatives of the oil industry, academic & research institutions, & government departments; *Committees:* Permanent Council; Executive Board; Scientific Program; Congress Arrangements; Environmental Affairs; Development

World Pheasant Association (WPA)

Biology Field Station, Newcastle University, Close House Estate, Heddon-on-the-Wall NE15 0HT United Kingdom
Tel: 44(0)1661 853397
office@pheasant.org.uk
www.pheasant.org.uk
Overview: A small international charitable organization founded in 1975
Mission: To develop & promote the conservation of all species in the order galliformes, which are, broadly speaking the game birds of the world
Chief Officer(s):
Zheng Guangmei, President
Richard Carden, Chairman
Finances: *Annual Operating Budget:* $50,000-$100,000; *Funding Sources:* Donations
Staff Member(s): 2
Membership: 2,000
Activities: Habitat Survey & Protection; Education; Aviculture; Species Studies; International Symposia; Reintroduction Programs; Conservation Strategy

World Ploughing Organization (WPO)

Grolweg2, Hall 6964 BL Netherlands
Tel: 31-313-619-634; *Fax:* 31-313-619-735
www.worldploughing.org
twitter.com/worldploughing
Overview: A small international charitable organization founded in 1952
Mission: To foster & preserve the art & improve the skill of ploughing the land; To urge the development & adoption of improved techniques & aids for all branches of agriculture
Affliation(s): Canadian Plowing Organization
Chief Officer(s):
Hans Spieker, General Secretary
hans.spieker@worldploughing.org
Finances: *Annual Operating Budget:* $50,000-$100,000
Staff Member(s): 1
Membership: 30; *Fees:* CHF 3,000; *Member Profile:* National ploughing championships organizations
Activities: World Championship Ploughing Contests; Tillage Clinics

World Presidents' Organization

c/o Young Presidents' Organization, #1000, 600 East Las Colinas Blvd., Irving TX 75039 USA
Tel: 972-587-1500; *Fax:* 972-587-1611
Toll-Free: 800-773-7976
info@wpo.org
www.wpo.org
Overview: A small international organization founded in 1970
Mission: To create an environment where the power of idea exchange enhances lives, enriches families & improves communities
Chief Officer(s):
Paul N. Summers, International Chair & CEO
Membership: 9,000

World Resources Institute (WRI)

#800, 10 G St. NE, Washington D.C. 20002 USA
Tel: 202-729-7600; *Fax:* 202-729-7610
www.wri.org
www.linkedin.com/groups?gid=69154
www.facebook.com/worldresources
twitter.com/worldresources
www.youtube.com/WorldResourcesInst
Overview: A small international organization founded in 1982
Mission: To generate accurate information about global resources & environmental conditions, analyze emerging issues & develop creative responses to both problems & opportunities; to bring the insights of scientific research, economic analysis & practical experience to political, business & other leaders around the world by publishing books, reports & papers
Chief Officer(s):
Andrew Steer, President & CEO
asteer@wri.org
Manish Bapna, Exec. Vice-President & Managing Dir
mbapna@wri.org
Steve Barker, CFO & Vice-President, Finance & Administration
sbarker@wri.org
Staff Member(s): 200
Activities: Policy studies to present accurate infromation about global resources & environmental conditions, analysis of emerging issues & development of creative yet workable policy responses; in developing countries, provides field services & technical support for governments & nongovernmental organizations that are working to ensure the sustainability of natural resources; *Internships:* Yes *Library* Open to public by appointment

World Safety Organization (WSO)

WSO World Management Centre, PO Box 518, 106 West Young Ave., #F, Warrensburg MO 64093 USA
Tel: 660-747-3132; *Fax:* 660-747-2647
info@worldsafety.org
www.worldsafety.org
www.facebook.com/WorldSafetyOrganization
twitter.com/WorldSafetyOrg
Overview: A medium-sized international organization founded in 1875
Mission: To protect people, property, resources & the environment & to internationalize occupational & environmental safety through exchange of knowledge, programs, etc.
Member of: Consultative Status Category II (non-governmental) with Economic & Social Council of the United Nations
Chief Officer(s):
Vlado Senkovich, President/Director General
Edward E. Hogue, Vice-President/Deputy Director General
Lon S. McDaniel, Chief Executive Officer
Membership: *Fees:* $55 associate; $80 affiliate; $35 student; $185 institution; $1,000 corporate; *Member Profile:* Open to all individuals & entities involved in the safety & accident prevention field; *Committees:* Aviation Transportation; Construction; Maritime Transportation; Highway Transportation; Rail Transportation; Transportation of Dangerous Goods
Activities: World Safety & Accident Prevention Congress (every 2-6 years); World Safety & Accident Prevention Educational Conference (annually); professional development courses & seminars; *Library*
Awards:
• WSO Concerned Company/Corporation Honorable Mention Certificate (Award)
• WSO Educational Award (Award)
• WSO Concerned Organization Award (Award)
• WSO Safety Person of the Year (Award)
• WSO James K. Williams Award (Award)
• WSO Concerned Citizen Award (Award)
• WSO Concerned Professional Award (Award)
• WSO Concerned Company/Corporation Award (Award)

World Society for Ekistics (WSE)
24, Strat. Syndesmou St., Athens 106 73 Greece
Tel: 30-210-3623-216; *Fax:* 30-210-3629-337
ekistics@otenet.gr
www.ekistics.org
Overview: A small international organization founded in 1965
Mission: To advance the science of ekistics (human settlements) by drawing on the research & experience of professionals in such fields as architecture, engineering, ekistics, regional & city planning & sociology
Chief Officer(s):
Suzanne Keller, President
Panayis Psomopoulos, Secretary General/Treasurer
Finances: *Annual Operating Budget:* Less than $50,000; *Funding Sources:* Membership dues; grants
5 volunteer(s)
Membership: 200; *Fees:* $40
Activities: Human settlements

World Tourism Organization (UNWTO)
Calle Capitán Haya, 42, Madrid 28020 Spain
Tel: 34-91-567-8100; *Fax:* 34-91-571-3733
omt@unwto.org
www.unwto.org
www.facebook.com/WorldTourismOrganization
twitter.com/unwto
vimeo.com/unwto
Overview: A medium-sized international organization founded in 1975
Mission: To promote responsibile & accessible world tourism
Chief Officer(s):
Taleb D. Rifai, Secretary General
Membership: 400 affiliate members; 156 member countries; 6 associate members; *Member Profile:* Executive Council comprised of 22 full members, one for every five in WTO plus host State Spain (as ex officio member), one Associate member, & one Affiliate member

World Trade Centres Association (WTCA)
#518, 420 Lexington Ave., New York NY 10170 USA
Tel: 212-432-2626; *Fax:* 212-488-0064
wtca@wtca.org
www.wtca.org
twitter.com/WTCAonline
Overview: A small international organization founded in 1968
Mission: To encourage expansion of world trade, promote international business relations & increase participation in world trade by less developed countries
Chief Officer(s):
Eric Dahl, CEO
edahl@wtca.org
Membership: *Member Profile:* Regular - organizations substantially involved in development or operation of World Trade Centre; *Committees:* Clubs & Associations; Industrializing Nations; Research & Development; Trade Policy; Legal; Facilities; Information & Communications

World Union of Catholic Women's Organizations ***Voir*** Union mondiale des organisations féminines catholiques

World University Roundtable (WUR)
Desert Sanctuary Campus, PO Box 2470, Benson AZ 85602 USA
Tel: 520-586-2985; *Fax:* 520-586-4764
info@worlduniversity.org
www.worlduniversity.org
Overview: A small international licensing organization founded in 1946
Mission: To set before the student a broad overview of man's extant learning & to suggest areas of research & study which will advance his comprehension of what lies within his immediate future
Member of: American Library Association
Affliation(s): World University Association of Schools
Finances: *Funding Sources:* Membership dues
Membership: *Member Profile:* All professional in science, education & culture
Activities: International promotion of national offices & affiliated schools; *Library:* World University Library; by appointment

World Veterinary Poultry Association (WVPA)
Merial, Lyon Gerland Laboratory, 254 rue Marcel Mérieux, BP 391, Lyon 69007 France
www.wvpa.net
Overview: A medium-sized international organization founded in 1959
Mission: WVPA carries out the following objectives: organizing meetings for studying diseases & conditions relating to the avian species; encouraging research; promoting the exchange of information; & establishing & maintaining liaison with other bodies with related interests.
Chief Officer(s):
T. Baqust, President
Francois-Xavier Le Gros, Sec.-Treas.
Membership: 1,000-4,999; *Member Profile:* Ordinary members are veterinarians interested in avian science & related subjects, or non-veterinarians engaged in research, advisory work or teaching concerned with avian science.
Awards:
- Houghton Lecture Award (Award)
- Bart Rispens Award (Award)
- Houghton Trust (Grant)

Provides grants to young research workers for attendance at scientific meetings, training courses, & educational visits to laboratories
Publications:
- Aerosols

Type: Newsletter; *Frequency:* Annually; *Editor:* Dr. C. Cardona
- Avian Pathology

Type: Journal; *Frequency:* Bimonthly; *Editor:* Dr. D. Cavanagh
Profile: Original research papers & occasional reviews related to infectious & non-infectious diseases of poultry & all other birds

World Wildlife Fund - USA (WWF-USA) / Fonds mondial pour la nature
PO Box 97180, 1250 - 24 St. NW, Washington DC 20090-7180 USA
Tel: 202-293-4800; *Fax:* 202-293-9211
Toll-Free: 800-960-0993
PIResponse@worldwildlife.org, www.worldwildlife.org
www.facebook.com/worldwildlifefund
twitter.com/world_wildlife
www.youtube.com/wwfus
Overview: A large international organization founded in 1961
Mission: The largest private US organization working worldwide to conserve nature; to preserve the diversity & abundance of life on Earth & the health of ecological systems by protecting natural areas & wild populations of plants & animals, including endangered species; to promote sustainable approaches to the use of renewable natural resources; to promote more efficient use of resources & energy & the maximum reduction of pollution; committed to reversing the degradation of natural environment & to building a future in which human needs are met in harmony with nature; strives to determine how best to manage individual species & habitats & to obtain critical data for setting conservation priorities
Affliation(s): WWF has national organizations, national associates & representatives in nearly 40 countries across five continents; affiliation with international WWF network headquarters in Gland, Switzerland
Chief Officer(s):
Carter S. Roberts, President
Neville Isdell, Chair
Finances: *Funding Sources:* Contributions from members; grants from foundations, corporations & government agencies
Membership: 1,000,000+; *Fees:* $25-$500
Activities: Golden Lion Tarmarin Project, Brazil; Hol Chan Marine Reserve, Belize; involved in over 50 projects involving protection of tropical rainforests; Osborn Center works to make the wise management & efficient use of renewable resources a more central element in the economic development plans of developing nations; conducts field work & policy research to promote sustainable & efficient approaches to community development in the US; *Library* Open to public

World Wildlife Fund for Nature ***See*** WWF International

World's Poultry Science Association
PO Box 31, Beekbergen 7360AA Netherlands
Tel: 31-6-515-19584; *Fax:* 31-207-508-941
www.wpsa.com
Overview: A medium-sized international organization founded in 1912
Mission: Strives to advance knowledge and understanding of all aspects of poultry science and the poultry industry. Its major role is to encourage, and help facilitate, liaison among research scientists and educators, and between those in research and education and those working in the many diverse sectors of the industry.
Affliation(s): World's Poultry Science Association - Canadian Branch
Chief Officer(s):
E.N. Silva, President
edit@fea.unicamp.br
F.A. Bradley, Treasurer
Membership: 7,000 in 60 countries; *Fees:* Schedule available

Worldwatch Institute
#800, 1776 Massachusetts Ave. NW, Washington DC 20036-1904 USA
Tel: 202-452-1999; *Fax:* 202-296-7365
worldwatch@worldwatch.org, www.worldwatch.org
www.facebook.com/WorldwatchInst
twitter.com/WorldwatchInst
www.youtube.com/user/WorldwatchInst;
flickr.com/photos/worldwatchag
Overview: A medium-sized international charitable organization founded in 1974
Mission: Research organization that works for an environmentally sustainable & socially just society; provides compelling, accessible fact-based analysis of critical global issues; informs people about the interaction between nature, people & economies; focuses on the underlying causes & practical solutions to the world's problems
Chief Officer(s):
Robert Engelman, President
rengelman@worldwatch.org
Finances: *Annual Operating Budget:* $3 Million-$5 Million
Staff Member(s): 30
Activities: *Internships:* Yes; *Rents Mailing List:* Yes *Library*

WWF International (WWF)
Avenue du Mont-Blanc, Gland CH-1196 Switzerland
Tel: 41-22-364-9111; *Fax:* 41-22-364-8836
wwf.panda.org, www.linkedin.com/groups/WWF-44458
www.facebook.com/WWF, twitter.com/wwf
www.youtube.com/wwf
Also Known As: World Wide Fund for Nature
Previous Name: World Wildlife Fund for Nature
Overview: A large international charitable organization founded in 1961
Mission: To stop the degradation of the planet's natural environment & to build a future in which humans live in harmony with nature by conserving the world's biological diversity, ensuring that the use of renewable & natural resources is sustainable, promoting the reduction of pollution & wasteful consumption
Affliation(s): The World Conservation Union; International Council for Bird Protection; International Waterfowl Research Bureau; Charles Darwin Foundation
Chief Officer(s):
Yolanda Kakabadse, President
James P. Leape, Director General
Finances: *Annual Operating Budget:* Greater than $5 Million; *Funding Sources:* Individuals & general donations; legacies & bequests; corporate subscriptions & donations
Staff Member(s): 3800
Membership: 4.7 million; *Fees:* Schedule available
Activities: Six international environmental issues: Climate Change, Endangered Seas, Forests, Fresh Water Programmes, Species, Toxics; sponsors educational & training programs for park & wildlife managers, ecologists & teachers; *Internships:* Yes
Awards:
- WWF Prince Bernhard Scholarships for Nature Conservation (Scholarship)

To help build conservation expertise and leadership in the developing world. *Amount:* Up to CHF 10,000
- The Kathryn Fuller Science for Nature Fund (Scholarship)
- The e8 Sustainable Energy Development Scholarship Programme (Scholarship)

Young Presidents' Organization (YPO)
#1000, 600 East Las Colinas Blvd., Irving TX 75039 USA
Tel: 972-587-1500; *Fax:* 972-587-1611
Toll-Free: 800-773-7976
askypo@ypo.org, www.ypo.org
www.linkedin.com/company/young-presidents%27-organization
www.facebook.com/youngpresorg
twitter.com/YPO
www.youtube.com/YPOvideo
Overview: A small international organization founded in 1950
Mission: To create better leaders through idea exchange
Affliation(s): 10 Chapters in Canada
Membership: 22,000 in 125 countries; *Member Profile:* Young global business leaders

Zero Population Growth ***See*** Population Connection

Indexes

Acronym Index

Acronym Index

Acronym Index

B

C

Acronym Index

Disponible sous forme de listes ou d'étiquettes:
416-644-6479, ou Ligne sans frais: 1-866-433-4739

Acronym Index

D

E

Acronym Index

F

G

H

Acronym Index

J

N

Acronym Index

O

Acronym Index

P

Q

R

S

T

U

V

W

Y

Z

Budget Index

- Canadian associations listed by annual budget size in eight ranges (less than $50,000; $50,000 - $100,000; $100,000 - $250,000; $250,000 - $500,000; $500,000 - $1,500,000; $1,500,000 - $3,000,000; $3,000,000 - $5,000,000; greater than $5 million)
- Each entry is accompanied by a page number which points you to the corresponding listing in the alphabetical listings of Canadian associations

Less than $50,000

Budget Index

$50,000-$100,000

$100,000-$250,000

Budget Index

$250,000-$500,000

Budget Index

$500,000-$1.5 Million

$1.5 Million-$3 Million

$3 Million-$5 Million

Budget Index

Greater than $5 Million

Conferenes & Conventions

- Conferences and conventions of both Canadian and foreign associations scheduled to take place in 2015, 2016, 2017, and several beyond 2018
- Canadian and foreign associations listed here together by year and month
- Name of conference, date, place, host organization or sponsor, scope, contact information, and an overview are included when available
- Conferences and conventions for which only the year is known are listed at the end of the respective year, sorted by conference name
- Since plans can change and the list of conferences is not comprehensive, please check with associations of interest to you, which are listed in alphabetical order under Canadian Associations and Foreign Associations

2015

January

34th Annual Guelph Organic Conference & Expo 2015
Date: January 29 - February 1, 2015
Location: Guelph University Centre
Guelph, ON
Sponsor/Contact: Ecological Agriculture Projects
Macdonald Campus of McGill University
Sainte-Anne-de-Bellevue, QC H9X 3V9
514-398-7771 *Fax:* 514-398-7621
E-mail: ecological.agriculture@mcgill.ca
URL: eap.mcgill.ca
Scope: Local
Anticipated Attendance: 830
Contact Information: Website: www.guelphorganicconf.ca; Twitter: twitter.com/GuelphOrganic; Phone: 519-824-4120 Ext. 56311

47th Canadian Mineral Processors Conference
Date: January 20-22, 2015
Location: Westin Hotel
Ottawa, ON
Sponsor/Contact: Canadian Mineral Processors Society
555 Booth St.
Ottawa, ON K1A 0G1
URL: www.cmpsoc.ca
Scope: National

130th Modern Language Association (MLA) Annual Convention
Date: January 8-11, 2015
Location: Vancouver Convention Centre
Vancouver, BC
Sponsor/Contact: Modern Language Association of America
26 Broadway, 3rd Fl.
New York, NY 10004-1789
646-576-5000 *Fax:* 646-458-0030
URL: www.mla.org
Scope: Provincial

2015 Manitoba Water Well Association Annual Conference & Trade Show
Date: January 11-14, 2015
Location: Keystone Centre/Canad Inn
Brandon, MB
Sponsor/Contact: Manitoba Water Well Association
P.O. Box 1648
Winnipeg, MB R3C 2Z6
204-479-3777
E-mail: info@mwwa.ca
URL: www.mwwa.ca
Scope: Provincial
Purpose: A review of the year's highlights & an opportunity to address new business
Contact Information: E-mail: info@mwwa.ca

2015 Ontario Golf Course Management Conference and Trade Show
Date: January 28-30, 2015
Location: Scotiabank Convention Centre
Niagara, ON
Sponsor/Contact: Ontario Golf Superintendents' Association
328 Victoria Rd. South
Guelph, ON N1L 0H2
519-767-3341 *Fax:* 519-766-1704
Toll-Free: 877-824-6472
E-mail: admin@ogsa.ca
URL: www.ogsa.ca
Scope: Provincial

2015 Public Education Symposium
Date: January 29-31, 2015
Location: Sheraton Centre Hotel
Toronto, ON
Sponsor/Contact: Ontario Public School Boards Association
#1850, 439 University Ave.
Toronto, ON M5G 1Y8
416-340-2540 *Fax:* 416-340-7571
E-mail: webmaster@opsba.org
URL: www.opsba.org
Scope: Provincial

2015 Western Canadian Association of Bovine Practitioners Conference
Date: January 15-17, 2015
Location: Sheraton Cavalier Hotel
Saskatoon, SK
Sponsor/Contact: Western Canadian Association of Bovine Practitioners
226E Wheeler St., 2nd Fl.
Saskatoon, SK S7P 0A9
Fax: 306-956-0607
Toll-Free: 866-269-8387
E-mail: info@wcabp.com
URL: www.wcabp.com
Scope: National

Alberta Association of Services for Children & Families 2015 Annual Conference
Date: January 29-30, 2015
Location: Fantasyland Hotel
Edmonton, AB
Sponsor/Contact: Alberta Association of Services for Children & Families
Bonnie Doon Mall
#255, 8330 - 82nd Ave.
Edmonton, AB T6C 4E3
780-428-3660 *Fax:* 780-428-3844
E-mail: aascf@aascf.com
URL: www.aascf.com
Scope: Provincial

Alberta Law Conference 2015
Date: January 29-30, 2015
Location: Fairmont Hotel Macdonald
Edmonton, AB
Sponsor/Contact: Law Society of Alberta
#500, 919 - 11th Ave. SW
Calgary, AB T2R 1P3
403-229-4700 *Fax:* 403-228-1728
Toll-Free: 800-661-9003
URL: www.lawsocietyalberta.com
Scope: Provincial

American Library Association 2015 Midwinter Meeting & Exhibits
Date: January 23-27, 2015
Location: Chicago, IL USA
Sponsor/Contact: American Library Association
50 East Huron St.
Chicago, IL 60611
Fax: 312-440-9374
Toll-Free: 800-545-2433
E-mail: ala@ala.org
URL: www.ala.org
Scope: International
Purpose: A meeting for librarians, support staff, trustees, & retirees, offering discussion groups, committee meetings, speakers, & exhibits
Contact Information: Registration Customer Service, Phone: 1-800-974-3084, E-mail: ala@experient-inc.com

American Philological Association 146th Annual Meeting
Date: January 8-11, 2015
Location: New Orleans, LA USA
Sponsor/Contact: American Philological Association
University of Pennsylvania
#201E, 220 South 40th St.
Philadelphia, PA 19104-3512
215-898-4975 *Fax:* 215-573-7874
E-mail: apaclassics@sas.upenn.edu
URL: apaclassics.org
Scope: International

Association of Canadian Publishers 2015 Mid-Winter PD & Meeting
Date: January 30-31, 2015
Location: Hyatt Regency Hotel
Toronto, ON
Sponsor/Contact: Association of Canadian Publishers
#306, 174 Spadina Ave.
Toronto, ON M5T 2C2
416-487-6116 *Fax:* 416-487-8815
E-mail: admin@canbook.org
URL: www.publishers.ca
Scope: National
Purpose: Themes include copyright law & the digital marketplace at an event featuring guest speakers, roundtables, & committee meetings
Contact Information: Meeting Contact: Inna Shepelska, Fax: 416-487-8815, E-mail: inna_shepelska@canbook.org

CFA Society Winnipeg 50th Annual Forecast Dinner
Date: January 29, 2015
Location: RBC Convention Centre
Winnipeg, MB
Sponsor/Contact: CFA Society Winnipeg
P.O. Box 2684
Winnipeg, MB R3C 4B3
204-471-3640
E-mail: info@cfawinnipeg.ca
URL: www.cfasociety.org/winnipeg/
Scope: Provincial

Calgary CFA Society - 38th Annual Forecast Dinner
Date: January 15, 2015
Location: Telus Convention Centre
Calgary, AB
Sponsor/Contact: CFA Society Calgary
P.O. Box 118
#100, 111 - 5th Ave. SW
Calgary, AB T2P 3Y6
403-249-2009 *Fax:* 403-206-0650
E-mail: admin@cfacalgary.com
URL: www.cfacalgary.com
Scope: Local

Canadian Accredited Independent Schools Advancement Professionals Biennial National Confernece 2015
Date: January 29-31, 2015
Location: Le Place d'Armes Hôtel & Suites
Montreal, QC
Sponsor/Contact: Canadian Accredited Independent Schools Advancement Professionals
E-mail: communications@caisap.ca
URL: www.caisap.ca
Scope: National

Canadian Arts Presenting Association / Association canadienne des organismes artistiques 2015 27th Annual Conference
Date: January 21-24, 2015
Location: Marriott Harbourfront Hotel
Halifax, NS
Sponsor/Contact: Canadian Arts Presenting Association
#200, 17 York St.
Ottawa, ON K1N 9J6
613-562-3515 *Fax:* 613-562-4005
E-mail: mail@capacoa.ca
URL: www.capacoa.ca
Scope: National

Canadian Association for Pharmacy Distribution Management 2015 Executive Conference
Date: January 19-20, 2015
Location: Montréal Airport Marriott Inn
Dorval, QC
Sponsor/Contact: Canadian Association for Pharmacy Distribution Management
#301A, 3800 Steeles Ave. West
Woodbridge, ON L4L 4G9
905-265-1706 *Fax:* 905-265-9372
URL: www.capdm.ca
Scope: National

Canadian Association of Farm Advisors 2015 Conference
Date: January 7-8, 2015
Location: Saskatoon, SK
Sponsor/Contact: Canadian Association of Farm Advisors

Conferences Index

P.O. Box 578
Blaine Lake, SK S0J 0J0
306-466-2294 *Fax:* 306-466-2297
Toll-Free: 877-474-2871
E-mail: info@cafanet.com
URL: www.cafanet.com
Scope: National
Purpose: Joint conference with SK Young Ag Entrepreneurs to maximize learning, engagement and networking.

Canadian Association of Nuclear Medicine Annual Scientific Meeting 2015
Date: January 29 - February 1, 2015
Location: Hotel Omni Mont-Royal
Montréal, QC
Sponsor/Contact: Canadian Association of Nuclear Medicine
P.O. Box 4383 Stn. E
Ottawa, ON K1S 2L0
613-882-5097
E-mail: canm@canm-acmn.ca
URL: www.canm-acmn.ca
Scope: National
Purpose: A day of dedicated nuclear medicine technologist sessions.

Canadian Association of Numismatic Dealers 2015 Annual Convention
Date: January 23-25, 2015
Location: Sheraton Hamilton Hotel
Hamilton, ON
Sponsor/Contact: Canadian Association of Numismatic Dealers
c/o Jo-Anne Simpson, Executive Secretary
P.O. Box 10272 Stn. Winona
Stoney Creek, ON L8E 5R1
905-643-4988 *Fax:* 905-643-6329
E-mail: email@cand.org
URL: www.cand.org
Scope: National
Contact Information: Contact: Tom Kennedy, Phone: 519-271-8825, E-mail: cand@cogeco.ca

Canadian Association of Optometrists Optometric Leaders' Forum 2015
Date: January 2015
Location: Ottawa, ON
Sponsor/Contact: Canadian Association of Optometrists
234 Argyle Ave.
Ottawa, ON K2P 1B9
613-235-7924 *Fax:* 613-235-2025
Toll-Free: 888-263-4676
E-mail: info@opto.ca
URL: www.opto.ca
Scope: National

Canadian Association of University Teachers 2015 9th Annual Forum for Presidents
Date: January 16-18, 2015
Location: Ottawa, ON
Sponsor/Contact: Canadian Association of University Teachers
2705 Queensview Dr.
Ottawa, ON K2B 8K2
613-820-2270 *Fax:* 613-820-7244
E-mail: acppu@caut.ca
URL: www.caut.ca
Scope: National
Purpose: Information for academic staff association presidents

Canadian Museums Association 2015 Museum Enterprises Conference
Date: January 22-24, 2015
Location: Hilton Toronto Hotel
Toronto, ON
Sponsor/Contact: Canadian Museums Association
#400, 280 Metcalfe St.
Ottawa, ON K2P 1R7
613-567-0099 *Fax:* 613-233-5438
Toll-Free: 888-822-2907
E-mail: info@museums.ca
URL: www.museums.ca
Scope: National
Purpose: Keynote sessions, educational presentations, workshops, & networking opportunities for museum professionals involved in operations, admissions, retail, & food services
Contact Information: Symposium Contact: Erin Caley, Phone: 613-567-0099, ext. 233; E-mail: ecaley@museums.ca

Canadian Nursing Students' Association 2015 National Conference
Date: January 28-31, 2015
Location: University of Saskatchewan - Regina Campus
Regina, SK
Sponsor/Contact: Canadian Nursing Students' Association
Fifth Ave. Court
#15, 99 - 5th Ave.
Ottawa, ON K1S 5K4
613-235-3150
E-mail: communications@cnsa.ca
URL: www.cnsa.ca
Scope: National
Purpose: Keynote speakers, panels, debates, professional development sessions, & networking opportunities
Anticipated Attendance: 500+
Contact Information: National Conference Planning Committee, E-mail: conference@cnsa.ca

Canadian Nutrition Society 2015 Protein Conference
Date: January 10, 2015
Location: Toronto Marriott Downtown Eaton Centre Hotel
Toronto, ON
Sponsor/Contact: Canadian Nutrition Society
#310, 2175 Sheppard Ave. East
Toronto, ON M2J 1W8
416-491-7188 *Fax:* 416-491-1670
Toll-Free: 888-414-7188
E-mail: info@cns-scn.ca
URL: www.cns-scn.ca
Scope: National
Contact Information: Phone: 416-491-7188, Fax: 416-491-1670, E-mail: info@cns-scn.ca

Canadian Quarter Horse Assocation 2015 Annual General Meeting
Date: January 17, 2015
Location: Holiday Inn
Cambridge, ON
Sponsor/Contact: Canadian Quarter Horse Association
c/o Sherry Clemens, Secretary
P.O. Box 2132
Moose Jaw, SK S6H 7T2
306-692-8393
E-mail: admin@huntseathorses.com
URL: www.cqha.ca
Scope: National

Canadian Society of Association Executives, Ottawa-Gatineau Chapter, Tête-à-Tête Tradeshow 2015
Date: January 29, 2015
Location: Shaw Centre
Ottawa, ON
Sponsor/Contact: Canadian Society of Association Executives
c/o Royal College of Physicians and Surgeons of Canada
773 Echo Dr.
Ottawa, ON K1S 5N8
613-730-6237
E-mail: tcohen@rcpsc.edu
URL: www.csae.com/ottawa
Scope: Local
Contact Information: Event Contact: Kathryn Cyr, Phone: 613-271-1476, E-mail: csae.ottawa-gatineau@rogers.com; URL: www.csaeteteatete.ca

Canadian Society of Hospital Pharmacists 2015 46th Annual Professional Practice Conference
Date: January 31 - February 5, 2015
Location: Sheraton Centre Toronto Hotel
Toronto, ON
Sponsor/Contact: Canadian Society of Hospital Pharmacists
#3, 30 Concourse Gate
Ottawa, ON K2E 7V7
613-736-9733 *Fax:* 613-736-5660
E-mail: info@cshp.ca
URL: www.cshp.ca
Scope: National
Purpose: Educational sessions for clinical practitioners & managers from across Canada
Anticipated Attendance: 650
Contact Information: E-mail: info@cshp.ca

Canadian Thoracic Society Better Breathing 2015: Global Threats, Local Responses
Date: January 29-31, 2015
Location: Toronto Marriott Downtown Eaton Centre
Toronto, ON
Sponsor/Contact: Canadian Thoracic Society
c/o National Office, The Lung Association
#300, 1750 Courtwood Cres.
Ottawa, ON K2C 2B5
613-569-6411 *Fax:* 613-569-8860
Toll-Free: 888-566-5864
E-mail: ctsinfo@lung.ca
URL: www.lung.ca/cts
Scope: National

Canadian Union of Public Employees (CUPE) Saskatchewan 2015 Winter School
Date: January 25-28, 2015
Location: Temple Gardens Mineral Spa
Moose Jaw, SK
Sponsor/Contact: Canadian Union of Public Employees
Saskatchewan Regional Office
3275 East Eastgate Dr.
Regina, SK S4Z 1A5
306-757-1009 *Fax:* 306-757-0102
E-mail: cupesask@sasktel.net
URL: www.sk.cupe.ca
Scope: Provincial
Purpose: Workshops for the Saskatchewan region
Contact Information: E-mail: cupesask@sasktel.net

Consulting Engineers of British Columbia 2015 Annual Transportation Conference
Date: January 28, 2015
Location: Hilton Metrotown
Burnaby, BC
Sponsor/Contact: Consulting Engineers of British Columbia
#1258, 409 Granville St.
Vancouver, BC V6C 1T2
604-687-2811 *Fax:* 604-688-7110
E-mail: info@acec-bc.ca
URL: www.acec-bc.ca
Scope: Provincial
Purpose: An event presenting educational & networking opportunities to enhance business development. Theme: Future Trends and Topics in the BC Transportation Industry
Contact Information: Coordinator, Accounting & Events: Alla Samusevich

Council of Outdoor Educators of Ontario (COEO) 2015 Conference
Date: January 16-18, 2015
Location: Mono Cliffs Outdoor Education Centre
Orangeville, ON
Sponsor/Contact: Council of Outdoor Educators of Ontario
c/o Sport Alliance Ontario
3 Concorde Gate
Toronto, ON M3C 3N7
E-mail: info@coeo.org
URL: www.coeo.org
Scope: National
Purpose: Theme: "Make Peace with Winter"

Dairy Farmers of Nova Scotia Annual General Meetin 2015
Date: January 7-8, 2015
Location: Best Western Glengarry
Truro, NS
Sponsor/Contact: Dairy Farmers of Nova Scotia
#100, 4060 Hwy. 236
Lower Truro, NS B6L 1J9
902-893-6455 *Fax:* 902-897-9768
E-mail: hboyd@dfns.ca
URL: www.dfns.ca
Scope: Provincial

Dairy Farmers of Ontario Annual Meeting 2015
Date: January 14-15, 2015
Location: Fairmont Royal York Hotel
Toronto, ON
Sponsor/Contact: Dairy Farmers of Ontario
6780 Campobello Rd.
Mississauga, ON L5N 2L8
905-821-8970 *Fax:* 905-821-3160
E-mail: questions@milk.org
URL: www.milk.org
Scope: Provincial

Elementary Teachers' Federation of Ontario 2015 ICT Conference: Technology for Teachers
Date: January 16-17, 2015
Location: ETFO Provincial Office and OISE
Toronto, ON
Sponsor/Contact: Elementary Teachers' Federation of Ontario
136 Isabella St.
Toronto, ON M4Y 1P6
416-962-3836 *Fax:* 416-642-2424
Toll-Free: 888-838-3836
URL: www.etfo.ca
Scope: Provincial
Purpose: A workshop designed to help members expand their presentation skills
Contact Information: Workshop Contacts: Ruth Dawson, Phone: 416-962-3836, ext. 2278, E-mail: rdawson@etfo.org; Jane Bennett, 416-962-3836, ext. 2277, E-mail:

Conferences Index

jbennett@etfo.org; Joanne Myers, Phone: 416-962-3836, ext. 2279, E-mail: jmyers@etfo.org

Engineers Without Borders 2015 National Conference
Date: January 16-18, 2015
Location: Montréal, QC
Sponsor/Contact: Engineers Without Borders
#601, 366 Adelaide St. West
Toronto, ON M5V 1R9
416-481-3696 *Fax:* 416-352-5360
Toll-Free: 866-481-3696
E-mail: info@ewb.ca
URL: www.ewb.ca
Scope: National

Forest Products Association of Nova Scotia 2015 81st Annual Meeting
Date: January 27-28, 2015
Location: Marriott Harbourfront Hotel
Halifax, NS
Sponsor/Contact: Forest Products Association of Nova Scotia
P.O. Box 696
Truro, NS B2N 5E5
902-895-1179 *Fax:* 902-893-1197
URL: www.fpans.ca
Scope: Provincial
Purpose: A yearly gathering of association members
Contact Information: Contact: Brenda Archibald, Phone: 902-895-1179, E-mail: barchibald@fpans.ca

Horse Breeders & Owners 33rd Annual Conference
Date: January 9-11, 2015
Location: Red Deer, AB
Sponsor/Contact: Horse Industry Association of Alberta
97 East Lake Ramp NE
Airdrie, AB T4A 0C3
403-420-5949 *Fax:* 403-948-2069
URL: www.albertahorseindustry.ca
Scope: Provincial
Purpose: Internationally recognized speakers of interest to horse breeders, owners, & professionals

Human Resources Professionals Association 2015 Annual Conference & Trade Show
Date: January 21-22, 2015
Location: Metro Toronto Convention Centre
Toronto, ON
Sponsor/Contact: Human Resources Professionals Association
#200, 150 Bloor St. West
Toronto, ON M5S 2X9
416-923-2324 *Fax:* 416-923-7264
Toll-Free: 800-387-1311
E-mail: info@hrpa.org
URL: www.hrpa.ca
Scope: Provincial

Keystone Agricultural Producers 2015 Annual Meeting
Date: January 27-29, 2015
Location: Delta Hotel
Winnipeg, MB
Sponsor/Contact: Keystone Agricultural Producers
#203, 1700 Ellice Ave.
Winnipeg, MB R3H 0B1
204-697-1140 *Fax:* 204-697-1109
E-mail: kap@kap.mb.ca
URL: www.kap.mb.ca
Scope: National

Manitoba Bar Association 2015 Mid-Winter Conference
Date: January 23-24, 2015
Location: Winnipeg, MB
Sponsor/Contact: Manitoba Bar Association
#1450, 363 Broadway
Winnipeg, MB R3C 3N9
204-927-1210 *Fax:* 204-927-1212
E-mail: admin@cba-mb.ca
URL: www.cba.org/manitoba
Scope: Provincial

Manitoba Percheron & Belgian Club 2015 Annual General Meeting
Date: January 31, 2015
Location: Royal Oak Inn
Brandon, MB
Sponsor/Contact: Manitoba Percheron & Belgian Club
c/o Brenda Hunter
P.O. Box 159
Kenton, MB R0M 0Z0
204-764-3789
E-mail: bhunterphoto@gmail.com
URL: www.manpercheronbelgianclub.com
Scope: Provincial
Purpose: Featuring a joint banquet & auction with the Clyde Club

Manitoba Restaurant & Foodservices Association LocalFare Trade Show
Date: January 20, 2015
Location: RBC Convnetion Centre
Winnipeg, MB
Sponsor/Contact: Manitoba Restaurant & Food Services Association
103-D Scurfield Blvd.
Winnipeg, MB R3Y 1M6
204-783-9955 *Fax:* 204-783-9909
Toll-Free: 877-296-2909
E-mail: info@mrfa.mb.ca
URL: www.mrfa.mb.ca
Scope: Provincial

Manitoba Water & Wastewater Association 2015 Annual Conference & Trade Show
Date: January 11-14, 2015
Location: Keystone Centre/Canad Inn
Brandon, MB
Sponsor/Contact: Manitoba Water & Wastewater Association
P.O. Box 1600
#215, 9 Saskatchewan Ave. West, 2nd Fl.
Portage la Prairie, MB R1N 3P1
204-239-6868 *Fax:* 204-239-6872
Toll-Free: 866-396-2549
E-mail: mwwa@mts.net
URL: www.mwwa.net
Scope: Provincial
Purpose: The presentation of technical papers plus the opportunity to view industry products & services
Contact Information: Executive Director: Iva Last: Phone: 204-239-6868, Toll-Free Phone: 1-866-396-2549, Fax: 204-239-6872, E-mail: mwwa@mts.net

Mineral Exploration Roundup 2015
Date: January 26-29, 2015
Location: British Columbia
Sponsor/Contact: Association for Mineral Exploration British Columbia
#800, 889 West Pender St.
Vancouver, BC V6C 3B2
604-689-5271 *Fax:* 604-681-2363
E-mail: info@amebc.ca
URL: www.amebc.ca
Scope: Provincial

Nova Scotia Fruit Growers' Association Annual Convention 2015
Date: January 27-28, 2015
Location: Old Orchard Inn
Wolfville, NS
Sponsor/Contact: Nova Scotia Fruit Growers' Association
Kentville Agricultural Centre
32 Main St.
Kentville, NS B4N 1J5
902-678-1093 *Fax:* 902-679-1567
URL: www.nsapples.com
Scope: Provincial

Ontario Camps Association 2015 Annual General Meeting
Date: January 20, 2015
Location: Vaughan Estates
Toronto, ON
Sponsor/Contact: Ontario Camps Association
70 Martin Ross Ave.
Toronto, ON M3J 2L4
416-485-0425 *Fax:* 416-485-0422
E-mail: info@ontariocamps.ca
URL: www.ontariocamps.ca
Scope: Provincial

Ontario Fruit and Vegetable Growers' Association Annual Meeting & Convention 2015
Date: January 13-14, 2015
Location: Crowne Plaza Hotel
Niagara Falls, ON
Sponsor/Contact: Ontario Fruit & Vegetable Growers' Association
#105, 355 Elmira Rd. North
Guelph, ON N1K 1S5
519-763-6160 *Fax:* 519-763-6604
E-mail: info@ofvga.org
URL: www.ofvga.org
Scope: Provincial

Ontario Health Libraries Association Annual General Meeting and Awards Presentations
Date: January 28-31, 2015
Location: Metro Toronto Convetion Centre
Toronto, ON
Sponsor/Contact: Ontario Health Libraries Association
c/o Karen Gagnon, Staff Library, Providence Care, Mental Health Servic
752 King St. West, Bag 603
Kingston, ON K7L 4X3
E-mail: askohla@accessola.com
URL: www.ohla.on.ca
Scope: Provincial

Ontario Library Association 2015 Super Conference
Date: January 28-30, 2015
Location: Metro Toronto Convention Centre
Toronto, ON
Sponsor/Contact: Ontario Library Association
#201, 50 Wellington St. East
Toronto, ON M5E 1C8
416-363-3388 *Fax:* 416-941-9581
Toll-Free: 866-873-9867
E-mail: info@accessola.com
URL: www.accessola.com
Scope: Provincial
Purpose: An annual gathering of delegates, speakers, & exhibitors for a continuing education event in librarianship. Theme: "Think it. Do it!"
Anticipated Attendance: 4,500+
Contact Information: Conference Coordinator: Liz Kerr, Phone: 416-363-3388, ext. 232, E-mail: lkerr@accessola.com; Education Coordinator: Michelle Arbuckle, Phone: 416-363-3388, ext. 230, E-mail: marbuckle@accessola.com; Manager, Member Services: Beckie MacDonald, Phone: 416-363-3388, ext. 226, E-mail: bmacdonald@accessola.com

Ontario Library Boards' Association 2015 Annual General Meeting
Date: January 28-31, 2015
Location: Metro Toronto Convention Centre
Toronto, ON
Sponsor/Contact: Ontario Library Boards' Association
c/o Ontario Library Association
#201, 50 Wellington St. East
Toronto, ON M5E 1C8
416-363-3388 *Fax:* 416-941-9581
Toll-Free: 866-873-9867
E-mail: info@accessola.com
URL: www.accessola.com/olba
Scope: Provincial
Purpose: AGM reports from executive members, the business of the association, statement of expenses, & the introduction of the new council

Ontario Processing Vegetable Industry Conference 2015
Date: January 20-21, 2015
Location: Four Points by Sheraton
London, ON
Sponsor/Contact: Ontario Processing Vegetable Growers
435 Consortium Ct.
Longon, ON N6E 2S8
519-681-1875 *Fax:* 519-685-5719
URL: www.opvg.org
Scope: Provincial

Ontario Public Library Association 2015 36th Annual General Meeting
Date: January 28-31, 2015
Location: Metro Toronto Convention Centre
Toronto, ON
Sponsor/Contact: Ontario Public Library Association
#201, 50 Wellington St. East
Toronto, ON M5E 1C8
416-363-3388 *Fax:* 416-941-9581
Toll-Free: 866-873-9867
E-mail: info@accessola.com
URL: www.accessola.com/opla
Scope: Provincial
Purpose: Featuring the introduction of the new council, as well as reports from the association's president, treasurer, & committees

Ontario Respiratory Care Society 2015 Annual Better Breathing Conference: Global Threats, Local Responses
Date: January 29-31, 2015
Location: Toronto Marriott Downtown Eaton Centre
Toronto, ON
Sponsor/Contact: Ontario Respiratory Care Society
#401, 18 Wynford Dr.
Toronto, ON M3C 0K8
416-864-9911 *Fax:* 416-864-9916
E-mail: orcs@on.lung.ca
URL: www.on.lung.ca
Scope: Provincial
Purpose: A forum for professional education to implement strategies for optimal respiratory health in Ontario
Contact Information: E-mail: orcs@on.lung.ca

Conferences Index

Ontario Tire Dealers Association 2015 National Trade Show & Conference
Date: January 17-24, 2015
Location: RIU Aruba Palace, Aruba
Sponsor/Contact: Ontario Tire Dealers Association
P.O. Box 516
34 Edward St.
Drayton, ON N0G 1P0
888-207-9059 *Fax:* 866-375-6832
URL: www.otda.com
Scope: Provincial

Ontario Trial Lawyers Association 2015 Long Term Disability Conference: Good Practices and Bad Faith From Coast to Coast
Date: January 23, 2015
Location: Twenty Toronto Street Conferences and Events
Toronto, ON
Sponsor/Contact: Ontario Trial Lawyers Association
1190 Blair Rd.
Burlington, ON L7M 1K9
905-639-6852 *Fax:* 905-639-3100
URL: www.otla.com
Scope: Provincial
Contact Information: Conference Chairs: Najma Rashid, Jason Singer & Brad Moscato

Promotional Product Professionals of Canada 2015 National Convention
Date: January 26-30, 2015
Location: Metro Toronto Convention Centre, South Building
Toronto, ON
Sponsor/Contact: Promotional Product Professionals of Canada Inc.
#100, 6700, Côte-de-Liesse
Saint-Laurent, QC H4T 2B5
514-489-5359 *Fax:* 514-489-7760
Toll-Free: 866-450-7722
E-mail: info@pppc.ca
URL: www.pppc.ca
Scope: National
Purpose: Educational seminars, business meetings, roundtable discussions, networking events, plus a trade show with over 600 exhibitors
Contact Information: Events Coordinator: Mara Welch, E-mail: shows@pppc.ca

Safety Services Manitoba SAFE Work Conference 2015
Date: January 21-22, 2015
Location: Victoria Inn & Conference Centre
Winnipeg, MB
Sponsor/Contact: Safety Services Manitoba
#3, 1680 Notre Dame Ave.
Winnipeg, MB R3H 1H6
204-949-1085 *Fax:* 204-949-2897
Toll-Free: 800-661-3321
E-mail: registrar@safetyservicesmanitoba.ca
URL: www.safetyservicesmanitoba.ca
Scope: Provincial
Purpose: Theme: "A Safety Odyssey"

SaskOutdoors' Annual General Meeting 2015
Date: January 24, 2015
Location: Saskatoon, SK
Sponsor/Contact: Saskatchewan Outdoor & Environmental Education Association
26 Corkery Bay
Regina, SK S4T 7K6
E-mail: soeea.sk@gmail.com
URL: www.soeea.sk.ca
Scope: Provincial

Saskatchewan Beef Industry 2015 6th Annual Conference: Harvesting the Future
Date: January 21-23, 2015
Location: Evraz Place
Regina, SK
Sponsor/Contact: Saskatchewan Livestock Association
Canada Center Building, Evraz Place
P.O. Box 3771
Regina, SK S4P 3N8
306-757-6133 *Fax:* 306-525-5852
E-mail: sla@accesscomm.ca
URL: www.sasklivestock.com
Scope: Provincial
Purpose: An event organized by the Saskatchewan Livestock Association, Saskatchewan Cattlemen's Association, Saskatchewan Cattle Feeders Association, Saskatchewan Beef & Forage Symposium Committee, & the Saskatchewan Stock Growers Association
Contact Information: E-mail: sla@accesscomm.ca

Scotia Horticultural Congress 2015
Date: January 26-27, 2015
Location: Old Orchard Inn
Greenwich, NS
Sponsor/Contact: Horticulture Nova Scotia
Kentville Agricultural Centre
32 Main St.
Kentville, NS B4N 1J5
902-678-9335 *Fax:* 902-678-1280
E-mail: info@horticulturens.ca
URL: www.hortns.com
Scope: Provincial

Sea Farmers Conference 2015
Date: January 28-30, 2015
Location: Delta Halifax
Halifax, NS
Sponsor/Contact: Aquaculture Association of Nova Scotia
c/o Starlite Gallery
#215, 7071 Bayers Rd.
Halifax, NS B3L 2C2
902-422-6234 *Fax:* 902-422-6248
E-mail: info@aansonline.ca
URL: www.aansonline.ca
Scope: Provincial
Purpose: Topic: The Case for Aquaculture

Toronto Gift Fair
Date: January 25-29, 2015
Location: The International Centre & Congress Centre
Toronto, ON
Sponsor/Contact: Canadian Gift Association
42 Voyager Ct. South
Toronto, ON M9W 5M7
416-679-0170 *Fax:* 416-679-0175
Toll-Free: 800-611-6100
E-mail: info@cangift.org
URL: www.cangift.org
Scope: Local
Purpose: The Toronto Gift Fair is Canada's largest temporary trade gift fair.
Anticipated Attendance: 24,600
Contact Information: Karen Bassels, Vice President, Toronto Gift Fair; PHone: 416.642.1024; Email: kbassels@cangift.org; URL: torontogiftfair.org; Email: toronto@cangift.org

Western Retail Lumber Association 2015 Prairie Showcase Buying Show & Convention
Date: January 21-23, 2015
Location: Calgary, AB
Sponsor/Contact: Western Retail Lumber Association
Western Retail Lumber Association Inc.
#1004, 213 Notre Dame Ave.
Winnipeg, MB R3B 1N3
204-957-1077 *Fax:* 204-947-5195
Toll-Free: 800-661-0253
E-mail: wrla@wrla.org
URL: www.wrla.org
Scope: Provincial
Contact Information: Caren Kelly, Marketing Manager, E-mail: Ckelly@wrla.org

Yukon Fish & Game Association 2015 Annual Banquet, Awards & Dance
Date: January 31, 2015
Location: High Country Inn Convention Center
Whitehorse, YT
Sponsor/Contact: Yukon Fish & Game Association
509 Strickland St.
Whitehorse, YT Y1A 2K5
867-667-4263 *Fax:* 867-667-4237
URL: www.yukonfga.ca
Contact Information: Yukon Fish & Game Association Office, Phone: 867-667-4263, E-mail: yfga@klondiker.com

February

10th International Chamber of Commerce International Mediation Competition
Date: February 6-11, 2015
Location: Paris, France
Sponsor/Contact: World Chambers Federation
38 cours Albert 1er
Paris, 75008
E-mail: wcf@iccwbo.org
URL: www.iccwbo.org/wcf
Scope: International

2015 12th Annual Canadian Critical Care Conference
Date: February 24-27, 2015
Location: Four Seasons Resort Whistler, BC
Sponsor/Contact: Canadian Critical Care Society
c/o Toronto General Hospital, 10 Eaton North, Room 220
200 Elizabeth St.
Toronto, ON M5G 2C4
416-340-4800 *Fax:* 416-340-4211
E-mail: info@canadiancriticalcare.org
URL: www.canadiancriticalcare.org
Scope: National
Contact Information: URL: www.canadiancriticalcare.ca

2015 Atlantic Universities Physics & Astronomy Conference (AUPAC)
Date: February 2-8, 2015
Location: Mount Allison University
Sackville, NB
Sponsor/Contact: Science Atlantic
P.O. Box 15000
1390 Le Marchant St.
Halifax, NS B3H 4R2
902-494-3421
E-mail: admin@scienceatlantic.ca
URL: www.scienceatlantic.ca
Scope: Provincial

2015 Beef Farmers of Ontario Annual General Meeting
Date: February 18-18, 2015
Location: International Plaza Hotel
Toronto, ON
Sponsor/Contact: Beef Farmers of Ontario
130 Malcolm Rd.
Guelph, ON N1K 1B1
519-824-0334 *Fax:* 519-824-9101
E-mail: info@ontariobeef.com
URL: www.ontariobeef.com
Scope: Provincial
Purpose: An opportunity for Ontario Cattlemen's Association members to help set policy direction on cattle industry issues
Contact Information: Communications Manager: Lianne Wuermli, E-mail: leaanne@ontariobeef.com

2015 British Columbia Art Teachers' Association Annual Conference
Date: February 19-22, 2015
Location: Vancouver, BC
Sponsor/Contact: British Columbia Art Teachers' Association
c/o B.C. Teachers' Federation
#100, 550 West 6th Ave.
Vancouver, BC V5Z 4P2
250-248-4662 *Fax:* 250-248-4628
Toll-Free: 800-663-9163
E-mail: psac41@bctf.ca
URL: bcata.ca
Scope: Provincial

2015 Certified Organic Associations of British Columbia Conference
Date: February 27- March 1, 2015
Location: Chilliwack, BC
Sponsor/Contact: Certified Organic Associations of British Columbia
#202, 3002 - 32nd Ave.
Vernon, BC V1T 2L7
250-260-4429 *Fax:* 250-260-4436
E-mail: office@certifiedorganic.bc.ca
URL: www.certifiedorganic.bc.ca
Scope: Provincial

2015 Claims Conference
Date: February 4, 2015
Location: Metro Toronto Convention Centre
Toronto, ON
Sponsor/Contact: Ontario Insurance Adjusters Association
29 De Jong Dr.
Mississauga, ON L5M 1B9
905-542-0576 *Fax:* 905-542-1301
Toll-Free: 888-259-1555
E-mail: manager@oiaa.com
URL: www.oiaa.com
Scope: Provincial

2015 Environmental Managers Association of British Columbia Workshop
Date: February 19, 2015
Location: Simon Fraser University, Segal Building
Vancouver, BC
Sponsor/Contact: Environmental Managers Association of British Columbia
P.O. Box 3741
Vancouver, BC V6B 3Z8
604-998-2226 *Fax:* 604-998-2226
E-mail: info@emaofbc.com
URL: www.emaofbc.com
Scope: Provincial
Purpose: Theme: Supporting BC's Resource Sectors Toward Successful Development

2015 Manitoba Cattle Producers Association Annual General Meeting
Date: February 5-6, 2015
Location: Victoria Inn Hotel & Convention Centre
Brandon, MB
Sponsor/Contact: Manitoba Cattle Producers Association
154 Paramount Rd.
Winnipeg, MB R2X 2W3
204-772-4542 *Fax:* 204-774-3264
Toll-Free: 800-772-0458
URL: www.mcpa.net
Scope: Provincial

2015 Ontario Coaches Conference
Date: February 20-22, 2015
Location: Sheraton Parkway North
Richmond Hill, ON
Sponsor/Contact: Coaches Association of Ontario
#108, 3 Concorde Gate
Toronto, ON M3C 3N7
Fax: 416-426-7331
Toll-Free: 888-622-7668
URL: www.ontariobobsleighskeleton.ca
Scope: Provincial

2015 ROMA/OGRA Combined Conference
Date: February 22-25, 2015
Location: Fairmont Royal York
Toronto, ON
Sponsor/Contact: Rural Ontario Municipal Association
#801, 200 University Ave.
Toronto, ON M5H 3C6
416-971-9856 *Fax:* 416-971-6191
Toll-Free: 877-426-6527
URL: www.roma.on.ca
Scope: Provincial
Purpose: Theme: CTRL+ALT+DEL

2015 Society for Research on Nicotine and Tobacco 20th Annual Meeting
Date: February 25-28, 2015
Location: Philadelphia Marriott Hotel
Philadelphia, PA
Sponsor/Contact: Society for Research on Nicotine & Tobacco
2424 American Lane
Madison, WI 53704
608-443-2462 *Fax:* 608-443-2474
E-mail: info@srnt.org
URL: www.srnt.org
Scope: International
Contact Information: Jane Shepard; Email: meetings@srnt.org

24th Annual Saskatchewan Home Based Educators (SHBE) Home Based Educators Convention
Date: February 20-21, 2015
Location: Evraz Place (Queensbury Centre)
Regina, SK
Sponsor/Contact: Saskatchewan Home Based Educators
P.O. Box 8541
Saskatoon, SK S7K 6K6
E-mail: help_desk@shbe.info
URL: www.shbe.info
Scope: Provincial

66th Annual Forests Ontario Conference 2015
Date: February 20, 2015
Location: Nottawasaga Inn
Alliston, ON
Sponsor/Contact: Forests Ontario
#700, 144 Front St. West
Toronto, ON MSJ 2L7
416-646-1193 *Fax:* 416-493-4608
Toll-Free: 877-646-1193
E-mail: info@treesontario.ca
URL: www.forestsontario.ca
Scope: Provincial

88th Ontario Road Builders' Association 2015 Annual General Meeting & Convention - "The Road Ahead"
Date: February 9-10, 2015
Location: The Fairmont Royal York
Toronto, ON
Sponsor/Contact: Ontario Road Builders' Association
#1, 365 Brunel Rd.
Mississauga, ON L4Z 1Z5
905-507-1107 *Fax:* 905-890-8122
URL: www.orba.org
Scope: Provincial
Purpose: Informative sessions of interest to members of the road building industry
Contact Information: Office Manager & Coordinator, Events: Kim Le Fort, E-mail: kim@orba.org

AFOA Canada 15th National Conference 2015
Date: February 17-19, 2015
Location: RBC Convention Centre Winnipeg
Winnipeg, MB
Sponsor/Contact: AFOA Canada
#301, 1066 Somerset St. West
Ottawa, ON K1Y 4T3
613-722-5543 *Fax:* 613-722-3467
Toll-Free: 866-722-2362
E-mail: info@afoa.ca
URL: www.afoa.ca
Scope: National

ANHIX (Alberta Network for Heath Information eXchange) and COACH (Canada's Health Informatics Association) Conference 2015
Date: February 5, 2015
Location: Delta Calgary South
Calgary, AB
Sponsor/Contact: COACH - Canada's Health Informatics Association
#301, 250 Consumers Rd.
Toronto, ON M2J 4V6
416-494-9324 *Fax:* 416-495-8723
Toll-Free: 888-253-8554
E-mail: info@coachorg.com
URL: www.coachorg.com
Scope: National
Contact Information: COACH Program Coordinator: Cheryl Cornelio, Email: ccornelio@coachorg.com

Alberta Association of Agricultural Societies 2015 Annual Meeting & Convention
Date: February 6-8, 2015
Location: Ramada Conference Center
Edmonton, AB
Sponsor/Contact: Alberta Association of Agricultural Societies
J.G. O'Donoghue Building
#200, 7000 - 113 St.
Edmonton, AB T6H 5T6
780-427-2174 *Fax:* 780-422-7755
E-mail: aaas@gov.ab.ca
URL: www.albertaagsocieties.ca
Scope: Provincial
Purpose: An event attended by members of the Alberta Association of Agricultural Societies, where agricultural societies can submit resolutions to the annual general meeting & vote
Contact Information: E-mail: aaas@gov.ab.ca

Alberta Fish & Game Association 2015 Annual General Meeting
Date: February 19-21, 2015
Location: Alberta
Sponsor/Contact: Alberta Fish & Game Association
6924 - 104 St.
Edmonton, AB T6H 2L7
780-437-2342 *Fax:* 780-438-6872
E-mail: office@afga.org
URL: www.afga.org
Scope: Provincial
Purpose: Voting on resolutions

Alberta Gift Fair
Date: February 22-25, 2015
Location: Edmonton Expo Centre, Northlands
Edmonton, AB
Sponsor/Contact: Canadian Gift Association
42 Voyager Ct. South
Toronto, ON M9W 5M7
416-679-0170 *Fax:* 416-679-0175
Toll-Free: 800-611-6100
E-mail: info@cangift.org
URL: www.cangift.org
Scope: Local
Purpose: The Alberta Gift Fair contains Western Canada's most comprehensive collection of products and services, catering to the specialized needs of retailers, sales representatives and manufacturers.
Anticipated Attendance: 16,000
Contact Information: Brenda Harrison, Show Manager; Phone: 416.642.1049; Email: bharrison@cangift.org; URL: albertagiftfair.org; Email: alberta@cangift.org

Alberta Percheron Club 2015 Annual Meeting
Date: February 7, 2015
Location: Westerner Park
Red Deer, AB
Sponsor/Contact: Alberta Percheron Club
c/o Julie Roy
RR#1
Markerville, AB T0M 1M0
403-728-3127
E-mail: sanlan@platinum.ca
URL: www.albertapercherons.com
Scope: Provincial
Contact Information: Julie Roy; Email: sanlan@platinum.ca

Alberta Weekly Newspapers Association 2015 Newspaper Symposium
Date: February 13-14, 2015
Location: Radisson Hotel Edmonton South
Edmonton, AB
Sponsor/Contact: Alberta Weekly Newspapers Association
3228 Parsons Rd.
Edmonton, AB T6H 5R7
780-434-8746 *Fax:* 780-438-8356
Toll-Free: 800-282-6903
E-mail: info@awna.com
URL: www.awna.com
Scope: Provincial
Purpose: A symposium for persons who work for newspapers, such as managers, editors, photographers, & sales people, featuring a keynote speaker, courses on a variety of topics, & the presentation of awards
Contact Information: Professional Development & Communications Coordinator: Maurizia Hinse, E-mail: maurizia@awna.com

Alzheimer Manitoba A Night to Remember in Brazil: Gala 2015
Date: February 12, 2015
Location: RBC Convention Centre
Winnipeg, MB
Sponsor/Contact: Alzheimer Manitoba
#10, 120 Donald St.
Winnipeg, MB R3C 4G2
204-943-6622 *Fax:* 204-942-5408
Toll-Free: 800-378-6699
E-mail: alzmb@alzheimer.mb.ca
URL: www.alzheimer.mb.ca/
Scope: Provincial

American Association for the Advancement of Science 2015 Annual Meeting
Date: February 12-16, 2015
Location: San Jose, CA USA
Sponsor/Contact: American Association for the Advancement of Science
1200 New York Ave. NW
Washington, DC 20005
202-326-6440
E-mail: membership@aaas.org
URL: www.aaas.org
Scope: International
Purpose: Information for scientists, engineers, educators, & policy-makers
Contact Information: Phone: 202-326-6450; Fax: 202-289-4021; E-mail: meetings@aaas.org; Director, Meetings & Public Engagement: Tiffany Lohwater, E-mail: tlohwate@aaas.org

Annual Forestry Conference and AGM 2015
Date: February 18-20, 2015
Location: Vancouver Island Conference Centre
Nanaimo, BC
Sponsor/Contact: Association of British Columbia Forest Professionals
#330 - 321 Water St.
Vancouver, BC V6B 1B8
604-687-8027 *Fax:* 604-687-3264
E-mail: info@abcfp.ca
URL: www.abcfp.ca
Scope: Provincial

Association of Ontario Land Surveyors 2015 Annual General Meeting
Date: February 25-27, 2015
Location: Deerhurst Resort
Huntsville, ON
Sponsor/Contact: Association of Ontario Land Surveyors
1043 McNicoll Ave.
Toronto, ON M1W 3W6
416-491-9020 *Fax:* 416-491-2576
Toll-Free: 800-268-0718
E-mail: info@aols.org
URL: www.aols.org
Scope: Provincial
Purpose: The theme is "Building Our Geospatial Future"
Contact Information: Lena Kassabian; Email: lena@aols.org; Phone: 416-491-9020 ext. 25

BC Fruit Growers Association 126th Annual General Meeting 2015
Date: February 20-21, 2015
Location: Penticton, BC
Sponsor/Contact: British Columbia Fruit Growers' Association

Conferences Index

1473 Water St.
Kelowna, BC V1Y 1J6
250-762-5226 *Fax:* 250-861-9089
E-mail: info@bcfga.com
URL: www.bcfga.com
Scope: Provincial
Contact Information: Email: info@bcfga.com

Brain Care Centre 2015 Defying Limitations Gala
Date: February 28, 2015
Location: DoubleTree by Hilton Hotel West Edmonton
Edmonton, AB
Sponsor/Contact: Brain Care Centre
Royal Alex Place
#229, 10106 - 111th Ave.
Edmonton, AB T5G 0B4
780-477-7575 *Fax:* 780-474-4415
Toll-Free: 800-425-5552
E-mail: admin@braincarecentre.com
URL: www.braincarecentre.com
Scope: Provincial

British Columbia Food Technologists 2015 Annual Suppliers' Night
Date: February 25, 2015
Location: Delta Burnaby Hotel & Conference Centre
Burnaby, BC
Sponsor/Contact: British Columbia Food Technolgists
c/o Nilmini Wijewickreme, SGS Canada
50-655 West Kent Ave. North
Vancouver, BC V6P 6T7
E-mail: info@bcft.ca
URL: www.bcft.ca
Scope: Provincial
Purpose: A learning event featuring over 100 supplier exhibits of interest to food scientists, research & development technologists, & senior managers & purchasers from food & beverage companies
Contact Information: Chair, Program Committee: Emilie Le Bihan, E-mail: elebihan@metaromneotech.com

British Columbia Nurses' Union Convention 2015
Date: February 24-26, 2015
Location: Hyatt Regency Vancouver
Vancouver, BC
Sponsor/Contact: British Columbia Nurses' Union
4060 Regent St.
Burnaby, BC V5C 6P5
604-433-2268 *Fax:* 604-433-7945
Toll-Free: 800-663-9991
E-mail: contactbcnu@bcnu.org
URL: www.bcnu.org
Scope: Provincial

British Columbia Recreation & Parks Association 2015 38th Annual ProvincialParks & Grounds Spring Training Conference
Date: February 25-26, 2015
Location: The Anvil Centre
New Westminster, BC
Sponsor/Contact: British Columbia Recreation & Parks Association
#101, 4664 Lougheed Hwy.
Burnaby, BC V5C 5T5
604-629-0965 *Fax:* 604-629-2651
Toll-Free: 866-929-0965
E-mail: bcrpa@bcrpa.bc.ca
URL: www.bcrpa.bc.ca
Scope: Provincial
Purpose: Continuing education sessions that cover a wide range of interests for parks & grounds professionals
Contact Information: Programs & Initiatives Coordinator: Natalie Korsovetski, Phone: 604-629-0965, ext. 229, E-mail: nkorsovetski@bcrpa.bc.ca

British Columbia Road Builders & Heavy Construction Association 2015 Annual General Meeting & Convention
Date: Februrary 8-11, 2015
Location: Westin Resort & Spa
Los Cabos, Mexico
Sponsor/Contact: British Columbia Road Builders & Heavy Construction Association
#307, 8678 Greenall Ave.
Burnaby, BC V5J 3M6
604-436-0220 *Fax:* 604-436-2627
E-mail: info@roadbuilders.bc.ca
URL: www.roadbuilders.bc.ca
Scope: Provincial
Contact Information: Manager, Communications & Membership: Parveen Parhar, E-mail: parveen@roadbuilders.bc.ca

Calgary City Teachers Convention 2015
Date: February 12-13, 2015
Location: Telus Convention Centre
Calgary, AB
Sponsor/Contact: Alberta Teachers' Association
Barnett House
11010 - 142 St.
Edmonton, AB T5N 2R1
780-447-9400 *Fax:* 780-455-6481
Toll-Free: 800-232-7208
E-mail: government@teachers.ab.ca
URL: www.teachers.ab.ca
Scope: Local

Canadian Advanced Technology Alliance National Public Alerting Summit
Date: February 17-18, 2015
Location: Edmonton, AB
Sponsor/Contact: Canadian Advanced Technology Alliance
National Headquarters
#416, 207 Bank St.
Ottawa, ON K2P 2N2
613-236-6550
E-mail: info@cata.ca
URL: www.cata.ca
Scope: National

Canadian Association of Agri-Retailers 2015 20th Annual Convention & Trade Show
Date: February 18-19, 2015
Location: Delta Grand Okanagan Resort
Kelowna, BC
Sponsor/Contact: Canadian Association of Agri-Retailers
#628, 70 Arthur St.
Winnipeg, MB R3B 1G7
204-989-9300 *Fax:* 204-989-9306
Toll-Free: 800-463-9323
E-mail: info@caar.org
URL: www.caar.org
Scope: National
Purpose: A conference & exhibition featuring the annual general meeting, educational workshops, guest speaker sessions, the presentation of awards, & networking events
Contact Information: Canadian Association of Agri-Retailers, Phone: 1-800-463-9323, E-mail: info@caar.org

Canadian Association of Environmental Law Societies 2015 Conference
Date: February 13-14, 2015
Location: Univeristy of Calgary
Calgary, AB
Sponsor/Contact: Canadian Association of Environmental Law Societies
E-mail: info@caels.org
URL: caels.org
Scope: National

Canadian Association of Hepatology Nurses 2015 Annual National Education Conference
Date: February 28, 2015
Location: Banff, AB
Sponsor/Contact: Canadian Association of Hepatology Nurses
c/o Dawn King
1 Campbell Ave.
St. Johns, NL A1E 2Z1
URL: www.livernurses.org
Scope: National
Contact Information: Co-Chair, Conference Committee: Sharon Bojarski, E-mail: sharonbojarski@hotmail.com; Co-Chair, Conference Committee: Sandi Mitchell, E-mail: sandi.mitchell@bccdc.ca

Canadian Association on Water Quality 2015 Central Canadian Symposium on Water Quality Research
Date: February 18-19, 2015
Location: Holiday Inn
Burlington, ON
Sponsor/Contact: Canadian Association on Water Quality
P.O. Box 5050
867 Lakeshore Rd.
Burlington, ON L7R 4A6
905-336-4513 *Fax:* 905-336-6444
URL: www.cawq.ca
Scope: National
Purpose: A gathering of people in diverse fields of water quality research to present innovations in engineering, science, & policy.

Canadian Bar Association Mid-Winter Meeting of Council 2015
Date: February 20-22, 2015
Location: Fairmont Chateau Laurier
Ottawa, ON
Sponsor/Contact: Canadian Bar Association
#500, 865 Carling Ave.
Ottawa, ON K1S 5S8
613-237-2925 *Fax:* 613-237-0185
Toll-Free: 800-267-8860
E-mail: info@cba.org
URL: www.cba.org
Scope: National

Canadian Council for Refugees 2015 Winter Working Group Meetings
Date: February 27-28, 2015
Location: Toronto, ON
Sponsor/Contact: Canadian Council for Refugees
#302, 6839, rue Drolet
Montréal, QC H2S 2T1
514-277-7223 *Fax:* 514-277-1447
E-mail: info@ccrweb.ca
URL: www.ccrweb.ca
Scope: National
Purpose: Meetings of the Overseas Protection & Sponsorship Working Group, the Immigration & Settlement Working Group, & the Inland Protection Working Group, for all Canadian Council for Refugees members, plus anyone who is interested in participating
Contact Information: E-mail: info@ccrweb.ca

Canadian Depression Research and Intervention Network Conference 2015
Date: February 24-25, 2015
Location: Ottawa Convention Centre
Ottawa, ON
Sponsor/Contact: Canadian Depression Research & Intervention Network
The Royal Ottawa Mental Health Centre
#5412, 1145 Carling Ave.
Ottawa, ON K1Z 7K4
E-mail: info@cdrin.org
URL: cdrin.org
Scope: National
Anticipated Attendance: 300

Canadian Digestive Diseases Week (CDDW) & the 2015 Annual Canadian Association for the Study of the Liver (CASL) Winter Meeting
Date: February 27 - March 2, 2015
Location: Banff, AB
Sponsor/Contact: Canadian Association for the Study of the Liver
c/o BUKSA Strategic Conference Services
#307, 10328 - 81st Ave.
Edmonton, AB T6E 1X2
780-436-0983 *Fax:* 780-437-5984
E-mail: casl@hepatology.ca
URL: www.hepatology.ca
Scope: National
Purpose: A February or March scientific conference of the Canadian Association of Gastroenterology (CAG) & the Canadian Association for the Study of the Liver (CASL), featuring lectures, symposia, small group sessions, exhibits, & opportunities for networking

Canadian Digestive Diseases Week: Canadian Association of Gastroenterology Annual Scientific Conference 2015
Date: February 27 - March 2, 2015
Location: Fairmont Banff Springs
Banff, AB
Sponsor/Contact: Canadian Association of Gastroenterology
#224, 1540 Cornwall Rd.
Oakville, ON L6J 7W5
905-829-2504 *Fax:* 905-829-0242
Toll-Free: 888-780-0007
E-mail: general@cag-acg.org
URL: www.cag-acg.org
Scope: National

Canadian Federation of Agriculture 2015 Annual General Meeting
Date: February 24-25, 2015
Location: Delta Ottawa City Centre
Ottawa, On
Sponsor/Contact: Canadian Federation of Agriculture
21 Florence St.
Ottawa, ON K2P 0W6
613-236-3633 *Fax:* 613-236-5749
E-mail: info@cfafca.ca
URL: www.cfa-fca.ca
Scope: National
Contact Information: Suzanne Lamirande; Email: suzanne@cfafca.ca; Phone: 613-236-3633 ext: 2327

Conferences Index

Canadian Health Food Association (CHFA) Québec 2015
Date: February 6-7, 2015
Location: Palais des congrès
Montreal, QC
Sponsor/Contact: Canadian Health Food Association
#302, 235 Yorkland Blvd.
Toronto, ON M2J 4Y8
416-497-6939 *Fax:* 905-479-3214
Toll-Free: 800-661-4510
E-mail: info@chfa.ca
URL: www.chfa.ca
Scope: Provincial
Purpose: A conference & trade show designed for owners & decision makers from both small & large establishments, such as natural & health food retail stores, specialty stores, food chains, & pharmacies
Anticipated Attendance: 875
Contact Information: Phone: 416-497-6939; Toll-Free Phone: 1-800-661-4510; E-mail: info@chfa.ca

Canadian International Turfgrass 2015 48th Annual Conference & Trade Show
Date: February 2-6, 2015
Location: Telus Convention Centre
Calgary, AB
Sponsor/Contact: Canadian Golf Superintendents Association
#205, 5520 Explorer Dr.
Mississauga, ON L4W 5L1
905-602-8873 *Fax:* 905-602-1958
Toll-Free: 800-387-1056
E-mail: cgsa@golfsupers.com
URL: www.golfsupers.com
Scope: International
Purpose: An international confernce & trade show featuring over 100 exhibitors
Contact Information: Manager, Member Services: Lori Micucci, E-mail: lmicucci@golfsupers.com; URL: golfsupers.com/en/calgary2015

Canadian Land Reclamation Association Alberta Chapter Annual General Meeting and Conference
Date: February 25-27, 2015
Location: Red Deer, AB
Sponsor/Contact: Canadian Land Reclamation Association
URL: www.clra.ca
Scope: Provincial

Canadian Memorial Chiropractic College Event: Practice OpportUnity 2015
Date: February 19, 2015
Location: Toronto, ON
Sponsor/Contact: Canadian Memorial Chiropractic College
6100 Leslie St.
Toronto, ON M2H 3J1
416-482-2340 *Fax:* 416-482- 362
E-mail: communications@cmcc.ca
URL: www.cmcc.ca
Scope: National
Purpose: An event for Canadian Memorial Chiropractic College students to meet industry professional, such as chiropractors & associated business vendors
Contact Information: General Information, Phone: 416-482-2340, ext. 200, E-mail: events@cmcc.ca; Sponsorship Information, E-mail: sponsorship@cmcc.ca

Canadian Nuclear Association Conference & Trade Show 2015
Date: February 25-27, 2015
Location: Westin Hotel
Ottawa, ON
Sponsor/Contact: Canadian Nuclear Association
#1610, 130 Albert St.
Ottawa, ON K1P 5G4
613-237-4262 *Fax:* 613-237-0989
URL: www.cna.ca
Scope: National
Contact Information: Email: conference@cna.ca

Canadian Pediatric Endocrine Group 2015 Scientific Meeting
Date: February 19-21, 2015
Location: Westin Nova Scotian
Halifax, NS
Sponsor/Contact: Canadian Pediatric Endocrine Group
c/o Robert Barnes, M.D., Montreal Children's Hospital
#316E, 2300, rue Tupper
Montréal, QC H3H 1P3
514-412-4315 *Fax:* 514-412-4264
URL: www.cpeg-gcep.net
Scope: National

Canadian Rheumatology Association 2015 Annual Scientific Meeting
Date: February 4-7, 2015
Location: Fairmont Chateau Frontenac
Québec, QC
Sponsor/Contact: Canadian Rheumatology Association
#244, 12 - 16715 Yonge St.
Newmarket, ON L3X 1X4
905-952-0698 *Fax:* 905-952-0708
E-mail: info@rheum.ca
URL: rheum.ca
Scope: National

Canadian Society of Association Executives, Trillium Chapter, 2015 6th Annual Winter Summit
Date: February 5-6, 2015
Location: Kitchener, ON
Sponsor/Contact: Canadian Society of Association Executives
39 River St.
Toronto, ON M5A 3P1
416-646-1600 *Fax:* 416-646-9460
URL: www.csae.com/trillium/
Scope: Provincial

Canadian Society of Professional Event Planners 2015 Annual Conference
Date: February 26-28, 2015
Location: Saskatoon, SK
Sponsor/Contact: Canadian Society of Professional Event Planners
312 Oakwood Court
Newmarket, ON L3Y 3C8
905-868-8008 *Fax:* 905-895-1630
Toll-Free: 866-467-2299
E-mail: infoc@cspep.ca
URL: www.canspep.ca
Scope: National

Canadian Teachers' Federation 2015 Annual Francophone Symposium / Symposium de l'enseignement en français
Date: February 5-6, 2015
Location: Shaw Convetion Centre
Edmonton, AB
Sponsor/Contact: Canadian Teachers' Federation
2490 Don Reid Dr.
Ottawa, ON K1H 1E1
613-232-1505 *Fax:* 613-232-1886
Toll-Free: 866-283-1505
E-mail: info@ctf-fce.ca
URL: www.ctf-fce.ca
Scope: National
Purpose: Held jointly with The Manitoba Teachers' Society / Éducatrices et éducateurs francophones du Manitoba
Contact Information: Contact: Johanne Deschamps, Address: 2490, promenade Don Reid, Ottawa, ON K1H 1E1

Canadian Union of Public Employees (CUPE) 2015 Manitoba Winter School
Date: February 26 - March 1, 2015
Location: Lakeview Resort
Gimli, MB
Sponsor/Contact: Canadian Union of Public Employees
Manitoba Regional Office
#703, 275 Broadway
Winnipeg, MB R3C 4M6
204-942-0343 *Fax:* 204-956-7071
Toll-Free: 800-552-2873
E-mail: cupemb@mts.net
URL: www.cupe.mb.ca
Scope: Provincial
Purpose: Workshops presented each winter for the Manitoba region
Contact Information: E-mail: cupemb@mts.net

Canadian Union of Public Employees 2015 Human Rights Conference
Date: February 5-8, 2015
Location: RBC Convention Centre
Winnipeg, MB
Sponsor/Contact: Canadian Union of Public Employees
1375 St. Laurent Blvd.
Ottawa, ON K1G 0Z7
613-237-1590 *Fax:* 613-237-5508
E-mail: cupemail@cupe.ca
URL: www.cupe.ca
Scope: National

Central Alberta Teachers Convention 2015
Date: February 19-20, 2015
Location: Red Deer College
Red Deer, AB
Sponsor/Contact: Alberta Teachers' Association
Barnett House
11010 - 142 St.
Edmonton, AB T5N 2R1
780-447-9400 *Fax:* 780-455-6481
Toll-Free: 800-232-7208
E-mail: government@teachers.ab.ca
URL: www.teachers.ab.ca
Scope: Local

Chartered Professional Accountants Canada 1st National SR&ED Symposium
Date: February 5-6, 2015
Location: Toronto, ON
Sponsor/Contact: Chartered Professional Accountants Canada
277 Wellington St. West
Toronto, ON M5V 3H2
416-977-3222 *Fax:* 416-977-8585
Toll-Free: 800-268-3793
E-mail: member.services@cpacanada.ca
URL: www.cpacanada.ca
Scope: National

Construction Safety Association of Manitoba 2015 The Safety Conference
Date: February 3-4, 2015
Location: RBC Convention Centre
Winnipeg, MB
Sponsor/Contact: Construction Safety Association of Manitoba
1447 Waverly St.
Winnipeg, MB R3T 0P7
204-775-3171 *Fax:* 204-779-3505
E-mail: safety@constructionsafety.ca
URL: www.constructionsafety.ca
Scope: Provincial
Purpose: A safety & health conference for construction owners, supervisors, foremen, safety committees, workers, & students, featuring workshops & a trade show with more than 100 exhibitors
Anticipated Attendance: 2,000+
Contact Information: Executive Director, Construction Safety Association of Manitoba: Sean Scott, Phone: 204-775-3171, Fax: 204-779-3505, E-mail: sean@constructionsafety.ca

East York-Scarborough Reading Association Reading for the Love of It Confernece 2015
Date: February 9-10, 2015
Location: Sheraton Centre Hotel
Toronto, ON
Sponsor/Contact: East York - Scarborough Reading Association
#309, 1315 Lawrence Ave. East
Toronto, ON M3A 3R3
416-444-7473 *Fax:* 416-444-9282
E-mail: eys@readingfortheloveofit.com
URL: www.readingfortheloveofit.com
Scope: Local

Easter Seals 2015 64th Annual Rogers Conn Smythe Sports Celebrities Dinner & Auction in Support of Easter Seals Kids
Date: February 18, 2015
Location: Royal York Hotel
Toronto, ON
Sponsor/Contact: Easter Seals Canada
#401, 40 Holly St.
Toronto, ON M4S 3C3
416-932-8382 *Fax:* 416-932-9844
Toll-Free: 877-376-6362
E-mail: info@easterseals.ca
URL: www.easterseals.ca
Scope: National
Purpose: An event to raise money for youth & young adults with physical disabilities
Contact Information: Development Officer, Special Events (Marketing): Catherine Harwood, Phone: 416-421-8377, ext. 309, E-mail: charwood@easterseals.org; Development Officer, Special Events (Volunteers): Lauren Squizzato, Phone: 416-421-8377, ext. 316; URL: connsmythedinner.com

Economic Developers Council of Ontario 2015 Conference
Date: February 10-12, 2015
Location: Hamilton Convention Center
Hamilton, ON
Sponsor/Contact: Economic Developers Council of Ontario Inc.
6506 Marlene Ave.
Cornwall, ON K6H 7H9
613-931-9827 *Fax:* 613-931-9828
E-mail: edco@edco.on.ca
URL: www.edco.on.ca
Scope: Provincial

Elementary Teachers' Federation of Ontario 2015 ... and still we rise
Date: February 25-27, 2015
Location: Fairmont Royal York Hotel
Toronto, ON
Sponsor/Contact: Elementary Teachers' Federation of Ontario
136 Isabella St.
Toronto, ON M4Y 1P6
416-962-3836 *Fax:* 416-642-2424
Toll-Free: 888-838-3836
URL: www.etfo.ca
Scope: Provincial
Purpose: Annual leadership conference for women
Contact Information: Conference Contact: Kalpana Makan, E-mail: kmakan@etfo.org

Environmental Services Association of Alberta Environment Business 2015
Date: February 10-12, 2015
Location: Edmonton, AB
Sponsor/Contact: Environmental Services Association of Alberta
#102, 2528 Ellwood Dr. SW
Edmonton, AB T6X 0A9
780-429-6363 *Fax:* 780-429-4249
Toll-Free: 800-661-9278
E-mail: info@esaa.org
URL: www.esaa.org
Scope: Provincial
Contact Information: URL: www.environmentbusiness.ca, Phone: 780-429-6363 x 223

Federation of Canadian Municipalities 2015 Sustainable Communities Conference and Trade Show
Date: February 10-12, 2015
Location: London Convention Centre
London, ON
Sponsor/Contact: Federation of Canadian Municipalities
24 Clarence St.
Ottawa, ON K1N 5P3
613-241-5221 *Fax:* 613-241-7440
E-mail: federation@fcm.ca
URL: www.fcm.ca
Scope: National
Purpose: This year's theme is "Building Momentum for Sustainability"

Geological Association of Canada, Newfoundland & Labrador Section 2015 Technicl Meeting
Date: February 16-17, 2015
Location: Johnson Geo Centre
St. John's, NL
Sponsor/Contact: Geological Association of Canada
c/o Heather Rafuse, Department of Natural Resources, Geological Survey
P.O. Box 8700
St. John's, NL A1B 4J6
URL: gac.esd.mun.ca/nl/nfsection.htm
Scope: Provincial
Purpose: An annual meeting featuring guest speakers & a general session for the presentation of papers
Contact Information: Technical Program Chair: James Conliffe, E-mail: jamesconliffe@gov.nl.ca

Hotel Association of Canada 2015 Annual Conference
Date: February 2-3, 2015
Location: Hilton Toronto
Toronto, ON
Sponsor/Contact: Hotel Association of Canada Inc.
#1206, 130 Albert St.
Ottawa, ON K1P 5G4
613-237-7149 *Fax:* 613-237-8928
E-mail: info@hotelassociation.ca
URL: www.hotelassociation.ca
Scope: National
Contact Information: Orie Berlasso, Director; Phone: 416-924-2002; Email: orieberlasso@bigpictureconferences.ca

Institute of Public Administration of Canada 2015 10th National Leadership Conference & Awards
Date: February 5-6, 2015
Location: King Edward Hotel
Toronto, ON
Sponsor/Contact: Institute of Public Administration of Canada
#401, 1075 Bay St.
Toronto, ON M5S 2B1
416-924-8787 *Fax:* 416-924-4992
URL: www.ipac.ca
Scope: National
Contact Information: URL: www.ipac.ca/Leadership2015, Email: ntl@ipac.ca

Manitoba Dental Assistants Association 2015 Annual General Meeting
Date: February 7, 2015
Location: Caboto Centre
Winnipeg, MB
Sponsor/Contact: Manitoba Dental Assistants Association
#17, 595 Clifton St.
Winnipeg, MB R3G 2X5
204-586-7378 *Fax:* 204-783-9631
E-mail: mdaa@mdaa.ca
URL: www.mdaa.ca
Scope: Provincial
Purpose: A review of the year & bylaws & results of the MDAA Wage Survey
Contact Information: E-mail: mdaa@mdaa.ca

Manitoba Environmental Industries Association Inc. 2015 Remediation & Renewal Conference
Date: February 25, 2015
Location: Victoria Inn
Winnipeg, MB
Sponsor/Contact: Manitoba Environmental Industries Association Inc.
#100, 62 Albert St.
Winnipeg, MB R3B 1E9
204-783-7090 *Fax:* 204-783-6501
E-mail: admin@meia.mb.ca
URL: www.meia.mb.ca
Scope: Provincial
Purpose: An annual one day conference with information about recent changes in provincial & federal environmental legislation & regulatory affairs
Contact Information: Coordinator, Education & Training: Rosemary Deans, Phone: 204-783-7090

Manitoba Non-Profit Housing Association 2015 Conference
Date: February 12-13, 2015
Location: Victoria Inn Hotel & Convention Centre
Winnipeg, MB
Sponsor/Contact: Manitoba Non-Profit Housing Association
#200A, 1215 Henderson Hwy.
Winnipeg, MB R2G 1L8
204-797-6746 *Fax:* 204-336-3809
E-mail: info@mnpha.com
URL: mnpha.com
Scope: Provincial

Modular Housing Association - Prairie Provinces 9th Annual Saskatchewan Industry Meeting
Date: February 4, 2015
Location: Executive Hotel & Resorts
Regina, SK
Sponsor/Contact: Modular Housing Association Prairie Provinces
P.O. Box 3538 Stn. main
Sherwood Park, AB T8H 2T4
780-429-1798 *Fax:* 780-429-1871
E-mail: mha@shawlink.ca
URL: mhaprairies.ca
Scope: Provincial

Newfoundland & Labrador Federation of Agriculture 2015 Annual General Meeting
Date: February 4-5, 2015
Location: Hotel Gander
Gander, NL
Sponsor/Contact: Newfoundland & Labrador Federation of Agriculture
P.O. Box 1045
308 Brookfield Rd., Bldg. 4
Mount Pearl, NL A1N 3C9
709-747-4874 *Fax:* 709-747-8827
E-mail: info@nlfa.ca
URL: www.nlfa.ca
Scope: Provincial
Purpose: An opportunity for members in good standing to vote & hold office
Contact Information: Phone: 709-747-4874; E-mail: info@nlfa.ca

North Central Teachers Convention 2015
Date: February 5-6, 2015
Location: Shaw Conference Centre
Edmonton, AB
Sponsor/Contact: Alberta Teachers' Association
Barnett House
11010 - 142 St.
Edmonton, AB T5N 2R1
780-447-9400 *Fax:* 780-455-6481
Toll-Free: 800-232-7208
E-mail: government@teachers.ab.ca
URL: www.teachers.ab.ca
Scope: Local

Northeast Teachers Convention 2015
Date: February 12-13, 2015
Location: Doubletree by Hilton
Edmonton, AB
Sponsor/Contact: Alberta Teachers' Association
Barnett House
11010 - 142 St.
Edmonton, AB T5N 2R1
780-447-9400 *Fax:* 780-455-6481
Toll-Free: 800-232-7208
E-mail: government@teachers.ab.ca
URL: www.teachers.ab.ca
Scope: Local

Ontario Association of Veterinary Technicians 2015 Conference
Date: February 26-28, 2015
Location: Scotiabank Convention Centre
Niagara Falls, ON
Sponsor/Contact: Ontario Association of Veterinary Technicians
#104, 100 Stone Rd. West
Guelph, ON N1G 5L3
519-836-4910 *Fax:* 519-836-3638
Toll-Free: 800-675-1859
E-mail: oavt@oavt.org
URL: www.oavt.org
Scope: Provincial

Ontario Good Roads Association / Rural Ontario Municipal Association 2015 Combined Conference
Date: February 22-25, 2015
Location: Fairmount Royal York
Toronto, ON
Sponsor/Contact: Ontario Good Roads Association
#22, 1525 Cornwall Rd.
Oakville, ON L6J 0B2
289-291-6472 *Fax:* 289-291-6477
E-mail: info@ogra.org
URL: www.ogra.org
Scope: Provincial
Purpose: Workshops, information about current municipal issues, a trade show, & social events
Anticipated Attendance: 1,500+
Contact Information: Ontario Good Roads Association, Phone: 905-795-2555; Fax: 905-795-2660

Ontario Parks Association 2015 59th Annual Educational Forum
Date: February 25, 2015
Location: Holiday Inn Burlington Hotel and Conference Centre
Burlington, ON
Sponsor/Contact: Ontario Parks Association
7856 - 5th Line South, RR#4
Milton, ON L9T 2X8
905-864-6182 *Fax:* 905-864-6184
Toll-Free: 866-560-7783
E-mail: opa@ontarioparksassociation.ca
URL: www.ontarioparksassociation.ca
Scope: Provincial
Purpose: Educational presentations of interest to park & green space managers & operational staff. This year's theme is "Parks for Life: Making the Connections."

Ontario Percheron Horse Association 2015 Annual Meeting
Date: February 7, 2015
Location: Holiday Inn Express
Newmarket, ON
Sponsor/Contact: Ontario Percheron Horse Association Inc.
c/o Michelle Campbell
2321 Cockshutt Rd.
Waterford, ON N0E 1Y0
519-443-6399
E-mail: Secretary@ontariopercherons.ca
URL: www.ontariopercherons.ca
Scope: Provincial
Contact Information: Meeting Contact: Hedy Edwards, Phone: 905-887-5485

Ontario Stone, Sand & Gravel Association 2015 Annual General Meeting
Date: February 25-27, 2015
Location: Hilton Toronto Hotel
Toronto, ON
Sponsor/Contact: Ontario Stone, Sand & Gravel Association
#103, 5720 Timberlea Blvd.
Mississauga, ON L4W 4W2
905-507-0711 *Fax:* 905-507-0717
URL: www.ossga.com
Scope: Provincial

Ontario Trial Lawyers Association 2015 Medical Malpractice Conference - Medical Malpractice: Strategies for Success
Date: February 6-9, 2015
Location: Atlantis Paradise Island
Nassau, Bahamas
Sponsor/Contact: Ontario Trial Lawyers Association

1190 Blair Rd.
Burlington, ON L7M 1K9
905-639-6852 *Fax:* 905-639-3100
URL: www.otla.com
Scope: Provincial
Contact Information: Conference Chairs: Richard Halpern and Maria Damiano

Ontario University Registrars' Association 2015 Conference
Date: February 11-13, 2015
Location: Toronto Marriott Downtown Eaton Centre Hotel
Toronto, ON
Sponsor/Contact: Ontario University Registrars' Association
900 McGill Rd.
Kamloops, BC V2C 0C8
250-828-5019
URL: www.oura.ca
Scope: Provincial

Palliser District Teachers Convention 2015
Date: February 19-20, 2015
Location: Telus Convention Centre
Calgary, AB
Sponsor/Contact: Alberta Teachers' Association
Barnett House
11010 - 142 St.
Edmonton, AB T5N 2R1
780-447-9400 *Fax:* 780-455-6481
Toll-Free: 800-232-7208
E-mail: government@teachers.ab.ca
URL: www.teachers.ab.ca
Scope: Local

Potatoes New Brunswick 2015 Conference & Trade Show
Date: February 5, 2015
Location: E.P. Senechal Center
Grand Falls, NB
Sponsor/Contact: Potatoes New Brunswick
P.O. Box 7878
Grand Falls, NB E3Z 3E8
506-473-3036 *Fax:* 506-473-4647
E-mail: gfpotato@potatoesnb.com
URL: www.potatoesnb.com
Scope: Provincial
Purpose: An event for New Brunswick potato growers & interested stakeholders to present happening in the industry
Anticipated Attendance: 200+
Contact Information: E-mail: gfpotato@potatoesnb.com

Saskatchewan Urban Municipalities Association (SUMA) 110th Annual Convention and Tradeshow 2015
Date: February 1-4, 2015
Location: TCU Place
Saskatoon, SK
Sponsor/Contact: Saskatchewan Urban Municipalities Association
#200, 2222 - 13th Ave.
Regina, SK S4P 3M7
306-525-3727 *Fax:* 306-525-4373
E-mail: suma@suma.org
URL: www.suma.org
Scope: Provincial
Contact Information: Email: registration@suma.org

Saskatchewan Wildlife Federation 2015 86th Annual Convention
Date: February 19-21, 2015
Location: Weyburn, SK
Sponsor/Contact: Saskatchewan Wildlife Federation
9 Lancaster Rd.
Moose Jaw, SK S6J 1M8
306-692-8812 *Fax:* 306-692-4370
Toll-Free: 877-793-9453
E-mail: sask.wildlife@sasktel.net
URL: www.swf.sk.ca
Scope: Provincial
Purpose: A yearly gathering of members, featuring the presentation of awards
Contact Information: Receptionist/Clerk: Dianne Bloski

Society of Plastics Engineers 2015 GPEC Conference
Date: February 23-25, 2015
Location: Hyatt Regency
Dallas, TX USA
Sponsor/Contact: Society of Plastics Engineers
13 Church Hill Rd.
Newtown, CT 06470
203-775-0471 *Fax:* 203-775-8490
E-mail: info@4spe.org
URL: www.4spe.org
Scope: International
Contact Information: URL: www.plasticsrecycling.com

Society of Plastics Engineers 2015 International Polyolefins Conference
Date: February 22-25, 2015
Location: Hilton Houston North Hotel
Houston, TX USA
Sponsor/Contact: Society of Plastics Engineers
13 Church Hill Rd.
Newtown, CT 06470
203-775-0471 *Fax:* 203-775-8490
E-mail: info@4spe.org
URL: www.4spe.org
Scope: International
Purpose: This year's theme is "Four Decades of Advancing Polyolefin Technology"
Anticipated Attendance: 600+
Contact Information: Sponsorship contact: Brandon Cleary, E-mail: brandon@birchplastics.com; Publicity contact: David Hansen, E-mail: david.hansen47@yahoo.com

Society of Plastics Engineers 2015 Thermoset Conference
Date: February 3-5, 2015
Location: Le Parker Méridien
Palm Springs, CA USA
Sponsor/Contact: Society of Plastics Engineers
13 Church Hill Rd.
Newtown, CT 06470
203-775-0471 *Fax:* 203-775-8490
E-mail: info@4spe.org
URL: www.4spe.org
Scope: International
Contact Information: RSVP contact: Shelane Nunnery, Phone: 630-247-6733, E-mail: shelane@gvineme.com; URL: www.spetopcon.com

South Western Alberta Teachers Convention 2015
Date: February 19-20, 2015
Location: University of Lethbridge
Lethbridge, AB
Sponsor/Contact: Alberta Teachers' Association
Barnett House
11010 - 142 St.
Edmonton, AB T5N 2R1
780-447-9400 *Fax:* 780-455-6481
Toll-Free: 800-232-7208
E-mail: government@teachers.ab.ca
URL: www.teachers.ab.ca
Scope: Local

South Western Alberta Teachers' Convention Association 116th Annual Convention
Date: February 19-20, 2015
Location: University of Lethbridge
Lethbridge, AB
Sponsor/Contact: South Western Alberta Teachers' Convention Association
c/o Roxane Holmes
1215 - 19 Ave.
Coaldale, AB T1M 1A4
403-308-8761
URL: www.swatca.ca
Scope: Provincial
Purpose: Theme: "Learning With E's"

Southeastern Alberta Teachers Convention 2015
Date: February 19-20, 2015
Location: Alberta
Sponsor/Contact: Alberta Teachers' Association
Barnett House
11010 - 142 St.
Edmonton, AB T5N 2R1
780-447-9400 *Fax:* 780-455-6481
Toll-Free: 800-232-7208
E-mail: government@teachers.ab.ca
URL: www.teachers.ab.ca
Scope: Local

The Maritimes Energy Association 2015 Annual General Meeting & Dinner
Date: February 10, 2015
Location: The Marriott Harbourfront
Halifax, NS
Sponsor/Contact: The Maritimes Energy Association
Cambridge Tower 1
#305, 202 Brownlow Ave.
Dartmouth, NS B3B 1T5
902-425-4774 *Fax:* 902-422-2332
E-mail: info@maritimesenergy.com
URL: www.maritimesenergy.com
Scope: Provincial
Purpose: An event featuring the induction of new members to the board of directors, plus a keynote speaker & networking opportunities

Toronto Field Naturalists 2015 Monthly Talks: Mosses, Mooses and Mycorrhizas
Date: February 1, 2015
Location: University of Toronto, Northrop Frye Building
Toronto, ON
Sponsor/Contact: Toronto Field Naturalists
#1519, 2 Carlton St.
Toronto, ON M5B 1J3
416-593-2656
E-mail: office@torontofieldnaturalists.org
URL: www.torontofieldnaturalists.org
Scope: Local
Purpose: This lecture discusses the connections between mosses, mooses, fungi & forest ecosystems
Contact Information: E-mail: office@torontofieldnaturalists.org

Water Environment Federation and American Water Works Association (AWWA) The Utility Management Conference 2015
Date: February 17-20, 2015
Location: Hyatt Regency Austin
Austin, TX USA
Sponsor/Contact: Water Environment Federation
601 Wythe St.
Alexandria, VA 22314-1994
703-684-2400 *Fax:* 703-684-2492
Toll-Free: 800-666-0206
E-mail: comments@wef.org
URL: www.wef.org
Scope: International
Purpose: Water and wastewater managers and utility professionals will gather to hear the latest in cutting edge approaches and practices, techniques and case studies in all aspects of utility management.
Contact Information: Phone: 703-684-2400 ext. 7010; Email: confinfo@wef.org

Western Barley Growers Association 38th Annual Convention
Date: February 11-13, 2015
Location: Deerfoot Inn
Calgary, AB
Sponsor/Contact: Western Barley Growers Association
Agriculture Centre
97 East Lake Ramp NE
Airdrie, AB T4A 0C3
403-912-3998 *Fax:* 403-948-2069
E-mail: wbga@wbga.org
URL: www.wbga.org
Scope: Provincial

Western Canada Roadbuilders and Heavy Construction Association's 2015 Annual Convention
Date: February 8-11, 2015
Location: Hapuna Beach Prince Hotel
Island of Hawaii, HI USA
Sponsor/Contact: Western Canada Roadbuilders Association
c/o Manitoba Heavy Construction Association
#3, 1680 Ellice Ave.
Winnipeg, MB R3H 0Z2
204-947-1379 *Fax:* 204-943-2279
URL: www.wcrhca.org
Scope: Provincial
Contact Information: Chris Lorenc, SHCA President; Phone: 204-947-1379; Email: clorenc@mhca.mb.ca

March

17th National Metropolis Conference: Broadening the Conversation: Policy and Practice in Immigration, Settlement and Diversity
Date: March 26-28, 2015
Location: Sheraton Wall Centre
Vancouver, BC
Sponsor/Contact: Association for Canadian Studies
1822A, rue Sherbooke ouest
Montréal, QC H3H 1E4
514-925-3099 *Fax:* 514-925-3095
E-mail: general@acs-aec.ca
URL: www.acs-aec.ca
Scope: National
Contact Information: URL: www.metropolisconference.ca

19th Annual Alberta Magazine Conference 2015
Date: March 5-6, 2015
Location: Calgary, AB
Sponsor/Contact: Alberta Magazine Publishers Association
#304, 1240 Kensington Rd. NW
Calgary, AB T2N 3P7

403-262-0081 *Fax:* 403-670-0492
E-mail: ampa@albertamagazines.com
URL: www.albertamagazines.com
Scope: Provincial

2015 Unifor National Retail and Wholesale Workers Conference
Date: March 13-15, 2015
Location: Unifor Family Education Centre
Port Elgin, ON
Sponsor/Contact: UNIFOR
205 Placer Ct.
Toronto, ON M2H 3H9
416-497-4110
Toll-Free: 800-268-5763
E-mail: communications@unifor.org
URL: www.unifor.org
Scope: National

2015 Water & Wastewater Leadership Center
Date: March 8-19, 2015
Location: University of North Carolina at Chapel Hill
Chapel Hill, NC USA
Sponsor/Contact: Water Environment Federation
601 Wythe St.
Alexandria, VA 22314-1994
703-684-2400 *Fax:* 703-684-2492
Toll-Free: 800-666-0206
E-mail: comments@wef.org
URL: www.wef.org
Scope: International

24th Annual Police Employment Conference
Date: March 2-3, 2015
Location: Delta Meadowvale
Mississauga, ON
Sponsor/Contact: Police Association of Ontario
#1-3, 6730 Davand Dr.
Mississauga, ON L5T 2K8
905-670-9770 *Fax:* 905-670-9755
E-mail: pao@pao.ca
URL: www.pao.ca
Scope: Provincial
Purpose: Labour relations

2nd Annual Back to the Bible Canada / Laugh Again ministry cruise
Date: 22-29
Location: Various, Caribbean
Sponsor/Contact: Good News Broadcasting Association of Canada
P.O. Box 246 Stn. A
Abbotsford, BC V2T 6Z6
Toll-Free: 800-663-2425
E-mail: bttb@backtothebible.ca
URL: www.backtothebible.ca
Scope: National
Purpose: Cruise conference including Bible teaching & engagement; inspirational speaking, worship & special music

4-H Ontario 2015 Conference & Annual Meeting
Date: March 27-29, 2015
Location: Waterloo Inn
Waterloo, ON
Sponsor/Contact: Canadian 4-H Council
P.O. Box 212
111 Main St. North
Rockwood, ON N0B 2K0
519-856-0992 *Fax:* 519-856-0515
Toll-Free: 877-410-6748
E-mail: inquiries@4-hontario.ca
URL: www.4-hontario.ca
Scope: Provincial

43rd Annual Conference of the Art Libraries Society
Date: March 19-23, 2015
Location: Fort Worth, TX USA
Sponsor/Contact: Art Libraries Society of North America
Technical Enterprises, Inc.
7044 - 13th St. South
Oak Creek, WI 53154
414-908-4954 *Fax:* 414-768-8001
Toll-Free: 800-817-0621
E-mail: info@arlisna.org
URL: www.arlisna.org
Purpose: The conference provides the opportunity for professionals involved in art librarianship to meet, learn and share their knowledge of the field. It also allows them to explore exhibitions & interact with vendors involved with art libraries.
Contact Information: Program Co-Chair: Catherine Essinger; Email: cwessinger@uh.edu; Program Co-Chair: Lynn Wexler; Email: lwexler@mfah.org

Aboriginal Youth 2015 13th Annual Gathering Our Voices Conference
Date: March 17-20, 2015
Location: Prince George Civic Centre
Prince George, BC
Sponsor/Contact: British Columbia Association of Aboriginal Friendship Centres
551 Chatham St.
Victoria, BC V8T 1E1
250-388-5522 *Fax:* 250-388-5502
Toll-Free: 800-990-2432
E-mail: admin@bcaafc.com
URL: www.bcaafc.com
Scope: Provincial
Purpose: Hosted by the British Columbia Association of Aboriginal Friendship Centres & Ooknakane Friendship Centre. For Aboriginal youth aged 14 to 24.
Contact Information: Youth Conference Coordinator: Della Preston, Phone: 250-388-5522, Toll-Free Phone: 1-800-990-2432, Fax: 250-388-5502, E-mail: dpreston@bcaafc.com

Accreditation Canada Quality Conference 2015
Date: March 23-24, 2015
Location: Westin Harbour Castle
Toronto, ON
Sponsor/Contact: Accreditation Canada
1150 Cyrville Rd.
Ottawa, ON K1J 7S9
613-738-3800 *Fax:* 613-738-7755
Toll-Free: 800-814-7769
E-mail: communications@accreditation.ca
URL: www.accreditation.ca
Scope: National
Contact Information: URL: www.accreditation.ca/quality-conference-2015

Alberta Association of Municipal Districts & Counties Spring 2015 Convention & Trade Show
Date: March 16-18, 2015
Location: Shaw Conference Centre
Edmonton, AB
Sponsor/Contact: Alberta Association of Municipal Districts & Counties
2510 Sparrow Dr.
Nisku, AB T9E 8N5
780-955-3639 *Fax:* 780-955-3615
Toll-Free: 855-548-7233
E-mail: aamdc@aamdc.com
URL: www.aamdc.com

Alberta Camping AssociationAnnual Conference 2015
Date: March 23-25, 2015
Location: Southern Alberta Bible Camp
Lomond, AB
Sponsor/Contact: Alberta Camping Association
Percy Page Centre
11759 Groat Rd.
Edmonton, AB T5M 3K6
780-427-6605 *Fax:* 780-427-6695
E-mail: info@albertacamping.com
URL: www.albertacamping.com
Scope: Provincial

Alberta Library Trustees Association 2015 Annual General Meeting
Date: March 20-21, 2015
Location: Lethbridge Lodge Hotel & Conference Centre
Lethbridge, AB
Sponsor/Contact: Alberta Library Trustees Association
#6-24, 7 Sir Winston Churchill Sq.
Edmonton, AB T5J 2V5
780-761-2582 *Fax:* 866-419-1451
E-mail: admin@librarytrustees.ab.ca
URL: www.librarytrustees.ab.ca
Scope: Provincial
Purpose: Financial statements, a proposed budget, nominations report, & special resolutions
Contact Information: Alberta Library Trustees Association Executive Director: Heather Mayor; President: Dwight Nagel, E-mail: mdnagel@telus.net; president@librarytrustees.ab.ca

Alberta Pharmacists' Association 2015 Spring Professional Development Conference
Date: March 6-7, 2015
Location: Fantasyland Hotel
Edmonton, AB
Sponsor/Contact: Alberta Pharmacists' Association (RxA)
Canadian Western Bank Building
#1725, 10303 Jasper Ave.
Edmonton, AB T5J 3N6
780-990-0326 *Fax:* 780-990-1236
E-mail: rxa@rxa.ca
URL: www.rxa.ca
Scope: Provincial

Alberta Psychiatric Association 2015 Scientific Conference and AGM
Date: March 19-22, 2015
Location: Rimrock Resort Hotel
Banff, AB
Sponsor/Contact: Alberta Psychiatric Association
#400, 1040 - 7 Ave. SW
Calgary, AB T2P 3G9
403-244-4487 *Fax:* 403-244-2340
E-mail: info@albertapsych.org
URL: www.albertapsych.org
Scope: Provincial

Alberta Recreation & Parks Association 2015 Parks Forum
Date: March 12-14th, 2015
Location: Canmore, AB
Sponsor/Contact: Alberta Recreation & Parks Association
11759 Groat Rd.
Edmonton, AB T5M 3K6
780-415-1745 *Fax:* 780-451-7915
Toll-Free: 877-544-1747
E-mail: arpa@arpaonline.ca
URL: arpaonline.ca
Scope: Provincial
Purpose: A staff development event, with keynote speakers, plenary workshops, & presentations, of interest to practitioners at municipal, provincial, & national parks, allied stakeholders, teachers, & students
Contact Information: E-mail: arpa@arpaonline.ca

Alberta Society of Professional Biologists 2015 Annual Conference & General Meeting
Date: March 31 - April 1, 2015
Location: Coast Canmore Hotel & Conference Centre
Canmore, AB
Sponsor/Contact: Alberta Society of Professional Biologists
P.O. Box 21104
Edmonton, AB T6R 2V4
780-434-5765 *Fax:* 780-413-0076
E-mail: pbiol@aspb.ab.ca
URL: www.aspb.ab.ca
Scope: Provincial
Purpose: Theme: "A Generation of Science, Regulation and Conservation"
Contact Information: Association & Event Coordinator: Shauna Prokopchuk, Phone: 780-434-5765, E-mail: shauna@managewise.ca

Allied Beauty Association Trade Show - Montréal 2015
Date: March 8-9, 2015
Location: Palais des congrès (Convention Centre)
Montréal, QC
Sponsor/Contact: Allied Beauty Association
#26-27, 145 Traders Blvd. East
Mississauga, ON L4Z 3L3
905-568-0158 *Fax:* 905-568-1581
E-mail: abashows@abacanada.com
URL: www.abacanada.com
Scope: National
Purpose: A trade show for beauty professionals to learn about the new happenings in the industry

Animal Care Expo 2015
Date: March 30 - April 2, 2015
Location: New Orleans, LA USA
Sponsor/Contact: The Humane Society of the United States
2100 L St. NW
Washington, DC 20037
202-452-1100
E-mail: membership@humanesociety.org
URL: www.humanesociety.org
Scope: National
Purpose: An educational conference meant to inspire people to help animals. Topics covered include factory farming & animal fighting.
Contact Information: URL: www.animalsheltering.org/expo

Annual Meeting of the Provincial Assembly (AMPA) 2015
Date: March 13-16, 2015
Location: The Sheraton Centre Toronto Hotel
Toronto, ON
Sponsor/Contact: Ontario Secondary School Teachers' Federation
60 Mobile Dr.
Toronto, ON M4A 2P3
416-751-8300 *Fax:* 416-751-3394
Toll-Free: 800-267-7867
URL: www.osstf.on.ca
Scope: Provincial
Anticipated Attendance: 500+

Association of British Columbia Land Surveyors 2015 110th Annual General Meeting
Date: March 19-20, 2015
Location: Penticton Lakeside Resort
Penticton, BC
Sponsor/Contact: Association of British Columbia Land Surveyors
#301, 2400 Bevan Ave.
Sidney, BC V8L 1W1
250-655-7222 *Fax:* 250-655-7223
Toll-Free: 800-332-1193
E-mail: office@abcls.ca
URL: www.abcls.ca
Scope: Provincial
Contact Information: Board & Administrative Coordinator, Vicki Pettigrew, E-mail: office@abcls.ca

British Columbia Teachers' Federation 2015 99th Annual General Meeting
Date: March 14-17, 2015
Sponsor/Contact: British Columbia Teachers' Federation
#100, 550 - 6th Ave. West
Vancouver, BC V5Z 4P2
604-871-2283 *Fax:* 604-871-2293
Toll-Free: 800-663-9163
E-mail: benefits@bctf.ca
URL: www.bctf.ca
Scope: Provincial
Purpose: A meeting to set the future directions of the Federation

CARFLEO Annual General Meeting & Conference
Date: March 26-27, 2015
Location: Queen of Apostles Retreat Centre
Mississauga, ON
Sponsor/Contact: Catholic Association of Religious & Family Life Educators of Ontario
E-mail: contact@carfleo.org
URL: www.carfleo.org
Scope: Provincial

Canadian Academy of Psychiatry & the Law 20th Annual Conference
Date: March 1-4, 2015
Location: Fairmont Château Frontenac
Quebec, QC
Sponsor/Contact: Canadian Academy of Psychiatry & the Law
c/o M. Bordeleau, Canadian Psychiatric Association
#701, 141 Laurier Ave.
Ottawa, ON K1P 5J3
613-234-2815 *Fax:* 613-234-9857
URL: www.capl-acpd.org
Scope: National
Purpose: Information for psychiatrists working in law & psychiatry, & for any physicians interested in furthering their knowledge of this field

Canadian Association for Dental Research 39th Annual Meeting
Date: March 11-14, 2015
Location: Boston, MA USA
Sponsor/Contact: Canadian Association for Dental Research
c/o Dr. C. Birek, Faculty of Dentistry, University of Manitoba
780 Bannatyne Ave.
Winnipeg, MB R3E 0W2
204-789-3256 *Fax:* 204-789-3913
E-mail: birek@ms.umanitoba.ca
URL: www.cadr-acrd.ca
Scope: International
Purpose: In conjunction with the 44th Annual Meeting of the American Association of Dental Research & the 93rd General Session & Exhibition of the International Association for Dental Research

Canadian Association of Accredited Mortgage Professionals 2015 Manitoba Regional Symposium & Trade Show
Date: March 19, 2015
Location: Winnipeg, MB
Sponsor/Contact: Canadian Association of Accredited Mortgage Professionals
Atria II
#1401, 2235 Sheppard Ave. East
Toronto, ON M2J 5B5
416-385-2333 *Fax:* 416-385-1177
Toll-Free: 888-442-4625
E-mail: info@caamp.org
URL: www.caamp.org
Scope: Provincial
Contact Information: E-mail: events@caamp.org

Canadian Association of Accredited Mortgage Professionals 2015 Ontario Regional Symposium & Trade Show
Date: March 12, 2015
Location: Toronto, ON
Sponsor/Contact: Canadian Association of Accredited Mortgage Professionals
Atria II
#1401, 2235 Sheppard Ave. East
Toronto, ON M2J 5B5
416-385-2333 *Fax:* 416-385-1177
Toll-Free: 888-442-4625
E-mail: info@caamp.org
URL: www.caamp.org
Scope: Provincial
Contact Information: E-mail: events@caamp.org

Canadian Association of Accredited Mortgage Professionals 2015 Saskatchewan Regional Symposium & Trade Show
Date: March 17, 2015
Location: Saskatoon, SK
Sponsor/Contact: Canadian Association of Accredited Mortgage Professionals
Atria II
#1401, 2235 Sheppard Ave. East
Toronto, ON M2J 5B5
416-385-2333 *Fax:* 416-385-1177
Toll-Free: 888-442-4625
E-mail: info@caamp.org
URL: www.caamp.org
Scope: Provincial
Contact Information: E-mail: events@caamp.org

Canadian Association of Business Incubation Leadership Summit 2015
Date: March 30-31, 2015
Location: Waterloo, ON
Sponsor/Contact: Canadian Association of Business Incubation
#2002A, 1 Yonge St.
Toronto, ON M5E 1E5
416-345-9937 *Fax:* 416-345-9044
E-mail: info@cabi.ca
URL: www.cabi.ca
Scope: National

Canadian Association of Geographers Western Division 2015 57th Annual Conference Meeting
Date: March 12-14, 2015
Location: University of Northern British Columbia
Prince George, BC
Sponsor/Contact: Canadian Association of Geographers
c/o H. Jiskoot, Water & Environmental Science Bldg., U. of Lethbridge
4401 University Dr.
Lethbridge, AB T1K 3M4
URL: www.geog.uvic.ca/dept/wcag
Scope: Provincial

Canadian Association of University Teachers 2015 Annual Forum for Chief Negotiators
Date: March 27-29, 2015
Location: Ottawa, ON
Sponsor/Contact: Canadian Association of University Teachers
2705 Queensview Dr.
Ottawa, ON K2B 8K2
613-820-2270 *Fax:* 613-820-7244
E-mail: acppu@caut.ca
URL: www.caut.ca
Scope: National
Purpose: An examination of collective bargaining challenges & strategies

Canadian Cattlemen's Association 2015 Annual General Meeting
Date: March 10-12, 2015
Location: Delta Ottawa
Ottawa, ON
Sponsor/Contact: Canadian Cattlemen's Association
#310, 6715 - 8 St. NE
Calgary, AB T2E 7H7
403-275-8558 *Fax:* 403-274-5686
E-mail: feedback@cattle.ca
URL: www.cattle.ca
Scope: National
Purpose: An opportunity for members to address industry issues & to elect officers

Canadian College & University Food Service Association 2015 Winter Workshop
Date: March 1-2, 2015
Location: Hyatt Regency - King St.
Toronto, ON
Sponsor/Contact: Canadian College & University Food Service Association
c/o Drew Hall, University of Guelph
Gordon St.
Guelph, ON N1G 2W1
519-824-4120 *Fax:* 519-837-9302
E-mail: mcollins@hrs.uoguelph.ca
URL: www.ccufsa.on.ca
Scope: National
Purpose: A workshop for institutional members & institutional members only

Canadian Construction Association 97th Annual Conference 2015
Date: March 22-26, 2015
Location: San Antonio, TX USA
Sponsor/Contact: Canadian Construction Association
#1900, 275 Slater St.
Ottawa, ON K1P 5H9
613-236-9455 *Fax:* 613-236-9526
E-mail: cca@cca-acc.com
URL: www.cca-acc.com
Scope: National

Canadian Energy Research Institute 2015 Natural Gas Conference
Date: March 2-3, 2015
Location: Calgary TELUS Convention Center
Calgary, AB
Sponsor/Contact: Canadian Energy Research Institute
#150, 3512 - 33 St. NW
Calgary, AB T2L 2A6
403-282-1231 *Fax:* 403-284-4181
E-mail: info@ceri.ca
URL: www.ceri.ca
Scope: National
Purpose: An exploration of issues facing the gas industry
Contact Information: General Inquiries, E-mail: conference@ceri.ca; Contact, Sponsorship Information: Deanne Landry, Phone: 403-220-2395, E-mail: dlandry@ceri.ca

Canadian Foundry Association 2015 Issues Meeting
Date: March 19, 2015
Location: The Waterfront Banquet & Conference Hall
Hamilton, ON
Sponsor/Contact: Canadian Foundry Association
#1500, 1 Nicholas St.
Ottawa, ON K1N 7B7
613-789-4894 *Fax:* 613-789-5957
URL: www.foundryassociation.ca
Scope: National
Purpose: Technical committees work on issues to represent members' interests
Contact Information: E-mail: info@foundryassociation.ca

Canadian Gas Association 2015 Operations Conference
Date: March 30-31, 2015
Location: Edmonton, AB
Sponsor/Contact: Canadian Gas Association
#809, 350 Sparks St.
Ottawa, ON K1R 7S8
613-748-0057 *Fax:* 613-748-9078
E-mail: info@cga.ca
URL: www.cga.ca
Scope: National
Contact Information: E-mail: help@canavents.com

Canadian Home Builders' Association 2015 72nd National Conference
Date: March 4-6, 2015
Location: Marriott Halifax Harbourfront
Halifax, NS
Sponsor/Contact: Canadian Home Builders' Association
#500, 150 Laurier Ave. West
Ottawa, ON K1P 5J4
613-230-3060 *Fax:* 613-232-8214
E-mail: chba@chba.ca
URL: www.chba.ca
Scope: National
Purpose: Featuring the Canadian Home Builders' Association Annual Meeting of Members, provincial caucus meetings, guest speakers, the association's annual economic session, presentation of the National SAM Awards, social events, & networking opportunities
Contact Information: Director, Conferences & Special Events: Lynda Barrett, Phone: 905-954-0730

Canadian Horticultural Council 91st Annual General Meeting 2015
Date: March 10-12, 2015
Location: Fairmont Château Frontenac
Québec City, QC
Sponsor/Contact: Canadian Horticultural Council
9 Corvus Ct.
Ottawa, ON K2E 7Z4
613-226-4880 *Fax:* 613-226-4497
E-mail: webmaster@hortcouncil.ca
URL: www.hortcouncil.ca

Scope: National
Purpose: Members come together to deal with the challenges and opportunities facing Canada's horticultural industry.

Canadian Manufacturers & Exporters 2015 Dare to Compete Conference
Date: March 24-26, 2015
Location: RBC Convention Centre Winnipeg
Winnipeg, MB
Sponsor/Contact: Canadian Manufacturers & Exporters
#1500, 1 Nicholas St.
Ottawa, ON K1N 7B7
613-238-8888 *Fax:* 613-563-9218
URL: www.cme-mec.ca
Scope: National

Canadian Media Production Association 2015 Conference: Prime Time in Ottawa
Date: March 4-6, 2015
Location: Westin Ottawa
Ottawa, ON
Sponsor/Contact: Canadian Media Production Association
601 Bank St., 2nd Fl.
Ottawa, ON K1S 3T4
613-233-1444 *Fax:* 613-233-0073
Toll-Free: 800-656-7440
E-mail: ottawa@cmpa.ca
URL: www.cmpa.ca
Scope: National
Purpose: A learning & networking opportunity for business leaders from the feature film, television, interactive media, broadcasting, & telecommunications industries
Contact Information: Web Site: www.primetimeinottawa.ca; Manager, Member Services & Special Events: Lisa Moreau, E-mail: lisa.moreau@cmpa.ca

Canadian Union of Public Employees (CUPE) Saskatchewan 2015 Annual Convention
Date: March 4-6, 2015
Location: Delta Hotel
Regina, SK
Sponsor/Contact: Canadian Union of Public Employees
Saskatchewan Regional Office
3275 East Eastgate Dr.
Regina, SK S4Z 1A5
306-757-1009 *Fax:* 306-757-0102
E-mail: cupesask@sasktel.net
URL: www.sk.cupe.ca
Scope: Provincial
Purpose: A meeting to debate & pass resolutions
Contact Information: E-mail: cupesask@sasktel.net

Canola Council of Canada 2015 Conference
Date: March 3-5, 2015
Location: Fairmont Banff Springs Hotel
Banff, AB
Sponsor/Contact: Canola Council of Canada
#400, 167 Lombard Ave.
Winnipeg, MB R3B 0T6
204-982-2100 *Fax:* 204-942-1841
Toll-Free: 866-834-4378
E-mail: admin@canolacouncil.org
URL: www.canolacouncil.org
Scope: National
Contact Information: Communications Manager: Crystal Klippenstein, Phone: 204-982-7762, Email: klippensteinc@canolacouncil.org; URL: convention.canolacouncil.org

Career Development Conference (CDC) 2015: Raising the Bar: In Practice and in Community
Date: March 6-7, 2015
Location: Executive Airport Plaza Hotel & Conference Centre
Richmond, BC
Sponsor/Contact: British Columbia Career Development Association
#728, 510 West Hastings St.
Vancouver, BC V6B 1L8
604-684-3638
URL: www.bccda.org
Scope: Provincial

Central East Alberta Teachers Convention 2015
Date: March 5-6, 2015
Location: Shaw Conference Centre
Edmonton, AB
Sponsor/Contact: Alberta Teachers' Association
Barnett House
11010 - 142 St.
Edmonton, AB T5N 2R1
780-447-9400 *Fax:* 780-455-6481
Toll-Free: 800-232-7208
E-mail: government@teachers.ab.ca
URL: www.teachers.ab.ca
Scope: Local

Credit Union Central of Manitoba - Conference and AGM 2015
Date: March 25-27. 2015
Location: Brandon, MB
Sponsor/Contact: Credit Union Central of Manitoba
#400, 317 Donald St.
Winnipeg, MB R3B 2H6
204-985-4700 *Fax:* 204-949-0217
E-mail: cuinfo@cucm.org
URL: www.creditunion.mb.ca
Scope: Provincial

Equine Canada 2015 Annual Convention & Awards Gala
Date: March 25-29, 2015
Location: Crowne Plaza Gatineau-Ottawa
Ottawa, ON
Sponsor/Contact: Equine Canada
#100, 2685 Queensview Dr.
Ottawa, ON K2B 8K2
613-248-3433 *Fax:* 613-248-3484
Toll-Free: 866-282-8395
E-mail: inquiries@equinecanada.ca
URL: www.equinecanada.ca
Scope: National
Purpose: Meetings & clinics, plus the Equine Canada Awards Gala, for persons involved in equestrian sport, recreations, & industry from across Canada
Contact Information: Manager, Events: Fleur Tipton, Phone: 613-287-1515, ext. 111, E-mail: ftipton@equinecanada.ca

Expo Hightex 2015
Date: March 25-26, 2015
Location: Boucherville, QC
Sponsor/Contact: Groupe CTT Group
3000, rue Boullé
Saint-Hyacinthe, QC J2S 1H9
450-778-1870 *Fax:* 450-778-3901
Toll-Free: 877-288-8378
E-mail: info@gcttg.com
URL: www.groupecttgroup.com
Scope: National

FRP Canada 2015 National Conference
Date: March 10-12, 2015
Location: Sheraton Hamilton Hotel
Hamilton, ON
Sponsor/Contact: Canadian Association of Family Resource Programs
#707, 331 Cooper St.
Ottawa, ON K2P 0G5
613-237-7667 *Fax:* 613-237-8515
Toll-Free: 866-637-7226
E-mail: info@frp.ca
URL: www.frp.ca
Scope: National
Purpose: A biennial conference, presenting a keynote speaker, a panel discussion, workshops, & exhibits
Contact Information: Phone: 613-237-7667, ext. 231; E-mail: conference@frp.ca

Festivals & Events Ontario 2015 Conference
Date: March 4-6, 2015
Location: Sheraton on the Falls
Niagara Falls, ON
Sponsor/Contact: Festivals & Events Ontario
#301, 5 Graham St.
Woodstock, ON N4S 6J5
519-537-2226 *Fax:* 519-537-2226
E-mail: info@festivalsandeventsontario.ca
URL: www.festivalsandeventsontario.ca
Scope: Provincial
Contact Information: URL: www.feo2015.com

Glass & Architectural Metals Association 2015 Annual General Meeting
Date: March 11, 2015
Location: Red Deer, AB
Sponsor/Contact: Glass & Architectural Metals Association
c/o Calgary Construction Association
2725 - 12 St. NE
Calgary, AB T2E 7J2
URL: www.pgaa.ca/gama
Scope: Provincial
Purpose: The yearly business meeting of the association

Grain Farmers of Ontario 2015 March Classic
Date: March 24, 2015
Location: Ontario
Sponsor/Contact: Grain Farmers of Ontario
Ontario AgriCentre
#201, 100 Stone Rd. West
Guelph, ON N1G 5L3
Fax: 519-767-9713
Toll-Free: 800-265-0550
E-mail: info@gfo.ca
URL: www.gfo.ca
Scope: Provincial
Purpose: A gathering of representatives from government, industry, & farms throughout Ontario to attend presentations about trade, world markets, & new oppotunities
Anticipated Attendance: 500+
Contact Information: E-mail: info@gfo.ca

Homeschool Conference 2015
Date: March 27-28, 2015
Location: Calvary Temple
Winnipeg, MB
Sponsor/Contact: Manitoba Association of Christian Home Schools
PO Box 13 RPO SO St Vital
Winnipeg, MB R2N 3X9
E-mail: info@machs.ca
URL: www.machs.mb.ca
Scope: Provincial

IFAI (Industrial Fabrics Association International) Canada Expo 2015
Date: March 12-13, 2015
Location: Vancouver, BC
Sponsor/Contact: Industrial Fabrics Association International Canada
1485 Laperriere Ave.
Ottawa, ON K1Z 7S8
613-792-1218 *Fax:* 613-729-6206
Toll-Free: 800-225-4324
E-mail: ifaicanada@ifai.com
URL: www.ifaicanada.com
Scope: International
Purpose: Featuring how-to workshops, technical symposiums, business & professional development sessions, & product launches
Contact Information: Ashleigh Esselman; Email: aeesselman@ifai.com; Phone: 1 651 225 6934

Independent Power Producers Society of Alberta 2015 21st Annual Conference
Location: Alberta
Sponsor/Contact: Independent Power Producers Society of Alberta
#2600, 144 - 4th Ave. SW
Calgary, AB T2P 3N4
Fax: 403-256-8342
URL: www.ippsa.com
Scope: Provincial
Purpose: An event featuring guest speakers, panel discussions, debates, a trade show, social events, & networking opportunities
Anticipated Attendance: 500+
Contact Information: Executive Director: Evan Bahry, Phone: 403-282-8811, E-mail: Evan.Bahry@ippsa.com

Institute of Transportation Engineers 2015 Technical Conference & Exhibit
Date: March 29 - April 1, 2015
Location: Westin La Paloma
Tucson, AZ USA
Sponsor/Contact: Institute of Transportation Engineers
#600, 1627 Eye St. NW
Washington, DC 20006
202-785-0060 *Fax:* 202-785-0609
E-mail: ite_staff@ite.org
URL: www.ite.org
Scope: International
Contact Information: Contact, Registration Information: Sallie C. Dollins, E-mail: sdollins@ite.org; Contact, Technical Program: Eunice Chege, E-mail: echege@ite.org; Contact, Exhibits: Christina Garneski, E-mail: cgarneski@ite.org; Contact, Paper Submittals: Eunice Chege, E-mail: echege@ite.org

Language Without Borders
Date: March 26, 2015
Location: Sheraton on the Falls & Crowne Plaza Niagara Falls - Fallsview
Niagara Falls, ON
Sponsor/Contact: Canadian Association of Second Language Teachers
2490 Don Reid Dr.
Ottawa, ON K1H 1E1
613-727-0994 *Fax:* 613-727-3831
Toll-Free: 877-727-0994
E-mail: admin@caslt.org
URL: www.caslt.org

Languages Canada 2015 8th Annual Conference & Annual General Meeting
Date: March 1-4, 2015
Location: Hilton Lac-Leamy Hotel
Gatineau, QC
Sponsor/Contact: Languages Canada
5886 - 169A St.
Surrey, BC V3S 6Z8
604-574-1532 *Fax:* 888-277-0522
E-mail: info@languagescanada.ca
URL: www.languagescanada.ca
Scope: National
Contact Information:
conference@languagescanada.ca

Le 50e Congrès annuel de l'Association québécoise du transport et des routes inc.
Date: 31 mars au 2 avril, 2015
Location: Palais des congrès de Montréal
Montréal, QC
Sponsor/Contact: Association québécoise du transport et des routes inc.
Bureau de Montréal
#200, 1255, rue University
Montréal, QC H3B 3B2
514-523-6444 *Fax:* 514-523-2666
URL: www.aqtr.qc.ca
Scope: National
Contact Information: Responsable: Öve Arcand, téléphone: 514-523-6444 ext. 325, courriel: congres@aqtr.qc.ca

Manitoba Heavy Construction Association 2015 4th Annual Expo
Date: March 24-26, 2015
Location: Winnipeg, MB
Sponsor/Contact: Manitoba Heavy Construction Association
#3, 1680 Ellice Ave.
Winnipeg, MB R3G 0Z2
204-947-1379 *Fax:* 204-943-2279
E-mail: info@mhca.mb.ca
URL: www.mhca.mb.ca
Scope: Provincial
Purpose: An educational event, to help train & educate workers in the heavy construction industry
Contact Information: Manager, Events & Membership: Christine Miller, Phone: 204-947-1379

Manitoba School Boards Association Convention 2015: Building Partnerships for Student Success
Date: March 19-21, 2015
Location: Delta Winnipeg
Winnipeg, MB
Sponsor/Contact: Manitoba School Boards Association
191 Provencher Blvd.
Winnipeg, MB R2H 0G4
204-233-1595 *Fax:* 204-231-1356
Toll-Free: 800-262-8836
E-mail: webmaster@mbschoolboards.ca
URL: www.mbschoolboards.ca
Scope: Provincial

Mighty Peace Teachers Convention 2015
Date: March 5-6, 2015
Location: Grande Prairie, AB
Sponsor/Contact: Alberta Teachers' Association
Barnett House
11010 - 142 St.
Edmonton, AB T5N 2R1
780-447-9400 *Fax:* 780-455-6481
Toll-Free: 800-232-7208
E-mail: government@teachers.ab.ca
URL: www.teachers.ab.ca
Scope: Local

Newfoundland & Labrador Construction Association 2015 47th Annual Conference & Annual General Meeting
Date: March 5-7, 2015
Location: Delta St. John's Hotel & Conference Centre
St. John's, NL
Sponsor/Contact: Newfoundland & Labrador Construction Association
#201, 333 Pippy Pl.
St. John's, NL A1B 3X2
709-753-8920 *Fax:* 709-754-3968
E-mail: info@nfld.com
URL: www.nlca.ca
Scope: Provincial
Purpose: Sessions & keynote addresses of interest to persons such as general, electrical, & mechanical contractors, manufacturers, suppliers, safety professionals, engineers, training providers, LEED accredited professionals, & municipalities
Contact Information: Chair, Conference 2015 Committee: Steve Hayward, Phone: 709-747-1159, Fax: 709-747-1169, E-mail: steve@extrememetals.ca; Executive Assistant/Events Coordinator: Adelle Connors, E-mail: aconnors@nlca.ca

One Full Circle Annual General Meeting & Gala 2015
Date: March 2015
Sponsor/Contact: One Full Circle
882, boul Décarie
Saint-Laurent, QC H4L 3L9
514-651-4545
E-mail: onefullcircleofc@gmail.com
URL: theofc.org

Ontario Automotive Recyclers Association 2015 Convention & Trade Show
Date: March 26-28, 2015
Location: Hilton Toronto/Markham Suites Conference Centre
Markham, ON
Sponsor/Contact: Ontario Automotive Recyclers Association
#1, 1447 Upper Ottawa St.
Hamilton, ON L8W 3J6
905-383-9788 *Fax:* 905-383-1904
Toll-Free: 800-390-8743
E-mail: admin@oara.com
URL: www.oara.com
Scope: Provincial

Ontario English Catholic Teachers' Association 2015 Annual General Meeting
Date: March 14-16, 2015
Location: Westin Harbour Castle
Toronto, ON
Sponsor/Contact: Ontario English Catholic Teachers' Association (CLC)
#400, 65 St. Clair Ave. East
Toronto, ON M4T 2Y8
416-925-2493 *Fax:* 416-925-7764
Toll-Free: 800-268-7230
E-mail: membership@oecta.on.ca
URL: www.oecta.on.ca
Scope: Provincial
Purpose: Delegates attend to the business of the association, elect Provincial Executive members, & listen to presentations by guest speakers
Anticipated Attendance: 600+
Contact Information: Ontario English Catholic Teachers' Association Office, Phone: 416-925-2493

Ontario Home Economics Association Annual General Meeting & Conference
Date: March 27-28, 2015
Location: Ontario
Sponsor/Contact: Ontario Home Economics Association
c/o Registrar/Office Administrator
1225 Meadowview Rd., RR#2
Omemee, ON K0L 2W0
705-799-2081 *Fax:* 705-799-0605
E-mail: info@ohea.on.ca
URL: www.ohea.on.ca
Scope: Provincial

Ontario Modern Language Teachers Association Spring Conference 2015
Date: March 26-28, 2015
Location: Sheraton On The Falls Hotel & Conference Centre
Niagara Falls
Sponsor/Contact: Ontario Modern Language Teachers Association
#246, 55 Northfield Dr. East
Waterloo, ON N2K 3T6
519-763-2099
E-mail: omlta@omlta.org
URL: www.omlta.org
Scope: Provincial

Ontario Physiotherapy Association 2015 Annual Conference: InterACTION 2015
Date: March 27-28, 2015
Location: Ottawa Marriott
Ottawa, ON
Sponsor/Contact: Ontario Physiotherapy Association
#210, 55 Eglinton Ave. East
Toronto, ON M4P 1G8
416-322-6866 *Fax:* 416-322-6705
Toll-Free: 800-672-9668
E-mail: physiomail@opa.on.ca
URL: www.opa.on.ca
Scope: Provincial

Ontario Real Estate Association 2015 Leadership Conference: Rock Solid Leadership
Date: March 10-12, 2015
Location: Westin Harbour Castle
Toronto, ON
Sponsor/Contact: Ontario Real Estate Association
99 Duncan Mill Rd.
Toronto, ON M3B 1Z2
416-445-9910 *Fax:* 416-445-2644
Toll-Free: 800-265-6732
E-mail: info@orea.com
URL: www.orea.com
Scope: Provincial
Purpose: Educational & networking opportunities for current & future leaders in the real estate industry, plus the Ontario Real Estate Association Annaul Assembly Meeting & elections
Contact Information: Event Coordinator: Christine Gruber, Email: christineg@orea.com

Ontario Retirement Communities Association "Together We Care" Convention 2015
Date: March 30 - April 1, 2015
Location: Metro Toronto Convention Centre
Toronto, ON
Sponsor/Contact: Ontario Retirement Communities Association
#202, 2401 Bristol Circle
Oakville, ON L6H 6P1
905-403-0500 *Fax:* 905-829-1594
Toll-Free: 888-263-5559
E-mail: info@orcaretirement.com
URL: www.orcaretirement.com
Scope: Provincial
Purpose: Canada's largest gathering of retirement and long term care professionals.
Contact Information: Email: maureen@orcaretirement.com; Phone: 905-403-0500 Ext. 231

Pacific Dental Conference 2015
Date: March 5-7, 2015
Location: Vancouver, BC
Sponsor/Contact: British Columbia Dental Association
#400, 1765 - 8th Ave. West
Vancouver, BC V6J 5C6
604-736-7202 *Fax:* 604-736-7588
Toll-Free: 888-396-9888
E-mail: post@bcdental.org
URL: www.bcdental.org
Scope: Provincial
Purpose: An opportunity for dental professionals to obtain continuing education credits
Anticipated Attendance: 12,000+
Contact Information: Address: Pacific Dental Conference, #305, 1505 West 2nd Ave., Vancouver, BC V6H 3Y4; Phone: 604-736-3781; E-mail: info@pdconf.com; URL: www.pdconf.com

Parks & Recreation Ontario / Parcs et loisirs de l'Ontario 2015 Educational Forum & Trade Show
Date: March 24-27, 2015
Location: Blue Mountain Resort
Collingwood, ON
Sponsor/Contact: Parks & Recreation Ontario
#302, 1 Concorde Gate
Toronto, ON M3C 3N6
416-426-7142 *Fax:* 416-426-7371
E-mail: pro@prontario.org
URL: www.prontario.org
Scope: Provincial

Pest Management Canada 2015
Date: March 19-21, 2015
Location: Westin Calgary
Calgary, AB
Sponsor/Contact: Canadian Pest Management Association
P.O. Box 1748
Moncton, NB E1C 9X5
Fax: 866-957-7378
Toll-Free: 866-630-2762
E-mail: cpma@pestworld.org
URL: www.pestworldcanada.org
Scope: National
Purpose: Educational sessions, networking opportunities, & exhibits of products, services & techniques
Contact Information: E-mail: cpma@pestworld.org

Prospectors & Developers Association of Canada (PDAC) 2015 83rd International Convention, Trade Show, & Investors Exchange Mining Investment Show
Date: March 1-4, 2015
Location: Metro Toronto Convention Centre
Toronto, ON
Sponsor/Contact: Prospectors & Developers Association of Canada
135 King St. East
Toronto, ON M5C 1G6
416-362-1969 *Fax:* 416-362-0101
E-mail: info@pdac.ca
URL: www.pdac.ca

Scope: International
Purpose: A four day event that attracts more than 1,000 exhibitors & attendees from 125 countries to participate in short courses, technical sessions, & networking opportunities
Anticipated Attendance: 30,300+
Contact Information: Director, Convention: Nicole Sampson, Phone: 416-362-1969, ext. 226, E-mail: nsampson@pdac.ca

Québec Gift Fair
Date: March 22-25, 2015
Location: Place Bonaventure
Montréal, QC
Sponsor/Contact: Canadian Gift Association
42 Voyager Ct. South
Toronto, ON M9W 5M7
416-679-0170 *Fax:* 416-679-0175
Toll-Free: 800-611-6100
E-mail: info@cangift.org
URL: www.cangift.org
Scope: Local
Anticipated Attendance: 10,000
Contact Information: Anne-Sophie Pelchat, Show Manager; PHone: 416.642.1051; Email: apelchat@cangift.org; URL: quebecgiftfair.org; Email: quebec@cangift.org

Registered Nurses' Association of Ontario 4th Annual Nurse Executive Leadership Academy
Date: March 1-4, 2015
Location: White Oaks Conference Centre
Niagara-on-the-Lake, ON
Sponsor/Contact: Registered Nurses' Association of Ontario
158 Pearl St.
Toronto, ON M5H 1L3
416-599-1925 *Fax:* 416-599-1926
Toll-Free: 800-268-7199
URL: www.rnao.org
Scope: Provincial
Purpose: The program features expert faculty from policy, practice and academic settings, providing up-to-date insights for knowledge and competence in governance, policy formulation, evidence-based accountability and leadership.

Restaurants Canada Annual Event: Atlantic Canada's Foodservice & Hospitality Trade Show 2015 (ApEx)
Date: March 29-30, 2015
Location: Cunard Centre
Halifax, NS
Sponsor/Contact: Restaurants Canada
1155 Queen St. West
Toronto, ON M6J 1J4
416-923-8416 *Fax:* 416-923-1450
Toll-Free: 800-387-5649
E-mail: info@restaurantscanada.org
URL: www.restaurantscanada.org
Scope: Provincial
Purpose: A showcase of the latest products, services, & trends for maritime foodservice operators
Anticipated Attendance: 2,000+
Contact Information: Toll-Free Phone: 1-877-755-1938; Canadian Restaurant & Foodservices Association, E-mail: info@crfa.ca

Restaurants Canada Show 2015
Date: March 1-3, 2015
Location: Direct Energy Centre
Toronto, ON
Sponsor/Contact: Restaurants Canada
1155 Queen St. West
Toronto, ON M6J 1J4
416-923-8416 *Fax:* 416-923-1450
Toll-Free: 800-387-5649
E-mail: info@restaurantscanada.org
URL: www.restaurantscanada.org
Scope: National
Purpose: A trend-setting event, featuring culinary demonstrations, seminars, workshops, presentations, more than 700 exhibitors, & numerous networking opportunities for members of Canada's foodservice sector
Anticipated Attendance: 13,000+
Contact Information: Toll-Free Phone: 1-800-387-5649; E-mail: info@crfa.ca

Saskatchewan Association of Rural Municipalities 2015 Annual Convention
Date: March 9-12, 2015
Location: Prairieland Park, SK
Sponsor/Contact: Saskatchewan Association of Rural Municipalities
2075 Hamilton St.
Regina, SK S4P 2E1
306-757-3577 *Fax:* 306-565-2141
Toll-Free: 800-667-3604
E-mail: sarm@sarm.ca
URL: www.sarm.ca
Scope: Provincial

Society for Research in Child Development 2015 Biennial Meeting
Date: March 19-21, 2015
Location: Philadelphia, PA USA
Sponsor/Contact: Society for Research in Child Development
#401, 2950 South State St.
Ann Arbor, MI 48104
734-926-0600 *Fax:* 734-926-0601
E-mail: info@srcd.org
URL: www.srcd.org
Scope: International
Contact Information: Biennial Meeting Planner: Hailey Buck, Phone: 734-926-0613, Fax: 734-926-0601, E-mail: hkbuck@srcd.org, biennialmeeting@srcd.org

Society of Cardiovascular Anesthesiologists Echo 18th Annual Comprehensive Review & Update of Perioperative Echo
Date: March 23-27, 2015
Location: Loews Atlanta Hotel
Atlanta, GA USA
Sponsor/Contact: Society of Cardiovascular Anesthesiologists
2209 Dickens Rd.
Richmond, VA 23230-2005
804-282-0084 *Fax:* 804-282-0090
E-mail: sca@societyhq.com
URL: www.scahq.org
Scope: International

Society of Christian Schools in British Columbia 2015 Business & Development Conference
Date: March 10-11, 2015
Location: Cedar Springs Conference Center
Sumas, WA USA
Sponsor/Contact: Society of Christian Schools in British Columbia
Fosmark Centre, Trinity Western University
7600 Glover Rd.
Langley, BC V2Y 1Y1
604-888-6366 *Fax:* 604-888-2791
E-mail: contact@scsbc.ca
URL: www.scsbc.ca
Scope: Provincial

Society of Plastics Engineers 2015 ANTEC Orlando Conference
Date: March 23-25, 2015
Location: Orange County Convention Center
Orlando, FL USA
Sponsor/Contact: Society of Plastics Engineers
13 Church Hill Rd.
Newtown, CT 06470
203-775-0471 *Fax:* 203-775-8490
E-mail: info@4spe.org
URL: www.4spe.org
Scope: International

Society of Toxicology 54th Annual Meeting & ToxExpo
Date: March 22-26, 2015
Location: San Diego Convention Center
San Diego, CA USA
Sponsor/Contact: Society of Toxicology
#300, 1821 Michael Faraday Dr.
Reston, VA 20190
703-438-3115 *Fax:* 703-438-3113
E-mail: sothq@toxicology.org
URL: www.toxicology.org
Scope: International
Purpose: Toxicology meeting & exhibition
Anticipated Attendance: 6,500
Contact Information: Phone: 703-438-3115; Fax: 703-438-3113; E-mail: sothq@toxicology.org

Special Education Association of British Columbia 2015 40th Annual Crosscurrents Conference
Date: March 5-6, 2015
Location: Sheraton Vancouver Airport Hotel
Richmond, BC
Sponsor/Contact: Special Education Association of British Columbia
c/o British Columbia Teachers' Federation
#100, 550 West 6th Ave.
Vancouver, BC V5Z 4P2
URL: www.seaofbc.ca
Scope: Provincial
Purpose: Sessions for regular & special education teachers, as well as administrators, teacher assistants, & parents
Contact Information: Conference Chair: Stephanie Koropatnick, E-mail: seaconferencechair@gmail.com

TRENDS: The Apparel Show 2015 (sponsored by the Alberta Men's Wear Agents Association)
Date: March 5-9, 2015
Location: Edmonton Expo Centre
Edmonton, AB
Sponsor/Contact: Alberta Men's Wear Agents Association
P.O. Box 66037 Stn. Heritage
Edmonton, AB T6J 6T4
780-455-1881 *Fax:* 780-455-3969
E-mail: amwa@shaw.ca
URL: www.trendsapparel.com
Scope: Provincial
Purpose: Wholesale sales representatives present men's, ladies', children's, sports, work, & western wear, as well as shoe lines
Contact Information: E-mail: amwa@shaw.ca

The Profile Show 2015
Date: March 1-4, 2015
Location: Toronto Congress Centre, North Building
Toronto, ON
Sponsor/Contact: Ontario Fashion Exhibitors
P.O. Box 218
#2219, 160 Tycos Dr.
Toronto, ON M6B 1W8
416-596-2401 *Fax:* 416-596-1808
Toll-Free: 800-765-7508
E-mail: info@profileshow.ca
URL: www.profileshow.ca
Scope: Provincial

Toronto Field Naturalists 2015 Monthly Talk: What the *#&! Is a Bioblitz?
Date: March 1, 2015
Location: University of Toronto, Northrop Frye Building
Toronto, ON
Sponsor/Contact: Toronto Field Naturalists
#1519, 2 Carlton St.
Toronto, ON M5B 1J3
416-593-2656
E-mail: office@torontofieldnaturalists.org
URL: www.torontofieldnaturalists.org
Scope: Local
Purpose: This lecture focuses on bioblitzes & the information they provide about our natural surroundings.
Contact Information: E-mail: office@torontofieldnaturalists.org

Water Environment Federation 2015 Design-Build for Water/Wastewater Conference
Date: March 11-13, 2015
Location: Henry B. Gonzalez Convention Center
San Antonio, TX USA
Sponsor/Contact: Water Environment Federation
601 Wythe St.
Alexandria, VA 22314-1994
703-684-2400 *Fax:* 703-684-2492
Toll-Free: 800-666-0206
E-mail: comments@wef.org
URL: www.wef.org
Scope: International

Westcoast Building & Hardware Trade Show & Conference 2015
Date: March 27, 2015
Location: Cloverdale, BC
Sponsor/Contact: Building Supply Industry Association of British Columbia
#2, 19299 - 94th Ave.
Surrey, BC V4N 4E6
604-513-2205 *Fax:* 604-513-2206
Toll-Free: 888-711-5656
URL: www.bsiabc.ca
Scope: Provincial
Purpose: A trade show for members of the building supply industry, presenting educational opportunities & new & innovative products & services
Contact Information: Registration & Sponsorship Information, Phone: 604-513-2205, E-mail: info@bsiabc.ca

Winnipeg Chamber of Commerce 2015 6th Annual Spirit of Winnipeg Awards
Date: March 13, 2015
Location: Winnipeg, MB
Sponsor/Contact: Winnipeg Chamber of Commerce
#100, 259 Portage Ave.
Winnipeg, MB R3B 2A9
204-944-8484 *Fax:* 204-944-8492
E-mail: info@winnipeg-chamber.com
URL: www.winnipeg-chamber.com
Scope: Provincial
Purpose: A presentation of awards to honour innvoation in Winnipeg

Contact Information: Events Coordinator: Yanik Ottenbreit, Phone: 204-944-3306, E-mail: yottenbreit@winnipeg-chamber.com

April

11th Annual BC Broadband Conference - BCBC 2015
Date: April 28-29, 2015
Location: Radisson Hotel Vancouver Airport
Richmond, BC
Sponsor/Contact: British Columbia Broadband Association
248 Reid St.
Quesnel, BC V2J 2M2
E-mail: info@bcba.ca
URL: bcba.ca
Scope: Provincial

2015 Alberta Association of Travel Health Professionals Annual Travel Health Symposium and General Meeting
Date: April 17-18, 2015
Location: Matrix Hotel
Edmonton, AB
Sponsor/Contact: Alberta Association of Travel Health Professionals
North Tower
#440, 10030-107 St.
Edmonton, AB T5J 3E4
URL: www.aathp.com
Scope: Provincial

2015 Annual Hospice Palliative Care Ontario Conference
Date: April 21, 2015
Location: Sheraton Parkway Toronto North Hotel & Convention Centre
Richmond Hill, ON
Sponsor/Contact: Hospice Palliative Care Ontario
#707, 2 Carlton St.
Toronto, ON M5B 1J3
416-304-1477 *Fax:* 416-304-1479
Toll-Free: 800-349-3111
E-mail: info@hpco.ca
URL: www.hpco.ca
Scope: Provincial
Anticipated Attendance: 500

2015 Annual Ontario Cooperative Education Association Spring Conference
Date: April 19-21, 2015
Location: Delta Meadowvale Hotel & Conference Centre,
Mississauga, ON
Sponsor/Contact: Ontario Cooperative Education Association
35 Reynar Dr.
Quispamsis, NB E2G 1J9
Fax: 506-849-8375
E-mail: ocea@rogers.com
URL: www.ocea.on.ca
Scope: Provincial

2015 Association for Healthcare Philanthropy Convene Canada
Date: April 29 - May 1, 2015
Location: Sheraton Wall Centre Hotel.
Vancouver, BC
Sponsor/Contact: Association for Healthcare Philanthropy (Canada)
c/o Stratford General Hospital Foundation
46 General Hospital Dr.
Stratford, ON N5A 2Y8
519-272-8210 *Fax:* 519-272-8238
URL: www.ahp.org
Scope: National

2015 BC Economic Summit
Date: April 26-28, 2015
Location: Sheraton Vancouver Airport Hotel
Richmond, BC
Sponsor/Contact: British Columbia Economic Development Association
#102, 9300 Nowell St.
Chilliwack, BC V2P 4V7
604-858-7199 *Fax:* 604-795-7118
E-mail: info@bceda.ca
URL: www.bceda.ca
Scope: Provincial

2015 BC Funeral Association Exhibitors' Showcase and Conference
Date: April 22-24, 2015
Location: Delta Grand Okanagan Resort & Conference Centre
Okanagan, BC
Sponsor/Contact: British Columbia Funeral Association
#211, 2187 Oak Bay Ave.
Victoria, BC V8R 1G1
250-592-3213 *Fax:* 250-592-4362
Toll-Free: 800-665-3899
E-mail: info@bcfunerals.com
URL: www.bcfunerals.com
Scope: Provincial

2015 BC Surgical Society Annual Spring Meeting
Date: April 30- May 2, 2015
Location: Fairmont Chateau Whistler
Whistler, BC
Sponsor/Contact: British Columbia Surgical Society
#115, 1665 West Broadway
Vancouver, BC V6J 5A4
604-638-2843 *Fax:* 604-638-2938
E-mail: athomas@bcma.bc.ca
URL: www.bcss.ca
Scope: Provincial

2015 Calgary Chamber of Voluntary Organizations Connections Conference
Date: April 13-14, 2015
Location: Mount Royal University, Ross Glen Hall
Calgary, AB
Sponsor/Contact: Calgary Chamber of Voluntary Organizations
#1070, 105 - 12 Ave. SE
Calgary, AB T2G 1A1
403-261-6655 *Fax:* 403-261-6602
E-mail: info@calgarycvo.org
URL: www.calgarycvo.org
Scope: Local

2015 Canadian Agency for Drugs & Technologies in Health Symposium
Date: April 12-14, 2015
Location: Saskatoon, SK
Sponsor/Contact: Canadian Agency for Drugs & Technologies in Health
#600, 865 Carling Ave.
Ottawa, ON K1S 5S8
613-226-2553 *Fax:* 613-226-5392
Toll-Free: 866-988-1444
E-mail: requests@cadth.ca
URL: www.cadth.ca
Scope: National

2015 Canadian Association of Pregnancy Support Services Conference
Date: April 14-17, 2015
Location: Coast Plaza Hotel
Vancouver, BC
Sponsor/Contact: Canadian Association of Pregnancy Support Services
#304 - 4820 Gaetz Ave.
Red Deer, AB T4N 4A4
403-347-2827 *Fax:* 403-343-2847
Toll-Free: 866-845-2151
URL: www.capss.com
Scope: National

2015 Canadian Association of Staff Physician Recruiters 11th Annual Conference
Date: April 26-28, 2015
Location: Niagara Falls, ON
Sponsor/Contact: Canadian Association of Staff Physician Recruiters
E-mail: info@caspr.ca
URL: caspr.ca
Scope: National

2015 Canadian Conference on Medical Education (CCME)
Date: April 25-28, 2015
Location: Fairmont Vancouver & Hyatt Regency Vancouver
Vancouver, BC
Sponsor/Contact: Medical Council of Canada
P.O. Box 8234 Stn. T
#100, 2283 St. Laurent Blvd.
Ottawa, ON K1G 3H7
613-521-6012 *Fax:* 613-521-9509
E-mail: MCC_Admin@mcc.ca
URL: www.mcc.ca
Scope: National
Contact Information: www.mededconference.ca/ccme2015

2015 Canadian Corporate Council Association National Conference
Date: April 19-21, 2015
Location: Hilton Toronto
Toronto, ON
Sponsor/Contact: The Canadian Corporate Counsel Association
#1210, 20 Toronto St.
Toronto, ON M5C 2B8
416-869-0522 *Fax:* 416-869-0946
E-mail: ccca@ccca-accje.org
URL: www.ccca-accje.org
Scope: National
Purpose: Theme - The Business of Law: Black Letter and Beyond

2015 Canadian Marketing Association Conference: CMAcreative
Date: April 2015
Sponsor/Contact: Canadian Marketing Association
#607, 1 Concorde Gate
Toronto, ON M3C 3N6
416-391-2362 *Fax:* 416-441-4062
E-mail: info@the-cma.org
URL: www.the-cma.org
Scope: National
Purpose: A day with the leading creative minds in marketing and beyond, exploring the standout ideas and newest ways of thinking to help inspire and motivate you to make the next breakthrough in your life.

2015 Human Resources Institute of Alberta Conference
Date: April 22-23, 2015
Location: Shaw Conference Centre
Edmonton, AB
Sponsor/Contact: Human Resources Institute of Alberta
#410, 1111 - 11 Ave. SW
Calgary, AB T2R 0G5
403-209-2420 *Fax:* 403-209-2401
Toll-Free: 800-668-6125
E-mail: info@hria.ca
URL: humanresourcesalberta.com
Scope: Provincial

2015 Insurance Brokers Association of Manitoba Convention
Date: April 29 - May 1, 2015
Location: Fairmont Winnipeg
Winnipeg, MB
Sponsor/Contact: Insurance Brokers Association of Manitoba
#600, 1445 Portage Ave.
Winnipeg, MB R3G 3P4
204-488-1857 *Fax:* 204-489-0316
Toll-Free: 800-204-5649
E-mail: info@ibam.mb.ca
URL: www.ibam.mb.ca
Scope: Provincial

2015 National Association of Career Colleges Conference
Date: April 29 - May 1, 2015
Location: Delta St. John's Hotel and Conference Centre
St. John's, NL
Sponsor/Contact: National Association of Career Colleges
#270, 44 Byward Market Sq.
Ottawa, ON K1N 7A2
613-800-0340 *Fax:* 613-789-9669
URL: www.nacc.ca
Scope: National

2015 Northwest Fire Conference
Date: April 29th to May 2, 2015
Location: Sawridge Inn and Conference Centre
Peace River, AB
Sponsor/Contact: Alberta Fire Chiefs Association
780-719-7939 *Fax:* 780-892-3333
URL: www.afca.ab.ca
Scope: Provincial

2015 OWWA/OMWA Joint Annual Conference and OWWEA Trade Show
Date: April 26-29, 2015
Location: Toronto, ON
Sponsor/Contact: Ontario Water Works Association
#100, 922 The East Mall Dr.
Toronto, ON M9B 6K1
416-231-1555 *Fax:* 416-231-1556
Toll-Free: 866-975-0575
E-mail: waterinfo@owwa.ca
URL: www.owwa.com
Scope: Provincial
Purpose: This annual industry highlight features a full slate of plenary and technical sessions focusing on the latest in technology and research affecting drinking water from source to tap. The Trade Show consistently has more than 100 exhibitors representing the manufacturers and suppliers of products and services for the water industry.

2015 Ontario Psychological Association Annual Conference
Date: April 24-25, 2015
Location: The King Edward Hotel
Toronto, ON
Sponsor/Contact: Ontario Psychological Association
#403, 21 St. Clair Ave. East
Toronto, ON M4T 1L8
416-961-5552
E-mail: opa@psych.on.ca
URL: www.psych.on.ca
Scope: Provincial

2015 Unifor Pride Conference
Date: April 24-26, 2015
Location: Unifor Family Education Centre
Port Elgin, ON
Sponsor/Contact: UNIFOR
205 Placer Ct.
Toronto, ON M2H 3H9
416-497-4110
Toll-Free: 800-268-5763
E-mail: communications@unifor.org
URL: www.unifor.org
Scope: National

24th Annual Canadian Conference on HIV/AIDS Research - Canadian Association for HIV Research 2015
Date: April 30 - May 3, 2015
Location: Metro Toronto Convention Centre
Toronto, ON
Sponsor/Contact: The Canadian Association for HIV Research
#1105, 1 Nicholas St.
Ottawa, ON K1N 7B7
613-241-5785
E-mail: info@cahr-acrv.ca
URL: www.cahr-acrv.ca
Scope: National

3rd Annual Adolescent Literacy Summit
Date: April 9-10, 2015
Location: Victoria Inn
Winnipeg, MB
Sponsor/Contact: Manitoba Reading Association
c/o Child Guidance Clinic, Winnipeg School Division
700 Elgin Ave.
Winnipeg, MB R2E 1B2
204-786-7841
URL: www.readingmanitoba.org
Scope: Provincial

46th Annual Saskatchewan Reading Conference 2015
Date: April 23-24, 2015
Location: Delta Hotel
Regina, SK
Sponsor/Contact: Saskatchewan Reading Council
c/o Good Spirit School Div., Fairview Education Centre
63 King St. East
Yorkton, SK S3N OT7
306-786-5500 *Fax:* 306-783-0355
Toll-Free: 866-390-0773
URL: saskreading.com
Scope: Provincial

68th Society of Architectural Historians Annual Conference
Date: April 15-19, 2015
Location: Chicago, IL USA
Sponsor/Contact: Society of Architectural Historians
1365 North Astor St.
Chicago, IL 60610-2144
312-573-1365 *Fax:* 312-573-1141
E-mail: info@sah.org
URL: www.sah.org
Scope: International

6ième Colloque Annuel sur l'Enveloppe du bâtiment du Québec
Date: April 22-23, 2015
Location: Palais des congrès de Montréal
Montréal, QC
Sponsor/Contact: Conseil de l'enveloppe du bâtiment du Québec
12465 - 94E av
Montréal, QC H1C 1H6
514-943-0251 *Fax:* 514-943-0300
URL: www.cebq.org
Scope: Provincial

70th BC Trappers' AssociationAnnual General Meeting & Convention
Date: April 17-19, 2015
Location: 100 Mile House Curling Club
100 Mile House, BC
Sponsor/Contact: BC Trappers' Association
c/o Alana Leclerc
P.O. Box 1063
Prince George, BC V2L 4V2
250-962-5452 *Fax:* 250-962-5462
E-mail: info@bctrappers.bc.ca
URL: bctrappers.bc.ca
Scope: Provincial

8th Annual Hydrogen + Fuel Cells 2015 International Conference
Date: April 27-28, 2015
Location: Four Seasons Hotel
Vancouver, BC
Sponsor/Contact: Canadian Hydrogen & Fuel Cell Association
#900, 1188 West Georgia St.
Vancouver, BC V6E 4A2
604-283-1040 *Fax:* 604-283-1043
E-mail: info@chfca.ca
URL: www.chfca.ca
Scope: International
Purpose: HFC2015 will feature prominent industry and government leaders as keynote speakers as well as plenary and parallel sessions focusing on key issues and new initiatives within the sector.
Contact Information: Michael Davis, Director, Client and Sponsor Services; Website: www.hfc2015.com; Email: hfc2015@chfca.ca; Phone: 604-688-9655 Ext. 2

Alberta Assessors' Association Annual Conference and General Meeting 2015
Date: April 22-24, 2015
Location: Sheraton Cavalier Hotel Calgary
Calgary, AB
Sponsor/Contact: Alberta Assessors' Association
10555 - 172 St.
Edmonton, AB T5S 1P1
780-483-4222
E-mail: membership@assessor.ab.ca
URL: www.assessor.ab.ca
Scope: Provincial

Alberta College of Medical Diagnostic & Therapeutic Technologists 2015 Annual Conference
Date: April 17-18, 2015
Location: Deerfoot Inn & Casino
Calgary, AB
Sponsor/Contact: Alberta College of Medical Diagnostic & Therapeutic Technologists
#800, 4445 Calgary Trail NW
Edmonton, AB T6H 5R7
780-487-6130 *Fax:* 780-432-9106
Toll-Free: 800-282-2165
E-mail: info@acmdtt.com
URL: acmdtt.com
Scope: Provincial
Purpose: Educational presentations & breakout sessions

Alberta Family Mediation Society 2015 Conference
Date: April 9-10, 2015
Location: Providence Renewal Centre
Edmonton, AB
Sponsor/Contact: Alberta Family Mediation Society
#1650, 246 Stewart Green SW
Calgary, AB T3H 3C8
403-233-0143
Toll-Free: 877-233-0143
E-mail: info@afms.ca
URL: www.afms.ca
Scope: Provincial

Alberta Home Education Association Convention 2015
Date: April 10-11, 2015
Location: Alberta
Sponsor/Contact: Alberta Home Education Association
URL: www.aheaonline.com
Scope: Provincial

Alberta Hotel and Lodging Association 95th Annual Convention and Trade Show 2015
Date: April 16-18, 2015
Location: Alberta
Sponsor/Contact: Alberta Hotel & Lodging Association
2707 Ellwood Dr. SW
Edmonton, AB T6X 0P7
780-436-6112 *Fax:* 780-436-5404
Toll-Free: 888-436-6112
URL: www.ahla.ca
Scope: Provincial

Alberta Land Surveyors' Association 2015 Annual General Meeting
Date: April 23-24, 2015
Location: Fairmont Chateau Lake Louise
Lake Louise, AB
Sponsor/Contact: Alberta Land Surveyors' Association
#1000, 10020 - 101A Ave.
Edmonton, AB T5J 3G2
780-429-8805 *Fax:* 888-459-1664
Toll-Free: 800-665-2572
E-mail: info@alsa.ab.ca
URL: www.alsa.ab.ca
Scope: Provincial

Alberta School Councils' Association 2015 Conference and AGM
Date: April 24-26, 2015
Location: Delta Edmonton South
Edmonton, AB
Sponsor/Contact: Alberta School Councils' Association
#1200, 9925 - 109 St.
Edmonton, AB T5K 2J8
780-454-9867 *Fax:* 780-455-0167
Toll-Free: 800-661-3470
E-mail: parents@albertaschoolcouncils.ca
URL: www.albertaschoolcouncils.ca
Scope: Provincial

Alberta Senior Citizens' Housing Association 2015 Convention and Tradeshow
Date: April 15-17, 2015
Location: Shaw Conference Centre
Edmonton, AB
Sponsor/Contact: Alberta Senior Citizens' Housing Association
9711 - 47 Ave.
Edmonton, AB T6E 5M7
780-439-6473 *Fax:* 780-433-3717
E-mail: ascha@ascha.com
URL: www.ascha.com
Scope: Provincial

AllerGen NCE Inc. 2015 10th Annual Conference
Date: April 29 - May 1, 2015
Location: Toronto, ON
Sponsor/Contact: AllerGen NCE Inc.
Michael DeGroote Centre for Learning & Discovery, McMaster University
#3120, 1200 Main St. West
Hamilton, ON L8N 2A5
905-525-9140 *Fax:* 905-524-0611
E-mail: info@allergen-nce.ca
URL: www.allergen-nce.ca
Scope: National
Purpose: Keynote speakers, discussion panels, research presentations, poster viewing, the presentation of awards, networking opportunities, & a social program
Contact Information: Coordinator, Highly Qualified Personnel & Events: Michelle Harkness, Phone: 905-525-9140, ext. 26633, E-mail: michelleharkness@allergen-nce.ca

Allied Beauty Association Trade Show - Toronto 2015
Date: April 19-20, 2015
Location: Metro Toronto Convention Centre
Toronto, ON
Sponsor/Contact: Allied Beauty Association
#26-27, 145 Traders Blvd. East
Mississauga, ON L4Z 3L3
905-568-0158 *Fax:* 905-568-1581
E-mail: abashows@abacanada.com
URL: www.abacanada.com
Scope: National
Purpose: A trade show for beauty professionals only to become aware of future trends in the beauty industry

American Academy of Neurology 2015 67th Annual Meeting
Date: April 18-25, 2015
Location: Walter E. Washington Convention Center
Washington, DC USA
Sponsor/Contact: American Academy of Neurology
201 Chicago Ave.
Minneapolis, MN 55415
612-928-6000 *Fax:* 612-454-2746
Toll-Free: 800-879-1960
E-mail: memberservices@aan.com
URL: www.aan.com
Scope: International
Purpose: Education, science, & practice programs & exhibits
Anticipated Attendance: 12,000+
Contact Information: Member Services, E-mail: memberservices@aan.com

American Association for Thoracic Surgery 95th Annual Meeting
Date: April 25-29, 2015
Location: Washington State Convention & Trade Ctr.
Seattle, WA USA
Sponsor/Contact: American Association for Thoracic Surgery
#221U, 900 Cummings Center
Beverly, MA
978-927-8330 *Fax:* 978-524-8890
URL: www.aats.org
Scope: International
Purpose: Education in the field of thoracic & cardiovascular surgery, for cardiothoracic surgeons, physicians in related specialties, allied health professionals, fellows & residents in

cardiothoracic & general surgical training programs, as well as medical students with an interest in cardiothoracic surgery
Anticipated Attendance: 4,000

American Concrete Institute Spring 2015 Convention: Concrete Endures
Date: April 12-15, 2015
Location: Marriott & Kansas City Convention Center
Kansas City, MO USA
Sponsor/Contact: American Concrete Institute
P.O. Box 9094
38800 Country Club Dr.
Farmington, MI 48333-9094
248-848-3700 *Fax:* 248-848-3701
URL: www.concrete.org
Scope: International

American Society of Neuroradiology 2015 53rd Annual Meeting
Date: April 25-30, 2015
Location: Sheraton Chicago Hotel & Towers
Chicago, IL USA
Sponsor/Contact: American Society of Neuroradiology
#207, 2210 Midwest Rd.
Oak Brook, IL 60523
630-574-0220 *Fax:* 630-574-0661
E-mail: jgantenberg@asnr.org
URL: www.asnr.org
Scope: International
Contact Information: Director, Scientific Meetings: Lora Tannehill, E-mail: ltannehill@asnr.org; Manager, Scientific Meetings: Valerie Geisendorfer, E-mail: vgeisendorfer@asnr.org

Archives Association of British Columbia Conference 2015
Date: April 23-24, 2015
Location: Coquitlam, BC
Sponsor/Contact: Archives Association of British Columbia
#249, 34A-2755 Lougheed Hwy.
Port Coquitlam, BC V3B 5Y9
E-mail: info@aabc.ca
URL: www.aabc.ca
Scope: Provincial

Arctic Observing Summit 2015
Date: April 24-30, 2015
Location: Cape Town, South Africa
Sponsor/Contact: World Meteorological Organization
Information & Public Affairs
P.O. Box 2300
7 bis, av de la Paix, Geneva 2
Geneva, CH-1211
E-mail: cpa@wmo.int
URL: www.wmo.int
Scope: International
Purpose: The Arctic Observing Summit (AOS) is a high-level, summit that aims to provide community-driven, science-based guidance for the design, implementation, coordination and sustained long-term (decades) operation of an international network of arctic observing systems.

Association of Kootenay Boundary Local Governments 2015 Annual General Meeting
Date: April 22-24, 2015
Location: Nakusp, BC
Sponsor/Contact: Association of Kootenay & Boundary Local Governments
c/o Arlene Parkinson
790 Shakespeare St.
Trail, BC V1R 2B4
250-368-8650
E-mail: akblg@shaw.ca
URL: www.akblg.ca
Scope: Local

Association of Medical Microbiology & Infectious Disease Canada 2015 Annual Conference
Date: April 16-18, 2015
Location: Delta Prince Edward Island & PEI Convention Centre
Charlottetown, PE
Sponsor/Contact: Association of Medical Microbiology & Infectious Disease Canada
#101, 298 Elgin St.
Ottawa, ON K2P 1M3
613-260-3233 *Fax:* 613-260-3235
E-mail: info@ammi.ca
URL: www.ammi.ca
Scope: National
Purpose: A yearly meeting presenting the latest information in the fields of infectious diseases and microbiology for microbiologists, physicians, researchers, laboratory technologists, & students in the areas of medical microbiology & infectious diseases

Association of Vancouver Island Coastal Communities 2015 Annual General Meeting & Convention
Date: April 10-12, 2015
Location: Courtenay, BC
Sponsor/Contact: Association of Vancouver Island Coastal Communities
Local Government House
525 Government St.
Victoria, BC V8W 0A8
250-356-5122 *Fax:* 250-356-5119
URL: www.avicc.ca
Scope: Local
Contact Information: Contact: Iris Hesketh-Boles, E-mail: iheskethboles@ubcm.ca

Association québécoise des infirmières et des infirmiers en recherche clinique Congrès 2015
Date: 30 avril et 1 mai 2015
Location: Québec, QC
Sponsor/Contact: Association québécoise des infirmières et des infirmiers en recherche clinique
4200, rue Molson
Montréal, QC H1Y 4V4
514-935-2501 *Fax:* 514-935-1799
E-mail: info@aqiirc.qc.ca
URL: aqiirc.qc.ca
Scope: Provincial

Atlantic Community Newspapers Association 2015 43rd Annual Conference
Date: April 24-25, 2015
Location: Hilton Hotel
Halifax, NS
Sponsor/Contact: Newspapers Atlantic
#216, 7075 Bayers Rd.
Halifax, NS B3L 2C2
902-832-4480 *Fax:* 902-832-4484
Toll-Free: 877-842-4480
E-mail: info@newspapersatlantic.ca
URL: newspapersatlantic.ca
Scope: Provincial
Purpose: A Maritime meeting with speakers, educational seminars, an awards banquet, networking opportunities with colleagues, & social events

Boys and Girls Clubs of Canada Pacific / Western Regional Conference 2015
Date: April 29 - May 1, 2015
Location: Saskatoon, SK
Sponsor/Contact: Boys & Girls Clubs of Canada
National Office
#400, 2005 Sheppard Ave. East
Toronto, ON M2J 5B4
905-477-7272 *Fax:* 416-640-5331
E-mail: info@bgccan.com
URL: www.bgccan.com
Scope: National

Brain Injury Association of Canada 2015 Annual Conference
Date: April 15-16, 2015
Location: Halifax, NS
Sponsor/Contact: Brain Injury Association of Canada
#200, 440 Laurier Ave. West
Ottawa, ON K1R 7X6
613-762-1222 *Fax:* 613-236-5208
Toll-Free: 866-977-2492
E-mail: info@biac-aclc.ca
URL: www.biac-aclc.ca
Scope: National

British Association for Canadian Studies (BACS) 2015 40th Annual Conference
Date: April 23-25, 2015
Location: British Library Conference Centre
London, United Kingdom
Sponsor/Contact: British Association for Canadian Studies
#212, South Block, Senate House, University of London
Malet St.
London, WC1E 7HU
E-mail: canstuds@gmail.com
URL: www.canadian-studies.net
Scope: International
Purpose: Distinguished speakers on a great range of topics
Contact Information: Conference Manager: Luke Flanagan, E-mail: lukeflanagan@btinternet.com

British Columbia Association of Medical Radiation Technologists 2015 Annual General Conference & Annual General Meeting
Date: April 24-25, 2015
Location: Executive Plaza Hotel
Coquitlam, BC
Sponsor/Contact: British Columbia Association of Medical Radiation Technologists
Central Office
#102, 211 Columbia St.
Vancouver, BC V6A 2R5
604-682-8171 *Fax:* 604-681-4545
Toll-Free: 800-990-7090
E-mail: office@bcamrt.bc.ca
URL: www.bcamrt.bc.ca
Scope: Provincial
Purpose: Speakers present on a variety of educational topics as well as tips for the workplace and health and wellness.

British Columbia Human Resources Management Association 2015 53rd Annual Conference & Tradeshow
Date: April 28-29, 2015
Location: Vancouver Convention Centre
Vancouver, BC
Sponsor/Contact: British Columbia Human Resources Management Association
#1101, 1111 West Hastings St.
Vancouver, BC V5E 2J3
604-684-7228 *Fax:* 604-684-3225
Toll-Free: 800-665-1961
E-mail: info@bchrma.org
URL: www.bchrma.org
Scope: Provincial
Purpose: A human resources professional development event, with guest speakers, educational sessions, exhibits, the presentation of awards, & networking events
Contact Information: Manager, Conference & Events: Erin Roddie, Phone: 604-694-6933, E-mail: eroddie@hrma.ca

British Columbia School Superintendents Association 2015 Spring Forum
Date: April 15, 2015
Location: Westin Bayshore
Vancouver, BC
Sponsor/Contact: British Columbia School Superintendents Association
#208, 1118 Homer St.
Vancouver, BC V6B 6L5
604-687-0590
E-mail: info@bcssa.org
URL: www.bcssa.org
Scope: Provincial
Purpose: Topics related to the British Columbia School Superintendents Association's Dimensions of Practice, featuring innovative & successful models of leadership
Contact Information: Professional Development Coordinator: Kim Young, E-mail: kimyoung@bcssa.org

CHHMA [Canadian Hardware & Housewares Manufacturers Association] Spring Conference & AGM 2015
Date: April 8, 2015
Location: International Centre (Conference Facility)
Mississauga, ON
Sponsor/Contact: Canadian Hardware & Housewares Manufacturers' Association
#101, 1335 Morningside Ave.
Toronto, ON M1B 5M4
416-282-0022 *Fax:* 416-282-0027
Toll-Free: 800-488-4792
URL: www.chhma.ca
Scope: National

CIO Peer Forum 2015
Date: April 14-15, 2015
Location: Vancouver Convention Centre
Vancouver, BC
Sponsor/Contact: CIO Association of Canada
National Office
#204, 7270 Woodbine Ave.
Markham, ON L3R 4B9
905-752-1899 *Fax:* 905-513-1248
Toll-Free: 877-865-9009
E-mail: national@ciocan.ca
URL: www.ciocan.ca
Scope: National
Purpose: The theme is "Action is Eloquence: Creating Value from Innovation." Hosted by the CIO Association's Toronto & Ottawa Chapters.
Contact Information: Alex Buhler, CIO Peer Forum Co-Chair; Email: national@ciocan.ca

Conferences Index

Canada Grains Council's Second Annual Canadian Global Crops Symposium
Date: April 13-15 2015
Location: Saskatoon, SK
Sponsor/Contact: Canada Grains Council
#1215, 220 Portage Ave.
Winnipeg, MB R3C 0A5
204-925-2130 *Fax:* 204-925-2132
E-mail: office@canadagrainscouncil.ca
URL: www.canadagrainscouncil.ca
Scope: National

Canadian Aeronautics & Space Institute 62nd Aeronautics Conference & Annual General Meeting 2015
Date: April 21-23, 2015
Location: Fairmont The Queen Elizabeth Hotel
Montréal, QC
Sponsor/Contact: Canadian Aeronautics & Space Institute
#104, 350 Terry Fox Dr.
Ottawa, ON K2K 2W5
613-591-8787 *Fax:* 613-591-7291
E-mail: casi@casi.ca
URL: www.casi.ca
Scope: International

Canadian Amateur Musicians, Ottawa-Gatineau Region, 2015 Annual General Meeting
Date: April 25, 2015
Sponsor/Contact: Canadian Amateur Musicians
309 Olmstead St.
Ottawa, ON K1L 7K2
613-860-1751
E-mail: ottawagatineau@cammac.ca
URL: www.cammac.ca
Scope: Local

Canadian Archaeological Association Annual Meeting 2015
Date: April 29 - May 3, 2015
Location: St. John's, NL
Sponsor/Contact: Canadian Archaeological Association
c/o William Ross
189 Peter St.
Thunder Bay, ON P7A 5H8
807-345-2733
URL: www.canadianarchaeology.com
Scope: National
Contact Information: Amanda Crompton, Conference Chair; Email: caa2015aca@gmail.com

Canadian Association for Clinical Microbiology and Infectious Diseases Annual Conference 2015
Date: April 16-18, 2015
Location: Prince Edward Island Convention Centre
Charlottetown, PE
Sponsor/Contact: Canadian Association for Clinical Microbiology & Infectious Diseases
c/o Heather Adam, Dept of Medical Microbiology & Infectious Diseases
University of Manitoba, MS675F-820 Sherbrook St.
Winnipeg, MB R3A 1R9
204-787-8678 *Fax:* 204-787-4699
URL: www.cacmid.ca
Scope: National

Canadian Association for Medical Education / Association canadienne pour l'éducation médicale 2015

Canadian Conference on Medical Education
Date: April 25-28, 2015
Location: Fairmont Vancouver & Hyatt Regency Vancouver
Vancouver, BC
Sponsor/Contact: Canadian Association for Medical Education
#800, 265 Carling Ave.
Ottawa, ON K1S 2E1
613-730-0687 *Fax:* 613-730-1196
E-mail: came@afmc.ca
URL: www.came-acem.ca
Scope: National
Contact Information: Social Media: www.facebook.com/CanadianConferenceOnMedicalEducation; twitter.com/MedEdConference; Web Site: www.mededconference.ca

Canadian Association of Accredited Mortgage Professionals 2015 Alberta Regional Symposium & Trade Show
Date: April 16, 2015
Location: Calgary, AB
Sponsor/Contact: Canadian Association of Accredited Mortgage Professionals
Atria II
#1401, 2235 Sheppard Ave. East
Toronto, ON M2J 5B5
416-385-2333 *Fax:* 416-385-1177
Toll-Free: 888-442-4625
E-mail: info@caamp.org
URL: www.caamp.org
Scope: Provincial
Contact Information: E-mail: events@caamp.org

Canadian Association of Gift Planners 2015 Conference
Date: April 22-24, 2015
Location: Halifax, NS
Sponsor/Contact: Canadian Association of Gift Planners
#201, 1188 Wellington St. West
Ottawa, ON K1Y 2Z5
613-232-7991 *Fax:* 613-232-7286
Toll-Free: 888-430-9494
E-mail: communications@cagp-acpdp.org
URL: www.cagp-acpdp.org
Scope: National
Purpose: An annual spring meeting, featuring educational workshops, experienced speakers, & exhibits
Contact Information: URL: www.cagpconference.org; Email: conference@cagp-acpdp.org

Canadian Association of Petroleum Producers (CAPP) Scotiabank Investment Symposium 2015
Date: April 8-9, 2015
Location: Sheraton Centre Hotel
Toronto, ON
Sponsor/Contact: Canadian Association of Petroleum Producers
#2100, 350 - 7 Ave. SW
Calgary, AB T2P 3N9
403-267-1100 *Fax:* 403-261-4622
E-mail: communication@capp.ca
URL: www.capp.ca
Scope: National
Purpose: High-profile speakers on energy and industry discussion panels.
Contact Information: Email: brenda.jones@capp.ca; Phone: 403-267-1174

Canadian Association of Psychosocial Oncology National Annual 2015 Conference
Date: April 22-24, 2015
Location: Montreal, QC
Sponsor/Contact: Canadian Association of Psychosocial Oncology
#1, 189 Queen St. East
Toronto, ON M5A 1S2
416-968-0207 *Fax:* 416-968-6818
E-mail: capo@funnel.ca
URL: www.capo.ca
Scope: National
Contact Information: Association Manager: Anthony Laycock, E-mail: capo@funnel.ca

Canadian Energy Research Institute 2015 Oil Conference
Date: April 20-21, 2015
Location: The Fairmont Palliser Hotel
Calgary, AB
Sponsor/Contact: Canadian Energy Research Institute
#150, 3512 - 33 St. NW
Calgary, AB T2L 2A6
403-282-1231 *Fax:* 403-284-4181
E-mail: info@ceri.ca
URL: www.ceri.ca
Scope: National
Contact Information: General Inquiries, E-mail: conference@ceri.ca; Contact, Sponsorship Information: Deanne Landry, Phone: 403-220-2395, E-mail: dlandry@ceri.ca

Canadian Federation of Independent Grocers Grocery & Specialty Food West 2015
Date: April 13-14, 2015
Location: Vancouver Convention Centre
Vancouver, BC
Sponsor/Contact: Canadian Federation of Independent Grocers
#902, 2235 Sheppard Ave. East
Toronto, ON M2J 5B5
416-492-2311 *Fax:* 416-492-2347
Toll-Free: 800-661-2344
E-mail: info@cfig.ca
URL: www.cfig.ca
Scope: National
Purpose: An annual two day event for grocery industry professionals & over 350 exhibitors, featuring innovative products & ideas
Anticipated Attendance: 4,500
Contact Information: General Information, E-mail: events@cfig.ca

Canadian Franchise Association 2015 National Convention
Date: April 12-14, 2015
Location: Niagara Falls, ON
Sponsor/Contact: Canadian Franchise Association
#116, 5399 Eglinton Ave. West
Toronto, ON M9C 5K6
416-695-2896 *Fax:* 416-695-1950
Toll-Free: 800-665-4232
E-mail: info@cfa.ca
URL: www.cfa.ca
Scope: National

Canadian Gas Association 2015 Engineering Conference
Date: Aptil 20-21, 2015
Location: Toronto, ON
Sponsor/Contact: Canadian Gas Association
#809, 350 Sparks St.
Ottawa, ON K1R 7S8
613-748-0057 *Fax:* 613-748-9078
E-mail: info@cga.ca
URL: www.cga.ca
Scope: National
Contact Information: E-mail: help@canavents.com

Canadian Geriatrics Society 35th Annual General Meeting
Date: April 16-18, 2015
Location: Hilton Bonaventure
Montréal, QC
Sponsor/Contact: Canadian Geriatrics Society
#6, 20 Crown Steel Dr.
Markham, ON L3R 9X9
905-415-9161 *Fax:* 905-415-0071
Toll-Free: 866-247-0086
URL: www.canadiangeriatrics.com
Scope: National
Contact Information: thecanadiangeriatricssociety.wildapricot.org

Canadian Health Food Association (CHFA) Expo West 2015
Date: April 9-12, 2015
Location: Vancouver Convention Centre
Vancouver, BC
Sponsor/Contact: Canadian Health Food Association
#302, 235 Yorkland Blvd.
Toronto, ON M2J 4Y8
416-497-6939 *Fax:* 905-479-3214
Toll-Free: 800-661-4510
E-mail: info@chfa.ca
URL: www.chfa.ca
Scope: Provincial
Purpose: A conference & trade show attended by owners, managers, employees, & nutrition & health care practitioners from pharmacies, health stores, grocery stores, specialty stores, & online retailers
Contact Information: Phone: 416-497-6939; Toll-Free Phone: 1-800-661-4510; E-mail: info@chfa.ca

Canadian Museums Association 2015 68th National Conference
Date: April 13-17, 2015
Location: Banff, AB
Sponsor/Contact: Canadian Museums Association
#400, 280 Metcalfe St.
Ottawa, ON K2P 1R7
613-567-0099 *Fax:* 613-233-5438
Toll-Free: 888-822-2907
E-mail: info@museums.ca
URL: www.museums.ca
Scope: National
Purpose: A conference & tradeshow for Canadian museum professionals, such as directors, administrators, & curators
Contact Information: Conference contact: Megan Lafrenière, Phone: 613-567-0099, ext. 233, E-mail: mlafreniere@museums.ca

Canadian Obesity Summit 2015
Date: April 28 - May 2, 2015
Location: Toronto, ON
Sponsor/Contact: Canadian Obesity Network
Li Ka Shing Centre for Health Research & Innovation, Univ. of Alberta
#1-116, 8602 - 112 St.
Edmonton, AB T6G 2E1
780-492-8361 *Fax:* 780-492-9414
E-mail: info@obesitynetwork.ca
URL: www.obesitynetwork.ca
Scope: National

Canadian Produce Marketing Association 2015 90th Annual Convention & Trade Show
Date: April 15-17, 2015
Location: Palais des congrès de Montréal Montréal, QC
Sponsor/Contact: Canadian Produce Marketing Association
162 Cleopatra Dr.
Ottawa, ON K2G 5X2
613-226-4187 *Fax:* 613-226-2984
E-mail: question@cpma.ca
URL: www.cpma.ca
Scope: International
Purpose: Featuring business sessions, a trade show, a keynote speaker, & awards
Anticipated Attendance: 2,700
Contact Information: Senior Manager, Convention & Trade Show: Carole Brault, CMP, Phone: 613-226-4187, ext. 219; E-mail: cbrault@cpma.ca; Manager, Trade Show & Events: Natalia Kaliberda, Phone: 613-226-4187, ext. 223; E-mail: nkaliberda@cpma.ca

Canadian Respiratory Conference 2015
Date: April 23-25, 2015
Location: Ottawa, ON
Sponsor/Contact: Canadian Lung Association
National Office
#300, 1750 Courtwood Cres.
Ottawa, ON K2C 2B5
613-569-6411 *Fax:* 613-569-8860
Toll-Free: 800-566-5864
E-mail: info@lung.ca
URL: www.lung.ca
Scope: National
Purpose: Jointly organized by the Canadian Lung Association, the Canadian Thoracic Society, the Canadian COPD Alliance, & the Canadian Respiratory Health Professionals
Contact Information: Web Site: www.lung.ca/crc; E-mail: crc@taylorandassociates.ca

Canadian Respiratory Conference 2015
Date: April 23-25, 2015
Location: Ottawa, ON
Sponsor/Contact: Canadian Respiratory Health Professionals
#300, 1750 Courtwood Cres.
Ottawa, ON K2C 2B5
613-569-6411 *Fax:* 613-569-8860
E-mail: crhpinfo@lung.ca
URL: www.lung.ca/crhp
Scope: National
Purpose: Jointly organized by the Canadian Thoracic Society, the Canadian Respiratory Health Professionals, the Canadian COPD Alliance and the Canadian Lung Association

Canadian Sanitation Supply Association's CanClean 2015
Date: April 28-29, 2015
Location: International Centre Mississauga, ON
Sponsor/Contact: Canadian Sanitation Supply Association
P.O. Box 10009
910 Dundas St. West
Whitby, ON L1P 1P7
905-665-8001 *Fax:* 905-430-6418
Toll-Free: 866-684-8273
URL: www.cssa.com
Scope: National

Canadian Self Storage Association 9th Annual Western Canadian Conference, Trade Show & Self Storage Facility Tours
Date: April 23, 2015
Location: Dalta Vancovuer Suites Vancouver, BC
Sponsor/Contact: Canadian Self Storage Association
P.O. Box 188
Coldwater, ON L0K 1E0
Fax: 519-941-0877
Toll-Free: 888-898-8538
E-mail: info@cssa.ca
URL: www.cssa.ca
Scope: National

Canadian Thoracic Society 2015 Annual General Meeting
Date: April 23-25, 2015
Location: Westin Ottawa Ottawa, ON
Sponsor/Contact: Canadian Thoracic Society
c/o National Office, The Lung Association
#300, 1750 Courtwood Cres.
Ottawa, ON K2C 2B5
613-569-6411 *Fax:* 613-569-8860
Toll-Free: 888-566-5864
E-mail: ctsinfo@lung.ca
URL: www.lung.ca/cts
Scope: National

Canadian Union of Public Employees (CUPE) New Brunswick 2015 52nd Annual Convention
Date: April 15-18, 2015
Location: New Brunswick
Sponsor/Contact: Canadian Union of Public Employees
Maritime Regional Office
91 Woodside Lane
Fredericton, NB E3C 0C5
506-458-8059 *Fax:* 506-452-1702
URL: nb.cupe.ca
Scope: Provincial
Contact Information: Secretary-Treasurer: Minerva Porelle, Phone: 506-466-6149, E-mail: oporelle@nbnet.nb.ca

Collection Systems 2015: Collection Systems Taking Center Stage - Seize the Opportunity
Date: April 19-22, 2015
Location: Duke Energy Convention Center
Cincinnati, OH USA
Sponsor/Contact: Water Environment Federation
601 Wythe St.
Alexandria, VA 22314-1994
703-684-2400 *Fax:* 703-684-2492
Toll-Free: 800-666-0206
E-mail: comments@wef.org
URL: www.wef.org
Scope: International

Community Planning Association of Alberta Planning Conference 2015
Date: April 15-17, 2015
Location: Black Knight Inn Red Deer, AB
Sponsor/Contact: Community Planning Association of Alberta
#205, 10940 - 166A St.
Edmonton, AB T5P 3V5
780-432-6387 *Fax:* 780-452-7718
E-mail: cpaa@cpaa.biz
URL: www.cpaa.biz
Scope: Provincial

Compressed Gas Association Canada Annual Meeting 2015
Date: April 19-23, 2015
Location: Palm Beach Gardens, FL USA
Sponsor/Contact: Compressed Gas Association, Inc.
#103, 14501 George Carter Way
Chantilly, VA 20151
703-788-2700 *Fax:* 703-961-1831
E-mail: cga@cganet.com
URL: www.cganet.com
Scope: National

Computer Human Interaction 2015 Conference on Human Factors in Computing Systems
Date: April 17-23, 2015
Location: Seoul, Korea
Sponsor/Contact: Special Interest Group on Computer Human Interaction
P.O. Box 93672 Stn. Nelson Park
Vancouver, BC V6E 4L7
604-876-8985
E-mail: chi-VanCHI@acm.org
URL: www.sigchi.org
Scope: International
Anticipated Attendance: 2,500+

Consulting Engineers of British Columbia 2015 Awards Gala
Date: April 10, 2015
Location: Vancover Convention Centre Vancouver, BC
Sponsor/Contact: Consulting Engineers of British Columbia
#1258, 409 Granville St.
Vancouver, BC V6C 1T2
604-687-2811 *Fax:* 604-688-7110
E-mail: info@acec-bc.ca
URL: www.acec-bc.ca
Scope: Provincial
Purpose: The presentation of the Awards for Engineering Excellence in categories such as buildings, municipal, transportation, natural resources, energy & industry, & soft engineering
Contact Information: Coordinator, Accounting & Events: Alla Samusevich

Council of Forest Industries 2015 Annual Convention
Date: April 8-10, 2015
Location: Prince George, BC
Sponsor/Contact: Council of Forest Industries
Pender Place I Business Building
#1501, 700 Pender St. West
Vancouver, BC V6C 1G8
604-684-0211 *Fax:* 604-687-4930
E-mail: info@cofi.org
URL: www.cofi.org
Scope: National
Purpose: A meeting about issues affecting the forestry industries of British Columbia.
Contact Information: Phone: 604-684-0211; Fax: 604-687-4930

Cruise3sixty 2015
Date: April 22-26, 2015
Location: Broward County Convention Center
Fort Lauderdale, FL USA
Sponsor/Contact: Cruise Lines International Association, Inc.
#400, 910 SE 17th St.
Fort Lauderdale, FL 33316
754-224-2200 *Fax:* 754-224-2250
E-mail: info@cruising.org
URL: www.cruising.org
Scope: International
Purpose: An annual cruise conference hosted by Cruise Lines International Association, Inc., including educational training & networking opportunities.
Contact Information: Registration Coordinator: Tim Chau, Phone: 949-457-1545 ext. 122, Fax: 949-457-1281, E-mail: tchau@mjpa.com; URL: www.cruise3sixty.com

Economic Developers Alberta 2015 Annual Conference
Date: April 8-10, 2015
Location: Delta Kananaskis Kananaskis, AB
Sponsor/Contact: Economic Developers Alberta
Suite 127
#406, 917 - 85 St. Southwest
Calgary, AB T3H 5Z9
403-214-0224 *Fax:* 403-214-0224
Toll-Free: 866-671-8182
URL: www.edaalberta.ca
Scope: Provincial

Environmental Services Association of Alberta 2015 Water Technology (WaterTech) Symposium
Date: April 20-22, 2015
Location: Delta Lodge Kananaskis Kananaskis, AB
Sponsor/Contact: Environmental Services Association of Alberta
#102, 2528 Ellwood Dr. SW
Edmonton, AB T6X 0A9
780-429-6363 *Fax:* 780-429-4249
Toll-Free: 800-661-9278
E-mail: info@esaa.org
URL: www.esaa.org
Scope: Provincial
Purpose: A water technology transfer event for environmental professionals.
Anticipated Attendance: 300+
Contact Information: URL: www.esaa-events.com/watertech; Director, Program & Event Development: Joe Chowaniec, Phone: 780-429-6363, ext. 223, E-mail: chowaniec@esaa.org; Exhibit Information, E-mail: exhibits@esaa-events.com; Sponsorship Information, E-mail: sponsors@esaa-events.com

Food & Consumer Products of Canada 3rd Annual Health & Wellness Forum - The Science of Sugar & Sugar Substitutes
Date: April 22, 2015
Sponsor/Contact: Food & Consumer Products of Canada
100 Sheppard Ave. East
Toronto, ON M2N 6Z1
416-510-8024 *Fax:* 416-510-8043
E-mail: info@fcpc.ca
URL: www.fcpc.ca
Scope: National

Gerontological Nursing Association of British Columbia 2015 Conference
Date: April 23-25, 2015
Location: Coast Capri Hotel Kelowna, BC
Sponsor/Contact: Gerontological Nursing Association of British Columbia
c/o 328 Nootka St.
New Westminster,, BC V3L 4X4
604-484-5698 *Fax:* 604-874-4378
E-mail: gnabc@shaw.ca
URL: gnabc.com
Scope: Provincial

Conferences Index

Gerontological Nursing Association of Ontario 2015 Annual General Meeting
Date: April 21-22, 2015
Location: Toronto, ON
Sponsor/Contact: Gerontological Nursing Association of Ontario
P.O. Box 368 Stn. K
Toronto, ON M4P 2E0
E-mail: info@gnaontario.org
URL: www.gnaontario.org
Scope: Provincial
Purpose: Conference Theme: Aging 2015: Innovations, Networks and Communities

Global Business Travel Association Canada Conference 2015
Date: April 20-22, 2015
Location: Toronto, ON
Sponsor/Contact: Global Business Travel Association (Canada)
#919, 105-150 Crowfoot Cres. NW
Calgary, AB T3G 3T2
Fax: 403-719-6336
E-mail: membercare@gbta.org
URL: www.gbta.org/canada
Scope: National
Purpose: Featuring over 50 exhibitors, 12 concurrent education sessions & 4 general session featured speakers

Health Sciences Association 2015 Convention
Date: April 30 - May 2, 2015
Location: Hyatt Regency
Vancouver, BC
Sponsor/Contact: Health Sciences Association of British Columbia
180 East Columbia St.
New Westminster, BC V3L 0G7
604-517-0994 *Fax:* 604-515-8889
Toll-Free: 800-663-2017
URL: www.hsabc.org
Scope: Provincial
Purpose: A gathering of health care & social services professionals
Contact Information: Director of Communications: Miriam Sobrino, E-mail: msobrino@hsabc.org

Healthcare Information & Management Systems Society 2015 Annual Conference
Date: April 12-16, 2015
Location: Chicago, IL USA
Sponsor/Contact: Healthcare Information & Management Systems Society
#1700, 33 West Monrnoe St.
Chicago, IL 60603-5616
312-664-4467 *Fax:* 312-664-6143
E-mail: himss@himss.org
URL: www.himss.org
Scope: International
Anticipated Attendance: 38,000+
Contact Information: URL: www.himssconference.org

Library Association of Alberta Annual Conference 2015
Date: April 30 - May 3, 2015
Location: Alberta
Sponsor/Contact: Library Association of Alberta
80 Baker Cres. NW
Calgary, AB T2L 1R4
403-284-5818 *Fax:* 403-282-6646
Toll-Free: 877-522-5550
E-mail: info@laa.ca
URL: www.laa.ca
Scope: Provincial
Purpose: A conference held each spring for members of the Alberta library community, featuring association annual general meetings, session presentations, networking opportunities, & a trade show. Beginning this year, the conference is no longer held jointly with the Alberta Library Trustees Association (ALTA).
Contact Information: Library Association of Alberta, Phone: 403-284-5818, Toll-Free Phone: 1-877-522-5550, Fax: 403-282-6646, E-mail: info@laa.ca, info@albertalibraryconference.com

Manitoba Dental Association 2015 131st Annual Meeting & Convention
Date: April 17-18, 2015
Location: Keystone Centre
Brandon, MB
Sponsor/Contact: Manitoba Dental Association
#103, 698 Corydon Ave.
Winnipeg, MB R3M 0X9
204-988-5300 *Fax:* 204-988-5310
E-mail: office@manitobadentist.ca
URL: www.manitobadentist.ca
Scope: Provincial
Purpose: A conference & trade show, with business meetings, educational presentations, & networking opportunities, for dentists, dental hygienists, the oral health team, lab personnel, practice consultants, & dental students
Contact Information: E-mail: office@manitobadentist.ca

Manitoba Society of Pharmacists Conference 2015
Date: April 17-19, 2015
Location: RBC Convention Centre
Winnipeg, MB
Sponsor/Contact: Manitoba Society of Pharmacists Inc.
#202, 90 Garry St.
Winnipeg, MB R3C 4H1
204-956-6681 *Fax:* 204-956-6686
Toll-Free: 800-677-7170
E-mail: info@msp.mb.ca
URL: www.msp.mb.ca
Scope: Provincial

Microwave Theory & Techniques Society IEEE Wireless & Microwave Technology Conference (WAMICON)
Date: April 13-15, 2015
Location: Hilton Cocoa Beach Oceanfront
Cocoa Beach, FL USA
Sponsor/Contact: IEEE Microwave Theory & Techniques Society
5829 Bellanca Dr.
Elkridge, MD 21075
410-796-5866 *Fax:* 410-796-5829
URL: www.mtt.org
Scope: International

Model Aeronautics Association of Canada 2015 Annual Meetings
Date: April 19, 2015
Location: Delta Edmonton Centre
Edmonton, AB
Sponsor/Contact: Model Aeronautics Association of Canada Inc.
#9, 5100 South Service Rd.
Burlington, ON L7L 6A5
905-632-9808 *Fax:* 905-632-3304
Toll-Free: 855-359-6222
URL: www.maac.ca
Scope: National
Contact Information: Phone: 780-429-3900

Municipal Equipment & Operations Association (Ontario) Inc. 2015 Annual Spring Meeting
Date: April 15-16, 2015
Location: Waterloo Motor Inn
Waterloo, ON
Sponsor/Contact: Municipal Equipment & Operations Association (Ontario) Inc.
38 Summit Ave.
Kitchener, ON N2M 4W2
519-741-2600 *Fax:* 519-741-2750
E-mail: admin@meoa.org
URL: www.meoa.org
Scope: Provincial
Purpose: An event to elect the new executive, to address the business of the association, to participate in a plant tour, to hear guest speakers, & to attend educational presentations

National Emergency Nurses Affiliation 2015 Conference
Date: April 30 - May 3, 2015
Location: Edmonton, AB
Sponsor/Contact: National Emergency Nurses Affiliation
112 Old River Rd., RR#2
Mallorytown, ON K0E 1R0
URL: www.nena.ca
Scope: National
Purpose: Theme: Prepare For The Unexpected
Contact Information: Email: conference2015@nena.ca; Phone: 604-594-5407

North America's Premier Natural Health Show 38th Annual Convention and Exhibition (Total Health 2015)
Date: April 17-19, 2015
Location: Metro Toronto Convention Centre
Toronto, ON
Sponsor/Contact: Consumer Health Organization of Canada
#1901, 355 St. Clair Ave. West
Toronto, ON M5P 1N5
416-924-9800 *Fax:* 416-924-6404
E-mail: info@consumerhealth.org
URL: www.consumerhealth.org
Scope: International
Purpose: Speakers will focus on creating good health and preventing disease using natural methods: energy medicine, organic gardening, traditional farming, agricultural biodiversity, healthy homes, ecologically based communities, renewable energy source and preserving a healthy environment for our children. We as consumers must choose foods and medicines which do no harm to people, animals or our planet.
Contact Information: Phone: 416-924-9800 or 1-877-389-0996; Fax: 416-924-6404; Website: www.totalhealthshow.com

Northeast Modern Language Associations 2015 46th Annual Convention
Date: April 30- May 3, 2015
Location: Toronto, ON
Sponsor/Contact: Northeast Modern Language Association
c/o Dr. Elizabeth Abele, Dept. of English, Nassau Community College
One Education Dr.
Garden City, NY 11530-6793
E-mail: nemlasupport@gmail.com
URL: www.nemla.org
Scope: International
Contact Information: Executive Director: Elizabeth Abele, E-mail: northeast.mla@gmail.com

Northwest Wall & Ceiling Bureau 2015 Annual Convention & Trade Show
Date: April 16-18, 2015
Location: Rancho Mirage, CA USA
Sponsor/Contact: Northwest Wall & Ceiling Bureau
1032A NE 65th St.
Seattle, WA 98115
E-mail: info@nwcb.org
URL: www.nwcb.org
Scope: International
Purpose: Informative seminars & exhibits, plus networking opportunities, for persons in the northwestern wall & ceiling industry
Contact Information: Director, Communications & Events: Tiina Freeman, E-mail: tiina@nwcb.org; Exhibitor & Sponsorship Information, Phone: 206-524-4243

Northwestern Ontario Municipal Association 2015 Annual General Meeting & Conference
Date: April 22-24, 2015
Location: Victoria Inn & Conference Centre
Thunder Bay, ON
Sponsor/Contact: Northwestern Ontario Municipal Association
P.O. Box 10308
Thunder Bay, ON P7B 6T8
807-683-6662
E-mail: admin@noma.on.ca
URL: www.noma.on.ca
Scope: Local
Purpose: A meeting which is held alternatively in the association's three districts (Kenora, Rain River, or Thunder Bay), featuring informative presentations & networking opportunities
Contact Information: NOMA Executive Director, Phone: 807-683-6662, E-mail: admin@noma.on.ca

Ontario Association of Non-Profit Homes & Services for Seniors 2015 Annual Meeting & Convention: Great Places to Live & Work
Date: April 13-15, 2015
Location: Sheraton Centre
Toronto, ON
Sponsor/Contact: Ontario Association of Non-Profit Homes & Services for Seniors
#700, 7050 Weston Rd.
Woodbridge, ON L4L 8G7
905-851-8821 *Fax:* 905-851-0744
URL: www.oanhss.org
Scope: Provincial
Purpose: A professional development event & trade show, featuring expert speakers, for senior staff from the long term care, seniors' housing, & community services sectors
Contact Information: Contact, Sponsorship Information: Ellen Maracle-Benton, Phone: 905-404-9545, E-mail: ellen@eventsinsync.com

Ontario Association on Developmental Disabilities 2015 Annual Conference
Date: April 14-17, 2015
Location: Four Points by Sheraton
Thorold, ON
Sponsor/Contact: Ontario Association on Developmental Disabilities
2 Surrey Pl.
Toronto, ON M5S 2C2

416-657-2267 *Fax:* 416-925-6508
E-mail: oadd@oadd.org
URL: www.oadd.org
Scope: Provincial
Purpose: Participants include front-line staff such as clinicians, therapists, & case-workers, as well as management, including program managers, supervisors, & human resources personnel
Contact Information: Ontario Association on Developmental Disabilities Conference Committee, E-mail: oadd@oadd.org

Ontario Gerontology Association's 34th Annual Conference
Date: April 21-22, 2015
Location: Toronto, ON
Sponsor/Contact: Ontario Gerontology Association
#216C, 351 Christie St.
Toronto, ON M6G 3C3
416-535-6034 *Fax:* 416-535-6907
E-mail: info@gerontario.org
URL: www.gerontario.org
Scope: Provincial
Purpose: Theme - Aging 2015: Innovation in Care, Networks and Communities

Ontario Municipal Human Resources Association Spring Workshop 2015
Date: April 15-17, 2015
Location: Delta Hotel & Conference Centre
Guelph, ON
Sponsor/Contact: Ontario Municipal Human Resources Association
#307, 1235 Fairview St.
Burlington, ON L7S 2K9
905-631-7171 *Fax:* 905-631-2376
E-mail: customerservice@omhra.on.ca
URL: www.omhra.ca
Scope: Provincial

Ontario Numismatic Association 2015 53rd Annual Convention
Date: April 17-19, 2015
Location: Crowne Plaza Niagara Falls-Fallsview
Niagara Falls, ON
Sponsor/Contact: Ontario Numismatic Association
c/o Bruce Raszmann
P.O. Box 40033 Stn. Waterloo Square
75 King St. South
Waterloo, ON N2J 4V1
URL: the-ona.ca
Scope: Provincial
Purpose: Education program, dealer participation, business meetings, & networking events

Ontario Professional Foresters Association 2015 58th Annual Meeting
Date: April 2015
Location: Ontario
Sponsor/Contact: Ontario Professional Foresters Association
#201, 5 Wesleyan St.
Georgetown, ON L7G 2E2
905-877-3679 *Fax:* 905-877-6766
E-mail: opfa@opfa.ca
URL: www.opfa.ca
Scope: National

Ontario Refrigeration & Air Conditioning Contractors Association 2015 AGM & Cruise
Date: April 2015
Location: Fort Lauderdale, FL USA
Sponsor/Contact: Ontario Refrigeration & Air Conditioning Contractors Association
#43, 6770 Davand Dr.
Mississauga, ON L5T 2G3
905-670-0010 *Fax:* 905-670-0474
E-mail: contact@oraca.ca
URL: www.oraca.ca
Scope: Provincial

Ontario Small Urban Municipalities 2015 62nd Annual Conference & Trade Show
Date: April 28 - May 1, 2015
Location: Belleville, ON
Sponsor/Contact: Ontario Small Urban Municipalities
c/o Association of Municipalities of Ontario
#801, 200 University Ave.
Toronto, ON M5H 3C6
416-971-9856 *Fax:* 416-971-6191
Toll-Free: 877-426-6527
E-mail: amo@amo.on.ca
URL: www.osum.ca
Scope: Provincial
Anticipated Attendance: 200+
Contact Information: OSUM Annual Conference & Trade Show Coordinator: Ted Blowes, Phone: 519-271-0250, ext. 241, E-mail: ted.b@quadro.net

Ontario Transportation Exposition 2015
Date: April 12-15, 2015
Location: Sheraton Toronto Airport Hotel and the International Centre
Toronto, ON
Sponsor/Contact: Ontario Public Transit Association
#400, 1235 Bay St.
Toronto, ON M5R 3K4
416-229-6222 *Fax:* 416-969-8916
URL: www.ontariopublictransit.ca
Scope: Provincial

Ontario Trial Lawyers Association 2015 Products Liability Conference: Products Liability Litigation
Date: April 1, 2015
Location: Twenty Toronto Street Conferences and Events
Toronto, ON
Sponsor/Contact: Ontario Trial Lawyers Association
1190 Blair Rd.
Burlington, ON L7M 1K9
905-639-6852 *Fax:* 905-639-3100
URL: www.otla.com
Scope: Provincial
Contact Information: Conference Chairs: Gary Will and Matt Lalande

Ontario Water Works Association / Ontario Municipal Water Association 2015 Annual Joint Conference & Trade Show
Date: April 26-29, 2015
Location: Toronto, ON
Sponsor/Contact: Ontario Municipal Water Association
c/o Doug Parker
43 Chelsea Cres.
Belleville, ON K8N 4Z5
613-966-1100 *Fax:* 613-966-3024
Toll-Free: 888-231-1115
URL: www.omwa.org
Scope: Provincial
Purpose: A conference featuring a plenary session, technical sessions, a trade show, & networking opportunities

Partners in Prevention 2015 National Conference: Health & Safety Conference & Trade Show
Date: April 28-29, 2015
Location: The International Centre
Mississauga, ON
Sponsor/Contact: Workplace Safety & Prevention Services
Centre for Health & Safety Innovation
5110 Creekbank Rd.
Mississauga, ON L4W 0A1
905-614-1400 *Fax:* 905-614-1414
Toll-Free: 877-494-9777
E-mail: customercare@wsps.ca
URL: www.wsps.ca
Scope: National

Pediatric Academic Societies' 2015 Annual Meeting
Date: April 25-28, 2015
Location: San Diego, CA USA
Sponsor/Contact: Academic Pediatric Association
6728 Old McLean Village Dr.
McLean, VA 22101
703-556-9222 *Fax:* 703-556-8729
E-mail: info@academicpeds.org
URL: www.ambpeds.org
Scope: International
Purpose: An international meeting focussing on research in child health
Contact Information: Address: #7B, 3400 Research Forest Dr., The Woodlands, TX, 77381, USA; Phone: 281-419-0052; Fax: 281-419-0082

Pediatric Endocrine Society 2015 Annual Meeting
Date: April 25-28, 2015
Location: San Diego, CA USA
Sponsor/Contact: Pediatric Endocrine Society
6728 Old McLean Village Dr.
McLean, VA 22101
E-mail: info@pedsendo.org
URL: www.pedsendo.org
Scope: International
Purpose: A conference for persons who represent the disciplines of pediatric endocrinology
Contact Information: E-mail: info@pedsendo.org

Physical & Health Education Canada National Conference 2015
Date: April 30 - May 2, 2015
Location: Banff, AB
Sponsor/Contact: Physical & Health Education Canada
#301, 2197 Riverside Dr.
Ottawa, ON K1H 7X3
613-523-1348 *Fax:* 613-523-1206
Toll-Free: 800-663-8708
E-mail: info@phecanada.ca
URL: www.phecanada.ca
Scope: National
Purpose: The conference is in partnership with the Manitoba Physical Education Teacher's Association (MPETA)

Pipe Line Contractors Association of Canada 2015 61st Annual Convention
Date: April 13-17, 2015
Location: Hyatt Regency Maui Resort & Spa
Maui, HI USA
Sponsor/Contact: Pipe Line Contractors Association of Canada
#201, 1075 North Service Rd. West
Oakville, ON L6M 2G2
905-847-9383 *Fax:* 905-847-7824
E-mail: plcac@pipeline.ca
URL: www.pipeline.ca
Scope: National
Purpose: A program about the special pipeline construction industry, including various speakers & the association's annual general meeting
Contact Information: E-mail: plcac@pipeline.ca

Planning Institute of British Columbia 2015 Annual Conference
Date: April 16-17, 2015
Location: Washington State Convention Center
Seattle, WA USA
Sponsor/Contact: Planning Institute of British Columbia
#1750, 355 Burrard St.
Vancouver, BC V6C 2G8
604-696-5031 *Fax:* 604-696-5032
Toll-Free: 866-696-5031
E-mail: info@pibc.bc.ca
URL: www.pibc.bc.ca
Scope: Provincial

Professional Photographers of Canada 2015 46th Canadian Imaging Conference & Trade Show
Date: April 25-28, 2015
Location: Sheraton Inn on the Falls
Niagara Falls, ON
Sponsor/Contact: Professional Photographers of Canada 1970 Incorporated
209 Light St.
Woodstock, ON N4S 6H6
519-537-2555 *Fax:* 519-537-5573
Toll-Free: 888-643-7762
URL: www.ppoc.ca
Scope: National
Purpose: An opportunity for the exchange of professional ideas
Contact Information: URL: conference.ppoc.ca

RIMS (Risk & Insurance Management Society Inc.) 2015 Annual Conference & Exhibition
Date: April 26-29, 2015
Location: New Orleans Ernest N. Morial Convention Center
New Orleans, LA USA
Sponsor/Contact: Risk & Insurance Management Society Inc.
c/o Thomas Oystrick, RIMS Canada Council, Mount Royal University
4825 Mount Royal Gate SW
Calgary, AB T3E 6K6
E-mail: canada@rims.org
URL: www.rimscanada.ca
Scope: International
Purpose: An international conference & exhibition presenting professional development & networking opportunities for risk professionals

Registered Nurses' Association of Ontario Annual General Meeting 2015
Date: Aptil 16-18, 2015
Location: Hilton Toronto
Toronto, ON
Sponsor/Contact: Registered Nurses' Association of Ontario
158 Pearl St.
Toronto, ON M5H 1L3
416-599-1925 *Fax:* 416-599-1926
Toll-Free: 800-268-7199
URL: www.rnao.org
Scope: Provincial

Conferences Index

Royal Winnipeg Ballet Diamond Gala
Date: April 18, 2015
Location: RBC Convention Centre
Winnipeg, MB
Sponsor/Contact: Royal Winnipeg Ballet
380 Graham Ave.
Winnipeg, MB R3C 4K2
204-956-0183 *Fax:* 204-943-1994
E-mail: customerservice@rwb.org
URL: www.rwb.org
Scope: Local

Rural & Remote 2015
Date: April 9-11, 2015
Location: Fairmont Queen Elizabeth
Montreal, QC
Sponsor/Contact: Society of Rural Physicians of Canada
P.O. Box 893
269 Main St.
Shawville, QC J0X 2Y0
Fax: 819-647-2485
Toll-Free: 877-276-1949
E-mail: info@srpc.ca
URL: www.srpc.ca
Scope: International
Purpose: Includes the 23rd Annual Rural and Remote Medicine Course and the Second World Summit on Rural Generalist Medicine

SCA/STS Critical Care Symposium
Date: April 10, 2015
Location: Washington Marriott Marquis
Washington, DC USA
Sponsor/Contact: Society of Cardiovascular Anesthesiologists
2209 Dickens Rd.
Richmond, VA 23230-2005
804-282-0084 *Fax:* 804-282-0090
E-mail: sca@societyhq.com
URL: www.scahq.org
Scope: International
Purpose: Hosted jointly by the Society of Cardiovascular Anesthesiologists & the Society of Thoracic Surgeons.

Safety Services New Brunswick Health & Safety Conference 2015
Date: April 23-24, 2015
Location: Deltra Brunswick
Saint John, NB
Sponsor/Contact: Safety Services New Brunswick
#204, 440 Wilsey Rd.
Fredericton, NB E3B 7G5
506-458-8034 *Fax:* 506-444-0177
Toll-Free: 877-762-7233
E-mail: info@safetyservicesnb.ca
URL: www.safetyservicesnb.ca
Scope: Provincial

SaskCentral 2015 Annual General Meeting
Date: April 8-9, 2015
Location: Saskatchewan
Sponsor/Contact: SaskCentral
P.O. Box 3030
2055 Albert St.
Regina, SK S4P 3G8
306-566-1200 *Fax:* 306-566-1372
Toll-Free: 866-403-7499
E-mail: info@saskcentral.com
URL: www.saskcentral.com
Scope: Provincial

Saskatchewan Waste Reduction Council Waste ReForum 2015
Date: April 22-24, 2015
Location: Sheraton Cavalier
Saskatoon, SK
Sponsor/Contact: Saskatchewan Waste Reduction Council
The Two-Twenty
#208, 220 - 20th St. West
Saskatoon, SK S7M 0W9
306-931-3242 *Fax:* 306-955-5852
E-mail: info@saskwastereduction.ca
URL: www.saskwastereduction.ca
Scope: Provincial
Purpose: Workshops & sessions on environmental issues

Society of Cardiovascular Anesthesiologists 37th Annual Meeting 2015
Date: April 11-15, 2015
Location: Washington Marriott Marquis
Washington, DC USA
Sponsor/Contact: Society of Cardiovascular Anesthesiologists
2209 Dickens Rd.
Richmond, VA 23230-2005
804-282-0084 *Fax:* 804-282-0090
E-mail: sca@societyhq.com
URL: www.scahq.org
Scope: International

Society of Cardiovascular Anesthesiologists 4th Annual Thoracic Anesthesia Symposium 2015
Date: April 10, 2015
Location: Washington Marriott Marquis
Washington, DC USA
Sponsor/Contact: Society of Cardiovascular Anesthesiologists
2209 Dickens Rd.
Richmond, VA 23230-2005
804-282-0084 *Fax:* 804-282-0090
E-mail: sca@societyhq.com
URL: www.scahq.org
Scope: International

Southern Interior Local Government Association 2015 Annual General Meeting & Convention
Date: April 29 - May 1, 2015
Location: Coast Hotel & Convention Centre
Kamloops, BC
Sponsor/Contact: Southern Interior Local Government Association
c/o Alison Slater
1996 Sheffield Way
Kamloops, BC V2E 2M2
250-374-3678 *Fax:* 250-374-3678
URL: www.silga.ca
Scope: Local

The Saskatchewan Hotel & Hospitality Association (SHHA) Hotel & Hospitality Conference
Date: April 13-14, 2015
Location: DoubleTree by Hilton Hotel
Regina, SK
Sponsor/Contact: Saskatchewan Hotel & Hospitality Association
#302, 2080 Broad St.
Regina, SK S4P 1Y3
306-522-1664 *Fax:* 306-525-1944
Toll-Free: 800-667-1118
URL: www.shha.co
Scope: Provincial

Toronto Field Naturalists 2015 Monthly Talk: Climate Change Effects on Pollinators
Date: April 12, 2015
Location: University of Toronto, Northrop Frye Building
Toronto, ON
Sponsor/Contact: Toronto Field Naturalists
#1519, 2 Carlton St.
Toronto, ON M5B 1J3
416-593-2656
E-mail: office@torontofieldnaturalists.org
URL: www.torontofieldnaturalists.org
Scope: Local
Purpose: This lecture examines the results that climate change has on bees, wildflowers blooming times & plant-pollinator interactions
Contact Information: E-mail: office@torontofieldnaturalists.org

Trauma 2015: Trauma Association of Canada Annual Scientific Meeting & Conference
Date: April 10-11, 2015
Location: Westin Calgary
Calgary, AB
Sponsor/Contact: Trauma Association of Canada
c/o Trauma Services, Foothills Medical Centre
1403 - 29 St. NW
Calgary, AB T2N 2T9
403-944-2888 *Fax:* 403-944-8799
E-mail: info@traumacanada.org
URL: www.traumacanada.org
Scope: National

Victorian Studies Association of Western Canada 2015 Conference
Date: April 10-11, 2015
Location: Manteo Lakeside Resort
Kelowna, BC
Sponsor/Contact: Victorian Studies Association of Western Canada
LLPA Department, Douglas College, University of Victoria
#2635, 700 Royal Ave.
New Westminster, BC V3M 5Z5
URL: web.uvic.ca/vsawc
Scope: National

Water Environment Association of Ontario 2015 44th Annual Technical Symposium & Exhibition
Date: April 19-21, 2015
Location: Toronto Congress Centre
Toronto, ON
Sponsor/Contact: Water Environment Association of Ontario
P.O. Box 176
Milton, ON L9T 4N9
416-410-6933 *Fax:* 416-410-1626
E-mail: julie.vincent@weao.org
URL: www.weao.org
Scope: Provincial
Purpose: A conference featuring technical sessions, a keynote speaker, a student program, an awards presentation, & networking opportunities
Contact Information: Chair, Conference Committee: Frank Farkas, E-mail: farkas.f@spdsales.com

Western Canada 24th Annual PD Days 2015
Date: April 9-10, 2015
Location: Renaissance Vancouver Hotel Harbourside
Vancouver, BC
Sponsor/Contact: British Columbia Provincial Renal Agency
#700, 1380 Burrard St.
Vancouver, BC V6Z 2H3
604-875-7340
E-mail: bcpra@bcpra.ca
URL: www.bcrenalagency.ca
Scope: Provincial
Purpose: A showcase of approaches to the delivery of peritoneal dialysis
Contact Information: E-mail: westernpddays@bcpra.ca

May

11th annual Advanced Palliative Medicine Conference "New Frontiers in Palliative Medicine"
Date: May 28-30, 2015
Location: Westin Calgary
Calgary, AB
Sponsor/Contact: Canadian Society of Palliative Care Physicians
c/o Fraser Health Authority
#400, 13450 - 102 Ave.
Surrey, BC V3T 0H1
604-341-3174 *Fax:* 604-587-4644
E-mail: office@cspcp.ca
URL: www.cspcp.ca
Scope: National

14th Annual Forum on Hydropower 2015
Date: May 14-15, 2015
Location: Ottawa, ON
Sponsor/Contact: Canadian Hydropower Association
#1402 - 150 Metcalfe St.
Ottawa, ON K2P 1P1
613-751-6655 *Fax:* 613-751-4465
E-mail: info@canadahydro.ca
URL: canadahydro.ca
Scope: National
Contact Information: Yvonne Jack, Email: yvonne@canadahydro.ca; URL: www.hydroforum.ca

16th Continuing Medical Education Conference
Date: May 8-10, 2015
Location: Delta Lodge at Kananaskis
Kananaskis, AB
Sponsor/Contact: Alberta Society of Radiologists
#110, 10350 - 124th St.
Edmonton, AB T5N 3V9
780-443-2615 *Fax:* 780-443-0687
E-mail: asr@radiologists.ab.ca
URL: www.radiologists.ab.ca
Scope: Provincial

19th Annual Vision Quest Conference & Trade Show 2015
Date: May 12-14, 2015
Location: RBC Covention Centre
Winnipeg, MB
Sponsor/Contact: Community Futures Manitoba Inc.
#559, 167 Lombard Ave.
Winnipeg, MB R3B 0V3
204-943-2905 *Fax:* 204-956-9363
E-mail: info@cfmanitoba.ca
URL: www.cfmanitoba.ca
Scope: Provincial
Purpose: An annual event for business leaders, innovators, & entrepreneurs, from Manitoba, Saskatchewan, Alberta, northern Ontario, Nunavut, Northwest Territories, & the United States, to discuss & promote Aboriginal business & community development, featuring interactive workshops, motivational keynote presentations from business leaders, a trade show with more than 80 booths, & social & networking events
Anticipated Attendance: 1,000+
Contact Information: Vision Quest Conferences Inc., Phone: 204-942-5049, Toll-Free Phone: 1-800-557-8242; URL: www.vqconference.com

2015 Annual Canadian Society of Hand Therapists Conference
Date: May 22-23, 2015
Location: Hyatt Regency Hotel
Montreal, QC
Sponsor/Contact: Canadian Society of Hand Therapists
URL: csht.org
Scope: National

2015 Annual Conference of the Canadian Blood & Marrow Transplant Group
Date: May 13-16, 2015
Location: Le Centre Sheraton
Montreal, QC
Sponsor/Contact: Canadian Blood & Marrow Transplant Group
#400, 570 West 7th Ave.
Vancouver, BC V5Z 1B3
604-874-4944 *Fax:* 604-874-4378
E-mail: cbmtg@malachite-mgmt.com
URL: www.cbmtg.org
Scope: National

2015 Archives Association of Ontario Conference
Date: May 27-29, 2015
Location: London, ON
Sponsor/Contact: Archives Association of Ontario
#202, 720 Spadina Ave.
Toronto, ON M5S 2T9
647-343-3334
E-mail: aao@aao-archivists.ca
URL: aao-archivists.ca
Scope: Provincial

2015 British Columbia Association of School Business Officials Annual General Meeting
Date: May 20-23, 2015
Location: Penticton, BC
Sponsor/Contact: British Columbia Association of School Business Officials
#208, 1118 Homer St.
Vancouver, BC V6B 6L5
604-687-0595 *Fax:* 604-687-8118
E-mail: executivedirector@bcasbo.ca
URL: www.bcasbo.ca
Scope: Provincial

2015 CAFE Family Business Symposium
Date: May 20, 2015
Location: Westin Harbour Castle
Toronto, ON
Sponsor/Contact: Canadian Association of Family Enterprise
#112, 465 Morden Rd.
Oakville, ON L6K 3W6
905-337-8375 *Fax:* 905-337-0572
Toll-Free: 866-849-0099
E-mail: info@cafecanada.ca
URL: www.cafecanada.ca

2015 Canadian Academic Accounting Association Annual Conference
Date: May 28-31, 2015
Location: Hilton Toronto Hotel
Toronto, ON
Sponsor/Contact: Canadian Academic Accounting Association
245 Fairview Mall Dr.
Toronto, ON M2J 4T1
416-486-5361 *Fax:* 416-486-6158
E-mail: admin@caaa.ca
URL: www.caaa.ca
Scope: National
Contact Information: Ron Baker, Chair, CAAA Annual Conference 2015; Email: annualconfchair@caaa.ca

2015 Canadian Association of Aquarium Clubs Convention
Date: May 15-17, 2015
Location: Burlington Holiday Inn & Conference Centre
Burlington, ON
Sponsor/Contact: Canadian Association of Aquarium Clubs
#223, 1717 60th St. SE
Calgary, AB T2A 7Y7
E-mail: amtowell@shaw.ca
URL: www.caoac.ca
Scope: National

2015 Canadian Association of Foodservice Professionals National Conference
Date: May 28-30, 2015
Location: Delta Fredricton
Fredericton, NB
Sponsor/Contact: Canadian Association of Foodservice Professionals
CAFP National Office
#130, 10691 Shellbridge Way
Richmond, BC V6X 2W8
604-248-0215 *Fax:* 604-270-3644
Toll-Free: 877-599-2237
E-mail: national@cafp.com
URL: www.cafp.com
Scope: National

2015 Canadian Association of Science Centres Annual Conference
Date: May 28-30, 2015
Location: Edmonton, AB
Sponsor/Contact: Canadian Association of Science Centres
P.O. Box 3443 Stn. D
Ottawa, OM K1P 6P4
613-566-4247
E-mail: casc.accs@gmail.com
URL: www.canadiansciencecentres.ca
Scope: National
Purpose: Theme: "True North"

2015 Canadian Federation of Humane Societies National Animal Welfare Conference
Date: May 2-5, 2015
Location: River Rock Hotel
Richmond, BC
Sponsor/Contact: Canadian Federation of Humane Societies
#102, 30 Concourse Gate
Ottawa, ON K2E 7V7
613-224-8072 *Fax:* 613-723-0252
Toll-Free: 888-678-2347
E-mail: info@cfhs.ca
URL: www.cfhs.ca
Scope: National

2015 Canadian Philosophical Association Congress
Date: May 31- June 3, 2015
Location: University of Ottawa
Ottawa, ON
Sponsor/Contact: Canadian Philosophical Association
c/o Louise Morel, Saint Paul University
223 Main St.
Ottawa, ON K1S 1C4
613-236-1393 *Fax:* 613-782-3005
E-mail: administration@acpcpa.ca
URL: www.acpcpa.ca

2015 Canadian Population Society Annual Meeting
Date: May 30 - June 5, 2015
Location: University of Ottawa
Ottawa, ON
Sponsor/Contact: Canadian Population Society
520-17 Aberdeen St.
Ottawa, ON K1S 3J3
E-mail: admin@canpopsoc.ca
URL: www.canpopsoc.org
Scope: National

2015 Canadian Society of Landscape Architects Congress
Date: May 21-23, 2015
Location: Hilton Mexico City Reforma
Mexico City, Mexico
Sponsor/Contact: Canadian Society of Landscape Architects
P.O. Box 13594
Ottawa, ON K2K 1X6
866-781-9799 *Fax:* 866-871-1419
E-mail: info@csla.ca
URL: www.csla.ca
Scope: National

2015 Conference of the Canadian Society of Animal Science and the Canadian Meat Council
Date: May 6-8, 2015
Location: The Westin Hotel
Ottawa, ON
Sponsor/Contact: Canadian Society of Animal Science
c/o University of Alberta, Agriculture & Forestry Centre, #4-10
Edmonton, AB T6G 2C8
780-248-1700 *Fax:* 780-248-1900
URL: www.csas.net
Scope: National

2015 Conference of the Hungarian Studies Association of Canada
Date: May 30 - June 1, 2015
Location: University of Ottawa
Ottawa, ON
Sponsor/Contact: Hungarian Studies Association of Canada
c/o Margit Lovrics
#1804, 75 Graydon Hall Dr.
Toronto, ON M3A 3M5
URL: www.hungarianstudies.org
Purpose: Held in conjunction with the Congress of the Humanities & Social Sciences

2015 Government Finance Officers Association of British Columbia Annual Conference
Date: May 27-29, 2015
Location: Penticton, BC
Sponsor/Contact: Government Finance Officers Association of British Columbia
#408 - 612 View St.
Victoria, BC V8W 1J5
250-382-6871
E-mail: office@gfoabc.ca
URL: www.gfoabc.ca
Scope: Provincial

2015 Inclusion BC Conference
Date: May 27-29, 2015
Location: Vancouver, BC
Sponsor/Contact: Inclusion BC
227 - 6th St.
New Westminster, BC V3L 3A5
604-777-9100 *Fax:* 604-777-9394
Toll-Free: 800-618-1119
E-mail: info@inclusionbc.org
URL: www.inclusionbc.org
Scope: Provincial

2015 Joint Assembly of the Canadian Geophysical Union
Date: May 3-7, 2015
Location: Palais des congrès de Montréal
Montréal, QC
Sponsor/Contact: Canadian Geophysical Union
c/o Dept. of Geology & Geophysics, University of Calgary
ES #278, 2500 University Dr. NW
Calgary, AB T2N 1N4
403-220-5596 *Fax:* 403-284-0074
E-mail: cgu@ucalgary.ca
URL: www.cgu-ugc.ca
Scope: Provincial

2015 Joint Congress on Medical Imaging and Radiation Sciences
Date: May 28-30, 2015
Location: Palais des congrès de Montréal
Montréal, QC
Sponsor/Contact: Canadian Association of Medical Radiation Technologists
#1000, 85 Albert St.
Ottawa, ON K1P 6A4
613-234-0012 *Fax:* 613-234-1097
Toll-Free: 800-463-9729
E-mail: editorialoffice@camrt.ca
URL: www.camrt.ca
Scope: National

2015 MAPC Annual General Meeting and Conference
Date: May 1-2, 2015
Location: Victoria Inn and Conference Centre
Winnipeg, MB
Sponsor/Contact: Manitoba Association of Parent Councils
#1005, 401 York Ave.
Winnipeg, MB R3C 0P8
204-956-1770 *Fax:* 204-948-2855
Toll-Free: 877-290-4702
E-mail: info@mapc.mb.ca
URL: www.mapc.mb.ca
Scope: Provincial

2015 for National Wildlife Federation's 79th Annual Meeting
Date: May 27-29, 2015
Location: National Conservation Training Center
Shepherdstown, WV USA
Sponsor/Contact: National Wildlife Federation
P.O. Box 1583
Merrifield, VA 22116-1583
703-438-6000 *Fax:* 703-438-6035
Toll-Free: 800-822-9919
URL: www.nwf.org
Scope: International

25e congrès annuel du Réseau de Soins Palliatifs du Québec
Date: 14 mai au 15 mai 2015
Location: Centre des congrès de l'Hôtel Universel à Rivière-du-Loup
Rivière-du-Loup, QC
Sponsor/Contact: Réseau des soins palliatifs du Québec
P.O. Box 321 Stn. Chef
Granby, QC J2G 8E5
514-826-9400 *Fax:* 438-238-1336
E-mail: info@reseaupalliatif.org
URL: www.aqsp.org
Purpose: La réunion accueille des médecins, des professionnels et des bénévoles qui sont intéressés par les soins palliatifs. Le but de la conférence est de partager les expériences et de connaissances entre ceux dans le milieu des soins palliatifs.
Contact Information: Courriel: congresrspq@pluricongres.com

26th Annual Conference and Meeting of the Canadian Bioethics Society
Date: May 27-29, 2015
Location: Winnipeg, MB
Sponsor/Contact: Canadian Bioethics Society
561 Rocky Ridge Bay NW
Calgary, AB T3G 4E7
403-208-8027
E-mail: info@bioethics.ca
URL: www.bioethics.ca
Scope: National

32nd Annual Meeting of the Canadian Biomaterials Societ 2015
Date: May 27-30, 2015
Location: Toronto, ON
Sponsor/Contact: Canadian Biomaterials Society
URL: www.biomaterials.ca

38th British Columbia Care Providers Association Annual Conference
Date: May 24-26, 2015
Location: The Fairmont Chateau Whistler Resort
Whistler, BC
Sponsor/Contact: British Columbia Care Providers Association
#301, 1338 West Broadway
Vancouver, BC V6H 1H2
604-736-4233 *Fax:* 604-736-4266
E-mail: info@bccare.ca
URL: www.bccare.ca
Scope: Provincial

3rd Annual Canadian Writing Centres Conference
Date: May 29 - June 1, 2015
Location: University of Ottawa
Ottawa, ON
Sponsor/Contact: Canadian Association for the Study of Discourse & Writing
c/o W. Brock MacDonald, Woodsworth College, University of Toronto
119 St. George St.
Toronto, ON M5S 1A9
URL: www.cs.umanitoba.ca/~casdw
Scope: National

43rd Annual Rady JCC Sports Dinner 2015
Date: May 7, 2015
Location: RBC Convention Centre
Winnipeg, MB
Sponsor/Contact: Rose & Max Rady Jewish Community Centre
123 Doncaster St.
Winnipeg, MB R3M 0S3
204-477-7510 *Fax:* 204-477-7530
E-mail: inquiry@radyjcc.com
URL: radyjcc.com
Scope: Provincial

44e Congrès de l'Association des archivistes du Québec
Date: 27 au 29 mai 2015
Location: Hôtel Tadoussac
Tadoussac, QC
Sponsor/Contact: Association des archivistes du Québec
P.O. Box 9768 Stn. Sainte-Foy
Québec, QC G1V 4C3
418-652-2357 *Fax:* 418-646-0868
E-mail: infoaaq@archivistes.qc.ca
URL: www.archivistes.qc.ca
Contact Information: Maude Leclerc, Courriel: congres2015@archivistes.qc.ca

49th Canadian Meteorological & Oceanographic Society Congress
Date: May 31 - June 4, 2015
Location: Whistler Conference Centr
Whistler, BC
Sponsor/Contact: Canadian Meteorological & Oceanographic Society
P.O. Box 3211 Stn. D
Ottawa, ON K1P 6H7
613-990-0300 *Fax:* 613-990-1617
E-mail: cmos@cmos.ca
URL: www.cmos.ca
Scope: National

4th Climate Change Technology Conference (CCTC 2015)
Date: May 25-27, 2015
Location: Hotel Omni Mont-Royal
Montreal, QC
Sponsor/Contact: The Engineering Institute of Canada
1295 Hwy. 2 East, RR#1
Kingston, ON K7L 4V1
613-547-5989 *Fax:* 613-547-0195
E-mail: jplant1@cogeco.ca
URL: www.eic-ici.ca
Scope: National

50th Annual Canadian Transportation Research Forum Conference
Date: May 24-26, 2015
Location: Marriott Chateau Champlain
Montréal, QC
Sponsor/Contact: Canadian Transportation Research Forum
P.O. Box 23033
Woodstock, ON N4T 1R9
519-421-9701 *Fax:* 519-421-9319
URL: www.ctrf.ca
Scope: National

52nd Annual Canadian Culinary Federation 2015 National Convention
Date: May 26-31, 2015
Location: Sheration St.John's
St. John's, NL
Sponsor/Contact: Canadian Culinary Federation
c/o Roy Butterworth, National Administrator
30 Hamilton Ct.
Riverview, NB E1B 3C3
E-mail: admin@ccfcc.ca
URL: www.ccfcc.ca
Scope: National

7th Annual Electric Vehicles Conference & Trade Show 2015
Date: May 25-27, 2015
Location: Westin Nova Scotian
Halifax, NS
Sponsor/Contact: Electric Mobility Canada
#309, 9-6975 Meadowvale Town Centre Circle
Mississauga, ON L5N 2V7
905-301-5950 *Fax:* 905-826-0157
URL: www.emc-mec.ca
Scope: National
Contact Information: Twitter: twitter.com/EVVEconf; Website: www.emc-mec.ca/evve2015

83e Congrès annuel de l'Association des bibliothécaires du Québec 2015
Date: 7 mai 2015
Location: Centre de Conférence Gelber
Montréal, QC
Sponsor/Contact: Association des bibliothécaires du Québec
P.O. Box 26717 Stn. Beaconsfield
Beaconsfield, QC H9W 6G7
514-697-0146 *Fax:* 514-697-0146
E-mail: abqla@abqla.qc.ca
URL: www.abqla.qc.ca
Scope: Provincial

87th Annual BC Cattlemen's Association Convention & AGM Trade Show
Date: May 21-23, 2015
Location: Merritt, BC
Sponsor/Contact: British Columbia Cattlemen's Association
#4, 10145 Dallas Dr.
Kamloops, BC V2C 6T4
250-573-3611 *Fax:* 250-573-5155
E-mail: info@cattlemen.bc.ca
URL: www.cattlemen.bc.ca
Scope: Provincial

9th Annual Canadian Neuroscience Meeting
Date: May 24-27, 2015
Location: Westin Bayshore
Vancouver, BC
Sponsor/Contact: Canadian Association for Neuroscience
URL: can-acn.org
Scope: National
Purpose: Neuroscientists meet to discuss neuroscience research in Canada.

ARMA 2015 Canada Region Conference & Expo
Date: May 25-27, 2015
Location: Westin Calgary
Calgary, AB
Sponsor/Contact: ARMA Canada
c/o Yvonne Perry-White
195 Summerlea Rd.
Brampton, ON L6T 4P6
905-792-7099
URL: www.armacanada.org
Scope: National
Contact Information: Conference Director: Ivan Saunders, E-Mail: isaunders@accesscomm.ca; URL: armacanadaconference.org

AUTO21 Annual Conference 2015
Date: May 26-27, 2015
Location: Westin Ottawa
Ottawa, ON
Sponsor/Contact: AUTO21 Network of Centres of Excellence
401 Sunset Ave.
Windsor, ON N9B 3P4
519-253-3000 *Fax:* 519-971-3626
E-mail: info@auto21.ca
URL: www.auto21.ca
Scope: National
Purpose: Theme: A Legacy of Collaborative Innovation
Anticipated Attendance: 350

Alberta Association of Library Technicians 2015 41st Annual Conference
Date: May 28-31, 2015
Location: Radisson Hotel and Conference Centre, Canmore
Canmore, AB
Sponsor/Contact: Alberta Association of Library Technicians
P.O. Box 700
Edmonton, AB T5J 2L4
Toll-Free: 866-350-2258
E-mail: marketing@aalt.org
URL: www.aalt.org
Scope: Provincial
Purpose: Keynote speakers, program sessions, & social events of interest to library technicians
Contact Information: Alberta Association of Library Technicians Conference Committee, Toll-Free Phone: 1-866-350-2258, E-mail: conference@aalt.org

Alberta Automotive Recyclers and Dismantlers Association Annual General Meeting & Conference 2015
Date: May 1-2, 2015
Location: Calgary, AB
Sponsor/Contact: Alberta Automotive Recyclers & Dismantlers Association
24650 - 33 St. NE
Edmonton, AB T5Y 6J1
780-478-5820 *Fax:* 780-628-6463
E-mail: admin@aarda.com
URL: aarda.com
Scope: Provincial

Alberta Fire Chiefs Association 2015 Conference and Trade Show
Date: May 22-27, 2015
Location: Sheraton Red Deer Hotel
Red Deer, AB
Sponsor/Contact: Alberta Fire Chiefs Association
780-719-7939 *Fax:* 780-892-3333
URL: www.afca.ab.ca
Scope: Provincial

Alberta Motor Transport Association 2015 Annual General Meeting & Conference
Date: May 1-2, 2015
Location: Chateau Lake Louise Hotel
Banff, AB
Sponsor/Contact: Alberta Motor Transport Association
#1, 285005 Wrangler Way
Rocky View, AB T1X 0K3
Fax: 403-243-4610
Toll-Free: 800-267-1003
E-mail: amtamsc@amta.ca
URL: www.amta.ca
Scope: Provincial
Purpose: An event for transportation leaders to learn about the latest issues facing the industry & to set the direction for the association for the upcoming year
Contact Information: E-mail: amtamsc@amta.ca

Alberta Public Housing Administrators' Association Spring AGM & Education Sessions 2015
Date: May 6-7, 2015
Location: Edmonton Marriott River Cree Resort
Edmonton, AB
Sponsor/Contact: Alberta Public Housing Administrators' Association
14220 - 109 Ave. NW
Edmonton, AB T5N 4B3
780-498-1971 *Fax:* 780-464-7039
URL: www.aphaa.org
Scope: Provincial

Allied Beauty Association Trade Show - Edmonton 2015
Date: May 3-4, 2015
Location: Edmonton Expo Centre
Edmonton, AB
Sponsor/Contact: Allied Beauty Association
#26-27, 145 Traders Blvd. East
Mississauga, ON L4Z 3L3
905-568-0158 *Fax:* 905-568-1581
E-mail: abashows@abacanada.com
URL: www.abacanada.com
Scope: National
Purpose: A trade show for beauty

professionals to learn about new happenings in the beauty industry

American Industrial Hygiene Conference & Exposition 2015
Date: May 30 - June 4, 2015
Location: Salt Lake City, UT USA
Sponsor/Contact: American Industrial Hygiene Association
#777, 3141 Fariview Park Dr.
Falls Church, VA 22042
703-849-8888 *Fax:* 703-207-3561
E-mail: infonet@aiha.org
URL: www.aiha.org
Scope: International
Contact Information: Assistant Manager, Meetings: Lindsay Padilla, Phone: 703-846-0754, Email: lpadilla@aiha.org

American Society for Aesthetic Plastic Surgery 2015 Annual Meeting
Date: May 14-19, 2015
Location: Palais des congrès (Convention Centre)
Montréal, QC
Sponsor/Contact: American Society for Aesthetic Plastic Surgery
c/o Renato Saltz, M.D., FACS
5445 South Highland Dr.
Salt Lake City, UT 84117
801-274-9500 *Fax:* 801-274-9515
Toll-Free: 888-272-7711
E-mail: findasurgeon@surgery.org
URL: www.surgery.org
Scope: International

American Society of Colon & Rectal Surgeons 2015 Annual Meeting
Date: May 30 - June 3, 2015
Location: Hynes Convention Center & Sheraton Boston Hotel
Boston, MA USA
Sponsor/Contact: American Society of Colon & Rectal Surgeons
#550, 85 West Algonquin Rd.
Arlington Heights, IL 60005
847-290-9184 *Fax:* 847-290-9203
E-mail: ascrs@fascrs.org
URL: www.fascrs.org
Scope: International
Purpose: Courses, workshops, symposia, lectures, & scientific sessions for surgeons
Anticipated Attendance: 1,500+
Contact Information: Director, Exhibits: Jean Foellmer, Email: jeanfoellmer@fascrs.org

Aquaculture Canada 2015: The Aquaculture Association of Canada's Annual Conference & General Meeting
Date: May 2015
Location: Nanaimo, BC
Sponsor/Contact: Aquaculture Association of Canada
16 Lobster Lane
St. Andrews, NB E5B 3T6
506-529-4766 *Fax:* 506-529-4609
E-mail: aac@dfo-mpo.gc.ca
URL: www.aquacultureassociation.ca
Scope: National
Purpose: Featuring presentations, special sessions, workshops, & posters
Contact Information: Office Administrator: Catriona Wong, Phone: 506-529-4766, Fax: 506-529-4609, E-mail: AAC@dfo-mpo.gc.ca

Association canadienne des relations industrielles 2015 Conférence
Date: Mai 25-27, 2015
Location: HEC Montréal
Montréal, QC
Sponsor/Contact: Association canadienne des relations industrielles
Département des relations industrielles, Université Laval
#3129, 1025, av. des Sciences-Humaines
Québec, QC G1V 0A6
E-mail: acri-cira@rlt.ulaval.ca
URL: www.cira-acri.ca
Scope: National

Association of Canada Lands Surveyors 2015 11th National Surveyor's Conference
Date: May 13-15, 2015
Location: Fairmont Winnipeg
Winnipeg, MB
Sponsor/Contact: Association of Canada Lands Surveyors
100E, 900 Dynes Rd.
Ottawa, ON K2C 3L6
613-723-9200 *Fax:* 613-723-5558
URL: www.acls-aatc.ca
Scope: National
Purpose: Topics include the Code of Ethics, risk management, social media, & geodetic information, plus business meetings, award presentations, & networking opportunities
Contact Information: Administrator, Communications & Membership Services: Martha Reeve, Phone: 613-723-9200

Association of Canadian Search, Employment & Staffing Services National Conference 2015
Date: May 13-15, 2015
Location: Marriott Ch†teau Champlain
Montréal, QC
Sponsor/Contact: Association of Canadian Search, Employment & Staffing Services
#100, 2233 Argentia Rd.
Mississauga, ON L5N 2X7
905-826-6869 *Fax:* 905-826-4873
Toll-Free: 888-232-4962
E-mail: acsess@acsess.org
URL: www.acsess.org
Scope: National

Association of Ontario Midwives 2015 Annual General Meeting & Conference
Date: May 4-6, 2015
Location: Delta Toronto East
Toronto, ON
Sponsor/Contact: Association of Ontario Midwives
#301, 365 Bloor St. E.
Toronto, ON M3W 3L4
416-425-9974 *Fax:* 416-425-6905
Toll-Free: 866-418-3773
E-mail: admin@aom.on.ca
URL: www.aom.on.ca
Scope: Provincial

Association of School Business Officials of Alberta 2015 Annual Conference and Trade Show
Date: May 3-6, 2015
Location: DoubleTree by Hilton
Edmonton, AB
Sponsor/Contact: Association of School Business Officials of Alberta
#1200, 9925 - 109 St.
Edmonton, AB T5K 2J8
780-451-7103 *Fax:* 780-482-5659
URL: www.asboa.ab.ca
Scope: Provincial

Atlantic Provinces Trial Lawyers Association Annual Spring Plaintiff Practice Conference 2015
Date: May 29-30, 2015
Location: Inverary Inn
Baddeck, NS
Sponsor/Contact: Atlantic Provinces Trial Lawyers Association
PO Box 2618, Central RPO
Halifax, NS B3J 3N5
902-446-4446 *Fax:* 902-425-9552
Toll-Free: 866-314-4446
URL: www.aptla.ca
Scope: Provincial

Automotive Recyclers Association of Atlantic Canada 2015 Mid-Year Meeting
Date: May 22-23, 2015
Location: Crowne Plaza Fredericton Lord Beaverbrook Hotel
Fredericton, NB
Sponsor/Contact: Automotive Recyclers Association of Atlantic Canada
519-858-8761
E-mail: araac@execulink.com
URL: araac.ca
Scope: Provincial

BPW Ontario 69th Provincial Conference
Date: May 22-24, 2015
Location: Nottawasaga Resort
Alliston, ON
Sponsor/Contact: Canadian Federation of Business & Professional Women's Clubs
#201, Bramalea Rd.
Brampton, ON L6T 2W4
URL: www.bpwontario.org
Scope: Provincial

Bakery Showcase 2015 Trade Show & Conference
Date: May 31 - June 1, 2015
Location: Palais des congrès de Montréal
Montréal, QC
Sponsor/Contact: Baking Association of Canada
#202, 7895 Tranmere Dr.
Mississauga, ON L5S 1V9
905-405-0288 *Fax:* 905-405-0993
Toll-Free: 888-674-2253
E-mail: info@baking.ca
URL: www.baking.ca
Scope: National

Boys and Girls Clubs of Canada 13th Annual ED Symposium
Date: May 20-22, 2015
Location: Intercontinental Toronto Centre
Toronto, ON
Sponsor/Contact: Boys & Girls Clubs of Canada
National Office
#400, 2005 Sheppard Ave. East
Toronto, ON M2J 5B4
905-477-7272 *Fax:* 416-640-5331
E-mail: info@bgccan.com
URL: www.bgccan.com
Scope: National

Boys and Girls Clubs of Canada National Youth Forum 2015
Date: May 6-10, 2015
Location: University of Manitoba
Winnipeg, MB
Sponsor/Contact: Boys & Girls Clubs of Canada
National Office
#400, 2005 Sheppard Ave. East
Toronto, ON M2J 5B4
905-477-7272 *Fax:* 416-640-5331
E-mail: info@bgccan.com
URL: www.bgccan.com
Scope: National

British Columbia Association of Broadcasters 68th Annual Conference
Date: May 13-15, 2015
Location: Penticton, BC
Sponsor/Contact: British Columbia Association of Broadcasters
URL: www.bcab.ca
Scope: Provincial

British Columbia Federation of Foster Parent Associations 2015 Conference & Annual General Meeting
Date: May 22-23, 2015
Location: Hilton Whistler Resort & Spa
Whistler, BC
Sponsor/Contact: British Columbia Federation of Foster Parent Associations
#207, 22561 Dewdney Truck Rd.
Burnaby, BC V2X 3K1
604-466-7487 *Fax:* 604-466-7490
Toll-Free: 800-663-9999
E-mail: office@bcfosterparents.ca
URL: www.bcfosterparents.ca
Scope: Provincial
Purpose: Workshops & a business meeting of the federation for members from all regions of British Columbia
Contact Information: E-mail (general information): office@bcfosterparents.ca

British Columbia Historical Federation 2015 Conference: Journey to the Cariboo
Date: May 21-23, 2015
Location: Quesnel, BC
Sponsor/Contact: British Columbia Historical Federation
P.O. Box 5254 Stn. B
Victoria, BC V8R 6N4
E-mail: info@bchistory.ca
URL: www.bchistory.ca
Scope: Provincial
Purpose: Informative lectures & presentations by local historians

British Columbia Institute of Agrologists 68th Annual General Meeting & Conference 2015
Date: May 7-9, 2015
Location: Coast Capri Hotel & Laurel Packinghouse
Kelowna, BC
Sponsor/Contact: British Columbia Institute of Agrologists
2777 Claude Rd.
Victoria, BC V9B 3T7
250-380-9292 *Fax:* 250-380-9233
Toll-Free: 877-855-9291
E-mail: p.ag@bcia.com
URL: www.bcia.com
Scope: Provincial

British Columbia Library Association 2015 Conference
Date: May 20-22, 2015
Location: Sheraton Vancouver Airport Hotel
Richmond, BC
Sponsor/Contact: British Columbia Library Association
#150, 900 Howe St.
Vancouver, BC V6Z 2M4
604-683-5354 *Fax:* 604-609-0707
Toll-Free: 888-683-5354
E-mail: office@bcla.bc.ca
URL: www.bcla.bc.ca
Scope: Provincial

Conferences Index

British Columbia Nature (Federation of British Columbia Naturalists) 2015 Nature Conference & Annual General Meeting
Date: May 7-10, 2015
Location: Salt Spring, BC
Sponsor/Contact: British Columbia Nature (Federation of British Columbia Naturalists)
c/o Parks Heritage Centre
1620 Mount Seymour Rd.
North Vancouver, BC V7G 2R9
604-985-3057
E-mail: manager@bcnature.ca
URL: www.bcnature.ca
Scope: Provincial
Purpose: An annual meeting of naturalists, environmentalists, biologists, & academics who are members of British Columbia Nature
Contact Information: Office Manager: Betty Davison, E-mail: manager@bcnature.ca

British Columbia Pharmacy Association 2015 Conference
Date: May 21-23, 2015
Location: Delta Victoria Ocean Pointe Resort and Spa
Victoria, BC
Sponsor/Contact: British Columbia Pharmacy Association
#1530, 1200 West 73rd Ave.
Vancouver, BC V6P 6G5
604-261-2092 *Fax:* 604-261-2097
Toll-Free: 800-663-2840
E-mail: info@bcpharmacy.ca
URL: www.bcpharmacy.ca
Scope: Provincial
Purpose: Information & exhibits related to pharmacy in British Columbia
Contact Information: Chief Operating Officer, Member & Corporate Services: Cyril Lopez, Phone: 604-269-2869, E-mail: cyril.lopez@bcpharmacy.ca

British Columbia Play Therapy Association 2015 Annual General Meeting & Workshops
Date: May 29-30, 2015
Location: Vancouver Public Library
Vancouver, BC
Sponsor/Contact: British Columbia Play Therapy Association
#335, 2818 Main St.
Vancouver, BC V5T 0C1
778-710-7529
URL: bcplaytherapy.ca
Scope: Provincial

British Columbia Principals & Vice-Principals Association Annual Conference 2015
Date: May 11-14, 2015
Location: Fairmont Chateau Whistler
Whistler, BC
Sponsor/Contact: British Columbia Principals & Vice-Principals Association
#200, 525 - 10 Ave. West
Vancouver, BC V5Z 1K9
604-689-3399 *Fax:* 604-877-5380
Toll-Free: 800-663-0432
URL: www.bcpvpa.bc.ca
Scope: Provincial

British Columbia Recreation & Parks Association 2015 Symposium
Date: May 6-8, 2015
Location: Victoria, BC
Sponsor/Contact: British Columbia Recreation & Parks Association
#101, 4664 Lougheed Hwy.
Burnaby, BC V5C 5T5
604-629-0965 *Fax:* 604-629-2651
Toll-Free: 866-929-0965
E-mail: bcrpa@bcrpa.bc.ca
URL: www.bcrpa.bc.ca
Scope: Provincial
Purpose: An annual meeting of interest to parks & recreation professionals & volunteers, as well as elected officials from across British Columbia
Anticipated Attendance: 400+
Contact Information: Corporate Account Coordinator: Matt Anderson, Phone: 604-629-0965, ext. 239, E-mail: corpsales@bcrpa.bc.ca

British Columbia Water & Waste Association 2015 43rd Annual Conference & Trade Show
Date: May 27-30, 2015
Location: Kelowna, BC
Sponsor/Contact: British Columbia Water & Waste Association
#221, 8678 Greenall Ave.
Burnaby, BC V5J 3M6
604-433-4389 *Fax:* 604-433-9859
Toll-Free: 877-433-4389
E-mail: contact@bcwwa.org
URL: www.bcwwa.org
Scope: Provincial
Purpose: A four day conference, including technical sessions & the chance to view current products at the trade show
Anticipated Attendance: 1,250
Contact Information: Manager, Conferences & Events: Carlie Thauvette, Phone: 604-630-0011, E-mail: cthauvette@bcwwa.org

CAMPUT, Canada's Energy & Utility Regulators 2015 Conference
Date: May 10-13, 2015
Location: Hyatt Regency Hotel
Calgary, AB
Sponsor/Contact: CAMPUT, Canada's Energy & Utility Regulators
#646, 200 North Service Rd. West
Oakville, ON L6M 2Y1
905-827-5139 *Fax:* 905-827-3260
E-mail: info@camput.org
URL: www.camput.org
Scope: National
Purpose: An annual event to address current regulatory issues & energy related subjects
Contact Information: E-mail: info@camput.org

CAPM&R 63rd Annual Scientific Meeting
Date: May 20-23, 2015
Location: Sheraton Vancouver Wall Centre
Vancouver, BC
Sponsor/Contact: Canadian Association of Physical Medicine & Rehabilitation
Ottawa, ON
613-707-0483 *Fax:* 613-707-0480
E-mail: info@capmr.ca
URL: www.capmr.ca
Scope: National

CAUCE 2015: The 62nd Annual Conference & General Meeting of the Canadian Association for University Continuing Education
Date: May 27-29, 2015
Location: University of Manitoba
Winnipeg, MB
Sponsor/Contact: Canadian Association for University Continuing Education
c/o Centre for Continuing & Distance Education, U. of Saskatchewan
#464, 221 Cumberland Ave. North
Saskatoon, SK S7N 1M3
306-966-5604 *Fax:* 306-966-5590
E-mail: cauce.secratariat@usask.ca
URL: www.cauce-aepuc.ca
Scope: National

CDSR 2015: International Conference of Control, Dynamic Systems, and Robotics
Date: May 7-8, 2015
Location: Ottawa, ON
Sponsor/Contact: International Academy of Science, Engineering & Technology
#414, 1376 Bank St.
Ottawa, ON K1H 7Y3
613-695-3040
E-mail: info@international-aset.com
URL: www.international-aset.com
Scope: National
Purpose: Annual conference in fields related to traditional and modern control and dynamic systems.
Contact Information: Website: dscconference.com

Canada's Venture Capital & Private Equity Association 2015 Annual Conference
Date: May 19, 2015
Location: Westin Bayshore
Vancouver, BC
Sponsor/Contact: Canada's Venture Capital & Private Equity Association
Heritage Bldg., MaRS Centre
#120J, 101 College St.
Toronto, ON M5G 1L7
416-487-0519 *Fax:* 416-487-5899
E-mail: cvca@cvca.ca
URL: www.cvca.ca

Canadian Association for Commonwealth Literature & Language Studies 2015 Annual Conference
Date: May 30 - June 1, 2015
Location: University of Ottawa
Ottawa, ON
Sponsor/Contact: Canadian Association for Commonwealth Literature & Language Studies
c/o Kristina Fagan, Department of English, University of Saskatchewan
9 Campus Dr.
Saskatoon, SK S7N 5A5
URL: www.caclals.ca
Scope: National
Purpose: Keynote speakers, roundtables, sessions, & readings

Canadian Association for Conservation 2015 41st Annual Conference & Workshop
Date: May 26-30, 2015
Location: Edmonton, AB
Sponsor/Contact: Canadian Association for Conservation of Cultural Property
c/o Danielle Allard
#419, 207 Bank St.
Ottawa, ON K2P 2N2
613-231-3977 *Fax:* 613-231-4406
E-mail: coordinator@cac-accr.com
URL: www.cac-accr.ca
Scope: National
Purpose: Educational sessions & a tradeshow
Contact Information: Conference Chair: Kateri Morin, E-mail: kateri.morin@mcc.gouv.qc.ca

Canadian Association for Enterostomal Therapy National Conference 2015
Date: May 21-24, 2015
Location: Halifax Marriott Harbourfront Hotel
Halifax, NS
Sponsor/Contact: Canadian Association for Enterostomal Therapy
66 Leopolds Dr.
Ottawa, ON K1V 7E3
Fax: 613-834-6351
Toll-Free: 888-739-5072
E-mail: office@caet.ca
URL: www.caet.ca
Scope: National

Canadian Association for Food Studies 10th Annual Assembly: Capital Ideas - Nourishing Debates, Minds and Bodies
Date: May 30 - June 2, 2015
Location: University of Ottawa
Ottawa, ON
Sponsor/Contact: Canadian Association for Food Studies
c/o Centre for Studies in Food Security, Ryerson University
350 Victoria St.
Toronto, ON M5B 2K3
416-979-5000 *Fax:* 416-979-5362
E-mail: cafsadmin@foodstudies.ca
URL: cafs.landfood.ubc.ca
Scope: National

Canadian Association for Health Services and Polivc ResearchConference 2015
Date: May 26-28, 2015
Location: Hilton Bonaventure
Montreal, QC
Sponsor/Contact: Canadian Association for Health Services & Policy Research
292 Somerset St. West
Ottawa, ON K2P 0J6
613-288-9239 *Fax:* 613-599-7805
E-mail: info@cahspr.ca
URL: www.cahspr.ca
Scope: National

Canadian Association for Music Therapy 2015 Conference
Date: May 22-24, 2015
Location: Calgary, AB
Sponsor/Contact: Canadian Association for Music Therapy
#320, 110 Cumberland St.
Toronto, ON M5R 3V5
416-944-0421 *Fax:* 416-944-0431
Toll-Free: 800-996-2268
E-mail: camt@musictherapy.ca
URL: www.musictherapy.ca
Scope: National

Canadian Association for Pharmacy Distribution Management 2015 Annual Conference
Date: May 2-6, 2015
Location: Omni Scottsdale Resort & Spa at Montelucia
Paradise Valley, AZ USA
Sponsor/Contact: Canadian Association for Pharmacy Distribution Management
#301A, 3800 Steeles Ave. West
Woodbridge, ON L4L 4G9
905-265-1706 *Fax:* 905-265-9372
URL: www.capdm.ca
Scope: National
Purpose: Information for pharmacy supply chain industry professionals

Contact Information: Canadian Association for Pharmacy Distribution Management, Phone: 905-265-1706

Canadian Association for Theatre Research 2015 Conference: "Capital Ideas"
Date: May 30 - June 2, 2015
Location: Ottawa, ON
Sponsor/Contact: Canadian Association for Theatre Research
c/o Peter Kuling
#2507, 140 Erskine Ave.
Toronto, ON M4P 1Z2
416-303-0441 *Fax:* 647-344-6198
E-mail: catr.membership@gmail.com
URL: www.catr-acrt.ca
Scope: National

Canadian Association for the Prevention of Discrimination and Harassment in Higher Education 2015 Conference
Date: May 20-22, 2015
Location: Toronto, ON
Sponsor/Contact: Canadian Association for the Prevention of Discrimination & Harassment in Higher Education
c/o University of British Columbia
Vancouver, BC V6T 1Z2
604-822-4859 *Fax:* 604-822-3260
E-mail: amlong@ubc.ca
URL: www.capdhhe.org
Scope: National

Canadian Association of Accredited Mortgage Professionals 2015 Québec Regional Symposium & Trade Show
Date: May 5, 2015
Location: Montréal, QC
Sponsor/Contact: Canadian Association of Accredited Mortgage Professionals
Atria II
#1401, 2235 Sheppard Ave. East
Toronto, ON M2J 5B5
416-385-2333 *Fax:* 416-385-1177
Toll-Free: 888-442-4625
E-mail: info@caamp.org
URL: www.caamp.org
Scope: Provincial
Contact Information: E-mail: events@caamp.org

Canadian Association of Defence & Security Industries 2015 Trade Show
Date: May 27-28, 2015
Sponsor/Contact: Canadian Association of Defence & Security Industries
#300, 251 Laurier Ave. West'
Ottawa, ON K1P 5J6
613-235-5337 *Fax:* 613-235-0784
E-mail: cadsi@defenceandsecurity.ca
URL: www.defenceandsecurity.ca
Scope: National
Anticipated Attendance: 11,000+

Canadian Association of Emergency Physicians (CAEP) 2015 Annual Conference
Date: May 30 - June 3, 2015
Location: Shaw Conference Centre
Edmonton, AB
Sponsor/Contact: Canadian Association of Emergency Physicians
#808, 180 Elgin St.
Ottawa, ON K2P 2K3
613-523-3343 *Fax:* 613-523-0190
Toll-Free: 800-463-1158
E-mail: admin@caep.ca
URL: www.caep.ca
Scope: National

Canadian Association of Law Libraries Annual General Meeting, 2015
Date: May 3-6, 2015
Location: Moncton, NB
Sponsor/Contact: Canadian Association of Law Libraries
P.O. Box 1570
#310, 4 Cataraqui St.
Kingston, ON K7L 5C8
613-531-9338 *Fax:* 613-531-0626
E-mail: office@callacbd.ca
URL: www.callacbd.ca
Scope: National

Canadian Association of Nurses in HIV/AIDS Care Conference 2015
Date: May 14-16, 2015
Location: Ottawa, ON
Sponsor/Contact: Canadian Association of Nurses in HIV/AIDS Care
St. Paul's Hospital
#B552, 1081 Burrard St.
Vancouver, BC V6Z 1Y6
E-mail: admin@canac.org
URL: www.canac.org
Scope: National
Contact Information: Email: canac2015@gmail.com

Canadian Association of Occupational Therapists 2015 Annual Conference
Date: May 27-30, 2015
Location: Winnipeg, MB
Sponsor/Contact: Canadian Association of Occupational Therapists
CTTC Building
#3400, 1125 Colonel By Dr.
Ottawa, ON K1S 5R1
613-523-2268 *Fax:* 613-523-2552
Toll-Free: 800-434-2268
E-mail: insurance@caot.ca
URL: www.caot.ca
Scope: National
Purpose: A scientific program & exhibits
Contact Information: Conference & Advertising Manager: Lisa Sheehan, E-mail: conference@caot.ca

Canadian Association of Pharmacy Technicians Professional Development Conference 2015
Date: May 1-3, 2015
Location: Delta Halifax
Halifax, NS
Sponsor/Contact: Canadian Association of Pharmacy Technicians
#164, 9-6975 Meadowvale Town Centre Circle
Mississauga, ON L5N 2V7
416-410-1142
E-mail: info@capt.ca
URL: www.capt.ca
Scope: National

Canadian Association of Pharmacy in Oncology Conference 2015
Date: May 21 - 24, 2015
Location: Delta St. John's Hotel and Conference Centre
St. John's, NL
Sponsor/Contact: Canadian Association of Pharmacy in Oncology
c/o Sea to Sky Meeting Management Inc.
#206, 201 Bewicke Ave.
Winnipeg, MB V7M 3M7
778-338-4142 *Fax:* 704-984-6434
E-mail: info@capho.org
URL: www.capho.ca
Scope: National

Canadian Association of Professional Academic Librarians 2015 Annual Conference
Date: May 31 - June 2, 2015
Location: Ottawa, ON
Sponsor/Contact: Canadian Association of Professional Academic Librarians
E-mail: capalibrarians@gmail.com
URL: capalibrarians.org
Scope: National

Canadian Association of Radiologists 78th Annual Scientific Meeting
Date: May 28-30, 2015
Location: Palais des congrès
Montréal, QC
Sponsor/Contact: Canadian Association of Radiologists
#310, 377 Dalhousie St.
Ottawa, ON K1N 9N8
613-860-3111 *Fax:* 613-860-3112
E-mail: membership@car.ca
URL: www.car.ca
Scope: National
Purpose: The theme of the event is Collaborative Care - Imaging and Treatment
Contact Information: URL: jointcongress.ca

Canadian Association of Research Libraries 2015 Spring Meeting
Date: May 12-14, 2015
Location: Toronto, ON
Sponsor/Contact: Canadian Association of Research Libraries
Morisset Library, University of Ottawa
#239, 65 University St.
Ottawa, ON K1N 9A5
613-562-5385 *Fax:* 613-562-5297
E-mail: carladm@uottawa.ca
URL: www.carl-abrc.ca
Scope: National
Purpose: A spring meeting to set the future direction of the association & Canadian research libraries
Contact Information: Program & Administrative Officer: Katherine McColgan, Phone: 613-482-9344, ext. 102, E-mail: Katherine.McColgan@carl-abrc.ca

Canadian Association of Slavists 2015 Annual Conference (in conjunction with the Canadian Federation for the Humanities & Social Sciences Congress)
Date: May 30 - June 1, 2015
Location: University of Ottawa
Ottawa, ON
Sponsor/Contact: Canadian Association of Slavists
Alumni Hall, Dept. of History & Classics, University of Alberta
#2, 28 Tory Bldg.
Edmonton, AB T6G 2H4
780-492-2566 *Fax:* 780-492-9125
E-mail: csp@ulberta.ca
URL: www.ualberta.ca/~csp/cas/contact.html
Scope: National
Purpose: A yearly meeting with roundtable discussions, panels, & the presentation of papers by members of the Canadian Association of Slavists

Canadian Association of University Research Administrators 2015 Annual General Meeting
Date: May 24-27, 2015
Location: Fairmont Royal York Hotel
Toronto, ON
Sponsor/Contact: Canadian Association of University Research Administrators
c/o JPDL Quebec
189 St. Paul Rd.
Québec, QC G1K 3W2
418-692-6636 *Fax:* 418-692-5587
E-mail: caura-acaru@jpdl.com
URL: www.caura-acaru.ca
Scope: National

Canadian Association of University Teachers 2015 Annual Workshop for New Presidents
Date: May 29-30, 2015
Location: Ottawa, ON
Sponsor/Contact: Canadian Association of University Teachers
2705 Queensview Dr.
Ottawa, ON K2B 8K2
613-820-2270 *Fax:* 613-820-7244
E-mail: acppu@caut.ca
URL: www.caut.ca
Scope: National
Purpose: An examination fo the role of faculty association presidents

Canadian Astronomical Society 2015 Annual Meeting
Date: May 24-27, 2015
Location: McMaster University
Hamilton, ON
Sponsor/Contact: Canadian Astronomical Society
c/o R. Hanes, Dept. of Physics, Engineering, Physics & Astronomy
64 Bader Lane, Stirling Hall, Queen's University
Kingston, ON K7L 3N6
613-533-6000 *Fax:* 613-533-6463
E-mail: casca@astro.queensu.ca
URL: www.casca.ca
Scope: National
Purpose: Annual meetings are open to all interested persons, but the presentation of scientific papers is restricted to members or applicants for membership & speakers invited by the Local Organizing Committee

Canadian Athletic Therapists Association's 49th National Conference
Date: May 28-30, 2015
Location: Westin Nova Scotian
Halifax, NS
Sponsor/Contact: Canadian Athletic Therapists Association
#300, 400 - 5th Ave. SW
Calgary, AB T2P 0L6
403-509-2282 *Fax:* 403-509-2280
E-mail: info@athletictherapy.org
URL: www.athletictherapy.org
Scope: National
Contact Information: URL: conference.athletictherapy.org

Canadian Authors Association, National Capital Region Branch 29th Annual National Capital Writing Contest Awards Night
Date: May 12, 2015
Location: Ottawa, ON
Sponsor/Contact: Canadian Authors Association
Ottawa, ON
E-mail: cdn-authors-ncr@live.ca
URL: www.canauthors-ottawa.org
Scope: Local
Purpose: Awards to recognize the best adult short story, youth short story or essay, & poetry

Conferences Index

Canadian Board of Marine Underwriters 2015 Semi-Annual Meeting
Date: May 20-21, 2015
Location: Delta St. John's Hotel & Conference Centre
St. John's, NL
Sponsor/Contact: Canadian Board of Marine Underwriters
#100, 2233 Argentia Rd.
Mississauga, ON L5N 2X7
905-826-4768 *Fax:* 905-826-4873
E-mail: info@cbmu.com
URL: www.cbmu.com
Scope: National
Purpose: A gathering of representatives from the marine insurance industry of Canada
Contact Information: Administrator: Halyna Troian, E-mail: cbmu@cbmu.com

Canadian Comparative Literature Association 2015 Annual Meeting (in conjunction with the Congress of the Humanities & Social Sciences)
Date: May 2015
Location: University of Ottawa
Ottawa, ON
Sponsor/Contact: Canadian Comparative Literature Association
c/o Markus Reisenleitner, Department of Humanities, York University
217 Vanier College
Toronto, ON M3H 1P3
URL: complit.ca
Scope: National
Purpose: Each yearly meeting of the Canadian Comparative Literature Association is held at the Congress of the Humanities & Social Sciences
Contact Information: Canadian Comparative Literature Association Treasurer: Paul D. Morris, E-mail: pdmorris@ustboniface.mb.ca

Canadian Council for Refugees 2015 Spring Consultation
Date: May 21-23, 2015
Sponsor/Contact: Canadian Council for Refugees
#302, 6839, rue Drolet
Montréal, QC H2S 2T1
514-277-7223 *Fax:* 514-277-1447
E-mail: info@ccrweb.ca
URL: www.ccrweb.ca
Scope: National
Purpose: A meeting of refugees, immigrants, representatives of NGOs, government, academics, community workers, youth advocates, & international guests to examine issues that affect newcomers to Canada
Contact Information: E-mail: info@ccrweb.ca

Canadian Council for Small Business & Entrepreneurship 2015 Conference
Date: May 28-30, 2015
Location: MacEwan University School of Business
Edmonton, AB
Sponsor/Contact: Canadian Council for Small Business & Entrepreneurship
c/o Pat Sargeant, Women's Enterprise Centre of Manitoba
#100, 207 Donald St.
Winnipeg, MB R3C 1M5
204-988-1873 *Fax:* 902-988-1871
E-mail: ccsbesecretariat@wecm.ca
URL: www.ccsbe.org
Scope: National

Canadian Council of Cardiovascular Nurses 2015 Spring Nursing Conference
Date: May 29, 2015
Location: Ottawa, ON
Sponsor/Contact: Canadian Council of Cardiovascular Nurses
#202, 300 March Rd.
Ottawa, ON K1P 5V9
613-599-9210 *Fax:* 613-595-1155
E-mail: info@cccn.ca
URL: www.cccn.ca
Scope: National

Canadian Counselling and Psychotherapy Association 2015 Annual Conference
Date: May 19-22, 2015
Location: Sheraton on the Falls Hotel
Niagara Falls, ON
Sponsor/Contact: Canadian Counselling & Psychotherapy Association
#114, 223 Colonnade Rd. South
Ottawa, ON K2E 7K3
613-237-1099 *Fax:* 613-237-9786
Toll-Free: 877-765-5565
E-mail: info@ccpa-accp.ca
URL: www.ccpa-accp.ca
Scope: National

Canadian Down Syndrome Society 2015 28th National Conference
Date: May 15-17, 2015
Location: Edmonton, AB
Sponsor/Contact: Canadian Down Syndrome Society
#103, 2003 - 14 St. NW
Calgary, AB T2M 3N4
403-270-8500 *Fax:* 403-270-8291
E-mail: info@cdss.ca
URL: www.cdss.ca
Scope: National

Canadian Educational Researchers' Association 2015 Annual Meeting & Reception
Date: May 30 - June 3, 2015
Location: University of Ottawa
Ottawa, ON
Sponsor/Contact: Canadian Educational Researchers' Association
c/o Don Klinger, Duncan McArthur Hall, Faculty of Education
Queen's University
Kingston, ON K7M 5R7
URL: www.csse-scee.ca/cera
Scope: National
Purpose: An event offering an annual review of the association's activities, plus professional interactions with other CERA members from across Canada.
Contact Information: URL: www.csse-scee.ca/conference

Canadian Engineering Education Association 2015 Conference
Date: May 31 - June 3, 2015
Location: McMaster University
Hamilton, ON
Sponsor/Contact: Canadian Engineering Education Association
c/o Design Engineering, University of Manitoba
E2-262 EITC, 75 Chancellors Circle
Winnipeg, MB R3T 5V6
204-474-7113 *Fax:* 204-474-7676
E-mail: ceea@umanitoba.ca
URL: ceea.ca
Scope: National

Canadian Federation for Humanities & Social Sciences' Congress of the Humanities & Social Sciences 2015
Date: May 30 - June 5
Location: University of Ottawa
Ottawa, ON
Sponsor/Contact: Canadian Federation for Humanities & Social Sciences
#300, 275 Bank St.
Ottawa, ON K2P 2I6
613-238-6112 *Fax:* 613-238-6114
E-mail: fedcan@fedcan.ca
URL: www.fedcan.ca
Scope: International
Purpose: Educational events, exhibits, & networking opportunities for researchers, policy makers, graduate students, & community members
Anticipated Attendance: 6,500+
Contact Information: E-mail: congress@fedcan.ca; Website: congress2015.ca

Canadian Gerontological Nursing Association 18th Biennial Conference
Date: May 27-30, 2015
Location: Charlottetown, PE
Sponsor/Contact: Canadian Gerontological Nursing Association
#1202, 71 Charles St. East
Toronto, ON M4Y 2T3
416-927-8654 *Fax:* 604-874-4378
E-mail: cgna@malachite-mgmt.com
URL: www.cgna.net
Scope: National
Contact Information: URL: cgnaconference.ca; Email: CGNA.conference@gmail.com

Canadian Group Psychotherapy Association's 35th Annual Conference
Date: May 6-9, 2015
Location: Toronto, ON
Sponsor/Contact: Canadian Group Psychotherapy Association
902-473-8604 *Fax:* 902-425-9699
E-mail: canadiangpa@gmail.com
URL: www.cgpa.ca
Scope: National

Canadian Hard of Hearing Association 2015 National Conference, Annual General Meeting, & Trade Show
Date: May 21-23, 2015
Location: The Westin Nova Scotia
Halifax, NS
Sponsor/Contact: Canadian Hard of Hearing Association
#205, 2415 Holly Lane
Ottawa, ON K1V 7P2
613-526-1584 *Fax:* 613-526-4718
Toll-Free: 800-263-8068
E-mail: chhanational@chha.ca
URL: www.chha.ca
Scope: National
Purpose: Educational workshops & plenary sessions
Contact Information: General Conference Information, Toll-Free Phone: 1-800-263-8068, TTY: 613-526-2692, Fax: 613-526-4718, E-mail: conference@chha.ca

Canadian Institute of Mining, Metallurgy & Petroleum 2015 Annual Conference & Exhibition
Date: May 9-13, 2015
Location: Palais des Congrès
Montréal, QC
Sponsor/Contact: Canadian Institute of Mining, Metallurgy & Petroleum
CIM National Office
#1250, 3500, boul de Maisonneuve ouest
Westmount, QC H3Z 3C1
514-939-2710 *Fax:* 514-939-2714
E-mail: cim@cim.org
URL: www.cim.org
Scope: National
Purpose: A mining event, featuring a technical program, workshops, field trips, a student program, & a social program
Contact Information: Events Director: Lise Bujold; Phone: 514-939-2710, ext. 1308; E-mail: lbujold@cim.org

Canadian Investor Relations Institute 28th Annual Conference
Date: May 31 - June 2, 2015
Location: Fairmont Banff Springs
Banff, AB
Sponsor/Contact: Canadian Investor Relations Institute
#601, 67 Yonge St.
Toronto, ON M5E 1J8
416-364-8200 *Fax:* 416-364-2805
E-mail: enquiries@ciri.org
URL: www.ciri.org
Scope: National

Canadian Nuclear Society 2015 Annual Conference & CNS/CNA Student Conference
Date: May 31 - June 3
Location: Saint John Trade & Convention Center
Saint John, NB
Sponsor/Contact: Canadian Nuclear Society
655 Bay St., 17th Fl.
Toronto, ON M5G 2K4
416-977-7620 *Fax:* 416-977-8131
E-mail: cns-snc@on.aibn.com
URL: www.cns-snc.ca
Scope: National
Purpose: A meeting open to all persons interested in nuclear science, nuclear engineering, & technology, featuring the presentation of Canadian Nuclear Society awards
Contact Information: Canadian Nuclear Society Office: Phone: 416-977-7620, E-mail: cns-snc@on.aibn.com; URL: www.cnsconference2015.org

Canadian Nutrition Society 2015 5th Annual Meeting
Date: May 28-30, 2015
Location: RBC Convention Centre
Winnipeg, MB
Sponsor/Contact: Canadian Nutrition Society
#310, 2175 Sheppard Ave. East
Toronto, ON M2J 1W8
416-491-7188 *Fax:* 416-491-1670
Toll-Free: 888-414-7188
E-mail: info@cns-scn.ca
URL: www.cns-scn.ca
Scope: National
Purpose: Conference sessions & the presentation of awards
Contact Information: Phone: 416-491-7188, Fax: 416-491-1670, E-mail: info@cns-scn.ca

Canadian Orthopaedic Nurses Association 2015 Annual Conference
Date: May 24-27, 2015
Location: Fredericton Convention Center
Fredericton, NB
Sponsor/Contact: Canadian Orthopaedic Nurses Association
2035 Rosealle In
West Kelowna, BC V1Z 3Z5

250-769-3640
URL: www.cona-nurse.org
Scope: National
Contact Information: Nancy Schuttenbeld, Conference Chair; Email: Nancy.schuttenbeld@horizonnb.ca

Canadian Pain Society 2015 36th Annual Scientific Meeting
Date: May 20-23, 2015
Location: Delta Hotel & Convention Centre
Charlottetown, PE
Sponsor/Contact: Canadian Pain Society
#202, 1143 Wentworth St. West
Oshawa, ON L1J 8P7
905-404-9545 *Fax:* 905-404-3727
E-mail: office@canadianpainsociety.ca
URL: www.canadianpainsociety.ca
Scope: National
Purpose: The exchange of current information about pain assessment, pain mechanisms, & pain management for healthcare professionals, scientists, & trainees from clinical, research, industry, & policy settings
Contact Information: Office Manager, Canadian Pain Society Office: Ellen Maracle-Benton, E-mail: ellen@canadianpainsociety.ca

Canadian Pension & Benefits Institute Forum 2015
Date: May 25-27, 2015
Location: New York Hilton Midtown
New York City, NY USA
Sponsor/Contact: Canadian Pension & Benefits Institute
CPBI National Office
1175, av Union
Montréal, QC H3B 3C3
514-288-1222 *Fax:* 514-288-1225
E-mail: info@cpbi-icra.ca
URL: www.cpbi-icra.ca
Scope: International
Purpose: Theme: Definig Our Future

Canadian Pharmacists Association 2015 103rd Annual National Conference
Date: May 30 - June 2, 2015
Location: The Westin Ottawa
Ottawa, ON
Sponsor/Contact: Canadian Pharmacists Association
1785 Alta Vista Dr.
Ottawa, ON K1G 3Y6
613-523-7877 *Fax:* 613-523-0445
Toll-Free: 800-917-9489
E-mail: info@pharmacists.ca
URL: www.pharmacists.ca
Scope: National
Purpose: An educational program, plus a trade show, & networking events for pharmacists from throughout Canada
Contact Information: E-mail: info@pharmacists.ca

Canadian Public Health Association 2015 Conference
Date: May 25-28, 2015
Location: Vancouver, BC
Sponsor/Contact: Canadian Public Health Association
#300, 1565 Carling Ave.
Ottawa, ON K1Z 8R1
613-725-3769 *Fax:* 613-725-9826
E-mail: info@cpha.ca
URL: www.cpha.ca
Scope: National
Purpose: A conference for policy-makers, researchers, environmental health professionals, academics, & students from across Canada
Contact Information: Conference Manager: Sarah Pettenuzzo, Phone: 613-725-3769, ext. 153; Conference Officer: Julie Paquette, Phone: 613-725-3769, ext. 126

Canadian Public Relations Society / La Société canadienne des relations publiques 2015 National Summit
Date: May 31 - June 2, 2015
Location: Montréal, QC
Sponsor/Contact: Canadian Public Relations Society Inc.
#346, 4195 Dundas St. West
Toronto, ON M8X 1Y4
416-239-7034 *Fax:* 416-239-1076
E-mail: admin@cprs.ca
URL: www.cprs.ca
Scope: National
Purpose: An education conference, with networking opportunities with public relations professionals from across Canada
Contact Information: E-mail: admin@cprs.ca

Canadian Science Writers' Association 44th Annual Conference
Date: May 28-31, 2015
Location: Saskatoon, SK
Sponsor/Contact: Canadian Science Writers' Association
P.O. Box 75 Stn. A
Toronto, ON M5W 1A2
Toll-Free: 800-796-8595
E-mail: office@sciencewriters.ca
URL: www.sciencewriters.ca
Scope: National

Canadian Society for Civil Engineering 2015 Annual General Meeting & Conference
Date: May 27-30, 2015
Location: Regina, SK
Sponsor/Contact: Canadian Society for Civil Engineering
4877, rue Sherbrooke ouest
Montréal, QC H3Z 1G9
514-933-2634 *Fax:* 514-933-3504
E-mail: info@csce.ca
URL: www.csce.ca
Scope: National

Canadian Society for Medical Laboratory Science / Société canadienne de science de laboratoire médical LABCON2015
Date: May 23-25, 2015
Location: Fairmont Queen Elizabeth
Montreal, QC
Sponsor/Contact: Canadian Society for Medical Laboratory Science
33 Wellington Ave. North
Hamilton, ON L8R 1M7
905-528-8642 *Fax:* 905-528-4968
Toll-Free: 800-263-8277
URL: www.csmls.org
Scope: National
Contact Information: Web Site: labcon.csmls.org; LABCON Hotline: 1-800-263-8277

Canadian Society for Pharmaceutical Sciences 2015 Annual Symposium
Date: May 26-28, 2015
Location: Eaton Chelsea Hotel
Toronto, ON
Sponsor/Contact: Canadian Society for Pharmaceutical Sciences
Katz Group Centre, University of Alberta
#2-020L, 11361 - 87 Ave.
Edmonton, AB T6G 2E1
780-492-0950 *Fax:* 780-492-0951
URL: www.cspscanada.org
Scope: National
Purpose: Educational sessions, networking opportunities, & the presentation of awards
Contact Information: Phone: 780-492-0950

Canadian Society for Transfusion Medicine Conference 2015
Date: May 21-24, 2015
Location: Fort Garry Hotel
Winnipeg, MB
Sponsor/Contact: Canadian Society for Transfusion Medicine
#6, 20 Crown Steel Dr.
Markham, ON L3R 9X9
905-415-3917 *Fax:* 905-415-0071
Toll-Free: 855-415-3917
E-mail: office@transfusion.ca
URL: www.transfusion.ca
Scope: National
Purpose: Theme: "Where Past and Future Meet"

Canadian Society for the History of Medicine & Canadian Association for the History of Nursing 2015 Annual Conference
Date: May 30 - June 1, 2015
Location: University of Ottawa
Ottawa, ON
Sponsor/Contact: Canadian Association for the History of Nursing
c/o Jayne Elliot, School of Nursing, University of Ottawa
451 Smyth Rd.
Ottawa, ON K1H 8M5
URL: www.cahn-achn.ca
Purpose: The theme of the conference is "Capital Ideas," asking attendees to consider the different ways ideas affect society

Canadian Society for the History of Medicine 2015 Annual Conference (In conjunction with the 2015 Congress of the Humanities & Social Sciences)
Date: May 30 - June 1, 2015
Location: University of Ottawa
Ottawa, ON
Sponsor/Contact: Canadian Society for the History of Medicine
c/o Brock University, Community Health Sciences
500 Glendridge Ave.
St. Catharines, ON L2S 3A1
905-688-5550 *Fax:* 905-688-8954
URL: www.cshm-schm.ca
Scope: National
Purpose: Events include the the annual AMS / Paterson Lecture by an historian of medicine, & the H.N. Segall Prize which honours the best student paper

Canadian Society for the Study of Religion Congress 2015
Date: May 30 - June 2, 2015
Location: University of Ottawa
Ottawa, ON
Sponsor/Contact: Canadian Society for the Study of Religion
c/o Dr. Arlene Macdonald
#2.104, 301 University Blvd.
Galveston, TX 77555-1311
URL: www.cssrscer.ca
Scope: Provincial
Purpose: Theme: "Capital Ideas"

Canadian Society of Association Executives, Ottawa-Gatineau Chapter, 2015 Annual General Meeting Luncheon
Date: May 27, 2015
Location: Fairmont Chateau Laurier
Ottawa, ON
Sponsor/Contact: Canadian Society of Association Executives
c/o Royal College of Physicians and Surgeons of Canada
773 Echo Dr.
Ottawa, ON K1S 5N8
613-730-6237
E-mail: tcohen@rcpsc.edu
URL: www.csae.com/ottawa
Scope: Local
Contact Information: E-mail: csae.ottawa-gatineau@rogers.com

Canadian Society of Biblical Studies 2015 Annual Meeting (in conjunction with the 2015 Congress of the Humanities & Social Sciences)
Date: May 30 - June 1, 2015
Location: University of Ottawa
Ottawa, ON
Sponsor/Contact: Canadian Society of Biblical Studies
c/o Prof. Robert A. Derrenbacker, Jr., Regent College
5800 University Blvd.
Vancouver, BC V6T 2E4
URL: www.ccsr.ca/csbs
Scope: National

Canadian Society of Church History 2015 Annual Meeting (in conjunction with the 2015 Congress of the Humanities & Social Sciences)
Date: May 30 - June 1 2015
Location: University of Ottawa
Ottawa, ON
Sponsor/Contact: Canadian Society of Church History
c/o Robynne R. Healey, Dept. of History, Trinity Western University
7600 Glover Rd.
Langley, BC V2Y 1Y1
E-mail: robynne.healey@twu.ca
URL: churchhistcan.wordpress.com
Scope: National

Canadian Society of Exploration Geophysicists GeoConvention 2015 (Focus 2015)
Date: May 4-8, 2015
Location: Calgary TELUS Convention Centre
Calgary, AB
Sponsor/Contact: Canadian Society of Exploration Geophysicists
#600, 640 - 8th Ave. SW
Calgary, AB T2P 1G7
403-262-0015
E-mail: cseg.office@shaw.ca
URL: www.cseg.ca
Scope: National
Purpose: Technical information for persons involved in earth sciences, from geologists to reservior engineers, & managers
Contact Information: URL: www.geoconvention.com

Canadian Society of Medievalists 2015 Conference
Date: May 30 - June 2, 2015
Location: University of Ottawa
Ottawa, ON
Sponsor/Contact: Canadian Society of Medievalists

104 Mount Aubrun St., 5th Fl.
Cambridge, MA 02138
617-491-1622 *Fax:* 617-492-3303
E-mail: csmtreasurer@gmail.com
URL: www.canadianmedievalists.ca
Scope: National

Canadian Society of Patristic Studies 2015 Annual Meeting
Date: May 2015
Location: University of Ottawa
Ottawa, ON
Sponsor/Contact: Canadian Society of Patristic Studies
c/o Dr. S. Muir, Religious Studies, Concordia University College of AB
7128 Ada Blvd.
Edmonton, AB T5B 4E4
URL: www.ccsr.ca/csps
Scope: National

Canadian Society of Respiratory Therapists 2015 Annual Education Conference & Trade Show
Date: May 21-23, 2015
Location: Hyatt Regency Hotel
Calgary, AB
Sponsor/Contact: Canadian Society of Respiratory Therapists
#400, 301 Cooper St.
Ottawa, ON K1G 3Y6
613-731-3164 *Fax:* 613-521-4314
Toll-Free: 800-267-3422
E-mail: info@csrt.com
URL: www.csrt.com
Scope: National
Purpose: Featuring internationally renowned speakers, workshops, & presentations for respiratory therapists
Anticipated Attendance: 400+
Contact Information: Education Conference & Trade Show Contact: Lindsey Naddaf, Phone: 613-731-3164, ext. 231

Canadian Society of Zoologists 2015 54th Annual Congress
Date: May 11-15, 2015
Location: University of Calgary
Calgary, AB
Sponsor/Contact: Canadian Society of Zoologists
c/o Biology Department, University of Western Ontario
London, ON N6A 5B7
519-661-3869
URL: www.csz-scz.ca
Scope: National
Purpose: A conference to advance the study of animals & their environment
Contact Information: Secretary: Helga Guderley, E-mail: helga.guderley@bio.ulaval.ca

Canadian Theological Society Conference (Congress)
Sponsor/Contact: Canadian Theological Society
c/o M. Beavis, St. Thomas More College
1437 College Dr.
Saskatoon, SK S7N 0W6
E-mail: secretary@cts-stc.ca
URL: cts-stc.ca
Scope: National

Canadian Union of Postal Workers National Convention 2015
Date: May 4-8, 2015
Sponsor/Contact: Canadian Union of Postal Workers
377 Bank St.
Ottawa, ON K2P 1Y3
613-236-7238 *Fax:* 613-563-7861
E-mail: feedback@cupw-sttp.org
URL: www.cupw-sttp.org
Scope: National

Canadian Union of Public Employees (CUPE) Ontario 2015 52nd Convention
Date: May 27-30, 2015
Location: Toronto Sheraton Centre
Toronto, ON
Sponsor/Contact: Canadian Union of Public Employees
Ontario Regional Office
#1, 80 Commerce Valley Dr. East
Markham, ON L3T 0B2
905-739-9739 *Fax:* 905-739-9740
E-mail: info@cupe.on.ca
URL: www.cupe.on.ca
Scope: Provincial
Anticipated Attendance: 1,200
Contact Information: CUPE Ontario, E-mail: info@cupe.on.ca

Canadian Urban Transit Association 2015 Annual Conference
Date: May 30 - June 3, 2015
Location: Winnipeg, MB
Sponsor/Contact: Canadian Urban Transit Association
#1401, 55 York St.
Toronto, ON M5J 1R7
416-365-9800 *Fax:* 416-365-1295
URL: www.cutaactu.ca
Scope: National
Purpose: Professional development activities & networking opportunities, held in May or June each year
Contact Information: Phone: 416-365-9800

Catholic Health Alliance of Canada 2015 Annual Conference: Standing Together at the Margins - Creating a Circle of Compassion
Date: May 6-8, 2015
Location: Sheraton Cavalier Hotel
Saskatoon, SK
Sponsor/Contact: Catholic Health Alliance of Canada
Annex C, Saint-Vincent Hospital
60 Cambridge St. North
Ottawa, ON K1R 7A5
613-562-6262 *Fax:* 613-782-2857
URL: www.chac.ca
Scope: National
Purpose: A conference featuring keynote speakers & the presentation of awards
Contact Information: Executive Director: James Roche, Phone: 613-562-6262, ext. 2164, E-mail: jroche@bruyere.org

Classical Association of Canada Annual Conference 2015
Date: May 20-22, 2015
Location: University of Toronto
Toronto, ON
Sponsor/Contact: Classical Association of Canada
Guy Chamberland, Classical Studies, Thorneloe College
Laurentian University
Sudbury, ON P3E 2C6
416-736-2100
URL: www.cac-scec.ca
Scope: National

College of Registered Nurses of Nova Scotia 2015 Education Forum
Date: May 13, 2015
Location: Nova Scotia
Sponsor/Contact: College of Registered Nurses of Nova Scotia
#4005, 7071 Bayers Rd.
Halifax, NS B3L 2C2
902-491-9744 *Fax:* 902-491-9510
Toll-Free: 800-565-9744
E-mail: info@crnns.ca
URL: www.crnns.ca
Scope: Provincial

Colleges and Institutes Canada 2015 Conference
Date: May 25-26, 2015
Location: RBC Convention Centre
Winnipeg, MB
Sponsor/Contact: Colleges and Institutes Canada
#701, 1 Rideau St.
Ottawa, ON K1N 8S7
613-746-2222 *Fax:* 613-746-6721
E-mail: info@collegesinstitutes.ca
URL: www.collegesinstitutes.ca
Scope: National
Purpose: Provides an opportunity for colleges, institutes, cégeps, university colleges and polytechnics to share their success stories and help shape a new direction for the future.
Anticipated Attendance: 800

Collège des médecins du Québec Colloque et assemblée générale annuelle 2015
Date: May 8, 2015
Location: Paliais des congrés de Montréal
Montréal, QC
Sponsor/Contact: Collège des médecins du Québec
2170, boul René-Lévesque ouest
Montréal, QC H3H 2T8
514-933-4441 *Fax:* 514-933-3112
Toll-Free: 888-633-3246
E-mail: info@cmq.org
URL: www.cmq.org
Scope: Provincial

Conference of the Canadian Society for the Study of Names
Date: May 30-31, 2015
Location: Ottawa, ON
Sponsor/Contact: Canadian Society for the Study of Names
P.O. Box 2164 Stn. Hull
Gatineau, QC J8X 3Z4
URL: www.csj.ualberta.ca/sco
Contact Information: Program Chair: Diane Dechief, Email: diane.dechief@mail.utoronto.ca

Congrès 2015 de l'Association des professeurs de français des universités et collèges canadiens
Date: 31 mai à 3 juin, 2015
Location: Université d'Ottawa
Ottawa, ON
Sponsor/Contact: Association des professeurs de français des universités et collèges canadiens
Département de Françaises, Université de Simon Fraser
8888 University Dr.
Burnaby, BC V5A 1S6
URL: www.apfucc.net

Congrès annuel de l'Association québécoise pour l'hygiène, la santé et la sécurité du travail 2015
Date: 20 mai, 2015
Location: Manoir Saint-Sauveur
St-Sauveur, QC
Sponsor/Contact: Association québécoise pour l'hygiène, la santé et la sécurité du travail
P.O. Box 52
89, boul de Bromont
Bromont, QC J2L 1A9
450-776-2169
Toll-Free: 888-355-3830
E-mail: info@aqhsst.qc.ca
URL: www.aqhsst.qc.ca
Scope: Provincial

Congrès annuel de Association du jeune barreau de Montréal 2015
Date: May 28-29, 2015
Location: Palais des congrès de Montréal
Montréal, QC
Sponsor/Contact: Association du jeune barreau de Montréal
#RC-03, 445, boul. St-Laurent
Montréal, QC H2Y 3T8
514-954-3450 *Fax:* 514-954-3496
E-mail: info@ajbm.qc.ca
URL: www.ajbm.qc.ca
Scope: Provincial

Construction Specifications Canada Conference 2015
Date: May 27-31, 2015
Location: Winnipeg, MB
Sponsor/Contact: Construction Specifications Canada
#312, 120 Carlton St.
Toronto, ON M5A 4K2
416-777-2198 *Fax:* 416-777-2197
E-mail: info@csc-dcc.ca
URL: www.csc-dcc.ca
Scope: National

Council of Post Secondary Library Directors, British Columbia, Spring 2015 Meeting
Date: May 20, 2015
Location: British Columbia
Sponsor/Contact: Council of Post Secondary Library Directors, British Columbia
c/o G. Makarewicz, Director, Library & Bookstore Svs., Langara College
100 West 49th Ave.
Vancouver, BC V5Y 2Z6
E-mail: admin@cpsld.ca
URL: www.cpsld.ca
Scope: Provincial
Purpose: A meeting of British Columbia's library directors of not-for-profit post secondary education institutions, with the goal to strengthen the post secondary library system in the province

Crane Rental Association of Canada 2015 Conference
Date: May 27-30, 2015
Location: Montréal, QC
Sponsor/Contact: Crane Rental Association of Canada
P.O. Box 26
Regina, SK S4P 2Z5
306-585-2722 *Fax:* 306-584-3566
Toll-Free: 855-680-2722
E-mail: info@crac-canada.com
URL: www.crac-canada.com
Scope: National

Credit Union Central of Canada 2015 Annual General Meeting & Canadian Conference for Credit Union Leaders
Date: May 2-6, 2015
Location: Banff, AB
Sponsor/Contact: Credit Union Central of Canada
Corporate Office
#1000, 151 Yonge St.
Toronto, ON M5C 2W7

416-232-1262 *Fax:* 416-232-9196
Toll-Free: 800-649-0222
E-mail: inquiries@cucentral.com
URL: www.cucentral.ca
Scope: National
Contact Information: Credit Union Central of Canada Communications Department Contact: Edith Wilkinson, Phone: 416-232-3421, Fax: 416-232-3734, E-mail: wilkinsone@cucentral.com

Electro-Federation Canada Annual Conference 2015
Date: May 25-29, 2015
Sponsor/Contact: Electro-Federation Canada Inc.
#300, 180 Attwell Dr.
Toronto, ON M9W 6A9
905-602-8877 *Fax:* 905-602-5686
Toll-Free: 866-602-8877
URL: www.electrofed.com
Scope: National
Contact Information: Nathalie Lajoie; Phone: 647-258-7484

Engineers Canada Board, Annual & Executive Committee Meetings 2015
Date: May 22-23, 2015
Location: Calgary, AB
Sponsor/Contact: Engineers Canada
#1100, 180 Elgin St.
Ottawa, ON K2P 2K3
613-232-2474 *Fax:* 613-230-5759
Toll-Free: 877-408-9273
E-mail: info@engineerscanada.ca
URL: www.engineerscanada.ca
Scope: National

Federation of Northern Ontario Municipalities 2015 55th Annual Conference
Date: May 6-8, 2015
Location: Holiday Inn
Sudbury, ON
Sponsor/Contact: Federation of Northern Ontario Municipalities
88 Riverside Dr.
Kapuskasing, ON P5N 1B3
705-337-4454 *Fax:* 705-337-1741
E-mail: fonom.info@gmail.com
URL: www.fonom.org
Scope: Local
Purpose: A meeting for northern Ontario's municipal decision makers, featuring exhibits by suppliers, vendors, & professionals who provide services to municipalities
Contact Information: E-mail: fonom.info@gmail.com

Funeral Service Association of Canada 2015 Convention
Date: May 20-23, 2015
Location: St. John's, NL
Sponsor/Contact: Funeral Service Association of Canada
#304, 555 Legget Dr.
Ottawa, ON K2K 2K3
613-271-2107 *Fax:* 613-271-3737
Toll-Free: 866-841-7779
E-mail: info@fsac.ca
URL: www.fsac.ca
Scope: National

Geological Association of Canada (GAC) & the Mineralogical Association of Canada (MAC) 2015 Joint Annual Meeting
Date: May 3-7, 2015
Location: Palais des congrès de Montréal
Montréal, QC
Sponsor/Contact: Geological Association of Canada
Department of Earth Sciences, Memorial University of Newfoundland
#ER4063, Alexander Murray Bldg.
St. John's, NL A1B 3X5
709-737-7660 *Fax:* 709-737-2532
E-mail: gac@mun.ca
URL: www.gac.ca
Scope: National
Purpose: Featuring exhibits, a technical program, & special events
Contact Information: Communications Chair, Mike Villeneuve, E-mail: mike.villeneuve@nrcan.gc.ca; URL: ja.agu.org/2015

Government Finance Officers Association 2015 109th Annual Conference
Date: May 31 - June 3, 2015
Location: Philadelphia, PA USA
Sponsor/Contact: Government Finance Officers Association
#2700, 203 North LaSalle St.
Chicago, IL 60601-1210
312-977-9700 *Fax:* 312-977-4806
E-mail: inquiry@gfoa.org
URL: www.gfoa.org
Scope: International
Anticipated Attendance: 4,100+
Contact Information: Manager, Communications: Natalie Laudadio, Phone: 312-977-9700, ext. 2298

Human Anatomy & Physiology Society 2015 29th Annual Conference
Date: May 23-28, 2015
Location: Hyatt Regency San Antonio Riverwalk
San Antonio, TX USA
Sponsor/Contact: Human Anatomy & Physiology Society
P.O. Box 2945
251 S.L. White Blvd.
LaGrange, GA 30241-2945
E-mail: admin@hapsweb.org
URL: www.hapsweb.org
Scope: International
Purpose: An international conference, featuring workshops & networking opportunities
Contact Information: Phone: 1-800-448-4277; Email: info@hapsconnect.org

Human Resources Association of Nova Scotia 2015 Conference
Date: May 26-27, 2015
Location: World Trade and Convention Centre
Halifax, NS
Sponsor/Contact: Human Resources Association of Nova Scotia
#102, 84 Chain Lake Dr.
Halifax, NS B3J 1A2
902-446-3660 *Fax:* 902-446-3677
E-mail: bffice@hrans.org
URL: www.hrans.org
Scope: Provincial

ICCSTE 2015: International Conference on Civil, Structural and Transportation Engineering
Date: May 4-5, 2015
Location: Ottawa, ON
Sponsor/Contact: International Academy of Science, Engineering & Technology
#414, 1376 Bank St.
Ottawa, ON K1H 7Y3
613-695-3040
E-mail: info@international-aset.com
URL: www.international-aset.com
Scope: International
Purpose: Conference topics focus on the areas of civil, structural & transportation engineering
Contact Information: URL: iccste.com

IPA Canadian Section Annual General Meeting 2015
Date: May 28-31, 2015
Location: Niagara Falls, ON
Sponsor/Contact: International Police Association
179 Greak Oak Trail
Binbrook, ON L0R 1C0
URL: www.ipa.ca
Scope: National
Contact Information: Garry Bulmer, Email: gbulmer@cogeco.ca

Institute of Industrial Engineers Annual IE Conference & Expo 2015
Date: May 30 - June 2, 2015
Location: Renaissance Nashville Hotel
Nashville, TN USA
Sponsor/Contact: Institute of Industrial Engineers
#200, 3577 Parkway Lane
Norcross, GA 30092
770-449-0461 *Fax:* 770-441-3295
E-mail: cs@iienet.org
URL: www.iienet2.org
Scope: International

Insurance Brokers Association of Alberta 2015 Convention
Date: May 3-6, 2015
Location: The Fairmont Chateau Lake Louise
Lake Louise, AB
Sponsor/Contact: Insurance Brokers Association of Alberta
3010 Calgary Trail NW
Edmonton, AB T6J 6V4
780-424-3320 *Fax:* 780-424-7418
Toll-Free: 800-318-0197
E-mail: ibaa@ibaa.ca
URL: www.ibaa.ca
Scope: Provincial
Contact Information: Margaret Buhay;Email: convention@ibaa.ca; Tel: 780-569-5121

International Society for Magnetic Resonance in Medicine 2015 23rd Scientific Meeting & Exhibition
Date: May 30 - June 5, 2015
Location: Toronto, ON
Sponsor/Contact: International Society for Magnetic Resonance in Medicine
2030 Addison St., 7th Fl.
Berkeley, CA 94704
510-841-1899 *Fax:* 510-841-2340
E-mail: info@ismrm.org
URL: www.ismrm.org
Scope: International
Purpose: Featuring the 24th Annual Meeting of the Section for Magnetic Resonance Technologists
Contact Information: Director, Meetings: Sandra Daudlin, E-mail: sandra@ismrm.org; Coordinator, Meetings: Melisa Martinez, E-mail: melisa@ismrm.org

Jasper Dental Congress 2015
Date: May 21-24, 2015
Location: Jasper, AB
Sponsor/Contact: Alberta Dental Association & College
#101, 8230 - 105 St.
Edmonton, AB T6E 5H9
780-432-1012 *Fax:* 780-433-4864
Toll-Free: 800-843-3848
E-mail: adaadmin@telusplanet.net
URL: www.abda.ab.ca
Scope: Provincial

Journées dentaires internationales du Québec (JDIQ) 2015
Date: 22 au 26 mai 2015
Location: Palais des congrès de Montréal
Montréal, QC
Sponsor/Contact: Ordre des dentistes du Québec
625, boul René-Lévesque ouest, 15e étage
Montréal, QC H3B 1R2
514-875-8511 *Fax:* 514-393-9248
Toll-Free: 800-361-4887
URL: www.odq.qc.ca
Scope: Provincial
Contact Information: Directeur, Dr Denis Forest, téléphone: 514-875-8511, poste 2222; adresse email: denis.forest@odq.qc.ca

Lower Mainland Local Government Association 2015 Annual General Meeting & Conference
Date: May 6-8, 2015
Location: Harrison Hot Springs Resort and Spa
Harrison, BC
Sponsor/Contact: Lower Mainland Local Government Association
#60, 10551 Shellbridge Way
Richmond, BC V6X 2W9
250-356-5122 *Fax:* 604-270-9116
URL: www.lmlga.ca
Scope: Local
Purpose: Tradeshow, workshops, & seminars for persons involved in local government

Manitoba Association of Library Technicians 2015 Annual General Meeting
Date: May 2015
Location: Manitoba
Sponsor/Contact: Manitoba Association of Library Technicians
P.O. Box 1872
Winnipeg, MB R3C 3R1
E-mail: malt.mb.ca@gmail.com
URL: www.malt.mb.ca
Scope: Provincial
Purpose: Each year between May 1st & May 31st, reports of the association's executive are presented & officers are elected

Manitoba Child Care Association 2015 38th Annual Early Childhood Educator Provincial Conference
Date: May 21-23, 2015
Location: Manitoba
Sponsor/Contact: Manitoba Child Care Association
2350 McPhillips St., 2nd Fl.
Winnipeg, MB R2V 4J6
204-586-8587 *Fax:* 204-589-5613
Toll-Free: 888-323-4676
E-mail: info@mccahouse.org
URL: www.mccahouse.org
Scope: Provincial
Purpose: Keynote speakers, a trade show, & an awards banquet
Contact Information: Manager, Professional Development: Karen Houdayer, Phone: 204-336-5062,

Toll-Free: 1-888-323-4676, ext. 224,
E-mail: khoudayer@mccahouse.org

Manitoba Federation of Labour 2015 Convention
Date: May 28-31, 2015
Location: Keystone Centre
Brandon, MB
Sponsor/Contact: Manitoba Federation of Labour
#303, 275 Broadway
Winnipeg, MB R3C 4M6
204-947-1400 *Fax:* 204-943-4276
URL: www.mfl.mb.ca
Scope: Provincial
Contact Information: Communications Coordinator: John Doyle, Phone: 204-782-8465, E-mail: jdoyle@mfl.mb.ca

Manitoba Magazine Publishers Association 2015 Conference
Date: May 27-28, 2015
Location: Viscount Gort
Winnipeg, MB
Sponsor/Contact: Manitoba Magazine Publishers Association
#606 - 100 Arthur St.
Winnipeg, MB R3B 1H3
204-942-0189 *Fax:* 204-257-2467
E-mail: exedir@manitobamagazines.ca
URL: manitobamagazines.ca
Scope: Provincial

Manitoba Operating Room Nurses Association 2015 Annual General Meeting
Date: May 21, 2015
Location: Norwood Hotel
Winnipeg, MB
Sponsor/Contact: Manitoba Operating Room Nurses Association
Scope: Provincial

Medical Library Association 2015 Annual Meeting & Exhibition
Date: May 15-20, 2015
Location: Austin, TX USA
Sponsor/Contact: Medical Library Association
#1900, 65 East Wacker Pl.
Chicago, IL 60601-7246
312-419-9094 *Fax:* 312-419-8950
E-mail: info@mlahq.org
URL: www.mlanet.org
Scope: International

Microwave Theory & Techniques Society International Microwave Symposia 2015
Date: May 15-22, 2015
Location: Phoenix, AZ USA
Sponsor/Contact: IEEE Microwave Theory & Techniques Society
5829 Bellanca Dr.
Elkridge, MD 21075
410-796-5866 *Fax:* 410-796-5829
URL: www.mtt.org
Scope: International
Purpose: Technical papers; Workshops; Trade show

Municipal Equipment & Operations Association (Ontario) Inc. 2015 Annual Professional Development Day
Date: May 20, 2015
Location: Forest City GC
London, ON
Sponsor/Contact: Municipal Equipment & Operations Association (Ontario) Inc.
38 Summit Ave.
Kitchener, ON N2M 4W2
519-741-2600 *Fax:* 519-741-2750
E-mail: admin@meoa.org
URL: www.meoa.org
Scope: Provincial
Purpose: A learning opportunity for members of the association

NAFSA's 2015 Annual Conference & International Education Expo
Date: May 24-29, 2015
Location: Boston, MA USA
Sponsor/Contact: NAFSA: Association of International Educators
1307 New York Ave. NW, 8th Fl.
Washington, DC 20005-4701
202-737-3699 *Fax:* 202-737-3657
E-mail: inbox@nafsa.org
URL: www.nafsa.org
Scope: International

National Initiative for the Care of the Elderly Annual Nice Knowledge Exchange 2015
Date: May 28, 2015
Location: Hart House, University of Toronto
Toronto, ON
Sponsor/Contact: National Initiative for the Care of the Elderly
#328, 263 McCaul St.
Toronto, ON M5T 1W7
416-978-0545 *Fax:* 416-978-4771
E-mail: nicenetadmin@utoronto.ca
URL: www.nicenet.ca
Scope: National

New Brunswick Federation of Labour 53rd Convention
Date: May 24-27, 2015
Location: Delta Brunswick
Saint John, NB
Sponsor/Contact: New Brunswick Federation of Labour
#314, 96 Norwood Ave.
Moncton, NB E1C 6L9
506-857-2125 *Fax:* 506-383-1597
E-mail: nbfl@nbnet.nb.ca
URL: www.nbfl-fttnb.ca
Scope: Provincial
Purpose: A biennial gathering where approximately sixty resolutions are normally submitted & handled
Contact Information: New Brunswick Federation of Labour, E-mail: nbfl_fttnb@bellaliant.com

Newspapers Canada 2015 Annual Conference & Trade Show
Date: May 22, 2015
Location: Sheraton Centre Toronto Hotel
Toronto, ON
Sponsor/Contact: Canadian Newspaper Association
c/o Newspapers Canada
#200, 890 Yonge St.
Toronto, ON M4W 3P4
416-923-3567 *Fax:* 416-923-7206
Toll-Free: 877-305-2262
E-mail: info@newspaperscanada.ca
URL: www.newspaperscanada.ca
Scope: National
Purpose: An annual spring event with speakers, presentations, & seminars covering a wide range of topics for both daily & weekly newspapers
Contact Information: Tina Ongkeko, E-mail: conference@newspaperscanada.ca

North American Society of Adlerian Psychology 2015 63rd Annual Conference
Date: May 28-31, 2015
Location: Philadelphia, PA USA
Sponsor/Contact: North American Society of Adlerian Psychology
614 Old West Chocolate Ave.
Hershey, PA 17033
717-579-8795 *Fax:* 717-533-8616
E-mail: info@alfredadler.org
URL: www.alfredadler.org
Scope: International
Purpose: Educational & networking opportunities for members of the North American Society of Adlerian Psychology
Contact Information: E-mail: info@alfredadler.org

North Central Local Government Association 2015 60th Annual General Meeting & Convention
Date: May 6-8, 2015
Location: Prince George Civic Centre
Prince George, BC
Sponsor/Contact: North Central Local Government Association
c/o Maxine Koppe
#206, 155 George St.
Prince George, BC V2L 1P8
250-564-6585 *Fax:* 250-564-6514
URL: www.nclga.ca
Scope: Local

Nova Scotia Ground Water Association 2015 Annual General Meeting
Location: Nova Scotia
Sponsor/Contact: Nova Scotia Ground Water Association
#417, 3 - 644 Portland St.
Dartmouth, NS B2W 2M3
Fax: 902-435-0089
Toll-Free: 888-242-4440
E-mail: nsgwa@ns.aliantzinc.ca
URL: www.nsgwa.ca
Scope: Provincial
Purpose: A yearly gathering featuring divisional meetings, presentations, & association business
Contact Information: Secretary-Treasurer: Noreene McGuire, E-mail: nsgwa@ns.aliantzinc.ca

Ontario Association of Architects 2015 Annual Conference: Urban Renewal
Date: May 6-8, 2015
Location: Hamilton, ON
Sponsor/Contact: Ontario Association of Architects
111 Moatfield Dr.
Toronto, ON M3B 3L6
416-449-6898 *Fax:* 416-449-5756
Toll-Free: 800-565-2724
E-mail: oaamail@oaa.on.ca
URL: www.oaa.on.ca
Scope: Provincial
Purpose: Continuing education sessions by speakers who excel in their field of expertise
Contact Information: Continuing Education Coordinator: Ellen Savitsky, E-mail: ellens@oaa.on.ca

Ontario Association of Fire Chiefs 2015 Conference
Date: May 2-6, 2015
Location: Toronto Congress Centre
Toronto, ON
Sponsor/Contact: Ontario Association of Fire Chiefs
#14, 530 Westney Rd. South
Ajax, ON L1S 6M3
905-426-9865 *Fax:* 905-426-3032
Toll-Free: 800-774-6651
URL: www.oafc.on.ca
Scope: Provincial
Anticipated Attendance: 600+
Contact Information: Mercedes Sturges, Conference and Event Manager; Phone: 905-426-9865 x224; Email: mercedes.sturges@oafc.on.ca

Ontario Association of Police Services Boards Annual General Meeting & Spring Conference 2015
Date: May 27-30, 2015
Location: Marriot Eaton Centre
Toronto, ON
Sponsor/Contact: Ontario Association of Police Services Boards
Suite A, 10 Peel Centre Dr.
Brampton, ON L6T 4B9
905-458-1488 *Fax:* 905-458-2260
Toll-Free: 800-831-7727
E-mail: admin@oapsb.ca
URL: www.oapsb.ca
Scope: Provincial

Ontario Association of School Business Officials 72nd Annual Conference & Education Industry Show
Date: May 6-8, 2015
Location: Blue Mountain Resort
Collingwood, ON
Sponsor/Contact: Ontario Association of School Business Officials
#207, 144 Main St.
Markham, ON L3P 5T3
905-209-9704 *Fax:* 905-209-9705
E-mail: office@oasbo.org
URL: www.oasbo.org
Scope: Provincial

Ontario Dental Association Annual Spring Meeting 2015
Date: May 7-9, 2015
Location: Metro Toronto Convention Centre
Toronto, ON
Sponsor/Contact: Ontario Dental Association
4 New St.
Toronto, ON M5R 1P6
416-922-3900 *Fax:* 416-922-9005
Toll-Free: 800-387-1393
E-mail: info@oda.ca
URL: www.oda.ca
Scope: Provincial
Anticipated Attendance: 11,700

Ontario Genealogical Society 2015 Annual Conference
Date: May 29-31, 2015
Location: Georgian College
Barrie, ON
Sponsor/Contact: Ontario Genealogical Society
#102, 40 Orchard View Blvd.
Toronto, ON M4R 1B9
416-489-0734 *Fax:* 416-489-9803
E-mail: provoffice@ogs.on.ca
URL: www.ogs.on.ca
Scope: Provincial
Purpose: Theme: Tracks through Time

Ontario Petroleum Institute 2015 54th Conference & Trade Show
Location: Oakwood Resort
Grand Bend, ON
Sponsor/Contact: Ontario Petroleum Institute Inc.
#104, 555 Southdale Rd. East
London, ON N6E 1A2

519-680-1620 *Fax:* 519-680-1621
E-mail: opi@ontariopetroleuminstitute.com
URL: ontariopetroleuminstitute.com
Scope: Provincial
Purpose: Presentation of papers about oil & natural gas exploration, production, & storage
Contact Information: E-mail: opi@ontpet.com

Ontario Pharmacists' Association 2015 Conference
Date: May 28-31, 2015
Location: Ottawa, ON
Sponsor/Contact: Ontario Pharmacists' Association
#800, 375 University Ave.
Toronto, ON M5G 2J5
416-441-0788 *Fax:* 416-441-0791
E-mail: mail@opatoday.com
URL: www.opatoday.com
Scope: Provincial
Purpose: An annual event for Ontario's pharmacists, featuring the annual general meeting of the association, an educational program, keynote speaker presentations, a showcase of new products & services, an awards presentation, networking opportunities, & social events
Anticipated Attendance: 600
Contact Information: Events & Development Specialist: Kristen Stamper, Phone: 416-441-0788, ext. 4247; Email: kstamper@opatoday.com

Ontario Rheumatology Association 2015 Annual Meeting
Date: May 22-24, 2015
Location: JW Marriott
Minett, ON
Sponsor/Contact: Ontario Rheumatology Association
#244, 12 - 16715 Yonge St.
Newmarket, ON L3X 1X4
905-952-0698 *Fax:* 905-952-0708
E-mail: admin@ontariorheum.ca
URL: ontariorheum.ca
Scope: Provincial

Operating Room Nurses Association of Canada National Conference 2015
Date: May 3-7, 2015
Location: Shaw Conference Centre
Edmonton, AB
Sponsor/Contact: Operating Room Nurses Association of Canada
604-466-7965
E-mail: info@ornac.ca
URL: www.ornac.ca
Scope: National
Purpose: Theme: "Bridging Excellence in Perioperative Practice"
Contact Information: Margot Walsh, Chair, National Conference; Email: nationalconference@ornac.ca

Paint & Decorating Retailers Association Canada Paint & Accessories Show at the National Hardware Show 2015
Date: May 5-7, 2015
Sponsor/Contact: Paint & Decorating Retailers Association Canada
1401 Triad Center Dr.
St. Peters, MO 63376
636-326-2636
E-mail: info@pdra.org
URL: www.pdra.org
Scope: National

Petroleum Safety Conference 2015
Date: May 5-7, 2015
Location: Banff, AB
Sponsor/Contact: Enform: The Safety Association for the Upstream Oil & Gas Industry
Head Office
5055 - 11th St. NE
Calgary, AB T2E 8N4
403-516-8000 *Fax:* 403-516-8166
Toll-Free: 800-667-5557
E-mail: customerservice@enform.ca
URL: www.enform.ca
Scope: National
Contact Information: URL: www.psc.ca

Project Management Institute Global Congress 2015
Date: May 11-13, 2015
Location: London, UK
Sponsor/Contact: Project Management Institute
14 Campus Blvd.
Newtown Square, PA 19073-3299
610-356-4600 *Fax:* 610-356-4647
Toll-Free: 855-746-4849
E-mail: customercare@pmi.org
URL: www.pmi.org
Scope: International
Purpose: Professional development, information sharing, exhibit viewing, & neworking opportunities

Psychologists Association of Alberta Connect 2015
Date: May 29, 2015
Location: Cochrane, AB
Sponsor/Contact: Psychologists Association of Alberta
#103, 1207 - 91 St. SW
Edmonton, AB T6X 1E9
780-424-0294 *Fax:* 780-423-4048
Toll-Free: 888-424-0297
E-mail: paa@psychologistsassociation.ab.ca
URL: www.psychologistsassociation.ab.ca
Scope: Provincial

Public Sector Management Workshop 2015
Date: May 24-26, 2015
Location: Victoria, BC
Sponsor/Contact: Financial Management Institute of Canada
#1107, 200 Elgin St.
Ottawa, ON K2P 1L5
613-569-1158 *Fax:* 613-569-4532
E-mail: national@fmi.ca
URL: www.fmi.ca
Scope: National

Real Estate Institute of Canada 2015 Annual Conference & Annual General Meeting: Opening Opportunities
Date: May 26-28, 2015
Location: Vancouver, BC
Sponsor/Contact: Real Estate Institute of Canada
#208, 5407 Eglinton Ave. West
Toronto, ON M9C 5K6
416-695-9000 *Fax:* 416-695-7230
Toll-Free: 800-542-7342
E-mail: infocentral@reic.com
URL: www.reic.ca
Scope: National
Purpose: A gathering of real estate professionals to participate in professional development programs, listen to guest speakers, & to network with industry experts, colleages, & suppliers

Responsible Investment Association 2015 Conference
Date: May 31 - June 2, 2015
Location: Banff Centre
Banff, AB
Sponsor/Contact: Responsible Investment Association
#300, 215 Spadina Ave.
Toronto, ON M5T 2C7
416-461-6042
E-mail: staff@riacanada.ca
URL: riacanada.ca
Scope: National

Royal Canadian Mounted Police Veterans Association 2015 Annual General Meeting
Date: May 28-31, 2015
Location: Québec, QC
Sponsor/Contact: Royal Canadian Mounted Police Veterans' Association
1200 Vanier Pkwy.
Ottawa, ON K1A 0R2
613-993-8633 *Fax:* 613-993-4353
Toll-Free: 877-251-1771
E-mail: rcmp.vets@rcmp-grc.gc.ca
URL: www.rcmpvetsnational.ca
Scope: National
Contact Information: URL: www.grc-rcmp-vets.qc.ca/en/agm-2015

Saskatchewan Association of Social Workers 2015 Annual General Meeting & Provincial Conference
Date: May 27-29, 2015
Location: Executive Royal Hotel
Regina, SK
Sponsor/Contact: Saskatchewan Association of Social Workers
Edna Osborne House
2110 Lorne St.
Regina, SK S4P 2M5
306-545-1922 *Fax:* 306-545-1895
Toll-Free: 877-517-7279
E-mail: sasw@accesscomm.ca
URL: www.sasw.ca
Scope: Provincial
Purpose: A conference usually held each April at one of the association's branch locations
Contact Information: E-mail: sasw@accesscomm.ca

Saskatchewan Emergency Medical Services Association 2015 Annual Convention & Trade Show
Date: May 11-13, 2015
Location: SHeraton Cavalier
Saskatoon, SK
Sponsor/Contact: Saskatchewan Emergency Medical Services Association
#105, 111 Research Dr.
Saskatoon, SK S7N 3R2
306-382-2147 *Fax:* 306-955-5353
E-mail: semsa@semsa.org
URL: www.semsa.org
Scope: Provincial
Purpose: An informative convention with a trade show that provides the opportunitiy for those working in emergency medicl services to meet with suppliers to discuss products & services
Contact Information: SEMSA Office, Phone: 306-382-2147, E-mail: semsa@semsa.org

Saskatchewan Library Association 2015 Annual Conference & Annual General Meeting
Date: May 7-9, 2015
Location: Doubletree Inn by Hilton
Regina, SK
Sponsor/Contact: Saskatchewan Library Association
#15, 2010 - 7th Ave.
Regina, SK S4R 1C2
306-780-9413 *Fax:* 306-780-9447
E-mail: slaexdir@sasktel.net
URL: www.saskla.ca
Scope: Provincial
Purpose: Featuring discussions of issues affecting library service in Saskatchewan, the Mary Donaldson Memorial Lecture, & networking occasions, held during a two or three day period
Contact Information: Saskatchewan Library Association, Phone: 306-780-9409, Fax: 306-780-9447, E-mail: slaprograms@sasktel.net

Saskatchewan Library Trustees Association 2015 Annual General Meeting
Date: May 7-9, 2015
Location: Doubletree Inn
Regina, SK
Sponsor/Contact: Saskatchewan Library Trustees Association
79 Mayfair Cres.
Regina, SK S4S 5T9
306-584-2495 *Fax:* 306-585-1473
URL: slta.ca
Scope: Provincial
Purpose: Featuring the president's report, auditor's report, library system reports, & elections
Contact Information: Saskatchewan Library Trustees Association Executive Director: Nancy Kennedy, E-mail: njk@sasktel.net

Saskatchewan Physical Education Association Conference 2015: Moving With Synergy
Date: May 6-8, 2015
Location: University of Regina and Ramada Plaza Hotel
Regina, SK
Sponsor/Contact: Saskatchewan Physical Education Association
P.O. Box 193
Harris, SK S0L 1K0
306-656-4423 *Fax:* 306-656-4405
E-mail: spea@xplornet.com
URL: www.speaonline.ca
Scope: Provincial

Society of Gynecologic Oncologists of Canada 14th Annual Continuing Professional Development Meeting
Date: May 1, 2015
Location: Toronto, ON
Sponsor/Contact: Society of Gynecologic Oncologists of Canada
780 Echo Dr.
Ottawa, ON K1S 5R7
613-730-4192 *Fax:* 613-730-4314
Toll-Free: 800-561-2416
URL: www.g-o-c.org
Scope: National

Sonography Canada 2015 National Conference & Annual General Meeting
Date: May 21-23, 2015
Location: Delta Beauéjour
Moncton, NB
Sponsor/Contact: Sonography Canada
P.O. Box 119
Kemptville, ON K0G 1J0
Fax: 613-258-0899
Toll-Free: 877-488-0788
E-mail: info@sonographycanada.ca
URL: www.sonographycanada.ca
Scope: National

Conferences Index

The 6th Canadian Association of Foot Care Nurses 2015 Annual General Meeting & Conference
Date: May 22-24, 2015
Location: Winnipeg, MB
Sponsor/Contact: Canadian Association of Foot Care Nurses
c/o Pat MacDonald, President
110 Linden Park Bay
Winnipeg, MB R2R 1Y3
URL: www.cafcn.ca
Contact Information: Email: conference@cafcn.ca

The Canadian Evaluation Society (CES) 2015 National Conference (C2015)
Date: May 24-27, 2015
Location: Montréal, QC
Sponsor/Contact: Canadian Evaluation Society
1485 Laperriere Ave.
Ottawa, ON K1Z 7S8
613-725-2526 *Fax:* 613-729-6206
E-mail: secretariat@evaluationcanada.ca
URL: www.evaluationcanada.ca
Scope: National

The International Trademark Association's 137th Annual Meeting 2015
Date: May 2-6, 2015
Location: San Diego, CA USA
Sponsor/Contact: International Trademark Association
655 Third Ave., 10th Fl.
New York, NY 10017-5617
212-642-1700 *Fax:* 212-768-7796
E-mail: info@inta.org
URL: www.inta.org
Scope: International
Contact Information: meetings@inta.org; URL: www.inta.org/2015AM

The National Space Society's 34th Annual International Space Development Conference
Date: May 20-24, 2015
Location: Hyatt Regency
Toronto, ON
Sponsor/Contact: National Space Society
#500, 1155 15th St. NW
Washington, DC 20005
202-429-1600 *Fax:* 202-530-0659
E-mail: nsshq@nss.org
URL: www.nss.org
Scope: International
Purpose: Discussions of the future of space exploration

Thermal Insulation Association of Alberta Annual General Meeting & Banquet 2015
Date: May 2015
Location: Red Deer, AB
Sponsor/Contact: Thermal Insulation Association of Alberta
#400, 1040 - 7 Ave. SW
Calgary, AB T2P 3G9
403-244-4487 *Fax:* 403-244-2340
E-mail: info@tiaa.cc
URL: www.tiaa.cc
Scope: Provincial

Titanium Europe 2015
Date: May 11-13, 2015
Location: Hilton Birmingham Metropole Hotel
Birmingham, UK
Sponsor/Contact: International Titanium Association
#100, 11674 Huron St.
Northglenn, CO 80234
303-404-2221 *Fax:* 303-404-9111
E-mail: ita@titanium.org
URL: www.titanium.org
Scope: International
Contact Information: Jennifer Cunningham, Planner; E-mail: jcunningham@titanium.org

Toronto Field Naturalists 2015 Monthly Talk: Toronto's Urban Forests
Date: May 3, 2015
Location: University of Toronto, Northrop Frye Building
Toronto, ON
Sponsor/Contact: Toronto Field Naturalists
#1519, 2 Carlton St.
Toronto, ON M5B 1J3
416-593-2656
E-mail: office@torontofieldnaturalists.org
URL: www.torontofieldnaturalists.org
Scope: Local
Purpose: This lecture explains the state of the forests in Toronto
Contact Information: E-mail: office@torontofieldnaturalists.org

Virée ornithologique Québec 2015
Date: May 23, 2015
Location: Four Points by Sheraton Québec
Québec, QC
Sponsor/Contact: Club des ornithologues de Québec inc.
Domaine de Maizerets
2000, boul Montmorency
Québec, QC G1J 5E7
418-661-3544
E-mail: coq@coq.qc.ca
URL: www.coq.qc.ca
Scope: Provincial

XVI International Council for Laboratory Animal Science General Assembly & 54th Annual Symposium
Date: May 3-June 2, 2015
Location: Palais des congrès de Montréal
Montréal, QC
Sponsor/Contact: International Council for Laboratory Animal Science
40 Washington St.
Brussels, 1050
E-mail: info@iclas.org
URL: www.iclas.org
Scope: International

June

106th Rotary International Convention
Date: June 6-9, 2015
Location: São Paulo, Brazil
Sponsor/Contact: Rotary International
One Rotary Center
1560 Sherman Ave.
Evanston, IL 60201
847-866-3000 *Fax:* 847-328-8554
Toll-Free: 866-976-8279
E-mail: contact.center@rotary.org
URL: www.rotary.org
Scope: International

10th Annual British Columbia Nurse Practitioner Association Conference
Date: June 12-14, 2015
Location: Hyatt Regency Hotel
Vancouver, BC
Sponsor/Contact: British Columbia Nurse Practitioner Association
27656 - 110th AVe.
Maple Ridge, BC V2W 1P6
E-mail: info@bcnpa.org
URL: www.bcnpa.org
Scope: Provincial

139th American Association on Intellectual & Developmental Disabilities Annual Meeting
Date: June 1-4, 2015
Location: Galt House of Louisville
Louisville, KY USA
Sponsor/Contact: American Association on Intellectual & Developmental Disabilities
#200, 501 - 3rd St. NW
Washington, DC 20001
URL: aaidd.org
Scope: International

2015 Annual General Meeting of the College of Dental Surgeons of British Columbia
Date: June 5, 2015
Location: Vancouver Marriott Pinnacle Downtown Hotel
Vancouver, BC
Sponsor/Contact: College of Dental Surgeons of British Columbia
#500, 1765 West 8th Ave.
Vancouver, BC V6J 5C6
604-736-3621 *Fax:* 604-734-9448
Toll-Free: 800-663-9169
E-mail: info@cdsbc.org
URL: www.cdsbc.org
Scope: Provincial

2015 Canadian Association for Studies in Co-operation Conference
Date: June 2-4, 2015
Location: Ottawa, ON
Sponsor/Contact: Canadian Association for Studies in Co-operation
c/o Centre for the Study of Co-operatives, University of Saskatchewan
101 Diefenbaker Pl.
Saskatoon, SK S7N 5B8
306-966-8509 *Fax:* 306-966-8517
E-mail: casc.acec@usask.ca
URL: www.coopresearch.coop
Scope: National

2015 Canadian Association of Career Educators & Employers National Conference
Date: June 7 - 10, 2015
Location: The Westin Ottawa
Ottawa, ON
Sponsor/Contact: Canadian Association of Career Educators & Employers
#202, 720 Spadina Ave.
Toronto, ON M5S 2T9
416-929-5156
Toll-Free: 866-922-3303
URL: www.cacee.com
Scope: National

2015 Canadian Association of Labour Media Conference
Date: June 18-20, 2015
Location: Victoria, BC
Sponsor/Contact: Canadian Association of Labour Media
P.O. Box 10624 Stn. Bloorcourt
Toronto, ON M6H 4H9
581-983-4397 *Fax:* 581-983-4397
E-mail: editor@calm.ca
URL: www.calm.ca

2015 Canadian Institute of Financial Planning National Conference
Date: June 3-6, 2015
Location: The Westin Bayshore
Vancouver, BC
Sponsor/Contact: Canadian Institute of Financial Planning
#600, 3660 Hurontario St.
Mississauga, ON L5B 3C4
647-723-6450 *Fax:* 647-723-6457
Toll-Free: 866-933-0233
E-mail: cifps@cifps.ca
URL: www.cifps.ca
Scope: National

2015 Canadian Mathematical Society Summer Meeting
Date: June 5-8, 2015
Location: University of Prince Edward Island
Charlottetown, PE
Sponsor/Contact: Canadian Mathematical Society
#209, 1785 St Laurent Blvd.
Ottawa, ON K1G 3Y4
613-733-2662 *Fax:* 613-733-8994
E-mail: office@cms.math.ca
URL: www.cms.math.ca
Scope: National

2015 Canadian Society of Clinical Chemists Canadian Congress of Laboratory Medicine (CLMC)
Date: June 19-24, 2015
Location: Hotel Le Westin
Montreal, QC
Sponsor/Contact: Canadian Society of Clinical Chemists
P.O. Box 1570
#310, 4 Cataraqui St.
Kingston, ON K7K 1Z7
613-531-8899 *Fax:* 866-303-0626
E-mail: office@cscc.ca
URL: www.cscc.ca
Scope: National
Purpose: Joint Conference of CSCC and the Canadian Association of Pathologists
Contact Information: www.clmc.ca/2015

2015 Canadian Society of Pharmacology & Therapeutics Meeting
Date: June 7, 2015
Location: Peter Gilgan Centre for Research and Learning Auditorium
Toronto, ON
Sponsor/Contact: Canadian Society of Pharmacology & Therapeutics
c/o PATH Research Institute
#200, 25 Main St. West
Hamilton, ON L8P 1H1
905-523-7284
URL: www.pharmacologycanada.org
Scope: National

2015 Canadian Water Resource Association 68th National Confernece
Date: June 2-4, 2015
Location: Radisson Hotel
Winnipeg, MB
Sponsor/Contact: Canadian Water Resources Association
c/o Membership Office
9 Covus Crt.
Ottawa, ON K2E 7Z4
613-237-9363 *Fax:* 613-594-5190
E-mail: services@aic.ca
URL: www.cwra.org
Scope: National

2015 Leaders & Innovators Conference
Date: June 22-23, 2015
Location: Kingbridge Conference Centre & Institute
King City, ON
Sponsor/Contact: Ontario College Administrative Staff Associations

P.O. Box 263
#201-202, 120 Centre St. North
Napanee, ON K7R 3M4
Fax: 866-742-5430
Toll-Free: 866-742-5429
E-mail: info@ocasa.on.ca
URL: www.ocpinfo.com
Scope: Provincial

2015 Manitoba Association of Fire Chiefs Annual Conference & Trade Show
Date: June 4-6, 2015
Location: South Beach Casino & Resort
Winnipeg, MB
Sponsor/Contact: Manitoba Association of Fire Chiefs
P.O. Box 1208
Portage La Prairie, MB R1N 3J9
204-857-6249
E-mail: mb.firechiefs@mymts.net
URL: mafc.ca
Scope: Provincial

2015 National Orchestras Meeting
Date: June 4-6, 2015
Location: Sheraton Vancouver Wall Centre Hotel
Vancouver, BC
Sponsor/Contact: Orchestras Canada
#700, 425 Adelaide St. West
Toronto, ON M5V 3C1
416-366-8834 *Fax:* 416-504-0437
E-mail: info@oc.ca
URL: www.orchestrascanada.org
Scope: National

2015 Volunteer Management Professionals of Canada National Conference
Date: June 17-18, 2015
Location: Edmonton, AB
Sponsor/Contact: Volunteer Management Professionals of Canada
#9, 380 Champlain St.
Dieppe, NB E1A 1P3
E-mail: info@vmpc.ca
URL: www.vmpc.ca
Scope: National

47th International Snowmobile Congress / CCSO Annual General Meeting
Date: June 10-13, 2015
Location: Niagara Falls Convention Center
Niagara Falls, NY
Sponsor/Contact: Canadian Council of Snowmobile Organizations
P.O. Box 21059
Thunder Bay, ON P7A 8A7
807-345-5299
E-mail: ccso.ccom@tbaytel.net
URL: www.ccso-ccom.ca
Scope: International

92nd Canadian Paediatric Society Annual Conference 2015
Date: June 24-27, 2015
Location: Toronto, ON
Sponsor/Contact: Canadian Paediatric Society
2305 St. Laurent Blvd.
Ottawa, ON K1G 4J8
613-526-9397 *Fax:* 613-526-3332
E-mail: info@cps.ca
URL: www.cps.ca
Scope: National
Contact Information: Phone: 613-526-9397 ext. 2148, Email: meetings@cps.ca, www.annualconference.cps.ca

98th Canadian Chemistry Conference & Exhibition
Date: June 13-17, 2015
Location: Ottawa Convention Centre
Ottawa, ON
Sponsor/Contact: Chemical Institute of Canada
#550, 130 Slater St.
Ottawa, ON K1P 6E2
613-232-6252 *Fax:* 613-232-5862
Toll-Free: 888-542-2242
E-mail: info@cheminst.ca
URL: www.cheminst.ca
Scope: National
Contact Information: Website: www.csc2015.ca; Email: info@csc2015.ca; Phone: 613-232-6252; Fax: 613-232-5862; Toll-free: 888-542-2242

9e Colloque de l'industrie éolienne québécoise / Québec's 9th Wind Energy Conference
Date: 15 juin au 17 juin 2015
Location: Carleton-sur-Mer, QC
Sponsor/Contact: TechnoCentre éolien
70, rue Bolduc
Gaspé, QC G4X 1G2
418-368-6162 *Fax:* 418-368-4315
E-mail: info@eolien.qc.ca
URL: www.eolien.qc.ca
Scope: Provincial
Purpose: Les enjeux de la filière éolienne et l'innovation sous toutes ses formes sont au cour même de l'événement.
Anticipated Attendance: 200
Contact Information: Twitter: twitter.com/TCEolien

Administrative Sciences Association of Canada 2015 Conference
Date: June 13-16, 2015
Location: World Trade & Convention Centre
Halifax, NS
Sponsor/Contact: Administrative Sciences Association of Canada
c/o Sobey School of Business
Saint Mary's University
Halifax, NS B3H 3C3
902-496-8139
E-mail: jean.mills@smu.ca
URL: www.asac.ca
Scope: National

Air & Waste Management Association 2015 Annual Conference & Exhibition
Date: June 22-25, 2015
Location: Raleigh Convention Center
Raleigh, NC USA
Sponsor/Contact: Air & Waste Management Association
One Gateway Center
420 Fort Duquesne Blvd., 3rd Fl.
Pittsburgh, PA 15222-1435
412-232-3444 *Fax:* 412-232-3450
Toll-Free: 800-270-3444
E-mail: info@awma.org
URL: www.awma.org
Scope: International
Contact Information: URL: ace2015.awma.org

Alberta School Boards Association 2015 Spring General Meeting
Date: June 1-2, 2015
Location: Sheraton Red Deer
Red Deer, AB
Sponsor/Contact: Alberta School Boards Association
#1200, 9925 - 109 St.
Edmonton, AB T5K 2J8
780-482-7311 *Fax:* 780-482-5659
E-mail: reception@asba.ab.ca
URL: www.asba.ab.ca
Scope: Provincial
Purpose: An Alberta School Boards Association professional development event
Contact Information: Administrative Assistant, Communications: Noreen Pownall, Phone: 780-451-7102, E-mail: npownall@asba.ab.ca

American Library Association 2015 Annual Conference
Date: June 25-30, 2015
Location: San Francisco, CA USA
Sponsor/Contact: American Library Association
50 East Huron St.
Chicago, IL 60611
Fax: 312-440-9374
Toll-Free: 800-545-2433
E-mail: ala@ala.org
URL: www.ala.org
Scope: International
Purpose: A program for people in the library & information services field, offering speakers, educational programs, committee meetings, & exhibits
Contact Information: Registration Customer Service, Phone: 1-800-974-3084, E-mail: ala@experient-inc.com

American Water Works Association 2015 134th Annual Conference & Exposition
Date: June 7-11, 2015
Location: Anaheim, CA USA
Sponsor/Contact: American Water Works Association
6666 West Quincy Ave.
Denver, CO 80235
303-794-7711 *Fax:* 303-347-0804
Toll-Free: 800-926-7337
E-mail: custsvc@awwa.org
URL: www.awwa.org
Scope: International
Purpose: An annual meeting providing technical sessions, an exhibit hall, & networking opportunities for water professionals
Contact Information: American Water Works Association, Phone: 800-926-7337, Fax: 303-347-0804, E-mail: awwamktg@awwa.org

Ancient, Free & Accepted Masons of Canada - Grand Lodge of Alberta 2015 Annual Communication
Date: June 12-13, 2015
Location: Red Deer Sheraton Hotel
Red Deer, AB
Sponsor/Contact: Ancient, Free & Accepted Masons of Canada - Grand Lodge of Alberta
330 - 12 Ave. SW
Calgary, AB T2R 0H2
403-262-1149 *Fax:* 403-290-0671
E-mail: grandsecretary@freemasons.ab.ca
URL: www.freemasons.ab.ca
Scope: Provincial

Appraisal Institute of Canada / Institut canadien des évaluateurs 2015 Annual Conference
Date: June 3-6, 2015
Location: Delta Grand Okanagan Resort and Conference Centre
Kelowna, BC
Sponsor/Contact: Appraisal Institute of Canada
#403, 200 Catherine St.
Ottawa, ON K2P 2K9
613-234-6533 *Fax:* 613-234-7197
E-mail: info@aicanada.ca
URL: www.aicanada.ca
Scope: National
Contact Information: Conference & Meetings Planner, Kevin Collins, Phone: 613-234-6533, ext. 231, E-Mail: kevinc@aicanada.ca

Association of Canadian Archivists 2015 40th Annual Conference & Annual General Meeting
Date: June 11-13, 2015
Location: Radisson Plaza, Hotel Saskatchewan
Regina, SK
Sponsor/Contact: Association of Canadian Archivists
P.O. Box 2596 Stn. D
Ottawa, ON K1P 5W6
613-234-6977 *Fax:* 613-234-8500
E-mail: aca@archivists.ca
URL: www.archivists.ca
Scope: National
Purpose: A meeting occurring in May or June each year, for archivists from across Canada, featuring educational presentations, trade show exhibits, networking opportunities, as well as workshops immediately prior or following conference sessions
Contact Information: Association of Canadian Archivists Board or Office, E-mail: aca@archivists.ca

Association of Canadian Map Libraries & Archives 2015 Annual Conference
Date: June 16-19, 2015
Location: Carleton University & University of Ottawa
Ottawa, ON
Sponsor/Contact: Association of Canadian Map Libraries & Archives
c/o Legal Deposit, Maps, Published Heritage, Library & Archives Canada
550, boul de la Cité
Gatineau, ON K1N ON4
E-mail: membership@acmla.org
URL: www.acmla-acacc.ca
Scope: National
Purpose: A yearly gathering of map librarians & archivists & other individuals with an interest in maps & geographic data who support the objectives of the association
Contact Information: First Vice-President Siobhan Hanratty, E-mail: vice.president1@acmla.org

Association of Canadian Publishers 2015 Annual General Meeting
Date: June 10-12, 2015
Location: Toronto Reference Library
Toronto, ON
Sponsor/Contact: Association of Canadian Publishers
#306, 174 Spadina Ave.
Toronto, ON M5T 2C2
416-487-6116 *Fax:* 416-487-8815
E-mail: admin@canbook.org
URL: www.publishers.ca
Scope: National
Purpose: An event featuring plenary sessions, professional development seminars, presentations, as well as committee meetings & reports

Conferences Index

Contact Information: Program Manager: Kate Edwards, Phone: 416-487-6116, ext 234, E-mail: kate_edwards@canbook.org

Association of Consulting Engineering Companies Leadership Summit 2015
Date: June 11-13, 2015
Location: Niagara Falls, ON
Sponsor/Contact: Association of Consulting Engineering Companies - Canada
#420, 130 Albert St.
Ottawa, ON K1P 5G4
613-236-0569 *Fax:* 613-236-6193
Toll-Free: 800-565-0569
E-mail: info@acec.ca
URL: www.acec.ca
Scope: National
Contact Information: Email: registration@unconventionalplanning.com

Association of Local Public Health Agencies 2015 Annual General Meeting & Conference
Date: June 7-9, 2015
Location: Ottawa, ON
Sponsor/Contact: Association of Local Public Health Agencies
#1306, 2 Carlton St.
Toronto, ON M5G 1T6
416-595-0006 *Fax:* 416-595-0030
E-mail: info@alphaweb.org
URL: www.alphaweb.org
Scope: Provincial

Association of Municipal Managers, Clerks & Treasurers of Ontario Annual Conference 2015
Date: June 7-10, 2015
Location: Thunder Bay, ON
Sponsor/Contact: Association of Municipal Managers, Clerks & Treasurers of Ontario
#610, 2680 Skymark Ave.
Mississauga, ON L4W 5L6
905-602-4294 *Fax:* 905-602-4295
E-mail: amcto@amcto.com
URL: www.amcto.com
Scope: Provincial

Association of Ontario Health Centres 2015 32nd Annual Conference & General Meeting
Date: June 2-3, 2015
Location: Sheraton Parkway Toronto North
Richmond Hill, ON
Sponsor/Contact: Association of Ontario Health Centres
#500, 907 Lawrence Ave. West
Toronto, ON M6A 3B6
416-236-2539 *Fax:* 416-236-0431
E-mail: mail@aohc.org
URL: www.aohc.org
Scope: Provincial
Purpose: The theme of this year's conference will be Shift the Conversation: Community Health & Wellbeing
Contact Information: Event Coordinator: John Boggan, E-mail: john.boggan@aohc.org

Association of Professional Community Planners of Saskatchewan 2015 Conference
Date: June 27-30, 2015
Location: Saskatoon, SK
Sponsor/Contact: Saskatchewan Professional Planners Institute
2424 College Ave.
Regina, SK S4P 1C8
306-584-3879 *Fax:* 306-352-6913
E-mail: msteranka@sasktel.net
URL: sppi.ca
Scope: Provincial
Purpose: A meeting of planners & related professionals to share new ideas, enhance professional practice, network & socialize
Contact Information: URL: www.thrive2015fleurir.ca

Association québécoise de pédagogie collégiale 35e colloque annuel
Date: 3 juin au 5 juin 2015
Location: Hôtel Le Montagnais
Saguenay, QC
Sponsor/Contact: Association québécoise de pédagogie collégiale
Cégep marie-victorin
7000, rue Marie-Victorin
Montréal, QC H2G 1J6
514-328-3805 *Fax:* 514-328-3824
E-mail: info@aqpc.qc.ca
URL: www.aqpc.qc.ca
Scope: National

Atlantic Provinces Library Association 2015 Annual Conference
Date: June 10-13, 2015
Location: Memorial University
St. John's, NL
Sponsor/Contact: Atlantic Provinces Library Association
c/o School of Information Management, Kenneth C. Rowe Management Bldg.
6100 University Ave.
Halifax, NS B3H 3J5
E-mail: executive@yahoo.ca
URL: www.apla.ca
Scope: Provincial
Purpose: An educational program to support the interests & concerns of the library community in the Atlantic provinces
Contact Information: Conference coordinator: Kathryn Rose, Email: 2015apla@gmail.com; URL: apla2015.wordpress.com

BC Municipal OH&S Conference
Date: June 14-16, 2015
Location: British Columbia
Sponsor/Contact: British Columbia Municipal Safety Association
20430 Fraser Hwy.
Langley, BC V3A 4G2
Fax: 778-278-0029
URL: www.bcmsa.ca
Scope: Provincial

Banff World Media Festival 2015
Date: June 7-10, 2015
Location: Fairmont Banff Springs Hotel
Banff, AB
Sponsor/Contact: Banff World Television Festival Foundation
c/o Achilles Media Ltd.
#202, 102 Boulder Cres.
Canmore, AB T1W 1L2
403-678-1216 *Fax:* 403-678-3357
E-mail: info@achillesmedia.com
URL: www.btvf.com
Scope: National

CAILBA 2015 Annual General Meeting
Date: June 2-4, 2015
Location: Westin Prince Hotel Toronto
Toronto, ON
Sponsor/Contact: Canadian Association of Independent Life Brokerage Agencies
105 King St. East
Toronto, ON M5C 1G6
416-548-4223 *Fax:* 416-340-9977
E-mail: info@cailba.com
URL: www.cailba.com
Scope: National

CHICA 2015 National Education Conference
Date: June 14-17, 2015
Location: Victoria, BC
Sponsor/Contact: Community & Hospital Infection Control Association Canada
P.O. Box 46125 Stn. Westdale
Winnipeg, MB R3R 3S3
204-897-5990 *Fax:* 204-895-9595
Toll-Free: 866-999-7111
E-mail: chicacanada@mts.net
URL: www.chica.org
Scope: National

Canada Green Building Council 2015 National Conference & Expo
Date: June 2-4, 2015
Location: Vancouver, BC
Sponsor/Contact: Canada Green Building Council
#202, 47 Clarence St.
Ottawa, ON K1N 9K1
613-241-1184 *Fax:* 613-241-4782
Toll-Free: 866-941-1184
E-mail: info@cagbc.org
URL: www.cagbc.org
Scope: International
Purpose: Educational sessions & exhibits devoted to green building.
Contact Information: General Inquiries, E-mail: info@greenbuildexpo.org

Canadian Anesthesiologists' Society 2015 71st Annual Meeting
Date: June 19-22, 2015
Location: Ottawa Convention Centre
Ottawa, ON
Sponsor/Contact: Canadian Anesthesiologists' Society
#208, One Eglinton Ave. East
Toronto, ON M4P 3A1
416-480-0602 *Fax:* 416-480-0320
E-mail: anesthesia@cas.ca
URL: www.cas.ca
Scope: National
Purpose: A convention, with an exhibition pharmaceutical companies & equipment manufacturers

Canadian Association for Information Science / Association canadienne des sciences de l'information 2015 43rd Annual Conference
Date: June 3-5, 2015
Location: University of Ottawa
Ottawa, ON
Sponsor/Contact: Canadian Association for Information Science
c/o Nadia Caidi, Faculty of Information
#335, 45 Willcocks St.
Toronto, ON M5S 1C7
416-978-4664
E-mail: nadia.caidi@utoronto.ca
URL: www.cais-acsi.ca
Scope: National
Purpose: Held in conjunction with the Congress of the Humanities & Social Sciences; Canadian information scientists & professionals have met to discuss the access, retrieval, production, value, use, & management of information.
Contact Information: Conference Co-Chair: Eric Meyers, Phone: 604-827-3945, E-mail: Eric.Meyers@ubc.ca; Conference Co-Chair: Heather O'Brien, Phone: 604-822-6365, E-mail: h.obrien@ubc.ca

Canadian Association for Social Work Education 2015 Annual Conference
Date: June 1-4, 2015
Location: University of Ottawa
Ottawa, ON
Sponsor/Contact: Canadian Association for Social Work Education
#410, 383 Parkdale Ave.
Ottawa, ON K1Y 4R4
613-792-1953
Toll-Free: 888-342-6522
E-mail: admin@caswe-acfts.ca
URL: caswe-acfts.ca
Scope: National
Purpose: A forum for the exchange of scientific & professional practice ideas. The theme is Le travail social à la croisée des idées, des langues et des cultures / Social Work at the Intersection of Ideas, Languages and Cultures
Contact Information: Phone: 613-792-1953, ext 221; E-mail: admin@caswe-acfts.ca

Canadian Association for Supported Employment 2015 Conference
Date: June 2-4, 2015
Location: Victoria, BC
Sponsor/Contact: Canadian Association for Supported Employment
c/o AiMHi Prince George Association for Community Living
950 Kerry St.
Prince George, BC V2M 5A3
250-564-6408 *Fax:* 250-564-6801
E-mail: info@supportedemployment.ca
URL: www.supportedemployment.ca
Scope: National

Canadian Association for the Study of Adult Education (CASAE) 2015 Annual National Conference
Date: June 9-11, 2015
Location: Université de Montréal
Montréal, QC
Sponsor/Contact: Canadian Association for the Study of Adult Education
#204, 260 Dalhousie St.
Ottawa, ON K1N 7E4
613-241-0018 *Fax:* 613-241-0019
E-mail: casae.aceea@csse.ca
URL: www.casae-aceea.ca
Scope: National
Contact Information: URL: www.casaeconference.ca

Canadian Association of Accredited Mortgage Professionals 2015 Atlantic Regional Symposium & Trade Show
Date: June 1, 2015
Location: Halifax, NS
Sponsor/Contact: Canadian Association of Accredited Mortgage Professionals
Atria II
#1401, 2235 Sheppard Ave. East
Toronto, ON M2J 5B5
416-385-2333 *Fax:* 416-385-1177
Toll-Free: 888-442-4625
E-mail: info@caamp.org
URL: www.caamp.org
Scope: Provincial
Contact Information: E-mail: events@caamp.org

Canadian Association of Accredited Mortgage Professionals 2015 British Columbia Regional Symposium & Trade Show
Date: June 17, 2015
Location: Vancouver, BC
Sponsor/Contact: Canadian Association of Accredited Mortgage Professionals

Atria II
#1401, 2235 Sheppard Ave. East
Toronto, ON M2J 5B5
416-385-2333 *Fax:* 416-385-1177
Toll-Free: 888-442-4625
E-mail: info@caamp.org
URL: www.caamp.org
Scope: Provincial
Contact Information: E-mail: events@caamp.org

Canadian Association of Geographers 2015 Annual Meeting & Conference
Date: June 1-6, 2015
Location: Simon Fraser University
Vancouver, BC
Sponsor/Contact: Canadian Association of Geographers
Department of Geography, McGill University
#425, 805, rue Sherbrooke ouest
Montréal, QC H3A 2K6
514-398-4946 *Fax:* 514-398-7437
E-mail: valerie.shoffey@cag-acg.ca
URL: www.cag-acg.ca
Scope: National
Purpose: A business meeting & educational conference for geographers & students, featuring the presentation of papers & posters, plus exhibits, & social activities

Canadian Association of Journalists 2015 Annual Conference
Date: June 5-7, 2015
Location: Atlantica Hotel
Halifax, NS
Sponsor/Contact: Canadian Association of Journalists
P.O. Box 280
Brantford, N3T 5M8
519-756-2020
URL: www.caj.ca
Scope: National

Canadian Association of Municipal Administrators 2015 44th Annual Conference & Annual General Meeting
Date: June 1-3, 2015
Location: Fairmont Jasper Park Lodge
Jasper, AB
Sponsor/Contact: Canadian Association of Municipal Administrators
P.O. Box 128 Stn. A
Fredericton, NB E3B 4Y2
866-771-2262
E-mail: admin@camacam.ca
URL: www.camacam.ca
Scope: National
Purpose: Information & a trade show for senior managers from Canadian municipalities throughout Canada
Contact Information: E-mail: admin@camacam.ca

Canadian Association of Neuroscience Nurses 2015 46th Annual Meeting & Scientific Sessions: Generating the Flow of Knowledge
Date: June 23-26, 2015
Location: Sheraton Hotel Newfoundland
St. John's, NL
Sponsor/Contact: Canadian Association of Neuroscience Nurses
c/o Aline Mayer, Membership Chairperson, CANN
30 Chantilly Gate
Stittsville, ON K2S 2B1
E-mail: canninfo@cann.ca
URL: www.cann.ca
Scope: National
Purpose: Scientific sessions offering professional development for neuroscience nurses.
Contact Information: Canadian Association of Neuroscience Nurses Professional Practice Chair (for information about the certification review workshop, held each year in conjunction with the annual scientific meeting), Newfoundland Scientific Chair, Jenny Slade, Email: jenny.slade@easternhealth.ca

Canadian Association of Student Financial Aid Administrators 2015 Annual Conference
Date: June 14-16, 2015
Location: Université Laval
Québec, QC
Sponsor/Contact: Canadian Association of Student Financial Aid Administrators
c/o Treasurer, University of Manitoba
422 University Centre
Winnipeg, MB R3T 2N2
204-474-9532
E-mail: info@casfaa.ca
URL: www.casfaa.ca
Scope: National
Contact Information: URL: www.casfaa2015.ulaval.ca

Canadian Association of University Business Officers 2015 Annual Conference
Date: June 14-16, 2015
Location: University of New Brunswick
Saint John, NB
Sponsor/Contact: Canadian Association of University Business Officers
#320, 350 Albert St.
Ottawa, ON K1R 1B1
613-230-6760 *Fax:* 613-563-7739
E-mail: info@caubo.ca
URL: www.caubo.ca
Scope: National

Canadian Authors Association 93rd Annual National Conference: CanWrite! 2015
Date: June 11-14, 2015
Location: Orillia, ON
Sponsor/Contact: Canadian Authors Association
74 Mississaga St. East
Orillia, ON L3V 1V5
705-653-0323
Toll-Free: 866-216-6222
E-mail: admin@canauthors.org
URL: www.canauthors.org
Scope: National
Purpose: Educational seminars, awards, readings, & networking opportunities
Contact Information: Email: admin@canauthors.org

Canadian Catholic School Trustees' Association Annual General Meeting
Date: June 11-13, 2015
Location: St. John's, NL
Sponsor/Contact: Canadian Catholic School Trustees' Association
Catholic Education Centre
570 West Hunt Club Rd.
Nepean, ON K2G 3R4
613-224-4455 *Fax:* 613-224-3187
E-mail: ccsta@ocsb.ca
URL: www.ccsta.ca

Canadian College & University Food Service Association 2015 National Conference
Date: June 27 - July 2, 2015
Location: Delta Grand Hotel
Kelowna, BC
Sponsor/Contact: Canadian College & University Food Service Association
c/o Drew Hall, University of Guelph
Gordon St.
Guelph, ON N1G 2W1
519-824-4120 *Fax:* 519-837-9302
E-mail: mcollins@hrs.uoguelph.ca
URL: www.ccufsa.on.ca
Scope: National
Purpose: A gathering of food service directors, managers, & senior administrators from self-operated & contracted schools

Canadian College of Neuropsychopharmacology 2015 Annual Meeting
Date: June 9-12, 2015
Location: Lord Elgin Hotel
Ottawa, ON
Sponsor/Contact: Canadian College of Neuropsychopharmacology
c/o Rachelle Anderson, Dept. of Psychiatry, University of Alberta
#IE7.19, 8440 - 112 St., Walter MacKenzie Centre
Edmonton, AB T6G 2B7
780-407-6543 *Fax:* 780-407-6672
E-mail: Rachelle@ccnp.ca
URL: www.ccnp.ca
Scope: National

Canadian Council for the Advancement of Education 2015 Annual Conference: Beyond Boundaries - Transformation, Collaboration and Trending
Date: June 10-12, 2015
Location: e Centre Sheraton Montreal Hotel
Montreal, QC
Sponsor/Contact: Canadian Council for the Advancement of Education
#310, 4 Cataraqui St.
Kingston, ON K7K 1Z7
613-531-9213 *Fax:* 613-531-0626
E-mail: admin@ccaecanada.org
URL: www.ccaecanada.org
Scope: National
Purpose: An annual national gathering, with keynote speakers, plenary sessions, roundtables, & the presentation of awards
Contact Information: Executive Director: Mark Hazlett, E-mail: haz@ccaecanada.org

Canadian Council of Motor Transport Administrators 2015 Annual Meeting
Date: June 16-19, 2015
Location: Whitehorse, YT
Sponsor/Contact: Canadian Council of Motor Transport Administrators
2323 St. Laurent Blvd.
Ottawa, ON K1G 4J8
613-736-1003 *Fax:* 613-736-1395
E-mail: ccmta-secretariat@ccmta.ca
URL: www.ccmta.ca
Scope: National
Purpose: Educational events, an exhibition, a working forum where important decisions are made, & an excellent networking opportunity for government decision-makers & members of the private sector
Contact Information: Phone: 613-736-1003 Fax: 613-736-1395, E-mail: ccmta-secretariat@ccmta.ca

Canadian Dermatology Association 2015 90th Annual Conference
Date: June 7-8, 2015
Location: Vancouver, BC
Sponsor/Contact: Canadian Dermatology Association
#425, 1385 Bank St.
Ottawa, ON K1H 8N4
613-738-1748 *Fax:* 613-738-4695
Toll-Free: 800-267-3376
E-mail: info@dermatology.ca
URL: www.dermatology.ca
Scope: National
Purpose: Oral & poster presentations on subjects relevant to practicing dermatologists

Canadian Energy Research Institute 2015 Petrochemical Conference
Date: June 7-9, 2015
Location: Delta Lodge at Kananaskis
Kananaskis, AB
Sponsor/Contact: Canadian Energy Research Institute
#150, 3512 - 33 St. NW
Calgary, AB T2L 2A6
403-282-1231 *Fax:* 403-284-4181
E-mail: info@ceri.ca
URL: www.ceri.ca
Scope: National
Contact Information: General Inquiries, E-mail: conference@ceri.ca; Contact, Sponsorship Information: Deanne Landry, Phone: 403-220-2395, E-mail: dlandry@ceri.ca

Canadian Environmental Grantmakers' Network Annual Conference and CFC Conference 2015
Date: June 9-11, 2015
Location: The Old Mill
Toronto, ON
Sponsor/Contact: Canadian Environmental Grantmakers' Network
#300, 70 The Esplanade
Toronto, ON M5E 1R2
647-288-8891 *Fax:* 416-979-3936
E-mail: pegi_dover@cegn.org
URL: www.cegn.org
Scope: National
Contact Information: Pegi Dover; Email: pegi_dover@cegn.org; Phone: 647-288-8891

Canadian Federation of Nurses Unions Convention 2015
Date: June 1-5, 2015
Location: Halifax, NS
Sponsor/Contact: Canadian Federation of Nurses Unions
2841 Riverside Dr.
Ottawa, ON K1V 8X7
613-526-4661 *Fax:* 613-526-1023
Toll-Free: 800-321-9821
URL: www.nursesunions.ca
Scope: National

Canadian Federation of University Women 2015 Annual General Meeting
Date: June 18-21, 2015
Location: Québec City, QC
Sponsor/Contact: Canadian Federation of University Women
Head Office
#502, 331 Cooper St.
Ottawa, ON K2P 0G5

Conferences Index

613-234-8252 *Fax:* 613-234-8221
E-mail: cfuwgen@rogers.com
URL: www.cfuw.org
Scope: National

Canadian Gaming Association 2015 19th Annual Canadian Gaming Summit
Date: June 16-18, 2015
Location: Caesars Windsor
Windsor, ON
Sponsor/Contact: Canadian Gaming Association
#503, 131 Bloor St. West
Toronto, ON M5S 1P7
416-304-7800 *Fax:* 416-304-7805
E-mail: info@canadiangaming.ca
URL: www.canadiangaming.ca
Scope: International
Purpose: A conference & trade show for representatives from gaming & regulatory agencies, First Nations gaming, provincial lotteries, casinos, race tracks, & charitable gaming organizations
Contact Information: URL: www.canadiangamingsummit.com

Canadian Health Libraries Association (CHLA) / Association des bibliothèques de la santé du Canada (ABSC) 2015 39th Annual Conference
Date: June 19-22, 2015
Location: Vancouver, BC
Sponsor/Contact: Canadian Health Libraries Association
39 River St.
Toronto, ON M5A 3P1
416-646-1600 *Fax:* 416-646-9460
E-mail: info@chla-absc.ca
URL: www.chla-absc.ca
Scope: National
Purpose: An annual May or June gathering of health science librarians to participate in continuing education courses & lectures, & to view products & services related to their work
Contact Information: Continuing Education, E-mail: ce@chla-absc.ca; Public Relations, E-mail: pr@chla-absc.ca

Canadian Historical Association 2015 Annual Meeting (held in conjunction with the Congress of the Humanities & Social Sciences)
Date: June 1-3, 2015
Location: University of Ottawa
Ottawa, ON
Sponsor/Contact: Canadian Historical Association
#501, 130 Albert St.
Ottawa, ON K1P 5G4
613-233-7885 *Fax:* 613-565-5445
URL: www.cha-shc.ca
Scope: National
Purpose: An event for historians to showcase their research & to discuss issues related to the discipline
Contact Information: Program Chair: Heather MacDougall, E-mail: hmacdoug@uwaterloo.ca; Liaison with Program Committee: James Opp, E-mail: james_opp@carleton.ca

Canadian Institute of Actuaries 2015 Annual Meeting
Date: June 17-18, 2015
Location: Ottawa, ON
Sponsor/Contact: Canadian Institute of Actuaries
Secretariat
#1740, 360 Albert St.
Ottawa, ON K1R 7X7
613-236-8196 *Fax:* 613-233-4552
E-mail: head.office@cia-ica.ca
URL: www.cia-ica.ca
Scope: National

Canadian Institute of Planners 2015 Conference: Thrive
Date: June 27-30, 2015
Location: Saskatoon, SK
Sponsor/Contact: Canadian Institute of Planners
#1112, 141 Laurier Ave. West
Ottawa, ON K1P 5J3
613-237-7526 *Fax:* 613-237-7045
Toll-Free: 800-207-2138
E-mail: general@cip-icu.ca
URL: www.cip-icu.ca
Scope: National
Purpose: Educational sessions & workshops for professional planners from across Canada
Contact Information: Phone: 613-237-7526; Fax: 613-237-7045; E-mail: conference@cip-icu.ca; URL: www.thrive2015fleurir.ca

Canadian Institute of Plumbing & Heating 2015 Annual Business Conference/Annual General Meeting
Date: June 14-16, 2015
Location: Fairmont Chateau Frontenac
Québec, QC
Sponsor/Contact: Canadian Institute of Plumbing & Heating
#504, 295 The West Mall
Toronto, ON M9C 4Z4
416-695-0447 *Fax:* 416-695-0450
Toll-Free: 800-639-2474
E-mail: info@ciph.com
URL: www.ciph.com
Scope: National

Canadian Institute of Transportation Engineers / Ontario Traffic Council 2015 Conference
Date: June 7-10, 2015
Location: Regina, SK
Sponsor/Contact: Canadian Institute of Transportation Engineers
P.O. Box PO Box 81009, Harbour Square PO
89 Queens Quay West
Toronto, ON M5J 2V3
202-785-0060 *Fax:* 202-785-0609
URL: www.cite7.org
Scope: National
Anticipated Attendance: 150-350

Canadian Institute of Underwriters Annual General Meeting 2015
Date: June 1-2, 2015
Location: Marriott Toronto Downtown
Toronto, ON
Sponsor/Contact: Canadian Institute of Underwriters
c/o Marian Kingsmill, DKCI Events (David Kingsmill Consultants Inc.)
P.O. Box 91516 Stn. Roseland Plaza
3023 New St.
Burlington, ON L7R 4L6
URL: www.ciu.ca
Scope: National

Canadian Land Reclamation Association / Association canadienne de réhabilitation des sites dégradés 2015 40th Annual General Meeting
Date: June 15-18, 2015
Location: Radisson Winnipeg Downtown
Winnipeg, MB
Sponsor/Contact: Canadian Land Reclamation Association
P.O. Box 61047 Stn. Kensington
Calgary, AB T2N 4S6
403-289-9435
E-mail: clra@telusplanet.net
URL: www.clra.ca
Scope: National
Purpose: Business affairs of the association
Contact Information: Lucie Labbe, Phone: 514-287-8500

Canadian Law & Society Association Annual Meeting 2015
Date: June 3-5, 2015
Location: Ottawa, ON
Sponsor/Contact: Canadian Law & Society Association
c/o Dept. of Law, Carleton University
1125 Colonel Bay Dr.
Ottawa, ON K1S 5B6
E-mail: info@acds-clsa.org
URL: www.acds-clsa.org
Scope: National

Canadian Library Association / Association canadienne des bibliothèques 70th National Conference & Trade Show 2015
Date: June 3-6, 2015
Location: Ottawa, ON
Sponsor/Contact: Canadian Library Association
#400, 1150 Morrison Dr.
Ottawa, ON K2H 8S9
613-232-9625 *Fax:* 613-563-9895
E-mail: info@cla.ca
URL: www.cla.ca
Scope: National
Purpose: Featuring keynote speakers, workshops, social events, & a trade show
Anticipated Attendance: 800+
Contact Information: Manager, Conference & Events: Wendy Walton, Phone: 613-232-9625, ext. 302, E-mail: wwalton@cla.ca; Manager, Marketing & Communications (Trade show & sponsorship opportunities): Judy Green, Phone: 613-232-9625, ext. 322, E-mail: jgreen@cla.ca

Canadian Medical & Biological Engineering Society 2015 38th Annual National Conference
Date: June 7-12, 2015
Location: Toronto, ON
Sponsor/Contact: Canadian Medical & Biological Engineering Society
1485 Laperrière Ave.
Ottawa, ON K1Z 7S8
613-728-1759
E-mail: secretariat@cmbes.ca
URL: www.cmbes.ca
Scope: National
Purpose: An annual gathering of Canadian biomedical engineering professionals for continuing education & networking opportunities. This year's conference is a collaboration with l'Association des physiciens et ingénieurs biomédicaux du Québec (APIBQ).
Contact Information: Chair, Long-Term Conference Planning: Sarah Kelso, E-mail: sarah.a.kelso@gmail.com

Canadian Neurological Sciences Federation 50th Annual Congress
Date: June 9-12, 2015
Location: Royal York Hotel
Toronto, ON
Sponsor/Contact: Canadian Neurological Sciences Federation
#709, 7015 Macleod Trail SW
Calgary, AB T2H 2K6
403-229-9544 *Fax:* 403-229-1661
E-mail: info@cnsfederation.org
URL: www.cnsfederation.org
Scope: National
Purpose: Courses, lectures, oral & digital poster presentations, plus exhibits & social events
Contact Information: Canadian Neurological Sciences Federation, Phone: 403-229-9544

Canadian Ophthalmological Society 2015 Annual Meeting & Exhibition
Date: June 18-21, 2015
Location: Victoria Conference Centre
Victoria, BC
Sponsor/Contact: Canadian Ophthalmological Society
#610, 1525 Carling Ave.
Ottawa, ON K1Z 8R9
613-729-6779 *Fax:* 613-729-7209
E-mail: cos@eyesite.ca
URL: www.eyesite.ca
Scope: National
Contact Information: Registration Contact: Rita Afeltra, E-mail: rafeltra@cos-sco.ca; URL: www.cos-sco.ca/victoria2015

Canadian Organization of Campus Activities 2015 National Conference
Date: June 8-12, 2015
Location: DoubleTree by Hilton West Edmonton
Edmonton, AB
Sponsor/Contact: Canadian Organization of Campus Activities
#202, 509 Commissioners Rd. West
London, ON N6J 1Y5
519-690-0207 *Fax:* 519-681-4328
E-mail: cocaoffice@coca.org
URL: www.coca.org
Scope: National
Purpose: Educational sessions, plus showcases featuring music, films, & comedy, plus the Campus Activities Biz Hall trade show

Canadian Organization of Campus Activities 2015 National Conference
Date: June 2015
Location: Alberta
Sponsor/Contact: Canadian Organization of Campus Activities
#202, 509 Commissioners Rd. West
London, ON N6J 1Y5
519-690-0207 *Fax:* 519-681-4328
E-mail: cocaoffice@coca.org
URL: www.coca.org
Scope: National
Purpose: Educational sessions, plus showcases featuring music, films, & comedy, plus the Campus Activities Biz Hall trade show

Canadian Orthopaedic Association 2015 70th Annual Meeting & Canadian Orthopaedic Research Society 49th Annual Meeting
Date: June 17-20, 2015
Location: Fairmount Hotel Vancouver
Vancouver, BC
Sponsor/Contact: Canadian Orthopaedic Association
#360, 4150, rue Ste-Catherine ouest
Montréal, QC H3Z 2Y5
514-874-9003 *Fax:* 514-874-0464
E-mail: cynthia@canorth.org
URL: www.coa-aco.org
Scope: National

Contact Information: Meghan Corbeil, Contact; Phone: 514-874-9003 ext. 4; Email: meghan@canorth.org; URL: www.coaannualmeeting.ca

Canadian Orthopaedic Residents Association 2015 Annual Meeting
Date: June 17-20, 2015
Location: Vancouver, BC
Sponsor/Contact: Canadian Orthopaedic Residents Association
#450, 4150, rue Sainte-Catherine ouest
Montréal, QC H3Z 2Y5
514-874-9003 *Fax:* 514-874-0464
E-mail: coraweb@canorth.org
URL: www.coraweb.org
Scope: National

Canadian Pediatric Foundation 92nd Annual Conference
Date: June 24-27, 2015
Location: Sheraton Centre Hotel
Toronto, ON
Sponsor/Contact: Canadian Pediatric Foundation
2305 St. Laurent Blvd.
Ottawa, ON K1G 4J8
613-526-9397 *Fax:* 613-526-3332
E-mail: cpf@cps.ca
URL: www.cps.ca
Scope: National
Contact Information: Email: meetings@cps.ca; URL: www.annualconference.cps.ca

Canadian Physiotherapy Association 2015 Congress
Date: June 18-21, 2015
Location: Halifax, NS
Sponsor/Contact: Canadian Physiotherapy Association
955 Green Valley Cres.
Ottawa, ON K2C 3V4
613-564-5454 *Fax:* 613-564-1577
Toll-Free: 800-387-8679
E-mail: information@physiotherapy.ca
URL: www.physiotherapy.ca
Scope: National
Purpose: Educational courses, workshops, the presentation of scientific research, private practice leadership information, & networking opportunities for physiotherapists from across Canada
Contact Information: Registration Contact: Hope Caldwell, Phone: 1-800-387-8679, ext. 247, E-mail: hcaldwell@physiotherapy.ca

Canadian Political Science Association 2015 Annual Conference (within the Congress of the Humanities & Social Sciences)
Date: June 3, 2015
Location: University of Ottawa
Ottawa, ON
Sponsor/Contact: Canadian Political Science Association
#204, 260 Dalhousie St.
Ottawa, ON K1N 7E4
613-562-1202 *Fax:* 613-241-0019
E-mail: cpsa@csse.ca
URL: www.cpsa-acsp.ca
Scope: National
Purpose: A conference including the association's business & committee meetings, special presentations, workshops, & exhibits
Contact Information: Canadian Political Science Association Secretariat, E-mail: cpsa-acsp@cpsa-acsp.ca

Canadian Poultry and Egg Processors Council (CPEPC) Convention 2015
Date: June 14-16, 2015
Location: Winnipeg, MB
Sponsor/Contact: Canadian Poultry & Egg Processors Council
#400, 1545 Carling Ave.
Ottawa, ON K1Z 8P9
613-724-6605 *Fax:* 613-724-4577
URL: www.cpepc.ca
Scope: National

Canadian Psychological Association 2015 76th Annual Convention
Date: June 4-6, 2015
Location: Westin Ottawa
Ottawa, ON
Sponsor/Contact: Canadian Psychological Association
#702, 141 Laurier Ave. West
Ottawa, ON K1P 5J3
613-237-2144 *Fax:* 613-237-1674
Toll-Free: 888-472-0657
E-mail: cpa@cpa.ca
URL: www.cpa.ca
Scope: National
Purpose: An educational conference & exhibition
Contact Information: E-mail: convention@cpa.ca

Canadian Remote Sensing Society 2015 36th Canadian Symposium on Remote Sensing
Date: June 9-11, 2015
Location: Delta Hotel
St. John's, NL
Sponsor/Contact: Canadian Remote Sensing Society
c/o Canadian Aeronautics & Space Institute
#104, 350 Terry Fox Dr.
Kanata, ON K2K 2W5
613-591-8787 *Fax:* 613-591-7291
E-mail: casi@casi.ca
URL: www.crss-sct.ca
Scope: National

Canadian Society for Brain, Behaviour & Cognitive Science Annual Meeting
Date: June 5-7, 2015
Location: Carleton University
Ottawa, ON
Sponsor/Contact: Canadian Society for Brain, Behaviour & Cognitive Science
c/o Dept. of Psychology, University of British Columbia
Vancouver, BC V6T 1Z4
E-mail: secretary@csbbcs.org
URL: www.csbbcs.org

Canadian Society for Chemistry 2015 98th Canadian Chemistry Conference & Exhibition
Date: June 13-17, 2015
Location: Ottawa, ON
Sponsor/Contact: Canadian Society for Chemistry
#550, 130 Slater St.
Ottawa, ON K1P 6E2
613-232-6252 *Fax:* 613-232-5862
Toll-Free: 888-542-2242
E-mail: info@cheminst.ca
URL: www.cheminst.ca
Scope: National
Contact Information: URL: www.csc2015.ca

Canadian Society for Immunology 28th Annual Conference
Date: June 4-7, 2015
Location: The Fairmount Winnipeg
Winnipeg, MB
Sponsor/Contact: Canadian Society for Immunology
c/o Dept. of Veterinary Microbiology, Univ. of Saskatchewan
52 Campus Dr.
Saskatoon, SK S7N 5B4
306-966-7214 *Fax:* 306-966-7244
E-mail: info@csi-sci.ca
URL: www.csi-sci.ca
Scope: National

Canadian Society for Italian Studies 2015 Annual Conference
Date: June 19-21, 2015
Location: Sant'Anna Institute
Sorrento, Italy
Sponsor/Contact: Canadian Society for Italian Studies
c/o Sandra Parmegiani, School of Languages & Literatures, U of Guelph
50 Stone Rd. East
Guelph, ON N1G 2W1
519-824-4120 *Fax:* 519-763-9572
E-mail: sparmegi@uoguelph.ca
URL: www.canadiansocietyforitalianstudies.camp7.org
Scope: International
Purpose: In conjunction with the 80th Congress of the Canadian Federation of the Humanities & Social Sciences

Canadian Society of Otolaryngology - Head & Neck Surgery 2015 69th Annual Meeting: "Taking Care of Your Patients and Yourself - Work / Life Balance"
Date: June 6-9, 2015
Location: RBC Convention Centre / Delta Hotel
Winnipeg, MB
Sponsor/Contact: Canadian Society of Otolaryngology - Head & Neck Surgery Administrative Office
221 Millford Cres.
Elora, ON N0B 1S0
519-846-0630 *Fax:* 519-846-9529
Toll-Free: 800-655-9533
E-mail: cso.hns@sympatico.ca
URL: www.entcanada.org
Scope: National
Purpose: Scientific presentations for graduates in medicine who hold a certificate in otolaryngology & professionals who work in areas related to otolaryngology
Contact Information: Canadian Society of Otolaryngology Administrative Office: Phone: 519-846-0630, E-mail: cso.hns@sympatico.ca

Canadian Society of Plastic Surgeons 2015 69th Annual Meeting
Date: June 2-6, 2015
Location: Fairmont Empress Hotel
Victoria, BC
Sponsor/Contact: Canadian Society of Plastic Surgeons
#4, 1469, boul St-Joseph est
Montréal, QC H2J 1M6
514-843-5415 *Fax:* 514-843-7005
E-mail: csps_sccp@bellnet.ca
URL: www.plasticsurgery.ca
Scope: National
Purpose: An opportunity for participants to learn during the scientific program & to view exhibits
Contact Information: Phone: 514-843-5415; Fax: 514-843-7005, E-mail: csps_sccp@bellnet.ca

Canadian Sociological Association Congress 2015
Date: June 1-5, 2015
Location: University of Ottawa
Ottawa, ON
Sponsor/Contact: Canadian Sociological Association
P.O. Box 98014
2126 Burnhamthorpe Rd. West
Mississauga, ON L5L 5V4
438-880-2182
E-mail: office@csa-scs.ca
URL: www.csa-scs.ca
Scope: National
Purpose: In conjunction with the Canadian Federation of Humanities and Social Sciences.

Canadian Standards Association 2015 Annual Conference & Committee Week
Date: June 14-19, 2015
Location: Niagara Falls, ON
Sponsor/Contact: Canadian Standards Association
#100, 5060 Spectrum Way
Mississauga, ON L4W 5N6
416-747-4000 *Fax:* 416-747-2473
Toll-Free: 800-463-6727
E-mail: member@csa.ca
URL: www.csa.ca
Scope: National
Purpose: Educational presentations & committee meetings
Anticipated Attendance: 600+

Canadian Urological Association 2015 70th Annual Meeting
Date: June 28-30, 2015
Location: Westin Hotel
Ottawa, ON
Sponsor/Contact: Canadian Urological Association
#1303, 1155, University St.
Montréal, QC H3B 3A7
514-395-0376 *Fax:* 514-395-1664
E-mail: cua@cua.org
URL: www.cua.org
Scope: National

Career Colleges Ontario & National Association of Career Colleges (NACC) Annual Conference 2015 - All In With CCO
Date: June 24-26, 2015
Location: Niagara Falls, ON
Sponsor/Contact: Career Colleges Ontario
#2, 155 Lynden Rd.
Brantford, ON N3R 8A7
519-752-2124 *Fax:* 519-752-3649
E-mail: info@careercolleges.ca
URL: careercolleges.ca
Scope: Provincial
Purpose: A keynote address, professional development sessions, a business meeting, & networking opportunities
Contact Information: Career Colleges Ontario Administrative Assistant: Dena Stuart, Phone: 519-752-2124, ext. 200, Fax: 519-752-3649, E-mail: denastuart@careercollegesontario.ca

Clean Nova Scotia 2015 Annual General Meeting
Location: Nova Scotia
Sponsor/Contact: Clean Nova Scotia

Conferences Index

126 Portland St.
Dartmouth, NS B2Y 1H8
902-420-3474 *Fax:* 902-424-5334
Toll-Free: 888-380-5008
E-mail: cns@clean.ns.ca
URL: www.clean.ns.ca
Scope: Provincial
Purpose: Reports from executives, a review of finances, & information about envrionmental programming
Contact Information: Coordinator, Communications: Leanna Grosvold, E-mail: lgrosvold@clean.ns.ca

Community Health Nurses of Canada 2015 10th National Community Health Nurses Conference
Date: June 22-24, 2015
Location: Winnipeg, MB
Sponsor/Contact: Community Health Nurses of Canada
182 Clendenan Ave.
Toronto, ON M6P 2X2
647-239-9554 *Fax:* 416-426-7280
E-mail: info@chnc.ca
URL: www.chnc.ca
Scope: National
Purpose: A meeting of persons interested in community health nursing for educational sessions, workshops, posters, & exhibits
Contact Information: E-mail: info@chnc.ca

Community Living Grimsby, Lincoln & West Lincoln 50th Annual General Meeting
Date: June 8, 2015
Sponsor/Contact: Community Living Grimsby, Lincoln & West Lincoln
Lincoln Kingsway Plaza
P.O. Box 220
#8-9, 5041 King St.
Beamsville, ON L0R 1B0
905-563-4115 *Fax:* 905-563-8887
E-mail: info@cl-grimsbylincoln.ca
URL: www.cl-grimsbylincoln.ca
Scope: Local

Continuing Care Association of Nova Scotia 2015 AGM
Date: June 7-9, 2015
Location: Liscomb Lodge
Marie Joseph, NS
Sponsor/Contact: Continuing Care Association of Nova Scotia
c/o Sunshine Personal Home Care
38A Withrod Dr.
Halifax, NS B3N 1B1
902-446-3140
E-mail: ccans@eastlink.ca
URL: www.nsnet.org/ccans
Scope: Provincial

Cooperative Housing Federation of Canada 2015 Annual General Meeting
Date: June 3-6, 2015
Location: Charlottetown, PE
Sponsor/Contact: Cooperative Housing Federation of Canada
#311, 225 Metcalfe St.
Ottawa, ON K2P 1P9
613-230-2201 *Fax:* 613-230-2231
Toll-Free: 800-465-2752
E-mail: info@chfcanada.coop
URL: www.chfc.ca
Scope: National
Purpose: Training for co-op volunteers & staff; Business meeting; Youth forum; Elections for the Board of Directors; Group caucuses
Anticipated Attendance: 850

Dietitians of Canada 2015 Annual National Conference
Date: June 4-6, 2015
Location: Québec City, QC
Sponsor/Contact: Dietitians of Canada
#604, 480 University Ave.
Toronto, ON M5G 1V2
416-596-0857 *Fax:* 416-596-0603
E-mail: centralinfo@dietitians.ca
URL: www.dietitians.ca
Scope: National
Purpose: A learning & networking event for dietitians
Contact Information: General information email: events@dietitians.ca

Doctors Nova Scotia 2015 Annual Conference
Date: June 5-6, 2015
Location: Membertou Trade & Convention Centre
Cape Breton, NS
Sponsor/Contact: Doctors Nova Scotia
25 Spectacle Lake Dr.
Dartmouth, NS B3B 1X7
902-468-1866 *Fax:* 902-468-6578
E-mail: info@doctorsns.com
URL: www.doctorsns.com
Scope: Provincial

Editors' Association of Canada Conference 2015-Editing Goes Global
Date: June 12-14, 2015
Location: Metro Toronto Convention Centre
Toronto, ON
Sponsor/Contact: Editors' Association of Canada
#505, 27 Carlton St.
Toronto, ON M5B 1L2
416-975-1379 *Fax:* 416-975-1637
Toll-Free: 866-226-3348
E-mail: info@editors.ca
URL: www.editors.ca
Scope: National

Federation of Canadian Municipalities 2015 Annual Conference & Trade Show
Date: June 5-8, 2015
Location: Shaw Conference Centre
Edmonton, AB
Sponsor/Contact: Federation of Canadian Municipalities
24 Clarence St.
Ottawa, ON K1N 5P3
613-241-5221 *Fax:* 613-241-7440
E-mail: federation@fcm.ca
URL: www.fcm.ca
Scope: National

Federation of Medical Regulatory Authorities of Canada 2015 AGM & Conference
Date: June 6-8, 2015
Location: Fredericton, NB
Sponsor/Contact: Federation of Medical Regulatory Authorities of Canada
#103, 2283 St. Laurent Blvd.
Ottawa, ON K1G 5A2
613-738-0372 *Fax:* 613-738-9169
E-mail: info@fmrac.ca
URL: www.fmrac.ca
Scope: National

Fenestration Canada's 2015 Annual General Meeting
Date: June 4-7, 2015
Location: Fairmont Hotel Vancouver
Vancouver, BC
Sponsor/Contact: Fenestration Canada
#1208, 130 Albert St.
Ottawa, ON K1P 5G4
613-235-5511 *Fax:* 613-235-4664
E-mail: info@fenestrationcanada.ca
URL: www.fenestrationcanada.ca
Scope: National
Purpose: A business meeting to keep current with industry trends & opportunities

Film Studies Association of Canada 2015 Annual Conference
Date: June 2-4, 2015
Location: University of Ottawa
Ottawa, ON
Sponsor/Contact: Film Studies Association of Canada
c/o Peter Lester, Brock University
500 Glenridge Ave.
St Catharines, ON L2S 3A1
E-mail: fsac@filmstudies.ca
URL: www.filmstudies.ca
Scope: National
Contact Information: Email: conference2015@filmstudies.ca

Financial Executives International Canada 2015 Conference
Date: June 10, 2015
Location: RBC Convention Centre Winnipeg
Winnipeg, MB
Sponsor/Contact: Financial Executives International Canada
#1201, 170 University Ave.
Toronto, ON M5H 3B3
416-366-3007 *Fax:* 416-366-3008
Toll-Free: 866-677-3007
URL: www.feicanada.org
Scope: National

Gymnastics Nova Scotia 2015 Annual General Meeting
Date: June 18-21, 2015
Location: Ottawa, ON
Sponsor/Contact: Gymnastics Nova Scotia
5516 Spring Garden Rd., 4th Fl.
Halifax, NS B3J 1G6
902-425-5450 *Fax:* 902-425-5606
E-mail: gns@sportnovascotia.ca
URL: www.gymns.ca
Scope: Provincial
Purpose: A yearly gathering to establish the general policy & direction of the association, consider committee reports, & elect the new executive committee
Contact Information: E-mail: gns@sportnovascotia.ca

Independent Telecommunications Providers Association 2015 50th Annual Convention
Date: June 7-9, 2015
Location: Taboo Muskoka Resort
Gravenhurst, ON
Sponsor/Contact: Independent Telecommunications Providers Association
29 Peevers Cres.
Newmarket, ON L3Y 7T5
519-595-3975 *Fax:* 519-595-3976
URL: www.ota.on.ca
Scope: Provincial
Purpose: An event featuring guest speakers, informative seminars, the annual general meeting, social events, & opportunities to meet with telecommunications industry representatives

International Association of Music Libraries, Archives & Documentation Centres 2015 64th Annual Conference
Date: June 21-26, 2015
Location: New York City, NY USA
Sponsor/Contact: International Association of Music Libraries, Archives & Documentation Centres
c/o Roger Flury, Music Room, National Library of New Zealand
P.O. Box 1467
Wellington, 6001
URL: www.iaml.info
Scope: International
Purpose: Educational sessions, social & cultural programs, & exhibits of interest to international music librarians, archivists, & documentation specialists

International Organization of Securities Commissions / Organisation internationale des commissions de valeurs Annual Conference 2015
Date: June 14-18, 2015
Location: London, UK
Sponsor/Contact: International Organization of Securities Commissions
C/ Oquendo 12
Madrid, 28006
E-mail: mail@iosco.org
URL: www.iosco.org
Scope: International

International Peat Society Annual Meetings and International Peat Technology Conference 2015
Date: June 7-12, 2015
Location: Tullamore Court Hotel
Tullamore, Ireland
Sponsor/Contact: International Peat Society
Kauppakatu 19 D 31
Jyväskylä, FIN-40100
E-mail: ips@peatsociety.org
URL: www.peatsociety.org
Scope: International
Contact Information: URL: www.peatsociety.org/tullamore2015

Local Government Management Association of British Columbia 2015 Annual General Meeting & Conference
Date: June 16-18, 2015
Location: Prince George Civic Centre
Prince George, BC
Sponsor/Contact: Local Government Management Association of British Columbia
Central Building
620 View St., 7th Fl.
Victoria, BC V8W 1J6
250-383-7032 *Fax:* 250-384-4879
E-mail: office@lgma.ca
URL: www.lgma.ca
Scope: Provincial
Purpose: A meeting & tradeshow held each year in May or June in British Columbia for members of the Local Government Management Association of British Columbia
Anticipated Attendance: 400-500
Contact Information: Program Coordinator: Ana Fuller, Phone: 250-383-7032, ext. 227, Fax: 250-383-4879, E-mail: afuller@lgma.ca

Motion Picture Theatre Associations of Canada ShowCanada 2015
Date: June 2-4, 2015
Location: Fairmont Le Château Frontenac
Québec City, QC

Sponsor/Contact: Motion Picture Theatre Association of Manitoba
c/o Empire Theatres
#127, 1120 Grant Ave.
Winnipeg, MB R2C 4J2
204-453-4536 *Fax:* 204-470-3104
E-mail: et084-gm@empiretheatres.com
Scope: National
Purpose: A program featuring speakers, seminars, information about digital issues & new technologies, the presentation of awards, a trade show, film screenings, & social & networking events
Contact Information: Head Coordinator, ShowCanada: Patricia Gariepy, Phone: 450-668-1346, E-mail: registration@showcanada.ca; URL: www.showcanada.ca

NOIA Conference 2015
Date: June 15-18, 2015
Location: Delta St. John's
St. John's, NL
Sponsor/Contact: NOIA
Atlantic Place
#602, 215 Water St.
St. John's, NL A1C 6C9
709-758-6610 *Fax:* 709-758-6611
E-mail: noia@noia.ca
URL: www.noia.ca
Scope: National
Purpose: The Annual Noia Conference is a key service that provides members and the general public with information on trends and business opportunities in the East Coast Canada oil & gas industry.

National Health Leadership Conference 2015
Date: June 15-16, 2015
Location: Charlottetown, PE
Sponsor/Contact: Canadian College of Health Leaders
292 Somerset St. West
Ottawa, ON K2P 0J6
613-235-7218 *Fax:* 613-235-5451
Toll-Free: 800-363-9056
E-mail: info@cchl-ccls.ca
URL: www.cchl-ccls.ca
Scope: National
Purpose: In partnership with HealthCareCAN.
Contact Information: Laurie Oman, Conference Services Coordinator; Phone: 613-235-7218 ext. 227; Email: loman@cchl-ccls.ca

North American Association of Central Cancer Registries 2015 Annual Conference: First in Flight: Launching a New Era in Cancer Surveillance
Date: June 13-19, 2015
Location: Westin Charlotte
Charlotte, NC USA
Sponsor/Contact: North American Association of Central Cancer Registries, Inc.
2121 West White Oaks Dr., #B
Springfield, IL 62704-7412
217-698-0800 *Fax:* 217-698-0188
E-mail: info@naaccr.org
URL: www.naaccr.org
Scope: International
Anticipated Attendance: 450

Ontario Association of Chiefs of Police 2015 Annual Meeting
Date: June 14-17, 2015
Location: Ontario
Sponsor/Contact: Ontario Association of Chiefs of Police
#605, 40 College St.
Toronto, ON M5G 2J3
416-926-0424 *Fax:* 416-926-0436
Toll-Free: 800-816-1767
E-mail: oacpadmin@oacp.ca
URL: www.oacp.on.ca
Scope: Provincial

Ontario College of Teachers 2015 Annual Meeting of Members
Date: June 4, 2015
Sponsor/Contact: Ontario College of Teachers
101 Bloor St. East
Toronto, ON M5S 0A1
416-961-8800 *Fax:* 416-961-8822
Toll-Free: 888-534-2222
E-mail: info@oct.ca
URL: www.oct.ca
Scope: Provincial
Purpose: Presentations of interest to teachers

Ontario Occupational Health Nurses Association 44th Annual Conference
Date: June 4-5, 2015
Location: Niagara Falls Mariott Gateway on the Falls
Niagara Falls, ON
Sponsor/Contact: Ontario Occupational Health Nurses Association
#605, 302 The East Mall
Toronto, ON M9B 6C7
416-239-6462 *Fax:* 416-239-5462
Toll-Free: 866-664-6276
E-mail: administration@oohna.on.ca
URL: www.oohna.on.ca
Scope: Provincial

Ontario Public School Boards' Association 2015 AGM
Date: June 11-13, 2015
Location: Westin Trillium House
Blue Mountain, ON
Sponsor/Contact: Ontario Public School Boards Association
#1850, 439 University Ave.
Toronto, ON M5G 1Y8
416-340-2540 *Fax:* 416-340-7571
E-mail: webmaster@opsba.org
URL: www.opsba.org
Scope: Provincial

Operating Room Nurses Association of Nova Scotia Annual General Meeting 2015
Date: June 5-6, 2015
Location: Old Orchard Inn Resort & Spa
Annapolis Valley, NS
Sponsor/Contact: Operating Room Nurses Association of Nova Scotia
URL: www.ornans.ca
Scope: Provincial

Ordre des ingénieurs du Québec Assemblée générale annuelle 2015
Date: June 11, 2015
Location: Palais des congrès des Montréal
Montréal, QC
Sponsor/Contact: Ordre des ingénieurs du Québec
Gare Windsor
#350, 1100, av des Canadiens-de-Montréal
Montréal, QC H3B 2S2
514-845-6141 *Fax:* 514-845-1833
Toll-Free: 800-461-6141
E-mail: info@oiq.qc.ca
URL: www.oiq.qc.ca
Scope: Provincial

Packaging Association of Canada PACKEX Toronto - Canada's Packaging Marketplace
Date: June 16-18, 2015
Location: Toronto Congress Centre
Toronto, ON
Sponsor/Contact: Packaging Association of Canada
#607, 1 Concorde Gate
Toronto, ON M3C 3N6
416-490-7860 *Fax:* 416-490-7844
E-mail: pacinfo@pac.ca
URL: www.pac.ca
Scope: National
Contact Information: URL: www.canontradeshows.com/expo/packex13

Quilt Canada 2015
Date: June 4-6, 2015
Location: University of Lethbridge
Lethbridge, AB
Sponsor/Contact: Canadian Quilters' Association
6 Spruce St.
Pasadena, NL A0L 1K0
E-mail: administration@canadianquilter.com
URL: www.canadianquilter.com
Scope: National
Purpose: National conference

Society for Existential & Phenomenological Theory & Culture 2015 Conference
Date: June 2-5, 2015
Location: Ottawa, ON
Sponsor/Contact: Society for Existential & Phenomenological Theory & Culture
URL: www.eptc-tcep.net

Society of Gynecologic Oncologists of Canada 36th Annual General Meeting
Date: June 12-13, 2015
Location: Québec City, QC
Sponsor/Contact: Society of Gynecologic Oncologists of Canada
780 Echo Dr.
Ottawa, ON K1S 5R7
613-730-4192 *Fax:* 613-730-4314
Toll-Free: 800-561-2416
URL: www.g-o-c.org
Scope: National

Special Libraries Association 2015 Annual Conference & INFO-EXPO
Date: June 14-16, 2015
Location: Boston, MA USA
Sponsor/Contact: Special Libraries Association
331 South Patrick St.
Alexandria, VA 22314-3501
703-647-4900 *Fax:* 703-647-4901
E-mail: cschatz@sla.org
URL: www.sla.org
Scope: International
Purpose: A meeting featuring educational sessions, keynote speakers, & exhibitors of interest to information professionals from around the world
Contact Information: Director, Events: Caroline Hamilton, Phone: 703-647-4949, E-mail: chamilton@sla.org; Director, Marketing & Exhibits: Jeff Leach, Phone: 703-647-4922, E-mail: jleach@sla.org

Speed Skating Canada 2015 Annual General Meeting
Date: June 26-28, 2015
Location: Winnipeg, MB
Sponsor/Contact: Speed Skating Canada
#402, 2781 Lancaster Rd.
Ottawa, ON K1B 1A7
613-260-3669 *Fax:* 613-260-3660
E-mail: ssc@speedskating.ca
URL: www.speedskating.ca
Scope: National
Purpose: A gathering of the organization's Board of Directors, branches, & committees

Statistical Society of Canada / Société statistique du Canada 2015 Annual Meeting
Date: June 15-18, 2015
Location: Dalhousie University
Halifax, NS
Sponsor/Contact: Statistical Society of Canada
#209, 1725 St. Laurent Blvd.
Ottawa, ON K1G 3V4
613-733-2662 *Fax:* 613-733-1386
E-mail: info@ssc.ca
URL: www.ssc.ca
Scope: National

Terrazzo Tile & Marble Association of Canada 2015 Annual Convention
Date: June 11-14, 2015
Location: Chateaux Frontenac
Québec City, QC
Sponsor/Contact: Terrazzo Tile & Marble Association of Canada
#8, 163 Buttermill Ave.
Concord, ON L4K 3X8
905-660-9640 *Fax:* 905-660-0513
Toll-Free: 800-201-8599
E-mail: association@ttmac.com
URL: www.ttmac.com
Scope: National
Contact Information: E-mail: association@ttmac.com

The Canadian Society of Microbiologists 65th Annual Conference
Date: June 15-18, 2015
Location: University of Regina
Regina, SK
Sponsor/Contact: Canadian Society of Microbiologists
CSM-SCM Secretariat
17 Dossetter Way
Ottawa, ON K1G 4S3
613-421-7229 *Fax:* 613-421-9811
E-mail: info@csm-scm.org
URL: www.csm-scm.org
Scope: National
Purpose: In conjunction with the IUMS 2015 Congress
Contact Information: Congress Manager: Marie Lanouette, iums2014@nrc-cnrc.gc.ca

The World Congress on Medical Physics & Biomedical Engineering: IUPESM 2015 (hosted by the Canadian Medical & Biological Engineering Society)
Date: June 7 - 12, 2015
Location: Toronto, ON
Sponsor/Contact: Canadian Medical & Biological Engineering Society
1485 Laperrière Ave.
Ottawa, ON K1Z 7S8
613-728-1759
E-mail: secretariat@cmbes.ca
URL: www.cmbes.ca
Scope: National
Purpose: Co-hosted with the Canadian Organization of Medical Physicists (COMP)

Contact Information: E-mail: secretariat@cmbes.ca; Chair, Long-Term Conference Planning: Sarah Kelso, E-mail: sarah.a.kelso@gmail.com

Travel Media Association of Canada 2015 Conference & AGM
Date: June 10-13, 2015
Location: Holiday Inn Peterborough Waterfront
Peterborough, ON
Sponsor/Contact: Travel Media Association of Canada
c/o TO Corporate Services
#255, 55 St. Clair Ave. West
Toronto, ON M4V 2Y7
416-934-0599 *Fax:* 416-967-6320
E-mail: info@travelmedia.ca
URL: www.travelmedia.ca
Scope: National

Vocational Rehabilitation Association of Canada 2015 National Conference
Date: June 16-19, 2015
Location: Delta Hotel Ottawa
Ottawa, ON
Sponsor/Contact: Vocational Rehabilitation Association of Canada
#310, 4 Cataraqui St.
Kingston, ON K7K 1Z7
613-507-5530 *Fax:* 888-441-8002
Toll-Free: 888-876-9992
E-mail: info@vracanada.com
URL: www.vracanada.com
Scope: National

Water Environment Federation Residuals and Biosolids 2015: The Next Generation of Science, Technology & Management
Date: June 7-10, 2015
Location: Walter E. Washington Convention Center
Washington, DC USA
Sponsor/Contact: Water Environment Federation
601 Wythe St.
Alexandria, VA 22314-1994
703-684-2400 *Fax:* 703-684-2492
Toll-Free: 800-666-0206
E-mail: comments@wef.org
URL: www.wef.org
Scope: International
Purpose: A specialty conference on residuals and biosolids management.

Western Association of Broadcasters Conference 2015
Date: June 3-4, 2015
Location: Fairmont Banff Springs Hotel
Banff, AB
Sponsor/Contact: Western Association of Broadcasters
#507, 918 - 16th Ave. NW
Calgary, AB T2M 0K3
Toll-Free: 877-814-2719
E-mail: info@wab.ca
URL: www.wab.ca
Scope: Provincial

Winnipeg Chamber of Commerce 2015 25th Annual Golf Clssic
Date: June 3, 2015
Location: Winnipeg, MB
Sponsor/Contact: Winnipeg Chamber of Commerce
#100, 259 Portage Ave.
Winnipeg, MB R3B 2A9
204-944-8484 *Fax:* 204-944-8492
E-mail: info@winnipeg-chamber.com
URL: www.winnipeg-chamber.com
Scope: Provincial
Purpose: An annual golf tournament since 1990.
Contact Information: Events Coordinator: Yanik Ottenbreit, Phone: 204-944-3306, E-mail: yottenbreit@winnipeg-chamber.com

World Congress on Medical Physics and Biomedical Engineering 2015
Date: June 7-12, 2015
Location: Toronto, ON
Sponsor/Contact: International Federation for Medical & Biological Engineering
E-mail: office@ifmbe.org
URL: www.ifmbe.org
Scope: International
Purpose: The Congresses are scheduled on a three-year basis and aligned with Federation's General Assembly meeting at which elections are held.

Young Brokers Council 2015 Annual Conference
Date: June 10-12, 2015
Location: Sheraton On The Falls Hotel & Conference Centre
Niagara Falls, ON
Sponsor/Contact: Insurance Brokers Association of Ontario
#700, 1 Eglinton Ave. East
Toronto, ON M4P 3A1
416-488-7422 *Fax:* 416-488-7526
Toll-Free: 800-268-8845
E-mail: contact@ibao.com
URL: www.ibao.org
Scope: Provincial

July

16th FINA World Championships 2015 - Kazan, Russia
Date: July 24 - August 9, 2015
Location: Kazan, Russia
Sponsor/Contact: International Amateur Swimming Federation
Av. de l'Avant-Poste 4
Lausanne, 1005
URL: www.fina.org
Scope: International

18th World Congress of the International Confederation for Plastic Reconstructive & Aesthetic Surgery 2015
Date: July 6-10, 2015
Location: Hofburg Palace
Vienna, Austria
Sponsor/Contact: International Confederation for Plastic Reconstructive & Aesthetic Surgery
Zita Congress SA
P.O. Box 155
1st km Peanias Markopoulou Ave
Peania Attica, 190 02
E-mail: zita@iprasmanagement.com
URL: www.ipras.org
Scope: International
Contact Information: URL: www.ipras2015.com

2015 Canadian Federation of Music Teachers' Associations Convention - "Pathways"
Date: July 8-11, 2015
Location: Sheraton Vancouver Airport Hotel
Richmond, BC
Sponsor/Contact: Canadian Federation of Music Teachers' Associations
#302, 550 Berkshire Dr.
London, ON N6J 3S2
519-471-6051
E-mail: admin@cfmta.org
URL: www.cfmta.org
Scope: National

2015 Canadian Society of Soil Science Annual Meeting
Date: July 5-10, 2015
Location: Montreal, QC
Sponsor/Contact: Canadian Society of Soil Science
Business Office
P.O. Box 637
Pinawa, MB R0E 1L0
204-753-2747 *Fax:* 204-753-8478
E-mail: sheppards@ecomatters.com
URL: www.csss.ca
Purpose: Joint meeting with Association Québécoise de Spécialistes en Sciences du Sol (AQSSS)

2015 Institute of Internal Auditors 2015 International Conference
Date: July 5-8, 2015
Location: Vancouver Convention Centre
Vancouver, BC
Sponsor/Contact: The Institute of Internal Auditors
247 Maitland Ave.
Altamonte Springs, FL 32701-4201
407-937-1111 *Fax:* 407-937-1101
E-mail: customerrelations@theiia.org
URL: www.theiia.org
Scope: International

2015 World Credit Union Conference
Date: July 12-15, 2015
Location: Denver, CO USA
Sponsor/Contact: World Council of Credit Unions, Inc.
P.O. Box 2982
5710 Mineral Point Rd.
Madison, WI 53705-4493
608-395-2000 *Fax:* 608-395-2001
E-mail: mail@woccu.org
URL: www.woccu.org
Scope: International
Contact Information: URL: cuindenver2015.org

American Association for Justice 2015 Annual Convention
Date: July 11-15, 2015
Location: Montréal Convention Center
Montréal, QC
Sponsor/Contact: American Association for Justice
#200, 777 - 6th St., NW
Washington, DC 20001
202-965-3500
Toll-Free: 800-424-2725
E-mail: membership@justice.org
URL: www.justice.org
Scope: International

Association of School Transportation Services of British Columbia 50th Annual Convention and Trade Show
Date: July 8-10, 2015
Location: Sun Peaks Grand Hotel and Conference Centre
Sun Peaks, BC
Sponsor/Contact: The Association of School Transportation Services of British Columbia
250-804-7892 *Fax:* 250-832-2584
E-mail: info@astsbc.org
URL: www.astsbc.org
Scope: Provincial

Bibliographical Society of Canada 2015 Annual General Meeting
Date: July 6-11, 2015
Location: Montreal, QC
Sponsor/Contact: Bibliographical Society of Canada
P.O. Box 19035 Stn. Walmer
360 Bloor St. West
Toronto, ON M5S 3C9
E-mail: secretary@bsc-sbc.ca
URL: www.bsc-sbc.ca
Scope: National

CSBE/SCGAB 2015 Annual General Meeting & Technical Conference
Date: July 5-8, 2015
Location: Delta Edmonton South Hotel & Conference Centre
Edmonton, AB
Sponsor/Contact: Canadian Society for Bioengineering
2028 Calico Crescent
Orleans, ON K4A 4L7
613-590-0975
E-mail: bioeng@shaw.ca
URL: www.bioeng.ca
Scope: National
Purpose: The conference will include workshops, technical sessions, networking receptions, tours, a guest program, the CSBE Awards Banquet and the CSBE Annual General Meeting.
Contact Information: Local Organizing Committee Chair: Rick Atkins, Email: rick.atkins@gov.ab.ca; URL: csbe-scgab.ca/edmonton2015

Canadian Association of Optometrists 2015 33rd Biennial Congress
Date: July 15-18, 2015
Location: Fredericton, NB
Sponsor/Contact: Canadian Association of Optometrists
234 Argyle Ave.
Ottawa, ON K2P 1B9
613-235-7924 *Fax:* 613-235-2025
Toll-Free: 888-263-4676
E-mail: info@opto.ca
URL: www.opto.ca
Scope: National

Canadian Association of School System Administrators 2015 Annual Conference
Date: July 2-4, 2015
Location: Montréal, QC
Sponsor/Contact: Canadian Association of School System Administrators
1123 Glenashton Dr.
Oakville, ON L6H 5M1
905-845-2345 *Fax:* 905-845-2044
URL: www.cassa-acgcs.ca
Scope: National

Canadian Phytopathological Society 2015 87th Annual Meeting
Date: July 25-29, 2015
Sponsor/Contact: Canadian Phytopathological Society
c/o Vikram Bisht
P.O. Box 1149
65 - 3 Ave. NE
Carman, MB R0G 0J0
204-745-0260 *Fax:* 204-745-5690
URL: www.cps-scp.ca
Scope: National
Purpose: The objectives of CPS are to encourage research, education, and the dissemination of knowledge on the nature, cause, and control of plant diseases.

Canadian Seed Growers' Association's 2015 Annual General Meeting
Date: July 8-10, 2015
Location: Marriott Chateau Champlain Hotel
Montréal, QC
Sponsor/Contact: Canadian Seed Growers' Association
P.O. Box 8455
#202, 240 Catherine St.
Ottawa, ON K1G 3T1
613-236-0497 *Fax:* 613-563-7855
E-mail: seeds@seedgrowers.ca
URL: www.seedgrowers.ca
Scope: National

Canadian Veterinary Medical Association 2015 Convention and Annual General Meeting
Date: July 16-19, 2015
Location: Calgary, AB
Sponsor/Contact: Canadian Veterinary Medical Association
339 Booth St.
Ottawa, ON K1R 7K1
613-236-1162 *Fax:* 613-236-9681
E-mail: admin@cvma-acmv.org
URL: www.canadianveterinarians.net
Scope: National

Controlled Release Society 2015 42nd Annual Meeting & Exposition
Date: July 26-29, 2015
Location: Edinburgh International Conference Centre
Edinburgh, Scotland
Sponsor/Contact: Controlled Release Society
3340 Pilot Knob Rd.
St. Paul, MN 55121
651-454-7250 *Fax:* 651-454-0766
E-mail: crs@scisoc.org
URL: www.controlledrelease.org
Scope: International
Contact Information: Meeting Manager: Tressa Patrias, Email: tpatrias@scisoc.org

Education International 7th World Congress
Date: July 21-26, 2015
Location: Ottawa Convention Centre
Ottawa, ON
Sponsor/Contact: Education International
5, boul du Roi Albert II, 8 étage
Brussels, B1210
E-mail: headoffice@ei-ie.org
URL: www.ei-ie.org
Scope: International

HTFF 2015: International Conference on Heat Transfer and Fluid Flow
Date: July 20-21, 2015
Location: Bracelona, Spain
Sponsor/Contact: International Academy of Science, Engineering & Technology
#414, 1376 Bank St.
Ottawa, ON K1H 7Y3
613-695-3040
E-mail: info@international-aset.com
URL: www.international-aset.com
Scope: International

ICEPR 2015: 5th International Conference on Environmental Pollution and Remediation
Date: July 15-17, 2015
Location: Barcelona, Spain
Sponsor/Contact: International Academy of Science, Engineering & Technology
#414, 1376 Bank St.
Ottawa, ON K1H 7Y3
613-695-3040
E-mail: info@international-aset.com
URL: www.international-aset.com
Scope: International
Contact Information: URL: icepr.org

ICMIE 2015: 4th International Conference on Mechanics & Industrial Engineering
Date: July 20-21, 2015
Location: Barcelona, Spain
Sponsor/Contact: International Academy of Science, Engineering & Technology
#414, 1376 Bank St.
Ottawa, ON K1H 7Y3
613-695-3040
E-mail: info@international-aset.com
URL: www.international-aset.com
Scope: International
Contact Information: URL: icmie.net

ICNFA 2015: 6th International Conference on Nanotechnology: Fundamentals and Applications
Date: July 15-17, 2015
Location: Barcelona, Spain
Sponsor/Contact: International Academy of Science, Engineering & Technology
#414, 1376 Bank St.
Ottawa, ON K1H 7Y3
613-695-3040
E-mail: info@international-aset.com
URL: www.international-aset.com
Scope: International
Contact Information: URL: icnfa.com

Institute of Food Technologists 2015 Annual Meeting & Food Expo
Date: July 11-14, 2015
Location: McCormick Place South
Chicago, IL USA
Sponsor/Contact: Institute of Food Technologists
#1000, 525 West Van Buren
Chicago, IL 60607
312-782-8424 *Fax:* 312-782-8348
Toll-Free: 800-438-3663
E-mail: info@ift.org
URL: www.ift.org
Scope: International
Purpose: The largest annual food science forum & exposition, featuring presentation from experts of research institutions, government agencies, & companies, of interest to food scientists, suppliers, & marketers from around the globe
Anticipated Attendance: 21,500+

International Association of Administrative Professionals 2015 International Education Forum & Annual Meeting
Date: July 25-29, 2015
Location: Kentucky International Convention Center
Louisville, KY USA
Sponsor/Contact: International Association of Administrative Professionals
P.O. Box 20404
10502 NW Ambassador Dr.
Kansas City, MO 64195-0404
816-891-6600 *Fax:* 816-891-9118
E-mail: service@iaap-hq.org
URL: www.iaap-hq.org
Scope: International
Purpose: Education workshops
Anticipated Attendance: 1,200+

MMME 2015: International Conference on Mining, Material and Metallurgical Engineering
Date: July 20-21, 2015
Location: Barcelona, Spain
Sponsor/Contact: International Academy of Science, Engineering & Technology
#414, 1376 Bank St.
Ottawa, ON K1H 7Y3
613-695-3040
E-mail: info@international-aset.com
URL: www.international-aset.com
Scope: International

MVML 2015: International Conference on Machine Vision and Machine Learning
Date: July 13-14, 2015
Location: Bracelona, Spain
Sponsor/Contact: International Academy of Science, Engineering & Technology
#414, 1376 Bank St.
Ottawa, ON K1H 7Y3
613-695-3040
E-mail: info@international-aset.com
URL: www.international-aset.com
Scope: International

Maritime Fire Chiefs' Association 2015 101st Annual Conference
Date: July 5-7, 2015
Location: Summerside, PE
Sponsor/Contact: Maritime Fire Chiefs' Association
P.O. Box 6
Dartmouth, NS B2Y 3Y2
URL: www.mfca.ca
Scope: Provincial
Purpose: Information about the latest trends & innovations within the fire service

National Conference on Music Education 2015
Date: July 9-11, 2015
Location: Winnipeg, MB
Sponsor/Contact: Canadian Music Educators' Association
#A-430A, Wilfrid Laurier University
Waterloo, ON N2L 3C5
778-896-7343
URL: www.cmea.ca
Scope: National

Ontario Horticultural Association 109th Convention in District 6
Date: July 3-5, 2015
Location: Redeemer University College
Ancaster, ON
Sponsor/Contact: Ontario Horticultural Association
448 Paterson Ave.
London, ON N5W 5C7
E-mail: secretary@gardenontario.org
URL: www.gardenontario.org
Scope: Provincial

Parents Without Parents Convention 2015
Date: July 8-11, 2015
Location: Nashville, TN USA
Sponsor/Contact: Parents Without Partners Inc.
1100-H Brandywine Blvd.
Zanesville, OH 43701-7303
Fax: 561-395-8557
Toll-Free: 800-637-7974
E-mail: Intl.pres@parentswithoutpartners.org
URL: www.parentswithoutpartners.org
Scope: National

Royal Canadian Numismatic Association 2015 Convention
Date: July 22-25, 2015
Location: Westin Nova Scotian
Halifax, NS
Sponsor/Contact: Royal Canadian Numismatic Association
#432, 5694 Hwy. 7 East
Markham, ON L3P 1B4
647-401-4014 *Fax:* 905-472-9645
E-mail: info@rcna.ca
URL: www.rcna.ca
Scope: National
Purpose: An annual event, presenting an education symposium, a bourse & display, business meetings, award presentations, plus social & networking activities
Contact Information: E-mail: 2015convention@rcna.ca

Soil & Water Conservation Society 69th Annual International Conference
Date: July 26-29, 2015
Location: Sheraton Four Seasons Hotel
Greensboro, NC USA
Sponsor/Contact: Soil & Water Conservation Society
945 SW Ankeny Rd.
Ankeny, IA 50023-9723
515-289-2331 *Fax:* 515-289-1227
E-mail: swcs@swcs.org
URL: www.swcs.org
Scope: International

Storytellers of Canada 2015 Conference
Date: July 2-5, 2015
Location: Levis, QC
Sponsor/Contact: Storytellers of Canada
#201, 192 Spadina Ave.
Toronto, ON M5T 2C2
E-mail: admin@storytellers-conteurs.ca
URL: www.storytellers-conteurs.ca
Scope: National
Contact Information: Email: conference@storytellers-conteurs.ca

The 39th Annual SSF-IIIHS Int'l Conference
Location: Montreal, QC
Sponsor/Contact: International Institute of Integral Human Sciences
P.O. Box 1387 Stn. H
Montréal, QC H3G 2N3
514-937-8359 *Fax:* 514-937-5380
E-mail: info@iiihs.org
URL: www.iiihs.org
Scope: International

August

2015 Couchiching Summer Conference
Date: August 7-9, 2015
Sponsor/Contact: Couchiching Institute on Public Affairs
#301, 250 Consumers Rd.
Toronto, ON M2J 4V6
416-642-6374 *Fax:* 416-495-8723
Toll-Free: 866-647-6374
E-mail: couch@couchichinginstitute.ca
URL: www.couchichinginstitute.ca
Purpose: The conference's theme is the politics & potential of sport. Issues will be discussed involving sports as entertainment, the violence of sports, sports & gender as well as sports & drugs
Contact Information: Phone: 416-642-6374; Email: couch@couchichinginstitute.ca

Academy of Management 2015 Annual Meeting
Date: August 7-11, 2015
Location: Vancouver Convention Centre Vancouver, BC
Sponsor/Contact: Academy of Management
P.O. Box 3020
Briarcliff Manor, NY 10510-8020
914-923-2607 *Fax:* 914-923-2615
URL: www.aomonline.org
Scope: International
Purpose: Sharing of research and expertise in all management disciplines through distinguished speakers, competitive paper sessions, symposia, panels, workshops, & special programs for doctoral students
Anticipated Attendance: 10,000+
Contact Information: Assistant Director of Meetings: Taryn Fiore, E-mail: tfiore@pace.edu

Ahmadiyya Muslim Jamaat Canada 2015 39th Annual Convention
Date: August 28-30, 2015
Sponsor/Contact: Ahmadiyya Muslim Jamaat Canada
10610 Jane St.
Maple, ON L6A 3A2
905-303-4000 *Fax:* 905-832-3220
E-mail: info@ahmadiyya.ca
URL: www.ahmadiyya.ca
Scope: National
Purpose: A Muslim convention, featuring religious addresses & the presentation of awards
Contact Information: Email: jalsa@ahmadiyya.ca, URL: jalsa.ahmadiyya.ca

American Association of Naturopathic Physicians 2015 Annual Conference
Date: August 5-8, 2015
Location: Oakland Marriott Oakland, CA USA
Sponsor/Contact: American Association of Naturopathic Physicians
#250, 818 - 18th St., NW
Washington, DC 20006
202-237-8150 *Fax:* 202-237-8152
Toll-Free: 866-538-2267
E-mail: member.services@naturopathic.org
URL: www.naturopathic.org
Scope: International

American Fisheries Society Annual Meeting
Date: August 16-21, 2015
Location: Portland, OR USA
Sponsor/Contact: American Fisheries Society
5410 Grosvenor Lane
Bethesda, MD 20814-2199
301-897-8616 *Fax:* 301-897-8096
URL: www.fisheries.org
Scope: International
Contact Information: URL: 2015.fisheries.org

American Psychological Association 2015 Convention
Date: August 6-9, 2015
Location: Toronto, ON
Sponsor/Contact: American Psychological Association
750 First St. NE
Washington, DC 20002-4242
202-336-5500 *Fax:* 202-335-5997
Toll-Free: 800-374-2721
E-mail: executiveoffice@apa.org
URL: www.apa.org
Scope: International

Association of Municipalities of Ontario 2015 Annual Conference
Date: August 16-19, 2015
Location: Scotiabank Conference Centre Niagara Falls, ON
Sponsor/Contact: Association of Municipalities of Ontario
#801, 200 University Ave.
Toronto, ON M5H 3C6
416-971-9856 *Fax:* 416-971-6191
Toll-Free: 877-426-6527
E-mail: amo@amo.on.ca
URL: www.amo.on.ca
Scope: Provincial
Purpose: A yearly gathering of municipal government officials to discuss current issues.
Contact Information: Special Events & Business Development Coordinator: Navneet Dhaliwal, Phone: 416-971-9856, ext. 330, Fax: 416-971-6191, E-mail: ndhaliwal@amo.on.ca

British Columbia School Superintendents Association 2015 Summer Leadership Academy
Date: August 19-21, 2015
Location: Delta Grand Okanagan Kelowna, BC
Sponsor/Contact: British Columbia School Superintendents Association
#208, 1118 Homer St.
Vancouver, BC V6B 6L5
604-687-0590
E-mail: info@bcssa.org
URL: www.bcssa.org
Scope: Provincial
Contact Information: Professional Development Coordinator: Kim Young, E-mail: kimyoung@bcssa.org

British Columbia Teachers' Federation 2015 Summer Leadershipo Conference
Date: August 26-28, 2015
Location: British Columbia
Sponsor/Contact: British Columbia Teachers' Federation
#100, 550 - 6th Ave. West
Vancouver, BC V5Z 4P2
604-871-2283 *Fax:* 604-871-2293
Toll-Free: 800-663-9163
E-mail: benefits@bctf.ca
URL: www.bctf.ca
Scope: Provincial

Canadian Association of Chiefs of Police 2015 110th Annual Conference
Date: August 16-19, 2015
Location: Québec, QC
Sponsor/Contact: Canadian Association of Chiefs of Police
#100, 300 Terry Fox Dr.
Kanata, ON K2K 0E3
613-595-1101 *Fax:* 613-383-0372
E-mail: cacp@cacp.ca
URL: www.cacp.ca
Scope: National
Purpose: Conference sessions & exhibits

Canadian Association of Insolvency & Restructuring Professionals 2015 Annual Conference
Date: August 20-22, 2015
Location: Fairmont Château Whistler Whistler, BC
Sponsor/Contact: Canadian Association of Insolvency & Restructuring Professionals
277 Wellington St. West
Toronto, ON M5V 3H2
416-204-3242 *Fax:* 416-204-3410
E-mail: info@cairp.ca
URL: www.cairp.ca
Scope: National
Purpose: Technical sessions plus networking opportunities & social events
Contact Information: Events Manager: Cristina Contesti, Phone: 416-204-3242, ext. 3245; Email: cristina.contesti@cairp.ca

Canadian Association of Police Governance Conference 2015
Date: August 27-29, 2015
Sponsor/Contact: Canadian Association of Police Governance
#302, 157 Gilmour St.
Ottawa, ON K2P 0N8
613-235-2272 *Fax:* 613-235-2275
URL: capg.ca
Scope: National

Canadian Bar Association Canadian Legal Conference & Expo 2015
Date: August 14-16, 2015
Location: St. John's, NL
Sponsor/Contact: Canadian Bar Association
#500, 865 Carling Ave.
Ottawa, ON K1S 5S8
613-237-2925 *Fax:* 613-237-0185
Toll-Free: 800-267-8860
E-mail: info@cba.org
URL: www.cba.org
Scope: National
Purpose: Continuing legal education programs, sessions, & networking opportunities for legal professionals in Canada

Canadian Cattlemen's Association 2015 Semi-Annual Meeting & Convention
Date: August 12-15, 2015
Location: Winnipeg, MB
Sponsor/Contact: Canadian Cattlemen's Association
#310, 6715 - 8 St. NE
Calgary, AB T2E 7H7
403-275-8558 *Fax:* 403-274-5686
E-mail: feedback@cattle.ca
URL: www.cattle.ca
Scope: National
Purpose: Information sessions, policy setting, networking opportunities, & a social program

Canadian Fertilizer Institute 70th Annual Conference
Date: August 16-20, 2015
Location: The Westin, Bayshore Vancouver, BC
Sponsor/Contact: Canadian Fertilizer Institute
#907, 350 Sparks St.
Ottawa, ON K1R 7S8
613-230-2600 *Fax:* 613-230-5142
E-mail: info@cfi.ca
URL: www.cfi.ca
Scope: National

Canadian Institute for Theatre Technology Rendez-vous 2015: Annual Conference & Trade Show
Date: August 20-22, 2015
Location: Vancouver, BC
Sponsor/Contact: Canadian Institute for Theatre Technology
P.O. Box 85041
345 Laurier Blvd.
Mont-Saint-Hilaire, QC J3H 5W1
613-482-1165 *Fax:* 613-482-1212
Toll-Free: 888-271-3383
E-mail: info@citt.org
URL: www.citt.org
Scope: National
Contact Information: CITT / ICTS Phone: 613-482-1165, Toll-Free Phone: 1-888-271-3383, E-mail: info@citt.org

Canadian Medical Association 2015 148th Annual Meeting
Date: August 23-25, 2015
Location: Halifax, NS
Sponsor/Contact: Canadian Medical Association
1867 Alta Vista Dr.
Ottawa, ON K1G 5W8
613-731-8610 *Fax:* 613-236-8864
Toll-Free: 888-855-2555
E-mail: cmamsc@cma.ca
URL: www.cma.ca
Scope: National
Purpose: General Council is open to delegates & observers who must be Canadian Medical Association members or invited guests
Contact Information: Registration Officer, Phone: 1-800-663-7336, ext. 2383, E-mail: gcregistrations@cma.ca

Canadian National Exhibition 2015
Date: August 21 - September 7, 2015
Location: Canadian National Exhibition Place Toronto, ON
Sponsor/Contact: Canadian National Exhibition Association
Exhibition Place
Toronto, ON M6K 3C3
416-263-3800 *Fax:* 416-263-3838
E-mail: info@theex.com
URL: www.theex.com
Scope: National

Canadian Nuclear Society 2015 17th International Conference on Environmental Degradation of Materials in Nuclear Power Systems - Water Reactors
Date: August 9-13, 2015
Location: Fairmont Château Laurier Ottawa, ON
Sponsor/Contact: Canadian Nuclear Society
655 Bay St., 17th Fl.
Toronto, ON M5G 2K4
416-977-7620 *Fax:* 416-977-8131
E-mail: cns-snc@on.aibn.com
URL: www.cns-snc.ca
Scope: National
Contact Information: Canadian Nuclear Society Office: Phone: 416-977-7620, E-mail: cns-snc@on.aibn.com; URL: www.envdeg2015.org

Canadian Security Traders Association 22nd Annual Conference
Date: August 20-23, 2015
Sponsor/Contact: Canadian Security Traders Association, Inc.
P.O. Box 3
31 Adelaide St. East
Toronto, ON M5C 2J6
E-mail: janice.cooper@canadiansta.org
URL: www.canadiansta.org
Scope: National

Canadian Society of Hospital Pharmacists 2015 Annual Summer Educational Sessions
Date: August 8-11, 2015
Location: London, ON
Sponsor/Contact: Canadian Society of Hospital Pharmacists
#3, 30 Concourse Gate
Ottawa, ON K2E 7V7
613-736-9733 *Fax:* 613-736-5660
E-mail: info@cshp.ca
URL: www.cshp.ca
Scope: National
Purpose: Workshops, plus the annual general meeting of the society
Anticipated Attendance: 250
Contact Information: E-mail: info@cshp.ca

Catholic Women's League of Canada 2015 National Convention
Date: August 16-19, 2015
Location: Vancouver, BC
Sponsor/Contact: Catholic Women's League of Canada
702C Scotland Ave.
Winnipeg, MB R3M 1X5
Fax: 888-831-9507
Toll-Free: 888-656-4040
E-mail: info@cwl.ca
URL: www.cwl.ca
Scope: National

Eastern Apicultural Society of North America 2015 Annual Conference & Short Course
Date: August 10-14, 2015
Location: University of Guelph
Guelph, ON
Sponsor/Contact: Eastern Apicultural Society of North America, Inc.
c/o Loretta Surprenant
P.O. Box 300
Essex, NY 12936
518-963-7593 *Fax:* 518-963-7593
E-mail: secretary@easternapiculture.org
URL: www.easternapiculture.org
Scope: International
Purpose: Annual business meeting, lectures, workshops, short courses, & vendor displays for beginning & advanced beekeepers
Anticipated Attendance: 500

Goldschmidt Conference 2015
Date: August 16-21, 2015
Location: Prague, Czech Republic
Sponsor/Contact: Geochemical Society
c/o Earth & Planetary Sciences Department, Washington University
#CB 11691, Brookings Dr.
St. Louis, MO 63130-4899
314-935-4131 *Fax:* 314-935-4121
E-mail: gsoffice@geochemsoc.org
URL: www.geochemsoc.org
Scope: International
Purpose: An international conference on geochemistry
Anticipated Attendance: 3,000+

Institute of Public Administration of Canada 2015 67th National Annual Conference: Governing in the Now
Date: August 23-26, 2015
Location: Halifax, NS
Sponsor/Contact: Institute of Public Administration of Canada
#401, 1075 Bay St.
Toronto, ON M5S 2B1
416-924-8787 *Fax:* 416-924-4992
URL: www.ipac.ca
Scope: National
Purpose: Conference participants & speakers include Canadian public decison makers from both municipal, provincial, & federal jurisdictions, as well as members of academia, senior policy advisors, & heads of schools of pubic policy
Anticipated Attendance: 500+
Contact Information: URL: www.ipac.ca/2015

Institute of Transportation Engineers 2015 Annual Meeting & Exhibit
Date: August 2-5, 2015
Location: Westin Diplomat
Hollywood, FL USA
Sponsor/Contact: Institute of Transportation Engineers
#600, 1627 Eye St. NW
Washington, DC 20006
202-785-0060 *Fax:* 202-785-0609
E-mail: ite_staff@ite.org
URL: www.ite.org
Scope: International
Contact Information: Contact, Registration Information: Sallie C. Dollins, E-mail: sdollins@ite.org; Contact, Technical Program: Eunice Chege, E-mail: echege@ite.org; Contact, Exhibits: Christina Garneski, E-mail: cgarneski@ite.org; Contact, Paper Submittals: Eunice Chege, E-mail: echege@ite.org

International Academy of Energy, Minerals, & Materials 2015 International Conference & Exhibition on advanced and nano materials
Date: August 10-12, 2015
Location: Ottawa, ON
Sponsor/Contact: International Academy of Energy, Minerals, & Materials
Esprit Dr.
Ottawa, ON K4A 4Z1
613-322-1029 *Fax:* 613-830-8371
E-mail: info@iaemm.com
URL: iaemm.com
Scope: International
Contact Information: URL: icanm2015.iaemm.com

International Confederation of Principals (ICP) 12th World Convention
Date: August 3-6, 2015
Location: Helsinki, Finland
Sponsor/Contact: International Confederation of Principals
ICP Secretariat
68 Martin St.
Heidelberg, Victoria, 3084
URL: www.icponline.org
Scope: International
Purpose: A convention of interest to principals vice-principals, education leaders, academics, researchers, policy makers, & government representatives from around the world
Anticipated Attendance: 2,000+
Contact Information: Executive Secretary: Toni Lehtinen, E-mail: icp2015@surefire.fi; URL: www.confedent.fi/icp2015

International Society for Environmental Epidemiology 27th Annual Conference
Date: August 30 - September 3, 2015
Location: Sao Paolo, Brazil
Sponsor/Contact: International Society of Indoor Air Quality & Climate
c/o Gina Bendy
2548 Empire Grade
Santa Cruz, CA 95060
831-426-0148 *Fax:* 831-426-6522
E-mail: info@isiaq.org
URL: www.isiaq.org
Scope: International
Contact Information: Email: contact@isee2015.org; URL: www.isee2015.org

Joint Statistical Meetings 2015
Date: August 8-13, 2015
Location: Seattle, WA USA
Sponsor/Contact: Statistical Society of Canada
#209, 1725 St. Laurent Blvd.
Ottawa, ON K1G 3V4
613-733-2662 *Fax:* 613-733-1386
E-mail: info@ssc.ca
URL: www.ssc.ca
Scope: International
Purpose: Held jointly with the Statistical Society of Canada, American Statistical Association, the International Biometric Society (ENAR & WNAR), the International Chinese Statistical Association, the Institute of Mathematical Statistics, & the International Indian Statistical Association

Kin Canada 2015 National Convention
Date: August 20-22, 2015
Location: Brandon, MB
Sponsor/Contact: Kin Canada
P.O. Box 3460
1920 Rogers Dr.
Cambridge, ON N3H 5C6
519-653-1920 *Fax:* 519-650-1091
Toll-Free: 800-742-5546
E-mail: kinhq@kincanada.ca
URL: www.kincanada.ca
Scope: National

Metallurgy & Materials Society of the Canadian Institute of Mining, Metallurgy & Petroleum COM 2015: 54th Annual Conference of Metallurgists
Date: August 23-26, 2015
Location: Fairmont Royal York Hotel
Toronto, ON
Sponsor/Contact: Metallurgy & Materials Society of the Canadian Institute of Mining, Metallurgy & Petroleum
#1250, 3500, boul de Maisonneuve ouest
Montréal, QC H3Z 3C1
514-939-2710
URL: www.metsoc.org
Scope: International
Purpose: A technical program, with short courses & industrial tours, plus a metals trade show, the poster session, plenary sessions, & student activities
Contact Information: E-mail: metsoc@cim.org

Oasis: Refreshment for the Journey
Date: August 20-23, 2015
Location: Acadia University
Wolfville, NS
Sponsor/Contact: Convention of Atlantic Baptist Churches
1655 Manawagonish Rd.
Saint John, NB E2M 3Y2
506-635-1922 *Fax:* 506-635-0366
E-mail: cabc@baptist-atlantic.ca
URL: www.baptist-atlantic.ca
Scope: Provincial
Contact Information: URL: oasis.baptist-atlantic.ca

Pacific Northwest Library Association 2015 Conference
Date: August 5-7, 2015
Location: Hilton Vancouver
Vancouver, BC
Sponsor/Contact: Pacific Northwest Library Association
c/o Michael Burris, Public Library InterLINK
7252 Kingsway
Burnaby, BC V5E 1G3
604-517-8441 *Fax:* 604-517-8410
URL: www.pnla.org
Scope: Provincial

Society of Plastics Engineers 2015 24th Annual Thermoforming Conference
Date: August 31 - September 3, 2015
Location: Renaissance Schaumburg Convention Center
Atlanta, GA USA
Sponsor/Contact: Society of Plastics Engineers
13 Church Hill Rd.
Newtown, CT 06470
203-775-0471 *Fax:* 203-775-8490
E-mail: info@4spe.org
URL: www.4spe.org
Scope: International
Contact Information: Conference Coordinator, Lesley Kyle, Phone: 914-671-9524, Email: thermoformingdivision@gmail.com

Uniform Law Conference of Canada 2015 Conference
Date: August 9-13, 2015
Location: Explorer Hotel
Yellowknife, NT
Sponsor/Contact: Uniform Law Conference of Canada
c/o 622 Hochelaga St.
Ottawa, ON K1K 2E9
613-747-1695 *Fax:* 613-941-9310
E-mail: conference@ulcc.ca
URL: www.ulcc.ca
Scope: National
Contact Information: Executive Director, Marie Bordeleau, Email: marie.bordeleau@ulcc-chlc.ca

September

18th Canadian Association of Thoracic Surgeons Annual Meeting
Date: September 17-20, 2015
Location: Québec, QC
Sponsor/Contact: Canadian Association of Thoracic Surgeons
#300, 421 Gilmour St.
Ottawa, ON K2P 0R5
E-mail: cats@canadianthoracicsurgeons.ca
URL: www.canadianthoracicsurgeons.ca
Scope: National

2015 Association des recycleurs de pièces d'autos et de camions Congress
Date: September 17-20, 2015
Location: Cacouna
Rivière-du-Loup, QC
Sponsor/Contact: Association des recycleurs de pièces d'autos et de camions
#101, 37, rue de la Gare
St-Jérôme, QC J7Z 2B7
450-504-8315 *Fax:* 450-504-8313
Toll-Free: 855-504-8315
E-mail: info@arpac.org
URL: arpac.org

Scope: Provincial

2015 Canadian Marketing Association Conference: CMAconnections
Date: September 2015
Sponsor/Contact: Canadian Marketing Association
#607, 1 Concorde Gate
Toronto, ON M3C 3N6
416-391-2362 *Fax:* 416-441-4062
E-mail: info@the-cma.org
URL: www.the-cma.org
Scope: National
Purpose: CMAconnections focuses on all aspects of interaction between brands and their audience and consumer.

2015 Canadian Society for Aesthetic (Cosmetic) Plastic Surgery 42nd Annual Meeting
Date: September 18-19, 2015
Location: Montréal, QC
Sponsor/Contact: Canadian Society for Aesthetic (Cosmetic) Plastic Surgery
2334 Heska Rd.
Pickering, ON L1V 2P9
905-831-7750 *Fax:* 905-831-7248
E-mail: info@csaps.ca
URL: www.csaps.ca
Scope: National

2015 Canadian Surgery Forum
Date: September 17-20, 2015
Location: Quebec, QC
Sponsor/Contact: Canadian Association of General Surgeons
P.O. Box 1428 Stn. B
Ottawa, ON K1P 5R4
613-882-6510
E-mail: cags@cags-accg.ca
URL: www.cags-accg.ca
Scope: National

2015 IPS-ISHS Peat in Horticulture
Date: September 7-11, 2015
Location: Vienna, Austria
Sponsor/Contact: International Peat Society
Kauppakatu 19 D 31
Jyväskylä, FIN-40100
E-mail: ips@peatsociety.org
URL: www.peatsociety.org
Scope: International

2015 Municipal Finance Officers' Association of Ontario Annual Conference
Date: September 23-25, 2015
Location: Ontario
Sponsor/Contact: Municipal Finance Officers' Association of Ontario
2169 Queen St. East, 2nd Fl.
Toronto, ON M4L 1J1
416-362-9001 *Fax:* 416-362-9226
E-mail: office@mfoa.on.ca
URL: www.mfoa.on.ca
Scope: Provincial

23rd Supply Chain Management Association - British Columbia Education Conference
Date: September 23-24, 2015
Location: Tigh-Na-Mara
Parksville, BC
Sponsor/Contact: Supply Chain Management Association - British Columbia
#300, 435 Columbia St.
New Westminster, BC V3L 5N8
604-540-4494 *Fax:* 604-540-4023
Toll-Free: 800-411-7622
E-mail: info@scmabc.ca
URL: www.scmabc.ca
Scope: Provincial

5th Annual Living with Wildlife 2015
Date: September 2015
Location: Vancouver, BC
Sponsor/Contact: Fur-Bearer Defenders
179 West Broadway
Vancouver, BC V5Y 1P4
604-435-1850
E-mail: fbd@furbearerdefenders.com
URL: furbearerdefenders.com
Scope: National
Purpose: Living With Wildlife conference brings together experts in their field to discuss a wide variety of solutions of how we can co-exist with urban wildlif
Contact Information: Email: info@furbearerdefenders.com

68th Canadian Geotechnical Conference and 7th Canadian Permafrost Conference
Date: September 20-23, 2015
Location: Quebec City Conference Centre
Quebec City, QC
Sponsor/Contact: Canadian Geotechnical Society
8828 Pigott Rd.
Richmond, BC V7A 2C4
604-277-7527 *Fax:* 604-277-7529
Toll-Free: 800-710-9867
URL: www.cgs.ca
Scope: National

6th IWA-ASPIRE Conference & Exhibition 2015
Date: September 20-24, 2015
Location: Beijing, China
Sponsor/Contact: International Water Association
Alliance House
12 Caxton St.
London, SW1H 0QS
E-mail: water@iwahq.org
URL: www.iwahq.org
Scope: International
Contact Information: Congress Web Site: www.iwaaspire2015.org

Alberta Rural Municipal Administrators' Association 2015 Conference
Date: September 9-11, 2015
Location: Best Western Wayside Inn
Wetaskiwin, AB
Sponsor/Contact: Alberta Rural Municipal Administrators Association
6027 - 4th St. NE
Calgary, AB T2K 4Z5
403-275-0622 *Fax:* 403-275-8179
URL: www.armaa.ca
Scope: Provincial
Purpose: 2015 theme: "Making Up Is Hard To Do"
Contact Information: Valerie Schmaltz; Email: d_vschmaltz@shaw.ca

Alberta Urban Municipalities Association Convention & AMSC Trade Show 2015
Date: September 23-25, 2015
Location: Telus Convention Centre
Calgary, AB
Sponsor/Contact: Alberta Urban Municipalities Association
#300, 8616 15 Ave.
Edmonton, AB T6E 6E6
780-433-4431 *Fax:* 780-433-4454
Toll-Free: 800-310-2862
E-mail: main@auma.ca
URL: www.auma.ca
Scope: Provincial

Association of Canadian Pension Management 2015 National Conference
Date: September 15-17, 2015
Location: Delta Grand Okanagan
Kelowna, BC
Sponsor/Contact: Association of Canadian Pension Management
#304, 1255 Bay St.
Toronto, ON M5R 2A9
416-964-1260 *Fax:* 416-964-0567
E-mail: info@acpm.com
URL: www.acpm.com
Scope: National
Contact Information: Member Loginrketing, Communications & Membership: Ric Marrero, Phone: 416-964-1260, ext. 223, E-mail: Ric.Marrero@acpm.com

Association of Great Lakes Outdoors Writers Fall Conference 2015
Date: September 28 - October 1, 2015
Location: Minneapolis, MN USA
Sponsor/Contact: Association of Great Lakes Outdoor Writers
P.O. Box 35
Benld, IL 62009
Toll-Free: 877-472-4569
URL: aglowinfo.org
Scope: Local

British Isles Family History Society of Greater Ottawa 2015 21st Annual Family History Conference
Date: September 18-20, 2015
Location: Ottawa, ON
Sponsor/Contact: British Isles Family History Society of Greater Ottawa
P.O. Box 38026
Ottawa, ON K2C 3Y7
613-234-2520
E-mail: queries@bifhsgo.ca
URL: www.bifhsgo.ca
Scope: Provincial

Building Owners & Managers Association 2015 Conference
Date: September 15-17, 2015
Location: Québec, QC
Sponsor/Contact: Building Owners & Managers Association - Canada
P.O. Box 61
#1801, 1 Dundas St. West
Toronto, ON M5G 1Z3
416-214-1912 *Fax:* 416-214-1284
E-mail: info@bomacanada.ca
URL: www.bomacanada.ca
Scope: National

CAMPUT, Canada's Energy & Utility Regulators 2015 Annual General Meeting
Date: September 2015
Location: Charlottetown, PE
Sponsor/Contact: CAMPUT, Canada's Energy & Utility Regulators
#646, 200 North Service Rd. West
Oakville, ON L6M 2Y1
905-827-5139 *Fax:* 905-827-3260
E-mail: info@camput.org
URL: www.camput.org
Scope: National
Purpose: A meeting held each August or September to deal with the administration of the association

Canadian Association for Pharmacy Distribution Management 2015 Annual September Member Forum
Date: September 14, 2015
Sponsor/Contact: Canadian Association for Pharmacy Distribution Management
#301A, 3800 Steeles Ave. West
Woodbridge, ON L4L 4G9
905-265-1706 *Fax:* 905-265-9372
URL: www.capdm.ca
Scope: National
Purpose: An educational & social event for pharmacy supply chain industry professionals
Contact Information: Canadian Association for Pharmacy Distribution Management, Phone: 905-265-1706

Canadian Association of Advanced Practice Nurses Conference & Biennial General Meeting
Date: September 23-25, 2015
Location: Winnipeg, MB
Sponsor/Contact: Canadian Association of Advanced Practice Nurses
P.O. Box 117
153 Frederick St.
Kitchener, ON N2H 2M2
519-579-1096 *Fax:* 519-578-9185
E-mail: adminassist@caapn-aciipa.org
URL: caapn-aciipa.org
Scope: National

Canadian Association of Burn Nurses 14th Biennial Conference
Date: September 16-18, 2015
Location: Moncton, NB
Sponsor/Contact: Canadian Association of Burn Nurses
c/o Shannon Bonn, IWK Health Centre
P.O. Box 9700
5850-5980 University Ave.
Halifax, NS B3K 6R8
E-mail: shannon.bonn@iwk.nshealth.ca
URL: www.cabn.ca
Scope: National
Contact Information: Sharon Brown; Email: sharon.brown@horizonnb.ca

Canadian Association of Fire Chiefs 2015 Fire Rescue Canada Conference
Date: September 20-24, 2015
Location: Victoria Conference Centre
Victoria, BC
Sponsor/Contact: Canadian Association of Fire Chiefs
#702, 280 Albert St.
Ottawa, ON K1P 5G8
613-270-9138
Toll-Free: 800-775-5189
URL: www.cafc.ca
Scope: International
Purpose: Speaker presentations, seminars, & workshops for the fire & emergency services community from across Canada & the United States

Canadian Association of Genetic Counsellors Annual Conference 2015
Date: September 9-12, 2015
Location: The Westin Ottawa
Ottawa, ON
Sponsor/Contact: Canadian Association of Genetic Counsellors
P.O. Box 52083
Oakville, ON L6J 7N5
905-847-1363 *Fax:* 905-847-3855
E-mail: CAGCOffice@cagc-accg.ca
URL: www.cagc-accg.ca
Scope: National

Canadian Association of Orthodontists 2015 67th Annual Scientific Session
Date: September 17-19, 2015
Location: Fairmont Empress Hotel
Victoria, BC
Sponsor/Contact: Canadian Association of Orthodontists
#310, 2175 Sheppard Ave. East
Toronto, ON M2J 1W8
416-491-3186 *Fax:* 416-491-1670
Toll-Free: 877-226-8800
E-mail: cao@taylorenterprises.com
URL: www.cao-aco.org
Scope: National
Purpose: A scientific session with exhibits
Contact Information: Chair, Communications Committee: Dr. Dan Pollit, E-mail: dpollit@rogers.com

Canadian Association of Radiation Oncology 2015 Annual Scientific Meeting
Date: September 9-12, 2015
Location: Delta Grand Okanagan
Kelowna, BC
Sponsor/Contact: Canadian Association of Radiation Oncology
774 Echo Dr.
Ottawa, ON K1S 5N8
613-260-4188 *Fax:* 613-730-1116
E-mail: caro-acro@rcpsc.edu
URL: www.caro-acro.ca
Scope: National
Purpose: Lectures, presentations, & exhibits for health professionals involved in radiation oncology

Canadian Call Management Association 51st Annual Convention & Trade Show
Date: September 28 - October 2, 2015
Location: Doubletree Hilton
Charleston, SC USA
Sponsor/Contact: Canadian Call Management Association
#10, 24 Olive St.
Grimsby, ON L3M 2B6
905-309-0224 *Fax:* 905-309-0225
Toll-Free: 800-896-1054
E-mail: info@camx.ca
URL: www.camx.ca
Scope: National

Canadian Chiropractic Association 2015 Conference
Date: September 17-20, 2015
Location: Scotiabank Convention Centre
Niagara Falls, ON
Sponsor/Contact: Canadian Chiropractic Association
#6, 186 Spadina Ave.
Toronto, ON M5T 3B2
416-585-7902 *Fax:* 416-585-2970
Toll-Free: 877-222-9303
URL: www.chiropracticcanada.ca
Scope: National

Canadian College of Medical Geneticists 39th Annual Scientific Meeting 2015
Date: September 10-12, 2015
Location: The Westin
Ottawa, ON
Sponsor/Contact: Canadian College of Medical Geneticists
774 Echo Dr.
Ottawa, ON K1S 5N8
613-730-6250 *Fax:* 613-730-1116
E-mail: ccmg@royalcollege.ca
URL: www.ccmg-ccgm.org
Scope: National

Canadian Employee Relocation Council 2015 Annual Conference
Date: September 27-29, 2015
Location: Le Centre Sheraton
Montréal, QC
Sponsor/Contact: Canadian Employee Relocation Council
#1010, 180 Dundas St. W.
Toronto, ON M5G 1Z8
416-593-9812 *Fax:* 416-593-1139
Toll-Free: 866-357-2372
E-mail: info@cerc.ca
URL: www.cerc.ca
Scope: National

Canadian Federation of Independent Grocers Grocery Innovations Canada 2015
Date: September 28-29, 2015
Location: Toronto Congress Centre
Toronto, ON
Sponsor/Contact: Canadian Federation of Independent Grocers
#902, 2235 Sheppard Ave. East
Toronto, ON M2J 5B5
416-492-2311 *Fax:* 416-492-2347
Toll-Free: 800-661-2344
E-mail: info@cfig.ca
URL: www.cfig.ca
Scope: National
Purpose: An annual event, featuring the Canadian Federation of Independent Grocers' annual general meeting, keynote presentations, panel presentations, informative conference sessions, over 500 grocery exhibits, the presentation of industry awards, & networking opportunities
Anticipated Attendance: 5,000
Contact Information: General Information, E-mail: events@cfig.ca

Canadian Health Food Association (CHFA) Expo East 2015
Date: September 17-20, 2015
Location: Metro Toronto Convention Centre, South Building
Toronto, ON
Sponsor/Contact: Canadian Health Food Association
#302, 235 Yorkland Blvd.
Toronto, ON M2J 4Y8
416-497-6939 *Fax:* 905-479-3214
Toll-Free: 800-661-4510
E-mail: info@chfa.ca
URL: www.chfa.ca
Scope: Provincial
Purpose: A trade event, featuring exhibits from leading suppliers, manufacturers, distributors, & brokers of natural health products & organics
Anticipated Attendance: 2,900
Contact Information: Phone: 416-497-6939; Toll-Free Phone: 1-800-661-4510; E-mail: info@chfa.ca

Canadian Healthcare Engineering Society 35th Annual Conference
Date: September 20-22, 2015
Location: Shaw Conference Centre
Edmonton, AB
Sponsor/Contact: Canadian Healthcare Engineering Society
#310, 4 Cataraqui St.
Kingston, ON K7K 1Z7
613-531-2661 *Fax:* 613-531-0626
E-mail: ches@eventsmgt.com
URL: www.ches.org
Scope: National
Purpose: Theme: Healthcare Facilities & the Technology Highway

Canadian Home Builders' Association - Alberta Conference: BUILD 2015
Date: September 17-20, 2015
Location: Jasper, AB
Sponsor/Contact: Canadian Home Builders' Association - Alberta
#328, 9707 - 110 St.
Edmonton, AB T5K 2L9
780-424-5890 *Fax:* 780-426-0128
Toll-Free: 800-661-3348
E-mail: info@chbaalberta.ca
URL: www.chbaalberta.ca
Scope: Provincial
Purpose: BUILD is the acronym for Being a United Industry in Leadership & Development
Contact Information: Email: conference@chbaalberta.ca

Canadian Institute of Planners / Alberta Professional Planners Institute 2015 Conference
Date: September 16-19, 2015
Location: Edmonton, AB
Sponsor/Contact: Alberta Professional Planners Institute
P.O. Box 596
Edmonton, AB T5J 2K8
780-435-8716 *Fax:* 780-452-7718
Toll-Free: 888-286-8716
E-mail: admin@albertaplanners.com
URL: www.albertaplanners.com
Scope: National
Purpose: An event for planners, architects, academics, engineers, & policy makers. This year's title is "Great Cities, Great Regions: Prairie-Urban Transformations"
Contact Information: Co-Chairs, 2015 Conference Organizing Committee: Peter Ohm RPP, MCIP & Nancy MacDonald RPP, MCIP

Canadian Insurance Accountants Association 2015 51st Annual Conference
Date: September 20-23, 2015
Location: San Francisco, CA USA
Sponsor/Contact: Canadian Insurance Accountants Association
c/o Taylor Enterprises Ltd.
#310, 2175 Sheppard Ave. East
Toronto, ON M2J 1W8
416-971-7800 *Fax:* 416-491-1670
E-mail: ciaa@ciaa.org
URL: www.ciaa.org
Scope: National
Purpose: CIAA members, speakers, presenters, & exhibitors from across Canada

Canadian Society for Vascular Surgery 2015 37th Annual Meeting
Date: September 25-26, 2015
Location: Delta Victoria
Victoria, BC
Sponsor/Contact: Canadian Society for Vascular Surgery
c/o Christiane Dowsing, Society Manager
774 Echo Dr.
Ottawa, ON K1S 5N8
613-730-6263 *Fax:* 613-730-1116
E-mail: csvs@royalcollege.ca
URL: canadianvascular.ca
Scope: National
Purpose: The annual general meeting of the society, plus continuing education sessions, lectures, exhibits, & social events

Canadian Society of Safety Engineering (CSSE) 2015 Professional Development Conference
Date: September 20-23, 2015
Location: Ottawa, ON
Sponsor/Contact: Canadian Society of Safety Engineering, Inc.
39 River St.
Toronto, ON M5A 3P1
416-646-1600 *Fax:* 416-646-9460
URL: www.csse.org
Scope: National

Canadian Student Leadership Association 2015 Conference
Date: September 22-26, 2015
Location: Halifax, NS
Sponsor/Contact: Canadian Student Leadership Association
2460 Tanner Rd.
Victoria, BC V8Z 5R1
URL: studentleadership.ca
Scope: National

Coal Association of Canada 2015 Association Conference & Trade Show
Date: September 16-18, 2015
Location: Westin Bayshore Hotel
Vancouver, BC
Sponsor/Contact: Coal Association of Canada
#150, 205 - 9th Ave. SE
Calgary, AB T2G 0R3
403-262-1544 *Fax:* 403-265-7604
Toll-Free: 800-910-2625
E-mail: info@coal.ca
URL: www.coal.ca
Scope: National
Contact Information: Linda Kool; Email: kool@coal.ca

Dynamics 2015: The Annual National Convention & Product Exhibition of the Canadian Association of Critical Care Nurses
Date: September 27-29, 2015
Location: RBC Convention Centre Winnipeg
Winnipeg, MB
Sponsor/Contact: Canadian Association of Critical Care Nurses
P.O. Box 25322
London, ON N6C 6B1
519-649-5284 *Fax:* 519-649-1458
Toll-Free: 866-477-9077
E-mail: caccn@caccn.ca
URL: www.caccn.ca
Scope: National
Purpose: Featuring programming to enhance education, clinical practice, research, & leadership.
Contact Information: Toll-Free Phone: 1-866-477-9077; E-mail: caccn@caccn.ca

Economic Developers Association of Canada 47th Annual Conference
Date: September 19-22, 2015
Location: Whitehorse, YT
Sponsor/Contact: Economic Developers Association of Canada
7 Innovation Dr.
Flamborough, ON L9H 7H9
905-689-8771 *Fax:* 905-689-5925
E-mail: info@edac.ca
URL: www.edac.ca
Scope: National

Foothills Library Association 2015 Annual General Meeting
Location: Alberta

Conferences Index

Sponsor/Contact: Foothills Library Association
P.O. Box 2985 Stn. M
Calgary, AB T2P 3C3
E-mail: flapresident@fla.org
URL: www.fla.org
Scope: Local
Purpose: A general meeting & social event.
Contact Information: Events Line Contact: Inesia Adolph, E-mail: events@fla.org

Hospice & Palliative Care Manitoba 2015 24th Provincial Conference
Date: September 17-18, 2015
Location: Victoria Inn
Winnipeg, MB
Sponsor/Contact: Hospice & Palliative Care Manitoba
2109 Portage Ave.
Winnipeg, MB R3J 0L3
204-889-8525 *Fax:* 204-888-8874
Toll-Free: 800-539-0295
E-mail: info@manitobahospice.mb.ca
URL: www.manitobahospice.ca
Scope: Provincial
Purpose: An opportunity to for persons working in the field of palliative care to advance their knowledge & skills, to network with others in the field, & to view displays by approximately 30 exhibitors
Anticipated Attendance: 400+
Contact Information: Conference Coordinator: Andrea Firth, E-mail: afirth2@manitobahospice.mb.ca

International Academy of Energy, Minerals, & Materials 2015 International Conference on Clean Energy
Date: September 14-16, 2015
Location: Ottawa, ON
Sponsor/Contact: International Academy of Energy, Minerals, & Materials
Esprit Dr.
Ottawa, ON K4A 4Z1
613-322-1029 *Fax:* 613-830-8371
E-mail: info@iaemm.com
URL: iaemm.com
Scope: International
Purpose: Conference topics include the following: Biomass energy, materials & technologies; Hydro energy, materials & technologies; Wind energy resources & technologies; Solar cells energy, materials & technologies; Fuel cells materials & hydrogen energy; Battery materials & technologies; Energy storage techniques; Nanotechnology & energy; Green buildings; Energy process & system simulation, modelling & optimization; & more
Contact Information: URL: icce2015.iaemm.com

International Association of Hydrogeologists 2015 42nd Congress: Hydrogeology: Back to the Future
Date: September 13-18, 2015
Location: Rome, Italy
Sponsor/Contact: International Association of Hydrogeologists
IAH Secretariat
P.O. Box 4130 Stn. Goring
Reading, KOA 1L0 RG8 6BJ
E-mail: info@iah.org
URL: www.iah.org
Scope: International
Purpose: Presented in partnership with the Ministry of Energy, Mines, Water & Environment & the International Institute for Water & Sanitation

Contact Information: Email: organizing@iah2015.org; URL: www.iah2015.org

International Society for Sexually Transmitted Diseases Research 21st Meeting
Date: September 13-16, 2015
Location: Brisbane Convention and Exhibition Centre
Brisbane, Australia
Sponsor/Contact: International Society for Sexually Transmitted Diseases Research
c/o Basil Donovan, The Kirby Institute, University of New South Wales
Sidney
URL: www.isstdr.org
Scope: International
Purpose: To address the range of the biomedical, behavioral, & social sciences related to all sexually transmitted diseases, including HIV infection
Anticipated Attendance: 1,000

International Society for Vascular Behavioural & Cognitive Disorders 2015 VasCog Congress
Date: September 17-19, 2015
Location: Tokyo, Japan
Sponsor/Contact: International Society for Vascular Behavioural & Cognitive Disorders
c/o Newcastle University Campus for Ageing & Vitality
NIHR Biomedical Research Building, 1st Fl.
Newcastle upon Tyne, NE4 5PL
E-mail: vascogsoc@gmail.com
URL: www.vas-cog.org
Scope: International

Metallurgy & Materials Society of the Canadian Institute of Mining, Metallurgy & Petroleum World Gold 2015 5th International Conference
Date: September 29 - October 1, 2015
Location: Misty Hills, Gauteng, South Africa
Sponsor/Contact: Metallurgy & Materials Society of the Canadian Institute of Mining, Metallurgy & Petroleum
#1250, 3500, boul de Maisonneuve ouest
Montréal, QC H3Z 3C1
514-939-2710
URL: www.metsoc.org
Scope: International
Purpose: Jointly convened by the Canadian Institute of Mining, Metallurgy & Petroleum (CIM), the Australasian Institute of Mining & Metallurgy (AusIMM), & the Southern African Institute of Mining & Metallurgy (SAIMM)

Money Laundering in Canada 2015 Conference
Date: September 27-29, 2015
Location: Banff Springs Hotel
Banff, AB
Sponsor/Contact: Canadian Anti-Money Laundering Institute
P.O. Box 427
629 St. Lawrence St.
Merrickville, ON K0G 1N0
613-269-2619 *Fax:* 613-526-9384
E-mail: contactus@camli.org
URL: www.camli.org
Scope: National

National Insurance Conference of Canada 2015
Date: September 30 - October 2, 2015
Location: Le Centre Sheraton Montréal
Montréal, QC
Sponsor/Contact: Insurance Bureau of Canada
P.O. Box 121
#2400, 777 Bay St.
Toronto, ON M5G 2C8
416-362-2031 *Fax:* 416-361-5952
URL: www.ibc.ca
Scope: National
Purpose: Sponsored by the Insurance Bureau of Canada, among other companies & organizations
Contact Information: Web Site: www.niccanada.com; Phone: 416-368-0777; Fax: 416-363-7454

Northern Finance Association 2015 Conference
Date: September 18-20, 2015
Location: Chateau Lake Louise
Banff, AB
Sponsor/Contact: Northern Finance Association
c/o Rotman School of Management
105 St. George St.
Toronto, ON M5S 3E6
URL: www.northernfinance.org
Scope: Local

Ontario Association of Consultants, Counsellors, Psychometrists & Psychotherapists 2015 Conference
Date: September 17-19, 2015
Location: Toronto, ON
Sponsor/Contact: Ontario Association of Consultants, Counsellors, Psychometrists & Psychotherapists
#410, 586 Eglinton Ave. East
Toronto, ON M4P 1P2
416-298-7333 *Fax:* 416-298-9593
Toll-Free: 888-622-2779
E-mail: oaccpp@oaccpp.ca
URL: www.oaccpp.ca
Scope: Provincial

Ontario Association of Pathologists 2015 Annual Meeting
Date: September 18-20, 2015
Location: Niagara Falls, ON
Sponsor/Contact: Ontario Association of Pathologists
c/o Mt. Sinai Hospital, Pathology & Laboratory Medicine
#600, 600 University Ave.
Toronto, ON M5G 1X5
416-586-1575 *Fax:* 416-586-8628
URL: www.ontariopathologists.org
Scope: Provincial

Ontario Municipal Human Resources Association Fall Conference 2015
Date: September 16-18, 2015
Location: Fern Resort
Orillia, ON
Sponsor/Contact: Ontario Municipal Human Resources Association
#307, 1235 Fairview St.
Burlington, ON L7S 2K9
905-631-7171 *Fax:* 905-631-2376
E-mail: customerservice@omhra.on.ca
URL: www.omhra.ca
Scope: Provincial

Ontario Municipal Tax & Revenue Association 2015 Fall Conference
Date: September 13-16, 2015
Location: JW Marriott The Rosseau Muskoka Resort & Spa
Minett, ON
Sponsor/Contact: Ontario Municipal Tax & Revenue Association
#119, 14845 - 6 Yonge St.
Aurora, ON L4G 6H8
E-mail: webmaster@omtra.ca
URL: www.omtra.ca
Scope: Provincial

Prevention Matters Conference 2015
Date: September 30 - October 20, 2015
Location: TCU Place
Saskatoon, SK
Sponsor/Contact: Saskatchewan Prevention Institute
1319 Colony St.
Saskatoon, SK S7N 2Z1
306-651-4300 *Fax:* 306-651-4301
E-mail: info@skprevention.ca
URL: www.skprevention.ca
Scope: Provincial
Contact Information: Contact: Lee Hinton, Education & Promotions Coordinator, Phone: 306-651-4318, Email: lhinton@skprevention.ca

Public Works Association of British Columbia 2015 Technical Conference & Trade Show
Date: September 21-23, 2015
Location: Penticton Trade & Conference Centre
Penticton, BC
Sponsor/Contact: Public Works Association of British Columbia
#102, 211 Columbia St.
Vancouver, BC V6A 2R5
Toll-Free: 877-356-0699
E-mail: info@pwabc.ca
URL: www.pwabc.ca
Scope: Provincial

Recycling Council of Alberta Waste Reduction 2015 Conference
Date: September 30 - October 2, 2015
Location: Banff, AB
Sponsor/Contact: Recycling Council of Alberta
P.O. Box 23
Bluffton, AB T0C 0M0
403-843-6563 *Fax:* 403-843-4156
E-mail: info@recycle.ab.ca
URL: www.recycle.ab.ca
Scope: Provincial
Purpose: Presentations, exhibits, & networking opportunities. Held jointly with the Conference on Canadian Stewardship.
Contact Information: Phone: 403-843-6563; E-mail: info@recycle.ab.ca

Scleroderma Society of Canada 16th Annual Conference
Date: September 17-19, 2015
Location: Hamilton Sheraton Hotel
Hamilton, ON
Sponsor/Contact: Scleroderma Society of Canada
#206, 41 King William St.
Hamilton, ON L8R 1A2
Toll-Free: 866-279-0632
E-mail: info@scleroderma.ca
URL: www.scleroderma.ca
Contact Information: Anna McCusker, Email: anna@sclerodermaontario.ca, URL: www.sclerodermaconference.ca

Sheet Metal and Air Conditioning Contractors' National Association (SMACNA) 72nd Annual Convention
Date: September 27-30, 2015
Location: The Broadmoor Hotel
Colorado Springs, CO USA
Sponsor/Contact: Sheet Metal & Air Conditioning Contractors' National Association
P.O. Box 221230
4201 Lafayette Center Dr.
Chantilly, VA 20153-1230
703-803-2980 *Fax:* 703-803-3732
E-mail: info@smacna.org
URL: www.smacna.org
Scope: National
Contact Information: Email: SMACNAConvention@cmrus.com; Phone: 800-336-9704

Society of Plastics Engineers 2015 ANTEC Brussels Conference
Date: September 8-9, 2015
Location: Brussels, Belgium
Sponsor/Contact: Society of Plastics Engineers
13 Church Hill Rd.
Newtown, CT 06470
203-775-0471 *Fax:* 203-775-8490
E-mail: info@4spe.org
URL: www.4spe.org
Scope: International

TRENDS: The Apparel Show 2015 (sponsored by the Alberta Men's Wear Agents Association)
Date: September 10-14, 2015
Location: Edmonton Expo Centre
Edmonton, AB
Sponsor/Contact: Alberta Men's Wear Agents Association
P.O. Box 66037 Stn. Heritage
Edmonton, AB T6J 6T4
780-455-1881 *Fax:* 780-455-3969
E-mail: amwa@shaw.ca
URL: www.trendsapparel.com
Scope: Provincial
Purpose: An event, held twice each year, featuring approximately 250 sales representatives
Contact Information: E-mail: amwa@shaw.ca

The 7th Canadian Quality Congress
Date: September 28-29, 2015
Location: Edmonton, AB
Sponsor/Contact: Canadian Society for Quality
c/o Dr. Madhav Sinha
Winnipeg, MB
204-261-6606
E-mail: csq@shaw.ca
URL: canadianqualitycongress.com
Scope: National

The American Association of Bovine Practitioners 2015 Annual Conference
Date: September 17-19, 2015
Location: New Orleans, LA USA
Sponsor/Contact: American Association of Bovine Practitioners
P.O. Box 3610
#802, 3320 Skyway Dr.
Auburn, AL 36831-3610
334-821-0442 *Fax:* 334-821-9532
E-mail: aabphq@aabp.org
URL: www.aabp.org
Scope: International

The Maritimes Energy Association 2015 Core Energy Conference & Trade Show
Date: September 29-30, 2015
Location: Halifax, NS
Sponsor/Contact: The Maritimes Energy Association
Cambridge Tower 1
#305, 202 Brownlow Ave.
Dartmouth, NS B3B 1T5
902-425-4774 *Fax:* 902-422-2332
E-mail: info@maritimesenergy.com
URL: www.maritimesenergy.com
Scope: Provincial
Purpose: A gathering of interest to decision makers in the offshore & onshore & the renewable & non-renewable energy sectors to participate in roundtable discussions & networking events

The Profile Show 2015
Date: September 18-21, 2015
Location: Toronto Congress Centre, North Building
Toronto, ON
Sponsor/Contact: Ontario Fashion Exhibitors
P.O. Box 218
#2219, 160 Tycos Dr.
Toronto, ON M6B 1W8
416-596-2401 *Fax:* 416-596-1808
Toll-Free: 800-765-7508
E-mail: info@profileshow.ca
URL: www.profileshow.ca
Scope: Provincial

Transportation Association of Canada 2015 Conference & Exhibition
Date: September 27-30, 2015
Location: PEI Convention Centre
Charlottetown, PE
Sponsor/Contact: Transportation Association of Canada
2323 St. Laurent Blvd.
Ottawa, ON K1G 4J8
613-736-1350 *Fax:* 613-736-1395
E-mail: secretariat@tac-atc.ca
URL: www.tac-atc.ca
Scope: National

Union of British Columbia Municipalities 2015 Annual Convention
Date: September 21-25, 2015
Location: Vancouver Convention & Exhibition Centre
Vancouver, BC
Sponsor/Contact: Union of British Columbia Municipalities
#60, 10551 Shellbridge Way
Richmond, BC V6X 2W9
604-270-8226 *Fax:* 604-270-9116
URL: www.ubcm.ca
Scope: Provincial

Water Environment Federation WEFTEC 2015: 88th Annual Water Environment Federation Technical Exhibition & Conference
Date: September 26-30, 2015
Location: McCormick Place
Chicago, IL USA
Sponsor/Contact: Water Environment Federation
601 Wythe St.
Alexandria, VA 22314-1994
703-684-2400 *Fax:* 703-684-2492
Toll-Free: 800-666-0206
E-mail: comments@wef.org
URL: www.wef.org
Scope: International
Purpose: Educational & training opportunities, plus an exhibition by more than 750 companies
Anticipated Attendance: 18,000
Contact Information: Membership Information, Toll-Free Phone: 1-800-666-0206, International Phone: +44 120-679-6351 or 571-830-1545

Western Canada Water 2015 67th Annual Conference & Exhibition
Date: September 15-18, 2015
Location: Winnipeg, MB
Sponsor/Contact: Western Canada Water
P.O. Box 1708
240 River Ave.
Cochrane, AB T4C 1B6
403-709-0064 *Fax:* 403-709-0068
Toll-Free: 877-283-2003
E-mail: member@wcwwa.ca
URL: www.wcwwa.ca
Scope: Provincial
Purpose: Information & a showcase of products & services for delegates from the Western Canada Water marketplace, such as utility managers & operators, municipal & provincial government representatives, & consulting engineers
Anticipated Attendance: 500+
Contact Information: Western Canada Water, Toll-Free Phone: 1-877-283-2003, Toll-Free Fax: 1-877-283-2007, E-mail: member@wcwwa.ca

October

11th Annual Canadian ADHD Resource Alliance Conference
Date: October 17-18th, 2015
Location: Vancouver, BC
Sponsor/Contact: Canadian ADHD Resource Alliance
#604, 3950 - 14th Ave.
Markham, ON L3R 0A9
416-637-8583 *Fax:* 416-385-3232
E-mail: info@caddra.ca
URL: www.caddra.ca
Scope: National

15th Annual Power of Water Caanada Conference 2015
Date: October 18-20, 2015
Location: White Oaks Conference Resort
Niagara-on-the-Lake, ON
Sponsor/Contact: Ontario Waterpower Association
#264, 380 Armour Rd.
Peterborough, ON K9H 7L7
Fax: 705-743-1570
Toll-Free: 866-743-1500
E-mail: info@owa.ca
URL: www.owa.ca
Scope: Provincial
Purpose: The largest gathering of the hydroelectric sector in Canada and will feature a tradeshow with more than 50 exhibitors.
Contact Information: Website: conference.owa.ca; Twitter: twitter.com/PowerofWaterCan

2015 Annual Breaking the ICE West Conference
Date: October 3, 2015
Location: Nikkei Centre
Burnaby, BC
Sponsor/Contact: Ontario March of Dimes
10 Overlea Blvd.
Toronto, ON M4H 1A4
416-425-3463 *Fax:* 416-425-1920
Toll-Free: 800-263-3463
E-mail: info@marchofdimes.ca
URL: www.marchofdimes.ca
Scope: Provincial
Purpose: A consumer-centered conference aimed at helping people who use Alternative and Augmentative Communication (AAC) systems to develop their lives to the best of their abilities
Contact Information: Phone: 800-263-3463

2015 Annual Breaking the ICE West Conference
Date: October 2015
Location: Burnaby, BC
Sponsor/Contact: March of Dimes Canada
10 Overlea Blvd.
Toronto, ON M4H 1A4
416-425-3463 *Fax:* 416-425-1920
Toll-Free: 800-263-3463
E-mail: info@marchofdimes.ca
URL: www.marchofdimes.ca
Scope: Provincial
Purpose: A consumer-centered conference aimed at helping people who use Alternative and Augmentative Communication (AAC) systems to develop their lives to the best of their abilities
Contact Information: Phone: 800-263-3463

2015 Canaidan Association of Physician Assistants Conference
Date: October 22-25, 2015
Location: Toronto, ON
Sponsor/Contact: Canaidan Association of Physician Assistants
#704, 265 Carling Ave.
Ottawa, ON K1S 2E1
613-248-2272 *Fax:* 613-521-2226
Toll-Free: 877-744-2272
E-mail: admin@capa-acam.ca
URL: capa-acam.ca
Scope: National

24th Annual Alberta Association of Family School Liaison Workers Conference
Date: October 1-2, 2015
Location: Calgary, AB
Sponsor/Contact: Alberta Association of Family School Liaison Workers
c/o Tonia Koversky, St. Albert Family & Community Support Services
#10, 50 Bellerose Dr.
St. Albert, AB T8N 3L5
780-459-1749 *Fax:* 780-458-1260
URL: www.aafslw.ca
Scope: Provincial

28th Annual Alberta Snowmobile & Powersports Show 2015
Date: October 16-18, 2015
Location: Edmonton, AB
Sponsor/Contact: Alberta Snowmobile Association
11759 Groat Rd.
Edmonton, AB T5M 3K6
780-427-2695 *Fax:* 780-415-1779
URL: www.altasnowmobile.ab.ca
Scope: Provincial

54th Annual Northwest Math Conference
Date: October 22-24, 2015
Location: Whistler, BC
Sponsor/Contact: British Columbia Association of Mathematics Teachers
c/o British Columbia Teachers' Federation
#100, 550 West 6th Ave.
Vancouver, BC V5Z 4P2

Conferences Index

604-871-2283
Toll-Free: 800-663-9163
URL: www.bcamt.ca
Scope: Provincial

65th Canadian Chemical Engineering Conference
Date: October 4-7, 2015
Location: Calgary, AB
Sponsor/Contact: Chemical Institute of Canada
#550, 130 Slater St.
Ottawa, ON K1P 6E2
613-232-6252 *Fax:* 613-232-5862
Toll-Free: 888-542-2242
E-mail: info@cheminst.ca
URL: www.cheminst.ca
Scope: National
Contact Information: URL: csche2015.ca

9th Annual Saskatchewan Association of Human Resource Professionals Conference
Date: October 6-7, 2015
Location: Saskatoon, SK
Sponsor/Contact: Saskatchewan Association of Human Resource Professionals
2106 Lorne St.
Regina, SK S4P 2M5
306-522-0184 *Fax:* 306-522-1783
E-mail: communications@sahrp.ca
URL: www.sahrp.ca
Contact Information: communications@sahrp.ca

Alberta Association of Optometrists - 2015 Annual Convention and Trade Show
Date: October 21-24, 2015
Location: Telus Convention Centre
Calgary, AB
Sponsor/Contact: Alberta Association of Optometrists
#100, 8407 Argyll Rd.
Edmonton, AB T6C 4B2
780-451-6824 *Fax:* 780-452-9918
Toll-Free: 800-272-8843
URL: www.optometrists.ab.ca
Scope: Provincial

Alberta Public Housing Administrators' Association Fall Conference 2015
Date: October 20-22, 2015
Location: The Banff Centre
Banff, AB
Sponsor/Contact: Alberta Public Housing Administrators' Association
14220 - 109 Ave. NW
Edmonton, AB T5N 4B3
780-498-1971 *Fax:* 780-464-7039
URL: www.aphaa.org
Scope: Provincial

Allied Beauty Association Trade Show - Calgary 2015
Date: October 4-5, 2015
Location: Calgary Stampede Park
Calgary, AB
Sponsor/Contact: Allied Beauty Association
#26-27, 145 Traders Blvd. East
Mississauga, ON L4Z 3L3
905-568-0158 *Fax:* 905-568-1581
E-mail: abashows@abacanada.com
URL: www.abacanada.com
Scope: National
Purpose: A trade show for beauty professionals to learn about current happenings in the beauty industry

American Association of Neuromuscular & Electrodiagnostic Medicine 2015 62nd Annual Meeting
Date: October 28-31, 2015
Location: Hawaii Convention Center & Hilton Hawaiian Village
Honolulu, HI USA
Sponsor/Contact: American Association of Neuromuscular & Electrodiagnostic Medicine
2621 Superior Dr. NW
Rochester, MN 55901
507-288-0100 *Fax:* 507-288-1225
E-mail: aanem@aanem.org
URL: www.aanem.org
Scope: International
Contact Information: Director, Meetings: Denae Brennan, E-mail: dbrennan@aanem.org

American College of Chest Physicians Conference: CHEST 2015
Date: October 24-29, 2015
Location: Palais des congrès (Convention Centre)
Montréal, QC
Sponsor/Contact: American College of Chest Physicians
3300 Dundee Rd.
Northbrook, IL 60062-2348
Toll-Free: 800-343-2227
URL: www.chestnet.org
Scope: International
Purpose: A chest medicine conference for health professionals such as cardiologists, critical care physicinas, general medicine physicians, ICU medical directors, pulmonologists, pediatric pulmonologists, sleep medicine physicians, anesthesiologists, practice administrators, respiratory therapists, advanced practice nurses, & registered nurses

American Thyroid Association 2015 85th Annual Meeting
Date: October 18-23, 2015
Location: Walt Disney Swan & Dolphin Resort
Orlando, FL USA
Sponsor/Contact: American Thyroid Association
#550, 6066 Leesburg Pike
Falls Church, VA 22041
E-mail: thyroid@thyroid.org
URL: www.thyroid.org
Scope: International
Purpose: Held each autumn, the meeting includes platform presentations, lectures, symposia, discussion groups, posters, exhibits, & opportunities for networking
Anticipated Attendance: 1,000+

Association for Financial Professionals 2015 Annual Conference
Date: October 18-21, 2015
Location: Denver, CO USA
Sponsor/Contact: Association for Financial Professionals
#750, 4520 East West Hwy.
Bethesda, MD 20814
301-907-2862 *Fax:* 301-907-2864
E-mail: afp@afponline.org
URL: www.afponline.org
Scope: National

Association of Family Health Teams of Ontario 2015 Conference
Date: October 28-29, 2015
Location: Westin Harbour Castle
Toronto, ON
Sponsor/Contact: Association of Family Health Teams of Ontario
#800, 60 St. Clair Ave. East
Toronto, ON M4T 1N5
647-234-8605
E-mail: info@afhto.ca
URL: www.afhto.ca
Scope: Provincial
Contact Information: Saleemeh Abdolzahraei, Membership and Conference Coordinator; Email: saleemeh@afhto.ca

Atlantic Canada Water & Wastewater Association 2015 68th Annual Conference
Date: October 4-7, 2015
Sponsor/Contact: Atlantic Canada Water & Wastewater Association
P.O. Box 41002
Dartmouth, NS B2Y 4P7
902-434-6002 *Fax:* 902-435-7796
E-mail: acwwa@hfx.andara.com
URL: www.acwwa.ca
Scope: Provincial
Purpose: The association's annual general meeting & the election of its executive committee, plus a trade show, educational events, & networking occasions
Anticipated Attendance: 260-340
Contact Information: Technical Director: Jennie Rand

Automotive Recyclers Association of Atlantic Canada 2015 Annual General Meeting
Date: October 16-17, 2015
Location: Radisson Suite Hotel Halifax
Halifax, NS
Sponsor/Contact: Automotive Recyclers Association of Atlantic Canada
519-858-8761
E-mail: araac@execulink.com
URL: araac.ca
Scope: Provincial

BC Kidney Days 2015
Date: October 1-2, 2015
Location: Vancouver Renaissance Harbourside Hotel
Vancouver, BC
Sponsor/Contact: British Columbia Provincial Renal Agency
#700, 1380 Burrard St.
Vancouver, BC V6Z 2H3
604-875-7340
E-mail: bcpra@bcpra.ca
URL: www.bcrenalagency.ca
Scope: Provincial
Purpose: Brings together clinicians & administrators from across BC & other parts of Canada & the United States to discuss current research, trends, clinical treatment & surgical breakthroughs in renal patient care.
Contact Information: Kidney Days Contact: Stephanie Allan, E-mail: sallan2@bcpra.ca

British Columbia Association of Teachers of Modern Languages 2015 Conference
Date: October 24, 2015
Location: Delta Burnaby Hotel and Conference Centre
Burnaby, BC
Sponsor/Contact: British Columbia Association of Teachers of Modern Languages
c/o BC Teachers' Federation
#100, 550 West 6th Ave.
Vancouver, BC V5Z 4P2
604-871-2283 *Fax:* 604-871-2286
E-mail: psac51@bctf.ca
URL: www.bcatml.org
Scope: Provincial

British Columbia Honey Producers 2015 Annual General Meeting, Convention & Trade Show
Date: October 16-18, 2015
Location: Courtney, BC
Sponsor/Contact: British Columbia Honey Producers Association
P.O. Box 1650
Comox, BC V9M 8A2
URL: www.bcbeekeepers.com
Scope: Provincial

British Columbia Museums Association Conference 2015
Date: October 25-28, 2015
Location: New Westminster, BC
Sponsor/Contact: British Columbia Museums Association
675 Belleville St.
Victoria, BC V8W 9W2
250-356-5700 *Fax:* 250-387-1251
E-mail: bcma@museumsassn.bc.ca
URL: museumsassn.bc.ca
Scope: Provincial

British Columbia Music Educators' Association 2015 Annual Conference
Date: October 2015
Location: British Columbia
Sponsor/Contact: British Columbia Music Educators' Association
c/o British Columbia Teachers' Federation
#100, 550 West 6th Ave.
Vancouver, BC V5Z 4P2
URL: www.bctf.ca/bcmea
Scope: Provincial
Purpose: Professional development activities & exhibits for British Columbia teachers
Contact Information: Alia Chua, Conference Co-chair, Email: alianicolechua@gmail.com; URL: www.bcmeaconference.com

British Columbia Recreation & Parks Association 2015 Provincial Ripple Effects Aquatics Conference
Date: October 22-23, 2015
Location: Pinnacle North Vancouver
Vancouver, BC
Sponsor/Contact: British Columbia Recreation & Parks Association
#101, 4664 Lougheed Hwy.
Burnaby, BC V5C 5T5
604-629-0965 *Fax:* 604-629-2651
Toll-Free: 866-929-0965
E-mail: bcrpa@bcrpa.bc.ca
URL: www.bcrpa.bc.ca
Scope: Provincial
Purpose: A two-day conference which occurs every two years, presenting operations, programming, & best practices for aquatics professionals
Contact Information: Parks & Recreation Program Coordinator: Natalie Korsovetski, Phone: 604-629-0965, ext. 229; E-mail: nkorsovetski@bcrpa.bc.ca

British Columbia Science Teachers' Association Catalyst Conference 2015
Location: British Columbia
Sponsor/Contact: British Columbia Science Teachers' Association

c/o Ashcroft Secondary School
P.O. Box 669
Ashcroft, BC V0K 1A0
250-453-9144 *Fax:* 250-453-2368
E-mail: bcscta@gmail.com
URL: www.bcscta.ca
Scope: Provincial
Contact Information: catalyst.bcscta.ca

British Columbia Teachers' Federation 2015 Provincial Specialist Associations Day
Date: October 23, 2015
Location: British Columbia
Sponsor/Contact: British Columbia Teachers' Federation
#100, 550 - 6th Ave. West
Vancouver, BC V5Z 4P2
604-871-2283 *Fax:* 604-871-2293
Toll-Free: 800-663-9163
E-mail: benefits@bctf.ca
URL: www.bctf.ca
Scope: Provincial
Purpose: An annual professional development day, offering a wide range of workshops for teachers across British Columbia
Contact Information: British Columbia Teachers' Federation Media Relations Officer: Rich Overgaard, E-mail: rovergaard@bctf.ca

Canadian AIDS Treatment Information Exchange Forum 2015
Date: October 15-16, 2015
Location: Toronto, ON
Sponsor/Contact: Canadian AIDS Treatment Information Exchange
P.O. Box 1104
#505, 555 Richmond St. West
Toronto, ON M5V 3B1
416-203-7122 *Fax:* 416-203-8284
Toll-Free: 800-263-1638
E-mail: questions@catie.ca
URL: www.catie.ca
Scope: National

Canadian Academy of Audiology 2015 18th Annual Conference & Exhibition
Date: October 21-24, 2015
Location: Niagara Falls, ON
Sponsor/Contact: Canadian Academy of Audiology
P.O. Box 62117
777 Guelph Line
Burlington, ON L7R 4K2
905-633-7114 *Fax:* 905-633-9113
Toll-Free: 800-264-5106
E-mail: caa@canadianaudiology.ca
URL: www.canadianaudiology.ca
Scope: National
Purpose: Annual general meeting, educational sessions, speaker presentations, exhibits, & networking opportunities
Contact Information: Phone: 1-800-264-5106; Fax: 905-633-9113; E-mail: conference@canadianaudiology.ca

Canadian Academy of Child and Adolescent Psychiatry 35th Annual Meeting
Date: October 4-6, 2015
Location: Quebec, QC
Sponsor/Contact: Canadian Academy of Child & Adolescent Psychiatry
#701, 141 Laurier Ave. West
Ottawa, ON KIP 5J3
613-288-0408 *Fax:* 613-234-9857
E-mail: info@cacap-acpea.org
URL: www.cacap-acpea.org
Scope: National

Canadian Association for Graduate Studies 2015 Annual General Meeting & Conference
Date: October 30 - November 2, 2015
Location: Hyatt Regency - Calgary
Calgary, AB
Sponsor/Contact: Canadian Association for Graduate Studies
#301, 260 St. Patrick St.
Ottawa, ON K1N 5K5
613-562-0949 *Fax:* 613-562-9009
E-mail: info@cags.ca
URL: www.cags.ca
Scope: National
Purpose: A yearly conference held at the end of October or the beginning of November, including plenary & breakout sessions, workshops, the presentation of awards, & the Killam Lecture related to graduate studies

Canadian Association of Communicators in Education Conference 2015
Date: October 17-20, 2015
Location: Charlottetown, PE
Sponsor/Contact: Canadian Association of Communicators in Education
2490 Don Reid Dr.
Ottawa, ON K1H 1E1
E-mail: info@cace-acace.org
URL: www.cace-acace.org
Scope: National
Purpose: Theme: "Sharing our Stories"

Canadian Association of Geographers, Atlantic Division 2015 27th Annual Meeting
Date: October 2015
Sponsor/Contact: Canadian Association of Geographers
c/o James Boxall, GIS Centre, Killam Library, Dalhousie University
6225 University Ave.
Halifax, NS B3H 4H8
URL: community.smu.ca/acag
Scope: Provincial
Purpose: Paper & poster presentations, plenary addresses, lectures, the presentation of awards, a field trip, social activities, & opportunities to network with other geographers & students from across Canada

Canadian Association of Nurses in Oncology 2015 Conference
Date: October 4-7, 2015
Location: Fairmont Royal York Hotel
Toronto, ON
Sponsor/Contact: Canadian Association of Nurses in Oncology
#201, 375 West 5th Ave.
Vancouver, BC V5Y 1J6
604-874-4322 *Fax:* 604-874-4378
E-mail: cano@malachite-mgmt.com
URL: www.cano-acio.ca
Scope: National
Purpose: The conference theme is People, Purpose, Passion

Canadian Association of Paediatric Health Centres Annual Conference 2015
Date: October 18-20, 2015
Location: Quebec City, QC
Sponsor/Contact: Canadian Association of Paediatric Health Centres
c/o Canadian Association of Paediatric Health Centres
#104, 2141 Thurston Dr.
Ottawa, ON K1G 6C9
613-738-4164 *Fax:* 613-738-3247
E-mail: info@caphc.org
URL: www.caphc.org
Scope: National

Canadian Association of Research Libraries 2015 Fall Meeting
Date: October 20-22, 2015
Location: Ottawa, ON
Sponsor/Contact: Canadian Association of Research Libraries
Morisset Library, University of Ottawa
#239, 65 University St.
Ottawa, ON K1N 9A5
613-562-5385 *Fax:* 613-562-5297
E-mail: carladm@uottawa.ca
URL: www.carl-abrc.ca
Scope: National
Contact Information: Program & Administrative Officer: Katherine McColgan, Phone: 613-482-9344, ext. 102, E-mail: Katherine.McColgan@carl-abrc.ca

Canadian Association of Wound Care 2015 21st Annual Wound Care Conference
Date: October 29 - November 1, 2015
Location: Westin Harbour Castle Hotel
Toronto, ON
Sponsor/Contact: Canadian Association of Wound Care
#608, 920 Yonge St.
Toronto, ON M4W 3C7
416-485-2292 *Fax:* 416-485-2291
Toll-Free: 866-474-0125
E-mail: info@cawc.net
URL: www.cawc.net
Scope: National
Purpose: Educational components of the conference include basic clinical, advanced clinical, research, & public policy & education
Contact Information: Business Manager: David Stein, E-mail: david@cawc.net

Canadian Association on Gerontology 2015 44th Annual Scientific & Educational Meeting: Landscapes of Aging
Date: October 23-25, 2015
Location: Calgary, AB
Sponsor/Contact: Canadian Association on Gerontology
#328, 263 McCaul St.
Toronto, ON M5T 1W7
Toll-Free: 855-224-2240
E-mail: cagacg@igs.net
URL: www.cagacg.ca
Scope: National
Purpose: A multi-discplinary conference for persons interested in individual & population aging

Canadian Chamber of Commerce 2015 AGM and Convention
Date: October 17-18, 2015
Location: Westin Ottawa
Ottawa, ON
Sponsor/Contact: The Canadian Chamber of Commerce
#420, 360 Albert St.
Ottawa, ON K1R 7X7
613-238-4000 *Fax:* 613-238-7643
E-mail: info@chamber.ca
URL: www.chamber.ca
Scope: National
Contact Information: Marley Ransom, Communications and Events Specialist; Email: mransom@chamber.ca; Phone: 613-238-4000 ext. 227

Canadian Council of Cardiovascular Nurses 2015 Fall Conference, Annual General Meeting & Scientific Session
Date: October 25-28, 2015
Location: Toronto, ON
Sponsor/Contact: Canadian Council of Cardiovascular Nurses
#202, 300 March Rd.
Ottawa, ON K1P 5V9
613-599-9210 *Fax:* 613-595-1155
E-mail: info@cccn.ca
URL: www.cccn.ca
Scope: National
Purpose: Plenary speakers & workshops address issues in the cardiovascular nursing field. This year's conference is a joint effort between the Canadian Cardiovascular Society, the Canadian Diabetes Association, the Heart & Stroke Foundation of Canada, & the Canadian Stroke Network.

Canadian Dam Association 2015 Annual Conference
Date: October 3-8, 2015
Location: Mississauga, ON
Sponsor/Contact: Canadian Dam Association
P.O. Box 2281
Moose Jaw, SK S6TH 7W6
URL: www.cda.ca
Scope: National
Purpose: Featuring technical paper presentations, workshops, tours, exhibitor presentations, & a social program

Canadian Fertility & Andrology Society 2015 61st Annual Meeting
Date: October 1-4, 2015
Location: Marriott Harbourfront Hotel
Halifax, NS
Sponsor/Contact: Canadian Fertility & Andrology Society
#1107, 1255, rue University
Montréal, QC H3B 3W7
514-524-9009 *Fax:* 514-524-2163
E-mail: info@cfas.ca
URL: www.cfas.ca
Scope: National
Purpose: Educational presentations, a trade show, & networking opportunities for persons involved in the field of reproductive medicine
Anticipated Attendance: 350

Canadian Hypertension Congress 2015
Date: October 22-24, 2015
Location: Hilton Toronto Airport Hotel and Suites
Toronto, ON
Sponsor/Contact: Hypertension Canada
c/o Judi Farrell
#211, 3780 - 14th Ave.
Markham, ON L3R 9Y5
905-943-9400 *Fax:* 905-943-9401
URL: www.hypertension.ca
Scope: National

Canadian Nuclear Society 2015 7th International Conference on Modelling & Simulation in Nuclear Science & Engineering
Date: October 18-21, 2015
Location: Ottawa Marriott Hotel
Ottawa, ON
Sponsor/Contact: Canadian Nuclear Society
655 Bay St., 17th Fl.
Toronto, ON M5G 2K4

Conferences Index

416-977-7620 *Fax:* 416-977-8131
E-mail: cns-snc@on.aibn.com
URL: www.cns-snc.ca
Scope: National
Contact Information: Canadian Nuclear Society Office: Phone: 416-977-7620, E-mail: cns-snc@on.aibn.com; URL: cns2015simulation.org

Canadian Parking Association 2015 Conference & Trade Show
Date: October 17-21, 2015
Location: Vancouver, BC
Sponsor/Contact: Canadian Parking Association
#350, 2255 St. Laurent Blvd.
Ottawa, ON K1G 4K3
613-727-0700 *Fax:* 613-727-3183
E-mail: info@canadianparking.ca
URL: www.canadianparking.ca
Scope: National

Canadian Power and Sail Squadrons 2015 Annual General Meeting & Conference
Date: October 20-24, 2015
Location: Niagara Falls, ON
Sponsor/Contact: Canadian Power & Sail Squadrons (Canadian Headquarters)
26 Golden Gate Ct.
Toronto, ON M1P 3A5
416-293-2438 *Fax:* 416-293-2445
Toll-Free: 888-277-2628
E-mail: hqg@cps-ecp.ca
URL: www.cps-ecp.ca
Scope: National

Canadian Psychiatric Association 65th Annual Conference / 65e Conférence annuelle de l'Association des psychiatres du Canada
Date: October 1-3, 2015
Location: The Fairmont Hotel Vancouver
Vancouver, BC
Sponsor/Contact: Canadian Psychiatric Association
#701, 141 Laurier Ave. West
Ottawa, ON K1P 5J3
613-234-2815 *Fax:* 613-234-9857
Toll-Free: 800-267-1555
E-mail: cpa@cpa-apc.org
URL: www.cpa-apc.org
Scope: National
Anticipated Attendance: 1200+
Contact Information: E-mail: conference@cpa-apc.org

Canadian Society for Eighteenth-Century Studies 2015 Conference
Date: October 14-17, 2015
Location: Vancouer, BC
Sponsor/Contact: Canadian Society for Eighteenth-Century Studies
c/o Department of French, University of Manitoba
427 Fletcher Argue Bldg.
Winnipeg, MB R3T 2N2
204-474-9206
URL: www.csecs.ca
Contact Information: Email: csecs@sfu.ca

Canadian Society of Association Executives / Société canadienne d'association 2015 Conference & Showcase
Date: October 28-30, 2015
Location: Calgary, AB
Sponsor/Contact: Canadian Society of Association Executives
#1100, 10 King St. East
Toronto, ON M5C 1C3
416-363-3555 *Fax:* 416-363-3630
Toll-Free: 800-461-3608
URL: www.csae.com
Scope: National
Anticipated Attendance: 500+
Contact Information: E-mail: events@csae.com

Canadian Society of Association Executives National Conference & Showcase 2015
Date: October 28-30, 2015
Location: Calgary, AB
Sponsor/Contact: Canadian Society of Association Executives
c/o British Columbia Bottle Depot Association
9850 King George Hwy.
Surrey, BC V3T 4Y3
604-930-0003 *Fax:* 604-930-0060
E-mail: bcbd@telus.net
URL: www.csae.com
Scope: National
Contact Information: Peter Gregus, Managing Director, Meetings and Conventions Calgary

Canadian Society of Clinical Perfusion 2015 Annual General Meeting & Scientific Sessions
Date: October 2015
Location: Toronto Convention Centre
Toronto, ON
Sponsor/Contact: Canadian Society of Clinical Perfusion
914 Adirondack Rd.
London, ON N6K 4W7
Fax: 866-648-2763
Toll-Free: 888-496-2727
E-mail: cscp@cscp.ca
URL: www.cscp.ca
Scope: National
Purpose: Continuing education sessions on product development involving the society's corporate members, a business meeting, Canadian Society of Clinical Perfusion cerification examinations held off site from the convention centre, the presentation of awards, & networking opportunities
Contact Information: Annual General Meeting Coordinator: Bill O'Reilly, E-mail: cscp@cscp.ca; Chair, Accreditation, Competency, & Examination: Manon Caouette, E-mail: cscp@cscp.ca; Contact, Professional Development: Philip Fernandes, E-mail: cscp@cscp.ca

Canadian Society of Transplantation 2015 Annual Scientific Conference
Date: October 5-10, 2015
Location: Vancouver, BC
Sponsor/Contact: Canadian Society of Transplantation
774 Echo Dr.
Ottawa, ON K1S 5N8
613-730-6274 *Fax:* 613-730-1116
E-mail: cst@rcpsc.edu
URL: www.cst-transplant.ca
Scope: National
Purpose: Co-hosted with the Banff Foundation of Allograft Pathology

Canadian Water & Wastewater Association 2015 National Water & Wastewater Conference
Date: October 25-28, 2015
Location: Whistler, BC
Sponsor/Contact: Canadian Water & Wastewater Association
#11, 1010 Polytek St.
Ottawa, ON K1J 9H9
613-747-0524 *Fax:* 613-747-0523
E-mail: admin@cwwa.ca
URL: www.cwwa.ca
Scope: National
Purpose: An exchange of news & views from Canadian utility conservation specialists
Contact Information: Phone: 613-747-0524; Fax: 613-747-0523; E-mail: admin@cwwa.ca

Canadian Wind Energy Association (CanWEA) 31st Annual Conference and Exhibition
Date: October 5-7, 2015
Location: Metro Toronto Convention Centre
Toronto, ON
Sponsor/Contact: Canadian Wind Energy Association Inc.
#710, 1600 Carling Ave.
Ottawa, ON K1Z 1G3
613-234-8716 *Fax:* 613-234-5642
Toll-Free: 800-922-6932
E-mail: info@canwea.ca
URL: www.canwea.ca
Scope: National
Purpose: To discuss the opportunities and latest developments in the wind energy industry.
Anticipated Attendance: 2000
Contact Information: Email: events@canwea.ca

Congrès de l'exploration minière du Québec
Date: 7 au 8 octobre 2015
Sponsor/Contact: Association de l'exploration minière de Québec
#203, 132, av du Lac
Rouyn-Noranda, QC J9X 4N5
819-762-1599 *Fax:* 819-762-1522
E-mail: info@aemq.org
URL: www.aemq.org
Purpose: Prospecteurs, géologues, investisseurs, fournisseurs, conférenciers et futurs diplômés pourront débattre des questions qui entourent l'industrie minérale. Les activités comprennent des ateliers, des conférences, une réception de réseautage et une foire commerciale.
Anticipated Attendance: 1500+
Contact Information: Numéro de téléphone: 819-762-1599; numéro sans frais: 1-877-762-1599; courriel: info@aemq.org

Earth Matters Conference 2015
Date: October 15-17, 2015
Location: Coast Hotel
Canmore, AB
Sponsor/Contact: Alberta Council for Environmental Education
911 Larch Place
Canmore, AB T1W 1S5
URL: abcee.org
Scope: Provincial
Contact Information: Email: conference@abcee.org

Environmental Services Association of Alberta 2015 Remediation Technologies (RemTech) Symposium
Date: October 14-16, 2015
Location: Fairmont Banff Springs Hotel
Banff, AB
Sponsor/Contact: Environmental Services Association of Alberta
#102, 2528 Ellwood Dr. SW
Edmonton, AB T6X 0A9
780-429-6363 *Fax:* 780-429-4249
Toll-Free: 800-661-9278
E-mail: info@esaa.org
URL: www.esaa.org
Scope: Provincial
Purpose: Remediation technology information for environmental professionals, such as engineering firms, pipeline companies, drill companies, energy marketers, natural gas producers, oil & gase services companies, environmental consulting firms, & mining companies
Contact Information: URL: www.esaa-events.com/remtech; Director, Program & Event Development: Joe Chowaniec, Phone: 780-429-6363, ext. 223, E-mail: chowaniec@esaa.org; Exhibit Information, E-mail: exhibits@esaa-events.com; Sponsorship Information, E-mail: sponsors@esaa-events.com

ICRP 2015
Date: October 20-22, 2015
Location: Mayfield Hotel & Resort
Seoul, Korea
Sponsor/Contact: International Commission on Radiological Protection
P.O. Box 1046 Stn. B
280 Slater St.
Ottawa, ON K1P 5S9
613-947-9750
E-mail: admin@icrp.org
URL: www.icrp.org
Scope: International
Contact Information: ICRP Scientific Secretary Christopher Clement, sci.sec@icrp.org

IDWeek 2015
Date: October 7-11, 2015
Location: San Diego, CA USA
Sponsor/Contact: Infectious Diseases Society of America
#300, 1300 Wilson Blvd.
Arlington, VA 22209
703-299-0200 *Fax:* 703-299-0204
E-mail: membership@idsociety.org
URL: www.idsociety.org
Scope: International
Contact Information: URL: www.idweek.org

International Bar Association 2015 Annual Conference
Date: October 4-9, 2015
Location: Vienna, Austria
Sponsor/Contact: International Bar Association
10 St. Bride St., 4th Fl.
London, EC4A 4AD
E-mail: member@int-bar.org
URL: www.ibanet.org
Scope: International
Purpose: An opportunity to network, generate new business & participate in professional development programs
Contact Information: Web Site: www.ibanet.org/Conferences/Vienna2015.aspx

International Continence Society (ICS) 2015 45th Annual Scientific Meeting
Date: October 7-9, 2015
Location: Palais des congrès de Montréal
Montréal, QC
Sponsor/Contact: International Continence Society
19 Portland Sq.
Bristol, BS2 8SJ
E-mail: info@icsoffice.org
URL: www.icsoffice.org

Scope: International
Purpose: Educational workshops & a scientific meeting for urological, gynaecological, physiotherapy, & nursing professionals. This year's meeting is held jointly with the International Urogynecological Association.

International Society for Pediatric & Adolescent Diabetes 2015 41st Annual Meeting
Date: October 7-10, 2015
Location: Brisbane, Australia
Sponsor/Contact: International Society for Pediatric & Adolescent Diabetes
c/o KIT, Kurfürstendamm 71
10709
Berlin
E-mail: secretariat@ispad.org
URL: www.ispad.org
Scope: International
Purpose: A scientific meeting featuring paper, poster, & plenary sessions, workshops, & symposia
Contact Information: URL: www.ispad-apeg.com

Master Brewers Association Annual Conference 2015
Date: October 7-10, 2015
Location: Jacksonville, FL USA
Sponsor/Contact: Master Brewers Association of The Americas
3340 Pilot Knob Rd.
St. Paul, MN 55121-2097
651-454-7250 *Fax:* 651-454-0766
E-mail: mbaa@mbaa.com
URL: www.mbaa.com
Scope: International

National Trust Conference 2015: Heritage Energized
Date: October 22-24, 2015
Location: Fairmont Palliser Hotel
Calgary, AB
Sponsor/Contact: Heritage Canada Foundation
190 Bronson Ave.
Ottawa, ON K1R 6H4
613-237-1066 *Fax:* 613-237-5987
Toll-Free: 866-964-1066
E-mail: heritagecanada@heritagecanada.org
URL: www.heritagecanada.org
Scope: National
Purpose: In association with the Canadian Association of Heritage Professionals and in collaboration with Alberta Historical Resources Foundation.

Ontario Field Ornithologists 2015 Annual Convention
Date: October 2-4, 2015
Location: Point Pelee, ON
Sponsor/Contact: Ontario Field Ornithologists
P.O. Box 116 Stn. F
Toronto, ON M4Y 2L4
E-mail: membership@ofo.ca
URL: www.ofo.ca
Scope: Provincial
Purpose: Activities include guest speakers, birding displays, field trips, & a social event
Contact Information: Lynne Freeman; Phone: 416-463-9540; Email: lynnef.to@gmail.com

Ontario Independent Meat Processors Meat Industry Expo 2015
Date: October 23-24, 2015
Location: Niagara Falls, ON
Sponsor/Contact: Ontario Independent Meat Processors
7660 Mill Rd., RR#4
Guelph, ON N1H 6J1
519-763-4558 *Fax:* 519-763-4164
E-mail: info@oimp.ca
URL: www.oimp.ca
Scope: Provincial

Ontario Non-Profit Housing Association 2015 Annual Conference, General Meeting & Trade Show
Date: October 23-25, 2015
Location: Toronto Sheraton Centre
Toronto, ON
Sponsor/Contact: Ontario Non-Profit Housing Association
#400, 489 College St.
Toronto, ON M6G 1A5
416-927-9144 *Fax:* 416-927-8401
Toll-Free: 800-297-6660
E-mail: mail@onpha.org
URL: www.onpha.on.ca
Scope: Provincial
Purpose: Featuring speakers, workshops, & company exhibitors
Anticipated Attendance: 1,400
Contact Information: Phone: 1-800-297-6660, ext. 110; E-mail: conference@onpha.org; Manager, Conference & IT: Patsy Duffy, Phone: 416-927-9144, ext. 110, E-mail: patsy.duffy@onpha.org

Pain Society of Alberta 9th Annual Conference
Date: October 16-17, 2015
Location: Banff Conference Centre
Banff, AB
Sponsor/Contact: Pain Society of Alberta
132 Warwick Rd.
Edmonton, AB T5X 4P8
780-457-5225 *Fax:* 780-475-7968
E-mail: info@painsocietyofalberta.org
URL: painsocietyofalberta.org
Scope: Provincial

Safety Saves Conference & Tradeshow 2015
Date: October 27-28, 2015
Location: Canad Inns Polo Park
Manitoba
Sponsor/Contact: Incident Prevention Association of Manitoba
#51, 162 - 2025 Corydon Ave.
Winnipeg, MB R3P 0N5
204-275-3727
E-mail: office@ipam-manitoba.com
URL: ipam-manitoba.com
Scope: Provincial
Contact Information: Kristin Petaski; Email: Kristin@workengsolutions.ca

Saskatchewan Home Economics Teachers Association Conference 2015
Date: October 15-17, 2015
Location: Regina, SK
Sponsor/Contact: Saskatchewan Home Economics Teachers Association
Saskatoon, SK
URL: www.sheta.ca
Scope: Provincial

Saskatchewan Parks & Recreation Association 2015 Conference & Annual General Meeting
Date: October 2015
Sponsor/Contact: Saskatchewan Parks & Recreation Association
#100, 1445 Park St.
Regina, SK S4N 4C5
306-780-9231 *Fax:* 306-780-9257
Toll-Free: 800-563-2555
E-mail: office@spra.sk.ca
URL: www.spra.sk.ca
Scope: Provincial
Purpose: Presentations on the themes of technology, issues affecting small town Saskatchewan, & current issues
Contact Information: SPRA Consultant: Kelly Skotnitsky, E-mail: kskotnitsky@spra.sk.ca

Society of Plastics Engineers 2015 RETEC Conference
Date: October 4-6, 2015
Location: Indianapolis Westin
Indianapolis, IN USA
Sponsor/Contact: Society of Plastics Engineers
13 Church Hill Rd.
Newtown, CT 06470
203-775-0471 *Fax:* 203-775-8490
E-mail: info@4spe.org
URL: www.4spe.org
Scope: International
Purpose: This year's theme is Show Your Colours

Society of Plastics Engineers Annual Blow Molding Conference 2015
Date: October 11-13, 2015
Location: Sheraton Station Square
Pittsburgh, PA USA
Sponsor/Contact: Society of Plastics Engineers
13 Church Hill Rd.
Newtown, CT 06470
203-775-0471 *Fax:* 203-775-8490
E-mail: info@4spe.org
URL: www.4spe.org
Scope: International

Sustainable Forestry Initiative 2015 Annual Conference
Date: October 6-8, 2015
Location: Lake Tahoe, CA USA
Sponsor/Contact: Sustainable Forestry Initiative Inc.
#700, 900 - 17th St. NW
Washington, DC 20006
E-mail: info@sfiprogram.org
URL: www.sfiprogram.org
Scope: International
Purpose: Educational sessions, business meetings, the presentation of annual SFI awards, & networking opportunities

The Canadian Greenhouse Conference (CGC) 2015
Date: October 7-8, 2015
Location: Ontario
Sponsor/Contact: Ontario Institute of Agrologists
Ontario AgriCentre
#108, 100 Stone Rd. West
Guelph, ON N1G 5L3
519-826-4226 *Fax:* 519-826-4228
Toll-Free: 866-339-7619
URL: www.oia.on.ca
Scope: National
Purpose: Held annually since 1979 the CGC is committed to providing a high quality conference experience for the extension of information through speakers, workshops, demonstration and exhibits.
Contact Information: Website: www.canadiangreenhouseconference.com

Titanium USA 2015
Date: October 4-7, 2015
Location: Rosen Shingle Creek Golf Resort
Orlando, FL USA
Sponsor/Contact: International Titanium Association
#100, 11674 Huron St.
Northglenn, CO 80234
303-404-2221 *Fax:* 303-404-9111
E-mail: ita@titanium.org
URL: www.titanium.org
Scope: International

Winnipeg Chamber of Commerce 2015 Annual General Meeting
Date: October 2, 2015
Location: Winnipeg, MB
Sponsor/Contact: Winnipeg Chamber of Commerce
#100, 259 Portage Ave.
Winnipeg, MB R3B 2A9
204-944-8484 *Fax:* 204-944-8492
E-mail: info@winnipeg-chamber.com
URL: www.winnipeg-chamber.com
Scope: Provincial
Purpose: An examination of the organization's goals & objectives & finances
Contact Information: Events Coordinator: Yanik Ottenbreit, Phone: 204-944-3306, E-mail: yottenbreit@winnipeg-chamber.com

November

2015 British Columbia Crime Prevention Association Training Symposium
Date: November 5-7, 2015
Location: British Columbia
Sponsor/Contact: British Columbia Crime Prevention Association
#120, 12414 - 82nd Ave.
Surrey, BC V3W 3E9
604-501-9222 *Fax:* 604-501-2261
Toll-Free: 888-405-2288
E-mail: info@bccpa.org
URL: www.bccpa.org
Scope: Provincial

2015 Canadian Marketing Association Conference: CMAfuture
Date: November 2015
Sponsor/Contact: Canadian Marketing Association
#607, 1 Concorde Gate
Toronto, ON M3C 3N6
416-391-2362 *Fax:* 416-441-4062
E-mail: info@the-cma.org
URL: www.the-cma.org
Scope: National
Purpose: A look at the newest methods, strategies and technology on the horizon; the best things you've never heard of.

2015 Canadian Pool & Spa Conference & Expo
Date: November 30 - December 3, 2015
Location: Scotiabank Convention Centre
Niagara Falls, ON
Sponsor/Contact: Pool & Hot Tub Council of Canada
5 MacDougall Dr.
Brampton, ON L6S 3P3
905-458-7242 *Fax:* 905-458-7037
Toll-Free: 800-879-7066
E-mail: info@poolcouncil.ca
URL: www.poolcouncil.ca
Purpose: The conference features seminars & courses, as well as the expo

Conferences Index

Contact Information: URL: www.poolandspaexpo.ca

2015 Prince Edward Island Veterinary Medical Association Annual General Meeting
Date: November 8, 2015
Location: Rodd Charlottetown Hotel
Charlottetown, PE
Sponsor/Contact: Prince Edward Island Veterinary Medical Association
P.O. Box 21097 Stn. 465 University Ave.
Charlottetown, PE C1A 9h6
902-367-3757 *Fax:* 902-367-3176
E-mail: admin.peivma@gmail.com
URL: www.peivma.com
Scope: Provincial

2015 Royal Winter Agricultural Fair
Date: November 6-15, 2015
Location: Ricoh Coluseum & Direct Energy Centre
Toronto, ON
Sponsor/Contact: Royal Agricultural Winter Fair Association
The Ricoh Coliseum
100 Prince's Blvd.
Toronto, ON M6K 3C3
416-263-3400
E-mail: info@royalfair.org
URL: www.royalfair.org
Scope: International
Purpose: The Royal is the largest combined indoor agricultural fair and international equestrian competition in the world.

Air Transport Association of Canada 2015 81st Annual General Meeting & Trade Show
Date: November 2-4, 2015
Location: Fairmont Queen Elizabeth Hotel
Montréal, QC
Sponsor/Contact: Air Transport Association of Canada
#700, 255 Albert St.
Ottawa, ON K1P 6A9
613-233-7727 *Fax:* 613-230-8648
E-mail: atac@atac.ca
URL: www.atac.ca
Scope: National
Purpose: A business meeting, the presentation of awards, the chance to view exhibits, & networking opportunities for manufacturers, service providers, flying club & school presidents, operation directors, directors of maintenance, program & procurement managers, chief pilots, & government representatives
Contact Information: E-mail: atac@atac.ca

Alberta Association of Municipal Districts & Counties Fall 2015 Convention & Trade Show
Date: November 17-19, 2015
Location: Shaw Conference Centre
Edmonton, AB
Sponsor/Contact: Alberta Association of Municipal Districts & Counties
2510 Sparrow Dr.
Nisku, AB T9E 8N5
780-955-3639 *Fax:* 780-955-3615
Toll-Free: 855-548-7233
E-mail: aamdc@aamdc.com
URL: www.aamdc.com

American Anthropological Association 2015 Annual Meeting
Date: November 18-22, 2015
Location: Colorado Convention Center
Denver, CO USA
Sponsor/Contact: American Anthropological Association
Stn. 600
2300 Clarendon Blvd.
Arlington, VA 22201
703-528-1902 *Fax:* 703-528-3546
URL: www.aaanet.org
Scope: International
Contact Information: Director, American Anthropological Association & Section Meetings: Jason G. Watkins, E-mail: jwatkins@aaanet.org; Meeting Planner: Carla Fernandez, E-mail: cfernandez@aaanet.org

American Concrete Institute Fall 2015 Conference: Spanning the Globe
Date: November 8-12, 2015
Location: Sheraton
Denver, CO USA
Sponsor/Contact: American Concrete Institute
P.O. Box 9094
38800 Country Club Dr.
Farmington, MI 48333-9094
248-848-3700 *Fax:* 248-848-3701
URL: www.concrete.org
Scope: International

American Society of Mechanical Engineers 2015 International Mechanical Engineering Congress & Exposition
Date: November 13-19, 2015
Location: Hilton of the Americas and George R. Brown Convention Center
Houston, TX USA
Sponsor/Contact: American Society of Mechanical Engineers
3 Park Ave.
New York, NY 10016-5990
800-843-2763
E-mail: customercare@asme.org
URL: www.asme.org
Scope: International
Contact Information: Jimmy Le, Phone: 212-591-7116; Fax: 212-591-7856; Email: LeJ2@asme.org

Annual Tax Conference 2015
Date: November 22-24, 2015
Location: Palais des congrès de Montréal
Montréal, QC
Sponsor/Contact: Canadian Tax Foundation
#1200, 595 Bay St.
Toronto, ON M5G 2N5
416-599-0283 *Fax:* 416-599-9283
Toll-Free: 877-733-0283
URL: www.ctf.ca
Scope: National

Association for Preservation Technology International 2015 Annual Conference
Date: November 1-5, 2015
Location: The Clubhouse on Baltimore
Kansas, MO
Sponsor/Contact: Association for Preservation Technology International
#200, 3085 Stevenson Dr.
Springfield, IL
E-mail: info@apti.org
URL: www.apti.org
Scope: International
Purpose: Training & networking opportunities plus exhibits of interest to an international audience of persons involved in the application of methods & materials to conserve historic structures
Anticipated Attendance: 1,000

Association of Manitoba Municipalities 17th Annual Convention
Date: November 23-25, 2015
Location: Brandon Keystone Centre
Brandon, MB
Sponsor/Contact: Association of Manitoba Municipalities
1910 Saskatchewan Ave. West
Portage la Prairie, MB R1N 0P1
204-857-8666 *Fax:* 204-856-2370
E-mail: amm@amm.mb.ca
URL: www.amm.mb.ca

Association of Power Producers of Ontario 2015: 27th Annual Canadian Power Conference & Power Networking Centre
Date: November 17-18, 2015
Location: Ontario
Sponsor/Contact: Association of Power Producers of Ontario
P.O. Box 1084 Stn. F
#1602, 25 Adelaide St. East
Toronto, ON M5C 3A1
416-322-6549 *Fax:* 416-481-5785
E-mail: appro@appro.org
URL: www.appro.org
Scope: Provincial
Purpose: An annual event held in the autumn, featuring speakers, educational sessions, exhibits, & a student program
Contact Information: E-mail: appro@appro.org

Atlantic Provinces Trial Lawyers Association 14th Annual Plaintiff Pracetice Conference 2015
Date: November 6, 2015
Location: Delta Halifax
Halifax, NS
Sponsor/Contact: Atlantic Provinces Trial Lawyers Association
PO Box 2618, Central RPO
Halifax, NS B3J 3N5
902-446-4446 *Fax:* 902-425-9552
Toll-Free: 866-314-4446
URL: www.aptla.ca
Scope: Provincial

Atlantic Provinces Trial Lawyers Association's Specialty MCPD Education Conference 2015
Date: November 7, 2015
Location: Delta Halifax
Halifax, NS
Sponsor/Contact: Atlantic Provinces Trial Lawyers Association
PO Box 2618, Central RPO
Halifax, NS B3J 3N5
902-446-4446 *Fax:* 902-425-9552
Toll-Free: 866-314-4446
URL: www.aptla.ca
Scope: Provincial

British Columbia Recreation & Parks Association 2015 In Your Face Youth Workers' Conference
Date: November 2015
Location: British Columbia
Sponsor/Contact: British Columbia Recreation & Parks Association
#101, 4664 Lougheed Hwy.
Burnaby, BC V5C 5T5
604-629-0965 *Fax:* 604-629-2651
Toll-Free: 866-929-0965
E-mail: bcrpa@bcrpa.bc.ca
URL: www.bcrpa.bc.ca
Scope: Provincial
Contact Information: Programs & Initiatives Coordinator: Natalie Korsovetski, Phone: 604-629-0965, ext. 229, E-mail: nkorsovetski@bcrpa.bc.ca

Canadian Association of Accredited Mortgage Professionals 2015 Annual General Meeting
Date: November 15-17, 2015
Location: Toronto, ON
Sponsor/Contact: Canadian Association of Accredited Mortgage Professionals
Atria II
#1401, 2235 Sheppard Ave. East
Toronto, ON M2J 5B5
416-385-2333 *Fax:* 416-385-1177
Toll-Free: 888-442-4625
E-mail: info@caamp.org
URL: www.caamp.org
Scope: Provincial
Contact Information: E-mail: events@caamp.org

Canadian Association of Aesthetic Medicine 12th Annual Conference
Date: November 6-7, 2015
Location: The Westin Prince Hotel
Toronto, ON
Sponsor/Contact: Canadian Association of Aesthetic Medicine
#220, 445 Mountain Hwy.
North Vancouver, BC V7J 2L1
604-988-0450 *Fax:* 604-929-0871
E-mail: info@caam.ca
URL: www.csa-sce.ca
Scope: National

Canadian Association of Perinatal & Women's Health Nurses National Conference 2015
Date: November 5-7, 2015
Location: Hilton Quebec
Quebec, QC
Sponsor/Contact: Canadian Association of Perinatal & Women's Health Nurses
780 Echo Dr.
Ottawa, ON K1S 5R7
613-730-4192 *Fax:* 613-730-4314
Toll-Free: 800-561-2416
E-mail: admin@capwhn.ca
URL: www.capwhn.ca
Scope: National
Contact Information: Executive Director: Rita Assabgui, E-mail: admin@capwhn.ca

Canadian Association of University Teachers 2015 Annual Forum for Aboriginal Academic Staff
Date: November 6-8, 2015
Location: Winnipeg, MB
Sponsor/Contact: Canadian Association of University Teachers
2705 Queensview Dr.
Ottawa, ON K2B 8K2
613-820-2270 *Fax:* 613-820-7244
E-mail: acppu@caut.ca
URL: www.caut.ca
Scope: National

Canadian Bureau for International Education 2015 Annual Conference
Date: November 22-25, 2015
Location: Niagara Falls, ON
Sponsor/Contact: Canadian Bureau for International Education
#1550, 220 Laurier Ave. West
Ottawa, ON K1P 5Z9
613-237-4820 *Fax:* 613-237-1073
E-mail: info@cbie.ca
URL: www.cbie-bcei.ca
Scope: National
Purpose: The Conference features professional development workshops, concurrent sessions and networking opportunities.

Canadian Network for Respiratory Care Biennial National Respiratory Education Conference
Sponsor/Contact: Canadian Network for Respiratory Care
16851 Mount Wolfe Rd.
Caledon, ON L7E 3P6
905-880-1092 *Fax:* 905-880-9733
Toll-Free: 855-355-4672
E-mail: info@cnrchome.net
URL: www.cnrchome.net

Canadian Society for International Health's 22nd Canadian Conference on Global Health
Date: November 5-7, 2015
Location: Hilton Bonaventure
Montréal, QC
Sponsor/Contact: Canadian Society for International Health
#1105, 1 Nicholas St.
Ottawa, ON K1N 7B7
613-241-5785
E-mail: csih@csih.org
URL: www.csih.org
Scope: National
Purpose: The conference is the largest meeting of researchers, academics, decision makers, NGOs, policy makers, students & health care providers involved with global health in Canada.
Contact Information: Conference Manager: Sarah Brown, Phone: 613-241-5785 ext. 326, Email: sbrown@csih.org

Canadian Society for Training & Development 2015 National Conference and Trade Show
Date: November 18-20, 2015
Location: Metro Toronto Convention Centre, North Building
Toronto, ON
Sponsor/Contact: Canadian Society for Training & Development
#315, 720 Spadina Ave.
Toronto, ON M5S 2T9
416-367-5900 *Fax:* 416-367-1642
Toll-Free: 866-257-4275
E-mail: info@cstd.ca
URL: www.cstd.ca
Scope: National

Canadian Society of Endocrinology & Metabolism (CSEM) & Canadian Diabetes Assocation Professional Conference & Annual Meetings
Date: November 2015
Location: Vancouver, BC
Sponsor/Contact: Canadian Society of Endocrinology & Metabolism
#1403, 222 Queen St.
Ottawa, ON K1P 5V9
613-594-0005 *Fax:* 613-569-6574
E-mail: info@endo-metab.ca
URL: www.endo-metab.ca
Scope: National
Purpose: Interactive workshops, oral abstract sessions, poster presentations, speakers addressing current diagnosis & treatment issues, a trade show, social activities, & networking opportunities
Contact Information: Chair, Program Planning Committee: Stephanie Kaiser, E-mail: CSEM@royalcollege.ca

Canadian Technical Asphalt Association 60th Annual Conference & Annual General Meeting
Date: November 15-18, 2015
Location: Ottawa, ON
Sponsor/Contact: Canadian Technical Asphalt Association
#300, 895 Fort St.
Victoria, BC V8W 1H7
250-361-9187 *Fax:* 250-361-9187
E-mail: admin@ctaa.ca
URL: www.ctaa.ca
Scope: National

Canadian Urban Transit Association 2015 Fall Conference & Trans-Expo
Date: November 20-25, 2015
Location: Montréal, QC
Sponsor/Contact: Canadian Urban Transit Association
#1401, 55 York St.
Toronto, ON M5J 1R7
416-365-9800 *Fax:* 416-365-1295
URL: www.cutaactu.ca
Scope: National
Purpose: An annual technical meeting which also features a display of products & services for sales opportunities & business to business marketing
Contact Information: Phone: 416-365-9800

Coaching Association of Canada Petro-Canada Sport Leadership Sportif Conference 2015
Date: November 12-14, 2015
Location: RBC Convention Centre and the Delta Winnipeg
Winnipeg, MB
Sponsor/Contact: Coaching Association of Canada
#300, 141 Laurier Ave. West
Ottawa, ON K1P 5J3
613-235-5000 *Fax:* 613-235-9500
URL: www.coach.ca
Scope: National
Purpose: An inpiring event for coaches, featuring guest speakers & the presentation of sport leadership awards
Contact Information: Phone: 613-235-5000

Helicopter Association of Canada 2015 20th Annual Convention & Trade Show
Date: November 13-15, 2015
Location: Vancouver Convention Centre
Vancouver, BC
Sponsor/Contact: Helicopter Association of Canada
#500, 130 Albert St.
Ottawa, ON K1P 5G4
613-231-1110 *Fax:* 613-369-5097
URL: www.h-a-c.ca
Scope: National
Purpose: Professional development programs & information sessions to help Helicopter Association of Canada members achieve in the present economic & regulatory climate
Anticipated Attendance: 800+
Contact Information: Office Manager & Contact, Member Services: Barb Priestley, Phone: 613-231-1110, ext. 237, Fax: 613-369-5097, E-mail: barb.priestley@h-a-c.ca

International Foster Care Organisation 2015 World Conference
Date: November 8-11, 2015
Location: Star Events Centre
Sydney, Australia
Sponsor/Contact: International Foster Care Organisation
26 Red Lion Square
London, WC1R 4AG
E-mail: ifco@ifco.info
URL: www.ifco.info
Scope: International
Purpose: A biennial conference, featuring a youth program, workshops, & plenary sessions about quality care solutions for children & youth living in out-of-home care
Contact Information: Website: www.ifco2015.com

Mechanical Contractors Association of Canada (MCAC) 74th Annual National Conference 2015
Date: November 16-19, 2015
Location: Omni Ranco las Palmas Resort & Spa
Palm Springs, CA USA
Sponsor/Contact: Mechanical Contractors Association of Canada
#601, 280 Albert St.
Ottawa, ON K1P 5G8
613-232-0492 *Fax:* 613-235-2793
E-mail: mcac@mcac.ca
URL: www.mcac.ca
Scope: National

Municipal Engineers Association 2015 Annual General Meeting & Workshop
Date: November 18-20, 2015
Location: Ontario
Sponsor/Contact: Municipal Engineers Association
#2, 6355 Kennedy Rd.
Mississauga, ON L5T 2L5
905-795-2555 *Fax:* 905-795-2660
E-mail: info@municipalengineers.on.ca
URL: www.municipalengineers.on.ca
Scope: Provincial
Purpose: A workshop & business meeting during three days each November

National Association of College Auxiliary Services 2015 47th Annual Conference
Date: November 1-4, 2015
Location: San Antonio, TX
Sponsor/Contact: National Association of College Auxiliary Services
P.O. Box 5546
7 Boar's Head Lane
Charlottesville, VA 22905-5546
434-245-8425 *Fax:* 434-245-8453
E-mail: info@nacas.org
URL: www.nacas.org
Scope: International

Ontario Waste Management Association Canadian Waste to Resource Confernece 2015
Date: November 4-5, 2015
Location: Palais des congrès de Montréal
Montréal, QC
Sponsor/Contact: Ontario Waste Management Association
#3, 2005 Clark Blvd.
Brampton, ON L6T 5P8
905-791-9500 *Fax:* 905-791-9514
E-mail: info@owma.org
URL: www.owma.org
Scope: Provincial

Saskatchewan Association of Rural Municipalities 2015 Midterm Convention
Date: November 5-6, 2015
Location: Regina, SK
Sponsor/Contact: Saskatchewan Association of Rural Municipalities
2075 Hamilton St.
Regina, SK S4P 2E1
306-757-3577 *Fax:* 306-565-2141
Toll-Free: 800-667-3604
E-mail: sarm@sarm.ca
URL: www.sarm.ca
Scope: Provincial

Saskatchewan Water and Wastewater Association 2015 Conference & Trade Show
Date: November 4-5, 2015
Location: TCU Place Saskatoon
Saskatoon, SK
Sponsor/Contact: Saskatchewan Water & Wastewater Association
P.O. Box 7831
Saskatoon, SK S7K 4R5
306-761-1278 *Fax:* 306-761-1279
Toll-Free: 888-668-1278
E-mail: office@swwa.ca
URL: www.swwa.sk.ca
Scope: National

Science Teachers' Association of Ontario 2015 Conference
Date: November 12-14, 2015
Location: Toronto, ON
Sponsor/Contact: Science Teachers' Association of Ontario
P.O. Box 771
Dresden, ON N0P 1M0
Fax: 800-754-1654
Toll-Free: 800-461-2264
E-mail: info@stao.org
URL: www.stao.org
Scope: Provincial

Society of Environmental Toxicology & Chemistry North America 2015 36th Annual Meeting
Date: November 1-5, 2015
Location: Salt Palace Convention Center
Salt Lake City, UT USA
Sponsor/Contact: Society of Environmental Toxicology & Chemistry SETAC Asia / Pacific, SETAC Latin America, & SETAC North America
1010 - 12th Ave. North
Pensacola, FL 32501-3370
850-469-1500 *Fax:* 850-469-9778
E-mail: setac@setac.org
URL: www.setac.org
Scope: International
Anticipated Attendance: 2,300

The Transplantation Society 2015 Transplant Science Symposium
Date: November 11-13, 2015
Location: Mantra Lorne
Lorne, Australia
Sponsor/Contact: The Transplantation Society
International Headquarters
#605, 1255, rue University
Montréal, QC H3B 3V9
514-874-1717 *Fax:* 514-874-1716
E-mail: info@tts.org
URL: www.tts.org
Scope: International
Contact Information: URL: www.tss2015.org

Win-Door North America 2015 (an event owned & produced by Fenestration Canada)
Date: November 3-5, 2015
Location: Metro Toronto Convention Centre
Toronto, ON
Sponsor/Contact: Fenestration Canada
#1208, 130 Albert St.
Ottawa, ON K1P 5G4
613-235-5511 *Fax:* 613-235-4664
E-mail: info@fenestrationcanada.ca
URL: www.fenestrationcanada.ca
Scope: International
Purpose: Meetings, demonstrations, &

seminars, plus an opportunity for suppliers to show their products & services to manufacturers & fabricators from across Canada, the United States, & international destinations
Anticipated Attendance: 3,500+

December

Canadian Association of University Teachers 2015 Workshop for Senior Grievance Officers
Date: December 11-13, 2015
Location: Ottawa, ON
Sponsor/Contact: Canadian Association of University Teachers
2705 Queensview Dr.
Ottawa, ON K2B 8K2
613-820-2270 *Fax:* 613-820-7244
E-mail: acppu@caut.ca
URL: www.caut.ca
Scope: National

Other Conferences in 2015

10th Annual Manitoba Association for Behaviour Analysis 2015 Conference
Location: Manitoba
Sponsor/Contact: Manitoba Association for Behaviour Analysis
P.O. Box 53017 Stn. South St. Vital
Winnipeg, MB R2N 3X2
E-mail: president@maba.ca
URL: www.maba.ca
Scope: Provincial

11e Congrès annuel de l'Association québécoise du lymphoedème
Location: Quebec
Sponsor/Contact: Association Québécoise du Lymphoedème
6565 St. Hubert
Montréal, QC H2S 2M5
514-979-2463
E-mail: aql@infolympho.ca
URL: www.infolympho.ca
Scope: Provincial

11th Annual Saskatchewan Nurse Practitioner Conference
Sponsor/Contact: Nurse Practitioners of Saskatchewan
c/o Kelly Hughes RN(NP)
69 Red River Rd.
Saskatoon, SK S7K 1G2
E-mail: npos@npos.ca
URL: www.npos.ca
Scope: Provincial

14th Annual Windfall Ecology Festival
Sponsor/Contact: Windfall Ecology Centre
93A Industrial Pkwy. South
Aurora, ON L4G 3V5
905-727-0491 *Fax:* 905-727-0491
Toll-Free: 866-280-4431
E-mail: info@windfallcentre.ca
URL: www.windfallcentre.ca
Purpose: Electric vehicles, infrastructure development and practical information on how to incorporate electric mobility into your organization and strategy planning.
Contact Information: Fraser Damoff, Program Coordinator; Email: fdamoff@windfallcentre.ca; Phone: 905-727-0491 ex.123.

15th Annual International Conference for Enhanced Building Operations (ICEBO)
Sponsor/Contact: American Society of Heating, Refrigerating & Air Conditioning Engineers
1791 Tullie Circle NE
Atlanta, GA 30329
404-636-8400 *Fax:* 404-321-5478
Toll-Free: 800-527-4723
E-mail: ashrae@ashrae.org
URL: www.ashrae.org
Scope: International
Purpose: A global forum providing technology transfer, best practices, education and excellent networking opportunities for those who insist upon using the latest innovative solutions to enhance operations and maximize the efficiency and productivity of their buildings.
Contact Information: Alissa Simpson, Conference Manager; Email: alissasimpson@tees.tamus.edu; Website: icebo.tamu.edu

15th Canadian Conference on Building Science and Technology
Sponsor/Contact: National Building Envelope Council
c/o 5041 Regent St.
Burnaby, BC V5C 4H4
604-473-9587
E-mail: nbec@cebq.org
URL: www.nbec.net
Scope: National
Purpose: Provides a forum for the presentation, discussion and sharing of practical building science research, knowledge and field experience.

17th International Labour & Employment Relations Association World Congress
Location: Cape Town, South Africa
Sponsor/Contact: International Labour & Employment Relations Association
c/o DIALOGUE
International Labour Office, 22
Geneva, CH-1211
E-mail: iira@ilo.org
URL: www.ilo.org/public/english/iira
Scope: International

18th Annual Canadian Diabetes Association Professional Conference & Annual Meeting 2015
Sponsor/Contact: Canadian Diabetes Association
#1400, 522 University Ave.
Toronto, ON M5G 2R5
416-363-3373 *Fax:* 416-363-7465
Toll-Free: 800-226-8464
E-mail: info@diabetes.ca
URL: www.diabetes.ca
Scope: National
Contact Information: Sonia Morgan; Phone: 416-408-7205; Email: professional.conference@diabetes.ca

2015 Alberta Association of Police Governance Conference and Annual General Meeting
Location: Alberta
Sponsor/Contact: Alberta Association of Police Governance
P.O. Box 36098 Stn. Lakeview Post Office
Calgary, AB T3E 7C6
587-892-7874
E-mail: admin@aapg.ca
URL: www.aapg.ca
Scope: Provincial

2015 Alberta Water Council Symposium
Sponsor/Contact: Alberta Water Council
Petroleum Plaza, South Tower
#1400, 9915 - 108 St.
Edmonton, AB T5K 2G8
780-644-7380
E-mail: info@awchome.ca
URL: www.albertawatercouncil.ca
Scope: Provincial

2015 Annual Breaking the ICE Conference
Sponsor/Contact: Ontario March of Dimes
10 Overlea Blvd.
Toronto, ON M4H 1A4
416-425-3463 *Fax:* 416-425-1920
Toll-Free: 800-263-3463
E-mail: info@marchofdimes.ca
URL: www.marchofdimes.ca
Scope: Provincial
Purpose: A consumer-centered conference aimed at helping people who use Alternative and Augmentative Communication (AAC) systems to develop their lives to the best of their abilities

2015 Annual Breaking the ICE Conference
Sponsor/Contact: March of Dimes Canada
10 Overlea Blvd.
Toronto, ON M4H 1A4
416-425-3463 *Fax:* 416-425-1920
Toll-Free: 800-263-3463
E-mail: info@marchofdimes.ca
URL: www.marchofdimes.ca
Scope: Provincial
Purpose: A consumer-centered conference aimed at helping people who use Alternative and Augmentative Communication (AAC) systems to develop their lives to the best of their abilities
Contact Information: Phone: 800-263-3463

2015 Annual General Meeting of Canada's National Firearms Association
Sponsor/Contact: Canada's National Firearms Association
P.O. Box 49090
Edmonton, AB T6E 6H4
780-439-1394 *Fax:* 780-439-4091
Toll-Free: 877-818-0393
E-mail: info@nfa.ca
URL: nfa.ca
Scope: National

2015 Annual Meeting of the British Columbia Society of Respiratory Therapists
Location: British Columbia
Sponsor/Contact: British Columbia Society of Respiratory Therapists
P.O. Box 4760
Vancouver, BC V6B 4A4
604-623-2227
URL: www.bcsrt.ca
Scope: Provincial

2015 Annual Ontario Podiatric Medical Association Conference
Location: Ontario
Sponsor/Contact: Ontario Podiatric Medical Association
#900, 45 Sheppard Ave. East
Toronto, ON M2N 5W9
416-927-9111 *Fax:* 416-927-9111
Toll-Free: 866-424-6762
E-mail: contact@opma.ca
URL: www.opma.ca
Scope: Provincial

2015 Auditing Canada Annual Conference
Location: Halifax, NS
Sponsor/Contact: Auditing Association of Canada
9 Forest Rd.
Whitby, ON L1N 3N7
905-404-9511
E-mail: admin@auditingcanada.com
URL: www.auditingcanada.com
Scope: National
Contact Information: Brenda Macdonald; Email: Brenda.MacDonald@nspower.ca

2015 BC Fairs Conference
Location: British Columbia
Sponsor/Contact: British Columbia Association of Agricultural Fairs & Exhibitions
18231 - 60th Ave.
Surrey, BC V3S 1V7
778-574-4082
E-mail: info@bcfairs.ca
URL: www.bcfairs.ca
Scope: Provincial

2015 British Columbia Saw Filers Association Annual General Meeting, Supplier's Fair & Conference
Location: British Columbia
Sponsor/Contact: British Columbia Saw Filers Association
6521 Orchard Hill Rd.
Vernon, BC V1H 1B6
250-546-2234 *Fax:* 604-585-4014
E-mail: info@bcsawfilers.com
URL: www.bcsawfilers.com
Scope: Provincial

2015 Building SustainABLE Communities Conference
Sponsor/Contact: Fresh Outlook Foundation
12510 Ponderosa Rd.
Lake Country, BC V4V 2G9
250-766-1777 *Fax:* 250-766-1767
URL: www.freshoutlookfoundation.org
Scope: National

2015 Canadian Aerospace Summit
Sponsor/Contact: Aerospace Industries Association of Canada
#703, 255 Albert St.
Ottawa, ON K1P 6A9
613-232-4297 *Fax:* 613-232-1142
E-mail: info@aiac.ca
URL: www.aiac.ca
Scope: National
Purpose: Visionaries and practitioners will speak on the new evolution and expectations in aerospace, meet leading industry decision-makers, and gain first-hand intelligence on key business opportunities.
Anticipated Attendance: 1200

2015 Canadian Association of Physicists Congress
Sponsor/Contact: Canadian Association of Physicists
MacDonald Bldg.
#112, 150 Louis Pasteur Priv.
Ottawa, ON K1N 6N5
613-562-5614 *Fax:* 613-562-5615
E-mail: cap@uottawa.ca
URL: www.cap.ca
Scope: National

2015 Canadian Association of Police Educators Conference
Sponsor/Contact: Canadian Association of Police Educators

c/o Wayne Jacobsen
1430 Victoria Ave. East
Brandon, MB R7A 2A9
204-725-8700
E-mail: cape.educators@gmail.com
URL: cape-educators.ca
Scope: National
Contact Information: Wayne Jacobsen; Email: JacobseW@assiniboine.net

2015 Canadian Cardiovascular Congress
Sponsor/Contact: Canadian Cardiovascular Society
#1403, 222 Queen St.
Ottawa, ON K1P 5V9
613-569-3407 *Fax:* 613-569-6574
Toll-Free: 877-569-3407
E-mail: info@ccs.ca
URL: www.ccs.ca
Scope: National

2015 Canadian Institute of Planners and Atlantic Planners Institute Annual Conference
Sponsor/Contact: Atlantic Planners Institute
35 Ascot Ct.
Fredericton, NB E3B 6C4
506-455-7203 *Fax:* 506-455-1113
E-mail: apiexecutivedirector@gmail.com
URL: www.atlanticplanners.org
Scope: Provincial

2015 Canadian Society for the Study of Practical Ethics Annual Meeting
Sponsor/Contact: Canadian Society for the Study of Practical Ethics
c/o Dept. of Philosophy, #618, Jorgenson Hall, Ryerson Univ.
350 Victoria St.
Toronto, ON M5B 2K3
416-979-5000 *Fax:* 416-979-5362
URL: www.csspe.ca
Scope: National

2015 Canadian Stuttering Association Conference
Sponsor/Contact: Canadian Stuttering Association
P.O. Box 3027
Sherwood Park, AB T8H 2T1
416-840-5169
Toll-Free: 866-840-5169
E-mail: csa@stutter.ca
URL: www.stutter.ca
Scope: National

2015 Canadian University Music Society Annual Meeting
Sponsor/Contact: Canadian University Music Society
c/o Secretariat
#202, 10 Morrow Ave.
Toronto, ON M6R 2J1
416-538-1650 *Fax:* 416-489-1713
E-mail: journals@interlog.com
URL: www.cums-smuc.ca
Scope: National

2015 Community Living Ontario 62nd Annual Conference
Location: Ontario
Sponsor/Contact: Community Living Ontario
#403, 240 Duncan Mill Rd.
Toronto, ON M3B 3S6
416-447-4348 *Fax:* 416-447-8974
Toll-Free: 800-278-8025
E-mail: info@communitylivingontario.ca
URL: www.communitylivingontario.ca
Scope: Provincial

2015 Down Syndrome Association of Ontario Conference
Location: Ontario
Sponsor/Contact: Down Syndrome Association of Ontario
#304, 300 Earl Grey Dr.
Ottawa, ON K2T 1C1
905-439-6644
E-mail: info@dsao.ca
URL: www.dsao.ca
Scope: Provincial

2015 Home Care Summit
Sponsor/Contact: Canadian Home Care Association
7111 Syntex Dr., 3rd Fl.
Mississauga, ON L5N 8C3
289-290-4389 *Fax:* 289-290-4301
E-mail: chca@cdnhomecare.ca
URL: www.cdnhomecare.ca
Scope: National

2015 Industrial Gas User's Association Spring Seminar
Sponsor/Contact: Industrial Gas Users Association Inc.
#502, 350 Sparks St.
Ottawa, ON K1R 7S8
613-236-8021 *Fax:* 613-230-9531
E-mail: info@igua.ca
URL: www.igua.ca
Scope: National

2015 L.I.V.E. Conference
Sponsor/Contact: March of Dimes Canada
10 Overlea Blvd.
Toronto, ON M4H 1A4
416-425-3463 *Fax:* 416-425-1920
Toll-Free: 800-263-3463
E-mail: info@marchofdimes.ca
URL: www.marchofdimes.ca
Scope: Provincial
Purpose: The Leadership in Volunteer Education (L.I.V.E.) Conference is Peer Support's annual 3-day training and networking event for active members, current and future volunteer leaders in stroke, polio and caregiver support groups across Canada.
Contact Information: Phone: 800-263-3463

2015 Manitoba Association of Health Information Providers Annual General Meeting
Location: Manitoba
Sponsor/Contact: Manitoba Association of Health Information Providers
c/o Neil John Maclean Health Sciences Library, University of Manitoba
727 McDermott Ave.
Winnipeg, MB R3E 3P5
URL: www.chla-absc.ca/mahip/
Scope: Provincial

2015 Ontario Community Support Association Annual Conference
Location: Ontario
Sponsor/Contact: Ontario Community Support Association
#104, 970 Lawrence Ave. West
Toronto, ON M6A 3B6
416-256-3010 *Fax:* 416-256-3021
Toll-Free: 800-267-6272
E-mail: reception@ocsa.on.ca
URL: www.ocsa.on.ca
Scope: Provincial

2015 Ontario Kinesiology Association Conference & AGM
Location: Ontario
Sponsor/Contact: Ontario Kinesiology Association
6519B Mississauga Rd.
Mississauga, ON L5N 1A6
905-567-7194 *Fax:* 905-567-7191
E-mail: info@oka.on.ca
URL: www.oka.on.ca
Scope: Provincial

2015 Ontario Museum Association Annual Conference
Location: Ontario
Sponsor/Contact: Ontario Museum Association
George Brown House
50 Baldwin St.
Toronto, ON M5T 1L4
416-348-8672 *Fax:* 416-348-0438
Toll-Free: 866-662-8672
URL: www.museumsontario.com
Scope: National

2015 Operating Room Nurses of Alberta Association Provincial Conference
Location: Alberta
Sponsor/Contact: Operating Room Nurses of Alberta Association
E-mail: info@ornaa.org
URL: www.ornaa.org

2015 Social Work Provincial Conference
Location: Ontario
Sponsor/Contact: Ontario Association of Social Workers
410 Jarvis St.
Toronto, ON M4Y 2G6
416-923-4848 *Fax:* 416-923-5279
E-mail: info@oasw.org
URL: www.oasw.org
Scope: Provincial

2015 Value of Generic Drugs Symposium
Sponsor/Contact: Canadian Generic Pharmaceutical Association
#409, 4120 Yonge St.
Toronto, ON M2P 2B8
416-223-2333 *Fax:* 416-223-2425
E-mail: info@canadiangenerics.ca
URL: www.canadiangenerics.ca
Scope: International

22nd Convention of the Ukrainian Fraternal Society of Canada
Sponsor/Contact: Ukrainian Fraternal Society of Canada
235 McGregor St.
Winnipeg, MB R2W 4W5
204-568-4482 *Fax:* 204-589-6411
Toll-Free: 800-988-8372
E-mail: info@ufsc.ca
URL: www.ufsc.ca
Scope: National

27th Annual British Columbia Association of School Psychologists Conference
Location: British Columbia
Sponsor/Contact: British Columbia Association of School Psychologists
#562, 162 - 2025 Corydon Ave.
Winnipeg, MB R3P 0N5
E-mail: executives@bcasp.ca
URL: www.bcasp.ca
Scope: Provincial

31st Annual Ontario Native Education Counselling Association Conference
Location: Ontario
Sponsor/Contact: Ontario Native Education Counselling Association
P.O. Box 220
37A Reserve Rd.
Naughton, ON P0M 2M0
705-692-2999 *Fax:* 705-692-9988
E-mail: oneca@oneca.com
URL: www.oneca.com
Scope: Provincial

38th Day in Primary Eye Care Conference
Location: Ontario
Sponsor/Contact: Ontario Medical Association
#900, 150 Bloor St. West
Toronto, ON M5S 3C1
416-599-2580 *Fax:* 416-340-2944
Toll-Free: 800-268-7215
E-mail: info@oma.org
URL: www.oma.org
Scope: Provincial
Contact Information: OMA Public Affairs & Communications Department Contact: Catherine Flaman, Phone: 416-340-2915

3rd Canadian Conference on Positive Psychology
Sponsor/Contact: Canadian Positive Psychology Association
#703, 1 Eglinton Ave. East
Toronto, ON M4P 3A1
416-481-8930
E-mail: info@positivepsychologycanada.com
URL: www.positivepsychologycanada.com
Scope: National

50th ISOCARP Congress
Location: The Netherlands
Sponsor/Contact: International Society of City & Regional Planners
P.O. Box 983
The Hague, 2501 CZ
E-mail: isocarp@isocarp.org
URL: www.isocarp.org
Scope: International

60th Annual Ontario Anesthesia Meeting
Location: Ontario
Sponsor/Contact: Ontario Medical Association
#900, 150 Bloor St. West
Toronto, ON M5S 3C1
416-599-2580 *Fax:* 416-340-2944
Toll-Free: 800-268-7215
E-mail: info@oma.org
URL: www.oma.org
Scope: Provincial
Contact Information: OMA Public Affairs & Communications Department Contact: Catherine Flaman, Phone: 416-340-2915

6th Annual Ontario Parks Association 2015 Equipment Education & Golf Forum
Location: Ontario
Sponsor/Contact: Ontario Parks Association
7856 - 5th Line South, RR#4
Milton, ON L9T 2X8
905-864-6182 *Fax:* 905-864-6184
Toll-Free: 866-560-7783
E-mail: opa@ontarioparksassociation.ca
URL: www.ontarioparksassociation.ca
Scope: Provincial

6th International Conference on Ocean Energy (ICOE) 2015
Sponsor/Contact: Marine Renewables Canada
121 Bird Sanctuary Dr.
Nanaimo, BC V9R 6H1

URL: www.marinerenewables.ca
Scope: International
Purpose: Global marine renewable energy event focused on the industrial development of marine renewable energy.

6th World Hydrogen Technology Convention (WHTC 2015)
Location: Sydney, Australia
Sponsor/Contact: International Association for Hydrogen Energy
#303, 5794 40th St. SW
Miami, FL 33155
E-mail: info@iahe.org
URL: www.iahe.org
Scope: International
Purpose: A conference of the International Association for Hydrogen Energy, for the hydrogen & fuel cell community, featuring an exhibition with hydrogen & fuel cell applications from research institutions & companies
Anticipated Attendance: 1,000+

72nd Truck Loggers Association Convention & Trade Show
Sponsor/Contact: Truck Loggers Association
#725, 815 Hastings St. West
Vancouver, BC V6C 1B4
604-684-4291 *Fax:* 604-684-7134
E-mail: contact@tla.ca
URL: www.tla.ca
Scope: National

89th Annual Ontario Trucking Association Convention
Location: Ontario
Sponsor/Contact: Ontario Trucking Association
555 Dixon Rd.
Toronto, ON M9W 1H8
416-249-7401 *Fax:* 866-713-4188
E-mail: publicaffairs@ontruck.org
URL: www.ontruck.org
Scope: Provincial

95th Annual Insurance Brokers Association of Ontario Convention
Location: Ontario
Sponsor/Contact: Insurance Brokers Association of Ontario
#700, 1 Eglinton Ave. East
Toronto, ON M4P 3A1
416-488-7422 *Fax:* 416-488-7526
Toll-Free: 800-268-8845
E-mail: contact@ibao.com
URL: www.ibao.org
Scope: Provincial

95th Association of Professional Engineers & Geoscientists of New Brunswick Annual Meeting
Location: New Brunswick
Sponsor/Contact: Association of Professional Engineers & Geoscientists of New Brunswick
183 Hanwell Rd.
Fredericton, NB E3B 2R2
506-458-8083 *Fax:* 506-451-9629
Toll-Free: 888-458-8083
E-mail: info@apegnb.com
URL: www.apegnb.com
Scope: Provincial

AFOA British Columbia Spring Conference 2015
Location: British Columbia
Sponsor/Contact: AFOA Canada
#1010, 100 Park Royal
West Vancouver, BC V7T 1A2
604-925-6370 *Fax:* 604-925-6390
E-mail: exec@afoabc.org
URL: www.afoabc.org
Scope: Provincial

AFOA British Columbia Winter Conference 2015
Location: British Columbia
Sponsor/Contact: AFOA Canada
#1010, 100 Park Royal
West Vancouver, BC V7T 1A2
604-925-6370 *Fax:* 604-925-6390
E-mail: exec@afoabc.org
URL: www.afoabc.org
Scope: Provincial

ARUCC 2015 Conference
Sponsor/Contact: Association of Registrars of the Universities & Colleges of Canada
c/o Angelique Saweczko, Thompson Rivers University
900 McGill Rd.
Kamloops, BC V2C 0C8
250-828-5019
URL: www.arucc.ca
Scope: National

Aboriginal Nurses Association of Canada 2015 Annual General Meeting
Sponsor/Contact: Aboriginal Nurses Association of Canada
#600, 16 Concourse Gate
Ottawa, ON K2E 7S8
613-724-4677 *Fax:* 613-724-4718
Toll-Free: 866-724-3049
E-mail: info@anac.on.ca
URL: www.anac.on.ca
Scope: National
Purpose: Featuring the election of the Board of Directors
Contact Information: E-mail: info@anac.on.ca

Aboriginal Nurses Association of Canada 2015 National Conference
Sponsor/Contact: Aboriginal Nurses Association of Canada
#600, 16 Concourse Gate
Ottawa, ON K2E 7S8
613-724-4677 *Fax:* 613-724-4718
Toll-Free: 866-724-3049
E-mail: info@anac.on.ca
URL: www.anac.on.ca
Scope: National
Contact Information: E-mail: info@anac.on.ca

Active Healthy Kids Canada / Jeunes en forme Canada 2015 Global Summit on the Physical Activity of Children
Sponsor/Contact: Active Healthy Kids Canada
#1205, 77 Bloor St. West
Toronto, ON M5S 1M2
416-913-0238 *Fax:* 416-913-1541
E-mail: info@activehealthykids.ca
URL: www.activehealthykids.ca
Scope: International
Purpose: Brings together those who are working to resolve the growing childhood physical inactivity crisis.
Contact Information: Communications Manager: Katherine Janson, Phone: 416-913-0238, E-mail: kjanson@participACTION.com

Adult Basic Education Association of British Columbia Conference 2015
Location: British Columbia
Sponsor/Contact: Adult Basic Education Association of British Columbia
5476 - 45th Ave.
Delta, BC V4K 1L4
604-296-6901
URL: www.abeabc.ca
Scope: Provincial
Contact Information: Email: abeabcnews@gmail.com

Agricultural Institute of Canada 2015 Annual General Meeting
Sponsor/Contact: Agricultural Institute of Canada
#900, 9 Corvus Crt.
Ottawa, ON K2E 7Z4
613-232-9459 *Fax:* 613-594-5190
Toll-Free: 888-277-7980
E-mail: office@aic.ca
URL: www.aic.ca
Scope: National

Alberta Animal Welfare Conference 2015
Location: Alberta
Sponsor/Contact: Alberta Society for the Prevention of Cruelty to Animals
10806 - 124 St.
Edmonton, AB T5M 0H3
780-447-3600 *Fax:* 780-447-4748
E-mail: info@albertaspca.org
URL: www.albertaspca.org
Scope: Provincial

Alberta Association of Academic Libraries 2015 Annual General Meeting
Location: Alberta
Sponsor/Contact: Alberta Association of Academic Libraries
c/o Leigh Cunningham, Medicine Hat College Library Services
299 College Dr. SE
Medicine Hat, AB TIA 3Y6
403-504-3654
URL: aaal.ca
Scope: Provincial

Alberta Association of Clinic Managers Annual Conference 2015
Location: Alberta
Sponsor/Contact: Alberta Association of Clinic Managers
c/o Jennifer Hendricks, Treasurer
30 Prestwick Row SE
Calgary, AB T2Z 3L7
E-mail: info@aacm.ca
URL: aacm.ca
Scope: Provincial

Alberta Association of Landscape Architects 2015 Annual General Meeting
Location: Alberta
Sponsor/Contact: Alberta Association of Landscape Architects
P.O. Box 21052
Edmonton, AB T6R 2V4
780-435-9902 *Fax:* 780-413-0076
E-mail: aala@aala.ab.ca
URL: www.aala.ab.ca
Scope: Provincial

Alberta Beef Producers Semi-Annual General Meeting 2015
Sponsor/Contact: Alberta Beef Producers
#320, 6715 - 8th St. NE
Calgary, AB T2E 7H7
403-275-4400 *Fax:* 403-274-0007
E-mail: abpfeedback@albertabeef.org
URL: www.albertabeef.org
Scope: Provincial

Alberta Chambers of Commerce 2015 Provincial Conference & Policy Session
Location: Alberta
Sponsor/Contact: Alberta Chambers of Commerce
#1808, 10025 - 102A Ave.
Edmonton, AB T5J 2Z2
780-425-4180 *Fax:* 780-429-1061
Toll-Free: 800-272-8854
E-mail: info@abchamber.ca
URL: www.abchamber.ca
Scope: Provincial

Alberta Chicken Producers 2015 Annual General Meeting
Location: Alberta
Sponsor/Contact: Alberta Chicken Producers
2518 Ellwood Dr. SW
Edmonton, AB T6X 0A9
780-488-2125 *Fax:* 780-488-3570
Toll-Free: 877-822-4425
URL: www.chicken.ab.ca
Scope: Provincial
Purpose: An interactive educational event focussing upon biosecurity & emergency preparedness, plus a business meeting, & a keynote speaker

Alberta Development Officers Association 2015 Conference
Location: Slave Lake, AB
Sponsor/Contact: Alberta Development Officers Association
P.O. Box 2232 Stn. Main
Stony Plain, AB T7Z 1X7
780-913-4214 *Fax:* 780-963-9762
E-mail: admin@adoa.net
URL: www.adoa.net
Scope: Provincial

Alberta Educational Facilities Administrators Association 2015 Annual Conference
Sponsor/Contact: Alberta Educational Facilities Administrators Association
7 White Pelican Way
Lake Newell Resort, AB T1R 0X5
403-376-0461
URL: www.aefaa.ca
Scope: Provincial

Alberta Federation of Labour 2015 Convention
Location: Alberta
Sponsor/Contact: Alberta Federation of Labour
10654 - 101 St.
Edmonton, AB T5H 2S1
780-483-3021 *Fax:* 780-484-5928
Toll-Free: 800-661-3995
E-mail: afl@afl.org
URL: www.afl.org
Scope: Provincial
Purpose: A convention held every two years, attended by delegates from every union affiliated to the federation

Alberta Forest Products Association 2015 73rd Annual General Meeting & Conference
Sponsor/Contact: Alberta Forest Products Association
#900, 10707 - 100 Ave.
Edmonton, AB T5J 3M1
780-452-2841 *Fax:* 780-455-0505
URL: www.albertaforestproducts.ca
Scope: Provincial
Purpose: A business meeting, sessions on topics relevant to the industry,

Conferences Index

networking opportunities, & a recognition dinner

Alberta Foster Parent Association 42nd Annual Conference & Awards Banquet
Sponsor/Contact: Alberta Foster Parent Association
9750 - 35th Ave.
Edmonton, AB T6E 6J6
780-429-9923 *Fax:* 780-426-7151
Toll-Free: 800-667-2372
E-mail: reception@afpaonline.com
URL: www.afpaonline.com
Scope: Provincial

Alberta Gerontological Nurses Association Annual Conference & AGM 2015
Location: Alberta
Sponsor/Contact: Alberta Gerontological Nurses Association
P.O. Box 67040 Stn. Meadowlark
Edmonton, AB T5R 5Y3
E-mail: info@agna.ca
URL: www.agna.ca
Scope: Provincial

Alberta Health & Safety 2015 14th Annual Conference & Trade Fair
Sponsor/Contact: Health & Safety Conference Society of Alberta
P.O. Box 38009
Calgary, AB T3K 5G9
403-236-2225 *Fax:* 780-455-1120
E-mail: info@hsconference.com
URL: www.hsconference.com
Scope: Provincial

Alberta Hospice Palliative Care Association 2015 Imagine Conference
Location: Alberta
Sponsor/Contact: Alberta Hospice Palliative Care Association
#1245, 70 Ave. SE
Calgary, AB T2H 2X8
403-206-9938 *Fax:* 403-206-9958
E-mail: director@ahpca.ca
URL: ahpca.ca
Scope: Provincial

Alberta Museums Association 2015 Annual Conference
Sponsor/Contact: Alberta Museums Association
#404, 10408, 124 St.
Edmonton, AB T5N 1R5
780-424-2626 *Fax:* 780-425-1679
E-mail: info@museums.ab.ca
URL: www.museums.ab.ca
Scope: Provincial
Anticipated Attendance: 250+

Alberta School Boards Association 2015 Fall General Meeting
Location: Alberta
Sponsor/Contact: Alberta School Boards Association
#1200, 9925 - 109 St.
Edmonton, AB T5K 2J8
780-482-7311 *Fax:* 780-482-5659
E-mail: reception@asba.ab.ca
URL: www.asba.ab.ca
Scope: Local
Purpose: An Alberta School Boards Association professional development event
Contact Information: Administrative Assistant, Communications: Noreen Pownall, Phone: 780-451-7102, E-mail: npownall@asba.ab.ca

Alberta Speleological Society 2015 Annual General Meeting
Location: Alberta
Sponsor/Contact: Alberta Speleological Society
c/o Andrea Corlett
#1606 924 - 14 Ave. SW
Calgary, AB T2R 0N7
E-mail: info@caving.ab.ca
URL: www.caving.ab.ca
Scope: Provincial
Purpose: A meeting of cavers, featuring the election of executive members, the presentation of awards
Contact Information: E-mail: info@caving.ab.ca

Alberta Water & Wastewater Operators Association 2015 40th Annual Operators Seminar
Location: Alberta
Sponsor/Contact: Alberta Water & Wastewater Operators Association
11810 Kingsway Ave.
Edmonton, AB T5G 0X5
780-454-7745 *Fax:* 780-454-7748
Toll-Free: 877-454-7745
E-mail: awwoa@telus.net
URL: www.awwoa.ab.ca
Scope: Provincial
Purpose: Speakers, including operators, supervisors, technical industry representatives, & other experts in their fields, bring operators up-to-date on numerous topics in the water & wastewater field
Anticipated Attendance: 500+
Contact Information: Training Program Coordinator: Cathie Monson, Phone: 780-454-7745, Fax: 780-454-7748, E-mail: cmonson@awwoa.ca

Alberta Weekly Newspapers Association 2015 95th Annual General Meeting & Convention
Sponsor/Contact: Alberta Weekly Newspapers Association
3228 Parsons Rd.
Edmonton, AB T6H 5R7
780-434-8746 *Fax:* 780-438-8356
Toll-Free: 800-282-6903
E-mail: info@awna.com
URL: www.awna.com
Scope: Provincial

Allied Beauty Association 2015 Annual General Meeting
Location: Niagara-on-the-Lake, ON
Sponsor/Contact: Allied Beauty Association
#26-27, 145 Traders Blvd. East
Mississauga, ON L4Z 3L3
905-568-0158 *Fax:* 905-568-1581
E-mail: abashows@abacanada.com
URL: www.abacanada.com
Scope: National

Amalgamated Transit Union Canadian Council Conference 2015
Sponsor/Contact: Amalgamated Transit Union (AFL-CIO/CLC)
#210, 61 International Blvd.
Toronto, ON M9W 6K4
416-679-8846 *Fax:* 416-679-9195
E-mail: director@atucanada.ca
URL: www.atucanada.ca
Scope: National

Ancient, Free & Accepted Masons of the Grand Lodge of British Columbia & Yukon 2015 Masonic Leadership & Ladies Conference
Sponsor/Contact: Ancient, Free & Accepted Masons of Canada - Grand Lodge of British Columbia & Yukon
1495 West 8th Ave.
Vancouver, BC V6H 1C9
604-736-8941 *Fax:* 604-736-5097
E-mail: grand_secretary@freemasonry.bcy.ca
URL: freemasonry.bcy.ca
Scope: Provincial
Purpose: Discussions of leadership skills, best practices in lodge leadership, & information about the Grand Lodge

Animal Nutrition Association of Canada Annual General Meeting & Convention 2015
Sponsor/Contact: Animal Nutrition Association of Canada
#1301, 150 Metcalfe St.
Ottawa, ON K2P 1P1
613-241-6421 *Fax:* 613-241-7970
E-mail: info@anacan.org
URL: www.anacan.org
Scope: National

Annual General Meeting of the Canadian Co-operative Wool Growers Ltd.
Sponsor/Contact: Canadian Co-operative Wool Growers Ltd.
P.O. Box 130
142 Franktown Rd.
Carleton Place, ON K7C 3P3
613-257-2714 *Fax:* 613-257-8896
Toll-Free: 800-488-2714
E-mail: ccwghq@wool.ca
URL: www.wool.ca
Scope: National

Arctic Change 2015 Annual Scientific Meeting
Sponsor/Contact: ArcticNet Inc.
Pavillon Alexandre-Vachon, Université Laval
#4081, 1045, av de la Médecine
Québec, QC G1V 0A6
418-656-5830 *Fax:* 418-656-2334
E-mail: arcticnet@arcticnet.ulaval.ca
URL: www.arcticnet.ulaval.ca
Scope: National

Assaulted Women's Helpline Training Programs for the Non-Profit Sector
Sponsor/Contact: Assaulted Women's Helpline
P.O. Box 369 Stn. B
Toronto, ON M5T 2E2
416-364-4144 *Fax:* 416-364-0563
Toll-Free: 888-364-1210
E-mail: admin@awhl.org
URL: www.awhl.org
Scope: Local
Purpose: Specially designed training programs or workshops for organizations & groups on subjects such as impacts of abuse on immigrant & refugee women, cross-cultural perspectives on violence against women, elder abuse, partner abuse, same sex partner abuse, sexual assault, resources for abused women
Contact Information: Assaulted Women's Helpline, Training, Resource, & Outreach Department, Toll-Free Phone: 1-888-364-1210

Assaulted Women's Helpline Training Programs for the Workplace
Sponsor/Contact: Assaulted Women's Helpline
P.O. Box 369 Stn. B
Toronto, ON M5T 2E2
416-364-4144 *Fax:* 416-364-0563
Toll-Free: 888-364-1210
E-mail: admin@awhl.org
URL: www.awhl.org
Scope: Local
Purpose: Customized workshops on topics such as working with abused women, developing non-discriminatory policies, EAP training on woman abuse, cross-cultural perspectives on violence against women, anti-violence initiatives, intervention strategies, & diversity training
Contact Information: Assaulted Women's Helpline, Training, Resource, & Outreach Department, Toll-Free Phone: 1-888-364-1210

Association de la construction du Québec 2015 congrès annuel
Location: Quebec
Sponsor/Contact: Association de la construction du Québec
9200, boul Métropolitain est
Anjou, QC H1K 4L2
514-354-0609 *Fax:* 514-354-8292
Toll-Free: 888-868-3424
E-mail: info@prov.acq.org
URL: www.acq.org
Scope: Provincial

Association des urologues du Québec 40e Congrès annuel
Location: Quebec
Sponsor/Contact: Association des urologues du Québec
#3000, 2, Complexe Desjardins, 32e étage
Montréal, QC H5B 1G8
514-350-5131 *Fax:* 514-350-5181
E-mail: info@auq.org
URL: www.auq.org
Scope: Provincial

Association for Canadian Studies in the United States (ACSUS) 23rd Biennial Conference
Sponsor/Contact: Association for Canadian Studies in the United States
#350, 2030 - M St. NW
Washington, DC 20036
E-mail: info@acsus.org
URL: www.acsus.org
Scope: International
Purpose: Speakers & panels presenting research & information about Canada across all disciplines
Contact Information: Executive Director: David Archibald, E-mail: info@acsus.org

Association of BC Drama Educators 2015 Spring Conference
Location: British Columbia
Sponsor/Contact: Association of BC Drama Educators
c/o BC Teachers' Federation
#100, #550 West 6 Ave.
Vancouver, BC V5Z 4P2
604-871-2283 *Fax:* 604-871-2286
Toll-Free: 800-663-9163
URL: www.bcdramateachers.com
Scope: Provincial

Association of Canadian Ergonomists 46th Annual Conference
Sponsor/Contact: Association of Canadian Ergonomists
#1003, 105-150 Crowfoot Cres. NW
Calgary, AB T3G 3T2
403-219-4001 *Fax:* 403-451-1503
Toll-Free: 888-432-2223

E-mail: info@ace-ergocanada.ca
URL: www.ace-ergocanada.ca
Scope: National

Association of Consulting Engineering Companies - New Brunswick 2015 17th Annual General Meeting, Trade Show, Conference, & Awards Gala
Location: New Brunswick
Sponsor/Contact: Association of Consulting Engineering Companies - New Brunswick
183 Hanwell Rd.
Fredericton, NB E3B 2R2
506-470-9211 *Fax:* 506-451-9629
E-mail: info@acec-nb.ca
URL: www.acec-nb.ca
Scope: Provincial
Purpose: Featuring a business meeting, speakers, conference seminars, exhibits, & the presentation of awards
Contact Information: E-mail: info@acec-nb.ca

Association of Early Childhood Educators Ontario 2015 65th Annual Provincial Conference
Location: Ontario
Sponsor/Contact: Association of Early Childhood Educators Ontario
#211, 40 Orchard View Blvd.
Toronto, ON M4R 1B9
416-487-3157 *Fax:* 416-487-3758
Toll-Free: 866-932-3236
E-mail: info@aeceo.ca
URL: www.aeceo.ca
Scope: Provincial
Purpose: A conference & exhibits for delegates from across Ontario
Contact Information: Professional Development, Marketing & Advertising: Lena DaCosta, E-mail: ldacosta@aeceo.ca

Association of Manitoba Museums Conference 2015
Location: Manitoba
Sponsor/Contact: Association of Manitoba Museums
#1040, 555 Main St.
Winnipeg, MB R3B 1C3
204-947-1782 *Fax:* 204-942-3749
URL: www.museumsmanitoba.com
Scope: Provincial

Association of Municipal Administrators of New Brunswick 2015 Annual Conference and Annual General Meeeting
Location: New Brunswick
Sponsor/Contact: Association of Municipal Administrators of New Brunswick
20 Courtney St.
Douglas, NB E3G 8A1
506-453-4229 *Fax:* 506-444-5452
E-mail: amanb@nb.aibn.com
URL: www.amanb-aamnb.ca
Scope: Provincial

Association of New Brunswick Land Surveyors 2015 Annual General Meeting
Location: New Brunswick
Sponsor/Contact: Association of New Brunswick Land Surveyors
#312, 212, Queen St.
Fredericton, NB E3B 1A8
506-458-8266 *Fax:* 506-458-8267
E-mail: anbls@nb.aibn.com
URL: www.anbls.nb.ca
Scope: Provincial

Association of New Brunswick Licensed Practical Nurses 2015 Annual General Meeting
Location: New Brunswick
Sponsor/Contact: Association of New Brunswick Licensed Practical Nurses
384 Smythe St.
Fredericton, NB E3B 3E4
506-453-0747 *Fax:* 506-459-0503
Toll-Free: 800-942-0222
URL: www.anblpn.ca
Scope: Provincial
Anticipated Attendance: 200+
Contact Information: Executive Director/Registrar: JoAnne Graham, LPN, E-mail: execdir@anblpn.ca

Association of Professional Biology 2015 10th Annual Professional Biology Conference
Sponsor/Contact: Association of Professional Biology
#300, 1095 McKenzie Ave.
Victoria, BC V8P 2L5
250-483-4283 *Fax:* 250-483-3439
URL: www.apbbc.bc.ca
Scope: Provincial
Purpose: Part of the event is the annual general meeting, featuring reports from the association executive & committee chairs, the auditor's report & financial statement, resolutions, & new business
Contact Information: Managing Director & Registrar: Megan Hanacek, E-mail: managingdirector@apbbc.bc.ca

Association of Professional Engineers & Geoscientists of British Columbia 2015 Conference & Annual General Meeting
Location: British Columbia
Sponsor/Contact: Association of Professional Engineers & Geoscientists of British Columbia
#200, 4010 Regent St.
Burnaby, BC V5C 6N2
604-430-8035 *Fax:* 604-430-8085
Toll-Free: 888-430-8035
E-mail: apeginfo@apeg.bc.ca
URL: www.apeg.bc.ca
Scope: Provincial
Purpose: A chance to learn & network with colleagues & suppliers during business & technical sessions, a trade exhibition, & social events
Anticipated Attendance: 700+
Contact Information: Sponsorship Information: Maria-Carmen Kelly, Email: mckelly@apeg.bc.ca; Exhibtor Booth Information: Tim Verigin, Email: tverigin@apeg.bc.ca

Association of Professional Engineers, Geologists & Geophysicists of Alberta 2015 Annual Conference & Annual General Meeting
Location: Alberta
Sponsor/Contact: Association of Professional Engineers & Geoscientists of Alberta
Scotia One
#1500, 10060 Jasper Ave. NW
Edmonton, AB T5J 4A2
780-426-3990 *Fax:* 780-426-1877
Toll-Free: 800-661-7020
E-mail: email@apega.ca
URL: www.apega.ca
Scope: Provincial
Purpose: An annual gathering in Calgary or Edmonton, featuring professional development activities & other conference events
Contact Information: Manager, Communications: Philip Mulder, Phone: 780-426-3990, ext. 2809, Fax: 780-425-1722, E-mail: pmulder@apegga.org; Manager, Human Resources & Professional Development: Nancy Toth, Phone: 780-426-3990, ext. 2811, Fax: 780-425-1722, E-mail: ntoth@apegga.org

Association of Registered Professional Foresters of New Brunswick Annual General Meeting 2015
Location: New Brunswick
Sponsor/Contact: Association of Registered Professional Foresters of New Brunswick
#221, 1350 Regent St.
Fredericton, NB E3C 2G6
506-452-6933 *Fax:* 506-450-3128
E-mail: arpf@nbnet.nb.ca
URL: www.arpfnb.ca
Scope: Provincial

Association of the Chemical Profession of Alberta 2015 Annual General Meeting
Sponsor/Contact: Association of the Chemical Profession of Alberta
P.O. Box 21017
Edmonton, AB T6R 2V4
780-413-0004 *Fax:* 780-413-0076
URL: www.pchem.ca
Scope: Provincial

Association provinciale des enseignantes et enseignants du Québec Congrés Annuel 2015
Location: Quebec
Sponsor/Contact: Association provinciale des enseignantes et enseignants du Québec
#1, 17035, boul Brunswick
Kirkland, QC H9H 5G6
514-694-9777 *Fax:* 514-694-0189
Toll-Free: 800-361-9870
E-mail: reception@qpat-apeq.qc.ca
URL: www.qpat-apeq.qc.ca
Scope: Provincial

Association pétrolière et gazière du Québec 2015 Conférence Annuelle
Location: Quebec
Sponsor/Contact: Association pétrolière et gazière du Québec
#200, 140, Grande Allée est
Québec, QC G1R 5P7
418-261-2941
E-mail: info@apgq-qoga.com
URL: www.apgq-qoga.com
Scope: Provincial
Contact Information: Email: conference@apgq-qoga.com

Association québécoise de lutte contre la pollution atmosphérique Coquetel bénéfice 2015
Sponsor/Contact: Association québécoise de lutte contre la pollution atmosphérique
484, rte 277
Saint-Léon-de-Standon, QC G0R 4L0
418-642-1322 *Fax:* 418-642-1323
Toll-Free: 855-702-7572
E-mail: info@aqlpa.com
URL: www.aqlpa.com
Scope: Provincial

Athletic Therapists Association for British Columbia 10th Annual General Meeting
Sponsor/Contact: Athletic Therapy Association of British Columbia
#200, 4170 Still Creek Dr.
Burnaby, BC V5C 6C6
604-918-5077
E-mail: info@athletictherapybc.ca
URL: www.athletictherapybc.ca
Scope: Provincial

Atlantic Respirology & Critical Care 2015 27th Annual Conference
Sponsor/Contact: The New Brunswick Association of Respiratory Therapists Inc.
500 St. George St.
Moncton, NB E1C 1Y3
506-389-7813 *Fax:* 506-389-7814
Toll-Free: 877-334-1851
E-mail: info@nbart.ca
URL: www.nbart.ca
Scope: Provincial
Purpose: A meeting of respiratory therapists, respirologists, intensivists, nurses, & educators from the Atlantic provinces, who are interested in the advancements in respirology & critical care
Contact Information: E-mail: info@nbart.ca

Automotive Parts Manufacturers' Association 2015 19th Annual Automotive Outlook Conference
Sponsor/Contact: Automotive Parts Manufacturers' Association
#801, 10 Four Seasons Pl.
Toronto, ON M9B 6H7
416-620-4220 *Fax:* 416-620-9730
E-mail: info@apma.ca
URL: www.apma.ca
Scope: National
Contact Information: Dongi Pranaitis, 905-940-2800 x404. Email: DongiP@autoshow.ca

BPW Canada [Canadian Federation of Business & Professional Women's Clubs] 2015 National Convention
Sponsor/Contact: The Canadian Federation of Business & Professional Women's Clubs
P.O. Box 62054
Orleans, ON K1C 7H8
URL: www.bpwcanada.com
Scope: National
Purpose: An opportunity to educate & empower Canadian women to improve economic, political, employment, & social conditions
Contact Information: Secretary: Tammy Richmond, E-mail: tlrich37@gmail.com

Bereavement Ontario Network 2015 25th Annual Fall Conference
Location: Ontario
Sponsor/Contact: Bereavement Ontario Network
174 Oxford St.
Woodstock, ON N4S 6B1
519-266-4747
E-mail: info@BereavementOntarioNetwork.ca
URL: www.bereavementontarionetwork.ca
Scope: Provincial

Black Law Students' Association of Canada 23rd Annual National Conference
Sponsor/Contact: Black Law Students' Association of Canada
E-mail: Admin@blsacanada.com
URL: www.blsacanada.com
Scope: National

Conferences Index

Contact Information: Email: Conference@blsacanada.com

Book & Periodical Council's 2015 Book Summit
Sponsor/Contact: Book & Periodical Council
#107, 192 Spadina Ave.
Toronto, ON M5T 2C2
416-975-9366 *Fax:* 416-975-1839
E-mail: info@thebpc.ca
URL: www.thebpc.ca
Scope: National
Purpose: An annual one day professional development conference, featuring workshops, panel discussions, & keynote speakers
Contact Information: Web Site: www.booksummit.ca; E-mail: publicity@theBPC.ca

Brain Injury Association of London & Region 2015 Annual Conference
Location: Ontario
Sponsor/Contact: Ontario Brain Injury Association
560 Wellington St., Lower Level
London, ON N6A 3R4
519-642-4539 *Fax:* 519-642-4124
E-mail: support@braininjurylondon.on.ca
URL: www.braininjurylondon.on.ca
Scope: Local
Purpose: A conference for professionals & survivors
Anticipated Attendance: 120

Breast Cancer Action Nova Scotia 2015 Annual General Meeting
Location: Nova Scotia
Sponsor/Contact: Breast Cancer Action Nova Scotia
#205, 967 Bedford Hwy.
Bedford, NS B4A 1A9
902-465-2685 *Fax:* 902-484-6436
E-mail: bcans@bca.ns.ca
URL: www.bcans.ca
Scope: Provincial
Purpose: A business meeting for members, featuring reports from committee chairs
Contact Information: E-mail (general information): bcans@bcans.ca

Britiish Columbia Veterinary Technologists Association 2015 Conference
Location: British Columbia
Sponsor/Contact: Britiish Columbia Veterinary Technologists Association
101 Todd Rd.
Kamloops, BC V5C 5A9
250-319-0027 *Fax:* 866-319-1929
URL: bcvta.com
Scope: Provincial

British Columbia Association for Charitable Gaming 2015 Symposium
Location: British Columbia
Sponsor/Contact: British Columbia Association for Charitable Gaming
#401, 151 - 10090 152nd St.
Surrey, BC V3R 8X8
604-568-8649 *Fax:* 250-627-1200
Toll-Free: 888-672-2224
URL: bcacg.com
Scope: Provincial

British Columbia Association of Social Workers Conference 2015
Location: British Columbia
Sponsor/Contact: British Columbia Association of Social Workers
#402, 1755 West Broadway
Vancouver, BC V6J 4S5
604-730-9111 *Fax:* 604-730-9112
Toll-Free: 800-665-4747
E-mail: bcasw@bcasw.org
URL: www.bcasw.org
Scope: Provincial

British Columbia Association of Speech-Language Pathologists & Audiologists 2015 Conference
Location: British Columbia
Sponsor/Contact: British Columbia Association of Speech-Language Pathologists & Audiologists
#402, 1755 Broadway West
Vancouver, BC V6J 4S5
604-420-2222 *Fax:* 604-736-5606
Toll-Free: 877-222-7572
E-mail: bcaslpa@telus.net
URL: www.bcaslpa.ca
Scope: Provincial

British Columbia Camping Association 2015 Conference
Location: British Columbia
Sponsor/Contact: British Columbia Camping Association
c/o Camp Luther
9311 Shook Rd.
Mission, BC V2V 7M2
URL: bccamping.org
Scope: Provincial

British Columbia Career College Association Annual Conference 2015
Location: British Columbia
Sponsor/Contact: British Columbia Career College Association
P.O. Box 40528
#11, 200 Burrard
Vancouver, BC V6C 3L0
604-874-4419 *Fax:* 604-874-4420
E-mail: thebccca@gmail.com
URL: www.bccca.com
Scope: Provincial

British Columbia College of Social Workers 2015 Annual Meeting
Location: British Columbia
Sponsor/Contact: British Columbia College of Social Workers
#302, 1765 West 8th Ave.
Vancouver, BC V6J 5C6
604-737-4916 *Fax:* 604-737-6809
E-mail: info@bccsw.bc.ca
URL: www.bccollegeofsocialworkers.ca
Scope: Provincial
Purpose: A business meeting featuring an election of social workers to the board
Contact Information: Office Coordinator: Christeen Young, E-mail: christeen.young@bccsw.ca

British Columbia Dance Educators' Association 2015 Conference
Location: British Columbia
Sponsor/Contact: British Columbia Dance Educators' Association
c/o BC Teachers' Federation
#100, 550 West 6th Ave.
Vancouver, BC V5Z 4P2
604-871-2283
Toll-Free: 800-663-9163
E-mail: psac73@bctf.ca
URL: www.bcdea.ca
Scope: Provincial

British Columbia Electrical Association 2015 Conference
Location: British Columbia
Sponsor/Contact: British Columbia Electrical Association
#224, 3989 Henning Dr.
Burnaby, BC V5C 6N5
604-291-7708 *Fax:* 604-291-7795
URL: www.bcea.bc.ca
Scope: Provincial

British Columbia Federation of Labour 2015 Policy Convention: The 59th Convention of the British Columbia Federation of Labour
Location: British Columbia
Sponsor/Contact: British Columbia Federation of Labour
#200, 5118 Joyce St.
Vancouver, BC V5R 4H1
604-430-1421 *Fax:* 604-430-5917
E-mail: bcfed@bcfed.ca
URL: www.bcfed.com
Scope: Provincial
Purpose: A policy conference held every other year for delegates from British Columbia's local unions, branches, lodges, & labour councils
Anticipated Attendance: 800
Contact Information: E-mail: admin@bcfed.ca

British Columbia Food Technologists 2015 Annual Speaker's Night
Sponsor/Contact: British Columbia Food Technolgists
c/o Nilmini Wijewickreme, SGS Canada
50-655 West Kent Ave. North
Vancouver, BC V6P 6T7
E-mail: info@bcft.ca
URL: www.bcft.ca
Scope: Provincial

British Columbia Hospice Palliative Care Association 2015 Conference
Location: British Columbia
Sponsor/Contact: British Columbia Hospice Palliative Care Association
#1100, 1200 West 73rd Ave.
Vancouver, BC V6P 6G5
604-267-7026 *Fax:* 604-267-7026
Toll-Free: 877-410-6297
E-mail: office@hospicebc.org
URL: www.bchpca.org
Scope: Provincial
Purpose: An annual meeting of members, with guest speakers, exhibits, regional meetings, the presentation of awards, & networking sessions
Contact Information: E-mail: office@hospicebc.org

British Columbia Library Trustees' Association 2015 Annual General Meeting
Location: British Columbia
Sponsor/Contact: British Columbia Library Trustees' Association
432 - 3 St.
Vancouver, BC V3L 2S2
604-913-1424 *Fax:* 604-913-1413
Toll-Free: 888-206-1245
E-mail: admin@bclta.ca
URL: www.bclta.org
Scope: Provincial
Contact Information: Administrative Assistant, British Columbia Library Trustees' Association: Jan Thomas, Phone: 604-913-1424, Fax: 604-913-1413, E-mail: admin@bclta.ca

British Columbia Lung Association 2015 12th Annual Air Quality & Health Workshop
Sponsor/Contact: British Columbia Lung Association
2675 Oak St.
Vancouver, BC V6H 2K2
604-731-5864 *Fax:* 604-731-5810
Toll-Free: 800-665-5864
E-mail: info@bc.lung.ca
URL: www.bc.lung.ca
Scope: Provincial

British Columbia Lung Association 2015 Annual General Meeting
Location: British Columbia
Sponsor/Contact: British Columbia Lung Association
2675 Oak St.
Vancouver, BC V6H 2K2
604-731-5864 *Fax:* 604-731-5810
Toll-Free: 800-665-5864
E-mail: info@bc.lung.ca
URL: www.bc.lung.ca
Scope: Provincial
Purpose: An annual meeting to determine the association's direction during the coming year
Contact Information: Phone: 604-731-5864; Toll-Free Phone: 1-800-665-5864

British Columbia Primary Teachers Association Conference & AGM 2015
Location: British Columbia
Sponsor/Contact: British Columbia Primary Teachers Association
#C27, RR#2, S120
Rock Creek, BC V0H 1Y0
250-446-2198 *Fax:* 250-446-2198
URL: www.bcpta.ca
Scope: Provincial

British Columbia Primary Teachers Association Spring Event 2015
Location: British Columbia
Sponsor/Contact: British Columbia Primary Teachers Association
#C27, RR#2, S120
Rock Creek, BC V0H 1Y0
250-446-2198 *Fax:* 250-446-2198
URL: www.bcpta.ca
Scope: Provincial

British Columbia Psychogeriatric Association 2015 Conference
Location: British Columbia
Sponsor/Contact: British Columbia Psychogeriatric Association
P.O. Box 47028
1030 Denman St.
Vancouver, BC V6G 3E1
Fax: 888-835-2451
URL: www.bcpga.com
Scope: Provincial

British Columbia School Superintendents Association 2015 Fall Conference & Annual General Meeting
Location: British Columbia
Sponsor/Contact: British Columbia School Superintendents Association
#208, 1118 Homer St.
Vancouver, BC V6B 6L5
604-687-0590
E-mail: info@bcssa.org
URL: www.bcssa.org
Scope: Provincial
Purpose: Themes include leadership, school effectiveness, & improvement
Contact Information: Professional Development Coordinator: Kim Young, E-mail: kimyoung@bcssa.org

British Columbia School Superintendents Association 2015 Winter Conference
Location: British Columbia

Sponsor/Contact: British Columbia School Superintendents Association
#208, 1118 Homer St.
Vancouver, BC V6B 6L5
604-687-0590
E-mail: info@bcssa.org
URL: www.bcssa.org
Scope: Provincial
Contact Information: Professional Development Coordinator: Kim Young, E-mail: kimyoung@bcssa.org

British Columbia Seniors Living Association 2015 Conference
Location: British Columbia
Sponsor/Contact: British Columbia Seniors Living Association
#300, 3665 Kingsway
Vancouver, BC V5R 5W2
604-689-5949 *Fax:* 604-689-5946
Toll-Free: 888-402-2722
E-mail: membership@bcsla.ca
URL: www.bcsla.ca
Scope: Provincial

British Columbia Social Studies Teachers Association 2015 Annual Conference
Location: British Columbia
Sponsor/Contact: British Columbia Social Studies Teachers Association
c/o BC Teachers' Federation
#100, 550 West 6th Ave.
Vancouver, BC V5Z 4P2
604-871-2283 *Fax:* 604-871-2286
Toll-Free: 800-663-9163
E-mail: bcssta@gmail.com
URL: bcssta.wordpress.com
Scope: Provincial

British Columbia Sustainable Energy Association Annual General Meeting 2015
Location: British Columbia
Sponsor/Contact: British Columbia Sustainable Energy Association
P.O. Box 44104 Stn. Gorge Plaza
2947 Tillicum Rd.
Victoria, BC V9A 7K1
250-744-2720
E-mail: info@bcsea.org
URL: www.bcsea.org
Scope: National
Contact Information: Email: watershow@shaw.ca; Website: www.watershow.ca; Phone: 778-432-2120

British Columbia Teacher-Librarians' Association 2015 Provincial Conference
Location: British Columbia
Sponsor/Contact: British Columbia Teacher-Librarians' Association
c/o British Columbia Teachers' Federation
#100, 550 West 6th Ave.
Vancouver, BC V5Z 4P2
604-871-2283 *Fax:* 604-871-2286
Toll-Free: 800-663-9163
E-mail: bctlamembership@gmail.com
URL: www.bctf.ca/bctla
Scope: Provincial
Purpose: A gathering of British Columbia's teacher-librarians for workshops, keynote presentations, & social events
Contact Information: Conference Chair: Sylvia Zubke, Phone: 604-713-4985, E-mail: szubke@gmail.com

British Columbia Trucking Association 2015 102nd Annual General Meeting & Management Conference
Location: British Columbia
Sponsor/Contact: British Columbia Trucking Association
#100, 20111 - 93A Ave.
Langley, BC V1M 4A9
604-888-5319
E-mail: bcta@bctrucking.com
URL: www.bctrucking.com
Scope: Provincial
Purpose: A meeting of members of the British Columbia motor carrier association
Contact Information: Administrative Coordinator: Jennifer Cameron, E-mail: bcta@bctrucking.com

British Columbia Welsh Pony & Cob Association 2015 Annual General Meeting
Location: British Columbia
Sponsor/Contact: British Columbia Welsh Pony & Cob Association
c/o Debbie Miyashita
11075 Hynes St.
Whonnock, BC V2W 1P5
604-462-7166
URL: www.bcwelshponyandcob.com
Scope: Provincial

Building Energy Management Manitoba 2015 Better Buildings Conference
Sponsor/Contact: Building Energy Management Manitoba
#309, 23 - 845 Dakota St.
Winnipeg, MB R2M 5M3
204-452-2098
E-mail: info@bemm.ca
URL: www.bemm.ca
Scope: Provincial
Contact Information: URL: www.betterbuildingsconference.com

CIAA's 31st Annual General Meeting & Conference
Sponsor/Contact: Canadian Independent Adjusters' Association
Centennial Centre
#100, 5401 Eglinton Ave. West
Toronto, ON M9C 5K6
416-621-6222 *Fax:* 416-621-7776
Toll-Free: 877-255-5589
E-mail: info@ciaa-adjusters.ca
URL: www.ciaa-adjusters.ca
Scope: National

CIVICUS: World Alliance for Citizen Participation 2015 World Assembly
Sponsor/Contact: CIVICUS: World Alliance for Citizen Participation
P.O. Box 933
24 Gwigwi Mrwebi St.
Johannesburg, 2135
E-mail: info@civicus.org
URL: www.civicus.org
Scope: International

CNIB 2015 National Braille Conference
Sponsor/Contact: Canadian National Institute for the Blind
1929 Bayview Ave.
Toronto, ON M4G 3E8
Fax: 416-480-7700
Toll-Free: 800-563-2642
E-mail: info@cnib.ca
URL: www.cnib.ca
Scope: National

CTEA 52nd Manufacturers Technical Conference
Sponsor/Contact: Canadian Transportation Equipment Association
#3B, 16 Barrie Blvd.
St. Thomas, ON N5P 4B9
519-631-0414 *Fax:* 519-631-1333
E-mail: transportation@ctea.ca
URL: www.ctea.ca

Calgary Law Library Group 2015 Annual General Meeting
Location: Calgary, AB
Sponsor/Contact: Calgary Law Library Group
c/o Law Society Library, Calgary Courts Centre
#501N, 601 - 5th St. SW
Calgary, AB T2P 5P7
URL: www.cllg.ca
Scope: Local
Purpose: An annual meeting of legal information professionals & law librarians from Calgary & the surrounding area

Calgary Zoological Society 2015 Annual General Meeting
Location: Alberta
Sponsor/Contact: Calgary Zoological Society
1300 Zoo Rd. NE
Calgary, AB T2E 7V6
403-232-9300 *Fax:* 403-237-7582
Toll-Free: 800-588-9993
E-mail: comments@calgaryzoo.ab.ca
URL: www.calgaryzoo.org
Scope: Provincial
Purpose: Members of the society receive voting rights at the annual meeting
Contact Information: Manager, Communications: Laurie Skene, E-mail: lauries@calgaryzoo.com

Canada East Equipment Dealers' Association 2015 Annual Meeting & Convention
Sponsor/Contact: Canada East Equipment Dealers' Association
580 Bryne Dr, #C1
Barrie, ON L4N 9P6
705-726-2100 *Fax:* 705-726-2187
URL: www.ceeda.ca
Scope: Provincial

Canada Green Building Council 2015 Annual General Meeting
Sponsor/Contact: Canada Green Building Council
#202, 47 Clarence St.
Ottawa, ON K1N 9K1
613-241-1184 *Fax:* 613-241-4782
Toll-Free: 866-941-1184
E-mail: info@cagbc.org
URL: www.cagbc.org
Scope: National
Purpose: Presentations of the financial report & the president's report, & a guest speaker
Contact Information: E-mail: info@cagbc.org

Canada's Health Informatics Association 2015 Annual Geenral Meeting
Sponsor/Contact: COACH - Canada's Health Informatics Association
#301, 250 Consumers Rd.
Toronto, ON M2J 4V6
416-494-9324 *Fax:* 416-495-8723
Toll-Free: 888-253-8554
E-mail: info@coachorg.com
URL: www.coachorg.com

Scope: National

Canada-Korea Conference on Science & Technology
Sponsor/Contact: Association of Korean Canadian Scientists & Engineers
#206, 1133 Leslie St.
Toronto, ON M3C 2J6
416-449-5204 *Fax:* 416-449-2875
E-mail: info@akcse.org
URL: www.akcse.org
Purpose: Organized by the Association of Korean-Canadian Scientists and Engineers & Korean Federation of Science and Technology Societies, the conference is an opportunity for scientists to showcase their research results, projects & innovations
Contact Information: URL: ckc.akcse.org

Canadian Acoustical Association / Association canadienne d'acoustique Annual Conference
Sponsor/Contact: Canadian Acoustical Association
c/o C. Laroche, Faculty of Health Sciences, University of Ottawa
#3062, 451 Smyth Rd.
Ottawa, ON K1H 8M5
613-562-5800 *Fax:* 613-562-5248
URL: www.caa-aca.ca
Scope: National
Contact Information: Technical Coordinator, Tim Kelsall, Phone: 905-403-3932, Fax: 905-855-8270, E-Mail: conference@caa-aca.ca

Canadian Agricultural Safety Association's Conference & AGM 2015
Sponsor/Contact: Canadian Agricultural Safety Association
3325-C Pembina Hwy.
Winnipeg, MB R3V 0A2
204-452-2272 *Fax:* 204-261-5004
Toll-Free: 877-452-2272
E-mail: info@casa-acsa.ca
URL: www.casa-acsa.ca
Scope: National
Purpose: A forum for members, supporters, researchers and innovators to network, share, and learn about important trends and developments in agricultural safety.
Contact Information: CASA Conference Coordinator: Diane Wreford, Phone: 204-930-4612; Emil: dwreford@casa-acsa.ca

Canadian Amateur Wrestling Association / Association canadienne de lutte amateur 2015 Annual General Meeting
Sponsor/Contact: Canadian Amateur Wrestling Association
#7, 5370 Canotek Rd.
Gloucester, ON K1J 9E6
613-748-5686 *Fax:* 613-748-5756
E-mail: info@wrestling.ca
URL: www.wrestling.ca
Scope: National

Canadian Animal Health Institute 2015 Annual Meeting
Sponsor/Contact: Canadian Animal Health Institute
#102, 160 Research Lane
Guelph, ON N1G 5B2
519-763-7777 *Fax:* 519-763-7407
E-mail: cahi@cahi-icsa.ca
URL: www.cahi-icsa.ca
Scope: National
Purpose: An exploration of predictions in

Conferences Index

the industry, plus strategies to prepare for change. The Board of Directors is elected annually.

Canadian Association for Community Living 2015 National Family Conference
Sponsor/Contact: Canadian Association for Community Living
Kinsmen Building, York University
4700 Keele St.
Toronto, ON M3J 1P3
416-661-9611 *Fax:* 416-661-5701
E-mail: inform@cacl.ca
URL: www.cacl.ca
Scope: National
Purpose: A discussion of issues that impact families, professionals, & self-advocates who help people with intellectual disabilities
Anticipated Attendance: 500+

Canadian Association for Japanese Language Education 2015 Annual Conference
Sponsor/Contact: Canadian Association for Japanese Language Education
P.O. Box 75133
20 Bloor St. East
Toronto, ON M4W 3T3
E-mail: cajle.pr@gmail.com
URL: www.cajle.info
Scope: National

Canadian Association for Laboratory Accreditation 2015 Annual General Meeting
Location: Winnipeg, MB
Sponsor/Contact: Canadian Association for Laboratory Accreditation Inc.
#310, 1565 Carling Ave.
Ottawa, ON K1Z 8R1
613-233-5300 *Fax:* 613-233-5501
URL: www.cala.ca
Scope: National

Canadian Association for Latin American & Caribbean Studies 2015 44th Congress
Sponsor/Contact: Canadian Association for Latin American & Caribbean Studies
c/o Juan Pablo Crespo Vasquez, York Research Tower, York University
#8-17, 4700 Keele St.
Toronto, ON M3J 1P3
416-736-2100 *Fax:* 519-971-3610
E-mail: calacs@yorku.ca
URL: www.can-latam.org
Scope: National
Purpose: Theme: Environments, Socieities Imaginaries: The Americas in Motion
Contact Information: Communications Contact: James Gaede, E-mail: admin@can-latam.org

Canadian Association for Population Therapeutics Annual Conference 2015
Sponsor/Contact: Canadian Association for Population Therapeutics
CHU - Ste-Justine, Research Center
3175, Cote-Ste-Catherine
Montréal, QC H3T 1C5
514-345-4931 *Fax:* 514-345-4801
URL: www.capt-actp.com
Scope: National

Canadian Association for Prosthetics and Orthotics 2015 Conference
Sponsor/Contact: Canadian Association for Prosthetics & Orthotics
#217, 294 Portage Ave.
Winnipeg, MB R3C 0B9
204-949-4970 *Fax:* 204-947-3627
E-mail: capo@mts.net
URL: www.prostheticsandorthotics.ca
Scope: National

Canadian Association for Sandplay Therapy 2015 Conference
Sponsor/Contact: Canadian Association for Sandplay Therapy
c/o Dave Rogers, Treasurer
#232, 220 Century Rd.
Spruce Grove, AB T7X 3X7
URL: www.sandplay.ca
Scope: National

Canadian Association of Accredited Mortgage Professionals Mortgage Forum 2015
Sponsor/Contact: Canadian Association of Accredited Mortgage Professionals
Atria II
#1401, 2235 Sheppard Ave. East
Toronto, ON M2J 5B5
416-385-2333 *Fax:* 416-385-1177
Toll-Free: 888-442-4625
E-mail: info@caamp.org
URL: www.caamp.org
Scope: Provincial
Contact Information: E-mail: events@caamp.org

Canadian Association of Ambulatory Care 2015 Conference
Location: Westin Prince Hotel Toronto, ON
Sponsor/Contact: Canadian Association of Ambulatory Care
#B602, 2075 Bayview Ave.
Ontario, ON M4N 3M5
E-mail: canadianambulatorycare@gmail.com
URL: www.canadianambulatorycare.com
Scope: National

Canadian Association of Animal Health Technologists & Technicians 2015 26th Annual General Meeting
Sponsor/Contact: Canadian Association of Animal Health Technologists & Technicians
339 Booth St.
Ottawa, ON K1R 7K1
800-567-2862
E-mail: info@caahtt-acttsa.ca
URL: www.caahtt-acttsa.ca
Scope: National
Purpose: A meeting usually held in partnership with the Canadian Veterinary Medical Association Convention, featuring full inclusion of technicians in the scientific program
Contact Information: Conventions & Special Programs Assistant: Sarah M. Cunningham, Phone: 613-236-1162, ext. 121, Fax: 613-236-9681, E-mail: scunningham@cvma-acmv.org

Canadian Association of Chemical Distributors 2015 29th Annual General Meeting
Sponsor/Contact: Canadian Association of Chemical Distributors
349 Davis Rd., #A
Oakville, ON L6J 2X2
905-844-9140 *Fax:* 905-844-5706
URL: www.cacd.ca
Scope: National
Purpose: An event featuring keynote speakers
Contact Information: Manager, Communications & Member Services: Catherine Wieckowska, Phone: 905-844-9140, E-mail: catherine@cacd.ca

Canadian Association of Chiefs of Police 2015 SMILE Conference
Sponsor/Contact: Canadian Association of Chiefs of Police
#100, 300 Terry Fox Dr.
Kanata, ON K2K 0E3
613-595-1101 *Fax:* 613-383-0372
E-mail: cacp@cacp.ca
URL: www.cacp.ca
Scope: National
Purpose: Participants gain technical hands-on skills & practical knowledge about social media

Canadian Association of College & University Student Services 2015 Annual Conference
Sponsor/Contact: Canadian Association of College & University Student Services
#202, 720 Spadina Ave.
Toronto, ON M5S 2T9
647-345-1116
E-mail: contact@cacuss.ca
URL: www.cacuss.ca
Scope: National
Contact Information: Email: conference@cacuss.ca

Canadian Association of Electroneurophysiology Technologists 2015 Annual General Meeting
Sponsor/Contact: Canadian Association of Electroneurophysiology Technologists Inc.
c/o University of Alberta Hospital
8440 - 112 St. NW
Edmonton, AB T6G 2B7
780-407-8822
URL: www.caet.org
Scope: National

Canadian Association of Fairs & Exhibitions Annual Convention 2015
Sponsor/Contact: Canadian Association of Fairs & Exhibitions
P.O. Box 13161
Ottawa, ON K2K 1X4
613-233-0012 *Fax:* 613-233-1154
Toll-Free: 800-663-1714
E-mail: info@canadian-fairs.ca
URL: www.canadian-fairs.ca
Scope: National

Canadian Association of Geographers, Prairie Division 2015 Annual Meeting & Conference
Sponsor/Contact: Canadian Association of Geographers
c/o D. Eberts, J.R. Brodie Science Ctr., Dept of Geography, Brandon U.
#4-09, 270 - 18th St.
Brandon, MB R7A 6A9
URL: pcag.uwinnipeg.ca
Scope: Provincial
Purpose: The business meeting of the division, plus paper & poster presentations & a field trip

Canadian Association of Importers & Exporters 2015 12th Annual Western Canada Conference
Sponsor/Contact: Canadian Association of Importers & Exporters
#200, 10 St. Mary St.
Toronto, ON M4Y 1P9
416-595-5333
E-mail: info@iecanada.com
URL: www.iecanada.com
Scope: National
Purpose: A yearly educational opportunity for presidents, general managers, directors of operations, controllers, customs specialists, & logistics managers
Contact Information: Western Region Coordinator: Paulette Niedermier, Phone: 403-808-2451, E-mail: pniedermier@iecanada.com

Canadian Association of Importers & Exporters 2015 83rd Annual Conference & Tradeshow
Sponsor/Contact: Canadian Association of Importers & Exporters
#200, 10 St. Mary St.
Toronto, ON M4Y 1P9
416-595-5333
E-mail: info@iecanada.com
URL: www.iecanada.com
Scope: National
Purpose: Sessions & workshops addressing current topics relevant to trade practitioners
Contact Information: General E-mail: conference@iecanada.com

Canadian Association of Internes and Residents 2015 Annual General Meeting
Sponsor/Contact: Canadian Association of Internes & Residents
#412, 151 Slater St.
Ottawa, ON K1P 5H3
613-234-6448
E-mail: cair@cair.ca
URL: www.cair.ca
Scope: National

Canadian Association of Medical Device Reprocessing 2015 Conference
Sponsor/Contact: Canadian Association of Medical Device Reprocessing
147 Parkside Dr.
Oak Bluff, MB R4G 0A6
E-mail: info@camdr.ca
URL: www.camdr.ca
Scope: National

Canadian Association of Midwives 15th Annual Conference & Exhibit
Sponsor/Contact: Canadian Association of Midwives
59 Riverview
Montréal, QC H8R 3R9
514-807-3668 *Fax:* 514-738-0370
E-mail: admin@canadianmidwives.org
URL: www.canadianmidwives.org
Scope: National

Canadian Association of Montessori Teachers 2015 Annual Conference
Sponsor/Contact: Canadian Association of Montessori Teachers
312 Oakwood Crt.
Newmarket, ON L3Y 3C8
416-755-7184 *Fax:* 866-328-7974
E-mail: info@camt100.ca
URL: www.camt100.ca
Scope: National

Canadian Association of Music Libraries, Archives & Documentation Centres 2015 Conference
Sponsor/Contact: Canadian Association of Music Libraries, Archives & Documentation Centres
c/o Music Section, Library & Archives Canada
395 Wellington St.
Ottawa, ON K1A 0N4
URL: caml.info.yorku.ca
Scope: National
Purpose: A national meeting covering

Conferences Index

issues & information of interest to music librarians, archivists, & researchers
Contact Information: Contact: Brian McMillan, E-mail: brian.mcmillan@mcgill.ca.

Canadian Association of Petroleum Landmen 2015 Annual Conference
Location: St. John's, NL
Sponsor/Contact: Canadian Association of Petroleum Landmen
#350, 500 - 5 Ave. SW
Calgary, AB T2P 3L5
403-237-6635 *Fax:* 403-263-1620
E-mail: reception@landman.ca
URL: www.landman.ca
Scope: National
Purpose: Presentations on the industry by guest speakers
Contact Information: Director, Communications: Joan Dornian, Phone: 403-531-4713

Canadian Association of Prosthetics & Orthotics 2015 National Conference
Sponsor/Contact: Canadian Association of Prosthetics & Orthotics
#217, 294 Portage Ave.
Winnipeg, MB R3C 0B9
204-949-4970 *Fax:* 204-947-3627
E-mail: capo@mts.net
URL: www.pando.ca
Scope: National

Canadian Association of Recycling Industries (CARI) 2015 18th Annual Consumer's Night
Sponsor/Contact: Canadian Association of Recycling Industries
#1, 682 Monarch Ave.
Ajax, ON L1S 4S2
905-426-9313 *Fax:* 905-426-9314
URL: www.cari-acir.org
Scope: National
Contact Information: Association Manager: Donna Turner, Phone: 905-426-9313

Canadian Association of Speech-Language Pathologists & Audiologists 2015 Annual General Meeting
Sponsor/Contact: Speech-Language & Audiology Canada
#1000, 1 Nicholas St.
Ottawa, ON K1N 7B7
613-567-9968 *Fax:* 613-567-2859
Toll-Free: 800-259-8519
E-mail: info@sac-oac.ca
URL: www.sac-oac.ca
Scope: National

Canadian Association of Statutory Human Rights Agencies (CASHRA) Annual Conference 2015
Sponsor/Contact: Canadian Association of Statutory Human Rights Agencies
#170, 99 - 5th Ave.
Ottawa, ON K1P 5P5
URL: www.cashra.ca
Scope: National
Purpose: A joint initiative with The Canadian Human Rights Commission

Canadian Association of Zoos & Aquariums 2015 Annual Conference
Sponsor/Contact: Canadian Association of Zoos & Aquariums
#400, 280 Metcalfe St.
Ottawa, ON K2P 1R7
613-567-0099 *Fax:* 613-233-5438
Toll-Free: 888-822-2907
E-mail: info@caza.ca
URL: www.caza.ca
Scope: National
Purpose: A meeting of members to vote on the business of the association.
Contact Information: Cathy Simon, Email: Cathy.Simon@moncton.ca, Phone: 506-877-7722; Bruce Dougan, Email: Bruce.Dougan@moncton.ca

Canadian Avalanche Association 2015 Spring Conference & Meetings
Sponsor/Contact: Canadian Avalanche Association
P.O. Box 2759
110 MacKenzie Ave.
Revelstoke, BC V0E 2S0
250-837-2435 *Fax:* 250-837-4624
Toll-Free: 800-667-1105
E-mail: info@avalanche.ca
URL: www.avalanche.ca
Scope: National
Purpose: An introduction for technicians & supervisors from transportation & utility & resource sectors, such as forestry, mining, & railways, who manage winter operations & avalanche hazard programs
Contact Information: Interim Operations Manager & Membership Services: Stuart Smith, E-mail: ssmith@avalanche.ca

Canadian Bar Association 2015 Annual National Environmental, Energy and Resources Law Summit
Sponsor/Contact: Canadian Bar Association
#500, 865 Carling Ave.
Ottawa, ON K1S 5S8
613-237-2925 *Fax:* 613-237-0185
Toll-Free: 800-267-8860
E-mail: info@cba.org
URL: www.cba.org
Scope: National
Purpose: Natural Resource and Energy Legal Developments: North and South of 60. Set against the backdrop of Canada's arctic region, join us in an engaging program designed to provide private practitioners, in-house corporate and government counsel, regulators, and other professionals with an annual update on the hottest issues in the environmental, energy and resources law field.

Canadian Bottled Water Association 2015 27th Annual Canadian Bottled Water Convention & Trade Show
Sponsor/Contact: Canadian Bottled Water Association
#203-1, 70 East Beaver Creek Rd.
Richmond Hill, ON L4B 3B2
905-886-6928 *Fax:* 905-886-9531
E-mail: info@cbwa.ca
URL: www.cbwa.ca
Scope: National
Purpose: Best practices, techniques, & tools to assist persons involved in the bottled water industry in Canada
Contact Information: E-mail: info@cbwa.ca

Canadian Cartographic Association 2015 Annual General Conference
Sponsor/Contact: Canadian Cartographic Association
c/o Paul Heersink
39 Wales Ave.
Markham, ON L3P 2C4
Fax: 416-446-1639
E-mail: treasurer@cca-acc.org
URL: www.cca-acc.org
Scope: National
Purpose: In partnership with the Association of Canadian Map Libraries and Archives.

Canadian Carwash Association 2015 Annual General Meeting
Sponsor/Contact: Canadian Carwash Association
#340, 4195 Dundas St. West
Toronto, ON M8X 1Y4
416-239-0339 *Fax:* 416-239-1076
E-mail: office@canadiancarwash.ca
URL: www.canadiancarwash.ca
Scope: National

Canadian Celiac Association National Conference 2015
Sponsor/Contact: Canadian Celiac Association
#400, 5025 Orbitor Dr., Bldg. 1
Mississauga, ON L4W 4Y5
905-507-6208 *Fax:* 905-507-4673
Toll-Free: 800-363-7296
E-mail: info@celiac.ca
URL: www.celiac.ca
Scope: National

Canadian Child Care Federation 2015 Annual General Meeting
Sponsor/Contact: Canadian Child Care Federation
#600, 700 Industrial Ave.
Ottawa, ON K1G 0Y9
613-729-5289 *Fax:* 613-729-3159
Toll-Free: 800-858-1412
E-mail: info@cccf-fcsge.ca
URL: www.cccf-fcsge.ca
Scope: National

Canadian Council for Refugees 2015 Fall Consultation
Sponsor/Contact: Canadian Council for Refugees
#302, 6839, rue Drolet
Montréal, QC H2S 2T1
514-277-7223 *Fax:* 514-277-1447
E-mail: info@ccrweb.ca
URL: www.ccrweb.ca
Scope: National
Purpose: An event featuring large plenary sessions, workshops, & working sessions that address issues that challenge refugees, immigrants, community workers, & advocates
Contact Information: E-mail: info@ccrweb.ca

Canadian Council for Refugees 2015 Summer Working Group Meetings
Sponsor/Contact: Canadian Council for Refugees
#302, 6839, rue Drolet
Montréal, QC H2S 2T1
514-277-7223 *Fax:* 514-277-1447
E-mail: info@ccrweb.ca
URL: www.ccrweb.ca
Scope: National
Purpose: An opportunity for Canadian Council for Refugees members & other refugee & immigrant rights advocates to exchange information & develop policy positions
Contact Information: E-mail: info@ccrweb.ca

Canadian Council of Technicians & Technologists (CTTT) 2015 National Technology Conference
Sponsor/Contact: Canadian Council of Technicians & Technologists
#155, 955 Green Valley Cres.
Ottawa, ON K2C 3V4
613-238-8123 *Fax:* 613-238-8822
Toll-Free: 800-891-1140
E-mail: ccttadm@cctt.ca
URL: www.cctt.ca
Scope: National

Canadian Crude Quality Technical Association (CCQTA) 2015 Annual General Meeting
Sponsor/Contact: Canadian Crude Quality Technical Association
URL: www.ccqta.com
Scope: National

Canadian Dairy Commission Annual Public Meeting 2015
Sponsor/Contact: Canadian Dairy Commission
NCC Driveway, Bldg. 55
960 Carling Ave.
Ottawa, ON K1A 0Z2
613-792-2000 *Fax:* 613-792-2009
E-mail: carole.cyr@cdc-ccl.gc.ca
URL: www.cdc-ccl.gc.ca
Scope: National

Canadian Economics Association 2015 49th Conference
Location: Toronto, ON
Sponsor/Contact: Canadian Economics Association
Département des Sciences Économiques, Université du Québec à Montréal
P.O. Box 8888 Stn. Centre-Ville
Montréal, QC H3C 3P8
514-987-3000
URL: www.economics.ca
Scope: National
Purpose: An annual conference held during the last week of May or the first week of June
Contact Information: Conference Organizer: Professor Thomas Lemieux, E-mail: cea2013@economics.ca

Canadian Environmental Network / Réseau canadien de l'environnement 2015 Annual Conference on the Environment
Sponsor/Contact: Canadian Environmental Network
39 McArthur Ave., Level 1-1
Ottawa, ON K1L 8L7
613-728-9810 *Fax:* 613-728-2963
E-mail: info@rcen.ca
URL: rcen.ca
Scope: National
Contact Information: E-mail: chair@rcen.ca

Canadian Farm Writers' Federation 2015 Annual General Meeting & Conference
Sponsor/Contact: Canadian Farm Writers' Federation
P.O. Box 250
Ormstown, QC J0S 1K0
Fax: 450-829-2226
Toll-Free: 877-782-6456
E-mail: secretariat@cfwf.ca
URL: cfwf.wildapricot.org
Scope: National

Canadian Federation of Apartment Associations Rental Housing Conference 2015
Sponsor/Contact: Canadian Federation of Apartment Associations
#640, 1600 Carling Ave.
Ottawa, ON K1Z 1G3

Conferences Index

613-235-0101 *Fax:* 613-238-0101
E-mail: admin@cfaa-fcapi.org
URL: www.cfaa-fcapi.org
Scope: National

Canadian Finance & Leasing Association 2015 Conference
Sponsor/Contact: Canadian Finance & Leasing Association
#301, 15 Toronto St.
Toronto, ON M5C 2E3
416-860-1133 *Fax:* 416-860-1140
Toll-Free: 877-213-7373
E-mail: info@cfla-acfl.ca
URL: www.cfla-acfl.ca
Scope: National

Canadian Fluid Power Association 2015 Annual General Meeting
Sponsor/Contact: Canadian Fluid Power Association
#310, 2175 Sheppard Ave. East
Toronto, ON M2J 1W8
416-499-1416 *Fax:* 416-491-1670
E-mail: info@cfpa.ca
URL: www.cfpa.ca
Scope: National

Canadian Foundation for Healthcare Improvement's CEO Forum 2015
Sponsor/Contact: Canadian Foundation for Healthcare Improvement
#700, 1565 Carling Ave.
Ottawa, ON K1Z 8R1
613-728-2238 *Fax:* 613-728-3527
E-mail: info@cfhi-fcass.ca
URL: www.cfhi-fcass.ca
Scope: National
Purpose: An invitation-only annual meeting for healthcare chief executive officers, senior leaders, deputy ministers, & experts to discuss issues in Canadian health services

Canadian Foundry Association 2015 Annual Meeting
Sponsor/Contact: Canadian Foundry Association
#1500, 1 Nicholas St.
Ottawa, ON K1N 7B7
613-789-4894 *Fax:* 613-789-5957
URL: www.foundryassociation.ca
Scope: National
Purpose: A gathering of members to address issues facing the Canadian foundry industry
Contact Information: Executive Director: Judith Arbour

Canadian GeoExchange Coalition 8th National Geoexchange Business & Policy Forum
Sponsor/Contact: Canadian GeoExchange Coalition
#304, 1030 Cherrier St.
Montréal, QC H2L 1H9
514-807-7559 *Fax:* 514-807-8221
URL: www.geo-exchange.ca
Scope: International

Canadian Global Campaign for Education 2015 Annual Learning Forum
Sponsor/Contact: Canadian Global Campaign for Education
321 Chapel St.
Ottawa, ON K1N 7Z2
613-232-3569 *Fax:* 613-232-7435
E-mail: info@cgce.ca
URL: www.cgce.ca
Scope: National
Purpose: An opportunity for policy makers, development practitioners, academics, & civil society organizations to share best practices & discuss future programming
Contact Information: E-mail: info@cgce.ca

Canadian Healthcare Assn & Canadian College of Health Leaders 2015 National Health Leadership Conference
Sponsor/Contact: HealthCareCAN
#100, 17 York St.
Ottawa, ON K1N 9J6
613-241-8005 *Fax:* 613-241-5055
E-mail: info@healthcarecan.ca
URL: www.healthcarecan.ca
Scope: National
Purpose: A meeting of health system decision-makers, such as chief executive officers, trustees, directors, managers, & department heads. The theme this year is "From rhetoric to action: Achieving person & family-centred health systems."
Contact Information: Coordinator, Conference Services: Laurie Oman, Phone: 613-235-7218, Toll-Free: 1-800-363-9056, ext. 237, E-mail: loman@cchl-ccls.ca

Canadian Healthcare Association 2015 Annual General Meeting
Sponsor/Contact: HealthCareCAN
#100, 17 York St.
Ottawa, ON K1N 9J6
613-241-8005 *Fax:* 613-241-5055
E-mail: info@healthcarecan.ca
URL: www.healthcarecan.ca
Scope: National
Purpose: The association's business meeting, including the presentation of the Marion Stephenson Award & the CHA Award for Distinguished Service by the Boarrd of Directors
Contact Information: Communications Specialist: Teresa Neuman, E-mail: tneuman@cha.ca

Canadian Heavy Oil Association Conference 2015
Sponsor/Contact: Canadian Heavy Oil Association
#400, 500 - 5th Ave. SW
Calgary, AB T2P 3L5
403-269-1755 *Fax:* 403-453-0179
URL: www.choa.ab.ca
Scope: National

Canadian Homeopathic Conference 2015
Sponsor/Contact: National United Professional Association of Trained Homeopaths
#102, 2680 Matheson Blvd.
Mississauga, ON L4W 0A5
905-267-8539 *Fax:* 905-267-3401
E-mail: info@nupath.org
URL: www.nupath.org
Scope: National
Contact Information: URL: www.chconference.ca

Canadian Horse Heritage & Preservation Society 2015 Annual General Meeting
Sponsor/Contact: Canadian Horse Heritage & Preservation Society
c/o Judi Hayward, Five Winds Farm
1697 Lockyer Rd.
Roberts Creek, BC V0N 2W1
E-mail: judihayward@dccnet.com
URL: www.chhaps.org
Scope: National

Canadian Industrial Transportation Association 58th Annual Convention & Golf Tournament
Sponsor/Contact: Freight Management Association of Canada
#405, 580 Terry Fox Dr.
Ottawa, ON K2L 4C2
613-599-3283 *Fax:* 613-599-1295
E-mail: info@fma-agf.ca
URL: www.cita-acti.ca
Scope: National

Canadian Insititute for the Administration of Justice 2015 Annual Conference
Location: Saskatoon, SK
Sponsor/Contact: Canadian Institute for the Administration of Justice
Faculté de droit, Univ. de Montréal
P.O. Box 6128 Stn. Centre-Ville
#A3421, 3101, chemin de la Tour
Montréal, QC H3C 3J7
514-343-6157 *Fax:* 514-343-6296
E-mail: ciaj@ciaj-icaj.ca
URL: www.ciaj-icaj.ca
Scope: National
Purpose: Theme: Aboriginal Peoples & the Law - "We're all in this together"

Canadian Institute for NDE NDT in Canada 2015 Conference
Sponsor/Contact: Canadian Institute for NDE
135 Fennell Ave. West
Hamilton, ON L8N 3T2
905-387-1655 *Fax:* 905-574-6080
Toll-Free: 800-964-9488
E-mail: info@cinde.ca
URL: www.cinde.ca
Scope: International
Contact Information: Phone: 905-387-1655 Ext. 238; Email: events@cinde.ca

Canadian Institute of Food Science & Technology, Manitoba Section, 2015 Annual General Meeting
Location: Manitoba
Sponsor/Contact: Canadian Institute of Food Science & Technology
c/o A. Tezcucano, Manitoba Agriculture, Food & Rural Initiatives
P.O. Box 100
229 Main St. South
Morris, MB R0G 1K0
E-mail: manitobasection@cifst.ca
URL: www.cifst.ca
Scope: Provincial

Canadian Institute of Forestry / Institut forestier du Canada 2015 107th Annual General Meeting & Conference
Sponsor/Contact: Canadian Institute of Forestry
c/o The Canadian Ecology Centre
P.O. Box 430
6905 Hwy. 17 West
Mattawa, ON P0H 1V0
705-744-1715 *Fax:* 705-744-1716
E-mail: admin@cif-ifc.org
URL: www.cif-ifc.org
Scope: National
Purpose: Meetings, presentations, poster sessions, displays, & field trips

Canadian Institute of Public Health Inspectors 2015 81st Annual Educational Conference
Sponsor/Contact: Canadian Institute of Public Health Inspectors
#720, 999 West Broadway Ave.
Vancouver, BC V5Z 1K5
604-739-8180 *Fax:* 604-738-4080
Toll-Free: 888-245-8180
E-mail: questions@ciphi.ca
URL: www.ciphi.ca
Scope: National
Purpose: Featuring the presentation of Institute awards

Canadian Italian Heritage Foundation Renaissance Gala
Sponsor/Contact: Canadian Italian Heritage Foundation
11 Director Ct.
Woodbridge, ON L4L 4S5
905-850-4500 *Fax:* 905-850-4516
Scope: National

Canadian Katahdin Sheep Association 2015 Annual General Meeting
Sponsor/Contact: Canadian Katahdin Sheep Association Inc.
c/o Canadian Livestock Records Corporation
2417 Holly Lane
Ottawa, ON K1V 0M7
613-731-7110 *Fax:* 613-731-0704
E-mail: katahdin@clrc.ca
URL: www.katahdinsheep.com
Scope: National

Canadian Law & Society Association Annual Mid-Winter Meeting 2015
Sponsor/Contact: Canadian Law & Society Association
c/o Dept. of Law, Carleton University
1125 Colonel Bay Dr.
Ottawa, ON K1S 586
E-mail: info@acds-clsa.org
URL: www.acds-clsa.org
Scope: National

Canadian Linguistic Association 2015 Conference (part of the Congress of the Humanities & Social Sciences)
Sponsor/Contact: Canadian Linguistic Association
c/o University of Toronto Press, Journals Division
5201 Dufferin Ave.
Toronto, ON M3H 5T8
URL: www.chass.utoronto.ca/~cla-acl
Scope: National
Purpose: Information from all areas of linguistics
Contact Information: Treasurer (travel grant information): Laura Colantoni
E-mail: laura.colantoni@utoronto.ca

Canadian Machinery Vibration Association 2015 Annual Seminar
Sponsor/Contact: Canadian Machinery Vibration Association
#1260, 225 The East Mall
Toronto, ON M9B 0A9
416-622-1170 *Fax:* 416-622-5376
E-mail: val@cmva.com
URL: www.cmva.com
Scope: National

Canadian Meat Council 2015 95th Annual Conference
Sponsor/Contact: Canadian Meat Council
#407, 1545 Carling Ave.
Ottawa, ON K1Z 8P9
613-729-3911 *Fax:* 613-729-4997
E-mail: info@cmc-cvc.com
URL: www.cmc-cvc.com
Scope: National
Purpose: A meeting with a technical symposium & exhibits, a general session, as well as the announcement of scholarship recipients

Conferences Index

Contact Information: Event Planner, Tanya Poirier, Phone: 613-729-3911 ext. 31

Canadian Meat Science Association 2015 Annual Meeting
Sponsor/Contact: Canadian Meat Science Association
Dept. of Agricultural, Food & Nutritional Science, Univ. of Alberta
#4-10, Agriculture / Forestry Centre
Edmonton, AB T6G 2P5
780-492-3651 *Fax:* 780-492-5771
E-mail: ruth.ball@ales.ualberta.ca
URL: www.cmsa-ascv.ca
Scope: National

Canadian Meat Science Association 2015 Technical Symposium
Sponsor/Contact: Canadian Meat Science Association
Dept. of Agricultural, Food & Nutritional Science, Univ. of Alberta
#4-10, Agriculture / Forestry Centre
Edmonton, AB T6G 2P5
780-492-3651 *Fax:* 780-492-5771
E-mail: ruth.ball@ales.ualberta.ca
URL: www.cmsa-ascv.ca
Scope: National

Canadian Mental Health Association 2015 Conference
Sponsor/Contact: Canadian Mental Health Association
#1110, 151 Slater St.
Ottawa, ON K1P 5H3
613-745-7750 *Fax:* 613-745-5522
URL: www.cmha.ca
Scope: National

Canadian Morgan Horse Association Convection and Annual General Meeting
Location: British Columbia
Sponsor/Contact: Canadian Morgan Horse Association
P.O. Box 286
Port Perry, ON L9L 1A3
905-982-0060 *Fax:* 905-982-0097
E-mail: info@morganhorse.ca
URL: www.morganhorse.ca
Scope: National

Canadian Network of National Associations of Regulators 2015 Conference
Sponsor/Contact: Canadian Network of National Associations of Regulators
528 River Rd.
Ottawa, ON K1V 1E9
613-739-4376
URL: www.cnnar.ca
Scope: National

Canadian Nurses Association 2015 Annual Meeting
Sponsor/Contact: Canadian Nurses Association
50 Driveway
Ottawa, ON K2P 1E2
613-237-2133 *Fax:* 613-237-3520
Toll-Free: 800-361-8404
E-mail: info@cna-aiic.ca
URL: www.cna-aiic.ca
Scope: National
Purpose: The highlights of the association's year
Contact Information: E-mail: info@cna-aiic.ca

Canadian Nursing Education Conference Anticipating and Shaping the Future of Nursing Education
Sponsor/Contact: Canadian Association of Schools of Nursing
#450, 1145 Hunt Club Rd.
Ottawa, ON K1V 0Y3
613-235-3150 *Fax:* 613-235-4476
E-mail: inquire@casn.ca
URL: www.casn.ca
Scope: National

Canadian Nursing Students' Association 2015 Annual Atlantic Regional Conference
Date: Spring 2015
Sponsor/Contact: Canadian Nursing Students' Association
Fifth Ave. Court
#15, 99 - 5th Ave.
Ottawa, ON K1S 5K4
613-235-3150
E-mail: communications@cnsa.ca
URL: www.cnsa.ca
Scope: Provincial
Purpose: A conference to promote professional & personal development & discussion in the field of nursing
Contact Information: E-mail: atlantic@cnsa.ca

Canadian Nursing Students' Association 2015 Annual Ontario Regional Conference
Location: Ontario
Sponsor/Contact: Canadian Nursing Students' Association
Fifth Ave. Court
#15, 99 - 5th Ave.
Ottawa, ON K1S 5K4
613-235-3150
E-mail: communications@cnsa.ca
URL: www.cnsa.ca
Scope: Provincial
Purpose: Registered nursing students & practical nursing students from across Ontario participate in the Ontario regional meeting, hospital tours, keynote speaker sessions, workshops, panel presentations, & social events
Anticipated Attendance: 400
Contact Information: E-mail: ontario@cnsa.ca

Canadian Nursing Students' Association 2015 Annual Québec Regional Conference
Location: Quebec
Sponsor/Contact: Canadian Nursing Students' Association
Fifth Ave. Court
#15, 99 - 5th Ave.
Ottawa, ON K1S 5K4
613-235-3150
E-mail: communications@cnsa.ca
URL: www.cnsa.ca
Scope: Provincial
Purpose: A professional development opportunity for Québec's nursing students, featuring a business meeting for the region
Contact Information: E-mail: quebec-conference@cnsa.ca

Canadian Nursing Students' Association 2015 Annual Western / Prairie Regional Conference
Sponsor/Contact: Canadian Nursing Students' Association
Fifth Ave. Court
#15, 99 - 5th Ave.
Ottawa, ON K1S 5K4
613-235-3150
E-mail: communications@cnsa.ca
URL: www.cnsa.ca
Scope: Provincial
Purpose: An event for nursing students showcasing keynote speakers, health panels, poster presentations, workshops, a career fair, regional executive meetings, & networking & social events
Contact Information: E-mail: prairie@cnsa.ca; west@cnsa.ca

Canadian Paint and Coating Association 102nd Annual Conference
Sponsor/Contact: Canadian Paint & Coatings Association
#608, 170 Laurier Ave. West
Ottawa, ON K1P 5V5
613-231-3604 *Fax:* 613-231-4908
E-mail: cpca@cdnpaint.org
URL: www.cdnpaint.org
Scope: National
Purpose: Paint & coasting professionals gather to discuss the state of the Canadian paint & coasting industries.

Canadian Payroll Association 2015 33rd Annual Conference & Trade Show: Payroll Champions
Location: Sheraton Centre Toronto Hotel
Sponsor/Contact: Canadian Payroll Association
#1600, 250 Bloor St. East
Toronto, ON M4W 1E6
416-487-3380 *Fax:* 416-487-3384
Toll-Free: 800-387-4693
E-mail: infoline@payroll.ca
URL: www.payroll.ca
Scope: National
Purpose: A payroll event, where compliance, employment standards, & strategic management leaders have the opportunity to advance their skills, to learn about the latest trends & issues, & to network with professionals from across Canada
Contact Information: Phone: 416-487-3380, ext. 111; E-mail: conference@payroll.ca

Canadian Political Science Students' Association 2015 Annual National Conference
Sponsor/Contact: Canadian Political Science Students' Association
University of Calgary, Dept. of Political Science
2500 Universtiy Dr. NW
Calgary, AB T2N 1N4
613-562-1202 *Fax:* 613-241-0019
E-mail: contact@cpssa.ca
URL: www.cpssa.ca
Scope: National

Canadian Propane Association (CPC) 2015 Leadership Summit
Sponsor/Contact: Canadian Propane Association
#616, 130 Albert St.
Ottawa, ON K1P 5G4
613-683-2270 *Fax:* 613-683-2279
E-mail: info@propane.ca
URL: www.propane.ca
Scope: National
Purpose: The summit provides the opportunity for leaders in the propane industy to share ideas & knowledge among each other

Canadian Public Relations Society, Prince George, 2015 Annual General Meeting
Location: British Columbia
Sponsor/Contact: Canadian Public Relations Society Inc.
c/o Matt Wood, City of Quesnel
410 Kinchant St.
Quesnel, BC V2J 7J5
URL: cprsnorthernlights.com
Scope: Local
Purpose: A review of the society's activities during the past year, a financial report, & the election of officers
Contact Information: Secretary-Treasurer: Reneé McCloskey, E-mail: cprsnl@gmail.com

Canadian Public Relations Society, Toronto, 2015 Annual General Meeting
Location: Toronto, ON
Sponsor/Contact: Canadian Public Relations Society Inc.
c/o Lois Marsh, CPRS Toronto Secretariat
#1801, 1 Yonge St.
Toronto, ON M5E 1W7
416-360-1988 *Fax:* 416-369-0515
URL: www.cprstoronto.com
Scope: Local

Canadian Public Relations Society, Vancouver Island, 8th Annual Beyond the Hype Conference
Sponsor/Contact: Canadian Public Relations Society Inc.
c/o Phil Saunders, Communications Officer, Royal Roads University
2005 Sooke Rd.
Victoria, BC V9Y 5Y2
E-mail: info@cprs-vi.org
URL: www.cprs-vi.org
Scope: Local
Purpose: A one day conference for public relations & communications professionals, featuring a variety of speakers
Contact Information: E-mail: beyondthehypeconference@gmail.com; URL: www.beyondthehype.ca

Canadian Quaternary Association (CANQUA) 2015 Biennial Meeting
Location: St. John's, NL
Sponsor/Contact: Canadian Quaternary Association
c/o Kathryn Hargan, Department of Biology, Queen's University
116 Barrie St.
Kingston, ON K7L 3N6
613-533-6000
URL: www.canqua.com
Scope: National
Contact Information: Secretary-Treasurer: Kathryn Hargan, E-mail: kathrynhargan@gmail.com

Canadian Renewable Fuels 2015 12th Annual Summit
Sponsor/Contact: Canadian Renewable Fuels Association
#605, 350 Sparks St.
Ottawa, ON K1R 7S8
613-594-5528 *Fax:* 613-594-3076
E-mail: l.ehman@greenfuels.org
URL: www.greenfuels.org
Scope: International
Purpose: A conference of interest to representatives from the ethanol & biodiesel industries, plus agricultural associations & petroleum companies
Contact Information: Director, Member Relations & Industry Promotions:

Deborah Elson, E-mail: d.elson@greenfuels.org

Canadian School Boards Association / Association canadienne des commissions/conseils scolaires 2015 Congress
Location: Saskatoon, SK
Sponsor/Contact: Canadian School Boards Association
#515, 1410 rue Stanley
Montréal, QC H3A 1P8
514-289-2988 *Fax:* 514-849-8228
E-mail: info@cdnsba.org
URL: www.cdnsba.org
Scope: National

Canadian Society for Epidemiology & Biostatistics 2015 Biennial Conference
Location: Toronto, ON
Sponsor/Contact: Canadian Society for Epidemiology & Biostatistics
c/o Pamela Wilson, The Willow Group
1485 Laperriere Ave.
Ottawa, ON K1Z 7S8
613-722-8796 *Fax:* 613-729-6206
E-mail: secretariat@cseb.ca
URL: www.cseb.ca
Scope: National

Canadian Society for Exercise Physiology 2015 Annual General Meeting
Sponsor/Contact: Canadian Society for Exercise Physiology
#370, 18 Louisa St.
Ottawa, ON K1R 6Y6
613-234-3755 *Fax:* 613-234-3565
Toll-Free: 877-651-3755
E-mail: info@csep.ca
URL: www.csep.ca
Scope: National
Contact Information: E-mail: info@csep.ca

Canadian Society for Mechanical Engineering 2015 25th Biennial Canadian Congress of Applied Mechanics (CANCAM)
Sponsor/Contact: Canadian Society for Mechanical Engineering
1295 Hwy. 2 East
Kingston, ON K7L 4V1
613-547-5989 *Fax:* 613-547-0195
E-mail: csme@cogeco.ca
URL: www.csme-scgm.ca
Scope: National
Purpose: Tech tracks at past conferences have included civil engineering, computational mechanics, dynamics & vibration, education in applied mechanics, fluid mechanics, manufacturing, mechatronics, micro-electro-mechanical systems, solid mechanics & materials, & thermodynamics & heat transfer
Contact Information: Canadian Society for Mechanical Engineering, E-mail: csme@cogeco.ca

Canadian Society for Mechanical Engineering 2015 Congress
Sponsor/Contact: Canadian Society for Mechanical Engineering
1295 Hwy. 2 East
Kingston, ON K7L 4V1
613-547-5989 *Fax:* 613-547-0195
E-mail: csme@cogeco.ca
URL: www.csme-scgm.ca
Scope: National
Purpose: A meeting of mechanical engineers, held every other year in a Canadian city, for discussion of research & issues important to the profession & related fields
Contact Information: Canadian Society for Mechanical Engineering, E-mail: csme@cogeco.ca

Canadian Society of Nephrology Annual General Meeting 2015
Sponsor/Contact: Canadian Society of Nephrology
P.O. Box 25255 Stn. RDP
Montreal, QC H1E 7P9
514-643-4985
E-mail: info@csnscn.ca
URL: www.csnscn.ca
Scope: National

Canadian Society of Questers Fall Conference 2015
Sponsor/Contact: Canadian Society of Questers
P.O. Box 1465
Salmon Arm, BC V1E 4P6
E-mail: pinkrose4233@gmail.com
URL: www.questers.ca
Scope: National

Canadian Society of Questers Spring Conference 2015
Sponsor/Contact: Canadian Society of Questers
P.O. Box 1465
Salmon Arm, BC V1E 4P6
E-mail: pinkrose4233@gmail.com
URL: www.questers.ca
Scope: National

Canadian Solar Industries Association 2015 Solar Canada Conference & Exposition
Sponsor/Contact: Canadian Solar Industries Association
#605, 150 Isabella St.
Ottawa, ON K1S 1V7
613-736-9077 *Fax:* 613-736-8938
Toll-Free: 866-522-6742
E-mail: info@cansia.ca
URL: www.cansia.ca
Scope: National
Purpose: The presentation of timely topics for solar industry professionals from across Canada, featuring more than 60 speakers & 225 exhibitors
Anticipated Attendance: 4000+
Contact Information: Web Site: www.solarcanadaconference.ca

Canadian Solar Industries Association 2015 Solar Ontario Conference & Showcase
Sponsor/Contact: Canadian Solar Industries Association
#605, 150 Isabella St.
Ottawa, ON K1S 1V7
613-736-9077 *Fax:* 613-736-8938
Toll-Free: 866-522-6742
E-mail: info@cansia.ca
URL: www.cansia.ca
Scope: National
Purpose: A one-day event for solar energy professionals, practitioners, stakeholders & advocates

Canadian Sport Massage Therapists Association 2015 Annual General Meeting & Conference
Sponsor/Contact: Canadian Sport Massage Therapists Association
1030 Burnside Rd. West
Victoria, BC V8Z 1N3
250-590-9861 *Fax:* 250-388-7835
E-mail: natoffice@csmta.ca
URL: www.csmta.ca
Scope: National

Canadian Stroke Congress 2015
Sponsor/Contact: Canadian Stroke Network
#301, 600 Peter Morand Cres.
Ottawa, ON K1G 5Z3
613-562-5696 *Fax:* 613-521-9215
E-mail: info@canadianstrokenetwork.ca
URL: www.canadianstrokenetwork.ca
Scope: National

Canadian Teachers' Federation 2015 Annual General Meeting
Sponsor/Contact: Canadian Teachers' Federation
2490 Don Reid Dr.
Ottawa, ON K1H 1E1
613-232-1505 *Fax:* 613-232-1886
Toll-Free: 866-283-1505
E-mail: info@ctf-fce.ca
URL: www.ctf-fce.ca
Scope: National
Purpose: Approval of a budget for the upcoming year, a discussion & determination of policy priorities, & an election of directors
Contact Information: Director of Communications: Francine Filion, Phone: 613-688-4314

Canadian Teachers' Federation, Yukon Teachers' Association & the Government of Yukon 2015 Women's Issues Symposium
Location: Yukon Territory
Sponsor/Contact: Canadian Teachers' Federation
2490 Don Reid Dr.
Ottawa, ON K1H 1E1
613-232-1505 *Fax:* 613-232-1886
Toll-Free: 866-283-1505
E-mail: info@ctf-fce.ca
URL: www.ctf-fce.ca
Scope: National

Canadian Tenpin Federation, Inc. / Fédération canadienne des dix-quilles, inc. 2015 Annual General Meeting
Sponsor/Contact: Canadian Tenpin Federation, Inc.
916 - 3 Ave. North
Lethbridge, AB T1H 0H3
403-381-2830 *Fax:* 403-381-6247
E-mail: ctf@gotenpinbowling.ca
URL: www.gotenpinbowling.ca
Scope: National

Canadian Union of Public Employees (CUPE) British Columbia Division 2015 51st Annual Convention
Location: British Columbia
Sponsor/Contact: Canadian Union of Public Employees
British Columbia Regional Office
#500, 4940 Canada Way
Burnaby, BC V5G 4T3
604-291-9119 *Fax:* 604-291-9043
Toll-Free: 800-664-2873
E-mail: info@cupe.bc.ca
URL: www.cupe.bc.ca
Scope: Provincial

Canadian Union of Public Employees (CUPE) Manitoba 2015 52nd Annual Convention
Location: Dauphin, MB
Sponsor/Contact: Canadian Union of Public Employees
Manitoba Regional Office
#703, 275 Broadway
Winnipeg, MB R3C 4M6
204-942-0343 *Fax:* 204-956-7071
Toll-Free: 800-552-2873
E-mail: cupemb@mts.net
URL: www.cupe.mb.ca
Scope: Provincial
Contact Information: E-mail: cupemb@mts.net

Canadian Union of Public Employees (CUPE) Saskatchewan 2015 Summer School
Location: Saskatchewan
Sponsor/Contact: Canadian Union of Public Employees
Saskatchewan Regional Office
3275 East Eastgate Dr.
Regina, SK S4Z 1A5
306-757-1009 *Fax:* 306-757-0102
E-mail: cupesask@sasktel.net
URL: www.sk.cupe.ca
Scope: Provincial
Purpose: An annual series of courses for the Saskatchewan region
Contact Information: E-mail: cupesask@sasktel.net

Canadian Water Quality Association 2015 Annual General Meeting
Sponsor/Contact: Canadian Water Quality Association
#330, 295 The West Mall
Toronto, ON M9C 4Z4
416-695-3068 *Fax:* 416-695-2945
Toll-Free: 866-383-7617
E-mail: k.wong@cwqa.com
URL: www.cwqa.com
Scope: National

Catholic Health Association of BC 75th Annual General Meeting and Conference
Location: British Columbia
Sponsor/Contact: Catholic Health Association of British Columbia
9387 Holmes St.
Burnaby, BC V3N 4C3
604-524-3427 *Fax:* 604-524-3428
E-mail: smhouse@shawlink.ca
URL: chabc.bc.ca
Scope: Provincial

Centre for Comparative Literature 2015 26th Annual Conference
Sponsor/Contact: Centre for Comparative Literature
c/o Isabel Bader Theatre
93 Charles St. West, 3rd Fl.
Toronto, ON M5S 1K9
417-813-4041 *Fax:* 416-813-4040
URL: www.complit.utoronto.ca
Scope: National
Contact Information: E-mail: conference@acla.org

Certified General Accountants Association of British Columbia 2015 65th Annual General Meeting, Conference, & Trade Show
Sponsor/Contact: Certified General Accountants Association of British Columbia
#300, 1867 West Broadway
Vancouver, BC V6J 5L4
604-732-1211 *Fax:* 604-732-1252
Toll-Free: 800-565-1211
E-mail: info@cga-bc.org
URL: www.cga-bc.org
Scope: Provincial
Purpose: A provincial conference about recent developments in the profession for Certified General Accountants & other professional accountants

Conferences Index

Chartered Professional Accountants of British Columbia Fall Leadership Conference 2015
Location: British Columbia
Sponsor/Contact: Chartered Professional Accountants of British Columbia
E-mail: info@bccpa.ca
URL: www.bccpa.ca
Scope: Provincial

Chartered Professional Accountants of British Columbia Spring Leadership Conference 2015
Location: British Columbia
Sponsor/Contact: Chartered Professional Accountants of British Columbia
E-mail: info@bccpa.ca
URL: www.bccpa.ca
Scope: Provincial

Children's Mental Health Ontario Annual Conference 2015
Location: Ontario
Sponsor/Contact: Children's Mental Health Ontario
#309, 40 St. Clair Ave. East
Toronto, ON M4T 1M9
416-921-2109 *Fax:* 416-921-7600
Toll-Free: 888-234-7054
E-mail: info@cmho.org
URL: www.kidsmentalhealth.ca
Scope: National

Church Library Association of Ontario 2015 Annual Fall Conference
Location: Ontario
Sponsor/Contact: Church Library Association of Ontario
c/o Margaret Godefroy, CLAO Membership Secretary
#603, 155 Navy St.
Oakville, ON L6J 2Z7
905-845-0222
E-mail: agodefroy@cogeco.ca
URL: www.churchlibraries.ca
Scope: Provincial
Purpose: A Saturday event in a southern Ontario location, featuring technical, administrative, & promotional workshops
Contact Information: Email: conference@clao.ca

Church Library Association of Ontario 2015 Annual Spring Conference
Location: Ontario
Sponsor/Contact: Church Library Association of Ontario
c/o Margaret Godefroy, CLAO Membership Secretary
#603, 155 Navy St.
Oakville, ON L6J 2Z7
905-845-0222
E-mail: agodefroy@cogeco.ca
URL: www.churchlibraries.ca
Scope: Provincial
Purpose: A Saturday conference, usually held in a southern Ontario location, featuring workshops, speakers, networking opportunities, exhibitors, & a book swap
Contact Information: Email: conference@clao.ca

Clean Energy BC 2015 13th Annual Conference
Location: British Columbia
Sponsor/Contact: Clean Energy BC
#354, 409 Granville St.
Vancouver, BC V6C 1T2
604-568-4778 *Fax:* 604-568-4724
Toll-Free: 855-568-4778
URL: www.cleanenergybc.org
Scope: Provincial
Purpose: An event featuring guest speakers, short courses, exhibits, & field trips
Contact Information: Coordinator, Events: Lisa Bateman, E-mail: lisa.bateman@cleanenergybc.org

College of Chiropractors of British Columbia 2015 Annual General Meeting
Location: British Columbia
Sponsor/Contact: College of Chiropractors of British Columbia
#125, 3751 Shell Rd.
Richmond, BC V6X 2W2
604-270-1332 *Fax:* 604-278-0093
Toll-Free: 866-256-1474
E-mail: info@bcchiro.com
URL: www.bcchiro.com
Scope: Provincial
Purpose: A meeting of College of Chriopractors of British Columbia registrants that is open to the public
Contact Information: Phone (attendance information): 604-270-1332, E-mail: info@bcchiro.com

College of Family Physicians of Canada / Collège des médecins de famille du Canada 2015 Annual General Meeting
Location: Ontario
Sponsor/Contact: College of Family Physicians of Canada
2630 Skymark Ave.
Mississauga, ON L4W 5A4
905-629-0900 *Fax:* 905-629-0893
Toll-Free: 800-387-6197
E-mail: info@cfpc.ca
URL: www.cfpc.ca
Scope: Provincial

College of Optometrists of BC 2015 Annual General Meeting
Location: British Columbia
Sponsor/Contact: College of Optometrists of BC
#1204, 700 West Pender St.
Vancouver, BC V6C 1G8
604-623-3464 *Fax:* 604-623-3465
E-mail: optometry_board@telus.net
URL: www.optometrybc.com
Scope: Provincial
Purpose: The presentation of financial statements, as well as reports from the chair, the registrar, the deputy registrar, & college board members
Contact Information: Chief Administrative Officer & Assistant to the Registrar: Stanka Jovicevic, E-mail (general information): college@optometrybc.ca

College of Registered Nurses of British Columbia 2015 Annual General Meeting
Location: British Columbia
Sponsor/Contact: College of Registered Nurses of British Columbia
2855 Arbutus St.
Vancouver, BC V6J 3Y8
604-736-7331 *Fax:* 604-738-2272
Toll-Free: 800-565-6505
E-mail: info@crnbc.ca
URL: www.crnbc.ca
Scope: Provincial

Community Futures Manitoba Inc. 2015 Annual Provincial Conference
Location: Manitoba
Sponsor/Contact: Community Futures Manitoba Inc.
#559, 167 Lombard Ave.
Winnipeg, MB R3B 0V3
204-943-2905 *Fax:* 204-956-9363
E-mail: info@cfmanitoba.ca
URL: www.cfmanitoba.ca
Scope: Provincial
Purpose: A yearly event to explore economic development issues in Manitoba, featuring keynote addresses
Anticipated Attendance: 150
Contact Information: E-mail: info@cfmanitoba.ca

Community Living Oshawa / Clarington 2015 Annual General Meeting
Location: Ontario
Sponsor/Contact: Community Living Oshawa / Clarington
39 Wellington St. East
Oshawa, ON L1H 3Y1
905-576-3011 *Fax:* 905-576-9754
URL: www.communitylivingoc.ca
Scope: Local

Compost Council of Canada 2015 25th Annual National Compost Conference
Sponsor/Contact: Compost Council of Canada
16 Northumberland St.
Toronto, ON M6H 1P7
416-535-0240 *Fax:* 416-536-9892
Toll-Free: 877-571-4769
E-mail: info@compost.org
URL: www.compost.org
Scope: National
Purpose: Current developments in the composting industry, such as research, processing improvements, & community developments
Contact Information: E-mail: info@compost.org

Congrès Association des médecins vétérinaires praticiens du Québec 2015
Location: Quebec
Sponsor/Contact: Association des médecins vétérinaires praticiens du Québec
#4500, 2336, ch Ste-Foy
Québec, QC G1V 1S5
418-651-0477 *Fax:* 450-261-9435
E-mail: amvpq@amvpq.org
URL: www.amvpq.org
Scope: Provincial

Congrès d'orientation de la FCSQ 2015
Sponsor/Contact: La Fédération des commissions scolaires du Québec
P.O. Box 10490 Stn. Sainte-Foy
1001, av Bégon
Québec, QC G1V 4C7
418-651-3220 *Fax:* 418-651-2574
E-mail: info@fcsq.qc.ca
URL: www.fcsq.qc.ca
Scope: National

Congrès des milieux documentaires du Québec 2015
Sponsor/Contact: Corporation des bibliothécaires professionnels du Québec
#215, 1453 Beaubien est
Montréal, QC H2G 3C6
514-845-3327 *Fax:* 514-845-1618
E-mail: info@cbpq.qc.ca
URL: www.cbpq.qc.ca
Scope: Provincial

Conservation Agriculture 2015 7th World Congress (hosted by Soil Conservation Council of Canada with Conservation Agriculture Systems Alliance)
Sponsor/Contact: Soil Conservation Council of Canada
P.O. Box 998
Indian Head, SK S0G 2K0
306-972-7293 *Fax:* 306-695-3442
E-mail: info@soilcc.ca
URL: www.soilcc.ca
Scope: International
Purpose: A gathering of world academic, industry, & producer leaders in conservation agriculture
Contact Information: Soil Conservation Council of Canada, Executive Director: Glen Shaw, E-mail: info@soilcc.ca

Conservation Council of Ontario 2015 Annual Meeting
Location: Ontario
Sponsor/Contact: Conservation Council of Ontario
#132, 215 Spadina Ave.
Toronto, ON M5T 2C7
416-533-1635 *Fax:* 416-979-3936
E-mail: cco@web.ca
URL: www.weconserve.ca/cco
Scope: Provincial
Purpose: An overview of strategic direction & the election of new members
Contact Information: E-mail: info@weconserve.ca

Construction Owners Association of Alberta Best Practices Conferences 2015
Location: Alberta
Sponsor/Contact: Construction Owners Association of Alberta
Sun Life Place
#800, 10123 - 99 St. NW
Edmonton, AB T5J 3H1
780-420-1145 *Fax:* 780-425-4623
E-mail: coaa-mail@coaa.ab.ca
URL: www.coaa.ab.ca
Scope: Provincial

Construction Safety Association of Manitoba 2015 21st Annual Westman Safety Conference
Location: Manitoba
Sponsor/Contact: Construction Safety Association of Manitoba
1447 Waverly St.
Winnipeg, MB R3T 0P7
204-775-3171 *Fax:* 204-779-3505
E-mail: safety@constructionsafety.ca
URL: www.constructionsafety.ca
Scope: Provincial
Purpose: An event that caters to industries in the Westman region, by offering specialized training in areas such as emergency preparedness & response, safety administration, as well as information about changes to workplace safety & health regulations
Contact Information: Westman Office, Phone: 204-728-3456, Fax: 204-571-0678

Consulting Engineers of Alberta 2015 18th Annual Tri-Party Transportation Conference & Trade Show Exhibition
Location: Alberta
Sponsor/Contact: Consulting Engineers of Alberta
Phipps-McKinnon Building
#870, 10020 - 101A Ave.
Edmonton, AB T5J 3G2
780-421-1852 *Fax:* 780-424-5225
E-mail: info@cea.ca
URL: www.cea.ca

Scope: Provincial
Purpose: Keynote speakers, forums, & workshops about transportation infrastructure in Alberta
Anticipated Attendance: 700+
Contact Information: Manager, Business Services/Events: Kary Kremer, E-mail: kkremer@cea.ca

Consulting Engineers of Alberta 2015 37th Annual General Meeting
Location: Alberta
Sponsor/Contact: Consulting Engineers of Alberta
Phipps-McKinnon Building
#870, 10020 - 101A Ave.
Edmonton, AB T5J 3G2
780-421-1852 *Fax:* 780-424-5225
E-mail: info@cea.ca
URL: www.cea.ca
Scope: Provincial
Purpose: Presentations by guest speakers plus the business meeting for consulting engineers in Alberta
Contact Information: Manager, Business Services/Events: Kary Kremer, E-mail: kkremer@cea.ca

Consulting Engineers of Nova Scotia (CENS) 2015 Annual General Meeting
Sponsor/Contact: Consulting Engineers of Nova Scotia
P.O. Box 613 Stn. M
Halifax, NS B3J 2R7
902-461-1325 *Fax:* 902-461-1321
E-mail: cens@eastlink.ca
URL: www.cens.org
Scope: Provincial

Consulting Engineers of Ontario 2015 Annual General Meeting
Location: Ontario
Sponsor/Contact: Consulting Engineers of Ontario
#405, 10 Four Seasons Pl.
Toronto, ON M9B 6H7
416-620-1400 *Fax:* 416-620-5803
URL: www.ceo.on.ca
Scope: Provincial

Council of Archives New Brunswick AGM 2015
Location: New Brunswick
Sponsor/Contact: Council of Archives New Brunswick
P.O. Box 1204 Stn. A
Fredericton, NB E3B 5C8
506-453-4327 *Fax:* 506-453-3288
E-mail: archives.advisor@gnb.ca
URL: www.canbarchives.ca/canb
Scope: Provincial

Council of Nova Scotia Archives Annual Conference 2015
Location: Nova Scotia
Sponsor/Contact: Council of Nova Scotia Archives
6016 University Ave.
Halifax, NS B3H 1W4
902-424-7093
E-mail: advisor@councilofnsarchives.ca
URL: www.councilofnsarchives.ca
Scope: Provincial

Council of Ontario Construction Associations Annual General Meeting 2015
Location: Ontario
Sponsor/Contact: Council of Ontario Construction Associations
#2001, 180 Dundas St. West
Toronto, ON M5G 1Z8
416-968-7200 *Fax:* 416-968-0362
E-mail: info@coca.on.ca
URL: www.coca.on.ca
Scope: Provincial

Council of Post Secondary Library Directors, British Columbia, Fall 2015 Meeting
Location: British Columbia
Sponsor/Contact: Council of Post Secondary Library Directors, British Columbia
c/o G. Makarewicz, Director, Library & Bookstore Svs., Langara College
100 West 49th Ave.
Vancouver, BC V5Y 2Z6
E-mail: admin@cpsld.ca
URL: www.cpsld.ca
Scope: Provincial
Purpose: A meeting held each autumn with a program of interest to library directors & chief librarians from not-for-profit post secondary education institutions in British Columbia

Council of Prairie & Pacific University Libraries Fall Meeting 2015
Sponsor/Contact: Council of Prairie & Pacific University Libraries
Bennett Library
8888 University Dr.
Burnaby, BC V5A 1S6
778-782-9404 *Fax:* 778-782-3023
URL: www.coppul.ca
Scope: National

Credit Union Central of Canada 2015 National Lending Conference
Sponsor/Contact: Credit Union Central of Canada
Corporate Office
#1000, 151 Yonge St.
Toronto, ON M5C 2W7
416-232-1262 *Fax:* 416-232-9196
Toll-Free: 800-649-0222
E-mail: inquiries@cucentral.com
URL: www.cucentral.ca
Scope: National
Contact Information: Credit Union Central of Canada Communications Department Contact: Edith Wilkinson, Phone: 416-232-3421, Fax: 416-232-3734, E-mail: wilkinsone@cucentral.com

Cross Country Ontario 2015 Annual General Meeting
Location: Ontario
Sponsor/Contact: Cross Country Ontario
738 River St.
Thunder Bay, ON P7A 3S8
807-768-4617
E-mail: admin@xco.org
URL: www.xco.org
Scope: Provincial
Purpose: Board meetings are held each month by telephone, & the annual general meeting takes place each May
Contact Information: Administrative Director: Liz Inkila, E-mail: admin@xco.org

EcoLinks 2015
Sponsor/Contact: Ontario Society for Environmental Education
P.O. Box 587
Lakefield, ON K0L 2H0
705-652-0923
URL: home.osee.ca
Scope: Provincial

Electricity Distributors Association Executive Symposium 2015
Sponsor/Contact: Electricity Distributors Association
#1100, 3700 Steeles Ave. West
Vaughan, ON L4L 8K8
905-265-5300 *Fax:* 905-265-5301
Toll-Free: 800-668-9979
E-mail: email@eda-on.ca
URL: www.eda-on.ca
Scope: Provincial

Elementary Teachers' Federation of Ontario 2015 Annual Meeting
Location: Ontario
Sponsor/Contact: Elementary Teachers' Federation of Ontario
136 Isabella St.
Toronto, ON M4Y 1P6
416-962-3836 *Fax:* 416-642-2424
Toll-Free: 888-838-3836
URL: www.etfo.ca
Scope: Provincial

Elementary Teachers' Federation of Ontario 2015 Women's Conference
Location: Ontario
Sponsor/Contact: Elementary Teachers' Federation of Ontario
136 Isabella St.
Toronto, ON M4Y 1P6
416-962-3836 *Fax:* 416-642-2424
Toll-Free: 888-838-3836
URL: www.etfo.ca
Scope: Provincial
Contact Information: Program Contact: Evelyn Doucett, Phone: 416-962-3836, ext. 2214, E-mail: edoucett@etfo.org

End Exclusion
Sponsor/Contact: Saskatchewan Voice of People with Disabilities, Inc.
984 Albert St.
Regina, SK S4R 2P7
306-569-3111 *Fax:* 306-569-1889
Toll-Free: 877-569-3111
E-mail: voice@saskvoice.com
URL: www.saskvoice.com
Scope: Provincial

Energy Council of Canada Annual General Meeting 2015
Sponsor/Contact: Energy Council of Canada
#608, 350 Sparks St.
Ottawa, ON K1R 7S8
613-232-8239 *Fax:* 613-232-1079
E-mail: krystal.piamonte@energy.ca
URL: www.energy.ca
Scope: National

Energy Psychology Conference 2015
Sponsor/Contact: Canadian Association for Integrative and Energy Therapies
416-221-5639 *Fax:* 416-221-7126
URL: www.caiet.org
Scope: National

Engineers Nova Scotia 2015 Annual General Meeting
Location: Nova Scotia
Sponsor/Contact: Engineers Nova Scotia
1355 Barrington St.
Halifax, NS B3J 1Y9
902-429-2250 *Fax:* 902-423-9769
Toll-Free: 888-802-7367
E-mail: info@engineersnovascotia.ca
URL: www.engineersnovascotia.ca
Scope: Provincial
Purpose: A business meeting with guest speakers for professional engineers & engineers-in-training in Nova Scotia
Contact Information: E-mail: info@engineersnovascotia.ca

Entomological Society of Canada 2015 Annual Meeting
Sponsor/Contact: Entomological Society of Canada
393 Winston Ave.
Ottawa, ON K2A 1Y8
613-725-2619
E-mail: entsoc.can@bellnet.ca
URL: www.esc-sec.ca
Scope: National

Entomological Society of Ontario 2015 152nd Annual General Meeting
Sponsor/Contact: Entomological Society of Ontario
c/o Vista Centre
P.O. Box 83025
1830 Bank St.
Ottawa, ON K1V 1A3
603-736-3393
URL: www.entsocont.ca
Scope: Provincial
Purpose: A gathering of entomologists of all disciplines

Environmental Education Ontario Spring Event and Annual General Meeting 2015
Location: Ontario
Sponsor/Contact: Environmental Education Ontario
32 Springdale Dr.
Kitchener, ON N2K 1P9
519-579-3097
E-mail: admin@eeon.org
URL: www.eeon.org
Scope: Provincial
Contact Information: Email: admin@eeon.org

Ex Libris Association 2015 Annual General Meeting & Conference
Location: Toronto, ON
Sponsor/Contact: Ex Libris Association
c/o Faculty of Information Studies, University of Toronto
140 St. George St.
Toronto, ON M5S 3G6
E-mail: ExLibris@fis.utoronto.ca
URL: exlibris.fis.utoronto.ca
Scope: National
Purpose: A one-day program with speakers on issues of current interest & trends in the library & archives community
Contact Information: Chair, Annual Conference: Richard Ficek, E-mail: exLibris@fis.utoronto.ca

Family Caregivers' Network Society 2015 Annual General Meeting
Location: British Columbia
Sponsor/Contact: Family Caregivers' Network Society
526 Michigan St.
Victoria, BC V8V 1S2
250-384-0408 *Fax:* 250-361-2660
E-mail: fcns@telus.net
URL: www.fcns-caregiving.org
Scope: Provincial

Federation of Ontario Cottagers' Associations 2015 Spring Annual General Meeting
Location: Ontario
Sponsor/Contact: Federation of Ontario Cottagers' Associations
#201, 159 King St.
Peterborough, ON K9J 2R8

705-749-3622 *Fax:* 705-749-6522
E-mail: info@foca.on.ca
URL: www.foca.on.ca
Scope: Provincial
Contact Information: Phone: 705-749-3622, ext. 5; E-mail: communications@foca.on.ca

Fenestration West Annual Conference 2015
Location: British Columbia
Sponsor/Contact: Fenestration Association of BC
#101, 20351 Duncan Way
Langley, BC V3A 7N3
778-571-0245 *Fax:* 866-253-9979
E-mail: info@fen-bc.org
URL: www.fen-bc.org
Scope: Provincial

Field Botanists of Ontario Annual General Meeting
Location: Ontario
Sponsor/Contact: Field Botanists of Ontario
c/o W.D. McIlveen
RR#1
Acton, ON L7J 2L7
URL: www.trentu.ca/fbo
Scope: Provincial

Fisheries Council of Canada 2015 70th Annual Conference
Sponsor/Contact: Fisheries Council of Canada
#900, 170 Laurier Ave. West
Ottawa, ON K1P 5V5
613-727-7450 *Fax:* 613-727-7453
E-mail: info@fisheriescouncil.org
URL: www.fisheriescouncil.ca
Scope: National
Purpose: Educational sessions, opportunities to network, & social programs
Contact Information: E-mail: info@fisheriescouncil.org

Food Processors of Canada Annual Executives Meeting 2015
Sponsor/Contact: Food Processors of Canada
#900, 350 Sparks St.
Ottawa, ON K1R 7S8
613-722-1000 *Fax:* 613-722-1404
E-mail: fpc@foodprocessors.ca
URL: www.foodnet.fic.ca
Scope: National

Foothills Library Association 2015 Calgary Libraries in Action
Location: Alberta
Sponsor/Contact: Foothills Library Association
P.O. Box 2985 Stn. M
Calgary, AB T2P 3C3
E-mail: flapresident@fla.org
URL: www.fla.org
Scope: Local
Purpose: Prominent issues for librarians are explored through presentations & discussions.
Contact Information: Events Line Contact: Inesia Adolph, E-mail: events@fla.org

Fraser Valley Labour Council 2015 Annual General Meeting
Location: British Columbia
Sponsor/Contact: Fraser Valley Labour Council
#202, 9292 - 200th St.
Langley, BC V1M 3A6
604-314-9867 *Fax:* 604-430-6762
E-mail: bharder@usw.ca
URL: www.fvlc.ca
Scope: Local
Contact Information: Secretary: Pamela Willingshofer, Phone: 604-837-3426

Gas Processing Association Canada 2015 Safety Conference & Awards Banquet
Location: Alberta
Sponsor/Contact: Gas Processing Association Canada
#400, 1040 - 7th Ave. SW
Calgary, AB T2P 3G9
403-244-4487 *Fax:* 403-244-2340
E-mail: info@gpacanada.com
URL: www.gpacanada.com
Scope: National
Contact Information: Email: conference@gpacanada.com

Golf Business Canada Conference & Trade Show 2015
Sponsor/Contact: National Golf Course Owners Association Canada
#105, 955 Green Valley Cres.
Ottawa, ON K2C 3V4
613-226-3616 *Fax:* 613-226-4148
Toll-Free: 866-626-4262
E-mail: ngcoa@ngcoa.ca
URL: www.ngcoa.ca
Scope: National

Green Building Symposium - Kingston
Location: Kingston, ON
Sponsor/Contact: Sustainable Kingston
184 Sydenham St.
Kingston, ON K7K 3M2
613-544-2075
E-mail: info@sustainablekingston.ca
URL: sustainablekingston.ca
Scope: Local

GrowCanada Conference 2015
Sponsor/Contact: CropLife Canada
#612, 350 Sparks St.
Ottawa, ON K1R 7S8
613-230-9881
URL: www.croplife.ca
Scope: National
Purpose: Provides a platform to connect with industry leaders from across the country, explore cutting edge insight and build a stronger and more vibrant Canadian agricultural sector that ultimately contributes to a better world.
Contact Information: URL: www.growcanadaconference.ca

Gymnastics Ontario Coaches Congress
Location: Ontario
Sponsor/Contact: Ontario Gymnastic Federation
#214, 3 Concorde Gate
Toronto, ON M3C 3N7
416-426-7100 *Fax:* 416-426-7377
Toll-Free: 866-565-0650
E-mail: info@ogf.com
URL: www.ogf.com
Scope: Provincial

Halifax Library Association 2015 Annual General Meeting
Location: Halifax, NS
Sponsor/Contact: Halifax Library Association
c/o 5940 South St.
Halifax, NS B3H 1S6
E-mail: halifaxlibraryassociation@gmail.com
URL: halifaxla.wordpress.com
Scope: Local

Health Sciences Association of Alberta 2015 44th Annual General Meeting
Location: Alberta
Sponsor/Contact: Health Sciences Association of Alberta
10212 - 112 St.
Edmonton, AB T5K 1M4
780-488-0168 *Fax:* 780-488-0534
Toll-Free: 800-252-7904
URL: www.hsaa.ca
Scope: Provincial
Contact Information: Communications Officer: Kim Adonyi-Keegan, E-mail: kima@hsaa.ca

Human Resource Management Association of Manitoba Human Resource & Leadership Conference 2015
Location: Manitoba
Sponsor/Contact: Human Resource Management Association of Manitoba
#1810, 275 Portage Ave.
Winnipeg, MB R3B 2B3
204-943-2836 *Fax:* 204-943-1109
E-mail: hrmam@hrmam.org
URL: www.hrmam.org
Scope: Provincial

Infectious Diseases Society of America Annual Meeting 2015
Sponsor/Contact: Infectious Diseases Society of America
#300, 1300 Wilson Blvd.
Arlington, VA 22209
703-299-0200 *Fax:* 703-299-0204
E-mail: membership@idsociety.org
URL: www.idsociety.org
Scope: International

Infrastructure Health & Safety Association 2015 Annual General Meeting
Location: Ontario
Sponsor/Contact: Infrastructure Health & Safety Association
Centre for Health & Safety Innovation
#400, 5110 Creekbank Rd.
Mississauga, ON L4W 0A1
905-625-0100 *Fax:* 905-625-8998
Toll-Free: 800-263-5024
E-mail: info@ihsa.ca
URL: www.ihsa.ca
Scope: Provincial
Purpose: A business meeting featuring a guest speaker & the presentation of awards
Contact Information: E-mail: info@ihsa.ca

Institute of Food Technologists 2015 Annual Wellness Conference
Sponsor/Contact: Institute of Food Technologists
#1000, 525 West Van Buren
Chicago, IL 60607
312-782-8424 *Fax:* 312-782-8348
Toll-Free: 800-438-3663
E-mail: info@ift.org
URL: www.ift.org
Scope: International
Purpose: Informative presentations plus exhibits of interest to food industry professionals in product development, brand management, & marketing

Institute of Public Administration of Canada 2015 Annual Book Colloquium
Sponsor/Contact: Institute of Public Administration of Canada
#401, 1075 Bay St.
Toronto, ON M5S 2B1
416-924-8787 *Fax:* 416-924-4992
URL: www.ipac.ca
Scope: Provincial

Institute of Public Administration of Canada 2015 Annual General Meeting
Sponsor/Contact: Institute of Public Administration of Canada
#401, 1075 Bay St.
Toronto, ON M5S 2B1
416-924-8787 *Fax:* 416-924-4992
URL: www.ipac.ca
Scope: National
Purpose: A yearly business meeting, presenting reports from the national president, treasurer, & secretary

Insurance Brokers Association of Alberta Fall Conference 2015
Location: Alberta
Sponsor/Contact: Insurance Brokers Association of Alberta
3010 Calgary Trail NW
Edmonton, AB T6J 6V4
780-424-3320 *Fax:* 780-424-7418
Toll-Free: 800-318-0197
E-mail: ibaa@ibaa.ca
URL: www.ibaa.ca
Scope: Provincial

Insurance Brokers Association of British Columbia 67th Annual Conference & Trade Show
Location: British Columbia
Sponsor/Contact: Insurance Brokers Association of British Columbia
#1300, 1095 West Pender St.
Vancouver, BC V6E 2M6
604-606-8000 *Fax:* 604-683-7831
URL: www.ibabc.org
Scope: Provincial

International Academy of Energy, Minerals, & Materials 2015 International Conference on Mining, Material and Metallurgical Education
Sponsor/Contact: International Academy of Energy, Minerals, & Materials
Esprit Dr.
Ottawa, ON K4A 4Z1
613-322-1029 *Fax:* 613-830-8371
E-mail: info@iaemm.com
URL: iaemm.com
Scope: International

International Heavy Haul Association 2015 Specialist Technical Session
Location: Perth, Australia
Sponsor/Contact: International Heavy Haul Association
2808 Forest Hills Crt.
Virginia Beach, 23454-1236
URL: www.ihha.net
Scope: International
Purpose: A conference offered every four years to examine heavy haul operation issues. This year's tentative theme is "Operational Excellence."

International Personnel Management Association - Canada 2015 Leadership Summit
Sponsor/Contact: International Personnel Management Association - Canada
National Office
20 Edwards Pl.
Mount Pearl, NL A1N 3V5
Fax: 613-226-2298
Toll-Free: 888-226-5002
E-mail: national@ipma-aigp.ca
URL: ipma-aigp.ca
Scope: National

International Society for Rock Mechanics 13th International Congress on Rock Mechanics
Location: Montréal, QC
Sponsor/Contact: International Society for Rock Mechanics
c/o Laboratório Nacional de Engenharia Civil
101 Av. do Brasil
Lisbon, 1700-066
E-mail: secretariat.isrm@lnec.pt
URL: www.isrm.net
Scope: International

International Union of Microbiological Societies 2015 XV Congress
Sponsor/Contact: International Union of Microbiological Societies
Centralbureau voor Schimmelcultures
P.O. Box 85167
Utrecht, 3508AD
URL: www.iums.org
Scope: International
Purpose: Meetings of the three divisions of the International Union of Microbiological Societies

Kidney Foundation of Canada / Fondation canadienne du rein 2015 Kidney Care Conference
Sponsor/Contact: Kidney Foundation of Canada
#300, 5165, rue Sherbrooke ouest
Montréal, QC H4A 1T6
514-369-4806 *Fax:* 514-369-2472
Toll-Free: 800-361-7494
E-mail: info@kidney.ca
URL: www.kidney.ca
Scope: National
Contact Information: Kidney Care Coordinator: Molly Diamond, Phone: 780-451-6900, ext. 222, E-mail: molly.diamond@kidney.ab.ca

LIMRA and LOMA Canada 2015 Annual Conference
Sponsor/Contact: LOMA Canada
675 Cochrane Dr., East Tower, 6th Floor
Markham, ON L3R 0B8
905-530-2309 *Fax:* 905-530-2001
E-mail: lomacanada@loma.org
URL: www.loma.org/canada
Scope: National
Purpose: This full-day event connects corporate leaders with industry pundits and innovative thinkers to examine current challenges, share strategic insights and get cutting-edge solutions for an unpredictable business environment.
Contact Information: askloma@loma.org

Landscape NL Annual General Meeting 2015
Sponsor/Contact: Landscape Newfoundland & Labrador
P.O. Box 8062
St. John's, NL A1B 3M9
Fax: 866-833-8603
Toll-Free: 855-872-8722
E-mail: lnl@landscapenl.com
URL: members.landscapenl.com
Scope: Provincial

Law Society of Upper Canada / Barreau du Haut-Canada 2015 Annual General Meeting
Sponsor/Contact: Law Society of Upper Canada
Osgoode Hall
130 Queen St. West
Toronto, ON M5H 2N6
416-947-3300 *Fax:* 416-947-3924
Toll-Free: 800-668-7380
E-mail: lawsociety@lsuc.on.ca
URL: www.lsuc.on.ca
Scope: Provincial
Contact Information: E-mail: lawsociety@lsuc.on.ca

Law Union of Ontario 2015 Annual Conference
Location: Ontario
Sponsor/Contact: Law Union of Ontario
31 Prince Arthur Ave.
Toronto, ON M5R 1B2
416-927-9662 *Fax:* 416-960-5456
E-mail: law.union.of.ontario@gmail.com
URL: www.lawunion.ca
Scope: Provincial

Libertarian Party of Canada 2015 Convention
Sponsor/Contact: The Libertarian Party of Canada
#205, 372 Rideau St.
Ottawa, ON K1N 1G7
613-288-9089
E-mail: info@libertarian.ca
URL: www.libertarian.ca
Scope: National

Library Boards Association of Nova Scotia 2015 Annual Conference
Location: Nova Scotia
Sponsor/Contact: Library Boards Association of Nova Scotia
c/o Janet Ness, Secretary, Library Boards Association of Nova Scotia
53 Sherwood Dr.
Wolfville, NS B4P 2K5
902-542-7386
E-mail: janet_ness@hotmail.com
URL: www.standupforlibraries.ca
Scope: Provincial
Purpose: An annual autumn meeting for anyone with an interest in public libraries in Nova Scotia
Contact Information: Library Boards Association of Nova Scotia Executive Assistant: Christina Pottie, Email: cpottie@southshorepubliclibraries.ca

Licensed Practical Nurses Association of British Columbia 2015 Conference and AGM
Location: British Columbia
Sponsor/Contact: Licensed Practical Nurses Association of British Columbia
#211, 3030 Lincoln Ave.
Coquitlam, BC V3B 6B4
604-434-1972
E-mail: info@lpnabc.ca
URL: www.lpnabc.ca
Scope: Provincial

LifeCanada / VieCanada 2015 National Conference
Sponsor/Contact: LifeCanada
P.O. Box 500
Ottawa, ON K0A 3P0
613-722-1552 *Fax:* 613-482-4937
Toll-Free: 866-780-5433
E-mail: info@lifecanada.org
URL: www.lifecanada.org
Scope: National
Purpose: A 3-day national gathering of experts and pro-life professionals from across the country and abroad.

Living & Thriving with a Disability Conferences 2015
Sponsor/Contact: Ontario March of Dimes
10 Overlea Blvd.
Toronto, ON M4H 1A4
416-425-3463 *Fax:* 416-425-1920
Toll-Free: 800-263-3463
E-mail: info@marchofdimes.ca
URL: www.marchofdimes.ca
Scope: Provincial

Maintenance & Engineering Society of The Canadian Institute of Mining, Metallurgy & Petroleum 2015 Maintenance Engineering/Mine Operators' Conference
Sponsor/Contact: Maintenance, Engineering & Reliability (MER) Society
c/o Secretary, Marcel M. Djivre
2058 Latimer Cres.
Sudbury, ON P3E 5L6
705-621-1945
URL: www.cim.org
Scope: National
Purpose: A technical conference of interest to persons involved in maintenance & engineering in the mining industry

Manitoba Association for Volunteer Administration Biennial Conference 2015
Location: Manitoba
Sponsor/Contact: Manitoba Association for Volunteer Administration
P.O. Box 3099
Winnipeg, MB R3C 4B3
E-mail: MAVAmanitoba@gmail.com
URL: www.mavamanitoba.ca
Scope: Provincial

Manitoba Association of Medical Radiation Technologists 2015 Annual General Conference
Sponsor/Contact: Manitoba Association of Medical Radiation Technologists
#202, 819 Sargent Ave.
Winnipeg, MB R3E 0B9
204-774-5346 *Fax:* 204-774-5346
E-mail: admin@mamrt.ca
URL: www.mamrt.ca
Scope: Provincial
Purpose: A conference providing educational sessions, held each spring

Manitoba Conservation Districts Association 40th Annual Conservation Conference
Location: Manitoba
Sponsor/Contact: Manitoba Conservation Districts Association
#4, 940 Princess Ave.
Brandon, MB R7A 0P6
204-570-0164
E-mail: info@mcda.ca
URL: www.mcda.ca
Scope: Provincial

Manitoba Council for International Cooperation's Annual General Meeting 2015
Sponsor/Contact: Manitoba Council for International Cooperation
#302, 280 Smith St.
Winnipeg, MB R3C 1K2
204-987-6420 *Fax:* 204-956-0031
E-mail: info@mcic.ca
URL: www.mcic.ca
Scope: Provincial
Purpose: Featuring a panel discussion, nominations for the board, bylaw changes, & the presentation of the Global Citizenship Awards for graduating Grade 12 students & Educators.
Contact Information: Email: info@mcic.ca; Phone: 204-987-6420

Manitoba Environmental Industries Association Inc. 2015 Annual General Meeting
Location: Manitoba
Sponsor/Contact: Manitoba Environmental Industries Association Inc.
#100, 62 Albert St.
Winnipeg, MB R3B 1E9
204-783-7090 *Fax:* 204-783-6501
E-mail: admin@meia.mb.ca
URL: www.meia.mb.ca
Scope: Provincial
Purpose: A gathering of members to address the business of the association & to provide networking opportunities
Contact Information: Executive Director: Margo Shaw, Phone: 204-783-7090

Manitoba Environmental Industries Association Inc. 2015 Conference
Sponsor/Contact: Manitoba Environmental Industries Association Inc.
#100, 62 Albert St.
Winnipeg, MB R3B 1E9
204-783-7090 *Fax:* 204-783-6501
E-mail: admin@meia.mb.ca
URL: www.meia.mb.ca
Scope: Provincial
Purpose: An annual one day conference to inform participants about recent environmental legislation & regulatory affairs at the provincial & federal levels
Contact Information: Coordinator, Education & Training: Rosemary Deans, Phone: 204-783-7090

Manitoba Home Builders' Association 2015 14th Annual Kitchen, Bath, & Renovation Show
Sponsor/Contact: Manitoba Home Builders' Association
#1, 1420 Clarence Ave.
Winnipeg, MB R3T 1T6
204-925-2560 *Fax:* 204-925-2567
E-mail: info@homebuilders.mb.ca
URL: www.homebuilders.mb.ca
Scope: Provincial
Purpose: A showcase of products & services, where appointments can be made with members of the Manitoba Home Builders' Association's Renovation Council to learn solutions to renovation dilemmas

Manitoba Home Builders' Association 2015 41th Annual Home Expressions Home & Garden Show
Sponsor/Contact: Manitoba Home Builders' Association
#1, 1420 Clarence Ave.
Winnipeg, MB R3T 1T6
204-925-2560 *Fax:* 204-925-2567
E-mail: info@homebuilders.mb.ca
URL: www.homebuilders.mb.ca
Scope: Provincial
Purpose: A consumer show owned & managed by the Manitoba Home Builders' Association

Manitoba Home Builders' Association 2015 Spring Parade of Homes
Sponsor/Contact: Manitoba Home Builders' Association
#1, 1420 Clarence Ave.
Winnipeg, MB R3T 1T6
204-925-2560 *Fax:* 204-925-2567
E-mail: info@homebuilders.mb.ca
URL: www.homebuilders.mb.ca
Scope: Provincial

Manitoba Hotel Association 2015 Annual General Meeting, Convention, & Tradeshow
Location: Manitoba
Sponsor/Contact: Manitoba Hotel Association
#200, 1534 Gamble Pl.
Winnipeg, MB
204-942-0671 *Fax:* 204-942-6719
Toll-Free: 888-859-9976
URL: www.manitobahotelassociation.ca
Scope: Provincial
Purpose: Presentations from government ministers, educational speakers, & others from the hospitality industry
Contact Information: Phone: 204-942-0671; Fax: 204-942-6719

Manitoba Institute of Agrologists 2015 65th Annual General Meeting & Professional Development Event
Location: Manitoba
Sponsor/Contact: Manitoba Institute of Agrologists
#201, 38 Dafoe Ave.
Winnipeg, MB R3T 2N2
204-275-3721 *Fax:* 888-315-6661
E-mail: mia@mts.net
URL: www.mia.mb.ca
Scope: Provincial
Purpose: The business meeting of the institute, plus presentations & networking opportunities

Manitoba Library Association 2015 Annual General Meeting
Location: Manitoba
Sponsor/Contact: Manitoba Library Association
#606, 100 Arthur St.
Winnipeg, MB R3B 1H3
204-943-4567 *Fax:* 866-202-4567
E-mail: manitobalibrary@gmail.com
URL: www.mla.mb.ca
Scope: Provincial
Purpose: A meeting of association members held each year between March 1st & May 31st, featuring reports from the president, treasurer, & each person chairing a standing or ad hoc committee established by the executive committee. Theme: Unlimited Potential
Contact Information: Co-Chair MLC Program Committee: Sarah Clark, Email: Sarah.Clark@umanitoba.ca

Manitoba Ozone Protection Industry Association 2015 22nd Annual General Meeting
Location: Winnipeg, MB
Sponsor/Contact: Manitoba Ozone Protection Industry Association
1980B Main St.
Winnipeg, MB R2V 2B6
204-338-0804 *Fax:* 204-338-0810
Toll-Free: 888-667-4203
E-mail: mopia@mts.net
URL: www.mopia.ca
Scope: Provincial
Purpose: The presentation of the annual report, featuring financial & executive reports

Manitoba Physical Education Teachers Association 2015 SAGE Conference
Location: Manitoba
Sponsor/Contact: Manitoba Physical Education Teachers Association
c/o Sport for Life Centre
#319, 145 Pacific Ave.
Winnipeg, MB R3B 2Z6
204-926-8357 *Fax:* 204-925-5703
E-mail: mpeta@sportmanitoba.ca
URL: mpeta.ca
Scope: Provincial

Manitoba Professional Planners Institute 2015 Annual General Meeting
Sponsor/Contact: Manitoba Professional Planners Institute
137 Bannatyne Ave., 2nd Fl.
Winnipeg, MB R3B 0R3
204-943-3637 *Fax:* 204-925-4624
E-mail: mppiadmin@shaw.ca
URL: www.mppi.mb.ca
Scope: Provincial

Manitoba School Library Association SAGE Conference: 2015 - Canadian Literature
Location: Manitoba
Sponsor/Contact: Manitoba School Library Association
c/o Claudia Klausen, Emerson Elementary School
323 Emerson Ave.
Winnipeg, MB R2G 1V3
URL: www.manitobaschoollibraries.com
Scope: Provincial
Purpose: A business meeting for school librarians from Manitoba
Contact Information: President, E-mail: mslapresident@gmail.com

Manitoba Society of Artists 2015 83rd Provincial Annual Open Juried Competition & Exhibition
Location: Manitoba
Sponsor/Contact: Manitoba Society of Artists
c/o Luba Olesky
2018 Henderson Hwy.
Winnipeg, MB R2G 1P2
URL: www.mbsa.ca
Scope: Provincial
Purpose: A major exhibition & the presentation of awards for both professional & amateur artists
Contact Information: Chairs, Juried Exhibition: Pat McCullough & Bonnie Taylor

Manitoba Society of Artists 2015 Art History Conference & Annual General Meeting
Location: Manitoba
Sponsor/Contact: Manitoba Society of Artists
c/o Luba Olesky
2018 Henderson Hwy.
Winnipeg, MB R2G 1P2
URL: www.mbsa.ca
Scope: Provincial
Contact Information: E-mail: president@mbsa.ca

Manitoba Speech & Hearing Association 2015 Annual Conference
Sponsor/Contact: Manitoba Speech & Hearing Association
#2, 333 Vaughan St.
Winnipeg, MB R3B 3J9
204-453-4539 *Fax:* 204-477-1881
E-mail: office@msha.ca
URL: www.msha.ca
Scope: Provincial
Purpose: A continuing education event, with speaker & poster presentations, & exhibits, as well as networking & social activities
Contact Information: E-mail: office@msha.ca

Manitoba Teachers' Society 2015 Annual General Meeting
Location: Manitoba
Sponsor/Contact: Manitoba Teachers' Society
McMaster House
191 Harcourt St.
Winnipeg, MB R3J 3H2
204-888-7961 *Fax:* 204-831-0877
Toll-Free: 800-262-8803
URL: www.mbteach.org
Scope: Provincial

Marine Renewables Canada 2015 Annual Conference
Sponsor/Contact: Marine Renewables Canada
121 Bird Sanctuary Dr.
Nanaimo, BC V9R 6H1
URL: www.marinerenewables.ca
Scope: National
Purpose: Multiple networking opportunities to meet leaders and experts from business, government, and academia that will help build connections and support emerging industry needs.

Maritech 2015
Sponsor/Contact: Prince Edward Island Society for Medical Laboratory Science
P.O. Box 20061 Stn. Sherwood
161 St. Peters Rd.
Charlottetown, PE C1A 9E3
URL: peismls.com
Scope: Provincial

Medical Council of Canada's 2015 Annual General Meeting
Sponsor/Contact: Medical Council of Canada
P.O. Box 8234 Stn. T
#100, 2283 St. Laurent Blvd.
Ottawa, ON K1G 3H7
613-521-6012 *Fax:* 613-521-9509
E-mail: MCC_Admin@mcc.ca
URL: www.mcc.ca
Scope: National

Municipal Equipment & Operations Association (Ontario) Inc. 2015 Annual Municipal & Contractor Fall Equipment Show
Sponsor/Contact: Municipal Equipment & Operations Association (Ontario) Inc.
38 Summit Ave.
Kitchener, ON N2M 4W2
519-741-2600 *Fax:* 519-741-2750
E-mail: admin@meoa.org
URL: www.meoa.org
Scope: Provincial
Purpose: An opportunity for suppliers to promote & demonstrate their products & services

Municipal Waste Association 2015 Annual General Meeting
Location: Ontario
Sponsor/Contact: Municipal Waste Association
#100, 127 Wyndham St. North
Guelph, ON N1H 4E9
519-823-1990 *Fax:* 519-823-0084
E-mail: carrie@municipalwaste.ca
URL: www.municipalwaste.ca
Scope: Provincial
Purpose: A yearly event featuring a business meeting, trade show, & networking opportunities
Contact Information: Executive Director: Ben Bennett, E-mail: ben@municipalwaste.ca

National Association for Environmental Management 2015 23rd Annual EHS Management Forum
Sponsor/Contact: National Association for Environmental Management
#1002, 1612 K St. NW
Washington, DC 20006
202-986-6616 *Fax:* 202-530-4408
Toll-Free: 800-391-6236
E-mail: programs@naem.org
URL: www.naem.org
Scope: International
Purpose: Environmental, health & safety, & sustainability practitioners gain the opportunity to exchange ideas, participate in interactive sessions, & hear timely keynote presentations
Anticipated Attendance: 500+
Contact Information: E-mail: programs@naem.org

National Association for Environmental Management 2015 Conference: Metrics and Materiality for EHS and Sustainability Reporting
Sponsor/Contact: National Association for Environmental Management
#1002, 1612 K St. NW
Washington, DC 20006
202-986-6616 *Fax:* 202-530-4408
Toll-Free: 800-391-6236
E-mail: programs@naem.org
URL: www.naem.org
Scope: International
Purpose: An international gathering of environmental, health & safety, & sustainability practitioners, with opportunities for benchmarking, best-practice sharing, & networking
Contact Information: E-mail: programs@naem.org

National Environmental Health Association 2015 79th Annual Conference & Exhibition
Sponsor/Contact: National Environmental Health Association
#1000N, 720 South Colorado Blvd.
Denver, CO 80246
303-756-9090 *Fax:* 303-691-9490
Toll-Free: 866-956-2258
E-mail: staff@neha.org
URL: www.neha.org
Scope: International
Contact Information: Toll-Free Phone: 866-956-2258; Fax: 303-691-9490; E-mail: staff@neha.org

National Home Inspectors' 2015 22nd Annual National Conference
Sponsor/Contact: Canadian Association of Home & Property Inspectors
P.O. Box 13715
Ottawa, ON K2K 1X6
Fax: 866-876-9877
Toll-Free: 888-748-2244
E-mail: info@cahpi.ca
URL: www.cahpi.ca
Scope: National
Contact Information: Conference Chair: Terry Gordon, E-mail: tegordon@ns.sympatico.ca

Natural Step Canada Accelerate: Collaborating for Sustainability Conference 2015
Sponsor/Contact: Natural Step Canada
#203, 4 Florence St.
Ottawa, ON K2P 0W7
613-748-3001 *Fax:* 613-748-1649
E-mail: info@naturalstep.ca
URL: www.naturalstep.ca

Scope: National

Nature Canada 2015 Annual General Meeting
Sponsor/Contact: Nature Canada
#300, 75 Albert St.
Ottawa, ON K1P 5E7
613-562-3447 *Fax:* 613-562-3371
Toll-Free: 800-267-4088
E-mail: info@naturecanada.ca
URL: www.naturecanada.ca
Scope: National
Purpose: The annual meeting usually features the election of the Board of Directors, the presentation of Nature Canada awards, & the adoption of resolutions
Contact Information: Nature Canada Executive Assistant & Office Manager: Sue Robertson, E-mail: srobertson@naturecanada.ca

Nature Manitoba 2015 Annual General Meeting
Location: Franco-Manitoban Cultural Centre
Winnipeg, MB
Sponsor/Contact: Nature Manitoba
Hammond Building
#401, 63 Albert St.
Winnipeg, MB R3B 1G4
204-943-9029 *Fax:* 204-943-9029
E-mail: info@naturemanitoba.ca
URL: www.naturemanitoba.ca
Scope: Provincial
Purpose: An opportunity for Nature Manitoba members to discuss & advance policy positions about nature in Manitoba
Contact Information: E-mail: info@naturemanitoba.ca

Nature Nova Scotia 2015 Annual General Meeting & Conference
Location: Nova Scotia
Sponsor/Contact: Nature Nova Scotia (Federation of Nova Scotia Naturalists)
c/o Nova Scotia Museum of Natural History
1747 Summer St.
Halifax, NS B3H 3A6
902-582-7176
E-mail: doug@fundymud.com
URL: www.naturens.ca
Scope: Provincial
Purpose: A weekend event, with an annual meeting featuring reports on the past year's activities to the membership, plus educational talks & field trips
Contact Information: Treasurer: Jean Gibson Collins, Phone: 902-678-4725, E-mail: ejgibson@ns.sympatico.ca

New Brunswick Environmental Network 2015 Annual General Meeting
Location: New Brunswick
Sponsor/Contact: New Brunswick Environmental Network
167 Creek Rd.
Waterford, NB E4E 4L7
506-433-6101 *Fax:* 506-433-6111
E-mail: nben@nben.ca
URL: www.nben.ca
Scope: Provincial
Purpose: Featuring the election of a Steering Committee by member groups
Contact Information: E-mail: nben@nben.ca

New Brunswick Federation of Labour Education Conference
Location: New Brunswick
Sponsor/Contact: New Brunswick Federation of Labour
#314, 96 Norwood Ave.
Moncton, NB E1C 6L9
506-857-2125 *Fax:* 506-383-1597
E-mail: nbfl@nbnet.nb.ca
URL: www.nbfl-fttnb.ca
Scope: Provincial
Contact Information: New Brunswick Federation of Labour, E-mail: nbfl_fttnb@bellaliant.com

New Brunswick Institute of Agrologists 2015 Annual General Meeting
Location: New Brunswick
Sponsor/Contact: New Brunswick Institute of Agrologists
P.O. Box 3479 Stn. B
Fredericton, NB E3B 5H2
506-459-5536 *Fax:* 506-454-7837
URL: www.ianbia.com
Scope: Provincial

New Westminster & District Labour Council 2015 Annual General Meeting
Location: British Columbia
Sponsor/Contact: New Westminster & District Labour Council
#105, 3920 Norland Ave.
Burnaby, BC V5G 4K7
604-291-9306 *Fax:* 604-291-0996
E-mail: nwdlc@shawcable.com
URL: www.nwdlc.ca
Scope: Local

Newfoundland & Labrador Association of Medical Radiation Technologists 2015 64th Annual Provincial Conference
Location: Newfoundland & Labrador
Sponsor/Contact: Newfoundland & Labrador Association of Medical Radiation Technologists
P.O. Box 29141 Stn. Torbay Rd. Post Office
St. John's, NL A1A 5B5
709-777-6036
E-mail: association@nlamrt.ca
URL: www.nlamrt.ca
Scope: Provincial

Newfoundland & Labrador Construction Association 2015 Annual Awards Gala
Sponsor/Contact: Newfoundland & Labrador Construction Association
#201, 333 Pippy Pl.
St. John's, NL A1B 3X2
709-753-8920 *Fax:* 709-754-3968
E-mail: info@nfld.com
URL: www.nlca.ca
Scope: Provincial
Purpose: An awards presentation to honour industry professionals, featuring a keynote address to delegates
Contact Information: Coordinator, Events Coordinator: Adelle Connors, Phone: 709-753-8920, E-mail: aconnors@nlca.ca

Newfoundland & Labrador Library Association Annual Conference & Annual General Meeting 2015
Location: Newfoundland & Labrador
Sponsor/Contact: Newfoundland & Labrador Library Association
PO Box 23192, RPO Churchill Sq.
St. John's, NL A1B 4J9
E-mail: secretary@nlla.ca
URL: www.nlla.ca
Scope: Provincial
Purpose: An annual spring meeting, presenting opportunities to learn about new services, current issues, & research in Newfoundland & Labrabor libraries

Nova Scotia Association of Medical Radiation Technologists 2015 75th Annual General Conference & Annual General Meeting
Location: Nova Scotia
Sponsor/Contact: Nova Scotia Association of Medical Radiation Technologists
P.O. Box 9410 Stn. A
Halifax, NS B3k 5S3
902-434-6525 *Fax:* 902-425-2441
Toll-Free: 866-788-6525
E-mail: info@nsamrt.ca
URL: www.nsamrt.ca
Scope: Provincial
Purpose: A gathering of association members held each spring, consisting of educational presentations, exhibitor booth viewing, a business meeting, & networking events
Contact Information: E-mail: info@nsamrt.ca

Nova Scotia Association of Medical Radiation Technologists 2015 Annual Fall Education Seminar
Location: Nova Scotia
Sponsor/Contact: Nova Scotia Association of Medical Radiation Technologists
P.O. Box 9410 Stn. A
Halifax, NS B3k 5S3
902-434-6525 *Fax:* 902-425-2441
Toll-Free: 866-788-6525
E-mail: info@nsamrt.ca
URL: www.nsamrt.ca
Scope: Provincial
Purpose: Held the weekend before Medical Radiation Technologists Week, the annual continuing education meeting consists of talks related to the disciplines of radiation therapy, nuclear medicine, & radiological technology, as well as a keynote address related to all medical radiation technology disciplines
Contact Information: Education Committee Chair: Ryan Duggan

Nova Scotia Automobile Dealers' Association 2015 Annual General Meeting, Automotive Conference, & President's Dinner
Location: Nova Scotia
Sponsor/Contact: Nova Scotia Automobile Dealers' Association
#700, 6009 Quinpool Rd.
Halifax, NS B3K 5S3
902-425-2445 *Fax:* 902-425-2441
E-mail: info@nsada.ca
URL: www.nsada.ca
Scope: National
Purpose: An event for association members from across Nova Scotia
Contact Information: E-mail: info@nsada.ca

Nova Scotia Library Association 2015 Annual Conference
Location: Nova Scotia
Sponsor/Contact: Nova Scotia Library Association
c/o Kelli WooShue, Halifax Public Libraries
60 Alderney Dr.
Dartmouth, NS B2Y 4P8
902-490-5710
E-mail: wooshuk@halifax.ca
URL: www.nsla.ns.ca
Scope: Provincial
Purpose: Hosted by Halifax Public Libraries in the autumn
Contact Information: E-mail: conference@nsla.ns.ca

Nurse Practitioners' Association of Ontario Annual Conference 2015
Location: Ontario
Sponsor/Contact: Nurse Practitioners' Association of Ontario
#1801, 1 Yonge St.
Toronto, ON M5E 1W7
416-593-9779 *Fax:* 416-369-0515
E-mail: admin@npao.org
URL: www.npao.org
Scope: Provincial

OMEA/CMIEC Soundscapes 2015
Location: Ontario
Sponsor/Contact: Ontario Music Educators' Association
URL: www.omea.on.ca
Scope: Provincial

Oil Sands and Heavy Oil Technologies Conference & Exhibition 2015
Sponsor/Contact: Canadian Crude Quality Technical Association
URL: www.ccqta.com
Scope: National
Purpose: Forum for oil sands innovation.
Contact Information: Gail Killough, Conference Manager, gailk@pennwell.com; Phone: 713-963-6251; Website: www.oilsandstechnologies.com; Twitter: twitter.com/ogjevents; Email: registration@pennwell.com

Older Adult Centres' Association of Ontario Annual Conference 2015
Location: Ontario
Sponsor/Contact: Older Adult Centres' Association of Ontario
P.O. Box 65
Caledon East, ON L7C 3L8
905-584-8125 *Fax:* 905-584-8126
Toll-Free: 866-835-7693
E-mail: sue@oacao.org
URL: www.oacao.org
Scope: Provincial

Ontario Art Education Association 2015 Annual Conference
Sponsor/Contact: Ontario Art Education Association
E-mail: membership@OAEA.ca
URL: www.oaea.ca
Scope: Provincial

Ontario Association for Behaviour Analysis Annual Conference 2015
Location: Ontario
Sponsor/Contact: Ontario Association for Behaviour Analysis
#413, 283 Danforth Ave.
Toronto, ON M4K 1N2
E-mail: contact@ontaba.org
URL: www.ontaba.org
Scope: Provincial

Ontario Association for Family Mediation Annual AGM & Conference 2015
Location: Ontario
Sponsor/Contact: Ontario Association for Family Mediation
P.O. Box 102
Almonte, ON K0A 1A0
416-740-6236 *Fax:* 866-352-1579
Toll-Free: 800-989-3025
URL: www.oafm.on.ca

Conferences Index

Scope: Provincial
Contact Information: Phone: 416-740-6236

Ontario Association for Geographic & Environmental Education Fall Conference 2015
Sponsor/Contact: Ontario Association for Geographic & Environmental Education
#202, 10 Morrow Ave.
Toronto, ON M6R 2J1
416-538-1650 *Fax:* 416-489-1713
URL: www.oagee.org
Scope: Provincial

Ontario Association for Geographic & Environmental Education Spring Conference 2015
Sponsor/Contact: Ontario Association for Geographic & Environmental Education
#202, 10 Morrow Ave.
Toronto, ON M6R 2J1
416-538-1650 *Fax:* 416-489-1713
URL: www.oagee.org
Scope: Provincial

Ontario Association of Broadcasters 2015 Annual General Meeting
Location: Ontario
Sponsor/Contact: Ontario Association of Broadcasters
P.O. Box 54040
5762 Hwy. 7 East
Markham, ON L3P 7Y4
905-554-2730 *Fax:* 905-554-2731
URL: www.oab.ca
Scope: Provincial

Ontario Association of Child & Youth Counsellors 2015 Conference
Location: Ontario
Sponsor/Contact: Ontario Association of Child & Youth Counsellors
#111, 290 North Queen St.
Toronto, ON M9C 5L2
E-mail: office@oacyc.org
URL: www.oacyc.org
Scope: Provincial

Ontario Association of Library Technicians / Association des bibliotechniciens de l'Ontario 2015 42nd Annual Conference
Location: Ontario
Sponsor/Contact: Ontario Association of Library Technicians
Abbey Market
P.O. Box 76010
1500 Upper Middle Rd. West
Oakville, ON L6M 3H5
E-mail: info@oaltabo.on.ca
URL: oaltabo.on.ca
Scope: Provincial
Purpose: Featuring educational sessions, speeches, the annual business meeting, & award presentations
Contact Information: Ontario Association of Library Technicians External Communications Coordinator: Dana Schwarz; Internal Communications Coordinator: Serena McGovern, E-mail: info@oaltabo.on.ca

Ontario Association of Medical Radiation Sciences 2015 Annual General Conference
Sponsor/Contact: Ontario Association of Medical Radiation Sciences
P.O. Box 1054 Stn. Main
#101, 233 Colborne St.
Brantford, ON N3T 5S7
519-753-6037 *Fax:* 519-753-6408
Toll-Free: 800-387-4674
E-mail: mbrshpcoord@oamrs.org
URL: www.oamrs.org
Scope: Provincial
Contact Information: Contact, Professional Services: Dana Steane, steaned@oamrs.org

Ontario Association of Naturopathic Doctors 2015 Convention & Tradeshow
Location: Ontario
Sponsor/Contact: Ontario Association of Naturopathic Doctors
#603, 789 Don Mills Rd.
Toronto, ON M3C 1T5
416-233-2001 *Fax:* 416-233-2924
Toll-Free: 877-628-7284
E-mail: info@oand.org
URL: www.oand.org
Scope: Provincial

Ontario Association of Radiology Managers 2015 Annual Fall Conference
Location: Ontario
Sponsor/Contact: Ontario Association of Radiology Managers
26 Gateway Crt.
Whitby, ON L1R 3M9
905-655-5645
E-mail: headoffice@oarm.org
URL: www.oarm.org
Scope: Provincial

Ontario College & University Library Association 2015 Annual General Meeting
Sponsor/Contact: Ontario College & University Library Association
c/o Ontario Library Association
2 Toronto St., 3rd Fl.
Toronto, ON M5C 2B6
416-363-3388 *Fax:* 416-941-9581
E-mail: info@accessola.com
URL: www.accessola.com/ocula/
Scope: Provincial
Purpose: OCULA's Annual General Meetings are held during the Ontario Library Association Superconference, usually in January or February of each year.

Ontario Community Newspapers Association 2015 Annual Spring Convention
Location: Ontario
Sponsor/Contact: Ontario Community Newspapers Association
#116, 3228 South Service Rd.
Burlington, ON L7N 3H8
905-639-8720 *Fax:* 905-639-6962
URL: www.ocna.org
Scope: Provincial
Purpose: A gathering of newspaper professionals & youth from throughout Ontario, featuring the Ontario Community Newspapers Association's Supplier Showcase

Ontario Energy Association 2015 Annual Conference & Annual General Meeting
Location: Ontario
Sponsor/Contact: Ontario Energy Association
#202, 121 Richmond St. West
Toronto, ON M5H 2K1
416-961-2339 *Fax:* 416-961-1173
E-mail: oea@energyontario.ca
URL: www.energyontario.ca
Scope: Provincial
Purpose: Examples of programming includes panel sessions, the presentation of awards, information sharing opportunities, & social events
Contact Information: Phone: 416-961-2339; E-mail: events@energyontario.ca

Ontario English Catholic Teachers' Association 2015 Beginning Teachers Conference
Location: Ontario
Sponsor/Contact: Ontario English Catholic Teachers' Association (CLC)
#400, 65 St. Clair Ave. East
Toronto, ON M4T 2Y8
416-925-2493 *Fax:* 416-925-7764
Toll-Free: 800-268-7230
E-mail: membership@oecta.on.ca
URL: www.oecta.on.ca
Scope: Provincial
Purpose: A conference for all Ontario English Catholic Teachers' Association members in their first five years of teaching
Contact Information: Ontario English Catholic Teachers' Association Office, Phone: 416-925-2493

Ontario English Catholic Teachers' Association 2015 GSN Seminar
Location: Ontario
Sponsor/Contact: Ontario English Catholic Teachers' Association (CLC)
#400, 65 St. Clair Ave. East
Toronto, ON M4T 2Y8
416-925-2493 *Fax:* 416-925-7764
Toll-Free: 800-268-7230
E-mail: membership@oecta.on.ca
URL: www.oecta.on.ca
Scope: Provincial
Contact Information: Ontario English Catholic Teachers' Association Office, Phone: 416-925-2493

Ontario English Catholic Teachers' Association 2015 Leadership Training Program
Location: Ontario
Sponsor/Contact: Ontario English Catholic Teachers' Association (CLC)
#400, 65 St. Clair Ave. East
Toronto, ON M4T 2Y8
416-925-2493 *Fax:* 416-925-7764
Toll-Free: 800-268-7230
E-mail: membership@oecta.on.ca
URL: www.oecta.on.ca
Scope: Provincial
Purpose: A workshop for association members
Contact Information: Ontario English Catholic Teachers' Association Office, Phone: 416-925-2493

Ontario Environment Network Conference & AGM 2015
Sponsor/Contact: Ontario Environmental Network
P.O. Box 1412 Stn. Main
North Bay, ON P1B 8K6
705-840-2888
E-mail: oen@oen.ca
URL: www.oen.ca
Scope: Provincial

Ontario Federation of Agriculture 2015 79th Annual Convention
Sponsor/Contact: Ontario Federation of Agriculture
Ontario AgriCentre
#206, 100 Stone Rd. West
London, ON N1G 5L3
519-821-8883 *Fax:* 519-821-8810
Toll-Free: 800-668-3276
E-mail: info@ofa.on.ca
URL: www.ofa.on.ca
Scope: Provincial
Contact Information: Ag Business Centre, Phone: 519-674-1500 ext. 63596, Toll-Free: 1-866-222-9682

Ontario Federation of Anglers & Hunters 2015 87th Annual General Meeting & Fish & Wildlife Conference
Location: Ontario
Sponsor/Contact: Ontario Federation of Anglers & Hunters
P.O. Box 2800
4601 Guthrie Dr.
Peterborough, ON K9J 8L5
705-748-6324 *Fax:* 705-748-9577
E-mail: ofah@ofah.org
URL: www.ofah.org
Scope: Provincial
Purpose: Presentations for anglers & hunters in Ontario
Contact Information: Communications Manager: Lezlie Goodwin, Phone: 705-748-6324, ext. 270

Ontario Federation of Anglers & Hunters 2015 Annual Get Outdoors Youth Leadership Conference
Location: Ontario
Sponsor/Contact: Ontario Federation of Anglers & Hunters
P.O. Box 2800
4601 Guthrie Dr.
Peterborough, ON K9J 8L5
705-748-6324 *Fax:* 705-748-9577
E-mail: ofah@ofah.org
URL: www.ofah.org
Scope: Provincial
Purpose: An opportunity for young people to participate in activities to promote interest in outdoor activities, hunting, & fishing
Contact Information: Communications Manager: Lezlie Goodwin, Phone: 705-748-6324, ext. 270

Ontario Food Protection Association (OFPA) Fall Meeting 2015
Location: Ontario
Sponsor/Contact: Ontario Food Protection Association
P.O. Box 51575
2140A Queen St. East
Toronto, ON M4E 1C0
519-265-4119 *Fax:* 416-981-3368
E-mail: info@ofpa.on.ca
URL: www.ofpa.on.ca
Scope: Provincial

Ontario Food Protection Association (OFPA) Spring Meeting 2015
Location: Ontario
Sponsor/Contact: Ontario Food Protection Association
P.O. Box 51575
2140A Queen St. East
Toronto, ON M4E 1C0
519-265-4119 *Fax:* 416-981-3368
E-mail: info@ofpa.on.ca
URL: www.ofpa.on.ca
Scope: Provincial

Ontario Gang Investigators Association 2015 Conference
Location: Ontario
Sponsor/Contact: Ontario Gang Investigators Association
P.O. Box 57085 Stn. Jackson Square
Hamilton, ON L8P 4W9
URL: ongia.org
Scope: Provincial

Ontario Geothermal Association's 2015 Conference
Location: Ontario
Sponsor/Contact: Ontario Geothermal Association
#201, 2800 Skymark Ave.
Mississauga, ON L4W 5A6
905-602-4700 *Fax:* 905-602-1197
Toll-Free: 800-267-2231
URL: www.ontariogeothermal.ca
Scope: Provincial
Contact Information: Heather Grimoldby-Campbell; Email: hgrimoldby@hrai.ca

Ontario Ground Water Association 62nd Annual Convention & Trade Show 2015
Sponsor/Contact: Ontario Ground Water Association
48 Front St. East
Strathroy, ON N7G 1Y6
519-245-7194 *Fax:* 519-245-7196
URL: www.ogwa.ca
Scope: Provincial
Purpose: Meetings, seminars, networking opportunities, & a social program

Ontario Home Builders' Association Conference 2015
Location: Ontario
Sponsor/Contact: Ontario Home Builders Association
#101, 20 Upjohn Rd.
Toronto, ON M3B 2V9
416-443-1545 *Fax:* 416-443-9982
Toll-Free: 800-387-0109
URL: www.ohba.ca
Scope: Provincial

Ontario Lacrosse Association 2015 Annual General Meeting
Location: Ontario
Sponsor/Contact: Ontario Lacrosse Association
#306, 3 Concorde Gate
Toronto, ON M3C 3N7
416-426-7066 *Fax:* 416-426-7382
URL: www.ontariolacrosse.com
Scope: Provincial

Ontario Minor Hockey Association 2015 Annual General Meeting & Hometown Hockey Consumer Show
Location: Ontario
Sponsor/Contact: Ontario Minor Hockey Association
#3, 25 Brodie Dr.
Richmond Hill, ON L4B 3K7
905-780-6642 *Fax:* 905-780-0344
E-mail: omha@omha.net
URL: www.omha.net
Scope: Provincial
Purpose: Addressing the business of the association, plus revisions to regulations, policies, & procedures for the upcoming season
Contact Information: Contact: Daniel Clement, Phone: 905-780-6642, ext. 247

Ontario Municipal Social Services Association 2015 Policy and Research Conference
Location: Ontario
Sponsor/Contact: Ontario Municipal Social Services Association
#2500, 1 Dundas St West
Toronto, ON M5G 1Z3
416-642-1659 *Fax:* 416-979-4627
E-mail: info@omssa.com
URL: www.omssa.com
Scope: Provincial

Ontario Professional Fire Fighters Association 2015 18th Annual Convention
Sponsor/Contact: Ontario Professional Fire Fighters Association
292 Plains Rd. East
Burlington, ON L7T 2C6
905-681-7111 *Fax:* 905-681-1489
URL: www.opffa.org
Scope: Provincial

Ontario Professional Fire Fighters Association 2015 Annual Legislative Conference
Location: Ontario
Sponsor/Contact: Ontario Professional Fire Fighters Association
292 Plains Rd. East
Burlington, ON L7T 2C6
905-681-7111 *Fax:* 905-681-1489
URL: www.opffa.org
Scope: Provincial
Purpose: An opportunity for representatives from across Ontario to meet with Members of Provincial Parliament to advocate issues of concern

Ontario Professional Planners Institute 2015 Conference
Sponsor/Contact: Ontario Professional Planners Institute
#201, 234 Eglinton Ave. East
Toronto, ON M4P 1K5
416-483-1873 *Fax:* 416-483-7830
Toll-Free: 800-668-1448
E-mail: info@ontarioplanners.on.ca
URL: www.ontarioplanners.on.ca
Scope: Provincial

Ontario Public Health Association 2015 Annual Conference & General Meeting
Sponsor/Contact: Ontario Public Health Association
#1850, 439 University Ave.
Toronto, ON M5G 1Y8
416-367-3313 *Fax:* 416-367-2844
Toll-Free: 800-267-6817
E-mail: info@opha.on.ca
URL: www.opha.on.ca
Scope: Provincial
Purpose: A review of association bylaws, presentation of the annual report, & the appointment of the Board of Directors

Ontario Rett Syndrome Association 2015 Conference
Location: Ontario
Sponsor/Contact: Ontario Rett Syndrome Association
P.O. Box 50030
London, ON N6A 6H8
519-474-6877 *Fax:* 519-850-1272
URL: www.rett.ca
Scope: Provincial

Ontario Society of Occupational Therapists Conference 2015
Sponsor/Contact: Ontario Society of Occupational Therapists
#210, 55 Eglinton Ave. East
Toronto, ON M4P 1G8
416-322-3011 *Fax:* 416-322-6705
Toll-Free: 877-676-6768
E-mail: osot@osot.on.ca
URL: www.osot.on.ca
Scope: Provincial

Ontario Soil & Crop Improvement Association 2015 Provincial Annual Meeting
Location: Ontario
Sponsor/Contact: Ontario Soil & Crop Improvement Association
1 Stone Rd. West
Guelph, ON N1G 4Y2
519-826-4214 *Fax:* 519-826-4224
Toll-Free: 800-265-9751
E-mail: oscia@ontariosoilcrop.org
URL: www.ontariosoilcrop.org
Scope: Provincial
Purpose: An opportunity for farmers & persons involved in agriculture in Ontario to bring local views to give direction to the association
Contact Information: & Conference Centre Improvement Association, E-mail: oscia@ontariosoilcrop.org

Ontario Sustainable Energy Association 2015 Annual All-Energy Canada Exhibition & Conference
Sponsor/Contact: Ontario Sustainable Energy Association
#400, 215 Spadina Ave.
Toronto, ON M5T 2C7
416-977-4441 *Fax:* 416-644-0116
E-mail: info@ontario-sea.org
URL: www.ontario-sea.org
Scope: Provincial
Contact Information: Executive Director: Kristopher Stevens, E-mail: kristopher@ontario-sea.org

Ontario Trails Council 2015 Trailhead Ontario
Location: Ontario
Sponsor/Contact: Ontario Trails Council
P.O. Box 500
Deseronto, ON K0K 1X0
E-mail: ontrails@gmail.com
URL: www.ontariotrails.on.ca
Scope: Provincial
Purpose: An event in Oxford County, Ontario for participants to discuss Ontario's trails, development, policy, & tourism, & to view displays
Contact Information: Web Site: trailheadontario.com; Facebook: www.facebook.com/TrailheadOntario; Twitter: twitter.com/trailheadon; E-mail: ontrails@gmail.com

Ordre des arpenteurs-géomètres du Québec 47e Congrès
Location: Quebec
Sponsor/Contact: Ordre des arpenteurs-géomètres du Québec
Iberville Quatre
#350, 2954, boul Laurier
Québec, QC G1V 4T2
418-656-0730 *Fax:* 418-656-6352
E-mail: oagq@oagq.qc.ca
URL: www.oagq.qc.ca
Scope: Provincial

Ottawa Chamber of Commerce 2015 Annual General Meeting
Location: Ottawa, ON
Sponsor/Contact: Ottawa Chamber of Commerce
328 Somerset St. West
Ottawa, ON K2P 0J9
613-236-3631 *Fax:* 613-236-7498
E-mail: info@ottawachamber.ca
URL: www.ottawachamber.ca
Scope: Provincial
Contact Information: E-mail: info@ottawachamber.ca

Ottawa Chamber of Commerce Ottawa Business Summit 2015
Location: Ottawa, ON
Sponsor/Contact: Ottawa Chamber of Commerce
328 Somerset St. West
Ottawa, ON K2P 0J9
613-236-3631 *Fax:* 613-236-7498
E-mail: info@ottawachamber.ca
URL: www.ottawachamber.ca
Scope: Provincial
Purpose: Featuring a guest speaker, take-away learning materials, & facilitated networking to help improve one's business
Contact Information: E-mail: info@ottawachamber.ca

Outdoor Writers of Canada 2015 National Conference & Annual General Meeting
Sponsor/Contact: Outdoor Writers of Canada
P.O. Box 934
Cochrane, AB T4C 1B1
403-932-3585 *Fax:* 403-851-0618
E-mail: outdoorwritersofcanada@shaw.ca
URL: www.outdoorwritersofcanada.com
Scope: National
Purpose: Craft improvement sessions for communicators with expertise in the outdoor field
Contact Information: Executive Director: T.J. Schwanky, E-mail: outdoorwritersofcanada@shaw.ca

Parkinson Society Canada Annual General Meeting
Sponsor/Contact: Parkinson Society Canada
#316, 4211 Yonge St.
Toronto, ON M2P 2A9
416-227-9700 *Fax:* 416-227-9600
Toll-Free: 800-565-3000
E-mail: general.info@parkinson.ca
URL: www.parkinson.ca
Scope: National

Parks & Recreation Ontario / Parcs et loisirs de l'Ontario 2015 Aquatics Conference and Exhibitors' Expo
Location: Ontario
Sponsor/Contact: Parks & Recreation Ontario
#302, 1 Concorde Gate
Toronto, ON M3C 3N6
416-426-7142 *Fax:* 416-426-7371
E-mail: pro@prontario.org
URL: www.prontario.org
Scope: Provincial

People First of Canada 2015 24th Annual General Meeting & Conference
Sponsor/Contact: People First of Canada
#5, 120 Maryland St.
Winnipeg, MB R3G 1L1
204-784-7362 *Fax:* 204-784-7364
E-mail: info@peoplefirstofcanada.ca
URL: www.peoplefirstofcanada.ca
Scope: National
Purpose: A meeting for People First representatives from across Canada, featuring the presentation of awards

Petroleum Services Association of Canada 2015 Annual General Meeting, Canadian Drilling Activity Forecast Session, & Industry Dinner
Sponsor/Contact: Petroleum Services Association of Canada
#1150, 800 - 6 Ave. SW
Calgary, AB T2P 3G3
403-264-4195 *Fax:* 403-263-7174
URL: www.psac.ca
Scope: National
Purpose: At the end of October each year, the Petroleum Services Association

Conferences Index

of Canada Annual Report is released, in conjunction with the Annual General Meeting & the Canadian Drilling Activity Forecast
Contact Information: Manager, Meetings & Events: Heather Doyle, Phone: 403-213-2796, E-mail: hdoyle@psac.ca

Petroleum Services Association of Canada 2015 Annual Mid-Year Update
Sponsor/Contact: Petroleum Services Association of Canada
#1150, 800 - 6 Ave. SW
Calgary, AB T2P 3G3
403-264-4195 *Fax:* 403-263-7174
URL: www.psac.ca
Scope: National
Purpose: A respected petroleum industry event to update the Canadian Drilling Activity Forecast
Contact Information: Manager, Meetings & Events: Heather Doyle, Phone: 403-213-2796, E-mail: hdoyle@psac.ca

Petroleum Services Association of Canada 2015 Annual Spring Conference
Sponsor/Contact: Petroleum Services Association of Canada
#1150, 800 - 6 Ave. SW
Calgary, AB T2P 3G3
403-264-4195 *Fax:* 403-263-7174
URL: www.psac.ca
Scope: National
Purpose: A gathering of petroleum service industry workers
Contact Information: Manager, Meetings & Events: Heather Doyle, Phone: 403-213-2796, E-mail: hdoyle@psac.ca

Pharmacists' Association of Newfoundland & Labrador 2015 Annual Conference
Sponsor/Contact: Pharmacists' Association of Newfoundland & Labrador
#203, 85 Thorburn Rd.
St. John's, NL A1B 3M2
709-753-7881 *Fax:* 709-753-8882
Toll-Free: 866-753-7881
E-mail: email@panl.net
URL: www.panl.net
Scope: Provincial
Purpose: Educational sessions & networking opportunities
Contact Information: E-mail: email@panl.net

Pharmacy Association of Nova Scotia 2015 Annual Conference
Location: Nova Scotia
Sponsor/Contact: Pharmacy Association of Nova Scotia
#225, 170 Cromarty Dr.
Dartmouth, NS B3B 0G1
902-422-9583 *Fax:* 902-422-2619
E-mail: pans@pans.ns.ca
URL: pans.ns.ca
Scope: Provincial
Purpose: Educational sessions on topics of interest to pharmacists in Nova Scotia
Contact Information: Pharmacy Association of Nova Scotia CEO: Allison Bodnar, E-mail: abodnar@pans.ns.ca

Plumbing Officials' Association of British Columbia 2015 Conference
Location: British Columbia
Sponsor/Contact: Plumbing Officials' Association of British Columbia
2328 Hollyhill Pl.
Victoria, BC V8N 1T9
250-361-0342 *Fax:* 250-385-1128
E-mail: bhusband@victoria.ca
URL: www.bcplumbingofficials.com
Scope: Provincial

Port Alberni & District Labour Council 2015 Annual General Meeting
Location: Port Alberni, BC
Sponsor/Contact: Port Alberni & District Labour Council
3940 Johnson Rd.
Port Alberni, BC V9Y 5N5
250-724-7966 *Fax:* 250-724-7966
URL: www.portalberni.ca/node/293
Scope: Local

Prince Edward Island Association of Medical Radiation Technologists 2015 Annual Meeting
Location: Prince Edward Island
Sponsor/Contact: Prince Edward Island Association of Medical Radiation Technologists
61 Queen Elizabeth St.
Charlottetown, PE C1A 3A8
URL: www.peiamrt.com
Scope: Provincial

Private Motor Truck Council of Canada Annual Conference 2015
Sponsor/Contact: Private Motor Truck Council of Canada
#115, 1660 North Service Rd. East
Oakville, ON L6H 7G3
905-827-0587 *Fax:* 905-827-8212
Toll-Free: 877-501-7682
E-mail: info@pmtc.ca
URL: www.pmtc.ca
Scope: National

Professional Locksmiths Association of Alberta Annual General Meeting
Location: Alberta
Sponsor/Contact: Professional Locksmith Association of Alberta
36 Sunridge Close
Airdrie, AB T4B 2G6
403-948-9997 *Fax:* 403-948-9997
Toll-Free: 877-765-7522
URL: www.plaa.org
Scope: Provincial

Provincial Intermediate Teachers' Association Annual Fall Conference
Sponsor/Contact: Provincial Intermediate Teachers' Association
c/o South Slope Elementary School
4446 Watling St.
Burnaby, BC V5J 5H3
604-664-8300 *Fax:* 604-664-8308
E-mail: rmyrtle@shaw.ca
URL: www.pita.ca
Scope: Provincial

Provincial Intermediate Teachers' Association Annual Whistler Conference
Location: Whistler, BC
Sponsor/Contact: Provincial Intermediate Teachers' Association
c/o South Slope Elementary School
4446 Watling St.
Burnaby, BC V5J 5H3
604-664-8300 *Fax:* 604-664-8308
E-mail: rmyrtle@shaw.ca
URL: www.pita.ca
Scope: Provincial

Public Health Association of British Columbia Conference and AGM 2015
Location: British Columbia
Sponsor/Contact: Public Health Association of British Columbia
#210, 1027 Pandora Ave.
Victoria, BC V8V 3P6
250-595-8422 *Fax:* 250-595-8622
E-mail: staff@phabc.org
URL: www.phabc.org
Scope: Provincial

RIMS (Risk & Insurance Management Society Inc.) Canada 2015 Conference
Sponsor/Contact: Risk & Insurance Management Society Inc.
c/o Thomas Oystrick, RIMS Canada Council, Mount Royal University
4825 Mount Royal Gate SW
Calgary, AB T3E 6K6
E-mail: canada@rims.org
URL: www.rimscanada.ca
Scope: National
Purpose: A risk management conference & exhibition, held each autumn, of interest to Canadian risk professionals
Anticipated Attendance: 1,000+

Recreation Facilities Association of British Columbia 2015 Conference
Location: British Columbia
Sponsor/Contact: Recreation Facilities Association of British Columbia
P.O. Box 112
Powell River, BC V8A 4Z5
Toll-Free: 877-285-3421
E-mail: info@rfabc.com
URL: www.rfabc.com
Scope: Provincial

Recycling Council of British Columbia 2015 Annual Zero Waste Conference & Annual General Meeting
Sponsor/Contact: Recycling Council of British Columbia
#10, 119 West Pender St.
Vancouver, BC V6B 1S5
604-683-6009 *Fax:* 604-683-7255
Toll-Free: 800-667-4321
E-mail: rcbc@rcbc.bc.ca
URL: www.rcbc.bc.ca
Scope: Provincial
Purpose: An event each spring about recycling & waste reduction in British Columbia
Contact Information: E-mail: conference@rcbc.bc.ca

Recycling Council of Ontario 2015 Annual General Meeting & Policy Forum
Location: Ontario
Sponsor/Contact: Recycling Council of Ontario
#225, 215 Spadina Ave.
Toronto, ON M5T 2C7
416-657-2797
Toll-Free: 888-501-9637
E-mail: rco@rco.on.ca
URL: www.rco.on.ca
Scope: Provincial
Purpose: Voting by members for the Board of Directors
Contact Information: Contact: Lucy Robinson, Phone: 416-657-2797, E-mail: lucy@rco.on.ca

Registered Professional Foresters Association of Nova Scotia 2015 Annual General Meeting
Sponsor/Contact: Registered Professional Foresters Association of Nova Scotia
P.O. Box 1031
Truro, NS B2N 5G9
902-893-0099
E-mail: contact@rpfans.ca
URL: www.rpfans.ca
Scope: Provincial
Purpose: A business meeting for Nova Scotia's professional foresters

Restaurants Canada Annual Event: Alberta Foodservice Expo 2015
Location: Alberta
Sponsor/Contact: Restaurants Canada
1155 Queen St. West
Toronto, ON M6J 1J4
416-923-8416 *Fax:* 416-923-1450
Toll-Free: 800-387-5649
E-mail: info@restaurantscanada.org
URL: www.restaurantscanada.org
Scope: Provincial
Purpose: An opportunity for Alberta's foodservice executives, restaurateurs, chefs, & qualified buyers to learn the latest trends from more than 200 food distributors & foodservice equipment manufacturers, suppliers, & dealers
Anticipated Attendance: 2,000+
Contact Information: MediaEdge Communications Inc. Contact: Chris Torry, Phone: 416-512-8186, ext. 280, E-mail: christ@mediaedge.ca

Restaurants Canada Annual Event: CONNECT 2015
Location: British Columbia
Sponsor/Contact: Restaurants Canada
1155 Queen St. West
Toronto, ON M6J 1J4
416-923-8416 *Fax:* 416-923-1450
Toll-Free: 800-387-5649
E-mail: info@restaurantscanada.org
URL: www.restaurantscanada.org
Scope: Provincial
Purpose: A trade show to highlight British Columbia's culinary excellence, with workshops, seminars, cooking competitions, & celebrity chef demonstrations
Anticipated Attendance: 5,000+
Contact Information: Canadian Restaurant & Foodservices Association Toll-Free Phone: 1-8800-387-5649; E-mail: bcexpo@crfa.ca, info@crfa.ca

Rhythmic Gymnastics Manitoba Inc. 2015 Annual General Meeting & Awards Presentation
Location: Manitoba
Sponsor/Contact: Rhythmic Gymnastics Manitoba Inc.
145 Pacific Ave.
Winnipeg, MB R3B 2Z6
201-492-5573
E-mail: rhythmic@sportmanitoba.ca
URL: www.rgmanitoba.com
Scope: Provincial
Contact Information: Phone: 204-925-5738; E-mail: rhythmic@sportmanitoba.ca

Royal Canadian Artillery Association 14th Annual Seminar & 129th Annual General Meeting
Sponsor/Contact: Royal Canadian Artillery Association
1346 Mitchell Dr.
Victoria, BC V8S 4P8
250-385-7922
URL: www.rcaa-aarc.ca
Scope: National

Royal College of Dentists of Canada 2015 Annual General Meeting
Sponsor/Contact: Royal College of Dentists of Canada
#2404, 180 Dundas St. West
Toronto, ON M3G 1Z8

416-512-6571 *Fax:* 416-512-6468
E-mail: office@rcdc.ca
URL: www.rcdc.ca
Scope: National

Royal College of Physicians & Surgeons of Canada 2015 Annual General Meeting
Sponsor/Contact: The Royal College of Physicians & Surgeons of Canada
774 Echo Dr.
Ottawa, ON K1S 5N8
613-730-8177 *Fax:* 613-730-8830
Toll-Free: 800-668-3740
E-mail: info@royalcollege.ca
URL: rcpsc.medical.org
Scope: National

Saskatchewan Association of Library Technicians 2015 Annual General Meeting & Fall Workshops
Location: Saskatchewan
Sponsor/Contact: Saskatchewan Association of Library Technicians, Inc.
P.O. Box 24019
Saskatoon, SK S7K 8B4
Fax: 306-543-4487
E-mail: sasksalt@gmail.com
URL: www.libraries.gov.sk.ca/salt
Scope: Provincial
Purpose: A business meeting, speakers, & networking opportunities for library technicians from Saskatchewan
Contact Information: E-mail: sasksalt@gmail.com

Saskatchewan Beekeepers Association 2015 93rd Annual Convention & Meeting
Location: Saskatchewan
Sponsor/Contact: Saskatchewan Beekeepers Association
P.O. Box 55
RR#3
Yorkton, SK S3N 2X5
306-743-5469 *Fax:* 306-743-5528
E-mail: whowland@accesscomm.ca
URL: www.saskatchewanbeekeepers.ca
Scope: Provincial
Purpose: Featuring speakers & research results

Saskatchewan Camping Association 2015 Annual General Meeting
Location: Saskatchewan
Sponsor/Contact: Saskatchewan Camping Association
3950 Castle Rd.
Regina, SK S4S 6A4
306-586-4026 *Fax:* 306-790-8634
E-mail: info@saskcamping.ca
URL: www.saskcamping.ca
Scope: Provincial
Purpose: Featuring the election of the board of directors of the association
Contact Information: Executive Director: Donna Wilkinson, Phone: 306-586-4026, E-mail: donnaw@sasktel.net

Saskatchewan Early Childhood Association 2015 Annual General Meeting
Location: Saskatchewan
Sponsor/Contact: Saskatchewan Early Childhood Association
#5, 3041 Sherman Dr.
Prince Albert, SK S6V 7B7
306-975-0875 *Fax:* 306-975-0877
Toll-Free: 888-658-4408
E-mail: saskcare@sasktel.net
URL: www.skearlychildhoodassociation.ca
Scope: Provincial

Saskatchewan Early Childhood Association 2015 Excellence in Early Learning Conference
Location: Saskatchewan
Sponsor/Contact: Saskatchewan Early Childhood Association
#5, 3041 Sherman Dr.
Prince Albert, SK S6V 7B7
306-975-0875 *Fax:* 306-975-0877
Toll-Free: 888-658-4408
E-mail: saskcare@sasktel.net
URL: www.skearlychildhoodassociation.ca
Scope: Provincial
Purpose: A conference offering demonstration classrooms, peer to peer learning, & hands-on activities

Saskatchewan Federation of Labour 2015 59th Annual Convention
Location: Saskatchewan
Sponsor/Contact: Saskatchewan Federation of Labour
#220, 2445 - 13th Ave.
Regina, SK S4P 0W1
306-525-0197 *Fax:* 306-525-8960
E-mail: sfl@sfl.sk.ca
URL: www.sfl.sk.ca
Scope: Provincial
Contact Information: Office Administration Contact: Debbie Lussier, E-mail: d.lussier@sfl.sk.ca

Saskatchewan Federation of Labour 2015 Pension Conference
Location: Saskatchewan
Sponsor/Contact: Saskatchewan Federation of Labour
#220, 2445 - 13th Ave.
Regina, SK S4P 0W1
306-525-0197 *Fax:* 306-525-8960
E-mail: sfl@sfl.sk.ca
URL: www.sfl.sk.ca
Scope: Provincial
Contact Information: Office Administration Contact: Debbie Lussier, E-mail: d.lussier@sfl.sk.ca

Saskatchewan Federation of Police Officers 2015 Annual Meeting
Location: Saskatchewan
Sponsor/Contact: Saskatchewan Federation of Police Officers
306-539-0960
URL: www.saskpolice.com
Scope: Provincial
Purpose: The Executive Board reports on matters dealt with for & on behalf of members of the Federation at a meeting held each year between April 1st & May 31st

Saskatchewan Parks & Recreation Association 2015 Spring Education & Training Symposium
Location: Saskatchewan
Sponsor/Contact: Saskatchewan Parks & Recreation Association
#100, 1445 Park St.
Regina, SK S4N 4C5
306-780-9231 *Fax:* 306-780-9257
Toll-Free: 800-563-2555
E-mail: office@spra.sk.ca
URL: www.spra.sk.ca
Scope: Provincial
Contact Information: SPRA Consultant: Kelly Skotnitsky, E-mail: kskotnitsky@spra.sk.ca

Saskatchewan School Library Association Conference 2015
Location: Saskatchewan
Sponsor/Contact: Saskatchewan School Library Association
c/o Saskatchewan Teachers' Federation
2317 Arlington Ave.
Saskatoon, SK S7J 2H8
E-mail: sasksla@gmail.com
URL: www.ssla.ca
Scope: Provincial

Saskatchewan Snowmobile Association 2015 Annual General Meeting & The Diamond in the Snow Awards Banquet
Location: Saskatchewan
Sponsor/Contact: Saskatchewan Snowmobile Association
P.O. Box 533
221 Centre St.
Regina Beach, SK S0G 4C0
306-729-3500 *Fax:* 306-729-3505
Toll-Free: 800-499-7533
E-mail: sasksnow@sasktel.net
URL: www.sasksnowmobiling.sk.ca
Scope: Provincial
Purpose: Reports from the chairman, president & chief executive officer, & discussions about finances & association issues

Saskatchewan Soil Conservation Association 2015 27th Annual Conservation Agriculture Conference
Location: Saskatchewan
Sponsor/Contact: Saskatchewan Soil Conservation Association
P.O. Box 1360
Indian Head, SK S0G 2K0
306-695-4233 *Fax:* 306-695-4236
Toll-Free: 800-213-4287
E-mail: info@ssca.ca
URL: www.ssca.ca
Scope: Provincial
Purpose: A meeting during Crop Production Week
Contact Information: Office Manager: Marilyn Martens, Phone: 306-695-4233

Saskatoon & District Labour Council 2015 Annual General Meeting
Location: Saskatchewan
Sponsor/Contact: Saskatoon & District Labour Council
#110B, 2103 Airport Rd.
Saskatoon, SK S7L 6W2
306-384-0303 *Fax:* 306-382-3642
E-mail: sdlc@sasktel.net
URL: www.saskatoondlc.ca
Scope: Local
Contact Information: Registrar: Donna Rederburg

Scandinavian Society of Nova Scotia 2015 Annual General Meeting
Location: Nova Scotia
Sponsor/Contact: Scandinavian Society of Nova Scotia
Box 31241, Gladstone RPO
Halifax, NS B3K 5Y1
E-mail: scansons@gmail.com
URL: www.scandinaviansociety.ca
Scope: Provincial
Purpose: The presentation of society reports, a summary of events from the previous year, & an award ceremony
Anticipated Attendance: 45

School Sports Newfoundland & Labrador Annual General Meeting
Sponsor/Contact: School Sports Newfoundland & Labrador
1296A Kenmount Rd.
St. John's, NL A1B 3W8
709-729-2795 *Fax:* 709-729-2705
E-mail: ssnl@sportnl.ca
URL: www.schoolsportsnl.ca

Sickle Cell Association of Ontario's 2015 Educational Conference
Location: Ontario
Sponsor/Contact: Sickle Cell Association of Ontario
#202, 3199 Bathurst St.
Toronto, ON M6A 2B2
416-789-2855 *Fax:* 416-789-1903
E-mail: sicklecell@look.ca
URL: www.sicklecellontario.ca
Scope: Provincial

Snowmobilers of Manitoba Inc. 2015 5th Annual Snoman Congress
Sponsor/Contact: Snowmobilers of Manitoba Inc.
2121 Henderson Hwy.
Winnipeg, MB R2G 1P8
204-940-7533 *Fax:* 204-940-7531
E-mail: info@snoman.mb.ca
URL: www.snoman.mb.ca
Scope: Provincial

Society Promoting Environmental Conservation Annual General Meeting 2015
Sponsor/Contact: Society Promoting Environmental Conservation
2060 Pine St.
Vancouver, BC V6J 4P8
604-736-7732 *Fax:* 604-736-7115
E-mail: admin@spec.bc.ca
URL: www.spec.bc.ca
Scope: Provincial

Society of Canadian Ornithologists / Société des ornithologistes du Canada 2015 33rd Annual Meeting
Location: Wolfville, NS
Sponsor/Contact: Society of Canadian Ornithologists
a/s Thérèse Beaudet, SCO Membership Secretary
1281, ch des Lièges
St-Jean de l'Ile d'Orléans, QC G0A 3W0
E-mail: beaudet.lamothe@sympatico.ca
URL: www.sco-soc.ca
Scope: National

Society of the Plastics Industry, Inc. Spring 2015 National Board Conference
Sponsor/Contact: Society of the Plastics Industry, Inc.
#1000, 1667 K St. NW
Washington, DC 20006
202-974-5200 *Fax:* 202-296-7005
URL: www.plasticsindustry.org
Scope: National

Spina Bifida & Hydrocephalus Association of British Columbia 2015 Conference
Location: British Columbia
Sponsor/Contact: Spina Bifida & Hydrocephalus Association of British Columbia
c/o BC Children's Hospital
4480 Oak St.
Vancouver, BC V6H 3V4
604-878-7000 *Fax:* 604-677-6608
E-mail: sbhabc@shaw.ca
URL: www.sbhabc.org

Scope: Provincial
Contact Information: Email: sbhabc@shaw.ca

The 18th Annual Supply Chain Management Association of Ontario Conference
Location: Ontario
Sponsor/Contact: Supply Chain Management Association - Ontario
P.O. Box 64
#2704, 1 Dundas St. West
Toronto, ON M5G 1Z3
416-977-7566 *Fax:* 416-977-4135
Toll-Free: 877-726-6968
E-mail: info@scmao.ca
URL: www.scmao.ca
Scope: Provincial
Anticipated Attendance: 400+

The Acadian Entomological Society 2015 Annual Meeting
Sponsor/Contact: The Acadian Entomological Society
Natural Resources Canada, Canadian Forest Service
P.O. Box 4000
Atlantic Forestry Centre, 1350 Regent St.
Fredericton, NB E3B 5P7
E-mail: b35ckp@mun.ca
URL: www.acadianes.org/aes.html

The Canadian Addison Society Annual General Meeting 2015
Sponsor/Contact: The Canadian Addison Society
193 Elgin Ave. West
Goderich, ON N7A 2E7
Toll-Free: 888-550-5582
E-mail: liaisonsecretary@addisonsociety.ca
URL: www.addisonsociety.ca
Scope: National

The Environmental Studies Association of Canada (ESAC) 2015 Conference
Sponsor/Contact: Environmental Studies Association of Canada
c/o Dean's Office, Faculty of Environmental Studies, Univ. of Waterloo
Waterloo, ON N2L 3G1
519-888-4442 *Fax:* 519-746-0292
Toll-Free: 866-437-2587
URL: www.esac.ca
Scope: National

The Leadership in Volunteer Education (L.I.V.E) Conference 2015
Sponsor/Contact: Ontario March of Dimes
10 Overlea Blvd.
Toronto, ON M4H 1A4
416-425-3463 *Fax:* 416-425-1920
Toll-Free: 800-263-3463
E-mail: info@marchofdimes.ca
URL: www.marchofdimes.ca
Scope: Provincial
Purpose: Peer Support's annual 3-day training and networking event for active members, current and future volunteer leaders in stroke, polio and caregiver support groups across Canada
Contact Information: Phone: 800-263-3463

The Navy League of Canada 2015 Annual General Meeting
Sponsor/Contact: Navy League of Canada
66 Lisgar St.
Ottawa, ON K2P 0C1
Fax: 613-990-8701
Toll-Free: 800-375-6289
E-mail: info@navyleague.ca
URL: www.navyleague.ca
Scope: National

The Provincial Towing Association Annual Trade & Tow Show
Sponsor/Contact: Provincial Towing Association (Ontario)
65 Keith Rd.
Bracebridge, ON P1L 0A1
705-646-0536 *Fax:* 705-645-0017
Toll-Free: 866-582-0855
URL: www.ptao.org
Purpose: The Trade & Tow Show features training sessions, the PTAO general meeting, competitions & the awards banquet

The Royal Canadian Geographical Society 2015 Annual General Meeting & Annual Dinner of the College of Fellows
Sponsor/Contact: The Royal Canadian Geographical Society
#200, 1155 Lola St.
Ottawa, ON K1K 4C1
613-745-4629 *Fax:* 613-744-0947
Toll-Free: 800-267-0824
E-mail: rcgs@rcgs.org
URL: www.rcgs.org
Scope: National
Purpose: A gathering of Society members, featuring the approval of the audited financial statement, a guest speaker, & the presentation of awards

The Society of Toxicology of Canada Annual Symposium 2015
Sponsor/Contact: Society of Toxicology of Canada
P.O. Box 55094
Montréal, QC H3G 2W5
E-mail: stcsecretariat@mcgill.ca
URL: www.stcweb.ca
Scope: National

Tire and Rubber Association 2015 Tire & Rubber Summit
Sponsor/Contact: Tire and Rubber Association of Canada
Plaza 4
#100, 2000 Argentia Rd.
Mississauga, ON L5N 1W1
905-814-1714 *Fax:* 905-814-1085
E-mail: info@rubberassociation.ca
URL: www.tracanada.ca
Scope: National

Toronto Health Libraries Association 2015 Annual General Meeting
Location: Toronto, ON
Sponsor/Contact: Toronto Health Libraries Association
c/o Melissa Paladines (Treasurer), Credit Valley Hospital
2200 Eglinton Ave. West
Toronto, ON L5M 2N1
URL: www.thla.ca
Scope: Local

Tourism Industry Association of PEI 2015 Annual General Meeting
Sponsor/Contact: Tourism Industry Association of PEI
P.O. Box 2050
25 Queen St., 3rd Fl.
Charlottetown, PE C1A 7N7
902-566-5008 *Fax:* 902-368-3605
Toll-Free: 866-566-5008
E-mail: tiapei@tiapei.pe.ca
URL: www.tiapei.pe.ca

Travel and Tourism Research Association Canada's 2015 Conference
Sponsor/Contact: Travel and Tourism Research Association
#600, 116 Lisgar St.
Ottawa, ON K2P 0C2
613-238-6378
E-mail: info@ttracanada.ca
URL: www.ttracanada.ca
Scope: National

Tunnelling Association of Canada 2015 Conference
Sponsor/Contact: Tunnelling Association of Canada
8828 Pigott Rd.
Richmond, ON V7A 2C4
604-241-1297 *Fax:* 604-241-1399
E-mail: admin@tunnelcanada.ca
URL: www.tunnelcanada.ca
Scope: National
Contact Information: Wayne Gibson, Conference Manager

United Steelworkers / International Association of Machinists 2nd Annual Canadian Airport Screeners Conference
Sponsor/Contact: United Steelworkers of America (AFL-CIO/CLC)
234 Eglinton Ave. East, 8th Fl.
Toronto, ON M4P 1K7
416-487-1571 *Fax:* 416-482-5548
Toll-Free: 877-669-8792
E-mail: info@usw.ca
URL: www.usw.ca
Scope: International

United Steelworkers National Human Rights Conference Fighting for Human Rights in a Low-Wage Economy
Sponsor/Contact: United Steelworkers of America (AFL-CIO/CLC)
234 Eglinton Ave. East, 8th Fl.
Toronto, ON M4P 1K7
416-487-1571 *Fax:* 416-482-5548
Toll-Free: 877-669-8792
E-mail: info@usw.ca
URL: www.usw.ca
Scope: National

Universities Art Association of Canada Conference 2015
Sponsor/Contact: Universities Art Association of Canada
189 Mill Ridge Rd.
Arnprior, ON K7S 3G8
613-622-5570 *Fax:* 613-622-0671
E-mail: uaac@gozoom.ca
URL: www.uaac-aauc.com
Scope: National

University of Alberta African Students' Association 2015 Conference
Sponsor/Contact: African Students Association - Univeristy of Alberta
c/o Student Group Services Office, Students' Union Bldg., Univ. of Alb
#040A, 8900 - 114 St. NW
Edmonton, AB
780-915-8151
E-mail: Afsa09@ualberta.ca
URL: www.afsaualberta.org
Scope: Local

Utility Contractors Association of Ontario 2015 Annual Convention
Location: Ontario
Sponsor/Contact: Utility Contractors Association of Ontario, Inc.
P.O. Box 762
Oakville, ON L6K 0A9
905-847-7305 *Fax:* 905-412-0339
URL: www.uca.on.ca
Scope: Provincial
Purpose: An event with guest speakers & networking activities for association members & their guests

West Coast Environmental Law 2015 Annual General Meeting
Sponsor/Contact: West Coast Environmental Law
#200, 2006 West 10th Ave.
Vancouver, BC V6J 2B3
604-684-7378 *Fax:* 604-684-1312
Toll-Free: 800-330-9235
E-mail: admin@wcel.org
URL: www.wcel.org
Scope: Provincial
Purpose: The appointment of board members takes place each year

Western Stock Growers' Association Annual General Meeting 2015
Sponsor/Contact: The Western Stock Growers' Association
P.O. Box 179
900 Village Lane
Okotoks, AB T1S 1Z6
403-250-9121
E-mail: office@wsga.ca
URL: www.wsga.ca
Scope: Provincial

Wilderness Tourism Association 2015 Summit & Annual General Meeting
Sponsor/Contact: Wilderness Tourism Association
P.O. Box 423
Cumberland, BC V0R 1S0
250-336-2862 *Fax:* 250-336-2861
E-mail: admin@wilderness-tourism.bc.ca
URL: www.wilderness-tourism.bc.ca
Scope: Provincial
Purpose: Informative sessions & workshops about nature based tourism

Winnipeg 2015 State of the City Address
Location: Winnipeg, MB
Sponsor/Contact: Winnipeg Chamber of Commerce
#100, 259 Portage Ave.
Winnipeg, MB R3B 2A9
204-944-8484 *Fax:* 204-944-8492
E-mail: info@winnipeg-chamber.com
URL: www.winnipeg-chamber.com
Scope: Provincial
Purpose: A presentation by Mayor Brian Bowman
Anticipated Attendance: 1,100
Contact Information: Events Coordinator: Yanik Ottenbreit, Phone: 204-944-3306, E-mail: yottenbreit@winnipeg-chamber.com

Women's Inter-Church Council of Canada 2015 Annual General Meeting
Sponsor/Contact: Women's Inter-Church Council of Canada
47 Queen's Park Cres. East
Toronto, ON M5S 2C3
416-929-5184 *Fax:* 416-929-4064
E-mail: wicc@wicc.org
URL: www.wicc.org
Scope: National

Wood Pellet Association of Canada 2015 Conference & AGM
Sponsor/Contact: Wood Pellet Association of Canada
P.O. Box 2989
1877 Upper McKinnon Rd.
Revelstoke, BC V0E 2S0

URL: www.pellet.org
Scope: National

Wycliffe Bible Translators of Canada Inc. 2015 Annual General Meeting
Sponsor/Contact: Wycliffe Bible Translators of Canada, Inc.
4316 - 10th St. NE
Calgary, AB T2E 6K3
403-250-5411 *Fax:* 403-250-2623
Toll-Free: 800-463-1143
E-mail: info@wycliffe.ca
URL: www.wycliffe.ca
Scope: National

Yukon Chamber of Mines 2015 43rd Annual Yukon Geoscience Forum & Trade Show
Sponsor/Contact: Yukon Chamber of Mines
3151B - 3rd Ave.
Whitehorse, YT Y1A 1G1
867-667-2090 *Fax:* 867-668-7127
E-mail: info@yukonminers.ca
URL: www.yukonminers.ca
Scope: Provincial
Purpose: A conference for the mining & exploration industry, featuring technical events, short courses, & exhibits
Contact Information: E-mail: admin@yukonminers.ca

Yukon Conservation Society 2015 Annual General Meeting
Location: Yukon Territory
Sponsor/Contact: Yukon Conservation Society
302 Hawkins St.
Whitehorse, YT Y1A 1X6
867-668-5678 *Fax:* 867-668-6637
E-mail: ycs@ycs.yk.ca
URL: www.yukonconservation.org
Scope: Provincial
Contact Information: Phone: 867-668-5678

2016

January

2016 Canadian Marketing Association Conference: CMAideas
Date: January 2016
Sponsor/Contact: Canadian Marketing Association
#607, 1 Concorde Gate
Toronto, ON M3C 3N6
416-391-2362 *Fax:* 416-441-4062
E-mail: info@the-cma.org
URL: www.the-cma.org
Scope: National
Purpose: Brings together a unique conference of creators, innovators and leaders with insights from unlikely places and undiscovered territories.

2016 Manitoba Water Well Association Annual Conference & Trade Show
Date: January 31 - Febraury 3, 2016
Location: Victoria Inn
Winnipeg, MB
Sponsor/Contact: Manitoba Water Well Association
P.O. Box 1648
Winnipeg, MB R3C 2Z6
204-479-3777
E-mail: info@mwwa.ca
URL: www.mwwa.ca
Scope: Provincial
Purpose: A review of the year's highlights & an opportunity to address new business
Contact Information: E-mail: info@mwwa.ca

American Library Association 2016 Midwinter Meeting & Exhibits
Date: January 22-26, 2016
Location: Boston, MA USA
Sponsor/Contact: American Library Association
50 East Huron St.
Chicago, IL 60611
Fax: 312-440-9374
Toll-Free: 800-545-2433
E-mail: ala@ala.org
URL: www.ala.org
Scope: International
Purpose: An annual gathering of those in the library & information services community, highlighting committee meetings, discussion groups, speakers, & exhibits
Contact Information: Registration Customer Service, Phone: 1-800-974-3084, E-mail: ala@experient-inc.com

American Philological Association 147th Annual Meeting
Date: January 7-10, 2016
Location: San Francisco, CA USA
Sponsor/Contact: American Philological Association
University of Pennsylvania
#201E, 220 South 40th St.
Philadelphia, PA 19104-3512
215-898-4975 *Fax:* 215-573-7874
E-mail: apaclassics@sas.upenn.edu
URL: apaclassics.org
Scope: International

Canadian Society of Hospital Pharmacists 2016 47th Annual Professional Practice Conference
Date: January 30 - February 3, 2016
Location: Sheraton Centre Toronto Hotel
Toronto, ON
Sponsor/Contact: Canadian Society of Hospital Pharmacists
#3, 30 Concourse Gate
Ottawa, ON K2E 7V7
613-736-9733 *Fax:* 613-736-5660
E-mail: info@cshp.ca
URL: www.cshp.ca
Scope: National
Purpose: Presentations about pharmacists' roles, pharmacy practice, & pharmacy programs
Anticipated Attendance: 650
Contact Information: E-mail: info@cshp.ca

Manitoba Water & Wastewater Association 2016 Annual Conference & Trade Show
Date: January 31 - February 3, 2016
Location: Victoria Inn
Winnipeg, MB
Sponsor/Contact: Manitoba Water & Wastewater Association
P.O. Box 1600
#215, 9 Saskatchewan Ave. West, 2nd Fl.
Portage la Prairie, MB R1N 3P1
204-239-6868 *Fax:* 204-239-6872
Toll-Free: 866-396-2549
E-mail: mwwa@mts.net
URL: www.mwwa.net
Scope: Provincial
Purpose: The presentation of technical papers plus the opportunity to view industry products & services
Contact Information: Executive Director: Iva Last: Phone: 204-239-6868, Toll-Free Phone: 1-866-396-2549, Fax: 204-239-6872, E-mail: mwwa@mts.net

Western Retail Lumber Association 2016 Prairie Showcase Buying Show & Convention
Date: January 20-22, 2016
Location: Calgary, AB
Sponsor/Contact: Western Retail Lumber Association
Western Retail Lumber Association Inc.
#1004, 213 Notre Dame Ave.
Winnipeg, MB R3B 1N3
204-957-1077 *Fax:* 204-947-5195
Toll-Free: 800-661-0253
E-mail: wrla@wrla.org
URL: www.wrla.org
Scope: Provincial
Contact Information: Caren Kelly, Marketing Manager, E-mail: Ckelly@wrla.org

February

American Association for Justice 2016 Winter Convention
Date: February 27 - March 2, 2016
Location: Boca Raton Beach Club
Boca Raton, FL USA
Sponsor/Contact: American Association for Justice
#200, 777 - 6th St., NW
Washington, DC 20001
202-965-3500
Toll-Free: 800-424-2725
E-mail: membership@justice.org
URL: www.justice.org
Scope: International

American Association for the Advancement of Science 2016 Annual Meeting
Date: February 11-15, 2016
Location: Washington, DC USA
Sponsor/Contact: American Association for the Advancement of Science
1200 New York Ave. NW
Washington, DC 20005
202-326-6440
E-mail: membership@aaas.org
URL: www.aaas.org
Scope: International
Purpose: Information for scientists, engineers, educators, & policy-makers
Contact Information: Phone: 202-326-6450; Fax: 202-289-4021; E-mail: meetings@aaas.org; Director, Meetings & Public Engagement: Tiffany Lohwater, E-mail: tlohwate@aaas.org

Association of Ontario Land Surveyors 2016 Annual General Meeting
Date: February 24-26, 2016
Location: London Convention Centre & London Hilton
London, ON
Sponsor/Contact: Association of Ontario Land Surveyors
1043 McNicoll Ave.
Toronto, ON M1W 3W6
416-491-9020 *Fax:* 416-491-2576
Toll-Free: 800-268-0718
E-mail: info@aols.org
URL: www.aols.org
Scope: Provincial
Contact Information: Lena Kassabian; Email: lena@aols.org; Phone: 416-491-9020 ext. 25

Canadian Centre for Occupational Health & Safety Forum V
Date: February 29 - March 1, 2016
Location: Vancouver, BC
Sponsor/Contact: Canadian Centre for Occupational Health & Safety
135 Hunter St. East
Hamilton, ON L8N 1M5
905-572-2981 *Fax:* 905-572-2206
Toll-Free: 800-668-4284
E-mail: clientservices@ccohs.ca
URL: www.ccohs.ca
Scope: National

Canadian Digestive Diseases Week (CDDW) & the 2016 Annual Canadian Association for the Study of the Liver (CASL) Winter Meeting
Date: February 21 - March 2, 2016
Location: Montreal, QC
Sponsor/Contact: Canadian Association for the Study of the Liver
c/o BUKSA Strategic Conference Services
#307, 10328 - 81st Ave.
Edmonton, AB T6E 1X2
780-436-0983 *Fax:* 780-437-5984
E-mail: casl@hepatology.ca
URL: www.hepatology.ca
Scope: National
Purpose: A February or March scientific conference of the Canadian Association of Gastroenterology (CAG) & the Canadian Association for the Study of the Liver (CASL), featuring lectures, symposia, small group sessions, exhibits, & opportunities for networking

Canadian Digestive Diseases Week: Canadian Association of Gastroenterology Annual Scientific Conference 2016
Date: February 21 - March 2, 2016
Location: Montreal, QC
Sponsor/Contact: Canadian Association of Gastroenterology
#224, 1540 Cornwall Rd.
Oakville, ON L6J 7W5
905-829-2504 *Fax:* 905-829-0242
Toll-Free: 888-780-0007
E-mail: general@cag-acg.org
URL: www.cag-acg.org
Scope: National

Canadian Rheumatology Association 2016 Annual Scientific Meeting
Date: February 17-20, 2016
Location: Lake Louise, AB
Sponsor/Contact: Canadian Rheumatology Association
#244, 12 - 16715 Yonge St.
Newmarket, ON L3X 1X4
905-952-0698 *Fax:* 905-952-0708
E-mail: info@rheum.ca
URL: rheum.ca
Scope: National

March

2016 Canadian Marketing Association Conference: CMAinsights
Date: March 2016
Sponsor/Contact: Canadian Marketing Association
#607, 1 Concorde Gate
Toronto, ON M3C 3N6
416-391-2362 *Fax:* 416-441-4062
E-mail: info@the-cma.org
URL: www.the-cma.org
Scope: National
Purpose: CMAinsights will feature multiple

Conferences Index

content streams; focusing on both the marketer and the data practitioner.

Alberta Association of Municipal Districts & Counties Spring 2016 Convention & Trade Show
Date: March 14-16, 2016
Location: Shaw Conference Centre
Edmonton, AB
Sponsor/Contact: Alberta Association of Municipal Districts & Counties
2510 Sparrow Dr.
Nisku, AB T9E 8N5
780-955-3639 *Fax:* 780-955-3615
Toll-Free: 855-548-7233
E-mail: aamdc@aamdc.com
URL: www.aamdc.com

American Counseling Association / Canadian Counselling and Psychotherapy Association 2016 Annual Conference
Date: March 30 - April 3, 2015
Location: Palais des congrès de Montréal
Montreal, QC
Sponsor/Contact: Canadian Counselling & Psychotherapy Association
#114, 223 Colonnade Rd. South
Ottawa, ON K2E 7K3
613-237-1099 *Fax:* 613-237-9786
Toll-Free: 877-765-5565
E-mail: info@ccpa-accp.ca
URL: www.ccpa-accp.ca
Scope: National

Canadian Association for Dental Research 40th Annual Meeting
Date: March 16-19, 2016
Location: Los Angeles, CA USA
Sponsor/Contact: Canadian Association for Dental Research
c/o Dr. C. Birek, Faculty of Dentistry, University of Manitoba
780 Bannatyne Ave.
Winnipeg, MB R3E 0W2
204-789-3256 *Fax:* 204-789-3913
E-mail: birek@ms.umanitoba.ca
URL: www.cadr-acrd.ca
Scope: International
Purpose: In conjunction with the 45th Annual Meeting of the American Association of Dental Research & the 94th General Session & Exhibition of the International Association for Dental Research

GLOBE 2016 13th Biennial Conference & Trade Fair on Business & the Environment
Date: March 2-4, 2016
Location: Vancouver Convention Centre - East Building
Vancouver, BC
Sponsor/Contact: GLOBE Foundation
World Trade Centre
#578, 999 Canada Pl.
Vancouver, BC V6C 3E1
604-695-5001 *Fax:* 604-695-5019
Toll-Free: 800-274-6097
E-mail: info@globe.ca
URL: www.globe.ca
Scope: International
Purpose: A global gathering of government leaders, senior executives, & NGO representatives, from more than seventy countries, to share experiences & explore new opportunities during conference sessions & interactive networking opportunities, & to see the most recent environmental & clean technologies at the international trade show
Anticipated Attendance: 10,000+
Contact Information: General Information: Phone: 604-695-5001, Toll-Free Phone: 1-800-274-6097, E-mail: info@globeseries.com; Exhibiting Information, E-mail: sales@globeseries.com; URL: www.globeseries.com

Pacific Dental Conference 2016
Date: March 17-19, 2016
Location: Vancouver, BC
Sponsor/Contact: British Columbia Dental Association
#400, 1765 - 8th Ave. West
Vancouver, BC V6J 5C6
604-736-7202 *Fax:* 604-736-7588
Toll-Free: 888-396-9888
E-mail: post@bcdental.org
URL: www.bcdental.org
Scope: Provincial
Anticipated Attendance: 12,000+
Contact Information: Address: Pacific Dental Conference, #305, 1505 West 2nd Ave., Vancouver, BC V6H 3Y4; Phone: 604-736-3781; E-mail: info@pdconf.com, exhibits@pdconf.com

Society of Toxicology 55th Annual Meeting & ToxExpo
Date: March 13-17, 2016
Location: Ernest N. Morial Convention Center
New Orleans, LA USA
Sponsor/Contact: Society of Toxicology
#300, 1821 Michael Faraday Dr.
Reston, VA 20190
703-438-3115 *Fax:* 703-438-3113
E-mail: sothq@toxicology.org
URL: www.toxicology.org
Scope: International
Purpose: Toxicology meeting & exhibition
Anticipated Attendance: 6,500
Contact Information: Phone: 703-438-3115; Fax: 703-438-3113; E-mail: sothq@toxicology.org

TRENDS: The Apparel Show 2016 (sponsored by the Alberta Men's Wear Agents Association)
Date: March 3-7, 2016
Location: Edmonton Expo Centre
Edmonton, AB
Sponsor/Contact: Alberta Men's Wear Agents Association
P.O. Box 66037 Stn. Heritage
Edmonton, AB T6J 6T4
780-455-1881 *Fax:* 780-455-3969
E-mail: amwa@shaw.ca
URL: www.trendsapparel.com
Scope: Provincial
Purpose: Items from more than 1,500 manufacturers are shown by 250 sales representatives
Contact Information: E-mail: amwa@shaw.ca

April

2016 Ontario Psychological Association Annual Conference
Date: April 8-9, 2016
Location: The King Edward Hotel
Toronto, ON
Sponsor/Contact: Ontario Psychological Association
#403, 21 St. Clair Ave. East
Toronto, ON M4T 1L8
416-961-5552
E-mail: opa@psych.on.ca
URL: www.psych.on.ca
Scope: Provincial

69th Society of Architectural Historians Annual Conference
Date: April 6-10, 2016
Location: Pasadena, CA USA
Sponsor/Contact: Society of Architectural Historians
1365 North Astor St.
Chicago, IL 60610-2144
312-573-1365 *Fax:* 312-573-1141
E-mail: info@sah.org
URL: www.sah.org
Scope: International

American Concrete Institute Spring 2016 Convention: Concrete Endures
Date: April 17-21, 2016
Location: Hyatt & Frontier Airlines Center
Milwaukee, WI USA
Sponsor/Contact: American Concrete Institute
P.O. Box 9094
38800 Country Club Dr.
Farmington, MI 48333-9094
248-848-3700 *Fax:* 248-848-3701
URL: www.concrete.org
Scope: International

Association of Vancouver Island Coastal Communities 2016 Annual General Meeting & Convention
Date: April 8-10, 2016
Location: Nanaimo, BC
Sponsor/Contact: Association of Vancouver Island Coastal Communities
Local Government House
525 Government St.
Victoria, BC V8W 0A8
250-356-5122 *Fax:* 250-356-5119
URL: www.avicc.ca
Scope: Local
Contact Information: Contact: Iris Hesketh-Boles, E-mail: iheskethboles@ubcm.ca

Canadian Air Traffic Control Association 2016 Convention
Location: Halifax, NS
Sponsor/Contact: Canadian Air Traffic Control Association
#304, 265 Carling Ave.
Ottawa, ON K1S 2E1
613-225-3553 *Fax:* 613-225-8448
E-mail: catca@catca.ca
URL: www.catca.ca
Scope: National
Purpose: A biennial convention attended by delegates from regions across Canada

Canadian Respiratory Conference 2016
Location: Halifax Convention Centre
Halifax, NS
Sponsor/Contact: Canadian Lung Association
National Office
#300, 1750 Courtwood Cres.
Ottawa, ON K2C 2B5
613-569-6411 *Fax:* 613-569-8860
Toll-Free: 800-566-5864
E-mail: info@lung.ca
URL: www.lung.ca
Scope: National
Purpose: Jointly organized by the Canadian Lung Association, the Canadian Thoracic Society, the Canadian COPD Alliance, & the Canadian Respiratory Health Professionals
Anticipated Attendance: 650
Contact Information: Web Site: www.lung.ca/crc; E-mail: crc@taylorandassociates.ca

Carl Orff Canada Music for Children 24th National Conference
Date: April 28 - May 1, 2016
Location: Sheraton Cavalier Hotel
Saskatoon, SK
Sponsor/Contact: Carl Orff Canada Music for Children
c/o Joan Linklater
88 Tunis Bay
Winnipeg, MB R3T 2X1
204-261-1893
URL: www.orffcanada.ca
Scope: National

Council of Forest Industries 2016 Annual Convention
Date: April 6-8, 2016
Location: Kelowna, BC
Sponsor/Contact: Council of Forest Industries
Pender Place I Business Building
#1501, 700 Pender St. West
Vancouver, BC V6C 1G8
604-684-0211 *Fax:* 604-687-4930
E-mail: info@cofi.org
URL: www.cofi.org
Scope: National
Purpose: A meeting about issues affecting the forestry industries of British Columbia.
Contact Information: Phone: 604-684-0211; Fax: 604-687-4930

Library Association of Alberta Annual Conference 2016
Date: April 28 - May 1, 2016
Location: Alberta
Sponsor/Contact: Library Association of Alberta
80 Baker Cres. NW
Calgary, AB T2L 1R4
403-284-5818 *Fax:* 403-282-6646
Toll-Free: 877-522-5550
E-mail: info@laa.ca
URL: www.laa.ca
Scope: Provincial
Purpose: A conference held each spring for members of the Alberta library community, featuring association annual general meetings, session presentations, networking opportunities, & a trade show. Beginning this year, the conference is no longer held jointly with the Alberta Library Trustees Association (ALTA).
Contact Information: Library Association of Alberta, Phone: 403-284-5818, Toll-Free Phone: 1-877-522-5550, Fax: 403-282-6646, E-mail: info@laa.ca, info@albertalibraryconference.com

Northwest Wall & Ceiling Bureau 2016 Annual Convention & Trade Show
Date: April 28-30, 2016
Location: San Diego, CA USA
Sponsor/Contact: Northwest Wall & Ceiling Bureau
1032A NE 65th St.
Seattle, WA 98115
E-mail: info@nwcb.org
URL: www.nwcb.org
Scope: International
Purpose: Informative seminars & exhibits, plus networking opportunities, for persons in the northwestern wall & ceiling industry
Contact Information: Director, Communications & Events: Tiina Freeman, E-mail: tiina@nwcb.org;

Exhibitor & Sponsorship Information, Phone: 206-524-4243

Pediatric Academic Societies' 2016 Annual Meeting
Date: April 30 - May 3, 2016
Location: Baltimore, MD USA
Sponsor/Contact: Academic Pediatric Association
6728 Old McLean Village Dr.
McLean, VA 22101
703-556-9222 *Fax:* 703-556-8729
E-mail: info@academicpeds.org
URL: www.ambpeds.org
Scope: International
Purpose: An international meeting focussing on research in child health
Contact Information: Address: #7B, 3400 Research Forest Dr., The Woodlands, TX, 77381, USA; Phone: 281-419-0052; Fax: 281-419-0082

Pediatric Endocrine Society 2016 Annual Meeting
Date: April 30 - May 3, 2016
Location: Baltimore, MD USA
Sponsor/Contact: Pediatric Endocrine Society
6728 Old McLean Village Dr.
McLean, VA 22101
E-mail: info@pedsendo.org
URL: www.pedsendo.org
Scope: International
Purpose: Original science abstract sessions, poster sessions, plenary sessions, business meetings, topic symposia, workshops, & exhibits
Contact Information: E-mail: info@pedsendo.org

Public Library Association (a division of the American Library Association) 2016 Biennial Conference
Date: April 5-9, 2016
Location: Denver, CO USA
Sponsor/Contact: American Library Association
50 East Huron St.
Chicago, IL 60611
Fax: 312-440-9374
Toll-Free: 800-545-2433
E-mail: ala@ala.org
URL: www.ala.org
Scope: International
Purpose: The multi-day event offers nearly 200 education programs, social events that include author luncheons and networking receptions, and an exhibits hall featuring the latest in products and services.
Contact Information: Registration Customer Service, Phone: 1-800-974-3084, E-mail: ala@experient-inc.com

Water Environment Association of Ontario 2016 45th Annual Technical Symposium & Exhibition
Date: April 10-12, 2016
Location: Scotiabank Convention Centre Niagara Falls, ON
Sponsor/Contact: Water Environment Association of Ontario
P.O. Box 176
Milton, ON L9T 4N9
416-410-6933 *Fax:* 416-410-1626
E-mail: julie.vincent@weao.org
URL: www.weao.org
Scope: Provincial
Purpose: A conference featuring technical sessions, a keynote speaker, a student program, an awards presentation, & networking opportunities
Contact Information: Chair, Conference Committee: Frank Farkas, E-mail: farkas.f@spdsales.com

May

2016 Bienniel Conference of the Pentecostal Assemblies of Canada
Date: May 2-5, 2016
Location: Palais des congrès de Montréal Montréal, QC
Sponsor/Contact: Pentecostal Assemblies of Canada
2450 Milltower Ct.
Mississauga, ON L5N 5Z6
905-542-7400 *Fax:* 905-542-7313
E-mail: info@paoc.org
URL: www.paoc.org
Scope: National

2016 British Columbia Association of School Business Officials Annual General Meeting
Date: May 25-27, 2016
Location: Penticton, BC
Sponsor/Contact: British Columbia Association of School Business Officials
#208, 1118 Homer St.
Vancouver, BC V6B 6L5
604-687-0595 *Fax:* 604-687-8118
E-mail: executivedirector@bcasbo.ca
URL: www.bcasbo.ca
Scope: Provincial

2016 OWWA/OMWA Joint Annual Conference and OWWEA Trade Show
Date: May 1-4, 2016
Location: Windsor, ON
Sponsor/Contact: Ontario Water Works Association
#100, 922 The East Mall Dr.
Toronto, ON M9B 6K1
416-231-1555 *Fax:* 416-231-1556
Toll-Free: 866-975-0575
E-mail: waterinfo@owwa.ca
URL: www.owwa.com
Scope: Provincial
Purpose: This annual industry highlight features a full slate of plenary and technical sessions focusing on the latest in technology and research affecting drinking water from source to tap. The Trade Show consistently has more than 100 exhibitors representing the manufacturers and suppliers of products and services for the water industry.

American Association for Thoracic Surgery 96th Annual Meeting
Date: May 14-18, 2016
Location: Baltimore Convention Center Baltimore, MD USA
Sponsor/Contact: American Association for Thoracic Surgery
#221U, 900 Cummings Center
Beverly, MA
978-927-8330 *Fax:* 978-524-8890
URL: www.aats.org
Scope: International
Purpose: Education in the field of thoracic & cardiovascular surgery, for cardiothoracic surgeons, physicians in related specialties, allied health professionals, fellows & residents in cardiothoracic & general surgical training programs, as well as medical students with an interest in cardiothoracic surgery
Anticipated Attendance: 4,000

American Society of Neuroradiology 2016 54th Annual Meeting
Date: May 21-26, 2016
Location: Washington Marriott Wardman Park
Washington, DC USA
Sponsor/Contact: American Society of Neuroradiology
#207, 2210 Midwest Rd.
Oak Brook, IL 60523
630-574-0220 *Fax:* 630-574-0661
E-mail: jgantenberg@asnr.org
URL: www.asnr.org
Scope: International
Contact Information: Director, Scientific Meetings: Lora Tannehill, E-mail: ltannehill@asnr.org; Manager, Scientific Meetings: Valerie Geisendorfer, E-mail: vgeisendorfer@asnr.org

Bibliographical Society of Canada 2016 Annual General Meeting
Date: May 28 - June 3, 2016
Location: University of Calgary Calgary, AB
Sponsor/Contact: Bibliographical Society of Canada
P.O. Box 19035 Stn. Walmer
360 Bloor St. West
Toronto, ON M5S 3C9
E-mail: secretary@bsc-sbc.ca
URL: www.bsc-sbc.ca
Scope: National

Biomaterials 2016 10th World Congress
Date: May 18-22, 2016
Location: Palais des congrès (Convention Centre)
Montréal, QC
Sponsor/Contact: International Union of Societies for Biomaterials Science & Engineering
c/o Prof. Nicholas A. Peppas, The University of Texas at Austin
#C-0400, 1 University Station
Austin, TX 78712-0231
512-471-6644 *Fax:* 512-471-8227
E-mail: peppas@che.utexas.edu
URL: www.worldbiomaterials.org
Scope: International

Canada's Venture Capital & Private Equity Association 2016 Annual Conference
Location: Halifax Convention Centre Halifax, NS
Sponsor/Contact: Canada's Venture Capital & Private Equity Association
Heritage Bldg., MaRS Centre
#120J, 101 College St.
Toronto, ON M5G 1L7
416-487-0519 *Fax:* 416-487-5899
E-mail: cvca@cvca.ca
URL: www.cvca.ca
Anticipated Attendance: 600

Canadian Association of Law Libraries Annual General Meeting, 2016
Date: May 14-18, 2016
Location: Vancouver, BC
Sponsor/Contact: Canadian Association of Law Libraries
P.O. Box 1570
#310, 4 Cataraqui St.
Kingston, ON K7L 5C8
613-531-9338 *Fax:* 613-531-0626
E-mail: office@callacbd.ca
URL: www.callacbd.ca
Scope: National

Canadian Association of Municipal Administrators 2016 45th Annual Conference & Annual General Meeting
Date: May 30 - June 1, 2016
Location: Winnipeg, MB
Sponsor/Contact: Canadian Association of Municipal Administrators
P.O. Box 128 Stn. A
Fredericton, NB E3B 4Y2
866-771-2262
E-mail: admin@camacam.ca
URL: www.camacam.ca
Scope: National
Purpose: Information & a trade show for senior managers from Canadian municipalities throughout Canada
Contact Information: E-mail: admin@camacam.ca

Canadian Health Libraries Association (CHLA) / Association des bibliothèques de la santé du Canada (ABSC) 2016 40th Annual Conference
Date: May 13-18, 2016
Location: Toronto, ON
Sponsor/Contact: Canadian Health Libraries Association
39 River St.
Toronto, ON M5A 3P1
416-646-1600 *Fax:* 416-646-9460
E-mail: info@chla-absc.ca
URL: www.chla-absc.ca
Scope: National
Purpose: A joint conference with the Medical Library Association
Contact Information: Continuing Education, E-mail: ce@chla-absc.ca; Public Relations, E-mail: pr@chla-absc.ca

Canadian Pain Society 2016 Annual Meeting
Date: May 8-10, 2016
Location: Winnipeg, MB
Sponsor/Contact: Canadian Pain Society
#202, 1143 Wentworth St. West
Oshawa, ON L1J 8P7
905-404-9545 *Fax:* 905-404-3727
E-mail: office@canadianpainsociety.ca
URL: www.canadianpainsociety.ca
Scope: National
Purpose: The exchange of current information about pain assessment, pain mechanisms, & pain management for healthcare professionals, scientists, & trainees from clinical, research, industry, & policy settings
Contact Information: Office Manager, Canadian Pain Society Office: Ellen Maracle-Benton, E-mail: ellen@canadianpainsociety.ca

Canadian Physiotherapy Association 2016 Congress
Date: May 26-29, 2016
Location: Victoria, BC
Sponsor/Contact: Canadian Physiotherapy Association
955 Green Valley Cres.
Ottawa, ON K2C 3V4
613-564-5454 *Fax:* 613-564-1577
Toll-Free: 800-387-8679
E-mail: information@physiotherapy.ca
URL: www.physiotherapy.ca
Scope: National
Purpose: Educational courses, workshops, the presentation of scientific research, private practice leadership information, & networking opportunities for physiotherapists from across Canada
Contact Information: Registration Contact: Hope Caldwell, Phone: 1-800-387-8679,

ext. 247, E-mail: hcaldwell@physiotherapy.ca

Canadian Society for Medical Laboratory Science / Société canadienne de science de laboratoire médical LABCON2016
Date: May 22-24, 2016
Location: Fairmont Queen Elizabeth Montréal, QC
Sponsor/Contact: Canadian Society for Medical Laboratory Science
33 Wellington Ave. North
Hamilton, ON L8R 1M7
905-528-8642 *Fax:* 905-528-4968
Toll-Free: 800-263-8277
URL: www.csmls.org
Scope: National
Contact Information: Staff Contact: Natalie Marino, Phone: 905-528-8642 ext. 8696

Canadian Urban Transit Association 2016 Annual Conference
Date: May 14-18, 2016
Location: Halifax, NS
Sponsor/Contact: Canadian Urban Transit Association
#1401, 55 York St.
Toronto, ON M5J 1R7
416-365-9800 *Fax:* 416-365-1295
URL: www.cutaactu.ca
Scope: National
Purpose: Professional development sessions & the presentation of Corporate Awards, held in May or June each year

Electro-Federation Canada Annual Conference 2016
Date: May 31-June 3, 2016
Sponsor/Contact: Electro-Federation Canada Inc.
#300, 180 Attwell Dr.
Toronto, ON M9W 6A9
905-602-8877 *Fax:* 905-602-5686
Toll-Free: 866-602-8877
URL: www.electrofed.com
Scope: National
Contact Information: Nathalie Lajoie; Phone: 647-258-7484

Government Finance Officers Association 2016 110th Annual Conference
Date: May 22-25, 2016
Location: Toronto, ON
Sponsor/Contact: Government Finance Officers Association
#2700, 203 North LaSalle St.
Chicago, IL 60601-1210
312-977-9700 *Fax:* 312-977-4806
E-mail: inquiry@gfoa.org
URL: www.gfoa.org
Scope: International
Anticipated Attendance: 4,100+
Contact Information: Manager, Communications: Natalie Laudadio, Phone: 312-977-9700, ext. 2298

International Society for Magnetic Resonance in Medicine 2016 24th Scientific Meeting & Exhibition
Date: May 7-13, 2016
Location: Singapore
Sponsor/Contact: International Society for Magnetic Resonance in Medicine
2030 Addison St., 7th Fl.
Berkeley, CA 94704
510-841-1899 *Fax:* 510-841-2340
E-mail: info@ismrm.org
URL: www.ismrm.org
Scope: International
Purpose: Featuring the 25th Annual Meeting of the Section for Magnetic Resonance Technologists
Contact Information: Director, Meetings: Sandra Daudlin, E-mail: sandra@ismrm.org; Coordinator, Meetings: Melisa Martinez, E-mail: melisa@ismrm.org

Journées dentaires internationales du Québec (JDIQ) 2016
Date: 27 au 31 mai 2016
Location: Quebec
Sponsor/Contact: Ordre des dentistes du Québec
625, boul René-Lévesque ouest, 15e étage
Montréal, QC H3B 1R2
514-875-8511 *Fax:* 514-393-9248
Toll-Free: 800-361-4887
URL: www.odq.qc.ca
Scope: Provincial
Contact Information: Directeur, Dr Denis Forest, téléphone: 514-875-8511, poste 2222; adresse email: denis.forest@odq.qc.ca

Lower Mainland Local Government Association 2016 Annual General Meeting & Conference
Date: May 11-13, 2016
Location: Fairmont Chateau Whistler Whistler, BC
Sponsor/Contact: Lower Mainland Local Government Association
#60, 10551 Shellbridge Way
Richmond, BC V6X 2W9
250-356-5122 *Fax:* 604-270-9116
URL: www.lmlga.ca
Scope: Local
Purpose: Tradeshow, workshops, & seminars for persons involved in local government

Manitoba Association of Library Technicians 2016 Annual General Meeting
Date: May 2016
Location: Manitoba
Sponsor/Contact: Manitoba Association of Library Technicians
P.O. Box 1872
Winnipeg, MB R3C 3R1
E-mail: malt.mb.ca@gmail.com
URL: www.malt.mb.ca
Scope: Provincial
Purpose: Each year between May 1st & May 31st, reports of the association's executive are presented & officers are elected

Medical Library Association 2016 Annual Meeting & Exhibition
Date: May 13-18, 2016
Location: Toronto, ON
Sponsor/Contact: Medical Library Association
#1900, 65 East Wacker Pl.
Chicago, IL 60601-7246
312-419-9094 *Fax:* 312-419-8950
E-mail: info@mlahq.org
URL: www.mlanet.org
Scope: International

Microwave Theory & Techniques Society International Microwave Symposia 2016
Date: May 22-27, 2016
Location: San Francisco, CA USA
Sponsor/Contact: IEEE Microwave Theory & Techniques Society
5829 Bellanca Dr.
Elkridge, MD 21075
410-796-5866 *Fax:* 410-796-5829
URL: www.mtt.org
Scope: International
Purpose: Technical papers; Workshops; Trade show

Ontario Dental Association Annual Spring Meeting 2016
Date: May 5-7, 2016
Location: Metro Toronto Convention Centre
Toronto, ON
Sponsor/Contact: Ontario Dental Association
4 New St.
Toronto, ON M5R 1P6
416-922-3900 *Fax:* 416-922-9005
Toll-Free: 800-387-1393
E-mail: info@oda.ca
URL: www.oda.ca
Scope: Provincial
Anticipated Attendance: 11,700

Ontario Small Urban Municipalities 2016 63rd Annual Conference & Trade Show
Date: May 3-6, 2016
Location: Stratford, ON
Sponsor/Contact: Ontario Small Urban Municipalities
c/o Association of Municipalities of Ontario
#801, 200 University Ave.
Toronto, ON M5H 3C6
416-971-9856 *Fax:* 416-971-6191
Toll-Free: 877-426-6527
E-mail: amo@amo.on.ca
URL: www.osum.ca
Scope: Provincial
Anticipated Attendance: 200+
Contact Information: OSUM Annual Conference & Trade Show Coordinator: Ted Blowes, Phone: 519-271-0250, ext. 241, E-mail: ted.b@quadro.net

Ontario Water Works Association / Ontario Municipal Water Association 2016 Annual Joint Conference & Trade Show
Date: May 1-4, 2016
Location: Windsor, ON
Sponsor/Contact: Ontario Municipal Water Association
c/o Doug Parker
43 Chelsea Cres.
Belleville, ON K8N 4Z5
613-966-1100 *Fax:* 613-966-3024
Toll-Free: 888-231-1115
URL: www.omwa.org
Scope: Provincial
Purpose: A conference featuring a plenary session, technical sessions, a trade show, & networking opportunities

June

2016 Canadian Society of Landscape Architects Congress
Date: June 23-25, 2016
Location: Fort Garry Hotel, Spa and Conference Centre
Winnipeg, MB
Sponsor/Contact: Canadian Society of Landscape Architects
P.O. Box 13594
Ottawa, ON K2K 1X6
866-781-9799 *Fax:* 866-871-1419
E-mail: info@csla.ca
URL: www.csla.ca
Scope: National

93rd Canadian Paediatric Society Annual Conference 2016
Date: June 22-25, 2016
Location: Charlottetown, PE
Sponsor/Contact: Canadian Paediatric Society
2305 St. Laurent Blvd.
Ottawa, ON K1G 4J8
613-526-9397 *Fax:* 613-526-3332
E-mail: info@cps.ca
URL: www.cps.ca
Scope: National
Contact Information: Phone: 613-526-9397 ext. 2148, Email: meetings@cps.ca, www.annualconference.cps.ca

ARMA Annual Conference & Expo 2016
Location: Halifax Annual Conference Halifax, NS
Sponsor/Contact: ARMA International
#450, 11880 College Blvd.
Overland Park, KS 66215
913-341-3808 *Fax:* 913-341-3742
Toll-Free: 800-422-2762
E-mail: hq@armaintl.org
URL: www.arma.org
Anticipated Attendance: 600

American Library Association 2016 Annual Conference
Date: June 23-28, 2016
Location: Orlando, FL USA
Sponsor/Contact: American Library Association
50 East Huron St.
Chicago, IL 60611
Fax: 312-440-9374
Toll-Free: 800-545-2433
E-mail: ala@ala.org
URL: www.ala.org
Scope: International
Purpose: A conference providing speakers, educational programs, committee meetings, & exhibits related to library & information services
Contact Information: Registration Customer Service, Phone: 1-800-974-3084, E-mail: ala@experient-inc.com

American Water Works Association 2016 135th Annual Conference & Exposition
Date: June 12-16, 2016
Location: Chicago, IL USA
Sponsor/Contact: American Water Works Association
6666 West Quincy Ave.
Denver, CO 80235
303-794-7711 *Fax:* 303-347-0804
Toll-Free: 800-926-7337
E-mail: custsvc@awwa.org
URL: www.awwa.org
Scope: International
Purpose: Offering a technical program, professional development activities, & exhibitors for the worldwide water community
Contact Information: American Water Works Association, Phone: 800-926-7337, Fax: 303-347-0804, E-mail: awwamktg@awwa.org

Association of Canadian Archivists 2016 41st Annual Conference & Annual General Meeting
Date: June 2-4, 2016
Location: Marriott Chateau Champlain Montréal, QC

Sponsor/Contact: Association of Canadian Archivists
P.O. Box 2596 Stn. D
Ottawa, ON K1P 5W6
613-234-6977 *Fax:* 613-234-8500
E-mail: aca@archivists.ca
URL: www.archivists.ca
Scope: National
Purpose: A meeting occurring in May or June each year, for archivists from across Canada, featuring educational presentations, trade show exhibits, networking opportunities, as well as workshops immediately prior or following conference sessions
Contact Information: Association of Canadian Archivists Board or Office, E-mail: aca@archivists.ca

Canadian Anesthesiologists' Society 2016 72nd Annual Meeting
Date: June 24-27, 2016
Location: Vancouver Convention Centre
Vancouver, BC
Sponsor/Contact: Canadian Anesthesiologists' Society
#208, One Eglinton Ave. East
Toronto, ON M4P 3A1
416-480-0602 *Fax:* 416-480-0320
E-mail: anesthesia@cas.ca
URL: www.cas.ca
Scope: National
Purpose: A convention, with an exhibition pharmaceutical companies & equipment manufacturers

Canadian Association for Enterostomal Therapy National Conference 2016
Date: June 4-8, 2016
Location: Palais Congres
Montreal, QC
Sponsor/Contact: Canadian Association for Enterostomal Therapy
66 Leopolds Dr.
Ottawa, ON K1V 7E3
Fax: 613-834-6351
Toll-Free: 888-739-5072
E-mail: office@caet.ca
URL: www.caet.ca
Scope: National
Purpose: In partnership with Wound, Ostomy Continence Nurses Society (WOCN).

Canadian Association of Emergency Physicians (CAEP) 2016 Annual Conference
Date: June 3-8, 2016
Location: Quebec City Convention Centre
Quebec City, QC
Sponsor/Contact: Canadian Association of Emergency Physicians
#808, 180 Elgin St.
Ottawa, ON K2P 2K3
613-523-3343 *Fax:* 613-523-0190
Toll-Free: 800-463-1158
E-mail: admin@caep.ca
URL: www.caep.ca
Scope: National

Canadian Association of University Business Officers 2016 Annual Conference
Date: June 12-14, 2016
Location: Université du Québec
Québec, QC
Sponsor/Contact: Canadian Association of University Business Officers
#320, 350 Albert St.
Ottawa, ON K1R 1B1
613-230-6760 *Fax:* 613-563-7739
E-mail: info@caubo.ca
URL: www.caubo.ca
Scope: National

Canadian Institute of Plumbing & Heating 2016 Annual Business Conference/Annual General Meeting
Date: June 26-28, 2016
Location: Fairmont Banff Springs
Banff, AB
Sponsor/Contact: Canadian Institute of Plumbing & Heating
#504, 295 The West Mall
Toronto, ON M9C 4Z4
416-695-0447 *Fax:* 416-695-0450
Toll-Free: 800-639-2474
E-mail: info@ciph.com
URL: www.ciph.com
Scope: National

Canadian Library Association / Association canadienne des bibliothèques 71st National Conference & Trade Show 2016
Date: June 1-4, 2016
Location: Halifax Convention Centre
Halifax, NS
Sponsor/Contact: Canadian Library Association
#400, 1150 Morrison Dr.
Ottawa, ON K2H 8S9
613-232-9625 *Fax:* 613-563-9895
E-mail: info@cla.ca
URL: www.cla.ca
Scope: National
Purpose: Conference program includes educational workshops, keynote speakers, networking opportunities, & exhibitors at the trade show
Anticipated Attendance: 1,500
Contact Information: Manager, Conference & Events: Wendy Walton, Phone: 613-232-9625, ext. 302, E-mail: wwalton@cla.ca; Manager, Marketing & Communications (Trade show & sponsorship opportunities): Judy Green, Phone: 613-232-9625, ext. 322, E-mail: jgreen@cla.ca

Canadian Nurses Association 2016 Annual Meeting & Biennial Convention
Date: June 20-22, 2016
Location: New Brunswick
Sponsor/Contact: Canadian Nurses Association
50 Driveway
Ottawa, ON K2P 1E2
613-237-2133 *Fax:* 613-237-3520
Toll-Free: 800-361-8404
E-mail: info@cna-aiic.ca
URL: www.cna-aiic.ca
Scope: National
Purpose: One of Canada's largest nursing conferences, featuring presentations, speakers, workshops, & the opportunity to view new products in the health-care marketplace
Anticipated Attendance: 1,000+
Contact Information: E-mail: conferences@cna-aiic.ca

Canadian Ophthalmological Society 2016 Annual Meeting & Exhibition
Date: June 17-20, 2016
Location: Shaw Centre
Ottawa, ON
Sponsor/Contact: Canadian Ophthalmological Society
#610, 1525 Carling Ave.
Ottawa, ON K1Z 8R9
613-729-6779 *Fax:* 613-729-7209
E-mail: cos@eyesite.ca
URL: www.eyesite.ca
Scope: National
Contact Information: cos@eyesite.ca

Canadian Organization of Campus Activities 2016 National Conference
Date: June 7-11, 2016
Location: Ottawa, ON
Sponsor/Contact: Canadian Organization of Campus Activities
#202, 509 Commissioners Rd. West
London, ON N6J 1Y5
519-690-0207 *Fax:* 519-681-4328
E-mail: cocaoffice@coca.org
URL: www.coca.org
Scope: National
Purpose: Educational sessions, plus showcases featuring music, films, & comedy, plus the Campus Activities Biz Hall trade show

Canadian Orthopaedic Association 2016 71st Annual Meeting & Canadian Orthopaedic Research Society 50th Annual Meeting
Location: Halifax Convention Centre
Halifax, NS
Sponsor/Contact: Canadian Orthopaedic Association
#360, 4150, rue Ste-Catherine ouest
Montréal, QC H3Z 2Y5
514-874-9003 *Fax:* 514-874-0464
E-mail: cynthia@canorth.org
URL: www.coa-aco.org
Scope: National
Anticipated Attendance: 600

Canadian Pharmacists Association 2016 104th Annual National Conference
Date: June 4-7, 2016
Location: Vancouver, BC
Sponsor/Contact: Canadian Pharmacists Association
1785 Alta Vista Dr.
Ottawa, ON K1G 3Y6
613-523-7877 *Fax:* 613-523-0445
Toll-Free: 800-917-9489
E-mail: info@pharmacists.ca
URL: www.pharmacists.ca
Scope: National
Purpose: Educational oral & poster presentations, a trade show, an awards presentation, & networking events
Contact Information: E-mail: info@pharmacists.ca

Canadian Psychological Association 2016 77th Annual Convention
Date: June 9-11, 2016
Location: Victoria Conference Centre & The Fairmont Empress Hotel
Victoria, BC
Sponsor/Contact: Canadian Psychological Association
#702, 141 Laurier Ave. West
Ottawa, ON K1P 5J3
613-237-2144 *Fax:* 613-237-1674
Toll-Free: 888-472-0657
E-mail: cpa@cpa.ca
URL: www.cpa.ca
Scope: National
Purpose: An educational conference & exhibition
Contact Information: E-mail: convention@cpa.ca

Canadian Public Health Association 2016 Conference
Date: June 13-16, 2016
Location: Toronto, ON
Sponsor/Contact: Canadian Public Health Association
#300, 1565 Carling Ave.
Ottawa, ON K1Z 8R1
613-725-3769 *Fax:* 613-725-9826
E-mail: info@cpha.ca
URL: www.cpha.ca
Scope: National
Purpose: A conference for policy-makers, researchers, environmental health professionals, academics, & students from across Canada
Contact Information: Conference Manager: Sarah Pettenuzzo, Phone: 613-725-3769, ext. 153; Conference Officer: Julie Paquette, Phone: 613-725-3769, ext. 126

Canadian Society for Chemistry 2016 99th Canadian Chemistry Conference & Exhibition
Location: Halifax Convention Centre
Halifax, NS
Sponsor/Contact: Canadian Society for Chemistry
#550, 130 Slater St.
Ottawa, ON K1P 6E2
613-232-6252 *Fax:* 613-232-5862
Toll-Free: 888-542-2242
E-mail: info@cheminst.ca
URL: www.cheminst.ca
Scope: National
Anticipated Attendance: 1,000

Canadian Society of Plastic Surgeons 2016 70th Annual Meeting
Date: June 14-19, 2016
Location: Westin Hotel
Ottawa, ON
Sponsor/Contact: Canadian Society of Plastic Surgeons
#4, 1469, boul St-Joseph est
Montréal, QC H2J 1M6
514-843-5415 *Fax:* 514-843-7005
E-mail: csps_sccp@bellnet.ca
URL: www.plasticsurgery.ca
Scope: National
Purpose: An opportunity for participants to learn during the scientific program & to view exhibits
Contact Information: Phone: 514-843-5415; Fax: 514-843-7005, E-mail: csps_sccp@bellnet.ca

Canadian Union of Public Employees (CUPE) Ontario 2016 53rd Convention
Date: June 1-4, 2016
Location: Caesars Windsor Hotel
Windsor, ON
Sponsor/Contact: Canadian Union of Public Employees
Ontario Regional Office
#1, 80 Commerce Valley Dr. East
Markham, ON L3T 0B2
905-739-9739 *Fax:* 905-739-9740
E-mail: info@cupe.on.ca
URL: www.cupe.on.ca
Scope: Provincial
Purpose: A gathering where convention delegates debate & vote on resolutions
Anticipated Attendance: 1,200
Contact Information: CUPE Ontario, E-mail: info@cupe.on.ca

Canadian Urological Association 2016 71st Annual Meeting
Date: June 26-28, 2016
Location: Westin Hotel
Vancouver, BC
Sponsor/Contact: Canadian Urological Association
#1303, 1155, University St.
Montréal, QC H3B 3A7
514-395-0376 *Fax:* 514-395-1664
E-mail: cua@cua.org
URL: www.cua.org
Scope: National

Coastal Zone Canada 2016
Date: June 2016
Location: Toronto, ON
Sponsor/Contact: Coastal Zone Canada Association
c/o Jennifer Barr, Dalhousie University
P.O. Box 15000
6414 Coburg Rd.
Halifax, NS B3H 4R2
902-494-4650 *Fax:* 902-494-1334
E-mail: czcadmin@dal.ca
URL: www.czca-azcc.org
Scope: National
Contact Information: Peter Zuzek; Email: pzuzek@baird.com

Goldschmidt Conference 2016
Date: June 26 - July 1, 2016
Location: Yokohama, Japan
Sponsor/Contact: Geochemical Society
c/o Earth & Planetary Sciences Department, Washington University
#CB 11691, Brookings Dr.
St. Louis, MO 63130-4899
314-935-4131 *Fax:* 314-935-4121
E-mail: gsoffice@geochemsoc.org
URL: www.geochemsoc.org
Scope: International
Purpose: An international conference on geochemistry
Anticipated Attendance: 3,000+

International Commission of Agricultural & Biosystems Engineering 2016 4th International Conference of Agricultural Engineering (CIGR-AgEng2016)
Date: June 26-29, 2016
Location: Aarhus, Denmark
Sponsor/Contact: International Commission of Agricultural & Biosystems Engineering
c/o Dr. Takaaki Maekawa, School of Life & Environmental Sciences
1-1-1 Tennodai, University of Tsukuba
Tsukuba, Ibaraki
E-mail: biopro@sakura.cc.tsukuba.ac.jp
URL: www.cigr.org
Scope: International

Local Government Management Association of British Columbia 2016 Annual General Meeting & Conference
Date: June 21-23, 2016
Location: Vancouver Island Conference Centre
Nanaimo, BC
Sponsor/Contact: Local Government Management Association of British Columbia
Central Building
620 View St., 7th Fl.
Victoria, BC V8W 1J6
250-383-7032 *Fax:* 250-384-4879
E-mail: office@lgma.ca
URL: www.lgma.ca
Scope: Provincial
Purpose: A meeting & tradeshow held each year in May or June in British Columbia for members of the Local Government Management Association of British Columbia
Anticipated Attendance: 400-500
Contact Information: Program Coordinator: Ana Fuller, Phone: 250-383-7032, ext. 227, Fax: 250-383-4879, E-mail: afuller@lgma.ca

North American Association of Central Cancer Registries 2016 Annual Conference
Date: June 11-17, 2016
Location: St. Louis, MI USA
Sponsor/Contact: North American Association of Central Cancer Registries, Inc.
2121 West White Oaks Dr., #B
Springfield, IL 62704-7412
217-698-0800 *Fax:* 217-698-0188
E-mail: info@naaccr.org
URL: www.naaccr.org
Scope: International
Anticipated Attendance: 450

XIIIth International Orthoptic Congress 2016
Date: June 27-30, 2016
Location: Westin Harbour Castle Hotel
Rotterdam, The Netherlands
Sponsor/Contact: International Orthoptic Association
c/o Moorfields Eye Hospital
City Rd.
London, EC1V 2PD
E-mail: webmaster@internationalorthoptics.org
URL: www.internationalorthoptics.org
Scope: International
Purpose: Plenary sessions, exhibitions, & educational activities
Contact Information: Web Site: www.ioacongress2016.org; E-mail: IOA2016@congrex.com

July

Association of Visual Language Interpreters of Canada Summer 2016 Biennial Conference: Interpreters & Human Rights
Date: July 12-16, 2016
Location: Fredericton Convention Centre
Fredericton, NB
Sponsor/Contact: Association of Visual Language Interpreters of Canada
#110, 39012 Discovery Way
Squamish, BC V8B 0E5
604-617-8502 *Fax:* 604-567-8502
E-mail: avlic@avlic.ca
URL: www.avlic.ca
Scope: National
Contact Information: Web Site: www.avlic2016.com; Co-Chair: Becky Schirato, E-mail: chairperson@avlic2016.com

Controlled Release Society 2016 43rd Annual Meeting & Exposition
Date: July 17-20, 2016
Location: Washington State Convention Center
Seattle, WA USA
Sponsor/Contact: Controlled Release Society
3340 Pilot Knob Rd.
St. Paul, MN 55121
651-454-7250 *Fax:* 651-454-0766
E-mail: crs@scisoc.org
URL: www.controlledrelease.org
Scope: International
Contact Information: Meeting Manager: Tressa Patrias, Email: tpatrias@scisoc.org

Institute of Food Technologists 2016 Annual Meeting & Food Expo
Date: July 16-19, 2016
Location: McCormick Place South
Chicago, IL USA
Sponsor/Contact: Institute of Food Technologists
#1000, 525 West Van Buren
Chicago, IL 60607
312-782-8424 *Fax:* 312-782-8348
Toll-Free: 800-438-3663
E-mail: info@ift.org
URL: www.ift.org
Scope: International
Purpose: An annual gathering of thousands of food professionals from around the world to participate in scientific sessions, poster sessions, the IFT Food Expo, an awards celebration, & networking events

International Association of Music Libraries, Archives & Documentation Centres 2016 65th Annual Conference
Date: July 3-8, 2016
Location: Rome, Italy
Sponsor/Contact: International Association of Music Libraries, Archives & Documentation Centres
c/o Roger Flury, Music Room, National Library of New Zealand
P.O. Box 1467
Wellington, 6001
URL: www.iaml.info
Scope: International
Purpose: Presenting association committee & national branch meetings, guest speakers, & informative sessions related to music librarianship

Joint Statistical Meetings 2016
Date: July 30 - August 4, 2016
Location: Chicago, IL USA
Sponsor/Contact: Statistical Society of Canada
#209, 1725 St. Laurent Blvd.
Ottawa, ON K1G 3V4
613-733-2662 *Fax:* 613-733-1386
E-mail: info@ssc.ca
URL: www.ssc.ca
Scope: International
Purpose: Held jointly with the Statistical Society of Canada, American Statistical Association, the International Biometric Society (ENAR & WNAR), the International Chinese Statistical Association, the Institute of Mathematical Statistics, & the International Indian Statistical Association

Soroptimist 43rd Biennial Convention 2016
Date: July 20-23, 2016
Location: Walt Disney World Dolphin Hotel
Orlando, FL USA
Sponsor/Contact: Soroptimist International of the Americas
1709 Spruce St.
Philadelphia, PA 19103-6103
215-893-9000 *Fax:* 215-893-5200
E-mail: siahq@soroptimist.org
URL: www.soroptimist.org
Scope: International

August

15th International Peat Congress: Peatland in Harmony - Agriculture, Industry, Nature
Date: August 15-19, 2016
Location: Kuching, Malaysia
Sponsor/Contact: International Peat Society
Kauppakatu 19 D 31
Jyväskylä, FIN-40100
E-mail: ips@peatsociety.org
URL: www.peatsociety.org
Scope: International

2016 World Congress of Food Science of Technology
Date: August 21-25, 2016
Location: Royal Dublin Society
Dublin, Ireland
Sponsor/Contact: Canadian Institute of Food Science & Technology
#1311, 3-1750 The Queensway
Toronto, ON M9C 5H5
905-271-8338 *Fax:* 905-271-8344
E-mail: cifst@cifst.ca
URL: www.cifst.ca
Scope: International
Purpose: IUFoST promotes the advancement of global food science and technology, fosters the worldwide exchange of scientific knowledge and ideas through the biennial World Congress and aims to strengthen food science and technology's role in helping secure the world's food supply and eliminate world hunger.
Contact Information: Email: iufost2016@conferencepartners.ie; URL: www.iufost2016.com

28th International Pediatric Association Congress of Pediatrics 2016
Date: August 17-22, 2016
Location: Vancouver, BC
Sponsor/Contact: International Pediatric Association
141 Northwest Point Blvd.
Elk Grove Village, IL 60007-1098
URL: www.ipa-world.org
Scope: International

Academy of Management 2016 Annual Meeting
Date: August 5-9, 2016
Location: Anaheim, CA USA
Sponsor/Contact: Academy of Management
P.O. Box 3020
Briarcliff Manor, NY 10510-8020
914-923-2607 *Fax:* 914-923-2615
URL: www.aomonline.org
Scope: International
Purpose: Sharing of research and expertise in all management disciplines through distinguished speakers, competitive paper sessions, symposia, panels, workshops, & special programs for doctoral students
Anticipated Attendance: 10,000+
Contact Information: Assistant Director of Meetings: Taryn Fiore, E-mail: tfiore@pace.edu

American Fisheries Society Annual Meeting
Date: August 20-25, 2016
Location: Kansas City, MO USA
Sponsor/Contact: American Fisheries Society

5410 Grosvenor Lane
Bethesda, MD 20814-2199
301-897-8616 *Fax:* 301-897-8096
URL: www.fisheries.org
Scope: International

Canadian Fertilizer Institute 71st Annual Conference
Date: August 12-19, 2016
Location: Fairmont Tremblant Quebec
Mont-Tremblant, QC
Sponsor/Contact: Canadian Fertilizer Institute
#907, 350 Sparks St.
Ottawa, ON K1R 7S8
613-230-2600 *Fax:* 613-230-5142
E-mail: info@cfi.ca
URL: www.cfi.ca
Scope: National

Canadian Medical Association 2016 149th Annual Meeting
Date: August 2016
Sponsor/Contact: Canadian Medical Association
1867 Alta Vista Dr.
Ottawa, ON K1G 5W8
613-731-8610 *Fax:* 613-236-8864
Toll-Free: 888-855-2555
E-mail: cmamsc@cma.ca
URL: www.cma.ca
Scope: National
Purpose: A meeting, featuring a business session to consider business & matters referred by the General Council
Contact Information: Registration Officer, Phone: 1-800-663-7336, ext. 2383, E-mail: gcregistrations@cma.ca

Catholic Women's League of Canada 2016 National Convention
Date: August 14-17, 2016
Location: Halifax Convention Centre
Halifax, NS
Sponsor/Contact: Catholic Women's League of Canada
702C Scotland Ave.
Winnipeg, MB R3M 1X5
Fax: 888-831-9507
Toll-Free: 888-656-4040
E-mail: info@cwl.ca
URL: www.cwl.ca
Scope: National

Institute of Transportation Engineers 2016 Annual Meeting & Exhibit
Date: August 14-17, 2016
Location: Anaheim Convention Center
Anaheim, CA USA
Sponsor/Contact: Institute of Transportation Engineers
#600, 1627 Eye St. NW
Washington, DC 20006
202-785-0060 *Fax:* 202-785-0609
E-mail: ite_staff@ite.org
URL: www.ite.org
Scope: International
Contact Information: Contact, Registration Information: Sallie C. Dollins, E-mail: sdollins@ite.org; Contact, Technical Program: Eunice Chege, E-mail: echege@ite.org; Contact, Exhibits: Christina Garneski, E-mail: cgarneski@ite.org; Contact, Paper Submittals: Eunice Chege, E-mail: echege@ite.org

International Board on Books for Young People 2016 35th International Congress
Date: August 25-28, 2016
Location: Auckland, New Zealand
Sponsor/Contact: International Board on Books for Young People
Nonnenweg 12, Postfach
Basel, CH-4003
E-mail: ibby@ibby.org
URL: www.ibby.org
Scope: International
Purpose: A biennial congress, hosted by an IBBY national section, for IBBY members & people involved in children's books & reading development from around the world. This year's theme is "Literature in a Multi-linguistic Society."

September

2016 Entomological Society of Canada Annual Meeting and International Congress of Entomology
Date: September 23-30, 2016
Location: Orlando, FL USA
Sponsor/Contact: Entomological Society of Canada
393 Winston Ave.
Ottawa, ON K2A 1Y8
613-725-2619
E-mail: entsoc.can@bellnet.ca
URL: www.esc-sec.ca
Scope: National

American Association of Neuromuscular & Electrodiagnostic Medicine 2016 63rd Annual Meeting
Date: September 14-17, 2016
Location: Hilton New Orleans
New Orleans, LA USA
Sponsor/Contact: American Association of Neuromuscular & Electrodiagnostic Medicine
2621 Superior Dr. NW
Rochester, MN 55901
507-288-0100 *Fax:* 507-288-1225
E-mail: aanem@aanem.org
URL: www.aanem.org
Scope: International
Contact Information: Director, Meetings: Denae Brennan, E-mail: dbrennan@aanem.org

Building Owners & Managers Association 2016 Conference
Date: September 20-22, 2016
Location: Regina, SK
Sponsor/Contact: Building Owners & Managers Association - Canada
P.O. Box 61
#1801, 1 Dundas St. West
Toronto, ON M5G 1Z3
416-214-1912 *Fax:* 416-214-1284
E-mail: info@bomacanada.ca
URL: www.bomacanada.ca
Scope: National

Canadian Association of Orthodontists 2016 68th Annual Scientific Session
Date: September 15-17, 2016
Location: Delta Prince Edward & PEI Convention Centre
Charlottetown, PE
Sponsor/Contact: Canadian Association of Orthodontists
#310, 2175 Sheppard Ave. East
Toronto, ON M2J 1W8
416-491-3186 *Fax:* 416-491-1670
Toll-Free: 877-226-8800
E-mail: cao@taylorenterprises.com
URL: www.cao-aco.org
Scope: National
Purpose: A scientific session with exhibits

Canadian Association of Radiation Oncology 2016 Annual Scientific Meeting
Date: September 14-17, 2016
Location: Fairmont Banff Springs
Banff, AB
Sponsor/Contact: Canadian Association of Radiation Oncology
774 Echo Dr.
Ottawa, ON K1S 5N8
613-260-4188 *Fax:* 613-730-1116
E-mail: caro-acro@rcpsc.edu
URL: www.caro-acro.ca
Scope: National
Purpose: Lectures, presentations, & exhibits for health professionals involved in radiation oncology

Canadian Fertility & Andrology Society 2016 62nd Annual Meeting
Date: September 22-24, 2016
Location: Sheraton Centre
Toronto, ON
Sponsor/Contact: Canadian Fertility & Andrology Society
#1107, 1255, rue University
Montréal, QC H3B 3W7
514-524-9009 *Fax:* 514-524-2163
E-mail: info@cfas.ca
URL: www.cfas.ca
Scope: National
Purpose: Educational presentations, a trade show, & networking opportunities for persons involved in the field of reproductive medicine

Canadian Psychiatric Association 66th Annual Conference / 66e Conférence annuelle de l'Association des psychiatres du Canada
Date: September 15-17, 2016
Location: The Westin Harbour Castle
Toronto, ON
Sponsor/Contact: Canadian Psychiatric Association
#701, 141 Laurier Ave. West
Ottawa, ON K1P 5J3
613-234-2815 *Fax:* 613-234-9857
Toll-Free: 800-267-1555
E-mail: cpa@cpa-apc.org
URL: www.cpa-apc.org
Scope: National
Anticipated Attendance: 1200+
Contact Information: E-mail: conference@cpa-apc.org

Canadian Society for Vascular Surgery 2016 38th Annual Meeting
Date: September 16-17, 2016
Location: The Westin Nova Scotian
Halifax, NS
Sponsor/Contact: Canadian Society for Vascular Surgery
c/o Christiane Dowsing, Society Manager
774 Echo Dr.
Ottawa, ON K1S 5N8
613-730-6263 *Fax:* 613-730-1116
E-mail: csvs@royalcollege.ca
URL: canadianvascular.ca
Scope: National
Purpose: The annual general meeting of the society, plus continuing education sessions, lectures, exhibits, & social events

Dynamics 2016: The Annual National Convention & Product Exhibition of the Canadian Association of Critical Care Nurses
Date: September 25-27, 2016
Location: Charlottetown, PE
Sponsor/Contact: Canadian Association of Critical Care Nurses
P.O. Box 25322
London, ON N6C 6B1
519-649-5284 *Fax:* 519-649-1458
Toll-Free: 866-477-9077
E-mail: caccn@caccn.ca
URL: www.caccn.ca
Scope: National
Purpose: Featuring programming to enhance education, clinical practice, research, & leadership.
Contact Information: Toll-Free Phone: 1-866-477-9077; E-mail: caccn@caccn.ca

International Association for Child & Adolescent Psychiatry & Allied Professions / Canadian Academy of Child and Adolescent Psychiatry Conference 2016
Date: September 18-22, 2016
Location: Calgary TELUS Convention Centre
Calgary, AB
Sponsor/Contact: Canadian Academy of Child & Adolescent Psychiatry
#701, 141 Laurier Ave. West
Ottawa, ON KIP 5J3
613-288-0408 *Fax:* 613-234-9857
E-mail: info@cacap-acpea.org
URL: www.cacap-acpea.org
Scope: International
Contact Information: URL: www.iacapap2016.org

International Society of Hypertension 26th Scientific Meeting
Date: September 24-29, 2016
Location: Seoul, Korea
Sponsor/Contact: International Society of Hypertension
ISH Secretariat, Hampton Medical Conferences Ltd.
113-119 High St.
Hampton Hill, Middlesex, TW12 1NJ
E-mail: secretariat@ish-world.com
URL: www.ish-world.com
Scope: International
Purpose: Scientific program & exhibition

International Water Association World Water Congress & Exhibition 2016
Date: September 25-30, 2016
Location: Brisbane, Australia
Sponsor/Contact: International Water Association
Alliance House
12 Caxton St.
London, SW1H 0QS
E-mail: water@iwahq.org
URL: www.iwahq.org
Scope: International
Purpose: Provides international water experts the change to explore the science & practice of water management

National Insurance Conference of Canada 2016
Date: September 28-30, 2016
Location: The Westin Bayshore
Vancouver, BC
Sponsor/Contact: Insurance Bureau of Canada
P.O. Box 121
#2400, 777 Bay St.
Toronto, ON M5G 2C8
416-362-2031 *Fax:* 416-361-5952
URL: www.ibc.ca
Scope: National
Purpose: Sponsored by the Insurance

Conferences Index

Bureau of Canada, among other companies & organizations
Contact Information: Web Site: www.niccanada.com; Phone: 416-368-0777; Fax: 416-363-7454

TRENDS: The Apparel Show 2016 (sponsored by the Alberta Men's Wear Agents Association)
Date: September 8-12, 2016
Location: Edmonton Expo Centre
Edmonton, AB
Sponsor/Contact: Alberta Men's Wear Agents Association
P.O. Box 66037 Stn. Heritage
Edmonton, AB T6J 6T4
780-455-1881 *Fax:* 780-455-3969
E-mail: amwa@shaw.ca
URL: www.trendsapparel.com
Scope: Provincial
Purpose: A semiannual show involving the participation of wholesale sales representatives showing clothing & shoes
Contact Information: E-mail: amwa@shaw.ca

The American Association of Bovine Practitioners 2016 Annual Conference
Date: September 15-17, 2016
Location: Charlotte, NC USA
Sponsor/Contact: American Association of Bovine Practitioners
P.O. Box 3610
#802, 3320 Skyway Dr.
Auburn, AL 36831-3610
334-821-0442 *Fax:* 334-821-9532
E-mail: aabphq@aabp.org
URL: www.aabp.org
Scope: International

Union of British Columbia Municipalities 2016 Annual Convention
Date: September 26-39, 2016
Location: Penticton Trade & Convention Centre
British Columbia
Sponsor/Contact: Union of British Columbia Municipalities
#60, 10551 Shellbridge Way
Richmond, BC V6X 2W9
604-270-8226 *Fax:* 604-270-9116
URL: www.ubcm.ca
Scope: Provincial

Water Environment Federation WEFTEC 2016: 89th Annual Water Environment Federation Technical Exhibition & Conference
Date: September 24-28, 2016
Location: New Orleans Morial Convention Center
New Orleans, LA USA
Sponsor/Contact: Water Environment Federation
601 Wythe St.
Alexandria, VA 22314-1994
703-684-2400 *Fax:* 703-684-2492
Toll-Free: 800-666-0206
E-mail: comments@wef.org
URL: www.wef.org
Scope: International
Purpose: An annual educational & networking event drawing water quality experts from around the world
Anticipated Attendance: 18,000
Contact Information: Membership Information, Toll-Free Phone: 1-800-666-0206, International Phone: +44 120-679-6351 or 571-830-1545

October

19th ISRRT World Congress in Seoul, South Korea
Date: October 17-22, 2016
Location: Coex Center
Seoul, South Korea
Sponsor/Contact: International Society of Radiographers & Radiological Technologists
143 Bryn Pinwydden, Pentwyn, Cardiff
Wales, CF2 7DG
URL: www.isrrt.org
Scope: International
Purpose: Hosted by the South Korean Society of Radiographers.
Contact Information: Email: isrrt.yule@btinternet.com, URL: isrrt2016.kr

2016 Canadian Cardiovascular Congress
Date: October 22-26, 2016
Location: Palais des congrès de Montréal
Montréal, QC
Sponsor/Contact: Canadian Cardiovascular Society
#1403, 222 Queen St.
Ottawa, ON K1P 5V9
613-569-3407 *Fax:* 613-569-6574
Toll-Free: 877-569-3407
E-mail: info@ccs.ca
URL: www.ccs.ca
Scope: National

Alberta Urban Municipalities Association Convention & AMSC Trade Show 2016
Date: October 5-7, 2016
Location: Edmonton, AB
Sponsor/Contact: Alberta Urban Municipalities Association
#300, 8616 15 Ave.
Edmonton, AB T6E 6E6
780-433-4431 *Fax:* 780-433-4454
Toll-Free: 800-310-2862
E-mail: main@auma.ca
URL: www.auma.ca
Scope: Provincial

American Concrete Institute Fall 2016 Conference: Spanning the Globe
Date: October 23-27, 2016
Location: Marriott Philadelphia
Philadelphia, PA USA
Sponsor/Contact: American Concrete Institute
P.O. Box 9094
38800 Country Club Dr.
Farmington, MI 48333-9094
248-848-3700 *Fax:* 248-848-3701
URL: www.concrete.org
Scope: International

Association for Preservation Technology International 2016 Annual Conference
Date: October 30 - November 1, 2016
Location: Hilton Palacio del Rio
San Antonio, TX USA
Sponsor/Contact: Association for Preservation Technology International
#200, 3085 Stevenson Dr.
Springfield, IL
E-mail: info@apti.org
URL: www.apti.org
Scope: International
Purpose: Training & networking opportunities plus exhibits of interest to an international audience of persons involved in the application of methods & materials to conserve historic structures
Anticipated Attendance: 1,000

Canadian Association of Paediatric Health Centres Annual Conference 2016
Date: October 23-25, 2016
Location: Halifax, NS
Sponsor/Contact: Canadian Association of Paediatric Health Centres
c/o Canadian Association of Paediatric Health Centres
#104, 2141 Thurston Dr.
Ottawa, ON K1G 6C9
613-738-4164 *Fax:* 613-738-3247
E-mail: info@caphc.org
URL: www.caphc.org
Scope: National

Canadian Dam Association 2016 Annual Conference
Date: October 15-20, 2015
Location: Halifax, NS
Sponsor/Contact: Canadian Dam Association
P.O. Box 2281
Moose Jaw, SK S6TH 7W6
URL: www.cda.ca
Scope: National
Purpose: Featuring technical paper presentations, workshops, tours, exhibitor presentations, & a social program

Canadian Parking Association 2016 Conference & Trade Show
Date: October 22-26, 2016
Location: Ottawa, ON
Sponsor/Contact: Canadian Parking Association
#350, 2255 St. Laurent Blvd.
Ottawa, ON K1G 4K3
613-727-0700 *Fax:* 613-727-3183
E-mail: info@canadianparking.ca
URL: www.canadianparking.ca
Scope: National

Canadian Society of Association Executives / Société canadienne d'association 2016 Conference & Showcase
Date: October 26-28, 2015
Location: Toronto, ON
Sponsor/Contact: Canadian Society of Association Executives
#1100, 10 King St. East
Toronto, ON M5C 1C3
416-363-3555 *Fax:* 416-363-3630
Toll-Free: 800-461-3608
URL: www.csae.com
Scope: National
Anticipated Attendance: 500+
Contact Information: E-mail: events@csae.com

Canadian Society of Association Executives National Conference & Showcase 2016
Date: October 26-28, 2016
Location: Toronto, ON
Sponsor/Contact: Canadian Society of Association Executives
c/o British Columbia Bottle Depot Association
9850 King George Hwy.
Surrey, BC V3T 4Y3
604-930-0003 *Fax:* 604-930-0060
E-mail: bcbd@telus.net
URL: www.csae.com
Scope: National

Sheet Metal and Air Conditioning Contractors' National Association (SMACNA) 73rd Annual Convention
Date: October 16-20, 2016
Location: JW Marriott Desert Ridge
Phoenix, AZ USA
Sponsor/Contact: Sheet Metal & Air Conditioning Contractors' National Association
P.O. Box 221230
4201 Lafayette Center Dr.
Chantilly, VA 20153-1230
703-803-2980 *Fax:* 703-803-3732
E-mail: info@smacna.org
URL: www.smacna.org
Scope: National
Contact Information: Email: SMACNAConvention@cmrus.com; Phone: 800-336-9704

Western Canada Water 2016 68th Annual Conference & Exhibition
Date: October 4-7, 2016
Location: Telus Convention Centre
Calgary, AB
Sponsor/Contact: Western Canada Water
P.O. Box 1708
240 River Ave.
Cochrane, AB T4C 1B6
403-709-0064 *Fax:* 403-709-0068
Toll-Free: 877-283-2003
E-mail: member@wcwwa.ca
URL: www.wcwwa.ca
Scope: Provincial
Purpose: Informative sessions, an exhibition, & networking opportunities for utility managers & operators, consulting engineers, & municipal & provincial government representatives
Anticipated Attendance: 500+
Contact Information: Western Canada Water, Toll-Free Phone: 1-877-283-2003, Toll-Free Fax: 1-877-283-2007, E-mail: member@wcwwa.ca

November

Alberta Association of Municipal Districts & Counties Fall 2016 Convention & Trade Show
Date: November 14-17, 2016
Location: Shaw Conference Centre
Edmonton, AB
Sponsor/Contact: Alberta Association of Municipal Districts & Counties
2510 Sparrow Dr.
Nisku, AB T9E 8N5
780-955-3639 *Fax:* 780-955-3615
Toll-Free: 855-548-7233
E-mail: aamdc@aamdc.com
URL: www.aamdc.com

American Anthropological Association 2016 Annual Meeting
Date: November 16-20, 2016
Location: Minneapolis Convention Center
Minneapolis, MN USA
Sponsor/Contact: American Anthropological Association
Stn. 600
2300 Clarendon Blvd.
Arlington, VA 22201
703-528-1902 *Fax:* 703-528-3546
URL: www.aaanet.org
Scope: International
Contact Information: Director, American Anthropological Association & Section Meetings: Jason G. Watkins, E-mail: jwatkins@aaanet.org; Meeting Planner: Carla Fernandez, E-mail: cfernandez@aaanet.org

Conferences Index

American Council for Québec Studies Biennial Conference
Date: November 3-6, 2016
Location: Westin Portland Harborview
Portland, ME USA
Sponsor/Contact: American Council for Québec Studies
c/o University of Maine
213 Little Hall
Orono, ME 04469
E-mail: acqs2@maine.edu
URL: www.southalabama.edu/acqs

American Society of Mechanical Engineers 2016 International Mechanical Engineering Congress & Exposition
Date: November 11-17, 2016
Location: Phoenix Convention Center
Phoenix, AZ USA
Sponsor/Contact: American Society of Mechanical Engineers
3 Park Ave.
New York, NY 10016-5990
800-843-2763
E-mail: customercare@asme.org
URL: www.asme.org
Scope: International
Contact Information: Jimmy Le, Phone: 212-591-7116; Fax: 212-591-7856; Email: LeJ2@asme.org

Association of Manitoba Municipalities 18th Annual Convention
Date: November 21-23, 2016
Location: RBC Convention Centre
Winnipeg, MB
Sponsor/Contact: Association of Manitoba Municipalities
1910 Saskatchewan Ave. West
Portage la Prairie, MB R1N 0P1
204-857-8666 *Fax:* 204-856-2370
E-mail: amm@amm.mb.ca
URL: www.amm.mb.ca
Anticipated Attendance: 600

Canadian Bureau for International Education 2016 Annual Conference
Date: November 13-16, 2016
Location: Ottawa, ON
Sponsor/Contact: Canadian Bureau for International Education
#1550, 220 Laurier Ave. West
Ottawa, ON K1P 5Z9
613-237-4820 *Fax:* 613-237-1073
E-mail: info@cbie.ca
URL: www.cbie-bcei.ca
Scope: National
Purpose: The Conference features professional development workshops, concurrent sessions and networking opportunities.

Canadian Urban Transit Association 2016 Fall Conference & Trans-Expo
Date: November 5-9, 2016
Location: Vancouver, BC
Sponsor/Contact: Canadian Urban Transit Association
#1401, 55 York St.
Toronto, ON M5J 1R7
416-365-9800 *Fax:* 416-365-1295
URL: www.cutaactu.ca
Scope: National
Purpose: A yearly technical conference, which also includes the presentation of Employee Awards based on accomplishments in areas such as attendance, safety, & acts of heroism

Helicopter Association of Canada 2016 21st Annual Convention & Trade Show
Date: November 11-13, 2016
Location: Shaw Convention Centre
Edmonton, AB
Sponsor/Contact: Helicopter Association of Canada
#500, 130 Albert St.
Ottawa, ON K1P 5G4
613-231-1110 *Fax:* 613-369-5097
URL: www.h-a-c.ca
Scope: National
Purpose: Professional development programs & information sessions to help Helicopter Association of Canada members achieve in the present economic & regulatory climate
Anticipated Attendance: 800+
Contact Information: Office Manager & Contact, Member Services: Barb Priestley, Phone: 613-231-1110, ext. 237, Fax: 613-369-5097, E-mail: barb.priestley@h-a-c.ca

International Forum on Disability Management
Date: November 22-24, 2016
Location: Kuala Lumpur Convention Centre
Kuala Lumpur, Malaysia
Sponsor/Contact: National Institute of Disability Management & Research
c/o Pacific Coast University for Workplace Health Sciences
4755 Cherry Creek Rd.
Port Alberni, BC V9Y 0A7
778-421-0821 *Fax:* 778-421-0823
E-mail: nidmar@nidmar.ca
URL: www.nidmar.ca
Scope: International
Contact Information: Email: enquiries@ifdm2016.com.my; Phone: +603 4264 5053

Ontario Non-Profit Housing Association 2016 Annual Conference, General Meeting & Trade Show
Date: November 3-5, 2016
Location: Toronto Sheraton Centre
Toronto, ON
Sponsor/Contact: Ontario Non-Profit Housing Association
#400, 489 College St.
Toronto, ON M6G 1A5
416-927-9144 *Fax:* 416-927-8401
Toll-Free: 800-297-6660
E-mail: mail@onpha.org
URL: www.onpha.on.ca
Scope: Provincial
Purpose: Featuring speakers, workshops, & company exhibitors
Anticipated Attendance: 1,400
Contact Information: Phone: 1-800-297-6660, ext. 110; E-mail: conference@onpha.org; Manager, Conference & IT: Patsy Duffy, Phone: 416-927-9144, ext. 110, E-mail: patsy.duffy@onpha.org

Society of Environmental Toxicology & Chemistry North America 2016 37th Annual Meeting
Date: November 12-16, 2016
Location: Minneapolis, MN USA
Sponsor/Contact: Society of Environmental Toxicology & Chemistry
SETAC Asia / Pacific, SETAC Latin America, & SETAC North America
1010 - 12th Ave. North
Pensacola, FL 32501-3370
850-469-1500 *Fax:* 850-469-9778
E-mail: setac@setac.org
URL: www.setac.org
Scope: International
Anticipated Attendance: 2,300

Other Conferences in 2016

10th Annual Canadian Neuroscience Meeting
Sponsor/Contact: Canadian Association for Neuroscience
URL: can-acn.org
Scope: National
Purpose: Neuroscientists meet to discuss neuroscience research in Canada.

15th Ostomy Canada Society National Conference
Sponsor/Contact: Ostomy Canada Society
#501, 344 Bloor St. West
Toronto, ON M5S 3A7
416-595-5452 *Fax:* 416-595-9924
Toll-Free: 888-969-9698
E-mail: info1@ostomycanada.ca
URL: www.ostomycanada.ca
Scope: National

2016 Biennial Canadian Police Association Conference
Sponsor/Contact: Canadian Police Association
#100, 141 Catherine St.
Ottawa, ON K2P 1C3
613-231-4168 *Fax:* 613-231-3254
E-mail: cpa-acp@cpa-acp.ca
URL: www.cpa-acp.ca
Scope: National

2016 Canadian Association of Science Centres Annual Conference
Location: Vancouver Aquarium
Vancouver, BC
Sponsor/Contact: Canadian Association of Science Centres
P.O. Box 3443 Stn. D
Ottawa, OM K1P 6P4
613-566-4247
E-mail: casc.accs@gmail.com
URL: www.canadiansciencecentres.ca
Scope: National

2016 Canadian Society of Clinical Chemists Conference
Sponsor/Contact: Canadian Society of Clinical Chemists
P.O. Box 1570
#310, 4 Cataraqui St.
Kingston, ON K7K 1Z7
613-531-8899 *Fax:* 866-303-0626
E-mail: office@cscc.ca
URL: www.cscc.ca
Scope: National

2016 International Summit of Cooperatives
Sponsor/Contact: International Cooperative Alliance
P.O. Box 2100
150, Route de Ferney
Geneva, 1211
E-mail: ica@ica.coop
URL: ica.coop
Scope: International
Contact Information: Email: info@intlsummit.coop

2016 National Association of Career Colleges Conference
Location: Edmonton, AB
Sponsor/Contact: National Association of Career Colleges
#270, 44 Byward Market Sq.
Ottawa, ON K1N 7A2
613-800-0340 *Fax:* 613-789-9669
URL: www.nacc.ca
Scope: National

21st World Hydrogen Energy Conference (WHEC 2016)
Location: Zaragoza, Spain
Sponsor/Contact: International Association for Hydrogen Energy
#303, 5794 40th St. SW
Miami, FL 33155
E-mail: info@iahe.org
URL: www.iahe.org
Scope: International
Purpose: A biennial conference of the International Association for Hydrogen Energy

24th World Mining Congress & Expo
Location: Centro Empresarial Sul América
Rio de Janeiro, Brazil
Sponsor/Contact: Canadian Institute of Mining, Metallurgy & Petroleum
CIM National Office
#1250, 3500, boul de Maisonneuve ouest
Westmount, QC H3Z 3C1
514-939-2710 *Fax:* 514-939-2714
E-mail: cim@cim.org
URL: www.cim.org
Scope: International
Anticipated Attendance: 1,500

32nd World Conference of the International Society for Music Education
Sponsor/Contact: International Society for Music Education
#148, 45 Glenferrie Rd.
Malvern, VA 3144
E-mail: isme@isme.org
URL: www.isme.org
Scope: International
Purpose: Listening to the Musical Diversity of the World

44th Annual Conference of the Art Libraries Society
Sponsor/Contact: Art Libraries Society of North America
Technical Enterprises, Inc.
7044 - 13th St. South
Oak Creek, WI 53154
414-908-4954 *Fax:* 414-768-8001
Toll-Free: 800-817-0621
E-mail: info@arlisna.org
URL: www.arlisna.org
Purpose: The conference provides the opportunity for professionals involved in art librarianship to meet, learn and share their knowledge of the field. It also allows them to explore exhibitions & interact with vendors involved with art libraries.

66th Canadian Chemical Engineering Conference
Location: Québec City, QC
Sponsor/Contact: Chemical Institute of Canada
#550, 130 Slater St.
Ottawa, ON K1P 6E2
613-232-6252 *Fax:* 613-232-5862
Toll-Free: 888-542-2242
E-mail: info@cheminst.ca
URL: www.cheminst.ca
Scope: National

7th International Conference on Fog, Fog Collection and Dew
Location: University of Wroclaw
Wroclaw, Poland
Sponsor/Contact: FogQuest

Conferences Index

448 Monarch Pl.
Kamloops, BC V2E 2B2
250-374-1745 *Fax:* 250-374-1746
E-mail: info@fogquest.org
URL: www.fogquest.org
Scope: International
Contact Information: Mietek Sobik; Email: sobikmie@meteo.uni.wroc.pl

84e Congrès annuel de l'Association des bibliothécaires du Québec 2016
Location: Quebec
Sponsor/Contact: Association des bibliothécaires du Québec
P.O. Box 26717 Stn. Beaconsfield
Beaconsfield, QC H9W 6G7
514-697-0146 *Fax:* 514-697-0146
E-mail: abqla@abqla.qc.ca
URL: www.abqla.qc.ca
Scope: Provincial

Alberta Association of Library Technicians 2016 42nd Annual Conference
Location: Alberta
Sponsor/Contact: Alberta Association of Library Technicians
P.O. Box 700
Edmonton, AB T5J 2L4
Toll-Free: 866-350-2258
E-mail: marketing@aalt.org
URL: www.aalt.org
Scope: Provincial
Purpose: Keynote speakers, program sessions, & social events of interest to library technicians
Contact Information: Alberta Association of Library Technicians Conference Committee, Toll-Free Phone: 1-866-350-2258, E-mail: conference@aalt.org

Alberta Forest Products Association 2016 74th Annual General Meeting & Conference
Location: Alberta
Sponsor/Contact: Alberta Forest Products Association
#900, 10707 - 100 Ave.
Edmonton, AB T5J 3M1
780-452-2841 *Fax:* 780-455-0505
URL: www.albertaforestproducts.ca
Scope: Provincial
Purpose: A business meeting, sessions on topics relevant to the industry, networking opportunities, & a recognition dinner

Alberta Library Trustees Association 2016 Annual General Meeting
Location: Alberta
Sponsor/Contact: Alberta Library Trustees Association
#6-24, 7 Sir Winston Churchill Sq.
Edmonton, AB T5J 2V5
780-761-2582 *Fax:* 866-419-1451
E-mail: admin@librarytrustees.ab.ca
URL: www.librarytrustees.ab.ca
Scope: Provincial
Purpose: Financial statements, a proposed budget, nominations report, & special resolutions
Contact Information: Alberta Library Trustees Association Executive Director: Heather Mayor; President: Dwight Nagel, E-mail: mdnagel@telus.net; president@librarytrustees.ab.ca

Alberta Recreation & Parks Association 2016 Biennial Youth Development Through Recreation Services Symposium
Sponsor/Contact: Alberta Recreation & Parks Association
11759 Groat Rd.
Edmonton, AB T5M 3K6
780-415-1745 *Fax:* 780-451-7915
Toll-Free: 877-544-1747
E-mail: arpa@arpaonline.ca
URL: arpaonline.ca
Scope: Provincial
Purpose: A three day educational forum, featuring presenters ranging from frontline staff involved in youth programs to youth policy makers
Contact Information: Coordinator, Children & Youth Programs: Allison Pratley, E-mail: apratley@arpaonline.ca

Allied Beauty Association 2016 Annual General Meeting
Location: Montréal, QC
Sponsor/Contact: Allied Beauty Association
#26-27, 145 Traders Blvd. East
Mississauga, ON L4Z 3L3
905-568-0158 *Fax:* 905-568-1581
E-mail: abashows@abacanada.com
URL: www.abacanada.com
Scope: National

American College of Chest Physicians Conference: CHEST 2016
Sponsor/Contact: American College of Chest Physicians
3300 Dundee Rd.
Northbrook, IL 60062-2348
Toll-Free: 800-343-2227
URL: www.chestnet.org
Scope: International
Purpose: Educational sessions, CME credits, clinical instruction, & networking opportunities for health professionals

Archives Society of Alberta 2016 Biennial Conference
Location: Alberta
Sponsor/Contact: Archives Society of Alberta
#407, 10408 - 124 St. NW
Edmonton, AB T5N 1R5
780-424-2697 *Fax:* 780-425-1679
E-mail: info@archivesalberta.org
URL: www.archivesalberta.org
Scope: Provincial

Association for Canadian Studies in the United States (ACSUS) 2016 Biennial Colloquium
Sponsor/Contact: Association for Canadian Studies in the United States
#350, 2030 - M St. NW
Washington, DC 20036
E-mail: info@acsus.org
URL: www.acsus.org
Scope: International
Purpose: An examination of an interdisciplinary topic during a meeting held at a Canadian location
Contact Information: Executive Director: David Archibald, E-mail: info@acsus.org

Association for Literature, Environment, & Culture in Canada 2016 Biennial Conference
Sponsor/Contact: Association for Literature, Environment, & Culture in Canada
c/o Department of English, University of Calgary
2500 University Dr. NW, 11th Fl.
Calgary, AB T2N 1N4
E-mail: contactus@alecc.ca
URL: www.alecc.ca
Scope: National

Association of Canadian Map Libraries & Archives 2016 Annual Conference
Sponsor/Contact: Association of Canadian Map Libraries & Archives
c/o Legal Deposit, Maps, Published Heritage, Library & Archives Canada
550, boul de la Cité
Gatineau, ON K1N ON4
E-mail: membership@acmla.org
URL: www.acmla-acacc.ca
Scope: National
Purpose: A yearly gathering of map librarians & archivists & other individuals with an interest in maps & geographic data who support the objectives of the association

Association of Power Producers of Ontario 2016: 28th Annual Canadian Power Conference & Power Networking Centre
Location: Ontario
Sponsor/Contact: Association of Power Producers of Ontario
P.O. Box 1084 Stn. F
#1602, 25 Adelaide St. East
Toronto, ON M5C 3A1
416-322-6549 *Fax:* 416-481-5785
E-mail: appro@appro.org
URL: www.appro.org
Scope: Provincial
Purpose: An annual event held in the autumn, featuring speakers, educational sessions, exhibits, & a student program
Contact Information: E-mail: appro@appro.org

Association of Professional Community Planners of Saskatchewan 2016 Conference
Sponsor/Contact: Saskatchewan Professional Planners Institute
2424 College Ave.
Regina, SK S4P 1C8
306-584-3879 *Fax:* 306-352-6913
E-mail: msteranka@sasktel.net
URL: sppi.ca
Scope: Provincial
Purpose: A meeting of planners & related professionals to share new ideas, enhance professional practice, network & socialize

Atlantic Canada Water & Wastewater Association 2016 69th Annual Conference
Sponsor/Contact: Atlantic Canada Water & Wastewater Association
P.O. Box 41002
Dartmouth, NS B2Y 4P7
902-434-6002 *Fax:* 902-435-7796
E-mail: acwwa@hfx.andara.com
URL: www.acwwa.ca
Scope: Provincial
Purpose: A trade show, plus educational sessions & networking opportunities for Atlantic Canada's water professionals
Contact Information: Technical Director: Jennie Rand

Atlantic Provinces Library Association 2016 Annual Conference
Sponsor/Contact: Atlantic Provinces Library Association
c/o School of Information Management, Kenneth C. Rowe Management Bldg.
6100 University Ave.
Halifax, NS B3H 3J5
E-mail: executive@yahoo.ca
URL: www.apla.ca
Scope: Provincial
Purpose: An educational program to support the interests & concerns of the library community in the Atlantic provinces

British Columbia Federation of Labour 2016 Convention: The 60th Convention of the British Columbia Federation of Labour
Location: Vancouver, BC
Sponsor/Contact: British Columbia Federation of Labour
#200, 5118 Joyce St.
Vancouver, BC V5R 4H1
604-430-1421 *Fax:* 604-430-5917
E-mail: bcfed@bcfed.ca
URL: www.bcfed.com
Scope: Provincial
Purpose: A meeting held every two years to set the direction of the labour movement in British Columbia, attended by rank & file trade union members
Anticipated Attendance: 1,000+
Contact Information: E-mail: admin@bcfed.ca

British Columbia Library Association 2016 Conference
Location: British Columbia
Sponsor/Contact: British Columbia Library Association
#150, 900 Howe St.
Vancouver, BC V6Z 2M4
604-683-5354 *Fax:* 604-609-0707
Toll-Free: 888-683-5354
E-mail: office@bcla.bc.ca
URL: www.bcla.bc.ca
Scope: Provincial

British Columbia Library Trustees' Association 2015 Annual General Meeting
Sponsor/Contact: British Columbia Library Trustees' Association
432 - 3 St.
Vancouver, BC V3L 2S2
604-913-1424 *Fax:* 604-913-1413
Toll-Free: 888-206-1245
E-mail: admin@bclta.ca
URL: www.bclta.org
Scope: Provincial

British Columbia Teacher-Librarians' Association 2016 Provincial Conference
Location: British Columbia
Sponsor/Contact: British Columbia Teacher-Librarians' Association
c/o British Columbia Teachers' Federation
#100, 550 West 6th Ave.
Vancouver, BC V5Z 4P2
604-871-2283 *Fax:* 604-871-2286
Toll-Free: 800-663-9163
E-mail: bctlamembership@gmail.com
URL: www.bctf.ca/bctla
Scope: Provincial
Purpose: A gathering of British Columbia's teacher-librarians for workshops, keynote presentations, & social events
Contact Information: Conference Chair: Sylvia Zubke, Phone: 604-713-4985, E-mail: szubke@gmail.com

British Columbia Water & Waste Association 2016 44th Annual Conference & Trade Show
Location: British Columbia
Sponsor/Contact: British Columbia Water & Waste Association

#221, 8678 Greenall Ave.
Burnaby, BC V5J 3M6
604-433-4389 *Fax:* 604-433-9859
Toll-Free: 877-433-4389
E-mail: contact@bcwwa.org
URL: www.bcwwa.org
Scope: Provincial
Purpose: A four day conference, including technical sessions & the chance to view current products at the trade show
Anticipated Attendance: 1,250
Contact Information: Manager, Conferences & Events: Carlie Thauvette, Phone: 604-630-0011, E-mail: cthauvette@bcwwa.org

CAMPUT, Canada's Energy & Utility Regulators 2016 Conference
Sponsor/Contact: CAMPUT, Canada's Energy & Utility Regulators
#646, 200 North Service Rd. West
Oakville, ON L6M 2Y1
905-827-5139 *Fax:* 905-827-3260
E-mail: info@camput.org
URL: www.camput.org
Scope: National
Purpose: An annual event to address current regulatory issues & energy related subjects
Contact Information: E-mail: info@camput.org

CAUCE 2016: The 63rd Annual Conference & General Meeting of the Canadian Association for University Continuing Education
Location: University of Waterloo
Waterloo, ON
Sponsor/Contact: Canadian Association for University Continuing Education
c/o Centre for Continuing & Distance Education, U. of Saskatchewan
#464, 221 Cumberland Ave. North
Saskatoon, SK S7N 1M3
306-966-5604 *Fax:* 306-966-5590
E-mail: cauce.secrataria t@usask.ca
URL: www.cauce-aepuc.ca
Scope: National

Canadian Arts Presenting Association / Association canadienne des organismes artistiques 2016 28th Annual Conference
Sponsor/Contact: Canadian Arts Presenting Association
#200, 17 York St.
Ottawa, ON K1N 9J6
613-562-3515 *Fax:* 613-562-4005
E-mail: mail@capacoa.ca
URL: www.capacoa.ca
Scope: National

Canadian Association for Co-operative Education (CAFCE) 2016 Conference
Sponsor/Contact: Canadian Association for Co-operative Education
#202, 720 Spadina Ave.
Toronto, ON M5S 2T9
416-929-5256
E-mail: cafce@cafce.ca
URL: www.cafce.ca
Scope: National

Canadian Association for Information Science / Association canadienne des sciences de l'information 2016 44th Annual Conference
Sponsor/Contact: Canadian Association for Information Science
c/o Nadia Caidi, Faculty of Information
#335, 45 Willcocks St.
Toronto, ON M5S 1C7
416-978-4664
E-mail: nadia.caidi@utoronto.ca
URL: www.cais-acsi.ca
Scope: National
Purpose: Held in conjunction with the Congress of the Humanities & Social Sciences; Canadian information scientists & professionals have met to discuss the access, retrieval, production, value, use, & management of information.
Contact Information: Conference Co-Chair: Eric Meyers, Phone: 604-827-3945, E-mail: Eric.Meyers@ubc.ca; Conference Co-Chair: Heather O'Brien, Phone: 604-822-6365, E-mail: h.obrien@ubc.ca

Canadian Association for Pharmacy Distribution Management 2016 Annual Conference
Sponsor/Contact: Canadian Association for Pharmacy Distribution Management
#301A, 3800 Steeles Ave. West
Woodbridge, ON L4L 4G9
905-265-1706 *Fax:* 905-265-9372
URL: www.capdm.ca
Scope: National
Purpose: A meeting of pharmacy supply chain industry professionals, featuring presentations by experts on timely & important topics for the industry
Contact Information: Canadian Association for Pharmacy Distribution Management, Phone: 905-265-1706

Canadian Association for Pharmacy Distribution Management 2016 Executive Conference
Sponsor/Contact: Canadian Association for Pharmacy Distribution Management
#301A, 3800 Steeles Ave. West
Woodbridge, ON L4L 4G9
905-265-1706 *Fax:* 905-265-9372
URL: www.capdm.ca
Scope: National
Contact Information: Canadian Association for Pharmacy Distribution Management, Phone: 905-265-1706

Canadian Association for Pharmacy Distribution Management 2016 September Member Forum
Sponsor/Contact: Canadian Association for Pharmacy Distribution Management
#301A, 3800 Steeles Ave. West
Woodbridge, ON L4L 4G9
905-265-1706 *Fax:* 905-265-9372
URL: www.capdm.ca
Scope: National
Contact Information: Allison Chan, Phone: 905-265-1706, ext. 223, Email: allison@capdm.ca

Canadian Association of Chiefs of Police 2016 111th Annual Conference
Sponsor/Contact: Canadian Association of Chiefs of Police
#100, 300 Terry Fox Dr.
Kanata, ON K2K 0E3
613-595-1101 *Fax:* 613-383-0372
E-mail: cacp@cacp.ca
URL: www.cacp.ca
Scope: National
Purpose: Conference sessions & exhibits

Canadian Association of Fire Chiefs 2016 Conference
Sponsor/Contact: Canadian Association of Fire Chiefs
#702, 280 Albert St.
Ottawa, ON K1P 5G8
613-270-9138
Toll-Free: 800-775-5189
URL: www.cafc.ca
Scope: International
Purpose: Speaker presentations, seminars, & workshops for the fire & emergency services community from across Canada & the United States

Canadian Association of Geographers 2016 Annual Meeting & Conference
Location: Halifax, NS
Sponsor/Contact: Canadian Association of Geographers
Department of Geography, McGill University
#425, 805, rue Sherbrooke ouest
Montréal, QC H3A 2K6
514-398-4946 *Fax:* 514-398-7437
E-mail: valerie.shoffey@cag-acg.ca
URL: www.cag-acg.ca
Scope: National
Purpose: A business meeting & educational conference for geographers & students, featuring the presentation of papers & posters, plus exhibits, & social activities

Canadian Association of Hepatology Nurses 2016 Annual National Education Conference
Sponsor/Contact: Canadian Association of Hepatology Nurses
c/o Dawn King
1 Campbell Ave.
St. Johns, NL A1E 2Z1
URL: www.livernurses.org
Scope: National
Contact Information: Co-Chair, Conference Committee: Sharon Bojarski, E-mail: sharonbojarski@hotmail.com; Co-Chair, Conference Committee: Sandi Mitchell, E-mail: sandi.mitchell@bccdc.ca

Canadian Association of Professional Academic Librarians 2016 Annual Conference
Sponsor/Contact: Canadian Association of Professional Academic Librarians
E-mail: capalibrarians@gmail.com
URL: capalibrarians.org
Scope: National

Canadian Association of Provincial Court Judges 2016 National Education Meeting
Location: Vancouver, BC
Sponsor/Contact: Canadian Association of Provincial Court Judges
c/o Judge Alan T. Tufts, Nova Scotia Provincial Court
87 Cornwallis St.
Kentville, NS B4N 2E5
902-679-6070 *Fax:* 902-679-6190
E-mail: capcp@judges-juges.ca
URL: www.judges-juges.ca
Scope: National

Canadian Association of Slavists 2016 Annual Conference (in conjunction with the Canadian Federation for the Humanities & Social Sciences Congress)
Location: University of Calgary
Calgary, AB
Sponsor/Contact: Canadian Association of Slavists
Alumni Hall, Dept. of History & Classics, University of Alberta
#2, 28 Tory Bldg.
Edmonton, AB T6G 2H4
780-492-2566 *Fax:* 780-492-9125
E-mail: csp@ulberta.ca
URL: www.ualberta.ca/~csp/cas/contact.html
Scope: National
Purpose: A yearly meeting with roundtable discussions, panels, & the presentation of papers by members of the Canadian Association of Slavists

Canadian Astronomical Society 2016 Annual Meeting
Sponsor/Contact: Canadian Astronomical Society
c/o R. Hanes, Dept. of Physics, Engineering, Physics & Astronomy
64 Bader Lane, Stirling Hall, Queen's University
Kingston, ON K7L 3N6
613-533-6000 *Fax:* 613-533-6463
E-mail: casca@astro.queensu.ca
URL: www.casca.ca
Scope: National
Purpose: Annual meetings are open to all interested persons, but the presentation of scientific papers is restricted to members or applicants for membership & speakers invited by the Local Organizing Committee

Canadian Athletic Therapists Association's 50th National Conference
Sponsor/Contact: Canadian Athletic Therapists Association
#300, 400 - 5th Ave. SW
Calgary, AB T2P 0L6
403-509-2282 *Fax:* 403-509-2280
E-mail: info@athletictherapy.org
URL: www.athletictherapy.org
Scope: National

Canadian Bar Association Mid-Winter Meeting of Council 2016
Sponsor/Contact: Canadian Bar Association
#500, 865 Carling Ave.
Ottawa, ON K1S 5S8
613-237-2925 *Fax:* 613-237-0185
Toll-Free: 800-267-8860
E-mail: info@cba.org
URL: www.cba.org
Scope: National

Canadian Dermatology Association 2016 91st Annual Conference
Sponsor/Contact: Canadian Dermatology Association
#425, 1385 Bank St.
Ottawa, ON K1H 8N4
613-738-1748 *Fax:* 613-738-4695
Toll-Free: 800-267-3376
E-mail: info@dermatology.ca
URL: www.dermatology.ca
Scope: National
Purpose: Oral & poster presentations on subjects relevant to practicing dermatologists

Canadian Dermatology Association 2016 91st Annual Conference
Sponsor/Contact: Canadian Dermatology Association
#425, 1385 Bank St.
Ottawa, ON K1H 8N4
613-738-1748 *Fax:* 613-738-4695
Toll-Free: 800-267-3376
E-mail: info@dermatology.ca
URL: www.dermatology.ca
Scope: National
Purpose: An educational experience with

Conferences Index

exhibits, networking opportunities, & the presentation of awards

Canadian History of Education Association 19th Biennial Conference
Date: Fall 2016
Location: Waterloo, ON
Sponsor/Contact: Canadian History of Education Association
University of Saskatchewan, College of Education
28 Campus Dr.
Saskatoon, SK S7N 0X1
URL: www.ache-chea.ca
Scope: National

Canadian Insitiute for the Administration of Justice 2016 Annual Conference
Sponsor/Contact: Canadian Institute for the Administration of Justice
Faculté de droit, Univ. de Montréal
P.O. Box 6128 Stn. Centre-Ville
#A3421, 3101, chemin de la Tour
Montréal, QC H3C 3J7
514-343-6157 *Fax:* 514-343-6296
E-mail: ciaj@ciaj-icaj.ca
URL: www.ciaj-icaj.ca
Scope: National

Canadian Institute of Mining, Metallurgy & Petroleum MassMin 2016: 7th Intl Conference & Exhibition on Mass Mining
Location: Sydney, Australia
Sponsor/Contact: Canadian Institute of Mining, Metallurgy & Petroleum
CIM National Office
#1250, 3500, boul de Maisonneuve ouest
Westmount, QC H3Z 3C1
514-939-2710 *Fax:* 514-939-2714
E-mail: cim@cim.org
URL: www.cim.org
Scope: International
Purpose: Topics include mine design, rock flow modeling & prediction, mine automation, & mining methods

Canadian Medical & Biological Engineering Society 2016 39th Annual National Conference
Location: Calgary, AB
Sponsor/Contact: Canadian Medical & Biological Engineering Society
1485 Laperrière Ave.
Ottawa, ON K1Z 7S8
613-728-1759
E-mail: secretariat@cmbes.ca
URL: www.cmbes.ca
Scope: National
Purpose: An annual gathering of Canadian biomedical engineering professionals for continuing education & networking opportunities. This year's conference is a collaboration with l'Association des physiciens et ingénieurs biomédicaux du Québec (APIBQ).
Contact Information: Chair, Long-Term Conference Planning: Sarah Kelso, E-mail: sarah.a.kelso@gmail.com

Canadian Neurological Sciences Federation 51st Annual Congress
Sponsor/Contact: Canadian Neurological Sciences Federation
#709, 7015 Macleod Trail SW
Calgary, AB T2H 2K6
403-229-9544 *Fax:* 403-229-1661
E-mail: info@cnsfederation.org
URL: www.cnsfederation.org
Scope: National
Purpose: Courses, lectures, oral & digital poster presentations, plus exhibits & social events
Contact Information: Canadian Neurological Sciences Federation, Phone: 403-229-9544

Canadian Produce Marketing Association 2016 91st Annual Convention & Trade Show
Sponsor/Contact: Canadian Produce Marketing Association
162 Cleopatra Dr.
Ottawa, ON K2G 5X2
613-226-4187 *Fax:* 613-226-2984
E-mail: question@cpma.ca
URL: www.cpma.ca
Scope: International
Purpose: Featuring business sessions, a trade show, a keynote speaker, & awards

Canadian Public Relations Society / La Société canadienne des relations publiques 2016 National Summit
Sponsor/Contact: Canadian Public Relations Society Inc.
#346, 4195 Dundas St. West
Toronto, ON M8X 1Y4
416-239-7034 *Fax:* 416-239-1076
E-mail: admin@cprs.ca
URL: www.cprs.ca
Scope: National
Purpose: An education conference, with networking opportunities with public relations professionals from across Canada
Contact Information: E-mail: admin@cprs.ca

Canadian Remote Sensing Society 2016 37th Canadian Symposium on Remote Sensing
Location: Winnipeg, MB
Sponsor/Contact: Canadian Remote Sensing Society
c/o Canadian Aeronautics & Space Institute
#104, 350 Terry Fox Dr.
Kanata, ON K2K 2W5
613-591-8787 *Fax:* 613-591-7291
E-mail: casi@casi.ca
URL: www.crss-sct.ca
Scope: National

Canadian School Boards Association / Association canadienne des commissions/conseils scolaires 2016 Congress
Sponsor/Contact: Canadian School Boards Association
#515, 1410 rue Stanley
Montréal, QC H3A 1P8
514-289-2988 *Fax:* 514-849-8228
E-mail: info@cdnsba.org
URL: www.cdnsba.org
Scope: National

Canadian Society for Pharmaceutical Sciences 2016 Annual Symposium
Sponsor/Contact: Canadian Society for Pharmaceutical Sciences
Katz Group Centre, University of Alberta
#2-020L, 11361 - 87 Ave.
Edmonton, AB T6G 2E1
780-492-0950 *Fax:* 780-492-0951
URL: www.cspscanada.org
Scope: National
Purpose: Educational sessions, networking opportunities, & the presentation of awards
Contact Information: Phone: 780-492-0950

Canadian Society of Biblical Studies 2016 Annual Meeting (in conjunction with the 2016 Congress of the Humanities & Social Sciences)
Location: Brock University
St Catharines, ON
Sponsor/Contact: Canadian Society of Biblical Studies
c/o Prof. Robert A. Derrenbacker, Jr., Regent College
5800 University Blvd.
Vancouver, BC V6T 2E4
URL: www.ccsr.ca/csbs
Scope: National

Canadian Society of Otolaryngology - Head & Neck Surgery 2016 70th Annual Conference
Location: Québec, QC
Sponsor/Contact: Canadian Society of Otolaryngology - Head & Neck Surgery
Administrative Office
221 Millford Cres.
Elora, ON N0B 1S0
519-846-0630 *Fax:* 519-846-9529
Toll-Free: 800-655-9533
E-mail: cso.hns@sympatico.ca
URL: www.entcanada.org
Scope: National
Purpose: Scientific information for those who specialize in head & neck surgery
Contact Information: Canadian Society of Otolaryngology Administrative Office: Phone: 519-846-0630, E-mail: cso.hns@sympatico.ca

Canadian Society of Respiratory Therapists 2016 Annual Education Conference & Trade Show
Sponsor/Contact: Canadian Society of Respiratory Therapists
#400, 301 Cooper St.
Ottawa, ON K1G 3Y6
613-731-3164 *Fax:* 613-521-4314
Toll-Free: 800-267-3422
E-mail: info@csrt.com
URL: www.csrt.com
Scope: National
Purpose: Featuring internationally renowned speakers, workshops, & presentations for respiratory therapists
Contact Information: Education Conference & Trade Show Contact: Lindsey Naddaf, Phone: 613-731-3164, ext. 231

Canadian Society of Transplantation 2016 Annual Scientific Conference
Sponsor/Contact: Canadian Society of Transplantation
774 Echo Dr.
Ottawa, ON K1S 5N8
613-730-6274 *Fax:* 613-730-1116
E-mail: cst@rcpsc.edu
URL: www.cst-transplant.ca
Scope: National
Purpose: Annual meeting of the society, group meetings, symposia, poster presentations, award presentations, exhibits, & social events

Canadian Wind Energy Association (CanWEA) 32nd Annual Conference and Exhibition
Sponsor/Contact: Canadian Wind Energy Association Inc.
#710, 1600 Carling Ave.
Ottawa, ON K1Z 1G3
613-234-8716 *Fax:* 613-234-5642
Toll-Free: 800-922-6932
E-mail: info@canwea.ca
URL: www.canwea.ca
Scope: National
Purpose: To discuss the opportunities and latest developments in the wind energy industry.
Contact Information: Email: events@canwea.ca

Church Library Association of Ontario 2016 Annual Fall Conference
Location: Ontario
Sponsor/Contact: Church Library Association of Ontario
c/o Margaret Godefroy, CLAO Membership Secretary
#603, 155 Navy St.
Oakville, ON L6J 2Z7
905-845-0222
E-mail: agodefroy@cogeco.ca
URL: www.churchlibraries.ca
Scope: Provincial
Purpose: A Saturday event in a southern Ontario location, featuring technical, administrative, & promotional workshops
Contact Information: Email: conference@clao.ca

Church Library Association of Ontario 2016 Annual Spring Conference
Location: Ontario
Sponsor/Contact: Church Library Association of Ontario
c/o Margaret Godefroy, CLAO Membership Secretary
#603, 155 Navy St.
Oakville, ON L6J 2Z7
905-845-0222
E-mail: agodefroy@cogeco.ca
URL: www.churchlibraries.ca
Scope: Provincial
Purpose: A Saturday conference, usually held in a southern Ontario location, featuring workshops, speakers, networking opportunities, exhibitors, & a book swap
Contact Information: Email: conference@clao.ca

Community Living Grimsby, Lincoln & West Lincoln 51st Annual General Meeting
Sponsor/Contact: Community Living Grimsby, Lincoln & West Lincoln
Lincoln Kingsway Plaza
P.O. Box 220
#8-9, 5041 King St.
Beamsville, ON L0R 1B0
905-563-4115 *Fax:* 905-563-8887
E-mail: info@cl-grimsbylincoln.ca
URL: www.cl-grimsbylincoln.ca
Scope: Local

Computer Human Interaction 2016 Conference on Human Factors in Computing Systems
Location: San José, CA USA
Sponsor/Contact: Special Interest Group on Computer Human Interaction
P.O. Box 93672 Stn. Nelson Park
Vancouver, BC V6E 4L7
604-876-8985
E-mail: chi-VanCHI@acm.org
URL: www.sigchi.org
Scope: International
Anticipated Attendance: 2,500+

Council of Archives New Brunswick AGM 2016
Location: New Brunswick
Sponsor/Contact: Council of Archives New Brunswick
P.O. Box 1204 Stn. A
Fredericton, NB E3B 5C8

Conferences Index

506-453-4327 *Fax:* 506-453-3288
E-mail: archives.advisor@gnb.ca
URL: www.canbarchives.ca/canb
Scope: Provincial

Council of Nova Scotia Archives Annual Conference 2016
Sponsor/Contact: Council of Nova Scotia Archives
6016 University Ave.
Halifax, NS B3H 1W4
902-424-7093
E-mail: advisor@councilofnsarchives.ca
URL: www.councilofnsarchives.ca
Scope: Provincial

Eating Disorder Association of Canada 5th Biennial Conference
Location: Winnipeg, MB
Sponsor/Contact: Eating Disorder Association of Canada
E-mail: edacatac@gmail.com
URL: www.edac-atac.ca
Scope: National

Editors' Association of Canada Conference 2016
Location: Vancouver, BC
Sponsor/Contact: Editors' Association of Canada
#505, 27 Carlton St.
Toronto, ON M5B 1L2
416-975-1379 *Fax:* 416-975-1637
Toll-Free: 866-226-3348
E-mail: info@editors.ca
URL: www.editors.ca
Scope: National

Federation of Medical Regulatory Authorities of Canada 2016 AGM & Conference
Sponsor/Contact: Federation of Medical Regulatory Authorities of Canada
#103, 2283 St. Laurent Blvd.
Ottawa, ON K1G 5A2
613-738-0372 *Fax:* 613-738-9169
E-mail: info@fmrac.ca
URL: www.fmrac.ca
Scope: National

Global Business Travel Association Canada Conference 2016
Sponsor/Contact: Global Business Travel Association (Canada)
#919, 105-150 Crowfoot Cres. NW
Calgary, AB T3G 3T2
Fax: 403-719-6336
E-mail: membercare@gbta.org
URL: www.gbta.org/canada
Scope: National
Purpose: Featuring over 50 exhibitors, 12 concurrent education sessions & 4 general session featured speakers

Horse Breeders & Owners 34th Annual Conference
Sponsor/Contact: Horse Industry Association of Alberta
97 East Lake Ramp NE
Airdrie, AB T4A 0C3
403-420-5949 *Fax:* 403-948-2069
URL: www.albertahorseindustry.ca
Scope: Provincial
Purpose: Internationally recognized speakers of interest to horse breeders, owners, & professionals

Institute of Transportation Engineers 2016 Technical Conference & Exhibit
Sponsor/Contact: Institute of Transportation Engineers
#600, 1627 Eye St. NW
Washington, DC 20006
202-785-0060 *Fax:* 202-785-0609
E-mail: ite_staff@ite.org
URL: www.ite.org
Scope: International

International Association of Administrative Professionals 2016 International Education Forum & Annual Meeting
Sponsor/Contact: International Association of Administrative Professionals
P.O. Box 20404
10502 NW Ambassador Dr.
Kansas City, MO 64195-0404
816-891-6600 *Fax:* 816-891-9118
E-mail: service@iaap-hq.org
URL: www.iaap-hq.org
Scope: International
Purpose: Education workshops

International Permafrost Association 2016 11th International Conference on Permafrost
Location: Potsdam, Germany
Sponsor/Contact: International Permafrost Association
c/o H. Lantuit, Alfred Wegener Institute for Polar & Marine Research
Telefrafenberg A43
Potsdam, 14473
E-mail: contact@ipa-permafrost.org
URL: ipa.arcticportal.org
Scope: International
Purpose: The conference will be held in early summer
Contact Information: E-mail: contact@ipa-permafrost.org

International Society for Affective Disorders 8th Biennial Conference 2016
Sponsor/Contact: International Society for Affective Disorders
c/o Caroline Holebrook, Institute of Psychiatry, King's College London
PO72 De Crespigny Park, Denmark Hill
London, SE5 8AF
E-mail: enquiry@isad.org.uk
URL: www.isad.org.uk
Scope: International

Liberal Party of Canada 2016 Biennial Convention
Sponsor/Contact: The Liberal Party of Canada
#600, 81 Metcalfe St.
Ottawa, ON K1P 6M8
613-237-0740 *Fax:* 613-235-7208
E-mail: info@liberal.ca
URL: www.liberal.ca
Scope: National
Purpose: An opportunity for Liberals across Canada to engage in preparations for the next election, to elect the Party's new executive, and to discuss policy resolutions that shape the party's next electoral platform.

Library Boards Association of Nova Scotia 2016 Annual Conference
Location: Nova Scotia
Sponsor/Contact: Library Boards Association of Nova Scotia
c/o Janet Ness, Secretary, Library Boards Association of Nova Scotia
53 Sherwood Dr.
Wolfville, NS B4P 2K5
902-542-7386
E-mail: janet_ness@hotmail.com
URL: www.standupforlibraries.ca
Scope: Provincial
Purpose: An annual autumn meeting for anyone with an interest in public libraries in Nova Scotia
Contact Information: Library Boards Association of Nova Scotia Executive Assistant: Christina Pottie, Email: cpottie@southshorepubliclibraries.ca

Maintenance & Engineering Society of The Canadian Institute of Mining, Metallurgy & Petroleum 2016 Maintenance Engineering/Mine Operators' Conference
Sponsor/Contact: Maintenance, Engineering & Reliability (MER) Society
c/o Secretary, Marcel M. Djivre
2058 Latimer Cres.
Sudbury, ON P3E 5L6
705-621-1945
URL: www.cim.org
Scope: National
Purpose: A technical conference of interest to persons involved in maintenance & engineering in the mining industry

Manitoba Libraries 2016 Bi-annual Conference
Location: Manitoba
Sponsor/Contact: Manitoba Library Association
#606, 100 Arthur St.
Winnipeg, MB R3B 1H3
204-943-4567 *Fax:* 866-202-4567
E-mail: manitobalibrary@gmail.com
URL: www.mla.mb.ca
Scope: Provincial
Purpose: Informative presentations, guest speakers, & a trade show for members of Manitoba's library community
Contact Information: Professional Development Director: Katherine Penner, Phone: 204-474-6846, E-mail: katherine_penner@umanitoba.ca

Manitoba School Library Association 2016 Annual General Meeting
Location: Manitoba
Sponsor/Contact: Manitoba School Library Association
c/o Claudia Klausen, Emerson Elementary School
323 Emerson Ave.
Winnipeg, MB R2G 1V3
URL: www.manitobaschoollibraries.com
Scope: Provincial
Contact Information: President, E-mail: mslapresident@gmail.com

Mechanical Contractors Association of Canada (MCAC) 75th Annual National Conference 2016
Sponsor/Contact: Mechanical Contractors Association of Canada
#601, 280 Albert St.
Ottawa, ON K1P 5G8
613-232-0492 *Fax:* 613-235-2793
E-mail: mcac@mcac.ca
URL: www.mcac.ca
Scope: National

Metallurgy & Materials Society of the Canadian Institute of Mining, Metallurgy & Petroleum COM 2016: 55th Annual Conference of Metallurgists
Sponsor/Contact: Metallurgy & Materials Society of the Canadian Institute of Mining, Metallurgy & Petroleum
#1250, 3500, boul de Maisonneuve ouest
Montréal, QC H3Z 3C1
514-939-2710
URL: www.metsoc.org
Scope: International
Purpose: A conference featuring short courses, industrial tours, a metals trade show, a poster session, plenary sessions, & student activities
Contact Information: E-mail: metsoc@cim.org

Newfoundland & Labrador Library Association Annual Conference & Annual General Meeting 2016
Location: Newfoundland & Labrador
Sponsor/Contact: Newfoundland & Labrador Library Association
PO Box 23192, RPO Churchill Sq.
St. John's, NL A1B 4J9
E-mail: secretary@nlla.ca
URL: www.nlla.ca
Scope: Provincial
Purpose: An annual spring meeting, presenting opportunities to learn about new services, current issues, & research in Newfoundland & Labrabor libraries

Northwestern Ontario Municipal Association 2016 Annual Regional Conference
Location: Ontario
Sponsor/Contact: Northwestern Ontario Municipal Association
P.O. Box 10308
Thunder Bay, ON P7B 6T8
807-683-6662
E-mail: admin@noma.on.ca
URL: www.noma.on.ca
Scope: Local
Purpose: A meeting, held each September or October, for both full & associate members of the Northwestern Ontario Municipal Association
Contact Information: NOMA Executive Director, Phone: 807-683-6662, E-mail: admin@noma.on.ca

Nova Scotia Library Association 2016 Annual Conference
Location: Nova Scotia
Sponsor/Contact: Nova Scotia Library Association
c/o Kelli WooShue, Halifax Public Libraries
60 Alderney Dr.
Dartmouth, NS B2Y 4P8
902-490-5710
E-mail: wooshuk@halifax.ca
URL: www.nsla.ns.ca
Scope: Provincial
Purpose: Hosted by Pictou Antigonish Regional Library in the autumn
Contact Information: E-mail: conference@nsla.ns.ca

Ontario Association of Library Technicians / Association des bibliotechniciens de l'Ontario 2016 43rd Annual Conference
Sponsor/Contact: Ontario Association of Library Technicians
Abbey Market
P.O. Box 76010
1500 Upper Middle Rd. West
Oakville, ON L6M 3H5
E-mail: info@oaltabo.on.ca
URL: oaltabo.on.ca
Scope: Provincial
Purpose: Featuring educational sessions, speeches, the annual business meeting, & award presentations
Contact Information: Ontario Association of Library Technicians External

Communications Coordinator: Dana Schwarz; Internal Communications Coordinator: Serena McGovern; E-mail: info@oaltabo.on.ca

Ontario College of Teachers 2016 Annual Meeting of Members
Sponsor/Contact: Ontario College of Teachers
101 Bloor St. East
Toronto, ON M5S 0A1
416-961-8800 *Fax:* 416-961-8822
Toll-Free: 888-534-2222
E-mail: info@oct.ca
URL: www.oct.ca
Scope: Provincial
Purpose: Presentations of interest to teachers

Ontario Library Boards' Association 2016 Annual General Meeting
Location: Ontario
Sponsor/Contact: Ontario Library Boards' Association
c/o Ontario Library Association
#201, 50 Wellington St. East
Toronto, ON M5E 1C8
416-363-3388 *Fax:* 416-941-9581
Toll-Free: 866-873-9867
E-mail: info@accessola.com
URL: www.accessola.com/olba
Scope: Provincial
Purpose: AGM reports from executive members, the business of the association, statement of expenses, & the introduction of the new council

Ontario Public Library Association 2016 37th Annual General Meeting
Location: Ontario
Sponsor/Contact: Ontario Public Library Association
#201, 50 Wellington St. East
Toronto, ON M5E 1C8
416-363-3388 *Fax:* 416-941-9581
Toll-Free: 866-873-9867
E-mail: info@accessola.com
URL: www.accessola.com/opla
Scope: Provincial
Purpose: Featuring the introduction of the new council, as well as reports from the association's president, treasurer, & committees

Pacific Northwest Library Association 2016 Conference
Sponsor/Contact: Pacific Northwest Library Association
c/o Michael Burris, Public Library InterLINK
7252 Kingsway
Burnaby, BC V5E 1G3
604-517-8441 *Fax:* 604-517-8410
URL: www.pnla.org
Scope: Provincial

Promotional Product Professionals of Canada 2016 National Convention
Sponsor/Contact: Promotional Product Professionals of Canada Inc.
#100, 6700, Côte-de-Liesse
Saint-Laurent, QC H4T 2B5
514-489-5359 *Fax:* 514-489-7760
Toll-Free: 866-450-7722
E-mail: info@pppc.ca
URL: www.pppc.ca
Scope: National
Purpose: Educational seminars, business meetings, roundtable discussions, networking events, plus a trade show with over 600 exhibitors
Contact Information: Events Coordinator: Mara Welch, E-mail: shows@pppc.ca

RIMS (Risk & Insurance Management Society Inc.) 2016 Annual Conference & Exhibition
Sponsor/Contact: Risk & Insurance Management Society Inc.
c/o Thomas Oystrick, RIMS Canada Council, Mount Royal University
4825 Mount Royal Gate SW
Calgary, AB T3E 6K6
E-mail: canada@rims.org
URL: www.rimscanada.ca
Scope: International
Purpose: A gathering of risk professionals from around the world to share experiences

RIMS (Risk & Insurance Management Society Inc.) Canada 2016 Conference
Sponsor/Contact: Risk & Insurance Management Society Inc.
c/o Thomas Oystrick, RIMS Canada Council, Mount Royal University
4825 Mount Royal Gate SW
Calgary, AB T3E 6K6
E-mail: canada@rims.org
URL: www.rimscanada.ca
Scope: National
Purpose: An annual risk management conference & exhibition held in the autumn for risk managers & the vendor community

RMCAO [Ready Mixed Concrete Association of Ontario] 56th Annual General Meeting & Convention
Sponsor/Contact: Ready Mixed Concrete Association of Ontario
#3, 365 Brunel Rd.
Mississauga, ON L4Z 1Z5
905-507-1122 *Fax:* 905-890-8122
URL: www.rmcao.org
Scope: Provincial

Royal Canadian Mounted Police Veterans Association 2016 Annual General Meeting
Location: Nova Scotia
Sponsor/Contact: Royal Canadian Mounted Police Veterans' Association
1200 Vanier Pkwy.
Ottawa, ON K1A 0R2
613-993-8633 *Fax:* 613-993-4353
Toll-Free: 877-251-1771
E-mail: rcmp.vets@rcmp-grc.gc.ca
URL: www.rcmpvetsnational.ca
Scope: National

Royal Canadian Numismatic Association 2016 Convention
Location: Ottawa, ON
Sponsor/Contact: Royal Canadian Numismatic Association
#432, 5694 Hwy. 7 East
Markham, ON L3P 1B4
647-401-4014 *Fax:* 905-472-9645
E-mail: info@rcna.ca
URL: www.rcna.ca
Scope: National
Purpose: An annual event, presenting an education symposium, a bourse & display, business meetings, award presentations, plus social & networking activities
Contact Information: E-mail: info@rcna.ca

Saskatchewan Association of Rural Municipalities 2016 Annual Convention
Sponsor/Contact: Saskatchewan Association of Rural Municipalities
2075 Hamilton St.
Regina, SK S4P 2E1
306-757-3577 *Fax:* 306-565-2141
Toll-Free: 800-667-3604
E-mail: sarm@sarm.ca
URL: www.sarm.ca
Scope: Provincial

Saskatchewan Library Association 2016 Annual Conference & Annual General Meeting
Sponsor/Contact: Saskatchewan Library Association
#15, 2010 - 7th Ave.
Regina, SK S4R 1C2
306-780-9413 *Fax:* 306-780-9447
E-mail: slaexdir@sasktel.net
URL: www.saskla.ca
Scope: Provincial
Purpose: Featuring discussions of issues affecting library service in Saskatchewan, the Mary Donaldson Memorial Lecture, & networking occasions, held during a two or three day period
Contact Information: Saskatchewan Library Association, Phone: 306-780-9413, Fax: 306-780-9447, E-mail: slaprograms@sasktel.net

Saskatchewan Library Trustees Association 2016 Annual General Meeting
Location: Saskatchewan
Sponsor/Contact: Saskatchewan Library Trustees Association
79 Mayfair Cres.
Regina, SK S4S 5T9
306-584-2495 *Fax:* 306-585-1473
URL: slta.ca
Scope: Provincial
Purpose: Featuring the president's report, auditor's report, library system reports, & elections
Contact Information: Saskatchewan Library Trustees Association Executive Director: Nancy Kennedy, E-mail: njk@sasktel.net

Saskatchewan Urban Municipalities Association (SUMA) 111th Annual Convention and Tradeshow 2016
Sponsor/Contact: Saskatchewan Urban Municipalities Association
#200, 2222 - 13th Ave.
Regina, SK S4P 3M7
306-525-3727 *Fax:* 306-525-4373
E-mail: suma@suma.org
URL: www.suma.org
Scope: Provincial

Society of Cardiovascular Anesthesiologists 19th Annual Comprehensive Review & Update of Perioperative Echo 2016
Sponsor/Contact: Society of Cardiovascular Anesthesiologists
2209 Dickens Rd.
Richmond, VA 23230-2005
804-282-0084 *Fax:* 804-282-0090
E-mail: sca@societyhq.com
URL: www.scahq.org
Scope: International

Sonography Canada 2016 National Conference & Annual General Meeting
Sponsor/Contact: Sonography Canada
P.O. Box 119
Kemptville, ON K0G 1J0
Fax: 613-258-0899
Toll-Free: 877-488-0788
E-mail: info@sonographycanada.ca
URL: www.sonographycanada.ca
Scope: National

Special Libraries Association 2016 Annual Conference & INFO-EXPO
Location: Philadelphia, PA USA
Sponsor/Contact: Special Libraries Association
331 South Patrick St.
Alexandria, VA 22314-3501
703-647-4900 *Fax:* 703-647-4901
E-mail: cschatz@sla.org
URL: www.sla.org
Scope: International
Purpose: A gathering of information professionals, providing informative educational sessions, keynote speakers, & exhibitors
Contact Information: Director, Events: Caroline Hamilton, Phone: 703-647-4949, E-mail: chamilton@sla.org; Director, Marketing & Exhibits: Jeff Leach, Phone: 703-647-4922, E-mail: jleach@sla.org

Statistical Society of Canada / Société statistique du Canada 2016 Annual Meeting
Sponsor/Contact: Statistical Society of Canada
#209, 1725 St. Laurent Blvd.
Ottawa, ON K1G 3V4
613-733-2662 *Fax:* 613-733-1386
E-mail: info@ssc.ca
URL: www.ssc.ca
Scope: National

Taking Action for Animals 2016
Sponsor/Contact: The Humane Society of the United States
2100 L St. NW
Washington, DC 20037
202-452-1100
E-mail: membership@humanesociety.org
URL: www.humanesociety.org
Scope: National
Purpose: An educational conference meant to inspire people to help animals. Topics covered include factory farming & animal fighting.
Contact Information: URL: takingactionforanimals.org

The Canadian Greenhouse Conference (CGC) 2016
Location: Ontario
Sponsor/Contact: Ontario Institute of Agrologists
Ontario AgriCentre
#108, 100 Stone Rd. West
Guelph, ON N1G 5L3
519-826-4226 *Fax:* 519-826-4228
Toll-Free: 866-339-7619
URL: www.oia.on.ca
Scope: National
Purpose: Held annually since 1979 the CGC is committed to providing a high quality conference experience for the extension of information through speakers, workshops, demonstration and exhibits.

The Maritimes Energy Association 2016 Annual General Meeting & Dinner
Sponsor/Contact: The Maritimes Energy Association
Cambridge Tower 1
#305, 202 Brownlow Ave.
Dartmouth, NS B3B 1T5
902-425-4774 *Fax:* 902-422-2332
E-mail: info@maritimesenergy.com
URL: www.maritimesenergy.com
Scope: Provincial
Purpose: Focus on innovation, leadership

and connecting with the WIT to get it done.

The Maritimes Energy Association 2016 Core Energy Conference & Trade Show
Sponsor/Contact: The Maritimes Energy Association
Cambridge Tower 1
#305, 202 Brownlow Ave.
Dartmouth, NS B3B 1T5
902-425-4774 *Fax:* 902-422-2332
E-mail: info@maritimesenergy.com
URL: www.maritimesenergy.com
Scope: Provincial
Purpose: An annual event during the first week of October for stakeholders in the onshore, offshore, wind, tidal, & policy sectors of the Maritime energy industry

Tire and Rubber Association 2016 Symposium
Sponsor/Contact: Tire and Rubber Association of Canada
Plaza 4
#100, 2000 Argentia Rd.
Mississauga, ON L5N 1W1
905-814-1714 *Fax:* 905-814-1085
E-mail: info@rubberassociation.ca
URL: www.tracanada.ca
Scope: National

Travel Media Association of Canada 2016 Conference & AGM
Sponsor/Contact: Travel Media Association of Canada
c/o TO Corporate Services
#255, 55 St. Clair Ave. West
Toronto, ON M4V 2Y7
416-934-0599 *Fax:* 416-967-6320
E-mail: info@travelmedia.ca
URL: www.travelmedia.ca
Scope: National

Win-Door North America 2016 (an event owned & produced by Fenestration Canada)
Sponsor/Contact: Fenestration Canada
#1208, 130 Albert St.
Ottawa, ON K1P 5G4
613-235-5511 *Fax:* 613-235-4664
E-mail: info@fenestrationcanada.ca
URL: www.fenestrationcanada.ca
Scope: International
Purpose: Meetings, demonstrations, & seminars, plus an opportunity for suppliers to show their products & services to manufacturers & fabricators from across Canada, the United States, & international destinations

2017

January

American Library Association 2017 Midwinter Meeting & Exhibits
Date: January 20-24, 2017
Location: Atlanta, GA USA
Sponsor/Contact: American Library Association
50 East Huron St.
Chicago, IL 60611
Fax: 312-440-9374
Toll-Free: 800-545-2433
E-mail: ala@ala.org
URL: www.ala.org
Scope: International
Purpose: A library & information service meeting presenting speakers, discussion groups, exhibits, & committee meetings
Contact Information: Registration Customer Service, Phone: 1-800-974-3084, E-mail: ala@experient-inc.com

American Philological Association 148th Annual Meeting
Date: January 5-8, 2017
Location: Toronto, ON
Sponsor/Contact: American Philological Association
University of Pennsylvania
#201E, 220 South 40th St.
Philadelphia, PA 19104-3512
215-898-4975 *Fax:* 215-573-7874
E-mail: apaclassics@sas.upenn.edu
URL: apaclassics.org
Scope: International

Western Retail Lumber Association 2017 Prairie Showcase Buying Show & Convention
Date: January 18-20, 2017
Location: Calgary, AB
Sponsor/Contact: Western Retail Lumber Association
Western Retail Lumber Association Inc.
#1004, 213 Notre Dame Ave.
Winnipeg, MB R3B 1N3
204-957-1077 *Fax:* 204-947-5195
Toll-Free: 800-661-0253
E-mail: wrla@wrla.org
URL: www.wrla.org
Scope: Provincial
Contact Information: Caren Kelly, Marketing Manager, E-mail: Ckelly@wrla.org

February

American Association for the Advancement of Science 2017 Annual Meeting
Date: February 16-20, 2017
Location: Boston, MA USA
Sponsor/Contact: American Association for the Advancement of Science
1200 New York Ave. NW
Washington, DC 20005
202-326-6440
E-mail: membership@aaas.org
URL: www.aaas.org
Scope: International
Purpose: Information for scientists, engineers, educators, & policy-makers
Contact Information: Phone: 202-326-6450; Fax: 202-289-4021; E-mail: meetings@aaas.org; Director, Meetings & Public Engagement: Tiffany Lohwater, E-mail: tlohwate@aaas.org

Canadian Digestive Diseases Week (CDDW) & the 2017 Annual Canadian Association for the Study of the Liver (CASL) Winter Meeting
Date: February 26 - March 8, 2017
Location: Banff, AB
Sponsor/Contact: Canadian Association for the Study of the Liver
c/o BUKSA Strategic Conference Services
#307, 10328 - 81st Ave.
Edmonton, AB T6E 1X2
780-436-0983 *Fax:* 780-437-5984
E-mail: casl@hepatology.ca
URL: www.hepatology.ca
Scope: National
Purpose: A February or March scientific conference of the Canadian Association of Gastroenterology (CAG) & the Canadian Association for the Study of the Liver (CASL), featuring lectures, symposia, small group sessions, exhibits, & opportunities for networking

Canadian Digestive Diseases Week: Canadian Association of Gastroenterology Annual Scientific Conference 2017
Date: February 26 - March 8, 2017
Location: Banff, AB
Sponsor/Contact: Canadian Association of Gastroenterology
#224, 1540 Cornwall Rd.
Oakville, ON L6J 7W5
905-829-2504 *Fax:* 905-829-0242
Toll-Free: 888-780-0007
E-mail: general@cag-acg.org
URL: www.cag-acg.org
Scope: National

March

Alberta Association of Municipal Districts & Counties Spring 2017 Convention & Trade Show
Date: March 20-22, 2017
Location: Shaw Conference Centre
Edmonton, AB
Sponsor/Contact: Alberta Association of Municipal Districts & Counties
2510 Sparrow Dr.
Nisku, AB T9E 8N5
780-955-3639 *Fax:* 780-955-3615
Toll-Free: 855-548-7233
E-mail: aamdc@aamdc.com
URL: www.aamdc.com

American Concrete Institute Spring 2017 Convention
Date: March 26-30, 2017
Location: Renaissance Center
Detroit, MI USA
Sponsor/Contact: American Concrete Institute
P.O. Box 9094
38800 Country Club Dr.
Farmington, MI 48333-9094
248-848-3700 *Fax:* 248-848-3701
URL: www.concrete.org
Scope: International

Association of Ontario Land Surveyors 2017 Annual General Meeting
Date: March 1-3, 2017
Location: Ottawa Convention Centre & Westin Ottawa
Ottawa, ON
Sponsor/Contact: Association of Ontario Land Surveyors
1043 McNicoll Ave.
Toronto, ON M1W 3W6
416-491-9020 *Fax:* 416-491-2576
Toll-Free: 800-268-0718
E-mail: info@aols.org
URL: www.aols.org
Scope: Provincial
Contact Information: Lena Kassabian; Email: lena@aols.org; Phone: 416-491-9020 ext. 25

Canadian Association for Dental Research 41st Annual Meeting
Date: March 22-25, 2017
Location: San Francisco, CA USA
Sponsor/Contact: Canadian Association for Dental Research
c/o Dr. C. Birek, Faculty of Dentistry, University of Manitoba
780 Bannatyne Ave.
Winnipeg, MB R3E 0W2
204-789-3256 *Fax:* 204-789-3913
E-mail: birek@ms.umanitoba.ca
URL: www.cadr-acrd.ca
Scope: International
Purpose: In conjunction with the 46th Annual Meeting of the American Association of Dental Research & the 95th General Session & Exhibition of the International Association for Dental Research

Pacific Dental Conference 2017
Date: March 9-11, 2017
Location: Vancouver, BC
Sponsor/Contact: British Columbia Dental Association
#400, 1765 - 8th Ave. West
Vancouver, BC V6J 5C6
604-736-7202 *Fax:* 604-736-7588
Toll-Free: 888-396-9888
E-mail: post@bcdental.org
URL: www.bcdental.org
Scope: Provincial
Anticipated Attendance: 12,000+
Contact Information: Address: Pacific Dental Conference, #305, 1505 West 2nd Ave., Vancouver, BC V6H 3Y4; Phone: 604-736-3781; E-mail: info@pdconf.com, exhibits@pdconf.com

Society of Toxicology 56th Annual Meeting & ToxExpo
Date: March 12-16, 2017
Location: Baltimore Convention Center
Baltimore, MD USA
Sponsor/Contact: Society of Toxicology
#300, 1821 Michael Faraday Dr.
Reston, VA 20190
703-438-3115 *Fax:* 703-438-3113
E-mail: sothq@toxicology.org
URL: www.toxicology.org
Scope: International
Purpose: Toxicology meeting & exhibition
Anticipated Attendance: 6,500
Contact Information: Phone: 703-438-3115; Fax: 703-438-3113; E-mail: sothq@toxicology.org

April

American Association for Thoracic Surgery 97th Annual Meeting
Date: April 29 - May 3, 2017
Location: Boston Hynes Convention Centre
Boston, MA USA
Sponsor/Contact: American Association for Thoracic Surgery
#221U, 900 Cummings Center
Beverly, MA
978-927-8330 *Fax:* 978-524-8890
URL: www.aats.org
Scope: International
Purpose: Education in the field of thoracic & cardiovascular surgery, for cardiothoracic surgeons, physicians in related specialties, allied health professionals, fellows & residents in cardiothoracic & general surgical training programs, as well as medical students with an interest in cardiothoracic surgery

American Society of Neuroradiology 2017 55th Annual Meeting
Date: April 22-27, 2017
Location: Long Beach Convention & Entertainment Center
Long Beach, CA USA
Sponsor/Contact: American Society of Neuroradiology
#207, 2210 Midwest Rd.
Oak Brook, IL 60523

630-574-0220 *Fax:* 630-574-0661
E-mail: jgantenberg@asnr.org
URL: www.asnr.org
Scope: International
Contact Information: Director, Scientific Meetings: Lora Tannehill, E-mail: ltannehill@asnr.org; Manager, Scientific Meetings: Valerie Geisendorfer, E-mail: vgeisendorfer@asnr.org

Council of Forest Industries 2017 Annual Convention
Date: April 5-7, 2017
Location: Prince George, BC
Sponsor/Contact: Council of Forest Industries
Pender Place I Business Building
#1501, 700 Pender St. West
Vancouver, BC V6C 1G8
604-684-0211 *Fax:* 604-687-4930
E-mail: info@cofi.org
URL: www.cofi.org
Scope: National
Purpose: A meeting about issues affecting the forestry industries of British Columbia.
Contact Information: Phone: 604-684-0211; Fax: 604-687-4930

International Society for Magnetic Resonance in Medicine 2017 25th Scientific Meeting & Exhibition
Date: April 20-28, 2017
Location: Honolulu, HI USA
Sponsor/Contact: International Society for Magnetic Resonance in Medicine
2030 Addison St., 7th Fl.
Berkeley, CA 94704
510-841-1899 *Fax:* 510-841-2340
E-mail: info@ismrm.org
URL: www.ismrm.org
Scope: International
Purpose: Featuring the 26th Annual Meeting of the Section for Magnetic Resonance Technologists
Contact Information: Director, Meetings: Sandra Daudlin, E-mail: sandra@ismrm.org; Coordinator, Meetings: Melisa Martinez, E-mail: melisa@ismrm.org

Library Association of Alberta Annual Conference 2017
Date: April 27-30, 2017
Location: Alberta
Sponsor/Contact: Library Association of Alberta
80 Baker Cres. NW
Calgary, AB T2L 1R4
403-284-5818 *Fax:* 403-282-6646
Toll-Free: 877-522-5550
E-mail: info@laa.ca
URL: www.laa.ca
Scope: Provincial
Purpose: A conference held each spring for members of the Alberta library community, featuring association annual general meetings, session presentations, networking opportunities, & a trade show. Beginning this year, the conference is no longer held jointly with the Alberta Library Trustees Association (ALTA).
Contact Information: Library Association of Alberta, Phone: 403-284-5818, Toll-Free Phone: 1-877-522-5550, Fax: 403-282-6646, E-mail: info@laa.ca, info@albertalibraryconference.com

Water Environment Association of Ontario 2017 46th Annual Technical Symposium & Exhibition
Date: April 2-4, 2017
Location: Ottawa Convention Centre
Ottawa, ON
Sponsor/Contact: Water Environment Association of Ontario
P.O. Box 176
Milton, ON L9T 4N9
416-410-6933 *Fax:* 416-410-1626
E-mail: julie.vincent@weao.org
URL: www.weao.org
Scope: Provincial
Purpose: A conference featuring technical sessions, a keynote speaker, a student program, an awards presentation, & networking opportunities
Contact Information: Chair, Conference Committee: Frank Farkas, E-mail: farkas.f@spdsales.com

May

2017 OWWA/OMWA Joint Annual Conference and OWWEA Trade Show
Date: May 8-11, 2016
Location: Niagara Falls, ON
Sponsor/Contact: Ontario Water Works Association
#100, 922 The East Mall Dr.
Toronto, ON M9B 6K1
416-231-1555 *Fax:* 416-231-1556
Toll-Free: 866-975-0575
E-mail: waterinfo@owwa.ca
URL: www.owwa.com
Scope: Provincial
Purpose: This annual industry highlight features a full slate of plenary and technical sessions focusing on the latest in technology and research affecting drinking water from source to tap. The Trade Show consistently has more than 100 exhibitors representing the manufacturers and suppliers of products and services for the water industry.

Bibliographical Society of Canada 2017 Annual General Meeting
Date: May 27 - June 2, 2017
Location: Ryerson University
Toronto, ON
Sponsor/Contact: Bibliographical Society of Canada
P.O. Box 19035 Stn. Walmer
360 Bloor St. West
Toronto, ON M5S 3C9
E-mail: secretary@bsc-sbc.ca
URL: www.bsc-sbc.ca
Scope: National

Canadian Association for Leisure Studies Canadian Congress on Leisure 2017
Date: May 1, 2017
Location: University of Waterloo
Waterloo, ON
Sponsor/Contact: Canadian Association for Leisure Studies
c/o Recreation & Leisure Studies, Faculty of Applied Health Sciences
University of Waterloo
Waterloo, ON N2L 3G1
URL: www.cals.uwaterloo.ca
Scope: National
Purpose: A triennial meeting at the Canadian Congress on Leisure Research. The theme in 2017 is Engaging Legacies, which will involve discussions focused on inclusive communities

Canadian Association of Municipal Administrators 2017 46th Annual Conference & Annual General Meeting
Date: May 29-31, 2017
Location: Gatineau, QC
Sponsor/Contact: Canadian Association of Municipal Administrators
P.O. Box 128 Stn. A
Fredericton, NB E3B 4Y2
866-771-2262
E-mail: admin@camacam.ca
URL: www.camacam.ca
Scope: National
Purpose: Information & a trade show for senior managers from Canadian municipalities throughout Canada
Contact Information: E-mail: admin@camacam.ca

Canadian Union of Public Employees (CUPE) Ontario 2017 54th Convention
Date: May 31 - June 3, 2017
Location: Toronto Sheraton Centre
Toronto, ON
Sponsor/Contact: Canadian Union of Public Employees
Ontario Regional Office
#1, 80 Commerce Valley Dr. East
Markham, ON L3T 0B2
905-739-9739 *Fax:* 905-739-9740
E-mail: info@cupe.on.ca
URL: www.cupe.on.ca
Scope: Provincial
Purpose: A gathering where convention delegates debate & vote on resolutions
Anticipated Attendance: 1,200
Contact Information: CUPE Ontario, E-mail: info@cupe.on.ca

Canadian Urban Transit Association 2017 Annual Conference
Date: May 13-17, 2017
Location: Montreal, QC
Sponsor/Contact: Canadian Urban Transit Association
#1401, 55 York St.
Toronto, ON M5J 1R7
416-365-9800 *Fax:* 416-365-1295
URL: www.cutaactu.ca
Scope: National
Purpose: Professional development sessions & the presentation of Corporate Awards, held in May or June each year

Government Finance Officers Association 2017 111th Annual Conference
Date: May 21-24, 2017
Location: Denver, CO USA
Sponsor/Contact: Government Finance Officers Association
#2700, 203 North LaSalle St.
Chicago, IL 60601-1210
312-977-9700 *Fax:* 312-977-4806
E-mail: inquiry@gfoa.org
URL: www.gfoa.org
Scope: International
Anticipated Attendance: 4,100+
Contact Information: Manager, Communications: Natalie Laudadio, Phone: 312-977-9700, ext. 2298

Journées dentaires internationales du Québec (JDIQ) 2017
Date: 26 au 30 mai 2017
Location: Quebec
Sponsor/Contact: Ordre des dentistes du Québec
625, boul René-Lévesque ouest, 15e étage
Montréal, QC H3B 1R2
514-875-8511 *Fax:* 514-393-9248
Toll-Free: 800-361-4887
URL: www.odq.qc.ca
Scope: Provincial
Contact Information: Directeur, Dr Denis Forest, téléphone: 514-875-8511, poste 2222; adresse email: denis.forest@odq.qc.ca

Local Government Management Association of British Columbia 2015 Annual General Meeting & Conference
Date: June 21-23, 2017
Location: Penticton Trade & Convention Centre
Penticton, BC
Sponsor/Contact: Local Government Management Association of British Columbia
Central Building
620 View St., 7th Fl.
Victoria, BC V8W 1J6
250-383-7032 *Fax:* 250-384-4879
E-mail: office@lgma.ca
URL: www.lgma.ca
Scope: Provincial
Purpose: A conference & tradeshow held in May or June each year for members of the Local Government Management Association of British Columbia
Contact Information: Program Coordinator: Ana Fuller, Phone: 250-383-7032, ext. 227, Fax: 250-383-4879, E-mail: afuller@lgma.ca

Medical Library Association 2017 Annual Meeting & Exhibition
Date: May 26-31, 2017
Location: Seattle, WA USA
Sponsor/Contact: Medical Library Association
#1900, 65 East Wacker Pl.
Chicago, IL 60601-7246
312-419-9094 *Fax:* 312-419-8950
E-mail: info@mlahq.org
URL: www.mlanet.org
Scope: International

Ontario Dental Association Annual Spring Meeting 2017
Date: May 4-6, 2017
Location: Metro Toronto Convention Centre
Toronto, ON
Sponsor/Contact: Ontario Dental Association
4 New St.
Toronto, ON M5R 1P6
416-922-3900 *Fax:* 416-922-9005
Toll-Free: 800-387-1393
E-mail: info@oda.ca
URL: www.oda.ca
Scope: Provincial
Anticipated Attendance: 11,700

Ontario Small Urban Municipalities 2017 64th Annual Conference & Trade Show
Date: May 2-5, 2017
Location: Niagara Falls, ON
Sponsor/Contact: Ontario Small Urban Municipalities
c/o Association of Municipalities of Ontario
#801, 200 University Ave.
Toronto, ON M5H 3C6
416-971-9856 *Fax:* 416-971-6191
Toll-Free: 877-426-6527
E-mail: amo@amo.on.ca
URL: www.osum.ca
Scope: Provincial
Anticipated Attendance: 200+

Contact Information: OSUM Annual Conference & Trade Show Coordinator: Ted Blowes, Phone: 519-271-0250, ext. 241, E-mail: ted.b@quadro.net

Pediatric Academic Societies' 2017 Annual Meeting
Date: May 6-9, 2017
Location: San Francisco, CA USA
Sponsor/Contact: Academic Pediatric Association
6728 Old McLean Village Dr.
McLean, VA 22101
703-556-9222 *Fax:* 703-556-8729
E-mail: info@academicpeds.org
URL: www.ambpeds.org
Scope: International
Purpose: An international meeting focussing on research in child health
Contact Information: Address: #7B, 3400 Research Forest Dr., The Woodlands, TX, 77381, USA; Phone: 281-419-0052; Fax: 281-419-0082

Pediatric Endocrine Society 2017 Annual Meeting
Date: May 6-9, 2017
Location: San Francisco, CA USA
Sponsor/Contact: Pediatric Endocrine Society
6728 Old McLean Village Dr.
McLean, VA 22101
E-mail: info@pedsendo.org
URL: www.pedsendo.org
Scope: International
Purpose: A yearly spring conference, featuring lectures, topic symposia, business meetings, plenary sessions, exhibits, & opportunities for networking
Contact Information: E-mail: info@pedsendo.org

June

70th Society of Architectural Historians Annual Conference
Date: June 7-11, 2017
Location: Glasgow, Scotland
Sponsor/Contact: Society of Architectural Historians
1365 North Astor St.
Chicago, IL 60610-2144
312-573-1365 *Fax:* 312-573-1141
E-mail: info@sah.org
URL: www.sah.org
Scope: International

94th Canadian Paediatric Society Annual Conference 2017
Date: June 14-17, 2017
Location: Vancouver, BC
Sponsor/Contact: Canadian Paediatric Society
2305 St. Laurent Blvd.
Ottawa, ON K1G 4J8
613-526-9397 *Fax:* 613-526-3332
E-mail: info@cps.ca
URL: www.cps.ca
Scope: National
Contact Information: Phone: 613-526-9397 ext. 2148, Email: meetings@cps.ca, www.annualconference.cps.ca

American Library Association 2017 Annual Conference
Date: June 22-27, 2017
Location: Chicago, IL USA
Sponsor/Contact: American Library Association
50 East Huron St.
Chicago, IL 60611
Fax: 312-440-9374
Toll-Free: 800-545-2433
E-mail: ala@ala.org
URL: www.ala.org
Scope: International
Purpose: Highlights include a variety of speakers, educational programs, committee meetings, & exhibits
Contact Information: Registration Customer Service, Phone: 1-800-974-3084, E-mail: ala@experient-inc.com

American Water Works Association 2017 136th Annual Conference & Exposition
Date: June 11-15, 2017
Location: Philadelphia, PA USA
Sponsor/Contact: American Water Works Association
6666 West Quincy Ave.
Denver, CO 80235
303-794-7711 *Fax:* 303-347-0804
Toll-Free: 800-926-7337
E-mail: custsvc@awwa.org
URL: www.awwa.org
Scope: International
Purpose: A technical program & exhibits for association members & associated professionals
Contact Information: American Water Works Association, Phone: 800-926-7337, Fax: 303-347-0804, E-mail: awwamktg@awwa.org

Association of Canadian Archivists 2017 42nd Annual Conference & Annual General Meeting
Date: June 8-10, 2017
Location: Ottawa Marriott Hotel Ottawa, ON
Sponsor/Contact: Association of Canadian Archivists
P.O. Box 2596 Stn. D
Ottawa, ON K1P 5W6
613-234-6977 *Fax:* 613-234-8500
E-mail: aca@archivists.ca
URL: www.archivists.ca
Scope: National
Purpose: A meeting occurring in May or June each year, for archivists from across Canada, featuring educational presentations, trade show exhibits, networking opportunities, as well as workshops immediately prior or following conference sessions
Contact Information: Association of Canadian Archivists Board or Office, E-mail: aca@archivists.ca

Canadian Anesthesiologists' Society 2017 73rd Annual Meeting
Date: June 23-26, 2017
Location: Scotiabank Convention Centre Niagara Falls, ON
Sponsor/Contact: Canadian Anesthesiologists' Society
#208, One Eglinton Ave. East
Toronto, ON M4P 3A1
416-480-0602 *Fax:* 416-480-0320
E-mail: anesthesia@cas.ca
URL: www.cas.ca
Scope: National
Purpose: A convention, with an exhibition pharmaceutical companies & equipment manufacturers

Canadian Association of University Business Officers 2017 Annual Conference
Date: June 11-13, 2017
Location: Carleton University Ottawa, ON
Sponsor/Contact: Canadian Association of University Business Officers
#320, 350 Albert St.
Ottawa, ON K1R 1B1
613-230-6760 *Fax:* 613-563-7739
E-mail: info@caubo.ca
URL: www.caubo.ca
Scope: National

Canadian Pharmacists Association 2017 105th Annual National Conference
Date: June 3-6, 2017
Location: Québec, QC
Sponsor/Contact: Canadian Pharmacists Association
1785 Alta Vista Dr.
Ottawa, ON K1G 3Y6
613-523-7877 *Fax:* 613-523-0445
Toll-Free: 800-917-9489
E-mail: info@pharmacists.ca
URL: www.pharmacists.ca
Scope: National
Purpose: A continuing education program, a trade show, as well as social events of interest to pharmacists
Contact Information: E-mail: info@pharmacists.ca

Canadian Public Health Association 2017 Conference
Date: June 12-15, 2017
Location: Ottawa, ON
Sponsor/Contact: Canadian Public Health Association
#300, 1565 Carling Ave.
Ottawa, ON K1Z 8R1
613-725-3769 *Fax:* 613-725-9826
E-mail: info@cpha.ca
URL: www.cpha.ca
Scope: National
Purpose: A conference for policy-makers, researchers, environmental health professionals, academics, & students from across Canada
Contact Information: Conference Manager: Sarah Pettenuzzo, Phone: 613-725-3769, ext. 153; Conference Officer: Julie Paquette, Phone: 613-725-3769, ext. 126

Canadian Urological Association 2017 72nd Annual Meeting
Date: June 25-27, 2016
Location: Westin Harbour Castle Hotel Toronto, ON
Sponsor/Contact: Canadian Urological Association
#1303, 1155, University St.
Montréal, QC H3B 3A7
514-395-0376 *Fax:* 514-395-1664
E-mail: cua@cua.org
URL: www.cua.org
Scope: National

Microwave Theory & Techniques Society International Microwave Symposia 2017
Date: June 4-9, 2017
Location: Honolulu, HI USA
Sponsor/Contact: IEEE Microwave Theory & Techniques Society
5829 Bellanca Dr.
Elkridge, MD 21075
410-796-5866 *Fax:* 410-796-5829
URL: www.mtt.org
Scope: International
Purpose: Technical papers; Workshops; Trade show

North American Association of Central Cancer Registries 2017 Annual Conference
Date: June 17-22, 2017
Location: Albuquerque, NM USA
Sponsor/Contact: North American Association of Central Cancer Registries, Inc.
2121 West White Oaks Dr., #B
Springfield, IL 62704-7412
217-698-0800 *Fax:* 217-698-0188
E-mail: info@naaccr.org
URL: www.naaccr.org
Scope: International
Anticipated Attendance: 450

July

17th FINA World Championships 2017
Date: July 15-30, 2017
Location: Guadalajara, Mexico
Sponsor/Contact: International Amateur Swimming Federation
Av. de l'Avant-Poste 4
Lausanne, 1005
URL: www.fina.org
Scope: International

Canadian Association of Chiefs of Police 2017 112th Annual Conference
Date: July 17-18, 2017
Location: Palais des congrès de Montréal Montréal, QC
Sponsor/Contact: Canadian Association of Chiefs of Police
#100, 300 Terry Fox Dr.
Kanata, ON K2K 0E3
613-595-1101 *Fax:* 613-383-0372
E-mail: cacp@cacp.ca
URL: www.cacp.ca
Scope: National
Purpose: Conference sessions & exhibits

Institute of Transportation Engineers 2017 Annual Meeting & Exhibit
Date: July 30 - August 2, 2017
Location: Sheraton Centre Toronto Toronto, ON
Sponsor/Contact: Institute of Transportation Engineers
#600, 1627 Eye St. NW
Washington, DC 20006
202-785-0060 *Fax:* 202-785-0609
E-mail: ite_staff@ite.org
URL: www.ite.org
Scope: International
Contact Information: Contact, Registration Information: Sallie C. Dollins, E-mail: sdollins@ite.org; Contact, Technical Program: Eunice Chege, E-mail: echege@ite.org; Contact, Exhibits: Christina Garneski, E-mail: cgarneski@ite.org; Contact, Paper Submittals: Eunice Chege, E-mail: echege@ite.org

Joint Statistical Meetings 2017
Date: July 30 - August 4, 2017
Location: Baltimore, MD USA
Sponsor/Contact: Statistical Society of Canada
#209, 1725 St. Laurent Blvd.
Ottawa, ON K1G 3V4
613-733-2662 *Fax:* 613-733-1386
E-mail: info@ssc.ca
URL: www.ssc.ca
Scope: International
Purpose: Held jointly with the Statistical

Conferences Index

Society of Canada, American Statistical Association, the International Biometric Society (ENAR & WNAR), the International Chinese Statistical Association, the Institute of Mathematical Statistics, & the International Indian Statistical Association

August

2017 American Sociological Association Annual Meeting
Date: August 11-14, 2017
Location: Palais des congrès de Montréal
Montréal, QC
Sponsor/Contact: American Sociological Association
#600, 1430 K St.
Washington, DC 20005
202-383-9005 *Fax:* 202-638-0882
E-mail: executive.office@asanet.org
URL: www.asanet.org
Scope: International

Academy of Management 2017 Annual Meeting
Date: August 4-8, 2016
Location: Atlanta, GA USA
Sponsor/Contact: Academy of Management
P.O. Box 3020
Briarcliff Manor, NY 10510-8020
914-923-2607 *Fax:* 914-923-2615
URL: www.aomonline.org
Scope: International
Purpose: Sharing of research and expertise in all management disciplines through distinguished speakers, competitive paper sessions, symposia, panels, workshops, & special programs for doctoral students
Anticipated Attendance: 10,000+
Contact Information: Assistant Director of Meetings: Taryn Fiore, E-mail: tfiore@pace.edu

International Union of Crystallography 24th Triennial Congress & General Assembly
Date: August 21-29, 2017
Location: Hyderabad International Convention Centre
Hyerabad, Indian
Sponsor/Contact: International Union of Crystallography
c/o Executive Secretariat
2 Abbey Sq.
Chester, CH1 2HU
E-mail: execsec@iucr.org
URL: www.iucr.org
Scope: International

September

American Academy for Cerebral Palsy & Developmental Medicine 71st Annual Meeting
Date: September 13-16, 2017
Location: Palais des congrès de Montréal
Montreal, QC
Sponsor/Contact: American Academy for Cerebral Palsy & Developmental Medicine
#1100, 555 East Wells St.
Milwaukee, WI 53202
414-918-3014 *Fax:* 414-276-2146
E-mail: info@aacpdm.org
URL: www.aacpdm.org
Scope: International

American Association of Neuromuscular & Electrodiagnostic Medicine 2017 64th Annual Meeting
Date: September 13-16, 2017
Location: JW Marriott Desert Ridge
Phoenix, AZ USA
Sponsor/Contact: American Association of Neuromuscular & Electrodiagnostic Medicine
2621 Superior Dr. NW
Rochester, MN 55901
507-288-0100 *Fax:* 507-288-1225
E-mail: aanem@aanem.org
URL: www.aanem.org
Scope: International
Contact Information: Director, Meetings: Denae Brennan, E-mail: dbrennan@aanem.org

Canadian Psychiatric Association 67th Annual Conference / 67e Conférence annuelle de l'Association des psychiatres du Canada
Date: September 14-16, 2017
Location: The Ottawa Convention Centre
Ottawa, ON
Sponsor/Contact: Canadian Psychiatric Association
#701, 141 Laurier Ave. West
Ottawa, ON K1P 5J3
613-234-2815 *Fax:* 613-234-9857
Toll-Free: 800-267-1555
E-mail: cpa@cpa-apc.org
URL: www.cpa-apc.org
Scope: National
Anticipated Attendance: 1200+
Contact Information: E-mail: conference@cpa-apc.org

Dynamics 2017: The Annual National Convention & Product Exhibition of the Canadian Association of Critical Care Nurses
Date: September 24-26, 2017
Location: Toronto, ON
Sponsor/Contact: Canadian Association of Critical Care Nurses
P.O. Box 25322
London, ON N6C 6B1
519-649-5284 *Fax:* 519-649-1458
Toll-Free: 866-477-9077
E-mail: caccn@caccn.ca
URL: www.caccn.ca
Scope: National
Purpose: Featuring programming to enhance education, clinical practice, research, & leadership.
Contact Information: Toll-Free Phone: 1-866-477-9077; E-mail: caccn@caccn.ca

The American Association of Bovine Practitioners 2017 Annual Conference
Date: September 14-16, 2017
Location: Omaha, NE USA
Sponsor/Contact: American Association of Bovine Practitioners
P.O. Box 3610
#802, 3320 Skyway Dr.
Auburn, AL 36831-3610
334-821-0442 *Fax:* 334-821-9532
E-mail: aabphq@aabp.org
URL: www.aabp.org
Scope: International

Union of British Columbia Municipalities 2017 Annual Convention
Date: September 25-29, 2017
Location: Vancouver Convention & Exhibition Centre
Vancouver, BC
Sponsor/Contact: Union of British Columbia Municipalities
#60, 10551 Shellbridge Way
Richmond, BC V6X 2W9
604-270-8226 *Fax:* 604-270-9116
URL: www.ubcm.ca
Scope: Provincial

Western Canada Water 2017 69th Annual Conference & Exhibition
Date: September 19-22, 2017
Location: TCU Place
Saskatoon, SK
Sponsor/Contact: Western Canada Water
P.O. Box 1708
240 River Ave.
Cochrane, AB T4C 1B6
403-709-0064 *Fax:* 403-709-0068
Toll-Free: 877-283-2003
E-mail: member@wcwwa.ca
URL: www.wcwwa.ca
Scope: Provincial
Purpose: A technical program, a keynote speaker, & a trade show for delegates from Western Canada Water
Anticipated Attendance: 500+
Contact Information: Western Canada Water, Toll-Free Phone: 1-877-283-2003, Toll-Free Fax: 1-877-283-2007, E-mail: member@wcwwa.ca

XXI Congress on Safety & Health at Work - Global Forum for Prevention
Date: September 2-6, 2017
Location: Singapore
Sponsor/Contact: International Labour Organization
4, route des Morillons
Geneva, CH-1211
E-mail: ilo@ilo.org
URL: www.ilo.org
Scope: International
Purpose: The World Congress is a forum for the exchange of knowledge, practices & experiences for anyone involved with or interested in health & safety in the workplace.

October

2017 International Council of Graphic Design Associations World Congress
Date: October 15-23, 2017
Location: Palais des congrès de Montréal
Montreal, QC
Sponsor/Contact: International Council of Graphic Design Associations
455, rue Saint-Antoine ouest, #SS10
Montréal, QC H2Z 1J1
514-448-4949 *Fax:* 514-448-4948
E-mail: info@icograda.org
URL: www.icograda.org
Scope: International

American Concrete Institute Fall 2017 Conference
Date: October 15-19, 2017
Location: Disneyland Hotel
Anaheim, CA USA
Sponsor/Contact: American Concrete Institute
P.O. Box 9094
38800 Country Club Dr.
Farmington, MI 48333-9094
248-848-3700 *Fax:* 248-848-3701
URL: www.concrete.org
Scope: International

Canadian Society of Association Executives / Société canadienne d'association 2017 Conference & Showcase
Date: October 25-27, 2017
Location: St. John's, NL
Sponsor/Contact: Canadian Society of Association Executives
#1100, 10 King St. East
Toronto, ON M5C 1C3
416-363-3555 *Fax:* 416-363-3630
Toll-Free: 800-461-3608
URL: www.csae.com
Scope: National
Anticipated Attendance: 500+
Contact Information: E-mail: events@csae.com

November

Alberta Association of Municipal Districts & Counties Fall 2017 Convention & Trade Show
Date: November 21-23, 2017
Location: Shaw Conference Centre
Edmonton, AB
Sponsor/Contact: Alberta Association of Municipal Districts & Counties
2510 Sparrow Dr.
Nisku, AB T9E 8N5
780-955-3639 *Fax:* 780-955-3615
Toll-Free: 855-548-7233
E-mail: aamdc@aamdc.com
URL: www.aamdc.com

Alberta Urban Municipalities Association Convention & AMSC Trade Show 2017
Date: November 22-24, 2017
Location: Calgary, AB
Sponsor/Contact: Alberta Urban Municipalities Association
#300, 8616 15 Ave.
Edmonton, AB T6E 6E6
780-433-4431 *Fax:* 780-433-4454
Toll-Free: 800-310-2862
E-mail: main@auma.ca
URL: www.auma.ca
Scope: Provincial

American Anthropological Association 2017 Annual Meeting
Date: November 29 - December 3, 2017
Location: Marriott Wardman Park Hotel & Omni Shoreham Hotel
Washington, DC USA
Sponsor/Contact: American Anthropological Association
Stn. 600
2300 Clarendon Blvd.
Arlington, VA 22201
703-528-1902 *Fax:* 703-528-3546
URL: www.aaanet.org
Scope: International
Contact Information: Director, American Anthropological Association & Section Meetings: Jason G. Watkins, E-mail: jwatkins@aaanet.org; Meeting Planner: Carla Fernandez, E-mail: cfernandez@aaanet.org

American Society of Mechanical Engineers 2017 International Mechanical Engineering Congress & Exposition
Date: November 2017
Sponsor/Contact: American Society of Mechanical Engineers
3 Park Ave.
New York, NY 10016-5990
800-843-2763
E-mail: customercare@asme.org
URL: www.asme.org
Scope: International

Harmony, Inc. 2017 International Convention & Contests
Location: Halifax Convention Centre
Halifax, NS
Sponsor/Contact: Harmony, Inc.
Toll-Free: 855-750-3341
E-mail: info@harmonyinc.org
URL: www.harmonyinc.org
Anticipated Attendance: 1,000

Helicopter Association of Canada 2017 22nd Annual Convention & Trade Show
Date: November 10-12, 2017
Location: Westin Ottawa
Ottawa, ON
Sponsor/Contact: Helicopter Association of Canada
#500, 130 Albert St.
Ottawa, ON K1P 5G4
613-231-1110 *Fax:* 613-369-5097
URL: www.h-a-c.ca
Scope: National
Purpose: Professional development programs & information sessions to help Helicopter Association of Canada members achieve in the present economic & regulatory climate
Anticipated Attendance: 800+
Contact Information: Office Manager & Contact, Member Services: Barb Priestley, Phone: 613-231-1110, ext. 237, Fax: 613-369-5097, E-mail: barb.priestley@h-a-c.ca

Other Conferences in 2017

12th International Energy Agency Heat Pump Conference
Sponsor/Contact: Canadian GeoExchange Coalition
#304, 1030 Cherrier St.
Montréal, QC H2L 1H9
514-807-7559 *Fax:* 514-807-8221
URL: www.geo-exchange.ca
Scope: International
Purpose: To promote heat pumping technologies through discussions, networking, and information exchange.

2017 Canadian Association of Science Centres Annual Conference
Location: Ontario Science Centre
Toronto, ON
Sponsor/Contact: Canadian Association of Science Centres
P.O. Box 3443 Stn. D
Ottawa, OM K1P 6P4
613-566-4247
E-mail: casc.accs@gmail.com
URL: www.canadiansciencecentres.ca
Scope: National

2017 International Play Association Conference
Sponsor/Contact: Alberta Recreation & Parks Association
11759 Groat Rd.
Edmonton, AB T5M 3K6
780-415-1745 *Fax:* 780-451-7915
Toll-Free: 877-544-1747
E-mail: arpa@arpaonline.ca
URL: arpaonline.ca
Scope: International
Purpose: Organized by IPA Canada, the City of Calgary, ARPA, and other partner organizations.

7th World Hydrogen Technology Convention (WHTC 2017)
Location: Prague, Czech Republic
Sponsor/Contact: International Association for Hydrogen Energy
#303, 5794 40th St. SW
Miami, FL 33155
E-mail: info@iahe.org
URL: www.iahe.org
Scope: International
Purpose: A conference of the International Association for Hydrogen Energy, for the hydrogen & fuel cell community, featuring an exhibition with hydrogen & fuel cell applications from research institutions & companies
Anticipated Attendance: 1,000+

Association of Manitoba Municipalities 19th Annual Convention
Location: Brandon, MB
Sponsor/Contact: Association of Manitoba Municipalities
1910 Saskatchewan Ave. West
Portage la Prairie, MB R1N 0P1
204-857-8666 *Fax:* 204-856-2370
E-mail: amm@amm.mb.ca
URL: www.amm.mb.ca

Association of Vancouver Island Coastal Communities 2017 Annual General Meeting & Convention
Sponsor/Contact: Association of Vancouver Island Coastal Communities
Local Government House
525 Government St.
Victoria, BC V8W 0A8
250-356-5122 *Fax:* 250-356-5119
URL: www.avicc.ca
Scope: Local

Atlantic Provinces Library Association 2017 Annual Conference
Sponsor/Contact: Atlantic Provinces Library Association
c/o School of Information Management, Kenneth C. Rowe Management Bldg.
6100 University Ave.
Halifax, NS B3H 3J5
E-mail: executive@yahoo.ca
URL: www.apla.ca
Scope: Provincial
Purpose: An educational program to support the interests & concerns of the library community in the Atlantic provinces

British Columbia Federation of Labour 2017 Convention: The 61st Convention of the British Columbia Federation of Labour
Sponsor/Contact: British Columbia Federation of Labour
#200, 5118 Joyce St.
Vancouver, BC V5R 4H1
604-430-1421 *Fax:* 604-430-5917
E-mail: bcfed@bcfed.ca
URL: www.bcfed.com
Scope: Provincial
Purpose: A meeting for trade union members from throughout British Columbia to set the direction for the labour movement
Anticipated Attendance: 1,000+

Building Owners & Managers Association 2017 Conference
Location: Toronto, ON
Sponsor/Contact: Building Owners & Managers Association - Canada
P.O. Box 61
#1801, 1 Dundas St. West
Toronto, ON M5G 1Z3
416-214-1912 *Fax:* 416-214-1284
E-mail: info@bomacanada.ca
URL: www.bomacanada.ca
Scope: National

CAUCE 2017: The 64th Annual Conference & General Meeting of the Canadian Association for University Continuing Education
Location: Simon Fraser University
Burnaby, BC
Sponsor/Contact: Canadian Association for University Continuing Education
c/o Centre for Continuing & Distance Education, U. of Saskatchewan
#464, 221 Cumberland Ave. North
Saskatoon, SK S7N 1M3
306-966-5604 *Fax:* 306-966-5590
E-mail: cauce.secratariat@usask.ca
URL: www.cauce-aepuc.ca
Scope: National

Canadian Association of Advanced Practice Nurses Conference & Biennial General Meeting 2017
Sponsor/Contact: Canadian Association of Advanced Practice Nurses
P.O. Box 117
153 Frederick St.
Kitchener, ON N2H 2M2
519-579-1096 *Fax:* 519-578-9185
E-mail: adminassist@caapn-aciipa.org
URL: caapn-aciipa.org
Scope: National

Canadian Association of Emergency Physicians (CAEP) 2017 Annual Conference
Location: Whistler Conference Centre
Whistler, BC
Sponsor/Contact: Canadian Association of Emergency Physicians
#808, 180 Elgin St.
Ottawa, ON K2P 2K3
613-523-3343 *Fax:* 613-523-0190
Toll-Free: 800-463-1158
E-mail: admin@caep.ca
URL: www.caep.ca
Scope: National

Canadian Association of Geographers 2017 Annual Meeting & Conference
Location: York University
Toronto, ON
Sponsor/Contact: Canadian Association of Geographers
Department of Geography, McGill University
#425, 805, rue Sherbrooke ouest
Montréal, QC H3A 2K6
514-398-4946 *Fax:* 514-398-7437
E-mail: valerie.shoffey@cag-acg.ca
URL: www.cag-acg.ca
Scope: National
Purpose: A business meeting & educational conference for geographers & students, featuring the presentation of papers & posters, plus exhibits, & social activities

Canadian Association of Slavists 2017 Annual Conference (in conjunction with the Canadian Federation for the Humanities & Social Sciences Congress)
Location: Ryerson University
Toronto, ON
Sponsor/Contact: Canadian Association of Slavists
Alumni Hall, Dept. of History & Classics, University of Alberta
#2, 28 Tory Bldg.
Edmonton, AB T6G 2H4
780-492-2566 *Fax:* 780-492-9125
E-mail: csp@ulberta.ca
URL: www.ualberta.ca/~csp/cas/contact.html
Scope: National
Purpose: A yearly meeting with roundtable discussions, panels, & the presentation of papers by members of the Canadian Association of Slavists

Canadian Bureau for International Education 2017 Annual Conference
Sponsor/Contact: Canadian Bureau for International Education
#1550, 220 Laurier Ave. West
Ottawa, ON K1P 5Z9
613-237-4820 *Fax:* 613-237-1073
E-mail: info@cbie.ca
URL: www.cbie-bcei.ca
Scope: National
Purpose: The Conference features professional development workshops, concurrent sessions and networking opportunities.

Canadian Fertilizer Institute 72nd Annual Conference
Sponsor/Contact: Canadian Fertilizer Institute
#907, 350 Sparks St.
Ottawa, ON K1R 7S8
613-230-2600 *Fax:* 613-230-5142
E-mail: info@cfi.ca
URL: www.cfi.ca
Scope: National

Canadian Health Libraries Association (CHLA) / Association des bibliothèques de la santé du Canada (ABSC) 2017 41st Annual Conference
Location: Edmonton, AB
Sponsor/Contact: Canadian Health Libraries Association
39 River St.
Toronto, ON M5A 3P1
416-646-1600 *Fax:* 416-646-9460
E-mail: info@chla-absc.ca
URL: www.chla-absc.ca
Scope: National
Purpose: An annual May or June gathering of health science librarians to participate in continuing education courses & lectures, & to view products & services related to their work
Contact Information: Continuing Education, E-mail: ce@chla-absc.ca; Public Relations, E-mail: pr@chla-absc.ca

Canadian Labour Congress 2017 National Convention
Sponsor/Contact: Canadian Labour Congress
National Headquarters
2841 Riverside Dr.
Ottawa, ON K1V 8X7
613-521-3400 *Fax:* 613-521-4655
URL: www.canadianlabour.ca
Scope: National
Purpose: A convention for members of the labour movement to develop an Action Plan, based on committee reports, resolutions, & the discussion of policies

Canadian Library Association / Association canadienne des bibliothèques 72nd National Conference & Trade Show 2017
Sponsor/Contact: Canadian Library Association
#400, 1150 Morrison Dr.
Ottawa, ON K2H 8S9
613-232-9625 *Fax:* 613-563-9895
E-mail: info@cla.ca
URL: www.cla.ca

Conferences Index

Scope: National
Purpose: Featuring keynote speakers, workshops, social events, & a trade show
Anticipated Attendance: 800+
Contact Information: E-mail: info@cla.ca

Canadian Marine Pilots' Association 5th Congress
Sponsor/Contact: Canadian Marine Pilots' Association
#1302, 155 Queen St.
Ottawa, ON K1P 6L1
613-232-7777 *Fax:* 613-232-7667
E-mail: cmpa@tnpa.ca
URL: www.marinepilots.ca
Scope: National

Canadian Nurses Association 2017 Annual Meeting
Sponsor/Contact: Canadian Nurses Association
50 Driveway
Ottawa, ON K2P 1E2
613-237-2133 *Fax:* 613-237-3520
Toll-Free: 800-361-8404
E-mail: info@cna-aiic.ca
URL: www.cna-aiic.ca
Scope: National
Purpose: A business meeting attended by members of the provincial & territorial nursing associations & interested parties
Contact Information: E-mail: info@cna-aiic.ca

Canadian Society of Biblical Studies 2017 Annual Meeting (in conjunction with the 2017 Congress of the Humanities & Social Sciences)
Sponsor/Contact: Canadian Society of Biblical Studies
c/o Prof. Robert A. Derrenbacker, Jr., Regent College
5800 University Blvd.
Vancouver, BC V6T 2E4
URL: www.ccsr.ca/csbs
Scope: National

Canadian Society of Hospital Pharmacists 2017 48th Annual Professional Practice Conference
Sponsor/Contact: Canadian Society of Hospital Pharmacists
#3, 30 Concourse Gate
Ottawa, ON K2E 7V7
613-736-9733 *Fax:* 613-736-5660
E-mail: info@cshp.ca
URL: www.cshp.ca
Scope: National
Purpose: Informative sessions to educate & motivate participants

Canadian Society of Hospital Pharmacists 2017 Annual Summer Educational Sessions
Sponsor/Contact: Canadian Society of Hospital Pharmacists
#3, 30 Concourse Gate
Ottawa, ON K2E 7V7
613-736-9733 *Fax:* 613-736-5660
E-mail: info@cshp.ca
URL: www.cshp.ca
Scope: National
Purpose: The annual general meeting of the society & educational workshops held each year in partnership with one of the society's branches
Contact Information: E-mail: info@cshp.ca

Canadian Urban Transit Association 2017 Fall Conference & Trans-Expo
Sponsor/Contact: Canadian Urban Transit Association
#1401, 55 York St.
Toronto, ON M5J 1R7
416-365-9800 *Fax:* 416-365-1295
URL: www.cutaactu.ca
Scope: National
Purpose: A yearly technical conference, which also includes the presentation of Employee Awards based on accomplishments in areas such as attendance, safety, & acts of heroism

Computer Human Interaction 2017 Conference on Human Factors in Computing Systems
Sponsor/Contact: Special Interest Group on Computer Human Interaction
P.O. Box 93672 Stn. Nelson Park
Vancouver, BC V6E 4L7
604-876-8985
E-mail: chi-VanCHI@acm.org
URL: www.sigchi.org
Scope: International

Goldschmidt Conference 2017
Sponsor/Contact: Geochemical Society
c/o Earth & Planetary Sciences Department, Washington University
#CB 11691, Brookings Dr.
St. Louis, MO 63130-4899
314-935-4131 *Fax:* 314-935-4121
E-mail: gsoffice@geochemsoc.org
URL: www.geochemsoc.org
Scope: International
Purpose: An international conference on geochemistry
Anticipated Attendance: 3,000+

International Heavy Haul Association 2017 International Conference
Location: Russia
Sponsor/Contact: International Heavy Haul Association
2808 Forest Hills Crt.
Virginia Beach, 23454-1236
URL: www.ihha.net
Scope: International
Purpose: An international conference, scheduled every four years, featuring meetings covering the complete spectrum of heavy haul subjects, as well as technical tours

International Society for Sexually Transmitted Diseases Research World STI & HIV Congress 2017
Location: Rio de Janeiro, Brasil
Sponsor/Contact: International Society for Sexually Transmitted Diseases Research
c/o Basil Donovan, The Kirby Institute, University of New South Wales
Sidney
URL: www.isstdr.org
Scope: International
Purpose: To address the range of the biomedical, behavioral, & social sciences related to all sexually transmitted diseases, including HIV infection

Lower Mainland Local Government Association 2017 Annual General Meeting & Conference
Sponsor/Contact: Lower Mainland Local Government Association
#60, 10551 Shellbridge Way
Richmond, BC V6X 2W9
250-356-5122 *Fax:* 604-270-9116
URL: www.lmlga.ca
Scope: Local
Purpose: Tradeshow, workshops, & seminars for persons involved in local government

Na'amat Canada National Triennial Convention
Sponsor/Contact: Na'amat Canada Inc.
#6, 7005 Kildare Rd.
Montréal, QC H4W 1C1
514-488-0792 *Fax:* 514-487-6727
Toll-Free: 888-278-0792
E-mail: naamat@naamatcanada.org
URL: www.naamat.com

Nova Scotia Library Association 2017 Annual Conference
Location: Nova Scotia
Sponsor/Contact: Nova Scotia Library Association
c/o Kelli WooShue, Halifax Public Libraries
60 Alderney Dr.
Dartmouth, NS B2Y 4P8
902-490-5710
E-mail: wooshuk@halifax.ca
URL: www.nsla.ns.ca
Scope: Provincial
Purpose: Hosted by Annapolis Valley Regional Library in the autumn
Contact Information: E-mail: conference@nsla.ns.ca

Royal Canadian Mounted Police Veterans Association 2017 Annual General Meeting
Location: Prince Edward Island
Sponsor/Contact: Royal Canadian Mounted Police Veterans' Association
1200 Vanier Pkwy.
Ottawa, ON K1A 0R2
613-993-8633 *Fax:* 613-993-4353
Toll-Free: 877-251-1771
E-mail: rcmp.vets@rcmp-grc.gc.ca
URL: www.rcmpvetsnational.ca
Scope: National

Royal Canadian Numismatic Association 2017 Convention
Location: Boucherville, QC
Sponsor/Contact: Royal Canadian Numismatic Association
#432, 5694 Hwy. 7 East
Markham, ON L3P 1B4
647-401-4014 *Fax:* 905-472-9645
E-mail: info@rcna.ca
URL: www.rcna.ca
Scope: National
Purpose: An annual event, presenting an education symposium, a bourse & display, business meetings, award presentations, plus social & networking activities
Contact Information: E-mail: info@rcna.ca; URL: www.boucherville2017.com

Sheet Metal and Air Conditioning Contractors' National Association (SMACNA) 74th Annual Convention
Sponsor/Contact: Sheet Metal & Air Conditioning Contractors' National Association
P.O. Box 221230
4201 Lafayette Center Dr.
Chantilly, VA 20153-1230
703-803-2980 *Fax:* 703-803-3732
E-mail: info@smacna.org
URL: www.smacna.org
Scope: National
Contact Information: Email: SMACNAConvention@cmrus.com; Phone: 800-336-9704

2018

January

American Philological Association 149th Annual Meeting
Date: January 4-7, 2018
Location: Boston, MA USA
Sponsor/Contact: American Philological Association
University of Pennsylvania
#201E, 220 South 40th St.
Philadelphia, PA 19104-3512
215-898-4975 *Fax:* 215-573-7874
E-mail: apaclassics@sas.upenn.edu
URL: apaclassics.org
Scope: International

February

American Association for the Advancement of Science 2018 Annual Meeting
Date: February 15-19, 2018
Location: Austin, TX USA
Sponsor/Contact: American Association for the Advancement of Science
1200 New York Ave. NW
Washington, DC 20005
202-326-6440
E-mail: membership@aaas.org
URL: www.aaas.org
Scope: International
Purpose: Information for scientists, engineers, educators, & policy-makers
Contact Information: Phone: 202-326-6450; Fax: 202-289-4021; E-mail: meetings@aaas.org; Director, Meetings & Public Engagement: Tiffany Lohwater, E-mail: tlohwate@aaas.org

American Library Association 2018 Midwinter Meeting & Exhibits
Date: February 8-13, 2018
Location: Denver, CO USA
Sponsor/Contact: American Library Association
50 East Huron St.
Chicago, IL 60611
Fax: 312-440-9374
Toll-Free: 800-545-2433
E-mail: ala@ala.org
URL: www.ala.org
Scope: International
Purpose: A library & information service meeting presenting speakers, discussion groups, exhibits, & committee meetings
Contact Information: Registration Customer Service, Phone: 1-800-974-3084, E-mail: ala@experient-inc.com

Association of Ontario Land Surveyors 2018 Annual General Meeting
Date: February 28 - March 2, 2018
Location: Sheraton On The Falls Hotel Niagara Falls, ON
Sponsor/Contact: Association of Ontario Land Surveyors
1043 McNicoll Ave.
Toronto, ON M1W 3W6
416-491-9020 *Fax:* 416-491-2576
Toll-Free: 800-268-0718
E-mail: info@aols.org
URL: www.aols.org
Scope: Provincial
Contact Information: Lena Kassabian; Email: lena@aols.org; Phone: 416-491-9020 ext. 25

March

Canadian Association for Dental Research 42nd Annual Meeting
Date: March 14-17, 2018
Location: Fort Lauderdale, FL USA
Sponsor/Contact: Canadian Association for Dental Research
c/o Dr. C. Birek, Faculty of Dentistry, University of Manitoba
780 Bannatyne Ave.
Winnipeg, MB R3E 0W2
204-789-3256 *Fax:* 204-789-3913
E-mail: birek@ms.umanitoba.ca
URL: www.cadr-acrd.ca
Scope: International
Purpose: In conjunction with the 47th Annual Meeting of the American Association of Dental Research & the 96th General Session & Exhibition of the International Association for Dental Research

Public Library Association (a division of the American Library Association) 2018 Biennial Conference
Date: March 20-24, 2018
Location: Philadelphia, PA USA
Sponsor/Contact: American Library Association
50 East Huron St.
Chicago, IL 60611
Fax: 312-440-9374
Toll-Free: 800-545-2433
E-mail: ala@ala.org
URL: www.ala.org
Scope: International
Purpose: The multi-day event offers nearly 200 education programs, social events that include author luncheons and networking receptions, and an exhibits hall featuring the latest in products and services.
Contact Information: Registration Customer Service, Phone: 1-800-974-3084, E-mail: ala@experient-inc.com

April

Council of Forest Industries 2015 Annual Convention
Date: April 11-13, 2018
Location: Kelowna, BC
Sponsor/Contact: Council of Forest Industries
Pender Place I Business Building
#1501, 700 Pender St. West
Vancouver, BC V6C 1G8
604-684-0211 *Fax:* 604-687-4930
E-mail: info@cofi.org
URL: www.cofi.org
Scope: National
Purpose: A meeting about issues affecting the forestry industries of British Columbia.
Contact Information: Phone: 604-684-0211; Fax: 604-687-4930

International Commission of Agricultural & Biosystems Engineering XIX 2018 World Congress
Date: April 22-26, 2018
Location: Antalya, Turkey
Sponsor/Contact: International Commission of Agricultural & Biosystems Engineering
c/o Dr. Takaaki Maekawa, School of Life & Environmental Sciences
1-1-1 Tennodai, University of Tsukuba
Tsukuba, Ibaraki
E-mail: biopro@sakura.cc.tsukuba.ac.jp
URL: www.cigr.org
Scope: International

International Society for Magnetic Resonance in Medicine 2018 26th Scientific Meeting & Exhibition
Date: April 14-20, 2018
Location: Paris, France
Sponsor/Contact: International Society for Magnetic Resonance in Medicine
2030 Addison St., 7th Fl.
Berkeley, CA 94704
510-841-1899 *Fax:* 510-841-2340
E-mail: info@ismrm.org
URL: www.ismrm.org
Scope: International
Purpose: Featuring the 26th Annual Meeting of the Section for Magnetic Resonance Technologists
Contact Information: Director, Meetings: Sandra Daudlin, E-mail: sandra@ismrm.org; Coordinator, Meetings: Melisa Martinez, E-mail: melisa@ismrm.org

Library Association of Alberta Annual Conference 2018
Date: April 26-29, 2018
Location: Alberta
Sponsor/Contact: Library Association of Alberta
80 Baker Cres. NW
Calgary, AB T2L 1R4
403-284-5818 *Fax:* 403-282-6646
Toll-Free: 877-522-5550
E-mail: info@laa.ca
URL: www.laa.ca
Scope: Provincial
Purpose: A conference held each spring for members of the Alberta library community, featuring association annual general meetings, session presentations, networking opportunities, & a trade show. Beginning this year, the conference is no longer held jointly with the Alberta Library Trustees Association (ALTA).
Contact Information: Library Association of Alberta, Phone: 403-284-5818, Toll-Free Phone: 1-877-522-5550, Fax: 403-282-6646, E-mail: info@laa.ca, info@albertalibraryconference.com

May

American Society of Neuroradiology 2018 56th Annual Meeting
Date: May 19-24, 2018
Location: Vancouver Convention Centre Vancouver, BC
Sponsor/Contact: American Society of Neuroradiology
#207, 2210 Midwest Rd.
Oak Brook, IL 60523
630-574-0220 *Fax:* 630-574-0661
E-mail: jgantenberg@asnr.org
URL: www.asnr.org
Scope: International
Contact Information: Director, Scientific Meetings: Lora Tannehill, E-mail: ltannehill@asnr.org; Manager, Scientific Meetings: Valerie Geisendorfer, E-mail: vgeisendorfer@asnr.org

Canadian Union of Public Employees (CUPE) Ontario 2018 55th Convention
Date: May 30 - June 2, 2018
Location: Caesars Windsor Hotel Windsor, ON
Sponsor/Contact: Canadian Union of Public Employees
Ontario Regional Office
#1, 80 Commerce Valley Dr. East
Markham, ON L3T 0B2
905-739-9739 *Fax:* 905-739-9740
E-mail: info@cupe.on.ca
URL: www.cupe.on.ca
Scope: Provincial
Purpose: A gathering where convention delegates debate & vote on resolutions
Anticipated Attendance: 1,200
Contact Information: CUPE Ontario, E-mail: info@cupe.on.ca

Government Finance Officers Association 2018 112th Annual Conference
Date: May 6-9, 2018
Location: St. Louis, MO USA
Sponsor/Contact: Government Finance Officers Association
#2700, 203 North LaSalle St.
Chicago, IL 60601-1210
312-977-9700 *Fax:* 312-977-4806
E-mail: inquiry@gfoa.org
URL: www.gfoa.org
Scope: International
Anticipated Attendance: 4,100+
Contact Information: Manager, Communications: Natalie Laudadio, Phone: 312-977-9700, ext. 2298

Journées dentaires internationales du Québec (JDIQ) 2018
Date: 25 au 29 mai 2018
Location: Quebec
Sponsor/Contact: Ordre des dentistes du Québec
625, boul René-Lévesque ouest, 15e étage
Montréal, QC H3B 1R2
514-875-8511 *Fax:* 514-393-9248
Toll-Free: 800-361-4887
URL: www.odq.qc.ca
Scope: Provincial
Contact Information: Directeur, Dr Denis Forest, téléphone: 514-875-8511, poste 2222; adresse email: denis.forest@odq.qc.ca

Medical Library Association 2018 Annual Meeting & Exhibition
Date: May 18-23, 2018
Location: Atlanta, GA USA
Sponsor/Contact: Medical Library Association
#1900, 65 East Wacker Pl.
Chicago, IL 60601-7246
312-419-9094 *Fax:* 312-419-8950
E-mail: info@mlahq.org
URL: www.mlanet.org
Scope: International

Pediatric Academic Societies' 2018 Annual Meeting
Date: May 5-8, 2018
Location: Toronto, ON
Sponsor/Contact: Academic Pediatric Association
6728 Old McLean Village Dr.
McLean, VA 22101
703-556-9222 *Fax:* 703-556-8729
E-mail: info@academicpeds.org
URL: www.ambpeds.org
Scope: International
Purpose: An international meeting focussing on research in child health
Contact Information: Address: #7B, 3400 Research Forest Dr., The Woodlands, TX, 77381, USA; Phone: 281-419-0052; Fax: 281-419-0082

Pediatric Endocrine Society 2018 Annual Meeting
Date: May 5-8, 2018
Location: Toronto, ON
Sponsor/Contact: Pediatric Endocrine Society
6728 Old McLean Village Dr.
McLean, VA 22101
E-mail: info@pedsendo.org
URL: www.pedsendo.org
Scope: International
Purpose: An annual gathering of persons from the disciplines of pediatric endocrinology, including business meetings, lectures, topic symposia, poster sessions, workshops, exhibits, & social activities
Contact Information: E-mail: info@pedsendo.org

June

American Library Association 2018 Annual Conference
Date: June 21-26, 2018
Location: New Orleans, LA USA
Sponsor/Contact: American Library Association
50 East Huron St.
Chicago, IL 60611
Fax: 312-440-9374
Toll-Free: 800-545-2433
E-mail: ala@ala.org
URL: www.ala.org
Scope: International
Purpose: A conference providing speakers, educational programs, committee meetings, & exhibits related to library & information services

American Water Works Association 2018 137th Annual Conference & Exposition
Date: June 11-15, 2018
Location: Las Vegas, NV USA
Sponsor/Contact: American Water Works Association
6666 West Quincy Ave.
Denver, CO 80235
303-794-7711 *Fax:* 303-347-0804
Toll-Free: 800-926-7337
E-mail: custsvc@awwa.org
URL: www.awwa.org
Scope: International
Purpose: Technical programs, workshops, poster sessions, seminars, continuing education units, & exhibits for the international water community
Contact Information: American Water Works Association, Phone: 800-926-7337, Fax: 303-347-0804, E-mail: awwamktg@awwa.org

Canadian Anesthesiologists' Society 2018 74th Annual Meeting
Date: June 15-18, 2018
Location: Palais de Congrès Montreal, QC
Sponsor/Contact: Canadian Anesthesiologists' Society
#208, One Eglinton Ave. East
Toronto, ON M4P 3A1
416-480-0602 *Fax:* 416-480-0320
E-mail: anesthesia@cas.ca
URL: www.cas.ca
Scope: National
Purpose: A convention, with an exhibition pharmaceutical companies & equipment manufacturers

Canadian Nurses Association 2018 Annual Meeting & Biennial Convention
Date: June 18-20, 2018
Location: Alberta
Sponsor/Contact: Canadian Nurses Association
50 Driveway
Ottawa, ON K2P 1E2
613-237-2133 *Fax:* 613-237-3520
Toll-Free: 800-361-8404
E-mail: info@cna-aiic.ca
URL: www.cna-aiic.ca
Scope: National
Purpose: An opportunity for delegates from across Canada to discuss challenges in the nursing profession, share successes, participate in workshops, listen to speakers, & view new products from the health-care marketplace
Anticipated Attendance: 1,000+
Contact Information: E-mail: conferences@cna-aiic.ca

Canadian Pharmacists Association 2018 106th Annual National Conference
Date: June 2-5, 2018
Location: Winnipeg, MB
Sponsor/Contact: Canadian Pharmacists Association
1785 Alta Vista Dr.
Ottawa, ON K1G 3Y6
613-523-7877 *Fax:* 613-523-0445
Toll-Free: 800-917-9489
E-mail: info@pharmacists.ca
URL: www.pharmacists.ca
Scope: National
Purpose: A yearly event for Canadian pharmacists, featuring educational workshops, a trade show, awards, & social events
Contact Information: E-mail: info@pharmacists.ca

Canadian Public Health Association 2018 Conference
Date: June 11-14, 2018
Location: Halifax, NS
Sponsor/Contact: Canadian Public Health Association
#300, 1565 Carling Ave.
Ottawa, ON K1Z 8R1
613-725-3769 *Fax:* 613-725-9826
E-mail: info@cpha.ca
URL: www.cpha.ca
Scope: National
Purpose: A conference for policy-makers, researchers, environmental health professionals, academics, & students from across Canada
Contact Information: Conference Manager: Sarah Pettenuzzo, Phone: 613-725-3769, ext. 153; Conference Officer: Julie Paquette, Phone: 613-725-3769, ext. 126

Canadian Urological Association 2018 73rd Annual Meeting
Location: Halifax Convention Centre
Halifax, NS
Sponsor/Contact: Canadian Urological Association
#1303, 1155, University St.
Montréal, QC H3B 3A7
514-395-0376 *Fax:* 514-395-1664
E-mail: cua@cua.org
URL: www.cua.org
Scope: National
Anticipated Attendance: 600

Federation of Canadian Municipalities 2018 Annual Conference & Trade Show
Attendees: 2,000
Location: Halifax Convention Centre
Halifax, NS
Sponsor/Contact: Federation of Canadian Municipalities
24 Clarence St.
Ottawa, ON K1N 5P3
613-241-5221 *Fax:* 613-241-7440
E-mail: federation@fcm.ca
URL: www.fcm.ca
Scope: National

Microwave Theory & Techniques Society International Microwave Symposia 2018
Date: June 11-15, 2018
Location: Philadelphia, PA USA
Sponsor/Contact: IEEE Microwave Theory & Techniques Society
5829 Bellanca Dr.
Elkridge, MD 21075
410-796-5866 *Fax:* 410-796-5829
URL: www.mtt.org
Scope: International
Purpose: Technical papers; Workshops; Trade show

September

American Society for Bone & Mineral Research 2018 Annual Meeting
Date: September 27 - October 1, 2018
Location: Palais des congrès de Montréal
Montréal, QC
Sponsor/Contact: American Society for Bone & Mineral Research
#800, 2025 M St. NW
Washington, DC 20036-3309
E-mail: asbmr@asbmr.org
URL: www.asbmr.org
Scope: International
Purpose: Plenary & poster sessions, panel discussions, & networking events
Contact Information: E-mail: asbmr@asbmr.org

Canadian Psychiatric Association 68th Annual Conference / 68e Conférence annuelle de l'Association des psychiatres du Canada
Date: September 27-29, 2018
Location: The Westin Harbour Castle
Toronto, ON
Sponsor/Contact: Canadian Psychiatric Association
#701, 141 Laurier Ave. West
Ottawa, ON K1P 5J3
613-234-2815 *Fax:* 613-234-9857
Toll-Free: 800-267-1555
E-mail: cpa@cpa-apc.org
URL: www.cpa-apc.org
Scope: National
Anticipated Attendance: 1200+
Contact Information: E-mail: conference@cpa-apc.org

The American Association of Bovine Practitioners 2018 Annual Conference
Date: September 13-15, 2018
Location: Phoenix, AZ USA
Sponsor/Contact: American Association of Bovine Practitioners
P.O. Box 3610
#802, 3320 Skyway Dr.
Auburn, AL 36831-3610
334-821-0442 *Fax:* 334-821-9532
E-mail: aabphq@aabp.org
URL: www.aabp.org
Scope: International

Western Canada Water 2018 70th Annual Conference & Exhibition
Date: September 18-21, 2018
Location: Winnipeg Convention Centre
Winnipeg, MB
Sponsor/Contact: Western Canada Water
P.O. Box 1708
240 River Ave.
Cochrane, AB T4C 1B6
403-709-0064 *Fax:* 403-709-0068
Toll-Free: 877-283-2003
E-mail: member@wcwwa.ca
URL: www.wcwwa.ca
Scope: Provincial
Purpose: A technical program, a keynote speaker, & a trade show for delegates from Western Canada Water
Anticipated Attendance: 500+
Contact Information: Western Canada Water, Toll-Free Phone: 1-877-283-2003, Toll-Free Fax: 1-877-283-2007, E-mail: member@wcwwa.ca

October

Canadian Association of Paediatric Health Centres Annual Conference 2018
Date: October 14-16, 2018
Location: Saskatoon, SK
Sponsor/Contact: Canadian Association of Paediatric Health Centres
c/o Canadian Association of Paediatric Health Centres
#104, 2141 Thurston Dr.
Ottawa, ON K1G 6C9
613-738-4164 *Fax:* 613-738-3247
E-mail: info@caphc.org
URL: www.caphc.org
Scope: National

Canadian Society of Association Executives / Société canadienne d'association 2018 Conference & Showcase
Date: October 24-26, 2018
Location: Ottawa, ON
Sponsor/Contact: Canadian Society of Association Executives
#1100, 10 King St. East
Toronto, ON M5C 1C3
416-363-3555 *Fax:* 416-363-3630
Toll-Free: 800-461-3608
URL: www.csae.com
Scope: National
Anticipated Attendance: 500+
Contact Information: E-mail: events@csae.com

Other Conferences in 2018

20th ISRRT World Congress
Sponsor/Contact: International Society of Radiographers & Radiological Technologists
143 Bryn Pinwydden, Pentwyn, Cardiff
Wales, CF2 7DG
URL: www.isrrt.org
Scope: International

71st Society of Architectural Historians Annual Conference
Sponsor/Contact: Society of Architectural Historians
1365 North Astor St.
Chicago, IL 60610-2144
312-573-1365 *Fax:* 312-573-1141
E-mail: info@sah.org
URL: www.sah.org
Scope: International

Alberta Association of Municipal Districts & Counties Fall 2018 Convention & Trade Show
Location: Alberta
Sponsor/Contact: Alberta Association of Municipal Districts & Counties
2510 Sparrow Dr.
Nisku, AB T9E 8N5
780-955-3639 *Fax:* 780-955-3615
Toll-Free: 855-548-7233
E-mail: aamdc@aamdc.com
URL: www.aamdc.com

Alberta Association of Municipal Districts & Counties Spring 2018 Convention & Trade Show
Location: Alberta
Sponsor/Contact: Alberta Association of Municipal Districts & Counties
2510 Sparrow Dr.
Nisku, AB T9E 8N5
780-955-3639 *Fax:* 780-955-3615
Toll-Free: 855-548-7233
E-mail: aamdc@aamdc.com
URL: www.aamdc.com

Association of Canadian Archivists 2018 43rd Annual Conference & Annual General Meeting
Sponsor/Contact: Association of Canadian Archivists
P.O. Box 2596 Stn. D
Ottawa, ON K1P 5W6
613-234-6977 *Fax:* 613-234-8500
E-mail: aca@archivists.ca
URL: www.archivists.ca
Scope: National
Purpose: A meeting occurring in May or June each year, for archivists from across Canada, featuring educational presentations, trade show exhibits, networking opportunities, as well as workshops immediately prior or following conference sessions
Contact Information: Association of Canadian Archivists Board or Office, E-mail: aca@archivists.ca

Association of Visual Language Interpreters of Canada Summer 2018 Biennial Conference
Location: Saskatchewan
Sponsor/Contact: Association of Visual Language Interpreters of Canada
#110, 39012 Discovery Way
Squamish, BC V8B 0E5
604-617-8502 *Fax:* 604-567-8502
E-mail: avlic@avlic.ca
URL: www.avlic.ca
Scope: National

CAUCE 2018: The 65th Annual Conference & General Meeting of the Canadian Association for University Continuing Education
Sponsor/Contact: Canadian Association for University Continuing Education
c/o Centre for Continuing & Distance Education, U. of Saskatchewan
#464, 221 Cumberland Ave. North
Saskatoon, SK S7N 1M3
306-966-5604 *Fax:* 306-966-5590
E-mail: cauce.secratariat@usask.ca
URL: www.cauce-aepuc.ca
Scope: National

Canadian Association of Municipal Administrators 2018 47th Annual Conference & Annual General Meeting
Sponsor/Contact: Canadian Association of Municipal Administrators

P.O. Box 128 Stn. A
Fredericton, NB E3B 4Y2
866-771-2262
E-mail: admin@camacam.ca
URL: www.camacam.ca
Scope: National
Purpose: Information & a trade show for senior managers from Canadian municipalities throughout Canada
Contact Information: E-mail: admin@camacam.ca

Canadian Health Libraries Association (CHLA) / Association des bibliothèques de la santé du Canada (ABSC) 2018 42nd Annual Conference
Location: St. John's, NL
Sponsor/Contact: Canadian Health Libraries Association
39 River St.
Toronto, ON M5A 3P1
416-646-1600 *Fax:* 416-646-9460
E-mail: info@chla-absc.ca
URL: www.chla-absc.ca
Scope: National
Purpose: An annual May or June gathering of health science librarians to participate in continuing education courses & lectures, & to view products & services related to their work
Contact Information: Continuing Education, E-mail: ce@chla-absc.ca; Public Relations, E-mail: pr@chla-absc.ca

Canadian Library Association / Association canadienne des bibliothèques 73rd National Conference & Trade Show 2018
Sponsor/Contact: Canadian Library Association
#400, 1150 Morrison Dr.
Ottawa, ON K2H 8S9
613-232-9625 *Fax:* 613-563-9895
E-mail: info@cla.ca
URL: www.cla.ca
Scope: National
Purpose: Keynote speakers, an educational program, poster sessions, exhibits, & social events
Anticipated Attendance: 800+
Contact Information: E-mail: info@cla.ca

Institute of Transportation Engineers 2018 Annual Meeting & Exhibit
Sponsor/Contact: Institute of Transportation Engineers
#600, 1627 Eye St. NW
Washington, DC 20006
202-785-0060 *Fax:* 202-785-0609
E-mail: ite_staff@ite.org
URL: www.ite.org
Scope: International

International Board on Books for Young People 2018 36th International Congress
Sponsor/Contact: International Board on Books for Young People
Nonnenweg 12, Postfach
Basel, CH-4003
E-mail: ibby@ibby.org
URL: www.ibby.org
Scope: International

International Society of Hypertension 27th Scientific Meeting
Sponsor/Contact: International Society of Hypertension
ISH Secretariat, Hampton Medical Conferences Ltd.
113-119 High St.
Hampton Hill, Middlesex, TW12 1NJ
E-mail: secretariat@ish-world.com
URL: www.ish-world.com
Scope: International
Purpose: Scientific program & exhibition

International Water Association World Water Congress & Exhibition 2018
Sponsor/Contact: International Water Association
Alliance House
12 Caxton St.
London, SW1H 0QS
E-mail: water@iwahq.org
URL: www.iwahq.org
Scope: International
Purpose: Provides international water experts the change to explore the science & practice of water management

Joint Statistical Meetings 2018
Sponsor/Contact: Statistical Society of Canada
#209, 1725 St. Laurent Blvd.
Ottawa, ON K1G 3V4
613-733-2662 *Fax:* 613-733-1386
E-mail: info@ssc.ca
URL: www.ssc.ca
Scope: International
Purpose: Held jointly with the Statistical Society of Canada, American Statistical Association, the International Biometric Society (ENAR & WNAR), the International Chinese Statistical Association, the Institute of Mathematical Statistics, & the International Indian Statistical Association

Manitoba Libraries 2018 Bi-annual Conference
Location: Manitoba
Sponsor/Contact: Manitoba Library Association
#606, 100 Arthur St.
Winnipeg, MB R3B 1H3
204-943-4567 *Fax:* 866-202-4567
E-mail: manitobalibrary@gmail.com
URL: www.mla.mb.ca
Scope: Provincial
Purpose: Informative presentations, guest speakers, & a trade show for members of Manitoba's library community
Contact Information: Professional Development Director: Katherine Penner, Phone: 204-474-6846, E-mail: katherine_penner@umanitoba.ca

Nova Scotia Library Association 2018 Annual Conference
Sponsor/Contact: Nova Scotia Library Association
c/o Kelli WooShue, Halifax Public Libraries
60 Alderney Dr.
Dartmouth, NS B2Y 4P8
902-490-5710
E-mail: wooshuk@halifax.ca
URL: www.nsla.ns.ca
Scope: Provincial
Purpose: Hosted by Cumberland Regional Library in the autumn
Contact Information: E-mail: conference@nsla.ns.ca

Pacific Dental Conference 2018
Sponsor/Contact: British Columbia Dental Association
#400, 1765 - 8th Ave. West
Vancouver, BC V6J 5C6
604-736-7202 *Fax:* 604-736-7588
Toll-Free: 888-396-9888
E-mail: post@bcdental.org
URL: www.bcdental.org
Scope: Provincial
Contact Information: Address: Pacific Dental Conference, #305, 1505 West 2nd Ave., Vancouver, BC V6H 3Y4; Phone: 604-736-3781; E-mail: info@pdconf.com; URL: www.pdconf.com

Royal Canadian Mounted Police Veterans Association 2018 Annual General Meeting
Location: New Brunswick
Sponsor/Contact: Royal Canadian Mounted Police Veterans' Association
1200 Vanier Pkwy.
Ottawa, ON K1A 0R2
613-993-8633 *Fax:* 613-993-4353
Toll-Free: 877-251-1771
E-mail: rcmp.vets@rcmp-grc.gc.ca
URL: www.rcmpvetsnational.ca
Scope: National

Society of Toxicology 57th Annual Meeting & ToxExpo
Sponsor/Contact: Society of Toxicology
#300, 1821 Michael Faraday Dr.
Reston, VA 20190
703-438-3115 *Fax:* 703-438-3113
E-mail: sothq@toxicology.org
URL: www.toxicology.org
Scope: International
Purpose: Toxicology meeting & exhibition
Contact Information: Phone: 703-438-3115; Fax: 703-438-3113; E-mail: sothq@toxicology.org

Union of British Columbia Municipalities 2018 Annual Convention
Location: British Columbia
Sponsor/Contact: Union of British Columbia Municipalities
#60, 10551 Shellbridge Way
Richmond, BC V6X 2W9
604-270-8226 *Fax:* 604-270-9116
URL: www.ubcm.ca
Scope: Provincial

Western Retail Lumber Association 2018 Prairie Showcase Buying Show & Convention
Sponsor/Contact: Western Retail Lumber Association
Western Retail Lumber Association Inc.
#1004, 213 Notre Dame Ave.
Winnipeg, MB R3B 1N3
204-957-1077 *Fax:* 204-947-5195
Toll-Free: 800-661-0253
E-mail: wrla@wrla.org
URL: www.wrla.org
Scope: Provincial

World Congress on Medical Physics and Biomedical Engineering 2018
Location: Prague, Czech Republic
Sponsor/Contact: International Federation for Medical & Biological Engineering
E-mail: office@ifmbe.org
URL: www.ifmbe.org
Scope: International
Purpose: The Congresses are scheduled on a three-year basis and aligned with Federation's General Assembly meeting at which elections are held.

2019

January

American Library Association 2019 Midwinter Meeting & Exhibits
Date: January 24-29, 2019
Location: Seattle, WA USA
Sponsor/Contact: American Library Association
50 East Huron St.
Chicago, IL 60611
Fax: 312-440-9374
Toll-Free: 800-545-2433
E-mail: ala@ala.org
URL: www.ala.org
Scope: International
Purpose: A library & information service meeting presenting speakers, discussion groups, exhibits, & committee meetings
Contact Information: Registration Customer Service, Phone: 1-800-974-3084, E-mail: ala@experient-inc.com

American Philological Association 150th Annual Meeting
Date: January 3-6, 2019
Location: San Diego, CA USA
Sponsor/Contact: American Philological Association
University of Pennsylvania
#201E, 220 South 40th St.
Philadelphia, PA 19104-3512
215-898-4975 *Fax:* 215-573-7874
E-mail: apaclassics@sas.upenn.edu
URL: apaclassics.org
Scope: International

April

Library Association of Alberta Annual Conference 2019
Date: April 25-28, 2019
Location: Alberta
Sponsor/Contact: Library Association of Alberta
80 Baker Cres. NW
Calgary, AB T2L 1R4
403-284-5818 *Fax:* 403-282-6646
Toll-Free: 877-522-5550
E-mail: info@laa.ca
URL: www.laa.ca
Scope: Provincial
Purpose: A conference held each spring for members of the Alberta library community, featuring association annual general meetings, session presentations, networking opportunities, & a trade show. Beginning this year, the conference is no longer held jointly with the Alberta Library Trustees Association (ALTA).
Contact Information: Library Association of Alberta, Phone: 403-284-5818, Toll-Free Phone: 1-877-522-5550, Fax: 403-282-6646, E-mail: info@laa.ca, info@albertalibraryconference.com

Pediatric Academic Societies' 2019 Annual Meeting
Date: April 27-30, 2019
Location: Baltimore, MD USA
Sponsor/Contact: Academic Pediatric Association
6728 Old McLean Village Dr.
McLean, VA 22101
703-556-9222 *Fax:* 703-556-8729
E-mail: info@academicpeds.org
URL: www.ambpeds.org
Scope: International
Purpose: An international meeting focussing on research in child health
Contact Information: Address: #7B, 3400 Research Forest Dr., The Woodlands, TX, 77381, USA; Phone: 281-419-0052; Fax: 281-419-0082

Pediatric Endocrine Society 2019 Annual Meeting
Date: April 27-30, 2019
Location: Baltimore, MD USA
Sponsor/Contact: Pediatric Endocrine Society
6728 Old McLean Village Dr.
McLean, VA 22101
E-mail: info@pedsendo.org
URL: www.pedsendo.org
Scope: International
Purpose: An annual opportunity for medical education for those engaged in the disciplines of pediatric endocrinology
Contact Information: E-mail: info@pedsendo.org

May

American Society of Neuroradiology 2019 57th Annual Meeting
Date: May 18-23, 2019
Location: Hynes Convention Center Boston, MA USA
Sponsor/Contact: American Society of Neuroradiology
#207, 2210 Midwest Rd.
Oak Brook, IL 60523
630-574-0220 *Fax:* 630-574-0661
E-mail: jgantenberg@asnr.org
URL: www.asnr.org
Scope: International
Contact Information: Director, Scientific Meetings: Lora Tannehill, E-mail: ltannehill@asnr.org; Manager, Scientific Meetings: Valerie Geisendorfer, E-mail: vgeisendorfer@asnr.org

International Society for Magnetic Resonance in Medicine 2019 27th Scientific Meeting & Exhibition
Date: May 11-17, 2019
Location: Montreal, QC
Sponsor/Contact: International Society for Magnetic Resonance in Medicine
2030 Addison St., 7th Fl.
Berkeley, CA 94704
510-841-1899 *Fax:* 510-841-2340
E-mail: info@ismrm.org
URL: www.ismrm.org
Scope: International
Purpose: Featuring the 26th Annual Meeting of the Section for Magnetic Resonance Technologists
Contact Information: Director, Meetings: Sandra Daudlin, E-mail: sandra@ismrm.org; Coordinator, Meetings: Melisa Martinez, E-mail: melisa@ismrm.org

Journées dentaires internationales du Québec (JDIQ) 2019
Date: 24 au 28 mai 2019
Location: Quebec
Sponsor/Contact: Ordre des dentistes du Québec
625, boul René-Lévesque ouest, 15e étage
Montréal, QC H3B 1R2
514-875-8511 *Fax:* 514-393-9248
Toll-Free: 800-361-4887
URL: www.odq.qc.ca
Scope: Provincial
Contact Information: Directeur, Dr Denis Forest, téléphone: 514-875-8511, poste 2222; adresse email: denis.forest@odq.qc.ca

Medical Library Association 2019 Annual Meeting & Exhibition
Date: May 3-8, 2019
Location: Chicago, IL USA
Sponsor/Contact: Medical Library Association
#1900, 65 East Wacker Pl.
Chicago, IL 60601-7246
312-419-9094 *Fax:* 312-419-8950
E-mail: info@mlahq.org
URL: www.mlanet.org
Scope: International

June

American Library Association 2019 Annual Conference
Date: June 20-25, 2019
Location: Washington, DC USA
Sponsor/Contact: American Library Association
50 East Huron St.
Chicago, IL 60611
Fax: 312-440-9374
Toll-Free: 800-545-2433
E-mail: ala@ala.org
URL: www.ala.org
Scope: International
Purpose: A conference providing speakers, educational programs, committee meetings, & exhibits related to library & information services

American Water Works Association 2019 138th Annual Conference & Exposition
Date: June 2019
Location: Denver, CO USA
Sponsor/Contact: American Water Works Association
6666 West Quincy Ave.
Denver, CO 80235
303-794-7711 *Fax:* 303-347-0804
Toll-Free: 800-926-7337
E-mail: custsvc@awwa.org
URL: www.awwa.org
Scope: International
Purpose: Presenting water research & best practices of interest to international water professionals
Contact Information: American Water Works Association, Phone: 800-926-7337, Fax: 303-347-0804, E-mail: awwamktg@awwa.org

Canadian Anesthesiologists' Society 2019 75th Annual Meeting
Date: June 21-24, 2019
Location: Telus Convention Centre Calgary, AB
Sponsor/Contact: Canadian Anesthesiologists' Society
#208, One Eglinton Ave. East
Toronto, ON M4P 3A1
416-480-0602 *Fax:* 416-480-0320
E-mail: anesthesia@cas.ca
URL: www.cas.ca
Scope: National
Purpose: A convention, with an exhibition pharmaceutical companies & equipment manufacturers

Microwave Theory & Techniques Society International Microwave Symposia 2019
Date: June 3-7, 2019
Location: Boston, MA USA
Sponsor/Contact: IEEE Microwave Theory & Techniques Society
5829 Bellanca Dr.
Elkridge, MD 21075
410-796-5866 *Fax:* 410-796-5829
URL: www.mtt.org
Scope: International
Purpose: Technical papers; Workshops; Trade show

September

Union of British Columbia Municipalities 2019 Annual Convention
Date: September 23-27, 2019
Location: Vancouver Convention & Exhibition Centre Vancouver, BC
Sponsor/Contact: Union of British Columbia Municipalities
#60, 10551 Shellbridge Way
Richmond, BC V6X 2W9
604-270-8226 *Fax:* 604-270-9116
URL: www.ubcm.ca
Scope: Provincial

Western Canada Water 2019 71st Annual Conference & Exhibition
Date: September 17-20, 2019
Location: Shaw Conference Center Edmonton, AB
Sponsor/Contact: Western Canada Water
P.O. Box 1708
240 River Ave.
Cochrane, AB T4C 1B6
403-709-0064 *Fax:* 403-709-0068
Toll-Free: 877-283-2003
E-mail: member@wcwwa.ca
URL: www.wcwwa.ca
Scope: Provincial
Purpose: A technical program, a keynote speaker, & a trade show for delegates from Western Canada Water
Anticipated Attendance: 500+
Contact Information: Western Canada Water, Toll-Free Phone: 1-877-283-2003, Toll-Free Fax: 1-877-283-2007, E-mail: member@wcwwa.ca

Other Conferences in 2019

Canadian Nurses Association 2019 Annual Meeting
Sponsor/Contact: Canadian Nurses Association
50 Driveway
Ottawa, ON K2P 1E2
613-237-2133 *Fax:* 613-237-3520
Toll-Free: 800-361-8404
E-mail: info@cna-aiic.ca
URL: www.cna-aiic.ca
Scope: National
Purpose: A review of the association's strategic initiatives during the past year
Contact Information: E-mail: info@cna-aiic.ca

Canadian Pharmacists Association 2019 107th Annual National Conference
Sponsor/Contact: Canadian Pharmacists Association
1785 Alta Vista Dr.
Ottawa, ON K1G 3Y6
613-523-7877 *Fax:* 613-523-0445
Toll-Free: 800-917-9489
E-mail: info@pharmacists.ca
URL: www.pharmacists.ca
Scope: National
Purpose: Professional development activities, workshops, & a trade show for pharmacists from across Canada

Canadian Union of Public Employees (CUPE) Ontario 2019 56th Convention
Sponsor/Contact: Canadian Union of Public Employees
Ontario Regional Office
#1, 80 Commerce Valley Dr. East
Markham, ON L3T 0B2
905-739-9739 *Fax:* 905-739-9740
E-mail: info@cupe.on.ca
URL: www.cupe.on.ca
Scope: Provincial
Contact Information: CUPE Ontario, E-mail: info@cupe.on.ca

Government Finance Officers Association 2019 112th Annual Conference
Sponsor/Contact: Government Finance Officers Association
#2700, 203 North LaSalle St.
Chicago, IL 60601-1210
312-977-9700 *Fax:* 312-977-4806
E-mail: inquiry@gfoa.org
URL: www.gfoa.org
Scope: International
Contact Information: Manager, Communications: Natalie Laudadio, Phone: 312-977-9700, ext. 2298

Pacific Dental Conference 2019
Location: British Columbia
Sponsor/Contact: British Columbia Dental Association
#400, 1765 - 8th Ave. West
Vancouver, BC V6J 5C6
604-736-7202 *Fax:* 604-736-7588
Toll-Free: 888-396-9888
E-mail: post@bcdental.org
URL: www.bcdental.org
Scope: Provincial
Contact Information: Address: Pacific Dental Conference, #305, 1505 West 2nd Ave., Vancouver, BC V6H 3Y4; Phone: 604-736-3781; E-mail: info@pdconf.com; URL: www.pdconf.com

Royal Canadian Mounted Police Veterans Association 2019 Annual General Meeting
Sponsor/Contact: Royal Canadian Mounted Police Veterans' Association
1200 Vanier Pkwy.
Ottawa, ON K1A 0R2
613-993-8633 *Fax:* 613-993-4353
Toll-Free: 877-251-1771
E-mail: rcmp.vets@rcmp-grc.gc.ca
URL: www.rcmpvetsnational.ca
Scope: National

2020

January

American Library Association 2020 Midwinter Meeting & Exhibits
Date: January 23-28, 2020
Location: Philadelphia, PA USA
Sponsor/Contact: American Library Association
50 East Huron St.
Chicago, IL 60611
Fax: 312-440-9374
Toll-Free: 800-545-2433
E-mail: ala@ala.org
URL: www.ala.org
Scope: International
Purpose: A library & information service meeting presenting speakers, discussion groups, exhibits, & committee meetings
Contact Information: Registration Customer Service, Phone: 1-800-974-3084, E-mail: ala@experient-inc.com

April

Library Association of Alberta Annual Conference 2020
Date: April 30 - May 3, 2020
Location: Alberta
Sponsor/Contact: Library Association of Alberta
80 Baker Cres. NW
Calgary, AB T2L 1R4
403-284-5818 *Fax:* 403-282-6646
Toll-Free: 877-522-5550
E-mail: info@laa.ca
URL: www.laa.ca
Scope: Provincial
Purpose: A conference held each spring for members of the Alberta library community, featuring association annual general meetings, session presentations, networking opportunities, & a trade show. Beginning this year, the conference is no longer held jointly with the Alberta Library Trustees Association (ALTA).
Contact Information: Library Association of Alberta, Phone: 403-284-5818, Toll-Free Phone: 1-877-522-5550, Fax: 403-282-6646, E-mail: info@laa.ca, info@albertalibraryconference.com

May

Cooperative Housing Federation of Canada 2020 Annual General Meeting
Location: Halifax Convention Centre Halifax, NS
Sponsor/Contact: Cooperative Housing Federation of Canada
#311, 225 Metcalfe St.
Ottawa, ON K2P 1P9
613-230-2201 *Fax:* 613-230-2231
Toll-Free: 800-465-2752
E-mail: info@chfcanada.coop
URL: www.chfc.ca
Scope: National
Purpose: Training for co-op volunteers & staff; Business meeting; Youth forum; Elections for the Board of Directors; Group caucuses

Journées dentaires internationales du Québec (JDIQ) 2020
Date: 22 au 26 mai 2020
Location: Quebec
Sponsor/Contact: Ordre des dentistes du Québec
625, boul René-Lévesque ouest, 15e étage
Montréal, QC H3B 1R2
514-875-8511 *Fax:* 514-393-9248
Toll-Free: 800-361-4887
URL: www.odq.qc.ca
Scope: Provincial
Contact Information: Directeur, Dr Denis Forest, téléphone: 514-875-8511, poste 2222; adresse email: denis.forest@odq.qc.ca

Pediatric Academic Societies' 2020 Annual Meeting
Date: May 2-5, 2020
Location: Philadelphia, PA USA
Sponsor/Contact: Academic Pediatric Association
6728 Old McLean Village Dr.
McLean, VA 22101
703-556-9222 *Fax:* 703-556-8729
E-mail: info@academicpeds.org
URL: www.ambpeds.org
Scope: International
Purpose: An international meeting focussing on research in child health
Contact Information: Address: #7B, 3400 Research Forest Dr., The Woodlands, TX, 77381, USA; Phone: 281-419-0052; Fax: 281-419-0082

Pediatric Endocrine Society 2020 Annual Meeting
Date: May 2-5, 2020
Location: Philadelphia, PA USA
Sponsor/Contact: Pediatric Endocrine Society
6728 Old McLean Village Dr.
McLean, VA 22101
E-mail: info@pedsendo.org
URL: www.pedsendo.org
Scope: International
Purpose: An annual continuing education event, featuring speaker presentations, a scientific program, poster sessions, exhibits, & networking occasions for persons who represent the field of pediatric endocrinology
Contact Information: E-mail: info@pedsendo.org

June

American Library Association 2020 Annual Conference
Date: June 25-30, 2020
Location: Chicago, IL USA
Sponsor/Contact: American Library Association
50 East Huron St.
Chicago, IL 60611
Fax: 312-440-9374
Toll-Free: 800-545-2433
E-mail: ala@ala.org
URL: www.ala.org
Scope: International
Purpose: A conference providing speakers, educational programs, committee meetings, & exhibits related to library & information services

American Water Works Association 2020 139th Annual Conference & Exposition
Date: June 2020
Location: Orlando, FL USA
Sponsor/Contact: American Water Works Association
6666 West Quincy Ave.
Denver, CO 80235
303-794-7711 *Fax:* 303-347-0804
Toll-Free: 800-926-7337
E-mail: custsvc@awwa.org
URL: www.awwa.org
Scope: International
Purpose: An annual meeting of water professionals, featuring technical programs & exhibits to foster sustainability
Contact Information: American Water Works Association, Phone: 800-926-7337, Fax: 303-347-0804, E-mail: awwamktg@awwa.org

Canadian Nurses Association 2020 Annual Meeting & Biennial Convention
Date: June 21-23, 2020
Location: Prince Edward Island
Sponsor/Contact: Canadian Nurses Association
50 Driveway
Ottawa, ON K2P 1E2
613-237-2133 *Fax:* 613-237-3520
Toll-Free: 800-361-8404
E-mail: info@cna-aiic.ca
URL: www.cna-aiic.ca
Scope: National
Purpose: A large Canadian nursing conference, featuring presentations, speakers, workshops, discussions, & the opportunity to see new products in the health-care marketplace
Anticipated Attendance: 1,000+
Contact Information: E-mail: conferences@cna-aiic.ca

Microwave Theory & Techniques Society International Microwave Symposia 2020
Date: June 14-19, 2020
Location: Los Angeles, CA USA
Sponsor/Contact: IEEE Microwave Theory & Techniques Society
5829 Bellanca Dr.
Elkridge, MD 21075
410-796-5866 *Fax:* 410-796-5829
URL: www.mtt.org
Scope: International
Purpose: Technical papers; Workshops; Trade show

Other Conferences in 2020

American Society of Neuroradiology 2020 58th Annual Meeting
Sponsor/Contact: American Society of Neuroradiology
#207, 2210 Midwest Rd.
Oak Brook, IL 60523
630-574-0220 *Fax:* 630-574-0661
E-mail: jgantenberg@asnr.org
URL: www.asnr.org
Scope: International
Contact Information: Director, Scientific Meetings: Lora Tannehill, E-mail: ltannehill@asnr.org; Manager, Scientific Meetings: Valerie Geisendorfer, E-mail: vgeisendorfer@asnr.org

International Society for Magnetic Resonance in Medicine 2020 28th Scientific Meeting & Exhibition
Sponsor/Contact: International Society for Magnetic Resonance in Medicine
2030 Addison St., 7th Fl.
Berkeley, CA 94704
510-841-1899 *Fax:* 510-841-2340
E-mail: info@ismrm.org
URL: www.ismrm.org
Scope: International
Purpose: Featuring the 29th Annual Meeting of the Section for Magnetic Resonance Technologists

Medical Library Association 2020 Annual Meeting & Exhibition
Sponsor/Contact: Medical Library Association
#1900, 65 East Wacker Pl.
Chicago, IL 60601-7246
312-419-9094 *Fax:* 312-419-8950
E-mail: info@mlahq.org
URL: www.mlanet.org
Scope: International

Western Canada Water 2020 72nd Annual Conference & Exhibition
Sponsor/Contact: Western Canada Water
P.O. Box 1708
240 River Ave.
Cochrane, AB T4C 1B6
403-709-0064 *Fax:* 403-709-0068
Toll-Free: 877-283-2003
E-mail: member@wcwwa.ca
URL: www.wcwwa.ca
Scope: Provincial
Purpose: A technical program, a keynote speaker, & a trade show for delegates from Western Canada Water
Anticipated Attendance: 500+
Contact Information: Western Canada Water, Toll-Free Phone: 1-877-283-2003, Toll-Free Fax: 1-877-283-2007, E-mail: member@wcwwa.ca

2021

January

American Library Association 2021 Midwinter Meeting & Exhibits
Date: January 21-26, 2021
Location: Indianapolis, IN USA
Sponsor/Contact: American Library Association
50 East Huron St.
Chicago, IL 60611
Fax: 312-440-9374
Toll-Free: 800-545-2433
E-mail: ala@ala.org
URL: www.ala.org
Scope: International
Purpose: A library & information service meeting presenting speakers, discussion groups, exhibits, & committee meetings
Contact Information: Registration Customer Service, Phone: 1-800-974-3084, E-mail: ala@experient-inc.com

June

American Library Association 2021 Annual Conference
Date: June 24-29, 2021
Location: San Francisco, CA USA
Sponsor/Contact: American Library Association
50 East Huron St.
Chicago, IL 60611
Fax: 312-440-9374
Toll-Free: 800-545-2433
E-mail: ala@ala.org
URL: www.ala.org
Scope: International
Purpose: A conference providing speakers, educational programs, committee meetings, & exhibits related to library & information services

Microwave Theory & Techniques Society International Microwave Symposia 2021
Date: June 21-25, 2021
Location: Atlanta, GA USA
Sponsor/Contact: IEEE Microwave Theory & Techniques Society
5829 Bellanca Dr.
Elkridge, MD 21075
410-796-5866 *Fax:* 410-796-5829
URL: www.mtt.org
Scope: International
Purpose: Technical papers; Workshops; Trade show

Other Conferences in 2021

American Water Works Association 2021 140th Annual Conference & Exposition
Sponsor/Contact: American Water Works Association
6666 West Quincy Ave.
Denver, CO 80235
303-794-7711 *Fax:* 303-347-0804
Toll-Free: 800-926-7337
E-mail: custsvc@awwa.org
URL: www.awwa.org
Scope: International
Purpose: An international gathering of thousands of water professionals,

featuring a technical program, workshops, seminars, & exhibits
Contact Information: American Water Works Association, Phone: 800-926-7337, Fax: 303-347-0804, E-mail: awwamktg@awwa.org

Canadian Nurses Association 2021 Annual Meeting
Sponsor/Contact: Canadian Nurses Association
50 Driveway
Ottawa, ON K2P 1E2
613-237-2133 *Fax:* 613-237-3520
Toll-Free: 800-361-8404
E-mail: info@cna-aiic.ca
URL: www.cna-aiic.ca
Scope: National
Purpose: A business meeting featuring a board report & a CEO update
Contact Information: E-mail: info@cna-aiic.ca

Journées dentaires internationales du Québec (JDIQ) 2021
Location: Quebec
Sponsor/Contact: Ordre des dentistes du Québec
625, boul René-Lévesque ouest, 15e étage
Montréal, QC H3B 1R2
514-875-8511 *Fax:* 514-393-9248
Toll-Free: 800-361-4887
URL: www.odq.qc.ca
Scope: Provincial
Contact Information: Directeur, Dr Denis Forest, téléphone: 514-875-8511, poste 2222; adresse email: denis.forest@odq.qc.ca

Pediatric Academic Societies' 2021 Annual Meeting
Sponsor/Contact: Academic Pediatric Association
6728 Old McLean Village Dr.
McLean, VA 22101
703-556-9222 *Fax:* 703-556-8729
E-mail: info@academicpeds.org
URL: www.ambpeds.org
Scope: International
Purpose: An international meeting focussing on research in child health
Contact Information: Address: #7B, 3400 Research Forest Dr., The Woodlands, TX, 77381, USA; Phone: 281-419-0052; Fax: 281-419-0082

Pediatric Endocrine Society 2021 Annual Meeting
Sponsor/Contact: Pediatric Endocrine Society
6728 Old McLean Village Dr.
McLean, VA 22101
E-mail: info@pedsendo.org
URL: www.pedsendo.org
Scope: International

Western Canada Water 2021 73rd Annual Conference & Exhibition
Sponsor/Contact: Western Canada Water
P.O. Box 1708
240 River Ave.
Cochrane, AB T4C 1B6
403-709-0064 *Fax:* 403-709-0068
Toll-Free: 877-283-2003
E-mail: member@wcwwa.ca
URL: www.wcwwa.ca
Scope: Provincial
Purpose: A technical program, a keynote speaker, & a trade show for delegates from Western Canada Water
Anticipated Attendance: 500+
Contact Information: Western Canada Water, Toll-Free Phone: 1-877-283-2003, Toll-Free Fax: 1-877-283-2007, E-mail: member@wcwwa.ca

2022

September

Western Canada Water 2022 74th Annual Conference & Exhibition
Date: September 20-23, 2015
Location: Calgary, AB
Sponsor/Contact: Western Canada Water
P.O. Box 1708
240 River Ave.
Cochrane, AB T4C 1B6
403-709-0064 *Fax:* 403-709-0068
Toll-Free: 877-283-2003
E-mail: member@wcwwa.ca
URL: www.wcwwa.ca
Scope: Provincial
Purpose: A technical program, a keynote speaker, & a trade show for delegates from Western Canada Water
Anticipated Attendance: 500+
Contact Information: Western Canada Water, Toll-Free Phone: 1-877-283-2003, Toll-Free Fax: 1-877-283-2007, E-mail: member@wcwwa.ca

Other Conferences in 2022

Microwave Theory & Techniques Society International Microwave Symposia 2022
Sponsor/Contact: IEEE Microwave Theory & Techniques Society
5829 Bellanca Dr.
Elkridge, MD 21075
410-796-5866 *Fax:* 410-796-5829
URL: www.mtt.org
Scope: International
Purpose: Technical papers; Workshops; Trade show

Executive Name Index

- Names of key contacts for Canadian associations, listed alphabetically by surname
- An executive name may appear more than once in cases where an individual is involved in more than one association
- Included are both volunteer and paid staff
- Each entry is accompanied by a page number which points you to the corresponding listing in the alphabetical listings of Canadian associations

A

Executive Name Index

Executive Name Index

Executive Name Index

Executive Name Index

Executive Name Index

Executive Name Index

Executive Name Index

Executive Name Index

Executive Name Index

Executive Name Index

Executive Name Index

Executive Name Index

Executive Name Index

C

Executive Name Index

Executive Name Index

Executive Name Index

Executive Name Index

Executive Name Index

Executive Name Index

Executive Name Index

Executive Name Index

Executive Name Index

D

Executive Name Index

Executive Name Index

Executive Name Index

Durston, Jerry, *Child Evangelism Fellowship of Canada*, 565

E

Executive Name Index

F

Executive Name Index

Fox-Alder, Judith, *The Terry Fox Foundation*, 1365

Fréchette, François-Régis, *Ordre des infirmières et infirmiers du Québec*, 1117

Executive Name Index

G

Executive Name Index

Executive Name Index

Executive Name Index

Executive Name Index

H

Executive Name Index

Executive Name Index

Executive Name Index

Executive Name Index

Executive Name Index

Executive Name Index

I

Executive Name Index

Executive Name Index

Executive Name Index

K

Executive Name Index

Executive Name Index

Executive Name Index

Executive Name Index

L

Executive Name Index

Executive Name Index

Executive Name Index

Executive Name Index

Executive Name Index

Executive Name Index

Executive Name Index

Executive Name Index

M

Executive Name Index

Executive Name Index

Executive Name Index

Executive Name Index

Executive Name Index

N

Executive Name Index

Executive Name Index

Executive Name Index

O

P

Executive Name Index

Executive Name Index

Executive Name Index

Executive Name Index

Executive Name Index

Executive Name Index

Executive Name Index

Q

R

Executive Name Index

Executive Name Index

S

Executive Name Index

Executive Name Index

Executive Name Index

Executive Name Index

Executive Name Index

Executive Name Index

Executive Name Index

Executive Name Index

Executive Name Index

T

Executive Name Index

Executive Name Index

U

V

Executive Name Index

Executive Name Index

W

Executive Name Index

Executive Name Index

Executive Name Index

Executive Name Index

Executive Name Index

Executive Name Index

X

Y

Executive Name Index

Z

Executive Name Index

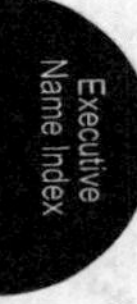
Executive Name Index

Geographic Index

- Canadian associations indexed only
- Headquarters, along with branches, divisions, chapters, etc. are listed
- Name of provinces are presented alphabetically, followed by constituent cities & towns, also in alphabetical order
- Each entry is accompanied by a page number which points you to the corresponding listing

Alberta

Geographic Index

Geographic Index

Camrose

Canmore

Cardston

Caroline

Carstairs

Carvel

Castor

Geographic Index

Geographic Index

Geographic Index

Edson

Elk Point

Evansburg

Fairview

Falher

Fawcett

Geographic Index

British Columbia

Geographic Index

Geographic Index

Pitt Meadows

Port Alberni

Port Clements

Port Coquitlam

Port Edward

Port Hardy

Port McNeill

Port Moody

Port Renfrew

Pouce Coupe

Powell River

Prince George

Prince Rupert

Princeton

Qualicum Beach

Quathiaski Cove

Queen Charlotte

Quesnel

Radium Hot Springs

Regina

Revelstoke

Richmond

Vanderhoof

Vernon

Victoria

Geographic Index

Wells

West Kelowna

West Vancouver

Westbank

Whistler

White Rock

Whonnock

Williams Lake

Winfield

Winlaw

Zeballos

Manitoba

Altona

Arborg

Ashern

Austin

Baldur

Beausejour

Birtle

Blumenort

Boissevain

Brandon

Carberry

Geographic Index

New Brunswick

Arthurette

Balmoral

Bathurst

Bayswater

Blacks Harbour

Bloomfield Station

Boiestown

Bouctouche

Burtts Corner

Campbellton

Cap-Pelé

Caraquet

Centre Village

Centreville

Charters Settlement

Chipman

Clair

Cocagne

Collette

Cookville

Dalhousie

Dartmouth

Dieppe

Dorchester

Douglas

Dow Settlement

Drummond

Edmundston

Elsipogtog

Erb Settlement

Florenceville

Florenceville-Bristol

Fredericton

Geographic Index

Fredericton Junction

Gagetown

Glassville

Grand Bay

Grand Bay-Westfield

Grand Falls

Grand Manan

Grand-Barachois

Hampton

Haut-Saint-Antoine

Havelock

Hillgrove

Hillsborough

Keswick Ridge

Kingsclear

Kingston

Lamèque

Letang

Lower Cove

Lower Coverdale

Lower Kingsclear

Lutes Mountain

McLeod Hill

Memramcook

Miramichi

Moncton

Geographic Index

Morrisdale

Nackawic

Nasonworth

New Brandon

New Denmark

New Maryland

Newcastle Centre

Old Ridge

Oromocto

Penobsquis

Petit-Rocher

Pine Glen

Pokemouche

Port Elgin

Quispamsis

Rexton

Richibucto

Ripples

Riverview

Rogersville

Rothesay

Rowena

Sackville

Saint John

Newfoundland & Labrador

Geographic Index

Geographic Index

St. Johns

St. Philips

Steady Brook

Stephenville

Stephenville Crossing

Torbay

Trinity

Upper Island Cove

Wabana, Bell Island

Winterton

Nova Scotia

Amherst

Annapolis Royal

Geographic Index

Northwest Territories

Nunavut

Geographic Index

Ontario

Geographic Index

Geographic Index

Hampton

Hanmer

Hannon

Hanover

Harley

Harriston

Harrow

Harrowsmith

Havelock

Hawkesbury

Hearst

Hillsburgh

Hillsdale

Holland Landing

Hornepayne

Huntsville

Huron Park

Ilderton

Ingersoll

Ingleside

Innerkip

Innisfil

Iroquois Falls

Jacksons Point

Jordan

Kagawong

Kakabeka Falls

Kanata

Lakefield

Lanark

Lansdowne

Leamington

Lefaivre

Lindsay

Lions Head

Listowel

Little Current

London

Geographic Index

Longlac

Lucknow

Lyn

Lyndhurst

Maberry

Madoc

Mallorytown

Manitouwadge

Manotick

Maple

Marathon

Markdale

Markham

Maryhill

Matheson

Mattawa

Maxville

McArthurs Mills

Meaford

Merrickville

Metcalfe

Midhurst

Midland

Millbrook

Milton

Mindemoya

Minesing

Mississauga

Mississippi Mills

Monetville

Moonbeam

Moosonee

Morpeth

Morrisburg

Geographic Index

Geographic Index

Geographic Index

Geographic Index

Geographic Index

Geographic Index

Geographic Index

Geographic Index

Geographic Index

Geographic Index

Geographic Index

Tottenham

Trenton

Tweed

Unionville

Uxbridge

Val Caron

Vaughan

Vernon

Vineland

Vineland Station

Wabigoon

Walkerton

Wallaceburg

Wardsville

Warsaw

Wasaga Beach

Washago

Waterdown

Waterford

Waterloo

Geographic Index

Wawa

Welland

Wellesley

Wellington

West Lorne

Westport

Whitby

White River

Whitney

Wiarton

Wikwemikong

Wilberforce

Willowdale

Wilsonville

Winchester

Windsor

Wolfe Island

Woodbridge

Geographic Index

Cornwall

Crapaud

Emerald

Fortune

Frenchfort

Glenfinnan

Hunter River

Kensington

Lennox Island

Montague

Mount Stewart

Murray River

North Wiltshire

Souris

Stratford

Summerside

Tignish

Wellington

Wellington Station

Wilsloe

York

York Point

Québec

Acton Vale

Alma

Amos

Amqui

Anjou

Le Moyne

LeGardeur

Lennoxville

Les Escoumins

Lévis

Listiguj First Nation

Longueuil

Loretteville

Louiseville

Magog

Malartic

Maniwaki

Mansonville

Maria

Marieville

Mascouche

Geographic Index

Geographic Index

Geographic Index

Geographic Index

Rawdon

Repentigny

Richmond

Rigaud

Rimouski

Geographic Index

Geographic Index

Geographic Index

Geographic Index

Saskatchewan

Geographic Index

Geographic Index

Geographic Index

Regina Beach

Rocanville

Rosetown

Rosthern

Saltcoats

Saskatoon

Geographic Index

Mailing List Index

- Canadian and foreign associations that rent mailing lists of members, listed by subject
- An entry may appear under more than one subject
- Each entry is accompanied by a page number which points you to the corresponding listing in the alphabetical listings of both Canadian and foreign associations
- Contact association for more information on rental fees, etc.

Mailing List Index

Registered Charitable Organizations Index

- Canadian and Foreign associations that identify themselves as registered charitable organizations, listed by subject
- An entry may appear under more than one subject
- Each entry is accompanied by a page number which points you to the corresponding listing in the alphabetical listings of both Canadian and Foreign associations

Charitable Organization Index

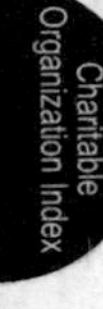
Charitable Organization Index

Charitable Organization Index

Developmentally Disabled Persons

Diabetes

Dietitians & Nutritionists

Diplomatic & Consular Service

Disabled Persons

Disarmament

Diseases

Charitable Organization Index

Food Industry

Food Science

Football

Footwear

Foreign Aid

Forest Industries

Forestry

Foster Parents

Foundations

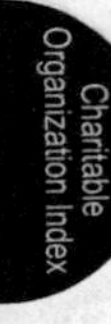

France

Francophones in Canada

Fraternal Organizations

Free-Nets

French Immersion Programs

French Language

French Media

Friedreich's Ataxia

Friends of Groups

Fruit & Vegetables

Charitable Organization Index

Charitable Organization Index

Hobbies

Hockey

Holocaust & Holocaust Studies

Home & School Associations

Home Care

Home Economics

Home Schooling

Homeopathy

Horse Racing

Horses

Horticulture

Hospice Care

Hospital Auxiliaries

Hospitals

Hostelling

Hotels & Motels

Housing

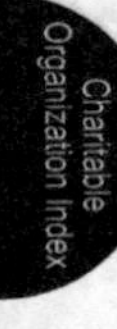

Charitable Organization Index

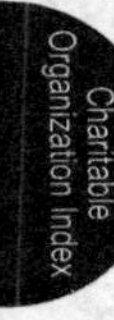
Charitable Organization Index

Charitable Organization Index

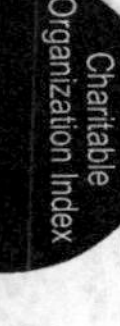

Charitable Organization Index

Charitable Organization Index

Charitable
Organization Index

Charitable Organization Index

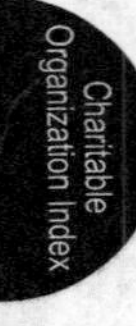
Charitable Organization Index

CANADA'S INFORMATION RESOURCE CENTRE (CIRC)

Access all these great resources online, all the time, at Canada's Information Resource Centre (CIRC)
http://circ.greyhouse.ca

Canada's Information Resource Centre (CIRC) integrates all of Grey House Canada's award-winning reference content into one easy-to-use online resource. With **90,130 Canadian organizations** and **over 140,600 contacts**, plus thousands of additional facts and figures, CIRC is the most comprehensive resource for specialized database content in Canada! Since last year, **two new databases have been added**; access all 11 now with Canada Info Desk Complete - it's the total package!

KEY ADVANTAGES OF CIRC:

- seamlessly cross-database search content from select databases
- save search results for future reference
- link directly to websites or email addresses
- clear display of your results make compiling and adding to your research easier than ever before

DESIGN YOUR OWN CUSTOM CONTACT LISTS!

CIRC gives you the option to define and extract your own lists in seconds. Find new business leads, do keyword searches, locate upcoming conference attendees; all the information you want is right at your fingertips.

CHOOSE BETWEEN QUICK AND EXPERT SEARCH!

With CIRC, you can choose between Expert and Quick search to pinpoint information. Designed for both beginner and advanced researchers, you can conduct simple text searches as well as powerful Boolean searches.

PROFILES IN CIRC INCLUDE:

- Phone numbers, email addresses, fax numbers and full addresses for all branches of the organization.
- Social media accounts, such as Twitter and Facebook.
- Key contacts based on job titles.
- Budgets, membership fees, staff sizes and more!

Search CIRC using common or unique fields, customized to your needs!

Careers & Employment Canada now available on CIRC!

ONLY GREY HOUSE DIRECTORIES PROVIDE SPECIAL CONTENT YOU WON'T FIND ANYWHERE ELSE!

- **Associations Canada:** finances/funding sources, activities, publications, conferences, membership, awards, member profile
- **Canadian Parliamentary Guide:** private and political careers of elected members, complete list of constituencies and representatives
- **Canadian Environmental Resouce Guide:** products/services/areas of expertise, working languages, domestic markets, type of ownership, revenue sources
- **Financial Services:** type of ownership, number of employees, year founded, assets, revenue, ticker symbol
- **Libraries Canada:** staffing, special collections, services, year founded, national library symbol, regional system
- **Governments Canada:** municipal population
- **Canadian Who's Who:** birth city, publications, education (degrees, alma mater), career/occupation and employer
- **Major Canadian Cities:** demographics, ethnicity, immigration, language, education, housing, income, labour and transportation
- **Health Guide Canada:** chronic and mental illnesses, general resources, appendices and statistics
- **Careers & Employment Canada:** employment websites, major employers, recruiters, summer jobs and internships

The new CIRC provides easier searching and faster, more pinpointed results of all of our great resources in Canada, from Associations and Government to Major Companies to Zoos and everything in between. Whether you need fully detailed information on your contact or just an email address, you can customize your search query to meet your needs.

Contact us now for a **free trial** subscription or visit **http://circ.greyhouse.ca**

For more information please contact Grey House Publishing Canada
Tel.: (866) 433-4739 or (416) 644-6479 Fax: (416) 644-1904 | info@greyhouse.ca | www.greyhouse.ca

Principales villes canadiennes

Comparaison et classement

Principales villes canadiennes offre à l'utilisateur de nombreuses manières de classer et de comparer 50 villes principales du Canada. Toute l'information statistique se trouve au bout de vos doigts : vous pouvez obtenir des détails sur les villes, chacune comptant 100 000 habitants ou plus. Dans le Centre de documentation du Canada (CDC), vous pouvez classer instantanément les villes selon vos préférences et créer vos propres tableaux analytiques à l'aide des données fournies. Ces tableaux de classement répondent à des centaines de questions, notamment : quelles villes comptent la population la plus jeune? À quel endroit la croissance économique est-elle la plus forte? Quelles villes présentent les meilleures statistiques en matière de main-d'œuvre?

Un profil de ville offre des renseignements supplémentaires afin de vous donner une idée de son emplacement, de son histoire, de ses activités récréatives et culturelles. Suivent des classements qui démontrent l'unicité de la ville dans un spectre de villes qui se trouvent partout au Canada. Vous trouverez également des remarques intéressantes au sujet de la ville et de son classement parmi les 50 principales villes, par exemple selon celle où il fait le mieux vivre, où se trouvent les plus riches et où il fait le plus froid. Ces rapports sont disponibles uniquement auprès de Grey House Publishing Canada et dans le cadre de votre abonnement à ce nouveau produit emballant!

PRINCIPALES VILLES CANADIENNES COMPREND CES TABLEAUX STATISTIQUES :

Données démographiques

- Croissance de la population
- Caractéristiques relatives à l'âge
- Ratio homme/femme
- État matrimonial

Logement

- Type et taille du logement
- Âge et valeur du logement

Main-d'œuvre

- Population active
- Emploi
- Industrie
- Lieu de travail

Ethnicité, immigration et langue

- Langue maternelle
- Connaissance des langues officielles
- Langue parlée à la maison
- Populations minoritaires
- Formation
- Niveau scolaire

Revenu

- Revenu médian
- Revenu médian après impôts
- Revenu médian par type de famille
- Revenu médian après impôts par type de famille

Transport

- Moyen de transport vers le travail

OFFERT EN VERSION ÉLECTRONIQUE!

Principales villes canadiennes est offert en version électronique sur le Web. Vous accédez donc instantanément aux faits dont vous avez besoin pour chaque ville, de même que des éléments intéressants qui illustrent la comparaison entre les villes.

Servez-vous de la version en ligne pour effectuer des recherches parmi les statistiques et créer vos propres tableaux, ou consulter les tableaux déjà prêts en format PDF. Elle peut vous aider dans le cadre de recherches pour des travaux universitaires, pour le développement d'infrastructures ou consultez-la par simple curiosité – autant de données réunies en une source modifiable.

For more information please contact Grey House Publishing Canada
Tel.: (866) 433-4739 or (416) 644-6479 Fax: (416) 644-1904 | info@greyhouse.ca | www.greyhouse.ca

Health Guide Canada

An Informative Handbook on Health Services in Canada

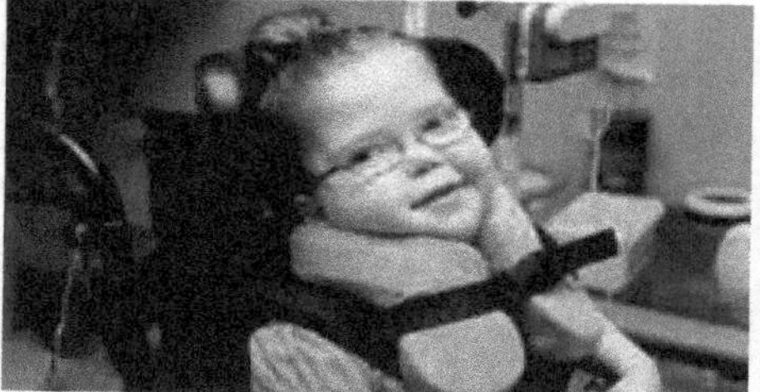

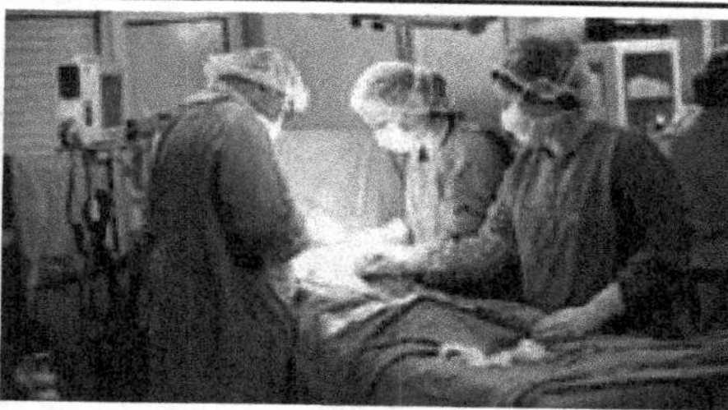

Health Guide Canada: An informative handbook on chronic and mental illnesses and health services in Canada offers a comprehensive overview of 99 chronic and mental illnesses, from Addison's to Wilson's disease. Each chapter includes an easy-to-understand medical description, plus a wide range of condition-specific support services and information resources that deal with the variety of issues concerning those with a chronic or mental illness, as well as those who support the illness community.

Health Guide Canada contains thousands of ways to deal with the many aspects of chronic or mental health disorder. It includes associations, government agencies, libraries and resource centres, educational facilities, hospitals and publications. In addition to chapters dealing with specific chronic or mental conditions, there is a chapter relevant to the health industry in general, as well as others dealing with charitable foundations, death and bereavement groups, homeopathic medicine, indigenous issues and sports for the disabled.

Specific sections include:

- Educational Material
- Section I: Chronic & Mental Illnesses
- Section II: General Resources
- Section III: Appendices
- Section IV: Statistics

Each listing will provide a description, address (including website, email address and social media links, if possible) and executives' names and titles, as well as a number of details specific to that type of organization.

In addition to patients and families, hospital and medical centre personnel can find the support they need in their work or study. *Health Guide Canada* is full of resources crucial for people with chronic illness as they transition from diagnosis to home, home to work, and work to community life.

PRINT OR ONLINE—QUICK AND EASY ACCESS TO ALL THE INFORMATION YOU NEED!

Available in softcover print or electronically via the web, *Health Guide Canada* provides instant access to the people you need and the facts you want every time. Whereas the print edition is verified and updated annually, ongoing changes are added to the web version on a monthly basis. The web version allows you to narrow your search by using index fields such as name or type of organization, subject, location, contact name or title and postal code.

HEALTH GUIDE CANADA HELPS YOU FIND WHAT YOU NEED WITH THESE VALUABLE SOURCING TOOLS!

Entry Name Index—An alphabetical list of all entries, providing a quick and easy way to access any listing in this edition.

Tabs—Main sections are tabbed for easy look-up. Headers on each page make it easy to locate the data you need.

Create your own contact lists! Online subscribers have the option to instantly generate their own contact lists and export them into spreadsheets for further use—a great alternative to high cost list broker services.

GREY HOUSE PUBLISHING CANADA For more information please contact Grey House Publishing Canada

Tel.: (866)-433-4739 or (416) 644-6479 Fax: (416) 644-1904 | info@greyhouse.ca | www.greyhouse.ca

Guide parlementaire canadien

Votre principale source d'information en matière de résultats d'élections fédérales!

Publié annuellement depuis avant la Confédération, le *Guide parlementaire canadien* est une source fondamentale de notices biographiques des membres élus et nommés aux gouvernements fédéral et provinciaux. Il y est question, notamment, d'établissements gouvernementaux comme la résidence du gouverneur général, le Conseil privé et la législature canadienne. Ce recueil exhaustif présente les résultats historiques et actuels accompagnés de données statistiques, provinciales et politiques.

LE GUIDE PARLEMENTAIRE CANADIEN EST DIVISÉ EN CINQ CATÉGORIES EXHAUSTIVES:

La monarchie—des renseignements biographiques sur Sa Majesté la reine Elizabeth II, la famille royale et le gouverneur général.

Le gouvernement fédéral—un chapitre distinct pour chacun des sujets suivants: Conseil privé, sénat, Chambre des communes (y compris une brève description de l'institution, son historique sous forme de textes et de graphiques et une liste des membres actuels) suivi de notes biographiques sans pareil.*

Les élections fédérales

1867–2008

- Les renseignements sont présentés en ordre alphabétique par province puis par circonscription.
- Les notes de chaque circonscription comprennent : La date d'établissement, la date d'abolition, l'ancienne circonscription, les circonscriptions ultérieures, etc. puis l'année d'élection ainsi que le nom et le parti des candidats élus.
- Viennent ensuite des renseignements sur l'élection partielle.

2011

- Les renseignements de l'élection 2011 sont organisés de la même manière, mais comprennent également de l'information sur tous les candidats qui se sont présentés dans chaque circonscription, leur appartenance politique et le nombre de voix récoltées.

Gouvernements provinciaux et territoriaux—Chaque chapitre portant sur le gouvernement provincial comprend :

- des renseignements statistiques
- une description de l'Assemblée législative
- des notes biographiques sur le lieutenant-gouverneur ou le commissaire
- une liste des ministres actuels
- les dates de périodes législatives depuis la Confédération
- une liste des membres et des circonscriptions
- des notes biographiques*
- les résultats des élections générales et partielles

Cours : fédérale—chaque chapitre comprend : une description de la cour (suprême, fédérale, cour d'appel fédérale, cour d'appel de la cour martiale et cour de l'impôt), son histoire, une liste des juges qui y siègent ainsi que des notes biographiques.*

* Les notes biographiques respectent un format concis, bien qu'approfondi :

Renseignements personnels—lieu de naissance, formation, renseignements familiaux

Carrière politique—cheminement politique et service public

Carrière privée—antécédents professionnels, membre d'organisations, antécédents militaires

OFFERT EN FORMAT PAPIER ET DÉSORMAIS ÉLECTRONIQUE!

Offert sous couverture rigide ou en format électronique grâce au web, le *Guide parlementaire canadien* donne invariablement un accès instantané aux représentants du gouvernement et aux faits qui font l'objet de vos recherches. Si la version imprimée est vérifiée et mise à jour annuellement, des changements continus sont apportés mensuellement à la base de données en ligne. Servez-vous de la version en ligne afin de circonscrire vos recherches grâce aux champs spéciaux de l'index comme l'institution, la province et le nom.

Créez vos propres listes! Les abonnés au service en ligne peuvent générer instantanément leurs propres listes de contacts et les exporter en format feuille de calcul pour une utilisation approfondie – une solution de rechange géniale aux services dispendieux d'un commissionnaire en publipostage!

Pour obtenir plus d'information, veuillez contacter Grey House Publishing Canada

par tél. : 1 866 433-4739 ou 416 644-6479 par téléc. : 416 644-1904 | info@greyhouse.ca | www.greyhouse.ca

Financial Services Canada

Unparalleled Coverage of the Canadian Financial Service Industry

With corporate listings for over 17,000 organizations and hard-to-find business information, *Financial Services Canada* is the most up-to-date source for names and contact numbers of industry professionals, senior executives, portfolio managers, financial advisors, agency bureaucrats and elected representatives.

Financial Services Canada is the definitive resource for detailed listings—providing valuable contact information including: name, title, organization, profile, associated companies, telephone and fax numbers, e-mail and website addresses. Use our online database and refine your search by stock symbol, revenue, year founded, assets, ownership type or number of employees.

POWERFUL INDEXES HELP YOU LOCATE THE CRUCIAL FINANCIAL INFORMATION YOU NEED.

Organized with the user in mind, *Financial Services Canada* contains categorized listings and 4 easy-to-use indexes:

Alphabetic—financial organizations listed in alphabetical sequence by company name

Geographic—financial institutions and their branches broken down by town or city

Executive Name—all officers, directors and senior personnel in alphabetical order by surname

Insurance class—lists all companies by insurance type

Reduce the time you spend compiling lists, researching company information and searching for e-mail addresses. Whether you are interested in contacting a finance lawyer regarding international and domestic joint ventures, need to generate a list of foreign banks in Canada or want to contact the Toronto Stock Exchange—*Financial Services Canada* gives you the power to find all the data you need.

PRINT OR ONLINE—QUICK AND EASY ACCESS TO ALL THE INFORMATION YOU NEED!

Available in softcover print or electronically via the web, *Financial Services Canada* provides instant access to the people you need and the facts you want every time.

Financial Services Canada print edition is verified and updated annually. Regular ongoing changes are added to the web version on a monthly basis. The web version allows you to narrow your search by using index fields such as name or type of organization, subject, location, contact name or title and postal code.

Create your own contact lists! Online subscribers have the option to instantly generate their own contact lists and export them into spreadsheets for further use—a great alternative to high cost list broker services.

ACCESS TO CURRENT LISTINGS FOR...

Banks and Depository Institutions
- Domestic and savings banks
- Foreign banks and branches
- Foreign bank representative offices
- Trust companies
- Credit unions

Non-Depository Institutions
- Bond rating companies
- Collection agencies
- Credit card companies
- Financing and loan companies
- Trustees in bankruptcy

Investment Management Firms, including securities and commodities
- Financial planning / investment management companies
- Investment dealers
- Investment fund companies
- Pension/money management companies
- Stock exchanges
- Holding companies

Insurance Companies, including federal and provincial
- Reinsurance companies
- Fraternal benefit societies
- Mutual benefit companies
- Reciprocal exchanges accounting and law
- Accountants
- Actuary consulting firms
- Law firms (specializing in finance)
- Major Canadian companies
- Key financial contacts for public, private and Crown corporations
- Government
- Federal, provincial and territorial contacts

Publications Appendix
- Leading publications serving the financial services industry

For more information please contact Grey House Publishing Canada

Tel.: (866)-433-4739 or (416) 644-6479 Fax: (416) 644-1904 | info@greyhouse.ca | www.greyhouse.ca

Mailing List Services

As a boutique provider of mailing lists, Grey House Publishing Canada specializes in the areas below to ensure a high level of accuracy. Our clients return to us time and time again because of the reliability of our information and great customer service. We'll work with you to develop a campaign that provides results. No other list services will work as closely as we do to meet your unique needs.

Associations—the most extensive list of Canadian associations available, featuring all professional, trade and business organizations together with not-for-profit groups.

Arts & Culture—the definitive source of key prospects in various Canadian arts and cultural outlets.

Education—the most comprehensive list of educational institutions and organizations in Canada.

Health Care / Hospitals—includes all major medical facilities with chief executives.

Lawyers—key prospects for a number of direct mail offers.

Media—the definitive source of key prospects in various Canadian media outlets, offering the top business managers and/or publishers.

Environmental—a complete profile of the Canadian Environmental scene, constantly revised for the annual Canadian Environmental Resource Guide.

Financial Services—a list of key contacts from the full range of Canada's financial services industry.

Government Key Contacts—a list of key Government contacts, maintained by the Canadian Almanac & Directory, Canada's standard institutional reference for 165 years.

Libraries—the most unique and complete list of government, special and public libraries available.

Major Canadian Companies—listings of Canada's largest private, public and Crown corporations with major key contacts of the top business decision-makers.

AVAILABILITY

Lists are available on CD, labels and via e-mail. They are provided on a one-time use basis or for a one-year lease. For a quotation on tailor-made lists to suit your needs, inquire using the contact information listed below.

For more information please contact Grey House Publishing Canada

Tel.: (866) 433-4739 or (416) 644-6479 Fax: (416) 644-1904 | info@greyhouse.ca | www.greyhouse.ca

Services de liste de distribution

En tant que point de service fournisseur de listes de distribution, Grey House Canada se spécialise dans les domaines ci-dessous pour assurer un degré supérieur de précision. Nos clients nous sont fidèles, car ils souhaitent bénéficier de notre fiabilité et de notre service à la clientèle. Nous collaborerons avec vous pour développer une campagne qui produit des résultats. Aucun autre service de création de listes ne collabore aussi étroitement que nous avec leurs clients pour satisfaire leurs besoins particuliers.

Associations—la liste la plus complète des associations canadiennes qui énumère toutes les associations professionnelles, corporatives et commerciales ainsi que les groupes sans but lucratif.

Arts et culture—la source manifeste des candidats clés des divers vecteurs artistiques et culturels au Canada.

Éducation—la liste la plus complète des établissements et des organismes d'enseignement au Canada.

Soins de santé/hôpitaux—comprend les principaux établissements médicaux et leurs directeurs.

Avocats—les principaux clients potentiels pour nombre d'offres de publipostage direct.

Médias—la source certaine des clients potentiels clés dans divers points de vente de médias canadiens; elle comprend les principaux dirigeants et éditeurs.

Environnement—un profil complet de la scène environnementale canadienne; constamment mis à jour pour le Guide des ressources environnementales canadiennes.

Services financiers—une liste des personnes-ressources clés de tout l'éventail de l'industrie des services financiers du Canada.

Coordonnées gouvernementales clés—une liste des contacts essentiels, entretenue par le Répertoire et almanach canadien, la référence institutionnelle au Canada depuis 165 ans.

Bibliothèques—la liste la plus unique et la plus complète des bibliothèques gouvernementales, spécialisées et publiques disponible.

Principales entreprises canadiennes—une liste des plus grandes sociétés privées, publiques et de la Couronne au Canada, y compris les coordonnées des principaux décideurs du monde des affaires.

DISPONIBILITÉ

Les listes sont offertes sur disque, étiquettes et par courriel. Elles sont fournies sur la base d'une utilisation unique ou d'un abonnement d'un an. Pour obtenir un devis pour une liste personnalisée selon vos besoins, contactez-nous.